THE
BROWN-DRIVER-BRIGGS
HEBREW AND ENGLISH LEXICON

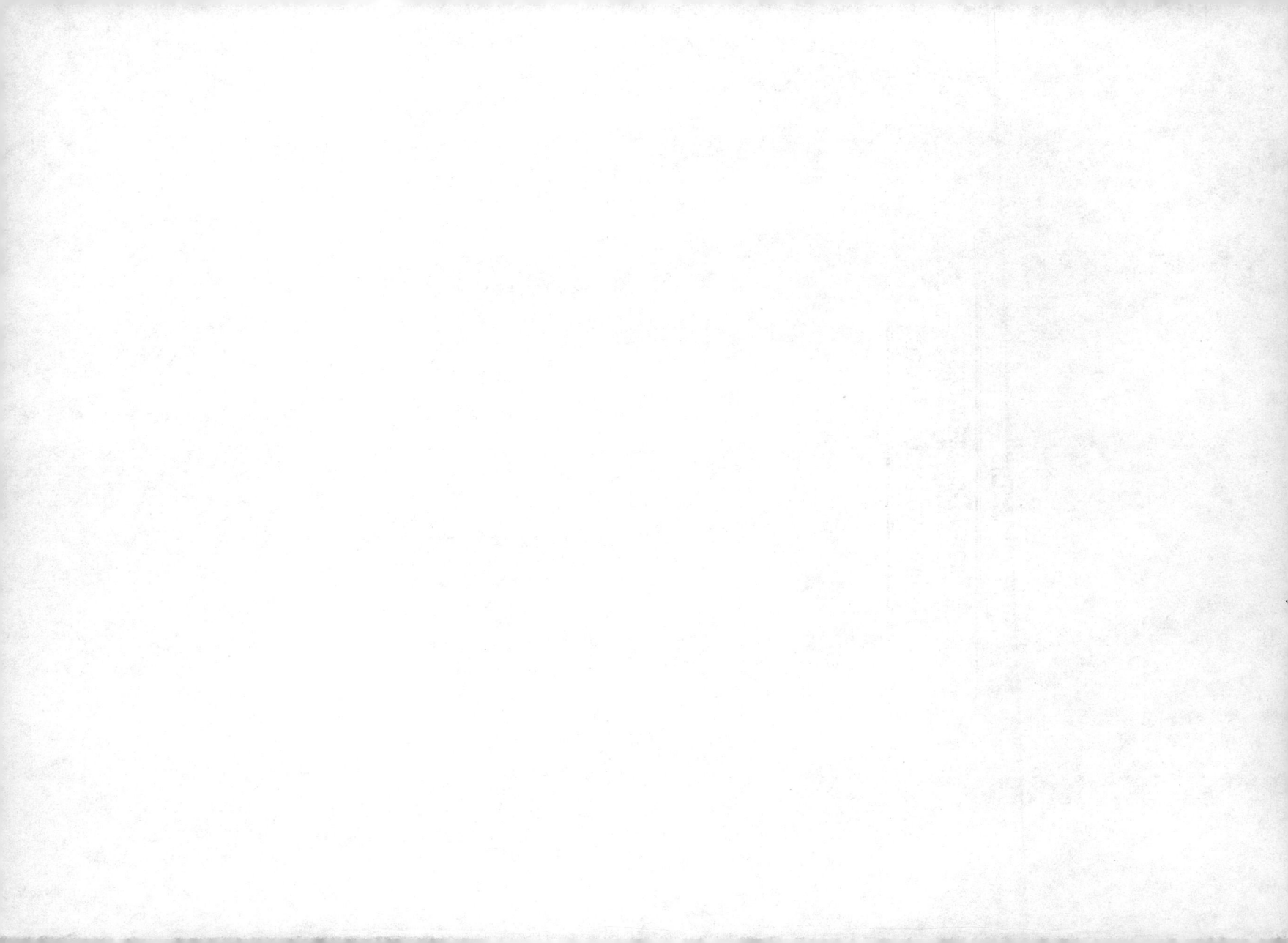

THE BROWN-DRIVER-BRIGGS HEBREW AND ENGLISH LEXICON

With an appendix containing the Biblical Aramaic

Coded with the numbering system from *Strong's Exhaustive Concordance of the Bible*

Based on the lexicon of William Gesenius, as translated by Edward Robinson, and edited with constant reference to the thesaurus of Gesenius as completed by E. Rödiger, and with authorized use of the German editions of Gesenius' Handwörterbuch über das Alte Testament

Francis Brown, D.D., D. Litt.

with the cooperation of

S. R. Driver, D.D., Litt.D. and Charles A. Briggs, D.D., D.Litt.

THE BROWN-DRIVER-BRIGGS HEBREW AND ENGLISH LEXICON:
WITH AN APPENDIX CONTAINING THE BIBLICAL ARAMAIC

by Francis Brown, with the cooperation of S. R. Driver and Charles A. Briggs

Hendrickson Publishers, Inc.
P. O. Box 3473
Peabody, Massachusetts 01961-3473

ISBN 1-56563-206-0

Reprinted from the 1906 edition originally published by Houghton, Mifflin and Company, Boston.

Strong's numbering was added by Hendrickson Publishers.

Eighth Printing — June 2004

Printed in the United States of America

PUBLISHER'S PREFACE TO THE NEW EDITION

A TRIO of eminent Old Testament scholars—Francis Brown, R. Driver, and Charles Briggs—spent over twenty years researching, writing, and preparing *The Brown-Driver-Briggs Hebrew and English Lexicon.* Since it first appeared in the early part of the twentieth century, BDB has been considered the finest and most comprehensive Hebrew lexicon available to the English-speaking student. Based upon the classic work of Wilhelm Gesenius, the "father of modern Hebrew lexicography," BDB gives not only dictionary definitions for each word, but relates each word to its Old Testament usage and categorizes its nuances of meaning. BDB's exhaustive coverage of Old Testament Hebrew words, as well as its unparalleled usage of cognate languages and the wealth of background sources consulted and quoted, render BDB an invaluable resource for all students of the Bible.

In order to make evident the etymology of each word, BDB organizes the Hebrew words according to their roots, rather than alphabetically. This organization by stem allows the student learning Hebrew vocabulary to see clearly the relationships among different words from the same root. This method of arrangement is also profitable for the student who wishes to study all the derivatives of a given root. However, a weakness of arrangement by root is that words can be difficult to locate. For more on this and the advantages of the *Strong's* numbering system, see below. BDB groups Aramaic words together in a section at the back of the volume for easy reference. Another section at the back contains Addenda and Corrigenda to the original edition.

The present volume is a reprinting of the 1906 American edition, with the addition of the numbering system from *Strong's Exhaustive Concordance* and correction of the numerous errors and misprintings found in the original text. This new edition, which gives the *Strong's* number for each Hebrew word, opens the invaluable store of word-study material found in BDB to the novice Hebrew student and even those who do not know Hebrew at all.

For those who are not familiar with Hebrew, a study on the different uses of the word "spirit" in the Old Testament, for instance, would begin in *Strong's Exhaustive Concordance. Strong's* assigns each biblical Hebrew word a number. In *Strong's* one finds a listing of all of the Old Testament occurrences of the word "spirit." To the right of each citation are the *Strong's* numbers corresponding to the four different Hebrew words translated as "spirit," namely 7307, 7308, 178, and 5397. With these numbers in hand, the search continues in the BDB index. The index is arranged in order of the *Strong's* numbers. Number 7307, the index indicates, is found on page 924, quadrant c. In the margin at the upper right hand side of page 924 in BDB is the *Strong's* number 7307. This entry for the word *rûwach* lists the common meanings for the word (breath, wind, spirit), and then discusses the various nuances of meanings as found in different passages, quoting material from other sources and scholars where relevant. The root word is listed preceding this entry, and entries discussing related words follow. According to the index, *Strong's* number 7307 is also found on page 1112d, as is number 7308. On page 1112, in the Aramaic section, 7307 is next to the root word, and the Aramaic occurrences of the word for "spirit" are listed next to 7308. The rest of this search on "spirit," with *Strong's* numbers 178 and 5397, would proceed in a similar fashion. It is important to check all of the page references listed in the index, as well as all of the cross references found within the entries, for complete information on a given word. Because of BDB's arrangement according to Hebrew stems, it is the index that allows the user to exhaustively search BDB for a given word. Additionally, hard-to-trace words are listed a second time in their alphabetical place with a cross reference to ease any inconvenience for the beginning student of Hebrew. At the end of such a word search, the user will have seen all of the possible shades of meaning of the Hebrew words translated into English in the KJV as "spirit," as well as the particular nuance emphasized in the biblical passages where the word occurs. This kind of study sheds invaluable light upon the biblical meaning and would not otherwise be possible without years of Hebrew study.

PREFACE

THE need of a new Hebrew and English Lexicon of the Old Testament has been so long felt that no elaborate explanation of the appearance of the present work seems called for. Wilhelm Gesenius, the father of modern Hebrew Lexicography, died in 1842. His *Lexicon Manuale Hebraicum et Chaldaicum in V. T. Libros*, representing a much riper stage of his lexicographical work than his earlier Hebrew dictionaries, was published in 1833, and the corresponding issue of his *Hebräisches und Chaldäisches Handwörterbuch über das Alte Testament*, upon which the later German editions more or less directly depend, appeared in 1834. The *Thesaurus philologicus Criticus Linguæ Hebrææ et Chaldææ Veteris Testamenti*, begun by Gesenius some years earlier, and not completed at his death, was substantially finished by Roediger in 1853, although the concluding part, containing Indices, Additions and Corrections, was not published until 1858. The results of Gesenius' most advanced work were promptly put before English-speaking students. In 1824 appeared Gibbs' translation of the *Neues Hebräisch-deutsches Handwörterbuch*, issued by Gesenius in 1815, and in 1836 Edward Robinson published his translation of the Latin work of 1833. This broad-minded, sound and faithful scholar added to the successive editions of the book in its English form the newest materials and conclusions in the field of Hebrew word-study, receiving large and valuable contributions in manuscript from Gesenius himself, and, after the latter's death, carefully incorporating into his translation the substance of the *Thesaurus*, as its fasciculi appeared.

But the last revision of Robinson's Gesenius was made in 1854, and Robinson died in 1863. The last English edition of Gesenius, prepared by Tregelles, and likewise including additions from the *Thesaurus*, dates as far back as 1859. In the meantime Semitic studies have been pursued on all hands with energy and success. The language and text of the Old Testament have been subjected to a minute and searching inquiry before unknown. The languages cognate with Hebrew have claimed the attention of specialists in nearly all civilized countries. Wide fields of research have been opened, the very existence of which was a surprise, and have invited explorers. Arabic, ancient and modern, Ethiopic, with its allied dialects, Aramaic, in its various literatures and localities, have all yielded new treasures; while the discovery and decipherment of inscriptions from Babylonia and Assyria, Phœnicia, Northern Africa, Southern Arabia, and other old abodes of Semitic peoples, have contributed to a far more comprehensive and accurate knowledge of the Hebrew vocabulary in its sources and its usage than was possible forty or fifty years ago. In Germany an attempt has been made to keep pace with advancing knowledge by frequent editions of the *Hand wörterbuch*, as well as by the brilliant and suggestive, though unequal, *Wörterbuch* of Siegfried and Stade (in 1892–93), but in England and America there has not been heretofore even so much as a serious attempt.

The present Editors consider themselves fortunate in thus having the opportunity afforded by an evident demand. Arrangements have been made whereby the rights connected with 'Robinson's Gesenius' are carried over to the present work, and exclusive authority to use the most recent German editions has been secured.[1] They have felt, however, that the task which they had undertaken could not be rightly discharged by merely adding new knowledge to the old, or by substituting more recent opinions for others grown obsolete, or by any other form of superficial revision. At an early stage of the work they reached the conviction that their first and perhaps chief duty was to make a fresh and, as far as possible, exhaustive study of the Old Testament materials, determine the actual uses of words by detailed examination of every passage, comparing, at the same time, their employment in the related languages, and thus fix their proper meanings in Hebrew.

In the matter of etymologies they have endeavoured to carry out the method of sound philology, making it their aim to exclude arbitrary and fanciful conjectures, and in cases of uncertainty to afford the student the means of judging of the materials on which a decision depends. They could not have been satisfied to pursue the course chosen by Professors Siegfried and Stade, in excluding the etymological feature almost entirely from their lexicon. This method deprives the student of all knowledge as to the extra-Biblical history and relationship of his words, and of the stimulus to study the cognate languages, and lessens his opportunity of growing familiar with the modes of word-formation. It greatly simplifies, of course, the task of the lexicographer. The Editors acknowledge, at once, that their labours would have ended much sooner if they had not included the etymology of words, and they are sensible of the exposure to criticism at a thousand points which results from their undertaking to do so. They have cheerfully assumed this burden, and are ready to accept this criticism, from which they hope to learn much. Here, if anywhere, it is certain that results must, in many cases, long remain provisional. They have preferred to make what contribution they could to the final settlement of these difficult questions. For like reasons they have been unwilling to follow Buhl in excluding the explanation of the meaning of proper names, hazardous as such explanations often are.

That the Editors have made use of the *Thesaurus* of Gesenius on every page, with increasing admiration for the tireless diligence, philological insight and strong good

[1] The eleventh German edition appeared in 1890, the year before the First Part of the present Lexicon was issued, under the editorship of Professors Mühlau and Volck, of Dorpat, who had prepared the eighth, ninth and tenth, also. The twelfth edition, in 1895, marked an era in the history of this useful dictionary, for with it began the careful editorship of Professor Frants Buhl, of Copenhagen, then at Leipzig, who issued the thirteenth edition, also, in 1899, and, after a very thorough revision, the fourteenth, in 1905. None of these editions had the exact scope of the present work, and none of them absolved the Editors in any degree from personal investigation of the entire material. The Editors have, however, derived much benefit from the German work, and especially from the contributions to it of Professor Buhl and his co-laborers, Professors Socin and Zimmern. Unfortunately the present Lexicon, with the exception of the Appendix, was almost entirely in type when the fourteenth edition appeared, and adequate use of its new material, especially its extensive references to current philological literature, must be reserved for a later opportunity.

sense of this great Lexicographer, and recognition of Robinson's wisdom in allowing him to speak directly to English students by the admirable translation and editorship of the *Lexicon Manuale*, need not be further emphasized. They have also made free reference to Gesenius' Hebrew Grammar in the successive editions prepared by Professor Kautzsch, follower of Gesenius at Halle, and, since 1898, to the excellent English translation of this book made by Messrs. Collins and Cowley, which appeared in that year. The Grammars of Ewald, Olshausen, Böttcher, Stade, August Müller and König, the *Syntax* of A. B. Davidson, and other grammatical works have been cited as occasion required. Nöldeke's contributions to Hebrew lexicography and grammar have been constantly used, with the works of Lagarde and Barth on the formation of nouns, of Gerber on denominative verbs, and many which cannot be catalogued here. All the critical commentaries and a great number and variety of textual, topographical and geographical works, with monographs and articles bearing on every possible aspect of Old Testament language, have been examined.

The published materials for the study of the languages cognate with Hebrew have reached such proportions as to tax even the most industrious in any extended comparison of kindred words. For the Arabic, constant use has been made of the Dictionaries of Lane, Freytag, Dozy, Wahrmund, the Beirût Fathers, and others besides. The Editors have found themselves sharing with peculiar keenness in the unavailing regret of scholars that Mr. Lane's magnificent plan of complete Arabic lexicography was not destined to be realized. Fränkel's *Aramäische Fremdwörter im Arabischen* has been constantly used. For the vast and increasing storehouse of Assyrian, — as yet most imperfectly explored, — the dictionaries of Delitzsch and — as far as the times of its appearance allowed — Muss-Arnolt have been employed, as well as Meissner's *Supplement*, and many special vocabularies. Paul Haupt, Bezold, Guyard, Strassmaier, Zimmern, Jensen, Winckler, Scheil, Sayce, King, Johns, R. F. Harper, and many writers in the *Zeitschrift für Assyriologie*, the *Beiträge zur Assyriologie und Semitischen Sprachwissenschaft*, and other publications, have been laid under contribution. A place of honour must here be given to Eberhard Schrader, the founder of Assyriology in Germany, whose fruitful work has been prematurely cut short by impaired health, and the *Keilinschriftliche Bibliothek*, begun by him, is mentioned here many times. Winckler is of course recognized as the chief editor of the inscriptions from Tel el-Amarna. For Syriac, the *Thesaurus* of R. Payne Smith and the *Lexicon* of Brockelmann have been always at hand, with Castell accessible in case of need. Constant reference has been made to Nöldeke's *Syrische Grammatik* (now, fortunately, translated), as well as his older works, the *Neusyrische Grammatik*, and the priceless *Mandäische Grammatik*. Duval and Nestle, also, have been laid under contribution. The Aramaic of the Targums and other Jewish-Aramaic documents, as well as the post-Biblical Hebrew, have been examined in the dictionaries of Buxtorf, J. Levy, Jastrow and Dalman, the collections of Bacher, the grammars of Strack, Marti and Dalman, the editions of Lagarde, Berliner and Merx, as well as the older publications. The Christian Aramaic of Palestine has been studied in the treatment of Schwally and Schulthess. In the Aramaic Appendix frequent references have been made not only to the grammars of Kautzsch and Dalman, but also to Krauss' *Griechische u. Lateinische Lehnwörter im Talmud*, and especially to the independent and valuable pamphlets of Scheftelowitz, *Arisches im Alten Testament* I and II. The Hebrew text of Ecclesiasticus has been used in the primary editions of Schechter, of Neubauer and Cowley, of Schechter and Taylor, of E. N. Adler, G. Margoliouth, I. Lévi and Gaster, as well as in the more compact editions of Strack and Lévi, and the admirable *facsimile* issued by the Clarendon Press. Dillmann has been the main authority for Ethiopic, with resort, from time to time, to Prätorius and Charles. North Semitic inscriptions have yielded their material through the *Corpus Inscription Semiticarum*, the *Répertoire d'Épigraphie Sémitique*, the collections of de Vogüé, Euting and others, and especially, in recent years, by the aid of the Handbooks of Lidzbarski and G. A. Cooke, and the Glossary of S. A. Cook. The important Aramaic texts from Egypt, of the fifth century B. C., which have been first published by Cowley and Sayce, have also been utilized for the Aramaic Lexicon. The lexical matter of Southern Arabia has been gathered from the *Corpus*, from the inscriptions published by Osiander, M. Levy, Halévy, Mordtmann, D. H. Müller (including the discoveries of Langer), Glaser and others. Egyptian parallels have been adduced mainly from Wiedemann, Bondi, Erman, Steindorff and Spiegelberg, with occasional reference to Lepsius, Brugsch and Ebers. In all these departments, where active work is going on, fugitive materials have of course been found in many places, often scattered and sometimes remote.

It has been the purpose to recognize good textual emendations, but not to swell the list by conjectures which appeared to lack a sound basis. There is still much to do in textual criticism, and much which has been done since the printing of this Lexicon began would receive recognition if extensive revision were now possible. Among the critical discussions of the Hebrew text which have been frequently used are those of Geiger, Graetz, Wellhausen (*Samuel*, *Minor Prophets*), Perles, Oort, Cornell, (*Ezekiel*, *Jeremiah*), Beer (*Job*), Driver (*Samuel*), Burney (*Kings*), the several Parts of the Polychrome Bible, the Notes by translators in Kautzsch's *Altes Testament*, as well as those found in the Commentaries (especially the two recently completed series published under the editorship of Nowack and Marti, respectively, and the Old Testament volumes of the International Critical Commentary edited by Professors Briggs and Driver), and in many periodicals.

As to the arrangement of the work, the Editors decided at an early stage of their preparations to follow the *Thesaurus*, and the principal dictionaries of other Semitic languages, in classifying words according to their stems, and not to adopt the purely alphabetical order which has been common in Hebrew dictionaries. The relation of Semitic derivatives to the stems is such as to make this method of grouping them an obvious demand from the scientific point of view. It is true that practical objections to it may be offered, but these do not appear convincing. One is that it compels the editor to seem to decide, by placing each word under a given stem, some questions of etymology which in his own mind are still open. The number of such cases, however, is comparatively small, and the uncertainty can always be expressed by a word of caution. And even if the objection were much more important it would be better to assume the burden of it, in order to give students of Hebrew, from the outset, the immense advantage of familiarity with the structure and formative laws of the Hebrew vocabulary in their daily work. Another objection incidental to this arrangement is thought to be the increased difficulty of reference. This difficulty will diminish rapidly as students advance in knowledge, and by the practice of setting words formed by prefix or affix, — or otherwise hard for the beginner to trace, — a second time in their alphabetic place, with cross-references, it is hoped to do away with the difficulty almost entirely.

The Aramaic of the Bible has been separated from the Hebrew, and placed by itself at the end of the book, as a separate and subordinate element of the language of the Old Testament. This is a change from the older practice, which, since it was adopted here, has been made also by Siegfried and Stade, and by Buhl, and which the Editors believe will commend itself on grounds of evident propriety.

The question of adding an English-Hebrew Index has been carefully considered. With reluctance, it has been decided, for practical reasons, not to do so. The original limits proposed for the Lexicon have already been far exceeded, and the additional time, space and cost which an Index would require have presented a barrier which the Editors could not see their way to remove.

The work of preparing the Lexicon has been divided as follows: — the articles written by Professor Driver include all pronouns, prepositions, adverbs, conjunctions, interjections, and other particles, together with some nouns whose principal use (with or without a preposition) is adverbial; also some entire stems of which only one derivative is used adverbially; *e. g.*, I. בדד, בלה (not בְּלִיַּעַל), יחד, I. כלל, מאם, רגע; but in the case of יוֹמָם, נֶגֶד, סָבִיב, I. עֵבֶר, מַעַל and עַל (sub עלה), עִם, עַתָּה, יען (sub ענה), among others, Professor Driver's responsibility does not go beyond the particular words. Under פָּנֶה he is responsible for the treatment of פְּנֵי with prepositions prefixed. He has prepared a few other articles, as well; *e. g.*, אֱלִיל; II. בדד, הֶבֶל, תּוּשִׁיָּה ישה, תָּמִיד, מחר, מְעַט, תֹּהוּ.

In addition to articles for which he is exclusively responsible, he has read all the proofs, and made many suggestions.

The following articles have been prepared by Professor Briggs;[1] they are in the main terms important to Old Testament Religion, Theology and Psychology, and words related to these: —

אֲבַדּוֹן, אדן, I. אהל, אוב, II. אוה, I. אול, I. און, אור, אֵל, אֱלֹהִים, אֱלוֹהַּ, II. אלה, I. אמן, אפד, II. ארן, ארר, אִשָּׁה, אשם, אשר (but not אֲשֶׁר); באש, בָּגַד, I. בַּד, בוש, בחר, I. בטח, בין (not [בֵּ֫ין], בֵּין), בכר, בְּלִיַּעַל, בָּמָה, בעל בקש, I. ברא, בְּרִית, ברד, I. בַּר, ברר, בשׂר, בתל; גאה, I. גאל, גָּבֹהַּ, גבר, גדל, גלה, גָּמַל (not גָּמָל),

[1] Except where words are pointed, or special restrictions made, it is generally to be understood that Professor Briggs is responsible for all words belonging to the stem whose letters are given. Proper names, and much of the etymological material, especially in the last two thirds of the book, form a standing exception, nor is Professor Briggs responsible for any part of the Biblical Aramaic.

גער; דבר, דין; הוה (incl. יהוה); זבח, I. זור, זנה, I. זנח, זעם, זרק; חגג, חוס, I. חזה, חטא, חיה, חכם, III. חלל II. חלם, I. חנן (not חִנָּם), I. חסד, חסה, חפץ, חקק, חרה, I. חרם, I. חרף, חשב, חשֶׁן; טהר, טוב, טמא; I. יאל, ידה, יטב, יכח, יסר, יעד, יצר, ירא, ירה, ישע, ישר; כבד, כהן, כסה, כסל, כעס, I. כפר, כְּרוּב, כרע, כרת; לאך, לבב, ליץ, למד; I. מאס, מות, I. מחה, מִנְחָה, מעל, מַצָּה, מַצּוֹת, מרה, משח, I. משל; נאם, נבא, נדב, נדר, I. נחל, נחם, נסה, I. נסך, נפש, I. נצח, נצל, I. נצר, נקה, נקם; סוד, סֶלָה, סלח; עבד, עוּד, II. עוה, III. עול, עזז, עלה (not מַ֫עַל, עַל), עלם, עמל, III. ענה, ערל; I. פאר, פדה, פלא, פלל, I. פסח, פשע; צבא, צדק, צוה; קדש, קהל, I. קטר, II. קִינָה, קנא, I. קנה, קסם, I. קצף; רהב, רוח, רוע, I. רחם, I. רעע, רצה, רשע; שׂטן; שְׁאוֹל, שבת, שגג, שגה, שַׁדַּי, I. שָׁוְא, שוע, שחה, שיר, שכן, שלם, שפט, שקר, שרת; תמם, תעב, תעה.

Professor Brown is responsible for all articles and parts of articles not included in the above statements, as well as for the arrangement of the book and the general editorial oversight.

The work has consumed a much longer time than was anticipated at the outset. Twenty-three years have passed since it was undertaken, and nearly fifteen since the issue of the First Part, in June, 1891. Several causes have prevented an earlier completion of it. Not only have the Editors been engaged in the active duties of their professorships, to which they were obliged to subordinate even so important a work as this, but they have more than once encountered serious interruptions from unforeseen circumstances of a personal nature. But, above all, the task itself has proved a greater one than they supposed it to be. The field has been large, the questions have been many, and often difficult, the consideration of usage, involved, as it is, with that of textual change and of fresh proposals in exegesis, has required an enormous amount of time. The study of etymologies is involved with masses of new material, rapidly increasing and as yet imperfectly published and digested; the critical discussion of the many related topics is of great extent and scattered through many books and periodicals. Even tentative conclusions can be reached often only through a weighing of careful facts yielded by prolonged investigation. And so the process has gone on year after year. The Editors are quite aware that the patience of purchasers has been put to a severe test. They would be glad to think that they may find in the result a partial compensation.

They know, indeed, that this result is far from perfect. Their most earnest care has not been able to exclude errors, the First Part, in particular, was printed under unfavourable conditions, and the years since the earlier Parts were issued have brought new knowledge at many points. It was not possible, nor would it have been just to owners of these Parts, to make considerable changes in the plates. Such changes have been limited, almost wholly, to obvious misprints, and occasional errors in citation. A selected and restricted list of some of the more important '*Addenda et Corrigenda*' is appended to the volume. The Editors venture to hope that in the future they may be able to utilize the additional material which is now in their hands.

caus. = causative.
Cels$^{\text{Hierob.}}$ = O. Celsius, Hierobotanicon.
cf. = *confer*, compare.
1 Ch, 2 Ch = 1 & 2 Chronicles.
Champoll = J. F. Champollion.
Che = T. K. Cheyne. Che^{Founders} = *Id.*, Founders of Old Testament Criticism; Che$^{\text{(Heb.) Hpt}}$ = *Id.*, Isaiah, in Hpt.'s Sacred Books of the O. T. ('Polychrome Bible'), Eng. Trans., and Heb. Text; Che$^{\text{Intr. Is.}}$ = *Id.*, Introduction to Isaiah; Che^{OP} = *Id.*, Origin and Religious Contents of the Psalter.
ChGn = G. Smith's Chald. Genesis, Germ. ed.
Chron = Chronicles; also Chronicon (*e.g.*, Euseb$^{\text{Chron.}}$).
Chr-Pal. = Christian-Palestinian Aramaic.
ChWB = J. Levy, Chaldäisches Wörterbuch.
Cilic. = Cilician (Aramaic).
CIS = Corpus Inscript. Semiticarum.
ClGann = Clermont-Ganneau.
Co = C. H. Cornill.
coll. = collective.
Comm. = Commentary, Commentaries, Commentators.
comp. = compare, compares, comparative.
concr. = concrete.
conj. = conjecture(s); also conjunction.
consec. = consecutive.
constr. = construction.
contr. = contract, contracted.
Cook = Stanley A. Cook.
Cooke = G. A. Cooke.
COT = The Cuneiform Inscr. & the Old Test. (Eng. Trans. of KAT^{2}, by O. H. Whitehouse).
Cowley = A. E. Cowley.
cp. = compare.
cpd. = compound, compounded.
CR = Comptes Rendus.
cstr. = construct.
Ct = Canticles = Song of Solomon.
Cuche = *Id.*, Dictionnaire Arabe-Français.

D = Deuteronomist in Dt., in other books Deuteronomic author or redactor.
D (in BAram. Appendix) = G. Dalman, usu. *Id.*, Aramäisches-Neuhebräisches Wörterbuch; D§ = *Id.*, Grammatik des Jüdisch-Aramäischen (2nd ed., 1905).
Da = A. B. Davidson. Da$^{\text{Synt.}}$ = *Id.*, Hebrew Syntax.
Dalm = G. Dalman. Dalm^{WB} = *Id.*, Aramäisches-Neuhebräisches Wörterbuch.
Dan. = Daniel.
DB = Dictionary of the Bible, ed. J. Hastings.
De = Franz Delitzsch. De$^{\text{Compl. Var.}}$ = *Id.*, Complutensische Varianten zum alttestamentlichen Texte; De$^{\text{HL und Koheleth}}$ = *Id.*, Comm. über das Hohelied und Koheleth.
del. = *dele*, strike out (also *delet*, *delent*).
Derenb = (usu.) H. Derenbourg; sts. J. Derenbourg; Derenb^{Études} = *Id.*, Études sur l'Épigraphie du Yémen.
DeW = W. M. L. De Wette.
DHM = D. H. Müller. DHM^{BS} = *Id.*, Burgen u. Schlösser Süd-Arabiens; DHM$^{\text{Epigr. Denkm. (Ar., or aus Abess.)}}$ = *Id.*, Epigraphische Denkmäler, or Epigr. Denkm. aus Arabien, or Epigr. Denkm. aus Abessinien; DHM$^{\text{Hofmus.}}$ = *Id.*, Inschriften des Hofmuseums; DHM$^{\text{Sendsch.}}$ = *Id.*, Inschriften von Sendschirli; DHM$^{\text{Stud.}}$ = *Id.*, Südarabische Studien; DHM^{SMB} = *Id.*, Sab. Alterthümer in d. Kön. Museen zu Berlin.
Di = A. Dillmann.
Dict.Bib. = Smith, Dictionary of the Bible.
Dietr = F. E. C. Dietrich, esp. *Id.*, Abhandlungen für semit. Wortforschung.
Diod = Diodorus Siculus.
Dioscor = Dioscorides; Dioscor$^{\text{De Mater. Med.}}$ = *Id.*, De Materia Medica.
div. = *divinum, divinitatis.*
Dl = Friedrich Delitzsch. Dl§ = *Id.*, Assyrian Grammar; Dl^{H} = *Id.*, Hebrew & Assyrian; Dl^{HWB} = *Id.*, Assyrisches Handwörterbuch; Dl^{K} = *Id.*, Sprache d. Kossäer; Dl^{L} = *Id.*, Assyrische Lesestücke; Dl$^{\text{Pa(r)}}$ = *Id.*, Wo lag das Paradies? Dl$^{\text{Pr(ol)}}$ = *Id.*, Prolegomena; Dl^{S} = *Id.*, Assyrische Studien; Dl^{W} = *Id.*, Assyrisches Wörterbuch.
DLZ = Deutsche Literatur-Zeitung.
Dn = Daniel.
Door = A. van Doorninck.
Doughty$^{\text{Arab. Des.}}$ = C. M. Doughty, Travels in Arabia Deserta.
Dozy = R. Dozy, (usu.) Suppl. aux Dict. Arabes.
DPV = Deutscher Palästina-Verein.
Dr = S. R. Driver. Dr§ = *Id.*, Hebrew Tenses; Dr$^{\text{Intr.}}$ = *Id.*, Introduction to Literature of O. T.; Dr$^{\text{Psalt.}}$ = *Id.*, Psalter; Dr^{Sm}, or ^{Sam} = *Id.*, Text of Samuel.
Dr-Wh = Driver and White, Leviticus (Hpt.).
Dt = Deuteronomy.
Du = B. Duhm.
dub. = dubious, doubtful.
Dvd = David.
DWAk = Denkschriften der Wiener Akademie d. Wiss.
Dy = J. Dyserinck.

E = Elohist.
Eb = G. Ebers. Eb^{AgM} = *Id.*, Aegypten u. d. Bücher Mosis; Eb^{GS} = *Id.*, Durch Gosen zum Sinai.
EB(i) = Encyclopaedia Biblica, edd. Black and Cheyne.
Ec = Ecclesiastes.
Ecclus = Ecclesiasticus; Ecclus, Oxford ed., = Heb. Fragments of Ecclesiasticus, edd. Neubauer and Cowley.
Eg. = Egyptian.
elsewh. = elsewhere.
EMey = Eduard Meyer, EMey^{Entstehung} = *Id.*, Entstehung des Judenthums, = *Id.*, Entstehung J., etc.
Enc.Brit. = Encyclopaedia Brittanica, 9th ed.
Ency(cl).Bib. = EB(i), q. v.
Eng.Tr(ans). = English Translation.
Ephr. = Ephraimitic source.
Ephr(em) = Ephrem Syrus.
Esar. = Esarhaddon.
Esdr. = Esdras.
esp. = especially.
Est = Esther.
E.T. = Eng. Trans.
Eth. = Ethiopic.
Eut = J. Euting. Eut^{K} = *Id.*, Sammlung Karthag. Inschriften; Eut^{Nab} = *Id.*, Nabatäische Inschriften; Eut$^{\text{Sin.}}$ = *Id.*, Sinaitische Inschriften.
E.V. = English Version(s).
Ew = H. Ewald. Ew§ = *Id.*, Heb. Gram.; Ew$^{\text{G(esch.)}}$ = *Id.*, Geschichte d. Volkes Israel; Ew^{H} = *Id.*, History of Isr. (Eng. Trans. of Ew$^{\text{G(esch.)}}$); Ew^{JBW}, or Ew$^{\text{Jahrb.}}$ = *Id.*, Jahrb. d. bibl. Wissenschaft; Ew^{BTh} = *Id.*, Biblische Theologie; Ew^{Ant} = *Id.*, Antiquities.
Ex = Exodus.
exc. = except.
exil. = exile.
Ez = Ezekiel.
Ezr = Ezra.

f., *f.* = feminine.
f, or ff = and following.

A list of abbreviations was issued with Part I. This has been now revised and enlarged, and it is hoped that by its aid the abbreviations made necessary by the fulness of reference, on the one hand, and the requirements of space, on the other, will be quite intelligible.

Thanks are due to many scholars who have shown an interest in the work, and have contributed to its value by their suggestions. Prominent among these are Professor Hermann L. Strack, D. D., of Berlin, Professor George F. Moore, D. D., of Harvard University, and, for the Biblical Aramaic, Stanley A. Cook, Esq., of Cambridge, who has kindly read the proofs of the Aramaic Appendix, and made various additions and improvements. Dr. Eberhard Nestle, of Maulbronn, Professor Theodor Nöldeke, of Strassburg, Henry Preserved Smith, D. D., of Amherst, Mass., Thomas Kelly Cheyne, D. D., of Oxford, Richard J. H. Gottheil, Ph. D., of Columbia University, New York, A. F. Kirkpatrick, D. D., and William Emery Barnes, D. D., of Cambridge, T. W. Davies, of the University College of North Wales, and Max Margolis, of the University of California, as well as Mr. H. W. Sheppard, of Bromley, Kent, and others, have laid the Editors under obligation by sending important comments or lists of corrections. Any further communications which may advance the cause of Hebrew scholarship, and promote a more thorough comprehension of the Old Testament Scriptures by supplying material for a possible future edition of the Lexicon, will be cordially welcomed.

It is impossible to bring this Preface to a close without especial reference to the relations between the Editors and their Publishers, in America and in England. The new Hebrew lexicon owes its origin to Messrs. Houghton, Mifflin and Company, of Boston, Mass., holders of the copyright of 'Robinson's Gesenius,' and long its publishers. The present Editors were authorized by them to undertake the work as a revision of that book. The late Mr. Henry O. Houghton, senior member of the firm, gave the project his especial attention, devoting much time to personal conference with the American editors, and making a visit to Oxford for a discussion of the matter with Professor Driver, and with the Delegates of the Clarendon Press, whose coöperation he received. It is a matter of deep regret that his life was not spared to see the completion of an enterprise in which he took so sympathetic an interest. We desire to record our appreciation of that interest, and of the considerate patience with which he, and the other members of this publishing-house, both before and since his death, have met the delays in finishing the work.

We are under similar obligations to the Delegates of the Clarendon Press. Since assuming a share in this enterprise they have shown unfailing regard for it as a serious contribution to Hebrew learning. The Editors have many courtesies to acknowledge from successive Secretaries of the Clarendon Press, the late Master of Pembroke, Professor Bartholomew Price, D. D., P. Lyttleton Gell, Esq., and C. Cannan, Esq.

We desire to express our thanks to the printers, to whose painstaking care in the composition, — made complicated and difficult by the great variety of type, including half a dozen fonts of foreign characters, — in the correcting and in the press-work,

the excellent appearance of the page is due, to Horace Hart, M. A., under whose direction they have worked, and not least to J. C. Pembrey, M. A., chief Oriental proof-reader, whose sharp eye little escapes, and whose personal enthusiasm is always concentrated upon the book in hand.

The merits of the work — if it have them — are dependent to a large degree on the hearty coöperation of all these, whose service we gratefully acknowledge.

In thus sending out into the world a book to which have gone many years of life and much persistent effort, our most earnest wish is that it shall be of real use to students, as a key with which they may unlock for themselves the rich treasure-house of the Old Testament.

The Editors.

March, 1906.

ABBREVIATIONS

A = Alexandrine MS. of Septuagint.
ABA = Abhandlungen d. Berliner Akademie d. Wissenschaften.
abs. = absolute.
abstr. = abstract.
Abulf = Abulfeda.
Ac = Academy (London).
acc. = accusative (direct obj. etc.).
acc. cogn. = acc. of cognate meaning with verb.
acc. pers. = acc. of person.
acc. rei = acc. of thing.
acc. to = according to.
act. = active.
adj. = adjective.
adv. = adverb.
AE = Aben Ezra.
AGG = Abhandlungen d. Göttinger Gesellsch. d. Wissenschaften.
AGI = Assyrian & English Glossary, Johns Hopkins University.
AJPh = American Journal of Philology.
AJSL = American Journal of Semitic Languages.
Ak. = Akkadian.
al. = *et aliter*, and elsewhere; also *et alii*, and others.
Albr = K. Albrecht.
alttest(am). = alttestamentliche(r,s).
alw. = always.
Am = Amos.
Am.J.Sem.Lang. = AJSL, q. v.
AmRV = American RV.
Andr = Andreas. Andr^{M} = *Id.*, in Marti's Aram. Grammatik.
Aq = Aquila.
AR = Andover Review.
Ar. = Arabic.
Aram. = Aramaic, Aramaism.
Arch. = Archaeology.
ARSK = A. R. S. Kennedy.
As. = Assyrian.
Asrb. = Assurbanipal.
Asrn. = Assurnasirpal.
A.T. = Altes Testament.
Ath. = Athenaeum (London).
Av. = Avesta, Avestan.
AV = Authorized Version.
AW = Abu 'l Walid.
A&W = Abel & Winckler, Keilschrifttexte, Glossary.
ÄZ = Ägyptische Zeitschrift.

B = Vatican MS. of Septuagint.
Ba = J. Barth. Ba$^{\text{Erkl. d. Jes.}}$ = *Id.*, Erklärung des Jesaias; Ba^{ES} = *Id.*, Etymologische Studien; Ba^{NB} = *Id.*, Nominalbildung.
Bä = K. C. Bähr.
Bab. = Babylonian.
Bacher = W. Bacher. Bacher$^{\text{Terminol.}}$ = *Id.*, Älteste Terminologie der jüdischen Schriftauslegung.
Bachm = J. Bachmann.
Bäd = K. Bädeker. Bäd$^{\text{Eg.}}$ = Bädeker's Egypt; Bäd$^{\text{Pal.}}$ = Bädeker's Palestine.
Bae = F. Baethgen. Bae$^{\text{Rel.}}$, or Bae$^{\text{Sem. Rel.}}$ = Beiträge zur Semitischen Religionsgeschichte.
Baen = B. Baentsch.
Bähr = K. C. Bähr. Bähr$^{\text{Symb.}}$ = Bähr, Symbolik des Mosaischen Cultus.
BAL = C. Bezold, Babylonisch-Assyrische Literatur.
B.Aram. = Biblical Aramaic.
BarHeb(r) = Bar Hebraeus.
BAS = Beiträge zur Assyriologie u. Semit. Sprachwissenschaft, edd. Dl. & Hpt.
Bau(d) = W. von Baudissin. Bau^{Rel} = *Id.*, Studien zur Semitischen Religionsgeschichte; Bau$^{\text{Priest.}}$ = *Id.*, Geschichte des Alttestamentlichen Priesterthums.
Bd. = Bäd, q. v.
BD = Baer & Delitzsch, Heb. Text.
Be = E. Bertheau.
beg. = beginning.
Behrm = G. Behrmann.
Belsh. = Belshazzar.
Benn = W. H. Bennett.
Benz = J. Benzinger. Benz$^{\text{Arch.}}$ = *Id.*, Hebräische Archaeologie.
Berggren = J. Berggren, Guide Français-Arabe Vulgaire.
Berliner$^{\text{T.Onk.}}$ = A. Berliner, Targum of Onkelos.
Berthol = A. Bertholet.
BeRy = Bertheau's Comm., ed. by Ryssel.
Bev = A. A. Bevan.
Bez = C. Bezold.
BH = Biblical Hebrew.

Bi = G. Bickell.
Bl = F. Bleek.
Bla = J. S. Black.
Bloch$^{\text{(Gl.)}}$ = A. Bloch, Phönizisches Glossar.
Bmg = A. J. Baumgartner.
Bo = S. Bochart. Bo$^{\text{Hieroz.}}$ = *Id.*, Hierozoicon.
Bö = F. Böttcher. Bö$^{\text{§}}$, or Bö$^{\text{i, ii}}$ = *Id.*, Lehrbuch d. Hebr. Sprache; Bö$^{\text{Ä, or NÄ.}}$ = *Id.*, Ährenlese, or Neue Ährenlese; Bö$^{\text{Inf.}}$ = *Id.*, De Inferis; Bö$^{\text{Prob.}}$ = *Id.*, Proben alttest. Schrifterklärung.
Bondi = J. H. Bondi, Hebr. Lehnwörter in Hieroglyphischen .... Texten.
BOR = Babylonian & Oriental Record.
Br = C. A. Briggs. Br$^{\text{Gen. Intr.}}$ = *Id.*, General Introduction to the Study of Holy Scripture; Br$^{\text{Hex.}}$ = *Id.*, Higher Criticism of the Hexateuch; Br^{MP} = *Id.*, Messianic Prophecy.
Braun$^{\text{de Vest. Sacerd.}}$ = J. Braunius, Vestitus Sacerdotum Hebraeorum.
Brd = C. Bredenkamp.
Brock = C. Brockelmann, esp. *Id.*, Lexicon Syriacum.
Bu = K. Budde. Bu^{RS} = *Id.*, Richter u. Samuel; Bu$^{\text{Urg.}}$ = *Id.*, Die biblische Urgeschichte.
Buhl = Frants Buhl, esp. as editor of eds.$^{\text{12-14}}$ of Gesenius's Handwörterbuch über das A. T.; Buhl$^{\text{G(eogr.)}}$ = *Id.*, Geographie des Alten Palästina; Buhl$^{\text{Edom.}}$ = *Id.*, Geschichte der Edomiter.
Bur = C. F. Burney.
Burckh = J. L. Burckhardt, esp. *Id.*, Travels in Syria, etc.
Bux = J. Buxtorf.
Bz = C. Bezold.

c. = *circa*, about; also *cum*, with.
Ca = C. P. Caspari.
Calv = John Calvin.
Cappad. = Cappadocia.
Castell = Edward Castell.
Castle = Castell.

F.B. = F. Brown.

fem. = feminine, *feminae*.

FFP = Flora and Fauna of Palestine (Survey).

Fi = Frederick Field, esp. *Id.*, Origenis Hexaplorum quae supersunt.

fig. = figurative.

fin. = finite, finitivum.

FJB = F. J. Bliss.

Fl = H. L. Fleischer. Fl$^{\text{Kl. Schr.}}$ *Id.*, Kleine Schriften.

Flora = Post, Flora of Syria.

fr. = from.

Fr = S. Frensdorff. Fr^{MM} = *Id.*, Massora Magna.

Frä = S. Fränkel, and (usu.) *Id.*, Aramäische Fremdwörter im Arabischen.

Frankenb(erg) = W. Frankenberg. Frankenb^{Spr} = *Id.*, Comm. Sprüche (ed. Nowack).

Frey = G. W. Freytag, Lex. Arab.; Frey$^{\text{Prov. Ar.}}$, or $^{\text{Prov.}}$ = *Id.*, Arabum Proverbia.

fs. = feminine singular.

Fü = J. Fürst.

𝔊 = Greek Version of the LXX. 𝔊L = LXX of Lucian (Lag).

GACooke = (usu.) G. A. Cooke, North Semitic Inscriptions; = GACooke$^{\text{Inscr.}}$

Gal. = Galilee.

Gann = Clermont-Ganneau.

GASm = George Adam Smith. GA Sm$^{\text{G(eogr.)}}$ = *Id.*, Historical Geography of the Holy Land.

Gei = A. Geiger. Gei$^{\text{Urschr.}}$ = *Id.*, Urschrift u. Übersetzungen der Bibel; Gei $^{\text{Nachgel. Schr.}}$ = *Id.*, Nachgelassene Schriften.

gent. = *gentis*, of a people, *gentilicium*.

geogr. = geography.

Gerber $^{\text{(Verb. Denom.)}}$ = W. T. Gerber, Verba Denominativa.

Ges = W. Gesenius. Ges§ = *Id.*, Heb. Gram. ed. by Kautzsch; Ges^{Lbg} = *Id.*, Lehrgebäude d. Heb. Sprache.

Gesch. = Geschichte.

Gf = K. H. Graf.

GFM = G. F. Moore.

GGA = Göttingsche Gelehrte Anzeigen.

GGAbh. = Gött. Gel. Abhandlungen.

GGN = Gött. Nachrichten.

Gie = F. Giesebrecht.

Gi(nsb) = C. D. Ginsburg.

Gl(as) = E. Glaser; Gl^{MSI} = *Id.*, Mittheilungen über Sab. Inschriften; Gl^{Skizze} = *Id.*, Skizze der Geschichte u. Geographie Arabiens.

Gloss., gl. = glossary, rarely = a gloss.

Gn = Genesis.

Gr = H. Grätz.

Gray = G. B. Gray. Gray$^{\text{Prop. N.}}$ = *Id.*, Hebrew Proper Names.

Gu = H. Guthe, rarely Stan. Guyard. Gu§ = Guyard, Notes de lexicogr. assyrienne.

Guérin = V. Guérin, Description géographique de la Palestine.

Guidi = Ignazio Guidi; Guidi$^{\text{Della Sede}}$ = *Id.*, Della Sede Primitiva dei Popoli Semitici.

Gunk = H. Gunkel. Gunk$^{\text{Schöpf.}}$ = *Id.*, Schöpfung u. Chaos.

Guy = Stan. Guyard.

𝔥 = Hebrew (Consonantal Text).

H = Code of Holiness.

Haev = Haevernick.

Hal = J. Halévy. Hal^{M} = *Id.*, Mélanges; Hal^{DR} = *Id.*, Documents Religieux; Hal^{MA} = *Id.*, Mission Archéol. dans le Yémen; Hal^{ÉS}, or $^{\text{Et. Sab.}}$ = *Id.*, Études Sabéennes.

Ḥamm = Ḥammurabi, esp. *Id.*, Code of Laws.

Hartm$^{\text{Plurilit.-bildungen}}$ = M. Hartmann, Pluriliteralbildungen in den semitischen Sprachen.

Hast = James Hastings. Hast(ings) ^{DB}, or $^{\text{Dict. Bib.}}$ = Dictionary of the Bible, ed. James Hastings.

Hb = Habakkuk.

Hbr = Hebraica.

HDerenb = H. Derenbourg.

Heb. = Hebrew.

He(ngst) = E. Hengstenberg.

Herod(ot.) = Herodotus.

Hex = Hexateuch.

Hg = Haggai.

Hi = F. Hitzig.

Hilg = A. Hilgenfeld.

Hilpr = H. V. Hilprecht.

Hirz = L. Hirzel.

Ho = Hosea.

Hoffm = G. Hoffmann.

Hollenb = W. A. Hollenberg.

Holz = H. Holzinger.

Hom = F. Hommel. Hom^{AA}, or $^{\text{A. u. A}}$, or ^{Aufsätze} = *Id.*, Aufsätze u. Abhandlungen; Hom^{Chr}, or $^{\text{Chrest(om.)}}$, or $^{\text{Südar. Chrest.}}$ = *Id.*, Südarabische Chrestomathie; Hom^{NS} = *Id.*, Namen der Säugethiere.

Houb = C. F. Houbigant.

HP = Holmes & Parsons, Septuagint.

HPS = H. P. Smith.

Hpt = Paul Haupt. Hpt^{C} = *Id.*, Akkadische Sprache; Hpt^{D} = *Id.*, Über einen Dialekt der Sumerischen Sprache [GGN. 1880, Nr. 17]; Hpt^{E} = *Id.*, E. vowel; Hpt^{F} = *Id.*, Sumer. Familiengesetze; Hpt^{L} = *Id.*, Beiträge z. Ass. Lautlehre; Hpt^{N} = *Id.*, Nimrodepos; Hpt$^{\text{Prol. As. Gr.}}$ = *Id.*, Prolegomena to an Assyrian Grammar; Hpt^{S} = *Id.*, Sintfluthbericht; Hpt^{T} = *Id.*, ASKT, Akkad. & Sum. Keilschrifttexte; Hpt, or ^{Hpt} (Che^{Hpt}, &c.) usu. = Sacred Books of the O. T, ed. Hpt (Polychrome Bible).

HSch = H. Schultz.

Hultsch = F. Hultsch, Griechische u. Römische Metrologie.

Hup = H. Hupfeld. Hup^{Ri}, Hup^{RiNow}, Hup-Now = *Id.*, Psalmen, edd. Riehm, Nowack.

Idiot. = Idioticon.

Impf. = Imperfect.

Imv. = Imperative.

ind. = indirect.

indef. = indefinite.

Inf. = Infinitive.

infr., *infr.* = *infra*, below.

Inschr. = Inschrift, Inschriften.

inscr. = inscription(s); Inscr. of Carpentr. = Inscription of Carpentras.

intr(ans). = intransitive.

i.q. = *id quod*, i. e. the same with.

Is = Isaiah.

J = Jehovist.

JA = Journ. of the Royal Asiatic Society.

Jacob = G. Jacob. Jacob$^{\text{Ar(ab.) Dichter}}$ = *Id.*, Studien in Arab. Dichtern; *Id.*$^{\text{Bed. Leben}}$ = *Id.*, Leben der vorislamischen Beduinen.

J. Aram. = Jewish-Aramaic (Jüdisch-Aramäisch).

JAs = Journal Asiatique.

Jastr = Marcus Jastrow, Dict. of Targumim, Talmud, etc.; also Morris Jastrow, Jr.; Jastr$^{\text{Rel. Bab.}}$ = M. Jastrow, Jr., Religion of Babylonia and Assyria.

J$^{\text{AT. im Licht d. AO}}$ = A. Jeremias, Das Alte Testament im Licht des Alten Orients.

Jb = Job.

JBL = Journal of Biblical Literature.

JBTh = Jahrbücher f. deutsche Theologie.

JDMich = J. D. Michaelis.

Je = Jeremiah.

Jen = P. Jensen. Jen$^{\text{Cosmol.}}$ = *Id.*, Cosmologie der Babylonier.

Jer = Jerome; also Jerusalem.

Jerem = A. Jeremias.

Jerus. = Jerusalem.

Jes = Jesaias.

JHC = Johns Hopkins Univ. Circulars.

JHMich = J. H. Michaelis.
JLZ = Jenaer Lit.-Zeitung.
Jo = Joel.
Jon = Jonah.
Jos = Joshua.
Jos^{Ant}, Jos^{BJ} = Fl. Josephus, Antiquities, or Bell. Jud.
Joseph = Fl. Josephus (sts.).
JosKi = Joseph Kimchi.
JPh(il). = Journal of Philology (Engl.).
JPTh = Jahrbücher für Prot. Theol.
JQ = Jewish Quarterly.
Jr = A. Jeremias, Leben nach dem Tode.
JThS = Journal of Theological Studies.
Ju = Judges.
Jud. = Judæa, Judæan.
Jüd. Zeitschr. = Monatsschrift für Gesch. u. Wiss. des Judenthums.
juss. = jussive.

K = E. Kautzsch (in B. Aram. Appendix). K$^{\text{§}}$ = *Id.*, Gramm. d. bibl. Aram.; K$^{\text{Aram.}}$ = *Id.*, Aramaismen im A.T.
1K, 2K = 1 & 2 Kings.
Ḳam. = al-Ḳamus (Arab. Dict.), by al-Fīrūzābādī.
KAT^{2} = E. Schrader, Keilinschr. u. d. Alte Testament. KAT^{3} = *Id.*, 3rd ed. by H. Winckler and H. Zimmern.
Kau = E. Kautzsch; Kau$^{\text{§}}$ = *Id.*, Gram. d. bibl. Aram.; Kau$^{\text{Aram(aismen) (im AT)}}$ = K $^{\text{Aram.}}$; Kau^{AT} = Die Heiligen Schriften d. Alten Testaments, ed. Kau.; Kau^{MN} = *Id.*, Mittheilungen u. Nachrichten d. DPV, 1904; ^{Kau} (So^{Kau}, etc.) = Kau^{AT}.
Kay = W. Kay.
KB = E. Schrader, Keilinschriftl. Bibliothek.
Ke = C. F. Keil.
Kenn = B. Kennicott.
Kennedy = (usu.) A. R. S. Kennedy.
KG = E. Schrader, Die Keilinschr. und die Geschichtsforschung.
kg. = king.
Kgs. = Kings.
Ki = David Kimchi (Qamchi).
Kiep(ert) = H. Kiepert.
Kirkp = A. F. Kirkpatrick.
Kit = R. Kittel. Kit^{Di} = Di, Jesaia, ed. Kit; Kit$^{\text{Gesch. (or Hist.)}}$ = Kit, Geschichte der Hebräer (or Eng. Trans.).
Kit-Di = Kit^{Di} = Dillmann's Comm. (Isaiah), ed. by Kit.
Klo = A. Klostermann. Kl^{S} = Die Bücher Sam. u. d. Könige.
Kmp = A. Kamphausen.
Kn = A. Knobel.
Knudtzon$^{\text{Ass. Gebete}}$ = J. A. Knudtzon, Assyrische Gebete an den Sonnengott.
Kö = E. König. Kö$^{\text{i, ii, iii}}$ = *Id.*, Heb. Gram.; Kö$^{\text{Synt.}}$ = Kö^{iii}; Kö$^{\text{§}}$ = *Id.*, Heb. Gram.; Kö$^{\text{Einl.}}$ = *Id.*, Einleitung in d. A.T.
Köh = A. Köhler.
Kohut-Memorial = Studies in Memory of A. Kohut; Kohut-Studies = *id.*
Kosters^{Herstel} = W. H. Kosters, Het Herstel van Israël in het Perzische Tijdvak.
Kp = A. F. Kirkpatrick.
Krae = R. Kraetzschmar.
Krauss = S. Krauss, esp. *Id.*, Griechische und Lateinische Lehnwörter im Talmud, etc.
Kremer = A. Kremer. Kremer$^{\text{Beitr.}}$ = *Id.*, Beiträge.
Krochm = A. Krochmal.
KSGW = Königl. Sächs. Ak. d. Wiss.
Kt = K^{e}thibh.
Kue = A. Kuenen. Kue$^{\text{Ges. Abh.}}$ = *Id.*, Gesammelte Abhandlungen.

La = Lamentations.
Lag = P. de Lagarde. Lag$^{\text{Agathang.}}$ = *Id.*, Agathangelus; Lag$^{\text{Arm. Stud.}}$, or ^{AS} = *Id.*, Armenische Studien; Lag ^{BN} = *Id.*, Bildung d. Nomina; Lag^{M}, or $^{\text{Mitth.}}$ = *Id.*, Mittheilungen; Lag$^{\text{Novi Psalt. spec.}}$ = *Id.*, Novi Psalterii Specim.; Lag$^{\text{Onom.}}$ = *Id.*, Onomastica Sacra; Lag^{Or} = *Id.*, Orientalia; Lag$^{\text{Pers. Stud.}}$ = *Id.*, Persische Studien; Lag^{Se} = *Id.*, Semitica; Lag^{Sy}, or $^{\text{Sym(m.)}}$ = *Id.*, Symmicta.
Landberg = C. Landberg. Landberg$^{\text{Prov.}}$ = *Id.*, Proverbes et Dictons.
Lane = E. W. Lane; usu. *Id.*, Arabic Dictionary. Lane$^{\text{(Mod.) Egypt.}}$ = *Id.*, Modern Egyptians.
Lay = A. H. Layard.
l.c. = *in loco citato.*
LCB = Litterarisches Centralblatt.
Ldzb = M. Lidzbarski; usu. *Id.*, Nordsemitische Inschriften.
Len = F. Lenormant. Len^{Beginnings} = *Id.*, Beginnings of History (Eng. Trans. of Origines de l'Histoire, I). Len$^{\text{Or(ig.)}}$ = *Id.*, Les Origines de l'Histoire.
(v.)Leng = C. von Lengerke.
Levy = Jacob Levy.
Lewy$^{\text{(Sem.) Fremdw(örter)}}$ = H. Lewy, Semitische Fremdwörter im Griechischen.
Liḥy. = Liḥyanian (language).
Lindberg$^{\text{Vergl. Sem. Gram.}}$ = Lindberg, Vergleichende semitische Grammatik.
Linn = C. Linnaeus (Carl von Linné).
Littm = Enno Littmann.
Lo = R. Lowth.
loc. = local, locality.
Loft = W. K. Loftus, esp. Loft^{CS} = *Id.*, Chaldaea and Susiana.
LOPh = Literaturblatt für Orientalische Philologie.
Löw = J. Löw, Aramäische Pflanzennamen.
Lu = Martin Luther.
Luz(z) = S. D. Luzzatto.
Lv = Leviticus.
Lyon = D. G. Lyon.
Lzb = M. Lidzbarski (v. Ldzb.). Lzb$^{\text{Eph(em).}}$ = *Id.*, Ephemeris für semitische Epigraphik.

M, M$^{\text{§}}$ = (in BAram. Appendix) K. Marti, Gram. d. bibl. Aram.
m., *m.* = masculine.
M-A = W. Muss-Arnolt. M-A^{CD} = *Id.*, Compendious Assyr. Dict.
Mal = Malachi.
Mand. = Mandean.
Marquart = J. Marquart. Marquart *Id.*, ^{Fundamente} = *Id.*, Fundamente israelitischer u. jüdischer Geschichte.
Marti = K. Marti.
Mas(s) = Masora.
MBAk = Monatsbericht d. Berliner Akad. d. Wissenschaften.
MDPV = Mittheilungen d. Deutschen Palästina-Vereins.
Me = A. Merx.
Meier^{WurzelWB} = E. Meier, Hebräisches Wurzelwörterbuch.
Meinh = J. Meinhold.
Meissn = B. Meissner. Meissn$^{\text{Suppl.}}$ = *Id.*, Supplement zum Assyr. Wörterb.
Mem. = Survey of W. Palestine, Memoirs.
metaph. = metaphor, metaphorically.
Mey = E. Meyer. Mey$^{\text{E. Jud.}}$, or ^{Entstehung}, or $^{\text{Enst. J.}}$, or $^{\text{Entstehung d. Jud.}}$, or $^{\text{Judenth(um)}}$ = *Id.*, Die Entstehung des Judenthums.
MGWJ = Monatsschr., q.v.
MI = Mesha-Inscription.
Mi = Micah.
Mich = J. D. Michaelis.
Min. = Minaean.
Mish(n). = Mishna.
mng. = meaning.
Mo = F. E. Movers.
Monatsschr. = Monatsschrift für Geschichte u. Wissen. d. Judenthums.
Mordt(m) = J. H. Mordtmann. Mordtm$^{\text{Him. Inschr.}}$ = *Id.*, Himjarische Inschriften.
mpl. = masculine plural.

ms. = masculine singular.
MT = Massoretic Text.
Müll = A. Müller.
Muss-Arn = W. Muss-Arnolt.
MV$^{11 (10,9,8)}$ = Gesenius, Handwörterbuch über das A.T., edd. F. Mühlau & W. Volck.
MVAG, or MVG = Mittheilungen d. Vorderasiatischen Gesellschaft.

n. = *nomen*, noun.
Na = Nahum.
Nab. = Nabataean.
Näg = C. W. E. Nägelsbach.
Nasar = Lexid. cod. Nasaraei, ed. M. Norberg.
NBab. = New Babylonian.
Nbr = A. Neubauer.
Ne = Nehemiah (rarely = E. Nestle).
Neb = Nebuchadnezzar.
Nes = E. Nestle. Nes§ = *Id.*, Syriac Gram.; Nes^{Eg} = Eigennamen; Nes$^{Marg.}$ = *Id.*, Marginalien u. Materialien.
NH = New (Late) Hebrew.
NHWB = Levy, Neuhebr. Wörterb.
NKZ = Neue kirchliche Zeitschrift.
Nö = T. Nöldeke. Nö§ = *Id.*, Syrische Grammatik; Nö$^{Beitr(äge)}$, or ^{BSW} = *Id.*, Beiträge z. semitischen Sprachwissenschaft; Nö^{M} = *Id.*, Mandäische Grammatik; Nö^{NS} = *Id.*, Neu-Syrische Grammatik; Nö$^{Untersuch.}$ = *Id.*, Untersuchungen zur Kritik des A.T.; Nö $^{Zur\ Gram.\ d.\ class.\ Ar.}$ = *Id.*, Zur Grammatik des classischen Arab. (in Denkschriften der Wiener Akademie, 1896).
no. = number.
nom. = *nomen*, noun.
nom. coll = *nom. collectivum*, collective noun.
nom. unit = *nom. unitatis*, noun of singular or individual meaning.
Nor = E. Norris, Assyrian Dictionary.
Norberg$^{Lexid.}$ = Nasar, q.v.
Norzi = J. S. ben Abraham Norzi.
Now = W. Nowack. Now$^{Arch.}$ = *Id.*, Hebräische Archäologie.
n.pr. = *nomen proprium*, proper name.
n.pr.loc. = *n. pr. loci*, proper name of place.
Nu = Numbers.

Ob = Obadiah.
obj. = object.
OBaktr. = Old Baktrian.
Oehl = Oehler.
oft. = often.
OH = Old Hebrew (Inscriptions).
OIran. = Old Iranian.
Ol = J. Olshausen. Ol§ = *Id.*, Heb. Gram.
OLZ = Orientalische Literaturzeitung.
Onk = Targum of Onkelos.
Oort = H. Oort.
op. cit. = *in opere citato*.
OP(ers.) = Old Persian. OP also (in Che^{OP}) = Origin of Psalter.
opp. = opposite, as opposed to, or contrasted with.
Opp(ert) = Jules Oppert.
Or(elli) = C. von Orelli.
Os = E. Osiander.
OT = Old Testament.
Öt = S. Öttli.

P = Priests' Code or Narrative.
Pal(est). = Palestine, Palestinian, etc.
Pal(m). = Palmyrene.
PAOS = Proceedings of the American Oriental Society.
Pap. = Papyrus.
part. = particle.
pass. = passive.
PB = Proceedings of Soc. of Bib. Archaeol.
Pe = J. J. S. Perowne.
PEF = Pal. Explor. Fund, usu. *Id.*, Quart. Statem'nt. PEF $^{Mem.}$ = Mem., q.v.
Pei = F. E. Peiser.
Perles = F. Perles. Perles$^{(Anal.)}$ = *Id.*, Analekten.
pers. = person, *personae*.
Pers. = Persian.
PESoc = American Palestine Explor. Society.
Pf. = Perfect.
Ph. = Phenician.
Phi = F. Philippi.
Pietschm = R. Pietschmann (also Pietschm$^{Phön(iz.)}$, or $^{Gesch.\ Ph.}$) = (usu.) *Id.*, Geschichte Phöniziens.
Pinsk = S. Pinsker.
pl. = plural.
Plin^{HN} = Pliny, Hist. Nat.
POS = Proceedings Am. Orient. Soc.
Post = G. E. Post. Post^{Flora} = *Id.*, Flora of Syria.
postB = post-Biblical.
postex = post-exilic.
post-pos. = post-positive.
Pr = Proverbs.
Prä(t) = F. Prätorius. Prä$^{Amh.\ Spr.}$ *Id.*, Amharische Sprache; Prä(t)$^{Neue\ Beiträge}$ = *Id.*, Neue Beiträge zur Erklärung der Himjarischen Inschriften.
PRE = Herzog's Prot. Real-Encycl.
Presb.Rev. = Presbyterian Review (New York).
Prol = Prolegomena.
PS = R. Payne Smith, Thesaurus Syriacus.
Ps = Psalms, Psalmen.
Ps.-J = Targum of Pseudo-Jonathan.
ψ = Psalm.
pt(cp). = participle.
Ptol = Ptolemy (usu. Claudius Ptolemy).
punct. = punctuation.

Qor = Qoran.
Qr = Q^{e}rê.
qu. = question.
q.v. = *quod vide*.
qy. = query.

R = Redactor (e.g. in Hexateuch). R^{D} = Deuteronomic redactor.
1 R, 2 R, 3 R, 4 R, 5 R = Cuneiform Inscr. of Western Asia (H. Rawlinson).
RA = Revue Archéologique.
Ra = Rashi.
rd. = read.
rdg. = reading.
Rd'A = Revue d'Assyriologie.
Re = E. Renan.
Reckend = S. Reckendorf.
refl. = reflexive.
RÉJ = Revue des Études Juives.
Rel = H. Reland.
RÉS = Répertoire d'Épigraphie Sémitique.
Rev.Bib. = Revue Biblique.
Ri = E. Riehm. Ri^{HWB} = Handwörterb. d. bibl. Alterth.
Rö = E. Rödiger.
Rob = E. Robinson. Rob^{BR} = *Id.*, Biblical Researches.
Rob-Ges. = Gesenius, Hebrew and English Lexicon, translated by E. Robinson.
Roo = T. Roorda.
Rosenm = E. F. C. Rosenmüller.
Rothst = W. Rothstein.
RP$^{2(1)}$ = Records of Past, 2nd (1st) Series.
RS = W. Robertson Smith. RS ^{OTJC} = *Id.*, Old Testament in Jewish Church; RS $^{Proph.}$ = *Id.*, Prophets of Israel; RS^{K} = *Id.*, Kinship & Marriage in Early Arabia; RS^{Sem} = *Id.*, Religion of Semites.
RTr = Recueil de Travaux.
Ru = Ruth.
RV = Revised Version.
RVm = Revised Version margin.
RWB = Bibl. Realwörterbuch, ed. Winer.
Ry = V. Ryssel.

𝔖 = Syriac Version. 𝔖^{Jerus} = Chr-Pal. Evang. (Lagarde).
1 S, 2 S = 1 & 2 Samuel.
Saad = Arabic Version of Saadya.
Sab. = Sabean.
SabDenkm = Sabäische Denkmäler, edd. Mordtmann & Müller.
SAC = Stanley A. Cook; esp. *Id.*, Aramaic Glossary.
Sam. = Samaria, Samaritan (rarely = Samuel).
Sarg = Sargon.

SahoSpr. = Saho Sprache.
SASm = S. A. Smith.
Say = A. H. Sayce. Say^{Monuments} = *Id.*, Higher Criticism and the Monuments; Say $^{\text{Rel. Bab.}}$ = *Id.*, Religion of Babylonia.
SB = SBAk.
SBAk = Sitzungsbericht d. Berl. Akademie der Wissenschaften.
S-C$^{\text{Pap.}}$ = A. H. Sayce and A. E. Cowley, Aram. Papyri.
Sch = F. W. Schultz.
Scheft = Scheftelowitz, usu. = Scheft, Arisches im A.T.; Scheft ^{MGWJ} = *Id.*, Monatsschrift für Gesch. u. Wiss. d. Jud. (1903); also pub. separately (Scheft^{ii}).
Schenkel^{BL} = D. Schenkel, Bibel-Lexicon.
Schl(ottm) = C. Schlottmann.
Schr = E. Schrader.
Schröd, Schroed = P. Schröder, esp. *Id.*, Phönizische Sprache.
Schu = A. Schultens.
Schü = E. Schürer, Gesch. des jüdischen Volkes im Zeitalter Jesu Christi.
Schulth = F. Schulthess. Schulth $^{\text{Hom. Wurz.}}$ = *Id.*, Homonymische Wurzeln im Syrischen; Schulth$^{\text{Lex.}}$ = *Id.*, Lexicon d. Chr. Pal. Aramäischen.
Schw = F. Schwally. Schw(ally)$^{\text{Idiot.}}$ = *Id.*, Idioticon d. Chr. Pal.
Seetzen^{Reise} = Seetzen, Reisen durch Syrien.
seld. = seldom, rare.
Sen = Sennacherib.
Sendsch. = Sendschirli (Zinjirli).
sf. = suffix, *or* with suffix.
sg. = singular.
Shlm = Shalmaneser II.
SI = Siloam Inscription.
si vera l. = *si vera lectio.*
Siegf = C. Siegfried.
sim. = simile.
SK = Studien u. Kritiken.
Skr. = Sanskrit.
Sm = R. Smend (rarely = Samuel). Sm$^{\text{Rel. Gesch.}}$ = Smend, Alttestamentliche Religionsgeschichte; Sm^{Listen} = *Id.*, Listen der Bücher Esra u. Nehemia.
So(c) = A. Socin.
Spi = W. Spitta. Spi§ = Gram. d. arab. Vulg. Dial.
Spieg = F. Spiegel; Spieg^{APK} = *Id.*, Altpersische Keilinschriften.
Spiegelb = W. Spiegelberg.
Spr = Sprache, or Sprüche.
sq. = followed by.
SS = C. Siegfried u. B. Stade, Hebräisches Wörterbuch.
st. = *status*, state, stative.
St = H. Steiner.
Sta = B. Stade; Sta§ = *Id.*, Heb. Gram.; Sta$^{\text{G(esch.)}}$ = *Id.*, Geschichte des Volkes Israel.
Steind = G. Steindorff.
Steuern = C. Steuernagel.
Str = H. L. Strack. Str§ = *Id.*, Gram. d. bibl. Aram.
Strassm = foll.
Strm = J. Strassmaier. Strm^{AV} = *Id.*, Alphabet. Verzeichniss.
sts. = sometimes.
Stu = G. Studer.
Stud. Bib. = Studia Biblica.
subst. = substantive.
Sum(er). = Sumerian.
supr., *supr.* = *supra*, above.
Surenh = W. Surenhusius, Mishna.
Survey, Survey^{WP} = Survey of Western Palestine (PEF); Survey^{EP} = *Id.* of Eastern Palestine.
Symm = Symmachus.
Syr. = Syriac.

𝔗 = Targum.
t. (following a number) = times.
TA = Tel el-Amarna; also Taj-al-'Arūs (Arab. Dict.).
Talm = Talmud.
Tariff = Palmyrene Tariff Inscription.
TB, TBA = Transactions of the Society of Biblical Archaeology.
TelAm. = TA, q.v.
Tg = Targum Tg^{Jer} = Targum of Jerusalem, etc.
Th(e) = O. Thenius.
Theod = Theodotion.
Theophr = Theophrastus; Theophr $^{\text{Hist. Plant.}}$ = *Id.*, Historia de Plantis.
Thes = W. Gesenius, Thesaurus Linguae Hebraeae.
Thes$^{\text{Add.}}$ = *Id.*, Additions by E. Rödiger.
ThT = Theologisch Tijdschrift.
ThLB = Theol. Literaturblatt.
ThLZ = Theol. Literaturzeitung.
Tiele = C. P. Tiele.
Tiph. = Tiphel (rare conjugation).
To = Tobler.
TP = Tiglath-Pileser.
Tpg. = Topography.
Tr = Transactions.
tr. = translate (translated, translation); rarely = transitive.
trans(it). = transitive.
Tristr = H. B. Tristram. Tristr^{NHB} = *Id.*, Natural History of the Bible; Tristr^{FFP} = *Id.*, Fauna and Flora of Palestine (Survey, Memoirs).
TSBA = TB, q. v.
TSWt = Theol. Studien aus Württemberg.
TTijdschr = ThT, q. v.
Tu = F. Tuch.
txt. = text.
txt.err. = textual error.
Univ.Pa.Exp. = Bab. Exped. of the Univ. of Pennsylvania.
usu. = usual, usually.

𝔙 = Vulgate.
v = verse; v. = *vide*, see.
van d. H. = E. van der Hooght, Heb. text of O.T.
var. = variant reading.
VB = Variorum Bible.
vb. = verb.
vdVelde = C. W. M. van de Velde, esp. *Id.*, Reis door Syrie en Palestina; E. T., Narrative of a Journey through Syria and Palestine; vdVelde$^{\text{Mem(oir)}}$ = *Id.*, Memoir to accompany Map of Holy Land constructed by C. W. M. van de Velde.
vid. = *vide*, see.
vir. = *viri*, of a man.
Vog = C. J. M. de Vogüé, Syrie Centrale. Vog$^{\text{Palm.}}$ = *Id.*
Vogelst$^{\text{Landwirthsch.}}$ = H. Vogelstein, Landwirthschaft in Palästina zur Zeit der Mišnâh.
VOJ = Vienna Oriental Journal (= Wiener Zeitschrift für die Kunde des Morgenlandes).
Vrss = Old Versions.
Vulg.Ar. = Vulgar Arabic.
Vullers = J. A. Vullers, Lexicon Persico-Latinum.

W = W. Wright. W^{AG} = *Id.*, Arabic Gram.; W^{SG}, or ^{CG} = *Id.*, Comp. Semit. Gram.
Wahrm = A. Wahrmund, esp. *Id.*, Arab. Handwörterbuch.
WAW = W. Aldis Wright.
wd. = word, also would.
We = J. Wellhausen. We$^{\text{Bl. Einl.}}$ = *Id.*, Bleek's Einleitung in d. A.T.; We$^{\text{Comp.}}$ = *Id.*, Composition des Hexateuchs; We$^{\text{de gent.}}$ = *Id.*, De gentibus et familiis Iudaeis; We$^{\text{Held. (or, Arab. Heidenthum)}}$ = *Id.*, Reste Arabischen Heidenthums (= We$^{\text{Skizzen iv, 2nd ed.}}$); We $^{\text{Hist.}}$ = *Id.*, History of Israel (trans. by Black); We$^{\text{Prol.}}$ = *Id.*, Prolegomena zur Geschichte Israels; We ^{Skizzen} = *Id.*, Skizzen und Vorarbeiten.
Weissb = F. H. Weissbach.
Wetzst = J. G. Wetzstein.
wi. = with, construed with.
Wied = A. Wiedemann. Wied^{Samml} *Id.*, Sammlung Altägyptische Wörter.
Wild(eb) = G. Wildeboer.
Wilkinson$^{\text{(Anc.) Egypt.}}$ = J. G. Wilkinson, Ancient Egyptians.
WisdLt = Wisdom Literature.
Wkl = H. Winckler.

WMM = W. Max Müller. WMM As. u. Eur(op.), or Asien = *Id.*, Asien u. Europa.
Wr = C. H. H. Wright.
Wü = A. Wünsche.
WZKM = VOJ, q. v.

Xen(oph). = Xenophon.

Z = Zeitschrift.
ZA = Zeitschr. für Assyriologie.
ZAW = Z. f. alttest. Wissenschaft.
Zc = Zechariah.
Zehnpf = R. Zehnpfund.
ZEthnol. = Zeitschrift für Ethnologie.
Zim = H. Zimmern. Zim[BP] = *Id.*, Babylonische Busspsalmen.
Zinj. = Inscriptions of Zinjirli (N. Syria).
ZK = Z. für Keilschriftforschung.
ZKM = Z. f. Kunde d. Morgenlandes.
ZKW, or ZKWL = Z. f. kirchl. Wiss. und kirchl. Leben.
ZLuth.Th. = Z. für Lutherische Theologie.
ZMG = Z. d. deutsch. Morgenländ. Gesellschaft.
Zö = O. Zöckler.
Zp = Zephaniah.
ZPV = Z. d. deutsch. Pal.-Vereins.
ZVölkerpsych. = Z. für Völkerpsychologie.
ZWTh., or ZWiss.Th. = Z. für Wissenschaftliche Theologie.

< over a letter, indicates the accented (tone-)syllable.

† prefixed, or added, or both, indicates 'All passages cited.'

> indicates that the preceding is to be preferred to the following.

< indicates that the following is to be preferred to the preceding.

‖ parallel, of words (synonymous or contrasted); also of passages; sometimes = 'see parallel,' or 'so also in parallel.'

= equivalent, equals.

+ plus, denotes often that other passages, etc., might be cited. So also where the forms of verbs, nouns, and adjectives are illustrated by citations, near the beginning of articles; while 'etc.' in such connexions commonly indicates that other forms of the word occur, which it has not been thought worth while to cite.

[ ] indicates that the form, etc., enclosed, is not actually found, or that the Hebrew offers no positive proof; *e.g.* n. [m.] denotes that the noun is presumably masculine, though the gender is not clearly exhibited in Hebrew.

√ = root *or* stem.

׳ = sign of abbreviation (in Hebrew words).

א׳ often = אֱלֹהִים, Elohim.

וגו׳ = וְגוֹמַר = *et caetera* (in Hebrew quotations).

י׳ = Yahweh.

‸ beneath a Hebrew word represents any accent that occasions vowel change.

Note. Scripture citations in small superior letters and figures, following **n.m.** or **n.f.**, refer to some passage where the gender is exhibited. Small inferior figures following Hebrew words, names of conjugations, etc., denote the (approximate) number of occurrences of such words, conjugations, etc.

א

א, *Âleph*, first letter; in post B Heb. = numeral 1 (and so in marg. of printed MT); א̈ = 1000; no evidence of this usage in OT times.

1 אָב v. II. אבה. p. 3

אבב (*fresh, bright*, As. *abâbu* Dl^{W}, AGl.)

3 †[אֵב] **n. [m.] freshness, fresh green** (Lag$^{BN\ 207}$ Inf. *ibb;* thence concr., cf. Ar. أَبٌّ; above stem & mng. better than √אנב (spring) cf. As. *inbu*, fruit, Aram. אִנְבָּה (q. v.) Dl$^{HA\ 65,\ Pr\ 114}$) עֹדֶנּוּ בְאִבּוֹ *while yet in its freshness* (i.e. אָחוּ, reed) Jb 8^{12}; concr., pl. *green shoots* בְּאִבֵּי הַנָּחַל Ct 6^{11} (‖ הַפָּרְחָה הַגֶּפֶן הֵנֵצוּ הָרִמֹּנִים:).

24 †אָבִיב **n.m.**$^{Lv\ 2,14}$ **coll.** (Lag$^{BN\ 207}$ Inf.) **1. fresh, young ears** of barley Ex 9^{31}; indef. Lv 2^{14} מִנְחַת בִּכּוּרִים ליהוה א׳ קָלוּי בָּאֵשׁ. **2.** חֹדֶשׁ הָאָבִיב month of ear-forming, or of growing green, **Abib**, month of Exodus & passover, Ex 13^{4} 23^{15} $34^{18.18}$ (JE), Dt $16^{1.1}$ (1st month = c. April = הַחֹדֶשׁ הָר׳, הָרִאשׁוֹן (q.v.) in P; v. Di Ex 12^{2}; = postexilic נִיסָן q.v.)

26 אֲבַגַיִל v. אֲבִיגַיִל sub II. אבה. p. 4

5 †אֲבַגְתָא **n. pr. m.** (Pers. cf. בִּגְתָא) eunuch of Ahasuerus Est 1^{10}.

6 †אָבַד **vb. perish** (MI אבד, As. *abâtu* Dl$^{W\ 184}$ Aram. אֲבַד, ܐܒܰܕ).—**Qal** *Pf.* א׳ Nu 21^{30}+; אָבְדוּ ψ 10^{16}+ (+ Ez 6^{3} 𝔊 Co) etc.; *Impf.* יֹאבַד Jb 3^{3} Je 4^{9}; יֹאבֵד Jb 20^{7} + 2 t.; 3 fs. תֹּאבַד Dt 22^{3} + 4 t.; תֹּאבֵד Jb 8^{13} + 3 t.; יֹאבְדוּ Ju 5^{31} + 3 t.; יֹאבֵדוּ Jb 4^{9}+; 3 fpl. וַתֹּאבַדְנָה 1 S 9^{3}; תֹּאבֵדוּן Dt 4^{26}+; נֹאבֵד Jn 1^{6} 3^{9}; נֹאבְדָה Jon 1^{14} etc.; *Inf. abs.* אָבֹד Dt 4^{26} + 2 t.; cstr. אֲבֹד Dt 7^{20} Pr 11^{10}; אֲבָדְךָ Dt 28^{20}; אָבְדֶךָ Dt 28^{22}; אֲבָדְכֶם Jos 23^{13}; אָבְדָם Ob^{12}
8 Pr 28^{28}; *Pt.* אוֹבֵד Dt 26^{5} + 7 t.; cstr. אֹבַד Dt 32^{28} (bef. ע? v. Di Bö$^{§ 378}$); etc. **1.** *perish, die*, of individuals (mostly late) Nu 17^{27} (‖ גוע & מות (v^{28})), (also Dt 26^{5}? cf. infr.) Jon $1^{6.14}$ Jb 31^{19} cf. 29^{13} Pr 31^{6} Est $4^{14.16.16}$ Mi 4^{9} Je 40^{15} cf. Is 57^{1} Pr 11^{10} 28^{28} Ec 7^{15} ψ 119^{92}; emphasis on mortality Jb 4^{20} ψ 146^{4} Ec 9^{6}; Saul & Jonath., under fig. of weapons 2 S 1^{27}; lion Jb 4^{11}; caravan Jb 6^{18} (cf. Di); cf. א׳ חָסִיד מִן־הָאָרֶץ Mi 7^{2}, וא׳ מֶלֶךְ מֵעַזָּה Zc 9^{5}; *perish, be exterminated* (judgment for sin), of Israel Lv 26^{38} Dt $8^{19.19.20}$ $28^{20.22}$ $30^{18.18}$ Je $27^{10.15}$ cf. 6^{21}, Ob^{12} cf. ψ 80^{17} Is 27^{13}; other nations Dt 7^{20} Je 10^{15} 51^{18} ψ 2^{12} 10^{16} 83^{18} cf. 9^{4} Am 1^{8} Is 41^{11} 60^{12} cf. Jon 3^{9} v. also Ex 10^{7} Nu $21^{29.30}$ (JE) Je 48^{46}; house of Ahab 2 K 9^{8}; wicked in general Ju 5^{31} Jb 4^{9} cf. v^{7}, ψ 37^{20} 49^{11} 68^{3} (‖ sim. of melting wax), 73^{27} 92^{10}; also Pr 19^{9} 21^{18}; לָנֶצַח א׳ Jb 20^{7}; cf. דֶּרֶךְ רְשָׁעִים א׳ ψ 1^{6}; sq. מֵעַל הָאָרֶץ (of annihilation of Isr.) Dt $4^{26.26}$ 11^{17} Jos $23^{13.16}$ (D); sq. מִתּוֹךְ הַקָּהָל (of Korah's company) Nu 16^{33} (JE); *perish, be ruined, destroyed*, of inanimate things, e.g. land Je 9^{11} (‖ נִצְּתָה כַמִּדְבָּר) cf. 48^{8}; harvest Jo 1^{11}; Jonah's gourd Jon 4^{10}; riches Je 48^{36} Ec 5^{13}; vessel ψ 31^{13}; houses Am 3^{15} (so oft. As. Dl^{W}); city Ez 26^{17} (but del. 𝔊 Co); cf. bamôth Ez 6^{3} 𝔊 Co; heavens & earth ψ 102^{27}. **2.** fig. *perish, vanish*, subj. memory Jb 18^{17} ψ 9^{7}; name ψ 41^{6} (i.e. be forgotten); vigour Jb 30^{2}; wisdom Is 29^{14}; cf. אֹבַד עֵצוֹת Dt 32^{28}; אֱמוּנָה Je 7^{28} (‖ נִכְרְתָה); חָזוֹן Ez 12^{22}; יוֹם Jb 3^{3} (i.e. be blotted out); לֵב Je 4^{9} (i.e. courage fail); תִּקְוָה ψ 9^{19} Pr 10^{28} 11^{7} Ez 19^{5} 37^{11} Jb 8^{13}; so תַּאֲוָה ψ 112^{10} (i.e. comes to naught); תּוֹחֶלֶת Pr 11^{7}, sq. מִן + agent La 3^{18}; תּוֹרָה + עֵצָה sq. מִן + persons negligent Je 18^{18} Ez 7^{26}, cf. Je 49^{7}; esp. א׳ מָנוֹס מִן־ (i.e. they could not escape) Am. 2^{14} Je 25^{35} Jb 11^{20} ψ 142^{5}. **3.** *be lost, strayed*, asses 1 S $9^{3.20}$; sheep Je 50^{6} Ez $34^{4.16}$ ψ 119^{176} (fig. of erring men); perh. Dt 26^{5}.

Pi. caus. of Qal.—*Pf.* אִבַּד 2 K 21^{3} + 2 t.;

sf. וְאִבֶּדְךָ Co Ez 28^{16} cf. infr.; אִבַּדְתִּי Je 15^{7}; וְאִבַּדְתִּי Ez 6^{3} (𝔊 Co וְנֶאֶבְדוּ) etc.; *Impf.* יְאַבֵּד Ec 9^{18}; וַיְאַבֵּד Ec 7^{7} Zp 2^{13}; 1 s. sf. וָאֲבֶדְךָ Ez 28^{16} (for וָאֲאַבֶּ׳ Ew^{§72c} Ol^{§79a} Kö I^{338} Ges$^{§68 fin}$; but Co 3 ms.; v. also Co 38^{14}); תְּאַבְּדוּן Dt 12^{2} etc.; *Inf. abs.* אַבֵּד Dt 12^{2}+3t.; *cstr. id.* Ez 22^{27}+etc.; *Pt.* מְאַבְּדִים Je 23^{1}. **1.** *cause to perish, destroy, kill,* obj. pers. (mostly late) 2 K 11^{1} Est 3^{9} 4^{7} 8^{5} 9^{24}; ‖ הרג 9$^{6.12}$; ‖ הרג + השמיד 3^{13} 7^{4} 8^{11}; ‖ המם 9^{24}; cf. ψ 119^{95}; obj. נְפָשׁוֹת Ez 22^{27} (del. 𝔊 Co); in judgment, subj. ׳י ψ 5^{7}; cf. Pr 1^{32}; sq. מִתּוֹךְ Ez 28^{16}; obj. a people 2 K 13^{7} 2 K 19^{18}=Is 37^{19}; Jb 12^{13}; in judgment Dt 11^{4} Je 12^{17} 15^{7} Zp 2^{13} ψ 9^{6} cf. 21^{11}; obj. inanimate things esp. idols, bamôth etc., Nu. 33$^{52.52}$ (J) Dt 12$^{2.2}$ 2 K 21^{3} Ez 6^{3} (but cf. 𝔊 Co supr.); bars of Zion La 2^{9} (‖ שִׁבַּר). **2.** fig. *cause to vanish, blot out, do away with* names of idols Dt 12^{3}; voice of Babylon Je 51^{55}; memory of dead Is 26^{14}; substance Pr 29^{3}; understanding Ec 7^{7}; good (טוֹבָה q.v.) Ec 9^{18}. **3.** *cause to stray, lose;* obj. Isr. under fig. of flock Je 23^{1} (‖ הֵפִיץ); abs. Ec 3^{6} (‖ בִּקֵּשׁ).

Hiph. *Pf.* וְהֶאֱבִיד Nu 24^{19}; הֶאֱבַדְתָּ Jb 14^{19} etc.; *Impf.* אֹבִידָה Je 46^{8} (Ges$^{§68,2 R.1}$). *Inf. cstr.* הַאֲבִיד 2 K 10^{19}+etc.; *Pt.* מַאֲבִיד Dt 8^{20}. **1.** *destroy, put to death,* in judgment, (subj. ׳י) obj. pers. Lv 23^{30} (sq. מִקֶּרֶב עַמָּהּ; ‖ כָּרַת v^{29}); Je 49^{38} (sq. מִשָּׁם); Ob^{8} (sq. מֵאֱדוֹם); obj. nation, Ammon Ez 25^{7} (sq. מִן־הארצות; ‖ כָּרַת), cf. v^{16}; Canaanites Dt 8^{20} (sq. מִפְּנֵיכֶם); Canaan = Philistines Zp 2^{5} (‖ כָּרַת); esp. Isr. Dt 28$^{51.63}$ (‖ הִשְׁמִיד), cf. Js 7^{7}; also abs. Je 18^{7} (‖ לִנְתוֹשׁ וְלִנְתוֹץ);=1^{10} (+ וְלַהֲרוֹס)=31^{28} (+ וּלְהָרֵעַ); animals Ez 32^{13} (sq. מֵעַל מַיִם רַבִּים); cf. Dt 7^{10}; ψ 143^{12} (‖ הִצְמִית); (human subj.), obj. servants of Baal 2 K 10^{19}, obj. nation Dt 9^{3}, cf. Nu 24^{19} (E; sq. מֵעִיר); 2 K 24^{2}; cf. Je 46^{8}; obj. inanimate, chariots Mi 5^{9}; idols Ez 30^{13} (del. BCo). **2.** fig., obj. name of kings Dt 7^{24} (sq. מִתַּחַת הַשָּׁמָיִם); hope Jb 14^{19}; voice of mirth etc. Je 25^{10} (cf. 51^{55} **Pi.** supr.)

8 †אֹבֵד **n.[m.]** destruction, עֲדֵי א׳ Nu 24$^{20.24}$ (JE; on form with abstract sense v. Ba$^{NB 149}$).

9 †אֲבֵדָה **n.f.** a lost thing—abs. exc. Dt 22^{3} cstr. אֲבֵדַת—Ex 22^{8}; with מָצָא Lv 5$^{22.23}$; with מָצָא + אָבַד Dt 22^{3};—(אבדה) Pr 27^{20} Kt cf. אֲבַדּוֹ infr.)

10 אֲבַדֹּה, אֲבַדּוֹ cf. אבדון infr.

12, 13 †אֲבַדָן, & אָבְדַן (cstr.) **n.[m.]** destruction (Syr. ܐܒܕܢܐ) Est 9^{5} (מַכַּת־חֶרֶב וְהֶרֶג וְא׳), 8^{6}; (on form v. BeRy; Ol$^{§215 b.1}$ Ba$^{NB 49, 487}$).

11 †אֲבַדּוֹן **n.f.**$^{? Pr 27,20}$ abstr. nearly = **n.pr.** (place of) **Destruction, Ruin, 'Abaddôn** (cf. 𝔖 ܐܒܕܢܐ
Jb 28^{22} etc.)—אֲבַדּוֹן Jb 26^{6} (+4t.); abbrev. אבדה 10
Kt אֲבַדּוֹ Qr †Pr 27^{20}.—Place of ruin in She'ôl for lost or ruined dead, as development of earlier distinction of condition in Sheʼôl (v. שְׁאוֹל). Only in WisdLt; Jb 31^{12}; ‖ שאול Jb 26^{6} Pr 15^{11} 27^{20}; ‖ מות Jb 28^{22}; ‖ קבר ψ 88^{12}.

†I. אָבָה **vb. be willing, consent** (cf. As. 14
abûtu, command, Dl^{W}, Eth. አበየ: *refuse,* Ar. أَبَى, id., Nejd *be willing* So$^{De Jes 3, p. 26; LCB 1880, 817}$)—

Qal (c. לֹא, אַל exc. Is 1^{19} Jb 39^{9}; in Hex. rare & only JED, incl. Lv 26^{21}); *Pf.* אָבָה Ex 10^{27}+ אָבוּ Ju 19^{25}+7t.; אָבוּא Is 28^{12} (Sta$^{§31 R.2}$; Kö$^{I.414}$); *Impf.* יֹאבֶה Dt 29^{19}+2t.; 2 ms. juss. תֹּבֵא Pr 1^{10} (Sta$^{§143e1 fin}$; Kö$^{I.576f}$) etc.; *Pt.* אֹבִים Ez 3^{7};—*be willing,* sq. Inf. with לְ Ex 10^{27}+29t.; without לְ Dt 2^{30}+8t.; subj. ׳י Dt 10^{10} 23^{6} 29^{19} Jos 24^{10} 2 K 8^{19} 13^{23} 24^{4} 2 Ch 21^{7}; human subj. Gn 24$^{5.8}$ Ju 19^{10} 2 S 2^{21} 13^{25} 14$^{29.29}$ 23$^{16.17}$=1 Ch 11$^{18.19}$ 1 Ch 19^{19}; in bad sense Ex 10^{27} Dt 2^{30} 25^{7} Ju. 19^{25} 20^{13} 2 S 13$^{14.16}$; esp. of perverse Isr. Lv 26^{21} Dt 1^{26} 1 S 15^{9} Is 28^{12} 30^{9} 42^{24} Ez 3$^{7.7}$ 20^{8}; subj. animal, רֵים Jb 39^{9}; abs. (no Inf.) 2 S 12^{17} 1 K 20^{8} 22^{50}; cf. Pr 6^{35}, of jealous man; bad sense Ju 11^{17} Is 30^{15}; good sense 1 S 22^{17} 26^{23} 31^{4}=1 Ch 10^{4} 2 S 6^{10} Pr 1^{10}; + vb. fin. Is 1^{19} (אִם תֹּאבוּ וּשְׁמַעְתֶּם); *consent, yield to,* sq. לוֹ Dt 13^{9} (good sense); sq. לִי ψ 81^{12}; sq. לַעֲצָתִי Pr 1^{30}; sq. acc. תּוֹכַחְתִּי v^{25} (all in bad sense).

†אֶבְיוֹן **adj. in want, needy, poor,**—so, 34
alw. abs., Dt 15^{4}+40t.; אֶבְיֹנְךָ Ex 23^{6} Dt 15^{11}; אֶבְיוֹנִים (אֶבְיֹנֵי) אֶבְיֹנֵי Ex 23^{11} Is 29^{19}; אֶבְיוֹנֶיהָ ψ 132^{15}—(Hex. only JED; mostly poet., 23t. ψ) *needy,* chiefly *poor* (in material things); as adj. Dt 15$^{7.7.9}$; 24^{14} ψ 109^{16} (both ‖ עָנִי); elsewhere subst.; ψ 49^{3} (‖ עָשִׁיר); Dt 15$^{4.11}$; subj. to oppression & abuse Am 2^{6} 5^{12} (both ‖ צַדִּיק) 4^{1} 8^{6} (all ‖ דַּל) Is 32^{7}; Am 8^{4} Ez 16^{49} 18^{12} 22^{29} ψ 37^{14} Jb 24$^{4.14}$ Pr 30^{14}—cf. ψ 109^{16} supr.—(all ‖ עָנִי) Je 5^{28} (‖ יָתוֹם) 2^{34}; cared for by good Jb 29^{16} 30^{25} (‖ קְשֵׁה־יוֹם) 31^{19} ψ 112^{9} Est 9^{22}; Pr 14^{31} (‖ דַּל) 31^{20} Je 22^{16} (‖ עָנִי); care of them enjoined, negatively Ex 23^{6};—cf. Dt 24^{14} supr.—positively Ex 23^{11} Dt 15^{11} Pr 31^{9} (both ‖ עָנִי)—cf. Dt 15$^{7.7.9}$ supr.—ψ 82^{4} (‖ דַּל); cared for by God Je 20^{13} ψ 107^{41} 132^{15} Jb 5^{15}; 1 S 2^{8}=ψ 113^{7} Is 14^{30} (all ‖ דַּל) ψ 35^{10} 140^{13} (both ‖ עָנִי), cf. Davidic king ψ 72^{12} (‖ עָנִי)=v^{4} (‖ *id.*), בְּנֵי אֶבְ׳ v$^{13.13}$ (‖ דַּל); *needing help,* deliverance from trouble, esp. as delivered by God ψ 9^{19} 12^{6} 40^{18}=70^{6} 74^{21} 86^{1} 109^{22} Is 29^{19} 41^{17} (all ‖ עָנִי) Is 25^{4} (‖ דַּל) ψ 69^{34} 109^{31}.

†אֲבִיּוֹנָה **n.f. caper-berry** (as stimulating 35

desire) Ec 12^{5} (v. GFM $^{JBL 1891, 55 ff.}$; so 𝔊 𝔙, Mish. אביונות, cf. NHWB; v. also 𝔖; i.e. *capparis spinosa*, cf. Ri^{HWB}; so Thes, Ew De, etc.; but Wetzst in De (Germ. ed. 1875) proposes אֶבְיוֹנָה (as fem. of אביון) *the poor soul* in sense=נִשְׁמָתוֹ הָאֶבְיוֹנָה cf. Symm 𝔖, where double translation).

16 †**אֵבֶה** **n.[m.] reed, papyrus** (etymology uncertain;=Ar. أَبَاءٌ, As. *abu* Dl^{W}, AGl) אֳנִיּוֹת אֵבֶה Jb 9^{26} (craft made of reeds, light & swift, Heliod. $^{Aethiop. X, 460}$)=כְּלֵי־גֹמֶא Is 18^{2}.

II. **אבה** (perh. at least formally justified as stem of אָב (cstr. אֲבִי), so Thes (cf. infr.), but existence & mng. wholly dub.; as real √ Ba $^{ZMG 1887, 609 ff.}$ Ol$^{§ 123 c}$; acc. to Dl$^{W p. 22}$ אבה As. *abû*= *decide*, אָב=*he who decides;* Thes (so RobGes Nö$^{ZMG xl, 737}$ & cf. Sta$^{§ 186}$ al.) makes אָב nom. prim. bilit., imitating infant's speech cf. πάππας, *pappa, papa* (cf. Ew$^{§ 106 a}$); also As. *bab* Jen$^{ZA 1886, 404}$).

1 **אָב** $_{1191}$ **n.m. father** (Ph. אב, As. *abu*, Ar. أَبٌ, Sab. אב CIS$^{iv, 1. 37 l. 2}$ al., Eth. አብ: Aram. אַבָּא, ܐܒܐ)—abs. אָב Gn 44^{19}+47 t.; cstr. אֲבִי Gn 17$^{4.5}$ (cf. in אַבְרָהָם *ib.* & elsewh. in n.pr. On Hal's prop. אֲבַר v. אברהם); אֲבִי (cf. Ge$^{§§ 90, 3b, 96}$) Gn 4^{20} +; sf. אָבִי Gn 19^{34}+ (MI אבי); אָבִיךָ Gn 12^{1}+; אָבִיו Gn 2^{24}+; אָבִיהוּ Ju 14^{10}+6 t.; pl. אָבוֹת Ex 12^{3}+; cstr. אֲבוֹת Ex 6^{25}+7 t.; sf. אֲבֹתַי (אֲבוֹתַי) Gn 47^{9}+15 t.; אֲבוֹתֵיהֶם 1 Ch 4^{38}+32 t. (late); אֲבוֹתָם Ex 4^{5}+106 t. etc.;—**1.** *father of individual* Gn 2^{24} (+ אֵם) 11$^{28.29.29}$ 19$^{31.32.33}$, + oft. (mostly JED); of father as commanding Gn 50^{16} (J) Je 35$^{6 f}$ Pr 6^{20} (cf. Gn 18^{19} J 28$^{1.6}$ P 1 S 17^{20} 1 K 2^{1}); instructing מוסר Pr 1^{8} 4^{1} (cf. Dt 8^{5}); specif. as begetter, *genitor* Pr 23^{22} Zc 13$^{3.3}$ (+אֵם) Is 45^{10}; cf. Gn 49^{4} (J) Lv 18$^{7.8.11}$ (P); rebuking Gn 37^{10}; loving Gn 37^{4} 44^{20} (JE; cf. 22^{2} 25^{28} 37^{3} 2 S 14^{1}); pitying ψ 103^{13} (in sim. cf. 2 S 18^{5}); blessing Gn 27^{41} (JE cf. 27^{4} also 28^{1} P+); as glad Pr 10^{1} 15^{20} cf. 29^{3}; grieving Gn 37^{35} (JE; cf. 2 S 12^{22} 19$^{1.2 f}$) etc. Also as obj. of honour, obedience, love Ex 20^{12} (E)=Dt 5^{16}; Ex 21$^{15.17}$ (E) Dt 21$^{18.19}$ Gn 28^{7} (P) 1 K 19^{20} (all + אֵם), 50$^{1.5}$ (J) Mal 1^{6} etc. Hence metaph. of *intimate connection* Jb 17^{14} *to corruption I cry, My father art thou* (אִמִּי וַאֲחֹתִי לָרִמָּה ||). **2.** of God as *father of his people* (v. RS$^{Sem 42}$), who constituted, controls, guides and lovingly watches over it: Dt 32^{6} Je 3$^{4.19}$ 31^{9} Is 63$^{16.16}$ 64^{7} Mal 1^{6} 2^{10} (cf. Ex 4^{22} 19^{4} (JE) Dt 32^{11} Ho 11^{1}); cf. Je 2^{27} (of idolatr. Isr.) אֹמְרִים לָעֵץ אָבִי אַתָּה וְלָאֶבֶן אַתְּ ילדתני׃; esp. God as *father of Davidic line* 2 S 7^{14} ψ 89^{27}; *f. of needy* (late) ψ 68^{6} (cf. 103^{13}) (in n.pr., *f. of individ.*, cf. infr.) **3.** *head of household*, family or clan; בֵּית אָבִי as abode Gn 38$^{11.11}$ Lv 22^{13}+;=family Gn 24^{40} (|| מִשְׁפַּחְתִּי) 41^{51} 46^{31} + cf. Nu 18$^{1.2}$ Jos 2$^{12.18}$ 6^{25}; esp. techn. of divisions of Isr. בֵּית אָב לְמִשְׁפָּחוֹת Nu 3$^{30.35}$=a father's house, i.e. a family or clan; more oft. pl. (אבותם, אבותיו) בֵּית אָבוֹת=fathers' houses= families, clans (cf. Di on Ex 6^{14}) Ex 6^{14} 12^{3} Nu 1$^{2.18 ff}$ (oft. in Nu) Jos 14^{1} 19^{51} 21$^{1.1}$ 22$^{14.14}$ (always P in Hex.); also 1 Ch 5$^{13.15}$+oft. in Ch; cf. ראשי אבות הלוים (=ר׳ בית א׳) Ex 6^{25} cf. 1 K 8^{1} 1 Ch 6^{4} 7^{11}+oft. Ch Ezr Ne. **4.** *ancestor* (**a**) of individual; grandfather (instead of precise term) Gn 28^{13} 32^{10} (J; where used by Jacob of Abr. & then of Isaac); greatgr. 1 K 15^{13}; great-greatgr. 1 K 15^{11} etc.; oft. pl. (=*fathers, forefathers*) Gn 15^{15} 46^{34} (JE) 1 K 19^{4} 21$^{3.4}$ 2 K 19^{12} 20^{17}+; particularly שכב עם אבותיו 1 K 1^{21} 2^{10} 11^{21} 22^{40}+; joined with אב׳ ויקבר עם 1 K 14^{31} 15^{24} 22^{51} 2 K 8^{24} 15^{38} cf. v^{7}, 16^{20} + (all of kings of Judah); intens., אֲבֹתֶיךָ וַאֲבוֹת אֲבֹתֶיךָ Ex 10^{6} cf. Dn 11^{24}; (**b**) of people Gn 10^{21} (J) 17$^{4.5}$ (P) 19$^{37.38}$ (J) 36$^{9.43}$ (P) Dt 26^{5} Is 51^{2} 43^{27} (where אביך הראשון *thy first father*, v. Che) cf. also Ez 16$^{3.45}$+ oft.; pl. Ex 3$^{13.15.16}$ (E) Dt 1^{8} Jos 1^{6} Ju 2^{1} 1 S 12^{6}+; 1 S 12$^{15\ ad\ fin}$ rd. וּבְמַלְכְּכֶם 𝔊 We Dr. **5.** *originator* or *patron* of a class, profession, or art Gn 4$^{20.21}$. **6.** fig. of *producer, generator* Jb 38^{28} הֲיֵשׁ לַמָּטָר אָב || מִי־הוֹלִיד אֶגְלֵי־טָל׃). **7.** fig. of *benevolence* & protection Jb 29^{16} אָב אָנֹכִי לָאֶבְיוֹנִים, cf. 31^{18}; of Eliakim Is 22^{21}; perh. also of gracious Mess. king אֲבִי עַד Is 9^{5} *everlasting father* (Ge Ew De Che Brd Di)—others *divider of spoil* (Abarb Hi Kn Kue Br^{MP}). **8.** term of *respect & honour* (*Abbas, Pater, Papa, Pope*); appl. to master 2 K 5^{13}; priest Ju 17^{10} 18^{19}; prophet 2 K 2$^{12.12}$ 6^{21} 13$^{14.14}$ cf. 8^{9}; counsellor Gn 45^{8} (E; cf. δευτέρου πατρός 𝔊 add. Est 3^{13}; τῷ πατρί 1 Mac 11^{32}); king 1 S 24^{12}; artificer 2 Ch 2^{12} 4^{16}. **9.** specif., *ruler, chief* (late) 1 Ch 2$^{24.42.42}$ etc. (cf. Ew$^{§ 273 b}$).

†**אֲבִי־עַלְבוֹן** **n.pr.m.** a hero of David 2 S 45
23^{31} rd. אֲבִיאֵל so 𝔊 1 Ch 11^{32}, cf. Dr^{s} (We^{s} אבי־בעל (v. sub אביאל); otherwise Klo^{s}.

†**אֲבִיאֵל** **n.pr.m.** (*Ēl is (my) father*, cf. אביהו 22
& Ph. אבבעל (*fem.*), also אביבעל; & אבנבעל *our father* etc.; Abi-ba'al KAT$^{2\ 355}$; v. RS$^{Sem 45}$. Nö$^{ZMG 1888, 480}$ makes אבי here, & in אביהו etc., cstr. but this seems unlikely; cf. also אליאב etc.; views differ much as to these n.pr. and uniform interpr. is impossible. Cf. in gen. Ol $^{§ 277 f}$). **1.** Saul's grandfather 1 S 9^{1} 14^{51}. **2.** =foregoing, 1 Ch 11^{32}.

23 †אֲבִיאָסָף **n.pr.m.** (*my father has gathered*) son (descendant) of Korah Ex 6^{24},
43 Sam. אביסף, so אֶבְיָסָף 1 Ch $6^{8.22}$ 9^{19} (cf. Nes[Eg 185]).

26 †אֲבִיגַ֫יִל **n.pr.f.** (*my father is joy* (?) orig. אבגל ? (אֲבִגַל?) cf. MT infr. & Nö[ZMG 1883, 537 Anm2]). **1.** wife of Nabal, then of David 1 S $25^{14.23.39.40.42}$ 27^{3} 30^{5} 2 S 2^{2} 1 Ch 3^{1}; = אֲבִגַיִל 1 S $25^{3.36}$ אֲבוּגַיִל v^{18}, אֲבִיגָל v^{32}, אֲבִיגַ֫ל 2 S 3^{3}. **2.** sister of David 1 Ch $2^{16.17}$ = אֲבִיגַל 2 S 17^{25}.

27 †אֲבִידָן **n.pr.m.** (*my father is judge*) a prince of Benj. Nu 1^{11} 2^{22} $7^{60.65}$ 10^{24}.

28 †אֲבִידָע **n.pr.m.** (*my father took knowledge*) a son of Midian Gn 25^{4} 1 Ch 1^{33}. Cf. Sab. אבידע, Hal[MA 192, 202], also ידעאב, DHM[ZMG '83, 399].

29 †אֲבִיָּהוּ **n.pr.m.** & **f.** (*Yah*(*u*) *is* (*my*) *father*)
38 —so †2 Ch $13^{20.21}$ = אֲבִיָּם †1 K 14^{31} $15^{1.7.7.8}$
21 (𝔊 'Αβιου, 'Αβια); = אֲבִי †2 K 18^{2} (𝔊 'Αβου,
29 'Αβουθ); = אֲבִיָּה 1 S 8^{2} + 22 t.—**1.** king of
Judah, son & successor of Rehoboam 1 K 14^{31} $15^{1.7.7.8}$ 1 Ch 3^{10} 2 Ch $11^{20.22}$ 12^{16} $13^{1.2.3.4.15.17.19.20.21.22.23}$. **2.** 2nd son of Samuel 1 S 8^{2} 1 Ch 6^{13}. **3.** son of Jerob. I 1 K 14^{1}. **4.** son of Becher, a Benjamite 1 Ch 7^{8}. **5.** head of a priestly house 1 Ch 24^{10}. **6.** *id.* Ne 10^{8} $12^{4.17}$. **7.** wife of Hezron 1 Ch 2^{24}. **8.** mother of Hezekiah 2 K 18^{2} 2 Ch 29^{1}.

30 אֲבִיהוּא **n.pr.m.** (*he is father*) a son of Aaron Ex 6^{23} $24^{1.9}$ 28^{1} Lv 10^{1} + 7 t.

31 †אֲבִיהוּד **n.pr.m.** (*my father is majesty*, cf. עַמִּיהוּד, הוד) son of Bela, a Benjamite 1 Ch 8^{3}.

32 †אֲבִיחַ֫יִל **n.pr.m.** & **f.** (*my father is might*, Sab. אבחיל Hal[MA 234])—prob. = אֲבִיהָיִל 2 Ch 11^{18}, אֲבִיהַיִל 1 Ch 2^{29} — **1.** a Levite Nu 3^{25}. **2.** a Gadite 1 Ch 5^{14}. **3.** father of Esther Est 2^{15} 9^{29}. **4.** wife of Abishur 1 Ch 2^{29}. **5.** wife of Rehoboam 2 Ch 11^{18}.

36 †אֲבִיטוּב **n.pr.m.** (*my father is goodness*) son of Shaharaim, a Benjamite 1 Ch 8^{11}.

37 †אֲבִיטַל **n.pr.f.** (*my father is* (*the*) *dew*) a wife of David 2 S 3^{4} 1 Ch 3^{3}.

39 †אֲבִימָאֵל **n.pr.m.** (*a father is Ēl;* South-Arab. name) son of Joktan Gn 10^{28} 1 Ch 1^{22}. Cf. Sab. אבמעתתר, *Abmi 'Attar* a father is *'Attar* ([עשתר] v. עַשְׁתֹּרֶת) Hal[M 86], DHM[ZMG 1883, 18].

40 אֲבִימֶ֫לֶךְ **n.pr.m.** (*Melek* (= Malik, Molech) *is father*)—אֲבִימֶלֶךְ Gn 20^{18} + —**1.** king of Gerar Gn $20^{2.3.4}$ +, $21^{22.25.25}$ +, $26^{1.8}$ + (24 t. Gn). †**2.** king of Gath ψ 34^{1} err. for אָכִישׁ, cf. 1 S $21^{11 f}$;—a better known Philist. name substituted for a less known (Hup[3]). > Others (Thes Ol De MV) think a *title* of Philist. kings, cf. Pharaoh. **3.** son of Gideon Ju 8^{31} $9^{1.3.4}$ +, 10^{1} (40 t. Ju), 2 S 11^{21}. †**4.** priest, son of Abiathar 1 Ch 18^{16} err. for אֲחִימֶלֶךְ q.v. (Sab. also **n.pr.f.** Osiander[ZMG 1865, 209]).

†אֲבִינָדָב **n.pr.m.** (*my father is noble*) 41
1. a man of Gibeah in whose house the ark tarried 1 S 7^{1} 2 S $6^{3.3.4}$ 1 Ch 13^{7}. **2.** a son of Jesse 1 S 16^{8} 17^{13}; 1 K 4^{11} (? perh. otherwise unknown; Klo prop. אֲבִינֵר בְּ). **3.** a son of Saul 1 S 31^{2} 1 Ch 8^{33} 9^{39} 10^{2}.

†אֲבִינֹ֫עַם **n.pr.m.** (*my father is delight*) 42
father of Barak Ju $4^{6.12}$ $5^{1.12}$.

אֲבִינֵר **n.pr.m.** (*my father is Nêr*, or *is a* 74
lamp cf. 2 S 21^{17}; acc. to Lag[BN 75] = אֲבֵן (= בֵּן) + נֵר = son of Ner; cf. 𝔊 'Αβεννηρ)—so only 1 S 14^{50}, elsewh. אַבְנֵר—cousin of Saul, and captain of his host 1 S $14^{50.51}$ $17^{55.55.55}$ + 52 t. 1 & 2 S + 1 K $2^{5.32}$ 1 Ch 26^{28} 27^{21}.

†אֲבִיעֶ֫זֶר **n.pr.m.** (*my father is help*)— 44
= אִיעֶזֶר Nu 26^{30} —**1.** a Manassite, called 'son' 372
of Gilead Nu 26^{30} (cf. Di) Jos 17^{2} Ju 6^{34} 8^{2}; and son of Gil.'s sister 1 Ch 7^{18}. **2.** a Benjamite, a warrior of David 2 S 23^{27} 1 Ch 11^{28} 27^{12}.

†אֲבִי הָעֶזְרִי **adj.gent.** Abiezrite Ju $6^{11.24}$ 33
8^{32} = אִיעֶזְרִי Nu 26^{30}. 373

†אֲבִירָם **n.pr.m.** ((*the*) *Exalted One is* (*my*) 48
father (v. Bae[Rel 156]) cf. As. *Aburamu* (?) KAT[2 479] cf. Dl[L2, p. 91, l. 225]). **1.** a Reubenite, son of Eliab Nu $16^{1.12.24.25.27.27}$ 26^{9} Dt 11^{6} ψ 106^{17}. **2.** son of Hiel the Bethelite 1 K 16^{34}. Cf. also following.

אַבְרָם **n.pr.m.** (*id.*, Thes al. *exalted father*) 87
Abram Gn $11^{26.27}$ + 57 t. Gn (to 17^{5}) + 1 Ch 1^{27}
Ne 9^{7}; = אַבְרָהָם **Abraham** Gn $17^{5.9.15}$ + 172 t. 85
OT. (אברהם connected Gn 17^{5} by word-play with הם of המון; really = אברם—רהם = רום which however is not found in Heb.—cf. Di > Hal RÉJ[1887, 177 f] who prop. אַבִר הַם גּוֹיִם cf. Gn 49^{24} with Is 41^{21}; so that אַבִר הָם *chief of multitude* is the new name of Gn 17^{5} (הָם) √המה).

†אֲבִישַׁג **n.pr.f.** (*my father is a wanderer* 49
(שׁגג?) a handmaid of David 1 K $1^{3.15}$ $2^{17.21.22}$.

†אֲבִישׁוּעַ **n.pr.m.** (*my father is rescue*, or 50
is opulence (cf. שׁוּעַ *rich* Jb 34^{19}; also שׁוּעַ Jb 36^{19}? but v. שׁוע); Lag[BN 75] thinks fr. אֲבֵן (= בֵּן) + שׁוּעַ cf. 𝔊 'Αβεσσουε 1 Ch 8^{4}) **1.** a son of Phinehas 1 Ch $5^{30.31}$ 6^{35} Ezr 7^{5}. **2.** a Benjamite, son of Bela 1 Ch 8^{4}.

†אֲבִישׁוּר **n.pr.m.** (*my father is a wall*, Sab. 51
אבשור Hal[MA 148], cf. As. *Abudûru* Dl[Pr 202]) son of Shammai 1 Ch $2^{28.29}$.

52 **אֲבִישַׁי** **n.pr.m.** (*my father is Jesse;* Lag$^{BN 75}$ thinks fr. אֲבֶן (=בֵּן) + ישי cf. 𝔊 Ἀβεσσα[ι] 1 S 26^6) —א׳ 1 S $26^{6.6}$ + 17 t. 1 & 2 S = אַבְשַׁי 2 S 10^{10} + 5 t. 1 Ch.—grandson of Jesse; son of Zeruiah & brother of Joab 1 S $26^{6.6.7.8.9}$ 2 S $2^{18.24}$ + 20^6 (where rd. יואב 𝔖 Th We Dr) + 12 t. 2 S + 20^7 (where insert אבישי 𝔊 We Dr) + 5 t. 1 Ch.

53 **אֲבִישָׁלוֹם** **n.pr.m.** (*my father is peace;* acc. to Lag$^{BN 75}$ = אֲבֶן (בֵּן) + שָׁלֵם, cf. 𝔊 Ἀβεσσαλωμ) —א׳ †1 K $15^{2.10}$ = אַבְשָׁלוֹם 2 S 3^3 +, 2 Ch $11^{20.21}$, אַבְשָׁלֹם 2 S 13^{14} + — **1.** Rehob.'s father-in-law †1 K $15^{2.10}$ 2 Ch $11^{20.21}$. **2.** 3rd son of Dvd 2 S 3^3 13^1 + 90 t. 2 S (insert 2 S 13^{27} 𝔊 Th We cf. Dr; del. v^{38} Dr cf. We), + †1 K 1^6 $2^{7.28}$ 1 Ch 3^2 ψ 3^1.

54 **אֶבְיָתָר** **n.pr.m.** (*the Great One is father* (?) so Bä$^{Rel. 156}$, cf. Sab. ותר) a priest, son of Ahimelech 1 S $22^{20.21.22}$ $23^{6.9}$ $30^{7.7}$ 2 S 8^{17} (rd. אב׳ בן־אחמלך so 𝔖 We Dr) + 22 t. 2 S 1 K 1 Ch.

26 **אבוגיל** Kt 2 S 25^{18} v. אֲבִיגַיִל sub II. אבה.

17 †**אֲבוֹי** **interj.** exclam. of pain, **Oh!** Pr 23^{29} (‖ אוֹי *woe!*). Prob. akin to Syr. ܐܘܒܝ *alas* . . . ! PS^{53} (AW Ges less prob. as a subst. *need* from אָבָה, cf. אֶבְיוֹן).

אבח (Dl$^{BD Ez. x, Pr 75}$ comp. As. [*abâḫu*], *torment*, but dub.)

19 [**אִבְחָה**] **n.f.** cstr. אִבְחַת חֶרֶב Ez 21^{20}; Dl, as above, *slaughter;* but prob. error for טבחת (v. טבח) Ges Co; 𝔊 σφάγια ῥομφαίας, cf. 𝔗.

20 **אֲבַטִּיחִים** v. בטח. p. 105

אָבִי v. ביה.

21 **אֲבִי** v. אֲבִיָּהוּ sub II. אבה. p. 4

33 **אֲבִי הָעֶזְרִי** v. אֲבִיעֶזֶר sub II. אבה. p. 4

29 **אֲבִיָּה** v. אֲבִיָּהוּ sub II. אבה. p. 4

32 **אֲבִיהַיִל** v. אֲבִיחַיִל sub II. אבה. p. 4

34 **אֲבִיּוֹנָה, אֶבְיוֹן** v. I. אָבָה. p. 2

38 **אֲבִיָּם** v. אֲבִיָּהוּ sub II. אבה. p. 4

43 **אֶבְיָסָף** v. אֲבִיאָסָף sub II. אבה. p. 4

55 †[**אָבַךְ**] **vb.** turn (?) (cf. As. *abâku* Dl^W = הָפַךְ; Thes MV al. compare בוך) **Hithp.** וַיִּתְאַבְּכוּ Is 9^{17}, *roll, roll up*, as volume of smoke (of Isr. under fig. of thickets of forest) v. De & cf. הִתְהַפֵּךְ Ju 7^3.

56 †I. **אָבַל**$_{39}$ **vb. mourn** (As. [*abâlu*] v. Dl^W) —**Qal** *Pf.* אָבַל Is 24^7 + 2 t. etc. *Impf.* 3 fs. תֶּאֱבַל Ho 4^3 + 3 t.—*mourn, lament* (poet. & higher style); abs., human subj. Jo 1^9 Am 8^8 9^5 Is 19^8 (‖ אנה) cf. Jb 14^{22} (subj. נַפְשׁוֹ); sq. על Ho 10^5; more oft. fig., inanim. subj., gates Is 3^{26}; land 24^4 33^9 Ho 4^3 Jo 1^{10} Je 4^{28} (sq. על) 12^4 23^{10} cf. 12^{11} (sq. על), יְהוּדָה 14^2; pastures Am 1^2. **Hithp.** —*Pf.* הִתְאַבֵּל 1 S 15^{35}; *Impf.* יִתְאַבָּל Ez $7^{12.27}$; וַיִּתְאַבֵּל Gn 37^{34} + 3 t. etc.; *Imv.* fs. הִתְאַבְּלִי 2 S 14^2; *Pt.* מִתְאַבֵּל 1 S 16^1 + 2 t. etc.;—**mourn** (mostly prose) esp. for dead, sq. על Gn 37^{34} 2 S 13^{37} 14^2 19^2 (‖ בכה) 2 Ch 35^{24}, cf. also Is 66^{10} (over Jerusalem); abs. 1 Ch 7^{22}; cf. 2 S 14^2 *play the mourner* (where indic. by dress); over unworthy Saul sq. אֶל 1 S 15^{35} 16^1; over sin sq. על Ezr 10^6 cf. (abs.) Ne 8^9; judgment of י׳ Ex 33^4 abs. (indic. by dress), Nu 14^{39} Ez 7^{27} (del. B Co); sq. כִּי 1 S 6^{19}; calamity Ne 1^4 Ez 7^{12} cf. Dn 10^2. **Hiph.** *Pf.* הֶאֱבַלְתִּי Ez 31^{15}; *Impf.* וַיַּאֲבֶל־ La 2^8; —*cause to mourn;* Ez 31^{15} abs. MT, but A B Co obj. תהום sq. על, *caused the deep to mourn over;* La 2^8 obj. wall etc.; (both these fig., cf. Qal).

†**אֵבֶל** **n.m.** $^{Gn 50,11}$ **mourning**—abs. Gn 50^{10} 60
+ 17 t.; cstr. 27^{41} + 3 t.; אֶבְלֵךְ Is 60^{20}; אֶבְלָם Je 31^{13}—for dead, cstr. Gn 27^{41} Dt 34^8 (‖ בכי) so א׳ יָחִיד sim. for grievous mourning Am 8^{10}, *id.* metaph. Je 6^{26} (‖ מִסְפַּד תַּמְרוּרִים); Gn $50^{11.11}$ Je 16^7 cf. 2 S 19^3 עשה א׳ Ez 24^{17} (v. Co) sq. לְ Gn 50^{10} (v. also II. אָבֵל ad fin.); for calamity, Est 4^3 9^{22} (‖ יָגוֹן; contr. יום טוב) Jb 30^{31} (‖ קול בכים) Is 60^{20} 61^3 (where appar. = mourning garb, sq. מַעֲטֵה תְהִלָּה, v. also Bi Che on txt.; ‖ רוּחַ כֵּהָה; contr. שֶׁמֶן שָׂשׂוֹן); Je 31^{13} (‖ שׂשׂון), La 5^{15} (‖ מָחוֹל), Am 5^{16} (‖ מִסְפֵּד); cf. א׳ כִּבְנוֹת יַעֲנָה Mi 1^8; = time, period of mourning 2 S 11^7; בֵּית א׳ Ec 7^2 (‖ ב׳ מִשְׁתֶּה, v^4 (‖ ב׳ שִׂמְחָה); בִּגְדֵי א׳ garments of mourning 2 S 14^2.

אָבֵל מִצְרַיִם v. אָבֵל מ׳ sub II. אבל. p. 6 67

†I. **אָבֵל** **adj.** **mourning**—א׳ Gn 37^{35} Est 57
6^{12}; cstr. אֲבֵל־ ψ 35^{14}; אֲבֵלִים Jb 29^{25} Is 61^2 etc.; —for dead Gn 37^{35}, calamity Est 6^{12}, cf. fig. La 1^4 (pred., inanim. subj.), elsewhere as subst. *mourner;* sg. ψ 35^{14} (cstr.) for dead (‖ קדר); pl. Jb 29^{25} abs.; for calamity Is 57^{18} $61^{2.3}$ (where mourners for Zion, or of Zion, v. Di).

II. **אבל** (perh. أَبَلَ *grow green,* cf. ܐܒܠܐ *grass;* Lag$^{BN 45}$ prop. أَبَلَ *withstand,* hence אָבֵל as withstanding scorching sun (protected by trees, springs, etc.), hence also (Lag) إِبِل *camel*).

†II. **אָבֵל** **n.f.** **1.** meadow (?) 1 S 6^{18} MT but 58
rd. אֶבֶן cf. $v^{14.15}$ 𝔊 𝔖 We Dr. **2.** **n.pr.loc.** city 59
in N. Isr. 2 S 20^{18}, near Beth Maacah v^{14}=

62 אָבֵל בֵּית מַעֲכָה v^{15} (so also v^{14} Ew Th We Klo Dr),
66 1 K 15^{20} 2 K 15^{29}; = א׳ מַיִם 2 Ch 16^{4} (=Abil el
Ḳamḥ, *wheat-meadow* NW. of Dan & S. of Mu-
63 tulleh Rob$^{BR\,III,\,372}$). **3.** אָבֵל הַשִּׁטִּים **n.pr.loc.** (=
acacia-meadow) in lowlands of Moab Nu 33^{49};
=שִׁטִּים Nu 25^{1} Mi 6^{5} (=Tel Kefrein (?) Tristr
64 & Merrill$^{PESoc.\ 4th\ Statement,\ 89}$). **4.** אָבֵל כְּרָמִים
n.pr.loc. (=*vineyard-meadow*) in Ammon Ju
65 11^{33} (v. Euseb. Ἀβελαμπελων). **5.** אָבֵל מְחוֹלָה
n.pr.loc. (=*dance-meadow*) Ju 7^{22} 1 K 4^{12};
Elisha's birthplace 19^{16} (v. Euseb. Ἀβελμαελαι).
67 **6.** אָבֵל מִצְרַיִם **n.pr.loc.** (=*meadow of Egypt*,
i.e. fertile as Egypt?) E. of Jordan Gn 50^{11}
(where interpr. as if אֵבֶל מ׳, so 𝔊 𝔙; v. Di).

61 †**אֲבָל** **adv.** **1.** in older Heb. with an asseverative force, **verily, of a truth** Gn 42^{21} 2 S 14^{5} 1 K 1^{43} 2 K 4^{14}, with a slight advers. force, **nay, but** Gn 17^{19} (P). **2.** in late Heb. as a decided adversative, **howbeit, but** Dn 10$^{7.21}$ Ezr 10^{13} 2 Ch 1^{4} 19^{3} 33^{17} (cf. Ar. بَلْ *of a truth*, sometimes, from the context, *nay rather* Qor 2$^{82.94.110.129.149.165.261}$ 3^{143} 4^{52} etc.)

III. **אבל** (cf. Ar. أَبِلَ *able to manage camels*, fr. إِبِل, coll., Sab. אבל *camel* DHM$^{ZMG\ 1883,\ 329}$).

179 †**אוּבִיל** **n.pr.m.** (? *camel-driver*), overseer of David's camels 1 Ch 27^{30}.

180 **אֵבֶל, אוּבָל** v. יבל. p. 385

68 **אֶבֶן**$_{274}$ **n.f.** $^{Gn\ 29,2}$ (**m.**$^{1\,S\,17,40?}$) **stone** (As. *abnu*, = the sharp, projecting? v. Dl$^{W,\ Pr\ 107}$; Ph. אבן; Aram. אֶבֶן, ܐܒܢܐ; Eth. አብን: Sab. אבנ[ם] DHM $^{ZMG\ 1883,\ 341}$)—א׳ abs. Gn 28^{22}+; אָ֑בֶן 11^{3}+; cstr. 49^{24}+; sf. אַבְנוֹ 2 K 3^{25}; אֲבָנִים Gn 31^{46}+, etc.; —a *stone* (large or small). **1.** in natural state, used as pillow Gn 28$^{11.18}$ (E); seat Ex 17^{12} (E); cover of well Gn 29$^{2.3.3.8.10}$ (J); causing one to stumble Is 8^{14}; marring good ground 2 K 3$^{19.25}$; hand-missile Ex 21^{18} (JE) Nu 35$^{17.23}$ (P) 2 S 16$^{6.13}$, esp. in judicial stoning, with vb. רָגַם Lv 20$^{2.27}$ 24^{23} Nu 14^{10} 15$^{35.36}$ Jos 7$^{25\,a}$ (all P), so also Dt 21^{21} 2 Ch 24^{21} Ez 16^{40} 23^{47}; cf. 1 K 12^{18}= 2 Ch 10^{18}; with vb. סָקַל Dt 13^{11} 17^{5} 22$^{21.24}$ 1 K 21^{13}; also Jos 7$^{25\,b}$ (JE or D); sling-stones Ju 20^{16} 1 S 17$^{40.49.49.50}$ 2 Ch 26^{14}; hurled by engines 2 Ch 26^{15}; set up for inscribing law Dt 27$^{2.4.8}$ Jos 8^{32} (all D); as memorial Jos 4$^{3.5.6.7.8.9.20.21}$ (JED) 1 S 7^{12}; as sacred pillar (מַצֵּבָה) Gn 28^{18} 35^{14} (anointed with oil), 28^{22} (=בֵּית־אֵל) cf. (רֹעֶה) א׳ יִשְׂרָאֵל Gn 49^{24} (v. Di); as witness 31^{45} cf. Jos 24$^{26.27}$ (all JE); pl. gathered into heap (גַּל) over dead, Jos 7^{26} (v. Di) 8^{29} cf. 10$^{18.27}$ (JE) 2 S 18^{17}; גַּל on which meal was eaten, in a compact Gn 31$^{46.46}$ (JE); built into altar Ex 20^{25} Dt 27$^{5.6}$ (JED) Jos 8^{31} 1 K 18$^{31.32.38}$; cf. 2 K 23^{15} 𝔊 Klo (for הבמה); of figured stone (forbidden) א׳ מַשְׂכִּית Lv 26^{1} (H); א׳ גדולה where ark rested 1 S 6$^{14.15}$ also v^{18} (MT אבל q.v.); (v. for other noteworthy stones **9.** infr.) **2.** *stone, as material*, of tablets Ex 24^{12} 31^{18} 34^{1} (pl.) v $^{4.4}$ (JE) Dt 4^{13} 5^{19} 9$^{9.10.11}$ 10$^{1.3}$; of vessels, hence prob. Ex 7^{19} (P; א׳=vessels of stone ‖ עצים) v. Di; idols (‖ עֵץ) Dt 4^{28} 28$^{36.64}$ 29^{16} 2 K 19^{18}=Is 37^{19}; also Je 3^{9} Ez 20^{32}; pavement 2 K 16^{17}; edifice 1 K 6^{7} cf. Gn 11^{3}; also 2 S 5^{11} 2 K 12^{13} 1 Ch 22^{15}; oft. pl. of (worked) stones Lv 14$^{40.42.42.43.45}$ (P; in wall of house) 2 K 22^{6}+, cf. of city-wall Ne 3^{35}; of (ruined) city 1 K 15^{22} Ne 3^{34}; tomb Is 14^{19}; אֲבָנִים יְקָרוֹת (costly building-stones) 1 K 5^{31} 7$^{9.10.11}$ (v. also sub **3**); אַבְנֵי־שַׁיִשׁ = *marble* (v. 𝔊) 1 Ch 29^{2}; אַבְנֵי גָזִית = *hewn stones* 1 K 5^{31} 1 Ch 22^{2} Ez 40^{42} (for altar-tables),—cf. גָּזִית; א׳ מַחְצֵב 2 K 12^{13} 22^{6} 2 Ch 34^{11}; foundation-stone, corner-stone Is 28^{16} Je 51^{26} Jb 38^{6} ψ 118^{22}; cap-stone, completing the building, הָא׳ הָרֹאשָׁה Zc 4^{7} (but v. רֹאשׁ פִּנָּה ψ 118^{22} as above), Zc 3^{9} *upon one stone seven eyes*, prob. refers to this cap- or head-stone; the eyes are symbol of God's watchfulness; perhaps explaining cup-stones found in Orient, v. Guthe $^{ZPV\ 1890,\ 129}$; *stone-cutters* חָרָשֵׁי א׳ 2 S 5^{11} 1 Ch 22^{15}; חֹצְבֵי הָא׳ 2 K 12^{13} cf. 1 Ch 22^{2}. **3.** *precious stone*, gen. with modifying word א׳ יְקָרָה coll. 2 S 12^{30} 1 K 10^{2}+oft. (v. **2**); א׳ הַשֹּׁהַם Gn 2^{12} (J) cf. Ex 25^{7} 28^{9} 35$^{9.27}$ 39^{6} (P) 1 Ch 29^{2}; א׳ מִלֻּאִים Ex 25^{7} 35$^{9.27}$ cf. 1 Ch 29^{2}; א׳ סַפִּיר Ez 1^{26} 10^{1}; אַבְנֵי פוּךְ וְרִקְמָה Is 54^{12}; א׳ חֵפֶץ *ib.*; אַבְנֵי אֶקְדָּח 1 Ch 29^{2}; א׳ חֵן Pr 17^{8}; on אַבְנֵי אֵשׁ (*stones of fire*) Ez 28$^{14.16}$ as precious stones = As. *aban išâti* (?) v. Dl$^{Pa\ 118}$ & $^{W\ 40}$; but Sm al. *thunderbolts*; also without distinctive modifier Ex 25^{7} 35^{9}; חָרַשׁ א׳ engraver in stone Ex 28^{11} cf. 31^{5} 35^{33} (P). †**4.** *stones containing metal*, = *ore*, Dt 8^{9} (v. Di) Jb 28^{2} cf. v^{3}. †**5.** *a weight*, as orig. stone (v. Pr 27^{3} cf. Eng. weight *stone* = 14 ℔) אַבְנֵי־כִיס Pr 16^{11} (cf. As. Dl$^{W\ 38}$); א׳ הַמֶּלֶךְ 2 S 14^{26} (i.e. acc. to royal standard; cf. COT $^{Gn\ 23,16}$); א׳ וָא׳ Dt 25^{13} Pr 20$^{10.23}$ (i.e. different weights, for dishonest use); כִּיס אַבְנֵי מִרְמָה Mi 6^{11}; just weights אַבְנֵי־צֶדֶק Lv 19^{36}; א׳ שְׁלֵמָה Pr 11^{1}; hence also heavy mass of metal (lead) Zc 5^{8}. †**6.** *plummet* Is 34^{11} (*stones of devastation*, or *emptiness*, cf. on sense 2 K 21^{13} Am 7$^{7.8}$); also made of metal הָא׳ הַבְּדִיל Zc 4^{10} (conversely plummet fr. *plumbum*). †**7.** objects like stones; partic. *hail*, explicitly, אַבְנֵי הַבָּרָד Jos 10^{11} cf. Is 30^{30}; א׳ אֶלְגָּבִישׁ Ez 13$^{11.13}$ 38^{22}; but also אֲבָנִים

גְּדֹלוֹת Jos 10[11] (E) (cf. As. Dl[W 38]); lime-stones אַבְנֵי־גִר Is 27[9]. **8.** in sim. (mostly poet.) of sinking in water Ex 15[5]=Ne 9[11]; motionlessness Ex 15[16]; strength Jb 6[12]; firmness 41[16]; solidity (of ice) 38[30]; in prose, of commonness 1 K 10[27] 2 Ch 1[15]; also metaph. of one in fear 1 S 25[37] (i.e. *petrified* with terror, cf. Ex 15[16] supr.); לֵב הָא׳ =perverse, hard heart Ez 11[19] 36[26]; אַבְנֵי־נֵזֶר Zc 9[16] (of ransomed Isr.)—א׳ personif. Hb 2[11] cf. v[19]; cf. Ez 13[11] (v. **7** supr.) †**9.** In topogr. terms (nearly=n.pr.); אֶבֶן בֹּהַן Jo 15[6] 18[17];
72 הָאֶ׳ הָעֵזֶר 1 S 5[1] cf. 7[12], also 4[1] (We Dr); הָאֶ׳ הָאָזֶל 1 S 20[19], rd. הָאַרְגָּב הַלָּאז v. 𝔊 here & v[41] (We Dr Klo); אֶ׳ הַזֹּחֶלֶת 1 K 1[9] (where We Skizzen III,171 comp. Ar. *Zuhal*=Saturn).

70 †[אֹבֶן] **n.[m.] wheel, disc.**—*Du.* הָאָבְנָיִם—**1.** potter's *wheel* Je 18[3] (two discs revolving one above the other; name from likeness to mill-stones; v. AW[18]). **2.** עַל־הָא׳ Ex 1[16] prob. =*sella parturientis*,=δίφροι λοχειαῖοι *bearing-stool, midwife's stool* (fr. likeness to potter's wheel; on custom of labor upon stool v. Ploss Das Weib, 2nd ed. ii, 35, 179 etc. & Cesnola Coll. fr. Cyprus, Metrop. Mus., N. York, No. 614, terra cotta fig. fr. 4th or 5th cent. B.C.; Descriptive Atlas of Cesn. Coll. I, pl. lxvi. No. 435; cf. W. H. W[ard] PESoc. 2nd Statement 1873, p. 76).

71 אבנה Kt 2 K 5[12] v. אֲמָנָה.

73 אַבְנֵט v. בנט. p. 126

74 אַבְנֵר v. אֲבִינֵר sub II. אָבָה. p. 4

75 †[אָבַס] **vb. feed, fatten** (Mish. *id.*; ? As. [*abâsu*] Dl[W 46]) **Qal** *Pt. pass. fattened,* אָבוּס of ox Pr 15[17]; אֲבוּסִים of fowl 1 K 5[3].

18 †אֵבוּס **n.m.** Pr 14,4 **crib** (=*feeding-trough,* on form v. Ges §84 a 12. R.) of ass Is 1[3] (cstr.); oxen Pr 14[4] (abs.); אִם־יָלִין עַל־אֲבוּסֶךָ Jb 39[9] (of wild-ox).

3965 †[מַאֲבוּס] **n.[m.] granary** (=*place of fodder;* ? As. *bit abûsâti* Dl[W 46]) pl. sf. מַאֲבֻסֶיהָ Je 50[26].

76 אֲבַעְבֻּעֹת v. בוע. p. 101

אבץ (meaning unknown).

77 †[אֶבֶץ] **n.pr.loc.** city in Issachar, אָבֶץ Jos 19[20].

78 †אִבְצָן **n.pr.m.** judge of Isr. Ju 12[8.10] (Lag GN 1891, 19 (אָ)בֶן צָן), 𝔊 Ἀβεσσαν, 𝔖 ܐܒܨܢ).

אבק (Ar. أَبَقَ *run away* (cf. Lag BN 51)).

80 †אָבָק **n.m.** Ez 26,10 **dust**—א׳ Dt 28[24]+3 t.; cstr. אֲבַק Na 1[3]; sf. אֲבָקָם Ez 26[10]—*dust* (? fleeing, flying; syn. עָפָר=oft. dust lying on or composing ground) Ex 9[9] Ez 26[10] Dt 28[24] (‖ עָפָר) Is 5[24] (‖ מֹק) 29[5] (‖ מֹץ); fig. of clouds under Yahweh's feet Na 1[3].

†[אֲבָקָה or אַבְקָה] **n.f.** prob. coll., cstr. אַבְקַת 81
רוֹכֵל Ct 3[6] **powders** *of merchant*=scent-powders. (On formation cf. Lag BN 81.)

†[אָבַק] **vb. denom. Niph. wrestle** (=*get* 79
dusty, cf. κόνις, κονίω, v. also Str Pirke Aboth, I, 4 מִתְאַבֵּק בַּעֲפַר רַגְלֵיהֶם=*sit at their feet;* others, e.g. Di, comp. חבק). וַיֵּאָבֵק עִם Gn 32[25]; *Inf.* sf. בְּהֵאָבְקוֹ עִם v[26].

אבר (cf. As. *abâru, be firm, strong* Dl[W]).

†אֵבֶר **n.[m.] pinions** (fr. strength, poet. & 83
fig., pl. in sense) as of dove ψ 55[7]; eagle Is 40[31]; אֶרֶךְ הָא׳ of king of Babyl. under fig. of eagle Ez 17[3] (‖ גְּדוֹל הַכְּנָפַיִם of broad, overshadowing wings).

†אֶבְרָה **n.f. pinion** (nom. unit., poet.) of 84
ostrich Jb 39[13]; אֶבְרָתוֹ of eagle, sim. for י׳ Dt 32[11]; metaph. of י׳ ψ 91[4]; אֶבְרוֹתֶיהָ of dove ψ 68[14]; (all ‖ כנף).

†[אָבַר] **vb. denom. Hiph. fly** (=*move* 82
pinions); of hawk יַאֲבֶר־נֵץ Jb 39[29].

†[אָבִיר] **adj. strong**; alw.=subst. *the* 46
Strong, old name for God (poet.); only cstr. in אֲבִיר יַעֲקֹב Gn 49[24] & thence ψ 132[2.5] Is 49[26] 60[16]; א׳ יִשְׂרָאֵל Is 1[24] (cf. Che crit. n.)—Ba NB 51 assigns this cstr. to אַבִּיר.

†אַבִּיר **adj. mighty, valiant**—א׳ Jb 34[20] 47
+ Is 10[13] Kt (Qr כַּבִּיר); cstr. *id.* 1 S 21[8]; pl. אַבִּירִים Jb 24[22]+;—*mighty* (alw.=subst. & poet. exc. 1 S 21[8]). **1.** men Ju 5[22] Jb 24[22] (=*violent*) 34[20] Je 46[15] 1 S 21[8] (rd. א׳ הָרָצִים Gr Dr, cf. 22[17]; but Lag Probebibel אביל הָעֲיָרִים v. *Id.* BN 45; Klo גִּבּוֹר), La 1[15]; אַבִּירֵי לֵב *stout of heart* Is 46[12] (=*obstinate*) ψ 76[6]. **2.** angels ψ 78[25] (cf. 103[20]). **3.** animals; bull, sim. of king of Assyr. Is 10[13] (rd. כְּאַבִּיר & v. Di); elsewh. pl.; metaph. for enemies אַבִּירֵי בָשָׁן ψ 22[13] (‖ פָּרִים); for princes ψ 68[31]; for Edomites Is 34[7]; hence even as sacrif. ψ 50[13] (‖ עַתּוּדִים); of horses Je 8[16] 47[3] 50[11].

אַבְרָהָם v. אַבְרָם sub II. אבה. p. 4 85

†אַבְרֵךְ proclaimed before Joseph Gn 41[43] 86
(mng. dub.; many Egypt. deriv. proposed; e.g. *a-bor-k*, Copt.=*prostrate thyself!* Benfey Verh. d. äg. Spr. z. Sem. 302 f; *āprek*,=*head bowed!* Chabas RA I, —but *ā*=ע, v. also Wiedemann Altäg. Wörter 1883, 8; *ap-reχ-u, head of the wise,* Harkavy Berl. äg. Zeitschr. 1869;

àb-rek, rejoice thou! Cook[Speaker's Comm. Gn. ad loc. and p. 482]; Lepage Renouf[PSBA Nov. 1888, 5 f] *àb(u)-rek, thy command is our desire,* i.e. we are at thy service; Say[Rel. Bab. 183] As. *abrikku* = Ak. *abrik, vizier* (unpub. tabl.), v. already Dl[W; L 134 c., l. 11.12] who cp. As. *abarakku* = title, perh. *grand vizier;* against Dl, v. COT & Nö[ZMG 1886, 734]).

52, 87 אַבְשַׁי, אַבְרָם v. אֲבִישַׁי, אֲבִירָם sub II. אבה. p. 5

53 אַבְשָׁלוֹם, אַבְשָׁלֹם v. אֲבִישָׁלוֹם sub II. אבה. p. 5

אגא (cf. Ar. أَجَا, *flee* Frey).

89 †אָגֵא **n.pr.m.** (*fugitive?*) father of a hero of David 2 S 23[11] (ins. also 1 Ch 11[13] Dr[Sm]).

90 †אֲגַג, (אֲגַג Nu 24[7]) **n.pr.m.** (*violent?* As. *agâgu* Dl[W]) king of Amalek 1 S 15[8.9.20.32.32.32.33], also Nu 24[7] (E), as symbol of might; (Is א׳ then title? v. Di).

91 †אֲגָגִי **adj.gent.** of Haman (= Amalekite? so Jew. trad. & cf. Jos.[Ant. xi. 6. 5]) Est 3[1.10] 8[3.5] 9[24].

אגד (*bind,* so Talm. אָגַד, Aram. אֲגַד).

92 †אֲגֻדָּה **n.f.** band (Mishn. אֲגוּדָּה cf. NHWB). **1.** pl. cstr. אֲגֻדּוֹת מוֹטָה *bands, thongs* (fastening ox-bow) metaph. of fetters of slavery Is 58[6]. **2.** אֲגֻדַּת אֵזוֹב *bunch* of hyssop Ex 12[22]. **3.** א׳ abs. *band* of men (cf. חֶבֶל. Eng. *band*) 2 S 2[25]. **4.** אֲגֻדָּתוֹ *vault* of the heavens (as fitted together, constructed, cf. Ar. إِجَادٌ) Am 9[6].

93 †אֱגוֹז **n.[m.]** nuts (coll.) (NH *id.*, אַמְגוּזָא, Ar. جَوْزٌ, Eth. ገውዝ: Aram. ܓܘܙܐ, אֱגוֹזָא; cf. Pers. گوز, whence prob. אֱגוֹז as loan-word) Ct 6[11].

אגל (Hoffm[Hiob. 86] comp. Ar. اجل *restrict,* Eth. ኢጐሌ: *a certain one* (name *withheld*), etc.)

96 אֵגֶל **n.[m.]** usually trans. **drop,** אֶגְלֵי־טָל *dew-drops* Jb 38[28] (‖ מָטָר) so Vrss De Di; Hoffm 'Rückstände,' 'Ansammlungen,' i.e. **collections, stores, reserve-supply.**

97 †אֶגְלַיִם **n.pr.loc.** town in Moab Is 15[8]; (meaning?); ? cf. Αἰγαλειμ (Euseb.) 9 m. S. of Areopolis; v. Lag[Onom. 228, 98; ed. 2, p. 244].

אגם (*troubled, sad,* As. *agâmu* Dl[W] cf. Ar. أَجَمَ *loathe;* also أَجَمَةٌ *marshy jungle;* v. עגם).

98 †אֲגַם **n.[m.]** **troubled pool** (Aram. *id.*, ܐܓܡܐ, As. *agammu* Dl[W])—א׳ abs. Is 35[7]; cstr. 41[18] + 2 t.; אֲגַמִּים Ex 8[1] + 2 t.; אַגְמֵי Is 14[23]; אַגְמֵיהֶם Ex 7[19]—**1.** *troubled* or *muddy* (gloomy) *pools* or *marshes,* pl. א׳ מַיִם Is 14[23]. **2.** any *pool, pond,* sg. א׳ מַיִם Is 41[18] ψ 107[35] 114[8]; pl. without מַיִם Ex 7[19] 8[1] (P) Is 42[15]. **3.** *swamp-reed, rush* (= אַגְמוֹן) Je 51[32].

†[אָגֵם] **adj. sad** (cf. Mish.) אַגְמֵי־נֶפֶשׁ Is 19[10]. 99

†אַגְמֹן, אַגְמוֹן **n.[m.] rush, bulrush. 1.** 100
used as cord or line Jb 40[26] (of twisted rushes, or spun of rush-fibre, cf. Di ad loc.); as fuel 41[12]; sim. of bending head Is 58[5]. **2.** metaph. of the lowly, insignif. (‖ כִּפָּה) Is 9[13] 19[15].

אגן (prob. *circular, round,* cf. Ar. أُجْنَةٌ *ball of cheek* & v. Talm. אוֹגֶן *curved rim of a vessel*).

†[אַגָּן] **n.[m.] bowl, basin** (Talm. אוֹגָן, Aram. 101
ܐܓܢܐ, אַגָּנָא; Ar. إِجَّانَةٌ, *vessel* in which clothes are washed; As. (pl.) *aganâtē* Dl[W]). **1.** *basins* used in ritual אַגָּנֹת Ex 24[6] (E). **2.** אַגַּן הַסַּהַר, sim. of curves of body Ct 7[3]. **3.** metaph. of family of Eliakim. כְּלֵי הָאַגָּנוֹת = *basin-vessels* Is 22[24] (= bowl-shaped vessels Che) opp. כְּלֵי הַנְּבָלִים; both ‖ כְּלֵי הַקָּטָן.

אגף (As. stem of *agappu, wing,* cf. Dl[W]).

†[אֲגַף] **n.[m.] band, army** (loan-word, orig. 102
wing of army; As. *agappu,* Aram. אגף, *wing.* Others, fr. נגף, Sta[§ 256 b])—All Ez. & all *pl.* (or *du.?*) אֲגַפֶּיךָ Ez 38[9] 39[4]; אֲגַפָּיו 12[14] + 3 t.; אֲגַפֶּיהָ 38[6] (all c. כָּל־ exc. 38[22])—*bands, armies* of king of Judah Ez 12[14] 17[21]; *hordes* (RV) of Gog 38[9.22] 39[4]; specif. of גֹּמֶר 38[6]; of תּוֹגַרְמָה *ib.*

†I. [אָגַר] **vb. gather** (food)—only **Qal**— 103
Pf. אָגְרָה, of ant Pr 6[8] (obj. מַאֲכָל); *Impf.* 2 ms. תֶּאֱגֹר of Isr. Dt 28[39] (obj. = grapes, not expr.); *Pt.* אֹגֵר בַּקַּיִץ subst. *one who gathers* (abs.) Pr. 10[5].

II. **אגר** (*pay, hire,* Ar. أَجَرَ, Aram. אֲגַר, ܐܓܪ, As. *agâru* Dl[W], Palm. אגר Reck[ZMG 1888, 396]).

†אָגוּר **n.pr.m.** (perh. *hireling,* Ar. أَجِيرٌ, 94
Aram. אֲגִירָא, ܐܓܝܪܐ v. PS, As. *agîru,* cf. Hpt[BAS i. 124]; others *gatherer,* fr. I. אגר) son of יָקֶה, an author of proverbs Pr 30[1].

†[אֲגוֹרָה] **n.f. payment,** אֲגוֹרַת כֶּסֶף 1 S 2[36]. 95

†אִגֶּרֶת **n.f. letter, letter-missive** (late, prob. 107
loan-word, As. *egirtu* Dl[W])—abs. Ne 2[8] + 2 t.; cstr. Est 9[29]; pl. אִגְּרוֹת abs. 2 Ch 30[1] + 3 t.; cstr. Ne 2[9]; אִגְּרֹתֵיהֶם Ne 6[17]—*letter,* esp. royal letter 2 Ch 30[1.6] Ne 2[7.8.9]; but also others Ne 6[5.17.19] Es 9[26.29] (‖ סֵפֶר vv[20.30]; other syn. נִשְׁתְּוָן, מִכְתָּב q.v.)

אֲגַרְטָל v. גרטל. p. 173 105

אֶגְרֹף v. גרף. p. 175 106

108 **אֵד, אֹדוֹת, אוֹדוֹת, אֹדֹת** v. אוד.

109 †**[אָדַב]** **vb.** **grieve**; **Hiph.** *Inf.* לַאֲדִיב (= לְהַאֲדִיב Ges$^{§53.3.R7}$) *to cause to grieve* 1 S 2^{33}. (But Dr prop. לְהָדִיב fr. דוב q.v.)

110 †**אַדְבְּאֵל** **n.pr.m.** 3rd son of Ishmael (cf. Ar. اَدَبَ *invite, discipline*?) Gn 25^{13} 1 Ch 1^{29} (As. *Idiba'il* etc., name of north. Ar. tribe Dl$^{Pa\,301}$; cf. Minæan אדבל DHM in MV).

אדד (? cf. Ar. اَدٌّ *strength*).

112 †**אִדּוֹ** **n.pr.m.** a chief Israelite Ezr 8$^{17.17}$.

111 **אֲדַד** **n.pr.m.** v. הדד. p. 212

118 **אֲדַלְיָא** **n.pr.m.** 5th son of Haman Est 9^{8} (Pers.?).

I. **אדם** (cf. As. [*adâmu*] *make, produce* (?) Dl$^{W\,\&\,Pr\,104}$).

120 **אָדָם** $_{560}$ **n.m.** $^{Gn\,1,27}$ **man, mankind** (Ph. אדם, Sab. *id.*, CIS$^{iv.\,1.\,1.\,4}$ al.; cf. As. *admu, young* (of bird) Dl^{W}, but Nö$^{ZMG\,1886,722}$ identif. with Ar. أَنَام coll. *creatures*)—Sg. abs. exc. cstr. Pr 6^{12} cf. Thes; (בְּנֵי (הָ)א׳ oft. = pl. of א׳ Gn 11^{5} + 39 t., cf. בְּנוֹת הָא׳ Gn 6$^{2.4}$)—**1.** *a man* (= Ger. *Mensch*) = human being Gn 2$^{5.7.7.8.15.16.18}$ +, 16^{12} (27 t. J) Lv 5^{4} (‖ נֶפֶשׁ) 13$^{2.9}$ (19 t. P) Ne 2^{10} Is 13^{12} (‖ אֱנוֹשׁ); א׳ בְּלִיַּעַל ‖ אִישׁ אָוֶן Pr 6^{12}; הָא׳ הַגָּדוֹל Jos 14^{15} (E); cf. 1 S 25^{25} & v. בליעל); = any one Lv 1^{2} Nu 9$^{6.7}$ Jb 20^{29} 27^{13} Pr 15^{20} 21$^{16.20}$ 24^{30} Ec 7^{20} + oft. WisdLt, Je 2^{6} 4^{25} Ne 2^{12}, cf. נֶפֶשׁ א׳ Nu 19$^{11.13}$ +; seld. *man* opp. woman Gn 2$^{22.22.23.25}$ 3$^{8.12.17.20.21}$ Ec 7^{28}. **2.** coll. *man, mankind* Gn 1^{26} 9$^{5.6.6.6}$ + (P 28 t.) 6$^{1.5.6.7}$ (JE 24 t.) Dt 4^{32} (D 6 t.) (on 2 S 7^{19} cf. 1 Ch 17^{17} v. Dr^{Sm}); distinctly = men + women Gn 1^{27} 5^{1} Nu 5^{6}; given as name Gn 5^{2}; but = warriors Is 22^{6} רֶכֶב א׳ (‖ פרשים); ‖ beasts (41 t.) בְּהֵמָה Gn 6^{7} 7^{23} (J?) Ex 8$^{13.14}$ 9$^{9.10}$ (P) 9$^{19.22.25}$ 12^{12} 13$^{2.13.15}$ (all J) +; late proph. Je 21^{6} 31^{27} 50^{3} 51^{62} Ez 14$^{13.17.19.21}$ 25^{13} 29$^{8.11}$ 32^{13} (del. Co) 36^{11} Jon 3^{8} Zp 1^{3} Hg 1^{11} Zc 2^{8} 8^{10}; ‖ בָּקָר Ez 4^{15}; ‖ צֹאן, חֲמֹרִים, ב׳ Nu 31^{28}; ‖ *id.* + מִכָּל־הַבְּהֵמָה v^{30} cf. Jon 3^{7}; ‖ חַיָּה Gn 9^{5} (P) cf. Ez 1$^{5.8.10.26}$, & descript. of כְּרוּבִים Ez 10$^{8.14.21}$ cf. 41^{19}; ‖ trees Dt 20^{19} (rd. הָאָדָם v. Di); opp. God 1 S 15^{29} 16$^{7.7}$ Is 31^{3} Ez 28$^{2.9}$ 1 Ch 21^{13} 29^{1} 2 Ch 6^{18} Mal 3^{8} cf. Ex 33^{20} Dt 5^{21}; so בֶּן־א׳ Nu 23^{19} (‖ איש) Ez 2$^{1.3.6.8}$ (87 t. Ez, alw. addressed to proph.); בְּנֵי הָא׳ 1 S 26^{19}; made in God's image Gn 1$^{26.27}$ 9^{6} cf. Ec 7^{29}; as feeble, earthly, mortal Nu 16$^{29.29}$ Ps 82^{7} 144$^{3.4}$ Jb 5^{7} 14$^{1.10}$ cf. 25^{6} (בֶּן־א׳) Ec 12^{5}; as sinful 1 K 8^{46} 2 Ch 6^{36} Je 10^{14} cf. Nu 5^{6} Jb 31^{33} Ho 6^{7}; of men in general, other men (opp. to particular ones) Ju 16^{17} (cf. אַחַד הָא׳ v$^{7.11}$) 18$^{7.28}$ ψ 73^{5} Je 32^{20} +; ‖ אִישׁ Is 2$^{9.11.17}$ 5^{15} cf. Ez 23^{42} (del. Co Vrss); בְּנֵי א׳ 2 S 7^{14} (‖ אֲנָשִׁים) Pr 8^{4} (‖ אִישִׁים); ψ 49^{3} 62^{10} (both ‖ בְּנֵי אִישׁ) = men of low opp. men of high degree—so oft. Ph. and = *vassal* Sab. DHM$^{ZMG\,1875,\,680\,cf.\,686}$; נֶפֶשׁ א׳ coll. Nu 31$^{35.40.46}$ 1 Ch 5^{21} Ez 27^{13}. †**3. n.pr.m.** 121
Adam, first man (without art., cf. שָׂטָן 1 Ch 21^{1} over ag. הַשּׂ׳ Jb 1^{6} etc.) Gn 4^{25} (J) 5$^{1.3.4.5}$ (P) 1 Ch 1^{1}. (Gn 2^{20} 3$^{17.21}$ rd. לְא׳ v. Di.) †**4. n.** 121
pr.loc. city in Jordan valley (as *built*?) Jos 3^{16}.

127 **אֲדָמָה** $_{224}$ **n.f. ground, land** (as *tilled*, Ger. *bebaut*? Dl$^{Pr\,105}$, but Fleisch. (Merx$^{Archiv\,I,\,236\,f}$) comp. Ar. أَدَمَة, *skin*, as smoothly covering & close-fitting; √דם cf. Ar. دَمَّ *smear* (spread over surface); cf. also Nö$^{ZMG\,1886,\,737}$)—א׳ Gn 1^{25} +; cstr. אַדְמַת Gn 47^{20} +; *sf.* אַדְמָתִי Jb 31^{38} + 2 t. etc.; *pl.* אֲדָמוֹת ψ 49^{12}—**1.** *ground* (as tilled, yielding sustenance) Gn 2$^{5.9}$ 3$^{17.23}$ 4$^{2.3.12}$ 5^{29} 8^{21} 19^{25} 47^{23} Ex 34^{26} (all J); Ex 23^{19} (E) Dt 7^{13} 11^{17} 26$^{2.10.15}$ 28$^{4.11.18.33.42.51}$ 30^{9} 2 S 9^{10} Is 1^{7} 28^{24} 30$^{23.23.24}$ Je 7^{20} 14^{4} 25^{33} Hg 1^{11} Mal 3^{11} ψ 83^{11} 105^{35} Pr 12^{11} 28^{19} 1 Ch 27^{26} Ne 10$^{36.38}$ cf. fig. Jb 5^{6} (‖ עפר); personif. 31^{38} Jo 1^{10}; also אִישׁ הָא׳ Gn 9^{20} (J) *tiller, husbandman;* meton. אֹהֵב א׳ 2 Ch 26^{10} i.e. *lover of husbandry* (or do these point to earlier meaning *tillage*? cf. Dl$^{Pr\,105}$) אִישׁ עֹבֵד א׳ Zc 13^{5}. †**2.** *piece of ground*, landed property Gn 47$^{18.19.19.19.20.22.22.23.26}$ (all J) ψ 49^{12} (pl.) †**3.** *earth* as material substance; of wh. man is made Gn 2^{7} (עָפָר מִן־הָא׳); so animals v^{19} (מִן־הָא׳); altar Ex 20^{24}; earthen vessels חַרְשֵׂי א׳ Is 45^{9}; on head, sign of woe 1 S 4^{12} 2 S 1^{2} 15^{32}; of contrition Ne 9^{1} (cf. עָפָר, אֵפֶר); מַעֲבֵה הָא׳ 1 K 7^{46} cf. 2 Ch 4^{17} (*firmness of earth*, firm earth, clay-ground, for casting-moulds; or *clay-moulds* (Be)? or is this *n.pr.*? Klo prop. בְּמַעֲרָה הָאֲדֻמָּה *in the red cave*); mule-loads of 2 K 5^{17}; in it lie the dead מִיְּשֵׁנֵי אַדְמַת־עָפָר Dn 12^{2} cf. Gn 3$^{19.23}$ ψ 146^{4}. **4.** *ground* as earth's visible surface; רֶמֶשׂ הָא׳ Gn 1^{25} 6^{20} (both P) Ho 2^{20} cf. Gn 7^{8} 9^{2} (J?) Lv 20^{25} (P) Dt 4^{18} Ez 38^{20}; also Gn 4^{10} (J) Is 24^{21} Am 3^{5} Zp 1$^{2.3}$; as wet with dew 2 S 17^{12}; rain 1 K 17^{14} 18^{1}; cf. personif. פָּצְתָה הָא׳ אֶת־פִּיהָ Nu 16^{30} (P) (‖ ארץ v^{32}), vid. v^{31}; of partic. place, spot א׳ קֹדֶשׁ Ex 3^{5} esp. as abode of man Gn 4^{11} Ex 10^{6} Dt 4$^{10.40}$ 12^{1} 1 S 20^{31} 2 S 14^{7}; oft. פְּנֵי הָא׳ Gn 2^{6} 4^{14} 6$^{1.7}$ 7$^{4.23}$ 8$^{8.13}$ Ex 32^{12} 33^{16} Nu 12^{3} Dt 6^{15} 7^{6} (all J, D) 1 S 20^{15} + 9 t. **5.** *land, territory, country* (= ארץ) Gn 47^{19} (J) Lv 20^{24} (J?—‖ ארץ) cstr. bef. n.pr. א׳ מִצְרַיִם Gn 47$^{20.26}$; א׳ יְהוּדָה Is 19^{17}; א׳ יִשְׂרָאֵל Ez 11^{17} + 16 t. Ez; esp. of land as promised or given by

׳י to his people=Canaan Gn 28^{15} Ex 20^{12} Nu 11^{12} 32^{11} (all J?) Dt 5^{16}+16 t. Dt, Jos; 1 K 8$^{34.40}$ +, Je 16^{15} 24^{10} 25^{5} 35^{15} Ez 28^{25} 2 Ch 6$^{25.31}$ 7^{20} 33^{8}; cf. also Dt 12^{19} 21^{23} 29^{27} 2 K 17^{23} Is 6^{11} 7^{16} 14^{1}+, Ez 34$^{13.27}$+, Ne 9^{25} (א׳ שְׁמֵנָה),—in all c. 41 t.; +Jo 2^{21} (personif.); א׳ הַקֹּדֶשׁ Zc 2^{16} (cf. sub **4** supr.); hence also as Yahweh's land Dt 32^{43} Is 14^{2} Zc 9^{16} 2 Ch 7^{20}. †**6.** whole *earth*, inhabited earth (seld.; cf. also פְּנֵי הָא׳ sub **4** supr.) Gn 12^{3} 28^{14} (both J cf. אֶרֶץ 18^{18} 22^{18} 26^{4}) Dt 14^{2} Am 3^{2}
128 Is 24^{21}. †**7. n.pr.loc.** city in Naphtali (as *built* cf. אָדָם **4**?=*ed-Dâme*?) W. of L. Gennes. Jos 19^{36} v. Di.

126 †אֲדָמָה **n.pr.loc.** city in Vale of Siddim Gn 10^{19} 14$^{2.8}$ Dt 29^{22} Ho 11^{8}.

129, 5346 אַדְמִי הַנֶּקֶב **n.pr.loc.** pass in Naphtali, Jos 19^{33} v. נקב.

II. אדם (أَدِمَ, أُدْمٌ *tawny*, Eth. አደመ: (only in derivatives), As. *adâmu*? Dl^{W}; cf. Lag$^{BN\ 28}$).

119 †[אָדֵם, אָדַם] **vb. be red** (on format. cf. Lag$^{BN\ 83\ cf.\ 120}$)—**Qal** *Pf.* 3 pl. אָדְמוּ *ruddy*, of Nazirites La 4^{7}; **Pu.** *Pt. reddened, dyed red*, מְאָדָּם Na 2^{4} (of shield), מְאָדָּמִים of rams' skins Ex 25^{5} 26^{14} 35$^{7.23}$ 36^{19} 39^{34} (all P). **Hithp.** *Impf. redden, grow* or *look red*, יִתְאַדָּם Pr 23^{31} (of wine); **Hiph.** *Impf. emit* (*show*) *redness* (cf. Lag^{BN120}) יַאְדִּימוּ כַתּוֹלָע Is 1^{18} (of sins) i.e. be glaring, flagrant (cf. also v^{15}).

122 †אָדֹם **adj. red**—א׳ Is 63^{2} Zc 1^{8}+Gn 25$^{30.30}$, v. infr.; אָדוֹם Ct 5^{10}; f. אֲדֻמָּה Nu 19^{2}, pl. אֲדֻמִּים 2 K 3^{22}+2 t.;—*ruddy, red*, of man Ct 5^{10}; horse Zc 1$^{8.8}$ (‖ שָׂרֹק cf. As. Dl^{W87}) 6^{2} (‖ שָׁחֹר); heifer Nu 19^{2}; water 2 K 3^{22} (א׳ כַּדָּם); cf. as subst. *red, redness* on garment Is 63^{2}; הָאָדֹם=*the* (*red*) *lentils* Gn 25$^{30.30}$, but rd. הָאֱדֹם v. infr.; cf. also מַעֲלֶה.

124 †אֹדֶם **n.**[**f.**] **carnelian** (fr. *redness*; 𝔊 σάρδιον; on format. cf. Lag^{BN144}) Ex 28^{17} 39^{10} (P) Ez 28^{13}.

123 †אֱדֹם **n.**[**m.**] **name of a condiment** (Ar. إِدَامٌ v. Anderson in Di; cf. As. *adumatu*? Dl^{W}) הָאֱ׳ Gn 25$^{30.30}$ (J; so rd. for הָאָ׳ MT; v. Di).

123 אֱדוֹם (†אֱדֹם Ez 25^{14}) **n.pr.m. 1. Edom** (name of a god? v. Sta$^{G.\ 1,\ 121}$ RS$^{Sem\ 43}$; vid. *n.pr.* עבדאדם; but Bae$^{Rel\ 10}$ thinks dial. var. of אָדָם, בְּנֵי אָדָם=בני אדום)=Esau, elder son of Isaac Gn 25^{30} (J) (where etym.=*red*, cf. v^{25} (E?) & sub אַדְמוֹנִי) 36$^{1.8.19}$ (P). **2.** coll. (**m.** but **f.** Mal 1^{4}) *Edomites, Idumeans* as descend. of Esau Gn 36$^{9.43}$ (P); also 1 S 14^{47}+31 t.+2 S 8^{13} (for MT ארם; 𝔊𝔖, v. 1 Ch 18^{12} ψ 60^{2}, We Dr); perh. also v^{12} (𝔊𝔖 1 Ch 18^{11}; MT ארם but v. We Dr); also 2 Ch 20^{2} (v. Be); א׳=king of Edom Nu 20$^{18.20.21}$; poet. בְּנֵי א׳ ψ 137^{7} בַּת א׳ La 4$^{21.22}$. **3.** *land of Edom, Idumaea* (*f.* Ez 32^{29} 35^{15} and 36^{5}) S. & SE. of Pal. Gn 36$^{32.43}$+32 t. (incl. שְׂדֵה א׳ Gn 32^{4}; אֶרֶץ א׳ Gn 36$^{16.17.21.31}$ Nu 20^{23} 21^{4} 33^{37} +);—uncertain whether **2** or **3** are Ex 15^{15} Nu 20^{14} 24^{18}+9 t. (chiefly in מֶלֶךְ א׳ etc.)

†אֲדֹמִי **adj. gent. Edomite** Dt 23^{8} 1 S 21^{8} 130
22$^{9.18.22}$ 1 K 11^{14} ψ 52^{2}; אֲדוֹמִים 2 Ch 25^{14} 28^{17};
so 2 K 16^{6} (Qr; Kt ארומים, v. ארם); אֲדֹמִיִּם 726
1 K 11^{17}; *f.* אֲדֹמִיּוֹת 1 K 11^{1}.

†אֲדַמְדָּם **adj. reddish** (cf. As. *ada(m)mumu*? Dl^{W}) of leprous sores Lv 13^{42} (־דָּם) v^{49} (־דָּם); *f.* אֲדַמְדֶּמֶת v$^{24.43}$; ־דֶּמֶת v^{19}; *f.pl.* אֲדַמְדַּמּוֹת 14^{37}. 125

†אַדְמוֹנִי **adj. red, ruddy,** of Esau as new-born babe Gn 25^{25} (whence name Edom acc. to E? cf. Di); of youth 1 S 16^{12} 17^{42} (אַדְמֹנִי). 132

אֲדֻמִּים **n.pr.loc.** v. מַעֲלֵה sub עלה p. 748 131

†אַדְמָתָא **n.pr.m.** a prince of Persia & Media Est 1^{14} (cf. Pers. *admâta, unrestrained*). 133

אדן (mng. disputed; (1) cf. As. [*adannu*] *firm, strong*; adv. *adanniš, strongly, exceedingly* Dl^{W}>(2) Fü. (*a*) *make firm, fasten* (cf. عدن) whence אֶדֶן; (*b*) *determine, command, rule*, whence אָדוֹן; (3) Thes Add., MV al. (*a*) intr. *be under, low, inferior* (cf. דּוּן, دان), whence אֶדֶן; (*b*) tr. *put under command, rule over* (cf. דִּין) whence אָדוֹן; v. also (4) Lag$^{M.\ i.\ 102}$, אָדוֹן fr. (ادى).

[אֶדֶן]$_{57}$ **n.m.** $^{Ex\ 26,19}$ **base, pedestal**—אָ֑דֶן Ex 38^{7}; pl. אֲדָנִים Ex 26^{19}+; cstr. אַדְנֵי Ct 5^{15}+, etc. 134 **1.** *pedestals* of fine gold, on wh. pillars of marble were set Ct 5^{15}. **2.** *pedestals* of the earth on wh. its pillars were placed Jb 38^{6} (‖ corner-stone). **3.** (metal) *pedestals, bases*, or *sockets* in wh. tenons of planks & pillars of tabernacle were set up; two for each plank & one for each pillar Ex 26$^{19.19.19}$+52 t. in Ex 26.27.35–40 Nu 3.4 (all P); cf. 𝔊 Sm Co for אַרְכּוֹ Ez 41^{22}, of altar.

אָדוֹן **n.m.** $^{Mal\ 3,1}$ **lord** (Ph. אדן)—א׳ ψ 12^{5}+ 113
cstr. אֲדוֹן Jos 3^{11}+; pl. אֲדֹנִים Is 26^{13}+; cstr. אֲדֹנֵי
Dt 10^{17}+; sf. אֲדֹנֵינוּ 1 S 25^{14}+ etc.; (אֲדֹנָי, אֲדֹנַי,
אֲדֹנִי are variations of Mass. pointing to distin- 136
guish divine reference fr. human. Pl., with few exc. an intens. pl. of rank; word takes sf. as pl. in all other pers.; so doubtless here. Orig. reading prob. in all cases אֲדֹנִי (v. Dalman Der Gottesname Adonaj; Lag$^{BN\ 188}$ makes אֲדֹנָי an Aram. format.); אֲדֹנִי now found in J 51 t.; in E

†Gn 31^{35} 32^{19} 42^{10} Ex 21^{5}; in P †Gn $23^{6.11.15}$ Nu $36^{2.2}$; often S & K; in Chr only in sources, 1 Ch $21^{3.3.3.23}$ (=2 S $24^{3.22}$) 2 Ch $2^{13.14}$; Is & Je only in hist. parts Is $36^{8.9.12}$ Je 37^{20} 38^{9}; elsewh. †Dn 1^{10} $10^{16.17.19}$ 12^{8} Zc 1^{9} $4^{4.5.13}$ 6^{4} ψ 110^{1} Ju 4^{18} 6^{13} Ru 2^{13}; בִּי אֲדֹנִי †Ex $4^{10.13}$ Jos 7^{8} (J) Ju 6^{15} 13^{8} is referred to God, but בִּי אֲדֹנִי †Gn 43^{20} 44^{18} Nu 12^{11} (J) 1 S 1^{26} 25^{24} 1 K $3^{17.26}$ ref. to human superiors. There is uncertainty as to אֲדֹנִי Gn 18^{3} 19^{18}; אֲדֹנִי 19^{2})—†**1.** sg. *lord, master* (1) ref. to men: (*a*) supt. of household, or of affairs Gn $45^{8.9}$ (E)=ψ 105^{21}; (*b*) master ψ 12^{5}; (*c*) king Je 22^{18} 34^{5}; (2) ref. to God, הָאָדֹן יהוה *the Lord Yahweh* (v. יהוה) Ex 23^{17} 34^{23} (Cov't codes); אֲדוֹן כָּל־הָאָרֶץ *Lord of the whole earth* Jos $3^{11.13}$ (J) ψ 97^{5} Zc 4^{14} 6^{5} Mi 4^{13}; הָא׳ י׳ צְבָאוֹת, earlier Is 1^{24} 3^{1} 10^{33} 19^{4} (אֲדֹנָי Is 10^{16} in common MT; not Massora, doubtless scrib. error); הָא׳ Mal 3^{1}; אֲדוֹן ψ 114^{7}. **2.** pl. *lords, kings* Dt 10^{17}=ψ 136^{3}; Is 26^{13}; elsewh. intens. pl. of rank, *lord, master,* (1) ref. to men: (*a*) *proprietor* of hill Samaria †1 K 16^{24}; (*b*) *master* Gn 40^{7} (E) Ex $21^{4.4.6.8.32}$ (Cov't code) Gn 24^{9}+ (J, 11 t.) Dt 23^{16} Ju $19^{11.12}$ + 13 t. S & K; Jb 3^{19} ψ 123^{2} Pr 25^{13} 27^{18} 30^{10} Is 24^{2} Am 4^{1} Zp 1^{9} Mal $1^{6.6}$; (*c*) *husband* Ju $19^{26.27}$ ψ 45^{12}; (*d*) *prophet* 2 K $2^{3.5.16}$; (*e*) *governor* Ne 3^{5}; (*f*) *prince* Gn $42^{10.30.33}$ (E) 44^{8} (J) 1 S 29^{10}; (*g*) *king* Gn 40^{1} (E) Ju 3^{25} + 40 t. S & K; Ch only in sources 1 Ch 12^{19} cf. 1 S 29^{4}; 2 Ch 13^{6} 18^{16}=1 K 22^{17}; Is 19^{4} 22^{18} 36^{12} $37^{4.6}$ Je 27^{4}; (2) ref. to God Mal 1^{6}; אֲדֹנֵי הָאֲדֹנִים *Lord of lords* Dt 10^{17}=ψ 136^{3}; אֲדֹנֵינוּ ψ 135^{5} 147^{5} Ne 8^{10}; י׳ אֲדֹנֵינוּ ψ $8^{2.10}$ Ne 10^{30}; אֲדֹנַיִךְ י׳ Is 51^{22} (prob.=*thy husband, Yahweh*); אֲדֹנָיו Ho 12^{15} (possibly error for אֲדֹנָי). **3.** sf. 1 s. אֲדֹנִי (אֲדֹנַי) (1) ref. to men: *my lord, my master,* (*a*) *master* Ex 21^{5} (Cov't code) Gn 24^{12} +, 44^{5} (J, 20 t.) 1 S $30^{13.15}$ 2 K $5^{3.20.22}$ 6^{15}; (*b*) *husband* Gn 18^{12} (J); (*c*) *prophet* 1 K $18^{7.13}$ 2 K 2^{19} $4^{16.28}$ 6^{5} 8^{5}; (*d*) *prince* Gn 42^{10} (E), $23^{6.11.15}$ (P), 43^{20} 44^{18} +, 47^{18}, + (J, 12 t.); Ju 4^{18}; (*e*) *king* 1 S 22^{12} + (S & K 75 t.); (*f*) *father* Gn 31^{35} (E); (*g*) *Moses* Ex 32^{22} Nu 11^{28} 12^{11} $32^{26.27}$ (J); $36^{2.2}$ (P); (*h*) *priest* 1 S $1^{15.26.26}$; (*i*) *theophanic angel* Jos 5^{14} Ju 6^{13}; (*j*) *captain* 2 S 11^{11}; (*k*) general recognition of superiority Gn 24^{18} 32^{5}+; 33^{8}+; 44^{7}+(J, 13 t.), Ru 2^{13} 1 S 25^{24}+(15 t.); (2) ref. to God: אֲדֹנָי **a.** *my Lord* Gn 20^{4} (?E) Ex 15^{17} (Sam. יהוה) elsewhere in Hex, J; Gn $18^{3(?).27.30.31.32}$ $19^{2.18(?)}$ Ex $4^{10.13}$ 5^{22} 34^{9} Nu 14^{17} Jos 7^{8}; also Ju 6^{15} 13^{8}; not S; 1 K 22^{6} 2 K 19^{23}; not Chron. exc. memorials Ezr 10^{3} (ref. to Ezra) Ne 1^{11} 4^{8}; WisdLt only Jb 28^{28} (doubtless scrib. error for יהוה of many MSS.); not Ho; Is 37^{24} $38^{14.16}$ (hist. part); exil. Is 49^{14} (cf. 51^{22}); Mi 1^{2} ψ 16^{2}+(47 t., chiefly this sense, exc. sub **b.**; cf. אֱלֹהַי וַאדֹנָי *my Lord and my God* ψ 35^{23}; (writers that use אֱלֹהִים seld. use אֲדֹנָי); **b.** *Adonay* **n.pr.** of God, parallel with *Yahweh*, substit. for it oft. by scrib. error, & eventually supplanting it. In earlier Is 3^{17}+(19 t. seeming to belong here), Am $7^{7.8}$ 9^{1} Ez $18^{25.29}$ $33^{17.20}$ 21^{14} (prob. אֲדֹנָי י׳ as in usual phrase); Zc 9^{4} Mal $1^{12.14}$ La 1^{14}+(14 t.) ψ 2^{4} 37^{13} 78^{65} 90^{17} (יהוה?) 110^{5} (Dalman puts most of these sub (*a*);—many cases are doubtful); 1 K $3^{10.15}$ (Mass. אדני for יהוה cf. Dalm. 2 K 7^{6}; Dalm. rightly questions; he rds. יהוה). The phrases אֲדֹנָי אֱלֹהַי ψ 38^{16} 86^{12}, *Adonay my God;* אֲדֹנָי הָאֱלֹהִים Dn 9^{3}, א׳ הָאֵל $9^{9.15}$, א׳ אֱלֹהֵינוּ Dn 9^{4} favour taking א׳ Dn 1^{2} $9^{7.8}$ (יהוה?) $v^{16.17.19.19.19}$ as the divine name. **4.** אֲדֹנָי יהוה (*a*) *my Lord Yahweh* (v. יהוה) Gn $15^{2.8}$ (JE) Jos 7^{7} (J, 𝔊 om. י׳) Dt 3^{24} 9^{26} Ju 6^{22} 16^{28} 2 S 7 (6 t.) 1 K 2^{26} 8^{53}; prob. Am $3^{7.8}$ $7^{2.4.5}$ 9^{8} Je 1^{6} 4^{10} 14^{13} $32^{17.25}$ Ez 4^{14} 8^{1} 9^{6} 11^{13} 20^{49} 37^{3} (יָדַע כִּי אֲנִי א׳ י׳) 13^{9} 23^{49} 24^{24} 28^{24}; 29^{16} inappropriate in mouth of God; del. אֲדֹנָי (Co) or rd. י׳ אֱלֹהֵיכֶם (Dalm.); Mi 1^{2} Zp 1^{7} Ob ^{1} Zc 9^{14} ψ $71^{5.16}$ 73^{28}; (*b*) appar. **n.pr.** *Adonay Yahweh* Is 25^{8} Je 44^{26}; exil. Is 40^{10}+(10 t., but $61^{1.11}$ rd. יהוה, 𝔊); (*c*) uncertain whether (*a*) or (*b*) in proph. formula אָמַר א׳ י׳ Is 7^{7} 28^{16} 30^{15} 49^{22} 51^{4} 65^{13} Je 7^{20} Am 1^{8} 3^{11} 5^{3} 7^{6} Ob ^{1} Ez (131 t.); נְאֻם א׳ י׳ Is 56^{8} Je 2^{22} Am 3^{13} 4^{5} $8^{3.9.11}$ Ez (80 t.); דִּבֶּר־א׳ י׳ Ez 6^{3} 25^{3} 36^{4}; כֹּה הִרְאַנִי א׳ י׳ Am 4^{2} 6^{8}; נִשְׁבַּע א׳ י׳ Am $7^{1.4}$ 8^{1}. **5.** יהוה אֲדֹנָי *Yahweh my Lord* ψ 68^{21} 109^{21} 140^{8} 141^{8} Hb 3^{9}. **6.** אֲדֹנָי יהוה צְבָאוֹת (*a*) *my Lord Yahweh Ṣ.* (v. צבאות) ψ 69^{7} Am 9^{5} Is 10^{23} $22^{5.12}$ 28^{22} cf. י׳ אֱלֹהֵי הַצְּבָאוֹת א׳, *Yahweh, the God of Hosts my Lord* Am 5^{16}; (*b*) a divine name, *Adonay, Yahweh Ṣ.* Je $46^{10.10}$ 50^{25}; (*c*) uncertain are כֹּה אָמַר א׳ י׳ צ׳ Is 10^{24} $22^{14.15}$; נְאֻם א׳ י׳ צ׳ Is 3^{15} Je 2^{19} 49^{5} 50^{31}.

†אַדָּן **n.pr.loc.** in Babylonia Ezr 2^{59} (v. 135
כְּרוּב n.pr.)

†אַדּוֹן *id.* Ne 7^{61}. 114

†אֲדֹנִי־בֶ֫זֶק **n.pr.m.** (or title) king of Can. 137
city Bezek Ju 1^{7}; without Maqq. $v^{5.6}$.

†אֲדֹנִי־צֶ֫דֶק **n.pr.m.** Canaan. king of Jeru- 139
salem Jos $10^{1.3}$ (*Lord of righteousness; my Lord is righteous*, or *my Lord is Ṣidiq*—divine name—cf. אֲדֹנִיָּהוּ, מַלְכִּי צֶדֶק, Ph. אדנבעל etc.)

אֲדֹנִיָּ֫הוּ (אֲדֹנִיָּה) **n.pr.m.** (*my Lord is* 138
Yahweh, cf. Ph. אדנשמש, אדנבעל, אדנאשמן etc., in As. *Adunibaʾal* Schr$^{KB\ II.\ 172}$) **1.** fourth son of David 1 K 1^{8}+11 t., 2^{13}+5 t. (=אֲדֹנִיָּה 2 S 3^{4} 1 K $1^{5.7.18}$ 2^{28} 1 Ch 3^{2}). **2.** a Levite †2 Ch 17^{8}. **3.** a chief of the people †Ne 10^{17} (=אֲדֹנִיקָם 7^{18} Ezr 2^{13} cf. 8^{13}).

140 †אֲדֹנִיקָם **n.pr.m.** (*my Lord has arisen*) head of a family Ezr 2[13] 8[13] Ne 7[18] (אֲדֹנִיָּהוּ Ne 10[17]).

141 †אֲדֹנִירָם **n.pr.m.** (*my Lord is exalted*) official of Solom. 1 K 4[6] 5[28]; so also 2 S 20[24] 1 K 12[18] 𝔊 We Dr[Sm].

151 †אֲדֹרָם (contr. or corrupt, cf. foregoing) same official, under David 2 S 20[24], & Rehob. 1 K 12[18] (= הֲדֹרָם 2 Ch 10[18]).

142 †[אָדַר] **vb.** (poet.) **wide, great,** (thence) **high, noble** (? As. *adâru* Dl[W])—**Niph.** *Pt. majestic, glorious,* of ׳י, נֶאְדָּר Ex 15[11]; cstr. נֶאְדָּרִי v[6] (v. Di); **Hiph.** *Impf.* יַאְדִּיר *make glorious* the teaching Is 42[21] (׳י subj.)

145 †אֶדֶר **n.**[**m.**] **1. glory, magnificence** (As. *aduru, adiru*) ironic. of price of shepherd (symbol.) Zc 11[13]. **2. mantle, cloak** (as *wide*) Mi 2[8] (∥ שַׂלְמָה), but rd. אדרת (ת lost bef. foll. ת), so WRS[Proph 427].

115 †אֲדוֹרַיִם **n.pr.loc.** (*two hills?*) city in Judah 2 Ch 11[9] (cf. Ἀδωρα, Δωρα, Jos.[Ant. viii. 10. 1, xiv. 5. 3]); now *Dûra*, W. of Hebron, Rob.[BR II, 215].

146 †אַדָּר **n.pr.m.** (*noble?*). **1.** son of Bela, grandson of Benjm. 1 Ch 8[3] (perh. error—cf. Be—for אַרְדְּ *q.v.* Nu 26[40] Gn 46[21]). **2.** city in Judah Jos 15[3] (אַדָּרָה); = חֲצַר אַדָּר (*q.v.*) Nu 34[4].

117 †אַדִּיר **adj. majestic**—׳א ψ 8[2]+; **f.** אַדֶּרֶת Ez 17[8]? (v. infr.) etc.—**1. majestic** (wide, lofty) of waters of sea Ex 15[10] ψ 93[4]; a ship Is 33[21]; a tree Ez 17[23]; a vine Ez 17[8] (גֶּפֶן אַדֶּרֶת, so Fü; or ׳א n. abstr. v. sub אַדֶּרֶת infr.); also fig. of kings ψ 136[18]; nations Ez 32[18]; gods 1 S 4[8]; of ׳י ψ 93[4] 76[5]; of name of ׳י ψ 8[2.10]. **2.** subst. *majestic one,* of nobles, chieftains, etc., Ju 5[13.25] Na 2[6] 3[18] Je 14[3] 25[34] (אַדִּירֵי הַצֹּאן fig. so) [35.36] 30[21] Zc 11[2] 2 Ch 23[20] Ne 3[5] 10[30]; of ׳י Is 10[34] 33[21]; of servants of ׳י ψ 16[3] (= priests? cf. 1 Ch 24[5] & v. Che).

155 †אַדֶּרֶת **n.f. glory, cloak**—׳א abs. Jos 7[24]; אַדָּ֑רֶת Ez 17[8]; cstr. Gn 25[25] + 4 t.; אַדַּרְתּוֹ 1 K 19[13] + 3 t.; אַדַּרְתָּם Zc 11[3]—**1.** *glory, magnificence,* of vine Ez 17[8] (so Thes MV, but < *adj.f.* fr. אַדִּיר q.v.), of shepherds Zc 11[3] (or *sub* **2**). **2.** *mantle, cloak* (wide garment) of hair שֵׂעָר Gn 25[25] Zc 13[4] (as proph. mantle, so perh. 11[3] of shepherds = false proph.) cf. of Elijah 1 K 19[13.19] 2 K 2[8.13.14]; but אַדֶּרֶת שִׁנְעָר טוֹבָה (fine mantle of Shinar = Babylonian mantle—doubtless costly) Jos 7[21.24] (J) & (late) ׳א alone Jon 3[6].

†אֲדָר **n.pr.**[**m.**] 12th (Babylonian) month = 143
Feb.–Mar. (late Heb. loan-word, = Bab. *A(d)daru* v. Dl[W p. 188, cf. Al[3] 93], meaning dub. perh. *adâru,* be darkened, *eclipsed,* but v. Dl[W p. 190]) Est 3[7.13] 8[12] 9[1.15.17.19.21]; cf. Palm. Nab. אדר Vog[8] Eut[Nab 24].

†אַדְרַמֶּ֫לֶךְ **n.pr.m.** (*Adar is prince,* As. 152
Adar-malik (?) v. KAT[2 284], cf. ABK[140]; or *A. is Counsellor, Decider,* cf. Dl[K 52 f]; otherwise Sayce [Rel. Bab. 7]; on Bab. god *Adar* v. Schr[KGW 1880, 19 f] Dl[K 52 f], but Sayce[Rel. Bab. 151 f]; Jen[Ko 457 f] al. rd. As. name *Ninib;* on Carth. יתנאדר v. Bae[Rel. 54]) **1.** a god of Sepharvaim 2 K 17[31]. **2.** parricidal son of Sennacherib 2 K 19[37] Is 37[38].

אֲדֹרָם v. אדנירם sub אדון. above 151

אֲדַרְכֹּון v. דרכמון. p. 204 150

אֶדְרְעִי v. דרע. p. 204 154

אדשׁ only *Inf. abs.* אָדוֹשׁ v. דושׁ. p. 190 156

אהב[216] **vb. love**—**Qal** *Pf.* אָהַב Gn 27[9] + 7 t.; 157
אָהֵ֑ב Gn 27[14]; אָהַב Gn 37[3] + 3 t.; אֲהֵבְךָ Dt 15[16]; 3 fs. אֲהֵבָה Ct 1[7] +, etc.; *Impf.* יֶאֱהַב (־הָ֑ב) Pr 3[12] +; 1 s. אֱהַב Pr 8[17] (cf. Ew[§ 192 d] Ges[§ 68.1]); וָאֹהַב Mal 1[2]; וָאֹהֲבֵהוּ Ho 11[1]; אֹהֲבֵם Ho 14[5]; וָאֹהֲבֵם ψ 119[167]; 2 mpl. תְּאֵהָבוּ Pr 1[22] (cf. Kö[I p. 394] Ges[§ 63 R 2]); תֶּאֱהָבוּ Zc 8[17]; תֶּאֱהָבוּן ψ 4[3]; *Imv.* אֱהַב־ Ho 3[1]; אֱהָבוּ ψ 31[24] Am 5[15]; אֱהָ֑בוּ Zc 8[19]; אֱהָבֶהָ Pr 4[6]; *Inf. cstr.* אֱהֹב Ec 3[8]; אַהֲבָה Dt 10[12] +; אַהֲבַת Mi 6[8] + etc.; cf. also sub **n.** אהבה infr.; *Pt.* אֹהֵב (אוֹהֵב) Dt 10[18] + 26 t.; f. cstr. אֲהֻבַת Ho 3[1] is prob. *active* cf. Ba[NB 174 ff]; sf. אֹהֲבִי Is 41[8] etc.; f. אֹהֶבֶת Gn 25[28]; אֹהֲבָתִי Ho 10[11] etc.; *Pt. pass.* אָהוּב Ne 13[26]; אֲהוּבָה Dt 21[15.15.16].—*love* (mostly c. acc., sq. לְ + obj. Lv 19[18.34] 2 Ch 19[2] (late), sq. בְּ Ec 5[9]; abs. Ec 3[8] & v. infr.), (affection both pure & impure, divine & human);—**1.** human love to human object; abs., opp. hate שָׂנֵא Ec 3[8]; of love to son Gn 22[2] 25[28] 37[3.4] 44[20] (JE) Pr 13[24]; so also 2 S 13[21] 𝔊 Ew Th We, cf. Dr, of Dvd's loving Amnon; never to parent, but mother-in-law Ru 4[15]; of man's love to woman; wife Gn 24[67] 29[20.30] (cf. v[18])[32] (JE), also Dt 21[15.15.16] Ju 14[16] 1 S 1[5] 2 Ch 11[21] Est 2[17] Ho 3[1] Ec 9[9]; but also Gn 34[3] (J) Ju 16[4.15] 2 S 13[1.4.15] (where of carnal desire) 1 K 11[1] cf. v[2] Ho 3[1]; אֹ׳ רֵעַ *loving a paramour,* v. Ba[NB 176]; woman's love to man 1 S 18[20] (so v[28] MT, but rd. וְכִי כָל־יִשְׂרָאֵל אֹהֵב אֹתוֹ 𝔊 We Dr) Ct 1[3.4.7] 3[1.2.3.4] (5 t. subj. נַפְשִׁי); cf. also fig. of adulterous Judah Je 2[25] Is 57[8] Ez 16[37]; of love of slave to master Ex 21[5] (JE) Dt 15[16]; inferior to superior 1 S 18[22] cf. v[16]; love to neighbour Lv 19[18] (וְאָהַבְתָּ לְרֵעֲךָ כָּמוֹךָ), partic. to stranger

Lv 19[34] (both P), Dt 10[18.19]; love of friend to friend 1 S 16[21] 18[1.3] 20[17.17] Jb 19[19] Pr 17[1] cf. 2 S 19[7.7] 2 Ch 19[2]; v. also Pr 9[8] 16[13] cf. 15[12]; v. esp. *Pt.* infr. **2.** less oft. of appetite, obj. food, Gn 27[4.9.14] (JE); drink Ho 3[1] Pr 21[17]; husbandry 2 Ch 26[10]; cf. fig. of Ephraim Ho 10[11] sq. inf.; length of life ψ 34[13]; of cupidity Ho 9[1] Is 1[23] Ec 5[9.9]; of love of sleep Pr 20[13] cf. fig. of sluggish watchmen (sq. inf.) Is 56[10]; also c. obj. abstr. wisdom (personif.), knowledge, righteousness, etc. Pr 4[6] 8[17.21] 12[1] 22[11] 29[3] Am 5[15] Mi 6[8] (inf. ‖ infinitives) Zc 8[19], cf. Pr. 19[8] קֹנֶה לֵב אֹהֵב נַפְשׁוֹ; obj. folly, evil, etc., Mi 3[2] 4[3] ψ 11[5] 52[5.6] 109[17] Pr 1[22] 8[36] 17[19.19], cf. 18[21] Zc 8[17], cf. א׳ כֵּן Am 4[5] Je 5[3], sq. Inf. Ho 12[8] Je 14[10], esp. of idolatry Ho 4[18] (where del. הֵבוּ cf. Kö [I. p. 395]) Je 8[2]. **3.** love to God Ex 20[6] (JE) elsewhere Hex only Dt 5[10] 6[5] 7[9] + 9 t. Dt + Jos 22[5] 23[11]; also Ju 5[31] 1 K 3[3] Ne 1[5] Dn 9[4]; esp. in (late) ψ 31[24] 116[1] 145[20], but usually sq. name, law, etc. of י׳ ψ 5[12] 26[8] 40[17] 69[37] 70[5] 97[10] 119[47] + 11 t. ψ 119; cf. Is 56[6]; cf. also of love to Jerusalem Is 66[10] ψ 122[6]. **4.** esp. *Pt.* אֹהֵב =(*a*) *lover,* La 1[2] (fig. of Jerus.); (*b*) *friend* Hiram of David 1 K 5[15], cf. Je 20[4.6] Est 5[10.14] 6[13] ψ 38[12] (‖רֵעַ) so 88[19], & Pr 14[20]; also 18[24] 27[6]; Abr. of God Is 41[8] 2 Ch 20[7]. **5.** of divine love (*a*) to individual men Dt 4[37] 2 S 12[24] Pr 3[12] 15[9] ψ 146[8] Ne 13[26]; (*b*) to people Israel, etc. Dt 7[8.13] 23[6] Ho 3[1] 9[15] 11[1] 14[5] 1 K 10[9] 2 Ch 2[10] 9[8] Is 43[4] 48[14] Je 31[3] Mal 1[2.2.2] ψ 47[5]; to Jerusalem ψ 78[68] 87[2]; (*c*) to righteousness, etc. ψ 11[7] 33[5] 37[28] 45[8] 99[4] Is 61[8] Mal 2[11]. †**Niph.** *Pt.* pl. הַנֶּאֱהָבִים 2 S 1[23] *lovely, loveable* of Saul & Jonath. (‖ הַנְּעִימִם). †**Pi.** *Pt.* pl. sf. מְאַהֲבַי (־בָ֑י) Ho 2[7] + 3 t.; מְאַהֲבַיִךְ (־בָ֑יִךְ) Je 22[20] + 6 t.; מְאַהֲבֶיהָ Ho 2[9] + 4 t. **1.** *friends* Zc 13[6]; **2.** *lovers* in fig. of adulter. Isr. Ho 2[7.9.12.14.15] Ez 23[5.9]; Judah Je 22[20.22] 30[14] La 1[19] Ez 16[33.36.37] 23[22].

158 †[אַ֫הַב] **n.[m.]** love only pl. אֲהָבִים, *loves, amours;* bad sense Ho 8[9], but אַיֶּלֶת א׳ loving hind Pr 5[19] (fig. of wife ‖ יַעֲלַת חֵן).

159 †[אֹ֫הַב] **n.[m.]** id.=loved object, sf. אֳהָבָם Ho 9[10] (=בַּעַל=בֹּשֶׁת v. Hi Now) i.e. the idol worshipped; pl.=*amours* (carnal sense) Pr 7[18].

160 † אַהֲבָה **n.f. love** (=Inf. of אהב q.v.)—abs. א׳ Pr 10[12] + 18 t.; cstr. אַהֲבַת Je 2[2] + 3 t.; sf. אַהֲבָתִי ψ 109[4.5]; אַהֲבָתְךָ 2 S 1[26]; אַהֲבָתוֹ Is 63[9] Zp 3[17]; אַהֲבָתָהּ Pr 5[19]; אַהֲבָתָם Ec 9[6]—*love,* esp. WisdLt & late. **1.** human (to human obj.) abs. Ec 9[1.6] (both ‖ שִׂנְאָה) so Pr 10[12] 15[17] cf. 27[5]; v. also 17[9]; of man toward man ψ 109[4.5]; love for one's self (נַפְשׁוֹ) 1 S 20[17]; between man & woman Ct 2[4.5] 5[8] 8[6.7.7]; Pr 5[19] cf. also 2 S 1[26] (א׳ נָשִׁים); personif. Ct. 2[7] 3[5] 7[7] 8[4]; cf. fig. use 3[10]; of mere sexual desire 2 S 13[15]; fig. of Jerusalem's love to י׳ Je 2[2] (א׳ כְּלוּלֹתַיִךְ), & of love of adulter. Jerus. v[33]. **2.** God's love to his people Ho 11[4] (עֲבֹתוֹת א׳) Je 31[3] Is 63[9] Zp 3[17].

אהד (=אחד? v. Thes.)

†אֹ֫הַד **n.pr.m.** son of Simeon Gn 46[10] Ex 6[15]. 161

†אֵהוּד **n.pr.m.** **1.** a Benjamite, son of Gera, deliverer of Isr. fr. Moab Ju 3[15.16.20.20.21.23.26] 4[1]. **2.** a Benjamite, son of Bilhan (=foregoing?) 1 Ch 7[10]. 164

†אֲהָהּ (אָהּ, 𝔄𝔚:) **interj. alas!** Ju 11[35] 2 K 3[10] 6[5.15]; with לְ Jo 1[15] אֲהָהּ לַיּוֹם *alas for the day! for* etc. In the combination אֲהָהּ אֲדֹנָי יֱהוִֹה Jos 7[7] Ju 6[22] Je 1[6] 4[10] 14[13] 32[17] Ez 4[14] 9[8] 11[13] 21[5]. 162

†אַהֲוָא **n.pr.loc.** town or district in Babylonia, by which a stream is designated Ezr 8[15.31], also the stream v[21] (הנהר א׳), v[31] (נְהַר א׳). 163

†אֱהִי Ho. 13[10.14.14] **adv. where?** = אֵי, אַיֵּה. 165
So 𝔊 𝔖 𝔙 𝔗 AW in Ho 13[10], & 𝔊 𝔖 (cf. 1 Cor 15[55]) AW in Ho 13[14]. Taken by many of the older interpreters, and even by Ges in 13[14], as 1 s. impf. apoc. of היה *I would be:* but this is less suited to the context, and the jussive form is an objection, being unusual with the 1 ps.

I. **אהל** (*settle down* (?), Ar. أَهَلَ *be inhabited,* cf. As. *âlu, settlement, city, ma'âlu, ma'âltu, bed;* Dl[W] & [Pr 105]).

אֹ֫הֶל [343] **n.m.** [Gn 13,3] tent (cf. As. *âlu,* supr., Ar. أَهْلٌ, *fellow-dwellers, family,* Sab. אהל DHM[ZMG 1883, 341] al., also in n.pr. Sab. & Ph. v. אהליאב)—abs. א׳ Gn 4[20] +; cstr. *id.* Ex 28[43] +; אֹ֫הֱלָה (ה loc.) Gn 18[6] +; sf. אָהֳלִי Jb 29[4] +; אָהָלְךָ ψ 61[5]; אָהֳלֹה Gn 9[21] + 3 t. (v. Dr[Sm xxxv]); pl. אֹהָלִים Gn 13[5] + (Ges [§ 23.3]); בְּאֹהָלִים Ju 8[11] +; cstr. אָהֳלֵי Nu 16[26] +; sf. אֹהָלַי Je 4[20]; אֹהָלֶיךָ Nu 24[5] +; אָהֳלֵיכֶם Jos 22[8] +, etc.—**1.** *tent* of nomad Ct 1[5] Je 6[3] 49[29]; יֹשֵׁב א׳ *dweller in tents* Gn 4[20] 25[27] (J); אָהֳלֵי מִקְנֶה *tents of cattle* 2 Ch 14[14]; of soldier 1 Sa 17[54] cf. Dr, Je 37[10]; 1 K 8[66] לְאֹהָלֶיךָ, ישׂראל, exclam., *to thy tents, Israel!* 1 K 12[16.16] cf. 2 Ch 10[16] 2 S 20[1] (but cf. Dr, 1 S 17[54]); of pleasure-tent on house-top 2 S 16[22] (=bridal-tent, bridal pavilion, cf. חֻפָּה ψ 19[5] Jo 2[16] v. RS [Kinship 168]). **2.** *dwelling, habitation;* ψ 91[10] לְאֹהָלֶךָ *home* (lit. *to thy tents,* pl.) Ju 19[9] (after הלך); א׳ בֵּיתִי *habitation of my house* ψ 132[3] cf. Dn 11[45]; 168-69

א׳ דוד *habitat.* or *palace* of David where throne erected Is 16^{5}; א׳ בַּת צִיּוֹן *h. of daughter of Zion* (=Jerusalem) La 2^{4}; אָהֳלֵי יַעֲקֹב Je 30^{18} Mal 2^{12} (|| מִשְׁכָּן); א׳ יְהוּדָה Zc 12^{7} (|| בית דוד); א׳ רְשָׁעִים *h. of wicked* Jb 8^{22}, cf. א׳ רֶשַׁע ψ 84^{11}, א׳ יְשָׁרִים Pr 14^{11}; א׳ שֹׁחַד Jb 15^{34}; א׳ צַדִּיקִים ψ 118^{15}; א׳ אֱדוֹם=Edom itself, ψ 83^{7} cf. א׳ קֵדָר ψ 120^{5} א׳ כוּשָׁן Hb 3^{7}. **3.** *the sacred tent* used in worship of God; הָאֹהֶל *the tent;* א׳ מוֹעֵד *tent of meeting* of God with his people (tent of congregation or assembly Ges MV al.) Acc. to E Moses so called the tent which he used to pitch without the camp, afar off, into which he used to enter, & where God spake with him face to face, Ex 33$^{7-11}$ Nu 12$^{5.10}$ Dt 31$^{14.15}$; J seems to have same conception of an א׳ מ׳ outside the camp, Nu 11$^{24.26}$; D has no allusion to such a tent; P mentions it 131 t. as א׳ מ׳; 19 t. as הָאֹהֶל (cf. Ez 41^{1}) & א׳ הָעֵדוּת, *tent of the testimony* Nu 9^{15} 17$^{22.23}$ 18^{2} (as containing ark & tables of the testimony) cf. 2 Ch 24^{6}; this tent sometimes confounded with the מִשְׁכָּן but distinguished in מִשְׁכַּן א׳ מ׳ Ex 39^{32} 40$^{2.6.29}$, cf. 1 Ch 6^{17}; אֶת־הַמִּשְׁכָּן וְאֶת־אָהֳלוֹ Nu 3^{25}; הַמִּשְׁכָּן וְהָאֹהֶל Ex 35^{11}; tent was of three layers of skins, goatskins, ramskins, & *tachash* skins, each layer of eleven pieces stretched in form of a tent, covering & protecting the מִשְׁכָּן, wh. was in form of parallelopip. (Ex 26). An אֹהֶל מוֹעֵד was at Shilo 1 S 2^{22} (om. 𝔊; v. Dr) cf. ψ 78^{60}, called א׳ יוֹסֵף v^{67}. The Mosaic א׳ מ׳ was later at Gibeon 2 Ch 1$^{3.6.13}$; courses of ministry arranged for service at א׳ מ׳ 1 Ch 6^{17} 23^{32} cf. 1 Ch 9^{19} (הָא׳), v$^{21.23}$ (בֵּית הָא׳); David erected an אֹהֶל for ark on Mt. Zion 2 S 6^{17} 1 Ch 15^{1} 16^{1} 2 Ch 1^{4}; Joab fled for refuge to א׳ יהוה 1 K 2$^{28-30}$; sacred oil brought fr. הָא׳ 1 K 1^{39}; the א׳ מוֹעֵד was taken up into temple 1 K 8^{4}= 2 Ch 5^{5}; י׳ had not previously dwelt in a בַּיִת, but had gone מֵאֹהֶל אֶל־אֹהֶל *fr. tent to tent,* fr. one to another, 1 Ch 17^{5}, cf. 2 S 7^{6}; א׳ יהוה (|| הַר קֹדֶשׁ & בַּיִת) is refuge & dwelling-place of righteous, ψ 15^{1} 27$^{5.6}$ 61^{5} (cf. ψ 90^{1}).

167 †[אָהַל] **vb.denom.** tent, move tent fr. place to place (cf. As. *âʾilu*(?) Dl$^{W\ No.4\ \&\ AGl}$) וַיֶּאֱהַל Gn 13$^{12.18}$ (J), cf. יֹשֵׁב אֹהֶל (v. אֹהֶל); **Pi.** *Impf.* יַהֵל (contr. for יְאַהֵל) *pitch one's tent* like nomad Is 13^{20}.

170 †אָהֳלָה **n.pr.f.** Ohŏla (for אָהֳלָהּ *she who has a tent, tent-woman,* i.e. worshipper at tent-shrine, v. Sm) of Samaria, adulteress with Assyria Ez 23$^{4.4.5.36.44}$.

171 †אָהֳלִיאָב **n.pr.m.** Ohŏliab (*Father's tent,* cf. Ph. אהלבעל, אהלמלך; Sab. אהלאל, אהלעתתר) chief assistant of Bezalel in construction of tabernacle, etc. Ex 31^{6} 35^{34} 36$^{1.2}$ 38^{23}.

†אָהֳלִיבָה **n.pr.f.** Ohŏliba (=אָהֳלִיבָהּ *tent* 172
in her=(in meaning) אָהֳלָהּ cf. Sm) of Jerusalem as adulterous wife of י׳ Ez 23$^{4.4.11.22.36.44}$.

†אָהֳלִיבָמָה **n.pr.** Ohŏlibama (*tent of the* 173
high place) **1. f.** wife of Esau Gn 36$^{2.5.14.18.25}$. **2. m.** an Edomite chief Gn 36^{41} 1 Ch 1^{52}.

†II. [אָהַל] **vb.Hiph.** be clear, shine, Impf. 166
3 ms. יַאֲהִיל (subj. moon יָרֵחַ) Jb 25^{5} (|| זַכּוּ subj. כוכבים, cf. also יִזְכֶּה v^{4}) (=יָהֵל, fr. הלל; (by text. error?) cf. Di so 𝔊 > =I. אָהַל Kö$^{I.373}$, after Ki).

†III. [אהל] **n.[m.]** odorif. tree, aloe (?) (? loan-word from Skr. *aguru, agaru,* dial. *aghil,* cf. Wilson$^{Skr.\ Dict.}$; M. Müller in Pusey Dn 2d ed. p. 647 f.; *aloëxylon agallochum* (cf. Sigismund Aromata, Leipz. 1884, p. 38 f, MV cite Kondracki Beitr.z.Kenntn. d.Aloe, Dorpat 1874 & Baer Reden III, 293 f); others *aloë succotrina* (Schenkel^{BL}, cf. Di ad Nu 24^{6}); Wetzst in De$^{Ct\ 2d\ ed.\ 167}$ brings under I. אהל; he proposes *cardamum,* Ar. هَيْل fr. أُهَيْل=*little tents,* from three-cornered shape of capsules) **1.** pl.
אֲהָלִים trees planted by י׳ Nu 24^{6} (|| ארזים) perh. 174
error for אֵילִים cf. Di. **2.** *aloes,* as sweet-smelling; perfume for bed, אֲהָלִים Pr 7^{17}
(|| מֹר, קִנָּמוֹן); for garments אֲהָלוֹת ψ 45^{9} (|| מֹר, 174
קְצִיעוֹת); of bride, under fig. of odorif. tree Ct 4^{14} (|| מֹר, כָּל־רָאשֵׁי בְשָׂמִים).

אַהֲרֹן$_{346}$ **n.pr.m.** Aaron, elder brother of 175
Moses Ex 7^{7}; the priest Ex 31^{10}+; mentioned Ex 4^{14} 15^{20} 17^{10} 24^{1} 28^{29}+(115 t. Ex); Lv 8$^{12.23}$+ (80 t. Lv); Nu 20^{24f} 33^{39}+(101 t. Nu); 1 Ch 5^{29} +; Mi 6^{4} (only here in proph.) ψ 77^{21} 105^{26}; called הַכֹּהֵן Ex 31^{10} 35^{19} 39^{41} Lv 7^{34}+, v. ψ 99^{6} מֹשֶׁה וא׳ בְּכֹהֲנָיו; also בֶּן־א׳ הַכֹּהֵן Ex 38^{21} Nu 3^{32}+(all P) called קְדוֹשׁ יהוה ψ 106^{16}; oft. named with his sons Lv 2$^{3.10}$ 6^{2}+; בְּנֵי א׳ in strict sense Ex 28$^{1.4.40}$+oft.; בְּנֵי א׳ הַכֹּהֲנִים Lv 1^{5}+ Nu 3^{3} 10^{8} Jos 21^{19} 1 Ch 6^{42}; of temple-priests in gen'l, as descendants of A., 2 Ch 26^{18} 29^{21} 31^{19} 35$^{14.14}$, v. also 13$^{9.10}$ & cf. הַכֹּהֵן בֶּן־א׳ Ne 10^{39}; so בֵּית א׳ ψ 115$^{10.12}$ 118^{3} 135^{19}; אַהֲרֹן alone (= בֵּית א׳) 1 Ch 12^{28} cf. 27^{17}.

אוֹ$_{320}$ (أَوْ, ܐܘ, አው፡), **conj.** or (whether *aut* or 176
vel). **1.** Gn 24^{49} 31^{43} Ex 4^{11} Ct 2^{9} Lv 13^{24} Nu 5^{30}+oft. (esp. in *laws*); sometimes implying a preference, nearly=*or rather* Gn 24^{55} יָמִים אוֹ עָשׂוֹר a few days *or* ten Ju 18^{19} 1 S 29^{3}.

Prefixed to the first as well as to the second alternative (rare) *either* (*whether*)...*or* Lv 5^{1} $13^{48.51}$;=*or, if not* Ez 21^{15} (si vera l.) Ke Mal 2^{17} Jb 16^{3} 22^{11}. **2.** introducing a sentence, esp. a particular case under a general principle, *or* =*or if* Ex 21^{31} או־בֵן יִגָּח וג׳ *or if* he gore a son, etc. v^{36} Lv $4^{23.28}$ (v. Di) $5^{21.22}$ 25^{49b} Nu 5^{14} 2 S 18^{13} *or if* I had dealt falsely against his life, then, etc., Ez $14^{17.19}$ *or if* I send, etc. **3.** *if perchance*, 1 S 20^{10} *if perchance* thy father answer thee with something hard, Lv 26^{41}. **4.** once, with the juss. (as in Ar. with the subjunct. v. Dr^{§175})=*except:* Is 27^{5} I would burn them together, אוֹ יַחֲזֵק בְּמָעֻזִּי *or else* let him take hold (=*except* he take hold) of my stronghold, etc.

177 †אוּאֵל **n.pr.m.** a Judæan (*will of God*, cf. II. אוה; or contr. fr. אֲבוּאֵל cf. ?אִיעֶזֶר) Ezr 10^{34}.

אוב (meaning? Thes comp. Ar. آبَ *return*, أَيَّابٌ *water-carrier;* but cf. Lag$^{BN 90}$). MV comp. אבב (with conjectural sense) to get meaning *have a hollow sound*. Deriv. and signif. totally uncertain).

178 אוֹב **n.m.** $^{Jb 32,19}$ skin-bottle, necromancer, etc.—abs. א׳ Lv 20^{27} + 8 t.; pl. אֹבוֹת Lv 19^{31} + 7 t.—**1.** *skin-bottle*, only pl. אֹבוֹת חֲדָשִׁים *new (wine-) skins* Jb 32^{19}. **2.** *necromancer*, in phr. אוֹב אוֹ יִדְּעֹנִי *necrom. or wizard* Lv 20^{27} (H; usually tr. 'a man also or woman that hath a familiar spirit or that is a wizard' RV; but better *a man or a woman, if there should be among them, a necromancer or wizard;* no suff. reason for exceptional use of phrase here); א׳ וְיִדְּעֹנִי Dt 18^{11} 2 Ch 33^{6}=2 K 21^{6} (where א׳ וידענים); הָאֹבוֹת וְהַיִּדְּעֹנִים Lv 19^{31} 20^{6} (H) 1 S $28^{3.9}$ 2 K 23^{24} Is 8^{19} (where repres. as chirping & muttering, in practice of their art of seeking dead for instruction, prob. ventriloquism, & so 𝔊) 19^{3}. **3.** ghost, Is 29^{4} וְהָיָה כְּאוֹב מֵאֶרֶץ קוֹלֵךְ וּמֵעָפָר אִמְרָתֵךְ תְּצַפְצֵף *and thy voice shall be as a ghost fr. the ground and fr. the dust thy speech shall chirp* (so Ge MV Ew De Che al., but chirping might be of necromancer, as 8^{19}). **4.** *necromancy* אֵשֶׁת בַּעֲלַת־אוֹב *a woman who was mistress of necromancy* 1 S $28^{7.7}$; (> RS$^{JPh xiv, 127 f}$ makes אוֹב primarily a subterranean spirit, and signif. **2** only an abbrev. of בעלת א׳ etc.); קסם בָּאוֹב *divine by necromancy* 1 S 28^{8}, which seems to be interpr. of 1 Ch 10^{13} שאל בא׳ *inquire by necromancy*. (In these three exx. אוֹב is usually interpreted as ghost or familiar spirit conceived as dwelling in necromancer; but this apparently not the ancient conception.)

88 †אֹבֹת **n.pr.loc.** (*water-skins*) station of Isr. in wildern. Nu 21^{10} 34^{43}; not yet determ., prob. on eastern skirts of Idumæa not far from Moab; acc. to Wetzst in De$^{Ct 168}$ *Wêba*, وَيْبَة in the Arabah, but identif. not prob.; cf. Di on Nu 21^{10}.

אוד (*be curved, bent*, also trans. *burden, oppress*, cf. Ar. أَوَدَ).

181 †אוּד **n.m.** brand, fire-brand (orig. perh. bent stick used to stir fire) א׳ מֻצָּל מִשְּׂרֵפָה Am 4^{11}=א׳ מֻ׳ מֵאֵשׁ Zc 3^{2}, pl. זַנְבוֹת הָאוּדִים הָעֲשֵׁנִים Is 7^{4}, *stumps of smoking firebrands*.

182 †[אוֹדָה] **n.f.** cause (perh. orig. *circumstance*, cf. Sab. אוד *enclosing wall*)—only pl. אוֹדֹת Gn 21^{11}+; אדוֹת Nu 12^{1}+; (8 t. + 2 S 13^{16} vid. infra); אוֹדֹתַי Jos 14^{6}; אוֹדֹתֶיךָ ib.;—*cause*, alw. with עַל, & cstr., exc. Je 3^{8}, where sq. אֲשֶׁר; עַל־א׳ *because of* Gn $21^{11.25}$ Ex 18^{8} Nu 12^{1} 13^{24} Ju 6^{7} Je 3^{8};=*concerning* (*on occasion of*) Gn 26^{32} Jos $14^{6.6}$; in 2 S 13^{16} rd., for אַל אָחִי כִּי, אַל־אודות 𝔊L It. We Dr.

343 †אֵיד **n.m.** $^{Jb 18, 12}$ distress, calamity (under wh. one bends, cf. Ar. آدَ *burdening*)—א׳ Jb 21^{30} +; cstr. *id.* Jb 31^{23}+; אֵידִי 2 S 22^{19}=ψ 18^{19} etc.;—*distress, calamity* (poet. chiefly WisdLt & late); Pr 17^{5} 27^{10}. **1.** national calam. of Isr. (apostate) Je 18^{17} Ez 35^{5} Ob $^{13.13.13}$; of Egypt Je 46^{21}; Moab 48^{16}; Edom (א׳ עֵשָׂו) 49^{8}; Hazor v^{32}. **2.** of righteous sufferer 2 S 22^{19}=ψ 18^{19} cf. א׳ אֵל i.e. *from* God Jb 31^{23} & אָרְחוֹת אֵידָם 30^{12} *their calamitous paths* (sf. ref. to bereavement, pain, etc.) **3.** oft. of wicked Jb 18^{12} 21^{17} 31^{3} Pr $1^{26.27}$ (wisd. mocks at; ‖ פַּחַד) 6^{15} 24^{22}; also יוֹם א׳ Dt 32^{35} Jb 21^{30} (cf. supr. 2 S 22^{19}=ψ 18^{19} Pr 27^{10} Je 18^{17} 46^{21} Ob $^{13.13.13}$ where ‖ יוֹם אֵבֶד יוֹם צָרָה v$^{12.14}$, cf. יוֹם יהוה v^{15}).

108 †אֵד **n.m.** mist (deriv. dub.; Ar. آدَ=*be strong;* إِيَاد that which affords protection, shade; otherwise Dl$^{W 125}$) Gn 2^{6}; אֵדוֹ Jb 36^{27}.

I. **אוה** **1.** Ar. أَوَى *betake oneself* to a place for dwelling, etc.; **2.** id., *be tenderly inclined*.

339 †I. אִי **n.m.** $^{Is 20, 5}$ (†**f.** $^{Is. 23, 2}$) coast, region (contr. fr. אֱוִי so Ol$^{§152 b}$; place whither one betakes oneself for resting, etc., orig. fr. mariner's standpoint)—אִי abs. Is 20^{6}+; cstr. Je 47^{4}; (Jb 22^{30} v. sub IV. אִי cf. Di) pl. אִיִּים ψ 72^{10}+; אִיִּן Ez 26^{18} (Co איים) אִיֵּי Gn 10^{5}+;—*coast, border, region* (mostly late), of Philistia & Phenicia with adjacent country Is 20^{6} $23^{2.6}$; so of Caph-

tor (=Crete) Je 47^{4} מַלְכֵי הָאִי אֲשֶׁר בְּעֵבֶר הַיָּם Je 25^{22}; elswh. pl., coasts of Chittim Je 2^{10} Ez 27^{6}, of Elishah v^{7}; different countries (on or in sea) v$^{3.15.35}$ 26$^{15.18.18}$ (last del. Co cf. 𝔊) cf. 39^{6}, so also אִיֵּי הַגּוֹיִם Gn 10^{5} (P); partic. אִיֵּי הַיָּם = *coast-lands & islands* Is 11^{11} 24^{15}, ‖ הָאָרֶץ Est 10^{1}; v. (without הַיָּם) Dn 11^{18}, & ψ 72^{10}; so oft. Is^{2} incl. inhabitants, 41$^{1.5}$ 42$^{4.10}$ (אִיִּים וְיֹשְׁבֵיהֶם ‖ הַיָּם וּמְלֹאוֹ) v^{12} 49^{1} 51^{5} 59^{18} 60^{9} 66^{19} cf. Je 31^{10} ψ 97^{1}, Zp 2^{11} (אִיֵּי הַגּוֹיִם); *islands*, distinctly (taken up by י׳ as little things) Is 40^{15}; *coasts, banks,* i.e. habitable lands Is 42^{15} (‖ נְהָרוֹת).

385 †אִיתָמָר **n.pr.m.** ((*is*) *land of palms*? Thes) youngest (4th) son of Aaron Ex 6^{23} 28^{1} 38^{21} Lv 10$^{6.12.16}$ Nu 3$^{2.4}$ 4$^{28.33}$ 7^{8} 26^{60} (all P) 1 Ch 5^{29} 24$^{1.2.3.4.4.5.6}$ Ezr 8^{2}.

183 †[אָוָה] **vb. incline, desire** (cf. Stem **2**). **Pi.** *Pf.* אִוָּה ψ 132^{13}; אִוְּתָה Mi 7^{1}+, etc.; *Impf.* 3 fs. תְּאַוֶּה Dt 12^{20}+4 t.—*desire* subj. usually נֶפֶשׁ, obj. fruit Mi 7^{1} (in metaph.); flesh (to eat) 1 S 2^{16}, cf. Dt 12^{20} (sq. inf. לֶאֱכֹל בָּשָׂר); food & drink Dt 14^{26}; of king desiring rule, וּמָלַכְתָּ בְּכֹל אֲשֶׁר־תְּאַוֶּה נַפְשֶׁךָ 2 S 3^{21} 1 K 11^{37}; obj. *evil* (רַע) Pr 21^{10}; once obj. י׳ Is 26^{9} נַפְשִׁי אִוִּיתִךָ בַּלַּיְלָה; of God וְנַפְשׁוֹ אִוְּתָה וַיָּעַשׂ Jb 23^{13}; as desiring Zion for dwelling-place (late, only cases without נפשׁ) ψ 132$^{13.14}$; **Hithp.** *Pf.* הִתְאַוָּה Pr 21^{26}; הִתְאַוֵּיתִי Je 17^{16}; הִתְאַוּוּ Nu 11^{4}; וְהִתְאַוִּיתֶם Nu 34^{10}; *Impf.* יִתְאַוֶּה Ec 6^{2}; וַיִּתְאַוֶּה 2 S 23^{15}; apoc. וְיִתְאָו ψ 45^{12}, וַיִּתְאָו 1 Ch 11^{17}, etc.—*Pt.* fs. מִתְאַוָּה Pr 13^{4}; mpl. מִתְאַוִּים Am 5^{18} Nu 11^{34}—*desire, long for, lust after,* of bodily appetites; for dainty food Nu 11^{4} (E; sq. acc. cogn.)=ψ 106^{14}, Nu 11^{34} (E); sq. לְ Pr 23$^{3.6}$ cf. Ec 6^{2} (sq. acc.), v. also Pr 13^{4} (abs., subj. נֶפֶשׁ); abs. of extreme thirst 2 S 23^{15}=1 Ch 11^{17}; of king desiring the beauty (יָפְי) of princess ψ 45^{12} (sq. acc.); of covetous man Pr 21^{26} (sq. acc. cogn.); obj. בֵּית רֵעֶךָ Dt 5^{18} (‖ חמד); sq. inf. Pr 24^{1} (of desiring evil companionship); obj. יוֹם י׳ Am 5^{18} (acc.; of presumptuous, reckless longing) cf. Je 17^{16}. (Nu 34$^{7.8}$ for תְּתָאוּ—Pi. of תאה—Di prop. תִּתְאַוּ, & queries whether this & הִתְאַוִּיתֶם v^{10} are not fr. אוה, =*desire for yourselves.*)

176 [אַו] **n.m.** cstr. אַו, Kt Pr 31^{4} **desire**, so Thes MV; but < Qr אֵי q. v.

185 †[אַוָּה] **n.f. desire**—cstr. אַוַּת Dt 12^{15}+5 t.; sf. אַוָּתִי Ho 10^{10}—*desire, will,* usually sq. נֶפֶשׁ; of natural human desire (morally indiff.), for meat Dt 12$^{15.20.21}$; of longing for sanctuary 18^{6}; of royal good pleasure 1 S 23^{20}; without נֶפֶשׁ, of wild-ass Je 2^{24}; of divine will Ho 10^{10}.

†אֱוִי **n.pr.m.** (*desire*?) one of five chiefs 189
of Midian Nu 31^{8} Jos 13^{21}.

†[מַאֲוַי] **n.[m.]** **desire** pl. cstr. מַאֲוַיֵּי רָשָׁע 3970
ψ 140^{9}.

†תַּאֲוָה **n.f. desire**—abs. Gn 3^{6}+; cstr. תַּאֲוַת 8378
ψ 10^{3}+etc.;—*desire, wish* Pr 13$^{12.19}$ 18^{1}; of physical appetite, longing for dainty food מַאֲכַל ת׳ Jb 33^{20}; distinctly good sense ψ 10^{17} 38^{10} Pr 11^{23} 19^{22} (? cf. infr.) Is 26^{8} (לְשִׁמְךָ וּלְזִכְרְךָ ת׳־נָפֶשׁ); bad sense, *lust, appetite, covetousness* ψ 10^{3} (ת׳ נַפְשׁוֹ) 112^{10}; Pr 21$^{25.26}$ (as acc. cogn.); particularly of longing for dainties of Egypt Nu 11^{4} ψ 106^{14} (both acc. cogn.) 78^{30} & in **n.pr.** given to place where it occurred קִבְרוֹת הַתַּאֲוָה (q.v.) Nu 11$^{34.35}$ 33$^{16.17}$ Dt 9^{22}. **2.** *thing desired,* in good sense Pr 10^{24}; bad sense ψ 78^{29} so ת׳ לִבּוֹ ψ 21^{3}; *thing desirable* (to senses) Gn 3^{6} (ת׳ לָעֵינַיִם); perhaps also Pr 19^{22} *the ornament of a man is his kindness* (Ra Ki, etc. but cf. supr.)

†II. [אָוָה] **vb. sign, mark, describe** 184
with a mark (so Ges (who compares תאה, תוה) Dl$^{Pr 116 (not W)}$) only **Hithp.** *Pf.* הִתְאַוִּיתֶם לָכֶם *mark you out, measure,* Nu 34^{10} (P), so Vrss (cf. תְּתָאוּ לָכֶם v$^{7.8}$; v. however Di, & sub I. אוה).

אוֹת **n.m.** $_{79}$ $^{Ex 4,8}$ (**f.** $^{Jos 24,17}$) **sign** (Ar. آيَةٌ, pl. 226
آيٌ, Aram. אָתָא, ܐܳܬܳܐ)—א׳ Gn 4^{15}+; cstr. 9^{12}+; pl. אוֹתוֹת Ex 4^{9}+etc.—**1.** *sign, pledge, token* Gn 4^{15} (J); אוֹת אֱמֶת *true token* Jos 2^{12} (J); of blood of passover Ex 12^{13} (P); אוֹת לְטוֹבָה *token for good* ψ 86^{17}; *pledges, assurances* of travellers Jb 21^{29}. **2.** *signs, omens* promised by prophets as pledges of certain predicted events 1 S 10$^{7.9}$ +v^{1} where א׳ ins. 𝔊 𝔙, vid. We Dr; esp. phr. זֶה הָאוֹת לְ Ex 3^{12} 1 S 2^{34} 14^{10} 2 K 19^{29} Je 44^{29} Is 7$^{11.14}$; prob. also Is 44^{25} (of false proph.). **3.** *sign, symbol* of prophets Is 8^{18} cf. Ez 4^{3}. **4.** *signs, miracles,* as pledges or attestations of divine presence & interposition Ex 4$^{8.8.9}$ (J) 7^{3} (P) 8^{19} (J) ψ 74^{9} 2 K 19^{29} 20$^{8.9}$=Is 37^{30} 38$^{7.22}$; c. עָשָׂה Ex 4$^{17.30}$ Nu 14$^{11.22}$ Jos 24^{17} (all JE) Dt 11^{3} Ju 6^{17}; c. צִוָּה Ex 4^{28} (J); c. שִׁית 10^{1} (J); c. שִׂים Ex 10^{2} (J) ψ 78^{43} Is 66^{19}; הָאוֹת וְהַמּוֹפֵת (v. מוֹפֵת) Dt 13^{3} cf. 28^{46} Is 20^{3}; א׳ אוֹ מ׳ Dt 13^{2}; אוֹתוֹת וּמוֹפְתִים Dt 4^{34} 7^{19} 26^{8} 29^{2} Je 32^{21}; c. נָתַן Dt 6^{22} Ne 9^{10}; c. שִׂים Je 32^{20} ψ 105^{27}; c. שָׁלַח Dt 34^{11} ψ 135^{9}. **5.** *signs, memorials,* stones fr. Jordan Jos 4^{6} (J); metal of censers Nu 17^{3} (P); Aaron's rod Nu 17^{25} (P); א׳ עוֹלָם Is 55^{13} prob. also Ez 14^{8} (‖ מָשָׁל); signs on hands, etc.,

Ex $13^{9.16}$ (J)=Dt 6^{8} 11^{18}, prob. belong here; also memorial pillar in Egypt Is 19^{20}. **6.** *sign, pledge* of covenant, א׳ הַבְּרִית (v. ברית) *e.g.* rainbow, of Noachian covenant Gn $9^{12.13.17}$ (P); circumcision, of Abrahamic covenant Gn 17^{11} (P); the sabbath Ex $31^{13.17}$ (P); Ez $20^{12.20}$. **7.** *ensigns, standards* Nu 2^{2} (P) ψ 74^{4}. **8.** *signs, tokens* of changes of weather & times Gn 1^{14} (P; of heavenly luminaries) אוֹתוֹת הַשָּׁמַיִם Je 10^{2} (changes of the heavens as omens to frighten the nations) cf. ψ 65^{9}.

186 †אוּזַי **n.pr.m.** a Judæan, Ne 3^{25}.

188 †אוֹי **interj.** (onomatop.; cf. أَوْه, أُوه) woe! an impassioned expression of grief and despair: usually with dative אוֹי לִי Is 6^{5} *woe to me!* for I am undone, so 24^{16} Je 10^{19} 15^{10}; אוֹי־נָא לִי Je 4^{31} 45^{3}; אוֹי לָנוּ *woe* to us! 1 S $4^{7.8}$ Je 4^{13} 6^{4}; אוֹי־נָא לָנוּ La 5^{16}. With the 2nd or 3rd ps. often implying a denunciation; אוֹי־לְךָ מוֹאָב Nu 21^{29} (=Je 48^{46}) Je 13^{27} Ez 16^{23} repeated אוֹי אוֹי לָךְ; Is 3^{9} אוֹי לְנַפְשָׁם v^{11} Ho 7^{13} 9^{12} (שֹׁד לָהֶם ||). With a voc. (or implicit accus.) Ez $24^{6.9}$ אוֹי עִיר הַדָּמִים; absol. Nu 24^{23}. Used as a subst. Pr 23^{29} לְמִי אוֹי (לְמִי אֲבוֹי ||).

190 †אוֹיָה = אוֹי ψ 120^{5} אוֹיָה לִי.

III. אוה (*to cry* אוֹי, *howl* cf. Ar. آهَ, *to cry* آهْ to be assumed prob. as source of two foll. words).

338 †II. [אִי] **n.m.** jackal (*howler*, for *אִוִי v. Ba$^{NB 188}$, cf. Ar. اِبْنُ آوَى, whence (بَنَاتُ آوَى)—pl. אִיִּים, Is 13^{22} 34^{14} Je 50^{39} (inhabitant of desert, ruin).

344 †I. אַיָּה **n.f.** hawk, falcon, kite (perh. fr. cry; cf. Ar. يُؤْيُؤ, a kind of hawk) Lv 11^{14} Dt 14^{13} generic, cf. לְמִינָהּ & Di; Jb 28^{7} (keen-sighted).

345 †II. אַיָּה **n.pr.m.** (*falcon*) **1.** a Horite Gn 36^{24} 1 Ch 1^{40}. **2.** father of Rizpah 2 S 3^{7} $21^{8.10.11}$.

192 †אֱוִיל מְרֹדַךְ **n.pr.m.** (Bab. *Avêl* (Amêl) *Maruduk, man of Merodach*) son & successor of Nebuchadnezzar, king of Babylon, B.C. 562–60, 2 K 25^{27} (v. COT)=Je 52^{31}.

I. אול (*be foolish*, cf. יאל, & Ar. آلَ *grow thick* (of fluids)).

191 אֱוִיל 26 **adj.** foolish—א׳ Jb 5^{2}+; *pl.* אֱוִילִים ψ 107^{17}+, etc.;—*foolish*, Pr 29^{9} (אִישׁ א׳) Ho 9^{7} (pred. of prophet); cf. Is 35^{8}, elsewhere **n.m. fool** (always morally bad), who despises wisdom & discipline Pr 1^{7} 15^{5}; mocks at guilt 14^{9}; is quarrelsome 20^{3}; licentious 7^{22}; it is folly & useless to instruct him 16^{22} 27^{22} (19 t. Pr); cf. also Je 4^{22} Jb $5^{2.3}$ Is 19^{11} ψ 107^{17}.

†אֱוִלִי **adj.** id. Zc 11^{15}. 196

אִוֶּלֶת 25 **n.f.** folly.—abs. Pr 12^{23}+; cstr. 200
14^{8}+; sf. אִוַּלְתִּי ψ 38^{6}, etc.;—*folly*, special product of כְּסִילִים (v. כָּסַל) Pr 12^{23}+ (12 t.); c. פְּתָאִים Pr 14^{18}; c. אֱוִילִים only 16^{22} 27^{22} for alliteration. It is bound up in mind of boy, to be removed only by rod of discipline Pr 22^{15}; א׳ personif. tears down house built by חַכְמוֹת נָשִׁים Pr 14^{1}; it is contrasted with תְּבוּנָה Pr 14^{29} 15^{21}.

II. איל, אול (*be in front of, precede, lead*; v. Thes Nö$^{MBA 1880, 774; SBA 1882, 1175}$, who comp. Ar. أَوَّلُ for آوَلُ, Targ. אוולא; cf. Sab. אול DHM $^{Epigr. Denkm. 33. 34}$; v. on the other hand Lag$^{Or ii. p. 3; M i. p. 100}$ & sub I. אלה infr.)

†I. [אוּל] **n.[m.]** body, belly; sf. אוּלָם (in 193
contempt) ψ 73^{4} (lit. *their front, prominent part*).

†II. [אוּל] **n.[m.]** leading man, noble; pl. 193
cstr. אוּלֵי הָאָרֶץ 2 K 24^{15} Kt (Qr אֵילֵי v. III. [איל]).

†I. אוּלָם **n.m.**$^{1 K 7, 8}$ **porch** (cf. אֵילָם)—א׳ abs. 197
1 K 6^{3}+; אֻלָם Ez $40^{48.49}$; cstr. אוּלָם 1 K 7^{6}+; אֻלָם Ez 40^{7}+ (marg. אֻלָם 1 K $7^{7.12.21}$); pl. cstr. אֻלַמֵּי Ez 41^{15} (Co sg. c. sf.; in Ez Co rds. everywhere אילם vid. אֵילָם infr.)—*porch* (only K Ch Ez & Jo). **1.** in Solomon's temple 1 K 7^{19} 2 Ch 29^{7}, א׳ יהוה v^{17}; 8^{12} (altar in front of); א׳ יהוה 15^{8} (id.), cf. בֵּין הָאוּלָם וּבֵין הַמִּזְבֵּחַ Ez 8^{16} & Jo 2^{17}; א׳ הַהֵיכָל 1 K 7^{21}; א׳ הַבַּיִת v^{12}; תַּבְנִית הָא׳ 1 Ch 28^{11}. **2.** in Sol.'s palace 1 K $7^{8.8}$; א׳ הָעַמּוּדִים 1 K 7^{6} cf. v^{6}; א׳ הַכִּסֵּא 7^{7}=א׳ הַמִּשְׁפָּט v^{7}. **3.** in temple of Ezek.'s vision, partic. א׳ הַשַּׁעַר Ez $40^{7.8}$ (del. Co vid. 𝔊 𝔖 𝔙) $^{9.9.15.39.40}$ 44^{3} $46^{2.8}$; א׳ הַבַּיִת 40^{48} cf. v$^{48.49}$ $41^{25.26}$; אֻלַמֵּי הֶחָצֵר Ez 41^{25} Co sg. אֵילָם v. ואילמו החיצון.—(III. אוּלָם, adv., v. p. 19.)

II. אוּלָם **n.pr.m.** only geneal. **1.** 1 Ch 198
$7^{16.17}$. **2.** 1 Ch $8^{39.40}$.

I. אַיִל 156 **n.m.** $^{Gn 22, 13}$ ram (as leader of flock, 352
NHeb. & Aram. *id.*, As. *ailu* Dl^{W}, Ph. איל, = אַיִל rather than אַיָּל, cf. CIS$^{i. p. 231}$)—אֵיל (אַיִל) Gn 15^{9} +; cstr. אֵיל Ex 29^{22}+; pl. אֵילִים (אֵלִים, אֵילִם) Gn 32^{15}+; cstr. אֵילֵי Gn 31^{38} Is 60^{7}.—*ram*, **1.** used as food Gn 31^{38} (E) Dt 32^{14} (cf. ram of sacrifice, infr. e.g. Ex 29^{32} cf. Lv 8^{31}); as yielding wool 2 K 3^{4}; as tribute 2 Ch 17^{11}; as merchandise Ez 27^{21}; as gift Gn 32^{15} (E); in sim. of leaping, skipping ψ 114^{4} (הֶהָרִים רָקְדוּ כְּא׳) v^{6}; in Dn.'s vision, ram with two horns symbol. kings of Media and Persia Dn $8^{3.4.6.7.7.7.7.20}$; fig. of rich and powerful in Isr. Ez 34^{17}. **2.** slain

in ceremony of ratification of covenant betw. 'י & Abr. Gn 15^{9} (J); in Abr.'s sacrif. Gn 22$^{13.13}$ (E); Balaam's sacrif. Nu 23^{1} + 5 t. Nu 23 (JE); so in ritual (P), (*a*) in consecration ceremony of Aaron & his sons Ex 29^{1} + 15 t. Ex 29 (א׳ מִלֻּאִים v^{22} cf. v$^{26.27.31}$) Lv 8^{2} + 8 t. Lv 8 (א׳ הַמִּלֻּאִים v$^{22.29}$ א׳ הָעֹלָה v^{18}); (*b*) in guilt-offering (אָשָׁם) Lv 5$^{15.16.18.25}$ 19$^{21.22}$ cf. Ezr 10^{19} & א׳ הַכִּפֻּרִים Nu 5^{8}; (*c*) burnt-offering (עֹלָה) Lv 9^{2} & Nu 15$^{6.11}$ & Ez 46$^{4.5.6.7.11}$, on day of atonement Lv 16$^{3.5}$, Pentecost 23^{18}; (*d*) peace-offering (שְׁלָמִים) Lv 9$^{4.18.19}$; beginning of month Nu 28$^{11.12.14}$ cf. 29$^{2.3}$; passover v$^{19.20}$ cf. Ez 45$^{23.24}$; day of firstfruits v$^{27.28}$; in 7th month 29^{8} + 18 t. Nu 29; (*e*) in law of Nazarite Nu 6$^{14.17.19}$; (*f*) in consecration of altar of tabernacle Nu 7^{15} + 25 t. Nu ^{7}, cf. consecr. of Ezek.'s temple-altar Ez 43$^{23.25}$; (*g*) more generally 1 S 15^{22} Is 1^{11} Mi 6^{7} Jb 42^{8} ψ 66^{15}, also Is 34^{6} 60^{7}; at bringing ark to Jerus. 1 Ch 15^{26}; other occasions 29^{21} 2 Ch 13^{9} 29$^{21.22.32}$ Ezr 8^{35}; cf. fig. Je 51^{40} Ez 39^{18}. **3.** עֹרֹת אֵילִים מְאָדָּמִים *rams' skins dyed red*, of covering of tabernacle Ex 25^{5} 26^{14} 35$^{7.23}$ 36^{19} cf. 39^{34} (all P).

352 II. **אַ֫יִל n.[m.] projecting pillar or pilaster**—א׳ abs. 1 K 6^{31} (but v. infr.) cstr. *id.* Ez 40^{14} (but del. Co) ^{16} (Co better אֵילָיו); אֵיל 41^{3}, אֵל 40^{48}; pl. אֵילִים 40^{14} +; אֵלִם 40^{10}; sf. אילו Kt 40^{9} + 7 t.; אלו Kt 40^{29} + 2 t. Qr (in all) אֵלָיו, אֵילָיו; אֵלֵיהֶמָּה 40^{16};—*pilaster* or projection in wall at each side of entrance (cf. Bö$^{Proben, 302; NÄ 927}$), in Sol.'s temple 1 K 6^{31} (Bö$^{NÄ 525}$ rds. אֵילָם), in Ezek.'s temple Ez 40$^{9.10}$ + 14 t. Ez 40.41 + 40^{14a} Ew Hi Co אילם cf. 𝔊B; 40^{38} rd. אילם so Sm Co cf. 𝔊; 40^{14b} Co del. א׳.

352 †III. [אַ֫יִל?] **n.m. leader, chief** (=ram, as leader of flock? cf. Di Ex 15^{15} Ol$^{§ 142 f}$ Lag$^{BN 170}$ & v. Ez 34^{17})—cstr. אֵל Ez 31^{11}; pl. cstr. אֵילֵי Ex 15^{15} Ez 17^{13} + 2 K 24^{15} Qr (Kt אולי v. אול); אֵלֵי Ez 32^{21} (del. Co, v. 𝔊).—*leader, chief* א׳ מוֹאָב Ex 15^{15}; א׳ הָאָרֶץ Ez 17^{13} 2 K 24^{15} Qr; א׳ גּוֹיִם Ez 31^{11} (אֵלִים Jb 41^{17} v. sub אלה; perh. אֵלֵיהֶם Ez 31^{14} but cf. infr. IV. איל & also אֵל Note 1).

352 †IV. [אַ֫יִל?] **n.m. terebinth** (prob. as prominent, lofty tree, v. Di Gn 12^{6} 14^{6})—cstr. אֵיל only n.pr. אֵיל פָּארָן vid. infr.; pl. אֵילִים Is 1^{29}; אֵלִים Is 57^{5} cstr. אֵילֵי Is 61^{3}; sf. אֵלֵיהֶם Ez 31^{14} (> del. Co vid. 𝔅𝔄).—*terebinth* (cf. אֵלָה); as marking idol-shrines Is 1^{29} 57^{5} (so Che Di etc. > *gods*); fig. of ransomed ones of Zion אֵילֵי הַצֶּדֶק; perh. of haughty ones Ez 31^{14}.

†אֵיל פָּארָן **n.pr.loc.** (*terebinth* (or *palm*? 364
v. Di) *of Paran*) town & harbour at head of Ælanitic Gulf Gn 14^{6} (v. Di); = אֵלָה 36^{41}; אֵילַת Dt 2^{8} 2 K 14^{22} 16^{6}; אֵילוֹת 1 K 9^{26} 2 K 16^{6}; close to Ezion Geber (v. עֶצְיוֹן גֶּבֶר).

†[אֵילִים], alw. אֵילִם **n.pr.loc.** (= place of 362
terebinths or other great trees, v. Di Gn 14^{6} & Ex 15^{27} (12 fountains & 70 palms)) 2nd station of Isr. in desert after passing sea Ex 16$^{1.1}$ Nu 33$^{9.10}$; אֵילִמָה Ex 15^{27} Nu 33^{9}; prob. = Wady Gharandel cf. Rob$^{BR\ i. 100, 105}$.

†I. אֵלָה **n.f. terebinth** (= אֵילָה (?) v. IV. 424
איל > Sta$^{Gesch. 455}$ wh. derives fr. אֵל = *divine*; but cf. *ib.* on lack of clear distinction betw. אֵלָה, אֵלוֹן & אַלּוֹן)—Gn 35^{4} + 15 t. + אֵילָה Gn 49^{21} (for MT אַיָּלָה v. infr.)—*terebinth* = *Pistacia terebinthus*, Linn., a deciduous tree with pinnate leaves & red berries; occasional in Palestine; grows to great age; always of single tree; near Shechem Gn 35^{4} (E) cf. †אַלָּה Jos 24^{26} (E, rd. אֵלָה ?), Ophrah Ju 6$^{11.19}$; in Jabesh 1 Ch 10^{12}; tree in which Absalom was caught 2 S 18$^{9.9.10.14}$; v. also 1 K 13^{14}; expressly of idol-shrine Ho 4^{13} (‖ אַלּוֹן, לִבְנֶה) Ez 6^{13}; as fading, withering, sim. of Judah Is 1^{30}; as hewn down, sim. *id.* 6^{13} (‖ אַלּוֹן); fig. of Naphtali אֵילָה שְׁלֻחָה Gn 49^{21} (𝔊 Ew Ol Di > MT אַיָּלָה *hind* q.v.) *a slender terebinth*, v. Di & cf. II. אֵלָה; in topogr. designat. עֵמֶק הָא׳ 1 S 17$^{2.19}$ 21^{10} (v. עֵמֶק).

†II. אֵלָה **n.pr.m.** (*terebinth*, cf. Gn 49^{21} 425
sub I. אֵלָה) **1.** a chief of Edom Gn 36^{41} = 1 Ch 1^{52} (= אֵילַת **n.pr.loc.**? v. Di). **2.** son of Baasha; reigned two years in Isr. 1 K 16$^{6.8.13.14}$. **3.** father of Hoshea who was last king of Isr. 2 K 15^{30} 17^{1} 18$^{1.9}$. **4.** a son of Caleb 1 Ch 4$^{15.15}$. **5.** a son of Uzzi 1 Ch 9^{8}.

†I. אֵלוֹן **n.[f.] terebinth** (= אֵלָה)—א׳ cstr. Gn 436
12^{6} + 4 t.; pl. cstr. אֵלוֹנֵי Gn 13^{18} + 3 t.—*terebinth* (or other tall tree, cf. infr. on 1 S 10^{3} Ju 4^{5}), marking shrine, & hence used in topogr. designations; א׳ מוֹרֶה (*teacher's terebinth*) Gn 12^{6} (v. Di) so Dt 11^{30}; א׳ מְעוֹנְנִים (*conjurors' tereb.*) Ju 9^{37}; distinguished by owner or ruler א׳ מַמְרֵא Gn 13^{18} 14^{13} 18^{1}; by neighbouring town (בצענים) Ju 4^{11}; cf. א׳ בְּצַעֲנַנִּים Jos 19^{33} (edd. אַלּוֹן, but v. Norzi Baer Di); א׳ מֻצָּב אֲשֶׁר בִּשְׁכֶם Ju 9^{6} (cf. אֵלָה Gn 35^{4}); א׳ תָּבוֹר 1 S 10^{3} rd. א׳ דְּבוֹרָה (& cf.
אַלּוֹן בָּכוּת Gn 35^{8}, & תֹּמֶר דְּבוֹרָה Ju 4^{5}) cf. Ew$^{Gesch.}$ 439
$^{iii. 31}$ Th Di Gn 35^{8} (v. also sub אַלּוֹן).

356 †II. אֵילוֹן **n.pr.m.** (=*id.* cf. אֵלָה **n.pr.**) **1.** a son of Zebulun Gn 46^{14} Nu 26^{26}. **2.** אֵילֹן Gn 26^{34}; אֵילוֹן 36^{2} a Hittite, father-in-law of Esau. **3.** אֵילוֹן Ju 12$^{11.12}$ a judge of Isr., of tribe of Zeb.
358 **4. n.pr.loc.** אֵילוֹן Jos 19^{43} a town of Dan; so 1 K 4^{9} (where rd. א׳ וּבֵית ח׳ Th Klo).

440 †אֵלֹנִי **adj.gent.** of אֵילוֹן **1.** (as n. coll.) Nu 26^{26}.

359 †אֵילַת **n.pr.loc.** (*lofty tree*(*s* coll.?) i.e. palms? cf. Di Gn 14^{6}) town & harbour, N.E. arm of Red Sea, hence called Ælanitic Gulf (=Gulf of Akaba, fr. neighbouring fortress) Dt 2^{8} 2 K 14^{22} 16$^{6.6}$ (perh. later designat. for fuller איל פארן q.v.) = 𝔊 Αἰλων, Αἰλαθ, Gr. Αἴλανα, etc.; = אֵלָה (? Gn 36^{41} v. Di), אֵילוֹת infr.

359 †אֵילוֹת **n.pr.loc.** id. (*grove of lofty trees* (palms?)) 1 K 9^{26} 2 K 16^{6} 2 Ch 8^{17} 26^{2} (cf. אֵילַת, אֵיל פָּארָן).

361 [אֵילָם] **n.m.** porch (=אוּלָם, q.v.; only Ez, where Co always for אולם, cf. 𝔊 αιλαμ; Bö$^{NÄ 929}$ makes אילם *vestibule*, אולם *porch*)—אֵילָם rd. for אֵילִים Ez 40^{37} (so Sm Co); sf. אילמו Kt Ez 40$^{22.22}$ + 4 t. (Qr אֵילַמָּיו) + 41^{15} Co (for MT אֵלָמֵי); אלמו Kt Ez 40^{21} + 6 t. (Qr אֵלַמָּיו).—Co all sg.:—pl. אֵלַמּוֹת Ez 40^{16} (Co sg.) v^{30} (del. Co cf. MSS. of 𝔊, B etc., also Ew Hi Sm).—*porch*, of Ezek.'s temple Ez 40$^{16.21}$ + 13 t.

354 †אַיָּל **n.**[**m.**] (**f.** ψ 42^{2}) **hart, stag, deer** (Aram. *id.*, ܐܝܠܐ, Ar. إِيَّلٌ, As. *ailu* Dl^{W}, but dub., v. Hpt$^{BAS i. 170}$, Eth. ሀየል: = *leader*? cf. אַיִל)—א׳ abs. Dt 12^{15} + 6 t.; pl. אַיָּלִים Ct 2^{9} + 3 t.;—*hart, stag*, allowed as food Dt 12$^{15.22}$ 15^{22} (all ‖ צְבִי); 14^{5} (‖ צְבִי, יַחְמוּר etc.); eaten in Sol.'s household 1 K 5^{3} (‖ as Dt 14^{5}); sim. of leaping Is 35^{6}; id. עֹפֶר הָא׳ Ct 2$^{9.17}$ 8^{14} (all ‖ צְבִי); as in search of pasture, sim. of princes of Judah La 1^{6}; as longing for water, sim. of longing for י׳ ψ 42^{2}.

355 †אַיָּלָה **n.f.** hind, doe—א׳ abs. Gn 49^{21} (but
365 rd. אֵילָה v. infr.); אַיֶּלֶת Je 14^{5}; cstr. אַיֶּלֶת ψ 22^{1} Pr 5^{19}; pl. אַיָּלוֹת ψ 29^{9} + 4 t.; cstr. אַיְלוֹת Ct 2^{7} 3^{5}—*hind, doe*, as calving Jb 39^{1} (לֶדֶת יַעֲלֵי ‖ חֹלֵל א׳) cf. ψ 29^{9} (קוֹל י׳ יְחוֹלֵל א׳; סָלַע) in adjuration בִּצְבָאוֹת אוֹ בְּא׳ הַשָּׂדֶה Ct 2^{7} 3^{5}; in sim. מְשַׁוֶּה רַגְלַי כָּא׳ ψ 18^{34} = 2 S 22^{34} cf. וַיָּשֶׂם ר׳ כָּא׳ Hb 3^{19} i.e. surefooted, secure, cf. ‖ וְעַל בָּמֹתַי יַעֲמִידֵנִי ψ 18^{34} 2 S 22^{34}; so Hb 3^{19} but vb. יַדְרִכֵנִי; metaph. of Naphtali Gn 49^{21} א׳ שְׁלֻחָה, but rd. אֵילָה, cf. sub I. אֵלָה; in name of a melody ψ 22^{1} עַל־אַיֶּלֶת הַשַּׁחַר cf. De, & for hind as fig. of dawn *Yom.*$^{29 a}$.

†אַיָּלוֹן **n.pr.loc.** (*Deer-field*) **Aijalon**— 357
א׳ Jos 10^{12} + 8 t.; אַיָּלֹנָה 1 S 14^{31}—**1.** city in Dan Jos 19^{42} 21^{24} (Levit. city) Ju 1^{35}; 1 S 14^{31} doubtless same; so 1 Ch 6^{54} (where Dan om.); app. later in Benj. 1 Ch 8^{13} 2 Ch 11^{10} 28^{18} (v. Be); עֵמֶק אַיָּלוֹן Jos 10^{12} almost certainly named from same; = Epiph. Ἰαλω, mod. *Jâlo* Rob$^{BR ii. 253}$, Survey$^{iii. 19}$. **2.** city in Zebulun Ju 12^{12}.

†I. [אוּלַי] **n.pr.fl. Ulai, Eulaeus** (As. *Ulâi*, 195
cf. Dl$^{Pa 329}$ Gr. Εὐλαιος) only אוּלָי, river of Elam Dn 8$^{2.16}$; = (at least in lower part) mod. *Karûn* (old *Pasitigris*) v. Dl$^{Pa 177.189.329}$; in upper part perh. also = mod. *Kerkhah* (= Choaspes), which was formerly connected with Karûn not far from Susa (Loftus $^{Trav. \& Researches, 423 ff}$ Schaff-Herz. $^{iii. 2178, art. Shushan}$).

II. אוּלַי $_{44}$ and (Gn 24^{39}) אֻלַי **adv.** (perh. 194
from אוֹ & לַי = לֵא, לֻא, as in לוּלֵא, = *or not?*) **1.** **peradventure, perhaps**; usually expressing a hope, as Gn 16^{2} Nu 22$^{6.11}$ 23^{3} 1 S 6^{5} Je 20^{10}; but also a fear or doubt, as Gn 27^{12} Jb 1^{5}, sq. לֹא Gn 24$^{5.39}$; in mockery Is 47^{12} Je 51^{8}. **2.** followed by another clause ἀσυνδέτως, it expresses virtually the protasis = *if peradventure* Gn 18$^{24.28}$ (cf. v$^{29-32}$) Ho 8^{7} the blade shall yield no meal; אוּלַי יַעֲשֶׂה זָרִים יִבְלָעֻהוּ *if perchance* it yield, strangers shall swallow it up. **3.** in Nu 22^{33} לוּלֵי (q.v.) must be read; *unless* she had turned aside from me, surely, etc.

I. & II. אוּלָם **n.m.** & **n.pr.m.** v. sub II. אוּל. 197-98
p. 17

†III. אוּלָם and (Jb 17^{10}, perhaps for sake 199
of assonance with following כֻּלָּם) אֻלָּם **adv. but, but indeed,** a strong adversative Jb 2^{5} 5^{8} 13^{3} (where 𝔊 excellently οὐ μὴν δὲ ἀλλά). More usually with וְ, וְאוּלָם Gn 28^{19} (cf. Ju 18^{29}) 48^{19} *howbeit* his younger brother shall be greater than he, Ex 9^{16} *but in very deed*, Nu 14^{21} (cf. 1 S 20^{3} 25^{34}) 1 K 20^{23} Mic 3^{8} Jb 1^{11} 11^{5} 12^{7} 13^{4} 14^{18} 17^{10} 33^{1}.

I. און (cf. Ar. آنَ (med. ى) *be fatigued, tired*, أَيْنٌ *weariness, sorrow, trouble*).

אָוֶן $_{85}$ **n.m.**$^{Jb 5,6}$ **trouble, sorrow, wickedness** 205
—abs. Nu 23^{21} +; sf. אוֹנִי Gn 35^{18} etc.; *pl.* אוֹנִים 206
Ho 9^{4}—**1.** *trouble, sorrow* בֶּן־אוֹנִי *son of my trouble* or *sorrow* Gn 35^{18} (E); לֹא הִבִּיט אָוֶן בְּיַעֲקֹב Nu 23^{21} (song of Balaam), *he doth not behold trouble in Jacob* (‖ he doth not see misery—

עָמָל—in Isr.); oft. ‖ עָמָל, ψ 7^{15} (הִנֵּה יְחַבֶּל־אָוֶן *lo he travaileth with trouble* ‖ וְהָרָה עָמָל וְיָלַד שָׁקֶר, *yea he hath conceived misery & brought forth a lie*), prob. thence Jb 15^{35} (הָרֹה עָמָל וְיָלֹד אָוֶן)= Is 59^{4}; cf. עָמָל וָאָוֶן ψ 10^{7} 55^{11} 90^{10} Jb 4^{8} 5^{6} Is 10^{1} (v. עָמָל); also זוֹרֵעַ עַוְלָה יִקְצָר־אָוֶן Pr 22^{8} *the sower of iniquity shall reap trouble;* in this sense elsewh. only Dt 26^{14} Pr 12^{21} Je 4^{15} Hb 3^{7} Am 5^{5}, pl. intens. לֶחֶם אוֹנִים *bread of trouble, sorrow, or mourning* Ho 9^{4}. **2.** *idolatry* Ho 12^{12} Is 41^{29}; אָוֶן וּתְרָפִים הַפְצַר *stubbornness is idolatry & (the use of) teraphim* 1 S 15^{23} (poet. source); בֵּית אָוֶן Ho 4^{15} (for בֵּית אֵל because Bethel, house of God, is given over to idolatry) so also 5^{8} 10^{5} cf. בָּמוֹת א׳ Ho 10^{8}; בִּקְעַת א׳ Am 1^{5} (Baalbek);
204 בַּחוּרֵי א׳ rd. אוֹן, אֹן=On, Heliopolis Ez 30^{17};—abstr. for concr.=*idols* Is 66^{3}. **3.** *trouble of iniquity, wickedness,* מְתֵי אָוֶן Jb 22^{15}; אַנְשֵׁי א׳ 34^{36}=*men of trouble, troublers, wicked men;* cf. אִישׁ א׳ Pr 6^{12} Is 55^{7}; פֹּעֲלֵי אָוֶן *workers of trouble, evil-doers, workers of iniquity* Jb 31^{3} 34$^{8.22}$ ψ 5^{6} + (16 t. chiefly late ψ) Pr 10^{29} 21^{15} Is 31^{2} Ho 6^{8}; מַחְשְׁבוֹת אָוֶן *thoughts of trouble, wicked imaginations* Pr 6^{18} Is 59^{7} Je 4^{14}; oft. of words & thoughts Jb 11^{11} + (5 t.) ψ 36^{5} + (9 t.) Pr 17^{4} 19^{28} 30^{20} Is 29^{20} 32^{6} 58^{9} 59^{6} Ez 11^{2} Mi 2^{1} Hb 1^{3} Zc 10^{2}; לֹא אוּכַל אָוֶן וַעֲצָרָה Is 1^{13} *I cannot bear iniquity with the solemn meeting* (RV & most mod.; AV *it is iniquity, even the solemn meeting*).

8383 †תְּאֻנִים **n.[m.]** toil Ez 24^{12} תּ׳ הֶלְאָת *she hath wearied* (me or herself) *with toil* (but Co del. as dittogr. cf. 𝔊).

II. אוֹן (cf. Ar. آنَ (med. و) *be at rest, at ease, enjoy life of plenty;* آيِّنٌ *one enjoying a life of ease, freedom from toil & trouble*).

202 †I. אוֹן **n.m. vigour, wealth**—abs. Ho 12^{9}, sf. אוֹנִי Gn 49^{3} + etc.; pl. אוֹנִים ψ 78^{51} +. **1.** *manly vigour* בְּאוֹנוֹ שָׂרָה אֶת־אֱלֹהִים Ho 12^{4} (of Jacob); רֵאשִׁית אוֹן *beginning of manly vigour* Gn 49^{3} (of Reuben, first-born of Jacob); Dt 21^{17} ψ 105^{36} (first-born of Egyptians), so 78^{51}, רֵאשִׁית אוֹנִים where א׳ is assim. to מִצְרַיִם, or intens. pl. **2.** *strength* of man Jb 18$^{7.12}$; behemoth Jb 40^{16}; pl. intens. מֵרֹב אוֹנִים Is 40^{26} *because of the abundance of great strength* (of God); of man אֵין אוֹנִים Is 40^{29} *one not having strength;* תּוֹחֶלֶת אוֹנִים Pr 11^{7} *hope in strength* (not *the hope of iniquity* RV, or *of unjust men* AV). **3.** *wealth* Jb 20^{10} Ho 12^{9} מָצָאתִי א׳ לִי (‖ עָשַׁרְתִּי).

203 †II. אוֹן **n.pr.m.** (*vigour*) a chief of tribe of Reuben Nu 16^{1}.

אוֹנוֹ **n.pr.loc.** (*vigorous,* for אונון) city in Benjamin Ezr 2^{33} Ne 7^{37} 11^{35} 1 Ch 8^{12}; valley of same name Ne 6^{2}; prob. *Kefr ʿAnâ*, NW. of Lydda, Survey$^{II. 251}$. 207

†אוֹנָם **n.pr.m.** (*vigorous*). **1.** chief of Horites Gn 36^{23} 1 Ch 1^{40}. **2.** chief of tribe of Judah 1 Ch 2$^{26.28}$. 208

†אוֹנָן **n.pr.m.** (*vigorous*) son of Judah Gn 38$^{4.8.9}$ 46$^{12.12}$ Nu 26$^{19.19}$ 1 Ch 2^{3}. 209

אוֹן **n.pr.loc.** v. אֹן. p. 58 204

אוניות 2 Ch 8^{18} Kt v. אֳנִי sub אנה.

†אוּפָז (**n.pr.loc.** unknown & dub.) whence came gold, זְהַב מֵא׳ Je 10^{9}; כֶּתֶם א׳ Dn 10^{5}; so Thes 1 K 10^{18} זָהָב מוּפָז (מֵא׳=מוּפָז); but 𝔊 δόκιμος, & 2 Ch 9^{17} טָהוֹר, whence MV Klo make מוּפָז Hoph. Pt. fr. פזז q.v. Klo rds. אוֹפִיר (q.v.) for אוּפָז Je 10^{9} Dn 10^{5}, in view of כֶּתֶם אוֹפִיר Is 13^{12}. 210

אוֹפִיר **n.pr. Ophir**—א׳ 1 K 10^{11} +; אוֹפִירָה 9^{28} + אוֹפִר †Gn 10^{29}; אֹפִיר †1 K 10^{11}—**1. n.pr.m.** 11th son of Joktan Gn 10^{29} (J)=1 Ch 1^{23}; 𝔊 Οὐφειρ, Ὠφειρ, name of an Arabian tribe, vid. Gn 10^{30} & Di. **2. n.pr.loc.** (land or city S. or SE. fr. Palestine, exact position unknown, cf. infr.; 𝔊 Σωφηρα, Σωφειρα, Σουφειρ, etc.; Jb 28^{16} Ὠφειρ AC, cf. 1 K 22^{49} A Ὠφειρδε, B om.) place whither Sol.'s ships went fr. Ezion Geber, bringing thence gold 1 K 9^{28}—cf. 22^{49}—2 Ch 8^{18}; gold, almug-(sandal-?) wood & gems 10$^{11.11}$, cf. 2 Ch 9^{10}; prob. 1 K 10^{22} ref. to same ships; they came once in three years with gold, silver, ivory, apes & peacocks (all fr. Ophir?); 2 Ch 9^{21} makes these ships go to Tarshish (but on Tarshish-ships, i.e. large, sea-going vessels, merchantmen, v. 1 K 22^{49} & sub תַּרְשִׁישׁ). **3.** characteristic of fine gold (poet. & late) זְהַב א׳ 1 Ch 29^{4}; כֶּתֶם א׳ Is 13^{12} Jb 28^{16} ψ 45^{10}. **4.** hence for fine gold itself Jb 22^{24} (‖ בֶּצֶר).—(If **2**=**1**, then southern, prob. south-eastern, Arabia (cf. Di Gn 10^{29}) furnished the gold; and other articles, which point farther E. (e.g. to India, toward which the words קוֹפִים *apes* & תֻּכִּיִּים *peacocks* seem to lead), were either brought to Ophir by traders, & so found there by Sol.'s men, or were found elsewhere by the latter, whose cruise may have taken them beyond Ophir, the name of Ophir alone, as source of gold-supply, being preserved. If (less likely) **1** & **2** are not the same, the only data for determining loc. of **2** are the articles brought, & one may look toward India, Ceylon or other islands, or even lower Africa. Particular theories have as yet no adequate support; e.g. (*a*) old city *Supara*, or *Uppara*, in the region of Goa, Malabar coast 211 (cf. 𝔊 supr. **2**, but also **1**; form with Σ said on Copt. authority to denote India, v. Jablonskii Opusc. ed. te Water i. 337; cf. also Jos[Ant. viii. 6. 4]; in that case its use by 𝔊 may indicate a theory of the location of Ophir); (*b*) peninsula *Malacca;* (*c*) island *Sumatra;* (*d*) *Sofâla*, with city Zimbabye (SE. Africa); (*e*) west coast of Arabia (where gold & silver formerly found), etc. On these & other theories, v. Di Gn 10[29] Ri[HWB], Herzog, Smith[Dict. Bib.]; cf. Glaser [Skizze ii. 367 ff.])

213 †[אוּץ] **vb.** press, be pressed, make haste —**Qal** *Pf.* אָץ Jos 10[13] 17[15]; אַצְתִּי Je 17[16] *Pt.* אָץ Pr 19[2] + 3 t. Pr; אָצִים Ex 5[13];—**1.** *press, hasten* (trans. but obj. not expr.) Ex 5[13] (E). **2.** (intr.) *be pressed, confined, narrow* Jos 17[15] כִּי אָץ לְךָ הַר־אֶפְרָיִם. **3.** *hasten, make haste,* sq. לְ + Inf. Jos 10[13] לֹא אָץ לָבוֹא (J, of sun); Pr 28[20] א׳ לְהַעֲשִׁיר; sq. מִן Je 17[16] לֹא א׳ מֵרֹעֶה; sq. בְּ (of particular in wh. one hastens) Pr 19[2] (בְּרַגְלַיִם); 29[20] (בִּדְבָרִים); cf. also Pr 21[5] וְכָל־אָץ אַךְ לְמַחְסוֹר. **Hiph.** *Impf.* וַיָּאִיצוּ Gn 19[15]; תָּאִיצוּ Is 22[4]—*hasten* (tr.) sq. בְּ Gn 19[15] (J); sq. לְ + Inf. אַל־תָּא׳ לְנַחֲמֵנִי Is 22[4]. (May be Qal Impf., & vb. ע׳׳י.)

215 [אוֹר][43] **vb.** be or become light (cf. Ar. أَوْرٌ *enkindle*, Aram. (Nasar.) ܐܘܪ Aph. *illumine*, & deriv. in As.)—**Qal** *Pf.* אוֹר Gn 44[3]+; אֹרוּ 1 S 14[29]; *Impf.* 3 fpl. וַתָּאֹרְנָה 1 S 14[27] Qr; *Pt.* אוֹר Pr 4[18] (Ges[§ 72 R. 1]); *Imv.* fs. אוֹרִי Is 60[1] Pr 4[18];—*become light, shine* of sun (esp. in early morn.) Gn 44[3] (J) 1 S 29[10] Pr 4[18] Is 60[1]; of eyes (owing to refreshment) 1 S 14[27 (Qr) 29]. **Niph.** *Impf.* וַיֵּאֹר 2 S 2[32]; *Inf.* לֵאוֹר Jb 33[30]; *Pt.* נָאוֹר ψ 76[5]—become *lighted up* of day-break 2 S 2[32]; by light of life, revival Jb 33[30]; by light of glory, enveloped in light ψ 76[5]. **Hiph.** *Pf.* וְהֵאִיר Ex 25[37], etc.; *Impf.* יָאִיר Jb 41[24]+; יָאֵר Nu 6[25]+; וַיָּאֶר ψ 118[27]+, etc.; *Imv.* הָאֵר ψ 80[20]+, הָאִירָה ψ 31[17]+; *Inf.* הָאִיר Gn 1[15]+; *Pt.* מֵאִיר Pr 29[13]; מְאִירַת ψ 19[9]; מְאִירוֹת Is 27[11]—**1.** *give light,* of sun, moon & stars Gn 1[15.17] (P), of moon Is 60[19]; of pillar of fire (sq. לְ) Ex 13[21] 14[20] (both JE) ψ 105[39] Ne 9[12.19]; of sacred lamp Ex 25[37] Nu 8[2] (both P); fig. of the words of God ψ 119[130]. **2.** *light up, cause to shine, shine,* sq. acc. הֵאִירוּ בְרָקִים תֵּבֵל *lightnings lighted up the world* ψ 77[19] 97[4]; abs. הָאָרֶץ הֵאִירָה מִכְּבֹדוֹ Ez 43[2]; *the earth shined with his glory* (of theophany); of leviathan, which makes path shine behind him Jb 42[24]; לַיְלָה כַּיּוֹם יָאִיר *night shineth as day* ψ 139[12]. **3.** *light* a lamp ψ 18[29]; wood Is 27[11]; altar(-fire) Mal 1[10]. **4.** *lighten,* of the eyes, הָאִיר עֵינַיִם, subj. י׳, his law, etc. Pr 29[13] ψ 13[4] 19[9] Ezr 9[8]. **5.** *make shine,* of face of God יָאֵר י׳ פָּנָיו אֵלֶיךָ *Yahweh make his face shine upon thee* Nu 6[25] (priest's blessing), reappearing ψ 31[17] (sq. עַל־), 67[2] (sq. אֶת־), 80[4.8.20]; 119[135] (sq. בְּ), Dn 9[17] cf. ψ 4[7]; without פָּנִים (sq. לְ) ψ 118[27]; once, of face of man, Ec 8[1] חָכְמַת אָדָם תָּאִיר פָּנָיו *the wisdom of a man lighteth up his face.*

אוֹר[121] **n.m.** [Gn 1,3] (**f.** [Jb 36,32; Je 13,16]) **light** (As. *urru* 216
= *ûru* Dl[W]).—abs. Gn 1[3]+; cstr. Ju 16[2]+; sf. אוֹרִי ψ 27[1], etc.; *pl.* אוֹרִים ψ 136[7];—**1.** *light* as diffused in nature, light of day Gn 1[3.4.5] (P) Jb 3[9] 38[19]+. **2.** *morning light, dawn,* אוֹר הַבֹּקֶר light of the morn. Ju 16[2] 1 S 14[36] 25[34.36] 2 S 17[22] 2 K 7[9] Mi 2[1]; א׳ בֹּקֶר 2 S 23[4] (poem of David); עַד־הָא׳ Ju 19[26] (cf. עַד־הַבֹּקֶר v[25]); לָאוֹר Jb 24[14]; מִן־הָאוֹר עַד מַחֲצִית הַיּוֹם *fr. dawn till mid-day,* Ne 8[3] cf. Pr 4[18]. **3.** *light* of the heavenly luminaries; א׳ הַחַמָּה ‖ א׳ הַלְּבָנָה *moonlight & sunlight* Is 30[26]; כּוֹכְבֵי אוֹר *stars of light* ψ 148[3]; מְאוֹרֵי אוֹר *luminaries of light* Ez 32[8]; אוֹרִים = מְאוֹרִים ψ 136[7]; so עֲלֵי־אוֹר *in sunshine* Is 18[4]; the sun itself Jb 31[26]. **4.** *daylight* אוֹר רְשָׁעִים *light of the wicked* Jb 38[15] (their work-day being the night); יוֹם אוֹר *a day of light* Am 8[9] (= a clear, sunshiny day). **5.** *lightning* Jb 36[32] 37[3.11.15] cf. Hb 3[11]. **6.** *light* of lamp Pr 13[9] Je 25[10]; of crocodile's hot breath Jb 41[10]. **7.** *light of life* א׳ חַיִּים Jb 33[30] ψ 56[14]; cf. אוֹר Jb 3[16.20]. **8.** *light of prosperity* Jb 22[28] 30[26] ψ 97[11] La 3[2]. **9.** *light of instruction* נֵר מִצְוָה וְתוֹרָה אוֹר Pr 6[23] *the commandment is a lamp and instruction a light;* so the Messian. servant is אוֹר גּוֹיִם Is 42[6] 49[6]; cf. א׳ עַמִּים Is 51[4]; the advent of Mess. is shining of great light Is 9[1.1]. **10.** *light* of face אוֹר פָּנִים = bright, cheerful face (of men) Jb 29[24]; betokening king's favour Pr 16[15] (cf. א׳ עֵינַיִם ψ 38[11]); of God = his shining, enlightening, favouring face ψ 4[7] 44[4] 89[16]. **11.** Yahweh is א׳ יִשְׂרָאֵל Is 10[17], as source of enlightenment & prosperity; light & salvation ψ 27[1]; light to guide Mi 7[8] cf. ψ 43[3]; everlasting light of Zion, instead of sun & moon Is 60[19.20]; house of Jacob is to walk in his light Is 2[5].

†I. אוֹרָה **n.f. light** (late, Mish. *id.*, cf. Aram. 219
אוּרְתָּא *evening-light, moon-light, star-light,* etc.) **1.** *light* (opp. חֲשֵׁיכָה) ψ 139[12]. **2.** *light* of joy & happiness Es 8[16]; pl. intens. אוֹרוֹת *light* of life Is 26[19] (light that quickens dead bodies as dew the plants Ew Hi De Che Di RVm; vid. Br[MP 303] cf. אוֹר חַיִּים; but Ki Ges MV Bö RV transl. *herbs*).

†II. [אוֹרָה] **n.f. herb** (so Mish., Ges cf. נִצָּן, 219
Ar. انوار = *lights & flowers,* & Sam. יאר = דֶּשֶׁא of Gn 1[11.12]) only *pl.* אוֹרוֹת *herbs* 2 K 4[39] (cf. Is 26[19] supr. sub I. אוֹרָה).

217 †I. אוּר **n.m. flame.** לְכוּ בְאוּר אֶשְׁכֶם *walk in the flame of your fire* Is 50^{11}, & so fire itself, whose light & flame were seen 44^{16} 47^{14}—exil. Is. + 31^{9} & Ez 5^{2} (Co אֵשׁ).

224 †אֻרִים **n.[m.]pl. region of light, East** Is 24^{15} (so Ges MV Ew De Di RV; Lo Hi Kn Che rd. איים = *coasts*, so Cdd. 𝔊;—𝔊 mostly om. 𝔙 *in doctrina*, thinking of *Urim*, vid. Br$^{MP 297}$).

224 †אוּרִים **n.m. Urim** (pl. intens., mostly c. art. *the Urim*, and mostly joined with תֻּמִּים q.v.) תֻּמֶּיךָ וְאוּרֶיךָ לְאִישׁ חֲסִידֶךָ Dt 33^{8} *thy Thummim and thy Urim has the man of thy favour*, i.e. the Levite tested at Massah & Meribah; הָאוּרִים וְהַתֻּמִּים were put into the חֹשֶׁן הַמִּשְׁפָּט of the high priest Ex 28^{30} Lv 8^{8} (P); this חֹשֶׁן (q.v.) was a little bag or pouch worn on breast of high priest, to hold the *Urim & Thummim;* the name ח׳ הַמִּשְׁפָּט was given because of decisions made by that which was within it; thus, Eleazar was to inquire of י׳ for Joshua בְּמִשְׁפַּט הָאוּרִים Nu 27^{21} (P); Saul prayed הָבָה אוּרִים, opp. הבה תֻּמִּים, 1 S 14^{41} 𝔊, so We Dr (MT om. former, and rds. תָּמִים in latter); י׳ did not answer Saul בָּאוּרִים, or by dreams or prophets 1 S 28^{6}; postex. Jews reserved difficult questions until there stood up a priest לְאוּרִים וּלְתֻמִּים Ezr 2^{63} Ne 7^{65} (here alone without art.) These passages give little information; 𝔊 δήλωσις καὶ ἀλήθεια, 𝔙 *doctrina et veritas*, Sym φωτισμοὶ καὶ τελεώτητες; Jos$^{Ant. iii. 8. 9}$ thinks of the twelve gems of face of bag as giving decision by shining; Philo$^{Vit. Mos. iii}$ thinks of two small images (א׳ & ת׳), prob. embroidered in the cloth of the bag, like oracle-images of Egypt (Diod$^{I, 48, 75}$ Aelian$^{Var. Hist. 14, 34}$); Ew$^{Gesch. iii, 309; Antiq. 295}$, of two stones of different colours for sacred lot, on this v. Dr 1 S 14^{41} where 𝔊 אוּרִים & תֻּמִּים as obj. of give, δος = הָבָה; cf. הַפִּילוּ v^{42}, וַיִּלָּכֵד v^{41} (used of taking by lot 10^{20} Is 7$^{14.16}$); v. also We & RS$^{OTJC\ Lect\ x.\ N\ 4}$; Bähr^{Symbolik}, of one thing within bag, a sacred pledge to high priest of the enlightenment & perfection he would receive fr. י׳ when called to make sacred decisions; Ka$^{Ex\ 544}$ sees the sacred pledge in the twelve sacred gems themselves, that stimulate priest to self-sacrifice & perfect sanctification.

218 †II. אוּר **n.pr.m.** (*flame*) father of one of David's heroes 1 Ch 11^{35} (III. אוּר n.pr.loc. v. infr.)

221 †אוּרִי **n.pr.m.** (*fiery*, or contr. for אוּרִיָּה) **1.** prince of Judah Ex 31^{2} 35^{30} 38^{22} 1 Ch 2^{20} 2 Ch 1^{5}; **2.** a porter Ezr 10^{24}; **3.** father of an officer of Solomon 1 K 4^{19}.

222 †אוּרִיאֵל **n.pr.m.** (*flame of Ēl* or *my light is Ēl*, v. אֵל sub אלה; cf. Ph. ארמלך in As. *Urumilki* (Sen$^{Taylor\ Cylind.\ ii.\ 50}$, cf. COT $^{2\ K\ 18,\ 13}$)) **1.** chief of Levit. line of Kohath, in time of David 1 Ch 6^{9} 15$^{5.11}$. **2.** maternal grandfather of Abijah 2 Ch 13^{2}.

אוּרִיָּה **n.pr.m.** (*flame of Yah* or *my light is Yah* v. יָהּ). **1.** Hittite husband of Bathsheba 2 S 11^{3f} 23^{39}. **2.** priest in reign of Ahaz Is 8^{2} 2 K 16^{10f}. **3.** priest in time of Nehemiah Ezr 8^{33} Ne 3$^{4.21}$ 8^{4}. 223

†אוּרִיָּהוּ **n.pr.m.** (*flame of Yahweh* or *my light is Yahweh* v. יהוה) a prophet slain by Jehoiakim Je 26^{20}. 223

†יָאִיר **n.pr.m.** (*he enlightens*, or *one giving light*). **1.** son of Manasseh Nu 32$^{41.41}$ Dt 3$^{14.14}$ Jos 13^{30} 1 K 4^{13} 1 Ch 2$^{22.23}$. **2.** a judge in Gilead Ju 10$^{3.4.5}$. **3.** father of Mordecai Est 2^{5}. 2971

†יָאִרִי **adj.gent. Jairite** 2 S 20^{26}. 2972

†מָאוֹר **n.m. luminary**—abs. Gn 1^{16} +; cstr. מְאוֹר Pr 15^{30} +; pl. מְאוֹרֹת Gn 1^{15}; מְאֹרֹת v $^{14.16}$; cstr. מְאוֹרֵי Ez 32^{8}—*light, light-bearer, luminary, lamp*, of sun & moon Gn 1$^{14.15.16.16.16}$ (P) Ez 32^{8}; moon ψ 74^{16}; מְנֹרַת הַמָּאוֹר *the lamp-stand of the luminary* or *light* (where הַמּ׳ is sum of seven sacred lamps on golden lamp-stand) Ex 35$^{14.14.28}$ 39^{37} Nu 4$^{9.16}$, cf. Ex 25^{6} 27^{20} 35^{8} Lv 24^{2} (all P); מְאוֹר־עֵינַיִם יְשַׂמַּח־לֵב Pr 15^{30} *the luminary of the eyes* (= the eyes as a lamp) *gives the light of joy to the heart;* מְאוֹר פָּנֶיךָ ψ 90^{8} *the luminary of thy face* (thy face as a lamp) in the light of which the secrets are exposed. 3974

†[מְאוּרָה] **n.f. light-hole**—only cstr. מְאוּרַת—= den of great viper Is 11^{8}, cf. מָאוֹר Mish. *Ohaloth* 13^{1} (others *eye-ball* 𝔗 Ew De Di). 3975

†III. אוּר **n.pr.loc. Ur** (Bab. *Uru;* seat of moon-god worship; hence Eupolemos in Euseb$^{Praep.\ Ev.\ ix.\ 17}$ says Καμαρίνη ἥν τινας λέγειν πόλιν Οὐρίην), ancient city in Southern Babylonia; OT alw. אוּר כַּשְׂדִּים, i.e. Ur of the Kasdim (Chaldeans) v. כַּשְׂדִּים sub כשׂד; home of Terah, Abram's father, & A.'s point of departure for Mesopotamia & Canaan Gn 11^{28} 15^{7} (both J), & hence Ne 9^{7}; also Gn 11^{31} (P);—mod. *Muqayyar*, south of Euphrates, c. 150 miles SE. of Babylon; v. KG^{94f} Dl$^{Pa\ 226f}$ COT on Gn 11^{28}. 218

אֻרְוֹת v. אֻרְיָה sub I. ארה. p. 71 220

אוֹרְנָה v. אֲרַוְנָה. p. 72 728

†[אוּת] **vb.** only **Niph.** *Impf.* **consent, agree** (cf. Rab. נֵיאוֹת Niph. Pt. esp. *enjoying* NHWB^{48}) sq. לְ Gn 34^{22} יֵאֹתוּ לָנוּ; v^{15} נֵאוֹת לָכֶם; 225

v^{23} נֶאוֹתָה לָהֶם; sq. Inf. 2 K 12^{9} וַיֵּאֹתוּ הַכֹּהֲנִים לְבִלְתִּי קְחַת־כֶּסֶף.

226 **אות** v. II. אוה. p. 16

227 **אָז adv.** (cf. إِذْ, إِذًا, إِذَنْ, Eth.: also BAram. אֱדַיִן, prop. a subst.=*time:* see מֵאָז) **at that time, then,** whether expressing duration, or inception (**=thereupon**). **1.** strictly temporal: **a.** of past time:—without a verb Gn 12^{6} 13^{7} Jos 14^{11} 2 S 23^{14}; with a pf. Gn 4^{26} Ex 4^{26} Jos 10^{33} Ju 8^{3} 13^{21} Je 22^{15} אָז טוֹב לוֹ *then* was it well to him (cf. v^{16} Ho 2^{9}); more usually (esp. when=*thereupon*) with an impf. (v. Dr^{§27}) Ex 15^{1} Nu 21^{17} Jos 8^{30} 10^{12} 22^{1} 1 K 3^{16} 8^{1} 9^{11} (v. Dr$^{Intr.192}$) al. **b.** of fut. time (usually where some emph. is intended), with impf. Is 35$^{5.6}$ 60^{5} Mi 3^{4}, rather differently Lv 26^{41} 1 S 20^{12}; rarely with pf. 2 S 5^{24b} (*will have* gone forth) Is 33^{23}: with an accompanying logical force, implying the fulfilment of a condition, *then=if* or *when this has been done* (with the impf.) Gn 24^{41} Ex 12$^{44.48}$ Dt 29^{19} Jos 1^{8} 1 S 6^{3} Is 58$^{8.9}$ Je 11^{15} Hi Ke ψ 19^{14} 51^{21} Pr 3^{23} Jb 11^{15} 13^{20} 22^{26}. **c.** in poetry אז is sometimes used to throw emphasis on a particular feature of the description Gn 49^{4} Ex 15^{15} Ju 5$^{8.11.13.19.22}$ Is 33^{23} 41^{1} Hb 1^{11} ψ 2^{5} 96^{12}. **d.** it points back with emphasis to an inf. with ב 2 S 5^{24a} ψ 126$^{2.2}$ Jb 28^{27} 33^{16}; to בַּיּוֹם הַהוּא (anomalously) 1 Ch 16^{7}. **2.** expressing logical sequence strictly: in the apod.:—after אם (rare) for sake of special emphasis Is 58^{14} Pr 2^{5} Jb 9^{31}; =*in that case,* after לוּ or לוּלֵא 2 S 2^{27} hadst thou not spoken, כִּי אָז surely *then* had the people, etc. 19^{7} ψ 119^{92}; after אחלי 2 K 5^{3} ψ 119^{6}; after a suppressed protasis 2 K 13^{19} Jb 3^{13} יָשַׁנְתִּי אָז יָנוּחַ לִי I had slept, *then* were there rest for me; Jos 22^{31} (strangely)=*now, as things are;* Ec 2^{15}=*that being so.* (122 t., besides מאז and מן־אז. Seldom used except where some special emphasis is desired. 'Then' of AV RV more commonly represents וְ, esp. in the apodosis.)

†**מֵאָז** (cf. مُنْذُ), once (Je 44^{18}) מִן־אָז, lit. *from that time:* used (*a*) absol., as adv.=in *time past,* *of old,* whether of a nearer 2 S 15^{34} Is 16^{13}, or of a remoter past Is 44^{8} 45^{21} 48$^{3.5.7.8}$ ψ 93^{2} Pr 8^{22}; (*b*) with foll. gen. or relat. clause, as prep. or conj.=*from time of, since.* With subst. Ru 2^{7} מֵאָז הַבֹּקֶר *from time of* morning ψ 76^{8}; with infin. Ex 4^{10} מֵאָז דַּבֶּרְךָ *since* thy speaking unto thy servant; with finite vb. Gn 39^{5} Ex 5^{23} וּמֵאָז בָּאתִי וגו׳ and *since* I came unto Pharaoh, etc. 9^{24} Jos 14^{10} Is 14^{8} Je 44^{18}.

233 †**אֱזַי** = אָז (prob. a dialectic form; cf. Aram. אֱדַיִן) **then, in that case** ψ 124$^{3.4.5}$, in apod. after לוּלֵי: cf. אָז ψ 119^{92}.

229 †**אֶזְבַּי n.pr.m.** father of one of David's men 1 Ch 11^{37} (where הָאַרְבִּי=בֶּן־אֶזְבָּי 2 S 23^{35}).

231 †**אֵזוֹב n.m.** $^{1 K 5,13}$**hyssop** (Mish. אזוב, Aram. ܙܘܦܐ, Ar. زُوفَا Frey., Eth. አዛብ: 𝔊 ὕσσωπος, herb of purging qualities, but perh. not precise botanical term, v. Di Lv 14^{6f}; v. also Löw^{93})—א׳ abs. Ex 12^{22}+4 t.; אֵזוֹב Lv 14^{4}+4 t.;—*hyssop,* little plant (contr. אֶרֶז *cedar*) 1 K 5^{13}, הָא׳ אֲשֶׁר יֹצֵא בַּקִּיר; Ex 12^{22} (J) אֲגֻדַּת א׳ a bunch of h. for sprinkling blood on doorposts; without אגדת, used in cleansing from leprosy Lv 14$^{4.6.49.51.52}$; burnt with red heifer Nu 19^{6}; used in cleansing with ashes of red heifer v^{18} (all P); cf. ψ 51^{9} תְּחַטְּאֵנִי בְאֵ׳ וְאֶטְהָר.

234 **אַזְכָּרָה** v. זכר. p. 272

235 †**אָזַל vb. go** (mostly poet.) (𝔗 *id.,* BAram. אֲזַל, Syr. ܐܙܠ)—**Qal** *Pf.* אָזַל 1 S 9^{7}; 3 fs. אָזְלַת (poet.) Dt 32^{36}; אָזְלוּ Jb 14^{11}; *Impf.* 2 fs. תֵּזְלִי (for תֵּאזְלִי) Je 2^{36}; *Pt.* אֹזֵל Pr 20^{14}—*go away* Pr 20^{14}; *go about* Je 2^{36} מַה־תֵּזְלִי מְאֹד לְשַׁנּוֹת אֶת־דַּרְכֵּךְ; *be gone, exhausted, used up* Dt 32^{36} (subj. יָד *strength*); sq. מִן 1 S 9^{7} הַלֶּחֶם אָזַל מִכֵּלֵינוּ; Jb 14^{11} אָזְלוּ מַיִם מִנִּי־יָם; **Pu.** *Pt.* מְאוּזָּל Ez 27^{19} (RV *yarn,* cf. Aram. עזל *spin* but) rd. מֵאוּזָל, v. sub אוזל infr., so 𝔊 𝔖 Hi Sm Co.

237 †[**אֶזֶל**] only הָאָזֶל 1 S 20^{19} rd. הַלָּז(א)ו q.v.

187 †**אוּזָל n.pr.m.** (Sam. איזל, 𝔊 Αἰζηλ) 6th son of Joktan Gn 10^{27} 1 Ch 1^{21}=**n.pr.loc.** Ez 27^{19}, rd. מֵאוּזָל 𝔊 𝔖 Hi Sm Co; old capital of Yemen, later *San'â,* cf. Di Gn 10^{27}.

I. **אזן** (*pointed, sharp?* cf. Eth. መአዝን: *edge, corner, peak, pinnacle;* v. also As. Dl^{W}, & אָזֵן infr.)

241 **אֹזֶן**$_{188}$ **n.f.** $^{Ex 29,20}$ **ear** (Ar. أُذُن, Aram. ܐܕܢܐ, אוּדְנָא, As. *uznu,* Eth. እዝን:)—abs. 2 S 22^{45}+; cstr. Ex 29^{20}+; sf. אָזְנִי 1 S 20^{2}+, etc.; du. אָזְנַיִם (נַ֫יִם) Dt 29^{3}+; cstr. אָזְנֵי Gn 23^{10}+; sf. אָזְנַי (־נַי) Nu 14^{28}+; (never with article).—**1.** *ear,* as part of body; of human being, as bearing earring Gn 35^{4} Ex 32$^{2.3}$ (all JE) Ez 16^{12}; pierced by a master Ex 21^{6} (E) Dt 15^{17}; touched with blood in consecration (תְּנוּךְ א׳ *tip of ear*) Lv 8$^{23.24}$ 14$^{14.17.25.28}$; cut off by enemy Ez 23^{25} (of אָהֳלִיבָה q.v.); ear of dog Pr 26^{17} מַחֲזִיק בְּאָזְנֵי־כָלֶב; of sheep Am 3^{12} (fragment rescued from lion). **2.** especially as *organ of hearing,* **a.** of man Dt 29^{3} 2 S 22^{45}=ψ 18^{45}, Jb 42^{5} Is 30^{21}; implanted (נטע)

by ׳י ψ 94^{9}; of idols (do not hear) ψ 115^{6} 135^{17}; שָׁמַע בא׳ 2 S 7^{22} + 8 t.; esp. בְּא׳ after vb. of saying = *in the ears, in the hearing of* Gn 20^{8} (E) 23$^{10.13.16}$ (P) 44^{18} 50^{4} (J) Dt 5^{1} 31$^{11.28.30}$ + 44 t.; cf. Is 5^{9} (vb. om.); after noun of utterance, sound 1 S 15^{14} Jb 13^{17} 15^{21}; cf. א׳ after verbal noun Ez 24^{26} (לְהַשְׁמָעוּת א׳) cf. Is 11^{3}; הִטָּה א׳ incline the ear = give attention ψ 45^{11} Pr 22^{17} + 9 t.; sq. לְ ψ 49^{5} + 4 t.; so הִקְשִׁיב א׳ Is 32^{3}; Pr 2^{2} (sq. ל); הֵבִיא א׳ ל׳ Pr 23^{2}; as receiving words א׳ תִּקַּח Jb 4^{12} cf. Je 9^{19}; as tingling (צלל) at dreadful news 1 S 3^{11} 2 K 21^{12} Je 19^{3}; as hearing with satisfaction, triumph ψ 92^{12} תִּשְׁמַעְנָה אָזְנָי (|| וַתַּבֵּט עֵינִי בְּ׳) but Che del.; as intelligent (involving mental process) שָׁמְעָה א׳ וַתָּבֶן לָהּ Jb 13^{1}; א׳ מִלִּין תִּבְחָן Jb 12^{11} cf. 34^{3}; as unsatisfied Ec 1^{8} לֹא תִמָּלֵא א׳ מִשְּׁמֹעַ; as seeking (בקש) knowledge Pr 18^{15}; as hearing & blessing Jb 29^{11}; cf. א׳ שֹׁמַעַת Pr 20^{12} 25^{12} *a hearing* (responsive, obedient) *ear*; cf. Pr 15^{31} Is 43^{8}; opp. *stopping the ears* (wilful ignorance) אֹטֵם א׳ מִן־ Pr 21^{13} cf Is 33^{15}; also of adder in simile of wicked ψ 58^{5} כְּמוֹ פֶתֶן חֵרֵשׁ יַאְטֵם אָזְנוֹ; מֵסִיר א׳ מִן־ Pr 28^{9} so עֲרֵלָה א׳ *their ear is uncircumcised* Je 6^{10}; הִכְבִּיד א׳ Zc 7^{11} cf. Is 48^{8} Je 5^{21} Ez 12^{2}; cf. also Is 42^{20}. **b.** of Yahweh, בְּא׳ י׳ after vb. of utterance Nu 11^{18} (J) 14^{28} (P) 1 S 8^{21} Ez 8^{18}; after עָלָה 2 K 19^{28} = Is 37^{29}; after בּוֹא ψ 18^{7} cf. 2 S 22^{7} where vb. om.; so also (after noun without vb.) Nu 11^{1} (J) בְּא׳ י׳ 1 Ch 28^{8} nearly = in presence of; incline the ear הִטָּה א׳ 2 K 19^{16} = Is 37^{17} Dn 9^{18} ψ 86^{1}; sq. לְ ψ 17^{6} 88^{3} 116^{2}; sq. אֶל־ ψ 31^{3} 71^{2} 102^{3}; הִקְשִׁיב א׳ ψ 10^{17}; א׳ קַשֻּׁבוֹת לְ 2 Ch 6^{40} 7^{15} cf. ψ 130^{2}; *id.* sq. אֶל־ Ne 1$^{6.11}$; vb. om. א׳ אֶל־ ψ 34^{16}; cf. Is 59^{1} לֹא כָבְדָה א׳; La 3^{56} אַל־תַּעְלֵם א׳ ל׳. **3.** + גָּלָה א׳ *open ears of, reveal to*, subj. man 1 S 20$^{2.12.13}$ 22$^{8.8.17}$ Ru 4^{4}; subj. י׳ 1 S 9^{15} 2 S 7^{27} 1 Ch 17^{25}; גּ׳ א׳ לַמּוּסָר Jb 36^{10}, cf. v^{15}; כָּרָה א׳ ψ 40^{7}; יָעִיר לִי א׳ לִשְׁמֹעַ Is 50^{4}; פָּתַח־לִי א׳ Is 50^{5}; cf. וְא׳ חֵרְשִׁים תִּפָּתַחְנָה Is 35^{5}; opp. judicial deafness Mi 7^{16} Is 6^{10}.

238 I. †[אָזַן] 42 **vb. denom. Hiph. give ear, listen, hear**, almost wholly poet.—*Pf.* הֶאֱזִין Dt 1^{45}; וְהַאֲזִין consec. ψ 77^{2} (v. De Kö$^{I. p. 390}$); וְהַאֲזַנְתָּ Ex 15^{26}; הֶאֱזִינוּ Is 64^{3} +; *Impf.* יַאֲזִין Jb 9^{16} +; אָזִין (for אַאֲזִין) Jb 32^{11}, etc.; *Imv.* ms. הַאֲזִינָה Nu 23^{18} +; fs. הַאֲזִינִי Is 1^{2}; fpl. הַאֲזֵנָּה Gn 4^{23} Is 32^{9}, etc.; *Pt.* מֵזִין (for מַאֲזִין, v. Kö$^{I, 391}$) Pr 17^{4};—**1.** *hear*, perceive by the ear, abs. Is 64^{3} (|| שמע) ψ 135^{17}; *give ear, listen*, abs. (of mts. personif.) Dt 32^{1}, cf. Is 1^{2} (of earth, personif.); of men Ju 5^{3} ψ 49^{2} Is 28^{23} Jo 1^{2} (all || שמע) Ho 5^{1} (|| הִקְשִׁיב, שמע) Is 8^{9}; sq. acc. rei Gn 4^{23} Jb 33^{1} Is 1^{10} 32^{9} (all || שמע) 42^{23} (|| הקשיב, שמע); Jb 37^{14} (|| הִתְבּוֹנֵן); ψ 78^{1} sq. על (rei) Pr 17^{4} (|| הִקְשִׁיב); sq. עַד (rei) Jb 32^{11} (|| הוֹחַלְתִּי); *hearken* to, = be obedient to, abs. Je 13^{15} (|| שמע) 2 Ch 24^{19} Ne 9^{30}; c. acc. rei Jb 9^{16}; לְ (rei) Jb 34^{16} (|| שמע) Ex 15^{26}; sq. לְ pers. Jb 34^{2} (|| שמע); sq. עֲדֵי pers. Nu 23^{18}; sq. אֶל־ pers. Is 51^{4}. **2.** *of God, listening* (*with favour*) to prayer, etc., abs. ψ 80^{2} 84^{9} (|| שמע), sq. אֶל־ pers. ψ 77^{2} Dt 1^{45} (|| שמע); c. acc. rei ψ 5^{2} (|| בִּין) 17^{1} (|| הקשיב, שמע), ψ 55^{2} (|| הקשיב v^{3}) 86^{6} (|| *id.*), 140^{7} 141^{1}; sq. אֶל־ (rei) ψ 39^{13} 143^{1} (both || שמע); sq. לְ (rei) ψ 54^{4} (|| שמע).

†[אָזֵן] **n.[m.] coll. implements, tools** (fr. 240
sharpness? Aram. אֲזֵנִין, ܙܝܢܐ weapons אֲזֵנֶךָ Dt 23^{14} (Cdd. אוניך 𝔊 𝔙 אֵזוֹר cf. Di).

†אָזְנִי **n.pr.m.** a son of Gad Nu 26^{16} (*my* 244
hearing, or *my ear*? Gn 46^{16} אֶצְבּוֹן q.v.)

†אָזְנִי **adj.gent.** fr. same, הָאָזְנִי Nu 16^{16}. 244

†אֲזַנְיָהוּ **n.pr.m.** (*Yahweh hath heard*) 245
father of Jeshua, a Levite Ne 10^{10}.

†אַזְנוֹת תָּבוֹר **n.pr.loc.** (*peaks* of Tabor? 243
pl.) Jos 19^{34} place in Naphtali cf. Di.

†יַאֲזַנְיָהוּ **n.pr.m.** (*Yahweh heareth*)—so 2970
2 K 25^{23} Ez 8^{11}; יַאֲזַנְיָה Je 35^{3} Ez 11^{1}; contr.
(וִ)יְזַנְיָהוּ Je 40^{8}, (וִ)יְזַנְיָה Je 42^{1}—**1.** a Judæan 3153
2 K 25^{23} Je 40^{8}. **2.** an elder of Isr., son of Shaphan Ez 8^{11}. **3.** son of Jeremiah Je 35^{3}. **4.** a leading Judæan, son of Azur Ez 11^{1}. **5.** a leading Judæan Je 42^{1} (= עֲזַרְיָה 43^{2}).

II. †[אָזַן] **vb.** only **Pi.** *Pf.* **weigh, test,** 239
prove (cf. Ar. وَزَنَ *weigh*, also Ar. & Aram. deriv.); וְאִזֵּן (conj.) Ec 12^{9} (|| חִקֵּר, תִּקֵּן).

†[מֹאזֵן] **n.[m.]du. balances, scales** (Ar. 3976
مِيزَانٌ, Aram. (Nasar.) ܡܘܙܢܐ)—(קָנִים) מֹאזְנַיִם Is 40^{15} + 4 t.; cstr. מֹאזְנֵי Lv 19^{36} + 9 t.—*balances*, for weighing money Je 32^{10} וָאֶשְׁקֹל הַכֶּסֶף בְּמ׳; hair Ez 5^{1} (מ׳ מִשְׁקָל); שַׁחַק מ׳ Is 40^{15} *dust of bal.*, sim. of insignif. of nations bef. י׳; fig., calamity Jb 6^{2}; men ψ 62^{10}; hills Is 40^{12} (שָׁקַל בַּפֶּלֶס, || הָרִים וּגְבָעוֹת בְּמ׳); מ׳ צֶדֶק (|| אַבְנֵי־צ׳) Lv 19^{36} (|| אֵיפַת צ׳, הִין צ׳), Ez 45^{10} (|| אֵיפַת־צ׳, בַּת־צ׳) cf. Pr 16^{11} (פֶּלֶס וּמ׳ מִשְׁפָּט); fig. Jb 31^{6} יִשְׁקְלֵנִי בְמ׳ צֶדֶק; opp. מ׳ מִרְמָה Pr 11^{1} (|| אֶבֶן שְׁלֵמָה); 20^{23}

(לְהַקְטִין אֵיפָה וּלְהַגְדִּיל שֶׁקֶל ‖) Am 8^{5} (‖ אֶבֶן וָאָבֶן) Ho 12^{8}; מֹ׳ רֶשַׁע Mi 6^{11} (‖ אַבְנֵי מִרְמָה).

242 †אֻזֵּן שֶׁאֱרָה† **n.pr.loc.** (*portion*—weighed & measured—*of She'ĕra*, Blau^ZMG 1873, 296^), place built by ש׳, daughter of Ephraim 1 Ch 7^{24}.

246 אֲזִקִּים v. זקק. p. 279

247 †[אָזַר] **vb. gird, encompass, equip** (Talm. *id.*, Ar. أَزَرَ, Aram. in deriv. Lag^BN 177 der. fr. وَزَرَ^). **Qal** *Pf.* אֲזַרְנִי 1 S 2^{4}; *Impf.* sf. יַאַזְרֵנִי Jb 30^{18}; 2 ms. תֶּאְזוֹר Je 1^{17}; *Imv.* אֱזָר־נָא Jb 38^{3} 40^{7}; *Pt. pass.* אָזוּר 2 K 1^{8};—*gird, gird on*, sq. acc. rei *loins* חֲלָצֶיךָ Jb 38^{3} 40^{7}, מָתְנֶיךָ Je 1^{17}; pass., subj. אֵזוֹר, וְאֵזוֹר עוֹר אָזוּר בְּמָתְנָיו 2 K 1^{8}; cf. act. c. acc. pers. Jb 30^{18} כְּפִי כֻתָּנְתִּי יַאַזְרֵנִי, subj. לְבוּשִׁי v. Di; fig. 1 S 2^{4} אָזְרוּ חָיִל. **Niph.** *Pt.* נֶאְזָר fig. ψ 65^{7} of God (נ׳ בִּגְבוּרָה) *girded with might.* **Pi.** *Impf.* 2 ms. sf. וַתְּאַזְּרֵנִי ψ 18^{40} 30^{12}; וַתַּזְרֵנִי 2 S 22^{40} (Ges^§ 68 R 2^); *Pt.* sf. הַמְאַזְּרֵנִי ψ 18^{33}; cstr. מְאַזְּרֵי Is 50^{11} but cf. infr.—*gird*, c. 2 acc. (pers. & rei) fig., ψ 18^{40} = 2 S 22^{40} ψ 18^{33} (חָיִל); ψ 30^{12} (שִׂמְחָה); acc. rei om. Is 45^{5}; acc. pers. om. מְאַזְּרֵי זִיקוֹת Is 50^{11}; but rd. rather מְאִירֵי cf. 27^{11} (𝔊 Kn Brd Di). **Hithp.** *Pf.* הִתְאַזָּר ψ 93^{1}; *Imv.* הִתְאַזְּרוּ Is $8^{9.9}$—*gird oneself*, for war Is $8^{9.9}$; with עֹז ψ 93^{1} (subj. י׳).

232 †אֵזוֹר† **n.m.** ^Is 5, 27^ **waistcloth** (NH *id.*, Ar. إِزَارٌ, cf. RS^JQ Jan. 1892, 289 ff.^)—א׳ abs. Jb 12^{18} + 8 t.; cstr. 2 K 1^{8} + 4 t.;—of skin 2 K 1^{8} (prophet.); of linen Je 13^{1} (v. Che) cf. v^2.4.6.7.7.10.11^ (symbol. of Isr. & Jud. cleaving to י׳); of Assyrian warriors' waistcloth, '*girdle of loins*' Is 5^{27}; in wall-images of Chaldeans, חֲגוֹרֵי א׳ בְּמָתְנַיִם Ez 23^{15} (cf. 2 K 1^{18} v. sub אָזַר) so fig. of Yahweh's power over kings וַיֶּאְסֹר אֵזוֹר בְּמָתְנֵיהֶם Jb 12^{18} (א׳ = fetter, cf. Di; but acc. to RS^l.c.^ ref. to slaves' garment); metaph. of righteousness & faithfulness Is $11^{5.5}$ (א׳ חֲלָצָיו, א׳ מָתְנָיו).

248 אֶזְרוֹעַ v. זרע. p. 284

249 אֶזְרָח v. זרח. p. 280

255 אַח v. I. אחח. p. 28

251, 256-57 I. אָח, אַחְאָב, אֶחָב, אַחְבָּן etc. v. אחה. p. 26

254 II. אָח v. II. אחח. p. 28

253 †III. אָהּ **interj.** (onomatop.) **ah! alas!** Ez 6^{11} 21^{20}.

305 †אַחֲלַי† ψ 119^{5} and אַחֲלֵי 2 K 5^{3} (perh. from אָח III. and לִי = Aram. לוּ = לְוַי: the varying punctuation is due doubtless to the word being treated by the punctuators as a subst. = *wish*, with suff. & in c. st., '*my wish* is that,' etc.; cf. Ki on ψ 119 (תַּחְנוֹתַי וּבַקָּשׁוֹתַי), **ah that!** (𝔊 ὄφελον).

[אָחַד] **vb.** v. יחד or חדד (Co Ez 21^{21}). 258

אֶחָד ^962^ **adj.num. one** (Ph. אחד, Sab. *id.*, cf. DHM^ZMG 1876, 707^, Ar. أَحَدٌ, Eth. አሐዱ: Aram. חַד, ܚܕ; on As. *edu*, *aḫadu*, cf. Dl^W No. 139^)—abs. א׳ Gn 1^{5} + cstr. אַחַד Gn 21^{15} +; so even bef. prep. 1 S 9^{3} al. v. Dr; f. abs. אַחַת Gn 2^{21} +; אֶחָת Gn 11^{1} +; cstr. אַחַת Dt 13^{13} +; pl. m. אֲחָדִים Gn 11^{1} + 4 t.; חַד Ez 33^{30} del. Co cf. 𝔊;—**1.** *one* Gn 1^{9} $27^{38.45}$ Ex 12^{49} Jos 23^{10} 1 S 1^{24} 2 S 12^{3} +, Zc 14^{9} Mal 2^{10} Jb 31^{15} +, so also (emph.) 2 S 17^{3} for MT אֲשֶׁר 𝔊 We Dr; *one or two* לֹא לְיוֹם אֶחָד וְלֹא לִשְׁנַיִם Ezr 10^{13}; as subst. sq. מִן Gn 2^{21} Lv $4^{2.13}$ Is 34^{16} +; הָא׳ Gn 19^{9} $42^{13.32}$ 2 K $6^{3.5}$ +; *one and the same* Gn 40^{5} Jb 31^{15}; pl. דְּבָרִים אֲחָדִים †Gn 11^{1} cf. Ez 37^{17} (abs.), but v. Co; = *few, a few* יָמִים א׳ †Gn 27^{44} 29^{20} Dn 11^{20}; כְּאִישׁ אֶחָד *as one man, together* Ju 20^{8} 1 S 11^{7}; also כְּאֶחָד late = Aram. כַּחֲדָא †Ezr 2^{64} (= Ne 7^{66}) 3^{9} 6^{20} Ec 11^{6}; v. esp. Is 65^{25} (‖ earlier יַחְדָּו $11^{6.7}$). **2.** = *each, every* Ex 36^{30} Nu $7^{3.85}$ 28^{21} 1 K 4^{7} 2 K 15^{20} +; also repeated, distrib. sense Nu 7^{11} 13^{2} 17^{21} Jos 3^{12} $4^{2.4}$. **3.** = *a certain* 1 S 1^{1} 2 S 18^{10} 2 K 4^{1} Est 3^{8} + cf. 2 S 17^{9} v. Dr 1 S 1^{1}; hence **4.** = indef. art. 1 S 6^{7} 24^{15} 26^{20} (but del. 𝔊 We Dr) 1 K $19^{4.5}$ +. **5.** *only* 1 K 4^{19}; & (fem.) *once* 2 K 6^{10} ψ 62^{12} 89^{36} (*once for all*); אַחַת לְשָׁלֹשׁ שָׁנִים 2 Ch 9^{21}, א׳ בַּשָּׁנָה Lv 16^{34} cf. Jb 40^{5}, פַּעַם אֶחָת Jos $6^{3.11}$ cf. v^{14}, בְּאַחַת Nu 10^{4} Jb 33^{14}; *at once* בְּאֶחָת Pr 28^{18} cf. וְאִנָּקְמָה נְקַם־אַחַת Ju 16^{28}. **6.** *one . . . another, the one . . . the other* א׳ . . . א׳ Ex 17^{12} $18^{3.4}$ Am 4^{7} 2 S 12^{1} Je 24^{2} 2 Ch 3^{17} Ne 4^{11} +; 2 S 14^{6} rd. הָאֶחָד אֶת־אָחִיו for האחד את־האחד 𝔊 We Dr; *one after another, one by one*, לְאַחַד אֶחָד Is 27^{12} cf. Ec 7^{27}. **7.** as ordinal, *first* (mostly P & late) Gn 1^{5} (P) 2^{11} (J) Ex 39^{10} (P); Ez 10^{14} esp. of first day of month Ex 40^{2} (P) Ezr 3^{6} $10^{16.17}$ Ne 8^{2} Hg 1^{1}; *first year*, שְׁנַת אַחַת 2 Ch 36^{22} Ezr 1^{1} Dn 1^{21} $9^{1.2}$ 11^{1} abs. Jb 42^{14}; cf. *first* (day, יוֹם om.) Gn $8^{5.13}$ בְּאֶחָד לַחֹדֶשׁ; so Ex 40^{17} Lv 23^{24} Nu $1^{1.18}$ 29^{1} 33^{38} (all P) Dt 1^{3} 2 Ch 29^{17} Ezr $7^{9.9}$ Ez 26^{1} 29^{17} 31^{1} 32^{1} 45^{18}. **8.** in combin., **a.** אַחַד עָשָׂר *eleven* (cf. עַשְׁתֵּי עָשָׂר) Gn 32^{23} 37^{9} (JE) Dt 1^{2}; so אַחַת־עֶשְׂרֵה Jos 15^{51} (P) 2 K 23^{36} 24^{18} 2 Ch $36^{5.11}$ Je 52^{1} (precedes noun, exc. Jos 15^{51}); as ordinal, *eleventh* אַחַת עֶשְׂרֵה שָׁנָה Ez 30^{20} 31^{1} cf. 1 K 6^{38} 2 K 9^{29}; **b.** with other numerals, as 259 cardinal אֶחָד וְאַרְבָּעִים אֶלֶף וַחֲמֵשׁ מֵאוֹת Nu 1[41] cf. 2[16.28] 31[34.39] (all P; א׳ precedes other numeral); but אַרְבָּעִים וְאַחַת שָׁנָה (א׳ following) 1 K 14[21] 15[10] 2 K 14[23] 2 Ch 12[13] cf. 2 K 22[1] = 2 Ch 34[1]; 2 K 24[18] = Je 52[1] = 2 Ch 36[11]; Jos 12[24] (D) Is 30[17] Ezr 2[26] = Ne 7[30] cf. v[37]; Dn 10[13]; as ordinal בְּאַחַת וְשֵׁשׁ מֵאוֹת שָׁנָה Gn 8[13] (P) Ex 12[18] (P), 1 Ch 24[17] 25[28] 2 Ch 16[13] (א׳ preceding); but 1 K 16[23] Hg 2[1] (א׳ following).

261 †אֵחוּד **n.pr.m.** (*union* fr. אָחוּד?) a Benjamite 1 Ch 8[6] = אֵחִי Gn 46[21].

2297 †חַד **adj.** = אֶחָד Ez 33[30] del Co, cf. 𝔊.

אחה (stem assumed for אָח; which however perh. bilit. & prim. so Thes Rob Ges al.; Dl[HA 59] prop. *surround, protect;* Dl[W] comp. *aḫu, side.* Zehnpfund[BAS I. 510] prop. *belong together*, cf. Schult. Thes. De Goeje in RS[Sem 256 N] suggests connection with *ḥayy, family, clan*).

251 I. **אָח** 630 **n.m.** **brother** (Ph. אח, Ar. أَخٌ (cstr. أَخُو etc.), Sab. אח (sf. אחיהו) CIS[iv. 1, 17 and 24] al., Eth. እኅው: As. *aḫu* cf. Dl[W], Aram. אַח, ܐܚܐ; Palm., Nab. sf. אחוהי, אחיה);—abs. אָח Gn 24[29] + (Ez 18[10] del. Co cf. 𝔊 𝔖 𝔙; Ew Sm אַךְ; Dl Ba[Ez x] defends as = *one* cf. As. *aḫu*) never c. art.; cstr. אֲחִי Gn 10[21] +; sf. אָחִי Gn 4[9] +; אָחִיךָ Gn 4[9] +; אָחִיו Gn 4[2] +; אָחִיהוּ Je 34[9] + 3 t. etc.; pl. אַחִים Gn 13[8] +; so rd. Ho 13[15] v. De[Compl. Var. 23] cf. sub אָחוּ; cstr. אֲחֵי Nu 27[10] +; sf. אַחַי Gn 19[7] +; אֶחָי 1 S 20[29] + (but 1 S 30[23] 𝔊 We אַחֲרֵי for אֶחָי את); אַחֶיךָ Gn 37[13] +; אֶחָיו Gn 44[14] + etc. **1.** *brother*, born of same mother (& father) Gn 4[2.8.9.10.11] 27[6.11] 44[20] 49[5]; cf. 28[2] 29[10.10] + Ex 4[14] + oft.; also of half-brother Gn 20[5.13.16] (on parentage cf. v[12]) 37[2.4.5] +, 2 S 13[4.7.8] +. **2.** indef. = relative; Lot, of Abr. Gn 13[8] 14[12.14.16]; Jacob, of Laban 29[12.15] (nephew); hence of kinship in wider sense; member of same tribe Nu 16[10] 18[2.6] 2 S 19[13]; of same people Ex 2[11.11] 4[18] Dt 15[12] Ju 14[3] Is 66[20] Ne 5[1.5.8] vid. esp. Lv 19[17] cf. v[18] (extended to incl. sojourner גֵּר v[34]); of Israel & Judah 2 S 19[42]; Isr. & Edom Nu 20[14]; cf. of Ishmael Gn 16[12] 25[18]; of friend 2 S 1[26] 1 K 9[13] 20[32.33]; of allies בְּרִית א׳ Am 1[9]. **3.** fig. of resemblance Jb 30[29] אָח הָיִיתִי לְתַנִּים || (רֵעַ לִבְנוֹת יַעֲנָה) i.e. by reason of his crying, cf. Di; Pr 18[9] מִתְרַפֶּה בִמְלַאכְתּוֹ אָח הוּא לְבַעַל מַשְׁחִית. **4.** in phr. *one ... another* אִישׁ אָחִיו Gn 9[5] Jo 2[8] Zc 7[10]; אִישׁ ... אָחִיו Gn 13[11] + 25 t. + Ex 32[27] (where also same phr. c. רֵעֵהוּ & קְרֹבוֹ—v. these words—& also אִישׁ, אֶחָד); for development of idiom cf. Dt 15[2] Is 19[2] Je 34[14 (cf. 15) 17] Ez 38[21] Hg 2[22]; usually of men; of faces of golden cherubim Ex 25[20] 37[9]; of scales of crocodile Jb 41[9]. (אָח *fire-pot* v. sub II. אחח.)

אַחְאָב 91 **n.pr.m.** **Ahab** (*father's brother*; = 256
אחיאב Nö[ZMG 1886, 172], Ἀχίαβος was a nephew of Herod; cf. like name in Syr., given *ob maximum cum patre suo similitudinem*, Bar Hebræus in Euseb.[Chron. ii. 23] cf. LCB[1879, 1339]. In many cases, however, the mng. of n.pr. comp. with אח is dub., & perfect consistency, especially in comparison with cpds. of אָב, seems impossible; cf. rem. sub אביאל, and further We[Skizzen, iii. 1 f], Dl[Pr. cap. vi])—אַחְאָב 1 K 16[28] +; וּכְאֶחָב Je 29[22]— **1.** son of Omri, king of Isr. 1 K 16[28.29] 18[1.2.3] 20[2.13.14] + 41 t. 1 K, 27 t. 2 K, 14 t. 2 Ch; Mi 6[16]. †**2.** false prophet, time of Jerem. Je 29[21.22].

אֶחָב v. אַחְאָב. 256

†**אַחְבָּן** **n.pr.m.** (*brother of an intelligent* 257
one) son of Abishur, of Judah 1 Ch 2[29].

†**אַחוּמַי** **n.pr.m.** descendant of Judah 1 Ch 4[2]. 267

†**אֲחִיאָם** **n.pr.m.** one of David's heroes 2 S 279
23[33] 1 Ch 11[35].

†**אֲחִיָּה, אֲחִיָּהוּ** (always, exc. where other 281
form noted), **אֲחִי** **n.pr.m.** (*brother of Yah(u)*, 277
cf. Ph. אחמלך *brother of Milk*, & esp. אחתמלך *sister of Milk*, where אחת must be cstr. since מלך is a male deity; cf. Carth. חתמלקרת Euting[213]). **1.** a priest 1 S 14[3.18]. **2.** a scribe 1 K 4[3]. **3.** a prophet 1 K 11[29.30] 12[15] 14[2.4] 2 Ch 9[29]; 1 K 14[4.5.6.18] 2 Ch 10[15] (last five אֲחִיָּהוּ). **4.** father of king Baasha 1 K 15[27.29.33] 21[22] 2 K 9[9]. **5.** grandson of Hezron 1 Ch 2[25], or perh. **n.pr.f.**, mother of preceding four, cf. Be. **6.** son of Ehud, of Benj. 1 Ch 8[7] = אֲחוֹחַ v[4]. **7.** one of Dvd's heroes 1 Ch 11[36]. **8.** a Levite, Dvd's time 1 Ch 26[20]. **9.** a chief man under Nehem. Ne 10[27]. **10.** a Gadite 1 Ch 5[15] (אֲחִי). **11.** a man of Asher 1 Ch 7[34] (*id.*)

†**אֲחִיהוּד** **n.pr.m.** prince of Asher Nu 34[27]; 282
(*brother of majesty*, cf. הוֹד, אֲבִיהוּד; v. also אֲחִיחֻד).

†**אַחְיוֹ** **n.pr.m.** (= אחיון, i.e. *fraternal*). **1.** 283
a son of Aminadab, brother of Uzzah 2 S 6[3.4] (𝔊 אֶחָיו, We אָחִיו, but v. Dr) 1 Ch 13[7] (𝔊 אֶחָיו). **2.** a Benjamite 1 Ch 8[14], but rd. אֶחָיו 𝔊 Be. **3.** a Benjamite 1 Ch 8[31] = 9[37] (> 𝔊 אֶחָיו).

†**אֲחִיחֻד** **n.pr.m.** (prob. = אחיהוד q.v.) son 284
of Ehud, a Benjamite 1 Ch 8[7].

†**אֲחִיטוּב** **n.pr.m.** (*my brother is goodness*) 285
1. grandson of Eli 1 S 14[3] 1 Ch 5[33.34.37.38]; father

of Ahimelech 1 S $22^{9.20}$ (אֲחִטוּב) $v^{11.12}$ (on identity of pers. v. Be 1 Ch 5^{33}). **2.** father of Zadok 2 S 8^{17} (=1 Ch 18^{16}), but We rds. Ahim, son of Ahitub; 1 Ch 5^{37} Ezr 7^{2}; grandfather of Zadok 1 Ch 9^{11} Ne 11^{11} (on all cf. We l.c.)

286 †אֲחִילוּד **n.pr.m.** (acc. to Thes = אֲחִי יָלוּד *child's brother* (?)) **1.** father of Jehoshaphat, David's chronicler 2 S 8^{16} 20^{24} 1 K 4^{3} 1 Ch 18^{15}. **2.** father of Baana, officer of Solomon 1 K 4^{12}.

287 †אֲחִימוֹת **n.pr.m.** (*my brother is death*) a Levite 1 Ch 6^{10} (cf. מַחַת 1 Ch 6^{20} 2 Ch 29^{12}).

288 †אֲחִימֶלֶךְ **n.pr.m.** (*brother of Melek*, Ph. חמלך, חמלכת; v. also אחיהו supr.) **1.** priest in Saul's (Dvd's) time 1 S $21^{2.2.3.9}$ $22^{14.16}$ (אֲחִימֶלֶךְ) 1 Ch 24^{31} ψ 52^{2} (title); son of Ahitub 1 S 22 $^{9.11 (cf. 12).20}$; father of Abiathar 1 S 23^{6} 30^{7}; so also 2 S 8^{17} 𝔊 Ew We Th Dr; where MT אחימ׳ בן־אביתר; whence *id.* wrongly 1 Ch 24^{6}, cf. v^{4} (אֲח׳ מִבְּנֵי אִיתָמָר) & 18^{16} (where rd. אֲח׳ for אֲב׳). **2.** a Hittite 1 S 26^{6}.

289 †אֲחִימַן **n.pr.m.** (*my brother is a gift?* so Thes; cf. Ar. مَنّ) **1.** a son of Anak Nu 13^{22} Ju 1^{10}; אֲחִימָן Jos 15^{14}. **2.** a Levite, אֲחִימָן, 1 Ch 9^{17}.

290 †אֲחִימַעַץ **n.pr.m.** (*my brother is wrath*) **1.** son of Zadok 2 S $15^{27.36}$ $17^{17.20}$ $18^{19.22.23.27.28.29}$ 1 Ch 5^{34} (אֲחִימָעַץ) v^{35} 6^{38}; perh. also 1 K 4^{15} (son-in-law of Sol.) **2.** אֲחִימָעַץ, father-in-law of Saul 1 S 14^{50}.

291 †אַחְיָן **n.pr.m.** (*fraternal*, Aram. ܐܚܝܢܐ) a Manassite 1 Ch 7^{19}.

292 †אֲחִינָדָב **n.pr.m.** (*my brother is noble*) an officer of Solomon 1 K 4^{14}.

293 †אֲחִינֹעַם **n.pr.f.** (*my brother is delight*) **1.** wife of Saul 1 S 14^{50} (daughter of Ahimaaz). **2.** Jezreelitess, wife of David 1 S 25^{43} 27^{3} 30^{5} 2 S 2^{2} 3^{2} 1 Ch 3^{1}.

294 †אֲחִיסָמָךְ **n.pr.m.** (*my brother has supported*) father of Oholiab, a workman on tabern. Ex 31^{6} 35^{34} 38^{23}.

295 †אֲחִיעֶזֶר **n.pr.m.** (*my brother is help*, cf. As. *Aḫulê'te, my brother is strength*, Dl $^{Pr 202}$) **1.** a chief of Dan Nu 1^{12} 2^{25} $7^{66.71}$ 10^{25}. **2.** one of David's heroes 1 Ch 12^{3}.

296 †אֲחִיקָם **n.pr.m.** (*my brother has arisen*) son of Shaphan, Josiah's time 2 K $22^{12.14}$ 2 Ch 34^{20}; protector of Jerem. Je 26^{24}; father of Gedaliah 2 K 25^{22} Je 39^{14} $40^{5.6.7.9.11.14.16}$ $41^{1.2.6.10.16.18}$ 43^{6}.

297 †אֲחִירָם **n.pr.m.** (*brother of (the) lofty* = Ph. חרם v. חִירָם; cf. אֲבִירָם) son of Benj. Nu 26^{38} (prob. = אחרח 1 Ch 8^{1} v. Be) (cf. אֵחִי וְרֹאשׁ Gn 46^{21}).

†חִירָם **n.pr.m.** Hiram (Ph. חרם; abbr. fr. 2438
foregoing)—ח׳ 2 S 5^{11} + 18 t. 1 K + Kt 1 Ch 14^{1} 2 Ch 4^{11} 9^{10} (all Qr חוּרָם); חִירוֹם 1 K $5^{24.32}$
7^{10}; also חוּרָם 1 Ch 8^{5} + 9 t. Ch.—**1.** king of 2361
Tyre, contemp. of David & Solomon 2 S 5^{11} 1 K $5^{15.15.16.21.22.24.25.26.26.32}$ $9^{11.11.12.14.27}$ $10^{11.22}$ 1 Ch 14^{1} 2 Ch $2^{2.10.11}$ $8^{2.18}$ $9^{10.21}$. **2.** an artificer of Tyre, sent by Hiram the king 1 K $7^{13.40.40.45}$ 2 Ch 2^{12} $4^{11.11.16}$. **3.** a Benjamite 1 Ch 8^{5}.

†אֲחִירָמִי **adj.gent.** הָא׳ as n.coll. Nu 26^{38}. 298

†אֲחִירַע **n.pr.m.** (*my brother is evil*) a chief 299
of Naphtali Nu 1^{15} 2^{29} $7^{78.83}$ 10^{27}.

†אֲחִישַׁחַר **n.pr.m.** (*brother of (the) dawn*, 300
As. *Aḫšêri* Dl $^{Pr 202}$) a Benjamite 1 Ch 7^{10}.

†אֲחִישָׁר **n.pr.m.** (*my brother has sung*) 301
over Solomon's household 1 K 4^{6}.

†אֲחִיתֹפֶל **n.pr.m.** (*my brother is folly?*) 302
David's trusted & traitorous counsellor 2 S $15^{12.31.31.34}$ $16^{15.20.21.23.23}$ $17^{1.6.7.14.14.15}$ 21^{23} 23^{34} 1 Ch $27^{33.34}$.

†אַחֲוָה **n.f.** brotherhood הָא׳ Zc 11^{14} (be- 264
tween Judah & Israel).

†חִיאֵל **n.pr.m.** (prob. (אֲ)חִיאֵל *brother of* 2419
Ēl, 𝔊 Ἀχειηλ; cf. חירם & Ph. חמלך, etc.; v. Bae $^{Rel 156}$) a Bethelite, rebuilder of Jericho 1 K 16^{34}.

אחות **אָחוֹת** $_{114}$ **n.f.** sister (Ph. אחת, Aram. אֲחָת, 269
ܚܳܬܳܐ, Ar. أُخْتٌ, As. *aḫâtu*, Dl ^{W}, Eth. እኅት: Sab. in n.pr. אחתאמהו Os $^{ZMG 1865, 273}$) — abs. אָ׳ 2 S 13^{1} + (never with art.); cstr. אֲחוֹת Gn 4^{22}+; sf. אֲחֹתִי (אֲחוֹתִי) Gn 12^{13}+, etc.; *pl.* sf. אַחְוֹתַי (Qr אַחְיוֹתַי) Jos 2^{13}; אֲחוֹתַיִךְ Ez 16^{51} (Qr; Kt אחותך) + 2 t. (Co all אחיו׳); אַחְיוֹתֵךְ Ez 16^{52} (Co ־תיך); אֲחוֹתֵךְ Ez 16^{52} (must be pl., but del. Co); אַחְיֹתָיו Jb 42^{11}; אֲחוֹתֵיכֶם Ho 2^{3}; אַחְיֹתֵיהֶם 1 Ch 2^{16} Jb 1^{4} — **1.** *sister* Gn 4^{22} $12^{13.19}$; $20^{2.5.12}$ (same father, diff. mother) so Lv 18^{11} cf. Ez 22^{11}; Gn $24^{30.30}$+, Ex $2^{4.7}$; Lv 18^{9} (either parent same) so Dt 27^{22} Nu 6^{7} 2 S $13^{1.2.4}$ +, Ct $8^{8.8}$; called upon, in mourning for dead Je 22^{18}; = near relative Gn $24^{59.60}$ (or because Laban prominent? so Di); woman of same nationality Nu 25^{18} cf. Ho 2^{3}. **2.** = beloved Ct $4^{9.10.12}$ $5^{1.2}$ (4 t. ∥ כַּלָּה *bride*; phr. orig. implying that marriage with half-sister — of same father — was allowed? cf. Nö $^{ZMG 1886, 150}$, & Gn 20^{12}). **3.** symbol. of Judah, Samaria,

Sodom & Jerusalem Je $3^{7.8.10}$ Ez $16^{45.52.52}$ (del. Co) +, $23^{4.11}$+. **4.** fig. of intimate connection קָרָאתִי...אִמִּי וַאֲחֹתִי לָרִמָּה Jb 17^{14}; אֱמֹר לַחָכְמָה אֲחֹתִי אָתְּ Pr 7^{4}. †**5.** *another*, אִשָּׁה אֶל־אֲחֹתָהּ, of curtains of tabern. Ex $26^{3.3.6}$, loops v^{5}, tenons v^{17}; of wings of living creatures, Ezek.'s vision Ez $1^{9.23}$ 3^{13}; not of persons, but vid. רְעוּת.

260 †אָחוּ **n.m.** [Jb 8,11] **coll. reeds, rushes** (Aram. אַחְוָא, orig. Egypt., cf. demot. αχὺ fr. ἀχὰ *be green*, v. Ebers[AG & BB Mos. 338]; Wied[Sammlung 16]) Gn $41^{2.18}$ (E) Jb 8^{11}; also Ho 13^{15} where rd. אָחִים pl. for אַחְוִים (cf. AW), or fr. a parall. form [אָחֶה], v. De[Compl.Var. 23 f].

262 אַחְוָה v. חוה. p. 296

270 †אָחַז 68 **vb. grasp, take hold, take possession** (Ar. أَخَذَ, Sab. אחד Sab. Denkm.[39], Aram. אֲחַד, ܐܚܕ, As. *aḫazu*, Eth. አኀዘ:)—**Qal** *Pf.* אָחַז Ex 15^{14}+; אֲחָזָה Jb 23^{11} Is 33^{14}; sf. אֲחָזַנִי 2 S 1^{9}; 1 s. sf. אֲחַזְתִּיו Ct 3^{4}, etc.; *Impf.* יֹאחַז Jb 17^{9}+; וַיֹּאחֶז 2 S 6^{6}; 3 fs. תֹּאחֵז Dt 32^{41}; וַתֹּאחֶז Ru 3^{15}; וַתֹּחֶז 2 S 20^{9}; וָאֹחֵז Ju 20^{6}; יֹאחֵזוּן Is 13^{8}; *sf.* יֹאחֲזֵמוֹ Ex 15^{15}; יֹאחֲזוּךְ Je 13^{21}, etc.;—† as פ׳ gutt. וַיֶּאֱחֹז Ju 16^{3} 1 K 6^{10}; 2 ms. תֶּאֱחֹז Ec 7^{18}; *Inf.* אֱחֹז 1 K 6^{6}; אֱחֹז 1 Ch 13^{9} + 3 t.; *Imv.* אֱחֹז Ex 4^{4} 2 S 2^{21}, אֶחֱזִי־ Ru 3^{15}; אֶחֱזוּ Ct 2^{15}; אֶחֱזוּ Ne 7^{3}; *Pt. act.* אֹחֵז 2 Ch 25^{5}; *pass.* אָחוּז Est 1^{6}, etc.;—*grasp, take hold of*, sq. בְּ Gn 25^{26} Ex 4^{4} (both J) Ju 16^{3} 20^{6} (= וַיַּחֲזֵק בְּ 19^{29}) 2 S 4^{10} 6^{6} 20^{9} 1 K 1^{51} Ru $3^{15.15}$; 1 K 6^{6} of beams having hold in a wall; (cf. בֵּית אֲבָנִים יֶחֱזֶה Jb 8^{17}; Hoffm rds. יֹאחֵזָה=יֶחֱזֶה); also Ct 7^{9} of taking hold of branches, in metaph.; poet. fig., of God's seizing man in wrath Jb 16^{12}; taking hold graciously ψ 73^{23}; taking hold of judgment Dt 32^{41}; subj. man בַּאֲשֻׁרוֹ אָחֲזָה רַגְלִי Jb 23^{11} (|| דַּרְכּוֹ שָׁמַרְתִּי cf. also 17^{9}); of taking hold of folly Ec 2^{3} cf. 7^{18}; subj. הַשַּׁחַר Jb 38^{13}, לֶאֱחֹז בְּכַנְפוֹת הָאָרֶץ; also sq. acc. Ju 1^{6} 12^{6} 16^{21} 2 S 2^{21} Is 5^{29} Ct 2^{15} 3^{4} 1 Ch 13^{9} 2 Ch 25^{5} ψ 56^{1} 137^{9}; cf. 1 K 6^{10} (cf. v^{6} supr.), subj. וַיֶּא׳ אֶת־הַיָּצוּעַ, הַבַּיִת בַּעֲצֵי אֲרָזִים; of a snare catching the heel, in metaph. Jb 18^{9}; fig., subj. God ψ 77^{5}; God's hand 139^{10}; subj. pain, sorrow, fear, etc. Ex $15^{14.15}$ 2 S 1^{9} Jb 21^{6} 30^{16} ψ 48^{7} 119^{53} Is 21^{3} 33^{14} Je 13^{21} 49^{24}; subj. man, obj. fear, etc. Jb 18^{20} Is 13^{8}; obj. דֶּרֶךְ *take one's way* Jb 17^{9} יֹאחֵז צַדִּיק דַּרְכּוֹ AV RV *hold on his way* (cf. 23^{11} supr., & As. *ṣabâtu urḫu*, e.g. V. R[I, 74]);—abs. Ne 7^{3} of barring gates; pt. pass. *caught* Ec 9^{12}; *fastened, held* Est 1^{6}; *taken* (by lot) 1 Ch $24^{6.6.6}$ (on text v. Öt); *taken out* of a number Nu $31^{30.47}$; pt. act. of same form אֲחֻזֵי חֶרֶב Ct 3^{8} cf. Thes Ba[NB 175] & Eth. pt.; similarly Aram. אָחִיד, e.g. 𝔗 Am 2^{5}; ܐܚܝܕ e.g. 𝔖 Ju 8^{10} 1 Ch 5^{18}; & Ez $41^{6.6}$ (but v. Co). **Niph.** *Pf.* 3 pl. נֹאחֲזוּ Jos 22^{9}; וְנֹא׳ (cons.) Nu 32^{30}; *Impf.* וַיֵּאָחֲזוּ Gn 47^{27}; *Imv.* הֵאָחֲזוּ Gn 34^{10} Jos 22^{19}; *Pt.* נֶאֱחָז Gn 22^{13}; נֶאֱחָזִים Ec 9^{12};—*be caught* Gn 22^{13} Ec 9^{12}; elsewhere *have possessions* Gn 34^{10} 47^{27} Nu 32^{30} Jos $22^{9.19}$ (P). **Pi.** *Pt.* מְאַחֵז Jb 26^{9} c. acc. *enclose, overlay* (so As. Dl[W, p. 294], cf. Aram. ܐܚܕ, *shut*). **Hoph.** *Pt.* pl. מָאֳחָזִים 2 Ch 9^{18} *fastened to* sq. לְ.

אָחָז **n.pr.m.** (*he hath grasped*, abbrev. for 271
יהואחז (q.v.) cf. As. *Ia-u-ḫa-zi* (i.e. Ahaz) COT on 2 K 16^{8}) **1.** king of Judah, son of Jotham, father of Hezekiah 2 K 15^{38} $16^{1.2.5.7.8}$ + 13 t. 2 K; Is 1^{1} $7^{1.3.10.12}$ 14^{28} 38^{18}; 1 Ch 3^{13} 2 Ch 27^{9} + 8 t. 2 Ch; Ho 1^{1} Mi 1^{1}. **2.** son of Micah, & great-grandson of Jonathan 1 Ch $8^{35.36}$ 9^{42} (+ 9^{41} cf. 𝔊L 𝔙).

†אֲחֻזָּה 66 **n.f. possession**—א׳ Gn 47^{11} + 272
11 t.; cstr. אֲחֻזַּת Gn 17^{8} + 21 t.; sf. אֲחֻזָּתֶךָ ψ 2^{8};—*possession*, P & late; of landed property Gn 47^{11} Lv 14^{34} $25^{10.13.25.27.28.33 (houses) 41.45.46}$ Nu 27^{4} $32^{5.22.29}$ 35^{8} Dt 32^{49} Jos $21^{12.39}$ Ez 44^{28} $45^{5.6.7.7.8}$ $46^{18.18.18}$ $48^{20.21.22.22}$ 1 Ch 7^{28} 9^{2} 2 Ch 11^{14} 31^{1} Ne 11^{3}; c. אֶרֶץ, א׳ אֲחֻזָּה=*land possessed, one's own land* Gn 36^{43} Lv 14^{34} 25^{24} Nu 35^{28} Jos $22^{4.9.19.19}$, cf. אֲחֻזַּת הָאָרֶץ Lv 27^{24}; c. שָׂדֶה, ש׳ אֲחֻזָּה Lv $27^{16.22.28}$, cf. v^{21}; c. עִיר, ע׳ אֲחֻזָּה Lv $25^{32.33}$; אֲחֻזַּת נַחֲלָה=*possession by right of inheritance* Nu 27^{7} 32^{32}, & א׳ נַחֲלַת 35^{2} cf. א׳ בְּנַחֲלָה Ez 46^{16} (but Co as Nu 27^{7} so B); אֲחֻזַּת קֶבֶר Gn $23^{4.9.20}$ 49^{30} 50^{13}; א׳ עולם Gn 17^{8} 48^{4} Lv 25^{34}; in promise to Davidic king וַאֲחֻזָּתְךָ אַפְסֵי־אָרֶץ ψ 2^{8} (|| נַחֲלָה); fig. of י׳ as portion of Levit. priests Ez 44^{28} (|| נַחֲלָה).

אַחְזַי, אֲחַזְיָה, אֲחַזְיָהוּ **n.pr.m.** (*Yah(u)* 273-74
hath grasped; 𝔊 Ὀχοζ(ε)ιας 1 K 22^{52} etc., cf. Lag[BN 53]) **1.** king of Isr., son of Ahab 1 K $22^{40.50.52}$ 2 K 1^{18} 2 Ch 20^{37} (אֲחַזְיָהוּ); + 2 K 1^{2} 2 Ch 20^{35} (אֲחַזְיָה). **2.** king of Judah, son of Joram 2 K $8^{24.25}$ 9^{21} 10^{13} 11^{1} 12^{19} 13^{1} 14^{13} 1 Ch 3^{11} 22^{1} + 15 t. 2 K 1 Ch (all אֲחַזְיָהוּ); 2 K $9^{16.23.27.29}$ 11^{2} (אֲחַזְיָה). **3.** אַחְזַי a priest Ne 11^{13} (for which יַחְזֵרָה 1 Ch 9^{12} v. Sm[Listen, Tafel]).

†אֲחֻזָּם **n.pr.m.** (*possessor*) a man of Judah 275
1 Ch 4^{6}.

†אֲחֻזַּת **n.pr.m.** (*possession*) friend of Abi- 276
melech Gn 26^{26}.

I. **אחח** (*cry, howl*, onomat., cf. Ar. اَحَّ).

†[אֹחַ] **n.[m.]** jackal (As. *aḫû* Dl[W]) pl. 255
אֹחִים Is 13^{21} וּמָלְאוּ בָתֵּיהֶם א׳ (|| צִיִּים).

II. **אחח**?

†II. אָח **n.f.** fire-pot, brasier (Ar. إِجَّ, in 254

Thes, is an error) alw. c. art. Je 36[22] הָא׳ לְפָנָיו מְבֹעָרֶת *the brasier before him was burning;* v[23] הָאֵשׁ אֲשֶׁר אֶל־הָא׳; v[23] הָאֵשׁ אֲשֶׁר עַל־הָא׳ (I. אָח, *brother* v. sub אחה; III. אָח interj., p. 25).

265 †אֲחוֹחַ **n.pr.m.** a Benjamite 1 Ch 8[4] (perh. corruption of אחיה v[7] q. v.)

266 †אֲחוֹחִי (אֲחֹחִי) **adj.gent.** 2 S 23[9] (where for בֶּן־א׳ rd. הָא׳ We Dr; ref. unknown: Klo prop. (בֶּן אִישׁ חַי(ל) cf. v[20]) v[28] = 1 Ch 11[12.29] 27[4].

278 אֲחִי **n.pr.m.** a son of Benjamin Gn 46[21] (P) (perh. corruption of אֲחִירָם Nu 26[38] (P); so also אַחְרַח 1 Ch 8[1] cf. אַחֵר 7[12] & comm.)

אחל (existence & meaning dub.)

304 †אַחְלַי **n.pr.** (Dl[Pr 210] trans. *O! would that!* (cf. אַחֲלַי sub III. אָח supr. p. 25) & comp. interjectional Bab. name *Aḫulapia, O! that I at last!* Zim[BP 116]; cf. Ol[§ 277]; otherwise Hal[JAS 7, x. 360]) **1. f.** daughter of Sheshan 1 Ch 2[31]; so Be Öt al. in view of v[34]. **2. m.** father of one of David's mighty men (not in 2 S 23) 1 Ch 11[41].

303 אַחְלָב v. חלב. p. 316

306 †אַחְלָמָה **n.f.** perh. **amethyst** (etym. dub.; sub חלם Thes q.v.; Hal[JAs 7, x. 426] fr. חלם *être fort, solide;* Di Kn comp. Talm. חַלָּמִית, *malva* & think of green malachite; Dl[HA 36 N] der. fr. Aram. land *Aḫlamû*), *amethyst* acc. to 𝔊 𝔙 Josephus; v. also Lag[GGA 1884, 285], but cf. Di; one of the gems on the ephod Ex 28[19] 39[12].

308 אֲחַסְבַּי **n.pr.m.** father of Eliphelet, one of David's heroes 2 S 23[34]. (Meaning dub.; 1 Ch 11[35] has אוּר:, sq. חֵפֶר; txt. prob. corrupt.)

309 †אָחַר **vb. to remain behind, delay, tarry** (Ar. أَخَّرَ *to put off,* also *to remain behind;* Aram. Pa. אַחַר, Aph. ܐܘܚܪ, Shaph. ܫܘܚܪ, Sab. אחר Osiander[ZMG 1865, 197]; אחחר DHM[Epigr. Denkm. 34]). †**Qal** once only Gn 32[5] וָאֵחַר (contr. fr. וָאֶאֱחַר cf. אֵהַב Pr 8[17]) *and I have tarried* until now. †**Pi.** *Pf.* אֵחַר Gn 34[19]; אֵחֲרוּ Ju 5[28]; *Impf.* יְאַחֵר, תְּאַחֵר (3 t. תְּאַחַר) etc. Gn 24[56] + 9 t.; *Pt.* (־רֵי) מְאַחֲרִים 3 t. **1.** intensive, *delay, tarry,* abs. Ju 5[28] (|| בֹּשֵׁשׁ לָבוֹא) Is 46[13] and my salvation לֹא תְאַחֵר Hb 2[3] ψ 40[18] = 70[6] Dn 9[19]; with לְ & inf. Gn 34[19].—Pr 23[30] מְאַחֲרִים עַל־הַיָּיִן *those tarrying* over the wine, Is 5[11] מְאַחֲרֵי בַנֶּשֶׁף, ψ 127[2] (מַשְׁכִּימֵי קוּם ||) מְאַחֲרֵי שֶׁבֶת. **2.** causat. of Qal, *cause one to delay, hinder* Gn 24[56]; *keep back* (= *bring late*) Ex 22[28]; with לְ & inf. *delay to . . .* Dt 23[22] quoted Ec 5[3]: ellipt. Dt 7[10] *he delayeth* (it, the recompense) not to his enemy.—2 S 20[5] Qr וַיּוֹחֶר is taken by Ol[§ 241 c] as Qal (cf. וַתֹּחֶז v[9] from אָחַז), by Sta[§ 498 c] Kö[I. 397] Ges[§ 68 2 Rem] as Hiph. (lit. *shewed, exhibited delay*): on the Kt (וַיְּיַחֶר ?) v. Dr[Sm].

I. אַחֵר **adj. another** (prop. *one coming behind*), f. אַחֶרֶת (with dag. f. implic.); pl. אֲחֵרִים (as if from sg. אָחֵר), once Jb 31[10] אֲחֵרִין, אֲחֵרוֹת (= Ar. آخَرُ, Sab. אאחר, As. *aḫru* future, fpl. as subst. *aḫrat ûmê* future of days) Gn 4[25] זֶרַע אַחֵר *another* seed 8[10] שִׁבְעַת יָמִים אֲחֵרִים seven *other* days Ex 22[4] בִּשְׂדֵה אַחֵר in the field of *another* + oft.; אִישׁ אַחֵר *another* man (husband) Gn 29[19] Dt 24[2] Je 3[1]; חָצֵר הָאַחֶרֶת 1 K 7[8] *the other* court, v. חָצֵר; הַחוֹמָה א׳ 2 Ch 32[5] the *other* wall, v. חוֹמָה. Appended to a n. pr. for distinction Ezr 2[31] = Ne 7[34] (see v[7] = Ne v[12]) Ne 7[33] (prob. here txt. err., v. Be Ry[18]: not in Ezr 2[29]). Often with the collat. sense of *different,* as בְּגָדִים א׳ *other* garments Lv 6[4] 1 S 28[8] Ez 42[14] 44[19]; אֲבָנִים, עָפָר Lv 14[42]; רוּחַ Nu 14[24]; וְנֶהְפַּכְתָּ לְאִישׁ אַ׳ 1 S 10[6]; לֵב v[9] Ez 11[19] (𝔊 Hi Sm); שֵׁם Is 65[15] (cf. 62[2] חָדָשׁ); with that of *strange, alien,* as אִישׁ אַ׳ Dt 20[5.6.7] 28[30] (so אַחֵר, אֲחֵרִים alone ψ 109[8] Jb 31[8.10] Is 65[22] Je 6[12] 8[10] al.); עַם Dt 28[32]; אֶרֶץ 29[27] Je 22[26]; אִשָּׁה Ju 11[2]; לָשׁוֹן Is 28[11] (|| בְּלַעֲגֵי שָׂפָה); esp. in the phrase אֱלֹהִים אֲחֵרִים *other gods* (63 t.) Ex 20[3] (= Dt 5[7]) 23[13] (both JE) Jos 24[2.16] (E) 1 S 26[19] Ho 3[1], & particularly in Dt (6[14] 8[19] + 15 t.) & Deut. writers, as Jos 23[16] Ju 2[12.17.19] Je (18 t.) & compiler of Kings; אֵל אַחֵר once Ex 34[14] (JE). So אַחֵר alone Is 42[8] ψ 16[4]. † Of time, *following, next* (rare) בַּשָּׁנָה הָא׳ Gn 17[21] (P) in the *next* year; 2 K 6[29] בַּיּוֹם הָאַ׳; דּוֹר אַ׳ Joel 1[3] ψ 109[13] poet. *the next* generation (Ju 2[10] in prose = *another* generation). 312

אַחַר prop. subst. *the hinder* or *following part* (cf. the pl.) **1. adv. a.** of place, **behind,** twice Gn 22[13] (many MSS. Sam. 𝔊 𝔖 Ol Ew read אֶחָד v. Di) ψ 68[26]. **b.** of time, **afterwards** Gn 10[18] 18[5] 24[55] 30[21] Ju 19[5] +; וְאַחַר in laws of P, as Lv 14[8.19] 15[28] 22[7] Nu 5[26] al. **2. prep. a.** of place, **behind, after** Ex 3[1] 11[5] 2 K 11[6] Ct 2[9] Is 57[8]: הָלַךְ אַחַר *to go after, follow* Gn 37[17] 2 K 13[2] 23[3] Is 65[2] Ez 13[3] Jb 31[7]; הָיָה אַחַר 1 S 12[14]; מֵאַחַר *from after* † 2 S 7[8] ψ 78[71] Is 59[13]. **b.** of time, **after** Gn 9[28] Lv 25[15] al; אַחַר הַדְּבָרִים הָאֵלֶּה *after* these things † Gn 15[1] 22[1] 39[7] 40[1] 1 K 17[17] 21[1] Ezr 7[1] Est 2[1] 3[1]; אַחַר כֵּן † Lv 14[36] Dt 21[13] 1 S 10[5]; אַחַר זֶה (late) 2 Ch 32[9]; sq. inf. † Nu 6[19] Je 40[1] 1 Ch 2[24] Jb 21[3]; עַד אַחַר *till after* † Ne 13[19]. **c.** Ne 5[15] strangely: Ew RV *besides;* but text prob. corrupt, v. Be Ry. **3.** †**conj.** אַחַר אֲשֶׁר 310

after that Ez 40^{1}; and without אשר Lv 14^{43} Je 41^{16} Jb 42^{7}. As prep. & conj. the pl. אַחֲרֵי is much more freq., which in any case must be used before suffixes. **Plur.** only cstr. אַחֲרֵי with sf. אַחֲרַי, אַחֲרֶיךָ, etc. **1. subst. hinder part** †2 S 2^{23} בְּאַחֲרֵי הַחֲנִית with the *hinder end* of the spear. **2. prep. a.** of place, **behind, after** Gn 18^{10} וְהוּא אַחֲרָיו and it *behind* him Dt 11^{30} Ju 5^{14} 1 S 14^{13} 21^{10}; Ho 5^{8} אַחֲרֶיךָ Behind thee! (sc. Look *or* The foe is); with a vb. as הִבִּיט to look Gn 19^{17} 1 S 24^{9}, הֵנִיעַ רֹאשׁ to shake the head 2 K 19^{21} (=Is 37^{22}), esp. verbs expressing or implying motion, as בָּא to enter in (v. Dr 2 S 20^{14}), פָּנָה, מִלֵּא, הָלַךְ, הָיָה, דָּלַק, דָּבַק, בִּעֵר, הִשְׁלִיךְ, רָדַף (see these words). **b.** of time, **after** Gn 9^{9} זַרְעֲכֶם אַחֲרֵיכֶם your seed *after* you; similarly 17$^{7-10.19}$ 35^{12} 48^{4} Ex 28^{43} Nu 25^{13} all P (also Dt 1^{8} 4^{37} 10^{15} 1 S 24^{22} 2 S 7^{12} ||), & with בָּנָיו Gn 18^{19} J (+בֵּיתוֹ) Ex 29^{29} P Lv 25^{46}H Dt 4^{40} 12$^{25.28}$ Je 32$^{18.39}$ 1 Ch 28^{8} Pr 20^{7}, דּוֹרוֹתֵינוּ Jos 22^{27}, בֵּיתוֹ Jb 21^{21}; Ex 10^{14} Ju 10^{3} etc.; with inf. Gn 5^{4} אַחֲרֵי הוֹלִידוֹ *after his begetting* Sheth, 13^{14} 14^{17} 18^{12} 25^{11}+oft.; אַחֲרֵי־כֵן *afterwards* Gn 6^{4} (אחרי כן אשר=*afterwards, when*, cf. 2 Ch 35^{20}) 15^{14} 23^{19} 25^{26} 32^{21} 41^{31} 45^{15} etc.; ויהי אחרי־כן as a formula of transition chiefly in 2 S (2^{1} 8^{1} || 10^{1} || 13^{1} 21^{18} ||) cf. 1 S 24^{6} Ju 16^{4} 2 K 6^{24} 2 Ch 20^{1} 24^{4}†; in late Heb. אַחֲרֵי זֹאת †Jb 42^{16} Ezr 9^{10} 2 Ch 21^{18} (+כָּל־) 35^{20} (do.); cf. Aram. אַחֲרֵי דְנָה Dn 2$^{29.45}$, and בָּאתַר דְּנָה Dn 7$^{6.7}$.—The local (metaph.) and temporal senses blend ψ 49^{14} וְאַחֲרֵיהֶם בְּפִיהֶם יִרְצוּ & *after* them (i.e. following, imitating them) men applaud their speech, cf. Jb 21^{33}. **3. conj.** אַחֲרֵי אֲשֶׁר **after that,** with the finite vb. Dt 24^{4} Jos 7^{8} 9^{16} 23^{1} 24^{20}+; without אשר †Lv 25^{48} 1 S 5^{9}†. (The most common constr. of אחרי is as a prep. with the inf. cstr.) Jos 2^{7} אַחֲרֵי כַּאֲשֶׁר יָצְאוּ must be an error, either for אחרי אשר or for כאשר alone (notice אחריהם twice in the same verse); 2 S 24^{10} rd. אַחֲרֵי סָפַר vid. Dr. **4.** with other preps.:—**a.** מֵאַחֲרֵי $_{57}$, 1 Ch 17^{7} מִן־אַחֲרֵי (|| 2 S 7^{8} מֵאַחַר); (*a*) *from behind* Gn 19^{26} 2 S 2^{23}; *from after* i.e. *from following after*, usually with שׁוּב or סוּר 1 S 24^{2} 2 S 2$^{22.26.30}$ 11^{15}; oft. with God as obj. as Nu 14^{43} 32^{15} Dt 7^{4} Jos 22$^{16.18.23.29}$ 1 S 15^{11}+; with other vbs. of motion, as עָלָה 1 S 14^{46} 2 S 20^{2}, נַעֲלָה 2 S 2^{27}, לָקַח Am 7^{15} 1 Ch 17^{7}, זָנָה Ho 1^{2}; pregn. Is 30^{21} thy ears shall hear a word מֵאַחֲרֶיךָ *coming from behind* thee, Je 9^{21} (sc. נָפַל, see v^{a}) 1 S 13^{7} 𝔊L We Dr חָרְדוּ מֵאַחֲרָיו. (*β*) denoting *position* (מִן=*off, on the side of*; see מִן) *behind* Ex 14$^{19.19}$ Jos 8$^{2.4.14}$ 1 K 10^{19} Ne 4^{7} (מֵאַחֲרַי לְ) 2 Ch 13^{13b}. (*γ*) of time (rare) †Dt 29^{21} Ec 10^{14}; מֵאַחֲרֵי כֵן †2 S 3^{28} 15^{1} 2 Ch 32^{23}. **b.** †אֶל־אַחֲרֵי 2 S 5^{23} 2 K 9^{18} v^{19} סֹב אֶל־אַחֲרַי Zc 6^{6}. **c.** †עַל־אַחֲרֵי Ez 41^{15} *beside, at the back of.*

†אַחֲרַי **adj.** Pr 28^{23} (si vera l.) אָדָם אַחֲרַי a 310
man **that turneth backwards** (cf. Je 7^{24}) so Jos Ki De Ol$^{p.429}$ (doubtfully) Now Sta^{§301b}: acc. to Ew^{§220a} Hi an abnormal adv.=*afterwards*, Lag^{Pr} conj. בְּאָרְחוֹ cf. 𝔊 ὁδούς.

אָחוֹר $_{41}$ **subst.** (Arab. أُخُرٌ) **the hinder** 268
side, back part, in the sg., mostly in adverbial phrases:—**a.** as accus., in poetry *backwards* 23 t. (=prose אֲחֹרַנִּית) with vbs. such as נָפַל *fall* Gn 49^{17}, נָשׁוֹג *be turned* 2 S 1^{22} (|| תָּשׁוּב רֵיקָם), שׁוּב ψ 9^{4} 56^{10}+, נָסוֹג 35^{4} 40^{15}+ (of enemies repulsed), 44^{19} Is 50^{5} (from obedience to God), נָזוֹר Is 1^{4}, הֵשִׁיב 44^{25} ψ 44^{11}, הִכָּה 78^{66}; *behind* (opp. קֶדֶם) ψ 139^{5} Jb 23^{8}; in the phrase פָּנִים וְאָחוֹר in front and *behind* †1 Ch 19^{10} (altered from מִפָּ׳ וּמֵאָ׳ in 2 S v. infr.) 2 Ch 13^{14} Ez 2^{10}. **b.** בְּאָחוֹר †Pr 29^{11}, וְחָכָם בְּאָחוֹר יְשַׁבְּחֶנָּה Ges Hi but a wise man stilleth it (רוּחַ anger) *backwards* (sc. when it would break forth), De *in the background*, sc. of his heart (|| כָּל־רוּחוֹ יוֹצִיא כְּסִיל). **c.** לְאָחוֹר (*a*) as **a.** †ψ 114$^{3.5}$ Je 7^{24}; (*β*) of time, *hereafter* (cf. לְפָנִים=before) †Is 41^{23} 42^{23}. **d.** מֵאָחוֹר *behind* (מִן=on the side of) †2 S 10^{9} מִפָּנִים וּמֵ׳ in front and *behind*, Is 9^{11} וּפְלִשְׁתִּים מֵאָ׳ and the Philistines *behind* (=on the West), opp. אֲרָם מִקֶּדֶם. †**Plur.** cstr. אֲחֹרֵי **hinder part** (of the tabernacle) Ex 26^{12}, (of a man or animal) 33^{23} 1 K 7^{25} (=2 Ch 4^{4}) Ez 8^{16}.

†אֲחֹרַנִּית **adv.** (prop. an adj. fem., cf. 322
קַדְרַנִּית Sta^{§367}) **backwards** (=poet. אָחוֹר) Gn 9$^{23.23}$ 1 S 4^{18} 1 K 18^{37} 2 K 20$^{10.11}$ Is 38^{8}.

אַחֲרוֹן $_{51}$ **f.** אַחֲרוֹנָה, pl. אַחֲרֹנִים (also אַחֲרוֹנִים), 314
adj. from אַחַר, **coming after** or **behind** (as a compar. or superl., acc. to the context); hence **a.** of place, *behind, hindermost* Gn 33$^{2.2}$; הַיָּם הָאַחֲרוֹן *the hinder* (=the Western) sea (i.e. the Mediterranean: opp. הַיָּם הַקַּדְמוֹנִי the front sea =the Dead Sea, the Semites, in defining the quarters of the heavens, turning naturally to the East, cf. קֶדֶם of the East, תֵּימָן, יָמִין of the South, above s.v. אָחוֹר **d.** and As. *mat aḫarru* 'the Western land,' of Phœnicia & Palestine) †Dt 11^{24} 34^{2} Jo 2^{20} Zc 14^{8}; Jb 18^{20} poet. אַחֲרֹנִים Ew Hi Di De *the dwellers in the West* (opp. קַדְמוֹנִים). More commonly **b.** of time, *latter* or *last* (acc. to context) Ex 4^{8} Dt 24^{3} 2 S 19^{12} Is 8^{23}, of God Is 44^{6} (|| רִאשׁוֹן) 48^{12} (do.) cf. 41^{4}; in genl. *subsequent* (vaguely), יוֹם א׳= time *to come* †Is 30^{8} Pr 31^{25} (but Ne 8^{18} הַיּוֹם הָאַ׳=*the last* day), (הַ)דּוֹר (הָ)אַ׳ *the following* generation †Dt 29^{21} ψ 48^{14} 78$^{4.6}$ 102^{19}, (הָ)אַחֲרֹנִים

they that come after Jb 18^{20} (Ges Schl) Ec 1^{11} 4^{16}, but Is 41^{4} *the last*, Jb 19^{25} וְאַחֲרוֹן עַל־עָפָר יָקוּם and as *one coming after* (me) (and so able to establish my innocence when I am dead) will he (גֹּאֲלִי my Vindicator) arise upon the dust.—The *fem.* is used adverbially (cf. רִאשֹׁנָה)=*afterwards* or *at the last* (acc. to context): (*a*) absol. †Dan 11^{29}; (*β*) בָּאַחֲרוֹנָה (opp. בָּרִאשֹׁנָה) † Dt 13^{10} 17^{7} 1 S 29^{2} 2 S 2^{26} 1 K 17^{13} Dn 8^{3}; (*γ*) לָאַ׳ †Nu 2^{31} (P) Ec 1^{11}.

319 **אַחֲרִית** 61 **n.f. after-part, end**;—**a.** of place, only ψ 139^{9} (late) א׳ יָם. **b.** of time, *latter part* or actual *close* (acc. to context), opp. רֵאשִׁית;—of year Dt 11^{12}; of a man's life Nu 23^{10} Pr 5^{11} Jb 8^{7} 42^{12}; of a people's existence Nu 24^{20}; =*final lot* Dt 32$^{20.29}$ Je 12^{4} 31^{17} ψ 73^{17}; *a future*, i.e. a happy close of life, suggesting sometimes the idea of a posterity, promised to the righteous Pr 23^{18} (‖ תִּקְוָה *hope*) 24^{14} Je 29^{11} (לָתֵת לָכֶם א׳ וְתִקְוָה), withheld from the wicked Pr 24^{20} (‖ נֵר יִדְעָךְ: v. infr.); the *end* or ultimate *issue* of a course of action Je 5^{31} Pr 14^{12} 23^{32} (of wine, i.e. of indulgence in it) 25^{8} Is 46^{10} (absol., but implicitly of a phase of history) 47^{7} (of the conduct described v^{6b-7a}) Dn 12^{8} Ec 7^{8}; of a prediction = the *event* Is 41^{22}. בְּאַחֲרִית הַיָּמִים *in the end of the days*, a prophetic phrase denoting the final period of the history so far as the speaker's perspective reaches; the sense thus varies with the context, but it often=the ideal or Messianic future; † Gn 49^{1} (of the period of Israel's possession of Canaan) Nu 24^{14} Dt 4^{30} (of the period of Israel's return to God after adversity) 31^{29} (of the period of Israel's rebellion) Ho 3^{5} Is 2^{2} (=Mi 4^{1}) Je 23^{20} (v. Graf)=30^{24} 48^{47} 49^{39} Ez 38^{16} (of the period of Gog's attack upon restored Israel) Dn 2^{28} (Aram.) 10^{14} (of the age of Antiochus Epiphanes): cf. בְּא׳ הַשָּׁנִים Ez 38^{8}. **c.** א׳ הַגּוֹיִם Je 50^{12} the *last, hindermost* of the nations (of Babylon), opp. ראשית הגוים Am 6^{1} (Israel) cf. Nu 24^{20} (Amalek) chief of the nations. **d.** concr. *posterity* (extension of usage noted above in Pr 24^{20}) ψ 37$^{37.38}$ (*possibly* not more than 'a future' here) 109^{13} (‖ בְּדוֹר אַחֵר יִמַּח שְׁמָם) Am 4^{2} 9^{1} Ez 23$^{25.25}$ (acc. to others, in these four passages, *remnant, residue*) Dn 11^{4}.

313 †II. **אַחֵר n.pr.m.** 1 Ch 7^{12} (ident. & meaning quite dub.; Be thinks=אַחֵר **adj.** *another*, to avoid naming Dan (cf. Gn 46^{23} Nu 26^{42}) on account of the narrative Ju 17 f. Öt identifies with שֻׁחָרִים 8^{8}).

315 †**אַחְרַח n.pr.m.** a son of Benjamin 1 Ch 8^{1} (perh. corruption of אֲחִירָם Nu 26^{38}, cf. also אֵחִי).

†**אֲחַרְחֵל n.pr.m.** app. a descendant of 316
Judah 1 Ch 4^{8} (deriv. & mng. dub.)

†**אֲחַשְׁדַּרְפְּנִים n.m.pl. satraps** (Pers. 323
Khshatrapâvan, protectors of the realm, v. Spieg APK 215 = ἐξατράπης, σατράπης, cf. Lag G. Abh. 68, 14; Sem. i. 42 f, who rds. אַחְשַׁדְרְפָן)—א׳ Est 8^{9} 9^{3}; cstr. אֲחַשְׁדַּרְפְּנֵי 3^{11} Ezr 8^{36}.

אֲחַשְׁוֵרוֹשׁ n.pr.m. Ahasuerus = Xerxes 325
(Pers. *Khshayârshâ=mighty + eye* or *man*, vid. Spiegel l.c. 216; in Aram. חשיארש, CIS II. i. 122 [B.C. 481]) king of Pers. Ezr 4^{6} Est 1$^{1.1.2.9.10}$ + 18 t. Est + Est 10^{1} Qr (Kt אחשרש); אֲחַשְׁרֹשׁ Est 1^{16} 2^{21} 3^{12} 8$^{7.10}$; also Dn 9^{1} where made father of 'Darius the Mede,' cf. Meinh.

†**אֲחַשְׁתָּרִי n.pr.m.** but in form *adj. gent.* 326
(cf. Be) הָאֲחַ׳ 1 Ch 4^{6} (perh. Pers. = *belonging to the realm, royal*, vid. infr.)

†[**אֲחַשְׁתְּרָן**] **adj.** (?) royal (fr. Pers. 327
Khshatra, lordship, realm, vid. Spiegel l.c. 215) pl. הָאֲחַשְׁתְּרָנִים agreeing with הָרֶכֶשׁ Est 8$^{10.14}$.

אַחַת v. אֶחָד. p. 31 259

אַט v. אטט. below 328

אטד (mng. dub.; perh. cf. Ar. وطد *make firm, strong*, cf. Thes MV).

†**אָטָד n.m.** Ju 9,15 **bramble, buck-thorn** 329
(cf. Che ψ 58^{10}) (*rhamnus*, Ar. أَطَد, As. *eṭidu* v. Dl W, No. 153, Aram אַטְדָּא, ܐܛܕܐ cf. Löw No. 15) contr. עֵצִים Ju 9$^{14.15.15}$ (personif., in fable); ψ 58^{10} as fuel (in fig., cf. Che); גֹּרֶן הָא׳, n.loc., Gn 50$^{10.11}$ (v. גֹּרֶן & אבל מצרים).

אטט Arab. أَطَّ *to emit a moaning* or *creaking sound* (cf. AW Lex. 36 Ges Jes. i. 604 f Lane i. 66).

†[**אִטִּי** Ol. 412] **n.m. mutterer**, pl. אִטִּים Is 19^{3} *mutterers* (‖ אֹבוֹת, יִדְּעֹנִים) i.e. either ventriloquists or whisperers of charms (cf. 8^{19} 29^{4}).

†**אַט subst. gentleness**, used only adver- 328
bially:—**a.** as adverb. accus. 1 K 21^{27} וַיְהַלֵּךְ אַט: and he (Ahab) went about *softly* (sc. in penitence); **b.** with לְ of norm or state (as in לָבֶטַח, v. לְ) 2 S 18^{5} לְאַט־לִי לַנַּעַר (deal) *gently* for me with the young man, Is 8^{6} the waters of Shiloah הַהֹלְכִים לְאַט that go *gently*; with pretonic qameṣ Jb 15^{11} דָּבָר לָאַט עִמָּךְ: a word (spoken) *gently* with thee; with sf. Gn 33^{14} and I אֶתְנַהֲלָה לְאִטִּי will lead on *gently* (lit. *according to my gentleness*).

†[**אָטַם**] **vb. shut, shut up** (Mish. אטם, cf. 331

אוֹטֵם *stoppage*, Aram. אֲטַם; Ar. أَطَمَ *contract, stop*, أُطُمٌ *fortress;* As. *aṭamu*, in list of headgear, etc.=*turban?* Dl$^{W. No. 155}$) —**Qal** *Pt. act.* אֹטֵם Pr 17^{28} + 2 t.; *pass.* אֲטֻמִים 1 K 6^{4}; אֲטֻמוֹת Ez 40^{16} + 2 t.;—*shut, stop*, obj. lips Pr 17^{28}; ears 21^{13} Is 33^{15}; pass.=*closed* (i.e. *narrowed, narrowing*, cf. 𝔖 in Co) חַלּוֹנוֹת א׳ Ez 40^{16} 41$^{16.26}$; cf. חַלּוֹנֵי שְׁקֻפִים אֲטֻמִים 1 K 6^{4}. **Hiph.** *Impf.* i.q. Qal יַאְטֵם ψ 58^{5} (juss. with sense of indic., cf. Dr$^{§173 obs.}$) of adder, stopping ears, sim. of wicked.

330 †אֲטוּן **n.[m.] thread, yarn** (etym. unknown; on form v. Ges$^{§84a. 12. R.}$ Talm. אֲטוּנָא, אַטְוּנָא, *cord, rope;* so 𝔗) cstr. א׳ מִצְרָיִם Pr 7^{16}.

332 †[אָטַר] **vb. shut up, close, bind** (Ar. أَطَرَ *bend, curve*, إِطَارٌ *what surrounds, encloses*) **Qal** *Impf.* 3 fs. תֶּאְטַר ψ 69^{16} (אַל תּ׳ עָלַי בְּאֵר פִּיהָ).

333 †אָטֵר **n.pr.m.** (*binder?*) a chief of Jews Ezr 2$^{16.42}$ Ne 7$^{21.45}$ 10^{18}.

334 †אִטֵּר **adj. shut up, bound** (NH אִטֵּר, *lame*) אִישׁ א׳ יַד־יְמִינוֹ Ju 3^{15} 20^{16} *a man bound, restricted, as to his right hand*, i.e. *left-handed*.

335 [אַי] (أَىٌّ, ܐܝ: in Syr. in cpds. as ܐܝܟܢ *how?* W$^{SG 120-2}$; cf. As. *aiu, who? what?*). †**1. interrog. adv. where? a.** so with sf. אַיֶּכָּה [a verbal form, v. Sta$^{§355 b. 3}$] Gn 3^{9}; אַיּוֹ Ex 2^{20}, poet. *where is he?*=he is nowhere Jb 14^{10} 20^{7} (Je 37^{19} rd. Qr אַיֵּה); אַיָּם Na 3^{17} (in indirect qu.) and the place thereof is not known, אַיָּם *where* they are. Idiomatically, with the sf. anticipating the noun to which it refers (Ew^{§309c}, cf. Dr$^{Sm. i. 21, 14}$) 2 K 19^{13} אַיּוֹ מֶלֶךְ־חֲמָת *where is he*, the king of Hamath? (|| Is 37^{13} אַיֵּה) Is 19^{12} Mi 7^{10}. When used alone, or with other adverbs (v. infr.), it is contracted to אֵי Gn 4^{9} Dt 32^{37} 1 S 26^{16} Pr 31^{4} Qr. (The more usual form is אַיֵּה.) **b.** strengthened by the enclitic זֶה (v. זֶה, 4) אֵי־זֶה$_{15}$ *where, then?* (never of a *person*, exc. Est 7^{5} (late), & only once 1 K 22^{24} [but v. 2 Ch 18^{23}] with a *verb*) Is 50^{1} 66$^{1.1}$ Je 6^{16}, in indirect qu. 1 S 9^{18}; in the phrase ... אֵי־זֶה הַדֶּרֶךְ *where is* the way (that) ...? †1 K 13^{12} 2 K 3^{8} 2 Ch 18^{23} Jb 38$^{19 a. 24}$. **2.** prefixed to other adverbs or prons., אֵי imparts to them an interrog. force: thus **a.** אֵי־זֶה *which* (of two or more)? only Ec 2^{3} 11^{6} (late), in indirect qu. **b.** †אֵי־מִזֶּה *whence?* (מִזֶּה=*hence;* v. sub זֶה) Gn 16^{8} אֵי־מִזֶּה בָאת 1 S 30^{13} 2 S 1$^{3.13}$ Jb 2^{2}; in indirect qu. Ju 13^{6} 1 S 25^{11}; with subst. annexed 2 S 15^{2} אֵי־מִזֶּה עִיר אַתָּה lit. *whence*, as regards city, art thou? Jon 1^{8}. **c.** †אֵי־לָזֹאת Je 5^{7} *upon what ground?* (𝔙 super quo?) *how?* With other adverbs, אֵי coalesces into one word, v. אֵיכָה, אֵיכָכָה, אֵיפֹה.

אַיֵּה$_{45}$ (lengthened from אֵי, cf. הֵן & הִנֵּה) 346
interr. adv. Where? Gn 18^{9} 19^{5} 22^{7}; the most gen. term expressing this idea, used of both persons & things (but never with a *verb* [contrast אֵיפֹה]); oft. in poet. or elevated style, where the answer *nowhere* is expected, Is 33^{18} 36^{19} 51^{13} Je 2^{28} (cf. Dt 32^{37} אֵי) 17^{15} 37^{19}, Jb 15^{23} he wandereth abroad for bread אַיֵּה (saying) *Where* is it? 21^{28} Zc 1^{5} (אַיֵּה־הֵם); in the (iron.) phrase *where is thy* (*their*) *God?* †ψ 42$^{4.11}$ 79^{10} 115^{2} (אַיֵּה־נָא) Jo 2^{17}; rhetorically, of an earnest inquiry Je 2$^{6.8}$ Job 35^{10}, or longing Is 63$^{11.15}$ Ju 6^{13}.

אֵיךְ$_{59}$ (Aram. אֵיךְ, ܐܝܟ [pron. *âch*]) **adv.** 349
1. interrog. How? Gn 26^{9} 2 S 1$^{5.14}$ 1 K 12^{6} Is 20^{6} al.; oft. with impf. (esp. in 1 ps.) in an expostulation Gn 39^{9} 44$^{8.34}$ Jos 9^{7} 2 S 2^{22} 12^{18} ψ 137^{4}, Is 48^{11} for *how* should it be profaned? (ו)איך תאמר *how canst* or *dost* thou (do you) say...? Ju 16^{15} Is 19^{11} Je 2^{23} (cf. 8^{8} אֵיכָה) 48^{14} ψ 11^{1}; in an indirect sentence 2 K 17^{28} Je 36^{17} Ru 3^{18}. **2. as an exclam. How!** whether of lamentation 2 S 1^{19} Je 2^{21} 9^{18} Mi 2^{4}; or of satisfaction Is 14$^{4.12}$ Je 48^{39} 51^{41} Ob^{5} al.; with intensive force=*how gladly!* Je 3^{19}, *how terribly!* 9^{6} (but others render here 'for how [else] should I do'? etc.)

†אֵיכָה (from אֵי and כֹּה=כָּה; cf. As. *ekiam*) 349
adv. 1. interrog. In what manner? *τίνι τρόπῳ*; (rather more definite than אֵיךְ=*πῶς*;) Dt 1^{12} 7^{17} 12^{30} 18^{21} 32^{30} Ju 20^{3} (indirect sentence) 2 K 6^{15} Je 8^{8} ψ 73^{11}. **2. exclam. How!** (slightly more emph. than אֵיךְ) Is 1^{21} Je 48^{17}
La 1^{1} 2^{1} 4$^{1.2}$. **3. Where?** (prob. north-Isr.; 351
cf. Aram. אֵיכָא, ܐܝܟܐ *where?* Cf. Dr$^{Intr. 178, 421}$) only 2 K 6^{13} Kt Ct 1$^{7.7}$,—each time in an indirect sentence.

†אֵיכוֹ 2 K 6^{13} Qr **where?** v. אֵיכָה **3.** above 351

†אֵיכָכָה (Ct) אֵיכָכָה (Est) (from אֵי & כָּכָה 349
thus) **How?** only Ct 5$^{3.3}$ Est 8$^{6.6}$.

I. [אַיִן] **adv.** (from אֵי; As. *aina, ainu*, Arab. 370
أَيْنَ *where?* مِنْ أَيْنَ *whence?*) only in the compound מֵאַיִן$_{17}$ **whence?** Gn 29^{4} 42^{7} (syn. אֵי־מִזֶּה e.g. Gn 16^{8} 1 S 30^{13}) Ju 17^{9} 19^{17} Jb 1^{7} (2^{2} אֵי־מִזֶּה); used in a rhet. or poet. style (where אֵי־מִזֶּה would be too prosaic) Nu 11^{13} מֵאַיִן לִי בָּשָׂר *whence* have I flesh etc.? 2 K 6^{27} Je 30^{7} Alas! for that day is great; מֵאַיִן כָּמֹהוּ *whence* is its like? (see also II. אַיִן ad fin.) Na 3^{7} ψ 121^{1} Jb 28$^{12.20}$; in an indirect sentence Jos 2^{4} (cf. אֵי־מִזֶּה 1 S 25^{11}).

575 אָן **adv.** (contracted fr. I. אַיִן) **where?** or
whither? 1 S 10^{14} (cf. 27^{10} 𝔊 𝔗, v. sub אַל ad
fin.); only besides in †מֵאָן *whence?* 2 K 5^{25} Kt
(Qr מֵאַיִן); †עַד־אָן of time *to what point? how
long?* Jb 8^{2}. With ה *locale*: אָ֫נָה (*a*) *whither?* Gn
16^{8} 32^{18} 2 S 2^{1} 13^{13} 2 K 6^{6} Is 10^{3} ψ 139$^{7.7}$ + 9 t.;
in indirect sentence Jos 2^{5} Ne 2^{16}; (*b*) = *where?*
†Ru 2^{19}; (*c*) in the phrase אָ֫נָה וָאָ֫נָה *any
whither* †1 K 2$^{36.42}$ 2 K 5^{25}; (*d*) of time, עַד־אָ֫נָה
how long? †Ex 16^{28} Nu 14$^{11.11}$ (c. לֹא) Jos 18^{3} Je
47^{6} (sq. לֹא) Hb 1^{2} ψ 13$^{2.2.3.3}$ 62^{4} Jb 18^{2} 19^{2} (less
common than the syn. עַד מָתַי).

375 †אֵיפֹה (from אֵי & פֹּה *here*) **adv. 1. where?**
Gn 37^{16} 1 S 19^{22} 2 S 9^{4} Is 49^{21} Je 3^{2} Jb 4^{7} 38^{4}
Ru 2^{19}; in indirect sentence Je 36^{19} (less common
than אַיֵּה, used of *persons* [contrast אֵי־זֶה] and
with a verb [contrast אַיֵּה]). **2. of what kind?**
(*qualis?*) only Ju 8^{18}.

337 †III. **אִי interj.** (so in Rabb., v. De$^{Koh\ 197}$ Wr
$^{Eccl\ 490}$) **alas!** (late) Ec 4^{10} אִי לוֹ (written in MT
as one word) *alas* for him (Ew ^{§309c}), the one,
who falleth, etc. (i.e. who falleth alone) 10^{16}.

336 †IV. **אִי adv. not** (frequently in Rabb., as
אִי אֶפְשַׁר *impossible*; and in Eth. the ordinary
negative; cf. Ph. אי CIS$^{I.\ 3,5}$, and in איבל $^{165,18;}$
^{167,11}; As. *ai*) Jb 22^{30} אִי־נָקִי *the non-innocent*.

350 †אִי כָבוֹד (1 S 4^{21}), אִי־כָבוֹד (1 S 14^{3}) **n.
pr.m.** (*inglorious*), son of Phinehas (explained
1 S 4^{21} by גָּלָה כָבוֹד מִיִּשְׂרָאֵל *glory is gone into
exile from Israel*).

348 אִיזֶבֶל **n.pr.f.** (sense uncertain, CIS$^{I.\ 158}$ there
occurs the n.pr.f. בעלאזבל *Baal exalts?* or *is
husband to?* [v. זָבַל], of which אִיזֶבֶל is conjectured by DHM to be an intentional alteration,
made for the purpose of avoiding the name Baal.
If so, א׳ perhaps suggested to the Hebrew ear
the idea of *un-exalted* or *un-husbanded*), queen
of Ahab, daughter of Ethbaal, king of Tyre
1 K 16^{31} 18$^{4.13.19}$ 19$^{1.2}$ 21^{5}+; 2 K 9^{7}+.

339 I. **אִי n.m.** *isle, coast*, v. I. אָוָה. p. 15

369 II. אַ֫יִן *nought*, v. p. 34.

44 אִיעֶזֶר v. אֲבִיעֶזֶר. p. 4

385 אִיתָמָר v. I. אָוָה. p. 16

340 [אָיַב]$_{283}$ **vb. be hostile to** (As. *aibu* (v. Dl^{W}),
341 *enemy* = אֹיֵב)—**Qal** *Pf.* †וְאָיַבְתִּי Ex 23^{22}; *Pt.* אוֹיֵב
341 (אֹיֵב) Ex 15^{6}+; sf. אֹיְבִי (אוֹיְבִי) 2 S 22^{18} = ψ 18^{18}+;
f. sf. אֹיַבְתִּי Mi 7$^{8.10}$; אֹיִבְךָ Ex 23^{4}+, etc.; pl.
אוֹיְבִים ψ 68^{24} 127^{5}; אֹיְבִים ψ 139^{22}, etc.;—*be hostile to, treat as enemy* Ex 23^{22} (E, Cov't code)
וְאָיַבְתִּי אֶת־אֹיְבֶיךָ וְצַרְתִּי אֶת־צֹרְרֶיךָ (subj. י׳); elsewhere *Pt.* 1 S 18^{29} וַיְהִי שָׁאוּל אֹיֵב אֶת־דָּוִד;
usually as subst. & mostly sf.; *enemy*, of personal foe Ex 23^{4} (E ‖ שֹׂנֵא v^{5}) Nu 35^{23} (P) 1 S
19^{17} (cf. 18^{29}) 24$^{5.20}$ 2 S 4^{8} 1 K 21^{20} Jb 27^{7} ψ 54^{9}
55^{13} (‖ מְשַׂנֵּא; opp. מְיֻדָּע, אַלּוּף v^{14}) Mi 2^{8} Pr 16^{7}
24^{17}+; in sim. Je 30^{14} (מַכַּת אוֹיֵב); of public
national enemy, sg. Ju 16$^{23.24}$; coll. Ex 15$^{6.9}$
Dt 33^{27} Na 3^{11} 2 Ch 6^{24}+; personif. Mi 7$^{8.10}$;
more oft. pl. Ex 23^{22} (E) Lv 26^{7f} (H) Nu 10^{9} (P)
Dt 1^{42} 6^{19} Je 15^{9} 34$^{20.21}$+; of enemies of God,
as protector of his people Nu 10^{35} (J) Ju 5^{31} 1 S
30^{26} 2 S 18^{19} ψ 66^{3} 68$^{1.22}$ Na 1$^{2.8}$ Is 66^{6}+; as
morally supreme Jb 13^{24} 33^{10} ψ 37^{20} 92$^{10.10}$+;
of God as enemy of rebellious people Is 63^{10},
in sim. La 2$^{4.5}$.

†אֵיבָה **n.f.** enmity—א׳ Gn 3^{15} + 2 t.; cstr. 342
אֵיבַת Ez 25^{15} 35^{5}—*enmity*, personal hostility,
betw. men Nu 35$^{21.22}$ (P), betw. serpent & woman
Gn 3^{15} (J), betw. peoples אֵיבַת עוֹלָם Ez 25^{15} 35^{5}.

אִיּוֹב **n.pr.m. Job** (meaning unknown; Thes 347
√איב; *obj. of enmity*, cf. for pass. sense יִלּוֹד; Ew
comp. Ar. أَوَّابٌ *he who turns* (to God); but cf.
Di on 1^{1}; all dub. cf. Lag$^{BN\ 90}$) Jb 1$^{1.5.5.5.8.9.14}$ +
48 t. Jb; Ez 14$^{14.20}$.

אִיד, אֵד v. אוד. p. 15 343

אַיָּה v. III. אוה, sub אוי. p. 17 344

אַיֵּה v. אֵי. אִיִּים v. III. אוה. p. 32 346

אֵיךְ, אֵיכָה, אֵיכָכָה v. *ib.* p. 32 349

אַיִל, אַיָּל, אַיָּלָה, אֵילוֹן, אֵילוֹן, אֵילָם, 352
אֵילָם, אֵילַת, אֵילוֹת etc. v. אול.

†אֱיָל **n.m. help** (loan-word from Aram. אֱיָל 353
אֱיָלָ *help*, so Lag$^{Or\ ii.7,\ BN\ 175}$, Nö$^{ZMG\ 1883,\ 526}$) only
in sim. כְּגֶבֶר אֵין אֱ׳ ψ 88^{5}.

†[אֱיָלוּת] **n.f.** id. sf. אֱיָלוּתִי ψ 22^{20} *my help* 360
(‖ יהוה).

אים (cf. 𝔗, Talm. אַיֵּם *terrify* Lag$^{BN\ 28}$).

†אָיֹם **adj. terrible, dreadful**—*terrible*, of 366
Chaldeans אָיֹם וְנוֹרָא הוּא Hb 1^{7}; of dignified
woman, *awe-inspiring* אֲיֻמָּה כַּנִּדְגָּלוֹת Ct 6$^{4.10}$.

†אֵימָה$_{17}$ **n.f. terror, dread** (Talm. *id.*, cf. 367
As. *imtu*, Dl^{W})—א׳ Gn 15^{12}+; אֵימָתָה Ex 15^{16}
(cf. Ges$^{§90,\ 2R.b}$); cstr. אֵימַת Pr 20^{2}; sf. אֵימָתִי Ex
23^{27}; אֵמָתִי Jb 33^{7}, etc.; pl. אֵימִים Je 50^{38}; אֵמִים 368

Jb 20^{25}; אִימוֹת ψ 55^{5}; sf. אֵמֶיךָ ψ 88^{16};—*terror, dread* (mostly poet.), inspired by ׳י Ex 15^{16} (song in E ‖ פַּחַד) 23^{27} (E) Dt 32^{25} Jb 9^{34} 13^{21} cf. 33^{7}; 20^{25} ψ 88^{16} (‖ בִּעוּתִים, חֲרוֹנִים v^{17}); cf. Gn 15^{12} אֵימָה חֲשֵׁכָה גְדֹלָה; occasioned by enemies Jos 2^{9} Is 33^{18} Ezr 3^{3}; by king Pr 20^{2}; cf. ψ 55^{5} אֵימוֹת מָוֶת (‖ יִרְאָה, רַעַד, פַּלָּצוּת v^{6}); pred. of snorting of a war-horse Jb 39^{20}, of teeth of crocodile Jb 41^{6}; pl. fig.=idols (i.e. dreadful, shocking things) Je 50^{38} (‖ פסלים).

368 †אֵימִים **n.pr.m.pl. Emim** (*terrors*) ancient inhab. of Moab Gn 14^{5} (הָאֵימִים); Dt 2^{10} (הָאֵמ׳); v^{11} (אֵמ׳).

370 I. [אַיִן], מֵאַיִן *whence?* v. sub אַי. p. 32

369 II. אַיִן, אָיִן cstr. אֵין **subst.** prop. **nothing, nought** (Moab. אן, As. *iânu*). **1.** †Is 40^{23} הַנּוֹתֵן רוֹזְנִים לְאָיִן who bringeth princes *to nothing;* †כְּאַיִן *as nothing*, ib. 40^{17} $41^{11.12}$ Hg 2^{3} ψ 39^{6}; *almost* (‖ כִּמְעַט) ψ 73^{2}; †מֵאַיִן *of nothing* Is 41^{24}. **2.** cstr. אֵין, very freq. as **particle of negation, is not, are not, was not, were not,** etc. (corresp. to the affirm. יֵשׁ q.v. Similar in usage, though not etym. akin, are לַיְסَ, לֵית, ܠܰܝܬ, አልቦ), prop. 'there is *nought of* . . .' sq. a subst. or a pron. suffix (אֵינֶנִּי [*verbal* form, Ges $^{§100,5;\ 152,1c}$], אֵינְךָ, אֵינֵךְ, אֵינֶנּוּ, אֵינֶנָּה, אֵינְכֶם, אֵינָם, also ψ 59^{14} אֵינֵמוֹ, 73^{5} אֵינֵימוֹ): twice abnormally, in late Heb., a nom. אֵין אֲנִי, אֵין אֲנַחְנוּ Ne 4^{17} (so sts. לֵית, ܠܰܝܬ, Nö $^{M.\ p.\ 295}$); once, incorrectly, את Hg 2^{17}. **a.** denying existence absolutely Is 44^{6} 47^{10} אֵין רֹאֵנִי *there is none* that seeth me, lit. *nought of* one seeing me! אֵין עוֹד *there is none* else Dt 4^{39} 1 K 8^{60} Is $45^{5.6.18.22}$. **b.** more commonly, in a limited sense, *there is none here* or *at hand* Ex 2^{12} and he saw כִּי־אֵין אִישׁ that *there was no* man (sc. there), Nu 21^{5}; Gn 5^{24} וְאֵינֶנּוּ and he *was not* (of Enoch's disappearance from earth) 42^{13} one (*cas.pend.* as oft.), *he is not*, v^{36}; oft.=*is* (or *has*) *vanished* Gn 37^{30} 1 K 20^{40} Is 17^{14} ψ 37^{10} 103^{16} Jb 8^{22} 24^{24} 27^{19}. **c.** with the sense determined by a predic. following: Gn 37^{29} Joseph *was not in the pit*, 41^{39} + oft.; Ex 5^{10} אֵינֶנִּי נֹתֵן לָכֶם תֶּבֶן *I am not giving* you straw; and so often with particip. where duration has to be expressed Gn 39^{23} Dt 21^{18} Is 1^{15} Je 7^{16}, or intention Gn 20^{7} אִם אֵינְךָ מֵשִׁיב דַּע . . . if thou *art not restoring* her, know, 43^{5} Ex 8^{17} 33^{15} (idiomatically, after אם; v. Dr ^{§137}) Ju 12^{3}. Foll. once pleon. by יֵשׁ ψ 135^{17}. Treated as a *mere* part. of negation, אֵין may vary its position in the sentence, the subst. which should strictly stand in the genitive being not only separated from it by a little word, as בּוֹ Gn 37^{24}, לוֹ Ex 22^{1}, שָׁם Ex 12^{30}, גַּם ψ 14^{3}, etc., but even for emphasis *prefixed* to it, as Gn 19^{31} 40^{8} וּפֹתֵר אֵין אֹתוֹ 41^{15} Ex 5^{16} Ju 13^{9} 14^{6} 16^{15} 19^{1} (so MI ^{24}): if however it be thus brought to the end of a sentence, or be disconnected with what follows, it stands in the absol. form, as Gn 2^{5} ואדם אַיִן לעבד האדמה and man *there was none* to till the ground, Lv 26^{37} וְרֹדֵף אָיִן, Nu 20^{5} 2 K 19^{3} Ho 13^{4} Mi 7^{2}. **d.** sometimes the subj. has to be supplied from the context: thus (*a*) †1 S 9^{4} and they passed through the land of Shaalim וָאַיִן *and they* (the asses) *were not* (lit. *and nought!*), esp. after vbs. of *waiting* or *seeking* Is 59^{11} ψ 69^{21} Jb 3^{9}; Is 41^{17} Ez 7^{25} Pr 14^{6}; 13^{4}; 20^{4}. (β) †Ex 17^{7} is ׳י in the midst of us אִם־אָיִן: *or not?* Nu 13^{20}. (γ) †Ju 4^{20} וְאָמַרְתְּ אָיִן: then thou shalt say, *There is not*, 1 K 18^{10} 1 S 10^{14}. (δ) Gn 30^{1} give me children, וְאִם־אַיִן *and if not*, I die, Ex 32^{32} Ju $9^{15.20}$ 2 S 17^{6} (v. Dr) 2 K 2^{10} Jb 33^{33}. **e.** with subj. not expressed, once (late), Dn 8^{5} וְאֵין נוֹגֵעַ בָּאָרֶץ and (it) *was not touching* the earth. **f.** once, Jb 35^{15} with the finite vb.; but rd. here כִּי אֵין פֹּקֵד (the usage of لَيْسَ, cited by De, does not justify the anomaly in Heb.) Je 38^{5} the impf. may be due to the fact that no ptcp. of יכל was in use, and a relat. must be tacitly supplied: 'The king *is not* (one that) can do aught against you.' On Ex 3^{2} see Ges $^{§52,2R.6}$; Ew ^{§169d}. **3.** אֵין לְ׳, with subst., or pron., *there is* (*was*) *not to* . . .=. . . *have, has, had*, etc. *not:* Gn 11^{30} אֵין לָהּ וָלָד *she had no* child, Nu 27^{9} וְאִם־אֵין לוֹ בַּת and if *he have no* daughter + oft.; with a ptcp. Dt 22^{27} Je 14^{16} 30^{17} 49^{5} 50^{32} ψ 142^{5} La $1^{2.9.17}$; Ex 22^{2} אִם־אֵין לוֹ if he *have nought*, Dn 9^{26} ואין לו and *have nought* (or *none*). **4.** in circumst. clauses (Dr ^{§164}):—(*a*) Ex 21^{11} she shall go out free אֵין כָּסֶף *without money*, 22^{9} אֵין רֹאֶה *none seeing it*, Nu 11^{6} Is 47^{1} Je 2^{32} Ho 3^{4} 7^{11} ψ 32^{9} 88^{5}+. (*b*) Dt 32^{4} a God of faithfulness וְאֵין עָוֶל *and no iniquity*, i.e. *without iniquity*, Je 5^{21} Jo 1^{6} ψ 104^{25}. (*c*) very oft., in such phrases as וְאֵין מַחֲרִיד *with none to affright* Lv 26^{6} (12 t.); וְאֵין מְכַבֶּה Is 1^{31} al.; וְאֵין מַצִּיל 5^{29} ψ 7^{3}, etc. (Dr ^{§159}). **5.** with inf. and לְ׳, *it is not to* . . .: i.e. (*a*) like οὐκ ἔστιν, *it is not possible to* . . . (cf. sub יֵשׁ and לֹא), but hardly exc. in late Heb.; 2 Ch 20^{6} וְאֵין עִמְּךָ לְהִתְיַצֵּב *it is not possible to* stand (in conflict) with thee, 22^{9} Ezr 9^{15} Ec 3^{14} Est 4^{2}. Once without ל, ψ 40^{6} אֵין עֲרֹךְ אֵלֶיךָ οὐκ ἔστι παραβάλλειν σοι. (β) *there is no need to* . . . 1 Ch 23^{26} וְגַם לַלְוִיִּם אֵין־לָשֵׂאת for the Levites also *there was no need* to bear 2 Ch 5^{11} 35^{15} (v. Dr $^{§202.1}$). **6.** with

prefixes:—**a.** † בְּאֵין prop. *in defect of:*—(*α*) *for want of, without*—Pr 5^{23} HE will die בְּאֵין מוּסָר *for lack of* instruction, 11^{14} בְּאֵין תַּחְבֻּלוֹת *without* guidance, 14^{4} 15^{22} 26^{20} 29^{18} Is 57^{1} Ez 38^{11}; cf. בְּלֹא. (*β*) of time=*when there was (were) not* Pr $8^{24.24}$. **b.** †כְּאַיִן Is 59^{10} כְּאֵין עֵינַיִם poet. for כַּאֲשֶׁר אֵין לוֹ עֵינַיִם (cf. Ew^{§286g} Ges$^{§152.1h}$). **c.** †לְאֵין (*α*) for לַאֲשֶׁר אֵין לוֹ Is 40^{29}; in late prose 2 Ch 14^{10} Ne 8^{10}. (*β*) *in the condition of not* . . . (ל of state, v. sub ל)=*without* or *so that not* . . . (peculiar to Ch), 1 Ch 22^{4} cedar trees לְאֵין מִסְפָּר *without* number, 2 Ch 14^{12} and there fell of the Cushites לְאֵין־לָהֶם מִחְיָה *so that they had none* remaining alive, 20^{25} לְאֵין מַשָּׂא *so that there was no* carrying away, 21^{18} Ezr 9^{14}. (*γ*) עַד־לְאֵין (see עד ל׳), 2 Ch 36^{16} *until there was no* remedy (cf. עַד אֵין . . . ψ 40^{13} Jb 5^{9}). **d.** מֵאַיִן (*α*) (מִן causal) *from lack of* . . . Is 50^{2} Je 7^{32} 19^{11}. (*β*) (מִן negative, v. מִן) prop. *away from there being no* . . . (with אין pleon., cf. מִבְּלִי, and מִבְּלִי אֵין), i.e. *so that not* . . ., *without*, mostly epexegetical of some term expressing desolation: Is 5^{9} Surely many houses shall be desolate מֵאֵין יוֹשֵׁב *without* inhabitant, 6^{11}+oft. Je & Zp; Is 6^{11} מֵאֵין אָדָם, Je 32^{43} מֵאֵין אָדָם וּבְהֵמָה $33^{10.12}$ Ez 33^{28}; La 3^{49}. Once sq. inf. Mal 2^{13} *so that there is no* regarding more. (*γ*) in Je $10^{6.7}$ מֵאֵין כָּמוֹךָ, מֵאֵין is supposed by some to=a strengthened אַיִן, *even none, none at all;* but it is difficult to justify this expl. logically; and it is preferable to point מֵאַיִן כָּמוֹךָ *whence* is any like thee? cf. 30^{7}. (So Hi: v. Dr$^{Hbr. ii. 34-7}$.)

371 †אִין† 1 S 21^{9} . . . וְאִין יֶשׁ prob. irreg. for אֵין (so Ki Ges Ew$^{§213e, 286h}$ Ol^{640} Sta^{§194c}) with יֵשׁ pleon. (as ψ 135^{17}); > dialect.=Aram. אִין, إِنْ, *num?* (De, but v. Dr^{Sm} *ad loc.*)

374 †**אֵיפָה, אֵפָה** $_{35}$ **n.f. ephah** (etym. dub., 𝔊 οιφι etc., cf. Copt. *ôipi*, Thes Lag$^{Or. ii. 2}$ & cit.)—א׳ Nu 5^{15}+; אֵפָה Ex 16^{36}+; cstr. אֵיפַת Lv 19^{36}+;—*ephah*, a grain-measure. **1.** a certain quantity of wheat, barley, etc.=ten omers (עֹמֶר) Ex 16^{36} (cf. in measure of offerings Lv 5^{11} 6^{13} Nu 5^{15} 28^{5}, all עֲשִׂירִית הָא׳; $=\frac{1}{10}$ chomer (חֹמֶר) Ez 45^{11} (=bath, בַּת, liqu. meas. *q.v.*) cf. Is 5^{10}; chiefly of offerings, v. supr. & 1 S 1^{24} Ez $45^{13.13.24.24.24}$ $46^{5.5.7.7.7.11.11.11.14}$; cf. Ju 6^{19}, but also of food 1 S 17^{17} cf. Ru 2^{17} & Is 5^{10} supr. **2.** receptacle or measure, holding an ephah, in proph. vision Zc $5^{6.7.8.9.10}$; just measure אֵיפַת־צֶדֶק Lv 19^{36} (|| מֹאזְנֵי־צ׳, אַבְנֵי־צ׳, הִין צ׳) cf. Ez $45^{10.11}$; אֵיפָה שְׁלֵמָה וָצֶ׳ Dt 25^{15} (|| אֶבֶן שׁ׳ וָצ׳); of unjust measure אֵיפָה וְאֵיפָה Dt 25^{14} Pr 20^{10}; הַקְטִין א׳ Am 8^{5}; אֵיפַת רָזוֹן Mi 6^{10}. (On the actual size of ephah, cf. בַּת).

אֵיפֹה v. sub אֵי. p. 33 375

אוש, איש (Stem assumed in Thes for אִישׁ; existence & mng. somewhat dub. Thes (Add) & most derive אִישׁ fr. [אִנְשׁ] √אנשׁ (q. v.) In favour are pl. אֲנָשִׁים, fem. אִשָּׁה=[אִנְשָׁה], lack of proven √אישׁ, & lack of clear parallels for אישׁ in cogn. lang. Against the deriv. of אִישׁ fr. *inš* is the vocalization (ִי—, and that fully written, not ִ—), maintained even with suff., the (rare) pl. אִישִׁים, the impossibility of deriving אִישׁ & אִשָּׁה from same √ (אִשָּׁה fr. انث), the existence of אֱנוֹשׁ as parallel form, and the (exceptional) parallel Aram. איש (Inscr. of Carpentras), also Ar. إِيسَانٌ (cf. Frey) || إِنْسٌ; MI, SI, Ph. אש are not decisive; Sab. has both אסם & אנסם; the former app.=אִישׁ, the latter אֱנוֹשׁ; but on former cf. DHM$^{ZK\ 1884,\ 360}$ & Sab. Denkm.^{37}. On the whole, probability seems to favour √אישׁ; Thes gave mng. *be strong;* Dl$^{HA\ 9,\ Pr\ 161}$ comp. As. *išanu*, *strong* (cf. Dl$^{W.\ p.244}$), & n.pr. יְהוֹאָשׁ; cf. also Prät$^{LOPh.\ Feb.\ 1884}$; otherwise DHM$^{l.c.\ \&\ ZMG\ 1883,\ 330}$ & esp. Nö$^{ZMG\ 1886,\ 739}$ Lag$^{BN\ 68}$; cf. also Wetzst in De$^{Psalmen,\ ed.\ 4,\ p.\ 888}$ al. v. also אֱנוֹשׁ, אנשׁ).

אִישׁ $_{2166}$ **n.m. man** (=*vir*) (MI, SI, Ph. אש, 376
perh. also Sab. אסם cf. Prät$^{l.c.}$, but DHM$^{ZMG\ 1883,\ 330}$)—א׳ abs. Gn 2^{23}+; cstr. Gn 25^{27}+; sf. אִישִׁי Gn 29^{32}+, etc.; pl. אִישִׁים ψ 141^{4}+2 t. (Ph. אשם); usually אֲנָשִׁים Gn 12^{20}+, fr. √אנשׁ q.v.; cstr. אַנְשֵׁי Ju 6^{27}+; sf. אֲנָשַׁי 1 S 23^{12} etc.;—*man*, opp. woman Gn $2^{23.24}$ Lv 20^{27} Nu 5^{6} Dt 17^{2f} Jos 6^{21} 8^{25} Je 40^{7}, emph. on sexual distinction & relation Gn 19^{8} 24^{16} 38^{25} Ex 22^{15} Lv 15^{16} (שִׁכְבַת זָרַע) v^{18} (וְאִשָּׁה) (אֲשֶׁר יִשְׁכַּב אִישׁ אֹתָהּ שׁ־ז׳) 20^{10f} Nu 5^{13f} Dt 22^{22f} Is 4^{1}+; thence=*husband*, esp. c. sf. Gn $3^{6.16}$ 16^{3} $29^{32.34}$ Lv 21^{7} Nu 30^{7f} Dt 28^{56} Ju 13^{8f} Ru 1^{3f} 1 S 25^{19} Je 29^{6} Ez 16^{45}+; fig. of י׳ as husb. of Isr. אִישִׁי Ho 2^{18} (opp. בַּעְלִי); *man* as procreator, father Ec 6^{3}; of *male child* Gn 4^{1} cf. זֶרַע אֲנָשִׁים 1 S 1^{11}; *man*, opp. beast Ex 11^{7} Lv 20^{15} (cf. אָדָם); cf. fig. ψ 22^{7} but also of male of animals Gn $7^{2.2}$ (אִישׁ וְאִשְׁתּוֹ); *man*, opp. God Gn 32^{29} Nu 23^{19} (וּבֶן־אָדָם וְיִתְנֶחָם || לֹא אִישׁ אֵל וִיכַזֵּב); Jb 9^{32} 32^{13} Ho 11^{9} cf. Is 31^{8} Jb 12^{10} (רוּחַ כָּל־בְּשַׂר אִישׁ); hence in phrases to denote ordinary, customary, common שֵׁבֶט אֲנָשִׁים 2 S 7^{14} (|| נִגְעֵי בְּנֵי אָדָם); אַמַּת־אִישׁ לֶחֶם אֲנָשִׁים Ez $24^{17.22}$ (cf. Is 8^{1}); Dt 3^{11}; but also contr. אָדָם ψ 49^{3} 62^{10}; *man*, as valiant 1 S $4^{9.9}$ (וִהְיוּ לַאֲנָשִׁים) so 1 K 2^{2} cf. 1 S
26^{15}; so אִישׁ חַיִל 31^{12} 2 S 24^{9} 1 K 1^{42}+; also 381
אִישׁ מִלְחָמָה Nu 31^{49} Dt $2^{14.16}$ Jos $5^{4.6}$+; even of י׳

Ex 15^{3} יהוה אִישׁ מִלְחָמָה; oft. prefixed to other nouns in app. אִ׳ אָדוֹן Gn 42$^{30.33}$, אִ׳ שַׂר וְשֹׁפֵט Ex 2^{14}, אִ׳ כֹּהֵן Lv 21^{9}, אִ׳ סָרִיס Je 38^{7}; partic. bef. adj. gent. אִישׁ מִצְרִי Gn 39^{1} Ex 2$^{11.19}$ cf. Gn 37^{28} 38$^{1.2}$ 39^{14} 1 S 17^{12} 30$^{11.13}$+; a *man* as resident in, or belonging to a place or people Nu 25^{6} Ju 10^{1}+(so Ph.); usually pl. אַנְשֵׁי יִשְׂרָאֵל 1 S 7^{11} 31$^{7.7}$ cf. Jos 7$^{4.5}$+; also sg. coll. Dt 27^{14} Jos 9$^{6.7}$ Ju
382 20^{11} 1 S 11^{8} (v. Dr)+; 2 S 10$^{6.8}$ (אִ׳ טוֹב); (so MI $^{10.13}$); *men*=retainers, followers, soldiers 1 S 18^{27} 23^{3f} 24^{3} 25^{13}+ cf. Dt 33^{8} sg. coll. v. Di; אִישׁ אֱלֹהִים *man of God*=proph. Dt 33^{1} Jos 14^{6} 1 S 9^{6f} 1 K 12^{13f}+(v. אלהים); in phrase sq. abstr. אִישׁ חַיִל, אִ׳ מִלְחָמָה v. supr.; אִ׳ שֵׂיבָה Dt 32^{25}, אִ׳ הַדָּמִים 2 S 16^{7} cf. v. 8, אִ׳ הַבְּלִיַּעַל 2 S 16^{7}, אִ׳ מָוֶת 1 K 2^{26}, אִ׳ חָמָס ψ 140^{12} Pr 3^{31}+; sq. word of occupation, etc. אִ׳ שָׂדֶה Gn 25^{27}, אִ׳ הָאֲדָמָה Gn 9^{20} (cf. Zc 13^{5}), אִ׳ הַבֵּנַיִם *champion* 1 S 17^{4} (cf. Dr) v^{23}, אִ׳ בְּשֹׂרָה 2 S 18^{20}, אִישׁ עֲצָתוֹ *his counsellor* Is 40^{13}, cf. אִישׁ חֶרְמִי 1 K 20^{42}, אִ׳ רֵעִים Pr 18^{24}; oft. distrib.=*each, every* Gn 9^{5} 10^{5} 40$^{5.5}$ Ex 12^{3}+; incl. women Jb 42^{11} 1 Ch 16^{3} וַיְחַלֵּק לְכָל־אִישׁ יִשְׂרָאֵל מֵאִישׁ וְעַד אִשָּׁה לְאִישׁ כִּכַּר־לֶחֶם; of inanim. things 1 K 7$^{30.36}$; also אִישׁ אִישׁ Ex 36^{4} Nu 4$^{19.49}$ Ez 14$^{4.7}$+; *any one* Ex 34$^{3.3.24}$+; also אִישׁ אִישׁ Lv 15^{2} 22$^{4.18}$+; of gods 2 K 18^{33}=Is 36^{18}; *one...another* וְהִרְגוּ אִישׁ־אֶת־אָחִיו וְאִישׁ אֶת־רֵעֵהוּ וְאִישׁ אֶת־קְרֹבוֹ Ex 32^{27}, אִישׁ...רֵעֵהוּ Dt 1^{16} Mi 7^{2} (v. אָח), אִישׁ...אָחִיו Gn 11$^{3.7}$+ (v. רֵעַ) of inanimate things Gn 15^{10}.

378 †אִישׁ־בֹּשֶׁת† **n.pr.m. Ishbosheth** (for אִישׁ בַּעַל *man of Baal* v. בֹּשֶׁת, בַּעַל & Di ἡ Βααλ MBAk, June 1881) **1.** son of Saul, & king of Isr., with David as rival 2 S 2$^{8.10.12.15}$ 3$^{8.14.15}$ 4$^{5.8.8.12}$, also v$^{1.2}$ 𝔊
792 Dr cf. We;=אֶשְׁבַּעַל 1 Ch 8^{33} 9^{39}; cf. also **2.** 2 S 23^{8}, where rd. אשבשת for ישב בשבת so 𝔊 We Dr; one of Dvd's heroes; v. יָשָׁבְעָם 1 Ch 11^{11} 27^{2}.

379 †אִישׁ הוֹד† **n.pr.m.** (*man of majesty*) a man of Manasseh 1 Ch 7^{18}

380 †אִישׁוֹן† **n.**[**m.**] **pupil** of eye (cf. Dl$^{HA\ 9}$ Prät LOPh, Feb. 1884, but also Ar. إِنْسَانُ الْعَيْنِ, & Nö ZMG 1886, 739)—א׳ all cstr.—אִ׳ עַיִן Dt 32^{10} Pr 7^{2}; אִ׳ בַּת־עַיִן ψ 17^{8} (in all, sim. of preciousness); =*middle, midst* of night בְּאִ׳ לַיְלָה וַאֲפֵלָה Pr 7^{9}; בְּאִ׳ חֹשֶׁךְ 20^{20} Kt i.e. *in deep darkness* (Qr בֶּאֱשׁוּן v. Now).

3448 אִישַׁי v. יִשַׁי. p. 445

2978 אִיתוֹן Ez 40^{15} Qr v. אתיון sub אתה. p. 87

384 אִיתִיאֵל, אִיתַי v. אֵת *with*. p. 87

385 אִיתָמָר v. אִי sub I. אוה. p. 16

386 אֵיתָן, אֵתָן v. יתן. p. 450

אַךְ$_{159}$ **adv.** (perh. from the same demonstr. 389
root found also in כִּי, כֹּה, כֵּן). **1. surely. 2.** with a restrictive force, emphasizing what follows: **a.** in contrast to what precedes, **howbeit**; **b.** in contrast with other ideas generally, **only**. **1.** asseverative, often introducing with emphasis the expression of a truth (or supposed truth) newly perceived, esp. in colloquial language, *surely, no doubt* (*doch wohl*); Gn 26^{9} אַךְ הִנֵּה אִשְׁתְּךָ הִוא *of a surety*, lo, she is thy wife! 29^{14} 44^{28} Ju 3^{24} 20^{39} 1 S 16^{6} *surely* the anointed of י׳ is before him! 25^{21} Je 5^{4} ψ 58^{12} 73$^{1.13}$; but also in other cases, though rarely, Is 34$^{14.15}$ Zp 3^{7} ψ 23^{6} 139^{11} 140^{14} Jb 16^{7} 18^{21}; & rather singularly Ex 12^{15} 31^{13} Lv 23$^{27.39}$ (all P). **2.** restrictive: **a.** in contrast to what precedes, *howbeit, yet, but*: Gn 9^{4} *howbeit*, flesh with the life thereof ... ye shall not eat, 20^{12} Ex 21^{21} Lv 21^{23} 27^{26} Nu 18$^{15.17}$ 2 S 3^{13}; Je 10^{24} correct me, אַךְ בְּמִשְׁפָּט *but* with judgment, Jb 2^{6} 13^{15}; sts. with an advers. force, as Is 14^{15} 43^{24}; before an imper. (minimizing the request), Gn 23^{13} *only*, if thou wilt, I pray thee, hear me! 27^{13} Ju 10^{15} 1 S 18^{17} 1 K 17^{13} al. So 1 S 8^{9} אַךְ כִּי (v. כִּי; and cf. πλὴν ὅτι). **b.** in contrast to other ideas generally:—(*a*) Gn 7^{23} 18^{32} אַךְ הַפַּעַם *only* this once (so Ex 10^{17} al.) 34^{15} Ex 12^{16} (note accents), 1 S 18^{8} וְעוֹד לוֹ אַךְ הַמְּלוּכָה and there yet remains for him *only* the kingdom, 21^{5} Isa 45^{14} אַךְ בָּךְ אֵל *only* in thee is God! ψ 62^{2} etc. Jb 14^{22}; ψ 37^{8} fret not thyself אַךְ לְהָרֵעַ (which leadeth) *only* to do evil, Pr 11^{24} he that withholdeth more than is meet אַךְ לְמַחְסוֹר (tendeth) *only* to penury, 14^{23} 21^{5} 22^{16}; (*β*) attaching itself closely to the foll. word (usually an adj., rarely a verb), *only*, i.e. *exclusively, altogether, utterly* Dt 16^{15} and thou shalt be אַךְ שָׂמֵחַ *altogether* rejoicing, 28^{29} (cf. v^{33} רַק) Isa 16^{7} אַךְ נְכָאִים *utterly* stricken, 19^{11} Je 16^{19} *nought but* lies, 32^{30} Ho 12^{12} Jb 19^{13} אַךְ זָרוּ are *wholly* estranged (with play on אַכְזָר *cruel*). **c.** as an adv. of time (with inf. abs.), twice: Gn 27^{30} אַךְ יָצֹא יָצָא יַעֲקֹב ... וְעֵשָׂו בָּא *only just* (or *scarcely*) had Jacob gone out, ... and (=when) Esau came in, Ju 7^{19}.—וְאַךְ thrice: Gn 9^{5} *and only* (second limitation of v^{3}); Nu 22^{20} *but only*; Jos 22^{19} *but howbeit*.

Note.—In some passages the affirmative and restrictive senses agree equally with the context; and authorities read the Hebrew differently. Thus *only*=*nought but, altogether*, is adopted by Ges Ew Hi De in ψ 23^{6} 62^{10} 73$^{1.13}$; by Ew Hi De in 39$^{6.7}$ (Che *surely*); by Ges Ew De in 39^{12} (but Hi Che *surely*); by Ew Hi in 73^{18} (De Che *surely*); by Ges Hi De in 139^{11} (Ew *doch*). Isa 45^{14} Ges Ew Hi Di *only*; but De Che *of a truth*.

390 †אַכַּד **n.pr.loc.** Akkad Gn 10^{10} וַתְּהִי רֵאשִׁית מַמְלַכְתּוֹ בָּבֶל וְאֶרֶךְ וְא׳ וְכַלְנֵה בְּאֶרֶץ שִׁנְעָר׃; name of a city in Northern (?) Babylonia; = Bab. *Akkadi*, mostly name of land or district, but also of city, v. Hilpr.$^{\text{Freibrief Neb. I, col. ii, l. 50}}$; location uncertain; on possible identif. or confusion with *Agade* (*Agate, Agane?*), city of Sargon I, cf. Dl$^{\text{Pa 198}}$ & $^{\text{K 19 f.}}$ COT Gn 10^{10} Tiele$^{\text{Gesch. i. 76 f.}}$

391-92 אַכְזָב, אַכְזִיב v. כזב. p. 469

393-95 אַכְזְרִיּוּת, אַכְזָרִי, אַכְזָר v. כזר. p. 470

397 אָכִישׁ **n.pr.m.** king of Gath 1 S 21$^{11.12.13.15}$ + 15 t. 1 S 27–29 + 1 K 2$^{39.40}$ (perh. cf. اكش *anger*).

398 אָכַל **vb. eat** (Ar. أَكَلَ, As. *akâlu* Dl^{W}, 806 Aram. אֲכַל, ܐܟܠ)—**Qal** *Pf.* אָכַל Ex 34^{28}+; אָֽכְלָה Nu 21^{28}+, etc. *Impf.* יֹאכַל Gn 49^{27}+; וַיֹּאכַל Gn 25^{34}+; וַיֹּאכַל Gn 3^{6}+; יֹאכֶל Lv 21^{22}+; אֹכַל Gn 24^{33}+; וָאֹכַל 27^{33}; וָאֹכֵל Is 44^{19}; וָאֹכֵל Gn 3$^{12.13}$; 3 pl. יֹאכְלוּ Gn 32^{33}+; יֹאכֵלוּ Dt 18^{18}+; etc. (for יוֹכְלוּ Ez 42^{5} rd. יוצלו, יאצלו 𝔊 Ew Co); sf. יֹאכְלֻנּוּ Lv 7^{6}+; תֹּאכַלְכֶם Is 33^{11}, etc., prob. also תְּאָכְלֵהוּ Jb 20^{26}, either as secondary form fr. תא׳ (Ew$^{\S\,253}$ Di) or text. error (Ges$^{\S\,68.1}$) >Pi., Thes Kö$^{\text{I. 389}}$; or Po'el, Ki De MV; *Imv.* אֱכוֹל 1 K 18^{41}+, etc.; *Inf. abs.* אָכוֹל Gn 2^{16}+; cstr. אֲכֹל Nu 26^{10} + 2 t.; לֶאֱכֹל Gn 24^{33}+; לְאָכְלָה Je 12^{9}; *Pt.* אֹכֵל (אוֹכֵל) Gn 39^{6} +, אֹכֶלֶת Ex 24^{17}+, etc.—**1.** *eat*, human subject Gn 3$^{11.18}$ + oft.; mostly c. acc. Ex 16^{35}+; also sq. מִן־ (*eat of,*—some of,—or *from*) Ex 34^{15} Ru 2^{14}+; sq. בְּ (*eat of* or *at*) Ex 12$^{43\,f}$; abs. Dt 2^{6}+; as act of worship Gn 31^{54} (cf. 46^{1}) Ex 18^{12} 24^{11} 34^{15} Dt 12$^{7.18}$ 14$^{23.26}$+; cf. of priests Ex 29^{32} Lv 10^{13} +; cf. אָכַל אֶל־הֶהָרִים Ez 18$^{6.11.15}$ 22^{9} + 33^{25} עַל־הֶהָרִים Co עַל־הַדָּם; (but RS$^{\text{Rel. Sem. i. 324 N}}$ would emend first 4 by last); *eat up*, finish eating Gn 43^{2} (c. כלה) 1 K 13^{28}+; אָכַל לֶחֶם = take a meal Gn 43^{25} Ex 2^{20} 1 S 20^{24} Je 41^{1}+; so א׳ alone Gn 43^{16} 1 S 20^{5}+; א׳ לֶחֶם = *eat, get food* Gn 3^{19} 2 K 4^{8}+; Am 7^{12} (i.e. spend one's life) cf. Ec 5^{16}; לֹא א׳ ל׳ i.e. *fast* 1 S 28^{20} 30^{12} Ezr 10^{6} cf. Dn 10^{3}; fig. א׳ אֶת־בְּשָׂרוֹ Ec 4^{5} (i.e. waste away); eat words Je 15^{16} (i.e. eagerly receive); of adultery, Pr 30^{20} אָכְלָה וּמָחֲתָה פִיהָ וְאָמְרָה לֹא־פָעַלְתִּי אָוֶן׃; eat (taste) good fortune, א׳ בַּטּוֹב Jb 21^{25}; לְפִי אָכְלוֹ *according to his eating*, i.e. acc. to his needs in eating Ex 12^{4} 16$^{16.18}$ also v^{21}; cf. Jb 20^{21} & sub אָכְלָה; אָכוֹל הַפְּרִי 2 K 19^{29} Am 9^{14}, of peaceful enjoyment of results of labour; fig. of receiving consequences of action, good or bad Pr 1^{31} 18^{21} Ho 10^{13} cf. וַיֹּאכַל גַּם־אָכוֹל אֶת־כַּסְפֵּנוּ Gn 31^{15} i.e. he has reaped all the benefit, cf. Ho 7^{9}; fig. of mourner, אֵפֶר כַּלֶּחֶם אָכָלְתִּי ψ 102^{10} (cf. 80^{6} Hiph., & As. *akâl al âkul, bikîtum kurmatî* = food I ate not, weeping (was) my refreshment Hpt$^{\text{ASKT 166 f. Obv. l. 21, 22}}$ Zim$^{\text{BP 34, 42}}$); of gods, partaking of sacrifices Dt 32^{38}; fig. = destroy Dt 7^{16} (cf. Nu 14^{9}); cf. Je 10^{25} 30^{16} 50^{7} Ho 7^{7}. **2.** of beasts, birds, etc., *eat, devour;* Gn 37$^{20.33}$ 40$^{17.19}$ 1 K 13^{28} 14^{11} 16^{4} 21$^{23.24}$ Ho 2^{14}+; specif. of locusts Jo 1^{4} 2^{25} 2 Ch 7^{13} cf. Am 4^{9}; moth Jb 13^{28}; flies ψ 78^{45}; worms Dt 28^{39}; also Ez 19$^{3.6}$ (of Isr. under fig. of lion), cf. Je 50$^{7.17}$ 51^{34}; also Ho 13^{8} (of י׳ under fig. of lion), Ez 22^{25} (נֶפֶשׁ אָכָלוּ, of false proph. under fig. of lion). **3.** fig. of fire, *devour, consume* Lv 6^{3} (sq. 2 acc. *consume offering* to *ashes*) Na 3^{13} Is 5^{24} (in sim.), partic. of fire fr. י׳ Lv 10^{2} 16^{25} Ju 9$^{15\,f}$ 1 K 18^{38} 2 K 1$^{10.12.14}$ 2 Ch 7^{1}; cf. Am. 1$^{4.7.10.12.14}$ 2$^{2.5}$ 5^{6}+; Dt 5^{22} of fire at Sinai; of י׳ as fire (in judgment) Dt 4^{24} כִּי י׳ אֱלֹהֶיךָ אֵשׁ אֹכְלָה הוּא; cf. Dt 9^{3} Is 10^{17} 30$^{27.30}$ 33^{14} (מוֹקְדֵי עוֹלָם ||) (בער ||). **4.** of sword, *devour, slay* Dt 32^{42} 2 S 2^{26} 11^{25} 18^{8} Ho 11^{6} Je 2^{30} 12^{12}; cf. of devastation of land Is 1^{7} Je 8^{16}. **5.** in genl. *devour, consume, destroy* (inanim. subj.) of drought Gn 31^{40}; of pestilence Ez 7^{15}; of forest 2 S 18^{8}; cf. Lv 26^{38} וְאָכְלָה אֶתְכֶם אֶרֶץ אֹיְבֵיכֶם; of הַבֹּשֶׁת Je 3^{24} (v. בֹּשֶׁת). **6.** fig. of oppression, *devour* the poor, etc. Pr 30^{14} Hb 3^{14} cf. ψ 14^{4}; of bitter enmity לֶאֱכֹל אֶת־בְּשָׂרִי ψ 27^{2}. (cf. Jb 19^{22}). †**Niph.** *Pf.* וְנֶאֱכַל cons. Ex 22^{5} *Impf.* יֵאָכֵל Gn 6^{21}+; וַיֵּאָכֵל Nu 12^{12}, etc.; *Inf. abs.* הֵאָכֹל Lv 7^{18} 19^{7}; *Pt.* f. נֶאֱכֶלֶת Lv 11^{47};—**1.** *be eaten* by man Ex 12^{46} 13$^{3.7}$ 21^{28} 29^{34} Lv 6$^{9.16.19.23}$ 7$^{6.15.16.16.18}$ 11^{41} 19$^{6.7.23}$ 22^{30} 28^{17} Ez 45^{21}; of custom, usage Gn 6^{21} Ex 12^{16} Dt 12^{22} Jb 6^{6}; of permission to eat Lv 7^{19} 11$^{13.34.47.47}$ 17^{13}; c. neg. *be uneatable* Je 24$^{2.3.8}$ 29^{17}. **2.** *be devoured* by fire, *consumed* Zp 1^{18} 3^{8} Zc 9^{4} Ez 23^{25}. **3.** *be wasted, destroyed*, of flesh Nu 12^{12} Je 30^{16}. **Pu.** *Pf.* אֻכְּלוּ *be consumed* with fire Ne 2$^{3.13}$ cf. Na 1^{10} (fig.); so *Pt.* אֻכָּל (= מְאֻכָּל Ew$^{\S\,169\,d}$) Ex 3^{2}; by sword Is 1^{20} תְּאֻכְּלוּ. †**Hiph.** *Pf.* 2 ms. sf. הֶאֱכַלְתָּם ψ 80^{6}, וְהַאֲכַלְתִּי Is 49^{26}; sf. וְהַאֲכַלְתִּיךָ cons. Is 58^{14}; הֶאֱכַלְתִּיךָ Ez 16^{19}; וְהַאֲכַלְתִּים cons. Je 19^{9}; *Impf.* sf. יַאֲכִלֻנוּ Nu 11$^{4.18}$, etc.; 2 ms. js. תַּאֲכֵל; 1 s. אוֹכִיל Ho 11^{4}; *Imv.* הַאֲכִילֵהוּ Pr 25^{21}, etc.; *Inf.* לְהָכִיל Ez 21^{33} (but Co להחל, q.v.); *Pt.* מַאֲכִיל Je 23^{15}, etc.;—**1.** *cause to eat, feed with*, sq. 2 acc. subj. mostly י׳; Ex 16^{32} Dt 8$^{3.16}$ Ez 3^{2} Je 19^{9}; abs. Ho 11^{4}; cf. Nu 11$^{4.18}$; fig. Je 9^{14} 23^{15} Is 49^{26} 58^{14} Ez 16^{19}; also ψ 80^{6} הֶאֱכַלְתָּם לֶחֶם

דִּמְעָה (cf. 102^{10} Qal supr.); sq. acc. pers. + מִן ψ 81^{17}, but also subj. man Pr 25^{21}; 1 K 22^{27} 2 Ch 18^{26} וְהַאֲכִלֻהוּ לֶחֶם לַחַץ of prison fare; sq. acc. pers. only 2 Ch 28^{15}, cf. Ez 2^{3}. **2.** *cause to devour*, obj. sword Ez 21^{33} (but on text vid. Co).

400 †אֹכֶל$_{40}$ **n.m.** $^{Gn 41, 36}$ **food** (Ar. أُكْلٌ, Aram. ܐܘܟܠܐ, אוּכְלָא, As. *akalu* Dl^{W}, Eth. አክል:)—א׳ abs. Gn 41^{35}+; cstr. Gn 41$^{35.48}$; sf. אָכְלְךָ Lv 25^{37}; אָכְלוֹ Mal 1^{12}, etc.;—Hex mostly JED, not Ez.—*food, food-supply*, esp. cereals of store in Egypt Gn 41$^{35.35}$ + 12 t. Gn 41–44; 47^{24} cf. 14^{11} (JE); also Lv 11^{34} 25^{37} (P) Dt 2$^{6.28}$ (D); נֶשֶׁךְ א׳ *usury of food* Dt 23^{20} (D) (|| נ׳ כֶּסֶף, etc.); לְעֵת הָאֹכֶל *at meal-time* Ru 2^{14}; †poet. 17 t.;—*food* ψ 107^{18}; of offerings Mal 1^{12}; partic. food Jb 12^{11} (as tasted); 36^{31} (as given by God) so ψ 145^{15}; א׳ לְהָשִׁיב נֶפֶשׁ La 1^{11} cf. v^{19}; esp. cereals Pr 13^{23} Jo 1^{16} Hb 3^{17}; but also flesh ψ 78$^{18.30}$; of food (prey) of wild animals ψ 104^{21} (|| טרף) ^{27}; of prey of eagles Jb 9^{26} 39^{29}; ravens 38^{41}.

402 †אָכְלָה$_{17}$ **n.f. food, eating** (with some verbal force, cf. Dr$^{JPh xi. 217}$) only P, & Ez; always לְאָכְלָה, **1.** esp. in phr. like לָכֶם יִהְיֶה לְאָ׳ Gn 1^{29} 6^{21} 9^{3} Lv 11^{39}; so 25^{6} וְהָיְתָה שַׁבַּת הָאָרֶץ לָכֶם לְאָכְלָה; cf. נָתַן לְא׳ Gn 1^{30} Ex 16^{15}. **2.** *devouring*, by wild beasts, only fig. of ravaged people Ez 29^{5} 34$^{5.8.10}$ 39^{4}, cf. 35^{12}. **3.** *consuming*, in fire Ez 15$^{4.6}$, of fire-sacrifice of children 23^{37}; fig. of judgment of י׳ Ez 21^{37}; (cf. also inf. of אָכַל).

401 וְאֻכָל Pr 30^{1} rd. וָאֵכֶל & v. כלה. p. 477

396 †אֲכִילָה **n.f. an eating, a meal** 1 K 19^{8} (on form v. Ba$^{NB 136}$).

3978 †מַאֲכָל$_{30}$ **n.m.** $^{Ju 14, 14}$ (**f.** Hb 1^{16}) **food**—מ׳ Gn 2^{9} + 21 t.; cstr. מַאֲכַל Gn 40^{7} + 3 t.; sf. מַאֲכָלְךָ Ez 4^{10}; מַאֲכָלוֹ Hb 1^{16}; מַאֲכָלָהּ Pr 6^{8}; מַאֲכַלְכֶם Dn 1^{10}—*food*, in genl. Gn 6^{21} 1 K 10^{5} = 2 Ch 9^{4} Hg 2^{12}; opp. drink Ezr 3^{7} 2 Ch 11^{11} Dn 1^{10}; מַאֲכַל תַּאֲוָה Jb 33^{20}; fig. of peoples as fishes, food for Chaldeans Hb 1^{16}; appl. to fruit Gn 2^{9} 3^{6} (of tree טוֹב לְמַ׳) cf. עֵץ־מ׳ Lv 19^{23} Dt 20^{20} Ne 9^{25} Ez 47$^{12.12}$; appl. to דָּגָן Is 62^{8}; appl. to honey Ju 14^{14}; to flour 1 Ch 12^{41} where appos. קֶמַח; to food of ants Pr 6^{8} (|| לֶחֶם); to baker's work Gn 40^{17} cf. Ez 4^{10}; appl. to carcasses, as food for beasts & birds of prey Dt 28^{26} ψ 79^{2} cf. 44^{12} (צֹאן מ׳, sim. of suffering people) Je 7^{33} 16^{4} 19^{7} 34^{20} ψ 74^{14}.

3979 †מַאֲכֶלֶת **n.f. knife** (as *cutting* instrum., or instrument for dividing, making small, cf. S[iegfr.]$^{ThLZ Nov. 17, '83}$) Ju 19^{29}; מַאֲכֶלֶת Gn 22$^{6.10}$, pl. מַאֲכָלוֹת Pr 30^{14}.

†מַאֲכֹלֶת **n.f. fuel** cstr., only מַא׳ אֵשׁ Is 9$^{4.18}$. 3980

†מַכֹּלֶת **n.f. food-stuff**, consisting in חִטִּים, 4361
1 K 5^{25} (on form v. Bö$^{§ 415}$ Sta$^{§ 112 a. 2}$).

†אָכֵן (perh. from אַךְ; cf. Aram. דְּכֵן & דֵּךְ) 403
adv. with strong asseverative force: **a. surely, truly,** esp. at beginning of a speech (stronger & more decided than אַךְ) Gn 28^{16} Ex 2^{14} 1 S 15^{32} Is 40^{7} 45^{15} Je 3$^{23.23}$ 4^{10} 8^{8}. In 1 K 11^{2} אָכֵן stands unusually; and פֶּן־ (cf. 𝔊 𝔖 𝔗) should prob. be read (so Klo). **b.** emphasizing a contrast, *but indeed, but in fact*, esp. after אָמַרְתִּי *I said* or *thought*, expressing the reality, in opp. to what had been wrongly imagined, Is 49^{4b} (opp. to v^{a}) 53^{4} (opp. to v$^{3 end}$) Je 3^{20} (opp. to the expectation v^{19b}) Zp 3^{7b} ψ 31^{23b} (opp. to v^{23a}) 66^{19} 82^{7} (opp. to v^{6}) Jb 32^{8} (opp. to v^{7}).

†אָכַף **vb. press, urge** (Mish. *id.*, Aram. 404
ܐܟܦ *be urgent*, cf. ܐܘܟܦܐ, Ar. إِكَافٌ *saddle*);—**Qal** *Pf.* Pr 16^{26} (נֶפֶשׁ עָמֵל עָמְלָה לּוֹ || א׳ עָלָיו פִּיהוּ) i.e. his hunger impels him to work.

†[אֶכֶף] **n.m. pressure**, sf. אַכְפִּי Jb 33^{7} (𝔊 405
al. rd. כַּפִּי cf. 13^{21}, but cf. Di).

אכר (Ar. أَكَرَ *dig, till* the ground).

†אִכָּר **n.m.** $^{Jo 1, 11}$ **ploughman, husband-** 406
man (Ar. أَكَّارٌ, Aram. ܐܟܪܐ, אִיכָּרָא, cf. Mish.) א׳ sg. abs. Je 51^{23} (+ וְצִמְדּוֹ) Am 5^{16}; pl. אִכָּרִים Je 14^{4} 31^{24} (|| וְנָסְעוּ בָּעֵדֶר) 2 Ch 26^{10} (|| כֹּרְמִים) Jo 1^{11} (|| *id.*), אִכָּרֵיכֶם Is 61^{5} (|| *id.*)

אַכְשָׁף v. כשף. p. 506 407

I. אַל (= اَلْ, Ar. article, preserved perh. in following words derived by Hebrews from (or through) Arabic-speaking tribes; cf. Eng. *algebra, Alhambra, alkali, alcohol, alcove,* etc.)

†אֶלְגָּבִישׁ **n.[m.] hail** (= Ar. اَلْجِبْسُ *gyp-* 417
sum; cf. sub גבשׁ) אַבְנֵי א׳ Ez 13$^{11.13}$ 38^{22}.

†אַלְגּוּמִּים **n.[m.] pl.** a tree (foreign & ob- 418
scure) alw. with עֲצֵי, perh. **sandal-wood**:—2 Ch 2^{7} עֲצֵי אֲרָזִים בְּרוֹשִׁים וְא׳ (fr. Lebanon); עֲצֵי א׳ 2 Ch 9^{10} (|| אֶבֶן יְקָרָה; both fr. Ophir); cf. v^{11}, vid. foll.

†אַלְמֻגִּים **n.[m.]pl.** *id.* עֲצֵי אַלְמֻגִּים 1 K 484
10$^{11.12}$ (fr. Ophir); ע׳ הָא׳ 1 K 10^{12}.

†אַלְמוֹדָד **n.pr.** of South-Arab. people (but 486
prob. rd. אֵל (Sab., *god*) for אַל, cf. Di Gn 10^{26}, & Glas$^{Sk. ii. 280}$ *God is loved* (?)) Gn 10^{26} 1 Ch 1^{20}.

510 †אַלְקוּם band of soldiers (=Ar. القَوْمُ, *people;* so E. Castle, Thes etc., cf. Che$^{\text{Job \& Sol. 175}}$; >text. error for אֱלֹהִים Hi cf. Now) Pr 30^{31}.

513 †אֶלְתּוֹלַד n.pr.loc. (cf. תּוֹלָד sub ילד) city in southern Judah Jos 15^{30} 19^{4}; cf. also תּוֹלָ֑ד (q.v.) 1 Ch 4^{29}.

408 II. **אַל adv. of negation** (so Ph. e.g. CIS i.$^{3,4.5.8}$, BAram., Sab. (DHM$^{\text{ZMG 1875, 596}}$), and in the Eth. አልቦ: *albo, is not*), denying however, not objectively as a fact (like לֹא, *οὐ*), but subjectively as a wish (like *μή*), expressing therefore a *deprecation* or *prohibition:* **a.** (*a*) with a verb, which is then always an impf. (never an imperative), by preference in the cohort. or jussive mood, where this is in use, and may be of any person or number; Gn 15^{1} and often אַל־תִּירָא *fear not!* 22^{12} אַל־תִּשְׁלַח יָֽדְךָ *put not forth* thy hand, 37^{27} וְיָדֵנוּ אַל־תְּהִי־בוֹ and *let not* our hand *be* upon him, 21^{16} אַל־אֶרְאֶה *let me not* look upon the death of the lad! ψ 25^{2} אַל־אֵבוֹשָׁה *let* me *not be* ashamed; with 1 pl. (rare) 2 S 13^{25} Je 18^{18} Jon 1^{14}. In an imprecation: Gn 49^{4} אַל־תּוֹתַר have not thou the excellency! ψ 109^{12} Jb $3^{4.6}$. Sometimes strengthened by נָא: Gn 13^{8} 18^{3} al. (*b*) without a verb, (*α*) 2 S 1^{21} *let* (there be) *not* dew & *not* rain upon you! Is 62^{6} ψ 83^{1}. (*β*) used absol., in deprecation Gn 19^{18} 2 S 13^{16} (v. sub אוֹדֹה) 2 K 3^{13} 4^{16} 6^{27} (v. RVm: but possibly to be expl. by Dr$^{\S\ 152\ \text{iii}}$; so Th Ke: hardly as Ew$^{\S\ 355\ \text{b}}$) Ru 1^{13} אַל בְּנֹתַי *Nay,* my daughters, cf. Ju 19^{23}; (*γ*) after a preceding imper. Am 5^{14} Jo 2^{13} Pr 8^{10}, a juss. 27^{2}, an inf. abs. 27^{2}. (*c*) in poetry אַל sometimes expresses vividly the emotion or sympathy of the poet (v. Dr$^{\S\ 56\text{-}8}$); Is 2^{9} וְאַל־תִּשָּׂא לָהֶם and *forgive* them *not!* (with a touch of passion), ψ 41^{3} Pr 3^{25} Jb 5^{22}; ψ 34^{6} (but 𝔊 𝔖 Ew Che here rd. וּפְנֵיכֶם, prob. rightly); $50^{3\text{a}}$ may our God come וְאַל־יֶחֱרַשׁ and *not be* silent! (the psalmist identifying himself with a spectator of the scene v$^{2.3\ \text{b-c}}$) 121^{3} (contrast v^{4} לֹא) Je 46^{6}+. **b.** once Pr 12^{28} joined closely to a subst. (cf. לֹא **2** *b*) to express with emph. its negation: In the way of righteousness is life, and in the pathway thereof אַל־מָוֶת there is *no-death!* i.e. *immortality.* **c.** once Jb 24^{25} used poet. as a subst., And bring my words לְאַל to *nought!* —N.B. 1 S 27^{10} אַל־פְּשַׁטְתֶּם הַיּוֹם, אַל with the pf. is against all analogy; and either אֶל־מִי (with 𝔊 𝔙), or better אָן *whither?* (with 𝔖 𝔗: v. 1 S 10^{14}) must be read.

413 **אֶל** (nearly always followed by Makkeph), poet. אֱלֵי (cf. עֲדֵי, עֲלֵי), but only in Job (†3^{22} 5^{26} 15^{22} 29^{19}), with suff. אֵלַי, אֵלֶיךָ, אֵלַיִךְ, etc. אֲלֵיהֶם & אֲלֵהֶם, אֲלֵכֶם (5 t.) & אֲלֵיכֶם, אֵלֵינוּ (both very often), once אֵלֵימוֹ ψ 2^{5}, אֲלֵיהֶן, once אֲלֵהֶן Ex 1^{19} (As. *ilî*, Ar. إِلَى), **prep.** denoting **motion to or direction towards** (whether physical or mental). **1.** of motion *to* or *unto* a person or place Gn $2^{19.22}$ 3^{19} 8^{9} 14^{22} 16^{9} etc., after every kind of verb expressing motion (הָלַךְ, בּוֹא, יָצָא, etc.) So with נָתַן *to give* (though לְ is here more common) Gn 21^{14} 35^{4} Dt 13^{2}+; מָכַר *to sell* 37^{36}, etc. Metaph. Je 2^{19} וְלֹא פַחְדָּתִי אֵלַיִךְ and that my fear (cometh) not *unto* thee (cf. Jb 31^{23}).—Peculiarly Gn 6^{16} אֶל אַמָּה *unto* the length of a cubit, etc. And metaph. in the phrase אֶל־(אֱלֵי־)גִּיל *unto* exultation †Ho 9^{11} Jb 3^{22}. Once, exceptionally (si vera l.)=*even:* Jb 5^{5} וְאֶל־מִצִּנִּים יִקָּחֵהוּ and *even* out of thorns he taketh it. Sometimes pregnant, as Is 66^{17} Je 41^{7} זָנָה אֶל commit whoredom (by going) *to* Nu 25^{1} Ez $16^{26.28.29}$; דָּרַשׁ אֶל seek (by resorting) *to* one (sc. for oracles) Dt 18^{11} Is 8^{19} 11^{10}+; חָבַר אֶל join together (& come) *unto* Gn 14^{3}; הִשְׁכִּים אֶל rise early (and go) *to* 19^{27}; 24^{11} הִבְרִיךְ אֶל made to kneel down *at;* 47^{18} תַּם אֶל i.e. has been made over *to;* פָּחַד אֶל to come in fear *to* Hos 3^{5} Mi 7^{17}. Opp. is מִן, as מִן־הַקָּצֶה אֶל־הַקָּצֶה from end *to* end Ex 26^{28}; מִפֶּה אֶל־פֶּה Ezr 9^{11} (syn. 2 K 21^{16} פֶּה לָפֶה). And of time (rare) †מִיּוֹם אֶל־יוֹם †1 Ch 9^{25}; מֵעֵת אֶל־עֵת †Nu 30^{15} (P) 1 Ch 16^{23} (in the ‖ ψ 96^{2} מִיּוֹם לְיוֹם).

2. Where the limit is actually entered, *into,* Gn 6^{18} and thou shalt enter *into* the ark 7^{1} 19^{3} 41^{21} 42^{17}; & so after verbs of throwing, casting, putting 37^{22} (הִשְׁלִיךְ) 39^{20} וַיִּתְּנֵהוּ אֶל־בֵּית הַסֹּהַר put him *into* the prison house, Ex 28^{30} (Lv 8^{8}) Dt 23^{25}; so after קָבַר to bury Gn 23^{19} 25^{9} 49^{29}; שָׂחַט to squeeze 40^{11}; מָחָה to blot out Nu 5^{23}, etc.; metaph. Gn 6^{6} was pained *into* or *unto* his heart, הֵשִׁיב, שָׂם אֶל־לֵב to place, bring *into* (=lay *to*) heart Dt 4^{39} 2 S 19^{20} al. In connexion with a number or multitude *into* which something enters, *in among:* 1 S 10^{22} behold he had hid himself אֶל־הַכֵּלִים *in among* the baggage, Je 4^{3} sow not אֶל־קֹצִים *in among* thorns.

3. Of direction *towards* anything: (*a*) of physical acts or states, as Gn 30^{40} נָתַן פְּנֵי הַצֹּאן אֶל, 39^{7} נָשָׂא עֵינָיו אֶל, Ex 25^{20}, Nu 6^{26} נָשָׂא פָנָיו אֶל (2 K 9^{32} differently), 24^{1} שָׁת פָּנָיו אֶל, Jos 8^{18} ψ 28^{2} 1 K $8^{29.30}$ (to pray *towards*) v^{38}; pregn. חָרֵד אֶל

to tremble (turning) *to* Gn 42^{28}, תָּמַהּ אֶל to wonder (turning) *towards* Gn 43^{33} Is 13^{8}, פָּחַד אֶל Je 36^{16}: without a vb. פָּנִים אֶל־פָּנִים face *to* face Gn 32^{31}+; פֶּה אֶל־פֶּה Nu 12^{8}; כִּי־אֵינֶנּוּ אֵלַי Gn 31^{5} the face of Laban, that he is not *toward* me; עֵינֵי י׳ אֶל־פ׳ the eyes of ׳י are *towards*... ψ 34^{16} (cf. 33^{18}). (*b*) with words such as אָמַר to say *to* Gn 3^{1}+oft., דִּבֶּר 8^{15}+oft., קָרָא 19^{5}, הִתְפַּלֵּל 20^{17} etc., שָׁמַע to hearken *to* 16^{11}, הִלֵּל to praise *to* 12^{15} (cf. Ez 13^{19} חִלֵּל אֶל to profane *to*), הִזְכִּיר 40^{14}. (*c*) with words expressing the direction of the mind, as קִוָּה *to wait* ψ 27^{14}+; יִחֵל *to hope* Is 51^{5}; נָשָׂא נֶפֶשׁ אֶל to lift up the soul (i.e. set the desire) *towards* Dt 24^{15} ψ 25^{1}; שִׁית, שָׂם לֵב אֶל to set the heart (mind) *to* Ex 9^{21} al.; לָמַד אֶל to accustom oneself *to* Je 10^{2}; חָרֵד אֶל to shew fear *towards* 2 K 4^{13}; Gn 43^{30}; Dt 28^{32} and thy eyes כָּלוֹת אֲלֵיהֶם failing (with longing) *towards* them, La 4^{17}; Is 63^{15} 2 S 3^{8} 1 K 14^{13} ψ 40^{6}; alone, as predic., *directed* or *disposed towards*, Gn 3^{16} 4^{7} 2 K 6^{11} who of ours *is towards* (i.e. favours) the king of Syria? Ho 3^{3} וְגַם־אֲנִי אֵלָיִךְ׃ Ez 36^{9} Hg 2^{17} Je 15^{1} (אֵין נַפְשִׁי אֶל).

4. Where the motion or direction implied appears from the context to be of a hostile character, אֶל = *against:* Gn 4^{8} וַיָּקָם ק׳ אֶל־הֶבֶל and Cain rose up *against* Abel (so 1 S 24^{8}) 22^{12} Ex 14^{5} Nu 32^{14}; with נִקְבַּץ Jos 10^{6}, הָלַךְ Ju 1^{10} 20^{30}; with בָּא of calamity, etc., coming *to* or *upon* any one Gn 42^{21} Ju 9^{57} 1 S 2^{34} 1 K 14^{10}+; Is 2^{4} 3^{8} their tongue and doings are אֶל־י׳ 32^{6} (לְדַבֵּר אֶל) Ho 7^{15} (cf. Na 1^{9}) 12^{5} וַיָּשַׂר אֶל־מַלְאָךְ and he strove *against* the angel. Here also belongs in partic. the phrase הִנְנִי אֶל... Behold I am *against* (thee, you, etc.) †Na 2^{14} 3^{5} Je 21^{13} (23$^{30-32}$ עַל) 50^{31} 51^{25} Ez 13$^{8.20}$ 21^{8} 29^{10} 30^{22} 34^{10} 35^{3} 38^{3} 39^{1} (5^{8} 26^{3} 28^{22} 29^{3} עַל: on 36^{9} v. supr.)

5. *Unto* sometimes acquires from the context the sense of *in addition to*, as Lv 18^{18} thou shalt not take אִשָּׁה אֶל אֲחֹתָהּ a woman *to, in addition to*, her sister, Jos 13^{22} (‖ Nu 31^{8} עַל); 1 S 14^{34} to eat אֶל־הַדָּם *together with* the blood (v^{32} & generally עַל); 1 K 10^{7} הוֹסִיף אֶל (generally עַל); Je 25^{26}; Ez 7^{26} שְׁמוּעָה אֶל שְׁמוּעָה (‖ עַל); 44^{7}; La 3^{41} let us lift up לְבָבֵנוּ אֶל־כַּפַּיִם our hearts *together with* the hands (cf. إِلَى, Qor 4^{2}; W$^{AG\ ii.\ §\ 51\ c}$).

6. Metaph. *in regard to, concerning, on account of:* thus הִתְאַבֵּל to mourn *concerning* 1 S 15^{35}; הִנָּחֵם to repent *as regards* 2 S 24^{16}; דָּרַשׁ to inquire 1 K 14^{5}; הִתְפַּלֵּל to pray *with regard to* 1 S 1^{27} 2 K 19^{20}; צָעַק to cry 2 K 8^{3} (v^{5} עַל); נֶעֱצַב be pained 1 S 20^{34}; נִחַם to comfort 2 S 10^{2}; more gen. 1 K 16^{13} 21^{22}; אֶל־נֶפֶשׁ *on account of, for the sake of*, one's life 1 K 19^{3} 2 K 7^{7} (Gn 19^{17} עַל). (עַל is more common in this sense.) And specially with verbs of saying, narrating, telling, etc. *with regard to*, as אָמַר Gn 20^{2} Is 29^{22} 37$^{21.33}$+; דִּבֶּר 2 S 7^{19} Je 40^{16b}; סִפֵּר ψ 2^{7} 69^{27}; צִוָּה Is 23^{11}; שָׁמַע Ez 19^{4}; הַשְּׁמוּעָה אֶל the report *regarding* ... 1 S 4^{19}. (Not freq., exc. in the case of אָמַר.)

7. Of rule or standard, *according to* (rare): אֶל־פִּי ... *according to* the command of, Jos 15^{13} 17^{4} 21^{3} (generally עַל־פִּי); אֶל־נָכוֹן *according to* what is fixed = of a certainty †1 S 23^{23} 26^{4} (v. Dr): perh. ψ 5^{1}; 80^{1} (45^{1} עַל).

8. Expressing presence at a spot, *against, at, by*, not merely after verbs expressing or implying motion (cf. **1**, Gn 24^{11}), as Jos 11^{5} and they came and encamped together אֶל־מֵי מֵרוֹם *at* the waters of Merom, 1 S 5^{4} cut off (and fallen) *on to* the threshold, 2 S 2^{23} al. and smote him אֶל־הַחֹמֶשׁ *in* or *on* the belly, Dt 33^{28} Ex 29^{12} Lv 4^{7}; but also in other cases, as Jos 5^{3} and he circumcised the Israelites אֶל *against, at* the hill of the foreskins, 22^{11} have built an altar אֶל גְּלִילוֹת הַיַּרְדֵּן *by* the districts of Jordan, Ju 12^{6} 2 S 3^{32}, 14^{30} & 18^{4} אֶל־יַד *at* the side of (elsewhere עַל יַד, לְיַד), 1 K 13^{20} as they were sitting אֶל־הַשֻּׁלְחָן *at* the table, 2 K 11^{14} אֶל־הַמֶּלֶךְ *by* the king, Je 41^{12} and found him *by* the great waters, etc., 46^{10} אֶל־נְהַר פְּרָת *by* the Euphrates, Ez 3^{15} 11^{11} 17^{8} 31^{7} 40^{18} 43^{3} 47^{7} 48^{12}.

9. Prefixed to other preps. it combines with them the idea of *motion* or *direction to:* thus אֶל־אַחֲרֵי 2 S 5^{23} 2 K 9$^{18.19}$ סֹב אֶל־אַחֲרַי turn *to* behind me, Zc 6^{6} (where אֶל is pleon., prob. due to clerical error; note יצא אל before & after); אֶל־בֵּין *in between* Ez 31$^{10.14}$; אֶל־בֵּינוֹת similarly Ez 10^{2}; אֶל־מִבֵּית לְ׳ *to* (the part) *within* (v. sub בַּיִת), *in within* Lv 16^{15}, 2 K 11^{15}‖ have her forth *in within* the ranks; אֶל־מוּל v. מוּל; אֶל־מִחוּץ לְ׳ אֶל־מִנֶּגֶב לְ׳ *unto* the south of Jos 15^{3}; *to* the outside of Lv 4$^{12.21}$+; אֶל־נֹכַח *to* the front of Nu 19^{4}; אֶל־תַּחַת Ju 6^{19} 1 K 8^{6} al. (v. sub תַּחַת).

Note 1.—In Gn 20^{13} אֶל־כָּל־הַמָּקוֹם אֲשֶׁר נָבוֹא שָׁמָּה אִמְרִי־לִי וגו׳; Nu 33^{54} אֶל־אֲשֶׁר וגו׳; Pr 17^{8} (cf. Dt 16^{6});—אֶל appears to be used by a species of attraction; the idea of motion involved in the relative clause influencing illogically the beginning of the sentence and causing אֶל to be used instead of בְּ. In Ez 31^{14} אֲלֵיהֶם, as pointed, can only be from אַיִל III or עַ (q.v.); if the word be taken as the pron. with suff. (Hi Ke), אֲלֵיהֶם must be read.

Note 2. There is a tendency in Hebrew, esp. manifest in S K Je Ez, to use אֶל in the sense of עַל; sometimes אֶל being used exceptionally in a phrase or construction which regularly, and in acc. with analogy, has עַל; sometimes, the two preps. interchanging, apparently without discrimination, in the same or parallel sentences. Thus (*a*) Jos 5^{14} וַיִּפֹּל אֶל־פָּנָיו; 1 S 13^{13} הֵקִים י׳ אֶת־מַמְלַכְתְּךָ אֶל־יִשְׂרָאֵל; 14^{34} (v. sub **5**); 17^{3} עֹמְדִים אֶל־הָהָר (contr. עַל Dt 11^{29}); 19^{16} 2 S 6^{3} 20^{23} (contr. 8^{16}) 1 K 13^{29} 18^{46} (contr. 2 K 3^{15} עַל) Je 35^{15} Ez 7^{18}. (*b*) Ju 6^{37} and upon (עַל) all the earth let there be dryness, v^{39} let there be dryness *on* (אֶל) the fleece; 1 S 14^{10} come up עָלֵינוּ, v^{12} come up אֵלֵינוּ; $16^{23\,\&\,16}$; 16^{13} & 18^{10} צָלַח אֶל, 10^{6} al. צָלַח עַל; 25^{17} evil is determined אֶל־אֲדֹנֵינוּ וְעַל כָּל־בֵּיתוֹ; v^{25}; 27^{10}; 2 S 2^{9} וַיַּמְלִכֵהוּ אֶל ...וְאֶל ...וְאֶל ...וְעַל ...וְעַל יְחִלוּ עַל... 3^{29} ...וְאֶל; 2 K $8^{3\,\&\,5}$; $9^{6\,\&\,3}$; Je 19^{15}; 25^{2}; 26^{15} ye lay innocent blood עֲלֵיכֶם וְאֶל־הָעִיר הַזּאת; 27^{19} 28^{8} 33^{14} 34^{7} 36^{31} $37^{13.14}$ Ez $18^{6.11\,\&\,15}$ 21^{12} etc. ψ 79^{6} (Je 10^{25} עַל twice). It is prob. that this interchange, at least in many cases, is not original, but due to transcribers.

Conversely, though not with the same frequency, עַל occurs where analogy would lead us to expect אֶל, or even in juxtaposition with אֶל, as 1 S 1^{10} הִתְפַּלֵּל עַל to pray *to* (v^{26} אֶל); v^{13}; 25^{25} אֶל...עַל; 1 K 20^{43} וַיֵּלֶךְ עַל־בֵּיתוֹ (21^{4} אֶל); Is 22^{15} Je 11^{2} 23^{35} 31^{12}. Cf. Dr[Sm i. 13, 13; ii. 8, 7; 15, 4].

454 †אֶלְיְהוֹעֵינַי **n.pr.m.** (*unto* י׳ *are mine eyes*) **1.** a Korahite 1 Ch 26^{3}. **2.** a returning exile Ezr 8^{4}.

454 †אֶלְיוֹעֵינַי **n.pr.m.** (*id.*) **1.** a descendant
462 of David 1 Ch $3^{23.24}$. **2.** a Simeonite אֶלְיוֹעֵנַי 1 Ch 4^{36}. **3.** a Benjamite (*id.*) 7^{8}. **4.** priests in time of Ezra (*a*) Ezr 10^{22}; (*b*) 10^{27} (אֶלְיוֹעֵנַי); (*c*) Ne 12^{41}.

411 †I. אֵל **pr. pl. m.** & **f.** = the more usual אֵלֶּה, *these* 1 Ch 20^{8}; with art. הָאֵל Gn $19^{8.25}$ $26^{3.4}$ Lv 18^{27} Dt 4^{42} 7^{22} 19^{11}. (Merely an orthogr. variation of אֵלֶּה, and doubtless pronounced similarly; the kindred dialects have in genl. a dissyllabic form: v. sub אֵלֶּה. Written similarly in Ph., e.g. CIS 3^{22} 14^{5} 93^{3} (האל), but ZMG [1875, 240] (Neo-Punic) אלא; in Plaut. Poen. v. 1. 9 transliterated *ily*; Schroed.[Ph. Gr. p. 81, 160, 286 ff.])

אֵלֶּה (أُولَى, አሉ: አላ: Rabb. אֵלּוּ, Aram. אִלֵּין, & compd. with ܗܠܝܢ and ܠܝܢ in ܗܠܝܢ, ܗܠܠܝܢ) **pr. pl. m.** & **f.** **these**, in usage the pl. of זֶה. **a.** Gn 2^{4} & oft.: in appos. to a subst. with a pron. suff. (always *without* the art.) Ex 9^{14} (rd. with Hi. אֵלֶּה בְּךָ for אֶל־לִבְּךָ) 10^{1} אֹתֹתַי אֵלֶּה *these* my signs, 11^{8} Dt 11^{18} 1 K 8^{59} 10^{8} 22^{23} 2 K 1^{13} Je 31^{21} Ezr 2^{65} Ne 6^{14}; in the genit. 2 K 6^{20} Is 47^{9} Dt 18^{12} ψ 15^{5}; and after כל Gn 14^{3} + oft. Standing alone in a neuter sense, *these things* (rare in best prose, & not very common in poetry), with עָשָׂה Dt 18^{12} 22^{5} 25^{16} 2 S $23^{17.22}$ ψ 15^{5}+; with other vbs. Ezr 9^{1} Is 44^{21} 47^{7} Je 13^{22} Ho 14^{10} ψ 42^{5} 50^{21} 107^{43} Jb 8^{2}; with אֶת־ Nu 15^{13} Is 48^{14}; with כָּל־ Ju 13^{23} Is 66^{2}+; v. also some of the cases with preps. sub **d.** אלה may point indifferently to what follows, Gn 6^{9} 10^{1} $25^{7.12.13}$ ψ 42^{5}; or to what has preceded, Gn 9^{19} $10^{20.31.32}$ 25^{4} Lv 21^{14} 22^{22} ψ 15^{5}; = *such as these* (τοιαῦτα), ψ 73^{12} Jb 18^{21}. **b.** repeated, אלה ... ואלה, *these ... those* Dt 27^{13} Jos 8^{22} Is 49^{12} (3 t.) ψ 20^{8}+. **c.** with the art. (but only after a subst. determined likewise by the art.) הָאֵלֶּה Gn 15^{1} + oft. **d.** with preps.: בְּאֵלֶּה Lv 25^{54} 26^{23} 1 K 22^{11} (7 t.), בָּאֵלֶּה †1 S 16^{10} 17^{39}; לָאֵלֶּה Lv 11^{24} (4 t.), לָאֵלֶּה 1 K 22^{17} (5 t.); מֵאֵלֶּה Gn 9^{19} (16 t.); עַד אֵלֶּה Lv 26^{18}; עַל־אֵלֶּה *on account of these things* Is 57^{6} 64^{11} Je 5^{9} al.; כְּאֵלֶּה †Jb 16^{2} Je 10^{16} = 51^{19}, כָּאֵלֶּה †Gn 27^{46} Lv 10^{19} (things like these, so Is 66^{8} Je 18^{13}) Nu 28^{24} P (cf. Ez 45^{25}) 2 K 25^{17} = Je 52^{22}, כְּמוֹ־אֵלֶּה †Jb 12^{3}. 428

II. אֵל *god*, אֶלְדָּד, אֶלְדָּעָה etc. v. I. אלה. 410

†אֵלָא **n.pr.m.** father of an officer of 414
Solomon 1 K 4^{18} (= II. אֵלָה *terebinth*?).

I. אלה (assumed as √ of אֵל, אֱלוֹהַּ (אֱלֹהִים) *god, God*, but question intricate, & conclusions dub. It is uncertain whether אֵל & אֱלֹהִים are from the same √. Following are the chief theories: **1. a.** Thes makes אֵל & אֱלֹהִים distinct, and both really primitive, but associates אֵל in treatment with אֵל *strong*, Pt. of √אול; *strong*, acc. to Thes, being derived from mng. *be in front of*; (different order in Lex. Man., RobGes); **b.** אֵל & אֱלֹהִים distinct; former fr. אול *strong;* latter pl. of אֱלוֹהַּ from √[אלה] = أَلِهَ (وَلِهَ) *go to and fro* in perplexity or fear, hence אֱלוֹהַּ *fear & object of fear*, reverence, *revered one;* פחד אל = أَلِهَ إِلَى *trepide confugere ad* Ho 3^{5}; פחד = אלהים Gn 31^{42} = מוֹרָא Is 8^{13}

De$^{Gn\ 18^{67.48}}$ (cf. σέβασμα, postB.Heb. יִרְאָה NHWB; Aram. דַּחֲלָא CWB); so De following Fl in De $^{Gn\ ed.\ 4,\ 57}$, cf. MV. **2.** אֵל & אֱלֹהִים possibly connected; אֵל = *leader, lord*, fr. √אול *be in front;* so Nö$^{MBAk\ 1880,\ 760\ f;\ SBAk\ 1882,\ 1175\ f}$. **3. a.** אֵל & אֱלֹהִים connected, & both fr. a √אלה (= אלהּ) to which is assigned mng. *strong;* so Ew$^{§\ 146\ d,\ 178\ b\ (v.\ also\ Jahrbücher\ d.\ bibl.\ Wiss.\ x.\ 11,\ Bibl.\ Theol.\ ii.\ 330)}$; **b.** אֵל fr. √אלה *strong* (not אלהּ), & אֱלֹהִים expanded from אֵל, cf. pl. אֲמָהוֹת fr. אמה etc.; so Di on Gn 1^{1}; he supports mng. *strong* by ref. to phrase יֶשׁ לְאֵל יָדִי Gn 31^{29} al.; **c.** similarly, אֵל, being very early & common Shemitic word, formed pl. אלהים, fr. which sing. אֱלוֹהַּ was afterwards inferred, Nes$^{Theol.\ Stud.\ a.\ Württ.,\ 1882,\ 243}$ (criticized by Nö$^{SBA\ l.c.}$). **4.** אֵל (אֱלוֹהַּ, אֱלֹהִים disregarded) fr. √אלה *stretch out to, reach after* (cf. prep. אֶל, אֱלֵי, also אָלָה *swear*), God as *the one whom men strive to reach*, 'das Ziel aller Menschensehnsucht und alles Menschenstrebens,' Lag$^{Or.\ ii.\ 3;\ GN\ 1882,\ 173 = M\ 96}$.—Cf. Spurrell $^{Heb.\ Text\ of\ Gn.,\ App.\ ii}$, where all these views are stated somewhat more fully, & briefly criticized; on the use of אֵל & אֱלֹהַּ in Shemitic languages vid., exhaustively, Nö$^{MBAk,\ SBAk,\ l.c.}$).

410 II. אֵל **n.m.** (also, in n.pr. אֵל, אֱלִי; Sam. אל, Ph. אל, אלן (i.e. prob. אֵלִן), Sab. אל, DHM $^{Or.\ Congr.\ Leiden,\ 1883}$, As. *ilu*, Dl^{W}; perhaps also Ar., Aram. cf. Nö$^{l.c.}$; on *goddess* אלת Ph. Palm. Nab. Sab. (also אלהת) DHM$^{l.c.}$, Ar. إِلَاهَةٌ (pl. إِلَاهَات) Fl$^{Kl.\ Schr.\ i.\ 154}$, As. *Allatu* Jr^{66}, Syr. ܐܠܳܗܬܳܐ, cf. also Bae$^{Rel\ 58,\ 90,\ 97,\ 271,\ 297}$) **god**, but with various subordinate applications to express idea of might;—hardly ever in prose exc. with defining word (adj. or gen.); its only suff. is ִי;—†**1.** applied to *men of might and rank*, אֵל גוים *mighty one of the nations* Ez 31^{11} (of Neb.; 𝔊 ἄρχων ἐθνῶν, איל some MSS. Co); אֵלִים *mighty men* Jb 41^{17} (אילים, many MSS. Di); אֵלֵי גִבּוֹרִים *mighty heroes* Ez 32^{21} (אֵילֵי MSS. Co); אֵילֵי הָאָרֶץ Ez 17^{13} 2 K 24^{15} (Kt אולי); אֵילִים Ex 15^{15} (prob. pl. of III. אַיִל, q.v.) These readings are uncertain because of an effort to distinguish these forms from the divine name. אֵל גִּבּוֹר *mighty hero* (as above) or *divine hero* (as reflecting the divine majesty) Is 9^{6}. †**2.** *angels*, בְּנֵי אֵלִים ψ 29^{1} 89^{7} = בְּנֵי הָאֱלֹהִים. †**3.** *gods of the nations*, אֵל אֵלִים *God of gods*, supreme God Dn 11^{36}; מִי כָמֹכָה בָּאֵלִם *who is like thee among the gods* Ex 15^{11}; *idols* Is 43^{10} 44$^{10.15.17}$ 46^{6}; מי אל בשמים *what God in heaven* Dt 3^{24}; אֵל אחר *another god* Ex 34^{14} (J); אֵל זר *foreign god* ψ 44^{21} 81^{10}; אל נכר Dt 32^{12} Mal 2^{11} ψ 81^{10}. †**4.** *Ēl* **n.pr.** אל ברית *Ēl Berith* Ju 9^{46} (= בעל ברית Ju 1286
8^{33} 9^{4}) cf. also **6** (*f*) infr. †**5.** as characterizing mighty things in nature, הררי אל *mighty mountains* ψ 36^{7} (lit. *mountains of Ēl*); also ψ 50^{10} Ol Bi Che v. sub II. אלף; ארזי אל *mighty cedars* ψ 80^{11}; כוכבי אל *lofty stars* Is 14^{13}.

6. God $_{217}$, the one only and true God of Israel: (*a*) הָאֵל *the God, the true God* Gn 31^{13} 35$^{1.3}$ 46^{3} (E) 2 S 22$^{31.33.48}$ (= ψ 18$^{31.33.48}$) ψ 68$^{20.21}$ 77^{15}; הָאֵל הַנֶּאֱמָן *the faithful God* Dt 7^{9}; האל הגדול *the great God* Dt 10^{17} = Je 32^{18} Dn 9^{4} Ne 1^{5} 9^{32}; האל הקדש *the holy God* Is 5^{17}; האל יהוה *the God Yahweh* Is 42^{5} ψ 85^{9}. †(*b*) אֵלִי *my God* Ex 15^{2} (poet.) ψ 18^{3} 22$^{2.2.11}$ 63^{2} 68^{25} 89^{27}
102^{25} 118^{28} 140^{7} Is 44^{17}. (*c*) cstr. אל בית אל 416
the God of Bethel, who had his seat there Gn 35^{7} (E); אל אביך God of thy fathers Gn 49^{25} (poet.); אל ישראל ψ 68^{36}; אל יעקב ψ 146^{5}; אל השמים *the God of heaven* ψ 136^{26}; אל סלעי *the God who is my rock* ψ 42^{10}; אל שמחת גילי *the God who is the joy of my exultation* ψ 43^{4}; אֵל רֳאִי *the God who lets himself be seen* Gn 16^{13} (J); אל הכבוד *the God of glory* ψ 29^{3}; אל דעות *the all-knowing God* 1 S 2^{3} (poet.); אֵל עוֹלָם *the everlasting God* Gn 21^{33} (J); אל ישועתי Is 12^{2}; אל חַיָּי ψ 42^{9}; אל אמת ψ 31^{6} = אל אֱמוּנָה Dt 32^{4} (poet.); אל נקמות ψ 94$^{1.1}$; אל גְּמֻלוֹת Je 51^{56}. (*d*) אֵל אֶחָד *one God* Mal 2^{10}; אל גדול *a great God* Dt 7^{21} ψ 77^{14} 95^{3}; אל מסתתר *a God hiding himself* Is 45^{15}; אל רחום *a compassionate God* Ex 34^{6} (J) Dt 4^{31} ψ 86^{15}; אל נשא *a forgiving God* ψ 99^{8}; אל חַנּוּן *a gracious God* Ne 9^{31} Jon 4^{2}; אל קנא *a jealous God* Ex 20^{5} 34^{14} (J) Dt 4^{24} 5^{9} 6^{15} Jos 24^{19} (D) = אל קנוא Na 1^{2}; אֵל חי *a living God* Jos 3^{10} (J) Ho 2^{1} ψ 42^{3} 84^{3}; אל צדיק Is 45^{21}; לא אֵל חפץ רשע ψ 5^{5}; לא אֵל Dt 32^{21} (poet.) Is 31^{3} Ez 28$^{2.2.9}$; מי אל כמוך Mi 7^{18} (cf. Ex 15^{11}). (*e*) **God** (the only true God, needing no article or predicate to define him) Nu 12^{13} (E rd. אַל Di) always in poetry, Jb 5^{8} + (55 t. Jb), ψ 7^{12} 10$^{11.12}$ 16^{1} 17^{6} 19^{1} 52$^{3.7}$ 55^{20} 57^{3} 73$^{11.17}$ 74^{8} 77^{10} 78$^{7.8.18.19.34.41}$ 82^{1} 83^{2} 90^{2} 104^{21} 106$^{14.21}$ 107^{11} 118^{27} 139$^{17.23}$ 149^{6} 150^{1} Is 40^{18} 43^{12} 45$^{14.20}$ 46^{9} La 3^{41} Ho 11^{9} 12^{1} Mal 1^{9}; עִמָּנוּאֵל *God is with us*, as name of child in prediction Is 7^{14} cf. 8$^{8.10}$. (*f*) *Ēl, a divine*
name אל אלהי ישראל Gn 33^{20} (E); אל אלהי 415
הרוחות Nu 16^{22} (P = יהוה אלהי הרוחות Nu 27^{16}); אל אלהים יהוה Jos 22^{22} (P) ψ 50^{1}. This is probable also in the ancient poems, Nu 23$^{8.19.22.23}$ 24$^{4.8.16.23}$ (poet. Balaam ‖ שדי & עליון) Dt 32^{18} 33^{26}

(poet. Moses ‖ צוּר & אֱלֹהֵי קֶדֶם) 2 S 22^{32} 23^{5} (poet. David ‖ צוּר) and in the combinations אל עליון (5 t.; vid. עליון) & אל שדי (10 t.; vid. שַׁדַּי).

†**7.** אֵל *strength, power* (on connection with I. אָלָה cf. Di Gn 1^{1} 31^{29}) in יֶשׁ־לְאֵל יָדִי *it is according to the power of my hand*=it is in my power, etc. Gn 31^{29} (E; sq. לְ + Inf.); בִּהְיוֹת לְאֵל יָדְיךָ Pr 3^{27} (sq. id.); יֶשׁ־לְאֵל יָדָם Mi 2^{1} (abs.); neg. וְאֵין לְאֵל יָדֶךָ Dt 28^{32} (abs.)=*thou shalt be powerless*, so Ne 5^{5}.

433 אֱלֹהַּ $_{57}$ so Dt 32^{17}; לֶאֱלֹהַּ Dn 11^{38} (vid. BD) sf. לֵאלֹהוֹ Hb 1^{11}; elsewhere אֱלוֹהַּ **n.m. god, God.** (Sam. *id.*, Aram. אֱלָהּ, ܐܠܳܗܳܐ, Ar. إِلٰهٌ, Sab. אלה DHM$^{l.c.}$;—אֱלֹהַּ as found in Heb. prob. a sg. formed by inference fr. pl. אֱלֹהִים: cf. Nes$^{l.c.}$)—**1.** *a heathen god*, late usage; כָּל־אֱלוֹהַּ 2 Ch. 32^{15} Dn 11^{37}; זוּ כחו לאלהו *whose power is his god* Hb 1^{11} 2 K 17^{31} (but Qr אֱלֹהֵי), אשר הביא אֱלוֹהַּ בְּיָדוֹ *who doth bring God in his hand* Jb 12^{6} (Ew Di RVm, etc.) **2. God**, used in ancient poems Dt $32^{15.17}$ ψ 18^{32}, and on their basis an archaism in later poetry Jb 3^{4} + (41 t. Jb), ψ 50^{22} 114^{7} 139^{19} Pr 30^{5} Is 44^{8} Hb 3^{3} Ne 9^{17} (citing Ex 34^{6} where אֵל is used).

430 אֱלֹהִים $_{2570}$ **n.m.pl. (f.** 1 K 11^{33}; on number of occurrences of אֵל, אֱלוֹהַּ, אֱלֹהִים cf. also Nes$^{l.c.}$) **1.** *pl.* in number. †**a.** *rulers, judges*, either as divine representatives at sacred places or as reflecting divine majesty and power: האלהים Ex 21^{6} (Onk 𝔖, but τὸ κριτήριον τοῦ Θεοῦ 𝔊) $22^{7.8}$; אלהים $22^{8.27}$ (𝔗 Ra AE Ew RVm; but *gods*, 𝔊 Josephus Philo AV; *God*, Di RV; all Covt. code of E) cf. 1 S 2^{25} v. Dr.; Ju 5^{8} (Ew, but *gods* 𝔊; *God* 𝔖 BarHeb.; יהוה 𝔙 Be) ψ $82^{1.6}$ (De Ew Pe; but *angels* Bl Hup) 138^{1} (𝔖 𝔗 Rab Ki De; but *angels* 𝔊 Calv; *God*, Ew; *gods*, Hup Pe Che). †**b.** *divine ones*, superhuman beings including God and angels ψ 8^{6} (De Che Br; but *angels* 𝔊 𝔖 𝔗 Ew; *God*, RV and most moderns) Gn 1^{27} (if with Philo 𝔗 Jer De Che we interpret נעשה as God's consultation with angels; cf. Jb 38^{7}). †**c. angels** ψ 97^{7} (𝔊 𝔖 Calv; but *gods*, Hup De Pe Che); cf. בני (ה)אלהים = *(the) sons of God*, or *sons of gods*=angels Jb 1^{6} 2^{1} 38^{7} Gn $6^{2.4}$ (J; so 𝔊 Bks. of Enoch & Jubilees Philo Jude v^{6} 2 Pet 2^{4} Jos$^{Ant. 1.3.1}$, most ancient fathers and modern critics; against usage are *sons of princes, mighty men*, Onk and Rab.; *sons of God*, the pious, Theod Chrys Jer Augustine Luther Calv Hengst; 𝔊L rd. οἱ υἱοὶ τοῦ Θεοῦ), cf. בני אלים. **d.** *gods* האלהים Ex 18^{11} 22^{19} (E) 1 S 4^{8} 2 Ch 2^{4} ψ 86^{8}; אלהי האלהים the *God of gods*, supreme God Dt 10^{17} ψ 136^{2}; אלהים Ex $32^{1.23}$ (JE) Ju 9^{13}; אלהים אחרים *other gods* Ex 20^{3} 23^{13} Jos $24^{2.16}$ (E) Dt $31^{18.20}$ (JE) 5^{7} + (17 t. in D, not P) Ju $2^{12.17.19}$ 10^{13} 1 S 8^{8} 26^{19} 1 K $9^{6.9}$ (= 2 Ch $7^{19.22}$) $11^{4.10}$ 14^{9} 2 K 5^{17} $17^{35.37.38}$ 22^{17} (= 2 Ch 34^{25}) 2 Ch 28^{25} Je 1^{16} + (18 t. Je) Ho 3^{1}; אלהי (ה)נכר *foreign gods* Gn $35^{2.4}$ Jos $24^{20.23}$ (E) Dt 31^{16} (JE) Ju 10^{16} 1 S 7^{3} 2 Ch 33^{15} Je 5^{19}; א׳ נחור Gn 31^{53} (E); א׳ מצרים Ex 12^{12} (P) Je $43^{12.13}$; א׳ האמרי Jos 24^{15} (E) Ju 6^{10}; א׳ ארם etc. Ju 10^{6}; אלהים מעשה ידי Dt 4^{28}; א׳ הגוים *gods of the nations* 2 K 18^{33} 19^{12} Dt 29^{17} 2 Ch $32^{17.19}$ Is 36^{18} 37^{12}; א׳ העמים Dt 6^{14} 13^{8} Ju 2^{12} ψ 96^{5} 1 Ch 5^{25} 16^{26} 2 Ch $32^{13.14}$; א׳ כסף Ex 20^{23} (E); א׳ זהב Ex 20^{23} (E) 32^{31} (JE); א׳ מַסֵּכָה Ex 34^{17} (J) Lv 19^{4} (H).

2. *Pl. intensive.* **a.** *god or goddess*, always with sf. 1 S 5^{7} (Dagon), Ju 11^{24} (Chemosh), 1 K 18^{24} (Baal), Ju 9^{27} Dn $1^{2.2}$; or cstr. לעשתרת א׳ צדנים לכמוש א׳ מואב to Ashtoreth goddess of the Zidonians, Chemosh god of Moab, etc. 1 K 11^{33}; א׳ הארץ god of the land 2 K $17^{26.26.27}$, and so the Syrians suppose that Yahweh is a mountain-god and not a god of valleys 1 K 20^{28}. **b.** *godlike one* Ex 4^{16} (J; Moses in relation to Aaron), Ex 7^{1} (P; in relation to Pharaoh), 1 S 28^{13} (the shade of Samuel), ψ 45^{7} (the Messianic king, *O God*, 𝔊 𝔖 Jer, most scholars ancient and modern, but *thy throne is God's*=God's throne AE Ki Thes Ew Hup, cf. 1 Ch 28^{5}). **c.** works of God, or things specially belonging to him (vid. אֵל **5**) הר אלהים ψ 68^{16}; Ez $28^{14.16}$; איש אלהים Jb 1^{16}; גן (ה)אלהים Ez 28^{13} $31^{8.9}$. **d. God** (vid. **3** & **4**).

3. הָאֱלֹהִים *the (true) God*, י׳ הוא האלהים *Yahweh is (the) God* Dt $4^{35.39}$ 7^{9} 1 K 8^{60} $18^{39.39}$ 2 Ch 33^{13}; הוא האלהים Is 45^{18}; י׳ האלהים Jos 22^{34} (P?) 1 K $18^{21.24}$ 2 Ch 32^{16}; אתה הוא האלהים 2 S 7^{28} 1 K 18^{37} 2 K 19^{15} 1 Ch 17^{26} Is 37^{16} Ne 9^{7}; האלהים as subj. or obj. is used in E 33 t., Chr 38 t., Ec 31 t., Jon 5 t., elsewhere Gn $5^{22.24}$ $6^{9.11}$ (sources of P) 17^{18} (P) Jos 22^{34} (P?) Gn 44^{16} (J) Dt $4^{35.39}$ 7^{9} Ju $6^{36.39}$ 7^{14} 10^{14} 16^{28} 21^{2} 1 S $10^{3.7}$ 14^{36} 2 S 2^{27} 6^{7} 7^{28} 12^{16} 1 K 8^{60} $18^{21.24.24.37.39.39}$ 19^{15} (Ephr) Jb 2^{10} Je 11^{12} Is 37^{16} 45^{18} ψ 108^{14} Dn $1^{9.17}$; י׳ הא׳ הקדוש 1 S 6^{20}; הא׳ הגדול Ne 8^{6}; הא׳ אשר בירושלם Ezr 1^{3}; ארני האלהים Dn 9^{3}; in many phrases, as איש האלהים *the man of God*, acting under divine authority and influence: = (*a*) *angel* Ju $13^{6.8}$, (*b*) *prophet* (the term coming into use in the Northern kingdom in the age of Elijah 1 S 9^{9-10}, cf. אִישׁ הָרוּחַ Hos 9^{7}): of *Moses* Dt 33^{1} Jos 14^{6} (E) 1 Ch 23^{14} 2 Ch 30^{16} Ezr 3^{2} ψ 90^{1};

of *Samuel* 1 S 9$^{6-10}$; of *David* 2 Ch 8^{14} Ne 12$^{24.36}$; *Shemaiah* 1 K 12^{22} (=2 Ch 11^{2}); *Elijah, Elisha,* and others of their time 1 K 13$^{1-31}$ 17$^{18-24}$ 20^{28} 2 K 1$^{9-13}$ 4$^{7-42}$ 5$^{8-20}$ 6$^{6-15}$ 7$^{2-9}$ 8$^{2-11}$ 13^{19} 23$^{16-17}$ (Ephr) 2 Ch 25$^{7.9}$; unnamed prophet 1 S 2^{27}; *Hanan* Je 35^{4}; a later title of prophet was עֶבֶד האלהים *the servant of God*, used of Moses 1 Ch 6^{34} 2 Ch 24^{9} Ne 10^{30} Dn 9^{11}. בית האלהים *the house of God*, Ju 18^{31}, esp. late, Chr (52 t.) Ec 4^{17} Dn 1^{2}; בית י׳ 1 Ch 22^{1}; ארון (ברית) האלהים *the ark* (*of the covenant*) *of God* Ju 20^{27} 1 S 4–5. 14, 2 S 6–7. 15 (23 t.) 1 Ch 13. 15. 16, 2 Ch 1^{4} (13 t.); מטה האלהים *the rod of God* Ex 4^{20} 17^{9} (E); הר האלהים *the mount of God* (Horeb) Ex 3^{1} 4^{27} 18^{5} 24^{13} (E) 1 K 19^{8} (Ephr); מלאך האלהים *the* (*theophanic*) *angel of God* Gn 31^{11} Ex 14^{19} (E) Ju 6^{20} 13$^{6.9}$ 2 S 14$^{17.20}$ 19^{28}; in other combinations Ex 18^{16} Nu 23^{27} (E) Ju 20^{2} 1 S 4^{8} 5^{11} 10^{5} 2 S 16^{23} 1 K 12^{22} 1 Ch 21^{7} + (14 t.) ψ 87^{3} Ec 9^{1}.

4. אֱלֹהִים=*God* י׳ אֱלֹהִים אֱמֶת=*Yahweh is God in truth* Je 10^{10}. **a.** אלהים (as subj. obj. direct or indirect) is used by P (50 t. in story of creation and deluge, elsewhere 28 t.), by E (91 t.), J chiefly in poetic sources Gn 3$^{1.3.5.5}$ 9^{27} 39^{9} Dt 32$^{17.39}$, by D (11 t.) Ju (21 t.) S (50 t.) K (29 t.) Chr (45 t.); in ψ 42–86 (180 t. often by editorial change for an original יהוה), elsewhere ψ 3^{3} 5^{11} 7$^{11.12}$ 9^{18} 10$^{4.13}$ 14$^{1.2.5}$ 25^{22} 36$^{2.8}$ 77^{14} 100^{3} 108$^{2.6.8.12.12}$ 149^{9} Jb 5^{8} 20^{29} 28^{23} 32^{2} 34^{9} (& in Prologue 6 t.) Pr 2^{5} 3^{4} 25^{2} Ec (7 t.) Hos (5 t.) Am 4^{11} (כמהפכת אלהים את סדם *as God overthrew Sodom* = Je 50^{40} = Is 13^{19}) Zc 8^{23} 12^{8} Mi 3^{7} (but אליהם 𝔊 𝔖) Is 35^{4} Is^{2} (9 t.) Je 10^{10} Ez (13 t.) Mal (5 t.) Jon (4 t.); the phrase היה ל׳ לאלהים Gn 28^{21} (E^{R}) 17$^{7.8}$ Ex 6^{7} 29^{45} Lv 11^{45} 22^{33} 25^{38} 26$^{12.45}$ Nu 15^{41} (P) Dt 26^{17} 29^{13} 2 S 7^{24} (=1 Ch 17^{22}) Zc 8^{8} Je (6 t.) Ez (6 t.); אלהים צדיק *righteous God* ψ 7^{10}; א׳ קדשים *holy God* Jos 24^{19} (E); א׳ חיים *living God* Dt 5^{23} 1 S 17$^{26.36}$ Je 10^{10} 23^{36}; א׳ חי 2 K 19$^{4.16}$ (=Is 37$^{4.17}$). For the phrases יהוה א׳, י׳ א׳ צבאות, י׳ אלהי, י׳ צבאות א׳, יה א׳, אל א׳ י׳, א׳ צבאות, אדני א׳ צבאות, vid. יהוה, יה, צבאות, & אדני. **b.** cstr. אֱלֹהֵי (*a*) *with persons* אֱלֹהֵי אַבְרָהָם= *God of Abraham*, a phrase of J, Gn 26^{24} 28^{13} 31^{53}, elsewhere ψ 47^{10} 1 K 18^{36} 1 Ch 29^{18} 2 Ch 30^{6}; א׳ אדני אברהם Gn 24$^{12.27.42.48}$ (J); אלהי אב *father's God* (various sf. & names), a phrase of E, Gn 31$^{5.29.42}$ 46^{3} 50^{17} Ex 3$^{6.13.15.16}$ 15^{2} 18^{4} Jos 18^{3}, elsewhere Gn 32^{10} 43^{23} (J) Ex 4^{5} (J ?) Dt (8 t.) Ju 2^{12} 2 K 21^{22} Chr (31 t.) Dn 11^{37}; אֱלֹהֵי יִשְׂרָאֵל *Israel's God*, phrase of E, Gn 33^{20} Ex 5^{1} 24^{10} 32^{27} Jos 8^{30} 14^{14} 22^{16} 24$^{2.23}$, elsewhere Ex 34^{23} Jos 7$^{13.19.20}$ (JE) Nu 16^{9} Jos 9$^{18.19}$ 22^{24} 10$^{40.42}$ 13$^{14.33}$ (R vid. Di Jos 7^{13}) Ju 4^{6} 5$^{3.5}$ 6^{8} 11$^{21.23}$ 21^{3} 1 S 1^{17} + (20 t.) K (26 t.) Chr (45 t.) ψ 41^{14} 106^{48} (doxol.) 59^{6} 69^{7} Is 17^{6} 21$^{10.17}$ 29^{23} Is^{3} 24^{15} 37$^{16.21}$ Is^{2} 41^{17} + (6 t.) Je 35^{17} + (48 t.), Ez 8^{4} + (7 t.) Zp 2^{9} Mal 2^{16} Ru 2^{12}; א׳ מערכות ישראל *God of the battle array of Israel* 1 S 17^{45}; א׳ יַעֲקֹב 2 S 23^{1} (poet.) ψ 20^{2} 46$^{8.12}$ 75^{10} 76^{7} 81$^{2.5}$ 84^{9} 94^{7} Is 2^{3} (=Mi 4^{2}); א׳ העבריים *God of the Hebrews* Ex 3^{18} 5^{3} 7^{16} 9$^{1.13}$ (JE); it is used with other proper names, Nahor Gn 31^{53} (E), Shem Gn 9^{26} (J), David 2 K 20^{5} 2 Ch 21^{12} 34^{3} Is 38^{5}, Hezekiah 2 Ch 32^{17}, Elijah 2 K 2^{14}; א׳ אדני המלך *the God of my lord the king* 1 K 1^{36}. (*β*) *with nouns of attributes or relationships,* א׳ קֶדֶם *ancient God* Dt 33^{27}; א׳ עולם *everlasting God* Is 40^{28}; א׳ אֱמֶת *true God* 2 Ch 15^{3}; א׳ אָמֵן Is 65^{16} (vid. אָמֵן); א׳ משפט Is 30^{18} Mal 2^{17}; א׳ מרום Mi 6^{6}; א׳ כָל בָּשָׂר *God of all flesh* Je 32^{27}; cf. א׳ הרוחות לכל בשר Nu 16^{22} 27^{16} (P); א׳ השמים *God of heaven* Gn 24^{7} (J^{R}) 2 Ch 36^{23} Ezr 1^{2} Ne 1$^{4.5}$ 2$^{4.20}$; cf. א׳ כל הארץ Is 54^{5}; י׳ א׳ השמים וא׳ הארץ Gn 24^{3} (J^{R}); א׳ מִקָּרֹב *a God at hand* opp. א׳ מֵרָחֹק Je 23^{23}, א׳ יִשְׁעִי, א׳ ישועתי *God of my salvation* ψ 18^{47} (=2 S 22^{47}) 24^{5} 25^{5} 27^{9} 65^{6} 79^{9} 85^{5} Is 17^{10} Mi 7^{7} Hb 3^{18} 1 Ch 16^{35}; א׳ ישועתי ψ 88^{2}; א׳ תשועתי ψ 51^{16}; א׳ צִדְקִי *God of my righteousness* ψ 4^{2}; א׳ חַסְדִּי ψ 59$^{11.18}$; א׳ צוּרִי *God who is my rock* 2 S 22^{3} (cf. ψ 18^{3}); א׳ מָעוּזִּי *God who is my stronghold* ψ 43^{2}; א׳ תְּהִלָּתִי *God who is my praise* ψ 109^{1}. **c.** *with sf.* in P (22 t. incl. phr. ויראת מאלהיך) Lv 19$^{14.32}$ 25$^{17.36.43}$ (H) Ex 8^{21} Jos 24^{27} (E) Dt 32^{37} (poet.) Jos 9^{23} (JE) Dt 10^{21} 31^{17} Ju 10^{10} 16$^{23.24}$ 1 S 10^{19} 2 S 10^{12} 22^{32} + (4 t. poet.) 1 K 12^{28} 20^{23} 2 K 19^{10} Chr (83 t.) ψ (62 t.) Pr 2^{17} 30^{9} Ru 1$^{15.16.16}$ Is 1^{10} 7^{13} 8$^{19.21}$ Is^{2} (29 t.) Je 5$^{4.5}$ 23^{36} 51^{5} Ez 34^{31} Dn (5 t.) Ho (12 t.) Am 2^{8} 4^{12} Jo 1$^{13.13.16}$ 2^{17} Mi 6^{8} 7^{7} Jon 1$^{5.6}$ Zp 3^{2} Na 1^{14} Zc 9^{7} 12^{5}; אלהים with sf. is also used with יהוה several hundred times (vid. יהוה).

†אֶלְדָּד† **n.pr.m.** (*God has loved*, cf. Sab. 419
ודדאל DHM$^{ZMG\ 1883,\ 15}$; v. also יְדִידְיָה) one of the
elders Nu 11$^{26.27}$; prob.=אֱלִידָד Nu 34^{21} where 449
called a prince of Benjamin.—On n.pr. with
אֵל cf. those with אָב & אָח, & esp. Nö$^{l.c.}$, v. p. 42,
& (Sab.) DHM$^{Epigr.\ Denkm.\ 88}$.

†אֶלְדָּעָה† **n.pr.m.** (*God has called?* cf. دعا 420
Ar.) son of Midian Gn 25^{4} 1 Ch 1^{33}.

†אֶלְזָבָד† **n.pr.m.** (*God has given*, cf. Θεόδω- 443
ρος, זְבַדְיָה, זְבַדִּיאֵל) **a.** one of David's band of
Gadites 1 Ch 12^{12}. **b.** a Korahite 1 Ch 26^{7}.

†אֶלְחָנָן† **n.pr.m.** (*God has been gracious,* 445

cf. Ph. בעלחנן ,אלחנן, in As. *Ba'alḫanunu* COT Gn 10^{18}) two of David's chiefs 2 S 21^{19}=1 Ch 20^{5}; 2 S 23^{24}=1 Ch 11^{26}.

446 †אֱלִיאָב **n.pr.m.** (*God is father*, cf. אֲבִיאֵל) **a.** prince of Zebulon Nu 1^{9} 2^{7} 7$^{24.29}$ 10^{16}. **b.** prince of Reuben Nu 16$^{1.12}$ 26$^{8.9}$ Dt 11^{6}. **c.** brother of David 1 S 16^{6} 17$^{13.28.28}$ 1 Ch 2^{13} 2 Ch 11^{18} (cf. אֱלִיהוּ 1 Ch 27^{18}). **d.** a Kohathite 1 Ch 6^{12}=אֱלִיאֵל v^{19} cf. אֱלִיהוּ 1 S 1^{1}. **e.** a Gadite 1 Ch 12^{9}. **f.** Levite singer 1 Ch 15$^{18.20}$ 16^{5}.

447 †אֱלִיאֵל **n.pr.m.** (*Ēl is God*, or *my God is God*) only Ch. **a.** two or three of David's chiefs 1 Ch 11$^{46.47}$ 12^{11}. **b.** chief of Manasseh 1 Ch 5^{24}. **c.** two chiefs of Benjamin 1 Ch 8$^{20.22}$. **d.** chief of the Hebronites 1 Ch 15$^{9.11}$. **e.** a chief Kohathite 1 Ch 6^{19}=אֱלִיאָב v^{12} cf. אֱלִיהוּ 1 S 1^{1}. **f.** a Levite 2 Ch 31^{13}.

448 †אֱלִיאָ֫תָה **n.pr.m.** (*God has come*) a Hemanite 1 Ch 25^{4}=אֱלִיָּתָה 1 Ch 25^{27}.

449 אֱלִידָד v. אֱלְדָּד supr. p. 44

450 †אֶלְיָדָע **n.pr.m.** (*God knows*, cf. דְּעוּאֵל, Sab. אלידע Hal ^{209}) **a.** son of David 2 S 5^{16} 1 Ch 3^{8} =בעלידע 1 Ch 14^{7} which perh. rd. here, cf. Dr^{Sm}. **b.** father of an adversary of Solomon 1 K 11^{23}. **c.** chief of Benjamin 2 Ch 17^{17}.

452 אֵלִיָּה 2 K 1^{3}+4 t.; אֵלִיָּ֫הוּ 1 K 17^{1}+62 t.; **n.pr.m.** (*Yah(u) is God*, cf. יוֹאֵל) **a.** Elijah, the great prophet of the reign of Ahab 1 K 17^{1} +65 t. K; 2 Ch 21^{12} Mal 3^{23}. **b.** Benjamite 1 Ch 8^{27}; **c.** a priest of Ezra's time Ezr 10^{21}; **c.** a son of Elam Ezr 10^{26}.

453 †אֱלִיהוּ Jb 32^{4}+3 t.; אֱלִיהוּא Jb 32^{2}+6 t.; **n.pr.m.** (*He is (my) God*) **a.** the young friend of Job Jb 32$^{2.4.5.6}$ 34^{1} 35^{1} 36^{1}. **b.** an Ephraimite, Samuel's great-grandfather 1 S 1^{1} cf. אֱלִיאָב 1 Ch 6^{12}, אֱלִיאֵל, v^{19}. **c.** chief of Manasseh 1 Ch 12^{20}. **d.** a Korahite 1 Ch 26^{7}. **e.** one of the brethren of David 1 Ch 27^{18} (cf. אֱלִיאָב 1 S 16^{6}).

455 †אֶלְיַחְבָּא **n.pr.m.** (*God hides*) one of David's chiefs 2 S 23^{32} 1 Ch 11^{33}.

456 †אֱלִיחֹ֫רֶף **n.pr.m.** (*Autumn God?* cf. Jb 29^{4}) one of Solomon's scribes 1 K 4^{3}.

458 †אֱלִימֶ֫לֶךְ (& ־מָ֑לֶךְ Ru 2^{1}) **n.pr.m.** (*God is king*, cf. מַלְכִּיאֵל) husband of Naomi Ru 1$^{2.3}$ 2^{3} 4$^{3.9}$.

460 †אֶלְיָסָף **n.pr.m.** (*God has added*) **a.** chief of Gad Nu 1^{14} 2^{14} 7$^{42.47}$ 10^{20}. **b.** chief of Gershon Nu 3^{24}.

†אֱלִיעֶ֫זֶר (־עָ֑זֶר Gn 15^{2}+) **n.pr.m.** (*God is* 461
help, cf. Ex 18^{4}; v. also אֶלְעָזָר infr., עֲזַרְאֵל, Ph. עזרבעל, בעלעזר, אשמנעזר) **a.** Abraham's steward (אֱלִיעָ֑זֶר), a Damascene Gn 15^{2}. **b.** a son of Moses Ex 18^{4} 1 Ch 23$^{15.17.17}$. **c.** Benjamite 1 Ch 7^{8}. **d.** several priests 1 Ch 15^{24} 1 Ch 26^{25} Ez 10^{18}. **e.** Reubenite 1 Ch 27^{16}. **f.** prophet in time of Jehoshaphat 2 Ch 20^{37}. **g.** Levite chief Ez 8^{16} 10^{23}. **h.** son of Harim Ezr 10^{31}.

†אֱלִיעָם **n.pr.m.** (*God is kinsman;* Ph. 463
אלעם) **a.** father of Bathsheba 2 S 11^{3}; cf. עַמִּיאֵל 1 Ch 3^{5}. **b.** one of David's heroes 2 S 23^{34} (acc. to some=**a**).

†אֱלִיפַז **n.pr.m.** (*God is fine gold?*) **a.** son 464
of Esau Gn 36$^{4.10.11.12.12.15.16}$ 1 Ch 1$^{35.36}$. **b.** friend of Job Jb 2^{11} 4^{1} 15^{1} 22^{1} 42$^{7.9}$.

†אֱלִיפָל **n.pr.m.** (*God has judged*) one of 465
David's heroes 1 Ch 11^{35} (but v. אֱלִיפֶלֶט 2 S 23^{34}).

†אֱלִיפְלֵ֫הוּ **n.pr.m.** (*may God distinguish* 466
him) one of the doorkeepers 1 Ch 15$^{18.21}$.

†אֱלִיפֶ֫לֶט (־פָּ֑לֶט 2 S 5^{16}+) **n.pr.m.** (*God is* 467
deliverance, cf. פְּלַטְיָאֵל) **a.** son of David 2 S 5^{16} 1 Ch 3$^{6.8}$ 14^{7}; =אֶלְפָּ֑לֶט 1 Ch 14^{5}. **b.** one of David's heroes 2 S 23^{34} (cf. also אֱלִיפָל 1 Ch 11^{35}). **c.** a Benjamite 1 Ch 8^{39}. **d.** one of the line of Adonikam Ezr 8^{13}. **e.** of the line of Hashum Ezr 10^{33}.

†אֱלִיצוּר **n.pr.m.** (צוּר *Rock is God*, cf. Dt 468
32^{4}; v. also צוּרִיאֵל) chief of Reuben Nu 1^{5} 2^{10} 7$^{30.35}$ 10^{18}.

†אֱלִיצָפָן **n.pr.m.** (*God has protected*, cf. Ph. 469
צפנבעל) **a.** chief of the Kohathites Nu 3^{30} 1 Ch 15^{8} 2 Ch 29^{13}; =אֶלְצָפָן Ex 6^{22} Lv 10^{4}. **b.** chief of Zebulun Nu 34^{25}.

†אֱלִיקָא **n.pr.m.** (?not in 𝔊, 1 Ch 11^{27} Dr) 470
one of David's heroes 2 S 23^{25}.

†אֶלְיָקִים **n.pr.m.** (*God sets up*, cf. Sab. 471
יקמאל, הקמאל Hal ^{615}) **a.** Hezekiah's prefect of the palace 2 K 18$^{18.26.37}$ 19^{2} Is 22^{20} 36$^{3.11.22}$ 37^{2}. **b.** son of Josiah, made king by Pharaoh 2 K 23^{34} 2 Ch 36^{4}; =יְהוֹיָקִים 2 K 24^{1} Je 1^{3} 1 Ch 3^{15}. **c.** a priest Ne 12^{41}.

†אֱלִישֶׁ֫בַע **n.pr.f.** (*God is an oath*, by which 472
one swears, cf. Is 19^{18} Am 8^{14} Zp 1^{5}) wife of Aaron Ex 6^{23}; ='Ελεισαβεθ 𝔊, cf. Lu 1^{7}.

474 †אֱלִישׁוּעַ **n.pr.m.** (*God is salvation*, cf. אֱלִישָׁע infr.; or *is opulence*, cf. אֲבִישׁוּעַ) son of David 2 S 5[15] 1 Ch 14[5].

475 †אֶלְיָשִׁיב **n.pr.m.** (*God restores*, cf. Nes[Eg 194] & Sab. תובאל DHM[ZMG 1883, 16]) **a.** a descendant of David 1 Ch 3[24]. **b.** priest of David's time 1 Ch 24[12]. **c.** high priest of Nehemiah's time Ezr 10[6] Ne 3[1.20.21.21] 12[10.10.12.23] 13[4.7.28]. **d.** a singer Ezr 10[24]. **e.** one of the line of Zattu Ezr 10[27]. **f.** one of the line of Bani Ezr 10[36].

476 †אֱלִישָׁמָע (*God has heard*, cf. יִשְׁמָעֵאל, & Sab. אלסמע, יסמעאל Hal[187, 193]) **a.** chief of Ephraim Nu 1[10] 2[18] 7[48.53] 10[22] 1 Ch 7[26]. **b.** son of David 2 S 5[16] 1 Ch 3[6.8] 14[7]. **c.** scribe of Jehoiakim Je 36[12.20.21]. **d.** one of the royal seed 2 K 25[25] Je 41[1]. **e.** a man of Judah 1 Ch 2[41]. **f.** a priest 2 Ch 17[8].

477 אֱלִישָׁע **n.pr.m.** (*God is salvation*, cf. אֱלִישׁוּעַ, Sab. יתעאל DHM[ZMG 1883, 15]) the prophet Elisha, the successor of Elijah 1 K 19[16] + 57 t. all K; Ἐλισα, Ἐλισαιε 𝔊; Ἐλισαιος Lu 4[27].

478 †אֱלִישָׁפָט **n.pr.m.** (*God has judged*, Ph. בעלשפט, שפטבעל) a captain in the time of Jehoiada 2 Ch 23[1].

448 אֱלִיָּתָה v. אֱלִיאָתָה. p. 45

486 אֶלְמוֹדָד v. sub I. אֵל. p. 38

493 †אֶלְנַעַם **n.pr.m.** (*God is pleasantness*) father of two of David's heroes 1 Ch 11[46] (not in S).

494 †אֶלְנָתָן (*God has given*, cf. נְתַנְאֵל, & As. *Ilu-iddin* Dl[Pr 207], Ph. בעליתן, יתנבעל, Palm. קסנתן, והבלת עתנתן Vog[Pal 30 & p. 31 f], Nab. והבאל, Eut[Nab 12, 1], Sab. אלוהב, והבאל DHM[ZMG 1883, 15. 361. 388] CIS[iv. 1, 1.2.6], Theodore, Diodate). **a.** the grandfather of Jehoiakim 2 K 24[8]; cf. Je 26[22] 36[12.25](?). **b.** Levites of the time of Ezra Ezr 8[16.16.16].

496 †אֶלְעָד **n.pr.m.** (*God has testified*) an Ephraimite 1 Ch 7[21].

497 †אֶלְעָדָה **n.pr.m.** (*God has adorned*, cf. עֲדִיאֵל) an Ephraimite 1 Ch 7[20].

498 †אֶלְעוּזַי **n.pr.m.** (*God is my strength* = אֶלְעֻזִּי, cf. עֻזִּיאֵל, Sab. אלעֹז (אלעז) DHM[ZMG 1883, 15]) one of the heroes of David 1 Ch 12[5].

499 אֶלְעָזָר **n.pr.m.** (*God has helped*, cf. אֱלִיעֶזֶר supr.) **a.** Eleazar the priest Ex 6[23] + (50 t. in Hex) Ju 20[28] 1 Ch 5[29.30] 6[35] 9[20] 24[1.2.3.4.4.5.6] Ezr 7. **b.** son of Abinadab 1 S 7[1]. **c.** one of David's heroes 2 S 23[9] 1 Ch 11[12]; ins. also 1 Ch 27[4] cf. Dr[Sm 280]. **d.** a Levite 1 Ch 23[21.22] 24[28]. **e.** priest of the time of Ezra Ezr 8[33] Ne 12[42]. **f.** one of the line of Parosh Ezr 10[25].

†אֶלְעָלֵא, ‖ אֶלְעָלֵה **n.pr.loc.** (*God doth* 500
ascend?) of a village in the tribe of Reuben, near Heshbon, in ruins, *el Âl* (vid. Rb[BR ii, 278]) Nu 32[3.37] Is 15[4] 16[9] Je 48[34].

†אֶלְעָשָׂה **n.pr.m.** (*God has made*, cf. עֲשָׂהאֵל, 501
יַעֲשִׂיאֵל etc.) **a.** descendant of Judah 1 Ch 2[39.40]. **b.** a Benjamite 1 Ch 8[37] 9[43]. **c.** of the line of Pashur Ezr 10[22]. **d.** son of Shaphan Je 29[3].

אֶלְפֶּלֶט v. אֱלִיפֶלֶט. p. 45 467

†אֶלְפַּעַל **n.pr.m.** (*God of doing*? cf. Ph. 508
פעלאבסת) a Benjamite 1 Ch 8[11.12.18].

אֶלְצָפָן v. אֱלִיצָפָן. p. 45 469

אֶלְקָנָה **n.pr.m.** (*God has created*, or *taken* 511
possession) **a.** father of Samuel 1 S 1–2 (8 t.) 1 Ch 6[12.19]. **b.** son of Korah Ex 6[24]. **c.** a ruler in Jerusalem in the time of Ahaz 2 Ch 28[7]. **d.** one of David's warriors 1 Ch 12[6]. **e.** several Levites (*α*) 1 Ch 6[8.10.21] (*β*) v[11.20] (*γ*) 9[16] (*δ*) 15[23].

†II. אָלָה **vb. swear, curse** (cf. I. אלה? so 422
Thes Lag[Or ii. 3])—**Qal** *Pf.* 1 K 8[31] (= 2 Ch 6[22] all Vrss Th Bö Bä Kp reading (וְ)אָלָה); אָלִית Ju 17[2]; *Inf. abs.* אָלֹה Ho 4[2]; אָלוֹת Ho 10[4]. **1.** *swear, take oath* before God 1 K 8[31] (= 2 Ch 6[22]); in covenants Ho 4[2] 10[4] (falsely). **2.** *curse* Ju 17[2]. **Hiph.** *Impf.* וַיֹּאֶל 1 S 14[24]; *Inf.* לְהַאֲלֹתוֹ 1 K 8[31] = 2 Ch 6[22] *adjure, put under oath.*

†אָלָה **n.f. oath** Gn 26[28] +; sf. אָלָתִי, אָלָתוֹ Gn 423
24[41] + (4 t.); pl. אָלוֹת Dt 29[20] + (4 t.) **1.** *oath* in testimony Lv 5[1] Nu 5[21.21] (P) Pr 29[23]; בא באלה *come into an oath* Ne 10[30]; הביא באלה *bring into an oath* Ez 17[13]; נשא אלה 1 K 8[31] (= 2 Ch 6[22]). **2.** *oath* of covenant Gn 24[41.41] 26[28] (J) Dt 29[11.13]; בזה אלה *despise an oath* Ez 16[59] 17[16.18.19]. **3.** *curse* (*a*) from God Nu 5[23] (P) Dt 29[18.19.20] 30[7] 2 Ch 34[24] Is 24[6] Je 23[10] Dn 9[11] Zc 5[3]; (*b*) from men Jb 31[30] ψ 10[7] 59[13]. **4.** *execration* in the phrase היה לאלה *become an execration* Nu 5[27] (P) Je 29[18] 42[18] 44[12].

†תַּאֲלָה, sf. תַּאֲלָתְךָ, **n.f. curse** La 3[65]. 8381

†III. [אָלָה] **vb. wail** (Aram. אֲלָא, ܐܠܐ) 421
only **Qal** *Imv.* fs. אֱלִי Jo 1[8] (v. אַלְלַי).

†אַלְיָה **n.f. fat tail** of sheep, still ac- 451
counted a delicacy in the East; (Mish. *id.* 𝔗,

אֱלִיתָא, אַלִּיתָא, etc., Ar. أَلْيَة, cf. Fl.[TWB i. 418a]) Ex 29[22] Lv 3[9] 7[3] 8[25] (all ‖ חֵלֶב); 9[19], prob. also 1 S 9[24] for הֶעָלֶיהָ v. Gei Dr (cf. Tristram[Nat. Hist. Bib. ch. vi] Ri[HWB Schafe] Smith[Dict. Bib. sheep]).

432 †אִלּוּ **conj.** (oft. in Mishnah; Aram. אִילּוּ, ܐܶܠܽܘ: from אִין, ܠܘ, and לוּ) **if, though,** only in late Heb., Ec 6[6] Est 7[4].

435 I. אֱלוּל **n.pr.** of 6th month, Aug.—Sept. Ne 6[15] (Mish. *id.*, Pal. אלול Vog[79], As. *Ululu* COT Ne 1[1], Ar. أَيْلُول, Aram. ܐܝܠܘܠ).

442 †אָלוּשׁ **n.pr.loc.** a station of Israel in the wilderness Nu 33[13.14].

444 †[אָלַח] **vb.** only **Niph.** **be corrupt morally;** *tainted* (Che ψ 14[3]) (cf. Ar أَلِخَ viii. *be confused* (of a thing), of milk, *turn sour*) *Pf.* 3 pl. נֶאֱלָחוּ ψ 14[3] 53[4]; *Pt.* נֶאֱלָח *a corrupt man* Jb 15[16].

195 אֱלַי Gn 24[39] v. אוּלַי. p. 19

473 †אֱלִישָׁה **n.pr.loc.** as *son of Javan* Gn 10[4] 1 Ch 1[7]; אִיֵּי א׳ Ez 27[7] (*Aeolis* Josephus Jer Kn; H. Derenbourg[Mélanges Graux, 235 f (Eng. trans. Hbr. Oct. 1887, 7)]; *Hellas* 𝔗[Jon] etc., Len[Orig. ii. 2. 34 f]; *Italy*, with *Sicily*, cf. מְדִינַת אִיטַלְיָא 𝔗 Ezek, Di Gn 10[4]; *Carthage* = Elissa, Sta[De Populo Javan, 8 f]; E. Meyer[Gesch. i. § 282]; decision difficult; last view very attractive).

I. [אלל] (*to be weak* or *insufficient*, assumed in Thes as root of אֱלִיל (as also of אַל): cf. Ar. أَلَّا *to fail* in a thing).

434 †II. אֱלוּל Je 14[14] Kt, i.q. אֱלִיל, q.v. below

457 †אֱלִיל **n.m.** (etym. uncertain: most prob. akin to Syr. ܠܝܠܐ *weak, feeble, poor;* perh. also in usage [cf. **b**] felt to suggest אַל *not;* cf. Che on Is 2[8]) *insufficiency, worthlessness.* **a.** Zc 11[17] רֹעִי הָאֱלִיל the shepherd of *worthlessness* = the worthless shepherd, Jb 13[4] רֹפְאֵי אֱלִל *worthless* physicians (‖ טֹפְלֵי־שֶׁקֶר), Je 14[14] Qr concr. *a thing of nought* (uttered by prophets), but here קֶסֶם אֱלִיל a *worthless* divin. (‖ חֲזוֹן שֶׁקֶר, תַּרְמִית לִבָּם) should perh. be read (cf. Gf). **b.** esp. pl. אֱלִילִים concr. *worthless gods, idols* (cf. הֲבָלִים) (*possibly* orig. an indep. word = *gods*, cf. Sab. אלאלת, & v. Nö[SBAk 1882, p. 1191], but even if so, associated by the prophets with idea of worthlessness, & used by them in iron. contrast with אֱלֹהִים, אֵלִים) Lv 19[4] (not to be *made*) 26[1] (both H), Is 2[8.18.20.20] (of silver & gold), 10[10] מַמְלְכוֹת הָאֱלִיל (coll.) kingdoms of *idolatrous worthlessness,* v[11] 19[1.3] (of Egypt) 31[7.7] Ez 30[13] (Egypt), Hb 2[18] א׳ אִלְּמִים *dumb* idols, ψ 96[5] (= 1 Ch 16[26]) all the gods of the nations are א׳ *vain, worthless gods* 97[7].

II. אלל (√ assumed for following words).

†אַלָּה **n.f.** oak (cf. אַלּוֹן, but 𝔊 here τερέμινθος) only Jos 24[26] *the oak which is in the sanctuary of* י׳; rd. however perh. אֵלָה, *terebinth* (v. 1. אֵלָה). 427

†אַלּוֹן **n.m.**[Gn 35, 8] **oak** (𝔊 βάλανος, δρῦς, etc.) 437
—א׳ abs. Gn 35[8]+; cstr. *ib.*; pl. אַלּוֹנִים Am 2[9] Ez 27[6]; cstr. אַלּוֹנֵי Is 2[13] Zc 11[12];—as marking grave of Deborah, Rebekah's nurse Gn 35[8] (E);
whence called *oak of weeping,* א׳ בָּכוּת *ib.* (v. Di 439
ad loc., & sub אֵלוֹן p. 18); elsewhere only in prophets; as marking illicit shrines Ho 4[13] (‖ לִבְנֶה, אֵלָה); as felled Is 6[13] (in sim.; ‖ אֵלָה); as furnishing material for making idols Is 44[14] (‖ אֶרֶז, תִּרְזָה, אֹרֶן); as sim. for strength (חסן) Am 2[9]; also אַלּוֹנֵי הַבָּשָׁן Is 2[13] (as lofty & majestic), cf. Ez 27[6] (as strong, for making oars); Zc 11[2], metaph. of prominent men.

†אַלּוֹן **n.pr.m.** (*oak*) a Simeonite 1 Ch 4[37] (on Jos 19[33] v. אֵלוֹן p. 18). 438

†אַלַּמֶּלֶךְ **n.pr.loc.** in Asher (= אַלַּת מֶלֶךְ? so Thes MV) Jos 19[26] (Baer אַלְּמֶ׳). 487

†אַלְלַי **interj.** (prob. onomatop.: cf. أَلَّ, אָלָה, ܝܠܠ *to wail,* አሌ: *woe!* Di[718]) **alas! woe!** sq. לִי *to me* Mi 7[1] Jb 10[15]. 480

†[אָלַם] **vb.** bind (perh. cf. As. [*alāmu*], *almattu, fortress* Dl in Zim[BP 114] & in BD Ezek.[xi]; Ar. أَلِمَ *be in pain,* Aram. ܐܠܡ *retain* anger). 481
Niph. (*be bound* =) **be dumb**, *Pf.* 3 fs. נֶאֱלָמָה Is 53[7]; וְנֶאֱלַמְתָּ Ez 3[26], etc.; *Impf.* 2 ms. תֵּאָלֵם Ez 24[27]; 3 fpl. תֵּאָלַמְנָה ψ 31[19].—**1.** *be dumb,* i.e. silent ψ 39[3] (‖ הֶחֱשֵׁיתִי, נ׳ דוּמִיָּה); cf. v[10] (‖ לֹא אֶפְתַּח־פִּי); sim. of sheep Is 53[7] (‖ *id.*); *be dumb,* i.e. unable to speak Ez 3[26] (result of וּלְשׁוֹנְךָ אַדְבִּיק אֶל־חִכֶּךָ) cf. 24[27] יִפָּתַח פִּיךָ ...; 33[22] וַיִּפָּתַח פִּי וְלֹא נֶאֱלַמְתִּי עוֹד; וּתְדַבֵּר וְלֹא תֵאָלֵם עוֹד; also Dn 10[15] (cf. v[16]); *be made dumb* subj. שִׂפְתֵי שָׁקֶר *lying lips* ψ 31[19] (‖ יִדְּמוּ לִשְׁאוֹל v[18]).

Pi. *Pt. bind* Gn 37[7] (E) מְאַלְּמִים אֲלֻמִּים *binding sheaves.*

485 †[אֲלֻמָּה] **n.f. sheaf**, in Joseph's dream Gn 37[7.7.7.7] (E) sq. sf. אֲלֻמָּתִי, pl. אֲלֻמִּים, אֲלֻמֹּתֵיכֶם; also ψ 126[6] אֲלֻמֹּתָיו (in fig. of ret. fr. captivity).

482 †אֵלֶם **n.[m.] silence**, ψ 56[1] (title) vid. Ol De, in name of melody עַל־יוֹנַת אֵלֶם רְחֹקִים; also ψ 58[2] (=adv. *in silence*?) but rd. אֵל(ִי)ם Ol De Che, etc.

483 †אִלֵּם **adj. dumb**, unable to speak; Ex 4[11] מִי שָׂם פֶּה לָאָדָם אוֹ מִי יָשׂוּם אִלֵּם; Is 56[10] כְּלָבִים אִלְּמִים fig. of false proph.; of idols אֱלִילִים א׳ Hb 2[8]; as subst. Pr 31[8] ψ 38[14] Is 35[6].

199 אֻלָם v. III. אוּלָם p. 19.

361 אֵלָם v. אֵילָם sub II. אול. p. 19

488 †אַלְמָן **adj. forsaken**, of Israel Je 51[5] (sq. מֵאֱלֹהִים).

489 †אַלְמֹן **n.[m.] widowhood**, fig. of Babylon Is 47[9] (‖ שְׁכוֹל, cf. v[9]; vid. Ba[NB 59]).

490 †אַלְמָנָה [54] **n.f. widow** (Mish. *id.*, As. *almattu* Dl in Zim[BP 114])—א׳ Gn 38[11]+; no cstr.; pl. אַלְמָנוֹת Ex 22[23]+; pl. sf. אַלְמְנוֹתָיו Jb 27[15], etc.—*widow* 1 K 17[20]; אִשָּׁה א׳ 2 S 14[5] (‖ וַיָּמָת אִישִׁי) 1 K 7[14] 11[26] 17[9.10]; Gn 38[11] (J; living in father's house) cf. Lv 22[13] (H; ‖ גְּרוּשָׁה); 21[14] (H), where widow forbidden as wife of h.p., like חֲלָלָה, גְּרוּשָׁה, זֹנָה cf. Ez 44[22.22.22] (*id.* of all priests, exc. widow of priest); Nu 30[10] (P; of widow's vow, ‖ גְּרוּשָׁה); נְשֵׁיכֶם אַלְמָנוֹת = ye shall be slain Ex 22[23] (‖ בְּנֵיכֶם יְתֹמִים) cf. ψ 109[9] Je 15[8] 18[21] Ez 22[25], also La 5[3] (sim.); of those snatched away by pestilence אַלְמְנוֹתָיו לֹא תִבְכֶּינָה Jb 27[15]; by sword, *id.*, ψ 78[64]; 𝔊 We rd. אַלְמְנוּת חַיּוּת 2 S 20[3] (v. אַלְמָנוּת infr.) of imprisoned concubines; fig. of Jerusalem La 1[1]; Babylon Is 47[8]; esp. widow as helpless, exposed to oppression & harsh treatment (oft. ‖ יָתוֹם, & גֵּר); Is 1[23] 10[2] Jb 22[9] 24[3] 31[16] ψ 94[6] Mal 3[5]; harshness forbidden, & care for them enjoined Ex 22[21] (E) Dt 14[29] 16[11.14] 24[17.19.20.21] 26[12.13] 27[19] Is 1[17] Je 7[6] 22[3] Zc 7[10], cf. Jb 29[13]; under esp. care of God Dt 10[18] Je 49[11] Pr 15[25] ψ 68[6] 146[9]; once of severity of judgment in not sparing widow Is 9[16]. (אַל׳ Is 13[22] vid. sub אַרְמוֹן; Ez 19[7] vid. *ib.* & also sub מעון.)

491 †[אַלְמָנוּת] **n.f. widowhood** (Mish. *id.*, Ph. אלמת) sf. בִּגְדֵי אַלְמְנוּתָהּ *her widow's garments* Gn 38[14.19]; cstr. אַלְמְנוּת חַיּוּת 2 S 20[3] (of David's imprisoned concubines; but text impossible; 𝔊 We אַלְמָנוֹת חַיּוֹת, cf. Dr; Klo thinks gloss); fig. of Jerusalem Is 54[4] אַלְמְנוּתַיִךְ.

†אַלְמֹנִי **adj. some one, a certain** (name 492
unspoken); מְקוֹם פְּלֹנִי א׳ 1 S 21[3] 2 K 6[8]; פ׳ א׳ alone, of person, = *such-an-one, so-and-so* Ru 4[1].

†אֶלָּסָר **n.pr.loc. Ellasar** Gn 14[1.9] (= Bab. 495
Larsa, mod. *Senkereh*, c. 28 miles NE. from Ur; cf. Loft[CS 240 f] Dl[Pa 223 f] Tiele[Gesch. i. 86], COT[ad loc.]).

†I. [אָלַף] **vb. learn** (Ar. أَلِفَ *keep*, 502
cleave to, become familiar with; Aram. אֲלַף, ܝܠܦ, *learn*, ܐܠܦ, Pa *teach*). **Qal** *Impf.* 2 ms. תֶּאֱלַף אֹרְחֹתָו Pr 22[25]; **Pi. teach**, sq. acc. יְאַלֵּף פִּיךָ Jb 15[5] (subj. עֲוֹנְךָ); so *Pt.* מַלְּפֵנוּ (for מְאַל׳ Sta[§111, 3] Kö[I. 388] Ge[§68 fin.], cf. Ew[§73 b]) Jb 35[11]; sq. 2 acc. אֲאַלֶּפְךָ חָכְמָה Jb 33[33].

†I. [אֶלֶף] **n.m.** [ψ 8, 8]; only pl. **cattle** 504
(Ph. אלף, As. *alpu*, COT[Gloss])—אֲלָפִים Pr 14[4] Is 30[24] used in tillage; subject to man ψ 8[8] (‖ צֹנֶה); their increase שְׁגַר אֲלָפֶיךָ a blessing Dt 7[13] 28[4.18.51] (‖ all עַשְׁתְּרֹת צֹאנֶךָ).

I. אַלּוּף **adj. tame**—א׳ abs. Mi 7[5]+; 441
cstr. Pr 2[17]+; sf. אַלּוּפִי ψ 55[14]; pl. אַלֻּפִים Je 13[21]; sf. אַלּוּפֵינוּ ψ 144[14], etc.;—**1.** *tame, docile*, כֶּבֶשׂ אַלּוּף *a docile* (gentle) *lamb* Je 11[19]. **2. n.m.** *friend, intimate* ψ 55[14] (‖ מְיֻדָּע) Mi 7[5] (‖ רֵעַ) Pr 16[28] 17[9] Je 13[21]; of a woman's husband א׳ נְעוּרֶיהָ Pr 2[17]; fig. of י׳ as husband of Judah, *id.*, Je 3[4]. **3.** i.q. I. אֶלֶף; אַלּוּפֵינוּ מְסֻבָּלִים ψ 144[14] (i.e. cows).

II. אֶלֶף **n.m.** [Ju 6, 15] **thousand** (אלף MI, SI, 503, 505
Sab. DHM[ZMG 1875, 615]; Ar. أَلْفٌ, Aram. ܐܠܦܐ, אלפיא, אֲלַף)—א׳ (אָ׳) Gn 20[16]+; sf. אַלְפִּי †Ju 6[15]; du. אַלְפַּיִם Nu 4[36]+; pl. אֲלָפִים Ex 18[21]+; cstr. אַלְפֵי Ex 32[28]+; אֲלָפֶיךָ Dt 7[13]+2 t.; אֲלָפָיו Qr 1 S 18[7]+2 t. (Kt ־פו)—*a thousand*. **1.** numeral: **a.** used with noun alone; mostly before noun Nu 35[4] Jos 7[3] Ne 3[13] 1 Ch 18[4]+; after noun (late) 1 Ch 12[35]+6 t. Ch Ezr Ne; א׳ בָּאַמָּה Nu 35[5.5.5.5] Ez 47[3] (del. Co); the noun always pl. when preceding, sometimes when following, 1 S 25[2] 1 K 3[4] 2 K 18[23] = Is 36[8] 2 Ch 30[24] ψ 90[4] Jb 42[12] Ec 6[6]; elsewh. sg. אִישׁ Ju 9[49] 15[15.16] Jos 7[3]+; אַמָּה Nu 35[4]+ (so SI); דּוֹר Dt 7[9]+, cf. 1 Ch 18[4] 19[6] 2 K 15[19] Jb 42[12] Ct 4[4] Is 7[23], noun sometimes coll.; א׳ pl. cstr. Mi 6[7] ψ 119[72] Gn 24[60]; noun not

expr. (or not fully) Gn 20[16] Nu 31[5.6]+; distrib. אֶלֶף . . . אֶלֶף Nu 31[4]; multipl. Dt 1[11] א׳ פְּעָמִים; indef. for great no. (pl.) Ex 20[6] 34[7] Dt 5[10] Je 32[18], (sg.) Dt 32[30] Ec 6[6]+. **b.** א׳ + other num. usually precedes it Ex 38[25]+ oft.; but foll. רִבּוֹא Ezr 2[64]+2 t.; it follows also smaller no. Nu 3[50] 1 K 5[12] (so SI); the noun foll. in sg. Ex 28[25]+8 t.; pl. 2 S 8[4]+2 t.; noun precedes, in pl. (late) Dn 12[12] +2 t.; noun not expr. Ex 38[28]+ oft. **c.** א׳ × other no. always foll. Ex 12[37]+; usual order is *no.* × א׳ + *additional no.* (if any) + *noun* (if expr.) Nu 31[52] Ju 20[35] cf. Ex 12[37] 2 K 3[4.4]+; less oft. *noun* + *no.* × א׳ Nu 31[33] 1 K 8[63]+; (other combin. v. Ex 38[26] Nu 26[51] 31[32] Ex 48[30] 1 Ch 29[7] etc.); א׳ usually sg. Nu 11[21]+; exc. after units, where pl. abs. Nu 1[46] Ju 20[34]+ (so MI); seld. pl. cstr. Ex 32[28] Ju 4[10] Jb 1[3.3]; (noun mostly sg. when foll. Ju 4[10] 1 K 12[21]+, yet pl. Jos 4[13] 1 S 13[5]+; when preceding it is pl. 1 Ch 5[21]+, or coll. Nu 31[33] 1 S 25[2] 1 K 8[63] 2 Ch 7[5]+); אֶלֶף אֲלָפִים 1 Ch 21[5] 22[14] 2 Ch 14[8]; אַלְפֵי שִׁנְאָן ψ 68[18], cf. שִׁנְאָן; בְּהַרְרֵי אָלֶף ψ 50[10], rd. אֵל cf. ψ 36[7], Ol Bi Che; yet v. Hup De.—*Note.* 10,000 = עֲשֶׂרֶת אֲלָפִים etc. Ju 1[4] 3[29] 1 K 5[28] 1 Ch 29[7]+; less oft. רִבּוֹ, רְבָבָה etc. q.v. **2.** *a thousand*, a company of 1000 men, as united under one superior, or leader, hence שַׂר א׳ (שָׂרֵי) Ex 18[21.25] cf. Nu 31[14]+; cf. רָאשֵׁי א׳ יִשְׂרָאֵל Nu 1[16] 10[4] Jos 22[21.30] & v. infr.; cf. also 1 S 29[2]; esp. *family*, etc. Ju 6[15] 1 S 10[19] (|| שֵׁבֶט & cf. מִשְׁפַּחַת v[21]); cf. Mi 5[2];—Nu 10[36] (רִבְבוֹת אַלְפֵי יִשְׂרָאֵל) 31[5] Jos 22[14] 1 S 23[23] apparently shew transit. to this technical use.

507 III. אֶ֫לֶף **n.pr.loc.** city in Benj., הָא׳ Jos 18[28]; perh. *Lifta* NW. fr. Jerus. Survey[iii. 18] (cf. II. אֶלֶף **2** for prob. meaning).

441 II. אַלּוּף **n.m.** [1 Ch 1, 51] **chief, chiliarch** (denom. fr. II. אֶלֶף v. Di Gn 36[15])—א׳ abs. Gn 36[15]+; pl. cstr. אַלּוּפֵי (אַלֻּפֵי) Ex 15[15]+; sf. אַלּוּפֵיהֶם Gn 36[19.30]—*chief* (tribal) of Edom Gn 36[15 (5 t.)]+38 t. Gn 36 (P); Ex 15[15] (E) 1 Ch 1[51 (4 t.)] +9 t.; of Judah Zc 12[5.6]; so אַלֻּף 9[7] (in sim.)

509 †[אָלַץ] **vb. Pi.** urge (Aram. ܐܠܨ, Sam. ...) 3 fs. וַתְּאַלְצֵהוּ Ju 16[6] (|| הֵצִיקָה לּוֹ בִדְבָרֶיהָ).

510 אַלְקוּם v. I. אַל. p. 39

512 †אֶלְקֹשִׁי **adj.gent.** c. art. Nahum the **Elkoshite** Na 1[1] (perhaps = *from Elkosh*, but locality unknown; identified by Jer[Comm.] with a village *Elcesi* in Galilee; cf. also Capernaum (= כְּפַר נַחוּם?); others (improbably) with an Elkosh on E. bank of Tigris, near Mosul).

†אֶלְתְּקֵה, אֶלְתְּקֵא **n.pr.loc.** Levitical city 514
in the tribe of Dan, between Ekron & Timna, As. *Altaku* (COT) Jos 19[44] 21[23].

†אֶלְתְּקֹן **n.pr.loc.** a city in the tribe of 515
Judah north of Hebron Jos 15[59].

אִם **conj.** (= Aram. אִן *if* [and in אִלָּא, אֶלָּא = 518
אִן לָא *if not, except*], Ar. إِنْ *if* [and in إِلَّا = إِنْ لَا *if not, except*], Eth. እመ: (*ĕmma*) *if* = אִם + מָה (إِنْ + مَا) [and in አላ: (*allâ*) *if not, but*], As. *umma*; also in Ar. أَمْ 'An ?' = הַאִם, cf. הַאִם: v. Nö[M p. 208, ZMG 1886, p. 739]; W AG i. § 367 e)

1. hypoth. part. if. **a.** *construction* (v. more fully Dr[§ 136-138, 143] Friedrich[Die Hebr. Condit. sätze 1884]): (1) with **impf.** (continued by pff. & waw consec.; apod. usually begins with pf. & waw consec. or bare impf.; or, if necess., with imper. or juss.) (*a*) of *future* time: Gn 18[26] אִם־אֶמְצָא if I shall find 50 righteous in Sodom, וְנָשָׂאתִי I will pardon, etc., 24[8] 32[9] Dt 19[8 f.] 1 K 1[52 b] 6[12] ψ 89[31-33]; Gn 42[37] Ju 13[16] 1 K 1[52 a] ψ 132[12]. (*b*) of *past* time (rare, but classical): Gn 31[8] אִם יֹאמַר *if ever* he said ... וְיָלְדוּ *then* they *used to* bear, etc., Ex 40[37]; & in the protestations Jb 31[7.13.16.25] etc. (alternating with pff., v. infr., & with jussives in apod.) (*c*) assuming a purely imaginary case (with impf. in both clauses, like the double opt. in Greek), *if, though:* Gn 13[16] so that אִם־יוּכַל *if* a man *were* able to number the stars, thy seed also יִמָּנֶה *might* be numbered, Nu 22[18] Is 1[18] אִם־יִהְיוּ ח׳ כַּשָּׁנִים יַלְבִּינוּ *though* your sins *were* as scarlet, they *should* become white as snow, Am 9[2-4] אִם־יַחְתְּרוּ *though* they *were* to dig into Sheôl, from thence תִּקָּחֵם *would* my hand fetch them, ψ 27[3] 139[8]+. (2) with **pt.** (expressing either a present process, or an approaching future: apod. as 1 *a*) Gn 24[42.49] Ju 6[36] 9[15] 11[9] אִם מְשִׁיבִים אַתֶּם if ye are going to bring me back ... וְנָתַן י׳ then י׳ will, etc.; similarly with יֵשׁ or אֵין Gn 44[26] Ex 22[2] 1 S 20[8] 23[23]; & with no explicit copula Dt 22[2] 25[2] Lv 1[3.14], etc. (3) with **perf.** (*a*) of *fut.* or *pres.* time (continued by pff. & waw consec., apod. as 1 *a*) Gn 43[9] אִם־לֹא הֲבִיאֹתִיו אֵלֶיךָ וְהִצַּגְתִּיו לְפָנֶיךָ if I do not bring him back (si eum non reduxero) and set him before thee, I will be guilty for ever, 47[6] *if* thou *knowest* that there are men of worth among them וְשַׂמְתָּם then make them, etc., Ju 16[17] 2 S 15[33] 2 K 7[4] ψ 41[7] 94[18] Jb 7[4] 9[30 f.] 10[14] אִם חָטָאתִי וּשְׁמַרְתָּנִי if I sin, thou watchest me. On אִם־נָא Gn 18[3] al. v. נָא. (*b*) of *past* time, whether (*α*) in actual fact, or (*β*) in an assumed case (the pf. is here continued by the *impf.* and waw consec.; apod. begins as before). (*a*) Ju 9$^{16-19}$ אִם ... עֲשִׂיתֶם *if ye have done* honestly וַתַּמְלִיכוּ *and have made* Abimelech king..., 1 S 26^{19}; esp. in protestations, as ψ 7^{4} אִם עָשִׂיתִי זאת *if I have* done this..., let the enemy pursue my soul, etc. Je 33$^{25f.}$ Jb 31$^{5f.9}$, etc. (*b*) Nu 5^{27} *if she have* defiled herself וַתִּמְעֹל *and been* faithless, וּבָאוּ *then shall* they come, etc., 15^{24} 35$^{22-24}$. (*c*) with bare pf. in apod., in sense of *If ... had...*, only Dt 32^{30} אִם־לֹא כִּי *were* it *not that...*, ψ 73^{15}. (לוּ is more usual in such cases.) (4) with **inf.** once (si vera l.) Jb 9^{27} אִם אָמְרִי = if I say (lit. if (there is) my saying).—Note that the vb. following אִם is often strengthened by the inf. abs., as Ex 15^{26} 19^{5} 21^{5} 22$^{3.12.16.22}$ Ju 11^{30} 14^{12} 16^{11} etc.; cf. Dr$^{Sm\ i.\ 20,\ 6}$.

b. *Special uses:* (1) repeated אִם ... אִם *whether ... or* (sive ... sive) Ex 19^{13} Dt 18^{3} 2 S 15^{21}; similarly אִם ... וְאִם Gn 31^{52} Je 42^{6} Ez 2^{5} Ec 11^{3} 12^{14} (cf. ܐܶܢ ... ܐܶܢ, ܐܶܢ ... ܐܶܢ PS^{250}; إِمَّا ... وَإِمَّا & إِنْ ... وَإِنْ).

(2) After an oath (expressed, or merely implied) אִם (the formula of imprecation being omitted) becomes an emph. negative, and אִם־לֹא an emph. affirmative: 2 S 11^{11} by thy life אִם־אֶעֱשֶׂה אֶת־הַדָּבָר הַזֶּה (may God bring all manner of evil upon me) *if* I do this thing! = *surely I will not* do this thing! (cf. the full phrases in 1 S 3^{17} 2 K 6^{31}) Gn 14^{23} 42^{15} Nu 14^{23} 1 S 3^{14} 19^{6} 2 K 2^{2} 3^{14} & oft.; Is 22^{14} ψ 89^{36} 95^{11} Jb 6^{28}; אִם־לֹא Nu 14^{28} Jos 14^{9} 1 K 20^{23} 2 K 9^{26} Is 5^{9} 14^{24} Je 15^{11} 49^{20} Jb 1^{11} + esp. Ez; after a neg. clause, emphasizing a contrasted idea, Gn 24^{38} (where the expl. by Aram. אֶלָּא is not supported by Heb. usage), cf. Je 22^{6}. Repeated, אִם ... וְאִם 2 S 20^{20} 2 K 3^{14} Is 62^{8} Je 38^{16}; Ez 14^{16}. In adjurations (with 2nd or 3rd ps.) = *that not* Gn 21^{23} 26^{29} 31^{50} 1 S 24^{22} 1 K 1^{51} Ct 2^{7} 3^{5} +. Of past or present time: 1 S 25^{34} as י׳ liveth (I say) that, unless thou hadst hastened..., כִּי אִם נוֹתַר that *surely there had not been* left...! 17^{55} as thy soul liveth אִם־יָדָעְתִּי *if* I know it! 1 K 17^{12} 18^{10}—both אִם־יֵשׁ (כִּי) here merely introduces the fact sworn to, & need not be translated; so 2 S 3^{35}: v. כִּי); ψ 121^{2} אִם־לֹא (after a neg. clause: cf. supr. Gn 24^{38}). Cf. Str^{§90}.

(3) Part. of wishing, *if but...! oh that...!* (rare) ψ 81^{9} *If thou wouldest* hearken to me! 95^{7} 139^{19} Pr 24^{11}. Cf. Ex 32^{32}. With an imv. (si vera l.) Jb 34^{16} וְאִם־בִּינָה; and with an anacoluthon, Gn 23^{13} (P) אִם־אַתָּה לוּ שְׁמָעֵנִי *if* thou!—oh that thou wouldst hear me!

(4) Nearly = *when*—with the pf.: (*a*) of past, Gn 38^{9} Nu 21^{9} וְהָיָה אִם־נָשַׁךְ ... וְרָאָה and it used to be, *if* or *when* a serpent had bitten a man, that he would look, etc., Ju 6^{3} ψ 78^{34} (v. Dr$^{§136\ \delta\ Obs.}$); Am 7^{2}. (*b*) of pres. or fut., Is 4^{4} אִם רָחַץ *when* the Lord shall have washed, 24^{13} 28^{25}; cf. Nu 36^{4} (with the impf.)

c. Compounded with other particles:—(*a*) בִּלְתִּי אִם *except if, except*, †Gn 47^{18} Ju 7^{14} Am 3$^{3.4}$. (β) הֲלוֹא אִם †2 K 20^{19} (for which Is 39^{7} has simply כִּי), perh. *Is it not* (good), *if...?* (De Di). (γ) כִּי־אִם, q.v. (δ) עַד אִם †Gn 24$^{19.33}$ Is 30^{17} Ru 2^{21}, & עַד אֲשֶׁר אִם †Gn 28^{15} Nu 32^{17} Is 6^{11}, *until*, prop. *until if* or *when*. (ε) רַק אִם *if only* (v. sub רַק). אִם־לֹא in Ez 3^{6b} is very difficult. The Vrss render *If I had sent*, etc., implying לֹא for אִם־לֹא (for Ew's אִלּוּ = אִם־לֹא, q.v., is precarious): Ges Hi Co 'but (אִם־לֹא after a neg., cf. supr. Gn 24^{38} ψ 131^{2}) unto *them* (Isr.) have I sent thee: *they* can understand thee' (but *understand* is a dub. rendering of שָׁמַע אֶל).

2. Interrog. part. a. in direct qu.: (*a*) alone (not freq. and usually = *Num?* expecting the answer *No*, esp. in a rhet. style): Gn 38^{17} 1 K 1^{27}; Ju 5^{8} מָגֵן אִם־יֵרָאֶה וָרֹמַח *was* there a shield to be seen or a spear...? Is 29^{16}; and repeated Am 3^{6} Je 48^{27} Jb 6^{12}. (*b*) more freq. in disjunctive interrogation: (*a*) הֲ ... אִם, expressing a real alternative Jos 5^{13} הֲלָנוּ אַתָּה אִם־לְצָרֵינוּ *art* thou for us, or for our enemies? Ju 9^{2} 1 K 22$^{6.15}$: more oft. expressing a merely formal alternative, esp. in poetry (a rhetorical *Num?*) Gn 37^{8} Nu 11$^{12.22}$ Ju 11^{25b} 2 S 19^{36} Is 10^{15} 66^{8} Je 3^{5} Hb 3^{8} ψ 77^{10} 78^{20} Jb 4^{17} 6$^{5.6}$ 10$^{4.5}$ 11^{7} etc. (β) הֲ ... וְאִם (rarer than הֲ ... אִם, but similar in use) 2 S 24^{13} (a real alt.); Is 49^{24} 50^{2} Je 5^{9} (v^{29} אִם) 14^{22} Jo 1^{2} 4^{4} Jb 8^{3} 11^{2} 21^{4} 22^{3} 34^{17} 40$^{8f.}$ (formal); Gn 17^{17} P (with an anacol.) וְאִם־שָׂרָה הֲבַת־תִּשְׁעִים שָׁנָה תֵּלֵד shall a child...? *or* Sarah,—shall she that is 90 years old bear? Pr 27^{24} (וְאִם after neg. clause). **b.** in oblique interrogation, *if, whether:* (*a*) alone, after verbs of seeing, inquiring, etc. 2 K 1^{2} Je 5^{1} 30^{6} Mal 3^{10} ψ 139^{24} Ct 7^{13} La 1^{12} Ezr 2^{59}; once מִי יוֹדֵעַ אִם *who knoweth if...?* i.e. (like *haud scio an*) *perhaps* Est 4^{14} (older syn. מִי יוֹדֵעַ alone: see 2 S 12^{22} Jo 2^{14} Jon 3^{9}). (*b*) disjunctively הֲ ... אִם Gn 27^{21} Nu 13$^{18-20}$; so אִם ... וְאִם Jos 24^{15}. **c.** compounded with הֲ, הַאִם †Nu 17^{28} הַאִם תַּמְנוּ לִגְוֹעַ prob. an emph. *Num? Shall we ever* have finished dying? Jb 6^{13} difficult: perh. *Is it* that my help is not in me? (a forcible means of expressing that that which might be thought impossible is nevertheless the case); Hi as an aposiop., If my help is not in me (am I still to wait)? (The view that הַאִם = הֲלֹא *nonne?* is inconsistent with the fact that אִם in a question has regularly the force of *Num?*)

517 **אֵם** v. אמם. below

520-22 **אַמָּה, אֻמָּה** v. אמם. p. 52

אמה (assumed as √ of foll., which however prob. bilit. cf. Sta[§ 188]; vid. also Lag[BN 82]).

519 †**אָמָה** **n.f. maid, handmaid** (Ph. אמת, Ar. أَمَةٌ, Sab. אמת in n.pr. Sab.Denkm.[20], Aram. ܐܡܬܐ, As. *amtu* Zim[BP 67])—א׳ abs. Gn 21[10]+; sf. אֲמָתִי Gn 30[3]+, etc.; pl. abs. אֲמָהֹת Gn 31[33] 2 S 6[22]; cstr. אַמְהוֹת 2 S 6[20]; אַמְהֹתַי Jb 19[5] etc. —*maid, handmaid.* **1.** lit. *maidservant* (= שִׁפְחָה q.v., wh. however sometimes more servile; rarely P in Hex) Gn 30[3] 31[33] (|| שִׁפְחָה 29[24.29] P 30[4f.] J etc.) Ex 2[5] (all E); 2 S 6[20.22] Jb 19[15] Na 2[8] (sf. refers to mistress, exc. Jb 19[15] cf. 2 S 6[20.22]); in legisl. (|| עֶבֶד) Ex 20[10.17] 21[20.26.27.32] (all E) Lv 25[6.44.44] (H) Dt 5[14.14.18] 12[12.18] 15[17 (cf. v. 12)] 16[11.14]; cf. also Jb 31[13] Ezr 2[65] Ne 7[67]; applied to *concubine* (sf. of master) Gn 20[17] 21[12] Ex 23[12] (all E) Ju 9[18] 19[19]; also Gn 21[10.10.13] (16[1 f.] P שִׁפְחָה q.v.) Ex 21[7] (all E), vid. on this Sta[Gesch i. p. 380]. **2.** fig. in address, אֲמָתְךָ etc., referring to speaker, in token of humility; Ru 3[9.9] (|| שפחה 2[13]) 1 S 1[16] (|| *id.* v[18]) 25[24.24.25.28.31.41] (|| *id.* v[27]) 2 S 14[15.16] (|| *id.* v[6.7.12.15.17.19]); 20[17]; 1 K 1[13.17] 3[20]; in addressing God (never שפחה) 1 S 1[11.11.11], cf. בֶּן־א׳ ψ 86[16] 116[16].

528 †I. **אָמוֹן** **n.pr. Amon**, an Egyptian god Na 3[8] Je 46[25], comp. by Greeks with Zeus (Herod.[ii. 42]; Diod.[i. 13]), Ἀμμῶν. He was originally the local deity of Thebes (=נֹא, called נֹא אָמוֹן Na 3[8], cf. א׳ מִנֹּא Je 46[25]), but subsequently became the supreme god of the Egyptian Pantheon, the successor of the sun-god *Ra* and so-called *Amon Ra.* He was the secret god, who hid himself and was difficult to find (Amon= concealment, hidden); v. Rawl.[Hist. Anc. Egypt, i. 322] Ebers Ri[HWB]. (II. III. אָמוֹן v. p. 54.)

526, 532 †**אָמִי** **n.pr.m.** Ezr 2[57] = III. אָמוֹן Ne 7[59].

535 †[**אָמַל**] **vb. be weak, languish** (cf. Ar. أَمَّلَ *hope, expect*). **Qal** *Pt.* pass. f. מָה אֲמֻלָה לִבָּתֵךְ *how weak is thy heart!* Ez 16[30] (but < Co מַה־לִּי וְלִבְרִיתֵךְ); **Pu'l.** *Pf.* אֻמְלַל Jo 1[10]+; אֻמְלְלָה Is 33[9]+; אֻמְלְלוּ Je 14[2] etc.;—*be* or *grow feeble, languish;* of loss of fertility (woman) 1 S 2[5] Je 15[9]; of fisherman whose trade fails Is 19[8] (|| אבל, אנה); in genl. of inhab. of smitten land Ho 4[3] (|| תֶּאֱבַל הָאָרֶץ); Is 24[4] cf. infr. usually subj. inanim., personif.; שַׁדְמוֹת חֶשְׁבּוֹן Is 16[8]; cf. Na 1[4.4]; תֵּבֵל Is 24[4] (|| אבל, נבל); אֶרֶץ 33[9] (|| אבל); subj. גֶּפֶן Is 24[7] (|| אָבַל תִּירוֹשׁ); יִצְהָר Jo 1[10] (|| שדד, אבל, הוביש; kindred subj.); תְּאֵנָה v[12] (|| הַגֶּפֶן הוֹבִישָׁה); שְׁעָרִים Je 14[2] (|| אָבְלָה יְהוּדָה); cf. La 2[8] וַיַּאֲבֶל־חֵל וְחוֹמָה יַחְדָּו אֻמְלָלוּ.

†[**אֻמְלָל**] **adj. feeble** (Mish. *id.*; on formation cf. Ew[§ 157 b] Sta[§ 232]); הַיְּהוּדִים הָאֲמֵלָלִים Ne 3[34]. 536

†**אֻמְלַל** **adj.** id. (Ew[ib.] Sta[§ 230]); א׳ אָנִי ψ 6[3] 537 (|| נִבְהֲלוּ עֲצָמָי).

I. **אמם** (perh. *be wide, roomy*, As. [*amāmu*] whence *ummu, womb, mother*=אֵם cf. Dl[Pr 109]; but אֵם n.prim. acc. to Thes Sta[§ 189 b] Lag[BN 22]).

אֵם [221] **n.f. mother** (Ph. אם, Ar. أُمٌّ, إِمٌّ, Eth. 517 እም, Sab. אם (only in n.pr. cf. e.g. Bae[Rel 118]) As. *ummu* COT[Gloss]; Aram. אֵם, אִימָּא, ܐܡܐ)—א׳ abs. Gn 32[12]+; cstr. Gn 3[20]+; sf. אִמִּי Gn 20[12] +etc.; †pl. only sf. אִמֹּתֵנוּ La 5[3]; אִמֹּתָם Je 16[3] La 2[12.12];—**1.** lit. (human) *mother,* as parent Gn 20[12] 32[12] 44[20] Ex 2[8] ψ 51[7] 113[9] (opp. עֲקָרָה) Je 15[8.10] 20[14] 22[26] 50[12] 1 Ch 4[9] Ct 6[9] 8[5]+; hence of Eve אֵם כָּל־חָי Gn 3[20]; poet. of birth, יָצָא מִבֶּטֶן אֵם Jb 1[21] Ec 5[14]; יָצָא מֵרֶחֶם אֵם Nu 12[12] cf. ψ 139[13] (Je 20[18] &) ψ 71[6] מִמְּעֵי אִמִּי גּוֹזִי (subj. י׳, cf. גחה 22[10]; > גּוֹזִי = *my benefactor* fr. birth Thes Ew Hup Pe); also וַתְּהִי אִמִּי קִבְרִי Je 20[17]; מִבֶּטֶן אֵם=fr. earliest existence Ju 16[17] Jb 31[18] ψ 22[11]; so מִמְּעֵי אֵם Is 49[1]; as giving suck Ct 8[1] (שְׁדֵי אֵם) ψ 22[10] cf. 131[2] (v. Ex 2[9] cf. v[8]); as exercising authority Gn 21[21] 24[28] 27[11.13.14] Ju 17[2 f] Ru 1[8] Ct 3[4] 8[2] etc.; esp. of queen-mother as possessing dignity & influence 1 K 1[11] 2[13.19.20] 2 Ch 22[2.3] Ct 3[11] Pr 31[1]; cf. names of mothers of kings of Judah 1 K 14[21.31] 15[2.10.13]+; as shewing love & care 1 S 2[19] 1 K 3[27] 17[23] 2 K 4[30] Is 66[13] (sim. of י׳'s comforting his people; cf. also Gn 27[45]); as beloved & lamented 1 K 19[20] (|| אָב) Gn 24[67] ψ 35[14]; בֶּן־אִמּוֹ=*own* (uterine) *brother* Gn 43[29]; & || אָח Gn 27[29] Dt 13[7] Ju 8[19] ψ 50[20] 69[9] Ct 1[6] cf. 8[1]; so בַּת־אִמּוֹ Lv 18[9] 20[17] Dt 27[22] (|| בַּת־אָבִיו) Gn 20[12]; oft. with אָב, as *parentes* Je 16[3] Zc 13[3.3] Is 8[4]; as rightfully claiming honour, authority, etc., cf. supr., Gn 28[7] (P) cf. 37[10] (E) Ju 14[2f], so in precept Pr 1[8] 6[20] 10[1] 15[20] etc. cf. Ez 22[7]; laws enjoining these Ex 20[12]=Dt 5[16] Lv 19[3] cf. Dt 22[15]; laws prohib. contrary Ex 21[15.17] (E) Lv 20[9.9] (H) Dt 21[18.19] 27[16]; laws as to mourning for Lv 21[2.11] (H) Nu 6[7] (P) cf. Je 16[7] Ez 44[25]; left for wife Gn 2[24]; for mother-in-law Ru 2[24]; for husband Dt 21[13] (law for captive women); cf. Dt 33[9] (of devoted service of Levites); loving, caring for children Pr 4[3] (on the opposite cf. ψ 27[10]); loved, cared for Jos 2[13] cf. v[18] 6[23]

1 S 22^{3} 1 K 19^{20} cf. 2 S 19^{38}. †**2.** fig. of Deborah as caring for her people אֵם בְּיִשְׂרָאֵל Ju 5^{7} (cf. אָב Is 22^{21} Jb 29^{16}); so of a city 2 S 20^{19} ('stock, race, community' RS$^{K 28}$ cf.$^{Proph. iv. n 8}$); of Israel Ho 2$^{4.7}$ 4^{5} cf. 10^{14}; of Judah Is 50$^{1.1}$; of Hittite as mother of Jerusalem אָבִיךְ הָאֱמֹרִי וְאִמֵּךְ חִתִּית Ez 16$^{3.45}$ cf. v$^{44.45}$; also 19$^{2.10}$ & vid. 23^{2}. †**3.** of animals, *dam* Ex 22^{29} (of ox & sheep) Lv 22^{27} (of bullock, sheep, or goat); Ex 23^{19}=34^{26} =Dt 14^{21} (of kid); *mother-bird* Dt 22$^{6.6.7}$; fig. Jb 17^{14} לַשַּׁחַת קָרָאתִי אָבִי אָתָּה אִמִּי וַאֲחֹתִי לָרִמָּה: †**4.** =*point of departure* or *division* אֵם הַדֶּרֶךְ Ez 21^{26} (|| רֹאשׁ שְׁנֵי הַדְּרָכִים).

522 †I. אַמָּה **n.f.** only **mother-city**, metropolis
4965 (cf. אֵם 2 S 20^{19} & Ph.); in phrase מֶתֶג הָאַמָּה *authority of mother-city* 2 S 8^{1}; v. מֶתֶג; cf. Dr.

520 II. אַמָּה $_{246}$ **n.f. ell, cubit** (SI אמה; so Sab. DHM$^{ZMG 1865, 613}$; Aram. ܐܡܬܐ, אַמָּא; As. *ammatu* Nor^{280}; Eth. አመት: etym. dub.; Thes al. *mater brachii*, i.e. length of fore-arm; others der. fr. √אמם, أَمَّ *precede*, be in front, & hence fore-arm cf. Di Is 6^{4}; Dl$^{Pr 109}$ MV der. immediately from √אמם be wide (v. supr.), אַמָּה= *distance*, & hence a particular distance, *ell, cubit*)—א׳ abs. Gn 6^{15}+; cstr. אַמַּת Dt 3^{11} Je 51^{13}; *du.* אַמָּתַיִם Ex 25^{10}+; *pl.* אַמּוֹת Ex 26^{16}+;— **1.** *cubit*, so אַמַּת־אִישׁ i.e. ordinary cubit, Dt 3^{11} (cf. Is 8^{1}); in Ez 40^{5} 43^{13} is a cubit one handbreadth longer, cf. 2 Ch 3^{3} א׳ בַּמִּדָּה הָרִאשׁוֹנָה; absol. length dub., cf. Smith$^{Dict. Bib., art. Weights and Measures}$; Lepsius$^{Längenmaasse der Alten, SBAk 1883, 1195 f.}$ identif. with Egyptian, longer cubit ·525 m., shorter ·450 m.; v. also *Id.*$^{Bab.-Assyr. Längenmaasse 1877; MBAk 1877, 741}$ Oppert$^{GGA 1878, 1055; Rev. d'Assyr. i. 124}$ (also on the Bab. 'half-cubit'=·270 m. Hpt$^{AJPh 1888, 419}$ Hom$^{Semiten i. 501}$); on א׳ אַצִּילָה Ez 41^{8} cf. Sm & Co (Co del.); חֲמֵשׁ אמות קָנִים Ez 42^{16} Kt, rd. מֵאוֹת so Qr Co; chiefly in Ex 25–27. 36–38 (56 t.) 1 K 6. 7 (45 t.) 2 Ch 3. 4 (21 t.) Ez 40–43 (86 t.); *a* (one) *cubit*=אַמָּה Gn 6^{16} Ex 25$^{10.23}$+; הָאַמָּה Ez 43^{14}; א׳ אַחַת Ez 40$^{12.12.42.42.42}$ 42^{4} 43^{14}; *two cubits*= אַמָּתַיִם שְׁתַּיִם Ex 25$^{10.17.23}$ 30^{2} 37$^{1.6.10.25}$ Nu 11^{31}; אַמּוֹת Ez 40^{9} 41$^{3.22}$ 43^{14}; c. num. 1–10 א׳ mostly follows num. in pl. Ex 26^{16} 27$^{1.1.1}$ 1 K 6^{10} Ez 40$^{5.7.9}$+; c. num. 11–1000+, it mostly foll. num. in sing. Gn 6$^{15.15.15}$ Ex 27$^{12.13}$ 38$^{13.14.15}$ Nu 35^{4} Jos 3^{4} 1 K 6$^{2.2.3}$ 7$^{15.15}$ Je 52$^{21.22}$ Ez 40$^{49.49}$+; seld. foll. in pl. Ez 40^{11} (del. Co) v^{27} (Co sg.) 42^{2}; so also חָמֵשׁ וְעֶשְׂרִים וְחָמֵשׁ אַמּוֹת Ez 40$^{13.29}$ but חָמֵשׁ וְעֶשְׂרִים אַמָּה Ez 40$^{25.30.33.36}$; (late) also in pl. precedes all num. 2 Ch 3$^{3.3.4.8.8}$+; 6^{13} Ez 42^{2}; also oft. בָּאַמָּה foll. all num. Ex 26$^{2.2.8.8}$ 27$^{9.18}$ 36$^{9.9.15.15.21}$ Nu 35$^{5.5.5.5}$ 1 K 6$^{6.6.6}$ 7$^{23.23.23}$ 2 Ch 4$^{2.2.2}$ Ez 40^{21} 47^{3} Zc 5$^{2.2}$+, cf. לְאַמּוֹת חָמֵשׁ 2 Ch 3^{11}; oft. א׳ וָחֵצִי Ex 25$^{10.10.10.17.17}$+, also א׳ וַחֲצִי הָא׳ Ex 26^{16} 36^{21} 1 K 7$^{31.32.35}$ etc.; cf. שֵׁשׁ אַמּוֹת וָזָרֶת 1 S 17^{4}; sq. בַּמִּדָּה *in measurement* Jos 3^{4} 2 Ch 3^{3}. **2.** †*measure*, full measure, limit, only אַמַּת בִּצְעֵךְ *the measure of thy gain-making* Je 51^{13} (|| קִצֵּךְ).

†III. [אַמָּה] **n.f.** (etym. & mng. dub.; Thes 520
foundation (cf. Talm. AW), fr. אֵם in metaph. sense, cf. MV; De on Is 6^{4} der. similarly, but makes *support* of *superliminaria* (cf. 𝔊 𝔖 𝔙); Ew Di der. fr. √אמם=أَمَّ *precede*, whence إِمَامٌ *front;* Dl$^{Pr 110}$ tr. *holder* fr. √אמם *be wide*, hence *contain, hold*) only אַמּוֹת הַסִּפִּים Is 6^{4}.

†IV. אַמָּה **n.pr.loc.** hill near Gibeon, 522
גִּבְעַת־אַמָּה 2 S 2^{24}.

[אֻמָּה†] **n.f. tribe, people** (Ar. أُمَّةٌ; As. 523
ummatu cf. Jen$^{Kosmol. 336}$, Aram. ܐܘܡܬܐ, אוּמָּא) only pl. אֻמּוֹת Nu 25^{15}; אֻמִּים ψ 117^{1}; sf. אֻמֹּתָם Gn 25^{16};—of tribes of Ishmaelites Gn 25^{16}; of Midian (|| בֵּית־אָב) Nu 25^{15}; || גּוֹיִם ψ 117^{1}.

†אֲמָם **n.pr.loc.** in southern Judah Jos 538
15^{26} (𝔊^{L} Ἀμαμ, so A, but B Σην).

†I. [אָמַן] **vb. confirm, support** (cf. Ar. 539
أَمِنَ, etc., v. infr.; Sab. אמן in deriv. & n.pr. cf. CIS$^{iv. 1, 10}$ DHM$^{ZMG 1885, 598}$; Aram. אֲמַן, ܐܡܢ in Haph. Eth. አምነ: As. in deriv.)—only **Qal** *Pt.* אֹמֵן;—**1.** as vb. *support, nourish* 2 K 10$^{1.5}$ Est 2^{7}. **2.** as subst. *foster-father* Nu 11^{12} (J) Is 49^{23}. **3.** אֹמֶנֶת *foster-mother, nurse* Ru 4^{16}
2 S 4^{4}. **4.** אֹמְנוֹת *pillars, supporters of the door* 547
2 K 18^{16}. *Pt. pass.* **a.** הָאֱמֻנִים *those brought up* (in scarlet) La 4^{5}. **b.** אֱמוּנִים intrans. *faithful* (as firm, stable) as subst. m. *faithful ones* ψ 12^{2} (>𝔊 𝔖 al. *faithfulness*) 2 S 20^{19} (cf. Ar. أَمُنَ *be faithful*, أَمَّنَ *trust in*, أَمِنَ *be secure*); ψ 31^{24} *faithful ones* י׳ *keepeth*, אֱמוּנִים נֹצֵר י׳; but א׳ is here taken by 𝔊 Ri De Che as n. abstr. v. אֵמֻן. **Niph.** נֶאֱמַן Pr 11^{13}+(6 t.); *Impf.* יֵאָמֵן, יֵאָמֵן 1 K 8^{26}+(9 t.); *Pt.* נֶאֱמָן Pr 25^{13}+(16 t.) נֶאֱמָנָה Is 1^{21}+(4 t.); נֶאֱמֶנֶת ψ 89^{29}; נֶאֱמָנִים Pr 27^{6}+(9 t.); נֶאֱמָנוֹת Dt 28^{59}. **1.** *carried by a nurse* Is 60^{4}. **2.** *made firm, sure, lasting:* place Is 22$^{23.25}$; name 1 Ch 17^{24}; waters Is 33^{16} Je 15^{18}; an event Ho 5^{9}; sickness Dt 28^{59}; mercy Is 55^{3}. **3.** *confirmed, established, sure:* kingdom 2 S 7^{16}; house, dynasty 1 S 2^{35} 25^{28} 1 K 11^{38} 1 Ch 17^{23}; prophet Samuel 1 S 3^{20}; cf.

word-play אִם לֹא תַאֲמִינוּ לֹא תֵאָמֵנוּ = *if ye believe not* (have not firm confidence) *ye will not be confirmed* Is 7[9]; הַאֲמִינוּ בי׳ וְתֵאָמֵנוּ = *believe in Yahweh and ye will be confirmed* 2 Ch 20[20]. **4.** *verified, confirmed:* words of God 1 K 8[26] 2 Ch 1[9] 6[17]; his precepts ψ 111[7]; testimonies ψ 19[8] 93[5]; covenant ψ 89[29]; words of men Gn 42[20] (E). **5.** *reliable, faithful, trusty:* persons 1 S 2[35] 22[14] Jb 12[20] ψ 89[38] 101[6] Pr 25[13] Is 8[2] Ne 13[13]; a city Is 1[21]; האל הנאמן *the faithful God* Dt 7[9] cf. Is 49[7]; נֶאֱמַן רוּחַ *faithful in spirit* (disposition) Pr 11[13]; לִבָבוֹ נֶאֱמָן *his heart faithful* Ne 9[8]; עֵד אֱמֶת וְנֶאֱמָן *true and faithful witness* Je 42[5]; נאמנים פצעי אוהב *faithful the wounds of a loving one* Pr 27[6]; c. אֵת ψ 78[8]; עִם Ho 12[1]; בְּ of thing ψ 78[37]; בְּכָל־בֵּיתִי *in all my house* (of Moses) Nu 12[7] (E). **Hiph.** הֶאֱמִין Gn 45[26] + (18 t.); *Impf.* יַאֲמִין, יַאֲמֵן Jb 15[31] + (30 t.); *Imv.* הַאֲמִינוּ 2 Ch 20[20] + (2 t.); *Pt.* מַאֲמִין Dt 1[32] Jos 25[16]. **1.** *stand firm* Jb 39[24] (c. neg. of the horse when the trumpet sounds Di De MV RVm; but *neither believeth* RV, *hardly trusts* Da). **2.** *trust, believe:* (*a*) abs. Ex 4[31] (J) Is 7[9] 28[16] Hb 1[5] ψ 116[10] Jb 29[24]; (*b*) with לְ of person, *trust to, believe* Gn 45[26] (E) Ex 4[1.8] (J) Je 40[14] 2 Ch 32[15]; with God Dt 9[23] Is 43[10]; לְ of thing Ex 4[8.9] (J) ψ 106[24] 1 K 10[7] 2 Ch 9[6] Is 53[1] Pr 14[15]; (*c*) with בְּ of person, *trust in, believe in* Ex 19[9] (J) 1 S 27[12] 2 Ch 20[20] Jb 4[18] 15[15] Pr 26[25] Je 12[6] Mi 7[5]; the usual construction with God Gn 15[6] (E) Ex 14[31] Nu 14[11] (J) 20[12] (P) Dt 1[32] 2 K 17[14] 2 Ch 20[20] ψ 78[22] Jon 3[5]; with בְּ of thing Dt 28[66] Jb 15[31] 24[22] 39[12] ψ 78[32] 106[12] 119[66]; (*d*) with כִּי *trust or believe that* Ex 4[5] (J) Jb 9[16] La 4[12]; (*e*) so with infin. Jb 15[22] ψ 27[13]; also *trust* to do a thing, almost = *allow*, Ju 11[20].

544 †אֹ֫מֶן **n.[m.] faithfulness;** אֱמוּנָה אֹמֶן *perfect faithfulness* (faithfulness, faithfulness) Is 25[1].

543 †אָמֵן **adv. verily, truly** Dt 27[15-26] (12 t.) 1 K 1[36] Ne 5[13] Je 11[5] 28[6] & doxologies 1 Ch 16[36] (= ψ 106[48]); אָמֵן (ו)אָמֵן Nu 5[22] (P) Ne 8[6], & in the doxologies ψ 41[14] 72[19] 89[53] 106[48]. ἀμήν = *Amen:* אֱלֹהֵי אָמֵן Is 65[16.16] *God of Amen* De Che RVm; cf. Rev 3[14], or *God of faithfulness, God of truth* (RV) (perh. rd. אֹמֶן Che Di).

542 †אָמָּן (*ommān*) **n.m. master-workman, artist** Ct 7[2] (Mish. Talm. אוּמָּן, אוּמָּנוּת *handiwork*, Syr. ܐܘܡܢܐ 𝔊 Ex 28[11], where = Heb. חָרָשׁ & is likewise used of gems; Nab. אמנא Vog[94], As. *mar ummâni*, Lyon [Sargontexte 65], cf. Zim [BP 12]; cf. II. אָמוֹן).

†אֵ֫מֻן **n.[m.] trusting, faithfulness** (on format. cf. Ges[§ 84a R.12]). **1.** בָּנִים לֹא אֵמֻן בָּם *children in whom there is no trusting* Dt 32[20] (poet.) **2.** אֱמוּנִים pl. abst. *faithfulness;* צִיר א׳ *messenger of faithfulness*, trusty messenger Pr 13[17]; עֵד א׳ *faithful witness* Pr 14[5]; cf. אִישׁ א׳ Pr 20[6]; שֹׁמֵר א׳ *keeping faithfulness* Is 26[2], perh. also ψ 31[24] נצר א׳ v. I. [אָמַן]. 529

†אֱמוּנָה **n.f. firmness, steadfastness, fidelity** Ex 17[12] + 46 t.; אֱמוּנוֹת Pr 28[20]. **1.** lit. *firmness, steadiness:* Ex 17[12] וַיְהִי יָדָיו א׳ *his hands were steadiness* (i. e. steady). **2.** *steadfastness*, אֱמוּנַת עִתֶּיךָ *steadfastness of thy times* Is 33[6]. **3.** *faithfulness, trust:* **a.** *of human conduct* ψ 37[3] Pr 12[22] Je 5[3] 7[28] 9[2] 2 K 12[16]; in office 2 K 22[7] 2 Ch 19[9] 31[12] 34[12]; בֶּאֱמוּנָה (על) *in trust* (over) 1 Ch 9[22.26.31] 2 Ch 31[15.18]; דֶּרֶךְ א׳ ψ 119[30]; אִישׁ אֱמוּנוֹת *man of great faithfulness* Pr 28[20]; associated with צֶדֶק in human character יָפִיחַ א׳ יַגִּיד צֶדֶק *who breatheth out faithfulness sheweth forth righteousness* Pr 12[17]; cf. 1 S 26[23] Is 59[4] Je 5[1]; צַדִּיק בֶּאֱמוּנָתוֹ יִחְיֶה *a righteous man by his faithfulness liveth* Hb 2[4] (> *faith* Luth AV RV). **b.** *as a divine attribute* ψ 88[12] 89[2.3.6.9] Is 25[1] Ho 2[22] La 3[21]; אֵל אֱמוּנָה Dt 32[4]; his faithfulness is shewn in his works ψ 33[4]; commands ψ 119[86]; in affliction ψ 119[75]; in his oath to David ψ 89[50]; it reacheth unto the skies ψ 36[6]; unto all generations ψ 100[5] 119[90]; he will not belie it ψ 89[34]. It is אֱמוּנָה אֹמֶן Is 25[1]; cf. אֱמוּנָה מְאֹד ψ 119[138]. It is closely associated with the divine חֶסֶד *mercy* ψ 89[25] 92[3] 98[3] Ho 2[22]; with the divine צֶדֶק, צְדָקָה ψ 96[13] 143[1] Is 11[5]; & salvation ψ 40[11]. 530

†אָמְנָה **n.f. bringing up, nourishment,** Est 2[20]. 545

†אָמְנָה **adv.** (fr. אָמֵן by affix ־ָה) **verily, truly, indeed** Gn 20[12] (E) Jos 7[20] (JE). 546

†אֲמָנָה **n.f. faith, support.** **1.** אֲנַחְנוּ כֹּרְתִים אֲמָנָה *we are plighting faith* (make a sure covenant AV RV) Ne 10[1]. **2.** א׳ עַל הַמ׳ *support, fixed provision*, for the singers Ne 11[23]. 548

†אֲמָנָה **n.pr.fl.** **1.** a river (*constant?* cf. Is 33[16]) flowing down from Antilebanon into the plain of Damascus 2 K 5[12] (Qr; אֲבָנָה Kt), the Gr. *Chrysorrhoas*, mod. Ar. *Nahr Baradâ*. **2.** the region from which it flows Ct 4[8]. 549

†אָמְנָם **adv.** (fr. אָמֵן by aff. ־ָם) **verily, truly, indeed, always in interrog.** Gn 18[13] (J), elsewh. הַאֻמְנָם Nu 22[37] (E) 1 K 8[27] 2 Ch 6[18] ψ 58[2]. 552

†אֻמְנָם **adv.** (= אָמְנָם) **verily, truly,** in 551

asseverations 2 K 19[17] (=Is 37[18]) Jb 19[4.5] 34[12] 36[4] Ru 3[12], also ironical Jb 9[2] 12[2].

571 †אֱמֶת **n.f. firmness, faithfulness, truth** (contr. for אֱמֶנֶת, fr. אָמַן) Gn 24[48] + 106 t.; sf. אֲמִתּוֹ, אֲמִתְּךָ ψ 91[4] + 18 t. **1.** *reliability, sureness:* דֶּרֶךְ אֱמֶת *sure way* Gn 24[48] (J); שׂכר אמת *sure reward* Pr 11[18]; אות אמת *sure token* Jos 2[12] (J); זֶרַע אמת Je 2[21]. **2.** *stability, continuance:* שָׁלוֹם וֶאֱמֶת *peace and stability* Is 39[8] (=2 K 20[19]) Est 9[30] Je 33[6] Zc 8[19], cf. שלום אמת Je 14[13]. **3.** *faithfulness, reliableness:* (*a*) *of men* אִישׁ אֱמֶת *faithful man* Ne 7[2]; אנשי אמת Ex 18[21] (E); הָלַךְ בֶּאֱמֶת *walk in faithfulness, faithfully* 1 K 2[4] 3[6] 2 K 20[3] Is 38[3] cf. 1 S 12[24]; of י׳, בַּאֲמִתֶּךָ ψ 25[5] 26[3] 86[11]; עיר האמת Zc 8[3]; of men ψ 45[5] 51[8] 2 Ch 31[20] 32[1] Pr 29[14] Is 10[20] 42[3] 48[1]; בא׳ ובתמים Ju 9[16.19] Jos 24[14]; חֶסֶד וֶא׳ *mercy and faithfulness* Pr 3[3] 14[22] 16[6] 20[28] Ho 4[1], & the phrase עשה חסד ואמת Gn 24[49] 47[29] Jos 2[14] (J) 2 S 15[20]. (*b*) *an attribute of God* ψ 54[7] 71[22] Is 38[18.19] 61[8]; נתן אמת Mi 7[20]; עשה אמת Ez 18[9] Ne 9[33]; עשה חסד ואמת Gn 32[11] (J) 2 S 2[6]; רב חסד ואמת *abundant in mercy and faithfulness* Ex 34[6] (J) ψ 86[15]; these attributes are also associated ψ 40[11.12] 61[8] 115[1] 138[2] Is 16[5] Gn 24[27] (J); they are messengers of God to men ψ 57[4] 85[11] 89[15] cf. ψ 43[3]; כל ארחות י׳ חסד ואמת ψ 25[10]; the faithfulness of God endureth for ever ψ 117[2]; he keepeth it for ever ψ 146[6]; it reacheth unto the skies ψ 57[11] 108[5]; it is shield & buckler ψ 91[4]; he is אל אמת ψ 31[6] = אלהי אמת 2 Ch 15[3]; אֱמֶת is also associated with the divine ישׁר ψ 111[8]; צֶדֶק ψ 85[12]; צְדָקָה Zc 8[8]; מִשְׁפָּט ψ 111[7] Je 4[2]; & salvation ψ 69[14]. **4.** truth (*a*) *as spoken:* דבר אמת *speak truth* 1 K 22[16] 2 Ch 18[15] Je 9[4] Zc 8[16] ψ 15[2]; דִּבְרֵי א׳ Ec 12[10]; אֱמֶת הַדָּבָר *the thing is true* Dt 22[20] 1 K 10[6] 2 Ch 9[5] Dn 10[1]; אמת נכון הדבר *the thing is certainly true* Dt 13[15] 17[4]; אמרים אמת = אִמְרֵי אֱמֶת Pr 22[21]; הגה אמת Pr 8[7]; הגיד א׳ Dn 11[2], אֲמִתֶּךָ ψ 30[10]; שפת אמת Pr 12[19]; אֱמֶת *it is true* Is 43[9]; האמת אתכם *whether truth* is with you Gn 42[16] (E) cf. Is 59[14.15]. (*b*) *of testimony and judgment* עֵד אֱמֶת *true witness* Pr 14[25]; עד אמת ונאמן Je 42[5]; משפט אמת Ez 18[8] Zc 7[9]; שְׁפַט אמת Zc 8[16]. (*c*) *of divine instruction* כְּתָב אֱמֶת Dn 10[21]; תורת אמת Mal 2[6] cf. Ne 9[13]; תורתך אמת ψ 119[142]; דבר י׳ בְּפִיךָ אמת 1 K 17[24] cf. 2 S 7[28]; משפטי י׳ אמת ψ 19[10]; ראש דברך אמת ψ 119[160]; מצותיך אמת ψ 119[151]. (*d*) *truth* as a body of ethical or religious knowledge Dn 8[12]; להשׂכיל באמתך Dn 9[13]. **5. adv.** *in truth, truly* ψ 132[11]; יהוה אלהים אמת *Yahweh is God in truth, truly* Je 10[10]; elsewhere בֶּאֱמֶת Ju 9[15] ψ 145[18] Je 26[15] 28[9] 32[41].

†II. אָמוֹן **n.m. artificer, architect, master-** 525
workman, as firm and sure in his workmanship: וָאֶהְיֶה אֶצְלוֹ אָמוֹן *I was at his side architect, master-workman* (𝔊 𝔖 𝔙 Ges Ew De MV RV, > *foster-son* AE Ki AV) Pr 8[30]; יֶתֶר הָאָמוֹן 527
rest of the master-workmen Je 52[15] (Hi Gf De RVm, but *rest of the multitude* Ges MV RV et al., אמון = המון)—**I.** אָמוֹן v. supr. p. 51.

†III. אָמוֹן **n.pr.m.** (*master-workman*) (*a*) 526
king of Judah 2 K 18[19.23.24.25] 1 Ch 3[14] 2 Ch 33[20.21.22.23.25] Je 1[2] 25[3]; (*b*) captain of a city 1 K 22[26] 2 Ch 18[25]; (*c*) one of the line of Solomon's
servants Ne 7[59] = אָמִי Ezr 2[57]. 532

†אַמְנוֹן **n.pr.m.** (*faithful*) **1.** eldest son of 550
David 2 S 3[2] 13[1-39]; = אֲמִינוֹן 2 S 13[20]; = אַמְנֹן 1 Ch 3[1]. **2.** a son of Shimon 1 Ch 4[20].

אֲמִינוֹן dimin., so Ew[§ 167 a] cf. W[I. § 269], or txt. 550
err.; cf. Dr 2 S 13[20], v. אַמְנוֹן.

†אֲמִתַּי **n.pr.m.** (*true*, fr. אֱמֶת by adj. affix 573
־ַי) father of the prophet Jonah 2 K 14[25] Jon 1[1].

†הֵימָן **n.pr.m. Heman** (*faithful*, cf. Aram. 1968
מְהֵימָן, ܡܗܝܡܢ) a wise man with whom Solomon is compared 1 K 5[11], where app. son of Mahol (Klo *sons of the dance*); named with 3 others, one being Ethan the Ezrahite; 1 Ch 2[6] a Heman is named with same 3 + 1 other, & all called sons of Zerah of Judah; Heman appears ψ 88[1] also as the Ezrahite (v. sub זרח), cf. Ethan supr.; in other passages Heman is a Levite; specif. Kohathite, son of Joel, called *the singer* (הַמְשׁוֹרֵר) 1 Ch 6[18] (|| Asaph v[24], Ethan v[29]); Heman, Asaph & Ethan named as the singers (הַמְשֹׁרְרִים) 1 Ch 15[17.19]; cf. Heman & Jeduthun 16[41.42] (|| Asaph v[37]); Heman, Asaph & Jeduthun 25[6] 2 Ch 5[12] 35[15]; elsewhere בְּנֵי אָסָף וְהֵימָן וידותון 1 Ch 25[1] cf. v[4.4.5.5]; בְּנֵי הֵימָן 2 Ch 29[14] (|| בְּנֵי ידותון);—25[5] Heman is called חֹזֵה הַמֶּלֶךְ בְּדִבְרֵי הָאֱלֹהִים (cf. Asaph 2 Ch 29[30], Jeduthun 2 Ch 35[15]).—On question of identity of Heman in these various connections, v. Thes Comm.

†מְהוּמָן **n.pr.m.** a eunuch of Ahasuerus 4104
(*id.*; but 𝔊 Ἀμαν) Est 1[10].

II. [אָמַן] v. יָמַן. 541

†[אָמֵץ] **vb. be stout, strong, bold, alert** 553
(acc. to Lag[BN 28 f.] fr. earlier אָמִץ cf. אֹמֶץ)—**Qal** *Pf.* 3 pl. אָמְצוּ 2 S 22[18] + 2 t.; *Impf.* יֶאֱמָץ Gn 25[23]; וַיֶּאֶמְצוּ 2 Ch 13[18]; *Imv.* אֱמָץ Jos 1[7] 1 Ch

28^{20}; אֱמָ֑ץ Jos 1^{6}; אֱמָ֫ץ Dt 31^{7} + 3 t.; אִמְצוּ Dt 31^{6} + 2 t.—**1.** *be strong*, of a people Gn 25^{23} (J); of personal enemies 2 S 22^{18} = ψ 18^{18}; ψ 142^{7} (all sq. מִן of compar.); also (without מִן) *prevail* 2 Ch 13^{18}. **2.** *Imv. be bold* (alw. ‖ חֲזַק, חִזְקוּ) Dt $31^{7.23}$ Jos $1^{6.7.18}$; (‖ id. + אַל־תִּירְאוּ וְאַל־תַּעַרְצוּ) Dt 31^{6}; ‖ id. + אַל־תַּעֲרֹץ וְאַל תֵּחָת) Jos 1^{9}; (‖ id. + אַל תִּירְאוּ וְאַל תֵּחָתּוּ) Jos 10^{25} 1 Ch 22^{13} 28^{20} 2 Ch 32^{7}. **Pi.** *Pf.* אִמֵּץ Dt 2^{30} etc.; *Impf.* יְאַמֵּץ Am 2^{14} etc.; וַיְאַמֶּץ־לוֹ Is 44^{14} 3 fs. sf. 3 ms. תְּאַמְּצֶנּוּ ψ 89^{22}; 1 s. sf. אֲאַמִּצְכֶם Jb 16^{5} etc.; *Imv.* אַמֵּץ Na 2^{2}; אַמֵּ֫צוּ Is 35^{3}; אַמְּצֵ֫הוּ Dt 3^{28}; *Inf.* sf. אַמְּצוֹ Pr 8^{28}; *Pt.* מְאַמֶּץ־ Pr 24^{5};—**1.** *make firm, strengthen*, sq. acc., of giving clouds their place Pr 8^{28} (subj. י׳); of repairing temple 2 Ch 24^{13}; of physical vigour Pr 31^{17} חָגְרָה בְעוֹז מָתְנֶיהָ וַתְּא׳ זְרוֹעֹתֶיהָ׃ (subj. אֵשֶׁת חַיִל); of strength for war Na 2^{2} (‖ חַזֵּק מָתְנַיִם) א׳ כֹּחַ Am 2^{14} (subj. חָזָק); cf. Pr 24^{5}; of royal power 2 Ch 11^{17} (‖ חִזֵּק); cf. Jb 4^{4} א׳ בִּ׳ כֹּרְעוֹת Is 35^{3}; א׳ בִּרְכַּיִם כֹּשְׁלוֹת (both ‖ חַזְּקוּ יָדַיִם רָפוֹת) fig. of encouragement; so א׳ alone Dt 3^{28} (‖ חַזֵּק) Jb 16^{5} (‖ חשׂך q.v.); ψ 89^{22} (subj. זְרוֹעַ י׳); of support Is 41^{10} (subj. י׳; ‖ עזר, תמך;—De Che sub **2**). **2.** *assure, secure* for one's self, alw. sq. לְ + sf.; of carpenter appropr. tree Is 44^{14}; cf. of י׳ appropriating Isr. under fig. of bough ψ 80^{16}; under fig. of chosen man v^{18}. **3.** sq. לֵבָב *harden, make obstinate* Dt 2^{30} (subj. י׳; ‖ הִקְשָׁה רוּחוֹ) Dt 15^{7} (of unkind man); 2 Ch 36^{13} (of king Zedekiah, ‖ הִקְשָׁה אֶת־עָרְפּוֹ). **Hithp.** *Pf.* הִתְאַמֵּץ 1 K 12^{18} = 2 Ch 10^{18}; *Impf.* וַיִּתְאַמְּצוּ 2 Ch 13^{7}; *Pt.* מִתְאַמֶּצֶת Ru 1^{18}; **1.** *strengthen oneself*, of conspirators 2 Ch 13^{7} (sq. עַל). **2.** *confirm oneself* in a purpose, *be determined* Ru 1^{18} (sq. לְ + Inf.) **3.** *make oneself alert*, make haste 1 K 12^{18} = 2 Ch 10^{18} (sq. לְ + Inf.) **Hiph.** *Impf. Juss. exhibit strength, be strong* חֲזַק ויא׳ לִבֶּ֑ךָ, וְיַאֲמֵץ ψ 27^{14}, so also 31^{25}.

555 †אֹ֫מֶץ **n.[m.]** strength, fig. טְהָר־יָדַיִם יֹסִיף אֹ֫מֶץ Jb 17^{9} *the clean of hands increaseth strength.*

556 †אַמְצָה **n.f.** strength, fig. Zc 12^{5}, but sense difficult, cf. Wr[Zech. p. 585]; Sta[ZAW 1881, 34] prop. אֶמְצְאָה לְיוֹשְׁבֵי (after 𝔊 𝔗) *may I be sufficient for.*

531 †אָמוֹץ **n.pr.m.** father of Isaiah (=following) Is 1^{1} 2^{1} 13^{1} 20^{2}; $37^{2.21}$ 38^{1} = 2 K $19^{2.20}$ 20^{1}; 2 Ch 26^{22} $32^{20.32}$.

554 †[אָמֹץ] **adj.** strong, only pl. אֲמֻצִּים of horses Zc $6^{3.7}$ (in v^{7} perh. rd. אֲדֻמִּים, cf. v^{2}, & Hi; see another view in Lag[BN 29]).

†אַמִּיץ (אַמִּץ) **adj.** mighty—א׳ abs. 2 S 533
15^{12} + 2 t.; cstr. Jb 9^{4} + 2 t.—*mighty*, of Absalom's conspiracy 2 S 15^{12}; elsewh. of persons; as subst., instrum. of י׳ (i.e. Assyrians) Is 28^{2} (‖ חָזָק); א׳ לִבּוֹ = valiant, conqueror Am 2^{16}; of י׳, חֲכַם לֵבָב וְא׳ כֹּחַ Jb 9^{4}; cf. א׳ כֹּחַ v^{19} (v. Di & RV), א׳ כֹּחַ Is 40^{26} (‖ רֹב אוֹנִים).

†אַמְצִי **n.pr.m.** **1.** a Levite 1 Ch 6^{31}. **2.** 557
man of priestly line Ne 11^{12} (not in ‖ 1 Ch 9^{12}).

אֲמַצְיָה, אֲמַצְיָהוּ **n.pr.m.** (י׳ *has been* 558
mighty). **1.** king of Jud., son of Joash, father of Azariah; אֲמַצְיָהוּ 2 K $14^{1.9}$ + 8 t. 2 K 14; 15^{3} 1 Ch 3^{12}; 2 Ch 24^{27} 25^{1} + 15 t. 2 Ch 24; $26^{1.4}$; אֲמַצְיָה 2 K 12^{22} 13^{12} 14^{8} 15^{1}. **2.** אֲמַצְיָה, a Simeonite 1 Ch 4^{34}. **3.** *id.*, a Levite 1 Ch 6^{30}. **4.** priest of Bethel, under Jerob. II, Am $7^{10.12.14}$.

†[מַאֲמָץ] **n.[m.]** power, strength, force, 3981
pl. cstr. מַאֲמַצֵּי־כֹחַ Jb 36^{19}.

אָמַר 5287 **vb.** utter, say (MI Ph. אמר, Aram. 559
אֲמַר, Eth. አመረ: I. 2 *shew, declare*, Ar. أَمَرَ *command*; perh. √ אמר orig. = *be* or *make prominent*, hence Hithp. infr., אָמִיר; Sab. אמר *lofty*, epith. of king JHMordtm[ZMG 1876, 37]; cf. Dl[Pr 28] who thinks orig. mng. *hell, sichtbar sein*, whence As. *amâru, see*, & *shew, declare, say*)—**Qal** *Pf.* א׳ Gn 3^{1} +, etc.; *Impf.* יֹאמַר Gn 31^{8} +; וַיֹּאמֶר Gn 1^{3} +; וַיֹּאמַ֫ר Gn 14^{19} +; in Jb alw. וַיֹּאמַר Jb 3^{2} +; 3 fs. תֹּאמַר Gn 21^{12} +; תֹּאמַ֫ר Pr 1^{21}; 1 s. אֹמַר Gn 22^{2} +; אֹמְרָה ψ 42^{10}; וָאֹמַר Gn 20^{13} +; וָאוֹמַר Ne $2^{7.17.20}$; 3 m. pl. יֹאמְרוּ Ex 4^{1} + etc.; sf. יֹמְרוּךָ ψ 139^{20}; 2 mpl. תֵּמְרוּ 2 S 19^{14} (cf. Kö[I. p. 385]); *Imv.* אֱמֹר (אֱמָר־) Gn 45^{17} +, etc.; *Inf. abs.* אָמוֹר Ex 21^{5} +; cstr. אֱמֹר Ez 25^{8} +; (הַ)אֱמֹר Jb 34^{18} but rd. הָאֹמֵר 𝔊 𝔙 Di, or better הָאָמֹר *Inf. abs.* c. ה interrog. cf. Ew[§ 328 d]; sf. אָמְרִי Jos 6^{10} +; אָמְרְכֶם Je 23^{38}; אֱמָרְכֶם Mal 1^{7} +; לֵאמֹר Gn 1^{22} +, etc.; *Pt. act.* אֹמֵר Gn 32^{10} +, etc.; *pass.* הֶאָמוּר Mi 2^{7}, but this grammatically indefensible, rd. הֶאָמוֹר, *Inf. abs.* c. ה interrog., v. Dr[Expositor, April, 1887, 263].

1. *Say* (subj. God Gn 3^{1} + or man 32^{5}, serpent 3^{1}, ass Nu 22^{28}, horse יֹאמַר הֶאָח Jb 39^{25} etc.; inanimate things, personif. Jb 28^{14} cf. v^{22} etc.; so in allegory or fable Ju 9^{8} 2 K 14^{9} etc.; esp. in narrat., וַיֹּאמֶר etc., Gn 4^{6} + very oft.): mostly sq. thing said, either subst. Je 14^{17} (c. cl. app.) Dt $27^{16f.}$ Ju 12^{6}; pronoun Gn 44^{16} 2 K 20^{14} +; or (usually) clause Gn 1^{3} 3^{1} 37^{20}

+oft. (*orat. recta*); with adv. *thus, so* Gn 32^{5} Nu 20^{14} 1 K 20$^{3.5}$+oft.; esp. כֹּה אָמַר י׳ Ex 5^{1} 7^{17} 8$^{1.20}$ 1 Ch 17^{4}+oft.; the person addressed usu. introduced by אֶל Gn 3^{1} 15^{7} 22^{7} Lv 21^{1} 2 S 3^{7} 1 K 12$^{5.23}$, or לְ Gn 3^{13} 4^{15} 1 S 20^{2} 2 S 2^{21} 1 K 14^{2}+oft.; rarer combinations are, א׳ בְּאָזְנֵי Is 49^{20} (cf. 5^{9} & vid. דבר); א׳ לִפְנֵי Ez 28^{9}; א׳ לְעֵינֵי Dt 31^{7} Jos 10^{12} Je 28^{11}; א׳ בְּ Jo 2^{17} ψ 126^{2}, where בְּ local; in all cases usually sq. dir. obj. of words said, Ex 19^{25} being very singular; Gn 4^{8} the object-clause has probably fallen out, cf. Vrss Di; =*mention, name, designate* Gn 22$^{2.3}$ 43$^{27.29}$ Ex 32^{13} Nu 14^{40} 1 S 10^{16} 16^{3} 2 S 6^{22} Ne 6^{19}; cf. ψ 139^{20} יֹמְרוּךָ לִמְזִמָּה *speak of thee for falsehood* (but many, as Hup Pe Dy Che, rd. יַמְרוּךָ); =*tell, declare, proclaim* (sq. dir. obj. only) ψ 40^{11} Ez 13^{7}; in reply to question=*answer* Ex 12^{27} Jos 4^{7} 1 K 9^{9} Je 5^{19} 22^{9}. The obj. spoken of may be referred to by אֶל 2 K 19^{32} Je 22^{18} 27^{19}, or לְ Gn 20^{13} אִמְרִי לִי say *of* me, etc. Dt 33^{9} Ju 9^{54} Is 5^{20} ψ 3^{3} 71^{10}, very rarely by a simple accus. Is 3^{10} (where rd. prob. for אִמְרוּ, אַשְׁרֵי), except after אֲשֶׁר where the words used follow (cf. אֲשֶׁר **4 d**) Gn 3^{17} Nu 10^{29} 14^{31} Dt 28^{68} Ju 7^{4} 1 S 9$^{17.23 b}$ 1 K 8^{29} La 4^{20}; cf. Nu 21^{16} 2 K 17^{12} 21^{4}, & (two extreme cases) Is 8^{12} La 2^{15} (v. Dr $^{Sm 1.24,5}$); הָאָמוֹר Mi 2^{7} rd. inf. abs. c. ה interrog. הֶאָמוֹר (v. supr.) *shall one say? shall it be said?* After another vb. of saying, introducing thing said: Dt 21^{7} 25^{9} 27^{15} Ct 2^{10}+, even after אמר Gn 22^{7} Lv 21^{1} Je 34^{2} Est 7^{5}+; esp. inf. לֵאמֹר, after דבר Gn 8^{15}, צוה 2^{16}, ענה 44^{16}, ברך 1^{22}, נשבע 24^{7}, נדר 28^{20}, etc.; after אמר 2 S 3^{18} 1 K 12^{23} Ru 4^{4} 1 Ch 21^{18}+; after שלח 2 Ch 35^{21}, שוב Gn 32^{7}; cf. also Gn 28^{6} Ex 5^{13} 9^{5} 13^{8} 17^{4} Nu 11^{20} Dt 1^{28} 13^{7} Ju 8^{15} 1 S 23^{2} 1 K 13^{3} Je 32^{3} 37^{9}+; also when subj. of לֵאמֹר differs from that of preceding clause Gn 31^{1} 38$^{13.24}$ etc.; after שמע Is 37^{9} =2 K 19^{9}.

2. *Say in the heart* (=think) א׳ בלבב Dt 8^{17} cf. 1 K 12^{26} ψ 10$^{6.11.13}$ 14^{1} 35^{25} Is 14^{13} 47$^{8.10}$ 49^{21} Ec 2$^{1.15}$ 3$^{17.18}$; א׳ אֶל־לִבּוֹ Ho 7^{2}; א׳ לִלְבָבָם Gn 8^{21} *said unto his heart* (to himself), subj. י׳, cf. 1 S 27^{1}; אָמְרָה נַפְשִׁי La 3^{24}; thence א׳ alone Gn 20^{11} 26^{9} Nu 24^{11} Ru 4^{4} 1 S 20^{26} 2 S 5^{6} 12^{22} 2 K 5^{11}; sq. cl. with כִּי Ju 15^{2}; in particular=*desire* מַה־תֹּאמַר נַפְשְׁךָ 1 S 20^{4} cf. Est 2^{13}; sq. inf. =*purpose*, Ex 2^{14} *thinkest thou to kill me, as thou killedst the Egyptian?* Jos 22^{33} 1 S 30^{6} 1 K 5^{19} 2 Ch 28$^{10.13}$; *expect* 2 S 21^{16} *he expected to slay David* 2 Ch 13^{8} 32^{1}.

3. *Promise* (sq. inf.) 1 Ch 27^{23} 2 Ch 21^{7} Est 4^{7}; (*id.*+לְ of pers.) 2 K 8^{19} Ne 9^{15}; (sq. acc. of dir. obj.+לְ of pers.+inf. of purpose) Ne 9^{23}.

4. *Command* (esp. late) sq. אֶל־ of person addressed, Nu 15^{38} 1 Ch 21^{18}; sq. לְ Jos 11^{9} 2 S 16^{11} 2 K 4^{24} Jb 9^{7} ψ 106^{34} (v. sub אֲשֶׁר **8 e**); sq. inf. 1 S 24^{11} 1 Ch 21^{17} 2 Ch 1^{18} 29$^{27.30}$ 31^{11} 35^{21} Est 1^{17} 4$^{13.15}$ 6^{1} 9^{14}; sq. inf.+לְ of pers. 2 Ch 14^{3} 29^{21} 31^{4} Est 1^{10}; sq. acc. dir. obj. 2 Ch 29^{24} *the king commanded the burnt-offering and the sin-offering*, cf. 1 K 5^{20} Est 2^{15}; sq. cl. with אשר=*that* Ne 13^{19}; *id.*+לְ of pers. v^{22}; sq. cl. with כִּי Jb 36^{10}; abs. 1 S 16^{16} (rd. however prob. יאמרו for יאמר, cf. Dr); also ψ 105$^{31.34}$ 107^{25} 1 Ch 14^{12} 2 Ch 24^{8} Ne 13$^{9.19}$ (all sq. vb. consec.); *command by letter* א׳ עִם־הַסֵּפֶר Est 9^{25} (sq. impf.); *appoint, assign* לֶחֶם א׳ לוֹ 1 K 11^{18}=*threaten* sq. inf. Dt 9^{25} ψ 106^{23}.

†**Niph.** *Pf.* נֶאֱמַר Dn 8^{26}; *Impf.* יֵאָמֵר Gn 22^{14}+; יֵאָמֶר לוֹ Is 4^{3}; יֵאָמַר Gn 10^{9}+; וַיֵּאָמַר Jos 2^{2}; *be said, told* Gn 10^{9} 22^{14} ψ 87^{5} Je 4^{11} 16^{14} (all abs., indef. subj., of current saying); so *said* in a book Nu 21^{14}; *be related, told*, of vision Dn 8^{26}; *said, told* to (sq. לְ ind. obj.) Jos 2^{2} Ho 2$^{1.1}$ Zp 3^{16}; either so, or *told concerning* Nu 23^{23}; Ez 13^{12} (אֶל־); יֵאָמֵר לָכֶם=*ye shall be called* (it shall be said to you) Is 61^{6} (‖ תִּקָּרֵאוּ), cf. 4^{3} 19^{18} 32^{5} 62$^{4.4}$ (‖ יִקָּרֵא לְ); hence *be called*, of Tophet לֹא־יֵאָמֵר עוֹד הַתֹּפֶת Je 7^{32}; subj. שֵׁם Gn 32^{29}; Jb 34^{31} כִּי אֶל־אֵל הֶאָמַר, Rabb. (cf. AV) treat הֶאָמַר as Niph. Inf. for לְהֵאָמֵר, but against grammar; the form as it stands is Qal Pf., אֶל־אֵל being prefixed to the interrog. for emphasis (cf. Je 22^{15} 23^{26} Ne 13^{27}), v. Dr^{§9} Di al.; Hoffm., however, reads הֶאָמֵר inf. abs.=imv. 'so must one speak (it be spoken) to God.' †**Hiph.** *Pf. avow, avouch* Dt 26^{17} אֶת־י׳ הֶאֱמַרְתָּ הַיּוֹם לִהְיוֹת לְךָ לֵאלֹהִים; v^{18} וי׳ הֶאֱמִירְךָ היום להיות לו לְעָם (*lit. cause to declare*, i.e. through agency of Moses; on this & other interpr. vid. Di). †**Hithp.** *Impf.* יִתְאַמְּרוּ ψ 94^{4} subj. כָּל־פֹּעֲלֵי אָוֶן *act proudly, boast* (‖ יַבִּיעוּ יְדַבְּרוּ עָתָק); prob. also 2 mpl. תִּתְיַמָּרוּ Is 61^{6} (in good sense, sq. בְּ of thing gloried in) 𝔖 𝔙 𝔗 & cf. 𝔊; Ges$^{Comm.}$ so De Che Kö$^{i. 457 f.}$ (fr. [ימר] *exchange* Thes Hi Kn Ew Di; but vid. ימר, מור).

†אֹמֶר **n.m.** ψ^{77,9} **utterance, speech, word,** 562
only poet., & Jos 24^{27} exalted style;—abs. א׳ Jb 22^{28}+5 t.; sf. אִמְרוֹ Jb 20^{29}; *Pl.* abs. אֲמָרִים Pr 19^{7} 22^{21}; cstr. אִמְרֵי Nu 24^{4}+; אֲמָרָיו Jb 22^{22}; אִמְרֵיכֶם Jb 32^{14} Is 41^{26} (on deriv. fr. אמר cf. Di

Jb 15^{33}) etc.;—**1.** *utterance, word*, esp. pl. Jb. 6^{26} (‖ מִלִּים) 32$^{12.14}$ (‖ מִלִּין) 33^{3} 34^{37}; ψ 5^{2} (‖ הָגִיג), 141^{6} (on this v. cf. Che); Pr 2^{1} (‖ מִצְוָה), v^{16} 4$^{10.20}$ (‖ דָּבָר), 7^{1} (‖ מִצְוָה), v^{5} 19^{7} Is 41^{26}; words of God Nu 24$^{4.16}$ cf. Jos 24^{27} Jb 6^{10} 22^{22} ψ 107^{11}; fig. of day ψ 19^{3} (sing.); cf. v^{4} (‖ דְּבָרִים) but vid. Che on v.; of wisdom (personif.) Pr 1^{21} (‖ קוֹל); oft. in phrase אִמְרֵי־פִי Dt 32^{1} ψ 19^{15} (‖ הֶגְיוֹן); 54^{4} (‖ תְּפִלָּה); 78^{1} (‖ תּוֹרָה); Pr 4^{5} 5^{7} 7^{24} 8^{8}; cf. Jb 8^{2} Pr 6$^{2.2}$; of י׳ Jb 23^{12} (‖ מִצְוַת שְׂפָתָיו); ψ 138^{4}; Ho 6^{5} (of Yahweh's words as weapon); in phrases אִמְרֵי־יֹשֶׁר Jb 6^{25}; א׳ בִינָה Pr 1^{2}; א׳ נֹעַם Pr 15^{26} 16^{24}; הָשִׁיב אֲמָרִים אֱמֶת א׳ אֱמֶת 22^{21}, cf. א׳ דַעַת 19^{27} 23^{12}; v^{21} *return answer;* תָּשִׁיב אֲמָרֶיהָ לָהּ Ju 5^{29} *she returneth* (i.e. *repeateth*) *her words to herself;* חָשַׂךְ א׳ *spare* (i.e. refrain fr.) *words* Pr 17^{27}. **2.** sg. *promise* ψ 77^{9}; *appointment, decree* Jb 20^{29}; *command* ψ 68^{12} (but v. Che); *plan, purpose* Jb 22^{28} גְּזַר־א׳; Hb 3^{9} Thes *sworn are the rods of appointment* (i.e. the chastisements decreed), but passage dub., v. Comm.;—Gn 49^{21} rd. אֲמִרֵי cf. אָמִיר; vid. Di.

561, 565 [אִמְרָה] **n.f. utterance, speech, word** (poet., mostly sg. coll., cf. pl. vb. ψ 119^{103}, but here rd. prob. pl.n. cf. 𝔊 Ol Hi De Che)—cstr. אִמְרַת Is 5^{24}+; אִמְרָתִי Gn 4^{23}+etc.; *Pl.* abs. אֲמָרוֹת ψ 12^{7}; cstr. אִמֲרוֹת ib.;—*utterance, speech* Gn 4^{23} (song of Lamech, ‖ קוֹל) so Is 28^{23} 32^{9}; Dt 32^{2} (‖ לֶקַח), ψ 17^{6} Is 29$^{4.4}$ (‖ also דִּבֵּר); esp. *saying(s), word(s)* of י׳ (command & promise) Dt 33^{9} (‖ בְּרִית); Is 5^{24} (‖ תּוֹרָה) 2 S 22^{31} = ψ 18^{31} ψ 12^{7} 105^{19} (‖ דָּבָר); esp. ψ 119$^{11.38.41}$ + 16 t.; 138^{2} 147^{15} (‖ דָּבָר), Pr 30^{5}.

565 †[אֶמְרָה] **n.f.** id., only אֶמְרָתוֹ אֲשֶׁר צִוָּה La 2^{17}.

201 †אוֹמָר **n.pr.m.** grandson of Esau (*eloquent?*) Gn 36$^{11.15}$ 1 Ch 1^{36}.

534 †אָמִיר **n.m. top, summit,** of tree Is 17^{6}; of mt. v^{9} (? so Ew Kn De Di; Lag Che Brd Or foll. 𝔊 & rd. הָאֱמֹרִי); *Pl.* cstr. אֲמִרֵי Gn 49^{21} (so rd. for אִמְרֵי, Ew Di al., cf. also 1. אֵלָה p. 18).

564 †אִמֵּר **n.pr.m. 1.** a priest assigned to Dvd's time 1 Ch 24^{14} perh. = **2.** ancestor of priest 1 Ch 9^{12} cf. Ne 11^{13} Ezr 2^{37} 10^{20} Ne 7^{40}. **3.** priest in Jerem.'s time Je 20^{1}. **4.** father of Zadok Ne 3^{29}. **5. n.pr.loc.** (?) Ezr 2^{59} = Ne 7^{61}.

567 אֱמֹרִי **n.pr.m.coll.** (construed as pl. Dt 3^{9} + 5 t.) **Amorites** (perh. = *mountain-dwellers*, cf. Nu 13^{29} Dt 1$^{7.19f.}$ etc. & Di Gn 10^{16} al.)—alw. c. art., exc. Nu 21^{29} Ez 16^{45}. **1.** called son of Canaan Gn 10^{16} (J) 1 Ch 1^{14} = **2.** a chief people dispossessed by Hebrews; (*a*) living E. of Jordan Nu 21$^{13.13.25}$ + 9 t. Nu + Jos 24^{8} (all E), cf. Jos 2^{10} 9^{10} (JE) Dt 1^{4} 3$^{2.9}$ + 7 t. D; also Ju 10$^{8.11}$ 11$^{19.21.23.23}$ 1 K 4^{19} ψ 135^{11} 136^{19} (Sihon their king Nu 21^{1}+; Sihon & Og Dt 3^{8}+); (*b*) living W. of Jordan Jos 10$^{5.6}$ 24$^{12.15.18}$ (all E), cf. 7^{7} (JE); 5^{1} 10^{12} (both D; cf. also 13^{4}, q. del. Di) Ju 1$^{34.35.36}$ 6^{10} 1 K 21^{26} 2 K 21^{11} cf. 1 S 7^{14} 2 S 21^{2}; (*c*) living in south Dt 1$^{7.19.20.27.44}$; cf. Gn 14^{7} (W. of Dead Sea); (*d*) in gen. = ancient inhabitants of Canaan Gn 15^{16} (J or R) 48^{22} (E) Am 2$^{9.10}$; (*e*) named in list of Canaanitish peoples, to be dispossessed by Isr. Ex 3$^{8.17}$ 13^{5} 33^{2} 34^{11} Jos 3^{10} 9^{1} (all J); Dt 7^{1} 20^{17} Jos 11^{3} 12^{8} (all D); Ex 23^{23} Nu 13^{29} Jos 24^{11} (all E); Ju 3^{5} 1 K 9^{20} 2 Ch 8^{7} Ezr 9^{1} Ne 9^{8}; cf. Ez 16$^{3.45}$; (on these lists cf. Bu Urgesch 344 ff. & We JBTh xxi. 602.) **3. adj.gent.** sg. Gn 14^{13} Dt 2^{24}.

†אִמְרִי **n.pr.m. 1.** a man of Judah 1 Ch 566
9^{4}; cf. **2.** Ne 3^{2} (= *tall?* or *eloquent?*).

אֲמַרְיָה, אֲמַרְיָהוּ **n.pr.m.** (*Yah(u) hath* 568
promised, cf. Palm. אמרשמשא, Sab. יתעאמר) long form only 1 Ch 24^{23} 2 Ch 19^{11} 31^{15}. **1.** a Levite 1 Ch 23^{19} 24^{23} (in Dvd's time), cf. 1 Ch 5$^{33.33}$ 6^{37} Ezr 7^{3}; vid. also **2.** 1 Ch 5$^{37.37}$; also **3.** Ezr 10^{42}. **4.** chief priest under Jehosh. 2 Ch 19^{11}. **5.** Levite under Hezekiah 2 Ch 31^{15}. **6.** son of Hezekiah & great-grandfather of Zephaniah Zp 1^{1}. **7.** a priest Ne 10^{4} 12$^{2.13}$. **8.** a man of Judah Ne 11^{4}.

†[מַאֲמָר] **n.m.** Est 9, 32 **word, command** 3982
(late; Mish. *id.*) cstr. מַאֲמַר Est 1^{15} 2^{20} 9^{32}. 3982

†אַמְרָפֶל **n.pr.m.** king of Shinar Gn 14$^{1.9}$ 569
(prob. = חמרבי, *Ḥammurabi* of Babylon, who reigned c. 2100 B.C., cf. Schr SBA 1887, xxxi (June 23) COT ii. 296 f. Dl in De Gen 1887, Excursus).

†אֶמֶשׁ **adv. yesterday** (etym. dub.; MV 570
after Fl De on Jb 30^{3} cf. Sta § 256 c der. fr. √משה = Ar. مسا, whence مَسَآءٌ, *evening;* v. also in Thes, & cf. As. *mušu, night* COT Gloss, Eth. ምሴት: but also Ar. أَمْسِ = As. *amšatu, yesterday*) = *last night* Gn 19^{34} 31$^{29.42}$ (אָמֶשׁ); = recently 2 K 9^{26}.—Jb 30^{3} א׳ שׁוֹאָה is difficult & uncertain Thes MV al. *darkness, gloom* of wasteness, so RV, but dub., cf. Di; G. Hoffm. rds. אֵם שׁ׳ = *the mother of* (*all*) *the ruined* (said of the desert).

אֱמֶת, אֲמִתַּי v. אמן. p. 54 571-73

אַמְתַּחַת v. מתח. p. 607 572

אָן **adv.** v. sub אַי. p. 33 575

204 †אֹן (Gn 41[45] 46[20]) אוֹן (Gn 41[50] Ez 30[17]) **n. pr.loc. On** (Egypt. *Ȧn* cf. Eb[GS 75] Wied[Samml 46]; perh.=As. *Unu*, Steindorff[BAS i. 610], contr. Dl[Pa 318]) city in lower Egypt, prob. on border of land of Goshen, residence of 'Potiphera, priest of On,' father-in-law of Joseph Gn 41[45.50] 46[20]; also Ez 30[17] (where MT אָוֶן); it was celebrated for worship of sun-god Ra, & hence called also *sun-city*, בֵּית שֶׁמֶשׁ Je 43[13], 𝔊 Ἡλίου πόλις; mod. *Matariye*, on E. bank of Nile, c. 7 miles E. of N. fr. Cairo & 18 fr. Memphis;—cf. Eb[GS 75, 507 f. & map] Wied[l.c.]

205 אֹן *sorrow*, v. אָוֶן. p. 19

577 †אָנָּא **interj.** (from אָהּ and נָא, q. v.) a strong part. of entreaty, **ah, now! I** (or **we**) **beseech thee!** oft. sq. an imper.; Gn 50[17] (to Joseph) אָנָּא שָׂא נָא וג׳ *Ah, now!* forgive, we pray, etc., Ex 32[31] (to God); elsewhere always sq. ׳י or אֲדֹנָי ψ 118[25.25] Ne 1[5.11] Dn 9[4]. Written אָנָּה 2 K 20[3] (=Is 38[3]) Jon 1[14] 4[2] ψ 116[4.16].

אנב (perh. *spring, leap*, so Dl[HA 65, Pr 114], inferred fr. As. *annabu, hare*; ag. this Nö[ZMG 1886, 734]).

768 †אַרְנֶבֶת **n.f. hare** (Ar. أَرْنَبٌ, Syr. ܐܪܢܒܐ, As. *annabu*, as *springer*?) eating of it forbidden Lv 11[6] (P) Dt 14[7].

335 אָנֶה, אָנָה v. sub אַי. p. 32

578 I. †[אָנָה] **vb. mourn—Qal** *Pf.* 3 pl. וְאָנוּ cons. Is 3[26] 19[8] (‖ אָבַל q.v.)

592 †אֲנִיָּה **n.f. mourning**; Is 29[2] La 2[5] (both times in combin. תַּאֲנִיָּה וַאֲנִיָּה).

8396 †תַּאֲנִיָּה **n.f.** id. *ib.*

593 †אֲנִיעָם **n.pr.m.** (*lament of people*) 1 Ch 7[19] a man of Manasseh.

II. **אנה** (√whence foll. nouns, cf. As. *ȧnu, unûtu, vessel, utensil*, v. Dl in Zim[BP 115] Hpt in KAT[2 Gloss i.]; Ar. إِنَآءٌ).

590 †אֳנִי **n.m.**[1 K 10, 11] & **f.**[v 22] **coll. ships, fleet**—abs. 1 K 9[26]+; cstr. 10[11]+;—of Sol. 1 K 9[26.27]; called א׳ תַּרְשִׁישׁ (i.e. large, sea-going vessels, such as sail to Tarshish) 10[22.22]; א׳ חִירָם 10[11.22]; propelled by oars א׳־שַׁיִט Is 33[21].

591 †אֳנִיָּה **n.f. unit. a ship**—abs. Jon 1[3]+3t.; *Pl.* abs. אֳנִיּוֹת Dt 28[68]+; אֳוֹנִיּוֹת 2 Ch 8[18]; cstr. =abs. 1 K 22[49]+, etc.;—*a ship* Pr 30[19] Gn 49[13] Dt 28[68] Ju 5[17] (where, however, cf. Bu[BB Richter u. Sam. p. 16] on text) 1 K 22[49.50] Is 43[14] 2 Ch 8[18] 20[36.37] Jon 1[4.5] ψ 104[26] 107[23] Dn 11[40]; א׳ הַיָּם Ez 27[9]; propelled by oars Ez 27[29]; esp. א׳ תַּרְשִׁישׁ (cf. אֳנִי) 1 K 22[49] 2 Ch 9[21] (cf. 1 K 10[22] supr. sub אֳנִי) ψ 48[8] Is 2[16] 23[1.14] 60[9] Ez 27[25]; late of ship going to Tarshish 2 Ch 9[21] 20[36] Jon 1[3]; *merchant-ship*, א׳ סוֹחֵר Pr 31[14]; א׳ אֵבֶה *swift ships* Jb 9[26] (cf. אבה); *seamen* אַנְשֵׁי־אֳנִיּוֹת 1 K 9[27].

579 †III. [אָנָה] **vb. be opportune, meet, encounter opportunely** (Ar. أَنَى *the right time is come*, or *it is come to the right time*, or *to maturity*, or *is opportune*). **Pi.** *Pf.* אִנָּה Ex 21[13] *cause* (*or allow*) *to meet* in הָאֱלֹהִים א׳ בְּיָדוֹ (obj. om.), i.e. without any purpose of the man to whom sf. ref. **Pu.** *be allowed to meet, be sent*, *Impf.* יְאֻנֶּה Pr 12[21] (c. לְ); 3 fs. תְאֻנֶּה ψ 91[10] (c. אֶל), subj. *evil.* **Hithp.** *cause oneself to meet, seek occasion* (=seek a quarrel with) sq. לְ 2 K 5[7].

8385 †[תַּאֲנָה] **n.f. occasion, time of copulation**; sf. תַּאֲנָתָהּ i.e. of wild ass Je 2[24].

†תֹּאֲנָה **n.f. opportunity**, i.e. ground of quarrel; of Samson, sq. מִן Ju 14[4].

אָנָּה v. אָנָּא. above 577

אֲנוּ Je 42[6] Kt: v. after אֲנִי. p. 59 580

†[אָנַח] **vb.** only **Niph. sigh, groan**, mostly poet. & late (Aram. אֲנַח, ܐܢܚ Ethp. cf. As. [*anāḫu*], *inḫu*, *sigh* Zim[BP 12, 30])—*Pf.* 3 fs. נֶאֶנְחָה La 1[8] Jo 1[18]; 3 pl. נֶאֶנְחוּ Is 24[7]; *Impf.* יֵאָנַח Pr 29[2] etc.; *Imv.* הֵאָנַח Ez 21[11]; *Pt.* נֶאֱנָח Ez 21[12]; נֶאֱנָחָה La 1[21] etc.;—**1.** *sigh*, in token of grief Is 24[7] Pr 29[2] La 1[4] (‖ נוּגוֹת) v[21] Ez 21[11.11]; of Jerus. La 1[8]; mostly abs. but sq. עַל־ Ez 9[4] (‖ נֶאֱנָק); sq. עַל־ & אֶל־ 21[12]. **2.** in physical distress La 1[11] (‖ בִּקֵּשׁ לֶחֶם); Ex 2[23] sq. מִן *by reason of* (‖ זָעַק). **3.** *groan* of cattle (בְּהֵמָה) Jo 1[18]. 584

†אֲנָחָה **n.f. sighing, groaning** (poet. & late);—*abs.* ψ 31[11]+; *sf.* אַנְחָתִי Jb 3[4]+; אַנְחָתָה Is 21[2] (sf. with Raphe), *Pl. sf.* אַנְחֹתַי La 1[22];—*sighing, groaning*, in distress, physical or mental Jb 3[24] (‖ שְׁאָגָה), 23[2] (‖ שִׂיחַ), ψ 6[7]; 38[10] (‖ תַּאֲוָה), Is 21[2], La 1[22]; ‖ יָגוֹן ψ 31[11] Is 35[10] 51[11] Je 45[3]; קוֹל א׳ ψ 102[6]. 585

אֲנַחְנוּ **pron. 1 pl.** we v. infr. p. 59 587

†אֲנָחֲרַת **n.pr.loc.** city in Naphtali Jos 19[19]. Kn (cf. Di) comp. *en-Na'ûra*, on E. side of Jebel Daḥi, little Hermon; cf. Rob[BR iii. 339]. 588

אֲנִי, אָנִי pron. 1 s. comm. I (أَنَا, אֲנָא, 589

ܐܢܐ, አነ:) Gn 6^{17} 9$^{9.12}$ + oft. Following a ptcp. as its subj. (to express mostly either a true present or the fut. instans) Gn 18^{17} הַמְכַסֶּה אֲנִי *Am I hiding* from Abraham that which, etc., Ju 15^{3} 1 S 3^{13} Je 1^{12} 38^{14} 44^{29} (v. Dr^{§135,4}). Appended to a verb, it expresses, in early Hebrew, a real emphasis, as Ju 8^{23} לֹא אֶמְשֹׁל אֲנִי בָּכֶם *I* will not rule over you, 2 S 12^{28} lest *I* take the city, 2 S 17^{15} thus and thus did Ahitophel counsel, and thus and thus יָעַצְתִּי אָנִי did *I* counsel; but in later Heb. it is sometimes pleonastic, Ec 2$^{11-15.18-20}$+. In response to a question, אָנִי alone =*I am, It is I*, Gn 27^{24} Ju 13^{11} 1 K 18^{8}+. With הֲ, הַאֲנִי †Is 66^{9}. (Syn. אָנֹכִי, q.v.)

580 †אֲנוּ **pron. 1 pl. comm. we** (common in postB. Heb.; cf. also Amh. *ĕnā*) may be regarded as the pl. of אֲנִי (W$^{SG\ 99}$), only Je 42^{6} Kt, for which Qr substitutes the normal אֲנַחְנוּ.

595 **אָנֹכִי, אָנֹכִי** (once Jb 33^{9} אָנֹכִי) **pron. 1 s. comm.** I; Gn 3^{10} 7^{4} 15$^{1.2}$ 16^{5}+oft. With הֲ, הֶאָנֹכִי †Nu 11^{12} Jb 21^{4}. (As. *anâku*, Ph. & Moab. אנך: not in Ar. Aram. Eth.; but *ku* appears as the affix of the 1 s. in the Eth. verb (e.g. *waladku*=Heb. יָלַדְתִּי). אָנֹכִי and אֲנִי appear to be two parallel formations (both containing the element *ani* [cf. the sf. ־נִי, ـنِي] or *ana*, & one strengthened by the addition of the demonst. basis *ku* [prob. akin to ܟܐ, כָּא, כֹּה *here*]: cf. Sta^{§179} W$^{SG\ 95\ f.\ 98-101}$), of which, in most of the Sem. languages, one prevailed to the exclusion of the other, but which in Heb. maintained their place side by side.) In some cases אני and אנכי appear capable of being used indifferently; in others the choice seems to have been determined, partly by rhythmical considerations, partly by a growing preference for אֲנִי among later writers. Thus when appended to the verb for emph. (whether with or without גַּם) the lighter form אֲנִי is nearly always used (Lv 20^{5} 26$^{24.32}$ Dt 12^{30} Ju 1^{3} 8^{23} 2 S 12^{28} 17^{15} 18$^{2.22}$ Je 17^{18} 21^{5} Ez 17^{22} Jb 13^{2}+; cf. the cases Gn 27^{34} 1 S 25^{24} 2 S 19^{1} 1 K 1^{26} Pr 23^{15}); on the contrary, in the emph. rhetorical style of Dt, אָנֹכִי is preferred (in the discourses, uniformly, exc. 12^{30}, in acc. with usage just noted, & 29^{5} in a standing expression; on 32$^{48.51}$ (P) cf. infr.) In partic. phrases, also, usage prefers sts. אני, sts. אנכי; thus there occurs חַי־אָנִי Nu 14^{21} & always, exc. Dt 32^{40}; (אָנִי) אִתְּךָ אֲנִי (Je 1$^{9.19}$ 30^{11} 46^{18} Is 43$^{2.5}$); אֲנִי יהוה Ex 6$^{2.6-8}$ & elsewh. in P, & esp. freq. in H (Lv 18$^{2.4.6}$ etc.) & Ez, also Gn 15^{7} 28^{13} Dt 29^{5} Ju 6^{10}+; (אנכי יהוה much less freq.; only JE & proph. writers, †Ex 20^{2}=Dt 5^{6}, Ho 12^{10} 13^{4} ψ 81^{11}, Ex 20^{5}=Dt 5^{9}, Is 43^{11} 44^{24} 51^{15} (Ex 4^{11} is diff.); cf. Dr$^{JPh\ xi.\ 224\ f.}$); אני אמרתי Is 38^{10} (Hez.) 49^{4} Je 5^{4} 10^{19} (3^{19} אנכי) Ru 4^{4} ψ 30^{7} 31^{23} 41^{5} 82^{6}+; ויאמר אָנִי (in response to a qu.) Gn 27^{24} Ju 13^{11} 2 S 20^{17} 1 K 13^{14} 18^{8} (ו׳ אנכי only 2 S 2^{20}; on the contrary, with a *predicate*, אָנֹכִי is regularly employed, Gn 24^{34} 1 S 30^{13} 2 S 1^{8} עֲמָלֵקִי אָנֹכִי 11^{5} 20^{17} Is 6^{5} Je 1^{6} Jon 1^{9}); (הִנְנִי) וַאֲנִי הִנֵּה Gn 6^{17} 9^{9} Ex 31^{6} Nu 3^{12}+ (but הִנֵּה אָנֹכִי Gn 24$^{14.43}$ 25^{32} Ex 3^{13} 19^{9}+; הִנֵּה אֲנִי is very uncommon; v. *ib.*^{226}). So far as the usage of partic. books is concerned, in the Pent. (exc. Dt) אֲנִי is used in P (incl. H) always (about 130 t.) exc. Gn 23^{4} (cf. Ez below); in JE אנכי is preferred, though not exclusively (81 : 48). In S there are 50 instances of each form. Je has some 54 instances of אני, 37 of אנכי. In later books the preponderance of אֲנִי is evident. Thus in Ez אני occurs 138 t., אנכי once 36^{28} (perh. a reminiscence of Je 11^{4b} 24^{7} 30^{22}); in La Hg Ezr Est Ec אני 45 t., אנכי never; in Ch אני 30 t., אנכי once 1 Ch 17^{1} (from 2 S 7^{2}); in Dn אני 23 t., אנכי once 10^{11}. Vid. more fully Giesebrecht $^{ZAW\ 1881,\ 251-8}$ Dr$^{l.\ c.\ 222-7}$.

אֲנַחְנוּ, אֲנָחְנוּ **pron. 1 pl. comm. we** 587
(the pl. corresp. to אָנֹכִי, as אֲנוּ to אֲנִי; v. W$^{SG\ p.\ 100}$; Ph. אנחן CIS$^{I.\ 3.\ 16.17}$, Aram. אֲנַחְנָא, 𝔗 also נַחְנָא, Syr. ܚܢܢ, ܢܚܢ, ܢܚܢܢ, ንሕነ:) Gn 13^{8} 29^{4} 37^{7} 42$^{11.13}$ Nu 9^{7} Dt 1$^{28.41}$ Jo 2$^{17.18}$, etc. Like אֲנִי, following a ptcp. as its subj. Gn 19^{13} Nu 10^{29} Ju 19^{18} 2 K 18^{26}; appended to a vb. for emph. Ju 9^{28} 2 K 10^{4} Is 20^{6}.

†נַחְנוּ, נָחְנוּ **pron. 1 pl. we** (abbrev. from 5168
אֲנַחְנוּ; cf. the forms نَحْنُ, ንሕነ: נַחְנָא, just cited; also As. *nîni*) Gn 42^{11} Ex 16$^{7.8}$ Nu 32^{32} La 3^{42}. (In 2 S 17^{12} נַחְנוּ is 1 pl. perf. Qal from נוּחַ.)

†אֲנָךְ **n.[m.] plummet** (cf. words in cogn. 594
lang. for *lead, tin*, etym. dub., perh. foreign; Ar. آنُكٌ (v. Frä^{153}) Syr. ܐܢܟܐ, Mand. אנכא, As. *anâku* Lyon$^{Sargontexte\ 92}$; v. Lag$^{Arm.\ Stud.\ §\ 103}$ cf. Id. $^{BN\ 175}$)—אֲנָךְ exc. once Am 7^{8}—*plummet* Am 7$^{7.8.8}$; חוֹמַת א׳, i.e. a vertical wall v^{7}.

אָנֹכִי **pron. 1 sg.** v. supr. sub אֲנִי. above 595

†[אָנַן] **vb.** only **Hithpo. complain, mur-** 596
mur (Mish. אנן, Aram. אֲנַן, Ar. أَنَّ, As. [*anânu*], whence *ênênu, unnînu, sigh* Zim$^{BP\ 22}$)—*Impf.* יִתְאוֹנֵן La 3^{39} (sq. עַל־ in ‖ member); *Pt.* מִתְאֹנְנִים בְּאָזְנֵי י׳ Nu 11^{1} (sq. acc.; vid. Di).

597 †[אָנַס] **vb.** **compel, constrain** (late, oft. Mish. *id.*, Aram. אֲנַס, ܐܢܣ)—**Qal** *Pt.* אֵין אֹנֵס viz., to drink Est 1^{8} (‖ כִּרְצוֹן אִישׁ וָאִישׁ).

599 †[אָנֵף, אָנַף] **vb.** (breathe, snort) **be angry** (MI *id.*, cf. Ar. أَنِفَ, As. etc. in deriv.) — **Qal** *Pf.* אָנַפְתָּ ψ 60^{3}, etc.; *Impf.* יֶאֱנַף ψ 2^{12}, etc.;—*be angry*, of ׳י; usually sq. בְּ 1 K 8^{46}=2 Ch 6^{36} Is 12^{1} ψ 85^{6} Ezr 9^{14}; abs. ψ 60^{3} 79^{5}; cf. also ψ 2^{12}. **Hithp.** id. alw. sq. בְּ, & alw. of ׳י, *Pf.* הִתְאַנַּף Dt 1^{37} 4^{21} 9^{20}; *Impf.* וַיִּתְאַנַּף Dt 9^{8} 1 K 11^{9} 2 K 17^{18}.

639 I. אַף $_{277}$ **n.m.**[Gn 30, 2] **nostril, nose, face, anger** (As. *appu, face* Flood[iii. 27, 29] cf. Hpt KAT²[Gloss], Ar. أَنْفٌ, Eth. አንፍ: *nose;* Aram. אַנְפִּין, ܐܦܐ, *face*)—abs. ψ 78^{21}+; cstr. Gn 27^{45}+; sf. אַפִּי Ex 22^{23}+, etc.; du. אַפַּיִם Pr 14^{17}+; אַפָּיו Gn 2^{7}+etc.;—In Hex JE (Jos 7^{1} P? 23^{16} D?). **1.** *nostril*, as organ of breathing Gn 2^{7} 7^{22} Jb 27^{3} cf. Nu 11^{20}; 2 S 22^{9}=ψ 18^{9} cf. Is 65^{5}; Is 2^{22} La 4^{20} Ez 38^{18} (del. Co) Am 4^{10}; רוּחַ אַפֶּיךָ (of ׳י) i.e. wind Ex 15^{8}; cf. נִשְׁמַת רוּחַ אַפּוֹ 2 S 22^{16}= ψ 18^{16} (vid. also sub **3**); *nose* sg. Ct 7$^{5.9}$ Ez 8^{17} 23^{25} Pr 30^{33} (where play upon diff. meaning of אַף & אַפַּיִם): (*a*) as organ of smelling Dt 33^{10} ψ 115^{6}; (*b*) as place of ring for ornament Gn 24^{47} Is 3^{21} Ez 16^{12}; (*c*) as place of ring or hook for captive 2 K 19^{28}=Is 37^{29}; for beasts, e.g. swine Pr 11^{22}; hippopot. Jb 40^{24}; crocod. v^{26}. **2.** Du. *face* (esp. in phrase אַפַּיִם אַרְצָה) Gn 19^{1} 42^{6} 48^{12} Nu 22^{31} 1 S 20^{41} 24^{9} 25^{41} 28^{14} 2 S 14^{4} 14^{33} 18^{28} 24^{20} 1 K 1$^{23.31}$ Is 49^{23} 1 Ch 21^{21} 2 Ch 7^{3} 20^{18} Ne 8^{6} also Gn 3^{19}; גֹּבַהּ אַפּוֹ *pride of his countenance* ψ 10^{4}; לְאַפֵּי *before*, loc. sense (cf. לִפְנֵי) 1 S 25^{23}; אַפָּיִם 1 S 1^{5} rd. אֶפֶס 𝔊 We Dr (q.v.) **3.** mostly *anger*, human Gn 27^{45} 49$^{6.7}$+(45 t.); oftener divine Ex 32^{12} Dt 9^{19} 2 K 24^{20}+(177 t.); oft. subj. חָרָה (וַיִּחַר etc.) *his anger was kindled* Gn 30^{2} 39^{19} Ex 4^{14} 22^{23} 32$^{10.11}$+; in various combinations, esp. חֲרוֹן אַף *fierceness of anger* Ex 32^{12} Nu 25^{4} 32^{14}+; cf. חֳרִי־אַף 1 S 20^{34}; בַּעַל־אַף Pr 22^{24} *one given to anger*, etc.; אֶרֶךְ אַפַּיִם *slow to anger* Ex 34^{6} Nu 14^{18} Ne 9^{17} + 7 t. of God; Pr 14^{29} 15^{18} 16^{32} 25^{15} of man.

649 †אַפַּיִם **n.pr.m.** a son of Nadab, 1 Ch 2$^{30.31}$.

601 †אֲנָפָה **n.f.** an unclean bird (cf. As. *anpatu* Dl[HA 33]; mng. quite dub.; on conjectures v. Di Lv 11^{19}) Lv 11^{19} Dt 14^{8}.

602 †[אָנַק] **vb. cry, groan** (Aram. אֲנַק, ܐܢܩ) — **Qal** *Impf.* יֶאֱנֹק Je 51^{52}; *Inf. cstr.* אֱנֹק Ez 26^{15}, both of groaning of wounded (חָלָל).

Niph. *id.*, in mourning, lamentation; *Inf. cstr.* הֵאָנֵק Ez 24^{17} (‖ עָשָׂה אֵבֶל); *Pt.* נֶאֱנָקִים 9^{4} (‖ נֶאֱנָחִים) sq. עַל.

†I. אֲנָקָה **n.f. crying, groaning,** in dis- 603
tress (Aram. ܐܢܩܬܐ) Mal 2^{13} (‖ בְּכִי, דִּמְעָה); *cstr.* אֶנְקַת ψ 12^{6} (of poor, אֶבְיוֹן); 79^{11} (of prisoner אָסִיר), so 102^{21}.

†II. אֲנָקָה **n.f. ferret, or shrew-mouse,** 604
unclean animal Lv 11^{30} (Tristr[FFP 24]; ܐܡܩܬܐ, 𝔗 אקמתא).

†I. [אָנַשׁ] **vb. be weak, sick** (As. *anâšu* 605
Zim[BP 56, 70]; Wetzst in De[Psalmen, ed. 4, 882] der. fr. II. אנשׁ *per antiphrasin;* Dl[Pr 160] identified with III. אנשׁ; v. also De[Psalmen, ed. 4, 904]; so Lag[BN 60], who comp. سَيْفٌ أَنِيثٌ, *weichliches* d.h. *stumpfes Schwert*. It seems safer at present to keep the three distinct). **Qal** *Pt. pass.* אָנוּשׁ Jb 34^{6}+; אֲנוּשָׁה Je 15^{18} Mi 1^{9} & so rd. ψ 69^{21} (Bi Che) etc.; as adj. *incurable*, of wound, but metaph. (מַכָּה) Mi 1^{9} Je 15^{18}; cf. Jb 34^{6} (חֵץ), Je 30^{12} (שֶׁבֶר ‖ נַחְלָה מַכָּה); so כְּאֵב אָנוּשׁ Is 17^{11}; cf. Je 30^{15} (מַכְאֹב); cf. יוֹם אָנוּשׁ 17^{16}; also in phr. עָקֹב הַלֵּב מִכֹּל וְאָנֻשׁ הוּא Je 17^{9}. **Niph.** *Impf.* וַיֵּאָנַשׁ 2 S 12^{15} *be sick*, of child.

II. אנשׁ (cf. Ar. أَنِسَ *be inclined to, friendly, social*, which however Nö[ZMG 1886, 739] thinks denom., cf. إِنْسٌ coll. *men, people;* v. on the other hand Wetzst[l.c.] Zim[BP 20], v. also Lag[BN 68];—hence אֲנָשִׁים pl. of אִישׁ; v. also sub אישׁ).

†אֱנוֹשׁ **n.m.**[Jb 15, 14] **man, mankind,** mostly 582
poet. (18 t. Jb, 13 t. ψ, etc.) (Ar. أُنَاسٌ (coll.), Aram. אֱנָשׁ, ܐ݈ܢܳܫܐ (coll.), Nab. אנושׁ, Palm. אנשׁ, Sab. אנס DHM[ZMG 1883, 330], also Ar. نَاسٌ, As. *nišu, people*, & cf. *tenišêtu, humanity, human race*, v. COT[Gloss] sub אנשׁ & נשׁ & Hpt[KAT 2.497])—*abs.* Is 8^{1}+; *cstr.* Je 20^{10};—**1.** of individ. Jb 5^{17} 13^{9} ψ 55^{14}, cf. Is 13^{12} (‖ אָדָם) 56^{2} (‖ בֶּן־אדם); Je 20^{10} אֱ׳ שְׁלֹמִי *man of my peace*, i.e. my friend. **2.** coll. *men* Is 24^{6} 33^{8} 51^{7} ψ 66^{12}; = men in general, ordinary men ψ 73^{5} cf. חֶרֶט אֱ׳ i.e. a common stylus Is 8^{1} (v. אַמַּת אִישׁ Dt 3^{11}). **3.** *man, mankind* Dt 32^{26} Jb 7^{1} 14^{19} 28$^{4.13}$ 32^{8} 33^{26} 36^{25} (‖ אָדָם & אֲנָשִׁים v^{24}) ψ 56^{2}; esp. opp. God Jb 4^{17} (‖ גֶּבֶר) 7^{17} 9^{2} 10$^{4.5}$ 15^{14} 25^{4} 33^{12} 2 Ch 14^{10}; ψ 8^{5} (‖ בֶּן־אָדָם) so Is 51^{12}; ψ 9$^{20.21}$, 90^{3} (‖ בְּנֵי־אָדָם); 103^{15}; 144^{3} (‖ אָדָם) בֶּן־א׳; cf. כִּי־א׳ רִמָּה וּבֶן־אָדָם תּוֹלֵעָה Jb 25^{6}; א׳ מִן־הָאָרֶץ ψ 10^{18}; כָּל־לְבַב א׳ Is 13^{7} cf. ψ 104$^{15.15}$.

†אֱנוֹשׁ **n.pr.m.** son of Seth Gn 4^{26} 5$^{6.7.9.10.11}$ 583
1 Ch 1^{1}.

III. **אנש** (*soft, delicate*, cf. Ar. أَنُثَ, *id.*, v. Lag[BN 68] Dl[Pr 160], also sub I. אנש; but cf. Nö[ZMG 1886, 780] who der. this mng. fr. *feminine*).

802 **אִשָּׁה** [775] **n.f. woman, wife, female** (Ar. أُنْثَى, Sab. אנתת etc. DHM[ZK 1884, 360], Aram. אִתְּתָא, אִנְתְּתָא, אִתָּא, ܐܢܬܬܐ, Palm. Nab. אנתתא, Eth. አንስት: Ph. אשת, As. *aššatu* COT[Gloss])—א׳ abs. Gn 2[23]+; cstr. אֵשֶׁת Gn 11[29]+ (appar. abs. Dt 21[11] 1 S 28[7] ψ 58[9] but cf. Bö[§728] Ges[§130.5]); sf. אִשְׁתִּי Gn 20[11]+; אִשְׁתְּךָ Gn 12[18]+ (אֶשְׁתְּךָ ψ 128[3]), etc.; *Pl.* †אִשֹּׁת Ez 23[44] (Co לעשות); נָשִׁים Gn 4[19]+; cstr. נְשֵׁי Gn 4[23]+; sf. נָשַׁי Gn 30[26] 1 K 20[7]; נְשֵׁיכֶם Ex 22[23]+, etc.;—**1.** *woman* Gn 3[1.2] 12[11]+; opp. man 2[22.23] Ex 35[29] 36[6] Dt 7[2.5]; 22[22] 1 S 21[5]+; א׳ emphat. *a genuine* (or ideal) *woman* Ec 7[28] (‖ אדם); sim. of men as feeble, timid Je 50[37] 51[30]; note esp. הַטַּף בַּנָּשִׁים *the children among the women, female children* Nu 31[18] (P); as conceiving Ex 2[2] Lv 12[2] 2 S 11[5]+; travailing Je 13[21]; bearing children Ju 13[24] 1 K 3[18]; cf. Jb 14[1] 15[14] 25[4]+, etc.; suckling Is 49[15]; דֶּרֶךְ נָשִׁים Gn 31[35]; ארח כַּנָּשִׁים Gn 18[11]; with adj., or app., א׳מֵינֶקֶת *nursing woman, nurse* Ex 2[7]; א׳ זוֹנָה *harlot* Jos 2[1] 6[22] Ju 11[1] 16[1] 1 K 3[16] Pr 6[26] Je 3[3] Ez 16[30] 23[44]; so א׳ זָרָה Pr 2[16] 7[5]; cf. also Ez 23[44] supr.; א׳ מְנָאֶפֶת *adulteress* Pr 30[20] (cf. אֵשֶׁת אִישׁ 6[26]), אֵשֶׁת זְנוּנִים Ho 1[2]; נָשִׁים נָכְרִיּוֹת *foreign women* 1 K 11[1.8] Ezr 10[2.10.11.14.17.18.44] Ne 13[26.27] (cf. v[23]); א׳ חֲכָמָה *wise woman*, one known as clever, shrewd 2 S 14[2] 20[16], etc.; also א׳ פִּילֶגֶשׁ *concubine* Ju 19[1.27]: א׳ אַלְמָנָה *widow* 2 S 14[5] 1 K 11[26] 17[9.10]; א׳ נְבִיאָה *prophetess* Ju 4[4]; also cstr. bef. noun of quality אֵשֶׁת רָע Pr 6[24]; א׳ כְּסִילוּת 9[13]; א׳ חֵן 11[16]; א׳ חַיִל 12[4] 31[10] Ru 3[11]; א׳ מִדְיָנִים Pr 21[9] 25[24] 27[15]; א׳ מ׳ וָכַעַס 21[19].

2. *Wife* (woman belonging to a man, usually cstr. or sf.) Gn 2[24.25] 3[8.17] 4[1.17]+oft.; of one betrothed (ארשׂ) Dt 20[7] 28[30]; בַּעַל (הָ)אִשָּׁה Ex 21[3.22]; אִישׁ הָאִשָּׁה Ju 20[4]; לְאִשָּׁה *to wife* Gn 2[22] 12[19] 16[3] 34[21]+oft. (after נָתַן, לָקַח husband or father subj.); *for wife* (after הָיְתָה, woman subj.) Gn 20[12] Nu 36[3.6.6.11.12] Dt 22[19.29]+; for unfaithful wife cf. **1**; cstr. in phr. אֵשֶׁת חֵיקֶךָ Dt 13[7] cf. 28[54]; א׳ נְעוּרֶיךָ Pr 5[18] Mal 2[14.15]; א׳ בְּרִיתֶךָ v[14]; אֵשֶׁת אָב=step-mother Lv 18[8.11] 20[11].

3. *Female* of animals Gn 7[2.2]; v. also sub **4.**

†**4.** With distrib. & recipr. sense, א׳ מֵאֵת רְעוּתָהּ *each woman from her neighbour* Ex 11[2] (E); cf. Ru 1[8.9] Je 9[19]; *each one*, of birds of prey Is 34[15] cf. v[16] (del. Bi Che); of cows (fig. of heartless women of Isr.) Am 4[3]; of sheep (fig. of Isr.) Zc 11[9]; & of inanimate things (P, & late) א׳ אֶל אֲחֹתָהּ Ex 26[3.3.5.6.17] (P) Ez 1[9] (del. Co) v[23] 3[13].

אנת (the root of the pron. 2 pers. in Shemitic: أَنْتَ, አንተ: *anta*; f. أَنْتِ, አንቲ: *antī*; BAram. Kt אַנְתָּה (m.), 𝔗 אַנְתְּ & אַתְּ (both m. & f.); Syr. ܐܢܬ, f. ܐܢܬܝ, the *n* being written but not pronounced; As. *atta*, f. *atti-e* Dl[§55a], the *nt* being merged in the double *t*; Heb. similarly. Pl. أَنْتُمْ, አንትሙ: f. أَنْتُنَّ, አንትን: Aram. אַנְתּוּן, ܐܢܬܘܢ, f. אַתֵּין, ܐܢܬܝܢ; As. *attunu*).

אַתָּה, אַתָּ֫ה (so regularly; but 26–7 t., with 859
different disj. accents, אָ֫תָּה: v. Fr[MM 228]; Sta[§178a (rd. 8 for 18)] **pron. 2 s.m. thou** (for *anta*, v. supr.; cf. נָתַתָּ for נָתַנְתָּ) Gn 3[11.19]+oft. Written אַתָּ †1 S 24[19] ψ 6[4] Jb 1[10] Ec 7[22] Ne 9[6]. Appended to a vb. for emph., Ex 18[19.19] 1 S 17[56] שְׁאַל אַתָּה inquire *thou*, 20[8] 22[18] Is 43[26] סַפֵּר אַתָּה. Added for the purpose of strengthening a gen. or accus. sf. 1 K 21[19] Pr 22[19] (Ges[§135.2]).

אתי, i.e. אַתִּי, the older & more original form 859
of אַתְּ *thou* (fem.), preserved, prob. dialectically, 7 t. in Kt, Ju 17[2] 1 K 14[2] 2 K 4[16.23] 8[1] Je 4[30] Ez 36[13]. (V. supr. As in Syr., the י may not have been fully sounded: the Massorites direct אַתְּ to be everywhere read.)

אַתְּ, אַתְּ pron. 2 s.f. thou (fem.) (shortened 859
from אַתִּי (q.v.); in Syr. the two genders are written differently, ܐܢܬ, ܐܢܬܝ, but, the ܝ not being sounded, are pronounced alike: in 𝔗 both are written אַתְּ or אַנְתְּ) Gn 12[11.13] 24[23]+oft. Thrice Nu 11[15] Dt 5[24] Ez 28[14] used as a masc. (as in Aram. of 𝔗); but prob. אַתָּ (v. sub אַתָּה) should be here read.

אַתֶּם pron. 2 m.pl. you (masc.) (for *antem*, 859
v. supr.) Gn 9[7] 26[27] 29[4]+oft. With הֲ, הַאַתֶּם †Ju 6[31]; following the vb. for emph. Ju 15[12] Je 34[15]; construed inaccurately with a fem. Ez 13[20].

†**אַתֵּן** Ez 34[31] (many edd. אַתֶּן), אַתֵּ֫נָה Gn 31[6] 859
Ez 13[11.20] (edd. אַתֵּ֫נָּה) 34[17] **pron. 2 f.pl. you** (fem.)

I. **אסה** (perh. cf. Ar. أَسَا *heal*, Aram. אֲסָא, ܐܣܐ).

אָסָא n.pr.m. (perh. *healer*) king of Judah, 609
son of Abijam and father of Jehoshaphat 1 K 15[8.9.11]+24 t. 1 K 15.16.22; 1 Ch 3[10] 9[16] 2 Ch 13[23]+28 t. 2 Ch 14–21; Je 41[9].

II. **אסה** (cf. Ar. أَسِيَ be sorrowful, distressed).

611 †אָסוֹן **n.m. mischief, evil, harm**; alw. abs. without art. Gn 42$^{4.38}$ (as subj. of קרא), 44^{29} (קרה), Ex 21$^{22.23}$ (היה).

610 אָסוּף v. סוּף. p. 692

אסם (*gather*, *store*, Aram. ܐܣܡ).

618 †[אָסָם] **n.m.** $^{Pr 3,10}$ *storehouse* (Aram. אסנא, *id.*, ܐܣܢܐ *store, supply*) pl. sf. אֲסָמֶיךָ Dt 28^{8} Pr 3^{10}.

619 †אַסְנָה **n.pr.m.** (Aram. אַסָּנָא *thorn-bush?*) head of a family of Nethinim Ezr 2^{50} (om. Ne 7^{52}).

621 †אָסְנַת **n.pr.f.** wife of Joseph (𝔊 Ἀσεννεθ, 𝔊L Ἀσσενεθ; Egyptian, = *belonging to* (goddess) *Neith* (Thes); Cook $^{Speaker's\ Comm.\ i.\ 479}$ prop. either *As-Neit, favourite of Neith*, or < *Isis-Neit*) Gn 41$^{45.50}$ 46^{20}.

622 **אָסַף** 200 **vb. gather, remove** (As. *asâpu*, Dl$^{Pr\ 45}$)—**Qal** *Pf.* אָסַף Gn 30^{23}+; אָסַפְתָּ ψ 85^{4}, etc.; *Impf.* יֶאֱסֹף 2 K 5^{3}; יַאַסְפֵנִי ψ 27^{10}, etc.; also וַיֹּסֶף 2 S 6^{1}; 2 ms. תֹּסֵף ψ 104^{29}; 1 s. אֹסְפָה Mi 4^{6}; so prob. (sf.) אֹסִפְךָ 1 S 15^{6} (rd. אֹסִפְךָ) v. Kö$^{i.\ 382}$ Dr^{Sm}; *Imv.* אֱסֹף Nu 21^{16}+ אֶסְפָה Nu 11^{16}; 2 fs. אִסְפִּי Je 10^{17}; אִסְפוּ ψ 50^{5}+; *Inf. abs.* אָסֹף Je 8^{13}+ (Hiph., fr. סוף acc. to Ba$^{NB\ 73}$); *cstr.* אֱסֹף 2 K 5^{7}+; אָסְפְּךָ Ex 23^{16}; אָסְפְּכֶם Lv 23^{39}; *Pt. act.* אֹסֵף Nu 19^{10}; אֹסִפְךָ 2 K 22^{20} 2 Ch 34^{28} (pointed אֹסִפְךָ i.e. Hiph.; cf. Kö$^{l.c.}$); אֹסְפָם ψ 39^{7};
624 *pass.* pl. cstr. אֲסֻפֵי Ez 34^{29};—**1.** *gather, collect* (*a*) persons Gn 29^{22} 42^{17} (sq. אֶל־) Ex 3^{16} 4^{29} Nu 11$^{16.24}$ 21^{16} Jos 2^{18} (sq. אֶל־ + ־ה loc.) 24^{1} (sq. ־ה loc.; all these JE); 1 S 5$^{8.11}$ 2 K 23^{1} (sq. אֶל־) Jos 2^{16} Is 11^{12} Zp 3^{8} Hb 2^{5} Ez 11^{17} (all ‖ קבץ) +; collect men, people, armies, etc., for fighting Nu 21^{23} (E) Ju 11^{20} 1 S 17^{1} 2 S 10^{17} 12^{29}+; cf. Zc 14^{2} (sq. עַל־ *against*); (*b*) once obj. beasts Je 12^{9}; (*c*) things, esp. fruits of earth Ex 23$^{10.16}$ (Cov't code) Lv 25$^{3.20.39}$ (H) Dt 11^{14} 16^{13} 28^{38} Is 17^{5} Je 40$^{10.12}$ Jb 39^{12} ψ 39^{7}; cf. Ru 2^{7} (‖ לקט *glean*); the quails Nu 11$^{32.32}$; food in gen. (מַאֲכָל) Gn 6^{21} (sq. אֶל־); eggs Is 10^{14}; money 2 K 22^{4} 2 Ch 24^{11}; ashes of red heifer Nu 19$^{9.10}$; chariots 1 K 10^{26} 2 Ch 1^{14}, etc.; of fisherman (בְּמִכְמַרְתּוֹ, in metaph.) Hb 1^{15}; of collecting wind Pr 30^{4} מִי אָ׳־רוּחַ בְּחָפְנָיו. **2.** *gather* an individual into company of others: (*a*) obj. pers. esp. *gather to one's fathers* 2 K 22^{20} (עַל־אֲבֹתֶיךָ) = 2 Ch 34^{28} (אֶל־; both ‖ Niph. of same vb. q. v.); hence also (*b*) *bring*, obj. pers. 1 S 14^{52} (on form here v. Dr) 2 S 11^{27} (both sq. אֶל־), association, responsibility, protection being implied; also of stray ox or sheep Dt 22^{2} (sq. אֶל־תּוֹךְ); hence also (*c*) *take up, care for*, subj. י׳ ψ 27^{10} (cf. perh. Is 40^{11} קבץ); (*d*) *draw up* the feet upon the bed (אֶל־) Gn 49^{33}. **3.** *bring up the rear of* Is 58^{8} כְּבוֹד י׳ יַאַסְפֶךָ i.e. be thy rear-guard (‖ הָלַךְ לְפָנֶיךָ צִדְקֶךָ)—52^{12} has Pi. מְאַסִּפְכֶם q. v. † **4.** *gather and take away, remove, withdraw* 1 S 14^{19} (obj. hand), Je 10^{17} (bundle, sq. מִן), leprosy 2 K 5^{11} (v. צרע); cf. also א׳ מִצָּרַעַת, remove (set free) a man from leprosy v$^{3.6.7}$; Gn 30^{23} Is 4^{1} (reproach), ψ 85^{4} (wrath, ‖ הֵשִׁיב), Je 16^{5} (peace, sq. מִן), Jo 2^{10} 4^{15} (light), ψ 26^{9} (נֶפֶשׁ) so Ju 18^{25}; ψ 104^{29} (רוּחַ) v. also Jb 34^{14} (sq. אֶל־); hence *destroy* 1 S 15^{6} obj. pers.);
pass. אֲסֻפֵי רָעָב *destroyed with hunger* Ez 34^{29}; 624
also *Inf. abs.* Je 8^{13} Zp 1^{2} (joined with הָסֵף fr. סוף, v. Kö$^{i.\ 445}$; considered Hiph. Inf. abs. by Ba$^{NB\ 73}$ v. supr.) **Niph.** *Pf.* נֶאֱסַף Nu 27^{13}+ נֶאֶסְפָה Je 48^{33} etc.; *Impf.* יֵאָסֵף Ex 9^{19}+; וַיֵּאָסֶף Gn 25^{8}+; יֵאָסֵפוּן ψ 104^{22} etc.; *Imv.* הֵאָסֵף Dt 32^{50}; הֵאָסְפִי Je 47^{6}; הֵאָסְפוּ Gn 49^{1}+; *Inf. abs.* הֵאָסֹף 2 S 17^{11} (on form cf. Ba$^{NB\ 74}$); *cstr.* הֵאָסֵף Gn 29^{7} Nu 12^{15}; *Pt.* נֶאֱסָף Gn 49^{29}; נֶאֱסָפִים 1 S 13^{11} Is 13^{14}; נֶאֱסָפִים Is 57^{1};—**1.** *assemble, be gathered*, reflex. (*a*) subj. men Gn 49^{1} (‖ קבץ v^{2}), Is 43^{9} (‖ קָבַץ), 2 Ch 30^{3} (sq. לְ) v^{13} (sq. acc. loc.), Ezr 3^{1} 9^{4} Ne 8$^{1.13}$ (all sq. אֶל־) 9^{1} 12^{28}; earlier mostly of assembling for war Gn 34^{30} (sq. עַל־), Jos 10^{5} Ju 6^{33} 9^{6} 10^{17} (‖ נצעק), 20^{11} (sq. אֶל־) v^{14} (sq. ־ה loc.), 1 S 13^{11} (sq. acc. loc.) +; (*b*) subj. flocks, etc. Gn 29^{3} (pass.; sq. שָׁמָּה) v$^{7.8}$ (all J); fish Nu 11^{22} (cf. Hb 1^{15} Qal); (*c*) inanim. subj. herbs Pr 27^{25}; water 2 S 14^{14} (in sim.); bones for burial Je 8^{2} cf. 25^{33} (bodies of slain) v. also Ez 29^{5} (‖ קבץ which Co rds. קבר), appar. = *compose, arrange* for burial. **2.** pass. of Qal **2**; (*a*) *be gathered to one's fathers* נֶא׳ אֶל־אֲבוֹתָיו Ju 2^{10}; elsewh. *to one's people* אֶל־עַמָּיו (all P) Gn 25$^{8.17}$ 35^{29} (‖ וַיִּגְוַע וַיָּמָת) 49$^{29.33}$ (‖ גוע), Nu 20$^{24.26}$ (‖ מות) 27$^{13.13}$ 31^{2} Dt 32$^{50.50}$ (both ‖ מות); also אֶל־קִבְרֹתֶיךָ 2 K 22^{20} = 2 Ch 34^{28} (both ‖ Qal q. v.); hence also (*b*) *be brought in* (into association with others, etc.) Nu 12$^{14.15}$ (E) of Miriam, after leprosy; also refl. *betake oneself*, of Moses 11^{30} (E), cf. 2 S 17^{13} (both sq. אֶל־); even with inanim. subj. Je 47^{6} הֵאָסְפִי אֶל־תַּעְרֵךְ (addressed to sword); of man & beast *brought home* (sq. ־ה loc.) for protection Ex 9^{19}.

3. Pass. of Qal **4**; *be taken away, removed, perish*, of men Is 57$^{1.1}$ (‖ אבד); fish Ho 4^{3}; *gladness* Is 16^{10} Je 48^{33} (sq. מִן); also reflex., *withdraw itself*, of moon Is 60^{20} (‖ בוא שמש). †**Pi.** *Pt.* מְאַסֵּף Nu 10^{25}+; מְאַסְּפָיו Is 62^{9} (so BD v.

Kö$^{i.201}$), כִּמְאַסִּפְכֶם Is 52^{12};—**1.** *gather* harvest Is 62^{9} (‖ קבץ); bodies for burial Je 9^{21}. **2.** *take in, receive into* (sq. בַּיְתָה) Ju 19$^{15.18}$. **3.** as subst. *rearguard, rearward* Nu 10^{25} (P) Jos 6$^{9.13}$ (both E); fig. of God Is 52^{12}. †**Pu.** *Pf.* וְאֻסַּף (cons.) Is 33^{4} Zc 14^{14} etc.; *Pt.* מְאֻסָּף Ez 38^{12}—*be gathered*, of men Is 24^{22} Ho 10^{10} (sq. עַל *against*), Ez 38^{12}; booty Is 33^{4}; wealth Zc 14^{14}. †**Hithp.** *Inf.* הִתְאַסֵּף Dt 33^{5} *gather themselves.*

625 †אֹסֶף **n.m.**$^{Is\ 32,10}$ **gathering** (on formation cf. Ba$^{NB\ 109}$) of summer fruit אָסְפֵּי־קַיִץ Mi 7^{1}; cf. abs. אֹסֶף Is 32^{10}; א׳ הֶחָסִיל *gathering of the locust*, i.e. as the locust devours, destroys Is 33^{4}.

623 אָסָף **n.pr.m.** (*gatherer*, cf. Ph. n.pr.f. אספת) †**1.** father of יוֹאָח the recorder 2 K 18$^{18.37}$=Is 36$^{3.22}$. **2.** one of David's chief musicians, a Levite, son of Berechiah 1 Ch 6$^{24.24}$ (‖ הֵימָן v^{18}, אֵיתָן v^{29} vid. these names); 15^{17} (‖ Heman & Ethan, all called) הַמְשֹׁרְרִים v^{19}; v. also 16$^{5.5.7}$ cf. v^{37} (‖ Heman & Jeduthun v$^{41.42}$); 25^{9}, named with Heman & Jeduthun also 25^{6} 2 Ch 5^{12} 35^{15}; ψ 50. 73–83 are ascribed to Asaph; cf. also בִּימֵי דָוִיד וְאָסָף Ne 12^{46}; he is called also הַחֹזֶה 2 Ch 29^{30}, cf. אָסָף הַנִּבָּא עַל־יְדֵי־הַמֶּלֶךְ 1 Ch 25^{2}; repeated mention is made also of *sons of Asaph* בְּנֵי־אָסָף, sons, descendants, and pupils, or those who sang and played after his manner 1 Ch 25^{1} (‖ Heman & Jeduthun) v$^{2.2}$; called הַמְשֹׁרְרִים 2 Ch 35^{15} Ezr 2^{41} Ne 7^{44} 11^{22}, cf. Ezr 3^{10}; performing service of purification, Hezekiah's time 2 Ch 29^{13}; one of them prophesying 2 Ch 20^{14};—1 Ch 26^{1} for בְּנֵי אָסָף rd. בְּנֵי אֶבְיָסָף, cf. 9^{19}; on זִכְרִי 9^{15}, זַבְדִּי Ne 11^{17}, זַכּוּר 12^{35}, called בֶּן־אָסָף, v. these names. †**3.** keeper of king's park Ne 2^{8}.

614 †אָסִיף **n.[m.] ingathering, harvest** (on formation cf. Lag$^{BN\ 173}$ Ba$^{NB\ 136}$) חַג הָאָסִיף Ex 34^{22} (J); ח׳ הָאָסִף Ex 23^{16} (E)—both Cov't codes.

†[אָסֹף] **n.[m.]** what is gathered, **store**, hence בֵּית הָאֲסֻפִּים *store-house*, near south gate of temple 1 Ch 26^{15} (cf. 2 Ch 25^{24}); v^{17} הָא׳ alone in same sense; cf. אֲסֻפֵּי הַשְּׁעָרִים Ne 12^{25}.

626 †אֲסֵפָה **n.f.verbal. a collecting, gathering**; אֻסְּפוּ א׳ אַסִּיר Is 24^{22} *they are collected, as a collecting captives* unto a pit (dungeon); or *they are gathered with a gathering* (as) *captives*, cf. 22^{18}; but perh. rd. אֹסֶף הָאַסִּיר (cstr.); v. Weir Che.

627 †[אֲסֻפָּה] **n.f. collection** (cf. Ph. אספת *assembly*) only בַּעֲלֵי אֲסֻפּוֹת Ec 12^{11} (דִּבְרֵי חֲכָמִים) compared to driven nails; *members of* learned *assemblies* Thes MV al.; so postB. Heb. NHWB $^{i.127}$; but Hitz-Now al. refer to the wise utterances, called *lords* (possessors) *of collection* because of their well-connected grouping.

†[אֲסַפְסֻף] **n.[m.] collection, rabble,** only 628
הָאסַפְסֻף Nu 11^{4} of the camp-followers attending Hebrews at the Exodus.

†אַסְפָּתָא **n.pr.m.** 3rd son of Haman Est 630
9^{7} (Pers. *aspadâta*, ab equo sacro datus acc. to Thes Add^{71}, after Pott & Benfey).

†[אָסַר] **vb. tie, bind, imprison** (Ar. 631
أَسَرَ, As. *asâru*, cf. COT^{Gloss}, Aram. אֲסַר, ܐܣܰܪ, Eth. አሰረ: አሥረ:)—**Qal** *Pf.* sf. אֲסָרָם Jb 36^{13}; 3 fs. אָסְרָה Nu 30^{5}+, etc.; *Impf.* יֶאְסֹר 1 K 20^{14}; וַיֶּאֱסֹר Gn 42^{24}; וַיֶּאְסֹר Gn 46^{29}+; pl. sf. יַאַסְרֻנִי Ju 16^{7} etc.; *Imv.* אֱסֹר 1 K 18^{44} 2 K 9^{21}; אִסְרוּ Je 46^{4} ψ 118^{27}; *Inf. abs.* אָסֹר Ju 15^{13}; אָסוֹר 16^{11}; *cstr.* לֶאְסֹר Nu 30^{3}+; לֶאֱסוֹר Ju 15^{10}; לְאָסְרְךָ 15^{12}; אָסְרָם Ho 10^{10}; *Pt. act.* cstr. אֹסְרִי Gn 49^{11}; *pass.* אָסוּר Gn 40^{3}+; pl. אֲסוּרִים 39^{20}+; also Ju 16$^{21.25}$ Qr (Kt אסירים); הָסוּרִים Ec 4^{14} (cf. Now); אֲסֻרוֹת 2 S 3^{34}; cstr. אסורי Gn 39^{20} Kt (Qr אֲסִירֵי);—**1.** *tie, bind,* for security, foal to vine (sq. לְ) Gn 49^{11} (blessing of Jacob); horses and asses 2 K 7$^{10.10}$; ψ 118^{27} is dub. De *bind the festal victim with cords;* Che *bind the procession with branches,* etc. **2.** *tie, harness,* kine to (בְּ) cart 1 S 6$^{7.10}$; so (metaph.) Ho 10^{10} *harness them to* (לְ) *their two iniquities* (but Jer Ew Now make א׳ here=יסר *chastise*, cf. אֶסֳּרֵם v^{a}); also sq. acc. *chariot* Gn 46^{29} (J) Ex 14^{6} (E) 2 K 9^{21}; abs. 1 K 18^{44} 2 K 9^{21}; even of making ready chargers א׳ הַסּוּסִים Je 46^{4} (‖ עֲלוּ הַפָּרָשִׁים). **3.** *bind,* with cords, fetters, etc., as prisoner, Simeon Gn 42^{24} (E), Samson Ju 15$^{10.12.13.13.13}$ 16$^{5.7.8.11.11.12}$; א׳ בַּנְחֻשְׁתַּיִם 2 K 25^{7} =2 Ch 36^{6}=Je 39^{7} 52^{11}; also 2 Ch 33^{11}; cf. (without בַּנ׳) 2 K 17^{4} (עָצַר ‖ א׳ בֵּית כֶּלֶא), 23^{33}; cf. of divine chastisement Jb 36^{13} & v. also Ez 3^{25} ψ 149^{8}; fig. of absolute authority ψ 105^{22}; esp. *Pt. pass.* 2 S 3^{34} *thy hands were not bound* (‖ *and thy feet not put in fetters*); א׳ בָּאזִקִּים Je 40^{1} cf. א׳ בַּזִּקִּים Jb 36^{8} (prob. fig. ‖ חַבְלֵי־עֹנִי); metaph. of king held captive by a woman's tresses Ct 7^{6}; perh. = *imprisoned* (whether bound or not) Gn 39^{20} 40$^{3.5}$ (all JE); as subst. pl. *prisoners* Gn 39^{20} (Kt, v. supr.); so (late) as distressed, & obj. of divine compassion Is 49^{9} 61^{1} ψ 146^{7}; בֵּית האסירים *prison* Ju 16$^{21.25}$; cf. Ec 4^{14}. **4.** *gird* (rare & late) א׳ אֵזוֹר בְּמָתְנֵיהֶם Jb 12^{18} (אֵזוֹר=slaves' waistcloth, RS p. 25 supr.; Hoffm rds. וַיֶּסֶר for וַיֶּאְסֹר) חַרְבּוֹ אֲסוּרִים עַל־מָתְנָיו;

Ne 4^{12}. **5.** sq. מִלְחָמָה *begin the battle, make the attack* (cf. Germ. *mit jemandem anbinden*) 1 K 20^{14} 2 Ch 13^{3}. **6.** fig. of obligation of oath or vow (only Nu 30, P) א׳ עַל־נֶפֶשׁ, usually sq.acc.cogn. אֱסָר, אִסָּר Nu $30^{3.5.5.6.8.9.11.12}$; without אֱסָר etc., $v^{7.10}$; cf. v^{4} אִסָּר א׳ (עַל־נֶפֶשׁ om.) **Niph.** pass. of Qal **3**, *be bound, imprisoned, Impf.* (juss.) יֵאָסֵר Gn 42^{19} (E); 2 ms. תֵּאָסֵר Ju $16^{6.10.13}$ (of Samson); *Imv.* הֵאָסְרוּ Gn 42^{16} (E).
612 **Pu.** *Pf. be taken prisoner* אֻסְּרוּ Is 22^{3}; אֻסָּ֑רוּ *ib.*

†אֵסוּר **n.m.** $^{Ju\,15,\,14}$ **band, bond** (Aram. אֱסוּר, ܐܣܘܪܐ); on the form v. Ges$^{§\,84a\,12.R.}$) אֱסוּרָיו, of Samson Ju 15^{14}; אֲסוּרִים Ec 7^{26} of hands of evil woman; בֵּית הָאֵסוּר = prison Je 37^{15}.

615 †אָסִיר **n.m.** $^{Gn\,39,\,20}$ **bondman, prisoner** (Ar. أَسِيرٌ, Aram. ܐܣܝܪܐ, MI אסר)—א׳ abs. ψ 79^{11} 102^{21}; pl. אֲסִירִם Gn 39^{22}+, cf. Ju $16^{21.25}$ Kt; cstr. אֲסִירֵי ψ 107^{10}+, Gn 39^{20} Qr; אֲסִירָיו ψ 69^{34}+, etc.;—*prisoner* Gn $39^{20.22}$ (J), elsewhere only poetic; Is 14^{17}; as having rest in grave from task-master Jb 3^{18}; esp. as obj. of divine compassion ψ 68^{7} (‖ יְחִידִ), 69^{34} (‖ אֶבְיוֹן); אֶנְקַת א׳ 79^{11} 102^{21} (both ‖ בְּנֵי תְמוּתָה), 107^{10} א׳ עֳנִי וּבַרְזֶל (‖ יֹשְׁבֵי חֹשֶׁךְ וְצַלְמָוֶת); cf. א׳ אָרֶץ La 3^{34}; specif. of liberated exiles of Isr. Zc 9^{11}, called *captives of hope* א׳ הַתִּקְוָה v^{12}.

616 †אַסִּיר **n.[m.]** mostly coll. **prisoners** (acc. to Ol$^{§\,185a}$ corruption of אָסִיר, cf. Lag$^{BN\,110}$) taken in battle Is 10^{4} (Lag$^{Symm\,i.\,105;\,GGA\,1884,\,259}$ rds. חַת אֹסִיר etc., *Osiris is broken*, but cf. Che$^{crit.\,n.}$), 24^{22} (sim. of judgment upon kings of earth); 42^{7} (‖ יֹשְׁבֵי חֹשֶׁךְ; ref. to exiled Isr., but v. also Hi Che Di); 1 Ch 3^{17} בְּנֵי יְכָנְיָה אַסִּר prob. = *sons of Jeconiah the captive* (yet note omission of art.) so Be Zö Öt al.; 𝔊 𝔙 trans. as n.pr.

617 †אַסִּיר **n.pr.m.** son of Korah Ex 6^{24} 1 Ch 6^{7}; called son of Ebiasaph $v^{8.22}$.

632 †אֱסָר **n.m.** $^{Nu\,30,\,8}$ **bond, binding obligation** (cf. BAram. אֱסָר, Syr. ܐܣܳܪܐ; so forms with suff. infr. v. Ba$^{NB\,62}$ cf. Sta$^{§\,208a}$; but perh. Aram. loan-word v. Lag$^{BN\,175}$)—א׳ abs. Nu 30^{3}+; cstr. v^{13}; sf. אֱסָרָהּ v^{5}; pl. sf. אֱסָרֶיהָ $v^{6.15}$, אֱסָרֶהָ v^{8}—only Nu 30 (P), *binding obligation* of oath or vow; mostly acc. cogn. with אָסַר (q.v.); Nu $30^{3.4.5.5.6.8.11.12}$; אִסַּר נַפְשָׁהּ v^{13}; שְׁבֻעַת אִסָּר *binding oath* v^{14}.

4562 †מָסֹ֫רֶת **n.f.** cstr. מ׳ הַבְּרִית *bond of the covenant* Ez 20^{37} (= מַאֲסֹרֶת; text dub. cf. Lag$^{GN\,1882,\,168\,f.\,M\,61}$; Co rds. מוּסַר, i.e. מוּסָר v. sub יסר; so 𝔖).

†[מוֹסֵר] **n.m.** $^{Is\,28,\,22}$ **band, bond**, poet. & late (= מַאֲסֵר; Eth. ማሠር: Syr. ܡܣܳܪܐ, cf. As. *mêsiru, sheathing, plating*, e.g. Lyon $^{Sargontexte,\,p.\,16,\,l.\,65\,\&\,p.\,80}$)—cstr. מוֹסַר Jb 12^{18} (so Di Hoffm al. for מוּסַר); pl. מוֹסֵרוֹת Je 5^{5} 27^{2}; cstr. מֹסְרוֹת Jb 39^{5}; מוֹסְרֵי Is 52^{2}; sf. מוֹסֵרָ֑י ψ 116^{16}; מוֹסְרוֹתֵימוֹ ψ 2^{3} etc.;—*bands* acc. after פִּתַּח Jb 39^{5} restraining-bands of wild ass; ψ 116^{16} bonds of distress; Is 52^{2} מ׳ צַוָּארֵךְ bonds of captivity of Zion, vb. Hithp.; cf. also Jb 12^{18} מוֹסַר מְלָכִים פִּתֵּחַ (so rd., v. supr. & AV RV); Di understands bonds imposed by kings; Hoffm girdles of kings, & rds. וַיָּסַר in ‖, for וַיֶּאְסֹר; more oft. acc. after נִתַּק ψ 2^{3} bonds imposed by י׳ & his anointed, cf. Je 5^{5} & 2^{20} (𝔊 𝔙, v. Comm.); of Yahweh's breaking bonds of Isr. Je 30^{8} Na 1^{13} (last four ‖ שָׁבַר עֹל), bonds of oppressed ψ 107^{14}; יְחַזְּקוּ מ׳ Is 28^{22}, i.e. bonds imposed by Assyria; cf. Je 27^{2} (‖ מֹט) lit., symbol. of rule of Nebuchadrezzar.

†מוֹסֵרָה **n.pr.loc.** station of Isr. in wilderness, where Aaron died (this was Mt. Hor acc. to Nu $20^{22\,f.}$ $33^{37\,f.}$) Dt 10^{6}; locality unknown. Another form is 4147

†מֹסֵרוֹת **n.pr.loc.** *id.*, Nu $33^{30.31}$. 4149

†אֵסַרְחַדֹּן **n.pr.m. Esarhaddon** (As. *Ašur-aḫ-iddina, Ashur hath given a brother*) king of Assyria B.C. 681–668, son & successor of Sennacherib Is 37^{38} = 2 K 19^{37} (van d. H. אֵסַר־חַדֹּן); Ezr 4^{2}; cf. COT. 634

אֶסְתֵּר **n.pr.f. Esther** (Pers. *stâra*, star) —daughter of Abihail, cousin and adopted daughter of Mordecai, of tribe of Benjamin; made queen in Vashti's place by Ahasuerus; her Jewish name הֲדַסָּה q.v. Est $2^{7.8.10.11.15.15.16.17}$ + 47 t. Est. 635

I. אַף v. sub אנף. p. 60 639

II. **אַף conj.** denoting addition, esp. of something greater, **also, yea** (so Ph. Aram. ܐܦ, אַף, אוּף; cf. فَ). **1.** very rare in plain prose (in which גַּם is more usual): Gn 40^{16}* (*with pron., as rather often) I *also* in my dream, Nu 16^{14} Dt $2^{11*.20*}$ 2 S 20^{14} (v. Dr) 2 K 2^{14*} Est 5^{12}; more freq. in poetry, esp. as introducing emphatically a new thought Dt $33^{3.20.28}$ 1 S 2^{7} ψ $16^{6.7.9}$ 18^{49} 65^{14} they shout for joy, *yea*, they sing! $68^{9.17}$ 74^{16} 89^{28*} 93^{1} Pr 22^{19*} 23^{28*}+; or in more elevated prose style, Lv $26^{16*.24*.28*.41*}$; and 25 t. in the impassioned rhetoric of Is² (40^{24}–48^{15}), e.g. 40^{24} $41^{10.26}$ 42^{13} $43^{7.19}$ 46^{11} *yea*, I have spoken, I will *also* bring it to pass; I have 637 purposed, I will *also* do it! $48^{12.15}$. Implying something surprising or unexpected, *even, indeed* Jb 14^3 15^4*. וְאַף *and also* Lv $26^{39.40.42.44}$ Dt 15^{17} Hb 2^{15} ψ 68^{19} 1 Ch 8^{32}*=9^{38}* 2 Ch 12^5* Ne 2^{18} 13^{15}; *and even* Jb 19^4 וְאַף־אָמְנָם שָׁגִיתִי *and even* indeed (if) I have erred . . . With הֲ, הַאַף *indeed . . . ? really . . . ?* †Gn $18^{13.23}$ wilt thou *indeed* sweep away the righteous with the wicked? v^{24} Am 2^{11} Jb 34^{17} 40^8. In contrast to a preceding thought (expressed or implied) *but, nay (imo)* ψ 44^{10} 58^3; cf. Ju 5^{29}*.

2. (Equally in prose and poetry) with ref. to a preceding sentence, *yea, à fortiori, the more so* (=*how much more!* after an affirm. clause; =*how much less!* after a neg. one): †2 S $4^{10 f.}$ when one told me, Saul is dead . . . I took hold of him and slew him . . . אַף כִּי־אֲנָשִׁים רְשָׁעִים הָרְגוּ וגו׳ *à fortiori, how much more* (should I do so), when wicked men have slain a righteous person, etc.! Ez 14^{21} (Ew Hi) 15^5 Pr 21^{27} (in all these passages כִּי=*when*) Jb 4^{19}. So וְאַף †1 S 23^3 2 K 5^{13} . . . וְאַף כִּי־אָמַר אֵלֶיךָ *and the more* (=*and how much rather*), when he hath said to thee, etc. More commonly in this sense strengthened by כִּי (q. v.), v. infr.

אַף כִּי **1.** *furthermore* †Ez 23^{40} Hb 2^5 (Ges *quin imo, quin etiam*). **2.** in a qu., *indeed* (is it) *that . . . ?* †Gn 3^1 אַף כִּי־אָמַר אֱלֹהִים *indeed, that* God has said . . . ? i.e. has God *really* said . . . ? (cf. הַאַף above). **3.** with ref. to a preceding sentence (which is often introduced by הֵן or הִנֵּה), *yea, that . . . !* i.e. *how much more* (or *less*)! †Pr 11^{31} lo, the righteous is recompensed in the earth אַף כִּי רָשָׁע וְחוֹטֵא *'tis indeed that* (=how much more) the wicked and the sinner! 15^{11} 17^7 $19^{7.10}$ Jb 9^{14} 15^{16} 25^6 1 S 14^{30} 1 K 8^{27} (=2 Ch 6^{18}) lo, the heavens . . . cannot contain thee אַף כִּי הַבַּיִת הַזֶּה *'tis indeed that* this house (cannot do so), i.e. *how much less* this house! 2 Ch 32^{15}. So וְאַף כִּי †Dt 31^{27} 1 S 21^6 (perh.; but v. RS $^{Sem. i. 436}$ Dr$^{Sm 293}$) 2 S 16^{11}. (In Jb 35^{14} (Hi De) Ne 9^{18} אַף כִּי is simply=*yea, when* . . .)

אפד (existence & mng. dub. Thes MV al. identify with אָפַד *gird on*, but this denom. v. infr.; Lag$^{BN 178; GN 1890, p. 15}$ prop. وفد, *come as ambassador*, as √ of אֵפוֹד).

646 **אֵפוֹד** (28 t.) & **אֵפֹד** (20 t.) **n.m.**$^{Ex 28,7}$ **ephod** (Eth. አፌድ: cf. Aram. ܦܘܕܐ *id.* (on mng. v. Lag$^{l. c.}$), perh. also As. *pid, pittu* Zim$^{BP 39}$; on form v. Ges $^{§ 84 a 12. R.}$ but Lag$^{l. c.}$ comp. وفاد, & thinks אֵפוֹד shortened from חֵשֶׁב הָא׳ *'robe of approach'* to God)—א׳ abs. Ex 25^7+; cstr. 1 S 2^{18}+;—**1.** *ephod*, priestly garment, shoulder-cape or mantle; **a.** as worn by ordinary priest made of white stuff (בַּד) 1 S 22^{18}; נֹשֵׂא א׳ cf. **2**; so Samuel as a temple-servant 2^{18}; חָגוּר א׳ *girt with an eph.*; so David when dancing before ark 2 S 6^{14} (*id.*) 1 Ch 15^{27} וְעַל דוד א׳; **b.** as prescribed in P for high priest, more costly, woven of gold, blue, purple, scarlet, & linen (שֵׁשׁ?) threads, provided with shoulder-pieces & breast-piece of like material, ornamented with gems and gold, Ex 25^7 $28^{4.6.12.15}$ 29^5 $35^{9.27}$ $39^{2.7}$+17 t. Ex 28, 39, also Lv 8^7; cf. prob. 1 S 2^{28} (נֹשֵׂא א׳) 14^3 21^{10} (v. sub **2**); חֵשֶׁב הָא׳ Ex $28^{27.28}$ 29^5 $39^{20.21}$ Lv 8^7; מְעִיל הָא׳ 29^5 39^{22} (cf. Lv 8^7); with vb. נָתַן אֶת־הָא׳ עַל־ *put the ephod on* Aaron Lv 8^7. **2.** *ephod used in consulting* י׳ 1 S 23^6 א׳ borne in hand (rd. יָרַד וְהָא׳ בְּיָדוֹ 𝔊 We Dr) v^9 $30^{7.7}$ (all c. הִגִּישׁ)+14^{18} (הגישׁ) & v^{18}, in both rd. הָא׳ for ארון & v^{18} also נֹשֵׂא 𝔊 Klo Dr; **a.** acc. to Thes MV Di Ex 28^6 al. properly sub **1 b**; consultation of י׳ in that case by Urim & Thummim in the breast-piece attached to the ephod (cf. Ex 28^{28-30} & v. אוּרִים); if so, in view of נשׂא א׳ 1 S 2^{28} $14^{3.18}$ (cf. supr.), not used elsewhere=*wear* exc. 22^{18}, & of 23^6, the word might be used by meton. for the breast-piece itself; **b.** others, e.g. Sta$^{Gesch. i. 466, 471}$ Bu$^{RS 115}$ al., think of an image representing י׳; cf. following. **3.** **a.** *ephod of gold* made by Gideon Ju 8^{27} for a local sanctuary, by which Isr. was ensnared; =**2 b** acc. to 𝔖 Thes ('sine controversia') Stu al.+Sta Bu l.c.; orig.=gold *sheathing* of an image (cf. etymol. supr. & Is 30^{22} sub אֲפֻדָּה); MV Be Kö$^{Hauptprobleme 59}$ think of garment, as sub **1** v. supr. **b.** made (material not given) for a private, local sanctuary Ju 17^5 $18^{14.17.18.20}$ (|| פֶּסֶל, תְּרָפִים, מַסֵּכָה in all, for 𝔊 gives מַסֵּכָה v^{20}, om. 𝔖); cf. Ho 3^4 Isr. shall abide without king, prince, sacrifice, pillar, ephod or teraphim; acc. to Thes al.+Sta Bu l.c.=**2 b**; Stu Be Ry al. regard as sub **1**; in view of distinction from פסל, מסכה & תרפים it seems more likely that this is not an image, but some means of consulting deity, perh. in imitation of Urim & Thummim.

†**אֵפֹד** **n.pr.m.** father of a chief of Ma- 641
nasseh Nu 34^{23}.

†**[אָפַד]** **vb.denom.** gird on ephod, **Qal** 640
Pf. וְאָפַדְתָּ לוֹ בְּחֵשֶׁב הָאֵפֹד Ex 29^5 *and thou shalt gird the ephod upon him with the cunningly-wrought band of the ephod;* so *Impf.* וַיֶּאְפֹּד לוֹ (|| חגר) בּוֹ Lv 8^7.

†**אֲפֻדָּה** **n.f.** ephod (=אֵפוֹד, for which it 642

supplies cstr. & sf. forms). **1.** of high-priest's ephod, cf. אֵפוֹד **1 b**, only חֵשֶׁב אֲפֻדָּתוֹ Ex 28^{8} 39^{5} the *cunningly-wrought band of his ephod.* **2.** of sheathing of idol-images, אֲפֻדַּת מַסֵּכַת זְהָבֶךָ Is 30^{22} (‖ צִפּוּי פְּסִילֵי כַסְפֶּךָ) cf. אֵפוֹד **3 a.**

643 †[אַפֶּדֶן] **n.[m.] palace** (Syr. ܐܦܕܢܐ; both from Pers. *apadâna*, cf. Spiegel $^{\text{Altpers. Keilschr. 128}}$, but this = *treasury, armoury*, M. Schultze $^{\text{ZMG 1885, 48 f.}}$) אָהֳלֵי אַפַּדְנוֹ Dn 11^{45}, of the 'king of the north,' i.e. Antiochus Epiphanes.

644 †אָפָה **vb. bake** (As. *êpû*, Zim $^{\text{BP 43}}$ Aram. אֲפָא, ܐܦܐ)—**Qal** *Pf.* א׳ Gn 19^{3}; אָפִיתִי Is 44^{19}; וְאָפוּ consec. Lv 26^{26} etc.; *Impf.* 3 fs. sf. וַתֹּפֵהוּ 1 S 28^{24}; יֹאפוּ Ez 46^{20}; תֹּאפוּ Ex 16^{23}; *Imv.* אֵפוּ Ex 16^{23}; *Pt.* אֹפֶה Gn 40^{1}+; אֹפֵהֶם Ho 7^{6}; pl. אֹפִים Gn 40^{16}+; אֹפוֹת 1 S 8^{13}, etc.—*bake*, obj. לֶחֶם Lv 26^{26} (H) Is $44^{15.19}$ (cf. Je 37^{21}); מַצּוֹת Gn 19^{3} (J) 1 S 28^{24}; עֻגֹת מַצּוֹת Ex 12^{39} (J); חַלּוֹת Lv 24^{5} (H); מִנְחָה Ez 46^{20}; מָן Ex $16^{23.23}$ (P;—c. 2nd obj. of material Ex 12^{39} בָּצֵק, Lv 24^{5} סֹלֶת, 1 S 28^{24} קֶמַח). *Pt.* alw. as subst. *baker* Gn $40^{1.2.5.16.17.20.22}$ 41^{10} (all E) Ho $7^{4.6}$; Je 37^{21} מִחוּץ הָא׳ *out of the bakers' street;* also 1 S 8^{13} (‖ טַבָּחוֹת, רַקָּחוֹת; only here fem.) Nowhere as a menial office, not even 1 S 8^{13} where despotic power & growth of court emphasized. **Niph.** *Impf.* 3 fs. תֵּאָפֶה Lv 6^{10} 7^{9}; 3 fpl. תֵּאָפֶינָה Lv 23^{17};—pass. of **Qal** *be baked, baken* of לֶחֶם Lv 23^{17}; מִנְחָה 7^{9} cf. 6^{10}.

3989 †[מַאֲפֶה] **n.[m.] thing baked**, cstr. מִנְחָה מַאֲפֵה תַנּוּר Lv 2^{4}.

645 †אֵפוֹ (Jb 17^{15} $19^{6.23}$ 24^{25}), elsewh. אֵפוֹא (cf. רִבּוֹ and רִבּוֹא), **enclitic part. then** (prob. from פוֹ, a part. with a demonstr. force, cf. פֹּה, פּוֹ *here*, with א prefixed. In the Targs. פּוּן is used somewhat similarly, e.g. Gn 26^{10} Nu 11^{29} Is 1^{9} $48^{18.19}$),—used **1.** in connexion with interrogatory pronouns or adverbs (like ἄρα, ποτε, *tandem*): מִי אֵפוֹא Gn 27^{33} who, *then*, ...? v^{37} וּלְכָה אֵפוֹא מָה אֶעֱשֶׂה and for thee, *then*, what shall I do, my son? Ex 33^{16} וּבַמֶּה יִוָּדַע אֵפוֹא and wherein shall it be known, *then*...? אַיֵּה אֵפוֹא where, then? Ju 9^{38} Is 19^{12} Jb 17^{15}; Ho 13^{10} אֱהִי מַלְכְּךָ אֵפוֹא; Is 22^{1} מַה־לָּךְ אֵפוֹא what is there to thee, *pray*...? **2.** in a command or wish: 2 K 10^{10} דְּעוּ אֵפוֹא know, *then;* (in apod.) Pr 6^{3} Jb 19^{6}; Jb 19^{23} מִי־יִתֵּן אֵפוֹ וְיִכָּתְבוּן מִלַּי would, *then*, that my words were written! **3.** after אִם, Gn 43^{11} אִם־כֵּן אֵפוֹא זֹאת עֲשׂוּ if it be so, *then*, do this, Jb 9^{24} if not *then*, who is it? 24^{25}.

†אֲפִיחַ **n.pr.m.** an ancestor of Saul 1 S 9^{1} 647
(etymology & meaning dubious).

אפל (Ar. أَفَلَ *disappear, depart, set* (of the sun)).

†אֹפֶל **n.m.** $^{\text{Jb 3,6}}$ **darkness, gloom** (only poet.) 652
—א׳ alw. abs.—**1.** *darkness*, of night ψ 91^{6} (opp. צָהֳרַיִם); deep in the earth, אֶבֶן א׳ Jb 28^{3} (‖ חֹשֶׁךְ, צַלְמָוֶת); *darkness, gloom* of underworld Jb $10^{22.22}$ (‖ צַלְמָוֶת, א׳ עֵיפָתָה, אֶרֶץ חֹשֶׁךְ); personif. Jb 3^{6} *that night—let darkness take it* יִקָּחֵהוּ א׳; fig. of spiritual darkness Is 29^{18} (‖ חֹשֶׁךְ); of secrecy, treachery ψ 11^{2}. **2.** esp. fig. of *calamity* Jb 23^{17} (‖ חשך q.v.), 30^{26} (opp. אור).

†אָפֵל **adj. gloomy**, of day of י׳ Am 5^{20} 651
(‖ חשך, opp. נֹגַהּ) cf. אֲפֵלָה.

†אֲפֵלָה **n.f. darkness, gloominess, calam-** 653
ity—א׳ Ex 10^{22}+; אֲפֵלָתְךָ Is 58^{10}; pl. אֲפֵלוֹת Is 59^{9}—**1.** *darkness* Dt 28^{29} Pr 7^{9} (‖ אִישׁוֹן לַיְלָה); of supernatural darkness in Egypt Ex 10^{22}; of day of י׳ (cf. Am 5^{20} sub אָפֵל) Jo 2^{2} Zp 1^{15} (both ‖ חשך, ענן, ערפל) sim. of wickedness Je 23^{18} Pr 4^{19}. **2.** fig. of *calamity* Is 8^{22} (‖ חֲשֵׁכָה), 58^{10} (‖ חשך, opp. צהרים), 59^{9} (‖ *id.*, opp. נגהות).

†[אָפִיל] **adj.** (darkened, concealed, thence) 648
late, of crops;—אֲפִילֹת Ex 9^{32} of wheat & spelt.

†מַאֲפֵל **n.[m.] darkness**, Jos 24^{7} (E) וַיָּשֶׂם 3990
מ׳ בֵּינֵיכֶם וגו׳, between Hebrews & Egyptians.

†מַאְפֵּלְיָה **n.f. deep darkness** (= מַאֲפֵל יָהּ 3991
acc. to Thes MV cf. Ct 8^{6} שַׁלְהֶבֶתְיָה; but Ew $^{\text{§165 b}}$ & on Je 2^{31} rds. מַאְפֵּלְיָה, fem. of [מאפלי], der. fr. Hiph. Pt.; cf. Sta $^{\text{§302 b}}$ מַאְפֵּלְיָה; Jäger $^{\text{BAS 471}}$ thinks this יָה an enclitic part. of emphasis, & comp. As.)—only אֶרֶץ מ׳ Je 2^{31} fig. of י׳ in dealing with his people (‖ מִדְבָּר).

אָפְלָל v. sub פלל. p. 813 654

אפן (meaning dub., perh. **turn**, cf. פנה).

†אוֹפַן, אֹפַן **n.m.** $^{\text{Ez 1,20}}$ **wheel.**—abs. אוֹפַן 212
1 K 7^{32}+; אֹפַן Ez 1^{16}+; cstr. אוֹפַן 1 K 7^{33} Is 28^{27}; אֹפַן Ex 14^{25}; pl. אוֹפַנִּים 1 K 7^{32}+; cstr. אוֹפַנֵּי 1 K 7^{30}; אוֹפַנֵּיהֶם Ez 10^{12}, etc.—**a.** *wheel* of chariot (מֶרְכָּבָה) Ex 14^{25} 1 K 7^{33} Na 3^{2}; of (threshing) cart (עֲגָלָה) Is 28^{27} cf. Pr 20^{26} (as instr. of punishment). **b.** wheels in Ezek.'s vision Ez $1^{15.16.16.19.19.20.20.21.\text{ (del. Co) }21}$ 3^{13} $10^{6.9.9.9.9.10.10.12.12.12.13.16.16.19}$ 11^{22}. **c.** wheels of the ten bases beneath the lavers in Sol.'s temple 1 K $7^{30.32.32.32.33}$.

655 †[אֹפֶן] **n.[m.]** **circumstance, condition** (perh. lit. *turning*) only du. (or pl.) sf. עַל־אָפְנָיו = *in* (right) *circumstances* Pr 25^{11} (cf. Str ad loc., also Orelli Syn. d. Zeit u. Ewigkeit 38 f.).

†אָפוּנָה ψ 88^{16} (ἅπ. λεγ. Dl Pr 135 f. comp. As. *appuna(ma)* adv. = *ma'diš, very, very much,*
6323 but dub.; Thes MV form fr. √פון, & comp. Ar. أَفَنَ *diminuit, mente diminuit* (Frey.), hence *be confused, helpless,* cf. 𝔊 ἐξηπορήθην; 𝔙 *conturbatus sum;* others emend אָפוּגָה fr. פוג q.v. A vb. however is not needed for parallelism).

656 †אָפֵס (cf. פָּסַס) **vb. cease, fail, come to an end:** only **Qal** *Pf.* 3 ms.; Gn $47^{15.16}$ (of money, כֶּסֶף), Is 16^4 (extortioner: ‖ תַּם, כָּלָה), 29^{20} (terrible one: ‖ כָּלָה, נִכְרַת), ψ 77^9 (חַסְדּוֹ: ‖ גָּמַר).

657 †אֶפֶס אָפֶס, **n.m.** prop. **ceasing,** hence **1. end, extremity,** only in the poet. phrase אַפְסֵי אָרֶץ (ψ 59^{14} א׳ הארץ) *ends, extreme limits,* of the earth, used esp. hyperbolically: Dt 33^{17} 1 S 2^{10} Mi 5^3 Je 16^{19} ψ 2^8 59^{14} 72^8 (= Zc 9^{10}); + כָּל־ Is 45^{22} 52^{10b} (= ψ 98^{3b}) ψ 22^{28} 67^8 Pr 30^4.

2. Expressing **non-existence: a.** as subst. (mostly a rare poet. syn. of אַיִן): Is 34^{12} and all his princes יִהְיוּ אָפֶס shall become *nought,* 41^{29}; 41^{12} יִהְיוּ כְאַיִן וּכְאֶפֶס; 40^{17} מֵאֶפֶס וָתֹהוּ (‖ כְּאַיִן) as made of *nought* and worthlessness are they accounted by him, 41^{24} (rd. פָּעָלְכֶם מֵאָפֶס, ‖ מֵאַיִן, v. אֶפַע); 52^4 and Asshur oppressed him בְּאֶפֶס *for nought.* **b.** as part. of negation, prop. *cessation of*...! (cf. אֵין ... *nought of*...), very rare in prose (2 S 9^3), chiefly a poet. syn. of אַיִן: Is 5^8 עַד אֶפֶס מָקוֹם till there is *an end of* place = till there is *no* place (cf. עַד אֵין ψ 40^{13}), Am 6^{10} (cf. אַיִן Ju 4^{20}), Dt 32^{36} (hence, in prose, 2 K 14^{26}), Is 45^6 (cf. אין 43^{11}) v^{14} 46^9 54^{15}; אֲנִי וְאַפְסִי עוֹד Zp 2^{15} Is $47^{8.10}$ is prob. to be rendered, 'I am, and *there is none* besides' (so Ges Ew Di etc.), the י being 'paragogic' as in זוּלָתִי etc. (Ges § 90, 3a Ew § 211b), cf. וְאֵין עוֹד Is $45^{5.6.18.21}$; but acc. to De the י is sf. of 1 s. 'I am, and *I am nought* besides' (i.e. and I am nought besides my all-sufficient self).—בְּאֶפֶס (like בְּאֵין, q.v.) *without:* Pr 14^{28} 26^{20} Jb 7^6 Dn 8^{25}. **c.** as adv. of limitation: (*a*) *only:* †Nu 22^{35} (cf. אַךְ v^{20}) 23^{13}. (*b*) אֶפֶס כִּי *save that, howbeit* (qualifying a preceding statement): †Nu 13^{28} Dt 15^4 Ju 4^9 Am 9^8 (+ 1 S 1^5 𝔊 We Sta Dr). So אֶפֶס alone †2 S 12^{14} (the foll. כִּי signifying *because*).

657 †[אֹפֶס] **n.[m.]** only in the **du.** אָפְסַיִם (not אַ׳; v. Baer), lit. **the two extremities,** i.e. either *the soles* of the feet (so AW Ges; cf. Aram. פִּיסְתָא, ܦܣܬܐ), or *the ankles* (so 𝔖 𝔗 𝔙, & most): only Ez 47^3 מֵי א׳ water of (i.e. reaching to) the *soles* (or *ankles*); cf. v^4 מֵי מָתְנַיִם water reaching to the loins.

†אֶפֶס דַּמִּים **n.pr.loc.** in Judah, c. 16 miles 658
SW. of Jerusalem, called in 1 Ch 11^{13} פַּס דַּמִּים, 6450
(meaning unknown; Lag BN 76 on basis of MSS. of 𝔊 would read ספר מים *edge* or *brink* (ܣܦܐ) *of water;* but such a pronounced Aramaism is not probable), only 1 S 17^1.

†[אֶפַע] מֵאָפַע Is 41^{24} txt. err. for מֵאָפֶס v. 659
אפס; so 𝔙 𝔗 Saad Thes Ew Di al.

אֶפְעֶה v. sub פעה. p. 821 660

†[אָפַף] **vb. surround, encompass** (As. 661
apâpu Zim BP 59)—**Qal** *Pf.* אֲפָפוּ ψ 40^{13}; אֲפָפוּנִי ψ 18^5 +;—*encompass* (poet.) lit. Jon 2^6 (subj. מַיִם); fig., subj. evils & misfortunes רָעוֹת ψ 40^{13} (sq. עָלַי); מִשְׁבְּרֵי מות 2 S 22^5, cf. חֶבְלֵי מ׳ ψ 18^5, also 116^3.

†[אָפַק] **vb. hold, be strong** (so Thes wh. 662
comp. Ar. أَفَقَ *excel = multum valuit;* MV comp. also فاق)—only **Hithp.** *Pf.* 3 pl. הִתְאַפָּקוּ Is 63^{15}; *Impf.* וַיִּתְאַפַּק Gn 43^{31} Est 5^{10}; 2 ms. תִּתְאַפַּק Is 64^{11}; אֶתְאַפָּק Is 42^{14}; וָאֶתְאַפַּק 1 S 13^{12}—**1.** *force, compel oneself* 1 S 13^{12}. **2.** *restrain oneself, refrain* Gn 43^{31} 45^1 Is 42^{14} Est 5^{10}; of י׳ Is 64^{11}; of Yahweh's compassion Is 63^{15}, מֵעֶיךָ וְרַחֲמֶיךָ אֵלַי הִתְאַפָּקוּ (almost passive).

†[אָפִיק] **n.m.** 2 S 22,16 **channel** (as holding, 650
confining waters; poet.)—cstr. אֲפִיק Jb 6^{15}; pl. אֲפִיקִים Ez 6^3 +; אֲפִקִים Ez 32^6; cstr. אֲפִיקֵי Jo 1^{20} +; sf. אֲפִיקֶיךָ Ez 35^8; אֲפִיקָיו Is 8^7—*channel = stream-bed, ravine, wady* א׳ מַיִם ψ 42^2 Jo 1^{20} cf. 4^{18} Ct 5^{12}; also ψ 18^{16}, but better א׳ יָם 2 S 22^{16}; א׳ נְחָלִים Jb 6^{15}; of river-bed Is 8^7; so also (without defining word) Ez 31^{12} 32^6 34^{13} ψ 126^4; ‖ גַּיְא Ez 6^3 35^8 $36^{4.6}$; fig. of bones of hippopotamus (as hollow) א׳ נְחֻשָׁה Jb 40^{18}; of furrows betw. scales of crocodile א׳ מָגִנִּים 41^7.—מְזִיחַ אֲפִיקִים Jb 12^{21} is dub.; Thes MV Di al. say *girdle of* the *strong* (אָפִיק = *firm, forceful,* or—Di—*capable, powerful*); ‖ נְדִיבִים.

†אֲפֵק, אֲפִיק (Ju 1^{31}) **n.pr.loc. Aphek** (perh. 663
enclosure, or *fortress*). **1.** city near Jezreel (As. *Apku,* cf. Dl Pa 287) Jos 12^{18} 1 S 29^1 (אֲפֵקָה, so) 1 K $20^{26.30}$ cf. 2 K 13^{17}. **2.** city in tribe of Asher Jos 19^{30} Ju 1^{31} (אֲפִיק). **3.** city NE. of

Beirût, mod. Afqa Jos 13^{4} אֲפֵקָה v. Di. **4.** place near Mizpah 1 S 4^{1} (cf. 7^{12}).

664 †אֲפֵקָה **n.pr.loc.** (mng. perh. *id.*) one of a group of cities including Hebron Jos 15^{53}.

I. **אפר** (cf. perh. أَفَرَ *leap*, أَفِرَ *be agile*; v. אבק).

665 †אֵפֶר **n.[m.] ashes** (as *light, flying*?)—א׳ abs. Gn 18^{27}+; cstr. Nu 19$^{9.10}$—*ashes* of red heifer, used in purifications Nu 19$^{9.10}$; on head, as sign of humiliation 2 S 13^{19}; contrition Dn 9^{3} (‖ שַׂק, צוֹם), Jon 3^{6} (‖ שַׂק) cf. Jb 42^{6} (עָפָר וא׳), Is 58^{5} (‖ שַׂק); mourning Est 4$^{1.3}$ (‖ שַׂק) cf. Jb 2^{8} (ישב בתוך הא׳), Je 6^{26} (‖ שַׂק), Ez 27^{30} (‖ עפר); in sim. *scattereth hoarfrost* כָּא׳ ψ 147^{16}; but also as filthy, loathsome כעפר וא׳ Jb 30^{19} (Di sim. of mourning, grief), as worthless, מִשְׁלֵי א׳ Jb 13^{12} *proverbs of ashes;* fig. of worthlessness Is 44^{20}; insignificance עפר וא׳ Gn 18^{27}; ignominy Ez 28^{18} Mal 3^{21}; distress & sorrow א׳ כַּלֶּחֶם אָכָלְתִּי ψ 102^{10} (so As. cf. Zim$^{BP 42}$) cf. La 3^{16} Is 61^{3} (פְּאֵר תַּחַת אֵפֶר).

II. **אפר** (*enclose, envelope,* As. *apâru, attire* Dl$^{Pr 54}$; Thes comp. Ar. غَفَرَ, *cover;* MV comp. Aram. ܡܥܦܪܐ, מעפרא, *mantle, turban;* but connection of √ פ׳ ע(غ) with אפר is dub.)

666 †אֲפֵר **n.[m.] covering, bandage** (As. *ipru, covering* Zim$^{BP 95}$, *êpartu, garment,* Id.$^{ib.}$ & Dl$^{Pr 54}$) א׳ עַל־עֵינָיו 1 K 20^{38} cf. v^{41}.

667 אֶפְרֹחַ v. פרח. p. 827

668 †אַפִּרְיוֹן **n.[m.] sedan, litter, palanquin** (so NH; origin dub.; no plausible Shemitic etymol.; perh. (so RS in Yule$^{Gloss. of Anglo-Indian Words, 502}$) Skr. *paryaṅka, litter-bed, 'palankeen;'* perh. (if poem be late) Gr. φορεῖον;—𝔊 has φορεῖον, 𝔙 *ferculum,* 𝔖 ܦܘܪܝܐ, 𝔗 פּוּרְיָא) Ct 3^{9} א׳ עָשָׂה לוֹ הַמֶּלֶךְ שְׁלֹמֹה.

669 אֶפְרַיִם **n.pr.m. Ephraim** (Gn 41^{52} connected with הִפְרָה, Hiph. of פרה, cf. פרא Hiph. Ho 13^{15}). **1.** 2nd son of Joseph Gn 41^{52} 46^{20}; reckoned among sons of Jacob, blessed by him, and given preference over Manasseh 48$^{1.5.13.14.17.17}$ (cf. v^{19}) v$^{20.20}$ 50^{23} Nu 1^{10} 1 Ch 7$^{20.22}$. **2.** בְּנֵי אֶפְרַיִם (=descendants, tribe of E.) Nu 1^{32} 2$^{18.18.24}$ 7^{48} 10^{22} 26$^{35.37}$ Jos 16$^{5.9}$ (boundaries of territory), 17^{8} 1 Ch 9^{3} 12^{31} 27$^{10.14.20}$ 2 Ch 28^{12}; less oft. מַטֵּה א׳ Nu 1^{33} 13^{8} Jos 21^{5} 1 Ch 6^{51}; מַטֵּה בְנֵי־א׳ Nu 34^{24} Jos 16^{8} cf. 14^{4}; שֵׁבֶט א׳ ψ 78^{67} (‖ אֹהֶל יוֹסֵף); בֵּית א׳ Ju 10^{9}; also א׳ alone, tribe *Ephraim* Nu 26^{28} Dt 33^{17} Jos 16^{10}+oft.; אֶרֶץ א׳ וּמְנַשֶּׁה Jos 17^{17} cf. Ju 12^{15} 2 Ch 30^{10} esp. **3.** הַר־אֶפְרַיִם *the mountain-country of Ephraim,* a ridge stretching from N. to S. through territory assigned to Ephr., with fruitful land on both slopes, esp. the western (cf. Di Jos 16^{1}) Jos 17^{15} 19^{50} 20^{7} Ju 2^{9} 3^{27} 4^{5}+26 t. **4.** by Ho & Is (rarely later) אֶפְרַיִם=kingdom of northern Israel (from Ephr. as largest & strongest tribe in it) Ho 4^{17} 5$^{3.3.5}$ (‖ יִשְׂרָאֵל) v$^{11.12}$+30 t. Ho; Is 7$^{2.5.8.9.17}$+9 t. Is; also Je 7^{15} 31$^{9.18.20}$ Ez 37^{16} (del. Co) v^{19} ψ 78^{9} 2 Ch 25$^{7.10}$ cf. 30^{1} ψ 60^{9}=108^{9}; עָרֵי א׳ 2 Ch 17^{2} cf. 34^{6}; שְׂדֵה א׳ Ob^{19}; hence א׳ alone in loc. sense 2 Ch 31^{1}; also Ho 5^{9}, where *fem.* (& perh. Is 7^{2}). †**5.** יַעַר אֶפְרַיִם 2 S 18^{6}, E. of Jordan; 𝔊L Klo rd. יער מַחֲנַיִם, cf. 17$^{24.27}$. †**6.** name of a city near Baal-hazor 2 S 13^{23} (='Εφραΐμ John 11^{54} & 1 Macc 11^{34}? Klo comp. 𝔊L Γοφραιμ & עפרון, Qr עֶפְרַיִן 2 Ch 13^{9}; so previously Bö Th Ke cf. Dr). †**7.** שַׁעַר אֶפְרַיִם a chief gate of Jerusalem 2 K 14^{13} 2 Ch 25^{23} Ne 8^{16} 12^{39}; perh. at NW. angle, near Holy Sepulchre, cf. Schick-Guthe$^{ZPV 1885}$.

אֶפְרָת v. אפרתה. below 672

†אֶפְרָתָה **n.pr.** (v. Sta$^{§ 308 d. 1; 342 d. 2; Morgenl.}$ 672
$^{Forsch. 215}$)—might in several cases, e.g. Gn 35^{16}, be אֶפְרָת+ה loc., but v. Ru 4^{11};—**1. n.pr.loc.** place near Bethel, where Rachel died & was
buried Gn 35$^{16.19}$ 48^{7} (אֶפְרָת only Gn 48^{7} where 672
ה perh. dropped on acc. of ה following (Ol); in last two passages הוא בית לחם is a gloss, v. Di; cf. 1 S 10^{2}). **2.** *id.*, a name of Bethlehem
Mi 5^{1} Ru 4^{11}; cf. perh. כָּלֵב אֶפְרָתָה 1 Ch 2^{24} (𝔊 3613
ἦλθεν Χαλὲβ εἰς 'Εφράθα). **3.** *id.* ψ 132^{6}, perh. applied to district where Kirjath Jearim lay, on the border of Judah & Benjamin, cf. De Che. **4. n.pr.f.** אֶפְרָת name given to wife of Caleb 1 Ch 2^{19}=אֶפְרָתָה v^{50} 4^{4}.

†אֶפְרָתִי **adj.gent. Ephrathite.** **1.** Eph- 673
raimite, cf. אֶפְרָתָה **1.** Ju 12^{5} 1 S 1^{1} (of ancestor of Elkanah) 1 K 11^{26} (of Jerob.) **2.** from א׳ **2**; א׳ מִבֵּית לֶחֶם 1 S 17^{12} (of Jesse); pl. אֶפְרָתִים מִבֵּית לֶחֶם Ru 1^{2}.

אפת (meaning dub. √ whence Ar. إِفْتٌ *calamity,* & also *wonder, portent;* acc. to Thes Ar. √=إِيفَ *suffer evil*).

†מוֹפֵת **n.m.**$^{Dt 29,2}$ **wonder, sign, portent** 4159
(=מאפת)—מוֹפֵת Ex 7^{9}+14 t.; מוֹפֶתְכֶם Ez 12^{11}; מוֹפְתִים Dt 4^{34}+4 t.; מֹפְתִים Dt 6^{22}+9 t.; מוֹפְתַי Ex 7^{3} 11^{9}; מוֹפְתָיו ψ 78^{43}; מֹפְתָיו 1 Ch 16^{12} ψ 105^{5}—**1.** *wonder,* as special display of God's power Ex 7^{3} 11^{9} ψ 105^{5} 1 Ch 16^{12} Jo 3^{3}; by Moses and Aaron Ex 4^{21} 11^{10} cf. 7^{9} (in mouth of

Pharaoh), by false proph. Dt $13^{2.3}$ (‖אות); usually ‖אות Dt 4^{34} 6^{22} 7^{19} 26^{8} 29^{2} 34^{11} ψ 78^{43} 105^{27} 135^{9} Je $32^{20.21}$ Ne 9^{10}; applied to effect of Yahweh's curse Dt 28^{46} (‖אות); to one protected by י׳ ψ 71^{7}. **2.** *sign* or *token* of future event (cf. אות) 1 K $13^{3.3.5}$ 2 Ch $32^{24.31}$; symbolic act Is 20^{3} (‖אות); as such the term is applied to persons Is 8^{18} (‖אות) Ez $12^{6.11}$ $24^{24.27}$; cf. אַנְשֵׁי מ׳ Zc 3^{8} *men who serve as a symbol or sign.*—Vb. used, of divine act, is נתן Ex 7^{9} etc., שׂים Je 32^{20}; שׂים also of entrusting to human power Ex 4^{21}, cf. דִּבֶּר 1 K 13^{3}; of human agency עשׂה Ex 4^{21} 11^{10}, נתן 1 K $13^{3.5}$.

675 †אֶצְבּוֹן **n.pr.m. 1.** אֶצְבֹּן a son of Gad (Sam. אצבעון, 𝔊 Θασοβαν) Gn 46^{16} = אָזְנִי Nu 26^{16} (𝔊 Ἀζενει, Ἀζαν), this shorter form less probable. **2.** אֶצְבּוֹן a grandson of Benjamin 1 Ch 7^{7} (𝔊 Ἀσεβων, Ἐσσεβων).

676 אֶצְבַּע v. II. צבע. p. 840

[אצל] prob. i.q. وَصَلَ *to join* (cf. on the א W ^{SG71}).

681 I. אֵ֫צֶל $_{61}$ **subst.** conjunction, proximity; with sf. אֶצְלִי, אֶצְלוֹ etc.; only used as a **prep. a.** (as an implicit accus.) **in proximity to** (as though وَصْلَ Lag $^{BN 68}$), **beside**: Gn $39^{10.15}$ 41^{3} and stood אֵצֶל הַפָּרוֹת *beside* the kine, 1 S 5^{2} אֵצֶל דָּגוֹן *beside* Dagon, 1 K $13^{24.25}$ 21^{1} Pr 8^{30} Ez $1^{15.19}$ 33^{30} 39^{15}; oft. in phrase אֵצֶל הַמִּזְבֵּחַ (מ׳ י׳) Lv 1^{16} 6^{3} Dt 16^{21} 1 K 2^{29} Am 2^{8}+; of a locality (cf. II. אֵת **2**) Dt 11^{30} *beside* the terebinths of Moreh, 1 K 1^{9} 4^{12} Je 41^{17}. After a vb. of motion (late) Dn $8^{7.17}$; cf. 2 Ch 28^{15b}. **b.** with מִן, מֵאֵצֶל *from proximity to, from beside* (cf. מֵעִם, מֵאֵת): †1 S 20^{41} (read with 𝔊 מֵאֵצֶל הָאַרְגָּב *from beside* the mound); Ez 40^{7} *contiguous to, beside* (מִן **3 c**); with suff. 1 S 17^{30} וַיִּסֹּב מֵאֶצְלוֹ and he turned about *from beside him,* 1 K 3^{20} 20^{36} Ez 10^{16}.

680 †[אָצַל] **vb. denom. lay aside, reserve, withdraw, withhold**—**Qal** *Pf.* אָצַלְתָּ Gn 27^{36}; אָצַ֫לְתִּי Ec 2^{10}; וְאָצַלְתִּ֫י cons. Nu 11^{17};—*reserve,* לִי בְּרָכָה Gn 27^{36}; (*withdraw*), *set apart* מִן־הָרוּחַ Nu 11^{17}; *withhold* מֵהֶם Ec 2^{10}. **Niph.** *Pf.* נֶאֱצַל Ez 42^{6} *be withdrawn,* i.e. *shortened* or *narrowed.* **Hiph.** *Impf.* וַיָּאצֶל Nu 11^{25} (Kö $^{i.390}$) = Qal Nu 11^{17}.

682 †II. אֵ֫צֶל in **n.pr.[m.]** בֵּית־הָאֵ֫צֶל Mi 1^{11}, acc. to Hi Ew Ca Ke = אָצֵ֑ל Zc 14^{5}, but dub.; cf. II. אָצַל infr.

682 †I. אָצַל, in pause אָצָ֑ל (Ges $^{§ 29.4c}$) **n.pr.m.** (perh. *noble*, cf. אָצִיל **2**) a descendant of Jonathan 1 Ch $8^{37.38}$ = $9^{43.44}$.

II. [אָצַל], in pause אָצָ֑ל Zc 14^{5}, acc. to 𝔊 𝔗 Thes Ew al., **n.pr.loc.** near Jerusalem; but no site found, & identification with בֵּית־הָאֵצֶל uncertain; hence Symm 𝔙 Köh Wr make subst., אֶל־אָצַל = *very near, hard by* (אָצֵל being the supposed abs. form of I. אֵצֶל; cf. Ol $^{§ 167 b}$). 682

†[אָצִיל] **n.[m.] side, corner, chief**—pl. cstr. אֲצִילֵי Ex 24^{11}; sf. אֲצִילֶיהָ Is 41^{9};—**1.** *sides* (borders) of earth Is 41^{9} (‖קצות); cf. ירכתי א׳ Je 6^{22} etc. **2.** fig. *nobles* (perh. as *sides, supports,* cf. sub פִּנּוֹת; so Ew Di: but perh. = أَصِيلٌ *noble*—from أَصُلَ *be rooted,* أَصْلٌ *root,* met. *origin, stock*—prop. a man having a (known) origin, sprung from an ancient and famous stock; so Ges, cf. Lag $^{BN 68}$) Ex 24^{11}. 678

†[אַצִּיל] **n.[f.] joining, joint** (cf. ܨܝܠܐ *elbow*)—pl. cstr. [י]אַצִּילֵי יד Ez 13^{18} (on יד cf. Sm Co);—*joint* of hand, i.e. *elbow* Ez 13^{18}; אַצִּלוֹת יָדֶיךָ Je 38^{12} *arm-joints.*—אַצִּ֫ילָה׃ Ez 41^{8} is obscure; perh. א׳ is here a technical architectural term *to the joining* (cf. Sm Ke). 679

†אֲצַלְיָ֫הוּ **n.pr.m.** (*Yahweh hath reserved,* or *set apart*) father of Shaphan the scribe 2 K 22^{3} 2 Ch 34^{8}. 683

אצם (meaning dub., cf. Ar. أَضِمَ *be angry*).

†אֹ֫צֶם **n.pr.m. 1.** elder brother of David 1 Ch 2^{15}. **2.** a descendant of Judah 1 Ch 2^{25}. 684

אֶצְעָדָה v. צעד. p. 858 685

†[אָצַר] **vb. lay up, store up** (Mish. *id.*, Aram. אֲצַר, ܐܨܪ, Ar. أَصَرَ *confine, restrict*)—**Qal** *Pf.* 3 pl. אָֽצְרוּ 2 K 20^{17} Is 39^{6}; *Pt.* הָאֹצְרִים Am 3^{10};—*store up* treasure 2 K 20^{17} = Is 39^{6}; obj. חָמָס וָשֹׁד Am 3^{10}, i.e. treasure gained by violence and robbery. **Niph.** *Impf.* יֵאָצֵר **be stored up,** of the merchandise of Tyre Is 23^{18}. **Hiph.** *Impf.* וָאוֹצְרָה (cf. Kö $^{i.391}$) (*denom.* from אוֹצָר) Ne 13^{13} *and I appointed treasurer,* sq. acc. pers. + עַל־אוֹצָרוֹת. 686

†אֵ֫צֶר **n.pr.m.** (*treasure;* or *covenant* Ar. إِصْرٌ) a chief of the Horites Gn $36^{21.27.30}$ 1 Ch $1^{38.42}$. 687

†אוֹצָר **n.m.** $^{Pr 15,16}$ **treasure, store, treasury, storehouse** (so Aram., also ܐܘܨܪܐ)—אוֹצָר Pr 15^{16}+; cstr. אוֹצַר Jos 6^{19}+; sf. אוֹצָרוֹ Dt 28^{12}+2 t.; pl. אוֹצָרוֹת Jo 1^{17}+; אֹצָרוֹת Pr 21^{6}+; 214

cstr. אוֹצְרוֹת Mi 6^{10}+; אֹצְרוֹת Jb 38^{22}+; pl. sf. אוֹצְרֹתָי׃ Dt 32^{34} Is 39^{4}; אֹצְרֹתָי׃ Dt 32^{34}; אוֹצְרוֹתֶיךָ Je 17^{3}; אוֹצְרֹתָם Is 30^{6}; אֹצְרֹתֵיהֶם Pr 8^{21}, etc.—**1.** *treasure(s)*, gen. pl. (gold, silver, costly utensils, etc.) Jos $6^{19.24}$ Is 2^{7} 30^{6} 45^{3} (א׳ חֹשֶׁךְ, i.e. concealed, hoarded) Ho 13^{15} Je 15^{13} 17^{3} 20^{5} 48^{7} 49^{4} 51^{13} 1 K $14^{26.26}$ 2 K $24^{13.13}$, perh. also Is $39^{2.4}$ = 2 K $20^{13.15}$; wealth Pr 15^{16} $21^{6.20}$; gathered for temple-building (sg.) א׳ בֵּית י׳ 1 Ch 29^{8}, א׳ הַמְּלָאכָה Ezr 2^{69}=Ne 7^{70}, also v^{69} (cf. 1 Ch 26^{27}). **2.** *store*, supply of food, drink, etc., 2 Ch 11^{11} 1 Ch $27^{27.28}$; fig. א׳ רֶשַׁע Mi 6^{10} Pr 10^{2}; יִרְאַת י׳ הִיא אוֹצָרוֹ Is 33^{6}. **3.** בֵּית אוֹצָר **a.** *treasure-house* Ne 10^{39} cf. Dn 1^{2}; **b.** *storehouse, magazine* Mal 3^{10}; & without בית **a.** *treasure-house* or *chamber, treasury* 1 K 7^{51} $15^{18.18}$ 2 K 12^{19} 14^{14} 16^{8} 18^{15} Je 38^{11} 50^{37} (?) 1 Ch 9^{26} $26^{20.20.22.24.26}$ $28^{12.12}$ 2 Ch 5^{1} 16^{2} (?) 32^{27} cf. Ez 28^{4}; **b.** *storehouse* Jo 1^{17} Pr 8^{21} 1 Ch $27^{25.25}$ Ne $13^{12.13}$; **c.** *magazine* of weapons, fig. of Yahweh's *armoury* Je 50^{25}; **d.** *storehouses* of God for rain, snow, hail, wind, sea Dt 28^{12} Jb $38^{22.22}$ Je 10^{13} 51^{16} ψ 135^{7} 33^{7}.

688 **אֶקְדָּח** v. קדח. p. 869

689 †**אַקּוֹ** **n.m.** **wild goat** (?) only Dt 14^{5} in list of clean animals אַיָּל וּצְבִי וְיַחְמוּר וְאַקּוֹ וְדִישֹׁן וּתְאוֹ וָזָמֶר (𝔊 ὄρυξ, 𝔖 𝔗 *ibex*; cf. Bo$^{\text{Hieroz. i. 900 f.}}$, Thes sub אנק cf. MV, with ref. to Ar. عناق *goat*; Thes comp. also Talm. אִיקָא, but NHWB MV refer this to *αἴξ*).

216 **אֹר** v. אוֹר, for Am 8^{8} v. יְאֹר. p. 20, 384

690 †**אֲרָא** **n.pr.m.** (meaning unknown, Thes conject.=אֲרִי *lion*) a descendant of Asher 1 Ch 7^{38}.

691-92 **אֲרִאֵל, אַרְאֵלִי** v. אֲרִיאֵל sub I. ארה. p. 72

693 † **אָרַב** **vb.** **lie in wait** (Ar. أَرِبَ *be crafty*, also أَرَّبَ *tie* (a knot) Frey)—**Qal** *Pf.* וְאָרַב consec. Dt 19^{11} Ju 21^{20}; אָרָבְתִּי׃ Jb 31^{9}; אָרְבוּ ψ 59^{4} La 4^{19}; *Impf.* יֶאֱרֹב ψ $10^{9.9}$; יֶאֶרְבוּ Pr 1^{18} Mi 7^{2}; וַיֶּאֶרְבוּ Ju 9^{34} 16^{2}; נֶאֶרְבָה Pr 1^{11}; *Imv.* אֱרֹב Ju 9^{32}; *Inf.* אֱרָב־ Pr 12^{6}; *Pt.* אֹרֵב Jos 8^{2}+11 t.; אוֹרֵב Jos 8^{12}+4 t.; אֹרְבִים Jos 8^{4}+2 t.;—*lie in wait* (with hostile purpose), abs. Ju $9^{32.43}$+ 21^{20} Jb 31^{9} ψ 10^{9} Pr 7^{12} 23^{28} 1 S $22^{8.13}$ La 3^{10} (of bear, cf. ψ 10^{9}); c. inf. of purpose ψ 10^{9}; c. acc. א׳ דָּם Pr 12^{6}; c. עַל, and pers. against whom Dt 19^{11} Ju 9^{34}; usually c. לְ Mi 7^{2} Ju 16^{2} ψ 59^{4} Pr $1^{11.18}$ 24^{15} La 4^{19} cf. Jos $8^{2.4.14}$; *Pt.* as subst.=*liers-in-wait* (pl.) Ju 20^{29}; usually sg. coll. *ambush* Jos $8^{2.12.14.19.21}$ Ju $16^{9.12}$ $20^{33.36.37.37.38}$ Ezr 8^{31}; pl. of this sing.=ambuscades Je 51^{12}; sg.=*place of lying-in-wait, ambush* (loc. sense) Jos 8^{7}.

Pi. *Pt.* pl. *liers-in-wait* i.q. **Qal** *Pt.* מְאָרְבִים Ju 9^{25} (c. לְ), 2 Ch 20^{22} (c. עַל). ? **Hiph.** *Impf.* וַיָּרֶב בנחל (for וַיֶּאֱרֹב) 1 S 15^{5} (cf. Dr Kö$^{\text{i. 390}}$; Ges-Kau$^{\text{§ 68. 2}}$ queries) but txt. dub.; cf. Ol$^{\text{§ 257 b}}$, & Klo, who prop. ויעבר בנחל.

†[**אֶרֶב**] **אֹרֶב** **n.[m.]**—**1.** *a lying-in-wait* Jb 38^{40}. **2.** *covert, lair* 37^{8} (‖ מְעוֹנֹת). 695

†**אֲרָב** **n.pr.loc.** city near Hebron Jos 15^{52} (𝔊 Ἐρεμ, 𝔊L Ἐρεβ; acc. to Onomast. Ἐρεμινθα Lag$^{\text{On. 254, 2nd ed. 260}}$ Ereb Id.$^{\text{119, 2nd ed. 152}}$, a village *Heromith* in Daroma; cf. Di Survey$^{\text{iii. 311}}$). 694

†**אַרְבִּי** **adj.gent.** הָא׳ 2 S 23^{35} (but cf. Dr). 701

†[**אֹרֶב**] **n.[m.]** **ambuscade** only fig.—**a.** יָשִׂים אָרְבּוֹ Je 9^{7} i.e. he planneth treachery. **b.** אָרְבָּם *their intrigue* Ho 7^{6} cf. Now$^{\text{p. 126}}$. 696

†[**אָרְבָּה**] **n.f.** **artifice**, pl. cstr. אָרְבּוֹת יָדָיו Is 25^{11} (lit. *tricks of his hands*). 698

†**אֲרֻבָּה** **n.f.** **lattice, window, sluice** (Mish. *id.*)—א׳ Ho 13^{3}; pl. אֲרֻבּוֹת 2 K 7^{2}+, cstr. *id.* Mal 3^{10}; אֲרֻבֹּת Gn 7^{11} 8^{2}; אֲרֻבֹּתֵיהֶם Is 60^{8};—*lattice*, latticed opening, where smoke escaped Ho 13^{3}; openings of dove-cote Is 60^{8}; metaph. of eyes Ec 12^{3} (as latticed by lashes ? Hi Now; only here of opening to look through); elsewhere of sluices in sky, opened by י׳, through which rain pours destructively, א׳ הַשָּׁמַיִם Gn 7^{11} 8^{2}, cf. Is 24^{18} (א׳ מִמָּרוֹם); but also fertilizing 2 K $7^{2.19}$ (א׳ בשמים); fig. of blessing Mal 3^{10} (א׳ השמים). 699

†**אֲרֻבּוֹת** **n.pr.loc.** (=אֲרָב? cf. Klo ad loc.) 1 K 4^{10} בָּאֲרֻבּוֹת. 700

†**מַאֲרָב** **n.m.** **ambush**—מַאֲרָב Jos 8^{9}+2 t.; מַאְרָב Ju 9^{35}; cstr. מַאֲרַב ψ 10^{8};—**1.** **a.** *ambush*, place of lying-in-wait Jos 8^{9} Ju 9^{35}; **b.** *lurking-place* ψ 10^{8} (‖ מִסְתָּרִים). **2.** *liers-in-wait* 2 Ch $13^{13.13}$ (cf. ארב *Pt.*) 3993

אַרְבְּאֵל cf. בֵּית אַרְבֵּאל, sub בית. p. 111 1009

אַרְבֶּה v. sub רבה. p. 916 697

אַרְבַּע, אַרְבָּעָה, אַרְבַּעַת, אַרְבָּעִים etc. v. רבע. pp. 916f 702, 704-05

†[**אָרַג**] **vb.** **weave** (Mish. *id.* cf. Ph. ארג *weaver*)—**Qal** *Impf.* 2 fs. תַּאַרְגִי Ju 16^{13}, 3 mpl. יֶאֱרֹגוּ Is 59^{5}; *Pt.* אֹרֵג Ex 28^{32}+4 t.; pl. אֹרְגִים Is 19^{9}+5 t.; אֹרְגוֹת 2 K 23^{7};—*weave* cloth, etc. Is 19^{9} (in Egypt) 2 K 23^{7}, Samson's locks Ju 16^{13}; metaph. weave spider's web=intrigue Is 59^{5}; most often Pt. used as subst.=*weaver* Is 38^{12}; 707

work of the weaver מַעֲשֵׂה א׳ Ex 28^{32} 39$^{22.27}$ cf. 35^{35}; weavers' beam (pl.) מְנוֹר א׳ 1 S 17^{7} 2 S 21^{19} 1 Ch 11^{23} 20^{5} (sim. of huge spear-shaft)—cf. also sub יַעֲרֵי ארגים.

708 †אֶ֫רֶג **n.[m.]** loom (v. GFM$^{POS\ Oct.\ 1889}$)—אֶרֶג Ju 16^{14} hand-loom to which Samson's hair was fastened, plucked up by him (א׳ obj. of וַיִּסַּע; del. הַיְתַד as gloss, cf. GFM supr.); Jb 7^{6} יָמַי קַלּוּ מִנִּי אָרֶג *my days are swifter than a loom.*

709 אַרְגֹּב v. רגב. p. 918

712 אַרְגָּז v. רגז. p. 919

710 †אַרְגְּוָן **n.[m.]** purple (of Aram. form, cf. Heb. infr.; perh. txt. err.)=*purple thread* 2 Ch 2^{6} (+ כַּרְמִיל וּתְכֵלֶת), cf. 2^{13} 3^{14} sub אַרְגָּמָן.

713 †אַרְגָּמָן **n.[m.]** **purple, red-purple,** i.e. **purple thread & cloth** (As. *argamannu* COT Ex 25^{4}, Ar. أُرْجُوَان, Aram. ܐܪܓܘܢܐ, cf. אַרְגְּוָן supr.; etym. dub.; possibly Skr. *râgaman*, adj. *red, reddish*, fr. *râga*, red colour, so Benary cf. Thes Add^{111} RobGes; vid. MV; Thes earlier, fr. רגם; but prob. loan-word, cf. also Lag $^{BN\ 205}$; Pers. ارغوان is also cited by PS)—form alw. as above—**1.** *purple thread*, cf. esp. Ex 35^{25} 39^{3} Est 1^{6}; **a.** mostly Ex (P) with ref. to the hangings of tabernacle, the ephod, etc.; seld. alone; c. תְּכֵלֶת, *violet* (q.v.), תּוֹלַעַת שָׁנִי, שֵׁשׁ (מָשְׁזָר), (also עִזִּים) Ex 25^{4} 26$^{1.31.36}$ 27^{16} 35$^{8.25.35}$ 36$^{8.35.37}$ 38$^{18.23}$ 39^{24} (on text v. Di) v^{29}; with these + זָהָב 28$^{5.6.8.15}$ 39$^{2.3.5.8}$; om. שֵׁשׁ מ׳ 28^{33} 39^{1}; also of temple-hangings, with כַּרְמִיל & בּוּץ, תְּכֵלֶת, 2 Ch 3^{14} cf. 2^{13} (v. also 2^{6} v. sub אַרְגְּוָן). **b.** as indicating wealth & luxury of Tyre, c. שֵׁשׁ, רִקְמָה, תְּכֵלֶת Ez 27^{7}; c. רִקְמָה & בּוּץ v^{16} (as articles of commerce); also in Persia, c. בּוּץ Est 1^{6}. **2.** *purple cloth*, chiefly of garments, בֶּגֶד א׳ Nu 4^{13} Ju 8^{26}; שֵׁשׁ וְא׳ לְבוּשָׁהּ Pr 31^{22}; וְתַכְרִיךְ בּוּץ וְא׳ Est 8^{15}, תְּכֵלֶת וְא׳ לְבוּשָׁם Je 10^{9}; also מֶרְכָּבוֹ א׳ Ct 3^{10}; in simile, of woman's hair Ct 7^{6}.

714 †אַרְדְּ **n.pr.m.** Gn 46^{21} son of Benjamin, but Nu 26^{40} *grand*son of Benjamin=אַדָּר 1 Ch 8^{3}.

716 †אַרְדִּי **adj.gent.** c. art. as n.pr.coll., מִשְׁפַּ׳ הָאַרְדִּי Nu 26^{40}.

720 †אֲרוֹד **n.pr.m.** son of Gad Nu 26^{17}=אֲרוֹדִי Gn 46^{16}.

722 †אֲרוֹדִי **adj.gent.** c. art. as n.pr.coll., מִשְׁפַּ׳ הָא׳ Nu 26^{17}; without art. as n.pr.=אֲרוֹד Gn 46^{16}.

715 †אַרְדּוֹן **n.pr.m.** son of Caleb, of tribe of Judah 1 Ch 2^{18}.

†אַרְוַד **n.pr.loc.** city of Phenicia (As. *Aruada*, etc. v. COT Gn 10^{18} Dl$^{Pa\ 281}$; 𝔊 'Αραδιοι; mod. *Ruâd*) on an island near main land, northward fr. Tripolis, mentioned with Sidon Ez 27$^{8\ cf.\ 11}$. 719

†אַרְוָדִי **adj.gent.** c. art. as n.coll. (As. *Arudai*, etc. COT^{Gloss}) mentioned among Canaanites, הָאַרְוָדִי Gn 10^{18}=1 Ch 1^{16}. 721

†אֲרִידַי **n.pr.m.** a son of Haman Est 9^{9} (Pers., perh.=*haridayas, delight of Hari*, v. Add Thes^{72}; but text very uncertain; cf. diff. tradition as to the names in 𝔊). 742

†אֲרִידָתָא **n.pr.m.** a son of Haman Est 9^{8} (Pers., perh.=*Hari-dâta, given by Hari*, v. *ib.*, but 𝔊 Φαραδαθα). 743

† I. [אָרָה] **vb.** **pluck, gather** (Eth. አረየ:) —**Qal** *Pf.* 1 s. אָרִיתִי Ct 5^{1}; 3 pl. sf. וְאָרוּהָ ψ 80^{13} *pluck* (grapes from) vine ψ 80^{13}, myrrh Ct 5^{1}. 717

†אֲרִי **n.m.**$^{Pr\ 28,\ 15}$ lion (As. *aria*, Eth. አርዌ: *wild beast*, cf. also אַרְיֵה infr.)—אֲרִי Am 3^{12}+ 13 t.+2 S 23^{20} Qr (Kt אריה), La 3^{10} (id.)+ ψ 22^{17} (כָּאֲרִי for wh. rd. כָּרוּ=כארו cf. De Pe Che crit. note); pl. אֲרָיִים 1 K 10^{20}; אֲרָיוֹת (also m.) Zp 3^{3}+16 t. (f. Je 51^{38}? but cf. Ju 14^{5});—*lion*, lit. in narrative Ju 14^{5} 1 S 17$^{34.36.37}$ 2 S 23^{20}=1 Ch 11^{22} 2 K 17$^{25.26}$ Pr 22^{13} 26^{13} Ct 4^{8} cf. Am 3^{12} 5^{19}; *lion-images* 1 K 7$^{29.29.36}$ 10$^{19.20}$=2 Ch 9$^{18.19}$; in comparison Nu 23^{24} 24^{9} Ju 14^{18} Is 38^{13} Je 51^{38} 2 S 1^{23} Ez 22^{5} La 3^{10}; metaph. Na 2^{12} Zp 3^{3} Je 50^{17} Ez 19$^{2.6}$ Pr 28^{15}. For כארי ψ 22^{17} rd. כארו, cf. above. Cf. also אַרְיֵה. 738

†[אֻרְיָה] **n.f.** **manger, crib** (Aram. אוּרְיָא, ܐܘܪܝܐ, Ar. آرِيّ *stall*, etc., As. *urû* Dl$^{BAS\ i.\ 211}$)—*Pl.* אֻרָוֹת 2 Ch 32^{28} (Aram. form for אֻרָוֹת; cf. Lag$^{BN\ 172}$); cstr. אֻרְוֹת 1 K 5^{6}, אֻרְיוֹת 2 Ch 9^{25}; —*crib* of horses 1 K 5^{6} (app. in enumeration of horses themselves, Eng. *head*, or *span*, cf. also 2 Ch 9^{25} with 1 K 10^{26}; so Th MV, but txt. here dub. cf. Klo), hence 2 Ch 9^{25}; of any animals (כל-בהמה) 2 Ch 32^{28} (on לְאֻ׳ v. Add.). 220, 723

†אַרְיֵה **n.m.**$^{Am\ 3,\ 8}$ lion (𝔗 *id.* Syr. ܐܪܝܐ, cf. also אֲרִי supr.)—only sg. as above Am 3^{4}+44 t. +2 S 23^{20} Kt (Qr אֲרִי) La 3^{10} (id.);—*lion*, lit. in narrative Ju 14$^{8.8.9}$ 2 S 23^{20} 1 K 13$^{24.24.25.26.28}$ (c. עמדים txt. err. acc. to Klo)^{28} 20$^{36.36}$ cf. Is 11^{7} 35^{9} 65^{25}; in simile Gn 49^{9} 2 S 17^{10} ψ 7^{3} 10^{9} 17^{12} 22^{14} Is 21^{8} 31^{4} Je 2^{30} 12^{8} 49^{19} 50^{44} La 3^{10} (Kt) Ez 1^{10} 10^{14} 1 Ch 12^{8} Ho 11^{10} Jo 1^{6} Mi 5^{7}, cf. Am 3$^{4.8}$ Ec 9^{4}; metaph. Gn 49^{9} Dt 33^{22} Jb 4^{10} ψ 22^{22} Is 15^{9} Je 4^{7} 5^{6} Na 2$^{12.12.13}$. 744

745 †אֲרִיֵה **n.pr.m.** so appar. 2 K 15^{25} an officer of Pekahiah, but c. art. הָאַרְיֵה, & on text with possible corruption & dittography v. Klo.

739-40 †אֲרִיאֵל **1. n.pr.f.** (prob., v. Ew) **Ariel** (*lioness of Ēl*) name applied to Jerusalem Is 29$^{1.2.2.7}$ (so Ges Ew Che Di al.; 𝔗 De Brd Or al.
741 say *hearth of Ēl*, cf. אֲרִאֵיל). **2. n.pr.m.** a chief man among returning exiles Ezr 8^{16}. **3.** אֲרִאֵל מוֹאָב 2 S 23^{20} = אֲרִיאֵל מ׳ 1 Ch 11^{26} taken by 𝔊 RV Dr^{Sm} al. as **n.pr.m.**, rd. *two sons of Ariel of Moab;* RS$^{Sem. i. 469}$ comp. אראל MI ^{12}, *altar-hearth* (so Sm & So, and Dr$^{Sm\ xci}$, v. sub אֲרִאֵיל) and transl. א׳ מוֹאָב *altar-hearths of Moab.* **4.** Ez 43^{15} & Qr v$^{15.16}$ vid. sub אֲרִאֵיל.

692 †אַרְאֵלִי **n.pr.m.** (app. n.gent. from foregoing, but 𝔊 Nu 26^{17} Ἀριηλ (Gn 46^{16} Ἀροηλεις, Ἀροηδις, Ἀπηδεις) = foregoing) a son of Gad Gn 46^{16} Nu 26^{17}; also **adj.gent.** c. art. as n.pr. coll. Nu 26^{17} מִשְׁפַּחַת הָאַרְאֵלִי 𝔊 Ἀριηλει.

691 †[אֶרְאֵל] **n.[m.]** (form & meaning dub. v. infr.)—only in אֶרְאֶלָּם Is 33^{7}; Ges אַרְאֵלָם *heroes;* cf. Thes Kn Che; Hi אֲרִאֵלָם; cf. De, who der. from אֲרִיאֵל, lit. = *lion of God*, coll. c. sf., & transl. *their heroes;* n.gent. fr. אֲרִיאֵל = Zion Nbr $^{Athen. 1886, p. 400}$ cf. Say$^{Ib. 466}$; Ew אַרְעֵל = אַרְאֵל *trembling*, cf. Di. Brd prop. הילילו 'cry pitifully.' 𝔖 𝔗 al. rd. some form of ראה, 𝔊 ירא. Wholly uncertain.

II. **ארה** (*burn*, cf. Ar. أَرَى, whence إِرَةٌ *hearth;* Ew$^{§ 163 g}$ al. v. infr.)

741 †אֲרִאֵיל **n.[m.] hearth, altar-hearth** (𝔊 Ἀριηλ; fr. ארה with ל aff. acc. to Ew$^{§ 163 g}$ Ol$^{§ 220}$ Sm Ez 43^{15} Di Is 29^{1} al.; but this formation very rare & here dub.; 𝔗 Hi De Brd Or Is 29^{1} der. fr. ארי + אל = *hearth of Ēl*, v. also RS $^{Sem. i. 469}$, who thinks of pillar-altars; cf. אראל דודה MI^{12} v. Sm & So, and Dr$^{Sm\ xci}$)—אראיל Kt Ez
2025 43$^{15.16}$; (Qr אֲרִיאֵל); = הַרְאֵל v^{15} (Vrss Co אריאל), all c. art.,—of altar-hearth in Ezekiel's temple.

725 †[אֲרוּמָה] **n.pr.loc.** home of Abimelek (Thes Add sub ארם) Ju 9^{41} בָּארוּמָה, prob. = רוּמָה 2 K 23^{36}, cf. Jer Lag $^{Onomast. 146, 2nd\ ed. 178}$. It must have lain near Shechem; identified by MV al. with *El 'Ormah*, 2 hours SE. from Shechem (van de Velde$^{Reisen\ ii. 268}$), but this place not otherwise known; cf. Survey$^{ii. 387}$.

728 †אֲרַוְנָה **n.pr.m. Araunah**, a Jebusite—א׳ 2 S 24$^{20.20.21.22.23}$ (but rd. עֶבֶד אֲדֹנַי cf. We Dr) v$^{23.24}$; Kt האורנה גֹּרֶן v^{16} (Qr הָאֲרַוְנָה) c. art. but cf. Dr; Kt ארניה ג׳ v^{18} (Qr אֲרַוְנָה); = אָרְנָן (q.v.) 1 Ch 21$^{15\,f}$; 𝔊 in S & Ch Ὀρνα.

ארז (cf. Ar. أَرَزَ *be firm*, also *withdraw*, 729
retreat).

†אֶרֶז **n.m.** $^{Ez 17, 23}$ **cedar;—f.** Ez 17^{22} א׳ הָרָמָה, 730
but del. הרמה 𝔊 Co;—(Ar. أَرْزٌ *pine-tree*, etc.; Eth. **አርዝ፡** Syr. ܐܪܙܐ)—א׳ abs. Lv 14^{4} + 19 t., אָרֶז Jb 40^{17} + 6 t.; pl. אֲרָזִים Is 9^{9} + 35 t.; cstr. אַרְזֵי Is 2^{13} + 5 t.; sf. אֲרָזֶיךָ Je 22^{17} Zc 11^{1}; אֲרָזָיו Is 37^{24} = 2 K 19^{23};—**1.** *cedar-tree*, (*a*) as *growing* Nu 24^{6} ψ 148^{9} Is 41^{19} 44^{14} cf. Ez 31^{8}; esp. as growing on Lebanon 1 K 5^{13}; 2 K 14^{9} = 2 Ch 25^{18} (both in fable of Jehoash); oft. אַרְזֵי (הַ)לְּבָנוֹן Ju 9^{15} Is 2^{13} 14^{8} ψ 29$^{5.5}$ (fig.) 104^{16}, cf. 1 K 5^{20} 2 K 19^{23} = Is 37^{24} ψ 92^{13} Ct 5^{15} Ez 27^{5} (sg. coll.) Zc 11$^{1.2}$ (fig.); Ct 1^{17} Ezr 3^{7} Je 22^{23} (fig.) Ez 17^{3} (fig.); (*b*) esp. in sim., of outward power, stateliness & majesty ψ 80^{11} (א׳ אֵל) cf. Ez 31^{3} (personif., but v. Co on text), Am 2^{9}; of individuals Je 22^{7} ψ 92^{13} Ez 17$^{22.23}$; cf. other exx. of fig. use, supr.; sim. of straightness & strength Jb 40^{17} (tail of hippopotamus). **2.** *cedar-timber, cedar-wood* for building, עֲצֵי אֲרָזִים 1 S 5^{11} 1 K 5$^{22.24}$ 6^{10} 9^{11} 1 Ch 14^{1} 22$^{4.4}$ 2 Ch 2^{7} Ezr 3^{7}; without עֵץ 2 S 7$^{2.7}$ 1 K 6$^{9.15.16.18.18.20.36}$ 7$^{2.2.3.7.11.12}$ 10^{27} 1 Ch 17$^{1.6}$ 2 Ch 1^{15} 2^{3} 9^{27} & Ct 8^{9} Is 9^{9} Je 22$^{14.15}$ (cf. also Is 44^{14} 1 K 5^{20} Ez 27^{5} Ezr 3^{7} supr.) **3.** *cedar-wood* used in purifications, c. עֵץ Lv 14$^{4.6.49.51.52}$ Nu 19^{6} (all P).

†אַרְזָה **n.f.coll. cedar-panels, cedar-** 731
work Zp 2^{14}.

†[אָרוּז] **adj. firm, strong** (cf. Ar. أَرَزَ supr.) 729
אֲרֻזִים Ez 27^{24}.

†מֵרוֹז **n.pr.loc.** Meroz, in northern Pales- 4789
tine Ju 5^{23} (expl. as = מְאֵרוֹז, مَأْرِز, *retreat* by Thes MV al.)

†אָרַח **vb. wander, journey, go** (Ph. ארח 732
in מארח, prob. = מְאָרֵחַ cf. Eth. **መርሐ፡** *lead, conduct*, v. Nö$^{ZMG\ 1888, 472}$; epithet of god Eshmun, Sab. ארח DHM$^{Epigr. Denkm. p. 70}$, Aram. אוֹרְחָא, ܐܳܘܪܚܳܐ *traveller*)—**Qal** *Pf.* וְאָרַח consec. Jb 34^{8}; *Pt.* אֹרֵחַ Ju 19^{17} +; pl. אֹרְחִים Je 9^{1};—**1.** *journey, go*, c. עִם fig. of association, companionship Jb 34^{8} וְא׳ לְחֶבְרָה עִם־פֹּעֲלֵי אָוֶן וְלָלֶכֶת עִם־אַנְשֵׁי־רֶשַׁע׃ (cf. also הלך ψ 1^{1}). **2.** *Pt. wandering, wayfaring, journeying*, הָאִישׁ הָאֹרֵחַ Ju 19^{17}; as subst. *wanderer, wayfarer, traveller* אֹרֵחַ 2 S 12^{4} (∥ הֵלֶךְ), Je 14^{8} (∥ גֵּר, in sim. of י׳); מְלוֹן אֹרְחִים *wayfarers' lodging-place* Je 9^{1}.

734 †אֹ֫רַח **n.m.** $^{Jb\ 6,18}$ (**f.** $^{Pr\ 15,19}$) way, path (As. *urḫu* COT^{Gloss}, Aram. אֹרַח, ܐܘܪܚܐ)—א׳ abs. ψ 19^{6}+; cstr. Pr 4^{18}+; sf. אָרְחִי Jb 19^{8} ψ 139^{3} etc.; pl. abs. אֳרָחוֹת Ju 5$^{6.6}$; cstr. אָרְחוֹת Jb 8^{13} +; sf. אָרְחֹתָי Jb 13^{27} 33^{11}; אָרְחוֹתָם Jo 2^{7} Pr 9^{15}; אָרְחֹתֵיהֶם Pr 2^{15}; also אֹרְחֹתָיו Is 2^{3}+; אֹרְחֹתֶיךָ ψ 119^{15}+ etc.;—*way, path* (in Heb. mostly poet.) **1.** lit. Ju 5$^{6.6}$ song of Deb. (alone = *highways*, opp. א׳ עֲקַלְקַלּוֹת *crooked (by-)paths;* cf. also הֹלְכֵי נְתִיבוֹת *ib.*); Is 33^{8} עֹבֵר א׳ = *wayfarer* (‖ מְסִלּוֹת), v. also Gn 49^{17} (blessing of Jacob) (‖ דֶּרֶךְ) & הַמְיַשְּׁרִים אָרְחוֹתָם *those who make straight their ways* (‖ עֹבְרֵי דָרֶךְ) Pr 9^{15}, בּוֹא א׳ *go* (tread) *a path* Is 41^{3}; of course of locusts Jo 2^{7} לֹא יְעַבְּטוּן א׳ *they confuse not their paths* (‖ דְּרָכִים); א׳ יַמִּים *paths of the seas* ψ 8^{9}; רוּץ אֹרַח *run along a path*, fig. of sun ψ 19^{6}. **2.** fig. *path, way,* of course & fortunes of life Jb 8^{13} 13^{27} = 33^{11} 19^{8} (‖ נְתִיבוֹת) ψ 139^{3} (‖ דֶּרֶךְ) 142^{4} (‖ נְתִיבָה) Pr 3^{6} (‖ דֶּרֶךְ) 4^{18} 15^{19} (both ‖ *id.*) Is 26^{7} (‖ מַעְגָּל) so דֶּרֶךְ אֹרְחֹתֶיךָ Is 3^{12}; *plain* or *even path* א׳ מִישׁוֹר ψ 27^{11}; in two cases with a special ref. (1) אֹרַח כַּנָּשִׁים Gn 18^{11} (J) of menstruation; (2) אֹרַח לֹא אָשׁוּב אֶהֱלֹךְ *a path (which) I shall not return, I am going* Jb 16^{22} i.e. to *Sheʾôl*, cf. As. name of lower world *irṣit lâ târat, land without return,* v. Jr^{10,65}. **3.** fig. *way,* of mode of living, or of character Jb 34^{11} (‖ פֹּעַל) ψ 119^{9}. Specif.: **a.** *ways of* י׳, his mode of action ψ 25^{10}; **b.** of man's righteousness, called *ways of* י׳ ψ 25^{4} (‖ דְּרָכִים) 44^{19} 119^{15} (‖ פִּקּוּדִים) Is 2^{3} = Mi 4^{2} (‖ דְּרָכִים) cf. א׳ מִשְׁפָּטֶיךָ Is 26^{8}; also *way of justice, uprightness,* etc. א׳ מִשְׁפָּט Pr 2^{8} (‖ דֶּרֶךְ) 17^{23} Is 40^{14} (‖ דֶּרֶךְ), א׳ יֹשֶׁר Pr 2^{13} (‖ *id.*), א׳ צְדָקָה 8^{20} (‖ נְתִיבוֹת), 12^{28} (‖ דֶּרֶךְ נְתִיבָה); so אֹרַח alone Is 30^{11} (‖ דֶּרֶךְ) Pr 15^{10}; note esp. אֹרַח חַיִּים, *path of life,* in righteousness & enjoyment of God ψ 16^{11} Pr 2^{19} 5^{6} 15^{24} (opp. שְׁאוֹל), also א׳ לְחַיִּים 10^{17} (on these cf. Str Pr 14^{32}); **c.** of wickedness, א׳ פָּרִיץ *way, path of the violent* ψ 17^{4}, cf. also Pr 22^{25}; א׳ רְשָׁעִים Pr 4^{14} (‖ דֶּרֶךְ), א׳ בֹּצַע 1^{19}; sq. abstr. א׳ שָׁקֶר ψ 119^{104}, so v^{128} (‖ פִּקּוּדִים), also c. adj. א׳ רָע ψ 119^{101} cf. Pr 2^{15} (עִקְּשִׁים *crooked*) called הָא׳ עוֹלָם Jb 22^{15}; note also א׳ אֵידָם *their destructive ways,* i.e. ways that cause destruction Jb 30^{12} (cf. 19^{12}). **4.** by meton. *traveller, wayfarer* Jb 31^{32} (cf. הֵלֶךְ 2 S 12^{4}) & in pl. *caravans* 6$^{18.19}$; but rd. perh. לָאֹרֵחַ 31^{32}, אֹרְחוֹת 6$^{18.19}$.

733 †אָרַח **n.pr.m.** (*traveller?*) **1.** a man of Asher 1 Ch 7^{39}. **2.** head of a family of returning exiles Ezr 2^{5} = Ne 7^{10}; perh. = אָרָה Ne 6^{18}.

†אֲרֻחָה **n.f.** meal, allowance (of food) abs. Je 40^{5}; cstr. אֲרֻחַת יָרָק Pr 15^{17} *a portion of herbs,* i.e. a slender meal; elsewh. of allowance given to captive king Jehoiachin, א׳ תָּמִיד *a continual allowance* 2 K 25^{30} = Je 52^{34}; אֲרֻחָתוֹ *ib.* = *id.* 737

†[אֹרְחָה] **n.f. travelling company, caravan** (strictly *Pt.* of אָרַח), cstr. אֹרְחַת Gn 37^{25}; pl. cstr. אֹרְחוֹת Is 21^{13}; cf. also sub אֹרַח, **4.** 736

אֲרִיאֵיל, אֲרִיאֵל etc., v. I. & II. ארה. 740-41

†אַרְיוֹךְ **n.pr.m.** king of Ellasar Gn 14$^{1.9}$, ally of Chedorlaomer in his western foray (prob. = *Rim-Aku,* Elamite king of Larsa = Ellasar; cf. COT$^{ii.\ 297\ f.}$). 746

†[אָרֵךְ, אָרַךְ] **vb. be long,** almost alw. of time (As. *arâku* COT^{Gloss}, Aram. אֲרַךְ, ܐܪܟ)—**Qal** *Pf.* אָרְכוּ Gn 26^{8}; *Impf.* יַאַרְכוּ Ez 12^{22}; 3 fpl. וַתֶּאֱרַכְנָה Ez 31^{5} (del. B Co)—*be long,* subj. הַיָּמִים (i.e. a long time passed Gn 26^{8} (J); cf. As. *urriku ûmî, days grew long,* Creation Tablet^{a} v. COT Gn 1^{1}); of delayed fulfilment of prophecy Ez 12^{22}; subj. פֹּארֹת Ez 31^{5} (but cf. supr.) **Hiph.** *Pf.* הֶאֱרִיךְ Pr 19^{11}; וְהַאֲרַכְתָּ Dt 22^{7}, etc.; *Impf.* יַאֲרִיךְ Dt 17^{20}+; יַאֲרִיכוּ Dt 25^{15}; יַאֲרִכוּן Ex 20^{12} cf. Dt 5^{16} 6^{2}; תַּאֲרִיכֻן Dt 4^{26} 30^{18}, etc.; *Imv.* fs. הַאֲרִיכִי Is 54^{2}; *Inf.* cstr. הַאֲרִיךְ Nu 9$^{19.22}$; *Pt.* מַאֲרִיךְ Ec 7^{15} 8^{12};—**1.** trans. *prolong,* (*a*) obj. יָמִים (i.e. live long) Dt 4$^{26.40}$ 5^{30} 11^{9} 17^{20} 22^{7} 30^{18} 32^{47} Jos 24^{31} = Ju 2^{7} (c. אַחֲרֵי = *survive*), Pr 28^{16} Is 53^{10} Ec 8^{13}; also (late) without ימים Ec 7^{15} 8^{12}; (*b*) *id.* 1 K 3^{14} subj. י׳ וְהַאֲרַכְתִּי אֶת־יָמֶיךָ *I will prolong thy days;* (*c*) *postpone* anger Is 48^{9} cf. Pr 19^{11} (i.e. shew oneself slow to anger); v. also Jb 6^{11} אַאֲרִיךְ נַפְשִׁי i.e. be patient; (*d*) lit. (but in fig.) *make long* furrows (c. לְ) ψ 129^{3}; tent-cords Is 54^{2}; tongue 57^{4} (stretch out in mockery). **2.** intrans. *grow long, continue long* (i.e. *display* length or continuance), subj. יָמִים Ex 20^{12} = Dt 5^{16} 6^{2} 25^{15}; *tarry long* Nu 9$^{19.22}$ (subj. הֶעָנָן), *last* (continue) *long,* subj. כֵּן Pr 28^{2}; *be long* (lit.) of staves of ark 1 K 8^{8} 2 Ch 5^{9}. 748

אֹ֫רֶךְ$_{94}$ **n.[m.] length**—only sg., א׳ abs. Ex 27^{1}+; cstr. Gn 6^{15}+; אָרְכּוֹ Ex 25^{10}+; אָרְכָּם 2 Ch 3^{11}; אָרְכָּן Ez 42^{11}, etc.—**a.** *length* of ark Gn 6^{15} (P), of land of Canaan 13^{17} (J); most oft. of ark & other measurements in tabernacle & temple Ex 25$^{10.17}$ 26$^{2.8}$ 27$^{1.9}$+ (22 t. Ex, P), 1 K 6$^{2.3.20}$+ (13 t. K & Ch), Ez 40$^{7.11.18}$+ (41 t. Ez), etc. **b.** of time א׳ יָמִים Dt 30^{20} Jb 12^{12} ψ 21^{5} 23^{6} 91^{16} 93^{5} Pr 3$^{2.16}$ La 5^{20}. **c.** א׳ אַפַּיִם *forbearance, self-restraint,* Pr 25^{15}.—(Ez 31^{7} 𝔊 𝔖 Co rd. רֹב for אֹרֶךְ, cf. v^{5} where Co del. vb. ארך; 41^{22} rd. prob. אדנו 𝔊 Sm, or ארניו Co = *base.*) 753

750 †[אָרֵךְ] **adj.** long—only cstr. אֶרֶךְ Ex 34^{6} + 14 t.—א׳ הָאֵבֶר *long of pinion* Ez 17^{3} (|| גְּדוֹל הַכְּנָפַיִם) of eagle, in metaph.; elsewhere always of feelings, as subst. Ec 7^{8} א׳ רוּחַ *the patient of spirit* (opp. גְּבַהּ ר׳); א׳ אַפַּיִם *one slow to anger* Pr 14^{29} (opp. קְצַר־רוּחַ), so 15^{18} (opp. אִישׁ חֵמָה), 16^{32} (|| מֹשֵׁל בְּרוּחוֹ); more oft. of ׳י, א׳ אַפַּיִם, Ex 34^{6} רַחוּם וְחַנּוּן א׳ אַפַּיִם וְרַב־חֶסֶד וֶאֱמֶת cf. Nu 14^{18} Ne 9^{17} ψ 86^{15} 103^{8} 145^{8}; so + וְנִחָם עַל־הָרָעָה Jo 2^{13} cf. Jon 4^{2} (where אֵל), א׳ אַפַּיִם וּגְדוֹל כֹּחַ Na 1^{3}; לְאֶרֶךְ אַפְּךָ only Je 15^{15}, א׳ appar. noun; rd. אֹרֶךְ? cf. Pr 25^{15}.

752 †[אָרֹךְ] **adj.** long—only fs. abs. אֲרֻכָּה;—**a.** of time, מִלְחָמָה א׳ *long war* 2 S 3^{1}; of the exile Je 29^{28}; **b.** fig. of God's wisdom א׳ מֵאֶרֶץ מִדָּהּ Jb 11^{9} (|| רְחָבָה מִנִּי־יָם).

724 †אֲרוּכָה **n.f. healing** of a wound, **restoration** (properly the new flesh that grows at the wounded spot, Ar. أَرِيكَةٌ; Fi $^{\text{JPh xiii. 114-6}}$, so Fl De on Is 58^{8}; v. also Di)—א׳ 2 Ch 24^{13} Ne 4^{1}; אֲרֻכָה Je 30^{17} 33^{6}; cstr. אֲרֻכַת Je 8^{22}; אֲרֻכָתְךָ Is 58^{8};—always fig. **a.** *healing, restoration* of Israel Is 58^{8}, here c. vb. צָמַח, elsewhere c. עָלָה; Je 8^{22} (|| רָפָא), c. עָלָה Hiph., subj. ׳י, 30^{17} 33^{6} (|| *id.*) **b.** *restoration* of walls of temple 2 Ch 24^{13}, of walls of Jerusalem (cf. Fi supr.) Ne 4^{1} (both c. עלה).

751 †אֶרֶךְ **n.pr.loc.** city in Babylonia (Bab. *Urûk* v. Dl infr.) on left bank of Euphrates, c. 40 miles NW. fr. Ur (אוּר) toward Babylon; mod. *Warka;* cf. Loftus $^{\text{CS 162 f.}}$ Dl $^{\text{Pa 221 f.}}$

757 †אַרְכִּי **adj.gent.** (deriv. unknown) applied to חוּשַׁי 2 S 15^{32} 16^{16} 17$^{5.14}$ 1 Ch 27^{33}; with art. =n. coll. גְּבוּל הָא׳ Jos 16^{2} (not far fr. Bethel).

758 **אֲרָם** 149 **n.pr.m. Aram** (As. *Aramu*, etc., v. Dl $^{\text{Pa 257}}$; Thes al. prop. √ארם = רום but cf. Nö as below)—**1.** 5th son of Shem Gn 10$^{22.23}$ 1 Ch 1^{17}. **2.** grandson of Nahor Gn 22^{21}. **3.** 1 Ch 2^{23}. **4.** a descendant of Asher 1 Ch 7^{34}.—Elsewhere only of Aramæan people & land (=**1** supr.), **f.**$^{\text{2 S 8,5}}$ **m.**$^{\text{2 S 10,14}}$. **a.** people, sg. coll.=*the Aramæans*, a leading branch of the Shemitic stock inhabiting Mesopotamia & northern Syria, in many tribes & settlements; 2 S 8$^{5.5.6}$ + 1 K 20$^{20.21}$ + 1 Ch 19$^{10.12}$ + (64 t. S K Ch) Am 9^{7} Is 7$^{2.4.5.8}$ 9^{11} 17^{3} Je 35^{11}; so Ez 16^{57} 27^{16}, but Co in both אדום; עַם אֲרָם Am 1^{5}; of particular divisions of Aram,
760 א׳ בֵּית רְחוֹב 2 S 10^{6}, א׳ צוֹבָא 2 S 10$^{6.8}$ ψ 60^{2} (title),
763 א׳ דַּמֶּשֶׂק 2 S 8^{5} cf. 1 Ch 18^{5}, even א׳ נַהֲרַיִם ψ 60^{2}
(title); (note that As. never gives name *Aramu* to people W. of Euphrates, but *Chatti* instead, with other particular names, COT Gn 10^{22}, also Dl $^{\text{l.c.}}$); on 2 S 8$^{12.13}$ 1 Ch 18^{11} v. אֱדוֹם. **b.** less often clearly of land, Aram Nu 23^{7} 2 S 15^{8} + 2 Ch 20^{2} (rd. however here אדום Thes Add al.), שְׂדֵה א׳ Ho 12^{13}; also of particular divisions of
the territory א׳ נַהֲרַיִם '*Mesopotamia*,' i.e. prob. 763
land between Euphrates & Chaboras, so Di after Kiep, Gn 24^{10} Dt 23^{5} Ju 3^{8} (cf. ψ 60^{2} supr.); cf. פַּדַּן א׳ *Paddan-Aram* Gn 25^{20} 31^{18} 33^{18} 35$^{9.26}$ 46^{15}, פַּדֶּנָה א׳ 28$^{2.5.6.7}$ v. פדן; א׳ דַּמֶּשֶׂק 2 S 8^{6} cf. 1 Ch 18^{6}. **c.** often indeterminate, esp. in מֶלֶךְ א׳ etc., perh. primarily land but often including people: so Ju 2^{11} 10^{6} (אֱלֹהֵי א׳) 1 K 10^{29} + 2 Ch 1^{17} + (41 t. K & Ch) Is 7^{1}.—(Cf. esp. Nö $^{\text{Schenkel BL, ZMG 1871, 113; Hermes v. 3, 443 f.}}$ Dl $^{\text{Pa 257}}$.)

†אֲרַמִּי **adj.gent. Aramæan**, c. art. הָא׳ 761
Gn 25$^{20.20}$ 28^{5} 31$^{20.24}$ 2 K 5^{20}; of Israel א׳ אֹבֵד 7421
Dt 26^{5}; pl. אֲרַמִּים 2 K 8$^{28.29}$ (|| אֲרָם) 9^{15} (|| *id.*); הָרַמִּים (=הָא׳) 2 Ch 22^{5} (|| *id.*); פִּילַגְשׁוֹ הָאֲרַמִּיָּה 1 Ch 7^{14} *his Aramæan concubine*.—(ארומים Kt 2 K 16^{6} rd. rather Qr אֲדוֹמִים.)

†אֲרָמִית **adv.** only of language **in Aramaic** 762
2 K 18^{26} = Is 36^{11} Ezr 4$^{7.7}$ Dn 2^{4}.

ארם (√ of following; cf. רום?).

†אַרְמוֹן **n.m.** $^{\text{Is 32,14}}$ **citadel**—א׳ abs. Je 30^{18} 759
+; cstr. Is 25^{2}; pl. אַרְמְנוֹת abs. Am 3$^{9.9}$; cstr. 1^{4} +; אַרְמְנוֹתֵינוּ Mi 5^{4} +, etc.—*citadel, castle, palace*, not used before royal period, mostly in prophets, esp. common in Am & Je; citadel as securely barred (in sim.) Pr 18^{19}; א׳ בֵּית הַמֶּלֶךְ i.e. the *citadel, stronghold* 1 K 16^{18}, cf. 2 K 15^{25}; usually more general, of *castles, palaces*, prominent buildings; esp. used in speaking of conquest, because the fine buildings would be esp. object of attack & plunder; palaces of Isr. Am 6^{8}; of Jerusalem Is 32^{14} (sg. coll.) La 2$^{5.7}$ 2 Ch 36^{19} ψ 48$^{4.14}$ 122^{7} cf. Ho 8^{14} Mi 5^{4} Am 2^{5} Je 17^{27}; of Samaria Am 3$^{10.11}$; also Je 6^{5} 9^{20} belonging to Benhadad (i.e. Aram) Am 1^{4} Je 49^{27}; of Tyre Is 23^{13} Am 1^{10}; of Babylon Is 25^{2} (sg. coll.), cf. 13^{22} where rd. אַרְמְנוֹתָיו for אלמנותיו so 𝔊 𝔗 𝔙 Che Di (|| היכלים; cf. Ez 19^{7} acc. to 𝔗 al., but v. rather מעון; Dl $^{\text{BD xi}}$ defends MT in Ez 19^{7} & comp. As. *almattu, fortress*); of Edom Is 34^{13}, of Gaza Am 1^{7}, of Rabbah 1^{14}, of Bozrah 1^{12}, of Kerioth 2^{2}, of Ashdod 3^{9}, of Egypt 3^{9}.

†אַרְמֹנִי **n.pr.m.** a son of Saul (*palatinus*) 764
2 S 21^{8}.

I. **ארן** (cf. Ar. أَرِنَ *alacer, lætus fuit;* possible √ of following).

765 †אֲרָן **n.pr.m.** a descendant of Esau (? Aram. ܝܥܠܐ *wild-goat*) Gn 36^{28} = 1 Ch 1^{42} (v. also דִּישָׁן).

766 †I. אֹ֫רֶן **n.[m.]** **fir** or **cedar** (As. *êrinu* COT^{Gloss}, Mish. pl. ארנים) Is 44^{14} (|| אֶרֶז, תִּרְזָה, עֲצֵי יַעַר, אַלּוֹן).

767 †II. אֹ֫רֶן **n.pr.m.** (*fir-tree*) a descendant of Judah 1 Ch 2^{25}.

†ארנבן **n.pr.loc.** whence wine, so Co Ez
835+3120 27^{19} for MT וְדָן וְיָוָן; cf. As. *wine of Aranabanim*.

770 †אַרְנָן **n.pr.m.** a descendant of David 1 Ch 3^{21}.

771 †אָרְנָן **n.pr.m.** a Jebusite, whose threshing-floor was bought by David to erect an altar 1 Ch $21^{15.18.20.20.21.21.22.23.24.25.28}$, & acc. to 2 Ch 3^{1} became site of temple; called אֲרַוְנָה 2 S $24^{16f.}$ q.v.

769 †אַרְנֹן, אַרְנוֹן† **n.pr.fl.** **Arnon**, wady & stream in Moab (MI ארנן, Thes Add Rob Ges MV der. fr. רנן, i.e. *the rushing, roaring* stream)—אַרְנוֹן Nu $21^{13.13}$ + 12 t., אַרְנֹן Nu 21^{14} + 10 t.—called boundary between Moab & Amorites Nu 21^{13} Ju $11^{18.22}$ cf. גְּבוּל אַרְנֹן Nu 22^{36}; oft. נַחַל אַרְנֹן Dt $2^{24.36}$ $3^{8.12.16}$ 4^{48} 2 K 10^{33}; נ׳ אַרְנוֹן Jos $12^{1.2}$ $13^{9.16}$; הַנְּחָלִים אַרְנוֹן Nu 21^{14}, i.e. the stream-ravines that unite to form Arnon, cf. Di; also בָּמוֹת אַרְנֹן *heights of Arnon* Nu 21^{28}; מעברות אַרְנוֹן *fords of Arnon* Is 16^{2}; elsewh. Nu $21^{13.24.26}$ Ju $11^{13.18.26}$; syn. of Moab Je 48^{20}; (cf. Tristr$^{Moab\ 125\ f.}$; mod. *Môjib*.)

II. ארן (√assumed for foll. word, cf. Sta $^{§\,208\,c}$; Dl$^{Pr\ 125}$ argues for √ארה (so Thes), on ground of an As. *êrû*, synon. of *êrênu*).

727 אָרוֹן, c. art. הָאָרוֹן, הָאָרֹן $_{203}$ **n.m.**$^{Ex\ 35,12}$ (**f.** $^{1\,S\,4,17;\,2\,Ch\,8,11}$) **chest, ark** (Ph. ארן, *sarcophagus*, As. *êrênu* (& *êrû*) *chest* Zim$^{BP\ 6,22}$, Ar. إِرَانٌ, *chest*, so Aram. ܐܪܘܢܐ, also Nab. ארנא, Vog$^{p.\ 102}$, Ph.; Mish. also pl. ארונות)—only sg.; abs. †אָרוֹן 2 K 12^{10} = 2 Ch 24^{8}; c. art. הָאָרוֹן Dt 10^{2} + alw. exc. Ex Lv Nu where הָאָרֹן (Ex $25^{14.14}$ + 13 t. Ex, Lv 16^{2} Nu 3^{31} 10^{35}); cstr. אֲרוֹן Ex 25^{10} +, †אֲרֹן Ex 30^{6} Nu 4^{5} 7^{89};—†**1.** *chest*, for money-offerings 2 K $12^{10.11}$ 2 Ch $24^{8.10.11.11}$. †**2.** *sarcophagus, mummy-case* of Joseph Gn 50^{26} (E). **3.** *chest, ark* in tabernacle & temple, containing tables of law, with cherubim above, the esp. seat of י׳ among his people, only Hex (71 t.) S (61 t.) K (12 t.) & Ch (48 t.) + Ju 20^{27} Je 3^{16} ψ 132^{8}; used alone & in various combinations (cf. Seyring$^{ZAW\ 1891,\ 114\ f.}$). **a.** indef. אֲרוֹן עֲצֵי שִׁטִּים *an ark of shittim-wood* Ex 25^{10} Dt 10^{3} cf. v^{1}. **b.** def. הָא׳ Ex 25^{14} + 54 t. (Hex P, exc. Jos JE; S K Ch). **c.** א׳ יהוה Jos 4^{11} + 32 t. Jos (JED) S K Ch. **d.** א׳ הָאֱלֹהִים † 1 S 3^{3} 4^{11}; א׳ הָאֱלֹהִים 1 S 4^{13} + 32 t. S Ch (but 1 S $14^{18.18}$ rd. הָאֵפוֹד 𝔊 We Dr), cf. א׳ אֱלֹהֵינוּ † 1 Ch 13^{3}. **e.** א׳ אלהי יִשְׂרָאֵל 1 S 5^{7} + 6 t. S, term used only by Philistines; א׳ יהוה אלהי יִשְׂרָאֵל † 1 Ch $15^{12.14}$; א׳ יהוה אֱלֹהֵיכֶם † Jos 4^{5} (JE); א׳ יהוה אֲדוֹן כָּל־הָאָרֶץ † 1 K 2^{26}; א׳ אֲדֹנָי יהוה † Jos 3^{13} (JED) cf. א׳ [הברית] אדון כל־הארץ v^{11}, where הברית (c. art.) is prob. interpol., v. Di; only once & late the long phrase א׳ האלהים יהוה יוֹשֵׁב הַכְּרֻבִים אֲשֶׁר נִקְרָא־שֵׁם 1 Ch 13^{6}. **f.** in combination with בְּרִית, largely D & under D's influence; ארון הַבְּרִית *ark of the covenant* † Jos $3^{6.6.8}$ 4^{9} 6^{6} (all JED); א׳ בְּרִית יהוה Nu 10^{33} 14^{44} (both J) Dt 10^{8} $31^{9.25}$ Jos $4^{7.18}$ 6^{8} 8^{33} Je 3^{16} + 17 t. S K Ch; once longer א׳ בְּרִית י׳ צְבָאוֹת יֹשֵׁב הַכְּרֻבִים † 1 S 4^{4}; also א׳ בְּרִית הָאֱלֹהִים † Ju 20^{27} 1 S 4^{4} 2 S 15^{24} 1 Ch 16^{6}; & א׳ בְּרִית י׳ אלהיכם Dt 31^{26} Jos 3^{3}. **g.** אֲרוֹן הָעֵדוּת *ark of the testimony*, only in P, corresponding to א׳ בְּרִית (cf. Di on Ex 25^{16}), Ex 25^{22} + 8 t. Ex, † Nu 4^{5} 7^{84} Jos 4^{16}. **h.** † א׳ הַקֹּדֶשׁ 2 Ch 35^{3}. **i.** א׳ עֻזֶּךָ *the ark of thy strength* 2 Ch 6^{41} ψ 132^{8}.—(Cf. also tables given by Seyring$^{l.c.}$ & his theory as to earliest designation of ark.)

אַרְנֶ֫בֶת v. אנב. p. 58 768

ארניה v. אֲרַוְנָה. p. 72 728

†אַרְפַּד **n.pr.loc.** city in northern Syria 774
(As. *Arpadda* Dl$^{Pa\ 275}$)—א׳ Is 10^{9} elsewh. אַרְפָּד; c. 15 miles N. of Aleppo, mod. *Tel Erfâd*; in OT only as conquered by Assyria, alw. named with Hamath, etc. 2 K 18^{34} 19^{13} = Is 36^{19} 37^{13} (on 𝔊 Ῥαφέθ = Ἀρφάθ cf. Lag$^{BN\ 78}$), also Is 10^{9} Je 49^{23}; (cf. Nö$^{ZMG\ 1871,\ 258}$ Kiep$^{ib.\ 655}$.)

†אַרְפַּכְשַׁד **n.pr.m.** 3rd son of Shem א׳ Gn 775
$10^{22.24}$ $11^{12.13}$ 1 Ch $1^{17.18.24}$; אַרְפַּכְשָׁד Gn $11^{10.11}$; doubtless a geogr. name (deriv. & mng. dub., Thes der. fr. أُرْفَةٌ *boundary* (stem أَرَفَ *define, limit*), cf. also Eth. አርፍት: *wall*, + כשד = כֶּשֶׂד, i.e. *Chaldean*; so Schr$^{COT\ Gn\ 10,22}$ who identifies with *Babylonia* (cf. Gn $11^{12f.}$ & אוּר כַּשְׂדִּים v$^{28.31}$); v. another interpr. Dl$^{Pa\ 255}$; acc. to most = *Arrapachitis* on Upper Zab, NE. fr. Nineveh, As. *Arbaḫa*, Armen. *Albak* Lag$^{Armen.\ Stud.\ 55\ \&\ reff.}$ so Bo MV, Di Gn 10^{22} Lag$^{Sy\ 1.54}$ Nö$^{ZMG\ 1882,\ 182}$; but As. *Arbaḫa* is unfavourable to this).

אֶ֫רֶץ $_{2407}$ **n.f.**$^{Gn\ 10,11}$ & (seld.) **m.**$^{Gn\ 13,16}$ **earth,** 776
land (Ph. MI ארץ, As. *irṣitu* COT^{Gloss}, Ar. أَرْضٌ, Sab. ארץ e.g. Os^{9} DHM$^{ZMG\ 1875,\ 594,\ 614;\ Sem.\ Sprachf.\ 12}$, cf. Prä$^{BAS\ i.\ 374\ n.}$, Aram. אֲרַע, ܐܪܥܐ)—א׳ abs.

Gn 1^{24}+; cstr. 2^{11}+; אָ֑רֶץ 1^{10}+; c. art. always הָאָ֫רֶץ 1^{11}+; c. ה ָ loc. אַ֫רְצָה 11^{31}+, (this form also poet. = אֶרֶץ Jb 34^{13}+); sf. אַרְצִי 20^{15}+; אַרְצְךָ (אַרְצֶ֑ךָ) 12^{1}+, etc.; pl. אֲרָצוֹת Je 28^{8}+65 t.; cstr. אַרְצוֹת Ez 39^{27}+6 t.; sf. אַרְצֹתָם Gn 10^{5}+2 t.;—**1. a.** *earth*, whole earth (opp. to a part) Gn 18$^{18.25}$ 22^{18}(= הָאֲדָמָה 12^{3}) Je 25$^{26.29.30}$ 26^{6} Is 37$^{16.20}$ = 2 K 19$^{15.19}$ Zc 4$^{10.14}$+. **b.** *earth*, opp. to heaven, sky Gn 1^{2} Ex 20^{4} Dt 5^{8} 30^{19} Ju 5^{4} La 2^{1} Is 37^{16} = 2 K 19^{15} ψ 146^{6} 1 Ch 21^{16} 29^{11} 2 Ch 2^{11}+; as permanent Ec 1^{4}; built on foundations, or pillars 1 S 2^{8} ψ 104^{5} Jb 38^{4} Is 48^{13} 51$^{13.16}$ cf. also Is 24^{18} ψ 82^{5}; firm, so that its shaking is something terrible, & token of terrible power 1 S 14^{4} 2 S 22^{8} = ψ 18^{8} Jb 9^{6} cf. ψ 46^{2} & v^{6}; so also Am 8^{8} Is 2$^{19.21}$ 24$^{18.19.20}$ ψ 60^{4} 77^{19} 99^{1} 114^{7}; as hung on nothing Jb 26^{7}; with waters under it Ex 20^{4} = Dt 5^{8} cf. Gn 7^{11}; personified, esp. as addressed, called to witness, etc. Dt 32^{1} Je 6^{19} 22^{29} Is 1^{2} Mi 1^{2} Jb 16^{18}. **c.** *earth* = inhabitants of earth Gn 6^{11} 11^{1} 1 K 2^{2} 10^{24} ψ 33^{8} 66^{4}+cf. תֵּבֵל א׳ Pr 8^{31} Jb 37^{12}. **2.** *land* = **a.** country, territory, א׳ שִׁנְעָר Gn 10^{10}, א׳ מִצְרַיִם 21^{21}; cf. also 10^{11} 11$^{28.31}$ 13^{10} 47$^{6.27}$ 50^{8} Is 7^{18} 23$^{1.13}$ 27^{13} ψ 78^{12} Je 25^{20} 1 Ch 1^{43}; personif. Is 62^{4} Ec 10$^{16.17}$. **b.** district, region Gn 19^{28} 22^{2} Jos 11^{3} ψ 42^{7}. **c.** tribal territory Dt 34^{2} Ju 21^{21} 1 S 9$^{4.16}$ 13^{7} 1 K 15^{20} Is 8^{23}; and still smaller territories 1 S 9$^{4.5}$. **d.** piece of ground Gn 23^{15}. **e.** specif. *land* of Canaan, or Israel Gn 11^{31} 12$^{1.5.6.7}$ 31^{3} Ex 14^{34} Dt 17^{14} 18^{9} 2 K 5$^{2.4}$+; esp. obj. of יָרַשׁ *possess* Dt 3^{20}+oft. Dt ψ al.; so after נָחַל Jos 19^{49}+; נָתַן Dt 1^{21}+. **f.** = inhabitants of land Lv 19^{29} Ez 14^{13}+cf. Dt 24^{4} Zc 12^{12} etc. **g.** used even of *Sheʾôl* Jb 10$^{21.22}$ (cf. As. *irṣit la târat, land without return*, in Descent of Ishtar, v. Jr $^{10.65}$); v. also ψ 139^{15} Is 44^{23}. **3. a.** *ground*, surface of ground = אֲדָמָה q.v. Gn 1$^{26.30}$ 18^{2} 33^{3} 38^{9} Ex 4^{3} 16^{4} Ru 2^{10} 1 S 5^{4}+very oft. in S. **b.** *soil*, as productive = אֲדָמָה Gn 1$^{11.12}$ Lv 19^{9} 25^{9} 26^{4} cf. Nu 14$^{7.8}$ Is 36^{7} = 2 K 18^{32} ψ 72$^{6.16}$ 107$^{34.35}$ Ezr 9^{12} Ne 9^{35}. **4.** אֶרֶץ in phrases: **a.** *people of the land* עַם־הָא׳ of non-Israelites Gn 23$^{7.12.13}$ (P) Nu 14^{9} (JE); as well as Isr. Lv 20^{4} (H) 2 K 15^{5} 16^{15} 21$^{24.24}$; esp. common people, opp. officials, princes Lv 4^{27} (P) Ez 7^{27} 2 K 11$^{18.19}$. †**b.** in measurements of distance, כִּבְרַת הָא׳ *the space* or *distance of country* (v. כברה) Gn 35^{16}, so כִּבְרַת א׳ *some distance* Gn 48^{7} 2 K 5^{19}. **c.** אֶרֶץ הַמִּישׁוֹר *the country of the plain, level* or *plain country* Dt 4^{33} Je 48^{21}; א׳ מִישׁוֹר fig. ψ 143^{10} (but rd. אֹרַח 𝔖 Bi Gr Che, cf. ψ 27^{11}). **d.** א׳ חַיִּים *land of the living* ψ 27^{13}; א׳ הַחַיִּים ψ 142^{6}. **e.** קְצֵה הָא׳ *end(s) of the earth* Is 42^{10} 43^{6} (‖ רָחוֹק) ψ 135^{7} Pr 17^{24}, so אַפְסֵי א׳ Pr 30^{4}+; קְצוֹת הָא׳ Is 40^{28} 41$^{5.9}$. **5.** pl. אֲרָצוֹת is almost wholly late, Je 16^{15}+6 t. Je; 23 t. Ez; Is 36^{20} 37^{11} = 2 K 18^{35} 19^{11} (Is 37^{18} rd. הַגּוֹיִם v. Che Di & cf. 2 K 19^{17}); 22 t. Chr; Dn 9^{7} 11$^{40.42}$; ψ 105^{44} 106^{27} 107^{3} 116^{9}; besides these only P Gn 10$^{5.20.31}$ Lv 26$^{36.39}$, exc. Gn 26$^{3.4}$ (J^{R}) 41^{54} (JE); it denotes *lands, countries*, often in contrast to Canaan, *lands of the nations*, etc., v. esp. abs. Ez 20^{32} 22^{4}; = the various petty divisions of Canaan afterward united under Israel's control Gn 26$^{3.4}$, cf. 1 Ch 13^{2} אַרְצוֹת יִשְׂרָאֵל, 2 Ch 11^{23} אַרְצוֹת יְהוּדָה.

†אַרְצָא **n.pr.m.** chamberlain of Zimri 777
1 K 16^{9}.

[אָרַר] **vb. curse** (As. *arâru* Zim$^{BP 68}$; on 779
relation of mngs. *bind & curse* in As. v. Dl$^{Pr 101}$) —**Qal** *Pf.* אָרוֹתִיהָ, וְאָרוֹתִ֫י Mal 2^{2}; *Impf.* 2 ms. תָּאֹר Ex 22^{27} Nu 22$^{6.12}$; אָאֹר Gn 12^{3}; *Imv.* אָ֫רָה־ Nu 22^{6} 23^{7}; אֹרוּ, אֹרוּ & *Inf. abs.* אָרוֹר all Ju 5^{23}; *Pt.* אֹרְרֵי Jb 3^{8}; אֹרְרֶיךָ Gn 27^{29} Nu 24^{9}; אָרוּר Gn 3^{14}+36 t. etc.;—*curse* ‖ בֵּרֵךְ *bless*, chiefly in poetic & legal sources of JED & later imitations: Gn 12^{3} 27^{29} (J) Nu 22$^{6.12}$ 23^{7} 24^{9} (E) Ex 22^{27} (E) Mal 2^{2}; אֹרוּ אָרוֹר יֹשְׁבֶיהָ = *curse for ever her inhabitants* Ju 5^{23}; אֹרְרֵי יוֹם *cursers of the day* (magicians whose imprecations made days unlucky) Jb 3^{8}. *Pt. pass.* אָרוּר, chiefly as exclamation, ‖ בָּרוּךְ Gn 3$^{14.17}$ 4^{11} 9^{25} 27^{29} 49^{7} Nu 22^{12} 24^{9} (E, poet.) Dt 27$^{15-26}$ Ju 21^{18} 1 S 14$^{24.28}$ 26^{19} Je 11^{3} 17^{5} 20$^{14.15}$ 48$^{10.10}$ Mal 1^{14}; אֲרוּרִים הַשֹּׁגִים מִמִּצְוֹתֶיךָ *cursed be those who wander from thy commands* ψ 119^{21} (𝔊 𝔖 Jer De Ri), הָאֲרוּרָה הַזֹּאת *this cursed woman* 2 K 9^{34}. †**Niph.** *Pt.* נֵאָרִים *cursed* Mal 3^{9}. †**Pi.** 3 ms. sf. אֵרְרָהּ *curse, lay under a curse* Gn 5^{29} (J); *Pt.* הַמַּיִם הַמְאָרֲרִים *the curse-bringing waters* Nu 5$^{18-27}$ (P 6 t. waters destroying the perjured adulteress drinking them). †**Hoph.** *Impf.* יוּאַר *be cursed* Nu 22^{6} (E).

†מְאֵרָה **n.f.** a curse Dt 28^{20} Mal 2^{2} 3^{9}; cstr. 3994
מְאֵרַת Pr 3^{33}; pl. מְאֵרוֹת Pr 28^{27}.

אֲרָרִי v. הֲרָרִי. p. 251 2043

†אֲרָרָט **n.pr.terr. Ararat** (As. *Urarṭu* 780
COT^{Gloss}, cf. Lag$^{Armen. Stud. § 100}$)—א׳ Je 51^{27}; אֲרָרָט Gn 8^{4}+3 t.—a district in Eastern Armenia between the river Araxes & lakes Van & Oroomiah, cf. KGF; to this prob. ref. in 2 K 19^{37} = Is 37^{38} אֶרֶץ א׳; also Gn 8^{4} הָרֵי א׳, where the ark rested; used perhaps with wider ref. Je 51^{27} מַמְלְכוֹת א׳ (‖ אַשְׁכְּנַז, מִנִּי).

†[אָרַשׂ] **vb.** betroth (Mish. ארס, Ph. ארש 781

in n.pr., Lag[Sem i. 50] connects with Ar. أَرَّشَ *a fine*, lit. *pay the price*, & so gain the right of possession; cf. Aram. אָרִיס *one who farms land*; As. *mirsu*, *tribute*, Zehnpf[BAS i. 518])—only **Pi. Pu.**; **Pi.** *Pf.* 3 ms. אֵרַשׂ Dt 20[7]; אֵרַשְׂתִּי 2 S 3[14]; sf. אֵרַשְׂתִּיךְ Ho 2[21.21.22]; *Impf.* 2 ms. תְּאָרֵשׂ Dt 28[30];—*betroth* (subj. man) obj. woman, אִשָּׁה Dt 20[7] 28[30]; sq. בּ of price paid to father & לְ of husband 2 S 3[14]; בּ of gift to bride & לְ of husband Ho 2[21.22], where fig. of Yahweh's covenant mercy to Israel. **Pu.** *Pf.* 3 fs. אֹרָשָׂה *be betrothed*, c. לֹא, subj. בְּתוּלָה Ex 22[15] Dt 22[28] (נער בתולה); *Pt.* f. מְאֹרָשָׂה Dt 22[23], where affirmed of נער בתולה (sq. לְ of husband) v[25.27] (in both subj. הַנַּעֲרָ).

ארשׂ (*to desire, request*, As. *êrêšu* Dl[Pr 55]).

782 †אֲרֶשֶׁת **n.f. desire, request** (As. *êrištu* Dl[l. c.]) only cstr. א׳ שְׂפָתָיו ψ 21[3] (||תַּאֲוַת לִבּוֹ) request granted by י׳.

219 **ארת** v. אוֹרָה. p. 21

783 †אַרְתַּחְשַׁשְׁתְּא **n.pr.m. Artaxerxes** (Pers. *Artakhshatrâ*, Spieg[APK 68, 207] 𝔊 Ἀρταξέρξης, cf. BeRy on Ezr 4[23] 7[1 f.] Ne 1[1]) א׳ Ezr 4[7] v. BD[102]; אַרְתַּחְשַׁשְׂתְּא Ezr 4[7], אַרְתַּחְשַׁסְתְּא Ezr 7[1.11] 8[1] Ne 2[1] 5[14] 13[6]; *Artaxerxes I*, or *Longimanus*, son & successor of Xerxes, reigned B.C. 465–424.

840 †אֲשַׂרְאֵל **n.pr.m.** a descendant of Judah 1 Ch 4[16] (the latter element in this & foll. may be אֵל *God*, but mng. of former part dub. Thes comp. אסר bind, *quem Deus obligavit sc. voto*).

841 †אֲשַׂרְאֵלָה **n.pr.m.** a son of Asaph 1 Ch 25[2] cf. יְשַׂרְאֵלָה v[14].

844 †אַשְׂרִיאֵל **n.pr.m.** a Manassite (Thes *votum Dei*, cf. supr.) Nu 26[31] Jos 17[2] 1 Ch 7[14].

845 †אַשְׂרִאֵלִי **adj.gent.** הָא׳ as n.coll. Nu 26[31].

784 **אֵשׁ** 377 **n.f.**[Ex 9, 23] (**m.**[Je 48, 45; ψ 104, 4]; **f. & m.**[Je 20, 9; Jb 20, 26]) **fire** (As. *išatu* COT[Gloss], Syr. ܐܶܫܳܬܳܐ, Eth. እሳት: deriv. fr. II. אנשׁ, أَنِسَ, sociable, friendly element (MV Wetzst in De[Psalmen, ed. 4, p. 888] Lag[BN 68] cf. مانوسة, انيسة), improb. esp. in view of As.; daghesh prob. secondary; cf. also Sta[§ 189 b])—א׳ abs. Ex 9[24]+; cstr. Lv 6[2]+ (seld.); †sf. אִשּׁוֹ Dt 4[36] Jb 18[5]; אֶשְׁכֶם Is 50[11]; אִשָּׁם Is 66[24];—**1.** *fire*, of conflagration, e.g. in briers, endangering or destroying crops תֵּצֵא אֵשׁ וּמָֽצְאָה קֹצִים Ex 22[5] cf. 3[2] הַסְּנֶה בֹּעֵר בָּאֵשׁ (both E); more often of deliberate destruction by fire, esp. שָׂרַף בָּאֵשׁ (בָּ c. qam. preton.) obj. golden calf Ex 32[20] (J), other idols Dt 7[5.25], Asherim 12[3], chariots Jos 11[6.9] 2 K 23[1], house Ju 12[1] 14[15], tower 9[52], city-gates Ne 1[3] 2[3.13.17], city Jos 6[24] Ju 18[27] cf. Is 1[7]+; also שִׁלַּח אֶת־הָעִיר בָּאֵשׁ Am 1[4.7.10]+; שִׁלַּח אֵשׁ בְּ †Ju 1[8] 20[48] cf. 2 K 8[12]; הִצִּית אֶת־הָעִיר בָּאֵשׁ Jos 8[8.19] Je 17[27]+, cf. Ju 9[49] 2 S 14[30.31] (of field, cf. Ex 22[5] supr.) **2.** of supernatural fire, attending theophany Ex 3[2] 19[18] (both JE) Dt 4[11.12.15.33.36]+; specif. עַמּוּד (הָ)אֵשׁ Ex 13[21.22] 14[24] (all JE) Ne 9[12.19] cf. Dt 1[33] (v. מַרְאֵה־אֵשׁ Nu 9[15.16] P); of destructive fire from י׳ Nu 11[1.2.3] (J) 26[10] (P) Lv 10[2] (P); cf. א׳ אֹכֶלֶת in sim. of Yahweh's glory Ex 24[17] (E) Dt 4[24] 9[3]; v. also 1 K 18[24.38] 2 K 1[10.10.12.12.14] Jb 1[16] (perh. lightning intended), cf. further of lightning Ex 9[23.24] (JE) ψ 18[13.14] 148[8] etc. **3.** fire for cooking, roasting, parching, etc. צְלִי אֵשׁ *roasted at a fire* Ex 12[8.9] (P) cf. Lv 2[14] 2 Ch 35[13] Is 44[16.19]; of tinder for lighting fire Gn 22[6.7] (E); of fire for melting (gold for the idolatrous calf) Ex 32[24]; for refining Je 6[29], where rd. with Qr מֵאֵשׁ תַּם עֹפֶרֶת; cf. Mal 3[2] (sim. of purifying work of messenger of cov't). **4.** esp. of altar-fire Lv 1[7.7] 6[2.3.5.6]+; in offering incense Lv 10[1], also אֵשׁ זָרָה *strange fire*, i.e. an incense not commanded, offered presumptuously 10[1] Nu 3[4] 26[61]; fire from י׳ consuming sacrifice (cf. **2**) Lv 9[24] 2 Ch 7[1.3]; of fire in child-sacrifice (usually הֶעֱבִיר בֵּן בָּאֵשׁ (לְ)) 2 K 16[3] 21[6] cf. 17[17] 23[10] 2 Ch 33[6]; also שָׂרַף בָּא׳ 2 K 17[31], בִּעֵר בָּא׳ 2 Ch 28[3]. **5.** fig. of Yahweh's anger ψ 89[47] (sim.) cf. Na 1[6] La 2[4] אֵשׁ־עֶבְרָתִי Ez 21[36] 22[31] 38[19], אֵשׁ־קִנְאָתִי Ez 36[5]; v. also Is 66[15] ψ 79[5] 89[47] etc.; of word of י׳ Je 23[29]; fig. of outbursting emotion ψ 39[4]; of flagrant wickedness Is 9[17], etc. **6.** in various combinations, לַפִּיד אֵשׁ Gn 15[17] (J) *a torch of fire* (cf. Di); לַבַּת־אֵשׁ Ex 3[2] *flame of fire*, לַהַב אֵשׁ Jo 2[5], לַפִּידֵי אֵשׁ (in sim.) Dn 10[6] cf. Zc 12[6], לַהֲבוֹת אֵשׁ ψ 29[7] לַהֲבֵי אֵשׁ Is 66[15] cf. א׳ לֶהָבוֹת ψ 105[32], נֹגַהּ א׳ לֶהָבָה Is 4[5] cf. Ho 7[6]; שְׁבִיב אִשּׁוֹ *spark of his fire* Jb 18[5] cf. כִּידוֹדֵי אֵשׁ 41[11]; תַּנּוּר אֵשׁ ψ 21[10] *oven of fire*, כִּיּוֹר אֵשׁ Zc 12[6]; אוֹר אֵשׁ *light of fire* ψ 78[14]; אֵשׁ לֹהֵט *flaming fire* ψ 104[4]; לְשׁוֹן אֵשׁ Is 5[24] *tongue of fire*, גַּחֲלֵי אֵשׁ Ez 1[13] *coals of fire*, so 10[2], cf. רִשְׁפֵּי אֵשׁ Ct 8[6]; on אַבְנֵי אֵשׁ Ez 28[14.16]
v. אֶבֶן; אֵשׁ דָּת Dt 33[2], lit. *fire of a law*, or *fire* 799
was a law, but דָּת *law* is Pers. & late; rd. perh. אֵשׁ [לַפִּ]דֹת cf. Ex 20[18] or אֵשׁ [יְקֹ]דֶת cf. Is 65[5].

†[אֶשָּׁה] **n.f. id.** Je 6[29] Kt מאשתם(מ) i.e. *from* 800
their fire, but Qr מֵאֵשׁ תַּם, v. sub אֵשׁ.

אִשֶּׁה **n.m.**[Jos 13, 14] **an offering made by fire** 801
(>Wetzst in De[Psalmen, ed. 4, 889] der. fr. √II. אנשׁ,

means to friendly relations betw. God & man; cf. Lag$^{BN 190}$) Ex 29^{18}+32 t.; cstr. אִשֵּׁה Lv 1^{9}+14 t.; pl. cstr. אִשֵּׁי Lv 4^{35}+15 t.; sf. אִשַּׁי Nu 28^{2}, אִשָּׁיו Lv 6^{10}; used chiefly of offerings of animals, but also of the מִנְחָה Lv 2^{11}, and of the sacred bread and frankincense Lv $24^{7.9}$ which was placed on the table as a memorial, and finally went to the priests. The word is used in Dt 18^{1} Jos 13^{14} (D) 1 S 2^{28}; elsewhere in P Lv 6^{10} 10^{15} 22^{22} Nu $28^{2.3}$, esp. in phrases אִשֵּׁי יהוה Lv 2^{3}+11 t., אִשֵּׁה רֵיחַ נִיחֹחַ ליהוה Lv 1^{9}+14 t., אשה ריח ניחח ליהוה Ex 29^{18}+6 t., אשה לריח ניחח Lv 23^{13}, אשה ריח ניחח ליהוה Lv 3^{16} Nu 18^{17}, אשה (הוא) ליהוה Ex 29^{25} Lv 2^{16}; אִשֶּׁה ליהוה acc. after verbs of offering Ex 30^{20}+14 t., אִשֶּׁה עֹלָה ליהוה Nu 28^{19}, קָרְבַּן אִשֶּׁה ליהוה Lv 22^{27} Nu 15^{25}.

786 †אִשׁ 2 S 14^{19} Mi 6^{10}, softer form for the usual יֵשׁ (q.v.), *there is, are.* (Cf. Aram. אִתַי, Ar. أَيْسَ; and on the softening of *ye, yi* to *'î*, see Ew$^{§ 53c}$ Ol$^{p. 425}$ Nö$^{§ 40c}$.)

788 †אַשְׁבֵּל **n.pr.m.** (=אַשְׁבְּאֵל? so Thes; more likely אֶשְׁבַּעַל) 2nd son of Benjamin Gn 46^{21} (𝔊 Ἀσβηλ) Nu 26^{38} (𝔊 Ἀσυβηρ) 1 Ch 8^{1} (𝔊 B Σαβα, A & 𝔊L Ἀσβηλ).

789 †אַשְׁבֵּלִי **adj.gent.** הָא' as n.coll. Nu 26^{38}.

790 †אֶשְׁבָּן **n.pr.m.** a chief of Edom Gn 36^{26} 1 Ch 1^{41} (etym. dub., 𝔊 Ἀσβαν, Ἐσεβαν, Ἀσεβων).

791 אַשְׁבֵּעַ v. שבע. p. 959f

792 אֶשְׁבַּעַל v. אִישׁ־בֹּשֶׁת. p. 36

אשׁד (√of following, cf. prob. As. *išdu, foundation*).

793 †אֶ֫שֶׁד **n.[m.] foundation, bottom, lower part** (slope) (As. *išdu* cf. Lotz$^{TP 186}$; >others fr. אָשַׁד, سفح *pour*, Sab. אסד=מסקי (משקה) DHM$^{ZMG 1883, 8}$, whence *fall, slope;* cf. Di Nu 21^{15}) אֶשֶׁד הַנְּחָלִים *the bottom of the ravines* Nu 21^{15}.

794 †[אֲשֵׁדָה] **n.f. foundation, (mountain-) slope** (cf. supr.)—only pl. abs. אֲשֵׁדוֹת Jos 10^{40} 12^{8}; cstr. אַשְׁדּוֹת Jos 12^{3} 13^{20}; אַשְׁדֹּת Dt 3^{17} 4^{49}—*mountain-slopes* Jos 10^{40} ההר והנגב והשפלה והא'; 12^{8} (|| id.+מדבר); elsewhere defined תַּחַת א' הַפִּסְגָּה Dt 3^{17} 4^{49} Jos 12^{3} cf. 13^{20}.

795 †אַשְׁדּוֹד **n.pr.loc. Ashdod** (As. *Asdudu*, COT^{Gloss} Dl$^{Pa 289}$; Thes MV der. fr. √ שדד q.v.) a powerful city of the Philistines on Mediterr. Sea, W. from Jerusalem, modern *Esdûd*, Jos 11^{22} $15^{46.47}$ (where assigned to Judah) 1 S $5^{5.6}$ (but del. Dr cf. 𝔊) 6^{17} Am 1^{8} 3^{9} Zp 2^{4} Zc 9^{6} Is 20^{1} Je 25^{20} 2 Ch 26^{6}; c. ־ָה loc. 1 S 5^{1} Is 20^{1}; אַנְשֵׁי א' 1 S 5^{7}; appar.=territory of Ashdod 2 Ch 26^{6} וַיִּבְנֶה עָרִים בְּאַשְׁדּוֹד. (Cf. Survey$^{J. 442}$.)

†אַשְׁדּוֹדִי **adj.gent. Ashdodite,** הָא' n.sg. 796
coll. Jos 13^{3}; usually pl. (הָ)אַשְׁדּוֹדִים 1 S $5^{3.6}$ Ne 4^{1}, and as adj. f. נָשִׁים אשדודיות Ne 13^{23} Kt (Qr אַשְׁדֳּדִיּוֹת).

†אַשְׁדּוֹדִית **adv. in the language of Ash-** 797
dod, i.e. of Philistines Ne 13^{24} מְדַבֵּר א'.

אשׁה (*support*, √whence following).

†[אָשְׁיָה] **n.f.** (support) **buttress** (Ar. آسِيَةٌ 803
column, support, AW Nö$^{M 113}$, 𝔗 אוּשָּׁא, pl. אוּשַּׁיָּיתָא, אוּשָּׁוָותָא) only pl. sf. *buttresses* of city of Babylon
Je 50^{15} אשויתיה Kt, אָשְׁיוֹתֶיהָ Qr (|| חוֹמוֹתֶיהָ). 803

יֹאשִׁיָּהוּ, יֹאשִׁיָּה **n.pr.m.** (י' *supporteth*) 2977
1. יֹאשִׁיָּהוּ king of Judah, son of Amon 1 K 13^{2} 2 K $21^{24.26}$ + 11 t. K, +19 t. Ch, +17 t. Je + Zp 1^{1}; also יאוֹשִׁיָּהוּ Je 27^{1}. **2.** יֹאשִׁיָּה a returned exile Zc 6^{10}.

אִשָּׁה v. sub III. אנשׁ. p. 61 802

אֱשׁוּן Qr Pr 20^{20} v. אִישׁוֹן sub איש. p. 36 380

אַשּׁוּר **n.pr.gent. & terr. Asshur, Assyria** 804, 838
(As. *Aššur*, land & city Dl$^{Pa 252}$ COT on Gn 2^{14}; Pers. *Athura*, Syr. ܐܬܘܪ; on the connection with name of god *Ašur*, & with √ אשר=ישר *good, gracious*, cf. COT$^{l.c.}$; v. also Jen$^{ZA, 1886, 1f.}$ Schr$^{ib. 209f.}$ Nö$^{ib. 268f.}$) **1.** *Asshur* as person, 2nd son of Shem Gn 10^{22} (P, in table of nations) 1 Ch 1^{17}. **2.** *people of Asshur* (oft. as invading army & even world-power) Nu $24^{22.24}$ (poem of Balaam) Ho 12^{2} 14^{4} Is 10^{5} 14^{25} $19^{23.23.24.25}$ 23^{13} 30^{31} 31^{8} 52^{4} La 5^{6} Ez 23^{5} 27^{23} 32^{22} (here fem.) Zc 10^{11};
ψ 83^{9} perh. rd. גְּשׁוּר, cf. 2 S 2^{9} sub אֲשׁוּרִי; or (if 805
ψ 83 be late) regard אַשּׁוּר (like עֲמָלֵק *ib.*) as used because of ancient significance; sts. personified as one Is 10^{5} Ez 31^{3} (but del. Co q.v.), cf. also Mi $5^{4.5}$ Zp 2^{13}; מַחֲנֵה א' 2 K 19^{32}=Is 37^{36}; בְּנֵי א' Ez 16^{28} $23^{7.9.12.23}$. **3.** *land of Assyria* Gn 2^{14} 10^{11} Ho 5^{13} 7^{11} 8^{9} 9^{3} 10^{6} Is $11^{11.16}$ 19^{23} Je $2^{18.36}$ Mi 7^{12} Zc 10^{10}; אַשּׁ֫וּרָה Gn 25^{18} Is 19^{23} 2 K 15^{29} $17^{6.23}$ 18^{11}; אֶרֶץ אַשּׁוּר Is 7^{18} 27^{13} Ho 11^{11} Mi 5^{5}. **4.** esp. מֶלֶךְ אַשּׁוּר Is 8^{4} 10^{12} $20^{1.4.6}$ (prob. gloss Is $7^{17.20}$ 8^{7}) 2 K 15^{19}+41 t. 2 K; 14 t. Is 36–38; 1 Ch 5^{6} (אַשֵּׁר)+13 t. Ch; also Je $50^{17.18}$ Na 3^{18} Ezr 4^{2}; (only Ezr 6^{22} of Persian or any king not strictly Assyrian); note also הַמֶּלֶךְ א' Is $36^{8.16}$ (א' perh. gloss, cf. Di who holds same view as to 2 K $18^{23.31}$); מַלְכֵי א' 2 K $19^{11.17}$=Is $37^{11.18}$ 2 Ch 28^{16} 30^{6} Ne 9^{32}.

†אַשּׁוּרִם **n.pr.gent.pl.** an Arab tribe 805

traced back to Abraham & Keturah Gn 25^{3} cf. Di.

805 †אַשּׁוּרִי **adj.gent.** הָא׳ as n.coll. 2 S 2^{9}, but rd. perh. הַגְּשׁוּרִי q.v., cf. also We Dr; Köh Klo al. rd. הָאָשֵׁרִי & comp. Ju 1^{32}.

806 אַשְׁחוּר v. שחר. p. 1007

807 †אֲשִׁימָא **n.pr.[m.]** a god of Hamath 2 K 17^{30}, otherwise wholly unknown.

810 †[אֶשֶׁךְ] **n.[m.]** testicle (Syr. ܐܫܟܐ, Eth. እስኪት: etym. unknown) only מְרוֹחַ אָשֶׁךְ Lv 21^{20}.

811 †אֶשְׁכּוֹל (אֶשְׁכֹּל Ct 7^{8}) **n.m.** $^{\text{Nu 13, 23}}$ **cluster** (Eth. አስካል: Ar. إِثْكَال, Aram. אִיתְכְּלָא; etym. dub.; Thes MV sub √שׁכל, but no suitable meaning proven; Sta$^{\text{§ 258, 300}}$ der. fr. √אשך c. afformat. ל)—א׳ abs. Nu 13^{24}+; cstr. v^{23}+; pl. אַשְׁכֹּלוֹת Ct 7^{8}; cstr. אַשְׁכְּלֹת Dt 32^{32}, אֶשְׁכְּלוֹת Ct 7^{9}; sf. אַשְׁכְּלֹתֶיהָ Gn 40^{10};—**1.** *cluster* of grapes, א׳ עֲנָבִים Nu 13^{23} cf. v^{24}; vid. also Gn 40^{10} הִבְשִׁילוּ א׳ עֲנָבִים *its clusters ripened grapes;* hence fig. of deeds of enemies of Israel, *clusters of gall have they* Dt 32^{32} (‖ עִנְּבֵי רוֹשׁ); fig. of Isr. Is 65^{8} יִמָּצֵא הַתִּירוֹשׁ בָּא׳; Mi 7^{1} אֵין אֶשְׁכּוֹל לֶאֱכוֹל fig. of desolation of Israel under Yahweh's judgment; Ct 7^{9} in sim. שָׁדַיִךְ כְּאֶשְׁכְּלוֹת הַגֶּפֶן cf. v^{8} (where Thes MV think of clusters of dates, v. תָּמָר *palm-tree, ib.*) **2.** *cluster* of henna-flowers, א׳ הַכֹּפֶר (v. כפר), metaph. of the beloved one Ct 1^{14}. (Cf. Grünwald$^{\text{Israel. Letterbode, Amst., xi. 148 f.}}$)

812 †אֶשְׁכֹּל **n.pr.** **1. m.** an Amorite, brother of Mamre, dwelling in neighbourhood of Hebron Gn 14$^{13.24}$. **2.** in combination נַחַל אֶשְׁכֹּל Nu 13^{23} Dt 1^{24}; נ׳ אֶשְׁכּוֹל Nu 13^{24} 32^{9};—*valley of Eshcol,* = *valley of a cluster,* region of Hebron (cf. 13^{22}); in 13^{24} der. fr. א׳ *cluster,* q. v.; see however Di *ad loc.*

813 אַשְׁכְּנַז **n.pr.m.** **1.** a descendant of Japhet Gn 10^{3} = 1 Ch 1^{6}; = **2.** a northern people Je 51^{27} מַמְלְכוֹת אֲרָרַט מִנִּי וְאַשְׁכְּנָז (perh. a people of Bithynia, = *Ascan(ians)* + *az* ending of Armen. patronymics, v. esp. Len$^{\text{Or. ii. 338 f.}}$, also Lag$^{\text{Ges. Abhandl. 254 f.}}$ Di Gn 10^{3}; but v. Lag$^{\text{Armen. Stud. 143}}$).

814 אֶשְׁכָּר v. II. שכר. p. 1016

אשל (*be firm, firmly rooted,* cf. Ar. أَثَلَ *be firm*).

815 †אֵשֶׁל **n.m.** *tamarisk-tree* (Ar. أَثْلٌ, Sab. אתל Sab. Denkm.^{65} cf. DHM$^{\text{BS ii. 958}}$; on an Aram. אַתְלָא v. Löw$^{\text{No. 38}}$; cf. Tristr$^{\text{FFP 250}}$) planted by Abraham Gn 21^{33} (J); in 1 S 22^{6} Saul is dwelling בַּגִּבְעָה תַּחַת־הָאֶשֶׁל בָּרָמָה; 31^{13} Saul and his sons are buried תַּחַת־הָא׳; it was perh. a sacred tree, marking shrine.

†אָשֵׁם, אָשַׁם **vb. offend, be guilty** (Ar. 816
أَثِمَ, *id.*, أَثَّمَ, *reum judicavit*, إِثْمٌ, أَثَامٌ, *fault, guilt, mulct*, cf. Eth. ኣሰመ:)—אָשַׁם Lv 5^{19} Nu 5^{7}; אָשֵׁם Hb 1^{11} + 7 t.; אָשְׁמָה Nu 5^{6}; אָשָׁמְתְּ Pr 30^{10}; אָשַׁמְתְּ Ez 22^{4}; אָשֵׁמוּ Lv 4^{13}; *Impf.* יֶאְשַׁם Ho 4^{15} + 13 t.; *Inf. abs.* אָשֹׁם Lv 5^{19}; אָשׁוֹם Ez 25^{12};—**1.** *commit an offence, a trespass, do a wrong,* or *an injury,* with לְ: אָשֹׁם אָשַׁם לַיהוה *he hath done a great wrong to Yahweh* (in violating the commands) Lv 5^{19} (P); וְנָתַן לַאֲשֶׁר אָשַׁם לוֹ *and he shall give it* (restitution) *to him to whom he did wrong* Nu 5^{7} (P), cf. 2 Ch 19$^{10.10}$; וַיֶּאְשְׁמוּ אָשׁוֹם *and they committed lasting wrong* (irreparable wrong, the Edomites against Judah) Ez 25^{12}. **2.** *be* or *become guilty* Ju 21^{22} Je 50^{7} Ho 4^{15} Hb 1^{11}; in offences requiring sin-offering Lv 4$^{13.22.27}$ (P), of trespass-offering Lv 5$^{2.3.17.23}$ Nu 5^{6} (P); with לְ *guilty of* Lv 5$^{4.5}$ (P), with בְּ *in* or *through* Ez 22^{4} Ho 13^{1}. **3.** *be held guilty, bear punishment* ψ 34$^{22.23}$ Pr 30^{10} Is 24^{6} Je 2^{3} Ho 5^{15} 10^{2} 14^{1} Zc 11^{5} Ez 6^{6} (but cf. שָׁמֵם). **Niph.** נֶאְשָׁמוּ *suffer punishment* Jo 1^{18}. **Hiph.** *Impf.* sf. הַאֲשִׁימֵם *declare them guilty* ψ 5^{11}.

†אָשֵׁם **adj. guilty,** א׳ abs. 2 S 14^{13}; pl. אֲשֵׁמִים 818
אֶל־אָחִינוּ Gn 42^{21} (E); *guilty*, and so bound to offer a trespass-offering Ezr 10^{19}; but rd. prob. וַאֲשָׁמָם, so Kue$^{\text{Chronol. v.h. Perzische Tijdvak, 1890, 43}}$.

אָשָׁם **n.m. offence, guilt**—א׳ Gn 26^{10} + 817
37 t., sf. אֲשָׁמוֹ Nu 5^{7} + 7 t.;—**1.** *offence, trespass, fault* ψ 68^{22} (*guiltiness* RV). **2.** *guilt* Gn 26^{10} (J) Pr 14^{9} Je 51^{5}. **3.** *compensation,* לְהָשִׁיב הָאָשָׁם אֵלָיו *to whom to return the compensation* (or satisfaction for injury) Nu 5$^{7.8}$ (P; *restitution for guilt* RV). **4.** *trespass-offering* (AV, but *guilt-offering* RV) used only in Lv 5, 6^{10} 7, 14, 19$^{21.22}$ Nu 5, 6^{12} 18^{9} (P), & Ez 40^{39} 42^{13} 44^{29} 46^{20}, cf. Ezr 10^{19}. This offering seems to have been confined to offences against God or man that could be estimated and so covered by compensation. The ordinary trespass-offering was a ram, together with restitution and a penalty of a fifth of its value. The trespass-offerings of the leper and Nazirite were he-lambs Lv 14 Nu 6^{12}; if the person who suffered wrong or his kinsmen were not living the fine went to the priests. The victims were offered, the blood and fat pieces going to the altar, the skin and flesh to the priests. There seems to have been no applica-

tion of the blood to the horns of the altar (the chief ceremony of the sin-offering) because the guilt was not expiated at the altar but by compensation to the wronged person or his representative. A part of the blood of the leper's trespass-offering was applied to his person to consecrate him (as in the case of the ram of consecration to consecrate the priests Lv 8^{23}). The trespass-offering is unknown to JED and the older Hebrew literature. However, the Philistines send an אשם of golden mice and tumours 1 S $6^{3.4.8.17}$, and an אשם of money was given to the priests 2 K 12^{17}, but these are entirely different from the trespass-offering of P. The Messianic servant offers himself as an אשם in compensation for the sins of the people, interposing for them as their substitute Is 53^{10} (incorrectly, *sin-offering* AV RV). See further Oehler$^{OT\ Theol.\ §137}$ Di Lv 5^{14}.

819 †אַשְׁמָה **n.f. wrong-doing, guiltiness** (properly *Inf.* cf. יִרְאָה, אַהֲבָה)—א׳ Lv 22^{16}+ 5 t., cstr. אַשְׁמַת Ezr 10^{10}+3 t.; sf. אַשְׁמָתוֹ Lv 5^{24}+6 t.; pl. אַשְׁמוֹת 2 Ch 28^{10}; sf. אַשְׁמוֹתַי ψ 69^{6};—**1.** *doing wrong, committing a trespass or offence* 2 Ch 24^{18} $28^{10.13.13.13}$ (‖ חטאת v^{13}) 32^{23} Ezr $9^{6.7.13.15}$ (‖ עָוֺן v^{13}) ψ 69^{6} (‖אִוֶּלֶת); מִכֹּל אֲשֶׁר יַעֲשֶׂה לְאַשְׁמָה בָהּ *of all that one may do wrong therein* Lv 5^{26} (P; ‖ לַחֲטֹא בָהֵנָּה v^{22}). **2.** *becoming guilty* 1 Ch 21^{3} Ezr $10^{10.19}$; יֶחֱטָא לְאַשְׁמַת הָעָם *sin to the becoming guilty of the people* (so that the people incur guilt) Lv 4^{3}; אַשְׁמַת שֹׁמְרוֹן *guilt of Samaria* (their idols) Am 8^{14}. **3.** *bringing a trespass-offering*, בְּיוֹם אַשְׁמָתוֹ *in the day of his bringing his trespass-offering* Lv 5^{24}; עֲוֺן אַשְׁמָה *iniquity requiring a trespass-offering* Lv 22^{16}.

821 אַשְׁמוּרָה (-מֹרֶת, -מֻרוֹת) v. שׁמר. p. 1038

820 אַשְׁמַנִּים v. שׁמן. p. 1032

אשן (√assumed for foll.; perh. *be hard, firm*, cf. Aram. אֻשּׁוּנָא, אֲשִׁינָא, something *firm*).

823 †אַשְׁנָה **n.pr.loc.** (*the firm ?*) name of two cities in Judah. **1.** Jos 15^{33}. **2.** v^{43}.

822 אֶשְׁנָב v. שׁנב. p. 1039

824 אֶשְׁעָן v. שׁען. p. 1043

825 †[אַשָּׁף] **n.m. conjurer, necromancer** (prob. Bab. loan-word, As. *ašipu* COT^{Gloss} cf. Dl$^{Pr\ 141}$, Aram. אָשַׁף, ܐܫܘܦܐ; v. also As. *šiptu, conjuration*) only pl. אַשָּׁפִים Dn 1^{20} (‖חַרְטֻמִּים), 2^{2} (‖ ח׳, מְכַשְּׁפִים, כַּשְׂדִּים).

אשף (√of dub. meaning, whence foll.)

827 †אַשְׁפָּה **n.f. quiver** for arrows (As. *išpatu* Dl^{K29}) א׳ lit. as part of warlike equipment Jb 39^{23} Is 22^{6}; fig. in sim. of sons of one's youth as arrows (weapons which the father may wield) ψ 127^{5} אַשְׁרֵי הַגֶּבֶר אֲשֶׁר מִלֵּא אֶת־אַשְׁפָּתוֹ מֵהֶם *the happiness of the man that hath filled his quiver with them!* of Yahweh's quiver, in metaph. of prophet as arrow of י׳ Is 49^{2} וַיְשִׂימֵנִי לְחֵץ בָּרוּר בְּאַשְׁפָּתוֹ הִסְתִּירָנִי *and he made me into a polished arrow, in his quiver he hid me;* also of quiver in which י׳ has his arrows of chastisement, בְּנֵי אַשְׁפָּתוֹ, i.e. *his arrows* La 3^{13} (‖ חֵץ v^{12}).

828 †אַשְׁפְּנַז **n.pr.m.** the רַב־סָרִיסִים, chief of eunuchs, of Nebuchadrezzar Dn 1^{3} (meaning unknown).

829 †אֶשְׁפָּר 2 S 6^{19} = 1 Ch 16^{3}; 𝔊 2 S 6^{19} Aq. Symm. *cake* or *roll;* other Verss. ancient & mod. have various conjectures, but actual etym. & mng. unknown; v. Lag$^{GGA\ 1884,\ No.\ 7,\ 262\ =\ M\ i.\ 214}$ Dr^{Sm}.

830 אַשְׁפֹּת, אַשְׁפַּתּוֹת v. שׁפת. p. 1046

831 †אַשְׁקְלוֹן **n.pr.loc.** a city of the Philistines (As. *Isqaluna* COT^{Gloss} Dl$^{Pa\ 290}$; Ph. adj.gent. cf. infr.) Ju 1^{18} 14^{19} 1 S 6^{17} 2 S 1^{20} Je 25^{20} $47^{5.7}$ Am 1^{8} Zp $2^{4.7}$ Zc $9^{5.5}$; on the Medit. Sea, S. of W. fr. Jerusalem, mod. *'Asqalân*, Survey$^{iii.\ 237\ f.}$ (with plan); cf. also ZPV$^{ii.\ 164\ f.}$

832 †אֶשְׁקְלוֹנִי **adj.gent.** c. art. as subst. הָא׳ Jos 13^{3} (Ph. אשקלני).

833 †[אָשַׁר] **vb. go straight, go on, advance** (As. *ašâru* Zim$^{BP\ 11}$; Ar. Aram. in deriv.)—**Qal** *Imv.* אִשְׁרוּ Pr 9^{6} אִשְׁרוּ בְּדֶרֶךְ בִּינָה *go straight on in the way of understanding.* **Pi.** *Pf.* אִשְּׁרוּ Mal 3^{12} Gn 30^{13}; *Impf.* תְּאַשֵּׁר Pr 4^{14}+4 t.; *Imv.* אַשֵּׁר Pr 23^{19}; *Pt.* pl. מְאַשְּׁרִים Mal 3^{15}+2 t.;—**1.** intensive *go straight on, advance* Pr 4^{14}. **2.** causative *lead on* Pr 23^{19} Is 3^{12} 9^{15}. **3.** *set right, righten* Is 1^{17}. **4.** *pronounce happy, call blessed* Gn 30^{13} (J) Jb 29^{11} ψ 72^{17} Pr 31^{28} Ct 6^{9} Mal $3^{12.15}$. **Pu.** *Impf.* יְאֻשַּׁר ψ 41^{3}; *Pt.* מְאֻשָּׁר Pr 3^{18} Is 9^{15}. **1.** *be led on* Is 9^{15}. **2.** *be made happy, blessed* ψ 41^{3} Pr 3^{18}.

835 †[אֶשֶׁר, or אָשָׁר, cf. Lag$^{BN\ 143}$] **n.[m.]** only *Pl.* cstr. אַשְׁרֵי **happiness, blessedness of** 1 K 10^{8}+32 t.&c.sf., v.infr.; abstr.intens.exclam. *O the happiness, blessedness of,* אַשְׁרֵי אֲנָשֶׁיךָ אַשְׁרֵי עֲבָדֶיךָ אֵלֶּה *happy thy men, happy these thy servants* 1 K 10^{8} (= 2 Ch 9^{7}); אַשְׁרֵי אֱנוֹשׁ יוֹכִחֶנּוּ אֱלוֹהַּ *blessed the man whom Eloah correcteth* Jb

5^{17}; אַשְׁרֵי תְמִימֵי דָרֶךְ *blessed the perfect in way* ψ 119^{1}; אַשְׁרֵי בָנָיו אַחֲרָיו *blessed his children after him* Pr 20^{7}; elsewhere cstr. with אָדָם ψ 32^{2} $84^{6.13}$ Pr 3^{13} 8^{34} 28^{14}; with הַגֶּבֶר ψ 34^{9} 40^{5} 94^{12} 127^{5}; (הָ)אִישׁ ψ 1^{1} 112^{1}; אֱנוֹשׁ Is 56^{2}; הַגּוֹי ψ 33^{12}; הָעָם ψ 89^{16} $144^{15.15}$; before ptcp. ψ 2^{12} 32^{1} 41^{2} 84^{5} 106^{3} 119^{2} 128^{1} Is 30^{18} Dn 12^{12}; before verbal clauses without relative ψ 65^{5} Pr 8^{32}; with שֶׁ ψ $137^{8.9}$ 146^{5}; with sf. אַשְׁרֶיךָ (for אֲשָׁרֶיךָ) *O thy happiness!* Dt 33^{29} ψ 128^{2}; אַשְׁרֵיךְ Ec 10^{17}; אַשְׁרֵיכֶם Is 32^{20}; אַשְׁרָיו Pr 14^{21} 16^{20}; אַשְׁרֵהוּ Pr 29^{18} (on these forms v. Ges[§ 93, R. 1, E]).

837 †[אֹשֶׁר] **n.[m.]** **happiness**, only sf. בְּאָשְׁרִי *in my happiness* Gn 30^{13} (J).

838 †[אָשׁוּר, אֲשֻׁר] **n.f.** [ψ 44, 19] **step, going** (cf. Ar. أَثَرٌ, إِثْرٌ, Eth. አሠር: *footstep*) only sf. אֲשֻׁרוֹ Jb 23^{11} Pr 14^{15}; אֲשׁוּרַי ψ 17^{5}; אֲשֻׁרָי ψ 40^{3} 73^{2}; אֲשֻׁרֵנוּ ψ 44^{19}; אֲשֻׁרָיו ψ 37^{31}, all poet. & fig. of mode of life, etc.

838 †[אַשֻׁר] **n.f.** [Jb 31, 7] **step, going**, same usage, אַשֻּׁרִי Jb 31^{7}; אַשֻּׁרֵנוּ ψ 17^{11}.

836 †אָשֵׁר **n.pr.m.** **Asher** (*happy one, Felix*, cf. Ph. אשרשלח, which however may contain (god) Asshur or Osiris, cf. Bae[Rel 161]). **1.** son of Jacob and Zilpah Gn 30^{13} 35^{26} 46^{17} Ex 1^{4} Nu 26^{46} 1 Ch 2^{2}. **2.** *the tribe* Gn 49^{20} Nu 1^{13} Dt 27^{13} $33^{24.24}$ Jos $17^{10.11}$ 19^{34} Ju 1^{31} 5^{17} 6^{36} 7^{23} 1 K 4^{16} 1 Ch 12^{36} 2 Ch 30^{11} Ez $48^{2.3.34}$; בְּנֵי אָשֵׁר Nu 1^{40} 2^{27} 7^{72} 10^{26} $26^{44.47}$ 34^{27} Jos $19^{24.31}$ 1 Ch $7^{30.40}$; מַטֵּה אָשֵׁר Nu 1^{41} 2^{27} 13^{13} Jos $21^{6.30}$ 1 Ch $6^{47.59}$. **3. n.pr.loc.** city E. of Shechem Jos 17^{7}.

843 †אָשֵׁרִי **adj.gent.** c. art. הָא׳ as n.coll. Ju 1^{32}.

8391 †אֲשֻׁרִים, in בַּת א׳ Ez 27^{6} (rd. בִּתְאַשֻּׁרִים *with box-wood* Bo Hi MV Co al., cf. foll.)

839, 8391 †תְּאַשּׁוּר **n.f.** **box-tree** (on form cf. Sta[§ 267]) Is 41^{19} 60^{13} Ez 27^{6} (cf. supr.) a small evergreen tree about 20 feet high, growing on Lebanon, Bo Tristr[Nat. Hist. Bib. 339], so 𝔙 𝔗 RV. (Others *sherbîn*, a species of cedar distinguished by the smallness of its cones and the upward direction of its branches, cf. Thes RobGes.)

842 †אֲשֵׁרָה, אֲשֵׁירָה 2 K 17^{16} **n.pr.f.** **Ashera** (As. n.pr.f. *Aš-ra-tu*, c. sign for deity, in Canaanitish n.pr. *Abad-Ašratum, servant of A.* Schr[ZA 1888, 363], cf. Wkl & Abel[Thontafelfund v. El Amarna ii. No. 77, l. 9], & Sayce[RP2. ii. 67, iii. 71]; on deriv. cf. As. *aširat*, adj. fem. *gracious*, COT[Gloss]):—usually with the art.: prob. **a.** a Canaanitish goddess of fortune & happiness; having prophets 1 K 18^{19}, an image 15^{13} = 2 Ch 15^{16} 2 K 21^{7}, sacred vessels 2 K 23^{4}, houses v^{7}. **b.** a symbol of this goddess, a *sacred tree* or *pole* set up near an altar 1 K 16^{33} 2 K 13^{6} 17^{16} 18^{4} 21^{3} $23^{6.15}$; prohibited Dt 16^{1}; burnt by Gideon Ju $6^{25.26.28.30}$. *Pl.* אֲשֵׁרוֹת **a.** the goddess Ju 3^{7} (prob. error for עַשְׁתָּרֹת 𝔙). **b.** *sacred trees* or *poles* 2 Ch 19^{3} 33^{3}; elsewhere אֲשֵׁרִים *id.* Is 27^{9} + 12 t.; sf. Mi 5^{14} + 5 t.;—Ex 34^{13} (J) Dt 7^{5} 12^{3} Is 17^{8} 27^{9} Je 17^{20} Mi 5^{13} 1 K $14^{15.23}$ 2 K 17^{10} 23^{14} 2 Ch 14^{2} 17^{6} 24^{18} 31^{1} 33^{19} $34^{3.4.7}$.—(Cf. also Sta[ZAW 1881, 344 f.] RS[Sem. i. 171 f., 175 n.] We[H 235], who think א׳ only the sacred pole.)

אֲשֶׁר **part. of relation** (Moab. *id.*; origin 834
dub.: **1.** acc. to Tsepreghi[Diss. Lugd. p. 171] Mühlau[Bö. Lb. ii. 79 n.] Sta[Morg. Forsch. 1875, 188; Lb. § 167] Hommel[ZMG 1878, 708 ff.] Müll[§ 153] Sayce[Hbr. ii. 51] Lag[M. i. 255] & esp. Kraetzschmar[Hbr. vi. 298 ff], orig. a subst. 'place' = أَثَرٌ *footstep, mark*, አሠር: (do.), אֲתַר, ܐܬܪ *place*, As. *ašru*, used (v. Kraetz.) both as a subst. 'there, where,' and as a relative of place 'where': in Heb. this development has advanced further, and it has become a relative sign generally. The chief objection to this explanation is that it would isolate Heb. from the other Semitic languages, in which pronouns are formed regularly from *demonstrative* roots (cf. also Nö[ZMG 1886, 738]). **2.** according to Phi[St. C. 73] Sperling[Nota Rel. im Hebr. 1876, 15-22] for אֲשֶׁל, developed from the relative שׁ (q.v.) by (1) the prefixing of either a merely prosthetic א, or, better, a pronominal א (giving rise to אש, the form of the relative in Ph.), and (2) the addition of the demonstr. root ל [found also in אֵל, אֵלֶּה, הַלָּזֶה (q.v.), اَلَّذِى *he who*, እለ: *who* (pl.)]: the main objection to this explanation is the change of ל to ר, which is hardly rendered probable by the comp. of Syr. ܗܪܟܐ by side of Targ. הָלְכָא. **1** seems preferable, the primitive root having acquired different significations in the different Semitic languages, and having been weakened in Heb. to a mere particle of relation). A **sign of relation**, bringing the clause introduced by it into relation with an antecedent clause. As a rule אֲשֶׁר is a mere **connecting link**, and requires to be supplemented (see the grammars) by a pron. affix, or other word, such as שָׁם, defining the nature of the relation more precisely: e.g. Gn 1^{11} אֲשֶׁר זַרְעוֹ־בוֹ lit. *as to which*, its seed is in it = in which is its seed, ψ 1^{4} like the chaff אֲשֶׁר־תִּדְּפֶנּוּ רוּחַ *as to which*, the wind drives it = which the wind drives, etc.; & so אֲשֶׁר . . שָׁם = *where*, אֲשֶׁר . . . מִשָּׁם = *whence*, Gn 2^{11} 3^{23} 20^{13} etc. Sometimes also (v. infr.) the relation

expressed by it is specifically temporal, local, causal, etc. More particularly

1. it includes its pronominal antecedent, whether in the nom. or obl. cases, as Nu 22^{6} וַאֲשֶׁר תָּאֹר יוּאָר and *he whom* thou cursest is cursed, Ex 4^{12} and I will teach thee אֲשֶׁר תְּדַבֵּר *that which* thou shalt say; and with particles or prepositions, as אֵת אֲשֶׁר (acc. to the context) *him who…*, *those who…*, *that which…*; לַאֲשֶׁר to *him who…* Gn 43^{16}, to *those who…* 47^{24}, to *that which* 27^{8}; מֵאֲשֶׁר Ju 16^{30} 2 S 18^{18} *than those* whom; Lv 27^{24} לַאֲשֶׁר קָנָהוּ מֵאִתּוֹ *to him* from whom he bought it, Nu 5^{7}; Is 24^{2} כַּאֲשֶׁר נֹשֵׁא בוֹ *like him* against whom there is a creditor. **2.** instances of אֲשֶׁר followed by a pron. affix, or by שָׁם, שָׁמָּה, מִשָּׁם, are so common that the exx. cited above will be sufficient. Very rarely there occurs the anomalous constr. עִם אֲשֶׁר Gn 31^{32} for אֲשֶׁר עִמּוֹ (see Gn 44^{9}), בַּאֲשֶׁר Is 47^{12} for אֲשֶׁר בָּהֶם, לַאֲשֶׁר for אֲשֶׁר...לָהֶם Ez 23^{40}: ψ 119^{49} see under על אשר. It is followed by the pron. in the *nomin.*, in the foll. cases:—(*a*) immediately, mostly before an adj. or ptcp., Gn 9^{3} all moving things אֲשֶׁר הוּא־חַי which are living, Lv 11^{26} Nu 9^{13} 14$^{8.27}$ 35^{31} Dt 20^{20} 1 S 10^{19} (v. Dr) 2 K 25^{19} (‖ Je 52^{25} היה) Je 27^{9} Ez 43^{19} Hg 1^{9} Ru 4^{15} Ne 2^{18} Ec 7^{26}; before a vb. 2 K 22^{13} (omitted 2 Ch 34^{21}). (*b*) in a *negative* sentence, at the end: Gn 7^{2} 17^{12} Nu 17^{5} Dt 17^{15} אֲשֶׁר לֹא אָחִיךָ הוּא who is not thy brother, 20^{15} Ju 19^{12} 1 K 8^{41}‖ 9^{20}‖. N.B. ψ 16^{3} אֲשֶׁר בָּאָרֶץ הֵמָּה is an unparalleled expression for 'who are in the land'; rd. אֲשֶׁר בָּאָרֶץ הֵמָּה אַדִּירֵי וג׳ 'the saints that are in the land, they (המה) are the nobles, in whom,' etc. **3.** sometimes (though rarely) the defining adjunct is a pron. of 1 or 2 ps. as well as of 3 ps. In such cases it is strictly to be rendered *I who…*, *thou who*, etc.; Ho 14^{4} אֲשֶׁר־בְּךָ יְרֻחַם יָתוֹם *thou by whom* the fatherless is compassionated! Je 31^{32} *I, whose* covenant they brake, 32^{19} Is 49^{23} Jb 37$^{17f.}$ *thou whose* garments are warm…, canst thou? etc., ψ 71$^{19.20}$ 144^{12} *we whose* sons, etc., 139^{15} my frame was not hidden from thee, אֲשֶׁר־עֻשֵּׂיתִי בַסֵּתֶר—*I who* was wrought in secret (=*though I* was wrought in secret), Ex 14^{13} for *ye who* have seen the Egyptians to-day,—ye shall not see them again for ever! (cf. ψ 41^{9}). **4.** the defining pron. adjunct is *dispensed with*—**a.** when אֲשֶׁר represents the simple subj. of a sentence, or the direct obj. of a vb.: so constantly, as Gn 2^{1} the work אֲשֶׁר עָשָׂה *which* he made, 3^{3} the tree אֲשֶׁר בְּתוֹךְ הַגָּן *which* is in the midst of the garden, etc. **b.** after words denoting time, place, or manner, so that אֲשֶׁר then becomes equivalent to *when*, *where*, *why*: (*a*) Gn 6^{4} אַחֲרֵי כֵן אֲשֶׁר afterwards, *when*, etc. (cf. 2 Ch 35^{20}) 45^{6} there are still 5 years אֲשֶׁר אֵין חָרִישׁ *when* there shall be no plowing, Jos 14^{10} 1 K 22^{25}; after יוֹם or הַיּוֹם Dt 4^{10} Ju 4^{14} 1 S 24^{5} (v. Dr) 2 S 19^{25} Je 20^{14} al.; similarly Gn 40^{13}. (*β*) Gn 35^{13} בַּמָּקוֹם אֲשֶׁר דִּבֶּר אִתּוֹ in the place *where* he spake with him, v^{14} 39^{20} Nu 13^{27} 22^{26} Dt 1^{31} in the desert which thou sawest, *where* (accents Ke Di), 8^{15} 1 K 8^{9} (unless לוּחוֹת הַבְּרִית has here fallen out: v. 𝔊 & Dt 9^{9}) Is 55^{11} 64^{10} ψ 84^{4}. So (*γ*) in אֶל אֲשֶׁר *to* (the place) *which* (or *whither*) Ex 32^{34} Ru 1^{16}; אֶל־כָּל־אֲשֶׁר *to* every (place) *whither* Jos 1^{16} Pr 17^{8}; בַּאֲשֶׁר *in* (the place) *where* †Ju 5^{27} 17$^{8.9}$ 1 S 23^{13} 2 K 8^{1} Ru 1$^{16.17}$ Jb 39^{30}, once only with שָׁם Gn 21^{17}; בְּכֹל אֲשֶׁר *wheresoever* Jos 1$^{7.9}$ Ju 2^{15} 1 S 14^{47} 18^{5} 2 S 7^{7} 2 K 18^{7}; מֵאֲשֶׁר *from* (the place) *where*=*whencesoever* †Ex 5^{11} Ru 2^{9}; עַל־אֲשֶׁר *to* (the place) *whither* (or *which*) 2 S 15^{20} 1 K 18^{12}; עַל־כָּל־אֲשֶׁר Je 1^{7}. (*δ*) זֶה הַדָּבָר אֲשֶׁר... this is the reason *that* or *why*... Jos 5^{4} 1 K 11^{27}. **c.** more extreme instances Lv 14$^{22.30.31}$ Nu 6^{21}, Dt 7^{19} (wherewith), 28^{20} 1 S 2^{32} (wherein), 1 K 2^{26} Ju 8^{15} (about whom), Is 8^{12} (where יאמר would be foll. normally by לוֹ), 31^{6} turn ye to (him as to) whom they have deeply rebelled, 47^{15} Zp 3^{11} Ec 3^{9}, 1 K 14^{19} (=how). **d.** it is dispensed with only in appearance after אֲשֶׁר אָמַר (אָמַרְתִּי וג׳) followed by the words used, its place being really taken by a pron. in the speech which follows, as Gn 3^{17} the tree *as to which* I commanded thee saying, Thou shalt not eat *from it*, Ex 22^{8} Dt 28^{68} Ju 7^{4} (זֶה) 8^{15} (where the noun repeated takes the place of the pron., cf. Dt 9^{2}) 1 S 9^{17} (זֶה) ^{23}+; cf. 2 S 11^{16} 2 K 17^{12} 21^{4}. **5.** אֲשֶׁר sts. in poet.=*one who*, *a man who* (*men who*), *ὅστις*, *οἵτινες*, ψ 24^{4} 55^{20} 95$^{4.5}$ Jb 4^{19} 5^{5} 9^{5} (Hi) 15^{17}. **6.** אֲשֶׁר occas. receives its closer definition by a subst. *following* it, in other words, its logical antecedent is inserted in the rel. clause: (*a*) in the phrase peculiar to Je., אֲשֶׁר הָיָה דְבַר י׳ אֶל יר׳ that which came (of) the word of י׳ to Je. †14^{1} 46^{1} 47^{1} 49^{34} (cf. Ew^{§334}); (*b*) Ex 25^{9} Nu 33^{4} 1 S 25^{30} 2 K 8^{12} 12^{6} לְכֹל אֲשֶׁר־יִמָּצֵא שָׁם בָּדֶק׃ Ez 12^{25}; cf. the Eth. usage Di^{§201}; (*c*) (antec. *repeated*) Gn 49^{30}=50^{13}, 1 S 25^{39} (י׳ repeated), Is 54^{9} (prob.) *as to which* I sware that, etc., Am 5^{1} which I take up over you (as) a dirge. **7.** אֲשֶׁר לְ׳ *that* (*belongs*, *belong*, belonged) *to*, is used **a.** either alone or preceded by כָּל־ to express (*all*) *that* (*belongs*) *to*, as Gn 14^{23} מִכָּל־אֲשֶׁר־לָךְ of all that is *thine*, 31^{1} מֵאֲשֶׁר לְאָבִינוּ of *that which was* our father's, 32^{24} & sent over אֶת־אֲשֶׁר־לוֹ *that which he had*, + oft. **b.** as a circumlocution of the genitive, as Gn 29^{9} עִם־הַצֹּאן אֲשֶׁר לְאָבִיהָ with the sheep *that were* her father's, 40^{5} 47^{4} Lv 9^{8} Ju 6^{11} 1 S 25^{7} הָרֹעִים אֲשֶׁר־לָךְ, 2 S 14^{31} אֶת־הַחֶלְקָה אֲשֶׁר־לִי, 23^{8} 1 K $1^{8.33}$ עַל הַפִּרְדָּה אֲשֶׁר־לִי upon mine own mule, v^{49} 4^{2} 2 K 11^{10} 16^{13} Ru 2^{21}; and esp. in the case of a compound expression depending on a single genit., as Gn 23^{9} 40^{5} 41^{43} מִרְכֶּבֶת הַמִּשְׁנֶה אֲשֶׁר־לוֹ the chariot of the second rank *which he had*, Ex 38^{30} Ju 3^{20} 6^{25} 1 S 17^{40} 21^{8} אַבִּיר הָרֹעִים אֲשֶׁר לְשָׁאוּל the mightiest of *Saul's herdmen*, 24^{5} אֶת־כְּנַף־הַמְּעִיל אֲשֶׁר־לְשָׁאוּל, 2 S 2^{8} Saul's captain of the host, 1 K 10^{28} 15^{20} 22^{31} Je 52^{17} Ru 4^{3}. **c.** with names of places (esp. such as do not readily admit the st. cstr.) Ju 18^{28} 19^{14} הַגִּבְעָה אֲשֶׁר לְבִנְיָמִין Gibeah (the hill) of Benjamin, 20^{4} 1 S 17^{1} 1 K 15^{27} 16^{15} 17^{9} 19^{3} 2 K 14^{11}. Comp. שֶׁל (q.v.) which in Rabb., like the Aram. דִּיל־, ܕܝܠ־, is in habitual use as a mark of the genitive.—N.B. In Aram. also דִּי, ܕ, without ל, expresses the gen. relation, as מִלְּתָא דִי־מַלְכָּא, lit. the word, *that of* the king = the word of the king. The few apparent cases of a similar use of אשר are, however, too foreign to the general usage of the language to be regarded otherwise than as due to textual error: 1 S 13^{8} read אֲשֶׁר אָמַר (or שָׂם Ex 19^{5}) שְׁמוּאֵל (𝔊 εἶπε); 1 K 11^{25} supply עָשָׂה (𝔊 ἣν ἐποίησεν); 2 K 25^{10} supply אֶת *with* (as || Je 52^{14}); 2 Ch 34^{22} read וַאֲשֶׁר אָמַר הַמֶּלֶךְ (cf. 𝔊) and those whom the king appointed (abbreviated from 2 K 22^{14}); cf. Ew $^{§ 292 a, b}$ with note.

8. אֲשֶׁר becomes, like Aram. דִּי, ܕ, a **conj.** approximating in usage to כִּי: thus **a.** = *quod*, ὅτι, *that*, subordinating an entire sentence to a verb of knowing, remembering, etc. (*α*) with אֵת Dt 9^{7} forget not אֵת אֲשֶׁר הִקְצַפְתָּ *the fact that* (= *how*) thou provokedst, etc., 29^{15} Jos 2^{10} 1 S $24^{11.19}$ 2 S 11^{20} know ye not אֵת אֲשֶׁר־יֹרוּ *how* they shoot from off the wall? 2 K 8^{12} Is 38^{3} + oft. As subj. (rare) 1 K 14^{19} 2 K 14^{15} 20^{20}. Of time (peculiarly) †2 S 14^{15} עַתָּה אֲשֶׁר now (is it) *that*... Zc 8^{20} (prob.) yet (shall it be) *that*... v^{23}; cf. כִּמְעַט שֶׁ Ct 3^{4}. (*β*) without אֵת (not very common, כִּי being usually employed): after יָדַע Ex 11^{7} Ez 20^{26} (very strange in Ez: v. Hi) Jb 9^{5} (Ew De Di) Ec 8^{12}, רָאָה Dt 1^{31} (RV) 1 S 18^{15}, הִתְוַדָּה to confess Lv 5^{5} $26^{40 b}$, הִשְׁבִּיעַ 1 K 22^{16} (caused to swear *that*...); after a noun Is 38^{7} הָאוֹת אֲשֶׁר the sign *that*... (|| 2 K 20^{9} כִּי): with growing frequency in late Hebrew, 2 Ch 2^{7}, and esp. Ne Est: Ne $2^{5.10}$ 7^{65} (= Ezr 2^{63}) $8^{14.15}$ 10^{31} $13^{1.19.22}$ Est 1^{19} 2^{10} 3^{4} 4^{11} 6^{2} 8^{11} Ec 3^{22} (מֵאֲשֶׁר) 5^{4} 7^{18} (with טוֹב: contrast Ru 2^{22}) $v^{22.29}$ $8^{12.14}$ 9^{1} Dn $1^{8.8}$. (*γ*) prefixed to a *direct* citation, like כִּי q.v. (= ὅτι *recitativum*) (rare) 1 S 15^{20} 2 S 1^{4} 2^{4} (v. Dr) ψ 10^{6} (prob.), Ne 4^{6}. **b.** it is resolvable into *so that*: Gn 11^{7} אֲשֶׁר לֹא יִשְׁמְעוּ *so that* they understand not, etc., 13^{16} 22^{14} אֲשֶׁר יֵאָמֵר so that it is said, Ex 20^{26} Dt $4^{10.40}$ אֲשֶׁר יִיטַב לְךָ 6^{3} $28^{27.51}$ 1 K $3^{12.13}$ 2 K 9^{37} Mal 3^{19}. **c.** it has a causal force, *forasmuch as, in that, since*: Gn 30^{18} 31^{49} and Mizpah, אֲשֶׁר אָמַר *for that* he said, $34^{13.27}$ 42^{21} we are guilty, אֲשֶׁר רָאִינוּ *we who* saw (or, *in that* we saw), Nu 20^{13} Meribah, *because* they strove there, Dt 3^{24} Jos $4^{7.23}$ 22^{31} Ju 9^{17} 1 S 2^{23} 15^{15} 20^{42} go in peace, אֲשֶׁר נִשְׁבַּעְנוּ *forasmuch as* we have sworn, 25^{26} *thou whom* (= or, *seeing that*) י׳ hath withholden, 2 S 2^{5} blessed are ye of י׳, אֲשֶׁר עֲשִׂיתֶם, *who* (οἵτινες) have done (or *in that ye* have done), 1 K 3^{19} 15^{5} 2 K 12^{3} 17^{4} 23^{26} Je 16^{13} Ec $8^{11.12}$ (Hi De Now). Here also belongs its use in אֲשֶׁר לָמָּה *since why*...? (= *lest*) Dn 1^{10}: v. sub לָמָּה. On אֲשֶׁר עַל כֵּן *forasmuch as* Jb 34^{27} v. sub כִּי עַל כֵּן. **d.** it expresses a *condition* (rare & peculiar): Lv 4^{22} אֲשֶׁר נָשִׂיא יֶחֱטָא in (case) that = *when* (or *if*) a ruler sinneth ($v^{3.13.27}$ אִם), Nu 5^{29} (explained differently by Ew $^{§ 334 a}$), Dt 11^{27} and the blessing אֲשֶׁר תִּשְׁמְעוּ *if* ye hearken (v^{28} אִם), 18^{22} Ges, Jos 4^{21} אֲשֶׁר יִשְׁאָלוּן ... *when* they ask..., then... (v^{6} כִּי), Is 31^{4}. In 1 K 8^{33} (|| 2 Ch 6^{24} כִּי, cf. K $v^{35.37}$) אֲשֶׁר may be rendered indifferently *because* or *when*. Once, similarly, אֵת אֲשֶׁר 1 K 8^{31} (|| אִם). **e.** perh. (exceptionally) = כַּאֲשֶׁר, *as*, Je 33^{22} Is 54^{9} (sq. כֵּן; but כֵּן q.v. sts. stands without כאשר, & אשר may in these passages connect with what precedes); acc. to some also Je 48^{8} ψ 106^{34} (in a connexion where כַּאֲשֶׁר would be more usual: אֲשֶׁר may however be the obj. of אָמַר). In 1 S 16^{7} אֲשֶׁר יִרְאֶה הָאָדָם rd. כַּאֲשֶׁר, v. Dr. **f.** combined with preps., אֲשֶׁר converts them into conjunctions: see below, מֵאֲשֶׁר, כַּאֲשֶׁר, בַּאֲשֶׁר. On its use similarly with לְמַעַן, יַעַן, עַל דְּבַר, בַּעֲבוּר, מִבְּלִי, (אַחֲרֵי) אַחַר, תַּחַת, מִפְּנֵי, עֵקֶב, עַל, עַד, כְּפִי, see these words.—הַאֲשֶׁר, with ה *interrog.*, occurs once, 2 K 6^{22}.

Note 1. אֲשֶׁר being a connecting link, without any perfectly corresponding equivalent in Engl., its force is not unfreq. capable of being represented in more than one way. See e.g. 2 S 2^{5} (above **8 c**), Is 28^{12} unto *whom* he said, or *for that* he said to *them*.

Note 2. The opinion that אֲשֶׁר has an asseverative force (like כִּי, q.v.), or introduces the apodosis, is not prob., being both alien to its general usage & not required by the passages alleged. Render Is 8^{20} either 'Surely acc. to this word will those speak *who* have no dawn,' or '. . . will they speak *when* (cf. supr. **8 d** Dt 11^{27} Jos 4^{21}) they have no dawn.'

834 **בַּאֲשֶׁר**$_{19}$ **a.** *in* (that) *which* . . . Is 56^{4} 65^{12} 66^{4} (supr. **1**); Ec 3^{9} *in* (that, in) *which* (**4 c**); Is 47^{12} (v. **2**). **b. adv.** *in* (the place) *where*: supr. **4 b** (γ). **c. conj.** *in that, inasmuch as*, †Gn $39^{9.23}$ Ec 7^{2} 8^{4}; cf. ܒ. **d.** †Jon 1^{8} בַּאֲשֶׁר לְמִי *on account of* whom? (בַּאֲשֶׁר לְ *on account of*, framed on model of Aram. בְּדִיל: v. sub שֶׁל).

834 **כַּאֲשֶׁר** v. sub כְּ. p. 455

834 **מֵאֲשֶׁר**$_{17}$ **a.** *from* (or *than*) *that which* (*him, them*, etc., *that* . . .) Gn 31^{1} Ex $29^{27.27}$ Nu 6^{11} (see Lv 4^{26}) Jos 10^{11} Ju 16^{30} Is 47^{13}+; *than that* . . . †Ec 3^{22}; לְבַד מֵאֲשֶׁר †Est 4^{11}. **b. adv.** *from* (the place) *where*: supr. **4 a** (β). **c. conj.** *from* (the fact) *that* . . ., *since* †Is 43^{4}.

377 †[**אשׁשׁ**] (cf. أَسَّسَ *found, establish*) **Hithpo.** וְהִתְאֹשָׁשׁוּ Is 46^{8} (der. fr. above by 𝔗 Jer Hi Kn De MV, *shew yourselves firm*, but) rd. perh. הִתְבֹּשָׁשׁוּ Lag Che, v. בּוֹשׁ (Thes expl. as denom. from אִישׁ; on other views cf. Di).

809 †**אֲשִׁישָׁה** **n.f.** (pressed) **raisin-cake**—א׳ 2 S 6^{19} 1 Ch 16^{3} distributed, with other viands, to people; esp. as stimulating, pl. אֲשִׁישׁוֹת Ct 2^{5}; more explicitly אֲשִׁישֵׁי עֲנָבִים Ho 3^{1} used in sacrificial feasts (cf. RS OTJC Lect. xi. n. 7); אֲשִׁישֵׁי קִיר חֲרֶשֶׂת Is 16^{7}, i.e. the raisin-cakes which were an article of trade at Qir-ḥareseth (taken by Thes al. = *foundations*, i.e. foundations exposed
808 by ruin, from [אָשִׁישׁ] with such a meaning).

802 **אֵשֶׁת** v. אִשָּׁה sub III. אנשׁ. p. 61

847 †**אֶשְׁתָּאוֹל** Jos 15^{33} + 2 t., **אֶשְׁתָּאֹל** Ju 13^{25} + 3 t. **n.pr.loc.** (in form like the inf. of the Arab. VIII. conj. from שָׁאַל: so אֶשְׁתְּמֹעַ from שָׁמַע. Perh. Arabic-speaking tribes may have settled in parts of S. of Judah) city of Danites in the שְׁפֵלָה of Judah, named with צָרְעָה Jos 15^{33} 19^{41} Ju 13^{25} 16^{31} $18^{2.8.11}$; perh. mod. *'Eshû'a* Survey iii. 25 Guerin Pal. ii. 13 f. 382.

848 †**אֶשְׁתָּאֻלִי** **adj.gent.** c. art. הָא׳ as n.coll. 1 Ch 2^{53}.

†**אֶשְׁתּוֹן** **n.pr.m.** a man of Judah (perh. fr. 850
אֵשֶׁת = *effeminate* or *uxorious*) 1 Ch $4^{11.12}$.

†**אֶשְׁתְּמוֹעַ** Jos 21^{14}, **אֶשְׁתְּמֹעַ** 1 S 30^{28} 1 Ch 851
$4^{17.19}$ 6^{42}, **אֶשְׁתְּמֹה** Jos 15^{50} **n.pr.loc.** Levitical city in mountain-country of Judah, south of Hebron, mod. *Semû'a* v. Rob BR i. 464, ii. 204 Survey iii. 403 Bd Pal. 153; 1 Ch $4^{17.19}$ it appears as **n.pr.m.** of a man of Judah. (On the form, cf. sub אֶשְׁתָּאוֹל.)

I. **אֵת**, with makk. אֶת־, with suff. אֹתִי; אֹתְךָ, 853
אֹתְכָה †Nu 22^{33}, אֹתָךְ, אֹתָ֑כָה †Ex 29^{35}, fem. אֹתָךְ; אֹתוֹ etc.; 2 pl. אֶתְכֶם, once אוֹתְכֶם Jos 23^{15}; 3 mpl. regularly אֹתָם, rarely אֶתְהֶם †Gn 32^{1} Ex 18^{20} Nu 21^{3} Ez 34^{12} 1 Ch 6^{50}, once אוֹתְהֶם Ez 23^{45}; 3 fpl., on the contrary, regularly אֶתְהֶן (13 t.), once אֹתָן Ez 16^{54} (also אוֹתְהֶן Ez 23^{47}, אֹתָ֫נָה Ex 35^{26}, אוֹתָ֫נָה Ez 34^{21}); forms with *cholem* also oft. written *plene*:—the **mark of the accusative**, prefixed as a rule only to nouns that are *definite* (Moab. *id.*, Ph. אית i.e. אִיַת (Schröd p. 213 f.); Aram. יָת freq. in 𝔗; Syr. ܝܳܬ very rare as mark of accus. (for which ܠ is preferred), but used often in the sense of *substance οὐσία*, also in that of *self*, e.g. ܒܝܳܬܶܗ *per se, reapse*, ܠܝܳܬܶܗ *sibi ipsi*, PS 1640 f., Sam. ࠀࠉࠕ; Ar. إِيَّا, only used with sf., when it is desired to emphasize the pronoun, e.g. Qor 1^{4} W AG i. § 189. [Eth. uses ኪያ: *kīyā* similarly, Di § 150 a; but it is dub. if this is etymologically akin.] The primitive form will have been *'iwyath*, orig. a subst. with foll. gen., Ol p. 432; whether ultim. a parallel development with אוֹת *sign* from √אוה is uncertain: Ol W AG i. § 188 Lag M i. 226 affirm, Nö ZMG 1886, 738 doubts. In Heb. the ground-form is אות; the forms with *ē*, *e* being abbreviated. In postB Heb., used in combination with another prep.: thus בְּאוֹתוֹ הַיּוֹם = Bibl. בַּיּוֹם הַהוּא, בְּאוֹתָהּ הַשָּׁעָה; or as a nomin., e.g. אוֹתוֹ הָאִישׁ = Bibl. הָאִישׁ הַהוּא).

1. As mark of the accus. prefixed to substs. defined either by the art. (or כֹּל), or by a genitive or pron. affix, or in virtue of being proper names: **a.** with transitive verbs, Gn $1^{1.16.29.30}$ 2^{11} $4^{1.2}$ 9^{3} (אֶת־כֹּל) etc. Similarly אֶת־מִי *whom* (in particular), Jos 24^{15} 1 S 12^{3} 28^{11} Is 6^{8} al. (but never אֶת־מָה); also with זֶה Gn 29^{33} 44^{29} 1 S 21^{16} 1 K 22^{27}+, זֹאת Gn 29^{27} 2 S 13^{27}+, אֵלֶּה Gn 46^{18} Lv 11^{18} Is 49^{21}+. So pretty uniformly in prose; but in poetry את is commonly dispensed with. By the use of את with the pron. affix, a pron. can at once, if required, be placed in a position of emphasis; let the order of words from this point of view be carefully noticed in the foll. passages: Gn 7^{1} 24^{14} 37^{4} Lv 10^{17} 11^{33} Nu 22^{32} *thee* I had slain, and *her* I had kept alive, Dt 4^{14} $6^{13.23}$ 13^{5} Ju 14^{3} אוֹתָהּ קַח לִי take for me *her*, 1 S 14^{35} 15^{1} 18^{17} 21^{10} אִם־אֹתָהּ תִּקַּח־לְךָ קָח if thou wilt take *that*, take it, 1 K 1^{35} 14^{9} Is 43^{22} 57^{11} Je 9^{2}. So הָאוֹתִי †Je 5^{22} 7^{19}. It also sometimes enables the reflexive sense to be expressed (elsewhere נַפְשָׁם) Je 7^{19} Ez 34^{2}. Rarely with a subst. which is undefined (Ew[§277 d 2] Ges[§117,1 R.2]), as Ex 21^{28} Nu 21^{9} Lv 20^{14} 1 S 24^{6} (but v. Dr) 2 S 4^{11} 18^{18} 23^{21}; or which, though definite, is without the art., Gn 21^{30} 2 S 15^{16} Lv 26^{5} 1 S 9^{3} (so Nu 16^{15}) Is 33^{19} 41^{7} Ez 43^{10} (for further exx. v. Ew *l.c.*) **b.** with a *passive* verb (Ges[§121.1] Ew[§295 b]) conceived as expressing neutrally the action in question, and construed accordingly with an *accus.* of that which is its real object: exx. occur with tolerable frequency from Gn 4^{18} (J) וַיִּקָּרֵא אֶת־שְׁמוֹ חֲנוֹךְ and there was called (= one called) his name Enoch, 17^{5} (P), 21^{5} (E), 27^{42} 2 S 21^{11} 1 K 18^{13} Ho 10^{6} etc., to Je 35^{18} 38^{4} 50^{20} Ez $16^{4.5}$ Est 2^{13} (cf. Dr[JPh xi. 227 f.]): also with pass. vbs. of filling (Ew[§281 b]), as Ex 1^{7}+. **c.** with *neuter* verbs or expressions, esp. such as involve the idea of *regarding*, or *treating*, appy. by a constr. κατὰ σύνεσιν (rare), Jo 22^{17} 2 S 11^{25} Ne 9^{32} (cf. 1 S 20^{13} Dr). Once after אֵין, Hg 2^{17} אֵין אֶתְכֶם אֵלַי. **d.** poet. (si vera l.), after an abstr. noun used with a verbal force, †Hb 3^{13} (Am 4^{11} Is 13^{19} Je 50^{40} מַהְפֵּכָה exerts a verbal force, like the Arab. *nom. verbi* [v. W[AG i. §196, 43]]; and Nu 10^{2} Ez 17^{9} לְמַשָּׂאוֹת, לְמַסַּע are Aramaizing infinitives: cf. Ew[§239 a]).

2. את marks an accus. in other relations than that of direct obj. to a verb: **a.** with verbs of motion (very rare) Nu 13^{17} Dt 1^{19} 2^{7} (to 'walk the wilderness'); denoting the goal Ju 19^{18} Ez 21^{25} (Ew[§281 d, n., 282 a 1]). **b.** denoting time (duration), also very rare: Ex 13^{7} Lv 25^{22} Dt 9^{25}. **c.** expressing the accus. of limitation (rare): Gn $17^{11.14}$ 1 K 15^{23}.

3. Chiefly in an inferior or later style, אֶת (or וְאֶת) is used irregularly, partly (*a*), as it would seem, to give greater definiteness (so esp. וְאֶת) at the mention of a new subject (when it may sometimes be rendered *as regards*), or through the influence of a neighbouring verb (a cstr. κατὰ σύνεσιν), or by an anacoluthon, partly (*β*) as resuming loosely some other prep. Thus (*a*) Ex 1^{14} Nu $3^{26.46}$ 5^{10} (with הָיָה: so Ez 35^{10}) Nu 18^{21b} Dt 11^{2} (anacol.), 14^{13} Jos 17^{11} Ju $20^{44.46}$ (contr. $v^{25.35}$) 1 S 17^{34} (v. Dr) 26^{16} 2 S 21^{22} 2 K 6^{5} Is 53^{8} (prob.), 57^{12} Je 23^{33} (but rd. rather with 𝔊 𝔙 אַתֶּם הַמַּשָּׂא) 27^{8} 36^{22} 38^{16} Kt, 45^{4b} Ez 16^{22} 17^{21} 20^{16} 29^{4b} 43^{7} (𝔊 Co prefix הַרְאִיתָ) 44^{3} Zc 8^{17} Ec 4^{3} Dn 9^{13} Ne $9^{19.34}$ 1 Ch 2^{9} 2 Ch 31^{17}. In 1 S 30^{23} Hg 2^{5} prob. some such word as *remember* is to be understood. (*β*) Je 38^{9} Ez 14^{22b} 37^{19b} Zc 12^{10}; סָבִיב אֶת 1 K 6^{5} Ez 43^{17} strangely (in 1 K 𝔊 om. the clause: so Sta ZAW 1883, 135).—In 1 K 11^{1} וְ is merely *and also, and especially* (v. וְ); v^{25} is corrupt (rd. with 𝔊 וזאת הָרָעָה אֲשֶׁר עָשָׂה הֲדַד); Ez $47^{17.18.19}$ rd. similarly for וְאֵת, זֹאת: see v^{20}.—For some particulars as to the use of את, see A. M. Wilson[Hbr. vi. 139 ff. 212 ff.] (who, however, confuses it sts. with II. אֵת). For denoting the pron. obj. of a vb., את with suff. preponderates relatively much above the verbal affix in P, as compared with JE Dt Ju S K (v. Giesebrecht ZAW 1881, 258 f.),—partly, probably, on account of the greater distinctness and precision which P loves.

II. **אֵת**, **prep.** with—with makk. אֶת־, with 854
suff. אִתִּי, אִתְּךָ, אִתְּכֶם etc. (also, however, אוֹתְךָ, אוֹתוֹ, and similarly מֵאוֹתְךָ, מֵאוֹתוֹ etc.), first in Jos 10^{25} 14^{12}, next 2 S 24^{24}; then repeatedly (but not exclusively) 1 K 20–2 K 8, & in Je Ez, e.g. 1 K 20^{25} (but v^{23} אִתָּם) $22^{7.8.24}$ (beside מֵאִתִּי) 2 K 1^{15} $3^{11.12.26}$ 6^{16} (beside מֵאִתּוֹ) 8^{8} Je 2^{35} 10^{5} 16^{8} 19^{10} 20^{11} Ez 2^{6} 10^{17} 23^{23} 37^{26} (v. infr. **1 d**; also Is 59^{21}, contr. Gn 17^{4}: on שָׁכַב אֹתָהּ Gn 34^{2} al., v. sub שָׁכַב, & cf. Dr[Sm ii. 13, 14]) prep. denoting **proximity** (syn. עִם; Ph. את, e.g. CIS[i. 3, 8] לא יכן לם משכב את רפאם let there not be for them a resting-place *with* the shades; As. *itti* (perh. akin to *ittu* 'side,' Dl[Pr 115] Hpt KAT[2. 498]; but cf. Nö[ZMG '86, 738 f.]). Not found as yet in the other cogn. languages: but cf. Eth. **እንተ፡** *'enta*, towards, which supports the view that אֵת is for *'int* [cf. תַּחַת, תַּחְתִּי], perh. from √אנה *to meet* Ol[p. 431] Prät[ZMG '73, 643], Lag[M i. 226]).

1. Of companionship, *together with*: Gn 6^{13} behold, I destroy them אֶת־הָאָרֶץ *together with* the earth, 11^{31} 12^{4} + oft., esp. with *verbs of* dwelling, abiding, going, etc., as Ju 1^{3} 14^{11} 19^{4}, & in the phrase הָעָם אֲשֶׁר אִתּוֹ Ju 4^{13} 7^{1} $9^{33.48}$ 1 S 14^{20} 30^{4} etc.; thou, and thy sons.... אִתָּךְ *with thee* Gn 6^{18}; similarly (3rd pers.) $7^{7.13}$ 8^{18} 9^{8} al. (charact. of P: Dr[Intr 124]); הִתְהַלֵּךְ אֶת־הָאֱלֹהִים to walk *with* God, i.e. to have him as a companion (sc. by adopting a course of life pleasing to him) Gn $5^{22.24}$ 6^{9} (cf. הִתְהַלֵּךְ אֵת lit. 1 S 25^{15}); —*by the side of, like* Is 45^{9}, *equally with* Lv 26^{39}, *in common with* Je 23^{28b} (cf. עִם **1 e**, **f**). Hence, in partic.—**a.** *with* for the purpose of help: Nu 14^{9} וי׳ אִתָּנוּ, Jos 14^{12} (אוֹתִי, as Je 20^{11}) Ju 1^{19} 2 K 6^{16} 9^{32} מִי אִתִּי מִי who is *on my side*, who?

אֲנִי כִּי אִתְּךָ Is 43^5 Je 1$^{18.19}$+; Is 63^3 ψ 12^5 our lips are *with us, on our side;* in the phrase (הָיְתָה) יַד פ׳ אֶת 2 S 14^{19} 2 K 15^{19} Je 26^{24}; נָשָׂא אֵת to bear *together with,* i.e. to assist Ex 18^{22} Nu 11^{17}. Exceptionally, = *with the help of:* Gn 4^1 for I have gotten a man אֶת־י׳ *with the help of* י׳ (cf. עִם 1 S 14^{45}) 49^{25} (where, however, the parallelism, & 𝔊 𝔖 Sam. favour וְאֵל שַׁדַּי for (וְאֵת שַׁדַּי) Mi 3^8; cf. Est 9^{29}. **b.** *beside* (Germ. *neben*): Gn 39^6 לֹא יָדַע אִתּוֹ מְאוּמָה he knew not *with* him, *beside* him, aught (i.e. Joseph managed everything), v^8 Ex 20^{23} לֹא תַעֲשׂוּן אִתִּי ye shall not make (aught) *beside* me. **c.** *beside* = *in the presence of* (rare): Gn 20^{16b} and *before* all thou shalt be righted, Is 30^8 Mi 6^1. In this sense אֶת־פְּנֵי פ׳ is more freq., v. sub פָּנִים. **d.** of intercourse of different kinds *with* another, e.g. after verbs of making a covenant or contract, or (less often) of speaking or dealing: (*a*) Gn 9^9 15^{18} 17^4 (Ez 16^{60} Is 59^{21} אוֹת-) Jos 10^4 1 K 3^1 etc.; cf. 1 S 2^{13} (but here הַכֹּהֵן מֵאֵת is prob. to be read with 𝔊 𝔖 𝔗 Ke We etc., cf. Dt 18^3). (*β*) Gn 17^3 42^{30} דִּבֶּר אִתָּנוּ קָשׁוֹת, 1 K 8^{15} ψ 109^2, & esp. in Je and Ez (as Je 1^{16} 4^{12} [52^9 אִתּוֹ] 5^5 12^1; Ez 2^1 3$^{22.24.27}$ 14^4 44^5—all אוֹת-); Gn 24^{49} to perform kindness אֵת (עִם is here more genl.), 2 S 16^{17} זֶה חַסְדְּךָ אֶת־רֵעֶךָ, Ru 2^{20} Zc 7^9; Ju 11^{27} וְאַתָּה עֹשֶׂה אִתִּי רָעָה, Dt 1^{30} 10^{21} 1 S 12^{7b}, (אוֹת-) Je 21^2 33^9 Ez 7^{27} 16^{59} 22^{14} 23$^{25.29}$ 39^{24}; abs. Ez 17^{17} 20^{44} ψ 109^{21} Zp 3^{19}; (*γ*) in a pregn. sense, (in dealing) *with*, i.e. *towards* (rare): Is 66^{14} ψ 67^2 יָאֵר פָּנָיו אִתָּנוּ make his face to shine *with* (=toward) us (varied from אֶל Nu 6^{25}) Dt 28^8; faithful *with* ψ 78^8 (cf. v^{37} נָכוֹן עִם); Ez 2^6 (אוֹתָךְ); Ju 16^{15} וְלִבְּךָ אֵין אִתִּי. (*δ*) often with verbs of fighting, striving, contending, as Gn 14$^{2.8.9}$ Nu 20^{13} Is 45^{9a} 50^8 ψ 35^1 Pr 23^{11}; with בָּא בְמִשְׁפָּט ψ 143^2 (Is 3^{14} al. עִם).

2. Of localities, esp. in the phrase אֲשֶׁר אֵת describing a site: Ju 3^{19} 4^{11} אֲשֶׁר אֶת־קֶדֶשׁ which is *near* Kedesh, 1 K 9^{26} 2 K 9^{27} (cf. עִם **2**, which is commoner in this sense); Ez 43^8; Ex 33^{21} הִנֵּה מָקוֹם אִתִּי. Perh., anomalously, 1 S 7^{16} *at* or *by* all those places (but v. Dr); in 2 S 15^{23} עַל־פְּנֵי דֶרֶךְ אֶת־הַמִּדְבָּר, אֵת = *towards* is against anal.: rd. with 𝔊L עַל־פָּנָיו דֶּרֶךְ הַזַּיִת אֲשֶׁר בַּמִּדְבָּר; 1 K 9^{25} אִתּוֹ *beside* it (sc. the altar); but עָלָיו 13^1 etc. would be idiomatic, & for אִתּוֹ אֲשֶׁר Klo proposes plausibly אֶת־אִשּׁוֹ (v. Ex 30^{20}).

3. אֵת פ׳ denotes specially, **a.** in one's possession or keeping: Gn 27^{15} 30^{29} thou knowest אֵת אֲשֶׁר הָיָה מִקְנְךָ אִתִּי ... how thy cattle fared *with* me, v^{33} Lv 5^{23} 19^{13} Dt 15^3 Ju 17^2 1 S 9^7 מָה אִתָּנוּ = what *have we?* 25^{29} Is 49^4 my right is *with* Jehovah (contr. 40^{27}), Je 8^8 ψ 38^{11} the light of mine eyes also אֵין אִתִּי i.e. is gone from me, Pr 3^{28} 8^{18}; in his power, Je 10^5 הֵיטֵיב אֵין אוֹתָם is not *in their power*, perh. ψ 12^5. A dream, or the word of י׳, is said to be אֵת *with* a prophet, 2 K 3^{12} Je 23^{28} 27^{18}. Metaph. of a mental quality, Pr 11^2 13^{10}. **b.** in one's knowledge or memory: Is 59^{12} פְּשָׁעֵינוּ אִתָּנוּ our transgressions are *with us*, i.e. present to our minds (וַעֲוֹנֹתֵינוּ יְדַעֲנוּם ‖), Jb 12^3 אֶת־מִי־אֵין כְּמוֹ־אֵלֶּה *with* whom are not (i.e. who *knoweth* not? τίς οὐ σύνοιδε;) things like these? 14^5 אִתָּךְ i.e. known to thee, Pr 2^1 Gn 40^{14} Je 12^3 (Ew Gf *towards* thee, as **1 d** γ). So אִם־יֵשׁ אֶת־נַפְשְׁכֶם Gn 23^8 [2 K 9^{15} נ׳ alone], אֶת־לְבָבְךָ 2 K 10^{15}. Comp. עִם **4 b**, which is more frequent in this sense.

4. מֵאֵת (מֵאִתִּי, etc.; also מֵאוֹת-, v. p. 85) *from proximity with* (like Gk. παρά with a genit., Fr. *de chez;* in Syr. Arab. ܡܢ ܥܡ, ܠܘܬ, مِنْ عِنْدَ correspond. Synon. מֵעִם; see below): coupled almost always with *persons* (contrast מֵעִם, **a**). Thus **a.** with קָנָה to buy Gn 25^{10} + oft. (cf. 17^{27}); לָקַח Gn 42^{24} Ex 25^2 Lv 25^{36} Nu 17^{17} + oft.; נָשָׂא ψ 24^5; שִׁלַּח, as Gn 8^8 וַיְשַׁלַּח אֶת־הַיּוֹנָה מֵאִתּוֹ and he sent forth the dove *from with him* 26^{27}; הָלַךְ Gn 26^{31} 1 K 18^{12} 20^{36} Je 9^1, of a wife deserting her husband Ju 19^2 וַתֵּלֶךְ מֵאִתּוֹ, Je 3^1 (cf. Is 57^8); with sim. words Gn 38^1 Dt 2^8 1 K 11^{23} Je 2^{37} (v. Ex 5^{20}); Is 54^{10} ψ 66^{20}; with שָׁאַל Ju 1^{14} 1 K 2^{16} ψ 27^4+, דָּרַשׁ 1 K 22^7 al., שָׁמַע 1 S 2^{23}.— מֵאֵת פְּנֵי פ׳ Gn 27^{30} 43^{34} Ex 10^{11} Jb 2^7; Lv 10^4 (הַקֹּדֶשׁ), 2 K 16^{14} (הַבַּיִת). Hence **b.** of rights or dues, handed over *from*, given *on the part of*, any one: Gn 47^{22} חֹק מֵאֵת פַּרְעֹה; oft. in P, as Gn 23^{20} Ex 27^{21} a perpetual due מֵאֵת בְּנֵי יִשְׂרָאֵל *from*, or *on the part of*, the children of Israel, Lv 7^{34b} 24^8 Nu 3^9 7^{84}+; Dt 18^3 1 S 2^{13} (𝔊, etc.; v. **1 d**) 2 S 15^3 וְשֹׁמֵעַ אֵין־לְךָ מֵאֵת הַמֶּלֶךְ but there is none to hear thee *deputed of* the king, 1 K 5^{14}. **c.** expressing origination: 1 K 1^{27} אִם מֵאֵת אֲדֹנִי הַמֶּלֶךְ נִהְיָה. Esp. מֵאֵת י׳—of a concrete object proceeding *from* him: Gn 19^{24} (brimstone), Nu 11^{31} (a wind), 16^{35} (fire), 1 S 16^{14} (evil spirit), Is 38^7 (a sign), Je 51^{53} (wasters), Mi 5^6 (dew); of wrath Zc 7^{12} (cf. Nu 17^{11}), teaching Is 51^4, the word of prophecy Je 7^1 (so 11^1 18^1 + oft. in Je) 37^{17} Ez 33^{30}; with 'have I (we) heard' Is 21^{10} 28^{22} Je 49^{14} (=Ob^1); of an event, or phase of history Jos 11^{20} מֵאֵת י׳ הָיְתָה *it came of* י׳ to . . ., 1 K 12^{24} Hb 2^{13} ψ 118^{23} מֵאֵת י׳ הָיְתָה זֹּאת (𝔊 παρὰ Κυρίου) Ezr 9^8 Ne 6^{16}; of trouble (רָעָה) 2 K 6^{33} Mi 1^{12} (יָרַד); of a good or evil lot, having its source in י׳ Je 13[25] Is 54[17] ψ 109[20], cf. Jb 2[10]; ψ 22[26] מֵאִתְּךָ תְהִלָּתִי *from thee* cometh my praise (thou art the source of it); Is 44[24] Qr מֵאִתִּי *of myself* (cf. ἀπ᾽ ἐμαυτοῦ John 5[30]; Kt is מִי אִתִּי who was with me?), 54[15] אֶפֶס מֵאוֹתִי not *at my instance* (cf. לֹא מִנִּי 30[1], לֹא מִמֶּנִּי Ho 8[4]). **d.** of a place †1 K 6[33] (corrupt: rd. with 𝔊 𝔖 𝔙 [partly] מְזוּזוֹת רְבֻעוֹת, & cf. Ez 41[21]).

Note. אֵת expresses closer association than עִם: hence while מֵעִם sts. denotes hardly more than *from the surroundings* or *belongings of*, מֵאֵת expresses *from close proximity to*. Thus Saul asks, מִי הָלַךְ מֵעִמָּנוּ who has gone *from* (those) *about* us? but Jacob, speaking of the loss of Joseph, says, Gn 44[28] וַיֵּצֵא הָאֶחָד מֵאִתִּי and the one is gone *from with* me. מֵאֵת is accordingly preferred to מֵעִם in the sense of origination or authorship; מאת is not usual in the sense of מֵעִם **c**, nor מֵעִם in the sense of מֵאֵת **b**.

856 †אֶתְבַּ֫עַל **n.pr.m. Ethbaal** (*with Baal,* i.e. living under B.'s favour; Ἰθόβαλος, Εἰθώβαλος Jos[Ant. viii. 13, 1. 2, c. Ap. 1, 18]; on later king of like name, in As. *Tuba'lu*, v. COT Gn 10[15]) king of Sidon, father of Jezebel 1 K 16[31].

863 †אִתַּי **n.pr.m.** (perh. from אֵת *with*=*companionable*)—**1.** one of David's captains, a native of Gath 2 S 15[19.21.22.22] 18[2.5.12]. **2.** one of David's 30 mighty men, a Benjamite 2 S 23[29] (in 1 Ch 11[31] אִתַי).

384 †אִיתִיאֵל **1.** Pr 30[1.1] נְאֻם הַגֶּבֶר לְאִיתִיאֵל לְאִיתִיאֵל וְאֻכָל:, in MT. **n.pr.m.** (prob. *with me is God:* v. Ol[§ 82 c]) usually taken as name of a son or pupil of Agur; but most moderns read לָאִיתִי אֵל לָאִיתִי אֵל וָאֵכֶל: *I have wearied myself* (v. לָאָה), *O God, I have wearied myself, O God, and am consumed.* **2.** a Benjamite Ne 11[7].

855 III. אֵת v. אתת. p. 88

859 אַתְּ, אַתִּי, אַתְּ, אַתָּה v. sub אנת. p. 61

857 †אָתָה **vb.** come (in Heb. only poet.) (Ar. أَتَى, Sab. אתו DHM[ZMG 1875, 597; 1883, 343], Aram. אֲתָא, ܐܬܐ)—**Qal** *Pf.* 'א Dt 33[2]; אָתָא Is 21[12] v. Ges[§ 75 R. 22]; 1 pl. אָתָנוּ Je 3[22]; *Impf.* יֶאֱתֶה Jb 37[22] Pr 1[27]; וַיֵּתֵא Dt 33[21] (=וַיֶּאֱתֶה cf. Di Kö[i. 577]), וַיֵּאת Is 41[25]; sf. יְאֶתָיֵנִי Jb 3[25]; 3 fs. תֵּאתֶה Mi 4[8]; 3 mpl. יֶאֱתָיוּ Jb 16[22]+2 t.; וַיֶּאֱתָיוּן Is 41[5]; *Imv.* mpl. אֵתָיוּ Is 21[12]+2 t.; *Pt.* fpl. אֹתִיּוֹת Is 41[23]+2 t.;—*come*, of men Dt 33[21] ψ 68[32] Is 41[25] 56[12] *Imv.*=*come now,* with hostile purpose Jb 30[14], of men unto י׳ Je 3[22] (sq. לְ) cf. Is 21[12]; of י׳ Dt 33[2]; of ends of earth, etc., personif. Is 41[5]; of time, morning Is 21[12], years Jb 16[22]; of weather Jb 37[22]; of beasts, to devour Is 56[9] (sq. inf.), of calamity Pr 1[27] Jb 3[25] *come upon*, c. sf., of dominion Mi 4[8] (sq. עַד). *Pt.* pl. fem. as subst. *things to come*, future things Is 41[23] 44[7] 45[11]. **Hiph.** *bring, Imv.* הֵתָיוּ מַיִם Is 21[14] *bring water* (on form, for הֵאֱתוּ cf. Di Ew[§ 141 a] Ges[§ 68, 2 R. 1]); Je 12[9] *bring beasts*, to devour.

†אִיתוֹן Qr, יאתון Kt, **n.m. entrance,** 2978
הָיִאתוֹן Ez 40[15]; Co rds. אתיון; cf. Sm Ol[§ 215 d]. 2978

אִיתִי, אִתַּי, אִיתִיאֵל v. sub II. אֵת.

†אֵתָם **n.pr.loc.** (perh.=Egypt. *Chetem,* 864
cf. Ebers[GS 521 f.] but 𝔊 Ὀθομ, Ὀθωμ, cf. Lag[BN 54]) Ex 13[20] in Egypt, place on edge of desert, so Nu 33[6.7]; מִדְבַּר אֵתָם Nu 33[8].

אַתֶּם v. sub אנת. p. 61 859

אֶתְמוֹל v. sub תמל. p. 1069 865

אתן (mng.? Thes comps. Ar. أَتَنَ *take short steps*, but this appy. only by-form of أَتَلَ).

†אָתוֹן **n.f.** [Gn 45, 23] **she-ass** (Ar. أَتَانٌ, Aram. 860
אֲתָנָא, ܐܬܢܐ, As. *atânu*)—אָתוֹן Nu 22[23]+10 t.; אֲתֹנְךָ Nu 22[30.32]; אֲתֹנוֹ Gn 49[11]+2 t.; pl. abs. אֲתֹנֹת Gn 12[16]+2 t.; אֲתֹנוֹת Ju 5[10]+12 t.; אתונות Jb 1[3] 42[12];—**she-ass**, as dam Gn 49[11] Zc 9[9]; as property (constituting wealth) Gn 12[16] 32[16] Jb 1[3.14] 42[12] cf. 1 Ch 27[30]; so of the asses of Kish 8 t. 1 S 9[3.3.5.20] 10[2.2.14.16]; as beasts of burden Gn 45[23]; for riding Ju 5[10] Nu 22[21.22] 2 K 4[22.24]; of Balaam's ass 14 t. Nu 22[21.22.23.23.23.25.27.27.28.29.30.30.32.33].

אַתֶּן, אַתֵּנָה v. sub אנת. p. 61 859

אֶתְנָה v. תנה. p. 1071 868

†אֶתְנִי **n.pr.m.** an ancestor of Asaph 1 Ch 6[26] 867
apparently identical with יְאָתְרַי v[6].

אֶתְנַן v. II. תנן. p. 1072 868

†[אתוק] **n.m. gallery, porch** (deriv. un- 862
certain) Ez 41[15] Kt ואתוקיהא, Qr וְאַתִּיקֶיהָא, Co (q.v.) וקירותיה.

†אַתִּיק **n.m.** *id.* Ez 42[3.3]; pl. אַתִּיקִים Ez 42[5]; 862
41[15] Qr, v. אתוק Kt; v[16] הָאַתִּיקִים (Co del.)

†אֲתָרִים **n.pr.loc.** only Nu 21[1] דֶּרֶךְ הָא׳; so 871
𝔊, perh. (Di) name of a caravan-route, cf. أَثَرٌ *vestige, footprint;* others (after 𝔗𝔖) transl. *way of the spies* (cf. 13[22]); but הָאֲתָרִים for הַתָּרִים is highly improbable, and a locality would hardly receive its designation from the spies.

אתת (? √of following, meaning dubious. Lag$^{M\ ii.\ 254}$ proposes √אנה, whence he derives also Ar. مَأْنٌ a tool used in tillage).

855 †III. [**אֵת**] **n.**[**m.**] a cutting instrument of iron, usually transl. **ploughshare**—sg. sf. אִתּוֹ 1 S 13^{20}; pl. אִתִּים 1 S 13^{21}, אִתִּים Is 2^{4}=Mi 4^{3}; sf. אִתֵּיכֶם Jo 4^{10}; acc. to Klo al. also 2 K 6^{5} אֶת־הַבַּרְזֶל, i.e. *the axe of iron.*

ב

ב, בּ, *Bêth,* 2nd letter; post B Heb.=numeral 2 (and so in margin of printed MT); בּ̈=2000; no evidence of this usage in OT times.

I. **בְּ, prep. in** (Moab. ב, Syr. ܒ, Ar. بِ, Eth. በ፡) before tone-syllables in certain cases (Ges $^{§\ 102.\ 2}$) בָּ, with suff. בִּי; בְּךָ (Ex 7^{29} 2 S 22^{30} ψ 141^{8} בְּכָה), in pause and fem. בָּךְ; בּוֹ (once, Je 17^{24} Kt בֹּה), בָּהּ; בָּנוּ; בָּכֶם, [בָּכֶן]; בָּם, בָּהֶם [also בָּהֵמָּה †Ex 30^{4} 36^{1} Hb 1^{16}], בָּהֶן †1 S 31^{7} Is 38^{16} Ez 42^{14} [15 times בָּהֵן (Fr$^{MM\ 235}$), and thrice, Lv 5^{22} Nu 13^{19} Je 5^{17}, בָּהֵנָּה]. Prep. denoting properly *in,* Gk. ἐν, but applied in many derived and fig. significations. The senses expressed by בְּ are grouped by the Rabbis in three classes, בֵּית הַכְּלִי *Beth vasculi,* בֵּית הַדִּיבּוּק וְהַנְּגִיעָה *Beth coniunctionis et viciniae,* בֵּית הָעֵזֶר *Beth auxilii;* and the same arrangement may be followed here, though the limits between the three classes are not clearly defined, and they sometimes overlap one another.

I. *In:* **1.** strictly, of position *in* a place (which often is expressed more precisely by בְּתוֹךְ, בְּקֶרֶב), as בַּבַּיִת *in* the house, בָּעִיר *in* the city, בַּדּוּד *in* the pot, בָּאָרֶץ *in* the land, etc. constantly. Heb. idiom also says בָּהָר *in* the mountain Ex 24^{18} etc., even in cases where we could hardly avoid saying *on,* as 1 K 11^{7} 19^{11}: so בֶּחָרֶב Dt 1^{16} al.; בְּרֹאשׁ הָהָר Ex 24^{17} ψ 72^{16}. Preceded by a verb of motion (esp. עָבַר) בְּ=*through,* as Gn 12^{6} and Abram passed through בָּאָרֶץ *in* the land=passed through it, 13^{17} 2 S 24^{2}+; *in* (=*through*) a gate, Is 62^{10} Je 17^{19} Mi 2^{13}. Fig. to speak בְּאָזְנֵי *in* the ears of...; to be good (*or* evil, etc.) בְּעֵינֵי *in* the eyes of... **2.** of presence in the midst of a multitude, *among,* Ex 14^{28} there was not left בָּהֶם *among* them even one, Lv 26^{36} 2 S 15^{31} Ahitophel בַּקֹּשְׁרִים is *among* the conspirators, 2 K 18^{5} בְּכֹל מַלְכֵי יְהוּדָה. So בְּךָ *in* thee (of Israel, coll.) Dt 7^{14} 15$^{4.7}$ 18^{10} 23^{11} 28^{54} (diff. from עִמְּךָ *beside* thee Lv 25^{35}).—Spec. **a.** of an individ., implying eminency among: Jos 14^{15} Je 46^{18} Tabor *among* the mountains, 49^{15} Pr 30^{30} Ct 1^{8} הַיָּפָה בַּנָּשִׁים the fair one (=the fairest) *among* women, La 1^{1}: cf. Luke 1^{42}. On 1 S 17^{12} v. Dr. **b.** hence with some verbs, when the action refers to only a part of the object, as הִכָּה בְּ to smite *among*... i.e. to smite some of... (diff. from הִכָּה with accus.); הָרַג בְּ ψ 78^{31}; נָשָׂא בְּ to bear *in,* i.e. to share in bearing, Nu 11^{17} al.; בָּנָה בְּ to build *in* or *at* Zc 6^{15} Ne 4^{4}; עָשָׂה בְּ Ex 5^{9}; עָמֵל בְּ to labour *on* Jon 4^{10}; אָכַל בְּ, שָׁתָה בְּ to eat or drink *of* Ju 13^{16} Pr 9^{5}; חָלַק בְּ to give a share *in* Jb 39^{17}. **c.** specifying the parts of which a whole consists (esp. in P) Gn 7^{21} 8^{17} 9$^{10.16}$ 17^{23} Ex 12^{19} Nu 31$^{11.26}$ Ho 4^{3}. **3.** with ref. to the limits enclosing a space, *within:* Ex 20^{10} בִּשְׁעָרֶיךָ *within* thy gates, Is 56^{5} בְּחוֹמֹתַי *within* my walls. **4.** often pregn. with verbs of motion, when the movement *to* a place results in rest *in* it, *into:* after בָּא בְּ Gn 19^{8} Is 19^{23}; נָתַן Gn 27^{17}; שָׁלַח *to send* Lv 16^{22}; *in among* Jos 23$^{7.12}$ 1 K 11^{2}.—Ho 12^{7} (an extreme case) שׁוּב בְּ to return (and rest) *in* thy God, 1 S 16^{3} (unless לִזְבֹּחַ should be read, as v^{7}).—עַיִן בְּעַיִן (with) eye (looking) *into* eye †Nu 14^{14} Is 52^{8}; פָּנִים בְּפָנִים †Dt 5^{4}; עֵינֵי פ׳ בְּ the eyes of... are *upon,* both in favourable (Dt 11^{12} ψ 101^{6}) and hostile (Am 9^{8} Jb 7^{8}) sense. **5.** applied to *time,* as Gn 1^{1} בְּרֵאשִׁית *in* the beginning; 2^{2} בַּיּוֹם הַשְּׁבִיעִי *on* the seventh day; Ju 10^{8} בַּשָּׁנָה הַהִיא *in* that year; & constantly. **6.** of a state or condition, whether material or mental, *in* which an action takes place: so oft., בְּשָׁלוֹם *in* peace Gn 15^{15}; בַּצָּרָה *in* distress ψ 91^{15}; הָלַךְ בְּתֻמּוֹ to walk *in* his integrity; Ex 5^{19} בְּרָע *in* evil case. **7.** בְּ introduces the *predicate,* denoting it as that *in* which the subj. consists, or *in* which it shews itself (the *Beth essentiae,*—common in Arabic, esp. with a ptcp. or adj. and in a negative sentence: Qor 2^{79} وَمَا ٱللّٰهُ بِغَافِلٍ and God (appears) not *as* one remiss; 2^{7} وَمَا هُمْ بِمُؤْمِنِينَ and they are not believers [comp. French *en*—*en honnête homme*]; v. W$^{AG\ ii.\ §\ 56\ a}$): viz. **a.** a primary pred., Ex 18^{4} the God of my fathers בְּעֶזְרִי was my help, ψ 146^{5} Ho 13^{9} (rd. כִּי מִי בְעֶזְרֶךָ: with 𝔊 𝔖 Che al.); ψ 68^{5} בְּיָהּ שְׁמוֹ his name consists in Yah, Jb 23^{13} 37^{10}. With the pred. in the pl. (as *pl. maj.*) ψ 118^{7} י׳ בְּעֹזְרָי J. is my great helper, 54[6] (v. Che), Ju 11[35]. **b.** a secondary pred., Ex 6[3] and I appeared unto them בְּאֵל שַׁדָּי *as* God Almighty, Nu 26[53] בְּנַחֲלָה *as* an inheritance, 34[2] Ez 46[16] 47[14] Dt 10[22] 26[14] I have not put away therefrom בְּטָמֵא *as* one unclean=while unclean, 28[62] Is 40[10] בְּחָזָק יָבוֹא he cometh *as* a strong one, ψ 35[2] (where v. De) and rise up *as* my help, v[16], 39[7] 55[19] Pr 3[26] Jb 36[32](De). **c.** a pred. as accus., Is 48[10] I have refined thee וְלֹא בְכֶסֶף but not *as though* silver, Ez 20[41]; Nu 18[26] 36[2] Jos 13[6.7] 23[4] Ez 45[1] 47[22.22] (rd. יַפִּלוּ) 48[29] (v. 𝔊 Co) all בְּנַחֲלָה (cf. **b**), ψ 78[55] & allotted it בְּחֶבֶל נַחֲלָה *as* a line of inheritance (i.e. as a measured inheritance). Is 26[4] כִּי בְּיָהּ יהוה צוּר עוֹלָמִים י׳ is different—for *in* Yah there is a rock of ages (cf. Qor 4[7.47] there is sufficiency *in* God as a patron). **d.** in comparisons, ψ 37[20] consume away בֶעָשָׁן *in the form of, as,* smoke 78[33] 102[4] Jb 34[36] 36[14].

II. Denoting proximity—**1.** *at, by* (not very common): 1 S 29[1] בָּעַיִן *by* the spring; Ez 10[15.20] בִּנְהַר כְּבָר *by* the river Chebar (1[3] עַל). **2.** *on:* Gn 8[20] Nu 23[2] בַּמִּזְבֵּחַ *on* the altar; Ju 8[21] *on* the necks of the camels; 1 K 2[5] al. בְּמָתְנָיו *on* his loins; Is 59[17] a helmet בְּרֹאשׁוֹ *on* his head. **3.** often with verbs of *touching, approaching, taking hold of, cleaving,* etc., as תָּפַשׂ, תָּמַךְ, פָּגַע, קָרַב, נָגַשׁ, נָגַע, חָשַׁק, דָּבַק, אָחַז (see these words). **4.** with words expressing or implying an act of hostility—**a.** *against:* Gn 16[12] יָדוֹ בַכֹּל וְיַד כֹּל בּוֹ his hand *against* all, and the hand of all *against* him; הָיְתָה יַד פּ׳ בּ Dt 13[10] 1 S 5[9] 18[17]+oft. Hence after verbs (q.v.) of *fighting* (רִיב, נִלְחַם), *going up* to invade (עָלָה), *being angry* (חָרָה אַף, אָנַף, הִתְעַבֵּר), *sinning* or *acting treacherously* (מָרַד, בָּגַד, חָטָא, כִּחֵשׁ, כִּזֵּב, שִׁקֵּר, פָּשַׁע, מָעַל, מָרָה), *testifying* (עָנָה, הֵעִיד), *mocking* (הֵתֵל, הִלְעִיג), *feeling loathing* (קוּץ), *rebuking* (גָּעַר: prop. to protest loudly), *speaking* (דִּבֶּר: Nu 12[8b]), etc., & even (an extreme case) Ho 7[14] יָסוּרוּ בִי they turn aside (so as to be) *against* me. In a weaker sense מַשְׁתִּין בַּקִּיר mingens *ad* parietem 1 S 25[22] al. **b.** *down to, upon* (*super* with accus.), esp. in such phrases as דָּמָיו בּוֹ Lv 20[9] al. his blood be *upon* him; דָּמוֹ בְרֹאשׁוֹ his blood be *upon* his head Jos 2[19]; שׁוּב (הֵשִׁיב י׳) בְּרֹאשׁוֹ Ju 8[57] (רָעָה), 1 K 2[33] (דָּם), v[44] (רָעָה), ψ 7[17] (עֲמָלוֹ); נָתַן דֶּרֶךְ פּ׳ בְּרֹאשׁוֹ 1 K 8[32] & oft. in Ez, as 9[10] 11[21].

III. 1. *With*—**a.** of accompaniment: Nu 20[20] בְּעַם כָּבֵד *with* much people, Jos 22[8] Ju 11[34] 1 K 10[2] 2 K 5[9] Je 41[15]; Ex 21[22] and he shall give בִּפְלִלִים *with arbitrators* (arbitrators being employed), Is 8[16] בְּלִמֻּדָי׃ *with* my disciples, i.e. having them present; Ex 8[1.13] Je 11[19] עֵץ בְּלַחְמוֹ a tree *with* its sap; 1 K 19[19] וְהוּא בִּשְׁנֵים הֶעָשָׂר and he *with* the 12th. **b.** often of what one takes or brings with one: Gn 32[11] בְּמַקְלִי *with* my staff I passed over Jordan, Ju 11[34] 15[1] 1 S 1[24], Is 7[24]; Mi 6[6] al. קִדֵּם בְּ to go to meet *with;* בָּא בְּ to come *with* Lv 16[3] ψ 66[13] 71[16]. (In Arabic this usage is developed more fully than in Hebrew, and أَتَى بِ lit. *to come with,* ذَهَبَ بِ lit. *to go away with,* are used idiomatically in the sense of *to bring,* and *to take away* respectively: W[AG ii. §56b].) Hence בְּאֵין, בְּלֹא, בִּבְלִי, בְּאֶפֶס=*without.* **c.** of concomitant (or surrounding) conditions, as בְּחִפָּזוֹן *with* (or *in*) haste; בְּצֶדֶק *with* (or *in*) righteousness; בִּשְׁגָגָה *in* error; בִּתְרוּעָה וּבְקוֹל שׁוֹפָר 2 S 6[15]; often in such phrases as בְּצִדְקָתְךָ ψ 31[2] *in* thy righteousness; בְּחַסְדְּךָ *in* thy mercy Ex 15[13];—בְּאָשְׁרִי *with* my happiness!=happy am I Gn 30[13]; ψ 29[4] the voice of י׳ is בַּכֹּחַ *with* power=is powerful; Ex 32[12] בְּרָעָה *with* evil purpose; ψ 73[8] בְּרָע *in* wickedness; 90[10] בִּגְבוּרֹת *with* strength. **2.** of the instrument or means: as **a.** בַּחֶרֶב *with* the sword Ex 5[3] etc.; בְּרַגְלַיִם *with* the feet Is 28[3]; בְּיַד ... *by* the hand of... (v. sub יָד); to stone בָּאֶבֶן or בָּאֲבָנִים *with* stones Lv 20[2] Nu 14[10] etc.; שָׁתָה בְּ to drink *with* a cup Gn 44[5] Am 6[6] (cf. in Aram. Dn 5[2]); to cry בְּגָרוֹן *with* the throat Is 58[1]; to burn בָּאֵשׁ *in* or *with* fire (oft.); to slay or to perish בָּרָעָב *through* hunger or בַּדֶּבֶר *through* pestilence Ex 16[3] Je 21[9]+oft. (cf. Jb 27[15] בַּמָּוֶת יִקָּבֵרוּ); to save *with* or *by* Ju 7[7] 1 S 14[6]. **b.** idiom., with certain verbs, as שִׂחֵק בְּ to play *with* Jb 40[29]; עָבַד בְּ to labour *with* a person (as with an instrument), i.e. to use him as a slave Ex 1[14] Je 22[13] 27[7] al.; עָשָׂה בְּ Je 18[23] Ne 9[24] Dn 11[7] Est 1[15] 2[11] 3[11] 6[6]; & perh. דִּבֶּר בְּ (of God) to speak *with* one Nu 12[2.8a] al. (v. Ew[§ 217 f. (3)]; Dr[Sm ii. 23, 2]). Further הִתְנַבֵּא ביהוה, בַּבַּעַל to prophesy *with* or *by* י׳ or Baal, י׳ or Baal being the inspirer; דָּרַשׁ, שָׁאַל בְּ to inquire or ask *by means of* a god (or oracle). **c.** ביהוה *through* י׳ (=by His aid) in many connexions, as ψ 18[30] 44[6] 56[5.11] 60[14] Is 26[13] 45[25] Ho 1[7] Zc 10[12]; with pass. verbs Dt 33[29] Is 45[17] (to be saved): and even of the immediate cause Nu 36[2] to be commanded ביהוה *by* י׳, Gn 9[6] בָּאָדָם *by* man shall his blood be shed (both unusual), Ho 14[4]. **d.** allied is the use of בְּ in such phrases as to bless, swear, speak, prophesy, etc., בְּשֵׁם *in* the name of ... (i.e. the name being used or appealed to in the act) Dt 6^{13} Je 11^{21}, etc. (so to swear ביהוה *by* י׳ Jos 2^{12} etc., בִּימִינוֹ Is 62^{8}; to bless בְּךָ *with thee* Gn 48^{20}, to swear *with me* ψ 102^{9}, i.e. using my name in oath, Je 29^{22}); almost = in the authority and power of 1 S 17^{45} 25^{5} 1 K 21^{8} Mi 4^{5} Zc 10^{12} ψ 20^{6} 44^{6} 89^{25}. **e.** בַּמָּה or בַּמֶּה *by means of what? how?* Gn 15^{8} Ju 6^{15} 16$^{5.6.10}$ 1 K 22^{21} Mal 2^{17}. בְּזֹאת *by means of this* Gn 42$^{15.33}$ Ex 7^{17} Nu 16^{28}; *with this = on this condition* Gn 34$^{15.22}$ 1 S 11^{2} Is 27^{9}. **3.** of cost or price (the *Beth pretii*), the price, whether given or received, being treated as the instrumental means by which the act is accomplished, *with, for, at the cost of:* thus regularly **a.** with שָׂכַר *hire* Gn 30^{16}, פָּדָה *redeem* Ex 34^{20}, אֵרַשׂ *betroth* 2 S 3^{14}, קָנָה *buy* 2 S 24^{24}; 1 K 2^{23} בְּנַפְשׁוֹ *at the cost of* his life hath A. spoken this word, 2 S 23^{17} who went בְּנַפְשׁוֹתָם *at peril of* their lives, Pr 7^{23} La 5^{9} Jos 6^{26} בִּבְכֹרוֹ יְיַסְּדֶנָּה *at the price of* his firstborn shall he lay its foundations, 1 Ch 12^{19} בְּרָאשֵׁינוּ *to the jeopardy of* our heads he will fall away, etc. **b.** with מָכַר *sell* Dt 21^{14}; עָבַד *serve* Gn 29$^{18.20}$ Ho 12^{13}; הֵמִיר *exchange* Lv 27^{10} Ho 4^{7} their glory I will exchange *for* ignominy, ψ 106^{20}; נָתַן בְּנֶשֶׁךְ to give *for* interest Lv 25^{37} ψ 15^{5}; in other connexions Gn 23^{9} 47$^{16 f.}$ Is 45^{13} La 1^{11} Ct 8$^{7.11}$; Dt 19^{21} נֶפֶשׁ בְּנֶפֶשׁ עַיִן בְּעַיִן life *for* life, eye *for* eye; Is 2^{22} בַּמֶּה נֶחְשָׁב הוּא *at what* is he to be accounted? 7^{23} a thousand vines בְּאֶלֶף כָּסֶף *at* a thousand (shekels of) silver.—Hence (perhaps) the idiom. usages שָׁנָה בְּשָׁנָה year *for* year, one year like another, annually Dt 15^{20} al.; יוֹם בְּיוֹם (late), כְּיוֹם בְּיוֹם † 1 S 18^{10}; כְּפַעַם בְּפַעַם (v. יוֹם, פַּעַם(בְּ)); חֹדֶשׁ בְּחֹדֶשׁ † 1 Ch 27^{1}. **4.** rather peculiarly, in certain cases where the object of an action may be treated as the *instrument* by which it is accomplished: as הֵנִיעַ בְּרֹאשׁ to shake *with* the head Je 18^{6} Jb 16^{4} (as well as הֵנִיעַ ראֹשׁ ψ 22^{8}); to open *with* the mouth Jb 16^{10}, *with* the lips ψ 22^{8}; to gnash *with* the teeth Jb 16^{9} (to gnash the teeth ψ 35^{16}); to wink *with* the eye Pr 6^{13} (to wink the eye, *ib.* 10^{10}); נָתַן בְּקוֹל to utter *with* the voice ψ 46^{7} 68^{34} Je 12^{8} (but נָתַן קוֹל is more common); to stretch out *with* the hand La 1^{17}; הֵרִים בַּמַּטֶּה (unusual) Ex 7^{20}. So קָרָא בְּשֵׁם to call *with* the name—in diff. senses, acc. to the context, viz. to *proclaim* Ex 33^{19} 34^{5} Is 44^{5} ψ 49^{12}; to *invoke* Gn 4^{26} 12^{8} 1 K 18$^{24-26}$ Is 12^{4}; to *name honourably* Is 43^{1} 45^{3}. Cf. Ew § 282 d Ges § 119. 3 b R. WAG ii. § 56 b β De Jb 31, 12; Pr 20, 30. **5.** with a causal force, *through, on account of:* Gn 18^{28} הֲתַשְׁחִית בַּחֲמִשָּׁה wilt thou destroy *on account of* five the whole city? Lv 26^{39} Nu 16^{26} Dt 9$^{4.5}$ 24^{16} אִישׁ בְּחֶטְאוֹ יוּמָתוּ׃ they shall be put to death, each *because of* his own sin (cf. Je 31^{30} Ez 3^{18}, v. 18^{17}) 2 S 3^{27} 14^{7} (cf. Jon 1^{14}) Is 7^{4} (|| מִן) 28^{7} (|| מִן) 50^{1} 53^{5} 57^{17} Je 51^{46} ψ 5$^{8.11}$ 6^{8} (|| מִן) 31^{10}, 32^{3} 42^{10} 90^{9} 94^{23}. So in בַּאֲשֶׁר, בִּגְלַל (v. אֲשֶׁר, גָּלָל), & (sts.) in בִּדְבַר *at, through,* the word of.... **6.** of the material *with* which a work is wrought, both absol. עָשָׂה בַּזָּהָב to work *with* gold Ex 31^{4} 1 K 7^{14}; and to make a thing *with* (in our idiom, *of*) gold Ex 38^{8} Ez 7^{20} 1 K 15^{22} (בָּנָה). Without a verb Lv 13^{52} 2 Ch 9^{18}. **7.** *with* for *although, in spite of* (cf. Germ. *bei* alle dem): Lv 26^{27} Nu 14^{11} בְּכֹל הָאֹתוֹת *in spite of* all the signs that I have wrought, Dt 1^{32} Is 47^{9} ψ 27^{3}; esp. in the phrase בְּכָל־זֹאת *for* all this Is 5^{25} 9$^{11.16.20}$ 10^{4} ψ 78^{32} al. (Cf. in Ar. بِمَا Qor 9^{25}.) **8.** of a standard of measurement or computation, *with, by:* Ex 12^{4} בְּמִכְסַת נְפָשֹׁת *by* the computation of souls; Lv 5^{25} al. בְּעֶרְכְּךָ *by* thy reckoning; Ez 4^{10}; בְּמִסְפָּר *by* number Dt 25^{2}+; ... בְּמִסְפַּר *by* the number of ... Lv 25$^{15.50}$ Nu 1^{2}, etc.; בְּשֶׁקֶל הַקֹּדֶשׁ Ex 30^{13} al. (in P); בָּאַמָּה often (v. אַמָּה); Dt 3^{11} בְּאַמַּת אִישׁ *by* the cubit of a man; 2 S 14^{26} בְּאֶבֶן הַמֶּלֶךְ. Of a model, Gn 1^{26} בְּצַלְמֵנוּ *in* our image, 5$^{1.3}$ Ex 25^{40}; בְּדַרְכֵי *with* the way (= in the manner) of ... Is 10$^{24.26}$ Am 4^{10}.

IV. בְּ is used also with certain classes of verbs, though the explanation of its use may be sometimes doubtful: viz. **a.** with verbs of *taking refuge, trusting, relying,* as בָּטַח, הֶאֱמִין, נִשְׁעַן, חָסָה. **b.** with verbs of *ruling, governing, restraining,* as מָלַךְ, מָשַׁל, נָגַשׂ, עָצַר, רָדָה, שָׁלַט. **c.** with verbs of *rejoicing, feeling pleasure* or *satisfaction,* etc., as חָפֵץ, שָׂמַח, שׂוּשׂ, עָלַץ, גִּיל, רָצָה, שָׂבַע (but with this verb מִן is more common). [Prob. a case of **III. 5.**] **d.** with verbs expressive of sensible perception, to denote the pleasurable or attentive exercise of the faculty concerned, as שָׁמַע בְּ to listen *to*, חָזָה, רָאָה, הִבִּיט בְּ, to look *upon*, הֵרִיחַ בְּ to smell *at* (see these words). **e.** occasionally also with verbs of *speaking, thinking, mentioning, knowing,* to denote the object of the action, as דִּבֵּר בְּ to speak *about* Dt 6^{7} ψ 87^{3} al. (v. sub דִּבֵּר); ψ 44^{9} 63^{7} 69^{13} שִׂיחַ, הָגָה, הִלֵּל בְּ; יָדַע Je 38^{24}; זָכַר once Je 3^{16}, הִזְכִּיר oft.; ψ 71^{6} בְּךָ תְהִלָּתִי *of* thee is my praise.

V. Followed by an inf. c., בְּ forms a periphrasis for the gerund, though in English it is commonly to be rendered by a verb and conj., viz.:—**1.** as a *temporal* conj., as Gn 2^{4} בְּהִבָּֽרְאָם *in* their *being created*=*when* they *were* created, 4^{8} בִּהְיוֹתָם *in* their *being* (=*when* they *were*) in the field; and constantly. Sometimes it has in appearance the force of *after that*, as Gn 33^{18} Ex 3^{12} 13^{17}; but as a rule this is really due to the action denoted by the inf. being treated as extending over a period *within* which the action of the principal verb takes place: so esp. in the phrase בְּצֵאת יִשְׂרָאֵל מִמִּצְרַיִם, even of events at the close of the 40 years, Dt 4^{45} 23^{5} Jos 5^{4}, the whole period being treated as that in which Egypt was left (comp. 2 K 2^{1}, where the time included is future). Cases, however, occur in which this explanation will hardly apply, as Dt $27^{4.12}$. **2.** as a *causal* conj. (cf. above **III. 5**), as Gn 19^{16} בְּחֶמְלַת י׳ עָלָיו *through* J.'s having compassion upon him, Ex 16^{7} 33^{16} 34^{29} Dt 1^{27} בְּשִׂנְאַת י׳ אֹתָנוּ *through* J.'s hating us, etc. (9^{28} similarly מִן), 1 K 18^{18} (=*in that* ye have...) Ez 9^{8} 43^{8} 44^{7} 2 Ch 28^{6}. **3.** as a *concessive* conj., *when*=*though*: Is 1^{15} ψ 46^{3} בְּהָמִיר אָרֶץ *though* the earth do change.

Note.—Ex 10^{12} בָּאַרְבֶּה can only be rendered '*with* the locusts,' the locusts being conceived as implicit in Moses' uplifted hand: but prob. לָאַרְבֶּה should be read. Thrice in late Heb. בְּ is used peculiarly: 1 Ch 7^{23} for *with* misfortune was it in his house (בְּרָעָה chosen for the purpose of explaining בְּרִיעָה); 9^{33} עֲלֵיהֶם בַּמְּלָאכָה it devolved upon them *with* the work; Ezr 3^{3} for *with* terror (was it) upon them from the peoples of the countries (the sentence without a verb as oft. in Chr.: Dr $^{Intr. 504 f.}$): cf. 8^{34}. Comp. Ew $^{§ 295 f.}$

1119 †בְּמוֹ poet. for בְּ (v. sub מוֹ: cf. Sab. בם, DHM $^{ZMG 1883, 344}$) Is 25^{10} Qr (<Kt בְּמֵי) 43^{2} $44^{16.19}$ ψ 11^{2} Jb 9^{30} Kt (>Qr בְּמֵי) $16^{4.5}$ 19^{16} 37^{8}.

II. בְּ, perh. abbrev. in **n.pr.** for בֶּן־, בֵּית q.v.

872 בָּאָה v. sub בּוֹא. p. 99

874 †[באר] **vb.** only **Pi.** **make distinct, plain** (so NH, Aram.; Lag $^{BN 58}$ prop. for Qal בָּאֵר, בָּאֹר, cf. deriv. infr.; Thes & most comp. Ar. بَأَرَ *dig a pit* or *well*, but this prob. denom. v. Lag $^{l.c.}$)—**Pi.** *Pf.* 3 ms. בֵּאֵר Dt 1^{5}, *Imv.* בָּאֵר Hb 2^{2}; *Inf. abs.* בַּאֵר Dt 27^{8} (cf. Bö $^{§ 393, 4}$)—*make distinct, plain*, of letters on tablets Hb 2^{2} כְּתֹב חָזוֹן וּבָאֵר עַל־הַלֻּחוֹת לְמַעַן יָרוּץ קוֹרֵא בוֹ, i.e. so that one may run past and (still) read; or, so that one may read swiftly; on stones Dt 27^{8} וְכָתַבְתָּ עַל־הָאֲבָנִים . . . . בַּאֵר הֵיטֵב *and thou shalt write upon the* [whitewashed] *stones* all the words of this law, *doing it plainly and well*; fig. *explain, expound* Dt 1^{5} הוֹאִיל מֹשֶׁה בֵּאֵר הַתּוֹרָה *Moses began* (and) *expounded the law*.

†בְּאֵר **n.f.** $^{Gn 26, 21}$ **well, pit**, mostly Hex, Gn 875
23 t. Ex 1 t. Nu 5 t., 37 t. in all; Ar. بِئْرٌ, Aram. בְּאֵרָא, בֵּיר, בֵּירָא, جُبٌّ, Sab. באר DHM $^{ZMG. 1875, 608}$, As. *bêru*, Lyon $^{Sargon 61}$ (connexion with above √ not clear; Lag $^{l.c.}$ *spring* of water, as *coming to light, appearing*; possible, although meaning in use rather *well*, than *spring*; v. however, Gn 16^{14} cf. v^{7} 26^{19} Nu 21^{17})—ב׳ abs. Gn 21^{30}+; cstr. 21^{19}+; sf. בְּאֵרְךָ Pr 5^{15}; Pl. abs. בְּאֵרֹת Gn 26^{15}; cstr. id. 26^{18}; cf. בֶּאֱרֹת בֶּאֱרֹת חֵמָר Gn 14^{10};—**1.** *a well*, often as made by digging (חָפַר) Gn $21^{25.30}$ (E), $26^{15.18.19.21.22.32}$ (all J), also poet. Nu 21^{18} (+כרה) vid. also $v^{16.17}$ (where the well addressed, in song, עֲלִי בְאֵר); also c. כרה in prose Gn 26^{25}; also with no ref. to its origin Gn 16^{14} (J; ‖ עַיִן v^{7}), 29^{2} Ex 2^{15} (J) Nu 20^{17} 21^{22} (E) 2 S $17^{18.21}$; בְּאֵר (הַ)מַּיִם Gn 21^{19} (E) 24^{11} (J; ‖ עַיִן $vv^{13.16.43.45}$); (cf. also 21^{25} 26^{18} supr. & esp. v^{19} בְּאֵר מַיִם חַיִּים); water taken from it by drawing (שָׁאַב) Gn $24^{11.20}$; flocks watered from it (הִשְׁקָה מִן־) $29^{2.3.8.10}$ (cf. esp. Ex 2^{16} *they drew*, דלה, and filled the troughs); also שְׁתֵה מַיִם . . . . מִתּוֹךְ בְּאֵרֶךָ Pr 5^{15} (‖ בּוֹר); the opening called פִּי הַבְּאֵר Gn $29^{2.3.3.8.10}$; cf. פְּנֵי הַבּ׳ 2 S 17^{19} (rd. prob. פִּי so Sam. 𝔗𝔖𝔙, cf. Dr); fig. of fresh delights of woman beloved Ct 4^{15} מַעְיַן גַּנִּים בְּאֵר מַיִם חַיִּים וְנֹזְלִים מִן־לְבָנוֹן. **2.** *pit* (=בּוֹר); *pits of bitumen* Gn 14^{10} (cf. supr.); בְּאֵר שַׁחַת ψ 55^{24} *pit of* (*the*) *grave*; cf. 69^{16} וְאַל־תֶּאְטַר עָלַי בְּאֵר פִּיהָ *and let not* (*the*) *pit shut its mouth over me* (‖ מְצוּלָה); fig. of strange woman בְּאֵר צָרָה *a narrow pit*, out of which rescue is difficult Pr 23^{27} (‖ שׁוּחָה
עֲמֻקָּה). **3.** as **n.pr.loc.** **a.** c. ה ָ loc. בְּאֵרָה 876
a station of Isr. in desert Nu 21^{16}, possibly=
בְּאֵר אֵילִים Is 15^{8}. **b.** same form Ju 9^{21}, acc. to 879
Euseb. Lag $^{Onom. 238, 2nd ed. 250}$ 8 miles north of Eleutheropolis; cf. Rob $^{BR i. 452}$ who comp. *el-Bîreh*, near Beth-shemesh.

בְּאֵר אֵילִים v. בְּאֵר **3. a.** above 879

†בְּאֵר לַחַי רֹאִי **n.pr.loc.** (lit. *well of the* 883
living One that seeth me) Gn 16^{14} (where explan., from story of Hagar) 24^{62} 25^{11} (all J); perh. name of ancient shrine or holy place, cf. Sta $^{ZAW ii. 347}$ & Di Gn 16^{14}; W. of Kadesh, cf. Jer sub Barad, Lag $^{Onom. 101, 2nd ed. 135}$, v. Rowlands in Williams $^{Holy City, 489}$ Trumbull $^{Kadesh-Barnea 64}$.

884 †בְּאֵר שֶׁבַע **n.pr.loc.** Beersheba (*well of seven*, explained Gn $21^{30.31}$ as place of *swearing by seven* lambs, or, *well of oath*, v. שְׁבֻעָה; cf. same meaning otherwise derived 26^{33})—בְּאֵר שֶׁבַע Gn 26^{33} + 13 t., בְּאֵר־שֶׁבַע Jos 19^{2}; בְּאֵר שָׁ֑בַע Gn 21^{14} + 18 t.; בְּאֵ֫רָה שֶּׁבַע (ָ־ה loc.) Gn 46^{1}—south from Hebron, acc. to Onom. c. 20 miles Lag $^{Onom. 103, 234, 2nd\ ed. 138, 248}$; mod. *Bîr-es-Seba*, 12 h. fr. Hebron Rob $^{BR\ i. 204\ f.}$ Survey $^{iii. 394}$ Gn $21^{14.31.32.33}$ $22^{19.19}$ $26^{23.33}$ 28^{10} $46^{1.5}$ Jos 15^{28} 19^{2} Ju 20^{1} 1 S 3^{20} 8^{2} 2 S 17^{11} 24^{7} 1 K 19^{3} 2 K 12^{2} 23^{8} Am 5^{5} 1 Ch 4^{28} 2 Ch 19^{4} 24^{1} Ne $11^{27.30}$; in phrase מִדָּן וְעַד־בּ׳ *from Dan to Beersheba* (i.e. all the territory of Israel, v. דָּן) Am 8^{14} Ju 20^{1} 1 S 3^{20} 2 S 3^{10} 17^{11} $24^{2.15}$ 1 K 5^{5}, & (only Ch) מִבְּאֵר שֶׁבַע וְעַד־דָּן *from Beersheba to Dan* 1 Ch 21^{2} 2 Ch 30^{5}.

878 †בְּאֵרָא **n.pr.m.** a man of Asher 1 Ch 7^{37}.

880 †בְּאֵרָה **n.pr.m.** a Reubenite 1 Ch 5^{6}.

881 †בְּאֵרוֹת **n.pr.loc.** (but only 2 S 4^{2} acc. to Masorah, v. BD $^{Ezr\ 2, 25}$ elsewh. בְּאֵרֹת), city of the Gibeonites Jos 9^{17}; assigned to Benjamin 2 S 4^{2} Jos 18^{25}; cf. also Ezr 2^{25} Ne 7^{29}; mod. *el-Bîreh* Rob $^{BR\ i. 452}$ Bd $^{Pal\ 214}$ Survey $^{iii. 88}$.

886 †בְּאֵרֹתִי **adj.gent.** always c. art. 2 S $4^{2.5.9}$, 23^{37} = הַבֵּרֹתִי 1 Ch 11^{39}; pl. הַבְּאֵרֹתִים 2 S 4^{3}.

885 †בְּאֵרֹת בְּנֵי־יַעֲקָן **n.pr.loc.** Dt 10^{6} (cf. Nu $33^{31.32}$, where בני יעקן), a station of Isr. in desert, prob. in country of Horites, cf. Di.

882 †בְּאֵרִי **n.pr.m.** (*my well*). **1.** a Hittite, Esau's father-in-law Gn 26^{34}. **2.** Hosea's father Ho 1^{1}.

877 †[באר] **n.m.** $^{Je\ 2, 13}$ **cistern, pit, well** (for בְּאֵר cf. בּוֹר)—sg. Kt באר בְּאֵר 2 S $23^{15.16.20}$ (Qr בֹּר); appar. *well* $v^{15.16}$ (rd. perh. בְּאֵר), *pit* v^{20}; pl. Je 2^{13} *me they have forsaken, the fountain of living water,* לַחְצֹב לָהֶם בֹּארוֹת בֹּארֹת נִשְׁבָּרִים, *to hew out for themselves cisterns, broken cisterns*, etc.

953 †בּוֹר **n.m.** $^{Gn\ 37, 20}$ **pit, cistern, well** (= בְּאֵר, MI בר, Ar. بُورَةٌ *hole* or *hollow* for cooking, As. *bûrtum* Dl $^{Pr\ 182}$, *bûru* Lotz $^{TP\ 169}$)—בּ׳ abs. Gn 37^{22} +; בֹּר Ex 21^{33} (2 S 23^{20} Qr, v. באר supr.); cstr. בּוֹר 2 K 10^{14} + (2 S $23^{15.16}$ Qr, v. באר supr.); בֹּ֫רָה (ָ־ה loc.) Gn 37^{24}; sf. בּוֹרוֹ Is 36^{16} = בֹּרוֹ 2 K 18^{31}; בּוֹרֶךָ Pr 5^{15}; pl. בֹּרוֹת Gn 37^{20} + 3 t.; בֹּרֹת Dt 6^{11}:—**1.** *cistern*, containing water, made by digging (חצב) Dt 6^{11} 2 Ch 26^{10} Ne 9^{25}; also (without ref. to origin) Pr 5^{15} (‖ בְּאֵר) Lv 11^{36} (‖ מַעְיָן), 1 S 19^{22} Is 36^{16} = 2 K 18^{31}. **2.** later appar. *well* (= בְּאֵר) 1 Ch $11^{17.18}$ = Qr 2 S $23^{15.16}$ (yet now no well at Bethlehem Rob $^{BR\ i. 470, 473}$ cf. also Survey $^{iii. 28}$ Guérin $^{Judée\ i. 130}$), cf. Ec 12^{6} & Je 6^{7} Kt כְּהָקִיר בּוֹר מֵימֶיהָ *as a well casteth out its water* (Qr בַּיִר); but הקיר perh. *keep cool, fresh* 𝔊 𝔙 Hi Gf. **3.** *pit* Ex 21^{33} (vb. פתח), v^{33} (כרה), cf. v^{34}; cf. fig. ψ 7^{16} of wickedness (‖ שַׁחַת; vb. חפר, כרה); 1 S 13^{6} as hiding-place; 2 S 23^{20} (Qr) = 1 Ch 11^{22} 2 K 10^{14} בּוֹר בֵּית עֵ֫קֶד; of pit into wh. Joseph was cast Gn $37^{20.22.24}$ (וְהַבּוֹר רֵק אֵין בּוֹ מָ֑יִם) $v^{28.29.29}$ (JE), cf. further Je $41^{7.9}$; fig. of Sarah as mother of Israel מַקֶּ֫בֶת בּ׳ Is 51^{1}; fig. of calamity ψ 40^{3} בּוֹר שָׁאוֹן; cf. ψ 88^{7} בּ׳ תַּחְתִּיּוֹת. **4.** *dungeon* (pit with no water in it Je 38^{6} Zc 9^{11} cf. Gn 37^{24} supr.) Gn 40^{15} 41^{14} (E) Is 24^{22} Je $38^{6.6}$ (בּ׳ אֵין מַיִם) $v^{7.9.10.11.13}$; also בֵּית הַבּוֹר *prison* Ex 12^{29} Je 37^{16}; fig. of exile Zc 9^{11} (מִבּוֹר אֵין מַיִם בּוֹ); cf. also La $3^{53.55}$. **5.** (poet. & late; never c. art.) *pit of the grave* Pr 28^{17}; so אַבְנֵי בּ׳ *stones of the pit* Is 14^{19} (of sepulchre, walled with stones) & of Sheʾôl ψ 30^{4} (‖ שאול); יַרְכְּתֵי בּ׳ *loins of (the) pit*, i.e. remotest pit Is 14^{15} (‖ שאול) Ez 32^{23} esp. in phrase יוֹרְדֵי בוֹר *those going down to (the) pit* ψ 28^{1} 143^{7} Is 38^{18} Ez 26^{20} $32^{25.29.30}$; also, (‖ שאול), ψ 88^{5} Pr 1^{12}; further Ez 26^{20} $32^{18.24}$ (all ‖ אֶרֶץ תַּחְתִּיּוֹת), $31^{14.16}$ (both ‖ אֶרֶץ תַּחְתִּית; v^{14} ‖ also מָוֶת, v^{16} שְׁאוֹל).

†בּוֹר הַסִּרָה **n.pr.loc.** 2 S 3^{26} (*cistern of Sirah*, Thes *cist. declinationis*, MV *of the pot*, v. סיר). 953, 5626

†בּוֹר עָשָׁן (so rd. for ordinary כּוֹר ע׳, v. 953, 6228
BD $^{Gn,\ p.\ vi.}$ 𝔊 𝔖) **n.pr.loc.** 1 S 30^{30} (*smoking pit*), in S.W. of Judah; elsewhere עָשָׁן q. v.

בַּיִר Qr Je 6^{7} v. בּוֹר. above 953

†בְּרִי **n.pr.m.** a descendant of Asher 1 Ch 1275
7^{36} (perh. = בְּאֵרִי).

†בֵּרוֹתָה **n.pr.loc.** near Hamath Ez 47^{16} 1268
(contr. fr. בְּאֵרוֹתָה?), cf. foll.;—hardly = Berytus (Beirût) with wh. form of name might agree v. Steph. Byzant. al. in Movers $^{Phen.\ ii. 1, 110\ n.}$; perh. *Bereitān* near Baalbek, v. Furrer $^{ZPV\ viii. 34}$.

†בֵּרֹתַי **n.pr.loc.** belonging to Hadadezer 1268
of Zoba 2 S 8^{8}; perh. = foregoing.

†בֵּרֹתִי **adj.gent.** 1 Ch 11^{39} v. הַבְּאֵרֹתִי supr. 1307

†בָּאַשׁ **vb. have a bad smell, stink** (Ar. 807
بَئِسَ *be evil*, Aram. בְּאֵשׁ, ܒܐܫ *be evil*, As. *bîšu* Lotz $^{TP\ 78}$)—**Qal** *Pf.* וּבָאַשׁ consec. Ex 7^{18}; *Impf.* וַתִּבְאַשׁ ־אַשׁ וַיִּבְאַשׁ v^{21}, 16^{20}; 3 fs. תִּבְאַשׁ Is 50^{2}; Ex 8^{10};—*stink*, of Nile, on account of dead fish Ex $7^{18.21}$ (E); of land of Egypt, owing to dead frogs 8^{10} (J); of manna kept over 16^{20} (P? or

R) וַיָּרֶם תּוֹלָעִים וַיִּבְאַשׁ *and it grew foul* (rotten, decayed) *with worms, and stank;* Is 50^{2} תִּבְאַשׁ דְּגָתָם מֵאֵין מַיִם וְתָמֹת בַּצָּמָא *their fish stink for lack of water*, etc. (𝔊 Lo Di rd. תִּיבַשׁ, *dry up* and die, which suits ||, but not the usage of יָבֵשׁ). **Niph.** *Pf.* נִבְאַשׁ 1 S 13^{4}; נִבְאֲשׁוּ 2 S 10^{6}; נִבְאַשְׁתָּ 2 S 16^{21};—only fig. *make oneself odious, become odious* (cf. Eng. *be in bad odour*), sq. אֶת *with=towards;* נִבְאַשְׁתָּ אֶת־אָבִיךָ 2 S 16^{21} *thou hast become odious with thy father;* also sq. בְּ (rather strangely) 1 S 13^{4} *Isr. made themselves odious to the Philistines;* 2 S 10^{6} Ammonites to David. **Hiph.** *Pf.* הִבְאִישׁ Ex 16^{24} 1 S 27^{12}; הִבְאִישׁוּ ψ 38^{6}; הִבְאַשְׁתֶּם Ex 5^{21}; *Impf.* יַבְאִישׁ Pr 13^{5} Ec 10^{1}; *Inf. abs.* הַבְאֵשׁ 1 S 27^{12}; *cstr. sf.* לְהַבְאִישֵׁנִי Gn 34^{30};—**1.** *emit a stinking odour* Ex 16^{24} of manna (cf. Qal v^{20}); ψ 38^{6} הִבְאִישׁוּ נָמַקּוּ חַבּוּרֹתָי *my wounds have grown stinking, they have festered* (of chastisement for sin); 1 S 17^{12} fig. of David הַבְאֵשׁ הִבְאִישׁ בְּעַמּוֹ *he hath become utterly abhorred among his people.* **2.** *cause to stink*, זְבוּבֵי מָוֶת יַבְאִישׁ יַבִּיעַ שֶׁמֶן רוֹקֵחַ *dead flies cause to stink* (and) *to ferment the oil of a perfumer;* usually fig. הִבְאַשְׁתֶּם אֶת־רֵיחֵנוּ Ex 5^{21} (J), i.e. ye have made us odious, sq. בְּעֵינֵי, cf. (c. acc. pers.) Gn 34^{30} sq. בְּ; also without obj. Pr 13^{5} *a wicked man makes odious and shameful* (De Now Str; Be Ew Hi Zö *acts odiously and shamefully*). **Hithp.** *Pf.* הִתְבָּאֲשׁוּ 1 Ch 19^{6} *they had made themselves odious* (=Niph. in || 2 S 10^{6}), sq. עִם.

889 †בְּאֹשׁ **n.m. stench**—בְּ׳ cstr. Am 4^{10}; sf. בָּאְשׁוֹ Jo 2^{20}; בָּאְשָׁם Is 34^{3};—בְּ׳ מַחֲנֵיכֶם, i.e. *stench* of corpses Am 4^{10}, also Is 34^{3}; cf. Jo 2^{20} of locusts (תַּעַל צַחֲנָתוֹ || עָלָה בְּ׳).

890 †בָּאְשָׁה **n.f.** (stinking things) **stinking** or **noxious weeds**, Jb 31^{40} תַּחַת חִטָּה יֵצֵא חוֹחַ וְתַחַת־שְׂעֹרָה בָאְשָׁה *instead of wheat may there spring forth bramble, and instead of barley stinking weeds* (cf. As. *bîšu* Zehnpfund$^{BAS\ i.\ 633}$).

891 †בְּאֻשִׁים **n.[m.]pl. stinking** or **worthless** things, **wild grapes** (NH n. unit. בְּאוּשָׁה) (perh. adj. om. עֲנָבִים cf. Di) Is 5$^{2.4}$ of Yahweh's vineyard, 𝔙 *labruscae* (v. further De).

892 †[בָּבָה] **n.f.** only בָּבַת עֵינוֹ Zc 2^{12} *the apple of his eye* (Aram. ܒܒܬܐ, ܒܒܐ; בָּבָא *gate* 𝔗 Est 5^{14}; Thes sub נבב to which Ges gives sense *perforate*, hence *opening of eye;* but cf. Ar. بُؤْبُؤ عين *pupil* of eye, perh.=بَبَّة Dozy^{49} *babe, baby, bébé* (imitating infant's prattle) i.e. child of the eye; v. Hi St, Fl in ChWB$^{i.\ 419\ b}$; cf. אִישׁוֹן ?).

†בֵּבַי **n.pr.m.** a chief of returning exiles בֵּבָי Ne 10^{16}; בְּנֵי בֵבַי Ezr 8^{11}; בֶּן־בֵּבָי Ezr 8^{11}; בְּנֵי בֵבָי Ezr 2^{11} 10^{28} Ne 7^{16}. 893

בָּבֶל $_{262}$ **n.pr.loc. Babel, Babylon** (in As. written *Bab-ilu, gate of god* Dl$^{Pa\ 212}$, cf. on other hand Jen$^{Kosmol.\ 498}$)—c. ־ָה loc. בָּבֶ֫לָה Ez 12^{13}+, בָּבֶ֫לָה 2 K 20^{17}+ once מִבָּבֶ֫לָה Je 27^{16};—the ancient capital of Babylonia, mod. *Hillah*, situated on Euphrates, in long. c. 44° 30′ E., and lat. c. 32° 50′ N.; Gn 10^{10} 11^{9} (where name connected with בלל *confuse, confound*), both J, not elsewh. in Hex; 2 K 17^{24}+31 t. 2 K; 18 t. Chr; Est 2^{6}; late ψ 87^{4} 137$^{1.8}$; Is$^{2.3}$, viz. 13$^{1.19}$ 14$^{4.22}$ 21^{9} 39$^{1.3.6.7}$ 43^{14} 47^{1} 48$^{14.20}$; Mi 4^{10} (but here prob. not orig., cf. RS$^{Proph.\ vii.\ n.\ 5}$ & reff.) Zc 2^{11} 6^{10} Dn 1^{1} Ez 12^{13} +19 t. Ez; Je 20$^{4.4.5.6}$+165 t. Je;—note esp. אֶרֶץ בּ׳ Je 50^{28}; also of land & people=realm, partic. in מֶלֶךְ בּ׳ 2 K 20^{12} of Merodach Baladan; v^{18} 24$^{1.7.11.12.12}$+oft. of Nebuchadrezzar; 2 K 25^{27}=Je 52^{31} cf. v^{34} of Evil-Merodach; Ne 13^{6} of Artaxerxes; the city personif. as בַּת בָּבֶל Is 47^{1} Je 50^{42}. (See Dl$^{Pa\ 212}$ COT Gn 11^{9} KG^{95}.) 894

בַּג Ez 25^{7} rd. בַּז v. בזז. p. 103 897

†[בָּגַד] **vb. act** or **deal treacherously**—**Qal** *Pf.* בָּגְדָה Je 3^{20}+14 t.; *Impf.* יִבְגֹּד Mal 2^{15}+5 t.; נִבְגַּד Mal 2^{10}; *Inf. abs.* בָּגוֹד Is 48^{8} Je 5^{11}; *cstr.* בְּגֹד Is 33^{1}; בְּגִדוֹ Ex 21^{8}; *Pt.* בֹּגֵד Pr 22^{12}+11 t.; בּוֹגֵד Is 33^{1}+10 t.;—*act* or *deal treacherously, faithlessly, deceitfully*, in the marriage relation, in matters of property or right, in covenants, in word and in general conduct. **a.** *abs.* 1 S 14^{33} Jb 6^{15} ψ 78^{57} Is 24^{16} 33$^{1.1}$ 48^{8} Mal 2^{11}. Cf. phrases אחי בגדו כמו נחל *my brethren have dealt deceitfully as a brook* Jb 6^{15}; בֹּגְדִים בָּגָדוּ וּבֶגֶד בּוֹגְדִים בָּגָדוּ *the treacherous have dealt treacherously, yea in treachery have the treacherous dealt treacherously* Is 24^{16} (striking alliteration); בֹּגְדֵי אָוֶן *treacherous in wickedness* ψ 59^{6}. **b.** with בְּ Ex 21^{8} (E), Ju 9^{23} Is 33$^{1.1}$ Je 3^{20} 5^{11} 12^{6} La 1^{2} Ho 5^{7} 6^{7} Mal 2$^{10.14.15.16}$. **c.** c. acc. ψ 73^{15}. **d.** c. מִן pregnant, בָּגְדָה אִשָּׁה מֵרֵעָהּ *acteth treacherously* (*in departing*) *from her friend* Je 3^{20}. The ptcp. is used Pr 2^{22}+8 t., ψ 25^{3} 59^{6} 119^{158} Is 21^{2} 24$^{16.16}$ 33^{1} Je 3$^{8.11}$ 9^{1} Hb 1^{13} 2^{5}; בֹּגְדֵי בָגֶד *dealers treacherously in treachery* (very *treacherously*) Je 12^{1}. 898

†I. בֶּ֫גֶד **n.[m.] treachery**, Is 24^{16} Je 12^{1}. 899

†בֹּגְדוֹת **pl.abst.** אַנְשֵׁי בֹּגְדוֹת *men of treachery* Zp 3^{4}. 900

†[בָּגוֹד] **adj. treacherous**, f. בָּגוֹדָה (on form cf. Ew$^{§\ 152\ b}$ Nö$^{§\ 107}$) Je 3$^{7.10}$. 901

II. בֶּ֫גֶד **n.m.** (except Lv 6^{20} עָלֶיהָ, but Sam. עליו, 899

cf. Di in *loco* Kö$^{\text{i. 182}}$) **garment, covering**—Gn 28^{2}+36 t.; *sf.* בִּגְדוֹ Ez 9^{3}+(14 t. without *dag. lene* Ges$^{\text{Lgb. 94}}$); pl. בְּגָדִים Lv 6^{4}+32 t.; cstr. בִּגְדֵי Gn 27^{15}+39 t.; sf. בְּגָדֶיךָ 1 K 22^{20}+81 t.; בִּגְדֹתֶיךָ ψ 45^{9};—**1.** *garment, clothing, raiment, robe* of any kind, from the filthy clothing of the leper to the holy robes of the high priest, the simplest covering of the poor as well as the costly raiment of the rich and noble, used throughout Heb. Lit.: Gn 24^{53} (J), 28^{20} (E; 14 t. JE), Ex 28^{2}+(P 90 t.), Dt 24^{17} Ju 8^{26}+4 t., 1 S 19^{13}+10 t., 1 K 1^{1}+23 t., 2 Ch 18^{9}+(Chr 9 t.), Est 4$^{1.4}$ Jb 13^{28} 22^{6} 37^{17} ψ 22^{19} 45^{9} 102^{27} 109^{19} Pr 6^{27} 20^{16} 25^{20} 27^{13} Ec 9^{8} Is^{2} 24^{16} 36^{22} 37^{1} Is^{3} 50^{9}+10 t., Je 12^{1}+3 t., Ez 16^{16}+13 t., Jo 2^{13} Am 2^{8} Hg 2^{12} Zc 3$^{3.4.5}$ 14^{14}; מְלֹא בִגְדוֹ *his lap-ful* 2 K 4^{39}. **2.** *covering, wrapping*, of furniture of tabernacle Nu 4$^{6-13}$ (6 t.); *coverlet* of a bed 1 S 19^{13}.

902 †בִּגְוַי **n.pr.m.** (cf. Skr. *bhagavân, happy*?) **1.** a companion of Zerubbabel Ezr 2^{2}=Ne 7^{7}; perh.=head of a family of returning exiles Ezr 2^{14} (בִּגְוָי)=Ne 7^{19}, cf. Ezr 8^{14}. **2.** a chief of the people in Nehemiah's time Ne 10^{17}; cf. Sm$^{\text{Listen 13}}$.

1556 בִּגְלַל v. גלל. p. 164ff

903 †בִּגְתָא **n.pr.m.** (Pers. cf. אֲבַגְתָא) a eunuch of Ahasuerus Est 1^{10}.

904 †בִּגְתָן **n.pr.m.** (Pers. *bagadâna, gift of God*?) a eunuch of Ahasuerus Est 2^{21}=בִּגְתָנָא 6^{2}.

בִּגְתָנָא v. foregoing.

906 †I. בַּד, בַּד **n.[m.]** **white linen** (deriv. unknown) pl. בַּדִּים—אֵפוֹד בַּד 1 S 2^{18} (Samuel), 22^{18} (priests of Nob), 2 S 6^{14}=1 Ch 15^{27} (David): in P as material of diff. priestly vestments Ex 28^{42} 39^{28} Lv 6$^{3.3}$ 16$^{4.4.4.4.23.32}$. *Pl.* (ה)לבוש (ה)בַּדִּים clad in (the) *linen garments*, of angel Ez 9$^{2.3.11}$ 10$^{2.6.7}$ Dn 10^{5} 12$^{6.7}$.

905, 907 II, III. בַּד v. sub I, II. בדד. p. 94-5

908 †בָּדָא **vb. devise, invent** (bad sense) (Mish. *id.*, Aram. בְּדָא, ܒܕܐ *invent*; cf. Ar. بَدَأَ *begin, make a beginning*)—**Qal** *Pf.* בָּדָא 1 K 12^{33}; *Pt. sf.* בּוֹדָאם (instead of בּוֹדְאָם) Ne 6^{8}—Jeroboam *devised* a feast in 8th month 1 K 12^{33}; *invent* accusation Ne 6^{8}.

909 †I. [בָּדַד] **vb. be separate, isolated** (Ar. بَدَّ *cause to withdraw*; II. *separate, disunite*, Gn 11^{8} Saad.; IV. *divide into parts*; X. *go alone, act independently*), only *Pt.* בּוֹדֵד Is 14^{31} (of straggler in army), Ho 8^{9} פֶּרֶא בּוֹדֵד לוֹ a wild-ass (sim. of Ephr.) *going alone* for itself (i.e. wilfully: v. sub לְ), ψ 102^{8} (of bird sitting solitarily).

II. בַּד, בַּד **n.m. separation**, concr. **part** 905
(بَدٌّ, بُدَّةٌ *portion*)—sf. (always with לְ) לְבַדּוֹ, לְבַדִּי etc., 3 f. pl. †Gn 21^{28} לְבַדְּהֶן, v^{29} לְבַדָּנָה;—**1.** with לְ, only in sg., לְבַד prop. *in a state of* (v. sub לְ) *separation, alone, by itself* (Fr. *à part*). **a.** Ex 26^{9} (=36^{16}) five curtains לְבַד *by themselves*, and six curtains לְבַד *by themselves*, Ju 7^{5} him shalt thou set לבד *apart*, Zc 12$^{12-14}$. **b.** with sf. (89 t.) to express the idea of *by oneself, alone* (prop. *in his, thy, my separation*), Gn 2^{18} it is not good for man to be לְבַדּוֹ *alone*, 21^{28} and A. set the seven lambs לְבַדְּהֶן *by themselves* (lit. in their separation), 32^{17} 43^{32} 2 S 10^{8} Is 5^{8}; Gn 42^{38} הוּא לְבַדּוֹ he *alone*, Ex 18^{14} אַתָּה לְבַדֶּךָ thou *alone*, Nu 11^{14} אָנֹכִי לְבַדִּי I *alone*, 1 K 19$^{10.14}$; Dt 8^{3} not upon bread *alone*, 29^{13} 2 S 13^{32} 18^{24} Is 44^{24} 49^{21} 63^{3}+; after an oblique case, as a dat. Ex 22^{19} Ju 3^{20} ψ 51^{6} לְךָ לְבַדְּךָ against thee *alone* have I sinned; a genit. 71^{16} I will make mention of צִדְקָתְךָ לְבַדֶּךָ׃ the righteousness of thee *alone*. **c.** as adv. of limitation, †Is 26^{13} *only* through thee do we celebrate thy name, Ec 7^{29}. **d.** followed by מִן it becomes a prep., *apart from, besides*, Ex 12^{37} Nu 29^{39} Dt 3^{5} 18^{8} (rd. מִמְּכָרָיו with 𝔊 𝔖 𝔗 Aq Ew Di) Ju 8^{26} 20^{15} al. (15 t.); once, Ezr 1^{6}, with עַל instead of מִן. **e.** מִלְּבַד$_{33}$ (prob. inverted for לְבַד מִן *besides*) (chiefly P and late): Gn 26^{1} 46^{26} Lv 9^{17} 23^{38} (4 t.) Nu 5^{8} 6^{21} 17^{14}+12 t. Nu 28–29; Dt 28^{69} Jos 22^{29} 1 K 10^{13} 1 Ch 3^{9} 2 Ch 9^{12} 17^{19} 31^{16} Ezr 2^{65}=Ne 7^{67} Dn 11^{4}. With sf. †Dt 4^{35} אֵין עוֹד מִלְּבַדּוֹ there is none else *besides* him (cf. מִבַּלְעָדַי Is 45^{21}).

†**2.** concr. *part* Ex 30^{34} (P) בַּד בְּבַד יִהְיֶה *part* for (i.e. like; cf. בְּ **III. 3.** end) *part* shall it be.

†**3.** בַּדִּים *parts*, spec. *extended from something*, i.e. (*a*) of a body, *members, limbs* Jb 18^{13} (of man), 41^{4} (of crocodile); (*b*) of a vine, *rods* or *shoots* Ez 17^{6} 19^{14}; (*c*) of *poles* or *staves* used for carrying the ark Ex 25$^{13.14.15}$ 35^{12} 37$^{4.5}$ 39^{35} 40^{20} Nu 4^{6} 1 K 8$^{7.8.8}$ (=2 Ch 5$^{8.9.9}$), or table of shewbread Ex 25$^{27.28}$ 35^{13} 37$^{14.15}$ Nu 4^{8}, or altar of B. O. Ex 27$^{6.6.7.7}$ 35^{16} 38$^{5.6.7}$ 39^{39} Nu 4^{14}, or altar of incense Ex 30$^{4.5}$ 35^{15} 37$^{27.28}$ Nu 4^{11}; (*d*) more gen. *bars* (of fortress) Ho 11^{6}, (of a gate) Jb 17^{16} fig. בַּדֵּי שְׁאֹל (v. Is 38^{10}).

†בָּדָד **n.[m.] isolation, separation**: Is 27^{10} 910
עִיר בְּצוּרָה בָּדָד the fenced city is *isolation*, i.e. is solitary (subst. for adj.: Dr$^{\text{§ 189. 2}}$); more usu. as adv. accus., to signify *alone*, Dt 32^{12}; esp. with vbs. of dwelling, Lv 13^{46} בָּדָד יֵשֵׁב he shall dwell *alone* (lit. *in isolation*), Je 15^{17} La 1^{1} 3^{28}: fig. of freedom from attack, security Dt 33^{28}

(of Isr.), Je 49^{31} (Kedar); so לְבָדָד Nu 23^{9} (Isr.) Mi 7^{14} ψ 4^{9} for thou לְבָדָד לָבֶטַח תּוֹשִׁיבֵנִי makest me dwell *solitarily,* in safety (v. Dt 33^{28}).

II. **בדד** (prob. i. q. בָּדָא q. v. *talk idly*).

907 †III. [בַּד] **n.m.** only *Pl.* בַּדִּים. **a.** *empty, idle talk* (Ph. CIS [3,6] listen not to בדנם = Heb. בַּדֵּיהֶם; cf. ﺑَﺪْﺍ *vain talk*), esp. with collat. idea of imaginary pretensions or claims: Jb 11^{3} בַּדֶּיךָ מְתִים יַחֲרִישׁוּ thy *idle talk* brings men to silence (וַתִּלְעַג‖), Is 16^{6} (of Moab) לֹא כֵן בַּדָּיו his *boastings* are not right (unfounded), hence Je 48^{30}. **b.** concr. *empty talkers, praters* (cf. NH בַּדָּאָה, Syr. ܒܕܝܐ, *liar*), of false prophets, Is 44^{25} Je 50^{36}.

911 †בְּדַד **n.pr.m.** father of an Edom. ruler (הֲדַד) Gn 36^{35} = 1 Ch 1^{46}.

1767 בְּדֵי v. דַּי. p. 191

912 †בֵּדְיָה **n.pr.m.** (= עֲבֵדְיָה *servant of* י׳?) 𝔊 Βαραια, 𝔊L Βαδαια) an Israelite Ezr 10^{35}.

914 [בָּדַל] **vb. be divided, separate** (Ar. بَدَّلَ *change, substitute,* Mish. בָּדַל *divide,* Syr. ܒܕܠ Ithp. Ethp.)—**Hiph.** *divide, separate; Pf.* הִבְדִּיל Nu 16^{9} Dt 10^{8}; sf. וְהִבְדִּילוֹ consec. Dt 29^{20}; 3 fs. וְהִבְדִּילָה Ex 26^{33}; וְהִבְדַּלְתָּ Nu 8^{14}; הִבְדִּילוּ Ez 22^{26}, etc.; *Impf.* יַבְדִּיל Lv 1^{17}+; וַיַּבְדֵּל Gn $1^{4.7}$ 1 Ch 25^{1}; sf. יַבְדִּילַנִי Is 56^{3}; וָאַבְדִּל Lv 20^{26}; וָאַבְדִּילָה Ezr 8^{24}, etc.; *Inf. abs.* הַבְדֵּל Is 56^{3}; *cstr.* לְהַבְדִּיל Gn 1^{14}+; *Pt.* מַבְדִּיל Gn 1^{6}; מַבְדִּילִים Is 59^{2};—**1.** *divide, separate,* subj. God Gn 1^{4} sq. בֵּין ... וּבֵין *between light and darkness,* cf. v^{7}; subj. heavenly bodies $v^{14.18}$; subj. firmament sq. בֵּין ... לְ Gn 1^{6} (all in P's source); Ex 26^{33} of the פָּרֹכֶת in tab., sq. בֵּין ... וּבֵין ... לָכֶם; of iniquities, separating men from God בֵּין ... לְבֵין Is 59^{2}. **2.** *separate, set apart,* sq. מִן, of י׳, setting off Isr. from other peoples Lv 20^{24} (H) Nu 16^{9} (P); Lv 20^{26} sq. also לִהְיוֹת לִי; cf. 1 K 8^{53} הִבְדַּ׳ לְךָ לְנַחֲלָה *separate them to thyself as an inheritance;* of Moses, setting apart Levites, sq. מִתּוֹךְ Nu 8^{14}; of separating an individual from the people, i.e. excluding him Dt 29^{20}, sq. also לְרָעָה; sq. מֵעַל Is $56^{3.3}$, i.e. excluding him; cf. also Ne 13^{3} sq. מִן; of setting apart (forbidding) beasts as unclean לָכֶם לְטַמֵּא Lv 20^{25}; of setting apart the tribe of Levi לָשֵׂאת וגו׳ Dt 10^{8} (subj. י׳); cf. also (hum. subj.) 1 Ch 25^{1}, sq. לַעֲבֹדָה, 2 Ch 25^{10} sq. Inf.; similarly Ezr 8^{24}; even sq. ptcp. Ez 39^{14} they shall set apart men עֹבְרִים, i.e. *to pass through,* or, *men that shall pass through* (RV); so of setting apart cities, **acc.** Dt 4^{41} cf. $19^{2.7}$. **3.** *make a distinction* between clean and unclean, holy and profane, sq. בֵּין ... וּבֵין Lv 20^{25} (H); 10^{10} 11^{47} (both P); sq. בֵּין ... לְ Ez 22^{26} 42^{20}. **4.** *divide into parts* Lv 1^{17} 5^{8} (P), prohibited in case of fowls offered in sacrifice. **Niph.** *Pf.* נִבְדְּלוּ 1 Ch 12^{8} Ezr 9^{1}; *Impf.* יִבָּדֵל Ezr 10^{8}; וַיִּבָּדֵל 1 Ch 23^{13}; וַיִּבָּדְלוּ Ezr 10^{16} Ne 9^{2}; *Imv.* הִבָּדְלוּ Nu 16^{21} Ezr 10^{11}; *Pt.* נִבְדָּל Ezr 6^{21} Ne 10^{29}. **1.** (reflex. of **Hiph. 2**) **a.** *separate oneself* from people of the land, heathen, and their practices, also from non-Jewish wives, sq. מִן Ezr 6^{21} 9^{1} 10^{11} Ne 9^{2}; abs. in same sense Ezr 10^{16} (cf. Sta [G. ii. 199 & 179 n.] Wl [Pharisäer u. Sadd. 76]). **b.** *withdraw from* (Moses & Aaron from Israel) Nu 16^{21} (P), sq. מִתּוֹךְ. **c.** *separate oneself* unto (אֶל) David 1 Ch 12^{8}. **d.** Ne 10^{29} combines **a.** & **c.** *separate oneself* מֵעַמֵּי הָאֲרָצוֹת אֶל־תּוֹרַת הָאֱלֹהִים. **2.** pass., *be separated.* **a.** *be excluded* from the people, sq. מִן Ezr 10^{8}. **b.** *be set apart,* of Aaron, sq. לְהַקְדִּישׁוֹ 1 Ch 23^{13}.—On הבדיל, & distinction fr. הפריד v. Dr [JPh. xi. 219].

†[בָּדָל] **n.[m.]** piece, severed piece, cstr. בְּדַל־אֹזֶן Am 3^{12}. 915

†[מִבְדָּלָה] **n.f. separate place,** הַמִּבְדָּלוֹת 3995
Jos 16^{9} (appos. הֶעָרִים); but rd. prob. הַמֻּבְדָּלוֹת **Hoph.** *Pt.* fr. בדל, or הַנִּבְדָּלוֹת **Niph.** *Pt.,* cf. Di.

†בְּדִיל **n.[m.]** alloy, tin, dross (orig. *that* 913
which is separated from precious metal; cf. Plin. [Hist. Nat. xxiv. 16, xxxiii. 9])—בְּ׳ abs. Nu 31^{22} + 4 t.; Pl. sf. בְּדִילָיִךְ Is 1^{25};—**1.** *alloy,* Is 1^{25} fig. of evil of Jerusalem, which י׳ will remove (הָסִיר; ‖ סִגַיִךְ). **2.** *tin* (*plumbum album*) Nu 31^{22} (P; + זָהָב, כֶּסֶף, נְחֹשֶׁת, בַּרְזֶל, עֹפֶרֶת); fig. of Isr. Ez 22^{18} (+ נְחֹשֶׁת, בַּרְזֶל, עוֹפֶרֶת); in simile v^{20} (+ id. + כֶּסֶף); as article of commerce brought to Tyre from Tarshish Ez 27^{12} (+ כֶּסֶף, בַּרְזֶל, עוֹפֶרֶת). **3.** *plummet,* הָאֶבֶן הַבְּדִיל (appos.) Zc 4^{10}.

†בְּדֹלַח **n.[m.]** prob. bdellium (𝔖 ܒܕܘܠܚܐ; 916
𝔗 בְּדוּלְחָא; etym. dub.; Lag [Ges. Abh. 20] prop. Skr. *udûkhala*) c. art. הַבְּ׳, apparently therefore well known; one of the products of the land Havilah Gn 2^{12}; used in simile of colour of manna וְעֵינוֹ כְּעֵין הַבְּדֹלַח Nu 11^{7}.—Meaning somewhat uncertain; 𝔊 Gn 2^{12} ἄνθραξ, Nu 11^{7} κρύσταλλος; Saad. AW Ki Bo al. *pearls,* cf. Lag [Or. ii. 44]; Jos [Ant. iii. 1. 6] Aq Theod Symm 𝔙 most *bdellium,*

an odoriferous transparent gum, of yellowish colour. (Cf. Smith $^{\text{Dict. Bible}}$ Sigismund $^{\text{Aromata, 18}}$.)

917 †בְּדָן **n.pr.m.** (=עַבְדּוֹן?). **1.** a judge of Israel 1 S 12^{11}; but rd. prob. בָּרָק, so 𝔊 𝔖 We, cf. Dr (v. Ju 4$^{6\,f.}$). **2.** a Manassite 1 Ch 7^{17}.

בדק (*penetrate, split?* cf. Aram. בְּדַק, ܒܕܩ *explore;* but these perh. denom. cf. Lag$^{\text{GN 1882, 400}}$).

919 †בֶּ֫דֶק **n.m.** $^{\text{2 K 12, 6}}$ **fissure, rent, breach** (Aram. בִּידְקָא, ܒܶܕܩܳܐ (Nasar.))—ב׳ abs. 2 K 12^{6}; cstr. *ib.* + 6 t.; sf. בִּדְקֵךְ Ez 27$^{9.27}$;—in a building; temple ב׳ הַבַּיִת 2 K 12$^{6.7.8.8.9}$ 22^{5}, cf. 12^{13} (ב׳ בֵּית י׳); v^{6} abs.; alw. c. חִזֵּק *repair;* cf. מַחֲזִיקֵי ב׳ *repairers of thy fissures* Ez 27$^{9.27}$ (of Tyre).

918 †[בָּדַק] **vb. denom. mend, repair,** only **Qal** *Inf. cstr.* לִבְדוֹק וּלְחַזֵּק הַבָּ֑יִת 2 Ch 34^{10}.

920 †בִּדְקַר **n.pr.m.** Isr. officer 2 K 9^{25} (v. בֵּן).

בהה (cf. Ar. بَهِىَ *be empty;* on a possible connexion in As. cf. Hpt$^{\text{BAS i. 18}}$).

922 †בֹּ֫הוּ **n.[m.] emptiness** (on form v. Ges $^{\S\,84\,a,\,1\,b}$ Sta$^{\S\,95,\,198\,a}$, on usage cf. Lag$^{\text{Or. ii. 60 f.}}$) alw. c. תֹּהוּ q.v.;—תֹהוּ וָבֹהוּ Gn 1^{2} of primæval earth; Je 4^{23} of earth under judgment of י׳; קַו־תֹהוּ וְאַבְנֵי בֹהוּ Is 34^{11}, *the line of wasteness and the stones of emptiness,* i.e. plummets, employed, not as usual for building, but for destroying walls; cf. Di & v. sub אבן **6.**

923 †בַּ֫הַט **n.[m.]** a costly stone, perh. **porphyry** (cf. Egypt. *behiti, behet, behat* Brugsch $^{\text{Dict. v. 438}}$ Dümichen $^{\text{Gesch. 167 f.}}$ Wendel $^{\text{Altäg. Bau- u. Edelsteine (1888) 77 f.}}$; 𝔊 has σμαραγδίτης), Est 1^{6} עַל רִֽצְפַת בַּהַט־וָשֵׁשׁ וְדַר וְסֹחָרֶת *upon a pavement of porphyry and marble,* etc.

926 †[בָּהַל] **vb.** (NH id. Pt. pass. בהול *disquieted;* Pi. *disquiet;* 𝔗 Pa. בַּהֵיל *hasten, be precipitate,* also *dismay:* but ܒܗܠ is *be quiet*)—**Niph.** *Pf.* נִבְהַל 1 S 28^{21}; נִבְהֲלָה ψ 6^{4}; נִבְהַלְתִּי Is 21^{3}; וְנִבְהָ֑לְתִּי consec. Jb 21^{6}; נִבְהֲלוּ Gn 45^{3}+, etc.; *Impf.* וַיִּבָּהֵל Ju 20^{41}; 2 ms. תִּבָּהֵל Ec 8^{3}; יִבָּהֵלוּן ψ 104^{29}, etc.; *Pt.* נִבְהָל ψ 30^{8}; נִבְהָל Pr 28^{22}; f. נִבְהָלָה Zp 1^{18};—**1.** *be disturbed, dismayed, terrified,* Gn 45^{3} (E) Ju 20^{41} 1 S 28^{21} 2 S 4^{1} (‖ וַיִּרְפּוּ יָדָיו, cf. Ez 7^{27} supr.); of bones of sufferer ψ 6^{3} (‖ cf. infr. v^{4}); of hands of dismayed people Ez 7^{27}; esp. at chastisements & judgments of י׳ Ex 15^{15} (song, in E) ψ 6^{4} (subj. נֶפֶשׁ, ‖ cf. supr. v^{3}) v^{11} (‖ בּוֹשׁ) 30^{8} cf. 104^{29}; 83^{18} (‖ בּוֹשׁ) 90^{7} Is 13^{8} 21^{3} (sq. מִן of occasion of fear) Jb 23^{15} (*id.*) Je 51^{32} Ez 26^{18} (del. 𝔊 Co); Jb 4^{5} (‖ לאה), cf. also 21^{6} as adj. *terrible* Zp 1^{18} כָּלָה אַךְ־נִבְהָלָה. **2.** *be in haste, hasty* (late, cf. Aram. above): Ec 8^{3} אַל־תִּבָּ׳ מִפָּנָיו תֵּלֵךְ *be not hasty* (*to*) *go from him;* Pr 28^{22} נִבְהָל לַהוֹן *hastening after riches.* **Pi.** *Impf.* וַיְבַהֵל Est 2^{9}; sf. יְבַהֲלֻהוּ Dn 11^{44}; וִיבַהֲלֻךָ Jb 22^{10}; יְבַהֲלֵמוֹ ψ 2^{5}; 2 ms. תְּבַהֲלֵם ψ 83^{16}; אַל־תְּבַהֵל Ec 5^{1} 7^{9}; *Inf.* sf. לְבַהֲלֵנִי 2 Ch 35^{21}; ־ם 32^{18}; *Part.* מבלהים Kt, מְבַהֲלִים Qr Ezr 4^{4} (BeRy pref. Kt, v. בלה);—**1.** *dismay, terrify,* sq. sf. 2 Ch 32^{18} (‖ ירא), Dn 11^{44} Jb 22^{10} (subj. פַּחַד), ψ 2^{5} (subj. י׳) 83^{16} (‖ רדף; subj. י׳); cf. also Ezr 4^{4} (v. sub בלה). **2.** *hasten, make haste, act hastily* (late), 2 Ch 35^{21} וֵאלֹהִים אָמַר לְבַהֲלֵנִי *God hath given command to speed me* (RVm); sq. inf. *make haste* Est 2^{9}; of hasty speech Ec 5^{1} אַל־תְּבַ׳ עַל־פִּיךָ (‖ וְלִבְּךָ אַל־יְמַהֵר לְהוֹצִיא דָבָר); of anger Ec 7^{9} אַל־תְּבַ׳ בְּרוּחֲךָ לִכְעוֹס. **Pu.** *Pt.* pl. מְבֹהָלִים Est 8^{14}, cf. מְבֹהֶלֶת Qr Pr 20^{21} (so rd. with Vrss Now Str; AV RV); Kt מבחלת v. בחל;—*hastened* Est 8^{14} of royal posts (‖ דְּחוּפִים); *hastily gained* נַחֲלָה מְבֹ׳ Pr 20^{21}. **Hiph.** *Pf.* sf. הִבְהִילָ֑נִי Jb 23^{16}; *Impf.* sf. וַיַּבְהִלוּהוּ 2 Ch 26^{20}; 3 mpl. וַיַּבְהִלוּ Est 6^{14};—**1.** *dismay, terrify,* sq. sf. Jb 23^{16} (subj. שַׁדַּי ‖ הֵרַךְ לִבִּי). **2.** (late) *hasten, hurry* (trans.), 2 Ch 26^{20} וַיַּבְהִלוּהוּ מִשָּׁם *and they hurried him thence* (‖ נִדְחַף); *make haste,* sq. inf. Est 6^{14} וַיַּבְ׳ לְהָבִיא *and they made haste to bring* Haman.

†בֶּהָלָה **n.f. dismay, sudden terror or ruin** 928
(cf. As. *bêltu, terror,* Dl$^{\text{Pr 32}}$)—ב׳ abs. Lv 26^{16} + 2 t.; pl. וּבֶהָלוֹת Je 15^{8};—*sudden terror* Lv 26^{16} וְהִפְקַדְתִּי עֲלֵיכֶם ב׳ (appositives follow); cf. Je 15^{8}; Is 65^{23} לֹא יֵלְדוּ לַבֶּהָלָה, ψ 78^{33} וַיְכַל־בַּהֶבֶל יְמֵיהֶם וּשְׁנוֹתָם בַּבֶּהָלָה *and he ended their days in a breath, and their years in sudden terror.*

בהם (Ar. بهم, IV. *shut,* X. *impeded in speech, tongue-tied;* Eth. ብህም: *be dumb*).

בְּהֵמָה$_{187}$ **n.f. beast, animal, cattle** (Ar. 929
بَهِيمَةٌ)—ב׳ Gn 1^{24} + 137 t.; cstr. בֶּהֱמַת Nu 3$^{41.41}$ + 10 t.; sf. בְּהֶמְתְּךָ Lv 19^{19} + 4 t.; בְּהֶמְתֶּךָ Ex 20^{10} + 4 t.; בְּהֶמְתּוֹ Gn 36^{6} Pr 12^{10}; pl. abs. בְּהֵמוֹת Dt 32^{24} + 6 t. + ψ 73^{22} (v. infr.); cstr. בַּהֲמוֹת ψ 8^{8} + 5 t.;—*beast,* & coll. *beasts* (Gn 8^{1} + very oft.) **1.** of living creatures other than man (אָדָם) Gn 8^{1} Ex 8$^{13.14}$ 9$^{9.10.22}$ 22^{18} Lv 18$^{23.23}$ (where ב׳ is male, so 20^{16}) Dt 27^{21} ψ 36^{7} etc.; מֵאָדָם וְעַד ב׳ (ב׳ including all the larger animals) Ex 9^{25} 12^{12} ψ 135^{8} Je 50^{3} etc.; as inferior to man Jb 18^{3} ψ 49$^{13.21}$, so also Ec 3$^{18.19.19.21}$; opp. also birds & reptiles Gn 6^{7} 7^{23} 8^{17} cf. Ez 44^{31} etc.; also to

fishes 1 K 5^{13} Jb 12^{7} cf. v^{8}, ψ 8^{9} Zp 1^{3}. **2.** opp. also to wild beasts ח׳ הַשָּׂדֶה, חַיַּת הָאָרֶץ Gn $1^{24.25.26}$ 2^{20} 3^{14} $7^{14.21}$ 9^{10} ψ 50^{10} 148^{10} Is 46^{1} etc.; esp. therefore *cattle*, as owned and used by man, Gn 47^{18} (מִקְנֵה הַבּ׳) Ex 20^{10}=Dt 5^{14}, Lv 19^{19} 26^{22} Nu $3^{41.41.45.45}$ Dt 2^{35} 11^{15} Jon 4^{11} Zc 2^{8} 8^{10} 14^{15} Ezr $1^{4.6}$ Ne 9^{37} 10^{37} etc.; in one (late) passage of animal for riding (horse? mule?) Ne $2^{12.12.14}$. **3.** rarely of *wild beasts*, esp. carnivora, בּ׳ יַעַר Mi 5^{7}; בּ׳ הָאָרֶץ Dt 28^{26} Is $18^{6.6}$ Je 7^{33} 15^{3} 16^{4} 19^{7} 34^{20}; בּ׳ הַשָּׂדֶה 1 S 17^{44}; alone, Pr 30^{30}; שֶׁן־בְּהֵמוֹת Dt 32^{24}; שֹׁד בּ׳ Hb 2^{17}.—On בְּהֵמוֹת ψ 73^{22} cf. infr.

930 †**בְּהֵמוֹת** **n.m. behemoth**, i.e. **hippopotamus** (appar. pl. intens. of foreg.; acc. to Di Jb 40^{15} cf. De Is 30^{6} fr. an (assumed) Egyptian *p-ehemau, ox of the water*) Jb 40^{15} (on identity, cf. further Bo [Hieroz. iii. 705]); prob. also ψ 73^{22} בְּהֵמוֹת הָיִיתִי עִמָּךְ *a behemoth was I with (toward) thee* (so Hi De; Che *beasts*); acc. to De Or also in בַּהֲמוֹת Is 30^{6} *the burden of the behemoth of the south* (supposed to be a designation of Egypt; but this unlikely, cf. Che Di, rd. therefore) rather *beasts of the south*, viz. of Judah.

בהן (cf. Ar. بَهَمَ IV. *shut, cover* (v. foregoing) whence also בֹּהֶן=إِبْهَام; as closing and covering the hand, cf. Lane).

931 †**בֹּהֶן** **n.[f.]** (cf. Sta [§ 310 c]) c. יָד **thumb**, c. רֶגֶל **great toe** (Ar. إِبْهَام, & (vulg.) بِهَام, بَاهِم)—בּ׳ only cstr. Ex $29^{20.20}$ + 12 t.; pl. cstr. בְּהֹנוֹת Ju $1^{6.7}$ (fr. sg. [בְּהוֹן] as alw. Cod. Sam. for MT בֹּהֶן);—*thumb* (יָדָם) בּ׳ יָדוֹ, & *great toe* (רַגְלָם) בּ׳ רַגְלוֹ (always named together) Ex $29^{20.20}$ Lv $8^{23.23.24.24}$ $14^{14.14.17.17.25.25.28.28}$; בְּהֹנוֹת י׳ וְר׳ Ju $1^{6.7}$.

932 †**בֹּהַן** **n.pr.m.** (*closing, covering?*) אֶבֶן בּ׳ בֶּן־רְאוּבֵן Jos 15^{6} 18^{17}, a mark of division between Judah & Benjamin.

בהק (NH בָּהַק *shine*, Aram. בְּהַק, ܒܗܩ, Aph. *id.*; hence בַּהֲקִיתָא, ܒܘܗܩܐ, an eruption, v. sq.)

933 †**בֹּהַק** **n.m.** a harmless eruption on the skin (NH *id.*, Aram. בּוֹהֲקָא; Ar. بَهَق) Lv 13^{39}.

בהר (NH Hiph. *be bright, shine;* cf. Aram. בְּהַר, ܒܗܪ (not Pe.) & deriv.; Eth. **በሀረ:** Ar. بَهَرَ *surpass*, esp. in brightness, *shine brightly*).

934 †**בַּהֶרֶת** **n.f. brightness, bright spot**, of eruption on skin (NH *id.*, Aram. בַּהְרָא)—בּ׳ abs. Lv 13^{2} + 7 t.; בַּהֶרֶת Lv 14^{56}; pl. abs. בֶּהָרוֹת Lv $13^{38.39}$;—*bright spot* (sore, scar, etc.), clean or unclean Lv 14^{56}; following a burn (from fire) Lv $13^{24.25.26.28}$; possible beginning of leprosy Lv $13^{2.4.19.23}$; but possibly a (passing) eruption מִסְפַּחַת v^{6}; or due to a boil שְׁחִין $v^{19.23}$; —due to בֹּהַק (q.v.) Lv $13^{38.39}$.

†**בָּהִיר** **adj. bright, brilliant**, of light; only 925
Jb 37^{21} לֹא רָאוּ אוֹר בּ׳ הוּא בַּשְּׁחָקִים.

בּוֹא 2569 **vb. come in, come, go in, go** 935
(As. *bâ'u* Hpt [KAT 499], Eth. **ቦአ:** Ar. بَآءَ *return*) —**Qal** *Pf.* בָּא Gn 6^{13} +; 3 fs. בָּ֫אָה Gn 15^{17} +; sf. בָּאַתְנוּ ψ 44^{18}; 2 ms. בָּ֫אתָ Jos 13^{1} +, בָּ֫אתָה 2 S 3^{7}; 2 fs. בָּאתְ Gn 16^{8} Ru 2^{12}, וּבָאתְ consec. Ru 3^{4} 2 S 14^{3} Mi 4^{10}; 3 pl. בָּאוּ Gn 7^{9} +; 1 pl. בָּאנוּ Gn 32^{7} + (בָּנוּ 1 S 25^{8}), etc.; *Impf.* יָבוֹא Gn 32^{9} +, יָבֹא Gn 49^{10} +; 3 fs. תָּבוֹא Gn 41^{50} +; sf. תְּבוֹאָתְךָ Jb 22^{21} (but text dub. v. Kö [i. 644]); 2 ms. תָּבוֹא Gn 15^{15} +; 2 fs. תָּבוֹאִי Ru 3^{17} +; 1 s. אָבוֹא Gn 33^{14} +; cohort. אָבֹ֫אָה Ju 15^{1}, אָבוֹ֫אָה Gn 29^{21} +, וַתָּבֹאתִי 1 S 25^{34} (Qr וַתָּבֹאת, but text prob. wrong, v. Kö [i. 647] Dr, rd. וַתָּבֹאִי); 3 pl. m. יָבוֹאוּ Gn 6^{20} +, also (by text err.) בָּאוּ Je 27^{18} cf. Kö [i. 645], יְבֹאֻן ψ 95^{11}; sf. יְבֹאוּנִי ψ 119^{77}, וִיבֹאֻנִי v^{41}; 3 f. pl. תָּבֹאןָ Gn 30^{38}, תָּבוֹאנָה 1 S 10^{7} +; תְּבֹאֶינָה 1 S 10^{7} ψ 45^{16}, etc.; *Imv.* בֹּא, בּוֹא Gn 7^{1} +, בֹּ֫אָה 1 S 20^{21} 1 K 13^{7}, בֹּ֫אִי, בּוֹ֫אִי 2 S 13^{11} +; mpl. בֹּ֫אוּ Gn 45^{17} +; *Inf.* בּוֹא, בֹּא Gn 39^{16} +; sf. בֹּאִי, בּוֹאִי Gn 48^{5} +, בּוֹאֲךָ 1 S 29^{6} +, בֹּאֲכָה Gn 10^{19} +, etc., בֹּאָם Gn 34^{5} +, בֹּאָן Gn 30^{38} cf. Ez 42^{12} (where Co for בְּבוֹאָן reads לבוא להנה); *Pt.* בָּא Gn 33^{1} +; f. בָּ֫אָה Gn 29^{6} +, הַבָּ֫אָה Gn 18^{21} + (accent wrong Ew [§ 331 b N.]); pl. בָּאִים Gn 18^{11} +; cstr. בָּאֵי Gn 23^{10} +; f. abs. בָּאוֹת Gn 41^{29}; (see further on forms Kö [i. 643 f.]);—**1.** *come in*, sq. אֶל Gn 6^{18} $7^{9.13}$, sq. בְּ Gn 19^{8} & so (subj. רוּחַ) Ez 2^{2} 37^{10}, sq. לְ Est 6^{4}, sq. הָ— loc. Gn 12^{11} 41^{57} Nu 14^{24}, sq. acc. (בית) Ju 18^{18} 2 K 11^{19} cf. ψ 100^{4} (שְׁעָרָיו), & בָּאֵי שַׁעַר עִירוֹ Gn $23^{10.18}$; even of lifeless things 2 K 18^{21}, וּבָא בְכַפּוֹ (of broken reed) = pierce; of food and drink (sq. אֶל־) Dn 10^{3} cf. Gn 41^{21} (fat kine when eaten by lean kine); v. also (sq. בְּ) Nu $5^{22.24.27}$; abs. Gn 7^{16} 24^{31} 1 K 1^{42} 14^{6} cf. 2 K $11^{5.9}$=2 Ch $23^{4.8}$ +; more partic. **a.** opp. יָצָא, *go out and come in* (Sab. וצאם או בהאם Hal [152]) Jos 6^{1} 2 K 11^{8} = 2 Ch 23^{7}; esp. in sense of going about one's affairs (including all one's undertakings) Dt $28^{6.19}$ Zc 8^{10} ψ 121^{8}; *id.* + ישׁב 2 K 19^{27}; also sq. לִפְנֵי הָעָם etc. = act as ruler (judge) of, Nu 27^{17} 2 Ch 1^{10} cf. 1 K 3^{7}; of leading an army 1 S $18^{13.16}$ cf. also Jos 14^{11}; v. further Dt 31^{2} 1 S 29^{6} & sub **c.** infr. **b.** of taking part in worship of congregation Dt $23^{2.3.3.4.4}$ + (sq. בְּ); or entering into tabernacle for priestly service Ex $28^{29.35}$ Lv 16^{23} (all sq.

-אֶל), Ex 28^{30} (sq. לִפְנֵי יהוה), Lv 16^{17} (sq. inf.) +. **c.** of entering on official duty 2 K 11^{9} = 2 Ch 23^{8} 1 Ch 27^{1} (all opp. יצא). **d.** of bride coming into her husband's house Jos 15^{18} = Ju 1^{14}. **e.** of entering a woman's tent or apartment (with implication *coire cum femina*, cf. Ar. أَتَى, NH בִּיאָה *coitio;* on origin of this use of word cf. RS K 90, 167, 291) Ju 15^{1} אֶל־אִשְׁתִּי הֶחָדְרָה, 16^{1} Gn 6^{4} 16^{2} 30^{3} $38^{8.9}$ 39^{14} Dt 22^{13} 2 S 12^{24} 16^{21} 20^{3} Ez $23^{44.44.44}$ Pr 6^{29} (all sq. -אֶל); sq. -עַל Gn 19^{31} Dt 25^{5} יָבֹא עָלֶיהָ וּלְקָחָהּ לוֹ לְאִשָּׁה; cf. בָּאֶיהָ Pr 2^{19};—subj. rarely woman Gn 19^{34} 2 S 11^{4}. **f.** of associating with (sq. בְּ) Jos $23^{7.12}$ cf. Gn 49^{6} בְּסֹדָם אַל תָּבֹא נַפְשִׁי (בִּקְהָלָם ‖ אַל־תֵּחַד). **g.** of entering into specific relations, בּוֹא (ברית, אלה .v) בּ׳ בִּבְרִית, בּ׳ בְּאָלָה; בּוֹא בְדָמִים *come into blood-guiltiness*, became guilty of murder 1 S 25^{26}. **h.** of burial, בּ׳ אֶל־קֶבֶר 1 K 13^{22} 14^{13} cf. תָּבוֹא אֶל־אֲבוֹתֶיךָ Gn 15^{15} (‖ תִּקָּבֵר). **i.** of sun, *set* (go in, enter, cf. As. *êrib šanši* COT Gn 19^{23}; opp. יצא *go forth, rise*) Gn $15^{12.17}$ 28^{11} Ex 17^{12} 22^{25} Lv 22^{7} Dt 16^{6} 23^{12} $24^{13.15}$ Jos 8^{29} $10^{13.27}$ Ju 19^{14} Ec 1^{5} 2 S 2^{24} 3^{35} 1 K 22^{36} 18^{34}; so also fig. Je 15^{9} of calamity באה שִׁמְשָׁהּ בְּעוֹד יוֹמָם (‖ אֻמְלְלָה יֹלֶדֶת הַשִּׁבְעָה etc.), cf. Is 60^{20}; Mi 3^{6} וּבָ׳ הַשֶּׁמֶשׁ עַל־הַנְּבִיאִים of ignorance and confusion. **j.** of harvest, *come in* = be gathered Lv 25^{22} (cf. תְּבוּאָה); so of revenue (*income*) 1 K 10^{14} = 2 Ch 9^{13} (sq. לְ pers.),—opp. יצא *be expended.* **k.** in other phrases: וַתָּבֹא הָעִיר בַּמָּצוֹר 2 K 24^{10} + *and the city came into siege;* cf. ψ 105^{18} בַּרְזֶל בָּאָה נַפְשׁוֹ *his soul came into iron* (v. AV RVm; Che *felt iron chains*, cf. Ew Ol Hup Pe; 𝔗 Hi De al. *iron came upon his soul*); בָּא בַּיָּמִים *come into (the) days*, = advanced in age Gn 24^{1} Jos 13^{1} 23^{1} (all ‖ זָקֵן); on 1 S 17^{12} v. Dr. **2.** *come* (approach, arrive) opp. הָלַךְ Gn 16^{8} 1 S 20^{21} (cf. v^{22}) Ne 6^{17} Ec $5^{14.15}$ (of birth opp. death); sq. -אֶל pers. vel rei Gn 14^{7} 37^{23}; sq. -עַל Ex 18^{23} 2 Ch 20^{24} (*come up upon*, almost = *ascend*); cf. also Lv 21^{11} Nu 6^{6}; sq. לְ 1 S 9^{12} 2 Ch 29^{17}; sq. עַד Nu 13^{22} Ju 15^{14} 2 S 16^{5}; cf. בָּאוּ בָנִים עַד־מַשְׁבֵּר 2 K 19^{3} = Is 37^{3} *children have come to the birth;* sq. אֶל + עַד 2 K 9^{20} בָּא עַד אֲלֵיהֶם; sq. ־ָה loc. Ju 11^{16} 2 K 6^{4}; sq. acc. 1 S 4^{12} 2 K 8^{7} Je 32^{24}; cf. also La 1^{4} בָּאֵי מוֹעֵד *those coming to an appointed feast;* abs. Gn 45^{16} *Joseph's brethren are come*, & oft.; also of lifeless things, ark of י׳ 1 S 4^{6}; wind Jb 1^{19}; so כַּסְפְּכֶם בָּא אֵלָי Gn 43^{23} *your money came unto me* = I received your money; *our inheritance has fallen to us* Nu 32^{19} (c. -אֶל); so 1 S 9^{16} *its cry is come unto me*, cf. Gn 18^{21} Ex 3^{9} La 1^{22}; of time, oft. of imminent future, esp. in phr. הִנֵּה יָמִים בָּאִים Is 39^{6} = 2 K 20^{17} Je 7^{32} 9^{24} 16^{14} 19^{6}; cf. also 1 S 26^{10} Ez 7^{7} +; of day of י׳ Jo 2^{1} 3^{4} Zc 14^{1} Mal $3^{2.19.23}$; also ptcp. as adj. הַיָּמִים הַבָּאִים Ec 2^{16} cf. Je 47^{4}; as subst. הַבָּאוֹת Is 41^{22} *things to come*, future things; & הַבָּאִים alone = adv. *in (days) to come* Is 27^{6}; partic. **a.** *come with*, i.e. come, bringing, sq. בְּ: אָבוֹא בֵיתְךָ בְעוֹלוֹת ψ 66^{13}; אָבוֹא בִּגְבֻרוֹת אדני י׳ ψ 71^{16} (‖ אַזְכִּיר צִדְקָתְךָ) so Lv 16^{3} & perh. Pr 18^{6}—cf. בְּ **III. 1. b.** **b.** *come upon, fall* or *light upon*, of enemy, *attack*, sq. -עַל Gn 34^{27} 1 S 11^{12} cf. Gn 32^{9} (sq. -אֶל); sq. sf. Jb 15^{21}, so also 20^{22} Ez 32^{11}; of calamity, etc. Pr 10^{24} 28^{32} ψ 44^{18} (all c. sf.); sq. לְ Jb 3^{25} (‖ אתה c. sf.) Is 47^{9} (‖ בוא על); of blessing, sq. -עַל Jos 23^{15}; sq. sf. Jb 22^{21} (cf. Di) ψ $119^{41.77}$. **c.** *come to pass*, of signs, wonders, predictions, etc. Dt 13^{3} Jos 23^{14} 1 S 9^{6} (בֹּא יָבֹא) Is 42^{9} Je 28^{9} Pr 13^{12} Jb 6^{8} +. **d.** Gn 6^{13} קֵץ כָּל־בָּשָׂר בָּא לְפָנַי perh. *has presented itself before me* (v. Kn), cf. La 1^{22} supr. & 2 Ch 7^{11} (where בוא for usual עלה); but perh. (cf. Di) *has come to pass before me*, i.e. in my mind it is already a fact. **e.**† in phr. עַד־בּוֹאֲךָ עַזָּה Ju 6^{4} cf. 11^{33} 1 S 17^{52} 2 S 5^{25} 1 K 18^{46} (עַד־בֹּאֲכָה) *until thou comest to* = as far as; so also בּוֹאֲךָ (בֹּאֲכָה) alone, = as far as, or in the direction of, Gn $10^{19.19.30}$ 13^{10} 25^{18} 1 S 27^{8} (all sq. ־ָה loc.) 1 S 15^{7}; so לְבֹא חֲמָת Nu 13^{21} 34^{8} Ez 48^{1}, cf. Ez 47^{15} (in a different connexion לָבוֹא אפרתה Gn 35^{16} 48^{7}); עַד לְבוֹא ח׳ Jos 13^{5} Ju 3^{3} 1 Ch 13^{5}, cf. 5^{9} 2 Ch 26^{8} Ez 47^{20}; מִלְּבוֹא ח׳ Am 6^{14} 1 K 8^{65} 2 K 14^{25} 2 Ch 7^{8}; of Isaac בָּא מִבּוֹא בְּאֵר לַחַי רֹאִי Gn 24^{62} (but text dub.) **f.** *attain to* וְעַד הַשְּׁלֹשָׁה לֹא בָא 2 S 23^{19} = 1 Ch 11^{21}. **g.** *be enumerated* הַבָּאִים בְּשֵׁמוֹת, lit. *those coming with names* 1 Ch 4^{38}. **3.** *go*, i.e. *walk, associate with* (עִם) ψ 26^{4}, so c. אֶת Pr 22^{24} (cf. הלך את 13^{20} & התהלך את Gn $5^{22.24}$ 6^{9}). **4.** *go* (cf. הלך) from speaker, but with limit of motion given Is 22^{15} לֶךְ־בֹּא אֶל־, so Ez $3^{4.11}$; Gn 45^{17} וּלְכוּ־בֹאוּ אַרְצָה כְּנָעַן; 1 S 22^{5} לֵךְ וּבָאתָ־לְּךָ אֶרֶץ יְהוּדָה; Is 47^{5} Jon 1^{3} אָנִיָּה בָּאָה תַרְשִׁישׁ *a ship going to Tarshish;* *go to war* יָבֹאוּ לַמִּלְחָמָה Nu 32^{6}. **Hiph.** *Pf.* הֵבִיא Gn 4^{4} +; sf. הֱבִיאַנִי Dt 9^{4} +, etc.; 2 ms. הֵבֵאתָ Is 43^{23}, הֵבֵאתָ Gn 20^{9} +, etc.; sf. הֲבִיאֹתַנִי 2 S 7^{18} 1 Ch 17^{16}, הֲבִיאֹתָנוּ Nu 16^{14}, הֲבֵתָנוּ ψ 66^{11}; 1 s. הֵבֵאתִי Gn 31^{39} +, והבאותי Je 25^{13} Kt (Qr וְהֵבֵאתִי); sf. וַהֲבִיאוֹתִיךָ Ez 38^{16} +, הֲבֵאתִיהָ Is 37^{26}, etc.; 3 pl. הֵבִיאוּ Gn 43^{2} +; sf. הֱבִיאוּהוּ 2 Ch 28^{27} etc.; 2 mpl. הֲבֵאתֶם Nu 20^{4} +; וַהֲבֵאתֶם 1 S 16^{17}; 1 pl. sf. הֲבִיאֹנֻם Nu 32^{17}; *Impf.* יָבִיא (יָבֵא) Lv 4^{32} +, וַיָּבֵא Gn 2^{19} +; sf. וַיְבִיאֵנִי Ez 40^{17}, etc.;

2 ms. תָּבִיא Jb 14^{3}; sf. תְּבִיאֵהוּ Jc 13^{1}, וַתְּבִיאֵם Ne 9^{23}, תְּבִאֵמוֹ Ex 15^{17}, אָבִיא Ex 11^{1} + (אָבִי 1 K 21^{29} Mi 1^{15}), etc.; *Imv.* הָבֵא Gn 43^{16} Ex 4^{6}, הָבִיא 1 S 20^{40}, הָבִיאָה Gn 27^{7} +; fs. הָבִיאִי 2 S 13^{10} +, etc.; *Inf. abs.* הָבֵא Hg 1^{6}; *cstr.* הָבִיא Gn 18^{19} +; *Pt.* מֵבִיא Ex 10^{14} +, מֵבִי 1 K 21^{21} + 3 t., מְבִיאֲךָ Dt 8^{7}; pl. מְבִיאִים (מְבִאִים) 1 K 10^{25} +; cstr. מְבִאֵי Je 17^{26}, מְבִיאֶיהָ Dn 11^{6};—**1.** *cause to come in, bring in* (conduct, lead, obj. persons and animals), sq. אֶל־ Gn 6^{19} Ct 2^{4} 3^{4}; sq. בְּ Lv 26^{41} ψ 66^{11}; sq. לְ Ju 19^{21} 1 S 9^{22}; sq. לִפְנֵי Est $1^{11.17}$; sq. ־ָה loc. Gn 24^{67} 46^{7}; sq. ־ָה + אֶל־ Gn 19^{10}; sq. acc. (חֶדֶר) Ct 1^{4} 2 K 9^{2}; also *bring, carry in* (lifeless things), sq. אֶל־ Nu 31^{54} Mal 3^{10}; sq. בְּ Je 17^{21}; *send*, of sending (shooting) arrows (fig.) La 3^{13}, cf. Lv 26^{36}; of sending breath (רוּחַ) into dry bones Ez 37^{5} (Co עַל); sq. לְ Ne 13^{12}; sq. ־ָה loc. Ex 26^{33} 2 K 20^{20} וַיָּבֵא אֶת־הַמַּיִם הָעִירָה; sq. acc. (חֶדֶר) 2 S 13^{10}; also 2 Ch 15^{18} (בֵּית); abs. 2 S 6^{17}; partic. **a.** opp. הוֹצִיא (*bring out*) Dt 9^{28} (sq. אֶל־); esp. in combination with הוֹצִיא *lead out and in* (to and from battle) Nu 27^{17} 1 Ch 11^{2}. **b.** *bring in* women as wives for sons (sq. מִן הַחוּץ) Ju 12^{9} (opp. שִׁלַּח הַחוּצָה). **c.** *bring into judgment* וְאֹתִי תָבִיא בְמִשְׁפָּט עִמָּךְ Jb 14^{3} cf. Ec 11^{9} 12^{14}. **d.** *cause* sun *to go down* Am 8^{9} (symbol of judgment). **e.** of harvest, *bring in, gather* 2 S 9^{10} Hg 1^{6} (opp. זרע) cf. Ne 13^{15}. **f.** *put* staves into (בְּ) rings Ex 25^{14} 37^{5} 38^{7} cf. 26^{11} Lv 14^{42}; hand into (בְּ) bosom Ex $4^{6.6}$; girdle into (בְּ) water Je 13^{1}. **g.** other phrases, הֵבִיאוּ צַוָּרָם בַּעֲבֹדַת אֲדֹנֵיהֶם Ne 3^{5} *put their necks to the work*, etc.; fig. הביאו את־צואריכם בְּעֹל Je 27^{12}; הָבִיאָה לַמּוּסָר לִבֶּךָ Pr 23^{12} *apply to instruction thy heart;* וְנָבִא לְבַב חָכְמָה ψ 90^{12} *that we may gain a heart of wisdom.* **2.** *cause to come, bring, bring near*, etc. (animate obj.), sq. אֶל־ Gn $2^{19.22}$ 43^{9} Lv 24^{11} Nu 5^{15}; oft. of bringing Isr. to Canaan Ex 6^{8} 23^{23} +, cf. Is 14^{2} 56^{7} Ne 1^{9}; abs. Dt 4^{38} 6^{23}; sq. לְ Gn $39^{14.17}$; sq. ־ָה loc. Ez 12^{13}; sq. הֲלֹם Ju 18^{3}, & עַד־הֲלֹם (fig. of Yahweh's prospering care) 2 S 7^{18} = 1 Ch 17^{16}; abs. Gn 46^{32}; also with lifeless obj., Gn 27^{10} (sq. לְ), so 2 Ch 36^{7}; Gn 31^{39} (sq. אֶל־); sq. acc. 2 K 12^{5} 2 Ch 36^{18} Dn $1^{2.2}$; sq. ־ָה loc. Ex 26^{33} Je 20^{5}; sq. לִפְנֵי 2 Ch 24^{14}; of ravens bringing food 1 K 17^{6} (sq. לְ); of bringing presents Gn 43^{26} 1 S 9^{7} 10^{27} (all sq. לְ); cf. 1 S 17^{18}; esp. offerings, sq. לְ Gn 4^{3} Nu 15^{25} Ne $10^{35.37}$ (לְבֵית), etc.; Lv 2^{2} sq. אֶל־ of priest; abs. Gn 4^{4} Lv 4^{32} $23^{14.15}$ Mal $1^{13.13}$ 2 Ch 31^{5}; cf. also Ex $35^{21.22.23.24.24.27.29}$ (sq. לְ *for*) so 36^{3} +; of time, *cause a day to come* La 1^{21}; *cause cry to come* (עַל־) Jb 34^{28}; = *carry* והב׳ בָּנַיִךְ בְּחֹצֶן Is 49^{22} (|| עַל־כָּתֵף נשׂא); *carry God in* (בְּ) *the hand* Jb 12^{6} (cf. אֱלֹהַּ p. 43); *allow to come*, almost = *invite* Est 5^{12} (sq. אֶל־) cf. v^{10}; partic. **a.** sq. עַל־ *bring against*, or *upon*, bring enemies against Je 25^{9} cf. Ez 23^{22}; obj. sword Lv 26^{25} Ez 5^{17} 11^{8} 14^{17} 33^{2}; plague Ex 11^{1}; curse or calamity Gn 27^{12} Dt 29^{26} 1 K 9^{9} = 2 Ch 7^{22} Jb 42^{11} cf. Je 25^{13} 36^{31} 44^{2} $49^{8.37}$ Ez 14^{22}; sin Gn 20^{9} 26^{10} Ex 32^{21}; cf. also sq. אֶל־ Je 32^{42} 49^{36}. **b.** *bring to pass* 2 K 19^{25} = Is 37^{26} cf. 1 Ch 4^{10} ψ 78^{29}. **c.** *bring, bring forward, bring on the scene* Mi 1^{15} Zc 3^{8}. **d.** *bring* for a purpose, sq. inf. ψ 78^{71} מֵאַחַר עָלוֹת הֱבִיאוֹ לִרְעוֹת בְּיַעֲקֹב עַמּוֹ. **e.** *bring, procure* בְּנַפְשֵׁנוּ נָבִיא לַחְמֵנוּ La 5^{9}. †**Hoph.** *Pf.* הוּבָא Lv 10^{18} +; 3 fs. הֻבָאת Gn 33^{11} (v. infr.); 2 ms. הֻבָאתָה Ez 40^{4}; 3 pl. הוּבְאוּ Gn 43^{18}; *Impf.* יוּבָא Lv 6^{23} +, יוּבָאוּ Je 27^{22}; *Pt.* מוּבָא 2 K 12^{10} +; pl. מוּבָאִים Gn 43^{18} Ez 30^{11} + 23^{42} (Co מרבדים), מוּבָאוֹת ψ 45^{15};—**a.** *be brought in* (of pers. and things), abs. Gn 43^{18}; sq. בית *into a house* Gn 43^{18}, temple 2 K $12^{5.10.14.17}$ 22^{4} 2 Ch $34^{9.14}$. **b.** *be brought*, sq. לְ Gn 33^{11} (but 𝔊 rd. Hiph. *I have brought*), ψ 45^{15}; sq. אֶל־ *unto* Lv 6^{23} 10^{18} $13^{2.9}$ 14^{2}; cf. Ez 23^{42} (but v. Co VB); sq. הֵנָּה Ez 40^{4}; sq. בָּבֶלָה Je 27^{22}; sq. inf. Lv 16^{27} Ez 30^{11}; sq. מִן Je 10^{9}. **c.** *be introduced, put*, sq. בְּ, staves into rings Ex 27^{7}; vessel into water Lv 11^{32}.

†בִּאָה **n.f.** entrance, entry, בַּבִּאָה Ez 8^{5}, 872
i.e. of temple (but del. B Co).

†מָבוֹא **n.m.** $^{\text{Je 38, 14}}$ **entrance, a coming** 3996
in, entering;—מ׳ abs. Je 38^{14} + 3 t. + Ez 42^{9} Kt (Qr מֵבִיא wrong, cf. Co); cstr. מְבוֹא Dt 11^{30} + 12 t.; sf. מְבוֹאוֹ ψ 104^{19} + 2 t.; מְבֹאוֹ ψ 50^{1}; מבואך 2 S 3^{25} Kt (Qr מוֹבָאֲךָ inexplicable
cf. Dr); pl. cstr. מְבוֹאֵי Ez 26^{10}, מְבוֹאֹת Ez 27^{3}; 3997
—**1.** *entrance*, i.e. place or way of entrance, into a city Ju $1^{24.25}$ 1 Ch 4^{39} Pr 8^{3} (מ׳ פְּתָחִים); into buildings 2 K 11^{16} 16^{18} 1 Ch 9^{19} (שֹׁמְרֵי הַמָּבוֹא), 2 Ch $23^{13.15}$ Je 38^{14} Ez 42^{9} 46^{19}; v. also מְבוֹאֹת יָם *entrance of (the) sea, gate of the sea*, of situation of Tyre Ez 27^{3}. **2.** *entering*, act of entrance, by violence, in storm of city Ez 26^{10}; *coming in* or together, making a crowd, כִּמְבוֹא עָם Ez 33^{31} sim. of eagerness to hear Yahweh's word; in phrase אֶת־מוֹצָאֲךָ וְאֶת־מבואך 2 S 3^{25} *thy going out and thy coming in; mode of entering temple*, or *the people who enter* Ez 44^{5}; particularly of *sunset* מְבוֹא הַשֶּׁמֶשׁ ψ 104^{19}; = *west* Dt 11^{30}; Jos 1^{4} 23^{4} הַיָּם הַגָּדוֹל מְבוֹא

הַשֶּׁמֶשׁ = Mediterranean, Zc 8[7] אֶרֶץ מְבוֹא הַשֶּׁמֶשׁ (‖ אֶרֶץ מִזְרָח), Mal 1[11] ψ 50[1] 113[3] *sunset=west*, opp. sunrise = east; in phr. *from E. to W.*, i.e. over the whole earth, everywhere on earth.

4126 †[מוֹבָא] **n.[m.] in-coming, entrance,** מוֹבָאֶךָ Qr 2 S 3[25], cf. Kt sub מבוא; וּמוֹבָאָיו Ez 43[11] *and its entrances* (‖ וּמוֹצָאָיו), del. B Co. In both, ungramm. form for assonance with מוצא.

8393 †תְּבוּאָה **n.f.** *proventus*, **product, revenue**—ת׳ abs. ψ 107[37] + 3 t.; cstr. תְּבוּאַת Lv 23[39] + 11 t.; sf. תְּבוּאָתִי Jb 31[12] Pr 8[19]; תְּבוּאָתְךָ Dt 14[28] + 2 t.; תְּבוּאָתֶךָ Pr 3[9]; תְּבוּאָתוֹ Lv 19[25] + Ez 48[18] Qr (Kt תבואתה), תְּבוּאָתֹה Je 2[3]; תְּבוּאָתָהּ Ex 23[10] + 7 t. + Ez 48[18] Kt (so Co); תְּבוּאָתֵנוּ Lv 25[20]; pl. תְּבוּאֹת Lv 25[15] + 4 t.; תְּבוּאוֹת Pr 14[4] 16[8]; תְּבוּאֹתֵיכֶם Je 12[13];—**1.** *product, yield*, usually of earth (=crops, etc.) ת׳ הָאָרֶץ Ex 23[10] Lv 19[25] 23[29] 25[3.7] (used as food for man & beast, cf. v[22]) Jos 5[12], cf. Ne 9[37] Lv 25[15.16], also Ez 48[18]; in Gn 47[24] בַּתּ׳ must=*of the crops* (בְּ partitive, cf. בְּ **I. 2. b**; 𝔊 del. בְּ); ת׳ שָׂדֶה 2 K 8[6] 2 Ch 31[5]; ת׳ כֶּרֶם Dt 22[9] cf. ψ 107[37]; לֶחֶם ת׳ הָאֲדָמָה Is 30[23]; ת׳ גֹּרֶן & ת׳ יֶקֶב Nu 18[30]; ת׳ זֶרַע Dt 14[22]; ת׳ דָּגָן 2 Ch 32[28]; as property of husbandmen, or people Lv 25[20] Dt 14[28] 16[15] 26[12] Pr 3[9]; crops as determined by season, ת׳ שֶׁמֶשׁ Dt 33[14] (‖ גֶּרֶשׁ יְרָחִים); *yield* of a year שָׁנָה Lv 25[12.22]; cf. v[21] עָשָׂה ת׳, subj. שָׁנָה. **2. a.** *income, revenue*, in general Jb 31[12] (almost = possessions) Pr 10[16] 14[4] 15[6] 16[8] Ec 5[9] cf. Is 23[3] (revenue of Tyre from trade with Egypt in bread stuffs). **b.** fig. *gain* of wisdom ת׳ חָכְמָה Pr 3[14] 8[19]; *product of lips* (ת׳ שְׂפָתָיו) Pr 18[20], i.e. results of his speech (‖ פְּרִי פִי־אִישׁ); of Isr. as Yahweh's product Je 2[3]; of Israel's wickedness Je 12[13].

936 †I. [בּוּז] **vb. despise** (NH *id.*)—**Qal** *Pf.* 3 ms. בַּז Zc 4[10] (cf. Kö [i. 439]); 3 pl. בָּזוּ Pr 1[7]; *Impf.* יָבוּז Pr 23[9]; 3 fs. וְתָבֻז Pr 30[17]; 2 ms. תָּבוּז (juss.) Pr 23[22]; pl. יָבוּזוּ Pr 6[30] Ct 8[7]; יָבֻזוּ Ct 8[1]; *Inf. abs.* בּוֹז Ct 8[7]; *Pt.* Pr 11[12] + 2 t.;—*despise, shew despite toward* (WisdLt & poet.) c. acc. Pr 1[7]; c. Inf. + לְ Pr 30[17]; elsewh. sq. לְ + noun, Pr 6[30] 11[12] 13[13] 14[21] 23[9.22] Ct 8[1.7.7] Zc 4[10].

937 †II. בּוּז **n.m.** [Pr 18, 3] **contempt**—בּ׳ abs. Gn 38[23] + 9 t.; cstr. Jb 31[34];—(WisdLt & poet., exc. Gn 38[23] J). **1.** *contempt* springing from pride and wickedness Jb 31[34] ψ 123[3.4] (‖ לַעַג); joined in one adverb. phr. with נאוה ψ 31[19] בְּגַ׳ וָב׳; springing from prosperity and ease Jb 12[5]; = object of contempt Gn 38[23] Pr 12[8]; ‖ חֶרְפָּה ψ 119[22] Pr 18[3]. **2.** judicial, poured out (שׁפך) by God, in judgment Jb 12[21] = ψ 107[40].

†בּוּזָה **n.f. contempt** Ne 3[36] הָיִינוּ ב׳ *we* 939
have become (an object of) *contempt*.

†III. בּוּז **n.pr.m.** (cf. As. n.pr.loc. *Bâzu* 938
Dl [Pa 307; ZK 1885, 93 f.]) **1.** 2nd son of Nahor, Abraham's brother Gn 22[21] J;=tribe named with דְּדָן & תֵּימָא Je 25[23]. **2.** a Gadite 1 Ch 5[14].

†I. בּוּזִי **adj.gent.** (=בעזי fr. בֹּעַז acc. to 940
J. Derenbourg [RÉJ i. 6]) of Elihu's father Jb 32[2.6].

†II. בּוּזִי **n.pr.m.** father of Ezekiel Ez 1[3]. 941

†בַּוַּי **n.pr.m.** a Jew of Nehem.'s time Ne 942
3[18] = בִּנּוּי v[24] which prob. rd. also v[18] (𝔊 Βεδει, Βενει, Βεζερ); cf. further Sm [Listen 12].

†בּוּךְ **vb. perplex, confuse** (? Ar. بَاكَ *stir* 943
up (water of spring) then *be disturbed, confused;* cf. As. *bâku, lead captive*, orig. *lead astray*? COT Ezr 4[2])—only **Niph.** *Pf.* 3 fs. נָבוֹכָה Est 3[15]; 3 mpl. נָבֹכוּ Jo 1[18]; *Pt.* pl. נְבֻכִים Ex 14[3];—*be confused, in confusion* (of a city) Est 3[15]; = wander aimlessly (of Isr.) Ex 14[3]; so of cattle Jo 1[18] (Merx prop. בָּכוּ, after 𝔊 ἔκλαυσαν, but בכה not elsewhere of cattle).

†מְבוּכָה **n.f. confusion, confounding,** Is 3998
22[5] יוֹם מְהוּמָה וּמְבוּסָה וּמְבוּכָה *a day of consternation and down-treading and confusion;* Mi 7[4] עַתָּה תִהְיֶה מְבוּכָתָם *now shall be their confusion.*

†I. בּוּל **n.[m.]** Bul, 8th month=*Marches-* 945
wan, As. *Araḫ samna*, 1 K 6[38] בְּיֶרַח בּוּל הוּא הַחֹדֶשׁ הַשְּׁמִינִי; (Canaanitish; Ph. ירח בל; a Palm. god is בול (in n.pr. עבדבול, Vog[93] זבדבול etc.) & ירחבול (Vog[93], moon-god), which DHM [Ber. Wien. Ak. cviii. 977] connects with Heb. בּוּל; Bae [Rel 87 f.] (q. v.) thinks=בעל, cf. Thes [p. 560]).

II. בּוּל **n.m.** *product, produce*, v. יבול. p. 385 944

בּוּנָה **n.pr.m.** v. בין. p. 107 946

בּוּנִּי **n.pr.m.** v. בנה. p. 125 1138

†[בּוּס] **vb. tread down, trample**—**Qal** 947
Impf. יָבוּס ψ 60[14]=108[14]; 3 *fs.* תָּבוּס Pr 27[7], אָבוּס Is 63[6]; *sf.* 3 s. אֲבוּסֶנּוּ Is 14[25]; 1 *pl.* נָבוּס ψ 44[6];—*tread down, trample* (of warriors), no obj. expr. Zc 10[5]; *id.*, fig. c. acc. (subj. י׳, as warrior) Is 14[25] cf. ψ 60[14]=108[14] Is 63[6]; (subj. men, with God's help) ψ 44[6]; fig. = *reject, loathe* Pr 27[7]. **Pol.** *Pf.* בּוֹסְסוּ Is 63[18]; בֹּסְסוּ Je 12[10]—*tread down*, in bad sense, subj. enemies of י׳, obj. acc. Je 12[10] (in metaph.); = *desecrate* (obj. מקדשׁ) Is 63[18]. **Hithpol.** *Pt. f.* מִתְבּוֹסֶסֶת

$16^{6.22}$—of the blind movements of infant's limbs, *kick out* (this way and that), fig. of Jerusalem. **Hoph.** *Pt.* מוּבָס Is 14^{19}—pass. *trodden down* Is 14^{19}, of corpse, sim. of king of Babylon.

2982 †יְבוּס **n.pr.loc. Jebus**, name of Jerusalem acc. to Ju 19^{10} יְבוּס הִיא יְרוּשָׁלָ͏ִם, cf. also v^{11}; 1 Ch 11^{4} יְרוּשָׁלַ͏ִם הִיא יְבוּס, cf. v^{5}.

2983 †יְבֻסִי, יְבוּסִי **1. adj.gent. Jebusite, Jebusites,** sg. אורנה הַיְבֻסִי 2 S $24^{16.18}$ cf. 1 Ch 21 $^{15.18.28}$ 2 Ch 3^{1}; as subst. *a Jebusite* Zc 9^{7}; usually c. art. הַיְ׳ coll. *the Jebusites,* in hist. statement Gn 10^{16} (J) = 1 Ch 1^{14} Nu 13^{29} (E) Jos 9^{1} 11^{3} 12^{8} 24^{11} (all D) Ju 3^{5} Ne 9^{8}, all in list of Canaanitish peoples; so also 1 K 9^{20} = 2 Ch 8^{7}, where remnant of these peoples referred to; also Ezr 9^{1}, which seems to shew that this list had become a standing expression for early inhabitants; cf. further in promises (JED) Gn 15^{21} Ex $3^{8.17}$ 13^{5} 23^{23} 33^{2} 34^{11} Dt 7^{1} 20^{17} Jos 3^{10}; specif. defined as inhabitants of Jebus-Jerusalem Jos $15^{63.63}$ (J) Ju $1^{21.21}$ 2 S $5^{6.8}$ (on which cf. Dr) 1 Ch 11^{4} (called also יוֹשֵׁב הָאָרֶץ 2 S 5^{6} & יֹשְׁבֵי הָאָרֶץ 1 Ch 11^{4}); v. also עִיר הַיְבוּסִי הַזֹּאת Ju 19^{11}; whence **2.** *Jerusalem,* Hex only P, Jos 15^{8} גֵּי בֶן־הִנֹּם אֶל־כֶּתֶף היבוסי מִנֶּגֶב הִיא יְרוּשָׁלָ͏ִם, cf. 18^{16}; 18^{28} וְהַיְבוּסִי הִיא יְרוּשָׁלַ͏ִם.—Cf. כנען.

4001 †מְבוּסָה **n.f. down-treading, subjugation,** גּוֹי קַו־קָו וּמְבוּסָה Is $18^{2.7}$ *a nation of might and of down-treading* (Che *all-subduing*); יוֹם מְהוּמָה וּמ׳ וּמְבוּכָה Is 22^{5}, cf. מְבוּכָה sub בוך.

8395 †[תְּבוּסָה] **n.f. down-treading = ruin, downfall,** cstr. תְּבוּסַת אחזיהו 2 Ch 22^{7} *the downfall of Ahaziah.*

בוע (assumed as √ of foll., cf. Lag $^{BN 10}$; but √ perh. בעע; acc. to Sta $^{§ 257}$ a quadrilit. Ar. بَغَّ, *efferbuit et commotus fuit* (sanguis), بُغْبُغ *puteus cujus aqua haurienti propinqua*).

76 †אֲבַעְבֻּעֹת **n.f.pl. blisters, boils** (𝔗 אֲבַעְבּוּעִין; cf. 𝔗 בֻּעְבֻּעַ, NH בַּעְבּוּעַ בּוּעָה, Syr. ܟܒܚܘܚܝܬܐ) Ex 9^{9} שְׁחִין פֹּרֵחַ אֲבַעְבֻּעֹת, cf. v^{10}.

בוץ so Thes, better **ביץ** (cf. Ar. بَاضَ *surpass in whiteness;* بَيَاضٌ *whiteness*).

1000 †[בֵּיצָה] **n.f.** $^{Is\ 10, 14}$ **egg** (NH *id.*, Ar. بَيْضَةٌ, Aram. בֵּיעְתָא, ܒܝܥܬܐ)—only *Pl.* בֵּיצִים Dt $22^{6.6}$ Is 10^{14}; cstr. בֵּיצֵי Is 59^{5}; sf. בֵּיצֶיהָ Jb 39^{14}, בֵּיצֵיהֶם Is 10^{14};—*eggs* Is 10^{14} (of small bird צפור) Dt $22^{6.6}$, cf. Is 10^{14} (in simil.); (of ostrich רננים) Jb 39^{14}; (of great viper צפעוני) Is $59^{5.5}$ (metaph.)

948 †בּוּץ, בֻּץ **n.[m.] byssus** (late), (Ph. בוץ, Aram. בוץ, ܒܘܨܐ; √ dub.; Birch, Wilkinson $^{Egyptians\ ii.\ 158\ f.}$ fr. Egypt. *hbos, clothe;* v. Say. Herodot $^{ii.\ 86}$; Thes fr. √ בוץ, but Nö $^{ZMG\ 1875,\ 650}$; Armen., acc. to Lag $^{Sem.\ i.\ 72\ al.}$) a fine white Egyptian linen, and cloth made of it, מִשְׁפְּחוֹת בֵּית־עֲבֹדַת הַבֻּץ 1 Ch 4^{21} *families of the house of byssus-working;* cf. 2 Ch 2^{13}; מְכֻרְבָּל בִּמְעִיל בּוּץ 1 Ch 15^{27} *clothed in a robe of byssus* (but rd. rather as ‖ 2 S 6^{14} מְכַרְכֵּר בְּכָל־עֹז *was dancing with all his might*); cf. תַּכְרִיךְ בּ׳ Est 8^{15}; מְלֻבָּשִׁים בּוּץ 2 Ch 5^{12}; חַבְלֵי בוּץ Est 1^{6}; 2 Ch 3^{14} material of פָּרֹכֶת; article of trade Ez 27^{16} (del. 𝔊 Co). Cf. also שֵׁשׁ.

בוק (= בקק).

†בּוּקָה **n.f. emptiness,** Na 2^{11} בּוּקָה וּמְבוּקָה וּמְבֻלָּקָה *emptiness and void and waste.* 950, 4003

†מְבוּקָה **n.f.** *id.*, Na 2^{11} v. supr. 4003

I. בּוֹר, *cistern,* v. sub באר. p. 92 953

II. בֹּר, *cleanness,* v. בֹּר sub ברר. p. 141 1252

†בּוּר **vb. Qal** *Inf. cstr.* לָבוּר Ec 9^{1} (c. acc.); prob. (si vera l.) **make clear, clear up, explain** (VB; so sts., in NH, ברר q.v.) but rd. perh. וְלִבִּי רָאָה 𝔊 𝔖 Bi; or לָתוּר Gr, cf. 1^{13} 2^{3} 7^{25}. 952

בּוֹשׁ $_{109}$ **vb. be ashamed** (Sab. בוס; מהבאס = *evil-doer* DHM $^{ZMG\ 1883,\ 375}$, ‖ Aram. בְּהַת, Syr. ܒܗܬ; Ar. بَاتَ, بَتَّ mean *disperse*)—**Qal** *Pf.* Je 48^{39}; בֹּשׁ Je 48^{13}; בּוֹשָׁה Je 15^{9}; בֹּשְׁתִּי Je 31^{19} + 25 t.; *Impf.* יֵבוֹשׁ Is 29^{22} + 57 t.; *Inf.* abs. בּוֹשׁ Je 6^{15} 8^{12}; *Imv.* בּוֹשִׁי Is 23^{4} Ez 16^{52}, בּוֹשׁוּ Ez 36^{32}; *Pt.* pl. בּוֹשִׁים Ez 32^{30};—**1.** abs. *feel shame* Je 6^{15} + 16 t., Is 19^{9} 23^{4} 37^{27} Is² 45^{16} + 14 t., Ez 16^{63} Mi 7^{16} Jo $2^{26.27}$ 2 K 19^{26} Ez 9^{6} Jb 6^{20} ψ 6^{11} (+ 27 t., chiefly in late Psalms). **2.** sq. מִן, *be ashamed of,* i.e. *disconcerted, disappointed by reason of* Je $2^{36.36}$ 12^{13} 48^{13} Is 1^{29} 20^{5} Ez 32^{30} 36^{32}. **3.** with obj. לֹא בֹשְׁתִּי לִשְׁאוֹל *I am ashamed to ask* Ez 8^{22}; לֹא תֵבֹשׁוּ תַּהְכְּרוּ לִי *ye are not ashamed to deal hardly with me* (impf. subj.) Jb 19^{3}. בּוֹשׁ often ‖ נכלם & חפר; בֹּשׁוּ וְהָכְלְמוּ *they are ashamed and confounded* Je 14^{3}, 22^{22} Is² 41^{11} $45^{16.17}$ Ez 16^{52} 36^{32} ψ 35^{4} 69^{7} Ez 9^{6}; וּבֹשׁוּ הַחֹזִים וְחָפְרוּ הַקֹּסְמִים *and the seers shall be ashamed and the diviners confounded* Mi 3^{7}, cf. Je 15^{9} Jb 6^{20} ψ 35^{26} 40^{15} 70^{3} 71^{24}; יֵבוֹשׁ מְקוֹרוֹ Ho 13^{15} (rd. יִיבַשׁ *be dry*); עַד־בּוֹשׁ † Ju 3^{25} 2 K 2^{17} 8^{11}. **Polel** *Pf.* בֹּשֵׁשׁ *delay* (in shame), בֹּשֵׁשׁ משֶׁה לָרֶדֶת *Moses delayed to descend* Ex 32^{1} (J), מַדּוּעַ בֹּשֵׁשׁ רִכְבּוֹ לָבוֹא *why delay his chariots to come?* Ju 5^{28}. **Hiph. 1.** הֱבִישׁוֹתָ ψ 44^{8}; הֱבִישׁתָה ψ 53^{6}; *Impf.* 2 ms. sf. תְּבִישֵׁנִי ψ $119^{31.116}$; תָּבִישׁוּ ψ 14^{6}; *put to shame, Pt.* מֵבִישׁ Pr 10^{5} 14^{35} 954

19^{26} 29^{15}; *one causing shame* or *acting shamefully*, || עֶבֶד מַשְׂכִּיל יִמְשֹׁל בְּבֵן מֵבִישׁ ; מַשְׂכִּיל *a servant acting wisely will rule over a son causing shame* Pr 17^{2}; אֵשֶׁת חַיִל || מְבִישָׁה Pr 12^{4}. **2.** הוֹבִישׁ 2 S 19^{6} Je 2^{26} 6^{15} Jo 1$^{10.12}$; הֹבִישׁ Je 10^{14} +7 t., Ho 2^{7} Jo 1$^{12.17}$ Is 30^{5} (but הבאיש Kt); הֹבִשׁוּ Je 8$^{9.12}$; *Imv.* הֹבִישׁוּ Jo 1^{11} (all the forms in Joel derived √יָבֵשׁ by ancient versions and some moderns, vid. Ew^{§122e} Ges^{§72,6}). **a.** *put to shame* 2 S 19^{6}. **b.** *act shamefully* Ho 2^{7}. **c.** *to be put to shame* Je 2^{26} 6^{15} 46^{24} 48$^{1.1.20}$ 50$^{2.2}$ Jo 1$^{10.12.17}$ (?). **d.** *be ashamed* Je 8$^{9.12}$ Jo 1$^{11.12}$ (?) Is 30^{5} (Qr); c. מִן Je 10^{14}=51^{17}. **Hithp.** *Impf.* יִתְבֹּשָׁשׁוּ *ashamed before one another* Gn 2^{25} (J).

955 †בּוּשָׁה **n.f.** shame ψ 89^{46} Mi 7^{10} Ob v^{10} Ez 7^{18}.

1317 †בָּשְׁנָה **n.f.** shame (בֹּשֶׁן Ew$^{§163f.}$) Ho 10^{6}.

1322 †בֹּשֶׁת **n.f.** shame Jb 8^{22} +20 t.; sf. בָּשְׁתִּי ψ 69^{20} +7 t. **1.** *shame* 1 S 20$^{30.30}$ ψ 40^{16} 69^{20} 70^{4} Is 30$^{3.5}$ 61^{7} Je 2^{26} 3^{25} 20^{18} Hb 2^{10} Zp 3$^{5.19}$; לָבַשׁ בֹּשֶׁת *clothe with shame* Jb 8^{22} ψ 35^{26} 132^{18}; || עטה בשת ψ 109^{29}; בֹּשֶׁת (ה)פָּנִים *shame* (or *confusion*) *of face* 2 Ch 32^{21} Ezr 9^{7} Dn 9$^{7.8}$, cf. ψ 44^{16} Je 7^{19}; בֹּשֶׁת עֲלוּמַיִךְ *shame of thy youth* Is 54^{4}; עֶרְיָה־בֹשֶׁת *nakedness* (*that is*) *shame* Mi 1^{11} cf. ψ 45^{5}; בֹּשֶׁת עֶרְוַת אמך 1 S 20^{30}. **2.** *shameful thing*, substituted for בַּעַל (q.v.) by later editors, Ho 9^{10} Je 3^{24}; מִזְבְּחוֹת לַבֹּשֶׁת Je 11^{13}, cf. יְרֻבֶּשֶׁת 2 S 11^{21}=יְרֻבַּעַל Ju 6^{32}; אִישׁ־בֹּשֶׁת 2 S 2^{8}=אֶשְׁבַּעַל 1 Ch 8^{33}.

4016 †[מְבוּשׁ] **n.[m.]** pl. sf. מְבֻשָׁיו, **his privates,** that excite shame, *pudenda*, Dt 25^{11}.

957 בַּז v. sub בזז. p. 102

958 †[בָּזָא] **vb.** divide, cut through (? cf. Aram. בְּזַע, ܒܙܥ *cleave*)—**Qal** *Pf.* בָּזְאוּ נהרים Is 18$^{2.7}$ whose land *rivers cut through* (of Cush).

959 †בָּזָה **vb.** despise (Pal. 𝔗 בְּזָא, cf. بَزَا *raise the head loftily and disdainfully*)—**Qal** *Pf.* Nu 15^{31}+; בָּזִיתָ 2 S 12^{9}; sf. בְּזִתָנִי 2 S 12^{10}, etc.; *Impf.* וַיִּבֶז Gn 25^{34} Est 3^{6}; sf. וַיִּבְזֵהוּ 1 S 17^{42}; 3 fs. וַתִּבֶז 2 S 6^{16} 1 Ch 15^{29}; 2 ms. תִּבְזֶה ψ 51^{19} 73^{20}; וַיִּבְזוּ Ne 2^{19}; וַיִּבְזֻהוּ 1 S 10^{27}; *Inf. cstr.* בְּזֹה Is 49^{7} (Di Ew^{§150b}); *Pt. act.* בּוֹזֶה Pr 15^{20} 19^{16}; בּוֹזֵהוּ Pr 14^{2}; בּוֹזִים 2 Ch 36^{16}; בּוֹזֵי Mal 1^{6}; sf. בֹּזַי 1 S 2^{30}; *pass.*
960 בָּזוּי Je 49^{15}+; f. בְּזוּיָה Ec 9^{16};—*despise, regard with contempt*, sq. acc. rei, birthright Gn 25^{34} (J); words of י׳ Nu 15^{31} (P; not elsewh. in Hex); 2 S 12^{9} cf. 2 Ch 36^{16}; name of י׳ Mal 1$^{6.6}$ (cf. infr.); oath (אָלָה) Ez 16^{59} 17$^{16.18.19}$; holy things Ez 22^{8}; one's own ways Pr 19^{16} (i.e. is careless of them, lives recklessly, opp. שֹׁמֵר נַפְשׁוֹ, cf. נֹצֵר דַּרְכּוֹ 16^{17}); distress of the distressed ψ 22^{25} (|| שִׁקֵּץ, subj. י׳); prayer, subj. *id.* ψ 102^{18}; broken & contrite heart ψ 51^{19} (c. לֹא), cf. on other hand 73^{20}; sq. acc. pers. Saul 1 S 10^{27}, David 17^{42} cf. Pr 15^{20}, י׳ 1 S 2^{30} 2 S 12^{10} Pr 14^{2}, his prisoners ψ 69^{34} (subj. י׳); sq. לְ, וַתִּבֶז לוֹ בְּלִבָּהּ 2 S 6^{16}=1 Ch 15^{29}, 2 K 19^{21}=Is 37^{22}; sq. עַל pers. Ne 2^{19}; sq. Inf. וַיִּבֶז בְּעֵינָיו לִשְׁלֹחַ יָד Est 3^{6}; note esp. בְּזֹה נֶפֶשׁ Is 49^{7} *a despising of soul*, i.e. *one despised from the soul, thoroughly despised;* on other views v. Che Di. *Pt.* pass. *despised*, of pers. cstr. בְּזוּי עָם *despised of people* (|| חֶרְפַּת אָדָם) ψ 22^{7}, cf. בָּזוּי בָּאָדָם Je 49^{15} also Ob v^{2}; of wisdom Ec 9^{16}. **Niph.** *Pt.* נִבְזֶה ψ 15^{4}+; f. נִבְזָה 1 S 15^{9} (so rd. for
נמבזה cf. We Dr); pl. נִבְזִים Mal 2^{9};—**1.** *despised* 5240
ψ 15^{4} 119^{141} Is 53$^{3.3}$ Je 22^{28}. **2.** *vile, worthless* 1 S 15^{9}. **3.** *despicable, contemptible* Mal 1^{7} said of table of י׳, cf. v^{12} 2^{9}; Dn 11^{21} as subst. of Antiochus Epiph. **Hiph.** *Inf.* לְהַבְזוֹת בַּעְלֵיהֶן Est 1^{17} *so as to cause to despise their lords* (cause their lords to be despised).

†בִּזָּיוֹן **n.[m.]** contempt Est 1^{18} (ב׳ וָקָצֶף). 963

בִּזָּה v. sub בזז. p. 103 961

†בָּזַז **vb.** spoil, plunder (Ar. بَزَّ, Aram. ܒܙ; 962
Amhar. ΠΗΠΗ: perh. Eth. በዘወ: *rescue* Prä$^{BAS\ i.\ 33}$)—**Qal** *Pf.* 3 ms. וּבָזַז (consec.) Ez 29^{19}; 3 pl. בָּזְזוּ Nu 31^{53}+7 t.; בָּזָזוּ Nu 31^{9}; sf. וּבְזָזוּם consec. Je 20^{5}; 1 pl. בָּזַזְנוּ Dt 2^{35}; בַּזּוֹנוּ 3^{7}; *Impf.* 2 ms. תָּבֹז Dt 20^{14}, pl. יָבֹזּוּ Is 10^{2}+2 t.; וַיָּבֹזּוּ Gn 34^{27}+4 t.; sf. יְבָזּוּם Zp 2^{9}; 2 mpl. תָּבֹזּוּ Jos 8^{2}; 1 pl. cohort. נָבֹזָּה 1 S 14^{36} (cf. Ges$^{§67R.11}$); *Imv.* בֹּזּוּ Na 2$^{10.10}$; *Inf. cstr.* בֹּז Is 10^{6}+3 t.; בּוֹז Est 3^{13} 8^{11}; *Pt. act.* pl. בֹּזְזִים Is 42^{24} 2 Ch 20^{25}; sf. בֹּזְזַיִךְ Je 30^{16}, בֹּזְזֵינוּ Is 17^{14}, בֹּזְזֵיהֶם Ez 39^{10}; *pass.* בָּזוּז Is 42^{22};—*spoil*=take as spoil, c. acc. rei Nu 31^{9} Dt 2^{35} (c. לְ & refl. suff.) Je 20^{5} Ez 26^{12} Na 2^{10} ψ 109^{11}; oftener c. acc. cogn., בַּז Nu 31^{32} Is 10^{6} (|| שָׁלַל שָׁלָל, as oft.) 33^{23} Ez 29^{19} 38$^{12.13}$; בִּזָּה 2 Ch 25^{13}; שָׁלָל Dt 3^{7} 20^{14} (both sq. לְ c. refl. suff.) 2 Ch 20$^{25.25}$ 28^{8} Est 3^{13} 8^{11}; בהמה & שלל Jos 8$^{2.27}$ 11^{14} (all sq. לְ c. refl. suff.); obj. pers. carried off (cf. בַּז) Gn 34^{29} (MT, but cf. Ol); *plunder, despoil*, c. acc. pers. robbed Is 10^{2} 11^{14} 17^{14} (שסה) 42^{22} (|| *id.*) Zp 2^{9} Je 30^{16} Ez 39$^{10.10}$; c. בָּהֶם (pers.) 1 S 14^{36}; c. acc. of place plundered Gn 34^{27} 2 K 7^{16} 2 Ch 14^{13}; *abs.* Nu 31^{53} Is 42^{24}. †**Niph.** *Pf.* וְנָבֹזּוּ consec. Am 3^{11}; *Impf.* 2 ms. תִּבּוֹז Is 24^{3}; *Inf. abs.* הִבּוֹז Is 24^{3}—*be spoiled, plundered*,

subj. ארמנות Am 3^{11}; הָבוֹז תִּבּוֹז הארץ Is 24^{3}; (הָבוֹק תִּבּוֹק ‖). †**Pu.** *Pf.* וּבֻזּוּ consec. Je 50^{37}—*be taken as spoil*, subj. אוצרת.

957 †בַּז **n.[m.] spoiling, robbery; spoil, booty**
897 —בַּ׳ abs. Nu 14^{3}+; so also Ez 25^{7} Qr (Kt בג meaningless); בַּז Je 2^{14}+; but הַבָּז Nu 31^{32} v. d. H; sf. בִּזָּהּ Ex 29^{19};—**1.** *spoiling, robbery*, לְב׳ i.e. to be plundered, despoiled Ez 7^{21} (of temple ‖ שָׁלָל) 23^{46}. **2.** *spoil, booty, plunder* Is 10^{6} 33^{23} Ez 29^{19} $38^{12.13}$ (all acc. cogn. ‖ שָׁלָל); cf. Nu 31^{32} Je 15^{13} 17^{3}; in phr. הָיָה לָבַז Je 49^{32} (of camels) Ez 36^{4} cf. v^{5}; also of human beings Nu $14^{3.31}$ Dt 1^{39} Je 2^{14} (all היה לב׳)+2 K 21^{14} (‖ מְשִׁסָּה) Is 42^{22} (‖ *id.*) Je 2^{14}, cf. 30^{16} (‖ מְשִׁסָּה); also Ez 25^{7} Qr, 26^{5} (היה לב׳; both in personif.); fig. of Isr. as sheep Ez $34^{8.22}$ (both היה לב׳) v^{28} היה בז (no לְ). On Is $8^{1.3}$ מַהֵר שָׁלָל חָשׁ בַּז v. מהר.

961 †בִּזָּה **n.f. spoil, booty** (late)—בִּזָּה 2 Ch 14^{13}+ 9 t.;—*spoil, prey*, of things 2 Ch 28^{14} Est $9^{10.15.16}$, cf. 2 Ch 14^{13} 25^{13} Dn 11^{24} (רכוש & שָׁלָל ‖); n. verb., *spoiling*, בַּב׳ Ezr 9^{7} Dn 11^{33}, cf. also לְב׳ Ne 3^{36}.

בִּזָּיוֹן v. sub בזה.

964 †בִּזְיוֹתְיָה **n.pr.loc.** acc. to MT place near Beersheba Jos 15^{28}; but rd. prob. וּבְנוֹתֶיהָ 𝔊 *and her daughters* (villages, cf. בת sub בן) v. Ne 11^{27} (We[Sm 215] Hollenb[Alex. Übers. Jos. 14] Di al.)

בזק (Aram. בְּזַק, ܒܙܰܩ *scatter;* Ar. بَزَقَ *rise* (of sun) is prob. erroneous v. Lane[199]).

965 †בָּזָק **n.[m.] lightning flash?** Ez 1^{14} Hi Co del.; verse om. in old MSS. of 𝔊; sense uncertain, possibly error for ברק.

966 †בֶּזֶק **n.pr.loc.** 1 S 11^{8} (בְּבָזֶק) rendezvous of Israel under Saul and Sam.; Ju $1^{4.5}$ home of Adoni-bezek; on loc. cf. Euseb. Lag[Onom. 105, 2nd ed. 139]; see also Stu. Ju 1^{4}; 17th (mile-)stone fr. Neapolis toward Scythopolis; mod. *Ḥirbet Ibzîk*, 14 Eng. m. fr. Nâblus, Survey[ii. 231].

967 †[בָּזַר] **vb. scatter** (Ar. بَذَرَ, Aram. בְּדַר)—**Qal** *Impf.* Dn 11^{24} בִּזָּה וְשָׁלָל וּרְכוּשׁ לָהֶם יִבְזוֹר *plunder and spoil and possessions he will scatter among them* (subj. Antiochus Epiph.) **Pi.** *Pf.* בִּזַּר, *id.*, ψ 68^{31}, but rd. *Imv.* בַּזֵּר (בַּזֵּר) (𝔊 𝔖 𝔙 so most; De follows MT), subj. ref. to י׳, obj. עַמִּים.

968 †בִּזְּתָא **n.pr.m.** a eunuch of Ahasuerus, Est 1^{10} (Thes comp. Pers. *beste, ligatus* sc. *membro*, e.g. *spado*, cf. Vullers[Dict. Pers.] sub بَسته).

973 †I. [בָּחַל] **vb. feel loathing** (cf. Syr. ܒܚܠ (so in lexx.) *nauseated* (yet v. Gei[Urschrift, 270]); NSyr. ܒܚܠ *envy* cf. Stoddard[Gram. 12, 57])—**Qal** *Pf.* 3 fs. בָּחֲלָה Zc 11^{8} וַתִּקְצַר נַפְשִׁי בָּהֶם וְגַם נַפְשָׁם ב׳ בִּי *felt a loathing* against me.

†II. [בָּחַל] **vb.** (Ar. بَخِلَ *be avaricious*); 973
only **Pu.** *Pt.* נַחֲלָה מְבֹחֶלֶת an inheritance *gotten by greed* Pr 20^{21} Kt; < Qr Vrss נ׳ מְבֹהֶלֶת, v. בהל.

†[בָּחַן] **vb. examine, try** (cf. Aram. בְּחַן, 974
Syr. ܒܚܰܢ, *try, examine;* Ar. محن I. VIII. *test*, cf. W[SG 65])—**Qal** *Pf.* sf. בְּחָנַנִי Jb 23^{10}, בָּחַנְתָּ ψ 17^{3}+ 7 t.; *Impf.* יִבְחָן ψ 11^{5}+5 t.; *Imv.* sf. בְּחָנֵנִי ψ 26^{2} +2 t.; *Inf.* בְּחֹן Zc 13^{9}; *Pt.* בֹּחֵן Je 11^{20}+5 t. (‖ נסה, צרף);—**1.** *examine, scrutinize, try* ψ 11^{5} 139^{23} Jb 7^{18}; עַפְעַפָּיו יִבְחֲנוּ בְּנֵי אָדָם *His eyelids try the children of men* (search them through and through) ψ 11^{4}. **2.** *prove, test, try.* **a.** with the metaphor of gold Jb 23^{10}; וּבְחַנְתִּים כִּבְחֹן אֶת־הַזָּהָב *and I will try them as one tries gold* Zc 13^{9}. **b.** without metaphor, of God testing persons ψ 26^{2} 66^{10} 81^{8} Je 9^{6}; their ways Je 6^{27}; the לֵב ψ 17^{3} Je 12^{3} Pr 17^{3} 1 Ch 29^{17}; reins Je 17^{10}; heart and reins ψ 7^{10} Je 11^{20} (= 20^{12}). **c.** of man testing or tempting God ψ 95^{9} Mal $3^{10.15}$. **d.** the ear trying words Jb 12^{11} = 34^{3}. **Niph.** *Impf.* יִבָּחֵן Jb 34^{36} Gn $42^{15.16}$, *to be tried, proved.* **Pu.** בֹּחַן Ez 21^{18} *the trial has been made* (𝔊 𝔖 𝔙 Ges MV Ew Ke, but noun בֹּחַן MT Symm Haev.; rd. בְּחֵן *with grace, favour*, Hi Co).

†בֹּחַן **n.[m.] testing,** Is 28^{16} אֶבֶן בֹּחַן *a tested,* 976
tried stone, i.e. approved for use as a foundation-stone. On Ez 21^{18} MT v. foreg. *ad fin.*

†בַּחַן **n.[m.] watch-tower,** Is 32^{14}. 975

†[בחון] sf. בַּחוּנָיו (dag. f. implic. Qr; בחיניו 971
Kt) Is 23^{13} *their siege-towers.*

†בָּחוֹן **n.[m.] assayer,** one who tries metals 969
Je 6^{27} (Ges[§84, 3] Ew[§152 b]).

בחיניו Is 23^{13} Kt; v. [בחון] supr. 971

†בָּחַר **vb. choose** (cf. Aram. בְּחַר, Syr. ܒܚܰܪ 977
‖ בחן, As. *bêru* (√ באר) Dl[Pr 76])—**Qal** *Pf.* בָּחַר Dt 7^{6}+66 t.; יִבְחַר Is 41^{24}+60 t.; אֶבְחַר Jb 29^{25} (Baer); *Imv.* בְּחַר Ex 17^{9}+5 t.; *Inf. abs.* בָּחוֹר 1 S 2^{28} Is $7^{15.16}$; *Inf. cstr.* sf. בָּחֳרִי Ez 20^{5}; *Pt.* בֹּחֵר 1 S 20^{30} Zc 3^{2}; *pass.* בָּחוּר Ex 14^{7}+18 t.;—**1.** with בְּ, **a.** *divine choice*, of Abraham Ne 9^{7}; Israel Dt 7^{7} Is 44^{1} Ez 20^{5}; to become his people Dt 7^{6} 14^{2}; Jeshurun Is 44^{2}; the seed of the patriarchs Dt 4^{37} 10^{15}; Levites Dt 18^{5} 21^{5} 1 Ch 15^{2} 2 Ch 29^{11}; Aaron ψ 105^{26}; Judah 1 Ch 28^{4} not Ephraim ψ 78^{67}; Levi and Judah Je 33^{24}; the king Dt 17^{15}, especially David 1 S 10^{24} $16^{8.9.10}$

2 S 6^{21} 1 K 8^{16} (=2 Ch 6^{6}) 1 Ch 28$^{4.5}$ 29^{1} 2 Ch 6^{5} ψ 78^{70}; others Nu 16^{5} 17^{20} (P) Hg 2^{23}; place of sacrifice Dt 12^{18} 14^{25} 16$^{7.15}$ 17^{8} 2 Ch 7^{12}; the city 1 K 8$^{16.44}$ (=2 Ch 6$^{5.34}$) 11^{32}; Jerusalem 2 Ch 6^{6} Is 14^{1} Zc 1^{17} 2^{16} 3^{2}; Zion ψ 132^{13}; delusions Is 66^{4}. **b.** *man's choice*, of ways Pr 3^{31} Is 66^{3}; good things Is 7$^{15.16}$; life Dt 30^{19}; gods Ju 10^{14} Is 41^{24}; God's pleasure Is 56^{4} 65^{12} 66^{4}. **2.** with אֲשֶׁר (alone, for אשר בחר ב׳): **a.** *divine choice*, of Israel Is 41^{8} יַעֲקֹב אֲשֶׁר בְּחַרְתִּיךָ, 43^{10}; the people 1 K 3^{8} ψ 33^{12}; men Nu 16^{7} (P) ψ 65^{5}; king 2 S 16^{18} 1 K 11^{34}; place of sacrifice Dt 12$^{14.26}$ 15^{20} 17^{10} 31^{11} (D) Jos 9^{27} (P), especially לָשׂוּם שְׁמוֹ שָׁם Dt 12$^{5.21}$ 14^{24}, לְשַׁכֵּן שְׁמוֹ שָׁם Dt 12^{11} 14^{23} 16$^{2.6.11}$ Ne 1^{9}; the city 1 K 8^{48} (=2 Ch 6^{38}), לשום שמי שם 1 K 11^{36} 14^{21} (= 2 Ch 12^{13}); Jerusalem 1 K 11^{13} 2 K 21^{7} (= 2 Ch 33^{7}) 23^{27}; fast Is 58$^{5.6}$; way ψ 25^{12}. **b.** *man's choice*, place to dwell in Dt 23^{7}; gardens Is 1^{29}; king 1 S 12^{13}; wives Gn 6^{2} (J); what to do 2 S 15^{15}. **3.** with acc. & לְ, *choose some one or something for*: **a.** *divine choice*, of Levi 1 S 2^{28}; Jacob ψ 135$^{4.5}$; inheritance ψ 47^{5}. **b.** *human choice*, persons Ex 17^{9} Jos 24$^{15.22}$ (E) 1 S 8^{18} 13^{12} 2 S 24^{12} (=1 Ch 21^{20}); things Gn 13^{11} (J) 1 S 17^{40} 1 K 18$^{23.25}$ Jb 34^{4}. **4.** with acc. and מִן, *choose, select from* 2 S 10^{9} (=1 Ch 19^{10}). **5.** acc. **a.** *divine choice*, temple 2 Ch 7^{16}; Judah ψ 78^{68}; servant Is 41^{9} 49^{7}. **b.** *man's choice*, persons Ex 18^{28} (E) Ju 5^{8} Jos 8^{3} (J) 2 S 17^{1}; things Jb 7^{15} 9^{14} 15^{5} 29^{25} 34^{33} 119$^{30.173}$ Pr 1^{29} Is 40^{20}. **6.** with עַל, כי על זה בחרת מעני *for this thou hast chosen rather than affliction* Jb 36^{21}; with acc. and על pregn. כל אשר תבחר עלי *all that thou choosest* (to lay) *upon me* 2 S 19^{39}. **7.** with לְ of acc. 1 S 20^{30} (many MSS. have בְּ; but 𝔊 We Dr read חָבֵר *companion*). The ptcp. בָּחוּר *chosen*, of a ruler ψ 89^{20}, warrior Je 49^{19} (=50^{44}); as cedars Ct 5^{15}; coll. רכב בחור *chosen chariots* Ex 14^{7} (E); איש בחור *chosen men, warriors* Ju 20$^{15.16.34}$ 1 S 24^{3} 2 Ch 13$^{3.17}$, for wh. בָּחוּר alone 1 K 12^{21} = 2 Ch 11^{1}, 2 Ch 25^{5}; בחורי ישׂראל 1 S 26^{2} ψ 78^{31}; 2 S 10^{9} בחורי בישׂראל (‖ 1 Ch 19^{10} בחור בישׂראל, doubtless the true reading, as 2 S 6^{1}). **8.** *test, try* (Aram.=בחן) בְּחַרְתִּיךָ בְּכוּר עֹנִי Is 48^{10} *I have tested thee in the furnace of affliction* 𝔖 𝔗 Ges Hi Ew De Che Dr, but *chosen* 𝔙 Rab Calv AV. **Niph.** נִבְחַר Je 8^{3}; *Pt.* נִבְחָר Pr 8^{10}+5 t.;—*to be chosen.* **a.** abs. *chosen, choice* Pr 8$^{10.19}$ 10^{20}. **b.** cstr. מִן, וְנִבְחַר מות מחיים *death will be chosen rather than life* Je 8^{3}; *choicer than* Pr 16^{16} 22^{1}; נבחר ליהוה מזבח *choicer* (more acceptable) *to Yahweh* than peace-offering Pr 21^{3}. **Pu.** יְבֻחַר *chosen, selected* Ec 9^{4} (יְחֻבַּר Qr).

†בָּחוּר **n.m.** young man Is 62^{5}+7 t.; pl. 970
בַּחוּרִים (intensive with dag. f. implic.) Pr 20^{29} +13 t.; cstr. בַּחוּרֵי Ez 23^{6}+4 t.; sf. בַּחוּרַי etc. La 1^{18}+16 t.;—*young man* (choice, in the prime of manhood) 1 S 9^{2} Ec 11^{9} Is 62^{5}; coll. *young men* Je 15^{8}; בָּחוּר וּבְתוּלָה *young men and virgins* Dt 32^{25} 2 Ch 36^{17} Je 51^{22} Ez 9^{6}; usually pl. Ju 14^{10} Ru 3^{10} 1 S 8^{16} 2 K 8^{12} 2 Ch 36^{17} Pr 20^{29} Is 9^{17} 31^{8} 40^{30} Je 6^{11} 9^{20} 11^{22} 18^{21} 48^{15} 49^{26} 50^{3} 51^{3} La 1^{15} 5$^{13.14}$ Ez 33$^{6.12.23}$ 30^{17} Jo 3^{1} Am 2^{11} 4^{10}; ‖ בתולות ψ 78^{63} 148^{12} Is 23^{4} Je 31^{13} La 1^{18} 2^{21} Am 8^{13} Zc 9^{17}.

†[בְּחוּרִים] **n.f.abstr.pl.** youth, pl. sf. 979
בְּחֻרָיו Nu 11^{28} (J; Onk 𝔖 Ges De Di; בחיריו 𝔊 Sam 𝔙 Lu Ke); בְּחוּרוֹתֶיךָ Ec 11^{9}, בְּחוּרֹתֶיךָ Ec 12^{1}.

†[בָּחִיר] **n.m.** chosen, cstr. בְּחִיר 2 S 21^{6} 972
(but We Dr בְּהַר י׳); sf. בְּחִירָיו 1 Ch 16^{13} ψ 89^{4} 105$^{6.43}$ 106$^{5.23}$ Is^{3} 42^{1} 43^{20} 45^{4} 65$^{9.15.22}$; always the *chosen* or *elect* of Yahweh.

†בַּחֻרִים **n.pr.loc.** (*young men's village*) of 980
a small town of Benjamin beyond the Mt. of Olives on the way to Jericho (cf. Rob$^{BR\ i.\ 433}$; Kasteren$^{ZPV\ 1890,\ 100\ ff.}$) 2 S 3^{16} 16^{5} 17^{18} 19^{17} 1 K 2^{8} (= עַלְמוֹן acc. to 𝔗^{Jon} Schwarz Marti-Schick$^{ZPV\ iii.\ 8\ f.}$).

†יִבְחָר **n.pr.m.** (*He* (*Ēl* or י׳) *chooses*) son 2984
of David 2 S 5^{15} 1 Ch 3^{6} 14^{5}.

†[מִבְחָר] **n.[m.]** (**f.** Ez 24^{5}) **choicest, best,** 4005
cstr. מִבְחַר Dt 12^{11}+10 t.; sf. מִבְחָרָיו Dn 11^{15}; vows Dt 12^{11}; valleys Is 22^{7}; fir trees Is 37^{24}; cedars Je 22^{7}; bones Ez 24^{4}; sepulchres Gn 23^{6} (P); of the flock Ez 24^{5}; of the Assyrians Ez 23^{7}; captains Ex 15^{4} (E poet.); young men Je 48^{15}; מבחר וטוב לבנון Ez 31^{16} (del. וטוב 𝔊 Co); עַם מִבְחָרָיו Dn 11^{15}= *his choice troops.*

†מִבְחוֹר **n.[m.]** choice, in the phrases עִיר 4004
מִבְחוֹר *choice city* 2 K 3^{19}; מִבְחוֹר בְּרֹשָׁיו *choice fir trees* 2 K 19^{23} = מִבְחַר בְּרוֹשָׁיו Is 37^{24} (prob. scribal error in both cases for מִבְחַר).

†מִבְחָר **n.pr.m.** (*choice*) one of David's 4006
warriors 1 Ch 11^{38}.

†בַּחֲרוּמִי **adj.gent.** Baharumite 1 Ch 978
11^{33}=בַּרְחֻמִי 2 S 23^{31}. Prob. בַּחֲרֻמִי Dr. 1273

†[בָּטָא, בָּטָה] **vb.** speak rashly, thought- 981
lessly (NH *id.*, בטי)—**Qal** *Pt.* בּוֹטֶה Pr 12^{18} *one that babbleth* (opp. לְשׁוֹן חֲכָמִים). **Pi.** *Impf.* יְבַטֵּא בִשְׂבוּעָה Lv 5^{4} *speak rashly, unadvisedly;* so וַיְבַטֵּא בִּשְׂפָתָיו (of Moses) ψ 106^{33}; *Inf.* לְבַטֵּא בִשְׂפָתַיִם Lv 5^{4} (P).

4008 †מִבְטָא n.[m.] rash utterance, מִבְטָא שׂפתיה Nu 30$^{7.9}$.

982 †I. בָּטַח vb. trust (cf. Ar. بَطَحَ *to throw one down upon his face* Thes, اِنْبَطَحَ *lie extended on the ground*, '*se reposer sur quelqu'un*' Fl MV)—**Qal** *Pf.* בָּטַח ψ 28^{7} + 35 t.; *Impf.* יִבְטַח Jb 40^{23} + 27 t.; *Imv.* בְּטַח ψ 37^{3} + 8 t.; *Inf. abs.* בָּטוֹחַ Is 59^{4}, *cstr.* בְּטֹחַ ψ 118^{8} + 2 t.; *Pt.* בֹּטֵחַ ψ 21^{8} + 35 t.; pass. בָּטוּחַ ψ 112^{7} Is 26^{3}. **I.** *trust.* **1.** abs. Is 12^{2}. **2.** with cogn. acc. מה הבטחון הזה אשׁר בטחת *what is this trust that thou dost trust?* 2 K 18^{19} = Is 36^{4}. **3.** with בְּ *trust in*—**a.** *God* 2 K 18^{5} 19^{10} 1 Ch 5^{20} ψ 9^{11} 21^{8} 22$^{5.6}$ 25^{2} 26^{1} 28^{7} 32^{10} 37^{3} 40^{4} 55^{24} 56$^{5.12}$ 62^{9} 84^{13} 91^{2} 112^{7} 115$^{9.10.11}$ 125^{1} 143^{8} Pr 16^{20} 29^{25} Is 26$^{3.4}$ 37^{10} Je 17^{7} 39^{18} Zp 3^{2}. **b.** *persons* Ju 9^{26} ψ 41^{10} 118$^{8.9}$ 146^{3} Pr 31^{11} Je 17^{5} 46^{25} Mi 7^{5}. **c.** *things* Dt 28^{32} Jb 39^{11} ψ 27^{3} 44^{7} 52^{9} 62^{11} 115^{8} 135^{18} Pr 11^{28} 28^{26} Is 30^{12} 42^{17} 47^{10} Je 5^{17} 7^{14} 12^{5} 13^{25} 48^{7} 49^{4} Ez 16^{15} Ho 10^{13} Am 6^{1}. **d.** in the name of God ψ 33^{21} Is 5^{10}; mercy of God ψ 13^{6} 52^{10}; word of God ψ 119^{42}; salvation of God ψ 78^{22}. **4.** with עַל, *trust* or *rely upon*—**a.** *God* ψ 31^{15} 37^{5} Pr 28^{25} Je 49^{11}. **b.** *persons* 2 K 18$^{20.21.24}$ = Is 36$^{5.6.9}$, Je 9^{3}. **c.** *things* 2 K 18^{21} = Is 36^{6} 2 Ch 32^{10}, ψ 49^{7} Is 31^{1} 59^{4} Ez 33^{13} Hb 2^{18}. **5.** with אֶל *trust to*—**a.** *God* 2 K 18^{22} (= Is 36^{7}) ψ 4^{6} 31^{7} 56^{4} 86^{2} Pr 3^{5}. **b.** *persons* Ju 20^{36}. **c.** *things* Je 7^{4} (= על דבר 7^{8}). **II.** *be confident* Jb 6^{20} 40^{23} Pr 14^{16}; צַדִּיקִים כִּכְפִיר יִבְטָח *the righteous are bold as a lion* Pr 28^{1}; *secure* Jb 11^{18} Pr 11^{15}; עַם בֹּטֵחַ *a people secure* Ju 18$^{7.10.27}$; בָּנוֹת בֹּטְחוֹת *careless daughters, (women)* Is 32^{9} cf. v$^{10.11}$. **Hiph.** *Pf.* הִבְטַחְתָּ Je 28^{15}; *Impf.* יַבְטַח Is 36^{15} + 2 t.; *Pt.* מַבְטִיחִי ψ 22^{10}; *cause to trust, make secure*, abs. ψ 22^{10}; with עַל Je 28^{15} 29^{31}; with אֶל 2 K 18^{30} = Is 36^{15}.

983 †I. בֶּ֫טַח n.[m.] security—Gn 34^{25} + 41 t.; הַשְׁקֵט וָבֶטַח Is 32^{17} *quietness and security* = בְּהַשְׁקֵט וּבְבִטְחָה Is 30^{15} (but prob. both infs.) elsewhere always adverb;—*securely*, ישׁב לבטח Lv 25$^{18.19}$ 26^{5} Ju 18^{7} 1 K 5^{5} ψ 4^{9} Pr 3^{29} Is 47^{8} Je 32^{37} 49^{31} Ez 28^{26} 34$^{25.28}$ 38$^{8.11.14}$ 39$^{6.26}$ Zp 2^{15} Zc 14^{11}; ישׁב בטח Dt 12^{10} 1 S 12^{11}; שׁכן לבטח Dt 33^{12} ψ 16^{9} Je 23^{6} 33^{16}; שׁכן בטח Dt 33^{28} Pr 1^{33}; (היה) לבטח Jb 24^{23} Ez 34^{27}; היה בטח Ju 8^{11}; הלך לבטח Pr 3^{23}; הלך בטח Pr 10^{9}; שׁכב לבטח Jb 11^{18} Ho 2^{20}; רבץ לבטח Is 14^{30}; נחה לבטח ψ 78^{53}; עבר בטח Mi 2^{8}; כושׁ בטח *Cush* (dwelling) *securely* Ez 30^{9} (pregnant construction, del. בטח Co); וַיָּבֹאוּ עַל הָעִיר בֶּטַח *and they came upon the city* (dwelling) *securely* Gn 34^{25} (J).

†בִּטְחָה n.f. trusting Is 30^{15} (prob. *inf. f.* = בֶּטַח Is 32^{17}). 985

†בִּטָּחוֹן n.m. trust 2 K 18^{19} = Is 36^{4}; *hope* Ec 9^{4}. 986

†בַּטֻּחוֹת n.f.pl. security, safety Jb 12^{6}. 987

†מִבְטָח n.[m.] confidence Ez 29^{16}—cstr. מִבְטַח Pr 14^{26} + 2 t.; sf. מִבְטַחִי Jb 31^{24} + 6 t. (dag. implicit); מִבְטֶחָם Je 48^{13}; מִבְטֶחָה Pr 21^{22}; pl. מִבְטַחִים Is 32^{18}; מִבְטַחַיִךְ Je 2^{37};—**1.** *the act* of confiding Pr 21^{22} 22^{19} 25^{19}. **2.** *the object* of confidence Jb 8^{14} 18^{14} 31^{24} ψ 40^{5} 65^{6} 71^{5} Je 2^{37} 17^{7} 48^{13} Ez 29^{16}. **3.** the state of confidence, *security* Pr 14^{26} Is 32^{18}. 4009

†II. בֶּ֫טַח n.pr.loc. city of Hadadezer king of Zobah 2 S 8^{8} (but read rather טִבְחַת so 1 Ch 18^{8}; 𝔊 Sm Μασβακ, 𝔊L Ματεβακ; 𝔊 Ch Μεταβηχας, 𝔊L ταβααθ; cf. also We Dr). 984

II. בטח (√ assumed for following).

†אֲבַטִּחִים n.[m.]pl. water-melons (Mish. אבטיח, Sam. ࠀࠁࠈࠇ; cf. Löw$^{No. 297}$; Ar. بِطِّيخ etc.; perh. loan-word in Heb. cf. Sta$^{§ 258}$; mod. Egypt. *battich, biṭṭich* cf. reff. in Di Nu 11^{5}; on formation cf. Lag$^{BN 10}$, who comp. Eth. *aqṭala*)—Egyptian fruit, הָא׳ Nu 11^{5} (‖ הַקִּשֻּׁאִים, הַשּׁוּמִים ,הַבְּצָלִים ,הֶחָצִיר); 𝔊 τοὺς πέπονας. 20

†[בָּטֵל] vb. cease (NH בָּטֵל, Ar. بَطَلَ, Eth. በጠለ: both *be futile, vain*, but As. *baṭâlu, cease* Lotz$^{TP 68}$, so Aram. בְּטֵיל, ܒܛܠ)—**Qal** *Pf.* וּבָטְלוּ consec. Ec 12^{3} *and* the grinders *cease.* 988

I. בטן (meaning dub.; √ of following).

†I. בֶּ֫טֶן n.f.$^{Nu 5, 25}$ belly, body, womb (Ar. بَطْنٌ—ב׳ abs. Ju 13^{7} +; בָּ֑טֶן v^{5} +; cstr. בֶּטֶן ψ 139^{13} +; sf. בִּטְנִי Jb 3^{10} +; בִּטְנְךָ Dt 7^{13} +; בִּטְנֵךְ Gn 25^{23}; בִּטְנוֹ Jb 15^{2} +, etc.;—**1. a.** *belly, abdomen*, of man Ju 3$^{21.22}$; of woman Nu 5$^{21.22.27}$; as beautiful in form Ct 7^{3}; as seat of hunger Pr 13^{25}; as eating Ez 3^{3} (‖ מֵעִים); cf. Pr 18^{20} (fig.); as seat of passion, avarice, etc. Jb 20$^{20.23}$; in fig. of God's casting riches out of extortioner's belly Jb 20^{15} (‖ וַיְקִאֶנּוּ), cf. also ψ 17^{14}; fig. of innermost part of a man = *inmost soul* Pr 18^{8} = 26^{22}, 20$^{27.30}$ (all חַדְרֵי ב׳); as seat of intell. faculties (= Eng. *breast* or *bosom*) 22^{18} (cf. מֵעִים ψ 40^{9}) Jb 15$^{2.35}$ 32^{18}, רוּחַ בִּטְנִי v^{19}; as trembling at theophany Hb 3^{16}. **b.** belly of hippopotamus Jb 40^{16}. **c.** בֶּטֶן שְׁאוֹל Jon 2^{3} (Jonah's prayer: ‖ מְצוּלָה בִּלְבַב יַמִּים). **2.** *body*, opp. soul ψ 31^{10} 990

(opp. נֶפֶשׁ), also 44[26] (opp. *id.*;—on this cf. Zim[BP 71]). **3.** *womb* Gn 25[23.24] 38[27] (all J) Ho 12[4] Jb 10[19] (‖ רֶחֶם v[18]) Ec 11[5] Jb 31[15] הֲלֹא בַבֶּטֶן עֹשֵׂנִי עָשָׂהוּ *did not he that made me in the womb make him* (‖ וַיְכֻנֶנּוּ בָּרֶחֶם אֶחָד); cf. ψ 139[13] תְּסֻכֵּנִי בְּבֶטֶן, & Je 1[5]; esp. פְּרִי ב׳ i.e. offspring Gn 30[2] (E) ψ 127[3] Is 13[18]; Pr 31[2] בַּר בִּטְנִי=*my son* (‖ בְּרִי) cf. בֶּן־בִּטְנָהּ Is 49[15]; of birth יָצָא מִבֶּטֶן Jb 1[21] 3[11] Ec 5[14]; בֶּטֶן alone=*birth* Ho 9[11] (‖ הֵרָיוֹן ,לֵדָה), cf. fig. מִבֶּטֶן מִי יָצָא הַקָּרַח Jb 38[29] *out of whose womb came the ice?* cf. לֹא סָגַר דַּלְתֵי בִטְנִי Jb 3[10] i.e. *of my* (mother's) *womb*; גֹּחִי מִבֶּטֶן *take, draw out of the womb*, subj. י׳ (i.e. cause to be born) ψ 22[10]; פְּרִי בֶטֶן used also of father Mi 6[7], cf. ψ 132[11] (David as ancestor of Messian. king); Jb 19[17] בְּנֵי בִטְנִי *sons of my body*, of doubtful interpr., perh.= *sons of my* (*mother's*) *womb*, cf. 3[10] (Ges De), i.e. my brothers or *men of my clan* RS[K 33 f.], others *my sons* (Ew), *my grandsons* (Di); also in addressing Isr. as a whole (masc. sf.) Dt 7[13] 28[4.11.18.53] 30[9], cf. מַחֲמַדֵּי בִטְנָם Ho 9[16] *beloved ones of their womb*; מִן־הַבֶּטֶן (מִבֶּטֶן)=*from birth* Ju 13[5.7] ψ 58[4] 71[6], cf. also Is 44[2.24] 46[3] (‖ רָחַם) 48[8] 49[1.5]; מִבֶּטֶן אִמִּי *id.* Ju 16[17] Jb 31[18] ψ 22[11] (‖ רֶחֶם). **4.** architectural word of some rounded projection connected with the two pillars Jachin & Boaz 1 K 7[20] (Klo rds. הבית).

991 †II. בֶּטֶן **n.pr.loc.** city in Asher Jos 19[25] (=*depression, basin, valley?* cf. Ar. بَطْنٌ, Lane[220 col. 3]) = Βατναί, called Βεθβετεν cf. Lag Onom. 236, 2nd ed. 249; 𝔊 Βαιθοκ, 𝔊L Βετελ.

II. בטן (assumed as √ of following; mng. unknown).

992 †בָּטְנִים **n.[m.]pl. pistachio**, an oval nut (cf. As. *buṭnu* COT[Gloss] & Schr[MBAk 1881, 419], Aram. בּוּטְנָא, ܒܛܡܐ, Ar. بُطْمٌ; on Punic βουτνούμ Blau[ZMG 1873, 527]) =*pistacia terebinthus* Rob[BR i. 208, ii. 222], Post[PEF Oct. 1888, 218, No. 214 f.; Tr. Vict. Inst. xxii. 271 etc.] (*pist. vera* Löw[No. 44]); Gn 43[11] one of the articles carried from Canaan to Egypt by sons of Jacob as present to Joseph; still a delicacy in Egypt and Syria, cf. Wetzst in Löw[p. 420].

993 †בְּטֹנִים **n.pr.loc.** city of Gad, E. of Jordan Jos 13[26], mod. *Baṭne*, W. of *Es-Salṭ* (v. d. Velde[Memoir 298])=Βοτνία cf. Lag[Onom. 234, 2nd ed. 247].

15 †[בָּיִי ,בָּי] **vb. entreat** (Ar. بَيَّ *come as suppliant, entreat*, still current in the Ḥauran: v. Wetzst in De[Jb 34, 36]), of which (prob.) אָבִי Jb 34[36] is 1 s. impf. (used dialectically): אָבִי יִבָּחֵן אִיּוֹב *would that* (lit. *I entreat that*) Job were tried!

†בִּי **part. of entreaty**, craving permission to address a superior, always foll. by אֲדֹנִי (or אֲדֹנָי), and always (exc. Jos 7[8]) at the beginning of a speech, **I pray, excuse me**—(not improb. from √ביי; so that בִּי אֲדֹנִי will be literally *a supplication of* (i.e. *to*) *my lord!* cf. Wetzst l. c., who compares the Ar. دَخْلُ سَيِّدِى lit. *a prayer to my lord!* a standing formula=*Pray, excuse me*, used exactly as בִּי אֲדֹנִי. Acc. to others contr. from בְּעִי, from בָּעָה *to ask*, and so lit. *a petition!* cf. Aram. בְּבָעוּ, ܒܒܥܘ (e.g. Gn 19[18] 𝔗, Nu 12[13] 𝔖); but ע is not often elided in Heb.)—Gn 44[18] בִּי אֲדֹנִי יְדַבֶּר־נָא *I pray*, my lord, let thy servant speak, etc.; so Nu 12[11] Ju 6[13] 1 S 1[26] 1 K 3[17.26], and foll. by a pl. subj. Gn 43[20] בִּי א׳ יָרֹד יָרַדְנוּ *Oh*, my lord, we came down, etc.; בִּי אֲדֹנָי (to God) Ex 4[10.13] Jos 7[8] Ju 6[15] 13[8] (𝔊 in Pent. and Jos. δέομαι, δεόμεθα: in other books absurdly ἐν ἐμοί). 994

†בִּין **vb. discern** (Nö[ZMG 1883, 532 f.]; Ar. بَانَ *become separated, be distinct*, IV. *speak perspicuously*; Eth. በየነ: I. 2 *consider, perceive*, Aram. ܒܝܢ *make to understand*, cf. Sab. בין (*the*) *wise*, as epith., Mordt[ZMG 1876, 37])—**Qal** *Pf.* בִּין Dn 10[1]; בִּינֹתִי Dn 9[2]; *Impf.* יָבִין ψ 19[13]+ בַּנְתָּה ψ 139[2]; אָבִינָה 25 t.; וַיָּבֶן Je 9[11]+2 t.; וַיָּבֶן 1 S 3[8]+2 t.; יָבִינוּ ψ 73[17]+4 t.; יָבִינוּ Pr 28[5]+12 t.; *Imv.* בִּין Dn 9[23]; בִּינָה ψ 5[2]; בִּינוּ Dt 32[7]+2 t.; *Inf.* abs. בִּין Pr 23[1]; *Pt.* בָּנִים Je 49[7];—**1.** *perceive* (with the senses):—**a.** *eyes*, acc. Pr 7[7], with לְ Jb 9[11] 14[21] 23[8] Pr 14[15]. **b.** *ears*, acc. Pr 29[19], with לְ Jb 13[1]. **c.** *touch*, acc. ψ 58[10]. **d.** *taste*, acc. Jb 6[30]. **2.** *understand, know* (with mind):—**a.** abs. Jb 18[2] 38[20] 42[3] ψ 49[21] 82[5] Pr 24[12] Is 6[9.10] 44[18] Dn 12[10] Ho 4[14] 14[10]; שמעתי ולא אבין *I heard but I could not understand* Dn 12[8]. **b.** acc. Jb 15[9] 23[5] 36[29] Pr 2[5.9] 20[24] 28[5] ψ 19[13] 92[7] Je 9[11]; יבין משפט Jb 32[9] Pr 28[5]; יבין דעת Pr 29[7]. **c.** with כִּי 1 S 3[8] 2 S 12[19] Is 43[10]. **d.** with inf. & לְ, יבין לָדַעַת Is 32[4]. **3.** *observe, mark, give heed to, distinguish, consider* (with attention):—**a.** acc. Dt 32[7] ψ 5[2] 50[22] 94[7.8] Pr 23[1] 21[29] (Qr) Dn 9[2] 10[1]. **b.** with לְ, ψ 73[17] 139[2] Dt 32[29]. **c.** with בְּ, Ezr 8[15] Ne 13[7] Dn 9[23]. **d.** with אֶל, ψ 28[5]. **e.** with עַל, Dn 11[30.37]. **4.** *have discernment, insight, understanding* Je 49[7]. **Niph.** נְבֻנוֹתִי Is 10[13]; *Pt.* נָבוֹן Gn 41[33]+15 t.; pl. נְבוֹנִים Je 4[22], elsewhere נְבֹנִים Dt 1[13] Is 5[22] (Baer) Ec 9[11]; נְבֹנָיו Is 29[14]; *be intelligent, discreet, discerning, have understanding* 1 S 16[18] Pr 1[5] 10[13] 14[6] 16[21] 17[28] 19[25] Ec 9[11] Is 3[3] 5[21] 10[13] 29[14] Je 4[22] Ho 14[10]; לֵב נָבוֹן intelligent mind Pr 14[33] 15[14] 18[15]; נָבוֹן וְחָכָם Gn 41[33.39]; 995

חכם ונבון Dt 4^{6} 1 K 3^{12}; חכמים ונבנים Dt 1^{13}. **Po.** יְבוֹנְנֵהוּ *he attentively considereth him* Dt 32^{10}. **Hiph.** *Pf.* הֵבִין Jb 28^{23} + 5 t.; *Impf.* יָבִין Is 28^{9} + 4 t.; וַיָּבֶן 2 Ch 11^{23} Dn 9^{22}; *Inf.* הָבִין ψ 32^{9} + 9 t.; *Imv.* הָבֵן Dn 8^{16} + 12 t.; *Pt.* מֵבִין Pr 28^{7} + 26 t.;—**1.** *understand:*—**a.** abs. Is 29^{16} 40^{21} 56^{11} 1 K 3^{11} ψ 32^{9} Dn 8^{17} 10^{12}. **b.** acc. 1 Ch 28^{9} Jb 28^{23} Pr 1$^{2.6}$ 8^{5} 14^{8} Is 28^{19} Dn 8^{23} Mi 4^{12}; מֵבִין one with understanding Pr 8^{9} 17$^{10.24}$ 28$^{2.7.11}$; מְבִינֵי מַדָּע Dn 1^{4}; able to understand (i.e. old enough) Ne 8^{3} 10^{29}, cf. 8^{2} (sq. לִשְׁמֹעַ). **2.** give heed to, attend to, observe, discern, abs. Is 57^{1} 2 Ch 11^{23} Dn 8^{5}; c. בְּ Ne 8^{12} Dn 9^{23} 10^{11}; מֵבִין בְּ skilled in 2 Ch 26^{5} 34^{12}; c. אֶל ψ 33^{15}; בין טוב לרע 1 K 3^{9}. **3.** *give understanding, make understand, teach:*—**a.** abs. Dn 8^{27} 9^{22}. **b.** with acc. pers. ψ 119$^{34.73.125.130.144.169}$ Jb 32^{8} Ne 8$^{7.9}$ Is
4000 40^{14}. **c.** with לְ pers. 2 Ch 35^{3} Dn 11^{33}; with לְ pers. & acc. rei Jb 6^{24} Dn 8^{16}. **d.** בְּ rei Ne 8^{8}, + acc. pers. Dn 1^{17}. **e.** double acc. Is 28^{9} ψ 119^{27} Dn 10^{14}; מֵבִין *teacher* 1 Ch 15^{22} 25$^{7.8}$ 27^{32} Ezr 8^{16}. **Hithp.** *Pf.* הִתְבּוֹנֵן Is 1^{3} + 6 t.; *Impf.* אֶתְבּוֹנֵן Jb 23^{15} + 3 t.; אֶתְבּוֹנָן Jb 32^{12} + 5 t.; יִתְבּוֹנָנוּ ψ 107^{43} + 2 t.; יִתְבּוֹנָנוּ Is 14^{16} 43^{18}. **1.** *shew oneself attentive, consider diligently:*—**a.** abs. Jb 11^{11} 23^{15} Is 1^{3} Je 2^{10} 9^{16}. **b.** acc. Jb 37^{14} ψ 107^{43} 119^{95} Is 43^{18} 52^{15}. **c.** with אֶל 1 K 3^{21} Is 14^{16}. **d.** with עַל Jb 31^{1} ψ 37^{10}. **e.** with עד Jb 32^{12} 38^{18}. **f.** with בְּ Jb 30^{20} Je 23^{20} (= 30^{24}). **2.** *get understanding, understand* Jb 26^{14} ψ 119^{104}. **3.** *shew oneself to have understanding* ψ 119^{100}.

946 †בּוּנָה **n.pr.m.** (*intelligence* = Palm. n.pr. בונא Vog$^{No.3}$) a man of Judah 1 Ch 2^{25}.

996 [בַּיִן] **subst.** prop. **interval, space between** (بَيْنٌ *id.*)—cstr. בֵּין, once Is 44^{4} (Baer) בֵּן; בֵּינִי, בֵּינְךָ, בֵּינֶךָ, בֵּינוֹ (בֵּינָיו †Jos 3^{4} 8^{11} Qr); with pl. sf. in pl. form בֵּינֵינוּ (בֵּנֵינוּ), etc.; also בֵּינוֹת †Ez 10$^{2.2.6.6.7.7}$ (+ 1^{13} 𝔊 Hi Ew etc. for דְּמוּת), בֵּינוֹתֵינוּ †Gn 26^{28} Jos 22^{34} Ju 11^{10}, בֵּינוֹתָם †Gn 42^{23} 2 S 21^{7} Je 25^{16}; dual בֵּנַיִם (v. infr.);—**1.** always (exc. dual) as **prep. in the interval of, between** (so Aram. בֵּין, & pl. בֵּינֵי, ܒܝܢܬ, ܒܝܢܝ; በበይናቲ:), as Gn 15^{17} בֵּין הַגְּזָרִים *between* the pieces, Ex 13^{9} al. בֵּין עֵינֶיךָ *between* thy eyes (v. עַיִן), Is 22^{11} al. *between* the two walls (v. חוֹמָה), Jb 24^{11} 30^{7} 40^{30} part him *between* merchants; rather more gen. *among* Ho 13^{15} Ct 2$^{2.3}$ Ez 19^{2} 31^{3} Jb 34^{37}; less exactly *within* Pr 26^{13} a lion is בֵּין הָרְחֹבוֹת *within* the broad places (cf. 23^{13} בְּתוֹךְ): once with a sing. (unusual) Dn 8^{16} בֵּין אוּלָי *between* the Ulai, i.e. between its banks. When the space separating two distinct objects is to be indicated, this is done **a.** most commonly by repeating בין, as Gn 13^{3} בֵּין בֵּית־אֵל וּבֵין הָעָי lit. *in the interval of* Bethel, and *in the interval of* ʿAi, i.e. *between* Bethel *and* ʿAi, 16^{14} 17^{7} 31$^{50.51}$ + oft. **b.** more rarely by בֵּין ... לְ, Gn 1^{6} dividing בֵּין מַיִם לָמָיִם lit. *in the interval of* waters *with reference to* waters, i.e. *between* the waters *and* the waters, Lv 20^{25} 27^{33} Dt 17$^{8.8.8}$ 2 S 19^{36} 1 K 3^{9} Ez 41^{18} 42^{20} 44$^{23.23}$ Jon 4^{11} Mal 3$^{18.18}$ 2 Ch 14^{10}. **c.** by בֵּין ... וּלְ †Jo 2^{17}. **d.** by בֵּין ... לְבֵין †Is 59^{2}. בֵּין is used not only of actual locality, but also with verbs of dividing (fig.) Gn 1^{14} Lv 10^{10}, and of judging, knowing, teaching, etc., if the idea of *distinguishing* be involved, as Gn 16^{5} 2 S 19^{36} הַאֵדַע בֵּין טוֹב לְרָע can I discern *between* good and evil? 1 K 3^{9} Jon 4^{11}; Gn 31^{49} (watch *between*), Ju 11^{10} (hear), Jos 22^{27} (witness), Is 2^{4} and he shall judge (arbitrate) *between* the nations, 5^{3}; Lv 27^{33}; Ez 44^{23}; Mal 3^{18}; 2 Ch 14^{10} (see RV); and in other metaph. applications, as of a covenant or sign *between* two contracting parties, Gn 9$^{12.15}$ Ex 31^{13} +; or an oath Gn 26^{28} 2 S 21^{7}; enmity or strife Gn 3^{15} 13^{7} Dt 25^{1} Pr 6^{19}; peace 1 K 5^{26}; good-will Pr 14^{9}.—It is used of *time* in the phrase of P בֵּין הָעַרְבַּיִם (v. sub עֶרֶב), & Ne 5^{18} בֵּין עֲשֶׂרֶת יָמִים *during the interval of* ten days, i.e. every ten days (unusual).

With other prepositions:—**a.** †אֶל־בֵּין, after a verb implying motion, *in between, in among* Ez 31$^{10.14}$. So אֶל־בֵּינוֹת לְ †ib. 10^{2}. **b.** †בְּבֵין Is 44^{4} *in the midst of, amongst* (𝔊 Ew Di Che כְּבֵין מַיִם חָצִיר). **c.** †עַל־בֵּין nearly as אֶל־בֵּין Ez 19^{11}. **d.** †מִבֵּין *from between:* Gn 49^{10} nor the ruler's staff מִבֵּין רַגְלָיו *from between* his feet (where, as the king sits in state, he holds it), Ex 25^{22} *from between* the cherubim (so Nu 7^{89}), Ho 2^{4} Zc 6^{1} 9^{7}; Dt 28^{57} the after-birth הַיּוֹצֵת מִבֵּין רַגְלֶיהָ that cometh forth *from between* her feet, i.e. from her womb (cf. Il. 19. 10 πεσεῖν μετὰ ποσσὶ γυναικός). Repeated 2 K 16^{14} to specify the two objects *from between* which a thing is moved. Ez 47^{18} is difficult and uncertain: v. Comm. Less precisely *from the midst of:* Nu 17^{2} מִבֵּין הַשְּׂרֵפָה *out of the midst of* the burning, ψ 104^{12} מִבֵּין עֳפָאִים *from amongst* the branches they utter their song, Je 48^{45} and a flame מִבֵּין סִיחוֹן *from the midst of* Sihon (Sihon representing his people: but expression is singular; rd. perh. מִבֵּית ס׳, cf. Nu 21^{28} מִקִּרְיַת ס׳: ‖ in both passages מֵחֶשְׁבּוֹן), Ez 37^{21}. **e.** †מִבֵּינוֹת לְ *from between* Ez 10$^{2.6.6.7}$.

996, 1143 **2.** †**Dual** בֵּנַיִם **space between two armies** (=Gk. *μεταίχμιον*), 1 S 17$^{4.23}$ אִישׁ הַבֵּנַיִם *man of the μεταίχμιον*, i.e. champion (of Goliath).

996 †בֵּינוֹת fem. of בַּיִן, בֵּין (Nö$^{M\ 194\ f.}$; Syr. ܒܝܢܬ oft., PS^{470}) **prep. between** Ez 41^{9b} (to be joined with v^{10}; see RVm), unless indeed a mere error for בֵּין (which Ez oft. uses); also Pr 8^{2} acc. to 𝔊 (*ἀνὰ μέσον*) 𝔗 𝔙 Hi Ew$^{§\ 217\ g}$; and Jb 8^{17} acc. to 𝔊 Ew Di^{1} (Di^{2} undecided).

998 †בִּינָה **n.f. understanding** 1 Ch 12^{32} + 28 t.; cstr. בִּינַת Pr 30^{2} Is 29^{14}; sf. בִּינָתִי Jb 20^{3} + 4 t.; pl. בִּינוֹת Is 27^{11};—**1.** *the act* Is 33^{19} Je 23^{20} Dn 1^{20} 8^{15} 9^{22} 10^{1}. **2.** *the faculty* Jb 20^{3} 39^{26} Pr 3^{5} 23^{4} 30^{2} Is 27^{11}; קנה בינה *get understanding* Pr 4$^{5.7}$ 16^{16}. **3.** *the object* of knowledge Dt 4^{6} 1 Ch 22^{12} Jb 28$^{12.20.28}$ 34^{16} 38^{36} 39^{17} Pr 9$^{6.10}$ 23^{23} Is 11^{2} 29^{14}; יָדַע בִּינָה 1 Ch 12^{32} 2 Ch 2$^{11.12}$ Jb 38^{4} Pr 1^{2} 4^{1} Is 29^{24}. **4.** personified Pr 2^{3} 7^{4} 8^{14}.

2985 †יָבִין **n.pr.m.** (*one who is intelligent, discerning*) two Canaanite kings of Hazor;—**1.** Jos 11^{1}. **2.** Ju 4$^{2.7.17.23.24.24}$ ψ 83^{10}. (But cf. Be Ju 4^{2} Bu$^{RS\ 66\ ff.}$)

4000 מבונים 2 Ch 35^{3} Kt; rd. מבינים (Qr) & v. sub בין Hiph. p. 107

8394 †תְּבוּנָה **n.f. understanding** Dt 32^{28} + 27 t.; sf. תְּבוּנָתִי Pr 5^{1} + 7 t.; תובנתו Jb 26^{12} Kt (Qr תְּבוּנָתוֹ); תְּבוּנָם Ho 13^{2} for תְּבוּנָתָם v. De ψ 27^{5}; תְּבוּנוֹת ψ 49^{4} + 4 t.; תְּבוּנוֹתֵיכֶם Jb 32^{11};—**1.** *the act* Jb 26^{12} ψ 78^{72} 136^{5} Pr 3^{19} 21^{30} 24^{3} Je 10^{12}(=51^{15}) Ez 28^{4} Ho 13^{2} Ob ^{7}. **2.** *the faculty* Ex 31^{3} 35^{31} 36^{1} (P) Dt 32^{28} (poet.) Jb 12$^{12.13}$ Pr 2$^{6.11}$ 28^{16} Is 44^{19}; אִישׁ תְּבוּנָה Pr 10^{23} 15^{21} 17^{27} 20^{5}; אִישׁ תְּבוּנוֹת Pr 11^{12} (=Ob ^{8} where אִישׁ omitted by scribal error); דֶּרֶךְ תְּבוּנָה Is 40^{14}. **3.** *the object of knowledge* Pr 2^{3} 3^{13} 5^{1} 14^{29} 18^{2} 19^{8} ψ 49^{4} 147^{5} Is 40^{28} 1 K 5^{9} 7^{14}; תטה לבך לתבונה *incline* thy mind to understanding Pr 2^{2}; *reasons* Jb 32^{11}. **4.** personified Pr 8^{1} as *teacher*.

8394 תְּבוּנָם, תובנתו v. sub תְּבוּנָה. above

בֵּיצָה v. sub בוץ. p. 101

בִּיר v. sub באר. p. 92

1002 †בִּירָה **n.f. castle, palace** (late & prob. loan-word; cf. As. *bîrtu, fortress* Dl$^{HA\ 22}$; Pers. *bâru*=Skr. *bura, bari*, v. Ry Ne 2^{8})—**1.** of *temple* at Jerusalem 1 Ch 29$^{1.19}$ הַבִּירָה; of fortress near temple Ne 2^{8} 7^{2} (cf. *βᾶρις* 𝔊L Ne 1^{1} 2^{8} 7^{2}—B *ἀβιρά, βειρά*—and later *βᾶρις* Jos Ant. xv. 11, 4). **2.** בְּשׁוּשַׁן הַבִּירָה Ne 1^{1} Est 1$^{2.5}$ 2$^{3.5.8}$ 3^{15} 8^{14} 9$^{6.11.12}$ Dn 8^{2}; in these passages it appar. means a fortress in the city bearing the same name (cf. esp. Est 3^{15} 8$^{14.15}$ 9$^{6.12.15.18}$).

†[בִּירָנִית] **n.f. fortress, fortified place** 1003
(late); only pl. abs. בִּירָנִיּוֹת וְעָרֵי מִסְכְּנוֹת 2 Ch 17^{12} built by Jehoshaphat; ב׳ וּמִגְדָּלִים 27^{4} built by Jotham.

בַּיִת$_{2034}$ **n.m.** $^{Dt\ 8,12}$ **house** (Ph. בת, MI. בת, 1004
sf. ביתה, Ar. بَيْتٌ, Aram. בַּיְתָא, ܒܝܬܐ, As. *bîtu*, COT^{Gloss}, Sab. בת, בית, *fortress* DHM$^{ZMG\ 1883,\ 387}$; *temple* Hal^{257} DHM$^{ZMG\ 1876,\ 697}$, Eth. ቤት: Palm. in בת עלמא, בת מקברתא *sepulchre* Vog$^{32,\ 64\ al.}$; etym. dub.; Thes √בות, Aram. בּוּת, ܒܬ *spend the night*, Ar. بَاتَ, Eth. ቤተ: but this perh. denom., & בית fr. √ל״י c. ת afform. cf. Sta$^{§\ 187\ a}$)—abs. בַּיִת Ex 12^{30} +; בָּיִת Gn 33^{17} +; בַּיְתָה (ה־ָ loc.) ψ 68^{7} +; cstr. בֵּית Gn 12^{15} +; sf. בֵּיתִי Gn 15^{2} +; בֵּיתְךָ Gn 7^{1} +, etc.; בַּיְתָה, הַבַּיְתָה (*in*)*to the house, homeward*, Gn 19^{10} ψ 68^{7} +; also בֵּיתָה (*in*)*to the house of* ...; pl. בָּתִּים Ex 1^{21} + (i.e. *bâttîm*, v. Nö in Me$^{Arch.\ i.\ 456\ f.}$, cf. Ges$^{§\ 96}$); cstr. בָּתֵּי Ex 8^{17} +; sf. בָּתֶּיךָ Ex 10^{6}; בָּתָּיו 1 Ch 28^{11}; בָּתֵּינוּ Ex 12^{27} +; בָּתֵּיכֶם Gn 42^{19}; בָּתֵּיהֶם Nu 16^{32} +; (בָּתֵּימוֹ ψ 49^{12}), etc.;—**1.** *house*, **a.** as dwelling, habitation Gn 19$^{2.3.4.11}$ 27^{15} 33^{17} (obj. of בָּנָה) Ex 12^{7} + oft.; ב׳ מוֹשָׁב Lv 25^{29} (cf. בֵּית לְשִׁבְתִּי 2 S 7^{5}); בֵּית=*in the house of*, when modifying word follows, cf. Dr$^{Sm\ 29,\ n.2}$ (after st. cstr. מוֹלֶדֶת בַּיִת אוֹ מוֹלֶדֶת חוּץ Lv 19^{9}); e.g. ב׳ אָבִיךָ Gn 24^{23}; ב׳ אִישָׁהּ Nu 30^{11}; ב׳ יהוה 2 K 23^{24}; so in n.pr. ביתאל Am 7^{13}; (ה)בַּיְתָה *into the house, home* Ex 9^{19} (of man & beast) cf. Ju 19^{18} 1 S 6^{7} (cf. v^{10}) 1 K 13$^{7.15}$ ψ 68^{7} Is 14^{17} etc.; cf. sub **7** infr.; partic. (*a*) in J occasionally of tent Gn 27^{15} cf. 33^{17} (c. בנה; here of nomad's hut); usually (*β*) house of solid materials, with doorposts, etc. Ex 12^{7} Dt 6^{9} 11^{20}, walls Lv 14$^{37.39}$, of stones, timber & mortar v^{45} (cf. v$^{40.42.43}$); so also Jos 2^{15}; supported by pillars Ju 16$^{26\ f.}$; with roof on which one could walk 2 S 11^{12} etc.; v. esp. temple and king's house in Jerusalem 1 K 5–7 etc.; cf. Ct 1^{17} Je 22^{14}; of Ezekiel's temple Ez 40 f.; בָּתֵּיכֶם סְפוּנִים of luxurious houses Hg 1^{4}; בנה בָּתִּים טֹבִים Dt 8^{12}; בנה בַּיִת־חָדָשׁ Dt 20^{5} cf. 22^{8}; also c. בנה Dt 28^{30} + oft.; (*γ*) cstr. before word of material, ב׳ אֲרָזִים 2 S 7$^{2.7}$=1 Ch 17^{1} (ב׳ הָא׳) v^{6}; ב׳ הַשֵּׁן 1 K 22^{39} cf. Am 3^{15}; ב׳ גָּזִית *house of hewn* stone Am 5^{11}; cf. בֵּית יַעַר הַלְּבָנוֹן 1 K 7^{2} 2 Ch 9^{20}, בֵּית הַיַּעַר Is 22^{8}; (*δ*) also before word of quality or characteristic, ב׳ מַרְזֵחַ ;ב׳ שִׂמְחָה || בֵּית אֵבֶל Ec 7^{2} || ב׳ מִשְׁתֶּה ;v^{4} Je 16^{5}; ב׳ מִשְׁתֶּה Je 16^{8}; בָּתֵּי חֶמְדָּתֵךְ Ez 26^{12}; בֵּית תַּעֲנֻגֶיהָ Mi 2^{9}; cf. ב׳ מְרִי *rebellious house* sub **5. d** infr.; (*ε*) in combinations, of structures for

various purposes:—(1) בֵּית הַמֶּלֶךְ=*palace* 1 K 9$^{1.10}$ 10^{12}+, etc.; בֵּית מַמְלָכָה Am 7^{13} cf. sub **2** infr.; ב׳ הַמַּלְכוּת Est 5^{1} cf. 2^{16}; ב׳ לְמַלְכוּתוֹ 2 Ch 1^{18}; (2) בֵּית הַסֹּהַר=*the prison* Gn 39$^{20.20.21.21.22.22.23}$ 40$^{3.5}$; cf. ב׳ מִשְׁמַרְכֶם Gn 42^{19}; ב׳ מִשְׁמֶרֶת 2 S 20^{3}; ב׳ הָאֵסוּר Je 37^{15}; ב׳ הָאֲסִירִים Ju 16$^{21.25}$; ב׳ הַסּוּרִים Ec 4^{14}; ב׳ הַכֶּלֶא 1 K 22^{27} 2 K 17^{4} 2 Ch 18^{26} Je 37$^{15.18}$ cf. Is 42^{7}; ב׳ כֶּלֶא 2 K 25^{27}; ב׳ הַמַּהְפֶּכֶת 2 Ch 16^{10}; ב׳ הַכְּלִיא Je 37^{4} 52^{31}; בָּתֵּי כְלָאִים Is 42^{22}; בֵּית הַפְּקֻדּוֹת Je 52^{31}; בֵּית־הַבּוֹר Je 37^{16}; (3) בֵּית הַנָּשִׁים *house of the women, harem* Est 2$^{9.11.13.14}$; (4) בֵּית מִשְׁתֵּה הַיַּיִן Est 7^{8}; ב׳ הַיַּיִן Ct 2^{4}; cf. בָּתֵּי מָשׂוֹשׂ Is 32^{13}; (5) בֵּית הַחֹרֶף Am 3^{15} Je 36^{22}; ב׳ הַקַּיִץ Am 3^{15}; (6) בֵּית נְכֹתֹה & בֵּית כֵּלָיו 2 K 20^{13}= Is 39^{2}; (7) בֵּית הַגָּן *garden-h.* (or n. pr.? cf. p. 111) 2 K 9^{27}; (8) בֵּית־עֵקֶד *binding-h.* (or n.pr.?) 2 K 10$^{12.14}$; (9) בֵּית עֲבָדִים *h. of slaves* (where slaves live), only fig. of Egypt Ex 13$^{3.14}$ 20^{2} Dt 5^{6} 6^{12} 7^{8} 8^{14} 13$^{6.11}$ Jos 24^{17} Ju 6^{8} Mi 6^{4} Je 34^{13};—on ב׳ הַחָפְשִׁית 2 K 15^{5}= 2 Ch 26^{21} cf. חפשית; esp. (10) בֵּית י׳= *temple* 1 K 7$^{12.40.45.51}$ & very oft.; also (mostly late) בֵּית הָאֱלֹהִים 1 Ch 9$^{11.13.26}$+ oft.; but also of earlier tent of worship Ju 18^{31}; v. also ב׳ הָאֹהֶל 1 Ch 9^{23}; cf. ב׳ אֱלֹהִים of local shrine 17^{5}; & also in mouth of Jacob, as explanation of name of Bethel Gn 28^{17} (cf. v^{19}), & as name of stone, or *Maççeba* v^{22} (all E); also ב׳ י׳ of earlier tent of worship Ju 19^{18} 1 S 1$^{7.24}$ 2 S 12^{20} (cf. further הֵיכַל הַבַּיִת (יהוה, אֱלֹהִים); ב׳ הָאוֹצָר Mal 3^{10}; cf. 1 K 6^{3}, & ב׳ alone in same sense, esp. 1 K 6 cf. 2 Ch 1^{18} 2$^{3.11}$+; v. 1 Ch 28^{2} ב׳ מְנוּחָה לַאֲרוֹן בְּרִית־י׳ וְלַהֲדֹם רַגְלֵי אֱלֹהֵינוּ; also בֵּית הַקֹּדֶשׁ 29^{3}; ב׳ קֹדֶשׁ הַקֳּדָשִׁים 2 Ch 3$^{8.10}$; ב׳ קָדְשֵׁנוּ וְתִפְאַרְתֵּנוּ Is 64^{10}; בֵּית־זְבֻל 2 Ch 6^{2}; בֵּית זָבַח 2 Ch 7^{12}; בֵּית מִקְדָּשָׁם 2 Ch 36^{17}; ב׳ תְּפִלָּה Is 56$^{7.7}$; ב׳ תִּפְאַרְתִּי 60^{7}; also of heathen temples ב׳ בַּעַל־בְּרִית Ju 9^{4}; ב׳־דָּגוֹן 1 S 5^{5}; ב׳ עַשְׁתָּרוֹת 1 S 31^{10}; ב׳ רִמּוֹן 2 K 5$^{18.18.18}$; ב׳ הַבַּעַל 2 K 10$^{21.21.23.25.26.27}$ 11^{18}; ב׳ עֲצַבֵּיהֶם 1 S 31^{9} (but rd. rather את־עצביהם as in ‖ 1 Ch 10^{9} so 𝔊 We Dr); בֵּית בָּמוֹת 1 K 12^{31} (cf. MI בת במת), v. also 13^{32} 2 K 17$^{29.32}$; בֵּית אוֹצַר אֱלֹהָיו Dn 1^{2}, etc.; made of woven material 2 K 23^{7}; אֲשֶׁר הַנָּשִׁים אֹרְגוֹת שָׁם בָּתִּים לָאֲשֵׁרָה perh.=*tent-shrines* but txt. dub. 𝔊 χεττιειν (כתנות?); 𝔊L στολάς; cf. Ew$^{H\ iii.\ 718}$ & Klo; (ζ) of portion of larger building (late), so pl. בָּתָּיו 1 Ch 28^{11} i.e. of the temple (‖ גַּנְזַכָּיו, עֲלִיֹּתָיו, חֲדָרָיו); cf. ב׳ הַכַּפֹּרֶת *ib.*; ב׳ הַמְבַשְּׁלִים Ez 46^{24}. **b.** as shelter or abode of animals 1 S 6$^{7.10}$ cf. Ex 9^{19}; בֵּית עַכָּבִישׁ Jb 8^{14} *spider's web* (cf. בָּנָה כָעָשׁ בֵּיתוֹ 27^{18}); of wild ass Jb 39^{6} שַׂמְתִּי עֲרָבָה בֵּיתוֹ; צִפּוֹר מָצְאָה בַיִת ψ 84^{4} (‖ קֵן); חֲסִידָה בְּרוֹשִׁים בֵּיתָהּ ψ 104^{17} (cf. ‖ & Che); Pr 30^{26} (of the שְׁפַנִּים 'conies'). **c.** fig. of human bodies בָּתֵּי־חֹמֶר Jb 4^{19} *houses of clay*, cf. in phr. שֹׁמְרֵי הַבַּיִת Ec 12^{3} *keepers of the house*, i.e. the arms; v. further בֵּית מְגוּרָי ψ 119^{54}. **d.** of Sh^{e}ʾôl, שְׁאוֹל בֵּיתִי Jb 17^{13}, cf. בֵּית מוֹעֵד לְכָל־חָי 30^{23} (‖ מָוֶת); בֵּית עוֹלָמוֹ Ec 12^{5} (perh.=tomb, v. De). **e.** of abode of light & darkness Jb 38^{20}. **f.** of land of Ephraim as ב׳ יהוה Ho 8^{1} 9^{15} (cf. אֶרֶץ י׳ 9^{3}). **2.** *place*, of Jerusalem בֵּית קִבְרוֹת אֲבֹתַי Ne 2^{3} (‖ עִיר v^{5}), cf. also n.pr. cpd. with בֵּית, infr., & בֵּית מַמְלָכָה Am 7^{13} (pred. of Bethel); בֵּית נְתִיבוֹת Pr 8^{2} i.e. where paths meet RV; ב׳ אֲבָנִים Jb 8^{17}; on both these v. בֵּית sub [בַּיִן] בֵּין p. 108. †**3.** *receptacle*, תְּעָלָה כְּבֵית סָאתַיִם 1 K 18^{32} *a trench like a receptacle of two seahs;* בָּתֵּי נֶפֶשׁ Is 3^{20} i.e. vials of perfume; esp. בָּתִּים לְבַדִּים Ex 25^{27} *holders for the staves*, i.e. rings, טַבָּעֹת *ib.*; so 37$^{14.27}$ 38^{5}; cf. בָּתִּים לִבְרִיחִם 26^{29} 36^{34} *holders for the bars* (all P, & all expl. by טבעת); בֵּית־לָהּ סָבִיב Ez 1^{27} (si vera l.) *its* [cstr. as ψ 58^{5}] *house* (=enclosing cage) *was round about* (del. BHi Co). **4.** of house as containing a family, hence in phr. of slaves belonging to household יְלִידֵי בֵיתוֹ Gn 14^{14} cf. 17^{12} (opp. מִקְנַת־כֶּסֶף) v^{13} (all ‖ *id.*); fig. of Israel Je 2^{14} (‖ עֶבֶד); cf. בֶּן־בֵּיתִי Gn 15^{3}; בְנֵי־בַיִת הָיָה לִי Ec 2^{7} (as token of wealth & prosperity); also of one's sister מוֹלֶדֶת בַּיִת Lv 18^{9} (‖ מ׳ חוּץ cf. infr.); אַנְשֵׁי בֵיתוֹ Gn 17^{27}; נַפְשׁוֹת ב׳ Gn 36^{6}; כָּל־הַנֶּפֶשׁ לְבֵית־יַעֲקֹב Gn 46^{27}. Hence **5.** *household, family* (592 t.) **a.** ordinary sense, those belonging to the same household Gn 7^{1} 12$^{1.17}$+, Dt 6^{22} 11^{6}+; Hex mostly JD; E Gn 35^{2} 42^{33} 50^{22} cf. Ex 1^{21} infr.; P Gn 36^{6} Ex 1^{1} 12^{4} Lv 16$^{6.11.17}$ Nu 16^{32} 18^{31} Jos 22^{15}; even where expressly said to inhabit *tents* Nu 16^{32} Dt 11^{6} אֶת־בָּתֵּיהֶם וְאֶת־אָהֳלֵיהֶם; specif. זְקַן־ב׳ Gn 24^{2} cf. 50^{7} (of rank & dignity in household); of a family of handicraftsmen מִשְׁפְּחוֹת בֵּית־עֲבֹדַת הַבֻּץ 1 Ch 4^{21} (v. בוץ); also, with fig. of house clearly in mind מִשְׁקֶלֶת ב׳ 2 K 21^{13}; מַפְתֵּחַ ב׳ Is 22^{22}. **b.** family of descendants, descendants as organized body Gn 18^{19} (J ‖ בָּנִים)+, & so c. בָּנָה (q. v.) יִבְנֶה ב׳ אחיו Dt 25^{9} cf. Ru 4^{11} &, subj. י׳, בָּנָה ב׳ לְ 2 S 7^{27}= 1 Ch 17$^{10.25}$; also 1 S 2^{35} 1 K 11^{38} (both ב׳ נֶאֱמָן), so עשׂה ב׳ לְ 2 S 7^{11} 1 K 2^{24}; also pl. וַיַּעַשׂ לָהֶם בָּתִּים Ex 1^{21}; עשׂה ב׳ נֶאֱמָן לְ 1 S 25^{28}; cf. esp. c. n.pr., e.g. **c.** בֵּית שָׁאוּל+ 2 S 3$^{1.1.6.6.8.10}$ 9$^{1.2.3.9}$ 16^{5} (מִשְׁפַּחַת ב׳ שׁ׳), v^{8} 19^{18} (cf. 21^{1} where rd. וְאֶל־בֵּיתֹה דָמִים, so 𝔊 We Dr) 1 Ch 12^{29}; בֵּית דָּוִד+ 2 S 3$^{1.6}$ 7^{26}= 1 Ch 17^{24} (cf. context in both), 1 K 12^{19}

=2 Ch 10^{19}, v$^{20.26}$ 13^{2} 14^{8} 2 K 17^{21} Is 7$^{2.13}$ 22^{22} Je 21^{12} Zc 12$^{7.8.10.12}$ (משפחת ב׳ ד׳) 2 Ch 21^{7} ψ 122^{5}; †ב׳ יָרָבְעָם† 1 K 13^{34} 14$^{10.10.13.14}$ 15^{29} 16^{3} 21^{22} 2 K 9^{9} 13^{6}; †ב׳ אַחְאָב† 2 K 8$^{18.27.27.27}$ (of Ahaziah חֲתַן ב׳ א׳), 9$^{7.8.9}$ 10$^{10.11}$ 21^{13} Mi 6^{16} 2 Ch 21$^{6.13}$ 22$^{3.4.7.8}$; etc. **d.** esp. of Hebrew people & subdivisions: (*a*) †בֵּית יִשְׂחָק† Am 7^{16}; (*β*) †ב׳ עֵשָׂו† Ob $^{18.18}$; (*γ*) †בֵּית יַעֲקֹב Gn 46^{27} (P) Ex 19^{3} (E) Am 3^{13} 9^{8} Mi 2^{7} 3^{9} Ob $^{17.18}$ Is 8^{17} 10^{20} 14^{1} 29^{22} 46^{3} 48^{1} 58^{1} Je 2^{4} 5^{20} ψ 114^{1}; also זֶרַע ב׳ יעקב Ez 20^{5} (del. Co); most frequently (*δ*) בֵּית יִשְׂרָאֵל (Vrss & var. sometimes בני v. בֵּן) †Hex Ex 16^{31} 40^{38} Lv 10^{6} Nu 20^{29} (all P) Lv 17$^{3.8.10}$ 22^{18} (H) Jos 21^{43} (D)†; 1 S 7^{2} + 8 t. S K; Ho 1$^{4.6}$ 5^{1} 6^{10} 12^{1}; Am 5^{1} + 7 t. Am; †Mi 1^{5} 3$^{1.9}$ Is 5^{7} 14^{2}, also 46^{3} 63^{7} Zc 8^{13}†; but esp. Je 2$^{4.26}$ + 17 t. Je; Ez 3$^{1.4.5.7.7.17}$ + 75 t. Ez; also זֶרַע ב׳ יִשְׂרָאֵל Je 23^{8} Ez 44^{22} (Co del. ב׳); †שְׁנֵי בָתֵּי יִשְׂרָאֵל Is 8^{14}; בֵּית יִשְׂרָאֵל ויהודה Ez 9^{9} + 25^{8} Co; further בֵּית מְרִי *rebellious house* (of Isr.) Ez 2$^{5.6}$ 3$^{9.26.27}$ 12$^{2.3}$, & ב׳ הַמֶּרִי Ez 2^{8} 12$^{2.9.25}$ 17^{12} 24^{3} [+ 44^{6} Co]; (*ε*) בֵּית יְהוּדָה 2 S 2$^{4.7.10.11}$ 1 K 12^{21} = 2 Ch 11^{1}, 2 K 19^{30} = Is 37^{31}, Is 22^{21} Ho 1^{7} 5$^{12.14}$ Zp 2^{7} Zc 8$^{13.15.19}$ 10$^{3.6}$ 12^{4}, & esp. Je 3^{18} + 9 t. Je; Ez 4^{6} + 4 t. Ez + 9^{9} supr.; also †ב׳ יְהוּדָה וּבִנְיָמִן 1 K 12^{23}; †ב׳ מֶלֶךְ יְהוּדָה† Je 21^{11} 22^{6}; (*ζ*) †ב׳ יוֹסֵף Gn 50^{8} Jos 17^{17} 18^{5} (all JE) Ju 1$^{22.23.35}$ 2 S 19^{21} 1 K 11^{28} Am 5^{6} Ob ^{18} Zc 10^{6}; (*η*) †ב׳ אֶפְרַיִם Ju 10^{9}; (*θ*) ב׳ בִּנְיָמִן 2 S 3^{19} cf. 1 K 12^{23} supr.; (*ι*) †ב׳ יִשָּׂשכָר† 1 K 15^{27}; (*κ*) †ב׳ לֵוִי Ex 2^{1} (E) Nu 17^{23} (P) Zc 12^{13} (משפחת ב׳ ל׳), ψ 135^{20}; & (*λ*) ב׳ אַהֲרֹן ψ 115$^{10.12}$ 118^{3} 135^{19}. **e.** technically, yet with some looseness of usage, בֵּית אָב *father's house,* of family or clan, pl. בֵּית אָבוֹת *father-houses, families* (e.g. Nu 1^{2}) (79 t.; only P & Chr) Ex 6^{14} 12^{3} Nu 1$^{2.4.18}$ + 41 t. Nu; Jos 22$^{14.14}$ 1 Ch 4^{38} 5^{13} + 25 t. Ch; Ezr 2^{59} 10^{16} Ne 7^{61} 10^{35}; = tribe Nu 17$^{17.17.18.21}$; = main division of tribe Nu 3$^{20.24}$ +, cf. 34$^{14.14}$ etc.; further subdivision Ex 12^{3} 1 Ch 7$^{2.7}$ +; cf. esp. 1 Ch 23^{11} *Jeush and Beriah had not many sons, therefore they became* לְבֵית אָב לִפְקֻדָּה אֶחָת (cf. ראשי אבות, sub אב). **6.** house, including *household affairs,* persons, property, etc. וַיַּפְקִדֵהוּ עַל־בֵּיתוֹ Gn 39^{4} cf. בְּבֵיתוֹ v^{5}; אֲשֶׁר עַל־בֵּיתוֹ Gn 44$^{1.4}$; hence אשר על הבית as title of governor of the palace (Ew $^{\text{H iii. 269}}$) Is 22^{15} 36^{3} cf. 1 K 4^{6} 2 K 15^{5}; in Israel 1 K 16^{9} 18^{3} 2 K 10^{5}: further 2 S 17^{23} 2 K 20^{1} = Is 38^{1}; hence of personal property אִם־תִּתֶּן־לִי אֶת־חֲצִי בֵיתֶךָ 1 K 13^{8}; family and property (everything on which one depends) Jb 8^{15}. **7.** בַּיְתָה, בָּ֫יְתָה, בָּ֫יְתָה, lit. *housewards,* hence metaph. *inwards,* †Ex 28^{26} = 39^{19} (sc. of the ephod), 1 K 7^{25} = 2 Ch 4^{4} (sc. of the circle of oxen supporting the molten sea); 2 S 5^{9} מִן־הַמִּלּוֹא וָבָיְתָה from the Millo and *inward,* Ez 44^{17}. **8.** מִבַּיִת **a.** adv. *on the inside* (of a building, chest, etc.: opp. מִחוּץ) †Gn 6^{14} Ex 25^{11} = 37^{2} Lv 14^{41} 1 K 6$^{15.16}$ 7^{9} 2 K 6^{30} (of a person's clothes), Ez 7^{15}; so with ה *loc.* מִבַּ֫יְתָה †1 K 6^{15}. **b.** †מִבֵּית לְ (cstr. Ges $^{\text{§ 130, 1 n.}}$) prep. *within* (opp. מִחוּץ לְ), מִבֵּית לַפָּרֹכֶת *within* the veil Ex 26^{33} Lv 16$^{2.12}$ Nu 18^{7} לְכָל־דְּבַר הַמִּזְבֵּחַ וּלְמִבֵּית לַפָּרֹכֶת for everything of the altar, and for (that) *within* the veil; 1 K 7$^{8.31}$ (rd. לַכְּתֵפֹת; see VB & Sta $^{\text{ZAW 1883, 165}}$); אֶל־מִבֵּית לְ (after a verb of motion) *in within* Lv 16^{15} 2 K 11^{15} = 2 Ch 23^{14}.

Note.—בית perh. occurs abbrev. into ב in n.pr. בְּעֶשְׁתְּרָה q.v. so Thes al.; cf. also Aram. בא=בית in like usage Lag $^{\text{Armen. Stud. § 339; Se i. 51; GGA 1884, 276}}$.

†בַּ֫יִת† c. art. הַבַּיִת Is 15^{2} acc. to Ew Brd Di 1006
al. **n.pr.loc.** but abbrev.; perh. for בֵּית דִּבְלָתַיִם Je 48^{22} (so Ew al.) or בֵּית בָּמוֹת cf. MI^{27} (cf. De Di); others (Ges De Che Or) take הַבּ׳ here = *the house,* i.e. temple or shrine.

†בֵּית אָ֫וֶן† **n.pr.loc.** (*house of iniquity* 1007
or *idolatry*? hardly likely unless as alteration of orig. בֵּית אוֹן, *house of wealth* or *strength*) eastward from Bethel Jos 7^{2} 18^{12} 1 S 14^{23}; 1 S 13^{5} בֵּית־א׳ (on Ho 4^{15} 5^{8} 10^{5} v. בֵּיתְאֵל infr.); site unknown.

בֵּיתְאֵל בֵּיתְ֑אֵל **n.pr.loc. Bethel** (so read, not 1008
בֵּית־אֵל as Jos 7^{2} + acc. to v. d. H; cf. Baer Gn 1008
12^{8}; *house of God,* or *house of Ēl*)—**1.** ancient place and seat of worship in Ephraim on border of Benjamin, identif. with *Luz* (former name) Gn 28^{19} 35^{6} Jos 18^{13} Ju 1^{23}; appar. distinguished from Luz Jos 16^{2} (yet cf. Di); name connected with vision of Jacob when journeying to Paddan-Aram (JE) Gn 28^{19} 35^{7} (where אֵל בֵּיתְאֵל, but 𝔊 𝔖 𝔙 Ol del. אֵל; Di maintains); cf. Ho 12^{5}; when journeying *from* P.-A. 35^{15} (P); name appar. given first to a stone (Gn 28^{18} 35^{14}) cf. We $^{\text{Skizzen iii. 70}}$; הַר בֵּיתְאֵל 1 S 13^{2}; later important place of worship 1 S 10^{3} עֹלֶה אֶל־הָאֱלֹהִים בֵּיתְאֵל; abode of prophet 1 K 13^{11} 2 K 2^{3}; Jeroboam set up one of the golden calves at Bethel 1 K 12$^{29 f.}$ cf. also 13$^{1 f.}$ 2 K 10^{29} 23^{15} Je 48^{13} v. further 2 K 17^{28}; 2 K 23^{15} Th prop. on internal grounds, בֵּית אַל *house of nothingness,* or ב׳ אָלָה *house of execration;* also Renan $^{\text{Hist. iii. 185}}$; in proph. Am 3^{14} 4^{4} 5$^{5.5.6}$ 7$^{10.13}$ Ho 10^{15}; note esp. Am 5^{5} ביתאל יִהְיֶה לְאָוֶן, &

בֵּית אָוֶן (*house of iniquity*) as substit. for ביתאל Ho 4[15] 5[8] 10[5] (עֶגְלוֹת בית און);—mod. *Beitîn* Rob[BR i. 448 f.] Guérin [Judée iii. 14-27] cf. Bd[Pal 215] Survey [ii. 305]. **2.** place in south country of Judah, not far from Beersheba & Ziklag 1 S 30[27] cf. We Dr; =MT כסיל Jos 15[30] (txt. err.; 𝔊 Βαιθηλ); also בְּתוּל Jos 19[4], בְּתוּאֵל 1 Ch 4[30].

1017 †בֵּית הָאֱלִי **adj.gent.** c. art. the Bethelite 1 K 16[34].

1018 †בֵּית הָאֵצֶל **n.pr.loc.** in Judah Mi 1[11]; dub., cf. sub אצל, p. 69.

1009 †בֵּית אַרְבֵאל **n.pr.loc.** Ho 10[14], perh. *Arbel* near Pella (E. of Jordan) Jer Euseb. in Lag [Onom. 88, 2nd ed. 123; 214, 2nd ed. 236], cf. Now *ad loc.*; but in Galilee Rob [BR ii. 399], mod. *Irbid*, cf. Furrer[ZPV ii. 1879, 57 f.]; Bd [Pal 257].

1010 †בֵּית בַּעַל מְעוֹן **n.pr.loc.** Jos 13[17], =בַּעַל מְעוֹן Nu 32[38] Ez 25[9] 1 Ch 5[8] (MI בת בעל מען &

1194 בעל מען)=בֵּית מְעוֹן Je 48[23] = בְּעֹן Nu 32[3] (rd. prob. מען; cf. Dr[Sm lxviii.]); city assigned to Reuben Jos 13[17] Nu 32[3.38] 1 Ch 5[8]; possessed by Moab Je 48[23] Ez 25[9];—mod. *Ma'în* Tristr [Moab 303 f.] Schick [ZPV ii. 1879, 5] Survey [EP i. 176] Bd [Pal 192].

1011 בֵּית בִּרְאִי **n.pr.loc.** v. בית לבאות infr. p. 111

1012 †בֵּית בָּרָה **n.pr.loc.** in combin. עַד בּ׳ בּ׳ וְאֶת־הַיַּרְדֵּן Ju 7[24.24] (?=בֵּית עֲבָרָה *place of ford*).

1013 †בֵּית גָּדֵר **n.pr.loc.** in Judah (*place of a wall*) 1 Ch 2[51] (as n.pr.m.) 𝔊 Βαιθγαιδων 𝔊L Βηθγεδδωρ; = גֶּדֶר Jos 12[13]?, cf. הַגְּדֵרִי 1 Ch 27[28], etc.

1019 †בֵּית הַגִּלְגָּל **n.pr.loc.** Ne 12[29]; cf. גִּלְגָּל.

1014 †בֵּית גָּמוּל **n.pr.loc.** in Moab Je 48[23] (*place of recompense*)—mod. *Umm ej-Jemâl*? Bd [Pal 203], 5 hours S. from Boṣra.

1004, 1588 †בֵּית הַגָּן **n.pr.loc.**? 𝔊 Βαιθαν (Βαιαγαν), 𝔊L Βαιθωρων, 2 K 9[27]; mod. *Jenîn*? v. גַּן, sub גנן, and עֵין גַּנִּים; cf. Sta [Gesch i. 542].

1015 †בֵּית דִּבְלָתַיִם **n.pr.loc.** in Moab Je 48[22] (MI בת דבלתן) v. ד׳. =עַלְמֹן דִּבְלָתָיְמָה Nu 33[46.47]

1016 †בֵּית־דָּגוֹן Jos 15[41], בֵּית דָּגֹן 19[27] **n.pr.loc.** **1.** in Judah (*house*, i.e. *temple of Dagon;* As. *Bit-Daganna* COT [Jos 15, 41, & i. p. 281]) Jos 15[41] (𝔊 Βαγαδιηλ, but 𝔊L Βηθδαγων)—name appears in mod. *Beit Dejân*, SE. of Jaffa, but loc. unsuitable, cf. Rob[BR ii. 232]. **2.** in Asher Jos 19[27] (𝔊 Βαιθεγενεθ, but 𝔊L Βηθδαγων) perh.=*Beit Dejen*, near Akko, cf. Di.

1027 †בֵּית הָרָם **n.pr.loc.** in Gad Jos 13[27] = בֵּית הָרָן Nu 32[36], mod. *Beit Harrân*, 1 hour E. of 1028
Jordan, opp. Jericho, Tristr[Moab 348]; name *Tell er-Ram(eh)* Merrill[PE Soc. iv. 1877] Schick[ZPV 1870, 3, 246] (cf. Lag [Onom. 103, 16, 2nd ed. 137] al.)

בֵּית הָרָן v. בֵּית הָרָם. p. 111 1028

†בֵּית חָגְלָה **n.pr.loc.** (*place of partridge*) 1031
in Benjamin, on border of Judah Jos 15[6]; בֵּית־ח׳ 18[19.21], mod. *'Ain Ḥajla* (or *Qaṣr Ḥajla* cf. Rob & Di Gn 50[11]) Rob [BR i. 544] Bd [Pal 172].

†בֵּית חוֹרֹן **n.pr.loc.** Jos 10[10.11], also בּ׳ חֹרוֹן, 1032, 358
בּ׳ חֹרֹן, & in Ch בּ׳ חוֹרוֹן, two cities in Ephraim, lower & upper B.H. (*place of a hole* or *hollow*(?) חֹר, perh. fr. a wady betw. the two, or near by; cf. also מַעֲלֶה Jos 10[10], מוֹרַד v[11] 1 Macc 3[16.24]) 1 Ch 7[24] אֶת־בֵּית־חוֹרוֹן הַתַּחְתּוֹן וְאֶת־הָעֶלְיוֹן; further, **a.** בּ׳ ח׳ עֶלְיוֹן Jos 16[5]; בּ׳ ח׳ הָעֶלְיוֹן 2 Ch 8[5]. **b.** 1 hour W. from **a.** בּ׳ ח׳ תַּחְתּוֹן Jos 16[3] 18[13] 1 K 9[17]; בּ׳ ח׳ הַתַּחְתּוֹן 2 Ch 8[5]; also Jos 10[10.11] 18[14]; prob. also 21[22] 1 S 13[18] 1 Ch 6[53] 2 Ch 25[13];—mod. *Beit 'Ûr el-fôqa & et-taḥta* Rob[BR ii. 250 f.] Bd[Pal 21] Survey[iii. 86];—cf. הַחֹרֹנִי **adj.gent.** Ne 2[10.19] 13[28], only of Sanballat; also du. חֹרֹנַיִם Jos 10[10.11] 𝔊 & 2 S 13[34] 𝔊 We Dr.

†בֵּית חָנָן **n.pr.loc.** in Dan (Judah? Philistine territory) 1 K 4[9] (where rd. וּב׳ ח׳ v. sub II. אֵלוֹן p. 19);—mod. *Beit Ḥanûn* cf. Rob[BR ii. 35].

†בֵּית הַיְשִׁימוֹת **n.pr.loc.** E. of Jordan 1020
(*place of the desert*, ישׁם) in Moab Ez 25[9]; בּ׳ הַיְשִׁמֹת Nu 33[49] Jos 12[3]; given to Reuben בּ׳ הַיְשִׁמוֹת Jos 13[20];—perh. mod. *es-Suweime*, De Saulcy[Voyage i. 315 f.], cf. Merrill[PE Soc. iv. 1877] Bd[Pal 172] Survey[EP i. 156].

†בֵּית כַּר **n.pr.loc.** (*place of a lamb*) appar. 1033
belonging to Philistines 1 S 7[11].

†בֵּית הַכֶּרֶם **n.pr.loc.** in Judah (*vineyard* 1021
place) Je 6[1], בּ׳ הַכָּרֶם Ne 3[14]; on location cf. Schick [ZPV iii. 83 f.], but v. editorial remarks *ib.*, & Bd[Pal 136].

†בֵּית לְבָאוֹת **n.pr.loc.** in Simeon (*place* 1034
of lionesses?) Jos 19[6]=בּ׳ בִּרְאִי (perh. text. err.) 1011
1 Ch 4[31];=לְבָאוֹת (in Judah) Jos 15[32].

בֵּית לֶחֶם[41] **n.pr.loc.** **1.** in Judah (*place* 1035
of bread (*food*), mod. Ar. بَيْت لَحْم, *place of meat*), 2 hours south of Jerusalem; birth-place of David;—בֵּית לָחֶם Ru 1[19] + 11 t.; בּ׳־לֶחֶם 1 S 20[6] + 9 t.; בֵּית לָחֶם Ju 12[8] + 11 t. + Gn 35[19] 48[7], where הוא בית לחם is a gloss, v. אֶפְרָתָה, p. 68; בּ׳־לָחֶם 1 S 17[15] + 3 t.;—as cstr. בּ׳ לֶחֶם יְהוּדָה Ju 17[7.8.9] 19[1.2.18.18] Ru 1[1.2] 1 S 17[12]; treated as n.pr.m. 1 Ch 2[51.54] 4[4]; *men of Bethlehem*

אַנְשֵׁי בּ׳ Ne 7^{26} = בְּנֵי בּ׳ Ezr 2^{21};—on אֶפְרָ֫תָה as name of Bethlehem, & confusion arising from gloss Gn 35^{19} 48^{7}, v. p. 68;—mod. *Beit Laḥm*, 5 m. S. of Jerus. Rob[BR i. 471] Bd[Pal 123] Survey[iii. 28, 83] Guérin[Judée i. 120-206]. **2.** בֵּית לֶחֶם in Zeb. Jos 19^{15}; perh. also Ju $12^{8.10}$; = *Beit Laḥm*, 7 m. NW. of Nazareth Rob[BR iii. 113] Survey[i. 301].

1022 †בֵּית הַלַּחְמִי **adj.gent.** the Bethlehemite 1 S 16^{18} 17^{51} 2 S 21^{19}, so read prob. also in ‖ 1 Ch 20^{5} for MT את לחמי cf. Be Th Ew[H iii. 70] We[H 266] Kue Dr[Sm]; בּ׳־הַלּ׳ 1 S 16^{1}.

1036 †בֵּית לְעַפְרָה **n.pr.loc.** appar. in Philistine territory Mi 1^{10}; site unknown, & txt. dub.

1037 בֵּית מִלּוֹא v. מִלּוֹא sub מלא. p. 571

1010 בֵּית מְעוֹן v. בֵּית בַּעַל מְעוֹן supr. p. 111

1038 †בֵּית מַעֲכָה **n.pr.loc.** so only אָבֵ֫לָה וּבּ׳ מ׳ 2 S 20^{14}, where rd. as in v^{15} and in אָבֵל בּ׳ מ׳ 1 K 15^{20} 2 K 15^{29} *Abel of Beth Maacah*; c. ה◌ָ loc.; אָבֵ֫לָה בּ׳ הַמַּעֲכָה 2 S 20^{15}; cf. sub II. אָבֵל.

1023 †בֵּית הַמֶּרְחָק possibly **n.pr.loc.** house or settlement on bank of Kidron 2 S 15^{17} (RV *Beth-merhak*, cf. MV RVm *Far House*; Ew The Ke Sta *the last house* of the city).

1024 †בֵּית מַרְכָּבוֹת **n.pr.loc.** in Simeon (*place of chariots*) 1 Ch 4^{31} = בּ׳־הַמַּרְכָּבֹת Jos 19^{5}; site unknown.

1039 †בֵּית נִמְרָה **n.pr.loc.** E. of Jordan, in Gad (*place of leopard*) Nu 32^{36} = Jos 13^{27}; 𝔊 Ναμραμ, Βαιθαναβρα, etc., v. also Lag[Onom. Sacr. 232, 2nd ed. 246];—mod. *Tel Nimrîn* Survey[EP i. 337] Bd[Pal 179], cf. also מֵי נִמְרִים Is 15^{6}, & Rob[BR i. 551].

1040 †בֵּית עֶ֫דֶן **n.pr.loc.** Am 1^{5} Aramaean city, or land = *Paradisus* (Ptol[Geogr. v. 14]); mod. *Jusieh* (cf. Rob[BR iii. 556])? or cuneif. *Bit-Adini*, in Mesopot. cf. Schr[KG 199] Dl[Pa 263 f.]; COT 2 K 19^{12} & v. sub עֶ֫דֶן; otherwise St, & Hoffm[ZAW iii. 1883, 97].

1041 †בֵּית־עַזְמָ֫וֶת **n.pr.loc.** near Jerusalem Ne 7^{28} = עַזְמָ֫וֶת Ezr 2^{24} & עַזְמָוֶת Ne 12^{29}; cf. 1 Ch 12^{13} (where n.pr.m.);—mod. *El-Ḥizmeh* c. 5 m. NNE. of Jerus. acc. to Ritter[Geogr. xvi. 519] Survey[iii. 9].

1025 †בֵּית הָעֵ֫מֶק **n.pr.loc.** on border of Asher (*valley-house*) Jos 19^{27}. Survey[i. 145] comp. *ʿAmka*, 7 m. NE. of Akko (but v. Rob[BR iii. 103, 108]).

1042 †בֵּית־עֲנוֹת **n.pr.loc.** in Judah (perh. = *temple of ʿAnât* Bae[Rel 53] Hal[JAs. 7, xiii. 1879, p. 208], cf. foll.) Jos 15^{59};—mod. *Beit ʿAnûn* Rob[BR iii. 280 f.] Guérin[Judée iii. 151 f.] Survey[iii. 351]. But 𝔊L Βηθαρωθ, cf. mod. *Bittîr*, c. 2½ hours SW. fr. Jerus. Bd[Pal 171].

†בֵּית־עֲנָת **n.pr.loc.** in Naphtali (*temple of ʿAnât* Nes[Eg 114] Bae[Rel 53] Mey[ZMG 1877, 718]) Jos 19^{38} Ju 1^{33}; בֵּית ע׳ v^{33};—perh. mod. *Ain-Ata* v. d. Velde[Narr. i. 170], 6 m. W. of Kedesh (name *ʿAnata* Guérin[Gal. ii. 374]; *ʿAinîtha*, Survey[i. 200]). 1043

†בֵּית־עֵ֫קֶד הָרֹעִים perh. **n.pr.loc.** (*binding-house of the shepherds*) 2 K 10^{12}; cf. v^{14} בּוֹר בּ׳־ע׳; *Bethacath* Jer Lag[Onom. 107. 17, 2nd ed. 141];—mod. *Beit Kâd* near Mt Gilboa (*Fuḳuʿa*) acc. to Survey[ii. 83]; but cf. בַּ֫יִת **1.** p. 109. 1044

†בֵּית הָעֲרָבָה **n.pr.loc.** (*place of the depression*) reckoned to Judah Jos $15^{6.61}$, to Benjamin 18^{22} = הָעֲרָבָה 18^{18}, הָעֲרָבָתָה v^{18}; cf. also 1026
adj.gent. הָעַרְבָתִי 2 S 23^{31} (perh. rd. בּ׳ית־הָע׳ 6164
Klo cf. Dr) = 1 Ch 11^{32};—site unknown.

†בֵּית פֶּ֫לֶט **n.pr.loc.** (*place of escape*) in 1046
south of Judah Jos 15^{27} Ne 11^{26}; cf. **adj.gent.**
הַפַּלְטִי 2 S 23^{26}, & so rd. also 1 Ch 11^{27} 27^{10} (Be). 6407

†בֵּית פְּעוֹר **n.pr.loc.** (= בּ׳ בַּעַל פּ׳, cf. sub 1047
בעל) E. of Jordan Dt 3^{29}, in land of Amorites 4^{46} cf. Jos 13^{20} (where assigned to Reuben); in land of Moab Dt 34^{6}. On site cf. Di Nu 23^{28} Lag[Onom. 232. 2nd ed. 246] Cond[Heth & Moab 142 f.] PEF[1882, 85 f.] Tristr[Moab 305].

†בֵּית פַּצֵּץ **n.pr.loc.** in Issachar (*place of dispersion*) Jos 19^{21}; site unknown. 1048

†בֵּית־צוּר **n.pr.loc.** in Judah (*house of rock*) Jos 15^{58} 2 Ch 11^{7} Ne 3^{16}; as n.pr.m. 1 Ch 2^{45};—mod. *Beit Ṣûr*, c. 12 m. S. fr. Jerusalem Rob[BR iii. 276 f.] Survey[iii. 311] Bd[Pal 138] (*Burj Ṣûr*). 1049

†בֵּית־רְחוֹב **n.pr.loc.** (*place of street*, or *market*?) near Dan on road to Hamath Ju 18^{28} 2 S 10^{6} (where אֲרַם בֵּית־רְחוֹב = רְחֹב Nu 13^{21}; cf. אֲרַם צוֹבָא וּרְחוֹב 2 S 10^{8};—loc. dub. (cf. Rob[iii. 371 f.]). 1050

†בֵּית רָפָא **n.pr.loc.**? in Judah; as **n.pr.m.** 1 Ch 4^{12}. 1051

†בֵּית שְׁאָן **n.pr.loc.** in Manasseh, W. of Jordan (*place of quiet*) 1 K $4^{12.12}$; בֵּית־שְׁאָן Jos $17^{11.16}$ Ju 1^{27} 1 Ch 7^{29}; = בֵּית שָׁן 1 S $31^{10.12}$; בֵּית־שַׁן 2 S 21^{12};—mod. *Beisân* (Scythopolis), NH בֵּישָׁן Rob[BR iii. 329] Bd[Pal 224] Survey[i. 101 f.] 1052

†בֵּית הַשִּׁטָּה **n.pr.loc.** (*place of the acacia*) Ju 7^{22} (on site cf. Rob[BR ii. 356]). 1029

†בֵּית שֶׁ֫מֶשׁ **n.pr.loc.** (*sun-temple*)—בּ׳ שׁ׳ 1053
Jos 19^{22} + 8 t.; בּ׳־שׁ׳ Jos 15^{10} + 6 t.; בּ׳ שָׁ֫מֶשׁ Jos 19^{38} + 4 t.;—**1.** city in SW. Judah Jos 15^{10} 1 S $6^{9.12.12.13.15.19.20}$ 1 K 4^{9} 2 K 14^{13} = 2 Ch 25^{23} 2 Ch

28[18]; distinguished from other places of same name as בֵּ׳ שׁ׳ אֲשֶׁר לִיהוּדָה 2 K 14[11] = 1 Ch 25[21]; assigned to Levites Jos 21[16] = 1 Ch 6[44];—ruin at mod. ʿ*Ain Shems* Rob [BR ii. 223 f.] Bd [Pal 163] Survey [iii. 35, 60]. **2.** city in Naphtali Jos 19[38] Ju 1[33.33]. **3.** city in Issachar Jos 19[22]; possibly ʿ*Ain esh-Shemsîyeh*, Jordan valley, S. of Beisân (Beth Shean) Survey [ii. 231]. **4.** = On-Heliopolis, in Egypt Je 43[13] Rob [BR i. 25] Eb [GS 505 f.] Dl [Pa 318 f.]

1030 †בֵּית־הַשִּׁמְשִׁי **adj.gent.** of foregoing **1,** c. art. 1 S 6[14.18].

1054 †בֵּית־תַּפּוּחַ **n.pr.loc.** in Judah (*place of apples*) Jos 15[53];—mod. *Taffûh* Rob [BR ii. 71] Bd [Pal 154] Survey [iii. 310, 379].

1055 †בִּיתָן **n.[m.]** house, palace—abs. הַבִּיתָן Est 7[7.8] (גִּנַּת הב׳); cstr. בִּיתַן Est 1[5] (גִּנַּת בּ׳ הַמֶּלֶךְ), all *garden of* ב׳; acc. to Dieulafoy [REJ 1888, cclxxvii.] *throne-room*, syn. of *apadâna* in mng., but cf. אַפֶּדֶן.

בֵּית **prep.** between, v. [בַּיִן] sub בין.

1057 †בָּכָא **n.[m.]** balsam-tree (v. Ar. بَكَأٌ Dozy [ZMG 1869, 188] but Löw [No. 47]; acc. to TA like جرجير, an *eruca*, cf. Lane s.v.; perh. cf. بَكَأَ *give little milk*, of camel, i.e. *drop, drip*); pl. בְּכָאִים
1056 2 S 5[23.24] = 1 Ch 14[14.15]; sg. in עֵמֶק הַבָּכָא ψ 84[7] *balsam-vale*, cf. De Che.

1058 †בָּכָה [114] **vb.** weep, bewail (Ar. بَكَى, Aram. בְּכָא, ܒܟܳܐ, As. *bakû* Zim [BP 23, 56], Eth. ብከየ:)—**Qal** *Pf.* ב׳ Gn 43[14] Ho 12[5]; וּבָכְתָה consec. Dt 21[13]; בָּכִיתִי Jb 30[25], etc.; *Impf.* וַיֵּבְךְּ Gn 37[35] + 16 t. (וַיֵּבְךְּ Gn 27[38] etc.); 3 fs. תִּבְכֶּה 1 S 1[10] + 2 t.; וַתִּבְכֶּה 1 S 1[7], וַתֵּבְךְּ Gn 21[16] (where 𝔊 masc. cf. Di) + 4 t.; 2 ms. תִּבְכֶּה Is 30[19] Ez 24[16]; וַתִּבְכֶּה 2 K 22[19], וַתֵּבְךְּ 2 S 12[21] 2 Ch 34[27]; 2 fs. תִּבְכִּי 1 S 1[8]; וְאֶבְכֶּה Ju 11[37] + 4 t.; אֶבְכֶּה 2 S 12[22] + 2 t.; יִבְכּוּ Lv 10[6] + 3 t.; יִבְכָּיוּן Jb 31[38] Is 33[7]; 3 fpl. תִּבְכֶּינָה Jb 27[15] ψ 78[64]; וַתִּב׳ Ru 1[9.14], etc.; *Imv.* pl. בְּכוּ Je 22[10] Jo 1[5]; בְּכֶינָה 2 S 1[24]; *Inf. abs.* בָּכוֹ Is 30[19] + 3 t. + Mi 1[10] (where rd. בְּעַכּוֹ, v. (עכו); בָּכֹה 1 S 1[10] + 3 t.; *cstr.* לִבְכּוֹת Gn 43[30] + 3 t.; לִבְכֹּתָהּ Gn 23[2]; *Pt.* בֹּכֶה (בּוֹכֶה) Ex 2[6] + 6 t.; fs. בּוֹכִיָּה La 1[16]; pl. בֹּכִים (בּוֹ׳) Ezr 3[12] +, etc.;—**1.** *weep* (in grief, humiliation, or joy), abs. Gn 42[24] 43[30.30] Ex 2[6] Nu 11[4.10] 14[1] 1 S 1[7.8.10] 11[5] 30[4.4] 2 S 1[12] 3[16] 13[36] 15[30.30] 19[1.2] 2 K 8[11.12] Is 30[19.19] Je 41[6] 50[4] Ez 24[16.23] La 1[2] Zc 7[3] Jo 1[5] 2[17] ψ 78[64] 126[6] cf. 69[11] (but on text v. Che) Jb 27[15] Ec 3[4] (opp. *laugh* שׂחק) Ezr 10[1] Ne 8[9] Est 8[3]; once c. inanim. subj. Jb 31[38] תְּלָמֶיהָ יִבְ׳ *its furrows weep;* on Ne 1[4] יָשַׁבְתִּי וָאֶבְכֶּה cf. As. *attašab abakî*, Flood 130 ed. Dl Gu [§77] Hpt [BAS i. 145]; of loud weeping נָשָׂא הַקּוֹל וַיֵּבְ׳ Gn 21[16] 27[38] 29[11] Ju 2[4] 21[2] 1 S 11[4] 24[17] 2 S 3[32] 13[36] Jb 2[12] Ru 1[9.14], cf. בּ׳ בְּאָזְנֵי י׳ Nu 11[18], also Jb 30[31]. **2.** c. acc. cogn. בְּכִי Ju 21[2] 2 S 13[36] 2 K 20[3] = Is 38[3], cf. בִּבְכִי Is 16[9], מִבְּכִי Je 48[32], & בּ׳ הַרְבֵּה בֶכֶה Ezr 10[1]; sq. קוֹל גָּדוֹל 2 S 15[33], cf. בּ׳ בקול גדול Ezr 3[12]; *weep bitterly* מַר יִבְ׳ Is 33[7]; also c. inf. abs. *weep intensely, grievously* 1 S 1[10] Je 22[10] La 1[2], cf. Is 30[19] & Mi 1[10] (but on text v. supr.) **3.** sq. עַל *weep upon*, i.e. embrace and weep, עַל־צוּארֵיו Gn 45[14] 46[29] cf. 45[15] 50[1]; also בּ׳ עַל־פָּנָיו 2 K 13[14]; v. further Gn 33[4] 45[14] & וַיִּבְכּוּ אִישׁ אֶת־רֵעֵהוּ 1 S 20[41]; also sq. עַל *weep over, for* Ju 11[37.38] 2 S 3[34] La 1[16]; sq. אֶל־ 2 S 1[24] 3[32] Ez 27[31]; sq. לְ Je 22[10] 48[32] Jb 30[25]; sq. מִפְּנֵי *because of* Je 13[17]; sq. temporal clause (of occasion of weeping) Gn 50[17] ψ 137[1] Ne 8[9]. **4.** sq. acc. *bewail* Gn 23[2] 37[35] 50[3] Lv 10[6] Nu 20[29] Dt 21[13] 34[8] Je 8[23], cf. Is. 16[9]. **5.** sq. עַל in sense of burden, annoy with weeping Nu 11[13] Ju 14[16.17] cf. לִפְנֵי Nu 11[20]. **6.** בּ׳ לִפְנֵי י׳ of penitent weeping Ju 20[23] (cf. Be; v. also 21[2]) Dt 1[45] 2 K 22[19] 2 Ch 34[27], cf. also Nu 25[6]; joined with fasting Ju 20[26] 2 S 12[21.22] cf. Ezr 10[1]; so of weeping in anxious entreaty Ho 4[5]; on pt. as n.pr. Ju 2[1.5] v. בֹּכִים infr. **Pi.** *Pt.* fs. מְבַכָּה *lament* Je 31[25] sq. עַל; *bewail*, pl. מְבַכּוֹת sq. acc. Ez 8[14].

†בֶּכֶה **n.[m.]** *a weeping*, only Ezr 10[1] בכו 1059
העם הַרְבֵּה בּ׳.

†בְּכִי **n.m.** [Ju 21, 2] weeping—בְּכִי Ju 21[2] + 1065
20 t. (also cstr. Dt 34[8], etc.); בִּבְכִי Gn 45[2]; בְּכִי Is 15[2] + 6 t.; sf. בִּכְיִי ψ 6[9];—*weeping* ψ 30[6] Is 15[2.5]; as acc. cogn. (c. בכה) Ju 21[2] 2 S 13[36] 2 K 20[3] = Is 38[3] cf. Is 16[9] (בבכי) Je 48[32] (מבכי); audible קוֹל בּ׳ ψ 6[9] Is 65[19] Ezr 3[13] cf. Je 3[21] 31[16] Is 15[3] (יֵילִיל יֹרֵד בבכי v. Je 9[17]); so also Gn 45[2] (ויתן את־קלו בב׳) & Je 48[5] (בבכי יעלה בכי i.e. the sound of it shall ascend)—but text here suspicious, cf. Is 15[5]; as disfiguring Jb 16[16]; ‖ words of mourning Est 4[3] (מִסְפֵּד, צוֹם, אֵבֶל), Je 31[9] (תחנונים cf. 3[21]), 9[10] 31[15] (נהי), cf. בכי אבל משה Dt 34[8] & Di *ad loc.;* contrition (humiliation) Jo 2[12] (מִסְפֵּד, צוֹם), Is 22[12] (מספד, קרחה, חגור שׂק), cf. Mal 2[13] (דמעה, אנקה); of bitter weeping Is 22[4] אֲמָרֵר בַּבֶּכִי, cf. Je 31[15] (& Is 33[7]); בכי יעזר Is 16[9] Je 48[32] i.e. Yaʿzer in Moab, cf. יעזר n.pr.; ψ 102[10] (שִׁקּוּי בב׳ מסכתי) cf. 42[4] 80[6] & Bab. *dîmtu maštîtî, tears (were) my drink* Zim [BP 34, 42]). Trop., of trickling streams (נהרות) in mines—hindrance to miners Jb 28[11].

†בָּכוּת **n.f.** weeping. Only in אַלּוֹן בָּכוּת 439
Gn 35[8] i.e. *mourning oak*, cf. אלון, p. 47.

1068 †[בְּכִית] **n.f.** weeping Gn 50^{4} יְמֵי בְכִיתוֹ, i.e. the appointed time of mourning for him.

1066 †בֹּכִים **n.pr.loc.** near Bethel, אֶל־הַבֹּכִים Ju 2^{1}, בֹּכִים v^{5} (cf. v^{4}); 𝔊 2^{1} τὸν Κλαυθμῶνα καὶ ἐπὶ Βαιθηλ; v^{5} Κλαυθμῶνες i.e. בְּכָיִם (𝔊L Κλαυθμών);—on poss. connex. with אַלּוֹן בָּכוּת Gn 35^{8} cf. Stu & We$^{Bleek's\ Einl.\ ed.\ 4,\ 183,\ Comp.\ Hex.\ 1889,\ 215}$; but perh. rd. ביתאל instead of בכים in v^{1}, cf. We Bu$^{RS\ 20}$.

1069 †[בָּכַר] **vb.** (NH בִּכֵּר, Aram. בַּכַּר, ܒܰܟܰܪ; cf. Ar. بَكَرَ *rise early, do anything early;* بِكْرٌ, *virgin, woman having her first child;* Eth. በኵር: *primogenitus;* As. *bukru, first-born,* Dl^{§65,5}) —**Pi.** *Impf.* יְבַכֵּר Ez 47^{12}; *Inf.* לְבַכֵּר Dt 21^{16};— **1.** *bear early, new fruit* Ez 47^{12}. **2.** *make* or *constitute as first-born* Dt 21^{16} (den. of בכור). **Pu.** *Impf.* יְבֻכַּר Lv 27^{26} *born* or *made a firstling.* **Hiph.** *Pt. f.* מַבְכִּירָה Je 4^{31} *one bearing her first child.*

1060 בְּכוֹר$_{122}$ **n.m.** first-born—Gn 35^{23} + 78 t.; בְּכֹר Gn 25^{13} + 14 t.; sf. בְּכֹרִי Gn 49^{3} + 14 t.; בְּכוֹרוֹ Gn 38^{6} + 3 t.; pl. cstr. בְּכוֹרֵי Ne 10^{37} + 2 t.; בְּכוֹרֵיהֶם ψ 136^{10}; pl. f. בְּכֹרוֹת Gn 4^{4} Ne 10^{37}; בְּכֹרֹת Dt 12$^{6.17}$ 14^{23};—**1.** *men and women:* **a.** *individuals* Gn 25^{13} + 69 t. **b.** coll. Nu 3$^{46.50}$ 8^{16} 18^{15}. **c.** pl. Ne 10^{37} ψ 135^{8} 136^{10}. **d.** כל בכור Ex 11^{5} 12$^{12.29}$ 13$^{2.13.15.15}$ 22^{28} 34^{2} Nu 3$^{12.12.12.13.40.42.43.45}$ 8$^{17.17.18}$ 33^{4} ψ 78^{51} 105^{36}. **2.** *animals:* **a.** *individuals* Lv 27^{26} Nu 18^{17} Dt 15$^{19.19}$ 33^{17}. **b.** coll. בכור בהמה Ex 11^{5} 12^{29} 13^{15} Nu 3^{41} 18^{15}; כל הבכור Dt 15^{19}. **c.** pl. בכרות Gn 4^{4} Dt 12$^{6.17}$ 14^{23} Ne 10^{37}. **3.** *figurative,* n. of relation בכור מות *first-born of death* Jb 18^{13} (deadly disease); בְּכוֹרֵי דַלִּים *first-born of the poor* (the poorest) Is 14^{30}; Israel is the first-born of Yahweh among the nations Ex 4^{22} cf. Je 31^{9}; and the seed of David among dynasties ψ 89^{28}.

1071 †בֶּכֶר **n.pr.m.** (*young camel,* Ar. بَكْرٌ, As. *bakru* Asrb$^{Annals\ ix.\ 65}$)—**1.** son of Ephraim Nu. 26^{35} = בֶּרֶד 1 Ch 7^{20}. **2.** son of Benjamin Gn 46^{21} 1 Ch 7$^{6.8}$ (בֶּכֶר).

1076 †בַּכְרִי **adj.gent.** c. art. as n. coll. Nu 26^{35}.

1074 †בֹּכְרוּ **n.pr.m.** a Benjamite (on form cf. גַּשְׁמוּ, מַלּוּכוּ, & Ol$^{§107\ ad\ fin.}$; on Nab. n.pr. in ו v. Eut Nab 24, 25, etc. & Nö$^{ib.\ 73\ ff.}$) 1 Ch 8^{38} = 9^{44}.

1075 †בִּכְרִי **n.pr.m.** (*youthful*)—**1.** a Benjamite 2 S 20$^{1.2.6.7.10.13.21.22}$; only in phr. שֶׁבַע בֶּן־בִּכְרִי. **2.** perh. **adj.gent.** pl. c. art. הַבִּכְרִים 2 S 20^{14} *the Bichrites* (i.e. family of Sheba'), MT הַבֵּרִים; cf. 𝔊 ἐν Χαρρει = (ב)כרי; so Klo Dr.

†בִּכְרָה **n.f.** young camel, dromedary (Ar. بَكْرَةٌ *young she-camel*) Je 2^{23}; pl. cstr. בִּכְרֵי Is 60^{6}. 1072, 1070

†בְּכֹרָה **n.f.** right of first-born Gn 25$^{32.34}$ (J) Dt 21^{17} 1 Ch 5$^{1.2}$; sf. בְּכֹרָתִי Gn 27^{36} (JE); בְּכֹרָתְךָ Gn 25^{31} (J); בְּכֹרָתוֹ Gn 25^{33} 43^{33} (J) 1 Ch 5^{1}. 1062

†בְּכוֹרַת **n.pr.m.** (*first-born*) Benjamite 1 S 9^{1}. 1064

†בְּכִירָה **n.f.** first-born, always of women Gn 19$^{31.33.34.37}$ 29^{26} (JE) 1 S 14^{49}. 1067

†בִּכּוּרָה **n.f.** first ripe fig, early fig (regarded as a delicacy) (Löw^{391}; cf. Ar. بَاكُورَةٌ, Span. *albacora,* Moorish *bokkôre*) Mi 7^{1} Ho 9^{10}; sf. בִּכּוּרָהּ = בִּכּוּרָתָהּ (rd. בִּכּוּרָה Di), Is 28^{4}; pl. 1063
בִּכֻּרוֹת Je 24^{2}. 1073

†בִּכּוּרִים **n.m.** first-fruits—Lv 2^{14} 23^{17} Nu 28^{26} (P) 2 K 4^{42} Ne 3^{12} 13^{31}; בִּכֻּרִים Lv 23^{20} (P); cstr. בִּכּוּרֵי Ex 23$^{16.19}$ (E) 34$^{22.26}$ (J) Nu 13^{20} (E) 18^{13} (P) Ne 10$^{36.36}$ Ez 44^{30}; sf. בִּכּוּרֶיךָ Lv 2^{14};—the first of grain and fruit that ripened and was gathered and offered to God according to the ritual; לֶחֶם הַבִּכּוּרִים bread made of the new grain offered at Pentecost Lv 23^{20}; יום הבכורים *day* of the first-fruits (Pentecost) Nu 28^{26}. 1061

בַּל v. sub בלה. p. 115 1077

בַּל, בֵּלְאשַׁצַּר v. sub בעל, p. 128. 1078

†בַּלְאֲדָן **n.pr.m.** (=Bab. *abal-iddina, he hath given a son* COT 2 K 20^{12}) father of מְרֹדַךְ בַּלְאֲדָן king of Babylon (v. sub מְרֹדַךְ) 2 K 20^{12} = Is 39^{1}; name prob. abbreviated by omission of name of god (v. *ib. Merodach-baladan* = *Marduk-abal-iddina, Marduk hath given a son;* cf. *Esarhaddon,* v. אֵסַרְחַדֹּן p. 64). 1081

†[בָּלַג] **vb.** gleam, smile (Ar. بَلَجَ)—only **Hiph.** *Impf.* 1 s. c. ו subord. וְאַבְלִיגָה Jb 9^{27} + 2 t.; *Pt.* מַבְלִיג Am 5^{9};—**1.** *shew a smile, look cheerful* ψ 39^{14} Jb 9^{27} 10^{20}. **2.** *cause to burst* or *flash* המב׳ שֹׁד עַל־עָז Am 5^{9} (cf. Ew St). 1082

†בִּלְגָּה **n.pr.m.** (*cheerfulness*)—**1.** priest of 15th course (David's time) 1 Ch 24^{14}. **2.** priest that went up with Zerubbabel Ne 12$^{5.18}$. 1083

†בִּלְגַּי **n.pr.m.** (*id.*) priest with Neh. Ne 10^{9}. 1084

†[מַבְלִיגִית] **n.f.** smiling, cheerfulness, source of brightening—מַבְלִיגִיתִי עֲלֵי יָגוֹן Je 8^{18} *a source of brightening to me in sorrow;* but text dub. cf. VB Che. 4010

1085 †בִּלְדַּד **n.pr.m.** (𝔊 Βαλδαδ; Nö ZMG 1888, 479 *Bel has loved*, cf. אֶלְדָּד; Dl Pa 298; ZK ii. 177 comp. cuneif. *Bir-Dadda*, cf. Hpt Hbr 1885, 224) 2nd friend of Job (הַשֻּׁחִי) ב׳ הַשּׁוּחִי Jb 2^{11} 8^{1} 18^{1} 25^{1} 42^{9}.

1088 †בָּלָה **n.pr.loc.** in Simeon Jos 19^{3}.

1086 †[בָּלָה] **vb. become old and worn out** (Ar. بَلِيَ, Aram. בְּלֵי, ܒܠܐ, Eth. ብልየ: *id.*)—**Qal** *Pf.* בָּלְתָה Dt 8^{4}, בָּלוּ 29^{4}+; *Impf.* יִבְלֶה Jb 13^{28} etc.; *Inf.* c. sf. בְּלֹתִי Gn 18^{12};—*wear out* (intr.), esp. of garments Dt 8^{4} 29$^{4.4}$, all c. מֵעַל pregn. *wear out* (and fall) *from upon*...(hence Ne 9^{21}), Jos 9^{13}; fig. of the heavens (with sim. of garment) Is 50^{9} ψ 102^{27} כַּבֶּגֶד יִבְלוּ, the earth Is 51^{6} כַּבֶּגֶד תִּבְלֶה; the bones (through suffering) ψ 32^{3}; afflicted man Jb 13^{28} וְהוּא כְּרָקָב יִבְלֶה || כְּבֶגֶד אֲכָלוֹ עָשׁ); of an aged and decrepit woman Gn 18^{12} (J) אַחֲרֵי בְלֹתִי after *I am worn out.* **Pi.** caus. of Qal. **a.** *wear out* (trans.), fig. La 3^{4} בִּלָּה בְשָׂרִי וְעוֹרִי, ψ 49^{15} and their form לְבַלּוֹת שְׁאוֹל is for She'ôl *to consume away* (others rd. לְבַלּוֹת is for *wasting away* [Dr §204], connecting ׳שׁ with foll.), 1 Ch 17^{9} לְבַלֹּתוֹ *to wear* it (Isr.) *out* (altered fr. לְעַנּוֹתוֹ 2 S 7^{10}), cf. Dn 7^{25} Aram. **b.** *wear out by use, use to the full,* Is 65^{22} and the work of their hands יְבַלּוּ they shall *use to the full, enjoy,* Jb 21^{13} they *wear out* their days in prosperity (Qr here יְכַלּוּ *complete,* which perh. is the true reading in both passages; cf. Ex 5^{13} Jb 36^{11}).—On בַּלֹּתִי ψ 92^{11}, v. sub בָּלַל.

1087 †[בָּלֶה] **adj. worn out**; f. בָּלָה Ez 23^{43} (of a woman, cf. Gn 18^{12} supr.); pl. בָּלִים Jos 9^{4} (sacks), v^{4} (wine-skins), בָּלוֹת v^{5} (sandals), v^{5} (garments).

1094 †[בְּלוֹא] **n.[m.] worn out things, rags** (Syr. ܒܠܘܝܐ *id.*) pl. cstr. בְּלוֹיֵ Je 38$^{11.11}$, בְּלוֹאֵי v^{12}.

8399 †[תַּבְלִית] **n.f. destruction**: c. sf. Is 10^{25} וְאַפִּי עַל־תַּבְלִיתָם and mine anger for *their destruction.*

1077 בַּל$_{69}$ **adv. not** (Ph. *id.*: e.g. CIS 1.165, 15 בל יכן לכהן shall *not* be for the priest; 3, 3 בל עתי = before my time) a poet. syn. of לֹא, of comparatively rare occurrence, Ho 7^{2} 9^{16} (Qr) Is 14^{21} 35^{9} 43^{17} Pr 9^{13} 14^{7} 19^{23} 22^{29} 23$^{7.35.35}$ 24^{23} 1 Ch 16^{30} (=ψ 96^{10}), only besides, except in the passages cited, in other Psalms: often repeated in the same context, as Is 26$^{10.10.11.14.14.18.18}$ 33$^{20.20.21.23.23.24}$ 44$^{8.9.9.9}$ ψ 10$^{4.6.11.15.18}$ 16$^{2.4.4.8}$ 17$^{3.3.5}$ 21$^{3.8.12}$; also used oft. with אָמוֹט, יִמּוֹט, תִּמּוֹט ψ 10^{6} 16^{8} 21^{8} 30^{7} 46^{6} 93^{1} 96^{10} 104^{5} Pr 10^{30} 12^{3} Jb 41^{15}. In Is 40^{24} it is prob. that it acquires from the context the sense of *hardly:* yea, *hardly* are they planted, yea, *hardly* are they sown..., when he even bloweth upon them, and they wither; cf. לֹא 2 K 20^{4}. Joined anomalously with an infin., ψ 32^{9} בַּל קְרוֹב אֵלֶיךָ (else) there is *not* coming nigh thee (i.e. else they will not approach thee).

†בְּלִי **subst. wearing out** (بَلًى, ܒܠܐ *wearing out* of a garment), hence **1.** fig. *destruction* Is 38^{17} שַׁחַת בְּלִי pit of destruction (of She'ôl). **2.** *defect, failure,* hence **adv. of negation** (cf. אֶפֶס), chiefly poet. for לֹא, אַיִן:—**a.** with finite vb. rare and only once in prose, Gn 31^{20} (E) עַל־בְּלִי הִגִּיד לוֹ because he told him not, Is 14^{6} 32^{10} Ho 8^{7} 9^{16} (Kt) Jb 41^{18}. **b.** used to negative an adj. or ptcp. 2 S 1^{21} בְּלִי מָשִׁיחַ *not* anointed, ψ 19^{4} Ho 7^{8}: more freq., esp. in Job, joined with a subst. in sense of *without,* Jb 8^{11} will the reed-grass grow בְּלִי־מָיִם *without* water? 24^{10} they go about naked בְּלִי לְבוּשׁ *without* clothing, 31^{39} 33^{9} 34^{6} 38^{2} words בְּלִי־דַעַת *without* knowledge, 39^{16} 42^{3} ψ 59^{5} בְּלִי־עָוֹן יְרוּצוּן *without* (my) iniquity they run (against me), cf. v^{4} לֹא, 63^{2} a dry land בְּלִי מָיִם *without* water, Is 28^{8}; Jb 30^{8} בְּנֵי בְלִי־שֵׁם children of (men of) *no* name. 1097

With preps. **a.** †בִּבְלִי, in בִּבְלִי דַעַת Dt 4^{42} 19^{4} Jos 20$^{3.5}$ D (=*unawares:* all in D's law of homicide); *without knowledge* Jb 35^{16} 36^{12}. **b.** †לִבְלִי *in a state of* (v. sub לְ) *no* ..., i.e. *without,* Is 5^{14} לִבְלִי־חֹק *regardless of, without* measure, Jb 38^{41} 41^{25} that is made לִבְלִי־חָת (to be) *in a state of no* fear, i.e. to be fear*less.* **c.** †מִבְּלִי (α) *from want of,* followed by a subst. or infin., מִן expressing *causation,* Dt 9^{28} מִבְּלִי יְכֹלֶת י׳ on account of Jehovah's *not* being able ... (in Nu 14^{16} מִבִּלְתִּי), 28^{55} (Ew 238d; but also RS JPh xvi. 72), Is 5^{13} *for want of* knowledge, Ho 4^{6} Ez 34^{5} La 1^{4} מִבְּלִי בָּאֵי מוֹעֵד *for lack of* comers to the stated feast. Followed by a pleon. אַיִן in the phrase הֲמִבְּלִי אֵין ... is it *on account of* there being *no* ...? (lit. is it *from the deficiency of no* ...? cf. ܡܢ ܕܠܐ ܕܠܐ in Syr.; PS 528), Ex 14^{11} 2 K 1$^{3.6.16}$. (β) *so that there is no* ... (lit. *away from* there being *no* ..., מִן expressing *negation,* and בְּלִי being pleon., as in מֵאֵין, v. sub אַיִן **6 d** β); Je 2^{15} its cities are burnt מִבְּלִי יֹשֵׁב *so that there is no* inhabitant, 9$^{9-11}$ Ez 14^{15} Zp 3^{6}. Once as a conj. מִבְּלִי אֲשֶׁר, with pleon. לֹא, *so that not* ... Ec 3^{11}. In Job מִבְּלִי is used more freely=

without, the connexion with a preceding verb being no longer distinctly felt: 4^{20} *without* any heeding, they perish for ever, 6^{6} $24^{7.8}$; prob. also 4^{11} 31^{19} (though here the sense (*a*) would be admissible). (γ) in Jb 18^{15} מִן ,תִּשְׁכּוֹן בְּאָהֳלוֹ מִבְּלִי־לוֹ is prob. *partitive* (so Hi): there shall dwell in his tent *what is naught* of his: Ew$^{§ 323a}$ De less probably *even naught*, cf. sub אַיִן **6 d γ**; Ges 'terror (supplied from v^{14}) shall dwell in his tent *so that it is no more* his.' **d.** †עַד־בְּלִי *till* there be *no* . . . ψ 72^{7} Mal 3^{10}.

1099, 1097 †בְּלִימָה† **n.[m.]** nothingness (from בְּלִי & מָה, lit. *not-aught*) Jb 26^{7} who hangeth the earth on בְּ׳.

1100 †בְּלִיַּעַל† 27 **n.[m.] worthlessness** (cpd. בְּלִי *not, without* and יַעַל *worth, use, profit*)—ב׳ Dt 13^{14} + 20 t.; בְּלִיָּעַל ψ 101^{3} + 5 t.;—the quality of *being useless, good for nothing*. **1.** abstr. אִישׁ (ה)בליעל, אַנְשֵׁי הבליעל, *worthless, good-for-nothing, base fellows* 1 S 25^{25} 2 S 16^{7} 20^{1} 1 K 21^{13} Pr 16^{27};=בֶּן־ב׳ 1 S 25^{17}, בְּנֵי ב׳ Dt 13^{14} Ju 19^{22} 20^{13} 1 S 2^{12} 10^{27} 1 K $21^{10.13}$ 2 Ch 13^{7}; בַּת ב׳ 1 S 1^{16} (drunken woman); עֵד ב׳ *base witness* Pr 19^{28}; דְּבַר ב׳ *base, wicked thing* ψ 41^{9} (yet cf. **3** infr.), 101^{3} (add prob. also 1 S 29^{10}, so 𝔊 We Dr); דָּבָר...ב׳ (elliptical and in apposition) Dt 15^{9}. **2.** concr. elliptical of אִישׁ ב׳ 2 S 23^{6} Jb 34^{18}; בְּל־אִישׁ רַע וּבְלִיַּעַל 1 S 30^{22}; אָדָם בְּלִיַּעַל Pr 6^{12}. **3.** *ruin, destruction:* so ψ 41^{9} acc. to De Che al., but v. supr.; יֹעֵץ ב׳ *counsellor of ruin* Na 1^{11}; ב׳ alone *a man of ruin, destroyer* Na 2^{1}; נַחֲלֵי ב׳ *floods of destruction* (‖ שְׁאוֹל) 2 S 22^{5}=ψ 18^{5}.

1107 †בִּלְעֲדֵי† (perh. from בַּל and עֲדֵי, עַד *unto;* Syr. ܒܠܥܕ=ἄνευ, χωρίς; Nab. בלעד *except*, Eut$^{Nab 3,9}$)—sf. בִּלְעָדַי (3 t.), בַּלְעָדַי (4 t.), בִּלְעָדֶיךָ (once)—prop. *not unto*, hence **apart from, except, without: a.** Jb 34^{32} בִּלְעֲדֵי אֶחֱזֶה *except, apart from* (what) I see myself, do thou instruct me. With sf. Gn 41^{44} בִּלְעָדֶיךָ *apart from* thee, *without* thee, no one shall lift up the head, Is 45^{6} for there is none בִּלְעָדָי *except* me. Also with sf., as a particle of deprecation, Gn 14^{24} בִּלְעָדַי *not to me!* i.e. I claim nothing, (in our idiom) *not at all!* 41^{16}. **b.** with מִן, מִבַּלְעֲדֵי (so ܡܢ ܒܠܥܕ *without*). (*a*) *apart from*, esp. with the collat. idea of without the knowledge and consent, Nu 5^{20} 2 K 18^{25} (=Is 36^{10}) am I now come up *apart from, without* י׳ against this place to destroy it? Je 44^{19} (cf. בִּלְעָדֶיךָ Gn 41^{44}). (β) *apart from, besides, except,* Jos 22^{19} 2 S 22^{32a} (=ψ 18^{32a}) for who is God *except* י׳? v^{32b}; similarly Is 43^{11} וְאֵין מִבַּלְעָדַי מוֹשִׁיעַ, $44^{6.8}$ 45^{21}.

[בֵּלֶת] **subst.** (from בָּלָה, of the form דֶּלֶת 1115
Ol$^{§ 146 b}$) prop. *failure*, hence used as **particle of negation, not, except** (cf. אֶפֶס, בְּלִי), twice with sf. (v. infr.), elsewhere always בִּלְתִּי (with binding vowel ִי—, as mark of cstr. state: Sta$^{§ 343}$ Ges$^{§ 90, 3}$), (Ph. בלת *only:* Tabnith-Inscr.^{5}) —†**1. adv. not**, with an adj. 1 S 20^{26} בִּלְתִּי טָהוֹר *not* clean, with a subst. Is 14^{6} מַכַּת בִּלְתִּי סָרָה a stroke of *non*-cessation, i.e. a never-ceasing stroke, with a finite vb. (si vera l.) Ez 13^{3} (RVm: but v. Dr$^{§ 41 Obs.}$). †**2.** after a preceding negation, *not*=**except** (syn. זוּלָתִי), Gn 21^{26} I have not heard בִּלְתִּי הַיּוֹם *except* to-day, Ex 22^{19} he that sacrificeth בִּלְתִּי לי׳ *except* unto י׳, Nu 32^{12} Jos 11^{19}: so בִּלְתִּי אִם Gn 47^{18} Ju 7^{14} (cf. כִּי אִם Gn 28^{17} Ne 2^{2}). With sf. (attached to the ground-form בֵּלֶת) בִּלְתִּי *except* me †Ho 13^{4}, בִּלְתֶּךָ *except* thee †1 S 2^{2}. †**3. conj.** (likewise after a neg., expressed or implied) Gn 43^{3} בִּלְתִּי אֲחִיכֶם אִתְּכֶם *except* your brother (be) with you, v^{5} Nu 11^{6} our soul is dry, there is nothing at all; *save that* our eyes are toward the manna, Is 10^{4} (and where will ye leave your glory?) *save that* they bow down under the prisoners, and fall under the slain! i.e. (iron.) their only refuge will be among the corpses of a battle-field. So בִּלְתִּי אִם Am $3^{3.4}$.—Dn 11^{18}, where no neg. precedes, it is difficult to extract a sense consistent with the gen. usage of בִּלְתִּי: Ges *besides that* his reproach he will return unto him, Ew *only, nothing but,* Hi *certainly,* Drechsler (on Is 10^{4}) *nay, even* (cf. RV).

4. With preps. **a.** לְבִלְתִּי 86 *so as not . . ., in order not...* (negation of לְ sq. inf.), usually sq. inf. cstr., as Gn 4^{15} gave a sign to Cain לְבִלְתִּי הַכּוֹת־אֹתוֹ *in order* that any finding him should *not* smite him, 19^{21} 38^{9} Ex $8^{18.25}$ 9^{17} Lv 18^{30} 20^{4} 26^{15} Dt 8^{11} 17^{12} the man that doeth presumptuously לְבִלְתִּי שְׁמֹעַ *so as not* to hearken etc. (cf. Je 16^{12} 17^{23} 18^{10} 42^{13} Dn 9^{11}) v^{20} Ju 2^{23}+; לְבִלְתִּי הוֹעִיל *in order not to* profit (the result represented forcibly as the design; cf. sub לְמַעַן) Is 44^{10} Je 7^{8}; after vbs. of commanding Gn 3^{11} which I commanded thee לְבִלְתִּי אֲכָל־מִמֶּנּוּ *not to* eat thereof, 2 K 17^{15} Je $35^{8f.14}$ Ru 2^{9}, swearing Dt 4^{21} Jos 5^{6} Ju 21^{7} Ez 20^{15}, agreeing 2 K 12^{9}, interceding Je 36^{25}. Once לְבִלְתִּי לְ 2 K 23^{10} (cf. לְמַעַן לְ Ez 21^{20}, בַּעֲבוּר לְ 1 Ch 19^{3}).

Twice as conj. with the impf., Ex 20^{20} 2 S 14^{14} (cf. בַּעֲבוּר, & מִן Dt 33^{11}). In Je 23^{14} 27^{18} sq. perf., which is inconsistent with the nature of a final conj.: rd. either יָבֹאוּ, יָשׁוּבוּ, or בּוֹא, שׁוּב (cf. Dr [§ 41 Obs.]). On Ez 13^3 v. supr. †**b.** מִבִּלְתִּי *an account of not*... (negation of מִן sq. inf.): sq. inf. Nu 14^{16} מִבִּלְתִּי יְכֹלֶת י׳; a verbal noun Ez 16^{28} מִבִּלְתִּי שָׂבְעָתֵךְ. †**c.** עַד־בִּלְתִּי *until not*..., sq. a perf. (Ges; RS [JPh xvi. 72]), or an inf. (Ew [§ 238 d]), in the phrase עַד־בִּלְתִּי הִשְׁאִיר־לוֹ (לָהֶם) שָׂרִיד *until* one left him (them) *not* a remnant, Nu 21^{35} Dt 3^3 Jos 8^{22} 10^{33} 11^8 2 K 10^{11}.—Jb 14^{12} עַד־בִּלְתִּי שָׁמַיִם *till* there be *no* heaven (cf. עַד־בְּלִי ψ 72^7).

1089 †[בָּלַהּ] **vb.** trouble (Aram. ܒܠܗ, cf. Ar. بَلِهَ *be weak in intellect;* v. also בהל)—only **Pi.** *Pt.* מְבַלְהִים אותם לִבְנוֹת Kt (Qr מְבַהֲלִים needless) Ezr 4^4 *troubled them in building.*

1091 †בַּלָּהָה **n.f.** terror, dreadful event, calamity, destruction—בַּלָּהָה Is 17^{14}; pl. בַּלָּהוֹת Jb 18^{11} + 7 t.; cstr. בַּלְהוֹת Jb 24^{17};—**1.** only pl. *terrors* Jb 18^{11} 27^{20} 30^{15}; מֶלֶךְ ב׳ Jb 18^{14} = death, cf. ב׳ צַלְמָוֶת Jb 24^{17}. **2.** *calamity* Is 17^{14}, pl. ψ 73^{19}; *calamity, destruction* Ez 26^{21} 27^{36} 28^{19}.

1090 †I. בִּלְהָה **n.pr.f.** (etym. dub.) handmaid of Rachel, concubine of Jacob Gn 29^{29} $30^{3.4.5.7}$ $35^{22.25}$ (sons Dan & Naphtali) 37^2 (prob. gloss, Ol) 46^{25} 1 Ch 7^{13}.

†II. בִּלְהָה **n.pr.loc.** a city of Simeon 1 Ch 4^{29}, prob. = בַּעֲלָה Jos 15^{29}, בָּלָה 19^3 cf. Di; site dub.

1092 †בִּלְהָן **n.pr.m.** **1.** descendant of Esau Gn 36^{27} = 1 Ch 1^{42}. **2.** a Benjamite 1 Ch $7^{10.10}$.

בְּלוֹא v. sub בלה.

1095 †בֵּלְטְשַׁאצַּר **n.pr.m.** Dn 1^7, בֵּלְטְאשַׁצַּר Dn 10^1 (prob. = Bab. *balâṭsu-uṣur, protect his life!* COT Dn 1^7 Dl in BD [Dn. p. ix]; Hoffm [ZA 1887, 56] conj. בלט ש[ר] אצר *Balaṭ* (= god Saturn?) *protect the king!*—Dn 4^5 conn. with *Bel*, but name then inexplicable), name given to Daniel by Neb.

בְּלִי, בְּלִימָה, בְּלִיַּעַל v. sub בלה.

1101 †I. בָּלַל **vb.** mingle, mix, confuse, confound (Ar. بَلَّ *moisten* (with water), cf. بَلَلٌ *moisture*, As. *balâlu*, Dl [Pr 70]; cf. Ph. בלל name of a sacrifice, & NH בִּלְבֵּל; Aram. בַּלְבֵּל, ܒܰܠܒܶܠ)—**Qal** *Pf.* בָּלַל Gn 11^9, בַּלֹּתִי ψ 92^{11} (but cf. infr.); *Impf.* 1 pl. נָבְלָה = נָבֹלָה Gn 11^7, cf. Kö [i. 325]; *Pt.* pass. בָּלוּל Ex 29^{40} + 3 t., בְּלוּלָה Lv 2^5 + 28 t., בְּלוּלֹת Ex 29^2 + 4 t.;—**1.** *mingle, confuse* (obj. שָׂפָה = speech, language, q.v.) Gn $11^{7.9}$ (J). **2.** *mix* (cakes or flour, etc. always with oil) term. techn. sacrif., only P (H Lv 23^{13}), cf. Di on Lv 2^4; usually as מנחה, סֹלֶת ב׳ בַּשֶּׁמֶן׳ Ex 29^{40} Lv 2^5 $14^{10.21}$ 23^{13} Nu $7^{13.19.25.31.37.43.49.55.61.67.73.79}$ Nu 8^8 $15^{4.6.9}$ $28^{5.9.12.12.13.20.28}$ $29^{3.9.14}$, מנחה ב׳ בשׁ׳, Lv 7^{10} (opp. חֲרֵבָה) 9^4, חַלּוֹת מַצּוֹת ב׳ בשׁ׳ Ex 29^2 Lv $7^{12.12}$, i.e. made by mixing with oil; סלת חלות ב׳ בשׁ׳ Lv 2^4, סלת חלות מצות ב׳ בשׁ׳ Nu 6^{15}, i.e. fine flour (in the form) of cakes so made. בַּלֹּתִי בְּשֶׁמֶן רַעֲנָן ψ 92^{11} *I shall be* (*am*) *anointed with fresh oil* AV RV; vb. not elsewhere in this sense; 𝔊 𝔙 Hup Che rd. בְּלֹתִי fr. בלה, inf. cstr. sf., abstr. for concrete, *my wasting* = *my wasting strength*, of declining age; Israel under figure of old man; this however is not favoured by context. The passage is therefore doubtful. **Hithpo.** *Impf.* יִתְבּוֹלָל Ho 7^8; אפרים בעמים הוא י׳ *Ephraim, among the peoples doth he mix himself;* but Ew Now derive here fr. בלה = בלל (or נבל) *waste away*, cf. Hiph. **Hiph.** *Impf.* וַנָּבֶל Is 64^5 *and we faded away*, but rd. perh. וַנִּבֹּל fr. נבל cf. Di (De, less probably, derives from בלל—cf. Ew Now Ho 7^8—or נבל = בול).

†בְּלִיל **n.m.** [Is 30, 24] fodder (Aram. ܒܠܝܠܐ; 1098
cf. Ar. بُلَّةٌ *moisture of fresh pasture*)—בְּלִיל Is 30^{24}; sf. בְּלִילוֹ Jb 6^5 24^6—*fodder* (strictly, *mixed fodder, farrago*) Jb 6^5; as growing in field 24^6 cf. Is 30^{24}.

†II. [בָּלַל] **vb. denom.** to give provender 1101
—**Qal** *Impf.* וַיָּבָל Ju 19^{21} Qr (Kt ויבול) sq. לְ *give provender to* the asses.

†שַׁבְּלוּל **n.m.** snail (Shaph. form, *causing* 7642
moisture, from notion of moisture or fluid in בלל);—name due to slimy trail ψ 58^9, שַׁבְּלוּל תֶּמֶס יַהֲלֹךְ.

†תֶּבֶל **n.[m.]** confusion, violation of nature, 8397
or the divine order—Lv 18^{23} 20^{12} (H) cf. Di on 18^{15}.

†תְּבַלֻּל **n.[m.]** confusion, obscurity (on 8400
form cf. Ar. conj. v. Inf. Sta [§ 267]) Lv 21^{20} (H) ת׳ בעינו i.e. defective sight? cf. Di. (‖ שֶׁבֶר, מְרוֹחַ אָשֶׁךְ, דַּק, גִּבֵּן, etc.)

†[בָּלַם] **vb.** curb, hold in (NH *id.*, Aram. 1102
בְּלַם, ܒܠܡ)—**Qal** *Inf.* לִבְלוֹם ψ 32^9, cf. Che.

בלס (cf. Eth. ባለስ: *fig*, Ar. بَلَسٌ a kind of *fig*, cf. Lag [M. i. 59 f. 68 f.]; hence following).

1103 †[בָּלַס] **vb. denom. gather figs, tend fig-trees, sycamores** (𝔊 *κνίζων*, 𝔙 *vellicans*, prob. properly to *nip* the sycamore fruit to fit it for eating, v. Tristr [Nat. Hist. Bib. 399] Bo [ii. cap. 39, p. 383 f.]; Theodoret ap. Fi [Hexapl. *ad loc.*] Theophrast [iv. 2])—**Qal** *Pt.* בּוֹלֵס, Am 7[14] בּ׳ שִׁקְמִים.

1104 †בָּלַע **vb. swallow down, swallow up, engulf** (idea of quickness, suddenness) (NH *id.*, Ar. بَلَعَ *swallow*, Eth. በልዐ: *eat*, Aram. בְּלַע, ܒܠܥ; As. *bêlû*, Pi. *destroy* Zim [BP 27])—**Qal** *Pf.* בָּלַע Jb 20[15], sf. בְּלָעַנִי Je 51[34] (Qr, cf. 𝔊 Kt -נוּ); 3 fs. בָּֽלְעָה Nu 16[30]; 3 pl. sf. בְּלָעוּנוּ ψ 124[3]; *Impf.* יִבְלָע Jb 20[18], וַיִּבְלַע Ex 7[12], sf. יִבְלָעֶנָּה Is 28[4]; 3 fs. וַתִּבְלַע Nu 16[32] + 2 t.; sf. תִּבְלָעֵנִי ψ 69[16], וַתִּבְלָעֵם Nu 16[34], וַתִּבְלָעֵם Dt 11[6], תִּבְלָעֵמוֹ Ex 15[12]; 3 mpl. sf. יִבְלָעֻהוּ Ho 8[7]; 3 fpl. וַתִּבְלַעְנָה Gn 41[7], וַתִּבְלַעְןָ Gn 41[24]; 1 pl. sf. נִבְלָעֵם Pr 1[12]; *Inf.* לִבְלֹעַ Jon 2[1]; sf. בִּלְעִי Jb 7[19];—**1.** *swallow down*, c. acc. Jb 7[19] Is 28[4], subj. דָּג Jon 2[1]; subj. שִׁבֳּלִים Gn 41[7.24]; מַטֶּה Ex 7[12]. **2.** *swallow up, engulf*, subj. אֶרֶץ Ex 15[12] Nu 16[30.32.34] 26[10] Dt 11[6] ψ 106[17]; fig. of greed Jb 20[15] (obj. חַיִל; opp. קיא *vomit*); of violence, extortion Pr 1[12] (כִּשְׁאוֹל); of devastation by enemy Ho 8[7] Je 51[34] ψ 124[3]; overwhelming by calamity ψ 69[16] (subj. מצולה); of full enjoyment, profit Jb 20[18] (no obj.) **Niph.** *Pf.* נִבְלַע Ho 8[8], נִבְלְעוּ Is 28[7];—*swallowed up*, i.e. devastated Ho 8[8]; engulfed by wine (yet cf. **Pi.** Is 3[12]) Is 28[7] (שָׁגוּ בַשֵּׁכָר ‖ נ׳ מִן־הַיַּיִן). **Pi.** *Pf.* בִּלַּע Is 25[8] + 3 t.; וּבִלַּע consec. Is 25[7]; 3 pl. בִּלֵּעוּ Is 3[12]; 1 pl. בִּלָּעְנוּ La 2[16], sf. בִּלַּעֲנוּהוּ ψ 35[25]; *Impf.* יְבַלַּע־ Pr 19[28], sf. 3 ms. יְבַלְּעֶנּוּ Jb 8[18] Pr 21[20]; יְבַלְּעֵם ψ 21[10]; 3 fs. sf. 3 ms. תְּבַלְּעֶנּוּ Ec 10[12]; 2 ms. תְּבַלַּע 2 S 20[19], sf. וַתְּבַלְּעֵנִי Jb 10[8]; 1 s. אֲבַלַּע 2 S 20[20], אֲבַלֵּעַ Is 19[3]; *Imv.* בַּלַּע ψ 55[10]; *Inf.* בַּלַּע Nu 4[20] Hb 1[13], בַּלֵּעַ La 2[8], sf. בַּלְּעוֹ Jb 2[3]; *Pt.* sf. מְבַלְּעָיִךְ Is 49[19];—**1.** *swallow* Nu 4[20] (כְּבַלַּע *as a swallowing*=for an instant); elsewhere **2.** *swallow up, engulf*, usually c. acc., **a.** fig. of destruction, ruin, Is 3[12] (obj. דֶּרֶךְ); (Ba from a √ II. בלע *confound*, cf. Di; v. also 9[15] 19[3] 28[7] ψ 55[10] 107[27]); subj. י׳ La 2[2.5.5.8] Jb 2[3] 10[8] ψ 21[10] (‖ אכל), Is 19[3] (obj. עֵצָה), i.e. *confuse, confound;* so ψ 55[10] בַּלַּע אֲדֹנָי פַּלַּג לְשׁוֹנָם *confuse, Lord, divide their speech* (cf. בלל Gn 11[7.9] & v. De Che); subj. wicked men, enemies ψ 35[25] Is 49[19] cf. La 2[16] (abs.) Hb 1[13]; obj. reflex. in sense Ec 10[12]; =annihilate Is 25[7.8]; **b.** lit.=*destroy* 2 S 20[19.20] (‖ הִשְׁחִית); indef. subj. Jb 8[18] יב׳ ממקמו; **c.** fig. for greedily (seize, adopt) practise Pr 19[28], for extravagance, squandering Pr 21[20]. **Pu.** *Impf.* יְבֻלַּע 2 S 17[16], יְבֻלָּע Jb 37[20]; *Pt.* מְבֻלָּעִים Is 9[15];—*be swallowed up*, i.e. destroyed Jb 37[20]; cf. פֶּן־יְבֻלַּע לַמֶּלֶךְ 2 S 17[16] (impers.); ruined Is 9[15] (yet cf. sub **Pi.**) **Hithp.** *Impf.* 3 fs. תִּתְבַּלָּע ψ 107[27] (subj. חכמה) their wisdom is all gone, 'they are at their wit's end' (cf. sub **Pi.**)

†I. בֶּ֫לַע **n.[m.] swallowing, devouring, thing swallowed. 1.** *swallowing*=*destruction*, דִּבְרֵי־בֶ֫לַע ψ 52[6] *devouring words* (‖ לְשׁוֹן מִרְמָה). **2.** *thing swallowed* בִּלְעוֹ, Je 51[44] וְהֹצֵאתִי את־ב׳ מִפִּיו *and I will bring forth that which he hath swallowed out of his mouth.* 1105

†II. בֶּ֫לַע **n.pr.m. 1.** בֶּ֫לַע Gn 36[32]=1 Ch 1[43]; בָּ֑לַע Gn 36[33]=1 Ch 1[44] a king of Edom, ב׳ בן בעור (cf. בִּלְעָם & Di Gn 36[32]). **2.** בֶּ֫לַע 1st son of Benjamin Gn 46[21] Nu 26[38.40] 1 Ch 7[6.7] 8[1.3] (בָּ֑לַע). **3.** בֶּ֫לַע a Reubenite 1 Ch 5[8]. 1106

†בַּלְעִי **adj.gent.** of **2,** הַבּ׳ n. coll. Nu 26[38]. 1108

†III. בֶּ֫לַע **n.pr.loc.** city=צֹעַר q. v. Gn 14[2.8]. 1106, p. 858 6820

בִּלְעֲדֵי v. sub בלה. p. 116 1107

I. בִּלְעָם **n.pr.m. Balaam** (acc. to Sta [§ 293]= בלע+ם; Nbr [Stud. Bib. i, 226] prop. בל=בעל+(god) עם), son of בְּעוֹר, prophet fr. פְּתוֹר (q.v.):—Nu 22[5.7.8.9] + 47t. Nu 22–24 (all JE) 31[8.16] (P) Dt 23[5.6] (D) (cf. R[D] Jos 13[22]) Jos 24[9.10] (E) Mi 6[5] Ne 13[2]. 1109

†II. בִּלְעָם **n.pr.loc.** town in Manasseh 1 Ch 6[55]; A Ιβλααμ, 𝔊L Ιεβλααμ=יִבְלְעָם (q.v.) Jos 17[11] + 2 t.; mod. *Bel'ame,* 6 hours N. of Nâblus, Bd [Pal 228], so Survey [ii. 47]. 1109

†[בָּלַק] **vb. waste, lay waste** (As. *balâḳu*, Pi. *destroy*, Lyon [Sargon 61]; cf. Ar. بَلُّوقَةٌ *a desert*) 1110
—**Po.** *Pt.* without מ, sf. בּוֹלְקָהּ Is 24[1] (‖ בּוֹקֵק, subj. י׳, obj. הארץ);—on form (which might also be Qal Pt.) cf. Ol [§ 254] Lag [GN 1882, 403]; also בקק Po. Je 51[2], and intensive use of Inf. abs. Niph. Is 24[3]; further Pu. (i.e. intens.) Pt. Na 2[11] (this however perhaps largely influenced by assonance). **Pu.** *Pt.* מְבֻלָּקָה Na 2[11] (בּוּקָה וּמְבוּקָה ומב׳), *devastated*, or as subst. *a devastated city.*

בָּלָק **n.pr.m.** (*devastator*) king of Moab, 1111

בּ׳ בֶּן צִפּוֹר Nu 22[2.4.7] + 37 t. Nu 22–24 (all JE) + Jos 24[9] (E) Ju 11[25] Mi 6[5].

בֵּלְשַׁאצַּר, בֵּלְאשַׁצַּר, בלשאצר v. בֵּל sub בעל.

1114 †בִּלְשָׁן **n.pr.m.** (= *inquirer*? NH & Aram. בלש; cf. sub בן) an Israelite who returned with Zerubbabel Ezr 2[2] = Ne 7[7].

[בַּלֶּת], בִּלְתִּי v. sub בלה. p. 115

1116 †בָּמָה[104] **n.f. high place** (√appar. בום on account of firm ⸗; cf. As. *bâmâtê* Zim[BP 48], Moab. במת במת MI[3, 27])—Je 48[35] + 18 t.; הַבָּמָ֫תָה 1 S 9[13]; pl. בָּמוֹת Nu 21[19] + 62 t.; cstr. בָּמֳתֵי Jb 9[8] Is 14[14] Am 4[13]; בָּמֳו̊תֵי Dt 32[13] Is 58[14] Mi 1[3] (Ew[§ 211 d] Ges[§ 87, 5] archaic fem. cstr. with retracted accent before monosyl. in poetry, *bâmŏ-thê* not *bŏm*); sf. בָּמוֹתַי 2 S 22[34] + 3 t.; בָּמוֹתַי ψ 18[34] + 10 t.; —**1.** *high place, mountain:* בָּמוֹת יַעַר *forest mountains* Mi 3[12] = Je 26[18]; במות עולם *ancient mountains* Ez 36[2]; במות ארנן Nu 21[28] (E poet.) **2.** *high places, battle-fields,* the chief places of the land giving possession, victory, dominion: על במותיך *on thy high places* (Gilboa, the battle-field) 2 S 1[19.25] (in v[19] 𝔊 has a doublet מֵתֶיךָ *thy dead,* v. We Dr). **a.** *of Israel:* רכב על במתי ארץ *ride upon the high places of the land* Dt 32[13] & Is 58[14] cf. Dt 33[29] ψ 18[34] = 2 S 22[34], Hb 3[19]. **b.** *of God:* דרך על במתי ארץ *tread upon the high places of the earth* Am 4[13] cf. Mi 1[3]; במתי ים Jb 9[8]; עלה על במתי עב (aspiration of the king of Babylon) Is 14[14]. **3.** *high places,* as places of worship, at first on hills and mountains, later on artificial mounds or platforms, under green trees, and in cities; still later for the chapels erected thereon, and once apparently for a portable sanctuary (decked with diverse colours) Ez 16[16]. The ancient worship of Israel was conducted on these high places. In the times of Samuel and David they ascended to them, descended from them, and offered sacrifices on them, 1 S 9[12-25] 10[5.13] (הבמה for הביתה We Dr). The custom continued in the reign of Solomon, but Gibeon was הבמה הגדולה 1 K 3[2-4] cf. 1 Ch 16[39] 21[29] 2 Ch 1[3.13]. High places of Baal were also used Nu 22[41] (E) Je 19[5] 32[35]; of Moab Is 15[2] 16[12] Je 48[35] (cf. MI[27]); these must be demolished Nu 33[52] (J). Solomon built במות (platforms or chapels) to Chemosh and Milkom on the Mt. of Evil Counsel opposite Jerusalem 1 K 11[7]: Jeroboam made temples on the ancient high places of Dan and Bethel 1 K 12[31.32] 2 Ch 11[15]; they are called במות און Ho 10[8], במות ישחק Am 7[9]: the kings of Israel built במות and בתי הבמות in all their cities 2 K 17[9], and the people worshipped there 2 K 17[11]; these were also used by the mixed population after the exile of Israel 2 K 17[29.32.32]: these various idolatrous high places were first destroyed by Josiah 1 K 13[2.32.33] 2 K 23[5-20] 2 Ch 34[3]. The worship of Yahweh on high places continued in Judah until the exile 1 K 22[44] 2 K 15[35]; the sanctity code predicts that Yahweh will destroy them Lv 26[30]; they were regarded as the reason for the rejection of Shiloh ψ 78[58]. The compiler of Kings, writing from the point of view of the Deut. code, complains רַק הַבָּמוֹת לֹא סָרוּ 2 K 12[4] 14[4] 15[4.35] cf. 2 Ch 15[17] 20[33], and praises the few pious kings who destroyed them. **a.** Rehoboam built במות with מצבות & אשרים on every high hill and under every green tree 1 K 14[23]. **b.** Asa did not remove the high places 1 K 15[14] (2 Ch 14[2.4] is incorrect unless במות בעל). **c.** Jehoshaphat in his reform on the basis of the covenant code did not remove them 1 K 22[44] (עוֹד הֵסִיר אֶת־הַבָּמוֹת 2 Ch 17[16] is doubtless incorrect, possibly rd. מצבות); Jehoram, his son, made high places in the cities of Judah 2 Ch 21[11] (𝔊 𝔙; not *mountains* 𝔖); and Ahaz sacrificed on high places on the hills and under every green tree and in every city of Judah 2 K 16[4] 2 Ch 28[4.25]; cf. Mi 1[5] (rd. חטאת? so 𝔊 𝔖 𝔗 Che al.; yet cf. JBL[1890, 73 f.]) **d.** Hezekiah removed them 2 K 18[4.22] 2 Ch 31[1] 32[12] Is 36[7]; but Manasseh rebuilt them 2 K 21[3] 2 Ch 33[3.19], and the people continued to sacrifice thereon to Yahweh 2 Ch 33[17]. **e.** Josiah, in his reform, based on the Deut. code, defiled them and brake them down from Geba to Beersheba 2 K 23[5.8.9]; but subsequently there were במות התפת in the valley of Ben Hinnom Je 7[31], and במות throughout Judah Je 17[3] cf. Ez 6[3.6] 20[29] (questioned by Ew & Co). **4.** *funereal mound*(?) Ez 43[7] (Thes, but *in their high places* AV RV; *in their death* 𝔗 Theod Ew Hi RVm), Is 53[9] (Lowth Ew Bö Rodwell Orelli; but *in his death* AV RV, or *martyr death* De Che Br).

†בָּמוֹת **n.pr.loc.** (*high place* or *great high* 1120,
place) place in Moab Nu 21[19.20] = בָּמוֹת בַּעַל Nu 1117
22[41] Jos 13[17] possibly on Mt. *ʿAṭṭarûs* cf. Di.

†בָּמְהָל **n.pr.m.** (= בֶּן־מ׳ *son of circum-* 1118
cision? cf. sub בן) descendant of Asher 1 Ch 7[33].

בְּמוֹ v. sub בְּ, p. 91. 1119

בָּמוֹת v. sub במה. above 1120

בֵּן[4870] **n.m. son** (MI Ph. בן; so Sab. CIS[iv. No. 2], 1121
cf. בני DHM[Sem. Sprachforsch. 6]; Ar. اِبْنٌ; As. *bin(u)*, Lyon[Sargon 9, 1. 57]; esp. in *bin-bin, grandson* COT[Gloss], cf. Dl infr.; Aram. בַּר, ܒܪ, pl. בְּנִין, ܒܢܝܢ; cf. Palm., esp. Vog[No. 21, 31, 36 a al.]; possibly orig. con-

nected with בנה *build*, so Thes, cf. As. *bânu, begetter* (Dl$^{Pr\ 104}$ & cf. Ba$^{ZMG\ 1887,\ 638\ ff.}$); but all traces of this √ lost in Heb. form; √ perh. orig. bilit. (בִּן, בֵּן) *בֵּן v. Sta$^{§\ 183}$)—abs. ב׳ Gn 4^{25}+; בֶּן־ Ez 18^{10}; cstr. בֶּן Gn 49$^{22.22}$; בֶּן־ Gn 5^{32}+; בֶּן Est 2^{5} Ne 6^{18}, & c. prefix Gn 17^{17} Nu 8^{25} 1 Ch 27^{23} 2 Ch 25^{5} 31$^{16.17}$; בְּנוֹ Nu 23^{18} 24$^{3.15}$; בְּנִי Gn 49^{11}; בִּן Dt 25^{2}; בִּן־ Ex 33^{11}+32 t. (29 t. in combination (יהושע (הושע, ישוע) בִּן־נוּן); sf. בְּנִי Gn 21^{10}+; בִּנְךָ Ex 20^{10}+; לִבְנֵךְ Dt 7^{3} 1 K 11^{13}; בְּנֵךְ Gn 30^{14}+; בְּנוֹ Gn 4^{17}+; בְּנָהּ Gn 21^{10}+; pl. בָּנִים Gn 3^{16}+; cstr. בְּנֵי Gn 6^{2}+; sf. בָּנַי Gn 31^{43}+; בָּנֵינוּ Jos 22^{25}+; בְּנֵיכֶם Ex 3^{22}+, etc.;—**1.** *son*, male child, born of a woman Gn 4^{25} 16$^{11.15}$ 17^{19} cf. v^{16} 18$^{10.14}$ 19$^{37.38}$+oft., cf. בֶּן־בִּטְנָהּ Is 49^{15}; begotten by a man Gn 5$^{4f.\ 28}$ 6^{10} 11$^{11f.}$+oft.; ‖ בַּת (בָּנוֹת) *daughter* Gn 5$^{4.7.10f.}$ 11$^{11.13.15f.}$ Ex 20^{10} Dt 5^{14} 16$^{11.14}$ 1 S 30$^{3.6}$ Jb 1^{2} 42^{13}+; of son as desired Gn 30^{2} (cf. 15^{2} 16^{2} 17^{17} 18$^{10f.}$ 1 S 1$^{5-11}$) 2 K 4$^{14.28}$ ψ 127^{3}+; rejoiced in Gn 30^{6}+; beloved Ex 21^{5} 2 S 19$^{1.3.5}$ 1 K 3^{26}; cared for Dt 1^{31}; spared Mal 3^{17}; disciplined & trained Dt 8^{5} Pr 3^{12} 13^{24} 19^{18} 29^{17}; owing reverence, obedience, etc. to parents Pr 6^{20} 10^{1} 13^{1}; בִּנְךָ בְכֹרְךָ *thy first-born son* Gn 27^{32}; הַבֵּן הַבְּכֹר Dt 21^{15} cf. 1 S 8^{2}; בְּנָהּ הַגָּדֹל *her elder son* Gn 27$^{15.42}$; בְּנוֹ הַגָּדֹל 27^{1}; בְּנָהּ הַקָּטָן *her younger son* Gn 27$^{15.42}$. In partic. **a.** בֶּן־אִמּוֹ *son of his mother*, i.e. own (uterine) brother Gn 43^{29}, cf. 27^{29} Ju 8^{19} ψ 50^{20} 69^{9}, & v. אֵם; בְּנֵי אָבִיךָ *sons of thy father*=brethren Gn 49^{8} (poet.) †**b.** בְּנֵי דֹדֵיהֶן=*cousins* Nu 36^{11}. **c.** בְּנִי *my son*, as term of kindliness or endearment, used by Eli to Samuel 1 S 3$^{6.16}$ cf. 4^{16} 24^{17} 26$^{17.21.25}$, v. also Pr 1$^{8.10}$ 2^{1}+; cf. בִּנְךָ, used by Ben-hadad of himself to Elisha 2 K 8^{9}; by Ahaz to Tiglath-pileser 16^{7}; esp. to express intimate and gracious relation with God: י׳ calls Israel בְּנִי בְכֹרִי Ex 4^{22} cf. v^{23} Ho 11^{1}, v. also ψ 80^{16} (but cf. Che); בָּנִים אַתֶּם ליהוה אלהיכם Dt 14^{1}; בְּנֵי עֶלְיוֹן ψ 82^{6} (‖ אלהים); בְּנֵי אֵל־חָי Ho 2^{1}; cf. further Dt 32^{5} (pl.) v^{20} (pl.) Is 1$^{2.4}$ 30$^{1.9}$ Je 3$^{14.22}$ 4^{22} 31^{20}; of future Davidic king 2 S 7^{14}=1 Ch 17^{13} cf. ψ 2^{7}; expressly referred to Solomon 1 Ch 22^{10} 28^{6}; also of children (offered in fire) Ez 16^{21}. **d.** בְּנֵי האלהים applied to supernatural beings Gn 6$^{2.4}$ Jb 1^{6} 2^{1}; בְּנֵי אלהים Jb 38^{7}; בְּנֵי אֵלִים ψ 29^{1} (on which cf. Che's note) 89^{7}. **e.** בֶּן־אָדָם *son of man*, cf. בְּנֵי א׳, v. אָדָם; †בְּנֵי אִישׁ ψ 4^{3} & (‖ בני אדם) 49^{3} 62^{10}. †**f.** בֶּן־בִּנְךָ=*thy grandson* Ex 10^{2} Dt 6^{2} Ju 8^{22} cf. Je 27^{7}; also pl. Ex 34^{7} Dt 4$^{9.25}$ Ju 12^{14} 2 K 17^{41} 2 Ch 8^{40} Jb 42^{16} ψ 128^{6} Pr 13^{22} 17^{6} Ez 37^{25}; also בֵּן alone with similar reference Gn 29^{5} (Laban son of Nahor); Laban calls his daughters' children his own sons Gn 31$^{28.43}$ cf. 32^{1}; so of Naomi Ru 4^{17}; בְּנֵי רִבֵּעִים 2 K 10^{30} *sons of the fourth generation*, and, in general, descendants Jos 22$^{24.25.27}$+; v. also sub **i.** infr. **g.** constantly, as more precise designation, added to personal name כָּלֵב בֶּן־יְפֻנֶּה Nu 14^{30} 32^{12} 34^{19}+; יְהוֹשֻׁעַ בִּן־נוּן Nu 11^{28} 14^{30} 32$^{12.28}$ 34^{17}+; יָרָבְעָם בֶּן־נְבָט 1 K 12$^{2.15}$+, etc.; also without personal name (often with implication of contempt) בֶּן־קִישׁ 1 S 10^{11}; בֶּן־יִשַׁי 1 S 20$^{27.30.31}$ 22$^{7.8.9.13}$ 25^{10} 2 S 20^{1}; בְּנֵי צְרוּיָה 2 S 16^{10}; בֶּן־רְמַלְיָהוּ Is 7$^{4.5.9}$ 8^{16}; בֶּן־טָבְאַל Is 7^{6}; cf. also בְּנֵי לֵוִי Nu 16$^{7.8}$. **h.** designated as בֶּן־זְקֻנִים i.e. born in old age of father Gn 37^{3}; opp. בְּנֵי הַנְּעוּרִים *sons of one's youth* ψ 127^{4}; also בֶּן־בֵּיתִי *one born in my house* Gn 15^{3} (i.e. slave) so בְּנֵי בַיִת Ec 2^{7}. **i.** in various combinations: (*a*) as expression of contumely, בֶּן־נַעֲוַת הַמַּרְדּוּת 1 S 20^{30}; בֶּן־הַמְרַצֵּחַ הַזֶּה 2 K 6^{32} *this son of a murderer*; cf. בְּנֵי־נָבָל Jb 30^{8}; בְּנֵי בְלִי־שֵׁם *ib.*; בְּנֵי עֹנְנָה Is 57^{3} (‖ זֶרַע מְנָאֵף); cf. בֶּן־אִשָּׁה אַחֶרֶת Ju 11^{2} (cf. v^{1}); (*β*) as term of respect, dignity, בֶּן־חוֹרִים *son of nobles* Ec 10^{17} (in Aram.=*free born*); בֶּן־חֲכָמִים Is 19^{11}; בֶּן־מַלְכֵי־קֶדֶם *ib.*; cf. בֶּן־מֶלֶךְ ψ 72^{1} (‖ מֶלֶךְ); בֶּן־אֲמָתֶךָ ψ 86^{16} in addressing י׳ (‖ עַבְדֶּךָ) & בְּנֵי־עֲבָדֶיךָ ψ 102^{29}; of noble appearance בְּנֵי הַמֶּלֶךְ Ju 8^{18}. **j.** oft. pl. with name of ancestor, people, land, or city, to denote descendants, inhabitants, membership in a nation or family, etc.: (*a*) e.g. בְּנֵי־עֵבֶר Gn 10^{21}; בְּנֵי־חֵת Gn 23$^{3.5.7.10.10.11.16.18.20}$ 25^{10} 49^{32} (all P); (בְּנֵי־שֵׁת) Nu 24^{17} v. sub **8**); בְּנֵי־חֲמוֹר Gn 33^{19} Jos 24^{32}; בְּנֵי עֵשָׂו Gn 36$^{5.15.19}$ Dt 2$^{4.8.12.22.29}$; בְּנֵי שֵׂעִיר Gn 36$^{20.21}$; בֶּן־(בני)הִנֹּם Jos 15^{8}+ (cf. sub גַּיְא); בְּנֵי לוֹט Dt 2$^{9.19}$ ψ 83^{9}; בְּנֵי־יוֹסֵף (lit. Gn 46^{27} 48^{8} 1 Ch 5^{1}) Nu 1^{32} 26$^{28.37}$ 34^{23} 36^{5} (מַטֵּה ב׳ י׳)+6 t. Jos, cf. ψ 77^{16}; even בְּנֵי חֲצִי שֵׁבֶט מְנַשֶּׁה 1 Ch 5^{23}; בְּנֵי דָוִיד (lit. 2 S 8^{18}=1 Ch 18^{17}, 1 Ch 3$^{1.9}$) 2 Ch 13^{8} 23^{3} 32^{33}; בְּנֵי אָסָף 2 Ch 29^{13} Ezr 2^{41} 3^{8}+ (v. אָסָף); בְּנֵי קֹרַח in titles of ψ 42–49, 84, 85, 87, 88; esp. (*β*) בְּנֵי־עַמּוֹן (standing designation of people of Ammon) Gn 19^{38}+81 t. (cf. עַמּוֹן & Nö$^{ZMG\ 1886,\ 171}$ Dr$^{Sm\ 66}$); בְּנֵי יַעֲקֹב (lit. Gn 34$^{7.13.25.27}$ 35$^{5.22.26}$ 49^{2}) 2 K 17^{34} ψ 105^{6} Mal 3^{6} cf. ψ 77^{16}; & chiefly (*γ*) בְּנֵי יִשְׂרָאֵל (lit. Gn 42^{5} 45^{21} 46^{5} Ex 1^{1}) Ex 1^{7}+613 t., incl. Hex 427 (of which 328 P, 49 E, 25 J, 25 D), Ju 61, S K Ch 73 (23 in ref. to ancient history, 10 in opp. to Judah); so also Vrss & var. sometimes for בֵּית יִשׂ׳, e.g. Jos 21^{43}+ v. Di, Ez 3^{1}+ v. Co; also the reverse Ez 2^{3} al.; note esp. עַם ב׳ יִשְׂרָאֵל Ex 1^{9}; עַמִּי ב׳ יִשְׂרָאֵל Ex 3^{10} 7^{4}; עֲדַת בְּנֵי יִשְׂרָאֵל Ex 16$^{1.2.9.10}$ 17^{1} Lv 16^{5} 19^{2} Nu 1$^{2.53}$ 8$^{9.20}$ 13^{26} 15$^{25.26}$

17^{6} 19^{9} 25^{6} 26^{2} 31^{12} (all P); דֹּרוֹת ב׳ יִשׂ׳ Ju 3^{2}; כָּל־ב׳ יִשׂ׳ וְכָל־הָעָם 20^{26}; ב׳ יִשׂ׳ וּבְנֵי הַלֵּוִי Ne 10^{40}; also (δ) בְּנֵי יְהוּדָה (lit. Gn 46^{12} 26^{19} 1 Ch 2$^{3.10}$ 4^{1}) Nu 1^{26} + 18 t. Nu Jos, Ju 1$^{8.9.16}$ (so rd. also v$^{21.21}$ cf. Jos 15^{53} & v. sub בנימן) 2 S 1^{18} 1 Ch 4^{27} + 8 t. Chr, Je 7^{30} + 4 t. Je; Ho 2^{2} Jo 4$^{6.8.19}$ Ob ^{12} (not in K, of Judah or of any other tribe, except בְּנֵי לֵוִי 1 K 12^{31}) incl. מַטֵּה בְּנֵי יהודה Jos 15$^{1.20.21}$ 21^{1} 1 Ch 6^{50}; for usage with other tribes of Isr., v. the articles;—but note (ε) †בְּנֵי לֵוִי (lit. Gn 46^{11} Ex 6^{16} Nu 3^{17} 1 Ch 5^{27} 6^{1} cf. 23^{6}) Ex 32^{28} Nu 3^{15} 16$^{7.8}$ 18^{21} Jos 21^{10} (as including sons of Aaron etc.); כָּל־בְּנֵי לֵוִי Ex 32^{26}; כָּל־אַחֶיךָ ב׳ ל׳ Nu 16^{10}; הַכֹּהֲנִים ב׳ ל׳ Dt 21^{5} 31^{9} cf. 1 K 12^{31} & Mal 3^{3}; 1 Ch 23$^{24.27}$ 24^{20} Ezr 8^{15} (distinguished from priests) Ne 12^{23} Ez 40^{46} (including בְּנֵי צָדוֹק the priests); also מַחֲנוֹת ב׳ ל׳ 1 Ch 9^{18}; בְּנֵי הַלֵּוִי 1 Ch 12^{27} Ne 10^{40}; בְּנֵי הַלְוִיִּם 1 Ch 15^{15} 24^{30} (cf. also לֵוִי); (ζ) בְּנֵי אַהֲרֹן (lit. Ex 28$^{1.40}$ 1 Ch 5^{29} 24^{1}; oft. Aaron and his sons lit. Ex 27^{21} 28$^{1.4}$ +) Lv 3$^{5.8.13}$ 6$^{7.11}$ 7$^{10.33}$ Jos 21^{10} 1 Ch 6$^{35.39.42}$ 15^{4} (+ Levites) 24$^{1.31}$ Ne 12^{47}; also בְּנֵי א׳ הַכֹּהֲנִים Lv 1$^{5.8.11}$ 2^{2} 3^{2} Nu 3^{3} 10^{8} & Jos 21^{19} 2 Ch 31^{19} cf. 26^{18} 29^{21} 35$^{14.14}$; בְּנֵי אַהֲרֹן הַכֹּהֵן Lv 1^{7} Jos 21^{4} (as subdivision of Levites) v^{13} cf. Lv 7^{34}; אֶת־כֹּהֲנֵי יהוה אֶת־בְּנֵי אַהֲרֹן 2 Ch 13^{9} cf. v^{10}; once in sing. הַכֹּהֵן בֶּן־אַהֲרֹן וְהַלְוִיִּם Ne 10^{39}; v. also sub אַהֲרֹן; (η) †בְּנֵי צָדוֹק Ez 40^{46}, 44^{15} הכהנים הלוים בני צדוק; הַמְקֻדָּשׁ 48^{11} מבני צדוק (𝔊 Sm Co join מ of מבני to preceding word, making pl.); (θ) בְּנֵי with names of peoples, lands, and cities, בְּנֵי כֻשִׁיִּים Am 9^{7}; בְּנֵי מִצְרַיִם Ez 16^{26}; בְּנֵי אַשּׁוּר Ez 16^{28} 23$^{7.9.12.23}$; ב׳ בָּבֶל Ez 23$^{15.17.23}$; ב׳ אֶרֶץ הַבְּרִית Ez 30^{5} (Co del. ארץ); ב׳ יְרוּשָׁלַםִ Jo 4^{6}; ב׳ צִיּוֹן Jo 2^{23} La 4^{2} ψ 149^{2} (cf. Zc 9^{13}). Vid. further (ι) בְּנֵי עַמְּךָ Lv 19^{18} cf. 20^{17} Nu 22^{5} Ju 14$^{16.17}$ Ez 3^{11} 33$^{2.12.17.30}$ 37^{18} Dn 12^{1}; בְּנֵי פָּרִיצֵי עַמְּךָ Dn 11^{14}; (κ) קֶבֶר בְּנֵי הָעָם 2 K 23^{6} 2 Ch 35$^{5.7.12}$; קִבְרֵי בְּנֵי הָעָם Je 26^{23}; (λ) בְּנֵי־קֶדֶם Gn 29^{1} Ju 7^{12} 8^{10} 1 K 5^{10} Jb 1^{3} Is 11^{14} Je 49^{28} Ez 25$^{4.10}$; †(μ) בְּנֵי הַמְּדִינָה Ezr 2^{1} = Ne 7^{6}; (ν) of bulls, בְּנֵי בָשָׁן Dt 32^{14} (song) cf. Klo$^{SK 1878, 801}$ Di. **2.** *children* (male and female) Gn 3^{16} 21^{7} Ex 21^{5} 22^{23}; hence בְּנֵי מְנַשֶּׁה הַזְּכָרִים Jos 17^{2} *male children,* בֵּן זָכָר Je 20^{15}. **3.** *youth, young men* (pl.) Pr 7^{7} Ct 2^{3}. **4.** *the young* of animals Lv 22^{28} (שׁוֹר אוֹ שֶׂה) cf. Dt 22$^{6.7}$ 1 S 6$^{7.10}$ Zc 9^{9} Jb 4^{11} 28^{8} 39$^{4.16}$;—בֶּן־בָּקָר etc. v. sub **7 b** infr. **5.** of plant-shoots בֵּן פֹּרָת Gn 49$^{22.22}$; also בֵּן ψ 80^{16}? (‖ כַּנָּה; see Che trans. & crit. n.) **6.** fig. of lifeless things, בְּנֵי רֶשֶׁף *sparks* Jb 5^{7}; *stars* עַיִשׁ עַל־בָּנֶיהָ Jb 38^{32}; *arrows* בֶּן־קָשֶׁת Jb 41^{2}; בְּנֵי אַשְׁפָּתוֹ La 3^{13}; cf. בֶּן־גָּרְנִי i.e. *corn of my threshing-floor* Is 21^{10}. **7. a.** *member* of a guild, order or class, †בְּנֵי הַנְּבִיאִים i.e. those belonging to the prophetic order 1 K 20^{35} 2 K 2$^{3.5.7.15}$ 4$^{1.38.38}$ 5^{22} 6^{1} 9^{1} (Hoffm RS$^{Proph. 85. 388, K 15 f.}$; Zehnpfund$^{BAS 1. 355}$ comp. As. *mâr šipri* (*šiprâtum*), *son of a messenger* = *messenger*, and explains from the son's succeeding to father's calling) & בֶּן־נָבִיא Am 7^{14}; prob. also †בְּנֵי הַכֹּהֲנִים 1 Ch 9^{30} Ezr 2^{61} 10^{18}; †בְּנֵי הַשֹּׁעֲרִים Ezr 2^{42}; cf. בְּנֵי הַגְּדוּד 2 Ch 25^{13} *men of the troop,* v. Palm. בני שירתא *men of the caravan* Vog$^{No. 4 al.}$; also †בְּנֵי הַגּוֹלָה = *exiles* †Ezr 4^{1} 6$^{19.20}$ 8^{35} 10$^{7.16}$ (v. גולה sub גלה); further, in בֶּן־נֵכָר = *foreigner* (only P, poet., & late) †Gn 17$^{12.27}$ Ex 12^{43} Lv 22^{25} Ez 44$^{9.9}$; ב׳־הַנּ׳ †Is 56^{3}; †בְּנֵי־נֵכָר 2 S 22$^{45.46}$ = ψ 18$^{45.46}$ Ne 9^{2} Is 60^{10} 61^{5} 62^{8} Ez 44^{7} ψ 144$^{7.11}$, בְּנֵי־הַנּ׳ Is 56^{6}; also בְּנֵי הַתּוֹשָׁבִים הַגָּרִים עִמָּכֶם Lv 25$^{4.5}$. **b.** of animals, בֶּן־בָּקָר *son of (the) herd,* i.e. young one of the herd, בָּקָר וּבְנֵי בָקָר 1 S 14^{32} cf. עֵגֶל בֶּן־בָּקָר Lv 9^{2} (P); then, in general, one of the herd: fit for food Gn 18$^{7.8}$ (J), for sacrifice Nu 15$^{8.9}$ (P); בן־הב׳ only Lv 12^{6} (P); esp. פַּר בֶּן־בָּקָר Ex 29^{1} Lv 4$^{3.14}$ 16^{3} 23^{18} Nu 7^{15} + 16 t. Nu (all P) + 2 Ch 13^{9} Ez 43$^{19.23.25}$ 45^{18} 46^{6}; פָּרִים בְּנֵי בָקָר Nu 28$^{11.19.27}$ 29$^{13.17}$ (P); also בְּנֵי אֲתֹנוֹ Gn 49^{11} (poem, J; ‖ עִירֹה); בְּנֵי־צֹאן ψ 114$^{4.6}$; בֶּן־רְאֵמִים ψ 29^{6}; בְּנֵי הָרַמָּכִים Est 8^{10}; בְּנֵי (הַ)יּוֹנָה Lv 1^{14} + 7 t. Lv + Nu 6^{10} cf. בֶּן־יוֹנָה Lv 12^{6} (all P); בְּנֵי־נֶשֶׁר Pr 30^{17}; בְּנֵי עֹרֵב ψ 147^{9}. **8.** ב׳ as n. relat. followed by word of quality, characteristic, etc. esp. †(a) בֶּן־(בני)חַיִל = *mighty man* 1 S 14^{52} 18^{17} 2 S 2^{7} 13^{28} 17$^{10.10}$ 1 K 1^{52} + 7 t. Ch; אֲנָשִׁים בני ח׳ Ju 18^{2} 2 K 2^{16}; אֶלֶף אִישׁ מִבְּנֵי הֶחָיִל Ju 21^{10}; †(β) בְּנֵי עַוְלָה *wicked men* 2 S 3^{34} 7^{10} 1 Ch 17^{9} Ho 10^{9}; בֶּן־ע׳ ψ 89^{23} (for בני בליעל v. בליעל); †(γ) בְּנֵי מֶרִי *rebels* Nu 17^{25} (cf. בַּיִת); †(δ) בְּנֵי הַתַּעֲרֻבוֹת *sons of pledges* = hostages 2 K 14^{14} = 2 Ch 25^{24}; †(ε) בְּנֵי מָוֶת i.e. those deserving of death 1 S 26^{16}; so בֶּן־מוֹת 2 S 12^{5}; בְּנֵי תְמוּתָה *appointed* or *exposed to death* ψ 79^{11} 102^{21}; cf. †(ζ) בִּן הַכּוֹת one worthy of smiting Dt 25^{2}; †(η) בְּנֵי עֳנִי Pr 31^{5}; †(θ) בְּנֵי חֲלוֹף Pr 31^{8}; †(ι) בְּנֵי שָׁאוֹן Je 48^{45} = *tumultuous ones;* so also (= שְׁאֵת) בְּנֵי שֵׁת Nu 24^{17} cf. RV Di al.; †(κ) בְּנֵי הַיִּצְהָר Zc 4^{14} i.e. anointed ones; †(λ) בֶּן־מֶשֶׁק Gn 15^{2} *son of possession,* i.e. heir; †(μ) הֵילֵל בֶּן־שָׁחַר Is 14^{12} *son of dawn;* †(ν) of animals בְּנֵי שַׁחַץ i.e. proud beasts Jb 28^{8} 41^{26}; (ξ) of Jonah's gourd בִּן־לַיְלָה Jon 4$^{10.10}$; †(ο) of a fertile hill קֶרֶן בֶּן־שָׁמֶן Is 5^{1}. **9.** n. relat. of age: **a.** of men, וַיְהִי נֹחַ בֶּן־חֲמֵשׁ מֵאוֹת שָׁנָה Gn 5^{32} cf. 7^{6} + 71 t. P; Gn 50^{26} Jos 14$^{7.10}$ 24^{29} (all E); Nu 32^{11} (J), Dt 31^{2}; also Ju 2^{8} 1 S 4^{15} 2 S 4^{4} 19$^{33.36}$ 1 Ch 2^{21}

23$^{3.24.27}$ 27^{3} 2 Ch 24^{15} 25^{5} 31$^{16.17}$ Ezr 3^{8} Is 65$^{20.20}$ Je 52^{1}; + 41 t. S K Ch of kings at accession; note esp. (incl. in above) the phrase מִבֶּן עֶשְׂרִים שָׁנָה וָמָ֫עְלָה Ex 30^{14} 38^{26} Nu 1^{3} + 21 t. Nu 1–3 + 26$^{2.4}$ 32^{11} 1 Ch 23$^{24.27}$ 2 Ch 25^{5} Ezr 3^{8}; cf. Lv 27^{7} Nu 8^{24} 26^{62} 1 Ch 23^{3} & without מעלה Nu 8^{25} 18^{16}; also מִבֶּן עשׂרים שנה וְעַד בֶּן־שִׁשִּׁים שָׁנָה Lv 27^{3} cf. v$^{5.6}$; מִבֶּן שלשים שנה ומעלה ועד בן־חמשים שנה Nu 4$^{3.3}$ + 12 t. Nu 4; מבן שלושׁ שנים וּלְמַ֫עְלָה 2 Ch 31^{16} cf. v^{17}; & לְמִבֶּן עשׂרים שנה וּלְמָ֫טָּה 1 Ch 27^{23}. **b.** of animals, (Hex all P, incl. H) בֶּן־שָׁנָה Ex 12^{5} 29^{38} Lv 9^{3} 23$^{18.19}$ Nu 7^{17} + 28 t. Nu 7, 28, 29; also Mi 6^{6}; בֶּן־שְׁנָתוֹ Lv 12^{6} 23^{12} Nu 6$^{12.14}$ + 12 t. Nu 7; also Ez 46^{13}.

Note.—בן appears perh. abbrev. as בּ in a few cpd. n.pr.; v. בִּדְקַר (= בֶּן־דקר?), בִּלְשָׁן, בִּמְהָל, בִּשְׁלָם, בִּרְשַׁע, בַּעֲנָה, בַּעֲלִים (so MV after Schol. Hamâsa^{3} ed. Freytag; Rö$^{de\ libr.\ hist.\ interpr.\ Arab.\ 20,\ 21}$; but this is very uncertain, cf. Ol$^{§\ 227\ b,\ p.\ 613}$).—On Lag.'s explan. of אבי in some n.pr. as for אבן = בן cf. Lag$^{BN\ 75}$ & v. אבינר p. 4, etc., but this is dub.

1122 †בֵּן **n.pr.m.** a Levite 1 Ch 15^{18}, but del. 𝔊 Be Öt cf. v^{20}.

1125 †בֶּן־אֲבִינָדָב **n.pr.m.** (?) (*son of Abinadab*) an officer of Solomon 1 K 4^{11}; but cf. אבינדב p. 4.

1126, 206 †בֶּן־אוֹנִ֫י **n.pr.m.** (*son of my sorrow*) Rachel's name for Benjamin (cf. infr.) Gn 35^{18}.

1127 †בֶּן־גֶּ֫בֶר **n.pr.m.** (*son of a man*, or *of Geber*) an officer of Solomon 1 K 4^{13}.

1128 †בֶּן־דֶּ֫קֶר **n.pr.m.** (?) (*son of Deker*) an officer of Solomon 1 K 4^{9}.

1130 †בֶּן־הֲדַד **n.pr.m.** (appar. *son of (god) Hadad* = Aram. ܒܰܪ ܗܰܕܰܕ, 𝔖 ܒܰܪ ܗܰܕܰܕ PS cf. Bae$^{Rel\ 68}$; also Bab. *Bin-addu-natan* etc., Pinches$^{PB\ Feb.\ 1883,\ 71}$; As. *Bir-Dadda* COT 1 K 20^{1} Hpt$^{Hbr\ 1885,\ 224}$, but cf. 𝔊 υἱὸς Ἄδερ, & Dl$^{ZK\ ii.\ 1885,\ 161\ f.}$; v. also Schr$^{KG\ 375\ ff.\ 538\ f.}$) name for king of Aram Je 49^{27}; in partic.;—**1.** time of Asa & Baasha 1 K 15$^{18.20}$ = 2 Ch 16$^{2.4}$. **2.** son of **1.** (cf. 1 K 20^{34}) As. *Dad-idri* COT (*Bir-idri* Dl$^{l.c.}$) 1 K 20$^{1.3.5.9.10.16.17.20.26.30.32.33.33}$ 2 K 6^{24} 8$^{7.9}$. **3.** son of Hazael 2 K 13$^{3.24.25}$ cf. Am 1^{4}.—Vid. הדד.

1132 †בֶּן־זוֹחֵת **n.pr.m.** one of tribe of Judah, 1 Ch 4^{20} וּבְנֵי יִשְׁעִי זוֹחֵת וּבֶן־זוֹחֵת.

1133 †בֶּן־חוּר **n.pr.m.** (*son of Chur*) an officer of Solomon 1 K 4^{8}. p. 301

1121 †בְּנוֹ 1 Ch 24$^{26.27}$ as **n.pr.m.** in AV RV, but render: the sons of Jaaziah *his son*, & the sons of Merari by Jaaziah *his son*, cf. VB & Be Öt.

†בֶּן־חַ֫יִל **n.pr.m.** (*son (man) of might*) a prince of Jehoshaphat 2 Ch 17^{7}. 1134

†בֶּן־חָנָן **n.pr.m.** one of tribe of Judah 1 Ch 4^{20}. 1135

†בֶּן־חֶ֫סֶד **n.pr.m.** (*son of mercy*) an officer 1136,
of Solomon 1 K 4^{10}. 2618

†בֶּן־עַמִּי **n.pr.m.** (*son of my people*) son of Lot by his younger daughter, and ancestor of the Ammonites (בְּנֵי־עַמּוֹן v. עַמּוֹן) Gn 19^{38}. 1151

†בְּנֵי־בְרַק **n.pr.loc.** city of Dan (in As. *Banai-barka* COT Jos 19^{45}) Jos 19^{45};—mod. *Ibn Abraḳ*, or *Ibraḳ*, c. 1¼ hour S. of E. from Jaffa, Scholz$^{Reise\ 256}$ Di, cf. Map Bd^{Pal} & Survey$^{ii.\ 251}$. 1139

†בְּנֵי יַעֲקָן **n.pr.loc.** a station of Israel in wilderness Nu 33$^{31.32}$ (= בְּאֵרֹת בני יעקן Dt 10^{6} q.v., p. 92; cf. also יַעֲקָן 1 Ch 1^{42} = וַעֲקָן Gn 36^{27}, & Di Nu 33^{31}). 1142

בִּנְיָמִין Gn 35^{18} +; usually בִּנְיָמִן **n.pr.m.** $_{166}$ 1144
(*son of (the) right hand*)—**1.** youngest son of Jacob, so called by him, but by Rachel, the mother, who died at Benjamin's birth, called בֶּן־אוֹנִי (q.v.) Gn 35^{18}; own brother of Joseph Gn 35^{24} 42^{4} 43^{29} 45^{12}; cf. 42^{36} 45$^{15.34}$ +; name of tribe of Benjamin Nu 1^{11} Dt 27^{12} 33^{12} Ju 5^{14} + 23 t. Ju; 32 t. S K Chr; Ho 5^{8} Ez 48^{23} Ob ^{19} ψ 68^{28} 80^{3}; בְּנֵי בנימן (lit. Gn 46^{21}) of tribe Nu 1^{36} 2^{22} 7^{60} 26$^{38.41}$ Jos 18$^{20.28}$ Ju 20$^{3.14.15.18.21.23.24.28.30.31.32.36.48}$ 21$^{13.20.23}$ 2 S 2^{25} 4^{2} 23^{29} 1 Ch 8^{40} 9$^{3.7}$ 11^{31} 12$^{17.30}$ Ne 11$^{4.7.31}$ Je 6^{1}; Ju 1$^{21.21}$ (but בני יהודה in ‖ Jos 15^{63} cf. Bu$^{RS\ 7}$); explicitly מַטֵּה בִנְיָמִן Nu 1^{37} 2^{22} 13^{9} 34^{21} Jos 21^{4} 1 Ch 6^{45} cf. Jos 21^{17}; מַטֵּה בְּנֵי ב׳ Nu 10^{24} Jos 18$^{11.21}$ 1 Ch 6^{50}; שֵׁבֶט ב׳ 1 S 10$^{20.21}$ 1 K 12^{21}; observe also כָּל־שִׁבְטֵי ב׳ Ju 20^{12} cf. 1 S 9^{21}; אִישׁ בִּנְיָמִן Ju 20^{41} 1 S 4^{12} cf. אִישׁ מִבֶּן־יָמִין 1 S 9^{1}; אֶרֶץ בִּנְיָמִן Ju 21^{21} 1 S 9^{16} 2 S 21^{14} Je 1^{1} 17^{26} 32^{44} 33^{13} 37^{12} cf. 32^{8}; גְּבוּל ב׳ 1 S 10^{2} Ez 48^{22} (del. Co) v^{24}; בֵּית בִּנְיָמִן 2 S 3^{19}; בֵּית יְהוּדָה וּב׳ 1 K 12^{23} 2 Ch 11^{1}; in name of a temple-gate שַׁעַר ב׳ הָעֶלְיוֹן Je 20^{2} cf. 37^{13} 38^{7} Ez 48^{32} Zc 14^{10}. †**2.** a son of Bilhan and great-grandson of Benjamin **1.** 1 Ch 7^{10}. †**3.** a Jew of Ezra's time Ezr 10^{32} cf. Ne 3^{23} 12^{34}.—בנימן בני פרץ 1 Ch 9^{4} Kt rd. with Qr בְּנֵי מִן־בְּנֵי פ׳.

†בֶּן־יְמִינִי **adj.gent.** from בִּנְיָמִן **1.** 1 S 9^{21} 1145
ψ 7^{1}; בֶּן־הַיְמִינִי Ju 3^{15} 2 S 16^{11} 19^{17} 1 K 2^{8}; pl. בְּנֵי יְמִינִי 1 S 22^{7} Ju 19^{16}; לַבֶּנְ יְמִינִי 1 Ch 27^{12} (Qr לַבֶּן יְמִינִי); = יְמִינִי (q.v.) 1 S 9^{4} +.

1148 †בְּנִינוּ† **n.pr.m.** (*our son?* Ol $^{§277 b, p. 613}$) a Levite Ne 10^{14}.

1323 I. בַּת$_{587}$ **n.f. daughter** (=*בִּנְתְּ fr. בן; Ph. בת, MI בנת pl. *maidens*, As. *bintu* Winckler Sargon, Gloss., Ar. بِنْتٌ; Sab. בת, בנת DHM $^{ZMG 1883, 391}$ CIS $^{iv. 1, No. 6. 21}$; Aram. ܒܪܬܐ)—ב׳ abs. Ex 1^{16} +; cstr. Gn 11^{29} +; sf. בִּתִּי Dt 22^{16} +; בִּתְּךָ Gn 29^{18} +; בִּתֵּנוּ Gn 34^{17} etc.; pl. בָּנוֹת Gn 5^{4} +; cstr. בְּנוֹת Gn 6^{2} +; sf. בְּנֹתַי Gn 31^{26} +; בְּנוֹתֶיךָ Gn 19^{12} +; בְּנֹתָם Gn 34^{21}; בְּנוֹתֵיהֶם Dt 12^{31} +, etc.; —**1.** *daughter*, female child, born of a woman Gn 30^{21} 34^{1} Ex 1$^{16.22}$ 21^{4} Lv 12^{6} Ho 1^{6} cf. Gn 20^{12} Lv 18^{9} Dt 27^{22} +; begotten by a man Gn 5$^{4.7.10}$ 11$^{11.13.15}$ cf. Gn 11^{29} 19^{8} 20^{12} 28^{2} Lv 19^{9} Dt 27^{22} +; oft. || בֵּן *son* Gn 5$^{4.7}$ + (v. בֵּן); cf. in allegory of Jehoash 2 K 14^{9} = 2 Ch 25^{18}; note esp. בְּנוֹת הָאָדָם i.e. human women Gn 6$^{2.4}$; בִּתְּךָ הַקְּטַנָּה *thy younger daughter* Gn 29^{18} (cf. הַצְּעִירָה v^{26} opp. הַבְּכִירָה); בִּתִּי הַגְּדוֹלָה *my eldest daughter* 1 S 18^{17}; בַּת־(הַ)מֶּלֶךְ = *princess* 2 Ch 22^{11} 2 K 9^{34} Dn 11^{6} cf. 2 S 13^{18} Je 41^{10} 43^{6} ψ 45^{10}; cf. as term of praise בַּת־נָדִיב Ct 7^{2}; in partic. †**a.** girl called בִּתֵּנוּ by father and brothers Gn 34^{17} cf. בִּתְּכֶם v^{8}. †**b.** of adopted daughter Est 2$^{7.15}$. †**c.** used in speaking to daughter-in-law Ru 1$^{11.12.13}$ 2$^{2.8.22}$ 3$^{1.16.18}$. †**d.** בַּת־אָבִיו = *sister* Ez 22^{11} (appos. אחותו); also *half-sister* Gn 20^{12} בַּת־אָבִי אַךְ לֹא בַּת־אִמִּי, cf. Lv 18^{9} & v^{11} בַּת־אֵשֶׁת אָבִיךָ, בַּת־דֹּדוֹ 20^{17}. †**e.** = *cousin* Est 2^{7}. †**f.** used in kindly address, בִּתִּי Ru 3$^{10.11}$ (Boaz to Ruth), cf. ψ 45^{11}; בְּנוֹתַי in mouth of י׳ Is 43^{6} (|| בָּנַי). †**g.** בְּנוֹת בָּנָיו = *granddaughters* Gn 46^{7} (P) cf. Lv 18^{10} & v^{17} (H); note also Gn 37^{35}, where בנותיו must include other than actual daughters. **h.** רִבְקָה בַּת־בְּתוּאֵל (as more precise designation) Gn 25^{20} cf. 24$^{23.24.47.47}$ also 26$^{34.34}$ 29^{10} +; note esp. †בַּת־פַּרְעֹה (without personal name) Ex 2$^{5.7.8.9.10}$ cf. 1 K 3^{1} 7^{8} 9^{24} 11^{1} 2 Ch 8^{11}; בַּת־אִישׁ כְּנַעֲנִי וּשְׁמוֹ שׁוּעַ Gn 38^{2} cf. v^{12} (but cf. 1 Ch 2^{3} sub בַּת־שׁוּעַ **n.pr.f.** infr.) †**i.** oft. pl. as designation of women of a particular city, land, or people: בְּנוֹת צִיּוֹן Is 3$^{16.17}$ 4^{4} Ct 3^{11} cf. Is 49^{22} 60^{4} La 3^{51}; בְּנוֹת יְרוּשָׁלִָם Ct 1^{5} 2^{7} 3$^{5.10}$ 5$^{8.16}$ 8^{4}; בְּנוֹת־שִׁילוֹ Ju 21$^{21.21}$; בְּנוֹת רַבָּה Je 49^{3}; observe transitional phrase בְּנוֹת אַנְשֵׁי הָעִיר Gn 24^{13}; further בְּנוֹת כְּנָעַן Gn 28$^{1.6.8}$ 36^{2} (all P) cf. ב׳ הַכְּנַעֲנִי Gn 24$^{3.37}$ (J); בְּנוֹת הָאָרֶץ Gn 27^{46} 34^{1} (both P); בְּנוֹת מוֹאָב Nu 25^{1} Is 16^{2} cf. Nu 21^{29}; ב׳ חֵת Gn 27$^{46.46}$ (P); ב׳ פְּלִשְׁתִּים Ju 14$^{1.2}$ 2 S 1^{20} || ב׳ הָעֲרֵלִים v^{20} (poet.); ב׳ יִשְׂרָאֵל Ju 11^{40} 1 S 1^{24} (poet.); ב׳ יְהוּדָה ψ 48^{12} 97^{8}; ב׳ מְנַשֶּׁה Jos 17^{6}; ב׳ דָּן 2 Ch 2^{13}; cf. בַּת־לֵוִי Ex 2^{1} i.e. a woman of tribe of Levi; also ב׳ אָחִיךָ Ju 14^{3}; ב׳ עַמֵּךְ Ez 13^{17}.—בַּת־צִיּוֹן etc. v. sub **3** infr. †**2.** *young women, women* Gn 30^{13} (J) Pr 31^{29} Ct 2^{2} 6^{9}; בָּנוֹת בֹּטְחוֹת Is 32^{9}; also בַּת הַנָּשִׁים Dn 11^{17}. †**3.** with name of city, land, or people, poet. personif. of that city or inhabitants, etc.: בַּת־צִיּוֹן Is 1^{8} 10^{32} 16^{1} 62^{11} Mi 1^{13} 4$^{8.10.13}$ Je 4^{31} 6$^{2.23}$ Zp 3^{14} Zc 2^{14} 9^{9} ψ 9^{15} La 1^{6} 2$^{1.4}$ 4^{22}; even זִקְנֵי בת־ציון La 2^{10}; חוֹמַת ב׳ צ׳ v$^{8.18}$; also שְׁבִיָּה ב׳־צ׳ Is 52^{2}; בְּתוּלַת ב׳־צ׳ 2 K 19^{21} = Is 37^{22} La 2^{13}; ב׳ יְרוּשָׁלִָם 2 K 19^{21} = Is 37^{22} Mi 4^{8} Zp 3^{14} Zc 9^{9} La 2$^{13.15}$; cf. בַּת־פּוּצַי Zp 3^{10} *daughter of my dispersed ones*; בַּת־צֹר ψ 45^{13}; ב׳ בָּבֶל Je 50^{42} 51^{33} ψ 137^{8}; בְּתוּלַת ב׳ בָּבֶל Is 47^{1}; v. further Zc 2^{11}; also of Tarshish Is 23^{10}, Sidon v^{12} (+ בְּתוּלַת), Dibon Je 48^{18} (+ יוֹשֶׁבֶת), Gallim Is 10^{30}; בְּתוּלַת בַּת־עַמִּי La 1^{15}; cf. בַּת יְהוּדָה 2^{2}; מִבְצְרֵי ב׳־יְהוּדָה *daughter of my people* Is 22^{4} Je 4^{11} 6$^{14.26}$ 8$^{11.19.21.22.23}$ 9^{6} La 3^{48} 4$^{3.6.10}$, בְּתוּלַת ב׳ ע׳ Je 14^{17}; בַּת־מִצְרָיִם Je 46^{24}; also 46^{11} (+ בְּתוּלַת), v^{19} (+ יוֹשֶׁבֶת); ב׳ אֱדוֹם La 4$^{21.22}$; ב׳ כַּשְׂדִּים Is 47$^{1.5}$; note הַבַּת הַשּׁוֹבֵבָה Je 31^{22} (|| בְּתוּלַת יִשְׂרָאֵל v^{21}) 49^{4} (= Ammon); on בַּת־אֲשֻׁרִים Ez 27^{6} v. sub אֲשֻׁרִים p. 81; less often in pl. בְּנוֹת הַגּוֹיִם Ez 32^{16}; ב׳ גּ׳ אַדִּרִם v^{18} (these perh. sub **1 i**); בְּנוֹת פְּלִשְׁתִּים Ez 16^{27} (in allegory); cf. also of Sodom, Samaria, Syria etc. v$^{44.45.46.46.53.55.55.57.57}$ 23^{2}. **4.** pl. = *villages*, after name of city, חֶשְׁבּוֹן וּבְכָל־בְּנֹתֶיהָ Nu 21^{25} cf. v^{32} 32^{42} (E) Jos 15$^{45.47.47}$ (JE?) + v^{28} 𝔊 Di, 17^{11} (6 t.) v^{16} (J) = Ju 1$^{27.27.27.27}$ 11$^{26.26}$ Je 49^{2} + 17 t. Ch + 6 t. Ne 11$^{25-31}$. On 1 Ch 18^{1} & its variation from || 2 S 8^{1} vid. We Dr. **5.** in phrases denoting character, quality, etc., בַּת־אֵל נֵכָר *daughter of a strange god*, i.e. idolatrous (woman or people) Mal 2^{11}; בַּת־גְּדוּד *daughter of a troop*, i.e. warlike city Mi 4^{14}; בְּנוֹת הַשִּׁיר Ec 12^{4} *the daughters of song*, i.e. songs, melodious notes; בַּת־בְּלִיַּעַל 1 S 1^{16} v. בְּלִיַּעַל sub בלה. †**6.** בַּת יַעֲנָה = *ostrich* Lv 11^{16} = Dt 14^{15}; pl. בְּנוֹת יַעֲנָה Jb 30^{29} Mi 1^{8} Is 13^{21} 34^{13} 43^{20} Je 50^{39} (v. יַעֲנָה); בַּת־עַיִן *pupil of the eye* La 2^{18} cf. Eth. ብንተ፡ ዐይን፡ v. also אִישׁוֹן. †**7.** fig. לַעֲלוּקָה שְׁתֵּי בָנוֹת Pr 30^{15} *two daughters* (i.e. She'ôl & the barren womb, cf. Comm.) †**8.** of vine = *branch* בָּנוֹת צָעֲדָה עֲלֵי־שׁוּר Gn 49^{22} cf. Di & v. sub בֵּן. †**9.** as n. relat. (all P), of age of woman בַּת־תִּשְׁעִים שָׁנָה Gn 17^{17}; of ewe-lamb בַּת־שְׁנָתָהּ Lv 14^{10} Nu 6^{14}; of she-goat *id.* Nu 15^{27}. Cf. בֵּן **9.**—II. בַּת v. sub בתת p. 144.

†בַּת־רַבִּים **n.pr.loc.** (*daughter of multi-* 1337
tudes) appellation of populous city of Heshbon, or of its gate, Ct 7^{5} (|| חֶשְׁבּוֹן).

1339 †בַּת־שֶׁ֫בַע **n.pr.f.** (*daughter of oath*? cf. אֱלִישֶׁ֫בַע) wife of Uriah 2 S 11^{3} ψ 50^{2}; afterwards of David, & mother of Solomon 12^{24} 1 K 1$^{11.15.16.31}$ 2$^{13.18.19}$; בַּת־שָׁ֑בַע 1 K 1^{28}; cf. also foll.

1340 †בַּת־שׁוּעַ **n.pr.f.** (?) (*daughter of opulence*?)—**1.** wife of David, mother of Solomon, etc. 1 Ch 3^{5}=בַּת־שֶׁ֫בַע q.v.; We Klo בַּת־שֶׁ֫וַע cf. Be; but prob. text. error v. Dr on 2 S 11^{3}. **2.** wife of Judah 1 Ch 2^{3} ב׳־שׁ׳ הַכְּנַעֲנִית, RV *Bath-shua* but in ‖ Gn 38$^{2.12}$ not a n.pr. (cf. v^{2}).

1332 †בִּתְיָה **n.pr.f.** (=בַּת יָהּ i.e. *worshipper of Yah*? cf. Ph. n.pr.f. בתבעל) 1 Ch 4^{18} wife of Mered of Judah, called בַּת־פַּרְעֹה.

1129 **בָּנָה** 373 **vb.** build (MI, Nab. Eut$^{\text{No.1}}$ בנה, Ph. בן, Ar. بَنَا, As. *banû* COT$^{\text{Gloss.}}$ cf. Ba$^{\text{ZMG 1887, 640}}$, Sab. בני CIS$^{\text{iv. 1, No. 56}}$, Aram. בְּנָא, ܒܢܳܐ, Palm. בנא Vog$^{\text{No. 31}}$)—**Qal** *Pf.* ב׳ Dt 20^{5}+, בָּֽנְתָה Pr 9^{1} 14^{1}, בָּנִיתָ Dt 6^{10}, בָּנִתָה 1 K 9^{3}; וּבָנִ֫יתָ consec. Dt 20^{20}+; בָּנִית Ez 16^{25}; בָּנִיתִי 1 K 8^{13}+; pl. בָּנוּ Gn 11^{5}+, etc.; *Impf.* יִבְנֶה Dt 25^{9}+; juss. וְיִבֶן Ezr 1^{3}, וַיִּבְנֶה Jos 19^{50} + 2 t., וַיִּ֫בֶן Gn 2^{22} +; sf. יִבְנֵ֫הוּ Jb 20^{19}; 3 fs. וַתִּ֫בֶן 1 Ch 7^{24} Zc 9^{3}; אֶבְנֶה 2 S 7^{27}+; pl. יִבְנוּ Is 65^{22}+, etc.; *Imv.* בְּנֵה Nu 23^{1}+; pl. בְּנוּ Nu 32^{24}+; *Inf. abs.* בָּנֹה 1 K 8^{13}; cstr. בְּנוֹת 1 Ch 6^{17} +, etc.; *Pt. act.* בֹּנֶה (בּוֹנֶה) Gn 4^{17} +; cstr. בֹּנֵה ψ 147^{2}; pl. בּוֹנִים (בֹּנִים) Ezr 4^{1}+; cstr. בֹּנֵי 1 K 5$^{32.32}$, etc.; *pass.* בָּנוּי Ct 4^{4} Ju 6^{28}; f. בְּנוּיָה ψ 122^{3}; pl. בְּנוּיִם Ne 7^{4};—*build*, **1.** (lit.) **a.** c. acc. (α) of city (Hex only JE) Gn 4^{17} 10^{11} 11$^{4.5}$ (+ tower) v^{8} (all J & his sources); Ex 1^{11} Nu 32^{24} Jos 24^{13} (all E) Ju 1^{26} 18^{28} + 22 t. K Ch + Je 32^{31} ψ 122^{3} (pt. pass.) cf. Hb 2^{12}; of village (חָצֵר) Ne 12^{29}; v. also sub *rebuild*, **i.** infr.; (β) house Gn 33^{17} (J), elsewhere in Hex only Dt 6^{10} 8^{12} 20^{5} 22^{8} 28^{30}; also 2 S 5^{11} 1 K 22^{39} 1 Ch 14^{1} 2 Ch 2^{2} Pr 24^{27} Am 5^{11} Zp 1^{13} Is 65^{21} Je 35$^{7.9}$ cf. Zc 5^{11}; as sign of security Ez 28^{26} cf. 11^{3}; of luxury Ec 2^{4} cf. Je 22^{14}; of permanent residence 1 K 2^{36} Je 29$^{5.28}$; esp. of temple 1 K 3^{1} 5^{32} 6^{2} + oft. S K Chr; fig. of wisdom's house Pr 9^{1}; esp. build temple ליהוה etc. 2 S 7$^{5.7}$ 1 K 6^{1} (=began to build) + 13 t. Chr + Is 66^{1}; לְשֵׁם י׳ etc. 2 S 7^{13} 1 K 5^{17} + 8 t. K, 13 t. Ch; לְךָ לְשִׁמְךָ 2 Ch 20^{8}; לִהְיוֹת שְׁמִי שָׁם 1 K 8^{16} 2 Ch 6^{5}; לָשׂוּם שְׁמִי שָׁם 1 K 9^{3}; obj. chambers, or stories 1 K 6$^{5.10}$, court 6^{36} Ho 8^{14} perh. of idol-temples; cf. 1 K 16^{32}; ψ 78^{69} of Yahweh's building his sanctuary, 147^{2} Jerusalem, ψ 127^{1} a house; also Am 9^{6} his chambers in the heavens; of Sol.'s palace 1 K 7$^{1.2}$ 9$^{1.10}$ + ; (γ) of a fortress 2 Ch 17^{12} 27^{4} cf. of Tyre Zc 9^{3} (מָצוֹר); (δ) of wall 1 K 3^{1} Is 60^{10} Ez 13^{10} 2 Ch 33^{14} (cf. 27^{3}) Ne 4^{4} 6^{1}+; (ε) gate 2 K 15^{35} = 2 Ch 27^{3}; (ζ) tower Is 5^{2} 2 Ch 26$^{9.10}$ 27^{4} cf. fig. Ct 8^{9} & pt. pass. Ct 4^{4} (in sim.); †(η) siege-works against (עַל־) a city Dt 20^{2} (מָצוֹר), Ec 9^{14} (מְצוֹדִים), 2 K 25^{1}=Je 52^{4} Ez 4^{2} (all דָּיֵק), & so (without עַל־) Ez 17^{17} 21^{27}; cf. בנה עָלַי, abs. La 3^{5} (in fig.); (θ) altar Gn 22^{9} 35^{7} Ex 17^{15} 20^{25} 24^{4} Nu 23$^{1.14.29}$ (all E), Gn 26^{25} Ex 32^{5} (both J), Jos 22^{11} + 6 t. Jos 22 (all P) Ju 6^{28} (pt. pass.) 21^{4} + 6 t. K Ch; oft. sq. ליהוה etc. Gn 8^{20} 12$^{7.8}$ 13^{18} (all J), Dt 27$^{5.6}$ Jos 8^{30} (E) Ju 6$^{24.26}$ + 8 t. S K Ch; †(ι) high places (בָּמָה) 1 K 11^{7} 14^{23} 2 K 17^{9} 21^{3} 23^{13} 2 Ch 33$^{3.19}$ Je 7^{31} 19^{5} 32^{35}; cf. גַּב Ez 16$^{24.31}$ (both ‖ רָמָה) & רָמָה v^{25}; †(κ) צִיּוּן Ez 39^{15}; also †(λ) גִּדְרֹת צֹאן Nu 32^{16} (E); †(μ) מֵיסַךְ הַשַּׁבָּת 2 K 16^{18}. †**b.** c. acc. of material Ex 20^{25} (E) 1 K 6^{36} 18^{32} 15^{22}= 2 Ch 16^{6} Ez 27^{5}; c. בְּ of material 1 K 6$^{15.16}$ 15^{17} 2 Ch 16^{6}; cf. †**c.** וַיִּבֶן אֶת־הַצֵּלָע לְאִשָּׁה Gn 2^{22} *and he* (Yahweh) *fashioned the rib into a woman.* †**d.** abs. 2 S 5^{9} 1 K 6^{16} Is 9^{9} Je 1^{10} 18^{9} 22^{13} 31^{28} Is 65^{22} + 12 t. Chr + Mal 1^{4} Ec 3^{3} (opp. פרץ); also **e.** Pt. act.=*builder* 1 K 5$^{32.32}$ + 6 t. Chr + Ez 27^{4} ψ 118^{22} 127^{1}. †**f.** c. indef. obj. 1 K 9^{19} =2 Ch 8^{6}. †**g.** וַיִּבֶן אֶת־הָהָר=*and he built* on *the hill* 1 K 16^{24}. †**h.** sq. בְּ *build at* Zc 6^{15} Ne 4^{11} (cf. בְּ **I 2 b**, p. 88). †**i.**=*rebuild* Jos 6^{26} 1 K 16^{34} Am 9^{14} Is 45^{13} ψ 69^{36} Ne 2^{5} Dn 9^{25} all of city; cf. phrase בנה חָרְבוֹת עוֹלָם Is 58^{12} 61^{4} & Ez 36^{36} Mal 1^{4} Jb 3^{14}; of walls Mi 7^{11} 2 Ch 32^{5} Ne 2^{17} 3$^{33.35.38}$ 6^{6} ψ 51^{20} (act. of י׳); of gate Ne 3$^{1.13.14.15}$; temple Zc 6$^{12.13}$ Ezr 1^{3}; altar 2 Ch 33^{16} (Qr וַיִּבֶן so Bö < Kt ויכן, fr. כון, so Öt), Ezr 3^{2}; high places 2 K 21^{3}=2 Ch 33^{3}; in some of these apparently an idea of merely repairing; so, sts. with added notion of enlarging etc., city Nu 32$^{34.37.38}$ (E) Jos 19^{50} (P) Ju 21^{23} 2 K 14^{22}=2 Ch 26^{2}, 1 Ch 11^{8} 2 Ch 8^{2} 11^{6} cf. Mi 3^{10}; Millo 1 K 9^{24} 11^{27}; cf. house Jb 20^{19}. **2.** fig. **a.** *build a house* (בית) = perpetuate and establish a family; subj. Leah & Rachel Ru 4^{11}; subj. a brother Dt 25^{9}; subj. י׳ (promise to David) 1 S 2^{35} 2 S 7^{27} 1 K 11^{38} 1 Ch 17^{10} and 17^{25}; (to Solomon) 1 K 11^{38}; cf. further סֻכַּת דָּוִד Am 9^{11} (*rebuild, restore*); = cause a household to flourish Pr 14^{1} cf. opp. 27^{18}; also of establishing David's throne ψ 89^{5}. **b.** build up Israel (after exile) subj. י׳ Je 24^{6} 31^{4} 33^{7} 42^{10} cf. 45^{4} & ψ 28^{5}; obj. Zion ψ 102^{17}. †**Niph.** *Pf.* נִבְנָה 1 K 3^{2} 6^{7}, נִבְנְתָה Nu 13^{22} Ne 7^{1}, וְנִבְנְתָה consec. Je 30^{18} + 2 t.; 2 fs. וְנִבְנֵית consec. Je 31^{4}; 3 pl. נִבְנוּ Mal 3^{15}; וְנִבְנוּ consec. Je 12^{16} Ez 36^{33}; *Impf.* יִבָּנֶה Jb 12^{14} + 4 t.; 3 fs. תִּבָּנֶה Nu 21^{27} +

3 t.; 2 ms. תִּבָּנֶה Jb 22^{23}, אִבָּנֶה Gn 16^{2}, וְאִבָּנֶה Gn 30^{3}; 3 fpl. תִּבָּנֶינָה Ez 36^{10}; 2 fpl. תִּבָּנֶינָה Is 44^{26}; *Inf.* לְהִבָּנוֹת Hg 1^{2} Zc 8^{9}, בְּהִבָּנֹתוֹ 1 K $6^{7.7}$; *Pt.* נִבְנֶה 1 Ch 22^{19};—**1. a.** *be built*, (lit.) of city Nu 13^{22}; of temple 1 K 3^{2} (לְשֵׁם י׳) 1 K $6^{7.7.7}$ (c. acc. mater.); Pt.=*to be built* (gerundive) 1 Ch 22^{19}. **b.** *be rebuilt:* of city of Sihon Nu 21^{27} cf. Is 25^{2} 44^{26}, of wall of Jerusalem Ne 7^{1}, of Jerusalem Je 30^{18} $31^{4.38}$ Is 44^{28} cf. Dn 9^{25} תָּשׁוּב וְנִבְנְתָה, & Ez 26^{14} (c. עוֹד), of ruinous places (הֶחֳרָבוֹת) Ez $36^{10.33}$, of a devoted city Dt 13^{17} (c. עוֹד), of temple Hg 1^{2} Zc 1^{16} 8^{9}, indef. subj. Jb 12^{14}. **2. a.** (fig.) of restored exiles, = *established* Je 12^{16}, of prosperous wicked Mal 3^{15}, of repentant offender Jb 22^{23}. **b.** *established*, made permanent, subj. חֶסֶד ψ 89^{3} (c. עוֹלָם), subj. בַּיִת Pr 24^{3} (by wisdom). **c.** of childless wife, by means of concubine אִבָּנֶה מִמֶּנָּה Gn 16^{2} 30^{3} *I shall be built up*, i.e. become the mother of a family, *from* or *through her;* cf. **Qal 2 a.**

1138 בּוֹנִּי v. בָּנִי infr. below

1131 †בִּנּוּי **n.pr.m. 1.** head of a family that returned with Zerubbabel Ne 7^{15} (=בָּנִי ‖ Ezr 2^{10} & perh. Ezr 10^{34} cf. Sm[Listen 14]; but BeRy prop. here בִּנּוּי). **2.** a Levite of Ezra's time Ezr 8^{33} Ne 10^{10} (prob.=בָּנִי 8^{7}, בָּנִי 9^{4}) 12^{8} cf. 3^{24} (בַּוַּי, text. err. v^{18}) v. BeRy; also Ezr 2^{40}=Ne 7^{43} לִבְנֵי rd. perh. לְבִנּוּי cf. Sm[Listen 16] but BeRy otherwise; cf. further Gr[Gesch. ii. 2, 389]. **3.** Israelites of Ezra's time, **a.** Ezr 10^{30}; **b.** Ezr 10^{38}.

1137 †בָּנִי **n.pr.m. 1.** one of David's heroes 2 S 23^{36} בָּנִי הַגָּדִי (‖ 1 Ch 11^{38} has בֶּן־הַגְרִי, but v. Dr[Sm]). **2.** Levites, **a.** 1 Ch 6^{31}; **b.** Ne 3^{17} cf. 8^{7} (=בִּנּוּי 10^{10}) $9^{4.4}$ (repeated prob. by error, cf. BeRy) v^{5} 10^{14} 11^{22}. On Ezr 2^{40}=Ne 7^{43} cf. Gr[Gesch. ii. 2, 389]; he reads קדמיאל בני for קדמיאל לבני, taking בני as n.pr., as 3 Ezr 5^{26} Καδμιηλου καὶ Βαννου. **3.** a man of Judah 1 Ch 9^{4} (מִן) בָּנִי Qr (>Kt בנימן). **4.** Ezr 2^{10} rd. בִּנּוּי cf. ‖Ne 7^{15}. **5.** heads of families of Isr. **a.** Ezr 10^{29}; **b.** Ne 10^{15}; **c.** Ezr 10^{34} but perh. rd. בִּנּוּי or בָּנִי cf. supr. **6.** an Israelite Ezr 10^{38}.—(בני as n.pr. Palm Vog[No. 34].)

1138 †בֻּנִּי **n.pr.m. 1.** Levites, **a.** Ne 9^{4}, but rd. perh. בִּנּוּי cf. BeRy & vid. 10^{10} 12^{8} Ezr 8^{33}; **b.** בּוּנִּי (בֶּן) Ne 11^{15}, but rd. perh. מִן בְּנֵי etc. cf. BeRy. **2.** a chief of people Ne 10^{16}, perh. repetit. of בָּנִי v^{15} cf. BeRy.

1140 †בִּנְיָה **n.f. structure, building** Ez 41^{13}, cf. also בִּנְיָן.

†בְּנָיָה, בְּנָיָהוּ **n.pr.m.** (*Yah hath built up*, 1141
cf. יבנאל, Sab. בנאל DHM[ZMG 1883, 15])—**1.** one of David's captains and heroes, son of Jehoiada, בניהו 2 S 8^{18} $23^{20.22}$ 1 K $1^{8.10.26.32.36.38.44}$ $2^{25.29.30.30.34.35.46}$ 4^{4} 1 Ch 11^{24} 18^{17} $27^{5.6}$ cf. v^{34} (v. Be); =בניה 2 S 20^{23} 1 Ch 11^{22}. **2.** one of David's thirty, בניהו 2 S 23^{30}=בניה 1 Ch 11^{31} 27^{14}. **3.** a Simeonite, בניה 1 Ch 4^{36}. **4.** Levites, **a.** בניהו 1 Ch $15^{18.20.24}$; **b.** (*id.*) 2 Ch 31^{13}; **c.** בניה 2 Ch 20^{14}. **5.** Israelites, בניה, **a.** Ezr 10^{25}; **b.** v^{30}; **c.** v^{35}; **d.** v^{43}; **e.** Ez 11^{13}=בניהו v^{1}.

†בִּנְיָן **n.m. structure** (loan-word = بُنْيَان 1146
acc. to Lag[BN 205]) applied **a.** to enclosing wall of Ezekiel's temple Ez 40^{5}; **b.** to rear-building of same $41^{12.12.15}$, but rd. prob. בִּנְיָה q.v.; so Sm Co; **c.** appar. to whole temple $42^{1.10}$ (Co rds. הבית); cf. v^{5} (del. Co);—Sm refers v^{1} to enclosing wall, vid. **a.**

†יַבְנְאֵל **n.pr.loc.** (*Ēl causeth to build;* cf. 2995
יַבְנֶה, בניהו)—**1.** town in Judah Jos 15^{11} (𝔊L Ἰαβνηλ)=יַבְנֶה (q.v.) 2 Ch 26^{6};=Gk. *Iamnia*, mod. Yebna Bd[Pal 161]. **2.** town in Naphtali Jos 19^{33}.

†יַבְנֶה **n.pr.loc.** (*he causeth to build*) a 2996
Philistine city 2 Ch 26^{6} 𝔊L Ἰαβνη (B Ἀβεννηρ) cf. Ἰεμναθ 𝔊L Jos 15^{46} (A Ἰεμναι); = יַבְנְאֵל **1**, q.v.

†I. יִבְנְיָה **n.pr.m.** (*Yah buildeth up*, cf. 2997
בניהו) a Benjamite 1 Ch 9^{8a} 𝔊 Βαναaμ, 𝔊L Ἰεβναα.

†II. יִבְנִיָּה **n.pr.m.** (*id.*; al. יִבְנְיָה but v. 2998
Baer's n.) a Benjamite 1 Ch 9^{8b} 𝔊 Βαναια, but 𝔊L Ἰεχονιου.

†[מִבְנֶה] **n.m. structure**, cstr. כְּמִבְנֵה־עִיר 4011
Ez 40^{2} *like the structure of a city*.

†מְבֻנַּי **n.pr.m.** one of David's heroes 2 S 4012
23^{27} rd. prob. סִבְּכַי ‖ 1 Ch 11^{29} cf. Dr[Sm].

†תַּבְנִית **n.f. construction, pattern, figure** 8403
—ת׳ abs. 1 Ch 28^{19}; cstr. Ex $25^{9.9}$ + 14 t. + Ez 8^{10} (del. Co); תַּבְנִיתוֹ 2 K 16^{10}, תַּבְנִיתָם Ex 25^{40};—**1.** app. originally *construction, structure*, yet only P & late: תַּבְנִית מִזְבַּח י׳ Jos 22^{28}; cf. ψ 144^{12} in sim. בְּנוֹתֵינוּ כְזָוִיֹּת מְחֻטָּבוֹת תַּ׳ הֵיכָל *carved acc. to the construction of a palace, palace-fashion.* **2.** *pattern*, acc. to which anything is to be constructed (P & late), of tabernacle Ex 25^{9}, utensils of tab. $v^{9.40}$; an altar 2 K 16^{10} תַּבְנִיתוֹ לְכָל־מַעֲשֵׂהוּ (disting. fr. דְּמוּת); temple 1 Ch 28^{11} cf. v^{12}; chariot, i.e. cherubim 1 Ch 28^{18}; מַלְאֲכוֹת הַתּ׳ 1 Ch 28^{19} i.e. objects of which the pattern is given. **3.** *figure, image*, Hex only D, of idols in form of animals Dt $4^{16.17.17.18.18}$; elsewhere late Is 44^{13} Ez 8^{10} (del. B Co) ψ 106^{20}; cf. ת׳ יָד Ez 8^{3} 10^{8} i.e. something like a hand.

בנט (assumed as √ of אַבְנֵט, Thes Sta[§257]).

73 †אַבְנֵט **n.[m.]** girdle—׳א abs. Ex 28^4+; אַבְנֵטְךָ Is 22^{21}; cstr. Ex 39^{29}; אַבְנֵטִים Ex 28^{40};—*girdle*, of high priest Ex $28^{4.39}$ 39^{29} Lv 8^7 16^4; of priests Ex 28^{40} 29^9 Lv 8^{13} (all P); of high official Is 22^{21}.—Josephus[iii. 7. 2] ἀβανήθ; cf. further Lag[Ges. Abh. 39].

996 בֵּנַיִם v. sub [בֵּין]. p. 107

1150 †בִּנְעָא **n.pr.m.** a descendant of Jonathan 1 Ch 8^{37} 9^{43}.

1152 †בְּסוֹדְיָה **n.pr.m.** (? *in the secret of Yah*) Israelite in Nehemiah's time Ne 3^6.

1153 †בֵּסַי **n.pr.m.** head of a family of Nethinim, בְּנֵי־בֵסַי Ne 7^{52}=ב׳־בֵסָי Ezr 2^{49}.

בסר (*be too early*, Ar. بَسَرَ, cf. Aram. בְּסִירָה *half-ripe*).

1155, 1154 †בֹּסֶר **n.m.**[Is 18, 5] **unripe or sour grapes** coll. (NH *id.*, Aram. בּוּסְרָא, ܒܘܣܪܐ; Ar. بُسْرٌ *unripe dates*)—בֹּסֶר Is 18^5+3t., בִּסְרוֹ Jb 15^{33};—*unripe grapes* Is 18^5 Jb 15^{33}; *sour g.* Je $31^{29.30}$ Ez 18^2.

בעד (Ar. بَعُدَ, بَعِدَ *be remote, distant*, Qor 9^{42}, بَعِيدٌ *distant;* Eth. በዐደ: *to change*, ψ 33 title, ብዑድ: *different, distinct*, በዐድ: *another*).

1157 בַּעַד$_{105}$ **subst.** prop. separation, with a gen., *in separation from*, in usage a **prep. away from, behind, about, on behalf of** (Ar. بَعْدُ, of time, *after*)—abs. †Ct $4^{1.3}$ 6^7, elsewhere cstr.

1157 בְּעַד, with sf. בַּעֲדִי Ex 8^{24}+, בַּעֲדֵנִי †ψ 139^{11}; בַּעַדְךָ Gn 20^7+; בַּעֲדוֹ etc.; 1 pl. בַּעֲדֵנוּ, †Am 9^{10} בַּעֲדֵינוּ; בַּעַדְכֶם 1 S 7^5+; בַּעֲדָם Lv 9^7+;—**1.** lit. **a.** with vbs. of falling, letting down, leaning forward so as to look out, *through* (lit. *away from*) a window, etc.: Jos 2^{15} and she let him down by a cord בְּעַד הַחַלּוֹן *away from* the window, i.e. *out through* it, 1 S 19^{12} 2 S 20^{21} 2 K 1^2 and A. fell בְּעַד הַשְּׂבָכָה *out through* the lattice; Gn 26^8 Ju 5^{28} *out through* the window נִשְׁקְפָה she *looked forth* (lit. *leant forward*), 2 S 6^{26}+; pregn. Jb 22^{13} will he judge בְּעַד עֲרָפֶל (looking) *out through* the thick clouds? Conversely Jo 2^9 *in through* the windows they come (the locusts) as a thief. **b.** idiom. with vbs. of *shutting*, esp. סָגַר בְּעַד to shut *behind* or *upon*—whether oneself, Ju 9^{51} and they entered the tower וַיִּסְגְּרוּ בַּעֲדָם and shut (the doors) *upon* themselves (sc. from the inside), 2 K $4^{4.5.33}$ Is 26^{20}; or another, Gn 7^{16} וַיִּסְגֹּר י׳ בַּעֲדוֹ and ׳י shut *behind* or *upon* him (sc. from the outside), i.e. shut him in, Ju 3^{23} (the sf. in בַּעֲדוֹ referring to Eglon), 2 K 4^{21} (but N.B. persons leaving a room shut the door אַחֲרֵי themselves Gn 19^6 2 S $13^{17.18}$): see also Ju 3^{22} 1 S 1^6 סָגַר י׳ בְּעַד רַחְמָהּ (cf. Gn 20^{18} עָצַר בְּעַד רֶחֶם), Jb 9^7 חָתַם בְּעַד to seal *up*, 1^{10} 3^{23} שׂוּךְ (הֵסַךְ) בְּעַד to make a hedge *about*, La 3^7 גָּדַר בְּעַד to fence *about*. Somewhat peculiarly Am 9^{10} (who say,) Evil will not draw near, or come in front בַּעֲדֵינוּ *so as to be about us* (but Gr עָדֵינוּ *unto* us), Jo 2^8 (of the locusts) בְּעַד הַשֶּׁלַח יִפֹּלוּ (prob.) *in among* the weapons they throw themselves (i.e. they pass about and between them without being injured or having their course impeded), 1 S 4^{18} and Eli fell backward בְּעַד יַד הַשַּׁעַר, i.e. (si vera l.) *about* the side of the gate: but text dub.; v. Dr. Without a vb. Jon 2^7 the earth, בְּרִיחֶיהָ בַעֲדִי her bars were *upon* me (or *about* me) for ever, ψ 139^{11} night shall be the light *about* me, ψ 3^4 thou מָגֵן בַּעֲדִי art a shield *about* me. Hence **c.** after a vb. of protecting, †Zc 12^8 in that day יָגֵן י׳ בְּעַד יוֹשֵׁב ירושלם will ׳י give protection *about*, etc. **2.** metaph. *on behalf of* (ὑπέρ); very freq. after הִתְפַּלֵּל Gn 20^7 Nu 21^7 1 S 7^5 ψ 72^{15}+; also with other vbs. of entreating Ex 8^{24} 1 S 7^9, or consulting (דָּרַשׁ) Is 8^{19} 2 K 22^{13} Je 21^2; with כִּפֶּר *atone* Ex 32^{30} Lv 9^7 $11^{6.11}$+, עָשָׂה (=offer) †Ez 45^{22}: see also 2 S 10^{12} 12^{16} Is 37^4 Je 7^{16} 11^{14} Ez 22^{30} Pr 20^{16} 27^{13} ψ 138^8 Jb 2^4 עוֹר בְּעַד עוֹר (v. עוֹר), 6^{22}. Almost=*for the sake of, on account of* Pr 6^{26} Je 11^{14} (but 𝔊 𝔖 𝔙 𝔗 and many MSS. בְּעֵת רָעָתָם, cf. v^{12} 15^{11}). Is 32^{14} hill and watchtower הָיָה בְעַד מְעָרוֹת are come to be *on behalf of* (i.e. take the place of, serve as) caves for ever: but use is singular, and בְּעַד is prob. only dittogr. from מער in מערות (so Gr).—With מִן, מִבַּעַד לְ׳ (cf. מִתַּחַת לְ׳, מִמַּעַל לְ׳): †Ct $4^{1.3}$ 6^7 thine eyes are doves מִבַּעַד לְצַמָּתֵךְ *from behind* thy veil. Cf. on בַּעַד Grätz[Monatsschrift, 1879, 49 ff.]

†[בָּעָה] **vb. inquire, cause to swell or** 1158
boil up (NH *id.*; Ar. بَغَى *seek, suppurate, swell;* Aram. בְּעָא, ܒܥܐ *seek*)—**Qal** *Impf.* 3 fs. תִּבְעֶה Is 64^1; 2 mpl. תִּבְעָיוּן Is 21^{12}; *Imv.* בְּעָיוּ Is 21^{12};—**1.** of rising desire, *seek, inquire*, abs., of inquiring of prophet Is $21^{12.12}$. **2.** *cause to boil up*, מַיִם תִּב׳־אֵשׁ Is 64^1 (but gloss Che). **Niph.** *Pf.* נִבְעוּ Ob ^{6} *searched out* (‖ נֶחְפְּשׂוּ); *Pt.* נִבְעֶה Is 30^{13} *swelling, swelling out* (of decaying wall; Di *swelling, enlarging*, of crack in wall).

בעז (*quick?* cf. Ar. بَغْزٌ *swiftness* (of horse)).

†בֹּעַז **n.pr.m.** (*quickness?*)—**1.** kinsman 1162
of Naomi, who married Ruth Ru $2^{1.3.4.5.8.11.}$

14.15.19.23 3$^{2.7}$ 4$^{1.1.5.8.9.13}$, also v$^{21.21}$ 1 Ch 2$^{11.12}$ (𝔊 Boos, Booζ). **2.** name of the left hand of two pillars set up before temple (cf. also יָכִין sub כון) 1 K 7^{21}=2 Ch 3^{17}; (mng. obscure; MT appar. ref. to **1**, cf. 𝔗 2 Ch 3^{17}; Thes supposes name of architect or donor; Ew perh. sons of Solomon, etc.; rd. possibly בְּעֹז *in strength*, 𝔊 2 Ch 3^{17} ἰσχύς; Th thinks יכין בעז a sentence, one word being engraved on each pillar, *he* (God) *establisheth in strength;* against him, however, Ke Be; Öt thinks an exclamation, *in strength!* expressing satisfaction of architect; Klo prop. for בעז, בַּעַל עֹז (cf. B 1 K 7^{21} Βαλαζ)).

1163 †[בָּעַט] **vb. kick** (so NH, Aram. בְּעַט, ܒܥܛ)—**Qal** *Impf.* וַיִּבְעַט Dt 32^{15}; 2 mpl. תִּבְעֲטוּ 1 Sa 2^{29};—*kick* (only fig. of refractory Israel) Dt 32^{15} (abs.); *kick at* (c. בְּ) 1 S 2^{29}.

1164 בְּעִי Jb 30^{24} v. עִי. p. 730

1166 †בָּעַל **vb. marry, rule over** (cf. Ar. بَعَلَ =*own, possess*, esp. a wife or concubine; Eth. በዐለ: *to be rich*, As. *bâlu, rule* COT^{Gloss}, Aram. בְּעַל *take possession of wife or concubine*)—**Qal** *Pf.* Mal 2^{11}+6 t.; *Impf.* יִבְעַל Is 62$^{5.5}$; *Pt.* sf. בֹּעֲלַיִךְ Is 54^{5}; pass. f. בְּעוּלָה Is 54^{1}+3 t.;—**1.** *marry* Gn 20^{3} (E) Dt 21^{13} 22^{22} 24^{1} Is 54$^{1.5}$ 62$^{4.5.5}$ Mal 2^{11}; sq. בְּ Je 3^{14} 31^{32} *be lord* (*husband*) *over.* **2.** *rule over* 1 Ch 4^{22} (sq. לְ) Is 26^{13}. **Niph.** *Impf.* תִּבָּעֵל Pr 30^{23} Is 62^{4} *be married.*

1167 †I. בַּעַל$_{166}$ **n.m. owner, lord** (Ph. בעל; Palm. *id. husband* Vog^{62} cf. Bae$^{\text{Rel 72 ff.}}$; As. *bêlu*$^{\text{l.c.}}$ Dl$^{\text{Gram. Gloss.}}$; Ar. بَعْلٌ *husband* etc., v. esp. Nö$^{\text{ZMG 1886, 174}}$, Sab. בעל CIS$^{\text{iv. 1, 2}}$)—Gn 20^{3}+92 t.; sf. בַּעְלִי Ho 2^{18}; בַּעְלָהּ Dt 24^{4}+5 t.; pl. בְּעָלִים Ju 2^{11}+17 t.; cstr. בַּעֲלֵי Gn 14^{13}+27 t.; sf. בְּעָלָיו Ex 21^{29}+14 t.; בְּעָלֶיהָ Jb 31^{39}+2 t.; בַּעְלֵיהֶן Est 1$^{17.20}$;—I. **1.** *owner* (oft. pl. c. sf. in sg. mng.): of ox Ex 21$^{28.29.29}$ 22$^{10.11.13.14}$ (E); ב׳ הבור of pit Ex 21$^{34.36}$ (E), of house Ex 22^{7} (E) Ju 19$^{22.23}$, debt Dt 15^{2}, the land Jb 31^{39}, the ass Is 1^{3}, goods Ec 5^{10}, riches Ec 5^{12}; ב׳ טוב one to whom good is due Pr 3^{27}, gain Pr 1^{19}; ב׳ שׂכל one having understanding Pr 16^{22}; ב׳ השחד receiver of the gift Pr 17^{8}. **2.** *husband* Gn 20^{3} Ex 21$^{3.22}$ (E) Dt 22^{22} 24^{4} 2 S 11^{26} Jo 1^{8} Pr 12^{4} 31$^{11.23.28}$ Est 1$^{17.20}$;
1180 בַּעְלִי Ho 2^{18} (*my Baal*, reference to the divine name used in the northern kingdom, here for the first time forbidden). **3.** *citizens, inhabi-*
1181 *tants:* בַּעֲלֵי of Jericho Jos 24^{11} (E), of the high places of Arnon Nu 21^{28} (E), of Shechem Ju 9^{2} +12 t., of the tower of Shechem Ju 9$^{46.47}$, of the city Ju 9^{51}, of Gibeah Ju 20^{5}, of Keilah 1 S 23$^{11.12}$, of Jabesh 2 S 21^{12}. **4.** *rulers, lords:* בַּעֲלֵי גוֹיִם Is 16^{8}. **5.** *n. of relation:* **a.** בַּעַל: ב׳ החלמות dreamer Gn 37^{19} (E); ב׳ דברים whosoever hath cases, complaints Ex 24^{14} (E); ב׳ שֵׂעָר an hairy man 2 K 1^{8}; ב׳ חמה wrathful Na 1^{2} Pr 29^{22}; ב׳ אף one given to anger Pr 22^{24}; ב׳ החכמה one having wisdom Ec 7^{12}; ב׳ משחית destroyer Pr 18^{9}; ב׳ כנף winged thing, bird Pr 1^{17} Ec 10^{20}; ב׳ נפשׁ one given to appetite Pr 23^{2}; ב׳ מזמות mischievous person Pr 24^{8}; ב׳ הלשון charmer Ec 10^{11}; ב׳ רשׁע one given to wickedness Ec 8^{8}; ב׳ פיפיות double-edged Is 41^{15}; ב׳ משפט adversary Is 50^{8}; ב׳ פקדת captain of the ward Je 37^{13}; ב׳ הקרנים two-horned Dn 8$^{6.20}$. **b.** בַּעֲלֵי: ב׳ בְּרִית confederates Gn 14^{13}; ב׳ חצים archers Gn 49^{23} (poet.); ב׳ הפרשים horsemen 2 S 1^{6}; ב׳ שׁבועה conspirators Ne 6^{18}; ב׳ אספות members of assemblies; or well-grouped sayings; or collectors (of wise sentences) Ec 12^{11}.—On 2 S 6^{2} v. II. בַּעֲלָה. (בַּעַל in Hex not J or P; בעל Lv 21^{4} 𝔊 ἐξάπινα = כבלע Nu 4^{20}: Di בְּאֵבֶל). Esp. II. *lord*, 1168
specif. as divine name, †**Baal**. **1.** *without article:* במות בעל Nu 22^{41} (poet. Balaam); בעל פעור Nu 25$^{3.5}$ (E) Dt 4^{3} (vid. below). This divine name is not used elsewhere in Hex. It probably originated from the sense of divine ownership, rather than sovereignty (RS$^{\text{Sem 92}}$). It seems to have been used in Northern Israel = אדון in the South. It was the special name of the God of the Canaanites, Philistines, etc., = Babylonian בֵּל, cf. Schr$^{\text{SK 1874, 335 ff.}}$ In later times scribes substituted בֹּשֶׁת, in n.pr. (ירבעל = ירבשׁת, אשׁבעל = אשׁבשׁת, vid. בֹּשֶׁת, Gei$^{\text{ZMG 1862, 728 ff.}}$), & also in the text for בעל Ho 9^{10} Je 11^{13} (hence ἡ βάαλ Je 2^{23} 7^{9} 11$^{13.17}$ 19^{5} Ho 2^{10} 13^{1}+, Rom 11^{4}, see Di$^{\text{Baal mit d. weib. Artikel, MBA 1881, June 16}}$ Dr 2 S 4^{4}). **2.** c. *art.*: הַבַּעַל Ju 2^{13} 6$^{25.28.30.31.32}$ 1 K 16$^{31.32.32}$ 18$^{19.21.22.25.26.26.40}$ 19^{18} 22^{54} 2 K 3^{2} 10$^{18.19.19.20.21.21.21.22.23.23.23.25.26.27.27.28}$ 11$^{18.18}$ 17^{16} 21^{3} 23$^{4.5}$ 2 Ch 23$^{17.17}$ Je 2^{8} 7^{9} 11$^{13.17}$ 12^{16} 19$^{5.5}$ 28$^{13.27}$ 32$^{29.35}$ Ho 2^{10} 13^{1} Zp 1^{4}. **3.** הַבְּעָלִים *emphatic pl.* (cf. האדונים, האלהים) *the great lord, the sovereign owner* Ju 2^{11} 3^{7} 8^{33} 10$^{6.10}$ 1 S 7^{4} 12^{10} 1 K 18^{18} 2 Ch 17^{3} 24^{7} 28^{2} 33^{3} 34^{4} Je 2^{23} 9^{13} Ho 2$^{15.19}$ 11^{2} (or local special Ba'als, vid. Dr$^{\text{Sm. p. 50}}$; pillars
of Baal MV). **4.** c. *attrib.*: בַּעַל בְּרִית *Lord of* 1170
covenant Ju 8^{33} 9^{4} (cf. אל ברית 9^{46}; Nö$^{\text{ZMG 1888, 478}}$);
ב׳ זְבוּב *Lord of flies* 2 K 1$^{2.3.6.16}$, Philistine god, 1176
𝔊 Βααλ μυῖαν (Beelzebub, Mt 12^{24}) cf. Bae$^{\text{Rel 25}}$.

†II. בַּ֫עַל **1. n.pr.loc.** city in the tribe of 1167
Simeon 1 Ch 4^{33}=בַּעֲלַת בְּאֵר. **2. n.pr.m. a.** a 1192
Reubenite 1 Ch 5^{5}; **b.** a Gibeonite 1 Ch 8^{30} 9^{36}.

1171 †בַּ֫עַל גָּד **n.pr.loc.** Jos 11^{17} 12^{7} 13^{5} (D), where Baal was worshipped as Gad, god of fortune, a city in the בִּקְעָה of Lebanon, under Mt. Hermon; either mod. *Bâniâs*, Gk. Paneas, NT Caesarea Philippi, where a grotto of Pan took the place of the ancient worship of Gad, Rob$^{\text{BR iii. 410}}$ Tristr$^{\text{Tpg 271}}$; or *Ḥâsbêyâ* Bd$^{\text{Pal 297}}$ Di; possibly = בעל חרמון cf. Thes Rob$^{\text{BR iii. 409}}$.

1174 †בַּ֫עַל הָמוֹן **n.pr.loc.** (*possessor of abundance;* or is ׳ב here n.pr. divin.?) Ct 8^{11}.

1177 †בַּ֫עַל חָנָן **n.pr.m.** (*Baal is gracious*, cf. Ph. חנבעל & (in As.) *Baalḫanunu*) **1.** king of Edom Gn $36^{38.39}$ 1 Ch $1^{49.50}$. **2.** a Gederite 1 Ch 27^{28}.

1178 †בַּ֫עַל חָצוֹר **n.pr.loc.** (*possessor of a court;* or ׳ב n.pr. divin.?) city on the border of Ephraim and Benjamin 2 S 13^{23}, prob. = חצור Ne 11^{33}; ?mod. *Tell ʿAsûr* (with ע) Rob$^{\text{BR ii. 264}}$ doubtfully; cf. Survey$^{\text{ii. 298}}$ (after de Saulcy).

1179 †בַּ֫עַל חֶרְמוֹן **n.pr.loc.** Ju 3^{3} 1 Ch 5^{23}, a city so named as seat of the worship of Baal. 'The crest of Hermon is strewn with ruins and the foundations of a circular temple of large hewn stones,' Tristr^{Tpg}, cf. on sacredness, Euseb. Lag$^{\text{Onom 217}}$: possibly = בעל גד q.v.

1186 †בַּ֫עַל מְעוֹן **n.pr.loc.** Nu 32^{38} 1 Ch 5^{8} Ez 25^{9} = בית בעל מעון Jos 13^{17} (cf. MI^{30}) = *Maʿîn* Tristr$^{\text{Moab 316}}$ Bd$^{\text{Pal 192}}$ Survey$^{\text{EP 176}}$.

1187 †בַּ֫עַל פְּעוֹר **n.pr.m.** Nu $25^{3.5}$ Dt $4^{3.3}$ ψ 106^{28} Ho 9^{10}, *Baal of Peor* (VB) i.e. worshipped at פְּעוֹר q.v.; or *Baal-P.* (whence *Peor* as n.pr.loc.); cf. Di Nu 25^{3} Baud$^{\text{Stud. ii. 233}}$ Bae$^{\text{Rel 14, 210}}$.

1188 †בַּ֫עַל פְּרָצִים **n.pr.loc.** (*possessor of breaches; or Baal of Peraṣim?*) where David defeated Philist. 2 S $5^{20.20}$ 1 Ch $14^{11.11}$; site unknown.

1189 †בַּ֫עַל צְפוֹן **n.pr.loc.** Ex $14^{2.9}$ Nu 33^{7}, near Red Sea in Egypt, prob. Mt. *ʿAtâka*, Eb$^{\text{GS 524}}$.

1190 †בַּ֫עַל שָׁלִשָׁה **n.pr.loc.** 2 K 4^{42}, place in Ephraim near Gilgal; = Βαιθσαρισαθ Lag$^{\text{Onom 239, 2nd ed. 250}}$ c. 15 m. fr. Diospolis. (? ׳ב n.pr. divin.)

1193 †בַּ֫עַל תָּמָר **n.pr.loc.** (*possessor of palms; or Baal of Tamar?*) Ju 20^{33}, near Gibeah.

1172 †I. [בַּעֲלָה] **n.f.** **1.** *mistress*, בַּעֲלַת הַבַּיִת mistress of the house 1 K 17^{17}. **2.** n. rel. ׳ב אוב necromancer 1 S $28^{7.7}$; ׳ב כשפים sorceress, Na 3^{4}.

1173 †II. בַּעֲלָה **n.pr.loc.** Jos $15^{9.10.11.29}$ 1 Ch 13^{6} = קִרְיַת בַּעַל Jos 15^{60} 18^{14} (*city of Baal*, from a high
1184 place of Baal there) = בַּעֲלֵי יְהוּדָה 2 S 6^{2} (We Dr read בעל; י added by dittogr.; so-called as seat of Baal-worship in Judah, in distinct. fr. like places elsewhere) = קִרְיַת יְעָרִים Jos 9^{17} v. 15^{9} 1 Ch 13^{6}; a city of Judah; ?*Kirjat el ʿEnab* Rob$^{\text{BR ii. 11}}$ Tristr^{Tpg}.

†בַּעֲלַת **n.pr.loc.** Jos 19^{44} 1 K 9^{18} 2 Ch 8^{6}, 1191
a city of Dan, possibly *Belʿaîn* Survey$^{\text{ii. 296}}$.

†בְּעָלוֹת **n.pr.loc.** pl. Jos 15^{24} 1 K 4^{16}, a city 1175
in the south of Judah, possibly the same as II. בַּעַל.

†בַּעֲלַת בְּאֵר **n.pr.loc.** (*mistress of a well*) 1192
= *Ramath Negeb* Jos 19^{8}, a city of Simeon = II. בַּעַל; mod. *Kurnub* acc. to Tristr^{Tpg} but dub.

†בְּעֶלְיָדָע **n.pr.m.** (*Baal knows*) son of 1182
David 1 Ch 14^{7}, the original name changed to אלידע 2 S 5^{16} (cf. We Dr).

†בְּעַלְיָה **n.pr.m.** (*Yah is lord*) one of 1183
David's heroes 1 Ch 12^{5}.

†בֵּל **n.pr.m.** a chief Babylonian deity (Bab. 1078
Bêlu = בַּעַל, *lord; Bêl* regarded as older form than בַּעַל by Hpt$^{\text{Hbr. i. 178; BAS i. 17}}$) = Merodach (cf. מרדך), tutelary god of Babylon (to be distinguished from older *Bêlu*, one of ancient Babylonian triad) Je 50^{2} (‖ מְרֹדָךְ) 51^{44}; Is 46^{1} (‖ נְבוֹ)—both writers of Babylonian period;—on Bel v. COT Gn 11^{4} Ju 2^{11}; Say$^{\text{Rel. Bab. 103, 110}}$ Jen $^{\text{Kosmologie 24, 134, 307, 391}}$.

†בֵּלְאשַׁצַּר **n.pr.m.** (*Bêl-šar-uṣur, Bel,* 1112
protect the king COT Dn 5^{1}) Dn 8^{1}; represented as king of Babylon, successor, and appar. son of Nebuchadrezzar ($5^{1.2.11}$ etc.); in cuneif. inscr. known only as prince, son of Nabonidus (last Shemitic king of Babylon), v. COT l.c.

†בְּעָלִיס **n.pr.m.** (Gr$^{\text{Monatsschrift, 1885, 471}}$ rds. 1185
בַּעֲלִים; = בֶּן־עֲלִים *son of delight?* cf. sub בְּ) king of Ammonites Je 40^{14} (Codd. & Jos$^{\text{Ant. x. 9, 2}}$ rd. בעלים).

†בְּעֹן v. בית בעל מעון sub בית. p. 111 1194

†בַּעֲנָא **n.pr.m.** (?בֶּן־עָנָה *son of distress*)— 1195
1. name of two officers of Solomon, **a.** 1 K 4^{12}; **b.** v^{16}. **2.** father (ancestor) of an Israelite of Nehemiah's time Ne 3^{4} cf. foll.

†בַּעֲנָה **n.pr.m.** (?*id.*)—**1.** a Benjamite, one 1196
of the murderers of Ishbosheth 2 S $4^{2.5.6.9}$. **2.** father of one of David's heroes 2 S 23^{29} = 1 Ch 11^{30}. **3.** head of a family of returning exiles Ezr 2^{2} = Ne 7^{7}; perh. also = בַּעֲנָא Ne 3^{4}. **4.** a chief of the people Ne 10^{28}.

†I. [בָּעַר] **vb. burn, consume** (𝔗 בְּעַר *burn;* 1197
ܒܥܰܪ *seek out, collect, glean;* this apparently

earlier mng.)—**Qal** *Pf.* 3 fs. בָּֽעֲרָה Nu 11^{3} + 2 t., וּבָֽעֲרָה consec. Is 10^{17} + 3 t., בָּֽעֲרוּ Ju 15^{14} + 2 t. + 2 S 22^{13} (but cf. De on ψ 18), וּבָֽעֲרוּ consec. Is 1^{31}; *Impf.* יִבְעַר Ex 3^{3} ψ 2^{12}, etc.; *Pt.* בֹּעֵר Ex 3^{2} + 6 t., בֹּעֲרָה Is 34^{9}, בּוֹעֵרָה Ho 7^{4}, בֹּעֵרָה Is 30^{33}, בֹּעֶרֶת Je 20^{9}, בֹּעֲרוֹת Ez 1^{13};—*burn*, **1.** (intr.) specif. *begin to burn, be kindled* ψ 18^{8} sq. מִן (subj. גֶּחָלִים) = 2 S 22^{9} (in v^{13} text. error cf. supr.), ψ 106^{18} (subj. אֵשׁ); fig. ψ 2^{12} (subj. אַפּוֹ) cf. Je 44^{6} (subj. חֵמָה); Is 30^{33} (c. בְּ, subj. נִשְׁמַת י׳), ψ 39^{4} (subj. אֵשׁ fig. of grief, distress) cf. Je 20^{9}. **2.** *be burning, burn*, Ju 15^{14} (subj. פִּשְׁתִּים, c. בָּאֵשׁ), Ex 3^{2} (הסנה, c. בָּאֵשׁ), v^{3} (subj. *id.*); Dt 4^{11} 5^{20} 9^{15} (all subj. הר, c. בָּאֵשׁ), cf. Is 34^{9} (זֶפֶת בערה), fig. of destruction Is 1^{31} (subj. חָסֹן & פֹּעֲלוֹ); of torch לַפִּיד Is 62^{1}; of oven תַּנּוּר Ho 7$^{4.6}$ (i.e. heated by fire within it). **3.** trans. *burn, consume* (subj. אשׁ, להבה etc., sq. בְּ) Nu 11$^{1.3}$ (אשׁ י׳), Jb 1^{16} (אשׁ אלהים); in simile Ez 1^{33} (נחלי אשׁ י׳), ψ 83^{15} (only here trans. c. acc.; should תבער be pointed as Pi.?); fig. (subj. wrath of י׳) Is 42^{25} cf. La 2^{5} (subj. fire = fiery trial) Is 43^{2}. **4.** act. but abs., fig., subj. wrath of י׳ Je 4^{4} 7^{20} 21^{12} ψ 89^{47} cf. Is 10^{17} ψ 79^{5} Is 30^{27} (שֵׁם י׳ . . . בֹּעֵר אַפּוֹ) Mal 3^{19} (היום בא); of human anger Est 1^{12}; subj. wickedness Is 9^{17}. **Pi.** *Pf.* בִּעֵר 1 K 22^{47} 2 K 23^{24}, וּבִעֵר consec. Lv 6^{5}, בִּעַרְתָּ 2 Ch 19^{3}, וּבִעַרְתָּ Dt 13^{6} + 9 t. in Dt; וּבִעֲרוּ cons. Ez 39$^{9.9}$ (9^{a} del. Co after Vrss), etc.; *Impf.* יְבַעֵר 1 K 14^{10}; 2 ms. תְּבַעֵר Dt 21^{9}, יְבַעֲרוּ Ez 39^{10}; 2 mpl. תְּבַעֲרוּ Ex 35^{3}, וּנְבַעֲרָה subord. Ju 20^{13}; *Pt.* מְבַעֲרִים Je 7^{18};—**1.** *kindle*, lit. c. acc. אשׁ Ex 35^{3} Je 7^{18} cf. Ez 39^{9} (v. supr.) v^{10}; fig. of י׳ sending destruction Ez 21^{4} cf. of human schemes Is 50^{11}; *light*, obj. lamps in temple 2 Ch 4^{20} cf. 13^{11}. **2.** *burn*, lit. c. acc. עֵצִים Lv 6^{5}, גָּלָל *dung* 1 K 14^{10}; abs. Is 44^{15} cf. 40^{16} Ne 10^{35}. **3.** fig. *consume*, utterly remove, partic. of evil and guilt, c. acc., esp. in Deuteronomic phrase (מישׂראל) ובערת הרע מקרבך Dt 13^{6} 17$^{7.12}$ 19$^{13.19}$ 21^{21} cf. v^{9} 22$^{21.22.24}$ 24^{7}, v. also Ju 20^{13}; further, 1 K 22^{47} 2 K 23^{24} 2 Ch 19^{3}; also of devoted (tabooed) things Dt 26$^{13.14}$; of persons (*exterminate*) 2 S 4^{11}; sq. אחרי pregn. 1 K 14^{10} 21^{21}; = devour, devastate, greedily enjoy the fruits of, Is 3^{14}; abs. היה לְבָעֵר *be for destruction, be destroyed* Nu 24^{22} Is 5^{5} 6^{13}; cf. רוּחַ בָּעֵר Is 4^{4}. **Pu.** *Pt.* מְבֹעֶרֶת Je 36^{22};—*burn* (i.e. be supplied with fire), of fire-jar, הָאָח. **Hiph.** *Pf.* וְהִבְעַרְתִּי Na 2^{14}; *Impf.* וַיַּבְעֵר Ju 15^{5} 2 Ch 28^{3}, וַיַּבְעֶר־ Ju 15^{5}; תַּבְעִיר Ez 5^{2}; *Pt.* מַבְעִיר 1 K 16^{3}, מַבְעִר Ex 22^{5};—**1.** *kindle* (c. acc. cogn.) Ex 22^{5}, cf. Ju 15^{5} ויב׳ אשׁ בלפידים *caused fire to burn among the brands.* **2.** *burn up*, c. acc. Ju 15^{5} 2 Ch 28^{3} (sacrifice of children בָּאֵשׁ) Ez 5^{2} (בָּאוּר but cf. Co) Na 2^{14} (בעשׁן). **3.** *consume=destroy* (cf. Pi.) 1 K 16^{3} (sq. אַחֲרֵי).

† בְּעֵרָה **n.f.** burning, only הַבּ׳ as acc. 1200
cogn. with הִבְעִיר Ex 22^{5}.

† תַּבְעֵרָה **n.pr.loc.** in the wilderness (*burn-* 8407
ing, cf. Nu 11^{3}) Nu 11^{3} Dt 9^{22}.

† [בְּעִיר] **n.m.** $^{Ex 22,4}$ **beasts, cattle, coll.** (NH 1165
id., Aram. *id.*, ܒܥܝܪܐ, Eth. ቡዐራዊ: etc., Sab. בער DHM $^{ZMG 1876, 674; 1883, 329}$; Ar. بَعِيرٌ of *camel;* also *ass*, etc., cf. Lane ^{227a}; connexion with above √ obscure)—sf. בְּעִירֹה Ex 22^{4}, בְּעִירֵנוּ Nu 20^{4}, בְּעִירְכֶם Gn 45^{17}, בְּעִירָם Nu 20^{8} + 2 t.;—*beasts* of burden Gn 45^{17} (i.e. asses 44$^{3.13}$); elsewhere general, *cattle* Ex 22^{4} Nu 20$^{4.8.11}$ ψ 78^{48}.

† II. [בָּעַר] **vb.denom.** be brutish—**Qal** 1197
Impf. יִבְעֲרוּ Je 10^{8} (|| יכסלו) *be stupid, dull-hearted, unreceptive;* cf. Pt. pl. בֹּעֲרִים ψ 94^{8} (|| כסילים); of *inhuman, cruel, barbarous* men Ez 21^{36}. **Niph.** *Pf.* נִבְעַר Je 10^{14} 51^{17}, נִבְעֲרוּ Je 10^{21}; *Pt.* נִבְעָרָה Is 19^{11};—*brutish, stupid* Is 19^{11} (|| אויל, עצה); *dull-hearted*, ignorant of God Je 10$^{14.21}$ 51^{17}. **Pi.** *Pf.* וּבִעֵר consec. Ex 22^{4} *feed, graze* (בשׂדה אחר). **Hiph.** *Impf.* יַבְעֶר־ Ex 22^{4} *cause to be grazed over*, sq. שׂדה.

† בַּעַר **n.m.** brutishness (only poet.)—abs. 1198
ב׳ ψ 49^{11} + 3 t., בָּעַר Pr 12^{1};—in combination, אִישׁ־ב׳ *brutish man* ψ 92^{7} (|| כסיל); elsewhere ב׳ alone in same sense (concrete) ψ 49^{11} (|| *id.*), & as pred. = adj., ψ 73^{22} Pr 12^{1} 30^{2}.

† בַּעֲרָא **n.pr.f.** wife of a Benjamite 1 Ch 8^{8}. 1199

† בְּעוֹר **n.pr.m.** (*a burning;* 𝔗 *torch*)—**1.** 1160
father of Balaam Nu 22^{5} 31^{8} Dt 23^{5} Jos 13^{22} 24^{9} Mi 6^{5}; בְּעֹר Nu 24$^{3.15}$ (בנו ב׳). **2.** father of בֶּלַע, a king of Edom Gn 36^{32} = 1 Ch 1^{43}.

† בַּעֲשֵׂיָה **n.pr.m.** (? = מַעֲשֵׂיָה; so Thes; cf. 1202
Dr$^{Sm. lxviii}$) a Levite 1 Ch 6^{25};—cf. מַעֲשֵׂיָה(וּ) sub עשׂה.

בַּעְשָׁא **n.pr.m.** a king of Israel 1 K 15$^{16.17.19}$ 1201
+ 18 t. 1 K 15–16 + 21^{22} 2 K 9^{9} 2 Ch 16$^{1.3.5.6}$ Je 41^{9}.

† בְּעֶשְׁתְּרָה **n.pr.loc.** (? = בֵּית עשׁתרה = 1203
house of Ashtoreth, cf. sub בית) a Levitical city in Manasseh Jos 21^{27}; = עַשְׁתָּרוֹת 1 Ch 6^{56}

† [בָּעַת] **vb.** fall upon, startle, terrify 1204
(Ar. بَغَتَ *come* or *happen suddenly*, NH בָּעַת

Hiph. *startle;* so Aram. בְּעֵת Pa. ܒܥܬ Aph.)—**Niph.** (late prose) *Pf.* נִבְעַת 1 Ch 21^{30}, נִבְעָת Est 7^{6}; נִבְעַ֫תִּי Dn 8^{17};—*be terrified,* abs. Dn 8^{17}; c. מפני 1 Ch 21^{30} Est 7^{6}. **Pi.** (mostly poet.) *Pf.* 3 fs. sf. בִּעֲתַ֫תְנִי Is 21^{4}, וּבִעֲתַ֫תּוּ 1 S 16^{14}; 3 pl. sf. בִּעֲתֻהוּ Jb 18^{11}; *Impf.* 3 fs. תְּבַעֵת Jb 13^{11}; sf. תְּבַעֲתַ֫נִי Jb 9^{34} 13^{21}, תְּבַעֲתֶ֫ךָּ Jb 33^{7}; 2 ms. sf. תְּבַעֲתַ֫נִּי Jb 7^{14}; 3 mpl. sf. יְבַעֲתוּנִי ψ 18^{5} = יְבַעֲתֻ֫נִי 2 S 22^{5}, יְבַעֲתֻ֫הוּ Jb 3^{5} 15^{24};—**1.** *fall upon* 1 S 16$^{14.15}$ (only here in prose); *overwhelm* Jb 3^{5} (cf. לקח v^{6}) 9^{34} 13^{11} (|| פחד נפל על) v^{21} (cf. ||) 15^{24} (|| תקף) 18^{11} (|| הפיץ) 33^{7} (|| כבד על) Is 21^{4}; *assail* ψ 18^{5} = 2 S 22^{5}. **2.** *terrify* Jb 7^{14} (|| חתת).

1205 †בְּעָתָה **n.f.** **terror, dismay** Je 8^{15} = 14^{19}.

1161 †[בִּעוּתִים] **n.m.pl.** **terrors, alarms,** occasioned by God בִּעוּתֵי אֱלוֹהַּ Jb 6^{4} (|| חִצֵּי שַׁדַּי); בִּעוּתֶ֫יךָ ψ 88^{17} (|| חֲרוֹנֶ֫יךָ).

1206 בֹּץ v. בצץ. p. 130

1209 †בֵּצָ֑י **n.pr.m.** Ne 10^{19} one of the chiefs of the people; Ezr 2^{17} Ne 7^{23} בְּנֵי ב׳ i.e. a family.

בצל (*strip, strip off,* Eth. በጸለ: I. 2; Ar. بَصَّلَ, appar. denom.)

1211 †[בָּצָל] **n.m.** **onion** (NH בָּצָל or בֶּ֫צֶל, Ar. بَصَلٌ, Eth. በጽል: Aram. בּוּצְלָא, ܒܘܨܠܐ)—בְּצָלִים Nu 11^{5} (אֶת הַקִּשֻּׁאִים וְאֵת הָאֲבַטִּחִים וְאֶת־הֶחָצִיר וְאֶת־הַבּ׳ וְאֶת־הַשּׁוּמִים).

1212 †בְּצַלְאֵל **n.pr.m.** (*in the shadow (protection) of Ēl;* cf. cuneif. *Ṣil-Bêl,* a king of Gaza, COT Jos 11^{22})—**1.** a skilled artisan of tribe of Judah Ex 31^{2} 35^{30} 36$^{1.2}$ 37^{1} 38^{22} (all P) 1 Ch 2^{20} 2 Ch 1^{5}. **2.** an Israelite Ezr 10^{30}.

1213 †בַּצְלוּת **n.pr.m.** (*stripping*)—head of Isr. fam. at return from exile; בני־ב׳ Ezr 2^{52} = Ne 7^{54} Kt; בַּצְלִית Ne 7^{54} Qr.

1214 †[בָּצַע] **vb.** **cut off, break off, gain by violence** (so NH, Ar. بَضَعَ, Eth. በፀዐ: Aram. בְּצַע)—**Qal** *Impf.* יִבְצַע Jb 27^{8}, יְבַצֵּ֑עוּ Jo 2^{8}; *Imv.* sf. בְּצָעַם בְּרֹאשׁ Am 9^{1}; *Inf.* בְּצֹעַ Ez 22^{27}; *Pt.* בּוֹצֵעַ Pr 15^{27} Je 6^{13}, בֹּצֵעַ ψ 10^{3} + 3 t.;—*cut off, break off* (c. acc. capitals of pillars) Am 9^{1} (but Lag$^{\text{Prov. v, vi}}$ בֹּזְעָם = בְּצָעַם Hb 3^{12} *in wrath*); so fig. Jb 27^{8} *when Eloah cutteth off, draweth out, his soul;* obj. om. *their course,* i.e. stop Jo 2^{8} (cf. Hi-St); usually *gain by violence* or in gen. *wrongfully* Ez 22^{27}; *Pt.* abs. ψ 10^{3} = *greedy getter, robber;* & c. acc. cogn. בֶּ֫צַע Pr 1^{19} 15^{27} Je 6^{13} 8^{10} Hb 2^{9}. **Pi.** *Pf.* בִּצַּע La 2^{17}; *Impf.* יְבַצַּע Is 10^{12}; sf. יְבַצְּעֵנִי Is 38^{12} Jb 6^{9}; 2 fs. וַתְּבַצְּעִי Ez 22^{12}; 3 fpl. תְּבַצַּ֫עְנָה Zc 4^{9};—*cut off, (dis)sever* (i.e. from life) Jb 6^{9} cf. Is 10^{19} (מִדַּלָּה); = *finish, complete* Is 10^{12} Zc 4^{9}; *accomplish* (= carry out, fulfil) La 2^{17} (obj. אמרתו); *violently make gain of,* obj. pers. Ez 22^{12} (instr. בעשׁק).

†בֶּ֫צַע **n.m.** **gain made by violence, unjust** 1215
gain, profit—בֶּ֫צַע Gn 37^{26} + 7 t. (cstr. Ju 5^{19} +); בָּ֑צַע Ex 18^{21} + 7 t.; sf. בִּצְעֵךְ Je 22^{17}; בִּצְעֵךְ Je 51^{13} Ez 22^{13}; בִּצְעוֹ Is 56^{11} 57^{17}; בִּצְעָם Ez 33^{31} Mi 4^{13};—*gain made by violence* (nearly = plunder) Ju 5^{19} Mi 4^{13}; more generally, *unjust gain* Ex 18^{21} 1 S 8^{3} ψ 119^{36} Pr 28^{16} Is 33^{15} 56^{11} 57^{17} Je 22^{17} 51^{13} Ez 22^{13} 33^{31}; as acc. cogn. c. בצע Pr 1^{19} 15^{27} Je 6^{13} 8^{10} Ez 22^{27} Hb 2^{9}; *profit* (with selfish suggestion) מה־ב׳ Gn 37^{26} Mal 3^{14} cf. ψ 30^{10} Jb 22^{3}.

†בצענים, בְּצַעֲנַנִּים, perh. **n.pr.loc.** in 6814
Naphtali: אֵלוֹן ב׳ Jos 19^{33} Ju 4^{11}. Cf. צענים. p. 858

בצץ (? cf. Ar. بَضَّ *be* بَضٌّ, i.e. *one soft, tender, impressible* in body, etc.)

†בֹּץ **n.[m.]** **mire** Je 38^{22}. 1206

†בִּצָּה **n.f.** **swamp,** Jb 8^{11} as place where 1207
rushes grow, cf. 40^{21}; בִּצֹּאתָו (Co ובצותיו) pl. sf. Ez 47^{11} (|| וּגְבָאָיו).

†בּוֹצֵץ **n.pr.loc.** a rock by Michmash 1 S 949
14^{4};—Βωσης Lag $^{\text{Onom. 238, 2nd ed. 250}}$.

†בָּצֵק **vb.** swell—**Qal** *Pf.* 3 fs. בָּצֵ֑קָה Dt 8^{4}; 1216
3 pl. בָּצֵ֑קוּ Ne 9^{21};—*swell,* or *receive swellings, blisters,* of foot, Di Dt 8^{4}, Ry Ne 9^{21}.

†בָּצֵק **n.[m.]** **dough**—בָּצֵק Ex 12^{39} + 4 t.; 1217
sf. בְּצֵקוֹ Ex 12^{34};—*dough,* not fermented Ex 12$^{34.39}$ (E); no restriction 2 S 13^{8} Ho 7^{4} Je 7^{18}.

†בָּצְקַת **n.pr.loc.** (?cf. Ar. بَصْقَةٌ an elevated 1218
region covered with volcanic stones) city of Judah toward Philistines, בָּצְקַת Jos 15^{39}; בָּצְקַ֑ת 2 K 22^{1} (home of Josiah's mother).

†[בָּצַר] **vb.** **cut off, make inaccessible** 1219
(esp. by fortifying), **enclose** (NH *id.,* Aram. בְּצַר, ܒܨܪ (Pa. *diminish, subtract*), perh. cf. Ar. بُصْرٌ *side, edge,* بِصْرٌ, etc., *rough stone,* أَرْضٌ بَصِرَةٌ *land in wh. are sharp stones* (cf. Lane))—**Qal** *Impf.* יִבְצֹר ψ 76^{13}; 2 ms. תִּבְצֹר Lv 25^{5} Dt 24^{21}, וַיִּבְצְרוּ Ju 9^{27}, תִּבְצְרוּ Lv 25^{11}; *Pt.* act. בּוֹצֵר Je 6^{9}, בֹּצְרִים Je 49^{9} Ob ^{5}; pass. m. בָּצוּר Zc 11^{2} Kt (Qr בָּצִיר), f. בְּצוּרָה Is 2^{15} + 3 t. + Ez 21^{25} v. infr.; pl. f. בְּצוּרוֹת Ez 36^{35}, בְּצֻרוֹת Nu 13^{28} + 14 t., בְּצוּרֹת Dt 1^{28} Ne 9^{25}, בְּצֻרֹת Dt 3^{5} 9^{1};—*cut off,* grape-clusters, ענבים Lv 25^{5}, cf. v^{11} (obj. נזיר), Dt 24^{21} Ju 9^{27} (obj.

in both, כרם); hence Pt. act. *grape-gathering, -gatherer* Je 6[9] 49[9] Ob[5]; fig. *cut off* (= take away) ψ 76[13] (obj. רוח נגידים); most often Pt. pass. *cut off, made inaccessible,* De Is 2[15] = *fortified,* always f.; generally adj. c. עיר, ערים; Nu 13[28] Dt 1[28] 3[5] 9[1] Jos 14[12] 2 S 20[6] 2 K 18[13] = Is 36[1] 2 K 19[25] = Is 37[26] 2 Ch 17[2] 19[5] 32[1] 33[14] Ne 9[25] Is 25[2] 27[10] Ez 36[35] Ho 8[14] Zp 1[16]; rarely c. חומה Dt 28[52] Is 2[15] Je 15[20]; יער הב׳ Zc 11[2] (rd. Kt); once, subst. of *secrets, mysteries* (= unattainable things) Je 33[3];—ב׳ Ez 21[25] 𝔊 Sm Co בְּתוֹכָהּ, doubtless right. **Niph.** *Impf.* יִבָּצֵר *be withheld* Gn 11[6] (מֵהֶם), Jb 42[2] (מִמְּךָ). **Pi.** *Impf.* 3 fs. תְּבַצֵּר Je 51[53] *fortify;* so *Inf.* לְבַצֵּר Is 22[10].

1220, 1222 †I. [בֶּ֫צֶר] **n.[m.]** precious ore (AW[105] Thes), > **gold, ring-gold** Hoffm[ZA 1887, 48 f. Hiob 70] (AW Thes *ore* as *that broken off;* Hoffm comp. Ar. بَطْرٌ *ring,* Heb. בִּצָּרָה *enclosure,* Talm. בטרא *finger-measure,* etc.; a √ II. בצר must then be assumed, = بطر)—בֶּ֫צֶר Jb 22[24] (|| אוֹפִיר q.v.); בְּצָרֶיךָ v[25] (|| כֶּסֶף) possibly also בִּצְרֵי כָ֫סֶף ψ 68[31] for MT בְּרַצֵּי־כ׳, cf. Che[crit. n.] Ne[JBL, 1891, 151].

1221 †II. בֶּ֫צֶר (*fortress*)—**1. n.pr.loc.** city in Reuben (MI בצר) Dt 4[43] Jos 20[8] 1 Ch 6[63]. **2. n.pr.m.** a descendant of Asher 1 Ch 7[37].

1223 †I. בָּצְרָה **n.f.** enclosure, i.e. (sheep-)fold, צאן ב׳ Mi 2[12].

1224 †II. בָּצְרָה **n.pr.loc. 1.** city of Edom (*fortress;* (v. Palm. n.pr.loc. בצרא Vog[No. 22] 𝔊 Βο-σ(σ)ορρα; cf. Βοσορ; Lag[Onom. Sacr. 102, 232, 2nd ed. 137, 247] = Βοστρα) Gn 36[33] = 1 Ch 1[44] Is 34[6] 63[1] (in both || (ארץ) אדום) Je 49[13.22] Am 1[12]. **2.** of Moab Je 48[24], prob. = II. בֶּצֶר **1**;—on Mi 2[12] cf. foregoing.

1225 †בִּצָּרוֹן **n.[m.]** stronghold, לַבִּ׳ Zc 9[12].

1226 †בַּצֹּ֫רֶת **n.f.** dearth (cf. foll.), שְׁנַת בּ׳ Je 17[8].

1226 †בַּצָּרָה **n.f.** dearth, destitution (i.e. *diminution,* cf. ܒܨܝܪܘܬܐ PS[572]; v. also vb. בצר 𝔗 Pr 14[28] *people reduced*)—*dearth* (= בצרת) עִתּוֹת בּ׳ ψ 9[10] 10[1]; pl. בַּצָּרוֹת Je 14[1].

1210 †בָּצִיר **n.m.**[Lv 26, 5] vintage (cf. בָּצַר)—בָּצִיר
1208 Lv 26[5] + 4 t. + Zc 11[2] Qr (but rd. בצור Kt); cstr. בְּצִיר Ju 8[2]; sf. בְּצִירֵךְ Je 48[32];—*vintage,* lit. Lv 26[5.5] Ju 8[2] Is 32[10] Je 48[32]; in simile Is 24[13] Mi 7[1]; Zc 11[2] rd. בצור (Kt) and cf. sub בָּצַר.

4013 †מִבְצָר **n.m.**[Is 17, 3] fortification—מִבְצָר Nu 32[71] + 18 t.; cstr. מִבְצַר Jos 19[29] + 2 t.; pl. מִבְצָרִים Nu 13[19] Dn 11[24]; מִבְצָרוֹת Dn 11[15]; מִבְצְרֵי La 2[2] Dn 11[39]; sf. מִבְצָרֶיךָ Ho 10[14] + 2 t.; מִבְצָרַיִךְ Na 3[12]; מִבְצָרֶיהָ v[14] Je 48[18]; מִבְצָרָיו ψ 89[41] La 2[5]; מִבְצָרֶיהָ Is 34[13]; מִבְצְרֵיהֶם 2 K 8[12];—*fortification,* esp. in phrase עיר (ערי) מ׳ (המ׳) = *fortified city* Nu 32[17.36] Jos 10[20] 19[29.35] 1 S 6[18] 2 K 3[19] 10[2] 17[9] 18[8] Je 4[5] 5[17] 8[14] 34[7] ψ 108[11] (עיר מ׳ = עִיר מָצוֹר ψ 60[11]), 2 Ch 17[19] Dn 11[15] (מ׳ in this connexion sing. exc. Je 5[17] & Dn 11[15] (מבצרות)); Je 1[18] fig. of prophet, so without עיר Je 6[27]; *fortress, stronghold,* lit. without עיר etc. Nu 13[19] 2 K 8[12] Je 48[18] Is 17[3] 25[12] (מ׳ משגב חומתיך) 34[13] (|| ארמנת), La 2[2.5] (|| *id.*) ψ 89[41] Ho 10[14] Am 5[9] Mi 5[10] Na 3[12.14] Hb 1[10] Dn 11[24.39]; sq. n.pr. מ׳ צֹר 2 S 24[7] (cf. Jos 19[29] עיר מ׳ צר).

בַּקְבּוּק, בַּקְבֻּק v. sub בקק. p. 132 1227-28

†בַּקְבַּקַּר **n.pr.m.** (form strange, mng. dub.) 1230
a Levite 1 Ch 9[15].

בַּקְבֻּקְיָה v. sub בקק. p. 132 1229

בקה (*test, prove,* cf. Aram. בְּקָא).

†בֻּקִּיָּ֫הוּ **n.pr.m.** (*proved of* י׳) Levite, son 1232
of Heman 1 Ch 25[4]; son of Asaph (?) v[13].

†בֻּקִּי **n.pr.m.** (*id.*)—**1.** a Danite chief Nu 1231
32[22]. **2.** a descendant of Aaron 1 Ch 5[31.31] 6[31] Ezr 7[4].

†בָּקַע **vb. cleave, break open or through** 1234
(NH *id.,* MI[15] מבקע השחרת *from break of dawn;* Aram. בְּקַע; cf. Eth. በቍዐ: *profit, be useful,* orig. *findere, aperire,* Di)—**Qal** *Pf.* בָּקַע ψ 78[13], בָּקְעָה Is 34[15], בָּקַעְתָּ Ne 9[11] ψ 74[15], וּבָקַעְתָּ Ez 29[7]; *Impf.* וַיִּבְקַע Ju 15[19] Is 48[21], וַיִּבְקְעוּ 2 S 23[16] = 1 Ch 11[18], וַיִּבְקָעוּהָ 2 Ch 21[17]; *Imv.* וּבְקָעֵהוּ Ex 14[16]; *Inf. cstr.* sf. בִּקְעָם Am 1[13] 2 Ch 32[1]; *Pt. act.* בּוֹקֵעַ Is 63[12] Ec 10[9], בֹּקֵעַ ψ 141[7];—**1.** *cleave, cleave open,* sq. acc., Ju 15[19] *God cleft open the hollow* (הַמַּכְתֵּשׁ), and water came out, cf. Is 48[21] (obj. צוּר), also ψ 74[15] *bring forth by cleaving,* obj. מַעְיָן וָנַחַל, all three of divine operation; *cleave* or *rip open* pregnant women Am 1[13]; of a broken staff, tearing the shoulder Ez 29[7] (but rd. כַּף *hand* for כָּתֵף, 𝔊 𝔙 Sm (?) Co); *cleave* wood Ec 10[9] (|| מַסִּיעַ אֲבָנִים); of ploughing (furrowing) the earth ψ 141[7] (|| פֹּלֵחַ; in sim.); esp. of *dividing* the sea, Ex 14[16] (P) Ne 9[11] ψ 78[13], cf. Is 63[12], obj. מַיִם;—in all these subj. י׳ exc. Ex 14[16] where he commands Moses; of *hatching out* (a brood, but no obj. expr.) Is 34[15], subj. קִפּוֹז *arrow-snake.* **2.** *break through* or *into,* sq. בְּ 2 S 23[16] = 1 Ch 11[18]; sq. acc. 2 Ch 21[17] וַיַּעֲלוּ בִיהוּדָה וַיִּבְקָעוּהָ; also 32[1], obj. suff. ref. to cities, ויאמר לְבִקְעָם אֵלָיו *and he thought to break into them* and so bring them *unto himself.*

Niph. *Pf.* נִבְקַע Jb 26^{8} Zc 14^{4} (וְ consec.); נִבְקְעוּ Gn 7^{11} Is 35^{6}, נִבְקָ֑עוּ 2 Ch 25^{11} Pr 3^{20}; *Impf.* יִבָּקַע Is 58^{8}, יִבָּקֵ֑עַ Jb 32^{19}; 3 fs. תִּבָּקַע Is 59^{5}, וַתִּבָּקַע Nu 16^{31}+3 t.; *Inf.* cstr. לְהִבָּקֵעַ Ez 30^{16};—**1.** *be cleft, rent open,* subj. the ground, הָֽאֲדָמָה Nu 16^{31} (J), הָאָ֫רֶץ 1 K 1^{40} (hyperb.); mountain Zc 14^{4}; *burst open,* of men hurled from rock 2 Ch 25^{12}; of cloud beneath its weight of water Jb 26^{8}; hyperb. of belly full of words seeking a vent, Jb 32^{19} *like new wine-skins it will burst open;* so of the water-receptacles (מעינות) of the great deep, at the flood Gn 7^{11}; of the water-masses themselves, תהומות Pr 3^{20}, מים ונחלים Is 35^{6}; also of the Red Sea, וַיִּבָּקְעוּ המים Ex 14^{21}; of light breaking forth Is 58^{8} (fig.); of serpent's egg *hatching out* as a viper Is 59^{5} הַזּוּרֶה תִּבָּקַע אֶפְעֶה. **2.** *be broken into,* of city captured by breaches in walls 2 K 25^{4}=Je 52^{7}, Ez 30^{16}. **Pi.** *Pf.* בִּקַּע 2 K 15^{16} Jb 28^{10}, וּבִקַּעְתִּ֫י Ez 13^{13}, בִּקֵּ֑עוּ Is 59^{5}; *Impf.* יְבַקַּע ψ 78^{15}, וַיְבַקַּע Gn 22^{3}; 3 fs. תְּבַקַּע Ez 13^{11}, תְּבַקְּעֵם Ho 13^{8}; 2 ms. תְּבַקַּע־ Hb 3^{9}, תְּבַקֵּ֑עַ 2 K 8^{12}; 2 fpl. וַתְּבַקַּ֫עְנָה 2 K 2^{24};—*cleave, cut to pieces,* or *rend open* (oft. more complete or more violent than Qal), sq. acc., of cleaving wood Gn 22^{3} i.e. cut it up for burning, so 1 S 6^{14}; of ripping open pregnant women 2 K 8^{12} 15^{16}; of tearing in pieces children 2 K 2^{24}; cf. also Ho 13^{8} (fig.); of cleaving open rocks, to bring forth water ψ 78^{15} (subj. God); of cutting mining-shafts Jb 28^{10} בַּצּוּרוֹת יְאֹרִים ב׳; נְהָרוֹת תְּבַקַּע־אָ֫רֶץ Hb 3^{9} *into rivers thou cleavest (the) earth; break through* or *down* (a wall, but no obj. expr.), Ez 13^{11} רוּחַ סְעָרוֹת תְּבַקֵּעַ (but Co תִּבָּקַע), cf. v^{13} וּבִקַּעְתִּי רוּחַ סְעָרוֹת בַּחֲמָתִי; of *hatching* eggs Is 59^{5} בֵּיצֵי צִפְעוֹנִי בִּקֵּ֑עוּ (fig.) **Pu.** *Impf.* יְבֻקָּ֑עוּ Ho 14^{1}; *Pt.* מְבֻקָּעָה Ez 26^{10}, מְבֻקָּעִים Jos 9^{4};—*be ripped open,* of women Ho 14^{1} (vb. of masc. form); *rent,* of old wine-skins Jos 9^{4}; *broken into,* of a city in whose walls a breach has been made Ez 26^{10}. **Hiph.** *Impf.* 1 pl. sf. וְנַבְקִעֶ֫נָּה Is 7^{6}; *Inf. cstr.* לְהַבְקִיעַ 2 K 3^{26};—*break into,* sq. sf. ref. to Judah, Is 7^{6} ונב׳ אֵלֵ֫ינוּ *let us break into it,* lay it open, and so bring it *unto ourselves* (cf. Qal 2 Ch 32^{1}); *break through* (abs.) with sword, שֹׁ֫לֵף חֶרֶב לְהַבְקִיעַ אֶל־מֶלֶךְ אֱדוֹם 2 K 3^{26}. **Hoph.** *Pf.* 3 fs. הָבְקְעָה הָעִיר Je 39^{2} *the city was broken into,* entrance was made by a breach. **Hithp.** *Pf.* הִתְבַּקָּ֑עוּ Jos 9^{13}, *Impf.* יִתְבַּקָּ֑עוּ Mi 1^{4};—*burst (themselves) open,* of wine-skins Jos 9^{13}; *cleave asunder,* of valleys Mi 1^{4}.

1235 †בֶּ֫קַע **n.[m.]** fraction, **half,** i.e. half-shekel, a weight; בֶּקַע מִשְׁקָלוֹ Gn 24^{22}, cf. Hesychius in Lag$^{Ges. Abh. 199, l. 18}$ βακαίον [Lag βέκαον] μέτρον τι; v. also בֶּקַע Ex 38^{26} (=מַחֲצִית הַשָּׁ֑קֶל).

†בִּקְעָה **n.f. valley** (cleft), **plain**—abs. ב׳ 1237
Gn 11^{2}+8 t.; cstr. בִּקְעַת Dt 34^{3}+7 t.; pl. בְּקָעוֹת Is 41^{18} ψ 104^{8}; בִּקְעֹת Dt 11^{11};—**1.** *valley* (opp. הַר mountain) Dt 8^{7} 11^{11} cf. Is 41^{18}; also 63^{14} כַּבְּהֵמָה בַּבִּקְעָה תֵרֵד; in creation-poem ψ 104^{8} יַעֲלוּ הָרִים יֵרְדוּ בְקָעוֹת. **2.** *plain* (sts. valley-plain, broad valley) Gn 11^{2}; also Ez 3$^{22.23}$ 8^{4} 37$^{1.2}$ (עַל־פְּנֵי הַבּ׳) as level, opp. הָֽרְכָסִים Is 40^{4} (|| מִישׁוֹר); elsewhere cstr., mostly with n.pr. Dt 34^{3} ב׳ יְרֵחוֹ (appos. הַכִּכָּר), ב׳ מִצְפֶּה Jos 11^{8}, ב׳ הַלְּבָנוֹן 11^{17} 12^{7}, ב׳ מְגִדּוֹ 2 Ch 35^{22} cf. Zc 12^{11}, ב׳ אוֹנוֹ Ne 6^{2}; ב׳־אָוֶן Am 1^{5} *plain of idolatry*=Baalbek (Damascus, acc. to Wetzst in De$^{Jes 3, 702}$; 𝔊 πέδιον Ὤν).

†[בָּקִיעַ, בְּקִיעַ] **n.[m.] fissure, breach,** 1233
Am 6^{11} בְּקִעִים, into which the small house is to be smitten (|| רְסִיסִים); בְּקִיעֵי עִיר־דָּוִד Is 22^{9}.

†I. [בָּקַק] **vb. be luxuriant** (Ar. بَقَّ *be* 1238
profuse, abundant (v. esp. Conjj. I. IV, Lane))—**Qal** *Pt.* בּוֹקֵק *luxuriant* Ho 10^{1} (fig. of Isr. as vine).

†II. [בָּקַק] **vb. empty** (cf. probably Ar. 1238
بَقَّ *make a gurgling noise,* of a mug dipped in water, or emptied of water)—**Qal** *Pf.* וּבַקֹּתִי Je 19^{7}, בְּקָקוּם Na 2^{3}; *Pt.* בּוֹקֵק Is 24^{1}, בֹּקְקִים Na 2^{3}; *empty, lay waste* land, acc., Is 24^{1} Na 2^{3}, also abs. v^{3}; fig. *make void* (obj. עֵצָה) Je 19^{7}. **Niph.** *Pf.* וְנָֽבְקָה (cf. Ges$^{§ 67. R. 11}$) Is 19^{3}; *Impf.* 3 fs. תִּבּוֹק Is 24^{3}; *Inf. abs.* הִבּוֹק Is 24^{3};—*be emptied* (laid waste) Is 24^{3} הִבּוֹק תִּבּוֹק, of land (|| הִבּוֹז תִּבּוֹז); fig. of spirit, courage Is 19^{3}. **Po.** *Impf.* יְבֹֽקְקוּ Je 51^{2} *empty out* (devastate) land.

†בַּקְבֻּק **n.[m.] flask** (from gurgling sound 1228
of emptying, cf. Ar. بَقْبَقَةٌ *gurgling sound;* also Syr. ܩܘܩܒܐ, *cantharus,* etc.)—abs. בַּקְבֻּק Je 19^{10}; cstr. *id.* 1 K 14^{3} Je 19^{1}.

†בַּקְבּוּק **n.pr.m.** head of a family of Ne- 1227
thinim; בני־ב׳ Ezr 2^{51} Ne 7^{53}.

†בַּקְבֻּקְיָה **n.pr.m.** a Levite Ne 11^{17} 12$^{9.25}$. 1229

†יַבֹּק **n.pr.fl.** (√ prob. בקק; so Thes after 2999
Simonis, Sam. Di) מַעֲבַר (ה)יבק Gn 32^{23} (where perhaps connected with (יאבק = אבק); נַחַל יַבּ׳ Dt 2^{37}, הַנַּחַל יַבּ׳ Dt 3^{16} Jos 12^{2}, יַבֹּק Nu 21^{24} (|| אַרְנֹן, cf. Dt 3^{16} Jos 12^{2}), הַיַּבֹּק Ju 11$^{13.22}$ (in both, || ארנון); it empties into Jordan from East, in latitude of Shechem; called (southern)

boundary of Ammon Dt 3^{16}, and (northern) of Amorites Jos 12^{2}; but some confusion (Di Nu 21^{24} Dt 2^{37});—mod. *Wady Zerqa*, Bd $^{Pal\ 181}$.

1239 †[בָּקַר] **vb. inquire, seek** (NH *id.*, Aram. בַּקַּר, ܒܰܩܰܪ; also Eth. በቀለ: in deriv.; orig. *divide, discern*, cf. Ar. بَقَرَ *slit, rip, split*)—only **Pi.** *Pf.* 1 s. sf. וּבִקַּרְתִּים consec. Ez 34^{11}; *Impf.* יְבַקֵּר Lv 13^{36} 27^{33}, אֲבַקֵּר Ez 34^{12}; *Inf. cstr.* לְבַקֵּר 2 K 16^{15} + 2 t.;—*seek, look for*, sq. לְ Lv 13^{36}; *seek* (to distinguish) sq. בֵּין־טוֹב לָרַע Lv. 27^{33}; *seek* (in order to care for) sq. acc. צֹאן Ez 34^{11} (|| דרשׁ v^{12}), fig. of י׳ seeking his people; *contemplate*, sq. בְּ ψ 27^{4} (|| חָזָה בְּ); *consider, reflect*, abs. Pr 20^{25} אַחַר נְדָרִים i.e. whether the vows were wise, or should be kept (cf. Str ad loc. & reff.); cf. perh. 2 K 16^{15} *consider* (what shall be done with the old altar); *look at* Klo, (so לְבַקֵּר 1 K 3^{21} for 2nd בַּבֹּקֶר), AV RV *to inquire by*, 𝔊 *for praying;* perh. denoting some religious service to be performed by king himself, cf. esp. RS $^{Sem.\ i.\ 467}$.

1241 בָּקָר $_{182}$ **n.m.** $^{1\ K\ 5,\ 3\ +}$ (**f.** $^{Gn\ 33,\ 16;\ Jb\ 1,\ 14\ cf.\ Dt\ 32,\ 14\ 2\ S\ 17,\ 29}$) **cattle, herd, ox** (Ar. بَقَرٌ, Aram. בַּקְרָא, ܒܩܪܳܐ, בַּקְרְתָא (cf. also Hom $^{NS\ 222\ ff.}$); name from *ploughing*, so Thes Lag $^{BN\ 51}$ al.)—abs. ב׳ Gn 12^{16} +; cstr. בְּקַר Nu 7^{88}; sf. בְּקָרְךָ Gn 45^{10} +; בְּקָרֶךָ Ex 20^{24} Je 5^{17}; בְּקָרוֹ 1 S 11^{7} 2 S 12^{4}; בְּקַרְכֶם Dt 12^{6}; בְּקָרָם Je 3^{24}+; pl. בְּקָרִים Am 6^{12} (al. rd. בבקר ים) 2 Ch 4^{3} (but rd. פְּקָעִים v. || 1 K 7^{24} infr.); sf. בְּקָרֵינוּ Ne 10^{37}; rd. בקריכם for בחוריכם 1 S 8^{16} 𝔊 We Dr;—**1.** mostly coll. **a.** *cattle*, generic (never pl. in form) Gn 12^{6} 13^{5} 20^{14} 21^{27} 24^{35} Lv 1^{2} Dt 8^{13} 1 S 11^{5} Ho 5^{6} Jo 1^{18} 1 Ch $27^{29.29}$ + oft. (frequently || צֹאן); as grazing, 1 Ch 27^{29} +; in sim. כַּבּ׳ Jb 40^{15} Is 11^{7} 65^{25}; as lowing (קוֹל הַבּ׳) 1 S 15^{14}; מִקְנֵה בָקָר *possession of* (i.e. property in) cattle Gn 6^{14} 47^{17} (both J); עֶדְרֵי ב׳ Jo 1^{18} *herds of cattle;* esp. בֶּן־בָּקָר *son of cattle* (i.e. *belonging to the* בקר), to denote a single ox, calf, etc.; as used for food Gn 18^{7} cf. v^{8} (J);—in these prob. = *calf* (v. also 1 S 14^{32} בָּקָר וּבְנֵי בָקָר); usually for sacrifice (Hex only P) Nu $15^{8.9}$; בֶּן־הַבּ׳ Lv 1^{5}; appos. עֵגֶל †Lv 9^{2};—cf. עֶגְלַת בָּקָר †Dt 21^{3} 1 S 16^{2} Is 7^{21};—mostly appos. פַּר Ex 29^{1} + 27 t.; also pl. †פָּרִים בני בקר Nu $28^{11.19.27}$ $29^{13.17}$ (on all these cf. בֵּן); also indef. *cattle, oxen*, of a number not specified Nu $7^{87.88}$ (in both enumerated as פָּרִים); 22^{40} 1 S 14^{32} 15^{21} 1 K 1^{9} $7^{29.29}$ (here of graven work) 8^{5} 1 Ch 12^{40} 2 Ch 5^{6} 18^{2} Is 22^{13} ψ 66^{15}; also as beasts of burden †1 Ch 12^{40}. **b.** a particular *herd* of cattle Gn 18^{7} (J); cf. pl. בְּקָרֵינוּ, *our herds*, only Ne 10^{37}. **2.** more individually, *head of cattle*,—yet alw. of more than one (Hex mostly P; pl. only Am 6^{12} + 2 Ch 4^{3} v. supr.); of two Nu 7^{17} + 11 t. Nu 7; †cf. also צֶמֶד ב׳ *yoke* (pair) *of oxen* 1 S 11^{7} cf. v^{7}, 1 K 19^{21} cf. v^{21} (ploughing, cf. v^{19}); also 2 S 6^{6} = 1 Ch 13^{9} (drawing a cart, cf. Nu $7^{3f.}$ 1 S $6^{7f.}$), 2 S 24^{22} = 1 Ch 21^{23}, 2 S $24^{22.24}$ 1 K 19^{20} Am 6^{12} (pl.); 500 *yoke of oxen* Jb 1^{3} cf. v^{14}; 1000 *yoke* 42^{12}; further, of four Nu 7^{7}; five Ex 21^{37} (תַּחַת הַשּׁוֹר); seven 2 Ch 29^{22} (|| פָּרִים v^{21}); eight Nu 7^{8}; ten 1 K 5^{3}; twelve Nu 7^{3} (singly called שׁוֹר) cf. v^{6}; of the twelve brazen bulls beneath the sea in Sol.'s temple 1 K $7^{25.44}$ = 2 Ch $4^{4.15}$ cf. 2 K 16^{17} 2 Ch 4^{3} (דְּמוּת בְּקָרִים) v^{3} (but rd. in both פְּקָעִים, as || 1 K 7^{24} cf. Be Öt) v^{4} Je 52^{20}; of twenty 1 K 5^{3}; seventy 2 Ch 29^{32}; hundreds or thousands 1 K 8^{63} = 2 Ch 7^{5}, 2 Ch 15^{11} 29^{33} $35^{7.8.9}$ (cf. v^{12}), & Nu $31^{33.38.44}$†. Note חֶמְאַת בָּקָר Dt 32^{14} (poem), מַלְמַד הַבּ׳ Ju 3^{31}, שְׁפוֹת ב׳ 2 S 17^{29}, כְּלִי הַבּ׳ 2 S 24^{22} 1 K 19^{21}, צְפוּעֵי הַבּ׳ Ez. 4^{15} (opp. גֶּלְלֵי הָאָדָם).

†בּוֹקֵר **n.m. denom. herdsman** Am 7^{14}; 941, 951
of Amos himself, cf. אֲשֶׁר־הָיָה בַנֹּקְדִים 1^{1}.

בֹּקֶר $_{214}$ **n.m.** $^{Ex\ 10,\ 13}$ **morning** (NH *id.*; from 1242
split, penetrate, as the dawn the darkness, light through cloud-rifts, etc.)—ב׳ Gn 1^{5} + (alw. abs.); pl. בְּקָרִים Jb 7^{18} + 4 t.;—**1.** *morning* (of point of time, time at which, never during which, Eng. *morning* = forenoon):—**a.** of end of night (opp. לַיְלָה) Ex 10^{13} (J) Lv 6^{2} (P) Ju 19^{25} Ru $3^{13.13}$ Is 21^{12} cf. 1 S 19^{11} (|| מחר, opp. לילה); opp. לֵילוֹת ψ 92^{3}; also (opp. לִין) Ex 23^{18} 34^{25} (both JE) Lv 19^{13} (H) Dt 16^{4}; opp. צלמות Am 5^{8}; cf. further Gn 40^{6} 41^{8} (both E) Ex 12^{22} $34^{2.2}$ (both JE) 1 S 3^{15}+. †**b.** implying the coming of dawn, and even daylight Gn 29^{25} (E) 44^{3} (J) 1 K 3^{21} (but Klo here for 2nd בַּבֹּקֶר, rds. לְבַקֵּר *by looking at* it v. בָּקַר) Jb 24^{17} 38^{12} (|| שַׁחַר); לִפְנוֹת הַבּ׳ Ex 14^{27} (JE) *at the turn of the morning*, so Ju 19^{26} (|| בַּעֲלוֹת הַשַּׁחַר v^{25}; sq. עַד־הָאוֹר, as something later, v^{26}); vid. Ru 3^{14} (|| בטרום יכיר איש את רעהו *before men could recognise each other*); cf. כּוֹכְבֵי בֹקֶר Jb 38^{7} *stars of morning;* but also c. אוֹר vb. Gn 44^{3} (J) הבקר אור; c. אור noun, באור הבקר Mi 2^{1}; & esp. עד אור הבקר Ju 16^{2} (opp. לילה) so 1 S 14^{36}; also 1 S $25^{22.34.36}$ 2 S 17^{22} 2 K 7^{9}; cf. 1 S 29^{10} (|| וְאוֹר לָכֶם). †**c.** of coming of sunrise Ju 9^{33} 2 S $23^{4.4}$ 2 K 3^{22} cf. מוֹצָאֵי ב׳ וערב ψ 65^{9} i.e. places of sunrise and sunset (|| קְצוֹת i.e. *ends* of earth). **d.** of beginning of day, מֵאָז הַבּ׳ וְעַד־עַתָּה Ru 2^{7} (cf. v^{14}) vid. 2 S 24^{15} (but

del. We Dr); time of prayer, & praise ψ $5^{4.4}$ (v. Hu) 59^{17} 88^{14} 92^{3}; ‖צהרים *noon* 1 K 18^{26} Je 20^{16}; of three hours of prayer, ערב ובקר וצהרים ψ 55^{18} (cf. Dn $6^{10.13}$); cf. also c. עֶרֶב infr. **e.** opp. עֶרֶב Gn 49^{27} (poem in J) Ex $16^{7.8.12.13}$ Lv 6^{13} Nu 9^{21} (all P) Dt $28^{67.67}$ 2 S 11^{14} 1 K 17^{6} Is 17^{14} Zp 3^{3} Ez $24^{18.18}$ 33^{22} Dn 8^{26} ψ 30^{6} $90^{5.6}$ Ec 11^{6} 1 Ch 16^{40} 2 Ch 2^{3} 13^{11} 31^{3} Ezr 3^{3} Est 2^{14}; opp. בֵּין הערבים Ex $29^{39.41}$ Nu $28^{4.8}$ (all P); esp. מִן־הבקר עד־הערב =*all day* Ex 18^{13} & (without art.) v^{14} (both E); מבקר לָעֶרֶב Jb 4^{20}=between morning and evening; also מֵעֶרֶב עַד־בֹּקֶר=*all night*, Ex 27^{21} (P) Lv 24^{3} (H) Nu 9^{21} & בָּעֶרֶב עַד־בּ׳ Nu 9^{15} (both P); note also the formula וַיְהִי ערב ויהי בקר *and evening came and then morning* Gn $1^{5.8.13.19.23.31}$ (all P), i.e. the day ended with evening, and the night with morning; peculiar is Dn 8^{14} of om. of daily sacrif. עַד עֶרֶב בֹּקֶר אַלְפַּיִם וּשְׁלֹשׁ מֵאוֹת, *until 2300 evening-mornings*, prob.=2300 half-days (Ew Hi Meinh Bev Dr $^{Intr. 464}$, cf. v^{26} & $3\frac{1}{2}$ times (years) 7^{25} $12^{11.17}$). **f.** oft. (above & elsewh.) c. prep. (+art. exc. Jb 7^{18}); *in the morning*, בַּבֹּקֶר Gn 19^{27} + 110 t., cf. also בִּהְיוֹת הַבּ׳ Ex 19^{16}; *in* (or *at*) *the morning*, לַבּ׳ Am 4^{4} + 7 t.; *for* (*against* or *by*) *the morning*, לַבּ׳ Ex 34^{2} cf. ψ 130^{6} (cf. Che crit. n.); nearly=*until* (עַד־) Ex 34^{25} Dt 16^{4} Zp 3^{3}; further בַּבּ׳ בַּבּ׳ *morning by morning, every morning* † Ex 16^{21} 30^{7} 36^{3} Lv 6^{5} (all P) 2 S 13^{4} 1 Ch 23^{30} 2 Ch 13^{11} Is 28^{19} 50^{4} Ez $46^{13.14.15}$ Zp 3^{5} also לַבּ׳ לַבּ׳, same sense, † 1 Ch 9^{27}; † pl. לַבְּקָרִים *every m.* afresh ψ 73^{14} Is 33^{2} cf. La 3^{23}; alm.=*continually* ψ 101^{8} (cf. Je 21^{12}); v. לִבְקָרִים † Jb 7^{18} (‖ לִרְגָעִים *every moment*); also without prep. or art. *in the morning* Ho 7^{6} cf. ψ $5^{4.4}$ ψ 55^{18}, **d.** supr., & sub **2.** **g.** fig. of bright joy after night of distress (poet.) Jb 11^{17}; cf. ψ 30^{6} 46^{6} (לִפְנוֹת ב׳) 49^{15} 59^{17} 90^{14} 143^{8}. **h.** in phrases, הִשְׁכִּים בַּבּ׳ (וַיַּשְׁכֵּם etc.) *he rose early in the morning* † Gn 19^{27} 20^{8} 21^{14} 22^{3} 26^{31} 28^{18} 32^{1} Ex 8^{16} 9^{13} 24^{4} 34^{4} Nu 14^{40} Jos 3^{1} 6^{12} 7^{16} 8^{10} (all JE) Ju 6^{28} $19^{5.8}$ 1 S 1^{19} 5^{4} cf. 15^{12}, 17^{20} $29^{10.10}$ cf. v^{11}, 2 K 3^{22} 19^{35}=Is 37^{36}, 2 Ch 20^{20} Jb 1^{5} Pr 27^{14} Is 5^{11}; (ויקומו etc.) ויקם בַּבּ׳ † Gn 24^{54} Nu $22^{13.21}$ (all JE) Ju 19^{27} 20^{19} 2 S 24^{11} 1 K 3^{21}; אַשְׁמֹרֶת הַבּ׳ *morning watch* † Ex 14^{24} 1 S 11^{11}. **2.** *morrow, next day* (cf. Germ. *Morgen, morgen*) without art. Ex $16^{19.20}$ Lv 7^{15} 22^{30} (opp. הַיּוֹם הַהוּא) Nu 16^{5} (‖ מָחָר v$^{7.16}$) cf. Ex $12^{10.10}$ Nu 9^{12}; with art. Ex $16^{23.24}$ 29^{34}; לַבּ׳ Ex 34^{25} Nu 22^{41} Zp 3^{3}; בַּבּ׳ 1 S 9^{19} (opp. הַיּוֹם *to-day*) cf. 20^{35}; *to-morrow morning* הַבּ׳ Ju 6^{31} (Stu); בַּבּ׳ Ex 7^{15} Jos 7^{14} Est 5^{14}; definitely מִמָּחֳרָת בַּבּ׳ 1 S 5^{4}; מֵהַבּ׳ 2 S 2^{27}; adverb. use in this sense (without prep. or art.) Ex 16^{7} Nu 16^{5}.

† [בַּקָּרָה] **n.f.verbal.** a seeking, כְּבַקָּרַת רֹעֶה 1243
עֶדְרוֹ Ez 34^{12} *like a shepherd's seeking his flock*.

† בִּקֹּרֶת **n.f.** punishment after examination 1244
(**inquisition**) Lv 19^{20}; (*scourging* 𝔙 AV after Jewish trad. Kerith ^{11a} Sifra Saad. AE Ki cf. Malbim ^{Sifra} Jastrow $^{Dict. 165}$.)

† [בִּקֵּשׁ] $_{224}$ **vb.** **seek** (Ph. בקשׁ)—**Pi.** *Pf.* 1245
בִּקֵּשׁ Dt 13^{11} + 15 t.; בִּקְשָׁה Ec 7^{28} Est 2^{15}; sf. בִּקַּשְׁתָּם Ho 2^{9}; בִּקַּשְׁתִּיו Ct $3^{1.2}$ cf. 5^{6}; בִּקְשׁוּ Ezr 2^{62} + 12 t.; sf. בִּקְשֻׁנִי Is 65^{1} + 2 t.; *Impf.* יְבַקֵּשׁ Jos 22^{23} + 37 t.; יְבַקֶּשׁ־ Pr 15^{14} + 2 t.; אֲבַקְשָׁה ψ 122^{9} + 3 t.; sf. יְבַקְשֵׁהוּ 1 S 23^{14} + 7 t.; יְבַקְשׁוּ 1 S 16^{16} + 23 t.; *Imv.* בַּקֵּשׁ 1 S 9^{3} + 3 t.; בַּקְשׁוּ 1 S 28^{7} + 8 t.; *Inf.* לְבַקֵּשׁ 1 S 10^{2} + 29 t.; *Pt.* מְבַקֵּשׁ Gn 37^{16} + 23 t.; pl. מְבַקְשִׁים Ex 10^{11} + 38 t.;—**1.** *seek to find:* **a.** abs. Ju 6^{29} 2 K 2^{17} Je 5^{1} Ez 34^{6} Ec 3^{6} 8^{17} (yet v. Ew). **b.** acc. Gn $37^{15.16}$ Jos 2^{22} (J) Ju 4^{22} 14^{4} 1 S 9^{3} $10^{2.14.21}$ 16^{16} 1 S $23^{14.25}$ 24^{3} 26^{2} $27^{1.4}$ + 26^{20} obj. *a flea*, but rd. נַפְשִׁי 𝔊 Th We Kirkp Klo Dr; 2 S $17^{3.20}$ 1 K 1^{3} 2^{40} 18^{10} 2 K 2^{16} 6^{19} 1 Ch 4^{39} 2 Ch 22^{9} Ezr 2^{62} (=Ne 7^{64}) Ne 12^{27} $37^{25.36}$ 119^{176} Pr 2^{4} 21^{6} 23^{35} 7^{28} Ct $3^{1.1.2.2}$ 5^{6} 6^{1} Is $41^{12.17}$ Je $2^{24.33}$ La 1^{11} Ez 7^{25} 22^{30} $34^{4.16}$ Ho 2^{9} Na 3^{11} Zc 11^{16} Mal 2^{15}. **c.** with לְ Jb 10^{6}. **d.** acc. rei לְ pers. Ju 18^{1} 1 S 13^{14} 28^{7} 1 K 1^{2} Ru 3^{1} Est 2^{2} ψ 122^{9} Is 40^{20} La 1^{19} Na 3^{7}. **2.** *seek to secure:* **a.** acc. the priesthood Nu 16^{10} (P); David for king 2 S 3^{17}; in battle 2 S 5^{17} (=1 Ch 14^{8}); ψ 27^{4} Je 45^{5} (cf. v^{5}); בקשׁ נפשׁ *seek to take one's life* Ex 4^{19} (J) 1 S 20^{1} $22^{23.23}$ 23^{15} 25^{29} 2 S 4^{8} 16^{11} 1 K $19^{10.14}$ ψ 35^{4} 38^{13} 40^{15} 54^{5} 63^{10} 70^{3} 86^{14} Pr 29^{10} Je 4^{30} 11^{21} $19^{7.9}$ 21^{7} 22^{25} $34^{20.21}$ 38^{16} $44^{30.30}$ 46^{26} 49^{37}. **b.** *aim at, practise:* בקשׁ רעה *seek hurt* of Nu 35^{23} (P) 1 S 24^{10} 25^{26} (אֶל) 1 K 20^{7} ψ $71^{13.24}$ Est 9^{2}; ב׳ כזב ψ 4^{3} cf. Pr 17^{11}, שׁבר Pr 17^{19}, רצון Pr 11^{27}, טובה Ne 2^{10}, אמונה Je 5^{1}, צדק, ענוה Zp $2^{3.3}$ שׁלום ψ 34^{15}, חכמה Pr 14^{6} Ec 7^{25}, בינה Dn 8^{15}, דעת Pr 15^{14} 18^{15}, תורה Mal 2^{7}, אהבה Pr 17^{9}, תאוה 18^{1} (לְ of dir. obj.), חשׁבנות Ec 7^{29}. **c.** *Inf.* Ex 4^{24} (J) Je 26^{21}. **d.** לְ & *Inf.* Gn 43^{30} Ex 2^{15} 10^{11} (JE) Dt 13^{11} 1 S 14^{4} $19^{2.10}$ 23^{10} 2 S 20^{19} 21^{2} 1 K $11^{22.40}$ Est 2^{21} 3^{6} 6^{2} ψ 37^{22} Ec 12^{10} Zc 6^{7} 12^{9}. **3.** *seek the face* **a.** *of rulers* 1 K 10^{24} (=2 Ch 9^{23}) Pr 29^{26}. **b.** *of God* (from resorting to sacred places) Ho 5^{15} 1 Ch 16^{11} (=ψ 105^{4}) 2 Ch 7^{14} 2 S 21^{1} ψ 24^{6} $27^{8.8}$; without פְּנֵי **c.** יהוה Dt 4^{29} Zp 1^{6} 2^{3} Ho 3^{5} 5^{6} Ex 33^{7} (J) 1 Ch 16^{10} (=ψ 105^{3}) 2 Ch 11^{16} 20^{4} Is 51^{1} Pr 28^{5} Zc $8^{21.22}$ Je 50^{4}; אלהים 2 S 12^{16}, cf. Ez 8^{22} Is 45^{19} 65^{1} 2 Ch $15^{4.15}$ Ho 7^{10} Je 29^{13} Mal 3^{1} ψ 40^{17} 70^{5} 69^{7} Dn 9^{3}; דבר י׳

Am 8^{12}; שִׁמְךָ ψ 83^{17}. **d.** sq. *Inf.* c. לְ, of resort to wizards, but obj. not expr. Lv 19^{34} (H). **4.** *desire, demand:* **a.** acc. 1 Ch 21^{3}. **b.** acc. rei מִן pers. Ez 7^{26} Dn 1^{20}. **5. a.** *require, exact,* acc. rei מִיַּד pers. Is 1^{12}; מִן pers. Ne 5^{12}, acc. rei v^{18}. **b.** *exact equivalent* or *penalty* for, acc. rei, מִיַּד pers. Gn 31^{39} 43^{9} (JE) 1 S 20^{16} 2 S 4^{11} Ez $3^{18.20}$ 33^{8}, cf. דרשׁ; no obj. expr. Jos 22^{23} (P). **6.** (late) *ask, request,* acc. rei Est 2^{15}; עַל rei Ne 2^{4}; עַל rei מִן pers. Est 7^{7} Ezr 8^{23}; עַל rei מִלִּפְנֵי pers. Est 4^{8}; acc. rei מִן pers. Dn 1^{8} (obj. cl. c. אשׁר), ψ 104^{21}; מִן pers. 2 Ch 20^{4}. **Pu.** *Impf.* יְבֻקַּשׁ Je 50^{20}, וַיְב׳ Est 2^{23}; תְּבֻקְשִׁי Ez 26^{21} *be sought.*

1246 †[בַּקָּשָׁה] **n.m. request, entreaty,** בַּקָּשָׁתִי Est $5^{7.8}$ 7^{3}; בַּקָּשָׁתֵךְ; Est 5^{3} 9^{12}; בַּקָּשָׁתוֹ Ezr 7^{6}.

1248 †I. בַּר **n.m. son** (Aram. בַּר, Syr. ܒܪܳܐ) only in late Heb. of Pr $31^{2.2}$ (both cstr.), v^{2} sf. בְּרִי; נַשְּׁקוּ בַר ψ 2^{12} *kiss the son,* 𝔖 Modern Vrss Ges De Pe et al.; *receive instruction* 𝔗; δράξασθε παιδείας 𝔊; *apprehendite disciplinam* 𝔙 Ew; *kiss purely, do sincere homage* Aq Sym Jer Br$^{MP 136}$; emend. Lag (מוֹסֵרוֹ) נַשְּׁקוּ מוֹסֵרוֹ *put on his bonds* (cf. v^{3}) so Kmp Che$^{OP 351}$.

1249-50 II. בַּר corn, III. בַּר pure, בָּר, I. II. בֹּר v. ברר.

1254 †I. בָּרָא$_{53}$ **vb. shape, create** (cf. Ar. بَرَى, *form, fashion by cutting, shape out, pare a reed for writing, a stick for an arrow,* but also بَرَأَ, *create;* Ph. הברא CIS$^{I. 347}$ *incisor, a trade involving cutting;* As. *barû, make, create,* COT^{Gloss} & Hpt KAT$^{2 Gloss 1}$ but dub.; Sab. ברא *found, build,* DHM$^{ZMG 1883, 413}$, synon. בנה; Ba$^{ZA. 1888, 58}$, comp. As. *banû, create, beget,* with change of liquid; Aram. בְּרָא, ܒܪܳܐ, *create*)—**Qal** *Pf.* Gn 1^{1}+19 t.; *Impf.* יִבְרָא Gn $1^{21.27}$ Nu 16^{30}; *Inf.* בְּרֹא Gn 5^{1}; *Imv.* בְּרָא ψ 51^{12}; *Pt.* בּוֹרֵא Is 42^{5} +10t.; sf. בֹּרַאֲךָ Is 43^{1}; בּוֹרְאֶיךָ Ec 12^{1};—*shape, fashion, create,* always of divine activity, with acc. rei, seldom except in P and Is². **1.** obj. heaven and earth Gn 1^{1} 2^{3} (P) Is $45^{18.18}$; mankind Gn $1^{27.27.27}$ $5^{1.2}$ (P) 6^{7} (J) Dt 4^{32} ψ 89^{48} Is 45^{12}; the host of heaven Is 40^{26}; heavens Is 42^{5}; ends of the earth Is 40^{28}; north and south ψ 89^{13}; wind Am 4^{13}; the תנינים Gn 1^{21} (P). **2.** the individual man Mal 2^{10} (‖ father) Ec 12^{1}; the smith and the waster Is $54^{16.16}$; Israel as a nation Is 43^{15}; Jacob Is 43^{1}; the seed of Israel Is 43^{7}. **3.** new conditions and circumstances: righteousness and salvation Is 45^{8}; darkness and evil Is 45^{7}; fruit of the lips Is 57^{19}; a new thing חֲדָשָׁה (a woman encompassing a man) Je 31^{22}; בְּרִיאָה (swallowing up the Korahites) Nu 16^{30} (J); cloud and flame over Zion Is 4^{5}. **4.** of transformations: a clean heart ψ 51^{12} (‖ חָדָשׁ), new heaven and earth Is 65^{17} (in place of old); transformation of nature Is 41^{20}; with double acc. בורא ירושלם גילה *transform Jerusalem into rejoicing* Is 65^{18}. **Niph.** *Pf.* 2 fs. נִבְרֵאת Ez 21^{35}; 3 pl. נִבְרָאוּ Ex 34^{10} + 2 t.; *Impf.* יִבָּרֵאוּן ψ 104^{30}; *Inf.* sf. הִבָּרְאֲךָ Ez 28^{13}; הִבָּרַאֲךָ Ez 28^{15}; הִבָּרְאָם Gn 2^{4} 5^{2}; *Pt.* נִבְרָא ψ 102^{19};—*Pass.* **1.** *be created:* heaven and earth Gn 2^{4} (P); creatures ψ 104^{30}; mankind Gn 5^{2} (P); heavens ψ 148^{5}. **2.** with reference to birth: במקום אשׁר נבראת *in the place where thou wast created* (i.e. native land) Ez 21^{35}; יום הבראך *day when thou wast created* (king of Tyre) Ez $28^{13.15}$ (cf. היום ילדתיך ψ 2^{7}); עַם נִבְרָא ψ 102^{19} (‖ עַם נוֹלָד ψ 22^{32}). **3.** of something new, astonishing: miracles Ex 34^{10} (J); new things, חדשׁות Is 48^{6}. **Pi.** *Pf.* בֵּרֵאתָ Jos 17^{15}; בֵּרֵאתוֹ Jos 17^{18}; *Inf.* abs. בָּרֵא Ez $21^{24.24}$ 23^{47};—**1.** *cut down:* a forest Jos $17^{15.18}$ (J); וּבָרֵא אוֹתְהֶן בְּחַרְבוֹתָם Ez 23^{47}. **2.** *cut out:* יָד hand, as an index Ez $21^{24.24}$.

†בְּרִיאָה **n.f. a creation, thing created,** 1278
as preternatural, unparalleled; acc. cogn. אִם־בּ׳ יִבְרָא י׳ Nu 16^{30}, cf. בָּרָא **Qal 3**, **Niph. 3.**

†בְּרָאיָה **n.pr.m.** (*י׳ hath created*) a Benjamite 1 Ch 8^{21}. 1256

†II. [בָּרָא] **vb. be fat** (Ar. بَرِئَ *be free of a thing, sound, healthy;* v. מרא)—**Hiph.** *Inf.* לְהַבְרִיאֲכֶם 1 S 2^{29} *to make yourselves fat.* 1254

†בָּרִיא **adj. fat**—ψ 73^{4} Ju 3^{17}; pl. בְּרִיאִים 1277, 1274
1 K 5^{3}; cstr. בְּרִיאֵי Dn 1^{15}; f. בְּרִיאָה Hb 1^{16} + 2 t. +
Ez 34^{20} בְּרִיָּה; Hi Ol$^{§ 171 a}$ בְּרִיָּה, < בריאה; pl. 1279
בְּרִיאוֹת Gn 41^{5} + 3 t.; בְּרִיאֹת Gn $41^{2.4}$;—*fat,* cattle Gn $41^{2.4.5.7.18.20}$ (E) 1 K 5^{3}; sheep Ez $34^{3.20}$ Zc 11^{16}; food Hb 1^{16}; אִישׁ בּ׳ *fat man* Ju 3^{17}; בריאי בשׂר Dn 1^{15}; בּ׳ אולם *their body fat* ψ 73^{4}.

בְּרֹאדַךְ בַּלְאֲדָן **n.pr.m.** v. sub מְרֹדַךְ. p. 597 1255

בְּרָאִי v. בית בראי sub בית. p. 111 1011

בַּרְבֻּרִים v. sub ברר. p. 141 1257

ברד (cf. Ar. بَرَدَ *be or become cold*).

†בָּרָד **n.m.**$^{Ex 9, 18}$ **hail** (Ar. بَرَدٌ, Aram. בְּרַד, 1259
ܒܪܳܕܳܐ; also Sab. ברדם, *cold* DHM$^{ZMG 1875, 607}$)—בָּרָד Ex 9^{18} + 28 t.;—*hail,* c. המטיר י׳ Ex $9^{18.23}$, c. נתן י׳ 9^{23}; also Ex $9^{19.22.24.25.25.26}$ $10^{5.12.15}$; ‖ קֹלֹת *thunder* Ex $9^{23.28.29.33}$, ‖ קֹלֹת & מָטָר Ex 9^{34}, ‖ אֵשׁ lightning 9^{24}; all JE, Egypt. plague; cf. ψ $78^{47.48}$ 105^{32}; another great hailstorm Jos 10^{11} (E), where אַבְנֵי הַבּ׳; further, in theoph. ψ 18^{13} (‖ גחלי־אשׁ) 2 S 22^{13} om. by error; del. however

in ψ 18^{14} cf. De Che etc.; אוצרות ב׳ Jb 38^{22}, ירקון וב׳ Hg 2^{17}; in אשׁ וב׳ שׁלג וקיטור ψ 148^{8}, sim. Is 28^{2} זרם ב׳ שׁער; fig. Is 28^{17} 30^{30} (אבן ב׳)—fig. of judgment of י׳.

1258 †בָּרַד **vb.denom.** hail, וּבָרַד בְּרֶדֶת הַיָּעַר consec. Is 32^{19} *it shall hail.*

1261 †[בָּרֹד] **adj.** spotted, marked (as if sprinkled with hail? so Ki cf. Lag$^{BN\ 29}$; Syr. ܒܪܘܕܐ, i.e. *grandinatus, grêlé,* PS), mpl. of sheep & goats עֲקֻדִּים נְקֻדִּים וּבְרֻדִּים Gn 31$^{10.12}$; horses Zc 6$^{3.6}$.

1260 †בֶּרֶד **1. n.pr.loc.** בֶּרֶד Gn 16^{14} near Kadesh. **2. n.pr.m.** בֶּרֶד an Ephraimite 1 Ch 7^{20}.

1262 †I. בָּרָה **vb. eat** (As. *barû* & deriv. Zim $^{BP\ 31}$)—**Qal** *Pf.* 2 S 12^{17}; *Impf.* אֶבְרֶה 2 S 13$^{6.10}$ *eat bread* (בְּרוּ־לָכֶם 1 S 17^{8} scribal error for בחרו לכם 1 K 18^{25} Dr$^{Sm\ 107}$). **Pi.** *Inf.* לְבָרוֹת La 4^{10} *for devouring.* **Hiph.** *Impf.* תַּבְרֵנִי 2 S 13^{5}; *Inf.* לְהַבְרוֹת 2 S 3^{35} *cause to eat bread.*

1279 †בִּרְיָה **n.f.** food 2 S 13$^{5.7.10}$; Ez 34^{20} v. בָּרִיא.

1267 †[בָּרוּת] **n.f.** food; בְּבָרוּתִי ψ 69^{22} *in* (or *as*) *my food.*

II. ברה (cf. As. *barû, bind,* whence *birîtu, fetter* Zim $^{BP\ 59,\ 82}$, & *treaty, covenant* Dl$^{K\ 7}$).

1285 בְּרִית $_{285}$ **n.f.** covenant (‖ Aram. קְיָם, διαθήκη; *constitutio*)—ב׳ Gn 9^{13} + 199 t.; sf. בְּרִיתִי Gn 6^{18} + 50 t.; בְּרִיתְךָ Dt 33^{9}; בְּרִיתֶךָ ψ 44^{18} + 11 t.; בְּרִיתְכֶם Is 28^{18}; בְּרִיתֵךְ Ez 16^{61}; בְּרִיתוֹ Ex 2^{24} + 18 t.;—*pact, compact, covenant.* **I.** *between men.* **1.** *treaty, alliance, league:* Abraham and Amorites Gn 14^{13}; Edom and its allies Ob ^{7}; with Philistines Gn 21$^{27.32}$ (E) 26^{28} (J); Jacob and Laban Gn 31^{44} (J); Joshua and Gibeonites Jos 9$^{6.7.11.15.16}$ (J); Israel and Canaanites Ex 23^{32} 34$^{12.15}$ (JE) Dt 7^{2} Ju 2^{2}; Ammonites and Jabesh 1 S 11^{1}; Solomon and Hiram 1 K 5^{26}; Ahab and Benhadad 1 K 20^{34}; Syria and Israel 1 K 15^{19} = 2 Ch 16^{3}; Nebuchadnezzar and Zedekiah Ez 17$^{13\text{-}19}$; nations against Israel ψ 83^{6}; nations with Egypt Ez 30^{5}; Ephraim and Assyria Ho 12^{2}; Judah and Israel Ez 16^{61}; Judah and Tyre Am 1^{9}; Assyria and Judah Is 33^{8}; נגיד ברית *a prince in league* (with him) Dn 11^{22} (so He Ew; Hi Meinh Bev ref. to h. p. Onias III, & translate *prince of cov't,* cf. AV RV); fig., with death Is 28$^{15.18}$; with stones of the field Jb 5^{23}. **2.** *constitution, ordinance,* between monarch and subjects: David and Abner 2 S 3$^{12.13.21}$; David and the elders of Israel 2 S 5^{3} = 1 Ch 11^{3}; Zedekiah and his people Je 34$^{8\text{-}18}$; hostile prince and Israelites Dn 9^{27}. **3.** *agreement, pledge:* Jehoiada and captains 2 K 11^{4} = 2 Ch 23^{1}; with oneself Jb 31^{1}; with Leviathan to be a servant Jb 40^{28}; between man and man Ho 10^{4}
cf. בעל ברית Ju 8^{33} 9^{4} = אל ברית Ju 9^{46}. **4.** *al-* 1286
liance of friendship between David and Jonathan 1 S 18^{3} 20^{8} 23^{18} cf. ψ 55^{21}. **5.** *alliance* of marriage Pr 2^{17} Mal 2^{14}.—In all cases כרת ברית is the technical phrase for making covenant except Je 34^{10} באו בברית; Dn 9^{27} הגביר ברית לְ. Various preps. are used, most oft. לְ Ex 23^{32} +, but also עִם Gn 26^{28} +, אֵת 2 S 3^{12} +, בֵּין 2 Ch 16^{3}. **II.** *between God and man.* **1.** *alliance* of friendship (‖ סוֹד) ψ 25^{14}. **2.** *covenant,* as a divine constitution or ordinance with signs or pledges (vid. אות). **a.** *with Noah* Gn 9$^{9\text{-}17}$ (P) Is 54^{10} Je 33$^{20.25}$; a divine promise that there would be no other deluge. **b.** *with Abraham, Isaac and Jacob* Gn 15^{18} (J) 17$^{2\text{-}21}$ Ex 2^{24} 6$^{4.5}$ Lv 26^{42} (P) 2 K 13^{23} 1 Ch 16^{15} = ψ 105$^{8.10}$, Ne 9^{8} Je 34^{18}; a promise to multiply their seed, give them the land of Canaan, and make them a blessing to the nations. **c.** *with Israel at Sinai* = Horeb, with a covenant sacrifice Ex 19^{5} 24$^{7.8}$ (E) 34$^{10.27.28}$ (J) 31^{16} Lv 2^{13} (P) 24^{8} 26$^{9.15.25.44.45}$ (H) Dt 4^{13}; renewed in plains of Moab Dt 28^{69}; with blessings and curses Dt 29^{20}; frequently referred to in other books 2 Ch 34^{32} ψ 25^{10} 44^{18} 50$^{5.16}$ 74^{20} 78$^{10.37}$ 103^{18} 106^{45} 111$^{5.9}$ Is 56$^{4.6}$ Je 1$^{2.3.6.8.10}$ 14^{21} 22^{9} 31^{32} Ez 16$^{8.59.60}$ 44^{7} Dn 9^{4} 11$^{28.30.32}$ Ho 6^{7} 8^{1} Zc 9^{11} 11^{10}; a divine constitution given to Israel with promises on condition of obedience and penalties for disobedience, in the form of tables of the covenant Dt 9$^{9.11.15}$, inscribed with the ten words, placed in ארון ברית (י׳) the ark of the covenant Nu 10^{33} + 40 t. (vid. ארון; in 1 S 4$^{3.4.4.5}$ om. ברית after ארון 𝔊 We Dr); set forth in דברי הברית *words of the covenant* Ex 34^{28} (J) Dt 28^{69} 29^{8} 2 K 23^{3} (= 2 Ch 34^{31}) Je 11$^{2\text{-}8}$; written in ספר הברית *the book of the covenant* Ex 24^{7} (E, cf. 34^{27} J) 2 K 23$^{2.21}$ (cf. 2 Ch 34^{30}). **d.** *with Phinehas* Nu 25$^{12.13}$ (P), a constitution, establishing an everlasting priesthood in his line; cf. ברית הכהנים Ne 13^{29} & ברית הלוי Mal 2$^{4.8}$. **e.** *with Joshua and Israel* Jos 24^{25} (E), an ordinance or constitutional agreement to serve Yahweh only. **f.** *with David* ψ 89$^{4.29.34.39}$ 132^{12} Je 33^{21} (cf. 2 S 7 = 1 Ch 17); a divine promise to the seed of David of an everlasting kingdom, the relation of sonship, and the superintendence of the temple (cf. ψ 2). **g.** *Jehoiada and the people* 2 K 11^{17} = 2 Ch 23^{3}, a constitutional agreement to be the people of Yahweh. **h.** *Hezekiah and the people* 2 Ch 29^{10}, a constitutional agreement to reform the worship. **i.** *Josiah and the people* 2 K 23^{3}, a constitutional agreement to obey the book of the covenant. **j.** *Ezra and the people*

Ezr 10[3], a constitutional agreement to put away foreign wives and observe the Law. **k.** *the prophetic covenant*, a divine promise through a series of prophets to establish a new constitution ברית חדשה Je 31[31], with new institutions and precepts Is 42[6] 49[8] 55[3] 59[21] 61[8] Je 31[31.33] 32[40] 50[5] Ez 16[60.62] 20[37] 34[25] 37[26] Ho 2[20]. In Is[2] the Messianic servant is ברית עם Is 42[6] 49[8], cf. מלאך הברית Mal 3[1]. **III.** Phrases. **1.** *covenant making:* כרת ברית Gn 15[18] Ex 34[10.27] (J) Jos 24[25] (E) Dt 5[2.3] 28[69] 29[13.24] 1 K 5[26] 2 K 11[17] 17[35.38] 23[3] 2 Ch 21[7] 23[3.16] 29[10] 34[30] Ezr 10[3] Ne 9[8] ψ 50[5] 89[4] Is 55[3] 61[8] Je 11[10] 31[31.32.33] 32[40] 34[13] Ez 34[25] 37[26] Hos 2[20]; הקים ברית *establish a covenant* Gn 6[18] 9[9.11.17] 17[7.19.21] Ex 6[4] (P) Ez 16[60.62], but *confirm covenant* Lv 26[9] (?; H) Dt 8[18]; נתן ברית Gn 17[2] Nu 25[12] (P); שׂם ברית 2 S 23[5] (poet.); עבר בברית Dt 29[11]; בא בברית 2 Ch 15[12] Ez 16[8]; צוה ברית ψ 111[9]; נשׂא ברית על פי ψ 50[16]. (Cf. further on these Dr[J Ph xi. 1882, 210 ff.]) **2.** *covenant keeping:* on the part of man שמר ברית 1 K 11[11] Ne 1[5] 9[32] ψ 78[10] 103[18] 132[12] Dn 9[4], נצר ברית Dt 33[9] ψ 25[10], מחזיקים בברית Is 56[4.6]; on the part of God זכר ברית Gn 9[15.16] Ex 2[24] 6[5] (all P), Lv 26[42.42.42] (H; on sf. cf. Di Ges[§ 128, 1 R b]) v[45] (H) ψ 105[8] 106[45] 111[5] 1 Ch 16[15] Ez 16[60]. Thus we have נאמנת ψ 89[29]; ברית עולם Gn 9[16] 17[7.13.18.19] Ex 31[16] Lv 24[8] Nu 18[19] 25[13] (P) 2 S 23[5] (poet.) 1 Ch 16[17] (=ψ 105[10]) Is 24[5] 55[3] 61[8] Je 32[40] 50[5] Ez 16[60] 37[26]; ברית מלח Lv 2[13] 2 Ch 13[5] 21[7] (a cov't. with sacrificial meal and salt; on cov't. with salt in Arabia cf. We[Skizzen iii. 124]); ברית שלום Nu 25[12] (P) Is 54[10] Ez 34[25] 37[26]; הברית והחסד Dt 7[9.12] 1 K 8[23] (=2 Ch 6[14]) Ne 1[5] 9[32] Dn 9[4]; ברית קדשׁ Dn 11[28.30]; מסרת הברית Ez 20[37]. **3.** *covenant violation:* עבר ברית Dt 17[2] Jos 7[11.15] 23[16] (D) Ju 2[20] 2 K 18[12] Ho 6[7] 8[1]; הפר ברית Gn 17[14] Lv 26[15.44] (H) Dt 31[16.20] (J) Ju 2[1] Is 24[5.5] Je 11[10] 14[21] 31[32] 33[20.21] Ez 16[59] 17[18.19] 44[7] Zc 11[10]; עזב ברית 1 K 19[10.14] Je 22[9] Dn 11[30]; מאס ברית 2 K 17[15]; נאר ברית ψ 89[39]; חלל ברית ψ 89[34] Mal 2[10]; שקר בברית ψ 44[18]; שכח ברית Dt 4[23.31] Je 50[5].

1265-66 בְּרוֹשׁ, בְּרוֹת v. sub ברשׁ. p. 141

1267 בָּרוּת v. sub I. ברה. p. 136

1268 בְּרוֹתָה, בֵּרֹתַי v. sub באר. p. 92

ברז (? cf. Aram. ברז *bore, pierce*, or Ar. بَرَزَ, *appear*).

1269 †**ברזות** **n.pr.f.** (?) descend. of Asher (perh. בִּרְזָא *foramen*, Thes., or بَرْزَةٌ woman whose beauties are *apparent*) 1 Ch 7[31] Kt (Qr בִּרְזָיִת).

1270 †**בַּרְזֶל** **n.m.**[Dt 19, 5] **iron** (c. ל afform.; fr. *piercing*? NH *id.*, Aram. *id.*, פַּרְזֶל, ܦܪܙܠܐ, Ph. ברזל, As. *parzillu* COT[Gloss], (Ar. فِرْزِلٌ *fetter* is loan-word))—alw. abs. ב׳ Gn 4[22] + 74 t. (בַּרְזֶ֑ל Gn 4[22] etc.);—**1.** *iron*, lit.: **a.** iron-ore, stone containing iron, Dt 8[9] Jb 28[2]; **b.** as raw material (to be worked) Gn 4[22] 1 Ch 22[3.14.16] 29[2.2.7] 2 Ch 2[6.13] 24[12] Is 44[12]; **c.** as article of commerce Ez 27[12.19]; **d.** as material of furniture, utensils, implements, etc., עֶרֶשׂ ב׳ Dt 3[11], רֶכֶב ב׳ Jos 17[16.18] Ju 1[19] 4[3.13], כְּלֵי ב׳ Jos 6[19.24] cf. 1 K 6[7] Nu 35[16], עֵט־ב׳ Jb 19[24] & fig. Je 17[1], חֲרִצֵי הַבּ׳ 2 S 12[31] = 1 Ch 20[3], מַגְזְרוֹת הַבּ׳ 2 S 12[31] *cutting instr. of iron*, vid. Am 1[3], כַּבְלֵי ב׳ ψ 149[8] (|| זִקִּים), קִיר ב׳ Jb 20[24], קַרְנֵי ב׳ 1 K 22[11] = 2 Ch 18[10], נֶשֶׁק ב׳ & מַחֲבַת ב׳ Ez 4[3]; בְּרִיחֵי ב׳, i.e. of Babylon, ag. Cyrus Is 45[2]; cf. 1 S 17[7] & Is 60[17.17] (fig.) **2.** *tool* of iron Dt 27[5] Jos 8[31] Pr 27[17.17] Ec 10[10] Is 10[34] (metaph.); head of an axe Dt 19[5] 2 K 6[5.6]; so *weapon* 2 S 23[7] Jb 41[19]; cf. also Nu 31[22] Jos 22[8] where iron as spoil of war. **3.** *iron* in fig. of unwatered earth Dt 28[23]; of Egyptian bondage, כּוּר הַבּ׳ Dt 4[20] 1 K 8[51] Je 11[4]; of oppression על ב׳ Dt 28[48] Je 28[14] cf. v[13]; of strength Je 15[12.12]; cf. ב׳ מִנְעָלֶיךָ Dt 33[25] & קַרְנֵךְ ב׳ Mi 4[13]; of prophet, firm through Yahweh's might, עַמּוּד ב׳ Je 1[18]; of distress, בְּרִיחֵי ב׳ ψ 107[16] cf. v[10] of judgments of י׳, & 105[18]; שֵׁבֶט ב׳ ψ 2[9]; of evil-doers, Je 6[28] Ez 22[18.20]; simile of scorching sky Lv 26[19]; מְטִיל ב׳ of bones of hippopotamus Jb 40[18]; גִּיד ב׳ of obstinate neck of Isr. Is 48[4].

†**בַּרְזִלַּי** **n.pr.m.** (*man of iron*)—**1.** a Gilead- 1271
ite 2 S 17[27] 19[32.33.35.40] 1 K 2[7]; בַּרְזִלָּ֑י 2 S 19[34]; Ezr 2[61] = Ne 7[63] בְּנֵי בַרְזִלַּי אֲשֶׁר לָקַח מִבְּנוֹת בַּרְזִלַּי הַגִּלְעָדִי וַיִּקָּרֵא עַל־שְׁמָם, where 2nd Barzillai = above, & former is **2.** a priest Ezr 2[61] = Ne 7[63], who adopted name בַּרְזִלַּי. **3.** 2 S 21[8] a Meholathite.

†**בָּרַח** **vb. go through, flee** (cf. Germ. 1272
durchgehen) (Ar. بَرِحَ *go away, withdraw, flee*) —**Qal** *Pf.* בָּרַח Gn 31[22] + 9 t., בָּרְחוּ Jb 9[25], בָּרָ֑חוּ Is 22[3]; *Impf.* יִבְרַח Jb 20[24], יִבְרָ֑ח Jb 27[22] Ne 6[11], וַיִּבְרַח Gn 31[21] + 13 t.; 3 fs. וַתִּבְרַח Gn 16[6], אֶבְרָ֑חָה ψ 139[7], יִבְרְחוּ Je 52[7], וַיִּבְרְחוּ 2 S 4[3] + 4 t., נִבְרָ֑חָה 2 S 15[14]; *Imv.* בְּרַח Gn 27[43] + 3 t., בִּרְחוּ Is 48[20]; *Inf. abs.* בָּרֹחַ Jb 27[22]; *cstr.* בְּרֹחַ 1 S 23[6] + 3 t., בְּרֹחוֹ Jon 1[3]; sf. בָּרְחִי 1 K 2[7], בָּרְחֲךָ Gn 31[5], בָּרְחוֹ Gn 35[7] + 2 t.;—**1.** *go* or *pass through*, of bar, וַיַּעַשׂ אֶת־הַבְּרִיחַ ... לִבְרֹחַ Ex 36[33] (P). **2.** *flee* Gn 31[20.21.22] (E) Ex 14[5] (J) Ju 9[21] 1 S 19[12.18] 22[17] 2 S 13[34.37.38] (del. Dr cf. We) 15[14] Is 22[3] Je 4[29] 26[21] 39[4] 52[7] Ne 6[11]; fig. of days fleeing away

Jb 9^{25}; of man, like a shadow Jb 14^{2}; c. מִן *flee from* a place 1 S 20^{1} 2 S 19^{10} (+ מֵעַל pers.) Is 48^{20}, a weapon Jb 20^{24}; a person, c. מֵאֵת 1 K 11^{23}, usually c. מִפְּנֵי Gn 16$^{6.8}$ 31^{27} 35$^{1.7}$ Ex 2^{15} (all JE) Ju 11^{3} 2 S 21^{11} 1 K 2^{7} 12^{2} = 2 Ch 10^{2} ψ 3^{1} 57^{1} (titles) 139^{7} Jon 1^{10}; מִיַּד י׳ fig. Jb 27^{22}; *flee to*, c. acc. place 1 S 27^{4} 1 K 11^{40} Ho 12^{13}; c. place & לְ Ne 13^{10}; c. place & ־ָה loc. Jon 1^{3} 4^{2} 2 S 4^{3}; c. place & אֶל־ Nu 24^{11} Am 7^{12}; c. אֶל־ & pers. 1 S 23^{6} Gn 27^{43} (J) 1 K 2^{39} 1 K 11^{40}; אַחֲרֵי & pers. 1 S 22^{20}; *flee*, sq. inf. 1 K 11^{17} Dn 10^{7}. **3.** flee=*hasten, come quickly* Ct 8^{14}. **Hiph.** *Pf.* הִבְרִיחוּ 1 Ch 8^{13}; *Impf.* יַבְרִיחַ Pr 19^{26}; sf. יַבְרִיחֶנּוּ Jb 41^{20}, וָאַבְרִחֵהוּ Ne 13^{28}, וַיַּבְרִיחוּ 1 Ch 12^{15}; *Pt.* מַבְרִחַ Ex 26^{28};—**1.** *pass through*, lit. Ex 26^{28} (P) cf. **Qal.** **2.** *cause to flee, put to flight*, animal Jb 41^{20}, men 1 Ch 8^{13} 12^{16}; *drive away* Pr 19^{16} Ne 13^{28} (sq. מֵעָלַי).

1281 †I. [בָּרִיחַ] **adj. fleeing** (= *בָּרִחַ): נָחָשׁ בָּרִחַ Jb 26^{13} of eclipse-dragon, לִוְיָתָן נָחָשׁ בָּרִחַ Is 27^{1} (prob. fig. of Assyrians); as subst. בָּרִיחִים Is 43^{14} *as fugitives* (for other views cf. Comm.); so prob. also Is 15^{5} בריחיה, v. בָּרִחַ.

1282 †II. בָּרִיחַ **n.pr.m.** son of Shemaiah 1 Ch 3^{22}.

1280 †בְּרִיחַ **n.m.** bar (cf. As. *burûḫu, spear-shaft, spear*, COT^{Gloss})—בְּרִיחַ Dt 3^{5} + 11 t. (cstr. Am 1^{5} etc.); בְּרִיחוֹ Ex 35^{11} 39^{33} Kt (Qr both ־חָיו needless); pl. בְּרִיחִם Ex 26^{26} + 8 t., בְּרִיחִים 2 Ch 14^{6}, בְּרִיחֵי Ex 36^{31} + 3 t., בְּרִיחַיִךְ Na 3^{13}, בְּרִיחָיו Ex 40^{18} + 7 t. (+ Qr Ex 35^{11} 39^{33}), בְּרִיחֶיהָ Je 51^{30} La 2^{9}, בְּרִחֶיהָ Jon 2^{7}, בְּרִיחֶהָ Is 15^{5} but cf. infr.;—**1. a.** *bar*, of wood, joining boards of tabern. Ex 26$^{26.27.27.28.29.29}$ 35^{11} 36$^{31.32.32.33.34.34}$ 40^{18} Nu 3^{36} 4^{31} (all P). **b.** *bar(s)* of city-gates Dt 3^{5} Ju 16^{3} 1 S 23^{7} 2 Ch 8^{5} 14^{6}; *id.* of gates of Jerusalem La 2^{9}; also (‖ מנעולים) Ne 3$^{3.6.13.14.15}$ cf. ψ 147^{13}; cf. Am 1^{5} Na 3^{13} Je 49^{31} Ez 38^{11} Je 51^{30}; bars of city-gates, ב׳ נחשת 1 K 4^{13}, ב׳ ברזל Is 45^{2} (of Babylon, broken bef. Cyrus); בְּרִיחֶהָ Is 15^{5} rd. prob. c. 𝔗 Di al. בָּרִ׳ v. בָּרִחַ; yet cf. Che's crit. n. **2.** fig. ב׳ בַּרְזֶל of distress, etc. ψ 107^{16}; of fortress, ב׳ אַרְמוֹן in simile Pr 18^{19}; fig. ב׳ of earth (pictured as house out of which Jonah is shut) Jon 2^{7}. (Older usage *sg.* of bar of door or gate, i.e. the great bar across the gate; so Dt 3^{5} Ju 16^{3} Am 1^{5} 1 S 23^{7} 1 K 4^{13} Je 49^{31} Pr 18^{9} Jb 38^{10} 2 Ch 8^{5} Ez 38^{11} Later *pl.* Is 45^{2} La 2^{9} 2 Ch 14^{6} Ne 3$^{3.6.13.14.15}$ ψ 147^{13}, but also Na 3^{13}.)

4015 † [מִבְרָח] **n.m.** (flight) fugitive—Ez 17^{21} מברחו Kt coll., מִבְרָחָיו Qr; Co rds. Qr, but del. as gloss; 𝔗 𝔖 Ew Sm rd. מִבְחָרָיו.

בַּרְחֻמִי 2 S 23^{31} = בַּחֲרוּמִי 1 Ch 11^{33}, rd. prob. 978, 1273
בַּחֲרֻמִי v. sub בחר & cf. Dr. p. 104

בֵּרִי **n.pr.m.** v. sub באר p. 92. 1275

בְּרִי Jb 37^{11} v. רִי sub רוה. p. 924 7377

[בְּרִי], בִּרְיָה v. בָּרִיא sub II. ברא. p. 135 1274, 1279

בֵּרִים 2 S 20^{14} obscure, many after 𝔅 rd. 1276
בַּחֻרִים; Klo prefers הַבִּכְרִים after 𝔊 & so Dr.

בְּרִית v. sub II. ברה; v. also אֵל 3, בַּעַל 4. p. 136 1285

בֹּרִית v. sub ברר. p. 141 1287

†[בָּרַךְ]$_{329}$ **vb. kneel, bless** (NH *id.*; Ar. 1288
بَرَكَ; Eth. በረከ: Aram. בְּרַךְ, ܒܪܟ (*praise*), Palm. esp. in בריך שמו לעלמא Vog$^{Palm. 74 ff. cf. 94, 144}$)—**Qal** *Impf.* יִבְרַךְ 2 Ch 6^{13}; נִבְרְכָה ψ 95^{6}; בָּרוּךְ (v.
Pi.); *Pt. pass.* בָּרוּךְ Gn 9^{26} + 70 t.;—**1.** *kneel* 1263
down (so Ar. Syr. Eth.): וַיִּבְרַךְ עַל־בִּרְכָּיו *and he kneeled upon his knees* 2 Ch 6^{13}; נִבְרְכָה לפני י׳ *let us kneel before Yahweh* ψ 95^{6}. **2.** *bless* (only pt. pass.). **a.** *of God:* בָּרוּךְ י׳ *blessed be* (or *is*) י׳ Ex 18^{10} (E) Gn 9^{26} 24^{27} (J) Ru 4^{14} 1 S 25$^{32.39}$ 2 S 18^{28} 1 K 1^{48} 5^{21} 8$^{15.56}$ 10^{9} 1 Ch 16^{36} 29^{10} 2 Ch 2^{11} 6^{4} 9^{8} Ezr 7^{27} ψ 28^{6} 31^{22} 41^{14} 72^{18} 89^{53} 106^{48} 119^{12} 124^{6} 135^{21} 144^{1} Zc 11^{5}; ב׳ אלהים ψ 66^{20} 68^{36}; ב׳ אדני ψ 68^{20} (prob. for an original יהוה); ב׳ אל עליון Gn 14^{20} (E); ב׳ צוּרִי 2 S 22^{47} (= ψ 18^{47}); ב׳ כבוד י׳ Ez 3^{12}; ב׳ שם כבודו ψ 72^{19}. **b.** *of men:* Gn 27^{33} (J) Nu 22^{12} (E) Dt 7^{14} 28$^{3.6}$ 33$^{20.24}$ 1 S 25^{33} 26^{25} Ju 17^{2} 1 K 2^{45} ψ 118^{26} Is 19^{25} Je 17^{7} 20^{14}; מברכך ברוך *blessed be the one blessing thee* Gn 27^{29} Nu 24^{9} (E); ב׳ ליהוה Ru 2$^{19.20}$ 3^{10} 1 S 15^{13} 23^{21} 2 S 2^{5} ψ 115^{15}; ב׳ לאל עליון Gn 14^{19}; בְּרוּךְ י׳ Gn 24^{31} 26^{29} (J); בְּרוּכֵי י׳ Is 65^{23}. **c.** *things:* בָּרוּךְ פרי בטנך *blessed be the fruit of thy womb* Dt 28^{4} cf. Dt 28^{5} 1 S 25^{33} Pr 5^{18}. **Niph.** *Pf.* נִבְרְכוּ Gn 12^{3} 18^{18} 28^{14} (J) *bless oneself* (cf. **Hithp.**). **Pi.**$_{233}$ *Pf.* בֵּרַךְ Gn 24^{1} + 29 t.; בֵּרֵךְ ψ 10^{3} Nu 23^{20}; בֵּרְכוּ 2 Ch 20^{26}; וּבֵרֲכוּ Jb 1^{5}; sf. בֵּרֲכוֹ, בֵּרֲכַנִי, etc., Gn 27^{27} + 5 t.; בֵּרַכְךָ Dt 2^{7} + 9 t.; *Impf.* וַיְבָרֶךְ, יְבָרֵךְ etc., Gn 28^{3} + 52 t.; אֲבָרְכָה Gn 12^{3} + 2 t.; pl. יְבָרֵכוּ Gn 24^{60} + 11 t.; sf. יְבָרֶכְךָ Gn 27^{10} + 21 t.; יְבָרְכֶךָּ Gn 49^{25} + 2 t.; יְבָרְכֵהוּ Gn 14^{19} + 16 t.; יְבָרֶכְכֶם Gn 48^{20} + 6 t.; אֲבָרֶכְכָה Gn 27^{7}; תְּבָרְכֵנִי Gn 27$^{19.31}$; יְבָרְכוּכָה ψ 145^{10}; יְבָרֲכֶנְהוּ ψ 72^{15}; *Imv.* בָּרֵךְ Dt 33^{11} + 29 t.; *Inf.* cstr. בָּרֵךְ Gn 22^{17} + 24 t.; *Inf.* abs. בָּרוֹךְ Jos 24^{10} (Ki, cf. Kö$^{i. 191}$, Ew$^{§ 240 b, 2}$ Ol Sta); *Pt.* מְבָרֵךְ Pr 27^{14} + 4 t.;—**1.** *bless God*, adore with

bended knees: acc. ברך י׳ Gn 24^{48} (J) Dt 8^{10} Ju $5^{2.9}$ 1 Ch $29^{10.20}$ 2 Ch 20^{26} 31^{8} Ne 9^{5} ψ 16^{7} 26^{12} 34^{2} 63^{5} $103^{20.21.22}$ 115^{18} $134^{1.2}$ $135^{19.20}$ $145^{2.10}$; ברכי נפשי את י׳ ψ $103^{1.2.22}$ $104^{1.35}$; ברך שם *bless the name of Yahweh* Ne 9^5 ψ 96^2 100^4 $145^{1.21}$; ברך אלהים Jos 22^{33} ψ 66^8 68^{27} (doubtless for an original יהוה), with לְ 1 Ch 29^{20}; מְבָרֵךְ אָוֶן Is 66^3 (of idolatrous worship). **2.** *God blesses* **a.** *men:* abs. Nu 23^{20} (E) ψ 109^{28}; with acc. Gn $32^{27.30}$ 48^{16} Ex 20^{24} Nu 24^1 Jos 24^{10} (E) Gn $12^{2.3}$ 22^{17} $24^{1.35}$ 26^{12} $30^{27.30}$ 39^5 49^{25} Jos 17^{14} (J) Gn $1^{22.28}$ 5^2 9^1 $17^{16.20}$ 25^{11} $26^{3.24}$ 28^3 35^9 48^3 Nu $6^{24.27}$ (P) Dt 1^{11} 2^7 7^{13} 12^7 $14^{24.29}$ $15^{4.6.10.14.18}$ $16^{10.15}$ 23^{21} $24^{13.19}$ 26^{15} 28^8 30^{16} Ju 13^{24} 2 S $6^{11.12}$ 7^{29} 1 Ch 4^{10} 13^{14} 17^{27} 26^5 2 Ch 31^{10} Ne 8^6 Ru 2^4 Jb 42^{12} ψ 5^{13} 28^9 29^{11} 45^3 $67^{2.7.8}$ 107^{38} $115^{12.13}$ 128^5 134^3 147^{13} Pr 3^{33} Is 19^{25} 51^2 61^9 Je 31^{23} Hg 2^{19}. **b.** *things:* sabbath Gn 2^3 Ex 20^{11} (P); field Gn 27^{27} (E); bread Ex 23^{25} (E); work Dt 28^{12} Jb 1^{10} cf. Dt 33^{11} ψ 65^{11} 132^{15}. **3.** *men bless men:* priests & kings בשם י׳ Dt 10^8 21^5 2 S 6^{18} 1 Ch 16^2 23^{13} ψ 129^8; Melchizedek Abraham Gn 14^{19}; Moses Dt 33^1 Ex 12^{32} 39^{43}; Joshua Jos 14^{13} $22^{6.7}$; priests Lv $9^{22.23}$ Nu 6^{23} Dt 27^{12} Jos 8^{33} 2 Ch 30^{27} ψ 118^{26}; Solomon 1 K $8^{14.55}$ (= 2 Ch 6^3); David 2 S 6^{20} (= 1 Ch 16^{43}) 19^{40}; Eli 1 S 2^{20}; Balaam Nu 22^6 $23^{11.20.25}$ 24^{10}; fathers, esp. on death-bed Gn 27^4 + 12 t. Gn 27 (all JE) $28^{1.6}$ (P) 32^1 (E) 48^9 (P) $48^{15.20}$ 49^{28} (J) 2 S 13^{25}; in consecrating a sacrifice 1 S 9^{13}. **4.** *salute, greet,* with an invocation of blessing (stronger than שלום): בך יברך ישראל *with thee will Israel bless* Gn 48^{20} (E). **a.** *in meeting* Gn 47^7 (P) 2 K 4^{29} 10^{15} 1 S 13^{10}. **b.** *in departing* Gn 24^{60} (J) 47^{10} (P) 1 K 8^{66}. **c.** *by messengers* 1 S 25^{14} 2 S 8^{10} 1 Ch 18^{10}. **d.** *in gratitude* Jb 31^{20} Pr 30^{11} Ne 11^2. **e.** *morning salutation* Pr 27^{14}. **f.** *congratulations* for prosperity Gn 12^3 (J) 27^{29} Nu 24^9 (E) 1 K 1^{47} ψ 49^{19} 62^5. **g.** *in homage* 2 S 14^{22} ψ 72^{15}. **h.** *in friendliness* 2 S 21^3. **5.** *bless,* with the antithetical meaning *curse* (Thes) from the greeting in departing, saying adieu to, taking leave of; but rather a blessing overdone and so really a curse as in vulgar English as well as in the Shemitic cognates: 1 K $21^{10.13}$ Jb $1^{5.11}$ $2^{5.9}$ ψ 10^3. **Pu.** *Impf.* יְבֹרַךְ 2 S 7^{29} + 3 t.; תְּבֹרַךְ Ju 5^{24} Pr 20^{21}; *Pt.* מְבֹרָךְ Nu 22^6 + 3 t.; f. מְבֹרֶכֶת Dt 33^{13}; מְבֹרָכָיו ψ 37^{22};—**1.** pass. *to be blessed, adored:* שם י׳ Jb 1^{21} ψ 113^2. **2.** *prospered by God:* **a.** persons 2 S 7^{29} 1 Ch 17^{27} ψ 37^{22} 112^2 128^4 Pr 20^{21}. **b.** things Dt 33^{13}. **3.** *have prosperity invoked,* by Balaam Nu 22^6. **4.** *in gratitude* Pr 22^9 Ju 5^{24}. **Hiph.** וַיַּבְרֵךְ הַגְּמַלִּים *and he made his camels kneel* Gn 24^{11} (J). **Hithp.** הִתְבָּרֵךְ Dt 29^{18} + 3 t.; *Impf.* יִתְבָּרֵךְ Is 65^{16} ψ 72^{17}; *Pt.* מִתְבָּרֵךְ Is 65^{16};—*bless oneself,* congratulate oneself בלבבו in his heart Dt 29^{18}; בזרעך with or by (cf. בְּ III. **2. d**) thy seed (invoke for oneself the blessing of the seed of Abraham) Gn 22^{18} 26^4 (J); by the Messianic king ψ 72^{17}; באלהי אמן Is 65^{16}; by י׳ Je 4^2.

†בֶּ֫רֶךְ **n.f.** Is. 45, 23 knee (As. *birku* COT Gloss; 1290
Eth. ብርክ: Aram. בְּרֵךְ, ܒܘܪܟܐ) Is 45^{23}; du. בִּרְכַּיִם Jb 3^{12} + 10 t.; sf. בִּרְכַּי etc. Gn 30^3 + 11 t.;—*knee, knees:* מים ברכים water reaching to the knees Ez 47^4; וַתְּנִיעֵנִי על ברכי Dn 10^{10}; יַכְּכָה בשחין רע על הברכים Dt 28^{35}; כרע על ברכים *kneel on knees* in worship 1 K 8^{54} Ezr 9^5 cf. Is 45^{23} 1 K 19^{18} 2 Ch 6^{13}, in entreaty 2 K 1^{13}, to drink of a fountain Ju $7^{5.6}$; שם פניו בין ברכיו *put his face between his knees* in prayer 1 K 18^{42}; על ברכים *upon the knees,* Gn 30^3 (E; on תֵּלֵד עַל ב׳ v. Ploss Das Weib Aufl. 2. ii. 180 ff. Sta ZAW 1886, 143 ff.) 50^{23} (E) Jb 3^{12} Ju 16^{19} 2 K 4^{20} Is 66^{12}; הוציא מעם ברכים Gn 48^{12} (E); knees as seat of strength, weak from terror Jb 4^4 Is 35^3 Ez 7^{17} 21^{12} Na 2^{11}; or fasting ψ 109^{24}.

†I. בְּרָכָה **n.f.** blessing (Ar. بَرَكَةٌ; Eth. በረከት: 1293
Aram. בִּרְכָּא, ܒܘܪܟܬܐ; NH as Heb.)—ב׳ Gn 12^2 + 39 t.; cstr. בִּרְכַּת Gn 28^4 + 9 t.; sf. בִּרְכָתוֹ Gn 49^{28} + 7 t.; pl. בְּרָכוֹת ψ 21^7 + 4 t.; cstr. בִּרְכֹת, בִּרְכוֹת Gn 49^{25} + 5 t.; sf. בִּרְכוֹתֵיכֶם Mal 2^2;—**1.** *blessing:* **a.** *of parent* Gn 27^{12-41} 49^{28} (JE), of Moses Dt 33^1. **b.** *of God* Ex 32^{29} (E) Lv 25^{21} (P) Dt $11^{26.27.29}$ 23^6 (= Ne 13^2) $28^{2.8}$ $30^{1.19}$ Jos 8^{34} (D) 2 S 7^{29} ψ 3^9 21^4 133^3 Is 44^3 Ez 34^{26} 44^{30} Jo 2^{14} Mal 3^{10}; ברכת יהוה Gn 39^5 (J) Dt 12^{15} 16^{17} 33^{23} ψ 129^8 Pr 10^{22}; ברכה מאת י׳ ψ 24^5; ברכת אברהם Gn 28^4 (P), the blessing given to Abraham. **c.** *of the people,* in recognition of good men ψ 109^{17} Pr 10^6 11^{26} 24^{25} 28^{20}. **d.** *of a poor man,* in recognition of benefits Jb 29^{13}. **2.** *source of blessing:* Abraham Gn 12^2 (J); Israel Is 19^{24} Ez 34^{26} Zc 8^{13}; seed of the righteous ψ 37^{26}; the king ψ 21^7; memory of the righteous Pr 10^7; new wine Is 65^8. **3.** *blessing, prosperity:* בברכת ישרים *by the prosperity of the upright* (the city is exalted) Pr 11^{11}; גם ברכות יעטה מורה *yea, the early rain covereth with blessings* ψ 84^7 cf. Gn $49^{25.26}$; וארותי את ברכותיכם *and I will curse your prosperity* Mal 2^2. **4.** *blessing, praise of God* Ne 9^5. **5.** *a gift, present* Gn 33^{11} (E) Jos 15^{19} (J) Ju 1^{15} 1 S 25^{27} 30^{26} 2 K 5^{15}; נֶפֶשׁ בְּרָכָה *a liberal person* Pr 11^{25} (cf. Syr. ܒܘܪܟܬܐ, Eth. በረከት:). **6.** *treaty of peace* 2 K 18^{31} = Is 36^{16}.

†II. בְּרָכָה **1. n.pr.loc.** valley in wilderness 1294
by Tekoa 2 Ch $20^{26.26}$; mod. *Bereikût* cf. Be & reff. **2. n.pr.m.** one of David's band 1 Ch 12^3.

1263 †בָּרוּךְ **n.pr.m.** (*blessed*) **1.** friend and amanuensis of Jeremiah Je 32[12.13.16] 36[4–32] 43[3.6] 45[1.2]. **2.** a priest, son of Zabbai (Zaccai) Ne 3[20] 10[7]. **3.** son of Colhozeh, of the tribe of Judah Ne 11[5].

1295 †בְּרֵכָה **n.f.** pool, pond (הברכה SI[5]; Ar. بِرْكَةٌ; Sab. ברכת Sab. Denkm.[73]; Aram. בְּרֵיכְתָא)—ב׳ 2 S 2[13.13] 4[12] 2 K 18[17] (=Is 36[2]) 20[20] Ne 3[16] Is 7[3] 22[9.11]; cstr. בְּרֵכַת 2 S 2[13] 1 K 22[38] Ne 2[14] 3[15] Na 2[9]; pl. בְּרֵכוֹת Ec 2[6] Ct 7[5].

1292 †בָּרַכְאֵל **n.pr.m.** (*Ēl doth bless*, cf. Ph. ברכבעל, Palm. בלברך Vog[117], Bab. *Bariki-ili* Opp[JAs 1887 Nov.-Dec., 536 f.]) father of Elihu Jb 32[2.6].

3000 †יְבֶרֶכְיָהוּ **n.pr.m.** (=יְבָרֶכְיָהוּ s. *Yah blesseth* Ges[§ 27, 3]) father of a Zechariah in Isaiah's time Is 8[2]; usually in abbreviated form as foll.: בֶּרֶכְיָה, **1.** son of Zerubbabel 1 Ch 3[20]. **2.** a Levite guard of the ark 1 Ch 9[16] 15[23]. **3.** father of Meshullam, one of Nehemiah's chiefs Ne 3[4.30] 6[18]. **4.** father of the prophet Zechariah Zc 1[1]=בֶּרֶכְיָהוּ v[7]; בֶּרֶכְיָהוּ also **5.** father of Asaph 1 Ch 6[24] 15[17]. **6.** Ephraimite chief 2 Ch 28[12].

1296 בֶּרֶכְיָה, בֶּרֶכְיָהוּ v. יְבֶרֶכְיָהוּ supra.

ברם (cf. Ar. بَرَمَ *twist a rope of two strands*).

1264 †בְּרֹמִים **n.[m.]** **variegated cloth** (Ar. بَرِيمٌ *rope* (or fabric) *of two strands* or *colours*; cf. As. *birmu*, a kind of clothing COT[Gloss], *burmu*, *iris*, Zim[BP 82]; on *burūmu* cf. Jen[Kosmol. 6 ff.]) וּבִגְנְזֵי בְּרֹמִים Ez 27[24].

6947 בַּרְנֵעַ cf. קָדֵשׁ ב׳. p. 873

1298 †בֶּרַע **n.pr.m.** king of Sodom Gn 14[2] (√ unknown; 𝔊 Βαλλα).

1283 †בְּרִיעָה **n.pr.m.** **1.** a son of Asher Gn 46[17.17] Nu 26[44.45] 1 Ch 7[30.31]. **2.** son of Ephraim 1 Ch 7[23] (where expl. as if fr. בְּרָעָה). **3.** a Benjamite בְּרִיעָה 1 Ch 8[13], בְּרִיעָה 1 Ch 8[16]. **4.** a Levite 1 Ch 23[10.11].

1284 †בְּרִיעִי **adj. gent.** c. art. as n.coll. מִשְׁפַּחַת הַבְּ׳ Nu 26[44].

1299 †בָּרַק **vb. flash**, of lightning (Ar. بَرَقَ *gleam, flash, lighten*, As. *barâḳu* Zim[BP 76], Aram. בְּרַק, ܒܪܰܩ, Eth. በረቀ: Sab. ברק Hal[252] cf. DHM[ZMG 1875, 597])—**Qal** *Pf.* בָּרָק so rd. after 𝔊 L 2 S 22[15] & also in ‖ ψ 18[15] (cf. Klo Che crit. n.); *Imv.* בְּרוֹק ψ 144[6];—all c.acc.cogn. בָּרָק, בְּרָקִים;—*flash*, trans. *flash lightning*, subj. י׳.

†בָּרָק **n.m.** [Ez 1, 13] **lightning** (chiefly in 1300
poetry) (Ar. بَرْقٌ, As. *birḳu* COT[Gloss], Zim[BP 76, 82] Aram. בְּרָק, ܒܶܪܩܳܐ)—abs. ב׳ Jb 20[25]+7 t.+2 S 22[15] (cf. infr.); cstr. בְּרַק Dt 32[41]+2 t.; pl. בְּרָקִים Ex 19[16]+7 t., בְּרָקָיו ψ 97[4];—*lightning*, **1.** lit. mostly pl.=*lightnings, lightning-flashes* Ex 19[16] ψ 18[15] (in theoph., on 2 S 22[15] v. infr.) 77[19] 97[4] 135[7] Jb 38[35] Je 10[13] 51[16]; so in sim. of swift brightness Na 2[5], sg. only ψ 144[6] 2 S 22[15] (where however rd. בְּרָקִים בָּרָק cf. בָּרַק—so 𝔊L Klo Che, cf. his crit. n. ψ 18[15]), Ez 1[13] (in vision), and in sim. of brightness Dn 10[6]; swift destruction Zc 9[14]. **2.** fig. (always sing.) of flashing arrow-head Jb 20[25], cf. ב׳ חרב Dt 32[41], ב׳ חנית Na 3[3] Hb 3[11]; cf. *glitter* of weapon Ez 21[15.20.33].

†בָּרָק **n.pr.m.** (*lightning-flash*, cf. Pun. 1301
Barcas, surname of Hamilcar, cf. Nepos[Hamilcar 1, 1]; Sab. ברקם DHM[ZMG, 1875, 592]; Palm. ברק Vog[Palm. 76]) son of Abinoam, & leader of Israel Ju 4[6.8.9.10.12.14.14.15.16.22] 5[1.12.15].

בְּרַק cf. בְּנֵי בְרַק. p. 122 1139

†בָּרֶקֶת **n.f.** a precious stone, **emerald**, acc. 1304
to 𝔊 𝔙 Josephus; (from *flashing, sparkling;* Lag[Rel. Jur. Eccl. x.] comp. Skr. *markata*, Gk. μάραγδος, ζμάραγδος) Ex 28[17] 39[10] (both P).

†בָּרְקַת **n.f.** id., Ez 28[13], cf. Ges[§ 80 R. 2] Pinsk 1304
Einl. 73.

†בַּרְקוֹס **n.pr.m.** (√ & mng. unknown; 1302
Bab. *Barḳûsu* Dl[Pr 212]) head of a family of Nethinim, בְּנֵי־ב׳ Ezr 2[53]=Ne 7[55].

†בַּרְקָנִים **n.m.pl.** **briers** (so Vrss Ki al., 1303
also Stu q.v., Be, √unknown; cf. ‖ קוֹצִים; >J. D. Michaelis, Thes al. *threshing-sledges*, furnished with sharp (*glittering*) stones) Ju 8[7] וְדַשְׁתִּי אֶת־בְּשַׂרְכֶם אֶת־קוֹצֵי הַמִּדְבָּר וְאֶת־הַבַּ׳ (vid. also דוש) *and I will thresh your flesh together with the thorns of the wilderness and the briers;* v[16] וַיִּקַּח אֶת־זִקְנֵי הָעִיר וְאֶת־קוֹצֵי הַמִּדְבָּר וְאֶת הַבַּ׳ וַיֹּדַע בָּהֶם אֵת אַנְשֵׁי סֻכּוֹת (rd. וַיָּדָשׁ for וַיֹּדַע 𝔊 Bu[RS 114]; cf. Stu Be) *and he took the thorns of the wilderness and the briers and threshed*, etc.

†[בָּרַר] **vb. purify, select** (cf. As. *barâru*, 1305
be shining, in deriv. Zim[BP 46.73] Belser[BAS ii. 154]; Ar. بَرٌّ *pious, kind, true;* بَرَّ *he was pious, good, virtuous, honest*)—**Qal** *Pf.* בָּרוֹתִי Ez 20[38]; *Inf.* sf. לְבָרָם Ec 3[18], Ges[§ 67 R. 3]; cf. לָבוּר 9[1] (si vera l.) as metaplastic form, but on text vid. בור supra p. 101; *Pt.* pass. m. בָּרוּר Jb 33[3]+4 t.; f. בְּרוּרָה Ne 5[18] Zp 3[9];—**1.** *purge out, purify:* וּבָרוֹתִי

מִכֶּם הַמֹּרְדִים *and I will purge out from among you the rebels* Ez 20^{38}; שָׂפָה בְרוּרָה *a purified lip* Zp 3^{9}; בָּרוּר מִלֵּלוּ *utter in a pure, sincere manner* Jb 33^{3}. **2.** *choose, select,* only *Pt.* and in Chronicler: chosen, valiant men 1 Ch 7^{40}; porters 1 Ch 9^{22}; musicians 1 Ch 16^{41}; sheep Ne 5^{18}. **3.** *cleanse, make shining, polish,* pt. pass. חֵץ בָּרוּר *polished arrow* Is 49^{2} (cf. De & Je 51^{11} infr.) **4.** *test, prove* Ec 3^{18} לְבָרָם הָאֱלֹהִים *that God may prove them* (RV);—on 9^{1} v. בּוּר. **Niph.** הִבָּרוּ Is 52^{11}; *Pt.* נָבָר 2 S 22^{27} (=ψ 18^{27});—*purify oneself:* **a.** ceremonially, the bearers of the sacred vessels Is 52^{11}. **b.** morally 2 S 22^{27}=ψ 18^{27}. **Pi.** *Inf.* לְבָרֵר Dn 11^{35} *purify* (‖ לִצְרוֹף, לְלַבֵּן). **Hiph. 1.** *Inf.* לְהָבַר Je 4^{11} *purify, cleanse.* **2.** *Imv.* הָבֵרוּ הַחִצִּים Je 51^{11} *polish arrows* (vid. **3** above). **Hithp. 1.** *Impf.* יִתְבָּרְרוּ Dn 12^{10} *purify oneself.* **2.** תִּתְבָּרָר ψ 18^{27}=תִּתָּבָר 2 S 22^{27} *shew oneself pure, just, kind.*

1249 †II. בַּר **adj.** pure, clean, Jb 11^{4} ψ 24^{4}; בָּר Pr 14^{4}; pl. cstr. בָּרֵי ψ 73^{1}; f. בָּרָה ψ 19^{9} Ct 6$^{9.10}$;—**1.** *pure, clear:* בר לבב *pure in heart* ψ 24^{4}; ברי לבב ψ 73^{1}; a pure damsel Ct 6$^{9.10}$, man Jb 11^{4}, commands of God ψ 19^{9}. **2.** *clean:* אֵבוּס בָּר *crib is clean* Pr 14^{4}. **3.** perh. adv. נַשְּׁקוּ־בַר *kiss purely,* of *sincere* homage ψ 2^{12} but cf. I. בַּר, p. 135.

1250 †III. בַּר **n.m.** grain, corn (cf. Ar. بُرّ *wheat, grain of wheat*), ψ 72^{16} Am 5^{11} 8$^{5.6}$; בָּר Gn 41$^{35.49}$ 42$^{3.25}$ 45^{23} (E) ψ 65^{14} Pr 11^{26} Je 23^{28} Jo 2^{24}.

1253 †I. בֹּר **n.m.** lye, potash, alkali used in smelting metals Is 1^{25} (see בֹּרִית).

1252 †II. בֹּר **n.m.** cleanness, pureness: בֹּר יָדַי *cleanness of my hands* 2 S 22^{21} (=ψ 18^{21}) ψ 18^{25} (=בֹּרִי *my cleanness* 2 S 22^{25}); בֹּר כַּף Jb 9^{30} 22^{30}.

1287 †בֹּרִית **n.f.** lye, alkali, potash, soap, used in washing Je 2^{22} Mal 3^{2}.

1250 †בַּר **n.m.** field (BAram. בָּרָא, Syr. ܒܪܐ, Ar. بَرّ *open country, land*)—יִרְבּוּ בַבָּר *they grow up in the open field* Jb 39^{4} (Aram. usage).

1257 †בַּרְבֻּרִים **n.m.pl.** birds fattened for table of Solomon 1 K 5^{3}; *capons* Ki, *geese* (from their pure white feathers) 𝔗^{Jer} Thes, *swans* Ew, *guinea-hens* Th, *fowls* Tristr. AV RV (ברברי=ינשוף water-birds Lv 11^{17} 𝔗^{Sam}).

ברשׁ (√ of foll., meaning unknown).

1265 †בְּרוֹשׁ **n.m.**$^{Ho\ 14,9}$ cypress or fir (As. *burâšu* COT^{Gloss}. Aram. ברותא, ܒܪܘܬܐ, cf. בְּרוֹת infr., v. also Gr. βράθυ, Lat. *bratum, cypress, juniper* (PS); in favour of *cypress,* also 𝔊 𝔖 & so Thes; in favour of *fir* or *pine,* 𝔙 Rob in RobGes (because cypress not now indigenous on Lebanon); cf. also RS$^{Proph.\ iv.\ n.\ 20}$ who lays stress on Ph. n.pr.loc. אי ברשם (=איברושים)=Gr. Πιτυοῦσαι i.e. *isle of firs;*—v. further Schroed$^{Phön.\ Spr.\ 99}$ Löw$^{No.\ 59}$ & *Brathu* as name of Hermon Philo Bybl. in Euseb$^{Praep.\ Evang.\ i.\ 10}$)—בְּרוֹשׁ Ho 14^{9}+4 t.; בְּרוֹשִׁים 2 S 6^{5}+11 t., בְּרֹשִׁים Na 2^{4}, בְּרוֹשָׁיו Is 37^{24}, בְּרֹשָׁיו 2 K 19^{23};—**1.** (lit.) a noble tree, usually ‖ ארז (exc. 2 S 6^{5} 1 K 6^{34} 2 Ch 3^{5} ψ 104^{17} Is 55^{13} Ho 14^{9} Na 2^{4}); as standing and growing Is 14^{8} 37^{24} = 2 K 19^{23}, Is 41^{19} 55^{13} (‖ הֲדַס) 60^{13} (‖ ארז=כבוד לבנון) ψ 104^{17}. **2.** sim. of luxuriance, stateliness Ez 31^{8}, productiveness Ho 14^{9} (Now thinks *cypress*), fig. for spear-shafts Na 2^{4} Hi-St, but 𝔊 𝔖 פרשים; fig. for mighty men Zc 11^{2}. **3.** as material (always pl.), for building temple (עצי ב׳) 1 K 5$^{22.24}$ 6^{34} cf. 9^{11} 2 Ch 2^{7}; עץ ב׳ (sing.) 2 Ch 3^{5} (cf. Baer's n.); צלעות ב׳ 1 K 6^{15}; for ships (no עץ) Ez 27^{5};—בְּכֹל עֲצֵי ברושים 2 S 6^{5} appar. = *with all musical instruments made of fir,* but ‖ 1 Ch 13^{8} בְּכָל־עֹז וּבְשִׁירִים & so here 𝔊 We Dr.

†[בְּרוֹת] **n.m.** id. (Aramaic (prob. North- 1266
Palest.) form of same) only pl. בְּרוֹתִים ‖ אֲרָזִים Ct 1^{17}; ref. to arbour of trees as their home, cf. אֶרֶז.

†בִּרְשַׁע **n.pr.m.** (√ & meaning unknown) 1306
king of Gomorrha Gn 14^{2}.

בְּרוֹתָה, בֵּרֹתִי, בֵּרֹתַי v. sub בארות, p. 92. 1307

בשׂם (*have a sweet odour,* cf. Aram. בְּסִים, ܒܣܡ *be sweet, pleasant,* Pa. ܒܣܡ *to delight,* בַּסִּימָא, *sweet;* Palm. בשימא (משחא) Vog$^{JAs\ 1883,\ Août.\ Sept.\ 153\ l.\ 12,\ 155\ l.\ 16,\ 18,\ 20\ etc.}$ *spiced (oil),* cf. Reckendorf$^{ZMG\ 1888,\ 405}$; As. *bašâmu,* Pa. *make fine, beautiful* COT^{Gloss}).

בֹּשֶׂם, [בָּשָׂם] v. בֹּשֶׂם. below 1314, 1313

†בֹּשֶׂם **n.m.**$^{1\ K\ 10,\ 10}$ spice, balsam, balsam- 1314
tree (Ar. بَشَامٌ, Aram. בּוּסְמָא, ܒܣܡܐ, Gk. βάλσαμον; cf. Löw^{53})—ב׳ Is 3^{24}+, בֹּשֶׂם Ex 30^{23} v. infr., בְּשָׂמִי Ct 5^{1} (as if fr. בָּשָׂם); pl. בְּשָׂמִים Ex 25^{6}+18 t., בְּשָׂמָיו Ct 4^{16};—**1.** *spice, perfume, sweet odour* Is 3^{24}; קִנְּמָן־בֶּשֶׂם Ex 30^{23} (ב׳ perh. so pointed to distinguish it from) קְנֵה־בֹשֶׂם v^{23};—with this cf. Aram. קני בוסמא, ܩܢܐ ܕܒܣܡܐ;—*spices* as costly, token of wealth 2 K 20^{13} = Is 39^{9} cf. 2 Ch 32^{27}; royal gifts 1 K 10$^{2.10.25}$ = 2 Ch 9$^{1.19.24}$; cf. sg. 1 K 10^{10} = 2 Ch 9^{9}; as article of commerce Ez 27^{22}; burnt at burial 2 Ch 16^{14};

appointed for ingredient of the anointing oil Ex 25^{6} 35^{8} cf. v^{28} (all P), cf. 1 Ch 9^{30} (Palm. v. supr.); stored in temple 1 Ch 9^{29}; used for purifying the women of Ahasuerus Est 2^{12}; elsewhere only Ct $4^{10.14}$ *spices*, v^{16} *balsam-juice*, gathered Ct 5^{1}; *balsam-tree* הָרֵי ב׳ Ct 8^{14}; *beds of balsam* עֲרוּגוֹת ב׳ Ct 6^{2}; cf. עֲרוּגַת ב׳ Ct 5^{13} sim. of lover's cheeks.

1315 †בָּשְׂמַת **n.pr.f.** (*perfume?*)—**1.** Hittite woman, a wife of Esau Gn 26^{34} (P); called daughter of Ishmael, and sister of Nebaioth Gn 36^{3} (but due prob. to R; this daughter of Ishmael is מַחֲלַת in 28^{9} P); v. also $36^{4.10.13.17}$ (all P) (Sam. has מחלת throughout Gn 36). **2.** daughter of Solomon, wife of Ahimaaz 1 K 4^{15}.

3005 †יִבְשָׂם **n.pr.m.** a descendant of Issachar 1 Ch 7^{2}.

4017 †מִבְשָׂם **n.pr.m.** **1.** a son of Ishmael Gn 25^{13} = 1 Ch 1^{29}. **2.** a descendant of Simeon 1 Ch 4^{25}.

1319 †[בָּשַׂר] **vb. bear tidings** (√*rub, smooth the face;* cf. Ar. بَشَرَ *remove the face or surface of a thing*, cf. Ar. بَشِرَ *be glad, joyful;* بَشَّرَهُ بِمَوْلُودٍ *he rejoiced him with the message of the birth of a son;* Eth. በሰረ: *bring a joyful message*, so As. *bussuru* (Pa.) Dl$^{\text{Pr 170}}$, Sab. תבשר DHM^{MV}, also בשר n.pr.dei, بشير DHM$^{\text{ZMG 1883, 358}}$, CIS$^{\text{iv. 1, 41, 1. 3}}$)—**Pi.** *Pf.* בִּשַּׂר Je 20^{15} + 2 t.; *Impf.* תְּבַשֵּׂר 2 S 18^{20} + 4 t.; אֲבַשְּׂרָה 2 S 18^{19}; *Imv.* בַּשְּׂרוּ 1 Ch 16^{23} = ψ 96^{2}; *Inf.* לְבַשֵּׂר 1 S 31^{9} + 2 t.; *Pt.* מְבַשֵּׂר Is 41^{27} + 6 t.; f. מְבַשֶּׂרֶת Is $40^{9.9}$; pl. מְבַשְּׂרוֹת ψ 68^{12};—**1.** *gladden with good tidings:* birth of a son Je 20^{15}; victory 1 S 31^{9} 2 S 1^{20} 1 Ch 10^{9} ψ 68^{12}; היה כמבשׂר בעיניו *he was in his eyes as a bearer of good tidings* 2 S 4^{10}. **2.** *bear tidings* 2 S $18^{19.20.20.26}$; even of evil 1 S 4^{17}, and so with acc. בשׂר טוב 1 K 1^{42}. **3.** *herald as glad tidings:* the salvation of God, *preach* (chiefly exilic usage) the advent of י׳ in salvation Na 2^{1} Is $40^{9.9}$ 41^{27} $52^{7.7}$; the praises of Yahweh 60^{6}; His righteousness in the great congregation ψ 40^{10}; His salvation daily ψ 96^{2} = 1 Ch 16^{23}; the Messianic servant preaches good tidings to the meek Is 61^{1}. **Hithp.** *Impf.* יִתְבַּשֵּׂר 2 S 18^{31} *receive good tidings* (so Kirkp. Klo; cf. Ar. بَشِرَ IV. X; otherwise AV).

1320 בָּשָׂר$_{266}$ **n.m. flesh** (cf. Ar. بَشَرٌ *skin*, Syr. ܒܶܣܪܳܐ, As. *bišru, blood-relation*, Dl$^{\text{As. Stud. i. 143, cf. Pr. 170}}$, Sab. בשר תורם *flesh of bulls*)—Gn 2^{21} + 126 t.; cstr. בְּשַׂר Gn 17^{11} + 40 t.; sf. בְּשָׂרִי etc. ψ 16^{9} + 96 t.; pl. בְּשָׂרִים Pr 14^{30};—**1.** *of the body:* **a.** *of animals* Gn 41^{2-19} Ex 21^{28} 22^{30} Nu 12^{12} (E) Nu 11^{4-33} (JE) Gn 9^{4} + (P 30 t.) Dt 12^{15} + (D 9 t.) Ju 6^{19-21} 1 S $2^{13.15}$ 1 K 17^{6} 19^{21} Jb 31^{31} 41^{15} ψ 50^{13} Pr 23^{20} Is 22^{13} $44^{16.19}$ 65^{4} 66^{17} Je 7^{21} 11^{15} Ez 4^{14} + 6 t. Dn 10^{3} Ho 8^{13} Mi 3^{3} Hg 2^{12} Zc $11^{9.16}$. **b.** *of men* Gn 40^{19} (E) 2^{21} Ex 4^{7} (J) Lv 12^{3} 13^{2} + 16 t. 26^{29} (P) Dt $28^{53.55}$ 32^{42} Ju 8^{7} 1 S 17^{44} 1 K 4^{34} $5^{10.14}$ 6^{30} 9^{36} Jb 2^{5} 4^{15} 6^{12} 7^{5} 10^{11} 13^{14} $19^{20.22}$ 21^{6} $33^{21.25}$ ψ 27^{2} $38^{4.8}$ 79^{2} 102^{6} 109^{24} Pr 4^{22} 5^{11} Is 9^{19} 17^{4} 49^{26} Je 19^{9} La 3^{4} Ez 32^{5} $37^{6.8}$ $39^{17.18}$ Dn 1^{15} Zc 14^{12}. The flesh of the body is contrasted with stone Ez 11^{19} 36^{26}. **2.** *flesh for the body itself* (esp. in P): על בשׂר אדם לא ייסך *upon the body of man it shall not be poured* Ex 30^{32} (P); מכנסי בד ילבש על בשׂרו *linen drawers shall he put on his body* Lv 6^{3} 16^{4} (P); וישׂם שׂק על בשׂרו 1 K 21^{27}; ורחץ את בשׂרו *and he shall bathe his body* Lv 14^{9} $15^{13.16}$ $16^{24.26.28}$ 17^{16} 22^{6} Nu $19^{7.8}$ (P); שׂרט לנפש לא תתנו בבשׂרכם *ye shall not put any cutting for any one in your body* Lv 19^{28} cf. Lv 21^{5} (P); והעבירו תער על כל בשׂרם *and they shall pass a razor over all their body* Nu 8^{7} (P). Ec. uses בשׂר only in this sense 2^{3} 4^{5} 5^{5} 11^{10} 12^{12}; elsewhere this usage only in poetry; the body antith. to נפשׁ Jb 14^{22} Is 10^{18} ψ 63^{2}; לב ψ 16^{9} 84^{3} Pr 14^{30} (only here emphatic pl. = *entire body* Bö$^{\text{§695}}$, *Leiblichkeit* De); מִבְּשָׂרִי *apart from my body*, in disembodied state Jb 19^{26}; סמר מפחדך בשׂרי *my body trembleth for fear of thee* ψ 119^{120}. **3.** *male organ of generation* (euphemism): בְּשַׂר עָרְלַתְכֶם Gn $17^{11.14.23.24.25}$ (P); בשׂר ערוה Ex 28^{42} (P), but בשׂר Gn 17^{14} Lv 15^{2-19} (P) Ez 16^{26} 23^{20} $44^{7.9}$. **4.** *flesh for kindred, blood-relations:* עצם מעצמי ובשׂר מבשׂרי *bone of my bone and flesh of my flesh* Gn 2^{23} (J); והיו לבשׂר אחד *and they shall become one flesh* Gn 2^{24} (J); עצמי ובשׂרי Gn 29^{14} (J) Ju 9^{2} 2 S 5^{1} $19^{13.14}$ 1 Ch 11^{1}; בשׂר with sf. in same sense Gn 37^{27} (J) Ne 5^{5} Is 58^{7}, for which שְׁאֵר בשׂרו *near of kin*, man or woman Lv 18^{6} 25^{49} (both H; 25^{49} ‖ מִשְׁפָּחָה, cf. RS$_{\text{K}}$$^{\text{149}}$). **5.** *man over against God as frail* or *erring* Gn 6^{3} (J) ψ 56^{5} 78^{39}; eyes of flesh Jb 10^{4}; arm of flesh 2 Ch 32^{8} Je 17^{5}; horses are flesh not spirit Is 31^{3}. **6.** the phrase כָּל־בָּשָׂר: **a.** *all living beings* Gn $6^{17.19}$ 7^{21} $9^{11.15.16.17}$ Lv 17^{14} Nu 18^{15} (P) Jb 34^{15} ψ 136^{25}. **b.** *animals* Gn $7^{15.16}$ 8^{17} (P). **c.** *mankind* Gn $6^{12.13}$ Nu 16^{22} 27^{16} (P) Dt 5^{23} ψ 65^{3} 145^{21} Is $40^{5.6}$ 49^{26} $66^{16.23.24}$ Je 12^{12} 25^{31} 32^{27} 45^{5} Ez $21^{4.9.10}$ Jo 3^{1} Zc 2^{17}; cf. כל בשׂר איש Jb 12^{10}.

†בְּשֹׂרָה **n.f. tidings** (cf. Ar. بِشَارَةٌ v. Ba 1309
$^{\text{NB 61}}$; Sab. בשרן DHM$^{\text{ZMG 1876, 672}}$), 2 S 4^{10} + 3 t.; בְּשׂוֹרָה 2 S $18^{25.27}$—**1.** *good tidings* 1 K

7^9. **2.** *tidings, news* 2 S $18^{20.25}$; with טובה 2 S 18^{27}. **3.** *reward for good tidings* 2 S 4^{10} 18^{22}.

1308 †בְּשׂוֹר **n.pr.** of brook in Philistine territory; alw. נַחַל הַבְּשׂוֹר 1 S $30^{9.10.21}$; 𝔊 Βοσορ (v^{21} Βεανα, but 𝔊L Βοσορ); mod. *Wady Razze* (Gaza) acc. to Guérin $^{Judée\ ii.\ 213}$;—it empties into sea SW of Gaza. (Connexion with above √ dub.)

1310 †בָּשֵׁל **vb. boil, seethe** (intr.), **grow ripe** (Aram. בְּשֵׁל, ܒܫܠ *ripen*, Nas. ܒܫܠ *boil*, NSyr. ܒܫܠ *be boiled, cooked*, cf. As. *bašâlu* (*bašlu*, *cooked*) Zim $^{BP\ 76}$)—**Qal** *Pf.* בָּשַׁל Jo 4^{13}, בָּשְׁלוּ Ez 24^5;—*boil, cook* (intr.) Ez 24^5; *grow ripe* (of קציר) Jo 4^{13};—**Pi.** *Pf.* 3 ms. sf. בִּשְּׁלָם 1 K 19^{21}; וּבִשַּׁלְתָּ Ex 29^{31} Dt 16^7, בִּשְּׁלוּ La 4^{10} + 2 t., וּבִשְּׁלוּ consec. Zc 14^{21}; *Impf.* 3 fs. וַתְּבַשֵּׁל 2 S 13^8; 2 ms. תְּבַשֵּׁל Ex 23^{19} + 2 t., וַיְבַשְּׁלוּ, יְבַשְּׁלוּ Ez $46^{20.24}$, 2 Ch 35^{13}, תְּבַשְּׁלוּ Ex 16^{23}, וַנְּבַשֵּׁל 2 K 6^{29}; *Imv.* בַּשֵּׁל 2 K 4^{38}, בַּשְּׁלוּ Lv 8^{31}, בַּשֵּׁלוּ Ex 16^{23}; *Inf.* בַּשֵּׁל 1 S 2^{13}; *Pt.* מְבַשְּׁלִים Ez 46^{24};—**1.** *boil* (tr.) obj. om. Nu 11^8, בָּשָׂר 1 S 2^{13}; גְּדִי Ex 23^{19} 34^{26} Dt 14^{21}; נזיד 2 K 4^{38}; of offerings, obj. הקדשים 2 Ch 35^{13}; obj. אשם Ez 46^{20}, זבח Ez 46^{24} (no obj.) v^{24}, cf. Zc 14^{21} (no obj.); Ex $16^{23.23}$ opp. אפה *bake*. **2.** *cook* (general), obj. בשר 1 K 19^{21} Ex 29^{31} Lv 8^{31} (both P); obj. בֵּן 2 K 6^{29} cf. יֶלֶד La 4^{10}; hence also of הפסח Dt 16^7 (cf. Di; ‖ Ex $12^{8.9}$ has צְלִי אֵשׁ opp. מְבֻשָּׁל בַּמָּיִם) 2 Ch 35^{13} (בָּאֵשׁ), cakes (הלבבות) 2 S 13^8. **Pu.** *Pf.* 3 fs. בֻּשָּׁלָה Lv 6^{21}; *Impf.* 3 fs. תְּבֻשַּׁל־ Lv 6^{21}; *Pt.* מְבֻשָּׁל Ex 12^9 1 S 2^{15};—*be boiled, sodden*, במים Ex 12^9 cf. Lv $6^{21.21}$ (all P) 1 S 2^{15}. **Hiph.** *Pf.* הִבְשִׁילוּ *ripened, brought to ripeness* Gn 40^{10} (a vine, its grape-clusters).

1311 †בָּשֵׁל **adj. cooked, boiled** (As. *bašlu, ripe* COT ^{Gloss})—Ex 12^9 בָּשֵׁל מְבֻשָּׁל במים; f. בְּשֵׁלָה Nu 6^{19}, (both P).

4018 †מְבַשְּׁלוֹת **n.f.pl. cooking-places** Ez 46^{23} (cf. בֵּית הַמְבַשְּׁלִים v^{24}).

1312 †בִּשְׁלָם **n.pr.m.** (= בֶּן־שָׁלֹם *son of peace?* cf. sub בן) a Persian officer in Canaan Ezr 4^7.

בשן (√ of foll. = *smooth, soft?* cf. Ar. بَثْنَةٌ, بِثْنَةٌ *soft and smooth ground*).

1316 בָּשָׁן $_{60}$ **n.pr.terr.m.** $^{Dt\ 3,3}$ (*smooth* (& fertile) land) **Bashan**, first mentioned as kingdom of Og, E. of Jordan, stretching from stream Jabbok (thus including northern Gilead) northward to Hermon, between Gennesaret (W) and mts of Hauran (E); cf. Di Nu 21^{33} Wetzst $^{Hauran\ 82}$; later a type of fertility;—usually c. art. הַבּ׳ Nu $21^{33.33}$ 32^{33} Dt 1^4 + 30 t. Dt Jos; 1 K $4^{13.19}$ 2 K 10^{33} 1 Ch $5^{11.12.16.23}$ $6^{47.56}$ Ne 9^{22} ψ 68^{23} 135^{11} 136^{20} Je 22^{20} 50^{19} (‖ הַכַּרְמֶל), Mi 7^{14} (‖ *id.*), Na 1^4 (‖ *id.*; personif., subj. of אֻמְלַל), Is 33^9 (‖ *id.*; personif. subj. of נֹעֵר); הַר־בָּשָׁן (i.e. range of Hauran) ψ $68^{16.16}$ (called הַר־אלהים,—from a sanctuary there?—& הַר־גַּבְנֻנִּים *many-peaked mt.*); of stately trees אַלּוֹנֵי הַבּ׳ Is 2^{13} (still seen on western slope of mts. of Hauran, Wetzst $^{Hauran\ 88}$); אַלּוֹנֵי ב׳ Zc 11^2 (fig. of prominent men); אַלּוֹנִים מִבּ׳ Ez 27^6; of bulls אַבִּירֵי ב׳ ψ 22^{13} (‖ פָּרִים, fig.); so בְּנֵי־ב׳ Dt 32^{14} (+ אֵילִים) כָּרִים also עַתּוּדִים, cf. בָּקָר & צֹאן v^a; vid. בֵּן **1. j.** (ν)); appar. more general is מְרִיאֵי ב׳ Ez 39^{18} (ref. to אֵילִים כָּרִים וְעַתּוּדִים פָּרִים . . . כֻּלָּם); once of kine (fem., fig. of luxurious and haughty women of Samaria) Am 4^1 פָּרוֹת הַבּ׳.

†בָּשָׁן־ **n.pr.loc.** in south. Judah הַבּ׳ Jos 15^{62}. 5044

בָּשְׁנָה v. sub בוש. p. 102 1317

†[בשס] **vb. Po.** *Inf.* sf. בּוֹשַׁסְכֶם Am 5^{11} prob. *your trampling* (by dissim. fr. בוס) sq. עַל. 1318

בֹּשֶׁת v. sub בוש. p. 102 1322

I. בַּת *daughter* v. sub בן. p. 123 1323

II. בַּת *bath* (a measure), בָּתָּה v. sub בתת. 1324

p. 144

†I. בְּתוּאֵל **n.pr.m.** (? = מְתוּאֵל *man of God*) Gn $22^{22.23}$ $24^{15.24.47.50}$ (J) son of Nahor, neph. of Abr., living in Aram-Naharaim, in city of Nahor; 25^{20} $28^{2.5}$ (P) Aramaean of Paddan-Aram. 1328

†II. בְּתוּאֵל **n.pr.loc.** in Simeon 1 Ch 4^{30} = 1328
בְּתוּל Jos 19^4; כְּסִיל 15^{30}; בֵּית־אֵל 1 S 30^{27} (v. p. 111 1329
supr.); yet cf. Lag $^{BN\ 64}$; site unknown.

בְּתוּל v. II. בְּתוּאֵל. above 1329

בִּתְיָה v. בַּת sub בן, p. 124. 1332

בָּתִּים v. בית. p. 108 1004

בתל (cf. Ar. بَتَلَ *sever, separate*).

†בְּתוּלָה $_{50}$ **n.f. virgin** (cf. Ar. بَتِيلٌ, بَتُولٌ, 1330
As. *batultu* (also *batûlu* of young man) 5 R 42^{56} v. Jer $^{ZA\ 1886,\ 399}$; NH בְּתוּלָה, ܒܬܘܠܬܐ)—Gn 24^{16} + 19 t.; cstr. בְּתוּלַת Dt 22^{19} + 12 t.; pl. בְּתוּלֹת Est 2^2 + 7 t.; בְּתֻלוֹת Zc 9^{17}; בְּתוּלֹת Ex 22^{16} + 2 t.; בְּתֻלֹת La 5^{11}; sf. בְּתוּלֹתָיו ψ 78^{63} + 3 t.;—one living apart in her father's house as *a virgin* Gn 24^{16} (J) Ex 22^{15} (E) Lv $21^{3.14}$ (P) Dt 22^{19} Ju 19^{24} 2 S 13^2 Jb 31^1 Is 62^5 Je 2^{32} 31^{13} Jo 1^8; נערה בתולה *a virgin damsel* Dt $22^{23.28}$ Ju 21^{12} 1 K 1^2 Est 2^3; בחור ובתולה Dt 32^{25} 2 Ch

36[17] Je 51[22] Ez 9[6]; personification of nations בתולת ישׂראל Je 18[13] 31[4.21] Am 5[2]; ב׳ בת ציון 2 K 19[21] (= Is 37[22]; on double st. cstr. v. Ges §130.5 Phi St. Cstr. 63) La 2[13]; ב׳ בת יהודה La 1[15]; ב׳ בת עמי Je 14[17]; ב׳ בת צידון Is 23[12]; ב׳ בת בבל Is 47[1]; ב׳ בת מצרים Je 46[11]; pl. *virgins* Ex 22[16] 2 S 13[18] Est 2[2.17.19] ψ 45[15] 78[63] La 1[4] 2[10] 5[11] Ez 44[22] Am 8[13]; בחורים ובתולות ψ 148[12] Is 23[4] Zc 9[17] La 1[18] 2[21].

1331 †בְּתוּלִים **n.f. virginity,** pl. abs. intens. Dt 22[14.17.20]; cstr. בְּתוּלֵי Dt 22[15.17], all concrete, *tokens of virginity;* abstr., sf. בְּתוּלַי Ju 11[37]; בְּתוּלֶיהָ Lv 21[13] Ju 11[38] Ez 23[8]; בְּתוּלֵיהֶן Ez 23[3].

1333 †[בָּתַק] **vb. cut, cut off, cut down** (As. *batâḳu*, COT Gloss. Zim BP 104 n.; cf. also Ar. بَتَكَ *secuit, amputavit*)—only **Pi.** *Pf.* consec. וּבִתְּקוּךְ בחרבותם Ez 16[40] *and they shall cut thee to pieces with their swords.*

1334 †[בָּתַר] **vb. cut in two** (Ar. بَتَرَ *cut off prematurely; extirpate by cutting*)—**Qal** *Pf.* בָּתַר Gn 15[10]; **Pi.** *Impf.* וַיְבַתֵּר Gn 15[10] *id.*

1335 †[בֶּתֶר] **n.m.** Gn 15, 10 **part, piece. 1.** בִּתְרוֹ Gn 15[10]; pl. sf. בְּתָרָיו Je 34[18], בִּתְרֵי הָעֵגֶל Je 34[19]; always of halves of animals cut in two in
1336 making covenants. **2.** הָרֵי בָתֶר Ct 2[17] *mountains of cutting,* i.e. *cleft mountains* 𝔊 Thes al.; or *of separation* (between us) Ew al.; acc. to We Prol. 415, Eng. Tr. 391 ב׳ = *malobathron.—Bether* as n.pr. AV RV.

†בִּתְרוֹן prob. **n.pr.terr.** (*cleft, ravine*) 1338
E. of Jordan; כָּל־הַבּ׳ 2 S 2[29].

בתת

(? *cut off, sever,* cf. Ar. بَتَّ, *secuit, resecuit, abrupit*).

†II. בַּת **n.m.** Ez 45, 14 (**f.** Is 5, 10) **bath** (Thes al. 1324
fr. above √ in sense of *define, measure;* cf. τέμνω; Lag Or. ii. 10 f. makes = בדת, = בד + fem. ת; cf. Syr. ܒܬ, instrument for pressing olives; cf. Epiphan. βάδος = ἐλαιοτριβεῖον; & βάδος also Hesych. Jos Ant. viii. 2. 9 but ed. Niese βάτους, βάτος)—ב׳ abs. Is 5[10] + 6 t.; (בָּ֑ת Ez 45[11]) cstr. Ez 45[10]; pl. בַּתִּים 2 Ch 2[9.9] + 3 t.;—a liquid measure = אֵיפָה of dry measure, each being $\frac{1}{10}$ חֹמֶר (q.v.) Ez 45[11.11.14.14]; also Is 5[10] 1 K 7[26.38] 2 Ch 2[9.9] 4[5] + Ez 45[14.14] (4 t. in this v., Co del. *a* & *d*). Ez 45[10] בַּת־צֶדֶק *a righteous* (right, accurate, full) *bath* (‖ אֵיפַת־צֶדֶק). The actual size of bath (= ephah) is appar. c. 40 litres (= Attic *metretes* cf. Jos Ant. viii. 2. 9; = 39.39 lit. cf. Boeckh Metrol. Untersuch. 259 f.; v. also J. Brandis Münz- Mass- u. Gewichtswesen 29 f. Smith Dict. Bible, art. Weights & Measures Ri HWB 934 f.).—I. בַּת v. sub בֵּן.

†[בַּתָּה] **n.f. precipice, steep** (as *cut off,* 1327
abrupt)—בְּנַחֲלֵי הַבַּתּוֹת Is 7[19] *in the ravines of the precipices.*

†בָּתָה **n.f. end, destruction** (for בַּתָּה, perh. 1326
on account of difference of meaning, perh. fr. analogy of כָּלָה with like sense; cf. Di)—וַאֲשִׁיתֵהוּ בָתָה Is 5[6] *and I will make it* (the vineyard) *a destruction,* a waste, or (Che) *make an end of it.*

ג

ג, גּ, *Gîmel,* third letter; in postB Heb. = numeral 3 (and so margin of printed MT); ג̈ = 3000; no evidence of this usage in OT times.

1341 גֵּא v. sub. גאה. below

1342 †גָּאָה **vb. rise up** (Aram. Pe. (𝔗 1 S 2[5]) & oft. Ethp. אִתְגָּאֵי, ܐܬܓܐܝ *be boastful, proud,* cf. also NH)—**Qal** *Pf.* ג׳ Ex 15[1.21], גָּאוּ Ez 47[5]; *Impf.* יִגְאֶה Jb 8[11] 10[16]; *Inf.* abs. גָּאֹה Ex 15[1.21];—**1.** *rise up,* of waters Ez 47[5]. **2.** *grow up,* of plants Jb 8[11]. **3.** *be lifted up, exalted,* of head Jb 10[16], of י׳ in triumph Ex 15[1.21].

1341 †גֵּא **adj.** proud, scribal error for גֵּאֶה Is 16[6] (as in Je 48[29]).

1343 †גֵּאֶה **adj. proud,** Jb 40[11.12] Is 2[12] Je 48[29]; pl. גֵּאִים ψ 94[2] 140[6] Pr 15[25] 16[19]; cstr. גְּאֵי ψ 123[4] Qr גאי יונים (> Kt גאיונים), yet cf. De al.

†גַּאֲוָה **n.f.** pride, Pr 8[13]. 1344

†גַּאֲוָה **n.f. majesty, pride** (cf. Syr. ܓܐܘܬܐ) 1346
—Jb 41[7] + 6 t.; cstr. גַּאֲוַת Pr 29[23] + 2 t.; sf. גַּאֲוָתִי Is 13[3] + 8 t.;—**1.** *rising up, swelling* of the sea ψ 46[4]. **2.** *majesty,* of Israel Dt 33[29], Moab Is 16[6] = Je 48[29], scales of crocodile Jb 41[7], of God Dt 33[26] ψ 68[35]. **3.** *pride, haughtiness* ψ 10[2] 31[19.24] 36[12] 73[6] Pr 14[3] 29[23] Is 9[8] 13[11] 25[11]; עליזי גאותי *my proudly exulting ones* Is 13[3] cf. Zp 3[11].

†גָּאוֹן **n.m.** Ho 5, 5 **exaltation**—Jb 40[10] + 5 t.; 1347
cstr. גְּאוֹן Lv 26[19] + 31 t.; sf. גְּאוֹנְךָ etc. Ex 15[7] + 9 t.; pl. sf. גְּאוֹנָ֑יִךְ Ez 16[56];—**1.** *exaltation, majesty, excellence,* **a.** of nations, their wealth, power, magnificence of buildings, e.g. Egypt Ez 32[12], Chaldeans Is 13[11.19] 14[11], Philistines Zc 9[6], Assyria Zc 10[11], Jacob ψ 47[5] Am

6^{8} 8^{7} Na 2^{3}, Israel Ho 5^{5} 7^{10} (prob. appellation of 'י), Na 2^{3}, Judah Je 13^{9}, Jerusalem v^{9} Ez 16^{56}; גְּאוֹן עֻזָּהּ *pride of her strength* Ez 30$^{6.18}$ 33^{28}; גאון עזים Ez 7^{24} (but 𝔊 Ew Hi Co rd. עזם); גאון עזכם Lv 26^{19} Ez 24^{21}; the fruit of land of Judah will become לגאון ולתפארת *majestic and beautiful* Is 4^{2}; גאון כל צבי *the majesty of all the splendour* (of Tyre) Is 23^{9}; Zion is to become גאון עולם *an everlasting excellency* Is 60^{15}. **b.** of God Ex 15^{7} Is 24^{14} Mi 5^{3}; הֲדַר גְּאוֹנוֹ Is 2$^{10.19.21}$; יַרְעֵם בְּקוֹל גְּאוֹנוֹ Jb 37^{4}; עֲדֵה נָא גָּאוֹן וָגֹבַהּ Jb 40^{10}. **c.** גאון הירדן *majesty of the Jordan*, referring to the green and shady banks, clothed with willows, tamarisks, and cane, in which the lions made their covert Je 49^{19} 50^{44} Zc 11^{3}, and therefore dangerous Je 12^{5} (Ew thinks of the *swelling* of its agitated waters); גְּאוֹן גַּלֶּיךָ *majesty of thy waves* Jb 38^{11}. **2.** *pride* (bad sense) Jb 35^{12} ψ 59^{13} Pr 8^{13} 16^{18} Ez 7^{20} 16^{49} Zp 2^{10}; of Moab Is 16$^{6.6}$=Je 48$^{29.29}$.

1348 †גֵּאוּת **n.f. majesty,** ψ 93^{1} + 7 t.;—**1.** *lifting up* גֵּאוּת עָשָׁן *column of smoke* Is 9^{17}; גֵּאוּת הַיָּם *swelling of the sea* ψ 89^{10}. **2.** *majesty* of God ψ 93^{1} Is 26^{10}; גֵּאוּת עָשָׂה *he hath done majestically* Is 12^{5}; עֲטֶרֶת גֵּאוּת *crown of majesty* Is 28$^{1.3}$ (Samaria, on a round hill majestically commanding the country). **3.** *pride* דִּבְּרוּ בְגֵאוּת *they speak proudly* ψ 17^{10}; so for גאות 74^{20} Bi Che.

1345 †גְּאוּאֵל **n.pr.m.** (*majesty of Ēl*) the spy of the tribe of Gad Nu 13^{15}.

1349 †[גַּאֲיוֹן] **adj. proud,** גאיונים ψ 123^{4} (Kt cf. Baer's note, yet rd. prob. גַּאֲיוֹנִים; but Qr better, גְּאֵי יוֹנִים *proudest oppressors*, v. גֵּאֶה).

גאיונים v. foregoing, and also גֵּאֶה.

1466 גֵּוָה **n.f. pride** (contr. for גַּאֲוָה Ew$^{§ 62 b, 73 b}$ cf. Aram. Dn 4^{34} & 𝔗)—**1.** *pride* Jb 33^{17} Je 13^{17}. **2.** *lifting up* Jb 22^{29} an exclamation, *up!* Ew Di De al.; but *pride* Hi Dr$^{§ 154 n. (ed. 3)}$.

גֵּאָיוֹת v. גַּיְא.

1350 †I. גָּאַל **vb. redeem, act as kinsman** (NH, Niph. *be redeemed*; also גואל, גאולה)—**Qal** *Pf.* גָּאַל, etc. Is 44^{23} + 14 t.; *Impf.* יִגְאַל, etc. Lv 25^{33} + 18 t.; *Imv.* גְּאַל, etc. Ru 4^{6} + 3 t.; *Inf.* abs. גָּאֹל Lv 27^{13} + 2 t.; cstr. לִגְאוֹל Ru 4^{4} + 2 t.; sf. לְגָאֳלֵךְ Ru 3^{13}; *Pt.* גֹּאֵל Lv 25^{26} + 24 t., גּוֹאֵל Is 59^{20} ψ 103^{4}; sf. גֹּאַלְךָ Is 48^{17}, גֹּאֲלֵךְ Is 54^{8} (sf. 19 t.); pass. pl. גְּאוּלִים, etc. Is 35^{9} + 4 t.;—**1.** *act as kinsman, do the part of next of kin* (chiefly in D H P Ru), גֹּאֵל *kinsman* Lv 25^{25} (H) Nu 5^{8} 35^{12} (P) Ru 2^{20} 3$^{9.12}$ 4$^{1.3.6.8.14}$ 1 K 16^{11}. **a.** in taking a kinsman's widow אם יגאלך טוב יגאל ואם לא יחפץ לגאלך וגאלתיך *if he will do thee the kinsman's part* (raise up children by the widow) *well, let him do the kinsman's part; but if he is not pleased to do thee the kinsman's part then I will do thee the kinsman's part* Ru 3^{13}; **b.** in redeeming from bondage Lv 25$^{48.49}$ (H); **c.** in redeeming a field Lv 25$^{26.33}$ (H) Ru 4$^{4.6}$; **d.** claim as kinsman Jb 3^{5}; **e.** גֹּאֵל הַדָּם *the avenger of blood* Nu 35$^{19.21.24.25.27.27}$ Jos 20$^{3.5}$ (?; not in 𝔊) v^{9} (P). Dt 19$^{6.12}$ (D) 2 S 14^{11}. **2.** *redeem*, by payment of value assessed, of consecrated things, by the original owner Lv 27$^{13.15.19.20.31}$ (P). **3.** *redeem*, with God as subj. implying personal relationship, chiefly in poetry:—**a.** individuals, from death ψ 103^{4} La 3^{58} Ho 13^{14}, מכל רע Gn 48^{16} (E poetry), נפש ψ 69^{19} 72^{14}, orphans Pr 23^{11} Je 50^{34}, ריבה ריבי וגאלני ψ 119^{154}, גֹּאֲלִי Jb 19^{25}, צוּרִי וְגֹאֲלִי ψ 19^{15}. **b.** Israel, from Egyptian bondage Ex 6^{6} (P?) 15^{13} (song) ψ 74^{2} 77^{16} 78^{35}, מיד אויב ψ 106^{10}. **c.** from exile (chiefly Is^{3}, the vb. not in Is^{1}) Is 43^{1} 44$^{22.23}$ 48^{20} 52^{9} 63^{9} Mi 4^{10}, מיד ψ 107^{2} Je 31^{11}; Yahweh is גֹּאֵל Is 41^{14} 43^{14} 44$^{6.24}$ 47^{4} 48^{17} 49$^{7.26}$ 54$^{5.8}$ 59^{20} 60^{16} 63^{16}; and the people גְּאוּלִים Is 35^{9} 51^{10} 62^{12} 63^{4} (cf. גְּאוּלַי infr.), ψ 107^{2}. **Niph.** *Pf.* נִגְאַל Lv 25^{49}; *Impf.* יִגָּאֵל Lv 25^{30} + 5 t.; תִּגָּאֵלוּ Is 52^{3};—**1.** refl. *redeem oneself* Lv 25^{49} (H). **2.** pass. *be redeemed*, **a.** field Lv 25^{30} (H), slave Lv 25^{54} (H); **b.** consecrated things Lv 27$^{20.27.28.33}$ (P); **c.** Jerusalem by Yahweh Is 52^{3}.

†גְּאוּלַי Is 63^{4}, in שְׁנַת ג׳, **n.abstr.** *redemption*, acc. to 𝔊 𝔖 𝔙 Ges Hi De MV Che Di RVm; then either pl. abstr. sf. *year of (my) redemption* (so most); or abstr. form. in ־ַי, after Syr. analogy, Lag$^{Symm. ii. 101 f. Sem. i. 19, 68. BN 192}$ (𝔊 om. *my*); but < Pt. pass. pl. sf. *my ransomed (released) ones* Ew Br Brd AV RV cf. sub גאל supra.

†גְּאֻלָּה^{14} **n.f. kin**(?), **redemption**—Lv 25^{24} 1353
+ 5 t.; cstr. גְּאֻלַּת Lv 25^{32}; sf. גְּאֻלָּתִי Ru 4^{6}, גְּאֻלָּתְךָ Ez 11^{15}, גְּאֻלָּתוֹ Lv 25^{26} + 4 t.;—**1.** *kin*, אַנְשֵׁי גְאֻלָּתֶךָ *men of thy kindred* Ez 11^{15}, RV Thes Hi al.; but 𝔊 𝔖 Ew Co א׳ גלותך *thy fellow-exiles*. **2.** *redemption*, of field Lv 25^{24} (H) Ru 4^{7}. **3.** *right of redemption* Lv 25$^{29.31.32.48}$ (H) Ru 4^{6} Je 32^{8}=משפט הגאלה Je 32^{7}. **4.** *price of redemption* Lv 25$^{26.51.52}$ (H).

†יִגְאָל **n.pr.m.** (*He redeems*)—**1.** one of the 3008
spies Nu 13^{7}. **2.** one of David's heroes 2 S 23^{36}. **3.** descendant of Zerubbabel 1 Ch 3^{22}.

1351 †II. [גָּאַל] **vb.** defile, late (cf. גָּעַל)—**Niph.** *Pf.* 3 mpl. נְגֹאֲלוּ Is 59^3 La 4^{14}, on form v. Ges$^{§ 51, 2}$, Kö$^{i. 265}$; *Pt.* נְגֹאָלָה Zp 3^1;—*be defiled*, hands with blood בַּדָּם, Is 59^3 cf. La 4^{14}; pt. as subst. *defiled, polluted one* Zp 3^1 of Jerusalem (‖ מֹרְאָה; appos. הָעִיר הַיּוֹנָה). **Pi.** *Pf.* 1 pl. sf. גֵּאַלְנוּךָ Mal 1^7 *pollute, desecrate*, obj. ׳י (desecrated in his altar). **Pu.** *Impf.* וַיְגֹאֲלוּ מִן־הַכְּהֻנָּה Ezr 2^{62} = Ne 7^{64} cstr. pregn. *and they were desecrated out of the priesthood*, i.e. deposed, as desecrated ones; *Pt.* מְגֹאָל of bread laid on Yahweh's altar Mal 1^7; of Yahweh's altar (table, שֻׁלְחָן) v^{12}. **Hiph.** *Pf.* 1 s. אֶגְאָלְתִּי Is 63^3 (on Aram. form v. Kö$^{i. 27}$ Ges$^{§ 53 R. 6}$ but) rd. perh. גֵּאַלְתִּי *Pi.*, v. GFM$^{ThLZ\ 1887, 292}$ cf. also Ges$^{l.c.\ N.}$ Ol$^{§ 255\ b}$ Sta$^{§ 159\ b, 3}$;—*I have polluted*, i.e. *stained, all my raiment*. **Hithp.** *Impf.* יִתְגָּאַל Dn 1^8; יִתְגָּאַל v^8;—*defile himself*.

1352 †[גֹּאַל] **n.[m.]** defiling, defilement, גָּאֳלֵי הַכְּהֻנָּה Ne 13^{29}.

1354 גַּב back, etc., v. sub גבב. below

1461 [גֵּב], גֵּבִים v. גוב p. 155.

1357 I. [גֵּב] *locust*, v. sub גבה. below

1356 II. [גֵּב] pit, III. [גֵּב] *beam*, v. sub גוב. p. 155

1359 גֹּב, גּוֹב **n.pr.loc.** v. sub גבב. below

גבא (cf. Ar. جَبَا, جَبِىَ *restrain* or *withhold oneself*; perh. = جَبَا *collect* (water in a cistern, also tribute), so Lane جَبَى I. ad fin., Fl NHWB$^{i. 431}$; v. also NH גבי, גָּבָה, Aram. גְּבָא, ܓܒܐ, *collect* debts, taxes, etc.)

1360 †גֶּבֶא **n.m.** $^{Ez\ 47, 11}$ cistern, pool (cf. Ar. جَابِيَةٌ *watering-trough*)—**1.** *cistern* מַיִם מִגֶּבֶא Is 30^{14}. **2.** *pool, marsh* גְּבָאָיו Ez 47^{11} (‖ בִּצֹּאתוֹ).

גבב (prob. *be curved, convex, elevated*, Aram. גַּבְּבָא *hill; be* or *make hollow, dig*, Ar. جَبَّ *cut off* or *out*, جُبٌّ, Aram. גֹּב, Eth. ገበ: As. *gubbu*,—all = *cistern*; cf. e.g. As. *gubbâni ša mê, cisterns of water*, Asrb$^{Annals\ Col.\ viii. 102}$, KB$^{ii. 220}$; v. n.pr. גֹּב infr.)

1354 †גַּב **n.m.** $^{?cf.\ Ez\ 43, 13}$ (**f.**$^{Ez\ 1, 18}$) anything convex, curved, gibbous, e.g. **back**, chiefly late;—abs. גַּב Ez 16^{24}; cstr. גַּב Ez 43^{13} (rd. גֹּבַהּ 𝔊 Ew Sm Co); sf. גַּבִּי ψ 129^3, גַּבֵּךְ Ez $16^{31.39}$; pl. cstr. גַּבֹּת Lv 14^9, גַּבֵּי Jb 13^{12} 15^{26}; sf. גַּבֵּיהֶם 1 K 7^{33}, גַּבֵּהֶם Ez 10^{12}, גַּבֵּיהֶן Ez 1^{18}, גַּבֹּתָם Ez 1^{18};—**1.** *back*, of man (fig. of Isr.) ψ 129^3; appar. of cherubim Ez 10^{12}, but Hi Sm emend v. so that ׳גּ ref. to wheels, *rim* v. **6** infr. **2.** *mound*, for illicit worship Ez $16^{24.31.39}$ (all ‖ רמה); 𝔊 𝔙 *lupanar, brothel*, after analogy of *fornix*, but this without sufficient proof, & needless. **3.** *boss*, or convex projection, of shield Jb 15^{26} (fig.) *he runneth against him . . . with the stout bosses of his shields* (i.e. wicked against ׳י); so ظهر in Ar. in similar phrase; cf. also Ar. جَوْبٌ, *shield*; also French *bouclier* fr. *boucle*. **4.** *bulwarks, breastworks*, fig. for arguments לְגַבֵּי־חֹמֶר גַּבֵּיכֶם Jb 13^{12} *breastworks of clay are your breastworks*. **5.** *brow*, only גַּבֹּת עֵינָיו Lv 14^9 *his eyebrows*. **6.** *rim* of wheel, *felloe* 1 K 7^{33} Ez $1^{18.18}$; so perh. 10^{12} v. **1** supr.—Ez 43^{13}; *elevation*, i.e. basement of altar, Da after MT., but v. גֹּבַהּ, cf. supr.

†גֹּב 2 S 21^{18}, גּוֹב v^{19} **n.pr.loc.** (cf. Aram. 1359
גֻּבָּא *den*, and ܓܘܒܐ, Ar. جُبٌّ, Eth. ገበ: As. *gubbu, well, cistern*, v. גבב)—field of battle with Philistines 2 S 21^{18} = גֶּזֶר in ‖ 1 Ch 20^4 (so here Th Ew; cf. Jos 10^{33}), but = גַּת 𝔊 𝔖 2 S 21^{18} (𝔊L Γαζεθ); 2 S 21^{19} (om. ‖ 1 Ch 20^5), 𝔊 Ρομ, Ροβ; Klo *Gath*; in v^{16} We Dr (q. v.) rd. בְּנֹב for בְּנֹב; site of Gob (si vera l.) unknown.

†גַּבַּי סַלָּי appar. **n.pr.m.** (cf. Aram. ܓܒܝܐ, 1373
Talm. גַּבַּי, *tax-gatherer*) a Benjamite Ne 11^8; but text dub. cf. 1 Ch 9^8 & Sm$^{Listen\ 7}$.

†גִּבְּתוֹן **n.pr.loc.** (*mound, height*, cf. 𝔗 גִּבְּבָא 1405
ridge) Philistine city 1 K $15^{27.27}$ $16^{15.17}$; assigned to Dan Jos 19^{44}, and to Levites 21^{23}: site unknown; cf. Lag$^{Onom.\ 246,\ 2nd\ ed.\ 255}$.

גבה (*collect*, Ar. جَبَا (= جَبَأَ?, cf. גבא supr.), NH גָּבָה, גַּבִּי, Aram. גְּבָא, ܓܒܐ; ‖ form גבא q.v.)

†I. [גֵּב] **n.[m.]** locust (name from *swarm*, 1357
collection, Eth. ጎበአ: cf. also Eth. አንበጣ: *locust* √ = Ar. نَبَطَ *scaturivit, manavit*), only pl. גֵּבִים Is 33^4 (in sim. of leaping).—גֵּב II, III, v. sub גוב.

†גּוֹב **n.[m.]** locusts, Na 3^{17}; cf. גֹּבַי. below 1462

†גֹּבַי, גּוֹבַי **n.m.** $^{Am.\ 7, 1,\ cf.\ v.\ 2}$ **coll. locusts** 1462
(*swarm, multitude*; Aram. גּוֹבָא, pl. גּוֹבָאֵי; on format. v. Ol$^{§ 216\ d}$), גֹּבַי symbol of Yahweh's judgment on Isr. Am 7^1; in sim. of disappearance of Assyrian leaders at destruction of Nineveh גּוֹב גּוֹבָי Na 3^{17} (*locust-*) *swarm of locusts* (‖ אַרְבֶּה); but del. גּוֹב as dittogr. We al.

†גָּבַהּ **vb.** be high, exalted (NH *id.* 1361
(Hiph.), Aram. גְּבַהּ, cf. Ar. جَبْهَةٌ *forehead*, جَبَهٌ *prominence of forehead*; compare perhaps also As. *gabâni, heights* (?) Lotz$^{TP\ 133}$)—**Qal** *Pf.* ׳ג 2 Ch 26^{16} + 5 t.; גָּבְהָא Ez 31^5 (ה = א); גָּבְהָה Ez

3 1[10], גָּבְהוּ Jb 35[5] + 3 t.; *Impf.* יִגְבַּהּ Pr 18[12] + 5 t.;
sf. יִגְבְּהוּ Ez 31[14], יִגְבָּ֑הוּ Jb 36[7], תִּגְבָּ֑הוּ Jc 13[15],
תִּגְבְּהֶ֫ינָה Ez 16[50]; *Inf.* כִּגְבֹהַּ ψ 103[11], לְגָבְהָה Zp 3[11];
—**1.** *be high, lofty, tall,* e.g. tree Ez 19[11] 31[5.10.14],
heavens Jb 35[5] Is 55[9] ψ 103[11], man 1 S 10[23].
2. *be exalted,* of man in dignity and honour Jb 36[7],
of servant of Yahweh Is 52[13], God Is 5[16], God's
ways Is 55[9]. **3.** *lofty* גָּבַהּ לִבּוֹ :—**a.** in a good
sense, *encouraged* in the ways of Yahweh 2 Ch
17[6]; **b.** elsewhere in a bad sense, *be haughty*
ψ 131[1] Pr 18[12] 2 Ch 26[16] 32[25] Ez 28[2.5.17], and so
without לב Is 3[16] Je 13[15] Ez 16[50] Zp 3[11]. **Hiph.**
Pf. הִגְבַּ֫הְתִּי Ez 17[24]; *Impf.* יַגְבִּיהַּ Jb 39[27] Je 49[16]
Ob[4]; וַיַּגְבִּיהֶ֫הָ 2 Ch 33[14]; יַגְבִּיהוּ Jb 5[7]; *Inf.*
הַגְבֵּהַּ Is 7[11] Ez 21[31]; *Pt.* מַגְבִּיהַּ Pr 17[19] ψ 113[5];—
make high, exalt, e.g. trees Ez 17[24], wall 2 Ch
33[14], gate Pr 17[19], nest Je 49[16] Ob[4], dwelling
ψ 103[5], a request Is 7[11], the lowly Ez 21[31];
יַגְבִּיהוּ עוּף *make their flight high, soar aloft* Jb 5[7],
without עוּף Jb 39[27].

1364, †גָּבֹהַּ **adj. high, exalted**—1 S 9[2] + 15 t.;
1362 גָּבוֹהַּ ψ 138[6]; cstr. גְּבֹהַּ 1 S 16[7]; גְּבַהּ (Ew[§ 213 d])
ψ 101[5] + 3 t.; pl. גְּבֹהִים Ec 5[7] + 5 t.; f. גְּבֹהָה Dt
3[5] + 6 t.; pl. גְּבֹהוֹת Dn 8[3] + 2 t.; גְּבֹהֹת Dt 28[52];
—**1.** *high, lofty, tall,* e.g. tree Ez 17[24], tower
Is 2[15] Zp 1[16], mountain Gn 7[19] ψ 104[18] Is 40[9] 57[7]
Ez 17[22] 40[2]; cf. phrases על כל גבעה גבהה *upon
every high hill* 1 K 14[23] 2 K 17[10] Je 2[20]; על גבעות
הגבהות Je 17[2]; עַל־כָּל־הַר גָּבֹהַּ Is 30[25] Je 3[6]; man
1 S 9[2]; tree גְּבַהּ קוֹמָה Ez 31[3]; horns Dn 8[3]; walls
Dt 3[5] 28[52]; gallows Est 5[14] 7[9]; gate Je 51[58];
altar Ez 41[22]; high things Jb 41[26] Ec 12[5]. **2.**
exalted in station Ez 21[31]; כִּי גָבֹהַּ מֵעַל גָּבֹהַּ שֹׁמֵר
וּגְבֹהִים עֲלֵיהֶם *for high one above high one is
watching, & the Most High over them* Ec 5[7] so
Ew Zö al., but Vrss De Now al. *higher* (earthly),
potentates *over them.* **3.** *haughty* ψ 138[6] Is 5[15]
10[33] 1 S 2[3]; גְּבַהּ־עֵינַיִם ψ 101[5]; ג׳ לֵב Pr 16[5]; ג׳ רוּחַ
Ec 7[8]. **4. n.**[**m.**] *loftiness,* גְּבֹהַּ קוֹמָתוֹ 1 S 16[7];
cf. גָּדוֹל **10,** p. 153.

1363 †גֹּ֫בַהּ **n.m. height**—Jb 22[12] + 9 t.; sf. גָּבְהוֹ
1 S 17[4] + 5 t.; pl. cstr. גָּבְהֵי Jb 11[8];—**1.** *height,*
of buildings and trees Ez 1[18] 19[11] 31[10.14] 40[42] 41[8]
2 Ch 3[4] Am 2[9]; prob. also Ez 43[13] (of altar), so
𝔊 Ew Co for MT גַּב (q. v.); of man 1 S 17[4];
heaven Jb 11[8] 22[12] (גבה cstr. SI[6] of rock). **2.**
exaltation, grandeur Jb 40[10]. **3.** *haughtiness,*
Je 48[29]; ג׳ אַף ψ 10[4]; ג׳־לִבּוֹ 2 Ch 32[26]; ג׳ רוּחַ
Pr 16[18].

1365 †גַּבְהוּת **n.f. haughtiness,** Is 2[11.17].

3011 †יָגְבְּהָה **n.pr.** (*exalted?* Ol[§ 277 k.4]) place in
the tribe of Gad Nu 32[35] Ju 8[11];—*Ḥirbet-
Ajbêhât,* NW. fr. 'Ammân, Bd[Pal 189].

גבול(ה) Jos 15[47] K†; rd. הַגָּדוֹל Vrss. Codd. 1366
cf. v[12].

גבח (only in foll. derivatives found in P;
cf. also NH גִּבֵּחַ, *giant*).

†גִּבֵּחַ **adj. having a bald forehead,** ג׳ הוּא 1371
Lv 13[41] (P ‖ קֵרֵחַ הוּא v[40]).

†גַּבַּ֫חַת **n.f.** bald forehead (NH *id.*, Aram. 1372
ܓܒܚܬܐ), only Lv 13—abs. Lv 13[42] (P; asson.
בְּקָרַ֫חַת אוֹ בְגַבַּ֫חַת); גַּבַּחְתּוֹ v[42.43] (both P & ‖ קָרַחְתּוֹ);
in all, as place of appearance of an eruption;
v[55] (P; ‖ id.) = *in its front,* i.e. front of garment.

גֵּבִי v. sub גבה. p. 146 1462

גֵּבִי, גֵּבִי סַלַּי v. sub גבב. p. 146 1373

גֵּבִים **n.pr.loc.** v. sub גוב. p. 155 1374

גבל (acc. to Thes orig. *twist, wind,* whence
not only גַּבְלֻת, מִגְבָּלֹת, but also גְּבוּל (*cord* and
then) *boundary,* as determined by measuring
cord, or line, whence vb. denom. גָּבַל *bound,
border,* q.v. infr.; NH גָּבַל, Aram. גְּבַל mean
mix, knead; Ar. جَبَلَ, Syr. ܓܒܠ = *create,
fashion;* MV assume meaning *massive,* whence
Ar. جَبَل *mountain* (cf. As. *gablu* HA[48]), and
גְּבוּל as originally earth-wall, etc., serving as
boundary; this explains גַּבְלֻת etc. less well).

גְּבוּל 240 **n.m.** [Nu 34, 3] **border, boundary, ter-** 1366
ritory (NH *id.*, Punic *gubulim* (pl., Plaut
Poen. i. 9)—גְּבוּל Gn 10[19] + 168 t. + Jos 15[47] Kt (but
rd. Qr גָּדוֹל); גְּבֻל Nu 21[13] + 9 t.; (both, in abs.
& cstr., e.g. abs. Nu 22[36] 34[8], cstr. Gn 10[19] 2 S
21[5]); sf. גְּבוּלִי 1 Ch 4[10], גְּבוּלְךָ Ex 7[27], גְּבֻלְךָ Ex
23[31] + 3 t., etc.; pl. (8 t.) only sf. גְּבוּלַ֫יִךְ Je 15[13]
17[3], etc.;—**1.** *border, boundary,* **a.** of a land or
people: Canaanites Gn 10[19] (J), Edom Nu 20[23]
Jos 15[1.21] (all P) cf. Ob[7], Amorites Nu 21[13] (E)
Jos 13[4] (D) cf. 12[5] (D) Ju 1[36], Moab Nu 21[13.15]
22[36] (E) 33[44] (P) Dt 2[18] Ju 11[18.18] 2 K 3[21] Is 15[8],
Ammon Nu 21[24] (E) Dt 3[16] Jos 12[2] 13[10] (all D)
Am 1[3], Bashan Jos 12[4] (D), Egypt 1 K 5[1] =
2 Ch 9[26], Is 19[19]; esp. of promised land Ex 23[31]
34[24] (JE) Nu 34[3] + 13 t. Nu 34 (all P) Dt 11[24]
12[20] 16[4] Jos 1[4] (D), cf. Ez 45[1] + 10 t. Ez 45–48;
also of Israel 2 K 14[25] Am 6[2] Mal 1[5]. **b.** *boundary* of smaller divisions, e.g. Geshurites Dt 3[14]
Jos 12[5] 13[11] (all D), cf. Jos 16[2.3] (J) 19[12] (P);
esp. of tribes of Israel Dt 3[16.17] Jos 13[30] (all D)
13[16] + 60 t. Jos 13–19 (P);—15[47] rd. גדול v. supr.;
Jos 22[25] (P) & 17[8] 18[11] 24[30] (JE), cf. 1 Ch 6[39.51]

2 Ch 11^{13} Ez 48^{1} + 15 t. Ez 48 (incl. v$^{22.22}$ q. del. Co);—in 1 S 13^{18} rd. for גְּבוּל, הַגֶּבַע 𝔊 We Dr. †**c.** *boundary* of territory belonging to an individual,—of field, piece of ground, etc. Gn 23^{17} (P) Dt 19^{14} 27^{17}, Jos 24^{30} (E) = Ju 2^{9} 1 Ch 4^{10} Pr 15^{25} 22^{28} 23^{10} Ho 5^{10}. †**d.** *border* of stream Nu 22^{36}. †**e.** *limit* to waters of deep ψ 104^{9} cf. Je 5^{22}. †**f.** a concrete object marking limit, (*a*) *barrier* in Ezekiel's temple Ez 40^{12} (del. 𝔊 𝔖 Co) v^{12}; (*β*) *border* of altar Ez 43$^{13.17.20}$; (*γ*) *surrounding wall* of restored Zion Is 54^{12} (so 𝔊 Ew Kn Che; De Brd *territory*, Di undecided). †**2.** *territory* (enclosed within boundary), **a.** of land or people Gn 47^{21} (J) Ex 7^{27} (P) 10$^{4.14}$ (‖ ארץ) v^{19} 13^{7} (all J), Nu 20$^{16.17.21}$ 21^{22} (E; ‖ ארץ) = Ju 11^{20}, Nu 21^{23} (E) Dt 2^{4} 19^{3} (גּ׳ אַרְצְךָ) v^{8} 28^{40} Jos 18$^{5.5}$ (E) Ju 11^{22} 19^{29} 2 S 21^{5} 1 K 1^{3} 2 K 10^{32} 1 Ch 21^{12} (‖ ארץ) ψ 105^{31} (= ארץ in ‖ Ez 8$^{16.17}$) v^{33} 147^{14} Je 31^{17} Ez 11$^{10.11}$ Jo 4^{6} Zp 2^{8}. **b.** *territory* of a city (or *limit* of such territory) Nu 35$^{26.27}$ Jos 13^{26} Ju 1$^{18.18.18}$ Ez 47$^{16.16.17.17}$ (del. 𝔊 Co) 48^{1} Am 6^{2}. †**c.** *territory* about Ezekiel's temple Ez 43^{12}. †**d.** pl. in like sense (only use of pl.), of land Mi 5^{5} Is 60^{18} (‖ ארץ) Je 15^{13} 17^{3}, of city 1 S 5^{6} 2 K 15^{16} 18^{8}; so Ez 27^{4} of Tyre. †**e.** fig. *territory* (region) *of darkness* Jb 38^{20}; *territory of wickedness* Mal 1^{4} (of Edom); *territory of his holiness* ψ 78^{54} (of Canaan).

1367 †[גְּבוּלָה] **n.f.** border, boundary—sf. גְּבֻלָתוֹ Is 28^{25}; *Pl.* abs. גְּבֻלֹת Nu 32^{33}, גְּבֻלוֹת Jb 24^{2}; cstr. גְּבוּלֹת ψ 74^{17}, גְּבוּלֹת Is 10^{13}, גְּבֻלֹת Dt 32^{8}; sf. גְּבוּלֹתֶיהָ Jos 18^{20} 19^{49}, גְּבֻלֹתֶיהָ Nu 34$^{2.12}$;—**1.** *border, boundary* of the earth (poet.) ψ 74^{17}; of peoples Is 10^{13} Dt 32^{8} (poem); of land of Canaan Nu 34$^{2.12}$ (P) Jos 19^{49} (JE); of a tribe Jos 18^{20} (P); of territory about cities Nu 32^{33} (P ?); of a piece of ground Jb 24^{2}; of barley-field Is 28^{25}.

1383 †גַּבְלֻת **n.f.** twisting—שַׁרְשֹׁת גַּבְלֻת Ex 28^{22}, שַׁרְשְׁרֹת גּ׳ 39^{15} (both P), *cords of twisting*, i.e. (well or tightly) twisted cords.

4020 †מִגְבָּלֹת **n.f.pl.** the twisted, i.e. cords, Ex 28^{14} cf. Di (appos. שַׁרְשְׁרֹת זָהָב ‖ (שׁ׳ הָעֲבֹתֹת).

1379 †גָּבַל **vb.denom.** bound, border—**Qal** *Pf.* גָּבְלוּ Dt 19^{14}; *Impf.* 3 ms. יִגְבּוֹל Jos 18^{20}, 3 fs. תִּגְבָּל־ Zc 9^{2};—*bound, border*, c. acc. Jos 18^{20} (P); c. בְּ *border upon, adjoin* Zc 9^{2}; trans. *set bounds* Dt 19^{14} (c. acc. cogn.). **Hiph.** *Pf.* 2 ms. *set bounds for*, c. acc. וְהִגְבַּלְתָּ Ex 19^{12}; *Imv. id.* הַגְבֵּל v^{23} (both JE), + *Pt.* מַגְבִּיל Ez 47^{18} 𝔊 𝔖 𝔙 Co.

1380 †גְּבַל **n.pr.loc.** maritime city on the Phenician coast Ez 27^{9}; (Ph. גבל = Byblus (Sm Di Jos 13^{5}); in As. *Gubli* COT^{Gloss}); mod. *Jebeil* Bd$^{Pal 358}$; v. also Furrer$^{ZPV\ viii.\ 20}$

†גִּבְלִי **adj.gent.** of foregoing, c.art. = n.coll. 1382
Jos 13^{5} והארץ הַגִּבְלִי, but rd. גְּבוּל הַגּ׳, cf. Di. 1 K 5^{32} הַגִּבְלִים (but prob. txt. err.; Th rds. וַיַּגְבִּלוּם *and they bordered them, made a border for them* (the stones); 𝔊 ἔβαλον, cf. also Klo).

†גְּבָל **n.pr.loc.** (= Ar. جِبَال, Γεβαληνη) 1381
mountainous region S. of Dead Sea, 𝔗 Seir, cf. Jos$^{Ant.\ ii.\ 1,\ 2;\ ix.\ 9,\ 1}$; ψ 83^{8} גבל ועמון ועמלק;—mod. *Jibâl*; Seetzen$^{ii.\ 357}$ Burckh$^{Travels\ 401}$ Rob$^{BR\ ii.\ 154}$.

גבן (prob. *be curved, contracted, coagulated;* Syr. Pa. ܓܒܶܢ *coagulate;* Ar. جَبُنَ is *be timid*, perh. from *shrinking, cowering*).

†גִּבֵּן **adj.** crook-backed, hump-backed 1384
(cf. Aram. גִּבִּין *id.*, NH גַּבָּן *highlander;* also NH גבין, Aram. גבינא, ܓܒܝܢܐ, all = *brow* (*eyebrow*, etc.); cf. Ar. جَبِين *side of forehead*), Lv 21^{20}.

†גְּבִינָה **n.f.** curd, or cheese (NH *id.*, 1385
Ar. جُبْن, Eth. ግብነት: Aram. גּוּבְנָא, ܓܘܒܢܐ, cf. ܓܒܬܐ)—וְכַגְּבִינָה תַּקְפִּיאֵנִי Jb 10^{10} (‖ חָלָב).

†[גַּבְנֹן] **n.[m.]** peak, rounded summit; 1386
pl. גַּבְנֻנִּים: ψ 68^{16} הַר־אֱלֹהִים הַר־בָּשָׁן הַר־גּ׳ הַר־בָּשָׁן; הָרִים גּ׳ v^{17} (appos., Thes Dr$^{§\ 188}$ al.; others adj. *many-peaked*). Cf. Wetzst$^{Batan.\ Giebelgeb.,\ 1884}$.

גבע (*convex, projecting, high;* cf. Aram. Pa. גַּבַּע *swell, swell up*, גְּבִיעַ *hump-backed*, גִּבְעֲתָא *hill;* v. also 1. גִּבְעָה infr.)

†גֶּבַע **n.pr.loc.**—גּ׳ abs. Jos 21^{17} +; cstr. 1387
Ju 20^{10} +; גָּבַע Jos 18^{24} +;—Levitical city, in Benjamin Jos 21^{17} = 1 Ch 6^{45} Jos 18^{24} cf. 1 Ch 8^{6}, 1 K 15^{22} Ne 11^{31}; also 1 S 13^{16} & Ju 20$^{10.33}$ MT, in all three rd. גִּבְעָה (גִּבְעַת), cf. context;—northernmost city in kingdom of Judah 2 K 23^{8} *from Geba to Beersheba*, cf. Zc 14^{10}; situated S. of pass of *Michmash* Is 10^{29} 1 S 14^{5} cf. 1 S 13^{3}; mentioned also 2 Ch 16^{6} Ezr 2^{26} Ne 7^{30} 12^{29}; in 1 S 13^{18} 𝔊 We Dr rd. הַגֶּבַע for MT גְּבוּל q. v.; (2 S 5^{25} rd. גבעון with 𝔊 and 1 Ch 14^{16}).—Mod. *Jebaʿ* Rob$^{BR\ i.\ 440\ f.}$ Bd$^{Pal\ 120}$.

†גִּבְעָא **n.pr.m.** a son of Caleb 1 Ch 2^{49}. 1388

†1. גִּבְעָה **n.f.** hill—abs. גִּבְעָה 2 S 2^{25} + 1389
13 t. + Ez 6^{13} (del. Co q.v.) 1 S 7^{1} 2 S 6$^{3.4}$ (cf. Dr); cstr. גִּבְעַת Jos 5^{3} + 8 t. + 1 S 10^{5} (cf. Dr); sf. גִּבְעָתִי Ez 34^{26} (but del. Co), גִּבְעָתָהּ Is 31^{4}; pl. abs. גְּבָעוֹת Dt 12^{2} + 35 t.; cstr. גִּבְעוֹת Dt 33^{15}

Hb 3^{6}, גִּבְעֹת Gn 49^{26}; sf. גִּבְעוֹתֶיךָ Ez 35^{8};—*hill, height, elevation*, both high and low, cf. ψ 148^{9} ההרים וכל גבעות, 65^{13};—**1.** in ordinary prose, *hill*, lower than mountain Ex 17$^{9.10}$ (E) 2 S 2^{25}; it may be n.pr. in 1 S 7^{1} 10^{10} 2 S 6$^{3.4}$ v. also sub II. גִּבְעָה. **2.** esp. as place of illicit worship על כָּל־ג׳ גְּבֹהָה ותחת כל עץ רענן 1 K 14^{23} 2 K 17^{10} Je 2^{20}; cf. Dt 12^{2} 2 K 16^{4} 2 Ch 28^{4} (these two +במות); also Ho 4^{13} Je 13^{27} 17^{2} Ez 6^{13} (v. supr.). **3.** very commonly ‖ הר in poet. & proph. Dt 33^{15} ψ 72^{3} 114$^{4.6}$ 148^{9} Ct 2^{8} 4^{6} Is 2$^{2.14}$ 30$^{17.25}$ 31^{4} 40$^{4.12}$ 41^{15} 42^{15} 54^{10} 55^{12} 65^{7} Je 3^{23} 4^{24} 16^{16} 50^{7} Ez 6^{3} 34^{6} 35^{8} 36$^{4.6}$ Ho 4^{13} 10^{8} Jo 4^{18} Am 9^{13} Mi 4^{1} 6^{1} Na 1^{5} Hb 3^{6}; rarely in prose Dt 12^{2}; sometimes as high and majestic (poet.) ג׳ עולם Gn 49^{26} Dt 33^{15} Hb 3^{6} ('everlasting hills'); cf. also Jb 15^{7} Pr 8^{25} (with adj. *high*, cf. supr.); v. also Je 49^{16}. **4.** hills with special names, some nearly or quite = n.pr.loc., which see under the respective words: ג׳ מֹרֶה Ju 7^{1} *teacher's hill*, in valley of Jezreel; ג׳ הָעֲרָלוֹת Jos 5^{3} *hill of the fore-skins;* ג׳ הָאֱלֹהִים 1 S 10^{5} (a designation of Gibeah); ג׳ הַחֲכִילָה 1 S 23^{19} 26$^{1.3}$; ג׳ אַמָּה 2 S 2^{24}; ג׳ הַלְּבוֹנָה Ct 4^{6} (i.e. hill where frankincense is grown); ג׳ גָּרֵב Je 31^{39}; ג׳ יְרוּשָׁלַםִ Is 10^{32} cf. 31^{4} (where ‖ הַר־צִיּוֹן), Ez 34^{26} (v. supr.) & הַגְּבָעוֹת Zp 1^{10} hills on which Jerusalem stands.

1390 II. גִּבְעָה **n.pr.loc.** (*hill*)—ג׳ Jos 15^{57}+; (הַ)גִּבְעָתָה Ju 20^{4} + 5 t.; גִּבְעַת Jos 18^{28}; cstr. גִּבְעַת 1 S 11^{4} + 9 t.; abs. alw. c. art. exc. Jos 15^{57} 18^{28} Ju 19^{12} 20^{31} 1 S 10^{26} 2 Ch 13^{2};—†**1.** a city of Judah Jos 15^{57} (perh. one of two villages called *Gabaa, Gabatha* in Onom. v. Lag [Onom. 246,
1394 128; 2nd ed. 255, 160]). **2.** city of Benj. Ju 19$^{14.16}$ + 20 t. Ju, 1 S 10^{26} 14^{2} 22^{6} 26^{1} 2 S 23^{29} = 1 Ch 11^{31}; also Ho 5^{8} 9^{9} 10$^{9.9}$ (cf. Ju 19$^{12 ff.}$) 2 Ch 13^{2}; perh. also 1 S 7^{1} 10^{10} 2 S 6$^{3.4}$ rd. also (for גבע) 1 S 13^{16} Ju 20$^{10.33}$; = גִּבְעַת Jos 18^{28}; called also גִּבְעַת בִּנְיָמִין 1 S 13$^{2.15}$ 14^{16}, & גִּבְעַת שָׁאוּל 1 S 11^{4} 15^{34} Is 10^{29}; 2 S 21^{6} rd. prob. גִּבְעוֹן, 𝔊 We Dr. †**3.** a city of Ephraim, called גִּבְעַת פִּינְחָס Jos 24^{33}.

1391 גִּבְעַת **n.pr.loc.** (Ges [§ 80, R. 2]) v. foregoing, **2.**

1395 †גִּבְעָתִי **adj.gent.** of גִּבְעָה of Benjamin (?) 1 Ch 12^{3}.

1375 †גָּבִיעַ **n.m.** [Gn 44, 12] **cup, bowl**—ג׳ Gn 44^{12} + 2 t.; cstr. גְּבִיעַ Gn 44^{2}; sf. גְּבִיעִי Gn 44^{2}; pl. גְּבִיעִים Ex 25^{34}, גְּבִעִים v$^{33.33}$ + 4 t.; sf. גְּבִיעֶיהָ Ex 25^{31} 37^{17};—*cup* (of Joseph) Gn 44$^{2.12.16.17}$; pl. *cups* (of golden candlestick in tab.) Ex 25$^{31.33.33.34}$ 37$^{17.19.19.20}$; *bowls* Je 35^{5} גְּבִעִים מלאים יין וכסות.

4021 †מִגְבָּעוֹת **n.f.pl.** head-gear, turban, of common priest (conical? cf. Di Ex 28^{40}), Ex 28^{40} Lv 8^{13}; מִגְבָּעֹת Ex 29^{9} 39^{28} (פַּאֲרֵי הַמּ׳).

†גִּבְעוֹן **n.pr.loc.**—ג׳ Jos 9^{17}+; c. ־ָה loc., 1391
גִּבְעוֹנָה 2 S 2^{12} cf. 1 K 3^{4};—Levitical city in tribe of Benjamin; formerly inhabited by Hivites Jos 9^{17} 10$^{2.4.5.10.12.41}$ 11^{19} 18^{25} 21^{17} 2 S 2$^{12.13}$ (*pool of Gibeon*) v^{16} 3^{30} 20^{8} Je 28^{1} 41^{12} (*great waters which are in Gibeon*) v^{16} 1 Ch 14^{16}; vid. esp. יֹשְׁבֵי ג׳, אַנְשֵׁי ג׳ Jos 9^{3} (called Hivites 9^{7}) 10$^{1.6}$ 11^{19} Ne 3^{7}, so בְּנֵי ג׳ Ne 7^{25} (= בְּנֵי גִבָּר Ezr 2^{20}, v. גִּבָּר); cf. also
as n.pr.m. 1 Ch 8^{29} וּבְגִבְעוֹן יָשְׁבוּ אֲבִי גִבְעוֹן = 9^{35}; 25
cf. מִדְבַּר ג׳ 2 S 2^{24}, עֵמֶק בְּג׳ Is 28^{21}; it was the site of a great *Bamah* 1 K 3$^{4.5}$ 9^{2}, where was 'the tabernacle of Yahweh in the high place' acc. to 1 Ch 16^{39}, cf. 21^{29} 2 Ch 1$^{3.13}$.

†גִּבְעֹנִי **adj.gent.**—alw. c. art. הַגִּבְעֹנִי Ne 3^{7}, הַגִּבְעוֹנִי 1 Ch 12^{4}, הַגִּבְעֹנִים 2 S 21$^{1.2.2.3.4.9}$. 1393

†גִּבְעֹל **n.[m.]** bud (Ol [§ 216 b])—Ex 9^{31} *the flax was bud* (i.e. in bud Dr [§ 188. (2)]), cf. RS [JPh xii. 299, 300]. 1392

†גָּבַר **vb.** be strong, mighty (NH *id.*, 1396
Aram. גְּבַר; Ar. جَبَرَ (conj. I. dial.; usually in derived conj.) *compel, force;* جَبَرِيَّةٌ *overbearing behaviour,* جَبْرٌ *constraint;* Eth. ገብረ: I, 1, *subigere;* II, 2, *cogere;* Syr. ܐܶܬܓܰܒܰܪ *play the man*, is denom. fr. ܓܰܒܪܳܐ *man*)—**Qal** *Pf.* ג׳ ψ 103^{11} + 5 t.; גָּבְרוּ Gn 7^{19} + 6 t.; גָּבֵרוּ 2 S 1^{23}; *Impf.* יִגְבַּר 1 S 2^{9}; וַיִּגְבְּרוּ Gn 7$^{18.24}$;—**1.** *be strong, mighty*, abs. גָּבְרוּ חַיִל *mighty in power* Jb 21^{7}; with מִן *stronger than* 2 S 1^{23} ψ 65^{4}; with בְּ *mighty among* 1 Ch 5^{2}. **2.** *prevail*:—**a.** abs. e.g. enemies Ex 17$^{11.11}$ (E) 1 S 2^{9} La 1^{16}, waters Gn 7$^{18.19.20.24}$ (P), power Je 9^{2}; **b.** with עַל *prevail over*, subj. enemies 2 S 11^{23}, blessings Gn 49^{26} (J), mercy of God ψ 103^{11} 117^{2}. **Pi.** *Pf.* גִּבַּרְתִּי Zc 10^{6}; sf. גִּבַּרְתִּים Zc 10^{12}; *Impf.* יְגַבֵּר Ec 10^{10} *make strong, strengthen.* **Hiph.** *Pf.* הִגְבִּיר בְּרִית לְ *confirm a covenant* Dn 9^{27}; *Impf.* נַגְבִּיר לִלְשֹׁנֵנוּ *we will confirm a covenant with our tongue* Ew Ol Che (or, to our tongue will we give strength Hi De) ψ 12^{5}. **Hithp.** *Impf.* יִתְגַּבָּר Jb 15^{25} Is 42^{13}; יִתְגַּבָּרוּ Jb 36^{9}:—of י׳, *shew himself a mighty one* against (עַל) Is 42^{13}; of wicked, *behave proudly* toward (אֶל) Jb 15^{25}; of erring righteous (abs.) 36^{9}.

גִּבָּר v. following. 1399

I. גֶּבֶר [66] **n.m.** man (NH *id.*, MI[16] גברן (pl.), 1397,
Aram. גְּבַר, ܓܰܒܪܳܐ; As. *gabru, rival* is Akk. loan- 1399
word acc. to Schr [JLZ 1874, 200] Dl [S 120, Sm. Chald. Gen. 286])—Dt 22^{5} + 39 t.; גָּבֶר Jb 3^{3} + 13 t.; cstr. גְּבַר

ψ 18^{26} (=2 S 22^{26} גִּבּוֹר but 𝔊 𝔖 rd. גֶּבֶר); pl. גְּבָרִים Je 41^{16}+10 t.;—man as strong, disting. fr. women, children, and non-combatants whom he is to defend, chiefly poetic Ex 10^{11} Nu 24$^{3.15}$ (E) Ex 12^{37} Jos 7$^{14.17.18}$ (J) Dt 22$^{5.5}$ Ju 5^{30} 2 S 23^{1} 1 Ch 23^{3} 24^{4} 26^{12} Jb 3^{3}+14 t. Jb; ψ 18^{26}+8 t. ψ; Pr 6^{34}+7 t. Pr; Is 22^{17} Je 17^{5}+8 t. Je; La 3$^{1.27.35.39}$ Dn 8^{15} Mi 2^{2} Hb 2^{5} Zc 13^{7}; also 1 S 10^{21} 𝔊 We Dr; =*each* (of locusts) Jo 2^{8}, cf. אִישׁ.

1398 †II. גֶּ֫בֶר **n.pr.m.** an official of Solomon 1 K 4^{19} (cf. בֶּן־גֶּבֶר v^{13}, p. 122 supr.)

1402 †גִּבָּר **n.pr.** (Aram. *id.*=*hero*) Ezr 2^{20} prob. =גִּבְעוֹן Ne 7^{25}.

1368 גִּבּוֹר$_{159}$ **adj.** strong, mighty (cf. Ar. جَبَّارٌ *one who magnifies himself, behaves proudly, a tyrant, who is bold, audacious*)—Gn 10^{9}+58 t.; גִּבֹּר Gn 10^{8}+2 t.; גִּבּוֹרִם 1 S 17^{51}; pl. גִּבּוֹרִים Je 46^{9}+27 t.; גִּבֹּרִים Jos 10^{2}+21 t.; cstr. גִּבּוֹרֵי 1 Ch 11^{27}+29 t.; גִּבֹּרֵי 1 Ch 9^{26}+4 t.; sf. גִּבּוֹרֶיךָ Ho 10^{13}+(var. sfs. 11 t.);—**1. adj.** גִּבּוֹר בַּבְּהֵמָה *mightiest among beasts* Pr 30^{30}; אִישׁ גִּבּוֹר 1 S 14^{52}; גִּבּוֹר בָּאָרֶץ ψ 112^{2}; גִּבּוֹר צַיִד *mighty in hunting* Gn 10^{9} (J); מלך גבור Dn 11^{3}; אֵל גִּבּוֹר the Messiah Is 9^{5}; attribute of God especially as fighting for his people ψ 24$^{8.8}$ Dt 10^{17} Ne 9^{32} Is 10^{21} Je 32^{18} (cf. Ar. اَلْجَبَّارُ). **2. n.m.** *strong, valiant man* Jos 10^{2} (E) Gn 6^{4} 10^{8} (J) Ju 5$^{13.23}$ 1 S 2^{4}+16 t. 1 K 1$^{8.10}$ 2 K 24^{16} 1 Ch 1^{10}+11 t. Ezr 7^{28} Jb 16^{14} ψ 19^{6} 33^{16} 45^{4} 52^{3} 78^{65} 89^{20} 120^{4} 127^{4} Pr 16^{32} 21^{22} Ct 3$^{7.7}$ 4^{4} Ec 9^{11} Is 3^{2} 13^{3} 21^{17} 42^{13} 49$^{24.25}$ Je 5^{16}+17 t. Ez 32^{12}+5 t. Ho 10^{13} Jo 2^{7} 4$^{9.10.11}$ Am 2$^{14.16}$ Ob ^{9} Na 2^{4} Zp 1^{14} 3^{17} Zc 9^{13} 10$^{5.7}$; cf. phrases גִּבּוֹר חיל *mighty man of valour* Ju 6^{12} 11^{1} 1 S 9^{1} 16^{18} 1 K 11^{28} 2 K 5^{1} (וְהָאִישׁ הָיָה גִּבּוֹר חַיִל מְצֹרָע so 𝔊 al.; but 𝔊L ὁ ἄνθρωπος ἦν λεπρός, cf. also Klo's dub. emend.), 1 Ch 12^{28} 28^{1} 2 Ch 13^{3} 17$^{16.17}$ 25^{6} 32^{21}; איש גבור חיל Ru 2^{1}; גבורי החיל Jos 1^{14} (D) 6^{2} 10^{7} (JE) 2 K 15^{20} 24^{14}; איש גבורי החיל Jos 8^{3}; גברי חיל 1 Ch 5^{24}+14 t. Ne 11^{14}; גבורי חילים 1 Ch 7$^{5.7.11.40}$; גבורי החילים 1 Ch 11^{26}; גברי כח ψ 103^{20}; גבורי מלחמה 2 Ch 13^{3}; גברי השׁערים 1 Ch 9^{26}; בית הגבורים Ne 3^{16}; (ה)צָבָא הגבורים 2 S 10^{7} 1 Ch 19^{8}; ראשׁי הגברים 1 Ch 11^{10}; גבורים לשׁתות *valiant to drink* Is 5^{22}.

1369 †גְּבוּרָה$_{61}$ **n.f.** strength, might—Ex 32^{18}+16 t.; cstr. גְּבוּרַת ψ 147^{10}; sf. גְּבוּרָתוֹ+(sfs. 32 t.); pl. גְּבוּרוֹת Jb 41^{4}+3 t.; גְּבֻרוֹת ψ 71^{16}; גְּבוּרֹתֶיךָ Dt 3^{24}+(sfs. 6 t.);—**1.** *strength*, of horse Jb 39^{19} ψ 147^{10}, crocodile Jb 41^{4}, sun Ju 5^{31}, body of man ψ 90^{10} Ec 9^{16} 10^{17}. **2.** *might, valour*, of warriors Ju 8^{21} Pr 8^{14} Is 3^{25} 28^{6} 30^{15} Je 9^{22} 23^{10} 49^{35} 51^{30} Ez 32$^{29.30}$ Mi 3^{8} 7^{16}; קוֹל עֲנוֹת גְּבוּרָה *noise of shouting in warlike strength* Ex 32^{18} (E); עֵצָה וּגְבוּרָה 2 K 18^{20} Is 11^{2} 36^{5}; cf. phrases of compiler of Kings כָּל גְּבוּרָתוֹ 1 K 15^{23} 2 K 10^{34} 20^{20}; אֲשֶׁר עָשָׂה וּגְבוּרָתוֹ 1 K 16$^{5.27}$ 22^{46} 2 K 13$^{8.12}$ 14$^{15.28}$; cf. also מַלְכוּתוֹ וּגְבוּרָתוֹ 1 Ch 29^{30}, תָקְפּוֹ וּגְבוּרָתוֹ Est 10^{2}. **3.** *might* of God Jb 26^{14} ψ 21^{14} 54^{3} 65^{7} 66^{7} 71^{18} 80^{3} 89^{14} 106^{8} 145^{11} Is 33^{13} Je 10^{6} 16^{21}; cf. phrases כח וגבורה 1 Ch 29^{12} 2 Ch 20^{6}, חכמה וג׳ Jb 12^{13}, משפט וג׳ Mi 3^{8}, הגדלה והג׳ 1 Ch 29^{11}; גְּבוּרוֹת *mighty deeds* of God Dt 3^{24} ψ 20^{7} 71^{16} 106^{2} 145$^{4.12}$ 150^{2} Is 63^{15}.

†גְּבִיר **n.m.** lord, Gn 27$^{29.37}$. 1376

†גְּבִירָה **n.f. 1.** lady, queen, 1 K 11^{19}; **2.** 1377
queen-mother, 1 K 15^{13}=2 Ch 15^{16}; וַיְסִרֶהָ מִגְּ׳ *he removed her from* (the position of) *queen-mother*; cf. 2 K 10^{13} Je 13^{18} 29^{2}.

†גְּבֶ֫רֶת **n.f. 1.** *lady, queen*, Is 47$^{5.7}$. **2.** 1404
mistress of servants, sf. גְּבִרְתִּי Gn 16^{8}; גְּבִרְתֵּךְ Gn 16^{9}; גְּבִרְתָּהּ Gn 16^{4} 2 K 5^{3} ψ 123^{2} Pr 30^{23}; (pl. גברת *women* MI^{16}).

†גַּבְרִיאֵל **n.pr.m.** (*man of Ēl*) an arch- 1403
angel Dn 8^{16} 9^{21} (cf. Lu 1^{19}).

גבשׁ (*be firm, massive*, cf. As. *gabâšu, be thick, massive*, Zim$^{BP 76}$, & deriv.; cf. also Aram. גַּבֵּשׁ Pa. *heap up*, & גַּבְשׁוּשִׁית *height, hill*).

†גָּבִישׁ **n.m.** crystal (cf. אֶלְגָּבִישׁ *hail*—on 1378
relation of meanings cf. Gk. κρύσταλλος, & Eth. usage of እብን: በረድ: Di$^{Lex. Aeth. 759}$—Ar. جِبْسٌ *gypsum*, As. *gibšu, mass, abundance*, COT^{Gloss})—רָאמוֹת וְגָבִישׁ Jb 28^{18} *coral and crystal*.

†מַגְבִּישׁ **n.pr.m.** Ezr 2^{30} בְּנֵי מ׳ 𝔊 Μαγεβως, 4019
etc., a family of returning exiles, om. ‖ Ne 7^{33}, but 𝔊A א Μαγεβως, etc., 𝔊L Μαγβεις; cf. Sm Listen 15.

גִּבְּתוֹן v. sub גבב. p. 146 1405

†גַּג **n.m.** roof, top (NH *id.*; Di comp. 1406
Eth. ጋግ: ጋጋ: *vinculum* (ferreum), *jugo* simil. *collare ferreum*; √dub.; Thes prop. גנג; perh. גנג (=גנן) *cover* Bö^{§292} Sta^{§189a} MV)—גָּג Jos 2^{6}+9 t.+1 S 9^{26} Kt (Qr הַגָּגָה), גָּגָה Jos 2^{6} 1 S 9^{26} Qr (Kt גג); cstr. Ju 9^{51}+2 t.+Ez 40^{13} (del. Co v. infr.); sf. גַּגֶּךָ Dt 22^{8}, גַּגּוֹ Ex 30^{3}+2 t.+Ez 40^{13} (del. Co v. infr.); pl. גַּגּוֹת Is 37^{27}+5 t.; sf. גַּגֹּתֶיהָ Is 15^{3}, גַּגּוֹתֵיהֶם Je 32^{29}, גַּגֹּתֵיהֶם Je 19^{13};—**1.** *roof* (of house) Dt 22^{8} Jos 2$^{6.6.8}$ 16^{27} 1 S 9$^{25.26}$ 2 S 11$^{2.2}$ 16^{22} 2 K 19^{26}=Is 37^{27}, Ne 8^{16} ψ 102^{8} 129^{6} Pr 21^{9} 25^{24} Is 15^{3} 22^{1} Je 48^{38}; as places of idolatrous worship (esp. of heavenly bodies) Je 19^{13} 32^{29} Zp 1^{5}; so הַגָּג עֲלִיַּת אָחָז 2 K

23^{12}, roof of tower Ju 9^{51}, over gate 2 S 18^{24}, of chamber Ez 40$^{13.13}$ (but 𝔊 Co קיר). **2.** top of altar of incense, in tabern. Ex 30^{3} 37^{26} (both P).

1407, 1410, 1412 גְּדִגְּדָה, גִּדְגָּד, גָּד, גַּד v. sub גדד. below

1413 †[גָּדַד] **vb. penetrate, cut** (NH *id., cut, cut out*, Aram. גְּדַד, ܓܕܰ, Ar. جَدَّ *cut, cut off;* Eth. ገደደ: in deriv.)—**Qal** *Impf.* ψ 94^{21} יָגוֹדּוּ עַל־נֶפֶשׁ צַדִּיק *they attack* (penetrate, make inroads upon) *the life of a righteous man* (Ol prop. יָגוּרוּ cf. 56^{7} 59^{4} where, however, Che יגודו; si vera l., perh. denom. fr. גְּדוּד cf. Ho 6^{9} & infr.; cf. also גוד & Kö$^{i. 356}$). **Hithpo.** *Impf.* יִתְגֹּדַד Je 16^{6}; 2 fs. תִּתְגֹּדֲדִי Mi 4^{14}, תִּתְגּוֹדָדִי Je 47^{5}; pl. וַיִּתְגֹּדְדוּ 1 K 18^{28}, יִתְגּוֹדָדוּ Je 5^{7} + Ho 7^{11} v. infr., תִּתְגֹּדְדוּ Dt 14^{1}; *Pt.* pl. מִתְגֹּדְדִים Je 41^{5};—**1.** *cut oneself*, as religious (heathen) practice 1 K 18^{28}; practised also by men of Shechem, etc. in worship of י׳ (late) Je 41^{5}; for the dead, forbidden Dt 14^{1} לֹא תִתְגֹּדְדוּ, וְלֹא תָשִׂימוּ קָרְחָה בֵּין עֵינֵיכֶם לָמֵת, Je 16^{6}; cf. 47^{5} (subject Philistia personified); also for MT יִתְגּוֹרָרוּ Ho 7^{14} Codd, *they cut themselves*, 𝔊 Gr Che RVm, or perh. (cf. גּוּר) sub. **2.** *gather in troops*, or *bands; go in troops* or *throngs, throng;* (denominative fr. גְּדוּד q.v.) cf. תִּתְגֹּדְדִי בַת־גְּדוּד Mi 4^{14} (addressed to Jerusalem); Je 5^{7} וּבֵית זוֹנָה יִתְגֹּ׳ *and to a harlot's house they throng.*

1416 I. גְּדוּד **n.m.**$^{Gn 49,19}$ band, troop (as *making inroads;* others, as a *division, detachment* (as severed), but this usually later in Heb.)—ג׳ abs. 1 S 30^{8} + 19 t.; cstr. 2 Ch 25^{9}; pl. גְּדוּדִים 2 S 4^{2} + 2 t.; cstr. גְּדוּדֵי 2 K 6^{23} + 6 t.; sf. גְּדוּדָיו Jb 19^{12} 25^{3};—**1.** *marauding band* (making *incursions, inroads*, cf. גדד) 1 S 30$^{8.15.15.23}$ cf. 1 Ch 12^{22}, also 2 Ch 22^{1} 1 K 11^{24} 2 K 5^{2} 6^{23} 13$^{20.21}$ 24$^{2.2.2.2}$ cf. 2 S 22^{30} = ψ 18^{30}, & Gn 49^{19} (v. גָּד 30^{11}) Ho 6^{9} 7^{1} Je 18^{22}; שָׂרֵי גְדוּדִים 2 S 4^{2}, cf. וַיִּתְּנֵם בְּרָאשֵׁי הַגְּדוּד 1 Ch 12^{19}; fig. of God's attacking forces, his chastisements Jb 19^{12} (cf. 25^{3} infr.) **2.** *troop*, of divisions of army of Isr. (late) גְּדוּדֵי צְבָא מִלְחָמָה 1 Ch 7^{4}, cf. 2 Ch 26^{11}; *band of Israel*, i.e. troop of mercenaries hired from Isr. by Amaziah 2 Ch 25$^{9.10}$; בְּנֵי הַגְּדוּד i.e. *soldiers of the band* 2 Ch 25^{13}; of army in general כְּמֶלֶךְ בַּגְּדוּד Jb 29^{25}, in sim.; also Mi 4^{14} בַּת־גְּדוּד of Zion. **3.** *foray, raid* 2 S 3^{22}.

1417-18 †II. [גְּדוּד, or גְּדוּדָה] **n.[m. or f.] furrow, cutting**—**1.** *furrow*, pl. defect. גְּדוּדֶהָ ψ 65^{11} (‖ תְּלָמֶיהָ). **2.** pl. גְּדֻדֹת, *cuttings* upon hands, cf. גדד Hithpo. **2**, sign of mourning Je 48^{37} (‖ שַׂק).

1407 †I. גַּד **n.m. coriander** (NH גִּיד, Aram. גִּידָא; connexion with above √ dub.; v. further Löw$^{No.155}$)—זֶרַע גַּד Ex 16^{31} Nu 11^{7}, sim. of manna.

†II. [גַּד] **1. n.[m.] fortune, good fortune** 1409
(Ar. جَدٌّ *id.*, Aram. גַּדָּא, ܓܰܕܳܐ)—Gn 30^{11} בגד Kt, i.e. בְּגָד (בָּא גָד Qr), 𝔊 ἐν τύχῃ, *by* or *with good*
fortune. **2. n.pr.m. god of fortune** (Ar. 1408
جَدّ We$^{Skizzen iii. 171}$; גד named often in Ph. & Aram. inscript., & found in Ph. & Aram. n.pr., Bae$^{Rel 76 f.}$ Nö$^{ZMG 1888, 479}$; v. esp. Siegf$^{JPTh 1875, 356 ff.}$)—c. לְ + art. לַגַּד Is 65^{11} cf. Che.

III. גָּד$_{71}$ **n.pr.m.** (*fortunatus*? perh. der. fr. 1410
foreg. divine name Siegf$^{JPTh 1875, 364}$ Sta$^{Gesch. i. 148}$; but v. also Bae$^{Rel 159 f.}$)—גָּד Gn 35^{26} +, as well as גָּד Gn 30^{11} +;—**1.** son of Jacob and Zilpah; **a.** strictly as personal name Gn 30^{11} 35^{26} 46^{16} Ex 1^{4} cf. Gn 49^{19} 1 Ch 2^{2}. **b.** as name of tribe Nu 1^{14} Dt 27^{13} 33$^{20.20}$ Jos 18^{7} Ez 48$^{27.28}$; cf. אֶרֶץ גָּד 1 S 13^{7} v. also Je 49^{1}, שַׁעַר גָּד Ez 48^{34}, on הַנַּחַל הַגָּד 2 S 24^{5} cf. We Dr; explicitly מַטֵּה גָד Nu 1^{25} 2^{14} 13^{15} Jos 13^{24} 20^{8} 21$^{7.36}$ 1 Ch 6$^{48.65}$; once, צְבָא מַטֵּה בְנֵי־גָד Nu 10^{20}; בְּנֵי גָד (MI^{10} אש גד) Nu 1^{24} + 12 t. Nu; Jos 4^{12} + 14 t. Jos; 1 Ch 5^{11} 12^{14}. †**2.** a prophet in David's time, called נָבִיא 1 S 22^{5}, but הַנָּבִיא חֹזֵה דָוִד 2 S 24^{11} & חֹזֵה דָוִיד ‖ 1 Ch 21^{9}, הַחֹזֶה 1 Ch 29^{29} & חֹזֵה־הַמֶּלֶךְ 2 Ch 29^{25}.

†I. גָּדִי **adj.gent.** of גָּד **1, Gadite** 2 S 23^{36} 1425
(so perh. also ‖ 1 Ch 11^{38} where MT הַגְּרִי q.v.; cf. Th Be Dr); elsewhere as n.pr. coll.: so 1 Ch 5^{18} (only here without art., rd. perh. גָּד so 𝔊), Dt 3$^{12.16}$ 4^{43} 29^{7} Jos 1^{12} 12^{6} 13^{8} 22^{1} 2 K 10^{33} 1 Ch 5^{26} 12$^{8.37}$ 26^{32}.

†II. גָּדִי **n.pr.m.** father of Menahem 2 K 1424
15$^{14.17}$ (cf. גדו (גדי?) n.pr.m. Eut$^{Nab No. 25}$; Palm. גדיא n.pr.m. Vog$^{No. 32}$).

גָּדָה in חֲצַר ג׳ v. sub חצר. p. 347 2693

†גַּדִּי **n.pr.m.** (*my fortune*) a man of Ma- 1426
nasseh Nu 13^{11}.

†גַּדִּיאֵל **n.pr.m.** (*Ēl is my fortune*) a man 1427
of Zebulun Nu 13^{10}.

גִּדְגָּד, in חֹר הַגִּ׳ v. following & sub חֹר. p. 301 2735

†גֻּדְגֹּדָה c. art. הַגֻּדְגֹּדָה **n.pr.loc.** (mng. dub.) 1412
station of Israel in wilderness Dt 10$^{7.7}$ (in ‖ Nu 33^{32} חֹר הַגִּדְגָּד v. sub חֹר).

†מְגִדּוֹ and (Zc 12^{11}) מְגִדּוֹן **n.pr.loc.** (con- 4023
nexion with above √ not clear; 𝔊 Μαγεδδω, Μεκεδω, Μαγεδω, etc.; 𝔙 Mageddo; As. *Magadû, Magidû*, COT^{Gloss} Dl$^{Pa 287}$) old Canaanitish city,

assigned to Manasseh 1 K 4^{12} 9^{15} 2 K 9^{27} $23^{29.30}$; מֶלֶךְ מ׳ Jos 12^{21}; יֹשְׁבֵי מ׳ Jos 17^{11}=Ju 1^{27}; מֵי מ׳ Ju 5^{19}; בִּקְעַת מ׳ Zc 12^{11} 2 Ch 35^{22};—mod. *Lejjûn* (=*Legio*) Rob [BR ii. 329 f. 364] Bd [Pal 229].

גדה (*cut, cut or tear away?*).

1415 †[גִּדָה] **n.f. bank** of river (cf. Ar. جُدَّةٌ, جِدَّةٌ *id.*, Aram. גּוּדָא, *wall*), גְּדוֹתָיו Jos 3^{15} 4^{18} 1 Ch 12^{16}
1428 Qr (Kt גדיתיו) Is 8^7.

1428 [גדיה] only pl. sf. Is 8^7 Kt, v. foregoing.

1423 †גְּדִי **n.m.** [Gn 27, 9] **kid** (NH *id.*, Ar. جَدْيٌ, Ph. גדא, Aram. גַּדְיָא, ܓܕܝܐ; cf. As. *gadû, gadiia*, Meissner [ZA iv. 1889, 286] Zehnpfund [BAS i. 505])—גְּדִי Gn 38^{17}+12 t. (abs. Gn 38^{23}+, & (generally) cstr. Gn 38^{17}+); pl. גְּדָיִים 1 S 10^3, cstr. גְּדָיֵי Gn $27^{9.16}$;—*kid*, almost always גּ׳ עִזִּים Gn $27^{9.16}$ $38^{17.20}$ Ju 6^{19} $13^{15.19}$ 15^1 1 S 16^{20}; abs. Ex 23^{19} 34^{26} Dt 14^{21} (all לא תבשל ג׳ בחלב אמו), & c. art. הַגּ׳ Gn 38^{23} Ju 14^6; abs. pl. 1 S 10^3;—cf. also עֵין גֶּדִי.

1429 †[גְּדִיָּה] **n.f.** only pl. **kids** sf. גְּדִיֹּתַיִךְ Ct 1^8 (‖ הצאן).

1431 †גָּדַל [115] **vb. grow up, become great** (Aram. גְּדַל (Ithpe.), ܓܕܠ *twist, twine*, Ar. جَدَلَ *twist a cord, make firm, strong, become strong*, so NH)—**Qal** *Pf.* ג׳ etc. Gn 38^{14}+14 t.; sf. גְּדֵלַנִי Jb 31^{18}; *Impf.* יִגְדַּל etc. ψ 35^{27}+34 t.;—**1.** *grow up*, **a.** child Gn $21^{8.20}$ 25^{27} $38^{11.14}$ Ex $2^{10.11}$ (JE) Ju 11^2 13^{24} Ru 1^{13} 1 S 2^{21} 3^{19} 1 K $12^{8.10}$ (=2 Ch $10^{8.10}$) 2 K 4^{18}; גְּדֵלַנִי כְאָב *he grew up to me as to a father* Jb 31^{18}; **b.** lamb 2 S 12^3. **2.** *become great*, **a.** in extent, wealthy Gn $26^{13.13}$ 41^{40} (JE) Je 5^{27}; **b.** in value, גָּדְלָה נַפְשׁ בְּעֵינֵי, בְּעֵינֵי י׳ *prized by* 1 S $26^{24.24}$; **c.** in intensity, grief Jb 2^{13}, mourning Zc 12^{11}, punishment La 4^6, trespass Ez 9^6; **d.** in sound, loud cry Gn 19^{13} (J); **e.** in importance, of a king Ec 2^9 1 K 10^{23} (=2 Ch 9^{22}) Dn $8^{9.10}$ (under fig. of horn), chief Gn 24^{35} 48^{19} (J), Messiah Mi 5^3, Jerusalem Ez 16^7; **f.** of God 2 S 7^{22} ψ 104^1, his works ψ 92^6, his power Nu 14^{17} (J). **3.** *to be magnified*, **a.** house of David Zc 12^7; **b.** Yahweh ψ 35^{27} 40^{17} 70^5 Mal 1^5, his name 2 S 7^{26} (=1 Ch 17^{24}). **Pi.** *Pf.* גִּדַּל Jos 4^{14} Est 3^1; גִּדֵּל Is 49^{21}; גִּדְּלָה Is 51^{18}, etc.; *Impf.* יְגַדֵּל Is 44^{14}+8 t.; *Imv.* גַּדְּלוּ ψ 34^4; *Inf.* גַּדֵּל Nu 6^5+3 t.; *Pt.* מְגַדְּלִים 2 K 10^6 (מְגַדְּלוֹת Ct 5^{13} 𝔊 𝔙 Hi Bö De);—**1.** *cause to grow*, e.g. hair Nu 6^5 (P), plants Jon 4^{10} Is 44^{14} Ez 31^4 Ct 5^{13}; *bring up children* 2 K 10^6 Is 1^2 23^4 49^{21} 51^{18} Dn 1^5 Ho 9^{12}. **2.** *make great, powerful* Gn 12^2 (J) Jos 3^7 4^{14} (D) 1 K $1^{37.47}$ 1 Ch $29^{12.25}$ 2 Ch 1^1 Est 3^1 5^{11} 10^2. **3.** *magnify*, **a.** man Jb 7^{17}; **b.** God ψ 34^4 69^{31}. **Pu.** *Pt.* pl. מְגֻדָּלִים *brought up* ψ 144^{12}. **Hiph.** *Pf.* הִגְדִּיל ψ 41^{10} +, etc.; *Impf.* יַגְדִּיל Is 42^{21} Dn 8^{25}, etc.; *Inf.* הַגְדִּיל 1 Ch 22^8 Am 8^5; *Pt.* מַגְדִּיל ψ 18^{51} (=מִגְדּוֹל in ‖ 2 S 22^{51}); pl. מַגְדִּילִים ψ 35^{26};—**1.** *make great*, e.g. shekel Am 8^5, pile for fire Ez 24^9, joy Is 9^2, counsel Is 28^{29}, wisdom Ec 1^{16}, works Ec 2^4, house of Yahweh 1 Ch 22^5; the heel ψ 41^{10} either *lifted high* (Ges), or (cf. De Now) *gave me insidiously a great fall*; cf. ג׳ פִּיךָ Ob ^{12} i.e. utter proud words (v. רחב Hiph.) **2.** *magnify*, salvation ψ 18^{51}, mercy Gn 19^{19} (J), teaching Is 42^{21}, the word of Yahweh ψ 138^2. **3.** *do great things* הִגְדִּיל לַעֲשׂוֹת, **a.** in a good sense, of God ψ $126^{2.3}$ Jo 2^{21}, also pregn. without Inf. 1 S 12^{24}. **b.** in bad sense, of 'the northern one' Jo 2^{20}, also pregn. without Inf. La 1^9 Zp $2^{8.10}$ Dn $8^{4.8.11.25}$; with עַל, of enemies ψ 35^{26} 38^{17} 55^{13} Jb 19^5 Je $48^{26.42}$; Ez 35^{13} of speaking ג׳ עָלַי בְּפִיכֶם. **c.** also, with Inf. implied, wept greatly 1 S 20^{41}. **Hithp.** *Pf.* וְהִתְגַּדִּלְתִּי Ez 38^{23} *I will magnify myself*, shew myself great and powerful (of God); *Impf.* יִתְגַּדֵּל, with עַל in a bad sense, *magnify oneself against* Is 10^{15} Dn 11^{36}; יִתְגַּדָּל Dn 11^{37}.

†גָּדֵל **pt.m.** or **adj.verbal. becoming** 1432
great, growing up, Gn 26^{13} (J) 1 S 2^{26} (cf. Dr) 2 Ch 17^{12}; also **great**, pl. cstr. גִּדְלֵי בָשָׂר Ez 16^{26} *great of flesh*.

†גֹּדֶל **n.m. greatness**—Dt 32^3+5 t.; sf. 1433
גָּדְלוֹ Dt 5^{21}+5 t.; גֻּדְלוֹ ψ 150^{11};—**1.** *greatness, magnitude*, tree Ez 31^7, arm of God ψ 79^{11}, mercy of God Nu 14^{19}. **2.** *magnificence*, **a.** king Ez $31^{2.18}$; **b.** God Dt 3^{24} 5^{21} 9^{26} 11^2 32^3 ψ 150^2. **3.** in a bad sense, גֹּדֶל לֵבָב = *pride, insolence of heart* Is 9^8 10^{12}.

†גְּדִלִים **n.[m.]pl. twisted threads** (NH 1434
גְּדִיל, Bab. *gidlu, cord* on which onions were strung, *a string* of onions, Zehnpfund [BAS i. 511]; Aram. גְּדִילָא, ܓܕܝܠܐ *thread, cord, rope*, also *plaited locks*, ܓܕܘܠܐ *id.*)—**1.** *tassels* Dt 22^{12} on border of garment (‖ צִיצִת Nu $15^{38.39}$). **2.** *festoons*, on capitals of columns 1 K 7^{17}.

גָּדוֹל [†522] **adj. great**—ג׳ Gn 4^{13}+279 t.; גָּדֹל Dt 1419
26^8+22 t.; cstr. גְּדוֹל Ez $17^{3.7}$, גְּדָל Ex 15^{16} Je 32^{19}, גְּדָל- Pr 19^{19}, גְּדָוֹל- ψ 145^8 Na 1^3; sf. גְּדוֹלָם Je 6^{13}+2 t.; pl. גְּדוֹלִים Ex 7^4+11 t., גְּדֹלִים Gn 12^{17}+22 t.; cstr. גְּדֹלֵי 2 K 10^6; sf. גְּדֹלָיו 2 K 10^{11} Jon 3^7; גְּדוֹלֶיהָ Na 3^{10}; f. גְּדוֹלָה Nu 22^{18}+96 t.; גְּדֹלָה Gn 15^{12}+31 t.; pl. גְּדוֹלֹת Ne 9^{26} 12^{31}, גְּדֹלוֹת

Dt 27^{2} + 30 t., גְּדֹלֹת Nu 13^{28} + 7 t.,—*great*, **1.** *in magnitude and extent*, e.g. sea Nu 34^{6}, river Gn 15^{18}, wilderness Dt 1^{19}, rain 1 K 18^{45}, mountain Zc 4^{7}, city Gn 10^{12}, house Je 52^{13}, altar Jos 22^{10}, throne 2 Ch 9^{17}, sea-monsters Gn 1^{21}, fish Jon 2^{1}, eagle Ez 17^{3}, terebinth 2 S 18^{9}, substance Gn 15^{14}, wealth Dn 11^{2}, victory 1 S 19^{5}; 1 S 19^{22} בּוֹר הַגָּדוֹל rd. בּ׳ הַגֹּרֶן acc. to 𝔊 We Dr. **2.** *in number*, e.g. nation Gn 12^{2}, congregation Je 31^{8}, camp 1 Ch 12^{22}, army Ez 17^{17}, sacrifice 2 K 10^{19}, slaughter Dt 28^{59} 1 S 4^{17}. **3.** *in intensity*, fear Dt 4^{34}, weeping Is 38^{3}, power כֹּחַ Ex 32^{11}, joy Jon 4^{6}, anger Dt 29^{23}, indignation Je 21^{5}, sin Gn 20^{9}, iniquity Gn 4^{13}, evil Gn 39^{9}, trespass Ez 9^{7}. **4.** *in sound, loud* voice Gn 39^{14}, cry Ex 11^{6}, shout Jos 6^{5}. **5.** *in age*, elder, eldest, son Gn 27^{1}, daughter Gn 29^{16}, brother Gn 10^{21}, sister Ez 16^{46}. **6.** *in importance*, **a.** *things* †(הַ)דָּבָר (הַ)גָּדֹל *an important thing* or *affair* Ex 18^{22} Dt 4^{32} 1 S 12^{16} 2 K 5^{13} 8^{13}; יום יהוה Je 30^{7} Ho 2^{2} Jo 2^{11} 3^{4} Zp 1^{14} Mal 3^{23}. **b.** *of men, great, distinguished*, Moses Ex 11^{3}, David 2 S 5^{10}, Job Jb 1^{3}, Mordecai Est 9^{4}, kings Ec 9^{14} Je 27^{7}; esp. of king of Assyr. הַמֶּלֶךְ הַגָּדוֹל 2 K $18^{19.28}$ = Is $36^{4.13}$, = As. *šarru rabbu, šarru dannu*, e.g. KB$^{i. 94, 1.1}$; הַכֹּהֵן הַגָּדוֹל *the h. p.* Lv 21^{10} + 20 t.; (הָ)אִישׁ גָּדוֹל 1 S 25^{2} 2 S 19^{33} 2 K 5^{1}; אִשָּׁה גְדוֹלָה 2 K 4^{8}; †גָּדוֹל *a great man* 2 S 3^{38} Mi 7^{3}; לֹא תֶהְדַּר פְּנֵי גָדוֹל *thou shalt not honour* (favour) *the person of a great man* (opp. דָּל) Lv 19^{15} (H); †(הַ)גְּדוֹלִים *the great* 2 S 7^{9} = 1 Ch 17^{8} Ne 11^{14} (vid. infr.) Pr 18^{16} 25^{6} Je 5^{5} (2 K 10^{11} 𝔊L ἀγχιστεύοντας, Klo גֹּאֲלָיו); further גְּדֹלֵי הָעִיר 2 K 10^{6}; (כָּל־)גְּדֹלָיו 2 K 10^{11}; Jon 3^{7}; כָּל־גְּדוֹלֶיהָ Na 3^{10}. **c.** †*of God, himself* 2 Ch 2^{4} Ne 4^{8} 8^{6} ψ 86^{10} 99^{2} 135^{5} 147^{5} Is 12^{6} Je 10^{6}; (הָ)אֵל (הַ)גָּדוֹל Dt 7^{21} 10^{17} Ne 1^{5} 9^{32} ψ 77^{14} 95^{3} Je 32^{18} Dn 9^{4}; גדול מכל האלהים Ex 18^{11}; גדול ומהלל מאד 1 Ch 16^{25} ψ 48^{2} 96^{4} 145^{3}; מלך גדול ψ 47^{3} 95^{3} Mal 1^{14}; †*his works* Dt 11^{7} Ju 2^{7} ψ 111^{2}, †*glory* ψ 21^{6} 138^{5}, †*name* Jos 7^{9} 1 S 12^{22} 1 K 8^{42} 2 Ch 6^{32} ψ 76^{2} 99^{3} Je 10^{6} 44^{26} Ez 36^{23} Mal $1^{11.11}$, *mercy* 1 K 3^{6} 2 Ch 1^{8} ψ 57^{11} 86^{13} 108^{5}, *goodness* Ne 9^{25}, *compassion* Is 54^{7}. **7.** in phrases †עוֹד הַיּוֹם גָּדוֹל *it is yet high day* (Fr. *grand jour*, Germ. *hoch am Tage*, the day is at its height) Gn 29^{7}; †כַּקָּטֹן כַּגָּדֹל (or reverse) *as well small as great* Dt 1^{17} 1 Ch 25^{8} 26^{13} 2 Ch 31^{15}; †(לְ)מִקָּטֹן וְעַד גָּדוֹל (or reverse) *from small to great* Gn 19^{11} 1 S 5^{9} $30^{2.19}$ 2 K 23^{2} 25^{26} 2 Ch 15^{13} 34^{30} Est $1^{5.20}$ Je 6^{13} 8^{10} 31^{34} $42^{1.8}$ 44^{12} Jon 3^{5}. **8.** cstr. גְּדֹל (הַ)כְּנָפַיִם *great* of wings Ez $17^{3.7}$, so of anger Pr 19^{19} (Qr); usually of God, in power Na 1^{3}, counsel Je 32^{19}, mercy ψ 145^{8}. **9.** as subst. concr. †עשׂה גדלות *do great things*, of God's great acts of redemption and judgment Dt 10^{21} Jb 5^{9} 9^{10} 37^{5} ψ 71^{19} 106^{21}; of the miracles of Elisha 2 K 8^{4}; of things *too great* and so presumptuous, haughty תבקשׁ ג׳ Je 45^{5}; מדברת ג׳ ψ 12^{4}; לא הלכתי בג׳ ψ 131^{1} (cf. BAram. Dn $7^{8.11.20}$; also Rev 13^{5}). **10.** †as subst. neut. *greatness* of arm Ex 15^{16}; cf. גָּבֹהַּ **4.**

†גְּדוּלָּה **n.f.** greatness—2 S 7^{21} + 3 t.; גְּדֻלָּה 1420
1 Ch 29^{11}; cstr. גְּדֻלַּת Est 10^{2}; sf. גְּדוּלָּתוֹ Est 1^{4}; גְּדֻלָּתוֹ ψ 145^{3}; גְּדֻלָּתִי ψ 71^{21}; גְדֻלּוֹתְךָ ψ 145^{6}; pl. intens. גְּדֻלּוֹת 1 Ch $17^{19.21}$;—chiefly late Heb. **a.** of Psalmist ψ 71^{21}, Mordecai Est 6^{3} 10^{2}, king Est 1^{4}; **b.** *of God's greatness*, as an attribute 1 Ch 29^{11} ψ $145^{3.6}$, or of his acts 2 S 7^{21} (cf. Dr) v^{23} = 1 Ch $17^{19.19.21}$.

†הַגְּדוֹלִים **n.pr.m.** father of Zabdiel Ne 11^{14} (RV & so most; but 𝔊 RVm al. *the great*).

†גִּדֵּל **n.pr.m.** (*very great*)—**1.** head of one 1435
of the families of Nethinim Ezr 2^{47} Ne 7^{49}. **2.** head of one of the families of Solomon's servants Ezr 2^{56} Ne 7^{58}.

†גְּדַלְיָה **n.pr.m.** (*Yah is great*)—**1.** go- 1436
vernor of Judea appointed by Nebuchadnezzar Je $40^{5.8}$ 41^{16}. **2.** son of Amariah, a son of Hezekiah Zp 1^{1}. **3.** priest of the sons of Jeshua Ezr 10^{18}.

גְּדַלְיָ֫הוּ **n.pr.m.** (*Yah(u) is great*)—**1.** 1436
governor of Judea = גדליה 2 K 25^{22-25} Je 39^{14} 40^{6-16} 41^{1-18} 43^{6} (24 t.) **2.** son of Pashur, one of the chiefs of Jerusalem in the time of Jeremiah Je 38^{1}. **3.** one of the sons of Jeduthun, in the time of David 1 Ch $25^{3.9}$.

†גִּדַּ֫לְתִּי **n.pr.m.** (*I magnify* (*God*)) son of 1437
Heman 1 Ch 25^{4} (cf. on this remarkable list of names Ew$^{§ 274 b}$ We RS$^{OTJC 422; 2nd ed. 143}$) v^{29}.

†יִגְדַּלְיָ֫הוּ **n.pr.m.** (*Yah(u) is great*) a pro- 3012
phet of the age of Josiah Je 35^{4}.

†מִגְדָּל **n.m.** tower, Gn 11^{5} + 11 t.; cstr. 4026
מִגְדַּל Ju 8^{17} + 21 t.; pl. מִגְדָּלִים 2 Ch 26^{9} + 6 t.; מִגְדָּלֶיהָ ψ 48^{13} Ez 26^{4}; pl.f. מִגְדָּלוֹת 2 Ch 32^{5} + 2 t.; cstr. מִגְדְּלוֹת Ct 5^{13} (?); sf. מִגְדְּלֹתַיִךְ Ez 26^{9} 27^{11};—**1.** *tower* Gn $11^{4.5}$ Ju 8^{9} $9^{51.51.52.52}$ 2 K 9^{17} 17^{9} 18^{8} 1 Ch 27^{25} 2 Ch 14^{6} $26^{9.10.15}$ 27^{4} 32^{5} Ne $3^{25.26.27}$ Is 2^{15} 30^{25} 33^{18} Ez $26^{4.9}$ 27^{11} ψ 48^{13}, watch-tower in vineyard Is 5^{2}; fig. of God as refuge ψ 61^{4} Pr 18^{10}; beautiful neck like tower of David

Ct 4[4]; an ivory tower 7[5]; breasts 8[10]. (Cf. MI[22] מגדלתה, Sab. (more precisely Liḥyân) מגדלנהן, Eut, v. DHM[Epigr. Denkm. 4, 1. 5]). Special towers mentioned on Lebanon Ct 7[5], Penuel Ju 8[17], Shechem Ju 9[46.47.49]; and at Jerusalem, the tower of David Ct 4[4] (the arsenal), מֵאָה Ne 3[1], חֲנַנְאֵל Ne 3[1] 12[39] Je 31[38] Zc 14[10], הַתַּנּוּרִים Ne 3[11] 12[38] (tower of the furnaces). **2.** *elevated stage, pulpit* of wood Ne 8[4]. **3.** *raised bed* ‖ עֲרוּגָה Ct 5[13], but 𝔊 𝔙 Hi Bö De rightly rd. מְגַדְּלוֹת.

4027 †מִגְדַּל־אֵל **n.pr.** (*tower of God*) stronghold in Naphtali Jos 19[38] prob. = Μαγδαλά Matt 15[39] = *Mejdel* in the plain of Gennesareth Rob [BR iii. 298] Bd[Pal 257].

4028 †מִגְדַּל־גָּד **n.pr.** (*tower of Gad*) stronghold in Judah Jos 15[37];—cf. *Magdala*, Lag[Onom. 139, 12, 2nd ed. 171]; possibly *Mejdel*, eastward of Askalon, Guérin[Judée ii. 130 f.] cf. Bd[Pal 162].

4029 †מִגְדַּל־עֵ֫דֶר **n.pr.** (*flock-tower*) shepherd's watch-tower near Bethlehem Gn 35[21] Mi 4[8].

4024 †מִגְדּוֹל **n.m.** tower, 2 S 22[51] Qr (Kt מגדיל = ψ 18[51] מַגְדִּל).

4024 †מִגְדֹּל **n.pr.** (מִגְדּוֹל only Je 46[14]) fortified city on the NE. border of Egypt Ex 14[2] Nu 33[7] Je 44[1] 46[14] Ez 29[10] 30[6]; Copt. *meschtôl* (Champoll. [L'Égypte sous les Pharaons ii. 79]), Egyptian *makθel* Eb[GS 522].

1438 †גָּדַע **vb.** hew, hew down or off (NH *id.* (rare), Aram. גְּדַע Ithp.; Ar. جَدَعَ *cut off* hand or other member, *mutilate*)—**Qal** *Pf.* גָּדַע La 2[3]; וְגָדַעְתִּי 1 S 2[31]; *Impf.* וָאֶגְדַּע Zc 11[10.14]; *Pt.* pass. גְּדוּעָה Is 15[2] (so many edd. but) Baer גְּרוּעָה; cf. infr., גְּדֻעִים Is 10[33];—*hew, cut in two,* a staff Zc 11[10.14]; metaph. *hew off,* an arm 1 S 2[31]; horns La 2[3]; *hew down,* trees Is 10[33]; if in Is 15[2] then = *shave off* (object זקן, beard), but no other indication of this meaning, and true MT גְּרוּעָה, cf. Baer's note & Je 48[37]; v. גרע. **Niph.** *Pf.* נִגְדַּע Ju 21[6], נִגְדַּע Je 50[23]; 3 fs. נִגְדְּעָה Je 48[25], וְנִגְדְּעָה consec. Is 22[25]; 2 ms. נִגְדַּעְתָּ Is 14[12]; 3 pl. וְנִגְדְּעוּ consec. Ez 6[6] Am 3[14];—*be hewn off,* of altar-horns Am 3[14], of idols Ez 6[6] (‖ נשבר); of severance of a tribe from nation Ju 21[6]; fig. of king of Babylon Is 14[12]; of Babylon as hammer Je 50[23] (‖ נשבר); of a minister, under fig. of secure peg or pin Is 22[25]; of horn of Moab Je 48[25] (‖ נשבר). **Pi.** *Pf.* גִּדַּע 2 Ch 34[7], גִּדֵּ֑עַ 2 Ch 34[4] ψ 107[16], וַיְגַדַּע 2 Ch 14[2], אֲגַדֵּ֑עַ ψ 75[11] Is 45[2], וַיְגַדְּעוּ 2 Ch 31[1]; 3 mpl. תְּגַדֵּעוּן Dt 7[5] 12[3];—*hew off, down, in two* (cf. Qal) of *Asherîm* Dt 7[5] 2 Ch 14[2] 31[1], of idols Dt 12[3] (פְּסִילִים) 2 Ch 34[4.7] (חַמָּנִים); fig. horns of wicked ψ 75[11]; bars of iron (i.e. of Babylon's gates) Is 45[2], cf. ψ 107[16]. †**Pu.** *Pf.* גֻּדָּ֑עוּ Is 9[9] *hew down* (of trees).

גִּדְעוֹן **n.pr.m.** judge of Israel Ju 6[11.13.19] + 1439
36 t. Ju 6–8;—called also יְרֻבַּעַל (q.v.) Ju 6[32] 7[1] etc., & יְרֻבֶּ֫שֶׁת (q.v.) 2 S 11[21].

†גִּדְעֹנִי **n.pr.m.** a Benjamite Nu 1[11] 2[22] 1441
7[60.65]; גִּדְעוֹנִי 10[24] (always אֲבִידָן בֶּן־ג׳).

†גִּדְעֹם **n.pr.loc.** marking limit of pursuit 1440
of Benjamites by rest of Israel Ju 20[45].

†[גָּדַף] **vb.** only **Pi.** revile, blaspheme 1442
(NH גָּדַף *cut, wound,* then (esp. Pi.) *revile;* Ar. جَدَفَ *cut, cut off,* II. *deny a favour, be ungrateful,* etc.; Aram. Pa. גַּדֵּף, ܓܰܕܶܦ, *revile*)—*Pf.* 2 ms. וְגִדַּפְתָּ 2 K 19[22] = Is 37[23]; 3 pl. גִּדְּפוּ 2 K 19[6] = Is 37[6]; *Pt.* מְגַדֵּף Nu 15[30] ψ 44[17];—**1.** *revile,* between man and man, (abs.) קוֹל מְחָרֵף וּמְגַדֵּף ψ 44[17] *the voice of* (him that) *reproacheth and revileth.* **2.** *blaspheme,* sq. acc. י׳ Nu 15[30] (P); 2 K 19[22] = Is 37[23] (‖ חֵרֵף; obj. אֶת־מִי, ref. to י׳ as above); Ez 20[27]; 2 acc. הַדְּבָרִים ... אֲשֶׁר ג׳ נַעֲרֵי מֶלֶךְ אַשּׁוּר אֹתִי 2 K 19[6] = Is 37[6] *the words* with *which the servants of the king of Assyria blaspheme me.*

†גִּדּוּפָה **n.f.** taunt, only Ez 5[15] וְהָיְתָה חֶרְפָּה 1422
וג׳ מוּסָר וּמְשַׁמָּה לַגּוֹיִם *and she shall become a reproach and a taunt, an admonition and an astonishment, to the nations.*

†גִּדּוּפִים **n.m.pl.** revilings, reviling words 1421
—ג׳ Is 43[28]; cstr. גִּדּוּפֵי Zp 2[8]; sf. גִּדֻּפֹתָם Is 51[7] between men, Is 43[28] (‖ חֵרֶם); 51[7] Zp 2[8] (both ‖ חֶרְפָּה).

גָּדַר **vb.** wall up or off, build a wall 1443
(denom.? NH *id.,* Ar. جَدَرَ and v. גָּדֵר infr.)—**Qal** *Pf.* גָּדַר Jb 19[8] + 2 t., וְגָדַרְתִּי Ho 2[8] Am 9[11]; *Impf.* 2 mpl. וַתִּגְדְּרוּ Ez 13[5]; *Pt.* גֹּדֵר Is 58[12] Ez 22[30]; pl. גֹּדְרִים 2 K 12[13] 22[6];—*wall up, shut off,* lit. only *Pt.*, abs. = *masons* (wall-builders) 2 K 12[13] 22[6]; also Is 58[12] (obj. פֶּרֶץ); fig. of Yahweh's dealings with men, obj. ארח Jb 19[8], דֶּרֶךְ La 3[9]; cf. Ho 2[8] (acc. cogn. גָּדֵר), in all = obstructing path of life, cf. also La 3[7] (c. בַּעֲדִי); of restoring fallen booth of David Am 9[11] (obj. פרצים); of repairing fortunes of Israel, a work neglected by prophets Ez 13[5], and by all in power 22[30] (both c. acc. cogn.)

†גָּדֵר **n.m.** [Ez 42, 7] wall (NH גָּדֵר, Aram. 1444,
גְּדֵירָא, גְּדֵירָא, Ar. جِدْرٌ, جَدْرٌ, and more com- 1447
monly جِدَارٌ *enclosing-wall* cf. Heb. גָּדוֹר infr.)

—abs. גָּדֵר Nu 22[24.24] + 5 t. + ψ 62[4] (rd. גדרה cf. infr.) + Ez 13[5] (Co גדרת cf. infr.); cstr. גְּדֵר Pr 24[31] Ez 42[10] (Co del.); sf. גְּדֵרוֹ Is 5[5], גְּדֵרָהּ Ho 2[8] (cf. Baer, note); pl. sf. גְּדֵרַיִךְ Mi 7[11], גְּדֵרֶיהָ ψ 80[13];—*wall, fence*, bordering a road Nu 2[24.24] cf. Ec 10[8]; connected with Ezekiel's temple Ez 42[7]; city wall Mi 7[11] cf. Ezr 9[9]; fig. of Yahweh's vineyard Is 5[5] ψ 80[13]; of fortunes of Israel Ez 22[30]; so also Ez 13[5] (Co גְּדֶרֶת cf. גְּדֵרָה); of hindrance in path of Israel (fig. as woman) Ho 2[8]; of man beset by enemies ψ 62[4] (ג׳ הַדְּחוּיָה, but rd. גְּדֵרָה ד׳ Ol De etc.)

1445 †גֶּ֫דֶר **n.pr.loc.** Canaanitish city Jos 12[13]. Γαδερ A & 𝔊L also Euseb Lag Onom. 244 2nd ed. 254 = בֵּית גָּדֵר? Lag BN 76; cf. גְּדֵרִי infr.; possibly = גָּדֵר 1 Ch 2[51] (v. p. 111).

1448 †I. גְּדֵרָה, גְּדֶ֫רֶת **n.f. wall**—גְּדֵרָה 1 Ch 4[23] + ψ 62[4] (MT גָּדֵר q.v.), גְּדֶרֶת Ez 13[5] (Co, cf. 𝔊; MT גָּדֵר) 42[12] (del. Co); pl. גְּדֵרוֹת Na 3[17] + 2 t., גְּדֵרֹת Nu 32[24]; cstr. גִּדְרוֹת Nu 32[26] + 2 t., Nu 32[16]; sf. גְּדֵרֹתָיו ψ 89[41];—*wall, hedge* 1 Ch 4[23] (or is this n.pr.loc.? cf. Öt) Na 3[17] (where grasshoppers alight), Je 49[3]; wall, connected with Ezekiel's temple Ez 42[12] (del. Co); defences ψ 89[41]; elsewhere ג׳ צאן *sheep-folds* Nu 32[16.36] 1 S 24[4] Zp 2[6] cf. Nu 32[24]; Ez 13[5] Co גְּדֶרֶת after 𝔊; ψ 62[4] MT גדר הדחויה, rd. גדרה ד׳ cf. גָּדֵר.

1452 †גְּדֵרָתִי **adj.gent.** of II. גְּדֵרָה; הַגְּדֵרָתִי 1 Ch 12[4].

1449 †II. גְּדֵרָה **n.pr.loc.** a city of Judah הַגְּדֵרָה Jos 15[36]; 𝔊 Γαδηρα, 𝔊L Γαδιρα; ? cf. Γεδουρ Lag Onom. 245, 2nd ed. 254.

1450 †גְּדֵרוֹת **n.pr.loc.** in Judah Jos 15[41]; הַגְּ׳ 2 Ch 28[18].

1453 †גְּדֵרֹתַ֫יִם **n.pr.loc.** in Judah Jos 15[36]; perh. del., so 𝔊; whole number too large, cf. Di.

1451 †גְּדֵרִי **adj.gent.** of גֶּ֫דֶר (q.v.) so Lag BN 77; cf. MV al.; others גְּדֵרָה; but 𝔊 Γεδωρειτης, 𝔊L Γεδδωριτης;—הַגְּדֵרִי 1 Ch 27[28].

1446 †גְּדוֹר, גְּדֹר **n.pr.** (Ar. جِدَارٌ *wall*);—**1. n.pr.loc.** city of Judah גְּדוֹר Jos 15[58]; also as n.pr.m., under fig. of genealogy גְּדֹר son of Penuel 1 Ch 4[4], גְּדוֹר son of Yered 1 Ch 4[18]; also הַגְּדוֹר 1 Ch 12[7] v. d. H.; הַגְּדוֹר Baer, cf. his note. **2. n.pr.loc.** גְּדֹר 1 Ch 4[39], but read Gerar, acc. to 𝔊 Ew Hi Be al. **3. n.pr.m.** גְּדוֹר 1 Ch 8[31] 9[37] a Benjamite, of Gibeon.

I. גדשׁ (NH גָּדַשׁ, Aram. גְּדַשׁ, *heap up*; cf. also Ar. كَدَسَ).

†I. גָּדִישׁ **n.m.** Jb 5, 26 heap, stack (NH *id.*, Aram. *id.*)—גָּדִישׁ Ex 22[5] + 3 t.;—*stack* of sheaves Ex 22[5] Ju 15[5] (‖ קָמָה in both) Jb 5[26]. 1430

II. גדשׁ (= جدث*; exact mng. unknown).

†II. גָּדִישׁ **n.[m.]** tomb (Ar. جَدَثٌ *id.*) Jb 1430
21[32]; Dr § 178, ed. 3, p. 229 suggests reading גָּדָשׁ.

†גֵּה Ez 47[13], rd. זֶה 𝔊 𝔗 𝔙 & all moderns. 1454

†[גָּהָה] **vb. depart**, i.e. **be cured, healed** 1455
(subj. wound) (cf. Aram. ܓܗܐ *be freed* (from guilt, pain, disease, etc.), Aph. *set free*, also *become free*) ולא־יִגְהֶה מִכֶּם מָזוֹר Ho 5[13].

†גֵּהָה **n.f.** healing, cure—גֵּהָה Pr 17[22] 1456
לֵב שָׂמֵחַ יֵיטִיב ג׳ cf. Now.

†[גָּהַר] **vb.** bend, crouch (so Vrss)— 1457
Qal *Impf.* וַיִּגְהַר 1 K 18[42] sq. אַרְצָה Elijah, with face between knees; 2 K 4[34.35] Elisha, over dead boy, sq. עליו (‖ וישכב v[34], cf. שׁכב).

גַּו, גֵּו v. sub גוה. p. 156 1458

גּוֹב, גּוֹבַי v. sub גבה. p. 146 1462

†[גּוּב] **vb. dig** (cf. Ar. جَابَ *pierce, bore,* 1461
hollow out)—**Qal** *Pt.* גֹּבִים *diggers* or *ploughmen* 2 K 25[12] Kt; but cf. Qr יֹגְבִים as Je 52[16] (v. יגב), and v. גֵּב infr.

†II. [גֵּב] **n.[m.]** pit, ditch, trench (Ar. 1356
جَوْبَةٌ *hollow, depression*; Syr. ܓܘܒܐ *cistern*)—only pl. גֵּבִים Je 14[3]; in 2 K 3[16] גבים גבים, i.e. *full of ditches*; further, *cisterns* (acc. to Klo 2 K 25[12]) Je 39[10] וִיגֵבִים (rd. וְגֵבִים); cf. also ‖ 2 K 25[12] (וּלְיֹגְבִים Kt, וּלְיוֹגְבִים Qr) = Je 52[16] (וּלְיֹגְבִים; both c. כֹּרְמִים); Klo prop. to emend these, so as to rd. in all וַיִּתֵּן לָהֶם כְּרָמִים וְגֵבִים *and gave to them vineyards and cisterns*; another view in Th; cf. further גוב, יגב.—I. גֵּב v. sub גבה.

†גֵּבִים **n.pr.loc.** (*trenches*) N. fr. Jerusalem, 1374
c. art. הַגּ׳ Is 10[31]; site unknown.

†III. [גֵּב] **n.[m.]** beam, rafter? (Thes sub 1356
גוב, but mng. & √ dub.), גֵּבִים 1 K 6[9]; but Lag Armen. Stud. § 499, M i. 212; BN 155 rds. גְּבָבִים (Pers. كنبد, Armen. γμβεθ) *vaulted roofs*.

†גּוֹג **n.pr.m.** (√ unknown)—**1.** 1 Ch 5[4] a 1463
Reubenite. **2.** *Gog of the land of Magog, prince of Rosh, Meshek, and Tubal*, גּוֹג אֶרֶץ מָגוֹג נְשִׂיא רֹאשׁ מֶשֶׁךְ וְתֻבָל Ez 38[2.3] (om. א׳ מגוג) 39[1] (om. id.)
cf. 38[14.16] (del. 𝔊 𝔖 Co) v[18] 39[1.11.11.11] (גֵּיא הֲמוֹן ג׳) 1996
v[15] (id.); cf. As. *Gâgu*, chief of a mountain tribe N. of Assyria Dl Pa 247 COT on Ez 38[2].

4031 †מָגוֹג **n.pr.terr.** (=*land of Gog*? cf. Dl $^{Pa\ 246}$ Len$^{Or\ ii.\ 1,\ 465}$)—Ez 38^{2} 39^{6}; in Gn 10^{2} = 1 Ch 1^{5} a son of Japhet, בְּנֵי יֶפֶת גֹּמֶר וּמָגוֹג וּמָדַי וְיָוָן וְתֻבָל וּמֶשֶׁךְ וְתִירָס; = Scythians? cf. Jos$^{Ant.\ i.\ 6.1}$; Lag $^{Ges.\ Abh.\ 158}$ refers name to mountainous region between Cappadocia and Media; cf. Di Gn 10^{2}, Kiep$^{MBAk\ Feb.\ 1889,\ 207}$ (N. & E. Armenia), Len (SE. Armenia), v. esp. Len$^{Or\ ii.\ 1,\ 412-476}$.

1464 †[גּוּד] **vb. invade, attack** (cf. גדד, whence יָגֻד etc. actually derived by Ki Bö Kö$^{i.\ 356}$ q.v.; SS, perh. better, denom. fr. גדוד)—**Qal** *Impf.* יָגֻד Gn 49^{19}, יְגוּדֶנּוּ v^{19}, יְגוּדֶנּוּ Hb 3^{16}; יגודו ψ 94^{21} Kt (v. גדד);—*attack* Gn 49^{19}, allit. c. גָּד n. pr. & גְּדוּד, גָּד גְּדוּד יְגוּדֶנּוּ וְהוּא יָגֻד עָקֵב: *Gad, a troop shall troop upon him, but he shall troop upon the heel* (i.e. pursue them in their retreat) VB; Hb 3^{16} לַעֲלוֹת לְעַם יְגוּדֶנּוּ cf. VB & Comm.

1466 I. גֵּוָה v. sub נאה. p. 145

גוה (*project, be convex?*).

1458 †[גֵּו] **n.[m.] back**—only sf. גֵּוְךָ 1 K 14^{9}, גֵּוֵךְ Ez 23^{35}, גֵּוָם Ne 9^{26};—alw. הִשְׁלִיךְ אַחֲרֵי ג׳ *cast behind the back*, i.e. put out of mind, ignore, reject י׳ 1 K 14^{9} Ez 23^{35}, and his law Ne 9^{26}.

1460 †I. גֵּו **n.[m.] back**—גֵּו abs. unused, cstr. Pr 10^{13} + 2 t., sf. גֵּוִי Is 50^{6}, גֵּוְךָ Is 38^{17}, 51^{23};—*back*, as beaten, lashed Pr 10^{13} 19^{29} 26^{3} cf. Is 50^{6}; in phr. הִשְׁלִיךְ אַחֲרֵי ג׳ (as גֵּו) Is 38^{17}, of Yahweh's casting sins of penitent behind his back, putting them out of mind; as trodden upon Is 51^{23}, fig. of extreme humiliation.

1460 †II. גֵּו **n.[m.] midst, Aramaism** (cf. Aram. גַּוָּא, גּוֹ *middle*, NH גּוֹ *midst, interior*; ܓܰܘ *id., belly*, Ar. جَوٌّ *midst*) Jb 30^{5} מִן־גֵּו יְגֹרָשׁוּ *from the midst* (of men) *they are driven*; Rosenmüller al. comp. Cicero$^{Off.\ iii.\ 8}$: *e medio pelluntur*.

1465 †II. גֵּוָה **n.f. back**—(so also Di Hoffm SS; 𝔊 Thes De AV RV *body* = גְּוִיָּה, cf. Ba$^{ZMG\ 1887,\ 605}$) Jb 20^{25} וַיֵּצֵא מִגֵּוָה *it comes out from the back* (of arrow which has struck a fugitive, and is then extracted; Hoffm rds. מִגֵּוָה).—I. גֵּוָה sub נאה.

1472 †גְּוִיָּה **n.f. body, corpse**—abs. ג׳ Na 3^{3}; cstr. גְּוִיַּת Ju 14^{8} + 2 t.; sf. גְּוִיָּתוֹ 1 S 31^{10} Dn 10^{6}, גְּוִיָּתֵנוּ Gn 47^{18}, גְּוִיָּתָם Na 3^{3}; pl. abs. גְּוִיּוֹת ψ 110^{6}; sf. גְּוִיֹּתֵנוּ Ne 9^{37}, גְּוִיֹּתֵיהֶם Ez 1^{23}, גְּוִיֹּתֵיהֶנָה v^{11};—**1.** living human *body* Gn 47^{18} (sg., of many persons), cf. pl. Ne 9^{37}; of man in Daniel's vision Dn 10^{6} (body apart from extremities); also of the living creatures in Ezek.'s vision Ez 1$^{11.23}$. **2.** *dead body, corpse, carcass*: **a.** of man 1 S 31^{10} (so orig. in ‖ 1 Ch 10^{10} v. We^{Sm} cf. Dr) v$^{12.12}$ (sg. of several persons), ψ 110^{6}; coll. Na 3$^{3.3}$; **b.** of lion Ju 14$^{8.9}$.

גּוֹי $_{561}$ **n.m.** $^{Gn\ 12,\ 2}$ **nation, people** (NH *id. Gentiles*, Ph. גו *community*, ܓܘܐ, Sab. גו *id.*, DHM$^{ZMG\ 1883,\ 348}$)—ג׳ Gn 12^{2} + 121 t.; sf. 1 s. גּוֹיִי 1471
Zp 2^{9}, גּוֹיֶךָ ψ 106^{5}, גּוֹיֵךְ Kt Ez 36$^{13.14.15}$ (Qr wrongly גּוֹיַיִךְ cf. Co, who del. v^{15}); pl. גּוֹיִם Gn 10^{5} + 410 t. + Qr Gn 25^{23} ψ 79^{10} (Kt גיים) + 6 t. Ez (var. emend. Co); cstr. גּוֹיֵי Gn 18^{18} + 8 t., גּוֹיֵ 2 Ch 32^{13} Ezr 6^{21} (cf. Baer's notes); sf. גּוֹיֵהֶם Gn 10$^{5.20.31.32}$;—**1.** *nation, people* Gn 10$^{5.5.20.31.32.32}$ (all P) + ; Is 2$^{2.4.4}$ = Mi 4$^{2.3.3}$; †Jb 12$^{23.23}$ 34^{29}†; Pr 14^{34}; כֹּל גּוֹיֵי הָאָרֶץ Gn 18^{18} 22^{18} 26^{4} (all J) Dt 28^{1}. **a.** specif. of descendants of Abraham, גּוֹי גָּדוֹל Gn 12^{2} cf. 18^{18} (both J), הֲמוֹן גּוֹיִם 17^{6}, גּוֹיִם 17$^{4.5}$ (all P); of Sarah גּוֹיִם 17^{16} (P); of Ishmael גּוֹי 21^{13}, גּוֹי גָּדוֹל v^{18} (both E), גּוֹי גָּדוֹל 17^{20} (P); of Jacob גּוֹי וּקְהַל גּוֹיִם Gn 35^{11} (P), גּוֹי גָּדוֹל 46^{3} (E); of Ephraim מְלֹא הַגּ׳ 48^{19} (J); of Moses גּוֹי גָּדוֹל Ex 32^{10} (J) cf. Nu 14^{12} (J) Dt 9^{14}; of Jacob and Esau as *two nations* Gn 25^{23} (J). **b.** definitely of Israel Ex 19^{6} (ג׳ קָדוֹשׁ) 33^{13} (both JE), Dt 4^{6} (הַגּוֹי הַגָּדוֹל הַזֶּה, said by heathen cf. v$^{7.8}$) v. also v^{34}, 26^{5} cf. ψ 33^{12}, ψ 83^{5} (said by enemies) Je 31^{36} 33^{24} Ez 37^{22}; in narrative Jos 3^{17} 4^{1} 5^{8} (JE), v^{6} (D), 10^{13} (poet., no art.); of Israel and Judah as *two nations* Ez 35^{10} (said by heathen) 37^{22}; of Judah Is 26$^{2.15.15}$ cf. 58^{2} 60^{22} Mi 4^{7}; once *my people* Zp 2^{9} (‖ עַם); *thy people* ψ 106^{5} (i.e. of י׳), cf. also Ez 36$^{13.14}$ (rd. Kt); esp. of Israel and (or) Judah as sinful, rebellious Dt 32^{28} Ju 2^{20} Is 1^{4} 10^{6} Je 5$^{9.29}$ 7^{28} 9^{8} 12^{17} Ez 2^{3} (del. 𝔊 Co) Hg 2^{14} Mal 3^{9}.—Note. This definite ref. to Israel and (or) Judah is comparatively rare; in Hex not P (yet v. Gn 17$^{4.5.6.16}$ 35^{11} P); seldom in exil. & post-exil. proph.; not Chr.—**c.** usually of non-Heb. peoples Ex 9^{24} 34^{10} (JE) Lv 25^{44} (H) Nu 14^{15} (J) Dt 15$^{6.6}$ 1 K 5^{11} 1 Ch 14^{17} 16^{20} Is 11$^{10.12}$ + oft.; opp. Israel as עַם י׳ 2 S 7^{23} 1 Ch 17$^{21.21}$ etc., v. עַם, cf. also Nu 23^{9}; note esp. גְּלִיל הַגּוֹיִם Is 8^{23} *circle* or *district of the nations* (v. גָּלִיל); also חֲרֹשֶׁת הַגּ׳ Ju 4$^{2.13.16}$ *Charosheth of the nations*, & מֶלֶךְ גּוֹיִם לְגִלְגָּל Jos 12^{23} *king of nations* (peoples, tribes) belonging *to Gilgal* (𝔊 Di *to the district*, i.e. 'Galilee'); esp. of these peoples as heathen: idolatrous Lv 8$^{24.28}$ (P) 20^{23} (H) 1 K 14^{24} 2 K 17$^{8.11.15.26.29.29}$ 2 Ch 28^{3} 32^{13} +, Ezr 6^{21} Ez 5^{6} + ; hostile Gn 15^{14} (J) Lv 26$^{33.38.45}$ (H) Dt 4^{27} 9$^{4.5}$ 18^{9} 1 Ch 16^{35} Je 5^{15} Ez 4^{13} + oft. Je Ez, etc.; in simile Ez 20^{32} 25^{8}; sometimes ‖ עַם ψ 33$^{10.12}$ Is 11^{10} Je 6^{18}, v. also Is 2$^{2.4}$ comp. with Mi 4$^{1.3}$. **2.** fig. of swarm of locusts Jo 1^{6}; of all species of beasts Zp 2^{14}. **3.** גּוֹיִם Gn 14$^{1.9}$ prob. mutilated n.pr. v. infr.

†I. [גּוּז] **vb. pass over, away** (Ar. جَازَ 1468

pass by, over; Aram. גּוּז *cross,* ܓܙ *pass away, fail*)—**Qal** *Pf.* גָּז ψ 90^{10}; *Impf.* וַיָּגָז Nu 11^{31}; —*pass away*, of the life of the aged, ψ 90^{10} גָּז חִישׁ; trans. *bring over*, subj. wind, obj. quails fr. sea, Nu 11^{31} (rd. perh. Hiph. וַיָּגֶז cf. Kö$^{i. 442}$ Di).

1470 †גּוֹזָן **n.pr.loc.** (As. *Guzana* COT 2 K 17^{6} Dl$^{Pa 184}$) city and district of Mesopotamia, on or near the middle course of the Euphrates, through which the river *Chabur* (חָבוֹר) flowed; thither some of the exiled Israelites were brought [by Sargon, B.C. 722–21]: גּוֹזָן 2 K 19^{12} = Is 37^{12}; חָבוֹר נְהַר גּוֹזָן 2 K 17^{6} 18^{11}; וְחָבוֹר וְהָרָא וּנְהַר גּוֹזָן 1 Ch 5^{26} where *Chabur* is separated entirely from the *river of Gozan* (v. חבור).

1518 גּוּחַ v. גיח. p. 161

1471 גּוֹי v. sub גוה. p. 156

1472 גְּוִיָּה v. sub גוה. p. 156

1471 †גּוֹיִם **n.pr.gent.** Gn 14$^{1.9}$, in phr. תִּדְעָל מֶלֶךְ גּוֹיִם *Tid'al king of Goim;* prob. a Babylonian (Elamitic, etc.) name corrupted; H. Rawlinson prop. *Gutî*, a people NE. of Babylonia, COT on Gn 14^{1}; also KGF$^{258 al.}$; cf. also Dl$^{Pa 233 f.}$

1523 גּוֹל v. גיל. p. 162

1474 †גּוֹלָן **n.pr.loc.** (? connected with √גול, Ar. جَالَ *go about, around;* جَوْلٌ *circuit;* cf. Ph. גול n.pr. insul.; also גְּלִילָה, גָּלִיל) city of Manasseh in Bashan, named as a city of refuge Dt 4^{43} cf. Jos 20^{9} 21^{27} both Qr (Kt גלון); given to sons of Gershom son of Levi acc. to 1 Ch 6^{56}; Euseb. knew it as a very large village Γαυλὼν ἢ Γωλάν Lag$^{Onom. 242, 2nd ed. 253}$; district of same name *ib.*, Josephus$^{Ant. viii. 2, 3 etc.}$ Gaulanitis, mod. Jaulân Rob$^{BR ii. 432}$ Bd$^{Pal 270}$ Schumacher$^{ZPV 1886 = Jaulân 1888}$, acc. to most, name applied first to city, thence to district, but perh. otherwise if above deriv. be correct.

גּוֹן (mng. dub., cf. perh. Aram. גְּוַן *tinge*, ܓܘܢܐ, ܓܘܢ; Ar. جَوْنٌ *reddish black*, cf. Hommel Säugethiere 64).

1476 †גּוּנִי **n.pr.m.** **1.** a Naphtalite Gn 46^{24} Nu 26^{48} 1 Ch 7^{13}. **2.** 1 Ch 5^{15} a Gadite.

1477 †גּוּנִי **adj.gent.** of foregoing **1**; c. art. as n. coll. הַגּוּנִי Nu 26^{48}; also of individ. 2 S 23^{32} acc. to 𝔊L (Ιεσσαι ὁ Γουνι) Klo Dr; rd. יִשַׁן הַגּוּנִי; also 1 Ch 11^{34} where rd. *id.* for השם הגזוני (𝔊L Εἰρασαι ὁ Γουνι).

1478 †גָּוַע **vb. expire, perish, die** (cf. Ar. جَاعَ *be empty, hungry*)—**Qal** *Pf.* גָּוַע Nu 20^{29} Jos 22^{20}, גָּוְעוּ La 1^{19}, גָּוַעְנוּ Nu 17^{27} 20^{3}; *Impf.* יִגְוַע Jb 34^{15}, יִגְוָע Gn 6^{17}, יִגְוְעוּ Jb 36^{12}, יִגְוָעוּ Zc 13^{8}, יִגְוָעוּן ψ 104^{29} etc.; *Inf.* cstr. גְּוַע Nu 20^{3}, גְּוֹעַ Nu 17^{28}; *Pt.* גֹּוֵעַ ψ 88^{16};—*expire* and die, only P & poet.; ג׳ וימת Gn 25$^{8.17}$ 35^{29} (all P); ‖ מות Jb 3^{11} 14^{10} cf. Nu 17^{28} (P); ‖ אבד Nu 17^{27} *we expire, we perish* (P); ‖ עָנִי ψ 88^{15} (progressive parall.) *distressed and about to die;* ‖ יאסף אל אבותיו Gn 49^{33}; ‖ על־עפר ישוב Jb 34^{15} cf. ψ 104^{29}; ‖ יִכָּרֵתוּ Zc 13^{8}; abs., both prose and (esp.) poetry Nu 20$^{3.3.29}$ Jos 22^{20} Gn 6^{17} 7^{21} (all P) Jb 10^{18} 13^{19} 27^{5} 36^{12} La 1^{19}; Jb 29^{18} עִם־קִנִּי אגוע *with my nest shall I die*, i.e. in full possession of what is mine, cf. Di.

†[גּוּף] **vb. shut, close** (NH *id.*, v. NHWB 1479
i. 314, 352)—**Hiph.** *Impf.* juss. יָגִיפוּ Ne 7^{3} *close* (doors, דלתות).

†[גּוּפָה] **n.f.** body, corpse (late; NH גּוּף, 1480
Aram. גּוּפָא; Ar. جِيفَةٌ)—cstr. sg. גּוּפַת 1 Ch 10^{12}; cstr. pl. גּוּפֹת 1 Ch 10^{12}, cf. Be (‖ 1 S 31^{12} has גְּוִיַּת).

†I. גּוּר **vb. sojourn** (cf. Ar. جَارَ *turn aside,* 1481
tarry, v. esp. III. IV. VIII. X; Aram. ܓܘܪ, Eth. in der.)—**Qal** *Pf.* גָּר Gn 35^{27} + 3 t., וְגָר consec. Is 11^{6}; גַּרְתָּה Gn 21^{23}; גַּרְתִּי Gn 32^{5} ψ 120^{5}; גָּרוּ Ex 6^{4}; *Impf.* יָגוּר Ex 12^{48} + 12 t., וַיָּגָר Gn 20^{1} + 2 t.; sf. יְגֻרְךָ ψ 5^{5}; 3 fs. וַתָּגָר 2 K 8^{2}; 2 fs. תָּגוּרִי 2 K 8^{1}; cohort. אָגוּרָה ψ 61^{5}, יָגוּרוּ Is 16^{4}; *Imv.* גּוּר Gn 26^{3}, גּוּרִי 2 K 8^{1}; *Inf. cstr.* גּוּר Gn 12^{10} + 17 t.; *Pt.* גָּר Dt 18^{6} Ju 17^{7} + 17 t.; f. cstr. גָּרַת Ex 3^{22}; pl. גָּרִים Lv 25^{6} + 8 t.; cstr. גָּרֵי Jb 19^{15};—**1.** *sojourn*, dwell for a (definite or indef.) time, dwell as a new-comer (cf. גֵּר) without original rights, v. esp. Gn 19^{9} (J) Dt 18^{6} & cf. Ju 17$^{7.8.9}$ 19^{1}; also Gn 12^{10} 20^{1} 21$^{23.34}$ 32^{5} 47^{4} (all JE); of patriarchs in Canaan Gn 26^{3} (J) 35^{27} Ex 6^{4} (both P) cf. ψ 105^{12} = 1 Ch 16^{19}, Ju 19^{16} 2 S 4^{3} 2 K 8$^{1.1.2}$ (seven years) Is 16^{4} Ru 1^{1} Ezr 1^{4} (in exile); cf. further Ex 3^{22} (E) גָּרַת בֵּית of a woman in another's house as lodger or guest (v. Di), גָּרֵי בֵיתִי Jb 19^{15}; so (poet.) of worshipper in Yahweh's house ψ 15^{1} 61^{5} cf. Is 33$^{14.14}$; fig. of evil לֹא יְגֻרְךָ רָע ψ 5^{5} *evil cannot be a guest of thine* (Che; sq. acc., as in Ar. جاوره III); particularly of the גֵּר (q.v.) in Israel Ex 12$^{48.49}$ Lv 16^{29} (all P) 17$^{8.10.12.13}$ 18^{26} 19$^{33.34}$ 20^{2} 25$^{6.45}$ (all H) Nu 9^{14} 15$^{14.15.16.26.29}$ 19^{10} Jos 20^{9} (all P) Ez 14^{7} 47$^{22.23}$; of Ephraim and Manasseh sojourning with Judah and Benjamin 2 Ch 15^{9}; of Rechabites sojourning in Judah Je 35^{7}; of Israelites sojourning in Egypt Dt 26^{5} Is 52^{4} ψ 105^{23}; so of Judah, to escape from

under Babylonian power Je 42$^{15.17.22}$ 43^{2} 44$^{8.12.14.28}$. **2.** *abide*, nearly or quite=*dwell* Je 43^{5} cf. La 4^{15}, Je 49$^{18.33}$ 50^{40}, also Jb 28^{4}; of wolf dwelling with lamb Is 11^{6}; *stay* (inactive) Ju 5^{17};—in Is 5^{17} rd. perh., for גָּרִים ,גְּדָיִם or כָּרִים cf. 𝔊 Lo Ew Di & Che crit. n. (> Stu גֵּרִים). **Hithpol.** *Pt.* מִתְגּוֹרֵר 1 K 17^{20} *seek hospitality with*, sq. עִם (cf. Ar. x); יִתְגּוֹרָרוּ Ho 7^{14} is dub. (cf. II. גור); AE Ki Thes Wü AV RV *they assemble themselves*, but txt. prob. err., v. גדד.

1483 †I. גּוּר **n.pr.loc.** (*sojourning, dwelling*) 2 K 9^{27} מַעֲלֵה־ג׳ אשׁר את־יִבְלְעָם, otherwise unknown.

1485 †גּוּר־בַּעַל **n.pr.loc.** (*dwelling* or *Gûr of Baal*) 2 Ch 26^{7} הָעַרְבִיִּים הַיֹּשְׁבִים בְּגוּר־בָּעַל.

1616 גֵּר$_{92}$ **n.m.**$^{\text{Ex 12, 48}}$ sojourner (Ar. جَارٌ, Eth. ጎዪር: ጊር: Aram. ܓܝܘܪܐ, גִּיּוֹר, *proselyte*, גַּיֵּר *proselytize*, Ph. גר in n.pr., & pl. גרם)—גֵּר Gn 15^{13} + 74 t.; sf. גֵּרְךָ Ex 20^{10} + 4 t., גֵּרוֹ Dt 1^{16}; pl. גֵּרִים Ex 22^{20} + 9 t., גֵּיּרִים 2 Ch 2^{16};—**1.** *sojourner*, temporary dweller, new-comer (no inherited rights), cf. Ex 12^{19} Lv 24^{16} Nu 15^{30} Jos 8^{33} (opp. *homeborn*); of Abraham at Hebron Gn 23^{4} (P; ‖ תּוֹשָׁב); Moses in desert Ex 2^{22} (J) 18^{3} (E; here explan. of name Gershom, Moses' son); as claiming hospitality Jb 31^{32}; perh. in above cases, and certainly in general, with technical sense; fig. of Yahweh Je 14^{8}; of Israel in Egypt Gn 15^{13} Ex 22^{20} 23^{9} (all JE) Lv 19^{34} (H) Dt 10^{19} 23^{8}; גֵּרִים with Yahweh Lv 25^{23} (H) 1 Ch 29^{15} ψ 39^{13} (in all ‖ תּוֹשָׁב) cf. 119^{19}. **2.** usually of גֵּרִים in Israel 2 S 1^{13} (Amalekite) cf. Jos 8$^{33.35}$ (E) 20^{9} (P) Is 14^{1}; dwellers in Israel with certain conceded, not inherited rights (cf. RS$^{\text{OTJC 434; 2nd ed. 342. n.; K 42; Sem 75 f.}}$ Sta$^{\text{Gesch. i. 400}}$). The גֵּר is to share in Sabbath rest Ex 20^{10} 23^{12} (both JE) Dt 5^{14}; otherwise he is to have like obligations with Israel Ex 12$^{19.48.49}$ Lv 16^{29} (all P) Lv 17$^{8.10.12.13.15}$ 18^{26} 20^{2} 22^{18} 24$^{16.22}$ (all H) Nu 9$^{14.14}$ 15$^{14.15.15.16.26.29.30}$ 19^{10} 35^{15} (all P) Ez 14^{7}; similar rights Dt 1^{16} Ez 47$^{22.23}$; and like privileges Dt 16$^{11.14}$ 26^{11} 29^{10} 31^{12} cf. 2 Ch 30^{25}; very rarely any distinction made, in obligation Lv 25$^{47.47.47}$ (H), in permissible food Dt 14^{21}; in future success Dt 28^{43}; kindness to גֵּר frequently enjoined: Lv 19^{10} (‖ עָנִי), 23^{22} (‖ *id.*) 19^{34} (all H); Dt 10$^{18.19}$ 14^{29} 24$^{19.20.21}$ 26$^{12.13}$ (all ‖ יָתוֹם וְאַלְמָנָה); oppression prohibited Lv 19^{33} (H) Dt 24^{14}; Ex 22^{20} 23$^{9.9}$ (JE) Dt 24^{17} 27^{19} Je 7^{6} 22^{3} Zc 7^{10} (these eight ‖ יָתוֹם וְאַלְמָנָה); obj. of care to י׳ ψ 146^{9} (‖ *id.*); charge that גֵּר has been oppressed Ez 22^{7} Mal 3^{5} (both ‖ *id.*); also Ez 22^{29} (‖ עָנִי וְאֶבְיוֹן), ψ 94^{6}; cf. also command that a poor brother be treated like גֵּר, i.e. kindly, Lv 25^{35} (H). Latest conception somewhat different: גֵּר 1 Ch 22^{2} 2 Ch 2^{16} (הַגֵּיּרִים) gathered for hard service; yet cf. 2 Ch 30^{25}. (Oft. c. verb. cogn. Ex 12$^{48.49}$ Lv 16^{29} 17$^{8.10.12.13}$ 18^{26} 19^{33} 20^{2} Nu 9^{14} 15$^{14.15.16.26.29}$ 19^{10} Jos 20^{9} Ez 47$^{22.23}$; oft. ‖ תּוֹשָׁב Gn 23^{4} Lv 25$^{23.35.47}$ 1 Ch 29^{15} ψ 39^{13}).

†גֵּרוּת **n.f.** lodging(-place)—וישׁבו בְּגֵרוּת 1628
כִּמְוֹהָם אשׁר אצל בית לחם Je 41^{17}, *inn, khan?* so 3643
Ew Gf; Hi al. גִּדְרוֹת *folds*, after Joseph. Aq.

†יָגוּר **n.pr.loc.** a southern city of Judah, 3017
toward Edom Jos 15^{21}.

†[מָגוֹר] **n.[m.]** sojourning-place, dwell- 4033
ing-place, sojourning—sf. מְגוּרָם ψ 55^{16}; pl. cstr. מְגוּרֵי Gn 37^{1}; sf. מְגוּרַי Gn 47^{9}, מְגוּרָי ψ 119^{54}, מְגֻרֶיךָ Gn 17^{8} 28^{4}, מְגוּרָיו Jb 18^{19}, מְגוּרֵיהֶם Gn 36^{7} + 2 t., מְגֻרֵיהֶם Ex 6^{4};—*dwelling-place* ψ 55^{16} Jb 18^{19};—*sojourning(-place)*, always pl., אֶרֶץ מ׳ Gn 17^{8} 28^{4} 36^{7} 37^{1} Ex 6^{4} (Hex always P) Ez 20^{38}; *sojourning* (pl.)=life-time, שְׁנֵי מ׳ Gn 47^{9} יְמֵי מ׳ Gn 47^{9}; cf. בֵּית מ׳ ψ 119^{54}.

†מְגוּרָה **n.f.** store-house, granary Hg 2^{19}. 4035

†מַמְּגֻרוֹת **n.f.pl.** *id.*, Jo 1^{17} (‖ אֹצָרוֹת; but 4460
𝔊 ληνοί, Me נתות).

†II. [גּוּר] **vb. stir up strife, quarrel** (cf. 1481
גרה)—so Ew Che Di RVm (Is 54^{15}); **gather together** Ges De Br cf. 𝔗 𝔙, so AV RV;—**Qal.** *Pf.* גָּר Is 54^{15}; *Impf.* יָגוּר v^{15}, יָגוּרוּ ψ 56^{7} 59^{4} 140^{3} (on all cf. infr.); *Inf.* abs. גּוֹר Is 54^{15};—**1.** *stir up strife*, abs. גּוֹר יָגוּר Is 54^{15}; cf. ψ 56^{7} (but AE Che rd. יָגוֹדּוּ *attack*, v. גדד); sq. עַל־ ψ 59^{4} (but Che *id.*; cf. ψ 94^{21}, wh. however Ol would emend by 56^{7} 59^{4}); sq. acc. מִלְחָמוֹת ψ 140^{3} (Hup Che rd. יְגָרוּ Pi. Impf. of גרה). **2.** *quarrel*, sq. אֶת־ *with* Is 54^{15}. Here also **Hithpol.** *Impf.* Ho 7^{14} יִתְגּוֹרָרוּ (cf. I. גור), acc. to Ew, *they excite themselves*, but unlikely; v. גדד.

†[גּוּר] **n.[m.]** whelp (as *quarrelsome?* 1484
or onomatop.? perhaps=As. *giru* Zehnpfund$^{\text{BAS i. 504}}$) of lion—גּוּרֵי אֲרָיוֹת Je 51^{38} (‖ כְּפִרִים) sim. of Babylonians; cf. גֹּרֹתָיו Na 2^{13} (‖ *id.* v^{14}) fig. of Assyrians.

†II. גּוּר **n.m.**$^{\text{Ez 19, 3. 5}}$ whelp, young—cstr. 1482
גּוּר (אַרְיֵה) Gn 49^{9} + 2 t.; sf. גּוּרֶיהָ Ez 19^{2}, גֻּרֶיהָ Ez 19$^{3.5}$, גּוּרֵיהֶן La 4^{3};—**1.** lion's *whelps*, fig. of Judah Gn 49^{9}; of Dan Dt 33^{22}; of Assyrian (prince?) Na 2^{12}; fig. of Israelites Ez 19$^{2.3.5}$ (‖ כְּפִיר). **2.** young of jackals (תַּנִּין) La 4^{3}.

†III. [גּוּר] **vb. dread** (cf. יָגֹר)—**Qal** *Impf.* 1481
אָגוּר ,וַיָּגָר Nu 22^{3} 1 S 18^{15}; 2 ms. תָּגוּר Dt 18^{22};

Dt 32^{27}; pl. יָגוּרוּ ψ 33^{8} Jb 41^{17} + Ho 10^{5}, תָּגוּרוּ Dt 1^{17}; *Imv.* גּוּרוּ ψ 22^{24} Jb 19^{29};—**1.** *be afraid* of, sq. מִפְּנֵי Nu 22^{3} Dt 1^{17} 1 S 18^{15}, גּוּרוּ לָכֶם מִפְּנֵי Jb 19^{29}; c. מִן 41^{17} Dt 18^{22}; c. acc. Dt 32^{27} (poet.) Ho 10^{5} rd. prob. ינודו *lament* (‖אבל, used c. לְ *e.g.* Na 3^{7} Je 15^{5} al.; cf. Che). **2.** *stand in awe* of, sq. מִן ψ 22^{24} 33^{8} (‖ יָרֵא).

4032 †מָגוֹר **n.m.** fear, terror—abs. מ׳ ψ 31^{14} + 6 t. + Je 20^{3} cf. infr.; pl. sf. מְגוּרַי La 2^{22};—*fear, terror* Is 31^{9}; = cause of terror Je 20^{4}; else-
4036 where in phrase, coined by Jerem., מ׳ מִסָּבִיב *terror on every side* Je 6^{25} 20^{3} (where as n.pr.), v^{10} 46^{5} 49^{29} ψ 31^{14} La 2^{22} (מְגוּרַי מִס׳).

4034 †[מְגוֹרָה] **n.f.** fear, terror—cstr. מְגוֹרַת Pr 10^{24}; pl. sf. מְגוּרֹתַי ψ 34^{5}, מְגוּרֹתָם Is 66^{4} (on these forms with ּ cf. Ges$^{§ 27.3. R. 1, \& 85. 48}$);—*terror* (= thing dreaded) ψ 34^{5} Pr 10^{24} Is 66^{4}.

1627 [גּוֹרֶן] Je 2^{25} גורנך Kt v. גָּרוֹן. p. 173

גוש (*be hard*, cf. Ar. جَسَأَ *be hard*, of hands, from toil).

1487 †גּוּשׁ **n.[m.]** clod, lump (NH *id.*, Aram. גּוּשָׁה; cf. Ar. جَسْءٌ etc., *rough ground*, also *ice*)—וְגִישׁ עָפָר Jb 7^{5}, Qr וְגוּשׁ ע׳.

1488 גֵּז v. sub גזז. below

1489 †גִּזְבָּר **n.m.** treasurer (loan-word; NH *id.*; cf. BAram. [גְּזָבַר], pl. גְּזָבְרַיָּא; Syr. ܓܙܒܪܐ, also ܓܙܘܪܐ, Pers. گنجور, cf. Lag$^{Ges. Abh. 27 f., Arm. Stud. § 454}$), Ezr 1^{8}.

1491 †[גָּזָה] **vb.** cut, (cut off, sever), √of גָּזִית (cf. Talm. גְּזָא *cut off*); hence perh. **Qal** *Pt. act.* sf. גּוֹזִי ψ 71^{6} thou art *he that severed me* from my mother's womb (De Che; 𝔊 σκεπαστής, De prop. ἐκσπαστής, v. 𝔊 ψ 22^{10}; 𝔙 *protector* cf. 𝔊, Thes Ew Hup Pe *benefactor*, cf. Ar. جَزَا *requite*, Jerus. Syr. ܓܙܐ, Talm. גְּזָא *id.*);—txt. and mng. dub.; ‖ψ 22^{10} has גֹּחִי; v. Che$^{crit. n. and OP 476}$; Du עֻזִּי.

1496 †גָּזִית **n.f.** a cutting, hewing—גָּזִית Ex 20^{25} + 10 t., always abs.;—*hewing*, אַבְנֵי ג׳ = *hewn stones* (building-stones) 1 K 5^{31} 1 Ch 22^{2} Ez 40^{42} (for tables), cf. אֲבָנִים יְקָרוֹת כְּמִדּוֹת ג׳ 1 K 7$^{9.11}$ (but Klo del. as gloss, cf. 𝔊); also without אבני = *hewn stones* Ex 20^{25} (altar) Am 5^{11} (בָּתֵּי ג׳) Is 9^{9} (opp. לְבֵנִים); טוּרֵי ג׳ 1 K 6^{36}, טוּרִים ג׳ 7^{12}; also La 3^{9} גָּדַר דְּרָכַי בְּג׳.

1492 גִּזָּה v. sub גזז. below

1493 †גִּזוֹנִי **adj. gent.** 1 Ch 11^{34} הַשֵּׁם הַגִּזוֹנִי, but rd. יָשֵׁן הַגּוּנִי (𝔊L Εἰρασαι ὁ Γουνι) cf. גּוּנִי.

†[גָּזַז] **vb.** shear (NH *id.*, Aram. גְּזַז, ܓܙ; Ar. جَزَّ, As. deriv.)—**Qal** *Impf.* וַיָּגָז Jb 1^{20}; 2 ms. תָגֹז Dt 15^{19}; *Imv.* 2 fs. גָּזִּי Je 7^{29}, גֹּזִּי Mi 1^{16}; *Inf.* 1494
cstr. גְּזֹז Gn 31^{19} (E) 1 S 25^{2}, גֹּז Gn 38^{13} (J); *Pt.* גֹּזֵז 1 S 25^{4}; pl. גֹּזְזִים 1 S 25^{7} + 2 t.; cstr. גֹּזֲזֵי Gn 38^{12}; sf. גֹּזֲזַי 1 S 25^{11}, גֹּזְזֶיהָ Is 53^{7};—*shear* sheep (obj. צֹאן) Gn 31^{19} 38^{13} Dt 15^{19} 1 S 25$^{2.4}$; cf. *Pt. shearer* (c. צאן) Gn 38^{12}, also גֹּזְזֶיהָ (i.e. רָחֵל) Is 53^{7}; abs. = *sheep-shearer*, 1 S 25$^{7.11}$ 2 S 13$^{23.24}$; obj. man's head (ראשׁו) Jb 1^{20}; of a woman's (fig. of Israel) Mi 1^{16} (no obj.; ‖קרחי), (fig. of Jerusalem) Je 7^{29} (obj. נֵזֶר q.v.) **Niph.** נָגֹזּוּ *be cut off* (= destroyed) of Assyrians Na 1^{12}.

†גֵּז **n.[m.]** shearing, mowing (As. *gizzu* 1488
Zehnpfund$^{BAS i. 530}$, Aram. גִּיזָּא, ܓܙܐ *fleece*)—גֵּז ψ 72^{6}, also cstr. Dt 18^{4} Jb 31^{20}; pl. cstr. גִּזֵּי Am 7^{1};—*shearing* = thing sheared off, *wool*, *fleece* ג׳ צֹאן Dt 18^{4}, ג׳ כְּבָשַׂי Jb 31^{20}; *mowing* Am 7^{1} (ג׳ הַמֶּלֶךְ cf. RS$^{Sem. i. 228}$); = land to be mown ψ 72^{6} (but *shearing* in both, acc. to Hoffm$^{ZAW 1883, 116 ff.}$ SS).

†גִּזָּה **n.f.** fleece—(Ar. جِزَّةٌ, Aram. ܓܙܬܐ) 1492
גִּזָּה Ju 6^{37} + 5 t.; cstr. גִּזַּת Ju 6^{37};—*fleece*, ג׳ צֶמֶר Ju 6^{37}; abs. Ju 6$^{37.38.38.39.39.40}$.

†גָּזֵז **n.pr.m.** son of עֵיפָה, concub. of Caleb 1495
1 Ch 2$^{46.46}$; v^{b} says that חָרָן son of עיפה (and Caleb?) begat Gazez.

גָּזִית v. sub גזה. above 1496

†I. גָּזַל **vb.** tear away, seize, rob (NH 1497
id., Ph. גזל Niph., Aram. גְּזַל, ܓܙܠ & (Nas.) ܓܙܠ; Ar. جَزَلَ *cut off*)—**Qal** *Pf.* גָּזַל Jb 20^{19} Ez 18^{18}, גָּזַל Lv 5^{23} + 2 t., גָּזַלְתִּי ψ 69^{5} etc.; *Impf.* יִגְזֹל Ez 18^{7}, וַיִּגְזֹל 2 S 23^{21} 1 Ch 11^{23} etc.; *Inf.* גָּזֹל Is 10^{2}; *Pt.* act. גֹּזֵל Pr 28^{24}; sf. גֹּזְלוֹ ψ 35^{10}; pl. cstr. גֹּזְלֵי Mi 3^{2}; pass. גָּזוּל Dt 28^{29} + 4 t.;—*tear away, rob*, c. obj. rei (movable), flock (עֵדֶר) Jb 24^{2}, ass Dt 28^{31}, women Ju 21^{23} cf. Gn 31^{31} (E), tear away orphan child from breast Jb 24^{9} יתום מִשֹּׁד, snatch a spear from enemy's hand 2 S 23^{21} = 1 Ch 11^{23}; fig. of drying up snow-water Jb 24^{19}; (obj. stationary) *take violent possession of*, well of water Gn 21^{25} (E), house Jb 20^{19}, fields Mi 2^{2}; (hyperb.) the skin Mi 3^{2}; **c. acc. cogn.** = *seize, plunder*, obj. גְּזֵלָה Lv 5^{23} (P) Ez 18$^{7.12.16}$, גָּזֵל Ez 18^{18} 22^{29}; indef. ψ 69^{5}; fig., obj. מִשְׁפָּט Is 10^{2}; c. obj. pers. robbed ψ 35^{10} Pr 22^{22} 28^{24}, prob. also Ju 9^{25} cf. Lv 19^{13} (H; abs.); cf. also pass. Dt 28^{29} (‖ עָשׁוּק); הצילו גָּזוּל מיד עושק Je 21^{12} cf. 22^{3}; Mal 1^{13} גָּזוּל (‖ פִּסֵּחַ *lame* and חוֹלֶה *sick*), prob. that rescued

after seizure by wild beasts, therefore mutilated. †**Niph.** *Pf.* 3 fs. וְנִגְזְלָה, subj. *sleep* Pr 4^{16} (יְשֵׁנוּ ‖ לֹא).

1498 †**גָּזֵל n.[m.] robbery**—abs. גָּזֵל Lv 5^{21} + 3 t. + Ez 18^{18} cf. infr.; cstr. גֵּזֶל Ec 5^{7} Ez 18^{18} (but cf. infr.);—*robbery* Lv 5^{21} (P) ψ 62^{11} (‖ עֹשֶׁק) Is 61^{8}; = *thing plundered*, taken as plunder, as acc. cogn. Ez 22^{29} (גָּזְלוּ גָּזֵל); fig. גֵּזֶל משפט = wresting

1499 of justice (cf. Is 10^{2}) Ec 5^{7}.—Ez 18^{18} has גֵּזֶל אָח, but 𝔊 Co del. אח; rd. then גָּזֵל.—Cf. Lag [BN 172].

1500 †**גְּזֵלָה n.f. plunder, spoil**—גְּזֵלָה Lv 5^{23} + 3 t.; cstr. גְּזֵלַת Is 3^{14}, גְּזֵלוֹת Ez 18^{12};—*thing seized, spoil* Lv 5^{23} (P) Ez 33^{15}; גְּזֵלַת הֶעָנִי Is 3^{14}; as acc. cogn. Ez $18^{7.12.16}$.

II. **גזל** (√ of foll., mng. dub.; acc. to Fl [NHWB i. 433] onomatop., cf. جَزَلَ Frey *crassa vox, vox columbi*, v. also Frä[115]).

1469 †**גּוֹזָל n.m.** [Dt 32, 11] **young of birds** (Syr. ܙܘܓܠܐ, cf. Ar. جَوْزَل)—תֹּר וְגוֹזָל Gn 15^{9} pigeon; גּוֹזָלָיו Dt 32^{11} eaglet (suff. ref. to נֶשֶׁר).

גזם (*cut off*, NH *id.*, Eth. **ገዘመ:** cf. Ar. جَزَمَ [= Aram. ܓܙܡ]; or possibly جَذَمَ [= Aram. ܓܕܡ]).

1501 †**גָּזָם n.m.** [Am 4, 9] **locusts** (coll.)—abs. גָּזָם Jo 1^{4} 2^{25} Am 4^{9};—always as devouring, devastating, Jo 1^{4} (‖ אַרְבֶּה, יֶלֶק, חָסִיל), 2^{25} (‖ *id.*); Am 4^{9} alone: *your gardens and your vineyards, and your fig-trees and your olive-trees* יֹאכַל הַגָּזָם.

1502 †**גַּזָּם n.pr.m.** head of a family of returned exiles בְּנֵי ג׳ Ezr 2^{48} = Ne 7^{51}.

גזע (√ of foll., cf. Ar. جَزَعَ *cut off*, & Eth. **ገዝዐ:** *saw in two*).

1503 †**[גֶּזַע] n.m.** [Jb 14, 8] **stock, stem** (NH *id.*, cf. Syr. ܓܘܙܥܐ *stem, trunk*)—cstr. גֶּזַע Is 11^{1}; sf. גִּזְעוֹ Jb 14^{8}, גִּזְעָם Is 40^{24};—*stock, stem* of a tree Jb 14^{8} (‖ שָׁרְשׁוֹ); fig. ג׳ ישי '*stem of Jesse*' Is 11^{1} (‖ שָׁרָשָׁיו); שֹׁרֵשׁ בָּאָרֶץ ג׳ Is 40^{24} (‖ זרע, נטע).

1504 †**גָּזַר vb. cut, divide** (Ar. جَزَرَ, NH גָּזַר *cut, determine, circumcise;* Eth. **ገዘረ:** Aram. גְּזַר, ܓܙܪ)—**Qal** *Pf.* גָּזַר Hb 3^{17}; *Impf.* וַיִּגְזֹר Is 9^{19}; 2 ms. תִּגְזַר Jb 22^{28}; וַיְגַזֵּרוּ 2 K 6^{4}; *Pt.* act. גֹּזֵר ψ 136^{13};—**1.** *divide, cut in two*, sq. acc. 1 K 3^{25} (ג׳ לִשְׁנַיִם) cf. v^{26} (obj. not expressed). **2.** *divide* the Red Sea (acc.) ψ 136^{13} sq. לִגְזָרִים. **3.** *cut down* הָעֵצִים 2 K 6^{4}. **4.** *cut off* (piece of meat to eat, but obj. not expr. ‖ אכל) Is 9^{19}. **5.** *cut off*, i.e. *destroy, exterminate* Hb 3^{17} (c. acc.; indef. subj.), sq. מִן loc. **6.** *decree* (Aramaism, cf. B Aram.) Jb 22^{28} c. acc. **Niph.** *Pf.* נִגְזַר 2 Ch 26^{21} Est 2^{1}, נִגְזַרְתִּי La 3^{24}, נִגְזָרוּ ψ 88^{6}, נִגְזָרְנוּ Ez 37^{11} Is 53^{8};—**1.** *be cut off*, separated, excluded from (מִן) temple 2 Ch 26^{21}, from (מִן) Yahweh's hand ψ 88^{6} (of the slain), from (מִן) the land of the living Is 53^{8} (of the suffering servant of י׳). **2.** *be cut off* = *destroyed* La 3^{54} Ez 37^{11}. **3.** *be decreed*, Est 2^{1} sq. עַל *against* (cf. **Qal 6**).

†I. **[גֶּזֶר] n.[m.]** part, only pl. הַגְּזָרִים Gn 15^{17} of halves of animals; גְּזָרִים ψ 136^{13} of divided portions of Red Sea. 1506

†II. **גֶּזֶר n.pr.loc.** (*portion*) Levitical city on border of Ephraim Jos 10^{33} 12^{12} 21^{21} 1 K 9^{16} 1507
1 Ch 6^{52} 7^{28} 20^{4}; גָּזֶר Jos $16^{3.10}$ Ju $1^{29.29}$ cf. 2 S 5^{25} 1 K $9^{15.17}$; c. ה— loc. גָּזְרָה 1 Ch 14^{16};—cuneiform *Gazri*, Bez [Tell el-Amarna Tabl. BM. 148]; mod. Tell-Jezer, c. 18 m. N. of W. fr. Jerus., S. of the Jaffa road; Gann in PEF [1873, 78 f.; 1875, 74 f.] cf. Bd [Pal 17].

†**גִּזְרִי adj.gent.** 2 S 27^{8} Qr (Kt והגרזי) cf. Dr. 1511

†**גְּזֵרָה n.f. separation**—אֶל־אֶרֶץ גְּזֵרָה Lv 16^{22} (P) *unto a land of separation*, of the goat for Azazel; *solitary land* RV; 'cut off,' i.e. *whence it would not readily find its way back* VB. 1509

†**גִּזְרָה n.f. cutting, separation**—גִּזְרָה Ez 41^{12} + 6 t.; sf. גִּזְרָתָם La 4^{7};—**1.** *cutting*, i.e. *polishing* (AV RV or *carving*, i.e. beauty of form, shape, cf. VB) סַפִּיר גִּזְרָתָם La 4^{7}; their *polishing* (or *beauty of form*) was as *sapphire*. **2.** *separation*, הַגִּזְרָה Ez $41^{12.13.14.15}$ $42^{1.10.13}$, separate place AV RV cf. Da; i.e. yard, or space adjoining temple on three sides. 1508

†**[מַגְזֵרָה] n.f. cutting instrument, axe**— 2 S 12^{31} of David's treatment of captives, וַיָּשֶׂם בַּמְּגֵרָה . . . וּבְמַגְזְרוֹת הַבַּרְזֶל. 4037

גֵּחֲזִי v. sub גַּיְא. p. 161 1522

גִּחִי v. [גּוּחַ, גִּיחַ]. p. 161 1518

גחל (prob. = *kindle, burn*).

†**גַּחֶלֶת n.f.** [Ez 1, 13] **coal** (cf. As. *guḫlu*, a shining precious stone? COT [Gloss] Zim [BP 45])— 1513
abs. גַּחֶלֶת Is 47^{14}; sf. גַּחַלְתִּי 2 S 14^{7}; pl. גֶּחָלִים ψ 18^{9} + 6 t.; cstr. גַּחֲלֵי Lv 16^{12} + 5 t. + ψ 18^{14} (del. 𝔊 De Che); sf. גֶּחָלָיו Is 44^{19}, גֶּחָלֶיהָ Ez 24^{11};—*coal*, pl. ג׳ אֵשׁ *coals of fire* Lv 16^{12} (P), 2 S 22^{13} = ψ 18^{13} [also ψ 18^{14} cf. supr.] Ez 10^{2} (in vision); cf. 2 S 22^{9} = ψ 18^{9} Jb 41^{13}, also Pr 6^{28} Is 44^{19}; in simile (of strife) Pr 26^{21} (opp. פֶּחָם *black coal*); Ez 1^{13} גַּחֲלֵי אֵשׁ (of the living creatures);

fig. of hope in posterity 2 S 14[7], of divine judgment, ג׳ רתם *coals of broom-plant* ψ 120[4], cf. 140[11], also (negat.) Is 47[14] Ez 24[11]; of kindness to enemy Pr 25[22].

גחם (? cf. Ar. جَحَمَ *kindle*, جَحِمَ, جَحُمَ *burn*).

1514 †**גַּ֫חַם** **n.pr.m.** (*flame?*) Gn 22[24] a son of Nahor, brother of Abraham, by רְאוּמָה his concubine.

גחן (cf. Aram. גְּחַן, Nasar. ܓܚܢ (Syr. ܓܚܢ PS) *curve, bend*).

1512 †**גָּחוֹן** **n.m.** belly, of reptiles (cf. perh. As. *giḫinnu, cord* (from twisting?) Zim[BP 104])—גְּחֹנְךָ Gn 3[14] (J) of the serpent, cf. גָּחוֹן Lv 11[42] (P).

גחר (? cf. Ar. جَحَرَ *retire, retreat*, etc.)

1515 †**גַּ֫חַר** **n.pr.m.** head of a family of returned exiles Ezr 2[47] בְּנֵי־ג׳ = Ne 7[49] בְּנֵי־גָחַר.

1516 †**גַּיְא** **n.m.** [Is 40, 4] (**f.** [Zc 14, 4]) **valley**—abs. גַּיְא Nu 21[20] + 8 t. + 1 S 17[52] (cf. infr.), גַּיְא 1 Ch 4[39], גֵּיא Zc 14[4], גֶּיא Is 40[4], גֵּי Dt 34[6] + 2 t.; cstr. גֵּיא Is 22[1] + 21 t.; גֵּי Jos 15[8] + 13 t.; pl. abs. גֵּאָיוֹת Ez 31[12] 36[4.6] + 7[16] 32[5] (del. Co) + 6[3] 2 K 2[16] Qr (so Co Ez 6[3]; Kt גיאות); sf. גֵּיאוֹתֶיךָ Ez 35[8];—*valley* Jos 8[11] (E) Mi 1[6] 1 S 17[3] 2 K 2[16] (opp. הַר) Is 40[4] (opp. הַר, גִּבְעָה), Ez 6[3] 35[8] 36[4.6] (in all c. הרים, גבעות אפיקים), 31[12] (opp. הַר), cf. 7[16] (del. B Co) 32[5]; specif., valley in Moab, a station of Isr. Nu 21[20] (E); over against Beth-Peor Dt 3[29] 4[46] 34[6]; a valley near גְּדוֹר 1 Ch 4[39]; ג׳ חִזָּיוֹן Is 22[1.5] near Jerus.; ג׳ שְׁמָנִים Is 28[1.4] *valley of fatness*, fertility, the valley surrounding Samaria; שַׁעַר הַגּ׳ 2 Ch 26[9] Ne 2[13.15] 3[13]; apocalyptic valley Zc 14[4], made by cleaving Mt. of Olives, cf. ג׳ הרים v[5.5]; valley of slaughter ג׳ ההרגה, a future name of valley of Hinnom Je 7[32] 19[6] 1 S 17[52] (גַּיְא) 𝔊 rds. גַּת cf. We Dr; Je 2[23] of valley of Hinnom, v. infr.; fig. ψ 23[4] ג׳ צלמות cf. צלמות; Ez 39[11] ג׳ הָעֹבְרִים, Co הָעֲבָרִים n.pr. cf. infr.; elsewhere in combination with n.pr.:—**a.** ג׳ יִפְתַּח־אֵל Jos 19[14.27] perh. = *Jotapata* Jos[BJ iii. 7, 7]; Rabbin. נופתחא Reland[Pal 816];—*Tell Jefât* Rob[BR iii. 107]. Guérin[Gal. i. 476 f.] cf. Bd[Pal 243]. **b.** ג׳ הַצְּבֹעִים 1 S 13[18]. **c.** ג׳־הַמֶּלַח 2 K 14[7] (Kt; Qr om. art.) 1 Ch 18[12] 2 Ch 25[11] = ג׳־מֶלַח 2 S 8[13] ψ 60[2] (title); S. of Dead Sea, in or bordering on Edom; *el-Ghôr*
2798 Rob[BR ii. 109]. **d.** ג׳ הַחֲרָשִׁים 1 Ch 4[14] Ne 11[35], appar. near Lod & Ono, NW. of Jerus., not far from the sea. **e.** ג׳ צְפַתָה לְמָרֵשָׁה 2 Ch 14[9] (? rd. צָפֹנָה, 𝔊 κατὰ βορρᾶν, *to the north of M.*) prob. near the great plain of Judah, W. of Jerus., toward the sea; ג׳ הָעֹבְרִים Ez 39[11], E. of Dead Sea (Hi Sm), Co rds. ג׳ הָעֲבָרִים. **f.** name to be changed to ג׳ הֲמוֹן־גּוֹג Ez 39[11.15]. Most frequently **g.** גֵּי הִנֹּם Jos 15[8] 18[16] Ne 11[30], גֵּי בֶן־הִנֹּם Jos 15[8] 18[16] 2 K 23[10] Qr (Kt גי בני ה׳) 2 Ch 28[3] 33[6] Je 7[31.32] 19[2.6] 32[35]; valley SW. & S. of Jerus. (Rob[BR ii. 273 f.]), where incense was burned, and children were offered in sacrifice to 'Molech.' Others identify with the Tyropœon valley, cf. RS[Sem. i. 353]; vid. further תֹּפֶת הִנֹּם.

†**גֵּיחֲזִי, גֵּחֲזִי** **n.pr.m.** (*valley of vision?*) 1522
servant of Elisha, גֵּיחֲזִי 2 K 4[12.14.25.27.29.36] 5[20.21]; גֵּחֲזִי 2 K 4[31] 5[25] 8[4.5].

גיד (√ of foll.; mng. dub.; ? cf. As. *gâdu, bind, fetter*, Jäger[BAS i. 589 f.])

†**גִּיד** **n.m.** [Gn 32, 33] **sinew** (NH *id.*, Aram. 1517
גִּידָא, ܓܝܕܐ; cf. Ar. جِيدٌ *neck*)—cstr. גִּיד Gn 32[33.33] Is 48[4]; pl. גִּידִים Jb 10[11] Ez 37[6], גִּדִים Ez 37[8]; cstr. גִּידֵי Jb 40[17];—*sinew*, in general of human body, ‖ בשׂר, עור, עצמות, Jb 10[11] cf. Ez 37[6.8]; of thigh Gn 32[33] (of beast) v[33]; iron sinew, fig. of obstinacy, Is 48[4] וג׳ בַּרְזֶל עָרְפֶּךָ וּמִצְחֲךָ נְחוּשָׁה; of hippopot., ג׳ פחדו, i.e. of his loins, Jb 40[17].

†[**גּוּחַ, גִּיחַ**] **vb. burst forth** (cf. Nö 1518
[ZMG 1883, 538]; NH *id.*, Aram. *id.*, and ܓܳܚ; Eth. ገሐ: *break forth*, of light, etc.)—**Qal** *Impf.* יָגִיחַ Jb 40[23], 2 ms. וַתָּגַח Ez 32[2]; *Imv.* fs. גֹּחִי Mi 4[10]; *Inf.* sf. (בְּ)גִיחוֹ Jb 38[8]; *Pt.* sf. גֹּחִי ψ 22[10] (but cf. infr.);—**1.** intrans. *burst forth*, of dashing river (a very Jordan) Jb 40[23]; of sea fig. as babe from womb Jb 38[8], cf. **2.** trans. **a.** *draw forth* from womb (subj. י׳) ψ 22[10] (where rd. גֹּחִי pt. fr. גּוּחַ, or regard גֹּחִי as metapl., as if fr. גחה*? v. De & Che[crit. note]) cf. ψ 71[6]; also **b.** *thrust forth, bring forth*, fig. of travail, applied to Jerusalem in distress Mi 4[10] (cf. Sta[§ 599 b] Kö[i. 505]); burst forth with rivers (fig. of Pharaoh under image of תַּנִּים) Ez 32[2], but for בנהרותיך (*rivers*) rd. prob. בְּנַחֲרוֹתֶיךָ Jb 41[12] (*nostrils*), i.e. snort with thy nostrils, so Ew Co; on fig. then cf. Jb 41[11-13].

†**גִּ֫יחַ** **n.pr.loc.** (fr. *a spring?*) near Gibeon 1520
in Benjamin 2 S 2[24].

†**גִּיחוֹן** **n.pr.fl.** (*a bursting forth*)—**1.** one of 1521
the rivers of Eden Gn 2[13] (on theories of identity v. Comm.; also Smith[Dict. Bible] Schaff-Herzog [Art. Eden] Spurrell[Text of Gen. ad loc.] Ri[HWB]). **2.** spring of water near Jerusalem: גִּחוֹן 1 K 1[33.38.45], מֵימֵי גִּיחוֹן 2 Ch 32[30], לְגִיחוֹן בַּנַּחַל 2 Ch 33[14];—there are two main theories as to locality: **a.** W. of Jerusalem, connected with *Birket Mamilla*, and aqueduct into city Rob[BR i. 239, 345 ff.]

Survey[Jerusalem] al.; **b.** E. of Jerusalem = Fountain of the Virgin, Furrer[Schenkel BL ii. 463] Bd[Pal 101], or Siloah water-system Guthe[ZPV, v., 1882, 359 ff.]

1522 גֵּיחֲזִי v. sub גַּיְא. p. 161

1523 † [גִּיל] **vb. rejoice** (Nö[ZMG 1883, 537]; cf. Ar. جَالَ *go round* or *about, be excited* to levity, etc.)—**Qal** *Pf.* גַּלְתִּי Is 65[19]; *Impf.* יָגִיל, תָּגִיל ψ 21[2] + 4 t. (ψ 21[2] Kt יגיל, Qr יָגֶל with retracted tone); יָגֵל, תָּגֵל ψ 13[6] + 11 t., וַיָּגֶל ψ 16[9], אָגִילָה, נָגִילָה ψ 9[15] + 5 t., יָגִילוּ ψ 13[5] + 5 t., יְגִילוּן ψ 89[17], תָּגֵלְנָה ψ 48[12] + 2 t.; יָגוֹל Pr 23[24]; *Imv.* גִּילוּ ψ 2[11] + 4 t., גִּילִי Is 49[13] + 2 t.;—**1.** *rejoice*, **a.** abs. ψ 13[5] 51[10] Zc 9[9]; ‖ שמח ψ 14[7] 16[9] 32[11] 48[12] 53[7] 96[11] 97[1.8] Pr 23[24.25] 1 Ch 16[31] Hb 1[15]; ‖ שׂוּשׂ, שִׂישׂ Is 35[1] 65[18]. **b.** c. בְּ ψ 149[2] Pr 2[14] 24[17] Is 9[2]; בירושלם Is 65[19] 66[10]; בישועתך ψ 9[15] 13[6] 21[2]; ביהוה ψ 35[9] Is 41[16] Zc 10[7]; באלהים Is 61[10] Hb 3[18]; בשם י׳ ψ 89[17]; בקדוש ישראל Is 29[19]; גיל ושמח ב׳ ψ 31[8] 118[24] Ct 1[4] Is 25[9] Jo 2[23]; גילי ושמחי כי Jo 2[21]. **c.** with על Zp 3[17]. Besides persons the subj. is לֵב ψ 13[6] Pr 24[17] Zc 10[7]; נפשׁ ψ 35[9] Is 61[10], כבוד (=נפשׁ) ψ 16[9], ארץ 1 Ch 16[31] ψ 96[11] 97[1] Is 49[13], ערבה Is 35[1.2]. **2.** *tremble* (cf. Ar. وَجِلَ) ψ 2[11] ‖ עבד (Thes Ew Hi Che, but 𝔊 Hu De Pe AV RV *rejoice*), Ho 10[5] ‖ אבל (Thes and most mod., but AV RV that *rejoiced* over it), possibly error for חיל Ew Gr Che.

1524 †I. גִּיל **n.[m.] rejoicing**—Jb 3[22] + 6 t., גּוֹל Pr 23[24]; sf. גִּילִי ψ 43[4];—*rejoicing* ψ 65[13] Pr 23[24]; ‖ שמחה ψ 45[16] Is 16[10] Je 48[33] Jo 1[16], שִׂמְחַת גִּילִי ψ 43[4], שמח אל גיל *glad unto rejoicing* Ho 9[1] Jb 3[22].

1524 †II. [גִּיל] **n.[m.] circle, age,** מן הילדים אשׁר כְּגִילְכֶם *of the youths which are of your age* Dn 1[10] (cf. Ar. جِيلٌ, Sam. גיל = Heb. דור = γενεά, Talm. בן גילו *one born at the same time, a contemporary*).

1525 †גִּילָה **n.f. rejoicing** Is 65[18], גִּילַת וְרַנֵּן Is 35[2] (nom. verbal. for Inf. abs. cf. De Di; cstr. before וְ Ges[§ 130. 2]; but rd. prob. גִּלָה); הַגִּילָה read Is 9[2] for הַגּוֹי לֹא by Krochm Che RS Di.

1542 †גִּלֹה **n.pr.loc.** city in mountains of Judah Jos 15[51] 2 S 15[12]; (on √ cf. Dr 2 S 15[12].)

1526 †גִּילֹנִי **adj.gent.** 2 S 15[12], 23[34] = 1 Ch 11[36], where also rd. הַגּ׳ (for MT הַפְּלֹנִי).

1527 גִּינַת v. sub גנן. p. 171

גיר (*boil, boil up?* cf. Aram. גִּיר *wave*, NH *id. foam*; Ar. جَيَّارٌ *quicklime*, also *heat in chest from rage or hunger* (Lane); *admodum aestuans* acc. to Fl NHWB[i. 433 b]; but cf. infr.)

†גִּר **n.[m.] chalk, lime** (perh. Aram. loan-word cf. Frä[9]; Aram. (also B Aram.) גִּיר, ܓܝܪܐ; Ar. جِيرٌ is loan-wd. Frä[l. c.])—מִזְבֵּחַ כְּאַבְנֵי גִר Is 27[9]. 1615

†[גִּיר] **n.m.** 2 Ch 2[16] v. גֵּר sub I. גור. p. 158 1616

†גישׁ Jb 7[5] Kt, v. גּוּשׁ. p. 159 1487

†גֵּישָׁן **n.pr.m.** a descendant of Judah through Caleb 1 Ch 2[47]. 1529

גַּל, גֵּל, גֹּל v. sub גלל. p. 164 1530

גלב (=*shear, shave*, As. [*galâbu*] Hpt[SFG]; Aram. גְּלַב *id.*, גַּלָּב *razor*; cf. ܡܓܠܒܐ 2 S 20[8] v. PS).

†[גַּלָּב] **n.[m.] barber** (Ph. גלב CIS[i, 257 ff.])—תַּעַר הַגַּלָּבִים Ez 5[1]. 1532

†גִּלְבֹּעַ **n.pr.loc. Gilboa'** (derivation unknown), mountain-ridge at S.E. end of plain of Jezreel, where Saul & Jonathan were killed; usually c. art. הַר הַגּ׳ 1 S 31[1.8] 2 S 1[6]; הָרֵי בַגִּלְבֹּעַ 2 S 1[21] (David's lament); בַּגּ׳ alone 1 S 28[4] 2 S 21[12]; without art. הַר גִּלְבֹּעַ 1 Ch 10[1.8] (‖ 1 S 31[1.8] supr.);—mod. *Jebel Fukû'a* Bd[Pal 244]. '1533

גַּלְגַּל, גִּלְגָּל, גֻּלְגֹּלֶת v. sub גלל. p. 165f 1534, 1536, 1538

גלד (√ of foll. mng. dub. perh. cf. Eth. ገለደ: *obducere, inducere*; Ar. جَلَدَ *scourge*).

†[גֶּלֶד] **n.m. skin** (Ar. جِلْدٌ, Aram. גִּלְדָּא, ܓܠܕܐ) of man Jb 16[15] שַׂק תָּפַרְתִּי עֲלֵי גִלְדִּי. 1539

גָּלָה[189] **vb. uncover, remove** (NH *id.*, cf. Ar. جَلَا *be or become clear, uncovered; display, reveal, declare; go forth, emigrate*; cf. Eth. ገለወ: *obducere, velare*, & II. ገለየ: in deriv. (rare) Di[1141]; Aram. גְּלָא, ܓܠܐ *reveal*)—**Qal**[51] *Pf.* ג׳ etc. 1 S 4[21] + (18 t. in all); *Impf.* יִגְלֶה 1 S 20[2] + 5 t., וַיִּגֶל 2 K 17[23] + 3 t., also juss. יִגֶל Jb 20[28] 36[15]; 3 mpl. יִגְלוּ Am 6[7]; *Imv.* ms. גְּלֵה Ez 12[3]; *Inf. abs.* גָּלֹה Am 5[5] + 2 t., *cstr.* גְּלוֹת Ju 18[30] Je 1[3]; *Pt.* גּוֹלֶה 2 K 24[14], גֹּלֶה 1 S 22[8] + 3 t., f. גּוֹלָה Is 49[21]; *pass.* גָּלוּי Est 3[14] + 2 t., cstr. גְּלוּי Nu 24[4.16];—**1.** גָּלָה אֹזֶן *uncover the ear* of one, i.e. *reveal* to him 1 S 9[15] 20[2.12.13] 22[8.8.17] 2 S 7[27] 1 Ch 17[25] Ru 4[4] Jb 33[16] 36[10.15]; גְּלוּי עינים *uncovered of eyes*, having the eyes open Nu 24[4.16]; גָּלָה סוד *reveal a secret* Am 3[7] Pr 20[19]; הגלוי *the revealed* opp. הֶחָתוּם Je 32[11]; גָּלוּי לְ *disclosed, published* Est 3[14] 8[13]. **2.** intr. *remove, depart*, גלה משׂושׂ 1540

הארץ *the mirth of the land is departed* Is 24^{11}; יגל
יבול ביתו *the increase of his house shall depart*
Jb 20^{28}; גלה חציר Pr 27^{25}. **3.** *go into exile*
Ju 18^{30} 2 K 17^{23} 25^{21} Is 5^{13} Je 1^{3} 52^{27} Ez 12^{3}
39^{23} Am 1^{5} 5^{5} 6^{7} 7$^{11.17}$ Mi 1^{16} La 1^{3}; גלה כבוד 1 S
4$^{21.22}$ Ho 10^{5}; pt. גֹּלָה *an exile* 2 S 15^{19} 2 K 24^{14}
Is 49^{21} Am 6^{7}. **Niph.** *Pf.* נִגְלָה 1 S 3^{21} + 9 t.,
נִגְלְתָה Is 53^{1}, נִגְלֵיתִי 1 S 2^{27}, נִגְלוּ Gn 35^{7} + 2 t.,
נִגְלֵינוּ 1 S 14^{8}; *Impf.* יִגָּלֶה, תִּגָּלֶה 1 S 3^{7} + 4 t.,
תִּגָּל Is 47^{3}, יִגָּלוּ 2 S 22^{16} + 2 t.; *Imv.* הִגָּלוּ Is 49^{9};
Inf. abs. נִגְלֹה 1 S 2^{27}; cstr. נִגְלוֹת 2 S 6^{20}, הִגָּלוֹת
2 S 6^{20} + 2 t.; *Pt.* pl. נִגְלֹת Dt 29^{28};—**1.** refl. **a.**
uncover oneself (one's nakedness) 2 S 6^{20}. **b.** *discover* or *shew oneself* Is 49^{9}, אֶל 1 S 14$^{8.11}$. **c.**
reveal himself (of God), אֶל Gn 35^{7} (E) 1 S 2^{27} 3^{21},
באזני Is 22^{14}. **2.** pass. **a.** *be uncovered* (one's nakedness), ערוה Ex 20^{26} (E) Is 47^{3} Ez 16^{36} 23^{29},
שולים Je 13^{22}. **b.** *be disclosed, discovered,* foundations 2 S 22^{16} (=ψ 18^{16}) Ez 13^{14}; gates of death
Jb 38^{17}, עון Ho 7^{1}, פשע Ez 21^{29}, רעה Pr 26^{26}
Ez 16^{57}. **c.** *be revealed* כבוד י׳ Is 40^{5}, זרוע י׳ Is 53^{1},
דבר י׳ 1 S 3^{7}, צדקה Is 56^{1}; with לְ Is 23^{1} Dn 10^{1},
הַנִּגְלֹת *the things revealed* Dt 29^{28}. **3.** *be removed,*
דּוֹרִי נִסַּע וְנִגְלָה מִנִּי *my habitation is plucked up and removed from me* Is 38^{12}. **Pi.**$_{56}$ *Pf.*
גִּלָּה Lv 20^{11}, גִּלִּית Is 57^{8}, גִּלֵּיתִי Je 33^{6}; *Impf.*
יְגַלֶּה Dt 23^{1}, תְּגַל Pr 25^{9}; *Imv.* גַּל ψ 119^{18}, גַּלִּי Is
47^{2}; *Inf.* גַּלּוֹת Lv 18^{6}; *Pt.* מְגַלֶּה Jb 12^{22};—**1.**
uncover, **a.** *nakedness* (oft = *contract marriage,*
RSLag$^{GN 1882, 408; JPh ix. 94}$) Lv 18$^{6-19}$ 20$^{11-21}$ (H 23 t.)
Ez 22^{10}; cf. כנף אביו Dt 23^{1} 27^{20}; of *exposure,*
as a reproach, Ez 16^{37} 23^{10}, cf. נבלת Ho 2^{12},
שולים Na 3^{5}; *immodesty* Ez 23^{18}, מקור דמיה
Lv 20^{18} (H), תזנותיה Ez 23^{18}; ג׳ alone Is 57^{8}
(all subj. fem.) **b.** in gen.: feet Ru 3$^{4.7}$, leg
Is 47^{2}, vail v^{2} (i.e. *remove* it) cf. 22^{8}, פני
לבושו Jb 41^{5}, eyes Nu 22^{31} (E) ψ 119^{18} (open
them so as to see). **2.** *disclose, discover, lay bare,* secret places Je 49^{10}, deep places Jb 12^{22},
foundations Mi 1^{6}, blood Is 26^{21}, iniquity Jb
20^{27}, secret Pr 11^{13} 25^{9}, a wanderer (betray)
Is 16^{3}. **3.** *make known, shew, reveal,* רִיב אֶל
make known a cause unto Je 11^{20} 20^{12}; with לְ
Jb 33^{6}; גִּלָּה צִדְקָתוֹ לעיני *shew his righteousness in the eyes of* ψ 98^{2}; with עַל: על עון, על חטאת
make known concerning, iniquity, sin La 2^{14}
4^{22}. **Pu.** *Pf.* גֻּלְּתָה *be uncovered* Na 2^{8}; *Pt.*
תוכחת מְגֻלָּה *open rebuke* Pr 27^{5}. **Hiph.**$_{39}$
Pf. הֶגְלָה 2 K 17^{11} +, הִגְלָה 2 K 24^{14}, הֶגְלָם 1 Ch
8^{7}, הִגְלָם Je 20^{4}; *Impf.* וַיֶּגֶל 2 K 17^{6} + 3 t.;
sf. וַיַּגְלֶהָ 2 K 16^{9}, וַיַּגְלֵם 2 K 15^{29}, 1 Ch 5^{26}, יַגְלוּם
1 Ch 8^{6}: *Inf.* הַגְלוֹת 1 Ch 5^{41} + 5 t., בַּגְלוֹתוֹ Je
27^{20};—*carry away into exile, take into exile* 2 K
15^{29} 16^{9} 17$^{6.11.26.27.28.33}$ 18^{11} 24$^{14.15}$ 25^{11} 1 Ch 5$^{6.26.41}$
8$^{6.7}$ 2 Ch 36^{20} Ezr 2^{1} Ne 7^{6} Est 2^{6} Je 20^{4} 22^{12} 24^{1}
27^{20} 29$^{1.4.7.14}$ 39^{9} 43^{3} 52$^{15.28.29.30}$ La 4^{22} Ez 39^{28}
Am 1^{6} 5^{27}. **Hoph.** *Pf.* הָגְלָה Est 2^{6}; f. הָגְלְתָה
Est 2^{6}, הָגְלוּ 1 Ch 9^{1} Je 40^{7}, הָגְלָת Je 13$^{19.19}$ (Ges
§ 75, R. 1); *Pt.* pass. מֻגְלִים Je 40^{1} *carried into exile.* **Hithp. 1.** *Impf.* וַיִּתְגַּל *was uncovered*
(naked) Gn 9^{21}. **2.** *Inf.* בְּהִתְגַּלּוֹת לִבּוֹ *that his heart may reveal itself* Pr 18^{2}.

† גּוֹלָה$_{42}$ **n.f. exiles, exile**—(cf. Ar. جَالٍ 1473
one emigrating, جَالِيَةٌ *a company of exiles*)—
Je 28^{6} + 38 t., הַגֹּלָה Is 49^{21} 1 Ch 5^{22} Est 2^{6} Na 3^{10};
—**1.** coll. *exiles,* Est 2^{6} Je 29^{1} Ez 1^{1} 3$^{11.15}$ 11$^{24.25}$
Na 3^{10}; כל־הגולה Je 28^{6} 29$^{4.20.31}$, קהל הגולה Ezr 10^{8}.
2. abstract, *exile,* Ezr 6^{21} 9^{4} 10^{6} Zc 6^{10}; הלך בגולה
go into exile Je 48^{11} 49^{3} Ez 12^{11} 25^{3} Am 1^{15};
יצא בג׳ Je 29^{16} 48^{7} Zc 14^{2}; הוליך גולה *carry into exile* 2 K 24^{15}, הביא ג׳ 2 K 24^{16}, הוציא ג׳ Ez
12^{4}, העלה ג׳ Ezr 1^{11}; כלי גולה *equipment for exile* Je 46^{19} Ez 12$^{3.4.7}$; עד הגלה *until the exile*
1 Ch 5^{22}; בני הגולה *exiles* Ezr 4^{1} 6$^{19.20}$ 8^{35} 10$^{7.16}$;
שבי הגולה *captivity of the exile* Ezr 2^{1} Ne 7^{6}.

† גָּלוּת **n.f. exile**—Is 20^{4} + 9 t.; גָּלֻת Ob$^{20.20}$; 1546
sf. גָּלוּתִי Is 45^{13}, גָּלוּתֵנוּ Ez 33^{21} 40^{1} (Qameṣ
unchangeable);—**1.** abs. *exile,* 2 K 25^{27} Je 52^{31}
Ez 1^{2} 33^{21} 40^{1} Am 1$^{6.9}$ Ob$^{20.20}$. **2.** coll. *exiles,*
גלות כוש Is 20^{4}, גלות יהודה Je 24^{5} 28^{4} 29^{22} 40^{1},
גלותי ישלח *he shall let my exiles* (*Yahweh's*) *go free* Is 45^{13}; vid. Lag$^{Arm. Stud. § 445}$.

† גִּלָּיוֹן **n.m. table, tablet** (Talm. גִּלָּיוֹן, the 1549
empty margin of page or roll, vid. Lag$^{GN 1881, 403, cf. BN 199}$)—קַח־לְךָ גִּלָּיוֹן גָּדוֹל וּכְתֹב עָלָיו *take thee a great tablet and write upon it* Is 8^{1}; pl. הַגִּלְיֹנִים
tablets of polished metal, mirrors Is 3^{23} 𝔗 𝔙 Ges
Che Di De; but *transparent garments, gauzes,*
𝔊 Ew (cf. Ar. جِلْوَةٌ *fine garment*).

† גָּלְיַת **n.pr.m.** (*conspicuous?* On ending ת 1555
cf. Dr 1 S 17^{4} & Nö in Eut$^{Nab 73}$) (גָּלְיָת 1 Ch 20^{5})
Philistine giant slain by David 1 S 17$^{4.23}$ 21^{10}
22^{10}, but acc. to 2 S 21^{19} slain by Elhanan of
Bethlehem (בֵּית הַלַּחְמִי; acc. to 1 Ch 20^{5} Elhanan slew לַחְמִי brother of Goliath).

† יָגְלִי **n.pr.m.** (*led into exile?*) chief of tribe 3020
of Dan Nu 34^{22}.

גִּלֹה **n.pr.loc.** v. sub גיל. p. 162 1542

גֻּלָּה v. sub גלל. p. 165 1543

1548 †[גָּלַח] **vb. be bald** (Ar. جَلَحَ); **Pi. shave, shave off** (so NH, Aram.)—*Pf.* וְגִלַּח consec. Lv 14^{3} + 2 t.; sf. וְגִלְּחוֹ consec. 2 S 14^{26}; 3 fs. וְגִלְּחָה consec. Dt 21^{12}; *Impf.* יְגַלַּח Lv 14^{9} Is 7^{20}, יְגַלֵּחַ Lv 13^{33} + 2 t., וַיְגַלַּח Gn 41^{14} 2 S 10^{4}; sf. (3 ms.) וַיְגַלְּחֵם, יְגַלְּחֶנּוּ 1 Ch 19^{4}; 3 fs. וַתְּגַלַּח Ju 16^{19}; 3 mpl. יְגַלְּחוּ Lv 21^{5} Ez 44^{20}; *Inf.* sf. of subj. גַּלְּחוֹ 2 S 14^{26};—**1.** *shave*, obj. the head, ראשׁ Nu $6^{9.9.18}$ (P) Dt 21^{12} (hair as containing impurity, cf. RS Sem i. 407), 2 S $14^{26.26\ cf.\ 26}$ Ez 44^{20}; Lv 13^{33} (P), obj. הַנֶּתֶק; obj. persons 1 Ch 19^{4}. **2.** *shave off*, the hair שֵׂעָר Lv $14^{8.9.9}$ (P) cf. Ju 16^{19}; the beard זָקָן Lv 21^{5} (H) 2 S 10^{4}. **3.** fig. of devastation by Assyrians Is 7^{20} (obj. שַׂעַר הָרַגְלָיִם, הָרֹאשׁ and הַזָּקָן). **4.** intrans. *he shaved* (himself) Gn 41^{14} (E). **Pu.** *Pf.* גֻּלָּח Ju 16^{22}, גֻּלַּחְתִּי Ju 16^{17}; *Pt.* cstr. מְגֻלְּחֵי Je 41^{5};—*be shaven*, subj. pers. (of Samson) Ju $16^{17.22}$; מְגֻלְּחֵי זָקָן Je 41^{5}. **Hithp.** *Pf.* וְהִתְגַּלָּח consec. Lv 13^{33}; *Inf.* sf. הִתְגַּלְּחוֹ Nu 6^{19};—*shave oneself* Lv 13^{33}; c. acc. אֶת־נִזְרוֹ Nu 6^{19} (both P).

I. גלל (جَلَّ *be great in rank* or *dignity* (often of God)).

1558 †I. [גָּלָל] **n.[m.] account**, only in cstr. st. with בְּ, בִּגְלַל *on account of, for the sake of* (جَلَلٌ *a great and momentous matter;* مِنْ جَلَلِكَ on thy *account;* cf. מִן בִּגְלַל דְּ *because that* in Palestinian 𝔗, as ψ 4^{9}, and ܒܓܠܠ in Jerus. Syriac PS^{731}) Gn 39^{5} ׳י blessed the house of the Egyptian בִּגְלַל יוֹסֵף *on account of* Joseph, Dt 15^{10} 18^{12} 1 K 14^{16} Je 11^{17} 15^{4}; with sf. בִּגְלָלֵךְ Gn 30^{27}; בִּגְלָלֵךְ 12^{13}; בִּגְלַלְכֶם Dt 1^{37} Mi 3^{12}.

1556 †II. [גָּלַל] **vb. roll, roll away** (NH *id.*, & deriv.; Aram. Pa. גַּלֵּל, Palp. גַּלְגֵּיל *roll*, Ithpalp. reflex., & deriv.; cf. ܐܬܓܠ Ethp., Ethpalp. (v. PS), ܓܠܓܠܐ *rota*, ܓܠܠܐ *fluctus*, etc.)—**Qal** *Pf.* 1 s. גַּלּוֹתִי Jos 5^{9}, וְגָלֲלוּ consec. Gn $29^{3.8}$; *Imv.* גֹּל ψ 22^{9} (MT De; but 𝔊 Bi Che rd. גַּל 3 ms. pf., so AV RVm) Pr 16^{3}, גּוֹל ψ 37^{5}, גַּל 119^{22} (but rd. גֹּל Ew Hi Ri Gr Che), גֹּלּוּ Jos 10^{18} 1 S 14^{33}; *Pt.* גֹּלֵל Pr 26^{27};—*roll* a stone Pr 26^{27}; *roll away* stone from upon (מֵעַל) the mouth of a well Gn $29^{3.8}$; *roll* stones unto (אֶל) the mouth of a cave Jos 10^{18}; stone unto (אֶל) Saul, at which to slay beasts 1 S 14^{33}; fig. reproach from upon (מֵעַל) the people Jos 5^{9} (subj. ׳י), cf. ψ 119^{22} (sq. מֵעַל); but also גּוֹל עַל־י׳ דַּרְכֶּךָ ψ 37^{5}, cf. 22^{9} Pr 16^{3} (both sq. אֶל־). **Niph.** *Pf.* וְנָגֹלּוּ consec. Is 34^{4}; *Impf.* וְיִגַּל (juss.) Am 5^{24};—*roll, roll up* or *along* (intrans.), וְנָגֹלּוּ כַסֵּפֶר הַשָּׁמַיִם Is 34^{4} *and the heavens shall roll up like a book;* יִגַּל כַּמַּיִם מִשְׁפָּט Am 5^{24} *let judgment roll along* (flow down) *as the waters.* **Pilp.** *Pf.* וְגִלְגַּלְתִּיךָ consec. Je 51^{25} *and I will roll thee down from* (מִן) the rocks (subj. ׳י; obj. Babylon under fig. of mt.) **Poʿal** *Pt.* שִׂמְלָה מְגוֹלָלָה בְדָמִים Is 9^{4} *garment rolled* (dabbled, rolled over and over) *in blood.* **Hithpo.** *Inf.* לְהִתְגֹּלֵל Gn 43^{8}; *Pt.* מִתְגֹּלֵל 2 S 20^{12}; *roll oneself over and over,* וַעֲמָשָׂא מִתְג׳ בַּדָּם 2 S 20^{12} *now Amasa was wallowing in his blood;* fig. Gn 43^{18} לְהִתְג׳ עָלֵינוּ *to roll himself upon us,* i.e. assail us with overwhelming force (‖ וּלְהִתְנַפֵּל עָלֵינוּ). **Hithpalp.** *Pf.* הִתְגַּלְגָּלוּ Jb 30^{14} (abs.; ‖ כְּפֶרֶץ רָחָב יֶאֱתָיוּ) cf. Hithpo. Gn 43^{8}. **Hiph.** *Impf.* וַיָּגֶל Gn 29^{10};—*roll away* stone from upon (מֵעַל) mouth of well; as **Qal** (which it really is, Impf. in *i*, acc. to Ba ZMG 1888, 178).

†גַּל **n.m.** Gn 31, 48 **heap, wave, billow** (as 1530
rolled together, rolling, rolling up), also **spring**, MT Ct 4^{12} cf. **3** infr.—abs. גַּל Jb 8^{17} + 5 t. (incl. הַגַּל Gn 31^{48} +); גָּל Gn 31^{46}; הַגָּל Gn 31^{46}; לְגָל Is 25^{2}; cstr. גַּל־ Jos 7^{26} + 2 t. + Gn $31^{47.48}$ q.v. infr.; pl. גַּלִּים 2 K 19^{25} + 6 t.; cstr. גַּלֵּי־ Is 48^{18}; sf. גַּלָּיו ψ 89^{10} + 6 t.; גַּלֵּיהֶם ψ 65^{8} + 2 t.;—**1.** *heap* of stones, **a.** ג׳ אבנים raised (הקים) over dead body Jos 7^{26} 8^{29}; cf. 2 S 18^{17} (c. הִצִּיב). **b.** גַּל alone Jb 8^{17} (roots wrapped about it). **c.** *heap* or *pile* made (עשׂה) for use in ratifying compact of Jacob with Laban Gn $31^{46.46.48.51.52.52.52}$ cf. also גַּלְעֵד **n.pr.** **d.** *heap* of ruins Is 25^{2}; elsewhere pl. Ho 12^{12} 2 K 19^{25} = Is 37^{26} Jb 15^{28} Jer. 9^{10} 51^{37}. **2.** *waves* (*rollers*) poet., only pl., waves of sea Je 5^{22} 31^{35} Is 51^{15} Jb 38^{11} ψ 65^{8} 89^{10} $107^{25.29}$; cf. also in simile Ez 26^{3} Is 48^{18} (גַּלֵּי־הַיָּם); fig. of chastisements from ׳י ψ 42^{8} (‖ מִשְׁבָּרִים) Jon 2^{3} (‖ id.); of army of Babylon's conqueror Je $51^{42.55}$; cf. Zc 10^{11} (VB; but Bev JPh xviii. 88 prop. גְּבָלִים cf. Ez 27^{9}). **3.** *spring*, Ct 4^{12} גַּן נָעוּל אֲחֹתִי כַלָּה גַּל נָעוּל מַעְיָן חָתוּם *a garden barred (is) my sister, bride, a spring barred, a fountain sealed;* but גַּן for גַּל 𝔊 𝔖 𝔙.

†גַּלִּים **n.pr.loc.** (*heaps*);—place N. of 1554
Jerus. 1 S 25^{44}; personified as בַּת־ג׳ Is 10^{30}.

1567 †גַּלְעֵד **n.pr.loc.** (*witness-pile*) name of pile of stones erected by Jacob and his company (Kit$^{Gesch. 129}$; by Laban We Di) Gn $31^{47.48}$ (v. גַּל **1 c**) appar. intended to explain גִּלְעָד q.v.; Di conj. also (as name of altar) Jos 22^{34} (cf. 𝔖).

1561 †[גֵּל] **n.[m.] dung** (*ball* of dung, Ar. جِلَّةٌ etc., dung of camels etc., cf. Aram. גֶּלָּא; on form v. Ew$^{§255\,b}$ 'Ol$^{§150.163}$)—sf. גֶּלְלוֹ Jb 20^{7}, pl. cstr. גֶּלְלֵי (צֵאת) הָאָדָם Ez $4^{12.15}$;—human dung used as fuel Ez $4^{12.15}$ ג׳ (צֵאת) הָאָדָם; perh. also Jb 20^{7}, but cf. Di, who thinks no ref. to fuel, & De who thinks of cattle-dung; (v. on Ar. word Wetzst in De).—See also II. גָּלָל.

1531 גֵּל, גֻּלָּה v. גֻּלָּה. below

1543 †גֻּלָּה **n.f. basin, bowl**—ג׳ Zc 4^{3} + v^{2} cf. infr.; cstr. גֻּלַּת Ec 12^{6}; pl. abs. גֻּלֹּת Jos $15^{19.19}$ + 2 t.; הַגֻּ׳ (-וֹת) 2 Ch 4^{12}; cstr. גֻּלֹּת (-וֹת) 1 K 7^{41} (הַגֻּ׳ Th, so ‖ 2 Ch 4^{12} cf. Be), v^{41} + 3 t.;—**1.** *basin* (*pool, well?*) גֻּ׳ מַיִם Jos 15^{19} = Ju 1^{15}; om. מ׳ Jos $15^{19.19}$ = Ju $1^{15.15}$ (prob. old **n.pr.loc.**, cf. Di). **2.** *bowl*, **a.** of lamp, i.e. oil-receptacle Zc 4^{3},
1531 also v^{2}, where MT גֻּלָּהּ as if fr. [גֹּל]; rd. גֻּלָּה Brd Ges$^{§91.1, R. 2.}$; (> Hi-St Bö$^{§734\,b}$ De on ψ 27^{5} Sta$^{§347\,c}$, who think גֻּלָּתָהּ = גֻּלָּהּ);—so also Ec 12^{6} גֻּלַּת הַזָּהָב. **b.** of bowl- or globe-shaped portion of capitals of the two pillars in temple 1 K $7^{41.41.42}$ = 2 Ch $4^{12.12.13}$.

1557 †II. גָּלָל **n.[m.] dung** (Ar. جَلَّةٌ), הַגָּ׳ 1 K 14^{10}.—See also [גֵּל]. above

1559 †III. גָּלָל **n.pr.m.** of two Levites;—**1.** 1 Ch 9^{15}. **2.** 1 Ch 9^{16} Ne 11^{17}.

1562 †גִּלֲלַי **n.pr.m.** a Levitical musician Ne 12^{36}.

1550 †I. [גָּלִיל] **adj. turning, folding** (= revolving), pl. גְּלִילִים of leaves of doors 1 K $6^{34.34}$.

1551 †II. גָּלִיל **n.m. cylinder, rod, circuit, district**;—**1.** *cylinder, rod*, only pl. cstr. גְּלִילֵי כֶסֶף Est 1^{6} of support of rich hangings (‖ עַמּוּדֵי שֵׁשׁ); & גְּלִילֵי זָהָב מְמֻלָּאִים בַּתַּרְשִׁישׁ Ct 5^{14}, sim. of (? fingers of) hands: *cylinders of gold set with topaz.* **2.** *circuit, district*, on northern border of Israel, in Naphtali (v. infr.), population largely heathen (NH *id.* Aram. גְּלִילָא, ܓܠܝܠܐ)—גְּלִיל הַגּוֹיִם Is 8^{23}; elsewhere = **n.pr.loc.** always c. art. Jos 20^{7} 21^{32} 1 Ch 6^{61} all קֶדֶשׁ בַּגּ׳; אֶרֶץ הַגּ׳ 1 K 9^{11}, so also 𝔊 Jos 12^{23} (cf. Di) for גִּלְגָּל q. v.—See also גְּלִילָה *ad fin.*

1552 †גְּלִילָה **n.f. circuit, boundary, territory**—ג׳ Ez 47^{8} 2 K 15^{29}; pl. cstr. גְּלִילוֹת Jos 13^{2} $22^{10.11}$ Jo 4^{4};—belonging to a people כָּל־גְּלִילוֹת הַפְּלִשְׁתִּים Jos 13^{2} cf. Jo 4^{4} (כֹּל ג׳ פְּלָשֶׁת); so ג׳ הַיַּרְדֵּן Jos $22^{10.11}$ acc. to some, but v. foll.; abs. Ez 47^{8} הַגּ׳ הַקַּדְמוֹנָה; as **n.pr.loc.** 2 K 15^{29} *Galilee*, 𝔊 Γαλιλαια (‖ כֹּל אֶרֶץ נַפְתָּלִי) cf. II. גָּלִיל.

†גְּלִילוֹת **n.pr.loc.** (strictly pl. of foreg.; 1553
prob. = *circles* of stones, 𝔙 *tumuli*, cf. Di) **1.** Jos 18^{17} (cf. הַגִּלְגָּל 15^{7}), place on border between Benj. & Judah. **2.** locality described as follows: **a.** אֶל־ג׳ הַיַּרְדֵּן אֲשֶׁר בְּאֶרֶץ כְּנָעַן Jos 22^{10} *unto Geliloth* (= *the circles*) *of Jordan which is in the land of Canaan*; (𝔊 Γαλγαλα, 𝔊L Γαλιλωθ). **b.** אֶל־מוּל אֶרֶץ כְּנַעַן אֶל־גְּלִילוֹת הַיַּרְדֵּן אֶל־עֵבֶר בְּנֵי יִשְׂרָאֵל v^{11} *in front of the land of Canaan, in Geliloth of Jordan, beyond the sons of Israel* (𝔊 Γαλααδ, 𝔊L om.) v. Di; yet cf. Dr$^{Intr. 106\,n.}$ Others render ג׳ here *circuit of Jordan* = כִּכַּר הַיַּרְדֵּן; *districts* VB, cf. גְּלִילָה.

†[גִּלּוּל] **n.m.** $^{Je\ 50,27}$ only pl. **idols** (= *logs,* 1544
blocks, shapeless things Ges Baud$^{Rel\ i.\ 95}$; Ew *doll-images* > *dungy things* Sm Ez 6^{4} SS after Rabb.)—גִּלּוּלִים Ez 22^{3} + 3 t. + Ez 30^{13} (del B Co); גִּלֻּלִים 1 K 15^{12} + 2 t.; cstr. גִּלּוּלֵי Ez 8^{10} + 6 t.; גִּלּוּלַיִךְ Ez 22^{4}; גִּלּוּלָיו 2 K 21^{11} + 4 t.; גִּלּוּלֶיהָ Je 50^{2}; -יכֶם Lv 26^{30} + 7 t.; -יכֶן Ez 23^{49}; -יהֶם Ez 6^{9} + 14 t. + Ez 6^{5} (del BA al Co); -יהֶן Ez 23^{37};—*idols* (39 t. Ez);—1 K 15^{12} 2 K 17^{12} 21^{21} Ez 6^{5} (del Co) v^{9} $6^{13.13}$ $14^{4.5}$ $18^{6.15}$ $20^{16.24.39}$ $23^{37.39.49}$ 33^{25} $44^{10.12}$; ‖ שִׁקּוּצִים Dt 29^{16} 2 K 23^{24} (‖ also תְּרָפִים), Ez $20^{7.18}$ (both c. vb. טמא) v^{8} 37^{23}, cf. also 8^{10} (שֶׁקֶץ, but שִׁקּוּצִים appar. 𝔊𝔖𝔗 & so Co); ‖ תּוֹעֵבָה Ez 14^{6} 2 K 21^{11}, cf. Ez 18^{12} 16^{36} (גִּלּוּלֵי ‖ תּוֹעֲבוֹתַיִךְ), & 1 K 21^{26} (where vb. תָּעַב); ‖ טֻמְאוֹת Ez 36^{25}; ‖ מִכְשׁוֹל עֲוֹנוֹ Ez $14^{3.4.7}$; ‖ עֲצַבִּים Je 50^{2}; ‖ אֱלִילִים Ez 30^{13} (Co אילים; cf. also supr.); ‖ חַמָּן Ez $6^{4.6}$ Lv 26^{30} (cf. infr.); ‖ תְּרָפִים 2 K 23^{24} (supr.); in phr. טִמֵּא בְּגִלּ׳ etc. Ez $20^{7.18.31}$ $22^{3.4}$ $23^{7.30}$ 36^{18} (del Co); תִּתְחַלְּלוּ בְּגִלּ׳ Ez 20^{39};—note especially the expression וְנָתַתִּי פִּגְרֵיכֶם עַל־פִּגְרֵי גִּלּוּלֵיכֶם Lv 26^{30} *and I will lay your carcases upon the carcases of your idols.*

†גַּלְגַּל **n.m.** $^{Ec\ 12,6}$ **wheel, whirl, whirlwind** 1534
(on format. cf. Ba$^{NB\ 204}$)—abs. ג׳ Ez 10^{2} + 7 t.; גַּלְגַּל ψ 83^{14}; pl. c. sf. גַּלְגִּלָּיו Is 5^{28} Je 47^{3};—**1.** *wheel*, **a.** of war-chariot Is 5^{28} Je 47^{3}, also coll. Ez 23^{24} 26^{10}; perh. also in Ezekiel's vision Ez $10^{2.6.13}$ (cf. *wheelwork*) but cf. infr. **b.** for drawing water Ec 12^{6}. **2. a.** *whirl* (of dust or

chaff) ψ 83^{14} Is 17^{13}, sim. of foes put to flight by God. **b.** perh. *whirling* of wheels Ez 10$^{2.6.13}$ Sm RV, but cf. supr. **c.** *whirlwind* ψ 77^{19}.

1536 †I. [גַּלְגַּל] **n.[m.]** wheel (on format. cf. Ba$^{NB\ 204}$) of cart, גַּלְגַּל עֶגְלָתוֹ Is 28^{28}.

1537 †II. גִּלְגָּל **n.pr.loc.** (= (sacred) *circle* of stones; cf. Di on Jos 5^{9}, where word-play on *roll away, off*)—c. art. exc. Jos 5^{9} 12^{23};—**1.** place E. of Jericho, where Isr. lay encamped Jos 4$^{19.20}$ 5$^{9.10}$ 9^{6} 10$^{7.9}$ 14^{6} cf. also Mi 6^{5} & Ju 3^{19} הַפְּסִילִים אֲשֶׁר אֶת־הַגִּ׳; ? mod. *Tell Jeljul* Bd$^{Pal\ 169}$; perh. also the place where sacrifices were offered 1 S 10^{8} 11$^{14.15.15}$ 13$^{4.7.8.12.15}$ (in v^{15} ins. also c. other words, Dr cf. We) 15$^{12.21.33}$; place of illicit sacrifice Ho 4^{15} 9^{15} 12^{12} Am 4^{4} 5$^{5.5}$, named also Ju 2^{1} 1 S 7^{16} 2 S 19$^{16.41}$; ? = בֵּית הַגִּלְגָּל Ne 12^{29}. **2.** place on border between Judah & Benjamin Jos 15^{17} (= גְּלִילוֹת 18^{17} cf. Di). **3.** place in N. Isr., dwelling of prophets 2 K 2^{1} 4^{38}, mod. *Jiljilie* S. from Nâbulus, SW. from *Seilûn* (Shiloh) cf. Di Ri$^{HWB\ 518}$. **4.** place in N. Isr. near Mt. Gerizim and Mt. Ebal Dt 11^{30}, identif. with **3** by Ke Ri $^{HWB\ 518}$ Schenkel^{BL} SS; but cf. Di. **5.** in phr. מֶלֶךְ גּוֹיִם לְגִלְגָּל Jos 12^{23}, in list of Canaanitish kings; prob. name of a (northern) district cf. Di (B βασιλέα Γεεὶ τῆς Γαλιλαίας—but 𝔊L & Codd. Γοειμ τῆς Γελγελ); Di comp. Is. 8^{23}.

1538 †גֻּלְגֹּלֶת **n.f.** skull, head, poll (person) (on format. cf. Ba$^{NB\ 205}$; Aram. גּוּלְגַּלְתָּא)—abs. גֻּ׳ 2 K 9^{35} + 3 t.; sf. גֻּלְגָּלְתּוֹ Ju 9^{53} 1 Ch 10^{10}; pl. sf. גֻּלְגְּלֹתָם Nu 1^{2} + 5 t.;—**1.** *skull*, as broken by a stone Ju 9^{53}; as severed from body 2 K 9^{35} 1 Ch 10^{10}. **2.** *head, poll* (in counting, taxing, etc.; only P and late) עֹמֶר לַגֻּ׳ Ex 16^{16} *an omer for every man;* cf. 38^{26} Nu 1$^{2.18.20.22}$ 3^{47} 1 Ch 23$^{3.24}$.

4039 †מְגִלָּה **n.f.** roll (writing, book; late)—מ׳ Je 36^{28} + 16 t.; cstr. מְגִלַּת־ ψ 40^{8} + 3 t.;—*roll* of writing, book מְגִלַּת־סֵפֶר Je 36$^{2.4}$ Ez 2^{9} ψ 40^{8}; מ׳ alone Je 36 $^{6.14.14.20.21.23.25.27.28.28.29.32}$ Ez 3$^{1.2.3}$ Ze 5$^{1.2}$.

1563 †[גָּלַם] **vb.** wrap up, fold, fold together (NH *id.*, Aram. in deriv.)—**Qal** *Impf.* וַיִּגְלֹם 2 K 2^{8} וַיִּקַּח אֵלִיָּהוּ אֶת־אַדַּרְתּוֹ וַיִּגְלֹם.

1545 †[גְּלוֹם] **n.[m.]** wrapping, garment (Aram. גְּלִימָא, ܓܠܝܡܐ = Pers. گليم acc. to Fl ChWB$^{i.\ 143}$ SFrä$^{LOPh.\ i.\ (1883-4)\ 410}$), בִּגְלוֹמֵי תְכֵלֶת Ez 27^{24}.

1564 †[גֹּלֶם] **n.[m.]** embryo (NH גּוֹלֶם, Aram. גּוֹלְמָא, *unfinished vessel*), גָּלְמִי רָאוּ עֵינֶיךָ ψ 139^{16} *mine imperfect substance* (RV) *did thine eyes see.*

†גַּלְמוּד **adj.** hard, barren (NH *id. lonely* NHWB; Ar. جَلْمَدٌ *rock*, جَلْمَدَةٌ *stony* (of land); Aram. גַּלְמוּדָה cf. Ba$^{NB\ 208}$)—גּ׳ Jb 3^{7} + 2 t. Jb; f. גַּלְמוּדָה Is 49^{21};—*hard, barren, unproductive,* mostly fig.: Jb 15^{34} of company of wicked men, where prob. a subst. v. De Di; Jb 30^{3} *through want and famine* (they are) *stiff* (*lifeless;* RV *gaunt*); of exiled Zion as bereaved and barren woman Is 49^{21}; so of night of Job's birth Jb 3^{7}. 1565

†[גָּלַע] **vb.** expose, lay bare (NH Pi. *disclose, make known;* cf. Ar. جَلَعَ (Frey) **a.** *exuit* (vestem), *removit* (praeputium); جُلُوعٌ *nuda fuit* (femina); **b.** جَلِعَ *patuit* (os) *labiis non tegentibus dentes; impudica fuit* (mulier); comp. also Syr. ܓܠܥ *circumcise* (in Lexx.); Eth. ገለፀ: *cortex, crusta, testa;* Gr $^{Monatsschr.\ 1884,\ 24\ f.}$; Schult Thes De Pr 17^{14} Fl in De, Now Str & most der. Heb. mng. from Ar. **b**; *shew the teeth,* then *snarl, quarrel* (cf. Ar. conj. III), but v. Gr$^{l.\ c.}$)—only **Hithp.** *Pf.* הִתְגַּלַּע Pr 17^{14}; *Impf.* יִתְגַּלָּע Pr 18^{1} 20^{3};—**disclose oneself, break out,** Pr 17^{14} subj. רִיב; *break* or *burst out* in contention, strife Pr. 20^{3} subj. כָּל־אֱוִיל; similarly 18^{1} (sq. בְּ *against;* Gr$^{l.\ c.}$ prop. יִלְעַג or יִלְעִיג). 1566

גִּלְעָד v. sub II. גלל. p. 165 1567

†גִּלְעָד **n.pr.loc.** of mountain-range or hill-country, land & city, E. of Jordan (cf. Ar. جَلْعَدٌ *durus, fortis* Frey, so Thes; Hi $^{Gesch.\ Isr.\ 26}$ comp. same √ used of *camel* (جَلْعَادٌ *camelus robustus ac firmus,* cf. Hom $^{NS\ 144}$), whence *camel hump,* orig. name of mt.)—גּ׳ Gn 37^{25} + 79 t. (mostly as **n.pr.m.** and in combin. with other **n.pr. loc.** cf. infr.); הַגִּ׳ Gn 31^{21} + 50 t. (so usually as name of mt. and land); גִּלְעָדָה Nu 32^{39} 1 Ch 27^{21}; הַגִּלְעָדָה 2 S 24^{6};—*Gilead*, used of territory between the Arnon and the Jabboḳ, mod. *Belḳa;* also of that between the Jabboḳ and the Jarmuk, mod. *Jebel Ajlûn;* also of the entire E.-Jordan land occupied by Israel, including both the parts just named (cf. Di Gn 31^{54} Stu Ju 10^{4}; Bd $^{Pal\ 178}$; also L. Oliphant $^{Land\ of\ Gilead,\ 1880}$);—**1.** territory S. of Jabboḳ, **a.** אֶרֶץ הַגִּ׳ Nu 32^{29} (P), אֶרֶץ גּ׳ v^{1} (JE), both connected with Reuben and Gad; so חֲצִי הַר הַגִּ׳ Dt 3^{12}; אֶרֶץ גּ׳ also 1 Ch 5^{9} (of Reuben); 1 K 4^{19} (of Sihon and Og); cf. אֶרֶץ גַּד וְגִ׳ 1 S 13^{7}; further, **b.** הַגִּ׳ alone, Ju 10^{17} (or possibly here name of city ?), 11^{29} (prob.); 1568

also 1 Ch 5[10] (of Reuben) v[10] (of Gad); cf. חֲצִי הַגּ׳ וְעַד יַבֹּק Jos 12[2] (of Sihon), so v[5] (both D); **c.** similarly ג׳ alone (without art.) in poet. ψ 60[9] (‖ Manasseh) = 108[9]; but also in prose in phrases זִקְנֵי ג׳ Ju 10[18], יֹשְׁבֵי ג׳ v[18] 11[8], שָׂרֵי ג׳ Ju 11[5.7.8.9.10.11], אַנְשֵׁי ג׳ Ju 12[4.4.5]; cf. also **d.** עָרֵי הַגּ׳ Nu 32[26] (JE; of Reuben and Gad); so of Jephthah's burial-place Ju 12[7]; even כָּל־עָרֵי הַגּ׳ Jos 13[25] (P; of Gad); besides these, of particular cities, esp. רָאמֹת בַּגּ׳ Dt 4[43] (of Gad); cf. רָאמוֹת בַּגּ׳ Jos 20[8] (P), 1 Ch 6[65] (of Gad), and רָמֹת בַּגּ׳ Jos 21[38] (P); usually רָמֹת ג׳ 1 K 4[13] 22[3.4.6.12.15.20.29] = 2 Ch 18[2.3.5.11.14.19.28]; 2 K 8[28] 9[1.4.14] 2 Ch 22[5]; also מִצְפֵּה ג׳ Ju 11[29.29]; further יַעְזֵיר ג׳ 1 Ch 26[31]. **2.** Northern Gilead, **a.** אֶרֶץ הַגּ׳ Jos 17[5.6] (JE; of Manasseh) cf. Ju 10[4] 1 Ch 2[22] (both of Jair); הַר הַגּ׳ Gn 31[21.23.25] (E); prob. also הַר ג׳ (no art.) Ct 4[1] (cf. 6[5] infr.). **b.** הַגּ׳ alone Nu 32[40] (JE; of Machir) Jos 17[1] (JE; *id.*) cf. 13[11] (D) Dt 2[36] 1 K 4[13] (of Jair); Dt 3[15.16] (boundary of Reuben and Gad); prob. also Ct 6[5] (cf. 4[1] supr.); cf. יֶתֶר הַגּ׳ Dt 3[13]; & חֲצִי הַגּ׳ Jos 13[31] (P; of Machir); הַגִּלְעָדָה 2 S 24[6] (prob.); cf. also **c.** ג׳ (no art.) prob. Je 8[22] 46[11] (in both ref. to צְרִי *balm*, prob. from the wooded Northern Gilead); similarly 22[6]; and גִּלְעָדָה 1 Ch 27[21], also Nu 32[39] (JE; of Machir). **d.** in combination יָבֵשׁ ג׳ (city) Ju 21[8.9.10.12.14] 1 S 11[1.9] (‖ יָבֵשׁ alone) 31[11] (‖ *id.*) = 1 Ch 10[11] 2 S 2[4.5] 21[12]; perh. also (מִ)תִּשְׁבֵּה ג׳ 1 K 17[1] (emend., after 𝔊, Ew Th al. see VB);—cf. further sub **6. n.pr.m.** infr. —Ju 7[3] וְיִצְפֹּר מֵהַר הַגּ׳ *and let him depart from Mt. Gilead*, appar. belongs here, but מֵהַר הַגִּלְבֹּעַ is read by Cler Hi Gr Ke Be; against this cf. Stu Bu[RS 112]. **3.** more generally, of all Gilead, **a.** אֶרֶץ הַגּ׳ Jos 22[9.13.15.32] (P; of Reuben, Gad and Manasseh; opp. land of Canaan); cf. 2 S 17[26]; so כָּל־אֶרֶץ הַגּ׳ 2 K 10[33]. **b.** אֶרֶץ ג׳ (no art.) Zc 10[10]; cf. הַר אֶפְרַיִם וְג׳ Je 50[19] (‖ Carmel and Bashan); ג׳ alone, also Gn 37[25]; likewise Mi 7[14] (‖ Carmel & Bashan, reference to fertility). **c.** הַגּ׳ alone, of Isr. territ. in gen. E. of Jordan, Ju 10[8]; cf. 2 S 2[9] 2 K 10[33] (of Reuben, Gad and Manasseh); כָּל־הַגּ׳ Dt 3[10]; אֶת־כָּל־הָאָרֶץ אֶת־הַגּ׳ Dt 34[1]; הַגּ׳ also in general sense Ez 47[18] 2 K 15[29] (?) Ob[19]. **4.** ג׳, name of a city Ho 6[8] (& Ju 10[17] ? cf. **1 a.** supr.);—on the ruined cities *Jilʿâd, Jilʿaud* on the *Jebel Jilʿâd*, N. of Es-Salṭ, and S. of Jabboḳ v. Di Gn 31[54] & reff. **5.** אֶרֶץ הַגּ׳ of Israelites living E. of Jordan (as a whole) Ju 20[1]; הַגּ׳ of people of Gilead Am 1[3.13]; so ג׳ Ju 5[17] (=גָּד), 12[4.5] (‖ אַנְשֵׁי ג׳ v[4.4.5]) Ho 12[12]. Cf. also גִּלְעָדִי infr. **6.** treated as **n.pr.m.** **a.** ג׳, son of Machir & grandson of Manasseh Nu 26[29.29.30] 27[1] 36[1] Jos 17[3] (all P) 1 Ch 2[21.23] 7[14.17]; once הַגּ׳ Jos 17[1] (JE) cf. Di;—ref. in all these to Northern Gilead. **b.** father of Jephthah Ju 11[1.2];—ref. to Gad (cf. supr. esp. sub **5**). **c.** 1 Ch 5[14] (a Gadite).

† גִּלְעָדִי **adj.gent.**;—**1.** of גִּלְעָד **6 a.** Nu 1569
26[29]. **2.** of **5.** Ju 11[1.40] 12[7]. **3.** of ג׳ **n.pr. loc.** Ju 10[3] 2 S 17[27] 19[32] 1 K 2[7] Ezr 2[61] = Ne 7[63]; cf. בְּנֵי גִלְעָדִים 2 K 15[25];—cf. also sub גִּלְעָד **5.**

† [גָּלַשׁ] **vb. sit, sit up,** possibly also re- 1570
cline (cf. Ar. جَلَسَ *sit up;* so Thes De al. (not Ew))—only **Qal** *Pf.* (שֶׁ)גָּלְשׁוּ Ct 4[1] 6[5] שֶׁגָּלְשׁוּ מ(הר) גִּלְעָד of flocks of goats, in sim. of a woman's hair; construction & sense rather awkward.

גַּם v. sub גמם. p. 168 1571

† [גָּמָא] **vb. swallow** (liquids), (NH *id.*; 1572
cf. Aram. גְּמָא, גְּמַע, ܓܡܰܥ; perh. cf. also Eth. ገምዕ: *jar, vessel* v. Di)—**Pi.** *Impf.* יְגַמֶּא־אֶרֶץ Jb 39[24] fig. of horse in swift gallop; (this, however, possibly denom. fr. גּוּמָּא NH, Aram. גּוּמְּתָא, ܓܘܡܬܐ *pit, hollow,* i.e. *he makes* [*paws* or *stamps*] *hollows in the earth*). **Hiph.** *Imv. fs. sf.* הַגְמִיאִינִי נָא מְעַט־מַיִם Gn 24[17] *let me drink a little water, pray.*

† גֹּמֶא **n.m.** [Jb 8, 11] **rush, reed, papyrus** (cf. 1573
Löw[p. 55]) (NH גּוֹמֶא, Eth. ገሚዕ: loan-word, acc. to Di;—name from *swallowing*, sucking up, water? so Thes, cf. Che Is 18[2] al.; = Copt. *gome*, v. Di Ex 2[3] whence others der. as loan-word)—גֹּמֶא Ex 2[3] + 3 t.;—*rush, paper-reed,* (Egypt.) Jb 8[11] (‖ אָחוּ); coll. Is 35[7] (‖ קָנֶה); as material, תֵּבַת ג׳ Ex 2[3] *chest of paper-reed;* כְּלֵי־ג׳ Is 18[2] *vessels of paper-reed.*

גמד (√ of foll.; cf. Ar. جَمَدَ *congeal, become solid; be hard, stern;* also *cut, cut off;* Aram. גְּמַד *contract;* Aph. *be bold, daring*).

† גֹּמֶד **n.m. cubit** (fr. elbow to knuckles 1574
of clenched (contracted) hand; Aq on Ez 27[11], Ra al.; Gk. πυγμή; NH גּוֹמֶד *cubit;* so Aram. גַּרְמִידָא Ch WB[1. 155], ܓܪܡܝܕܐ (lexx.))—Ju 3[16] of Ehud's sword ג׳ אָרְכָּהּ (v. GFM).

† גַּמָּדִים **n.pr.gent.** Ez 27[11]; *valorous men* 1575
Thes[Add. 79] Ew RVm; but n.pr. apparently needed; גמדים not elsewhere; Lag[Onom. Sacr. 2, 95, 2nd ed. 367] prop. גמרים v. גֹּמֶר; < Co צמרים cf. Gn 10[18].

1579 †גִּמְזוֹ **n.pr.loc.** (cf. Syr. [Syriac] (Lexx.) *sycamore;* Ar. جُمَّيْز is loan-wd. Frä[140]; cf. As. n.pr.loc. *Gamuzanu* Pinches[Hbr. July, 1886, 222]), city of Judah toward Philistines 2 Ch 28^{18}; mod. *Jimzu*, E. from Lydda Rob[BR ii. 249] Bd[Pal 21].

1580 †גָּמַל **vb. 1. deal fully or adequately with, deal out to. 2. wean. 3. ripen** (As. *gamâlu, deal with, benefit*, e.g. VR 35^{19}; NH גָּמַל, Aram. גְּמַל; v. Palm. n.pr. אגמלא Vog[No. 124], Nab. n.pr.f. גמלת Vog.[Nab. sub No. 7]; perh. orig. *complete, accomplish*, cogn. גמר;—Ar. جَمَلَ is *collect*, جَمُلَ *be beautiful, goodly*)—**Qal** *Pf.* ψ 13^6+; *Impf.* יִגְמֹל Nu 17^{23}+; *Imv.* גְּמֹל ψ 119^{17}; *Inf.* גְּמָלְךָ, גָּמְלָה 1 S 1^{23}; *Pt.* גֹּמֵל Pr 11^{17}+; pass. גָּמוּל Is 11^8; גָּמֻל ψ 131$^{2.2}$;—**1. a.** *deal out to, do to*, c. 2 acc. גְּמָלַתְהוּ טוֹב וְלֹא רָע *she doeth him good and not evil* Pr 31^{12}; כִּי אַתָּה גְּמַלְתַּנִי הַטּוֹבָה וַאֲנִי גְּמַלְתִּיךָ הָרָעָה *for thou hast done unto me the good but I have done unto thee the evil* 1 S 24^{18}; *do* evil (ה)רע *unto* Gn 50$^{15.17}$ Pr 3^{30}; c. לְ pers. Is 3^9; *do* good *unto*, 2 acc. Is 63$^{7.7}$; cf. also גֹּמֵל נַפְשׁוֹ אִישׁ חָסֶד Pr 11^{17}. **b.** with עַל pers. *deal bountifully with* ψ 13^6 116^7 119^{17} 142^8; c. acc. pers. *reward* 2 S 22^{21} (=ψ 18^{21}), perh. also לָמָּה יִגְמְלֵנִי הַגְּמוּלָה הַזֹּאת *why should he reward me with this reward?* 2 S 19^{37}. **c.** *recompense, repay, requite*, in a bad sense, with 2 acc. ψ 7^5; with לְ pers. Dt 32^6 ψ 137^8; with עַל pers. 2 Ch. 20^{11} ψ 103^{10} Jo 4^4. **2.** *wean a child* (complete his nursing) 1 S 1$^{23.23.24}$ 1 K 11^{20} Ho 1^8; גָּמוּל *weaned child* ψ 131$^{2.2}$ Is 11^8; גְּמוּלֵי מֵחָלָב *weaned from milk* Is 28^9. **3.** trans. *ripen, bear ripe* (almonds) Nu 17^{23}; intrans. *become ripe* (grapes) Is 18^5. **Niph.** *Impf.* יִגָּמֵל 1 S 1^{22}; וַיִּגָּמַל Gn 21^8; *Inf.* הִגָּמֵל Gn 21^8;—*be weaned.*

1576 †גְּמוּל **n.m. dealing, recompence, benefit**—ג׳ ψ 94^2+11 t.; sf. גְּמֻלְךָ Ob^{15}, etc.; pl. sf. גְּמוּלָיו ψ 103^2;—**1.** גְּמוּל יָדַיִם *dealing of the hands* Ju 9^{16} Pr 12^{14} (יָשׁוּב לְ) Is 3^{11} (יֵעָשֶׂה לְ). **2.** *dealing*, hence (from context) *equivalent of dealing, recompence:* c. suff. Ob^{15} גמלך ישוב בראשך, Jo 4$^{4.7}$ (הֵשִׁיב), so with הֵשִׁיב לְ ψ 28^4; שִׁלֵּם לְ 137^8 Pr 19^{17}; absolutely שִׁלֵּם (הֵשִׁיב) גְּמוּל לְ Is 59$^{18.18}$ 66^6 Je 51^6 La 3^{64}; עַל Jo 4^4 ψ 94^2; Is 35^4 ג׳ אֵל אלהים *the recompence of God.* **3.** *benefit:* תשכחי כל גמוליו ψ 103^2; כגמול עליו *according to the benefit* (done) *unto him* 2 Ch. 32^{25}

†גָּמוּל **n.pr.m.** (*weaned*) a chief of the 1577
Levites 1 Ch 24^{17}. Vid. also בֵּית גָּמוּל (Je 48^{23}).

†גְּמוּלָה **n.f.** [2 S 19, 37] **dealing, recompence** 1578
—ג׳ 2 S 19^{37} cf. גָּמַל; pl. גְּמוּלוֹת *dealings* Is 59^{18}; Je 51^{56} אֵל גְּמֻלוֹת *God of recompence.*

†[תַּגְמוּל] **n.m. benefit**—pl. c. Aram. sf. 1583
כָּל־תַּגְמוּלוֹהִי עָלָי *all his benefits unto me* ψ 116^{12}.

†גַּמְלִיאֵל **n.pr.m.** (*reward of God*) a prince 1581
of Manasseh Nu 1^{10} 2^{20} 7$^{54.59}$ 10^{23}, cf. Mishn. גמליאל, Palm. Vog[No. 124], 𝔊 Γαμαλιήλ Acts 5^{34}.

†גָּמָל **n.m.** Gn 24^{10} + 9 t., **f.** & **m.** Gn 32^{16} (cf. infr.), **camel** (NH *id.* Ar. جَمَلٌ (جُمْلٌ), Eth. ገመል: As. *gammalu* COT[Gloss] Aram. גַּמְלָא, [Syriac]; Palm. Tariff pl. גמלין Reckendorf[ZMG 1888, 401]; √גמל but mng. of √ dub.; Bo[Hieroz i. 73] der. fr. גמל *requite*, so Lag[BN 20, 49] (camel as μνησίκακος); v. also conject. in MV, Dl in Hpt[F. 70] Hpt[BAS i. 171]; A. v. Kremer[Semit. Culturentlehn., 2], Hom[NS 144 ff.])—abs. גָּמָל Gn 24^{64} + 7 t.; pl. גְּמַלִּים Gn 12^{16} + 30 t.; cstr. גְּמַלֵּי Gn 24^{10}; *sf.* גְּמַלֶּיךָ Gn 24^{14} + 3 t.; גְּמַלָּיו Gn 24^{20}; גְּמַלֵּיהֶם Gn 37^{25} + 6 t.;—*camel*, **1.** as property (in Hex only J) Gn 12^{16} (‖ אתנות) 24$^{10.35}$ (‖ חמורים etc.) 30^{43} (‖ *id.*) 32^8 (‖ בקר, צאן) Ex 9^3 (Egyptian ‖ סוסים, חמורים, בקר, צאן, etc.) Ju 6^5 7^{12} 1 S 15^3 (‖ חמור etc.) 27^9 1 Ch 5^{21} 27^{30} (all ‖ *id.*) 2 Ch 14^{14} (‖ צאן) Ezr 2^{67} (‖ פרדים, סוסים, חמורים) = Ne 7^{68} Jb 1^3 (‖ אתנות, בקר, צאן) cf. v^{17} 42^{12} (‖ *id.*) Je 49^{29} (‖ צאן) v^{32} Zc 14^{15} (‖ סוס, פרד, חמור) [4 t. ‖ סוס and other words, Ex 9^3 (Egyptians), Zc 14^{15} (enemies of Israel), Ezr 2^{67} = Ne 7^{68} (returned exiles)]. **2.** as beasts of burden Gn 24^{10} cf. v$^{11.14.19.20.22.30.31.32.32.44.46.46}$ 37^{25} (all J), 1 K 10^2 2 K 8^9 1 Ch 12^{41} 2 Ch 9^1 Is 30^6 (עַל־דַּבֶּשֶׁת ג׳), Is 60^6 (‖ בִּכְרֵי מִדְיָן). **3.** for riding Gn 24$^{61.63.64}$ (all J), 31$^{17.34}$ (both E) 1 S 30^{17}, cf. also Ju 8$^{21.26}$, and particularly Is 21^7 רֶכֶב גמל; a riding-company of camels i.e. a troop of camels with riders; נְוֵה גמלים an abode for camels, in prediction against Ammon Ez 25^5, (‖ מִרְבַּץ צאן). **4.** forbidden as food Lv 11^4 (P) Dt 14^7.

†גְּמַלִּי **n.pr.m.** a Danite Nu 13^{12}. 1582

גמם (Ar. جَمَّ *become much* or *abundant*, جَمٌّ *abundance, much*, جُمَّةٌ *collection* (of water), *company* (of people)).

גַּם$_{768}$ **adv.** denoting *addition*, also, more- 1571
over, yea (Moab. *id.*: prob. akin to √ جَمَّ; cf.

جَمًّا (accus.) *in a mass, altogether*)—**1.** *also, moreover*, emphasizing sts. the thought of an entire sentence, but more usually the word immediately following, as Gn 3^{6} וַתִּתֵּן גַּם לְאִישָׁהּ and gave *also* to her husband, v^{27} and take *also* of the tree of life, 7^{3} 19^{21} 24^{19} 26^{21} 29^{27} 30^{15} 32^{21}(גַּם הִנֵּה...: so Est 7^{9}) 48^{11} Ex 8^{28} 12^{32b} Dt 1^{37} 1 S 28^{20} 2 S 11^{12} 2 K 9^{27} Is 7^{13}+. Often before pronouns, Gn 4^{4} וְהֶבֶל הֵבִיא גַם הוּא and Abel, *he* also brought, 20^{5} וְהִיא־גַם־הִוא (so only here) and she herself *also*, v^{6} 27^{31} וַיַּעַשׂ גַּם הוּא, 30^{3} Dt 3^{20} Ju 3^{31} 6^{35} 9^{19} 1 S 19^{20-24} Je 12^{6} 48^{26} etc. (cf. MI ^{6} ויאמר גם הא): esp. in genealogies of J (Bu$^{Urg. 220}$) Gn $4^{22.26}$ 10^{21} 19^{38} $22^{20.24}$ cf. Ju 8^{31}. גַּם sq. pron. also begins a sentence with emph. in an elevated style, *thou* (*they*) *also*, Is 14^{10} Je $12^{6.6}$ 48^{7} Ez 16^{52} Na $3^{11.11}$. After a pron. in an oblique case (Ges$^{\S 135,2}$) Gn 27^{34} 1 S 19^{23} 2 S 17^{5} Je 25^{14} 27^{7}+. וְגַם *and also* (more often than גַּם alone attaching a sentence) Gn 6^{4} 14^{16} 15^{14} 17^{16} 20^{12} $24^{14.46}$ 30^{6} 37^{7} 38^{24} 42^{28} Ex 2^{19} 3^{9} 4^{14} Jos 7^{11} (5 t.) 1 S 4^{17} 1 K 21^{19}+oft.; with a negative = *neither* Ex 5^{2} 34^{3} al.—גַּם . . . גַּם (like *et . . . et*) *both . . . and* Gn 44^{16} $47^{3.19}$ Nu 18^{3} Je 51^{12} ψ 49^{3}+: גַּם . . . גַּם . . . Gn 24^{25} Ju 8^{22} Ec 9^{6}: with a negative *neither . . . nor* Nu 23^{25} 1 S 20^{27} 1 K 3^{26}, and (3 t.) Gn 43^{8} Ex 4^{10} 1 S 28^{6}. So (but seldom) גַּם . . . וְגַם Gn 24^{44} Ex $10^{25 f.}$ 1 S 2^{26} 12^{14} 26^{25}: with neg. 1 S 21^{9}.—N.B. In poetry independence and emphasis is sts. given by גַּם to a new idea, where in English we should be satisfied with *and:* ψ 107^{5} 137^{1} Jb 24^{19} Ct 7^{14} La 4^{15}. **2.** with stress on a particular word, *even*, Ex 4^{9} Nu 22^{33} גַּם אוֹתְךָ *even* thee I had slain, and kept her alive, 2 S 17^{10} Je 2^{33} ψ 132^{12} Pr 14^{13} *even* in laughter the heart is sorrowful, v^{20} 17^{28} 20^{11} Ru 2^{15} Ne 3^{35}; and so often after כִּי, Dt 12^{31} for *even* their sons they burn in the fire to their gods, 1 S 22^{17} Is 26^{12} Je 6^{11} 12^{6} 14^{5} Ho 9^{12} כִּי־גַם־אוֹי לָהֶם for *even* woe is it to them when I depart from them; הֲגַם †Gn 16^{13} 1 S $10^{11.12}$ = 19^{24} 1 K 17^{20} ψ 78^{20} Jb 41^{1} Est 7^{8}. Other cases:—1 S 24^{12} רְאֵה גַּם רְאֵה see, *yea* see! (but Hup$^{Qu. Job vi.}$ גַּם רָאֹה: cf. infr.) ψ 118^{11}; Jb 2^{10} גַּם אֶת־הַטּוֹב נְקַבֵּל shall we receive *good* (emph.) from God and not evil? 21^{7}; interposed once between a subst. and adj. Gn 20^{4} gentemne *etiam* justam interficies? emphasizing כֹּל, Dt 28^{61} Ju 9^{49b} 1 S 22^{7} גַּם־לְכֻלְּכֶם to *all* (emph.) of you will he give . . . ? 2 S 19^{31} גַּם אֶת־הַכֹּל יִקָּח *yea*, the whole let him take! Is 26^{12}; אֶחָד 2 S 17^{12b} and we will not leave ...גַּם אֶחָד *even* one (similarly v^{13b}), ψ 14^{3} (= 53^{4}) אֵין גַּם אֶחָד; an inf. or cogn. accus. attached to a verb, †Gn 31^{15} 46^{4} Nu 11^{15} 16^{13} 1 S 1^{6}. גַּם שְׁנֵיהֶם lit. *even both* i.e. the one as well as the other (Germ. *alle beide*) is said idiomatically, †Gn 27^{45} (שְׁנֵיכֶם), Dt 22^{22} 23^{19} 1 S 25^{43} (שְׁתֵּיהֶן), Pr 17^{15} $20^{10.12}$ Ru 1^{5}. **3.** introducing a climax, *yea*, esp. in a rhetorical style, Gn 27^{33} Dt $23^{3.4}$ Ju $5^{4.4}$ Is 13^{3} 14^{8} 43^{13} *yea*, from to-day I am the same, 44^{12} גַּם רָעֵב *yea*, he is hungry, and has no strength, 47^{3} $48^{8.8.8}$ 57^{7} Je 46^{16} 48^{2} 51^{44} Ho 7^{9} ψ 41^{10} 84^{7} 139^{12}; Is 66^{8} כִּי־חָלָה גַּם־יָלְדָה צִיּוֹן אֶת־בָּנֶיהָ, Je 5^{28} 12^{2} Ez 24^{5} Jb 21^{7} Ct 8^{1}: emphasizing an extreme, or aggravated, case, *yea, even*, Is 49^{15} *yea*, these may forget, Je 8^{17} *yea*, the stork knoweth, etc., Is 23^{12} גַּם שָׁם *even* there no rest shall be for thee (so ψ 139^{10}), 49^{25} 57^{6} Je 23^{11b} Mal 3^{15} ψ 84^{4}. **4.** expressing *correspondence*, esp. in the matter of *retribution* (the גַּם *correlativum*), so frequently גַּם אֲנִי, גַּם אָנֹכִי I *also* (on my part):—Gn 20^{6} I *also* [as well as thyself] know that thou hast done this innocently, Jos 24^{18} Ju 2^{21} 1 S 1^{28} (cf. Dr) 28^{22} גַּם אַתָּה thou *also* (as I have done v^{21}), 2 S 12^{13} 'י *also* [responding to thy confession] hath removed thy sin, 2 K $2^{3.5}$ Is 31^{2} 66^{3-4} (גם . . . גם, emphasizing the action of both parties), Je 2^{36} 4^{12} now will I *also* [in correspondence with their deeds] speak judgments with them, 7^{11} 51^{49} (גם...גם), Ez $5^{8.11}$ 16^{43} (וְגַם = therefore *also*), 23^{35} Ho 4^{6} because thou hast forgotten the direction of thy God, I *also* (on my part) will forget thy children, ψ 52^{7} (thou lovest evil, etc.) גַּם אֵל יִתָּצְךָ God *also* (on his part) will pluck thee up, 71^{22} 133^{1} Pr 1^{26} Jb 7^{11} 12^{3} 16^{4}; so וְגַם Ju 2^{3} Am $4^{6.7}$ Mi 6^{13} Mal 2^{9}. In the apodosis (uncommon): Gn 13^{16} if a man could number the dust of the earth, גַּם זַרְעֲךָ יִמָּנֶה thy seed *also* should be numbered, Je $31^{36.37}$ $33^{21.26}$ Zc 8^{6}. The correspondence is sometimes of the nature of a climax: Gn 27^{33} 30^{8} I have wrestled, גַּם יָכֹלְתִּי (cf. 1 K 22^{22} וְגַם תּוּכָל, Je 50^{24}), Is 66^{8}. **5.** connecting two ideas which express (or imply) a contradiction, גַּם acquires sts. an adversative force (cf. אַף **1** end), *yet, but, though:* ψ 95^{9} they tried me, *but also* (Che) saw my work (viz. of judgment), 129^{2} Je 6^{15} = 8^{12} Ez 20^{23} Ec $4^{8.16}$ 5^{18} Ne 6^{1}. So וְגַם Ez 16^{28} 20^{15} Ec 3^{13} 6^{7} Ne 5^{8}. **6.** גַּם כִּי (with impf.) *yea, when* La 3^{8}, *even when* Pr 22^{6}; *yea though* (stating an imagined case) Is 1^{15} Ho 8^{10} 9^{16} ψ 23^{4} (so גַּם אִם Ec 8^{17}); *also* (is it) *that* Ru 2^{21} (v. כִּי **1 d**). כִּי גַם = *for even* (v. supr. **2**); = *though even, although* (conceding a fact) Ec 4^{14} (v. De) 8^{12}.

†[מְגַמָּה] **n.f.** Hb 1^{9} (of the Chaldaeans) 4041
מְגַמַּת פְּנֵיהֶם קָדִימָה, of uncertain meaning: Ges the *assembling* of their faces is (directed) for-

wards; Ew De Ke *eagerness*, comparing (questionably) גָּמָא *swallow* Jb 39[24], and جَامَ (Freyt.) *seek* (whence St prop. מְגַמַּת). Text prob. erron.

גמץ (√ of foll., Aram. גְּמַץ *dig* (perh. denom.)).

1475 †גּוּמָּץ **n.m.** pit (Aram. loan-wd., cf. גּוּמְצָא, ܓܘܡܨܐ; NH גּוּמָּצָא cf. Ba[NB 66, Anm. 1]), Ec 10[8] חֹפֵר ג׳ בּוֹ יִפּוֹל *he that diggeth a pit shall fall into it;* so also Pr 26[27] 𝔗 𝔖 where 𝔊 כֹּרֶה שַׁחַת.

1584 †גָּמַר **vb. end, come to an end, complete** (only ψ) (NH *id. complete;* As *gamâru* Lotz [TP. Register] & deriv. COT[Gloss] al.; Aram. גְּמַר, ܓܡܰܪ; Eth. ገመረ: (II); cf. also Ar. جَمَّرَ *collect, assemble*)—**Qal** *Pf.* ג׳ ψ 12[2] 77[9]; *Impf.* יִגְמֹר ψ 138[8]; יִגְמָר־ ψ 7[10]; *Pt.* גֹּמֵר ψ 57[3];—**1.** *come to an end, be no more* ψ 7[10] 12[2] (‖ [פָּסַס]); 77[9] (‖ אָפֵס). **2.** trans. *bring to an end, complete,* אֵל גֹּמֵר עָלָי ψ 57[3] God that *completeth, accomplisheth, for me* (𝔊 Gr Bi גמל, & so Che doubtfully), י׳ יִגְמֹר בַּעֲדִי 138[8].

1586 †גֹּמֶר **n.pr. 1. m. a.** son of Japhet Gn 10[2.3] = 1 Ch 1[5.6]; Ez 38[6]; Lag[Onom. Sacr. 2, 95, 2nd ed. 367, v. BN 77] prop. גמרים for גמדים Ez 27[11] q.v.; he identif. גֹּמֶר with Cappadocia (cf. 𝔗 Ez 27[11], Kiep[Lb. d. alt. Geogr. 91]) = Armen. *Gamir* -χ (with pl. ending) v. also Lag[Arm. Stud. 32 § 448]; cf. further As. *Gimirrai*, Schr[KG 157 ff.] Dl[Pa 245 f.] also Len[Or. ii. 1, 332 ff.] **2. f.** wife of Hosea, Ho 1[3].

1587 †גְּמַרְיָהוּ, גְּמַרְיָה **n.pr.m.** (י׳ *hath accomplished*)—**1.** גמריהו son of Shaphan Je 36[10.11.12.25]. **2.** גמריה son of Hilkiah Je 29[3].

1588 גַּן, גַּנָּה v. sub גנן. p. 171

1589 †[גָּנַב] **vb. steal** (NH *id.*, Aram. גְּנַב, ܓܢܰܒ; Ar. جَنَّبَ is *hurt the side,* or *put aside,* den. fr. جَنْبٌ *side*)—**Qal** *Pf.* 3 fs. sf. גְּנָבַתּוּ Jb 21[18] 27[20], גְּנַבְתָּם Gn 31[32]; 2 ms. גָּנַבְתָּ Gn 31[30]; 1 s. וְגָנַבְתִּי consec. Pr 30[9]; גָּנְבוּ Jos 7[11] 2 S 21[12]; sf. גְּנָבוּךָ 2 S 19[42]; *Impf.* יִגְנֹב־ Ex 21[37], יִגְנוֹב Pr 6[30], וַיִּגְנֹב Gn 31[20]; 3 fs. וַתִּגְנֹב Gn 31[19] + 2 t.; 2 ms. תִּגְנֹב Ex 20[15] Dt 5[17], וַתִּגְנֹב Gn 31[26.27], יִגְנְבוּ Ob[5], תִּגְנֹבוּ Lv 19[11], נִגְנֹב Gn 44[8]; *Inf. abs.* גָּנֹב Ex 22[11] + 2 t.; *Pt.* גֹּנֵב Ex 21[16] + 2 t., גָּנוּב Gn 30[33]; f. cstr. גְּנֻבְתִי Gn 31[39.39]; pl. גְּנוּבִים Pr 9[17]; in Hexateuch always JED, exc. Lv 19[11] (H);—*steal* c. acc. rei Gn 31[19.30.32] 44[8] Ex 21[37] 2 S 21[12] cf. pass. Gn 30[33] 31[39] Pr 9[17]; c. obj. pers. Ex 21[16] Dt 24[7] 2 S 19[42];=*take by stealth* (for good purpose) 2 K 11[2] = 2 Ch 22[11]; abs. Ex 20[15] = Dt 5[17], Lv 19[11] Jos 7[11] Pr 6[30] 30[9] Ob[5] Zc 5[3], cf. *Inf. abs.* Ho 4[2] Je 7[9] & (c. Niph.) Ex 22[11]; גנב לֵב = *deceive* Gn 31[20.26] cf. Di; ג׳ אֹתִי Gn 31[27] *id.*; of sudden sweeping off by storm, in simile Jb 21[18]; fig. of destruction of wicked 27[20]. **Niph.** *be stolen,* subj. rei גָּנֹב יִגָּנֵב Ex 22[11]. **Pi.** *steal away* (trans.) וַיְגַנֵּב אבשלום את־לֵב 2 S 15[6]; מְגַנְּבֵי דְבָרַי Je 23[30]. **Pu.** *be stolen away* subj. pers. גֻּנֹּב גֻּנַּבְתִּי Gn 40[15]; subj. rei וְגֻנַּב consec. Ex 22[6]; *be brought by stealth* Jb 4[12] יְגֻנָּב. **Hithp.** *go by stealth, steal away* יִתְגַּנֵּב 2 S 19[4], וַיִּתְגַּנֵּב 2 S 19[4]. (Syr. ܓܢܰܒ ܢܰܦܫܶܗ *steal* oneself *away;* so ܐܶܬܓܰܢܰܒ Gn 31[27].)

†גְּנֵבָה **n.f. thing stolen** (on format. cf. Ba[NB 161, 166])—גְּנֵבָה Ex 22[3] (an animal); בִּגְנֵבָתוֹ Ex 22[2], ב׳ pret. cf. Di. 1591

†גַּנָּב **n.m.** [Ex 22, 1] **thief**—גַּנָּב Ex 22[1] + 12 t.; גַּנָּבִים Is 1[23] + 3 t.—*thief* that breaks in Ex 22[1.6.7] (JE); by window Jo 2[9] (in simile); *thief* as one who steals Is 1[23] ψ 50[18] Pr 6[30] 29[24] Je 2[26] 48[27] Ho 7[1] (‖ גְּדוּד) Zc 5[4]; coming by night Je 49[9] cf. Jb 24[14] (in simile), Ob[5] (‖ שׁוֹדְדֵי לַיְלָה); Jb 30[5]; stealer of men (slave-dealer) Dt 24[7]. 1590

†גְּנֻבַת **n.pr.m.** (cf. Palm. גנבא Vog[No. 137]) son of Hadad the Edomite 1 K 11[20.20] (on the ת, cf. Dr[§ 181 N]). 1592

גנז (*cover up, hide,* cf. NH *hide,* Ar. جَنَزَ *cover up,* Aram. גְּנַז Ithpa, ܓܢܰܙ Ethp. *be hidden,* Eth. ገነዘ: *enwrap*).

†[גְּנָזִים] **n.[m.]pl. 1. chests**(?); **2. treasury** —only pl. cstr. גִּנְזֵי;—**1.** perh. *chests* of variegated cloth ג׳ בְּרֹמִים Ez 27[24] so Thes AV RV; Sm Co al. *cloths, carpets,* Ew *Taschen.* **2.** *treasury* (NH גְּנָז, Aram. גִּנְזָא, גְּנַז, BAram. cstr. pl. גִּנְזֵי; Pers. loan-word from گنجه *treasure*? cf. Vullers[ii. 1032] Lag[Ges. Abh. 27]); גִּנְזֵי הַמֶּלֶךְ Est 3[9] 4[7]. 1595

†[גִּנְזַךְ] **n.[m.] treasury** (NH גנזכה *treasure;* loan-wd. fr. or through Pers. cf. supr. & Lag[Ges. Abh. 28]), וְגַנְזַכָּיו 1 Ch 28[11]. 𝔊 τῶν ζακχὼ αὐτοῦ; but 𝔊L τῶν ἀποθηκῶν αὐτοῦ. 1597

†[גָּנַן] **vb. cover, surround, defend** (Ar. جَنَّ, Aram. אַגֵּן (Aph.), Palm. אגן Vog[Palm. 132 ff.]) —**Qal** *Pf.* וְגַנּוֹתִי Is 37[35] + 3 t.; *Inf. abs.* גָּנוֹן Is 31[5] (c. Hiph. q.v.)—*defend,* subj. always י׳; obj. the city Jerusalem c. על Is 37[35] 38[6] = 2 K 20[6]; 2 K 19[34] c. אֶל־ (‖ הוֹשִׁיעַ). **Hiph.** *Impf.* —or **Qal** acc. to Ba[ZMG 1889, 178], who comp. Ar. يَجِنُّ—יָגֵן Is 31[5] + 2 t.—*defend* (= Qal), Jeru- 1598

salem Is 31^{5} יגן . . . גָּנוֹן c. על (|| הִצִּיל); obj. Yahweh's people Zc 9^{15} c. עַל, 12^{8} c. בְּעַד.

1588 † גַּן **n.m.** $^{Ct\ 4,12}$ & (Gn 2^{15}) **f. enclosure, garden** (NH *id.*, גִּנָּה, Ar. جَنَّةٌ, Eth. ገነት: As. *ginû* COT^{Gloss}, also *gannatu* Dl$^{Pr\ 84}$; Aram. גִּנְּתָא, גִּנָּא, ܓܢܬܐ; Ph. פר אגנן אם צ[צ]ץ CIS$^{i.\ 165,\ 11\ \&\ p.\ 232\ f.}$ *birds of enclosure* (domestic fowls) *or of wing*) — abs. גַּן Gn 2^{8} + 3 t.; cstr. id. Gn 2^{15} + 19 t.; c. art. הַגָּן Gn 2^{9} + 9 t., but כַּגַּן La 2^{6}; *sf.* גַּנִּי Ct 4^{16} 5^{1}, גַּנּוֹ Ct 4^{16} 6^{2}; *Pl.* גַּנִּים Ct 4^{15} + 2 t.—*garden* as enclosure La 2^{6} (simile); הַיּוֹשֶׁבֶת בַּגַּנִּים Ct 8^{13}; cf. Ct 4^{12} (fig. of bride גַּן נָעוּל); *g. of herbs* (יָרָק) Dt 11^{10} 1 K 21^{2}; fig. of bride, *g. of plants, fruits, and spices* Ct 4$^{16.16}$ 5^{1} 6$^{2.2}$ cf. מַעְיַן גנים Ct 4^{15}; *g. of* (*king's*) *house* 2 K 21^{18} = גַּן־עֻזָּא 2 K 21$^{18.26}$; גַּן הַמֶּלֶךְ 2 K 25^{4} Je 39^{4} 52^{7} Ne 3^{15}, cf. בֵּית הַגָּן 2 K 9^{27} (at Jezreel? but this perhaps **n.pr.loc.** v. sub בית p. 111); most often of garden (orchard?) in Eden (Hex only Gn & only J) Gn 2$^{8.9.10.16}$ 3$^{1.2.3.8.8.10}$, called גַּן־עֵדֶן Gn 2^{15} 3$^{23.24}$ Ez 36^{35} Jo 2^{3}, cf. גַּן־י׳ Gn 13^{10} Is 51^{3} (both in simile); גן־אלהים Ez 28^{13} (עֵדֶן גן־אל׳), 31$^{8.8.9}$ (|| עֵדֶן); in last three the trees of the garden are comp. with Assyrian under fig. of cedar of Lebanon.

1593-94 † גַּנָּה **n.f. garden** (cf. foregoing)—גַּנָּה Is 1^{30} 61^{11}; cstr. גַּנַּת Ct 6^{11} + 3 t.; sf. גַּנָּתוֹ Jb 8^{16}; pl. גַּנֹּת Nu 24^{6}, גַּנּוֹת Ec 2^{5} + 6 t.; sf. גַּנּוֹתֵיכֶם Am 4^{9}; *garden, orchard,* Am 4^{9} (|| כֶּרֶם, תְּאֵנָה, זַיִת), 9^{14} (fruit-garden; || כְּרָמִים), Je 29$^{5.28}$ Ec 2^{5} (|| פַּרְדֵּס), גִּנַּת אֱגוֹז Ct 6^{11} nut-garden; cf. גִּנַּת־בִּיתָן Est 1^{5} 7$^{7.8}$; in simile, of prosperous Isr. Nu 24^{6} (poem in JE; ג׳ עֲלֵי נָהָר), of chastised Isr. Is 1^{30} (ג׳ אשר מים אין לָהּ), of Yahweh's blessing Is 61^{11}; in Jb 8^{16} עַל־גַּנָּתוֹ in fig. of prosperity of wicked, as a luxuriant plant; gardens as places of idolatrous worship Is 1^{29} (|| אֵילִים), 65^{3} (|| לְבֵנִים), 66^{17} (i.e. groves).

1527 † גִּינַת **n.pr.m.** father of Tibni 1 K 16$^{21.22}$.

1599 † גִּנְּתוֹי Ne 12^{4} = following.

1599 † גִּנְּתוֹן **n.pr.m.** a priest among the returned exiles Ne 10^{7} 12^{16} cf. foregoing.

4043 † מָגֵן **n.m.**$^{1\ K\ 14,\ 27}$, & **f.** $^{1\ K\ 10,\ 17}$, **shield** (Ar. مِجَنّ, Aram. מְגִנָּא, ܡܓܢܐ) — מָגֵן Gn 15^{1} + 33 t. (also cstr. Dt 33^{29} Na 2^{4}); sf. מָגִנִּי ψ 7^{11} + 5 t.; מָגִנֵּנוּ ψ 33^{20} + 3 t.; מָגִנָּם ψ 115$^{9.10.11}$; pl. מָגִנִּים 1 K 10^{17} + 6 t.; מָגִנּוֹת 2 Ch 23^{9}; cstr. מָגִנֵּי 1 K 14^{26} + 4 t.; sf. מָגִנָּיו Jb 15^{26}; מָגִנֶּיהָ Ho 4^{18};—*shield, buckler,* carried by warrior for defence Ju 5^{8} 2 S 1$^{21.21}$ 2 K 19^{32} = Is 37^{33}, 1 Ch 5^{18} 14^{7} 17^{17} 23^{9} 26^{14} 32^{5} Ne 4^{10} ψ 76^{4} Je 46$^{3.9}$ Ez 23^{24} 38$^{4.5}$ 39^{9} Na 2^{4} Is 22^{6} cf. 21^{5} (anoint the shield, to make it slippery), so also ψ 35^{2} (where י׳ fig. as warrior); אִישׁ מָגֵן = armed man Pr 6^{11} 24^{34}; laid up for show, or as treasure 1 K 10$^{17.17}$ 14$^{26.27}$ (= 2 Ch 9$^{16.16}$ 12$^{9.10}$) 2 Ch 32^{27} cf. Ct 4^{4} Ez 27^{10}; of scales of crocodile (leviathan) אֲפִיקֵי מָגִנִּים Jb 41^{7}; fig. of wicked's defence against judgments of י׳, עֲבִי גַּבֵּי מָגִנָּיו Jb 15^{26}; fig. of king ψ 89^{19} (cf. Che); fig. of rulers of Ephraim Ho 4^{18}; fig. of rulers of earth ψ 47^{10}; fig. (very often) of י׳, as defence of his servants, ψ 3^{4} 7^{11} (rd. מָגִנִּי עָלַי אל׳ cf. Che crit. note) 18$^{3.31.36}$ (= 2 S 22$^{3.31.36}$) 28^{7} 33^{20} 59^{12} 84$^{10.12}$ 115$^{9.10.11}$ 119^{114} 144^{2} Pr 2^{7} 30^{5}, and v. esp. Gn 15^{1} (E).

† [מְגִנָּה] **n.f. covering,** מְגִנַּת־לֵב La 3^{65} 4044
covering of heart, i.e. a hard shell about the heart = *obstinacy,* so Ges (cf. Qor 6^{25} وَجَعَلْنَا عَلَىٰ قُلُوبِهِمْ أَكِنَّةً) RV; or, *covering of the understanding, blindness of heart,* so Ew Ke Näg Che.

† [מִגֵּן] **vb.** only **Pi. deliver up, deliver** 4042
(denom. fr. מָגֵן; on connex. of meanings cf. סָגַר) —*Pf.* מִגֵּן Gn 14^{20}; *Impf.* 3 fs. sf. תְּמַגְּנֶךָּ Pr 4^{9} אֲמַגֶּנְךָ Ho 11^{8};—*deliver up* to adversary Gn 14^{20} Ho 11^{8} + Is 64^{6} 𝔊 𝔖 𝔗 Ew Che al. וַתְּמַגְּנֵנוּ for MT וַתְּמוּגֵנוּ; also *deliver, give,* c. acc. & sf. of indirect obj. Pr 4^{9}.

† גָּעָה **vb. low** (of cattle) (NH *id.,* Aram. 1600
גְּעָא, ܓܥܐ)—יִגְעֶה־שּׁוֹר Jb 6^{5}; הָלֹךְ וְגָעוֹ 1 S 6^{12}.

† [גֹּעָה] **n.pr.loc.** close to Jerusalem גֹּעָתָה 1601
Je 31^{39};—site unknown.

† [גָּעַל] **vb. abhor, loathe** (NH געל Nithpa. 1602
be fouled, Hiph. *rinse out* with hot water; גְּעִילָה *rejection;* Aram. געל Ithpe. *be fouled, soiled*)—**Qal** *Pf.* 3 fs. גָּעֲלָה Lv 26^{43} Je 14^{19}, וְגָעֲלָה cons. Lv 26^{30}; גְּעַלְתִּים Lv 26^{44}; גָּעֲלוּ Ez 16^{45}; *Impf.* 3 fs. תִּגְעַל Lv 26$^{11.15}$; *Pt.* f. גֹּעֶלֶת Ez 16^{45};—*abhor, loathe,* (usually c. acc.), Yahweh, his people Lv 26$^{11.30.44}$ (H) Je 14^{19} (c. בְּ); the people, Yahweh's statutes, Lv 26$^{15.43}$ (H); Ez 16$^{45.45}$ women their husbands (fig., in proph. ag. Jerusalem). **Niph.** נִגְעַל מָגֵן גִּבּוֹרִים 2 S 1^{21} *the shield of heroes was defiled* RVm VB Kirkp. but < *is rejected, cast away* (*with loathing*) Dr, cf. Klo; 𝔊 προσωχθίσθη. **Hiph.** *Impf.* שׁוֹרוֹ עִבַּר וְלֹא יַגְעִל Jb 21^{10}; *and doth not cause,* or *allow,* (the cow) *to reject as loathesome* Ra De, cf. Di^{1}; Di^{2}, however, of bull, *cast away* (semen), or *shew aversion.*

1604 †גֹּ֫עַל **n.m.** loathing, בְּגֹעַל נַפְשֵׁךְ Ez 16^{5}.

1603 †גַּ֫עַל **n.pr.m.** appar. a Canaanite, son of עֶבֶד (but cf. VB) Ju 9$^{26.28.30.31.35.36.37.39.41}$.

1605 †גָּעַר **vb. rebuke** (Aram. גְּעַר, ܓܥܰܪ id., Eth. ገዐረ: *cry out*, Sab. יגער n.pr., Sab. Denkm. p. 29.30)—Is 17^{13}; גָּעַרְתָּ ψ 9^{6} + 2 t., etc.; *Impf.* יִגְעַר Zc 3^{2} + 3 t., תִּגְעֲרוּ Ru 2^{16}; *Imv.* גְּעַר ψ 68^{31}; *Inf.* מִגְּעָר־ Is 54^{9}; *Pt.* גּוֹעֵר Na 1^{4}, גֹּעֵר Mal 2^{3};—c. בְּ except ψ 9^{6} 68^{31} 119^{21} Mal 2^{3} where acc.;—**1.** *rebuke*, father his son Gn 37^{10} (E), reapers Ruth Ru 2^{16}, priest Jeremiah Je 29^{27}. **2.** of God rebuking nations ψ 9^{6} Is 17^{13}, proud ψ 119^{21}, Satan Zc 3$^{2.2}$, חית קנה ψ 68^{31}, בָּאֹכֵל (the devouring swarm of locusts, restraining them) Mal 3^{11}, the sea drying it up ψ 106^{9} Na 1^{4}, Zion Is 54^{9}; הַזֶּרַע the *seed* (prevent the usual harvest) Mal 2^{3} (𝔊 Aq 𝔙 הַזְּרֹעַ, *the arm*, viz., of priests, that they may not extend it to bless).

1606 †גְּעָרָה **n.f. rebuke**—Pr 13^{1} + 2 t.; גַּעֲרַת Ec 7^{5} + 5 t.; sf. גַּעֲרָתְךָ ψ 18^{16} + (sfs. 6 t.);—**1.** of man Pr 13$^{1.8}$ 17^{10} Ec 7^{5} Is 30$^{17.17}$. **2.** of God Jb 26^{11} ψ 18^{16} (=2 S 22^{16}) 76^{7} 80^{17} 104^{7} Is 50^{2} 51^{20} 66^{15}.

4045 †מִגְעֶ֫רֶת **n.f. rebuke** Dt 28^{20}.

1607 †[גָּעַשׁ] **vb. shake, quake** (NH *id.*)—**Qal** *Impf.* וַתִּגְעַשׁ ψ 18^{8a} = 2 S 22^{8a} Kt (Qr Hithp.);—*quake* of earth at theoph., ψ 18^{8} = 2 S 22^{8} (rd. Kt; ‖ רעשׁ). **Pu.** *Impf. be shaken up, convulsed* יְגֹעֲשׁוּ־עָם Jb 34^{20} *a people are convulsed.* **Hithp.** *shake back and forth, toss* or *reel to and fro* וַיִּתְגָּעַשׁ Qr 2 S 22^{8a} (< Kt **Qal**); יִתְגָּעֲשׁוּ Je 46^{7}, וַיִּתְגָּעֲשׁוּ ψ 18^{8b} + 2 t.;—of mountains ψ 18^{8b} = 2 S 22^{8b}; of waves of sea, Je 5^{22}; of waters of Nile Je 46^{7} (cf. v^{8}). **Hithpo.** *Pf.* וְהִתְגֹּעֲשׁוּ consec. Je 25^{16}; *Impf.* יִתְגֹּעֲשׁוּ Je 46^{8}; *id.* of waters of Nile Je 46^{8}; of drunken men, *reel to and fro*, Je 25^{16} (fig. of nations confounded by י׳).

1608 †[גַּ֫עַשׁ] **n.pr.loc.** הַר־גָּ֑עַשׁ Jos 24^{30} Ju 2^{9} mt. in Ephraim, S. of תִּמְנַת־סֶרַח (חֶרֶס) q. v.; נַחֲלֵי גָ֑עַשׁ 2 S 23^{30} = 1 Ch 11^{32} of ravines thereon, or near by.

1609 †גַּעְתָּם **n.pr.m.** a chief of Edom, son of Eliphaz Gn 36$^{11.16}$ 1 Ch 1^{36}.

1610 גַּף v. sub גפף. below

גפן (√ of following; meaning ?).

1612 †גֶּ֫פֶן **n.f.** $^{Ju\ 9,\ 13+}$ (**m.** only Ho 10^{1}, perh. infl. of יִשְׂרָאֵל, 2 K 4^{39}) **vine** (NH *id.*, Ar. جَفْنٌ (Yemen), As. *gapnu*, cf. Zehnpfund$^{BAS\ i.\ 633}$; Aram. גּוּפְנָא, גֻּפְנָא, ܓܽܘܦܢܳܐ, pl. ܓܽܘܦ̈ܢܶܐ)—ג׳ Gn 40^{9} + 38 t. (also cstr., as Nu 6^{4} Dt 32^{32} Is 16$^{8.9}$), גָּ֑פֶן Ju 9^{12} + 2 t.; *sf.* גַּפְנִי Jo 1^{7}, גַּפְנְךָ Je 5^{17}, גַּפְנוֹ 1 K 5^{5} + 3 t., גַּפְנָהּ Ho 2^{14}, גַּפְנָם Dt 32^{32} + 2 t.; pl. גְּפָנִים Ct 2^{13} Hb 3^{17}—*vine* (always grape-bearing exc. 2 K 4^{39}) Gn 40$^{9.10}$ (in dream) 49^{11} Nu 20^{5} Dt 8^{8} Ju 9$^{12.13}$ (in allegory) 1 K 5^{5} 2 K 18^{31} = Is 36^{16}, ψ 78^{47} 105^{33} Ct 2^{13} 6^{11} 7^{13} Is 7^{23} 24^{7} 32^{12} Je 5^{17} 8^{13} Ho 2^{14} Jo 1$^{7.12}$ 2^{22} Mi 4^{4} Hb 3^{17} Hg 2^{19} Zc 2^{10} 8^{12} Mal 3^{11}; גֶּפֶן שָׂדֶה a vine bearing poisonous gourds 2 K 4^{39}; גֶּפֶן הַיַּיִן Nu 6^{4} (cf. Gn 40^{10} Ju 9^{13}) Ju 13^{14}; אֶשְׁכְּלוֹת הַגֶּפֶן Ct 8^{9}; עֵץ הַגֶּפֶן Ez 15$^{2.6}$; in simile of stars fading away at Yahweh's judgment Is 34^{4}; in simile of wicked losing early promise Jb 15^{33}; in simile of wife ψ 128^{3}; fig. of Israel ψ 80$^{9.15}$ Ez 17$^{6.6.7.8}$ Ho 10^{1} cf. Ez 19^{10}, Je 2^{21} 6^{9}; also Ho 14^{8}; fig. of Israel as easily destroyed Ez 15$^{2.6}$; fig. of godless enemies of Israel Dt 32^{32} cf. Di; גֶּפֶן שִׂבְמָה fig. for prosperity of Moab Is 16$^{8.9}$ Je 48^{32}.—On the vine in Syria cf. Anderlind$^{ZPV\ 1888,\ 160\ ff.}$

גפף (√ of foll.; cf. Syr. ܓܦܦ in deriv., ܓܦܝܦܳܐ *curved, convex;* also Ar. جَفْجَفٌ both *hilly country* and *depression*, Frey.)

†[גַּף] **n.m. body, self, height, elevation** 1610
(cf. NH גּוּף) — sg. sf. גַּפּוֹ Ex 21$^{3.3.4}$; pl. cstr. גַּפֵּי Pr 9^{3};—**1.** *body, self*, only in phr. יָבֹא (יֵצֵא) בְּגַפּוֹ *he shall come in* (*go out*) *by himself* (with his body) Ex 21$^{3.3.4}$; in law of slave (cf. Di). **2.** *height, elevation* עַל־גַּפֵּי מְרֹמֵי קָ֑רֶת Pr 9^{3}.

†גֹּ֫פֶר **n.[m.] gopher**, only in עֲצֵי־גֹפֶר Gn 6^{14} 1613
(P), wood of which the ark was made (word dub.; Thes comp. כֹּפֶר & so Rob Ges (hence '*pitch-wood*, resinous wood'), cf. Di; Lag Semitica i. 64; Symmict. ii. 93, BN 217 ff. thinks word not original, but inferred from גפרית, and substituted here for גפרית by copyist, or editor. Cf. following).

†גָּפְרִית **n.f. brimstone** (Aram. גּוּפְרִיתָא, 1614
also כבריתא, כובריתא, ܟܶܒܪܺܝܬܳܐ, ܟܽܘܒܪܺܝܬܳܐ; Ar. كِبْرِيت (certainly foreign wd.); der. from (כֹּפֶר), גֹּפֶר by Thes RobGes, cf. Di Gn 6^{14}; i.e. *pitch*, and then other combustibles, esp. *sulphur;* Lag$^{l.\ c.}$ thinks fr. Bactr. *vohûkereti*)—גָּפְרִית Gn 19^{24} + 6 t.—*brimstone*, after הִמְטִיר Gn 19^{24} (J), fig. of judgment ψ 11^{6} Ez 38^{22} (in all ‖ אֵשׁ etc.), cf. also Jb 18^{15} Is 34^{9}, & Dt 29^{22}; נַחַל ג׳ simile for the destroying breath of י׳ Is 30^{33}.

1616 גֵּר v. sub I. גור. p. 158

1615 גֵּר v. sub גיר. p. 162

1617 † גֵּרָא **n.pr.m.** (Ph. גרא) son of Benjamin Gn 46^{21} (lacking Nu 26^{38-40}); son of Bela‘, & grandson of Benj., acc. to 1 Ch $8^{3.5}$ cf. v^{7}; designation of a Benjamite family or clan; hence Ehud called בֶּן־הַגֵּרָא Ju 3^{15}, & so Shimei, 2 S 16^{5} $19^{17.19}$ 1 K 2^{8}.

גרב (√ of foll.; Ar. جَرِبَ, Aram. ܓܪܒ (*have the scab* etc.), are appar. denom.)

1618 † גָּרָב **n.[m.] itch, scab** (Ar. جَرَبٌ, Aram. גַּרְבָּא, ܓܰܪܒܳܐ, As. *garabu* Dl § 162)—גָּרָב Lv 21^{20} 22^{22} Dt 28^{27}.

1619 † גָּרֵב **1. n.pr.m.** (cf. Palm. n.pr.m. גריבא Vog 141) one of David's heroes 2 S 23^{38} = 1 Ch 11^{40}. **2. n.pr.loc.** (cf. Sab. n.pr.loc. גרבם Hal No. 379, 382) only in גִּבְעַת גָּרֵב Je 31^{39} *hill of Gareb*, appar. close to Jerusalem on the SW. cf. Gf; v. also Hi Che.

1620-21 גַּרְגַּר, גַּרְגְּרוֹת v. sub גרר. p. 176

1622 † גִּרְגָּשִׁי **adj.gent.** only הַגִּ׳ as n.pr.coll.; 'begotten' by Canaan Gn 10^{16} = 1 Ch 1^{14}; in list of Canaanitish peoples displaced by Isr.; territ. unknown; Gn 15^{21} Dt 7^{1} Jos 3^{10} 24^{11} Ne 9^{8}; cf. Gn 10^{16} 1 Ch 1^{14} supr. (Hex only JED).

1623 † [גָּרַד] **vb. scrape, scratch** (NH *id.*, Aram. גְּרַד, ܓܪܰܕ & Ph. מגרדם *flesh-scrapers* CIS 338.4; cf. also Ar. جَرَدَ *peel* or *strip off* bark, *shave* hair fr. a hide etc.)—**Hithp.** *Inf.* לְהִתְגָּרֵד *scrape one's self* Jb 2^{8}.

1624 † [גָּרָה] **vb.** only **Pi. stir up strife, Hithp. engage in strife** (cf. NH Pi. *stir up, excite, against* (בְּ) Hithp.; Aram. Pa. גָּרֵא, ܓܰܪܺܝ; esp. As. *garû*, Qal *attack, be at war with, garû, girû, enemy*, etc. Asrb Annals iv. 49, 50 (KB ii. 190) also SASmith Asrb. i. ii. Gloss.; Ar. جَرَى is *run*, esp. of water, *flow*, etc.)—**Pi.** *Impf.* 3 ms. יְגָרֶה Pr 15^{18} 28^{25} 29^{22}, all c. obj. מָדוֹן *excite, stir up, strife.*—On גָּרָה Dt 14^{8} v. I. גֵּרָה sub גרר. **Hithp.** *Pf.* 2 fs. הִתְגָּרִית Je 50^{24}; *Impf.* 3 ms. יִתְגָּרֶה Dn 11^{25}, וְיִתְגָּרֶו v^{10}; 2 ms. תִּתְגָּרֶה 2 K 14^{19} 2 Ch 25^{19}; juss. apoc. תִּתְגָּר Dt $2^{9.19}$; 3 mpl. יִתְגָּרוּ Pr 28^{4} Dn 11^{10}, cf. Dn 11^{10} Kt., v. supr.; 2 mpl. תִּתְגָּרוּ Dt 2^{5} (juss.); *Imv.* ms. הִתְגָּר Dt 2^{24};—**1.** *excite oneself* against (בְּ pers.), *engage in strife* with, lit. Dt $2^{5.19}$, 2 K 14^{19} = 2 Ch 25^{19} (sq. בְּרָעָה—רעה; personif. as challenged opponent); also + acc. of manner, מִלְחָמָה Dt $2^{9.24}$; fig. וְשֹׁמְרֵי תוֹרָה יִתְגָּרוּ בָם Pr 28^{4} *while they that keep the law are at strife with them*, i.e. with those that forsake it. **2.** abs., *excite oneself* (against foe), *wage war*, only Dn 11: יִתְגָּרוּ וְאָסְפוּ הֲמוֹן חֲיָלִים רַבִּים v^{10} *they shall wage war*, etc.; וְיָשֹׁב וְיִתְגָּרֶו עַד־מָעֻזֹּה v^{10} *and he shall return and war, even to his stronghold;* v^{25} sq. בְּחַיִל גָּדוֹל + לַמִּלְחָמָה (instr.)

† גָּרוֹן **n.m.** ψ 69, 4 **neck, throat** (connexion 1627
with above √dub.; Thes RobGes (cf. MV) from גרה in (assumed) sense of גרר of a *dragging, scraping* sound; cf. מְגֵרָה; yet √perh. גרן q.v.; Ar. جِرَانٌ (sub جَرَنَ Frey Lane) *front part of neck* of camel, etc.)—ג׳ Is 3^{16} 58^{1}; sf. גְּרוֹנִי ψ 69^{4}; גְּרוֹנֵךְ Ez 16^{11} + Je 2^{25} Qr (Kt גורנך); גְּרוֹנָם ψ 115^{7} 149^{6}, גְּרֹנָם ψ 5^{10};—*throat;* **1.** of the visible exterior (front) of throat, *neck* נְטוּוֹת ג׳ Is 3^{16} *outstretched of neck* (= with outstretched neck); וְרָבִיד עַל־גְּרוֹנֵךְ Ez 41^{19} *and a chain upon thy neck.* **2.** *throat*, as capable of thirst Je 2^{25}; as organ of speech קְרָא בְגָרוֹן Is 58^{1} (‖ הָרֵם קוֹלֶךָ), לֹא יֶהְגּוּ בִּג׳ ψ 115^{7}; also רוֹמְמוֹת אֵל בִּגְרוֹנָם ψ 149^{6} *high songs to God (be) in their throat;* cf. נִחַר גְּרוֹנִי ψ 69^{4} *my throat is parched* (‖ יָגַעְתִּי בְקָרְאִי); so also קֶבֶר־פָּתוּחַ גְּרֹנָם ψ 5^{10} *their throat is an opened sepulchre.*

† [תִּגְרָה] **n.f. contention, strife, hostility** 8409
(cf. Aram. תִּגְרָא, oft. 𝔗; v. Thes; תִּגְרָה NHWB & Fl in ChWB ii. 581)—only cstr. sg. מִתִּגְרַת יָדְךָ ψ 39^{11} *from* (i.e. *through*) *the hostility of thy hand I am consumed.*

I. גֵּרָה, II. גֵּרָה v. sub גרר. p. 176 1625-26

גֵּרוּת v. sub I. גור. p. 158 1628

† [גָּרַז] **vb. cut, cut off** (Ar. جَرَزَ *cut, cut* 1629
off, exterminate)—**Niph.** *Pf.* נִגְרַזְתִּי ψ 31^{23} = destroyed out of Yahweh's sight.

† גַּרְזֶן **n.m.** Is 10, 15 **axe** (*pick, pick-axe*, 3 t. 1631
in SI; on format. cf. Sta 294 a Ges § 85, xi. 54)—Dt 19^{5} 20^{19} Is 10^{15} 1 K 6^{7} (Co conj. also Ez 31^{11}).

† גִּרְזִי Kt, גִּזְרִי (q.v.) Qr **adj.gent.** 1 S 27^{8}. 1511

† גְּרִזִּים **n.pr.loc.** mt. in N. Israel, S. of 1630
Sichem (Nabulus), opp. *Ebal* (עֵיבָל), which was on N.; only הַר ג׳ Dt 11^{29} 27^{12} Jos 8^{33} Ju 9^{7}; mod. *Jebel eṭ-Ṭôr* Rob BR ii. 274 ff. Bd Pal 220, 222.

גרטל (possibly quadrilit. √, whence foll. c. א prosthet. Cf. however infr.)

† [אֲגַרְטָל] **n.m.** a kind of vessel, **basin** 105
or **basket** (?; others *basket-like, basket-shaped*

vessel); only pl. cstr. אֲגַרְטְלֵי זָהָב, & א׳ כֶסֶף, both Ezr 1^{9}, denoting vessels from temple at Jerus. restored by Cyrus. (Etym. & mng. dub. cf. supr.; A 𝔊L Codd. 𝔊 ψυκτῆρες, *wine-coolers;* B om.; now commonly compared with Aram. קַרְטָלִיתָא Levy NHWB$^{iv. 376}$, ܩܪܛܠܐ, Ar. قِرْطَلَّة, قِرْطَالَة, supposed to be loan-word fr. Hellenist. Gk. κάρταλος, κάρταλλος (e.g. 𝔊 2 K 10^{7}, Heb. דּוּדִים), all = *basket, fruit-basket,* etc., *canistrum* (so MV BeRy SS); but κάρταλλος itself is possibly a Pers. or Shemit. loan-word; cf. esp. Frä$^{77 f.}$; further conject. in Thes BeRy.)

גרל (cf. Ar. جَرَلٌ, pl. أَجْرَالٌ *stones,* or *stony place* planted with trees; جَرِلٌ *stony;* جَرْوَلٌ, جُرَوِلٌ *stony ground, stones;* hence foll., because stones were used in casting lots; cf. Gk. ψῆφος *pebble, vote;* κύαμος *bean, lot*).

1486 **גּוֹרָל**$_{77}$ **n.m.** $^{Lv\ 16,8}$ & (†Jos 21^{10}, but v. infr.) **f. lot,** (NH *id.* & denom. Hiph. הִגְרִיל *cast lots*)—abs. ג׳ Jos 16^{1} + 51 t.; cstr. גּוֹרַל Jos 18^{11} + 2 t., גֹּרַל Nu 36^{3}; sf. גּוֹרָלִי ψ 16^{5}, גֹּרָלִי Ju 1^{3}, גּוֹרָלְךָ Pr 1^{14}, גֹּרָלְךָ Dn 12^{13}, גּוֹרָלֶךְ Ju 1^{3}, גּוֹרָלֵךְ Je 13^{25} Is 57^{6}, גּוֹרָלוֹ 1 Ch 26^{14}, גּוֹרָלָם Jos 18^{11} + 2 t.; pl. גּוֹרָלוֹת Jon 1^{7} + 8 t., גֹּרָלוֹת Lv 16^{8};—*a lot* cast for the decision of questions Pr 18^{18}, designation of persons, etc., for service or punishment, assignment of property, etc.; prob. stones put into the bosom-fold of a garment, Pr 16^{33} (בַּחֵיק יוּטַל אֶת־הַגּ׳), or into a vessel, and shaken until one springs out (יָצָא, עָלָה, or—late—נָפַל); this was regarded originally as divine decision (cf. on Urim & Thummim p. 22, supr.); for the agent, the usual verbs are נָתַן, יָרָה, הִשְׁלִיךְ, and הִפִּיל. Particularly:—**1.** *lot* for dividing land, esp. that which Joshua cast at Shiloh לִפְנֵי י׳ Jos 18^{6} (יָרָה) v$^{8.10}$ (both הִשְׁלִיךְ; all three sq. לְ of pers. for whom; all JE); cf. 19^{51} (P); so of lot coming up, or forth, עָלָה Jos 18^{11} (cstr.; P), also sq. לְ pers. 19^{10} (P), & foll. c. יָצָא 16^{1} (JE), Nu 33^{54} Jos 19$^{1.17.24.32.40}$ 21^{4} (all P); *be divided by lot* יֵחָלֵק בְּג׳ Nu 26^{55}, or *according to lot* עַל־פִּי הַגּ׳ תֵּחָלֵק v^{56}; *apportion by lot* הִתְנַחֲלוּ בְּג׳ 33^{54} 34^{13}, נִחַל בְּג׳ Jos 19^{51}; *give by lot* נָתַן בְּג׳ Nu 36^{2} Jos 21^{8} (all P) 1 Ch 6^{50}; *have by lot* הָיָה לְ׳ בַּגּ׳ Jos 21^{4}, & (היה om.) v$^{5.6}$ (all P) cf. 1 Ch 6$^{46.48}$; also Jos 21^{10} (P; הַגּ׳ רִאשֹׁנָה, only here f.; 𝔊—not 𝔊L—om. ראישנה, & so) ‖ 1 Ch 6^{39}; cf. further Is 34^{17} (הִפִּיל לְ). **2.** *lot* for assigning to service, duty or punishment, **a.** concerning the goats on day of atonement, Lv 16^{8} (נָתַן עַל) v$^{8.8}$ (sq. לְ); cf. v$^{9.10}$ (עָלָה עַל; all P). **b.** assigning priests to their courses, singers, musicians & porters to their duties, by lot חִלֵּק בְּג׳ 1 Ch 24^{5}; הִפִּיל ג׳ v^{31} 25^{8} 26^{13} (sq. לְ of position) v^{14}; of lot coming forth (יָצָא לְ pers.) 24^{7} (cf. v$^{7-18}$) 25^{9} (cf. v$^{9-31}$) 26^{14} cf. וַיֵּצֵא גוֹרָלוֹ v^{14}. **c.** *cast lots* for dwelling in Jerus. (הִפִּיל ג׳) Ne 11^{1} (sq. inf.) **d.** for supplying wood for altar-fire Ne 10^{35} (הִפִּיל עַל); here belongs prob. also **e.** Ju 20^{9} עָלֶיהָ בְּג׳, ref. to v^{10} (determining who shall go up, and who supply provision) 𝔊 ἀναβησόμεθα ἐπ᾽ αὐτὴν ἐν κλήρῳ so Stu (insert perh. נעלה), cf. AV RV, Bu$^{RS\ 151}$ (who rds. נַפִּילָה בְּג׳); > 𝔖 Be Ke who ref. ג׳ here to division of land of captured city. **f.** to determine guilty persons Jon 1$^{7.7}$ (both הִפִּיל) v^{17} (נָפַל עַל); so appar. Ez 24^{6} of inhab. of Jerus. under fig. of flesh in pot לֹא־נָפַל עָלֶיהָ ג׳ *no lot is fallen over it,* i.e. no discrimination is made, destruction is to include the whole city; (cf. also Jos 7$^{14 ff.}$ 1 S 14$^{41 ff.}$ where divine agency in detection is prominent but word גּוֹרָל not used). **g.** in allotting slaves Jo 4^{3} אֶל־עַמִּי יַדּוּ ג׳; Na 3^{10} (יַדּוּ עַל); so Ob^{11} וְעַל־יְרוּשָׁלַםִ יַדּוּ ג׳, —all c. vb. ידד q.v. **h.** in distributing plundered garments ψ 22^{19} (הִפִּיל עַל). **i.** to determine favourable day for a scheme, הִפִּיל Est 3^{7} (לִפְנֵי הָמָן) 9^{24} (sq. inf.; v. also פּוּר). **3.** *thing assigned, apportioned, allotted* esp. of land assigned by lot, *allotment* Jos 15^{1} 17^{1} 21^{38} (all P), 17$^{14.17}$ = *portion, share* (‖ נַחֲלָה; JE); cf. גֹּרַל נַחֲלָתֵנוּ Nu 36^{3} (P), גּוֹרַל נַחֲלָתָם Jos 14^{2} (P; but perh. rd. abs. גּוֹרָל cf. Di); also גְּבוּל גּוֹרָלָם 18^{11} (P) *the boundary of their allotment;* עָרֵי גוֹרָלָם 21^{20} (P); v. further Ju 1$^{3.3}$; so prob. Mi 2^{5} הִשְׁלִיךְ חֶבֶל בְּג׳ (Hi Che; cf. also Ew); ψ 125^{3}, land, exposed to oppressive exaction; also fig. of י׳ as portion, allotment of his people ψ 16^{5} (so Che, & on תָּמִיד for תּוֹמִיךְ cf. his crit. n.; v. also Ew; otherwise De al.;—‖ מְנָת חֶלְקִי); on the other hand, of idols Is 57^{6} (‖ חֵלֶק); also עֲמֹד לְג׳ Dn 12^{13}, of *allotted portion, share,* in the Messianic consummation; more generally, one's *portion, lot, fortune* גּוֹרָלְךָ תַּפִּיל בְּתוֹכֵנוּ Pr 1^{14} *cast thy fortune into the midst of us, in with us* (‖ כִּיס אֶחָד יִהְיֶה לְכֻלָּנוּ). **4.** *portion = recompence, retribution* Is 17^{14} (‖ חֵלֶק), Je 13^{25} (‖ מְנָת מִדַּיִךְ), both implying divine agency.

1632 †[גְּרֹל] **adj.** גְּרָל־חֵמָה Pr 19[19] Kt; < Qr גְּדָל־ cf. Vrss, AV RV Now Str al.

1633 I. [גָּרַם] **vb. lay aside, leave, save** (NH גָּרַם is *shorten, occasion, bring about, to pass,* Aram. גְּרַם Pa. *occasion, bring about,* ܓܪܡ *abscidit, decrevit,* cf. also Ar. جَرَمَ *cut off* (fruit), *shear* (sheep);—on connexion of ideas v. Fl NHWB[i. 437]) **Qal** *Pf.* 3 pl. לֹא גָֽרְמוּ לַבֹּקֶר Zp 3[3] *they have left nothing for the morrow,* in fig. of cruel judges (dub.: al. fr. II. [גָּרַם], v. Kau[AT] Dr).

1634 †גֶּ֫רֶם **n.[m.] bone, strength, self** (?) (Ar. جِرْمٌ *body,* Aram. גְּרַם, ܓܪܡܐ *bone, self*)—abs. גָּ֑רֶם Gn 49[14] + 2 t.; cstr. גֶּ֫רֶם 2 K 9[13]; sf. גְּרָמָיו Jb 40[18];—**1.** *bone* Pr 17[22] (coll.) 25[15]; of behemoth (hippopot.) Jb 40[18] (‖עצם q.v.) **2.** *strength* Gn 49[14] חֲמֹר גָּ֑רֶם *strong ass* (lit. *bony,* so VB). **3.** *self* (cf. עצם), 2 K 9[13] גֶּ֫רֶם הַמַּעֲלוֹת so Ges Ew Ke, but text dub., v. conjectures in Klo.

1633 †II. [גָּרַם] **vb. denom. break bones, break,**—**Pi.** *Impf.* וְעַצְמֹתֵיהֶם יְגָרֵם Nu 24[8] (JE); but also וְאֶת־חֲרָשֶׂיהָ תְּגָרֵמִי Ez 23[34] (yet on txt. v. Co.)

1636 †גַּרְמִי **adj. gent.** c. art. 1 Ch 4[19].

גרן (✓of foll.; ? cf. Ar. جَرَنَ, *become accustomed, worn smooth* (of skin, garment, etc.); also *grind grain vehemently;* vid. further جَرِينٌ *what one has ground,* of grain; & *place in which dates are dried*=مِجْرَنٌ).

1637 †גֹּ֫רֶן **n.m. threshing-floor** (cf. further vulg. Ar. جُرْنٌ *stone basin, trough, mortar,* etc. Dozy Lane, v. Moḥiṭ[243 b. 7])—גֹּרֶן Gn 50[10] + 27 t. (cstr. e.g. Gn 50[10.11] 2 S 6[6]); גָּֽרְנָה: Mi 4[12]; sf. גָּרְנִי Is 21[10]; גָּרְנְךָ Dt 15[14] 16[13]; pl. הַגֳּרָנוֹת 1 S 23[1], הַגְּרָנוֹת Jo 2[24]; cstr. גָּרְנוֹת Ho 9[1]—**threshing-floor,** (on form v. Rob[BR i. 550] cf. Fl NHWB[i. 437]) Gn 50[10.11] (גֹ׳ האטד) Nu 18[27] (דָּגָן מִן־הגֹ׳) Dt 15[14] 16[13] Ju 6[37] Ru 3[2] (הוּא זֹרֶה גֹ׳ הַשְּׂעֹרִים) v[3.6.14] 2 S 6[6] 24[16.18.21.24] 1 Ch 13[9] 21[15.18.21.22.28] 2 Ch 3[1] Ho 9[1] (גֹ׳ דָּגָן) v[2] Mi 4[12] Jb 39[12] cf. Di; תְּרוּמַת גֹ׳ Nu 15[20]; תְּבוּאַת גֹ׳ Nu 18[30]; of these, three may be n.pr.loc.:—גֹּרֶן הָאָטָד Gn 50[10.11]; גֹּרֶן נָכוֹן 2 S 6[6] (cf. We Dr)=גֹּרֶן כִּידֹן 1 Ch 13[9]; place of storing corn, etc. 1 S 23[1] 2 K 6[27] Jo 2[24]; open place at city-gate גֹּרֶן פֶּתַח שַׁעַר שֹׁמְרוֹן 1 K 22[10]=2 Ch 18[9], where kings of Isr. & Jud. sat (but this peculiar & text dub.; 𝔊 (in K) ἔνοπλοι; We om.; 𝔖 Th Be בְּרֻדִּים, agreeing with בְּגָדִים preceding; yet this elsewh. in Heb. only of animals); in simile of daughter of Babylon, Je 51[33] (trodden smooth) cf. fig. of Israel בֶּן־גָּרְנִי ‖ מְדֻשָׁתִי Is 21[10]; ....מִגֹּ׳ Ho 13[3].

גָּרוֹן, גָּרֹן v. sub גרה. p. 173 1627

גָּרַס **vb.** v. sub גרשׂ. p. 176 1638

†[גָּרַע] **vb. diminish, restrain, withdraw** (NH *id.,* Aram. גְּרַע, ܓܪܥ *shave head,* etc.; cf. جَرِعَ *swallow*)—**Qal** *Impf.* יִגְרַע Jb 36[7], יִגָּרַע Ex 21[10]; 2 ms. תִּגְרַע Dt 13[1] + 3 t.; אֶגְרַע Ez 5[11] (but cf. *infr.*), וָאֶגְרַע Ez 16[27]; תִּגְרְעוּ Ex 5[8] + 2 t.; *Inf.* לִגְרֹעַ Ec 3[14]; *Pt.* גְּרוּעָה Is 15[2] (so Baer; v.d.H. גְּדוּעָה v. גדע), גְּרֻעָה Je 48[37];—**1.** *diminish,* usually sq. מִן Ex 5[8.19] (the tale of bricks), Dt 4[2] 13[1] (in both, word of י׳; opp. הוסיף) cf. Ec 3[14], and also Je 26[2] (c. acc.); c. acc. also Ex 21[10] (food etc.) cf. Ez 16[27]; *Pt. pass. diminished, clipped,* of beard, Je 48[37] and Is 15[2] (so Baer, rightly, cf. his note and **v.** גדע). **2.** *restrain* Jb 15[4] (c. acc. שִׂיחָה meditation, devotion), Jb 15[8] (c. acc. חָכְמָה, sq. אֵלֶיךָ, i. e. *unto, for thyself,* monopolize; De Di Da render *draw unto thyself,* appropriate; Schult. comp. Ar. *swallow,* cf. Ew *saugst zu dir ein Weisheit*). **3.** *withdraw* Jb 36[7] (obj. עַיִן, *eye,* sq. מִן); Ez 5[11] absol. (si vera l.); Co. reads אֶתְגָּרֶה, for אֶגְרַע, on intern. grounds; others: *withdraw* (thy needs) Sm (cf. 16[27]); *withdraw* (mine eye) Ges Ke. **Niph.** *Pf.* consec. וְנִגְרַע Lv 27[18]; וְנִגְרְעָה Nu 36[3]; *Impf.* יִגָּרַע Nu 27[4] 36[4], יִגָּרֵ֑עַ Nu 36[3]; 1 pl. נִגָּרַע Nu 9[7]; *Pt.* נִגְרָע Ex 5[11];—**1.** *be withdrawn* c. מִן Nu 36[3.3.4] (inheritance, נחלה); Nu 27[4] a name out of a family; Ex 5[11] (מֵעֲבֹדַתְכֶם דָּבָר); impers. Lv 27[18] (*abatement shall be made*). **2.** *be restrained* sq. inf. Nu 9[7]. **Pi.** *Impf.* יְגָרַע Jb 36[27] *withdraw = draw up* c. acc. נִטְפֵי־מָיִם cf. Di (on other hand, De al. *draw down, let down*).

†[מִגְרָעָה] **n.f. recess, rebatement** (RV), i. e. **ledge,** only pl., נָתַן מִגְרָעוֹת לבית 1 K 6[6]. 4052

†[גָּרַף] **vb. sweep away** (orig. *shovel* or 1640
scoop up, away, cf. NH *id.,* Ar. جَرَفَ; Aram. גְּרַף, ܓܪܦ, Eth. in deriv.)—גְּרָפָם (נַחַל קִישׁוֹן) Ju 5[21].

†[אֶגְרֹף] **n.[m.] fist** (𝔊 πυγμή, so 𝔙; but 106
𝔗 *club, staff* (?), & so SS, cf. esp. Ex 21[18];—NH אֶגְרוֹף)—וְהִכָּה אִישׁ אֶת־רֵעֵהוּ בְּאֶבֶן אוֹ בְאֶגְרֹף Ex 21[18]; (cstr.) לְהַכּוֹת בְּאֶגְרֹף רֶ֑שַׁע Is 58[4].

†[מַגְרֵפָה] **n.f. shovel** (NH *id.;* Aram. 4053
מַגְרוֹפִיתָא; Ar. مِجْرَفَةٌ (v. Lane)) only pl. מֶגְרְפֹתֵיהֶם Jo 1[17] (Thes *clods,* after Jewish interpreters, so AV RV, cf. however Me[Joel 100 f.]; 𝔊 Me ארותיהם *their cribs,* of cattle; mng. of clause dubious).

1641 †[גָּרַר] **vb.** drag, drag away (NH *id.*, Ar. جَرَّ, Aram. גְּרַר, ܓܪܰ; As. *garâru*, *run*, Zim[BP 102]; etc.)—**Qal** *Impf.* sf. יְגֹרֵהוּ Hb 1^{15}, יְגוֹרֵם Pr 21^{7}—*drag away*, fishes in net, fig. Hb 1^{15} (Chaldeans, their opponents); violence, the wicked Pr 21^{7}. **Niph.** (rd. **Qal**? Sam. יָגוֹר cf. Di) *Impf.* יִגָּר Lv 11^{7} c. acc. cogn. גֵּרָה לֹא־יִגָּר = (the) *cud he cheweth not*, cf. also Dt 14^{8} Sam. 𝔊 (Di). **Po'al** *Pt.* (denom.; so NH Qal & Niph.) מְגֹרָרוֹת בַּמְּגֵרָה 1 K 7^{9} *sawn with the saw*. **Hithpo.** סַעַר מִתְגּוֹרֵר Je 30^{23} *a* (sweeping) *roaring whirlwind* (|| 23^{19} has מִתְחוֹלֵל). On יִתְגּוֹרָרוּ Ho 7^{14}, v. I. גור, גדד.

1625 †I. גֵּרָה **n.f.** cud (Ar. جِرَّةٌ, so called fr. sound of rumination?)—גֵּרָה Lv 11^{3} + 10t.—*cud*, only in legislation of clean and unclean animals, and almost always c. (ـִי, ـַת, ـָה) מַעֲלֵה Lv 11$^{3.4.4.5.6.26}$ (P) Dt 14$^{6.6.7}$; ג׳ יִגָּר (cf. גרר Niph.) Lv 11^{7}; Dt 14^{8} has גֵּרָה without vb., but read there as Lv 11^{7} (so Sam. 𝔊 Di).

1626 †II. גֵּרָה **n.f.** a weight, 20th part of shekel, **gerah** (As. *girû*, Zehnpfund [BAS i. 506])—גֵּרָה Ex 30^{13} + 4 t.—Only in definition of שֶׁקֶל, c. num. עֶשְׂרִים Ex 30^{13} Lv 27^{25} Nu 3^{47} 18^{16} Ez 45^{12}.

1620 †[גַּרְגַּר] **n.m.** berry (NH *id.*), גַּרְגְּרִים בְּרֹאשׁ אָמִיר Is 17^{6}.

1621 †גַּרְגְּרוֹת **n.f.pl.** neck (on format. cf. Ba [NB 204])—גַּרְגְּרֹתֶיךָ Pr 1^{9} 3^{22}, גַּרְגְּרוֹתֶךָ Pr 3^{3}, 6^{21}—always in fig., instruction of parents an ornament, a chain *upon neck* Pr 1^{9}, *bind them upon thy neck* 6^{21}; so of mercy & truth 3^{3}, cf. v^{22}.

4050 †מְגֵרָה **n.f.** saw (NH *id.*, perh. from its harsh *dragging* sound)—מְגֵרָה 2 S 12^{31a} + 2 t.; pl. מְגֵרוֹת 1 Ch 20^{3} (< מַגְזְרוֹת 2 S 12^{31b})—*saw*, used in cutting stone מְגֹרָרוֹת בַּמְּגֵרָה 1 K 7^{9}; used in torture (or as tools for enforced labour) of captives 2 S 12^{31a} 1 Ch 20^{3a}.

1642 †גְּרָר **n.pr.loc.** south of Gaza, usually identif. with mod. *Umm Jerâr* Bd [Pal 159] Guérin [Judée ii. 257 ff.]; but *Wady Jerūr* W. of *'Ain Ḳadīs* acc. to Trumbull [Kadesh Barnea 61 ff.] cf. Guthe [ZPV viii. 1885, 215]; Gn 20^{2} 26$^{6.20.26}$ 2 Ch 14$^{12.13}$; גְּרָרָה Gn 10^{19} 26^{1}; נַחַל גְּרָר Gn 26^{17}; וַיָּגָר בִּגְרָר Gn 20^{1}.

גרשׂ (Ar. جَرَشَ *bray, pound, grind coarse*, Aram. גְּרַס (rare) *crush*, ܓܪܝܣ *crushed*, ܓܪܰܣ *crush, destroy*; cf. following).

1638 †[גָּרַס] **vb.** be crushed (Aram. ܓܪܰܣ [*be crushed*,] *perish*)—**Qal** *Pf.* 3 fs. גָּרְסָה ψ 119^{20} fig. ג׳ נַפְשִׁי לְ *my soul is crushed* (i.e. perisheth: cf. Syr.) with longing *for* (cf. כָּלָה לְ). **Hiph.** *Impf.* וַיַּגְרֵס בֶּחָצָץ שִׁנָּי La 3^{16} *and he hath crushed my teeth with gravel*, fig. of divine chastisement.

†גֶּרֶשׂ **n.[m.]** a crushing, but only concrete 1643
of that which is crushed, *groats, grits* (cf. Ar. جَرِيشٌ, NH גְּרִיס, Aram. (rare) גְּרִיסְיָא, גְּרִשָׂא, ܓܪܽܣܳܐ)—אָבִיב קָלוּי בָּאֵשׁ גֶּרֶשׂ כַּרְמֶל Lv 2^{14} *young ears parched with fire, groats (&) fresh fruit* (v. Sifra ad loc.); מִגִּרְשָׂהּ (וּמִשַּׁמְנָהּ) Lv 2^{16}.

†[גָּרַשׁ] **vb.** drive out, cast out (NH *id.*, 1644
Aram. גְּרַשׁ Pa. Ithp. of divorce, MI^{19} ויגרשה)—**Qal** *Impf.* וַיִּגְרְשׁוּ Is 57^{20}; *Inf.* sf. מִגְרָשָׁהּ Ez 36^{5} infr.; *Pt.act.* גֹּרֵשׁ Ex 34^{11}; *pass.* f. גְּרוּשָׁה Lv 21^{7} + 4 t.;—*cast out, thrust out*, י׳, the Amorites Ex 34^{11} (JE; c. מִפְּנֵי); waters, mire and dirt רֶפֶשׁ וָטִיט Is 57^{20}; pass. only of divorced woman Lv 21^{7} (sq. מֵאִישָׁהּ; elsewh. with אַלְמָנָה *widow*), v^{14} 22^{13} (all H), Nu 30^{10} (P) Ez 44^{22}. On מִגְרָשָׁהּ Ez 36^{5} as Aram. *Inf.* cf. Ges [§ 45, 1. c.] Kö [i. 166]; Co del., on intern. grounds, cf. 𝔊. **Niph.** *Pf.* נִגְרָשׁ Is 57^{20}; 3 fs. וְנִגְרְשָׁה consec. Am. 8^{8}; נִגְרַשְׁתִּי Jon 2^{5};—*be driven* away, sq. מִנֶּגֶד עֵינֶיךָ, i.e. from the presence of Yahweh Jon 2^{5}; *be driven, tossed*, as the Nile Am 8^{8}; of the sea Is 57^{20} rel. cl., אֲשֶׁר om., *like the sea that is tossed*. **Pi.** *Pf.* 3 fs. וְגֵרְשָׁה consec. Ex 23^{28}; גֵּרַשְׁתָּ Gn 4^{14}, sf. 3 mpl. וְגֵרַשְׁתָּמוֹ consec. Ex 23^{31}; וְגֵרַשְׁתִּי Ex 33^{2}, sf. גֵּרַשְׁתִּיהוּ Ez 31^{11} (so 𝔗 𝔙, not 𝔊; cf. Co's conj.); וְגֵרַשְׁתִּיו consec. Nu 22^{11}; 3 pl. sf. גֵּרְשׁוּנִי 1 S 26^{19}; *Impf.* יְגָרֵשׁ Ex 11^{1}, וַיְגָרֶשׁ Gn 3^{24} + 6 t.; sf. וַיְגָרְשֵׁהוּ ψ 34^{1}, יְגָרְשֵׁם Ex 6^{1}; 2 ms. תְּגָרֵשׁ ψ 80^{9}, וַתְּגָרֶשׁ Jos 24^{12}; אֲגָרֵשׁ Ju 2^{3}, וָאֲגָרֵשׁ Ju 6^{9}; sf. 3 ms. אֲגָרְשֶׁנּוּ Ex 23$^{29.30}$ Nu 22^{6}; אֲגָרְשֵׁם Ho 9^{15}; וַיְגָרְשׁוּ Ju 11^{2}; יְגָרְשׁוּהָ Zp. 2^{4}, וַיְגָרְשׁוּם Ex 2^{17}; 2 mpl. תְּגָרְשׁוּן Mi 2^{9}, וַתְּגָרְשׁוּנִי Ju 11^{7}; *Inf.* cstr. לְגָרֵשׁ 1 Ch 17^{21} + || 2 S 7^{23} Gei We Dr, for MT לארצך; לְגָרְשֵׁנוּ 2 Ch 20^{11}; abs. *id.* Ex 11^{1}; *Imv.* גָּרֵשׁ Gn 21^{10} Pr 22^{10};—*drive out, away*, Hex all JE, incl. poem Dt 33; (י׳ subj.), Adam fr. garden Gn 3^{24} cf. Cain Gn 4^{14} (sq. מִן loc., & so 21 t.), David (men subj.) 1 S 26^{19}, id. (Abimelech subj.) ψ 34^{1} (title), Hagar (Abr. subj.) Gn 21^{10} cf. scorner, Pr 22^{10} daughters of Reuel (subj. shepherds) Ex 2^{17}; Moses and Aaron fr. Pharaoh's presence (indef. subj.) Ex 10^{11}; Gaal etc. (subj. Zebul) Ju 9^{41} (sq. מִן c. Inf.), Jephthah (Gil. subj.) Ju 11$^{2.7}$; Abiathar (subj. Sol.) 1 K 2^{27} (sq. מִן c. Inf.) wicked fr. temple (י׳ subj.) Ho 9^{15}; women fr. houses (nobles subj.) Mi 2^{9}; oft. of Canaanites

(hornet subj.) Ex 23^{28} Jos 24^{12} cf. Ex 23^{31} (Israel subj.); also (′י subj.; cf. MI^{19}) Ex 23$^{29.30}$ 33^{2} Dt 33^{27} Jos 24^{18} Ju 2^{3} 6^{9} ψ 78^{55} 80^{9} 1 Ch 17^{21}; of Israel from Egypt (subj. Pharaoh) Ex 6^{1} 11$^{1.1}$; from land of Moab (subj. Balak) Nu 22$^{6.11}$; Judah from Canaan (subj. Moab & Ammon) 2 Ch 20^{11}; Egypt from her land (′י subj.) Ez 31^{11} (but cf. text, supr.); Ashdod (indef. subj.) Zp 2^{4}. †**Pu.** *Pf.* גֹּרְשׁוּ subj. Israelites Ex 12^{39}; *Impf.* יְגֹרָ֑שׁוּ subj. despised and miserable outcasts Jb 30^{5} both sq. מִן loc.

1645 †[גֶּ֫רֶשׁ] **n.[m.] thing thrust or put forth, yield**; cstr. גֶּ֫רֶשׁ יְרָחִים Dt 33^{14} *yield, produce* of moons ‖ תְּבוּאֹת שָׁ֑מֶשׁ; i.e. produce in its seasons, cf. Di.

1646 †[גְּרוּשָׁה] **n.f. expulsion, violence.** Only pl. sf. גְּרֻשֹׁתֵיכֶם Ez 45^{9} *your acts of expulsion* (cf. Ew Da; '*Raubereien*' Sm Co).

1647 †גֵּרְשֹׁם **n.pr.m.** **1.** son of Moses & Ṣipporah Ex 2^{22} (expl. as if fr. גור) = 18^{3}; גֵּרְשׁוֹם 1 Ch 23$^{15.16}$ 26^{24}; so also גֵּרְשֹׁם Ju 18^{30} MT בֶּן־מְנַשֶּׁה cf. VB. **2.** a son of Levi גֵּרְשֹׁם 1 Ch 6$^{1.28}$ 15^{7} (cf. גֵּרְשׁוֹן); גֵּרְשׁוֹם 1 Ch 6$^{2.5.47.56}$. **3.** a son of Phinehas Ezr 8^{2}.

1648 †גֵּרְשׁוֹן **n.pr.m.** son of Levi (= גרשם 1 Ch 6$^{1.28}$ 15^{7} גרשום 1 Ch 6$^{2.5.47.56}$) Gn 46^{11} Ex 6$^{16.17}$ Nu 3$^{17.18.21.25}$ 4$^{22.38.41}$ 7^{7} 10^{17} 26^{57} Jos 21$^{6.27}$ 1 Ch 5^{27} 23^{6} (particularly in expression *sons of Gershon*, i.e. family, descendants of Gershon Nu 3^{25} 4$^{22.38.41}$ 7^{7} 10^{17} Jos 21$^{6.27}$; cf. *sons of Gershom* 1 Ch 6$^{47.56}$ 15^{7}).

1649 †גֵּרְשֻׁנִּי **adj.gent.** c. art. as subst. collect. Nu 3$^{21.23.24}$ 4$^{24.27.28}$ 26^{57} Jos 21^{33} 1 Ch 23^{7} 26^{21} 2 Ch 29^{12}; c. art. as adj. sing. m. 1 Ch 26^{21} 29^{8}.

4054 מִגְרָשׁ **n.m.**$^{Nu 35,2}$ **common, common-land, open land** (perhaps orig. *pasture-land*, as place of [cattle] *driving*)—abs. ′מ Ez 45^{2} + 2 t. + Ez 48^{15} (Co מִגְרָשָׁה); cstr. מִגְרַשׁ Lv 25^{34} 2 Ch 31^{19}; (on מִגְרָשָׁה Ez 36^{5} cf. גרשׁ); elsewh. pl., abs. מִגְרֹשׁוֹת Ez 27^{28} (Baer); Co מרעשׁת assumed fr. רָעַשׁ, cf. 𝔊; cstr. מִגְרְשֵׁי Nu 35^{4} + 2 t.; sf. מִגְרָשֶׁיהָ Jos 21$^{13.13}$ + 42 t.; מִגְרָשָׁהּ Jos 21^{11} + 46 t. in Jos 21 (generally ‸ or ˙ but also ˛ v^{21}); מִגְרְשֵׁיהֶם Nu 35^{3} + 4 t.; מִגְרְשֵׁיהֶן Nu 35^{7} + 8 t.—*common-land*, usually pl., and usually as attached to a city or town, esp. as surrounding Levitical cities Nu 35$^{2.3.4.5.7}$ Jos 14^{4} 21^{2} + 55 t. Jos 21 (all P; in Codd. & old Vrss. are two vv. Jos 21, betw. v$^{35.36}$, with ′מ 4 t.; om. Mass., Edd., Baer, but cf. Theile, & Di ad loc.); 1 Ch 6^{40} + 40 t. 1 Ch 6; 13^{2} 2 Ch 11^{14}; so also ′שְׂדֵה מ Lv 25^{34} (H), ′שְׂדֵי מ 2 Ch 31^{19}; lands surrounding the holy city Ez 48$^{15.17}$; *open land* or *space* about the temple Ez 45^{2}; only 1 Ch 5^{16} כָּל־מִגְרְשֵׁי שָׁרוֹן of (pasture-)lands in a district, cf. שָׁרוֹן.—Ez 27^{28} מגרשׁות, if true text, = open country about Tyre (opp. sea, cf. context), but v. Da & cf. supr.

גֵּרֹתִיו v. גּוּר sub II. גור. p. 158 1484

גשׁם (√of foll.; cf. Ar. جَسُمَ *be bulky, massive*, جِسْمٌ *body*, Syr. ܓܘܫܡܐ *id.*)

†I. גֶּ֫שֶׁם **n.pr.m.** an opponent of Nehemiah 1654
Ne 2^{19} 6^{1} (in both called הָעַרְבִי); v^{2}; also גַּשְׁמוּ 6^{6}; ו as in Nab. n.pr. cf. Nö in Eut$^{Nab 73}$.

†II. גֶּ֫שֶׁם **n.m.**$^{Gn 7,12}$ **rain, shower** (NH *id.*, 1653
conn. wi. above √ dub.)—abs. ′ג Gn 7^{12} +; גָּ֑שֶׁם 1 K 18^{41} +; cstr. גֶּשֶׁם Jb 37$^{6.6}$ +; pl. גְּשָׁמִים Ezr 10$^{9.13}$; cstr. גִּשְׁמֵי Ez 34^{26}; sf. גִּשְׁמֵיכֶם Lv 26^{4}; גִּשְׁמֵיהֶם ψ 105^{32};—*rain, shower* Gn 7^{12} 8^{2} (both J) Lv 26^{4} (H) Ho 6^{3} Am 4^{7} Je 5^{24} 14^{4} Is 44^{14} 55^{10} Ez 1^{28} Jo 2^{23} (‖ מַלְקוֹשׁ, מוֹרֶה); 1 K 17$^{7.14}$ 18^{45} (′ג גדול) 2 K 3^{17} Pr 25$^{14.23}$ Ec 11^{3} Ct 2^{11} ψ 105^{32}, וּמֵהַגּ׳ Ezr 10^{9} *and because of the rains*, cf. v^{13}; קוֹל הֲמוֹן הַגּ׳ 1 K 18^{41} cf. v^{44} Zc 14^{17} Ec 12^{2}; גֶּשֶׁם מָטָר וְג׳ מִטְרוֹת עֻזּוֹ Jb 37^{6}; מְטַר־גֶּשֶׁם Zc 10^{1}; cf. ג׳ נְדָבוֹת ψ 68^{10}; fig. of blessing Ez 34^{26}, ג׳ בְּרָכָה v^{26}; of destruction ג׳ שֹׁטֵף Ez 13$^{11.13}$ cf. 38^{22}.

†[גשׁם] **vb.denom.** (cf. NH Qal Pt. pass. 1652
& Hoph.)—**Pu.** *Pf.* 3 fs. גֻּשְּׁמָה Ez 22^{24} *be rained upon* (גֻּשְׁמָהּ Baer, but v. Ke Sm). **Hiph.** *cause* or *send rain*, *Pt.* מַגְשִׁמִים Je 14^{22}.

†[גֹּ֫שֶׁם] **n.[m.]** גָּשְׁמָהּ Ez 22^{24} (or גֻּשְּׁמָה from 1656
גֶּשֶׁם ?) acc. to punct.; but cf. sub גשׁם **vb.**

גַּשְׁמוּ **n.pr.**, v. I. גֶּשֶׁם. above 1654

†גֹּ֫שֶׁן **n.pr.loc.** (on etym. cf. Di Gn 45^{10})— 1657
1. district in Egypt E. of lower Nile, v. Eb$^{GS 500 ff.}$; Naville$^{Goshen, 1887}$, who rds. hierogl. *Kesem*, but cf. Groff$^{JAs xiv. 527}$ (𝔊 Γεσεμ ('Αραβίας)) — אֶרֶץ גֹּשֶׁן Gn 45^{10} (JE) 46^{34} 47$^{1.4.6.27}$ 50^{8} Ex 8^{18} 9^{26} (all J); אַ֫רְצָה גֹּשֶׁן Gn 46^{28} (J); גֹּ֫שְׁנָה v$^{28.29}$ (both J), in both 𝔊 καθ' Ἡρώων πόλιν cf. Di. (P has land רעמסס 47^{11} etc., cf. Di Gn 45^{10}). **2.** אֶרֶץ הַגֹּשֶׁן Jos 11^{16} (D), אֶרֶץ גֹּשֶׁן Jos 10^{41} (D), גֹּשֶׁן Jos 15^{51} (P) (𝔊 in all Γοσομ) a city named with גִּלֹה & חֹלֹן cf. Di.—not clearly located, but on southern border of Judah.

†גִּשְׁפָּא **n.pr.m.** named after צִיחָא as an 1658
officer of Nethinim Ne 11^{21}; v. om. B; 𝔊L & Codd. Γεσφα; name not elsewhere in OT, not even ‖ 1 Ch 9; possibly corrupted from חֲשֻׂפָא

Ne 7^{46} (following צִחָא; in ‖ Ezr 2^{43} חֲשׂוּפָא, צִיחָא), 𝔊 ʿΑσφα (B; Codd. Ασειφα, etc.); cf. BeRy.

גשר (√ of foll. Cf. As. *gašâru, strengthen, make firm* Lotz TPRegister; Ar. جَسَرَ *be bold,* also *arch a bridge,* cf. جِسْرٌ, جَسْرٌ *bridge,* NH גֶּשֶׁר *id.,* Aram. גִּישְׁרָא, ܓܶܫܪܳܐ, ܓܶܫܪܳܐ).

1650 **†גְּשׁוּר n.pr.m.** (*bridge? or land of bridges?* cf. Wetzst Hauran, 82). **1.** of people, = הַגְּשׁוּרִי Jos 13^{13} cf. 1 Ch 2^{23}. **2.** of land מֶלֶךְ גְּשׁוּר 2 S 3^{3} 13^{37} cf. v^{38} (but text in disorder cf. 𝔊 We Dr) 14^{32} 15^{8} בְּנֵי ג׳ בַּאֲרָם 1 Ch 3^{2}, גְּשׁוּרָה 2 S 14^{23}; a territory E. of the upper Jordan, exact limits unknown; acc. to Guthe ZPV xii. 1889, 232 f. between Gilead and Hermon, in *Jaulân;* acc. to Furrer ib. xiii. 1890, 198 = the *Ledjah,* district E. of Jaulân, with town *Jisre;* against him Guthe ib. 285 f.

†גְּשׁוּרִי adj.gent. = subst. הַגּ׳; **1.** people 1651
dwelling in Geshûr (supr.) Dt 3^{14} Jos 12^{5} $13^{11.13}$. **2.** a tribe of, or near, the Philistines Jos 13^{2}, also 1 S 27^{8}, but del 𝔊 (not 𝔊L) cf. We Dr; rd. possibly אשורי Hom Aufsätze i. (1892), 9; 2 S 2^{9} rd. האשורי for הגּ׳.

†[גָּשַׁשׁ] vb. feel with the hand, feel, 1659
stroke (NH *id.,* Ar. جَسَّ, Aram. גַּשֵּׁשׁ Pa., ܓܰܫ; Eth. **ገሰሰ:** or ገሠሠ: *stroke, touch*)—**Pi.** *Impf.* 1 pl. coh. נְגַשְׁשָׁה Is 59^{10}, נְגַשֵּׁשָׁה *ib., grope, grope for* cf. Che.

גַּת wine-press. **גַּת n.pr.** **גִּתִּי adj.gent.** 1660-61, 1663
גִּתַּיִם n.pr.loc. **גִּתִּית adj.** v. sub ינן. p. 387f 1664-65

†גֶּתֶר n.pr.m. (√ unknown) a son of Aram 1666
Gn 10^{23} = 1 Ch 1^{17}.

ד

ד, דּ, *Dāleth,* fourth letter; in modern Heb. = numeral 4; ד̈ = 4000; no evidence of this usage in OT times.

1669 **†[דָּאַב] vb. become faint, languish** (NH *id.* Hiph.; cf. Ar. دَأَبَ *toil, weary oneself;* v. also דְּאָבָה, דְּאָבוֹן & cf. דוב)—**Qal** *Pf.* 3 fs. דָּאֲבָה ψ 88^{10} (subj. עַיִן); *Inf.* לְדַאֲבָה Je 31^{12} לֹא יוֹסִיפוּ לְד׳ (subj. ransomed Israel);—Je 31^{25} has נֶפֶשׁ דָּאֵבָה, of hunger (‖ נֶפֶשׁ עֲיֵפָה), where adj. or pt. seems needed; Hi Gf דָּאֲבָה or דְּאֵבָה (the punctuators had, acc. to them, the Aram. participle in mind); Thes. makes relative clause.

1670 **†דְּאָבָה n.f. faintness, failure of mental energy, dismay** Jb 41^{14} וּלְפָנָיו תָּדוּץ דְּאָבָה *and before him* (i.e. the crocodile) *danceth dismay.*

1671 **†[דְּאָבוֹן] n.[m.] faintness, languishing,** cstr. וְכִלְיוֹן עֵינַיִם וְדַאֲבוֹן נָפֶשׁ Dt 28^{65} (cf. Lv 26^{16} & Syr. ܕܘܳܒܳܐ ܘܢܰܦܫܳܐ v. דוב).

1672 **†דָּאַג vb. be anxious, concerned, fear** (Talm. דְּאַג, דְּאֵיג *id.*)—**Qal** *Pf.* 3 ms. וְדָאַג consec. 1 S 9^{5} 10^{2}; 2 fs. דָּאַגְתְּ Is 57^{11}; *Impf.* 3 ms. יִדְאָג Je 17^{8}; אֶדְאַג ψ 38^{19}; *Pt.* דֹּאֵג Je 38^{19}, דֹּאֲגִים Je 42^{16};—**1.** *be anxious, concerned,* with reference to, in behalf of, c. לְ 1 S 9^{5} 10^{2}; *id.* c. מִן Je 42^{16} (famine personif.); sq. מֵחַטָּאתִי ψ 38^{19}; *be anxious,* abs. Je 17^{8} (‖ יִרָא). **2. fear, dread,** sq. acc. of pers. feared Is 57^{11} (‖ יָרֵא) Je 38^{19} (where also sq. cl. with פֶּן).

†דֹּאֵג n.pr.m. an Edomite, servant of 1673
Saul 1 S 21^{8} $22^{9.18.18.22}$ ($v^{18.18.22}$ Kt דויג cf. Dr) דּוֹאֵג ψ 52^{2} (title).

†דְּאָגָה n.f. anxiety, anxious care—דְּאָגָה 1674
Jos 22^{24} + 5 t.; *anxiety* for = for fear of, c. מִן Jos 22^{24}; *anxiety* Pr 12^{25} (where c. verb. masc. cf. Now), Je 49^{23} בַּיָּם ד׳; *anxious care* Ez 4^{16} 12^{19} (in both ‖ שִׁמָּמוֹן), 12^{18} (‖ רַעַשׁ and רָגְזָה).

דָּאג *fish,* cf. דָּג sub דגה. p. 185 1709

†[דָּאָה] vb. fly swiftly, dart through 1675
the air (cf. perhaps Ar. دَأْدَأَ *run vehemently* (of camel))—**Qal** *Impf.* יִדְאֶה Dt 28^{49} + 2 t.; וַיֵּדֶא ψ 18^{11} (> ‖ 2 S 22^{11} וַיֵּרָא); *fly swiftly, dart,* of eagle Dt 28^{49}, in simile of swift army; of Chaldaeans comp. with eagle, in judgment against Moab & Edom Je 48^{40} 49^{22} (in both ‖ פרש כנפיו); of י׳ in theoph. ψ 18^{11} (cf. 2 S 22^{11}) (וַיִּרְכַּב עַל־כְּרוּב וַיָּעֹף ‖ וַיֵּדֶא עַל־כנפי רוח).

†דָּאָה n.f. a bird of prey, possibly **kite** 1676
(𝔙 Saad. Bo Hieroz. ii. 191 Di Lv 11^{14}; Aram. דַּיְתָא, ܕܰܝܬܳܐ; NH דַּיָּה of diff. birds of prey; name prob. fr. flying, swooping), Lv 11^{14} forbidden as food; cf. also Dt 14^{13} וְהָרָאָה ואת־הָאַיָּה וְהַדַּיָּה, where for הראה rd. הַדָּאָה & del. הַדַּיָּה; so Sam 𝔊; cf. Di *l.c.*

†[דַּיָּה] n.f. id.—frequenting ruins, cf. Di 1772
l.c.; דַּיּוֹת Is 34^{15} (on הַדַּיָּה Dt 14^{13} cf. foregoing).

דֹּאר n.pr. v. sub II. דור. p. 190 1756

1677 דֹּב, דּוֹב v. דבב. below

דבא (? √ of foll.; existence & mng. dub.)

1679 †[דֹּבֶא] **n.[m.]** perh. **rest,** but sense very doubtful (? Ar. دَبَا *rest,* Ḳamus; 𝔊 𝔖 𝔗 Onk *strength,* reading perh. רבאך cf. Sam. רביך, vid. Di) וּכְיָמֶיךָ דָּבְאֶךָ׃ Dt 33^{25}.

1680 †[דָּבַב] **vb. move gently, glide, glide over** (NH דָּבַב *flow slowly, drop;* Ar. دَبَّ *walk leisurely, gently,* دَابَّةٌ *any animal that walks* or *creeps,* cf. דֹּב; As. *dabâbu, plot, plan,* COT ^{Gloss}, cf. דִּבָּה)—only **Qal** *Pt.* דּוֹבֵב שִׂפְתֵי יְשֵׁנִים Ct 7^{10}, of wine *gliding over the lips of sleepers;* (ד׳ שְׂפָתַי וְשִׁנָּי i. e. *my lips and teeth* 𝔊 𝔖 Aq Gei $^{Urschrift\ 405}$).

1677 †דֹּב **n.m.** $^{Pr\ 28,15}$, **f.** $^{2K\ 2,24\ (seld.)}$ **bear** (from soft or gliding motion, NH *id.,* Eth. ድብ፡ As. *dabû*(?) Dl $^{S\ 55}$; Aram. דּוּבָּא, ܕܶܒܳܐ; Ar. دُبّ, دُبَّةٌ, is however a loan-word cf. Hom $^{NS\ 301\ f.}$);—abs. דֹּב Am $5^{19}+5$ t.; דּוֹב 1 S $17^{34}+2$ t.; pl. דֻּבִּים 2 K 2^{24} Is 59^{11};—*bear,* female 2 K 2^{24} 2 S 17^{8} Pr 17^{12} Ho 13^{8} cf. Is 11^{7}; undetermined 1 S $17^{34.36.37}$ Am 5^{19} Pr 28^{15} Is 59^{11} La 3^{10} (on art. 1 S 17^{34} Am 5^{19} cf. RS $^{Sem.\ i.\ 119\ n.}$)

1681 †דִּבָּה **n.f. whispering, defamation, evil report** (? as that which glides stealthily)—abs. ד׳ Nu 14^{36} Pr 10^{18}; cstr. דִּבַּת Je $20^{10}+4$ t.; sf. דִּבָּתְךָ Pr 25^{10} דִּבָּתָם Gn 37^{2};—**1.** *whispering* ψ 31^{14} Je 20^{10} (Hi Hup De Gf VB; yet cf. Che ψ). **2.** *defamation* Pr 10^{18} (c. הוציא). **3.** *evil report,* specif. **a** (true) report of evil doing Gn 37^{2} (P) וַיָּבֵא אֶת־דִּבָּתָם רָעָה; cf. also Pr 25^{10} & Ez 36^{3} וַתֵּעֲלוּ עַל־שְׂפַת לָשׁוֹן וְדִבַּת־עָם, unfavourable report of spies Nu 13^{32} $14^{36.37}$ (all P & all c. הוֹצִיא; adj. רעה only 14^{37}).

1686 †דִּבְיוֹנִים **n.[m.]** so Qr; =דב יונים *dove's dung*(?) 2 K 6^{25} for Kt חרייונים; 𝔊 κόπρου περιστερῶν (Klo gives conject. emend.)

דבל (Ar. دَبَلَ *collect,* also *make into lumps, gobbets* (Lane); Eth. & cogn. in deriv.)

1690 †דְּבֵלָה **n.f. lump** of pressed figs, **pressed (fig-) cake** (NH דְּבֵילָה, Aram. *id.,* ܕܒܶܠܬܳܐ, = Greek παλάθη; Ar. دُبْلَةٌ *lump, large gobbet* or *mouthful;* cf. As. *dublu, foundation,* & Heb. synon. אֲשִׁישָׁה Dl $^{HA\ 58}$)—דְּבֵלָה 1 S 30^{12}; cstr. דְּבֶלֶת 2 K 20^{7}=Is 38^{21}; pl. דְּבֵלִים 1 S 25^{18} 1 Ch 12^{40};—used as food 1 S 25^{18} 30^{12} 1 Ch 12^{40}; דְּבֶלֶת תְּאֵנִים, as application to boil, or eruption 2 K 20^{7}=Is 38^{21}.

†[דִּבְלָה] **n.pr.loc.** only c. ה loc. דִּבְלָתָה 1689
Ez 6^{14} but rd. רִבְלָתָה JDMich Hi Sm Co Da.

†[דִּבְלַיִם] **n.pr.m.** father of Gomer wife of 1691
Hosea דִּבְלָיִם Ho 1^{3}.

דִּבְלָתַיִם in **n.pr.loc.** v. עלמן ד׳, בית ד׳ 1015
(possibly fr. √ דבל in sense of *collect, assemble,* Eth. ተደበለ፡ III. 3 *se colligere,* መድበል፡ *coetus, chorus, conventus, concilium*)—Je 48^{22}; דִּבְלָתָיְמָה Nu $33^{46.47}$.

†דָּבֵק, דָּבַק **vb. cling, cleave, keep** 1692
close (NH *id.,* Ar. دَبِقَ, Aram. דְּבַק, דְּבֵק, ܕܒܶܩ, ܕܒܰܩ)—**Qal** *Pf.* דָּבַק 1 K $11^{2}+2$ t.; וְדָבַק consec. Gn 2^{24}; דָּבֵק 2 K 3^{3}; 3 fs. דָּבְקָה Ru 1^{14} $+5$ t.; דָּבֵקָה Job 29^{10}; 1 s. דָּבַקְתִּי ψ 119^{31}; 3 pl. דָּבְקוּ 2 S 20^{2}; וְדָבְקוּ consec. Dt 28^{60}; דָּבֵקוּ Jb 41^{15}; וּדְבַקְתֶּם consec. Jos 23^{12}; *Impf.* יִדְבַּק Dt $13^{18}+3$ t.; 3 fs. תִּדְבַּק 2 K 5^{27} ψ 137^{6}; וַתִּדְבַּק Gn $34^{3}+2$ t.; sf. תִּדְבָּקַנִי Gn 19^{19}; 2 ms. תִּדְבָּק Dt 10^{20} Ez 29^{4} (del. B Co); 2 fs. תִּדְבָּקִין Ru $2^{8.21}$; 3 pl. יִדְבְּקוּ Nu $36^{7.9}$; 2 mpl. תִּדְבָּקוּ Jos 23^{8}; תִּדְבָּקוּן Dt 13^{5}; *Inf. cstr.* וּלְדָבְקָה־בוֹ Dt $11^{22}+2$ t.;—in Hexateuch only JD, except Nu $36^{7.9}$ (P);—**1.** *cling, cleave to,* **a.** lit. sq. בְּ Jb 19^{20} (bone to skin), so sq. לְ ψ 102^{6}; sq. אֶל 2 S 23^{10} (hand to sword; accidentally om. with other words 1 Ch 11^{13} cf. Dr 2 S 23^{11}), Je 13^{11} (girdle to loins), La 4^{4} (tongue to roof of mouth, in thirst), so sq. לְ Jb 29^{10} ψ 137^{6} (as a judgment); so also in metaph. ψ 44^{26} דָּבְקָה לָאָרֶץ בִּטְנֵנוּ *our belly cleaveth to the earth* (|| שָׁחָה לֶעָפָר נַפְשֵׁנוּ), 119^{25} דָּבְקָה לֶעָפָר נַפְשִׁי; fish to scales of crocodile (fig. of Pharaoh), sq. בְּ Ez 29^{4} (but cf. supr.); abs. (recipr.) of folds of crocodile's belly Jb 41^{15}; further of the חֵרֶם remaining in (*sticking to*) the hand sq. בְּ Dt 13^{18}; so of spot, stain Jb 31^{7}. **b.** so also of abiding on the land of one's tribe Nu $36^{7.9}$ (sq. בְּ). **c.** = *remain with, close to* sq. עִם Ru $2^{8.21}$ sq. בְּ v^{23}. **2.** *cling, cleave to,* **a.** fig. of loyalty, affection etc., sts. with idea of physical proximity retained, sq. בְּ Gn 2^{24} (J; man to wife) cf. 34^{3} (J) 1 K 11^{2} Jos 23^{12} (D); further Ru 1^{14} (Ruth to Naomi); 2 S 20^{2} (people to king); esp. (sq. בְּ) of cleaving to י׳ Dt 11^{22} (|| אָהֵב, הָלַךְ בְּכָל־דְּרָכָיו) 30^{20} (|| אָהֵב, שָׁמַע בְּקֹלוֹ), Jos 22^{5} (|| אָהֵב, הָלַךְ וגו׳, שָׁמַר מִצְוֹתָיו); cf. further Dt 10^{20} 13^{5} Jos 23^{8} (all D), 2 K 18^{6}; ψ 63^{9} (sq. אַחֲרֵי) & ψ 119^{31} דָּבַקְתִּי בְעֵדְוֹתֶיךָ; so **b.** of the opposite בְּחַטֹּאות יָרָבְעָם ... דָּבֵק 2 K 3^{3}; **c.** subj. disease, calamity, sq. בְּ pers. Dt 28^{60} 2 K

5^{27}; sq. אַחֲרֵי Je 42^{16}; sq. acc. Gn 19^{19} (J); subj. sin ψ 101^{3} (sq. בְּ pers.) **Pu.** *Impf.* 3 mpl. יְדֻבָּ֑קוּ pass. of Hiph. **1** sq. בְּ, of crocodile's scales, *they are joined together* Jb 41^{9} (‖ יִתְלַכְּדוּ); abs. of earth-clods Jb 38^{38}. **Hiph.** *Pf.* 3 fs. sf. הִדְבִּיקַ֫תְהוּ Ju 20^{42}; 3 pl. sf. הִדְבִּיקֻ֫הוּ 2 S 1^{6}; 1 s. הִדְבַּ֫קְתִּי Je 13^{11}; וְהִדְבַּקְתִּ֫י Ez 29^{4}; *Impf.* juss. יַדְבֵּק Dt 28^{21}; וַיַּדְבֵּק Gn 31^{23}; אַדְבִּיק Ez 3^{26}; וַיַּדְבִּיקוּ Ju 18^{22} 20^{45}; וַיַּדְבְּקוּ 1 S 14^{22} + 2 t. (cf. Ges §53 R 4 Kö I. 210). **1.** *cause to cling* or *cleave* to, sq. acc. + אֶל, lit. וּלְשׁוֹנְךָ אַדְבִּיק אֶל־חִכֶּ֫ךָ Ez 3^{26}; v. also 29^{4} (sq. acc. + בְּ; lit., but in metaph.); fig. of causing to cleave to י׳ Je 13^{11} (sq. acc. + אֶל); cf. further Dt 28^{21} (subj. י׳, sq. acc. of disease + בְּ). **2.** *pursue closely*, sq. אַחֲרֵי Ju 20^{45} 1 S 14^{22} 1 Ch 10^{2} = 1 S 31^{2} (sq. acc.); so also 2 S 1^{6} (sq. acc.) **3.** *overtake*, sq. acc. Gn 31^{23} (E), Ju 18^{22}; cf. 20^{42} (subj. הַמִּלְחָמָה). **Hoph.** *Pt.* וּלְשׁוֹנִי מֻדְבָּק מַלְקוֹחָ֑י ψ 22^{16} *and my tongue is made to cleave (to) my gums;* cf. sub **Qal 1.**

1695 †דָּבֵק **adj.** clinging, cleaving (to), ד׳ abs. וְיֵשׁ אֹהֵב דָּבֵק מֵאָח Pr 18^{24}; דְּבֵקָה לְ 2 Ch 3^{12} (of cherub's wing); of cleaving to י׳ הַדְּבֵקִים בְּ Dt 4^{4}.

1694 †דֶּ֫בֶק **n.m.** Is 41,7 joining, soldering, appendage—**1.** ד׳ *joining, soldering* Is 41^{7}. **2.** pl. הַדְּבָקִים *appendages* of breastplate (?) 1 K 22^{34} = 2 Ch 18^{33} בֵּין הַדּ׳ ובין הַשִּׁרְיָן. (The Be al. cf. VB: the jointed *attachment* or *appendage* to the rigid breast-armour, which covered the abdomen; >Klo prop. appendage of helmet; Thes suggests armpits, lit. *joints* (cf. מַדְבְּקֵי יָד Je 38^{12} 𝔗); Ew the soft muscles etc. *connecting* the chest with the bottom of the back.)

1696 [דָּבַר] 1142 **vb. speak** (original mng. dub.; *range in order* Thes is conjectural and not comprehensive enough; *treiben* MV does not explain Ar. or Heb. usage, but only Aram. A mng. *go away*, sustained by Ar. دَبَرَ بِهِ *go away with it*, would best explain the four branches of usage:—(1) Ar. دَبَرَ *depart, perish*, IV. *retreat*, fig. *retrograde, decline;* دَبْرٌ *passing away, death;* As. *dabâru*, Pi. *drive away*, Bez Orient. Diplom. Vocab., *Dibbara*, pest-god, Hpt. in KAT 2.500, דֶּ֫בֶר *pestilence.* (2) Ar. دَبَرَ *follow behind*, in time, place, or station; دُبْرٌ *part behind*, دُبُرٌ *back*, דְּבִיר *hindmost chamber of temple.* (3) Syr. ܕܒܰܪ *lead, guide*, cattle, sheep, government, *take* a wife, = Aram. דְּבַר; Syr. ܕܳܒܽܘܪܳܐ, Aram. דָּבַר *leader;* Syr. ܕܽܘܒܳܪܳܐ, Aram. דֻּבָּרָא *guidance;* Syr. ܕܒܳܪܳܐ, Aram. דִּבְרָא, Heb. דֹּבֶר; Syr. ܡܰܕܒܪܳܐ, Aram. מַדְבְּרָא, Heb. מִדְבָּר *pasture, wilderness;* Ar. دَبْرٌ, Syr. ܕܰܒܽܘܪܳܐ, Aram. דַּבַּרְתָּא, Heb. דְּבוֹרָה *swarm of bees*, may be in this line, as led by their queen, so Thes. (4) Ar. دَبَّرَ *consider the end* or *issue* (of an affair), *relate* (a story or tradition); دَبَّرَ فِى *consider*, دَبَّرَ عَلَى *plan against;* Ph. דבר *speak;* Heb. דִּבֶּר etc. Syn. of אָמַר *say*, as Aram. מַלֵּל with אֲמַר; Gk. λαλεῖν, λέγειν; Lat. *loqui, dicere;* Germ. *reden, sagen*)—†**Qal** 41 only inf. (once ?) & pt.: *Inf.* sf. בְּדָבְרֶ֫ךָ (by attraction to בְּשָׁפְטֶ֫ךָ for usual Piel) ψ 51^{6}; *Pt.* דֹּבֵר Ex 6^{29} + 30 t.; pl. דֹּבְרִים Nu 36^{5} ψ 109^{20}; cstr. דֹּבְרֵי ψ 5^{7} + 3 t.; f. דֹּבְרוֹת Nu 27^{7} ψ 31^{19}; pass. דָּבֻר Pr 25^{11};—*speak*, abs. Nu 27^{7} 32^{27} 36^{5} (P) ψ 51^{6} (?); דָּבָר דָּבֻר *word spoken* Pr 25^{11}; with acc. rei דֹּבֵר דָּבָר *speaking a word* Jb 2^{13}; אמת ψ 15^{2}, תמים Am 5^{10}, (מ)ישרים Pr 16^{13} Is 33^{15}, צדק Is 45^{19}, שלום Est 10^{3} ψ 28^{3}, שקר(ים) ψ 63^{12} 101^{7} Je 40^{16}, כזב ψ 5^{7} 58^{4}, רע ψ 109^{20}, נבלה Is 9^{16}, הַוַּת נפשו Mi 7^{3}; with אֶל of *person, unto* Gn 16^{13} (J) Ex 6^{29} (P) Je 38^{20} 40^{16} Dn 10^{11} Jon 3^{2}; בְּאָזְנֵי *in the ears of* Dt 5^{1} Je 28^{7}; עַל *concerning, about* ψ 31^{19} 109^{20} Je 32^{42} (sometimes rendered *against*, but dub.); עִם *with* ψ 28^{3}; הַמַּלְאָךְ הַדֹּבֵר בִּי *the angel that spake with me* (as a prophet, an instrument of communicating with Israel) Zc 1$^{9.13.14}$ 2$^{2.7}$ 4$^{1.4.5}$ 5$^{5.10}$ 6^{4} (vid. prep. בְּ **III. 2** Ew §217 f. (3)). †**Niph.** 4 *Pf.* נִדְבְּרוּ Mal 3^{16}, נִדְבָּ֑רוּ ψ 119^{23}, נִדְבַּרְנוּ Mal 3^{13}; *Pt.* הַנִּדְבָּרִים Ez 33^{30}; reciprocal sense, *speak with one another, talk*, abs. Mal 3^{16}; with בְּ, *against* ψ 119^{23} Ez 33^{30}; with עַל, *concerning, about* Mal 3^{13} (RV *against*, vid. Ew §217 i.) **Pi.** 1089 *Pf.* דִּבֶּר Gn 12^{4}+, דִּבֵּר Gn 21^{1} + (on דִּבֶּר Ex 12^{25} Dt 26^{19} v. Bö §1021 d (1) Kö I. 188); *Impf.* יְדַבֵּר Gn 44^{7}+, יְדַבֶּר־ Gn 44^{18}+; תְּדַבְּרוּן Gn 32^{20}, תְּדַבֵּרוּן ψ 58^{2}; *Imv.* דַּבֵּר Gn 24^{33}+, דַּבֶּר־ Ex 11^{2}+; *Inf.* דַּבֵּר Gn 24^{50} +, דַּבֶּר־ Is 59^{13} +; *Pt.* מְדַבֵּר Gn 27^{6}+; f. מְדַבֶּ֫רֶת 1 S 1^{13}+;—(הַדִּבֵּר) Je 5^{13}, inf. Ki 48, prob. Ol §182 e Kö §23 (5), perhaps MV; but more prob. a noun, as Ges §52 (2), Anm. 3 Ew §156 a, dub. pf. as Sta §222; בְּיוֹם דִּבֶּר Ex 6^{28} Nu 3^{1} Dt 4^{15}; תְּחִלַּת דִּבֶּר־ Ho 1^{2}, inf. Ki 48 Bö §987 (7) Kö §23 (5); but more prob. pf., as Ges §52 (2), Anm. 3);—*speak*, **1.** abs. Dt 18^{17} + (throughout the literature) usu. with לֵאמֹר, less freq. וַיֹּאמֶר: 2 K 18^{28}+, cf. the phrases †אני (י׳) דברתי† Ez 5^{13} + 18 t. Ez; †כי י׳ דבר† Is 1^{2} 21^{17} 22^{25} 24^{3} 25^{8} Je 13^{15} Jo 4^{8} Ob 18; †כי פי י׳ דבר† Is 1^{20} 40^{5} 58^{14} Mi 4^{4}; †פי ידבר† ψ 49^{4}; †(י)דבר פי† ψ 66^{14} 145^{21}; †עוד זה מדבר† Jb 1$^{16.17.18}$. **2.** with acc. rei, very frequently, ד׳ את הדברים האלה Ex 20^{1} Dt 5^{19}+; לָ֫מָּה תְּדַבֵּר עוֹד דְּבָרֶ֫יךָ *why speakest thou any more of thy affairs?* 2 S 19^{30}; עַד אִם־דִּבַּ֫רְתִּי דְּבָרָי *until I* *have told my errand* Gn 24^{33}; seld. sq. דָּבָר indef.; as ד׳ דָּבָר Is 58^{13} *speak a* (mere, empty) *word;* so prob. also ד׳ דְּבָרִים Ho 10^{4}; with other nouns, e.g. דבר קשות *spake rough words* Gn 42$^{7.30}$ (E); ד׳ גבהה *proud words* 1 S 2^{3}; טבות *friendly words* Je 12^{6}; טוב 1 S 19^{4} 1 K 22^{13} Est 7^{9}; שקר Is 59^{3}+, כזב Dn 11^{27}, אמת Je 9^{4}+, שוא ψ 12^{3}+; דבר שיר *utter, sing a song* Ju 5^{12}; משל 1 K 5^{12}; יְהוּדִית *the Jewish language* Ne 13^{24}; †סרה *rebellion* Dt 13^{6} Je 28^{16} 29^{32}. **3.** *with persons:* **a.** rarely acc. יָכְלוּ דַּבְּרוֹ לְשָׁלֹם *they could* [*not*] *speak unto him peaceably* Gn 37^{4} (J; but Ew § 282 a *about him*); וַיְדַבֵּר...אֹתָם Nu 26^{3} (P, but text corrupt vid. Di; no satisfactory explanation yet given, possibly rd. אִתָּם vid. **d**). **b.** most frequently with אֶל throughout the literature: Gn 8^{15}+; cf. phrases וַיְדַבֵּר י׳ אֶל מֹשֶׁה לֵּאמֹר Ex 6^{10} + 87 t. P; but †וידבר י׳ אל משה לך Ex 32^{7} 33^{1} (JE); דבר אל אהרן Lv 6^{18} + 8 t. (P); דבר אל בני ישׂראל Ex 6^{9} + 38 t. (P); elsewhere, Ex 19^{6} (E) Dt 1^{3} 4^{45} (D); ד׳ אל (כל) העדה Ex 12^{3} Lv 19^{2} Nu 16$^{24.26}$ (P); ד׳ אל לב *speak unto one's heart* Gn 24^{45}, i.e. to oneself, cf. also ד׳ על לִבָּהּ 1 S 1^{13}, v. **5** infr.; אל is used inexactly for על 1 S 3^{12} 1 K 16^{12} Is 16^{13} Je 27^{13} 30^{4} 33^{14} 36$^{7.31}$ 40^{2} 50^{1} 51$^{12.62}$ where it is rendered *concerning* or *against.* **c.** with לְ, *speak to* 1 K 2^{19} Ez 32^{21} Dn 2^{4}; ליהוה *speak, sing to Yahweh* words of a song Jos 10^{12} (D) 2 S 22^{1} (= ψ 18^{1} title); in D, דבר ל *promise to,* in phrases †כאשר דבר(י׳) ל Dt 1$^{11.21}$ 6^{3} 9^{3} 10^{9} 11^{25} 12^{20} 15^{6} 18^{2} 26^{18} 27^{3} 29^{12} Jos 13$^{14.33}$ 22^{4} 23$^{5.10}$ (all D); אשר דבר ל Dt 9^{28} 1 K 8$^{24.25.26}$ (= 2 Ch 6$^{15.16.17}$).—דבר ל Gn 24^{7} 28^{15} 49^{28} Ex 32^{34} (J) Jos 9^{21} (P) Ju 14^{7} 2 S 23^{3} Is 30^{10} Zc 9^{10} usu. rendered *speak to,* but oft. rather *promise to.* הֲיֵשׁ לְדַבֶּר־לָךְ אֶל־הַמֶּלֶךְ *is it possible to speak for thee unto the king?* 2 K 4^{13} (by attraction to לַעֲשׂוֹת לָךְ). **d.** with †אֶת *speak with* Gn 17$^{3.22.23}$ 21^{2} 23^{8} 34$^{6.8}$ 35$^{13.15}$ Ex 25^{22} 31^{18} 34$^{29.33.34.35}$ Nu 3^{1} 7^{89} Jos 22$^{15.21}$ (all P) Gn 35^{14} 41^{9} 42^{7} 45^{15} Jos 17^{14} (all E) Dt 5^{21}; sources of S K Ch 2 S 3^{27} 7^{7} = 1 Ch 17^{6} 1 K 8^{15} = 2 Ch 6^{4} 1 K 22^{24} = 2 Ch 18^{23} 2 Ch 10^{10} (= אל 1 K 12^{10}) Je 5^{5} 7^{22} 9^{7} 35^{2} 38^{25} Ez 2^{1} 3$^{22.24.27}$ 14^{4} 20^{3} 44^{5} Dn 1^{19} Zc 8^{16}; cf. phrases †דבר חד את אחד *speak one with another* Ez 33^{30}; †דבר משפטים את *speak judgments with,* usu. = *give judgment against,* (not Je 12^{1}), Je 1^{16} 4^{12} 12^{1} 39^{5} 52^{9} (= 2 K 25^{6}); דבר טבות את *speak kindly with* 2 K 25^{28} = Je 52^{32}. **e.** c. †עִם *speak with,* (not P), Gn 29^{9} 31$^{24.29}$ Ex 19^{9} 20$^{19.19.22}$ 33^{9} Nu 11^{17} 22^{19} Jos 24^{27} (all JE) Dt 5^{4} 9^{10} Ju 6^{17} 1 S 9^{25} (𝔊 Th We Dr וַיִּרְבְּדוּ לָ *spread a couch for*) 17^{23} 2 S 13^{22} 1 K 1$^{14.22}$ 2 K 6^{33} 18^{26} 2 Ch 9^{1} (= אֶל 1 K 10^{2}) Ne 9^{13} Est 6^{14} Je 32^{4} Dn 8^{18} 9^{22} 10$^{11.15.17.19}$ Ho 12^{5}; דִּבַּרְתִּי אֲנִי עִם לִבִּי *I spake, communed with my heart* Ec 1^{16}. **f.** †לִפְנֵי *before, in the presence of* Ex 6^{12} Nu 36^{1} (P) Ju 11^{11} 1 K 3^{22} Est 8^{3}. **4.** with בְּ: **a.** *instrumental,* דבר בְּ *speak with, by,* or *by means of a person* (vid. supr. **Qal** ad fin.) Nu 12$^{2.2.6.8}$ (E) 2 S 23^{2} (cf. Dr), 1 K 22^{28} = 2 Ch 18^{27}, Hb 2^{1}; †דִּבֶּר בְּשֵׁם *speak in the name of* Ex 5^{23} (J) Dt 18$^{19.20.20.22}$ 1 Ch 21^{19} Je 20^{9} 26^{16} 29^{23} 44^{16} Dn 9^{6} Zc 13^{3}; †ביד *by the hand of* Nu 17^{5} 27^{23} Jos 20^{2} (P) 1 S 28^{17} 1 K 8^{53} + 13 t. K, 2 Ch 10^{15} (= 1 K 12^{15}) Is 20^{2} Je 37^{2} 50^{1} Ez 38^{17}. **b.** *local* (fig.), בְּאָזְנֵי *in the ears of* Gn 20^{8} (E) Ex 11^{2} Dt 32^{44} (J) Gn 23^{16} Nu 14^{28} Jos 20^{4} (P) Dt 31$^{28.30}$ Ju 9$^{2.3}$ 1 S 8^{21} 11^{4} 25^{24} 2 S 3$^{19.19}$ Je 26^{15} Pr 23^{9}; †דבר בלב *speak in the heart* Ec 2^{15}. **c.** *of the object, speak of, about* (prep. בְּ **IV. e** Ew § 217 f. (2)) Dt 6^{7} 11^{19} 1 S 19$^{3.4}$ ψ 119^{46} 122^{8}; *propose for* (a wife) 1 S 25^{39} (cf. Ct 8^{8}). **d.** *of hostility, against* (Ew § 217 f. (1)) Nu 12$^{1.8}$ 21$^{5.7}$ (E) Jb 19^{18} ψ 50^{20} 78^{19}. **e.** *of price,* בְּנַפְשׁוֹ *at the cost of his life* 1 K 2^{23} (vid. בְּ **III. 3**). **5.** with †עַל, of the object *concerning* or *about which* one speaks Gn 18^{19} Nu 10^{29} (J) Jos 23^{14} (D) Ju 9^{3} 1 S 25^{30} 1 K 2$^{4.27}$ 5$^{13.13}$ 14^{2}, 22^{23} (= 2 Ch 18^{22}), 2 K 10^{10}, 19^{21} = Is 37^{22}, 1 Ch 22^{11} 2 Ch 23^{3} Je 1^{16} 18$^{7.8.9}$ 42^{19}. It may have this sense in most if not all of the following, where RV renders 1 K 2$^{18.19}$ Est 7^{9} Je 18^{20} *for;* 2 Ch 32^{16} Ne 6^{12} Je 11^{17} 16^{10} 25^{13} 26$^{13.19}$ 35^{17} Ez 36^{5} Dn 9^{12} 11^{36} Ho 7^{13} Am 3^{1} *against;* and 1 K 9^{5} 2 K 22^{19} Je 10^{1} 19^{15} *unto* (על is used for אל *unto* 2 Ch 32^{19} Je 6^{10} 25^{2} 26^{2} Ho 12^{11}); cf. the phrase †דבר על לב *speak upon the heart, speak kindly, comfort* Gn 34^{3} 50^{21} (E) Ju 19^{3} Ru 2^{13}, 1 S 1^{13} (seemingly from context על for אל, *to her heart, to herself,* vid. Dr), 2 S 19^{8} 2 Ch 30^{22} 32^{6} Is 40^{2} Ho 2^{16}. **6.** with infin. †דבר לעשׂות *promise to do* Ex 32^{14} (J) Dt 1^{14} Ez 6^{10} Jon 3^{10}; †דבר לתת *promise to give* Dt 19^{8}; †דבר למחות *threaten to blot out* 2 K 14^{27}; cf. †דבר להזהיר i.e. so as to warn Ez 3^{18} 33^{8}.

Note.—וַתָּקָם וַתְּדַבֵּר אֶת־כָּל־זֶרַע הַמַּמְלָכָה 2 Ch 22^{10} 𝔊 ἀπώλεσε, 𝔙 *interfecit,* scribal error for וַתְּאַבֵּד 2 K 11^{1}. Other explanations: *plot against, waylay* (Ar. دَبَّرَ) Thes MV; *pronounce sentence,* ellipt. וַתְּדַבֵּר מִשְׁפָּטִים Ges Hdw Rob; but cf. VB.—†**Pu.** *Impf.* בַּיּוֹם שֶׁיְּדֻבַּר־בָּהּ *in the day when she may be spoken for* Ct 8^{8} (vid. **Pi. 4 c**); *Pt.* נִכְבָּדוֹת מְדֻבָּר בָּךְ *glorious things are being spoken in thee* (RV Pe MV *of thee*) ψ 87^{3}. †**Hithp.** *Pt.* מִתְדַּבֵּר = מִדַּבֵּר with acc. מִדַּבֵּר הַדָּבָר הַזֶּה *speaking this word* 2 S 14^{13};

שֹׁמֵעַ (אֶת הַקּוֹל) מִדַּבֵּר אֶל׳ *heard* (*the voice,* or) *one speaking unto* Nu 7^{89} (P) Ez 2^{2} 43^{6} (Di Nu 7^{89} would rd. מְדַבֵּר after 𝔊; the meaning not appreciably different from Piel; the Hithp. difficult to reconcile with אֶל). † **Hiph.** *Impf.* וַיַּדְבֵּר עַמִּים תַּחְתָּי ψ 18^{48} (2 S 22^{48} has ומוֹריד for rare וַיַּדְבֵּר), יַדְבֵּר עַמִּים תַּחְתֵּינוּ 47^{4}; either (cf. Aram. דַּבַּר) *leads* subject (so Ges *coegit,* De Now), or (cf. Ar. أَدْبَرَ *turn the back, retreat*) *puts to flight,* fig. for *subdues* (so Hi).

1697 דָּבָר$_{1439}$ **n.m. speech, word**—Gn 18^{14} + 446 t.; cstr. דְּבַר Gn 12^{17} + 361 t.; sf. דְּבָרִי Nu 11^{23} + (sfs. 66 t.); sg. in all 875 t.; pl. דְּבָרִים Ex 4^{10} + 182 t.; cstr. דִּבְרֵי Gn 24^{30} + 253 t.; sf. דְּבָרָיו Gn 37^{8} (sfs. 127 t.); pl. in all 564 t.;—**I.** sg. *speech, discourse, saying, word,* as the sum of that which is spoken: **1.** *of men,* **a.** נְבוֹן דָּבָר *discreet in speech* 1 S 16^{18}; ד׳ שְׂפָתַיִם *speech of lips* ψ 59^{13}, *mere talk* Is 36^{5} (= 2 K 18^{20}) Pr 14^{23} (cf. ψ 17^{4} speech of God's lips); דָּבָר מַר *bitter speech* ψ 64^{4}; ד׳ כָּזָב *lying speech* Pr 30^{8}; טוֹב דְּבָרְךָ *thy saying is good* 1 S 9^{10}; וּדְבַר אַבְנֵר הָיָה עִם *and the speech of Abner had been with* the elders of Israel 2 S 3^{17} (cf. 1 K 1^{7}); †אמר הדבר הזה *say this saying* Je 23^{38} 31^{23} cf. 13^{12} 14^{17} (of God), 1 S 8^{10} (דִּבְרֵי י׳). **b.** *word of command,* ד׳ (הַ)מֶּלֶךְ 1 Ch 21$^{4.6}$ Est 1^{12} + 6 t. Est, Ec 8^{4} cf. 2 Ch 30^{5} 31^{5} Dn 9$^{23.25}$; †ד׳ מַלְכוּת *royal edict* Est 1^{19}; עָשָׂה כדבר *do according to the command of* Gn 44^{2} 47^{30} Ex 8$^{9.27}$ 12^{35} 32^{28} (J) Lv 10^{7} (P) Ju 11^{10} Ezr 10^{5} Ne 5$^{12.13}$; cf. 2 S 17^{6} (word of counsel), 1 K 3^{12} (request), 1 K 17^{13} (proposal; on these mngs. v. infr.) **c.** *message, report, tidings,* וַיִּשְׁמַע הָעָם אֶת־הַדָּבָר הָרָע הַזֶּה *and the people heard this evil report* Ex 33^{4} (JE) cf. 1 K 20^{12}; אמת (היה) הדבר *the report was true* 1 K 10^{6} = 2 Ch 9^{5}; עַד בּוֹא דָבָר מֵעִמָּכֶם *until word come from you* 2 S 15^{28}; ויגע הדבר אל מלך נינוה Jon 3^{6}; †הֵשִׁיב דָּבָר *return* or *bring word, report* Gn 37^{14} Nu 13^{26} 22^{8} (J) Dt 1$^{22.25}$ Jos 14^{7} 22^{32} (D) 1 K 2^{30} 20^{9} 2 K 22$^{9.20}$ (= 2 Ch 34$^{16.28}$), but *answer* 1 S 17^{30} 2 S 3^{11} 24^{13} (= 1 Ch 21^{12}), 1 K 12$^{6.9}$ (= 2 Ch 10$^{6.9}$), 12^{16} Ne 2^{20} Pr 18^{13} 27^{11} Is 41^{28} Ez 9^{11} (Dr $^{Sm.\ p.\ 190}$ explains the phrase as *turn back with a word*); cf. ענה (לא) דבר *answer something* or *nothing* 1 K 18^{21} 2 K 18^{36} ψ 119^{42} Is 36^{21} Je 44^{20} vid. **IV. 6**; השיב דברים *return words* Ex 19^{8} (E) Pr 24^{26} vid. **III. 1. d.** *advice, counsel,* בדבר בלעם *by advice of Balaam* Nu 31^{16} (P), cf. Ju 20^{7} 2 S 19^{44} Est 5^{5}. **e.** *request,* אמתו *of his maid,* עבדו *of his servant* 2 S 14$^{15.22}$. **f.** *promise,* לא יחל דברו *he shall not break his word* Nu 30^{3} (P), cf. הקים דבר *perform a promise* Ne 5^{13}, vid. also **2 b.** **g.** *charge, complaint,* אם אמת היה הדבר הזה *if this charge be true* Dt 22^{20} cf. 13^{15} 17^{4}, שׂים דבר בְּ 1 S 22^{15}, שׂים עלילות דברים לְ Dt 22$^{14.17}$. **h.** *decision, sentence,* דְּבַר הַמִּשְׁפָּט *the sentence of judgment* Dt 17^{9} cf. v$^{10.11}$. **i.** *theme, story,* רָחַשׁ לִבִּי דָּבָר טוֹב my heart swells with a *good theme* ψ 45^{2}; דְּבַר גְּבוּרוֹת *the story of his great might* Jb 41^{4}. **2.** *word of God,* as a divine communication in the form of commandments, prophecy, and words of help to his people, used 394 times. This word is communicated in several ways: **a.** ויהי דבר י׳ אל *then the word of Yahweh came unto* 1 S 15^{10} 2 S 7^{4} (cf. אלהים 1 Ch 17^{3}), 1 K 6^{11} 13^{20} 16^{1} 17$^{2.8}$ 21$^{17.28}$ 2 Ch 11^{2} (cf. האלהים 1 K 12^{22}); cf. 1 Ch 22^{8} (על by confusion), Is 38^{4} Je 1^{4} + 20 t. Je, Ez 3^{16} + 41 t. Ez, Jon 1^{1} 3^{1} Hg 2^{20} Zc 4^{8} 6^{9} 7$^{4.8}$ 8^{1} (without אל) v^{18}; †היה ד׳ י׳ אל Gn 15^{1} 2 Ch 12^{7} Je 25^{3} + 4 t. Je, Ez 1^{3} + 7 t. Ez, Dn 9^{2} Zc 1$^{1.7}$ 7^{1}; †הנה ד׳ י׳ אל Gn 15^{4} 1 K 19^{9}; †ד׳ י׳ היה אל 2 S 24^{11} 1 K 16^{7} 18^{1} 2 K 20^{4} Ez 24^{20}; †היה ד׳ י׳ ביד Hg 1^{1} 2$^{1.10}$; †ויהי ד׳ י׳ ביד Hg 1^{3}; †ד׳ י׳ אשר היה אל Ho 1^{1} Jo 1^{1} Mi 1^{1} Zp 1^{1}; †ד׳ י׳ אשר היה אליו 1 K 18^{31} Je 1^{2}; †ד׳ י׳ אשר היה אל יר׳ Je 14^{1} 46^{1} 47^{1} 49^{34} (vid. אשר **6 a**); הדבר אשר היה אל Je 7^{1} + 11 t. Je; †את ד׳ י׳ 2 K 3^{12} Je 23^{28} 27^{18}; cf. אֵלַי דָּבָר יְגֻנָּב *unto me a word was brought by stealth* Jb 4^{12}, cf. וְטֶרֶם יִגָּלֶה אֵלָיו דְּבַר י׳ *and the word of Yahweh was not yet revealed unto him* 1 S 3^{7}. Yahweh also sends his word שלח ψ 107^{20} 147^{18} Is 9^{7} Je 42^{5} (cf. pl. Zc 7^{12}) and makes it an object of vision ראה Je 2^{31} 38^{21} (cf. pl. Ez 11^{25}), חזה Is 2^{1}; it is also commanded צוה Ex 16$^{16.32}$ 35^{4} Lv 8^{5} 9^{6} 17^{2} Nu 30^{2} 36^{6} (P) Dt 4^{2} 13^{1} 15^{15} Jos 1^{13} 4^{10} (D) 1 Ch 16^{15} (= ψ 105^{8}) Ne 1^{8} Je 7^{23}, cf. הדברים אשר צוה Ex 35^{1} Lv 8^{36} (P) Ex 19^{7} (E) Dt 6^{6}. **b.** Yahweh confirms his word of promise Dt 9^{5} 1 S 1^{23} (where read דְּבָרְךָ *thy word* acc. to 𝔊 𝔖 & Dr), 1 K 2^{4} 6^{12} 8^{20} Je 29^{10} 33^{14}, and his word of warning 1 K 12^{15} Dn 9^{12}; his word stands for ever Is 40^{8}; it is settled for ever in heaven ψ 119^{89}; he remembers his *holy word* דבר קדשׁו ψ 105^{42} (cf. דִּבְרֵי קָדְשׁוֹ Je 23^{9}); he himself Jo 2^{11}, the angels ψ 103^{20}, and forces of nature ψ 148^{8} עשׂה דברו do his word of command; by his word the heavens were made ψ 33^{6}; it is near his people, in their mouth and heart Dt 30^{14}; a lamp to their feet ψ 119^{105}. **II.** *saying, utterance, sentence,* as a section of a discourse:—**1.** *of men,* **a.** דָּבָר בְּעִתּוֹ *a word in due season* Pr 15^{23} cf. Jb 4^{2} Pr 12^{25}; commonly in plural, †דִּבְרֵי (הַ)שִּׁיר(ה) *words of the song* (i.e. its lines of poetry) Dt 31^{30} 32^{44} ψ 18^{1} (= 2 S 22^{1}) 137^{3}; הלל בדברי דויד *to sing praises with the words of David* (his psalms) 2 Ch 29^{30}; דִּבְרֵי חֲכָמִים *sentences of the wise* Pr 1^{6} 22^{17} Ec

9^{17} 12^{11}; these sayings are commonly *written*, cf. דברי האגרת *words of the letter* Est 9^{26}; הדברים עתיקים *the records are ancient* 1 Ch 4^{22}; דִּבְרֵי (ה)סֵּפֶר Is 29$^{11.18}$ Je 29^{1}. **b.** *title of writings:* דִּבְרֵי קֹהֶלֶת Ec 1^{1}, ד׳ אגור Pr 30^{1}, ד׳ למואל Pr 31^{1}, ד׳ ירמיהו Je 1^{1}, so Am 1^{1} Ne 1^{1}; cf. in appended phrase or clause, Je 51^{64}, ד׳ איוב Jb 31^{40}. **c.** in Ch *name of a work:* ד׳ החזים 2 Ch 33$^{18.19}$, בד׳ שמעיה 2 Ch 12^{15}, בד׳ יהוא 2 Ch 20^{34}, על ד׳ שמואל 1 Ch 29^{29}; על ד׳ נתן 1 Ch 29^{29} 2 Ch 9^{29}, על ד׳ גד 1 Ch 29^{29}. (It is not certain whether writings of prophets or histories about them are referred to; in the latter case they are *acts*, **IV. 2,** vid. Dr$^{Intr\ 497}$.) **2.** *of God:* עֲשֶׂרֶת הַדְּבָרִים *the ten words* (sentences in the tables) Ex 34^{28} (JE) Dt 4^{13} 10^{4}, referred to as הדברים Ex 34^{1} (JE) Dt 4$^{10.36}$ 5^{19} 9^{10} 10^{2}; of commands of covenant code Ex 24$^{3.4.8}$ cf. 34^{27} (JE); of Deuteronomic code Dt 17^{19} (+ 16 t. D) 2 K 22^{11} 23$^{3-24}$ (cf. 2 Ch 34$^{19-31}$) Je 11$^{2-8}$ 34^{18}; the law-book of Joshua Jos 24^{26} (E); of the code of Ezra Ezr 7^{11} 9^{4} Ne 8$^{9.13}$; the words of Yahweh written by Jeremiah Je 25^{13} 36$^{4-32}$ 51^{61}; the words of the book of Daniel Dn 12$^{4.9}$; commands in general 1 S 15^{11} ψ 50^{17} 119$^{57.130.139}$; promises 2 S 7^{28} Ne 9^{8}, cf. 1 Ch 25^{5} 2 Ch 36^{16}. **III.** *a word, words:*—**1.** *of men:* שָׂפָה אֶחָת וּדְבָרִים אֲחָדִים *one lip, and one and the same words* Gn 11^{1} (J); אֵין אֹמֶר וְאֵין דְּבָרִים *no speech and no words* ψ 19^{4}; אִישׁ דְּבָרִים *man of words*, ready in speech, Ex 4^{10} (J); רב דברים *multitude of words* Jb 11^{2} Pr 10^{19} Ec 5^{2}; קְחוּ עִמָּכֶם דְּבָרִים *take with you words* Ho 14^{3}; דבר(י) (ה)שקר *lying word(s)* Ex 5^{9} 23^{7} (E) Pr 13^{5} 29^{12} Is 59^{13} Je 7$^{4.8}$; דִּבְרֵי רוּחַ *words of wind*, vain words Jb 16^{3}; וּמַה־שֵּׁמֶץ דָּבָר נִשְׁמַע־בּוֹ *and what a whisper of a word we hear of him!* Jb 26^{14}. **2.** *of God.* It is difficult to determine how many of the following should come under **II. 2.** The pl. for *words of God* is relatively seldom: Gn 20^{8} Ex 19^{6} Nu 12^{6} Jos 3^{9} (E) Ex 4$^{28.30}$ Nu 11^{24} (J) Dt 18^{19} Jos 23^{14} (D) 1 S 3^{18} 8^{10} 15^{1} 2 Ch 11^{4} Jb 42^{7} Pr 30^{6} Is 31^{2} Dn 10^{11} Am 8^{11} Mi 2^{7}, apart from Je 3^{12} + 30 t. Je, Ez 2^{7} + 4 t. Ez, Zc 1^{6} + 4 t. Zc. **IV.** *matter, affair*, thing about which one speaks:—**1.** *business, occupation:* דְּבַר הַמֶּלֶךְ *king's business* 1 S 21^{9}; לְכָל־דְּבַר *for every matter of* 1 Ch 26^{32} 27^{1} 2 Ch 19^{11}; לְכָל־דְּבָרֶיךָ *for all thine affairs* 1 Ch 28^{21}; דבר המזבח Nu 18^{7}; דָּבָר אֵין־לָהֶם עִם *they had no dealings with* Ju 18$^{7.28}$; †דְּבַר־יוֹם בְּיוֹמוֹ *the task or portion of a day in its day, daily duty or due* Ex 5$^{13.19}$ (E) 16^{4} (J) Lv 23^{37} (P) 1 K 8^{59} 2 K 25^{30} 1 Ch 16^{37} 2 Ch 8^{13} (ביום) v^{14} 31^{16} Ezr 3^{4} Ne 11^{23} 12^{47} Je 52^{34} Dn 1^{5}; †דבר שנה בשנה 1 K 10^{25} 2 Ch 9^{24}. **2.** pl. *acts* cstr. דִּבְרֵי 1 K 11$^{41.41}$ 1 Ch 29^{29} 2 Ch 12^{15} 16^{11}; †דְּבָרָיו *his acts* 2 Ch 13^{22} 35^{27}; especially in phrases, וְיֶתֶר דִּבְרֵי ... עַל־סֵפֶר דִּבְרֵי הַיָּמִים *and the rest of the acts of ... in the book of the chronicles* (*daily record of events*) *of* 1 K 14^{29} + 32 t. K.; וְיֶתֶר דִּבְרֵי 2 Ch 13^{22} + 8 t. Ch, וְיֶתֶר דְּבָרָיו 2 Ch 28^{26}, שְׁאָר דִּבְרֵי 2 Ch 9^{29} are referred to various sources; cf. also במספר דברי הימים 1 Ch 27^{24}, בדברי דויד 1 Ch 23^{27}, על־דברי מלכי ישׂראל 2 Ch 33^{18}: דברים טובים *good deeds* 2 Ch 12^{12} 19^{13}; דִּבְרֵי עֲוֹנֹת *acts of iniquity* ψ 65^{4} (De, *Fälle von Missethaten*); דִּבְרֵי־רָע *evil deeds* Je 5^{28}. It is used of God, only in כל דבריו לא יענה Jb 33^{13}, ד׳ נִפְלְאֹתֶיךָ ψ 105^{27}, ד׳ אתותיו ψ 145^{5}. **3.** *matter, affair:* דבר אוריה *affair of Uriah* 1 K 15^{5}; שרש דבר *root of the matter* Jb 19^{28}; מה היה הדבר *how went the matter?* 1 S 4^{16} 2 S 1^{4} cf. Ru 3^{18}; סבב את פני הדבר *change the face of the matter* 2 S 14^{20}; דִּבְרֵי הָאֲתֹנוֹת *the matter of the asses* 1 S 10^{2}; זה דבר הרצח *this is the case of the slayer* Dt 19^{4}; לְכָל־דְּבָרָיו 1 K 6^{38} *as to all its particulars.* **4.** *events, things:* in the phrase, †אחר הדברים האלה *after these things* (events in time) Gn 15^{1} 22^{1} 40^{1} (E) 39^{7} (J) 1 K 17^{17} 21^{1} Ezr 7^{1} Est 2^{1} 3^{1}; †אחרי הדברים האלה Gn 48^{1} Jos 24^{29} (E) Gn 22^{20} (J) 2 Ch 32^{1}. **5.** *cause, case* for judicial investigation: כִּי־יִהְיֶה לָהֶם דָּבָר *if they have a case* Ex 18^{16} cf. 18^{22} 22^{8}; בעל דברים *one having a case* Ex 24^{14}, cf. בדבר משפט 2 Ch 19^{6}; דְּבָרֶיךָ טוֹבִים וּנְכֹחִים *pleas, good and right* 2 S 15^{3} cf. Jos 20^{4}. **6.** *something, anything* (indefinite): עשׂה דבר *do a thing* Gn 22^{16} + (frequent); עשׂה דברים Is 42^{16} + (less frequent); היפלא מי׳ דבר Gn 18^{14} cf. Je 32$^{17.27}$; לא...דבר *nothing* 1 K 5^{7} 10^{3} Is 39^{2} Je 42^{4} + (frequent), אין דבר Ex 5^{11} (E) Nu 20^{19} 1 S 20^{21}; לא דבר מ׳ *nothing of* Ex 9^{4} (J) Jos 8^{35} 11^{15} 21^{45} 23^{14} (D); כל דבר *anything* Nu 31^{23} Dt 23^{20} +; דבר רע ψ 141^{4} +; ד׳ טוב 1 K 14^{13} +; דְּבַר־מָה *whatsoever* Nu 23^{3} (E); עֶרְוַת דבר Dt 23^{15} *nakedness of a thing*, i.e. unclean or unseemly thing (indecency in camp); so of a wife 24^{1}. **7.** *way, manner:* זֶה דְּבַר הַשְּׁמִטָּה *this is the manner of the release* Dt 15^{2} (cf. SI^{1}); כֵּן דְּבַר הַמֶּלֶךְ *so was the way of the king* Est 1^{13}; כדבר הזה *after this manner, thus* †Gn 18^{25} 32^{20} 44^{7} (JE) 2 S 15^{6} Ezr 10^{5} Ne 5$^{12.13}$ with (עשׂה), 1 S 9^{21} 2 S 14^{3} 17^{6} (דבר), 1 S 17$^{27.30}$ Is 8^{20} (אמר), Ne 6$^{4.5}$ (שלח), Ne 6^{4} (השיב) cf. 1 S 17^{30}, 2 K 7^{19} (היה); (peculiar to D, כדבר הרע הזה *such a wicked deed as this* Dt 13^{12} 19^{20}, כדבר הגדול הזה Dt 4^{32}); כדברים האלה עשׂה *thus and thus did he* Gn 39^{19}

(J) 1 S 2^{23} (but usually the pl. = *these words*). **8.** *reason, cause:* זֶה דְּבַר־הַמַּס 1 K 9^{15}; זה הדבר אשׁר *this is the reason why* Jos 5^{4} (D) 1 K 11^{27}; so 1 S 17^{29} AV RV, *was it not but a word?* Th Ke RVm VB Dr; . . . עַל דְּבַר *because of, for the sake of* Gn 20$^{11.18}$ (E) 12^{17} 43^{18} Ex 8^{8} (J) Nu 17^{14} (P) ψ 45^{5} 79^{9}, עַל דִּבְרֵי Je 14^{1}; עַל־דִּבְרֵיכֶם *for your sakes* Dt 4^{21}, עַל דְּבַר אשׁר Dt 22$^{24.24}$ 23^{5} 2 S 13^{22}.

1698 דֶּ֫בֶר$_{49}$ **n.m.** **pestilence** (cf. Ar. إِدْبَارٌ, دَبْرٌ, *departure, death*)—Ex 9^{3}+; דָּ֑בֶר Hb 3^{5}; sf. דְּבָרֶיךָ Ho 13^{14};—**1.** *plague, pestilence,* in general Ex 5^{3} 9^{15} Nu 14^{12} (J) Lv 26^{25} (H) Dt 28^{21}, 2 S 24$^{13.15}$ (+ v^{15a} 𝔊 We Dr) = 1 Ch 21$^{12.14}$, 1 K 8^{37} = 2 Ch 6^{28}, 2 Ch 7^{13} 20^{9} ψ 91$^{3.6}$ Je 14^{12} + 16 t. Je, Ez 5^{12} + 11 t. Ez, Ho 13^{14} Am 4^{10} Hb 3^{5}. Rd. וּבַדָּ֑בֶר, or the like, 1 S 4^{8}, for MT בַּמִּדְבָּר, We Klo Dr. †**2.** *cattle-plague, murrain* Ex 9^{3} (J) = ψ 78^{50}.

1699 †[דֹּ֫בֶר] **n.[m.]** **pasture** (cf. Aram. דַּבְרָא, Syr. ܕܒܪܐ)—sf. כְּעֵדֶר בְּתוֹךְ הַדָּבְרוֹ *as a flock in the midst of its pasture* Mi 2^{12} (art. with sf., cf. Ges §127.4b, who attaches ו as conj. to foll. word); וְרָעוּ כְבָשִׂים כְּדָבְרָם *and lambs shall feed as (in) their pasture* Is 5^{17}.

1702 †דֹּבְרוֹת **n.f.pl.** **floats, rafts** 1 K 5^{23}.

1700 †[דִּבְרָה] **n.f.** **cause, reason, manner**—cstr. עַל דִּבְרַת *because of, for the sake of* Ec 3^{18} 7^{14} 8^{2}; עַל־דִּבְרָתִי מַלְכִּי־צֶדֶק *after the order, or manner, of Melchizedek* ψ 110^{4} (י ancient genit. ending, to soften transition in poetry, Ges §90(3)a); sf. דִּבְרָתִי *my cause, suit* Jb 5^{8}.

1682 †I. דְּבוֹרָה **n.f.** **bee** (cf. Ar. دَبْرٌ, *swarm of bees,* Aram. דַּבַּרְתָּא, Syr. ܕܒܘܪܬܐ) Is 7^{18}; pl. דְּבֹרִים Dt 1^{44} Ju 14^{8} ψ 118^{12}. Rd. also דְּבֹרוֹ *its bees* 1 S 14^{26} for MT דְּבַשׁ cf. 𝔊 We Dr.

1683 †II. דְּבוֹרָה **n.pr.f.** (*bee*)—**1.** the nurse of Rebekah Gn 35^{8}. **2.** the prophetess Ju 4$^{4.5.9.10.14}$ 5$^{1.7.12.15}$.

1705 †דָּבְרַת **n.pr.loc.** Levitical city in Issachar, the present *Debûrîje* at the foot of Mt. Tabor (Rob$^{BR\ iii.\ 210}$ Bd$^{Pal\ 249}$) Jos 19^{12} (הַדָּבְרַת) 21^{28} 1 Ch 6^{57}.

1687 †I. דְּבִיר **n.m.** (cf. Ar. دُبُرٌ *back,* دَبْرٌ *part behind*) *hindmost chamber, innermost room of the temple of Solomon* = קדשׁ הקדשׁים *holy of holies, most holy place,* the place of the ark and the cherubic images, the throne-room of Yahweh 1 K 6$^{5.16.19.20.21.22.23.31}$ 7^{49} (= 2 Ch 4^{20}) 8$^{6.8}$ (= 2 Ch 5$^{7.9}$) 2 Ch 3^{16} ψ 28^{2}. Prob. rd. דְּבִיר 2 K 10^{25} also, for MT עִיר; so Klo after 𝔊L. (It is translated *oracle* in AV RV after Aq Sym χρηματιστήριον, 𝔙 *oraculum,* on the incorrect theory that it was derived from דִּבֶּר *speak.*)

†II. דְּבִיר **1. n.pr.m.** king of Eglon Jos 10^{3}. 1688

2. n.pr.loc. a. דְּבִ֫רָה c. ה‑ loc., N. border Judah Jos 15^{7} (*westward* Hup ψ 28^{2}). **b.** לִדְבִר town of the Gadites Jos 13^{26}, perh. *Lôdebâr* 2 S 9^{4} vid. לֹא דְבָר Di MV. **c.** דְּבִיר Ju 1$^{11.11}$ 1 Ch 6^{43}, דְּבִרָה Jos 10$^{38.39}$, elsewhere דְּבִר Jos 15^{15} +, a royal city of Canaanites anciently called קִרְיַת סֵפֶר Jos 15^{15} Ju 1^{11}, קִרְיַת סַנָּה Jos 15^{49}; on the mountains of Judah, in region of Hebron Jos 11^{21} 15^{49}, assigned to the Aaronite priests Jos 21^{15} as a city of refuge 1 Ch 6^{43}; mod. *Dhoherîye,* 5 hours SW. fr. Hebron, acc. to Kn, so Survey iii. 402; other conject. in Di Jos 10^{39} Ri$^{HWB\ 265}$.

†דִּבֵּר **n.[m.]** **speaking** (so Ew §156) Je 5^{13} 1699'
וְהַדִּבֵּר אֵין בָּהֶם; acc. to Hi Gf Ki (less prob.) vb. with art. for relat. (vid. [דָּבַר] **Pi.**): but rd. rather הַדָּבָר, *and the word is not in them.*

†[דַּבֶּ֫רֶת] **n.f.** **word**—יִשָּׂא מִדַּבְּרֹתֶיךָ *he receiveth of thy words* Dt 33^{3} (poem). 1703

†דִּבְרִי **n.pr.m.** a Danite Lv 24^{11}. 1704

†I. [מִדְבָּר] **n.m.** **mouth,** as organ of speech,—מִדְבָּרֵךְ נָאוֶה *thy mouth is lovely* Ct 4^{3} 4057
‖ שִׂפְתוֹתַיִךְ, 𝔊 λαλιά, Jer *eloquium.*

II. מִדְבָּר$_{270}$ **n.m.** **wilderness**—Dt 32^{10} +; 4057
c. ה loc. מִדְבָּרָה Jos 18^{12} + 15 t.; cstr. Ex 15^{22} +; מִדְבָּ֫רָה 1 K 19^{15}; sf. מִדְבָּרָהּ Is 51^{3};—**1.** tracts of land, used for the pasturage of flocks and herds, דָּשְׁאוּ נְאוֹת מִדְבָּר *the pastures of the wilderness put forth green grass* Jo 2^{22}; יִרְעֲפוּ נ׳ מ׳ *the pastures of the wilderness drop* (fertility) ψ 65^{13}; יָבְשׁוּ נ׳ מ׳ *are dried up* Je 23^{10}, cf. Je 9^{9} Jo 1$^{19.20}$. **2.** *uninhabited land,* מִדְבָּר לֹא־אָדָם בּוֹ *wilderness in which is no man* Jb 38^{26}; the abode of pelicans ψ 102^{7}; wild asses Jb 24^{5} Je 2^{24}; jackals Mal 1^{3}; ostriches Lam 4^{3}; מִי־יִתְּנֵנִי בַמִּדְבָּר מְלוֹן אֹרְחִים וְאֶעֶזְבָה אֶת־עַמִּי *O that I had in the wilderness a lodging place of wayfarers, that I might leave my people* Je 9^{1}; טוֹב שֶׁבֶת בְּאֶרֶץ מִדְבָּר *better to dwell in a desert land,* than with a contentious woman Pr 21^{19}; בְּאֶרֶץ מִדְבָּר וּבְתֹהוּ יְלֵל יְשִׁמֹן *in a desert land, and in a waste howling wilderness* Dt 32^{10}. **3.** *large tracts* of such land bearing various names, in certain districts of which there might be towns and cities: יִשְׂאוּ מִדְבָּר וְעָרָיו חֲצֵרִים תֵּשֵׁב קֵדָר *let the wilderness and its cities lift up* (their voice), *the villages that Kedar doth inhabit* Is 42^{11}. There were six cities in the wilderness of Judah Jos 15$^{61.62}$; הַמִּדְבָּר usually = wilderness of the wanderings

Gn 14^{6} Nu 14$^{16.29.32.33.33}$+, or the great Arabian desert Ju 11^{22}+; but may also refer to any other Ct 3^{6} 8^{5}. Special tracts—(a) of the wilderness of the wanderings were מ׳ שׁוּר Ex 15^{22}, סין Ex 16^{1}+, סיני Ex 19^{1}+, פארן Nu 13^{26}+, צן Nu 20^{1}+, קדשׁ ψ 29^{8}, אתם Nu 33^{8}; (b) in W. Pal. מ׳ יהודה Ju 1^{16} ψ 63^{1} cf. Jos 15^{61}, מעון 1 S 23$^{24.25}$, זיף 1 S 23^{15} 26^{2}, באר שׁבע Gn 21^{14}, עין גדי 1 S 24^{2}, תקוע 2 Ch 20^{20}, ירואל 2 Ch 20^{16}, גבעון 2 S 2^{24}; (c) in East. Palestine מואב Dt 2^{8}, אדום 2 K 3^{8}, קדמות Dt 2^{26}. **4.** fig. וְשַׂמְתִּיהָ כַמִּדְבָּר וְשַׁתִּהָ כְּאֶרֶץ צִיָּה *and (lest I) make her as a wilderness and set her like a dry land* Ho 2^{5}; הֲמִדְבָּר הָיִיתִי לְיִשְׂרָאֵל *have I been a wilderness to Israel?* Je 2^{31}.

דבשׁ (√ of foll.; cf. Ar. ادبسّ IX. *become black* or *brown*, of a colour between black and red; vid. deriv.; so Fl v. infr.; yet vb. in this mng. perh. denom. fr. دِبْسٌ i.e. having the colour of *dibs*).

1706 †דְּבַשׁ $_{54}$ **n.m.** $^{1 S 14, 29}$ **honey** (named from colour acc. to Fl NHWB$^{i. 439}$; Ar. دِبْسٌ (دُبْسٌ, دِبِسٌ) *date-honey*; NH דְּבַשׁ, Aram. דּוּבשׁא, ܕܒܫܐ, ܕܶܒܫܳܐ, *honey* both of fruits and of bees; cf. also As. *dišpu* COT^{Gloss} Zim$^{BP 84}$ Dl$^{Pr 70}$)—abs. ד׳ Gn 43^{11}+33 t.; דְּבָשׁ Ex 3^{8}+18 t.; sf. דִּבְשִׁי Ct 5^{1};—*honey*, product of bees, used as food Ju 14$^{8.9.18}$ (in lion's carcass); found in (clefts of) rock Dt 32^{13} (ד׳ מִסֶּלַע, in song, JE), ψ 81^{17} (מִצּוּר ד׳); in forest, on ground 1 S 14^{25} (על־פני השׂדה) v^{26} (הֵלֶךְ ד׳; but read rather הָלַךְ דְּבֹרוֹ *its bees had departed*, We Dr after 𝔊) v$^{29.43}$; transported in jar or bottle בַּקְבֻּק ד׳ 1 K 14^{3}; contrib. to priests and Levites 2 Ch 31^{5}; ‖ חֶמְאָה 2 S 17^{29} Is 7$^{15.22}$ (in last two the being limited to such food is apparently token of destitution); kept in store Je 41^{8}; a choice gift Gn 43^{11} (J); article of trade Ez 27^{17} (in these two perh. =*grape syrup*, mod. *dibs*, cf. Di Gn 43^{11} v. Rob$^{BR ii. 81}$); forbidden as burnt offering Lv 2^{11} (‖ שְׂאֹר); *honey comb*=יַעְרַת הַדּ׳ 1 S 14^{27} (cf. יַעְרִי Ct 5^{1}); also צוּף ד׳ Pr 16^{24} (cf. נֹפֶת צוּפִים ψ 19^{11}); most often in phrase describing abundance in land of Canaan אֶרֶץ זָבַת חָלָב וּד׳ Ex 3$^{8.17}$ 13^{5} 33^{3} (all JE) Lv 20^{24} (H) Nu 13^{27} 14^{8} 16$^{13.14}$ (all JE) Dt 6^{3} 11^{9} 26$^{9.15}$ 27^{3} 31^{20} (all D) Jos 5^{6} (D) Je 11^{5} 32^{22} Ez 20$^{6.15}$; cf. Dt 8^{8} 2 K 18^{32} (of land of captivity, words of the Rabshak); v. also Ez 16$^{13.19}$ Jb 20^{17} נַחֲלֵי ד׳ וְחֶמְאָה; *honey*, used to illustrate moral teachings Pr 24^{13} (‖ נֹפֶת), 25$^{16.27}$ (danger of surfeit); sim. of sweetness of taste Ez 3^{3} (the roll), cf. כְּצַפִּיחִת בִּדְ׳ Ex 16^{31} (P; description of manna); of sweetness of the law ψ 19^{11} (‖ נֹפֶת צוּפִים) cf. 119^{103}; (of pleasant words Pr 16^{24} cf. supr.); sweetness of lips ד׳ וְחָלָב Ct 4^{11}; fig. of love דִּבְשִׁי Ct 5^{1} (‖ חֲלָבִי, יֵינִי, יַעְרִי).

†[דַּבֶּ֫שֶׁת] **1. n.f.** hump (of camel) (etymol.?) 1707
cstr. Is 30^{6} עַל־דַּבֶּשֶׁת גְּמַלִּים. **2. n.pr.loc.** on 1708
border of Zebulun Jos 19^{11} דַּבָּ֑שֶׁת.

†יְדַבָּשׁ **n.pr.m.** a son of Etam? 1 Ch 4^{3}; 3031
MT has וְאֵלֶּה אֲבִי עֵיטָם יִזְרְעֶאל...וְיִדְבָּשׁ 𝔊 οὗτοι υἱοὶ Αἰτάν, cf. 𝔙;=וְאֵלֶּה בְּנֵי ע׳ cf. Be Öt (< אלה בני אבי ע׳, as some MSS.) On real significance of names cf. עֵיטָם.

†[דָּגָה] **vb. multiply, increase** (intr.); 1711
—**Qal** *Impf.* 3 mpl. וְיִדְגּוּ לָרֹב בקרב הארץ Gn 48^{16} (E).

†דָּג **n.m.**$^{Jon 2, 1}$ **fish** (NH *id.*)—דָּג Jon 2$^{1.1.11}$+ 1709
Ne 13^{16} Qr (Kt דָּאג); דָּגִים 1 K 5^{13}+6 t.; דְּגֵי Gn 9^{2}+7 t.;—*fish* of sea Jon 2$^{1.1.11}$ (in v^{1} ד׳ גָּדוֹל); Ne 13^{16} (דָּג Kt דָּאג) article of Tyrian trade; only here coll., rd. perh. דָּגָה; or regard as late usage, cf. converse דָּגָה of individual Jon 2^{2});—elsewhere always pl.: as subj. of Solomon's utterance 1 K 5^{13}; fish-spear צִלְצַל דגים Jb 40^{31}; most often דְּגֵי הַיָּם Gn 9^{2} (P), ψ 8^{9} Ho 4^{3} Zp 1^{3} Ez 38^{20} Jb 12^{8} (in all opp. to beasts & birds, & appar. used with them, +רֶמֶשׂ Ez. cf. vb. רמשׂ Gn, for animal creation in general; also Hb 1^{14} cf. infr.); Nu 11^{22} (JE) of fish (with beasts) as food (cf. Gn 9$^{2f.}$) in simile of men ensnared, like fish taken in net (מְצוֹדָה) Ec 9^{12} cf. Hb 1^{14} (דְּגֵי הַיָּם); 4 t. שַׁעַר הַדָּגִים *fish-gate* 2 Ch 33^{14} Zp 1^{10} Ne 3^{3} 12^{39} (on situation cf. שַׁעַר).

†דָּגָה **n.f. fish** (NH *id.*)—דָּגָה Nu 11^{5}+5 t.; 1710
cstr. דְּגַת Gn 1^{26}+4 t.+Ez 29^{4b} (del. B Co); sf. דְּגָתוֹ Ez 47^{10} 𝔊 𝔙 Co; (MT דגתם), דְּגָתָם Is 50^{2} ψ 105^{29}+Ez 47^{10} MT cf. supr.—*fish*, almost always coll.; fish of sea דְּגַת הַיָּם Gn 1$^{26.28}$(P) Ez 47^{10} (in sim.); in Nile (יְאֹר) Ex 7$^{18.21}$(E) cf. ψ 105^{29}; דְּגַת יְאֹרֶיךָ Ez 29$^{4.4}$ (cf. supr.) v^{5}; in sea and rivers Is 50^{2} Ez 47$^{9.10}$; food in Egypt Nu 11^{5} (JE); image of fish forbidden in worship, as of beasts and birds Dt 4^{18} (on sacredness of fish, and use in sacrifice cf. Selden$^{De Diis Syris, ii. 3}$; RS$^{Sem. i. 274}$); of single fish only Jon 2^{2} (2$^{1.1.11}$ דָּג) by late usage; cf. conversely דָּגָה=דָּאג coll. Ne 13^{16}.

†[דּוּג, דִּיג] **vb. denom. fish for, catch**— 1770
Qal *Pf.* 3 mpl. sf. וְדִיגוּם consec. Je 16^{16} (but as **Qal** dub. Ges$^{§ 73. 2}$; Sta$^{§ 160 b. 2}$ regards as **Hiph.** (abbrev.), Nö$^{ZMG. 1883, 540}$ conj. **Pi.**)

1728,1771 †[דַּיָּג] **n.m.**[Ez 47, 10] **fisher, fisherman,** only pl. דַּיָּגִים Is 19[8], דַּיָּגִים Qr Je 16[16] (Kt דוגים), דַּוָּגִים Ez 47[10] & Kt Je 16[16].

1729 †דּוּגָה **n.f. fishing, fishery,** only in וְנִשָּׂא בְּסִירוֹת דּוּגָה Am 4[2] (‖ בְּצִנּוֹת) of י׳, metaph. for dragging Isr. captive (cf. for practice referred to, in case of fish, Ez 29[4] & Jb 40[26] scornful summons to do it with crocodile, if possible! v. Herod[II. 70] on mode of capturing crocodiles).

1712 †דָּגוֹן **n.pr.m.**[18 5, 4] god & idol of Philistines (cf. As. *Dagan, Dakan(nu)*, name perh. non-Shemitic COT Ju 16[23] Dl[Pa 139] Sayce[Rel. Bab. 188 f.] but v. Jen infr.)—god of Ashdod, exc. Ju 16[23] (Gaza) & 1 Ch 10[10] (but cf. infr.);—דגון אֱלֹהֵיהֶם Ju 16[23] cf. דגון אֱלֹהֵינוּ 1 S 5[7], בֵּית ד׳ 1 S 5[2.5] 1 Ch 10[10] (here hardly orig. cf. ‖ 1 S 31[10] & We Dr); כֹּהֲנֵי ד׳ 1 S 5[5], מִפְתַּן ד׳ v[5]; as name of image (אֶצֶל) ד׳ v[2.3.4], דגון נֹפֵל v[3.4], רַק ד׳ נִשְׁאַר עָלָיו v[4] (but sense difficult; We prop. דָּגוֹ *only his fish*, i.e. fishy part, *was left upon him*, v. also Dr;—but was Dagon a fish-god? Cf. works cited above & Scholz[Götzendienst 238 ff.], Baud in PRE[2 iii. 460 ff.], esp. Jen[Kosmol. 449 ff.]). Vid. בֵּית דָּגוֹן p. 111.

1713 †[דָּגַל] **vb. look, behold** (As. *dagâlu*, Lotz[TP 131]; Thes RobGes MV SS De make דָּגוּל a denom. fr. דֶּגֶל = *lifted up like a banner*, or *furnished with a banner*, i.e. *exalted, distinguished*, AV RV *chiefest*);—*Pt. pass.* דָּגוּל מֵרְבָבָה Ct 5[10] *looked at, conspicuous*, acc. to Dl[HA 40].

1714 †[דֶּגֶל] **n.m.**[Nu 10, 14] **standard, banner** (As. *diglu* Dl[HA 40 Pr 58]; cf. also Di Nu 2[2]); cstr. דֶּגֶל Nu 2[3] + 7 t.; sf. דִּגְלוֹ Nu 1[52] + 2 t.; pl. sf. דִּגְלֵיהֶם Nu 2[17.31.34];—*standard*, partic. of separate tribes of Isr. ד׳ מחנה יהודה etc. Nu 2[3.10.18.25] 10[14.18.22.25]; cf. also 1[52] 2[2] (‖ אֹתֹת) v[17.31.34] (all P); fig. Ct 2[4] ודגלו עלי אהבה.

1713 †[דָּגַל] **vb. denom. carry,** or **set up standard, banner**—**Qal** *Impf.* 1 pl. נִדְגֹּל ψ 20[6] (Gr Che נָגִיל; Bi נְגַדֵּל, after 𝔊 𝔖; Now נִגְדַּל; poss. נַגְדִּל?) *set up standard* in battle, cf. Dl[Pr 61]. **Niph.** *Pt.* fpl. נִדְגָּלוֹת Ct 6[4.10] *bannered, supplied with standards*, pt. as subst., of *bannered hosts*, cf. De.

דגן (√of foll. mng. dub.; NH דַּגֵּן Pa. *heap up* etc. seems to be denom.; Ol[§ 215 b. 4] der. דָּגָן fr. דָּגָה, cf. MV; We[Skizzen iii. 170] inclines to regard דָּגָן as der. fr. n.pr. divin. דגן (cf. דָּגוֹן), as *cereal* fr. *Ceres*).

1715 †דָּגָן **n.m. corn, grain** (of cereals) (NH *id.*, Sam. 𐡃𐡂𐡍 v. Thes.; cf. Ph. ארצת דגן)—דָּגָן Gn 27[28] + 29 t.; cstr. דְּגַן ψ 78[24]; sf. דְּגָנִי Ho 2[11], דְּגָנְךָ Dt 7[13] 12[17] 14[23] 18[4], דְּגָנֶךָ Dt 11[14], דְּגָנֵךְ Is 62[8], דְּגָנָם ψ 4[8] 65[10]—*corn*, c. תִּירוֹשׁ *must*, q.v., Gn 27[28.37] (both J) ψ 4[8] Is 62[8] Ho 2[11] 7[14] 9[1] Zc 9[17]; cf. also Nu 18[27] (P; here, for תירוש, מְלֵאָה מִן־הַיָּקֶב), La 2[12] (where יַיִן), Ho 14[8] (where גֶּפֶן & יֵין לְבָנוֹן); ארץ דגן ותירוש of land of Canaan Dt 33[28]; of land of captiv. (words of the Rabshak) 2 K 18[32] = Is 36[17] (other products, also, named in both); usually c. תירוש & יצהר Nu 18[12] Dt 7[13] 11[14] 12[17] 14[23] 18[4] 28[51] 2 Ch 31[5] (+ דבש) 32[28] Ne 5[11] 10[40] 13[5.12] Je 31[12] Ho 2[10.24] Jo 1[10] 2[19] Hg 1[11]; also Jo 1[17] Me; (cf. 2 K 18[32] Is 36[17] supr.); alone, rare and late Ne 5[2.3.10] ψ 65[10] Ez 36[29]; דְּגַן־שָׁמַיִם ψ 78[24];—of the above the following refer to firstfruits offered to the priests Nu 18[12] (cf. v[27]) Dt 18[4] 2 Ch 31[5]; to tithe Dt 12[17] 14[23] Ne 13[5.12]; to both generally Ne 10[40]; to loaning on usury Ne 5[10.11].

†[דָּגַר] **vb. gather together as a brood** (cf. Aram. דְּגַר *heap together*; so دجر Nasar.)—**Qal** *Pf.* 3 ms. דָּגַר Je 17[11]; 3 fs. דָּגְרָה Is 34[15]—*gather together* into its shadow Is 34[15] (of קִפּוֹז, q.v.), דָּגַר וְלֹא יָלָד Je 17[11] (of partridge; sim. of one getting riches unjustly). 1716

†[דַּד] **n.m.** [Pr 5, 19] **breast,** better **teat, nipple** (τιτθοί Aq Pr 5[19] Symm Ez 23[3.21]; NH & Aram. דַּד; primit. caressing word; acc. to Fl in NHWB[i. 439])—Du. cstr. דַּדֵּי Ez 23[3.8] (both del. 𝔊 𝔖 Co); sf. דַּדַּיִךְ Ez 23[21] (rd. בתוליך 𝔖 Co); דַּדֶּיהָ Pr 5[19];—of breasts of woman Pr 5[19] (Hi Bi rd. דֹּדֶיהָ *her love* cf. 7[18]); of Samaria & Jerusalem under fig. of young women Ez 23[3] (דַּדֵּי בְּתוּלֵיהֶן) cf. v[8]; דַּדַּיִךְ v[21]; but prob. del. ד׳ in Ez cf. supr. & Gei[Urschrift 397].—Vid. also שַׁד sub שדה. 1717

דֹּד, דֹּדָה v. sub דוד. p. 187 1730, 1733

†[דָּדָה] **vb.** [**move slowly**] (NH Pi. דִּדָּה *lead slowly*, Hithp. הִדַּדָּה; Aram. דַּדִּי, אִידַּדִּי; Ar. دَأْدَأَ is *run quickly* (of a camel): on form, cf. Kö[i. 587]; SS der. fr. דאה cf. Sta[§ 112 a, 150 a, 129 b, 581 d])—**Pi.** *Impf.* 1 s. sf. אֲדַדֵּם (so read for MT אֶדַּדֵּם Dy Bi & Che, cf. his crit. note) *lead slowly* (in procession) ψ 42[5]. **Hithp.** *Impf.* 1 s. אֶדַּדֶּה Is 38[15]; also sf. אֶדַּדֵּם ψ 42[5] MT but cf. supr.;—*walk deliberately*, at ease (De Che Di), or as in procession (Ew), Is 38[15] (cf. Che Di VB). 1718

דֹּדַי Kt v. דּוֹדוֹ sub דוד. p. 187 1734

†דְּדָן **n.pr.loc. & gent.**;—ד׳ Gn 10[7] + 8 t. 1719

\+ Ez 27^{20} (but v. infr.) c. ה loc. דְּדָ֫נֶה Ez 25^{13} cf. Ges[§ 90, 2 ad fin.];—**1.** under fig. of son of רַעְמָה and grandson of כּוּשׁ (v. these arts.) Gn 10^{7} (brother of שְׁבָא) = 1 Ch 1^{9} Ez 27^{20}; cf. בְּנֵי ד׳ v^{15} (but rd. here perh. רדן 𝔊 υἱοὶ Ῥοδίων, cf. Sta[De Pop. Javan. 11], also 𝔖 ܪܘܕܝ̈, Co; v. sub דֹּדָנִים infr.) cf. also Ez 38^{13}, שְׁבָא וּד׳; also Je 25^{23}; south-Arabian tribe on Persian Gulf, = Sab. בנו דדן acc. to DHM[ZMG 1876, 122; Sab. Denkm. 28] (dubit. Mordt); but in NW. of Arabian peninsula, Glaser[Skizze ii. 391 ff.]; perhaps orig. further south cf. Di Gn 10^{7}. **2.** as son of יָקְשָׁן, father of אַשּׁוּרִם etc., Gn 25$^{3.3}$ (here also brother of שְׁבָא) = 1 Ch 1^{32}; Je 49^{8} יֹשְׁבֵי ד׳. This is appar. a northern branch of **1**, cf. Di Gn 25^{3}.—On דדן in MI[31.31] cf. Sm & So[MI p. 29] Nö[LCB Jan. 8, 1887] Cl Gann[JAs. Jan. 1887, 107].

1719 דְּדָ֫נֶה v. דְּדָן. p. 186

1720 †[דְּדָנִי] **adj.gent.** only pl. as subst. אֹרְחוֹת דְּדָנִים Is 21^{13}.

1721 †דֹּדָנִים **n.pr.gent.pl.** Gn 10^{4}; but = רוֹדָנִים 1 Ch 1^{7}; rd. here רדנים, so 𝔊 Sam Di Sta[De Pop. Javan. 11]; cf. Ez 27^{15} supr. sub דְּדָן.

1724 †[דָּהַם] **vb. astonish, astound** (Ar. دَهِمَ, دَهَمَ)—**Niph.** *Pt.* כְּאִישׁ נִדְהָם Je 14^{9} *like a man astounded* (‖ כְּגִבּוֹר לֹא יוכל להושיע); 𝔊 ὑπνῶν = נִרְדָּם.

1725 †[דָּהַר] **vb. rush, dash,** of horse (onomat.? perh. cf. Ar. دَهَرَ *befall, fall upon, overcome, conquer*)—**Qal** *Pt.* סוּס דֹּהֵר Na 3^{2}.

1726 †[דַּהֲרָה] **n.f. rushing, dashing,** of riders—*Pl.* cstr. דַּהֲרוֹת דַּהֲרוֹת אַבִּירָיו Ju 5^{22}; repetition for intensity, *furious dashing.*

8410 †תִּדְהָר **n.[m.]** name of a tree, prob. **elm** (Syr. ܕܪܕܪܐ (or ܕܕܪܐ PS) Lag[BN 130] Löw[71]; Ar. دَرْدَارٌ Lane[864] Dozy[i. 432] (also *ash*, v. Dozy[ib.]); so Symm & 𝔙 Is 41^{19}; cf. Di, where also other views, e.g. *plane-tree* (Rabb. Che), or *pine*;—√ dub.; Ges Is 41^{19} Thes der. from דהר *endure* inferred from Ar. دَهْرٌ *time*, but this questionable; perh. a loan-word), בְּרוֹשׁ תִּדְהָר וּתְאַשּׁוּר יַחְדָּו Is 41^{19} = 60^{13}.

1727 †[דּוּב] **vb. pine away** (cf. דאב, דאבון)—**Hiph.** *Pt.* f. pl. מְדִיבֹת נפשׁ Lv 26^{16} (diseases) *causing to pine away the soul* (life), cf. Di; in 1 S 2^{33} read prob. *Inf.* לְהָדִיב את נפשׁך (for MT לַאֲדִיב) so Dr; trans. *to cause thy* (al. *his*) *soul to pine away* (cf. VB).

1677 דֹּב *bear*, v. sub דבב. p. 179

1728-29 דּוּג, דַּוָּג, דּוּגָה v. sub דגה. p. 186

דוד (√ assumed for foll., wh. however perh. primitive caressing word, Fl NHWB[i. 439] *swing, rock, dandle, fondle, love*; > Thes Dietr[Sem. Wortforsch. 277] MV, who connect with דּוּד (cf. infr.) cf. Syr. ܕܘܕ *disturb*).

†דּוֹד **n.m.**[Ct 1, 2] **beloved, love** (pl.), **uncle** 1730
(NH *id.*, Syr. ܕܕ, ܕܕܐ; As. *dâdu* Dl[HA 19])—abs. דּוֹד Ct 5$^{9.9}$; cstr. דּוֹד 1 S 10^{14} + 3 t.; דֹּד Lv 10^{4} Est 2^{15}; sf. דּוֹדִי Is 5^{1} (but cf. infr.) + 26 t. all Ct; דֹּדִי Je 32^{8} + 2 t.; דֹּדְךָ Je 32^{7}; דּוֹדֵךְ Ct 5$^{9.9}$ + 2 t.; דּוֹדוֹ Am 6^{10} 1 S 10^{16}, דֹּדוֹ Lv 20^{20} + 4 t.; דּוֹדָהּ Ct 8^{5}; pl. דּוֹדִים Ct 5^{1}; דֹּדִים Pr 7^{18} Ez 16^{8} 23^{17}; pl. sf. דֹּדַי Ct 7^{13}; דֹּדֶיךָ Ct 1$^{2.4}$; דֹּדַיִךְ Ct 4$^{10.10}$; דֹּדֵיהֶן Nu 36^{11}—**1.** most often *loved one, beloved* (lover, betrothed) Ct 1$^{13.14.16}$ 2$^{3.8.9.10.16.17}$ 4^{16} 5$^{2.4.5.6.6.8.9.9.10.16}$ 6$^{1.1.2.3.3}$ 7$^{10.11.12.14}$ 8$^{5.14}$; *beloved one, friend,* שִׁירַת דּוֹדִי Is 5^{1} (where Lo Che שׁ׳ דודים *love-song*, v. **3** infr.) **2.** specif. *uncle*, Lv 10^{4} (father's brother, *patruus*; Syr. = also *avunculus*) Nu 36^{11} 1 S 14^{50} 2 K 24^{17} Lv 20^{20} 25$^{49.49}$ 1 S 10$^{14.15.16}$ Est 2$^{7.15}$ Je 32$^{7.8.9.12}$; perhaps also 1 Ch 27^{32} Jonathan, David's דּוֹד, so AV RV; = kinsman (?, so St RVm) Am 6^{10}. **3.** pl. abstr. *love* Pr 7^{18} Ct 1$^{2.4}$ 4$^{10.10}$ 5^{1} (5^{1} al. concr. *beloved ones*, so AV RV, 𝔊 ἀδελφοί); so עֵת דדים Ez 16^{8}; מִשְׁכַּב דדים Ez 23^{17}.

†[דּוֹדָה] **n.f. aunt**—only *sf.* דֹּדָתְךָ Lv 18^{14} 1733
father's brother's wife; דֹּדָתוֹ Lv 20^{20} Ex 6^{20} father's sister [cf. Nu 26^{59}].

†דּוֹדוֹ **n.pr.m.** (*his beloved*, cf. דודוהו; or 1734
comp. דודה n.pr.divin. MI^{12}, cf. דָּוִד infra)—**1.** man of tribe of Issachar Ju 10^{1}. **2.** דדי Kt 2 S 23^{9} (= דּוֹדַי 1 Ch 27^{4}), דּוֹדוֹ Qr = דּוֹדוֹ 1 Ch 11^{12}. **3.** father of אֶלְחָנָן 2 S 23^{24} = דּוֹדוֹ 1 Ch 11^{26}.

†דּוֹדַי **n.pr.m.** = דּוֹדוֹ (q.v.) 1 Ch 27^{4} (cf. 1737
דדי 2 S 23^{9} Kt).

†דּוֹדָוָהוּ **n.pr.m.** (< 𝔊 τοῦ Ὠδεια, 𝔊L 1735
Δουδιου, i.e. דּוֹדִיָּהוּ, *beloved of* י׳, cf. Nes[Eg 70]) father of Eliezer 2 Ch 20^{37}.

דָּוִד, דָּוִיד$_{1066}$ **n.pr.m. David,** son of יִשַׁי, 1732
king of Israel, whose dynasty remained on the throne of Jerusalem till the Babylonian exile (cf. 2 S 7$^{11-15}$ etc.) (*beloved one*? cf. Ba[NB 189]; acc. to Sayce[Mod. Rev. 1884, 158 ff. Rel. Bab. 53, 56 f.] orig. *Dodo*, title of sun-god worshipped in Isr. cf. דודה n.divin. among E. Jordan Israelites MI^{12})—דָּוִד alw. Ru Sa Ki (exc. 1 K 3^{14} 11$^{4.36}$) ψ Pr Ec Is Je; also 1 Ch 13^{6} Ez 34^{24} 37$^{24.25}$ (c. 790 t.); דָּוִיד alw. Zc Ch (exc. 1 Ch 13^{6}) Ezr Ne; also

Am 6^{5} (where gloss acc. to Peters Hbr. Apr. 1886, p. 175) 9^{11} Ho 3^{5} Ez 34^{23} 1 K 3^{14} $11^{4.36}$ Ct 4^{4} (c. 276 t.);—first named 1 S 16^{13}; cf. also Ru $4^{17.22}$ 2 S 1^{1}+, 1 K 1^{1}+, 2^{1}+, etc. (v. supra); in titles of ψ 3–9, 11–32, 34–41, 51–65, 68–70, 86, 101, 103, 108–110, 122, 124, 131, 133, 138–145 (73 in all); also in ψ 18^{51} (=2 S 22^{51}) 72^{20} $89^{36.50}$ 122^{5} $132^{1.11.17}$; ד׳ עַבְדִּי (י׳ speaks) 2 S 3^{18} $7^{5.8}$ = 1 Ch $17^{4.7}$ cf. v^{26} = 1 Ch 17^{24}, also 1 K $8^{24.25.26.66}$ = 2 Ch $6^{15.16.17.42}$, 1 K $11^{13.32.34.36.38}$ 14^{8} 2 K 8^{19} 19^{34} = Is 37^{35}, 2 K 20^{6}; cf. further ψ 18^{1} 36^{1} (both titles cf. supr.) 78^{70} $89^{4.21}$ 132^{10} 144^{10} Je $33^{21.22.26}$; so also as represented in coming (Messianic) ruler Ez $34^{23.24}$ $37^{24.25}$, cf. Ho 3^{5} Je 30^{9} (v. עֶבֶד). Phrases are: **a.** עִיר ד׳ (acc. to Sayce Mod. Rev. l.c. orig. *city of god Dod[o]*) = stronghold or citadel of Zion, 2 S $5^{7.9}$ = 1 Ch $11^{5.7}$, 2 S $6^{10.12.16}$ = 1 Ch 13^{13} $15^{1.29}$, cf. Is 22^{9}; esp. of burial of kings 1 K 2^{10} 3^{1}, 8^{1} = 2 Ch 5^{2}, 1 K 9^{24} = 2 Ch 8^{11}, 1 K 11^{27} v^{43} = 2 Ch 9^{31}, 1 K 14^{31} 15^{8} = 2 Ch 12^{16} 13^{23}, 1 K 15^{24} = 2 Ch 16^{14}, 1 K 22^{50} = 2 Ch 21^{1}, 2 K 8^{24} = 2 Ch 21^{20}, 2 K 9^{28} 12^{22} = 2 Ch 24^{25}, 2 K 14^{20} 15^{7}, v^{38} = 2 Ch 27^{9}, 2 K 16^{20}; burial of Jehoiada 2 Ch 24^{16}; further 2 Ch $32^{5.30}$ 33^{14} Ne 12^{37}; cf. also קִרְיַת חָנָה ד׳ Is 29^{1}. **b.** בֵּית ד׳ 2 S $3^{1.6}$+ (cf. בַּיִת **5 c**). **c.** אֹהֶל ד׳ Is 16^{5} (cf. אֹהֶל **2**). **d.** סֻכַּת ד׳ Am 9^{11} (cf. סֻכָּה sub סכך). **e.** כִּסֵּא ד׳ 2 S 3^{10} cf. 1 K 1^{37} $2^{12.24.45}$ Is 9^{6} Je 17^{25} $22^{2.30}$ 29^{16} 36^{30} cf. 13^{13} 22^{4}, (cf. also כִּסֵּא). **f.** קִבְרֵי ד׳ Ne 3^{16} cf. 2 Ch 32^{33} קִבְרֵי בְנֵי־ד׳ (cf. קֶבֶר). **g.** מִגְדַּל ד׳ Ct 4^{4}. **h.** כְּלֵי־שִׁיר ד׳ איש האלהים Ne 12^{36}. **i.** אֱלֹהֵי ד׳ 2 K 20^{5}+ (cf. אֱלֹהִים **4 b**). **j.** חַסְדֵי ד׳ 2 Ch 6^{42} Is 55^{3} (cf. 2 S 7^{15} 1 K 3^{6} ψ 89^{50} 2 Ch 1^{8} etc.).—(On txt. note the foll.:—דָּוִד 1 S 30^{20a} del. 𝔊 𝔙 We Dr; 2 S 3^{5} rd. prob. name of a former husband of Eglah We Dr; 2 S 13^{39} rd. רוּחַ We p. 223 Dr; 2 S 19^{44} rd. בְּכוֹר (for בדוד) 𝔊 The We Dr; insert דָּוִד 2 S 9^{11} 15^{32} & 24^{15} 𝔊 We Dr; in 1 Ch 18^{12} ψ 60^{1} אבשי & יואב are less orig. than דָּוִד 2 S 8^{13} We Dr).

1736 †[דּוּדַי] **n.m.** Gn 30, 14 **mandrake** (as love-producing, cf. Di Gn 30^{14})—pl. דּוּדָאִים (cf. Ew 189 g Sta §§ 301. 122) Gn 30^{14} Ct 7^{14}; cstr. דּוּדָאֵי Gn 30^{14} + 3 t.;—*mandrakes*, as exciting sexual desire, and favouring procreation Gn $30^{14.14.15.15.16}$ (J); also Ct 7^{14} where odour referred to. On דּוּדָאֵי Je 24^{1} *vessels, baskets*, v. דּוּד.

1731 †דּוּד **n.m.** Je 24, 2 **pot, jar** (Aram. דּוּדָא, ܕܘܕܐ; perh. cf. Syr. ܕܘܕ *disturb*, from the idea of boiling)—abs. דּוּד 1 S 2^{14} + 4 t.; pl. דּוּדִים 2 K 10^{7}, דְּוָדִים 2 Ch 35^{13}; pl. cstr. דּוּדָאֵי Je 24^{1}—**a.** *pot, kettle* or cooking (בִּשֵּׁל) 1 S 2^{14} (|| כִּיּוֹר, קַלַּחַת, פָּרוּר), 2 Ch 35^{13} (vb. בִּשֵּׁל, || סִירוֹת, צֵלָחוֹת), cf. Jb 41^{12}; **b.** receptacle for carrying, all Vrss *basket*, 2 K 10^{7} (heads of king's sons), Je $24^{2.2}$ (figs) cf. דּוּדָאֵי Je 24^{1}, as if fr. a II. [דּוּדַי]; ψ 81^{7} (clay or bricks, || סֵבֶל).

†[דָּוָה] **vb. be ill, unwell** (NH ד׳ *sorrow-* 1738
ful, miserable, not in physical sense; cf. Ar. [دَاءَ] دَوِىَ *be ill*; Eth. ደዌ: As. perh. deriv. *di'û, illness* Zim BP 96, 97; Aram. דְּוָא, דְּוֵי, ܕܘܐ, ܕܘܝ *be sad*)—**Qal** *Inf. cstr.* אִשָּׁה ... כִּימֵי נִדַּת דְּוֹתָהּ Lv 12^{2}.

†דְּוַי **n.[m.] illness**, עֶרֶשׂ דְּוָי ψ 41^{4} *bed of* 1741
languishing (Che); sg. cstr. (Ew De Di) הֵמָּה כִּדְוֵי לַחְמִי Jb 6^{7} *they* (i.e. my sufferings) *are like disease* (VB *loathsomeness*) *in my meat*, cf. Di; but txt. dub.

†דָּוֶה **adj. faint, unwell**—דָּוֶה La 5^{17}, f. דָּוָה 1739
Lv 15^{33} + 3 t.; **1.** *faint*, La 1^{13} (|| שֹׁמֵמָה) 5^{17}. **2.** *unwell, menstruous* Lv 15^{33} 20^{18}; Is 30^{22} דָּוָה perh. = כְּלִי דָוֶה De.

†[מַדְוֶה] **n.m.** Dt 7, 15 **sickness**—cstr. sg. 4064
מַדְוֵה מִצְרַיִם Dt 28^{60} (rd. מַדְוֵי pl., as 7^{15}?); cstr. pl. מַדְוֵי מִצְרַיִם Dt 7^{15} (both || חֳלִי).

†[דַּוָּי] **adj. faint** (on form cf. Ba NB 487)— 1742
דַּוָּי Is 1^{5} + 2 t.—*faint*, always of heart Is 1^{5} (|| לָחֳלִי fig. of condition of people); Je 8^{18} La 1^{22} of sorrow and distress.

†דְּיוֹ **n.m. ink** (NH *id.*, Aram. דְּיוֹתָא, ܕܝܘܬܐ; 1773
Ar. دَوَاةٌ *inkbottle, inkhorn*; Ges-Dietr Fl NHWB i. 41 der. fr. √דוה in assumed sense of *slowly flowing*; Fl comp. Ar. دواية دُواية *thin skin on surface of milk*, cf. also Ol § 173 g), וַאֲנִי כֹּתֵב עַל־הַסֵּפֶר בַּדְּיוֹ Je 36^{18}, cf. Lag Ges. Abh. 216. —On erasible quality of Hebrew ink cf. RS OTJC, 400 f. ed. 2, 71; v. further L. Löw Graphische Requisiten etc. bei den Juden, 1870, i. 145 ff.

†[דִּיחַ, דּוּחַ] **vb. rinse, cleanse away** 1740
by rinsing, washing (NH Hiph., Aram. Aph. *id.*; cf. As. *dîḫu* Dl Pr 177)—**Hiph.** *Pf.* sf. הדיחנו Kt Je 51^{34} Qr הֱדִיחָנִי but rd. הִדִּיחַנִי fr. נדח (Hi, cf. 50^{17}); *Impf.* 3 ms. יָדִיחַ Is 4^{4}; 3 mpl. יָדִיחוּ 2 Ch 4^{6} + Ez 40^{38} (Co conj. הַקְּדֵמִים);—**1.** *rinse*, victims to be offered in sacrifice Ez 40^{38}, so 2 Ch 4^{6} (cf. supr.) **2.** fig. *cleanse* by washing Is 4^{4}, of removing guilt.

דִּיג Kt v. דָּאג sub דאג. p. 178 1637

†[דּוּךְ] **vb. pound, beat** (in mortar) (NH 1743
& Aram. *id.*, Ar. دَاكَ; cf. also As. *dâku, kill*

COT^{Gloss}).—**Qal** *Pf.* 3 pl. דָּכוּ בַּמְּדֹכָה (milraʿ) Nu 11^{8} (|| טָחֲנוּ בָרֵחַיִם).

4085 †מְדֹכָה **n.f. mortar**, Nu 11^{8}.

1744 †דּוּכִיפַת **n.f.** an unclean bird, perh. **hoopoe**, 𝔊 𝔙 Saad al. (cf. Di Kn Lv 11^{19}) Lv 11^{19} Dt 14^{18}.

דום (NH דום *spread slander*, perh. orig. *whisper*, cf. דממה, דמם).

1745 †I. **דּוּמָה** **n.f. silence**;—ד׳=שְׁאוֹל ψ 94^{17}, יֹרְדֵי ד׳ ψ 115^{17}; also Is 21^{11} מַשָּׂא דּוּמָה *oracle of silence*, i.e. of concealment, hidden meaning, acc. to Ew Di, but v. II. ד׳, **3.**

1746 †II. **דּוּמָה** **n.pr. 1. m.** son of Ishmael Gn 25^{15}=1 Ch 1^{30}, cf. prob. *Dumath al-Jandal* in Northern Arabia in *Jôf* v. Burckhardt$^{Travels\ in\ Syria\ 662\ f.}$ Di; also Ges$^{Comm.}$ on Is 21^{11}, Glaser$^{Skizze\ ii.\ 392,440}$. **2.** city in mountains of Judah Jos 15^{52}, comp. Δοῦμα in the Daroma, 17 miles fr. Eleutheropolis Lag$^{Onom.\ 250,\ 2nd\ ed.\ 258}$, = mod. *Daume*, SW. fr. Hebron van de Velde$^{Memoir\ 308}$ Guérin$^{Judée\ iii.\ 359\ ff.}$ cf. Di. **3.** name of Edom with mystic mng. Is 21^{11} *Duma=silence* of death, desolation, De Che al. (JDMich Ges Hi think **3=1**; 𝔊 has Ἰδουμαια; Jer interpr. as *part* of Idumea; still another view sub I. דּוּמָה).

1747 †דּוּמִיָּה, דֻּמִיָּה (ψ 65^{2}) **n.f. silence, still waiting, repose**—ψ 39^{3} *silence;* 62^{2} *still waiting, resignation* (Dr$^{§189.2}$; but rd. prob., as v^{6}, דֹּמִי, Bi Gr Che); 65^{2} *id.* (but Ew Che Bä al. דֹּמִיָּה *is meet?* fr. I. דָּמָה, 𝔊 πρέπει, v. Che); 22^{3} *repose* (fr. grief and tears: Je 14^{17}).

1748 †דּוּמָם **n.[m.] silence** Hb 2^{19} אֶבֶן ד׳ *stone of silence=dumb stone;* **adv. in silence, silently,** Is 47^{5} La 3^{26} (? rd. here וְדָמַם fr. דמם).

דּוּמֶּשֶׂק 2 K 16^{10} cf. דַּמֶּשֶׂק. p. 199

1777 [דּוּן] **vb.** dub.; only in יָדוֹן Gn 6^{3}, v. דִּין. p. 192

1779 †[דּוּן] **n.[m.]** dub.; Qr Jb 19^{29} שַׁדּוּן; v. דִּין **n.** p. 192

1750 †[דּוּץ] **vb. spring, leap, dance** (Aram. דּוּץ *be joyous*, ܕܳܨ, *leap, dance, be joyous;* Ar. داص med. ى, *decline, slip* or *move about, glide to and fro;* Dl$^{Pr\ 65,66}$ comp. As. *dâṣu, withdraw, retreat,* but cf. Nö$^{ZMG\ 1886,\ 730}$)—**Qal** *Impf.* 3 fs. תָּדוּץ דְּאָבָה Jb 41^{14} before him *danceth dismay.*

דוק (? √ of foll.; mng. dub. cf. Sm Ez 4^{2} Lag$^{Ges.\ Abhandl.\ 36}$).

1785 †דָּיֵק **n.m. bulwark, siege-wall**—דָּיֵק 2 K 25^{1} + 5 t.—בנה ד׳ עליה סביב 2 K 25^{1} = Je 52^{4}; cf. Ez 4^{2} 17^{17} 21^{27} (all || שׁפך סֹלְלָה); נתן ד׳ על Ez 26^{8} (|| *id.*)

1752 **דּוּר** **vb. 1. heap up, pile. 2. dwell** (orig. *move in a circle, go about, surround*, cf. Ar. دَارَ; دَارٌ *house*, esp. as group of buildings about a court; As. *dûru, wall, fortress*, COT^{Gloss}; thence (denom. Fl NHWB$^{i.\ 440}$) *dwell* Aram. דּוּר, ܕܳܪ (pt. & Pa), hence in Heb. cf. Giesebr$^{ZAW\ i.\ 304}$ Fl$^{l.c.}$ Che$^{OP\ 479}$; Eth. ትውልድ *generation* (=דּוֹר: prob. loan-word); acc. to Hpt KAT$^{2\ Gloss.\ i.}$ As. [*darû, endure*], *dârû, everlasting* (cf. Bez$^{Orient.\ Diplom.}$) = Ar. دَهْرٌ *long time, age*)—**Qal** in *Inf.* מִדּוּר באהלי־רשׁע ψ 84^{11} *than to dwell in tents of wickedness. Imv.* (or *Inf. abs.* irreg. for דּוּר, cf. || לְקוֹחַ) דּוּר העצמים Ez 24^{5} *heap up.*—In Gn 6^{3} some rd. *Impf.* 3 ms. יָדוּר *shall dwell*, for יָדוֹן; v. דין.

1754 †דּוּר **n.[m.] circle, ball—1.** *circle* וְחָנִיתִי כַדּוּר עליך Is 29^{3} (>𝔊 Brd כְּדָוִד). **2.** *ball* צָנוֹף יִצְנָפְךָ צְנֵפָה כַּדּוּר Is 22^{18} (so most; but Bö$^{NÄ\ ii.\ 134}$ De Or Jastr$^{PAOS\ 1888,\ xcv.\ ff.}$ regard noun as כַּדּוּר, *ball*, as Talm., cf. also MV SS s.v.; vid. כדר). [**3.** *heap, pile* Ez 24^{5} Thes Ke MV cf. מְדוּרָה v^{9}; but v. supr. sub דּוּר **vb.**]

1755 †I. **דּוֹר, דֹּר** **n.m.** $^{Dt\ 32,\ 5}$ **period, generation, dwelling** (cf. sub **vb.** supr.; also NH דּוֹר, Aram. (incl. B Aram.) דָּר, ܕܳܪ, *age, generation;* Ar. دَوْرٌ *gyrus, orbis, periodus;* Sab. דר, *one time, once,* דרם דרם *each once* in a year DHM in MV)—abs. דּוֹר Gn 7^{1} + 68 t.; דֹּר Ex 3^{15} + 36 t.; cstr. דּוֹר Dt 32^{20} + 7 t., דֹּר Ex 3^{15}; sf. דּוֹרִי Is 38^{12}, דּוֹרוֹ Is 53^{8}; pl. דּוֹרִים ψ 72^{5} + 2 t., דֹּרוֹת abs. Jb 42^{16} Is 41^{4}; cstr. Ju 3^{2}; דּוֹרוֹת cstr. Is 51^{9}, דֹּרֹת Gn 9^{12}; sf. דֹּרֹתָיו Gn 6^{9} Lv 25^{30}, דּוֹרֹתֵינוּ Jos 22^{27}, דֹּרֹתֵינוּ v^{28}, דֹּרֹתֵיכֶם Gn 17^{12} + 27 t., דֹּרֹתָם Gn 17^{7} + 10 t.;—**1.** *period, age, generation*, mostly poet.: **a.** of duration in the past, *former age*(*s*) דּוֹרוֹת עוֹלָמִים Is 51^{9} (|| ימי קדם); שְׁנוֹת דֹּר וָדֹר Dt 32^{7} (song; || ימות עולם); בְּדֹר וָדֹר ψ 90^{1} (cf. v^{2}); מוֹסְדֵי דוֹר־וָדוֹר Is 58^{12} (|| חרבות עולם); שֹׁמְמוֹת דּוֹר וָדוֹר 61^{4} (|| *id.*) **b.** usually of duration to come, *future age*(*s*), לְדֹר דֹּר Ex 3^{15} (E; || לעולם) cf. Pr 27^{24} Kt (Qr לְדוֹר וָדוֹר; || *id.*); מִדֹּר דֹּר Ex 17^{16} (E), =לְדוֹר Is 34^{10}; לְדֹר וָדֹר ψ 10^{6} 33^{11} (|| לעולם) 49^{12} 79^{13} 85^{6} 102^{13} 119^{90} 135^{13} 146^{10} Jo 4^{20} (all || *id.*); ψ 89^{2} (|| עולם) 89^{5} (|| עד־עולם) 106^{31} (|| *id.*) Is 34^{17} (|| *id.*); ψ 77^{9} (|| לנצח); עַד־דֹּר וָדֹר ψ 100^{5} (|| לעולם) Is 13^{20} (|| לנצח) Je 50^{39} (|| *id.*); בְּכָל־דֹּר וָדֹר ψ 45^{18} (|| לעולם ועד) cf. Est 9^{28}; שְׁנוֹתָיו כְּמוֹ דֹר וָדֹר ψ 61^{7} cf. שְׁנֵי דּוֹר וָדוֹר Jo 2^{2} (|| העולם); as modifying phrase מְשׂוֹשׂ דּוֹר וָדוֹר Is 60^{15} (|| גאון עולם); further דּוֹר דּוֹרִים ψ 72^{5}; יְשׁוּעָתִי לְדוֹר דּוֹרִים

Is 51^{8} (||לעולם). **c.** apparently including both past and future בְּדוֹר דּוֹרִים שְׁנוֹתֶיךָ ψ 102^{25}; לְדֹר וָדֹר ψ 145^{13}; בְּכָל דּוֹר וָדֹר La 5^{19}. **2.** of men living at a particular time (period, age), *generation*, as transitory דּוֹר הֹלֵךְ וְדוֹר בָּא Ec 1^{4}: specific. **a.** in the present, and (or) the past Gn 7^{1} (J) Ex 1^{6} (P) Nu 32^{13} (JE) Dt 1^{35} 2^{14} Ju 2$^{10.10}$ Is 53^{8} (cf. Che crit. n.) Je 2^{31}; also ψ 95^{10} Jb 8^{8} Is 41^{4}. **b.** Ju 3^{2} (present & future); cf. pl. דֹּרֹתָיו Gn 6^{9} (i.e. his own gen. and those immediately contiguous, before and after). **c.** esp. of a future generation Gn 15^{16} (JE), with numeral, cf. Dt 23$^{3.4.9}$; also Dt 29^{21} ψ 48^{14} 71^{18} 78$^{4.6}$ 102^{19} 109^{13} Jo 1^{3} cf. ψ 22$^{31.32}$ (Che crit. n.); of a succession of generations דּוֹר לְדוֹר יְשַׁבַּח מַעֲשֶׂיךָ ψ 145^{4}; בְּכָל־דּוֹר וָדוֹר Est 9^{28}; usually pl. לְדֹרֹת עוֹלָם Gn 9^{12} (P); with num. לְאֶלֶף דּוֹר ψ 105^{8} (|| עולם)=1 Ch 16^{15} (||לעולם); Dt 7^{9}; v. further, of posterity, אַרְבָּעָה דֹּרוֹת Jb 42^{16}; usually pl. c. sf. Gn 17$^{7.9.12}$ Ex 12$^{14.17.42}$ 16$^{32.33}$ 27^{21} 29^{42} 30$^{8.10.21.31}$ 31$^{13.16}$ 40^{15} Lv 3^{17} 6^{11} 7^{36} 10^{9} (all P); 17^{7} 21^{17} 22^{3} 23$^{14.21.31.41.43}$ 24^{3} 25^{30} (all H); Nu 9^{10} 10^{8} 15$^{14.15.21.23.38}$ 18^{23} 35^{29} Jos 22$^{27.28}$ (all P). **3.** generation characterized by quality or condition, *class* of men: דּוֹר עִקֵּשׁ *crooked generation* Dt 32^{5} (song) cf. v^{20} ψ 78$^{8.8}$ Je 7^{29}; of diff. classes of wicked, Pr 30$^{11.12.13.14}$ cf. ψ 12^{8}; of the righteous, as a class ψ 14^{5} 24^{6} 73^{15} (דור בָּנֶיךָ) 112^{2} (cf. 22^{31} MT, but < Che joins לדור to v^{32} cf. supr. sub **2 c**); so also דּוֹר אֲבוֹתָיו i.e. the dead ψ 49^{20} (so most; yet v. infr. sub **4**). **4.** *dwelling-place, habitation* Is 38^{12} cf. דּוּר vb., so Saad Ki Ges De Che RVm (Ew *life* || חַיַּי); so also ψ 49^{20} De Witt, cf. Che$^{OP 479}$.

1756, 5299, 5316 †II. דֹּאר, דֹּר, דּוֹר **n.pr.loc.** (Ph. דאר; cuneif. *Du'ru* KG^{121} COT on Jos 17^{11}) city in Manasseh, on Mediterr., S. of Carmel (9 Roman miles N. of Caesarea, cf. Lag$^{Onom. 115, 2nd ed. 149}$), דּוֹר Jos 12^{23}; דּוֹר וּבְנוֹתֶיהָ Ju 1^{27} 1 Ch 7^{29}=דאר וב׳ Jos 17^{11}; נָפַת דּוֹר Jos 12^{23}=נָפַת דאר 1 K 4^{11}; נָפוֹת דּוֹר Jos 11^{2} (cf. נפה); mod. *Ṭanṭura* (*Ṭorṭura*) Wilson$^{Lands of Bible ii. 249}$ van de Velde$^{Narrat. i. 333}$ Bd$^{Pal 238}$ cf. Di Jos 11^{2}. On עֵין־דֹּר(דּוֹר) v. sub עַיִן.

4071 †מְדוּרָה **n.f.** pile (of wood, etc.) מ׳ Ez 24^{9}; מְדֻרָתָהּ אֵשׁ ועצים הרבה Is 30^{33}=*pyre* (so Ges Hi De Che Brd; Ew Di *its circuit, compass*).

1758 †דִּישׁ, דּוּשׁ **vb.** tread, thresh (Ar. دَاسَ, As. *dâšu*, Impf. 1 s. *adîš* Dl$^{Pr 191}$ COT^{Gloss} Hom$^{NS 391}$; cf. NH דּוּשׁ, Aram. *id.*, ܕܳܫ; v. further Nö$^{ZMG 1883, 538}$)—**Qal** *Pf.* דָּשׁ 1 Ch 21^{20}, וְדַשְׁתִּי Ju 8^{7}; *Impf.* וַיָּדָשׁ so rd. for וַיֹּדַע Ju 8^{16} cf. Be Door Bu Vrss; 2 ms. תָּדוּשׁ Is 41^{15} Hb 3^{12}; 3 ms. sf. יְדוּשֶׁנּוּ Is 28^{28}; 3 fs. sf. תְּדוּשֶׁהָ Jb 39^{15}; *Imv.* fs. דּוּשִׁי Mi 4^{13}; *Inf. cstr.* לָדוּשׁ 2 K 13^{7}, לָדוֹשׁ Ho 10^{11}, sf. דּוּשָׁם Am 1^{13}; דִּישׁוֹ Dt 25^{4}; *abs.* אָדוֹשׁ Is 28^{28} as if 156
fr. אדשׁ cf. Kö$^{I. 444}$; yet אדשׁ nowhere else & form very possibly textual error, cf. Ol$^{§ 245 k}$; *Pt.* f. דָּשָׁה Je 50^{11};—*tread on, trample on,* c. acc. Jb 39^{15} (beast on eggs, || זור); *thresh,* lit. c. acc. חִטִּים 1 Ch 21^{20} Je 50^{11}, לֶחֶם (*i.e.* its material) Is 28^{28} (in sim.); abs. 2 K 13^{7} (in sim.); Ho 10^{11} (metaph. of Ephraim as heifer); *tread* or *thresh* Ju 8^{7} *with* (אֶת=*together with,* cf. Stu; Ew$^{§ 234 e}$ takes as acc., & vb. as abbrev. Hiph.) *thorns,* קוֹצִים and בַּרְקָנִים q.v.; and also in Ju 8^{16} (rd. וידשׁ cf. supr.) sq. בָּהֶם, *with them,* ref. to קוצים and ברקנים; fig. of devastation of land Am 1^{3} (Gilead), destruction of peoples Hb 3^{12} (גוים); espec. Mi 4^{13}(abs.), where full metaph.; hyperbol. of Israel Is 41^{15} c. acc. הרים.—**Niph.** *be trampled down,* Pf. וְנָדוֹשׁ consec. Is. 25^{10} fig., subj. Moab; *Inf.* הִדּוֹשׁ *ib.* (simile, subj. מתבן *straw-heap;* on form cf. Ol$^{§ 193 a}$ Ba$^{NB 156}$)—**Hoph.** *be threshed, Impf.* יוּדַשׁ Is 28^{27} (subj. קֶצַח).

†דַּיִשׁ **n.m.** threshing, i.e. the process of 1786
threshing, Lv 26^{5} (H) וְהִשִּׂיג לָכֶם ד׳ אֶת־בָּצִיר.

†[מְדֻשָׁה] **n.f.** that which is threshed; sf. 4098
מְדֻשָׁתִי Is 21^{10} (|| בֶּן־גָּרְנִי) fig. in address to Israel by prophet.

†I. דִּישֹׁן **n.**[**m.**] a clean animal, 𝔊 πύγαργος 1788
cf. 𝔙; hence AV RV & most **pygarg**, a kind of antelope or gazelle, cf. Di Lv 11$^{2 f.}$; perh. rather **mountain-goat**, Hom$^{NS 391}$ cf. Eth. Vrs.; only Dt 14^{5}—(Hom$^{l. c.}$ der. fr. √דושׁ with kindred meaning of *spring, leap* & comp. As. *daššu*; so already Dl$^{S i. 54}$).

†II. דִּישֹׁן **n.pr.m.** **1.** a son of Seir דִּישׁוֹן 1787
Gn 36^{21}=דִּישׁוֹן 1 Ch 1^{38}; **2.** a son of Anah & grandson of Seir דִּשֹׁן Gn 36^{25} cf. v^{30} so also v^{26} (for דִּישָׁן q.v.)=דִּישׁוֹן 1 Ch 1$^{41.41.42}$, cf. also foll.

†דִּישָׁן **n.pr.m.** a son of Seir דִּישָׁן Gn 36^{21} 1789
(𝔊 Ῥισών; so v$^{28.30}$ cf. Di) 1 Ch 1^{38}; (v^{42} rd. דִּישׁוֹן q.v.) Gn 36^{26} (rd. דִּישׁוֹן 𝔊 𝔖 𝔙 Ol Di) v^{30} דִּישָׁן Gn 36^{28}.

דָּחָה **vb.** push, thrust (NH *id.*, Aram. 1760
דְּחָא, ܕܚܳܐ, דְּחֵי; cf also Ar. دَحَا, *spread, extend,* also *throw, propel*)—**Qal** *Pf.* 2 ms. sf. דְּחִיתַנִי ψ 118^{13}; *Inf. cstr.* לִדְחוֹת ψ 140^{5}; *abs.* דָּחֹה ψ 118^{13}; *Pt. act.* דֹּחֶה ψ 35^{5} (rd. דֹּחָם 𝔊 De Che); *pass.* f. הַדְּחוּיָה ψ 62^{4};—*push,* דָּחֹה דָחָה *push*

violently fig. c. acc. ψ 118[13] sq. cl. of purpose לִנְפֹּל, cf. לִדְחוֹת פעמי ψ 140[5] (Che *trip up my feet*), & ψ 35[5] (transp. דחה with רדפם v[6] and rd. דֹּחָם 𝔊; cf. יְהִי־דרכם חשך וַחֲלַקְלַקּוֹת v[a], and Je 23[12]); *pushed in* (Che), in sim., pt. pass., said of גָּדֵר *wall* ψ 62[4] (‖קיר נטוי). **Niph.** *Impf.* יִדָּחֶה Pr 14[32]; (3 mpl. יִדַּ֫חוּ Je 23[12] is fr. דחח, if rightly pointed; נִדְחֵי Is 11[12] 56[8] ψ 147[2], v. sub נדח);—*be thrust* or *cast down*, fig. of wicked Pr 14[32], cf. ψ 35[6] supr. **Pu.** *Pf.* 3 *pl.* דֹּחוּ ψ 36[13] *they are thrust down* (‖לא יכלו קום & נפלו).

1762 †[דְּחִי] **n.[m.]** stumbling, הִצַּלְתָּ... רַגְלַי מִדֶּחִי ψ 56[14]=116[8].

4072 †מִדְחֶה **n.m.** means or occasion of stumbling, Pr 26[28] פֶּה־חָלָק יַעֲשֶׂה מ׳ (‖ לְשׁוֹן־שֶׁקֶר יִשְׂנָא דַכָּיו).

1760 [דָּחַח] **vb.** only **Niph.** *Impf.* 3 mpl. יִדַּ֫חוּ (Kö [i. 377]) Je 23[12] *they shall be thrust down*, fig., of wicked; rd. perh. יִדָּ֫חוּ, fr. דחה q. v.

דחן (√ of following; perh. cf. Ar. دَخَنَ *smoke arose*, hence *become dusky, dingy, inclining to black*).

1764 †דֹּ֫חַן **n.m.** millet (NH דּוֹחַן, Aram. דּוֹחִינָא), Ez 4[9] in the series חִטִּין וּשְׂעֹרִים וּפוֹל וַעֲדָשִׁים וד׳ וְכֻסְּמִים v. Löw[72].

1765 †[דָּחַף] **vb.** drive, hasten (late) (NH *id.*, Aram. דְּחַף)—**Qal** *Pt. pass.* pl. דְּחוּפִים of runners Est 3[15] 8[14] (‖מְבֹהָלִים). **Niph.** *Pf.* *hasten one's self, hurry* נִדְחַף לָצֵאת Est 6[12]; נִדְחַף אֶל־ 2 Ch 26[20] (‖בהל).

4073 †[מַדְחֵפָה] **n.f.** thrust, ψ 140[12] יְצוּדֶנּוּ לְמַדְחֵפֹת (*evil*) *shall hunt him with thrust upon thrust* (Che, cf. De).

1766 †[דָּחַק] **vb.** thrust, crowd, oppress (NH *id.*, Ar. دَحَقَ *drive away, remove*, Aram. דְּחַק, ܕܚܩ)—**Qal** *Impf.* יִדְחָקוּן *thrust, crowd*, of locusts in swarm Jo 2[8]; *Pt. act.* pl. sf. לֹחֲצֵיהֶם וְדֹחֲקֵיהֶם Ju 2[18] (because of) *them that maltreated and oppressed them.*

1767 †דַּי **subst.** sufficiency, enough (NH, but not known in other cogn. languages)—cstr. דֵּי, with sf. (v. infr.) דַּיֶּ֫ךָּ, דַּיָּם:—**1.** absol. thrice only Mal 3[10] I will pour you out a blessing עַד־בְּלִי־דָי until there is not *sufficiency*, i.e. until my abundance can be exhausted, or, as this can never be, for ever (cf. ψ 72[7]), Est 1[18] וּכְדַי בִּזָּיוֹן וָקָצֶף and (there will be) *as enough* (i.e. in plenty) contempt and wrath, 2 Ch 30[3] לְמַדַּי=לְמַה־דַּי for what was *sufficient*. With a gen. of the person or thing *for* which anything suffices: Ex 36[5] מִדֵּי הָעֲבֹדָה (more) than *enough for* the work, Lv 5[7] and if his hand do not reach (if he do not command) דֵּי שֶׂה *enough for* (i.e. to buy) a lamb, 12[8] 25[28] דֵּי הָשִׁיב לוֹ *enough for* recovering it, Dt 15[8] דֵּי מַחְסֹרוֹ *enough for* his need, Is 40[16.16]. With suff. Pr 25[16] אֱכֹל דַּיֶּ֫ךָּ eat *that which is sufficient for* thee; דַּיָּם Ex 36[7] Je 49[9] Ob v[5]. Once with gen. of the thing which is sufficient, Pr 27[27] דֵּי חֲלֵב עִזִּים *enough of* goats' milk.

2. Combined with בְּ, כְּ, and esp. מִן (דֵּי, מִדֵּי) has a tendency to form compound prepositions, used idiomatically in certain applications:—**a.** בְּדֵי (*a*) *for* (the בְּ *pretii*) *what suffices for:* Na 2[13] the lion tare in pieces בְּדֵי גֹרוֹתָיו *for the need of* his whelps (‖ לְלִבְאֹתָיו; but ? כְּדֵי, v. **b**); iron. Hb 2[13] Je 51[58] the peoples labour בְּדֵי־אֵשׁ *for* fire (only to satisfy the fire), and the nations weary themselves בְּדֵי־רִיק *for* what is empty. (*β*) *in the abundance of*, i.e. *as often as* Job 39[25] בְּדֵי שֹׁפָר *in the abundance of* the trumpet, i.e. as often as the trumpet sounds (מִדֵּי elsewhere in this sense). **b.** כְּדֵי *according to the sufficiency*, or *abundance, of* Lv 25[26] and find כְּדֵי גְאֻלָּתוֹ *acc. to the sufficiency of* his redemption, i.e. *as much as* it demands, Dt 25[2] Ne 5[8] כְּדֵי בָנוּ (*st. c.* before בְּ: Ges[§ 130. 1]) 'quantum in nobis erat,' after our ability, Ju 6[5] they came כְּדֵי אַרְבֶּה לָרֹב *acc. to the abundance of* the locust in multitude (for which כְּאַרְבֶּה לָרֹב would ordinarily be said: cf. 7[12]). **c.** מִדֵּי *out of the abundance of*, hence *as often as*;—(*a*) sq. inf. 1 S 1[7] מִדֵּי עֲלֹתָהּ=*as often as* she went up, 18[30] 1 K 14[28] (=2 Ch 12[11]) 2 K 4[8] Is 28[19] מִדֵּי עָבְרוֹ *as often as* it passeth over, Je 31[20]; (*β*) sq. subst., Je 48[27] מִדֵּי דְבָרֶיךָ בּוֹ *as often as* thy words (are) of him; and in the idiom. phrases מִדֵּי שָׁנָה בְּשָׁנָה=*yearly* (a combination of מִדֵּי שָׁנָה and שָׁנָה בְּשָׁנָה: v. sub שָׁנָה) 1 S 7[16] (v. Dr) Zc 14[16] 2 Ch 24[5]; and מִדֵּי חֹדֶשׁ בְּחָדְשׁוֹ Is 66[23] *as often as* month (comes) in its month (i.e. in its own time: חֹדֶשׁ made more precise by the add. of בְּחָדְשׁוֹ; cf. the phrase דְּבַר יוֹם בְּיוֹמוֹ): so מִדֵּי שַׁבָּת בְּשַׁבַּתּוֹ *ib.*; (*γ*) as conj., with the finite verb (אֲשֶׁר being understood: cf. בַּעֲבוּר etc.), Je 20[8] מִדֵּי אֲדַבֵּר *as often as* I speak.

†דִּי זָהָב **n.pr.loc.** appar. on border of 1774
Moab Dt 1[1] (𝔊 Καταχρύσεα).

1769 †**דִּיבוֹן, דִּיבֹן n.pr.loc.—1.** city in Moab
(MI$^{21.28}$ דיבן, cf. ib.^{1} adj. gent. דיבני(ה)—) דִּיבֹן
Nu 21^{30} 32$^{3.34}$ (built up or at by Gad) Is 15^{2};
in territory of Gad, hence דִּיבֹן גָּד Nu 33$^{45.46}$ (cf.
on these vv. & 32^{34} MI$^{10\,f.}$); also דִּיבוֹן Jos
1775 13$^{9.17}$ Je 48^{22}; יֹשֶׁבֶת בַּת דִּיבוֹן Je 48^{18};=דִּימוֹן Is
1775 15^{9}, vid. also מֵי דִימוֹן v^{9}=Arnon, cf. Che & Hpt
$^{ZA\,1887,\,268}$;—mod. *Dîbân*, north of Arnon, cf.
Seetzen $^{Reisen\ i.\ 409}$ Tristr $^{Land\ of\ Moab\ 132\ ff.}$ Bd $^{Pal\ 193}$.
2. דִּיבֹן Ne 11^{25} place in Judah, toward south
1776 =דִּימוֹנָה Jos 15^{22}, cf. Hpt$^{l.c.}$; conject. by Kn
Ke (cf. Di) to be *Tell ed Dheib* (van de Velde
$^{Mem.\ 252}$) called also Ehdeib (Rob$^{BR\ ii.\ 102}$).

1770-71 **דָּיֵג, דַּיָּג** v. sub דגה. p. 185f

1772 **דַּיָּה** v. sub דאה. p. 178

1773 **דְּיוֹ** v. sub דוה. p. 188

1775 †**דִּימוֹן n.pr.loc.**=דִּיבוֹן **1,** q. v. above

1776 †**דִּימוֹנָה n.pr.loc.**=דִּיבוֹן **2,** q. v. above

1777 †**דִּין vb.** judge (cf. Ar. دَانَ intrans. *to be obedient, submissive,* trans. *requite, compensate, rule, govern,* دِينٌ *obedience, abasement, recompense,* دَيَّانٌ *requiter, governor,* مَدِينَةٌ *city;* As. *dânu,* Impf. *idin, judge* Asrb$^{Ann.\ x.\ 120}$ Dl$^{HA\ 49}$; Aram. דִּין, ܕܳܢ *judge, exercise judgment, punish,* דַּיָּינָא, ܕܰܝܳܢܳܐ *judge,* דִּינָא, ܕܺܝܢܳܐ *judgment,* ܡܕܺܝܢܬܳܐ *city;*—on √ע״ו v. Nö$^{ZMG\ 1883,\ 533}$), syn. שָׁפַט—**Qal** *Pf.* דָּן Je 22^{16}, etc.; *Impf.* יָדִין Gn 49^{16}+9 t., יָדוֹן Gn 6^{3} cf. infr., etc.; *Imv.* דִּין Pr 31^{9} Jb 35^{14}; דִּינוּ Je 21^{12}; *Inf.* לָדִין ψ 50^{4}+2 t.; *Pt.* דָּן Gn 15^{14} Je 30^{13};—**1.** *act as judge, minister judgment,* of God ידין עמו Dt 32^{36} (poet. = ψ 135^{14}) ψ 50^{4}; ידין עמים ψ 7^{9} 96^{10} Is 3^{13}; יָדִין לְאֻמִּים בְּמֵישָׁרִים ψ 9^{9}; Messianic king ψ 72^{2}. **2.** *plead the cause,* **a.** of men, usu. c. acc. cogn., אֵין־דָּן דִּינֵךְ *there is none to plead thy cause* Je 30^{13}; ד׳ דִּין יָתוֹם *plead cause of orphan* Je 5^{28}; ד׳ דין עני ואביון Je 22^{16}; also, acc. cogn. om., Pr 31^{9}. **b.** of God, דָּנַנִּי אֱלֹהִים *God has pled my cause* Gn 30^{6} (E). **3.** *execute judgment, vindicate,* in battle against enemies, דָּן יָדִין עַמּוֹ *Dan will judge* (vindicate as a warrior) *his people* (v. Di) Gn 49^{16} (poet.); the Messianic king בגוים ψ 110^{6}; God, בִּגְבוּרָתְךָ תְדִינֵנִי *in thy might judge me* (vindicate me) ψ 54^{3}. **4.** *execute judgment, requite,* of man, דִּינוּ לַבֹּקֶר מִשְׁפָּט *execute judgment every morning* Je 21^{12}; of God, upon Egypt Gn 15^{14} (E); עמים by means of powers of nature Jb 36^{31}; אפסי ארץ 1 S 2^{10} (poet.) **5.** *govern,* אַתָּה תָּדִין אֶת־בֵּיתִי *thou shalt govern my house* Zc 3^{7}. **6.** לֹא־יוּכַל לָדִין עִם *he cannot contend with* one mightier than he Ec 6^{10}. **Niph.** *Pt.* וַיְהִי כָל־הָעָם נָדוֹן בְּכָל־שִׁבְטֵי יִשְׂרָאֵל *and all the people were at strife throughout all the tribes of Israel* 2 S 19^{10} (reciprocal, cf. Dr.)

Note.—לֹא־יָדוֹן רוּחִי בָאָדָם לְעֹלָם Gn 6^{3} is difficult. (1) 𝔊 𝔙 𝔖 Onk rd. ידור or (Kue) ילון *abide in, dwell,—My spirit will not abide in man for ever;* this best suits the context, but ידור, as Aramaism, is dub. (2) Kn De Schr RVm render *rule in,* supported by Zc 3^{7} only. (3) Thes Ew Di render *be humbled in,* sustained by Ar. usage, but not by Heb. (4) *strive with* of AV RV (cf. **6** supr.) is hardly justified.

†**דִּין n.[m.]** judgment—Dt 17^{8} + 16 t.; 1779
sf. דִּינִי ψ 9^{5}, דִּינֵךְ Je 30^{13};—**1.** כסא דין *throne of judgment* Pr 20^{8}; משמים השמעת דין *from heaven thou didst cause judgment to be heard* ψ 76^{9}. **2.** *cause, plea,* בין דין לדין *between plea and plea* Dt 17^{8}; דין דין *plead a cause* Je 5^{28} 22^{16} 30^{13}; עשה דין *maintain the cause* ψ 9^{5} 140^{13}; ידע דין *consider the cause* Pr 29^{7}; דין לפניו *the cause is before him* Jb 35^{14}; שנה דין *change the cause* Pr 31^{5}; לְהַטּוֹת מִדִּין דַּלִּים Is 10^{2}; דין יתום Je 5^{28}; דין כל בני חֲלוֹף Pr 31^{8}. **3.** *judgment, condemnation,* דין רשע *judgment of the wicked* Jb 36^{17}; דין ומשפט *judgment and justice* v^{17}. **4.** *strife,* דין וקלון Pr 22^{10} (*legal strife, law-suit* Str). **5.** *government,* דת ודין *law and government* Est 1^{13}.

Note.—לְמַעַן תֵּדְעוּן שַׁדּוּן Jb 19^{29} is variously explained. (1) AV RV *that ye may know there is a judgment* follow Aq Symm Theod, so De Da, in interpreting שׁ relative + דִּין *judgment,* but שׁ is unknown to the dialect of Job and דִּין is used only in Elihu section. (2) 𝔊 rds. ὕλη, or ἴσχυς (i.e. שַׁדַּי (cf. 29^{5} 𝔊) ? or שׁד ?), & Qr שַׁדִּין, indicating ancient uncertainty and a corrupt text. (3) Ew Di rd. שַׁדַּי *the Almighty,* which accords with usage of Job. (4) Siegf כִּי שֵׁדֵהוּ (doubtfully).

†**דִּינָה n.pr.f.** daughter of Jacob Gn 30^{21} 1783
34$^{1.3.5.13.25.26}$ 46^{15}.

†**דָּן n.pr.m.** (*judge*)—**1.** son of Jacob and 1835
Bilhah Gn 30^{6} 35^{25} Ex 1^{4} Jos 19^{47} Ju 18^{29} 1 Ch 2^{2}. **2.** the tribe of Dan, מַטֵּה דָן Ex 31^{6} 35^{34} 38^{23} Lv 24^{11} Nu 1^{39} 13^{12} Jos 21$^{5.23}$ (all P); בְּנֵי דָן Gn 46^{23} Nu 1^{38} 2^{25} 7^{66} 10^{25} 26^{42} 34^{22} Jos 19$^{40.47.47.48}$ (all P) Ju 1^{34} 18$^{2.16.22.23.25.26.30}$; מַחֲנֵה דָן Nu 2$^{25.31}$ (P)—on Ju 13^{25} 18^{12} v. מַחֲנֶה; מִשְׁפַּחַת דָּן Nu 26^{42} (P); דָּן alone in poetry Gn 49$^{16.17}$ Dt 33$^{22.22}$ Ju 5^{17}, elsewhere Nu 1^{12} (P) Dt 27^{13} 1 Ch 27^{22} 2 Ch 2^{13} Ez 48$^{1.2.32}$. **3.** a city on northern frontier of

Israel at one of the sources of the Jordan, originally לַיִשׁ Ju 18^{29} (cf. v^{7}); = לֶשֶׁם Jos 19^{47}; captured by a colony of Danites; named Dan, and made a sacred place with rites of worship that lasted until the exile (Ju 18^{30}); = *Tell el Kâḍî*, Rob$^{BR\ iii.\ 351,\ 358}$ Bd$^{Pal\ 265}$. This place is frequently referred to: Gn 14^{14} Dt 34^{1} 1 K 12$^{29.30}$ 15^{20} 2 K 10^{29} 2 Ch 16^{4} Je 4^{15} 8^{16} Am 8^{14}; rd. also וּבְדָן for וְכֵן 2 S 20^{18} 𝔊 Ew We cf. Dr; and v. the phrase מִדָּן וְעַד־בְּאֵר שֶׁבַע Ju 20^{1} 1 S 3^{20} 2 S 3^{10} 17^{11} 24$^{2.15}$ 1 K 5^{5}; given by Chr מִבְּאֵר שֶׁבַע וְעַד־דָּן 1 Ch 21^{2} 2 Ch 30^{5}. (Ez 27^{19} v. ודן.)

1842 *Note.*— דָּנָה יַעַן 2 S 24^{6}. As no such place is known, the text is usually regarded as corrupt, and, 𝔊 being uncertain, is variously changed: (1) דָּנָה יַעַר *to Dan in the wood*, Thes after 𝔙 *silvestria.* (2) דָּנָה וְעִיּוֹן (וַיָּסֹבּוּ) *to Dan and Ijon* Klo (cf. 1 K 15^{20}). (3) דָּן וּמִדָּן (סָבְבוּ) We Dr cf. 𝔊.

1839 †הַדָּנִי **adj.gent.** alw. c. art. as n.pr. coll. הַדָּנִי 1 Ch 12^{35}; שֵׁבֶט הַדָּנִי Ju 18$^{1.30}$; מִשְׁפַּחַת הַדָּנִי Ju 13^{2} 18^{11}.

1781 †דַּיָּן **n.m.** judge 1 S 24^{16}; cstr. דַּיַּן ψ 68^{6}.

1840 דָּנִאֵל, later דָּנִיֵּאל **n.pr.m.** (cf. Ew$^{\S\ 45\ d}$; *Ēl is my judge;* on a possible connexion with Zend *dânu, wise,* or *wisdom* cf. Che$^{OP\ 107}$; v. Palm. דנאל Vog^{93})—**1.** son of David 1 Ch 3^{1}, דָּנִיֵּאל, but dub. cf. Che$^{OP\ 106}$; 𝔊 Δαμνιηλ, 𝔊L & Codd. Δαλουια; ‖ 2 S 3^{3} כִּלְאָב, 𝔊 Δαλουια; Klo^{Sm} prop. הֹדִיָּה, & in Ch הֹדִיאֵל, but grounds precarious. **2.** דָּנִיֵּאל, priest of the line of Ithamar Ezr 8^{2} Ne 10^{7}. **3.** דָּנִאֵל a great sage Ez 28^{3}; classed with Noah and Job as models of righteousness Ez 14$^{14.20}$; perh. the same as **4.** דָּנִיֵּאל, one of the noble young men taken into captivity by Nebuchadrezzar acc. to Dn 1$^{1-6}$, the hero of the book of Daniel, Dn 1^{6} + 22 t. (also frequently in Aramaic section).

4066 †I. מָדוֹן **n.m.**$^{Pr\ 22,10}$ **strife, contention**—
4079 ψ 80^{7} + 9 t.; pl. מְדָנִים Pr 18^{18}, מְדוֹנִים Pr 18^{19}
4090 + 7 t.; contracted into מִדְיָנִים Pr 6^{19} 10^{12}, מְדָנִים Pr 6^{14}; cstr. מִדְיְנֵי Pr 19^{13}. **1.** *strife, contention,* alm. wholly Pr:—Pr 18^{19} 23^{29} 26^{20}; also 17^{14} (‖ריב), 22^{10} (‖ דִּין וְקָלוֹן); מ׳ יִשָּׂא Hb 1^{3} *contention ariseth* (‖ ריב); שִׁלַּח מ׳ *let loose strife* Pr 6^{14} 16^{28}; יְגָרֶה מ׳ *he stirreth up strife* 15^{18} 28^{25} 29^{22}; note esp. אִישׁ מִדְוָנִים 26^{21} = *a contentious, quarrelsome man;* oftener אֵשֶׁת מ׳ = *a contentious woman* 21^{9} 25^{24} 27^{15}, cf. אשת מ׳ וָכָעַס 21^{19}. **2.** *object of contention* ψ 80^{7}, cf. אִישׁ מָדוֹן Je 15^{10} (‖ אִישׁ רִיב).—On מָדוֹן 2 S 21^{20} Qr, v. 4067
I. מִדָּה sub מדד. p. 551 4060

†II. מָדוֹן **n.pr.loc.** a royal city of the 4068
Canaanites Jos 11^{1} 12^{19}; 𝔊 **Μαρρων, Μαδων,** Λαμορων; = *Madîn,* close to *Hattîn,* Survey$^{i.\ 365}$, dub.; a village *Maron* lies 2 hours WSW. fr. Kedesh, van de Velde$^{Mem.\ 146}$, cf. Di.

†מְדָן **n.pr.m.** son of Abraham and Keturah 4091
Gn 25^{2} 1 Ch 1^{32}.

מִדְיָן **n.pr.m. 1.** son of Abraham and 4080
Keturah Gn 25$^{2.4}$ (J) 1 Ch 1$^{32.33}$. **2.** an Arabian tribe Gn 36^{35} (= 1 Ch 1^{46}) Nu 31$^{3.3.7.8.8.9}$ (P) Ju 6–9 (31 t.); having a כֹּהֵן (as chieftain?) Ex 2^{16} 3^{1} 18^{1} (E); זקנים Nu 22$^{4.7}$ (JE), נשיא(ים) Nu 25^{18} (P) Jos 13^{21} (P), שׂרים Ju 7^{25} 8^{3}, מלכים Nu 31$^{8.8}$ Ju 8$^{5.12.26}$; בִּכְרֵי מִדְיָן *dromedaries of Midian* Is 60^{6}; יוֹם מִדְיָן *day of Midian* Is 9^{3} (the victory over Midian Ju 7–8) cf. 10^{26} ψ 83^{10}. **3.** אֶרֶץ מִדְיָן *the land of Midian* Ex 2^{15} (E) Hb 3^{7}; מִדְיָן Ex 4^{19} (J) Nu 25^{15} (P) 1 K 11^{18}; land on Ælanitic gulf (where Arab. geographers still place town مدين). Cf. on Midian, Glaser$^{Skizze\ ii.\ 447\ ff.}$; Hom Aufsätze i. (1892), 4 f.

†מִדְיָנִי **adj.gent.** Midianite—Nu 10^{29} (J); 4084
f. מִדְיָנִית Nu 25$^{6.14.15}$ (P); pl. מִדְיָנִים Gn 37^{28} (JE)
Nu 25^{17} 31^{2} (P), מְדָנִים Gn 37^{36} (E). 4092

מְדִינָה **n.f. province** (an Aramaic word, 4082
cf. Syr. ܡܕܝܢܬܐ, Ar. مَدِينَةٌ *city*)—Est 1^{1} + 28 t.; pl. מְדִינוֹת 1 K 20^{14} + 23 t.;—a district of an empire, **1.** districts of realm of Ahab with שׂרים over them 1 K 20$^{14.15.17.19}$. **2.** of the Babylonian empire: Ez 19^{8}; Dn 8^{2} (of Elam); שָׂרָתִי בַּמְּדִינוֹת *princess among the provinces* La 1^{1} (of Judea). **3.** of the Persian empire Est 1^{1} + oft.; one of which was Palestine, Ne 1^{3}; the returning exiles, בְּנֵי הַמְּדִינָה *children of the province* Ezr 2^{1} Ne 7^{6}, having רָאשֵׁי הַמְּדִינָה Ne 11^{3}. **4.** provinces in general Ec 2^{8} 5^{7}; בְּמִשְׁמַנֵּי מְדִינָה *in the fat places of the province* Dn 11^{24} (fertile regions, prob. Egypt; other trans. vid. in Bev.)

†יָדוֹן **n.pr.m.** a Meronothite, one of the 3036
builders of the walls of Jerusalem Ne 3^{7}.

†דִּיפַת **n.pr.m.** a son of Gomer son of 7384
Japhet 1 Ch 1^{6}; but rd. prob. רִיפַת (q. v.); 𝔊 7384
Ἐρειφαθ, Ῥιφαε; 𝔊L Ῥιφαθ; ‖ Gn 10^{3} רִיפַת 𝔊 Ῥιφαθ, Ἐριφαθ.

דָּיֵק v. sub דוק. p. 189 1785

דִּישׁ, דַּיִשׁ, דִּישׁוֹן, דִּישָׁן v. דושׁ. p. 190 1785-89

†[דָּכָא] **vb. crush,** poet. (As. *dakû, crush,* 1792
Muss-Arnolt$^{Hbr.\ Oct.\ 1890,\ 66}$) not in **Qal;—Niph.**

Pt. נִדְכָּאִים Is 57[15];—*crushed*, fig. = *contrite ones*. **Pi.** *Pf.* דִּכָּא ψ 143[3]; 2 ms. דִּכֵּאתָ ψ 89[11]; *Impf.* וַיְדַכֵּא ψ 72[4]; 2 ms. תְּדַכֵּא Pr 22[22] (juss.); יְדַכְּאוּ ψ 94[5], תְּדַכְּאוּ Is 3[15]; sf. וִידַכְּאֵנִי Jb 6[9], יְדַכְּאוּם Jb 4[19]; 2 mpl. וּתְדַכְּאוּנַנִי Jb 19[2] (so Baer, v. his ed. p. 44, cf. Norzi); *Inf.* לְדַכֵּא La 3[34]; *sf.* דַּכְּאוֹ Is 53[10];—*crush*, (fig.) c. acc. one's life to the earth ψ 143[3], Egypt ψ 89[11] (cf. De Che; י׳ subj.), servant of Yahweh Is 53[10] (י׳ subj.), Jb 6[9] וְיֹאֵל אֱלוֹהַּ ויד׳; oppressor ψ 72[4], God's people ψ 94[5] (‖ יְעַנּוּ), Is 3[15], cf. Pr 22[22] illegally in tribunal, La 3[34] ד׳ תחת רגליו (in all human oppressor subj.); *crush me* בְּמִלִּים Jb 19[2] (Job's friends, subj.; ‖ תּוֹגְיוּן נַפְשִׁי); never lit., not even Jb 4[19] (יְדַכְּאוּם, with indef. subj.), for suff. ref. not to בָּתֵּי־חֹמֶר, but rather to שֹׁכְנֵי, i.e. men inhabiting the clay houses, bodies, cf. Di. **Pu.** *Pf.* דֻּכְּאוּ Je 44[10]; *Impf.* יְדֻכָּא Jb 22[9]; *Pt.* מְדֻכָּא Is 53[5], מְדֻכָּאִים Is 19[10];—*crushed*, broken in pieces, shattered Jb 22[9] c. obj. fem. זרועות; Is 19[10] subj. שָׁתוֹת (here metaphor. for nobles); fig. of servant of י׳ Is 53[5]; made humble, contrite Je 44[10]. **Hithp.** *Impf.* יִדַּכְּאוּ Jb 5[4], יִדַּכָּאוּ Jb 34[25];—*must let themselves be crushed*, i.e. maltreated Jb 5[4] (in court בשער, cf. **Pi.** Pr 22[22]); *are crushed* Jb 34[25] (the mighty, by God).

1793 †I. **דַּכָּא** **adj.** contrite (crushed)—דַּכָּא Is 57[15]; דַּכְּאֵי ψ 34[19]—*contrite* Is 57[15] (‖ שְׁפַל־רוּחַ); ד׳ רוּחַ ψ 34[19] (‖ נִשְׁבְּרֵי־לֵב).

1793 †II. **דַּכָּא** **n.[m.]** dust (as pulverized), תָּשֵׁב אֱנוֹשׁ עַד־דַּכָּא ψ 90[3] (on form cf. Ba[NB 143]).

1794 †[**דָּכָה**] **vb.** id. (only ψ);—**Qal** dub.; ודכה (יָשֹׁחַ) ψ 10[10] Kt is rd. as **Qal** *Pf.* וְדָכָה consec. by RobGes Ol De al., i.e. *and he is crushed*, or *and he croucheth* (Qr יִדְכֶּה *Impf.* so AV RV *he croucheth*); others rd. וְדָכֶה יָשֹׁחַ (adj. intrans. or passive) *and crushed he sinketh down*, cf. VB Che; possible wd. be יִדָּכֶה Niph. (‖ יָשֹׁחַ and ונפל). **Niph.** *Pf.* וְנִדְכֵּיתִי ψ 38[9]; *Pt.* נִדְכֶּה ψ 51[19];—*be crushed, broken*, of physical distress ψ 38[9] (‖ נְפוּגוֹתִי); *be contrite* (לֵב נִדְכֶּה) ψ 51[19] (‖ נִשְׁבָּר). **Pi.** *Pf.* דִּכִּיתָ ψ 51[10]; sf. דִּכִּיתָנוּ ψ 44[20]; *crush down*, of divine wrath; c. acc. ψ 44[20], and *crush to pieces*, obj. ref. to עצמות, in metaph. ψ 51[10].—דָּכוּ Nu 11[8] v. דוך.

1796 †[**דֳּכִי**] **n.[m.]** (crushing), crashing, dashing, sf. יִשְׂאוּ נהרות דָּכְיָם ψ 93[3] of ocean (waves).

דכך (√ of foll.; cf. Ar. دَكَّ, Aram. דְּכַךְ, NH in deriv.; v. also דכא, דכה).

†**דַּךְ** **adj.** crushed, oppressed—דַּךְ ψ 74[21], 1790
דָּךְ ψ 9[10] 10[18]; pl. sf. דַּכָּיו Pr 26[28] (Baer; edd. al. דַּכָּיו)—poet.; always fig., *oppressed, distressed* ψ 9[10], 10[18] (‖ יתום) 74[21] (‖ עָנִי and אביון); Pr 26[28] דַּכָּו = *those crushed by it* (a lying tongue).

†**דַּכָּה** **n.f.** crushing, פְּצוּעַ־דַּכָּה Dt 23[2] *one* 1795
wounded by crushing (viz. of testicles).

דַּל, דָּל **n.** *door*, v. sub דלה. below 1817

דַּל **adj.** v. sub דלל. p. 195 1800

†[**דָּלַג**] **vb.** leap (NH *spring over, skip* 1801
(a verse), omit)—**Qal** *Pt.* דּוֹלֵג Zp 1[9] *leap*, c. art. *one leaping* עַל־הַמִּפְתָּן; 𝔊 1 S 5[5] ὑπερβαίνοντες ὑπερβαίνουσιν = דָּלֹג יִדְלְגוּ cf. Dr. **Pi.** *Impf.* יְדַלֵּג Is 35[6]; אֲדַלֶּג־ ψ 18[30] = 2 S 22[30]; *Pt.* מְדַלֵּג Ct 2[8];—*leap, leap over* c. acc. שׁוּר ψ 18[30] = 2 S 22[30]; abs. *leap as the stag*, יְד׳ כָּאַיָּל פִּסֵּחַ Is 35[6]; sq. על of locality Ct 2[8] (‖ מְקַפֵּץ).

†**דָּלָה** **vb.** draw (water) (NH *id.*, Aram. 1802
דְּלָא, דְּלָ֑א; Ar. دَلَا *pull up* bucket; II, IV *let down;* V *hang down;* cf. دَلْوٌ *bucket;* Eth. ደለወ: *weigh;* As. *dalû, draw water*, cf. Dl[§ 108] C Adler PAOS Oct. 1888, xcix.; also *dilûtu, bucket*, Id[ib.], *dalâni* COT[Gloss])—**Qal** *Pf.* דָּלָה Ex 2[19]; *Impf.* 3 ms. sf. יִדְלֶנָּה Pr 20[5]; דַּלְיוּ Pr 26[7] v. infr.; 3 f. pl. וַתִּדְלֶנָה Ex 2[16]; *Inf. abs.* דָּלֹה Ex 2[19];—*draw* (water, but no obj. expr.) Ex 2[6.19.19]; fig. of drawing counsel (עֵצָה) out of heart, c. acc. (sf.) Pr 20[5].—דַּלְיוּ Pr 26[7] is difficult; rd. perh. 3 m. pl. דָּלְיוּ intrans., a lame man's legs *hang down* (helpless) so Ew Sta[§ 413 a]; other views in De Now. **Pi.** *Pf.* 2 ms. sf. דִּלִּיתָנִי ψ 30[2] fig. (cf. Pa. in Syr.) subj. י׳ *thou hast drawn me up* (out of Sheʾôl, cf. v[4]).

†[**דַּל**] **n.[m.]** door (Ph. דל) only fig.: cstr. 1817
דַּל שְׂפָתָי ψ 141[3].

†[**דֶּלֶה**] **n.f.** door, only Qr דְּלָתֶךָ (Kt דלתיך) 1817
Is 26[20] fig., door of chamber in which people (personified) hides (cf. also דֶּלֶת du.) p. 195

†**דְּלִי** **n.[m.]** bucket, כְּמַר מִדְּלִי *like a drop* 1805
(hanging) *from a bucket* Is 40[15]; Du. sf. יזל מים מִדָּלְיָו Nu 24[7] cf. Di (on form dolyāw cf. Ew [§ 180 a & Anm. 3], also Sta[§ 52 a]); fig. of Israel's prosperity.

†[**דָּלִיּוֹת**] pl. of [**דָּלִית**] **n.f.** branch, 1808
bough, metaph. of Israel under figure of olive tree דָּלִיּוֹתָיו Je 11[16] Ez 17[6.7] (figure of vine); v[23]

(under figure of cedar); 31[7.9.12] of Asshur as a cedar, דָּלִיּוֹתָיו Ez 19[11] Isr. as a vine (cf. Löw[65]).

1817 † דֶּלֶת **n.f.** (? **m.**[Ne 13, 19]) **door** (NH *id.*; As. *daltu(m)* Strm [AV 1843] Schr[COT Gloss]; Ph. pl. דלהת CIS[1, 7, 3];—acc. to Ba[ZMG 1887, 607] fr. √ידל, As. *edilu, to bolt, bar*)—דֶּלֶת (always abs., and c. art. exc. Ct 8[9] + Ez 41[24] but here Co art.) Gn 19[10] + 18 t.; דָּלֶת Gn 19[9] Ju 19[22]; *sf.* דַּלְתּוֹ 2 K 12[10]; Du. דְּלָתַיִם (cf. Sta[§ 187 a]) Dt 3[5] + 9 t., דְּלָתָיִם Jb 38[10]; cstr. דַּלְתֵי Jos 2[19] + 6 t. + Ez 26[2] Co; *sf.* דְּלָתַי Jb 31[32], דְּלָתֶיךָ Zc 11[1] + Is 26[20] Kt (cf. דָּלָה n.f.), דְּלָתֶיהָ Jos 6[26] 1 K 16[34]; pl. דְּלָתוֹת Je 36[23] + 10 t.; cstr. דַּלְתוֹת Ju 3[23] + 19 t. + Ez 26[2] (Co דלתי); *sf.* דַּלְתֹתַי Pr 8[34], דַּלְתוֹתָיו 2 Ch 3[7] 4[22]; דַּלְתֹתָיו Ne 3[1.3.6.13.14.15]; דַּלְתוֹתֵיהֶם 2 Ch 4[9]; **1.** *door* of house (disting. fr. door-way, cf. 1 K 6[31] פֶּתַח Gn 19[6]) Gn 19[9.10] Ex 21[6] (all JE) Dt 15[17] Jos 2[19] (JE) Ju 11[31] 19[22.27] 1 S 21[14] (דלתות השער) 2 K 4[4.5] 6[32.32] Is 57[8] Jb 31[32]; so fig. of wisdom's house Pr 8[34] לִשְׁקֹד עַל־דַּלְתֹתַי; partic. *doors* of house of 'י 1 S 3[15] (הֵיכַל 'י v[3]); temple 1 K 6[34.34.34] 7[50] 2 K 18[16] 1 Ch 22[3] 2 Ch 3[7] 4[22] 28[24] 29[3] Ne 6[10] Mal 1[10]; so of Ezek.'s temple, Ez 41[23.24.24.24.24.24.25]. **2.** *door* of room Ju 3[23.24.25] 2 S 13[17.18] 2 K 4[33] 9[3.10], esp. *doors* of דביר or ק׳ קדשים 1 K 6[31.32] 7[50] 2 Ch 4[22] cf. also Ez 41[23]; also of court עֲזָרָה 2 Ch 4[9.9], and of porch אוּלָם 2 Ch 29[7]. **3.** *gates of city* Dt 3[5] Jos 6[26] (cf. 1 K 16[34]) Ju 16[3] 1 S 23[7] 2 Ch 8[5] 14[6] Ne 3[1.3.6.13.14.15] 6[1] 7[1] (ד׳ then generally distinct fr. שַׁעַר, wh. denotes the whole structure of gate, incl. posts, open space, etc., while ד׳ is swinging door), 7[3] 13[19] (where also sense narrower than ‖ שער) Is 45[1] (‖ שערים) cf. v[2] and ψ 107[16]; Je 49[31] Ez 38[11]. **4.** in other senses (mostly fig.): door (prob. *lid*) of chest 2 K 12[10]; aperture of womb Jb 3[10] (ד׳ בטני); jaws of crocodile Jb 41[6] (ד׳ פניו); lips of man Ec 12[4]; doors enclosing and shutting off sea Jb 38[8.10]; doors of heaven through wh. comes rain ψ 78[23] (cf. אֲרֻבֹּת הַשׁ׳ Gn 7[11]); of column of MS. (from shape) Je 36[23]; fig. of easily accessible woman, Ct 8[9]; in simile Pr 26[14]; of Jerus. as gate of people Ez 26[2]; of Lebanon Zc 11[1].

1806 † דְּלָיָה, דְּלָיָהוּ **n.pr.m.** (*Yah(u) hath drawn*)—**1.** דְּלָיָהוּ, **a.** a priest, contemp. David, 1 Ch 24[18]. **b.** a prince of Judah, contemp. Jerem. Je 36[12.25]. **2.** דְּלָיָה, **a.** head of a family contemp. with Zerubb. Ezr 2[60] = Ne 7[62]. **b.** descendant of Zerubb. 1 Ch 3[24]. **c.** father of contemp. of Neh. Ne 6[10].

† [דָּלַח] **vb. make turbid** (As. *dalâḫu, disturb*, Zim[BP 81] also in deriv.; Pal. ℑ דְּלַח fig. *be anxious, fear*, ܕܠܚ *turbavit, conturbavit*) —**Qal** *Impf.* 2 ms., וַתִּדְלַח Ez 32[2]; 3 fs. sf. תִּדְלָחֵם Ez 32[13] + v[13] (Co תרפשׂם); — *stir up, trouble, make turbid* (always with *feet*) sq. מים Ez 32[2] (‖ תִּרְפֹּס,—ס Baer, and not שׂ); so 32[13a, b] (but v[13b] Co rds. תרפשׂ (cf. v[2]) for תדלחם). 1804

† [דָּלַל] **vb. hang, be low, languish** (NH Hiph. *thin, thin out* vines, etc.; As. *dalâlu, be weak, humble* Zim[BP 74.97]; Ar. دَلَّ *direct, guide,* دُلَّ *be directed, guided;* دَلْدَلَ *put in motion, commotion;* تَدَلْدَلَ *be in motion, hang, dangle;* also دَلٌّ *amorous, coquettish, gesture* or *behaviour* of women)—**Qal** *Pf.* דַּלֹּתִי ψ 116[6], דַּלּוֹתִי 142[7]; 1 pl. דַּלּוֹנוּ ψ 79[8], דַּלְלוּ Is 19[6], דַּלּוּ Is 38[14] Jb 28[4] (on דַּלְיוּ Pr 26[7] cf. דָּלָה);—*hang, 'depend,'* Jb 28[4] (of one descending a miner's shaft ‖ נָעוּ); *be low*, of streams Is 19[6] (‖ חָרְבוּ); *be low, brought low*, metaph. of distress ψ 79[8] 116[6] 142[7]; *languish*, of eyes, *look languishingly* (Che) Is 38[14]. — **Niph.** *Impf.* יִדַּל Is 17[4], וַיִּדַּל Ju 6[6], — *be brought low, laid low* Ju 6[6] fig. of Israel; Is 17[4] of glory of Jacob. 1809

† דַּל **adj. low, weak, poor, thin** (especially common in Wisd. lit. and poet.)—דַּל Lv 14[21] + 8 t., דָּל Ex 23[3] + 17 t. + דָּל ψ 82[3]; דַּלִּים Am 2[7] + 17 t.; דַּלּוֹת Gn 41[19];—*weak, thin*, of kine Gn 41[19] (E); of Amnon 2 S 13[4]; *weak*, of family of Saul 2 S 3[1] (opp. חָזָק) cf. Ju 6[15]; *reduced, poor* (opp. rich) Lv 14[21] (P) Ru 3[10] (opp. עָשִׁיר) Je 5[4] (opp. to הגדולים, v[5]) Pr 28[15] Zp 3[12] (עַם עָנִי וָדָל); mostly subst., *a poor* (man), *the poor* Ex 23[3] (JE); opp. to עָשִׁיר Ex 30[15] (P) Pr 10[15] 22[16] 28[11]; opp. הוֹן Pr 19[4]; ‖ אביון 1 S 2[8] Jb 5[16] ψ 72[13] 82[4] 113[7] Pr 14[31] Is 14[30] 25[4] Am 4[1] 8[6]; cf. also Jb 20[10.19] Pr 22[9] Je 39[10]; *reduced, weak, helpless* (‖ עני) Jb 34[28] ψ 82[3] (‖ also יתום), Pr 22[22] Is 10[2] 11[4] 26[6] Am 2[7]; ‖ אלמנה Jb 31[16]; opp. שׁוֹעַ Jb 34[19];—cf. also ψ 41[2] Pr 19[17] 21[13] 28[3.8] 29[7.14]. 1800

† I. דַּלָּה **n.f.** coll., **hair, thrum** (both from hanging down)—דַּלָּה Is 38[12]; cstr. דַּלַּת Ct 7[6];—*hair*, ד׳ ראשך Ct 7[6]; *thrum* (threads of warp hanging in loom) in sim. of premature death מִדַּלָּה יְבַצְּעֵנִי Is 38[12]. 1803

† II. [דַּלָּה] **n.f. the poor**—cstr. דַּלַּת Je 40[7] + 2 t.; pl. דַּלּוֹת Je 52[15.16];—*the poor* (coll., weak, helpless ones) Je 40[7] 2 K 24[14] 25[12] (in ‖ Je 52[16], as also v[15], MT has strangely the pl.) 1803

1807 †דְּלִילָה **n.pr.f.** Delila, Philistine woman, mistress of Samson Ju 16$^{4.6.10.12.13.18}$.

1810 †דִּלְעָן **n.pr.loc.** a city of Judah, Jos 15^{38}.

1811 †[דָּלַף] **vb.** drop, drip (WisdLt.) (NH *id.* (זלף more common), דֶּלֶף *trough*, etc., Aram. דְּלַף, ܕܠܦ, *drip*)—**Qal** *Pf.* 3 fs. אֶל־אֱלוֹהַּ דָּֽלְפָה עֵינִי Jb 16^{20} i.e. weeps (*drops* in tears); דָּֽלְפָה נַפְשִׁי מִתּוּגָה ψ 119^{28} i.e. weeps (itself away Che cf. De); *Impf.* בְּשִׁפְלוּת יָדַיִם יִדְלֹף הַבָּֽיִת׃ Ec 10^{18} *the house drips*, i.e. leaks, because cracks are not mended.

1812 †דֶּלֶף **n.m.** a dropping (of rain, cf. Wetzst ZPV xiv. 1891, 5), fig. דֶּלֶף טֹרֵד מִדְיְנֵי אִשָּׁה Pr 19^{13} etc.; ד׳ טוֹרֵד בְּיוֹם סַגְרִיר וְאֵשֶׁת מִדְוָנִים נִשְׁתָּוָה׃ Pr 27^{15}.

1813 †דַּלְפוֹן **n.pr.m.** a son of Haman, Est 9^{7}.

1814 †[דָּלַק] **vb.** burn (intrans.), hotly pursue (NH *id.*, Aram. דְּלַק, ܕܠܩ, all intrans. *burn, kindle;* Hiph., Aph. transitive)—**Qal** *Pf.* 2 ms. דָּלַקְתָּ Gn 31^{36}; 3 mpl. וְדָֽלְקוּ consec. Ob^{18}; sf. דְּלָקֻנִי La 4^{19}; *Impf.* יִדְלַק ψ 10^{2}; *Inf. cstr.* דְּלֹק 1 S 17^{53}; *Pt. act.* pl. דֹּלְקִים ψ 7^{14} Pr 26^{23};—**1.** *burn,* וְדָֽלְקוּ בָהֶם Ob^{18} (fig. of Isr. ravaging among Edomites, ∥ וַאֲכָלוּם; on construction c. בְּ cf. 2 K 17^{25}); also in חִצָּיו לְדֹלְקִים יִפְעָל ψ 7^{14} *his arrows he maketh burning ones* (subj. God) RV De Che al.; & שְׂפָתַיִם דֹּלְקִים Pr 26^{23} *burning* (*fervent*) *lips* (opp. לֵב רָע). **2.** *hotly pursue* Gn 31^{36} (E; sq. אַחֲרֵי) 1 S 17^{53} (sq. id.); ψ 10^{2} La 4^{19} (both sq. acc.) **Hiph.** *Impf.* sf. יַדְלִיקֵם Is 5^{11}; *Imv.* הַדְלֵק Ez 24^{10};—*inflame,* c. acc., subj. wine Is 5^{11}; *kindle* obj. הָאֵשׁ Ez 24^{10}.

1816 †דַּלֶּקֶת **n.f.** inflammation, Dt 28^{22}.

1817 דֶּלֶת v. sub דלה. p. 195

1818 †דָּם$_{360}$ **n.m.**$^{Gn 9,6}$ blood (NH *id.*, Ar. دَمٌ, Eth. ደም: As. *damu* Nor^{239} Zim$^{BP 72, 76}$; Aram. דַּם, דְּמָא, ܕܡܐ, ܕܡ)—abs. ד׳ Gn 37^{22} + 154 t.; cstr. דַּם Gn 9^{6} + 62 t.; sf. דָּמִי 1 S 26^{20} + 3 t.; דָּמְךָ 2 S 1^{16} (Qr; Kt דמיך) + 4 t.; דָּמֵךְ Ez 16^{22} + 3 t.; דָּמוֹ Gn 9^{4} + 30 t.; דָּמָהּ Lv 4$^{30.30}$ + 11 t.; דִּמְכֶם Gn 9^{5}; דָּמָם Lv 16^{27} + 11 t.; pl. דָּמִים Ex 4^{25} + 35 t.; cstr. דְּמֵי Gn 4^{10} + 18 t.; sf. דָּמֶיךָ 2 S 1^{16} Kt (Qr דָּֽמְךָ); דָּמַיִךְ Ez 16$^{6.6.6.9}$; דָּמָיו Lv 20^{9} + 3 t.; דָּמֶיהָ Lv 12^{7} + 2 t.; דְּמֵיהֶם Lv 20^{11} + 5 t.;—**1.** *blood* of man or animal, = the life (נֶפֶשׁ) Gn 9^{4} (P) Dt 12^{23} Lv 17$^{14.14}$ (H); cf. נֶפֶשׁ הַבָּשָׂר בַּדָּם הִוא v^{11} (H) & דִּמְכֶם לְנַפְשֹׁתֵיכֶם Gn 9^{5} (P); see also ψ 72^{14} וְיֵיקַר דָּמָם בְּעֵינָיו; hence blood of animals not to be eaten Lv 3^{17} 7$^{26.27}$ (all P) 17$^{10.10.12.12.14}$ 19^{26} (all H) Dt 12$^{16.23}$ 15^{23} 1 S 14$^{32.33.34}$ Ez 33^{25} (cf. RS$^{K 310}$), but to be poured out & covered with dust Lv 17^{13} (cf. RS$^{Sem. i. 216 f.}$). **2.** usually blood become visible, **a.** as from a wound ד׳ הַמַּכָּה 1 K 22^{35} (cf. חֲתַן דָּמִים Ex 4$^{25.26}$ v. infr. **h**); licked by dogs 1 K 21$^{19.19}$ 22^{38} Ez 32^{6}; from the nose Pr 30^{33}; bloody issue of a woman Lv 15^{19} cf. v^{25}; pl. דְּמֵי טָהֳרָה 12$^{4.5}$, & מְקֹר דָּמֶיהָ v^{7} (all P) 20^{18} (H); blood in which child welters Ez 16$^{6.6.22}$ + v^{6} (del. AB𝔊 Co al.); of goat Gn 37^{31} (JE); of slain bird Lv 14$^{6.51.52}$. **b.** oft. obj. of שָׁפַךְ *spill, shed* Gn 9^{6} (P) 37^{22} (E) Nu 35^{33} (P) Lv 17^{4} (H) Dt 21^{7} 1 S 25^{31} 1 K 18^{28} 2 K 21^{16} 24^{4} 1 Ch 22^{8} Ez 16^{38} 22$^{4.6.9.12.27}$ 23^{45} 33^{25} 36^{18} (del. B Co) Pr 1^{16}; also ψ 79^{3} שָׁפְכוּ דָמָם כַּמַּיִם; שֹׁפֵךְ דָּם *a blood-shedder* Ez 18^{10}; עִיר שֹׁפֶכֶת דָּם Ez 22^{3} cf. v^{4} (also 1 K 2^{31} Je 22$^{3.17}$ 1 Ch 22^{8} 28^{3} Pr 6^{17} La 4^{13}); less oft. subj. of pass. נִשְׁפַּךְ, שָׁפוּךְ, etc. Gn 9^{6} Nu 35^{33} (both P) Dt 19^{10} Zp 1^{17} ψ 79^{10}. **c.** דַּם חָלָל Dt 32^{42} (song) *blood of slain;* ד׳ חֲלָלִים 2 S 1^{22} so Nu 23^{24} (JE), obj. of שָׁתָה, of Isr. under fig. of lion; cf. also Ez 39$^{17.18.19}$, & 2 S 23^{17} = 1 Ch 11^{19} (דַּם הָאֲנָשִׁים hyperbol. for imperilled life); as food of young eagles Jb 39^{30}. **d.** oft. of *innocent blood,* i.e. blood shed with injustice & cruelty, דָּם נָקִי Dt 21$^{8.9}$ 1 S 19^{5} 2 K 21^{16} 24^{4} ψ 94^{21} 106^{38} cf. v^{38} Pr 6^{17} Is 59^{7} Je 7^{6} 22^{3} (also 26^{15}); דָּם נָקִיא Jo 4^{19} Jon 1^{14}; also in cstr. דַּם נָקִי Dt 19^{10}; cf. 27^{25} לְהַכּוֹת נֶפֶשׁ דַּם נָקִי; ד׳ נ׳ דַּם הַנָּקִי Dt 19^{13} Je 22^{17} 2 K 24^{4}; דַּם נְקִיִּים Je 19^{4}; דַּם נַפְשׁוֹת אֶבְיוֹנִים נְקִיִּים Je 2^{34}; further דַּם צַדִּיקִים La 4^{13}; דְּמֵי חִנָּם 1 K 2^{31}; in ψ 30^{10} דָּמִי = *my death* (∥ רִדְתִּי אֶל־שַׁחַת). **e.** *avenger of blood* גֹּאֵל הַדָּם Nu 35$^{19.21.24.25.27.27}$ (all P); Dt 19$^{6.12}$ Jos 20$^{3.5.9}$ 2 S 14^{11}. **f.** pl. דָּמִים of abundance, blood in quantity, hence sts. of blood shed by rude violence, and of blood-stains;—Gn 4$^{10.11}$ (J) as crying from the ground for vengeance (cf. RS$^{Sem. i. 397}$), comp. also 2 S 3^{28} 16^{8} 2 K 9$^{26.26}$; Is 1^{15} 9^{4} 26^{21} Ez 16$^{6.6.6.9.36}$ (on txt. of v^{6} vid. supr.) Zc 9^{7} 2 Ch 24^{25}; דְּמֵי אָדָם Hb 2$^{8.17}$, and in other connexions; but interchangeably with sg. 2 S 3^{27} 20^{12} 2 K 9^{33} Is 34$^{3.6.6.7}$ Ez 21^{37} 22^{13} (pl. Co) 24$^{8.8}$ al.; v. esp. אֶרֶץ אַל־תְּכַסִּי דָמִי Jb 16^{18}; דְּמֵי ירושלם *blood-stains of Jerusalem* Is 4^{4}; = slaughter, sg. Gn 37^{26} (J) Je 48^{10} Ez 5^{17} 28^{23} (∥ דֶּבֶר) 38^{22} (∥ id.); דַּם־עֲבָדָיו Dt 32^{43} (song: cf. ψ 79^{10}); pl. דְּמֵי עֲבָדַי 2 K 9$^{7.7}$; דְּמֵי יִזְרְעֶאל Ho 1^{4} *bloodshed at Jezreel;* cf. דָּמִים בְּדָמִים נָגָעוּ Ho 4^{2}; דְּמֵי מִלְחָמָה 1 K 2$^{5.5}$; in Ez 9^{9} וַתִּמָּלֵא הָאָרֶץ חָמָס (Baer) rd. דָּמִים for חָמָס v. d. H

Vrss Co Comm.; אָרַב לְדָם *lie in wait for blood* Pr 1^{11} cf. v^{18} 12^{6} Mi 7^{2}; דָּמִים of a *plan of murder* Is 33^{15} (obj. of שׁמע); מִשְׁפַּט דָּמִים Ez 7^{23} *bloody crime;* as symbol of oppression, violence Mi 3^{10} (‖ עַוְלָה), Hb 2^{12} (‖ id.) **g.** דָּמִים = *guilt of bloodshed, blood-guiltiness* Ex 22^{1}, then more generally, *mortal sin* (RS$^{\text{OTJC 417, 2nd ed. 441}}$, cf. Ez 18^{13}) ψ 51^{16} (cf. Ho 12^{15}); also בּוֹא בְדָמִים 1 S 25$^{26.33}$. **h.** pl. also in phrases: חֲתַן דָּמִים *bloody bridegroom* Ex 4$^{25.26}$; also those denoting character, chiefly poet., אִישׁ דָּמִים *bloody man* (sanguinary) 2 S 16^{8} ψ 5^{7} אִישׁ הַדָּמִים 2 S 16^{7}; אַנְשֵׁי דָמִים ψ 26^{9} 55^{24} 59^{3} 139^{19} Pr 29^{10}; ואל־בֵּית הַדָּמִים *bloody house* 2 S 21^{1} but rd. with 𝔊 We Dr ואל בֵּיתֹה דמים, *& on his house is blood;* עִיר דָּמִים Na 3^{1}; עִיר הַדָּמִים Ez 22^{2} 24^{6} + v^{9} (del. B Co). **i.** דָּמָיו בּוֹ *his blood is in (upon) him,* he is responsible for his own death Lv 20^{9} cf. v$^{11.12.13.16.27}$ (all H), Ez 18^{13} (+ יִהְיֶה); דָּמוֹ בְּרֹאשׁוֹ Ez 33^{5}; Jos 2$^{19.19}$; so with שָׁבוּ 1 K 2^{33}, יִהְיֶה v^{37} Ez 33^{4}; דָּמְךָ עַל רֹאשֶׁךָ 2 S 1^{16}, and הֵשִׁיב י׳ אֶת־דָּמוֹ עַל־רֹאשׁוֹ 1 K 2^{32}; also לֹא תָשִׂים דָּמִים בְּבֵיתֶךָ Dt 22^{8}; and דָּמָם לָשׂוּם עַל אֲבִימֶלֶךְ Ju 9^{24}; נָתַן דָּם על (אל) Je 26^{15} Jon 1^{14}; וְהָיָה עָלֶיךָ דָּמִים Dt 19^{10}, v. 2 S 21^{1} supr.; also sg. Ez 22^{4} בְּדָמֵךְ אָשַׁמְתְּ, and as subj. of יֵחָשֵׁב לְ *shall be imputed to* Lv 17^{4} (H); אֵין לוֹ דָּמִים Ex 22^{1} cf. v^{2} (both JE) & (sg.) Nu 35^{27} (P). **j.** of judicial process in case of bloodshed דְּבַר לֹא תַעֲמֹד לַמִּשְׁפָּט בֵּין־דָּם לְדָם Dt 17^{8} cf. 2 Ch 19^{10}; עַל־דַּם רֵעֶךָ Lv 19^{16} (H). **k.** in phrase *require blood at the hand of,* exact vengeance (for it) from, דָּרַשׁ דָּמוֹ מִיַּד Ez 33^{6} Gn 9^{5}; דָּמוֹ נִדְרָשׁ Gn 42^{22} (E); abs. דֹּרֵשׁ דמים ψ 9^{13}; אֲבַקֵּשׁ אֶת־דָּמוֹ מִיֶּדְכֶם 2 S 4^{11} cf. Ez 3$^{18.20}$ 33^{8}; פָּקַד ד׳ עַל־ Ho 1^{4}; וְנִקֵּיתִי ד׳ Jo 4^{21}; Ez 35$^{6.6.6.6}$; cf. on the other hand אַל־יִפֹּל דָּמִי אַרְצָה מִנֶּגֶד פְּנֵי י׳ 1 S 26^{20} i.e. let it not be unavenged. **l.** of blood as defiling a land Nu 35^{33} (P) cf. ψ 106^{38} (pl. בדמים); עֲקֻבָּה מִדָּם Ho 6^{8} of a city *foot-printed* (VB) *with blood;* defiling hands Is 1^{15} 59^{3} La 4^{14} cf. Ez 23$^{37.45}$; further, of blood as oppressing one who has shed it עָשֻׁק בְּדַם נָפֶשׁ Pr 28^{17}. **m.** atonement for blood-guilt is expressed by וְנִכַּפֵּר לָהֶם הַדָּם Dt 21^{8} (on form of vb. cf. Ges$^{\S 55.9}$ & Di). **n.** blood (-shedding) as connected with divine wrath וְשָׁפַכְתִּי חֲמָתִי עָלֶיהָ בְּדָם Ez 14^{19}; דַּם חֵמָה וְקִנְאָה Ez 16^{38}; v. further אַשְׁכִּיר חִצַּי מִדָּם Dt 32^{42}, cf. Je 46^{10}; cf. also of human vengeance by divine help יִרְחַץ בְּדַם הָרָשָׁע ψ 58^{11}; תִּמְחַץ רַגְלְךָ בְּדָם 68^{24}; note further Is 49^{26} Ez 39^{19} (in both fig. of being drunk with blood); then of simple human vengeance וְהוֹרַדְתָּ אֶת־שֵׂיבָתוֹ בְּדָם שְׁאוֹל 1 K 2^{9}. **o.** of water turned into blood (sg.) in Egypt, by divine power Ex 4^{9} (J) 7$^{17.20}$ (JE) v$^{19.19.21}$ (P) ψ 78^{44} 105^{29}; cf. Is. 15^{9} & Ez 32^{6}; further, of appearance of blood in sky Jo 3^{3}, & of colour of moon v^{4}; specifically of red colour of water אֲדֻמִּים כַּדָּם 2 K 3^{22} cf. v^{23}. **3.** blood used with religious significance, **a.** blood of passover-lamb Ex 12$^{7.13.13}$ (all P) v$^{22.22.23}$ (all JE); note also דַּם הַבְּרִית, i.e. blood by which covenant was ratified Ex 24^{8} (JE) Zc 9^{11}. **b.** blood used in ritual, Lv 17^{11} הַדָּם הוּא בַּנֶּפֶשׁ יְכַפֵּר (H); cf. 2 Ch 29^{24}; also Ez 44$^{7.15}$ (both ‖ חֵלֶב); further Lv 1^{5} Is 1^{11} ψ 50^{13}; thrown on altar, vb. זָרַק usually c. עַל Ex 24^{6} (JE) 29$^{16.20}$ Lv 1$^{5.11}$ 3$^{2.8.13}$ 7$^{2.14}$ 8$^{19.24}$ 9$^{12.18}$ (all P) 17^{6} (H) Nu 18^{17} (P) Ez 43^{18} 2 K 16$^{13.15.15}$ 2 Ch 29$^{22.22.22}$ cf. 30^{16}; sprinkled, vb. הִזָּה Lv 5^{9} 16^{19} (both P); sprinkled toward tent of meeting (vb. הִזָּה) Nu 19$^{4.4}$ (P); brought into tent of meeting Lv 4$^{5.16}$ 6^{23} cf. 10^{18} (all P); sprinkled toward the holy of holies (vb. הִזָּה) Lv 4$^{6.6.17}$ 16$^{14.14}$ (all P); brought within the veil on day of atonement Lv 16$^{15.15.15}$ (cf. v^{14}) v^{27} (all P); thrown on people Ex 24^{8} (JE; זָרַק); sprinkled on priests (הִזָּה) Ex 29^{21} Lv 8^{30} (both P); on garment (in sanctuary, הִזָּה) Lv 6^{20} (P); applied with finger to horns of altar Ex 29^{12} Lv 4$^{7.18.25.30.34}$ 8^{15} 9$^{9.9.9}$ 16$^{18.18}$ (all P; cf. also Ez 45^{19}) Ez 43^{20}; applied to tip of right ear of priest Ex 29^{20} Lv 8$^{23.24}$ (all P; also Lv 14$^{14.25}$ P); poured out at base of altar (שָׁפַךְ אֶל־) Ex 29^{12} Lv 4$^{7.18.25.30.34}$ (all P); cf. with מָצָה (Niph.) Lv 1^{15} 5^{9}; with יָצַק 8^{15} (all P); half of blood put in basons Ex 24^{6} (JE); blood poured out on altar Dt 12$^{27.27}$; blood of red heifer burned Nu 19^{5} (P); vid. further such terms as דַּם זִבְחִי Ex 23^{18} 34^{25} (both JE) (cf. Dt 12^{27} 2 K 16^{15}); דַּם הַשְּׁלָמִים Lv 7^{33} (P; cf. v^{14}); דַּם חַטַּאת הַכִּפֻּרִים Ex 30^{10} (P) cf. Ez 45^{19}; דַּם הָאָשָׁם Lv 14$^{14.17.25.28}$; (v. זֶבַח, שֶׁלֶם, אָשָׁם, חַטָּאת); דַּם־חֲזִיר, *swine's blood,* as heathen offering Is 66^{3}; cf. נִסְכֵּיהֶם מִדָּם ψ 16^{4} (v. Che). **4.** fig. of wine דַּם־עֲנָבִים Gn 49^{11} (blessing of Jacob ‖ יַיִן); cf. Dt 32^{14} (song) דַּם עֵנָב תִּשְׁתֶּה־חָמֶר.—בְּדָמְךָ Ez 19^{10} prob. text. error cf. VB; Da prop. בְּרוּמָהּ *in her height.*

†I. דָּמָה **vb. be like, resemble** (NH *id.*, 1819
Aram. דְּמָא, דְּמֵי, ܕܡܐ; cf. דמין, ܕܡܝܐ *price,* Nab. דמי *id.* (Nö in Eut$^{\text{Nab. Inscr. p. 35}}$); also ܕܡܘܬܐ, and ܕܘܡܝܐ *likeness* (whence Ar. دُمْيَة *image, effigy,* as loan-wd. Frä^{272}) cf. דְּמוּת)—**Qal** *Pf.* 3 ms. ד׳ Ez 31^{8} ψ 144^{4}; 3 fs. דָּמְתָה Ct 7^{8}; 2 ms.

דָּמִית Ez $31^{2.18}$; 1 s. דָּמִיתִי ψ 102^{7}; 3 pl. דָּמוּ Ez 31^{8}; 1 pl. דָּמִינוּ Is 1^{9}; *Impf.* 3 ms. יִדְמֶה ψ 89^{7}; 1 pl. וְנִדְמֶה consec. Is 46^{5}; *Imv.* ms. דְּמֵה Ct 2^{17} 8^{14}; *Pt.* דּוֹמֶה Ct 2^{9};—*be like, resemble,* of external appearance, sq. לְ, Ct 7^{8} $2^{9.17}$ 8^{14}; sq. אֶל־ Ez $31^{8.8.18}$ (all of tree, fig. of Pharaoh); of condition or quality sq. לְ Is 1^{9} ψ 102^{7} 144^{4}; so מִי . . . יִדְמֶה לַיהוה ψ 89^{7}; also abs. Is 46^{5}; sq. אֶל Ez 31^{2}. **Pi.** *Pf.* דִּמָּה 2 S 21^{5}, דִּמִּיתָ ψ 50^{21}; דִּמִּיתִי Nu 33^{56}, Is 14^{24}; sf. דִּמִּיתִיךְ Ct 1^{9}, דִּמּוּ 2 S 21^{5}; *Impf.* יְדַמֶּה Is 10^{7}; 2 fs. תְּדַמִּי Est 4^{13} (juss.); אֲדַמֶּה La 2^{13} Ho 12^{11}; 2 mpl. תְּדַמְּיוּן Is 40^{18}; sf. תְּדַמְּיוּנִי Is 40^{25} 46^{5};—*liken, compare; imagine, think, devise;*—**1.** *liken,* i.e. *consider to be like, compare,* causat. of **Qal**, sq. לְ of external appearance Ct 1^{9}; of quality or condition Is 46^{5} (obj. 'י) La 2^{13}; sq. אֶל of external appearance Is $40^{18.25}$ (both obj. God in ref. to idols); abs. *use comparisons* or *similitudes* (parables, symbols, etc.) Ho 12^{11} (subj. 'י). **2.** *imagine, form an idea, devise* 2 S 21^{5} (on context cf. Dr); *think, intend,* sq. Inf. Nu 33^{56} (J or H) Ju 20^{5} Est 4^{13}; abs. Is 10^{7} cf. 14^{24}; *think that,* sq. obj. cl. (Impf. without conj.) ψ 50^{21}; *think of,* sq. acc. ψ 48^{10}. **Hithp.** *make oneself* or *become like; Impf.* אֶדַּמֶּה לְעֶלְיוֹן Is 14^{14} *I will make myself like the Most High* (on form cf. Ges $^{§ 54.2}$).

1823 †דְּמוּת **n.f. likeness, similitude** (mostly late) (acc. to Lag $^{BN 12, 147 ff.}$ mispunct. for דְּמֻת fr. דְּמָיָה; acc. to We $^{Prol. 413, Eng. Tr. 389}$ an Aram. loan-word, but v. Di Gn 5^{1}, Dr $^{JPh xi. 216}$ Che $^{OP. 474}$)—abs. ד' Is 40^{18} + 3 t.; cstr. ד' Gn 5^{1} + 16 t.; sf. דְּמוּתוֹ Gn 5^{3}; דְּמוּתֵנוּ 1^{26};—**1.** *likeness, similitude,* of external appearance, chiefly in Ezek.: Ez 1^{5} (*likeness,* i.e. something that appeared like) so v^{26} 8^{2} (דְּמוּת כְּמַרְאֵה (אֵשׁ) (cf. Co), 10^{1} כְּמַרְאֵה ד' כִּסֵּא; cf. also Dn 10^{16} כִּדְמוּת בְּנֵי אָדָם i.e. *one like the sons of man; similitude, resemblance* Ez $1^{5.10.16.22.26}$ $10^{10.21.22}$; מַרְאֵה ד' 1^{26}; דְּמוּת כְּמַרְאֵה אָדָם; כְּבוֹד י' v^{28}; also 2 K 16^{10} (pattern of altar), 2 Ch 4^{3} (images of oxen); of son in likeness of father Gn 5^{3} (P); so also of man in likeness of God Gn 1^{26} (|| צֶלֶם) 5^{1} (both P); cf. Is 40^{18} *what* ד' *will ye compare to him* (אֵל)? || דִּמָּה q.v. **2.** adverbially, *in likeness of, like as* Is 13^{4} cf. Ez 23^{15} & כְּד' ψ 58^{5}.—Ez 1^{13} rd. בֵּין, v. וּבֵינוֹת and J P Peters $^{JBL 1892. 40.42}$. On דְּמוּת אֶחָד Ez 1^{16} 10^{10} (apparently masc.) cf. Thes & Sm who trans. *the likeness of one had they all four;* Co rds. אחת.

1825 †[דִּמְיוֹן] **n.[m.] likeness,** דִּמְיֹנוֹ כְּאַרְיֵה ψ 17^{12} *his likeness is as a lion,* i.e. he is like a lion.

†II. [דָּמָה] **vb. cease, cause to cease,** 1820
cut off, destroy—**Qal** *Perf.* 1 s. דָּמִיתִי Je 6^{2}, וְדָמִיתִי consec. Ho 4^{5}; *Impf.* 3 fs. תִּדְמֶה La 3^{49}; 3 fpl. juss. תִּדְמֶינָה Je 14^{17};—**1.** intr. *cease* Je 14^{17} (eyes from weeping) La 3^{49} (*id.*) **2.** *cause to cease, cut off, destroy,* c. acc. Israel (under fig. of בַּת־צִיּוֹן) Je 6^{2}; (under fig. of אִמֶּךָ) Ho 4^{5}. **Niph.** *Pf.* נִדְמָה Is $15^{1.1}$ +; 3 fs. נִדְמְתָה Je 47^{5}; 2 ms. נִדְמֵיתָה Ob^{5}, נִדְמֵיתָ Ez 32^{2}; 1 s. נִדְמֵיתִי Is 6^{5}; 3 pl. נִדְמוּ Ho 4^{6} +; *Inf. abs.* נִדְמֹה Ho 10^{15}; *Pt.* נִדְמֶה Ho 10^{7}; *be cut off, destroyed, ruined,* of a city Is $15^{1.1}$ (|| שֻׁדַּד) Je 47^{5}; of people Ho 4^{6} Zp 1^{11} Ob^{5}; of king Ho $10^{7.15.15}$ cf. Ez 32^{2}; of beasts ψ $49^{13.21}$; *be ruined, undone,* prophet at sight of Yahweh Is 6^{5}.

†דֳּמִי **n.[m.] cessation, pause, quiet, rest;** 1824
ד' Is 62^{6} + 2 t.; cstr. דְּמִי Is 38^{10} (but v. infr.);—**1.** *quiet,* in phr. אַל־ד' לָכֶם Is 62^{6} *keep not quiet* (let there be *no quiet to you*); in prayer to God אַל־ד' לָךְ ψ 83^{2} *keep not quiet* (inactive; || שׁקט, חרשׁ); cf. וְאַל־תִּתְּנוּ ד' לוֹ Is 62^{7} *and give no rest to him* ('י). **2.** in phr. בִּדְמִי יָמַי, appar. *quiet, peacefulness,* even tenour, of my days (so De Or SS); others, as Hi Ew Che Di, *pause, resting-time,* i.e. *noon-day* (cf. 𝔖𝔙, & *height* 𝔊), fig. of middle life, but usage dub.; Klo $^{SK 1884, 157}$ *cessation, pause,* of natural end of life, Hezekiah's natural expectation, in contrast with the speedy death implied in v^{b}; but parallelism of v^{11a} is ag. this; Brd emends בְּרֹם after 𝔊; Klo $^{l.c.}$ suggests בְּתֹם or כְּתֹם as poss., though not necessary;—but view stated first is on the whole best.

†I. [דָּמַם] **vb. be or grow dumb, silent,** 1826
still (NH *id.*; Eth. in II. አደመመ፡ *stupefy;* III., 1 & 2 ተደመ፡ ተደመመ፡ *be astounded, stupefied*)—**Qal** *Pf.* דַּמּוּ Jb 30^{27}, דָּמוּ ψ 35^{15}; *Impf.* יִדֹּם Am 5^{13} + 2 t., וַיִּדֹּם Lv 10^{3} Jos 10^{13}; 3 fs. תִּדֹּם La 2^{18}; 2 fs. תִּדְּמִי Je 48^{2} (so Ki Ol & Kö^{327} q.v.; others Niph.); וָאֶדֹּם Jb 31^{34}; יִדְּמוּ Ex 15^{16} + 3 t.; 1 pl. cohort. נִדְּמָה Je 8^{14} (so Thes Ol Bö Kö^{327} q.v.; others Niph.);—**1.** *be silent* ψ 4^{5} 30^{13} 35^{15} (prob., cf. De Che), Ez 24^{17} Lv 10^{3} (P) Am 5^{13}; in grief La 2^{10} 3^{28}. **2.** *be still* (opp. to both speech and motion) Jb 31^{34}; = perish Je 8^{14} 48^{2} ψ 31^{18} (ד' לשׁאול); c. לְ *be silent to* i.e. be resigned to ψ 37^{7} 62^{6}, sq. לְמוֹ עֲצָתִי Jb 29^{21} (|| לִי שָׁמְעוּ); *be still,* motionless, stand still Jos $10^{12.13}$ (of sun || עמד); 1 S 14^{9} (men); Je 47^{6} (of sword || הֵרָגְעִי); so also of bowels, as seat of mental excitement Jb 30^{27};

La 2[18] אַל־תִּדֹּם בַּת־עֵינֵךְ, i.e. cease not to weep (הוֹרִידִי כַנַּחַל דִּמְעָה ||). **3.** *be struck dumb, astounded,* in amazement and fear Ex 15[16] (כאבן) Is 23[2] (but cf. II. דמם). **Niph.** *Pf.* 3 pl. וְנָדַמּוּ consec. Je 25[37]; *Impf.* יִדַּמּוּ Je 49[26] 50[30], יִדַּמּוּ 1 S 2[9]; 2 mpl. תִּדַּמּוּ Je 51[6]—*be made silent,* i.e. destroyed; the wicked 1 S 2[9] (בַּחֹשֶׁךְ), cf. Je 51[6]; men of war Je 49[26] 50[30]; dwellings Je 25[37]. **Po.** *Pf.* 1 s. שִׁוִּיתִי וְדוֹמַמְתִּי נַפְשִׁי ψ 131[2] '*composed and quieted my soul*' Che (as a weaned child). **Hiph.** *Pf.* 3 ms. sf. הֲדִמָּנוּ *he* (God) *hath silenced us* (= caused to perish) Je 8[14].

1827 †דְּמָמָה **n.f.** (silence) **whisper** (on format. cf. Ba[NB 87])—וְאַחַר הָאֵשׁ קוֹל דְּמָמָה דַקָּה 1 K 19[12]; דְּמָמָה וָקוֹל אֶשְׁמָע Jb 4[16] *a whisper* and a voice, i.e. an articulate whisper (cf. Di); יָקֵם סְעָרָה לִדְמָמָה ψ 107[29] *he settleth storm into whisper.*

1822 †דֻּמָה **n.f.** **one silenced, brought to silence** (?; **destroyed**?) מִי כְצוֹר כְּדֻמָה בְּתוֹךְ הַיָּם Ez 27[32] (form pecul. & sense dub.: Baer כְּדֻמָּה; Co כְּבֻדָּה fr. כָּבֹד adj., cf. 23[41] ψ 45[14]) AV *What city is like Tyrus, like the destroyed* (as though for מְדֻמָּה cf. ההללה 26[1]; but Pi. Pu. not elsewh.) *in the midst of the sea?* RV *like her that is brought to silence.*—Dl[Baer Ezech p. xi. & Pr 64] der., hesitantly, fr. II. דמם.

1826 †II. [דָּמַם] **vb. wail** (?; cf. As. *damâmu, groan, wail, lament,* Dl[Baer's Ezech xi; Pr 64])—only **Qal** *Imv.* דֹּמּוּ יֹשְׁבֵי אִי Is 23[2] *wail, ye coast dwellers* (cf. Dl[l.c.]), || הֵילִילוּ v[1], & הֵילִילוּ יֹשְׁבֵי אִי v[6]; most, however, assign this to I. דמם q.v. (**3**).

דמן (√of foll., mng. dub.; Ar. دَمَنَ, *prepare, improve, manure land,* appar. denom.)

1828 †דֹּמֶן **n.m.** dung (Ar. دِمْنٌ) always in this form and always of corpses, lying on ground as offal 2 K 9[37] Je 8[2] 9[21] 16[4] 25[33] ψ 83[11].

1829 †דִּמְנָה **n.pr.loc.** Levitical city in Zebulun Jos 21[35] (but rd. perh. רִמּוֹנָה +; cf. 1 Ch 6[62] Jos 19[13], and v. Di).

4086 †מַדְמֵן **n.pr.loc.** in Moab Je 48[2] (on text, however, cf. Che Is 25[10]).

4087 †I. מַדְמֵנָה **n.f.** **dung-place, dung-pit,** במי מ׳ Is 25[10] (Qr בְּמוֹ מ׳).

4088 †II. מַדְמֵנָה **n.pr.loc.** in Benjamin, N. of Jerusalem Is 10[31].

4089 †מַדְמַנָּה **1. n.pr.loc.** city of southern Judah Jos 15[31]; loc. dub., Onom. Μηδεβηνα = Μηνοεις near Gaza Lag[Onom. 279, 2nd ed. 276]; cf. *Minyay* S. of Gaza Rob[BR i. 602]; on other proposed identif. cf. Di. **2. n.pr.m.** descendant of Caleb 1 Ch 2[49].

†[דָּמַע] **vb.** weep (NH *id.*, Ar. دَمَعَ & 1830
دَمِعَ; Aram. דְּמַע, ܕܡܰܥ: As. in deriv., v. infr.), **Qal** *Impf.* 3 fs., and *Inf. abs.*, וְדָמֹעַ תִּדְמַע וְתֵרֵד עֵינִי דִּמְעָה Je 13[17].

†[דֶּמַע] **n.[m.]** (weeping, trickling) **juice,** 1831
i.e. wine or (&) oil (cf. foll.) דִּמְעֲךָ Ex 22[28] (|| מְלֵאָתְךָ), cf. Di; Ar. دَمْعَةُ الكَرْمِ = *wine.*

†דִּמְעָה **n.f.** coll. **tears** (chiefly poet. and 1832
late; freq. in Je. and contemp.) (Ar. دَمْعٌ; As. *dimu, dimtu* Hpt[KAT 2 Gloss i.] Zim[BP 23, 95]; Aram. דִּמְעָא, ܕܶܡܥܬܳܐ; NH דֶּמַע, דִּמְעָה)—abs. ד׳ ψ 80[6] + 10 t.; cstr. דִּמְעַת Ec 4[1]; *sf.* דִּמְעָתִי ψ 6[7] + 4 t.; דִּמְעָתֶךָ 2 K 20[5] = Is 38[5] + Ez 24[16] (del. 𝔊 Co); דִּמְעָתָהּ La 1[2]; pl. דְּמָעוֹת ψ 80[6] La 2[11]—*tears* ψ 6[7] Ec 4[1] La 1[2] 2[11]; esp. in Je. in phrase תֵּרֵד עֵינִי ד׳ etc. Je 9[17] 13[17] 14[17], cf. La 2[18]; Je 8[23] וְעֵינִי מְקוֹר ד׳; אֲרַיֶּוְךְ דִּמְעָתִי of weeping over, in behalf of one Is 16[9]; as appealing to God's compassion 2 K 20[5] = Is 38[5] ψ 39[13]; ψ 56[9] שִׂימָה ד׳ בְנֹאדֶךָ (cf. Che); v. also ψ 116[8] Je 31[16] Is 25[8]; opp. רִנָּה ψ 126[5]; of hypocritical tears Mal 2[13]; fig. tears as food ψ 42[4] (דִּמְעָתִי לחם); לחם ד׳ 80[6]; as drink 80[6], cf. Babyl. *dimtu maštîti, tears (were) my drink* (Zim[BP 42]; || *bikîtum kurmatî, weeping (was) my sustenance*).—Ez 24[16] וְלֹא תָבוֹא דִּמְעָתֶךָ del. 𝔊 Co cf. v[23].

†דַּמֶּשֶׂק **n.pr.loc. Damascus** (As. *Dimašķi,* 1834
Dimaski, Dl[Pa 280] Schr[COT Gn 15, 2 & ABK 323] Jäger[BAS II. 281 f.]; Ar. دِمِشْقُ, دَمَشْقُ; Aram. 𝔗 Onk, etc. דמשק, Ps-Jon דרמשק; ܕܰܪܡܣܽܘܩ)—דַּמֶּשֶׂק 1 K 11[24] + 28 t.; דַּמֶּשֶׂק Gn 14[15] + 8 t.; דַּרְמֶשֶׂק 1 Ch 18[5] + 3 t. Ch; דַּרְמֶשֶׂק 2 Ch 24[23] 28[5]; דּוּמֶּשֶׂק 2 K 16[10]; דְּמֶשֶׁק Am 3[12] v. foll., Vrss. דַּמֶּשֶׂק;—ancient Aramaean city, situated lat. 33° 30′ N., long. 36° 15′ E., in plain E. of Hermon & SE. of Anti-Lebanon; on the *Nahr Baradâ* (Gk. Chrysorrhoas); mod. *Dimishk & Esh-Sham,* Rob[BR iii. 440 ff.] Bd[Pal 307]; *Damascus* Gn 14[15] Am 5[27] 1 K 11[24.24] 2 K 14[28] Ct 7[5]; so also prob. Gn 15[2] (perh. gloss cf. Di), (Am 3[12] v. foll.); a trading-centre Ez 27[18]; as capital & residence of king of Aram 1 K 15[18] = 2 Ch 16[2], cf. 1 K 20[34] 2 K 16[9.10.10.11.11.12] 2 Ch 28[5] Is 7[8.8] 8[4] 10[9] (cf. Peters[Hbr. April 1885, 242]) 17[1.1.3] Je 49[23.24.27]; including also surrounding territory Ez 47[16.17] cf. v[18] 48[1], v. מִדְבַּר ד׳ 1 K 19[15]; נַהֲרוֹת ד׳ 2 K 5[12]; = kingdom Am 1[3.5] cf. Zc 9[1];

once (late) מֶלֶךְ ד׳ 2 Ch 24^{23}; note also אֲרַם ד׳ 2 S $8^{5.6}$ = 1 Ch $18^{5.6}$; further אֱלֹהֵי ד׳ 2 Ch 28^{23} (‖ אֱלֹהֵי מַלְכֵי אֲרָם).

1833 †[דְּמֶשֶׁק] **n.[m.]**? Am 3^{12} וּבִדְ׳ עָרֶשׂ; punct. & mng. dub.: all ancient Vrss דַּמֶּשֶׂק, and so Pusey Hoffm[ZAW iii. 102] ('in Damascus on a couch') al., yet this hardly suitable in context; Thes Hi Ew Baur Ke Gunning RV al. follow MT, & render *damask, silk*, etc. (Ar. دِمَقْسٌ, connex. with city דַּמֶּשֶׂק (Ar. دِمَشْقُ) disputed; acc. to Frä[40.288] Ar. دِمَقْسٌ is by metath. from مِدَقْسٌ, & this a loan-word from Syr. ܡܛܟܣܐ, & this from Gk. μέταξα (Old Lat. *metaxa*)).

1835 דָּן v. sub דין. p. 192

1840 דָּנִאֵל v. sub דין. p. 193

דנג (√of foll., mng. unknown).

1749 †דּוֹנַג **n.m. wax,** דּוֹנַג Mi 1^{4} + 2 t.; דּוֹנָג ψ 22^{15} —always in simile, of melting; at theophany hills melt like wax ψ 97^{5}; like wax before fire Mi 1^{4}; wicked perish as wax melteth before fire ψ 68^{3}; heart melteth like wax ψ 22^{15} (simile of fear, despair). On ד׳ in ψ 118^{12} cf. Bae Che[crit. n.]

1837 †דַּנָּה **n.pr.loc.** a city of Judah 'in the hill country,' named just before *Ḳiryath Sanna* = *Debîr* (= *Ḳ. Sepher*), Jos 15^{49} 𝔊 Ῥεννα.

1838 †דִּנְהָבָה **n.pr.loc.** capital city of king Bela in Edom Gn 36^{32} = 1 Ch 1^{43}; identif. with *Tennib* (perh. = *Thenib*, near the edge of the Belka, ENE. from Heshbon, described by Tristr[Moab 222]) by Neubauer[Acad. 1891, 260] cf. Tomkins[ib. 284].

1840 דָּנִיֵּאל v. דָּנִאֵל sub דין. p. 193

1843-44 דֵּעַ, דֵּעָה v. sub ידע. p. 395

1845 דְּעוּאֵל (רְעוּאֵל) v. sub רעה, ידע. p. 396, 944ff

1846 †[דָּעַךְ] **vb. go out, be extinguished** (poet. & esp. Wisd. lit.) (Aram. דְּעֵיךְ, ܕܥܟ)—**Qal** *Pf.* 3 mpl. דָּעָ֑כוּ Is 43^{17}; *Impf.* יִדְעַךְ Pr 20^{20}, יִדְעָ֑ךְ Jb 18^{5} + 4 t.;—*go out, be extinguished*, of lamp, always fig., lamp of wicked (i.e. prosperity) אוֹר רְשָׁעִים Jb 18^{5}, נֵר ר׳ Jb 18^{6} 21^{17} Pr 13^{9} 20^{20} 24^{20}; of hostile armies Is 43^{17} (‖ כָּבוּ). **Niph.** *Pf.* 3 pl. נִדְעֲכוּ *be made extinct, dried up*, Jb 6^{17} (of brooks). **Pu.** *Pf.* 3 pl. דֹּעֲכוּ of assailants, *be extinguished, quenched* כְּאֵשׁ קוֹצִים ψ 118^{12}; but rd. perh. בערו with 𝔊 Bae & Che, v. Che[crit. n.]

1847 דַּעַת v. sub ידע. p. 395

דפה (√of foll., mng. unknown; NH דּוֹפִי is *blemish, fault*).

†[דֳּפִי] **n.[m.] blemish, fault** בְּבֶן־אִמְּךָ 1848
תִּתֶּן־דֹּפִי ψ 50^{20} *against thy mother's son thou dost allege a fault* (‖ בְּאָחִיךָ תְדַבֵּר).

†[דָּפַק] **vb. beat, knock** (Ar. دَفَقَ *pour* 1849
out, also *drive* (beasts))—**Qal** *Perf.* 3 mpl. sf. וּדְפָקוּם consec. Gn 33^{13}, but rd. 1 s. sf. וּדְפַקְתִּים 𝔊 𝔖 Sam Di *beat* (in driving, drive severely or cruelly); *Pt.* דּוֹפֵק Ct 5^{2} abs. *knocking* (at door). **Hithp.** *Pt.* מִתְדַּפְּקִים עַל־הַדָּ֑לֶת Ju 19^{22} *beat violently* (beat themselves tired) against the door.

†דָּפְקָה **n.pr.loc.** first station of Isr. after 1850
מדבר סין Nu $33^{12.13}$ 𝔊 Ῥαφακα; situation unknown, cf. views in Di. (On an interpret. of name from a stone or metal *Mafkat, Ta-Mafkat* = *Mafkat*-district, v. Eb[GS 148 f. 552 ff.])

דַּק, דֹּק v. sub דקק. p. 201 1851-52

דקל (√ of foll. cf. دَقَلٌ a kind of *palm*; NH דֶּקֶל, *date-tree, palm*, Aram. דִּיקְלָא, ܕܩܠܐ).

†דִּקְלָה **n.pr.m.(loc.)** a son of Joktan, i.e. 1853
an Arabian territory or people Gn 10^{27} = 1 Ch 1^{21}; unknown, cf. Di Gn 10^{27}.

†[דָּקַק] **vb. crush, pulverise, thresh;** 1854
be fine (Ar. دَقَّ *be* or *become thin, minute*; Eth. ደቀቀ: As. *daḳâḳu* Pa. *break in pieces* COT[Gloss]; Ph. דק *id.*, Aram. דְּקַק Pa. *id.*, ܕܩ)—**Qal** *Pf.* 3 ms. דַּק Dt 9^{21}, דָּק Ex 32^{20}; *Impf.* 3 ms. sf. יְדֻקֶּנּוּ Is 28^{28}; 2 ms. תָּדוּק Is 41^{15};—**1.** *crush* (trans.) sq. acc. לֶחֶם *bread-stuff, corn* Is 28^{28}; of threshing ‖ דּוּשׁ Is 41^{15} (fig. of pulverizing mts.) **2.** only Pf.; *be fine*, of state to wh. Moses reduced the golden calf by grinding וַיִּטְחַן עַד אֲשֶׁר־דָּק Ex 32^{20}; וָאֶכֹּת אֹתוֹ טָחוֹן הֵיטֵב עַד אֲשֶׁר־דַּק לְעָפָר Dt 9^{21}. **Hiph.** *Pf.* הֵדַק 2 K 23^{15} 2 Ch 34^{4}; 2 fs. וַהֲדִקּוֹת consec. Mi 4^{13}; *Impf.* וַיָּ֫דֶק 2 K 23^{6} 2 Ch 15^{16}; 1 s. sf. אֲדִקֵּם 2 S 22^{43} (but אֲרִיקֵם ‖ ψ 18^{43}); *Inf. abs.* הָדֵק Ex 30^{36}; *cstr.* לְהָדֵק 2 Ch 34^{7} (form anomalous cf. Ew[§ 238 d] Ol[§ 258 b] Be; rd. perh. לְהָדֵק Ki; or לָדֹק [v. כַּדֹּק Is 40^{15}] cf. Öt);—*make dust of, pulverize* וַיָּ֫דֶק לְעָפָר 2 K 23^{6} (i.e. the Ashera), ‖ 2 Ch $34^{4.7}$ (כִּתַּת לְהָדֵק); so of the *bamah* הֵדַק לְעָפָר 2 K 23^{15}; of the מִפְלֶצֶת 2 Ch 15^{16}; fig. Mi 4^{13} (obj. עַמִּים רַבִּים); Ex 30^{36} (P) has וְשָׁחַקְתָּ מִמֶּנָּה הָדֵק *and thou shalt beat some of it fine*

(i.e. the incense); 2 S 22^{43} rd. אֲרִיקֵם (‖ ψ 18^{43}) for אֲדִקֵּם. **Hoph.** *Impf.* יוּדַק Is 28^{28} *be crushed,* subj. לֶחֶם *bread corn* (cf. supr. **Qal**);—on sense cf. Che Di.

1851 †דַּק **adj. thin, small, fine**—abs. m. ׳ד Ex 16^{14}+4 t.; דַּק Lv 13^{30}; f. דַּקָּה Lv 16^{12} 1 K 19^{12}; pl. f. abs. דַּקּוֹת Gn 41^{6}+2 t.; דַּקֹּת 41^{24}; cstr. דַּקּוֹת 41^{3}, דַּקֹּת v^{4};—**1.** *thin,* of kine ׳ד בָּשָׂר Gn 41^{3} cf. v^{4} (Sam has in both רַקּוֹת cf. MT $v^{19.20.27}$); of ears of corn $v^{6.7.23.24}$ (all E); *thin, shrunk, withered,* of man Lv 21^{20} (H). **2.** *small, fine,* of the manna דַּק מְחֻסְפָּס דַּק כַּכְּפֹר Ex 16^{14}; of incense Lv 16^{12}, hair 13^{30} (all P); of dust אָבָק דַּק Is 29^{5}; in sim. of isles in hand of ׳י, אִיִּים כַּדַּק יִטּוֹל Is 40^{15} (דַּק = subst. *fine thing, fine dust*); once of a low whisper קוֹל דְּמָמָה דַקָּה 1 K 19^{12}.

1852 †דֹּק **n.[m.] veil, curtain** (as thin), הַנּוֹטֶה כַדֹּק שָׁמַיִם Is 40^{22} *he who spreadeth out, like a veil, the heavens.*

1856 †[דָּקַר] **vb. pierce, pierce through** (NH *id.*, Aram. דְּקַר, ܕܩܪ)—**Qal** *Pf.* 3 *pl.* דָּקָרוּ Zc 12^{10}; *sf.* וּדְקָרֻנִי consec. 1 S 31^{4}, וּדְקָרֻהוּ consec. Zc 13^{3}; *Impf.* וַיִּדְקֹר Nu 25^{8}, וַיִּדְקְרֵהוּ Ju 9^{54}—*pierce, run through* (always c. acc.): as retributive act, Israelite and Midianit. woman Nu 25^{8}; false prophet Zc 13^{3}; but also as speedy death Ju 9^{54} (Abimelech); 1 S 31^{4a} (Saul) = 1 Ch 10^{4}, also 1 S 31^{4b} (but del. Be We after 1 Ch 10^{4} & so 𝔊L 1 S 31^{4b}), see also Zc 12^{10} (cf. John 19^{37}). **Niph.** *Impf.* יִדָּקֵר *be pierced through,* slain Is 13^{15} (in conquest of Bab. by Medes). **Pu.** *Pt.* pl. מְדֻקָּרִים *pierced, riddled,* (i.e. desperately wounded) warriors, Je 37^{10}, slain Je 51^{4} (‖ חללים); by hunger La 4^{9} (‖ חַלְלֵי רָעָב).

1857 †דֶּקֶר **n.pr.m.** (*piercing,* i.e. *sharp weapon?* Talm. *pick, mattock*) 1 K 4^{9} בֶּן־דֶּקֶר cf. sub. בן.

4094 †[מַדְקָרָה] **n.f. piercing, stab, thrust,** only *pl. cstr.* כְּמַדְקְרוֹת חָרֶב Pr 12^{18} *like thrusts of a sword,* sim. of rash speaking.

1858 דַּר v. דרר. p. 201

1755 דֹּר v. דור. p. 189

דרא (√of foll. cf. Ar. دَرَا *repel*).

1860 †דֵּרָאוֹן **n.m. aversion, abhorrence,** abs. ׳ד Is 66^{24} *object of abhorrence;* cstr. דִּרְאוֹן עולם *everlasting abhorrence* Dn 12^{2} (on form cf. Lag$^{BN\,200,202}$).

דרב (√of foll. cf. Ar. دَرِبَ *become accustomed, trained,* دَرَّبَ *train,* cf. Fl NHWB$^{I.\,444}$; also Eth. ደረበ: (quadrilit.) *jaculando infigere, etc.*; or, since דָּרְבָן Aram. in form, & 1 S 13^{21} perh. secondary, possibly regard as Aram. loan-word & connect with Ar. ذَرِبَ *be sharp, penetrating* (GFM, note of Apr. 1892)).

†דָּרְבָן **n.[m.] goad** (NH *id.*), לְהַצִּיב הַדָּרְבָן 1 S 13^{21} (on form cf. Ol$^{§\,215\,b.\,3}$ al. Dr). 1861

[דָּרְבֹנָה] **n.[f.] goad,** only abs. pl., in sim. דִּבְרֵי חֲכָמִים כַּדָּרְבֹנוֹת Ec 12^{11} (cf. De$^{Koh\,434}$). 1861

דרג (√of foll. cf. Ar. دَرَجَ *go on foot, step by step, walk,* دَرَّجَ *rise in grade, rank;* NH דרג Hiph. *raise, make high;* Eth. ደረገ: is *be connected;* Aram. ܕܪܓ (verb denom. acc. to PS); also As. *darâgu, be high, lift,* Lyon$^{Sargontexte\,80}$, *durgu, daragu, path, way* (of steep mountain paths) COT^{Gloss} (cf. also דרך); Ar. دَرَجَةٌ *a step, stair,* Aram. דַּרְגָּא, ܕܪܓܐ, ܕܘܪܓܐ, *id.*)

†מַדְרֵגָה **n.f. steep place, steep,**—׳מ Ct 2^{14} (‖ סֶלַע), pl. הַמַּדְרֵגוֹת Ez 38^{20} (‖ ההרים and חומה). 4095

†דַּרְדַּע **n.pr.m.** (etym. dub.; possibly = דַּרְדַּר, belonging then sub דרר, cf. Thes Add^{83}) 1862
—only 1 K 5^{11} *Ethan the Ezrahite, and Heman, and Calcol, and Darda, the sons of Mahol* (types of wise men, but Solomon wiser than they); = דָּרַע 1 Ch 2^{6}, where rd. דַּרְדַּע with 𝔖 𝔗 1873
& Codd.

דַּרְדַּר v. דרר. p. 205 1863

דְּרוֹם, דְּרוֹר v. דרר. p. 204 1864

†דָּרְיָוֶשׁ **n.pr.m. Darius** (Old Pers. *Dârayava'ush* cf. Spieg$^{APK\,81}$)—**1.** Darius Hystaspis, 522–485 Ezr 4^{5} Hg $1^{1.15}$ 2^{10} Zc $1^{1.7}$ 7^{1}. **2.** Darius Codomannus, 336–332 Ne 12^{22}. **3.** 'Darius the Mede,' Dn 9^{1} 11^{1}, cf. Bev$^{Dan.\,p.\,19}$. 1867

דַּרְיוֹשׁ Ezr 10^{16} v. דרשׁ. p. 205 1875

†דָּרַךְ **vb. tread, march** (Aram. דְּרַךְ, ܕܪܟ; 1869
NH Hiph. *lead, conduct;* Ar. IV. ادرك *reach, overtake;* Eth. ደረከ: *be rough, severe* (from *calcavit,* Di); መድረክ: *threshold, vestibule*)—**Qal** *Pf.* 3 ms. דָּרַךְ Nu 24^{17}+6 t.; 3 fs. דָּרְכָה Jos 14^{9}; 2 ms. דָּרַכְתָּ Hb 3^{15}; 1 s. דָּרַכְתִּי Is 63^{3} Zc 9^{13}; pl. דָּרְכוּ Jb 22^{15}+3 t.; *Impf.* 3 ms. יִדְרֹךְ Mi 5^{4} +6 t.+ ידרך Je 51^{3} (כתיב ולא קרי); 3 fs. תִּדְרֹךְ Dt 11^{24} Jos 1^{3}; 2 ms. תִּדְרֹךְ Dt 33^{29}+2 t.; 2 fs. תִּדְרְכִי Ju 5^{21}; 1 s. sf. וְאֶדְרְכֵם Is 63^{3}; 3 mpl. יִדְרְכוּ 1 S 5^{5}, יִדְרְכוּן ψ 11^{2}, וַיִּדְרְכוּ Ju 9^{27}; 2 mpl. תִּדְרְכוּ Dt 11^{25}; *Pt.* act. דֹּרֵךְ Am 4^{13}+5 t.; דּוֹרֵךְ Jb 9^{8}; דֹּרְכִים Je 25^{30} Ne 13^{15}; דֹּרְכֵי Je 46^{9}+5 t.;

pass. f. דְּרוּכָה Is 21^{15}; דְּרֻכוֹת 5^{28};—**1.** *tread, march, march forth*, abs., תִּדְרְכִי נַפְשִׁי עֹז Ju 5^{21}; cf. דָּרַךְ כּוֹכָב מִיַּעֲקֹב Nu 24^{17} (poem) *a star hath marched forth from Jacob.* **2.** *tread upon* (land), sq. בְּ Dt 1^{36} 11^{25} (subj. pers.), Jos 14^{9} (subj. רֶגֶל) cf. Dt 11^{24} = Jos 1^{3} (subj. כַּף רַגְלְכֶם); tread in a path, sq. בְּ Is 59^{8} (fig. of mode of life); tread in (on) the sea, sq. בְּ Hb 3^{15} (but txt. dub. cf. VB); of an invader יִדְרֹךְ בְּאַרְמְנוֹתֵינוּ Mi 5^{4} (|| יָבוֹא בְּאַרְצֵנוּ), יִד׳ בִּגְבוּלֵנוּ v^{5} (|| *id.*); sq. עַל 1 S 5^{5} (עַל־מִפְתַּן דָּגוֹן); ψ 91^{3} (עַל־שַׁחַל וָפֶתֶן); esp. (poet.) עַל־בָּמֳתֵי אָרֶץ Mi 1^{3}, of י׳, so Am 4^{13}, & (עַל־בָּמֳתֵי יָם) Jb 9^{8}; of Isr. treading on heights of enemies, i.e. subduing them Dt 33^{29}. Once sq. acc. (אֲשֶׁר ref. אֹרַח) Jb 22^{15}. In technical senses **3.** *tread* wine- (or oil-) press, sq. acc. יְקָבִים Jb 24^{11} (|| יַצְהִירוּ), גִּתּוֹת Ne 13^{15}; sq. acc. of thing pressed ד׳ עֲנָבִים Am 9^{13}; also of product תִּדְרֹךְ־זַיִת . . . וְתִירוֹשׁ Mi 6^{15}; יַיִן בַּיְקָבִים לֹא יִדְרֹךְ הַדֹּרֵךְ Is 16^{10}; sq. גַּת Is 63^{2} (in sim.); abs. Je 25^{30} (sim.) 48^{33}; fig. of judgment Is 63^{3} sq. acc. פּוּרָה *winepress*, subj. י׳, cf. v^{3} וְאֶדְרְכֵם בְּאַפִּי (|| רמס), i.e. *tread them down;* so גַּת דָּרַךְ אֲדֹנָי לִבְתוּלַת בַּת־יְהוּדָה La 1^{15}. **4.** *tread* (i.e. bend) the bow, sq. acc. קֶשֶׁת Je 51^{3} (אֶל־יִדְרֹךְ ידרך הַדֹּרֵךְ קַשְׁתּוֹ); fig. of assaults of wicked ψ 11^{2} 37^{14}, of judgments of י׳ ψ 7^{13} La 2^{4} 3^{12}; also fig. of Judah as bow in hand of י׳, כִּי דָרַכְתִּי לִי יְהוּדָה Zc 9^{13} (|| קֶשֶׁת מִלֵּאתִי אֶפְרַיִם); twice in like mng. c. obj. חֵץ *arrow* ψ 58^{8} (but on txt. cf. Che$^{\text{crit. n.}}$) 64^{4}; דֹּרְכֵי קֶשֶׁת = *bow-benders, archers* Je $50^{14.29}$ 1 Ch 5^{18} 8^{40} 2 Ch 14^{7}; קֶשֶׁת דְּרוּכָה *bent bow* Is 21^{15}, קַשְּׁתֹתָיו דְּרֻכוֹת 5^{28}. **Hiph.** *Pf.* וְהִדְרִיךְ Is 11^{15}; sf. הִדְרִיכָהּ Je 51^{33} (where many Inf. cstr.) cf. RS$^{\text{J Ph xvi. (1888) 72}}$; 1 s. sf. הִדְרַכְתִּיךָ Pr 4^{11}; 3 pl. sf. הִדְרִיכֻהוּ Ju 20^{43}, הִדְרִיכוּהוּ Jb 28^{8}; *Impf.* יַדְרֵךְ ψ 25^{9}, sf. יַדְרִכֵנִי Hb 3^{19}; וַיַּדְרִיכֵם ψ 107^{7}; 1 s. sf. אַדְרִיכֵם Is 42^{16}; וַיַּדְרְכוּ Je 9^{2} (cf. Ges$^{\S 53, 3, R 4}$); *Imv.* ms. sf. הַדְרִיכֵנִי ψ 25^{5} 119^{35}; *Inf. cstr.* v. supr.; *Pt.* sf. מַדְרִיכְךָ Is 48^{17};—**1.** *tread, tread down*, of treading down enemy in battle Ju 20^{43}; of treading a path Jb 28^{8}; levelling threshing-floor Je 51^{33} (all sq. sf.). **2.** *tread* (bend) the bow (= **Qal 4**), only fig. וַיַּדְרְכוּ אֶת־לְשׁוֹנָם קַשְׁתָּם שֶׁקֶר Je 9^{2} *and they have bent their tongue as their bow in falsehood.* **3.** causat., *cause to tread* or *march, lead*, returning exiles Is 11^{15} (subj. י׳; no obj. expressed); cf. וַיַּדְרִיכֵם בְּדֶרֶךְ יְשָׁרָה ψ 107^{7} *and he led them in a straight way;* v. also Is 42^{16} (|| הוֹלִיךְ); with a moral application הִדְרַכְתִּיךָ בְּמַעְגְּלֵי־יֹשֶׁר Pr 4^{11}; cf. ψ 119^{35} הַדְרִיכֵנִי בִּנְתִיב מִצְוֺתֶיךָ *lead me in the path of thy commandments;* ψ 25^{5} בַּאֲמִתֶּךָ (|| לַמְּדֵנִי) cf. v^{9} בַּמִּשְׁפָּט (|| יְלַמֵּד דַּרְכּוֹ), Is 48^{17} בְּדֶרֶךְ תֵּלֵךְ (|| מְלַמֶּדְךָ לְהוֹעִיל); once of giving security & triumph עַל־בָּמוֹתַי יַדְרִכֵנִי Hb 3^{19} *upon mine heights he maketh me tread* (cf. **Qal 2**).

דֶּ֫רֶךְ $_{715}$ **n.m.** $^{\text{Dt 17, 16}}$ & (less often) **f.** $^{\text{Ex 18, 20}}$ 1870
way, road, distance, journey, manner—abs. ד׳ Gn 38^{16}+; דָּ֑רֶךְ v^{21}+; cstr. דֶּרֶךְ 3^{24}; sf. דַּרְכִּי 24^{42}+4 t.+2 S 22^{33} דַּרְכּוֹ; דַּרְכְּךָ Ho 10^{13} 1 K 19^{15}; דַּרְכֶּךָ ψ 5^{9}+9 t.; דַּרְכֵּךְ Je 2^{23}+8 t.; דַּרְכּוֹ Gn 6^{12}+; דַּרְכְּכֶם 1 S 1^{18} Jb 28^{23}; דַּרְכֵּנוּ Ju 18^{5}+2 t.; דַּרְכָּהּ Gn 19^{2}+3 t.; דַּרְכָּם 1 K 2^{4}+; du. דְּרָכַיִם Pr $28^{6.18}$; pl. דְּרָכִים Dt 28^{7}+6 t.; cstr. דַּרְכֵי Pr 3^{17}+24 t.; sf. דְּרָכַי Jb 13^{15}+17 t., דְּרָכָ֑י ψ 95^{10}+4 t.; דְּרָכֶיךָ Dt 28^{29}+16 t.; דְּרָכֶךָ Ex 33^{13}+2 t.; דְּרָכַיִךְ Je 3^{13}+4 t.; דְּרָכַיִךְ Ez 7^{3}+3 t.; דְּרָכָיו Dt 10^{12}+; דְּרָכֶיהָ Pr 3^{17}+3 t.; דְּרָכֵינוּ La 3^{40} Zc 1^{6}; דַּרְכֵיכֶם Lv 26^{22}+17 t.; דַּרְכֵיהֶם Je 16^{17}+5 t.; דַּרְכֵיהֶן Ez 16^{47};—**1.** *way, road, path* Gn 35^{3} (E) $38^{16.21}$ (both J) 48^{7} (P), 49^{17} (J; poem) Lv 26^{22} (H, only here in Lv) Nu $22^{22.23.23.23.31.34}$ (all JE) Dt 6^{7} $22^{4.6}$ 23^{5} 24^{9} $25^{17.18}$ Jos 3^{4} (D) Ru 1^{7} 1 S 4^{13} (on text cf. Dr) 15^{2} 24^{4} 2 S 16^{13} 1 K $13^{9.10.10.12.17.24.24.25.26.28}$ $18^{6.6.7}$ 20^{38} 2 K 2^{23} 3^{8} 6^{19} 7^{15}, $19^{28.33}$ = Is $37^{29.34}$, Ho 6^{9} 13^{7} Is $43^{16.19}$ $49^{9.11}$ 51^{10} $57^{14.14}$ Je 6^{25} La 1^{5} Ez $21^{24.25}$ $42^{11.12}$ Jo 2^{7}, Ezr $8^{22.31}$ Jb 12^{24} ψ 107^{40} 110^{7} Pr 7^{8} 8^{2} 26^{13} Ec 10^{3} 12^{5}; cstr. *way of* (oft. = to, toward) ד׳ עֵץ הַחַיִּים Gn 3^{24} (J) ד׳ שׁוּר 16^{7} (J) ד׳ אֶרֶץ פְּלִשְׁתִּים Ex 13^{17} (E) ד׳ הַבָּשָׁן Nu 21^{33} (JE); cf. Dt $1^{2.19}$ 3^{1} Jos 2^{7} (JE) 12^{3} 1 S $6^{9.12}$ $13^{17.18.18}$ 17^{52} 2 K 3^{20} Is 15^{5} Je $2^{18.18}$ 50^{5} Ez 47^{15} 48^{1}; ד׳ הַמִּדְבָּר (of different ways) Ex 13^{18} (E) Jos 8^{15} (JE) Ju 20^{42}, cf. Dt 2^{8} 2 S 2^{24} 2 K 3^{8}; ד׳ הַזַּיִת אֲשֶׁר ד׳ אֶת־הַמִּדְבָּר 2 S 15^{23} is corrupt; rd. בַּמִּדְבָּר 𝔊L Dr cf. We: *the way of the olive-tree which*, etc.; ד׳ הָעֲרָבָה Dt 2^{8} and (with diff. reference) 2 S 4^{7} 2 K 25^{4} = Je 52^{7}, Je 39^{4}; ד׳ הַכִּכָּר 2 S 18^{23}; ד׳ יַם־סוּף Nu 14^{25} 21^{4} (JE) Dt 1^{40} 2^{1}; oft. of gateway, as ד׳ הַשַּׁעַר 2 S 15^{2} cf. 2 K 11^{19} 25^{4} = Je 52^{7}; Ez 9^{2} 43^{4} $44^{1.4}$ $46^{9.9.9.9.9}$ 47^{2}; ד׳ אוּלָם הַשַּׁעַר 44^{3} $46^{2.8}$; ד׳ בֵּית הַגָּן 2 K 9^{27}, ד׳ גַּן־הַמֶּלֶךְ Je 39^{4}; ד׳ הַיָּם Is 8^{23} (cf. Comm. & Schumacher$^{\text{Jaulân 63 and PEF Apr. 1889, 78}}$); ד׳ מְבוֹא הַסּוּסִים 2 K 11^{16}; sq. ־ָה loc. Gn 35^{19} (E), 38^{14} (J) 48^{7} (P; rd. אפרתה Ol); ד׳ הַמֶּלֶךְ נֵלֵךְ + Nu 20^{17} 21^{22} (both JE; Ar. درب السلطان of diff. highroads, cf. Seetzen i. 61, 132, ii. 336 Rob$^{\text{BR iii. 141}}$ Di; = מְסִלָּה 20^{19}) i.e. the *highway*, used by king with his army; cf. || בַּדֶּרֶךְ בַּדֶּרֶךְ Dt 2^{27} i.e. straight (or steadily) along the way; in particular of path, way, in

which God moves †בַּיָּם דַּרְכֶּךָ ψ 77^{20} (‖ וּשְׁבִילְךָ); בְּמִדְבָּר פְּנוּ Na 1^{3}; cf. וּבִשְׂעָרָה דַּרְכּוֹ (בְּמַיִם רַבִּים; ד׳ י׳ Is 40^{3} (‖ יַשְּׁרוּ בָּעֲרָבָה מְסִלָּה לֵאלֹהֵינוּ); also Mal 3^{1}, comp. Is 43$^{16.19}$ (way made by י׳) & 51^{10}; path of lightning Jb 28^{26} 38^{25}; of light 38$^{19.24}$, of camel (בִּכְרָה) Je 2^{23}, of locusts Jo 2^{7} (pl.); v. further the four wonderful things Pr 30^{19} *the way of an eagle in the air, the way of a serpent upon a rock, the way of a ship in the heart of the sea,* and *the way of a man with a maid* (i.e. no trace is left in any case); cf. also v^{20} כֵּן דֶּרֶךְ אִשָּׁה מְנָאָפֶת; figure of death אָנֹכִי הוֹלֵךְ הַיּוֹם בְּדֶרֶךְ כָּל־הָאָרֶץ Jos 23^{14} *I am going to-day in the way of all the earth* (D); so also 1 K 2^{2} (cf. Gn 19^{31} **4 a**). **2.** *journey* Gn 24$^{21.40.42.56}$ (all J) Nu 9$^{10.13}$ (P) Jos 9$^{11.13}$ (both JE) 1 K 18^{27}, 19^{7} רַב מִמְּךָ הַד׳ ;לַעֲשׂוֹת ד׳ Ju 17^{8}; ד׳ בְּאֵר שָׁבַע Am 8^{14} (*journey of—to—Beersheba* cf. Hi St; but txt. dub., 𝔊 ὁ θεός, cf. Gunning; Hoffm ZAW$^{1883, 123}$ prop. דֹּדְךָ, We בְּאֵרְךָ cf. Bu$^{ThLz\ 1892,\ 62}$); דֶּרֶךְ חֹל 1 S 21^{6} *a common* (not sacred) *journey;* esp. c. temp. modif. ד׳ שְׁלֹשֶׁת יָמִים Gn 30^{36} (J) Ex 3^{18} 5^{3} 8^{23} Nu 10$^{33.33}$ (all JE), 33^{8} (P) cf. also Gn 31^{23} (E) Nu 11$^{31.31}$ (JE), 1 K 19^{4}, 2 K 3^{9}; *go one's way* †הָלַךְ לְדַרְכּוֹ Gn 19^{2} (J), 32^{2} (E), 33^{16} (J), Nu 24^{25} Jos 2^{16} (both JE), Ju 18^{26} 19^{27} 1 S 1^{18} 26^{25} 30^{2} 1 K 1^{49} Je 28^{11}, vid. הלך; also †הָפַךְ לְד׳ 1 S 25^{12}, & (fig.) †פָּנָה לְד׳ Is 53^{6} (so 56^{11} **5** infr.); of זוֹנָה, fig. of Israel, וַתְּפַזְּרִי אֶת־דְּרָכַיִךְ לַזָּרִים Je 3^{13}. **3.** of *direction,* almost or quite=*toward,* 1 K 8$^{44.48}$= 2 Ch 6$^{34.38}$ *pray toward the city,* etc.; 18^{43} *look toward the sea;* esp. in Ezek. of looking, going, etc. ד׳ צָפוֹנָה Ez 8$^{5.5}$ cf. 21^{2} 40^{6}; cstr. ד׳ הַקָּדִים Ez 40^{10} (del. 𝔊 Hi Co) v^{22} 43^{1}; ד׳ הַצָּפוֹן v^{20} cf. ד׳ הַדָּרוֹם v$^{24.24}$, ד׳ הֶחָצֵר 41^{12}, ד׳ הַיָּם 42^{7} etc. (c. 28 t. Ez); (v. also מִדֶּרֶךְ Ez 9^{2} cf. 43^{2} 44^{3}; on ד׳ אַמָּה אֶחָת Ez 42^{4} v. VB Co Da) cf. לֹא־יִפְנֶה דֶּרֶךְ כְּרָמִים Jb 24^{18}. †**4.** *way, manner:* **a.** *usage* ד׳ כָּל־הָאָרֶץ Gn 19^{31} (J; cf. also Jos 23^{14} 1 K 2^{2} supr.) **b.** =customary experience, or condition ד׳ נָשִׁים Gn 31^{35} (E). **c.** ד׳ מִצְרַיִם Am 4^{10} *the manner of Egypt,* i.e. as was done in Egypt; Is 10$^{24.26}$. **d.** *habit* of animals, ants Pr 6^{6} (pl.) †**5.** fig. of course of life, or action, undertakings, etc. לֹא תַצְלִיחַ אֶת־דְּרָכֶיךָ Dt 28^{29} cf. Jos 1^{8} (D) 1 S 18^{14} 2 S 22^{33}=ψ 18^{33}; Jb 3^{23} 8^{19} 17^{9} 22^{28} 24^{23} 31^{4} 34^{21} ψ 10^{5} 35^{6} 37$^{5.7.23}$ 91^{11} 102^{24} 119^{37} 128^{1} 139^{3} 146^{9} Pr 2^{8} 3$^{6.23}$ 11^{5} 20^{24} 29^{27} 31^{3}; Is 40^{27} 45^{13} 48^{15} 55$^{8.9}$ Je 2^{36} 10^{23} 12^{1} 23^{12} La 3$^{9.11}$ Ho 2^{8} 9^{8} 10^{13} Am 2^{7} (ד׳ עֲנָוִים); thrice (Ch) in summary of a king's life, of Abijah וּדְרָכָיו וּדְבָרָיו 2 Ch 13^{22}; of Jotham וְכָל־מִלְחֲמֹתָיו וּדְרָכָיו 2 Ch 27^{7}; of Ahaz

וְכָל־דְּרָכָיו הָרִאשֹׁנִים וְהָאַחֲרוֹנִים 2 Ch 28^{26}; ד׳ אֹרְחֹתֶיךָ Is 3^{12} cf. also Is 30^{11} and 57^{18}; =gain Is 56^{11}, pleasure, etc. Is 58^{13}. †**6. a.** of moral action and character הִשְׁחִית כָּל־בָּשָׂר אֶת־דַּרְכּוֹ עַל־הָאָרֶץ Gn 6^{12} (P); cf. Je 3^{21}; יִשְׁמְרוּ אֶת־דַּרְכָּם 1 K 2^{4} 8^{25}=2 Ch 6^{16}; cf. v^{39}=2 Ch 6^{30}; הֵכִין דְּרָכָיו לִפְנֵי י׳ 2 Ch 27^{6}; ψ 5^{9} 39^{2} 49^{14} 50^{23} 119$^{5.26.59.168}$ Pr 4^{26} 5$^{8.21}$ 10^{9} 14$^{2.8.12}$ 16$^{2.7.9.17.25}$ 19$^{3.16}$ 21$^{2.29}$ Je 2^{33} 6^{27} 7$^{3.5}$ 16^{17} 17^{10} 18$^{11.15}$ 26^{13} 32$^{19.19}$ La 3^{40} Ez 7$^{3.8.9.27}$ 14$^{22.23}$ 18$^{25.29.30}$ 24^{14} 28^{15} 33$^{17.20}$ 36^{19} Hg 1$^{5.7}$ Zc 1^{6}; דַּרְכֵי לִבְּךָ Ec 11^{9} cf. Is 57^{17} (& Je 32^{39} **c.** infr.) **b.** of duty (commanded by י׳, etc.) הַד׳ יֵלְכוּ בָהּ Ex 18^{20} (E) cf. 32^{8} (JE) Dt 9$^{12.16}$ 13^{6} 31^{29} Ju 2^{17} Jb 31^{7} ψ 25$^{8.12}$ 32^{8} 119^{1} 143^{8} Pr 21^{16} 22^{6} 23^{19} Is 30^{21} 48^{17} Je 7^{23} Mal 2^{8}; so, too, of wisdom דְּרָכֶיהָ Pr 3^{17}, ד׳ חָכְמָה 4^{11} 8^{32} cf. 23^{26}; ד׳ בִּינָה דַּרְכֵי־נֹעַם 9^{6} cf. Is 40^{14}. †**c.** specif.: in good sense ד׳ הַטּוֹבָה וְהַיְשָׁרָה 1 S 12^{23} 1 K 8^{36}=2 Ch 6^{27}; cf. Pr 16^{31} Je 6^{16}; תֹּם דְּרָכֶיךָ Jb 4^{6} cf. 22^{3} Pr 13^{6}; ד׳ צַדִּיקִים (i.e. of light) Jb 24^{13} (‖ נְתִיבֹתָיו); דְּרָכָיו ψ 1^{6}, Pr 2^{20}, ד׳ טוֹבִים ψ 37^{14}, יִשְׁרֵי־דָרֶךְ תְּמִימֵי דָרֶךְ Pr 11^{20} ψ 119^{1}; ד׳ תָּמִים ψ 101$^{2.6}$, ד׳ אֱמוּנָה ψ 119^{30}, ד׳ שָׁלוֹם Is 59^{8}; ד׳ עוֹלָם ψ 139^{24}, ד׳ חַיִּים Pr 6^{23}, cf. 12^{28} Je 21^{8} (opp. ד׳ המות v. infr.); without modifier 1 S 8$^{3.5}$ Jb 13^{15} 23^{10}, לֵב אֶחָד וְד׳ אֶחָד Je 32^{39}; cf. also **a.** supr.; esp. cstr. before names of good kings 1 K 22^{43} 2 K 22^{2} 2 Ch 11^{17} 20^{32} 21$^{12.12}$ (pl.) so 34^{2}; cf. דַּרְכֵי דָּוִיד הָרִאשֹׁנִים 2 Ch 17^{3} *the first ways of David;* also דַּרְכֵי עַמִּי Je 12^{16}. †**d.** oftener in bad sense דַּרְכָּם הַקָּשָׁה Ju 2^{19}, דַּרְכּוֹ הָרָעָה 1 K 13^{33}, ד׳ רָע Pr 2^{12} 8^{13} 28^{10}; cf. 2 K 17^{13} 2 Ch 7^{14} Je 18^{11} 23^{22} 25^{5} 26^{3} 35^{15} 36$^{2.7}$ Ez 3$^{18.19}$ 13^{22} 20^{44} 33^{11} Jon 3$^{8.10}$ Zc 1^{4}; ד׳ לֹא טוֹב ψ 36^{5} Pr 16^{29} Is 65^{2}; דַּרְכֵּךְ וְזִמָּה Ez 16^{27}; cf. with completed metaph. ד׳ לֹא סְלוּלָה Je 18^{15}; further ד׳ שֶׁקֶר ψ 119^{29}, ד׳ עֹצֶב ψ 139^{24}, ד׳ פִּשְׁעָם ψ 107^{17}; דרך דַּרְכֵי־חֹשֶׁךְ Pr 2^{13}; דַּרְכֵי מָוֶת Pr 14^{12}=16^{25}; ד׳ המות Je 21^{8}, cf. supr. **c**; ד׳ עָצֵל Pr 15^{19} (cf. 6^{6}); ד׳ חַטָּאִים ψ 1^{1} cf. v^{6} Pr 1^{15} 3^{31} 4^{19} (ד׳ רְשָׁעִים), 12^{15} (ד׳ אֱוִיל), 13^{15} (ד׳ בֹּגְדִים), also 15^{9} 21^{8} Is 55^{7}; ד׳ עִקֵּשׁ Pr 22^{5}, cf. עִקֵּשׁ דְּרָכַיִם Pr 28^{6} cf. v^{18}; further, without modifier, Ho 4^{9} 12^{3} Pr 7^{25} 14^{14} Is 53^{6} 66^{3} Je 2^{23} (of idolatry רְאִי דַרְכֵּךְ בַּגַּיְא) v^{33} 4^{11} (cf. Hi Gf) v^{18} 15^{7} 22^{1} Ez 16$^{47.47.61}$ 18^{23} 20^{43} 23$^{13.31}$ 33$^{8.9.9.11}$ 36$^{17.17.31.32}$ cf. also sub **a.** supr.; לָתֵת דַּרְכּוֹ בְּרֹאשׁוֹ 1 K 8^{32} *to place his way upon his head,* i.e. requite it on him = 2 Ch 6^{23}, cf. Ez 7^{4} 9^{10} 11^{21} 16^{43} 22^{31}; פְּרִי דַרְכָּם Pr 1^{31}; esp. cstr. before names of bad kings ד׳ יָרָבְעָם 1 K 15^{34} (cf. v^{26}) 16$^{2.19.26}$ 22^{53} cf. v$^{53.53}$; also ד׳ מַלְכֵי יִשְׂרָאֵל 2 K 8^{18} 16^{3} 2 Ch 21$^{6.13}$ 28^{2} (pl.); דַּרְכֵי בֵּית אַחְאָב

2 K 8^{27} = 2 Ch 22^{3} (of Ahaziah, grandson of Ahab); ד׳ הָעָם הַזֶּה Is 8^{11}, ד׳ הַגּוֹיִם Je 10^{2}, ד׳ אֲבוֹתֵיכֶם Ez 20^{30} cf. 2 K 21^{21}. †**e.** way of י׳: (*a*)=his creative activity Jb 26^{14}; applied in concrete sense to behemoth (hippopotamus) הוּא רֵאשִׁית דַּרְכֵי־אֵל Jb 40^{19} (hyperb.); cf. of wisdom רֵאשִׁית דַּרְכּוֹ Pr 8^{22}; (*b*) = his moral administration, Ex 33^{13} (pl.; JE); Dt 32^{4} 2 S 22^{31}=ψ 18^{31} Jb 21^{31} 36^{23}; אלהים בַּקֹּדֶשׁ דַּרְכֶּךָ ψ 77^{14} (מִי אֵל גָּדוֹל כֵּאלֹהִים ‖); ψ 85^{14} 103^{7} 138^{5} 145^{17}; Pr 10^{29} Is $55^{8.9}$ Je $5^{4.5}$ Ez $18^{25.25.29.29}$ $33^{17.20}$ Ho 14^{10}. (*c*)=his commandments וְשָׁמְרוּ ד׳ י׳ לַעֲשׂוֹת צְדָקָה וּמִשְׁפָּט Gn 18^{19} (J); כָּל־הַדֶּרֶךְ אֲשֶׁר צִוָּה י׳ Dt 5^{30} cf. (pl.) 8^{6} 10^{12} $11^{22.28}$ 19^{9} 26^{17} 28^{9} 30^{16} Jos 22^{5} (D) Ju 2^{22} 2 S 22^{22} = ψ 18^{22}, 1 K 2^{3} 3^{14} 8^{58} $11^{33.38}$ 2 K 21^{22} 2 Ch 6^{31} Jb 21^{14} 23^{11} 34^{27} ψ $25^{4.9}$ 27^{11} 37^{34} 51^{15} 67^{3} 81^{14} 86^{11} 95^{10} 119^{3} Is 2^{3}=Mi 4^{2}, Is 42^{24} 58^{2} 63^{17} 64^{4} Zc 3^{7} Mal 2^{9}; cf. וַיִּגְבַּהּ לִבּוֹ בְּדַרְכֵי י׳ 2 Ch 17^{6}; v. also ד׳ עֵדְוֹתֶיךָ ψ 119^{14}; ד׳ פִּקּוּדֶיךָ v ^{27}, ד׳ מִצְוֹתֶיךָ v ^{32}, ד׳ חֻקֶּיךָ v ^{33}.

4096 †[מִדְרָךְ] **n.[m.] treading- or stepping-place**, place for the foot to tread on, only cstr. מִדְרַךְ כַּף־רָגֶל Dt 2^{5} *a treading-place for the sole of a foot* (cf. 11^{24}=Jos 1^{3}).

150, 1871 †[אֲדַרְכּוֹן, דַּרְכְּמוֹן (א prosthet.)] **n.[m.]** unit (appar. of weight, certainly) of value, rare & late, perh. **drachma**, others **daric**, v. infr.:—only pl. דַּרְכְּמוֹנִים of gold Ezr 2^{69} (‖ מָנִים of silver) =Ne 7^{70} (‖ *id.*); so דַּרְכְּמֹנִים Ne $7^{69.71}$; also אֲדַרְכֹּנִים of gold money 1 Ch 29^{7} (‖ כִּכָּרִים; כ׳ also in same v. of silver, brass & iron); of weight (or worth) of gold utensils Ezr 8^{27}.—Weight of Gk. δραχμή=4.32 grammes (= 66.5 Eng. gr.); value of silver dr.=c. $9\frac{3}{4}$ *d.* Eng.; value of gold dr. ($\frac{1}{2}$ stater)=c. 9*s.* 5*d.* Eng., cf. Hultsch [Gr. u. Röm. Metrol. (1882) 224, 227, 230-250, & Tab. xiv, xvi].—(If ד׳=*drachma*, then perhaps edit. insertion in Ne Ezr (regarded as loan-word in both Gk. & Heb. fr. some Asiatic source by Ew [GGA 1855, 1392 ff.; 1856, 798; Gesch. i. 274, H. i. 189] cf. Sm [Listen 18, N. 24], but on Gk. deriv. cf. Lex. Lidd. & Sc., also Brandis [Münz-Mass-u. Gewichtssytem 58 f.] Hultsch [l. c. 131]); cf. Ph. pl. דרכנם, דרכמנם=*drachmæ* acc. to Re [RA 1888, 7] Berger [Mém. Soc. Ling. de Paris, 1889, 385] Hoffm [AGG xxxvi Mai, 1889, 8]. Acc. to view commonly current hitherto ד׳=*daric*, Gk. δαρεικός, cf. Syr. ܙܘܙܐ, Pers. gold coin=c. Eng. sovereign (weight= c. 2 drachm.): Brandis [l. c. 62, 244 ff.] Hultsch [l. c. 466] Schr in Ri [HWB Art. Darike] Erman [ZPV ii, 75] Hoffm [ZA 1887, 49 ff.] (Hoffm [l. c.] abandons), cf. Ryle Ezr 2^{69}.)

1834 דַּרְמֶשֶׂק v. דַּמֶּשֶׂק. p. 199

†דרע (acc. to Thes connected with Aram. אֶדְרָע, דְּרָע *arm*, Heb. זְרוֹעַ, whence foll. in sense *strong*, of fortified city; this, however, is dub.)

†אֶדְרֶעִי **n.pr.loc.** a chief city of Bashan 154
אֶדְרֶעִי Jos 19^{37}; אֶדְרֶעִי Nu 21^{33}=Dt 3^{1}, Dt 3^{10}; בְּעַשְׁתָּרֹת בְּאֶדְרֶעִי Dt 1^{4}; בְּעַשְׁתָּרוֹת וּבְאֶדְרֶעִי Jos 12^{4} 13^{12} cf. 13^{31};—on identity of all these cf. Di Dt 3^{10}; modern *Derʿât*, $7\frac{1}{2}$ hours WNW. of Bosra; Euseb. Ἀδραά (Lag [Onom. 213, 86, 2nd ed. 235]) cf. Di Nu 21^{33} Wetzst [Hauran 47, 77, 123] Bd [Pal 201].

דַּרְדַּע 1 Ch 2^{6} v. דרדע. p. 201 1873

דרק (√of foll. mng. dub.; Ar. دَرَقَ= *walk rapidly, hasten*, دَرَقَةٌ *shield*).

†דַּרְקוֹן **n.pr.m.** head of a family of 1874
Nethinim, who went up with Zerubbabel, בְּנֵי־ד׳ Ezr 2^{56}=Ne 7^{58}.

דרר (√of foll. words: Ar. دَرَّ;—**1.** *stream, flow abundantly* (of milk, tears, rain, etc.), cf. I. דְּרוֹר. **2.** *be abundant, luxuriant* (of herbage), cf. دَرْدَار a kind of tree, now *elm* (Lane), & דַּרְדַּר. **3.** *run vehemently, easily* (of horse), cf. دِرِّير *swift* horse, or other beast, & II. דְּרוֹר. **4.** *give light, shine* (of lamp), cf. كَوْكَبٌ دُرِّيٌّ *shining star*, دُرِّيّ *glistening* or *shining* of sword, دُرّ *pearls* (coll.) & דַּר; hence prob. דָּרוֹם).

†דַּר **n.[m.]** pearl? mother of pearl? 1858
(Ar. دُرّ *pearls*, دُرَّةٌ *a pearl*) Est 1^{6}.

†I. דְּרוֹר **n.[m.]** a flowing; free run, 1865
liberty;—**1.** מָר־דְּרוֹר Ex 30^{23} (P) i.e. *myrrh of flowing*, fine-flowing m. cf. מֹר & Di. **2.** c. קרא *proclaim liberty*, וּקְרָאתֶם דְּרוֹר בָּאָרֶץ לְכָל־יֹשְׁבֶיהָ Lv 25^{10} (H) in Jubilee year, cf. Is 61^{1} (‖ פְּקַח־קוֹחַ); Je $34^{8.15.17}$ all ref. to liberty of Sabbatical year; v ^{17} (iron.) *lo! I proclaim to you liberty unto the sword, unto pestilence & unto famine*, i.e. liberty to be destroyed by sword, pestilence and famine, (a judgment of Yahweh); שְׁנַת־הַד׳ Ez 46^{17} i.e. year of Jubilee (cf Lv 25^{10}).

†II. דְּרוֹר **n.f.** [ψ 84, 4] swallow ψ 84^{4} (‖ צִפּוֹר), 1866
Che (q.v.) makes simile of quiet, peace, security, and supplies ellipsis; in simile, Pr 26^{2} כַּצִּפּוֹר לָנוּד כַּדְּרוֹר לָעוּף (of groundless curse, which does not alight, i.e. is not fulfilled).

†דָּרוֹם **n.m. south** (poet. & late) (on for- 1864
mation cf. Ol [§ 216 a] Sta [§ 295])—דָּרוֹם Jb 37^{17} + 14 t. + Ez $40^{27b.28b}$ (del. 𝔊 Co in v ^{27b}; AB 𝔙 Co in v ^{28b}—*south*, Ez 42^{18} (over against צָפוֹן ,קָדִים,

יָם); 12 t. more in Ezek. (of wh. Co del. 2, cf. supr.) 21^{2} (=תֵּימָנָה and נֶגֶב); דֶּרֶךְ הַדּ׳ *toward south* 40$^{24.24.27}$, rd. also דֶּרֶךְ הַדּ׳ 42^{10} for ד׳ הַקָּדִים 𝔊 Ke Co; שַׁעַר הַדּ׳ *south gate* 40$^{[27].28.[28]}$ cf. Co supr., 40^{44} (opp. צפון; also קדים), v^{45} (opp. צפון) 42^{12}=לַדּ׳ 41^{11} (opp. צפון), לִשְׁכוֹת הד׳ 42^{13} (opp. צפון). Elsewhere only Dt 33^{23} (‖ יָם), Jb 37^{17}; Ec 1^{6} 11^{3} (both opp. צפון).

1863 †**דַּרְדַּר** **n.[m.] thistles** (coll.) (Ar. دردار, still current in Pal., Löw$^{p. 100}$; Eth. **ደንደር፡**) קוֹץ וְדַרְדַּר Gn 3^{18} (J) Ho 10^{8} symbol of wildness, desert.

1875 †**דָּרַשׁ**$_{162}$ **vb. resort to, seek** (cf. Ar. دَرَسَ *rub over, efface* (a site), *tread* (wheat), fig. *read repeatedly, study*; ܕܪܫ *beat* (a path), *discuss*, Pa. *practise in*; NH *search out* (a meaning), *expound*)—**Qal** *Pf.* 1 Ch 10^{14}; *Impf.* יִדְרֹשׁ ψ 10^{4}+, אֶדְרְשָׁה 1 S 28^{7}, נִדְרְשָׁה 1 K 22^{7}+, יִדְרְשׁוּן Is 55^{2}; *Imv.* דְּרָשׁ־ 1 K 22^{5}+; *Inf.* abs. דָּרֹשׁ Lv 10^{16} Dt 23^{22}; cstr. דְּרֹשׁ Dt 22^{2}+ לִדְרָשׁ־ Ez 14^{7}, לִדְרִיוֹשׁ (scribal error for לִדְרוֹשׁ Ew$^{§ 239 a}$ Ol$^{§ 245 g}$) Ezr 10^{16}; *Pt.* דֹּרֵשׁ Dt 11^{12}+10 t., דּוֹרֵשׁ 1 Ch 28^{9}+3 t.; pass. דְּרוּשִׁים ψ 111^{2}, דְּרוּשָׁה Is 62^{12}; syn. בקשׁ;—**1.** (*tread* a place,) *resort to, frequent*, with religious obj., c. acc. loc. Am 5^{5} 2 Ch 1^{5}, לְ loc. Dt 12^{5}. **2.** *seek, consult, inquire of*: **a.** acc. אֱלֹהִים, י׳ Gn 25^{22} (J) Ex 18^{15} (E) 1 S 9^{9} 1 K 22^{8} 2 K 3^{11} 8^{8} 22$^{13.18}$ 1 Ch 15^{13} 21^{30} 2 Ch 18^{7} 34^{21} ψ 24^{6} 78^{34} Je 21^{2} 37^{7} Ez 20$^{1.3}$; *the ark of God* 1 Ch 13^{3}; *word of Yahweh* 1 K 22^{5} (=2 Ch 18^{4}) cf. 1 K 14^{5}; with בְּ Yahweh 1 Ch 10^{14} 2 Ch 34^{26} Ez 14^{7}; his word 2 K 1^{16}; with אֶל, אֶל־אֵל Jb 5^{8}; their God Is 8^{19}, Messianic king Is 11^{10}; מֵעַל־סֵפֶר י׳ *out of the book of* י׳ Is 34^{16} (in gloss, acc. to Che$^{JQ Jan. 1892, 332}$); c. מֵאוֹתוֹ of a נָבִיא לי׳ 1 K 22^{7} (=2 Ch 18^{6}) cf. (supr.) v^{8} 2 K 3^{11} and 1 K 14^{5} (מֵעִמְּךָ). **b.** *heathen gods* and *necromancers*, הַדֹּרֵשׁ *the inquirer* Ez 14^{10}; with בְּ, בְּבַעַל זְבוּב 2 K 1$^{2.3.6.16}$; בָּאוֹב 1 Ch 10^{13}, בְּבַעֲלַת אוֹב 1 S 28^{7}, with אֶל, אֶל־הָאֹבוֹת Is 8^{19}, אֶל־הַמֵּתִים Dt 18^{11}, אֶל־הָאֱלִילִים Is 19^{3}. **3.** *seek deity in prayer and worship*: **a.** *the true God* (cf. בקשׁ **3**) דרשׁ י׳ Dt 4^{29} Ho 10^{12} Am 5$^{4.6}$ Is 9^{12} 31^{1} 55^{6} 58^{2} 65^{10} Je 10^{21} 29^{13} Zp 1^{6} La 3^{25} 1 Ch 16^{11} (=ψ 105^{4}) 28^{9} 2 Ch 12^{14} 14$^{3.6}$ 15$^{2.12}$ 16^{12} 22^{9} 26^{5} ψ 9^{11} 22^{27} 34$^{5.11}$ 119$^{2.10}$; דרשׁ (ה)אלהים 2 Ch 19^{3} 26^{5} 30^{19} ψ 14^{2} (=53^{3}) 69^{33}; אֲדֹנָי ד׳ ψ 77^{3}; with לְ, only in Chronicler, ליהוה 1 Ch 22^{19} 2 Ch 15^{13} 20^{3} Ezr 6^{21}; לאלהים 2 Ch 17^{4} 31^{21} 34^{3} Ezr 4^{2}; Dr$^{Intr. 503}$ finds in Chr weakened mng., *revere*. **b.** *seek heathen deities*, c. acc. Je 8^{2} 2 Ch 25$^{15.20}$; with לְ, Dt 12^{30} 2 Ch 17^{3}. **4. a.** *seek*, with idea of demanding, *require* (בקשׁ is *seek*, simply), with acc. lost sheep Dt 22^{2} Ez 34$^{6.8.11}$; goat Lv 10$^{16.16}$ (P); with אחר, after green fodder Jb 39^{8}. **b.** *inquire, investigate* (a matter), abs. Ju 6^{29} Dt 13^{15} 17$^{4.9}$ 19^{18}; with acc. כָּל־לְבָבוֹת דּוֹרֵשׁ י׳ *all hearts Yahweh searches* 1 Ch 28^{9}; לִדְרֹשׁ הַמּוֹפֵת *to inquire into the wonder* 2 Ch 32^{31}; with לְ, *to inquire about* 2 S 11^{3} Jb 10^{6}; sq. עַל pers. + inf. 2 Ch 24^{6} *apply to the Levites to bring*, etc., cf. 31^{9} (עַל both pers. and rei). **5.** *ask for, require, demand*, c. acc. rei Ez 20^{40}; + מִן pers. Dt 23^{22} Mi 6^{8}; *exact*, oft. with collat. idea of *avenging*, מֵעִם Dt 18^{19}, so with מִיַּד Ez 34^{10}, דָּרַשׁ דָּם מִיַּד Gn 9^{5} (P) Ez 33^{6}; acc. only, דֹּרֵשׁ דמים ψ 9^{13}, ד׳ רִשְׁעוֹ 10^{15}; abs. v$^{4.13}$ 2 Ch 24^{22}. **6.** *seek with application, study, follow, practise*, abs. by wisdom Ec 1^{13}; with acc. ד׳ מִשְׁפָּט *study* or *practise justice* Is 1^{17} 16^{5}; מַעֲשֵׂי י׳ ψ 111^{2}; טוב וְאַל־רָע Am 5^{14}; commands of God ψ 119$^{45.94.155}$ 1 Ch 28^{8}; the law Ezr 7^{10}; †ד׳ שָׁלוֹם *seek* or *study the peace, welfare* of any one Dt 23^{7} Je 29^{7} Ezr 9^{12}, לשלום Je 38^{4}, ד׳ טוב Est 10^{3}, ד׳ רעה Pr 11^{27} ψ 38^{13} (cf. בקשׁ **2**, where this use is more common). **7.** *seek with care, care for*, ארץ אשׁר יהוה אלהיך דֹּרֵשׁ אתהּ *land which Yahweh thy God careth for* Dt 11^{12}; אַל־יִדְרְשֵׁהוּ אֱלוֹהַּ *let not Eloah care for it* Jb 3^{4}; אוֹתָךְ לֹא יִדְ׳ Je 30^{14}; דָּרְשָׁה צֶמֶר Pr 31^{13}; with לְ Je 30^{17}; אֵין דּוֹרֵשׁ לְנַפְשִׁי *no one careth for me* ψ 142^{5}; but in both these לְ perh. belongs to אֵין, cf. ‖ אֵין לִי מַכִּיר ψ 142^{5}, also La 4^{4} etc.; דְּרוּשָׁה *cared for* (of Jerus.) Is 62^{12}. **Niph.** *Pf.* נִדְרַשׁ Gn 42^{22}, נִדְרַשְׁתִּי Is 65^{1}, נִדְרָשׁוּ 1 Ch 26^{31}; *Impf.* אִדָּרֵשׁ Ez 14^{3} 20$^{3.31.31}$ 36^{37}; *Inf.* abs. הַאִדָּרֹשׁ Ez 14^{3} (for ההדרשׁ);—**1.** *let oneself be inquired of, consulted*, only of God Ez 14$^{3.3}$ 20$^{3.31.31}$ 36^{37} Is 65^{1}. **2.** *be sought out* 1 Ch 26^{31}. **3.** *be required*, of blood (cf. **Qal 5**) Gn 42^{22} (E).

Note.—וְדָרְשׁוּ מֵחָרְבוֹתֵיהֶם *and beg out of their desolate places* ψ 109^{10} (Ki al. *wedŏršu*, vid. Baer); many MSS. rd. דָּרְשׁוּ, so most interpr.; 𝔊 Hup Bi Che rd. גֹּרְשׁוּ *be driven from*.

†[**מִדְרָשׁ**] **n.[m.] study, exposition, midrash**, only cstr. מִדְרַשׁ (late; common in NH, in sense of *imaginative exposition* or *didactic story*)—מִדְרַשׁ סֵפֶר הַמְּלָכִים *midrash of the book of Kings* 2 Ch 24^{27}; מִדְרַשׁ הַנָּבִיא עִדּוֹ *midrash of the prophet Iddo* 2 Ch 13^{22}. These were prob. of a didactic character, cf. Dr$^{Intr 497}$. 4097

†[**דָּשָׁא**] **vb. sprout, shoot, grow green** 1876
(As. *dašû* Pi *make abundant* Lyon$^{Sargontexte 77}$; cf. also sub דֶּשֶׁא, whence, acc. to others, vb. denom.)—**Qal** *Pf.* דָּשְׁאוּ Jo 2^{22} (subj. נְאוֹת מִדְבָּר).

Hiph. *Impf.* 3 fs. תַּדְשֵׁא (juss.) Gn 1^{11} *cause to sprout* or *shoot forth* דֶּשֶׁא.—תַּדְשֵׁא הָאָרֶץ דֶּשֶׁא Je 50^{11} v. sub דּוּשׁ.

1877 †דֶּשֶׁא **n.m.** [Is 15, 6] **grass** (NH *id.*, As. *dišu*, *herb*, Lyon[Sargontexte 69]; Sab. דתא *fresh shoots* DHM[ZMG 1875, 597] = *springtime* CIS[iv. p. 11]; Aram. דִּתְאָה, ܕܬܐܐ (cf. Lag[BN 130]))—ד׳ abs. Gn 1^{11} + 13 t.—acc. cogn. תַּדְשֵׁא Gn 1^{11}; cf. v^{12} (in both, produced by earth); springing out of earth 2 S 23^{4}; of a second crop of grass Pr 27^{25} (opp. חָצִיר); caused to spring forth by God לְהַצְמִיחַ מֹצָא דֶשֶׁא Jb 38^{27}; refreshed by rain Dt 32^{2}; נְאוֹת ד׳ ψ 23^{2}; as food of wild ass Jb 6^{5}; as failing (withered) Is 15^{6}; lacking for animals Je 14^{5}; וִירַק דֶּשֶׁא sim. of weakness 2 K 19^{26} (‖ עֵשֶׂב שָׂדֶה) = Is 37^{27}; of transitoriness (withering) ψ 37^{2} (יֶרֶק ד׳); of growth and prosperity, Is 66^{14}.

1878 †דָּשֵׁן **vb. be fat, grow fat** (Ar. دَسِمَ; whence also دَسَمٌ *grease, fat;* NH דִּשֵּׁן *make fat*, cf. NH דָּשֵׁן *fat*)—**Qal** *Pf.* 3 ms. וְדָשֵׁן consec. Dt 31^{20} (JE) fig. of Isr.'s prosperity. **Pi.** *Pf.* דִּשַּׁנְתָּ ψ 23^{5}; וְדִשְּׁנוּ consec. Nu 4^{13}; *Impf.*: יְדַשְּׁנֶה־סֶּלָה ψ 20^{4} volunt. (cf. Ges[§ 48, 3] De; but perh. rd. sf. -נָּה, -נֶהָ v. Ki Ges[l.c.]); 3 fs. תְּדַשֶּׁן־ Pr 15^{30}; *Inf.* לְדַשְּׁנוֹ Ex 27^{3}—causat. *make fat* ד׳ בשמן ראשי i.e. anoint, symbol of festivity and joy ψ 23^{5}; ד׳ עָצֶם Pr 15^{30} of bodily effect of good news; ד׳ עולה *find* a burnt-offering *fat* = acceptable ψ 20^{4}; elsewhere *denom.* fr. דֶּשֶׁן (fat ashes);—*take away, clear away the fat ashes* (acc. of altar cleared) Nu 4^{13} (P), so סירות לְדַשְּׁנוֹ Ex 27^{3} (P). **Pu.** *Impf.* יְדֻשָּׁן Pr 28^{25} Is 34^{7}; 3 fs. תְּדֻשָּׁן Pr 11^{25} 13^{4}—pass. of causat. Pi. *be made fat*, of dust saturated מֵחֵלֶב Is 34^{7}; fig. of prosperity of the liberal Pr 11^{25}, the diligent 13^{4}, the trustful 28^{25}. **Hothp.** *Pf.* 3 *fs.* הֻדַּשְּׁנָה (cf. Ol[§ 271] Ges[§ 54.3]) Is 34^{6}, of Yahweh's sword:—*it hath fattened itself* מֵחֵלֶב (‖ מָלְאָה דָּם).

1880 †דֶּשֶׁן **n.m. fatness, fat ashes**—abs. ד׳ ψ 63^{6} + 8 t., דָּשֶׁן Lv 1^{16} + 3 t.; cstr. דֶּשֶׁן ψ 36^{9}; sf. דִּשְׁנִי Ju 9^{9}—**1.** *fatness*, abundance, luxuriance, oil, Ju 9^{9} (of olive tree); abundance, fertility ψ 63^{6} (in simile ‖ חֵלֶב), 65^{12}, of food and drink, Jb 36^{16} Je 31^{14}; passing over into fig. of spiritual blessing ψ 36^{9} (ד׳ ביתך), Is 55^{2}. **2.** *fat ashes*, i.e. ashes of victims, mixed with the fat Lv 1^{16} 4$^{12.12}$ 6$^{3.4}$ (all P) Je 31^{40} 1 Ki 13$^{3.5}$.

†דָּשֵׁן **adj. fat,** דָּשֵׁן Is 30^{23} (‖ שָׁמֵן), of לֶחֶם 1879
as product of ground; fig. of righteous as trees דְּשֵׁנִים ψ 92^{15} (‖ רעננים) fat, full of oil (?) or sap (Che; cf. דֶּשֶׁן Ju 9^{9}); as subst. *vigorous, stalwart ones* (opp. יוֹרְדֵי עָפָר cf. Che) ψ 22^{30} דִּשְׁנֵי־אֶרֶץ (Brüll שְׁכֵנֵי, Renan[Hist. iii. 134] יֹשְׁבֵי).

†דָּת **n.f.** [Est 3, 15] **decree, law, usage,** only 1881
in Persian period (B Aram. NH *id.*, Syr. ܕܳܬܳܐ or ܕܳܬ; Pers. loan-w., Old Pers. *dâta*, *law*, Spieg[APK 225])—ד׳ abs. Est 1^{8} + 9 t.; cstr. דַּת Est 2^{12}, 9^{13}; דָּת; sf. דָּתוֹ Est 2^{8} + 4 t.; pl. cstr. דָּתֵי Ezr 8^{36} + 2 t.; sf. דָּתֵיהֶם Est 3^{8};—**1.** *decree, edict, commission* of Pers. king Ezr 8^{36} (word elsewhere only in Est) Est 2^{8} (‖ דְּבַר הַמֶּלֶךְ), 4^{3} (‖ *id.*) 8^{17} (‖ *id.*) 9^{1} (‖ *id.*; c. עשׂה *execute*) cf. also 9^{13}; c. vb. נִתַּן 3$^{14.15}$ 8$^{13.14}$ 9^{14}; written כְּתָב־הַדָּת 4^{8} (cf. 3^{14} 8^{13}). **2.** *law*, permanently valid and applicable, וְיִכָּתֵב בְּדָתֵי פָרַס־וּמָדַי וְלֹא יַעֲבוֹר Est 1^{19} cf. v^{15} 4$^{11.16}$; יֹדְעֵי דָּת וָדִין 1^{13} *those that understood law and judgment;* דָּתֵי הַמֶּלֶךְ 3^{8}; of laws of the Jews in Persia 3^{8}; even of rules for drinking at a feast 1^{8}; for purifying of women 2^{12}.—The distinction between **1** & **2** is not absolute. The king's will was law, and the royal edict (דְּבַר מַלְכוּת) concerning Vashti was reckoned among the laws (דָּתֵי) of the Persians & Medes (1^{19}).—In Dt 33^{2} MT אֵשׁ דָּת לָמוֹ *fire was a law for them* is corrupt; many emend. proposed, cf. Di; Di suggests אֵשׁ [לַפִּ]ד׳ת *fire of flames*, flaming fire, cf. הַלַּפִּידִם Ex 20^{18} (but לַפִּדֹת pl. in ־ֹת not in OT unless as n.pr.), or (better), אֵשׁ [יֹקֶ]דֶת *a burning fire*, cf. Is 65^{5} (diff. sense).

†דָּתָן **n.pr.m.** (cf. As. *Datana* Shlm[Obelisk, 1.161]) 1885
a Reubenite, son of Eliab Nu 16$^{1.12.24.25.27.27}$ 26$^{9.9}$ Dt 11^{6} ψ 106^{17}.

†דֹּתָן **n.pr.loc.** (𝔊 Δωθαειμ)—in N. Israel, 1886
north of Samaria; דֹּתָן Gn 37^{17} 2 K 6^{13}; דֹּתַיְנָה Gn 37^{17} cf. Di; mod. *Tel Dotân*, Bd[Pal 228].

ה

ה, *Hē*, fifth letter; = numeral 5 in postB. Heb.; no evidence of this usage in OT times.

הַ·, הַ, הָ, הֶ (on the use of these different forms, see the Grammars: e.g. Ges[§ 35]), **definite article, the** (so Moab. Ph. (Schröd[§ 62-4]), Liḥyan (NW. Arabia) *ha* (DHM[Epigr. Denkm. 4. 13. 58 ff.]); not As. Aram. or Eth.: Arab. اَلْ, of which, before dentals, sibilants, and liquids, the *l* is written but not pronounced, thus اَلشَّمْسُ pron. *'ash-shamsu*=Heb. הַשֶּׁמֶשׁ)—in gen. the use of the art. in Heb. is analogous to its use in Greek or German: but naturally there are applications peculiar to Hebrew (comp. with what follows Ges[§ 126] Ew[§ 277]):—**1.** joined with *substantives:* **a.** to mark a definite concrete object, as Gn 1[1] *the* heavens and *the* earth, הַמֶּלֶךְ the king, etc. Never, however (as in Greek e.g. ὁ Πλάτων), before true proper names, though it is used with certain terms, chiefly geographical, of which the orig. appellative sense has not been lost, as הַבַּעַל 'Baal,' lit. 'the lord,' in pl. הַבְּעָלִים i.e. the various local Baals, הַשָּׂטָן *the* Adversary Jb 1[6 ff.] (as a pr. n. שָׂטָן, 'Satan,' only 1 Ch 21[1]); הַלְּבָנוֹן (but not הַחֶרְמוֹן), הַיַּרְדֵּן (but not הָאַרְנֹן), הַכַּרְמֶל, הַשָּׁרוֹן the Sharon, הַשְּׁפֵלָה the (Judaean) lowland, הַמִּישׁוֹר, הַכִּכָּר the (Moabite) table-land, הָעֲרָבָה, הָעַי ''Ai,' הַגִּבְעָה 'Gibeah,' Ju 20[5 ff.], הַגָּלִיל 'Galilee,' הַגִּלְגָּל, הַגִּלְבֹּעַ, הַבָּשָׁן, הַגִּלְעָד (oft.), הַשִּׁטִּים, הַמִּצְפָּה, הָרָמָה, הַיְשִׁימוֹן, הָעֹפֶל, הַפִּסְגָּה. **b.** with an adjective to denote one who exhibits a quality κατ' ἐξοχήν, i.e. to express the compar. or superl. degree: so oft., as Gn 1[16] המאור הגדל the *greater* light, המאור הקטן the *lesser* light, 27[1] בנו הגדול=his *elder* son, 48[14] הצעיר the *younger*, 42[13] הַקָּטֹן the little one, i.e. the *youngest* (of Joseph's brethren), Lv 21[10] הַגָּדוֹל מֵאֶחָיו the *chiefest* of his brethren, Nu 35[25]+ הכהן הגדול the *chief* priest, הצעיר ב׳ the *least* among Ju 6[15], הצעירה מן the *least* of 1 S 9[21], הַיָּפָה ב׳ the *fairest* among Ct 1[8], 2 K 10[3] Pr 30[30], cf. Jos 14[15]. **c.** with nouns which are not definite in themselves, but *acquire their definition from the context, or from the manner in which they are introduced:* thus (*a*) in the standing phrases הַיּוֹם *to-day*, Gn 4[14] 21[26]+oft.; הַלַּיְלָה *to-night*, Gn 19[5] 30[15]+, once 1 S 15[16] *last night;* so הַשָּׁנָה *this* year, 2 K 19[29] Jer 28[16]; הַפַּעַם *this* time, Gn 18[32]+. (β) הַנָּהָר *the* river (κατ' ἐξοχήν), i.e. the Euphrates; Ex 2[15] *the well*, the well viz. of the district, Jos 8[11] *the* valley, 1 S 17[3]; 1 S 19[10] *the* wall, v[13] *the* bed, 20[21] הַנַּעַר *the* lad (whom Jonathan would naturally take with him), v[34] *the* table. Hence occas. where a suffix would define the noun more precisely, as הַחֲמוֹר 2 S 19[27]+=*my* ass, Ju 3[20] 1 S 1[9] הַכִּסֵּא=*his* seat, Ju 4[15] 1 K 22[35] 2 K 10[15]+ הַמֶּרְכָּבָה, 1 S 18[10] 20[33] הַחֲנִית. **d.** it is a peculiarity of Hebrew thought to conceive an object as defined by its being *taken for a particular purpose*, and thus by a kind of prolepsis to prefix the art. to the noun denoting it: 1 S 10[1] and Samuel took אֶת־פַּךְ הַשֶּׁמֶן lit. *the* cruse of oil, not, however, a cruse which had been defined previously, but one rendered definite by *being now taken;* in English idiom '*a* cruse of oil,' v[25] בַּסֵּפֶר lit. in *the* scroll or book, the one, viz. taken for the purpose, i.e. in *a* scroll (so Ex 17[14] Nu 5[23] Jb 19[23]), 21[10] בַּשִּׂמְלָה, Ju 4[18] וַתְּכַסֵּהוּ בַּשְּׂמִיכָה, v[19] 7[13] הָאֹהֶל *a* tent, 8[25] 9[48] אֶת־הַקַּרְדֻּמּוֹת *hatchets*, 20[16] every one able to sling בָּאֶבֶן אֶל־הַשַּׂעֲרָה with *a* stone at *a* hair, 1 S 6[8] בָּאַרְגָּז (unless indeed the אַרְגָּז was an understood appendage in every cart), Nu 11[27] הַנַּעַר *a* young man, 13[23] בַּמּוֹט on *a* pole, Jos 2[15] בַּחֶבֶל with *a* cord, 2 S 17[17] השפחה *a* girl (cf. Dr[1 S 1. 4; 19. 13]). Sts. it is uncertain whether an art. is to be referred to **c** or **d**: e.g. 1 S 2[13] *his* prong or *a* prong, 2 S 18[9] *his* mule or *a* mule, etc. **e.** with nouns that denote *objects or classes of objects that are known to all*, as הַצֹּאן, הַזָּהָב, הַמַּיִם; Gn 13[2] Abram was very rich בַּמִּקְנֶה בַּכֶּסֶף וּבַזָּהָב, Ex 31[4] לַעֲשׂוֹת בַּזָּהָב וּבַכֶּסֶף, Dt 14[26] and thou shalt lay out the money בַּבָּקָר וּבַצֹּאן וּבַיַּיִן וּבַשֵּׁכָר, 2 K 9[30] וַתָּשֶׂם בַּפּוּךְ עֵינֶיהָ, in French 'elle mit *du* fard à ses yeux.' It is, however, remarkable that this usage depends mostly on the punctuation, הַלֶּחֶם, הַיַּיִן, הַכֶּסֶף etc. (except as applied to denote *definite* quantities of gold, wine, etc., as Jos 6[24]) being far less common than כֶּסֶף, יַיִן etc., but בַּכֶּסֶף, לַכֶּסֶף etc. being much more freq. than בְּכֶסֶף, לְכֶסֶף etc.: for instances in which the art. forms part of the consonantal text, see Gn 6[20] 7[8]+ העוף and הבהמה, Dt 8[3] הַלֶּחֶם, 1 K 5[8.13] Is 28[7] הַיַּיִן and הַשֵּׁכָר, 60[17] Ez 15[4.7] הָאֵשׁ, Hb 2[5] Pr 20[1] ψ 65[14] הַצֹּאן, Ct 1[11] Ec 7[12]. Cf. below, **h.** **f.** in *comparisons*, the object compared being, as a rule, not an individual as such, but one exhibiting the characteristics of a class: Is 1[18] כַּתּוֹלָע, כַּשָּׁנִים like scarlet, like crimson (both meant generally), 5[24] כַּמֹּץ יִהְיֶה, v[28] כַּצַּר and כַּסּוּפָה, 10[14] כַּקֵּן, 13[8] כַּיּוֹלֵדָה (as always with this word, e.g. 42[14] ψ 48[7]), 11[7] כַּבָּקָר; + oft. (The usage is not, however, quite uniform, at least acc. to the punctuation: there occurs e.g. כְּקַשׁ Jb 41[21] Is 47[14]; כְּאַרְיֵה ψ 7[3] al.: and we find both כְּלָבִיא Is 5[29] and כַּלָּבִיא Ho 13[8]; כָּאֲרִי Is 38[13] and כַּאֲרִי Nu 24[9]; כַּגִּבּוֹר Is 42[13] and כְּגִבּוֹר Jb 16[14]; etc.) Similarly Gn 19[28] כְּקִיטֹר הַכִּבְשָׁן as the smoke of *a* furnace, Nu 11[8.12] כַּאֲשֶׁר יִשָּׂא הָאֹמֵן אֶת־הַיֹּנֵק, Dt 28[29] (הָעִוֵּר), Ju 8[18 b] כְּתֹאַר בְּנֵי הַמֶּלֶךְ, 14[6] כְּשַׁסַּע הַגְּדִי like (a lion's) rending *a* kid, 16^{9} 1 K 14^{15} Zc 12^{10} כְּמִסְפֵּד עַל הַיָּחִיד as mourning over *an* only child, 13^{9}+. Where, however, the standard of comparison is not the class in general, but only a particular part of it, defined by a special epithet (whether adj. or verb), the art. is naturally omitted: thus כַּמֹּץ like chaff (in general) Is 41^{15}, but כְּמֹץ עֹבֵר like chaff passing away 29^{5}; כַּצֵּל Jb 14^{2}, but כְּצֵל נָטוּי ψ 102^{12}; כַּקַּשׁ Is 40^{24}, but כְּקַשׁ נִדָּף 41^{2}; כָּאַיָּל Is 35^{6}, but כְּאַיָּל תַּעֲרֹג על וג׳ like *a hind* (*that*) *longeth for streams of water* ψ 42^{2}; כָּאֵשׁ Is 9^{17}, but כְּאֵשׁ תבער יער like *fire* (*that*) *kindleth a wood* ψ 83^{15}; כֶּעָשָׁן Is 51^{6}, but כְּעָשָׁן מֵאֲרֻבָּה like *smoke from a chimney* Ho 13^{3}: so Is 62^{1b} Jb 9^{26} 11^{16} כְּמַיִם עָבָרוּ like *waters* (*that*) *have passed by*, etc.; Dt 32^{2a} כַּטַּל ,כַּמָּטָר, but v^{2b} כִּשְׂעִירִים עֲלֵי־דֶשֶׁא, כִּרְבִיבִים עֲלֵי־עֵשֶׂב. Where the art. is found, although a rel. clause follows (as ψ 1^{4} 49^{13} Is 61^{10}), this is prob. to be regarded not as *limiting* the class of object compared, but as *describing* it. **g.** prefixed to *generic* nouns (in the singular) it designates the *class*, i. e. it imparts to the noun a *collective* force, as Ex 1^{22} כָּל־הַבֵּן all (lit. the whole of) *the sons*, כָּל־הַבַּת all *the daughters*, Lv $17^{8.10}$ מִן־הַגֵּר of *the strangers*, who sojourn in their midst, Nu 21^{7} הַנָּחָשׁ *the serpents;* Gn 14^{13} Ez 24^{26} 33^{21} הַפָּלִיט those who escaped; Jos 6^{7}+ הֶחָלוּץ, v 9^{13} הַמְאַסֵּף; 8^{19} הָאוֹרֵב; 1 S 13^{17} הַמַּשְׁחִית; Mi 2^{13}; Is 6^{4} הַקּוֹרֵא the choir of criers; 1 S 24^{14} הַקַּדְמֹנִי the ancients; Ec 7^{26} אֶת־הָאִשָּׁה woman, and oft. with gentile names, as הַיְבוּסִי the Jebusites, הַכְּרֵתִי וְהַפְּלֵתִי 2 S 8^{18} al., הַדָּנִי Ju 18^{1} etc., הַלֵּוִי the Levites, Nu 3^{20} 18^{23} Mal 2^{8} ψ 135^{20}+. **h.** with nouns denoting abstract ideas, esp. the names of moral qualities (cf. Gk. ἡ δίκη, Fr. la justice), chiefly in two cases—(*a*) where the art. is recognizable in the consonantal text, exceptionally, when some emphasis or definiteness is intended, as Dt 7^{9} שׁומר הברית והחסד; 2 S 2^{5} החסד הזה 1 K 3^{6}; את החסד והרחמים Je 16^{5} (contr. Zc 7^{9}); הצדק †Is 1^{26} 61^{3} Ec 3^{16}; הַצְּדָקָה †Is $32^{17.17}$ (contrast v^{16}) Dn 9^{7} (emph.); הַדַּעַת Ho 4^{6}; הָאֱמֶת Gn 32^{11} (sq. אֲשֶׁר), Is 59^{15} (contrast v^{14}) Zc $8^{3.19}$; הָאֱמוּנָה †Is 11^{5b} (contr. v^{a}) Je 7^{28}; הַחָכְמָה Jb $28^{12.20}$; הַחַיִּים Gn 2^{9}+; הָאַהֲבָה †Ct 2^{7} 3^{5} $8^{4.7}$; הָרֶשַׁע †Je $7^{4.8}$ 23^{26}; הַמָּוֶת Is 25^{8} Ru 1^{17}+; הַשֶּׁקֶר †ψ 125^{3} Ec 3^{16}; הָרִשְׁעָה †Zc 5^{8}; הַחֹשֶׁךְ Is 60^{2} Ec 2^{13}; see also Dt $30^{15.19}$ (Je 21^{8}), 1 K 7^{14} Je 32^{19} Mal 2^{5} החיים והשלום, ψ 123^{4} 130^{4} Dn 9^{9} 1 Ch 29^{11} 2 Ch 1^{12} Pr 31^{30} Ec $2^{13.17}$ $7^{12.19}$ 10^{6} 11^{10}: but in all such cases אֱמֶת, צֶדֶק, חֶסֶד, etc. are far more common. (β) where the art. depends on the punctuation, after preps., esp. בְּ, but with much irregularity, as בַּחֶסֶד Is 16^{5} Pr 20^{28} (but בְּח׳ Ho 2^{21} Pr 16^{6}), בַּצֶּדֶק Pr 25^{5} (elsewhere always בְּצ׳: בִּצְדָקָה also always); בֶּאֱמֶת and בֶּאֱמוּנָה always; בַּשֶּׁקֶר †Is 28^{15} (but ‖ כָּזָב, not הַכָּזָב) Je 5^{31} 13^{25} 20^{6} 23^{14} (בְּשֶׁקֶר †Je 3^{10} 29^{9}); בַּשָּׁלוֹם †ψ 29^{11} Jb 15^{21} (elsewhere בְּשָׁלוֹם); Zc 12^{4} to smite בַּשִּׁגָּעוֹן וּבַעִוָּרוֹן (but Dt 28^{28} בְּשִׁגעון וּבְעורון), cf. Gn 19^{11} Dt 28^{22}; to enter with one בַּמִּשְׁפָּט Jb 9^{32} 22^{4} (but בְּמשפט ψ 143^{2}), contrast also Pr 18^{5} with 24^{23}; לַמִּשְׁפָּט Is 59^{11} ψ 9^{8} (but לְמ׳ Is 5^{7} ψ 122^{5}); Pr 2^{2} 7^{4} לַחָכְמָה (but never החכמה in Pr 1–9, or indeed in the whole book); Pr 2^{3} 7^{4} לַבִּינָה, Jb 39^{17} בַּבִּינָה (but never הַבִּינָה); Pr $2^{2.3}$ לַתְּבוּנָה (but הַתְּבוּנָה only 1 K 7^{14} emph.); to perish בַּצָּמָא Ju 15^{18}+; Is 29^{21} בַּתֹּהוּ, 32^{19} בַּשִּׁפְלָה תִּשְׁפַּל הָעִיר Germ. in *die* Niedrigkeit sinkt die Stadt, 45^{16} together they go בַּכְּלִמָּה (in die Schmach), 46^{2} בַּשְּׁבִי into captivity, 47^{5} בֹּאִי בַחֹשֶׁךְ (so always: never בְּחשך). The living language may have used the art. more readily after a prep., where it did not lengthen the word by an entire syll.; still the disparity of usage between *a* and β makes it not improb. that the art. in β is in many cases not original but due to the punctuators. **i.** to mark the *vocative:* 1 S 17^{55} חֵי־נפשך הַמֶּלֶךְ as thy soul liveth, *O* king, I do not know, v^{58} בן מי אתה הַנַּעַר Whose son art thou, *lad?* 2 S 14^{4} Help, *O* king! 1 K 18^{26} הַבַּעַל עֲנֵנוּ, 2 K 9^{5} אֵלֶיךָ הַשָּׂר, Is 42^{18} הַחֵרְשִׁים שְׁמָעוּ, Je 2^{31} הַדּוֹר אַתֶּם רְאוּ וג׳, Ez 37^{4} הָעֲצָמוֹת הַיְבֵשׁוֹת *O* dry bones, Mal 3^{9} הַגּוֹי כֻּלּוֹ (Dr$^{\S 198\ Obs. 2}$).

N. B. In poetry, the article is frequently dispensed with before words which would naturally take it in prose: thus ψ $2^{2.8.10}$ & oft. אֶרֶץ; 8^{9} 18^{10} 33^{6} + שָׁמַיִם; (rarely in prose, Gn 1^{8} 2^{4} 1 K 8^{35}); 21^{2} $45^{14.16}$ 61^{7} al. מֶלֶךְ; 66^{6} 72^{8}+ יָם; $59^{7.15}$ עִיר; Ju 5^{2} ψ 18^{44} עָם etc.; ψ $9^{6.17}$ & oft. רָשָׁע; Is $1^{2.6.21}$ $3^{10.11}$ $11^{6.7.8}$.

2. With *adjectives, participles*, and *demonstrative pronouns* (הוא, היא, המה, הם, זה, אלה, זאת): viz. **a.** (so regularly) when the subst. qualified by these words *is defined by it likewise*, as המלך הגדול = ὁ βασιλεὺς ὁ μέγας, Gn 2^{12} הארץ ההוא, 20^{1} הַדָּבָר הַזֶּה, Jos 2^{3} האנשים הבאים אליך = οἱ ἄνδρες οἱ ἐλθόντες πρὸς σέ, Gn 13^{5} 16^{13} 24^{65} 32^{21} Ju 6^{28} Is $65^{3.4.5}$ 66^{24} ψ 31^{9}. So also with adjj. & ptcpp., if the subst. be defined by a sf. (as Dt 4^{37} בְּכֹחוֹ הַגָּדֹל, 1 S 8^{14}

וַיִּתֵּיכֶם הַטֹּבוֹת); and with a pron., if it be defined by a gen. (as Dt 29^{20} 1 S 14^{29} 15^{14} 2 K 6^{32} בֶּן־הַמְרַצֵּחַ הַזֶּה *this* son of a murderer), but not if it be defined by a sf., as Ex 10^{1} אֹתֹתַי אֵלֶּה (not אתתי הָאֵלֶּה), Jos 2^{14} דְּבָרֵנוּ זֶה *this* our word (not ד׳ הַזֶּה): v. Dr$^{§209\ Obs.}$ Similarly when the art. with the ptcp. has a *resumptive* force, ψ 33^{15} (v^{14} he looketh forth from the place, &c.), הַיֹּצֵר יַחַד לִבָּם *he that formeth*, etc., 19^{11} הַנֶּחֱמָדִים מִזָּהָב *which* (v^{10}b) *are more desirable* than gold, 49^{7} (^{6b} the iniquity of my aggressors surroundeth me), הַבֹּטְחִים *who trust* in their riches, etc., Gn 49^{21} Is 46^{6} 51^{20} Jb 6^{16}+ (v. Dr$^{§135.7}$). **b.** (rare) when the subst. qualified by the adj. or ptcp. was felt to be sufficiently definite for its own art. to be dispensed with, as sts. with the word *day* Gn 1^{31} יום הששי, 2^{3} יום השביעי, Ex $12^{15.18}$ 20^{10} (=Dt 5^{14}) Lv 19^{6} 22^{27}: so with מָבוֹא *entrance* Je 38^{14}, שַׁעַר Zc 14^{10}; חָצֵר *court* 1 K $7^{8.12}$ Ez 40^{28} al.; also in certain phrases (peculiar to P) where the subst. is defined by כל, as Gn 1^{21} כָּל־נֶפֶשׁ הַחַיָּה *all* living souls, v^{28} כָּל־חַיָּה הָרֹמֶשֶׂת all living things *that creep*, etc., 7^{21} 9^{10} Lv $11^{10.46}$; further in isolated cases, hardly reducible to rule, Lv 24^{10} 1 S 12^{23} דֶּרֶךְ הַטּוֹבָה, 16^{23} רוּחַ הָרָעָה, 2 S 12^{4} לְאִישׁ העשיר Je 6^{20} 17^{2} Zc 4^{7} ψ 104^{18} Ezr 10^{9} חֹדֶשׁ הַתְּשִׁיעִי (quite exceptional in OT). (With prons. this use is so rare that, where it occurs, it is dub. if the text be sound: 1 S $17^{12.17}$ Je 40^{3} Kt Mi 7^{11}). And with the ptcp.: 1 S 25^{10} רַבִּים עֲבָדִים הַמִּתְפָּרְצִים many are the slaves who break away etc., Is 7^{20} Je 27^{3} 46^{16}=50^{16} חֶרֶב הַיּוֹנָה the oppressing sword, Ez 2^{3} (but 𝔊 Co om. הגוים), 14^{22} $32^{22.24}$ ψ 62^{4} Pr 26^{18} Ju 21^{19} (very anomal., rd. prob. לַמְּסִלָּה). This usage is somewhat more freq. in the later parts of OT; and in postB. Heb. it is very general (e.g. יֵצֶר הָרַע the evil inclination): v. further Dr^{§209}. **c.** with the ptcp., where the ptcp. with the art. forms really the *subject:* Gn 2^{11} הוּא הַסֹּבֵב not 'it was encompassing,' but 'it is *that which encompassed,*' 45^{12} פִּי הַמְדַבֵּר my mouth is *that which* speaketh, Dt 3^{21} עֵינֶיךָ הָרֹאֹת thine eyes were *those which saw,* 4^{3} 8^{18} ὅτι οὗτός ἐστιν ὁ διδοὺς σοί, Is 14^{27} 66^{9} (v. Dr$^{§135.7}$).

3. The article is prefixed exceptionally—mostly in the latest Hebrew—with the force of a relative to the *verb:* †Jos 10^{24} הֶהָלְכוּא אִתּוֹ *that* went with him, Ez 26^{17}, הָעִיר הַהֻלָּלָה, 1 Ch 26^{28} וְכֹל הַהִקְדִּישׁ שְׁמוּאֵל and all *that* Samuel had dedicated, $29^{8.17}$ 2 Ch 1^{4} בַּהֵכִין in (the place) *that* he had prepared, 29^{36} Ezr 8^{25} $10^{14.17}$. Acc. to the punctuation, it occurs similarly elsewhere, as Gn 18^{21} הַבָּאָה (so 46^{27} Jb 2^{11}), 21^{3} הַנּוֹלַד־לוֹ, 1 K 11^{9} & Dn 8^{1} הַנִּרְאָה, Is 51^{10} הַשָּׂמָה, 56^{3} הַנִּלְוָה, Ru 1^{22} 2^{6} 4^{3} (all הַשָּׁבָה): but in all these passages, the change of a point, or even sts. of an accent, would restore the normal participial construction (as הַנּוֹלָד לוֹ, הַבָּאָה, cf. Gn 48^{5}, הַנִּרְאָה), which is, no doubt, what was intended by the orig. writers, and is recognised elsewhere by the Massorah, e.g. Gn 12^{7} 35^{1} הַנִּרְאֶה, 46^{26} & Ru 4^{11} הַבָּאָה (cf. Ew^{§331b} Ges^{138,3b}). Once, still more anomalously, before a prep. 1 S 9^{24} וְהֶעָלֶיהָ (as though καὶ τὸ ἐπ' αὐτῆς): but rd. prob. וְהָאַלְיָה *and the fat tail*, v. Dr. (In Arab. اَلْ also occurs, though very rarely, as a relative: W$^{AG\ i.\ §345b,\ CG\ 117}$).—On the anomalous use of the art. with a word in the *st. c.*, v. Gramm., as Ew^{§290d}, Ges$^{§127\ R.4}$, also Dr$^{§190\text{-}1}$.

הֲ, הַ, הָ, הֶ (on the different forms, see Ges$^{§100.4}$: on Dt 32^{6}, v. הַל, p. 210), **interrog. part.** (BAram. and 𝔗 הֲ, Arab. أ), prefixed, as a rule, to the first word of a sentence (or clause). **1.** in *direct* questions: **a.** as a simple interrogative, where the answer expected is uncertain, Ex 2^{7} הַאֵלֵךְ *shall I go* and call thee a nurse? 1 S 23^{11} הֲיַסְגִּרֻנִי *will* the men of Keilah deliver me into his hand? הֲיֵרֵד שָׁאוּל *will* Saul come down? Jb 1^{8}; and frequently. **b.** often in questions, expressed in a tone of surprise, or put rhetorically, to which a *negative* answer is expected (=Lat. *num?*): Gn 4^{9} הֲשֹׁמֵר אָחִי אָנֹכִי *Am* I my brother's keeper? 18^{17} *shall* I hide from Abraham that which I am about to do? 30^{2} 50^{19} Nu 11^{23a} Dt 4^{33} הֲשָׁמַע עָם . . . *Did* a people ever hear the voice of God speaking out of the midst of the fire, . . . and live? 20^{19} (rd. with 𝔊𝔗𝔖𝔙 Ew Ke Di etc. הָאָדָם for הַאָדָם), 2 S 7^{5} הַאַתָּה תִּבְנֶה־לִּי בַיִת (altered in 1 Ch 17^{4} to the neg. לֹא אַתָּה תִּבְנֶה וגו׳), 2 K 6^{22} הַאֲשֶׁר שָׁבִיתָ . . . those whom thou hast taken captive with thy sword and with thy bow, wilt thou smite? Is 28^{24} 36^{12a} 57^{6} 58^{5} Je 15^{12} 16^{20} Am 5^{25} ψ 50^{13} Jb 8^{11} $15^{7.8.11}$ $38^{12.16.17.22}$ etc.; before an inf. absol. (Ew^{§328a}) Je 7^{9} Jb 40^{2} and prob. Mi 2^{7} (rd. הֶאָמוֹר: see p. 55). After a protasis, הִנֵּה . . . הֲ Nu 22^{38} 2 K $7^{2.19}$ Je 32^{27} Ez 17^{10}; after הֵן Je 3^{1} Hg 2^{12}: cf. after אוּלַי Gn 24^{5}; after אִם Jb 14^{14} אִם יָמוּת גֶּבֶר הֲיִחְיֶה if a man dieth, shall he live? Occasionally, one or more words precede הֲ (in the same clause) for special emphasis: 2 S 7^7 Jb 34^{31} כִּי אֶל־אֵל הֶאָמַר for *to God* did one ever say . . .? Ne 13^{27}; Je 22^{15} (הֲלֹא), cf. 23^{26}. **c.** it is used in questions which, by seeming to make doubtful what cannot be denied, have the force of an impassioned or indignant affirmation: Gn 27^{36} ('dubitantis speciem prae se fert Esavus, ut eo acerbius affirmet,' Maurer, cited by Ges), 1 S 2^{27} הֲנִגְלֹה נִגְלֵיתִי וגו׳ *Did I reveal* myself to the house of thy father, when they were in Egypt? etc. (i.e. of course I did, although thy sons, by their actions, appear to belie it), 1 K 16^{31} (expressing astonishment), 21^{19} הֲרָצַחְתָּ וְגַם־יָרָשְׁתָּ *Hast thou* slain, and also taken possession? Je 31^{20} Jb 20^4 41^1 (cf. Hi); also Gn 16^{13}, and the phrases הַרְּאִיתֶם *do ye see?* 1 S 10^{24} 2 K 6^{32}; הֲרָאִיתָ *dost thou see?* 1 K 20^{13} Ez $8^{12.15.17}$ al. **d.** in disjunctive questions, the first question being introduced usually by הֲ, the second by אִם or (more rarely) וְאִם: see exx. under אִם **2** (p. 50). The disjunctive question may express a real alternative (as Jos 5^{13}), or (as esp. in poetry) the same thought may be repeated in a different form, in two parallel clauses (e.g. Is 10^{15}): in the latter case, the answer *No* is usually expected (v. p. 50). Only very rarely is the second question introduced by הֲ Ju 14^{15} (where, however, הֲלֹם ought no doubt to be read, with MSS., 𝔗 Be al., for הֲלֹא), or אוֹ Ju 18^{19} Jb 16^3 $38^{28.31}$.

2. In *indirect* interrogation, *whether* (Germ. *ob* . . .?)—**a.** singly, after verbs of *seeing* Gn 8^8 לִרְאוֹת הֲ to see *whether*, 18^{21} Ex 4^{18} Ct 6^{11}, *telling* Gn 43^6, *trying* Dt 13^4, *knowing* Ju 3^4 Ec 3^{21} (rd. הַעֹלָה and הַיֹּרֶדֶת: v. De or Wr *ad loc.*) **b.** disjunctively,—usually הֲ . . . אִם, Nu $13^{18\,end,\,19a}$ (and see the land) . . . הֲטוֹבָה הִיא אִם רָעָה *whether* it be good *or* bad, $v^{19b.20.20}$; הֲ . . . אִם לֹא Gn 24^{21} 27^{21} 37^{32} Ex 16^4 that I may try it (the people) הֲיֵלֵךְ בְּתוֹרָתִי אִם לֹא *whether* it will walk in my law or not, Nu 11^{23} Dt 8^2 Ju 2^{22}; הֲ . . . הֲ Nu 13^{18} (by side of הֲ . . . אִם); הֲ . . . אוֹ Ec 2^{19} 11^6.

518, 637, It is prefixed to other particles, as הַאִם,
1571, 3588, הֲלֹא, הֲכִי, הֲגַם, הַאַף: see אִם, אַף, etc. p. 49, etc.
3808

1973 †הַל Dt 32^6 הַל יְהוָה תִּגְמְלוּ־זֹאת (so V.d.H and other edd.) The reading here became early a subject of dispute, and MSS. and edd. vary accordingly. Some follow the school of Nehardea, and read הַל יְהוָה; others (so Norzi) follow the school of Sora, and read הַ לַיהוָה; others (so Hahn) have הַלַיהוָה. Were הַל original, it would be an interrog. part. = Ar. هَلْ, for which elsewhere הֲ is always found. The other punctuations would also each be highly irregular. The true reading is undoubtedly הַלַיהוָה (הַלַ־יְהוָה). Cf. De Rossi $^{Var.\ Lect.\ ad\ loc.}$; and on the possible origin of the anomaly, Gei $^{Jüd.\ Ztschr.\ 1864\text{-}65,\ p.\ 89\ f.}$

†**הֵא interj.** (Aram. הָא, Dn 2^{43} הָא (q.v.), هَا; Arab. هَا) lo, behold! Gn 47^{23} Ez 16^{43}. 1887

†**הֶאָח interj.** (onomatop.) expressing joy, **Aha!** always introduced by אָמַר, Is 44^{16} 1889
he says, *Aha,* I am warm, I have seen the fire. Of satisfaction over the misfortune of an enemy or rival, ψ $35^{21.25}$ let them not say in their heart הֶאָח נַפְשֵׁנוּ *Aha,* so would we have it! (*lit.* our desire!) 40^{16} (= 70^4), Ez 25^3 26^2 36^2. Metaph., of the neighing of a war horse in the battle, Jb 39^{25}.

הָאֲרָרִי 2 S 23^{33b} v. הֲרָרִי. p. 251 2043

הַב v. יהב. p. 396 3051

הַבְהָבִים v. sub יהב. p. 396 1890

I. **הֶבֶל** n.m. **vapour, breath** (NH *id.*, 1892
Syr. ܗܒܠܐ *id.*) fig. **vanity** (so NH, Syr. ܗܒܠܐ)—הֶבֶל Ec 1^2+; cstr. הֲבֵל †Ec $1^{2.2}$ 12^8, sf. הֶבְלִי etc. Ec 6^{12} 7^{15} $9^{9.9}$; pl. הֲבָלִים Je 10^8+; cstr. הַבְלֵי Je 8^{19}+, sf. הַבְלֵיהֶם Dt 32^{21}+;—**1.** lit. Is 57^{13} all of them (the idols) יִשָּׂא־רוּחַ יִקַּח הָבֶל *a breath* (𝔙 aura) will carry away, Pr 21^6 the getting of treasures by a lying tongue is הֶבֶל נִדָּף a *vapour* driven away. Elsewhere always **2.** fig. of what is evanescent, unsubstantial, worthless, **vanity,** as of idols Je 10^{15} = 51^{18} 16^{19} הֶבֶל וְאֵין בָּם מוֹעִיל (‖ שֶׁקֶר), heathen observances 10^3, and in phr. הָלַךְ אַחֲרֵי הַהֶבֶל 2^5 2 K 17^{15}; Pr 13^{11} הוֹן מֵהֶבֶל wealth (gotten) *out of vanity* (i.e. not by solid toil, opp. קֹבֵץ עַל יָד) is minished (but 𝔊 𝔙 Ew מְבֹהָל, v. 20^{21} Qr), 31^{30} שֶׁקֶר הַחֵן וְהֶבֶל הַיֹּפִי, La 4^{17} אֶל עֶזְרָתֵנוּ הָבֶל to our *vain* (Dr $^{§\,193\,n.}$) help; of life Jb 7^{16} כִּי הֶבֶל יָמָי, ψ 78^{33} וַיְכַל בַּהֶבֶל יְמֵיהֶם consumed their days *as* (בְּ **I**,**7d**) *vanity,* man ψ $39^{6.12}$ 62^{10} הֶבֶל בְּנֵי אָדָם . . . הֵמָּה מֵהֶבֶל יָחַד they are altogether (made) *of vanity,* 94^{11} 144^4, esp. in Ec (31 t. + הֲבֵל הֲבָלִים $1^{2.2}$ 12^8) of the fruitlessness of all human enterprise and endeavour, 1^2 הַכֹּל הָבֶל, v^{14} הַכֹּל הֶבֶל וּרְעוּת רוּחַ all was *vanity* and the pursuit of wind, $2^{1.14.15}$ etc., 6^4 (of an abortion) בַּהֶבֶל בָּא i.e. into a lifeless existence, v^{11} יֵשׁ דְּבָרִים הַרְבֵּה מַרְבִּים הָבֶל (of discussions lead-

ing to no result), note also the phrases יְמֵי (הֶבְלוֹ, הֶבְלְךָ) יְמֵי חַיֵּי ה׳ הֶבְלִי 7^{15} 9^{9}, 6^{12} 9^{9}; Jb 27^{12} (v. הָבַל), Is 49^{4} לְתֹהוּ וָהֶבֶל for nought and *vanity* have I spent my strength; as adv. accus. *vainly, to no purpose* Is 30^{7} הֶבֶל וָרִיק יַעְזֹרוּ, ψ 39^{7} אַךְ הֶבֶל יֶהֱמָיוּן they disquiet themselves *to no purpose*, Jb 9^{29}: הֶבֶל אִיגָע 35^{16}, with נִחַם to comfort 21^{34} Zc 10^{2}. *Pl.* †הֲבָלִים of false gods, Dt 32^{21} (בְּלֹא־אֵל ‖) כִּעֲסוּנִי בְהַבְלֵיהֶם 1 K $16^{13.26}$ Je 8^{19} (בִּפְסִלֵיהֶם ‖) הַבְלֵי נֵכָר, 10^{8} 14^{22} הַבְלֵי הַגּוֹיִם, ψ 31^{7} הַשֹּׁמְרִים הַבְלֵי־שָׁוְא empty *vanities* Jon 2^{9}; in more general sense Ec $1^{2.2}$ 12^{8} הֲבֵל הֲבָלִים, 5^{6}.

1891 †**הָבַל** **vb. denom. act emptily, become vain**—**Qal** Je 2^{5} = 2 K 17^{15} they went after vanity וַיֶּהְבָּלוּ and *became vain*, ψ 62^{11} וּבְגָזֵל אַל־תֶּהְבָּלוּ do not *become vain* (i.e. be demoralized) by robbery; with cogn. acc. Jb 27^{12} לָמָּה זֶּה הֶבֶל תֶּהְבָּלוּ why do ye *become vain* with vanity (i.e. shew yourselves utterly vain)? **Hiph.** *cause to become vain* Je 23^{16} (of false prophets) מַהְבִּלִים הֵמָּה אֶתְכֶם i.e. fill you with vain hopes.

1893 †II. **הָבֶל, הֶבֶל** **n.pr.m.** (perh. i.q. As. *ablu*, son, COT[Gloss]; cf. also We[Skizzen iii. 70]: der. from I. הֶבֶל not prob.) second son of Adam Gn $4^{2.2.4.4.8.8.9.25}$.

1894 †[**הָבְנִי**] **n.[m.]** ebony (so Symm 𝔙 Ki & moderns; otherwise 𝔊 𝔖; Egypt. *heben*, Lieblein[ÄZ 1886, 13] cf. Pinsker[Einleitung 83]; Gk. ἔβενος, Lat. *hebenum*)—only pl. הָבְנִים Ez 27^{15} Qr (Kt הובנים) קַרְנוֹת שֵׁן והבנים; it was brought fr. India, & (finer) fr. Ethiopia, cf. Sm & reff.

1895 †[**הָבַר**] **vb.**? **divide** (so most, but dub.; Ar. هَبَرَ *cut into large pieces, cut up*, is perh. denom. fr. هَبْرَةٌ *a 'chunk'* of meat; comparison of Ar. خَبَرَ *be acquainted with, skilled in* (AW Kn Di) is also doubtful; if correct, then rd. חבר; but cf. infr.)—**Qal** *Pf.* 3 pl. הררו Is 47^{13} Kt, *Pt.* הֹבְרֵי Qr; הֹבְרוּ שָׁמַיִם הַחֹזִים בַּכּוֹכָבִים *they that divide the heavens, that gaze at the stars* (Kt would be rel. cl. without אֲשֶׁר); ה׳ then refers to the distinguishing of signs of zodiac, or other astrological division of sky, cf. Che; on zodiac in Babylon v. Jen[Kosmologie 57 ff.]; & on planets & constellations Id[ib. 95 ff.] Epping & Strm[Astronomisches aus Bab. 109 ff.];—but text prob. corrupt; GFM (June, 1892) suggests חֹקְרֵי (cf. חקר את־הארץ Ju 18^{2}).

1896 †**הֵגֶא** **n.pr.m.** eunuch of Ahasuerus (prob. Pers.; cf. Ἡγίας, courtier of Xerxes, Ctesias[Pers 24]; also Herodot[ix. 33]; Roed. in Thes Add) Est 2^{3}; = הֵגַי $2^{8.15}$, הֵגֶא 2^{8}.

הגג (*murmur*, then *muse*; cf. Ar. هَجَّ *burn, blaze* (of fire), *make a murmuring noise* in burning; PS gives Syr. ܗܓ *phantasma vidit, somniavit*; Ethpe. & esp. Ethpa. *mente concepit, imaginatus est*; cf. also הָגָה).

†[**הָגִיג**] **n.m. murmuring** (Che), **whisper, musing** (on form cf. Ba[NB 136])—only sf. הֲגִיגִי **1.** ψ 5^{2} בִּינָה ה׳ *understand my murmuring* (whispering, faint utterance), addressed to י׳. **2.** ψ 39^{4} בַּהֲגִיגִי *in my musing* i.e. while I was musing. 1901

הַגְּדֹּדָה v. sub גדד p. 151. 1412

†I. **הָגָה** **vb. moan, growl, utter, speak, muse** (only poet.) (onomatop.; NH הָגָה *muse, speak, spell* a word, so Aram. הֲגָא; ܗܓܐ *muse*, esp. Ethpa.; Ar. هَجَا *satirize, insult, scold*, also *spell* (borrowed mng.))—**Qal** *Perf.* 2 ms. וְהָגִיתָ consec. Jos 1^{8}; 1 s. הָגִיתִי ψ 143^{5}, וְהָגִיתִי consec. ψ 77^{13}; *Impf.* יֶהְגֶּה Jb 27^{4} + 8 t.; 3 fs. תֶּהְגֶּה ψ 35^{28} + 2 t., אֶהְגֶּה ψ 63^{7} Is 38^{14}, יֶהְגּוּ ψ 2^{1} + 2 t., תֶּהְגּוּ Is 16^{7}; נֶהְגֶּה Is 59^{11}; *Inf. abs.* הָגוֹ Is 59^{11};— **1.** of inarticulate sounds: **a.** *growl*, of lion growling over prey, sq. עַל Is 31^{4}. **b.** *groan, moan*, in distress (like dove), abs., Is 38^{14} 59^{11} (הָגוֹ נֶהְגֶּה); *sigh for* (לְ) in sorrow, mourning, *moan for* Is 16^{7} (‖ יְיֵלִיל לְ), so also Je 48^{31}. **2.** *utter*, sq. acc. rei, ψ 38^{13}; subj. לָשׁוֹן Jb 27^{4} (‖ דִּבֵּר) ψ 35^{28} 71^{24} Is 59^{3}; subj. פֶּה ψ 37^{30} Pr 8^{7}—cf. also sub **Po.** infr.; *speak* (abs.) ψ 115^{7} (בְּ instr.) **3. a.** (*soliloquize*) *meditate, muse*, c. בְּ rei, Jos 1^{8} ψ 1^{2} 63^{7} 77^{13} 143^{5}; c. acc. Is 33^{18}, subj. לֵב. **b.** *imagine, devise*, c. acc. ψ 2^{1} Pr 24^{2} (subj. לֵב); c. Inf. Pr 15^{28} (subj. *id.*) **Po.** *Inf. abs.* only הֹרוֹ וְהֹגוֹ מִלֵּב דִּבְרֵי־שָׁקֶר Is 59^{13} *a conceiving and an uttering, out of the heart, lying words* (‖ דַּבֵּר עֹשֶׁק וְסָרָה);—on form cf. Kö[i. 600]; but rd. rather הָרוֹ וְהָגוֹ **Qal** *Inf. abs.* cf. Di; Ba[NB 77] retains MT & expl. as Qal Inf. pass. **Hiph.** *Pt.* pl. הַמְצַפְצְפִים וְהַמַּהְגִּים Is 8^{19} *those that make chirpings and mutterings*, of necromancers and wizards. 1897

†**הֶגֶה** **n.m.** [Jb 37, 2] **a rumbling, growling, moaning**:—ה׳ abs. Ez 2^{10} + 2 t.;—**1.** *a rumbling, growling sound* וְה׳ מִפִּיו יֵצֵא Jb 37^{2} of thunder, as sound going forth from God's mouth. **2.** *a moaning* קִינִים וָה׳ וָהִי Ez 2^{10} *lamentations and moaning and woe*. 1899

3. *a sigh* or *moan*, as transient, כִּלִּינוּ שָׁנֵינוּ כְמוֹ־הֶגֶה ψ 90^{9} *we bring our years to an end as a sigh*, i.e. *a fleeting sound* (cf. RVm VB).

1900 †הָגוּת **n.f.** meditation, musing, only cstr. (with firm ָ cf. Sta[§ 304 c]) פִּי יְדַבֵּר חָכְמוֹת וְה׳ לִבִּי תְבוּנוֹת ψ 49^{4} *my mouth shall speak wisdom, and the musing of my heart* shall be *understanding*.

1902 †הִגָּיוֹן **n.m.** resounding music, meditation, musing;—ה׳ abs. ψ 9^{17} 92^{4}; cstr. הֶגְיוֹן ψ 19^{15}; sf. הֶגְיוֹנָם La 3^{62};—**1.** *resounding music;* עֲלֵי הִגָּיוֹן בְּכִנּוֹר ψ 92^{4} *with sounding music upon the lyre* (Che); cf. ה׳ סֶלָה ψ 9^{17} (a musical direction, v. סלה). **2.** *meditation, musing* אִמְרֵי־פִי וְהֶגְיוֹן לִבִּי ψ 19^{15} *the words of my mouth and the meditation of my heart;* also in bad sense = *plotting* שִׂפְתֵי קָמַי וְהֶגְיוֹנָם עָלַי La 3^{62} *the lips of those rising against me, and their imagining against me* (‖ מַחְשְׁבֹתָם v^{61}; cf. I. הָגָה **3 b**).

1898 †II. הָגָה **vb.** remove (Thes comp. יגה)—**Qal** *Pf.* הָגָה Is 27^{8} (Di rds. הָגָה); *Inf. abs.* הָגוֹ Pr 25$^{4.5}$;—הָגוֹ סִיגִים מִכָּסֶף Pr 25^{4} *remove* (lit. *a removing*) *dross from silver;* as sim. of following הָגוֹ רָשָׁע לִפְנֵי מֶלֶךְ Pr 25^{5} *remove (the) wicked before a king;* הָגָה בְּרוּחוֹ הַקָּשָׁה Is 27^{8}, acc. to Di (v. supr.) *he* (י׳) *hath removed her* (i.e. sent into exile; his people under fig. of faithless wife) *by his harsh wind;* so transl. also Ew Che (*he scared her away*) Brd RV VB; De follows MT, regards as ellipt. rel. cl., and renders by ptcp., ‘sichtend (i.e. *sifting, winnowing*) heftigen Hauches,’ but conjectures הָגֹה (Inf. abs.)

1896 הָגִי, הֵגַי **n.pr.m.** v. הֵגֶא. p. 211

הגן (NH הָגַן, Aram. הֲגַן *be suitable, fit, worthy:* on orig. mng. cf. Fl in NHWB, s.v.)

1903 †[הָגִין] **adj.** appropriate, suitable? (cf. NH Aram., supr.)—הַגִּדֶרֶת הֲגִינָה Ez 42^{12} *the corresponding* (?) *wall*, Ke; otherwise Vrss (𝔊 καλάμου, 𝔙 *separatum*, etc.); Thes connects הגין with preceding דֶּרֶךְ, ‘*aptus, idoneus* (de via),’ AV RV ‘the way *directly* before the wall;’ in neither connexion does it give good sense, and the text is doubtless wrong cf. Sm Da.; Co conj. החצר החיצונה *the outer court.*

הגר (√of foll.; ? cf. Ar. هَجَرَ *forsake, retire;* هِجْرَةٌ *emigration, Hegira*).

1904 †הָגָר **n.pr.f.** Hagar, Sarah's Egyptian maid, mother of Ishmael, Gn 16$^{1.4.8}$ (all J), v$^{3.15.15.16}$ 25^{12} (all P), 21$^{9.14.17.17}$ (all E).

1905 †הַגְרִי **1. n.pr.gent.** only pl. הַגְרִים ψ 83^{7}; הַהַגְרִאִים 1 Ch 5^{10}, הַהַגְרִיאִים 1 Ch 5$^{19.20}$; a tribe (Aramaean? Arabian?) with which the E. Jordan Israelites waged successful war; v. dub. conj. as to identity in Glas[Skizze ii. 407]. **2. adj.gent.** of an officer of David יָזִיז הַהַגְרִי 1 Ch 27^{31}. **3. n.pr.m.** father of one of David's warriors בֶּן־הַגְרִי 1 Ch 11^{38} (but ‖ 2 S 23^{36} בָּנִי הַגָּדִי, so here Öt, cf. Be Th[Sm] Dr[Sm]).

הַגְרִאִים, הַגְרִיאִים v. foregoing. 1905

הֵד v. sub הדד. below 1906

הדד (perh. *make a loud noise;* so Ar. هَدَّ (of a falling building, rain, the sea, a braying camel); هَدَّةٌ *crash* (of a falling wall, etc.), هَادَّةٌ *thunder*).

הֵידָד **n.m.**[Is 16,9] shout, shouting, cheer (of a multitude; on formation compare Ol[§ 181 a] 1959
Sta[§ 218 b]);—ה׳ only abs., Is 16^{9} + 6 t. Is & Je;—**1.** *shouting* in harvest Is 16^{10}, Je 48$^{33.33.33}$ where לֹא יִדְרֹךְ הֵידָד הֵידָד לֹא הֵידָד, i.e. the shouting is no vineyard-shouting, but that of the foe, cf. infr.; comp. 25^{30} י׳ *shall utter* (עָנָה) *a shout like the* (*grape-*) *treaders* (sq. אֶל כָּל־יֹשְׁבֵי הָאָרֶץ). Hence also **2.** *shout* of the foe Is 16^{9} (נָפַל עַל), Je 51^{14} (וְעָנוּ עָלַיִךְ הֵידָד); cf. 25^{30} 48^{33} supr.

†הֵד **n.[m.]** id., only Ez 7^{7} הֵד הָרִים (*joyous*) 1906
shout on mountains (opp. מְהוּמָה *noise of battle*).

†הֲדַד **n.pr.m.** Hadad (𝔊 Ἀδερ but v. הדר 1908
Aram. n.pr.div. DHM[Altsem. Inschr. von Sendschirli 56], and n.pr. הדדנדאח עבדהדד Scholz[Götzendienst 245], Eut[SBAk 1887, 410] cf. Bae[Rel 68] & sub בֶּן־הֲדַד p. 122; also *Adda*, etc., in cpd. n.pr. Bez[Tell el-Amarna BM 155]; *Hadad, Adad, Addu* is known as an Aram. deity, weather- or storm-god, cf. Bae[Rel 67.68]; perh. = *thunderer* Dl[ZK 1885, 166] Bae[l.c.], cf. רִמּוֹן; on Hadad in Arabia cf. We[Skizzen iii. 51]; Sab. הדד Hal[27]; as **n.pr.div.** Heb. only in cpd. **n.pr.m.**, v. infr.)—**1.** name of kings of Edom, **a.** Gn 36^{35} = 1 Ch 1^{46}, Gn 36^{36} = 1 Ch 1^{47} (הֲדַד); **b.** 1 Ch 1^{47} (‖ Gn 36^{39} הֲדַר), v^{51} (הֲדַד). **2.** an Edomite (ה׳ הָאֲדֹמִי) 1 K 11$^{14.17.19.21.21.25}$ (הֲדַד); =
אֲדַד v^{17}. 111

†הֲדַדְעֶזֶר **n.pr.m.** Hadadezer (so Aram. 1909
inscr. הדדעזר Eut[SBAk 1885, 679] cf. Bae[Rel 67]; 𝔊 throughout (erroneously) Ἀδρα(α)ζαρ;—*Hadad is help(er)*, cf. COT 1 K 20^{1} & Ph. אשמנעזר); king of צוֹבָה (q.v.), son of רְחֹב, defeated by David 2 S 8$^{3.5.10.12}$; הֲדַרְעֶזֶר v$^{7.8.9.10}$ (= הֲדַדְעֶזֶר q.v. 10$^{16.16.19}$ 1 Ch 18$^{3.5.7.8.10.10}$ 19$^{16.19}$, all erron., v. inscr. supr., & cf. Bae[l.c.] Dr on 2 S 8^{3} 10^{16}); also 1 K 11^{23}.

1910 †**הֲדַדְרִמּוֹן n.pr.divin.** (or **n.pr.loc.** der. fr. **n.pr.divin.**), **Hadadrimmon** (=**n.pr.divin.** *Hadad* (cf. supr.) + **n.pr.divin.** *Rimmon*, *Rammân*, v. רִמּוֹן; cf. COT Zc 12[11] Dl ZK 1885, 175 & on question of nom. loc. or divin. Brd[Zc] Baud Stud. i. 293 f. Hi-St[Zc] Ri[HWB] RS Sem. i. 392)—in simile of mourning in Jerusalem כְּמִסְפַּד הֲדַדְרִמּוֹן בְּבִקְעַת מְגִדּוֹן Zc 12[11]; on ה׳ for ההרמונה Am 4[3], v. הרמון; & cf. Hi-St Gunning.

1911 †**הָדָה vb. stretch out** the hand (cf. Ar. هَدَى *lead, guide*, Aram. Pa. ܗܰܕܺܝ) Is 11[8] יָדוֹ הָדָה, sq. עַל, the weaned child *shall stretch out his hand upon*.

3056 †[**יֶהְדַּי**] **n.pr.m.** one of the family of Caleb (acc. to Thes = יהדיה, י׳ *leads* cf. Ol § 277 h, p. 621;
3056 but dub.) יֶהְדָּ֑י 1 Ch 2[47] (Baer; al. יֶהְדָּ֑י).

1935 **הדה** v. הוד. p. 217

1912 †**הֹדּוּ n.pr.loc. India** (Old Pers. *Hiñd'u* Spieg Altpers. Keilinschr. 246 Skr. *Sindhu, sea, great river*, v. reff. in Rö Thes Add 83, Yule Anglo-Indian Glossary, 329 ff.; cf. in Ar. هِنْد, Aram. ܗܶܢܕܽܘ, etc.) only מֵהֹדּוּ וְעַד־כּוּשׁ (הַמֶּלֶךְ) Est 1[1] 8[9] (𝔊 in both ἀπὸ τῆς Ἰνδικῆς).

1913 †**הֲדוֹרָם n.pr.m. 1.** Arabian tribe, called son of Joktan Gn 10[27] (cf. Di) = 1 Ch 1[21]; Glas ii. 435 comp. *Dauram* near Ṣan'â in Yemen (Sab. הדרום CIS iv. 1, p. 1; 𝔊 Ὀδοῤῥα Gn 10[27], 𝔊L Οδορραμ; 1 Ch 1[21] 𝔊B om, 𝔊L Αδωραμ). **2.** son of Tou (תֹּעוּ) king of Hamath 1 Ch 18[10] (𝔊 Ἰδουρααμ, 𝔊L Αθωραμ); so rd. prob. in ‖ 2 S 8[10], for יוֹרָם, cf. 𝔊 Ἰεδδουραν, v. We Dr).—הֲדֹרָם v. p. 214.

1914 †**הִדַּי n.pr.m.** one of David's heroes 2 S
2360 23[30] = חוּרַי 1 Ch 11[32]. p. 301

1915 †[**הָדַךְ**] **vb. cast** or **tread down** (Ar. هَدَكَ *tear down* (a building), synon. of هَدَمَ)—**Qal** *Imv.* הֲדֹךְ רְשָׁעִים Jb 40[12] *cast* or *tread down wicked men*.

הדם (√ of foll., cf. Ar. هَدَمَ *overthrow, overturn, cast down*).

1916 †**הֲדֹם n.m. stool, footstool,** always joined with רַגְלַיִם; only in poet. and late writings, (properly something *cast down, low*)—ה׳ abs. ψ 110[1] (or cstr. bef. לְ, cf. Ges § 130, 1); cstr. La 2[1] + 4 t.:—*footstool*, never lit., usually of י׳ Is 66[1] הַשָּׁמַיִם כִּסְאִי וְהָאָרֶץ ה׳ רַגְלָי; elsewh. with ref. to sanctuary ה׳ רַגְלָיו (cf. מְקוֹם רַגְלַי Is 60[13]) La 2[1], or perhaps of ark (as place on which God rests) בֵּית מְנוּחָה לַאֲרוֹן בְּרִית־י׳ וְלַה׳ רַגְלֵי ψ 99[5] 132[7], אֱלֹהֵינוּ 1 Ch 28[2]; of conquest of enemies of Messianic king by Yahweh's agency אָשִׁית אֹיְבֶיךָ הֲדֹם לְרַגְלֶיךָ ψ 110[1].

†**הֲדַס n.m.** Is 55, 13 **myrtle** (-tree), only late 1918
(NH, Aram. *id.*; Ar. هَدَس (in the dialect of Yemen); also آس, Aram. אָסָה, ܐܳܣܳܐ; cf. Löw No. 25)—abs. ה׳ Is 41[19] Ne 8[15]; הֲדַס Is 55[13]; pl. הַהֲדַסִּים Zc 1[8] + 2 t. (on form cf. Ges § 93, R. 4)—Is 41[19] (‖ אֶרֶז, שִׁטָּה, עֵץ שֶׁמֶן, בְּרוֹשׁ, תִּדְהָר, תְּאַשּׁוּר); Is 55[13] (‖ בְּרוֹשׁ; opp. הַסִּרְפָּד), עֲלֵי הֲדַס Ne 8[15] (‖ עֲלֵי־זַיִת, ע׳ עֵץ־שֶׁמֶן, ע׳ תְּמָרִים, ע׳ עֵץ עָבֹת); pl. Zc 1[8.10.11].

†**הֲדַסָּה n.pr.f.** Jewish name of Esther 1919
(= *myrtle*, on form cf. Sta § 199 a) Est 2[7] (cf. אֶסְתֵּר).

†[**הָדַף**] **vb. thrust, push, drive** (הֲדַף in 1920
𝔗; Ar. هَدَفَ is *ingressus* ad aliquem *fuit*, *propinquus fuit*, also of time *prope accessit*)—**Qal** *Pf.* 3 ms. sf. הֲדָפוֹ Nu 35[22] Je 46[15]; 1 s. sf. וַהֲדַפְתִּיךָ consec. Is 22[19]; *Impf.* 3 ms. יֶהְדֹּף Pr 10[3]; sf. 3 ms. יֶהְדֳּפֶנּוּ Nu 35[20]; sf. 3 mpl. יֶהְדָּפֵם Jos 23[5]; 3 mpl. sf. יֶהְדְּפֻהוּ Jb 18[18]; 2 mpl. תֶּהְדֹּפוּ Ez 34[21]; *Inf.* הֲדֹף Dt 6[19] 9[4]; sf. הָדְפָהּ 2 K 4[27];—**1.** *thrust, push*, subj. man, sq. acc. Nu 35[20.22] (here fatally); subj. cattle, fig. of men, Ez 34[21] (instr. בְּכָתֵף ‖ נָגַח); *push away* 2 K 4[27] (Gehazi, the Shunammite); *thrust away* (fr. oneself) fig. = *reject*, הַוַּת רְשָׁעִים Pr 10[3] (subj. י׳). **2.** *thrust out, drive out*, sq. מִן of place whence & acc. pers.; of י׳ driving out enemies of Isr. fr. Canaan Dt 6[19] 9[4] Jos 23[5]; cf. also indef. subj. יֶהְדְּפֻהוּ מֵאוֹר אֶל־חֹשֶׁךְ Jb 18[18] (‖ וּמִתֵּבֵל יְנִדֻּהוּ); & Je 46[15] (where no pl. whence). Hence **3.** = *depose* Is 22[19] of י׳ deposing Shebna (sq. מִן of station).

†[**הָדַר**] **vb. swell** (?), **honour, adorn,** 1921
(NH הִדֵּר *adorn*; Aram. הַדַּר, ܗܰܕܰܪ Pa. *adorn, honour*; perh. all denom.; cf. Palm. n.pr.f. הדירת *ornata, honorata* Vog No. 55; Ar. هَدَرَ *be of no account*; but also *ferbuit* (vinum) & اِهْدَرَّ *inflatus, tumens* (venter))—**Qal** *Pf.* 2 ms. וְהָדַרְתָּ Lv 19[32]; *Impf.* 2 ms. תֶּהְדַּר Ex 23[3] Lv 19[15]; *Pt. pass.* הָדוּר Is 63[1], pl. הֲדוּרִים Is 45[2] (poss. הררים 𝔊 ὄρη, cf. Di, but v. הר):—**1.** *swell*, only pt. pass. pl. Is 45[2] (si vera l.) in neuter sense, of hills, *swelling places, swells* of land (made level before Cyrus). **2.** *honour, pay honour to*, sq. acc.; in good sense וְהָדַרְתָּ פְּנֵי זָקֵן Lv 19[32] (H) *and thou shalt honour the face of an old*

man (|| מִפְּנֵי שֵׂיבָה תָּקוּם); in bad sense (of partiality, favouritism) לֹא תֶהְדַּר פְּנֵי גָדוֹל Lv 19^{15} (H) (|| לֹא תִשָּׂא פְנֵי־דָל); cf. וְדָל לֹא תֶהְדַּר בְּרִיבוֹ Ex 23^{3} (JE; either rd. גָּדֹל for ודל, — ו not needed at beginning of v.,—so Kn SS al., yet 𝔊 πένητα;—or suppose balancing cl., as Lv 19^{15}, to have fallen out, cf. Di). **3.** *adorn,* only pt. pass. *adorned, made splendid* הָדוּר בִּלְבוּשׁוֹ Is 63^{1}. **Niph.** *Pf.* נֶהְדָּרוּ La 5^{12} *were* (not) *honoured,* subj. פְּנֵי זְקֵנִים. **Hithp.** *Impf.* juss. 2 ms. תִּתְהַדַּר Pr 25^{6} *honour oneself,* i.e. *claim honour.*

1925 †הֶ֫דֶר **n. [m.] ornament, adornment, splendour,** only cstr. ה׳ מַלְכוּת Dn 11^{20} *splendour of (the) kingdom,* cf. AV RV, i.e. Judaea, or perh. Jerusalem acc. to Leng Hi Meinh; but rather *royal splendour,* cf. Gr, & esp. Bev who reads נוֹגֵשׂ מַעֲבִיר ה׳ (for 𝔐 מעביר נוגשׂ), i.e. *an exactor who shall cause the royal splendour to pass away.*

1926 †הָדָר **n.m.** $^{\psi\ 149,\ 9}$ **ornament, splendour, honour** (chiefly poet.)—abs. ה׳ Dt 33^{17} + 12 t.; cstr. הֲדַר Is 2^{10} + 7 t.; sf. הֲדָרִי Mi 2^{9} (but cf. infr.) Ez 16^{14}; הֲדָרְךָ ψ 45^{5} 90^{16}; הֲדָרֶ֑ךָ ψ 45^{4}; הֲדָרֵךְ Ez 27^{10}; הֲדָרָהּ Is 5^{14} La 1^{6}; pl. cstr. הַדְרֵי ψ 110^{3} (but rd. prob. הררי so Symm Jer edd.; Ol Hup Gr Bi Che);—**1.** *ornament* Pr 20^{29} (grey hair, for old men; || תִּפְאֶרֶת), Ez 16^{14} (fig. of ornaments of Jerus. as bride of י׳); פְּרִי עֵץ הָדָר Lv 23^{40} (H) i.e. *fruit of goodly* (ornamental, beautiful) *trees,* so AV RV & most, or *goodly tree-fruit,* 𝔊 καρπὸν ξύλου ὡραῖον, so Di;—here would come also בהדרי קדשׁ ψ 110^{3}, ref. to sacred, festal garments, acc. to Thes al. cf. RVm; but read prob. *on the holy mountains,* vid. supr. **2.** *splendour, majesty* Dt 33^{17} of Ephraim under figure of a noble bull (cf. Di); of Jerusalem Is 5^{14} cf. La 1^{6}; of Carmel Is 35^{2} (|| כָּבוֹד); of *majesty & dignity* conferred by י׳ on man ψ 8^{6} (|| כָּבוֹד), on king 21^{6} (|| *id.*, הוֹד), cf. 45^{4} (|| הוֹד) & v^{5} (but txt. perh. erron. Che$^{\text{crit. n.}}$); denied of suffering servant of י׳ Is 53^{2} (|| תֹּאַר); of *dignity* of good & capable woman (אֵשֶׁת חַיִל) Pr 31^{25} (|| עֹז); of *splendour* due to warlike equipment Ez 27^{10}; especially of *majesty* of י׳ 1 Ch 16^{27} = ψ 96^{6}, cf. Jb 40^{10} ψ 111^{3} (all || הוֹד); also ψ 104^{1} (|| *id.*, under fig. of garment); further ψ 29^{4} (|| כֹּחַ), 90^{16} (|| פֹּעַל); in combination הֲדַר כְּבוֹד הוֹדֶךָ ψ 145^{5}; כְּבוֹד ה׳ v^{12}; הֲדַר גְּאֹנוֹ Is $2^{10.19.21}$. **3.** *honour, glory* ψ 149^{9} for saints of י׳; cf. Mi 2^{9} of י׳'s glory as possession of his people, lost by exile & slavery: but perh. txt. err.; Hoffm ZAW$^{1882,\ 103}$ prop. הֲדִרוֹר, fr. their children ye take *freedom* (yet מֵעַל then hardly suitable).

†[הֲדָרָה] **n.f. adornment, glory**—only 1927
cstr. הַדְרַת;—**1.** ה׳־קֹדֶשׁ *holy adornment* (Che$^{\psi}$), always in connexion with public worship of י׳ 1 Ch 16^{29} 2 Ch 20^{21} ψ 29^{2} 96^{9}. **2.** ה׳־מֶלֶךְ *the glory of a king,* fig. of רָב־עָם, Pr 14^{28}.

†הֲדַר **n.pr.m.** a king in Edom (Aram. 1924
form) Gn 36^{39} = הֲדַד (q.v.) 1 Ch 1^{50} (so here Codd., 𝔖 Sam. no doubt rightly, cf. Di).

†הֲדֹרָם **n.pr.m.** an official of Rehoboam 1913
2 Ch 10^{18} (𝔊 Ἀδωνειραμ) = אֲדֹרָם 1 K 12^{18} (𝔊
Ἀραμ, Ἀδωνιραμ), & אֲדֹנִירָם, q.v.—הֲדוֹרָם v.p. 213. 1913

†הֲדַרְעֶ֫זֶר **n.pr.m.** a king of Aram (צוֹבָה) 1928
defeated by David 2 S $10^{16.16.19}$ = 1 Ch $19^{16.19}$; also 1 Ch $18^{3.5.8.9.10}$ & הֲדַרְעָזֶר $v^{7.10}$; all erron. for הֲדַדְעֶזֶר (q.v.), although 𝔊 throughout Ἀδρααζαρ.

†הָהּ **interj.** expressing woe, **alas!** Ez 1929
30^{2} howl ye הָהּ לַיּוֹם *alas* for the day! AV *Woe* worth the day! (cf. אֲהָהּ לַיּוֹם Joel 1^{15}.)

†הוֹ **interj.** i.q. the more usual הוֹי (q.v.) 1930
Ah! Am 5^{16} of mourners וּבְכָל־חוּצוֹת יֹאמְרוּ הוֹ־הוֹ.

הו Je 29^{23} Kt, v. הוּא. 1931

הוּא **m.** הִיא **f.** (pl. m. הֵם, הֵ֫מָּה; fem. 1931
הֵן, הֵ֫נָּה [the latter only with prefixes]; see these words), **pron. of the 3rd ps. sing., he, she,** used also (in both genders) for the neuter *it,* Lat. *is, ea, id.* (The א is not orthographic merely, but radical, being written on Moab. and Ph. inscriptions, though dropped in some of the later dialects. [In Heb. only Je 29^{23} Kt, and in the pr. n. אֱלִיהוּא.] Moab. (MI$^{6.27}$) and Ph. (often) הא; Aram. of Zinjirli הא, once הו (DHM$^{\text{Inschr. von Sendschirli 55}}$); 𝔗 הוּא, הִיא, Syr. ܗܘ, ܗܝ; Ar. هُوَ, هِيَ (for *hūʼa, hīʼa,* W$^{\text{SG 104}}$); Eth. ውእቱ፡ ይእቲ፡ *weʼĕtū, yeʼĕtī;* perh. also As. *šû, šî, himself, herself,* suff. *šu, ši,* cf. demonstr. *šuatu, šiati* (v. Kraetzschmar $^{\text{BAS. i. 383}}$ & reff., W$^{\text{SG 98, 105}}$ Dl$^{\S\ 55\text{b}, 57}$). In the Pent., הוא is of common gender, the fem. form הִיא occurring only 11 times, viz. Gn 14^{2} 20^{5} 38^{25} (v. Mass. here), Lv 11^{39} $13^{10.21}$ 16^{31} 20^{17} 21^{9} Nu $5^{13.14}$. The punctuators, however, sought to assimilate the usage of the Pent. to that of the rest of the OT, and accordingly wherever הוא was construed as a fem. pointed it הִוא (as a *Qrê perpetuum*). Outside the Pent. the same Qrê occurs 1 K 17^{15} Is 30^{33} Jb

31$^{11\,a}$—prob. for the sake of removing gramm. anomalies: five instances of the converse change, viz. of היא to be read as הוא, occur for a similar reason, 1 K 17^{15} (וַתֹּאכַל הוא־וָהִיא to be read as וַתֹּאכַל הִיא־וָהוּא, on account of the fem. verb) ψ 73^{16} Jb 31$^{11\,b}$ (כי הוא זמה והיא עָוֹן פלילים to be read as כי היא זמה והוא עון פלילים), Ec 5^{8} 1 Ch 29^{16}. The origin of the peculiarity in the Pent. is uncertain. It can hardly be a real archaism: for the fact that Arab., Aram., & Eth. have distinct forms for masc. & fem. shews that both must have formed part of the original Semitic stock, and consequently of Hebrew as well, from its earliest existence as an independent language. Nor is the peculiarity confined to the Pent.: in the MS. of the Later Prophets, of A.D. 916, now at S. Petersburg, published in facsimile by Strack (1876), the fem. occurs written הוא (see the passages cited in the *Adnotationes Criticae*, p. 026). In Ph. both masc. and fem. are alike written הא (CIS i. 1^{9} מלך צדק הא, l.^{13} מלאכת הא, 3^{10} אדם הא, l.^{11} ממלכת הא, 93^{2} 94^{2}), though naturally this would be *read* as *hu'* or *hi'* as occasion required. Hence, as 𝔊 shews that in the older Heb. MSS. the *scriptio plena* was not yet generally introduced, it is prob. that originally הא was written for both genders in Hebrew likewise, and that the epicene הוא in the Pent. originated at a comparatively late epoch in the transmission of the text—perh. in connexion with the assumption, which is partly borne out by facts (cf. De ZKWL 1880, pp. 393-399), that in the older language fem. forms were more sparingly used than subsequently.)

In usage הוא (f. הִיא; pl. הֵמָּה, הֵם, הֵנָּה: v. הֵמָּה) is **1.** an emph. he (she, it, they), sometimes equivalent to **himself (herself, itself, themselves)**, or (esp. with the art.) **that (those)**: **a.** Gn 3^{15} הוא ישופך ראש *he* (𝔊 αὐτός) shall bruise thee as to the head (opp. to the foll. אתה *thou*), v^{20} for *she* (and no one else) was the mother of all living (so oft. in causal sentences, where some emph. on the subject is desirable, as Ju 14^{3} ψ 24^{2} 25^{15} 33^{9} 91^{3} 103^{14} 148^{5} Jb 5^{18} 11^{11} 28^{24} Je 5^{5} 34$^{7\,b}$ Ho 6^{1} 11^{10}: Dr $^{1\,S\,14,18}$), 4^{20} Adah bare Jabal הוא היה אבי ישב אהלים *he* (ἐκεῖνος) was the father of tent-dwellers, v^{21} 10^{8} *he* began to be a mighty one in the earth, 20^{5} (αὐτός), Ju 13^{5} Is 32^{7} 33^{22} 2 K 14$^{7.22.25}$; Ho 10^{2} *he*—the unseen observer of their thoughts and deeds (Che), 13$^{15\,b}$ (*he*, the foe figured by the E. wind). (For its use thus in circ. clauses v. Dr$^{\S\,157,\,160,\,168,\,169}$.) And where the predic. is a subst. or ptcp., Gn 2^{11} . . . הוא הַסֹּבֵב *that* is the one which encompasseth etc., v$^{13.14}$ 10^{12} *that* is the great city. So in the explanatory notices, Gn 14^{3} הוא יָם הַמֶּלַח *that* is the salt sea, v^{8} הוא־צֹעַר *that* is Zoar, 36^{1} + oft. **b.** pointing back to the subj. and contrasting it with something else: Gn 4^{4} הבל גם־הוא Abel, *he* also . . . v^{26} 10^{21} 20^{5} וְהִיא־גַם־הִוא and she, *herself* also said, Ex 1^{10} + oft. **c.** appended alone to a *verb* (more rarely, but always with intentional emphasis), Ex 4^{14} I know כי דבר ידבר הוא that *he* can speak, v^{16} 1 S 22^{18} ויפגע הוא בכהנים and *he* (though none else would do it) smote the priests, 23^{22} for one hath told me, עָרֹם יַעְרִם הוא *He* can deal subtilly, Ez 12^{12} (peculiarly), cf. Dr$^{\S\,160\,n.}$: very rarely indeed to a noun Nu 18^{23} הַלֵּוִי הוא, Is 7^{14} י׳ הוא, Est 9^{1} (הֵמָּה) being probably all the exx. in the OT. **d.** Gn 13^{1} and Abram came up out of Egypt, הוא וְאִשְׁתּוֹ *himself* and his wife, and all that he had, 14^{15} הוא וַעֲבָדָיו *he* and his servants, 19^{30}; so very oft. **e.** *prefixed* to a noun (very rare, and mostly late), Ex 12$^{42\,b}$ Ez 3^{8} & 33^{8} הוא רָשָׁע: to pr. names Ex 6^{27} הוא משה ואהרן, 1 Ch 26^{26} *that* Shelomoth, 27^{6} 2 Ch 28^{22} 32^{12} (diff. from 2 K 18^{22}), v^{30} 33^{23} Ezr 7^{6}: cf. הֵם Ne 10^{38} (comp. in Syr. ܗܘ, Nö$^{\S\,227}$): cf. ψ 87^{5} 1 S 20^{29}.

2. It resumes the subj. with emph.: **a.** when the predic. is a *verb* (esp. if it be separated from its subject by an intervening clause), Gn 15^{4} but one that shall come forth out of thine own bowels, הוא יִירָשֶׁךָ *he* shall be thy heir, 3^{12} the woman whom thou gavest to be with me, הוא נתנה לי *she* gave to me, 24^{7} 44^{17} etc. Ju 7^{4} 2 S 14^{19} (throwing stress on יוֹאָב) 1 Ch 11^{20} Is 33$^{15\text{-}16}$ 34^{16} 38^{19} 47^{10} 59^{16} 63^{5} Ho 7^{8}; oft. in Pr, as 10$^{18.22.24}$ 11^{28} 13^{13} 19^{21} 22^{9} 24^{12}; 1 S 1^{13} (v. Dr), ψ 68^{36}. **b.** when the predic. is a *noun*, Gn 2^{14} and the fourth river, הוא פְרָת *it* was the Euphrates, v^{19} 9^{18} 15^{2} 42^{6} וְיוֹסֵף הוא הַשַּׁלִּיט and Joseph, *he* was the ruler etc.: in sentences of the type י׳ הוא הָאֱלֹהִים, י׳ הוא הַנִּלְחָם לָכֶם, י׳ הוא נַחֲלָתוֹ, Dt 3^{22} 4^{35} 7^{9} 10^{9} Jos 13$^{14.33}$ Is 9^{14} 33^{6} Ho 11^{5} (in these cases, to avoid stiffness, it is convenient often to drop the pron. in translating, as 'And the fourth river *was* the Euphrates:' the pronoun, however, though it then corresponds to the substantive verb in English, does not really *express* it, the copula, as the exx. shew, being in fact understood. Sts. in AV the pron. is retained for emphasis, as Dt. *ll. cc.*) So **c.** after אֲשֶׁר in an *affirmative* sentence, Gn 9^{3} all creeping things אֲשֶׁר הוא־חַי which are living, Lv 11^{39} Nu 9^{13} 14^{8} 35^{31} אֲשֶׁר הוא רָשָׁע לָמוּת who is guilty of death, Dt 20^{20} 1 S 10^{19} Hg 1^{9} al. (On **2**, cf. Dr$^{\S\,199,\ \text{with Obs.}}$)

3. Where, however, the pron. *follows* the

pred., its position gives it the minimum of emphasis, and it expresses (or resumes) the subject as unobtrusively as possible: thus **a.** Gn 12^{18} why didst thou not tell me כי אשתך הוא that she was thy wife? 20^{13} 21^{13} כי זרעך הוא for he is thy seed, 31^{20} because he told him not כִּי בֹרֵחַ הוּא, 37^{3} + oft. (the opp. order rare and emph.: Gn 24^{65} Dt 4^{6} 30^{20} Jos 10^{2} 1 K 2^{22} 3^{4} 21^{2} Ho 2^{4} ψ 45^{12}). **b.** resuming the subj., Gn 31^{16} all the wealth which God hath taken etc., לנו הוא ולבנינו *it is* ours and our children's, v^{43} and all that thou seest, לי הוא *it is* mine (or, omitting the pronoun, as not required in our idiom, simply) *is* mine, 41^{25} חלום פרעה אחד הוא the dream of Pharaoh *is* one, 48^{5} (לי הם), Ex 3^{5} for the place whereon thou standest, אַדְמַת קֹדֶשׁ הוּא *it* is holy ground, Nu 13^{32} 21^{26} Dt 1^{17} Jos 5^{15} 6^{19} Jb 3^{19} + oft.; Gn 23^{15} ארץ ... מַה־הוּא, so ψ 39^{5} Is 41^{22} (הֵנָּה); אַתֶּם .... הֵמָּה (unusual) Zp 2^{12}. (In all such cases the predicate is not referred directly to the subject, but, the subject being made a casus pendens, it is resumed by the pron., and the pred. thus referred to it indirectly. By this means the sentence is lightened and relieved, esp. if the subject consist of many words: in Gn 31^{16} for instance, the direct form of predicate כִּי לָנוּ וּלְבָנֵינוּ כָּל־הָעֹשֶׁר אֲשֶׁר הִצִּיל אֱלֹהִים מֵאָבִינוּ would have been heavy and inelegant.) So **c.** after אֲשֶׁר לֹא in a *negative* sentence, Gn 7^{2} 17^{12} אֲשֶׁר לֹא מִזַּרְעֲךָ הוּא which is not of thy seed, Nu 17^{5} Dt 17^{15} 1 K 8^{41} (cf. הֵמָּה **3 c**). **d.** peculiarly, as the subject of לֹא, Je 5^{12} לוא הוא *He* is not; and as embracing its predicate in itself, Is 18$^{2.7}$ a nation terrible מִן־הוּא (= מֵאֲשֶׁר הוּא) from (the time that) *it was*, Na 2^{9} מִימֵי הִיא from the days that (*st. c.* Ges$^{§ 130.4}$) *it was*, 2 K 7^{7} they left the camp כַּאֲשֶׁר הִיא as *it was* (cf. כַּאֲשֶׁר הֵמָּה v^{10}). (On **3**, cf. Dr$^{§ 198, with Obs.}$)

4. It *anticipates* (as it seems) the subject viz. **a.** (rare) Ct 6^{9} אַחַת הִיא יוֹנָתִי תַמָּתִי one is *she*, my dove my perfect one, Lv 25^{11} Ez 11^{15} 21^{16}, La 1^{18} צַדִּיק הוּא י׳ (oft. so in NH); Ec 6^{10} וְנוֹדָע אֲשֶׁר הוּא אָדָם and that which he, even man, is, is known (De Now); cf. 1 S 6^{19} מִקְרֶה הוּא הָיָה לָנוּ an accident is *it*, (that) hath befallen us. (Cf. הֵמָּה **4 a.**) **b.** after pronouns—(*a*) 2 S 7^{28} אַתָּה הוּא הָאֱלֹהִים Thou art *he*—God, ψ 44^{5} אתה הוא מלכי thou art *he*—my king, Is 37^{16} 43^{25} (אנכי), 51$^{9.10.12}$ 52^{6} Je 14^{22} 29^{23} Kt +; cf. Je 49^{12} וְאַתָּה הוּא נָקֹה תִּנָּקֶה and art thou he (that) shall be unpunished? (with change of pers. κατὰ σύνεσιν, cf. Ju 13^{11} 1 Ch 21^{17} Ez 38^{17}.) So Ew$^{§ 297 b}$ Müll$^{§ 499}$. But others, as Ges^{Thes} Roo$^{§ 563}$ De$^{Is 37, 16; ψ 44, 5}$, treat הוא as emphasizing the pronoun, 'Thou, he, art God' i.e. Thou and none else art God; '*Thou* (emph.) art my king.' (β) מִי הוּא, sq. a ptcp. or subst. Gn 27^{33} ψ 24^{10} מִי הוּא זֶה מֶלֶךְ הַכָּבוֹד who is he, then—the king of glory? (acc. to others, as before, '*Who* (emph.), then, is the king of glory?'); sq. a verb Is 50^{9} מִי הוּא יַרְשִׁיעֵנִי who is he (that) will condemn me? (al. '*Who* (emph.) will condemn me?') Jb 4^{7} 13^{19} 17^{3} 41^{2} Je 30^{21} (so with הֵנָּה Gn 21^{29}, הֵמָּה Zc 1^{9} 4^{5}). (γ) זֶה־הוּא †1 Ch 22^{1} Ec 1^{17} (freq. in NH, where the two words coalesce into one זְהוּ). On the analogous אֵלֶּה הֵם ..., v. הֵמָּה **4 b** (γ). (Cf. Dr$^{§ 200, 201}$.)

5. As an emph. predicate, of God, 'I am He,' i.e. I am He Who *is* (opp. to unreal gods, named in context, or to transitory world), the Unseen, yet Omni-present, and Self-consistent, Ruler of the world, †Dt 32^{39} אֲנִי אֲנִי הוּא I, I am *he*, and beside me there is no God, Is 41^{4} (v. Che) 43$^{10.13}$ even from to-day I am *he*, 46^{4} 48^{12} ψ 102^{28} (v. Che) thou art *he*, and thy years have no end (𝔊 usu. ἐγώ εἰμι: in ψ σὺ δὲ ὁ αὐτὸς εἶ). So also, acc. to many, Jb 3^{19}, but is הוא a *mere* predicate of identity? v. rather **3 b.**

6. In a neuter sense, *that, it* (of an action, occurrence, matter, etc.)—**a.** Jos 2^{21} כְּדִבְרֵיכֶם כֶּן־הוּא acc. to your words, so be *it;* Gn 42^{14} הוא אשר דברתי *that* is what I said, Ex 16^{23} Lv 10^{3} 2 K 9^{36}; Jb 8^{19} הן הוא משוש דרכו lo *that* (what has just been described) is the joy of his way, 13^{16} 15^{9} 31^{28} Pr 7^{23} Ec 2^{1} 3^{22} 9^{9} Est 9$^{1 b}$; similarly the fem. הִיא, Ju 14^{4} they knew not כי מי׳ היא that *it* was from י׳, Nu 14^{41} Jos 10^{13} Is 14^{24} ψ 77^{10} חַלּוֹתִי הִיא *it* (this perplexity) is my sickness, Jb 9^{22} Pr 18^{13} Je 22^{16} 2 Ch 25^{20} Ec 3^{13}; ref. to זאת Am 7^{6} ψ 118^{23} Jb 5^{27}, זֹה Ec 2^{24}. (Where there is a predicate, the gender of this usually regulates the choice of *m.* or *f.*: hence הִוא Gn 34^{14} Ex 8^{15} Nu 15^{25} (Ec 5^{5}) Dt 4^{6} +.) **b.** affirming the presence or existence of something (rare): 2 K 18^{36} = Is 36^{21} כִּי מִצְוַת הַמֶּלֶךְ הִיא for *it was* the king's command, saying etc., 1 S 20^{33} (text dub.), Je 50$^{15.25}$ 51$^{6.11}$ Mi 2^{3}, perh. Jb 32^{8}.

p. 241

7. With the art. הַהוּא, הַהִיא, הָהֵמָּה, הָהֵם, הַהֵנָּה: 1992, 2007
so regularly when joined to a subst. defined itself by the art.: Gn 2^{12} הָאָרֶץ הַהוּא *that* land, 19^{35} ובלילה ההוא and in *that* night, 21^{22} בָּעֵת הַהִוא at *that* time, Dt 1^{19} המדבר הגדול והנורא ההוא. Only four times does there occur the anomalous construction בַּלַּיְלָה הוּא Gn 19^{33} 30^{16} 32^{23} 1 S 19^{10}.

†[הָוָא] **vb. fall** (Ar. هَوَى *id.* e.g. of a 1933

star Qor 53[1])—**Qal** *Imv.* Jb 37[6] for he saith to the snow הֱוֵא־אָרֶץ *Fall* earthwards (an Arabizing usage).

1834 **הובנים** v. [הָבְנִי]. p. 211

הוד (√of foll.; De Jb 39[20] comp. Bed. هَوِيدٌ *crash, roar, resonance;* 'weithin hallende Selbstverkündigung' Id. ψ 8[6]; but هَادَ ordinarily means *be gentle, quiet*, esp. in speech).

1935 †I. **הוֹד n.m.** [Jb 37, 22] **splendour, majesty, vigour** (chiefly poet.) (NH *id.*)—ה׳ abs. Jb 37[22] + 8 t. (הַה׳ 1 Ch 29[11]); cstr. Is 30[30] + 3 t.; sf. הוֹדִי Dn 10[8]; הוֹדְךָ Nu 27[20] + 2 t.; הוֹדֶךָ Pr 5[9] ψ 145[4]; הוֹדוֹ Ho 14[7] + 3 t.; הֹדֹה Je 22[18];—**1.** *splendour, majesty*, of king הוֹדְךָ וַהֲדָרֶךָ ψ 45[4]; גָּדוֹל כְּבוֹדוֹ || י׳ הוֹד וְהָדָר תְּשַׁוֶּה עָלָיו ψ 21[6], subj. (בִּישׁוּעָתֶךָ); foretold of the צֶמַח Zc 6[13] וְהוּא־יִשָּׂא הוֹד וְיָשַׁב וּמָשַׁל עַל־כִּסְאוֹ; cf. וַיִּתֵּן עָלָיו הוֹד מַלְכוּת 1 Ch 29[25] (י׳ confers on Sol.); וְלֹא נָתְנוּ עָלָיו ה׳ מַלְכוּת Dn 11[21] (of usurper); v. also וְהוֹי הֹדֹה Je 22[18] in lament for king. Hence also **2.** divine *splendour, majesty*, light & glory which God wears as king: הוֹד וְהָדָר לָבָשְׁתָּ ψ 104[1] (7 t. joined with הָדָר); cf. Jb 40[10] where י׳ addresses Job in irony; עַל־אֱלוֹהַּ נוֹרָא הוֹד Jb 37[22]; הוֹד וְהָדָר לְפָנָיו ψ 96[6] = 1 Ch 16[26]; also הַגְּדֻלָּה וְהַגְּבוּרָה וְהַתִּפְאֶרֶת וְהַנֵּצַח וְהַה׳ 1 Ch 29[11]; see further כִּסָּה שָׁמַיִם הוֹדוֹ Hb 3[3] (|| וּתְהִלָּתוֹ מָלְאָה הָאָרֶץ); מָה־אַדִּיר שִׁמְךָ || ψ 8[2] אֲשֶׁר־תְּנָה הוֹדְךָ עַל־הַשָּׁמָיִם (בְּכָל־הָאָרֶץ); also הוֹדוֹ עַל־אֶרֶץ וְשָׁמָיִם ψ 148[13] (|| נִשְׂגָּב שְׁמוֹ לְבַדּוֹ); הֲדַר כְּבוֹד הוֹדֶךָ 145[4]; of Yahweh's actions הוֹד וְהָדָר פָּעֳלוֹ 111[3]; of his voice וְהִשְׁמִיעַ י׳ אֶת־הוֹד קוֹלוֹ Is 30[30]. **3. a.** *splendour* of Israel under divine blessing וִיהִי כַזַּיִת הוֹדוֹ Ho 14[7]. **b.** *majesty, dignity, authority* of Moses Nu 27[20] (P; only here in Hex) וְנָתַתָּה מֵהוֹדְךָ עָלָיו. Also, **c.** manly *vigour* פֶּן־תִּתֵּן לַאֲחֵרִים הוֹדֶךָ Pr 5[9], in warning against licentiousness; as displayed in outward appearance וְהוֹדִי נֶהְפַּךְ עָלַי לְמַשְׁחִית Dn 10[8] (|| כֹּחַ). **4.** of a horse, *majesty, majestic force* הוֹד נַחְרוֹ אֵימָה Jb 39[20] *the majesty of his snorting (majestic snorting*, VB) *is a terror;* also in sim. of Yahweh's dealings with Judah, וְשָׂם אוֹתָם כְּסוּס הוֹדוֹ בַּמִּלְחָמָה Zc 10[3] *and he will make them like the horse of his majesty in battle.*

1936 †II. **הוֹד n.pr.m.** (*splendour, vigour*)—a man of Asher 1 Ch 7[37].

1937 †**הודוה** Kt, הוֹדְיָה Qr, **n.pr.m.** only in
1938 בְּנֵי לְה׳ Ne 7[43] of a Levitical family; = הוֹדַוְיָה Ezr 2[40] q.v. sub ידה. p. 392

†**הוֹדִיָּה n.pr.m.** (*my splendour is Yah*)—**1.** a man of Judah 1 Ch 4[19]. **2.** Levites **a.** Ne 8[7] 9[5] 10[11]; **b.** Ne 10[14]. **3.** a chief of the people Ne 10[19]. 1940-41

†**הוֹדְיָה** Qr Ne 7[43] v. הודוה supr. 1937

†**הודיוהו, הוֹדַוְיָהוּ, הוֹדַוְיָה n.pr.m.** v. sub ידה. p. 392f 1938-39

†[**הָוָה**] **vb. become** (Ar. هَوَى *to fall* (v. הָוָא), also *to gape* or *yawn*, and *to desire* (cf. הַוָּה): cf. Fl[De Jb 6, 2]; Aram. הֲוָא, ܗܘܳܐ the usual word for *to be* (prob. orig. *to fall out, accidit*, hence *come to pass, come to be*, γίγνεσθαι), Mish. *id.* very common) a rare syn. of הָיָה q.v.:—**Qal** *Impf.* apoc. יְהוּא Ec 11[3] (for יְהִי with א *otiosum;* Ges[§75 R 13 e] Kön[p. 597 f.]; but Gr. plausibly הוּא); *Imv.* ms. הֱוֵה Gn 27[29], fs. הֱוִי Is 16[4], *Pt.* הֹוֶה Ec 2[22] Ne 6[6]:—Gn 27[29] הֱוֵה גְבִיר לְאַחֶיךָ *become* lord to thy brethren, Is 16[4] (perh. in imit. of Moab. dialect) הֱוִי סֵתֶר לָמוֹ *become* thou (Zion) a defence to them, Ec 2[22] 11[3] Ne 6[6]. 1933

†**הַוָּה n.f. 1. desire; 2. chasm**, fig. **destruction** (cf. هَوًى *desire*, هَوَاءٌ *atmosphere, emptiness*, هَاوِيَةٌ *a deep pit, hell* (cf. sub הָוָה); Aram. ܗܘܳܬܳܐ *gulf, chasm* (Lu 16[26] ܣ)) cstr. הַוַּת Mi 7[3] +, sf. הַוָּתִי Jb 6[2] +, pl. הַוּוֹת ψ 5[10] +;—**1.** *desire* (in bad sense) Mi 7[3] דֹּבֵר הַוַּת נַפְשׁוֹ speaketh *the desire of* his soul, Pr 10[3] הַוַּת רְשָׁעִים, 11[6] ה׳ בֹּגְדִים, ψ 52[9] יָעֹז בְּהַוָּתוֹ became strong through his (evil) *desire* (but read rather with ܣ ܛ Lag Gr Bi Che Now בְּהוֹנוֹ : || בְּעָשְׁרוֹ). **2.** *engulfing ruin, destruction* Jb 6[2] Qr 30[13] (cf. Baer's note) הַוָּתִי of Job's great calamity; pl. (intens.) הַוּוֹת, esp. as wrought, or meditated, by one against another, ψ 5[10] קִרְבָּם הַוּוֹת their inward part is *engulfing ruin* (Che), 38[13] דִּבְּרוּ הַוּוֹת, 52[4] ה׳ תַּחְשֹׁב, 55[12] ה׳ בְּקִרְבָּהּ (cf. Pr 17[4] לְשׁוֹן הַוֹּת), 57[2] לְשׁוֹנֶךָ עַד יַעֲבֹר ה׳ till *the storm of ruin* (Che) pass by, 91[3] דֶּבֶר ה׳ *destructive* pestilence, 94[20] כִּסֵּא ה׳ the seat (tribunal) of destruction (i.e. which ruins the innocent by injustice), Pr 19[13] a foolish son is הַוֹּת לְאָבִיו, Jb 6[30] (cf. v[2] supr.) 1942

הַיָּה n.f. destruction, sf. הַיָּתִי Jb 6[2] Kt, i.q. הַוָּתִי (Qr), and prob. an error for it: v. הַוָּה **2.** p. 228 1962

†**הֹוָה n.f. ruin, disaster** (cf. sub הַוָּה) Ez 7[26] הֹוָה עַל הֹוָה תָּבוֹא *disaster* shall come upon *disaster*, Is 47[11] וְתִפֹּל עָלַיִךְ הֹוָה *disaster* shall fall upon thee (|| שֹׁאָה, רָעָה). 1943

יהוה [c. 6823] i.e. **יַהְוֶה n.pr.dei Yahweh**, the proper name of the God of Israel—(**1.** MT יְהוָֹה [c518] (Qr אֲדֹנָי), or יֱהוִֹה [c 305] (Qr אֱלֹהִים), in 3068-69 the combinations יהוה אדני & אדני יהוה (vid. אֲדֹנָי), and with prep. מֵיהוָֹה, לַיהוָֹה, בַּיהוָֹה (Qr מֵאדֹנָי, לַאדֹנָי, בַּאדֹנָי), do not give the original form. 𝔊 and other Vrss follow the Qr. On the basis of Ex 20^{7} Lv 24^{11} יהוה was regarded as a *nomen ineffabile* (vid. Philo$^{\text{de Vita Mosis iii. 519, 529}}$), called by the Jews הַשֵּׁם and by the Samaritans שׁימא. The pronunciation *Jehovah* was unknown until 1520, when it was introduced by Galatinus; but it was contested by Le Mercier, J. Drusius, and L. Capellus, as against grammatical and historical propriety (cf. Bö$^{\S\,88}$). The traditional Ἰαβέ of Theodoret and Epiphanius, the יְהוֹ־, ־יָהוּ of compound n.pr. and the contracted form יָהּ, all favour יַהְוֶה (cf. יַהַלְמוֹן ψ 74^{6}; תַּהֲרוּ Is 33^{11}), v. Lag$^{\text{Sym. i. 14}}$ Baudissin$^{\text{Studien i. 179 ff.}}$; Dr$^{\text{Stud. Bib. i. 1 ff.}}$ For *Jeve* v. Sta$^{\text{ZAW 1881, 346}}$ De$^{\text{ib. 1882, 173 f. \& Gn. Excurs. ii.}}$ **2.** on liter. of interpret. v. Nes$^{\text{Eg. 67}}$ Dr$^{\text{l.c.}}$.—Many recent scholars explain יַהְוֶה as Hiph. of הוה (=היה) *the one bringing into being, life-giver* (cf. חַוָּה Gn 3^{20}) Schr HSch; *giver of existence, creator*, Kue Tiele; *he who brings to pass* (so already Le Clerc), *performer of his promises*, Lag, Nes$^{\text{Eg. 88}}$ (but Nes$^{\text{Eg. 91}}$ inclines to Qal as RS$^{\text{Brit. \& For. Ev. Rev.}}$ v. infr.); or from הוה *he who causes to fall*, rain or lightning RS$^{\text{OTJC ed. 1, 423; om. ed. 2, 245}}$, cf. We$^{\text{Skizzen iii. 175}}$; *'Fäller,'* destroying foes, Sta$^{\text{G. i. 429}}$ (dubiously). But most take it as Qal of הוה (= היה); *the one who is:* i.e. *the absolute and unchangeable one*, Ri; *the existing, ever-living*, as self-consistent and unchangeable, Di; or *the one ever coming into manifestation* as the God of redemption, De Oehl; cf. also RS$^{\text{Brit. \& For. Ev. Rev. 1876}}$, *he will be* it, i.e. all that his servants look for (cf. Ew$^{\text{infr.}}$), *he will approve himself* (*give evidence of being, assert his being* Dr$^{\text{l.c. 17}}$)).

I. יהוה is not used by E in Gn, but is given Ex 3$^{12\text{-}15}$ as the name of the God who revealed Himself to Moses at Horeb, and is
1961 explained thus: אֶהְיֶה עִמָּךְ *I shall be with thee* (v^{12}), which is then implied in אֶהְיֶה אֲשֶׁר אֶהְיֶה *I shall be the one who will be* it v^{14a} (i.e. with thee v^{12}) and then compressed into אֶהְיֶה v^{14b} (i.e. with thee v^{12}), which then is given in the nominal form יהוה *He who will be* it v^{15} (i.e. with thee v^{12}). Cf. Ew$^{\text{BTh ii. 337, 338}}$ RS$^{\text{l.c., Proph. 385 ff.}}$ Other interpretations are: *I am he who I am*, i.e. it is no concern of yours (Le Clerc Lag$^{\text{Psalt. Hieron. 156}}$); *I am*, (this is my name), *inasmuch as I am* (כִּי=אֲשֶׁר; AE JDMich We$^{\text{JD Th xxi, 540 = Comp. Hex. 72}}$); Di al. *I am who I am*, he who is essentially unnameable, inexplicable.—E uses יהוה sparingly by the side of אלהים and האלהים in his subsequent narrative. The Ephraimitic writers in Ju S K use it in similar proportions. P abstains from the use of יהוה until he gives an account of its revelation to Moses Ex 6^{3}; but subsequently uses it freely. He gives no explanation of its meaning. He represents that אֵל שַׁדַּי was the God of the patriarchs. J uses יהוה from the beginning of his narrative, possibly explaining it, Gn 21^{33} by אל עולם, the evergreen tamarisk being a symbol of the ever-living God; cf. De Gn 21^{33}. Elsewhere יהוה is the common divine name in pre-exilic writers, but in post-exilic writers gradually falls into disuse, and is supplanted by אלהים and אדני. In Job it is used 31 t. in prose parts, and 12^{9} (a proverb); not elsewhere in the poem. Chr apart from his sources prefers אלהים and האלהים. Dn uses יהוה only in chap. 9 (7 t.); Ec not at all. In the Elohistic group of ψ 42–83 it is used 39 t. (see אלהים). It occurs as the name of Israel's God MI^{18}. It is doubtful whether it was used by other branches of the Shemitic family, cf. COT Gn 2^{4b} Dl$^{\text{Pa 158 ff.}}$ Dr$^{\text{Stud. Bib. i. 7 ff.}}$

II. 1. יהוה is used with אלהים and suf- 430
fixes, especially in D; **a.** with אֱלֹהֶיךָ in the Ten Words Ex 20$^{2\text{-}12}$ (5 t.) = Dt 5$^{6\text{-}16}$; in the law of worship of JE, Ex 23^{19} 34$^{24.26}$; in D 234 t.; Jos 1$^{9.17}$ 9$^{9.24}$ (D^{2}); elsewhere Gn 27^{20} Ex 15^{26} (JE), Ju 6^{26}; S & K 20 t. 1 Ch 11^{2} 22$^{11.12}$ 2 Ch 9$^{8.8}$ 16^{7} Is 7^{11} 37$^{4.4}$ 41^{13} 43^{3} 51^{15} 55^{5} Je 40^{2} + (3 t.) Ho 12^{10} 13^{4} 14^{2} Am 9^{15} ψ 81^{11}. **b.** with אֱלֹהֵיכֶם in D 46 t.; D^{2} 28 t.; H 15 t.; P 15 t.; elsewhere Ex 23^{25} (E); 8^{24} 10$^{8.16.17}$ (JE); Ju 6^{10} 1 S 12$^{12.14}$ 2 K 17^{39} 23^{21} 1 Ch 22^{18} + (10 t. Chr) ψ 76^{12} Je 13^{16} + (5 t.) Ez 20$^{5.7.19.20}$ Jo 2^{13} + (6 t.) Zc 6^{15}. **c.** with אֱלֹהֵינוּ in D 23 t.; in D^{2} 5 t.; Ex 8^{6} (JE) Ex 3^{18} 5^{3} 8$^{22.23}$ 10$^{25.26}$ (E) Ju 11^{24} 1 S 7^{8} 1 K 8$^{57.59.61.65}$ 2 K 18^{22} 19^{19} = Is 36^{7} 37^{20}, 1 Ch 13^{2} + (15 t. Chr) Mi 4^{5} 7^{17} Is 26^{13} Je 3^{22} + (17 t.) ψ 20^{8} 90^{17} (?; Baer אֲדֹנָי) 94^{23} 99$^{5.8.9.9}$ 105^{7} 106^{47} 113^{5} 122^{9} 123^{2} Dn 9$^{10.13.14}$. **d.** c. אֱלֹהֵיהֶם Ex 10^{7} (J) Ex 29$^{46.46}$ Lv 26^{44} (P) Ju 3^{7} 8^{34} 1 S 12^{9} 1 K 9^{9} 2 K 17$^{7.9.14.16.19}$ 18^{12} 2 Ch 31^{6} 33^{17} 34^{33} Ne 9$^{3.3.4}$ Je 3^{21} 22^{9} 30^{9} 43$^{1.1}$ 50^{4} Ez 28^{26} 34^{30} 39$^{22.28}$ Ho 1^{7} 3^{5} 7^{10} Zp 2^{7} Hag 1$^{12.12}$ Zc 9^{16} 10^{6}. **e.** with אֱלֹהָיו Nu 23^{21} (E) Ex 32^{11} (J) Lv 4^{22} (P) Dt 17^{19} 18^{7} 1 S 30^{6} 1 K 5^{17} 11^{4} 15$^{3.4}$ 2 K 5^{11} 16^{2} 2 Ch 1^{1} + 13 t. Chr; Mi 5^{3} Je 7^{28} ψ 33^{12} 144^{15} 146^{5} Jon 2^{2}. **f.** with אֱלֹהַי Nu 22^{18} (JE) Dt 4^{5} 18^{16} 26^{14} Jos 14$^{8.9}$ 2 S 24^{24} 1 K 3^{7} 5$^{18.19}$

8^{28} 17$^{20.21}$ 1 Ch 21^{17} 22^{7} 2 Ch 2^{3} 6^{19} Ezr 7^{28} 9^{5} ψ 7$^{2.4}$ 13^{4} 18^{29} 30$^{3.13}$ 35^{24} 40^{6} 104^{1} 109^{26} Is 25^{1} Je 31^{18} Dn 9$^{4.20}$ Jon 2^{7} Hab 1^{12} Zc 11^{4} 13^{9} 14^{5}. **g.** with אֱלֹהַיִךְ Is 60^{9} Je 2$^{17.19}$ 3^{13} Mi 7^{10} Zp 3^{17}. **h.** with אלהים, probably always due to later editors, or to a Qr which has crept into the text Gn 2^{4b}—3^{23} (J, 20 t. either אלהים inserted by R^{P} as Di De; or יהוה inserted by J in an older source); Ex 9^{30} (J, but not in 𝔊 Sam.; Sam. אדני יהוה; possibly MT from earlier Qr, & Sam. from later Qr); 2 S 7$^{22.25}$ (𝔊 אדני יהוה and 1 Ch 17$^{20-23}$ only יהוה); 1 Ch 17$^{16.17}$ (but 2 S 7$^{18.19}$ אדני יהוה) 1 Ch 28^{20} 29^{1} 2 Ch 1^{9} 6$^{41.41.42}$ 26^{18} (but in the original ψ 132^{8} stood יהוה (so 𝔖), or else no divine name); ψ 72^{18} (the late doxology) 84^{12} (but it makes the line too long); Jon 4^{6}. For the combinations with other divine names see those names. **2.** the
589 phrase †אֲנִי יהוה is noteworthy:—**a.** after אמר
either alone Ex 6$^{2.29}$ (P) or before relative and other clauses: Gn 28^{13} (J) 15^{7} (R) Ex 6^{6} (P) with אלהיכם Ju 6^{10} Ez 20^{5}. **b.** after ידע כי (α) Ex 7^{17} 8^{18} 10^{2} (J); Ex 7^{5} 14$^{4.18}$ (P); 1 K 20$^{13.28}$ Je 24^{7} Ez 6^{7} + 48 t. Ez; (β) with אלהיכם Ex 6^{7} 16^{12} Dt 29^{5} (P) Ez 20^{20} Jo 4^{17}; (γ) with אלהיהם Ex 29^{46} (P) Ez 28^{26} 34^{30} 39$^{22.28}$; (δ) before relative and other clauses Is 45^{3} 49$^{23.26}$ 60^{16} Ez 7^{9} 17^{24} 21^{10} 22^{22} 35^{12} 36^{36}; (ε) with various forms of קדשׁ Ex 31^{13} (P) Ez 20^{12} 37^{28} 39^{7}; (ζ) with דברתי Ez 5^{13} 17^{21}, cf. יֵדְעוּ אשר אני י׳ Ez 20^{26}. **c.** after כִּי in various combinations Lv 11$^{44.45}$ Nu 35^{34} (P), Lv 20$^{7.26}$ 21$^{8.15.23}$ 22^{16} 24^{22} 25^{17} 26$^{1.44}$ (all H); Ex 15^{26} (R) Is 41^{13} 43^{3} 61^{8} Je 9^{23} Ez 12^{25} 21^{4} Zc 10^{6} Mal 3^{6}. **d.** emphatic Ex 6^{8} 12^{12} Lv 26$^{2.45}$ Nu 3$^{13.41.45}$ (all P); Lv 18$^{5.6.21}$ 19$^{12.14.16.18.28.30.32.37}$ 21^{12} 22$^{2.3.8.30.31.33}$ (all H) Is 43^{15}; with אלהיהם Ex 29^{46}; with אלהיך Is 48^{17}; with אלהיכם Lv 23^{43} 25$^{38.55}$ Nu 10^{10} 15$^{41.41}$ (P) Lv 18$^{2.4.30}$ 19$^{2.3.4.10.25.31.34.36}$ 20^{24} 23^{22} 26^{13} (all H) Ez 20$^{7.19}$ Jo 2^{27}; with מְקַדֵּשׁ Lv 20^{8} 22$^{9.32}$ (H), with דברתי Nu 14^{35} (P) Ez 5^{15} + (11 t. Ez); with clauses Is 27^{3} 41$^{4.17}$ 42$^{6.8}$ 45$^{5.6.7.8.18.19.21}$ 60^{22} Je 17^{10} 32^{27} Ez 14$^{4.7.9}$ 34^{24}; †אָנֹכִי יהוה is used in the Ten Words Ex 20$^{2.5}$ = Dt 5$^{6.9}$ cited ψ 81^{11} Ho 12^{10} 13^{4}; elsewhere only Ex 4^{11} (J) Is 43^{11} 44^{24} 51^{15}. **3.** יהוה is also used with several predicates, to form sacred names of holy places of Yahweh יהוה יראה Gn 22^{14} (J); יהוה נסי Ex 17^{15} (E) יהוה שָׁלוֹם Ju 6^{24} יהוה צדקנו Je 33^{16} (cf. 23^{6} where it is applied to the Messiah); יהוה שָׁמָּה Ez 48^{35}.—On combinations such as י׳ צְבָאוֹת, הַר י׳,
2022, 6635 etc., v. הַר, צָבָא, etc. p. 249, 838

Note.—Bonk ZAW 1891, 126 ff. seems to shew that as prefix, in comp. n.pr., יְהוֹ is the oldest and the latest form and that יוֹ is intermediate, belonging to the earlier post-exilic period until the time of Chr; occasional copyists' mistakes being taken into the account.

†יָהּ$_{T50}$ **n.pr.dei** contr. fr. יהוה, first appears 3050
in early poems; Ex 15^{2} עָזִּי וְזִמְרָת יָהּ *My strength and song is Yah* (cited Is 12^{2} ψ 118^{14}), cf. the poetic extract יָד עַל כֵּס יָהּ = *hand to the throne of Yah* Ex 17^{16} (E), the song of Hezekiah Is 38^{11} (repeated by dittography), (א)שׁ להבת יה (so read in preference to the MT שַׁלְהֶבֶתְיָה) = *flame of fire from Yah* Ct 8^{6}; ביה יהוה Is 26^{4} (יהוה sustained by Aq and the rhythmical movement, unless it be a mistake for שׁמו, cf. ψ 68^{5}), יה אלהים ψ 68^{19}. Elsewhere יָהּ is used only in late ψ, especially in the Hallels, in the phrase הַלְלוּ־יָהּ *praise ye Yah* ψ 104^{35} 105^{45} 106$^{1.48}$ 111^{1} 112^{1} 113$^{1.9}$ 115^{18} 116^{19} 117^{2} 135$^{1.3.21}$ 146$^{1.10}$ 147$^{1.20}$ 148$^{1.14}$ 149$^{1.9}$ 150$^{1.6}$, cf. also יהלל יה 102^{19} יהללו יה 115^{17} תהלל יה ψ 150^{6} (v. הלל); in var. other phrases ψ 77^{12} 89^{9} 94$^{7.12}$ 115^{18} 118$^{5.5.17.18.19}$ 122^{4} 130^{3} 135^{4}.

יֵהוּא **n.pr.m.** (prob. contr. fr. יהוהוא = י׳ 3058
is He, cf. יֵשׁוּעַ and reff.; cuneif. *Ia-u-a* COT 1 K 16^{23} 2 K 9^{2} (further Schr MBAW 1880, 277, ZA iii. 3 Hpt BAS i. 296, 329 Jäger ib. 468); cf. also אֱלִיהוּ)—**1.** king of Israel who overthrew the dynasty of Omri (𝔊 Εἰου, A oft. Ἰηου, 𝔊L Ἰου) 1 K 19$^{16.17.17}$ 2 K 9^{2} + 36 t. 2 K 9 & 10 + 12^{2} 13^{1} 14^{8} 15^{12}; 2 Ch 22$^{7.8.9}$ 25^{17} Ho 1^{4}. †**2.** prophet of N. Israel in time of Baasha & Jehoshaphat (𝔊 Εἰου, A Εἰηου 𝔊L Ἰου in K; 𝔊 Ἰου, Ἰησου, A 𝔊L Ἰηου in Ch) 1 K 16$^{1.7.12}$ 2 Ch 19^{2} 20^{34}. †**3.** one of David's heroes 1 Ch 12^{3} (𝔊 Ἰηουλ, 𝔊L Ἰηουδ). †**4.** a Judaite 1 Ch 2$^{38.38}$ (𝔊 Ἰησους, A 𝔊L Ἰηου). †**5.** a Simeonite prince 1 Ch 4^{35} (𝔊 οὗτος i.e. (י)הוּא; A 𝔊L Ἰηου).

†**יְהוֹאָחָז, יוֹאָחָז** **n.pr.m.** (י׳ *hath grasped;* 3059, 3099
𝔊 Ἰωαχας, & Ἰωαχαζ; cf. also אֲחַזְיָהוּ, & cuneif. *Ia-u-ḫa-zi* for Ahaz, v. אָחָז, and cf. further Jäger BAS i. 467 f.)—**1.** יְהוֹאָחָז king of Judah, son of Josiah 2 K 23$^{30.31.34}$ 2 Ch 36^{1}, = יוֹאָחָז v$^{2.4}$ (appar. = יוֹחָנָן 1 Ch 3^{15}). **2.** יְהוֹאָחָז king of Isr., son of Jehu 2 K 10^{35} 13$^{1.4.7.8.9.10.22.25.25}$ 14$^{8.17}$ 2 Ch 25$^{17.25}$ = יוֹאָחָז 2 K 14^{1}. **3.** יְהוֹאָחָז king of Judah, son of Jehoram of Judah 2 Ch 21^{17} 25^{23} = אֲחַזְיָהוּ (אֲחַזְיָה) **2,** q.v. **4.** יוֹאָחָז father of יוֹאָח Josiah's chronicler 2 Ch 34^{8}.

†**יְהוֹאָשׁ, יוֹאָשׁ** **n.pr.m.** 𝔊 Ἰωας (י׳ *is strong,* 3060, 3101
cf. אישׁ; or *hath bestowed*, cf. Ar. آسَ bestow; Ph. יאשׁ n.pr.f.; Sab. אלאוס Hal^{150}, אוסאל Hal^{144}, יאוסאל Hal^{192}, cf. DHM ZMG 1883, 15);—**1.** יְהוֹ׳ king

of Judah, son of Ahaziah (Jehoahaz **3**) 2 K 12$^{1.2.3.5.7.8.19}$ 14^{13},=יוֹאָשׁ 2 K 11^{2} 12$^{20.21}$ 13$^{1.10}$ 14$^{1.3.17.23}$ 1 Ch 3^{11} 2 Ch 22^{11} 24$^{2.4.22.24}$ 25$^{23.25}$;= יֹאָשׁ 2 Ch 24^{1}. **2.** יְהוֹ׳ king of Israel, son of Jehoahaz **2**, 2 K 13$^{10.25}$ 14$^{8.9.11.13.15.16.17}$=יוֹאָשׁ 2 K 13$^{9.12.13.13.14.25}$ 14$^{1.23.27}$ 2 Ch 25$^{17.18.21.23.25}$ Ho 1^{1} Am 1^{1}. **3.** יוֹ׳ father of Gideon (Jerubbaal) Ju 6$^{11.29.30.31}$ 7^{14} 8$^{13.29.32.32}$. **4.** יוֹ׳ a prince of Ahab's house, called בֶּן־הַמֶּלֶךְ 1 K 22^{26}=2 Ch 18^{25}. **5.** יוֹ׳ one of David's heroes 1 Ch 12^{3} (𝔊 Ἰωα, Ἰωας, A Ἰωρας). **6.** יוֹעָשׁ a Judaite prince 1 Ch 4^{22} (𝔊 Ἰωαδα, Ἰωας).

3075, †יְהוֹזָבָד, יוֹזָבָד **n.pr.m.** 𝔊 usu. Ἰωζαβαδ
3107 (י׳ *hath bestowed;* cf. Palm. נבוזבד Vog^{73}; v. also זְבַדְיָהוּ, זַבְדִּיאֵל)—**1.** יְהוֹזָבָד servant & murderer of Joash of Judah 2 K 12^{22} (𝔊 Ἰεζεβουθ) =2 Ch 24^{26} (𝔊 Ζωζαβεδ, Ἰωζαβεδ, Ἰωζαβεθ). **2.** יוֹזָבָד three of David's mighty men, **a.** 1 Ch 12^{5}; **b.** v^{21}; **c.** v^{21} (𝔊 Ἰωζαβειθ, Ἰωζαβειδ). **3.** יְהוֹזָבָד a Benjamite chief 2 Ch 17^{18}. **4.** priests & Levites, **a.** יְהוֹזָבָד 1 Ch 26^{4}; **b.** יוֹזָבָד 2 Ch 31^{13} (𝔊 Ἐζαβαθ, Ἰωαζαβαθ; 𝔊L Ἰωαζαβαδ); **c.** 35^{9} (𝔊 Ἰωζαβαδ; 𝔊L as foreg.); **d.** Ezr 8^{33}; **e.** Ezr 10^{22}; **f.** Ezr 10^{23}; **g.** Ne 8^{7}; **h.** Ne 11^{16}; (**d. f. g.** & **h.** perh. the same man).

3076, †יְהוֹחָנָן, יוֹחָנָן **n.pr.m.** 𝔊 mostly Ἰωαναν,
3110 Ἰωναν (י׳ *hath been gracious,* cf. אֶלְחָנָן, חֲנַנְאֵל & reff.; also Ph. יחנבעל בעליחן)—**1. a.** יְהוֹ׳ a priest Ne 12^{13}; **b.** high priest Ezr 10^{6}=יוֹחָנָן Ne 12$^{22.23}$ appar.=יוֹנָתָן Ne 12$^{11.11}$ (𝔊 Ἰωναθαν). **2.** יְהוֹ׳ Levite Ne 12^{42}. **3.** יְהוֹ׳ son of Tobiah Ne 6^{18} (𝔊 Codd. Ἰωναθαν). **4.** יְהוֹ׳ porter in David's time 1 Ch 26^{3} (𝔊 Ἰωνας, 𝔊L Ἰωναθαν). **5.** יְהוֹ׳ a Judaite captain 2 Ch 17^{15} appar. also 23^{1}. **6.** יְהוֹ׳ an Ephraimite 2 Ch 28^{12}. **7.** יְהוֹ׳ an Israelite, Ezra's time Ezr 10^{28}. **8.** יוֹ׳ (& so all foll.) a Jewish captain, after fall of Jerus. 2 K 25^{23} Je 40$^{8.13.15.16}$ 41$^{11.13.14.15.16}$ 42$^{1.8}$ 43$^{2.4.5}$ **9.** eldest son of king Josiah 1 Ch 3^{15} 𝔊L Ἰωαχας (appar.=יְהוֹאָחָז 2 K 23^{30}+). **10.** a post-exilic prince of the line of David 1 Ch 3^{24}. **11.** father of Azariah, priest in Sol.'s time 1 Ch 5$^{35.36}$. **12.** two of David's mighty men: **a.** a Benjamite 1 Ch 12^{5}; **b.** a Gadite 1 Ch 12^{13}. **13.** a returning exile Ezr 8^{12}.

3077, †יְהוֹיָדָע, יוֹיָדָע **n.pr.m.** (י׳ *knoweth;* cf.
3111 אֶלְיָדָע, יְדַעְיָה & reff., בְּעֶלְיָדָע)—**1.** יְהוֹ׳; 𝔊 usu. Ἰωδαε, A sts. Ἰωιαδαε (2 S 23^{30}+), 𝔊L Ἰωαδ (2 S 20^{23} Ἰωαδδαι), father of Benaiah (David's time), in combin. בְּנָיָהוּ בֶּן־יְהוֹ׳ 2 S 8^{18} 20^{23} 23$^{20.22}$ 1 K 1$^{8.26.32.36.38.44}$ 2$^{25.29.34.35.46}$ 4^{4} 1 Ch 11$^{22.24}$ 18^{17} 27^{5}; יְהוֹיָדָע בֶּן־בְּנָיָהוּ 1 Ch 27^{34} is prob. erron. inversion of the usual order; יְהוֹ׳ alone only 1 Ch 12^{28} (where called הַנָּגִיד לְאַהֲרֹן). **2.** יְהוֹ׳, 𝔊 usu. Ἰωδαε A sts. Ἰωιαδαε etc., (chief) priest at Jerus. in time of Joash 2 K 11$^{4.9.9.15.17}$ 12$^{3.8.10}$ 2 Ch 22^{11} 23$^{1.8.8.9.11.14.16.18}$ 24$^{2.3.6.12.14.14.15.17.20.22.25}$ Je 29^{26}. **3.** יוֹיָדָע a builder at wall of Jerus., with Nehemiah, Ne 3^{6} (𝔊 Ἰοειαα, Ἰοειδα, Ἰωδαε, etc.) **4.** יוֹ׳ son of h. p. Eliashib Ne 12$^{10.11.22}$ 13^{28} (𝔊 Ἰωδα, Ἰωδαε, Ἰωιαδα).

†יְהוֹיָכִין, יְהוֹיָכִן, יוֹיָכִין **n.pr.m.** (י׳ *ap-* 3078,
pointeth) last king but one of Judah, son of 3112
Jehoiakim (𝔊 Ἰωακειμ; in K, 𝔊L Ἰωακειν; 𝔊 in Je (usu.) & Ch Ἰεχονίας); יְהוֹיָכִין 2 K 24$^{6.8.12.15}$ 25$^{27.27}$ 2 Ch 36$^{8.9}$ Je 52^{31}=יְהוֹיָכִן v^{31};=יוֹיָכִין Ez 1^{2}; =יְכוֹנְיָה Je 27^{20}; =יְכָנְיָה 28^{4} 29^{2} 1 Ch 3$^{16.17}$
Est 2^{6}; =יְכָנְיָהוּ Je 24^{1}=כָּנְיָהוּ Je 22$^{24.28}$ 37^{1}. 3204,
3659

יְהוֹיָקִים, יוֹיָקִים, יוֹקִים **n.pr.m.** 𝔊 Ἰωακειμ 3079,
(י׳ *raiseth up;* cf. אֶלְיָקִים & reff.; also יָקִים, 3113,
יְקַמְיָה)—**1.** יְהוֹ׳ one of the last kings of Judah, 3137
son of Josiah 2 K 23$^{34.35.36}$ 24$^{1.5.6.19}$ 1 Ch 3$^{15.16}$ 2 Ch 36$^{4.5.8}$ Je 1^{3} 22$^{18.24}$ 24^{1}+19 t. Je, Dn 1$^{1.2}$; name changed fr. orig. אֶלְיָקִים 2 K 23^{34}=2 Ch 36^{4}. †**2.** יוֹיָקִים priest, son of Jeshua Ne 12$^{10.10.12.26}$. †**3.** יוֹקִים a Judaite 1 Ch 4^{22}.

†יְהוֹיָרִיב, יוֹיָרִיב **n.pr.m.** 𝔊 Ἰωιαρειβ, 3080,
Ἰωαρειβ, Ἰωαρειμ, etc. (י׳ *pleadeth,* or *contendeth*) 3114
—**1.** name of a priestly family יְהוֹ׳ 1 Ch 9^{10} 24^{7}; =יוֹ׳ Ne 11^{10} 12$^{6.19}$. **2.** teacher in Ezra's time Ezr 8^{16}. **3.** a Judaite Ne 11^{5}.

†יְהוּכַל, יוּכַל **n.pr.m.** 𝔊 Ἰωαχαλ (Codd. 3081,
have ζ, χ, s, for λ) (prob. contr. fr. יהויוכל, י׳ *is able*) 3116
a courtier of king Zedekiah, יְהוּ׳ Je 37^{3}=יוּ׳ 38^{1}.

†יְהוֹנָדָב, יוֹנָדָב **n.pr.m.** (י׳ *is noble,* or 3082,
is liberal, or *hath impelled,* cf. נְדַבְיָה)—**1.** יְהוֹ׳ 3122
son of Rechab & chief of the Rechabites (𝔊 Ἰωναδαβ) 2 K 10$^{15.15.23}$ Je 35$^{8.14.16.18}$;=יוֹ׳ Je 35$^{6.10.19}$. **2.** יְהוֹ׳ nephew of David (𝔊 Ἰωναδαβ, Ἰωναδαμ; 𝔊L Ἰωναθαν) 2 S 13^{5};=יוֹ׳ 2 S 13$^{3.3.32.35}$; (appar. called Jonathan 2 S 21^{21} 1 Ch 20^{7}, cf. יְהוֹנָתָן **3.**)

יְהוֹנָתָן, יוֹנָתָן **n.pr.m.** 𝔊 Ἰωναθαν through- 3083,
out, with occasional var. (י׳ *hath given;* cf. 3129
אֶלְנָתָן, נְתַנְיָהוּ, נְתַנְאֵל, & reff., Temanite רמננתן Hal$^{RÉJ\ 1884,\ ix.\ 7\ f.}$ Nbr$^{Stud.\ Bib.\ i.\ 211}$; Sab. והבאום Hal^{10})—**1.** יְהוֹ׳ son of Saul 1 S 14$^{6.8}$ 18$^{1.1}$+40 t. 1 S; 2 S 1^{4}+18 t. 2 S; 1 Ch 8$^{33.34}$ 9$^{39.40}$;=יוֹ׳ 1 S 13$^{2.3}$+27 t. 1 S, 1 Ch 10^{2}. †**2.** יְהוֹ׳ son of Abiathar 2 S 15$^{27.36}$ 17$^{17.20}$;=יוֹ׳ 1 K 1$^{42.43}$. †**3.** יְהוֹ׳ nephew of David 2 S 21^{21}=1 Ch 20^{7}; appar. called Jonadab 2 S 13$^{3\,ff.}$ where 𝔊L Ἰωναθαν, cf.

יהונדב **2.** †**4.** יְהוֹ׳ דּוֹד of David, i.e. his uncle? 1 Ch 27^{32}. †**5.** יְהוֹ׳ one of David's heroes 2 S 23^{32} (cf. Dr)=יוֹנָתָן 1 Ch 11^{34}. †**6.** יְהוֹ׳ one of David's treasurers 1 Ch 27^{25}. †**7.** יְהוֹ׳ a scribe Je $37^{15.20}$ 38^{26}. †**8.** Levites **a.** יְהוֹ׳ 2 Ch 17^{8}; **b.** יוֹ׳ Ne 12^{35}. †**9.** יְהוֹ׳ a priest Ne 12^{18}. †**10.** יְהוֹ׳ priest to the tribe of Dan, son of Gershom Ju 18^{30}. †**11.** יוֹ׳ a Judaite captain, after fall of Jerus. Je 40^{8}. †**12.** יוֹ׳ a Judaite 1 Ch $2^{32.33}$. †**13.** יוֹ׳ father of Ebed Ezr 8^{6}. †**14.** יוֹ׳ son of Asahel Ezr 10^{15}. †**15.** יוֹ׳ a priest Ne 12^{14}. †**16.** יוֹ׳ son of Joiada Ne $12^{11.11}$ appar.=יְהוֹחָנָן **2.**

3085 †**יְהוֹעַדָּה** **n.pr.m.** (mng. dub.; Thes י׳ *hath adorned* (as Heb. עדה Hiph.; vb. of *Pa.* form); MV י׳ *is equipment*, cf. Ar. عُدَّةٌ; possibly י׳ *hath carried off spoil*, or *hath deposed* (𝔗 עדא Pe Pa Aph; cf. Haph. Dn 2^{21}); or perh. י׳ *hath numbered* Ar. عَدَّ)—a descendant of Saul 1 Ch $8^{36.36}$ (𝔊 Ἰαδα, A Ἰωιαδα, 𝔊L Ἰωδα)=יַעְרָה $9^{42.42}$ (for יַעְדָּה? cf. Be; 𝔊 Ἰαδα, 𝔊L Ἰωδα).

3086 **יהועדין** 2 K 14^{2} Kt v. foll.

3086 †**יְהוֹעַדָּן** **n.pr.f.** (? du. (cf. Kt 2 K 14^{2}) or f.pl. of יהועדה, (עדה as noun) Aram. form; Klo 2 K 14^{2} cf. עַד־אָנָה יהוה ψ 13^{2}; comp. Bab. n.pr. *Aḫulapia*, v. אַחְלַי p. 29 supr.) mother of Amaziah, king of Judah 2 K 14^{2} Qr (Kt יהועדין, 𝔊 Ἰωαδειμ, A Ἰωαδειν), 2 Ch 25^{1} (𝔊 Ἰωναα, A Ἰωαδεν, 𝔊L Ἰωαδειν).

3087, 3136 †**יְהוֹצָדָק, יוֹצָדָק** **n.pr.m.** (י׳ *is righteous*; cf. צִדְקִיָּהוּ Sab. צדקאל Hal[193]) father of Joshua the high-priest, יְהוֹ׳ Hg $1^{1.12.14}$ $2^{2.4}$ Zc 6^{11} 1 Ch $5^{40.41}$;=יוֹ׳ Ezr $3^{2.8}$ 5^{2} 10^{18} Ne 12^{26} (𝔊 Ἰωσαδακ, Ἰωσεδεκ).

3088, 3141 †**יְהוֹרָם, יוֹרָם, יֹרָם** **n.pr.m.** (י׳ *is exalted*; cf. מַלְכִּירָם; further, Ph. רמבעל, בעלרם; Sab. אלרם DHM[ZMG 1876, 686])—**1.** יְהוֹ׳ (𝔊 Ἰωραμ) king of Judah, son of Jehoshaphat 1 K 22^{51} 2 K 1^{17} $8^{16.25.29}$ 12^{19} 2 Ch $21^{1.3.4.5.9.16}$ $22^{1.6.11}$;=יוֹ׳ 2 K $8^{21.23.24}$ 11^{2} 1 Ch 3^{11}. **2.** יְהוֹ׳ (𝔊 Ἰωραμ) king of Israel son of Ahab 2 K 1^{17} $3^{1.6}$ $9^{15.17.21.21.22.23}$ 2 Ch $22^{5.6.7}$; =יוֹ׳ 2 K $8^{16.25.28.28.29.29}$ $9^{14.14.16.16.29}$ 2 Ch $22^{5.7}$. **3.** יְהוֹ׳ priest in time of Jehoshaphat 2 Ch 17^{8} (𝔊 Ἰωραμ, Ἰωραν). **4.** יוֹ׳ son of Tou, king of Hamath 2 S 8^{10} (𝔊 Ἰεδδουραν) prob. err. for הֲדוֹרָם ‖ 1 Ch 18^{10}. **5.** יֹרָם a Levite 1 Ch 26^{25} (𝔊 Ἰωραμ).

3089-90 †**יְהוֹשַׁבְעַת, יְהוֹשֶׁבַע** **n.pr.f.** (י׳ *is an oath*; cf. אֱלִישֶׁבַע)—daughter of Joram of Judah, & wife of Jehoiada the priest; יְהוֹשֶׁבַע 2 K 11^{2} (𝔊 Ἰωσαβεε, Ἰωσαβεθ);=יְהוֹשַׁבְעַת 2 Ch $22^{11.11}$ (𝔊 Ἰωσαβεε).

יְהוֹשַׁבְעַת v. foregoing. 3090

יְהוֹשׁוּעַ, יְהוֹשֻׁעַ, and (later) **יֵשׁוּעַ**, **n.pr.m.** 3091, 3442
(& **loc.**, v. **9** infr.) (י׳ *is salvation*, or י׳ *is opulence*, cf. אֱלִישָׁע, אֱלִישׁוּעַ, אֲבִישׁוּעַ, & Nes SK 1892, 573 f.; in any case it came to be associated with ישׁע, cf. Mat 1^{21}; on יֵשׁוּעַ v. esp. Frä VOJ iv, 1890, 332 f. Müll SK 1892, 177 f. who cite analog. for change of וֹ to later ֵ, & Nes l.c.)—**1.** Moses' successor, son of Nun, (𝔊 Ἰησοῦς) יְהוֹשׁוּעַ Dt 3^{21} Ju 2^{7};=יְהוֹשֻׁעַ Ex $17^{9.10.13.14}$ 24^{13} 32^{17} 33^{11} Nu 11^{28} 13^{16} $14^{6.30.38}$ 26^{65} $27^{18.22}$ $32^{12.28}$ 34^{17} Dt 1^{38} 3^{28} $31^{3.7.14.14.23}$ 34^{9} Jos 1^{1}+167 t. Jos; Ju 1^{1} $2^{6.7.8.21.23}$ 1 K 16^{34} 1 Ch 7^{27};=יֵשׁוּעַ Ne 8^{17} (𝔊 Ἰησοῦς); acc. to P, name changed by Moses fr. הוֹשֵׁעַ q.v. Nu $13^{8.16}$ (𝔊 Αὐση) Dt 32^{44} (𝔊 Ἰησοῦς). †**2.** יְהוֹשֻׁעַ a Bethshemite 1 S $6^{14.18}$ (𝔊 Ὡσηε, A Ἰησοῦς, 𝔊L Ἰωσηε). †**3.** h.p. after the restoration, son of Jehozadak יְהוֹשֻׁעַ (𝔊 Ἰησοῦς) Hg $1^{1.12.14}$ $2^{2.4}$ Zc $3^{1.3.6.8.9}$ 6^{11};=יֵשׁוּעַ (𝔊 Ἰησοῦς) Ezr 2^{2} $3^{2.8}$ 4^{3} 5^{2} 10^{18} Ne 7^{7} $12^{1.7.10.26}$. †**4.** יְהוֹשֻׁעַ governor of Jerusalem under Josiah 2 K 23^{8} (𝔊 Ἰησοῦς, 𝔊L Ἰωσηε). †**5.** יֵשׁוּעַ (𝔊 Ἰησοῦς) head of one of the classes of priests 1 Ch 24^{11}, possibly also Ezr 2^{36}=Ne 7^{39}. †**6.** יֵשׁוּעַ (𝔊 Ἰησοῦς, etc.), a Levitical family-name of frequent occurrence: **a.** Ezr 2^{40} 3^{9}=Ne 7^{43} 8^{7} $9^{4.5}$ 10^{10} 12^{8}. **b.** 2 Ch 31^{15} Ezr 8^{33} Ne 12^{24}. †**7.** יֵשׁוּעַ (𝔊 *id.*), father of a builder at the wall Ne 3^{19}, perh.=†**8.** a Judaite family-name (𝔊 *id.*), Ezr 2^{6}=Ne 7^{11} (cf. Sm[Listen 12]). †**9.** **n.pr.loc.** in south of Judah Ne 11^{26} בְּיֵשׁוּעַ (𝔊 ἐν Ἰησοῦ, 𝔊L ἐν Σουα).

†**[יְהוֹשָׁמָע]** only abbrev. (or txt. err.)
הוֹשָׁמָע **n.pr.m.** (י׳ *hath heard*, cf. אֱלִישָׁמָע & 1953
reff.)—a descendant of the royal house of Judah 1 Ch 3^{18} (𝔊 Ὡσαμω(θ), 𝔊L Ωσαμά).

יְהוֹשָׁפָט, יוֹשָׁפָט **n.pr.m.** 𝔊 Ἰωσαφαθ, Ἰωσα- 3092, 3146
φατ (י׳ *hath judged*, cf. שְׁפַטְיָהוּ, אֱלִישָׁפָט & reff.)—**1.** יְהוֹ׳ (so all exc. **5.** & **6**) king of Judah, son of Asa 1 K 15^{24} 22^{2}+21 t. 1 K; 2 K 1^{17} $3^{1.7.11.12.12.14}$ $8^{16.16}$ 12^{19} 1 Ch 3^{10} 2 Ch 17^{1}+40 t. 2 Ch. †**2.** father of Jehu king of Israel 2 K $9^{2.14}$. †**3.** chronicler under David & Solomon, son of Ahilud 2 S 8^{16} 1 K 4^{3} 1 Ch 18^{15}; also 2 S 20^{24} (𝔊L Σαφαν). †**4.** one of Sol.'s 12 officers who provided victuals for the royal household 1 K 4^{17} (𝔊L Ἰωασαφατ). †**5.** יוֹ׳ one of David's heroes 1 Ch 11^{43}. †**6.** יוֹ׳ a priest & trumpeter in David's time 1 Ch 15^{24}. †**7.** in **n.pr.loc.** עֵמֶק יְהוֹשָׁפָט Jo $4^{2.12}$, symbolical name

of a valley near Jerusalem, place of ultimate judgment.

3097 **יוֹאָב** **n.pr.m.** (*׳י is father;* cf. אֲבִיָּהוּ, אֲבִיאֵל, אֱלִיאָב & reff.)—**1.** David's sister's son & captain of his host (𝔊 Ἰωαβ) 1 S 26^{6} 2 S 2^{13} + 100 t. 2 S (also 2 S 20^{6} for MT אֲבִישַׁי cf. 𝔖 We Dr); 1 K 1^{7} + 14 t. 1 K; 1 Ch 2^{16} + 22 t. 1 Ch; ψ 60^{2}. †**2.** a descendant of Judah 1 Ch 4^{14} (but 𝔊B 𝔊L Ἰωβαβ). †**3.** a family-name after the exile Ezr 2^{6} = Ne 7^{11} (𝔊 Ἰωβαβ, Ἰωαβ) Ezr 8^{9} (𝔊 Ἰωαβ).

3098 †**יוֹאָח** **n.pr.m.** (*׳י is brother;* cf. אֲחִיָּהוּ & reff.)—**1.** son of Asaph the chronicler in Hezekiah's time 2 K 18$^{18.26.37}$ (𝔊 Ἰωας, 𝔊L Ἰωαχ), = Is 36$^{3.11.22}$ (𝔊 Ἰωαχ). **2.** Levites **a.** son of Zimmah 1 Ch 6^{6}; **b.** id. 2 Ch 29$^{12.12}$ (𝔊 Ἰωα, Ἰωαχ(α) Ἰωδααθ). **3.** son of Joahaz the chronicler in Josiah's time 2 Ch 34^{8} (𝔊 Ἰωαχ, Ἰωας). **4.** a Levite, son of Obed-edom 1 Ch 26^{4} (𝔊 Ἰωαθ, Ἰωαα, Ἰωαδ).

3099 **יוֹאָחָז** v. יְהוֹאָחָז. p. 219

3100 †**יוֹאֵל** **n.pr.m.** 𝔊 Ἰωηλ (usu. interpr. as *׳י is God,* cf. אֵלִיָּהוּ; but Ph. . . . יאל CIS$^{\text{i. 132 l. 4}}$ & in יאלפעל (Louvre) appar. n.pr. dei, perh. = *Iolaos,* CIS$^{\text{i. p. 163}}$ & reff.; v. also Nes$^{\text{Eg 86}}$ RS$^{\text{K 301}}$; Nes *strong-willed,* cf. ויל, ואל Sin. Inscr. وائل, v. ואלו Eut$^{\text{Sin. Inschr. No. 5 + oft.}}$, yet cf. Dr$^{\text{Stud. Bib. i. 5 n.}}$; W in RS$^{\text{l.c.}}$ prop. connex. with Ar. *Wâil* in n. pr. trib. Bakr Wâil (√ وَأَلَ *take refuge*) cf. RS$^{\text{K 194}}$)—**1.** Samuel's first-born 1 S 8^{2}, 1 Ch 6^{18}; ins. also v^{13} after 𝔊L Ἰωηλ (cf. Dr 1 S 8^{2}). **2.** a Simeonite prince 1 Ch 4^{35}. **3.** a Reubenite 1 Ch 5$^{4.8}$. **4.** a Gadite chief 1 Ch 5^{12}. **5.** a chief man of Issachar 1 Ch 7^{3}. **6.** one of David's heroes 1 Ch 11^{38}. **7.** a chief of Manasseh 1 Ch 27^{20}. **8.** a Jew of Ezra's time Ezr 10^{43}. **9.** a Benjamite Ne 11^{9}. **10.** the prophet, son of Pethuel Jo 1^{1}. **11.** Levites **a.** 1 Ch 6^{21}; **b.** 2 Ch 29^{12}; **c.** 1 Ch 15$^{7.11.17}$, perh. = **d.** 1 Ch 23^{8} 26^{22}.

3101 **יוֹאָשׁ** v. יְהוֹאָשׁ. p. 219

3107 **יוֹזָבָד** v. יְהוֹזָבָד. p. 220

3108 †**יוֹזָכָר** **n.pr.m.** (*׳י hath remembered;* cf. זְכַרְיָהוּ; Sab. ידכראל Hal^{187})—servant & murderer of Joash king of Judah 2 K 12^{22} (𝔊 Ἰεζειχαρ, A 𝔊L Ἰωζαχαρ); = זָבָד 2 Ch 24^{26} (𝔊 Ζαβελ, Ζαβεθ, Ζαβαθ).

3110 **יוֹחָנָן** v. יְהוֹחָנָן. p. 220

3111 **יוֹיָדָע** v. יְהוֹיָדָע. p. 220

יוֹיָכִין v. יְהוֹיָכִין. p. 220 3112

יוֹיָקִים v. יְהוֹיָקִים. p. 220 3113

יוֹיָרִיב v. יְהוֹיָרִיב. p. 220 3114

†**יוֹכֶבֶד** **n.pr.f.** 𝔊 Ἰωχαβεδ (*׳י is glory;* 3115
cf. Ph. כבדמלקרת) daughter of Levi, wife of Amram and mother of Moses Ex 6^{20} Nu 26^{59} (both P).

יוּכַל v. יְהוּכַל. p. 220 3116

יוֹנָדָב v. יְהוֹנָדָב. p. 220 3122

יוֹנָתָן v. יְהוֹנָתָן. p. 220 3129

†**יוֹעֵד** **n.pr.m.** 𝔊 Ἰωαδ (*׳י is a witness*) a 3133
Benjamite Ne 11^{7}.

†**יוֹעֶזֶר** **n.pr.m.** (*׳י is a help;* cf. עֲזַרְיָהוּ, 3134
עֲזַרְאֵל, עֲזָרְאֵל, אֱלִיעֶזֶר & reff.) one of David's mighty men 1 Ch 12^{7} (𝔊 Ἰωζαρα, Ἰωζααρ, 𝔊L Ἰεζρααρ).

†**יוֹעָשׁ** **n.pr.m.** 𝔊 Ἰωας (*׳י hath aided* (?; cf. 3135
Ar. غَاثَ); comp. Sab. אלעוֹת DHM in MV)—**1.** a Benjamite, son of Becher 1 Ch 7^{8}. **2.** an officer under David 1 Ch 27^{28}.

יוֹצָדָק v. יְהוֹצָדָק. p. 221 3136

יוֹקִים v. יְהוֹיָקִים. p. 220 3137

יוֹרָם v. יְהוֹרָם. p. 221 3141

יוֹשָׁפָט v. יְהוֹשָׁפָט. p. 221 3146

†**יוֹתָם** **n.pr.m.** (*׳י is perfect*)—**1.** king of 3147
Judah, son of Azariah (𝔊 Ἰωαθαμ, Ἰωαθαν, Ἰωναθαν) 2 K 15$^{5.7.30.32.36.38}$ 16^{1} 1 Ch 3^{12} 5^{17} 2 Ch 26$^{21.23}$ 27$^{1.6.7.9}$ Is 1^{1} 7^{1} Ho 1^{1} Mi 1^{1}. **2.** youngest son of Jerubbaal (Gideon) Ju 9$^{5.7.21.57}$ (𝔊 ut supr.; Codd. Ἰωθαμ, Ἰωαθαμ). **3.** a descendant of Caleb 1 Ch 2^{47} (𝔊 Ἰωαθαμ).

יֵשׁוּעַ v. יְהוֹשׁוּעַ. p. 221 3442

†**הוֹהָם** **n.pr.m.** Canaanitish king of Heb- 1944
ron Jos 10^{3}.

הוֹי$_{51}$ **interj.** (onomatop.; cf. ܘܘ = הוֹ הוֹ 1945
Am 5^{16} 𝔖, = הֵידָד Je 51^{14} 𝔖; also Mod. Aram. *ú hú, ú hú* (in a lament), So$^{\text{Urmia-Dial. 102.4}}$)—expressing usually dissatisfaction and pain, **Ah, Alas, Ha** (not distinctly *Woe!* which is אוֹי): used in lamentations, 1 K 13^{30} and they mourned over him (saying) הוֹי אָחִי *Ah,* my brother! Je 22^{18} הוֹי אָחִי וְהוֹי אָחוֹת . . . הוֹי אָדוֹן וְהוֹי הֹדֹה, 34^{5} וְהוֹי אָדוֹן יִסְפְּדוּ לָךְ (cf. הוֹ־הוֹ Am 5^{16}): hence Is 1^{4} הוֹי גּוֹי חֹטֵא *Ah!* sinful nation, v^{24} *Ah!* I will ease me of my adversaries; esp.

preparatory to a declaration of judgment, Is 10^{5} הוֹי אַשּׁוּר שֵׁבֶט אַפִּי, 17^{12} 28^{1}, oft. sq. a ptcp. *Ah!* those that . . ., $5^{8.11.18}$ 29^{15} 31^{1} $45^{9.10}$ Je 22^{13} Am 5^{18} 6^{1} Hb $2^{6.9.12.15.19}$ Zc 11^{17}+ (more sympathetic than אוֹי לְ): sq. כִּי Je 30^{7}, אֶל 48^{1}, עַל 50^{27} Ez 13^{3}, לְ 13^{18}. Sts. hardly more than an exclam. arousing attention *Ha!* (though perh. with a touch of sympathy or pity) Is 18^{1} 55^{1} Zc $2^{10.10.11}$ Je 47^{6}.

1949 †[הוּם, הִים] **vb. murmur, roar, discomfit** (Ar. هَامَ (med. ى) is *rush about madly* (lit., or in passion, love, &c.), fig. *be distracted;* on √ הִים v. Hi$^{\psi 55,3}$ Nö$^{ZMG 1883, 540}$)—**Qal** *Pf.* 3 ms. sf. וְהָמָם consec. Dt 7^{23} וְה׳ מְהוּמָה גְדֹלָה (י׳ subj.) *and he shall discomfit them (with) a great discomfiture* (acc. to Di וה׳ is fr. הָמַם, here pointed as ע״ו because of מְהוּמָה; but v. Kö$^{i. 486}$ & reff.); here, acc. to Nö$^{l.c.}$, belongs *Impf.* 1 s. cohort. אָהִימָה (i. e. √ע״י) ψ 55^{3} *am driven about* (Hi De), or *distracted.* **Niph.** *Impf.* 3 fs. וַתֵּהֹם 1 S 4^{5} + 2 t. (on form cf. Ges$^{§ 72 R 5}$); *be in a stir,* of a city Ru 1^{19} (sq. עַל *over, on account of*), 1 K 1^{45}; of ground *re-echoing* shout 1 S 4^{5}. **Hiph.** *Impf.* 1 s. אָהִימָה ψ 55^{3} *shew disquietude* (so most, cf. supr.); but Ol Che וְאֶהֱמָיָה (77^{4}); Lag$^{Proph. Chald. xlviii. 2, BN 27}$ אֶהֱמֶה (v^{18}); 3 fpl. תְּהִימֶנָה (? תְּהֱמֶינָה) Mi 2^{12} *they* (i.e. fold & pasture) *shall murmur* with men.

4103 †מְהוּמָה **n.f. tumult, confusion, disquietude, discomfiture**—abs. מ׳ Dt 7^{23} + 7 t.; cstr. מְהוּמַת 1 S 5^{11} Ez 22^{5}; pl. abs. מְהוּמוֹת 2 Ch 15^{5}, מְהוּמֹת Am 3^{9};—**1.** *tumult, confusion* Am 3^{9} (‖ עֲשׁוּקִים *oppression*), *disturbance, turmoil* (opp. peace) 2 Ch 15^{5} (‖vb. המם v^{6}), cf. Ez 22^{5}; *disquietude* (of mind) Pr 15^{16}; esp. *tumult & confusion, panic,* as due to divine judgment מְהוּמַת־י׳ Zc 14^{13} cf. Ez 7^{7}; also 1 S 5^{9} and מְהוּמַת מָוֶת v^{11}. **2.** *discomfiture* (due to י׳) in war 1 S 14^{20} (cf. $v^{15.22}$); Dt 7^{23} (acc. cogn. c. הום q.v.), 28^{20} (‖ מְאֵרָה, מִגְעֶרֶת); cf. יוֹם מ׳ Is 22^{5} (‖ מְבוּסָה, מְבוּכָה) *a day of discomfiture & down-treading & confusion.*

1950 הוֹמָם **n.pr.** v. sub המם. p. 243

1951 †[הוּן] **vb. be easy** (Ar. هَانَ *be light, easy,* cf. هَيْنٌ, هَوْنٌ (v. און), Aram. NH הוֹן *gentleness,* ܗܘܢܐ, ܗܘܢ is *mind, sense;* vid. conject. on development of mngs. Fl ChWB$^{i. 423}$)—only **Hiph.** *Impf.* וַתָּהִינוּ sq. Inf. Dt 1^{41} *regard as easy* to go up, or *make light* of going up; so Thes Kn Ke Di RVm (construct. as Nu 14^{44} וַיַּעְפִּלוּ לַעֲלוֹת, though ‖ to this in Dt is v^{43}).

1952 †הוֹן **n.m.** $^{Pr 8.18}$, **wealth, sufficiency** (poet., almost wholly WisdLt, especially Pr; cf. I. און p. 20 supr.)—abs. הוֹן Pr 1^{13} + 15 t. + Ez $27^{12.18}$ (where 𝔊 𝔖 Co הוֹנֵךְ); cstr. Pr 6^{31} + 3 t.; sf. הוֹנֶךָ Pr 3^{9}; הוֹנֵךְ Ez 27^{27} + $v^{12.18}$ Co; הוֹנוֹ Pr 28^{8}; pl. sf. הוֹנַיִךְ Ez 27^{33}—**1.** *wealth* ψ 112^{3} (‖ עֹשֶׁר) Pr 8^{18} (‖ *id.*) 1^{13} (‖ שָׁלָל) cf. הוֹן עָשִׁיר Pr 10^{15} (opp. דַּלִּים), 18^{11}; Pr 3^{9} (‖ רֵאשִׁית כָּל־תְּבוּאָתֶךָ) הוֹן בֵּיתוֹ Pr 6^{31} Ct 8^{7}, בַּיִת וָהוֹן Pr 19^{14}; see 19^{4} (opp. דָּל) 28^{8} (opp. דַּלִּים); also ψ 119^{14} Pr 11^{4} 12^{27} $13^{7.11}$ 24^{4} 28^{22} (opp. חֶסֶר) 29^{3}; Ez $27^{12.18.27.33}$. **2.** with בְּ + מְכַר pretii, = *high value,* or *price* תִּמְכֹּר עַמְּךָ בְּלֹא הוֹן ψ 44^{13}—i.e. cheaply, = 'for no price at all' (‖ מחיר). **3.** *sufficiency, enough!* in exclam. Pr $30^{15.16}$ (so also 𝔖 𝔗, Aq Sym Theod ἀρκεῖ).

†[הוֹר], assumed by Thes al. as ancient form for הַר *mountain,* to explain הוֹרַי Gn 49^{26}, rd. הוֹרֵי־עַד; but better הַרֲרֵי־עַד *everlasting mountains,* v. הַר sub הרר. p. 249 2022

1953 הוֹשָׁמָע **n.pr.m.** = יְהוֹ׳ v. יהוה sub היה. p. 221

1954 הוֹשֵׁעַ v. sub ישׁע. p. 448

3467 הוֹשַׁעְיָה v. sub ישׁע. p. 446

2050 †[הוּת] **vb. shout at,** si vera l. (Ar. هَوَّتَ c. على *shout at, threaten,* dialect. for هَيَّتَ, cf. De ψ 62^{4} who comp. Damascene هَوَّتَ عَلَى فُلَانٍ *rush upon one* with cries and raised fist, cf. further Wetzst in De; so MV SS: Thes al. assign to [התת], *attack;* txt. dub.)—only **Po.** *Impf.* תְּהוֹתְתוּ עַל־אִישׁ ψ 62^{4}; but Hup Che rd. תְּהוֹלְלוּ *be frantic* against, cf. 102^{9}.

1956 הוֹתִיר **n.pr.m.** v. יתר. p. 452

1957 †[הָזָה] **vb. dream, rave** (Ar. هَذَى *talk deliriously,* Syr. ܗܕܐ, in Lexx., *id.,* cf. also Vrss; v. esp. Bo$^{Hieroz. ii. 56, p. 680; ed. Rosenm. vol. i. 782}$);—only **Qal** *Pt. act.* pl. הֹזִים Is 56^{10} לֹא יוּכְלוּ לִנְבֹּחַ ה׳ שֹׁכְבִים of dogs, metaph. of false prophets.

1958 †הִי (?) **n.[m.] lamentation, wailing,** only Ez 2^{10} וְכָתוּב אֵלֶיהָ קִנִים וָהֶגֶה וָהִי *and written in it were lamentations and mourning and wailing* (𝔊 οὐαί, *woe!* Ew$^{§ 101 c}$ comp. אִי, cf. III. אִי p. 33 supr.; acc. to Thes Sta$^{§ 125 b}$ al. הִי = נְהִי, נ being dropped; Ol$^{§ 77 g, 144 c}$ would emend נְהִי & so Co; v. נְהִי sub נהה. Text very dubious).

1931 הִיא v. הוּא. p. 214

1959 הֵידָד v. sub הדד. p. 212

1960 **הֵידוֹת** v. sub ידה. p. 392

1961 **הָיָה**$_{3570}$ **vb. fall out, come to pass, become, be** (SI$^{1.6}$ היה, ib^{3} הית; parallel form of הוה, Ar. هَوِىَ, Aram. הֲוָא, ܗܘܐ; v. הָוָה supr.) —**Qal** *Pf.* 3 ms. הָיָה Gn 3^{1}+; וְהָיָה consec. Gn 4^{14}+; 3 fs. הָיְתָה Gn 1^{2}+; הָיָתָה Is 14^{24}+3 t.; וְהָיְתָה consec. Gn 9^{13}+; והית 2 K 9^{37} Kt (Qr וְהָיְתָה); 2 ms. הָיִיתָ Dt 5^{15}+; 1 s. הָיִיתִי Gn 31^{40}; 3 pl. הָיוּ Gn 6^{4}+; 2 mpl. הֱיִיתֶם Ex 22^{20}+; וִהְיִיתֶם consec. Gn 3^{5}+; 1 pl. הָיִינוּ Is 1^{9}+; etc.; *Impf.* 3 ms. יִהְיֶה Gn 1^{29}+; juss. יְהִי Gn 1^{3}+; יֶהִי Ez 16^{15}; וִיהִי Gn 1^{6}+; וַיְהִי Gn 1^{3}+; וַיֶּהִי ψ 33^{9} Ez 16^{19}; 3 fs. תִּהְיֶה Gn 21^{30}+; 1 s. אֶהְיֶה Ex 3^{12}+; וָאֶהְיֶה 2 S 7^{6}+9 t.; וָאֱהִי Ju 18^{4}+12 t.; 3 mpl. יִהְיוּ Gn 6^{19}+; 3 fpl. תִּהְיֶינָה Is 16^{2}+19 t.; וַתִּהְיֶינָה Gn 41^{36}+11 t.; וְתִהְיֶנָה Je 18^{21} 48^{6}; תִּהְיֶיןָ, 2 S 20^{3}+6 t.; וַתִּהְיֶיןָ Gn 26^{35} 1 S 25^{43}; וַתִּהְיֶנָה 1 Ch 7^{15}; 2 mpl. תִּהְיוּ Gn 34^{15}+; תִּהְיוּן Ex 22^{20}; 1 pl. נִהְיֶה Gn 38^{23}+; וַנִּהְיֶה 2 S 11^{23} Je 44^{17}; וַנְּהִי Nu 13^{33} Is 64^{5}, etc.; *Imv.* ms. הֱיֵה Ex 18^{19}+; fs. הֲיִי Gn 24^{60}; mpl. הֱיוּ Ex 19^{15} Nu 16^{16}, וִהְיוּ 1 S 4^{9}+6 t.; *Inf. abs.* הָיוֹ Gn 18^{18}+3 t.; הָיֹה 1 K 13^{32} Ez 1^{3}; *cstr.* הֱיוֹת Gn 2^{18}+, so rd. prob. also for הֱיֵה Ez 21^{15} cf. Sm Kö i. p. 600 f. (Co em. היה־לה to הָהֵל *shine, glitter*); with pref. בִּהְיוֹת Ex 5^{13}+, בִּהְיֹת Ex 19^{16}+; לִהְיוֹת Gn 10^{8}+, לִהְיֹת Ex 23^{1}+; sf. הֱיוֹתִי Jon 4^{2}; הֱיוֹתְךָ Ju 18$^{19.19}$; לִהְיֹתְךָ Dt 26^{19}, etc.; *Pt.* f. הוֹיָה Ex 9^{3}.

I. 1. a. *Fall out, happen* מֶה־הָיָה הַדָּבָר 1 S 4^{16} *how has the matter fallen out, (gone, turned out)?* so 2 S 1^{4}; מֶה־הָיָה לוֹ Ex 32$^{1.23}$ (both JE) *what has happened to him?* cf. 1 S 10^{12}; מִקְרֶה הוּא הָיָה לָנוּ 1 S 6^{9} *a chance it is that has befallen us;* also וַיְהִי־לוֹ כֵּן 2 K 7^{20} *and so it happened to him,* cf. וַיְהִי־כֵן infr. **b.** *occur, take place, come about, come to pass:*—מַגֵּפָה גְדוֹלָה הָיְתָה בָּעָם 1 S 4^{17} *a great slaughter has taken place among the people,* cf. 2 S 17^{9}; וַתְּהִי הַמִּלְחָמָה בְּיַעַר אֶפְרָיִם 2 S 18^{6} *and the battle took place in the wood of Ephraim* (on אפרים cf. Klo Dr); Jos 22^{17} (P; of plague); תְּהִי נָא אָלָה Gn 26^{28} (J) *let an oath take place* (be taken) so Ju 21^{5}; cf. 2 K 17^{7} (si vera l.), Ez 16^{34}; esp. late, 2 Ch 29^{36} 32^{31} Ec 1$^{9.10}$ 3^{22} 8^{7} 10^{14} etc.; oft. of fulfilment of prediction, command, expectation, etc.:—כֵּן הָיָה Gn 41^{13} (E) *so it came to pass,* 2 S 13^{25}, וַיְהִי־כֵן Ju 6^{38} 2 K 15^{12} Is 29^{5}, & esp. וַיְהִי־כֵן Gn 1$^{7.9.11.15.24.30}$ (all P)+; יְהִי כִדְבָרֶךָ Gn 30^{34} *let it be as thou sayest,* Zc 6^{15}, v. also לֹא תָקוּם וְלֹא תִהְיֶה Is 7^{7} *it shall not arise* (be realized) *& shall not come* about, 14^{34}; (so oft. בּוֹא q.v. **2 c,** p. 98 supr.) **2.** esp. & very oft., *come about, come to pass* sq. substantive (subj.) cl. almost alw. + modifying (usu. temporal) cl. or phr.: **a.** (1) וַיְהִי *and it came to pass* that, most often (c. 292 t.) foll. by (*a*) Impf. consec.: *α.* with Inf. c. בְּ temp. Gn 12^{14} 19^{17} (both J)+75 t.+Est 3^{4} Qr (Hex chiefly J,—so alw. Gn,—& JE; P only Ex 16^{10}, D only Dt 5^{20} 31^{24} Jos 5^{1} 9^{1}; 27 t. in K), —somewhat diff. is 2 K 7^{18}; *β.* with Inf. c. כְּ Gn 4^{8} 11^{2} (both J)+29 t.+Est 3^{4} Kt (in Hex 10 t. JE; 3 t. P, Gn 19^{29} Ex 34^{29} Nu 17^{7}; not in D); *γ.* with בְּ sq. nom. temp. (יוֹם, בֹּקֶר, etc.) Gn 21^{22} (E) 26^{32} (J)+45 t. (Hex 14 t. JE; 3 t. P, Ex 6^{28} 16^{13} Nu 7^{1}; not D); *δ.* לְ temp. 1 S 1^{20} 2 S 13^{23} 1 K 20^{26} 1 Ch 20^{1}; *ε.* כְּ temp. Gn 39^{11} 1 S 25^{38}; *ζ.* מִן temp. viz.: מֵאָז Gn 39^{5}, מִיּוֹם 1 S 7^{2} cf. 30^{25}, מִיָּמִים Ju 11^{4} 15^{1}, מִקֵּץ Gn 4^{3} 8^{6} +6 t., מִקְצֵה Jos 3^{2} 2 K 8^{3} Ez 3^{16}, esp. מִמָּחֳרָת Gn 19^{34} Ex 18^{13} + 11 t.; *η.* כַּאֲשֶׁר temp. Gn 12^{11} (J) 20^{13} (E)+31 t. (Hex 13 t. JE, Dt 2^{16}, not P), characteristic of Neh.'s memoirs, †Ne 3^{33} 4$^{1.6.9}$ 6$^{1.16}$ 7^{1} 13^{19}; *θ.* with כִּי temp. Gn 6^{1} (J) Ex 3^{21} (E)+14 t.+Ju 16^{25} Kt; *ι.* אַחֲרֵי temp. Gn 22^{20} (J)+13 t., אַחַר Gn 39^{7} Jb 42^{7}, אַחֲרֵי־כֵן Ju 16^{14}+6 t.; *κ.* sq. עַד temp. 1 S 14^{19} (on which cf. Dr); comp. עַד־כֹּה וְעַד־כֹּה 1 K 18^{45}; *λ.* with combinations; as בְּ c. nom. temp. + בְּ Inf. Gn 34^{25} Ex 19^{16} 1 S 25^{37}; בְּ Inf.+כְּ Inf. Jos 3^{14}; double prep. כְּמִשְׁלֹשׁ חֳדָשִׁים Gn 38^{24}; מִקְצֵה+מִיָּמִים Jos 9^{16}; אַחֲרֵי אֲשֶׁר+id. 23^{1}; *μ.* other unusual constructions under this head are: those where temporal idea is expr. by a circumst. cl. Is 22^{7} 1 K 13^{20} 2 K 8^{21} (Dr § 165, & Obs.) =2 Ch 21^{9}; those with indef. כֹּל 1 S 10^{11} 2 S 2^{23} 15^{2}, or with pt.=rel. cl. 1 S 11^{1} (on all v. Dr § 78 n. & Sm); quite unique is 1 K 16^{31}, with הֲנָקֵל לֶכְתּוֹ וגו׳ in place of temp. cl. (*b*) וַיְהִי sts. sq. simple Pf., with a negative Gn 39^{10} (c. כְּ Inf.), Ex 13^{17} (c. בְּ Inf.) 2 K 12^{7} 17^{25} (both c. בְּ temp.); & without neg., Gn 8^{13} (P) 14^{1}+, usu. c. בְּ temp. (38 t.), Hex chiefly P; rarely c. other prep. & adv. as above; note esp. מִדֵּי sq. Inf. 1 S 18^{30} 2 Ch 12^{11}; sts. the subj. of foll. Pf. precedes it c. וְ, as Gn 22^{1} 41^{1} 1 S 18^{19} 30^{1} 2 K 2^{9} 4^{40}+; note esp. 2 S 17^{27} where several subj. & also several objects precede the Pf. (cf. Dr); in these cases the temporal modifier is occasionally a circumst. cl. 2 S 13^{30} 1 K 8^{10} 2 K 19^{37}=Is 37^{38}; rarely subj. precedes Pf. without וְ 1 K 11^{4} 21^{1}, comp. subj. preceding Pt. without וְ Ne 4^{10}; in 2 Ch 8^{1} the obj. (with וְ) precedes what is appar. the principal vb. (*c*) וַיְהִי sq. וְהִנֵּה Gn 24^{15} (J; טֶרֶם in temp.

cl.), 29^{25} (E), 38^{27} (J, both בְּ temp.) v^{29} (כְּ Pt.), 1 S 13^{10} (כְּ Inf.); also 2 S 1^{2} 13^{36} 15^{32} (circumst. cl.) 2 K 2^{11} (*id.*), 3^{20}, 13^{21} (circumst. cl.). (*d*) rarely וַיְהִי (in this sense) sq. other constructions: אָז יִתֵּן 1 K 9^{10} (c. מִקְצֵה); Impf. frequentat. 14^{28} (c. מִדֵּי־בֹא), 2 K 4^{8} (c. מִדֵּי עָבְרוֹ) Je 36^{23} (c. כְּ Inf.); Pf. consec. frequentat. 2 Ch 24^{11} (c. בְּ temp.). (2) rarely also Pf. c. וְ conj. וְהָיָה (cf. Dr^{§133}) sq. Impf. consec. as subj. cl.: 1 S 1^{12} (c. several circumst. cl.), 10^{9} (c. כְּ Inf.) 2 K 3^{15} (*id.*), 1 S 17^{48} (c. כִּי), Je 37^{11} (c. בְּ Inf.), Am 7^{2} (c. אִם temp.); also Je 3^{9} (appar. c. מִן causat., but obscure); 1 S 13^{22} (c. בְּ temp.) is foll. by וְלֹא & Pf. as well as Impf. consec. **b.** less oft. וְהָיָה Pf. consec. *and it shall come to pass*, or frequentat., *came to pass* (repeatedly, etc.) usu. (*a*) sq. simple Impf. (c. 100 t.): *α.* c. בְּ temp. Dt 21^{16} 25^{19} + 37 t., (esp. בַּיּוֹם הַהוּא Ho $2^{18.23}$ Is $7^{18.21.23}$ + 21 t.); *β.* c. בְּ loc. Ez 47^{23} Zc 13^{8} cf. also Ho 2^{1} (בִּמְקוֹם אֲשֶׁר, but perh. = *instead of*, cf. VB); *γ.* c. indef. rel. cl., or its equiv. (כֹּל indef., etc.), cf. Dr$^{§121, Obs. 1}$: Gn 4^{14} Nu 17^{20} Dt 12^{11} 18^{19} Jos $7^{14.15}$ Ju 7^{4} 1 S 2^{36} 17^{25} 2 S 15^{35} 1 K 19^{17} 20^{6} Is 4^{3} 24^{18} Na 3^{7} Je 27^{8} 42^{4} Ez 47^{9} Zc 14^{17} Jo 3^{5}; *δ.* c. כַּאֲשֶׁר Nu 33^{56} Dt 28^{63} Jos 23^{15} Ju 7^{17} Is 29^{8} Je 31^{28} Zc 8^{13}; *ε.* less often with other modif. phr.: כְּ Inf. Ex $33^{8.9}$ (both frequentat.), Jos 3^{13} 8^{8} Je 25^{12} 51^{63}; בְּ Inf. Gn 9^{14} (P) 2 K 4^{10} Ez 44^{17}; אִם condit. Dt 20^{11} (+ v^{11} Dr$^{§118 n.}$), also Jos 22^{18}, where the arrangement is peculiar, & the condit. is expressed without אִם (cf. Dr^{§155}); לְ temp. Dt 23^{12}; מִקֵּץ Is 23^{17}; טֶרֶם Is 65^{24}; מִדֵּי חֹדֶשׁ בְּחָדְשׁוֹ Is 66^{23}, etc. (*b*) וְהָיָה sq. Pf. consec. (c. 85 t.): *α.* most often + cl. c. כִּי temp. Gn 12^{12} 46^{33} (both J) Ex 1^{10} (E) Dt 11^{29} Is 8^{21} + 25 t.; *β.* c. אִם Ex $4^{8.9}$ Nu 15^{24}; Dt 11^{13} + 14 t.; also Gn 38^{9} Nu 21^{9} (both frequentat.); *γ.* c. בְּ temp. Gn 30^{41} (frequentat.) 47^{24} (but cf. Ol Di) Ex 16^{5} + 11 t.; *δ.* c. indef. rel. cl. or equivalent (Dr$^{§121 Obs. 1}$): Gn 24^{14} Nu 10^{32} (Dr$^{§118 n.}$) 21^{18} Dt 21^{3} Ju 11^{31} 19^{30} Zc 14^{16}; *ε.* occas. with other modif. phr.: כַּאֲשֶׁר Gn 27^{40} +; כְּ Inf. Gn 44^{31} +; בְּ Inf. Ex 33^{22} +; מִקֵּץ 2 S 14^{26}; עֵקֶב causat. Dt 7^{12}; also (*c*) sq. וְלֹא + simple Impf. Ex 3^{21} (c. כִּי temp.). (*d*) וְהָיָה sq. *Imv.* (very rare) Dt 6^{10} (c. כִּי temp.), 1 S 10^{7} (c. כִּי), cf. 29^{10}, cf. Pf. consec. in command 1 S 3^{9} (c. אִם). (*e*) וְהָיָה sq. simple Pf. (also very rare) Dt 8^{19} (c. אִם). (*f*) וְהָיָה sq. cl. without vb.: Gn 24^{43} Jos 2^{19} 1 K 18^{24} (all c. indef. rel. modifier, or equiv., v. (*a*) *γ*, (*b*) *δ*, supr.). (*g*) וְהָיָה (ו conj.) sq. Impf. consec. v. **a.** (*e*) supr.

II. *Come into being, become*:—**1. a.** abs., in lively narrative, *arise, appear, come* וַתְּהִי צְעָקָה גְדֹלָה Ex 12^{30} (J) *and there arose a great cry* in Egypt; וַיְהִי־קוֹל Ez 1^{25} (del. Co cf. Da), 37^{7} (del. קוֹל 𝔊 Co); כִּי הָיְתָה הָרְוָחָה Ex 8^{11} (J) Pharaoh saw *that respite had come*; Mi 7^{4} *now shall come their confusion* (‖ בוא); also of concrete objects וְהָיְתָה הַקֶּשֶׁת בֶּעָנָן Gn 9^{16} (P) *and the bow shall appear in the clouds* (‖ וְנִרְאֲתָה); וְרִמָּה לֹא הָיְתָה בּוֹ Ex 16^{24} (P) *and worms did not appear in it*; of condition or action begun & continuing, as: famine Gn 12^{10} $26^{1.1}$ (all J), 41^{54} (E), Ru 1^{1} 2 S 21^{1} 2 K 6^{25}; strife Gn $13^{7.8}$ (J), Hb 1^{3} (‖ מָדוֹן יִשָּׂא); oft. of action of the elements, as the coming of hail Ex $9^{18.24.26}$ (all J), thunder & lightning, etc., Ex 19^{16} (E), rain 1 K 18^{45}, storm Jon 1^{4}; esp. of creative fiats יְהִי אוֹר וַיְהִי אוֹר Gn 1^{3} *let light appear, and light appeared*, cf. v$^{5.8.13.19.23.31}$ (all P); also *arise, come on the stage* or *scene*, וְאַחֲרָיו הָיָה שַׁמְגַּר Ju 3^{31} *and after him arose Shamgar* (= וַיָּקָם 10^{1}); further וַעֲלָטָה הָיָה Gn 15^{17} (JE) *and darkness came on*; הַבֹּקֶר הָיָה Ex 10^{13} (J) *the morning came*, 19^{16} (E); וַיְהִי הַיּוֹם †1 S 1^{4} *and the day came*, when (v. Dr), 14^{1} 2 K $4^{8.11.18}$ Jb $1^{6.13}$ 2^{1}. **b.** sq. prep.: בְּ, וְיָדֵנוּ אַל־תְּהִי־בוֹ Gn 37^{27} (J) *but our hand, let it not come upon him*, of hand of י׳ 1 S 5^{9} 7^{13} 12^{15} + (all in hostile sense); וַיְהִי בִּרְכַּת י׳ בְּכָל־אֲשֶׁר יֶשׁ־לוֹ Gn 39^{5} (J) *and the blessing of* י׳ *came into* (on) *all that he had*; but also of plague Ex 12^{13} (P); sq. עַל, וּמֵי הַמַּבּוּל הָיוּ עַל־הָאָרֶץ Gn 7^{10} (J) *that the waters of the flood came upon the earth*; עָלַי הָיוּ כֻלָּנָה Gn 42^{36} (E) Gn 9^{2} (P) *fear shall come upon*, cf. 35^{25} (P) 2 Ch 14^{13} 17^{10} 20^{29} +; of wrath Jos 22^{20} 1 K 3^{27}; so of Saul's evil spirit fr. God 1 S $16^{16.23}$ 19^{9} (אֶל); but sq. עַל also in good sense וַתְּהִי עָלָיו רוּחַ י׳ conferring strength & efficiency Ju 3^{10} 11^{29} (צלח = היה Ju 14^{6} + oft.), cf. Nu 24^{2} (JE) of prophetic power; (on וַתְּהִי עָלָיו יַד י׳ 2 K 3^{15} Ez 3^{22} and the like, vid. יָד); יַד אֱלֹהֵינוּ הָיְתָה עָלֵינוּ Ezr 8^{31}, so ψ 80^{18}; even וַתְּהִי עַל־רֹאשׁ דָּוִד 2 S 12^{30} *and it* (the crown, עֲטֶרֶת) *came* (i.e. was put, set) *on David's head*; with a diff. mng. וַנִּהְיֶה עֲלֵיהֶם עַד־פֶּתַח הַשַּׁעַר 2 S 11^{23} *and we were* close *upon them even to the gateway* (cf. We Dr); *come, go, follow* (sq. אַחֲרֵי) i.e. take the side of, adhere to, Ex 23^{2} (JE) 1 S 12^{14} 2 S 2^{10} 1 K 12^{20} 16^{21}; sq. לְ, of blessings Gn 49^{26} (poem); of judgment, punishment Je 40^{3}; esp. וַיְהִי דבר . . . אֶל *and the word of . . . came unto*: word of Samuel 1 S 4^{1}; usually word of God (or י׳) Gn 15^{1} 1 S 15^{10} +; constantly in prophets: Ho 1^{1} Mi 1^{1} etc.; esp. Je & Ez: Je 1$^{4.11.13}$ 2^{1} 13^{8}+; Ez 3^{16} 6^{1} 7^{1} 11$^{14.17.21.26}$ 12$^{1.8}$+; so also abs. הָיָה הַמַּשָּׂא הַזֶּה Is 14^{28} in the death-year of king Ahaz *came this utterance;* also sq. מִן; מַלְכֵי עַמִּים מִמֶּנָּה יִהְיוּ Gn 17^{16} (P), וּקְהַל גּוֹיִם יִהְיֶה מִמֶּךָּ 35^{11} (P), וְהָיָה אַדִּירוֹ מִמֶּנּוּ Je 30^{21} (|| מִקִּרְבּוֹ יֵצֵא); הַכֹּל הָיָה מִן־הֶעָפָר וְהַכֹּל שָׁב אֶל הֶעָפָר Ec 3^{20} *all came from the dust, & all return unto the dust;* וַיְהִי קֶצֶף גָּדוֹל מֵאֵת י׳ צְבָאוֹת Zc 7^{12}. **2.** *become:* **a.** sq. pred. noun (to be viewed as implicit accus. Dr$^{§ 161, 3 n.}$, according to the Arab. usage W$^{AG ii, § 41.44.74}$): הִוא הָיְתָה אֵם כָּל־חָי Gn 3^{20} (J) *it was she that became the mother of all living;* וַיְהִי הֶבֶל רֹעֵה צֹאן וְקַיִן הָיָה עֹבֵד אֲדָמָה 4^{2} (J) *and Abel became a shepherd of flocks, while Cain became a tiller of ground;* 2 S 8^{14} Mi 2^{11}+oft. **b.** sq. pred. adj. Gn 38^{7} Ex 36^{13}+; cf. Gn 37^{20} *let us see what his dream will become* (turn out to be, signify); **c.** *become like* (כְּ), וִהְיִיתֶם כֵּאלֹהִים Gn 3^{5} *and ye shall become like gods* cf. v^{22}, Nu 11^{1} (JE), Ho 2^{1} 7^{11} Is 9^{18} 1 K 7^{8} Zc 9^{7}+; cf. Gn 15^{5} *so* (כֹּה) *shall thy seed become;* specif. of likeness in punishment Is 1^{9} 1 S 17^{36}+; also with כְּ repeated וְהָיָה כָעָם כַּכֹּהֵן Ho 4^{9} *and the people shall become like the priest* (lit., and the like of the people shall become the like of the priest), so esp. Is 24^{2} (6 pairs of words as above); וְהָיָה כַצַּדִּיק כָּרָשָׁע Gn 18^{25} (J), v. כְּ. **b+c** Gn 27^{32} *his hands had become like the hands of Esau his brother, hairy.* **d.** sq. pred.+לְ pers. וּתְהִי אִשָּׁה לְבֶן־אֲדֹנֶיךָ Gn 24^{51} (J) *and let her become wife to the son of thy lord,* 1 S 16^{21} 1 K 11^{25} ψ 89^{42} 1 Ch 18^{6}+; = *be instituted, established,* וְהָיְתָה לָהֶם חָק־עוֹלָם Ex 30^{21} (P) *and it shall be established for them as a perpetual ordinance* (cf. **f** infr.). **e.** sq. לְ pred.: וַיְהִי הָאָדָם לְנֶפֶשׁ חַיָּה Gn 2^{7} (J) *and the man became a living soul;* וְהָיָה לְאַרְבָּעָה רָאשִׁים Gn 2^{10} (J) *and it became four heads;* גַּם־הוּא יִהְיֶה־לְּעָם Gn 48^{19} (J) *he too shall become a people;* וִהְיוּ לַאֲנָשִׁים 1 S 4^{9} *and become* (shew yourselves to be) *men* (|| הִתְחַזְּקוּ; cf. with double לְ, **f** infr.); Zp 1^{13} Ez 17^{6} 47^{12} Jb 16^{8}; וְהָיָה י׳ לְמֶלֶךְ עַל־כָּל־הָאָרֶץ Zc 14^{9}; וַיְהִי לְמַס עֹבֵד +Gn 49^{15} Jos 16^{10}; so oft.; also in sense of *turn into,* be changed so as to become, וַיְהִי לְנָחָשׁ Ex 4^{3} *and it became a serpent,* v^{4} 7^{10} Is 1^{22} Dt 26^{5}+; fig. וַיְהִי לְמָיִם Jos 7^{5} *and it* (their heart) *turned to water,* so וְהוּא הָיָה לְאָבֶן 1 S 25^{37}; or, *serve as* וְהָיוּ לִמְאוֹרֹת Gn 1^{15} (P) *and they shall become* (fulfil the function of, serve as) *luminaries,* cf. v^{14}; וְהָיְתָה לְאוֹת בְּרִית Gn 9^{13} 17^{11} (both P). **f.** oft. c. לְ pred.+לְ pers.: וַתְּהִי לָהֶם הַלְּבֵנָה לְאָבֶן Gn 11^{3} (J) *and the bricks became* (served as) *stone for them;* וַתְּהִי לִי לְאִשָּׁה Gn 20^{12} (E) cf. 24^{67} (J)+, וַתִּהְיֶינָה מַחְלָה וְחָגְלָה . . . לִבְנֵי דֹדֵיהֶן לְנָשִׁים Nu 36^{11}; וְהָיָה לְךָ וְלָהֶם לְאָכְלָה 6^{21} (P), Ex 2^{10} 15^{2} Ju 8^{27}; וְהָיָה י׳ לִי לֵאלֹהִים Gn 28^{21} (E); אֲנִי אֶהְיֶה לּוֹ לְאָב וְהוּא יִהְיֶה־לִּי לְבֵן 1 Ch 17^{3}+; = *shew or prove oneself as* הֱיֵה־לִי לְבֶן־חַיִל 1 S 18^{17} *shew thyself for me a valiant man* (cf. 1 S 4^{9} **e** supr.); = *be instituted, established* (cf. **e** supr.) וְהָיְתָה לְאַהֲרֹן וּלְבָנָיו לְחָק־עוֹלָם Ex 29^{28} *and it shall be instituted for Aaron and his sons as a perpetual ordinance;* cf. v^{9} Lv 10^{15}; וְהָיְתָה לִהְיֹת לָהֶם מָשְׁחָתָם לִכְהֻנַּת עוֹלָם לְדֹרֹתָם Ex 40^{15} (all P). **g.** with עַל and לְ 1 S 22^{2} וַיְהִי עֲלֵיהֶם לְשָׂר *and he became over them prince.* **h.** sts. c. לְ pers. only = *become the property of, come into the possession of* וַיְהִי־לוֹ צֹאן־וּבָקָר וגו׳ Gn 12^{16} (J), *and he came to have flocks and herds* etc., 26^{14} 30^{43}; לֹא לוֹ יִהְיֶה הַזָּרַע Gn 38^{9} *not his should the seed become;* וְהָיָה לַי׳ Ju 11^{31} *it shall become Yahweh's;* Dt 10^{9} Jos 13^{29} 1 K 10^{26} 11^{3}+oft.; so of a woman, as wife תְּהִי־נָא לְךָ Ju 15^{2} *pray let her become thine,* cf. also וַתְּהִי אֵשֶׁת שִׁמְשׁוֹן לְמֵרֵעֵהוּ 14^{20}, Ho 3^{3} Ru 1^{13} Lv 21^{3} Dt 24^{2} Je 3^{1} Ez 16^{8} (and also + לְאִשָּׁה, לְנָשִׁים v. **f** supr.)

III. *Be* (often with subordinate idea of becoming);—**1.** *exist, be in existence* (i.e. orig. *have come into existence*), כָּל־הַיָּמִים אֲשֶׁר הָיָה 1 S 1^{28} *all the days which he shall have been* (lived, = חַי Gn 5^{5} etc., cf. Dr^{Sm}), Jb 3^{16}, Is 23^{13}; oft. c. בְּ loc. וְכֹל שִׂיחַ הַשָּׂדֶה טֶרֶם יִהְיֶה בָאָרֶץ Gn 2^{5} (J) *and there was not yet in the earth any shrub of the field;* וּבְאֵלֶּה לֹא הָיָה אִישׁ וגו׳ Nu 26^{64} (P) *and among them there was not a man to be found,* etc.; also וְלֹא הָיָה כַּיּוֹם הַהוּא לְפָנָיו וְאַחֲרָיו Jos 10^{14} (JE) *& there hath not been a day like that before it nor since,* cf. 2 S 14^{25} 1 K 18^{5} 21^{25} 23^{25} Ne 13^{26}+; somewhat weaker, in the freq. introductory clause וַיְהִי אִישׁ *now there was a man* Ju 13^{2} 1 S 1^{1} 9^{1} Nu 9^{6} (P), Jb 1^{1}+; on אֶהְיֶה אֲשֶׁר אֶהְיֶה Ex 3^{14} v. יהוה. **2.** *abide, remain, continue* (with word of place or time) וַיְהִי מֹשֶׁה בָּהָר Ex 24^{18} *and Moses remained in the mount* forty days, etc., so 34^{28} (both JE), Ju 17$^{4.12}$ 1 S 6^{1} 1 K 11^{20} 2 K 11^{3}=2 Ch 22^{12}+; also Lv 22^{27} 25^{28} (both H), etc.; sq. עַד temp. *remain until* Dt 22^{2} 1 K 11^{40} 2 K 15^{5} 2 Ch 5^{9} 26^{21} Dn 1^{21} etc.; cf. הוּא יִהְיֶה לְעוֹלָם Ec 3^{14}; so also of space sq. עַד *extend unto, as far as,* Jos 19^{10}: of net beneath altar, Ex 27^{5} *shall reach as far as* (עַד) *the middle of the altar.* **3.** with word of locality, *be in* or *at a place, be situated, stand, lie;* בִּהְיוֹתָם בַּשָּׂדֶה Gn 4^{8} (J) *when they were in the field,* הַמָּקוֹם אֲשֶׁר־הָיָה שָׁם אָהֳלֹה בַּתְּחִלָּה 13^{3} (J) *the place where his tent had stood at first;* וְהָאָרֶץ תִּהְיֶה לִפְנֵיכֶם 34^{10} *and the land, it lieth before you;* cf. Jos 19^{1} Ju $7^{1.8}$ Mi $5^{6.7}$; sq. עַל *be, be found or situated upon* Is 30^{25} *and there shall be upon every high mountain* etc., *streams, water-courses;* Ez 37^{27} *and my dwelling-place shall be over them;* fig. of guilt וְהָיָה עָלֶיךָ דָּמִים Dt 19^{10} *and blood* (-guilt) *be upon thee.* **4.** as copula, joining subj. & pred.:—**a.** sq. pred. adj. וַיִּהְיוּ שְׁנֵיהֶם עֲרוּמִּים Gn 2^{25}, וְהַנָּחָשׁ הָיָה עָרוּם 3^{1}, בִּהְיוֹתָם כֹּאֲבִים 34^{25}, וַיְהִי יוֹסֵף יְפֵה־תֹאַר 39^{6}; Dt 23^{15} Jos 19^{9} Ju 11^{1} Jb $1^{1.3b}$ 2 Ch 7^{21}. **b.** sq. pred. noun Gn 1^{2} 9^{18} 25^{3} 36^{14} 40^{13} 1 S $17^{34.42}$ 2 S 8^{10} 20^{25} 1 K 10^{6} 2 K 3^{4} $5^{1.1}$ 1 Ch 9^{20} 11^{20} 18^{10} 26^{10} 2 Ch 13^{7}; כִּי לֹא־הָיָה מֶלֶךְ יִשְׂרָאֵל 2 Ch 18^{32} (|| 1 K 22^{33} כִּי־לֹא־מֶלֶךְ ישׂראל הוּא)+; oft. of age: וַיְהִי אַבְרָם בֶּן־תִּשְׁעִים שָׁנָה וְתֵשַׁע שָׁנִים Gn 17^{1} (P) 2 K 8^{17} 14^{2} $15^{2.33}$ 18^{2} 2 Ch 21^{20} 27^{8}+; sq. pred. Inf. abs. (very anomal.) וְהַמַּיִם הָיוּ הָלוֹךְ וְחָסוֹר Gn 8^{5};=*amount to, come to,* in enum. of days of life, number of people, amounts of money, etc.: Gn $5^{4.5.8.11.14}$ 9^{29} 11^{32} 23^{1}+; Ex 38^{24} Nu 1^{46}, etc. **c.** sq. adv. & adverbial phr.: לֹא־טוֹב הֱיוֹת הָאָדָם לְבַדּוֹ Gn 2^{18} (J) *it is not good that the man be alone;* חָדַל לִהְיוֹת לְשָׂרָה אֹרַח כַּנָּשִׁים 18^{11} (J). **d.** sq. prep.: (*a*) *be with, accompany* c. עִם, subj. most oft. י׳ or אלהים with added idea of protection, aid Gn 26^{3} 31^{3} 39^{10} 48^{21} Jos 1^{3} 6^{27} Ju 1^{19} 2^{18} 1 S 3^{19} 18^{12} 20^{13} 1 K 1^{37} 1 Ch 11^{13} 2 Ch 17^{3}; sq. עִמָּדִי Gn 28^{20} 31^{5} 35^{3}; sq. עִם, human subj., of accompaniment וְהָיָה הַכֹּהֵן בֶּן־אַהֲרֹן עִם־הַלְוִיִּם Ne 10^{39}; 1 Ch 11^{12}, rd. also in || 2 S 23^{9} (Th We Dr);=*be on the side of* 1 K 1^{8}; c. עִם also=*be near* וּמַלְאַךְ י׳ הָיָה עִם־גֹּרֶן האורנה 2 S 24^{16} (cf. Dr); also 2 S 13^{20} implying sexual intercourse, so Gn 39^{10} (perh. gloss, cf. Di); peculiar uses with עִם are: וּדְבַר־אַבְנֵר הָיָה עִם־זִקְנֵי יִשְׂרָאֵל 2 S 3^{17} *and the speech of A. had been with the elders of Isr.,* cf. 1 K 1^{7}; וַיְהִי עִם־לְבַב דָּוִד אָבִי לִבְנוֹת 1 K 8^{17} *and it was with* (i.e. in) *the heart of David my father to build,* =2 Ch 6^{7} cf. 1 K $8^{18.18}$ 1 Ch 22^{7} 2 Ch $6^{8.8}$ 24^{4}; also 1 K 10^{2}=2 Ch 9^{1}; (*b*) *be with,* sq. אֶת, subj. י׳, אלהים, Gn 21^{20} $39^{2.21}$ but also c. human subj. וּבָנָיו הָיוּ אֶת־מִקְנֵהוּ Gn 34^{5}, cf. 1 S 29^{3}+; (*c*) sq. לְ of possessor כֶּרֶם הָיָה לִידִידִי Is 5^{1} *a vine-yard had my beloved,* Gn 30^{30} cf. Ex 20^{3}=Dt 5^{7}, Ju 18^{27} 1 S 9^{2} 1 K 5^{6}+oft. (cf. I. **2 d, f, h**); (*d*) sq. לְ+other prep.: of boundary וַיְהִי לָהֶם הַגְּבוּל מֵעֲרוֹעֵר Jos 13^{16}, cf. וַיְהִי גְבוּלָם מִמַּחֲנַיִם v^{30}; וַיְהִי לָהֶם הַגְּבוּל לִפְאַת צָפוֹנָה מִיַּרְדֵּן 18^{12}, etc.; (*e*) sq. בְּ *be among,* or *of,* Am 1^{1} *who was* one *of the herdsmen,* 1 K 2^{7} *let them be among those eating,* Pr 22^{26} 23^{20}. **5.** periphrastic conjug.: **a.** היה+pt., of continuous state, or condition, sts., esp. late (cf. NH), of habit, c. וַיְהִי also of beginning and continuance (cf. Dr$^{§135,(5)}$): pt. act. Gn 39^{22} (J), Ex 3^{1} (E), 1 S 2^{11} 7^{10} 18^{9} (cf. Dr) v$^{14.29}$ 2 S 8^{15}=1 Ch 18^{14}, Dt 28^{29} Is 30^{20} 1 K $5^{1.15.24}$ 2 K 6^{5} 9^{14} 2 Ch 9^{26} Ezr 4^{4} Ne 1^{4} 2^{13} Dn 1^{16}+; Gn 1^{6} (P); הָיָה יָרֵא אֶת־י׳ 1 K 18^{3} 2 K 4^{1} 2 Ch 26^{1}; pt. pass. Jos 10^{26} 1 K 13^{24} 22^{35} וְהַמֶּלֶךְ הָיָה מָעֳמָד בַּמֶּרְכָּבָה (|| 2 Ch 18^{34} הָיָה מַעֲמִיד), Is 2^{2}=Mi 4^{1}, וְהָיָה סָגוּר Ez 44^{2}, ה׳ נַעֲשָׂה Ne 5^{18}, וְאָהוּב לֵאלֹהָיו ה׳ 13^{26};—on 2 S 13^{32} cf. Dr. **b.** sq. Inf. c. לְ (Dr$^{§203, 204}$): וְהָיָה לְבָעֵר Is 5^{5} *and it shall be to burn* (is to be, is destined to be burned) etc.; וַיְהִי הַשֶּׁמֶשׁ לָבוֹא Gn 15^{12} *and the sun was about to set;* וַיְהִי הַשַּׁעַר לִסְגּוֹר Jos 2^{5} *and the gate was about to be shut;* but also וַיְהִי לִדְרֹשׁ אֱלֹהִים 2 Ch 26^{5} (nearly =וַיְהִי+Pt.) †**Niph.** *Pf.* נִהְיָה 1 K 1^{27}+6 t.+Mi 2^{4} (cf. infr. ad fin.); 3 fs. נִהְיְתָה Ju 19^{30}+5 t., נִהְיָתָה Ex 11^{6} Je 48^{19}, וְנִהְיָתָה consec. Ez 39^{8}+21^{12} (del. B Codd 𝔊 Co); 2 ms. נִהְיֵיתָ Dt 27^{9}; 1 s. נִהְיֵיתִי Dn 8^{27}; *Pt.* fs. נִהְיָה Pr 13^{19};—**1.** either, *be done, be brought about,* or *occur, come to pass:* in the strong expressions אֲשֶׁר כָּמֹהוּ לֹא נ׳ וְכָמֹהוּ לֹא תֹסִף Ex 11^{6} (J) a cry *such as hath not occurred* (been raised), *and will not be again,* cf. Dt 4^{32} (*be done;* || נִשְׁמַע), & Ju 19^{30} (|| נִרְאֲתָה);—but simply intrans. Jo 2^{2} Dn 12^{1} & appar. Ez 21^{12} (|| בָּאָה; on txt., however, v. supr.) 39^{8} (|| *id.*);—also אֵיכָה נִהְיְתָה הָרָעָה הַזֹּאת Ju 20^{3} *how hath this wickedness been done?* cf. v^{12} Je 5^{30} 48^{19} also Ne 6^{8}; c. לֹא, existence denied לֹא נ׳ Zc 8^{10} (|| אֵינֶנָּה); in all the above (exc. Jo 2^{2} Dn 12^{1} & Ez 21^{12} 39^{8}) personal agency is clearly implied; it is expressed מֵאֵת אֲדֹנִי הַמֶּלֶךְ נ׳ הַדָּבָר הַזֶּה 1 K 1^{27}, so of divine agency (מֵאִתִּי) 1 K 12^{24}=2 Ch 11^{4}; further *be attained, secured,* of wages Zc 8^{10} (c. לֹא, || אֵינֶנָּה); תַּאֲוָה נִהְיָה Pr 13^{19} *a desire come to pass, realized.* **2.** *be done, finished, gone,* only Dn וּשְׁנָתוֹ נִהְיְתָה עָלָיו Dn 2^{1} *and his sleep was finished upon him,* i.e. left him (cf. Aram. Dn 6^{19}); נִהְיֵיתִי 8^{27} *I came to an end, was exhausted* (si vera l., del. 𝔊; || נֶחֱלֵיתִי);

נִהְיָה, in וְנָהָה נְהִי נִהְיָה Mi 2[4], is dub.; *it is done, over, the ruin is come* RobGes Ew Hi Ca Che RVm; ? < om. as dittogr. Sta[ZAW 1886, 122 f.] cf. JBL[1890, 74.77].

1962 †[הַיָּה] **n.f.** only הַיָּתִי Jb 6[2] Kt v. הַוָּה. p. 217

1963 †הֵיךְ **adv.** *how?* (הֵיךְ, ܐܝܟ, *id.*, in Palest. Aram., as Jb 21[34] 𝔗, Gn 3[9] Dt 1[12] 𝔗[Ps.-J.], Mat 22[12] 𝔖[Jerus.] (though usu. these words have the force of *as*), and in הֵיכְדֵין *how, then?* ψ 73[11] + 𝔗; cf. Bevan[Dan. p. 29])—only twice, in late Heb., 1 Ch 13[12] (‖ 2 S 6[9] אֵיךְ), Dan 10[17].

1964 †הֵיכָל **n.m.**[Na 2, 7] (on Is 44[28] cf. Che Di) **palace, temple** (v. also NH *id. temple*, Aram. הֵיכְלָא, הֵיכָלָא, ܗܝܟܠܐ, *palace, temple*, Palm. הכלא *temple* Vog[16]; cf. Ar. هَيْكَل (prob. Aram. loan-wd. acc. to Frä[274]), Eth. **ሀይከል፡** *temple;* As. *ekallu, palace, temple;*—prob. loan-wd. fr. Akk. *e-gal, great house,* cf. Schr[HI 148] COT 2 K 20[18] Hpt[E-vowel 11 f.] Lehmann[Šamaššumukîn 126], and on usage Dl[338]; > fr. יכל (וכל) = כול *contain* Ew[§ 162 b] Thes Add[84]; cf. Ol[§ 191 b] Hoffm[AGG xxxvi. Mai 1889, 25] Dl[W]; fr. an orig. יכל Lag[BN 121], but cf. Hom[ZMG 1890, 547]) abs. ה׳ Am 8[3] + 27 t. (הה׳ 1 K 6[17] +); cstr. הֵיכַל Mi 1[2] + 35 t.; sf. הֵיכָלֶךָ ψ 48[10] + 2 t.; הֵיכָלוֹ Je 50[28] + 7 t.; pl. הֵיכָלוֹת Ho 8[14]; cstr. הֵיכְלֵי Is 13[22] + 2 t.; sf. הֵיכְלֵיכֶם Jo 4[5];—never in Hex, rarely in S & pre-exil. prophets; esp. freq. in Ki Ez & late proph., also Chr; occasionally in ψ;—**1.** rather seld. (royal) *palace* (so alm. always in As.); of Ahab 1 K 21[1], of king of Babylon 2 K 20[18] = Is 39[17], 2 Ch 36[7], cf. Dn 1[4], and pl. הֵיכְלֵי עֹנֶג Is 13[22] *luxurious palaces;* at Nineveh וְהַה׳ נָמוֹג Na 2[7]; not clearly defined are הֵיכַל מֶלֶךְ ψ 45[16] and הֵיכְלֵי שֵׁן v[9]; הֵיכָלוֹת Ho 8[14] (in N. Israel); vid. also וְהֵילִילוּ שִׁירוֹת הֵיכָל בַּיּוֹם הַהוּא Am 8[3] *and palace-songs shall be howlings in that day;* cf. also (prob.) of Phœnician palaces Jo 4[5]; quite general הֵיכְלֵי מֶלֶךְ Pr 30[28], & תַּבְנִית הֵיכָל ψ 144[12] (sim. of well-proportioned daughters);—usual term for royal palace in Heb. is בֵּית הַמֶּלֶךְ, v. בית. **2.** of palace of God considered as king, = *house of God* or *of* י׳, *temple* (cf. הה׳ Is 6[1] **e** infr. where proph. sees אדני ישֵׁב עַל־כִּסֵּא): **a.** of early, pre-Solomonic house at Shiloh פֶּתַח אֹהֶל מוֹעֵד 1 S 1[9] 3[3] (= בֵּית י׳ 1[7] 3[15]; הֵיכַל י׳ 2[22] om. 𝔊 We Klo Dr) with doors (דלתות, 3[15]) & a doorpost (מזוזה 1[9]) (cf. 2 S 22[7] = ψ 18[7] **e** infr.). **b.** of Solomon's temple: specif. the *hall* or *nave* of the temple (the holy place, distinguished from the דְּבִיר the inner sanctuary, the Holy of Holies, and with this included in the more general term בֵּית י׳ or הַבַּיִת, 1 K 6[1.2] + oft.) 1 K 6[17] (cf. v[19.20] & v[2]) also v[5.33] 1 K 7[50] = 2 Ch 4[22]; further 2 Ch 4[7.8] Ez 8[16.16] הָאוּלָם עַל־פְּנֵי הֵיכַל הַבַּיִת 1 K 6[3]; אֻלָם הַהֵיכָל 1 K 7[21] ‖ עַל־פְּנֵי הַהֵיכָל 2 Ch 3[17]; הֵיכַל י׳ 2 K 18[16]; also in wide sense (appar. = בֵּית י׳), הֵיכַל י׳ 2 K 23[4] 24[13] (‖ בֵּית י׳), Je 7[4.4.4] (‖ בֵּית י׳ v[2]), 24[1] v. also נִקְמַת הֵיכָלוֹ Je 50[28] 51[11] (both ‖ נִקְמַת י׳); 2 Ch 26[16] 27[2], cf. 29[16] (‖ פְּנִימָה בֵית י׳; opp. חֲצַר ב׳ י׳), in all three הֵיכַל י׳. **c.** *hall* or *nave* of Ezek.'s temple, the holy place (v. supr.) (included in הַבַּיִת, the general term embracing the whole group of buildings) Ez 41[1.4.15.21.23.25] (cf. v[20]) 42[8]. **d.** general designation of *2nd temple,* הֵיכַל י׳ Zc 8[9] (‖ בֵּית י׳ צְבָאוֹת); oftener הַהֵיכָל Hg 2[15.18] Zc 6[12.13.14.15] Ezr 3[6.10], הֵיכָלוֹ Mal 3[1] ψ 27[4]; (הַ)הֵיכָל Ezr 4[1]; בּוֹנִים הֵיכָל ליהוה אֱלֹהֵי יִשְׂרָאֵל Ne 6[10.10] (‖ בֵּית הָאֱלֹהִים), v[11]; Is 44[28], cf. also 66[6].—הֵיכָל occurs occasionally in ψ, without conclusive evidence, in all cases, to what temple ref. is had; appar. distinguished fr. בֵּית י׳ (as sub **b**) ψ 5[8] (הֵיכַל קָדְשְׁךָ; v. בֵּיתֶךָ v[7]); perhaps also ψ 68[30] (disting. from Holy of Holies by De Che; yet verse obscure); but no distinction evident ψ 79[1] 138[2] Jon 2[5.8] (all הֵיכַל קָדְשֶׁךָ); cf. קְדשׁ הֵיכָלֶךָ ψ 65[5] (‖ בֵּיתֶךָ); as containing the worshipping assembly ψ 48[10]. **e.** of the heavenly temple where י׳ sits enthroned Is 6[1]; his abode in the heavens 2 S 22[7] = ψ 18[7], ψ 11[4] (‖ שָׁמַיִם; cf. זְבֻל קָדְשׁוֹ Is 63[15], ‖ *id.*), 29[9]; אֲדֹנָי מֵהֵיכַל קָדְשׁוֹ Mi 1[2], cf. Hb 2[20] ויהוה בְּהֵיכַל קָדְשׁוֹ.

הֵילֵל Is 14[12] v. sub הלל. p. 237 1966

הִים v. הוּם. p. 223 1949

הֵימָם **n.pr.** v. הוֹמָם sub המם. p. 243 1967

הֵימָן **n.pr.** v. אמן. p. 54 1968

†הִין **n.m.**[Lv 19, 36] **hin,** a liquid measure (𝔊 εἶν (ἴν; 𝔊L ἵν); but χοῦς Lv 19[36]; Gk. ἴνιον, Egypt. measure, = *sextarius,* acc. to Böckh[Metrol. Unters. 244] cf. Brandis[Münz- Mass- & Gewichtswesen 29, 30]; the Heb. hin (6.06 litres) was, however, much larger than the Egypt. hin (0.456 litre), v. Hultsch[Metrol., Tab. xxi. p. 714, & pp. 368, 450 ff.]; v. further Ri[HWB] Smith[Dict. Bib.] E. Meyer[Gesch. i. 228])—abs. הִין Ex 30[24] + 4 t. Ez 45, 46; הַהִין Ex 29[40.40] + 14 t.; cstr. הִין Lv 19[36];—**1.** a measure, used of quantity of water for drinking Ez 4[11]; usually in connexion with offerings: **a.** of oil used with meal-offering Ex 29[40] Nu 15[4.6.9] 28[5] 1969

(all P), Ez 45^{24} $46^{5.6.11.14}$;—usually $\frac{1}{4}$ hin to $\frac{1}{10}$ ephah (of meal-offering); Nu 15^{6} $\frac{1}{3}$; v^{9} $\frac{1}{2}$; in Ez a (whole) hin, exc. 46^{14} $\frac{1}{3}$ hin to $\frac{1}{6}$ ephah. **b.** used in mixing the anointing oil Ex 30^{24}. **c.** of wine as drink-offering Lv 23^{13} (H); elsewh. P, Ex 29^{40} Nu 15^{5} 28^{14} (all $\frac{1}{4}$ hin) 15^{7} 28^{14} (both $\frac{1}{3}$ hin), 15^{10} 28^{14} (both $\frac{1}{2}$ hin; all with $\frac{1}{10}$ to $\frac{3}{10}$ ephah in case of meal-offering). **d.** once of שֵׁכָר as drink-offering Nu 28^{7} (P; $\frac{1}{4}$ hin; cf. Di). **2.** vessel with capacity of hin Lv 19^{36} (H) הִין־צֶדֶק *a just hin* (‖ אַבְנֵי־צ׳, מֹאזְנֵי צ׳, אֵיפַת צ׳).—The hin $=\frac{1}{6}$ bath acc. to Joseph. Ant. iii. 8, 3; 9, 4, = 6.06 litres (Hultsch$^{l.c.}$), v. II. בַּת. On order of words in above passages, note that הִין (רְבִיעִת ה׳ etc.) is usually appos. of liquid measured, & either precedes it Ex 29^{40} Nu 15^{4} 28^{14}, or, more oft., follows it Ex 30^{24} + 10 t.; Nu 28^{7} they are in diff. clauses; in Ex 29^{40} we find רֶבַע הַהִין ... בְּשֶׁמֶן, cf. Nu $15^{6.9}$ 28^{5};—Nu 28^{14} is peculiar: וְנִסְכֵּיהֶם חֲצִי הַהִין יִהְיֶה לַפָּר וּשְׁלִישִׁת הַהִין לָאַיִל וּרְבִיעִת הַהִין לַכֶּבֶשׂ יָיִן (יין only at end).

1970 †[הָכַר] **vb.** only **Qal** or **Hiph.** (Ges$^{§ 53 R. 4}$ Kö$^{i. 251}$) *Impf.* 2 mpl. תַּהְכְּרוּ in phrase לֹא־תֵבֹשׁוּ תַּהְכְּרוּ־לִי Jb 19^{3}, sense very dubious; Schult Thes De al. (as Hiph.) *ye cause me* (לִ=acc.) *to wonder* (cf. Ar. هَكِرَ); others (as Qal) *ye deal hardly with, wrong me* (so context seems rather to require, v. Ges in Add^{84} RobGes Ew Di Da RV; cf. Ar. حَكَرَ *wrong, detract from;* Codd. rd. תחכרו, which is preferable, if this mng. be adopted; 𝔊 ἐπίκεισθέ μοι, 𝔙 *opprimentes*); conjectures are תַּחְרְפוּ Ol^{Hiob}; תַּחַבְרוּ אֵלָי Me; Siegf תִּתְחַבְּרוּ.

1971 הַכָּרַת Is 3^{9} v. נכר. p. 648

1973 הַל Dt 32^{6} v. sub הֲ p. 210 supr.

1972 הָלְאָ v. sub foll.

1973 †הָלְאָה (i.e. *hā-le'āh*, the final *-āh*, the ה *locale*, being toneless), **adv. out there, onwards, further** (𝔗 הָלְאָ, always with לְ or מֵ prefixed; Syr. ܠܗܿܠ, ܠܗܿܠ PS^{1009} *id.*; Ar. هَلَا *forward! on!* Fl$^{Kl. Schr. i. 355}$)—**a.** of *place* Gn 19^{9} גֶּשׁ־הָלְאָה *approach out there!* i.e. *make way, get back* (𝔊 ἀπόστα ἐκεῖ: 𝔙 *recede illuc*), Nu 17^{2} and the fire זְרֵה־הָלְאָה scatter *yonder;* מֵהָלְאָה לְ *beyond* (lit. *off the yonder side of;* v. מִן **4 c**) Gn 35^{21} Je 22^{19} Am 5^{27} *beyond* Damascus: וָהָלְאָה attached to an indication of place, to mark direction, 1 S 10^{3} and thou shalt pass on מִשָּׁם וָהָלְאָה thence *and onwards;* 20^{22} מִמְּךָ וָהָלְאָה from thee *and onwards* i.e. beyond thee (opp. to מִמְּךָ וָהֵנָּה v^{21}), v^{37} Nu 32^{19} on the side of Jordan *forwards* (opp. to 'on the side of Jordan eastwards'). **b.** of *time*, Lv 22^{27} from the 8th day וָהָלְאָה *and onwards*, Nu 15^{23} 1 S 18^{9} מהיום ההוא והלאה from that day *and onwards*, Ez 39^{22} 43^{27} Is $18^{2.7}$. Hence

†[הָלָא] **vb.denom.** only **Ni. ptcp.** *fem.* Mi 4^{7} הַנַּהֲלָאָה (of sheep) **removed far off.** 1972

†הַלָּז **pron.comm. this**, a rare synonym of זֶה or הַזֶּה, *this* (Ar. اَلَّذِى (also اَلَّذْ), pl. اَلَّذِينَ, *who, which* (cf. זֶה, which is used also sts. as rel.), formed from اَلْ the def. art., and the pron. ذَا, זֶה, זוּ, with the insertion of the demonstr. element *la*, and thus in fact=הַזֶּה: W$^{AG i. § 347, CG p. 117}$)—usually with a subst. defined by the art., Ju 6^{20} הַסֶּלַע הַלָּז *this* rock, 1 S 14^{1} מֵעֵבֶר הַלָּז off *this* side-across, 17^{26} אֶת־הַפְּלִשְׁתִּי הַלָּז, (+ 20^{19} 𝔊 Th We Dr τὸ ἐργαβ ἐκεῖνο, i.e. הָאַרְגֹּב הַלָּז (or הַלָּאז) *this* mound (*or* cairn), for האבן האזל) 2 K 23^{17} Zc 2^{8}; with a *fem.*, 2 K 4^{25} הַשּׁוּנַמִּית הַלָּז: without a subst. Dn 8^{16} לְהַלָּז to *this one* (=normal לָזֶה). The fuller form is 1975

†הַלָּזֶה Gn 24^{65} הָאִישׁ הַלָּזֶה, 37^{19} בַּעַל הַחֲלֹמוֹת הַלָּזֶה *this* dreamer (contemptuously). Once also there occurs 1976

†הַלֵּזוּ Ez 36^{35} (*fem.*) הָאָרֶץ הַלֵּזוּ. 1977

הלחות Je 48^{5} Kt v. לוּחִית. p. 532 3872

הָלַךְ 1545 **vb.** go, come, walk (MI ואהלך, 1980, 3212
לך; SI וילכו; NH הָלַךְ (rare), Aram. הֲלַךְ, הַךְ (also BAram.), oftener הַלֵּיךְ Pa., ܗܰܠܶܟ, Palm. Ithp. אתילכא Vog$^{No. 15, l. 4}$; As. *alâku* Dl^{W}; also Ar. هَلَكَ *perish*)—**Qal** *Pf.* 3 ms. ה׳ Gn 26^{26}+; הָלַךְ 2 S 8^{6}+; 3 pl. הָלְכוּ Gn 14^{24}+; (הָ)הָלְכוּא Jos 10^{24} (Ges$^{§ 23, 3; 138, 3 b}$ Kö$^{i. 414 f.}$), etc.; *Impf.* rarely **a.** 3 ms. יַהֲלֹךְ Je 9^{3} + 4 t. Jb ψ; וַיַּהֲלֹךְ Jb 14^{20}; 3 fs. תִּהֲלַךְ ψ 73^{9}; וַתִּהֲלַךְ Ex 9^{23} (Ew$^{§ 138 b}$ Ges$^{§ 69, R. 8}$ Kö$^{i. 415}$); 1 s. אֶהֱלֹךְ Jb 16^{22} 23^{8} (cf. MI$^{14.15}$); יַהַלְכוּ Jb 41^{11}; usually **b.** (629 t.) as if fr. ילך (ולך; vid. **Hiph.** Ges$^{§ 69, 2 R. 8}$ Kö$^{i. 414 ff.}$ Prät$^{ZAW 1882, 310 ff.}$; cf. also יָלַד etc.) 3 ms. יֵלֵךְ Ex 10^{24}+; יֵלֶךְ Ec 5^{15}+; וְיֵלֵךְ Jb 27^{21}; יֵלֶךְ־ Ex 34^{9}+; וַיֵּלֶךְ Gn $12^{4.4}$ + 210 t., וַיֵּלַךְ Gn 24^{61} + 6 t.; 3 fs. תֵּלֵךְ Gn 24^{39} תֵּלֶךְ ψ 97^{3}; וַתֵּלֶךְ Gn 7^{18}+; 2 ms. תֵּלֵךְ etc. Gn 3^{14}+; 2 fs. תֵּלְכִי etc. Ju $4^{8.8}$+;

1 s. אֵלֵךְ Ex 3[11] +; וָאֵלֵךְ Ju 19[18] +; וָאֵלֵךְ Jb 19[10]; אֵלְכָה Gn 45[28] +, אֵילְכָה Mi 1[8]; 3 mpl. יֵלְכוּ Ex 5[7] +; יֵלֵכוּן ψ 89[31] + 2 t.; וַיֵּלְכוּ Gn 9[23] (וילכו also SI[4]) +; 3 fpl. תֵּלַכְנָה Ju 11[40] +; 2 mpl. תֵּלְכוּ Gn 42[38] +; תֵּלְכוּן Dt 6[14]; תֵּלֵכוּן Ex 3[21] Is 52[12]; 2 fpl. תֵּלַכְנָה Ru 1[11]; 1 pl. נֵלֵךְ Ex 8[23] +; וַנֵּלֶךְ Dt 1[19], etc.; *Imv.* rarely **a.** הֲלוֹךְ Pr 13[20] (Kt.; Qr הֹלֵךְ, cf. De Now); mpl. הִלְכוּ Je 51[50]; usu. **b.** (241 t.) ms. לֵךְ Gn 26[16] + (לך also MI[14]), לֶךְ־ Gn 27[9] +; לְכָה Gn 19[32] +; לְךָ Nu 23[13] Ju 19[13] 2 Ch 25[17]; לְכָה 1 S 23[27]; fs. לְכִי Ju 9[10] +; mpl. לְכוּ Gn 37[20] +; fpl. לֵכְנָה Ru 1[8], לֵכְןָ Ru 1[12], etc.; *Inf. abs.* הָלוֹךְ Gn 8[3] +; הָלֹךְ Gn 31[30] +; *cstr.* rarely **a.** הֲלֹךְ Ex 3[19] + 4 t.; הֲלָךְ־ Ec 6[9]; usu. **b.** (129 t.) לֶכֶת Mi 6[8] +; לָכֶת Pr 15[21] + 2 t.; sf. לֶכְתִּי 1 K 2[8]; לֶכְתְּכֶם 2 S 17[21] + 7 t. (6 Ez); לֶכְתָּן Ez 1[9.12.17], etc.; *Pt.* הֹלֵךְ Gn 18[16] +; הוֹלֵךְ Gn 15[2] +; f. הֹלְכָה Je 3[6]; הֹלֶכֶת Gn 32[21] + 2 t. + הֹלַכְתִּי 2 K 4[23]; pl. הֹלְכִים Ex 33[15] +, etc.; cstr. הֹלְכֵי Ju 5[6] + 3 t.; fpl. הֹלְכֹת etc. Ex 2[5] + 3 t.;—found in all documents of Hex, esp. JE (240 t.; D 65 t., P 30 t. + H 14 t.);—**I.** lit. **1.** of persons, **a.** *go, proceed, move, walk* Gn 22[6.8] Ex 17[5] Am 3[3] Zp 1[17] + oft.; of cherubim Ez 10[16] = living creatures 1[9.12.19.20.21.24]; opp. to sitting (ישב) Dt 6[7] 11[19] (both c. בַּדֶּרֶךְ); ‖ running (רוץ) Pr 4[12] Is 40[31], cf. also 2 Ch 30[6]; distinguished from riding, driving Gn 24[65] (J; sq. בַּשָּׂדֶה לִקְרָאתֵנוּ), Ju 5[10] (עַל־הַדֶּרֶךְ), Is 41[3] (בְּרַגְלָיו), cf. Ec 5[1] (sq. אֶל), 10[7] (sq. עַל־הָאָרֶץ); on usage with prep. v. infr.; but also ‖ וַיִּרְכַּב 1 K 13[13] 18[45] cf. 2 K 9[16]; וַיֵּלֶךְ רֹכֵב הַסּוּס v[18] (sq. לִקְרָאתוֹ); נְהַג וָלֵךְ ... וַתֵּלֶךְ וַתָּבֹא 4[24] *drive and go forward ... and she went, and came.* **b.** *depart, go away:* Gn 18[33] (J), *and* י׳ *departed,* Gn 34[17] (P) *then we will take our daughter and depart;* cf. 1 S 14[3] 15[27] Ex 3[19] (J), 12[28] (P) 2 K 5[25] +; *go, go out* (to a specific duty etc.): of Samuel 1 S 7[16], Barak Ju 4[8.8]; *go out, forth* (opp. שׁוּב) Ru 1[21] +; = *go into exile* (without modifier) 1 Ch 5[41] cf. Je 22[10] (הֹלֵךְ of one going into exile; opp. death); v. further אֲשֶׁר הָלְכוּ שָׁם Ez 37[21]. **c.** less oft. where Eng. idiom requires or prefers *come,* (approach, arrive), vb. in Heb. being referred to starting point; mostly c. prep. (on usage c. prep. in gen. v. infr.):—לְכָה אֵלַי 1 S 17[44]; so in prayer to י׳, וּלְכָה לִישֻׁעָתָה לָּנוּ ψ 80[3]; also in Yahweh's exhortations to Isr. Is 55[1] (לַמַּיִם), v[3] (אֵלַי); *come to, arrive at* a land (ה ָ loc.) Gn 29[1]; *come unto* (אֶל) a people Ru 2[11]; but cf. esp. (without prep.) Imv. followed by another Imv., etc., v. infr. **5 f**, & partic. cases like Nu 22[6.11.17] 23[7.7] Is 55[1.1] etc., where actual summons to approach the speaker. **d.** with modifiers: (1) *a.* of space traversed: אֶת כָּל־הַמִּדְבָּר Dt 1[19] (cf. I. אֵת **2**), כָּל־הַבִּתְרוֹן 2 S 2[29]; esp. c. acc. דֶּרֶךְ *way,* Gn 35[3] (E) Nu 20[17] (JE) Dt 1[31] 2 S 4[7] 1 K 13[12.12]; Je 52[7] cf. וְלֹא תָשׁוּב בַּדֶּרֶךְ אֲשֶׁר הָלָכְתָּ 1 K 13[9]; הֹלֵךְ דֶּרֶךְ = *traveller* Is 35[8]; sq. אֳרָחוֹת Ju 5[6] (song), ptcp. cstr. הֹלְכֵי נְתִיבוֹת v[6] *goers of paths* (wayfarers); c. acc. דֶּרֶךְ = *journey* Pr 7[19]; *β.* c. acc. of time Dt 2[14] 2 S 2[32], cf. Jos 5[6] 14[10]; also, with combination of ideas of space & time דֶּרֶךְ שְׁלֹשֶׁת יָמִים Ex 3[18] (+ בַּמִּדְבָּר v. infr.) cf. 5[3] 8[23] 15[22] (all JE), Nu 33[8] (P) 1 K 19[4]. (2) c. prep.: *a.* sq. בְּ of space (territory, country, etc.) in which בַּמִּדְבָּר Ju 11[16.18]; cf. וַיֵּלֶךְ בַּבַּיִת אַחַת הֵנָּה וְאַחַת הֵנָּה 2 K 4[35] *and he walked in the house once hither, once thither;* esp. + acc. of time or distance (cf. supr.) Jos 5[6] 14[10] (both D) 1 K 19[4]; בָּעֲרָבָה 2 S 2[29]; cf. בַּיַּבָּשָׁה Ex 14[29] = 15[19] (P ?); בְּתוֹךְ הָעֵמֶק Jos 8[13] (JE); sq. בְּ of way, path בְּדַרְכּוֹ 1 K 18[6.6] בד׳ Nu 21[22] (JE) Jos 24[17] (E) Dt 1[33] 2[27] Ju 18[6] 1 S 28[22]; לֹא תָשׁוּב לָלֶכֶת בַּדֶּרֶךְ אֲשֶׁר הָלַכְתָּ בָּהּ 1 K 13[17] (הָלַךְ of both going & coming); so oft. fig., cf. infr. **II. 3**; *walk in the streets* בִּרְחֹבֹת La 4[18], *walk by the way* בַּד׳ (opp. יָשַׁב *sit*) Dt 6[7] 11[19]; *β.* sq. עַל, *go* or *walk on (by)* עַל־יַד הַיְאֹר Ex 2[5]; עַל־הַדֶּרֶךְ 1 S 9[6] (i.e. *set out, start, upon* cf. Dr); cstr. sq. עַל Ju 5[10]. (3) *go to, unto: a.* sq. acc., in general בְּכֹל־אֲשֶׁר תֵּלֵךְ Gn 28[15] (J) *whithersoever thou goest* Jos 1[7.9] (D), cf. 2 S 7[9] 8[6.14] = 1 Ch 17[8] 18[6.13]; more definitely, to a land, with or without ארץ Ju 1[26] 21[21] Je 37[12]; so fig. Ho 7[11] *resort to* (acc.) *Asshur* (‖ קרא); to a city 1 S 11[14.15] 23[5] 1 K 2[8] 11[24] 12[1] 14[2.4] 2 K 9[1] 1 Ch 11[4] 2 Ch 8[3] Ezr 8[31]; to a house בַּיִת 2 S 13[7.8], house of י׳ ψ 122[1]; a field, Gn 27[5] (J; + Inf. of purpose); valley of salt 2 Ch 25[11]. *β.* sq. ה ָ loc., אַרְצָה Gn 11[31] 12[5], פַּדֶּנָה אֲרָם 28[2.5.7] (all P) cf. 29[1] (E) Nu 32[39] (JE) 2 S 14[23]; of city Gn 18[22] 28[10] (both J) Ju 9[1] 1 S 15[34] 16[13] 19[22] 2 S 15[9] 1 K 3[4] 18[45] 2 Ch 10[1]; of river Euphrates Je 13[4.6.7]; of a wood 1 S 23[16]; a mountain Jos 2[16] (JE); cf. also אָנָה הָלְכוּ *whither have they gone* Gn 16[8] 32[18] Jos 2[5] (all JE) cf. Ne 2[16] Ct 6[1] Ju 19[17], אָנֶה וָאָנָה 1 K 2[42] (but also אָן ה׳ 1 S 10[14]); שָׁמָּה Je 40[4] but also שָׁם 1 S 9[6] Je 45[5]; הֵנָּה 2 K 4[35]. *γ.* c. prep.: (*a*) most often sq. אֶל־ *unto,* e.g., *unto the place,* הַמָּקוֹם, Gn 22[3] (E) 30[25] (J),

etc.; of land Gn 22^{2} (E) 24$^{4.10}$ (J) 36^{6} (P) Jos 22^{9} (D), etc.; of city Gn 22^{19} (E) 1 S 9^{10} Jon 3^{3}, etc.; of house Gn 24^{38} (J) Ec 7$^{2.2}$; house of God Ec 4^{17}; of people Ex 19^{10} (E) etc.; in other designations of place, Jos 8^{9} (JE), Ezr 10^{6} Ru 2^{9}, etc.; also sq. אֶל = *against*, of military expedition: Ju 1^{10} against Canaanites; a city Ju 9^{1} 1 K 22^{15} = 2 Ch 18$^{5.14}$; also sq. אֶל of individual persons Gn 26$^{1.26}$ (both J), 41^{55} (E) 2 K 6$^{22.23}$ 22^{14} = 2 Ch 34^{22} Je 41^{14}+; once with implic. *coire cum femina* Am 2^{7} (cf. בוא **1 e,** p. 98); vid. esp. לַהֲלֹךְ אֶל־אֵל בַּמִּשְׁפָּט Jb 34^{23} of judicial inquiry by God; *come unto* the speaker Nu 22$^{16.37}$ (both JE), unto the one addressed Is 60^{14}. (*b*) rarely sq. עַל־ *unto* (Je K Ez) c. בַּיִת 1 K 20^{43}, שָׂדֶה 1 K 2^{26} (+ acc. loc.), cf. עַל־כָּל אֲשֶׁר Je 1^{7}, עַל־אֲשֶׁר יִהְיֶה שָׁם Ez 1^{12} (of the רוּחַ; cf. אֶל־אֲשֶׁר יִהְיֶה שָׁמָּה v^{20}); also וַאֲנִי הוֹלֵךְ עַל אֲשֶׁר־אֲנִי הוֹלֵךְ 2 S 15^{20} = *I am going I know not where* cf. Lag$^{\text{Psalt. Hieron. 1874, 156 f.}}$ Dr^{Sm}; v. further Je 3^{6} (sq. both אֶל & עַל; on confusion of אֶל and עַל vid. these words); sq. עַל *against* city 1 K 22^{6}, king 2 Ch 22^{5}. (*c*) sq. עַד *as far as, unto,* place עַד־כֹּה Gn 22^{5} (E), cf. 1 K 12^{30} (וַיֵּלְכוּ הָעָם לִפְנֵי הָאֶחָד עַד דָּן), 2 K 6^{2} 10^{25} 7^{15} cf. 2 Ch 26^{8}; persons 1 S 9^{9}. (*d*) sq. לְ, *to* a land 1 K 10^{13} etc.; a city 2 Ch 8^{17}; a mountain 1 Ch 4^{42}; a bamah 2 Ch 1^{3}; cf. לִמְבוֹא גְדֹר 1 Ch 4^{39} & v. infr.; also before n.pr. of pers. Gn 24^{56} (J); further לַמִּלְחָמָה Ez 7^{14}; לְסִבְלֹתֵיכֶם Ex 5^{4} (J) *go to your burdens* cf. Is 60^{3}, וְהַתּוֹדָה הַשֵּׁנִית הַהוֹלֶכֶת לְמוֹאל Ne 12^{38} *the second thanksgiving* choir, *that went the opposite way;* frequently לְדַרְכּוֹ etc., *go (to, on) one's way* Gn 19^{2} (J) 32^{2} (E) Nu 24^{25} Jos 2^{16} (both JE) Ju 18^{26} 1 S 1^{18} 26^{25}+; לְמַסָּעָיו Gn 13^{3} (J); cf. הַהוֹלֵךְ לְמֶרְחֲבֵי־אֶרֶץ Hb 1^{6} *that marcheth through the breadth of the land* (of invader); note esp. in sense of *depart to, go away to,* almost = *return to;* וְהָלַכְתָּ לְאֹהָלֶיךָ Dt 16^{7} *and thou shalt go* (back) *to thy tents,* so Ju 19^{6} 20^{8} 1 K 8^{66} 12^{16} = 2 Ch 10^{16}; לְבֵיתוֹ 1 S 10^{26} cf. 14^{8} 23^{18} 1 K 14^{12} 1 Ch 16^{43}; לִמְקוֹמוֹ 1 S 2^{20} (cf. VB Dr) 14^{46}; v. also *go away* or *off to* 1 Ch 4^{42} 2 Ch 8^{17}. (*e*) sq. בְּ *into* בַּשָּׂדֶה Nu 22^{23} (of Balaam's ass); esp. in ה׳ בַּשְּׁבִי *go into captivity* Am 9^{4} Na 3^{10} Dt 28^{41} Je 20^{6} 22^{22} 30^{16} La 1^{18} (= ה׳ שְׁבִי v^{5}) cf. Ez 30$^{17.18}$ Is 46^{2} 48^{11} ה׳ בַּגּוֹלָה Je 48^{11} Ez 25^{3}; v. also ה׳ בַּכְּלִמָּה Is 45^{16}; ה׳ בַּמִּלְחָמָה 1 S 17^{13}; ה׳ בַּקְּרָב 2 S 17^{11} (but v. Dr). (4) *go from, depart from,* sq. מִן, e.g. 1 K 2^{41}, etc., מִשָּׁם Gn 42^{26} (E) 1 K 19^{19}; cf. ψ 139^{7} אָנָה אֵלֵךְ מֵרוּחֶךָ; note esp. Ju 6^{21} וּמַלְאַךְ י׳ הָלַךְ מֵעֵינָיו cf. 1 S 14^{17} (מֵעִמָּנוּ), Ho 9^{6} (מִשֹּׁד, *from destruction*); also sq. מֵאֵת of divorced woman Je 3^{1} (מֵאִתּוֹ), cf. also Gn 26^{31} (J), Jos 22^{9} (? P) מֵאֵצֶל 1 K 20^{36}. (5) c. prep. denoting other relations:—*a.* אֵת of accompaniment, ה׳ אִתִּי (on warlike expedition) Gn 14^{24} cf. 2 S 15^{11} Jos 10^{24} Ju 1^{3} (sq. בְּ *into*), 7$^{4.4}$, v. also 1 S 23^{23} 2 S 16^{17}+. *β.* עִם Ju 4$^{8.8.9.9}$ 7^{4} 11^{8} 1 S 30$^{22.22}$ 2 S 19^{26} Nu 22$^{13.14}$ (JE)+. *γ.* בְּ *with* (cf. בְּ **III. 1,** p. 89), esp. Ex 10^{9}, cf. Ho 5^{6} בְּצֹאנָם וּבִבְקָרָם יֵלְכוּ לְבַקֵּשׁ אֶת־י׳, of vain sacrifices; 2 Ch 30^{6} *the runners went with* (בְּ) *letters.* *δ.* בְּקֶרֶב *in the midst of,* Ex 34^{9} (JE). *ε.* לִפְנֵי *in front of, before,* before Cyrus Is 45^{2}, (cf. of fire & pestilence, infr. **3**); of י׳ going before Isr. Ex 13^{21} Nu 14^{14}, cf. also Ex 23^{23} 32^{34} & (in mng.) 33^{14} (פָּנַי יֵלֵכוּ), v^{15}, Is 52^{12}, with which comp. וה׳ לְפָנֶיךָ צִדְקֶךָ 58^{8}; of other gods Ex 32$^{1.23}$ (all JE); לְנֶגְדֶּךָ Gn 33^{12} (J). *ζ.* c. אַחַר *go after, follow,* persons Gn 37^{17} (J) 2 K 7^{15}; אַחֲרֵי Gn 24$^{5.8.39.61}$ (all J), Jos 3^{3} (D), Nu 16^{25} (JE)+; cf. also **II. 3 d** (going after false gods, etc.); מֵאַחֲרֵיהֶם Ex 14^{19} (J). *η.* לְ with sense of dativ. ethic.: וַיֵּלֶךְ לוֹ אֶל־אַרְצוֹ Ex 18^{27} (E) *and he gat him* (betook himself) *to his country;* אֵלֶךְ לִי אֶל Ct 4^{6} *I will get me unto;* וְנֵלְכָה־לָּנוּ 1 S 26^{11} *and let us be gone,* cf. v^{12}, Ct 2^{11} (of rain cf. infr. **3**); Imv. in same construction: לֶךְ־לְךָ אֶל Gn 22^{2} (E) *get thee unto,* לְכוּ לָכֶם לְאָהֳלֵיכֶם Jos 22^{4} (D) also לֶךְ־לְךָ מִן Gn 12^{1} (J), & לְכִי־לָךְ Ct 2$^{10.13}$ *get thee away, come away.* *θ.* adverbial phrases of manner c. prep.: (*a*) בְּ, ה׳ בְּשָׁלוֹם *go in peace* Gn 26^{31} (J) 1 S 29^{7} 2 S 3$^{21.22.23}$ 15^{9}; ה׳ בְּכֹחַ הָאֲכִילָה הַהִיא 1 K 19^{8}, ה׳ בְּחֵמָה 2 K 5^{12}; cf. also 1 S 17^{39} Is 52^{12}; וה׳ בְּסַעֲרוֹת תֵּימָן Zc 9^{14} of י׳, *and he shall go in* (or with) *storms of the south;* בְּ pretii, הַהֹלְכִים בְּנַפְשׁוֹתָם 2 S 23^{17} *who went at risk of their life* (otherwise in ‖ 1 Ch 11^{19}); cf. (*b*) אֶל, ה׳ אֶל־נַפְשׁוֹ 1 K 19^{3} *he went for his life.* (*c*) לְ, ה׳ לְרַגְלָהּ 1 S 25^{42} *go according to her foot,* i.e. follow, attend her; לֵךְ לְשָׁלוֹם *go to, for* (in) *peace* Ex 4^{18} (E) Ju 18^{6} 1 S 1^{17} 20$^{13.42}$ 2 K 5^{19}; וְהֹלְכִים לְתֻמָּם 2 S 15^{11}. *κ.* with adj. or noun, agreeing with subj. of vb., in acc. (Ges$^{\text{§ 118.5}}$), sometimes where Lat. & Eng. use an attributive or appositive: *walk barefoot* 2 S 15^{30}; *walk naked and barefoot* Is 20^{3} (c. acc. of duration); וַתֵּלַכְנָה נְטוּוֹת גָּרוֹן וגו׳ Is 3^{16}; cf. 1 K 8^{66}; also לֹא תֵלֵךְ רָכִיל בְּעַמֶּךָ Lv 19^{16} (H) *thou* *shalt not walk as a slanderer among thy people,* Je 9[3], הוֹלֵךְ רָכִיל Pr 11[13] 20[19]; and even הֹלְכֵי רָכִיל Je 6[28] (yet רכיל poss. abstr., ה׳ ר׳ *walk in slander*); with adv. accus., construed more generally (Ges[§ 118, 5. c], Ew[§ 279 c]): *ye shall not walk loftily* (רוֹמָה) Mi 2[3]; *they shall come bending* (שְׁחוֹחַ) Is 60[14]; *and Agag came delicately* (מַעֲדַנֹּת) 1 S 15[32]; cf. also Lv 26[23] (II. **3b**) Ex 3[21] 2 S 17[18].

2. Also of animals, in similar meanings and combinations: הָלַךְ Na 2[12] *walk about, prowl* (lions, fig. of rulers of Assyria); Pr 30[29] (vid. v[30.31], of three beasts & a king); *walk, go, move* בִּמְסִלָּה אַחַת ה׳ 1 S 6[12] (of cows bringing ark), horses in Zec.'s vision Zc 6[7] וַיְבַקְשׁוּ לָלֶכֶת לְהִתְהַלֵּךְ בָּאָרֶץ; of beasts & birds Je 9[9], cf. 50[3] *both man & beast, they are fled, they are gone;* of flocks and herds (מִקְנֶה) יֵלֵךְ עִמָּנוּ Ex 10[26] *they shall go with us;* ה׳ מֵהַר אֶל־גִּבְעָה Je 50[6] *they have gone fr. mt. to hill* (Isr. under fig. of wandering sheep); in 1 S 14[26] rd. prob. הָלַךְ for הֵלֶךְ q.v.; esp. in laws of clean & unclean Lv 11[20.21] *every swarming winged thing that goeth on* (הַהֹלֵךְ עַל) *all fours,* cf. v[27.42]; also v[27] *everything that goeth on its paws,* & v[42] *everything that goeth on* (*its*) *belly,* (all P), so of serpent Gn 3[14] *on thy belly* (עַל־גְּחֹנְךָ) *shalt thou go* (J), cf. also Je 46[22] קוֹלָהּ כַּנָּחָשׁ יֵלֵךְ; (where appar. rel. cl., *her voice like the serpent that moves,* i.e. like the rustling sound of a gliding serpent, cf. VB); locusts Jo 2[7] (אִישׁ בִּדְרָכָיו), v[8] (גֶּבֶר בִּמְסִלָּתוֹ). **3.** in like manner of inanimate things, as: the ark (הַתֵּבָה) Gn 7[18] (P; sq. עַל־פְּנֵי הַמָּיִם); ships 1 K 22[49] (sq. ־ָה loc.) = 2 Ch 20[36] (sq. acc. of limit), cf. 2 Ch 9[21] (sq. acc.) 20[37] (אֶל); of אֳנִי־שַׁיִט Is 33[21] '*galley with oars*' (sq. בְּ of place in which); wheels (in Ezekiel's vision) Ez 1[17.17.19.21] 10[11.11.11.11]; moon Jb 31[26]; wind ψ 78[39] Ec 1[6.6]; of streams (הַנְּחָלִים) =*flow* אֶל־הַיָּם Ec 1[7]; cf. אֶל־מְקוֹם שֶׁהַנְּחָלִים הֹלְכִים שָׁם הֵם שָׁבִים לָלָכֶת v[7] *unto the place whither the streams flow, thither they flow again;* also אֲפִיקִים, sq. מַיִם as accus. of that with wh., Jo 4[18] ‖ of hills *flowing* חָלָב, *with milk;* cf. further fig. כָּל־בִּרְכַּיִם תֵּלַכְנָה מַּיִם Ez 7[17] 21[12] *all knees shall flow down in water,* i.e. be as weak as water; נְהָרוֹת Ez 31[4] (sq. סָבִיב); וְהָלַךְ עַל־כָּל־גְּדוֹתָיו Is 8[7] i.e. *overflow* (‖ עָלָה עַל־כָּל־אֲפִיקָיו) cf. Jos 4[18] (JE); so of water (as SI[4]) Is 8[6], 1 K 18[35] (וַיֵּלְכוּ הַמַּיִם סָבִיב לַמִּזְבֵּחַ), ψ 105[41] (הָלְכוּ בַּצִּיּוֹת נָהָר, *they flowed through dry regions* as *a river*); (on Inf. abs. used of waters of flood, Gn 8[3.5], cf. infr. **4 c** (4), (5)); of the sea הַיָּם הוֹלֵךְ וְסֹעֵר Jon 1[11.13] *was going on and being stormy = was growing more and more stormy* (cf. infr. **4 d**); of wine (יַיִן) Ct 7[10] *that goeth down, for my beloved, smoothly* (simile); also of lightning *go, dart* (בָּרָק) Jb 38[35], so אֵשׁ Ex 9[23] (E) וַתִּהֲלַךְ אֵשׁ אָרְצָה *and fire darted to earth* (on form, here & ψ 73[9] infr., as intens., of rapid motion, cf. Thes Ew[§ 138 b] Kö[I. 415]); אֵשׁ לְפָנָיו תֵּלֵךְ ψ 97[3]; of torches, in fig. of violent breathing of crocodile מִפִּיו לַפִּידִים יַהֲלֹכוּ Jb 41[11]; of sword אַחֲרַיִךְ תֵּלֶךְ חָרֶב Je 48[2], of arrow בָּרָק Jb 20[25] drawn from a wound; of pestilence דֶּבֶר (personified) ψ 91[6] (בָּאֹפֶל), Hb 3[5] (לְפָנָיו); of fame שָׁמְעוֹ הוֹלֵךְ בְּכָל־הַמְּדִינוֹת Est 9[4]; of the tongue (bad sense) וּלְשׁוֹנָם תִּהֲלַךְ בָּאָרֶץ ψ 73[9] (cf. Ex 9[23] supr.; ‖ שַׁתּוּ בַשָּׁמַיִם פִּיהֶם); of sound of trumpet Ex 19[19] (Pt. cf. infra **4 d**); of letters אִגְּרוֹת Ne 6[17] (sq. עַל, unto); of dew (טַל ‖ עֲנַן־בֹּקֶר) sim. of Isr.'s חֶסֶד Ho 6[4] cf. 13[3] *like dew that passeth away;* so of עָנָן Jb 7[9] כָּלָה עָנָן וַיֵּלַךְ; of rain הַגֶּשֶׁם חָלַף הָלַךְ לוֹ Ct 2[11] *the rain is over, it hath taken itself away;* of ark of י׳ (אֲרוֹן י׳) 1 S 6[8] *depart* (cf. also **5 d**); of shadow on dial *go forward* 2 K 20[9] (opp. שׁוּב ‖ נָטָה v[20] & יָרַד Is 38[8]); *grow,* of wicked under fig. of trees, יֵלְכוּ גַּם־עָשׂוּ פֶרִי Je 12[2]; cf. יֵלְכוּ יוֹנְקוֹתָיו Ho 14[3] *his branches shall spread,* said of Isr. under fig. of tree; of name (= fame) 2 Ch 26[8] (sq. עַד־לְבוֹא מִצְרַיִם); also of a thing that does not actually move; וְהָלַךְ הַגְּבוּל אֶל Jos 17[7] *and the boundary went unto* etc., cf. 16[8] (sq. מִן & ־ָה loc.);—in 2 K 13[21] *and it* (the dead body) *went* i.e. was let down into the grave, rd. וַיֵּלְכוּ for וַיֵּלֶךְ 𝔊L Th Klo, *and they went away.*

†**4.** The Inf. abs. is often used **a.** as in other vbs., quite independently (Ges[§ 113, 1]): הֲגָנֹב . . . . וְהָלֹךְ אַחֲרֵי אֱלֹהִים אֲחֵרִים Je 7[9] (series of 6 Inf. abs.) (are there) stealing, murdering, and adultery and false swearing and incense-burning to the Baal, *and going after other gods . . .?* as obj., וְלֹא־אָבוּ בִדְרָכָיו הָלוֹךְ Is 42[24] *and they desired not walking in his ways;* as appos. of obj., Je 23[14] *I have seen . . . . an abominable thing, committing adultery and walking in lies* (נָאוֹף וְהָלֹךְ בַּשֶּׁקֶר); cf. וַיַּעַשׂ כֵּן הָלֹךְ עָרוֹם וְיָחֵף Is 20[2] *and he did so, a walking naked and barefoot,* where also two adverb. accus. modifying the Inf. abs. (Ges[§ 113, 2]). **b.** to intensify meaning of finite form of הָלַךְ (Ges[§ 113, 3]): (1)

before finite vb. הָלֹךְ אֵלֵךְ עִמָּךְ Ju 4^{9} *I will surely go with thee*, cf. Je 37^{9}; הָלֹךְ הָלַכְתָּ Gn 31^{30} concessive, *thou art indeed gone*, הָלוֹךְ הָלְכוּ הָעֵצִים Ju 9^{8} introductory, *the trees went forth on a time* to anoint them a king. (2) after finite vb. וַיֵּלֶךְ הָלוֹךְ 2 S 3^{24} *and he is actually gone!* (a grave imprudence to permit it!), נֵלְכָה הָלוֹךְ לְחַלּוֹת אֶת־פְּנֵי י׳ Zc 8^{21} *let us by all means go to seek the favour of* י׳. **c.** most noteworthy is the joining of the Inf. abs. (1) with a following Inf. abs. denoting a simultaneous action or process, and so emphasizing duration or continuance: *a.* both Infs. preceding the finite vb., הָלוֹךְ וְטָפֹף תֵּלַכְנָה Is 3^{16} *a going and a tripping they go*, i.e. they keep tripping as they go; so הָלוֹךְ וּבָכוֹ יֵלֵכוּ Je 50^{4} *continually weeping they shall go*; *β.* one Inf. before, & one after the fin. vb. הָלוֹךְ יֵלֵךְ וּבָכֹה ψ 126^{6} *continually may* one *go weeping*; *γ.* elsewhere both after fin. vb. Jos 6^{9} *the rearguard* was *going* (הֹלֵךְ) *after the ark, continually blowing on the trumpets* (הָלוֹךְ וְתָקוֹעַ בַּשּׁוֹפָרוֹת), cf. v^{13} (where הָלֹוךְ cf. infr.; both JE), וַיֵּלֶךְ ... הָלוֹךְ וּבָכוֹ 2 S 3^{16}, of cows הָלְכוּ הָלוֹךְ וְגָעוֹ 1 S 6^{12} *they went continually lowing*, וַיֵּלֶךְ הָלוֹךְ וְאָכֹל Ju 14^{9} *and he went on, eating as he went*; הֹלְכִים הָלוֹךְ וְדַבֵּר 2 K 2^{11} *they were going on, talking as they went*; in הֹלֵךְ הָלֹךְ וּבֹכֶה Je 41^{6}, the pt. בֹּכֶה is peculiar, rd. perh. בָּכֹה, and for הֹלֵךְ rd. הֹלְכִים 𝔊 Hi cf. Gf. (2) with a foll. vb.fin.c. ו consec. (rare): הֹלְכִים הָלוֹךְ וְתָקְעוּ Jos 6^{13} (JE) they were *going along continually blowing* on the trumpets; וַתֵּלֶךְ הָלוֹךְ וְזָעָקָה 2 S 13^{19} *and she went, crying out as she went*; הָלוֹךְ ... הֹלֵךְ וַיְקַלֵּל 2 S 16^{13} he *went along ... cursing as he went*; so 1 S 19^{23} *and he went on, prophesying as he went*, until he came, etc. (3) in cases where vb. fin. is foll. by Inf. abs. + adj. denoting progress, advance: וַיֵּלֶךְ הָלוֹךְ וְקָרֵב 2 S 18^{25} *and he came continually nearer* (nearer & nearer); elsewh. with idea of actual motion lost fr. vb. fin.: וַיֵּלֶךְ הָלוֹךְ וָרָב 1 S 14^{19} *and the tumult kept growing greater and greater*; so וַיֵּלֶךְ דָּוִד הָלוֹךְ וְגָדוֹל 2 S 5^{10} = 1 Ch 11^{9}; cf. Ju 4^{24} *and the hand of the sons of Israel kept growing more and more severe* (וַתֵּלֶךְ ... הָלוֹךְ וְקָשָׁה) *upon Jabin*; note esp. וַיִּגְדַּל הָאִישׁ וַיֵּלֶךְ הָלוֹךְ וְגָדֵל עַד־כִּי־גָדַל מְאֹד Gn 26^{13} (J) *and the man grew great and kept on growing greater and greater until* etc. (גָּדֵל partic. adj.). (4) twice, where vb. fin. is not הלך, but another vb. denoting motion: וַיָּשֻׁבוּ הַמַּיִם ... הָלוֹךְ וָשׁוֹב Gn 8^{3} (J) *and the waters retired continually more and more*; וַיִּסַּע אַבְרָם הָלוֹךְ וְנָסוֹעַ הַנֶּגְבָּה Gn 12^{9} (J) *and Abram journeyed on continually further toward the south country*. (5) quite by itself is Gn 8^{5} (P) וְהַמַּיִם הָיוּ הָלוֹךְ וְחָסוֹר *and the waters, they continually diminished* (were a going and a diminishing; the Infs. abs. being predicate). (6) 13 t. the Inf. abs. = Imv. & is followed by Pf. consec. (chiefly in Je): הָלוֹךְ וְדִבַּרְתָּ 2 S 24^{12} *go and speak*, so Je 35^{2}; ה׳ וְאָמַרְתָּ *go and say*, Is 38^{5} Je 28^{13} 34^{2} 35^{13} 39^{16}; ה׳ וְקָרָאתָ Je 2^{2} 3^{12}; also ה׳ וְרָחַצְתָּ 2 K 5^{10} *go and wash*, ה׳ וְקָנִיתָ Je 13^{1} 19^{1} *go and buy*, ה׳ וְעָמַדְתָּ 17^{19} *go and stand*. **d.** akin to the use of Inf. abs. are some instances of Pt. הֹלֵךְ + adj. (or pt.): וַיֵּלֶךְ הַפְּלִשְׁתִּי הֹלֵךְ וְקָרֵב 1 S 17^{41} *and the Philistine came continually nearer* (cf. 2 S 18^{25} supr.); in other cases as predicate, with same idea of *growing, increasing*: וְדָוִד הֹלֵךְ וְחָזֵק וּבֵית שָׁאוּל הֹלְכִים וְדַלִּים 2 S 3^{1} *and David was growing stronger and stronger, while the house of Saul were growing weaker and weaker*, cf. 2 Ch 17^{12} Est 9^{4} (of individuals), 2 S 15^{12} (of people); + 2 adj. וְהַנַּעַר שְׁמוּאֵל הֹלֵךְ וְגָדֵל וָטוֹב 1 S 2^{26}; cf. (with different order) of wind, Ec 1^{6} *goeth* (הוֹלֵךְ) *toward* the south, and turneth about (סוֹבֵב) unto the north, *the wind turneth about and about continually* (סוֹבֵב סֹבֵב הוֹלֵךְ הָרוּחַ); of sea הַיָּם הוֹלֵךְ וְסֹעֵר Jon 1$^{11.13}$ *the sea was growing more and more stormy*; also וַיְהִי קוֹל הַשֹּׁפָר הוֹלֵךְ וְחָזֵק מְאֹד Ex 19^{19} *and the sound of the trumpet kept growing louder and louder*; & in metaph. אֹרַח צַדִּיקִים כְּאוֹר נֹגַהּ הוֹלֵךְ וָאוֹר עַד־נְכוֹן הַיּוֹם Pr 4^{18} *the path of just men is like a shining light, growing lighter and lighter until the full day.*

5. In combination with other verbal forms: **a.** sq. Inf. of purpose (c. לְ) Gn 25^{22} 31^{19} 37^{25} (all JE) Nu 14^{38} (P) 24^{1} (JE), Ju 8^{1} 9$^{8.9.11.13}$ + oft.; esp. ה׳ לִקְרַאת *go to meet* Jos 9^{11} (JE), 2 S 19^{16} 1 K 18$^{16.16}$ +; sometimes with hostile sense 1 S 23^{28} 1 K 20^{27} 2 K 23^{29}; also ה׳ לָשׁוּב *go to return*, Ex 4^{21} (RV *go back*), cf. also שׁוּב לָלֶכֶת *return again* Ec 1^{7} 5^{14}; ה׳ לָבוֹא *go to come* (*enter*, etc.) Je 41^{17} cf. 2 Ch 26^{8}. **b.** sq. finite vb. *go and do* so and so: Gn 22^{13} 27^{14} Ex 2^{8} 4$^{27.29}$ (all JE), Dt 13$^{7.14}$ 17^{3} 24^{2} Is 2^{3} = Mi 4^{2} Je 11^{12} + oft.; וַיֵּלֶךְ וַיָּשָׁב Ex 4^{18} (E), יֵלֵךְ וְיָשֹׁב Dt 20$^{5.6.7.8}$, וַיֵּלְכוּ וַיָּשׁוּבוּ Ju 21^{23} cf. Ho 2^{9} 5^{15}; ה׳ וַיָּבוֹא *went & came* Nu 13^{26} (P), Ru 2^{3} 1 S 22^{5}

2 S 11[22] 2 K 4[25]; notably וַיֵּלֶךְ וַיִּשְׁלַח 2 K 3[7] *and he went and sent.* **c.** following other verbs: וַיָּקֻמוּ וַיֵּלְכוּ Gn 22[19] (E) cf. 24[10] (J) 43[8] (J) Nu 16[25] (JE) Ju 4[9]; נִסְעָה וְנֵלֵכָה Gn 33[12] (J). **d.** esp. as result of action expr. in preced. vb., such as vb. of sending, etc.: וַיְשַׁלַּח אֶת־אֶחָיו וַיֵּלֵכוּ Gn 45[24] (E) cf. Jos 1[16] (D) 1 S 6[8] Jb 38[35]; also יִשָּׂאֵהוּ קָדִים וְיֵלַךְ 27[21] *an east wind shall carry him off, and he shall depart;* וַיְגָרְשֵׁהוּ וַיֵּלַךְ ψ 34[1] (title). (Cf. *depart* also of inanimate things **3** supr.) **e.** in longer series: וַיֵּלֶךְ וַיִּבְרַח וַיִּמָּלֵט 1 S 19[12]; וַיִּסַּע וַיֵּלֶךְ וַיָּשָׁב . . . וַיֵּשֶׁב 2 K 19[36] = Is 37[37]; cf. Nu 24[25] (JE); וַיָּקָם וַיֵּלֶךְ וַיָּבֹא Ju 19[10]; also וַיָּקָם וַיָּבֹא וַיֵּלֶךְ 2 K 10[12]. **f.** oft. in Imv. foll. by 2nd Imv. or equiv., (1) לֵךְ קַח־לִי Gn 27[13] (J) *go, bring me* (them), cf. Ho 1[2]; לְכוּ רְעוּ Gn 29[7] (J) *go, feed* (them), cf. 37[14] 42[19] Ex 4[19] +(in all c. 57 t.; only JED in Hex); but also (2) weakened to mere introductory word (as also supr. passim: esp. 2 K 3[7] etc.), *go to,* or *come, do* (*let us do*) so & so; לְכָה נִכְרְתָה בְרִית Gn 31[44] *come, let us make a compact,* cf. לְכָה נַשְׁקֶה 19[32] (where subj. fem.); לְכוּ וְנֵלְכָה 1 S 9[9] *come, and let us go,* so v[10], 11[14] Is 2[3] = Mi 4[2], cf. Zc 6[7] +; even לֵךְ בֹּא וְאֶשְׁלְחָה 2 K 5[5] *go to, come, and let me send,* cf. Is 22[15] 26[20] Ez 3[4.11]; further Ju 19[11.13] 1 S 9[5] 1 K 1[12] ψ 34[5] + (in all c. 49 t.; only JE in Hex). (3) apparently intermediate, and shewing transition fr. (1) to (2) are: לֶךְ־רֵד Ex 19[24] 32[7] cf. Ju 18[2]; לְכוּ סֹרוּ רְדוּ 1 S 15[6]; לֵךְ עֲלֵה מִזֶּה Ex 33[1]; לְכוּ וְהִתְהַלְּכוּ בָאָרֶץ Jos 18[8] & לְכוּ בֹּאוּ אַרְצָה Gn 47[17] cf. 1 S 22[5] 1 K 1[13] 2 K 7[9]; v. further לֵכְנָה שֹּׁבְנָה Ru 1[8] & שֹׁבְנָה לֵכְןָ v[12]; also 2 S 3[16] 1 K 19[15.20] + (in all c. 36 t.)

II. Fig.; the most common uses follow; in most the origin in a literal meaning is evident: † **1.** *pass away, die;* in phrases denoting or implying death (cf. Ar. هَلَكَ *perish*); וְהִנֵּה אָנֹכִי הוֹלֵךְ הַיּוֹם בְּדֶרֶךְ כָּל־הָאָרֶץ Jos 23[14] (D) *lo, I am going to-day the way of all the earth* cf. 1 K 2[2]; perh. also Gn 15[2] (JE) *I pass away childless,* but possibly sub **2** infr.; also 2 S 12[23] *I am going* (אֲנִי הֹלֵךְ) *to him* 2 S 12[23]; so of mankind דּוֹר הֹלֵךְ וְדוֹר בָּא Ec 1[4]; more explicitly, הַכֹּל הוֹלֵךְ אֶל־מָקוֹם אֶחָד הַכֹּל הָיָה מִן הֶעָפָר וְהַכֹּל שָׁב אֶל־הֶעָפָר Ec 3[20] cf. 6[6]; also בִּשְׁאוֹל אֲשֶׁר אַתָּה הֹלֵךְ שָׁמָּה 9[10], & הֹלֵךְ הָאָדָם אֶל־בֵּית עוֹלָמוֹ 12[5]; cf. בְּטֶרֶם אֵלֵךְ וְאֵינֶנִּי ψ 39[14] *before I depart and be not;* so acc. to some 2 Ch 21[20] but cf. infr. **3 a** (2); once with weaker sense sq. inf., הִנֵּה אָנֹכִי הוֹלֵךְ לָמוּת Gn 25[32] (J). **2.** *live* (‘*walk*’), in general (cf. **Pi. Hithp.**) (usu. poet., with modifying words): כִּי־אֵלֵךְ בְּגֵיא צַלְמָוֶת ψ 23[4] *though I walk in a valley of deep darkness;* cf. 138[7] & אֵלֶךְ חֹשֶׁךְ Jb 29[3]; קֹדֵר אֵלֵךְ ψ 42[10]; ה׳ חֲשֵׁכִים Is 50[10], v. also Ez 3[14]; perh. also Gn 15[2] cf. **1** supr.; יֵלְכוּ מֵחַיִל אֶל־חָיִל ψ 84[8] *they go from strength to strength;* הוֹלֵךְ בַּתֹּם יֵלֶךְ בֶּטַח Pr 10[9]; esp. **3.** of moral and religious life; יְיַשֶּׁר־לָכֶת Pr 15[21] *he maketh straight to walk* (walketh straight, upright); partic. **a.** *walk in* (בְּ) *ways* (counsels, statutes, etc.), (1) in good sense: (*a*) ה׳ בְּדֶרֶךְ תָּמִים ψ 101[6], cf. Is 30[21] Je 6[16] 1 K 8[36] = 2 Ch 6[27]; (*β*) in (בְּ) ways of י׳, esp. D: Dt 8[6] (|| לְיִרְאָה אֹתוֹ) cf. 10[12], 11[22] (|| לְאַהֲבָה אֶת־י׳ etc.), 28[9] (|| שָׁמַר מִצְוֹת י׳); v. also 13[15] +; 1 K 11[33] (sq. לַעֲשׂוֹת), v[38] (sq. וְעָשִׂיתָ) 2 K 21[22] ψ 119[3] 128[1]; בְּאֹרְחֹתָיו Is 2[3] = Mi 4[2]; further (sq. דֶּרֶךְ) Ju 2[17]; (*γ*) †in commandments of י׳ 2 Ch 17[4]; (*δ*) in his law(s) (תּוֹרָה) Ex 16[4.14] (J) 2 K 10[31] Je 9[12] 44[23] (+ בְּחֻקֹּת & בְּעֵדְוֹת), 2 Ch 6[16] Dn 9[10], cf. Ne 10[30] (of אֱלֹהִים); (*ε*) †in his ordinances, statutes (חֻקּוֹת) Lv 26[3] 1 K 6[12] Je 44[10.23] (v. supr.), Ez 5[6.7] 11[20] 18[9.17] 20[13.16.19.21], cf. בְּחֻקּוֹת חַיִּים 33[15]; also בְּחֻקַּי 1 K 8[61] Ez 11[12] 36[27]; (*ζ*) †in his judgments (מִשְׁפָּטִים) ψ 89[31] Ez 37[24]; (*η*) †in ordinances of David 1 K 3[3], cf. also infr.; (*θ*) in way(s) of good man 1 S 8[3.5] 2 Ch 21[12], of David 2 Ch 11[17] 34[2], of David & Sol. 17[3]. (2) in bad sense, (*a*) in (evil) ways c. בְּ 2 K 21[21] Ez 16[47] 23[31] 2 Ch 22[3]; cf. also (prob.) 2 Ch 21[20] וַיֵּלֶךְ בְּלֹא חֶמְדָּה *and he lived undesirably* (cf. 𝔊 𝔙 Kmp Öt); > others *he departed* (died) *unregretted,* so AV RV; (*β*) sq. acc. 2 K 21[21] Je 18[15] (ה׳ נְתִיבוֹת); (*γ*) c. adverb. acc. הוֹלֵךְ עִקְּשׁוּת פֶּה Pr 6[12] *one walking in perversity* (falseness) *of mouth* (cf. צְדָקוֹת Is 33[15]); (*δ*) in (בְּ) ordinances, statutes (חֻקּוֹת) of bad men Lv 18[3] 20[23] (both H) 2 K 17[8.19] Ez 20[18] (בְּחוּקֵּי). **b.** *walk with* (עִם, אֶת) i.e. associate, be familiar with: בְּשָׁלוֹם וּבְמִישׁוֹר ה׳ אִתִּי Mal 2[6] *in peace and uprightness he walked with me* (י׳); הַצְנֵעַ לֶכֶת עִם־אֱלֹהֶיךָ Mi 6[8]; but also of people at variance with י׳ וַהֲלַכְתֶּם עִמִּי קֶרִי Lv 26[23] cf. v[27.40]; & of י׳ at variance with people וְהָלַכְתִּי . . . עִמָּכֶם בְּקֶרִי v[24] cf. v[28] (all H); with men, אֶת־חֲכָמִים Pr 13[20]; עִם אַנְשֵׁי רֶשַׁע Jb 34[8]; cf. *walk with* (עִם) *vanity* Jb 31[5]. **c.** *walk before* י׳ (לִפְנֵי י׳; c. בֶּאֱמֶת, בְּכָל־לְבָם etc.) 1 K 2[4] 3[6] 8[23.25] 9[4] 2 Ch 6[16] 7[17] cf.

ה׳ קְדֹרַנִּית מִפְּנֵי י׳ Mal 3^{14}; *walk before the living* (i.e. walk *aright* before them) Ec 6^{8}. **d.** *walk, go, after* (אַחֲרֵי) (1) י׳ Dt 13^{5} 1 K 14^{8} Je 2^{2} Ho 11^{10}+; (2) other gods, Ju 2^{12} esp. D: Dt 4^{3} 6^{14} 8^{19} 13^{3} 28^{14} Je 2^{23} 7^{6} 8^{2} 11^{10} 16^{11} 25^{6}+; cf. *go & serve other gods* Jos 23^{16} Dt $13^{7.14}$ 17^{3} 29^{17} (cf. 28^{14} supr.); (3) things which do not profit Je 2^{8}; (4) vanity Ho 5^{11} (reading שָׁוְא cf. VB); v. also Am 2^{4}. **e.** *walk* in (1) one's integrity, etc., בְּתֻמִּי ψ 26^{11} cf. 84^{12} Pr 10^{9}, v. also תָּמִים ψ 15^{2}, הֹלְכֵי תֹם Pr 2^{7}; (2) bad sense, in (בְּ) sin 1 K $15^{3.26.34}$ $16^{2.26}$ 2 K $13^{6.11}$+ (esp. of wicked kings); (evil) counsel 2 Ch 22^{5} cf. ψ 1^{1}. **f.** (1) לֵב as subj., (*a*)=*thoughts,* לֹא לִבִּי הָלַךְ 2 K 5^{26} *did not my thoughts go forth;* (β) *evil inclination,* Jb 31^{7}; אֶל־לֵב שִׁקּוּצֵיהֶם . . . לִבָּם הֹלֵךְ Ez 11^{21}; sq. אַחֲרֵי גִּלּוּלֵיהֶם 20^{16}, אַחֲרֵי בִצְעָם 33^{31}; (2) נֶפֶשׁ=*desire,* טוֹב מַרְאֵה עֵינַיִם מֵהֲלָךְ־נָפֶשׁ Ec 6^{9} *better is sight of the eyes than outgoing of desire.* **4.** other fig. uses: *depart from* מִפְּנֵי Ho 11^{2} (from prophets as God's messengers; opp. קָרָא); *go into,* הָלְכוּ בַכְּלִמָּה Is 45^{16} *they have gone into confusion* (judgment on idol-makers); etc. †**Niph.** *Pf.* 1 s. כְּצֵל כִּנְטוֹתוֹ נֶהֱלָכְתִּי ψ 109^{23} *like a shadow when it stretches out I am gone* (cf. היה **Niph.**)

†**Pi.** (chiefly poet. & late) *Pf.* הִלַּכְתִּי Jb 30^{28} ψ 131^{1}; הִלָּכְתִּי ψ 38^{7}; 3 pl. הִלְּכוּ Jb 24^{10} La 5^{18}; *Impf.* יְהַלֵּךְ Ez 18^{9}+2 t.; וַיְהַלֵּךְ 1 K 21^{27}; 1 s. אֲהַלֵּךְ ψ 86^{11}+2 t.; 3 mpl. יְהַלְּכוּ Hb 3^{11}+2 t.; יְהַלֵּכוּן ψ 89^{16}+2 t.; 1 pl. נְהַלֵּךְ ψ 55^{15} Is 59^{9}; *Imv.* הַלֵּךְ Ec 11^{9}; *Pt.* מְהַלֵּךְ Pr 6^{11} ψ 104^{3}; מְהַלְּכִים Ec 4^{15};—**1.** *walk* in or with a throng sq. בְּ loc.: בְּבֵית א׳ נְהַלֵּךְ בְּרָגֶשׁ ψ 55^{15}; *walk, tread on coals* עַל־הַגֶּחָלִים Pr 6^{28}; of idols ψ 115^{7} *they do not walk,* have not the power of walking (cf. יִצְעָדוּ Je 10^{5}); of one *tramping,* formidable, sim. of poverty וּבָא־כִמְהַלֵּךְ רֵאשֶׁךָ Pr 6^{11},—a highwayman acc. to Ges Ew Hi Now, cf. 𝔊; || מַחְסֹרְךָ כְּאִישׁ מָגֵן (cf. also Hithp. 24^{34}); of י׳, *walking* (in majesty), *marching,* עַל־כַּנְפֵי רוּחַ ψ 104^{3} *on the wings of the wind;* of righteousness, personified, צֶדֶק לְפָנָיו יְהַלֵּךְ ψ 85^{14}; of wisdom בְּאֹרַח צְדָקָה אֲהַלֵּךְ Pr 8^{20} *in the path of righteousness do I walk* (stedfastly, unswervingly); of animals, *go about, prowl,* עַל הַר־צִיּוֹן שֶׁשָּׁמֵם שׁוּעָלִים הִלְּכוּ בוֹ (Qr שֶׁשָּׁמֵם) La 5^{18}, of ships, in (stately) movement ψ 104^{26}; of springs 104^{10} *between mountains they go (run, flow)*; of arrows Hb 3^{11} *at the light of thine arrows* that go (*fly, shoot;* cf. **Hithp.** ψ 77^{18}). **2.** also of *walking about* = living הַמְהַלְּכִים תַּחַת הַשָּׁמֶשׁ Ec 4^{15}; עָרוֹם הִלְּכוּ בְּלִי לְבוּשׁ Jb 24^{10} *naked they keep going about* (freq.), *without clothing;* so of going about as mourner קֹדֵר הִלַּכְתִּי Jb 30^{28} ψ 38^{7} (cf. **Qal** ψ 42^{10}); בָּאֲפֵלוֹת נְהַלֵּךְ Is 59^{9} *in darkness we walk* (of distress); on the other hand בְּאוֹר פָּנֶיךָ יְהַלֵּכוּן ψ 89^{16} (of blessedness & prosperity). **3.** *depart, go entirely away* (מִן) מִמְּקוֹם קָדוֹשׁ יְהַלֵּכוּ Ec 8^{10} *from the holy place they must depart* (on text cf. VB; || וְיִשְׁתַּכְּחוּ בָעִיר). **4.** fig. of mode of life, action, etc.: of particular path of one's life בְּאֹרַח־זוּ אֲהַלֵּךְ ψ 142^{4}; specif. in good sense וַיְהַלֵּךְ אַט 1 K 21^{27} *and he* (Ahab) *walked softly* (as a penitent); oftener c. בְּ of path in which: בִּדְרָכַי יְהַלֵּכוּ ψ 81^{14} *that in my ways they would walk!* cf. 86^{11} (בַּאֲמִתֶּךָ), Ez 18^{9} (בְּחֻקּוֹתַי); in bad or doubtful sense וְהַלֵּךְ בְּדַרְכֵי לִבְּךָ וּבְמַרְאֵי עֵינֶיךָ Ec 11^{9}; cf. also לֹא הִלַּכְתִּי בִּגְדֹלוֹת ψ 131^{1} *I do not walk (move, tread) among great things* (|| וּבְנִפְלָאוֹת מִמֶּנִּי; fig. of humility, cf. also v^{a}). †**Hithp.** *Pf.* הִתְהַלֶּךְ־ Gn 6^{9} 1 S 30^{31}; וְהִתְהַלֵּךְ consec. Ex 21^{19} 1 S 2^{35}; 2 ms. הִתְהַלַּכְתָּ Ez 28^{14} Jb 38^{16}; 1 s. הִתְהַלַּכְתִּי Gn 24^{40}+5 t., etc.; *Impf.* יִתְהַלֵּךְ Pr 23^{31}; יִתְהַלָּךְ Jb 18^{8} 22^{14}; 1 s. אֶתְהַלֵּךְ ψ 43^{2}+2 t.; וְאֶתְהַלְּכָה ψ 119^{45}; 3 mpl. יִתְהַלְּכוּ 1 S 2^{30}+2 t.; וַיִּתְהַלְּכוּ Ju 21^{24}+3 t.; יִתְהַלָּכוּ 1 S 23^{13}+3 t.; יִתְהַלָּכוּן ψ 12^{9}; 3 fpl. וַתִּתְהַלַּכְנָה Zc 6^{7}, etc.; *Imv.* הִתְהַלֵּךְ Gn 13^{17} 17^{1}; הִתְהַלְּכוּ Jos 18^{8} Zc 6^{7}; *Inf.* (לְ)הִתְהַלֵּךְ ψ 56^{14}+4 t.; sf. הִתְהַלֶּכְךָ Pr 6^{22}; *Pt.* מִתְהַלֵּךְ Gn 3^{8}+7 t.; fs. מִתְהַלֶּכֶת Ez 1^{13}; mpl. מִתְהַלְּכִים 1 S 25^{27};—*walk, walk about, move to and fro:* **1.** lit. **a.** *traverse,* in this direction and that, Gn 13^{17} (J; בָּאָרֶץ) Jos 18^{4} (JE), v^{8} (*id.;* לְכוּ וְהִתְה׳ בָּאָרֶץ); cf. Jb 1^{7}=2^{2} (both || שׁוּט) Zc $1^{10.11}$; similarly also 1 Ch 21^{4}; of fiery appearance in Ezek.'s vision מִתְה׳ בֵּין הַחַיּוֹת Ez 1^{13}; of horses in Zec.'s vision Zc 6^{7} (לָלֶכֶת לְהִתְ׳ בָּאָרֶץ), v^{7} (לְכוּ הִתְהַלְּכוּ בָא׳), v^{7}; *go in different directions* וַיִּתְה׳ מִשָּׁם בְּנֵי יִשְׂרָאֵל . . . . אִישׁ לְשִׁבְטוֹ Ju 21^{24} (|| וַיֵּצְאוּ מִשָּׁם etc.); so of lightning flashes as *arrows* of י׳ ψ 77^{18} *went hither & thither;* of water running off different ways 58^{8} (sim. of vanishing of wicked). **b.** *walk, walk about* הִתְהַלֵּךְ בַּחוּץ עַל־מִשְׁעַנְתּוֹ Ex 21^{19} (JE) i.e. leaning upon his staff; Pr 6^{22} (distinguished fr. שָׁכַב, הֵקִיץ); 2 S 11^{2} (עַל־גַּג בֵּית הַמֶּלֶךְ); וּבְחֵקֶר תְּהוֹם הִתְהַלַּכְתָּ Jb 38^{16} *and in the farthest ground of*

the deep hast thou walked? בְּתוֹךְ אַבְנֵי־אֵשׁ הִתְהַלָּ֑כְתָּ Ez 28^{14}; so also of ׳י, walking on earth, in anthropomorphic conception קוֹל י׳ אֱלֹהִים מִתְהַלֵּךְ בַּגָּן Gn 3^{8} (J) *the sound of* ׳י *Elohim walking about in the garden;* of God (*Ēl*) וְחוּג שָׁמַיִם יִתְהַלָּךְ Jb 22^{14} *and the vault of heaven he walketh; walk about in front of* (לִפְנֵי) Est 2^{11}; *attend, follow,* of retainers הַמִּתְהַלְּכִים בְּרַגְלֵי אֲדֹנִי 1 S 25^{27}; *wander,* of Israel ψ מִגּוֹי אֶל־גּוֹי 105^{13} = 1 Ch 16^{20}; *rove about,* of David and his band אֲשֶׁר־הִתְהַלֶּךְ־שָׁם 1 S 30^{31}; וַיִּתְהַלְּכוּ בַּאֲשֶׁר יִתְהַלָּ֑כוּ 23^{13} (on this phr. cf. Lag$^{\text{Psalt. Hieron. 1874, 156 f.}}$ Dr^{Sm}); *walk about, prowl,* of Jehoiachin under fig. of lion, וַיִּתְה׳ Ez 19^{6}; cf. also וּבָא־מִתְהַלֵּךְ רֵישֶׁ֑ךָ בְּתוֹךְ־אֲרָיוֹת Pr 24^{34} *and thy poverty cometh marching* (cf. **Pi.** 6^{11}); *glide, flow* of wine יִתְה׳ בְּמֵישָׁרִים Pr 23^{31} *glideth down smoothly* (VB; cf. **Qal 3** Ct 7^{10}); note esp. the foll., where emphasis lies not on verb, but on an auxiliary word; these cases form the natural transition to the figurative use:—ψ 12^{9} *on every side wicked men are walking;* בְּצֶלֶם יִתְהַלֶּךְ־אִישׁ 39^{7} *in appearance* (*semblance,* lit. *image* cf. Che$^{\text{crit. n.}}$) *walketh a man;* also לָמָּה קֹדֵר אֶתְהַלֵּךְ 43^{2} (cf. **Qal** 42^{10}, **Pi.** 38^{7} Jb 30^{28}). **2.** fig. *walk about* = *live;* the king before (לִפְנֵי) his people 1 S 12^{2}, so of Samuel v^{2}; of priest 2^{35} (לִפְנֵי מְשִׁיחִי); of friendly intercourse with (אֶת) men 1 S 25^{15}; cf. כְּרֵעַ כְּאָח־לִי הִתְהַלָּ֑כְתִּי ψ 35^{14}; of man's relation to God: especially sq. לִפְנֵי, ה׳ לְפָנַי וֶהְיֵה תָמִים, לְפָנַי Gn 17^{1} (P) *walk before me* (live constantly in my presence) *and* (*so*) *be perfect,* cf. 24^{40} (J), 48^{15} (E); ה׳ לְפָנֶיךָ בֶּאֱמֶת וּבְלֵבָב שָׁלֵם 2 K 20^{3} = Is 38^{3}; as token of divine favour יִתְהַלְּכוּ לְפָנַי עַד־עוֹלָם 1 S 2^{30} (v. esp. Dr, on sense here & elsewh.); ψ 116^{9} אֶתְהַלֵּךְ לִפְנֵי י׳ בְּאַרְצוֹת הַחַיִּים, 56^{14} (בְּאוֹר הַחַיִּים); יִתְה׳ בִּשְׁמוֹ Zc 10^{12} *they shall walk in his name;* c. אֶת, of Enoch and Noah ה׳ אֶת־הָאֱלֹהִים Gn 5$^{22.24}$ 6^{9} (denoting intimacy, fellowship: all P); further ψ ה׳ בַּאֲמִתֶּךָ 26^{3} *I have walked in thy faithfulness;* מִתְה׳ בְּתֻמּוֹ צַדִּיק Pr 20^{7} *he that walketh justly in his* (own) *integrity;* אֶתְה׳ בְּתָם־לְבָבִי בְּקֶרֶב בֵּיתִי ψ 101^{2}; cf. also ψ 119^{45} *and let me walk in a large place* (untrammelled, undismayed); of the wicked מִתְהַלֵּךְ בַּאֲשָׁמָיו ψ 68^{22} *one going on in his guilty deeds;* בַּחֲשֵׁכָה יִתְה׳ ψ 82^{5} they *walk in darkness* (‖ לֹא יָדְעוּ וְלֹא יָבִינוּ); of their exposure עַל־שְׂבָכָה יִתְה׳ Jb 18^{8} *he walketh on net-work,* (snare, cf. שׂבכה; ‖ שֻׁלַּח בְּרֶשֶׁת בְּרַגְלָיו); מִתְה׳ בְּקֶרֶב מַחֲנֶךָ esp. of ׳י as accompanying Israel Dt 23^{15} *walk in the midst,* etc., בְּתוֹכְכֶם Lv 26^{12}; 2 S 7^{7} *wherever* (בְּכֹל אֲשֶׁר) *I have walked with* (*among* בְּ) *all* (*the sons of*) *Isr.* = 1 Ch 17^{6}; as inhabiting a tent, on the march, וָאֶהְיֶה מִתְהַלֵּךְ בְּאֹהֶל וּבְמִשְׁכָּן 2 S 7^{6} *and I was walking in a tent and in a tabernacle.*

†**Hiph.** *Pf.* 3 ms. הוֹלִיךְ (as if from ילך, i.e. a verb פ״י, cf. reff. sub **Qal** *Impf.* supr.) 2 K 24^{15}; sf. הוֹלִיכְךָ Dt 8^{2}, וְהוֹלִיכוּ consec. Pr 16^{29}, etc.; *Impf.* יוֹלִיךְ Ec 10^{20}, יוֹלֵךְ Je 32^{5}; juss. יוֹלֵךְ Dt 28^{36}; שֶׁיֹּלֶךְ Ec 5^{14}; וַיּוֹלֶךְ Ex 14^{21} וַיֹּלֶךְ 2 K 6^{19} + 2 t.; אוֹלִיךְ וַיֹּלֶךְ La 3^{2}; sf. וַיּוֹלִכֵנִי Ez 40^{24} 43^{1} 47^{6} 1 s. וָאוֹלֵךְ 2 S 13^{13} Ez 32^{14}, cohort. וְאוֹלִיכָה 2 K 6^{19}, Am 2^{10} + 3 t., etc.; *Imv.* הוֹלֵךְ Nu 17^{11}; fs. הֵילִיכִי Ex 2^{9} (Bö$^{\text{ii. 461, § 1103}}$; but rd. prob. הוֹלִיכִי Ol$^{\text{§ 256, b}}$ Ges$^{\text{§ 69, 2, R 8}}$); mpl. הוֹלִיכוּ 2 K 17^{27}; *Inf.* sf. לְהֹלִיכוּ 2 Ch 36^{6}; *Pt.* מוֹלִיךְ Je 2^{6} + 4 t.; sf. מוֹלִיכֵךְ Dt 8^{15}, מוֹלִכֵךְ Je 2^{17}; מוֹלִיכָם Is 63^{13}; fpl. מוֹלְכוֹת Zc 5^{10};—**1.** *lead, bring:* sq. acc. usually of person; **a.** c. בְּ of space or region through which, Dt 8^{15} (Isr. in wilderness) Je 2^{6} ψ 136^{16}, so also Is 48^{21}; בַּדֶּרֶךְ Je 2^{17}; cf. Jos 24^{3} (E), Is 63^{13} ψ 106^{9}; also fig. Is 42^{16} *and I will lead* (*the*) *blind in a way* (בְּדֶרֶךְ) *they know not;* **b.** c. acc. pers., בְּ of space + acc. of time וָאוֹלֵךְ אֶתְכֶם אַרְבָּעִים שָׁנָה בַּמִּדְבָּר Dt 29^{4}; so Am 2^{10} (sq. Inf. of purpose c. לְ). **c.** sq. acc. pers. + acc. of *way, road,* Dt 8^{2}, cf. דֶּרֶךְ הַדָּרוֹם Ez 40^{24} (acc. of direction). **d.** sq. acc. pers. + acc. of place or condition to which . . . אֶת־נְשֵׁי הַמֶּלֶךְ הוֹלִיךְ גּוֹלָה 2 K 24^{15} *the women of the king,* etc., *he led into exile* (מִירוּשָׁלַםִ בָּבֶלָה); so also, of exile וְהוֹלַכְתִּיהָ הַמִּדְבָּר Ho 2^{16}; בָּבֶל Je 32^{5}; cf. of Yahweh's chastisement, La 3^{2} *me hath he driven and brought,* into *darkness and not* into *light;* sq. acc. pers. + אֶל: אֶל־גּוֹי etc. Dt 28^{36} (of exile); אֶל־נַחֲלֵי־מַיִם Je 31^{9}; אֶל־הַשַּׁעַר Ez 43^{1}; אֶל־הָעֵדָה Nu 17^{11} (P; implic. obj. being censer); אֶל of pers. 2 K 6^{19} Je 52^{26}, עַל in ‖ 2 K 25^{20}; עַל also 1 K 1^{38} וַיֹּלִכוּ אֹתוֹ עַל־גִּיחוֹן (see sub עַל **7 c** *β*). **e.** sq. acc. pers. + ה ָ— loc.: שֹׁמְרֹנָה 2 K 6^{19}; בָּבֶלָה 2 Ch 33^{11} 36^{6} (cf. 2 K 24^{15} supr.); cf. שָׁמָּה 2 K 17^{27}. **2.** *lead away* sq. acc. pers. + appos.; מוֹלִיךְ יוֹעֲצִים שׁוֹלָל Jb 12^{17} *he* (׳י) *leadeth away counsellors despoiled* cf. v^{19}; of Yahweh's judgment on the wicked ψ 125^{5} ׳י *will lead them away with* (אֶת) *the workers of iniquity.* **3.** *carry, bring:* c. obj. help-

less, or inanimate: **a.** + acc. loc., Josiah to Jerusalem (יְרוּשָׁלִָם) 2 Ch 35[24] (וַיְבִיאֻהוּ in ‖ 2 K 23[30]); cf. Zc 5[10] *whither are these carrying the ephah?* אָ֫נָה אוֹלִיךְ אֶת־חֶרְפָּתִי 2 S 13[13]. **b.** *carry, take, take away,* הֵילִ֫יכִי אֶת־הַיֶּ֫לֶד Ex 2[9] (E; on form cf. supr.); also carry away בְּיָדוֹ, in his hand, Ec 5[14]; of the spread of a careless speech Ec 10[20] *fowl of the heavens shall carry the voice* (‖ בַּעַל הכְּנָפַיִם יַגִּיד דָּבָר). **4.** fig., of influence on character: c. acc. pers. + בְּ *into:* Pr 16[29] *and he will lead him into a way* that is *not good* (i.e. sinful). **5. a.** *cause to walk, go,* men (i.e. עַמִּי יִשְׂרָאֵל) on (עַל) the mountains of Israel Ez 36[12] (‖ וִירֵשׁוּךָ, וְהָיִיתָ לָהֶם לְנַחֲלָה); cf. וָאוֹלֵךְ אֶתְכֶם קוֹמְמִיּוּת Lv 26[13] *and I caused you to walk upright* (fig.; opp. to being bowed down by a yoke); Is 63[12] *that caused his glorious arm to go at* (לְ) *the right hand of Moses.* **b.** *cause to flow, run* Ez 32[14] *and rivers like oil will I cause to flow.* **c.** *cause to depart, retire, go back,* י׳, the sea, Ex 14[21] (בְּ instr., בְּרוּחַ קָדִים).

1982 †הֵ֫לֶךְ **n.m. traveller** (properly *a going, journey,* whence *wayfarer, traveller*) only וַיָּבֹא הֵלֶךְ לְאִישׁ הֶעָשִׁיר 2 S 12[4] (‖ הָאֹרֵחַ הַבָּא לוֹ, הָאִישׁ הַבָּא לוֹ);—in MT 1 S 14[26] הֵלֶךְ דְּבַשׁ, ה׳ must be cstr. & = *flowing,* or *dropping* (*of honey*), but rd. rather הָלַךְ 𝔊 The Klo We Dr (& דְּבֹרוֹ for דְּבַשׁ q.v., 𝔊 We Dr).

1978 †[הָלִיךְ] **n.[m.]** *step,* only pl. sf. בִּרְחֹץ הֲלִיכַי בְּחֵמָה Jb 29[6] *when my steps were bathed in cream* (חֶמְאָה = חֵמָה) hyperb. of abundance, wealth.

1979 †[הֲלִיכָה] **n.f. a going, way, travelling-company,** sf. הֲלִיכָתָם Na 2[6] Qr (הלוכתם Kt); elsewh. only pl., cstr. הֲלִיכוֹת ψ 68[25], so Pr 31[27] Qr (הילכות Kt), הֲלִכוֹת Hb 3[6], הֲלִיכֹת Jb 6[19]; sf. הֲלִיכוֹתֶיךָ ψ 68[25];—**1.** *going, walk,* **a.** Na 2[6] *they shall stumble in their going;* elsewh. pl. *goings:* **b.** ψ 68[25.25] of *going, marching, progress of God into the sanctuary* (בַּקֹּדֶשׁ; so Hup Pe Che; Ew Hi De *in holiness*) ref. either to solemn processions of worshippers (e.g. De) or, perh. better, to the theophanic progress of God himself (e.g. Che); also **c.** of goings = *doings* צוֹפִיָּה הֲלִיכוֹת בֵּיתָהּ Pr 31[27] *watching the doings of her household;* of God Hb 3[6] הֲלִכוֹת עוֹלָם לוֹ *ways of eternity* (al. *of old*) *are his.* **2.** *travelling-company, caravan* הֲלִיכֹת שְׁבָא Jb 6[19] (‖ אָרְחוֹת תֵּמָא).

4108-09 †[מַהֲלָךְ] **n.m.**[Ne 2, 6] *walk, journey, going* (late); cstr. מַהֲלַךְ Ez 42[4] + 2 t.; sf. מַהֲלָכְךָ Ne 2[6]; pl. מַהְלְכִים Zc 3[7];—**1.** *walk* 'of 10 cubits' breadth before the chambers' in Ezekiel's temple Ez 42[4] (cf. Da). **2.** *journey* fr. Bab. to Jerusalem Ne 2[6]; of dimension of Nineveh, *a journey of three days* Jon 3[3] i.e. diameter or length, cf. v[4]; (acc. to Herodot[v. 53] one day's journey = 150 stadia, = length of Nineveh acc. to Diod[ii. 3]). **3.** pl. *goings,* i.e. *free access* (VB) Zc 3[7].

†[תַּהֲלוּכָה] **n.f. procession,** only pl. 8418
תַּהֲלֻכֹת Ne 12[31] of thanksgiving-processions at dedication of wall.

†I. [הָלַל] **vb. shine** (acc. to Thes al. = 1984
II. הלל (*splenduit,* from *sonuit acute, clare,* so Thes; these mngs., however, merely assumed); but v. Lag[Or. ii. 19] & sub foll.; cf. Ar. هَلَّ *begin to shine,* هِلَالٌ *new moon;* As. *êllu, bright* COT[Gloss])—**Qal** only *Inf.* sf. בְּהִלּוֹ נֵרוֹ עֲלֵי רֹאשִׁי Jb 29[3] *when it,* viz. *his lamp, shone upon my head* (cf. Ew[§ 309 c]), fig. of God's favour. **Hiph.** *Impf.* יָהֵל Jb 31[26], 3 fs. תָּהֶל Jb 41[10]; 3 mpl. יָהֵלּוּ Is 13[10];—*flash forth light,* of heavenly bodies, אוֹר = *sun* Jb 31[26] (‖ יָרֵחַ יָקָר הֹלֵךְ); sq. acc. cogn. כּוֹכְבֵי הַשָּׁמַיִם וּכְסִילֵיהֶם לֹא יָהֵלּוּ אוֹרָם Is 13[10] (‖ חָשַׁךְ הַשֶּׁמֶשׁ, & יָרֵחַ לֹא־יַגִּיהַּ אוֹרוֹ); also of crocodile עֲטִישֹׁתָיו תָּהֶל אוֹר Jb 41[10] *his sneezings flash forth light* (shining water-drops).

†הֵילֵל **n.m. appell. shining one,** epith. of 1966
king of Babylon, אֵיךְ נָפַלְתָּ מִשָּׁמַיִם ה׳ בֶּן־שָׁחַר Is 14[12] *how art thou fallen, shining one, son of dawn!* i.e. star of the morning. (Cf. As. *muštilil,* epith. of (Venus as) morning-star III R 57[60] Opp[JAS 1871, 448] Schr[SK 1874, 337] COT[ad loc.])

†II. [הָלַל] **vb. be boastful, Pi. praise** 1984
(Ar. هَلَّ *shout,* both in joy & (if conject. of Nö RS be right, v. cit. infr.) in terror; esp. II. in formula of worship; Syr. Pa. ܗܰܠܶܠ *cecinit, laudavit;* cf. NH הִלּוּל *praise,* הַלֵּל *id., Hallel* (ψ 113–118); Aram. הִילּוּלָא *marriage-song,* &c.; on As. *alâlu, shout for joy, rejoice* v. Lyon[Sargontexte 66 (Cylinder, l. 36)] also Winckler[Sargontexte 134, l. 194; 156, l. 149] KB[44, l. 36; 80, l. 194]; all variations of *cry aloud,* cf. Nö[ZMG 1887, 723] RS[Sem. 411]; perh. orig. *break through,* or *out* (in a cry), cf. We[Skizzen iii. 107 ff., esp. 109]; comp. also (acc. to Prät[BAS i. 369 f.]) Eth. ተማህለለ: *implore* (cf. Amhar. Tigr.), & መሐለ: *swear*)—**Qal** *Impf.* 2 mpl. תָּהֹ֫לּוּ ψ 75[5]; *Pt.* הוֹלְלִים ψ 5[6] + 2 t.;—*be boastful* אַל־תָּהֹ֫לּוּ ψ 75[5] (‖ אַל־

(תְּרִימוּקְרֶן); pt. *boastful ones, boasters* ψ 5^{6} (פֹּעֲלֵי אָוֶן‖); 73^{3} 75^{5} (both ‖ רְשָׁעִים). **Pi.** *Pf.* הִלֵּל ψ 10^{3}, 1 s. sf. הִלַּלְתִּיךָ ψ 119^{164}; 3 mpl. וְהִלְּלוּ consec. Is 62^{9}, sf. הִלְלוּךָ Is 64^{10}, etc.; *Impf.* יְהַלֵּל־ ψ 63^{6} 102^{19}; sf. יְהַלֶּלְךָ Pr 27^{2}, יְהַלְלֶךָּ Is 38^{18}, וַיְהַלְלָהָ Pr 31^{28}; 1 s. אֲהַלֵּל ψ 56^{5} + 2 t., cohort. אֲהַלְלָה ψ 69^{31} + 2 t., etc.; *Imv.* fs. הַלְלִי ψ 146^{1} 147^{12}; mpl. הַלְלוּ ψ 104^{35} + 30 t. ψ + Je 20^{13} 31^{7}; sf. הַלְלוּהוּ ψ 22^{24} + 15 t. ψ; *Inf. abs.* הַלֵּל 1 Ch 16^{36}; *cstr.* הַלֵּל 2 S 14^{25} + 16 t. Chr; *Pt.* pl. מְהַלְלִים 1 Ch 23^{5} + 4 t. Ch;—**1.** *praise* man or woman, acc. וַיְהַלְלוּ אֹתָהּ אֶל־פַּרְעֹה Gn 12^{15} (J) *and they praised her to Pharaoh*, cf. Pr 27^{2} $31^{28.31}$ Ct 6^{9}; וְהַמְהַלְלִים אֶת־הַמֶּלֶךְ 2 Ch 23^{12} *and those praising* (shouting acclamations to) *the king;* v. also לְהַלֵּל מְאֹד 2 S 14^{25} (of Absalom's beauty); in bad sense עֹזְבֵי תוֹרָה יְהַלְלוּ רָשָׁע Pr 28^{4} *deserters of law praise a wicked man.*
430, 3050 **2.** usually praise אֱלֹהִים ,י׳, etc.: **a.** sq. acc. of heathen god Ju 16^{24}. **b.** obj. י׳ (אֱלֹהִים); ψ 119^{164} (עַל *on account of*), subj. heaven, earth, seas, etc., ψ 69^{35}; תְּחִי נַפְשִׁי וּתְהַלְלֶךָּ ψ 119^{175}; in summons to all creatures to praise $148^{5.13}$; Is 38^{18} לֹא שְׁאוֹל תּוֹדֶךָּ מָוֶת יְהַלְלֶךָּ (cf. ψ 115^{17}); often of public worship in sanctuary, Is 62^{9} (thanksgiving in sanctuary after harvest), cf. 64^{10} ψ 22^{23} (אֲסַפְּרָה שִׁמְךָ‖), v^{27} 35^{18} 109^{30} (both ‖ אוֹדְךָ) 107^{32} (יְרוֹמְמוּהוּ‖) 84^{5}, v. also 146^{2} (אֲזַמְּרָה לֵא׳‖) 149^{3} (c. בְּ instr.; ‖ יְזַמְּרוּ לוֹ); also obj. שֵׁם י׳ (in some cases of public worship) ψ 74^{21} 148^{5}, Jo 2^{26} (thanksgiving after harvest); וַאֲגַדְּלֶנּוּ בְתוֹדָה‖) ψ 69^{31} שֵׁם־אֱלֹהִים בְּשִׁיר), 145^{2} (אֲבָרְכֶךָּ‖); further, ψ 56^{5} בֵּאלֹהִים אֲהַלֵּל דְּבָרוֹ, also v^{11} + v^{11b} ביהוה וגו׳, but cf. Hup Che on 11^{b} as editorial addition; obj. not expressed וְשִׂפְתֵי הַשְׁמִיעוּ הַלְלוּ וְאִמְרוּ הוֹשַׁע י׳ אֶת־עַמְּךָ Je 31^{7}, רְנָנוֹת יְהַלֶּל־פִּי ψ 63^{6}. **c.** use of Imv. deserves special notice: הַלְלוּהוּ ψ 22^{24} (כַּבְּדוּהוּ‖); of temple-worship cf. $v^{23.25}$); also in summons to angels, sun, moon, etc. (all created things) to praise י׳ $148^{2.2.3.3.4}$ 150^{1}; of temple-worship 150^{2} (בְּ *on account of*) v^{2} (בְּ), $v^{3.3.4.4.5.5}$ (all c. בְּ instr.); further Je 20^{13} (‖ שִׁירוּ לי׳) הַלְלוּ אֶת־י׳ ψ 117^{1} (addressed to nations, ‖ שַׁבְּחוּהוּ), 148^{7} (created things), שַׁבְּחִי יְרוּשָׁלַםִ‖) 147^{12} הַלְלִי אֱלֹהַיִךְ צִיּוֹן
3050 (אֶת־י׳). **d.** note esp.: *praise ye Yah!* הַלְלוּ־יָהּ ψ 135^{3}, liturgical (‖ זַמְּרוּ לִשְׁמוֹ); elsewh. always one word v. Baer$^{ψ\ p. 115}$, & alw. at beginning or end of ψ (chiefly late), appar. liturgical; הַלְלוּיָהּ ψ 104^{35} (‖ בָּרְכִי נַפְשִׁי אֶת־י׳), elsewh. הַלְלוּיָהּ: (1) at beginning ψ 106^{1} 111^{1} (both ‖ הודה) 112^{1} 113^{1} (‖ הַלְלוּ & הַ׳ אֶת־שֵׁם י׳), 135^{1} (‖ *id.*), 146^{1} (הַלְלִי נַפְשִׁי אֶת־י׳‖), 147^{1} (sq. זַמְּרָה in cl. with כִּי), 148^{1} (הַלְלוּהוּ, הַלְלוּ אֶת־י׳‖), 149^{1} (שִׁירוּ לי׳‖), 150^{1} (הַלְלוּהוּ, הַלְלוּ־אֵל‖); (2) at end ψ 104^{35} (supr.), 105^{45} 106^{48} 113^{9} 115^{18} (נְבָרֵךְ יָהּ‖), 116^{19} 117^{2} 135^{21} (‖ בָּרוּךְ י׳) 146^{10} 147^{20} 148^{14} 149^{9} 150^{6} (כֹּל הַנְּשָׁמָה תְּהַלֵּל יָהּ‖); add to these (not liturgical) כֹּל נְשָׁמָה תְּהַלֵּל יָהּ יְהַלֶּל־יָהּ ψ 102^{19}, 150^{6}, לֹא הַמֵּתִים יְהַלְלוּ־יָהּ 115^{17}. **e.** also sq. ליהוה, in Chr, of technical Levitical function (cf. Lag$^{Or.\ ii.\ 16\ ff.}$, who limits this technical הלל to priests, using חֲצֹצְרוֹת, for a signal to the people; v. e.g. Ne 12^{24} cf. v^{27}), 1 Ch 16^{4} (with instrumental music, cf. בִּכְלֵי נְבָלִים וּבְכִנֹּרוֹת & בִּמְצִלְתַּיִם, all v^{5}, and Ne 12^{27}) 23^{30} 25^{3} (all ‖ הודות); exercised (apparently) by both priests and Levites Ezr 3^{11} (‖ הודות) cf. v^{11}; by Levites 2 Ch 20^{19} (בְּקוֹל גָּדוֹל), 29^{30} (בְּדִבְרֵי דָוִיד) in which the people also joined 1 Ch 16^{36}; also 2 Ch 5^{13} (בַּחֲצֹצְרוֹת וּבִמְצִלְתַּיִם וּבִכְלֵי הַשִּׁיר) cf. also v^{12}; ‖ הוֹדוֹת), v^{13} (appar. of Levites & priests), מְהַלְלִים לי׳ בַּכֵּלִים 1 Ch 23^{5} (Levites) cf. 2 Ch 30^{21} (Levites & priests בִּכְלֵי עֹז לי׳); sq. לְשֵׁם תִּפְאַרְתֶּךָ 1 Ch 29^{13} (‖ מוֹדִים; David speaks in name of people); sq. לְהַדְרַת־קֹדֶשׁ 2 Ch 20^{21} (before the army; ‖ מְשֹׁרְרִים לי׳; prob. of Levites, cf. v^{19}). **f.** sq. acc. י׳ Ezr 3^{10} (priests & Levites: עַל־יְדֵי דָּוִיד), Ne 5^{13} (people). **g.** other forms, with like technical sense, but abs.: לְהַלֵּל לְהוֹדוֹת בְּמִצְוַת דָּוִיד Ne 12^{24} (Levites) cf. 1 Ch 23^{5} 2 Ch 8^{14} 29^{30} (עַד־לְשִׂמְחָה) 2 Ch 31^{2} (appar. priests & Levites; בְּשַׁעֲרֵי מַחֲנוֹת י׳ ‖ לְשָׁרֵת וּלְהֹדוֹת); v. also מְשׁוֹרְרִים בִּכְלֵי הַשִּׁיר‖) 2 Ch 23^{13} מוֹדִיעִים לְהַלֵּל); הוֹדוֹת ליהוה‖) 2 Ch 7^{6} בְּהַלֵּל דָּוִיד בְּיָדָם). **3.** appar. *boast, make one's boast* cf. **Qal 2** (sq. בְּ *in, of*), בֵּאלֹהִים ψ 44^{9} (שִׁמְךָ לְעוֹלָם נוֹדֶה‖); so, acc. to most, in bad sense, הִלֵּל רָשָׁע עַל־תַּאֲוַת נַפְשׁוֹ ψ 10^{3} *a wicked man boasteth of the desire of his soul,* but Che *praiseth* (י׳) *for* (i.e. in a mercenary spirit). **Pu.** *Pf.* 3 pl. הוּלָּלוּ ψ 78^{63}; *Impf.* יְהֻלַּל־ Pr 12^{8}; *Pt.* מְהֻלָּל 2 S 22^{4} + 6 t.; f. הַהֻלָּלָה Ez 26^{17} (cf. Ol$^{§\ 250\ c}$ Sta$^{§\ 220,\ 617\ b}$; MT, however, accents as Pf., regarding הַ as = relative, v. Sta$^{§\ 176\ c}$ Ges$^{§\ 52.\ 2,\ R.\ 6}$);—*be praised,* **1.** human subj., be *praised, commended* Pr 12^{8} (opp. יִהְיֶה לָבוּז); of maidens, *praised, celebrated* (in song) ψ 78^{63}; pt. (v. supr.) of city, *renowned* Ez 26^{17}. **2.** of י׳, only pt. = gerundive, *to be praised, worthy*

of praise 2 S 22^{4} = ψ 18^{4}; ψ 48^{2} גָּדוֹל י׳ וּמְה׳ מְאֹד 96^{4} = 1 Ch 16^{25}, ψ 145^{3}; so מְה׳ שֵׁם י׳ 113^{3}.
Hithpa. *Impf.* יִתְהַלֵּל 1 K 20^{11} + 5 t.; יִתְהַלֵּל Pr 20^{14}; 3 fs. תִּתְהַלֵּל ψ 34^{3}, תִּתְהַלָּל Pr 31^{30}; 2 ms. תִּתְהַלֵּל ψ 52^{3} Pr 27^{1}; תִּתְהַלָּל Is 41^{16}; 2 fs. תִּתְהַלְלִי Je 49^{4}; 3 mpl. יִתְהַלְלוּ ψ 64^{11} Is 45^{25}; יִתְהַלָּלוּ ψ 49^{7} Je 4^{2}; *Imv.* mpl. הִתְהַלְלוּ 1 Ch 16^{10} ψ 105^{3}; *Inf.* לְהִתְהַלֵּל ψ 106^{5}; *Pt.* מִתְהַלֵּל Pr 25^{14} Je 9^{23}; pl. מִתְהַלְלִים ψ 97^{7};—*glory, boast, make one's boast:*—**1.** of self-confident boasting, abs. 1 K 20^{11} cf. Pr 20^{14}; sq. בְּ of ground of boast Je 9$^{22.22.22}$ 49^{4} ψ 49^{7} 52^{3} Pr 25^{14}, אַל־תִּתְהַלֵּל בְּיוֹם מָחָר Pr 27^{1}; of glorying in idols הַמִּתְהַלְלִים בָּאֱלִילִים ψ 97^{7}. **2.** of glorying, making one's boast in (בְּ, on the ground of) י׳: בי׳ תִּתְהַלֵּל נַפְשִׁי ψ 34^{3}, cf. Is 45^{25} Je 4^{2} (‖ וְהִתְבָּרְכוּ בוֹ); sq. בִּקְדוֹשׁ יִשְׂרָאֵל Is 41^{16}; v. also ψ 105^{3} = 1 Ch 16^{10} sq. בְּשֵׁם קָדְשׁוֹ (‖ יִשְׂמַח לֵב מְבַקְשֵׁי י׳), cf. further Je 9^{23}; less oft. abs. Je 9^{23} ψ 63^{12} 64^{11} & 106^{5} sq. עִם־נַחֲלָתֶךָ *together with thine heritage* (‖ לִשְׂמֹחַ בְּשִׂמְחַת גּוֹיֶךָ). **3.** once, late = pass. *be praised, commended,* of God-fearing woman Pr 31^{30}. **Poʿel** *Impf.* יְהוֹלֵל Is 44^{25} + 2 t.;—*make into a fool, make fool of,* obj. שֹׁפְטִים Jb 12^{17} (subj. י׳; ‖ מוֹלִיךְ יוֹעֲצִים שׁוֹלָל); obj. קֹסְמִים Is 44^{25} (subj. י׳ ‖ מֵפֵר אֹתוֹת בַּדִּים); obj. חָכָם Ec 7^{7} (subj. הָעֹשֶׁק; ‖ וִיאַבֵּד אֶת־לֵב מַתָּנָה). **Poʿal** *Pt.* לִשְׂחוֹק אָמַרְתִּי מְהוֹלָל Ec 2^{2} *of laughter I said,* It is *mad* (folly); מְהוֹלָלַי ψ 102^{9} *those mad against me* (‖ אוֹיְבַי). **Hithpo.** *Impf.* וַיִּתְהֹלֵל 1 S 21^{14}; 3 mpl. יִתְהוֹלָלוּ Je 51^{7}, יִתְהוֹלְלוּ Na 2^{5}, יִתְהֹלָלוּ Je 50^{38}; *Imv.* mpl. הִתְהֹלְלוּ Je 46^{9}, הִתְהוֹלָלוּ Je 25^{16};—*act madly,* or *like a madman,* וַיִּתְהֹלֵל בְּיָדָם 1 S 21^{14} (of David) *and he acted like a madman in their hands;* of idolatrous worship by Chaldeans וּבָאֵימִים יִתְה׳ Je 50^{38}; of nations, as drunken men, fig. of terror at Yahweh's judgments, Je 25^{16} (‖ הִתְגֹּעֲשׁוּ) 51^{7}; also of madly driving & jolting chariots Na 2^{5} Je 46^{9}.

1985 †**הִלֵּל** **n.pr.m.** (*he hath praised;* cf. NH n.pr. הִלֵּל, *Hillel*) father of a judge of Israel Ju 12$^{13.15}$, called הַפִּרְעָתוֹנִי v. פִּרְעָתוֹן.

1974 †[**הִלּוּל**] **n.[m.]** (NH *id.*) only pl. הִלּוּלִים **rejoicing, praise:** **1.** וַיַּעֲשׂוּ הִלּוּלִים Ju 9^{27} i.e. a vintage-rejoicing, merry-making, connected with thanksgiving וַיָּבֹאוּ בֵּית אֱלֹהֵיהֶם, etc. (i.e. god Baal-Berith, see v^{4}). **2.** of praise to י׳, קֹדֶשׁ ה׳ Lv 19^{24} (H) *holiness of praise,* i.e. a consecrated thing in token of thanksgiving for fruit, offered in 4th year (cf. NH).

†[**הוֹלֵלָה**] **n.f. madness** (on txt. v. infr.), 1947
only pl. הוֹלֵלוֹת, הֹלֵלוֹת, and only Ec: Ec 1^{17} *and I set my heart* (וָאֶתְּנָה לִבִּי) *to know wisdom, and to know madness and folly* (הֹלֵלוֹת וְשִׂכְלוּת), cf. 2^{12} (‖ *id.*); וְלָדַעַת רֶשַׁע כֶּסֶל וְהַסִּכְלוּת הוֹלֵלוֹת 7^{25}, i.e. to know folly to be madness; possibly rd. הוֹלֵלוּת, cf. סִכְלוּת & foll.; the moral evil of it is specif. recognised in Ec 9^{3} (‖ רָע).

†**הוֹלֵלוּת** **n.f. id.** (formed unusually from 1948
the ptcp., an Aram. formation, cf. Ba$^{NB\ 414\ f.}$) תְּחִלַּת דִּבְרֵי־פִיהוּ סִכְלוּת וְאַחֲרִית פִּיהוּ הוֹלֵלוּת רָעָה Ec 10^{13} *the beginning of the words of his mouth is folly, and the end of his mouth* (his speech) *is evil madness.*

הַלְלוּיָהּ, הַלֲלוּיָהּ v. הלל **Pi.** p. 238 1984, 3050

†**יְהַלֶּלְאֵל** **n.pr.[m.]** (*he shall praise God,* 3094
cf. מַהֲלַלְאֵל infr.);—**1.** a man of Judah 1 Ch 4^{16}.
2. a Levite 2 Ch 29^{12}.

†[**מַהֲלָל**] **n.[m.] praise**;—only in וְאִישׁ 4110
לְפִי מַהֲלָלוֹ Pr 27^{21} the refining pot for silver, and the furnace for gold, *and a man according to his praise,* i.e. prob. acc. to the praise of him by others, which tests him; so De Str al.; perh. however *so let a man be to the mouth of his praise,* i.e. *that praises him,*—testing the praise to determine its worth, Thes RobGes; other views are: *according to the measure of his boasting* Ew, i.e. is judged according to his success or failure in that of which he boasts; Hi *according to the thing of which he boasts.*

†**מַהֲלַלְאֵל** **n.pr.m.** (*praise of God,* cf. 4111
יְהַלֶּלְאֵל supr.);—**1.** great-grandson of Seth acc. to genealogy of P, Gn 5$^{12.13.15.16.17}$ 1 Ch 1^{2}. **2.** a man of Judah Ne 11^{4}.

†**תְּהִלָּה** **n.f. praise, song of praise** (cf. 8416
Ar. تَهْلِيل, the shouting of a sacred formula; Sprenger$^{Muhammad\ iii.\ 527}$ We$^{Skizzen\ iii.\ 107\ ff.\ 114.117.214}$ Nö$^{ZMG\ 1887,723}$ RS$^{Sem.\ i.\ 411}$ Che$^{OP\ 460}$) abs. ת׳ Is 60^{18} + 19 t. + Je 49^{25} Kt, v. infr.; cstr. תְּהִלַּת Je 48^{2} + 2 t.; sf. תְּהִלָּתִי Je 17^{14} + 6 t.; תְּהִלָּתְךָ Dt 10^{21}, ψ 48^{11}, תְּהִלָּתֶךָ ψ 35^{28} + 6 t.; תְּהִלָּתֶיךָ ψ 9^{15}; תְּהִלָּתוֹ Is 42^{10} + 10 t.; pl. abs. תְּהִלֹּת Ex 15^{11}; cstr. תְּהִלּוֹת ψ 22^{4} + 3 t.;—**1.** *praise, adoration, thanksgiving,* paid to י׳:—ψ 48^{11} כשמך אלהים כן תהלתך על קצוי ארץ *as thy name, O God, so is thy praise to the ends of the earth,* 111^{10} תהלתו עמדת

לְעַד, תָּמִיד תְּהִלָּתוֹ בְּפִי ψ 34^{2} *continually is his praise in my mouth* (|| אֲבָרְכָה אֶת־י׳) cf. 71^{6}, also יִמָּלֵא פִי תְּהִלָּתֶךָ 71^{8}, פִּי יַגִּיד ת׳ 51^{17}, תַּבַּעְנָה שְׂפָתַי ת׳ 119^{171}, ת׳ י׳ יְדַבֶּר פִּי 145^{21} (|| וִיבָרֵךְ כָּל־בָּשָׂר שֵׁם קָדְשׁוֹ); as sung, *song of praise* יָשִׁירוּ תְּהִלָּתוֹ 106^{12}; הַמְשֹׁרְרִים וְשִׁיר־תְּהִלָּה וְהוֹדוֹת לֵאלֹהִים Ne 12^{46}; cf. ת׳ לֵאלֹהֵינוּ ψ 40^{4} (appos. שִׁיר חָדָשׁ) & Is 42^{10} (appos. *id.*), also לַיְשָׁרִים נָאוָה ת׳ 33^{1} (|| רַנְּנוּ צַדִּיקִים בי׳); vid. perh. ψ 148^{14} (Che; yet see De VB); note further אֱלֹהֵי תְהִלָּתִי ψ 109^{1}; יוֹשֵׁב תְּהִלּוֹת יִשְׂרָאֵל ψ 22^{4} *inhabiting the praises of Isr.;* וּמְרוֹמָם עַל־כָּל־בְּרָכָה וּתְהִלָּה Ne 9^{5} *exalted above all blessing and praise;* cf. also תְּהִלָּתִי Is 48^{9} (|| שְׁמִי), & of *praise due to* י׳ Is 42^{8}. **2.** the act of *general, public, praise* (cf. also supr. esp. ψ 22^{4} 33^{1} 106^{12} Ne 12^{46});—בֹּאוּ שְׁעָרָיו בְּתוֹדָה חֲצֵרֹתָיו בִּת׳ ψ 100^{4} *enter his gates with thanksgiving, his courts with praise;* שִׁירוּ לי׳ שִׁיר חָדָשׁ תְּהִלָּתוֹ בִּקְהַל חֲסִידִים ψ 149^{1}; cf. ψ 22^{26} 65^{2} 66^{2} 147^{1}; before the army הַחֲלוּץ בְּרִנָּה וּתְהִלָּה 2 Ch 20^{22}; in exhortation to the peoples הַשְׁמִיעוּ קוֹל תְּהִלָּתוֹ ψ 66^{8} (|| בָּרְכוּ עַמִּים אֱלֹהֵינוּ), cf. Is 42^{12}. **3.** *praise-song*, as title, תְּהִלָּה לְדָוִד ψ 145^{1} (so NH ספר תהלות & תְּהִלִּים, תִּילִּים, = *Psalms*). **4.** qualities, deeds, etc., of י׳, demanding praise:—נוֹרָא תְהִלֹּת Ex 15^{11} (song), i.e. terrible in attributes that call for praise (|| נֶאְדָּר בַּקֹּדֶשׁ & עֹשֵׂה פֶלֶא); oft. (both sg. and pl.) of Yahweh's deeds c. vb. סִפֵּר ψ 9^{15} 78^{4} 79^{13} Is 43^{21}, also + שֵׁם י׳ ψ 102^{22}; c. יַשְׁמִיעַ ψ 106^{2} (|| יְמַלֵּל גְּבוּרוֹת י׳); + צִדְקֶךָ c. יֶהְגֶּה ψ 35^{28}; c. יְבַשֵּׂרוּ Is 60^{6}; + חַסְדֵי י׳, c. אַזְכִּיר Is 63^{7}; vid. also לְהוֹדוֹת לְשֵׁם קָדְשֶׁךָ לְהִשְׁתַּבֵּחַ בִּתְהִלָּתֶךָ ψ 106^{47} = 1 Ch 16^{35} *to give thanks unto thy holy name, to glory in thy praises* (= praiseworthy deeds). **5.** *renown, fame, glory:* **a.** of Damascus עִיר תְּהִלָּה Je 49^{25} (on Qr תְּהִלַּת v. Hi Ges §80. 2 b); comp. perhaps מַעֲטֵה תְהִלָּה Is 61^{3} *mantle of renown* (*renown as a mantle*, cf. De VB; > Di *splendid garment;* but Bi Che Du read מַעֲטֵה אֵבֶל and translate ת׳ *praise, song of praise*, cf. **1. 2**). **b.** of י׳, כִּסָּה שָׁמַיִם הוֹדוֹ וּת׳ מָלְאָה הָאָרֶץ Hb 3^{3} *his splendour hath covered (the) heavens, and of his renown the earth is full.* Also **c.** fig., *praise, renown*, = obj. of praise, possessor of renown; used (*a*) of Israel Dt 26^{19} (abs.), Je 13^{11} (+ לִי), 33^{9} (+ לִי and לְכֹל גּוֹיֵי הָאָרֶץ)—all || שֵׁם, תִּפְאֶרֶת; v. also Is 61^{11}, & perh. ψ 148^{14} (see sub **1** supr.); (*b*) of Jerusalem Is 62^{7}, also Zp $3^{19.20}$ (both || שֵׁם), all these c. vb. הָיָה or שִׂים; cf. וְקָרָאת יְשׁוּעָה חוֹמֹתַיִךְ וּשְׁעָרַיִךְ ת׳ Is 60^{18}; (*c*) of Babylon וַתִּתָּפֵשׂ תְּהִלַּת כָּל־הָאָרֶץ Je 51^{41}; (*d*) of Moab אֵין עוֹד ת׳ מוֹאָב Je 48^{2}; (*e*) of י׳, הוּא תְהִלָּתְךָ וְהוּא אֱלֹהֶיךָ Dt 10^{21}, כִּי תְהִלָּתִי אָתָּה Je 17^{14} (no vb.)

†[הָלַם] **vb. smite, hammer, strike down** 1986
(cf. Ph. מהלם infr. sub מַהֲלֻמוֹת);—**Qal** *Pf.* 3 fs. וְהָלְמָה consec. Ju 5^{26}; 3 pl. הָלְמוּ Ju 5^{22} Is 16^{8}; sf. הֲלָמוּנִי Pr 23^{35}; *Impf.* 3 ms. sf. יֶהֶלְמֵנִי ψ 141^{5}; 3 mpl. יַהַלְמוּן ψ 74^{6}; *Pt. act.* הוֹלֶם פָּעַם Is 41^{7} (cf. Ges §29, 3 b); *pass.* cstr. הֲלוּמֵי Is 28^{1};—*smite* (with hammer), sq. acc. pers. Ju 5^{26} (fatally; || מָחַק, מָחֲצָה); also fig. of correction, discipline ψ 141^{5} (|| הוֹכִיחַ); of intoxicating wine גֶּפֶן שִׂבְמָה בַּעֲלֵי גוֹיִם הָלְמוּ שְׂרוּקֶּיהָ Is 16^{8} *the vine of Sibma, its choice branches smote down lords of nations* (so Hi De Che Brd Di al., RVm; *lords* subj. acc. to Ges Ew al. AV RV); also הֲלוּמֵי יָיִן *smitten down by wine* Is 28^{1}; cf. further Pr 23^{35}; sq. acc. rei. הוֹלֶם־פָּעַם Is 41^{7} *one striking an anvil; smite down*, or *strike off* ψ 74^{6} (obj. פִּתּוּחִים *carved work*); also abs. of horses' hoofs Ju 5^{22}.—On וַהֲלֹם 1 S 14^{16} v. הֲלֹם.

†הֶלֶם **n.pr.m.** a man of Asher 1 Ch 7^{35}. 1987

†הַלְמוּת **n.f. hammer, mallet**, only cstr. 1989
ה׳ עֲמֵלִים Ju 5^{26} *a workman's hammer.*

†יַהֲלֹם **n.[m.]** a precious stone, **jasper?** 3095
(so 𝔊 𝔙), or **onyx?** (cf. Di Ex 28^{18}) (appar. fr. √ הלם; owing to its hardness, as able to *smite, hammer?*)—mentioned in lists of precious stones Ex 28^{18} 39^{11} Ez 28^{13}.

†מַהֲלֻמוֹת **n.f.pl. strokes, blows** (cf. Ph. 4112
מהלם *stroke, stamp, impression*, once on a coin מהלם אגדר *coinage of Gader* (Gades), = *percussura, κόμμα*, Ges Mon. pl. 40, xv. c also p. 307)—Pr 18^{6} (cf. Baer) 19^{29}, both times of blows on the body.

†הֲלֹם **adv.** of place, **hither** (Ar. هَلُمَّ 1988
hither!)—Ex 3^{5} אַל־תִּקְרַב הֲלֹם approach not *hither*, Ju 18^{3} 20^{7} 1 S 10^{22} 14^{16} and lo, the camp melted away וַיֵּלֶךְ וַהֲלֹם rd. with 𝔊 (ἔνθεν καὶ ἔνθεν) Th We Dr הֲלֹם וַהֲלֹם *hither and thither* i.e. in different directions (cf. הֵנָּה וָהֵנָּה Jos 8^{20}), $v^{36.38}$ Ru 2^{14}; עַד הֲלֹם fig. *hitherto, thus far* (i.e. to this point of dignity and greatness) 2 S 7^{18} (= 1 Ch 17^{16}). ψ 73^{10}, if text be sound, הֲלֹם must mean *thither* (sc. after the persons described v^{3-9}); but such sense questionable; rd. prob. with Houb La for ישיב עמו הלם, יַשְׂבִּעֵמוֹ

לֶחֶם satisfies them with bread: cf. Che Hup[Now]. Gn 16[13] = *here;* but here also text is dub.: v Di. Ju 14[15] rd. הֲלֹם for הֲלֹא: v. הֲ **1** *end.*

1990 †הָם **n.pr.loc.** only in הַזּוּזִים בְּהָם Gn 14[5]; not otherwise known; Vrss בָּהֶם; Jer[Quaest. in libr. Genes.] בְּהֹם; Ol conj. בַּחֲמַת; Tu Di think perh. old name of Rabbath Ammon.

1991 †[הָם?, המה?] only in מֶהֱמֵהֶם Ez 7[11] Ew nothing *of their moaning, wailing;* Thes RV *wealth,* cf. הָמוֹן **5,** but precarious; form very suspicious; prob. dittogr. for preceding מֵהֶם; del. B Co.

4099 †הַמְּדָתָא **n.pr.m.** father of Haman (Pers. *mâh, moon* (*mâha, month,* Spieg[APK 236]) + *data, given?* so (written *hamaodata*) Öt; 𝔊 Ἀμαδαθου (alw. Genit.); in Gk. perh. Μαδάτης [Μαδάτας, Μαδέτης], cf. Xenoph[Cyr. v. 3. 41] Diod[xvii. 67] Pott[ZMG 1859, 424]);—הַמְּדָתָא הָאֲגָגִי Est 3[1.10] 8[5] 9[24]; without האגגי 9[10].

1992 הֵ֫מָּה and הֵם (without appreciable distinction in usage, except prob. in so far as the longer or shorter form was better adapted to the rhythm of particular sentences: on the whole הֵמָּה (alone) is somewhat more freq. than הֵם, הָהֵם on the contrary is said regularly, הָהֵמָּה occurring only 12 t., viz. Nu 9[7] (P), Je 14[15] Zc 14[15], and in the phr. בַּ(הַ)יָּמִים הָהֵמָּה 2 K 18[4] Je 3[16.18] 5[18] 50[4] Jo 3[2] 4[1] Zc 8[23] Ne 13[15], though בַּיָּמִים הָהֵם is much more common) **pron. 3 pl. masc.** (הֵמָּה used incorrectly for the fem. Zc 5[10]
2007 Ru 1[22] Ct 6[8]), **fem.** הֵ֫נָּה [NH also הֵן, which occurs however in Bibl. Heb. only after a prefix: v. infr. **8**], **pr. 3 pl. they** (BAram. הִמּוֹ, q.v.; هُمْ, هُنَّ; Eth. (one form) እሙንቱ: እማንቱ: *'emūn-tū, 'emān-tū;* cf. also for the dissyl. form, the sf. *-ōmū* [fem. *-ōn*]; perh. also As. suff. *šunu, šina[ni],* cf. reff. sub הוּא). In usage not different in genl. from הוּא, הִיא (which see, under the corresponding headings, for fuller explanations), thus:—

1. a. Gn 6[4] Ex 5[7] הֵם יֵלְכוּ let *them* (emph.) go and gather straw, Nu 31[16] Is 24[14] Ho 4[14] 7[3] etc.; after כִּי Je 5[5] 34[7]. (For the use in circumst. clauses v. Dr[§ 160, 169].) **b.** Ju 1[22] ויעלו . . . גַם הֵם, Dt 2[11] (אַף הֵם), 3[20] Jos 9[4] Ez 30[17]. **c.** Ex 18[22] every small matter יִשְׁפְּטוּ־הֵם let them judge *themselves,* v[26] Je 15[19] 17[18] ψ 109[28]; Est 9[1]. **d.** Gn 33[6] 44[3] Jud 6[5] etc. **e.** cf. Ne 10[38].

2. a. (Resuming the subj. with emph.) Gn 14[24] (note accents), Dt 1[39] ψ 23[4] 27[2] (accents), 37[9] 107[24] Ez 36[7] 44[15]. **b.** Is 30[7] Ez 27[13.17.21]; cf. Is 44[11]. **c.** Nu 14[27a] Je 27[9] Ez 43[19] אֲשֶׁר הֵם מִזֶּרַע צָדוֹק, Ec 4[2] Ne 2[13].

3. a. Gn 3[7] Ex 5[8] כִּי נִרְפִּים הֵם for *they* are idle, 14[3] 15[23] 29[33] etc. (the opp. order rare: Nu 11[16] Is 61[9], cf. De[ψ 94, 11]). **b.** Gn 34[21.23] 41[26] 48[5] שני בניך . . . לִי הֵם thy two sons . . ., they are mine, Ex 32[16] + oft.: Is. 41[22] הָרִאשֹׁנוֹת מָה הֵנָּה, 49[21] אֵלֶּה אֵיפֹה הֵם these—where were they? Zp 2[12] after אַתֶּם, peculiarly (cf. Dr[§ 198 Obs. 2]). **c.** Dt 20[15] אֲשֶׁר לֹא־מֵעָרֵי הַגּוֹיִם הָאֵלֶּה הֵנָּה, Ju 19[12] 1 K 9[20]. **d.** 2 K 7[10] כַּאֲשֶׁר הֵמָּה. (Pr 19[7] Kt לֹא־הֵמָּה is prob. corrupt: v. Comm.)

4. a. Pr 30[24] אַרְבָּעָה הֵם קְטַנֵּי־אָרֶץ four things are *they,* the little ones of the earth, v[29] (cf. before a rel. clause v[15.18] 6[16]) Ct 6[8] Is 51[19] שְׁתַּיִם הֵנָּה קֹרְאֹתַיִךְ, 1 Ch 9[26] (v. הוא **4 a**). **b.** (β) Gn 21[29] מָה הֵנָּה שֶׁבַע . . . *lit.* What are they—these seven sheep? Zc 1[9] 4[5]. (γ) אֵלֶּה . . . הֵם + Gn 25[16] (= 1 Ch 1[36]) Lv 23[2] Nu 3[20.21.27.33] 1 S 4[8] 1 Ch 8[6] 12[15] (v. Dr[§ 201, 3]).

6. a. In a neuter sense (rare), Jb 6[7] הֵמָּה כִּדְוֵי לַחְמִי *they* (i.e. such sufferings as mine) are as loathsomeness in my meat, Je 7[4] הֵיכַל י׳ הֵמָּה *they* (i.e. these buildings) are the temple of י׳; and in the fem., Lv 5[22] of all that a man doeth to sin בָּהֵנָּה *therein,* 1 Ch 21[10] מֵהֵנָּה (‖ 2 S 24[12] מֵהֶם); 2 S 12[8] Jb 23[14] כָּהֵנָּה things *such as these.*

7. With art. הָהֵם, Gn 6[4] Ex 2[11] Nu 14[38] + oft.; הָהֵמָּה 12 t. (v. supr.); הָהֵנָּה + 1 S 17[28].

N.B.—Ez 8[6] Kt מֵהֵם stands for מָה הֵם (so Qr), cf. מַזֶּה for מַה־זֶּה Ex 4[2]; 2 K 9[18] עַד־הֵם is irreg. for עֲדֵיהֶם; 2 S 4[6] וְהֵנָּה וגו׳ is textual error for וְהִנֵּה שֹׁעֶרֶת הַבַּיִת סֹקֶלֶת חִטִּים וגו׳ v. We Dr (𝔊 & RVm).

8. With preps. (in lieu of the normal, and more usual, forms with suffixes לָהֶם, בָּהֶם, מֵהֶם etc. [כָּהֵן & כָּהֶם, however, each once only, כְּמוֹהֶם thrice: v. כְּ])—**a.** בָּהֵמָּה + Ex 30[4] 36[1] (both P), Hb 1[16]; כָּהֵמָּה + Je 36[32]; לָהֵמָּה + Je 14[16]; מֵהֵמָּה + Je 10[2] Ec 12[12]. **b.** כָּהֵם + 2 S 24[3] Yahweh add to the people כָּהֵם וְכָהֵם מֵאָה פְעָמִים *the like of themselves* and *the like of themselves* 100 times, = 1 Ch 21[3] (but כָּהֵם here only once, cf. Dt 1[11] כָּכֶם), 2 Ch 9[11] Ec 9[12]. **c.** כָּהֵנָּה + Lv 5[22] (P) Nu 13[19] (JE) Je 5[17]: כָּהֵנָּה + Gn 41[19] 2 S 12[8] וְאֹסִפָה לְּךָ כָּהֵנָּה וְכָהֵנָּה, Jb 23[14]: לָהֵנָּה + Ez 1[5.23.23] 42[9] Zc 5[9]: מֵהֵנָּה + Lv 4[2] (P) Is 34[16] Je 5[6] Ez 16[51] 42[5] ψ 34[21] 1 Ch 21[10] (‖ 2 S
24[12] מֵהֶם). **d.** בָּהֵן + Gn 19[29] (P) 30[26.37] Ex 25[29] 2004
37[16] (both P) Lv 10[1] 11[21] 14[40] Nu 10[3] 16[7] (all

P) Dt 28^{52} Je 4^{29} 48^{9} 51$^{43.43}$ (בָּהֵן thrice only,
3860-61 v. p. 88); כָּהֵן †Ez 18^{14} (edd.; Baer כָּהֶן); לָהֵן
(=*therefore*) †Ru 1$^{13.13}$ (also BAram.); מֵהֵן †Ez 16$^{47.52}$ (edd.; Baer מֵהֶן). (With the exception of כָּהֵנָּה, these forms are found mostly in P and writers not earlier than Je.; **b** and **d**, however, depend solely on the punctuation.)

1993 †[הָמָה] **vb. murmur, growl, roar, be boisterous** (𝔗 הֲמָא, but rare, and perh. not genuine Aram.; cf. Ar. هَمْهَمَ *murmur*);—**Qal** *Pf.* 3 mpl. הָמוּ ψ 46^{7} + 2 t.; וְהָמוּ consec. Je 5^{22} + 2 t.; *Impf.* יֶהֱמֶה Je 6^{23} + 3 t.; 2 fs. תֶּהֱמִי ψ 42^{12} 43^{5}; יֶהֱמוּ 42^{6}; וַתֶּהֱמִי 55^{18}; אֶהֱמֶה 77^{4}; אֶהֱמָיָה 46^{4} + 3 t.; וַיֶּהֱמוּ Is 51^{15} Je 31^{35}; יֶהֱמָיוּן ψ 39^{7} + 2 t.; 1 pl. נֶהֱמֶה Is 59^{11}; *Inf.* הֲמוֹת Is 17^{12}; *Pt.* הֹמֶה Pr 20^{1} Je 4^{19}; f. הוֹמָה 1 K 1^{41}, הֹמִיָּה Pr 7^{11} 9^{13}, הוֹמִיָּה Is 22^{2}; fpl. הֹמִיּוֹת Pr 1^{21}, הֹמוֹת Ez 7^{16} (Co הַמּוֹת cf. 𝔊 𝔖);—**1.** *growl* like a dog כַּכֶּלֶב ψ 59$^{7.15}$, subj. wicked men; *groan* (in distress, lamentation), like bears כַּדֹּבִּים Is 59^{11} (‖ הגה כיונה); of doves (also in sim.) Ez 7^{16} cf. Da (si vera l., vid. supr.). **2.** *murmur*, fig. of soul (נֶפֶשׁ) in discouragement ψ 42$^{6.12}$ 43^{5}; in prayer 55^{18} 77^{4} (both ‖ אָשִׂיחָה); also subj. מֵעַיִם, of the *thrill* of deep-felt compassion or sympathy, sq. לְ of person pitied, Je 31^{20} (‖ רחם ארחמנו), sq. עַל, Ct 5^{4}; further כַּכִּנּוֹר, *like the lyre* (*zither*) Is 16^{11}; כַּחֲלִלִים, *like flutes*, subj. לֵב Je 48^{36} (sq. לְ) v^{36} (sq. אֶל); cf. Je 4^{19} לִבִּי הֹמֶה־לִי. **3.** *roar*, of waves, subj. גַּלִּים Je 5^{22} 31^{35} Is 51^{15} cf. ψ 46^{4}; sim. of roar of multitudes Is 17^{12} Je 6^{23} 50^{42}; metaph. *id.*, Je 51^{55}; *be tumultuous*, of peoples ψ 46^{7} (‖ מָטוּ); 83^{3} (‖ נָשְׂאוּ ראשׁ). **4.** *be in commotion, stir*, of city 1 K 1^{41} Is 22^{2}; so pt. fpl. as subst. ראשׁ הֹמִיּוֹת Pr 1^{21} *head of stirring, bustling* streets (‖ פתחי שערים); of man, אַךְ־הֶבֶל יֶהֱמָיוּן ψ 39^{7} *surely to no purpose they bustle about* (‖ אַךְ־בְּצֶלֶם יִתְהַלֶּךְ־אִישׁ). **5.** *be boisterous, turbulent*, as with wine Zc 9^{5} (but rd. perh. דָּמָם, cf. Fi$^{Hexapl. 11, 3, 1024}$ Klo$^{Th LZ, 1879, 564}$ Sta$^{ZAW 1881, 18}$); also pt. as adj., of שֵׁכָר (by meton.) Pr 20^{1}; of shameless woman Pr 7^{11} 9^{13}.

1995 †הָמוֹן **n.m.**$^{1 S 4, 14}$ (**f.** †Jb 31^{34}) **sound, murmur, roar, crowd, abundance**;—abs. ה׳ 1 S 4^{14} + 27 t. (+ 2 K 25^{11} = אָמוֹן in ‖ Je 52^{15}, v. II. אָמוֹן p. 54 supr.); cstr. הֲמוֹן Gn 17^{14} + 30 t.
1996 + Ez 39$^{11.15}$ (גֵּיא הֲמוֹן גּוֹג); sf. הֲמוֹנוֹ Is 5^{13} + 2 t.
+ Ez 31^{18} Qr + 3 t. (Kt המונה); so also Co for n.pr. (?) הֲמוֹנָה (q.v.) 39^{16}; הֲמוֹנָהּ Is 5^{14} + 6 t. + Ez 7$^{12.13}$ 30^{4} (all del. B Co; in 7^{13} also Da), הֲמֹנָהּ Ez 29^{19}; הֲמוֹנָם Is 31^{4} Ez 7^{11}; pl. הֲמֹנִים Jo 4$^{14.14}$; sf. הֲמוֹנֶיהָ Ez 32^{30};—הֲמָנְכֶם Ez 5^{7} v. sub המן infr.;—**1.** *sound, murmur, rush, roar*, esp. sound made by a crowd of people, *murmur, roar* ψ 65^{8} (שְׁאוֹן יַמִּים ‖ ה׳ לְאֻמִּים etc.); cf. קוֹל ה׳ Is 13^{4} *sound of a roaring* (‖ קוֹל שְׁאוֹן), 33^{3} Dn 10^{6}; הֲמוֹן עַמִּים Is 17^{12} (‖ שְׁאוֹן לְאֻמִּים) where again compared with הֲמוֹת יַמִּים; also 31^{4} of throng of shepherds (‖ קוֹל); of a city ה׳ קִרְיָה Jb 39^{7} (‖ תְּשֻׁאוֹת נֹגֵשׂ); cf. ה׳ עִיר = *noisy city* Is 32^{14}, הֲמוֹנָהּ Is 5^{14}; of *sound* of songs ה׳ שִׁירַיִךְ Ez 26^{13} (‖ קוֹל כִּנּוֹרַיִךְ), cf. Am 5^{23} (‖ זִמְרַת נְבָלֶיךָ); of crying קוֹל ה׳ 1 S 4^{14} (‖ קוֹל צְעָקָה); v. further הֲמוֹן מֵעִים fig. of sympathy Is 63^{15} (‖ רַחֲמִים), cf. הָמָה **2**; of rain קוֹל ה׳ הַגָּשֶׁם 1 K 18^{41}, cf. Je 10^{13} = 51^{16};—of *rumbling* of chariot-wheels ה׳ גַּלְגִּלָּיו Je 47^{3} (‖ קוֹל שַׁעֲטַת פַּרְסוֹת & רַעַשׁ לְרִכְבּוֹ). **2.** *tumult, confusion* (as occasioning a roar) 1 S 14^{19} 2 S 18^{29}. **3.** *crowd, multitude* (esp. freq. in Ez Ch):—**a.** frequently of great army Ju 4^{7} 1 S 14^{16} 1 K 20$^{13.28}$ Is 29$^{5.5}$ 2 Ch 13^{8} 14^{10} 20$^{2.12.15.24}$ 32^{7}; cf. Ez 39^{11}; also 7$^{12.13}$ 30^{4} (cf. emend. supr.); on Je 3^{23} cf. VB; v. further גֵּיא הֲמוֹן גּוֹג Ez 39$^{11.15}$; Dn 11^{10} (ה׳ חֲיָלִים רַבִּים) v$^{11.11.12.13}$ (‖ חַיִל גָּדוֹל); also pl. Jo 4$^{14.14}$. **b.** of a whole people 2 S 6^{19} Is 5^{13} 16^{14} Ez 7$^{11.14}$ 29^{19} 30$^{10.15}$ 31$^{2.18}$ 32$^{12.12.16.18.20.24.25.26.31.32}$. **c.** of any great throng 2 K 7$^{13.13}$ (so MT 25^{11}, but ‖ Je 52^{15} הָאָמוֹן) ψ 42^{5} Jb 31^{34} (ה׳ רַבָּה) Ez 23^{42}; ה׳ גּוֹיִם Gn 17$^{4.5}$ (P) cf. Is 29$^{7.8}$; so, under fig. of overwhelming mass of waves Je 51^{42}. **4.** *great number, abundance* (late) ה׳ נָשִׁים 2 Ch 11^{23}; of cattle Je 49^{32}; of things: materials for temple-building 1 Ch 29^{16}; tithes & gifts 2 Ch 31^{10}. Hence **5.** *abundance, wealth*, ψ 37^{16} cf. Ec 5^{9} (‖ כֶּסֶף), Is 60^{5} (ה׳ יָם ‖ חֵיל גּוֹיִם).

†[הֶמְיָה] **n.f. sound, music,** of instru- 1998
ments הֶמְיַת נְבָלֶיךָ Is 14^{11}.

†הֲמוֹנָה **n.pr.loc.** a city appar. to be 1997
founded to commemorate defeat of Gog, וְגַם שֶׁם־עִיר ה׳ Ez 39^{16}, but txt. dub. cf. Da; Co prop. וגמר המונו v. הָמוֹן supr.

המל (√ of foll.; cf. Ar. هَمَلَ *shed tears* (sc. the eye); *rain steadily* (sc. the sky)).

†הֲמוּלָּה, הֲמֻלָּה **n.f. rain-storm** (?), 1999
rushing or roaring sound (?): קוֹל הֲמוּלָּה גְדֹלָה Je 11^{16} *sound of a great storm*, of wind fanning flames in tree (in fig. of Yahweh's judgment on Judah); > AV RV Da *tumult*; קוֹל הֲמֻלָּה כְּקוֹל

מַחֲנֶה Ez 1^{24} of noise of wings of living creatures in Ezekiel's vision (del. B Co cf. Hi).

2000 †**הָמַם vb. make a noise, move noisily, confuse, discomfit** (cf. [הוּם])—**Qal** *Pf.* וְהָמַם consec. Is 28^{28}; sf. הֲמָמַנִי Je 51^{34} Qr (Kt הֲמָמָנוּ), הֲמָמָם 2 Ch 15^{6}; 1 s. וְהַמֹּתִי Ex 23^{27}; *Impf.* וַיָּהָם Ex 14^{24} Ju 4^{15}; sf. וַיְהֻמֵּם Jos 10^{10} 1 S 7^{10} ψ 18^{15} + 2 S 22^{15} Kt (doubtless right; Qr וַיָּהֹם); 2 ms. sf. וּתְהֻמֵּם ψ 144^{6}; *Inf. sf.* לְהֻמָּם Dt 2^{15} Est 9^{24};—**1.** *move noisily*, trans., drive a wagon in threshing ה׳ גִּלְגַּל עֶגְלָתוֹ וּפָרָשָׁיו Is 28^{28} (‖דוש). **2.** *confuse, discomfit*, c. acc. Ex 14^{24} 23^{27} Jos 10^{10} Ju 4^{15} 1 S 7^{10} ψ 18^{15} = 2 S 22^{15} (‖הפיץ), ψ 144^{6} (‖*id.*); *discomfit, vex*, 2 Ch 15^{6} c. acc. & בְּכָל־צָרָה of instr.; c. acc. also Dt 2^{15} (sq. עַד תֻּמָּם), Est 9^{24} (sq. לְאַבְּדָם); prob. also Je 51^{34} (‖אָכַל), cf. הוּם Dt 7^{23}.

1950 †**הוֹמָם n.pr.m.** son of Seir the Horite
1967 1 Ch 1^{39} 𝔊 Αἱμαν 𝔊L Ημαν; = הֵימָם Gn 36^{22}.

†**[הָמַן] vb. rage, be turbulent** (? denom. fr. המון Thes, after Rabb.; cf. Ke RV; AV *multiply;* but very dub.)—only **Qal** *Inf.* sf. יַעַן הֲמָנְכֶם מִן־הַגּוֹיִם Ez 5^{7} (Sm queries; Ew, after 𝔖 Aq, הֶמְיָנְכֶם fr. מנה); rd. rather, with Bö Co Da, המרותכם (fr. מרה) *because ye rebelled.*

2001 הָמָן **n.pr.m. Haman,** favourite of Ahasuerus (etym. dub.; acc. to Jen$^{VOJ\ 1892,\ 58\ ff.}$ = Elamit. n.pr.div. *Humban*, or *Humman*)—Est 3^{1} + 53 t. in Esther.

המס (√ of foll.; meaning dubious).

2003 †**[הֶמֶס] n.[m.]** only pl. הֲמָסִים **brushwood** (cf. De Che Di RV; some such mng. prob. fr. context) כִּקְדֹחַ אֵשׁ הֲמָסִים Is 64^{1} *as fire kindleth brushwood* (VB).

המר (√ of foll.; cf. Ar. هَمَرَ *pour, pour out*).

4113 †**[מַהֲמֹרָה] n.f. flood** (cf. Ar. √), or **watery pit** (prop. *place of flowing waters;* cf. Symm βοθύνους, and NH, NHWB$^{iii.\ 40}$)—only pl. מַהֲמֹרוֹת ψ 140^{11} (Gr Che מכמרות, *nets*, v. sub כמר; comp. רֶשֶׁת v^{6}).

2004 I. [הֵן] **pron. 3 pl. fem.,** oft. in NH, in
3860 Bibl. Heb. only with prefixes, בָּהֵן, etc.: see under הֵמָּה **8 d.** p. 241f

2005 II. הֵן 100 (הֶן־ †Nu $23^{9.24}$ Jb $8^{19.20}$ 13^{1} 26^{14} $33^{6.12.29}$ $36^{5.22.26}$; הֶן־ Jb 13^{15} 36^{30} 41^{1}+) **demonstr. adv.** or **interj.** lo! behold (on etym. v. הִנֵּה), less widely used than הִנֵּה, and in prose mostly confined to calling attention to some fact upon which action is to be taken, or a conclusion based; **a.** Gn 3^{22} הֵן הָאָדָם הָיָה *behold*, the man is become as one of us, & now lest, etc., 4^{14} *behold*, thou hast driven me forth etc., 11^{6} 15^{3} 19^{34} 27^{11} 29^{7} 30^{34} (nearly = *yea*), Ex 5^{5} $6^{12.30}$ Lv $10^{18.19}$ Nu 17^{27} Dt 5^{21} (in prose only in Pent. (23 t.) and Ez 18^{4} in this usage); in poetry, used more freely, but chiefly in Is² & Jb,—Nu $23^{9.24}$ (Balaam) Is 23^{13} 32^{1} 33^{7} ψ $51^{7.8}$ 68^{34} 78^{20} 139^{4} Pr 11^{31} (stating the premiss to a conclusion introduced by אַף כִּי, q.v.), 24^{12}: elsewhere (except in senses **b, c**) only in Is² (23 t.) & Jb (31 t.), as Is $40^{15.15}$ $41^{11.24.29}$ $50^{1.2.9.9.11}$ Jb 4^{18} 15^{15} 25^{5} (in these three passages before אַף or אַף כִּי), $9^{11.12}$ etc. (v. supr.). †**b.** as a **hypoth. part.,** propounding a possibility, **if** (so NH BAram., Mand. Palm. (ZMG 1888, 404); on the contr. Syr. ܐܢ, Pal. 𝔗 אִין, also Palm. (*ib.* p. 415), Ar. إِنْ, with א), a special application or development of the use **a**: Ex 4^{1} והן לא יאמינו לי and *behold* (= and *suppose*) they will not believe me? etc., Lv 25^{20} and if (וְכִי) ye say, What shall we eat the 7th year? הֵן לֹא נִזְרָע *behold*, we shall not sow etc. (i.e. *supposing* we do not sow), Is 54^{15} Jb 40^{23} 2 Ch $7^{13.13}$ (v^{13b} וְאִם); stating the ground on which a qu. is based, Ex 8^{22} (הֲלֹא=וְלֹא), Je 3^{1} Hg 2^{12} (v. הֵן Aram. **b**). †**c. if, whether,** in an indirect question, Je 2^{10} רְאוּ הֵן הָיְתָה כָּזֹאת (but
Gr הֲנִהְיְתָה); cf. אִם **2 b**, and הֵן Aram. **3.** 518, 2006
p. 50, 1090

הִנֵּה, once הִנֶּה־ Gn 19, 2, **demonstr. part.** 2009
lo! behold! (إِنَّ *certainly, surely,* lit. *lo!*), with sf. (the pron. being conceived as accus., Ew § 262 c; cf. إِنَّ, which takes an accus., whether of a noun or pron. sf.) הִנְנִי Gn 6^{13} + oft. (also הִנֵּנִי Gn 22^{7}), הִנֵּנִי Gn $22^{1.11}$+, (הִנֶּנִּי Gn 27^{18}), †Is 65^{1} הִנֵּנִי הִנֵּנִי (but הִנֵּה אָנֹכִי is also said Gn $24^{13.43}$ 25^{32} 48^{21} Ex 4^{23} 7^{17}+; and, more rarely, הִנֵּה אֲנִי Ez $37^{5.12.19.21}$ 2 Ch 2^{3}, cf. 2 K 10^{9} Je 32^{27}); הִנְּךָ Gn 20^{3} + (†2 K 7^{2} הִנְּכָה), הִנֶּךָ †ψ 139^{8}, fem. הִנָּךְ Gn 16^{11} + 6 t.; הִנּוֹ †Nu 23^{17} Jb 2^{6} 1 Ch 11^{25}, הִנֵּהוּ †Je 18^{3} Kt (הִנֵּה הוּא is more usual, as Gn 20^{16} 42^{27} 1 S 10^{22} Je 38^{5} Ru 3^{2}): 1 pl. הִנְנוּ †Jos 9^{25} 2 S 5^{1} Je 3^{22} Ezr 9^{15}, הִנֶּנּוּ †Gn 44^{16} 50^{18} Nu 14^{40}, הִנֵּנוּ Jb 38^{35}; הִנְּכֶם †Dt 1^{10} Je 16^{12}; הִנָּם Gn 40^{6} + oft. (37 t.)—*lo! behold!* **a.** pointing to persons or things, Gn 12^{19} and now הִנֵּה אִשְׁתְּךָ *behold* thy wife! 18^{9} הִנֵּה בָאֹהֶל *behold* (she is) in the tent (the suffix, when the noun to which הנה refers has immediately pre-

ceded, being not unfrequently omitted, 16^{14}: cf. Dr$^{§ 135. 6, 2}$), 30^{3} 31$^{51.51}$ Ex 24^{8} etc. With sf. of 1 ps., esp. in response to a call, indicating the readiness of the person addressed to listen or obey, *Here I am!* (lit. *Behold me!*) Gn 22$^{1.7.11}$ 27$^{1.18}$ 31^{11} 37^{13} 46^{2} Ex 3^{4} 1 S 3$^{4.5.6.8.16}$ 22^{12} 2 S 1^{7} Is 6^{8}, cf. 1 S 12^{3} הִנְנִי עֲנוּ בִי *here I am*, answer against me, 14^{43} (cf. Dr$^{p.292}$), 2 S 15^{26} (in resignation: cf. Gn 44^{16} 50^{18} Jos 9^{25} Ezr 9^{15}): of God Is 52^{6} 58^{9} 65$^{1.1}$ (repeated for emphasis). In the pl. הננו Nu 14^{40} Je 3^{22} Jb 38^{35}.—Emph. הִנְנִי אָנִי Ez 34$^{11.20}$, cf. 6^{3}. On הִנְנִי אֶל..., v. אל **4**, p. 40. **b.** introducing clauses involving predication: (*a*) with ref. to the past or present, it points generally to some truth either newly asserted, or newly recognised, Gn 1^{29} *behold!* I have given to you all herbs etc. 17^{20} 27^{6} 1 S 14^{33} etc.; often one upon which some proposal or suggestion is to be founded, Ex 1^{9} (cf. הן Gn 11^{6}) 1 S 20$^{2.5}$ 2 K 5^{20}. When the proposal is to be of the nature of an entreaty or request, הִנֵּה־נָא is often used, instead of the simple הִנֵּה Gn 12^{11} 16^{2} 18^{7} 1 K 20^{31} 22^{13} al. (v. נָא). (*b*) with ref. to the future. Here it serves to introduce a solemn or important declaration Ex 32^{34} 34^{10} Is 7^{14}; and is used esp. with the ptcp. (the *fut. instans*, Dr$^{§ 135.3}$) in predictions or threats, Gn 20^{3} הִנְּךָ מֵת (lit.) *behold* thee (accus.) about to die, thou art about to die, Ex 4^{23} 7^{17} 9^{3} Dt 31^{17} 1 S 3^{11} 1 K 20^{36} 22^{25} Is 3^{1} 10^{33} 17^{1} 19^{1} 22^{17} 24^{1}+oft.; in the phrase הנה ימים באים †1 S 2^{31} 2 K 20^{17}=Is 39^{6} Am 4^{2} 8^{11} 9^{13} + Je 15 t.; very often with the suffix of 1 ps. sg., as הִנְנִי מֵבִיא *Behold*, I bring (lit. *behold me bringing*, or *about to bring*) ... Gn 6^{17} Ex 10^{4} & often, esp. in Je; Gn 9^{9} Ex 8^{17} 9^{18} 34^{11} 2 K 22^{20} Is 13^{17} 29^{14} 43^{19} Je 8^{17} 11^{22} (הִנְנִי פֹקֵד; so 23^{2}+) 16^{16} 20^{4}, etc.; anomalously, with change of person, Is 28^{16} הִנְנִי יִסַּד (acc. to points) *behold me*, one who *has founded*, 29^{14} הִנְנִי יוֹסִף *behold me*, one who *will add* (so 38^{5}); but it is dub. whether the ptcp. יֹסֵד, יוֹסֵף should not be read. **c.** וְהִנֵּה... very freq. in historical style, esp. (but not exclusively) after verbs of *seeing* or *discovering*, making the narrative graphic and vivid, and enabling the reader to enter into the surprise or satisfaction of the speaker or actor concerned: Gn 1^{31} and *behold*, it was very good, 6^{12} 8^{13} 15^{12} 18^{2} 37^{29} Ex 2^{6} Dt 9^{13} etc.: in the description of a dream Gn 37$^{7.9}$ 40$^{9.16}$ 41$^{1.2.3}$ Is 29^{8}, or of a vision Am 7$^{1.4}$ 8^{1} etc. With a ptcp. (the context fixing the sense to the past), Gn 24^{30} 37^{15} (both without suffix); Ju 9^{43} 11^{34} 1 K 19$^{5.11}$+. **d.** like II. הֵן (**b**), nearly=*if* (rare): Lv 13$^{5.6.7.8.9}$ (& elsewhere in this and the next ch.) וְהִנֵּה *and behold=and if*, Dt 13^{15} and 17^{4} וְהִנֵּה אֱמֶת *and behold* it is true=*and if* it be true, 19^{18} 1 S 20^{12}; cf. 1 S 9^{7} 2 S 18^{11} Ho 9^{6}.

I. הֵ֫נָּה $_{49}$ **adv.** hither (perh. from II. הֵן, 2008
used δεικτικῶς, with ה-*loc.*, prop. *lo hitherwards!* or perh. akin to هُنَا, هَنَّا, هِنَّا *here*)—**a.** of *place*: (*a*) hither Gn 15^{16} יָשׁוּבוּ הֵנָּה, 42^{15} 45^{5} that you have sold me הֵנָּה *hither*, v$^{8.13}$ Jos 2^{2} 3^{9} 18^{6} 2 S 1^{10} Is 57^{3} וְאַתֶּם קִרְבוּ הֵנָּה, Je 31^{8} 51^{5}+; 1 S 20^{21} מִמְּךָ וָהֵנָּה from thee *and hitherwards*, i.e. on this side of thee (opp. מִמְּךָ וָהָלְאָה): repeated 2 K 4^{35} אַחַת הֵנָּה וְאַחַת הֵנָּה once *hither* and once *thither*=once *to and fro*; הֵנָּה וָהֵנָּה *hither and thither* i.e. in different (or opposite) directions, †Jos 8^{20} 2 K 2$^{8.14}$ 1 K 20^{40} strangely וַיְהִי עַבְדְּךָ עֹשֶׂה הֵנָּה וָהֵנָּה *lit.* and thy servant was a *doer of hitherwards and thitherwards*, i.e. was engaged in different directions (Ew$^{§ 360. c}$ treats ה׳ here as the pron. 3 pl. fem. construed irregularly, cf. עֹשֶׂה אֵלֶּה: but rd. prob. with 𝔊 𝔗 𝔖 𝔙 Th Klo פֹּנֶה *was turning* or *looking* (Ex 2^{12}) for עֹשֶׂה); עַד־הֵנָּה *even hither*, Nu 14^{19} 1 S 7^{12} 2 S 20^{16} קְרַב עַד־הֵנָּה, 2 K 8^{7}, *to this point* (in a book) Je 48^{47} 51^{64} (note of compiler or scribe). (*β*) *here* (cf. שָׁמָּה=*there*) Gn 21^{23} swear to me הֵנָּה *here*, Dn 12^{5} הֵנָּה לְ׳ ... הֵנָּה לְ׳ *on this side* of ... *on that side* of ... †**b.** of *time*, in עַד הֵנָּה *hitherto* Gn 15^{16} (with a neg., =not *yet*) 44^{28} Ju 16^{13} ψ 71^{17} & *until now* do I keep declaring thy wonders, 1 Ch 9^{18} 12^{9} *until now* (the point reached in the narrative). In late Heb., contracted to עֲדֶנָּה *hitherto, still* †Ec 4^{2}, עֲדֶן †Ec 4^{3} אֲשֶׁר עֲדֶן לֹא הָיָה=who has not *yet* been (cf. Mish. עֲדַיִן *hitherto, still*, עֲדַיִן לֹא =*not yet*).

II. הֵ֫נָּה **pron. 3 pl. fem.** they: v. הֵ֫מָּה. p. 241 2007

הֲנָחָה v. sub נוח. p. 629 2010

†הִנֹּם **n.pr.m.** (deriv. & mng. dub.; acc. 2011
to Sim Bö Gf al.=*wailing*, Ar. هَنَّ, fr. cries of children (v. infr.), but this improbable)—only in גֵּי(גֵּיא)בֶן־ה׳, & abbrev. ג׳ ה׳, **n.pr.loc.** of valley S. of Jerusalem, (𝔊 φάραγγα Ὀνομ Jos 15$^{8.8}$ Σονναμ 18^{16}; Γαιεννα v^{16}; Γαιβενθομ 2 Ch 28^{3}, 𝔊L φάρ. Βενεννομ; γὲ βανὲ Ἐννομ 33^{6}, 𝔊L γῇ Βενεννομ; elsewh. usu. φάρ. (υἱοῦ) Ἐννομ) —cf. sub גַּיְא;—as mere topographical term גֵּי בֶן־הִנֹּם, boundary between Judah & Benjamin

Jos 15^{8} 18^{16}; also ה׳ גֵּי 15^{8} 18^{16} (all P) cf. Ne 11^{30}; elsewhere alw. גּ׳ בֶן־ה׳ (2 K 23^{10} Kt has גי בני הנם, Qr & 𝔊 𝔙 sing.), & alw. with ref. to the sacrifice of children by fire, 2 K 23^{10} 2 Ch 28^{3} 33^{6} Je $7^{31.32}$ $19^{2.6}$ 32^{35}; on account of this inhuman & idolatrous practice it was abhorred by priest & prophet, & defiled by Josiah; this conception afterward developed, through Is 66^{24}, into Jewish *Gehinnom* (cf. Weber$^{\text{Synagog. Theol. 326 ff.}}$ Di$^{\text{Buch Henoch. 131 f.}}$) & NT γέεννα. On locality cf. Rob$^{\text{BR ii. 273 f.}}$ Tobler$^{\text{Topogr. ii 39 ff.}}$ Bd$^{\text{Pal 103}}$; mod. name (of lower half of valley, toward SE.) *Wady er-Rabâbi.*

2012 †הֵנַע **n.pr.** *loc.* named betw. *Sepharvaim* and *Iwwa;* site unknown, yet cf. Dl$^{\text{Pa 279}}$; 2 K 18^{34} 19^{13}=Is 37^{13}.

5130 הֲנָפָה v. sub נוף. p. 632

2013 †הַס, הָס **interj. hush! keep silence** (prob. onomatop.) Ju 3^{19} and he said, I have a secret errand unto thee, O king, וַיֹּאמֶר הָס and he said, *Keep silence!* Am 6^{10} וְאָמַר הָס (while burying men in a pestilence), 8^{3} (ellipt.) in every place הִשְׁלִיךְ הָס: they cast them (the corpses) forth, (saying) *Hush!* sq. מִפְּנֵי י׳ (מִפָּנָיו) Hb 2^{20} Zp 1^{7} Zc 2^{17}. Inflected, as though a verb, *imv. pl.* הַסּוּ Ne 8^{11} (Ges compares Arab. هَلُمَّ [=הֲלֹם] *hither!* inflected as an imv., e.g. هَلُمُّوا, هَلُمِّي: W$^{\text{AG i. § 368}}$). Hence as denom.

2013 †**Hiph.** *impf. apoc.* וַיַּהַס Nu 13^{30} and Caleb *stilled* the people.

2014 הֲפֻגָה v. sub פוג. p. 806

2015 †הָפַךְ **vb. turn, overturn** (NH *id.*, Aram. הֲפַךְ, ܗܦܰܟ, Ar. أَفَكَ W$^{\text{SG 47}}$, As. *abâku, apâku* Dl^{W})—**Qal** *Pf.* Lv 13^{3} + 13 t.; וְהָפַךְ consec. 2 K 21^{13} Jb 34^{25}; 3 mpl. הָפְכוּ ψ 78^{9}; הֲפַכְתֶּם Am 6^{12} Je 23^{36}, etc.; *Impf.* יַהֲפֹךְ La 3^{3} Je 13^{23}; וַיַּהֲפֹךְ Gn 19^{25} + 6 t.; וַיַּהֲפָךְ־ 1 S 10^{9}; sf. אֶהְפֹּךְ וַיַּהַפְכֵהוּ Ju 7^{13}; 3 fs. וַתַּהֲפֹךְ 2 Ch 9^{12}; Zp 3^{9}; וַיַּהַפְכוּ 1 S 25^{12} Jb 12^{15}; *Imv.* הֲפֹךְ 1 K 22^{34} = 2 Ch 18^{33}; *Inf. abs.* הָפוֹךְ Pr 12^{7}; *cstr.* הֲפֹךְ Gn 19^{29} 1 Ch 19^{3}; sf. הָפְכִּי Gn 19^{21}; הָפְכָּה 2 S 10^{3};—on הַפְּכְּכֶם (so Baer, q.v.) Is 29^{16}, v. הֶפֶךְ; *Pt. act.* הֹפֵךְ Am 5^{8}; הַהֹפְכִי ψ 114^{8}; pl. הַהֹפְכִים Am 5^{7}; *pass.* הֲפוּכָה Ho 7^{8} La 4^{6}.—**1.** trans. **a.** *turn, turn about, turn over,* c. acc.: e.g. turn the back (עֹרֶף) Jos 7^{8} (JE); a dish (צַלַּחַת) עַל־פָּנֶיהָ 2 K 21^{13}; the hand, & so the horses of a chariot 1 K 22^{34} = 2 Ch 18^{33}, 2 K 9^{23}; but also (sq. בְּ) of hostility La 3^{3}; turn a cake (pass.) Ho 7^{8}; of י׳, ה׳ שָׂפָה בְרוּרָה Zp 3^{9} i.e. restore speech of a pure kind, sq. אֶל־עַמִּים; לֵב אַחֵר 1 S 10^{9} *another heart,* sq. לוֹ; turn a wind (רוּחַ; i.e. bring from different quarter) Ex 10^{19} (J). **b.** *overturn, overthrow,* sq. acc. Sodom, etc., Gn $19^{21.25.29}$ (J), Dt 29^{22} Je 20^{16} La 4^{6} (cf. מַהְפֵּכַת וגו׳ Am 4^{11} v. infr.; also הֲפֵכָה, [מַהְפֵּכָה]); 4114
city of Ammon 2 S 10^{3} = 1 Ch 19^{3} (obj. om.); mountains Jb 9^{5} 28^{9}; throne Hg 2^{22} (‖ הִשְׁמִיד), chariots v^{22}; tent (אֹהֶל), ה׳ לְמַעְלָה Ju 7^{3}; obj. earth (ה׳ = *devastate*) Jb 12^{15}; wicked men Am 4^{11} הָפַכְתִּי בָכֶם כְּמַהְפֵּכַת אֱלֹהִים אֶת־סְדֹם וְאֶת־עֲמֹרָה) Pr 12^{7} Jb 34^{25} (obj. om.). **c.** *turn* = *change, transform* (1) sq. acc. = *alter;* a colour (עֵינוֹ) Lv 13^{55} (P); skin Je 13^{33}; bed (מִשְׁכָּבוֹ v. מ׳; Che *his lying down*) ψ 41^{4} i.e. restore to health; (2) *pervert* דִּבְרֵי אֱלֹהִים Je 23^{36}; (3) sq. acc. c. Inf. ψ 105^{25} *he turned their heart to hate his people;* (4) *turn to, into,* sq. two acc. Lv 13^{10} ψ 114^{8} rock into pool of water; usu. sq. acc. + לְ, ψ 66^{6} sea into dry land, ψ 78^{44} rivers into blood, cf. 105^{29}; Je 31^{13} mourning into joy, so ψ 30^{12}; Am 5^{7} justice into wormwood, cf. 6^{12}; 8^{10} feasts into mourning; Dt 23^{6} = Ne 13^{2} curse into blessing; Am 5^{8} death-shade into morning. **2.** *intrans.* **a.** *turn, turn back,* Ju $20^{39.41}$ 2 K 5^{26} ψ 78^{9} 2 Ch 9^{12}; sq. לדרך 1 S 25^{12}; **b.** *turn = change, change into,* sq. pred. adj. ה׳ לָבָן turn white Lv $13^{3.4.13.20}$ (all P). **Niph.** *Pf.* נֶהְפַּךְ Ex 7^{15} + 10 t.; נֶהְפָּךְ Jb 20^{14}; וְנֶהְפַּךְ consec. Lv 13^{16}; נֶהֶפְכָה La 5^{2}; 3 mpl. נֶהְפְּכוּ Jb 19^{19} + 3 t., נֶהֶפְכוּ 1 S 4^{19} Dn 10^{16}, וְנֶהֶפְכוּ consec. Ex 7^{17} Is 34^{9}, etc.; *Impf.* יֵהָפֵךְ Is 60^{5} Jo 3^{4}; וַיֵּהָפֵךְ Ex 14^{5} Is 63^{10}; 2 ms. תֵּהָפֵךְ Jb 30^{21} Ez 4^{8}; וַיֵּהָפְכוּ Ex 7^{20}; *Inf. abs.* נַהֲפוֹךְ Est 9^{1}; *Pt.* נֶהְפָּךְ Pr 17^{20}; נֶהְפֶּכֶת Jon 3^{4};—**1.** reflex. & intrans. **a.** *turn oneself, turn, turn back* (cf. **Qal 2 a**) Jos 8^{20} (JE); *turn aside* ψ 78^{57}; *turn* from side to side Ez 4^{8}; *pains turned upon* (עַל) *her* 1 S 4^{19} (i.e. came suddenly upon her) cf. Dn 10^{16}; *turn against* sq. בְּ Jb 19^{19}; *turn to(ward),* sq. עַל, Is 60^{5} (‖ בא לְ). **b.** *turn = change* (oneself) sq. pred. adj. Lv 13^{25} (P); sq. pred. noun (?), vine turns into degenerate plant Je 2^{21}; no pred. expressed Jb 20^{14} (cf. v^{b}); of heart turned in compassion Ho 11^{8} (‖ נִכְמְרוּ נִחוּמָי), in sorrow, distress, La 1^{20}; of heart changed, so as to be favourably disposed *toward* (sq. אֶל) Ex 14^{5} (J) = change of mind; sq. לְ, of plague spots changing colour Lv $13^{16.17}$ (P); rod changing to serpent

Ex 7[15] (P); faces to paleness Je 30[6]; dance to mourning La 5[15]; comeliness to corruption Dn 10[8]; וַיֵּהָפֵךְ לָהֶם לְאוֹיֵב Is 63[10] Jb 30[21]. **c.** *be perverse*, only pt. used subst. נֶהְפָּךְ בִּלְשׁוֹנוֹ Pr 17[20] *he that is perverse with his tongue.* **2.** pass., **a.** *be turned, turned over to* sq. לְ, an inheritance to strangers La 5[2]. **b.** *be reversed* Est 9[1]. **c.** *be turned, changed*, sq. לְ, waters into blood Ex 7[17.20] (E); Saul into another man 1 S 10[6]; streams into pitch Is 34[9]; sun to darkness Jo 3[4]; stones to chaff Jb 41[20]; month changed from sorrow to gladness Est 9[22]; cf. ψ 32[4] where complem. om. **d.** *be overturned, overthrown*, of city Nineveh Jon 3[4]. **e.** *be upturned*, of subterran. work of miners Jb 28[5] = *there is an upturning.* **Hithp.** *Impf.* 3 fs. תִּתְהַפֵּךְ Jb 38[14]; *Pt.* מִתְהַפֵּךְ Ju 7[13] Jb 37[12]; מִתְהַפֶּכֶת Gn 3[24];—reflex. & intrans.: **1.** *turn this way & that, every way*, of the flaming sword Gn 3[24] (J); storm-cloud Jb 37[12]; *turn over & over* Ju 7[13], of bread-cake tumbling into the host of Midian. **2.** *transform oneself*, Jb 38[14] of earth under rising dawn. **Hoph.** *Pf.* הָהְפַּךְ עָלַי בַּלָּהוֹת Jb 30[15] *there have been turned upon me terrors* (cf. הִתְגַּלְגָּלוּ v[14], of foes).

2016-17 †הֵ֫פֶךְ **n.m. the contrary, contrariness, perversity**;—abs. ה׳ Ez 16[34]; הָ֑פֶךְ v[34]; sf. הַפְכְּכֶם Is 29[16] (v. Baer);—**1.** *the contrary, opposite thing* וַיְהִי־בָךְ הֶפֶךְ מִן־הַנָּשִׁים Ez 16[34] *& there hath occurred in thee the contrary from other women;* v[34] וַתְּהִי לְהָ֑פֶךְ *so thou hast become the contrary.* **2.** הַפְכְּכֶם Is 29[16] *Oh, your perversity!*

2018 †הֲפֵכָה **n.f. overthrow** (cf. esp. As. *abiktu* Dl[W]), of the cities (of the plain) Gn 19[29]; cf. [מַהְפֵּכָה] and הֶפֶךְ **1 b.**

2019 †הֲפַכְפַּךְ **adj. crooked,** הֲפַכְפַּךְ דֶּרֶךְ אִישׁ וָזָר Pr 21[8] *crooked is the way of a guilty man.*

4114 †[מַהְפֵּכָה] **n.f. overthrow**—always cstr. מַהְפֵּכַת; & always of overthrow of Sodom, Gomorrah etc., exc. Is 1[7] מ׳ זָרִים, where rd. סְדֹם (Ew Che RS [Proph. 345] Di al.; also Lag [Sem. i. 3]); yet even so prob. gloss, cf. Stud. [JPTh 1877, 714]; מ׳ סְדֹם Dt 29[22] Je 49[18]; and with force of verbal noun, governing acc., מ׳ אלהים את־סדם Is 13[19] Je 50[40] Am 4[11]. Cf. also הֶפֶךְ **1 b,** הֲפֵכָה.

4115 †מַהְפֶּ֫כֶת **n.f. stocks** or similar instrum. of punishment (compelling *crooked* posture, or *distorting*), mentioned rather late; as punishment for Jeremiah הַמ׳ אֲשֶׁר בְּשַׁעַר בִּנְיָמִן Je 20[2] (𝔊 εἰς τὸν καταράκτην κ.τ.λ.), cf. אֶל־הַמ׳ 29[26] (𝔊 εἰς τὸ ἀπόκλεισμα; ‖ אֶל־הַצִּינֹק, 𝔊 εἰς τὸν καταράκτην, but order of words perhaps reversed in 𝔊); בֵּית הַמַּהְפֶּכֶת 20[3]; בֵּית הַמַּהְפֶּכֶת assigned also to Asa's time 2 Ch 16[10] (𝔊 εἰς φυλακήν; 𝔊L εἰς οἶκον φυλακῆς; cf. Acts 16[24], where εἰς τὴν ἐσωτέραν φυλακήν, + εἰς τὸ ξύλον).

†[תַּהְפֻּכָה] **n.f. perversity, perverse** 8419
thing (only Pr exc. Dt 32[20])—Pl. abs. תַּהְפֻּכוֹת Dt 32[20] + 8 t.; cstr. id. Pr 2[14];—*perverse things*, particularly utterances Pr 2[12] 10[32] 23[33], cf. פִּי ת׳ 8[13], לְשׁוֹן ת׳ 10[31], and even אִישׁ ת׳ Pr 16[28] (‖ נִרְגָּן *slanderer*); but also thoughts, devices Pr 6[14] 16[30]; דּוֹר ת׳ Dt 32[20] = *perverse generation* (‖ לֹא־אֵמֻן בָּם), ת׳ רָע Pr 2[14] (‖ עֲשׂוֹת רָע).

הֻצַּב Na 2[8] dub.; perhaps txt. err.; v. נצב. 5324
p. 662

הַצָּלָה v. sub נצל. p. 665 2020

†הֹ֫צֶן **n.[m.]** deriv. & mng. dub.; only 2021
Ez 23[24] וּבָאוּ עָלַיִךְ הֹצֶן רֶכֶב וְגַלְגַּל; txt. prob. in error: 𝔊 מִצָּפוֹן so Co (cf. 26[7]); 𝔖 𝔗 *with arms;* Hi הָצֵן, Inf. Hiph. of √צנן, *with rattling;* Ew חֹצֶן (so Codd.) *with shoulder* as place of carrying weapon; Bö Sm הָמוֹן *multitude;* Dl [Baer's Ezech. xi.] gains like sense without emend. by comparing As. *êṣin* (-*ši*) *collect, gather,* Flood Tabl. [ii. 25 ff.], but this very dubious.

הַר v. sub הרר. p. 249 2022

†הֹר **n.pr.mont. 1.** mt. on border of Edom, 2023
alw. הֹר הָהָר, named as stage in Isr.'s journey to Canaan Nu 20[22] 21[4] 33[37] Dt 32[50]; as place of Aaron's death Nu 20[23.25.27] 33[38.39.41] Dt 32[50] (all P); = mod. *Jebel Nebi Hârûn* c. 50 miles S. of Dead Sea, just S. (SW.) of Petra, acc. to Rob [BR ii. 125, 152, cf. 519 ff.] Bd [Pal 153]; disputed by Ew Kn Di, & esp. Trumbull [Kadesh Barnea 128 ff.], who thinks of *J. Madurah*, NW. of Edom. **2.** a NE. spur of Lebanon Nu 34[7.8] (P); mod. *Jebel Akkar* cf. Porter [Damascus, ed. 2, p. 333] Nbr [Géogr. du Talm. p. 9] Furrer [ZPV viii. 27]; yet v. Di.

†הָרָא **n.pr.loc.** 1 Ch 5[26] but rd. עָרֵי מָדַי 2024
cf. Schr [KGF 430], v. ‖ 2 K 17[6] 18[11].

הַרְאֵל Ez 43[15] v. אֲרִאֵיל sub II. ארה. p. 72 2025

†הָרַג **vb. kill, slay** (NH *id.*, ואהרג MI 2026
(1 s. Impf. consec.); Ar. هَرَجَ *fall into war, conflict, disorder, slaughter;* Sab. הרג *fight* Os[4, 1. 17], *kill* Sab Denkm[24.25])—**Qal** *Pf.* 3 ms. ה׳ Ju 9[24] + 4 t., הָרָ֑ג 2 S 14[7] + 2 t., וְהָרַג consec. Is 27[1]; sf. וַהֲרָגָנִי consec. 1 S 16[2] + 2 t.; הֲרָגוֹ Gn 4[25]; etc.; *Impf.* יַהֲרֹג ψ 10[8] + 4 t.; יַהֲרָג־ Jb 5[2]; וַיַּהֲרֹג Ex 13[15] + 14 t.; sf. יַהַרְגֵנִי Gn 4[14]; 1 s. אֶהֱרוֹג Am 2[3], אֶהֱרֹג Am 9[1]; cohort. וְאַהַרְגָה Gn 27[41]; sf.

וָאֶהֶרְגֵהוּ 2 S 4^{10} 2 K 10^{9}; 3 mpl. יַהַרְגוּ ψ 94^{6} Ez 23^{47}; וַיַּהַרְגוּ Gn 34^{25} + 4 t.; sf. יַהַרְגֻנִי Gn 26^{7}, etc.; *Imv.* הֲרֹג Ju 8^{20}; sf. הָרְגֵנִי Nu 11^{15}; pl. הִרְגוּ Nu 25^{5} + 2 t.; הִרְגוּ Nu 31^{17}; *Inf. abs.* הָרֹג Nu 11^{15} + 2 t.; הָרוֹג Est 9^{16}; *cstr.* הֲרֹג Ex 2^{15} + 11 t.; הֲרוֹג Ec 3^{3} Est 7^{4}; *sf.* הָרְגֵנִי Ex 2^{14}; הָרְגֵנוּ Ex 5^{21}; הָרְגוֹ 1 S 24^{11}; הָרְגֶךָ Gn 27^{42} + 2 t.; הָרְגוֹ Ex 21^{14}; *Pt. act.* הֹרֵג Gn 4^{15} + 4 t.; הוֹרֵג Ez 21^{16}; הֹרְגֶךָ Ez 28^{9}; הֹרְגִים Je 4^{31} 2 K 17^{25}; *pass.* הֲרוּגִים Is 10^{4} + 2 t.; הֲרֻגִים Is 14^{19}; cstr. הֲרֻגֵי Je 18^{21}; הֲרוּגָיו Is 27^{7}; הֲרוּגֶיהָ Is 26^{21}; הֲרֻגֶיהָ Pr 7^{26};—**1. a.** *kill, slay*, implying ruthless violence, esp. private violence Gn 4$^{8.14.15.23.25}$ 12^{12} (all J), 20^{11} (E) 26^{7} 27$^{41.42}$ 34$^{25.26}$ 37$^{20.26}$ (all J), 49^{6} (poem in J), Ex 2$^{14.14.15}$ (E), 5^{21} (J) 21^{14} 23^{7} (both JE), Nu 31^{19} (P) Ju 9$^{5.18.24.24.56}$ 16^{2} 20^{5} 1 S 16^{2} 22^{21} 24$^{11.12.18}$ 2 S 3^{30} 4$^{10.11.12}$ 12^{9} 14^{7} 23^{21} 1 K 2$^{5.32}$ 18$^{12.13.14}$ 19$^{1.10.14}$ 2 K 9^{31} 10^{9} 1 Ch 7^{21} 11^{23} 2 Ch 21$^{4.13}$ 22^{8} 24$^{23.25}$ 25^{3} Ne 4^{5} 6$^{10.10}$ Zc 11^{5} ψ 10^{8} 94^{6} (|| רִצֵּחַ); cf. Ju 8$^{18.19.20.21}$ 9^{54} 1 K 12^{27} Is 14^{20} 2 Ch 22^{1} Ne 9^{26}; so of massacre of Jews planned by Haman Est 3^{13} 7^{4} (both לְהַשְׁמִיד לַהֲרֹג וּלְאַבֵּד), and of slaughter of Jews' enemies in defence and revenge Est 8^{11} (same combin.) 9$^{6.10.12.15.16}$ cf. v^{11} (pt. pass. *the slain*). **b.** hence of wholesale slaughter after battle Nu 31$^{7.8.8.17.17}$ (all P), Jos 8^{24} 10^{11} (both JE), 13^{22} (P), Ju 7$^{25.25}$ 8^{17} 9^{45} 2 S 10^{18} 1 K 9^{16} 11^{24} 2 K 8^{12} 1 Ch 19^{18} 2 Ch 28$^{6.7.9}$ 36^{17} Ez 26$^{8.11}$, cf. Ju 9^{26}; pt. pass. *the slain* Is 10^{4} 14^{19} cf. Ez 23$^{10.47}$ 37^{9}, Je 18^{21} הֲרֻגֵי מָוֶת (|| מֻכֵּי־חֶרֶב); further Ho 9^{13} Hb 1^{17} Je 4^{31} Ez 21^{16} 28^{9}; also of slaughter in a revolt 2 K 11^{8} = 2 Ch 23^{17}. **2.** of God's slaying in judgment (stern and inscrutable), Gn 20^{4} (E), Ex 4^{23} 13^{15} 22^{23} (all JE), Am 2^{3} 4^{10} 9$^{1.4}$ La 2$^{4.21}$ 3^{43} ψ 59^{12} 78$^{31.34}$ 135^{10} 136^{18} cf. Nu 11$^{15.15}$ (JE), 22^{33} (J), Is 14^{30}, 26^{21} (pass. *the slain*, so 27^{7}), Je 15^{3}; fig. הֲרַגְתִּים בְּאִמְרֵי־פִי Ho 6^{5} (|| חָצַבְתִּי בַּנְּבִיאִים). **3.** rarely of judicial killing by men (at God's command), Ex 32^{27} (JE), Lv 20$^{15.16}$ (H), Nu 25^{5} (JE), Dt 13$^{10.10}$ cf. Ez 9^{6} תַּהַרְגוּ לְמַשְׁחִית. **4.** of killing beasts, Nu 22^{29} (J; Balaam's ass), Lv 20^{15} cf. supr., Is 22^{13} (oxen; || שָׁחֹט), הַתַּנִּין אֲשֶׁר בַּיָּם Is 27^{1}; also of killing vines, by hail ψ 78^{47}. **5.** of killing by beasts: lions 2 K 17^{25}, viper Jb 20^{16}. **6.** quite general is עֵת לַהֲרוֹג וְעֵת לִרְפּוֹא Ec 3^{3}. **7.** *destroy, ruin* לֶאֱוִיל יַהֲרָג־כָּעַשׂ וּפֹתֶה תָּמִית קִנְאָה Jb 5^{2}; מְשׁוּבַת פְּתָיִם תַּהַרְגֵם וְשַׁלְוַת כְּסִילִים תְּאַבְּדֵם Pr 1^{32}; also of those ruined by shameless woman Pr 7^{26}.—Regular construction is c. acc.; obj. sometimes om., as La 2^{21}; used abs. Ho 9^{13} Je 4^{31} 15^{3} La 3^{43} Ez 21^{16} Ec 3^{3}; sq. בְּ *slay among*, i.e. some of, 2 K 17^{25} 2 Ch 28$^{6.9}$ ψ 78^{31}; sq. מִן (part of), + acc., 1 Ch 19^{18}; sq. dir. obj. c. לְ †2 S 3^{30} Jb 5^{2} ψ 135^{11} = 136$^{19.20}$ (but in last 3 first obj. is acc.). **Niph.** *Impf.* **1.** pass. of **Qal 1 a,** יֵהָרֵג La 2^{20} *shall priest and prophet be slain in the sanctuary?* **2.** pass. of **Qal 1 b,** 3 fpl. תֵּהָרַגְנָה Ez 26^{6}; also Ez 26^{15} בֵּהָרֵג הֶרֶג (= בְּהֵהָרֵג), but 𝔊 Co בַּהֲרֹג חֶרֶב. **Pu.** *Pf.* 3 ms. הֹרָג Is 27^{7} *be slain* (pass. of **Qal 1 b**); cf. 1 pl. הֹרַגְנוּ ψ 44^{23} (|| נֶחְשַׁבְנוּ כְּצֹאן טִבְחָה).

†[הֶרֶג] n.m. Is 30.25 **slaughter**—ה׳ abs. Pr 24^{11} 2027
+ 2 t. + Ez 26^{15} (𝔊 Co חֶרֶב); cstr. Is 27^{7}—of Jews' slaughter of their enemies Est 9^{5} (|| אַבְדָן); כְּהֶרֶג הֲרוּגָיו הֹרָג Is 27^{7}; מָטִים לַהֶרֶג Pr 24^{11} (|| לְקֻחִים לַמָּוֶת); ביום הֶרֶג רָב Is 30^{25} (cf. ביום חֲבֹשׁ י׳ אֶת־שֶׁבֶר עַמּוֹ v^{26}). Ez 26^{15} rd. with 𝔊 Co supr.

†הֲרֵגָה n.f. slaughter; only abs. in foll. 2028
combinations, גֵּיא ה׳ Je 7^{32} 19^{6} new name for גֵּיא בֶן־הִנֹּם; יוֹם ה׳ Je 12^{3} of the wicked, i.e. day of judgment; צֹאן ה׳ Zc 11$^{4.7}$ i.e. Judah and Israel, slaughtered by their shepherds.

†I. הָרָה vb. conceive, become pregnant 2029
(As. *êrû* cf. Dl $^{Pr\ 21}$ Muss. Arnolt $^{Hbr.\ Oct.\ 1890,\ 67}$ Jäger $^{BAS\ i.\ 473}$);—**Qal** *Pf.* 3 ms. וְהָרָה consec. ψ 7^{15}; 3 fs. הָרָתָה Gn 16$^{4.5}$; 2 fs. וְהָרִית consec. Ju 13^{3}; 1 s. הָרִיתִי Nu 11^{12}; 1 pl. הָרִינוּ Is 26^{18}; *Impf.* וַתַּהַר Gn 4^{1} + 26 t. (וַתַּהַר Gn 16^{4}); 3 fpl. וַתַּהֲרֶיןָ Gn 19^{36}; 2 mpl. תַּהֲרוּ Is 33^{11}; *Inf. abs.* הָרֹה Jb 15^{35}, הָרוֹ Is 59^{4} cf. also v^{13} sub **Po.** infr.; *Pt.* f. sf. הוֹרָתִי Ct 3^{4}; הוֹרָתָם Ho 2^{7};—**1.** lit. *conceive, become pregnant* Gn 16$^{4.4.5}$ 19^{36} 25^{21} 38^{18} (all J), 2 S 11^{5} (agency of man expressed by מִן Gn 19^{36}, לְ 38^{18}); usu. in phr. וַתַּהַר וַתֵּלֶד Gn 4$^{1.17}$ 21^{2} 29$^{32.33.34.35}$ 30$^{5.7}$ (all J), v$^{17.19.23}$ (all E), 38$^{3.4}$ (both J), Ex 2^{2} (E), 1 S 1^{20} 2^{21} 2 K 4^{17} 1 Ch 7^{23} Is 8^{3} Ho 1$^{3.6.8}$, prob. also 1 Ch 4^{17} ותהר [ותלד] אֶת־מִרְיָם cf. Be; further Ju 13^{3}, and cf. Moses' question הֶאָנֹכִי הָרִיתִי אֵת כָּל־הָעָם הַזֶּה אִם אָנֹכִי יְלִדְתִּיהוּ Nu 11^{12} *have I conceived all this people, or have I brought it forth?* Pt. f. || אֵם Ho 2^{7} Ct 3^{4}. **2.** metaph. הָרִינוּ חַלְנוּ כְּמוֹ יָלַדְנוּ רוּחַ Is 26^{18} of anxious and disappointed waiting; תַּהֲרוּ חֲשַׁשׁ תֵּלְדוּ קַשׁ Is 33^{11}, of futile planning, cf. Che; elsewhere of evil, mischief וְהָרָה עָמָל וְיָלַד שָׁקֶר ψ 7^{15} (subj. wicked man), cf. Jb 15^{35} Is 59^{4}, so also v^{13}, read הָרוֹ (Inf. abs.) cf. Di. **Pu.** *Pf.* 3 ms. הֹרָה גָבֶר Jb 3^{3} *a man hath been conceived* (Bö $^{ii.\ p.\ 103}$ Ba $^{NB\ 77}$ regard as **Qal** pass.). **Po.** *Inf. abs., conceive, contrive, devise* הֹרוֹ וְהֹגוֹ

הָרוּ וְהָגוּ מִלֵּב דִּבְרֵי שָׁקֶר Is 59^{13}, but rd. rather **Qal** *Inf. abs.* v. supr. (Ba$^{l.c.}$ expl. MT as **Qal** *Inf. pass.*).—On הוֹרַי Gn 49^{26} v. הוֹר and הַר **1 c.**

2030 †II. הָרָה **adj.f. pregnant**—; abs. ה׳ Gn 16^{11} + 10 t.; cstr. הָרַת Je 20^{17}; pl. cstr. הָרוֹת Am 1^{13}; sf. הָרוֹתֶיהָ 2 K 15^{16}; הָרֹתֵיהֶם 2 K 8^{12};—*pregnant*, as attrib., אִשָּׁה ה׳ Ex 21^{22}; as pred. Gn 38^{24} (לִזְנוּנִים), v^{25} (לְאִישׁ), 1 S 4^{19} 2 S 11^{5} Is 7^{14} (+וְיֹלֶדֶת); in phr. הִנָּךְ הָרָה וְיֹלַדְתְּ Gn 16^{11} (on resemblance to Is 7^{14} cf. Peters$^{Hbr.\ Apr.\ 1885,\ 243;\ Apr.\ 1886,\ 175}$), Ju $13^{5.7}$; = subst. *pregnant women, women with child* Am 1^{13} 2 K 8^{12} 15^{16} Je 31^{8}, and, in sim., Is 26^{17}; once of womb וְרַחְמָהּ הֲרַת עוֹלָם Je 20^{17}.

2032 הֵרוֹן v. הֵרָיוֹן. below

2030 †[הָרִיָּה] **adj.f. pregnant**, only pl. as subst. וְהָרִיּוֹתָיו Ho 14^{1} (cf. As. *êriûtê* Jäger$^{BAS\ i.\ 473}$).

2032 †הֵרָיוֹן **n.[m.] conception, pregnancy**;—ה׳ abs. Ho 9^{11} Ru 4^{13}; sf. הֵרֹנֵךְ Gn 3^{16}, either contr., so Ew$^{§\ 214\ a}$, or erron. for הריונך which stands in Sam. cf. Di;—*conception*, in combin. מִלֵּדָה וּמִבֶּטֶן וּמֵהֵרָיוֹן Ho 9^{11}; וַיִּתֵּן י׳ לָהּ ה׳ וַתֵּלֶד Ru 4^{13}; עִצְּבוֹנֵךְ וְהֵרֹנֵךְ Gn 3^{16} (‖תֵּלְדִי).

2033 †הָרוֹרִי **adj. gent.** 1 Ch 11^{27} הַהֲרוֹרִי; but
2733 read prob. הַחֲרוֹדִי (cf. ‖ 2 S 23^{25}) q.v. p. 353

2036 †הֹרָם **n.pr.m.** a Canaanitish king ruling in Gezer Jos 10^{33}.

2037 †הָרֻם **n.pr.m.** a Judaite (DHM $^{Epigr.\ Denkm.\ 59}$ comp. Sab. n. pr. הרם, הרמה, Ar. n.pr. هَرِمٌ, etc.) 1 Ch 4^{8}.

1027 הָרָם v. בֵּית הָרָם p. 111 supr.

2038 †[הַרְמוֹן] **n.m.** mng. dub.; text perhaps corrupt; only Am 4^{3} וְהִשְׁלַכְתֶּנָה הַהַרְמ֫וֹנָה and *ye shall cast* them (your אחרית, posterity, AE; Hi RV *cast* [yourselves], but read rather with Vrss as pass. וְהָשְׁל׳ *shall be cast*) *into Harmon;* if text be sound, some locality must be meant, though the nature of the allusion is lost (AV, *into the palace*, treats הרמון improb. as=ארמון). 𝔗 𝔖 have *mountain(s) of Armenia* (הַר מוֹנָה), Symm *Armenia*, cf. Lag$^{Ges.\ Abh.\ 172}$, Hoffm$^{ZAW\ iii.\ 1882,\ 102}$, of exile; Hi-St for ה׳ rd. הֲדַדְרִמּוֹנָה *to Hadadrimmon*, n.pr.loc. in plain of Jezreel, so Gunning; 𝔊 εἰς τὸ ὄρος τὸ Ῥομμαν, whence Ew ingeniously ההר רמונה and ye shall cast *Rimmonah* (name of idol, supposed fem. of Rimmon 2 K 5^{18}) *to the mountains.*

הַרְמִּים v. אֲרַמִּי p. 74 supr. 761

†הָרָן **n.pr.m.** (*mountaineer;* i.e. moun- 2039
tain-people (or land)? cf. Di Gn 11^{27});—**1.** son of Teraḥ, brother of Abram and father of Lot Gn $11^{27.27.31}$ (all P), v^{28} (J); also father of Milcah (Nahor's wife) & Iscah v^{29} (J). **2.** a Levite (Gershonite) 1 Ch 23^{9}.—On הָרָן in **n.pr.loc.** v. sub בית הרם, p. 111.

†הָרַס **vb.** throw down, break or tear 2040
down (MI הרס; ? Ar. هَرَسَ, *bruise, bray, pound, crush* (grain))—**Qal** *Pf.* הָ׳ La $2^{2.17}$; הָרַס Is 14^{17}; וְהָרַסְתָּ Ju 6^{25} וְהָרַסְתִּי Ez 13^{14} Mi 5^{10}; וְהָרְסוּ Ez 16^{39} $26^{4.12}$ הָרָ֑סוּ 1 K $19^{10.14}$; *Impf.* יַהֲרוֹס Jb 12^{14}; sf. יֶהֶרְסְךָ Is 22^{19}; וַיֶּהֶרְסֶהָ 1 Ch 20^{1}; תֶּהֶרְסֶנּוּ Pr 29^{4} יֶהֶרְסֵם ψ 28^{5}; 3 fs. sf. 3 ms. יֶהֶרְסֶנָּה Pr 14^{1}; 2 ms. תַּהֲרֹס Ex 15^{7}; אֶהֱרֹס Je 24^{6} 42^{10} אֶהֱרוֹס Mal 1^{4}; 3 mpl. יֶהֶרְסוּ Ex $19^{21.24}$; יַהֲרֹסוּ 2 K 3^{25}; *Imv.* הֲרָס־ ψ 58^{7}; sf. הָרְסָהּ 2 S 11^{25}; *Inf.* הֲרֹס Je 31^{28}, הֲרוֹס Je 1^{10}; *Pt. act.* הֹרֵס Je 45^{4}; *pass.* הָרוּס 1 K 18^{30};—**1.** *throw down, tear down*, c. acc.: altar(s) Ju 6^{25} 1 K 18^{30} $19^{10.14}$; height (גַּב, where idol-altar stood? cf. גַּב sub גבב) Ez 16^{39}; city (cities) Is 14^{17} 2 S 11^{25} 2 K 3^{25} 1 Ch 20^{1} (cf. MI^{27}) Mal 1^{4} (obj. not expr.); wall(s) Ez 13^{14} 26^{12}; house Pr 14^{1} (fig. of foolish woman's action); strongholds (מִבְצָרִים) La 2^{2} Mi 5^{10}; tower(s) Ez 26^{4}; fig. *overthrow* (i.e. *ruin*) land Pr 29^{4} (opp. יַעֲמִיד); obj. men Ex 15^{7} (poem in E) Is 22^{19} (*cast down* Shebna from office); fig., opp. building up, of Yahweh's dealings with men ψ 28^{5}, cf. (without obj.) Je 24^{6} 42^{10}; obj. indef. אשר בָּנִיתִי אֲנִי הֹרֵס Je 45^{4}; abs. Je 1^{10} 31^{28} La 2^{17} Jb 12^{14}. **2.** *break down, break away* ה׳ שִׁנֵּימוֹ בְּפִימוֹ ψ 58^{7} *break away their teeth in their mouth!* fig., addressed to God. **3.** *break through*, intr., sq. אֶל־י׳ Ex 19^{21}; sq. לַעֲלֹת אֶל־י׳ v^{24} (both J). **Niph.** *Pf.* 3 fs. נֶהֶרְסָה Pr 24^{31}; 3 pl. נֶהֶרְסוּ Je 50^{15} Jo 1^{17}; וְנֶהֶרְסוּ consec. Ez 30^{4} 38^{20}; *Impf.* יֵהָרֵס Je 31^{40}; 3 fs. תֵּהָרֵס Pr 11^{11}; יֵהָרֵסוּן ψ 11^{3}; *Pt.* הַנֶּהֱרָסוֹת Ez $36^{35.36}$;—*be thrown* or *torn down;* wall(s) of vineyard Pr 24^{31}, of city Je 50^{15}; cities Ez 36^{35} cf. v^{36}; fig. *ruined* Pr 11^{11} (opp. תָּרוּם); foundations, יְסוֹדֹת Ez 30^{4}; שָׁתוֹת ψ 11^{3}; mountains Ez 38^{20}; storehouses מַמְּגֻרוֹת Jo 1^{17} [v. מ׳]; valley E. of Jerus. לֹא־יִנָּתֵשׁ וְלֹא־יֵהָרֵס Je 31^{40} *it shall not be plucked up nor thrown down*, appar. proverb. expression, implying destruction, removal. **Pi.** *Impf.* 2 ms. sf. תְּהָרְסֵם Ex 23^{24}; *Inf. abs.* הָרֵס Ex 23^{24}; *Pt.* pl. sf. מְהָרְסַיִךְ Is 49^{17};—*overthrow, tear down* הָרֵס תְּהָרְסֵם Ex 23^{24} *thou shalt utterly tear them down* (JE; obj. = idols cf. Di); pt. *destroyers*, of Zion Is 49^{17} (‖ מַחֲרִיבַיִךְ).

2041 †הֶ֫רֶס **n.[m.]** overthrow, destruction, only Is 19^{18} one shall be called עִיר הַהֶרֶס *city of destruction*, i. e. (as usually explained) with punning allusion to On-Heliopolis: it shall be called no longer עִיר הַחֶרֶס *city of the sun*, but עיר ההרס *city of destruction*, city whose temples, etc., of the sun have been destroyed; but perh. < 𝔊 πόλις ασεδεκ=עִיר הַצֶּדֶק *city of righteousness*, so Gei$^{Urschrift\ 79}$ Brd Di (change intentional? cf. id.); on other views v. id. & De Che.

2034 †[הֲרִיסָה] **n.f.** ruin (concr.);—וַהֲרִסֹתָיו אָקִים Am 9^{11} *and its ruins* (i.e. of סֻכַּת דָּוִיד) *will I raise up* (‖ פִּרְצֵיהֶן).

2035 †[הֲרִיסוּת] **n.f. overthrow, destruction, ruin**;—אֶרֶץ הֲרִסֻתֵךְ Is 49^{19} *the land of thine overthrow*, i.e. thy ruined land (‖ חָרְבֹתַיִךְ וְשֹׁמְמֹתַיִךְ).

הרר (√of foll.; meaning dubious).

2022, 2042 הַר $_{558}$ **n.m.** $^{Gn\ 7,\ 19}$ **mountain, hill, hill-country** (NH *id.*, pl. הָרִים, הֲרָרִים; Ph. הר †CIS $^{1,\ 3,\ 17}$; Sab. sf. הרתהמו DHM $^{ZMG\ 1876,\ 673}$);—הַ abs. Jos 17^{18}+; c. art. הָהָר Ex 3^{12}+; c. ה ־ָה loc. הָ֫רָה Gn 14^{10}, הָהָ֫רָה Gn 12^{8}+12 t.; cstr. הַר Gn 10^{30}+; sf. הַרְרִי ψ 30^{8}, הֲרָרִי Je 17^{3}; הַרְכֶם ψ 11^{1}; הַרְרָם Gn 14^{6}; pl. הָרִים Dt 11^{11}+; c. art. הֶהָרִים Gn 7^{19}+; cstr. הָרֵי Gn 8^{4}+27 t.; הַרְרֵי Dt 33^{15}+8 t. (all poet.); sf. הָרַי Is 14^{25} 49^{11} Zc 14^{5}+Ez 38^{21} (B Co חרדה), הָרָיו Is 65^{9}; הָרָיו Ez 35^{8} Mal 1^{3}; הֲרָרֶיהָ Dt 8^{9};—**1.** *mountain, hill* (these often not sharply distinguished, but): **a.** specif. *mountain, high elevation*, oft. in all the literature;—e.g. הַר סִינַי *Mount Sinai* (properly, the Mount of Sinai; so always) †Ex $19^{11.18.20.23}$ 24^{16} 31^{18} $34^{2.4.29.32}$ Lv 7^{38} 25^{1} 26^{46} 27^{34} Nu 3^{1} 28^{6} Ne 9^{13} (v. סִינַי); also הָהָר =*id.*, Ex 19^{2}+10 t. Ex 19 (v^{18} rd. הָעָם, so Codd. 𝔊 Di) 20^{18} 24^{4}+6 t. Ex 24; 25^{40} 26^{30} 27^{8} $32^{1.15.19}$ $34^{2.3.3.29}$;=הַר חוֹרֵב †Ex 33^{6} (v. חֹרֵב), also עַד הַר הָאֱלֹהִים חֹרֵבָה אֶל־הַר הָאֱלֹהִים חֹרֵב Ex 3^{1}, 1 K 19^{8}; further הָהָר=*id.*, Dt $4^{11.11}$ $5^{4.5.19.20}$ 9^{9}+10 t. Dt 9.10, 1 K 19^{11};=הַר הָאֱלֹהִים Ex 4^{27} 18^{5} 24^{13} (all JE)=הַר יהוה Nu 10^{33} (cf. Di); v. further הֹר הָהָר *Hor the mount* (so always) Nu 20^{22}+10 t. Nu; Dt 32^{50};=הָהָר Nu $20^{28.28}$; הַר נְבוֹ Dt 32^{49} 34^{1}=הָהָר 32^{50};=הַר הָעֲבָרִים הַזֶּה Nu 27^{12} Dt 32^{49}, cf. (לִפְנֵי נְבוֹ) הָרֵי הָעֲבָרִים Nu $33^{47.48}$; הַר גְּרִזִּים *Mt. Gerizim* †Dt 11^{29} 27^{12} Jos 8^{33}; רֹאשׁ הַר־גְּרִזִּים Ju 9^{7}; הַר עֵיבָל *Mt. Ebal* †Dt 11^{29} $27^{4.13}$ Jos $8^{30.33}$; also הַר חֶרְמוֹן *Mt. Hermon* Dt 3^{8} Jos 11^{17} $12^{1.5}$ $13^{5.11}$ 1 Ch 5^{23}; cf. Dt 4^{48} הַר בַּעַל חֶרְמוֹן (v. חֶרְמוֹן), & הַר שִׂיאֹן הוּא חֶרְמוֹן (v. *id.*, & בעל חרמון sub בעל); הַר הַלְּבָנוֹן *Mt. Lebanon* Ju 3^{3}, cf. מְרוֹם הָרִים יַרְכְּתֵי לְבָנוֹן 2 K 19^{23} =Is 37^{24} (v. לבנון); הַר הַכַּרְמֶל *Mt. Carmel* 1 K $18^{19.20}$ 2 K 2^{25} 4^{25} (v. כרמל); הָהָר=*id.*, 4^{27}, appar. also 1^{9}; הַר תָּבוֹר *Mt. Tabor*, Ju $4^{6.12.14}$, cf. Je 46^{18} תָּבוֹר בֶּהָרִים (opp. כַּרְמֶל בַּיָּם); הַר הַגִּלְבֹּעַ 1 S $31^{1.8}$ 2 S 1^{6}, also (poet.) הָרֵי בַגִּ׳ v^{21} (cf. Dr); הַר הַזֵּיתִים Ju 1^{35} (Stu עִר חֶרֶס) cf. חֶרֶס; הַר־חֶרֶס Zc $14^{4.4}$ *Mount of Olives*, (opp. גַּיְא) cf. הָהָר אֲשֶׁר מִקֶּדֶם לָעִיר Ez 11^{23}; also בָּהָר אֲשֶׁר עַל־פְּנֵי יְרוּשָׁלַםִ 1 K 11^{7} (place of Sol.'s idolatry)=הַר־הַמַּשְׁחִית 2 K 23^{13} *mt. of the destroyer* (same combin. in another, fig. sense Je 51^{25}), others der. הַמ׳ here fr. משׁח *anoint*, and render as=*Mt. of Olives* (cited as הר המשחה Talm., Shabb. 56 b), cf. Hoffm $^{ZAW\ 1882,\ 175}$; אַחַד הֶהָרִים in land of Moriah Gn 22^{2}; mts. about Jerus. in gen., יְרוּשָׁלַםִ הָרִים סָבִיב לָהּ ψ 125^{2}; cf. also ψ 121^{1} (‖ יהוה); הָהָר of citadel of Jerus. Is 22^{5}; of temple hill הַר הַבַּיִת Mi 3^{12}=Je 26^{18}; הַר בֵּית־י׳ Is 2^{2}=Mi 4^{1}, 2 Ch 33^{15}; also הֲרָרִי בַּשָּׂדֶה Je 17^{3}; further הַר צִיּוֹן *Mt. Zion* Is 4^{5} 8^{18} 10^{12} 18^{7} 24^{23} 29^{8} 31^{4} 37^{32} Mi 4^{7} La 5^{18} Ob ^{17}. Jo 3^{5} ψ $48^{3.12}$ 74^{2} 78^{68} 125^{1} (v. also צִיּוֹן); comp. הַר בֵּית־צִיּוֹן Is 10^{32}, הַר בַּת צ׳ 16^{1}; הַר־י׳ Is 2^{3}=Mi 4^{2}, Is 30^{29} ψ 24^{3}; (*id.* of Horeb Nu 10^{33} JE); הַר־י׳ צְבָאוֹת Zc 8^{3}, הַר הַקֹּדֶשׁ הַר־קָדְשִׁי Zp 3^{11} Ob ^{16} Ez 20^{40} Is 11^{9}=65^{25}, cf. 56^{7} 57^{13} 65^{11} Jo 2^{1} (‖ צִיּוֹן) 4^{17} (‖ *id.*) ψ 2^{6} (‖ *id.*) 3^{5} 15^{1} 43^{3} 48^{2}; v. further הַר הַקֹּדֶשׁ הַר־קָדְשִׁי יְרוּשָׁלַםִ Is 66^{20} cf. Dn 9^{16} & הַר צְבִי־קֹדֶשׁ Dn 11^{45}; יְרוּשָׁלַםִ Is 27^{13}; also הַר־הַקֹּדֶשׁ Je 31^{23}; even הַר קֹדֶשׁ אֱלֹהַי Dn 9^{20}; other designations of temple-hill are הָהָר חָמַד ψ 68^{17}, & הַר מְרוֹם יִשְׂרָאֵל Ez 17^{23} 20^{40} (‖ הַר־קָדְשִׁי); הַר קֹדֶשׁ אֱלֹהִים Ez 28^{14} of the distant abode of God (or gods?) so הַר אֱלֹהִים v^{16} (הַר־אֱלֹהִים ψ 68^{16} is general, *a God's mountain*, i.e. a majestic mt., likewise in simile כְּהַרְרֵי־אֵל ψ 36^{7});—הַר הָאֱלֹהִים elsewh. of Horeb (Sinai) Ex 4^{27} 18^{5} 24^{13} 1 K 19^{8} (v. supr.). Note partic. †הַר־מוֹעֵד Is 14^{13} *mountain of meeting* or *of assembly*, i.e. the dwelling-place of the gods, acc. to Babylonian conception, here represented as in the far north, v. esp. Che De Di, Dl $^{Pa\ 117\ ff.}$ COT $^{ad\ loc.}$ Jr $^{57\ ff.}$ Jen $^{Kosmologie\ 23}$. *Upon the mt.* is עַל־הָהָר cf. וַתֵּבְךְּ עַל־בְּתוּלֶיהָ עַל־הֶהָרִים Ju 11^{38}, & the peculiar phr. וְאֵלְכָה וְיָרַדְתִּי עַל־הֶהָרִים v^{37}; *go up upon* עָלָה אֶל־ Ex 19^{23} 24^{13} 34^{4} (all JE); cf. acc. in הַעַל אֹתָם הֹר הָהָר Nu 20^{25};

speak with one *upon* is דבר בהר Ex 31^{18} 34^{32} Nu 3^{1} (all P), Lv 25^{1} (H), cf. *command, give commands, law,* etc., בהר Lv 7^{38} 26^{46} 27^{34} (all P or H); other phrases with בְּ *upon* (lit. *in*, i.e. in the midst of a group of mts.) Ex 34^{3} בְּכָל (JE) 25^{40} 26^{30} 27^{8} Nu 28^{6} (all P), Is 13^{4}; but בְּחֹרֵב ψ 106^{19} = *at Horeb*, בְּהֹר הָהָר Nu 33^{37} *at Mt. Hor; go down from the mt.* is יָרַד מִן־הָהָר Ex 32$^{1.15}$ (both JE) 34$^{29.29}$ (both P), cf. Ju 9^{36} etc. **b.** *mountain-range* הַר־בָּשָׁן ψ 68$^{16.16}$ = הַר־אֱלֹהִים v^{16}; = הַר־גַּבְנֻנִּים v^{16}, הָרִים גַּבְנֻנִּים v^{17} (of the Jebel Hauran: v. בשן). **c.** *mountain*, indef., Jb 14^{18} (‖ צור); usu. pl. *mountains*, in general, or *the mountains*, esp. in poet. & the higher style; oft. fig.; הָרִים, הֶהָרִים, covered by flood Gn 7^{20} cf. v^{19} 8^{5}; covered by waters & freed therefrom by word of God (at creation) ψ 104^{6}; a chief work of God (in creation) Am 4^{13} ψ 65^{7} 90^{2} Pr 8^{25} (‖ גְּבָעוֹת); weighed by God Is 40^{12}; removed and overturned in anger of God Jb 9^{5} cf. ψ 46$^{3.4}$; devastated by God Is 42^{15} (‖ גְּבָעוֹת) cf. Je 9^{9}; smoking at God's touch ψ 104^{32} 144^{5}; melting at presence of י׳ Ju 5^{5} Mi 1^{4} ψ 97^{5} Is 63^{19} 64^{2}; trembling Is 5^{25} cf. Je 4^{24} (‖ גְּבָעוֹת), Na 1^{5} (‖ *id.*), Hb 3^{10}; called to witness Yahweh's dealings with his people Mi 6^{2} (‖ הָאֵתָנִים מֹסְדֵי אָרֶץ) cf. v^{1} (‖ הַגְּבָעוֹת), entreated to cover the guilty Ho 10^{8} (‖ גְּבָעוֹת); addressed by י׳ also Ez 6^{3} (‖ גְּבָעוֹת, opp. אֲפִיקִים, גֵּאָיוֹת); specif., mts. of Israel summoned to hear י׳ and addressed by him Ez 36$^{1.1.4.8}$ 37^{22} 38^{8} 39$^{2.4}$; summoned to praise י׳ ψ 148^{9} (‖ גְּבָעוֹת) cf. Is 44^{23} 49^{13} 55^{12} (‖ גְּבָעוֹת); leaping in praise of י׳ ψ 114$^{4.6}$ (both ‖ גְּבָעוֹת); הַרְרֵי־קֶדֶם Dt 33^{15} (‖ גִּבְעוֹת עוֹלָם); הַרְרֵי־עַד Hb 3^{6} (‖ *id.*); also ψ 76^{5} (acc. to 𝔊 Bi Che; MT has טָרֶף for עַד), and prob. Gn 49^{26} for MT הוֹרַי עַד (‖ גִּבְעֹת עוֹלָם) cf. Di. **d.** *high mt.* הַר גָּבֹהַּ Is 30^{25} (‖ גִּבְעָה נִשָּׂאָה) cf. 40^{9} 52^{7}; הַר גָּבֹהַּ מְאֹד Ez 40^{2}; הַר גָּבֹהַּ וְתָלוּל Ez 17^{22}; pl. הֶהָרִים הַגְּבֹהִים Gn 7^{19} ψ 104^{18} (‖ סְלָעִים), הֶה׳ הָרָמִים Is 2^{14} as symbol of strength and pride (‖ הַגְּבָעוֹת הַנִּשָּׂאוֹת), cf. הֶהָרִים Ez 38^{20} (‖ חוֹמָה, מַדְרֵגוֹת). **e.** opp. valley or plain Jos 12^{8} (D; opp. עֲרָבָה, אֲשֵׁדוֹת, מִדְבָּר, שְׁפֵלָה), cf. Dt 1^{7}, also Je 17^{26} (opp. שְׁפֵלָה); Gn 19^{17} (J; opp. כִּכָּר); oft. opp. גַּיְא 2 K 2^{16} Ez 31^{12} (fig.) 32^{5} (*id.*) 35^{8} (‖ גִּבְעָה), 36^{4} (‖ *id.*), Is 40^{4} (‖ *id.*), opp. בִּקְעָה Dt 8^{7} 11^{11} ψ 104^{8}; opp. מִדְבָּר La 4^{19} (cf. Jos 12^{8} supr.); בֵּין הָרִים ψ 104^{10} is ‖ בַּנְּחָלִים; see also אֱלֹהֵי הָרִים י׳ וְלֹא־אֱלֹהֵי עֲמָקִים 1 K 20^{28}, cf. v^{23} (opp. מִישׁוֹר); note also הַר הָעֵמֶק Jos 13^{19} (P), & גֵּיא־הָרַי, גֵּי־הָרִים Zc 14$^{5.5}$; further מִדְבַּר הָרִים ψ 75^{7} *mountainous desert* Vrss. & most mod. (Baer מִדְבָּר but cf. De); *mountain-ward* is הָ֫רָה Gn 14^{10}. **f.** mts. as hiding-places:—הַמִּנְהָרוֹת אֲשֶׁר בֶּהָרִים Ju 6^{2} *the burrows* (Stanley, VB) *which are in the mts.*; cf. ψ 11^{1} Je 16^{16} (‖ גִּבְעָה); הָפַךְ מִשֹּׁרֶשׁ הָרִים Jb 28^{9} (of mining), v. also Dt 8^{9}. **g.** mts. as running-place of gazelles 1 Ch 12^{8}; of leopards הַרְרֵי נְמֵרִים Ct 4^{8}; hunting-ground for partridges 1 S 26^{20}; עוֹף הָרִים ψ 50^{11} cf. 11^{1} (fig.); wandering-place of lost sheep (fig.) Na 3^{18} 1 K 22^{17} Je 50^{6} cf. v^{6} (‖ גִּבְעָה), Ez 34^{6} (‖ כָּל־גִּבְעָה רָמָה) 2 Ch 18^{16}. **h.** grazing-places for cattle בְּהֵמוֹת בְּהַרְרֵי־אָלֶף ψ 50^{10} (rd. אֵל for אלף Ol Bi Che), cf. יְתוּר הָרִים Jb 39^{8} of pasture of wild ass; also (si vera l.) בּוּל הָרִים Jb 40^{20}, i.e. mts. as furnishing food for hippopot.; v. further Ct 4^{6} 8^{14} Pr 27^{25}. **i.** as place of field and vineyards 2 Ch 26^{10} (opp. שְׁפֵלָה, מִישׁוֹר) Is 7^{25}; v. also הַמַּצְמִיחַ הָרִים חָצִיר ψ 147^{8} cf. Hg 1^{11}; fig. ψ 72^{3} (‖ גְּבָעוֹת); in promise יִטְּפוּ הֶהָרִים עָסִיס וְהַגְּבָעוֹת תֵּלַכְנָה חָלָב Jo 4^{18} cf. Am 9^{13}; **j.** as kindled into flame (i.e. their forests; in sim.) ψ 83^{15}. **k.** as scene of massacre, (fig.) Is 34^{3} *melting with blood*; as place of battle array, *height* 1 S 17$^{3.3}$. **l.** as places of illicit worship Is 65^{7} (‖ גְּבָעוֹת) cf. Je 3^{6} & appar. v^{23} (‖ *id.*) so הַר־גָּבֹהַּ וְנִשָּׂא Is 57^{7}, הֶהָרִים הָרָמִים Dt 12^{2} (‖ הַגְּבָעוֹת); but Ez 18$^{6.15}$ rd. perh. הַדָּם for הרים cf. RS$^{K\ 310}$ & Ez 33^{25}. **m.** in various combinations צַד הָהָר 1 S 23$^{26.26}$ 2 S 13^{34} *side of the mt.*, צֶלַע הָהָר 16^{13} *id.*; מֹץ הָרִים Is 17^{13} *chaff of mts.*; זֶרֶם הָרִים Jb 24^{8} *mountain-shower*; צֵל הֶהָרִים Ju 9^{36} *shadow of the mts.*; מִבֵּין שְׁנֵי הָרִים וְהֶהָרִים הָרֵי נְחֹשֶׁת Zc 6^{1}; *top of mt.* usu. רֹאשׁ הָהָר Nu 14$^{40.44}$ 1 S 26^{13} 2 K 1^{9}; as place for beacon Is 30^{17} (‖ גִּבְעָה), (cf. נְשָׂא־נֵס הָרִים 13^{2} & הַר־נִשְׁפֶּה Is 18^{3}), רֹאשׁ הֶהָרִים Is 2^{2} = Mi 4^{1}, רֹאשׁ הָרִים Is 42^{11} (‖ סֶלַע as dwelling-place) v. also ψ 72^{16}; רָאשֵׁי הֶהָרִים Gn 8^{5}; as lurking-places for ambuscade Ju 9$^{25.36}$, places for altars Ez 6^{13} (‖ גִּבְעָה רָמָה), for sacrifice Ho 4^{13} (‖ הַגְּבָעוֹת); רֹאשׁ הָהָר Jos 15^{8} = *mt.-ridge*, cf. v^{9} Ju 16^{3}; תּוֹעֲפוֹת הָרִים ψ 95^{4}; *foundations of mts.* מוֹסְדֵי הָרִים Dt 32^{22} ψ 18^{8} (‖ מוֹסְדוֹת הַשָּׁמַיִם 2 S 22^{8}); cf. לְקִצְבֵי הָרִים יָרַדְתִּי Jon 2^{7}. **n.** in fig. uses: תָּדוּשׁ הָרִים וְתָדֹק וּגְבָעוֹת כַּמֹּץ תָּשִׂים Is 41^{15} fig. of Isr.'s overcoming its foes; יִתְנַגְּפוּ רַגְלֵיכֶם עַל־הָרֵי נָשֶׁף Je 13^{16} of encountering hopeless calamities; הֶהָרִים Is 54^{10} as less permanent & changeless than Yahweh's kindness (‖ גְּבָעוֹת); הַר הַמַּשְׁחִית Je 51^{25} & הַר שְׂרֵפָה v^{25} fig. of Babylon. **2.** *hill-country, mountain-*

region, **a.** opp. plain, etc.:—dwelling-place of Canaanites, הָהָר Nu 13$^{17.29}$ (of promised land; opp. בָּעֲרָבָה בָּהָר; (יַד־הַיַּרְדֵּן & הַיָּם, אֶרֶץ הַנֶּגֶב) בָּהָר וּבָעֲרָבָה נֶגֶב Dt 1^{7}; וּבַשְּׁפֵלָה וּבַנֶּגֶב וּבְחוֹף הַיָּם בָּהָר כִּנְּרוֹת וּבַשְּׁפֵלָה וּבְנָפוֹת דּוֹר מִיָּם Jos 11^{2}; וּבַשְּׁפֵלָה וּבָעֲרָבָה וּבָאֲשֵׁדוֹת וּבַמִּדְבָּר וּבַנֶּגֶב 12^{8}; cf. 9^{1} 10^{40} Ju 1^{9}; הָהָר indef. (*the hill-country, the mountains*, in gen.) 2 Ch 2^{1} (place for hewing wood) so v^{17}; Ne 8^{15} (place for cutting boughs), etc. **b.** of a particular mountain-region, hill-country: הַר הָאֱמֹרִי Dt 1^{7} (cf. v^{7}) v^{19} (cf. v^{24}), also Jos 10^{6}; of Amalekites Ju 12^{15}; of Ephraim Jos 17^{15} 19^{50} 20^{7} 21^{21} 24$^{30.33}$ Ju 3^{27} 4^{5} 7^{24} 9^{48} 17^{1} + 6 t. Ju 17, 1 S 1^{1} 9^{4} 14^{22} 2 S 20^{21} 1 K 4^{8} 12^{25} 2 K 5^{22} 1 Ch 6^{52} 2 Ch 13^{4} 15^{8} 19^{4} Je 4^{15} 31^{6}; Ephraim and Gilead 50^{19} (cf. also הר(ה) Jos 17$^{16.18}$ Ju 3^{27}); of Israel Jos 11$^{16.21}$, cf. הָרֵי יִשְׂרָאֵל Ez 6^{2} 19^{9} 33^{28} 34^{13} 35^{12}; הָרֵי מָרוֹם יִשְׂרָאֵל Ez 17^{23} 20^{40} (הַר־קָדְשִׁי ‖) 34^{14}; עָרֵי הָהָר i.e. in mountain-country Dt 2^{37} (of Ammonites), Je 32^{44} 33^{13}; hill-country of Judah Jos 11^{21} 15^{48} 18^{12} 20^{7} 21^{11} 2 Ch 21^{11} (הָרֵי יהודה) 27^{4}; abode of Jebusites Jos 11^{3}.

2022 הַרְרֶיהָ, הַרְרֵי, הַרְרָם, הַרְרֵי, הֲרָרֵי v. הר. p. 249

2043 †הֲרָרִי, הָרָרִי, הַהֲרָרִי **adj. gent.** (= *mountain-dweller* (Thes)? or deriv. fr. some unknown **n.pr.loc.**);—used only in defining certain of David's heroes: **1. a.** שַׁמָּה הַהֲרָרִי 2 S 23^{33a} (cf. Dr) = 1 Ch 11^{34b} (where rd. prob. שַׁמָּה for שָׁגֵה, (𝔊L Σαμαια). **b.** שַׁמָּה בֶן־אָגֵא הָרָרִי 2 S 23^{11} (rd. perh. הַהֲרָרִי cf. Dr; but 𝔊 ὁ Ἀρουχαῖος, 𝔊L ὁ Αραχι, i.e. הָאַרְכִּי? cf. Klo). On שַׁמּוֹת הַהֲרוֹרִי 1 Ch 11^{27} (𝔊 ὁ Ἀδι, 𝔊L ὁ Αρωρι) v. הֲרוֹרִי supr. p. 248. **2.** אֲחִיאָם בֶּן־שָׂרָר הָאֲרָרִי 2 S 23^{33b} (rd. prob. הַהֲרָרִי) = אֲחִיאָם בֶּן־שָׂכָר הַהֲרָרִי 1 Ch 11^{35}.

†הָשֵׁם **n.pr.m.** father of one (or more?) of David's heroes 1 Ch 11^{34}, but rd. prob. יָשֵׁן 2 S 23^{32} and del. בני; cf. Dr^{Sm} and v. further sub יָשֵׁן. 2044

הַשְׁמָעוּת v. sub שׁמע. p. 1036 2045

הָשְׁפּוֹת v. אַשְׁפֹּת sub שׁפת. p. 1047 827, 8199

הִתּוּךְ v. sub נתך. p. 678 2046

הִתְחַבְּרוּת v. sub חבר. p. 288 2266

†הֲתָךְ **n.pr.m.** a Persian official at court of Ahasuerus Est 4$^{5.6.9.10}$. 2047

†[הָתַל] **vb.**—only **Pi. deceive, mock,** *Impf.* וַיְהַתֵּל בָּהֶם 1 K 18^{27} (secondary formation fr. תלל Hiph., q.v.; cf. Thes Ol$^{§ 257 \text{ f. ad fin.}}$ Sta$^{§ 145 \text{ e}}$; otherwise Kö$^{\text{I. 352}}$; v. further sub תלל). 2048

†הֲתֻלִּים **n.[m.]pl.** mockery:—אִם־לֹא ה׳ עִמָּדִי Jb 17^{2} *truly mockery surroundeth me* (De Di Da cf. VB). 2049

התת √of תְּהוֹתְתוּ ψ 62^{4} acc. to Thes al., but v. הות. p. 223 2050

ו

ו, *Wāw*, sixth letter; in modern Heb. = numeral 6; no evidence of this usage in OT times.

וְ, וּ, וָ demonstr. adv. and **conj. so, then, and** (Ph. Moab. Aram. ו; Ar. وَ; Eth. ወ: As. *u* Dl^{W} (but between vbs. the usu. connective is the enclitic *ma* KAT$^{2.508}$, Dl$^{§§ 82, 150}$). The use in Heb. shews that orig. וְ was not a merely copulative conj., but that it possessed a *demonstrative* force (cf. Dr$^{§ 122}$), which is often perceptible as such, though in other cases, from its being applied to denote mere juxtaposition or connexion [cf. Gk. τε, and Lat. *tum* . . . . *tum* = 'both . . . . and,' both properly demonstratives: As. *ma* has also a demonstr. force, Dl$^{§ 79}$], it is less palpable)—וְ before shwa' mobile or a labial is vocalized וּ; often before a tone-syll., when the word itself has a disj. accent, וָ (as וָמֵתִּי׃ Gn 19^{19}; וָמֵת 33^{13}; 44^{9}; וָחָיָה׃ Ex 1^{16}; וָיָמָּה Jos 15^{46}; וָלֹא 2 S 13^{26}; וָאָרֶץ Is 26^{19}; וָקָמוּ 49^{7}; וָחָתָּה׃ Je 48^{1}; וָרָע ψ 10^{15}); esp. when it forms with the preceding word a *pair*, whether of parallel or opposed ideas (as כֹּה וָכֹה Ex 2^{12}, מִי וָמִי 10^{8}, אֶבֶן וָאָבֶן Dt 25^{13}; 32^{7} + דֹּר וָדֹר; Gn 1^{2} תֹהוּ וָבֹהוּ, 1^{24} בְּהֵמָה וָרֶמֶשׂ, 8^{22} וְקַיִץ וָחֹרֶף וְיוֹם וָלַיְלָה, 4^{12} נָע וָנָד, 2^{19} טוֹב וָרָע׃, 12^{19} קַח וָלֵךְ׃, 14^{19} שָׁמַיִם וָאָרֶץ׃, 31^{44} אֲנִי וָאָתָּה, 41^{11} אֲנִי וָהוּא Ex 32^{27} עִבְרוּ וָשׁוּבוּ, אַתָּה וָהֵם Nu 16^{16}, אֱלֹהִים וָמֶלֶךְ 1 K 21^{13}, נִין וָנֶכֶד Is 14^{22},

שֹׁד וָשֶׁבֶר 59^{7}; and often: v. more fully Bö$^{§ 600}$); occas. also with a conj. accent (as וָחַי לְעֹלָם: Gn 3^{22} cf. Lv 18^{5}, וָמַתְנוּ שָׁם 2 K 7^{4}, וָאָרֶץ חֲדָשָׁה Is 65^{17}, Pr 25^{3}, שֹׁד וָשֶׁבֶר גָּדוֹל: Je 48^{3}, cf. 32^{29}).—וְ is used very freely and widely in Heb., but also with much delicacy, to express relations and shades of meaning which Western languages would usu. indicate by distinct particles. But in Heb. particles such as אוֹ, אָז, אַךְ, אָכֵן, אוּלָם, בַּעֲבוּר, לְמַעַן, לָכֵן, etc., were reserved for cases in which special emph. or distinctness was desired: their frequent use was felt instinctively to be inconsistent with the lightness and grace of movement which the Hebrew ear loved; and thus in AV, RV, words like *or, then, but, notwithstanding, howbeit, so, thus, therefore, that,* constantly appear, where the Heb. has simply וְ.

1. *And,* connecting both words (v. supra), and sentences (Gn 1^{5} וְלַחֹשֶׁךְ קָרָא וגו׳). When three, four, or more words follow, the conj. may connect them all, as Gn 7^{21} 10^{2} (6 t.) 24^{35} (7 t.) Jos 7^{24} (10 t.) 2 S 17$^{28\,f.}$: often however it is prefixed only to the last, as Gn 5^{32} 10^{1} Dt 18^{10} etc.; occas. even it connects only the first two, 1 K 8^{47} Is 1^{13} ψ 45^{9} Jb 42^{9}. Remarkably, however, וְ as a *mere* conj. is, as a rule, not in classical Hebrew attached directly to *verbs* (esp. in the perf.), the construction with וְ consec. (v. **2**) being (as in Moab.) preferred: thus יָצָא וַיִּבֶן is said, not יָצָא וּבָנָה. Exceptions in class. Heb. are (*a*) sts. where *synonyms* are coupled, as Nu 23^{19} אָמַר ... וְדִבֶּר, Dt 2^{30} Ju 5^{26} 1 S 12^{2} Is 1^{2} גדלתי ורוממתי 2^{11} 5^{14} 8^{8} 19^{6} 29^{20}; (*b*) isolated cases, difficult to reduce to rule (perh. sts. due to text. error), as Gn 28^{6} 38^{5} Jud 3^{23} 7^{13} 16^{18} 1 S 1^{12} 3^{13} 4^{19} 5^{7} 10^{9} 17$^{38.48}$ 25^{20} al. (in other passages, appar. similar, the pf. and וְ has a frequent. force (v. **2**), as Gn 37^{3} Ex 36$^{29\,f.}$ Nu 10$^{17\,f.}$ 21$^{15.20}$ 1 S 2^{22} 16^{14} 17$^{34\,f.}$ (v. Dr) 27^{9} 2 S 16^{13} 17^{17}, perh. also Gen. 15^{6} 21^{25} 34^{5}). In later parts of OT, prob. through Aram. influence, the pf. with simple וְ occurs more freq.: so esp. in Ec., where it is all but universal (e.g. 2$^{11.12.13.15}$ etc.). With the impf., the simple וְ is not so unidiomatic, even in class. Heb. (cf. **3**); v. Gen 1$^{9.26}$ 9^{27} 17^{2} 22^{17} 27^{29} Ex 23^{8} (freq.) 24^{7} Nu 14^{12} Dt 17^{13} 30$^{12.13}$ Jos 3^{13} 7^{3} Ju 7^{3} 13^{8} Is 5^{29} 14^{10}; oft. also in Je Is^{2} Jb ψ, e.g. Is 40^{30} 41^{20} (Dr$^{§ 116}$: contrast 28^{13}). Vid. more fully Dr$^{§ 130-4}$ Ges$^{§ 112.6}$. Special senses:—**a.** it sts. = *and specially,* Gn 3^{16} 1 K 11^{1} many strange women, *and specially* the daughter of Ph., Is 1^{1} Judah *and* (= *and particularly*) Jerusalem, 2^{1} 9^{7} ψ 18^{1}. **b.** *and in particular* ('und zwar'), *and that* (explicative), Gn 4^{4} Ju 7^{22} 1 S 17^{40} וּבַיַּלְקוּט, 28^{3} in Ramah, *and that* in his city (unusual: text suspicious), 2 S 13^{20} וְשֹׁמֵמָה *and that* desolate, Is 57^{11} I have been silent וּמֵעוֹלָם *and that* from of old, Is 32^{7} Je 15^{13} Am 3^{11} (si vera l.), 4^{10} Zc 9$^{9\,b}$ Mal 1^{11} ψ 68^{10} Pr 3^{12} La 3^{26} Ec 8^{2} Dn 1^{3} 8^{10} 9$^{25.27}$ Ne 8^{13} 1 Ch 9^{27} 2 Ch 8^{13} 29^{27} (but 'even' for וְ, before ל and inf., e.g. in Is 44^{28} Je 17^{10} 19^{12}, is wrong; v. Ew$^{§ 351\,c}$, Dr$^{§ 206}$). **c.** sts. it introduces an idea which so exceeds or adds to what has preceded, that it is nearly equivalent to *also,* 1 S 25^{43} 1 K 2^{22} ask *also* the kingdom for him; unusually Ho 8^{6} כי מישׂראל והוא for of Isr. is it *also,* Ec 5^{6} והבלים (v. De) 2 Ch 27^{5} (but v. 𝔊). Or it may be rendered *yea:* so esp. in the ascending numerations 3–4 Am 1$^{3.6.9.11.13}$ 2$^{1.4.6}$ Pr 30$^{18.21.29}$, 6–7 Pr 6^{16} Jb 5^{19}, 7–8 Mi 5^{4}—the first number being aggravated, or augmented, by a higher. In one idiom וּגְבוּל, occurring in geogr. descriptions, it is used peculiarly, seemingly = *at the same time:* †Nu 34^{6} and as for the W. border, וְהָיָה לָכֶם הַיָּם הַגָּדוֹל וּגְבוּל the great sea shall be to you *also* (Germ. 'zugleich') a border, Dt 3^{16} תּוֹךְ הַנַּחַל וּגְבוּל the middle of the stream being *at the same time* the border, v^{17} Jos 13$^{23.27}$ 15$^{12.47}$ (but these, exc. Nu 34^{6}, might be cases of **5 c** γ). **d.** it connects *alternative* cases, so that it = *or:* Ex 20$^{10.17}$ 21^{16} he that stealeth a man וּמְכָרוֹ וְנִמְצָא בְיָדוֹ and selleth him, *and* (= *or if*) he be found in his hand, v^{17} Lv 21^{14} 22$^{23.24}$ Pr 29^{9} (Fl Ew RV: *whether ... or*) Jb 31$^{13.16.26}$, etc. **e.** it connects *contrasted* ideas, where in our idiom the contrast would be expressed explicitly by *but;* in such cases prominence is usu. given to the contrasted idea by its being placed immed. after the conj.: Gn 2^{17} *but* of the tree of the knowledge ... thou shalt not eat, 4$^{2.5}$ 6^{8} 17^{21} 31^{10} etc., 1 K 2^{26} 10^{7} 11$^{32.34}$ 15^{14} Pr 10$^{1.2.3.4}$ + oft.; even after לֹא (where כִּי or כִּי אִם might be expected), as Gn 42^{10} Ex 21^{18} Lv 26^{45} Dt 11^{11} Ju 19^{12} 1 K 3^{11}. **f.** it introduces a contrasted idea in such a way as to suggest a *question,* esp. before a pron., Ju 14^{16} I told it not to my father or my mother, וְלָךְ אַגִּיד and shall I tell it *unto thee?* 2 S 11^{11} Je 25^{29} וְאַתֶּם הִנָּקֵה תִנָּקוּ and shall *ye* be guiltless? 45^{5} Ez 20^{31} 33$^{25\,b}$ Jon 4^{11}. So the וְ consec. and pf. (see **2 a**), Ex 5^{5} וְהִשְׁבַּתֶּם *and* will ye make them rest from their burdens? Nu 16^{10} וּבִקַּשְׁתֶּם *and* seek ye the priesthood also? 1 S 25^{11} Is 66^{9} ψ 50^{21} *and* shall I keep silence? Jb 32^{16} (cf. Dr$^{§ 119 γ}$). **g.** attaching a fresh subj. (or obj.) to a clause already grammatically complete, it = *and also*, Gn 2^{9b} Nu 16$^{2.18}$ and they stood at the entrance of the tent of meeting, ומשה ואהרן *and* Moses and Aaron (stood also), v^{27} Ex 35^{22} Ju 6^{5}; Gn 1^{16b} 12^{17} 44^{2} 46^{15} Ex 29^{3} Je 32^{29} (cf. Dr$^{Sm. i. 6, 11, \& p. 293}$): when the idea thus attached is subordinate, or not logically embraced in the principal pred., it approximates to the Arab. وَاوُ ٱلْمَعِيَّةِ or 'waw of association' (foll. by an *accus.*: W$^{AG ii. § 37}$), Est 4^{16} אֲנִי וְנַעֲרֹתַי אָצוּם I will fast (*sing.*) *and* (= with) my maidens, Ex 21^{4} 1 S 25^{42} 29^{10b} (but insert here אַתָּה with 𝔊) 2 S 12^{30} (but read וְבָהּ, as 1 Ch 20^{2}) 20^{10} Ne 6^{12}; Gn 4^{20} Is 42^{5} Je 19^{1} (but read וְלָקַחְתָּ מזקני with 𝔊) 2 Ch 2^{3} 13^{11}; cf. Je 22^{7} (אִישׁ וְכֵלָיו), Jb 41^{12}. Whether Is 48^{16} ורוחו belongs here, is dub. **h.** וְ repeated = *both* . . . *and* (but גַּם . . . גַּם is more usual in this sense); Gn 34^{28} Nu 9^{14} Jos 9^{23} 2 S 5^{8} (txt. dub.), Is 16^{5} 38^{15} Je 13^{14} 21^{6} 32^{14} (txt. dub.) v^{20} 40^{8} ψ 76^{7} Jb 34^{29} Dn 8^{13} Ne 12^{28}. **i.** a repetition of the *same* word with וְ interposed expresses (*a*) *diversity* (rare), Dt 25^{13} אֶבֶן וָאָבֶן a weight *and* a weight, i.e. different weights (explained by גְּדוֹלָה וּקְטַנָּה), v^{14} Pr 20^{23}; ψ 12^{3} בְּלֵב וָלֵב with a heart and a heart = with a double heart, 1 Ch 12^{33} בְּלֹא לֵב וָלֵב; (*b*) *distribution* (exc. in דֹּר וָדֹר Dt 32^{7} Is 13^{20} + oft. exclusively a late usage: cf. Dr$^{Intr. 505}$) †ψ 87^{5} 1 Ch 26^{13} לְשַׁעַר וָשָׁעַר: = for *every* gate, 28$^{14.14}$ 2 Ch 8^{14} 34^{13} 35^{15} Ezr 10^{14} זִקְנֵי עִיר וָעִיר elders of *every* city, Ne 13^{24}, Est 1$^{8.22.22}$ 2^{12} 3$^{4.12.12.12.12}$ 8$^{9.9}$; strengthened by כָּל־ 2 Ch 11^{12} בכל עיר ועיר in *every several city*, 19^{5} 28^{25} 31^{19} 32^{28} Est 2^{11} בכל־יום ויום, 3^{14} 4^{3} 8$^{11.13.17.17}$ 9$^{21.27.28}$ ψ 45^{18} 145^{13} (common in postB. Heb., esp. with כל). **j.** it is used in the formulation of proverbs (the *Vav adaequationis*, וָו הַשְׁוָאָה) as Pr 17^{3} 25$^{3.20.25}$ cold waters to a thirsty soul *and* good news from a far country (i.e. they are like each other), 26$^{3.9.14.20}$ 27^{21} Ec 5^{2} 7^{1} 8^{8} cf. 9^{11}; ψ 19^{5} 125^{2} Jb 14$^{11 f. 19}$ (cf. in Arab. 'every man *and* his cares [*accus.*],' 'every thing *and* its price,' i.e. they go together: 'merchants *and* dogs [*accus.*] of Seleucia,' i.e. they are like one another: v. Fl$^{Kl. Schr. iii. 535 f.}$). More rarely in the opp. order, Jb 5^{7} 12^{11}. But 1 S 12^{15b} cannot be thus explained: rd. with 𝔊 וּבְמַלְכְּכֶם, and v. Dr. **k.** in *circumstantial* clauses וְ introduces a statement of the *concomitant conditions* under which the action denoted by the principal verb takes place: in such cases, the relation expressed by וְ must often in Engl. be stated explicitly by a conj., as *when, since, seeing, though*, etc., as occasion may require. So very often, as Gn 11^{4} let us build a tower וְרֹאשׁוֹ בַשָּׁמַיִם *and* its top in the heavens (= *with* its top in etc.), 18^{12} shall I have pleasure, וַאדֹנִי זָקֵן *and* my lord is old (= my lord *being* old)? Ju 16^{15} How sayest thou, I love thee, וְלִבְּךָ אֵין אִתִּי *and* (= *when*) thy heart is not with me? and esp. with a pers. pron., Gn 15^{2} what wilt thou give me וְאָנֹכִי הוֹלֵךְ עֲרִירִי *and* I (= *the case being that* I) am going hence childless? 18^{13} 20^{3} lo, thou wilt die because of the woman thou hast taken וְהִוא בְּעֻלַת בָּעַל: = *seeing* she is married, 24^{62} וְהוּא יֹשֵׁב = *since* or *for* he was dwelling (different from וַיֵּשֶׁב = *and he proceeded* to dwell), 26^{27} וְאַתֶּם *seeing* ye hate me, Ju 13^{9} and came to her וְהִיא יוֹשֶׁבֶת = *as* she was sitting, 1 S 18^{23} 1 K 19^{19} + oft. Of a more except. type are ψ 72^{12} the afflicted וְאֵין־עֹזֵר לוֹ *and* (= *when*) he has no helper (cf. Jb 29^{12}), 104^{25} וְאֵין מִסְפָּר, 105^{34} Jb 5^{9}. Vid. more fully Dr$^{§ 156-60}$ Ges$^{§ 141, R 2}$. (The analogous use of the وَاوُ ٱلْحَالِ is very common in Arabic: W$^{ii. § 183}$.) Introducing an appeal to a fact *confirmatory* of some statement or promise, it almost = *as truly as* (cf. Ew$^{§ 340 c}$) Ho 12^{6} *and* J. is God of hosts, J. is his name! Jo 4^{20} Am 9$^{5-6}$ Is 51^{15} *and* I [who promise this] am J. thy God, who . . . . ! Je 29^{23} ψ 89$^{38 b}$ (comp. in Qor. the freq. 'And God is . . . . [the mighty, the merciful, etc.]').

2. The ו **consecutive** (formerly called the Waw 'conversive');—**a.** with the **impf.** (וַ with foll. daghesh; before א, וָ), as וַיֹּאמֶר prop. = *and he proceeded* to say, chiefly in contin. of a preceding *perfect* tense (so Moab.); **b.** with the **perf.** (וְ,—in 1 & 2 sg., the tone, with certain exceptions [v. Dr$^{§ 110}$], being thrown forward to the ultima), as וְיָשַׁבְתָּ prop. *so* [*viz.* as limited by a verb, or other term, preceding] *hadst thou sat*, chiefly in continuation of a preceding *imperfect* tense, in its various senses of future, jussive, or frequentative. The further analysis of these idioms belongs to the grammar; see on **a** Dr$^{Ch. vi.}$, Ges$^{§ 111}$, and on **b** Dr$^{Ch. viii.}$ Ges$^{§ 112}$. Here it must suffice to note—(*a*) ו consec. (esp. with the impf.) freq. couples two *verbs* in such a manner that the first, indicating the *general* character of the action, receives its closer definition in the second: in such cases, the first may often be represented in Engl. by an *adv.*, as Gn 26^{18} וַיָּשָׁב וַיַּחְפֹּר and he turned *and* dug = and he dug *again;* so oft.; and similarly with הוֹסִיף Gn 25^{1}, מִהֵר 24^{18}, הוֹאִיל Jos 7^{7}, etc.; more exceptionally, Gn 30^{27} Est 8^{6}, and (not consec.) Gn 47^{6} Jb 23^{3} Ct 2^{3} La 3^{26} (v. Ges$^{§ 120.2a}$; cf. in Syr. Nö$^{§ 335-6}$. In Arab. the stronger form of the conj. فَ here corresponds: W$^{ii. § 140}$). (*b*) וַ with the impf. sts. expresses a contrast = *and yet,* Gn 32^{31} I have seen God face to face וַתִּנָּצֵל *and yet* my soul is delivered, Dt 4^{33} 2 S 3^{8} 19^{29} Is 51^{12} ψ 73^{14} 144^{3} Jb 10^{8}+ (cf. Dr$^{§ 74 β}$). (*c*) there is a tendency in the later books of the OT to use the pf. with simple וְ, where the classical language would employ the impf. with וַ (cf. supr. **1**); so esp. in Ec, where וַ occurs thrice only, 1^{17} $4^{1.7}$. (*d*) a double pf. with ו consec. is sts. used, informally but neatly, with a hypoth. force; thus (*α*) in past or present time Ex 16^{21} וְחַם הַשֶּׁמֶשׁ וְנָמָס׃ and the sun used to be warm, and it used to melt = and *if* (or *when*) the sun was warm, it melted, 33^{10} 1 K 18^{10} Je $18^{4.8}$ וְשָׁב וְנִחַמְתִּי = and *if* it turns, I repent, 20^{9} (v. RV); (*β*) in fut. time, Gn 44^{22} ועזב אביו ומת and he will leave his father, and he will die = and *if* he leaves his father, he will die, 33^{13} 42^{38} Ex 4^{14} 12^{13} 1 S 16^{2} 19^{3} Ez 33^{3} 39^{15} etc. (Dr$^{§ 147-9}$, Ges$^{§ 159.2e}$).

3. With a **voluntative** (cohort. or juss.) וְ expresses an intention, **that** or **so that** (an elegancy by which the too frequent use of לְמַעַן or בַּעֲבוּר is avoided): Ex 10^{17} entreat God, וְיָסֵר *so may he* remove (= *that he may* remove) this death, Gn 27^{4} and bring it me וְאֹכֵלָה *so let me* eat (= *that I may* eat); and without the modal form being externally indicated, Ex 14^{1} speak . . . וְיָשֻׁבוּ *that* they return, v^{15}; and oft. Sts. even of past time, as 1 K 13^{33} whom he would, he consecrated וִיהִי *that* there might be priests of the high places, 2 K 19^{25} Is 25^{9a} La 1^{19}. After a neg., ψ 51^{18} thou desirest not sacrifice, וְאֶתֵּנָה *so* [= in that case] *would I* give it (or, *that I might* give it), 55^{13} וְאֶשָּׂא *so* could I bear it (or, *that I might* bear it), Is 53^{2} RVm Nu 23^{19} Je 5^{28} RV. Sts. also before an imv., Gn 12^{2} *and be* (= that thou mayest be) a blessing, 2 S 21^{3}+. See more fully Dr$^{§ 59-65}$, Ges$^{§ 108.2; 109.2; 110.2}$. (In Arabic فَ with the *subjunctive* is used similarly: W$^{ii. § 15d}$.) A volunt. is also sts. attached by וְ to a preceding volunt. or imv., so as to form a virtually hypothetical sentence, as Gn 42^{18} זאת עֲשׂוּ וִחְיוּ = *if* you do this, you shall live, 30^{28} 34^{12} Pr $3^{9f.}$ $4^{4.8}$ Is 55^{2}: v. Dr$^{§ 152}$.

4. It expresses often an informal inference, or consequence, **so, then,** esp. at the beginning of a speech: Gn 27^{8} ψ 2^{10} and often וְעַתָּה now, *therefore;* וְלָמָּה and וּמַדּוּעַ why, *then?* Gn 29^{25} Nu 12^{8} 16^{3}+; Ex 2^{20} וְאַיּוֹ where, *then,* is he? Gn 34^{21} 1 S 15^{14} 26^{22} וְיַעֲבֹר let, *then,* . . . come over, 2 S 24^{3} 2 K 4^{41} וּקְחוּ קֶמַח *then* bring meal, Ez 18^{32}. So the וְ consec. and the pf., as Dt 2^{4} וְנִשְׁמַרְתֶּם take heed, *therefore,* 4^{15} 7^{9} וְיָדַעְתָּ know, *therefore,* 30^{19} 1 S 6^{5} 1 K 2^{6} Ru 3^{9}; Jos 15^{19} Is 49^{6b} (Dr$^{§ 119δ}$).

5. ו introduces the *predicate* or *apodosis:* viz. **a.** וְ consec. and the *pf.*—in answer to אִם or כִּי constantly, as Ex 19^{5} 23^{22} if thou hearkenest to my voice, וְאָיַבְתִּי *then* am I (= I will be) enemy to thy enemies (v. Dr$^{§ 136-8}$); after the *casus pendens,* Ex 12^{44} every servant that is bought for money, וּמַלְתָּה thou shalt circumcise him, etc. Nu 14^{31} 24^{24} 1 S 25^{27} 2 S 14^{10} he that spake unto thee, וַהֲבֵאתוֹ אֵלַי *so hast thou* brought him (= *thou shalt* bring him) unto me, Is 9^{4} $56^{6f.}$+; Ex 12^{15} 31^{14} Dt 17^{12}+; after various time-determinations, as Gn 3^{5} in the day of your eating from it וְנִפְקְחוּ *then* shall your eyes be opened, Ex 16^{6} עֶרֶב וִידַעְתֶּם at even, *then* shall ye know, v^{7} 32^{34} 2 S 15^{10} 1 K 13^{31} בְּמוֹתִי וּקְבַרְתֶּם אֹתִי when I die, *so* ye shall bury me, etc., + oft.; after conjs., as כִּי Gn 29^{15}, יַעַן 1 K 20^{28} Is $3^{16f.}$, תַּחַת 60^{15}, etc., (v. Dr$^{§ 123}$). **b.** וַ consec. and the *impf.* (but much less frequently than the pf.), as Gn 30^{30} the little that thou hadst, וַיִּפְרֹץ *it* hath increased, Ex 9^{21} 2 S 4^{10} 1 K $9^{20f.}$ 15^{13}+; after time-determinations, Gn 22^{4} on the third day וַיִּשָּׂא *then* Abraham lifted up his eyes, 19^{15} 27^{34} 37^{18} 1 S 6^{6} 12^{8} Is 6^{1} Ho 11^{1} when Isr. was a child, וָאֹהֲבֵהוּ *then* I loved him, +; occas. after conjs., as כַּאֲשֶׁר Ex 16^{34}, יַעַן 1 S 15^{23}, לְמַעַן Is 45^{4}, אִם ψ 59^{16} (Dr$^{§ 127}$). **c.** in other cases (not 'consecutive')—all more or less uncommon: viz. *α.* וְ closely joined to the impf. Gn 13^{9} if to the left, וְאֵימִנָה *then* I will take the right (cf. 2 S 12^{8}) Ex 12^{3} on the 10th of the month וְיִקְחוּ *then* let them take, Nu 16^{5} Is 43^{4} Ho 4^{6} 10^{10} ψ 69^{33} Jb 15^{17}; 2 S 22^{41} Pr 23^{24} Kt (Dr$^{§ 125}$); *β.* separated fr. the vb., Ex 8^{22} Lv 7^{16} וּמִמָּחֳרָת וְהַנּוֹתָר יֵאָכֵל and on the morrow, *then* the remainder shall be eaten, Jos 3^{3} 1 K 8^{32} Is 8^{7}

48^{7} Jb 14^{7} 20^{19b} 23^{12} 25^{5} 32^{14}+; γ. without a vb., Gn 40^{9} בַּחֲלוֹמִי וְהִנֵּה in my dream, *behold*, a vine was before me, v^{16} 2 S $23^{3f.}$ Pr 10^{25}, and the extreme cases 2 S 15^{34} thy father's slave, וַאֲנִי מֵאָז I was *that* of old,—but now וַאֲנִי עַבְדֶּךָ *well*, I will be thine, Is 34^{12} (si vera l.), Jb 4^{6b} תִּקְוָתְךָ וְתֹם דְּרָכֶיךָ thy confidence—*it is* the uprightness of thy ways, 36^{26} מִסְפַּר שָׁנָיו וְלֹא חֵקֶר Ges. seine Jahre, *da* ist kein Zählen (cf. Dr [§ 124-5, 128-9]).—With **4, 5** comp. the Arab. ف, W [i. § 366 b, 367 c; ii. § 187]; Dr [§ 185 end].

2051 †וְדָן†, appar. **n.pr.loc.**, only in וְדָן וְיָוָן Ez 27^{19} *Wedān and Yāwān* (cf. VB and reff.) but identif. wholly dub.; = *Waddân* near Medina acc. to Glas [Skizze ii. 428]: 𝔊 om.; text prob. corrupt, cf. Sta [Javan. 11 ff.] Da al.; Ew Hi rd. דְּדָן, but דְּדָן is in following v., and anticipation improb., cf. Sta [l. c.]; Co rds. (for ודן ויון) וְאַרְנָבָן, on the basis of Bab. & As. *Aranabanim*, *Arnabani*, n.pr.loc., following *Ḫilbunim* (חֶלְבּוֹן) in lists of places whence wine was brought (cf. יֵין חֶלְבּוֹן v^{18}, & 𝔊 καὶ οἶνον for ויון; also COT Ez 27^{18}).

2052 †וָהֵב†, appar. **n.pr.loc.**, אֶת־וָהֵב בְּסוּפָה Nu 21^{14}, obj. of a vb. now lost out of the text (cf. RV & esp. Di VB), situation unknown; 𝔊 Ζωοβ, Ζοοβ; so Lag [BN 54] Say [Ac. Oct. 22, 1892] (זָהָב).

2053 †[וָו] **n.[m.] hook, pin** or **peg** (etym. unknown)—pl. abs. וָוִים Ex 38^{28}; cstr. וָוֵי Ex 27^{10} + 5 t.; וָוֵיהֶם Ex 26^{32} + 5 t.;—only P, in description of tabernacle Ex $26^{32.37}$ $27^{10.11.17}$ $36^{36.38}$ $38^{10.11.12.17.19.28}$, the *hooks* or *pegs* of gold and silver, fastened on, or in, the posts of the tabernacle, to support the various hangings (curtains, screens, etc.)

וזר (√of foll.; cf. Ar. وَزَرَ *bear a burden*, or وَزِرَ *be guilty*, yet v. Fl in De Pr 21^{8}).

†וָזָר **adj. criminal, guilty** הֲפַכְפַּךְ דֶּרֶךְ אִישׁ וָזָר Pr 21^{8} *crooked* is *the way of a guilty man* (si vera l.; txt. dub.; possible dittogr. in וְזָר וַזַּךְ?). 2054

†וַיְזָתָא **n.pr.m.** (perhaps=Pers. n.pr.m. *Vahyazdâta* Benfey [Pers. Keilinschr. (1847) 18, 93] cf. Spieg [APK 240], who conjectures meaning *given-of-the-Best-One* (vom Besten gegeben)),—a son of Haman Est 9^{9}. 2055

וָלָד, וְלַד v. sub ילד. p. 409 2056

†וַנְיָה **n.pr.m.** one of those with strange wives, Ezr 10^{36} (text dubious; 𝔊B Οὐιεχωα, א Οὐιερεχω, A Οὐουνια, 𝔊L Οὐανια). 2057

†וָפְסִי **n.pr.m.** a man of Naphtali, in נַחְבִּי בֶּן־וָפְסִי Nu 13^{14} (text dubious; 𝔊 Ναβει υἱὸς Ἰαβει). 2058

†וַשְׁנִי acc. to MT appar. **n.pr.m.** son of Samuel, only הַבְּכֹר וַשְׁנִי וַאֲבִיָּה 1 Ch 6^{13}, but rd. הַבְּכֹר יוֹאֵל וְהַשֵּׁנִי אביה cf. 𝔊L, and ‖ 1 S 8^{2}; v. Th [Sm] Be [Ch] Dr [Sm] al. 2059

†וַשְׁתִּי **n.pr.f.** (=Pers. (Zend) *vahista*, *best*, cf. Justi [Hdb. d. Zendsprache, 272]) queen of Ahasuerus (Xerxes) king of Persia, Est $1^{9.11.12.15.16.17.19}$ $2^{1.4.17}$. 2060

ז

ז, *Zâyin*, seventh letter; used as numeral 7 in modern Heb.; no evidence of this usage in OT times.

זאב (√of foll.; acc. to Fl [Bericht d. sächs. G. d. W. i. (1846-47) 430 f. = Kleinere Schriften iii. 212 f.] i.q. Ar. ذَأَبَ *drive away, and despise, drive* or *frighten away*, whence ذِئْب, ܕܺܐܒܳܐ, זְאֵב wolf, as *driven* or *chased away*; cf. Hom [NS 304] MV al.)

2061 †I. זְאֵב **n.m.** [Is 11, 6] **wolf** (NH *id.*, Ar. ذِئْب (*jackal* according to Hom [NS 303 ff.]; but see RS [ZMG 1880, 373] and Doughty [Arab. Deserta i. 327; ii. 144, 145]) Aram. דֵּיבָא, ܕܺܐܒܳܐ, As. *zību* Dl [S 47]; Eth. ዝእብ: *hyena* Di [1056] (on format. cf. Lag [BN 58]); Ph. in cpd.n.pr. זאבקם)—זְאֵב abs. Gn 49^{27} + 2 t.; cstr. Je 5^{6}; pl. זְאֵבִים Ez 22^{27}; cstr. זְאֵבֵי Hb 1^{8} Zp 3^{3};—*wolf*, never in narrative; in predictions of peace in Messian. age וְגָר זְאֵב עִם כֶּבֶשׂ Is 11^{6} זְאֵב וְטָלֶה יִרְעוּ כְאֶחָד Is 65^{25}; in simile, of Benjamin's fierceness בִּ׳ זְאֵב יִטְרָף Gn 49^{27}; of fierce horses of Chaldeans חַדּוּ מִזְּאֵבֵי עֶרֶב Hb 1^{8} (‖ קַלּוּ מִנְּמֵרִים); of princes of Judah כִּזְאֵבִים טֹרְפֵי טָרֶף Ez 22^{27}; metaph. of enemies of Judah Je 5^{6} זְאֵב עֲרָבוֹת (‖ אַרְיֵה, נָמֵר); of corrupt and oppressive judges שֹׁפְטֶיהָ זְאֵבֵי עֶרֶב Zp 3^{3} (‖ אֲרָיוֹת שֹׁאֲגִים).

†II. זְאֵב **n.pr.m.** (*wolf*)—a prince of 2062

Midian, Ju $7^{25.25.25}$ 8^3 ψ 83^{12}; also in **n.pr.loc.** יֶקֶב־זְאֵב Ju 7^{25} *wine-vat of Zeeb.*

2063 **זאת pron.f.** v. זֶה. p. 260

זבב (√of foll.; cf. Ar. ذَبَّ *go hither and thither* (of a man); ذَبْذَبَ *make to dangle*, or *move to and fro*, of a thing suspended in the air; but in this sense perhaps denom.)

2070 †**זְבוּב n.m.**$^{Ec\ 10,1}$ **fly** (as *moving to and fro* in the air? cf. Fl NHWB$^{i.\ 438\ b}$; NH *id.*, As. *zumbu*, Dl$^{S\ 63\ f.}$; Ar. ذُبَابٌ, Aram. דִּיבָבָא, ܕܒܒܐ, ܕܒܘܒܐ);—lit. only זְבוּבֵי מָוֶת Ec 10^1 i.e. *dead flies;* so AV RV Hi Now al.; >𝔊 De al. *death-bringing, deadly flies;* זְבוּב metaph. of Egyptian army Is 7^{18} (‖ דְּבוֹרָה, *bee*, of Assyrian); on בַּעַל זְבוּב v. בַּעַל II. **4,** p. 127 supr.

2079 †**זַבַּי n.pr.m.** (Palm. זבי Vog$^{No.\ 28}$ (but this perh.=*loricatus*, cf. زَغْفٌ *lorica*); connex. with above √ uncertain)—Jew in Ezra's time Ezr 10^{28}; 𝔊 Ζαβου(θ); cf. also Ne 3^{20} Kt (𝔊 Ζαβου etc., but Qr זַכַּי; v. זַכַּי Ezr 2^9=Ne 7^{14}).

2064 †[**זָבַד**] **vb. bestow upon, endow with** (Ar. زَبَدَ; Aram. זְבַד, ܙܒܰܕ +Gn 30^{20}, ܙܶܒܕܳܐ *dowry;* in Sab. n.pr., v. sub זָבָד infr.; also in Palm. n.pr. נבוזבד Vog^{73} and many others (זבד, זבדא, זבידא, זבדבל, זבדעתא = Ζαβδιβηλος, etc.): see Euting Sechs Inschr. aus Idalien p. 15), זְבָדַנִי אֱלֹהִים אֹתִי זֵבֶד טוֹב Gn 30^{20a} (E), appar. in expl. of name Zebulun, cf. Thes Di; another expl. in v^b, v. sub זבל.

2065 †**זֶבֶד n.m. endowment, gift,** Gn 30^{20a} cf. foregoing.

2066 †**זָבָד n.pr.m.** (*he hath given,* or, *a gift;* cf. Sab. n.pr. זבדם Hal^{168} DHM$^{ZMG\ 1883,\ 15}$, זביד DHM Epigr. Denkm. 50=زُبَيْد; also NH n.pr. זביד)—**1.** a descendant of Judah 1 Ch $2^{36.37}$. **2.** an Ephraimite 1 Ch 7^{21}. **3.** one of David's valiant men 1 Ch 11^{41}. **4.** one of the murderers of Joash of Judah 2 Ch 24^{26} (𝔊 Ζαβελ, Ζαβεθ, Ζαβαθ), called יוֹזָכָר (q.v. sub יהוה, הוה) 2 K 12^{22}. **5.** name of three returned exiles who had taken strange wives: **a.** Ezr 10^{27}; **b.** v^{33}; **c.** v^{43}.

2071 †**זָבוּד n.pr.m.** (*bestowed*) an officer of Solomon 1 K 4^5.

2072 †**זבוד n.pr.m.** a returned exile Ezr 8^{14} Kt; Qr זַכּוּר, q.v. (B om.; A Ζαβουδ, i.e. זָבוּד; 𝔊L Ζακχουρ).

2080 †**זבידה** Kt, **זְבוּדָּה** Qr, **n.pr.f.** mother of Jehoiakim 2 K 23^{36} זְבִידָּה בַת־פְּדָיָה מִן־רוּמָה; (‖ 2 Ch 36^5 om. MT); quite otherwise 𝔊B Ἰελλα, daughter of Ἐδειλ; in A the names are Ειελδαφ & Ειεδδιλα; 𝔊 2 Ch 36^5 Ζε(κ)χωρα & Νηρειου; 𝔊L (K & Ch) Ἀμιταλ & Ἱερεμιου (confusion with Zedekiah's mother 24^{18}).

†**זַבְדִּי n.pr.m.** (cf. Ar. زَبْدٌ *gift;* ? *gift of* י׳, vid. Dr$^{Stud.\ Bib.\ i.\ 5\ \&\ reff.}$; perh. *my gift, gift to me:* cf. זַבְדִּיאֵל; in NH n.pr. זבדי (זַבְדַּי or זַבְדִּי?); NT Ζεβεδαῖος, e.g. Mk 1^{19}, 𝔖 ܙܒܕܝ, *Zebedee*)—**1.** grandfather of Achan, of Judah (𝔊 Ζαμβρ(ε)ι etc., 𝔊L Ζαβδ(ε)ι) Jos 7^1 (app.=זִמְרִי 1 Ch 2^6, 𝔊 Ζαμβρ(ε)ι v$^{17.18}$. **2.** a Benjamite 1 Ch 8^{19}. **3.** an officer of David 1 Ch 27^{27}. **4.** a Levite Ne 11^{17} (om. B; A Ζεχρι, 𝔊L Ζεχρει) prob. rd. זִכְרִי, as ‖ 1 Ch 9^{15}. 2067

†**זַבְדִּיאֵל n.pr.m.** (*my gift is God*)—**1.** father of one of David's officers 1 Ch 27^2. **2.** a prominent Hebrew in Nehemiah's time Ne 11^{14}. 2068

זְבַדְיָה, זְבַדְיָהוּ n.pr.m. (י׳ *hath bestowed,* cf. יְהוֹזָבָד, & reff., also זַבְדִּיאֵל supr.)—זְבַדְיָהוּ **1.** Levites, **a.** 1 Ch 26^2; **b.** 2 Ch 17^8. **2.** an officer of Jehoshaphat 2 Ch 19^{11}. זְבַדְיָה **3.** Benjamites, **a.** 1 Ch 8^{15}; **b.** 1 Ch 8^{17}. **4.** one of David's men 1 Ch 12^8. **5.** an officer of David 1 Ch 27^7. **6.** a returning exile Ezr 8^8. **7.** one of priestly house Ezr 10^{20}. 2069

זָבַח$_{134}$ **vb. slaughter for sacrifice** (NH *id.*, Ph. זבח; As. *zibû* Dl$^{Pr\ 174}$ cf. Lotz$^{TP\ 174}$; Ar. ذَبَحَ, Sab. דבח CIS$^{iv.\ 1,\ 2,\ No.\ 74\ l.\ 11,\ 12}$; Aram. דְּבַח, ܕܒܰܚ, Eth. ዘብሐ:) **Qal**$_{112}$ *Pf.* 1 K 8^{63} 'ז 13^2, זָבַחְתָּ Ex 20^{24}+3 t., זָבַחְתִּי Ez 39^{19}, זָבְחוּ Ex 34^{15} Lv 17^5, זְבַחְתֶּם Ex 8^{24}, זָבַחְנוּ Ex 8^{23}; *Impf.* וַיִּזְבַּח Gn 31^{54}+14 t.; 2 ms. sf. תִּזְבָּחֶנּוּ Dt 15^{21}, 2 fs. sf. וַתִּזְבָּחִים Ez 16^{20}, 1 s. אֶזְבַּח ψ 116^{17}, אֶזְבְּחָה ψ 27^6 54^8 Jon 2^{10}; 2 mpl. תִּזְבָּחוּ Lv 19^5 +2 t., תִּזְבָּחוּ Lv 22^{29}+2 t.; 1 pl. נִזְבְּחָה Ex 3^{18}+, etc. (61 t. Impf.); *Imv.* זְבַח ψ 50^{14}, זִבְחוּ Ex 8^{21} ψ 4^6; *Inf. cstr.* זְבֹחַ 1 S 15^{15}+14 t., לִזְבּוֹחַ 2 Ch 11^{16}, בְּזָבְחוֹ 2 S 15^{12}; *Pt. act.* זֹבֵחַ Ex 13^{15}+8 t., זוֹבֵחַ Is 66^3, pl. זֹבְחִים Lv 17^5+(20 t. Pt.)—**I.** *slaughter for sacrifice* **1.** c. acc. of **a.** kind of sacrifice זֶבַח ז׳ Gn 31^{54}+, +פֶּסַח Dt $16^{2.5.6}$, +עֹלוֹת שְׁלָמִים Dt 27^7 Jos 8^{31}, +תּוֹדָה ψ $50^{14.23}$, +עלות ושלמים Ex 20^{24} (E). **b.** victims, (*a*) animals +בָּקָר וָצֹאן 1 K 8^{63} Nu 22^{40}, +צאן ובקר 2 Ch 18^2, +הַבְּרִיאָה Ez 34^3, +כָּל־פֶּטֶר רֶחֶם Ex 13^{15} (J); +פָּרִים וְאֵילִים 1 Ch 15^{26}, +שׁוֹר וָשֶׂה Dt 17^1; (*β*) mankind +בָּנִים וּבָנוֹת ψ 106^{37} Ez 16^{20}, +זֹבְחֵי אָדָם *sacrificers of mankind* Ho 13^2 (so Ra AE Hi Wü MV; *men that sacrifice* AV RV after Ki, so Pu Ew Ke Now Che SS). **c.** +תּוֹעֲבַת מִצְרַיִם 2076

Ex $8^{22.22}$ (E), †מָשְׁחָת Mal 1^{14}. **2.** absolute 1 S 1^{5}+oft. **3.** c. לְ of deity, †לְדָגוֹן Ju 16^{23}, †לַשְּׂעִירִם Lv 17^{7} (H), †לַשֵּׁדִים Dt 32^{17} ψ 106^{37}; *other gods* Ex 34^{15} (JE)+; but usually ליהוה Ex 3^{18}+9 t. JE, Lv 17^{5} 19^{5} 22^{29} (all H, not elsewh. in P), Dt 15^{21} 16^{2} 17^{1} 1 S 1^{3}+; †לֵאלֹהֵי אָבִיו Gn 46^{1} (E), לאלהים ψ 50^{14}, †לאדני Mal 1^{14}. **4.** with local prep. בְּ Gn 31^{54} (E)+, עַל Ex 20^{24} (E)+; לפני Lv 9^{4} (P)+, על פני השדה Lv 17^{5}(H). **II.** *slaughter for eating* (connected also with sacrifice, as all eating of flesh among ancient Hebrews was sacrificial, RS$^{Sem. 219}$) 1 S 28^{24} (fat calf for Saul), Ez 34^{3} (fat sheep for shepherds), 2 Ch 18^{2} (sheep and oxen for Jehoshaphat, c. לְ of person); cf. Dt 12^{15} v^{21} (abs.), 1 K 19^{21}. **III.** *slaughter in divine judgment* Ez 39^{17-19} c. acc. זְבְחִי (Gog and Magog as feast for vultures), 1 K 13^{2} 2 K 23^{20} (priests of high-places on their own altars).

†**Pi.**$_{22}$ *Pf.* זִבַּח 2 Ch 33^{22}, זִבְּחוּ ψ 106^{38}, זִבֵּ֑חוּ Ho 12^{12}; *Impf.* יְזַבֵּחַ Hb 1^{16}, יְזַבֵּ֫חוּ Ho $4^{13.14}$ 11^{2} (7 t. Impf.); *Inf. cstr.* לְזַבֵּחַ 1 K 12^{32}; *Pt.* מְזַבֵּחַ 1 K 3^{3}, pl. מְזַבְּחִים 2 Ch 5^{6}+8 t., מְזַבְּחוֹת 1 K 11^{8};—*sacrifice*, **1.** of the abundant sacrifices made to Yahweh by Solomon 1 K 8^{5} = 2 Ch 5^{6}, and Hezekiah 2 Ch 30^{22}, and prob. intensive; but **2.** elsewhere of sacrifice to other deities, possibly iterative in some cases, but certainly not in all: לַבְּעָלִים Ho 11^{2}, לֵאלֹהֵיהֶן 1 K 11^{8}, לָעֲגָלִים 12^{32}, לְחֶרְמוֹ Hb 1^{16}, לַעֲצַבֵּי כְנָעַן ψ 106^{38}, לְכָל־הַפְּסִילִים 2 Ch 28^{23}, לֵאלֹהֵי דַרְמֶשֶׂק 33^{22}; or in unlawful places עַל־רָאשֵׁי הֶהָרִים Ho 4^{13} cf. v^{14}, בַּגִּלְגָּל 12^{12}, בַּבָּמוֹת 1 K $3^{2.3}$ 22^{44} 2 K 12^{4} 14^{4} $15^{4.35}$, 16^{4} = 2 Ch 28^{4}. It is used without direct obj. Ho 4^{14} and oft.; also c. acc. of victim שְׁוָרִים Ho 12^{12} צֹאן וּבָקָר 1 K 8^{5} = 2 Ch 5^{6}; sons and daughters ψ 106^{38}, זִבְחֵי שְׁלָמִים 2 Ch 30^{22}.

2077 I. זֶ֫בַח$_{162}$ **n.m.**$^{Ju\ 16,\ 23}$ sacrifice, ז׳ abs. Gn 31^{54}+; cstr. Ex 34^{25}+; זֶבַח Lv 17^{8}+16 t.; sf. זִבְחוֹ Lv 7^{16} Ez 34^{15}, זִבְחֲכֶם Lv 19^{6}; pl. זְבָחִים Gn 46^{1}+; cstr. זִבְחֵי Lv 17^{5}+; sf. 3 mpl. זִבְחֵיהֶם Lv 17^{5}, זְבָחֵימוֹ Dt 32^{38}, זִבְחֹתָם †Ho 4^{19} etc.;—the common and most ancient sacrifice, whose essential rite was eating the flesh of the victim at a feast in which the god of the clan shared by receiving the blood and fat pieces. In the older literature it is distinguished from מִנְחָה and עֹלָה, in the later literature from חַטָּאת and אָשָׁם. †**I.** general name for all sacrifices eaten at feasts:—**1.** of the God of Israel Gn 46^{1} Ex 10^{25} 18^{12} (E) Ho 3^{4} 6^{6} 9^{4} Am 5^{25} Is 1^{11} 19^{21} Dt 12^{27} 18^{3} 1 S $2^{13.29}$ 3^{14} 6^{15} $9^{12.13}$ $15^{22.22}$ $16^{3.5.5}$ 2 S 15^{12} 1 K 8^{62} 12^{27} 2 K 5^{17} 16^{15} ψ 4^{7} 50^{8} $51^{18.19}$ Pr 15^{8} $21^{3.27}$ Is $43^{23.24}$ 56^{7} Je 6^{20} $7^{21.22}$ 17^{26} 33^{18} Ez 40^{42} 44^{11} 1 Ch $29^{21.21}$ 2 Ch $7^{1.4.5.12}$ Ne 12^{43} Dn 9^{27} Ec 4^{17}. They should be זִבְחֵי צֶדֶק *sacrifices of righteousness* (offered in righteousness by the righteous) Dt 33^{19} ψ 4^{6} 51^{21}; זִבְחֵי הַבְהָבַי *sacrifices of gifts to me* (י׳) Ho 8^{13}; the temple is בֵּית זָ֑בַח 2 Ch 7^{12}; they should not be ז׳ רִיב *sacrifices of strife*, where strife prevails Pr 17^{1}. **2.** of other deities Ex 34^{15} Nu 25^{2} Dt 32^{38} (JE) Ju 16^{23} 2 K $10^{19.24}$ Ho 4^{19} Is 57^{7} Ez 20^{28}; these are זִבְחֵי מֵתִים *sacrifices to dead things* (lifeless gods, opp. to י׳ as living) ψ 106^{28}. **II.** there are several kinds of זְבָחִים which are gradually distinguished: †**1.** *the covenant sacrifice*, between Jacob and Laban Gn 31^{54} (E), with God ψ 50^{5} (cf. Ex 24^{5} 1 S 11^{15}). †**2.** *the passover* זֶבַח חַג הַפָּסַח Ex 34^{25} (JE), זבח פסח Ex 12^{27} (J); and prob. also זבחי Ex 23^{18} (JE) = 34^{25} (*id.*) †**3.** *annual sacrifice* זֶבַח הַיָּמִים 1 S 1^{21} 2^{19} 20^{6}, cf. ז׳ מִשְׁפָּחָה sacrifice of the clan 1 S 20^{29}. †**4.** *thank offering* ז׳ (הַ)תּוֹדָה Lv 7^{12} 22^{29} ψ 107^{22} 116^{17}, which is given as הַזָּבַח, זִבְחוֹ, ז׳ קָרְבָּנוֹ Lv $7^{16.17}$; and as a variety of שְׁלָמִים Lv $7^{13.15}$; it is implied in זִבְחֵי תְרוּעָה ψ 27^{6}; yet זֶבַח is generic with תּוֹדָה 2 Ch $29^{31.31}$. **5.** in ritual of H & P זבחים are defined by שלמים (q.v.) Lv 3^{1}+39 t. Lv Nu, 1 S 10^{8} 1 K 8^{63} 2 Ch 30^{22}/33^{16} Pr 7^{14}, but sometimes (rarely) ז׳ alone is used in this sense, with or without suffix, where the meaning is plain from the context: Lv $17^{5.7.8}$ 19^{6} 23^{37} (H) Nu $15^{3.5.8}$ Jos $22^{26.29}$ (all P). These ritual offerings are of three varieties תּוֹדָה, נֶדֶר and נְדָבָה Lv $7^{12.16}$ (P); in the several lists זבחים are distinguished from תודות Am $4^{4f.}$ 2 Ch 29^{31}, from נדרים Nu 15^{8} (P) Dt $12^{6.11}$ Jon 1^{16}, from נדבות Am $4^{4f.}$ Dt 12^{6} and from the more comprehensive שלמים Nu 15^{8} Jos 22^{27} (P). So also the sacrifice at the institution of the covenant at Horeb Ex 24^{5} (JE) and the sacrifice at the installation of Saul 1 S 11^{15} are defined as †זבחים שלמים. Thus ז׳ seems not only to be used for all these special forms but also to include other festal sacrifices not defined in the codes of law. The ritual was the same for the entire class. They were all sacrifices for feasts in which the flesh of the victim was eaten by the offerers, except so far as the officiating priests had certain choice pieces and the blood and fat pieces went to the altar for God. The sacrifice at the institution of the covenant at Horeb, the Passover victim, and the ram of consecration, were special, in that there was an application of a portion of the blood to the persons and things which were to be consecrated, Ex 12^{22} 24^{8} Lv 8^{23}. †**6.** the slaughter of hostile nations is also a זֶבַח offered by God Himself, in which the vultures devour the flesh of the victims Is 34^{6} Je 46^{10} Ez 39$^{17.17.19}$ Zp 1$^{7.8}$. **7.** the verb used with זֶבַח is ordinarily זָבַח but others also are found e.g. †עָשָׂה Nu 6^{17} 15$^{3.5.8}$ Jos 22^{23} (P) 1 K 12^{27} 2 K 5^{17} 10^{24} Je 33^{18} (cf. Sab. עסי דבח Hal^{148} DHM$^{ZMG\ 1888,\ 374}$); †הֵבִיא Am 4^{4} Dt 12$^{6.11}$ Je 17^{26}, †הִגִּישׁ Am 5^{25}, †הִקְרִיב Lv 7$^{11.16}$ 22^{21} (all P), †עָבַד Is 19^{21}, †נָתַן Ec 4^{17}, יַעֲלֶה עֹלָה אוֹ זָבַח Lv 17^{8} (H), בִּשֵּׁל ז׳ Ez 46^{24}, שָׁחַט אֶת־הָעוֹלָה וְהַזָּבַח Ez 40^{42} cf. 44^{11}.

2078 †II. **זֶבַח** **n.pr.m.** a Midianite king Ju 8$^{5.6.7.10.12.12.15.15.18.21.21}$ ψ 83^{12}, 𝔊 Ζεβεε.

4096 **מִזְבֵּחַ**$_{401}$ **n.m.**$^{Jos\ 22,10}$ **altar** (Ar. مَذْبَحٌ, *place of slaughter, trench made by torrent*, Sab. מדֿבח DHM$^{Epigr.\ Denkm.\ 24}$); מ׳ abs. 2 K 18^{22} + 223 t., הַמִּזְבֵּחָה Ex 29^{13} + 31 t.; cstr. מִזְבַּח Ex 20^{24} + 76 t., sf. מִזְבְּחִי Ex 20^{26} + 7 t., מִזְבַּחֲךָ 1 K 8^{31} + 3 t., מִזְבְּחֶךָ Dt 33^{10}; מִזְבְּחוֹ Ju 6^{31} + 2 t.; pl. מִזְבְּחֹת Nu 23^{1} + 5 t., מִזְבְּחוֹת 2 K 21^{3} + 23 t., sf. מִזְבְּחוֹתֶיךָ ψ 84^{4}, other sfs. 21 t.;—**1.** JE narrate that altars were built by Noah after leaving the ark Gn 8^{20}; by Abraham at Shechem 12^{7}, Bethel 12^{8}, Hebron 13^{18}, mt. in land Moriah 22^{9}; by Isaac at Beersheba 26^{25}; by Jacob at Shechem 33^{20} (yet this perh. mistake for מַצֵּבָה, being obj. of וַיַּצֶּב־שָׁם, not elsewhere with מזבח, cf. also Di), at Bethel 35^{7}, by Moses at Rephidim Ex 17^{15}, Horeb 24^{4}, by Balak at Bamoth Baal, Pisgah, & Peor Nu 23$^{1.14.29}$; by Joshua on Mt. Ebal Jos 8^{30}: the prophetic histories narrate that altars were built by Gideon at Ophra Ju 6^{24}; by a man of God at Bethel Ju 21^{4}; by Samuel at Ramah 1 S 7^{17}; by Saul after Michmash 1 S 14^{35}; by David on the threshing floor of Ornan 2 S 24^{25} = 1 Ch 21^{18}, 1 Ch 22^{1}; that Solomon sacrificed on the altar at Gibeon 1 K 3^{4} and built altars in the temple at Jerusalem 1 K 6^{20} 8^{64}; that Jeroboam built an altar at Bethel 1 K 12^{32} (which was destroyed by Josiah 2 K 23^{15}); and that Elijah repaired an ancient altar on Carmel 1 K 18^{30}. An altar in Egypt is predicted Is 19^{19}. All this accords with the law of the Covenant code Ex 20$^{24-26}$ which recognises a plurality of altars and prescribes that they shall be built of אֲדָמָה, or of unhewn stones, and without steps. So אֲבָנִים Dt 27^{6} (JE), אֲבָנִים שְׁלֵמוֹת Jos 8^{31}, and twelve stones 1 K 18$^{30.32}$; cf. Is 27^{9}. The altar was also a place of refuge Ex 21^{14} (JE) 1 K 1$^{50.51}$ 2^{28}. **2.** D prescribes one central altar Dt 12$^{5\ f.\ 27}$; but no attempt to enforce this principle appears before Hezekiah (2 K 18$^{4.22}$), and Josiah, whose reform is more effectual, 2 K 23$^{8-20}$. **3.** P limits sacrifices to the altars of the tabernacle. A great altar was built E. of the Jordan, but it was according to P only as an עֵד after the pattern of the altar before the Tabernacle Jos 22$^{10-34}$. P describes two altars: **a.** the מִזְבַּח הָעֹלָה Ex 30^{28} 31^{9} 35^{16} 38^{1} 40$^{6.10.29}$ Lv 4$^{7.10.25.25.30.34}$ = מ׳ הַנְּחֹשֶׁת Ex 38^{30} 39^{39}, made of acacia wood plated with brass, 5 × 5 × 3 cubits in size, with four horns and a network of brass, on which all sacrifices by fire were made Ex 27$^{1-8}$ 38$^{1-7}$; **b.** מ׳ מִקְטַר קְטֹרֶת made of acacia wood plated with gold, 1 × 1 × 2 cubits in size, with four horns and a crown of gold Ex 30$^{1-6}$ = מ׳ הקטרת Ex 30^{27} 31^{8} 35^{15} 37^{25} = מ׳ הזהב Ex 39^{38} 40$^{5.26}$ Nu 4^{11} = מ׳ קטרת הַסַּמִּים Lv 4^{7}; these altars are named elsewhere only in Chr. 1 Ch 6^{34} 16^{40} 21^{29} 2 Ch 1$^{5.6}$. **4.** Solomon made two altars for the temple at Jerusalem: **a.** מ׳ הַנְּחֹשֶׁת for the court 1 K 8^{64} (which was laid aside by Ahaz 2 K 16$^{14.15}$, who made an altar after the model of one he saw in Damascus 2 K 16^{11}); in v^{14} הַמִּזְבַּח הַנ׳ (cstr. form c. art.) is erron., rd. prob. מִזְבַּח cf. Ges $^{§\ 127.\ 4\ a\ ad\ fin.}$; this altar, according to Chr, measured 20 × 20 × 10 cubits 2 Ch 4^{1}; this מזבח (ה)נחשת also 7^{7} & Ez 9^{2}; = מ׳ העולה 2 Ch 29^{18}, repaired by Asa 2 Ch 15^{8}; **b.** an altar of cedar, plated with gold, in the temple before the דְּבִיר 1 K 6$^{20.22}$ 7^{48}; = מ׳ הזהב 2 Ch 4^{19}; = מ׳ הַקְּטֹרֶת 1 Ch 28^{18} 2 Ch 26^{16}. **5.** Ezekiel plans two altars for the new temple: **a.** a table of wood 3 × 2 cubits Ez 41^{22}; **b.** an altar for the court, prob. same dimensions as **4 a**, with stairs Ez 43$^{13-17}$. **6.** after the return Jeshua built an altar on the ancient site in the court of the temple Ezr 3^{2}. **7.** besides these altars used in the worship of Yahweh, Ahab built an altar to Baal in Samaria 1 K 16^{32}; Ahaz made an altar on the roof of the upper chamber, and other kings of Judah made altars in the two courts, all of which were destroyed by Josiah 2 K 23^{12}. **8.** the ancient and most common term for making altars was בָּנָה Gn 35^{7} (E) 8^{20} (J) Dt 27$^{5.6}$ Ex 32^{5} (JE) +, implying building material; other vbs. are הֵקִים 2 S 24^{18} 1 K 16^{32} 2 K 21^{3} 1 Ch 21^{18} 2 Ch 33^{3}; הֵכִין Ezr 3^{3} (sq. עַל־מְכוֹנָתוֹ); שִׂים Je 11^{13}; וַיַּצֶּב־ Gn 33^{20} (but cf. **1**); Nu 23^{4} (E) has עָרַךְ *arrange*, *prepare;* עָשָׂה Gn 35$^{1.3}$ Ex 20^{24} (E) Gn 13^{4} (J) Ju 22^{28} 1 K 12^{33} 18^{26}; this becomes usual in P, Ex 27^{1} 30^{1} 37^{25} 38$^{1.30}$, so 2 Ch 4$^{1.19}$ 7^{7} 28^{24}. **9.** the dedication of the altar was חֲנֻכַּת המזבח Nu 7$^{10.11.84.88}$ 2 Ch 7^{9}; it was anointed with oil מָשַׁח Ex 40^{10} Lv 8^{11} Nu 7^{10} (all P). **10.** removal of unlawful altars is expr. by נָתַץ Ex 34^{13} (JE) Dt 7^{5} Ju 2^{2} 6$^{30.31.32}$ 2 K 11^{18} 23$^{12.15}$; נִתַּץ (Pi) Dt 12^{3} 2 Ch 31^{1} 34$^{4.7}$; נֻתַּץ Ju 6^{28}; הָרַס Ju 6^{25} 1 K 19$^{10.14}$; שִׁבֵּר 2 Ch 23^{17}; הֵסִיר 2 K 18^{22} = Is 36^{7}, 2 Ch 14^{2} 30^{14} 32^{12} 33^{15}. **11.** ministry at the altar was מִשְׁמֶרֶת הַמּ׳ Nu 18^{5} Ez 40^{46}, cf. Nu 3^{31} (P), מְשָׁרְתֵי מ׳ Jo 1^{13}; עָמַד עַל is said of officiating priest 1 K 13^{1}, עָלָה עַל Ex 20^{26} 1 S 2^{28} 1 K 12^{33} + (cf. יָרַד Lv 9^{22}); sacrifices were usually offered עַל־הַמִּזְבֵּחַ Gn 22^{9} Dt 12^{27} +; v. especially the phrases with זָרַק Ex 29$^{16.20}$ + (v. זרק); הִקְטִיר Lv 4^{10} (v. קטר **Hiph.**); הֶעֱלָה Lv 6^{3} + (v. עלה **Hiph.**) לְבַעֵר Ne 10^{35}; but בַּמִּזְבֵּחַ Gn 8^{20} (J) Nu 23$^{2.4.14.30}$ (E); one touching the altar is הַנֹּגֵעַ בַּמּ׳ Ex 29^{37} (P); לפני המ׳ of placing, or standing *before* altar Dt 26^{4} 1 K 8^{22}; as **acc.loc.** הַמִּזְבֵּ֫חָה in phrases esp. c. הִקְטִיר Ex 29^{13} +, and הֶעֱלָה Lv 14^{20}. **12.** the horns of the altar were especially for the application of the blood of the sin-offering in the ritual; sin is represented as graven לְקַרְנוֹת מִזְבְּחוֹתֵיכֶם Je 17^{1}; therefore of blood for cleansing it was said †נָתַן על קרנות המ׳ Ex 29^{12} Lv 4$^{7.18.25.30.34}$ 8^{15} 9^{9} 16^{18} (all P). An ancient custom is referred to, ψ 118^{27} אִסְרוּ־חַג בַּעֲבֹתִים עַד־קרנות המזבח *bind the festal victim with cords, unto the horns of the altar:* Ainsworth paraphrases: 'that is, all the court over, untill you come even to the hornes of the altar, intending hereby many sacrifices,' so De; but Che 'bind the procession with branches, (step on) to the altar-horns,' that is in sacred procession round the altar. **13.** the יְסוֹד (q. v.) is also referred to in the ritual of the sin-offerings in the phrases יָצַק אל יסוד Lv 8^{15} 9^{9} & שָׁפַךְ אל יסוד Ex 29^{12} Lv 4$^{7.18.25.30.34}$ (all P) יִמָּצֵה אל יסוד Lv 5^{9}. **14.** the altar was קֹדֶשׁ קָדָשִׁים Ex 29^{37} 40^{10} (P); but repeated sin-offerings were necessary to keep it pure and cleanse it from the pollution of the people in whose midst it was situated. This is expressed by חִטֵּא Lv 8^{15} (P) Ez 43^{22}; כִּפֶּר Lv 16$^{20.33}$ (P) Ez 43^{26}; קִדֵּשׁ Ex 29^{44} 40^{10} Lv 8^{15} Nu 7^{1} (P); טִהַר 2 Ch 29^{18}.

2079 זַבַּי v. sub זבב. p. 256

2081 †זְבִינָא **n.pr.m.** (*bought;* Aram., fr. √זְבַן, *buy,* cf. BAram. Dn 2^{8})—name of one who had taken a strange wife Ezr 10^{43}.

†[זָבַל] **vb.** prob. **exalt, honour** (As. 2082
zabâlu COT^{Gloss} and id. on Gn 30^{20} 1 K 8^{13}, cf. Dl$^{Pr 62 f.}$ so De; Ph. n.pr.f. בעלאזבל (prob. = *Baal has exalted*) cf. אִיזֶבֶל p. 33 supr.; cf. Ar. زَبَلَ *take up and carry;* > Nö$^{ZMG 1886, 729}$, who connects these vbs. with Syr. ܣܒܰܠ *bear, carry,* cf. Heb. סָבַל)—**Qal** *Impf.* יִזְבְּלֵנִי אִישִׁי Gn 30^{20b} (J), *my husband will honour me* (in expl. of name Zebulun (v. infr.); on another appar. expl. in v^{a} cf. זבד); > AV al. *dwell with me,* cf. Thes RobGes who derive *dwell with* fr. an assumed mng. *be round* (cf. דור); and others (cf. MV$^{s. 9}$), who derive *dwell* as denom. from זְבֻל in sense *dwelling.*

†I. זְבֻל **n.[m.] elevation, height, lofty** 2073
abode (NH זְבוּל *temple*);—בָּנֹה בָנִיתִי בֵּית זְבֻל לָךְ 1 K 8^{13} = 2 Ch 6^{2} (poet.; prob. from book of Jashar, cf. 𝔊 We$^{Comp. 271}$ Dr$^{Intr. 182}$; on בֵּית־זְבֻל = As. *bît zabal, lofty house* cf. COT 1 K 8^{13} Dl$^{Pr 62 f.}$); ψ 49^{15} לְבַלּוֹת שְׁאוֹל מִזְּבֻל לוֹ text dub.; Ew Hi Ri Now rd. מַזְבּוּל (or מִזְבּוּל, Ew) as n. = *dwelling;* Che prop. for מִזְּבֻל, [לְעוֹלָ]ם ז׳ Che$^{crit. n.}$; זְבֻל קָדְשְׁךָ Is 63^{15} (|| שָׁמַיִם) *the high abode of thy holiness* (cf. Che$^{crit. n.}$); of the lofty abode of sun and moon: שֶׁמֶשׁ יָרֵחַ עָמַד זְבֻלָה Hb 3^{11}.

†II. זְבֻל **n.pr.m.** an officer of Abimelech 2083
Ju 9$^{28.30.36.36.38.41}$.

†זְבֻלוּן, זְבוּלֻן **n.pr.m. Zebulun** (on expl. 2074
of name given in E and J cf. זבד, זבל);—זְבוּלֻן Gn 49^{13} + 25 t.; זְבֻלוּן Ju 5^{18} + 17 t.; זְבוּלוּן Ju 1^{30};—**1.** sixth son of Jacob and Leah Gn 30^{20} 35^{23} 46^{14} 49^{13} Ex 1^{3} 1 Ch 2^{1}. **2.** the tribe of Zebulun Nu 1^{9} Dt 27^{13} 33$^{18.18}$ Ju 1^{30} 4^{10} 5$^{14.18}$ Ez 48^{26} 1 Ch 12$^{34.41}$ 27^{19} 2 Ch 30$^{11.18}$; cf. ψ 68^{28} שָׂרֵי ז׳; שַׁעַר ז׳ Ez 48^{33}; בְּנֵי ז׳ Nu 1^{30} 2^{7} 7^{24} 26^{26} Jos 19$^{10.16}$ Ju 4^{6}; מַטֵּה ז׳ Nu 1^{31} 2^{7} 13^{10}; מַטֵּה בְנֵי ז׳ Nu 10^{16} 34^{25}. **3.** territory of the tribe אֶרֶץ ז׳ Ju 12^{12}, אַרְצָה ז׳ Is 8^{23}, גְּבוּל ז׳ Ez 48^{27}; also ז׳ alone Jos 19$^{27.34}$ 2 Ch 30^{10}, מַטֵּה ז׳ Jos 21$^{7.34}$ 1 Ch 6$^{48.62}$.

†זְבוּלֹנִי **adj. gent.** Ju 12$^{11.12}$; c. art. = 2075
n. coll. *the Zebulonites* Nu 26^{27}.

זוג, זיג (appar. √of foll.; 𝔗 NH זוג, זיג is *be clear, bright, transparent* (ChWB Jastr^{391a}); others (so Thes) derive foll. from √זגג with same meaning, v. infr. & Fl NHWB$^{i. 560 b}$).

2085 †**זָג** **n.[m.]** name of some comparatively insignif. product of vine (גֶּפֶן הַיַּיִן), the eating of which was included in prohibition to Nazirite; **skin** of grape, so Thes (after Onk Mishna Maaser. 5 ^{§4}, Orla 1 ^{§8}, cf. Sifre *ad loc.*): מֵחַרְצַנִּים וְעַד־זָג לֹא יֹאכֵל Nu 6^{4} (NH זוג, זג; so called as *transparent?* cf. Aram. זְגוּגִיתָא, ܙܓܘܓܝܬܐ *glass*, NH זַגָּג *glazier* (Ar. زُجَاج *glass*, is a loan-wd. acc. to Frä^{64}); cf. theory of √in Lag $^{Ges. Ath. 41}$, Fl $^{l.c.}$: but in Heb. *glass* is זְכוֹכִית).

2086-88 **זֵד, זָדוֹן** v. sub זיד. p. 267-68

2063 **זֶה** **demonstr. pron.** and **adv.**; fem. זֹאת, once זֹאתָה, Jer 26^{6} Kt (also זֹה and זוֹ, q.v.); comm. זוּ (q.v.): **this, here** (the element ז = ذ = ܕ is widely diffused in the Semitic languages, as a demonstr. particle, often acquiring, like Engl. *that*, Germ. *der, die, das*, the force of a **relative.** Thus **a.** Ph. ז *this* (e.g. קבר ז *this grave*), also sts. זן, f. זא, comm. אז (v. CIS I. i. 1$^{4.5.6.12}$ 44^{1} 88^{2} etc.); Aram. of Nineveh, Babylon, Têma, Egypt, זי as mark of the genit. [lit. *that of*] (CIS II. i. 1, 2, 3, 4, etc., 65, 69–71, 113, 114, 141, 142, etc.), זנה *this* (*ib.* 113^{22} 145 C^{2}), f. זא 113^{15} 145 B^{5}; Aram. of Zinjirli ז, זן, זנה *this*, זי *which* (DHM $^{Sendsch. 56}$); Eth. **ዝ:** *ze, this*, f. **ዛ:** *zā*, **ዘ:** *za, who* (masc.), also (like זִי, and דִּי, דְּ [v. infr.]) in common use as a mark of the genitive; **b.** Arab. ذَا *this*, fem. ذِى ذُو (gen. ذِى, acc. ذَا, fem. ذَاتُ), *possessor of* (lit. *that of* . . ., i.e. one who owns), or in the Ṭayyite dialect, *who, which*: from ذَا, with هَا *lo!* prefixed, هَاذَا *this*, f. هَاذِهِ, with the pron. element *-k* affixed, ذَاكَ = *this*: with *'al* (= the art.) + a demonstr. element *la* prefixed, اَلَّذِى *who, which* (in origin = Heb. הַלָּזֶה *this*, q.v.); Sab. דן *this*, f. דת, ד *who, which*, f. דת (Prä $^{ZMG. 1872, 419}$, DHM $^{ZMG. 1883, 338 f.}$, also $^{Epigr. Denkm. 65}$); **c.** BAram. דִּי *which*, דְּךְ, דִּכֵּן, דְּנָה (q.v.) *this*, f. דָּא (= זֹאת), דָּךְ; Palm. and Nab. די *which*, דנה *this*; 𝔗 דְּ *which*, דֵּין, דֵּיכִי *this*, f. דָּא; with הא *lo!* prefixed, הָדֵין, הָדָא (Syr. ܗܳܢܳܐ, contr. from ܗܳܕܶܐ), ܗܳܕܶܐ; Syr. ܕ *who, which*; Sam. ࠃ *who, which*, ࠃࠍ *this*, f. ࠆࠃ; Mand. ד *who, which*, דה *this* (rare), more commonly האזין, האדין (Nö $^{Mand § 80, 81}$). Alike in Heb. and the other dialects, the corresp. plur. is derived from a different source: Heb. אֵלֶּה, Ph. אל, Eth. *'ellū, 'ellā, these, 'ella, who*, Arab. أُولَى, أُولَى, *these*, أُولُوا, *owners of*, Sab. אלן *these*, אל, אלי *who, which*, Aram. אִלֵּין, with הא *lo!* prefixed, ܗܳܠܶܝܢ, Sam. ࠀࠋࠉࠍ, Mand. עלין. Only the Arab. اَلَّذِى forms its own pl. اَلَّذِينَ. V. further W $^{SG 107 ff.}$)—**1.** standing alone: **a.** *this one*, sts. contemptuously (esp. with אֶת), Gn 2^{23} לְזֹאת יִקָּרֵא אִשָּׁה, 5^{29} . . . זֶה יְנַחֲמֵנוּ, כִּי מֵאִישׁ לֻקֳחָה־זֹּאת, 12^{12} 38^{28} Ex 10^{7} עַד מָתַי יִהְיֶה זֶה לָנוּ לְמוֹקֵשׁ, 1 S 10^{27} מַה יֹּשִׁעֵנוּ זֶה how shall *this man* save us? 16$^{8.9}$ 21^{16} that ye have brought אֶת־זֶה *this fellow* to play the madman against me? 25^{21} in vain have I kept אֶת־כָּל־אֲשֶׁר לָזֶה all that *this fellow* hath etc. 2 S 13^{17} אֶת־זֹאת, 1 K 22^{27} אֶת־זֶה, Mi 5^{4} Is 66^{2}; as a genit., Gn 29$^{27.28}$ 1 K 21^{2}; with a *collective* force Lv 11$^{4.9}$ (= Dt 14$^{7.9}$), v$^{21.29}$ Ju 20$^{16.17}$ (כָּל־זֶה), Jb 19^{19} (with a *plural* verb). In a purely *neuter* sense (of an act, event, announcement, etc.) זאת is most common, as with עשׂה to do *this* Gn 3^{14} 20$^{5.6}$ 45^{19} and oft., שמעו זאת Am 8^{4} Is 47^{8} 48$^{1.16}$ 51^{21} al.; Gn 41^{39} Ex 17^{14} Dt 32^{6} Ju 7^{14} 21^{3} לָמָה . . . הָיְתָה זאת (cf. Jb 1^{13} ψ 118^{23}) 1 K 11^{39} 2 S 7^{19} 2 K 3^{18}+; אֵין זאת 1 S 20^{2b} cf. Am 2^{11}; rarely so with אֶת־ †Jos 22^{24} Je 9^{11} ψ 92^{7}; as an accus. of limit., *as regards this, in this*, Ez 20^{27} 36^{37} Jb 19^{26} (si vera l.), 33^{12} *in this* thou art not just; (late) אַחֲרֵי זאת †Jb 42^{16} Ezr 9^{10}, א׳ כל־זאת †2 Ch 21^{18} 35^{20}; pointing forward to a foll. clause, Gn 42^{18} 43^{11} Nu 8^{24} 14^{35} Is 56^{2} Jb 10^{13} etc.; Ex 9^{16} 1 S 25^{31} Is 1^{12} מִי בִקֵּשׁ זאת מִיֶּדְכֶם רְמֹס חֲצֵרָי; to one introduced by כִּי 2 S 19^{22} ψ 102^{19} 119$^{50.56}$ (see also בְּזֹאת **6 b** β): but זֶה also sts. occurs similarly Ex 13^{8} Pr 24^{12} Jb 15^{17} Ne 2^{2} Ec 1^{17} 2^{15} גם זה הבל (so v$^{19.21.23}$+), 7$^{18.18}$; of a concrete obj., Ex 30^{31} 2 K 4^{43} מָה אֶתֵּן זֶה לִפְנֵי מֵאָה אִישׁ: in late Heb., Ne 13^{6} בְּכָל־זֶה during all this, 2 Ch 32^{9} אַחַר זֶה; pointing forwards La 5$^{17 f.}$, to כִּי ψ 56^{10} Je 22^{21}. (See also below, **6 g.**) **b.** repeated זֶה . . . זֶה, *this . . . that, the one . . . the other* or (if indefinite) *another*, Gn 29^{27} (זאת), Ex 14^{20} וְלֹא קָרַב זֶה אֶל זֶה, 1 K 3^{23} 22^{20} Is 6^{3} 44^{5} (3 t.), ψ 75^{8} זֶה יַשְׁפִּיל וְזֶה יָרִים, Jb 1$^{16-18}$ 21$^{23.25}$+.

2. In appos. to a subst.: **a.** preceding it (rare) Ex 32$^{1.23}$ זֶה משֶׁה, Ju 5^{5} (= ψ 68^{9}) זֶה סִינַי *this* Sinai, Jos 9^{12} זֶה לַחְמֵנוּ *this* our bread, 1 K 14^{14} 2 K 6^{33} Is 23^{13} זֶה הָעָם, ψ 34^{7} 49^{14} 104^{25} זה הים גדול וג׳ *this* sea *there* is great and broad, 118^{20} Ct 7^{8} Ezr 3^{12}. (Cf. זוּ Hb 1^{11}.) **b.** following it:—(*a*) when the subst. is determined by a pron. affix, Gn 24^{8} שְׁבֻעָתִי זאת, *this* my oath, Dt 5^{16} O that לְבָבָם זֶה *this their* *heart* (their present temper) might continue always! 21^{20} Jos 2$^{14.20}$ דְּבָרֵנוּ זֶה, Ju 6^{14} go בְּכֹחֲךָ זֶה in *this* thy strength, Dn 10^{17} 2 Ch 24^{18}. (Cf. אֵלֶּה, **a.**) Rarely when it is undetermined, 2 K 1^{2} חֳלִי זֶה (so 8$^{8.9}$), ψ 80^{15}. (β) with the art., הַזֶּה, הַזֹּאת, after a subst. determined also by the art., Gn 7^{1} בַּדּוֹר הַזֶּה, v^{13} הַיּוֹם הַזֶּה, 12^{7} הָאָרֶץ הַזֹּאת, 15^{7} 17$^{21.23}$ Dt 4^{6} הגוי הגדול הזה, and continually. Not however after a n.pr., except such as are construed with the art., as הַיַּרְדֵּן הַזֶּה Gn 32^{11} Dt 3^{27} 31^{2} Jos 1$^{2.11}$ 4^{22}, הַלְּבָנוֹן הַזֶּה Jos 1^{4}, cf. Nu 27^{12}=Dt 32^{49} (2 K 5^{20} הַזֶּה belongs to הָאֲרַמִּי): and hardly ever (2 Ch 1^{10}) after a noun with a pron. affix (Jos 2^{17} מִשְּׁבֻעָתֵךְ הַזֶּה the gender of הזה shews that the text is in error: v. Dr$^{§ 209\ Obs.}$).

3. More oft. as pred., as 1 S 24^{17} הֲקוֹלְךָ זֶה, 2 K 3^{23} דָּם זֶה *this* is blood, 9^{37} זֹאת אִיזָבֶל:, Ez 5^{5} etc.; הֲזֶה Is 14^{16}, הֲזֹאת 23^{7} La 2^{15}; oft. at the beginning or close of enumerations (esp. P), descriptions, injunctions, etc., as Gn 5^{1} זה ספר *this* is the book . . ., 9^{12} זֹאת אוֹת הַבְּרִית, 17^{10} 20^{13} זֶה חַסְדֵּךְ אֲשֶׁר תַּעֲשִׂי עִמָּדִי, Lv 6$^{2.13.18}$ 7$^{1.11}$ Dt 6^{1} 33^{1} Jos 13^{2} Jb 27^{13} Is 58^{6} etc.; . . . זה הדבר אשר Ex 16^{16} 35^{4} Jos 5^{4} Ju 20^{9} 21^{11} Is 27^{22} Je 38^{21}+, cf. . . . זה אשר *this* is what (*or* how) . . . Gn 6^{15} Ex 29^{38} Je 33^{16}; זֶה לְּךָ הָאוֹת Ex 3^{12} 1 S 2^{34}+; at the end, Lv 7^{37} 11^{46} 13^{50} Nu 5^{21} 7$^{17.23}$ etc., Jos 19$^{8.16.23}$ etc., Is 14^{26} 16^{13} (זֶה הַדָּבָר אֲשֶׁר . . .), 17^{14} 54^{17} Je 13^{25} ψ 109^{20} Ct 5$^{16.16}$ Jb 5^{27}, in the latter case sts. with the force of *such* (i.e. such as has been described), 18^{21} 20^{29} (cf. אֵלֶּה ψ 73^{12}), ψ 24^{6} 48^{15} *such* (=such a one) is God, our God, for ever (Hi De) Zp 2^{15}; cf. Jb 14^{3} אַף־עַל־זֶה upon one *such as this* (v$^{1.2}$) dost thou open thy eyes?

4. It is attached enclitically, almost as an adv., to certain words, esp. interrog. pronouns, to impart, in a manner often not reproducible in Engl. idiom, directness and force, bringing the question or statement made into close relation with the speaker. (Contrast from this point of view מי זה and מי הוא: v. הוא **4 b.**) Thus **a.** אֵי־זֶה$_{15}$ where, *then?* Jb 28^{12} אֵי־זֶה מְקוֹם בִּינָה, v^{20} 38^{19b} (v. other exx. sub אֵי **1 b**, p. 32). **b.** מִי־זֶה, †1 S 17$^{55.56}$ בֶּן־מִי־זֶה הָעָלֶם: the son of *whom, here,* is the lad? Je 49^{19} (=50^{44}) וּמִי זֶה רֹעֶה אֲשֶׁר וג׳ and *who* (emph.) is the shepherd that etc., La 3^{37} ψ 24^{8} *Who* is the King of glory? (for which in v^{10} the stronger מִי הוּא זֶה is said: so Je 30^{21} Est 7^{5}), 25^{12}. Elsewhere, the rend. *Who* is *this* . . . is admissible: Is 63^{1} Je 46^{7} Jb 38^{2} 42^{3}; cf. מִי־זֹאת Ct 3^{6} 6^{10} 8^{5}. **c.** מַה־זֶּה *how, now?* Gn 27^{20} Ju 18^{24} וּמַה־זֶּה תֹּאמְרוּ אֵלַי and *how, now,* do ye say to me . . . ? 1 K 21^{5} 2 K 1^{5}; *what, now?* (τί ποτε;) 1 S 10^{11} מַה־זֶּה הָיָה לְבֶן־קִישׁ; עַל־מַה־זֶּה *for what?* Ne 2^{4}: contracted into מַזֶּה Ex 4^{2}. (Cf. Aram. מָדֵין *why?* ܡܟܝܠ used as a conj. *therefore*, e.g. 2 S 18^{22} 𝔖, PS^{2013}: both formed similarly.) **d.** מַה־זֹּאת in the phrase (עָשִׂית, עֲשִׂיתֶם) מַה־זֹּאת עָשִׂיתָ Gn 3^{13} 12^{18} 26^{10} 29^{25} 42^{28} Ex 14^{11} Ju 2^{2} 15^{11}+. Either *What, now,* hast thou (have ye) done? (Fl De) or *What* is *this* (that) thou hast (ye have) done? (The Arab. grammarians dispute on the precise construction of the corresp. phrase in Arabic مَا ذَا صَنَعْتَ; De$^{Gen.\ 3,\ 13\ (ed.\ 4)}$, and esp. Fl$^{Kl\ Schr.\ i.\ 356}$ Lane$^{p.\ 948}$.) **e.** לָמָּה־זֶּה *wherefore, now?* Gn 18^{13} 25^{22} 32^{30} Ex 5^{22} Nu 11^{20}+oft. Cf. Arab. لِمَا ذَا. **f.** הַאַתָּה זֶה †2 S 2^{20} האתה זה עשהאל Art thou Asahel? 1 K 18$^{7.17}$, without הֲ Gn 27^{24}; in an indirect question Gn 27^{21}. **g.** הִנֵּה זֶה *behold, here* . . . †1 K 19^{5} (in narrative), Is 21^{9} Ct 2$^{8.9}$. Cf. Nu 13^{17} (unusual) עֲלוּ זֶה בַּנֶּגֶב go up *here* in the South. **h.** עַתָּה זֶה, †1 K 17^{24} עַתָּה זֶה יָדַעְתִּי *now* I know that . . ., 2 K 5^{22} *just now*. Also **i.** prefixed to expressions denoting a period of time: Gn 27^{36} he hath supplanted me זֶה פַעֲמַיִם *now* two times (so 43^{10}), 31^{38} *now, already* twenty years, v^{41} (זֶה־לִּי . . .), 45^{6} Nu 14^{22} *now* ten times, 22$^{28.32}$ זֶה שָׁלֹשׁ רְגָלִים, Dt 8$^{2.4}$ Jos 22^{3} זֶה יָמִים רַבִּים, 2 S 14^{2}+; Zc 7^{3} זֶה כַּמֶּה שָׁנִים *already* how many years! cf. Ru 2^{7}.

5. In poetry, as a *relative* pron. (rare: but see also זוּ, זוֹ): ψ 74^{2} the hill of Zion זה שכנת בו *wherein* thou dwellest, 78^{54} 104^{8} אל־מְקוֹם זה to the place (*st. c.* Ges$^{§ 130.3}$) *which* . . . v^{26} Pr 23^{22} Is 25^{9};=*that which* Jb 15^{17}, *those who* 19^{19} (so once, Ex 13^{8}, even in prose). In some of the passages cited the punctuators, by coupling זה with the preceding subst., and separating it from what follows by a disj. accent (as הַר־זֶה), appear not to have recognised its relative sense, but to have construed, '*this* mountain, (which) thy right hand,' etc.

6. With prefixes (in special senses):— **a.** בָּזֶה$_{15}$ *in this* (place), *here,* Gn 38$^{21.22}$ Ex 24^{14} Nu 23$^{1.1}$ 1 S 1^{26} 9^{11}+; of time, *then,* †Est 2^{13}. Once בַּזֶּה 1 S 21^{10}. **b.** בְּזֹאת (α) *with this*= *on these conditions,* Gn 34$^{15.22}$ 1 S 11^{2} Is 27^{9};= *herewith, thus provided* Lv 16^{3}. (β) *by* or *through this* (esp. with יָדַע), Gn 42$^{15.33}$ Ex 7^{17} Nu 16^{28} Jos 3^{10} ψ 41^{12}; so בָּזֹאת Mal 3^{10}. (γ) *in spite of this,* Lv 26^{27} ψ 27^{3}, for which the fuller בְּכָל־זֹאת occurs, Is 5[25] 9[11.16.20] 10[4] ψ 78[32] Je 3[10] Ho 7[10]. (δ) בְּזֹאת *for this cause* (late style) † 1 Ch 27[24] 2 Ch 19[2]; *in this matter* 20[17]. **c.** כָּזֶה (α) † Gn 41[38] הֲנִמְצָא כָזֶה אִישׁ אשר . . ., Is 56[12] 58[5] Je 5[9] גּוֹי אֲשֶׁר כָּזֶה (so v[29] 9[8]). (β) כָּזֹה וְכָזֶה *thus and thus*, † Ju 18[4] 2 S 11[25] 1 K 14[5]. **d.** כָּזֹאת *the like of this = as follows*, † Gn 45[23]; כָּזֹאת *the like of this = things such as these* Ju 13[23] (c. השמיע), 15[7] 19[30] לא נראתה כָּזֹאת, 1 S 4[7] (cf. Je 2[10] 2 Ch 30[26]), 2 S 14[13] (c. חשב), Is 66[8] (c. שׁמע), Ezr 7[27]; = *accordingly, to that effect* (c. דִּבֶּר) 2 Ch 34[22]; = *in like manner* Ju 8[8]; = *thus* (as has been described) 1 K 7[37] 1 Ch 29[14] 2 Ch 31[20] 32[15]: כָּזֹאת וְכָזֹאת *thus and thus* † Jos 7[20] 2 S 17[15.15] 2 K 5[4] 9[12]. **e.** מִזֶּה *from here, hence* Gn 37[17] 42[15] 50[25] Ex 11[1.1] 13[3] Dt 9[12] + oft.: מִזֶּה . . . מִזֶּה *on one side . . . on the other side* Ex 17[12] מזה אחד ומזה אחד, 25[19] 26[13] 32[15] מזה ומזה הם כתובים, Nu 22[24] 1 S 14[4] 1 K 10[19.20] Zc 5[3] +; מִזֶּה וּמִזֶּה לְ *on one side and on the other side of* . . . Ex 38[15] Jos 8[33] Ez 45[7] 48[21]. **f.** עַל זֶה *on this account* (rare), La 5[17] (pointing forwards), Est 6[3]. So עַל זֹאת Am 8[8] Mi 1[8] Je 2[12] (Jb 17[8]) 4[8.28] ψ 32[6]; in late prose Ezr 8[23] 9[15] 10[2] Ne 13[14] 2 Ch 16[9.10] 29[9] 32[20]. **g.** עִם זֶה *in spite of this* † Ne 5[18].—On אֵי זֶה *which?* אֵי מִזֶּה *whence?* אֵי לָזֹאת *how?* v. sub אַי **2**, p. 32; and on הַלָּז, הַלָּזֶה, הַלֵּזוּ, v. p. 229.

Note.—זֶה in 1 S 17[34] (in many edd.) is a typographical error (not a Kt) of Jacob b. Chayim's Rabbin. Bible of 1525 for שֶׂה *sheep*, which has been perpetuated hence in other subseq. edd. The reading of MSS. and of the best ancient edd. is שֶׂה (cf. de Rossi [Var. Lect. ii. 151]).

2090 † זֹה *this* (f.) = זאת (cf. זוֹ, in Mish. the regular fem. of זֶה)—2 K 6[19] Ez 40[45] Ec 2[2.24] 5[15.18] 7[23] 9[13] (זאת does not occur in Ec); also in the phr. כָּזֹה וְכָזֶה (v. זה **6 c** β).

2097 † זוֹ i.q. זה (q.v.): only Ho 7[16 b] זוֹ לַעְגָּם *this* (i.e. the falling by the sword, v[a]) is their derision; and (as relat.) ψ 132[12] וְעֵדֹתִי זוֹ and my testimony *which* . . . (neglecting the accentuation: v. De, and cf. the remark under זֶה **5**).

2098 † זוּ **pron.** (poet.), indeclinable. **1.** a **demonstr.** Hb 1[11] זוּ כֹחוֹ *this* his strength, ψ 12[8] מִן־הַדּוֹר זוּ (unusual, for הַזֶּה), 62[12] שְׁתַּיִם־זוּ שָׁמָעְתִּי *these* two things &c. (but better (Wickes [Poet. Acc. 64]) שְׁתַּיִם זוּ two things (are there) *which* &c.: v. **2**). **2.** a **relative,** Ex 15[13] עַם־זוּ גָּאָלְתָּ the people *which* thou hast redeemed, v[16] Is 42[24] זוּ חָטָאנוּ לוֹ *against whom* we sinned, 43[21] ψ 9[16] (fem.) רֶשֶׁת־זוּ טָמָנוּ so 31[5], 10[2] 17[9] (with a *plural* antecedent) מִפְּנֵי רְשָׁעִים זוּ שַׁדּוּנִי, 32[8] 68[29] (thou) *who* hast wrought for us! 142[4] 143[8]. To most of these passages the remark made under זה **5** respecting the intention of the punctuators also applies: comp. De on ψ 9[16]. (Cf. ذُو, used as an indeclin. relat. pron. = ٱلَّذِى in the Ṭayyite dialect: thus أَتى عليهم ذو أَتى there has come upon them *that which* has come: نحن ذو فعلنا كذا it is we *who* have done this. See Schu [Hariri Cons. ii. 75], Thes[406], W [AG. i. 347, e], Lane [p. 986], Fl [Kl. Schr. i. p. 359].)

זהב (√ of foll.; meaning dubious; cf. Lag [BN 55 Anm]).

זָהָב 385 **n.m.** [Gn 2, 12] gold (NH *id.*; Ar. ذَهَبٌ, 2091
Sab. דהב e.g. Os[29] DHM [ZMG 1883, 338]; Aram. דְּהַב, ܕܗܒܐ, Palm. דהבא Vog [No. 23])—ז׳ abs. Gn 2[11] + 364 t.; cstr. Gn 2[12] + 6 t.; sf. זְהָבִי 1 K 20[7] + 2 t.; זְהָבְךָ 1 K 20[3.5]; זְהָבֵךְ Is 30[22]; זְהָבוֹ Is 2[20] 31[7]; זְהָבָם Ho 8[4] + 4 t.;—*gold*, **1.** = gold-ore, gold in a raw state, Gn 2[11.12] Je 10[9] Pr 17[3] 27[21] Jb 28[1] +; perh. also 1 K 9[28] 10[11] 22[49] etc.; cf. עַפְרֹת ז׳ Jb 28[6] *gold-dust;* v. also Zc 13[9] (sim. of tried people of י׳) and cf. Mal 3[3]; likewise Jb 23[10] (sim. of Job's purity, as shewn by divine tests); מִצָּפוֹן זָהָב Jb 37[22] is dub.; Ew De al. *out of the North comes gold;* others, however, *golden light, brightness,* of sun after clouds dispersed by north wind, 𝔊 Rabb. Da al.; or *golden splendour* of God coming from north Bö [Ä 76] Hi al.; Siegf conj. יהוה for זהב. **2.** gold as wealth Gn 13[2] (J; + כֶּסֶף, מִקְנֶה) 24[34] (J; + כֶּסֶף, בָּקָר, צֹאן, עֲבָדִם, שְׁפָחֹת, גְּמַלִּים, חֲמֹרִים) cf. Ho 2[8] Is 2[7] Dt 8[13] 17[17] Jb 3[15] 31[24] Zc 14[14] Ezr 1[4.6] +; in gen., as precious: נִבְחָר שֵׁם מֵעֹשֶׁר רָב מִכֶּסֶף וּמִזָּהָב חֵן טוֹב Pr 22[1] *to be chosen is a name more than great riches, and good favour more than silver and than gold;* Jb 28[17] (of wisdom) *gold and glass do not equal it;* ψ 19[10] (ordinances of י׳) *which are more to be desired than gold;* cf. 119[72.127]; also metaph. of princes and chief men of Zion La 4[1] (cf. v[2]). **3.** gold as spoil of war Jos 6[19] (+ כֶּסֶף, כְּלֵי־נְחֹשֶׁת, בַּרְזֶל) so v[24], cf. 7[21.24] 22[8] 2 K 7[8] +. **4.** gold as merchandise Ez 27[22] (+ רֹאשׁ כָּל־בֹּשֶׂם, אֶבֶן יְקָרָה), cf. also gold from Ophir 1 K 9[28] etc. (v. sub **7** infr.) **5.** gold as costly gift: to a prophet מְלֹא בֵיתוֹ כֶּסֶף וְז׳ (hypothet.), Nu 22[18] 24[13] (both E); brought by queen of Sheba to Solomon 1 K 10[2.10] (both + בְּשָׂמִים and אֶבֶן יְקָרָה) = 2 Ch 9[1.9]; as tribute 2 K 23[35.35] (cf. v[33]; all + כֶּסֶף); as satisfaction for murder 2 S 21[4] (+ כֶּסֶף). **6.** gold as

material: of (nose- or ear-)ring, נֶזֶם Gn 24^{22} Ex $32^{2.3}$ Ju $8^{24.26}$ Pr 11^{22} 25^{12} Jb 42^{11}; of chain Gn 41^{42}, shields 2 S 8^{7}, images of emerods 1 S $6^{4.17}$ and mice $v^{4.11.18}$; תַּפּוּחֵי ז׳ בְּמַשְׂכִּיּוֹת כָּסֶף Pr 25^{11}; גֻּלַּת ז׳ Ec 12^{6}; כְּלֵי־ז׳ Ex 3^{22} 11^{2} 12^{35} 1 S 6^{8} ψ 105^{37} etc.; כְּלֵי־כֶסֶף וּכְלֵי זָהָב Gn 24^{53} as presents to a bride (+ בְּגָדִים); so of presents to secure king's favour 2 S 8^{10} (+ כְּלֵי נְחֹשֶׁת), and in list of yearly gifts or tribute to Sol. 1 K 10^{25} = 2 Ch 9^{24}; as material of idols אֱלֹהֵי ז׳ כֶּסֶף וֵאלֹהֵי ז׳ Ex 20^{23} cf. 32^{31} Ho 8^{4} Is 2^{20} 30^{22} 31^{7} Dt 29^{16} ψ 115^{4} 135^{15}; as plating of idols Dt 7^{25}; especially as material of the furnishings of Solomon's temple, or (oftener) the platings of temple, or parts thereof, or of its furnishings 1 K $6^{20.21.21.21.22.22.28}$ 7^{48} + 10t. 1 K 6. 7; also 2 Ch $3^{5.5.6}$ + 14t. 2 Ch 3. 4; cf. 1 Ch $28^{14.14}$ + 14 t. 1 Ch 28. 29 (David's preparation for temple); v. also 2 K 24^{13} cf. 14^{14} = 2 Ch 25^{24}, 2 K 25^{15} = Je 52^{19} (in accounts of plundering temple etc.); but more often still of furnishing and utensils of tabernacle, insignia of high-priest etc., Ex $25^{3.11.24}$ + 97 t. Ex 25–40, Lv 8^{9} Nu 4^{11} 8^{4}; (in case of large objects frequently of plating or sheathing, cf. **12 c** infr.) Note the expressions תְּנוּפַת ז׳ ליהוה Ex 35^{22} *a wave-offering of gold*, זְהַב הַתְּנוּפָה 38^{24}; also זְהַב הַתְּרוּמָה Nu 31^{52} (all P) cf. Ezr 8^{25}, and (of offering to heathen god) יְכַבֵּד בְּזָהָב Dn 11^{38}. †**7.** gold described by its source, esp. gold from Ophir (cf. Glas$^{\text{Skizze ii. 357 ff. 368}}$) 1 K 9^{28} 10^{11} 22^{49} 1 Ch 29^{4} 2 Ch 8^{18} 9^{10}; so perh. Je 10^{9} (rd. אוֹפִיר for אוּפָז Ew Klo al.); זְהַב שְׁבָא ψ 72^{15}; on ז׳ פַּרְוָיִם 2 Ch 3^{6} v. פרוים; cf. further Gn $2^{11.12}$. **8.** gold defined by var. adj. and pts.: ז׳ שָׁחוּט *beaten gold* (v. שָׁחַט) 1 K $10^{16.17}$ = 2 Ch $9^{15.15.16}$; ז׳ סָגוּר 1 K $6^{20.21}$; also $7^{49.50}$ 10^{21} = 2 Ch $4^{20.22}$ 9^{21} (on mng. v. סָגַר); esp. (but only P & Ch) ז׳ טָהוֹר *pure gold* Ex $25^{11.17.24}$ + 21 t. Ex 25. 28. 30. 37. 39 (of equipments of tabernacle and high priest's insignia), 1 Ch 28^{17} 2 Ch 3^{4} 9^{17}; cf. ז׳ טוֹב 2 Ch $3^{5.8}$; on ז׳ מוּפָז 1 K 10^{18}, AV *best gold*, cf. פָּז, אוּפָז. **9.** ז׳ as measure of weight and value: **a.** = *gold-shekel*, עֲשָׂרָה ז׳ מִשְׁקָלָם Gn 24^{22}; כַּף אַחַת עֲשָׂרָה ז׳ Nu 7^{14} + 11 t. Nu 7; אֶלֶף וּשְׁבַע־מֵאוֹת ז׳ Ju 8^{26}, cf. 1 K 10^{16} 2 K 5^{5} 2 Ch $9^{15.16}$; אַלְפֵי ז׳ וָכָסֶף ψ 119^{72}; comp. further Jos 7^{21}; but also (only Ch) שֶׁקֶל expressed: שִׁקְלֵי ז׳ מִשְׁקַל שֵׁשׁ מֵאוֹת 1 Ch 21^{25} (50 shekels of silver in ‖ 2 S 24^{24}); וּמִשְׁקָל לְמִסְמְרוֹת לִשְׁקָלִים חֲמִשִּׁים ז׳ 2 Ch 3^{9}. **b.** שְׁלֹשֶׁת מָנִים ז׳ 1 K 10^{17} *three minas of gold* (v. מָנֶה). **c.** כִּכַּר ז׳ *talent of gold* 2 S 12^{30} 1 K 9^{14} + (v. כִּכָּר). **d.** זָהָב דַּרְכְּמוֹנִים שֵׁשׁ־רִבֹּאוֹת וָאֶלֶף Ezr 2^{69} cf. Ne $7^{69.70.71}$; also וּכְפֹרֵי ז׳ עֶשְׂרִים לַאֲדַרְכֹנִים אָלֶף Ezr 8^{27} (v. דַּרְכְּמוֹן); —with the above should perh. be compared הַזָּלִים ז׳ מִכִּיס Is 46^{6} i.e. the gold used in making the god was the coin carried in the bag. **10.** ז׳ = *golden oil*, from colour, Zc 4^{12}. **11.** ז׳ often named with כֶּסֶף, and then, in earlier and sts. in later writings, follows it: בַּכֶּסֶף וּבַזָּהָב Gn 13^{2} (J), cf. $24^{35.53}$ 44^{8} (all J), Ex 3^{22} 11^{2} 12^{35} Nu 22^{18} 24^{13} (all E), Jos $6^{19.24}$ (JE), Dt 7^{25} 17^{17} 29^{16} 2 S 8^{11} 21^{4} 1 K 7^{51} $15^{15.18.19}$ 2 K 7^{8} 16^{8} 18^{14} 20^{13} $23^{33.35.35}$ Ho 2^{10} 8^{4} Is 2^{7} 60^{9} Je 10^{4} Zp 1^{18} Ez 7^{19} 38^{13} Zc 6^{11} Jo 4^{5}, Pr 22^{1} ψ 105^{37} 115^{4} 135^{15} 2 Ch 1^{15} 5^{1} Ezr 1^{4} 8^{25} Dn 11^{8} Ec 2^{8}+; in later writings ז׳ oft. precedes Ez 28^{4} Zc 14^{14} Mal 3^{3} 1 Ch 18^{10} $22^{14.16}$ $28^{15.16}$ $29^{3.4.5.7}$ 2 Ch $9^{14.21}$ 24^{14} 25^{24} Ezr 1^{11} ψ 119^{72} Ct 1^{11} Dn 11^{38}+, and so in P, Ex 25^{3} 31^{4} $35^{5.32}$ Nu 31^{32}; yet also as early as Hb 2^{19} 1 K 10^{22} 2 K 25^{15}. **12.** the chief vbs. used with ז׳ are: **a.** עָשָׂה *make* of (c. 2 acc.) 1 K 7^{48} (cf. $v^{49.49.50.50}$) 10^{16} 12^{28} 14^{26} 2 Ch $4^{7.8.19}$ 12^{9} 13^{8}, and esp. in P (tabern.) Ex $25^{11.17.18}$ + 35 t. Ex 25–39; also sq. בְּ *work in* gold, לַעֲשׂוֹת בַּז׳ וּבַכֶּסֶף וּבַנְּחֹשֶׁת Ex 31^{4} 35^{32}, also (+ בַּבַּרְזֶל, etc.), 2 Ch $2^{6.13}$; **b.** יָצַק (obj. טַבְּעֹת ז׳) Ex 25^{12} $37^{3.13}$ (all P); **c.** צִפָּה *overlay with* (c. 2 acc.) 1 K $6^{20.21.21.22.28.30.32.35}$ ($v^{32.35}$ one acc. om.), 10^{18} 2 Ch $3^{4.10}$ 9^{17}, and esp. P (tabern.) Ex $25^{11.13.24.28}$ + 15 t. Ex 26–37; in same sense **d.** וַיְחַפֵּהוּ ז׳ 2 Ch 3^{5} cf. $v^{7.8.9}$, and **e.** תָּפוּשׂ ז׳ וָכֶסֶף Hb 2^{19} *encased in gold and silver;* also **f.** בַּז׳ יְרַקְּעֶנּוּ Is 40^{19}; **g.** רדד Hiph., וַיָּרֶד עַל־הַכְּרוּבִים וְעַל־הַתִּמֹּרוֹת אֶת־הַזּ׳ 1 K 6^{32} *and he spread upon the cherubim and upon the palm-trees the gold;* further **h.** בָּחַן *try*, Zc 13^{9}, cf. **i.** זִקֵּק Mal 3^{3}.—On דִּי זָהָב, n.pr. v. p. 191; on מֵי זָהָב n.pr. v. sub מַיִם.

†[זָהַם] **vb. be foul, loathsome,** but only 2092
Pi., causat. (NH *id.*, *be foul*, Pi. *make foul;* Aram. זְהִים *foul*, ܙܗܡ *make foul, fetid;* Ar. زَهِمَ *stink, be greasy*)—**Pi.** *Pf.* 3 fs. sf. 3 ms. וְזִהֲמַתּוּ חַיָּתוֹ לָחֶם (consec.) Jb 33^{20} *his life maketh it, bread, loathsome* to him (‖ ונפשו מַאֲכַל תַּאֲוָה). (On sf. v. Ges$^{\text{§ 131, 2, R. 4}}$; Dr$^{\text{1 S 21, 14}}$: acc. to Siegf the word is hopelessly corrupt.)

†זַהַם **n.pr.m.** (fr. above √?) a son of 2093
Rehoboam, 2 Ch 11^{19}.

†I. [זָהַר] **vb. be light, shining** (Ar. زَهَرَ, 2094
زَهَرَ *shine*, adj. أَزْهَرُ *bright* (cf. Lag$^{\text{BN 120}}$); Aram.

זְהַר, ܙܗܰܪ; NH in deriv.; v. also sub II. זהר)—**Hiph.** intrans. (late) *send out light, shine*, fig. of everlasting glory of teachers of righteousness: וְהַמַּשְׂכִּלִים יַזְהִרוּ כְּזֹהַר הָרָקִיעַ Dn 12^{3} *and they that make wise shall shine like the shining of the firmament* (‖ וּמַצְדִּיקֵי הָרַבִּים כַּכּוֹכָבִים לְעוֹלָם וָעֶד).

2096 †**זֹ֫הַר n.[m.] shining, brightness** (Ar. زُهْرَةٌ, NH זוֹהַר, cf. Aram. זִיהֲרָא);—abs. Ez 8^{2} כְּמַרְאֵה ז׳ *like an appearance of shining* (explained, v^{b}, as resembling amber, חַשְׁמַל cf. 1^{27}); also cstr. Dn 12^{3} v. foregoing.

2094 †II. [**זָהַר**] **vb.** only **Hiph.**, **Niph.** (NH Hiph., *admonish*, cf. Aram. זְהַר (Aph. Pa. etc.), ܙܗܰܪ (Ar. زَهَرَ VIII. *take care of, be mindful of* is perh. Aram. loan-word, so TA cf. Lane).—Most identify with I. זהר = *give light, enlighten, instruct, admonish;* this possible, but not certain, mng. *shine* is late in Heb.; usual sense as given below is not *enlighten, illumine* mentally, but *warn;* v. also construction with two accusatives Ex 18^{20});—**Hiph.** *Pf.* וְהִזְהִיר consec. Ez 33^{3}; sf. וְהִזְהִירֹה 2 K 6^{10}; 2 ms. הִזְהַרְתָּ Ez 3^{19} 33^{9}, וְהִזְהַרְתָּ Ez 3^{17} 33^{7}, וְהִזְהַרְתָּה Ex 18^{20}, sf. הִזְהַרְתּוֹ Ez 3$^{18.20.21}$, וְהִזְהַרְתָּ consec. Ez 3^{17} 33^{7}; וְהִזְהַרְתֶּם consec. 2 Ch 19^{10}; *Inf. cstr.* לְהַזְהִיר Ez 3^{18} 33^{8};—*instruct, teach, warn:* Ex 18^{20} (E) *teach them ordinances* (2 acc.); 2 K 6^{10} the place *which* (אֲשֶׁר) *the man of God told him of* (אָמַר־לוֹ) and *warned him* (sf.) *of;* elsewh. only Ez Ch; *warn, give a warning to*, alw. sq. acc. pers. only: Ez 3$^{18.19.20}$ 33^{3}; *give them* (acc.) *a warning from me* (מִמֶּנִּי, ׳י speaks) Ez 3^{17} 33^{7}; *warn the wicked* (רָשָׁע) *from* (away from, מִן) *his way* Ez 3^{18} 33$^{8.9}$; *warn the righteous* (צַדִּיק) Ez 3^{21} sq. Inf. *in order that the righteous sin not*, cf. 2 Ch 19^{10} sq. acc. pers. + final cl. c. וְ.

Niph. *Pf.* 3 ms. נִזְהָר Ez 3^{21} 33$^{4.5.6}$; also נִזְהָר v^{5} (rd. perh. הִזְהִיר, so We Sm Co); *Imv.* הִזָּהֵר Ec 12^{12}; *Inf. cstr.* לְהִזָּהֵר Ec 4^{13}; Pt. נִזְהָר ψ 19^{12};—*be instructed, admonished, warned* (pass. of Hiph.):—גַּם־עַבְדְּךָ נִזְהָר בָּהֶם ψ 19^{12} *yea thy servant, he is instructed* (or *warned*) *by them* (i.e. lets himself be instructed or warned by the מִשְׁפְּטֵי ׳י v^{10}); in Ez distinctly *take warning*, abs. Ez 3^{21} (cf. **Hiph.**) 33$^{4.5a}$; so Ec 12^{2} and, more generally, אֲשֶׁר לֹא יָדַע לְהִזָּהֵר Ec 4^{13} *who knoweth not how to take admonition; be warned, receive warning* Ez 33^{6} (of people, c. לֹא, i.e. if no warning be given them), also MT v^{5b}, but rd. perh. Hiph. (v. supr.) *but he* (i.e. the watchman) *gave warning, he hath delivered his (own) soul.*

†**זִו** appar. **n.pr.** of 2nd month, = c. April–May, named as month of beginning the temple-building; בְּחֹדֶשׁ זִו הוּא הַחֹדֶשׁ הַשֵּׁנִי 1 K 6^{1} = בְּיֶרַח זִו v^{37}; 𝔊B v^{1} has simply ἐν μηνὶ τῷ δευτέρῳ, v^{37} (in 𝔊 v^{4}) ἐν μηνὶ Νεισῶ καὶ τῷ δευτέρῳ μηνί; 𝔊 codd. ἐν μηνὶ Ζιου μηνὶ τῷ δευτέρῳ; 𝔊L (only v^{37}) ἐν δευτέρῳ μηνί, ἐν μηνὶ Ζιου;—(si vera l. comp. perh. Aram. זִיו ܙܝܘܳ *brightness, freshness*, so B Aram. Dn 2^{31} +; cf. 𝔗 יֶרַח זִיו נִיצָנַיָּא *month of brightness of flowers;* As. *zîmu* (*zîvu*), Dl$^{Pr\ 152\ f.}$ cf. Nö$^{ZMG\ 1886,\ 732}$; Thes al. der. זִיו, זִו (= זִהְיו) fr. זהה in sense *be bright, splendid*, etc., cf. Ar. زَهَا *increase, thrive* (of seed-produce), زَهْوٌ *a beautiful and bright*, or *fresh*, plant; Aram. זְהָא, adj. זָהוֹהָא *haughty, proud;* ܙܗܳܐ *glory, boast, be magnificent;* yet cf. Ol$^{§\ 174\ ad\ fin.}$) 2099

זוֹ, זוּ, v. p. 262. 2097-98

†[**זוּב**] **vb. flow, gush** (NH *id.*, Aram. דּוּב, דִּיב, ܕܳܒ, all used oft. in sense **4** infr.; Ar. ذَابَ (med. و) *melt, dissolve, flow*)—only **Qal** *Impf.* יָזוּב Lv 15^{25} etc.; *Pt.* זָב Je 49^{9} f. זָבָה Lv 15^{19} etc.;—**1.** *flow, gush* (poet.), of water from the smitten rock ψ 78^{20} (‖ שָׁטַף), 105^{41} (‖ הָלַךְ), Is 48^{21} (‖ נָזַל). **2.** *Pt.* freq. in (אֶרֶץ) זָבַת חָלָב וּדְבַשׁ, always of promised land, Ex 3$^{8.17}$ 13^{5} (all J) 33^{3} Nu 13^{27} 14^{8} 16$^{13.14}$ (all JE) Dt 6^{3} 11^{9} 26$^{9.15}$ 27^{3} 31^{20} Jos 5^{6} (D) Lv 20^{24} (H) Je 11^{5} 32^{22} Ez 20$^{6.15}$ (in last two ins. ארץ 𝔊 Co); זָב עִמְקֵךְ Je 49^{4} (fertile valley of Ammon). **3.** fig. *flow away = pine away* (from hunger) La 4^{9}. **4.** *flow*, of issue from woman (all P), Lv 15^{25} יָזוּב זוֹב דָּמָהּ (v. זוֹב); esp. *have an issue* (*flux, gleet*), of woman Lv 15^{25} and 15^{19} (תִּהְיֶה זָבָה); usu. of man, 2 S 3^{29} (‖ מְצֹרָע); elsewhere P, Lv 15^{2} זָב מִבְּשָׂרוֹ; with cogn. acc. 15^{33}; ordinarily *Pt.* זָב *one that has an issue* Lv 15$^{4.6.7.8.9.11.12.13.32}$ (all P), 22^{4} (H; ‖ צָרוּעַ); also Nu 5^{2} (P; ‖ *id.*) 2100

†**זוֹב n.m. issue** (Ar. ذَوْبٌ *fluid, liquid;* NH זוֹב, Aram. דּוֹבָא in specif. sense of Heb.); —*issue, flux*, alw. fr. genitals (cf. Di Lv 15^{2}); only P: of man or woman Lv 15^{33};—of man Lv 15$^{2.3.3.3.13.15}$; of woman Lv 15^{19} (דָּם יִהְיֶה זֹבָהּ בִּבְשָׂרָהּ, of monthly period); also v$^{25.25.26.28.30}$ (of morbid issue of blood, sts. connected with the other; cf. Mat 9^{20} etc.) 2101

זוד v. זיד. p. 267 2102

זוה (√of foll.; cf. Ar. زَوَى *put aside* or *away, draw together, contract*).

2106 †[זָוִית] **n.f.** corner (late) (Aram. זָוִיתָא, ܙܳܘܺܝܬܳܐ (oft. for Heb. פִּנָּה, מִקְצֹעַ), hence, as loan-word (Frä Aram. Fremdw. 11, 168) Ar. زَاوِيَةٌ);—Pl. abs. זָוִיּוֹת ψ 144[12]; cstr. זָוִיּוֹת Zc 9[15];—וּמָלְאוּ כַּמִּזְרָק כְּזָוִיּוֹת מִזְבֵּחַ Zc 9[15] simil. of warriors streaming with blood, v. Lv 1[5.11] etc.; בְּנוֹתֵינוּ כְזָ׳ וגו׳ ψ 144[12] *our daughters like corner* (-pillar)*s*, carved (so Che al., but v. II. חטב) in palace-fashion.

4200 †[מָזוּ] **n.m.** garner (on format. cf. Ol § 144 b, 197 b)—only Pl. sf. מְזָוֵינוּ מְלֵאִים ψ 144[13] *our garners* are *full* (word inflected as if מְ were radical; cf. Ol l.c.)

I. **זוז** (NH זוז *move*, As. *zâzu*, *move, rise, come forth* cf. COT gloss.; also *be agitated, enraged*, V R 64, i, l. 11).

2123 †I. **זִיז** **n.m.** ψ 80, 14 **coll. moving things** (i.e. beasts) (etym. & exact meaning still rather dub., cf. Che OP 472 and on ψ 50[11]; Thes al. √זוז; De ψ 50[11] comp. As. *zizânu*, coll. *reptiles*, Dl S. 74 f. from a זאזא cf. زَعْزَعَ *move to and fro, agitate* (cf. זוע); others comp. As. *zâzu, abundance* v. II. זוז, so even Di Is 66[11]; this hardly suits ψ 80[14]; 𝔗 זִיזָא *worm*);—only cstr. זִיז שָׂדַי ψ 50[11] *the moving things of the field*, as all known to י׳ (|| עוֹף הָרִים; also in v[10] חַיְתוֹ־יָעַר, etc.); fig. of enemies of Isr. ψ 80[14] (|| חֲזִיר מִיָּעַר).

2124 †**זִיזָא** **n.pr.m.**—**1.** a Simeonite 1 Ch 4[37]. **2.** a son of Rehoboam 2 Ch 11[20].

2125-26 †**זִיזָה** **n.pr.m.** a Levite 1 Ch 23[11], = זִינָא
2124 v[10] (rd. prob. זִיזָא, 𝔊 Ζιζα in both).

2117 †**זָזָא** **n.pr.m.** (perh. belongs under this √; comp. As. n.pr. Zazâ Zim BP 97 cf. Strm AV No. 2816)—a descendant of יְרַחְמְאֵל of Judah 1 Ch 2[33].

4201 †**מְזוּזָה** **n.f. door-post, gate-post**, abs. מ׳ Ex 21[6] Is 57[8]; cstr. מְזוּזַת 1 S 1[9] Ez 46[2]+ Ez 41[21] (del. 𝔖 Co cf. 𝔊 Hi), 45[19.19] (in both 𝔊 𝔖 𝔙 Co); sf. מְזוּזָתִי Ez 43[8], מְזוּזָתָם v[8]; pl. מְזוּזוֹת 1 K 6[31] + 2 t. (+ Ez 45[19.19] Co v. supr.), מְזוּזֹת Ex 12[7] + 4 t., מְזֻזוֹת Dt 6[9] Ju 16[3];—*door-post, gate-post*, **1.** of dwelling-house Ex 12[7] (P), v[22.23] 21[6] (all JE), Dt 6[9] 11[20] cf. Is 57[8]; also מ׳ פְּתָחָי Pr 8[34], מְזוּזָתָם Ez 43[8]; of Sol.'s house 1 K 7[5]. **2.** of house of י׳: **a.** of the pre-Solomonic sanctuary of י׳ 1 S 1[9]. **b.** of Sol.'s temple 1 K 6[33]; of the דְּבִיר v[31]. **c.** of Ezek.'s temple Ez 41[21] (del. Co v. supr.), 43[8] (מְזוּזָתִי), מ׳ הַבַּיִת Ez 45[19], מ׳ שַׁעַר v[9], cf. 46[2]. **3.** of city-gates Ju 16[3].

3151 †**יָזִיז** **n.pr.m.** an officer of David יָזִיז הַהַגְרִי 1 Ch 27[31].

II. **זוז** (*be abundant*, cf. esp. As. *zâzu, abundance*, Dl Pr. 67 f. Zim BP 94, 97; only as √of foll.; perh. related to I. זוז (cf. Thes), but this very dubious).

2123 II. **זִיז** **n.[m.] abundance, fulness**: only מִזִּיז כְּבוֹדָהּ Is 66[11] that ye may suck out and be delighted, *from the abundance of her glory* (i.e. of Jerusalem) (so Di al.; > Che crit. n., and OP 472 f. Brd (cf. Ew '*Euter*'), who comp. vulg. Ar. *zîza, udder* (breast, teat); this suits vb. תָּמֹצּוּ and || תִּינְקוּ וּשְׂבַעְתֶּם מִשֹּׁד, but is dub. in Heb., perh. not Shemit., v. Dozy i. 619 a and reff.; also Lag Proph. Chald. who proposes, plausibly, מִבִּיז, cf. Aram. ܒܺܝܙܳܐ PS 502, ביזא; Ar. بِزّ *pap*).

2104 †**זוּזִים** **n. pr. gent.** an ancient trans-Jordanic people, dwelling in הָם Gn 14[5]; otherwise unknown; abode appar. in (later) land of Ammon, between Bashan and Moab; commonly supposed = זַמְזֻמִּים q.v., in that case perh. txt. error in one case or the other, cf. Nö Untersuchungen z. Kritik d. A. T. 162.—(𝔊 ἔθνη ἰσχυρά).—On n.pr. loc. Ζιζα, زيزا, between Boṣra and Lejûn, cf. Kn Di ad loc., Tristr Moab 182 ff.

2105 †**זוֹחֵת** **n.pr.m.** a descendant of Judah (etym. and mng. unknown) 1 Ch 4[20] (v. also בֶּן־זוֹחֵת), 𝔊 Ζωαν, Ζωαβ, A Ζωχαθ, 𝔊L Ζαωθ.

2106 **זָוִית** v. sub זוה. above

I. **זול** (prob. √of foll., Ar. زَالَ *remove, depart*).

2108 †[**זוּלָה**] **n.[f.]** prop. **removal**, only found in the *st. c.* as **prep.** and **conj. except, only, save that**—cstr. זוּלַת 2 K 24[14] and (with the obsolete case-ending (ִ—) זוּלָתִי Dt 1[36] 4[12] Jos 11[13] 1 K 3[18] 12[20] ψ 18[32]; with sf. זוּלָתִי Ho 13[4] Is 45[5.21], זוּלָתְךָ, זוּלָתֶךָ 2 S 7[22] = 1 Ch 17[20] Is 26[13] 64[3] Ru 4[4], זוּלָתָהּ 1 S 21[10];—**1. prep.** *except, besides*, lit. *with removal of*...(syn. מִבַּלְעֲדֵי ψ 18[32] Is 45[21]; בִּלְתִּי Ho 13[4]; and cf. Dt 1[36] with Nu 32[12]), Dt 1[36] זולתי כלב *with the exception of* Caleb, 1 S 21[10] אֵין אַחֶרֶת זוּלָתָהּ there is none other *except* it, 1 K 12[20] 2 K 24[14] Ru 4[4]: oft. in such phrases as, There is no God (or, Who is God?) *except* me (or thee), 2 S 7[22] ψ 18[32] Ho 13[4] Is 45[5.21] 64[3]. Always after a neg. or qu., exc. Is 26[13] אדנים זולתך lords *other than* thou. Connected inexactly with what precedes,

ˈז acquires the force of *only*, Dt 4^{12} ye saw no form זוּלָתִי קוֹל *save* a voice = (there was) *only* a voice, 1 K 3^{18}. **2.** conj. Jos 11^{13} *except that* he burnt Hazor alone.

2107 †II. [זוּל] **vb. lavish** (cf. Aram. זוּל, *be cheap, of little value, lightly esteem;* similarly זלל q.v.)—**Qal** *Pt.* הַזָּלִים זָהָב מִכִּיס Is 46^{6} (‖ כֶּסֶף בַּקָּנֶה יִשְׁקֹלוּ).

2109 †[זוּן] **vb. feed** (NH. BAram. *id.*; Syr. ܙܳܢ; Sam. [Samaritan]);—**Hoph.** *Pt.* סוּסִים מוּזנים Je 5^{8} (Kt; i.e. מוּזָנִים; Qr מְיֻזָּנִים from יזן q.v.) *well-fed horses,* fig. of adulterers; Dl $^{Pr\ 73\ f.}$ comp. As. *zanânu, be full* (i.e. of sexual desire).

4202 †מָזוֹן **n.m. food, sustenance** (so Talm. BAram. Syr.)—בָּר וָלֶחֶם וּמָזוֹן Gn 45^{23} (Di ׳מ rather an Aram. word; perh. later gloss for orig. צֵדָה v^{21} 42^{25} ׳); הַמָּזוֹן לָרֹב 2 Ch 11^{23}.

2181 זוֹנָה v. זנה. p. 275

2111 †זוּעַ **vb. tremble, quake** (Aram. (incl. BAram.) *id.,* ܙܳܥ; cf. also Ar. زَاعَ *impel,* زَعْزَعَ *move, agitate, shake* (on these v. Nö $^{ZMG\ 1886,\ 725}$), As. *zû, storm-wind* (= Aram. זוֹעָא) Zim $^{BP\ 94}$);—**Qal** (late) *Pf.* 3 ms. זָע Est 5^{9}; *Impf.* 3 mpl. c. rel. שֶׁיָּזֻעוּ Ec 12^{3};—*tremble, quake,* in presence of powerful superior Est 5^{9} (sq. מִמֶּנּוּ); said of שֹׁמְרֵי הַבַּיִת in descr. of infirm old man Ec 12^{3}. **Pilp.** *Pt.* sf. מְזַעְזְעֶיךָ Hb 2^{7}; causat. and intens. they that shall *violently shake thee,* fig. of foes of Babylon, instruments of Yahweh's judgment.

2113, 2189 †זְוָעָה, and, by transpos., זַעֲוָה (Di Dt 28^{25} cf. Sta $^{§192\ a}$) **n.f. a trembling,** i.e. **object of trembling, terror:** זְוָעָה Is 28^{19}, also Kt Je 15^{4} + 4 t.; זַעֲוָה Dt 28^{25} Ez 23^{46} (also Qr Je 15^{4} + 4 t.);—*object of trembling, terror, fright;* וְהָיִיתָ לְזַעֲוָה Dt 28^{25} *and thou shalt become a terror* to all (לְכֹל) the kingdoms of the earth; וּנְתַתִּים לְז׳ וגו׳ Je 15^{4} 29^{18}, 34^{17} (‖ לְאָלָה וּלְשַׁמָּה וְלִשְׁרֵקָה וּלְחֶרְפָּה), also וּנְתַתִּים לְז׳ וגו׳ 24^{9} (‖ לְחֶרְפָּה וּלְמָשָׁל לִשְׁנִינָה וְלִקְלָלָה), Ez 23^{46} 2 Ch 29^{8}.

2127 †זִיעַ **n.pr.m.** a Gadite, 1 Ch 5^{13}, 𝔊 Ζουε, Ζεα.

2190 †זַעֲוָן **n.pr.m.** a Horite Gn 36^{27} = 1 Ch 1^{42}.

2114 †I. [זוּר] **vb. be a stranger** (Ar. زَارَ (med. و) *incline toward, repair to, visit;* II. *honour as visitor or guest;* IX. *decline, turn aside;* زَائِرٌ *visitor;* Aram. זוּר, oft. = Heb. סוּר *turn aside, turn aside to visit*)—**Qal** *Pf.* 3 pl. זֹרוּ ψ 58^{4} (Kö $^{I.\ 445}$), זָרוּ ψ 78^{30} Jb 19^{13}; *Pt.* זָר Ex 30^{33} + 27 t.; f. זָרָה Ex 30^{9} + 7 t.; mpl. זָרִים Ho 5^{7} + 30 t.; fpl. זָרוֹת Pr 22^{14} 23^{33}; sf. זָרַיִךְ Is 29^{5}; **1.** Pf. *become estranged* ψ 58^{4}, c. מן *from* Jb 19^{13} ψ 78^{30}. **2.** Pt. as adj. *strange,* or as noun *stranger:* **a.** to the family, of another household, אִישׁ זָר Dt 25^{5}, elsewhere זָר 1 K 3^{18} Jb 19^{15} Pr 6^{1} 11^{15} 20^{16} 27^{13}; זָרִים ψ 109^{11} Pr 5$^{10.17}$; בנים זרים, children of another household than God's Ho 5^{7}; especially of another family than priests' אִישׁ זָר Lv 22^{12} (H) Nu 17^{5} (P); זָר Lv 22$^{10.13}$ (H) Ex 29^{33} 30^{33} Nu 3$^{10.38}$ 18^{7} (P); not belonging to the tribe of Levi, Nu 1^{51} 18^{4} (P). **b.** to the person, *another* Jb 19^{27} Pr 14^{10} 27^{2}; (אִשָּׁה) זָרָה *strange woman, harlot* Pr 2^{16} 5$^{3.20}$ 7^{5} 22^{14} 23^{33}. **c.** to the land, *foreign,* זָרִים *foreigners* (as such usu. enemies) Ho 7^{9} 8^{7} Is 1$^{7.7}$ 25$^{2.5}$ 29^{5} 61^{5} Je 5^{19} 30^{8} 51$^{2.51}$ La 5^{2} Ez 7^{21} 11^{9} 16^{32} 28$^{7.10}$ 30^{12} 31^{12} Jo 4^{17} Ob ^{11} Jb 15^{19} ψ 54^{5}; אֵל זָר *foreign god* ψ 44^{21} 81^{10} = זָר Is 43^{12}; so זָרִים Dt 32^{16} and (in fig.) Je 2^{25} 3^{13}; מַיִם זָרִים *foreign waters* 2 K 19^{24} Je 18^{14}; זְמֹרַת זָר Is 17^{10} *vine-slip of a stranger;* כְּמוֹ־זָר נֶחְשָׁבוּ Ho 8^{12} *they are regarded as foreign;* מַעֲשֵׂהוּ זָר Is 28^{21} *his work is foreign* (as if dealing with enemies). **d.** *strange* to the law; קְטֹרֶת זָרָה *strange incense* Ex 30^{9} (P); אֵשׁ זָרָה *strange fire* Lv 10^{1} Nu 3^{4} 26^{61} (P). **Niph.** *Pf.* נָזֹרוּ Is 1^{4} Ez 14^{5}; *be estranged* Is 1^{4}, pregn., sq. אָחוֹר (cf. RV); מֵעַל Ez 14^{5}. **Hoph.** *Pt.* מוּזָר *estranged* ψ 69^{9}.

†II. [זִיר, זוּר] **vb. be loathsome,** Bö ^{§1142} 2114
(Ar. ذَارَ *fastidivit, abhorruit;* As. *zâru, resist, Impf. izîru,* Dl $^{Pr\ 65}$ Schr $^{COT\ Gloss}$)—only 3 fs. זָרָה Jb 19^{17} רוּחִי זָרָה לְאִשְׁתִּי *my breath is loathsome to my wife* (וְחַנֹּתִי לְ in ‖ cl.); > most, who derive fr. I. זוּר, *become strange* and so *repugnant.*

†זָרָא **n.[f.] loathsome thing,** עַד אֲשֶׁר יֵצֵא 2214
מֵאַפְּכֶם וְהָיָה לָכֶם לְזָרָא Nu 11^{20} (JE) *and it* (the flesh) *become to you a loathsome thing* (𝔊 εἰς χολέραν, 𝔙 *in nauseam*), prob. err. for זָרָה (Sam.)

†III. [זוּר] **vb. press down and out** (Aram. 2115
זִיר *press together,* Syr. ܙܳܪ, ܙܘܪ *compress;* cf. Ar. زَيَّرَ *twist* the lip of a beast)—**Qal** *Pf.* 3 pl. זֹרוּ Is 1^{6} (pass.; > √זרר, Ar. زَرَّ *draw forcibly together* Ol $^{§233c,\ 245\ I}$ Kö $^{I.\ 333}$); *Impf.* 3 ms.
וַיָּזַר Ju 6^{38}, 3 fs. sf. תְּזוּרֶהָ Jb 39^{15}; *Pt. pass.* f. זוּרָה 2116
(= זוּרָה Ges $^{§80,\ 2,\ d}$) Is 59^{5};—*press* (twist or

wring) *out* a fleece Ju 6[38]; *not pressed out*, of sore (fig. of continued disaster) Is 1[6]; *press under foot* an egg, Jb 39[15] (‖ דוּשׁ), Is 59[5] (pass.)

2213 †**זֵר n.m. circlet, border** (orig. *that which presses, binds*, cf. also Aram. ܙܝܪܐ *bracelet*, זִירָא *wreath, crown*, NH זִיר *id.*, זִירָה *ring, wrestler's ring*; others fr. a √זרר)—זֵר זָהָב Ex 25[11.24.25] 30[3] 37[2.11.12.26]; זֵרוֹ Ex 30[4] 37[27] (all P).

2223 †**זַרְזִיר adj. girded, girt** (cf. Ba [NB 206])—only cstr. Pr 30[31] זַרְזִיר מָתְנַיִם אוֹ־תַיִשׁ *that which is girt in the loins*, etc., named with lion, he-goat, and king, as stately in motion. Perh. =*greyhound* Ew Bö De al., or *war-horse* Bo Ges Hi al.; Vrss. *cock*, Talm. *raven*, v. De Now (NH זַרְזִיר *starling* (*war-horse* only in interpr. of Pr 30[31]), Aram. ܙܪܙܝܪܐ; Lexx. also ܙܘܙܙܐ *starling*, in Ar. زُرْزُور, perh. loan-wd. Others der. fr. a √זרר, v. supr.)

4205 †**מָזוֹר n.[m.] wound** (as needing to have its matter *pressed out*)—fig. of injury to, or sufferings of, Isr. and Judah: מָזוֹר Ho 5[13] also Je 30[13] (Gf Che RVm; but accents Ew Ges Gie AV RV *for pressing*, i.e. binding up); מְזֹרוֹ Ho 5[13] (cf. III. זור Is 1[6]).—מָזוֹר Ob[7] v. sub מזר.

2117 †**זָזָא** v. sub זוּז. p. 265

2118 †**[זָחַח] vb. remove, displace** (Ar. زَحَّ *push, thrust away*; comp. also Aram. זוּחַ, ܙܘܚ *move, move away* (intrans.))—**Niph.** *Impf.* וְלֹא יִזַּח הַחֹשֶׁן מֵעַל הָאֵפוֹד Ex 28[28] *and that the breast-piece be not displaced* etc., 39[21] (both P).

2119 †**I. [זָחַל] vb. shrink back, crawl away** (Aram. זְחַל *crawl* (also *drop, drip*, of water: so NH זָחַל), זָחִיל *worm*; Syr. ܙܚܠܐ *locust* (as *crawling*); Ar. زَحَلَ *withdraw, retire to a distance* (v. Lane, Wetzst in De [Hiob 2, 428]), and Sab. זחל *withdraw, humble oneself* DHM [ZMG 1875, 610])—**Qal** only *Pt.* pl. cstr. זֹחֲלֵי Dt 32[24] Mi 7[17];—*crawl*, of reptiles (pt.) זֹחֲלֵי עָפָר Dt 32[24] i.e. serpents (as poisonous), instruments of Yahweh's judgment on Isr.; ז׳ ארץ Mi 7[17] *id.* (as crawling into the earth to hide), sim. of nations in fear of י׳.

2120 †**זֹחֶלֶת n.f.** mng. dub.; perh. **crawling thing, serpent** (We [Skizzen iii. 171] cites Ar. *Zuḥal* =*Saturn*, in connex. with 1 K 1[9]; cf. Lane & Wetzst in De [Hiob 2, 428] on view that Zuḥal=*he who withdraws*, because of planet Saturn's remoteness)—only c. art., in design. loc. עִם אֶבֶן הַזֹּחֶלֶת 1 K 1[9] (cf. אֶבֶן ad fin.)

†II. **[זָחַל] vb. fear, be afraid** (Aram. דְּחַל, 2119
ܕܚܠ; cf. Ar. دَخْلٌ *rancour, malevolence*; Nö [ZMG. 1886, 741])—only **Qal** *Pf.* 1 s. זָחַלְתִּי Jb 32[6] *therefore I feared* (‖ וָאִירָא); > most, who derive fr. I. זָחַל=*shrink away* in fear, *hold back* (RV), cf. 𝔗 אִסְתְּפִיתִי Fl ChWB [ii. 571].

†**[זוּד, זִיד] vb. boil up, seethe, act** 2102
proudly, presumptuously, rebelliously (NH Hiph. הזיד as Heb.; Aram. of Zinjirli זד *presumptuous*, DHM [Sendsch. 56]; Ar. زَادَ (med. ى) *increase, exceed, exaggerate*, e.g. in talk; also Sab. n.pr. זיד (زَيْد) DHM [Epigr. Denkm. 44] זידאל Id [ib. 52] (on distinct. betw. זוד and זיד in Sab. v. Sab.Denkm.[64]); perh. also Sab. מזודן *great one, prince*, e.g. Sab.Denkm.[89])—**Qal** *Pf.* 3 fs. זָדָה Je 50[29]; 3 pl. זָדוּ Ex 18[11];—of Egyptians, בַּדָּבָר אֲשֶׁר זָדוּ עֲלֵיהֶם Ex 18[11] (E) *in the matter as to which they acted presumptuously against them*; of Babylon, אֶל־י׳ זָדָה Je 50[29] *against* י׳ *hath she acted presumptuously*. **Hiph.** *Pf.* 3 pl. הֵזִידוּ Ne 9[10] + 2 t.; *Impf.* 3 ms. יָזִיד Dt 18[20], יָזִד Ex 21[14]; וַיָּזֶד Gn 25[29]; 3 mpl. יְזִידוּן Dt 17[13]; 2 mpl. וַתָּזִדוּ Dt 1[43]; **1.** *boil, seethe*, trans., וַיָּזֶד יַעֲקֹב נָזִיד Gn 25[29] *and Jacob boiled pottage*. **2.** *act presumptuously, insolently*, Ex 21[14] (JE) כִּי יָזִד אִישׁ עַל־רֵעֵהוּ לְהָרְגוֹ בְעָרְמָה *when a man acteth presumptuously against his neighbour to slay him*; usually against י׳; sq. vb. fin. Dt 1[43] *and ye acted presumptuously and went up*; sq. inf. 18[20] the prophet who *shall presume to speak* a word in my name; also abs. 17[13]; elsewh. only Ne; of Egyptians 9[10] sq. עַל (=**Qal** Ex 18[11]); abs. v[16] (‖ וַיַּקְשׁוּ אֶת־עָרְפָּם וְלֹא שָׁמְעוּ וגו׳); v[29] (‖ וְלֹא שָׁמְעוּ וגו׳).

†**זֵד adj. insolent, presumptuous**:—ז׳ 2086
Pr 21[24]; pl. זֵדִים Je 43[2] + 11 t.;—alw. masc., and alw. of opposition to י׳, wickedness; with qualified noun expressed, only הָאֲנָשִׁים הַזֵּדִים Je 43[2], of opponents of Jerem.; elsewh. used substantively, as term. techn. for godless, rebellious men; once sg. זֵד יָהִיר לֵץ שְׁמוֹ Pr 21[24] *a haughty insolent one, scorner is his name* (‖ עוֹשֶׂה בְּעֶבְרַת זָדוֹן); usu. pl. Is 13[11] (גְּאוֹן ז׳ ‖ גַּאֲוַת עָרִיצִים); Mal 3[13] (‖ עֹשֵׂי רִשְׁעָה), v[19] (‖ עֹשֵׂה רִשְׁעָה); and in ψ 86[14] (‖ עָרִיצִים), 119[21] (‖ הַשֹּׁגִים מִמִּצְוֹתֶיךָ), v[51.69.78.85.122]; so prob. also ψ 19[14] גַּם מִזֵּדִים חֲשֹׂךְ עַבְדֶּךָ *also from presumptuous men hold back thy servant* (Ew Ol Hup Che RVm); >*presumptuous sins* De al. (AV RV).

2087 †זָדוֹן **n.m.** $^{Pr\ 11,\ 2}$ **insolence, presumptuousness** (on format. cf. Lag$^{BN\ 204,\ Anm.}$), abs. ז׳ Dt 17^{12} + 7 t.; cstr. זְדוֹן Je 49^{16} Ob^{3}; sf. זְדֹנְךָ 1 S 17^{28};—**1.** *insolence, presumption* toward men; affirmed of David by Eliab 1 S 17^{28} (‖ רֹעַ לְבָבֶךָ); usu. **2.** of presumptuous godlessness (cf. זוד, זֵד), exhibited in disobedience to priest or judge Dt 17^{12}; in false prediction 18^{22}; in gen. Pr 11^{2} (opp. צְנוּעִים), 13^{10}; עֶבְרַת ז׳ Pr 21^{24} (cf. זֵד); ז׳ לִבֶּךָ Je 49^{16} (=Ob^{3}) *presumption of thine heart;* of Babylon personif. under fig. of ז׳ Je 50$^{31.32}$; dub. is פָּרַח הַזּ׳ Ez 7^{10} *insolence hath blossomed* (preceded by צָץ הַמַּטֶּה) i.e. either of Isr. as demanding punishment, or of Babylon as instr. of punishment.

2121 †[זֵידוֹן] **adj. insolent, raging,** only pl. and fig. הַמַּיִם הַזֵּידוֹנִים ψ 124^{5}.

5138 †נָזִיד **n.[m.] thing sodden or boiled, pottage**; abs. נ׳ Gn 25^{29} + 4 t.; cstr. נְזִיד Gn 25^{34};—a kind of boiled leguminous food, obj. of וַיָּזֶד Gn 25^{29} (v. זוד **Hiph.**); defined v^{34} as נְזִיד עֲדָשִׁים (v. עדש); obj. of בִּשֵּׁל 2 K 4^{38}; boiled in a סִיר v^{39} cf. v^{40}; mentioned, appar. as a common food, Hg 2^{12}.

2123-25 זִיז, זִיזָא, זִיזָה v. sub I. זוז. p. 265

2124 זִיזָא v. זִיזָה sub I. זוז. p. 265

2126 †זִינָא **n.pr.m.** 1 Ch 23^{10} = זִיזָה v^{11} q.v. p. 265

2127 זִיעַ v. sub זוע. p. 266

2128 †זִיף **n.pr. 1. n.pr.loc. a.** city S.E. from Hebron, Jos 15^{55} 1 Ch 2^{42} 2 Ch 11^{8}, mod. *Tell Zîf;* Rob$^{BR\ i.\ 492,\ 498}$ Guérin$^{Judée\ iii.\ 159\ ff.}$: מִדְבַּר־ז׳ 1 S 23$^{14.15}$ 26$^{2.2}$; c. ה loc., זִיפָה 1 S 23^{24}. **b.** city of southern Judah Jos 15^{24}, site unknown. **2. n.pr.m.** a son of יְהַלֶּלְאֵל of Judah 1 Ch 4^{16}, whether related to **n.pr.loc.** supr. does not appear. 𝔊 Ζαφα, Ζιφ(αι). (1 Ch 2^{42} v. supr.)

2130 †[זִיפִי] **adj.gent.** of זִיף **1. a**; only mpl. as n.pr.gent. זִפִים 1 S 23^{19} 26^{1}; זִיפִים ψ 54^{2} (title).

2129 †זִיפָה **n.pr.m.** a son of יְהַלֶּלְאֵל 1 Ch 4^{16} (זִיף וְזִיפָה) (𝔊 Ζαιρα, Ζ(α)ιφα), cf. זִיף supr.)

2131 זִיקוֹת v. I. [זֵק]. p. 278

2114 זִיר v. זור. p. 266

2132 †זַיִת **n.m.** $^{ψ\ 52,\ 10}$ **olive-tree, olive** (NH *id.;* Aram. ܙܰܝܬܳܐ, זֵיתָא; Eth. ዘይት: Ar. زَيْتُون *olive-tree, olive,* زَيْت *olive-oil;* v. Lag $^{M\ iii.\ 215\ ff.}$ Hom $^{Aufsätze\ u.\ Abh.,\ 1892,\ 94,\ 99\ ff.}$; √dub.; Thes and most der. fr. assumed זהה *be bright, fresh, luxuriant* (v. sub זִו) + ת afformat. which is then treated as radical, cf. Sta$^{§\ 187\ a}$; but this not certain, cf. Ol$^{§\ 119\ b,\ 142\ a}$; acc. to Lag$^{Armen.\ Stud.\ §\ 1347}$ ז׳ is Armen. loan-word, v. also Lag $^{M\ l.\ c.;\ BN\ 219,\ Anm.}$);—abs. ז׳ Gn 8^{11}, cstr. זֵית Dt 8^{8} 2 K 18^{32}; sf. זֵיתְךָ Dt 24^{20}, זֵיתֶךָ Ex 23^{11} Dt 28^{40}; pl. זֵיתִים Dt 6^{11}, etc.;—**1.** *olive-tree* Ju 9$^{8.9}$ (personif., in Jotham's fable), Ho 14^{7} (sim. of beauty), Jb 15^{33} (as casting off its flowers, sim. of wicked man); in 2 S 15^{23} ins. הַזּ׳ אֲשֶׁר (before הַמִּדְבָּר, read בַּמּ׳) 𝔊L Dr; also pl. of two *olive-trees* Zc 4$^{3.11}$; ז׳ רַעֲנָן ψ 52^{10} *fresh,* (thriving) *olive-tree* (sim. of prosperity), so Je 11^{16}; עֲלֵה־ז׳ Gn 8^{11} (J) *olive-branch, sprig,* cf. Ne 8^{15} (here + עֲלֵי עֵץ־שֶׁמֶן, etc.); also pl. שְׁתִלֵי זֵיתִים ψ 128^{3} *olive-shoots* (sim. of children); שִׁבֲּלֵי זֵיתִים Zc 4^{12} *olive-branches* (in Zech.'s vision); זַיִת in representative or coll. sense, = *olive-trees,* groups of growing olive-trees, as property, source of wealth, *olive-yards* Ex 23^{11} (JE; + כֶּרֶם), Ju 15^{5} (+ *id.*); עֵץ־הַזַּיִת Hg 2^{19} (+ הַגֶּפֶן וְהַתְּאֵנָה וְהָרִמּוֹן); also in phr. כִּחֵשׁ מַעֲשֵׂה־זַיִת Hb 3^{17} *the bearing, yield,* of *olive-trees* (‖ וּשְׁדֵמוֹת לֹא־עָשָׂה אֹכֶל, cf. also תְּאֵנָה and יְבוּל גֶּפֶן v^{a}); specif. זֵית שֶׁמֶן, *oil-yielding olive-trees* Dt 8^{8} cf. 2 K 18^{32}; נֹקֶף ז׳ *striking* or *beating of olive-trees* Is 17^{6} 24^{13} (sim. of desolation at judgment of י׳), cf. כִּי תַחְבֹּט זֵיתְךָ Dt 24^{20}; rather more often pl.; Am 4^{9} (‖ גַּנּוֹת, כְּרָמִים, תְּאֵנִים), 1 S 8^{14} (‖ שָׂדוֹת, כְּרָמִים), cf. also Dt 6^{11} 28$^{40\ a}$ Jos 24^{13} 2 K 5^{26} 1 Ch 27^{28} Ne 5^{11} 9^{25}. **2.** of fruit of olive-tree, *olives:* Dt 28$^{40\ b}$ (c. שֶׁמֶן); תִּדְרֹךְ זַיִת Mi 6^{15} (‖ שֶׁמֶן); also שֶׁמֶן זַיִת *olive-oil* Ex 27^{20} 30^{24} (P) Lv 24^{2} (H). **3.** in designations of place: מַעֲלֵה הַזֵּיתִים 2 S 15^{30} *the ascent of the olive-trees* (𝔊 ἐν τῇ ἀναβάσει τῶν ἐλαιῶν = Mount of Olives); הַר־הַזֵּיתִים Zc 14$^{4.4}$ (𝔊 τὸ ὄρος τῶν ἐλαιῶν); the well-known hill E. of Jerus. (NT usu. as Zc 14^{4} 𝔊, e.g. Mk 13^{3}; cf. also הָהָר 1 K 11^{7} Ez 11^{33} Ne 8^{15}; 𝔗 טוּר זֵיתַיָּא 2 K 23^{13} cf. 2 S 15^{30} Zc 14^{4} etc.; 𝔗 Ct 8^{5} טוּר מִשְׁחָא, and so Talm. etc.)

†זֵיתָן **n.pr.m.** (? *olive-tree*)—a Benjamite 2133
1 Ch 7^{10}, 𝔊 Ζαιθαν, 𝔊L Ζηθα.

†זֵתָם **n.pr.m.** (sub זית in Thes, = foregoing) 2241
—a Levite (Gershonite) 1 Ch 23^{8}, appar. son of לַעְדָּן and brother of יְחִיאֵל and יוֹאֵל; 26^{22} appar. grandson of לַעְדָּן, and son of יְחִיאֵלִי (expressly called brother of יוֹאֵל); 𝔊 Ζεθομ, Ζοθομ, 𝔊L Ζηθαν.

2134 זַךְ, זַךְ, v. sub זכך. below

2135 †[זָכָה] **vb. be clear, clean, pure**, alw. in moral sense (As. *zakû* Zim^{BP}; Aram. זְכָא, ܙܟܳܐ, ܙܟܺܝ; cf. Ar. ذَكَا *be bright* (of a fire), *pungent* (of an odour); *be acute, quick of mind*)—**Qal** *Impf.* 3 ms. יִזְכֶּה Jb 15^{14} 25^{4}; 2 ms. תִּזְכֶּה ψ 51^{6}; 1 s. interrog. הַאֶזְכֶּה Mi 6^{11};—**1.** *be clean, pure,* of man, in the sight of God, Jb 15^{14} 25^{4} (in both ‖ יצדק; cf. also זַכּוּ 15^{15} 25^{5}). **2.** *be clear, be justified* = be regarded as just, righteous, of God, ψ 51^{6} (‖ תצדק), Mi 6^{11}. **Pi.** *Pf.* 1 s. זִכִּיתִי ψ 73^{13} Pr 20^{9}; *Impf.* יְזַכֶּה־ ψ 119^{9}:—*make* or *keep clean, pure,* obj. לְבָבִי ψ 73^{13} (‖ אֶרְחַץ כַּפָּי), obj. לִבִּי Pr 20^{9} (‖ טָהַרְתִּי); obj. אֶת־אָרְחוֹ ψ 119^{9}. **Hithp.** *Imv.* m.pl. הִזַּכּוּ Is 1^{16} *make yourselves clean* (‖ רַחֲצוּ);—on form cf. Ges$^{§ 54, 2, b, Rem.}$ Kö$^{Lgb. i, 345, 534}$ Sta$^{§ 129 d.}$

2137 זְכוֹכִית v. sub זכך. below

2141 †[זָכַךְ] **vb. be bright, clean, pure** (kindred with foregoing. Only La Jb)—**Qal** *Pf.* only 3 mpl. זַכּוּ;—**1.** *be bright, shining,* fig. of splendour of nobles זַכּוּ נְזִירִים מִשֶּׁלֶג La 4^{7} (‖ צַחוּ מֵחָלָב). **2.** *be clean, pure* in God's sight, of heavens Jb 15^{15}, of stars 25^{5} (‖ יַאֲהִיל of moon; cf. also יִזְכֶּה 15^{14} 25^{4}). **Hiph.** *cleanse,* only *Pf.* 1 s. וַהֲזִכּוֹתִי בְּבֹר כַּפָּי׃ Jb 9^{30}, fig. of making morally spotless (‖ הִתְרָחַצְתִּי).

2134 † זַךְ **adj. pure, clean**; abs. זַךְ Jb 8^{6} + 5 t.; זָךְ Ex 27^{20} Lv 24^{2}; f. זַכָּה Ex 30^{34} + 2 t.;—**1.** lit., *pure,* i.e. unmixed, free from foreign substances, of olive oil Ex 27^{20} Lv 24^{2}, of frankincense Ex 30^{34} Lv 24^{7} (all P and H). **2.** fig., *pure, clean, righteous* (only Jb Pr):—of man Jb 8^{6} (‖ יָשָׁר), 33^{9} (+ בְּלִי פָשַׁע; ‖ חַף); as subst. = *the pure, righteous* וְזַךְ יָשָׁר פָּעֳלוֹ Pr 21^{8} (opp. וָזָר q.v.); of mode of life כָּל־דַּרְכֵי־אִישׁ זַךְ בְּעֵינָיו Pr 16^{2}; of mode of action (פָּעֳלוֹ) 20^{11} (‖ יָשָׁר); of doctrine (לִקְחִי) Jb 11^{4} (‖ בַּר הייתי); of prayer 16^{17} (‖ לֹא חָמָס בְּכַפָּי).

2137 †זְכוֹכִית **n.[f.] glass** (ᵀ זכוכיתא; but v. Frä^{64}); as precious (‖ זָהָב), yet of less value than wisdom
2137 Jb 28^{17}. (Baer as above; זְכוּכִית van d. H, al.)

2140 †זַכַּי **n.pr.m.** head of a family of returned exiles, זַכָּי Ezr 2^{9} (𝔊 Ζακχου, 𝔊L Ζακχαιου) = Ne 7^{14} (𝔊 Ζαθου, A Ζακχουρ, 𝔊L Ζακχαιου); perh. = זַבַּי Ne 3^{20} Qr (Kt זכי q.v.; 𝔊 Ζαβ(ρ)ου, 𝔊L Ραββαι).

† זָכַר **vb. remember** (As. *zikâru, name,* 2142
mention, cf. n. *zikru*, Hpt in KAT$^{2\ Gloss.1}$ Lyon$^{Sarg.}$; Zinj. זכר, Ar. ذَكَرَ, Aram. דְּכַר, ܕܟܰܪ, Palm. דרכנא *monument*, Vog$^{No. 36\,b}$, דכיר *memorial*, Vog$^{No. 62}$, Sab. in n.pr. ידכראל DHM$^{Epigr.\ Denkm.\ 43}$, but Eth. ዘከረ)—**Qal** *Pf.* 3 ms. ׳ז Gn 40^{23} +; 3 fs. זָכְרָה La 1$^{7.9}$; 2 ms. וְזָכַרְתָּ Dt 5^{15} +; sf. זְכַרְתַּנִי Gn 40^{14} cf. 1 S 1^{11}, וְזָכַרְתָּם ψ 88^{6}; 2 fs. זָכַרְתְּ Is 47^{7} 57^{11} cf. 17^{10} + Ez 16$^{22.43}$ Qr (both Kt זכרתי), וְזָכַרְתְּ consec. Ez 16^{61}; 3 pl. זָכְרוּ Ju 8^{34} +, etc.; *Impf.* 3 ms. יִזְכֹּר Ho 8^{13} +; יִזְכָּר־ 2 S 14^{11} Pr 31^{7}; וַיִּזְכֹּר Gn 8^{1} +; sf. וַיִּזְכְּרֶהָ 1 S 1^{19}; 2 fs. תִּזְכְּרִי Is 54^{4} + 2 t.; 1 s. אֶזְכֹּר Lv 26$^{42.42}$ Is 43^{25} (ψ 77^{12} Qr v. infra), אֶזְכָּר־ Je 31^{34}, וָאֶזְכֹּר Ex 6^{5}; sf. 2 ms. אֶזְכָּרְךָ ψ 42^{7}, sf. 2 fs. אֶזְכְּרֵכִי ψ 137^{6} (v. Ges$^{§ 58, 3, R, 1}$ Sta$^{§§ 356.a, 2, 634\,a, 2}$), etc.; *Imv.* ms. זְכֹר Ex 32^{13} +; זְכָר־ ψ 25^{7} +; זָכְרָה Ne 6^{14} +; sf. זָכְרֵנִי Ju 16^{28} + 2 t.; mpl. זִכְרוּ Is 46^{9} +, זָכְרוּ Ne 4^{8}; *Inf. abs.* זָכוֹר Ex 13^{3} +; זָכֹר Je 31^{20} +; *cstr.* לִזְכֹּר Gn 9^{16} Ez 23^{19}, etc.; sf. בְּזָכְרֵנִי ψ 137^{1}; *Pt.* act. pl. cstr. וּלְזֹכְרֵי ψ 103^{18}; זָכוּר ψ 103^{14} v. infr.—**I.** human subj. **1.** *remember, recall, call to mind,* usu. as affecting present feeling, thought, or action: **a.** *remember* past experiences (acc.) Gn 42^{9} (E), 2 K 9^{25} (acc. pers. agent); sq. cl. with מִי Jb 4^{7}; things formerly known (acc.) Je 17^{2}; sq. cl. with כִּי Ju 9^{2}; with implied regret, longing Nu 11^{5} (JE), ψ 42^{5} 137^{1} La 1^{7} cf. ψ 77^{7}, neg. 137^{6} (‖ שכח v^{5}); so (sq. בְּ Je 3^{16} (‖ עלה על לב and פקד). **b.** *recall* past distress, etc.; obj. not expressed, La 3^{20} (זכור זכר), Jb 11^{16} (שכח in ‖ cl.); neg., sq. acc. Is 54^{4} (‖ שכח), Pr 31^{7} (‖ *id.*). **c.** *remember* sins, (1) to repent of them Dt 9^{7} (+ אל־תשכח, sq. cl. with את־אשר), elsewh. only Ezek., usu. c. acc. Ez 16^{61} (+ וְנִכְלַמְתְּ), v^{63} (obj. not expressed), 20^{43} 36^{21}; (2) to renew and repeat them Ez 23^{19}, neg. v^{27}. **d.** esp. *remember* the dealings of ׳י, expressed in great variety of terms in acc., Dt 7^{18} 8^{2} 24^{9} 32^{7} (‖ בין), Is 46^{9} 63^{11} ψ 77^{12} Qr (Kt Hiph. q.v.) v^{12} 105^{5} 143^{5} (‖ הגיתי, אָשׂוֹחֵחַ) 1 Ch 16^{12}; negatively, Is 43^{18} (‖ אַל תִּתְבֹּנָנוּ), Ez 16$^{22.43}$ ψ 78^{42} 106^{7} Ne 9^{17} (‖ וַיְמָאֲנוּ לִשְׁמֹעַ); obj. cl. with כִּי esp. D, Dt 5^{15} 15^{15} 16^{12} 24$^{18.22}$ ψ 78^{35}. **2.** *remember* persons (human subj.), **a.** to their advantage:—sq. acc. Gn 40^{14} (E), v^{23} (E; neg., ‖ שכח), 1 S 25^{31}. **b.** to make use of them (acc.) Na 2^{6}. **c.** their acts (acc.), to their advantage 2 Ch 24^{22}, to their disadvantage 2 S 19^{20} (neg.); to take vengeance Dt 25^{17}. **d.** *remember* human obligations, acc. rei: בְּרִית אַחִים Am 1^{9}; cf. perh. Est 2^{1} (acc. pers. and also of deed); neg. Ec 9^{15} (acc. pers.), ψ 109^{16} (sq. עשות חסד). **3.** *remember* ׳י: **a.** *call* him *to mind*

2 S 14^{11} (i.e. recall a specific command of his). **b.** *recall*, and (esp.) *keep* 'י *in mind* Dt 8^{18} Je 51^{50} Is 64^{4} (‖ עשה צדק), Ez 6^{9} Zc 10^{9} Jo 2^{8} ψ 42^{7} 63^{7} (‖ אהגה), 77^{4} Ne 4^{8}; negatively Ju 8^{34} Is 17^{10} (opp. שכח), 57^{11} (‖ לֹא שַׂמְתְּ עַל־לִבֵּךְ); cf. also ז׳ אֶת־בּוֹרְאֶךָ Ec 12^{1}, and (no obj. expressed) ψ 22^{28} (+ וישובו אל י׳); remember י׳'s name ψ 119^{55}. **4.** *remember*: **a.** words of Moses Jos 1^{13} (D) Mal 3^{22}; י׳'s instructions through prophet Is 44^{21} 46^{48} (‖ השיבו על לב), also Mi 6^{5} (sq. cl. with מה). **b.** commandments of י׳ (so as to do them) Nu 15^{39} (P, or H), v^{40} (P; + ועשיתם), ψ 103^{18} (+ לעשותם), 119^{52} (משפטים); his covenant 1 Ch 16^{15}. **5.** *think of* or *on*, *call to mind* something present or future:—sq. acc., issue of conduct Is 47^{7}, La 1^{9} (end of Jerusalem); fight with crocodile Jb 40^{32}; obj. a general truth, prosperity of wicked Jb 21^{6} (obj. not expr.); (fleeting) days of life Ec 5^{19}; (coming) days of darkness, 11^{8}; a duty Jb 36^{24} (sq. cl. with כִּי). **6.** *remember* a day, to observe, commemorate it:—day of Exodus Ex 13^{3} (J) Dt 16^{3}; sabbath Ex 20^{8} (E; ‖ שמר Dt 5^{12}). **7.** *remember*, with implied *mention of*, obj. י׳ Je 20^{9} (‖ דִּבֶּר בִּשְׁמוֹ); מַשָּׂא י׳ 23^{36}.

II. Subj. י׳ (אלהים). **1.** *remember* persons: **a.** individuals, with kindness, granting requests, protecting, delivering etc., c. acc. pers., Gn 30^{22} (E), 1 S 1^{11} (opp. שכח), v^{19}, Ju 16^{28} (sq. וְחַזְּקֵנִי); Je 15^{15} (‖ פָּקְדֵנִי), ψ 106^{4} (‖ *id.*), Jb 14^{13} (+ תשית לי חק), also Gn 8^{1} (P), 19^{29} (P); neg. ψ 88^{6} (‖ מידך נִגְזָרוּ); sq. לְ pers. ψ 25^{7} (yet cf. Che); sq. acc. rei + לְ pers. (dat. commod.) Ne 5^{19} 13$^{14.22.31}$. **b.** individuals, to punish, sq. לְ pers. Ne 6^{14} 13^{29}. **c.** his servants, people, the afflicted, (graciously) sq. לְ Ex 32^{13} (JE), Dt 9^{27} ψ 136^{23}; sq. acc. ψ 9^{13} (opp. שכח), 74^{2} 115^{12} (sq. יְבָרֵךְ); cf. Je 31^{20} (זכור זכר). **d.** his land Lv 26^{42} (H), and neg. La 2^{1} (his footstool). **e.** mankind ψ 8^{5} (‖ פקד). **2. a.** *remember* the distress of his servants, La 3^{19} (sq. cl. with מה), 5^{1} (‖ הַבִּיטָ וּרְאֵה). **b.** their devotion, acc., ψ 20^{4} Je 2^{2} (+ לְ pers.), ψ 132^{1} (+ *id.*); sq. cl. with את אשר 2 K 20^{3} = Is 38^{3}. **c.** their intercession Je 18^{20} (sq. inf. c. sf.) **3. a.** *remember* his own covenant (with them), acc., Gn 9$^{15.16}$ Ex 2^{24} 6^{25} (all P), Lv 26$^{42.42}$ (H, as also) v^{45} (+ לְ pers.); Je 14^{21} (+ אַל־תָּפֵר), Ez 16^{60} ψ 105^{8}, cf. v^{42} (obj. דְּבַר קָדְשׁוֹ), and 119^{49} Ne 1^{8}, ψ 106^{45} (+ לְ pers.), 111^{5}. **b.** his mercy, etc., acc., ψ 25^{6} 98^{3} 2 Ch 6^{42}; also Hb 3^{2}. **c.** extenuating circumstances, sq. cl. with כִּי, Jb 7^{7} 10^{9} ψ 78^{39} 103^{14} (זָכוּר *be-thinketh him*, Che, cf. De Kö$^{§20.14}$ Ba$^{NB 175}$); also ψ 89^{48} (sq. אֲנִי + epex. cl. with מה). **4.** *remember* sins, idolatries etc., sq. acc., Ho 7^{2} 8^{13} (‖ פקד), 9^{9} (‖ *id.*), Je 14^{10} (‖ *id.*); neg. Je 44^{21} (‖ עלה על לבו), Is 43^{25} 64^{8} ψ 25^{7} 79^{8} (+ לְ pers.); sq. לְ Je 31^{34}; also (obj. reproach) ψ 74$^{18.22}$ 89^{51}; and (obj. day of Jerusalem) ψ 137^{7} (+ לִבְנֵי אֱדוֹם, i.e. against them). **Niph.** *Pf.* 2 mpl. consec. וְנִזְכַּרְתֶּם Nu 10^{9}; *Impf.* 3 ms. יִזָּכֵר Je 11^{19}+; 3 fs. תִּזָּכֵר Ez 25^{10}, (תִּזָּכֵר) Ex 34^{19} rd. הַזָּכָר v. זָכָר); 2 fs. תִּזָּכְרִי Is 23^{16} Ez 21^{37}; 3 mpl. יִזָּכְרוּ Ho 2^{19}+; 3 fpl. תִּזָּכַרְנָה Is 65^{17}+; תִּזָּכַרְןָ Ez 3^{20}; *Inf. cstr.* sf. הִזָּכֶרְכֶם Ez 21^{29} (om. 𝔊 Co); *Pt.* pl. נִזְכָּרִים Est 9^{28}.—**1.** *be brought to remembrance, remembered, thought of*, usu. c. neg.:—**a.** in general, subj. Baalim Ho 2^{19} (+ בִּשְׁמָם), cf. Zc 13^{2} (‖ אכרית); former heaven and earth Is 65^{17} (‖ עלה על לב); (wicked) dead Jb 24^{20} (‖ ישכחהו v^{a}); coral (not to be thought of [others, *be mentioned*] in comparison with wisdom) Jb 28^{18}; of *attention paid* to Tyre under fig. of harlot Is 23^{16} (opp. נשכחה). **b.** *brought to* י׳*'s remembrance*, subj. the people, (1) with gracious result Nu 10^{9} (P; לפני י׳, ‖ וְנוֹשַׁעְתֶּם); (2) for judgment Ez 21^{29} (om. 𝔊 Co). **c.** *be remembered* by י׳, neg. of deeds, as affecting י׳'s judgment, (1) righteous Ez 3^{20} 18^{24} 33^{13} (sq. לְ of advantage, acc. to Co); (2) wicked 18^{22} (sq. לְ, om. A B 𝔙 etc., Co) 33^{16} (sq. לְ). **d.** *be remembered* אֶל־י׳ ψ 109^{14} (‖ אַל־תִּמָּח). **2.** neg. *be not remembered* = no longer exist, of name of Israel, as nation Je 11^{19} (‖ נכרת), ψ 83^{5} (‖ נַכְחִידֵם מִגּוֹי); of Ammonites Ez 21^{37} 25^{10}. **3.** *be remembered*, of particular days, in order to be observed, commemorated, Est 9^{28} (sq. וְנַעֲשִׂים *observe, celebrate*). **Hiph.** *Pf.* 3 ms. הִזְכִּיר Is 49^{1}; 2 ms. sf. 1 s. וְהִזְכַּרְתַּנִי consec. Gn 40^{14}; *Impf.* 3 ms. יַזְכִּיר Is 19^{17}; 1 s. אַזְכִּיר Ex 20^{24}+, etc.; *Imv.* ms. sf. 1 s. הַזְכִּירֵנִי Is 43^{26}; mpl. הַזְכִּירוּ Is 12^{4} Je 4^{16}; *Inf. cstr.* (לְ)הַזְכִּיר 2 S 18^{18}+; sf. 3 ms. כְּהַזְכִּירוֹ 1 S 4^{18}; sf. 2 mpl. הַזְכַּרְכֶם Ez 21^{29} (cf. Sta^{§245} Kö$^{§29.11}$); *Pt.* מַזְכִּיר Gn 41^{9}+, etc.; fs. מַזְכֶּרֶת Nu 5^{15};—**1.** *cause to remember, remind*, c. acc. pers. Is 43^{26}. **2.** *cause to be remembered, keep in remembrance*, c. acc. rei, a person's name 2 S 18^{18} ψ 45^{18}; of י׳, causing his name to be remembered, by some token, Ex 20^{24} (JE). **3.** *mention*, **a.** sq. acc. pers. Gn 40^{14} (E; sq. אֶל־ pers.), י׳, = *call upon* Is 62^{6}, name of י׳ 26^{13} 49^{1} (‖ קראני), name of other gods, neg., Ex 23^{13} (JE; ‖ יִשָּׁמַע); sq. בְּשֵׁם Am 6^{10}, cf. ψ 20^{8} (De Che al. *boast of, praise*, 𝔊 μεγαλυνθησόμεθα, whence Hup Bae prop. נַגְבִּיר (= *we display strength*), neg. Jos 23^{7} (D; || ולא תשביעו), so באלהי ישראל Is 48^{1} (|| הַנִּשְׁבָּעִים בְּשֵׁם). **b.** sq. acc. rei: faults Gn 41^{9} (E), the ark 1 S 4^{18}, land of Judah Is 19^{17}, Rahab (= Egypt) ψ 87^{4}, works of ׳י ψ 77^{12} (Kt, Qr Qal q.v.), his righteousness ψ 71^{16}, lovingkindness, Is 63^{7}; human love Ct 1^{4}; also in technical sense, apparently = *accuse* before God, alw. sq. עָוֺן, 1 K 17^{18} Nu 5^{15} (P) Ez 21^{28} v^{29} (sq. בְּהִגָּלוֹת פִּשְׁעֵיכֶם), 29^{16}. **c.** sq. cl., with כִּי Is 12^{4}; no conjunction Je 4^{16} (לְ indir. obj.; || הַשְׁמִיעוּ). **d.** abs. *commemorate, praise* 1 Ch 16^{4} (לְהַ׳, appar. Levitical function, sq. ולהודות ולהלל ליהוה), so perh. also לְהַזְכִּיר in titles ψ 38^{1} 70^{1} (others sub **5**). **4.** *record*, only pt. מַזְכִּיר as subst. (title of public officer) = *recorder* 2 S 8^{16} 20^{24} 1 K 4^{3} 2 K 18$^{18.37}$ = Is 36$^{3.22}$, 1 Ch 18^{15} 2 Ch 34^{8}. **5.** of sacrifice, *make a memorial*, i.e. offer an אַזְכָּרָה q.v.; sq. לְבֹנָה Is 66^{3}.—JPPeters [JBL, 1893, xii, 58] rds. אַזְכָּרָה ψ 42^{5} (v. **Qal I. 1**), 'let me make my *azkara*, and pour out libation for (עָלַי) my life.'

2144 †I. [זֶכֶר] **n.pr.m.** only זָ֑כֶר 1 Ch 8^{31} (𝔊 Ζαχουρ) = זְכַרְיָה 9^{37} q.v. (cf. Ph. n.pr. זכר).

2143 II. זֶ֫כֶר **n.m.** Ex 17^{14}, vid. following.

2143 †זֵ֫כֶר **n.m.**[ψ 9, 7] **remembrance, memorial** (cf. Hpt [Hbr. 1885, 230])—׳ז abs. ψ 111^{4}, cstr. Dt 25^{19}+; זֶכֶר cstr. Ex 17^{14} van d. H; sf. זִכְרִי Ex 3^{15}, זִכְרְךָ Is 26^{8}+, זִכְרֶ֑ךָ ψ 6^{6}, זִכְרוֹ Ho 12^{6}+, זִכְרָם Dt 32^{26}+:—**1.** *remembrance, memory:* **a.** of persons or people, blotted out by their destruction, Ex 17^{14} (E; c. מחה) = Dt 25^{19}, Dt 32^{26} (השבית) ψ 34^{17} 109^{15} (both הכרית), ψ 9^{7} (אבד), Jb 18^{17} (|| שֵׁם; אבד), Is 26^{14} (אבד); cf. on other hand ׳ז עוֹלָם as portion of righteous. **b.** of ׳י ψ 6^{6} 102^{13} (|| יהוה = אַתָּה). **c.** of ׳י's character and works ψ 30^{5} 97^{12} 111^{4}. **d.** *remembrance* of particular days, i.e. their observance Est 9^{28} (יְמֵי הַפּוּרִים). **2.** *memorial*, by which one is remembered: **a.** nearly = שֵׁם, ׳ז צַדִּיק לִבְרָכָה Pr 10^{7} (|| שֵׁם), cf. also Ec 9^{5} (c. נשכח); esp. of ׳י Ex 3^{15} (E), Ho 12^{6} Is 26^{8} ψ 135^{13} (all || שֵׁם). **b.** = renown (of Israel) Ho 14^{8} (cf. VB).

2145 †זָכָר **n.m. & adj.** male (As. *zikaru, zikru*, COT [Gloss] Lyon [Manual, Gloss]; Ar. ذَكَرٌ; Aram. דִּכְרָא, ܕܶܟܪܳܐ; Sab. ד[כ]רם DHM [ZMG 1876, 675]; relation to above √ obscure; male as *mentioned, talked of*, Lane [969 f.]; fr. assumed orig. sense *be sharp* (traces of this in Arab.: v. Lane), Bö [Prob 207] Fl in ChWB [i. 422], cf. Ar. ذَكَرٌ *male organ;* Schwally ZAW [1891, 176 ff.] fr. זָכַר = *call upon* in worship; hence *male* as *competent to worship*)—alw. abs. ׳ז Gn 1^{27}+; pl. (ה)זְכָרִים Ex 13^{12}+; vid. also [זָכוּר]:—**I.** subst. *male*, offspring of men and animals Ex 13$^{12.15}$ (pl., both JE); opp. נְקֵבָה Dt 4^{16}; specif. **1.** of men: **a.** in phr. אשר לא יָדְעָה אִישׁ לְמִשְׁכַּב זָכָר Ju 21^{12} (Bu [RS 153] Dr [Intr. 151]), cf. v^{11}, Nu 31$^{17.18.35}$ (all 3 P); צַלְמֵי זָכָר Ez 16^{17}. **b.** alone = *man* Je 30^{6} (גֶּבֶר || רְאוּ אִם־יֹלֵד זָכָר); usu. coll., *men, male persons* (of all ages) Ju 21^{11} 1 K 11$^{15.16}$, Gn 34^{25} Lv 6$^{11.22}$ 7^{6} Nu 1$^{2.20.22}$ 3$^{28.34.39}$ 18^{10} 26^{62} 31$^{7.17}$ (all P); pl. (ה)זכרים 2 Ch 31^{16} Ezr 8$^{3.4.5.6.7.8.9.10.11.12.13.14}$, so also Jos 5^{4} (|| כל־העם, and כל־אנשי המלחמה), 17^{2} (gloss? cf. Dr [Intr. 104]); esp. of individ., in connex. with circumcision Gn 17$^{10.12.14.23}$ 34$^{15.22.24}$ Ex 12^{48} (all P); of male child Lv 12^{2} (P) Is 66^{7}; opp. נְקֵבָה Gn 1^{27} 5^{2} Lv 12^{7} (child) 15^{33} 27$^{3.5.6.7}$ Nu 5^{3} (all P; cf. Sab. אנתים פאו ד(כ)רם DHM [l. c.]); opp. אִשָּׁה in command ag. sodomy Lv 18^{22} 20^{13} (both H). **2.** of animals, esp. for sacrifice Ex 34^{19} (JE; rd. הַזָּכָר for MT תִּזָּכָר); Ex 12^{5} Lv 1$^{3.10}$ 4^{23} (all P) 22^{19} (H), Mal 1^{14}; opp. נְקֵבָה Gn 6^{19} 7$^{3.9.16}$ Lv 3$^{1.6}$ (all P). **II.** adj. sg. *male* (only human beings) ׳יֻלַּד־לְךָ בֵּן ז Je 20^{15}; ׳כָּל־בְּכֹר ז Nu 3$^{40.43}$ (both P).

†[זָכוּר] **n.m.** male, i.q. זָכָר, but only c. sf.; 2138
—coll. כָּל־זְכוּרְךָ Ex 23^{17} = 34^{23} (both JE), = Dt 16^{16}, of attendance at feasts; כָּל־זְכוּרָהּ (of city refusing terms of peace) Dt 20^{13} commanded to be slain (opp. הַנָּשִׁים, הַטַּף, etc., v^{14}).

†זִכְרִי **n.pr.m.** 𝔊 Ζεχρει, Ζαχρι, etc., exc. as 2147
below:—**1.** a Reubenite 1 Ch 27^{16}. **2.** a Judahite 2 Ch 17^{16}. **3.** Levites: **a.** Ex 6^{21} (P). **b.** 1 Ch 26^{25}. **c.** an Asaphite 1 Ch 9^{15} || Ne 11^{17} where rd. זכרי (for זַבְדִּי, q.v.); cf. also *infr.* זַכּוּר **3 b.** **4.** a priest Ne 12^{17} (𝔊L Ζαχαριας). **5.** Benjamites: **a.** 1 Ch 8^{19}. **b.** v^{23}. **c.** v^{27}. **d.** Ne 11^{9}. **6.** father of a captain in Jehoiada's time 2 Ch 23^{1} (𝔊 Ζαχαρια, 𝔊L Ζεχρι). **7.** mighty man of Ephraim 2 Ch 28^{7} (𝔊 Ἐζεχρει, 𝔊L Ζαχαριας).

†זַכּוּר **n.pr.m.** 𝔊 Ζακχυρ, Ζακχουρ, etc.:— 2139
1. a Reubenite Nu 13^{4} (P). **2.** a Simeonite 1 Ch 4^{26}. **3.** Levites: **a.** 1 Ch 24^{27}. **b.** an Asaphite 1 Ch 25^{2} (Σακχους), v^{10} (Ζαχχουθ), Ne 12^{35} (Ζακχουρ), cf. זִכְרִי supr. **3 c.** **c.** Ne 10^{13} cf. 13^{13}. **4.** companion of Ezra, Ezr 8^{14} Qr (Kt זבוד, cf. supr. p. 256 a). **5.** contemp. of Nehemiah, Ne 3^{2}.

2146 †זִכָּרוֹן, זִכְּרֹן **n.m.**$^{Ec 1, 11}$ **memorial, remembrance** (cf. Lg$^{BN 199, 200}$)—abs. זִכָּרוֹן זִכָּרֹן Jos 4^{7}+; Ex 28$^{12.12.29}$; cstr. זִכְרוֹן Ec 1^{11}+2 t.; sf. זִכְרוֹנֵךְ Is 57^{8}; pl. הַזִּכְרֹנוֹת Est 6^{1}; sf. זִכְרֹנֵיכֶם Jb 13^{12};—**1.** *memorial, reminder:* **a.** memorial-day Ex 12^{14} (P). **b.** memorial-usage Ex 13^{9} (JE). **c.** memorial-objects, altar-plates Nu 17^{5}(P); stones in Jordan Jos 4^{7} (JE); crowns in temple Zc 6^{14}; ז׳ in Is 57^{8} is symbol of strange god (Di), or perh. phallus-image, as sign of harlot (Che), cf. >Du (who prop. זִכָּרוֹן, from זָכָר). **d.** memorial-record; in a book Ex 17^{14} (E); cf. סֵפֶר זִכָּרוֹן Mal 3^{16}, ס׳ הַזִּכְרֹנוֹת דברי הימים Est 6^{1}; memorial, as proof of citizenship Ne 2^{20} (|| צְדָקָה, חֵלֶק); reminder of Israel, לִפְנֵי י׳, of כֶּסֶף הַכִּפֻּרִים Ex 30^{16}; spoils of war Nu 31^{54}; inscribed stones of ephod Ex 28$^{12.29}$, called אַבְנֵי ז׳ v^{12}=39^{7}; blowing of trumpets Nu 10^{10} (foregoing all P), cf. זִכְרוֹן תְּרוּעָה Lv 23^{24} (H; where, however, no לִפְנֵי י׳, v. Di); מִנְחַת (ה)זכרון Nu 5$^{15.18}$ (P); *memorial-sentence, apophthegm* Jb 13^{12}. **2.** *remembrance* Ec 1^{11} (cstr. before prep. Ges$^{§ 130, 1}$), v^{11} 2^{16}.

2148 †זְכַרְיָהוּ, oftener זְכַרְיָה **n.pr.m.** (Sab. ידכראל DHM$^{Epigr. Denkm. 43}$) 𝔊 Ζαχαρια(ς), etc.:—**1.** זכריהו, king of Isr., son of Jerob. II, 2 K 15^{8} = זכריה 14^{29} 15^{11}. **2.** זכריהו, father of Hezekiah's mother 2 Ch 29^{1} = זכריה 2 K 18^{2}. **3.** זכריהו, contemporary of Isaiah Is 8^{2}. **4.** זכריהו, a Reubenite 1 Ch 5^{7}. **5.** זכריה, a Benjamite 1 Ch 9^{37} (𝔊 Ζαχαρια, A Ζαχχουρ 𝔊L Ζεχρει) = זָכֶר 1 Ch 8^{31} (v. I. [זָכַר]). **6.** זכריהו, a Manassite 1 Ch 27^{21} (𝔊 Ζαβδειου, 𝔊L Ζαχαριου). **7.** זכריהו, a son of Jehoshaphat 2 Ch 21^{2}. **8.** זכריה, a captain of Jehosh. 2 Ch 17^{7}. **9.** זכריהו, teacher of Uzziah 2 Ch 26^{5}. **10.** Levites, זכריהו: **a.** 1 Ch 15^{18} = זכריה v^{20}, 16^{5}. **b.** 1 Ch 24^{25}. **c.** 1 Ch 26$^{2.14}$. **d.** 1 Ch 26^{11}. **e.** 2 Ch 20^{14}. **f.** 2 Ch 29^{13} (𝔊 Ἀζαριας, A Ζαχαριας, so 𝔊L). זכריה: **g.** 1 Ch 9^{21}. **h.** 2 Ch 34^{12}. **i.** an Asaphite Ne 12^{35}. **11.** priests, זכריהו: **a.** 1 Ch 15^{24}. **b.** 2 Ch 35^{8}. זכריה: **c.** 2 Ch 24^{20} (𝔊 Ἀζαριαν; 𝔊L Ζαχαριαν; prob. referred to Matt 23^{35}, where appar. confusion with **f**). **d.** Ne 11^{12}. **e.** Ne 12^{41}. **f.** the well-known prophet Zc 1$^{1.7}$ 7$^{1.8}$ Ne 12^{16} [cf. Aram. Ezr 5^{1} 6^{14}]. **12.** returned exiles, זכריה: **a.** Ezr 8^{3} and perh. v^{16}, cf. Ne 8^{4}. **b.** Ezr 8^{11} (𝔊 Ἀζαριας, A Ζαχαριας, so 𝔊L). **c.** Ezr 10^{26}. **d.** a man of Judah Ne 11^{4}. **e.** *id.* Ne 11^{5} (𝔊 Θηζεια, א Θηδεια, A Ζαχαριου, so 𝔊L).

234 †אַזְכָּרָה **n.f. memorial-offering**, only P (an Aram. inf. form; cf. Ba$^{NB 90}$ Sta$^{§ 244}$)—abs. א׳ Lv 24^{7}; sf. אַזְכָּרָתָהּ Lv 2^{2}+5 t.;—used of the frankincense burned for the shew-bread והיתה ללחם לאז׳ אִשֶּׁה לי׳ Lv 24^{7}; elsewh. alw. after הקטיר, only c. sf., referring to מִנְחָה Lv 2$^{2.9.16}$ 6^{8} Nu 5^{26}; of the meal used as חַטָּאת by the very poor Lv 5^{12}; alw. connected with אִשֶּׁה, exc. Lv 6^{8} Nu 5^{26}.

מַזְכִּיר **n.m.** recorder, v. זָכַר **Hiph.** p. 270 2142

זלא (√ of foll.; meaning unknown).

†יִזְלִיאָה **n.pr.m.** a Benjamite 1 Ch 8^{18} (𝔊 3152
Ζαρεια, A Εζλια, 𝔊L Ἰεζελια).

זלג (Ar. زَلَجَ *glide, slip;* of arrow, *skim, slide along;* مِزْلَاجٌ a kind of *latch, sliding bolt;* Aram. זְלַג is *pour forth* (tears), *flow down*).

†מַזְלֵג **n.m.** appar. a sacrificial implement, 4207
three-pronged fork הַמַּ׳ שְׁלֹשׁ הַשִּׁנַּיִם 1 S 2^{13}, cf. v^{14} (v. Dr$^{Sm. pp. 23, 291}$).

†[מִזְלָגָה] **n.[f.]** id., only pl. הַמִּזְלָגֹת Ex 38^{3} 4207
Nu 4^{14}; הַמִּזְלָגוֹת 1 Ch 28^{17} 2 Ch 4^{16}; sf. מִזְלְגֹתָיו Ex 27^{3};—a sacrificial implement, belonging to altar in tabernacle, Ex 27^{3} 38^{3} Nu 4^{14} (all P); belonging to temple 1 Ch 28^{17} 2 Ch 4^{16}.

†I. [זָלַל] **vb. shake** (Ar. زَلَّ *slip,* زَلْزَلَ *agi-* 2151
tate, shake; تَزَلْزَلَ *be agitated, quake,* esp. of earth-quake)—**Niph.** *Pf.* נָזֹלּוּ *shake, quake* Is 63^{19} of mts. at י׳'s presence (Ges De Che Di Du; 𝔊 𝔙 as if fr. נזל *flow down*); so 64^{2} (but here prob. not original Che Di Du); read נָזֹלּוּ likewise Ju 5^{5} (𝔊 Thes Stu Be Bla MV SS; MT נָזְלוּ, fr. נזל).

†[זַלְזַל] **n.[m.]** (quivering) **tendrils**;— 2150
only pl. *tendrils* of vine הַזַּלְזַלִּים Is 18^{5} (|| הַנְּטִישׁוֹת), in fig. of Yahweh's destroying the Assyrians.

†II. [זָלַל] **vb. 1. be light, worthless, 2.** 2151
make light of (As. *zalâlu, be in ruins,* COT^{Gloss} (Asrn$^{Standard Inscr. 15}$), Ar. ذَلَّ = Aram. ܙܠ (rare), ܙܠܝܠ, *easy;* but זְלַל, ܙܠ, are more common (all intrans.))—**Qal** only *Pt.* act. זוֹלֵל Dt 21^{20}+2 t.; זוֹלֵלָה La 1^{11}; pl. זוֹלְלִים Pr 28^{7}, cstr. זֹלְלֵי Pr 23^{20}—**1.** *be worthless, insignificant* Je 15^{19} (opp. יָקָר) La 1^{11} (of Jerusalem in distress). **2.** trans. *make light of=be lavish with, squander* (cf. II. זול), esp. of gluttony ז׳ בשׂר Pr 23^{20} (|| סֹבְאֵי יַיִן), abs. v^{21} Dt 21^{20} (both || סֹבֵא), Pr 28^{7}.

Hiph. *Pf.* sf. הֱזִילוּהָ La 1[8] causat. of **Qal 1** *make light of, despise* (opp. כִּבֵּד); on form cf. Ges§ 67, R. 8 RobGes, MV SS (>assigned to זול by Thes Kö Lgb. i. 471).

2149 †**זֻלּוּת** **n.f. worthlessness**, only כְּרֻם זֻלֻּת לִבְנֵי אָדָם ψ 12[9] [van d. H. זֻלּוֹת] cf. De & Che crit. n.

זלעף (quadrilit. √ of foll.; v. reff. infr.)

2152 †**זַלְעָפָה** **n.f. raging heat** (on format. cf. Ges Lbg 863 Ol § 196 a. 1. 2)—ז׳ ψ 119[53]; pl. abs. זַלְעָפוֹת ψ 11[6]; cstr. זַלְעֲפוֹת La 5[10];—**1.** of fever heat of famine ז׳ רָעָב La 5[10]. **2.** of burning wind רוּחַ ז׳ ψ 11[6] (in fig. of י׳'s judgment, with אֵשׁ, גָּפְרִית). **3.** fig. of zeal ז׳ אֲחָזַתְנִי ψ 119[53].

2153 **זלף** (√ of foll.; Thes comp. Aram. זְלַף Pa. *drop, drip;* cf. ܙܠܰܦ; also NH זִלּוּף *sprinkling,* ܙܠܳܦܳܐ *dropping, pouring,* زَلَفَةٌ a *full bowl,* etc.)

†**זִלְפָּה** **n.pr.f.** Leah's maid, one of Jacob's wives, mother of Gad and Asher Gn 29[24] 30[9.10.12] (all J), 35[26] 37[2] 46[18] (all P).

2161 †**זָמַם** **vb. consider, purpose, devise** (Aram. זְמַם in der. conjj.; cf. Ar. زَمَّ *speak, talk* (rare); Aram. ܙܳܡ is *sonuit, resonavit,* the n. ܙܡܳܡܳܐ is *tinnitus, strepitus*) — only **Qal** *Pf.* זָמַם Dt 19[19] + 2t.; זָמַם La 2[17]; זָֽמְמָה Pr 31[16]; זַמּוֹתָ Pr 30[32]; זַמֹּתִי Je 4[28] but also זָמַמְתִּי Zc 8[14.15]; זַמֹּתִי ψ 17[3] either belongs here with irreg. accent (v. De), or is Inf. after anal. of ל״ה e.g. חֲנוֹת cf. 77[10] (Hi Ri); Che crit. n. rds. זַמֹּתִי; זָמְמוּ ψ 31[14]; *Impf.* יָזְמוּ Gn 11[6] (Ges § 67, R. 11); on poss. *Inf.* זַמֹּתִי ψ 17[3] v. supr.; *Pt.* זֹמֵם ψ 37[12];—**1.** *consider, fix thought upon,* c. acc. of concrete obj. שָׂדֶה Pr 31[16]. **2.** *purpose, devise:* **a.** esp. of Yahweh's purpose in punishment Je 4[28] (abs.), 51[12] sq. עשׂה + acc. (|| מְזִמָּה), La 2[17] (sq. אשׁר) Zc 1[6] (c. כֵּן sq. inf.), 8[14] (*id.*); of blessing only כאשׁר שַׁבְתִּי זָמַמְתִּי לְהֵיטִיב Zc 8[15] (opp. v[14]). **b.** of evil purpose of wicked men אשׁר יז׳ לעשׂות Gn 11[6] Dt 19[19] (c. כאשׁר + inf.), ψ 31[14] (sq. inf.); abs. Pr 30[32] (|| נבל), ψ 17[3] *have I* (i.e. if I have) *devised evil* (so De); sq. לְ pers. (= *against*) ψ 37[12].

2162 †**[זָמָם]** **n.[m.] plan, device** (bad sense), only זְמָמוֹ ψ 140[9] (|| מַאֲוַיֵּי רָשָׁע).

2154 †I. **זִמָּה** **n.f. plan, device, wickedness**—abs. ז׳ Lv 18[17] + 17 t.; cstr. זִמַּת Pr 24[9] + 2 t.; sf. זִמָּתֵךְ Ez 16[58] + 3t.; זִמַּתְכֶנָה Ez 23[48.49]; pl. זִמּוֹת Is 32[7], sf. זִמֹּתַי Jb 17[11];—**1.** *plan, purpose* Jb 17[3]; elsewhere always **2.** in bad sense: **a.** *evil device* Is 32[7] (c. יעץ, sq. לְחַבֵּל); זִמַּת אִוֶּלֶת Pr 24[9]; cf. ψ 26[10] (|| שֹׁחַד), 119[150]. **b.** *wickedness* in act עשׂה ז׳ Ho 6[9] (where murder in context), Pr 10[23] 21[27] cf. Now. Esp. **c.** of unchastity: incest Lv 18[17] 20[14.14], licentiousness 19[29] (all H), Ju 20[6] (|| נְבָלָה), adultery Jb 31[11]; freq. (mostly Ez) metaph. of idolatry of people under fig. of harlotry and adultery Je 13[27] (זִמַּת זְנוּתֵךְ), Ez 16[27] (דַּרְכֵּךְ זִמָּה), v[43.58] (both || תּוֹעֵבָה), 22[9] (c. עשׂה), v[11] (|| תועבה, טִמֵּא בְזִמָּה), 23[21.27] (|| זְנוּתֵךְ), v[29] (|| עֶרְוַת זְנוּנַיִךְ וְזִמָּתֵךְ וְתַזְנוּתַיִךְ), v[35] (|| תַּזְנוּתַיִךְ), v[44] (אִשֹּׁת הַז׳), Co (לעשׂות ז׳), v[48.48.49] (|| חֲטָאֵי גִלּוּלֵיכֶן), 24[13]. [In Ez 16[27.43] 24[13] del. Co, chiefly on intern. grounds.]

†II. **זִמָּה** **n.pr.m.** of several Levites (Gershonites)—**1.** 1 Ch 6[5]. **2.** 1 Ch 6[27]. **3.** 2 Ch 29[12]. 2155

†**מְזִמָּה** **n.f. purpose, discretion, device** (Je and WisdLt), מְזִמָּה Jb 42[2] + 5 t.; הַמְזִמָּתָה Je 11[15] (but rd. for הַמְּ׳ רַבִּים with 𝔊 הַמְזִמּוֹת הַנְּדָרִים); מְזִמָּתוֹ Je 51[11]; pl. abs. מְזִמּוֹת ψ 37[7] + 7 t.; cstr. id. Je 23[20] 30[24]; sf. מְזִמּוֹתָיו ψ 10[4];—**1.** of י׳'s *purposes* Jb 42[2]; chiefly in punishment (cf. זָמַם, זִמָּה) Je 23[20] 30[24] 51[11] (|| זמם v[12]). **2.** *power of devising, discretion* Pr 1[4] (|| דַּעַת), 2[11] (|| תְּבוּנָה), 3[21] (|| תֻּשִׁיָּה), 5[2] (|| דַּעַת); דַּעַת מְזִמּוֹת 8[12]. **3. a.** evil *thoughts* of men ψ 10[4], evil *devices* of men Jb 21[27] (|| מחשׁבות), ψ 10[2] 21[12] (both c. חָשַׁב). **b.** *wickedness* in act Je 11[15] ψ 37[7] (both c. עָשָׂה), 139[20] לִמְזִמָּה = *wickedly;*—note phrases: אִישׁ מְזִמּוֹת *a man of (evil) devices* (or *practices*) Pr 12[2] (opp. טוֹב) 14[17]; בַּעַל־מְזִמּוֹת Pr 24[8] (|| מְחַשֵּׁב לְהָרֵעַ; v. בַּעַל). 4209

†**זַמְזֻמִּים** **n.pr.gent.** said to be a name given to רְפָאִים by the Ammonites who dispossessed them Dt 2[20] (cf. Ar. زَمْزَمَ *talk gibberish?*), 𝔊 Ζοχομμιν, Ζομζομμειν, and Ζομμειν (so 𝔊L); cf. Gn 14[5] זוּזִים q.v. (𝔊 ἔθνη ἰσχυρά). 2157

†**[זָמַן]** **vb.** (Aram. and late) only **Pu.** *Pt.* **be fixed, appointed,** of time (Ar. زَمِنَ *continue,* Aram. Pa. זַמֵּן, ܙܰܡܶܢ *summon to fixed time* or *place, invite, appoint;* cf. זְמָן infr.)—עִתִּים מְזֻמָּנִים Ezr 10[14] Ne 10[35]; עִ׳ מְזֻמָּנוֹת Ne 13[31]. 2163

†**זְמָן** **n.m.** (late) **appointed time, time** (Ar. زَمَن, Eth. ዘመን: BAram. 𝔗 זְמַן, but Syr. ܙܒܰܢ, Mand. זיבנא, Sam. ࠆࠁࠍ, Palm. זבנא, cf. Reckendorf ZMG 1888, 394)—sg. זְמָן Ne 2[6] Ec 3[1]; sf. 2165

וְבִזְמַנָּם Est 9^{27}, בִּזְמַנֵּיהֶם v^{31} (on Dagh. cf. Ges $§20.2.c$).

2167 †I. [זמר] **vb.** only **Pi.** **make music** in praise of God ('י), only poet. (Ar. زَمَرَ *pipe, play* on a reed; Aram. ܙܡܰܪ, זַמֵּר and deriv.; Eth. ዘመረ: in der. conjj.; on an orig. mng. *hum, murmur*, cf. Hup ZKM iii, (1840) 394 ff. iv, 139 ff. Id Psalm. Einl. §7.2 De[4] on ψ 3) — **Pi.** *Impf.* 3 ms. sf. יְזַמֶּרְךָ ψ 30^{13}; 1 s. אֲזַמֵּר Ju 5^{3} 2 S 22^{50}; אֲזַמְּרָה(!) ψ 7^{18} + 7 t., אֲזַמְּרָה ψ 18^{50} + 3 t.; sf. אֲזַמֶּרְךָ ψ 57^{10} 108^{4}, וַיְזַמְּרוּ אֲזַמְּרֶךָּ ψ 131^{1}; 3 mpl. יְזַמְּרוּ ψ 66^{4} 149^{3}; ψ 66^{4}; 1 pl. נְזַמְּרָה ψ 21^{14}; *Imv.* mpl. זַמְּרוּ ψ 9^{12} + 14 t., זַמֵּרוּ ψ $47^{7.7}$; *Inf.* לְזַמֵּר ψ 92^{2}, זַמְּרָה ψ 147^{1}; —*make music, melody* (only ψψ, exc. Ju 5^{3} Is 12^{5});—**1.** of *singing* to (ל) God (Yahweh) Ju 5^{3} ψ 27^{6} 101^{1} 104^{33} 105^{2} = 1 Ch 16^{9} (all ‖ שׁיר vb.), ψ 9^{12} 30^{5} (both ‖ הודו), 47^{7} (לְמַלְכֵּנוּ), 66^{4} 71^{23} (with תְּרַנֵּנָּה שְׂפָתַי), 75^{10} (‖ הגיד), 146^{2} (‖ הלל); sq. אֶל־ 59^{18}; to his name לְשֵׁם, ψ 18^{50} = 2 S 22^{50} (‖ אודך), ψ 92^{2} (‖ לְהֹדוֹת), 135^{3} (‖ הללויה); sq. sf. = *sing thee, praise thee in song* ψ 30^{13} 57^{10} 108^{4} 138^{1} (all ‖ אודך); sq. acc 'י Is 12^{5}, אלהים ψ 47^{7}, אלהינו 147^{1}, אדני 68^{33} (‖ שירו), sq. שְׁמוֹ 7^{18} (‖ אודה), 9^{3} 61^{9} 66^{4} 68^{5} (‖ שירו); sq. כְּבוֹד שְׁמוֹ 66^{2}, גבורתך 21^{14} (‖ נשירה); sq. acc. of the song, מַשְׂכִּיל ψ 47^{8} (v. מ' sub שׂכל); abs. 57^{8} (‖ אשירה), 98^{4} (‖ רַנְּנוּ, פִּצְחוּ, הָרִיעוּ), 108^{2} (‖ אשירה); instrumental accomp. v^{3}; cf. also v^{4} *supr.*), $47^{7.7}$. **2.** of playing musical instruments בְּנֵבֶל עָשׂוֹר זַמְּרוּ־לוֹ ψ 33^{2} (‖ הודו לי' בְּכִנּוֹר), cf. 144^{9} (‖ אשירה); אזמרה ז' לי' בכנור בכנור 71^{22} (‖ אודך בִכְלִי־נֶבֶל); ז' 147^{7} (‖ ענו לי' בתודה) ז' לא' בכנור; 98^{5} בכנור וקול זמרה יזמרו לו בְּתֹף וכנור 149^{3} (‖ יהללו שמו בְמָחוֹל).

2172 †I. זִמְרָה **n.f. melody, song,** in praise of
2176 'י—abs. ז' ψ 81^{3} + 2 t.; זִמְרָת Ex 15^{2} ψ 118^{14} Is 12^{2}, rd. (י)זִמְרָתִ (v. Di[Ex] SS); cstr. זִמְרַת Am 5^{23}, on Gn 43^{11} v. infr.;—**1.** of instrumental music וְזִמְרַת נְבָלֶיךָ Am 5^{23} (‖ המון שִׁרֶיךָ). **2.** of singing תּוֹדָה וקול ז' Is 51^{3}; as *subject* of song עָזִּי וְזִמְרָתִי יָהּ (so rd.) Ex 15^{2} Is 12^{2} ψ 118^{14}. **3.** not clearly determined שְׂאוּ־ז' וּתְנוּ־תֹף כנור נעים עִם־נָבֶל: ψ 81^{3}; בכנור וקול ז' 98^{5} (cf. III. זמר ad fin.).—On מִזִּמְרַת הארץ Gn 43^{11} v. II. זמרה infr.

2176 זִמְרָת v. I. זִמְרָה. above

2158 †I. [זָמִיר] **n.m.** Is 25, 5 **song** (cf. Ba[NB 136])—cstr. זְמִיר Is 25^{5}; pl. abs. זְמִרוֹת Jb 35^{10} + 2 t., זְמִרֹת Is 24^{16}; cstr. זְמִרוֹת 2 S 23^{1};—*song* נְעִים זְמִרוֹת יִשְׂרָאֵל 2 S 23^{1} in epith. of David; Jb 35^{10} Is 24^{16}; of (hostile) song of triumph זְמִיר עָרִיצִים Is 25^{5} (‖ שְׁאוֹן זָרִים); song in praise of 'י ז' היו לי חֻקֶּיךָ ψ 95^{2} (‖ תודה), cf. בִּזְמִרוֹת נָרִיעַ לוֹ 119^{54}, i.e. they are the subject of my song.—On Ct 2^{12} v. II. זמיר sub II. זמר.

†מִזְמוֹר **n.[m.] melody** (techn. design. of psalms; cf. Hup Psalm. Einl. §7, 2 De[4] on ψ 3, Bae Psalmen, xiii; ܡܙܡܘܪܐ, مَزَامِير, መዝሙር: loan-wds., all = *Psalm(s)*; on מ', in relation to תהלה cf. Lg Or ii. 22 f.), always in this form; in 57 ψ-titles:—מ' alone ψ 98^{1}, מ' שיר ליום הַשַּׁבָּת 92^{1}, מ' לְתוֹדָה 100^{1}; usu. with pers. name or title; מ' לְדָוִד ψ 3^{1} 15^{1} 23^{1} 29^{1} 63^{1} 141^{1} 143^{1}, שיר מ' 108^{1}, מ' לדוד לְהַזְכִּיר 38^{1}, מ' שִׁיר־חֲנֻכַּת הבית 30^{1}, לדוד מ' 24^{1} 101^{1} 110^{1}, לַמְנַצֵּחַ מ' לדוד לַמְנַצֵּחַ . . . 13^{1} 19^{1} 20^{1} 21^{1} 31^{1} 41^{1} 51^{1} 64^{1} 140^{1}; לַמְנַצֵּחַ מ' לדוד 4^{1} 5^{1} 6^{1} 8^{1} 9^{1} 12^{1} 22^{1} 39^{1} 62^{1}, למנצח לדוד מ' 40^{1} 109^{1} 139^{1}, למנצח לדוד מ' שיר 65^{1}, למנצח לדוד מ' שיר 68^{1}; also simply לַמְנַצֵּחַ מ' שיר ψ 67^{1}, לַמְנַצֵּחַ שיר מ' 66^{1}; but also שיר מ' לבני־קֹרַח ψ 48^{1}, לִבְנֵי־קֹרַח מ' שיר 87^{1}, שיר מ' לבני קרח לַמְנַצֵּחַ לבני־ 88^{1} . . . מַשְׂכִּיל לְהֵימָן הָאֶזְרָחִי לַמְנַצֵּחַ . . . לבני־קרח מ' 47^{1} 49^{1} 85^{1}, למנצח . . . קרח מ' 84^{1}; further מ' לְאָסָף ψ 50^{1} 73^{1} 79^{1} 82^{1}, שיר מ' לאסף 83^{1}, לַמְנַצֵּחַ . . . מ' לאסף שיר 75^{1} 76^{1}, לַמְנַצֵּחַ . . . לאסף מ' 77^{1} 80^{1}. [Summary:—מ' in 34 ψψ with לַמְנַצֵּחַ, of wh. 23 have לדוד also, 5 לבני קרח also, 4 לאסף, and 2 no n.pr.; in addit., in 13 ψψ with לדוד, 2 with לבני קרח, 5 with לאסף; in only 3 without either n.pr. or title; מ' is preceded by שִׁיר 5 t., and foll. by שִׁיר 8 t.] 4210

II. [זָמַר] **vb. trim, prune** (NH *id.*; relation to ✓I. obscure)—**Qal** *Impf.* 2 ms. תִּזְמֹר Lv $25^{3.4}$ of pruning a vineyard (כֶּרֶם; H). **Niph.** *Impf.* יִזָּמֵר Is 5^{6} *be pruned*, subj. כֶּרֶם (‖ יֵעָדֵר). 2168

†II. זָמִיר **n.[m.] trimming, pruning** (cf. Lg[BN 173])—only עֵת הַזָּמִיר Ct 2^{12} (> others *singing*).—I. זמיר v. sub I. זמר supr. 2159

†זְמוֹרָה **n.[f.] branch, twig, shoot**—abs. ז' Nu 13^{23}, הַזּ' Ez 8^{17} 15^{2}; cstr. זְמֹרַת Is 17^{10}; sf. זְמֹרֵיהֶם Na 2^{3};—*branch* of grape-vine Nu 13^{23} (JE), Ez 15^{2}; *branch, twig* (Co *Reissigbündel*) used in idolatrous worship הַזּ' אֶל־אַפָּם Ez 8^{17} (v. Sm and most), but custom obscure (v. Da), and txt. dub.; זְמֹרַת זָר (cf. Ew § 287 b) Is 17^{10} *twigs of a strange one* (i.e. of a strange god) fig. of idolatrous cults adopted by Isr.; ז' pl. in fig. of Israelites Na 2^{3}. 2156

4211 †[מַזְמֵרָה] **n.f. pruning-knife**, only pl. לְמַזְמֵרוֹת וְכָרַת הַזַּלְזַלִּים בַּמַּזְמֵרוֹת Is 18[5]; לְמַזְמֵרוֹת Is 2[4] Mi 4[3] (both ‖ לְאִתִּים); וּמַזְמְרֹתֵיכֶם Jo 4[1] (‖ אִתֵּיכֶם).

4212 †[מְזַמֶּרֶת] **n.f. snuffers**, as utensil of Sol.'s temple, only pl. abs. מְזַמְּרוֹת 2 K 12[14], הַמְזַמְּרוֹת 1 K 7[50] = 2 Ch 4[22], 2 K 25[14] = Je 52[18].

III. **זמר** (√of foll.; mng. dub.; DHM in MV[10. 983] comp. Ar. ذِمَارٌ *thing to be protected, thing sacred, inviolable*, Lane[978], Sab. דמר *protect;* Aram. ܬܡܰܗ *wonder at, admire*, ܬܡܺܝܗܳܐ *mirus, admirabilis*, etc.; hence זמרת Gn 43[11] 'die Merkwürdigkeiten des Landes').

2173 †II. **זִמְרָה n.f.** of uncertain meaning, perh. **choice products** (cf. DHM supr.), of various fruits, etc. מִזִּמְרַת הארץ Gn 43[11]; 𝔊 οἱ καρποί, so MV Str.; > *music*, or *praise of the land*, fig. for produce (√I. זמר) Thes Tu Kn SS.—I. ז׳ v. sub I. זמר

Uncertain in deriv. are the five foll.:—

2169 †[זֶמֶר] **n.[m.]** a certain animal allowed as food, most prob. some kind of *mountain-sheep* or *-goat* (𝔊 تَيْتَل) וָזָמֶר Dt 14[5]. (AV RV *chamois:* but see Tristram[DB 2. s.v.], who points out that this is not a native of any Bible land.)

2174 †I. **זִמְרִי n.pr.m.** 𝔊 Ζαμβρ(ε)ι—**1.** a Simeonite Nu 25[14] (P). **2.** grandson of Judah 2 Ch 2[6] (app. = זַבְדִּי Jos 7[1] q.v.) **3.** king of Isr. before Omri 1 K 16[9. 10. 12. 15. 16. 18. 20] 2 K 9[31]. **4.** a Benjamite 1 Ch 8[36. 36] = 9[42. 42].

2174 †II. **זִמְרִי n.pr.gent.** vel **patr.**, only מַלְכֵי ז׳ Je 25[25] (+ מלכי עֵילָם and מלכי מָדָי); = Ζεμβρῖται in Ethiopia (Strabo[xvii. i. 786])? cf. Gf; om. 𝔊; interpol. acc. to Kue Gie.

2175 †**זִמְרָן n.pr.m.** son of Abraham & Keturah, 𝔊 Ζε(μ)βραν Gn 25[2] and 1 Ch 1[32] (𝔊L here Ζεμραμ). On locality referred to v. Di.

2160 †**זְמִירָה n.pr.m.** a Benjamite, 1 Ch 7[8], 𝔊 Ἀμαριας; 𝔊A, 𝔊L Ζαμαρια(ς).

2177 †**זַן n.[m.]** (late) **kind, sort** (Aram. ܙܢܳܐ, זַן; √ dub.; cf. De ψ 144[13])—מִזַּן אֶל זַן ψ 144[13] *from kind to kind*, i.e. *all sorts, kinds;* pl. וּזְנִים 2 Ch 16[14] (various) *sorts*.

זנב (√of foll.; meaning unknown).

2180 †**זָנָב n.m.**[Ju 15, 4] **tail**, also (fig.) **end, stump** (NH *id.*, As. *zibbatu* Hom[NS 368], Eth. ዝነብ: Ar. ذَنَبٌ, Aram. ܕܽܘܢܒܳܐ, דּוּנְבָא, דְּנַבָּא)—ז׳ abs. Ju 15[4. 4] + 5 t.; sf. זְנָבוֹ Jb 40[17]; pl. זְנָבוֹת Ju 15[4]; cstr. זַנְבוֹת Is 7[4];—**1. a.** *tail* of fox Ju 15[4. 4. 4], of serpent Ex 4[4] (J), of hippopot. Jb 40[17]; **b.** fig. of common people, opp. to rulers Is 9[13] 19[15] (in both, רֹאשׁ וְזָנָב ‖ כִּפָּה וְאַגְמוֹן; Is 9[14] is incorrect gloss); of subject-people (opp. ראשׁ) Dt 28[13. 44]. **2.** *end, stump* (of firebrand, אוּד) in metaph. Is 7[4].

†[זִנֵּב] **vb.denom. Pi. cut off**, or **smite, the tail**, only fig., of hostile attack in war; 2179
Pf. consec. 2 mpl. וְזִנַּבְתֶּם Jos 10[19] (sq. אֹתָם); *Impf.* 3 ms. וַיְזַנֵּב בְּךָ כָּל־הַנֶּחֱשָׁלִים Dt 25[18]; in both = *attack* or *smite in the rear.*

†**זָנָה vb. commit fornication, be a harlot** (Ar. زَنَى *commit fornication*, Aram. ܙܢܳܐ, זנא; cf. Eth. ዝንየት: *effusio seminis virilis, semen effusum*, Di[1055]; on this and ዘመወ: (comp. by Ges al.) v. Prät[BAS i. 32, Anm.])—**Qal** *Pf.* ז׳ Dt 31[16], זָנְתָה Gn 38[24] + 3 t., etc.; *Impf.* יִזְנֶה (Kt) Ez 23[43]; תִּזְנֶה Lv 19[29] + 4 t.; וַתִּזֶן Je 3[8] Ez 23[5]; תִּזְנִי Ho 3[3]; וַתִּזְנִי Je 3[6] (but rd. prob. וַתִּזֶן: וַתִּזְנִי is *not* Aram. form of 3 fs., v. Kö[i. 540] Kau[§ 47 & b]) Ez 16[15] + 4 t.; וַתִּזְנִים Ez 16[28]; יִזְנוּ (Qr) Ez 23[43]; וַיִּזְנוּ Ju 8[27] + 4 t.; תִּזְנֶינָה Ho 4[13. 14]; וַתִּזְנֶינָה Ez 23[3]; *Inf. abs.* זָנֹה Ho 1[2]; cstr. לִזְנוֹת Lv 20[5] + 3 t.; לִזְנֹת Lv 20[6]; sf. בִּזְנוּתֵךְ Ez 23[30]; *Pt.* זוֹנֶה ψ 73[27] Ez 6[9]; זֹנָה Ho 4[15]; pl. זֹנִים Lv 17[7] + 3 t.; זוֹנָה Dt 23[19] + 25 t.; זֹנָה Lv 21[7] + 2 t.;
זונות Pr 29[3]; זֹנוֹת Ho 4[14] + 4 t.—**1.** *be* or *act as* 2185
a harlot, abs. Gn 38[24] (J), Dt 22[21] (D), Lv 21[9] (H), Ho 4[13. 14] Am 7[17]; (ה)אשׁה + זונה Jos 2[1] 6[22] (J), Lv 21[7] (H), Ju 11[1] 16[1] Pr 6[26] Je 3[3] Ez 16[30] 23[44]; זוֹנָה Gn 34[31] 38[15] Jos 6[17. 25] (all J), Dt 23[19] Lv 21[14] (H), Pr 7[10] 23[27] Is 23[15. 16] Jo 4[3] Mi 1[7. 7] Ez 16[31]; נָשִׁים זונות 1 K 3[16]; ז(ו)נות 1 K 22[38] Pr 29[3] Ho 3[3] 4[14] Ez 16[33]; בית זונה Je 5[7]; *commit fornication*, man's act ז׳ אל Nu 25[1] (J); of woman's act Ju 19[2]; of a land given to harlotry Lv 19[29]. **2.** fig. *of improper intercourse with foreign nations* (religious reference sometimes involved) ז׳ את Is 23[17]; אחרי Ez 23[30]; אל Ez 16[26. 28. 28]; ז׳ תַּזְנוּתֶיהָ Ez 23[43] Na 3[4]; וַתִּזֶן אָהֳלָה תַּחְתָּי *and Ohola committed fornication* (whilst) *under me* Ez 23[5] (cf. Nu 5[19]). **3.** *of intercourse with other deities*, considered as harlotry, sts. involving actual prostitution, ז׳ אחרי Ex 34[15. 16] Dt 31[16] (all J), Lv 17[7] 20[5. 5] (all H), Ju 2[17] 8[27. 33] 1 Ch 5[25] Ez 6[9] 20[30]; after אֹבֹת, etc. Lv 20[6] (H), one's own heart & eyes Nu 15[39] (H); esp. of Isr., Judah, and Jerus. under fig. of lewd woman Ez 16[15]

(abs.) v^{16} (על במות), v^{17} (ז׳ בְּ), 23$^{3.3.19}$ (abs.), Je 3^{1} (c. acc.); v$^{6.8}$ (abs.); abs. elsewh. Ho 2^{7} 4^{15} Is 57^{3} ψ 106^{39}; as leaving י׳, sq. מֵעַל Ho 9^{1}; מאחרי 1$^{2.2}$; מתחת 4^{12}; sq. מן alone ψ 73^{27}; ז(ו)נה Je 2^{20} Ez 16$^{35.41}$; בית זונה Je 5^{7}; לִבָּם הַזּוֹנֶה *their whorish heart* Ez 6^{9}. **4.** זונה of moral defection Is 1^{21}. **Pu.** *Pf.* 3 ms. אַחֲרַיִךְ לֹא זוּנָּה *fornication was not done* (in going) *after thee* Ez 16^{34} (but del. Co). **Hiph.** *Pf.* 2 ms. הִזְנֵיתָ Ho 5^{3}; 3 pl. הִזְנוּ Ho 4$^{10.18}$ Ex 34^{16}; *Impf.* וַיֶּזֶן 2 Ch 21^{11}; וַתַּזְנֶה 2 Ch 21^{13}; *Inf. abs.* הַזְנֵה Ho 4^{18}; *cstr.* הַזְנוֹת 2 Ch 21^{13}; sf. לְהַזְנוֹתָהּ Lv 19^{29}. **1.** *cause to commit fornication:* **a.** sexual Lv 19^{29} (H). **b.** religious Ex 34^{16} (J), 2 Ch 21$^{11.13.13}$. **2.** *commit fornication:* **a.** sexual Ho 4^{10}. **b.** religious Ho 4$^{18.18}$ 5^{3}.

2183 †זְנוּנִים **n.[m.] fornication,** *pl. abstr. intens.* (Ol ^{§215a}; Dl $^{Pr 74}$, der. fr. √זנן, As. *zanânu, fill full,* cf. Dl $^{ib. 73}$)—ז׳ Ho 1^{2} + 5 t., cstr. זְנוּנֵי Na 3^{4} + 2 t., זְנוּנַיִךְ Ez 23^{29}, זְנוּנֶיהָ Ho 2^{4} Na 3^{4}. **a,** sexual Gn 38^{24} (J) Ho 1$^{2.2}$. **b.** international Na 3$^{4.4}$. **c.** religious 2 K 9^{22} Ez 23$^{11.29}$ Ho 2$^{4.6}$ 4^{12} 5^{4}.

2184 †זְנוּת **n.f.abstr. fornication;**—ז׳ Ho 4^{11} 6^{10}; sf. זְנוּתֵךְ Je 13^{27} Ez 23^{27}; זְנוּתָהּ Je 3^{9}; זְנוּתָם Ez 43$^{7.9}$; זְנוּתַיִךְ Je 3^{2}; זְנוּתֵיכֶם Nu 14^{33}. **a.** sexual Ho 4^{11}. **b.** international Ez 23^{27}. **c.** religious Nu 14^{33} (J) Je 3$^{2.9}$ 13^{27} Ez 43$^{7.9}$ Ho 6^{10} (where We $^{Kl. Proph.}$ suggests זְנֻנִית); cf. זָנָה **3.**

8457 †[תַּזְנוּת] **n.f.abstr. fornication;** — sf. תַּזְנוּתֵךְ Ez 16^{20} (Kt) v^{25} (Kt) v^{29}; תַּזְנֻתֵךְ Ez 16^{26}; תַּזְנוּתָם Ez 23$^{8.17}$; תַּזְנֻתַיִךְ Ez 16$^{15.34.36}$; תַּזְנֻתַיִךְ Ez 16^{22}; תַּזְנוּתַיִךְ Ez 16^{20} (Qr) v^{25} (Qr) v^{33} 23$^{29.35}$; תַּזְנוּתֶיהָ Ez 23$^{7.8.11.14.18.19.43}$. These are all international mingled with religious references.

2186 †I. זָנַח **vb. reject, spurn** (perh. cf. As. *zinû, be angry,* esp. of gods Gu ^{§105} Zim $^{BP 23 ff.}$)—**Qal** *Pf.* ז׳ Ho 8$^{3.5}$ La 2^{7}; זָנַחְתָּ ψ 44^{10} + 2 t.; sf. זְנַחְתַּנִי ψ 43^{2}; זְנַחְתָּנוּ ψ 60$^{3.12}$ 108^{12}; זְנַחְתִּים Zc 10^{6}; *Impf.* יִזְנַח ψ 77^{8} La 3^{31}; תִּזְנַח ψ 44^{24} + 2 t.;—*reject,* Isr. rejects good Ho 8^{3}; Samaria's calf rejects her Ho 8^{5} (others make י׳ subj.; We $^{Kl. Proph.}$ rds. אזנח *I reject*), elsewh. God rejects people ψ 43^{2} 60^{3} 77^{8} 88^{15} Zc 10^{6}; לָנֶצַח ψ 44^{24} 74^{1}; לעולם La 3^{31}; ז׳ ולא תצא בצבאתינו ψ 44^{10} 60^{12} 108^{12}; נַפְשִׁי מִשָּׁלוֹם La 3^{17}; king ψ 89^{39}; altar La 2^{7}. **Hiph.** *Pf.* הִזְנִיחַ 2 Ch 29^{19}; sf. הִזְנִיחָם 2 Ch 11^{14}; 3 pl. הֶאֶזְנִיחוּ Is 19^{6}, v. II. זנח; *Impf.* יַזְנִיחֲךָ 1 Ch 28^{9};—(late) *reject* (=earlier **Qal**), Jeroboam *rejects* the Levites מכהן לי׳ 2 Ch 11^{14}; Ahaz the sacred vessels 2 Ch 29^{19}; י׳ rejects Solomon 1 Ch 28^{9}.

†II. [זָנַח] **stink, emit stench** (cf. Ar. زَنِخَ 2186
become rancid, of oil, etc., Lane);—only **Hiph.** *Pf.* 3 mpl. הֶאֶזְנִיחוּ נְהָרוֹת *rivers stink* Is 19^{6} (rd. הִזְנִיחוּ Ges $^{§53.6}$ Ol ^{§255b} Sta ^{§420a} Kö $^{i. 293}$; but Ew ^{§126b} De Di derive from elative אַזְנָח or אֶזְנָח).

זָנוֹחַ **n.pr.loc. 1.** *Zanuʿa,* SE. Ṣorea (Rob 2182
$^{BR ii. 61}$ Bd $^{Pal 163}$) Jos 15^{34} Ne 3^{13} 11^{30} 1 Ch 4^{18}. **2.** a place in the mts. Jos 15^{56}, possibly *Zânûta,* SW. of Hebron, Guérin $^{Judée iii. 200}$ Survey $^{iii. 404}$; but Di thinks this is too far south.

†[זָנַק] **vb.** only **Pi. leap** (NH זִנֵּק *cause to* 2187
spring, spurt; Aram. ܙܢܩ *throw, shoot,* also *bind*)—*Impf.* 3 ms. יְזַנֵּק מִן־הַבָּשָׁן Dt 33^{22} *he leapeth forth from Bashan* (of Dan under fig. of lion's whelp).

זֵעָה v. יָזַע. p. 402 2188

זַעֲוָה v. זְוָעָה sub זוע. p. 266 2189

†זַעֲוָן **n.pr.m.** a descendant (branch or 2190
tribe) of Seir (𝔊 Ζουκαμ, but Ζαυαν 𝔊L 1 Ch 1^{42}; Sam. זועין)—Gn 36^{27} = 1 Ch 1^{42}. p. 266

†[זָעַךְ] **vb. extinguish,** only **Niph.** *be* 2193
extinguished יָמַי נִזְעָכוּ Jb 17^{1} (|| רוּחִי חֻבָּלָה). Elsewhere always דעך (q.v.), and so in cogn. languages. Prob. error for נדעכו.

†זָעַם **vb. be indignant** (cf. Aram. (rare) 2194
ܙܥܡ *blame,* & n. ܙܘܥܡܐ; Ar. تَزَغَّمَ onomatop., of *roar* of camel, *angry speech,* v. Frey, De on ψ 7^{12}) — *Pf.* ז׳ Nu 23^{8} + 3 t.; זָעַמְתָּה Zc 1^{12}; *Impf.* אֶזְעֹם Nu 23^{8}; 3 pl. sf. יִזְעָמוּהוּ Pr 24^{24}; *Imv.* זֹעֲמָה Nu 23^{7} (for זְעָמָה Ges $^{§64.(2)}$); *Pt. act.* זֹעֵם ψ 7^{12}; *pass.* cstr. זְעוּם Pr 22^{14}; f. זְעוּמָה Mi 6^{10};—**1.** *be indignant, have indignation,* of hostile prince עַל בְּרִית קוֹדֶשׁ Dn 11^{30}; elsewhere of Yahweh, who is אֵל זֹעֵם ψ 7^{12} (|| שׁוֹפֵט), c. acc. of enemy Is 66^{14}; cities of Judah Zc 1^{12}; people Mal 1^{4}; a man Pr 22^{14}. **2.** *express indignation in speech, denounce, curse* || יִקְּבֻהוּ Pr 24^{24}; || אֶקֹּב and אָרָה־ Nu 23$^{7.8.8}$ (E); אֵיפַת רָזוֹן זְעוּמָה Mi 6^{10} *an ephah of scantiness, denounced,* or *cursed.* **Niph.** *Pt.* pl. פָּנִים נִזְעָמִים Pr 25^{23} *face stirred with indignation.*

†זַעַם **n.m.** $^{Is 10, 25}$ **indignation;**—ז׳ Is 10^{25} + 2195
7 t.; זָעַם Is 26^{20} + 2 t.; sf. זַעְמִי Is 10^{5} + 3 t.; זַעַמְךָ ψ 102^{11}; זַעְמֶךָ ψ 38^{4} 69^{25}; זַעְמוֹ Is 13^{5} + 3 t.;—*indignation* of men Ho 7^{16} Je 15^{17}; elsewh. of י׳ Is 26^{20} 30^{27} Na 1^{6} Hb 3^{12} ψ 38^{4} 102^{11} Dn 11^{36}; || חרון אף ψ 69^{25} Zp 3^{8}; || עברה ψ 78^{49} Ez 21^{36} 22^{31}; || קצף Je 10^{10} ψ 102^{11}; || אף Is 10$^{5.25}$ 30^{27};

cf. בזעם אפו La 2^{6}; שפך ז׳ על ψ 69^{25} Ez 21^{36} 22^{31} Zp 3^{8}; כְּלֵי זַעַם Is 13^{5} Je 50^{25}; יום זעם Ez 22^{24}; אחרית הזעם Dn 8^{19}.

2196 †[זָעַף] **vb.** **be out of humour, vexed; be enraged** (Aram. ܙܥܦ *rage against*, זְעַף *to storm*, זַעְפָּא *storm;* cf. Sam. ࠆࠏࠐ *blow, breathe*)—**Qal** *Impf.* יִזְעַף Pr 19^{3}; וַיִּזְעַף 2 Ch 26^{19}; *Inf.* זַעְפּוֹ 2 Ch 26^{19}; *Pt.* pl. זֹעֲפִים Gn 40^{6} Dn 1^{10};—**1.** *be out of humour* Gn 40^{6} (E); *dejected*, of face Dn 1^{10}; sq. על Pr 19^{3} *fret against* (AV). **2.** *be enraged* (late: cf. Aram. above) 2 Ch 26^{19}; sq. עִם v^{19}.

2197 †זַעַף **n.m.** **storming, raging, rage** (poet. and late)—ז׳ abs. 2 Ch 16^{10} 28^{9}; cstr. Is 30^{30} + 2 t.; sf. זַעְפּוֹ Jon 1^{15};—**1.** *rage* of king, leading to violence Pr 19^{12} (‖ נַהַם כַּכְּפִיר), 2 Ch 16^{10} (‖ כעס), 28^{9} (בְּז׳ עִמּוֹ עַל־זאת); ז׳ אַף Is 30^{30} *raging* of anger (of י׳); ז׳ י׳ Mi 7^{9}. **2.** *raging* of sea Jon 1^{15}.

2198 †זָעֵף **adj.** **out of humour, vexed,** only of Ahab 1 K 20^{43} 21^{4} (‖ סַר).

2199 †[זָעַק] **vb.** **cry, cry out, call** (‖ form of צעק q.v.; Ar. زَعَقَ, Aram. ܙܥܩ)—**Qal** *Pf.* 3 fs. וְזָעָקָה 2 S 13^{19}; 1 s. זָעַקְתִּי ψ 142^{6}; 3 pl. זָעֲקוּ Ju 6^{7} + 3 t.; וְזָעֲקוּ consec. Ju 11^{11} + 2 t.; 2 mpl. וּזְעַקְתֶּם consec. 1 S 8^{18}; *Impf.* 3 ms. יִזְעַק Is 15^{5}; וַיִּזְעַק 1 S 7^{9} + 5 t., etc.; *Imv.* זְעַק Ez 21^{17}; fs. זַעֲקִי־ Is 14^{31}, cf. Je 48^{20} Kt; וְזַעֲקוּ Ju 10^{14} + 2 t.; וּזְעָקוּ Je 48^{20} Qr; *Inf. cstr.* מִזְּעֹק 1 S 7^{8}; וְלִזְעֹק 2 S 19^{29}; sf. זַעֲקֵךְ Is 30^{19}; בְּזַעֲקֵךְ Is 57^{13} (Ol. § 245 b Ges § 61. 1. R 1);—**1.** *call*, to one's aid, sq. acc. pers. Ju 12^{2}. **2.** *cry, cry out*, in need: **a.** unto God (י׳), sq. אֶל־ Ju $3^{9.15}$ $6^{6.7}$ 10^{10} 1 S $7^{8.9}$ (+ בעד of intercession), $12^{8.10}$ 15^{11} Mi 3^{4} Je 11^{11} Hb 1^{2} (c. acc. חמס, cf. Ho 8^{2} infr.), 2 Ch 20^{9} ψ 22^{6} $107^{13.19}$ 142^{6} Jo 1^{14}; sq. בְּקוֹל גָּדוֹל + אֶל־י׳ Ne 9^{4}; + קוֹלִי ψ 142^{2} (‖ התחנן); + בְּלִבָּם Ho 7^{14} (opp. הֵילִיל); sq. לְ Ho 8^{2} (+ obj. of words uttered), 1 Ch 5^{20}; sq. sf. Ne 9^{28}; sq. הַשָּׁמַיִם (without divine name) 2 Ch 32^{20} (‖ התפלל); abs., but with implication of cry to י׳ 1 S 8^{18} Is 30^{19}. **b.** unto other gods, sq. אֶל־ Ju 10^{14} Je 11^{12} Jon 1^{5}. **c.** unto king, sq. אֶל־ 2 S 19^{29}. **d.** abs., utterance of horror, anxiety, alarm, distress, sorrow, etc. 1 S 4^{13} 5^{10} 28^{12} (+ בקול גדול), 2 S 13^{19} 19^{5} (+ קול גדול), 1 K 22^{32} = 2 Ch 18^{31}, Is 15^{4} 26^{17} 57^{13} Je 20^{8} (‖ קרא, cf. Hb 1^{2} supr.), La 3^{8} (‖ אֲשַׁוֵּעַ) Ez 9^{8} 11^{13} 27^{30}; also of cry heard by God Ex 2^{23} (P); sq. לְ of that in behalf of, or for which one cries Is 15^{5} Je 48^{31}; so sq. עַל־ Je 30^{15}; sq. acc. cogn. זְעָקָה Est 4^{1}; ‖ היליל Je 47^{2}; and esp. Imv. Is 14^{31} Je 25^{34} 48^{20} Ez 21^{17}. **e.** *cry out* against one, sq. עַל־ Jb 31^{38} *if my land cry out against me* (‖ יִבְכָּיוּן); cf. also (abs., and without prep.) Hb 2^{11} *the stone shall cry out of* (מִן) *the wall.* **Niph.** *Pf.* 2 ms. נִזְעַקְתָּ Ju 18^{23}; 3 mpl. נִזְעֲקוּ Ju 18^{22}; *Impf.* וַיִּזָּעֵק Ju 6^{34} + 2 t.; וַיִּזָּעֲקוּ Jos 8^{16};—*be called together, assemble, join* Jos 8^{16} (JE), Ju $18^{22.23}$ 1 S 14^{20}; sq. אַחֲרָיו Ju $6^{34.35}$ *assembled after him*, i.e. joined him as his followers. **Hiph.** *Impf.* וַיַּזְעֵק Ju 4^{10} + 3 t.; יַזְעִיקוּ Jb 35^{9}; *Imv.* הַזְעֶק־ 2 S 20^{4}; *Inf. cstr.* לְהַזְעִיק 2 S 20^{5};—**1.** *call, call out*, or *together*, for military service, sq. acc. Ju $4^{10.13}$ 2 S $20^{4.5}$. **2.** *make a crying* Jb 35^{9} (יְשַׁוְּעוּ in ‖ cl.) **3.** *have proclamation made* ויז׳ ויאמר Jon 3^{7}. **4.** *call out to, or at*, sq. acc. וַיַּזְעֵק אֹתִי וַיְדַבֵּר Zc 6^{8} (si vera l.; Gr queries וַיָּעַר ?).

†זְעָקָה **n.f.** **cry, outcry,** abs. ז׳ Je 18^{22} + 2201
5 t.; cstr. זַעֲקַת Gn 18^{20} + 3 t.; sf. זַעֲקָתִי Jb 16^{18}; זַעֲקָתָם Is 15^{5} + 3 t.;—**1.** *outcry*, against, זַעֲקַת סְדֹם וגו׳ Gn 18^{20} (J). **2.** *cry of distress*, concerning something זַעֲקַת־שֶׁבֶר Is 15^{5} (obj. of יְעֹעֵרוּ; cf. בִּבְכִי in prev. cl.); abs. v^{8} (subj. of הִקִּיפָה, ‖ יְלָלָה); Je 18^{22} (תִּשָּׁמַע ז׳), 20^{16} 48^{4} 50^{46} Ne 5^{6} 9^{9} (all c. שמע), Je 48^{34} (joined with נתן קול), Jb 16^{18} Est 9^{31} (lamentation), cf. 4^{1} (ז׳ גְּדוֹלָה וּמָרָה, acc. cogn. c. זעק); specif. זעקת־דַּל Pr 21^{13} *cry of poor;* קול ז׳ Is 65^{19} (‖ קול בכי), Je 51^{54} Ez 27^{28}. **3.** *outcry, clamour* זעקת מושל בַּכְּסִילִים Ec 9^{17} (opp. דברי חכמים בְּנַחַת נשמעים).

זער (Ar. زَعِرَ *be scanty*, of hair, plumage, etc.; Aram. ܙܥܪ, זְעַר *be* or *grow small;* cf. **צער**).

†זְעֵיר **n.[m.]** a little (diminutive form 2191
Ol § 180 Lag BN 85)—**1.** of quantity, amount (of instruction) ז׳ שָׁם ז׳ שָׁם Is $28^{10.13}$ (in both ‖ צַו, קַו). **2.** of time, כַּתַּר־לִי ז׳ וַאֲחַוֶּךָּ Jb 36^{2}.

†מִזְעָר **n.[m.]** **a little, a trifle, a few.** **1.** 4213
of time עוֹד מְעַט מִזְעָר Is 10^{25} 29^{17} *yet a trifle, a little* = a very little while. **2.** of number שְׁאָר מְעַט מִזְעָר Is 16^{14} *a remnant, a very few* (opp. לוֹא כַבִּיר). In Is³ without מעט:—ונשאר אנוש מִזְעָר Is 24^{6}.

†[זִפְרֹן] **n.pr.loc.** only c. ה loc. זִפְרֹנָה Nu 2202
34^{9}, place on northern boundary of Canaan;

𝔊 Δεφρωνα, Ἐφρωνα; 𝔊L Ζεφρωνα; site dub., Wetzst [Hauran 88] prop. *Zifrân*, NE. fr. Damascus; Furrer [ZPV viii. 28] Bd [Pal 397] ('perh.') *Za'ferâne*, between Ḥumṣ and Hamath; Di rejects both.

2203 † זֶ֫פֶת **n.f.** [Is 34, 9] **pitch** (cf. on format. Ol [§ 164 c] Sta [§ 187 a]. Word is Armenian acc. to Lag [Arm. Stud. 1351, BN 219]; on Egypt. deriv. cf. Cook [Speaker's Comm. i. 484]; Ar. زِفْتٌ acc. to Frä [151], if Shemit., is Aram. loan-wd.; v. also Eth. ዘፍት: Di [1068])—*pitch*:—וַתַּחְמְרָה בַחֵמָר וּבַזָּ֑פֶת Ex 2[3] of ark of bulrushes; Is 34[9 a] וְנֶהֶפְכוּ נְחָלֶיהָ לְזֶפֶת וַעֲפָרָהּ לְגָפְרִית, v[9 b] והיתה אַרְצָהּ לְזֶפֶת בֹּעֵרָה׃.

2131 † I. [זִק] **n.[m.] missile, spark** (√dub.; cf. NH זִיקִין *fiery arrows*, Aram. זִיקָא *id.*, זִיקוּקָא *id.* + *spark*, ܙܝܩܐ *shooting star*, *ray of light*, ܙܝܩܬܐ *shooting star*)—only pl. זִקִּים of (fire-?) missiles Pr 26[18] (‖ חִצִּים, c. ירה); so זיקות *sparks, brands* (as leaping, springing forth?) Is 50[11] מְאַזְּרֵי ז׳ (v. אזר) (‖ קֹדְחֵי אֵשׁ), v[11] בְּעַרְתֶּם ז׳ (‖ אוּר אֶשְׁכֶם).

2131 II. [זִק], זִקִּים *fetters*, v. sub II. זקק. p. 279

זקן (√of foll.; meaning dubious).

2206 † זָקָן **n.m.** [2 S 10, 5 +] and **f.** [Is 15, 2 +] **chin, beard** (As. *ziḳnu*, Asrb [Annals iv. 29]; Ar. ذَقَنٌ, Aram. דִּקְנָא, ܕܩܢܐ)—abs. ז׳ Lv 13[20] +; cstr. זְקַן 2 S 20[9] +; sf. זְקָנִי Ezr 9[3]; זְקָנְךָ Lv 19[27] Ez 5[1]; זְקָנוֹ 1 S 21[14] + 2 t.; זְקַנְכֶם 2 S 10[5] 1 Ch 19[5]; זְקָנָם 2 S 10[4] Lv 21[5]; never pl.—**1.** *chin* (opp. ראשׁ, top of head) Lv 13[29.30] 14[9] (all P), 2 S 20[9] Ez 5[1]; cf. also 1 S 21[14] ψ 133[4] (where however chin as *bearded* may be meant); chin, or lower jaw, of lion and bear 1 S 17[35]. **2.** *beard*, as growing (צמח) 2 S 10[5] = 1 Ch 19[5]; as cut off Is 7[20] (ספה), 15[2] = Je 48[37] (גרע); cf. מְגֻלְּחֵי זָקָן Je 41[5] 2 S 10[4] (גלח); שְׂעַר ראשׁי וּזְקָנִי Ezr 9[3]; here belongs פאת זקנ(ך) Lv 19[27] 21[5] (both H; opp. ראשׁ).

2204 † זָקֵן **vb. be or become old** (cf., acc. to Thes, Ar. ذَقُونٌ *a she-camel that lets her lower lip hang down*, v. Lane [968]; ذِقْنٌ *decrepit man*)—**Qal** *Pf.* 3 ms. זָקֵן Gn 18[12] + 14 t. (often hard to disting. fr. pred. adj. זָקֵן q.v.); 3 fs. זָקְנָה Pr 23[22]; 2 ms. זָקַנְתָּ 1 S 8[5]; זָקַ֫נְתָּה Jos 13[1]; 1 s. זָקַנְתִּי Jos 23[2] + 3 t.; זָקַ֫נְתִּי Gn 18[13] 27[2]; *Impf.* וַיִּזְקַן 2 Ch 24[15];—*be* (or *become*) *old* Gn 18[12.13] 19[31] 27[1.2] (all J), 1 S 2[22] 4[18] 8[1.5] 12[2] 17[12] 2 S 19[33] 1 K 1[1.15] 2 K 4[14]; also Gn 24[1] (‖ בא בימים), so Jos 13[1.1] 23[1.2] (‖ here בָּאתִי בימים), 1 Ch 23[1] (‖ שְׂבַע ימים), 24[15] (‖ *id.*); Pr 23[22] ψ 37[25] (opp. ‖ היה נער); note esp. זָקַנְתִּי מִהְיוֹת לְאִישׁ Ru 1[12] *I am too old to belong to a man* (*husband*). **Hiph.** only *Impf.* 3 ms. יַזְקִין inchoat. *shew age, grow old* = senescere Ew [§ 122 c], cf. Di; of youth Pr 22[6]; of tree-root Jb 14[8].

זָקֵן **adj.** old, abs. ז׳ Gn 19[4] + 30 t. (on distinct. 2205
fr. vb. v. supr.); cstr. זְקַן Gn 24[2]; pl. זְקֵנִים Gn 18[11] + 44 t.; זְקֵנוֹת Zc 8[4]; cstr. זִקְנֵי Gn 50[7] + 85 t.; sf. זְקֵנַי La 1[19], זְקֵנֶיךָ Dt 21[2] 32[7], זְקֵנָיו Jos 8[33] + 3 t., זְקֵנֶיהָ Ju 8[14], זְקֵנֵינוּ Ex 10[9] Jos 9[11], זִקְנֵיכֶם Dt 5[20] + 2 t.;—**1.** *old*, of human beings, as adj. pred. Gn 18[11] (J), Jb 32[4] (ז׳ מִמֶּנּוּ לְיָמִים, in compar.), or attrib. אָב זָקֵן Gn 44[20] (J), אִישׁ ז׳ Ju 19[16.17.20.22], נָבִיא ז׳ 1 K 13[11.25.29], מֶלֶךְ ז׳ Ec 4[13]; prob. also ז׳ וּשְׂבַע ימים Gn 35[29] (P), Jb 42[17] and Gn 25[8] (P) acc. to 𝔊 Sam Di; cf. also Ezr 3[12]. **2.** usu. as subst.: **a.** *old man* (or woman), **b.** *elder*; **a.** *old man* Gn 43[27] (J), Lv 19[32] (H), Dt 28[50] 32[7] (‖ אָב), 1 S 2[31.32] 28[14] Is 47[6] Jb 12[20] 32[9] Pr 17[6] 20[29] ψ 119[100] Jo 1[2]; *old men and old women* Zc 8[4.4]; cf. זְקַן בֵּיתוֹ Gn 24[2] (J), זִקְנֵי בֵיתוֹ 2 S 12[17]; esp. opp. נַעַר Ex 10[9] (E), Is 3[5] 20[4] Je 51[22] La 2[21] ψ 148[12], and in phr. מִנַּעַר וְעַד זָקֵן Gn 19[4] (J), Jos 6[21] (JE), Est 3[13]; opp. ילדים 1 K 12[6.8.13] = 2 Ch 10[6.8.13]; opp. בַּחוּרִים Je 31[13] Ez 9[6] Jo 3[1], cf. 2 Ch 36[17] (+ יָשֵׁשׁ) and Je 6[11] (+ מְלֵא ימים); opp. עויל ימים Is 65[20]; opp. יונקי שדים and עוללים Jo 2[16]. **b.** usu. pl. *elders*, as having authority, term techn. (100 t. +); elders of a people, esp. Israel Ex 3[16.18] 12[21] (all J), 17[5.6] 18[12] 19[7] 24[1.9.14] Jos 24[1] (all E), Nu 11[16.16] (שֹׁטְרָיו), v[24.25.30] 16[25] Jos 7[6] 8[10] 9[11] (all JE), Dt 5[20] (‖ רָאשֵׁי שִׁבְטֵיכֶם), 27[1] 29[9] (‖ שֹׁטְרֵיכֶם, ראשי שבטיכם), 31[9.28] Jos 8[33] (‖ שֹׁטְרִים וְשֹׁפְטָיו), 23[2] (‖ שֹׁטְרָיו, שֹׁפְטָיו, רָאשָׁיו); cf. also prob. Jos 24[31] = Ju 2[7] (all D); Lv 9[1], cf. זִקְנֵי הָעֵדָה Lv 4[15] († both P), Ju 21[16]; see also 1 S 4[3] 8[4] 15[30] 2 S 3[17] 5[3] = 1 Ch 11[3], 2 S 17[4.15] 1 K 8[1.3] = 2 Ch 5[2.4], also 1 Ch 15[25] 21[16]; cf. Is 3[2] (גִּבּוֹר וְאִישׁ מִלְחָמָה שׁוֹפֵט וְנָבִיא וְקֹסֵם וז׳), 9[14] (‖ נְשׂוּא־פָנִים, but v. prob. gloss, cf. Ew Che Di Du al.); elders of one tribe (Judah) 1 S 30[26] 2 S 19[12], so of Gilead Ju 11[5.7.8.9.10.11]; after the division of the kingdoms, of N. Isr. זקני הארץ 1 K 20[7] cf. v[8], also 2 K 6[32.32] 10[1] (‖ שָׂרִים etc.) cf. v[5]; under Josiah זקני יְהוּדָה 2 K 23[1] = 2 Ch 34[29]; see also ז׳ הארץ Je 26[17], cf. זקני ארץ Pr 31[23], cf. La 1[19] 2[10] 4[16] 5[12.14] (‖ שָׂרִים; + שַׁעַר); oft. in Ezek.: Ez 7[26] (‖ כהן), of Judah 8[1], of Isr. 8[11.12] 14[1] 20[1.3], also 9[6] (but del. Co). Exil. ז׳ הַגּוֹלָה Je 29[1] (‖ הכהנים, הנביאים); post-exil. Ezr 10[8] (‖ שָׂרִים), poss. also Jo 1[14]; elders of י׳ Is 24[23] (cf. Ex 24[1.9]), זִקְנֵי הַכֹּהֲנִים 2 K 19[2] = Is 37[2], so Je 19[1] (‖ זקני העם); of other peoples,

Midian Nu 22$^{4.7}$, Moab v^{7} (all E), Egypt ψ 105^{22} (|| שׂרים); of Gebal Ez 27^{9}; elders of a city, esp. as sitting in the gate to judge Dt 19^{12} 21^{2} (+ שֹׁפְטֶיךָ) v$^{3.4.6.19}$ (+ שַׁעַר־מְקֹמוֹ), v^{20} 22^{15} (+ הַשָּׁעְרָה), v$^{16.17.18}$ 25^{7} (+ הַשַּׁעְרָה), v$^{8.9}$ (all in Dt. code, and only so therein), Ru 4$^{2.4.9.11}$ (cf. שַׁעַר v$^{1.11}$), מוֹשַׁב זְקֵנִים ψ 107^{32} (|| קְהַל־עָם); Ju 8^{14} (|| שׂרים), v^{16} 1 S 11^{3} 16^{4} 1 K 21$^{8.11}$ Ezr 10^{14}.

2207 †זֹקֶן **n.[m.] old age**—עֵינֵי ישׂראל כָּבְדוּ מִזֹּקֶן Gn 48^{10} (E).

2209 †זִקְנָה **n.f. old age**—זִקְנָה ψ 71^{9} + 2 t.; cstr. זִקְנַת 1 K 11^{4}; sf. זִקְנָתוֹ 1 K 15^{23}; זִקְנָתָהּ Gn 24^{36};—*old age*, || שֵׂיבָה ψ 71^{18} Is 46^{4}; *in the time of old age* לְעֵת ז׳ 1 K 11^{4} 15^{23} ψ 71^{9}; אַחֲרֵי ז׳ (i.e. after she had become old) Gn 24^{36} (J).

2208 †זְקֻנִים **n.pl.[m.] old age**—בֶּן־ז׳ Gn 37^{3} i.e. a late-born son; יֶלֶד ז׳ Gn 44^{20} *id.*; (ילדה) בֵּן לִזְקֻנָיו Gn 21$^{2.7}$ (all JE).

2210 †[זָקַף] **vb.** (late) **raise up** (NH *id.*; Aram. זְקַף, ܙܩܰܦ; As. *zaḳâpu*, Asrb[Hunting Inscr. IR 7, ix. A, 3]; Nö[ZMG 1886, 725] suggests Ar. زَقَفَ *carry off* (Ḳam.), orig. *lift up*)—only **Qal** *Pt. act.* and only fig. of י׳'s dealing with prostrate men:—וְזוֹקֵף לְכָל־הַכְּפוּפִים ψ 145^{14} (|| סוֹמֵךְ); זֹקֵף כְּפוּפִים 146^{8} י׳ *raiseth up prostrate ones.*

2212 †I. [זָקַק] **vb. refine, purify** (Aram. זְקַק; perh. kindr. with As. *zaḳiḳu*, *wind*, Asrb[Annals vi. 64] and Aram. ܙܰܩܳܐ, זִיקָא *violent wind, violent rain with whirlwind*)—**Qal** *Impf.* 3 mpl. יָזֹקּוּ Jb 28^{1} obj. זָהָב, 36^{27} obj. מָטָר (v. Di). **Pi.** *Pf.* consec. וְזִקַּק Mal 3^{3} (|| וְטִהַר) fig., of purifying sons of Levi, like gold and silver כַּזָּהָב etc. **Pu.** *Pt.* מְזֻקָּק *refined*, of gold 1 Ch 28^{18}, of silver 1 Ch 29^{4}: ψ 12^{7} (מ׳ שבעתים); of settled wines שְׁמָרִים מְזֻקָּקִים Is 25^{6}.

2212 II. זקק (NH זָקַק *bind, fetter*, Aram. זְקַק *id.*; comp. (perh. fr. idea of *restraint*) Ar. زِقٌّ, Aram. ܙܶܩܳܐ, זִיקָא, זִיקוּקָא, Eth. ዝቅ: all = (wine-)*skin*, etc.; also NH זִיקָה, *obligation*; Aram. ܙܩܳܩܳܐ *ring*).

2131 †II. [זֵק] **n.[m.] fetter,** only pl. זִקִּים:—*fetters* of captives רֻתְּקוּ בַזִּ׳ Na 3^{10}; בַּזִּ׳ יַעֲבֹרוּ Is 45^{14}; בַּז׳ ψ 149^{8} (c. אסר; || כַּבְלֵי בַרְזֶל); fig. בַּזּ׳ Jb 36^{8} (c. אסר; || חַבְלֵי עֹנִי).

246 †[אֵזֵק] **n.[m.]** id., specif. **manacle**, only pl. *manacles* אָסוּר בָּאזִקִּים Je 40^{1}, and מִן־הָאזִקִּים אֲשֶׁר עַל־יָדֶךָ v^{4}.

זָר v. I. זור, זָרָא v. sub II. זור. p. 266 2214

זָר v. III. זור. p. 267 2213

†[זָרַב] **vb.** only **Pu.**, meaning dub.; prob. 2215
(from context) **be burnt, scorched**—**Pu.** *Impf.* in rel. cl., בְּעֵת יְזֹרְבוּ נִצְמָתוּ Jb 6^{17} (|| בְּחֻמּוֹ נִדְעֲכוּ מִמְּקוֹמָם), of brooks *scorched* and drying up (|| form of צָרַב q.v.; so Ew Di De Hoffm Kau AV RV MV; > Thes RobGes who comp. Ar. زَرِبَ *flow away*, cf. NH זְרִיבָה; and Mich Dl[Pr 36 f.] VBm (*are straitened*) RVm (*shrink*) cf. Aram. ܙܪܰܒ *compress*, (Ar. زَرَبَ is to *make a wooden enclosure*), As. *zarâbu*, Zim[BP 32 n. 56, 70, 95]).

†זְרֻבָּבֶל **n.pr.m.** (acc. to MV perh. = זְרוּעַ בָּבֶל 2216
begotten in Babylon, v. also Thes)—grandson of king Jehoiachin, and son of Pedaiah 1 Ch 3$^{19.19}$ (but son of Shealtiel Ezr 3$^{2.8}$ etc., cf. שְׁאַלְתִּיאֵל brother(?) of פְּדָיָה 1 Ch 3^{17}); leader of first returning exiles Ezr 2^{2} = Ne 7^{7}, Ezr 3$^{2.8}$ 4$^{2.3}$ Ne 12$^{1.47}$ Hg 1^{12} 2^{4} Zc 4$^{6.7.9.10}$; called פַּחַת יְהוּדָה Hg 1$^{1.14}$ 2$^{2.21}$, called עַבְדִּי (by י׳) Hg 2^{23}.—𝔊 Ζοροβαβελ.

†זֶרֶד **n.pr.fl.** (√ dub.; on form cf. Lg[BN 77])— 2218
נַחַל זֶרֶד Dt 2^{13}; נַחַל זָרֶד Nu 21^{12} (JE), Dt 2$^{13.14}$; identification disputed; Rob[BR ii. 157] prop. *Wady-el-Aḥsy* (= נַחַל הָעֲרָבִים Is 15^{7}), between Moab & Edom; < either *Sail Sa'îde* (Kn), chief source of Arnon fr. SE. (Burckh[Syrien, 635]), or W. *Kerak* (Ges Ke Di); so also GASm[Geog. 557].

†[זָרָה] **vb. scatter, fan, winnow** (Ar. ذَرَا 2219
cause to fly, scatter (of wind), *winnow*; Aram. דְּרָא, ܕܪܳܐ; Eth. ዘረወ:)—**Qal** *Impf.* וַיִּזֶר Ex 32^{20}; 2 ms. תִּזְרֶה Ez 5^{2}; sf. תִּזְרֵם Is 30^{22} 41^{16}; וָאֶזְרֵם Je 15^{7}; *Imv.* זְרֵה Nu 17^{2}; *Inf.* לִזְרוֹת Je 4^{11}; *Pt.* זֹרֶה Ru 3^{2} Is 30^{24};—**1.** *scatter*, the powder into which golden calf was ground Ex 32^{20} (E, obj. not expr.); c. acc. (strange) fire from censers Nu 17^{2} (P); hair (symbol. act) Ez 5^{2}; Is 30^{22}. **2.** *fan, winnow*, obj. גֹּרֶן הַשְּׂעוֹרִים Ru 3^{2} Is 30^{24} (where *pt.* has indef. subj.), 41^{16} metaph., obj. mountains and hills, fig. of winnowing; fig. fan, winnow, in purification Je 4^{11} (|| לְהָבַר); in chastisement Je 15^{7} (בְּמִזְרֶה ז׳). **Niph.** *Impf.* וְיִזָּרוּ Ez 36^{19} *be scattered, dispersed*, of Israel; *Inf.* בְּהִזָּרוֹתֵיכֶם Ez 6^{8} *when ye shall be dispersed* (on pl. sf. Ew[§ 259 b], but Co del. י). **Pi.** *Pf.* sf. וְזֵרָם 1 K 14^{15}; זֵרִיתָ ψ 139^{3}, sf. זֵרִיתָנוּ ψ 44^{12}; וְזֵרִיתִי Ez 5^{10} etc.; *Inf.* זָרוֹת Ez 20^{23}

etc.;—**1.** (intens. of Qal) *scatter*, *disperse*, esp. of peoples, c. acc. (Israel and Judah) 1 K 14[15] Lv 26[33] (H), ψ 44[12] Je 31[10] Ez 5[10.12] 12[14.15] 20[23] 22[15] cf. Zc 2[2.4.4] ψ 106[27]; bones of Israel Ez 6[5]; people of Hazor Je 49[32]; of Elam 49[36]; of Babylon 51[2] (זָרִים = strangers?); Egyptians Ez 29[12] 30[26] + 30[23] (del. Co, intern. grounds); in general the wicked Pr 20[26]; evil 20[8]; pt.

4215 מְזָרִים = subst. *scatterers*, epith. of winds Jb 37[9] (cf. Qor 51[1]); וְזֵרִיתִי פֶּרֶשׁ עַל־פְּנֵיכֶם Mal 2[3] *scatter* dung on your faces (token of shame and curse); fig. *disperse* knowledge (of lips) Pr 15[7]. **2.** *winnow, sift* (cf. **Qal 2**) only fig. אָרְחִי וְרִבְעִי זֵרִיתָ ψ 139[3] *my path and my couch thou siftest* (Che; Ba[ZMG 1887, 607] *measurest, determinest*, whence זֶרֶת, q.v.) **Pu.** *be scattered, Impf.* יְזֹרֶה Jb 18[15], subj. גָּפְרִית, sq. עַל; *Pt.* f. מְזֹרָה (agreeing with רֶשֶׁת *net*) Pr 1[17].

4214 †מִזְרֶה **n.[m.] pitch-fork**, with six prongs (= مذراة) used in winnowing, cf. Wetzst[ZPV 1891, xiv. 2]; for winnowing provender זֹרֶה בָרַחַת וּבַמִּ׳ Is 30[24]; fig. for winnowing, i.e. chastising the people וָאֶזְרֵם בְּמִ׳ Je 15[7].

2222 זַרְזִיף ψ 72[6] v. זרף. p. 284

2223 זַרְזִיר Pr 30[31] v. sub III. זור. p. 267

2224 †[זָרַח] **vb. rise, come forth** (NH *id.*, As. *zarâḫu* Dl[Pr 180]; Sab. זרח *lofty*, *majestic* (of king) and in cpd. n.pr. DHM[ZMG 1875, 605; 1883, 327] Mordt[ZMG 1876, 37])—**Qal** *Pf.* ׳ז Dt 33[2] ψ 112[4]; זָרַח Is 60[1]; וְזָרַח consec. Is 58[10] Ec 1[5]; 3 fs. זָרְחָה Ex 22[2] + 3 t.; וְזָרְחָה consec. Mal 3[20]; *Impf.* יִזְרַח 2 S 23[4] Is 60[2]; יִזְרַח Jb 9[7]; וַיִּזְרַח Gn 32[32]; 3 fs. תִּזְרַח ψ 104[22]; *Inf. cstr.* זְרֹחַ Ju 9[33] Jo 4[8]; *Pt.* זוֹרֵחַ Ec 1[5];—**1.** *rise:* **a.** (of sun) Ju 9[33] Na 3[7] 2 S 23[4] Jon 4[8] Jb 9[7] ψ 104[22] Ec 1[5.5]; sq. עַל Ex 22[2] (JE), 2 K 3[22]; sq. לְ Gn 32[32] (J). **b.** fig., sq. לְ, שֶׁמֶשׁ צְדָקָה Mal 3[20]; of ׳י, וְזָרַח מִשֵּׂעִיר לָמוֹ Dt 33[2]; sq. עַל, Is 60[2] (‖ כבודו יראה); כבוד י׳ Is 60[1]; subj. אוֹר, fig. (= happiness, blessedness) Is 58[10] ψ 112[4] (sq. לְ). **2.** *come out, appear*, of appearance of leprosy (הַצָּרַעַת) 2 Ch 26[19].

2225 †I. [זֶרַח] **n.[m.] dawning, shining**;—only fig., נֹגַהּ זַרְחֵךְ i. e. of Zion, Is 60[3] (‖ אוֹר).

2226 †II. זֶרַח **n.pr.m.** (on form cf. Lg[BN 77, and Anm.])—**1.** Ⓖ *Ζαρα*, son of Judah and Tamar Gn 38[30] 46[12] (both J), 1 Ch 2[4] (all זָרַח), v[6]; as head of a family Nu 26[20] Jos 7[1] (both P), v[18.24] (JE), 22[20] (P) 1 Ch 9[6] (ⒼL *Ζηρα*), Ne 11[24] (cf. Sm[Listen 7]).

2. Edomites: **a.** Ⓖ *Ζαρε* Gn 36[13.17] (both P) = 1 Ch 1[37]. **b.** Ⓖ *Ζαρα* Gn 36[33] (P) = 1 Ch 1[44] (**b** = **a**?). **3.** ⒼL *Ζαρα*, Levites: **a.** (var. *Ιααρα*) 1 Ch 6[6]. **b.** (var. *Ζααραι*) 1 Ch 6[26]. **4.** head of a Simeonite family, Ⓖ *Ζαρα* Nu 26[13] (P), 1 Ch 4[24] (var. *Ζαρες*) (= צֹחַר Ⓖ *Σααρ* Gn 46[10] Ex 6[15], cf. Di Nu 26[13]). **5.** a Cushite, Ⓖ *Ζαρε*, foe of king Asa 2 Ch 14[8].

†זַרְחִי **adj. gent.** alw. c. art. as subst. coll. 2227
הַזּ׳: **1.** fr. זֶרַח **1**:—Jos 7[17.17] (JE), Nu 26[20] (P), cf. לַזּ׳ 1 Ch 27[11.13]. **2.** fr. זֶרַח **4**:—Nu 26[13].

†זְרַחְיָה **n.pr.m.** (׳י *hath risen*, or *shined;* 2228
Sab. זרחאל Hal[49])—Ⓖ *Ζαραια*:—**1.** priest 1 Ch 5[32.32] 6[36] Ezr 7[4]. **2.** head of a family of returned exiles Ezr 8[4] (= **1**?).

†אֶזְרָח **n.m.**[ψ 37, 35] a native (*one arising* 249
from the soil; = 'free tribesman' RS[Sem. i. 75])—abs. ׳א Lv 19[34] + 13 t.; cstr. אֶזְרַח Ex 12[19] + 2 t.;—**1.** *a native* Israelite, usu. coll., c. art., כָּל־הָא׳ בְּיִשְׂרָאֵל Lv 23[42] (H), cf. Nu 15[13] (P); elsewh. opp. גֵּר (q.v.):—הָא׳ בִּבְנֵי ישׂר׳ Nu 15[29] (P), cf. Ez 47[22]; אֶזְרַח הָאָרֶץ Ex 12[19.48] Nu 9[14] (all P); א׳ מִכֶּם Lv 19[34] v. also 17[15] 18[26] 24[16.22] (all H); Ex 12[49] Lv 16[29] Nu 15[30] (all P), Jos 8[33] (D). **2.** *a native* tree, growing in its natural soil א׳ רַעֲנָן ψ 37[35] (fig. of prosperous wicked).

†אֶזְרָחִי **adj. gent.** i.e. of family of זֶרַח, 250
only in אֵיתָן הָא׳ 1 K 5[11] (ⒼL Ἰσραηλίτης), ψ 89[1] (Ⓖ *id.*), and 88[1] הֵימָן הָא׳, both sons of זֶרַח (1 Ch 2[6]).

†יִזְרָח **adj. gent.** only in שַׁמְהוּת הַיִּ׳ 1 Ch 3155
27[8] Ⓖ *Εσραε*, ⒼL *Ιεσρα*; rd. הַיִּזְרָחִ(י) (= הַזַּרְחִי? cf. v[11.13]).

†יִזְרַחְיָה **n.pr.m.** (׳י *will arise*, or *shine*)— 3156
1. Ⓖ *Ζαρεια*, A *Ιεζρια*, ⒼL *Ιεζερια*:—a man of Issachar 1 Ch 7[3.3]. **2.** overseer (הַפָּקִיד) of the singers Ne 12[42], ⒼL al. *Ιεζριας*.

†מִזְרָח **n.[m.] place of sunrise, east**— 4217
abs. ׳מ Jos 11[3] + 21 t.; cstr. מִזְרַח Nu 21[10] + 19 t., c. ה loc. מִזְרָחָה Ex 27[13] + 28 t., cstr. מִזְרְחָה Dt 4[41] Jos 12[1] Ju 21[19] (not in Gn Lv Sa Ez etc.);—**1.** *sunrise*, always of quarter of the heavens = *east* מ׳ (ה)שֶׁמֶשׁ Nu 21[11] (P), Dt 4[41.47] Jos 1[15] 12[1] 13[5] (all D), 19[12.27.34] (all P), Ju 20[43] 21[19] 2 K 10[33] Is 41[25] 45[6] 59[19], cf. מ׳ שמשׁ לארץ Ju 11[18]; מִמִּז׳ שמשׁ וְעַד־מְבוֹאוֹ ψ 50[1] 113[3] Mal 1[11]; more often **2.** without שֶׁמֶשׁ: **a.** *the east* כִּרְחֹק מ׳ מִמַּעֲרָב ψ 103[12]. **b.** ׳מִמִּ *from the east* Is 41[2] 43[5] (opp. מִמַּעֲרָב), 46[11] Dn 11[44] (+ מִצָּפוֹן); ׳מִמִּ

וּמִמַּעֲרָב מִצָּפוֹן וּמִיָּם ψ 107^{3}. **c.** *to or toward the place of sunrise, to the east, eastward:* (1) מִזְרָ֫חָה Nu 32^{19} (P), Dt $3^{17.27}$ (יָ֫מָּה וְצָפ֫וֹנָה וְתֵימָ֫נָה וּמ׳), 4^{49} Jos 11^{8} 16^{1} (JE), $12^{1.3.3}$ 13^{8} (all D), $v^{27.32}$ 16^{5} 18^{7} 20^{8} (all P), 1 Ch 9^{18} 26^{14}; ‖ קֵ֫דְמָה Nu 3^{38} Jos 19^{13} (both P) Je 31^{40}; ‖ יָ֫מָּה, נֶ֫גְבָּה, צָפ֫וֹנָה 1 K 7^{25}, cf. Jos 16^{6} (P) 1 Ch 26^{17}; + קֵ֫דְמָה Ex 27^{13} 38^{13} Nu 2^{3} 34^{15} (all P); מִקֶּדֶם Zc 14^{4} (opp. יָ֫מָּה); מ׳ יָ֫מָּה צָפ֫וֹנָה וָנֶ֫גְבָּה (2) מִזְרָח (without ה loc.), 1 Ch 9^{24}, cf. Ne 12^{37}; מ׳ לַמִּזְבֵּחַ 2 Ch 5^{12}; (3) לַמִּז׳ 1 Ch 5^{9} 7^{28} (opp. לַמַּעֲרָב) 12^{16} (so Baer; v^{15} van d. H; opp. *id.*), 26^{17} (+ לַנֶּ֫גְבָּה, לַצָּפ֫וֹנָה), Ne 3^{26}; לַמִּזְרָ֫חָה 2 Ch 31^{14}; (4) אֶל־הַמּ׳ Dn 8^{9} (+ אֶל־הַנֶּגֶב, אֶל־הַצֶּ֫בִי); (5) מִיָּם עַד־יָם וּמִצָּפוֹן עַד־מִזְרָח Am 8^{12}. **d.** (on) *the east side* of, cstr. קְצֵה מִזְרַח יְרִיחוֹ Jos 4^{19} (P); also c. לְ, לְמִזְרַח הַגַּיְא 1 Ch 4^{39}, לְמ׳ הַיַּרְדֵּן 6^{63}; c. מִן, מִמִּז׳ Jos 11^{3} (opp. מִיָּם) cf. 17^{10} (+ מִצָּפוֹן; both JE), also 16^{6} (P). **e.** after a cstr. רְחוֹב הַמּ׳ 1 Ch 5^{10}; עַל־כָּל־פְּנֵי מ׳ לגלעד 2 Ch 29^{4}; שַׁעַר הַמּ׳ Ne 3^{29}; אֶרֶץ מ׳ Zc 8^{7} (opp. ארץ מְבוֹא הַשָּׁ֫מֶשׁ).

2229 †[**זָרַם**] **vb. pour forth in floods, flood away** (As. *zarâmu, overwhelm*, VR[36, 57 c] Dl[Pr 73] & in Zim[BP 119])—**Qal** *Pf.* 2 ms. sf. זְרַמְתָּם ψ 90^{5} *thou floodest them with rain, sweepest them* (men) *away.* **Po.** *Pf.* 3 pl. זֹ֫רְמוּ מַ֫יִם עָבוֹת ψ 77^{18} the *cloud masses* (Che) *poured forth water.*

2230 †**זֶ֫רֶם** **n.m.** [Hb. 3, 10] **flood of rain, rain-storm, downpour** (Aram. זַרְמִית *id.*)—abs. ז׳ Is 4^{6} + 2 t.; זָ֑רֶם Is 32^{2}; cstr. זֶרֶם Jb 24^{8} + 4 t.; Is 4^{6} (‖ מָטָר); ז׳ מַיִם Is 28^{2} Hb 3^{10}; ז׳ הָרִים Jb 24^{8}, i.e. such as falls among mts. cf. Di; ז׳ בָּרָד Is 28^{2}; מַחְסֶה מִזֶּרֶם 25^{4}, זֶרֶם קִיר v^{4} i.e. such as dashes against a wall, 32^{2} (‖ רוּחַ), נֶפֶץ וָזֶרֶם וְאֶבֶן בָּרָד 30^{30}.

2231 †**זִרְמָה** **n.f. issue** (of *semen virile*), in fig. of the paramours of Jerusalem וְזִרְמַת סוּסִים זִרְמָתָם Ez 23^{20}.

2232 †I. **זָרַע** **vb. sow, scatter seed** (NH *id.*; As. *zirû* TP[Prism vi. 15]; Ar. زَرَعَ; Aram. זְרַע, ܙܪܰܥ; Eth. **ዘርአ: ዘርዐ:** but in Sab. דרא DHM[ZMG 1883, 15] and in n.pr., Id. in MV[10, pp. 242, 983])—**Qal** *Pf.* 3 ms. זָרַע Ju 6^{3}; 1 s. וְזָרַעְתִּי Je 31^{27}; sf. וּזְרַעְתִּיהָ consec. Ho 2^{25}; 3 pl. זָֽרְעוּ Je 12^{13}; 2 mpl. זְרַעְתֶּם Hg 1^{6}; וּזְרַעְתֶּם consec. Gn 47^{23} + 2 t.; *Impf.* יִזְרָע Ec 11^{4}; וַיִּזְרַע Gn 26^{12}; sf. וַיִּזְרָעֶהָ Ju 9^{45}; 1 s. אֶזְרְעָה Jb 31^{8}; sf. וְאֶזְרָעֵם Zc 10^{9}, etc.; *Imv.* ms. זְרַע Ec 11^{6}; mpl. זִרְעוּ Ho 10^{12} + 2 t.; *Inf.* לִזְרֹעַ Is 28^{24}; *Pt. act.* זֹרֵעַ Is 55^{10} + 3 t.; זוֹרֵעַ Pr 22^{8} Je 50^{16}, etc.; *Pt. pass.* זָרֻעַ ψ 97^{11} (but on text v. infr.); f. זְרוּעָה Je 2^{2};—**1.** lit. *sow:* **a.** abs. *sow* (seed), do one's sowing Ju 6^{3} Gn 26^{12} (J), Is 28^{24} (after ploughing חרשׁ); זִרְעוּ וקצרו ונטעו כרמים Is 37^{30} = 2 K 19^{29}; ‖ קצר also Mi 6^{15} Lv 25^{11} (H), Ec 11^{4}; ‖ אסף Lv 25^{20} (H); opp. אכל Jb 31^{8}; זֹרְעֵי עַל־כָּל־מַיִם Is 32^{20} (on cstr. cf. Ges [§130, 1]); c. את־השׁנה השׁמינת Lv 25^{22}; sq. הַרְבֵּה Hg 1^{6} (opp. הָבֵא מְעָט). **b.** c. acc. of land אדמה Ex 23^{10} (JE; ‖ אסף), Gn 47^{23} (J); field (שׂדה) Lv 25^{3} (‖ אסף), cf. v^{4} ψ 107^{37}; as pt. pass. אֶרֶץ לֹא זְרוּעָה Je 2^{2} (‖ מִדְבָּר). **c.** c. acc. of seed ז׳ אֶת־זַרְעֲךָ Dt 11^{10}, cf. 22^{9} Je 35^{7} Lv 26^{16} (H) Ec 11^{6}; sq. חִטִּים Je 12^{13} (‖ קצר); cf. also בִּכּוּרֵי מַעֲשֶׂיךָ אשׁר תזרע בַּשָּׂדֶה Ex 23^{16} (JE). **d.** sq. 2 acc. שָׂדְךָ לֹא תִזְרַע כִּלְאָיִם cf. Dt 22^{9}; לֹא תזרע כַּרְמְךָ כִּלְאָיִם Lv 19^{19} (H); זַרְעֲךָ אשׁר־תזרע את־האדמה Is 30^{23}; also of destroyed city וַיִּזְרָעֶהָ מֶלַח Ju 9^{45}. **e.** pt. act. as subst. זוֹרֵעַ Je 50^{16} (‖ תֹּפֵשׂ מַגָּל בְּעֵת קָצִיר); לַזֹּרֵעַ Is 55^{10} (‖ לָאֹכֵל). **2.** of shrub and tree *producing, yielding seed,* c. acc. cogn. Gn $1^{29.29}$ (P), cf. **Hiph.** **3.** fig.: **a.** of Yahweh's *sowing* (planting) Isr. in the land וזרעתיה לי בָּאָרֶץ Ho 2^{25} (We וזרעתיהו, obj. being Jezreel); on the other hand וְאֶזְרָעֵם בָּעַמִּים Zc 10^{9}. **b.** c. 2 acc., of Yahweh's fructifying Isr. and Judah וזרעתי את־בית ישׂראל ואת־ב׳ יהודה זֶרַע אדם וזרע בהמה Je 31^{27}. **c.** of moral action, זִרְעוּ לָכֶם לִצְדָקָה Ho 10^{12} (‖ קצר); ז׳ צדקה Pr 11^{18}; אַל־תִּזְרְעוּ אֶל־קֹצִים Je 4^{3} *sow not in among thorns* (said of a few righteous deeds amid much wickedness); esp. of evil-doing רוּחַ יזרעו וְסוּפָתָה יִקְצֹרוּ Ho 8^{7}; זֹרְעֵי עָמָל Jb 4^{8} (‖ קצר); זורע עַוְלָה יקצור־אָוֶן Pr 22^{8}. **d.** of Israel's practising idolatry זְמֹרַת זָר תִּזְרָעֶנּוּ Is 17^{10} (2 acc.) **e.** הזרעים בדמעה בְּרִנָּה יִקְצֹרוּ ψ 126^{5} metaph. of distress followed by joy. **f.** אוֹר זָרֻעַ לַצַּדִּיק ψ 97^{11} rd. prob. זָרַח, Vrss Ol Hu Bae Che al.

Niph. **be sown, fructified,** *Pf.* 3 fs. וְנִזְרְעָה consec. Nu 5^{28}; 2 mpl. וְנִזְרַעְתֶּם consec. Ez 36^{9}; *Impf.* 3 ms. יִזָּרַע Na 1^{14}; יִזָּרֵ֑עַ Dt 21^{4} Lv 11^{37}; 3 fs. תִּזָּרַע Dt 29^{22};—**1.** *be sown:* **a.** subj. אֶרֶץ, לֹא תִזָּ׳ ולא תַצְמִחַ Dt 29^{22}, cf. (of נַחַל אֵיתָן) לֹא יֵעָבֵד בּוֹ ולא יִזּ׳ Dt 21^{4}; in address to הָרֵי ישׂראל, וְנֶעֱבַדְתֶּם וְנִזְרַעְתֶּם Ez 36^{9}. **b.** subj. זֶרַע, זֶרַע זֵרוּעַ אשׁר יִזָּרֵעַ Lv 11^{37} (P); fig. לֹא יִזָּ׳ מִשִּׁמְךָ עוֹד Na 1^{14} *no more of thy name be sown,* in judgment against Nineveh. **2.** *be fructified, made pregnant*

וְנִזְרְעָה זָ֑רַע Nu 5^{28} (P; of woman). **Pu.** *Pf.* 3 pl. זֹרָ֑עוּ Is 40^{24} of princes and judges under fig. of trees (|| שֹׁרֵשׁ בָּאָרֶץ גִּזְעָם, נִטָּ֑עוּ). **Hiph.** *Impf.* 3 fs. תַּזְרִיעַ Lv 12^{2}; *Pt.* מַזְרִיעַ Gn 1$^{11.12}$;—**1.** *produce seed,* of herb, c. acc. cogn. Gn 1$^{11.12}$; appar. denom. fr. זֶרַע; cf. **Qal 2.** **2.** of a woman, =*bear a child* תַּזְרִיעַ וְיָלְדָה זָכָר Lv 12^{2}.

2233 †זֶ֫רַע† **n.m.** $^{Dt. 28, 38}$ **sowing, seed, offspring** (NH *id.*, Aram. זְרַע, ܙܰܪܥܳܐ; Ph. זרע; Zinj. *id.;* Ar. زَرْعٌ *seed-produce, seed;* Eth. ዘርእ: As. *zêru, cultivated land,* Belser $^{BAS ii. 130}$, cf. Ar. زَرْعَةٌ)—abs. ז׳ Gn 47^{23}+; זָ֑רַע Gn 1^{29}+; cstr. זֶרַע Is 5^{10}+; זֶרַע־ Nu 11^{7}; sf. זַרְעִי 1 S 20^{42} 24^{22}; זַרְעֲךָ Dt 11^{10}+; זַרְעֶ֑ךָ Ec 11^{6}+, etc.; pl. sf. זַרְעֵיכֶם 1 S 8^{15};—**1.** lit.: **a.** a *sowing* לְז׳ הַשָּׂדֶה Gn 47^{24} (J; +אָכְלְכֶם; otherwise Lv 27$^{16 b}$, v. infr. **2 c**); לֹא מְקוֹם ז׳ Nu 20^{5} *no place for sowing* (JE; +וּתְאֵנָה וְגֶפֶן וְרִמּוֹן); cf. שְׂדֵה ז׳ Ez 17^{5} *a field suitable for sowing;* hence **b.** *sowing* as regularly recurring at its season Gn 8^{22} (J; || קָצִיר, +קֹר וָחֹם וְקַיִץ וָחֹרֶף וְיוֹם וָלַיְלָה), Lv 26^{5} (H; || בָּצִיר, דַּיִשׁ;—cf. Am 9^{13} infr. **2 a**). **2.** *seed:* **a.** lit., sown, to raise crops for food, usu. corn (wheat, barley, etc.) Gn 47$^{19.23}$ (J; cf. v$^{14 f.}$), Nu 24^{7} (JE); נָתַן ז׳ לַזֹּרֵעַ Is 55^{10} (|| לֶחֶם), Dt 28^{38} (ז׳ רַב), Lv 26^{16} (H; c. זָרַע), 27$^{16 a}$, ז׳ חֹמֶר שְׂעֹרִים v$^{16 b}$ (both P), cf. Is 5^{10}. **b.** fig., of idolatry of Judah Is 17^{11} (|| קציר); of fortunes of Zion מֶשֶׁךְ הַז׳ ψ 126^{6} *the dropping of seed,* i.e. the proper quantity for sowing (opp. אֲלֻמֹּת); Je 35^{7} (c. זָרַע || כֶּרֶם לֹא תִטָּ֑עוּ), cf. v^{9} (|| שדה, כרם); מְטַר ז׳ Is 30^{23} (c. זָרַע, || לֶחֶם תְּבוּאַת הָאֲדָמָה); also Dt 11^{10} (c. זָרַע), Ec 11^{6} (c. *id.*); ז׳ זֵרוּעַ Lv 11^{37}, cf. v^{38} (both P); as yielding the crop תְּבוּאַת זַרְעֶךָ Dt 14^{22} *the product of thy seed,* cf. **d** infr.; וְנִגַּשׁ חוֹרֵשׁ בַּקֹּצֵר וְדֹרֵךְ עֲנָבִים בְּמֹשֵׁךְ הַז׳ Am 9^{13}, in fig. of rapid and plentiful growth in the coming time; ז׳ הָאָרֶץ producing a vine Ez 17^{5}, of growth and prosperity of Isr.; הַז׳ Mal 2^{3}, rd. perh. הַזְּרֹעַ (cf. VB). **c.** *seed* as product; the manna is comp. with ז׳ גַּד, *coriander seed* in Nu 11^{7} (JE), Ex 16^{31} (P); seed of herbs and trees Gn 1$^{11.11.12.12.29.29}$ (all P). Esp. **d.** *seed* as *corn-product, corn-crop,* so (although not quite clearly) Dt 22^{9} (c. זָרַע; || תְּבוּאַת הַכָּ֑רֶם); pl. 1 S 8^{15} (perh. better *arable lands,* cf. supr. As. *zêru;* || כרמים), ז׳ הָאָרֶץ Lv 27^{30} (|| פְּרִי־עֵץ; otherwise Gn 47^{24}, cf. supr. **1 a**); ז׳ שִׁחֹר Is 23^{3} (|| קְצִיר יְאוֹר); הַעוֹד הַז׳ בַּמְּגוּרָה Hg 2^{19} (|| עֵץ הַזַּיִת, רִמּוֹן, תְּאֵנָה, גֶּפֶן); יָשׁוּב זַרְעֶךָ וְגָרְנְךָ יֶאֱסֹף Jb 39^{12} (of harvest); so perh. ז׳ כְּבֵית סָאתַיִם 1 K 18^{32}. **e.** זֶרַע הַשָּׁלוֹם הַגֶּפֶן Zc 8^{12}, rd. perh. הַז׳ שָׁלוֹם *the crop is security* (= secure), so 𝔖 Or al.; > Ew Hi al. who transl. ז׳ הַשׁ׳ *the growth of peace,* making הַגֶּפֶן appos.—Vbs. used c. ז׳ in these senses are:—usu. זָרַע Gn 1^{11} Lv 26^{16} Je 35^{7}+; נָתַן בְּ הִפְרִיחַ Is 17^{11}; =*plant, sow* Ez 17^{5}; נָתַן *yield* Is 55^{10}; מָשַׁךְ Am 9^{13}. **3.** *seed*=semen virile, וְנִזְרְעָה זָ֑רַע Nu 5^{28}, *and she shall be made pregnant* with *seed;* usu. שִׁכְבַת־ז׳, *flow of semen* Lv 22^{4} (H), Lv 15$^{16.32}$ (P; all c. תֵּצֵא), 15^{17} (P; c. הָיָה); as *acc. modi* שכב אֶת־אִשָּׁה שׁ׳ ז׳ Lv 19^{20} (H), 15^{18} Nu 5^{13} (both P); so also נתן שְׁכָבְתּוֹ לְזרע Lv 18^{20} (לְ genitiv.); cf. ז׳ אָדָם וז׳ בְּהֵמָה Je 31^{27} (as 2nd acc. after זָרַע q.v. **3 b**). **4.** *seed*=*offspring:* **a.** rarely of animals, coll. Gn 3^{15} 7^{3} (both J). Usu. **b.** of mankind, coll. =*descendants, posterity; seed of the woman* Gn 3^{15} (J); seed of the patriarchs (esp. Abr.) 12^{7} 13$^{15.16.16}$ 16^{10} 22$^{17.17.18}$ 24^{7} 26$^{3.4.4.4.24}$ 28$^{13.14.14}$ 32^{13} (all J), 15$^{13.18}$ Ex 32$^{13.13}$ 33^{1} (all JE), Gn 21^{12} Jos 24^{3} (both E; in both promised seed of Abr. restricted to line of Isaac), Dt 11^{9} 34^{4} Ne 9^{8};=a son as involving posterity Gn 15^{3,5} (JE) cf. infr.; phr. זַרְעָם אַחֲרֵיהֶם Dt 1^{8}, cf. 4^{37} 10^{15}, so P, Gn 17$^{7.7.8.9.10.19}$ 35^{12} 48^{4}; זַרְעֲךָ אִתָּךְ Gn 28^{4} (P; cf. Nu 18^{19}); v. also infr. **c.** **c.** *seed* (=posterity) of other individuals Gn 21^{13} (E; of Ishmael) 24^{60} 48^{19} (both J), Nu 14^{24} (JE), Lv 21^{21} 22$^{3.4}$ (all H), Nu 17^{5} (P), 1 S 20$^{42.42}$ 24^{22} 2 S 4^{8} 1 K 2$^{33.33}$ 11^{39} 2 K 5^{27} Je 29^{32} Ez 43^{19} Jb 5^{25} (|| צֶאֱצָאֶיךָ), 21^{8} (|| *id.*); esp. of seed of David as anointed to reign ψ 18^{51}=2 S 22^{51} (|| לִמְשִׁיחוֹ), as sitting on throne Je 33^{21}, cf. v$^{22.26}$, ψ 89$^{5.30.37}$; of Jehoiachin Je 22$^{28.30}$, Jehoiakim 36^{31} (cf. v^{30}); of child (son) as involving posterity Gn 38$^{8.9.9}$ (of Er's seed by Onan), 48^{11} (all J), cf. 19$^{32.34}$ (J), 2 S 7^{12} Ru 4^{12} Lv 21^{15} (H); phr. זַרְעָם אַחֲרֵיהֶם of seed of Noah and his sons Gn 9^{9}; of Aaron Ex 28^{43}; of Phinehas Nu 25^{13} (all P); of David 1 Ch 17^{11}; לְזַרְעוֹ לְדֹרֹתָם Ex 30^{21} (P), cf. Lv 21^{17} (H; both of Aaron), v. also **b** supr. ז׳, of *seed* of righteous, esp. ψψ:—ψ 25^{13} 37$^{25.26}$ 69^{37} 102^{29} (|| בָּנִים), 112^{2} (|| דור ישרים), cf. 22^{31} (on txt. v. Che); of wicked ψ 21^{11} 37^{28}. **d.** specif. of a *particular child* (son) ז׳ אַחֵר Gn 4^{25} (J); ז׳ אֲנָשִׁים 1 S 1^{11}; of children Lv 18^{21} 20$^{2.3.4}$ 22^{13} (all H), 1 S 2^{20} (cf. בָּנוֹת, בָּנִים v^{21}); children and grandchildren Gn 46$^{6.7}$ (P). **e.** =*family* Gn 17^{12} (P; cf. As. *zêr bit abišu* Asrb $^{Annals iii. 10}$); note esp. *of royal family* ז׳ הַמֶּלֶךְ 1 K 11^{14}; ז׳ הַמַּמְלָכָה 2 K 11^{1}= 2 Ch 22^{10}; ז׳ הַמְּלוּכָה 2 K 25^{25}=Je 41^{1}, Ez 17^{13} Dn 1^{3}; =*pedigree* בית אבותם וְזַרְעָם Ezr 2^{59}= Ne 7^{61}; =one's *nation,* as of same blood Est 10^{3} (|| עַם).—Some vbs. used c. ז׳ in these senses are:—נָתַן, God subj. Gn 15^{3} Ru 4^{12} (sq. מִן of woman); שִׂים 1 S 2^{20}; c. man as subj. נתן Gn 38^{9}; הֵקִים v^{8}; חִיָּה ז׳, *keep alive*, or *give life to*, of animals Gn 7^{3}; of woman 19$^{32.34}$ (sq. מִן of man). **f.** esp. as name for people of Isr., *seed of Abr.* Is 41^{8} 2 Ch 20^{7} (|| עַמְּךָ יִשְׂרָאֵל), Je 33^{26} ψ 105^{6} (|| בְּנֵי יעקב); of Isr. or Jacob 2 K 17^{20} Ne 9^{2} (|| בני ישׂראל v^{1}), Is 43^{5} 45$^{19.25}$ Je 31$^{36.37}$ 33^{26} ψ 22$^{24.24}$ 1 Ch 16^{13} (|| בני יעקב); so ז׳ בֵּית ישׂראל Je 23^{8} Ez 44^{22} (𝔖 𝔊 codd. Co del. בית); ז׳ בית יעקב Ez 20^{5}; in Est. ז׳ הַיְּהוּדִים Est 6^{13}; so of Edom (seed of Esau) Je 49^{10}, cf. מִזֶּרַע מָדַי Dn 9^{1}. **g.** *seed* of Isr. (or Jacob, or the people), is used also, by (later) prophets, of *future generations*, in addressing the people:—Dt 28$^{46.59}$ 30$^{6.19}$ 31^{21}, cf. Nu 18^{19} (P; לְזַרְעֲךָ אִתָּךְ || וּלְבָנֶיךָ וְלִבְנֹתֶיךָ), Je 30^{10}=46^{27} (Jacob and Isr. here=people), ψ 106^{27}; || צֶאֱצָא(יך) Is 44^{3} (Jacob and Jeshurun), 48^{19}, cf. 61^{9}; also Je 7^{15} Is 54^{3} 66^{22} (|| שִׁמְכֶם); מִפִּי זַרְעֲךָ וּמִפִּי זֶרַע זַרְעֲךָ Is 59^{21}; of Jews (יהודים) Est 9$^{27.28.31}$. **5.** *seed* as marked by moral quality = persons (or community) of such a quality; transition to this through such cases as those of ז׳ בְּרוּכֵי י׳ Is 65^{23} (|| צֶאֱצָאִים), cf. 61^{9} 65^{9}; ז׳ הַקֹּדֶשׁ Ezr 9^{2} (of Isr.), cf. Is 53^{10}; note, in good sense ז׳ צַדִּיקִים Pr 11^{21} (opp. רַע); ז׳ אֱמֶת Je 2^{21} (|| שׂוֹרֵק); ז׳ אלהים Mal 2^{15};—ז׳ קֹדֶשׁ Is 6^{13} is a gloss;—in bad sense ז׳ מְרֵעִים Is 1^{4} *community of evil-doers* (|| גּוֹי־חֹטֵא, עַם כֶּבֶד עָוֺן, בָּנִים מַשְׁחִיתִים), 14^{20}; ז׳ מְנָאֵף 57^{3} (|| בני עֹנְנָה); ז׳־שָׁקֶר v^{4} (|| יִלְדֵי־פֶשַׁע).

2221 †**זֵרוּעַ n.[m.] sowing, thing sown** (intensive format. acc. to Ol $^{§ 186 b}$ Sta $^{§ 228}$, yet on this and foll. cf. Ba $^{NB 42, 178 Anm. 4}$)—ז׳ זֵרוּעַ Lv 11^{37} (P), כְּגַנָּה זֵרוּעֶיהָ תַצְמִיחַ Is 61^{11} in sim. of Yahweh's causing righteousness to spring up.

2235 †[**זֵרֹעַ**] **n.[m.] vegetable** (cf. foregoing; on this and foll. cf. Bev $^{Dn 62, and n. 2}$)—only pl. מִן־הַזֵּרֹעִים Dn 1^{12}.

2235 †[**זֵרְעֹן**] **n.[m.]** id., only pl. זֵרְעֹנִים Dn 1^{16}.

3157 †**יִזְרְעֶאל 1. n.pr.loc.** (*God soweth;* Sab. אלדרא Mordt $^{ZMG 1879, 489}$; v. Lag $^{BN 131}$)—י׳ Jos 15^{56} 2 S 2^{9}+; יִזְרְעֶאל 1 S 25^{43} Jos 17^{16}+; יִזְרְעֶאלָה Jos 19^{18}+6 t.: **a.** city in the Negeb of Judah Jos 15^{56} 1 S 25^{43} (home of Ahinoam, one of David's wives), site unknown; cf. n.pr.m. 1 Ch 4^{3}. **b.** city in Issachar Jos 19^{18} on NW. spur of Mt. Gilboa 2 S 4^{4} (cf. 1 S 31$^{1.8}$) 1 K 4^{12} (cf. 1 S 31$^{10.12}$), mod. *Zer'în* (Rob $^{BR ii. 318 ff.}$ Bd $^{Pal 244}$), close to scene of great battle with Philistines 1 S 29^{1} (בָּעַיִן אשׁר בְּיִז׳, cf. Rob $^{BR ii. 323}$) v^{11}; subject to Ishbosheth 2 S 2^{9} (yet v. infr.), residence of Ahab and Jehoram of Isr. 1 K 18$^{45.46}$ 21^{1} (Naboth) 2 K 8$^{29.29}$=2 Ch 22$^{6.6}$, 2 K 9$^{15.15.16.17.30}$ 10^{11} cf. דְּמֵי יִז׳ Ho 1^{4}, and symbolical name of Hosea's son Ho 1^{4} (cf. Che);—in 2 K 10^{1} for שָׂרֵי יִז׳ rd. שָׂרֵי שֹׁמְרוֹן so 𝔊. Used by Hosea as representing Isr., with play on etymol., Ho 2^{24} (cf. וּזְרַעְתִּיהָ לִּי בָּאָרֶץ v^{25}), cf. also גָּדוֹל יוֹם יִז׳ v^{2}. Territory immediately about the city is חֵלֶק יִז׳ 2 K 9$^{10.36.37}$; cf. חֵל יִז׳ 1 K 21^{23} (rd. prob. חלק, v. Th Klo after 𝔖 𝔙; the adjacent plain is עֵמֶק יִז׳ (cf. Di Jos 17^{16} Bd $^{Pal 229}$) Jos 17^{16} Ju 6^{33} Ho 1^{5} (perh. also = יִז׳ 2 S 2^{9} supr., || Gilead, Ephr., Benj., etc.) **2. n.pr.m. a.** Hosea's son Ho 1^{4}, cf. **1 b** supr. **b.** Judahite name 1 Ch 4^{3}, cf. **1 a** supr.

†**יִזְרְעֵאלִי m., יִזְרְעֵאלִית f., adj.gent.** 3158-59
1. m. fr. יִזְרְעֶאל **1 b**; alw. נָבוֹת הַיִּז׳ 1 K 21$^{1.4.6.7.15.16}$ 2 K 9$^{21.25}$. **2. f.** fr. יִזְרְעֶאל **1 a**; alw. אֲחִינֹעַם הַיִּז׳ a wife of David; ending ־ִית 1 S 30^{5} 2 S 2^{2} 1 Ch 3^{1}; ending ־ֹת 1 S 27^{3} 2 S 3^{2} (=1 Ch 3^{1}).

†[**מִזְרָע**] **n.[m.] place of sowing, seed-** 4218
land, only cstr. כֹּל מִזְרַע יְאוֹר Is 19^{7} (|| עָרוֹת יְאוֹר); >Du who tr. *seed* (cf. מאכל etc.) on acc. of foll. vb. נִדַּף.

II. **זרע** (cf. Ar. ذَرَعَ *stretch out, extend,* esp. arm or leg; ذَرْعٌ *power,* ذِرَاعٌ *forearm*).

†**זְרֹעַ, זְרוֹעַ n.f.** $^{Ex 6, 6}$ and (rare) **m.** $^{Is 51, 5, cf.}$ 2220
$^{infr.}$ **arm, shoulder, strength** (NH *id.;* As. (Tel el Amarna $^{102, 1. 12, etc.}$) *zurû*, cf. Jastrow $^{JBL, xi, 1892, 123}$; Ar. ذِرَاعٌ; Aram. דְּרָעָא, ܕܪܳܥܳܐ; Eth. መዝራዕት:)—abs. זְרוֹעַ Ex 6^{6}+, זְרֹעַ Dt 7^{19}+; cstr. זְרוֹעַ ψ 10^{15}+, זְרֹעַ ψ 89^{11}+; sf. זְרוֹעִי Je 27^{5} ψ 89^{2}, זְרֹעִי Is 51^{5} 63^{5}; זְרוֹעֲךָ ψ 71^{18}+, זְרֹעֲךָ 1 S 3^{31}+, etc.; pl. זְרֹעִים Dn 11^{31}; cstr. זְרֹעֵי Gn 49^{24}; sf. זְרֹעַי Is 51^{5}, זְרֹעָיו 2 K 9^{24}; elsewh. fem. form, cstr. זְרֹעֹת ψ 37^{17}, זרעות Jb 22^{9}+6 t., זְרֹעֹת Dt 33^{27}; sf. זְרוֹעֹתָי ψ 18^{35}, זְרֹעֹתַי 2 S 22^{35}, etc. (In abs. and cstr. sg. more oft. *plene*, in pl. and c. sf. more oft. *defect.* In three instances where ז׳ is masculine it means a political or military *force* Dn 11$^{15.22.31}$).—**1.** *arm*, **a.** lit., of a man Ju 15^{14} 16^{12} 2 S 1^{10} Is 9^{19} 17^{5} (prob. acc. instr.), Dt 33^{20} Zc 11$^{17.17}$ Ct 8^{6} Dn 10^{6}; Ez 13^{30} (del. Co); ז׳ כֹּחוֹ Is 44^{12} (of a smith, forging); ז׳ חֲשׂוּפָה Ez 4^{7} (of prophet); in fig. of י׳ teaching Ephr. to walk Ho 11^{3}; זְרֹעֵי יָדָיו Gn 49^{24} *arms of his hands,* i.e. arms that by their strength enable him (Joseph)

to draw the bow; וַיַּךְ אֶת־יְהוֹרָם בֵּין זְרֹעָיו 2 K 9^{24}, i.e. his arms seen from behind, *his shoulders*. **b.** *arm* as *seat of* (human) *strength* ψ 18^{35} = 2 S 22^{35}; ז׳ לֹא עֹז Jb 26^{2}, כּוֹחַ הַז׳ Dn 11^{6} cf. v^{6}; ז׳ לֹא עֹז Jb 26^{2}; חִזַּקְתִּי ז׳ Ho 7^{15} cf. Ez 30$^{24.25}$; also c. שׁבר ψ 10^{15} 37^{17} Je 48^{25} (‖ קֶרֶן), Ez 30$^{21.22.24}$ cf. v^{25}; ז׳ רָמָה תִּשָּׁבֵר Jb 38^{15}.—On Mal 2^{3} cf. VB. Esp. **c.** *Yahweh's arm* as instrument of deliverance and judgment (oft. Dt Je Is^{2} ψ):—ז׳ נְטוּיָה Dt 4^{34} 5^{15} 26^{8} Ez 20$^{33.34}$ ψ 136^{12}, cf. Dt 7^{19} 11^{2} 1 K 8^{42} = 2 Ch 6^{32} (all ‖ יָד חֲזָקָה), Dt 9^{29} 2 K 17^{36}; (of creation) Je 27^{5} 32^{17} (all ‖ כֹּחַ גָּדוֹל); בִּז׳ נְטוּיָה Ex 6^{6} (P, or D's revision; no ‖); ז׳ חֲזָקָה Je 21^{5} (‖ יָד נְטוּיָה); גְּדֹל זרועך Ex 15^{16} (song), גֹּדֶל ז׳ ψ 79^{11}; ז׳ ψ 44^{4}; בִּז׳ ψ 77^{16}; זְרוֹעִי תְאַמְּצֶנּוּ ψ 89^{22} (‖ יָדִי); ז׳ עֻזֶּךָ ψ 89^{11} cf. Is 62^{8} (‖ יְמִינוֹ); ז׳ קָדְשׁוֹ ψ 98^{1} (‖ יְמִינוֹ), cf. Is 52^{10}; לְךָ ז׳ (‖ יְמִינְךָ), לִבְשִׁי־עֹז זְרוֹעַ י׳ Is 51^{9}; עִם־גְּבוּרָה ψ 89^{14}; ז׳ תִּפְאַרְתּוֹ Is 63^{12}; as support of weak Is 40^{11} (fig. of shepherd), cf. זְרֹעֹת עוֹלָם Dt 33^{27}; נַחַת זְרוֹעוֹ יַרְאֶה Is 30^{30} (of lightning stroke, ‖ השמיע הוד קולו of thunder); also אִם־זְרוֹעַ כָּאֵל לָךְ Jb 40^{9}.

Hence, **2.** *arm*, as symbol of *strength*: **a.** human 1 S 2$^{31.31}$ (𝔊 rd. זַרְעֲךָ and זֶרַע, but v. Klo Dr), Ez 22^{6} 31^{17}; וַתְּאַמֵּץ זְרוֹעֹתֶיהָ Pr 31^{17}; ז׳ בָּשָׂר 2 Ch 32^{8}; שָׂם בָּשָׂר זְרֹעוֹ Je 17^{5} (‖ יִבְטַח בָּאָדָם); cf. ψ 44^{4} (‖ חַרְבָּם); איש זרוע Jb 22^{8}; זְרֹעוֹת יְתֹמִים Jb 22^{9} (i.e. strength, resources); זְרֹעַ גְּדוֹלָה; ז׳ רַבִּים Jb 35^{9}; הָיוּ זרוע לִבְנֵי־לוֹט ψ 83^{9}; Ez 17^{9} (for pulling up a tree, in metaph.). **b.** = divine strength ψ 71^{18} (‖ גְּבוּרָה), זְרֹעוֹ מֹשְׁלָה לוֹ Is 40^{10} (‖ חָזָק); זְרֹעַי עַמִּים יִשְׁפֹּטוּ 51^{5} [Str thinks masc. to avoid verbal ending נָה, cf. 49^{11}]; and help Is 33^{2} (‖ יְשׁוּעָה) cf. 59^{16} 63^{5}; see also 53^{1}.

3. Pl. *forces*, political and military, c. יַעֲמֹדוּ Dn 11$^{15.31}$; v^{22} (see Bev).

4. *Shoulder* of animal sacrificed, belonging to priest Nu 6^{19} (P) Dt 18^{3}.

248 †אֶזְרוֹעַ **n.f. arm** (= foregoing c. א prosthet.)—*arm* of man כְּתֵפִי מִשִּׁכְמָה תִפּוֹל וְאֶזְרֹעִי מִקָּנָה תִשָּׁבֵר: Jb 31^{22}; of י׳ וּבְיָד חֲזָקָה וּבְאֶזְרוֹעַ נְטוּיָה Je 32^{21}, cf. זְרוֹעַ **1 c.**

†[זָרַף] **vb.** prob. **drip** (cf. either Ar. ذَرَفَ *shed* tears, or Aram. ܙܪܘܦܐ *imber vehemens*)—**Hiph.** יַזְרִיף rd. in ψ 72^{6} by Hup Bi Che (for
2222 זַרְזִיף) sq. אֶרֶץ *cause to drip, irrigate*.

2222 †זַרְזִיף **n.[m.]** drop, dripping (NH *id.*; on form (if genuine) cf. Nö$^{M\,85,\,NS\,191}$)—ψ 72^{6} כִּרְבִיבִים ז׳ אָרֶץ as showers, a *dripping* of the earth, but v. foregoing.

†זָרַק **vb. to toss or throw** (in a volume), **scatter abundantly** (NH *id.*; Aram. זְרַק *id.*, ܙܪܩ *disperse*; As. *zarâḳu* Lotz$^{TP\,138}$ Jäger$^{BAS\,ii.\,292\,Anm.**}$; cf. also Ar. زَرَقَ *cast at, pierce*, زُرَاقَةٌ and مِزْرَاقٌ *javelin* = Eth. ሞዝራቅ:)—**Qal** *Pf.* ז׳ Ex 24^{6} Lv 17^{6}, sf. זְרָקוֹ Ex 9^{8}, זָרְקָה Ho 7^{9} (12 t. Pf.); *Impf.* יִזְרֹק Lv 7^{2} + 16 t.; *Inf.* לִזְרֹק Ez 43^{18}; *Imv.* זְרֹק Ez 10^{2}; *Pt.* זֹרֵק Lv 7^{14}, pl. זֹרְקִים 2 Ch 30^{16}; **1.** *toss* (in handfuls, v. Ex 9^{8}; or from a *bowl*, מִזְרָק; opp. הִזָּה to *sprinkle* with the finger): **a.** cummin Is 28^{25}, dust, sq. עַל 2 Ch 34^{4} Jb 2^{12}, ashes השמימה, heavenward, Ex 9$^{8.10}$ (P), coals of fire על העיר Ez 10^{2}. **b.** blood, על (ה)מזבח *throw* (from a bowl) against the altar Ex 24^{6} (JE), Lv 17^{6} (H), Nu 18^{17} (P), 2 K 16$^{13.15}$ Ez 43^{18}, esp. in the ritual, על המזבח סביב against the altar round about Ex 29$^{16.20}$ Lv 1$^{5.11}$ 3$^{2.8.13}$ 7^{2} 8$^{19.24}$ 9$^{12.18}$ (all P); sq. על העם Ex 24^{8} (JE), sq. המזבחה 2 Ch 29$^{22.22.22}$; without designation of place Lv 7^{14} (P), 2 Ch 30^{16} 35^{11}. **c.** *water* for purification, sq. עַל, Ez 36^{25}. **2.** intrans. (si vera l.) Ho 7^{9} גַּם שֵׂיבָה זָרְקָה בּוֹ grey hairs are *profuse* upon him (? rd. זָרְחָה, as in 2 Ch 26^{19}). **Pu.** *Pf.* זֹרַק, of water of purification *poured* over (עַל) one defiled by a corpse Nu 19$^{13.20}$ (P). 2236

†מִזְרָק **n.m.**$^{Nu\,7,\,84}$ bowl, bason (prop. vessel for *throwing* or *tossing* a liquid); מ׳ Nu 7^{13} + 13 t., pl. מִזְרָקִים Zc 14^{20}, cstr. מִזְרְקֵי Nu 7^{84} + 2 t., מִזְרָקוֹת Ne 7^{70} + 9 t., מִזְרְקֹת Ex 38^{3} + 2 t., sf. מִזְרְקֹתָיו Ex 27^{3};—**1.** *bowl* for wine Am 6^{6}. **2.** elsewh. for use in ritual of sacrifice: **a.** for use at altar Ex 27^{3} 38^{3} Nu 4^{14} (all P), 1 K 7$^{40.45}$ Je 52^{18} Zc 9^{15} 14^{20}. **b.** given by the princes full of flour mingled with oil for a מנחה Nu 7$^{13.19.25.31.37.43.49.55.61.67.73.79.84.85}$ (P). **c.** golden basons for use in the temple 1 K 7^{50} 2 K 12^{14} 25^{15} 1 Ch 28^{17} 2 Ch 4$^{8.11.22}$ Je 52^{19}. **d.** golden basons for the second temple Ne 7^{70}. 4219

†[זָרַר] **vb.** only **Po. sneeze** (cf. זְרִירוֹ(ה)י׳ 2237
𝔗 Jb 41^{10} for Heb. עֲטִישֹׁתָיו; vb. prob. onomatop.);—וַיְזוֹרֵר הַנַּעַר עַד שֶׁבַע פְּעָמִים 2 K 4^{35}.

†זֶרֶשׁ **n.pr.f.** wife of Haman Est 5$^{10.14}$ 6$^{13.13}$ 2238
(acc. to Opp$^{Esth.\,25}$ = Pers. *zaris*, Zend *zairis*, *la dorée*, cf. زرشته *aurum ductile*, Vull$^{ii.\,128\,b}$; Jen$^{VOJ,\,1892,\,64}$ comp. Elamit. goddess *Kiriša*).

†זֶרֶת **n.f.** span (NH *id.* (𝔗 זַרְתָּא, Syr. 2239
ܙܪܬܐ; appar. fr. Heb.), etym. dub.; Thes and most der. fr. √ זרה, vid. Ol$^{§\,146\,b}$ but also Sta$^{§\,187\,a}$; Ba$^{ZMG\,1887,\,607}$ prop. √ זרה *measure off, determine*,

cf. p. 280)—*span*, as standard of measurement, שָׁמַיִם בַּזֶּ׳ תִּכֵּן Is 40^{12}; elsewh. of actual size, *a span*, distance between ends of thumb and little finger of spread hand; $=\frac{1}{2}$ cubit (v. אַמָּה & reff.; cf. Ex 25^{10} with Joseph$^{Ant. iii. 6,5}$), ז׳ Ex 28$^{16.16}$ 39$^{9.9}$ (all P) Ez 43^{13}; זָ֑רֶת 1 S 17^{4} six cubits and *a span*. Vid. Hultsch$^{Metrol. 1882, 443}$ Benz$^{Archäol. 179}$.

†זַתּוּא **n.pr.m.** head of a family of returned 2240
exiles Ezr 2^{8} = Ne 7^{13}; cf. also Ezr 10^{27}
Ne 10^{15}.

†זֵתָם **n.pr.m.** a Levite 1 Ch 23^{8} 26^{22}. p. 268 2241

†זֵתַר **n.pr.m.** an eunuch of Ahasuerus Est 2242
1^{10} (Opp$^{Esth. 25}$ comp. Pers. *zaitar, conqueror*).

ח

ח, *Ḥêth*, 8th letter; = numeral 8 in post BHeb.

2243 [חֹב], חֻבִּי v. sub חבב. below

2244 †[חָבָא] **vb. withdraw, hide** (not in **Qal**); cf. also חבה (NH *id.*; Ar. خَبَأَ; Eth. ኀብአ: As. *ḫabû* Dl$^{Pr 175}$; 𝔗 Ethpa. *hide oneself*)—**Niph.** *Pf.* 3 ms. נֶחְבָּא Ju 9^{5} + 1 S 10^{22} 2 S 17^{9} (both may be *pt.*); נַחְבֵּאתָ Gn 31^{27}; וְנֶחְ׳ consec. 1 S 19^{2}; נֶחְבְּאוּ Jos 10^{27}; נֶחְבָּ֑אוּ Jb 29$^{8.10}$; *Impf.* 2 ms. תֵּחָבֵא Jb 5^{21}; *Inf. cstr.* הֵחָבֵא 2 Ch 18^{24} Dn 10^{7}; *Pt.* pl. (cf. also *supr.*) נֶחְבְּאִים Jos 10^{17}, etc.—*hide oneself* in fear Gn 3^{10} (J), Jos 10$^{16.17.27}$ (all JE), Ju 9^{5} 1 S 19^{2} 2 S 17^{9} Am 9^{3} 2 Ch 18^{24} Dn 10^{7}; from modesty 1 S 10^{22}; cf. Jb 29^{8}; also לָ֫מָּה נַחְבֵּאתָ לִבְרֹחַ Gn 31^{27} (E), i.e. why didst thou flee secretly? pass., *be hidden* Jb 29^{10} קוֹל נְגִידִים נֶחְבָּ֑אוּ (‖ וּלְשׁוֹנָם לְחִכָּם דָּבֵ֑קָה, cf. also v. 9) i.e. in reverence, = *hushed* (so we speak of a *veiled* voice); be hidden for protection בְּשׁוֹט לָשׁוֹן Jb 5^{21}. **Pu.** *Pf.* 3 pl. חֻבָּ֑אוּ *have been hidden* (= are made to hide themselves, Di *ad loc.*) Jb 24^{4}. **Hiph.** *Pf.* 3 ms. sf. הֶחְבִּיאָ֑נִי Is 49^{2}; 3 fs. הֶחְבִּ֫אָתָה Jos 6^{17}, cf. Ges$^{§ 75. Rem. 21 a}$ Kö$^{i. 624 ff.}$ etc.; *Impf.* וַיַּחְבִּיאֵם 1 K 18^{4}; 3 fs. וַתַּחְבִּא 2 K 6^{29}; וָאַחְבִּא 1 K 18^{13};—*hide*, trans., c. acc. Jos 6$^{17.25}$ 1 K 18$^{4.13}$ 2 K 6^{29}; metaph., of divine protection Is 49^{2} בְּצֵל יָדוֹ ה׳. **Hoph.** *Pf. be hidden* הָחְבָּ֑אוּ Is 42^{22} (בְּבָתֵּי כלאים), i.e. imprisoned. **Hithp.** *Pf.* הִתְחַבְּאוּ 1 S 14^{11}; *Impf.* יִתְחַבֵּא 1 S 23^{23}; וַיִּתְ׳ Gn 3^{8}; יִתְחַבָּ֑אוּ Jb 38^{30}; וַיִּתְחַבְּאוּ 1 S 13^{6}; *Pt.* מִתְחַבֵּא 2 K 11^{3} + 2 t.; מִתְחַבְּאִים 1 S 14^{22} 1 Ch 21^{20};—**1.** *draw back, hide oneself*, usu. c. בְּ loc.; Gn 3^{8} (J), 1 S 13^{6} 14$^{11.22}$ 23^{23} 2 K 11^{3} 1 Ch 21^{20} 2 Ch 22$^{9.12}$. **2.** *draw together, thicken, harden*, of water becoming ice Jb 38^{30} כָּאֶבֶן מַיִם יִתְחַ׳.

†מַחֲבֵא **n.[m.] hiding-place,** only cstr. 4224
כְּמַחֲבֵא רוּחַ וְסֵתֶר זָרֶם Is 32^{2} *hiding-place from wind.*

†[מַחֲבֹא] **n.[m.]** id., pl. abs. מִכֹּל הַמַּחֲבֹאִים 4224
אשר יתחבא שם 1 S 23^{23}.

†[חָבַב] **vb. love** (NH Pi. *id.*; Ar. حَبَّ 2245
be loved; Eth. ተሐበበ: *amore alicujus incendi* Di; Aram. ܚܒ *kindle, be set on fire*, ܚܘܒܐ, חוּבָּא *love, embrace*, חוּבָּא *bosom*)—**Qal** *Pt.* אַף חֹבֵב עַמִּים Dt 33^{3} (Di rds. עַמּוֹ, cf. 𝔊).

†[חֹב] **n.[m.] bosom** (Aram.) לִטְמוֹן בְּחֻבִּי 2243
עֲוֺנִי Jb 31^{33} (cf. חֵיק).

†חֹבָב **n.pr.m.** (cf. Ph. n.pr. חב; We^{Skizzen} 2246
$^{iii, 171. 217}$ suggests compar. with حُبَاب *serpent*)—son of Reuel, חֹתֵן of Moses (v. חתן), Nu 10^{29} (JE), Ju 4^{11}; ins. ח׳ prob. also Ju 1^{16}, **v. GFM.**

†חֻבָּה **n.pr.m.** a descendant of Asher, 1 Ch
7^{34} (rd. וְחֻבָּה, so Qr; > Kt יְחֻבָּה). 3160

†[חָבָה] **vb. withdraw, hide,** cf. חבא;— 2247
Qal *Imv.* ms. חֲבִי Is 26^{20} (Aram. form, Ol$^{§ 235, 3}$ Ew$^{§ 224 c}$ Du; Di rds. חֲבִי = חֲבֵה), *withdraw* into privacy (‖ בֹּא בַחֲדָרֶיךָ). **Niph.** *Pf.* וְנֶחְבָּה consec. Je 49^{10}; וְנֶחְבֵּתֶם consec. Jos 2^{16} (JE); *Inf.* לְהֵחָבֵה (as ל״א) 1 K 22^{25} 2 K 7^{12}; *withdraw, hide oneself*, lit. Jos 2^{16} (JE), sq. שָׁ֫מָּה; 2 K 7^{12} c. בְּ loc.; 1 K 22^{25}; of Esau = Edom, *hiding* from judgment of י׳, וְנֶחְבָּה לֹא יוּכָל Je 49^{10}, as pointed, meant no doubt as pf., but constr. then hard; rd. rather inf. abs. נַחְבֹּה; so Gf Gie al. (v. Kö$^{i. 624}$).

†חֶבְיוֹן **n.[m.] hiding, hiding-place,** or 2253
< **veil, envelope,** only cstr. וְשָׁם ח׳ עֻזֹּה Hb 3^{4} (< 𝔊 𝔖 Hi-St Gr וְשָׂם *and he maketh*, cf. ψ 18^{12}).

†חֲבַיָּה **n.pr.m.** head of a priestly family 2252
Ezr 2^{61} = Ne 7^{63} (van d. H. Ezr חֲבַיָּה; Ne חֳבַיָּה,

marg. חֲבָיָּה; cf. Baer's note on Ezr 2^{61}; 𝔊 Ezr
Λαβεια, 𝔊L Ωδουια, A Οβαια, 𝔊 Ne Εβεια, 𝔊L
Αβια, א Αβεια).

2252 **חֲבָיָה, חֲבַיָּה** v. foregoing. p. 285

3160 **יְחֻבָּה** v. חֻבָּה sub חבב. p. 285

5147 †**נַחְבִּי** **n.pr.m.** a Naphtalite, one of the
Hebrew spies Nu 13^{4} (P).

2251 †**[חָבַט]** **vb.** **beat off, beat out** (NH *id.*,
strike, beat, Ar. خَبَطَ, Aram. ܚܒܛ, חֲבַט)—**Qal**
Impf. יַחְבֹּט Is 27^{12}; 3 fs. וַתַּחְבֹּט Ru 2^{17}; 2 ms.
תַּחְבֹּט Dt 24^{20}; *Pt.* חֹבֵט Ju 6^{11};—**1.** *beat off*,
זֵיתְךָ Dt 24^{20}. **2.** *beat out* (grain), Gideon
חֹבֵט חִטִּים בַּגַּת Ju 6^{11}, so Ru 2^{17}, of small quantities;—distinct fr. threshing on open floor, with
cattle; fig. of י׳'s judgment, and subsequent
gathering of Isr. Is 27^{12} (no obj. expr.), so Che
Di Du; Ges Hi Kn Brd place sub **1**; VB undecided. **Niph.** *Impf.* יֻחְבַּט Is 28^{27} fennel
(קֶצַח) beaten out בַּמַּטֶּה.

2252 **חֲבָיָה, חֲבַיָּה, חֲבִיָּה** v. sub חבה. p. 285

2253 **חֶבְיוֹן** v. sub חבה. p. 285

2254 †I. **[חָבַל]** **vb.** **bind, pledge** (Ar. حَبَلَ
bind; cf. Aram. ܚܒܠ, ܚܒܠܐ *travail;* חֲבַל
pledge (but rare and dub.); esp. ܚܒܠܐ *cord, field*,
חַבְלָא *cord*, ܚܒܠܐ, חֶבְלָא *pain*, esp. of travail;
Sab. חבל *border-territory*, or *field*, Sab.Denkm.
48.49; Eth. ሐበለ: Zim$^{BP\ 93n.}$, comp. As. *naḫbalu*,
rope, snare (but ḫ = خ))—**Qal** *Pf.* חָבַל Ez 18^{16}
Impf. יַחֲבֹל Dt 24^{6}; 2 ms. תַּחֲבֹל Dt 24^{17};
תַּחְבֹּל Ez 22^{25} Jb 22^{6}; יַחְבֹּלוּ Jb 24^{3}; יַחְבֹּלוּ Jb
24^{9}; *Imv.* sf. חַבְלֵהוּ Pr 20^{16} 27^{13}; *Inf. abs.* חָבֹל
Ex 22^{25}; *Pt. act.* חֹבֵל Dt 24^{6}, cf. חֹבְלִים Zc
$11^{7.14}$ (name of מַקֵּל); *pass.* חֲבֻלִים Am 2^{8};—
1. *bind*, only in חֹבְלִים, name of one of Zec.'s
symbolic staves, Zc $11^{7.14}$ symbol. of fraternity.
Esp. **2.** *bind* by taking a pledge of, *hold by a
pledge*, sq. acc. pers. Pr 20^{16} 27^{13} Jb 22^{6}; *take* or
hold in pledge, sq. acc. rei Ex 22^{25} (JE), Dt $24^{6.6.17}$
Jb 24^{3}; sq. acc. cogn. חֲבֹל Ez 18^{16}; עַל־עָנִי יַחְבֹּלוּ
Jb 24^{9} prob. pregn. (v. Di) *take pledges* (getting
power) *over the poor;* בְּגָדִים חֲבֻלִים Am 2^{8} *garments
taken in pledge.* **Niph.** *Impf.* יֵחָבֶל לוֹ Pr 13^{13}
becometh pledged to it (i.e. pledged to pay the
penalty, opp. יְשֻׁלָּם), so Ew Hi De Now Str RV^{m}
VB. > sub II. חָבַל q.v. **Pi.** *Pf.* 3 fs. חִבְּלָה
Ct 8^{5}; חִבְּלַתְךָ Ct 8^{5}; *Impf.* יְחַבֶּל־ ψ 7^{15};—*writhe,
twist*, hence *travail;* of mother Ct $8^{5.5}$ (c. acc.
of child; ‖ יְלָדַתְךָ); metaph. of wicked man
יְחַבֶּל־אָוֶן וְהָרָה עָמָל וְיָלַד שָׁקֶר: ψ 7^{15}.

†I. **חֶבֶל** **n.m.**$^{Jos\ 2,14}$ **f.**$^{\dagger Zp\ 2,6}$ (but v. infr.) **cord,** 2256
territory, band; ח׳ abs. Jos 2^{15}+; cstr. Dt 3^{4}+,
חֲבֶל Jos 19^{29}; sf. חַבְלוֹ Jb 18^{10}; pl. חֲבָלִים 2 S 8^{2}
+ 10 t. + Ez 47^{13} Jb 21^{7} v. infr.; cstr. חַבְלֵי Jos
17^{5} + 5 t.; חֶבְלֵי ψ 116^{3} + 2 t. + ψ 18^{5} (rd. משברי
v. infr.); sf. חֲבָלָיִךְ Is 33^{23}; חֲבָלָיו Is 33^{20};—**1.**
cord, rope, by which men were lowered Jos 2^{15}
(JE), Je $38^{6.11.12.13}$, or stones dragged 2 S 17^{13};
of tents Is 33^{20}; tackling of ship v^{23}; for binding Ez 27^{24} Jb 40^{25} Est 1^{6}; symbol of captivity
or subjection 1 K $20^{31.32}$; fig. of snare for wicked
Jb 18^{10} (‖ מַלְכֻּדְתּוֹ), set by wicked ψ 140^{6} (‖ פַּח);
ψ 119^{61} *cords of wicked men have surrounded
me;* of wicked held בחבלי חַטָּאתוֹ Pr 5^{22}; ח׳
הַשָּׁוְא Is 5^{18} *cords (ropes) of wickedness* (‖ כַּעֲבוֹת
הָעֲגָלָה); of cords of distress (עֳנִי) Jb 36^{8} (‖ זִקִּים);
so חֶבְלֵי מָוֶת (prob.) ψ 116^{3}, חֶבְלֵי שאול ψ 18^{6} =
2 S 22^{6} (‖ מוֹקְשֵׁי מָוֶת);—for חֶבְלֵי מות ψ 18^{5} rd.
מִשְׁבְּרֵי, v. 2 S 22^{5} and ‖ נַחֲלֵי בְלִיַּעַל, De Che Bae;
to draw בְּחַבְלֵי אָדָם Ho 11^{4} (i.e. *humanely,
kindly*); of cord of life חֶבֶל הַכֶּסֶף Ec 12^{6}. **2.**
measuring-cord, line ח׳ מִדָּה Zc 2^{5}; so ח׳ alone
2 S $8^{2.2.2}$ Am 7^{17} Mi 2^{5} ψ 78^{55}; fig. (of favoured
life) ψ 16^{5}; in gen. of one's portion, fortune Jb
21^{17} acc. to 𝔗 Thes Add. Ew Di al., but < v.
חֵבֶל. Thence **3.** *measured portion, lot, part,
region*, ח׳ נַחֲלָה *inherited portion* Dt 32^{9} 1 Ch 16^{18}
= ψ 105^{11}; also ח׳ alone Jos $17^{5.14}$ 19^{9} Ez 47^{13}
(חבלים; 𝔙 𝔗 rd. as dual, v. Ew Sm Da al.; Co
del. on intern. grounds); of particular regions
ח׳ אַרְגֹּב Dt $3^{4.13.14}$ 1 K 4^{13}; ח׳ אַכְזִיב Jos 19^{29} (si
vera l., v. WMM$^{Asien\ 194}$); ח׳ הַיָּם Zp 2^{5}; also v^{6}, but
ח׳ היתה here dub.; Sta prop. 2 fs. הָיִת, and del.
ח׳ הים; without הים, v^{7}. **4.** *band, company* of
prophets 1 S $10^{5.10}$.—II. **חֶבֶל** v. sub II. חָבַל. 2256
p. 287
†**חֵבֶל** **n.m.** $^{Is\ 66,7}$ (but v. Je 49^{24}) **pain,** 2256
pang;—ח׳ abs. Is 66^{7}; elsewh. pl. חֲבָלִים Is 13^{8}
+ 3 t. + Jb 21^{17} v. infr.; cstr. חֶבְלֵי Ho 13^{13}; sf.
חֲבָלֶיהָ Is 26^{17}; חֶבְלֵיהֶם Jb 39^{3} (on sf. v. Ges
§ 135, 5, R1);—*pain, pang:* **1.** *pains of travail:*
a. obj. of תְּשַׁלַּחְנָה Jb 39^{3} meton. for *offspring*
(‖ יַלְדֵיהֶן; v. Di; of goats and hinds). **b.** sim.
of distress of exiles Is 26^{17}; fig. of anguish of

nations (כַּיּוֹלֵדָה יְחִילוּן || צִירִים וַחֲבָלִים יֹאחֵזוּן Is 13^{8}), also Je 13^{21} 22^{23} 49^{24}; of crisis of redemption Ho 13^{13} (|| חֶבְלֵי יוֹלֵדָה), of birth of new Isr. Is 66^{7}. **2.** of other than birth-pangs only חבלים Jb 21^{17}; *pains, pangs, sorrows* (so 𝔊 𝔙 Thes,—otherwise Add.—RobGes Hi Da al.; || נֵר יִדְעָךְ, יָבֹא אֵידָם); > others, *portion, fortune*, v. חֵבֶל.

p. 286

2258 † חֲבֹל **n.[m.] pledge** (as *binding*)—יָשִׁיב ח׳ Ez 18^{12} 33^{15}; as cogn. acc. c. חָבַל Ez 18^{16}.

2258 † [חֲבֹלָה] **n.f. id.** (on format. cf. Lg$^{BN\ 179}$)—חֲבֹלָתוֹ Ez 18^{7}.

2260 † חִבֵּל **n.[m.]** prob. **mast** (as *corded* or *roped* in place; denom. fr. חֶבֶל)—only in sim. of drunken man שֹׁכֵב בְּרֹאשׁ ח׳ Pr 23^{34} (opp. שֹׁכֵב בְּלֶב־יָם) i.e. in the lookout-basket at the mast-head, cf. Thes *in carchesio.*—𝔊 𝔙 read חֹבֵל.

2259 † חֹבֵל **n.m. sailor** (denom. fr. חֶבֶל; i.e. *rope*-puller)—חֹבְלֵי הַיָּם Ez 27^{29}; חֹבְלָיִךְ Ez $27^{8.27.28}$; coll. רַב הַחֹבֵל i.e. the captain Jon 1^{6}.

2256 † חֹבְלִים **n.[m.]pl. union** (lit. *binders*) name of Zec.'s second symbolic staff Zc 11^{7} and c. art. v^{14}. See חָבַל **1.**

8458 † [תַּחְבֻּלָה] **n.f. direction, counsel** (prob. orig. of *rope*-pulling, i.e. *steering, directing* a ship, v. חֹבֵל, so Thes; v. De Pr 1^{5});—only pl. and only WisdLt. תַּחְבֻּלוֹת abs. Pr 1^{5} + 3 t.; cstr. Pr 12^{5}; *sf.* תַּחְבּוּלֹתָו Jb 37^{12}—*direction, guidance* (i.e. by God) Jb 37^{12} (of thunder cloud); *counsels* of wicked (רשׁעים) Pr 12^{5} (opp. מַחְשְׁבוֹת צדיקים); gen. *good, wise counsels* Pr 1^{5}; 11^{14} (|| רֹב יוֹעֵץ), 24^{6} (|| *id.*); 20^{18} (|| עֵצָה).

2254 II. חָבַל **vb. act (ruinously) corruptly** (NH *id. wound, injure;* Ar. خَبَلَ *corrupt* or *render unsound* (the mind, a limb, etc.), خَبِلَ *be deranged* (in mind); As. *ḫabâlu, injure,* VR^{62,11}; Aram. ܚܰܒܶܠ, חַבֵּל *corrupt, ruin;* Eth. ተኀበለ: *be arrogant, audacious;* Sab. חבל DHM$^{Epigr.\ Denkm.\ 48}$; cf. Palm. חבל *mortuus* Vog$^{No.\ 161}$ and oft.)—**Qal** *Pf.* 1 pl. חָבַלְנוּ Ne 1^{7}; *Impf.* 1 s. אֶחְבֹּל Jb 34^{31}; *Inf. cstr.* (used as *abs.*) Ne 1^{7};—*act corruptly* against, לְ חֲבֹל חבלנו Ne 1^{7}; abs. Jb 34^{31}. **Niph.** *Impf.* יֵחָבֶל לוֹ Pr 13^{13} *shall be ruined* (לְ reflex.), Thes RobGes AV RV, but < I. חָבַל (q. v.) **Pi.** *ruin, destroy: Pf.* 3 ms. consec. וְחִבֵּל את מעשה ידיך Ec 5^{5}, subj. God. *Impf.* 3 fs. תְּחַבֵּל וְחֶבֶל נִמְרָץ Mi 2^{10} *that destroyeth,* even with sore destruction; but rd. rather תֵּחָבְלוּ ח׳ נ׳ *ye shall be destroyed with* etc., so 𝔊 Roorda Che. *Inf. cstr.* לְחַבֵּל c. acc., the poor Is 32^{7}, the land 13^{5}; abs. 54^{16}; cf. *Pt.* pl. מְחַבְּלִים Ct 2^{15} c. acc. of foxes ruining vineyards. **Pu.** *Pf.* 3 ms. וְחֻבַּל consec. Is 10^{27} of yoke, *be ruined, broken,* si vera l.; RS$^{JPh\ xiii.\ 1885,\ p.\ 62}$ prop. יחדל, cf. also Che$^{crit.\ n.}$; and rem. by Di Du; 3 fs. חֻבָּלָה Jb 17^{1} *my spirit is broken* (|| יָמַי נִזְעָכוּ); *Impf.* 2 mpl. תְּחַבְּלוּ Mi 2^{10} (emend.: v. supr.)

†II. חֶבֶל **n.m. destruction**—חֶבֶל נִמְרָץ Mi 2256
2^{10}; cf. II. חָבַל **Pi.** above

† חֲבַצֶּלֶת **n.f. meadow-saffron** or **crocus** 2261
(*colchicum autumnale,* Linn.) (Syr. ܚܰܡܒܰܨܠܰܝܬܳܐ, v. Ges$^{Comm.\ Is\ 35,1}$ Löw$^{p.\ 174,\ No.\ 128}$; As. *ḫabaṣillatu* VR$^{32,\ 62}$ is a marsh-plant, reed; cf. Zim$^{BP\ 59}$ Dl$^{HA\ 34;\ Pr\ 82}$; also Che$^{l.c.}$ and crit. n.);—ח׳ הַשָּׁרוֹן שׁוֹשַׁנַּת הָעֲמָקִים Ct 2^{1} (fig. of Shulamite), וְתָגֵל עֲרָבָה וְתִפְרַח כַּחֲבַצָּלֶת׃ Is 35^{1} (*narcissus* Che$^{Is\ 35,1}$ cf. Conder$^{PEF,\ 1878,\ 46}$ Tristr$^{NHB\ 476}$ al.)

† חֲבַצִּנְיָה **n.pr.m.** a Rechabite Je 35^{3}, 𝔊 2262
Χαβασ(ε)ιν.

† [חָבַק] **vb. clasp, embrace** (NH *id.;* 𝔗 2263
חֲבַק; Mand. ܚܒܩ, NSyr. ܚܒܩ; Ar. حَبَقَ II. *collect* one's possessions, etc., Frey)—**Qal** *Inf.* לַחֲבוֹק Ec 3^{5}; *Pt.* חֹבֵק Ec 4^{5}; חֹבֶקֶת 2 K 4^{16};—*embrace,* c. acc. בֵּן 2 K 4^{16}; יָדָיו Ec 4^{5} (said of הַכְּסִיל = fold his arms, i.e. be idle; cf. חִבֻּק); no obj. expr. Ec 3^{5} (|| **Pi**). **Pi.** *Pf.* חִבְּקוּ Jb 24^{8} La 4^{5}; *Impf.* וַיְחַבֵּק Gn 48^{10}; וַיְחַבֶּק־ Gn 29^{13}; וַיְחַבְּקֵהוּ Gn 33^{4}; 3 fs. sf. תְּחַבְּקֵנִי Ct 2^{6} 8^{3}; 2 ms. וּתְחַבֵּק Pr 5^{20}, sf. תְּחַבְּקֶנָּה Pr 4^{8}; *Inf.* חַבֵּק Ec 3^{5};—*embrace* of pers., no obj. עת לִרְחֹק מֵחַבֵּק Ec 3^{5} (|| **Qal**); sq. לְ Gn 29^{13} (J), 48^{10} (E); sq. sf. 33^{4} (J), Pr 4^{8} Ct 2^{6} 8^{3}; c. acc. Pr 5^{20}; embrace צוּר for want of shelter Jb 24^{8} (of poor); embrace refuse-heaps אשׁפתות La 4^{5}, i.e. are outcasts.

† חִבֻּק **n.[m.] a clasping, folding** of the 2264
hands, only cstr. מְעַט ח׳ יָדַיִם לִשְׁכָּב Pr 6^{10} 24^{33} (cf. חָבַק **Qal**).

† חֲבַקּוּק **n.pr.m.** the prophet Habakkuk 2265
Hb 1^{1} 3^{1}; 𝔊 Ἀμβακουμ (As. *ḫambakûku* is name of a plant, Dl$^{HA\ 36,\ Pr\ 84}$, so حبقبق in Yemen (Schweinfurth) v. Hom$^{Aufsätze\ u.\ Abh.\ 1892,\ 27,\ 28}$).

† [חָבַר] **vb. unite** (usu. intr.), **be joined,** 2266
tie a magic knot or spell, charm (NH *id.;*

Eth. ኀበረ: yet As. [*abâru*], *ubburu*, *bind*, *ban* (of spells), *êbru*, friend, and many deriv., Dl W $^{51 ff.}$; Aram. ܚܰܒܰܪ, חֲבַר and many deriv.; cf. Ph. n. חבר *associate*)—**Qal** *Pf.* 3 mpl. חָבְרוּ Gn 14^{3}; *Pt. act.* m. חֹבֵר Dt 18^{11}, חוֹבֵר ψ 58^{6}; fpl. חֹבְרֹת Ex 26$^{3.3}$ + 2 t. + Ez 1^{9} (cf. infr.), חוֹבְרוֹת Ez 1^{11}; *Pt. pass.* cstr. חֲבוּר Ho 4^{17} (yet v. infr.); —**1.** *unite, be joined:* **a.** of allies, sq. אֶל־ loc. Gn 14^{3}, constr. praegn. = *came as allies unto;* pt. pass. fig. חֲבוּר עֲצַבִּים אֶפְרָיִם Ho 4^{17} *Ephr. is joined to idols* (but We rds. חבר, v. חָבֵר **2 d**, and cf. חֲבֵרָיו Is 44^{11}, חֲבֶרְתְּךָ Mal 2^{14}). **b.** of one thing reaching to, touching another; wings of Ezek.'s living creatures sq. אֶל־ rei, Ez 1^{9} (del. 𝔊 B Co, but v. Sm); cf. ח׳ איש v^{11}, i.e. *joining each one* (trans.), < 𝔊 𝔖 Co ח׳ אשה אל־אחותה (as v^{9}), *united each to the other;* so of curtains of tabernacle, sq. אֶל־ rei Ex 26$^{3.3}$; abs. *joined together*, of shoulderpieces of ephod Ex 28^{7} (all P; cf. also **Pu**). **2.** *tie magic knots, charm* (RS $^{JPh\ xiv.1885,\ 123}$ thinks mng. *charm* is der. fr. *nectere verba*, and comp. Ar. خَبَر, *narrative*); only c. acc. cogn. ח׳ חָבֶר Dt 18^{11} (in a long series of kindred phrases), specif. of charming serpents ψ 58^{6} (‖ מְלַחֲשִׁים). **Pi.** *Pf.* 3 ms. חִבַּר Ex 36^{10}; 2 ms. וְחִבַּרְתָּ Ex 26^{6} + 2 t.; *Impf.* וַיְחַבֵּר Ex 36^{10} + 2 t.; sf. וַיְחַבְּרֵהוּ 2 Ch 20^{36}; *Inf. cstr.* לְחַבֵּר Ex 36^{18};—**1.** *make an ally of, unite* one with, only ויחברהו עִמּוֹ 2 Ch 20^{36} *and he united him with himself*, sq. Inf. of purpose. **2.** *unite, join* (trans.), only Ex (P), of tabern., obj. the curtains, sq. acc. + אֶל־ rei Ex 26^{6} 36$^{10.10.13}$; sq. acc. only 26^{9} 36^{16}; obj. את־האהל *join the tent together*, 26^{11} 36^{18}. **Pu.** *Pf.* 3 ms. חֻבַּר Ex 39^{4}, וְחֻבָּר consec. Ex 28^{7} (but v. infr.), 3 fs. שֶׁחֻבְּרָה־ ψ 122^{3}; *Impf.* 3 ms. יְחֻבַּר Ec 9^{4} Qr (Kt יבחר v. infr.); sf. הַיְחָבְרְךָ ψ 94^{20} (Kö $^{i.\ 257 f.}$; Ges Ew Bö De al. as **Qal**); —**1. a.** *be allied with* thee (sf. ref. to י׳) ψ 94^{20}; **b.** *be united to* = be one of, מי אשר יְחֻ׳ אל כל־הַחַיִּים *whoever is united to all the living* (Kt יבחר is meaningless). **2.** *be joined together*, of ephod עַל־שְׁנֵי קְצוֹתָו ח׳ Ex 39^{4} *by its two edges was it joined together;* cf. ‖ 28^{7} (where MT עַל־שׁ׳ ק׳ < 𝔊 Sam which rd. אֶל־שְׁנֵי קְצוֹתָיו וְחֻבָּר (יְחֻבָּר); ψ עִיר שֶׁח׳־לָהּ 122^{3} *joined together for itself*, i.e. compactly built (of Jerusalem). **Hiph.** *Impf.* 1 s. אַחְבִּירָה עליכם בְּמִלִּים Jb 16^{4} *I could make a joining with words* (i.e. *join words together* RV VB) *against you.* **Hithp.** (late) *Pf.* אֶתְחַבֵּר (Ges $^{§ 54,\ 1 n.}$) 2 Ch 20^{35}; *Impf.* יִתְחַבָּרוּ Dn 11^{6}; *Inf.* sf. הִתְחַבֶּרְךָ 2 Ch 20^{37}; Aram. form הִתְחַבְּרוּת Dn 11^{23} (Ges $^{§ 54,\ 3\ R.\ 1}$);—*join oneself* to, *make an alliance* with, sq. עִם pers. 2 Ch 20$^{35.37}$, sq. אֶל־ pers. Dn 11^{23}; recipr. *league together* (abs.) Dn 11^{6}.

† I. חֶ֫בֶר **n.[m.]** **company, association, spell**—abs. חָ֑בֶר Dt 18^{11} + 2 t.; cstr. חֶבֶר Ho 6^{9}; pl. חֲבָרִים ψ 58^{6}, sf. חֲבָרַיִךְ Is 47$^{9.11}$;—**1.** *company, band* of (bad) priests Ho 6^{9}. **2.** *association, society* (abstr.), only in בֵּית חָ֑בֶר Pr 21^{9} = 25^{24} *house of association*, i.e. shared with a contentious woman (*house in common*, v. RV^{m} VB). **3. spell: a.** as acc. cogn. c. חָבַר (q.v.) Dt 18^{11} ψ 58^{6}. **b.** alone, of Babylonian magic Is 47$^{9.11}$ (v. Len $^{Chald.\ Magic\ [1878];\ Magie\ u.\ Wahrsagekunst,\ 1878}$; Scholz $^{Götzendienst\ u.\ Zauberwesen,\ 1877,\ 80\ ff.}$ Say $^{TBA\ iii.\ 145\ ff.\ and\ Rel.\ Bab\ 396\ ff.,\ 440\ ff.}$). 2267

† II. חֶ֫בֶר, חֵ֫בֶר **n.pr.m.** **1.** חֶבֶר (𝔊 Χαβερ) 2268
the Kenite, husband of Deborah Ju 4$^{11.17.17.21}$ 5^{24}. **2.** a man of Asher חֶבֶר Gn 46^{17} (P) 𝔊 Χοβωρ 1 Ch 7$^{31.32}$ 𝔊 Χαβερ 𝔊L Ιεχοβερ; חֵבֶר Nu 26^{45} 𝔊 Χοβερ; on poss. identif. with *Ḫabiri* of Tel el Amarna v. Jastr $^{JBL\ 1892,\ xi.\ 118\ ff.;\ 1893,\ xii.\ 61\ ff.}$ **3.** חֶבֶר name in Judah 1 Ch 4^{18} 𝔊 Αβεισα, 𝔊L Αβερ. **4.** חָ֑בֶר a Benjamite 1 Ch 8^{17} 𝔊 Αβαρ, 𝔊L Αβερ.

† חֶבְרִי **adj.gent.** of **2** supr., only c. art. 2277
= n. coll. מִשְׁפַּחַת הַחֶבְרִי Nu 26^{45} (𝔊 Χοβερ(ε)ι).

† חֶבְרָה **n.f.** **association, company** (abstr.) 2274
וְאָרַח לְח׳ עִם פֹּעֲלֵי אָוֶן Jb 34^{8} *and he goeth for company with doers of wickedness* (‖ וְלָלֶכֶת עִם־אַנְשֵׁי־רֶשַׁע).

† חָבֵר **adj.** and **n.m.** $^{Ct\ 8,\ 13}$, **united, associate,** 2270
companion—ח׳ abs. Pr 28^{24} ψ 119^{63}; sf. חֲבֵרוֹ Ec 4^{10} (+ 3 t. Ez Kt; Qr חבריו, v. infr.); pl. חֲבֵרִים Ju 20^{11} Ct 8^{13}; cstr. חַבְרֵי Is 1^{23}; sf. חֲבֵרֶךָ ψ 45^{8}, חֲבֵרַיִךְ Ct 1^{7}; חֲבֵרָיו Is 44^{11} + 3 t. Ez Qr;—**1.** adj. *united* כְּאִישׁ אֶחָד חֲבֵרִים Ju 20^{11} *knit together as one man* (AV RV). **2. n.** *associate, fellow:* **a.** of children (tribes) of Isr. assoc. with Judah as head Ez 37^{16}; id. assoc. with Joseph (Ephr.) as head v$^{16.19}$ (in all these rd. Qr חֲבֵרָיו). **b.** of like rank ψ 45^{8}. **c.** of like calling Ct 1^{7}. **d.** *worshippers* (associates, belonging to the society or guild) of idols Is 44^{11} (v. Che; > others *priests*, Geiger $^{Urschr.\ 121,\ 493}$ SS, cf. חֶבֶר Ho 6^{9}; Du rds. חֲבָרִים *enchantments*). **e.** in gen. Ct 8^{13}. **f.** implying likeness of character Is 1^{23} Pr 28^{24} ψ 119^{63}. **3.** *companion* at a particular time Ec 4^{10}.

2278 †[חֶבֶ֫רֶת] **n.f. consort**, i.e. wife וְהִיא חֲבֶרְתְּךָ Mal 2[14] (|| אֵשֶׁת בְּרִיתֶךָ).

2279 †חֹבֶ֫רֶת **n.f. a thing that joins or is joined**, only of the *curtain-pieces* of the tabernacle, as *joined together*:—הַח׳ Ex 26[10] 36[17]; בַּחֹבָ֑רֶת Ex 26[4.10].

2271 †[חַבָּר] **n.m. associate, partner** in a trade or calling, only יִכְרוּ עָלָיו חַבָּרִים Jb 40[30] *will partners* (i.e. those engaged in the catch) *make traffic upon it* (the crocodile)?

2250 †חַבּוּרָה, [חַבֻּרָה, חַבֻּרָה] **n.f. stripe, blow**;—abs. חַבּ׳ Is 1[6] + 2 t.; sf. חַבֻּרָתִי Gn 4[23]; חֲבֻרָתוֹ Is 53[5]; pl. cstr. חַבֻּרוֹת Pr 20[30]; sf. חַבּוּרֹתָי ψ 38[6]:—*stripe, blow, stroke*, Gn 4[23] *my blow*, i.e. for *striking me* (J), cf. Ex 21[25.25] (JE), also of injury to land of Judah (under fig. of human body) Is 1[6] (all || פֶּצַע, v. infr.); of blows (sg. coll.) inflicted on suffering servant of י׳ Is 53[5]; (pl.) ψ 38[6], חַבֻּרוֹת פֶּצַע Pr 20[30], i.e. *blows that cut in* (|| מַכּוֹת).

2272 †[חֲבַרְבֻּרָה] **n.f. stripe, mark**, only pl. sf. חֲבַרְבֻּרֹתָיו Je 13[23] of stripes on a panther (tiger? cf. נָמֵר;—|| עוֹרוֹ of a Cushite).

2275 †I. חֶבְרוֹן **n.pr.loc. Hebron** (*association, league*)—ח׳ Gn 13[18] +; c. ה loc. חֶבְרוֹנָה Jos 10[36] + 6 t.; חֶבְרֹ֫נָה 2 S 2[1];—𝔊 Χεβρων; mod. *El-Ḫalîl* (v. Rob [BR i. 213 f., ii. 73 ff.] Guérin [Judée iii. 214 ff.]); ancient city in southern Judah, where (or near which) Abr. built an altar Gn 13[18] (J), and where was a sanctuary in Dvd.'s time 2 S 15[7], cf. לִפְנֵי י׳ בְּח׳ 2 S 5[3] = 1 Ch 11[3]; built 7 yrs. bef. Ṣoan in Egypt acc. to Nu 13[22 b] (JE); under a king Jos 10[3.5.23] (JE) 12[10] (D); assigned to Caleb Jos 14[13.14] (JED) Ju 1[20] yet v. 1 Ch 6[40] (cf. v[41]); older name קִרְיַת (הָ)אַרְבַּע acc. to Jos 14[15] (JED), cf. Gn 23[2] 35[27] Jos 15[54] 20[7] (all P) Ju 1[10b]; v. also Jos 15[13] 21[11] (both P); called also מַמְרֵא Gn 23[19] (and 35[27], both P); a city of refuge Jos 21[13] (P) = 1 Ch 6[42]; עֵמֶק ח׳ Gn 37[14] (J); named elsewhere Nu 13[22a] (JE) Jos 10[36.39] 11[21] (all D) Ju 1[10a] 16[3] 2 S 2[32] 15[9] 2 Ch 11[10]; a resort of David, and for 7 yrs. his royal city 1 S 30[31] 2 S 2[1.11] 3[2.5.19.20.22.27.32] 4[1.8.12.12] 5[1.3.13] 1 K 2[11] 1 Ch 3[1.4] 11[1.3] 12[24.39] (van d. H. v[23.38]) 29[27]; rd. also perh. for תחתו 2 S 3[12], 𝔊L εἰς Χεβρων, cf. Dr; seat of Absalom's rebellion 2 S 15[10]; עָרֵי ח׳ 2 S 2[3] abode of David's men.

2275 II. חֶבְרוֹן **n.pr.m.** (𝔊 Χεβρων). **1.** grandson of Levi Ex 6[18] Nu 3[19] (both P) = 1 Ch 5[28] = 6[3], 23[12.19], cf. 15[9]. **2.** name in Caleb's family 1 Ch 2[42.43].

†חֶבְרֹנִי, חֶבְרוֹנִי **adj.gent.** of II. חֶבְרוֹן **1**:— 2276
alw. c. art. as subst. coll.; לַחברוני 1 Ch 26[23.30.31.31]; מִשְׁפַּחַת הַחֶבְרֹנִי Nu 3[27] 26[58].

†מַחְבֶּ֫רֶת **n.f. thing joined, place of joining**;—abs. מ׳ Ex 26[4] + 3 t.; מַחְבָּ֑רֶת Ex 36[11.17]; sf. מַחְבַּרְתּוֹ Ex 28[27] 39[20];—**1.** *thing joined*, of curtain-pieces of tabernacle (cf. חֹבֶרֶת), Ex 26[4.5] 36[11.11.12]. **2.** *place of joining*: **a.** of the curtains Ex 36[17]. **b.** of shoulder-pieces of the ephod Ex 28[27] 39[20] (all P). 4225

†[מְחַבְּרָה] **n.f. binder, clamp, joint**, only pl. abs. מְחַבְּרוֹת, of iron, *clamps* or the like, 1 Ch 22[3]; of wood, *binder*, or *coupling*, 2 Ch 34[11]. 4226

†חָבוֹר **n.pr.fl.** called נְהַר גּוֹזָן 2 K 17[6] = 18[11]; erron. 1 Ch 5[26] וְח׳ וְהָרָא וּנְהַר גּוֹזָן; 𝔊 (Χ)αβωρ, Gk. Χαβωρας, etc., Assyr. *Ḫabur*, flowing into Euphrates fr. E. (Dl [Pa 183 ff.] KAT[2 275. 614] COT[i. 267]); v. גּוֹזָן. 2249

חֲבֻרָתוֹ v. חַבּוּרָה supr. 2250

†[חָבַשׁ] **vb. bind, bind on, bind up** (NH *id.*; As. *abâšu*, acc. to Dl [W 70, Pr 174]; Ar. حَبَسَ *confine, restrict*; yet on As. *ḫibšu 'Kopfbinde'* (c. ח), etc., v. Zehnpfund [BAS i. 499, 526]; Aram. ܚܒܫ; cf. ܚܒܘܫܝܐ, חֲבוּשְׁיָא *imprisonment*, etc.)—**Qal** *Pf.* 2 ms. וְחָבַשְׁתָּ Ex 29[9]; 2 mpl. חֲבַשְׁתֶּם Ez 34[4]; *Impf.* יַחֲבוֹשׁ Jb 34[17]; וַיַּחֲבֹשׁ Gn 22[3] + 4 t.; וַיַּחֲבָשׁ־ 1 K 13[23]; וְיַחְבְּשׁ Jb 5[18]; וַיַּחְבְּשֵׁנוּ Ho 6[1]; 3 fs. וַתַּחֲבֹשׁ 2 K 4[24]; אֶחֱבֹשׁ Ez 34[16]; cohort. אֶחְבְּשָׁה־ 2 S 19[27] (but cf. infr.); וָאֶחְבָּשֵׁךְ Ez 16[10]; וַיַּחְבְּשׁוּ־ 1 K 13[13]; וַיַּחְבְּשׁוּ 1 K 13[27]; *Imv.* חֲבשׁ Jb 40[13]; חֲבוֹשׁ Ez 24[17]; חִבְשׁוּ 1 K 13[13.27]; *Inf. cstr.* חֲבשׁ Is 30[26] 61[1]; לְחָבְשָׁהּ Ez 30[21] (del. Co, cf. 𝔊). *Pt. act.* חֹבֵשׁ Is 3[7]; *pass.* חָבוּשׁ Jon 2[6]; חֲבוּשִׁים Ju 19[10]; חֲבֻשִׁים 2 S 16[1] Ez 27[24];—**1.** *bind, bind on*: **a.** headgear, c. acc. rei, לְ pers. Ex 29[9] Lv 8[13] (both P); c. עַל pers. Ez 24[17] (P); *pass.* of seaweeds clinging about head סוּף חָבוּשׁ לְרֹאשִׁי Jon 2[6]; c. sf. pers. et בְּ rei וָאֶחְבְּשֵׁךְ Ez 16[10] *and I bound* (or *wound*) *about thee* (i.e. thy head, Sm VB) שֵׁשׁ (in metaph. of י׳'s care for Jerus.; || אֶנְעֲלֵךְ, אַלְבִּישֵׁךְ); fig. of punishment for wicked פְּנֵיהֶם חֲבשׁ בטמון Jb 40[13] *bind their faces in darkness* (|| טָמְנֵם בֶּעָפָר) v. Di. **b.** pass. prob. *twined, twisted* in חֲבָלִים חֲבֻשִׁים וַאֲרֻזִים Ez 27[24], *cords twisted and strong*, v. Sm Da. Esp. **c.** of equipping a beast for riding; ass, in acc. Gn 22[3] Nu 22[21] (both E), 2 S 17[23] & 19[27] (where however rd. לוֹ חָבְשָׁה־לִּי, so 𝔊 𝔖 𝔙 Th We Dr),

1 K 2^{40} 13$^{13.13.23.27.27}$ (v^{27b} no dir. obj. expressed) 2 K 4^{24}; pass., also of asses, Ju 19^{10} 2 S 16^{1}. **d.** fig. = *restrain, control* (Germ. *bändigen*), abs. Jb 34^{17}. **2.** *bind up*, viz. a wound, usually in fig., of comforting the distressed, etc.; c. sf. pers. Ho 6^{1} (|| רָפָא, opp. הִכָּה); sq. לְ pers. לַחֲבשׁ לְנִשְׁבְּרֵי־לֵב Is 61^{1}; cf. Ez 34^{4} (sq. לַנִּשְׁבֶּרֶת; || רִפֵּא, חִזֵּק), v^{16} (sq. *id.*; || חִזֵּק); sq. acc. rei בְּיוֹם חֲבשׁ י׳ אֶת־שֶׁבֶר עַמּוֹ Is 30^{26} (|| רָפָא); c. acc. of Pharaoh's broken arm Ez 30^{21} (si vera l., v. supr.; cf. **Pu.**); abs. Jb 5^{18}; also Is 3^{7} of repairing fortunes of people (opp. הַכָּאִיב; || רָפָא=רָפָה). **Pi.** *Pf.* חִבֵּשׁ *bind, restrain* מִבְּכִי נהרות Jb 28^{11}; *Pt.* מְחַבֵּשׁ *bind up* לְעַצְּבוֹתָם ψ 147^{3}. **Pu.** *Pf.* *be bound up* חֻבָּשָׁה Ez 30^{21} (metaph.) Pharaoh's broken arm; חֻבָּ֫שׁוּ Is 1^{6} (wounds of land of Judah).

חבת (√of foll.; cf. Ar. خَبِتَ *be obscure*, IV. *be lowly, submissive*, خَبْتٌ *low ground*).

2281 † חֲבִתִּים **n.[m.]pl.** (NH *id.*)—some kind of **flat cakes**, or **bread-wafers**, only מַעֲשֵׂה הַח׳ 1 Ch 9^{31}.

4227 † מַחֲבַת† **n.f. flat plate, pan,** or **griddle** for baking, only P and late; abs. מ׳ Lv 2^{5} + 2 t.; מַחֲבָ֑ת Lv 7^{9}; cstr. מַחֲבַת Ez 4^{3};—**1.** used in preparing the (baken) *mincha*, preceded by עַל־ Lv 2^{5} 6^{14} 7^{9} (all P), cf. 1 Ch 23^{29}. **2.** מ׳ בַּרְזֶל Ez 4^{3} *a plate of iron*, signifying an iron wall, in prediction of siege of city.

2282-83 חָג, חָגָּא v. sub חגג. below, p. 291

חגב (√of foll.; mng. dub.; poss. cf. Ar. حَجَبَ *prevent, intervene, hide*, حِجَابٌ *that which veils, conceals, hides;* Syr. ܚܘܓܒܐ *shrine;* hence *locusts* as *concealing* the sky?).

2284 †I. חָגָב **n.m.**$^{\text{Ec 12, 5}}$ **locust, grasshopper** (NH *id.*; cf. 𝔗), prob. a non-flying species, v. Kn in Di$^{\text{Lv 11, 22}}$; הֶחָגָב allowed as food Lv 11^{22} (P; || חַרְגֹּל, סָלְעָם, אַרְבֶּה), כַּחֲגָבִים Nu 13^{33} (JE; sim. of insignificance), so Is 40^{22}; as agent of Yahweh's wrath חָגָב לֶאֱכוֹל הארץ 2 Ch 7^{13}; וְיִסְתַּבֵּל הֶחָגָב Ec 12^{5} *and the grasshopper shall be a burden;* better *shall drag itself along*, De Hi Now RV^{m}; De thinks ח׳ here fig. of the back part of the pelvic cavity (Ar. حَجَبَةٌ is *point of hip-bone*, Bo, cf. Lane), and refers to stiffness of aged joints, so Now; but the meaning is dubious; v. other views in Comm.

†II. חָגָב **n.pr.m.** head of a family of returning exiles Ezr 2^{46} 𝔊 Ἀγαβ (no || in Ne 7 H; but 𝔊L Ne 7^{48} has both Αγαβ and Αγαβα, cf. חֲגָבָא). 2285

† חֲגָבָא **n.pr.m.** head of a family of returning exiles Ne 7^{48}, 𝔊 Ἀγαβα (cf. also foregoing) prob. = following. 2286

† חֲגָבָה **n.pr.m.** head of a family of returning exiles Ezr 2^{47}, prob. = foregoing; 𝔊 Ἀγαβα. 2286

†[חָגַג] **vb. make pilgrimage, keep a pilgrim-feast** (Ar. حَجَّ *betake oneself to or towards an object of reverence; make a pilgrimage to Mecca;* Sab. חגג *make pilgrimage* Sab. Denkm.$^{\text{86, cf. 85}}$; Syr. ܚܓ *celebrate a feast*. In Palm. חגגו is n.pr. Vog$^{\text{No. 61}}$; cf. also Ph. n.pr. חגי, חגת);—**Qal** *Pf.* 2 mpl. חַגֹּתֶם Ex 12^{14} + 2 t.; *Impf.* 2 ms. תָּחֹג Ex 23^{14} Dt 16^{15}; 3 mpl. יָחֹ֫גּוּ ψ 107^{27} (Bö$^{\text{§ 1118 (2)}}$); וְיָחֹ֫גּוּ Ex 5^{1}; 2 mpl. תָּחֹ֫גּוּ Lv 23$^{39.41}$; *sf.* תְּחָגֻּ֫הוּ Ex 12^{14}; *Imv.* f. חָגִּי Na 2^{1}; *Inf.* cstr. חֹג Zc 14^{18} + 2 t.; *Pt.* חוֹגֵג ψ 42^{5}; pl. חֹגְגִים 1 S 30^{16};—**1.** *keep a pilgrim-feast*, abs. Ex 5^{1} (JE) of one proposed by Moses; שלשׁ רגלים תחג לי *three times shalt thou make pilgrimage unto me* (in the year) Ex 23^{14} (covt. code); of pilgrim-feasts in general Na 2^{1}, the Passover Ex 12^{14} (P); elsewh. feast of Booths; all celebrated in part by sacred processions and dances; המון חוגג ψ 42^{5} *multitude keeping festival* (led by the Psalmist in procession); חגג חג Lv 23^{39} (H), Nu 29^{12} (P), Na 2^{1} Zc 14$^{16.18.19}$; חגג אתו חג Ex 12^{14} (P), Lv 23^{41} (H); אתו Lv 23^{41} (H); sf. Ex 12^{14} (P). **2.** behave as at a חַג 1 S 30^{16} (of the Amalekites when surprised by David i.e. *enjoying themselves merrily*, Dr; others, *circling in the sacred dance*). **3.** *reel*, in giddiness on the sea ψ 107^{27} (cf. חָגָּא Is 19^{17}); this either points to an earlier meaning of √; or better, the ψ being late, means *reel* as from festival excesses (|| וְיָנוּעוּ כַּשִּׁכּוֹר). 2287

† חַג **n.m.**$^{\text{Is 29, 1}}$ **festival-gathering, feast, pilgrim-feast** (NH *id.*; Aram. ܚܓܐ, חַגָּא; Ar. حَجّ *pilgrimage;* Sab. חג DHM$^{\text{Epigr. Denkm. 31}}$; Nö$^{\text{ZMG 1887, 719}}$; RS$^{\text{Proph. Lect. ii. n. 6}}$; > We$^{\text{Skizzen iii. 106, 165}}$ *sacred dance*)—חַג abs. and cstr. Ex 10^{9} + 36 t.; חָג Nu 28^{17} + 13 t.; sf. חַגִּי Ex 23^{18}; חַגֶּ֫ךָ Dt 16^{14}; חַגָּהּ Ho 2^{13}; חַגֵּנוּ ψ 81^{4}; pl. חַגִּים Is 29^{1} + 2 t.; sf. חַגַּיִךְ Na 2^{1}; חַגֵּיכֶם Am 5^{21} + 2 t.;—**1.** *feast*, esp. one observed by a *pilgrimage* (Ex 23$^{14.17}$): **a.** *special feast* to the golden calf Ex 32^{5} (J; where there was a 2282

sacred dance v^{19}); a feast in the 8th month observed by Jeroboam in place of the feast of the 7th month in Judah 1 K 12$^{32.33}$; pilgrim feast proposed by Moses Ex 10^{9} (JE); feast at Shiloh Ju 21^{19}. Elsewhere **b.** apparently always of the three great pilgrim feasts, celebrated by processions and dancing: (1) *in general* Is 30^{29} Am 8^{10} Na 2^{1}; חגים ינקפו *let feasts come round* Is 29^{1}; ‖ עצרות Am 5^{21}; חג לי׳ Lv 23^{41} (H); disting. fr. the more gen. מועדים (sacred seasons) Ez 45^{17} 46^{11} Ho 9^{5} (יום חג), and fr. specif. שבתות, חדשים as well, Ho 2^{13}; (2) in particular: unleavened cakes and Passover חג (ה)מצות Ex 23^{15} = 34^{18} (JE); Lv 23^{6} (P), Dt 16^{16} 2 Ch 8^{13} 30$^{13.21}$ 35^{17} Ezr 6^{22}; חג Ex 12^{14} (P); first day of the seven Nu 28^{17} (P); the last day Ex 13^{6} (J); the seven Ez 45$^{21.23}$; חג הפסח Ex 34^{25}, חגי Ex 23^{18} (both JE); בַּכֶּסֶה לְיוֹם חַגֵּנוּ ψ 81^{4} (probably the full moon of Passover); חג הקציר Ex 23^{16} = חג שבעת Ex 34^{22} (JE), cf. Dt 16$^{10.16}$ 2 Ch 8^{13}; חג האס(י)ף Ex 23^{16} = 34^{22} (JE) = חג הסכ(ו)ת Lv 23^{34} (P), Dt 16$^{13.16}$ 31^{10} 2 Ch 8^{13} Ezr 3^{4} Zc 14$^{16.18.19}$; also חג י׳ Lv 23^{39} (H), הֶחָג 1 K 8$^{2.65}$ = 2 Ch 5^{3} 7$^{8.9}$, Ez 45 Ne 8^{14}; חַגֶּךָ (i.e. of people) Dt 16^{14}; 7 days Nu 29^{12} (P), Ne 8^{18}.—Vbs. c. חג are: חגג Lv 23$^{39.41}$ (H), Ex 12^{14} Nu 29^{12} (P), Na 2^{1} Zc 14$^{16.18.19}$; שמר Ex 23^{15} = 34^{18} (JE); התקדש Is 30^{29}; but usually עשׂה Ex 34^{22} (JE), Dt 16$^{10.13}$ 1 K 8^{65} 12$^{32.33}$ 2 Ch 7$^{8.9}$ 30$^{13.21}$ 35^{17} Ezr 3^{4} 6^{22} Ne 8^{18}. **2.** *festival sacrifice* (cf. NH חֲגִיגָה) ψ 118^{27} (see מזבח **12**); Mal 2^{3} (RV after Thes Ke al.: but AV Ew Or *feast*).

2283 †חָגָּא **n.[f.] reeling** (Aramaism for חגה Ew $^{\S 173b}$, by copyist's err. Di)—וְהָיְתָה...למצרים לח׳ Is 19^{17} and the land of Judah *shall become to Egypt a reeling*, i.e. Egypt shall reel in terror at the sight of it (‖ יִפְחָד); this mng. may either be fr. an orig. sense of חגג, or = be excited as at a חָג, cf. חגג **3**).

2292 †חַגַּי **n.pr.m.** (*festal*; Ph. חגי, חגת; Palm. חגגו Vog$^{No. 61}$)—the prophet Haggai Hg 1$^{1.3.12.13}$ 2$^{1.10.13.14.20}$ Ezr 5^{1} 6^{14}; 𝔊 Ἀγγαῖος.

2291 †חַגִּי **n.pr.m.** (*festal*) **1.** 𝔊 Ἀγγις, son of Gad Gn 46^{16} Nu 26^{15} (both P). **2. adj. gent.** as subst. coll., c. art. Nu 26^{15} (P).

2293 †חַגִּיָּה **n.pr.m.** (*feast of Yah*) a Levite, son of Shimea 1 Ch 6^{15}; 𝔊 Ἀγγια.

2294 †חַגִּית **n.pr.f.** (*festal*) wife of David and mother of Adonijah 2 S 3^{4} 1 K 1$^{5.11}$ 2^{13} 1 Ch 3^{2}; 𝔊 Ἀγγιθ.

חגה (√ of foll.; cf. Ar. حَجَا *conceal*; حَجًا, حَجًى *place of refuge, protection*).

†[חֲגָוִים] **n.m.pl. places of concealment, retreats**, as abode of dove יוֹנָתִי בְּחַגְוֵי הַסֶּלַע Ct 2^{14} (in metaph.); also, hyperbol., as abode of Edom שֹׁכְנִי בח׳ (ה)סלע Je 49^{16} Ob^{3}. 2288

חגל (√ of foll.; Ar. حَجَلَ, *hobble, hop*, whence حَجَلٌ *partridge*, cf. Syr. ܚܓܠܐ, ܚܓܠܐ, *id.*)

†חָגְלָה **n.pr.f.** (=*partridge*, v. supr.)—a daughter of Ṣelophchad of Manasseh Nu 26^{33} 27^{1} 36^{11} Jos 17^{3} (all P); 𝔊 Ἑγλα, A Αιγλα(μ). On n.pr.loc. בֵּית ח׳ v. p. 111 b. 2295

†[חָגַר] **vb. gird, gird on, gird oneself** (NH *id.*, Aram. חֲגַר; Ar. حَجَرَ *hinder, restrain*, so Syr. ܚܓܰܪ; As. *agâru, surround*, in deriv., Dl$^{W\ 105\ ff.}$; Sab. מחגרת (cf. Ar. مَحَاجِر, مَحْجِر *enclosed space, district*, etc.), DHM in MV; also n.pr. dei and loc. חגר, Sab. Denkm.$^{3.81.93}$ CIS$^{iv.\ 1,\ No.\ 49\ etc.}$)—**Qal** *Pf.* 3 fs. חָגְרָה Pr 31^{17}; 2 ms. וְחָגַרְתָּ Ex 29^{9}; 3 pl. חָגְרוּ Is 15^{3} La 2^{10}; וְח׳ consec. Ez 7^{18} 27^{31}; *Impf.* 3 ms. יַחְגֹּר Lv 16^{4}, וַיַּחְגֹּר Lv 8$^{7.7}$ + 4 t.; sf. יַחְגְּרֶהָ ψ 109^{19}; 2 ms. תַּחְגֹּר ψ 76^{11} (but on txt. v. infr.); 3 mpl. יַחְגְּרוּ Ez 44^{18} 2 S 22^{46} (but on txt. of both v. infr.), וַיַּחְגְּרוּ 1 S 25^{13} 1 K 20^{32}; 3 fpl. תַּחְגֹּרְנָה ψ 65^{13}; 2 mpl. וַתַּחְגְּרוּ De 1^{41}; *Imv.* ms. חֲגֹר 2 K 4^{29} 9^{1}, חֲגוֹר ψ 45^{4}; fs. חִגְרִי־ Je 6^{26}; mpl. חִגְרוּ 1 S 25^{13} + 3 t.; fpl. חֲגֹרְנָה Je 49^{3}, cf. חֲגוֹרָה Is 32^{11} (v. infr.); *Inf. cstr.* לַחֲגֹר Is 22^{12}; *Pt. act.* חֹגֵר 1 K 20^{11} 2 K 3^{21}; *pass.* m. חָגוּר Ju 18^{11} + 5 t.; f. cstr. חֲגֻרַת־ Jo 1^{8}; pl. חֲגוּרִים Ex 12^{11} Ju 18^{16}; חֲגֻרִים Dn 10^{5};—**1.** trans., *gird* some one, with girdle; c. 2 acc. Ex 29^{9} Lv 8^{13} (both P); pass., *girded* with ephod (acc.) 1 S 2^{18} 2 S 6^{14}; sq. בְּ Dn 10^{5}, c. acc. and בְּ, fig. Pr 31^{17}, חגרה בְּעוז מתניה Lv 8$^{7.7}$ (P), c. acc. מתנים *gird up thy loins*, i.e. make ready to go 2 K 4^{29} 9^{1}, pass. Ex 12^{11} (P); cf. prob. also חֲגוֹרָה עַל־חֲלָצַיִם Is 32^{11} *gird upon the loins* (2nd acc. om.); on verb. form as Imv. fpl. v. AE Ki Ew$^{\S 226a}$ Di Du; > as ms. Ol $^{\S 234a}$ Ges$^{\S 48.5}$ Sta$^{\S 591d}$ Kö$^{\S 20.12}$. **2.** *gird on, bind on* (= gird oneself with), a girdle ψ 109^{19} (in sim.); so esp. c. acc. שַׂק, שׂקים of mourning Is 15^{3} 22^{12} La 2^{10} Ez 7^{18} 27^{31} 2 S 3^{31} Je 4^{8} 6^{26} 49^{3}; also 1 K 20^{32} (c. acc. שׂק + ב bef. מתנים); pass., sq. על bef. obj. of mourning Jo 1^{8} (sim.); abs. (שׂק om.) Jo 1^{13} (‖ ספדו); sq. חֶרֶב 1 S 25$^{13.13.13}$ Dt 1^{41}; ψ 45^{4} ח׳ חרב על יָרֵךְ, so Ju 3^{16}, 1 S 17^{39} (sq. acc. + מֵעַל); c. acc. cogn. ח׳ חגורה 2 K 3^{21};

abs. 1 K 20[11]; pass. Ju 18[11.16.17] 2 S 20[8b] (where rd. חֶרֶב Klo Dr—not We), 21[16]; rd. perh. also חָגוּר for חֲגוֹר 20[8c], so Klo Dr. **3.** intr. *gird oneself*, sq. בְּ rei Lv 16[4] (P), so לֹא יַח׳ בַּיָּזַע *they shall not gird themselves with sweat* (?), but del. 𝔖 Co Sgfr; c. acc. rei (fig.) גִּיל גְּבָעוֹת תַּח׳ ψ 65[13] *with rejoicing the hills gird themselves*; cf. שְׁאֵרִית חֵמֹת תַּח׳ ψ 76[11] *with a remnant (residue) of wraths thou girdest thyself*, so Hi Hup De VB; but very doubtful; 𝔊 Bö Ew rd. תְּחָגֶּךָּ for תַּחְגֹּר; Bae Ka omit line as corrupt; cf. further Che and crit. n.—וְיַחְגְּרוּ 2 S 22[46] is txt. err. for וְיַחְרְגוּ, cf. ‖ ψ 18[46]; so Now Hup Kit al.

2290 †חֲגוֹר **n.[m.]** **belt, girdle** (distinct fr. אֵזוֹר *waist-cloth*, Che[Je. in Pulpit Comm. (1883) 333; Jerem., Life and Times (1888) 161] RS[JQ Jan. 1892, 289 ff.])—חֲגוֹר for sword 2 S 20[8] (yet rd. prob. חָגוּר, Th We Klo Dr), cf. 1 S 18[4]; article of commerce Pr 31[24] (coll.? or of a richly adorned girdle?).

2289 †[חָגוּר] **adj.** **girt, girded,** only pl. cstr.; חֲגוּרֵי אֵזוֹר Ez 23[15] *girded with a waist-cloth.*

2290 †חֲגוֹרָה **n.f.** **girdle, loin-covering, belt** —חֲגוֹרָה Is 3[24]; חֲגֹרָה 2 S 18[11] 2 K 3[21]; sf. חֲגֹרָתוֹ 1 K 2[5]; Pl. חֲגֹרֹת Gn 3[7];—*girdle, loin-covering* Gn 3[7] (J); as article of women's dress Is 3[24]; *belt* of warrior 1 K 2[5] 2 K 3[21] (חֹגֵר ח׳), cf. 2 S 18[11].—On חֲגוֹרָה Is 32[11] v. חָגַר **1.**

4228 †מַחֲגֹּרֶת **n.f.** **a girding, cincture,** only cstr.; תַּחַת פְּתִיגִיל מַחֲגֹּרֶת שָׂק Is 3[24] *instead of a mantle a girding of sackcloth.*

2297 I. חַד Ez 33[30] v. אֶחָד. p. 26

2299 II. חַד v. sub חדד. below,

2300 †[חָדַד] **vb.** **be sharp, keen** (Aram. חֲדַד; NH חִדֵּד *sharpen*; Ar. حَدَّ *be sharp* and *sharpen*; As. Pi. *uddudu, sharpen*, Dl[Pr 174, W 121])—**Qal** *Pf.* וְחַדּוּ מִזְּאֵבֵי עֶרֶב consec. Hb 1[8] *are keener than evening wolves* (of impetuous Chaldean horses). **Hiph.** הֵחַד (Che Or Brd) or יַחַד (Näg cf. Dr[§ 123 a, R]), ins. Is 44[12] after 𝔊 𝔖: the smith *sharpeneth* an axe. **Hoph.** *Pf.* 3 fs. הוּחַדָּה Ez 21[14.15.16] *be sharpened* (in all, subj. חֶרֶב).—Vid. also I. חדה.

2299 †II. [חַד] **adj.** **sharp**—only fs. חַדָּה, of חֶרֶב Ez 5[1]; in fig. of tongue ψ 57[5]; sim. of mouth Is 49[2]; fig. of end of (i.e. final experience with) strange woman מָרָה כַלַּעֲנָה ‖ ח׳ כְּחֶרֶב פִּיּוֹת Pr 5[4].
—I. חַד v. sub אֶחָד.

חַדָּה v. עֵין חַדָּה. p. 745 5876

†[חַדּוּד] **adj.** **sharpened, sharp, pointed,** 2303
only cstr., with superlat. sense = subst.: תַּחְתָּיו חַדּוּדֵי חָרֶשׂ Jb 41[22] *beneath him the sharpest of potsherds*, of scales of crocodile, cf. Di VB.

†חֲדַד **n.pr.m.** (on this and foll. cf. Palm. 2301
n.pr. חדודן Vog[No. 96], Sab. חדד Hal[27]);—a son of Ishmael Gn 25[15] (cf. Baer's n.; van d. H. חֲדַר) 𝔊 Χοδδαν, 𝔊L Χοδδαδ; = 1 Ch 1[30] 𝔊 Χουδαν, A Χοδδαδ, 𝔊L Αδαδ.

†חָדִיד **n.pr.loc.** in Benj., mentioned with 2307
לֹד and אוֹנוֹ Ezr 2[33] = Ne 7[37]; with these and other places Ne 11[34]; prob. = Ἀδιδά 1 Macc 12[38], Ἀδίδοις 13[13]; mod. *El-Ḥadite* c. 3¼ miles N. of E. from Lydda, Guérin[Judée i. 320] (cf. Rob[BR iii. 143]).

†I. [חָדָה] **vb.** **be** or **grow sharp**;—**Qal** 2300
grow sharp, *Impf.* apoc. = juss. יִחַד Pr 27[17a]; **Hiph.** *sharpen* (fig.), *Impf. apoc.* יַחַד Pr 27[17b]; בַּרְזֶל בְּבַרְזֶל יָחַד וְאִישׁ יַחַד פְּנֵי־רֵעֵהוּ *let iron by means of iron grow sharp, and let a man sharpen the countenance* (presence, bearing) *of his friend*;—so Ki[Michl. 126 a] De Now Kö[Lgb i. 373 f.], cf. Str. (who however makes both forms Hiph.)

†II. [חָדָה] **vb.** **rejoice** (As. *ḫadû* Dl[Pr 153]; 2302
Aram. ܚܕܐ, חֲדָא)—**Qal** *Impf.* 3 ms. וַיִּחַדְּ Ex 18[9] (E), and Jethro *rejoiced* over (עַל rei); juss. אַל־יִחַדְּ Jb 3[6] *let it not rejoice* among (בְּ) the days of the year, i.e. not take its place joyfully among them (fig. of day of Job's birth).—Klo prop. וְלֹא חָדוּ . . . בְּ 1 S 6[19] for וַיַּךְ . . . בְּ cf. also Dr. **Pi.** *Impf.* sf. (causat.) תְּחַדֵּהוּ בְשִׂמְחָה ψ 21[7] *thou makest him joyful* (Che *cheerest him*) *with gladness* (‖ תְּשִׁיתֵהוּ בְרָכוֹת).

†חֶדְוָה **n.f.** (late) **joy** (Aram. חדוא).—ח׳ 2304
1 Ch 16[27] (in the sanctuary); חֶדְוַת י׳ Ne 8[10] (‖ אַל־תֵּעָצֵבוּ).

†יַחְדִּיאֵל **n.pr.m.** (*God giveth joy*) a chief 3164
man in Manasseh 1 Ch 5[24], 𝔊 Ιελιηλ, A 𝔊L Ιεδιηλ.

†יֶחְדְּיָהוּ **n.pr.m.** (*May* י׳ *give joy!*) **1.** a 3165
Levite 1 Ch 24[20], 𝔊 Ιεδεια, 𝔊L Ιαδαια. **2.** officer of David 1 Ch 27[30] 𝔊 Ιαδ(α)ιας.

†חָדַל **vb.** **cease** (Sab. חדל *be negligent*, 2308
Sab. Denkm.[76])—**Qal** *Pf.* חָדַל Gn 18[11] + 4 t.; וְחָדַל consec. Nu 9[13] ψ 49[9]; 2 ms. וְחָדַלְתָּ Ex 23[5];

pl. חָדְלוּ Ju 5[6] + 4 t.; חָדֵ֑לּוּ (cf. Kö[I, 243]) Ju 5[7] 1 S 2[5]; 1 pl. חָדַלְנוּ Je 44[18]; *Impf.* יֶחְדַּל Dt 15[11] + (Jb 10[20] Kt יחדל jussive > Qr וַחֲדָ֑ל *Imv.*); אֶחְדָּ֑ל Ju 15[7] + 3 t.; וְאֶחְדָּ֑לָה Jb 16[6]; pl. יֶחְדָּ֑לוּ Ez 2[5] + 2 t.; יֶחְדָּלוּן Ex 9[29]; וַיֶּחְדְּלוּ Gn 11[8] Ex 9[33], נֶחְדָּ֑ל 1 K 22[15], etc.; *Inf. cstr.* חֲדֹל 1 S 12[23]; *Imv.* חֲדַל Ex 14[12] +, etc.; חִדְלוּ Is 1[16] 2[22]; חֲדָ֑לוּ Zc 11[12];— **1.** *cease, come to an end* Ex 9[29.33.34] (J), Is 24[8]; impers. חָדַל לִהְיוֹת לְשָׂרָה Gn 18[11] (J); *cease to be* Dt 15[11] (sq. מִן), and poet. Ju 5[6.7.7] 1 S 2[5] Jb 14[7]; = *be lacking, fail* Jb 19[14] Pr 10[19]. **2.** *cease, leave off*, sq. inf. c. לְ Gn 11[8] (J), 41[49] (E), Nu 9[13] (P), 1 S 12[23] 23[13] Je 44[18] 51[30] Dt 23[23] ψ 36[4] Pr 19[27] Ru 1[18]; inf. alone Is 1[16]; so also Ho 8[10], where read וְחָדְלוּ for וַיָּחֵ֫לּוּ 𝔊 Che We; sq. inf. c. מִן Ex 23[5] (JE), 1 K 15[21] = 2 Ch 16[5]; sq. subst. c. מִן (*cease regarding*) Is 2[22] (but Che Du al. treat v. as interpol.; om. 𝔊), 1 S 9[5] Pr 23[4]; sq. מֵאלהים 2 Ch 35[21], i.e. leave off provoking God; Ex 14[12] (J), sq. מִמֶּנּוּ *desist from us*, let us alone; Jb 7[16]; sq. acc. Jb 3[17] ח׳ רֹגֶז; Jb 14[6] *have rest* (i.e. cease from being troubled, see Di; cf. v[1]); no complem. expressed, *cease, forbear* Ju 15[7] 20[28] Am 7[5] 1 K 22[6.15] = 2 Ch 18[5.14], Je 40[4] 41[8] Zc 11[12] ψ 49[9] Jb 16[6] 2 Ch 25[16]; specif. of refusal to hear Ez 2[5.7] 3[11.27] (all opp. שָׁמַע). **Hoph.** *Pf.* (contracted) c. interrog. part. הֶחֳדַלְתִּי Ju 9[9.11.13] *should I be made to leave*, sq. acc. (cf. Kö[I, 240 ff.]); but perh. rd. הֶחָדַלְתִּי, **Qal** *Pf.* Stu Be, cf., for acc. sq., Jb 3[17].

2310 †חָדֵל **adj. forbearing, lacking,** הֶחָדֵל as subst. Ez 3[27] *he that forbeareth* (opp. שׁמע, cf. חָדַל **Qal** ad fin.); cstr. חֲדַל אִישִׁים Is 53[3] *lacking men* (i.e. forsaken by them);—*ceasing, transient* מֶה־חָדֵל אָ֑נִי ψ 39[5], but rd. rather חֶלֶד, v. Che[crit. n.]

2309 †[חֶ֫דֶל] **n.[m.] cessation,** only יוֹשְׁבֵי חָ֑דֶל Is. 38[11] (so Baer) *inhabitants of* (land of) *cessation*, i. e. of She'ôl; v. Di; but rd. rather חָ֑לֶד, v. חֶלֶד.

2311 †חַדְלָ֑י **n.pr.m.** an Ephraimite, 2 Ch 28[12], 𝔊 Χοαδ, A Αδδι, 𝔊L Αδλι.

חדק (√of foll.; NH חִדֵּק *press* or *thrust in*, Aram. חַדֵּק *id.* (denom.?)).

2312 †חֵ֫דֶק **n.[m.] brier** (NH *id.*; Aram. חִדְקָא Löw[p. 147, No. 104]; cf. Ar. حَدَقٌ a kind of nightshade, v. Lane[532]);—טוֹבָם כְּחֵדֶק Mi 7[4] *the best of them* (si vera l.) *is like the brier* (|| יָשָׁר מִמְּסוּכָה); דֶּרֶךְ עָצֵל כִּמְשֻׂכַת חָדֶק Pr 15[19] *the way of a sluggard is like a brier-hedge.*

†חִדֶּ֫קֶל **n.pr.fl. Tigris** (As. *Idiḳlat, Di-* 2313
ḳlat, Old Pers. *Tigrâ* Spieg[APK, Gloss.], etc.), the famous Assyr. river; v. esp. Dl[Pa 110 f. 170 ff.]; ח׳ Gn 2[14]; חִדָּ֑קֶל Dn 10[4].

†[חָדַר] **vb. surround, enclose** (Ph. in 2314
deriv.; Ar. خَدَّرَ II. *conceal*, خِدْرٌ *curtain* concealing a person, *chamber, house, or tent* as concealing some one; Eth. ኀደረ: *dwell*; v. also foll.)—only **Qal** *Pt.* fs. הַחֹדֶ֫רֶת לָהֶם Ez 21[19] *that which surroundeth them* (of the sword),—so 𝔖 Thes Sm Co Da VB.

†חֶ֫דֶר **n.m.** [1 Ch 28, 11] **chamber, room** (NH 2315-16
id.; Ph. חדר, חדרת; Sab. חדר Mordt[ZMG, 1876, 24]; Eth. መኅደር:)—abs. חֶדֶר 2 S 13[10] + 11 t.; הַחַ֫דְרָה Gn 43[20] 1 K 1[15]; הֶחָ֑דְרָה Ju 15[1] 2 S 13[10]; cstr. חֲדַר Ct 3[4]; חֲדַר Ex 7[28] + 5 t.; sf. חֶדְרוֹ Jo 2[16]; pl. חֲדָרִים Dt 32[25] Pr 24[4]; cstr. חַדְרֵי Pr 7[27] + 8 t.; sf. חֲדָרֶיךָ Is 26[20]; חֲדָרָיו Ct 1[4] 1 Ch 28[11];—*room, chamber*, usually private, as bedroom Gn 43[30] (J), Ju 15[1] 16[9.12] 2 S 13[10.10] 1 K 1[15] Ct 1[4] Is 26[20]; Ju 14[18] rd. prob. הַחַדְרָה *bridal-chamber* for הַחַרְסָה Sta[ZAW 1884, 253], cf. Jo 2[16] (|| חֻפָּתָהּ of bride), ח׳ הוֹרָתִי Ct 3[4] (|| בֵּית אִמִּי); of kings (of Egypt) ψ 105[30]; specif.: ח׳ מִשְׁכָּב *bed-chamber* Ex 7[28] (J), 2 S 4[7] 2 K 6[12] Ec 10[20]; other combinations:—ח׳ הַמְּקֵרָה Ju 3[24] = *cool chamber*; ח׳ הַפְּנִימִים 1 Ch 28[11] *inner chamber*; חדרי מַשְׂכִּיתוֹ Ez 8[12] *his chambers of imagery* (del. Hi Co Sgfr.); ח׳ בְּח׳ *a chamber within a chamber*, i.e. an innermost chamber 1 K 20[30] 22[25] = 2 Ch 18[24], 2 K 9[2]; pl. = *store-rooms* Pr 24[4]; so ח׳ הַמִּטּוֹת 2 K 11[2] = 2 Ch 22[11], i.e. room where beds were stored (Ke Th); metaph. ח׳ מָוֶת Pr 7[27] (|| דַּרְכֵי שְׁאוֹל); חדרי תֵמָן Jb 9[9] *chambers of south* (where constellations are treasured up, v. Di; Hoffm. thinks of n.pr. of star or constell.); cf. Jb 37[9] a *chamber* whence comes storm-wind (סוּפָה); חַדְרֵי בֶטֶן i.e. inner parts of body, only fig. Pr 18[8] = 26[22], 20[27.30]; in Dt 32[25] מֵחֲדָרִים = *within*, poet. for מִבַּיִת || מחוּץ *without*.

†חַדְרָ֑ךְ **n.pr.terr.** only Zc 9[1] אֶרֶץ ח׳ 2317
(|| דַּמֶּשֶׂק); perh. = As. *Ḫatarakka, Ḫatari(k)ka*, a district near Damascus and Hamath; v. Schr[COT ad loc.], Dl[Pa 279].

†[חָדַשׁ] **vb.** only **Pi.** (and **Hithp.**) **renew,** 2318
repair (poet. and late) (NH *id.*, Ph. חדש; n. חדש *new moon*, also in קרתחדשת *new-city* =

Carthage ; Aram. ܚܕܬ and חַדֵּשׁ; Ar. حَدَثَ *be new*, Eth. ሐደሰ: I. 2. *renew ;* Sab. החדת, v. Os (Levy)$^{ZMG 1865, 204}$ Mordt$^{ZMG 1876, 30}$; As. [*addâšu*], *uddiš, renew, eššu, new*, etc. Dl$^{W 199 ff.}$)—**Pi.** *Pf.* וְחִדְּשׁוּ consec. Is 61^{4}; *Impf.* וַיְחַדֵּשׁ 2 Ch 15^{8}; 2 ms. תְּחַדֵּשׁ Jb 10^{17} ψ 104^{30}; וּנְחַדֵּשׁ 1 S 11^{14}; *Imv.* חַדֵּשׁ ψ 51^{12} La 5^{21}; *Inf.* לְחַדֵּשׁ 2 Ch 24$^{4.12}$;—**1.** *renew, make anew* הַמְּלוּכָה 1 S 11^{14} (editorial); פני אדמה ψ 104^{30}, רוּחַ 51^{12} (‖ ברא);=bring back יָמֵינוּ כְּקֶדֶם La 5^{21}; ח׳ עדיך Jb 10^{17} i.e. *bringest fresh (new) witnesses.* **2.** *repair*, cities Is 61^{4}, temple 2 Ch 24$^{4.12}$, altar 2 Ch 15^{8}. **Hithp.** *Impf.* 3 fs. תִּתְחַדֵּשׁ c. pl. subj. ת׳ כַּנֶּשֶׁר נְעוּרָיְכִי ψ 103^{5} *thy youth reneweth itself, like the eagle.*

2319 †חָדָשׁ **adj. new** (on format. v. Lg$^{BN 48}$)—ח׳ abs. Ex 1^{8} + 19 t.; f. חֲדָשָׁה Lv 23^{16} + 19 t.; pl. חֲדָשִׁים Dt 32^{17} + 10 t.; f. חֲדָשׁוֹת Is 42^{9} 48^{6};—*new*, usu. **a.** attrib. Ex 1^{8} (E) *a new king ;* so of house Dt 20$^{5.22}$, wife 24^{5}, cords Ju 15^{13} 16$^{11.12}$, cart 1 S 6^{7} 2 S 6$^{3.3}$ (but del. in v^{b}, cf. We Dr)=1 Ch 13^{7}, garment 1 K 11$^{29.30}$, vessel 2 K 2^{20}, wine-skins Jos 9^{13} (JE) Jb 32^{19}, threshing instr. Is 4^{15}; meal-offering Lv 23^{16} (H) Nu 28^{26} (P); esp. (poet.) שִׁיר ח׳ *a new song* (of praise) ψ 33^{3} 40^{4} 96^{1} 98^{1} 144^{9} 149^{1} Is 42^{10}; בְּרִית ח׳ Je 31^{31}; שָׁמַיִם חדשים וארץ חדשה Is 65^{17} cf. 66^{22}; שֵׁם ח׳ Is 62^{2}; רוּחַ ח׳ *a new spirit* Ez 11^{19} 18^{31} 36^{26}, + לֵב ח׳ 18^{31} 36^{26}; פֶּתַח שַׁעַר־י׳ הֶח׳ Je 26^{10} *new gate* of (house of) י׳, cf. 36^{10} (v. Gf Je 20^{2}); also הֶחָצֵר הַח׳ 2 Ch 20^{5} *the new court* (v. Be Öt); אלהים חדשים Ju 5^{8} *new gods? judges?* txt. prob. corrupt, cf. Nö$^{ZMG 1888, 477}$, Müll$^{Königsb. Stud. i.}$, GACooke$^{Deb. 34 ff.}$ and conj. by Bu$^{RS, 103}$, RS in Bla^{Judges}; in gen. אֵין כָּל־ח׳ Ec 1^{9} *there is nothing new ;* with no subst. expr. חָגוּר חֲדָשָׁה 2 S 21^{16} *girt with a new* (sword : but txt. perh. corrupt, cf. We Klo Dr), of (food-)products of earth (opp. יָשָׁן) Lv 26^{10} (H) Ct 7^{14}; חֲדָשִׁים Dt 32^{17} *new ones* (i.e. gods ; ‖ מִקָּרֹב בָּאוּ); in gen. f. חֲדָשָׁה *a new thing* Is 43^{19} Je 31^{22}, fpl. Is 42^{9} (opp. הָרִאשֹׁנוֹת), 48^{6}. **b.** very rarely predicate : of י׳'s compassions חדשים לַבְּקָרִים La 3^{23} they are *new every morning ;* כְּבוֹדִי ח׳ עִמָּדִי Jb 29^{20} *my glory* shall be *fresh with me ;* רְאֵה זֶה ח׳ הוּא Ec 1^{10} *see, this is new !*

2320 I. חֹדֶשׁ$_{282}$ **n.m.**$^{Gn 7, 11}$ (**f.** MT 38^{24} but **m.** Sam Di) (**newness**), **new moon, month** (on format. cf. Lg$^{BN 144}$; on usage, names, etc., Muss-Arnolt$^{JBL 1892, 72 ff., 160 ff.}$)—ח׳ abs. Gn 7^{11} +; cstr. (rare) Gn 29^{14} +; sf. חָדְשׁוֹ Nu 28^{14} + 2 t.; חָדְשָׁהּ Ho 2^{13} Je 2^{24}; pl. חֳדָשִׁים Gn 38^{24} +; cstr. חָדְשֵׁי Ex 12^{2} + 2 t.; sf. חֳדָשָׁיו Jb 14^{5} + 2 t.; חָדְשֵׁיכֶם Is 1^{14} Nu 28^{11}; חָדְשֵׁכֶם Nu 10^{10};—† **1.** *new moon*=day, time, of new moon, as religious festival 1 S 20$^{5.18.24.27.34}$ (Dr); cf. יֹאכְלֵם ח׳ Ho 5^{7} *a new moon shall devour them*, Hi St VB, but on txt. v. We; usu. ‖ שַׁבָּת Am 8^{5} 2 K 4^{23} Is 1^{13} (+ קְרֹא מִקְרָא), מִדֵּי חֹדֶשׁ בְּחָדְשׁוֹ 66^{23}, Ez 46$^{1.6}$ (both יוֹם הַח׳), 1 Ch 23^{31} 2 Ch 2^{3} 8^{13} 31^{3} Ne 10^{34} (all + מוֹעֵד), Ho 2^{13} Ez 45^{17} (both + חג, מועד); ‖ מוֹעֵד alone Is 1^{14} Ez 3^{5}; ‖ יוֹם חַגֵּנוּ ψ 81^{4}; (cf. ראשׁ הַח׳ Nu 10^{10} 28^{11}; on religious observance of new moon cf. Di$^{Lv p. 578 f}$ Benz$^{Archäol. § 69}$); as time of augury in Babylon (astrolog. prognost.) Is 47^{13}.† **2.** *month* (as beginning with new moon, lunar month ; cf. Benz$^{Archäol. § 30}$, but then, without ref. to day of beginning): †**a.** as measure of time during which Gn 38^{24} (J), Nu 11$^{20.21}$ (JE), 9^{22} (P), Ju 11$^{37.38.39}$ 20^{47} 1 S 6^{1} 27^{7} 2 S 2^{11} 5^{5} 6^{11} 24$^{8.13}$ = 1 Ch 21^{12}, Am 4^{7} 1 K 4^{7} 5$^{7.28.28.28}$ 11^{16} 2 K 15^{8} 23^{31} 24^{8} Ez 39$^{12.14}$ 1 Ch 3^{4} 13^{14} 2 Ch 36$^{2.9}$ Est 2$^{12.12.12}$. In 1 S 10$^{27 b}$ rd. prob. כְּמֵחֹדֶשׁ for MT כמחריש, and join to 11^{1}, so 𝔊 We Dr (cf. Gn 38^{24}); in combinations, ח׳ יָמִים *a month* (of) *time* (cf. יֶרַח ימים Dt 21^{1} 2 K 15^{13}) Gn 29^{14} (J), Nu 11$^{20.26}$ (JE), ח׳ ימים ארבעה Ju 19^{2}; of age מִסְפַּר־ח׳ *number of his months*=length of his life Jb 14^{5} 21^{21}; cf. esp. בֶּן־ח׳ Lv 27^{6} Nu 3$^{15.22.28.34.39.40.43}$ 18^{16} 26^{62} (all P).† **b.** *calendar months*, †(1) with names ח׳ הָאָבִיב Ex 13^{4} 23^{15} 34$^{18.18}$ (all JE ; = 1st mo. 12^{2} P), Dt 16^{1}; ח׳ זִו 1 K 6^{1} (=2nd mo. ib.; = יֶרַח זִו v^{37}); cf. 8^{2} (יֶרַח הָאֵתָנִים=הַח׳ הַשְּׁבִיעִי), 6^{38} (יֶרַח בּוּל=הַח׳ הַשְּׁמִינִי); in the postex. books occur Babyl. names (v. the several words):—ח׳ נִיסָן Ne 2^{1} Est 3^{7} (=1st mo. Est 3^{7}); ח׳ סִיוָן Est 8^{9}=3rd mo.; ח׳ כִּסְלֵו Zc 7^{1} Ne 1^{1} (=9th mo. Zc 7^{1}); ח׳ טֵבֵת Est 2^{16}=10th mo.; ח׳ שְׁבָט Zc 1^{7}=11th mo.; ח׳ אֲדָר Est 3$^{7.13}$ 8^{12} 9^{1} in all=12th mo., 9$^{15.17.19.21}$; (cf. also אֱלוּל Ne 6^{15}, without ח׳ or יֶרַח; this was 6th mo.; v. further Schr$^{COT Ne 1, 1}$ Benz$^{l. c.}$).† (2) merely numbered (chiefly P and late) e.g. בַּח׳ הַשֵּׁנִי Gn 7^{11}, cf. 8$^{4.5.14}$ Lv 16^{29} Nu 1$^{1.18}$ (all P) + oft. P; Dt 1^{3} (P), 1 K 12$^{32.33}$ 25$^{1.3.8.25.27}$ Je 1^{3} + 11 t. Je, Ez 24^{1} 32^{1} Hg 1$^{1.15}$ Zc 1^{1} 7$^{1.3}$; 1 Ch 12^{15}, cf. entire list 27$^{2-15}$ 2 Ch 3^{2} + 12 t. 2 Ch; Ezr 3^{1} + 10 t. Ezr; Ne 7^{72} 8$^{2.14}$ Est 3^{12}; note esp. הַח׳ הַזֶּה לָכֶם ראשׁ חֳדָשִׁים רִאשׁוֹן הוּא לָכֶם Ex 12^{2} (P), as implying that the 1st mo. was formerly *not* in the spring ; observe also usage of omitting ח׳, e.g. בַּח׳ הָרִ׳=בָּרִאשׁוֹן Gn 8^{13}, cf. v^{5}; so commonly in Ezek.:—Ez 1^{1} 8^{1} 20^{1} 29$^{1.17}$ 30^{20} 31^{1} 33^{21} 45$^{18.21.25}$ + 26^{1} 32^{17} 45^{20} Co ; (ח׳ sts. expr., v. Ez 24^{1} 32^{1} supr.; on like usage with יוֹם v. יום). (3) special phrases and usages are:—

+עֹלַת חֹדֶשׁ בְּחָדְשׁוֹ לְחָדְשֵׁי שָׁנָה Nu 28^{14} (P; cf. יום, and Is 66^{23} supr. **1**); מִיּוֹם לְיוֹם וּמֵחֹדֶשׁ לְחֹדֶשׁ Est 3^7 *from day to day and from month to month;* חָדְשָׁהּ Je 2^{24} of wild she-ass's mating time.†

2321 †II. חֹדֶשׁ **n.pr.f.** a wife of Shaharaim of Benj. 1 Ch 8^9, 𝔊 Ἀδα, 𝔊L Βαδαα (so v^8=בַּעֲרָה).

2322 †חֲדָשָׁה **n.pr.loc.** town in Judah Jos 15^{37} (site unknown, cf. Di).

8483 †חָדְשִׁי in **n.pr.loc.** אֶרֶץ תַּחְתִּים ח׳ 2 S 24^6, rd. א׳ הַחִתִּים קָדְשָׁה v. Hi Gesch. Isr. i. 29, 𝔊L εἰς γῆν Χεττιειμ Καδης; cf. Dr ad loc. and (in part) Klo; v. also קָדֵשׁ.

2325 †[חוּב] **vb.** be guilty (NH *id., be under obligation, guilty;* Aram. ܚܳܒ, חוּב, *be defeated, guilty;* Ar. خَابَ *be disappointed, fail;*—Ar. حُوبٌ, حَوْبٌ *sin,* is loan-wd. acc. to Bev Dn 1^{10});—**Qal** not in MT; but rd. perh. חַבְתִּי (for סַבֹּתִי) 1 S 22^{22} *I am guilty,* so 𝔖 Th We Dr. **Pi.** *Pf. inculpate* וְחִיַּבְתֶּם אֶת־רֹאשִׁי לַמֶּלֶךְ consec. Dn 1^{10} *and inculpate my head with the king.*

2326 †חוֹב **n.[m.]** debt (NH *id.;* Aram. ܚܘܒܐ, חוֹבָא);—חֲבֹלָתוֹ ח׳ יָשִׁיב Ez 18^7 *his pledge as to indebtedness he restores,* v. Hi-Sm Ew § 291 b Ges § 132 R 5, b Kö Lgb. i. 497 f. and cf. Dr § 193 (but constr. hard: Co שׁוּב; dittogr. fr. חבל׳ Bev Dn 1, 10, cf. $v^{12.16}$).

2327 †חוֹבָה **n.pr.loc.** Gn 14^{15}, north of Damascus; mod. *Ḥoba,* 20 hours N. of Dam., acc. to Wetzst Del Gn. ed. 4, 561 ff. so Di.

2328 †[חוּג] **vb.** draw round, make a circle (Aram. ܚܳܓ *circumivit;* n. ܚܘܓܬܐ, חוּגְתָּא, *circle, vault of heavens*)—**Qal** *Pf.* חֹק חָג עַל־פְּנֵי מַיִם Jb 26^{10} (cf. Pr 8^{27}), *hath drawn as a circle* a bound, etc., of the horizon-line.

2329 †חוּג **n.[m.]** vault;—only of vault of the heavens חוּג שָׁמַיִם יִתְהַלָּךְ Jb 22^{14}; בְּחֻקוֹ חוּג עַל־פְּנֵי תְהוֹם Pr 8^{27}; הַיֹּשֵׁב עַל־חוּג הָאָרֶץ Is 40^{22}.

4230 †מְחוּגָה **n.f.** circle-instrument, compass, used by carvers of idols וּבַמְּחוּגָה יְתָאֳרֵהוּ Is 44^{13}.

I. חוד (√of foll.; Ar. حَادَ is *decline, turn aside, avoid,* hence perh. *riddle,* as *indirect, obscure*).

2420 †חִידָה **n.f.** riddle, enigmatic, perplexing saying or question;—abs. ח׳ Ju 14^{12}+6t.; sf. חִידָתִי Ju 14^{18} ψ 49^5; חִידָתְךָ Ju 14^{13}; pl. abs. חִידוֹת 1 K 10^1+4t.; חִידֹת Nu 12^8; sf. חִידֹתָם Pr 1^6;—**1.** *riddle*=dark, obscure utterance Nu 12^8 (JE; opp. פֶּה אֶל־פֶּה and מַרְאֶה); of something put indirectly and needing interpretation;—an allegory חוּד ח׳ Ez 17^2 (‖ מָשָׁל); allegor. and fig. sayings Pr 1^6 (‖ מְלִיצָה מָשָׁל and דִּבְרֵי חֲכָמִים); enigmat. sentences and comparisons, declaring fate of Chaldeans Hb 2^6 (+ מְלִיצָה ‖ מָשָׁל), perplexing moral problem ψ 49^5 (c. פָּתַח *open, propound;* ‖ מָשָׁל), a lesson taught indirectly ψ 78^2 (c. הִבִּיעַ, ח׳ מִנֵּי קֶדֶם; ‖ מָשָׁל). **2.** *riddle, enigma,* to be guessed, in Ju 14: **a.** with vb. חוּד Ju $14^{12.13.16}$ *propound a riddle.* **b.** with vb. הִגִּיד *tell* (give answer to) *a riddle* Ju $14^{14.15.17.19}$. **c.** with vb. מצא *find out a riddle* Ju 14^{18}. **3.** *perplexing questions* by which queen of Sheba put Sol. to the test (נִסָּה) 1 K 10^1=2 Ch 9^1. **4.** with הֵבִין skilled in *double-dealing* Dn 8^{23} (Bev).

†II. [חוּד] **vb. denom.** propound a riddle; 2330
—**Qal** *Pf.* 2 ms. חַדְתָּה Ju 14^{16}; *Impf.* אָחוּדָה Ju 14^{12}; *Imv.* חוּד (חִידָה וּמְשֹׁל מָשָׁל) Ez 17^2; חוּדָה Ju 14^{13}; always c. חידה acc. cogn.

I. חוה (Ph. חוא *live*=Heb. חָיָה q. v.) p. 310 2421

†I. חַוָּה **n.pr.f.** (*life,* vid. Di Gn 3^{20}; >We 2332
Prol. 1886, 322; Skizzen iii. 217 after Nö who suggests *serpent* as poss. mng., cf. Ar. حَيَّةٌ; but RS K 177 'mother of every *ḥayy,*' v. II. חַי sub חיה)—Gn 3^{20} *and the man called his wife* חַוָּה, because she was: אֵם כָּל־חָי; cf. ח׳ אִשְׁתּוֹ 4^1 (both J).—II. חַוָּה *village,* v. infr. sub II. חוה.

†יחואל **n.pr.m.** 2 Ch 29^{14} Kt; Qr יְחִיאֵל q.v. 3171
sub חיה.

II. חוה (√of foll.; Ar. حَوَى, *collect, gather;* حِوَاءٌ *circle of tents* cf. II. חַי sub חיה, Ar. حَيٌّ).

†II. [חַוָּה] **n.f.** tent-village—Pl. חַוֹּתֵיהֶם 2333
Nu 32^{41} (JE), cf. Di. Elsewh. in cpd. appella-
tive, almost=n.pr. חַוֹּת יָאִיר Dt 3^{14} Jos 13^{30} (D), 2334
Ju 10^4 1 K 4^{13} 1 Ch 2^{23}.—I. חַוָּה n.pr.f. v. supr.

†חִוִּי **adj. gent.** (=*villagers?*)—**1.** שְׁכֶם 2340
בֶּן־חֲמוֹר הַח׳ Gn 34^2 (P), cf. צִבְעוֹן הַח׳ 36^2 (but rd. rather הַחֹרִי Ol Di cf. 𝔊 Jos 9^7). **2.** c. art. as n.pr. coll. הַחִוִּי *the Hivvites* 'begotten' by Canaan Gn 10^{17}=1 Ch 1^{15}; esp. in list of Canaanit. peoples displaced by Hebrews Ex $3^{8.17}$ 13^5 $23^{23.28}$ 33^2 34^{11} Dt 7^1 20^{17} Jos 3^{10} 9^1 12^8 24^{11} (all JED), Ju 3^5 1 K 9^{20}=2 Ch 8^7; cf. עָרֵי הַח׳ וְהַכְּנַעֲנִי 2 S 24^7 (note צִידוֹן, מִבְצַר־צֹר, just preceding); applied specif. to Gibeonites Jos 9^7 (JE), 11^{19} (D).—In Jos 11^3 Ju 3^3 rd. prob. הַחִתִּי for הַחִוִּי We Mey Bu Urg 350 v. (partly) 𝔊, Dr on Dt 7^1.

4233 †מַחֲוִים appar. **adj. gent.**, only אֱלִיאֵל הַמַּ׳ 1 Ch 11[46], but rd. prob. הַמַּחֲנִי (Be), v. מַחֲנַיִם n.pr.loc. sub חנה; Öt suggests also הַמְּעוֹנִי; 𝔊 ὁ Μιει, A ὁ Μαωειν, 𝔊L ὁ Μαωθε.

2331 †III. [חָוָה] **vb.** only **Pi.** (poet. & late), **tell, declare** (Aram. ܚܘܝ, חַוֵּי)—**Pi.** *Impf.* 3 ms. יְחַוֶּה־ ψ 19[3]; 1 s. אֲחַוֶּה Jb 32[10.17]; sf. אֲחַוְּךָ Jb 15[17], אֲחַוֶּךָּ Jb 36[2]; *Inf. cstr.* חַוּוֹת;—*declare, make known*, c. acc. דָּעַת ψ 19[3] (subj. לַיְלָה, sq. לְלַיְלָה ‖ יַבִּיעַ אֹמֶר); c. acc. דֵּעִי Jb 32[10.17]; c. 2 acc. וָאִירָא מֵחַוֹּת דֵּעִי אֶתְכֶם 32[6], sq. sf. pers. + obj. cl., וַאֲחַוְּךָ כִּי־עוֹד לֶאֱלוֹהַּ מִלִּים: 36[2] *and I will shew thee that* (there are) *yet words for God;* sq. sf. pers. only Jb 15[17];—rd. prob. also וַאֲחַוֶּה for וַאֲקַוֶּה ψ 52[11] Hi Che al.

262 †[אַחֲוָה] **n.f. declaration** (in form, an Aram. Aphel Inf.)—only sf. וְאַחֲוָתִי בְּאָזְנֵיכֶם: Jb 13[17] (in ‖ line שִׁמְעוּ שָׁמוֹעַ מִלָּתִי).

2335 חוֹזָי 2 Ch 33[19] v. sub חזה. p. 302

חוח (√of foll., meaning dubious).

2336-37 †חוֹחַ **n.m.**[2 K 14,9] **1. brier, bramble. 2. hook, ring, fetter;**—ח׳ abs. Ho 9[6] + 8 t.; pl. חֹחִים 1 S 13[6] (but v. infr.), חוֹחִים Ct 2[2]; חַוָחִים 2 Ch 33[11];—**1. a.** *brier, bramble* 2 K 14[9.9] = 2 Ch 25[18.18] (allegory of Jehoash); coll., sign of desolation Ho 9[6] (‖ קִמּוֹשׂ), Is 34[13] (‖ קִמּוֹשׂ, סִירִים), Jb 31[40] (opp. חִטִּים); in sim. of fool's parable ח׳ עָלָה בְיַד־שִׁכּוֹר Pr 26[9] *a brier cometh into the hand of a drunken man* (De Now Str); כְּשׁוֹשַׁנָּה בֵּין הַחוֹחִים Ct 2[2]; *briers* = *thickets* as hiding-places 1 S 13[6] (but Ew We Dr חוֹרִים *holes*, cf. 14[11]; v. sub III. חרר ‖ מְעָרוֹת, סְלָעִים, בֹּרוֹת, צְרִחִים; 𝔊 here ἐν τ. μάνδραις; 14[11] ἐκ τ. τρωγλῶν). **2.** late, **a.** *hook* or *ring*, in jaw of crocodile c. תִּקֹּב Jb 40[26] (‖ הֲתָשִׂים אַגְמֹן בְּאַפּוֹ); of captive וַיִּלְכְּדוּ אֶת־מְנַשֶּׁה בַּחֹחִים 2 Ch 33[11] (cf. חַח).

2397 †חַח **n.m. hook, ring, fetter;**—חַח abs. Ex 35[22]; sf. חַחִי Is 37[29] 2 K 19[28]; pl. חַחִים Ez 19[4] + 2 t. + Ez 29[4] Qr (Kt erron. חחיים, v. infr.);—**1.** *hook, ring*, in nose of captive וְשַׂמְתִּי חַחִי בְּאַפֶּךָ Is 37[29] = 2 K 19[28] (cf. בַּחֹחִים 2 Ch 33[11], v. חוֹחַ supr.); so of princes of Judah, under fig. of young lions Ez 19[4.9] (in v[9] transp., so that בחחים foll. הביא as v[4]; so Co); in jaws of crocodile (metaph. of Pharaoh), c. נתן Ez 29[4], cf. 38[4] (but 𝔊 om. and sense opposes, cf. Co and—dub.—Da). **2.** *hook, ring* as ornament, perhaps *nose-ring* (others *brooch*, see VB), Ex 35[22] (P; ‖ כּוּמָז, טַבַּעַת, נֶזֶם).

חוט (of foll.; Ar. خَاطَ, Aram. ܚܛ, חֵיט *sew*).

†חוּט **n.m.**[Jos 2,18] **thread, cord, line** (NH *id.*; 2339
Ar. خَيْطٌ, Aram. ܚܘܛܐ, חוּטָא)—ח׳ abs. Gn 14[23] + 2 t.; cstr. Jos 2[18] + 3 t.;—**1.** *thread*, as easily broken Ju 16[12] (sim.); as composing a rope or cord; תִּקְוַת ח׳ הַשָּׁנִי הַזֶּה Jos 2[18] (JE) *this cord of scarlet thread* (lit. the cord of this thread of scarlet); prob. also מִחוּט וְעַד שְׂרוֹךְ נַעַל Gn 14[23] *from a thread to a sandal-thong;* in sim. כְּח׳ הַשָּׁנִי Ct 4[3] *like a thread of scarlet* are thy lips. **2. cord,** הַח׳ הַמְשֻׁלָּשׁ Ec 4[12] *a three-fold cord.* **3.** *line*, as measure of length 1 K 7[15] *and a line of twelve cubits surrounded* (i. e. would surround) *it* (cf. קָו v[23]), so Je 52[21].

חִוִּי v. sub II. חוה. p. 295 2340

†חֲוִילָה **n.pr.terr.** (√dub. Dl[Pa 12] suggests 2341
חול *sand-land, downs*, as Heb. popular etym., MV[11] give it as actual etym.; Sta[ThLZ Apr. 28, 1894, 235] compares this, as well as חול *sand*, with Ar. وَحَلٌ *soft mud, [damp sand]*)—אֶרֶץ הַחֲוִילָה Gn 2[11] (surrounded or bordered—סבב—by river Pishon; noted for excellent gold, bdellium and *shoham*-stone); elsewhere without art. חֲוִילָה 10[7] = 1 Ch 1[9] as a 'son' of Cush (between סְבָא and סַבְתָּה); but also as a 'son' of יָקְטָן, a descendant of Shem Gn 10[29] = 1 Ch 1[23] (between אוֹפִיר and יוֹבָב); מֵח׳ עַד־שׁוּר Gn 25[18] said of limits of Ishmaelitish territory; cf. same limits of Amalek 1 S 15[7] (but dub.; We rds. טֵלָם, cf. v[4] and vid. Dr; Glaser[Skizze ii. 326] rds. חֲכִילָה as 23[19] 26[1.3]).—Most have supposed several regions named ח׳ to be indicated in these passages:—e.g. Thes 1. Arabian shore of Pers. Gulf Gn 10[29] etc. 2. Ethiopian coast Gn 10[7] etc. 3. India Gn 2[11] (regarded as indef. extension of 1). Di[Gn 10,7] distinguishes 1 and 2 either as quite distinct, or as different settlements of one great people, and (on Gn 2[14]) thinks that כל ארץ ח׳ Gn 2[11] implies vague extension eastward. Dl[Pa 12 ff. 57 ff.] identif. ח׳ in all passages with NE. part of Syrian desert, so E. Meyer[Gesch. Alterth. i. 224]; Glaser[Skizze ii. 323 ff.] with central and NE. Arabia. The question is still undecided.

†I. חול [חִיל] **vb. whirl, dance, writhe** 2342
(NH, Aram. *id.*, *dance*; Ar. حَالَ *change, turn;* As. *ḫîlu, writhe* in fear Dl[Pr 191] (on *ḫ* = ح v. DHM[ZK i. 357]); on form of Heb. **vb.** v. Nö[ZMG. 1883, 536])—**Qal** *Pf.* 3 fs. חָלָה Mi 1[12] + 2 t.; וְחָלָה consec. Ho 11[6]; חַלְתִּי Is 23[4]; חָלוּ Je 5[3] (but v. infr.), La 4[6]; וְחָלוּ

Dt 2^{25}; חַ֫לְנוּ Is 26^{18}; *Impf.* יָחוּל Je 23^{19} 30^{23}; 3 fs. תָּחוּל Ez 30^{16} Qr (Kt Co תחיל); וַתָּ֫חֶל Je 51^{29}; אחולה Je 4^{19} Kt (Qr אוֹחִילָה, Hiph. יחל); יָחֻ֫לוּ 2 S 3^{29}; but also יָחִיל ψ 55^{5} (Jb 20^{21} v. II. חול); וַיָּ֫חֶל 1 S 31^{3} = 1 Ch 10^{3} + Gn 8^{10} (where rd. prob. וַיַּ֫חֶל as v^{12}; = וַיִּחֵל Ol Di); 3 fs. תָּחִיל Is 26^{17} + 2 t. + Ez 30^{16} Kt (cf. *supr.*); וַתָּ֫חֵל ψ 97^{4}; 2 fs. תְּחִלִין Is 45^{10}; יָחִילוּ ψ 77^{17} + 3t. (ψ 10^{5} v. II. חול); וַיָּחִילוּ Ju 3^{25}; יְחִילוּן Is 13^{8}; תָּחִילוּ Je 5^{22}; *Imv.* fs. חוּלִי Mi 4^{10} ψ 114^{7}; mpl. חִילוּ ψ 96^{9} 1 Ch 16^{30}; *Inf. cstr.* לָחוּל) Ju 21^{21} Ez 30^{16} (= Inf. abs.); *Pt.* fs. חוֹלָה Je 4^{31} vid. Gf Gie and Ges$^{§ 72 R. 1}$;—**1.** *dance* Ju 21^{21} (לָחוּל בַּמְּחֹלוֹת). **2.** *twist, writhe:* **a.** in pain, esp. childbirth Is 26^{17} 45^{10} (מַה־תּוֹלִיד ‖ מַה־תח׳); metaph., of sea Is 23^{4} (ילד ‖); Israel 26^{18} (הרה ‖), 54^{1} (ילד ‖); Zion $66^{7.8}$ (‖ *id.*), Mi 4^{10} (גֹּחִי ‖, sim. כיולדה; cf. v. 9), Je 4^{31}. **b.** fig., *be in severe pain,* or *anguish* (mostly poet. and elevated prose), sq. מפני Dt 2^{25} (רגז ‖, cf. also פַּחַד and יִרְאָה v^{a}); Ez 30^{16} ψ 96^{9} Je 5^{22} (ירא ‖); sq. מִלִּפְנֵי 1 Ch 16^{30} ψ 114^{7}; abs. ψ 55^{5} (אימות מָוֶת נפלו עלי ‖), Je 4^{19} Kt, ψ 77^{17} (רגז ‖) 97^{4} Is 13^{8} 23^{5} Je 51^{29} (רָעַשׁ ‖), Jo 2^{6} Zc 9^{5} (ירא ‖), prob. also 1 S 31^{3} (cf. 28^{5}) = 1 Ch 10^{3}, cf. Öt; fig. of mts. Hb 3^{10}. **c.** in contrition Je 5^{3}, חָ֫לוּ der. fr. חול Ew Gf Gie; < 𝔖 Ra Hi Ke al. fr. חלה (wrongly accented; vid. חלה **Qal 2**). **d.** in anxious longing עַד בּוֹשׁ Ju 3^{25}, sq. לְ Mi 1^{12} (on Gn 8^{10}, cf. supr.) **3.** *whirl, whirl about* עַל־רֹאשׁ יוֹאָב (i.e. blood—דמים—of Abner, from sword) 2 S 3^{29}; of attack of sword itself Ho 11^{6} (אכל, כִּלָּה ‖), cf. La 4^{6} לֹא חָלוּ בה ידים; of tempest על ראש רשעים יחול Je 23^{19} (v^{a} סער מִתְחוֹלֵל) = 30^{23} (v^{a} סַעַר מִתְגּוֹרֵר). **Po'lel.** *Impf.* יְחוֹלֵל ψ 29^{9}; 3 fs. תְּחוֹלֵל Pr 25^{23}; sf. תְּחוֹלֶלְכֶם Is 51^{2}; 2 ms. תְּחוֹלֵל Jb 35^{14}; וַתְּחוֹלֵל ψ 90^{2}; *Inf.* cstr. חֹלֵל Jb 39^{1}; *Pt.* מְחוֹלֵל Pr 26^{10}; מְחֹלְלֶךָ Dt 32^{18}; מְחוֹלֶלֶת Is 51^{9}; מְחֹלְלוֹת Ju 21^{23};—1 S 18^{6} ψ 87^{7} v. infr.; on חֹלְלָה Jb 26^{13} v. חלל;—**1.** *dance* Ju 21^{23}, so perh. also 1 S 18^{6} (rd. הַמְּחֹלְלוֹת 𝔊 We Dr; and חֹלְלִים pt. (מ om.) ψ 87^{7} RV Pe De Che Bae; cf. **Qal 1**). **2.** *writhe* in travail *with, bear, bring forth* (poet.), of Sarah, mother of Isr., Is 51^{2} (אַבְרָהָם אֲבִיכֶם ‖); of hinds Jb 39^{1} ψ 29^{9} (caus.); fig. of י׳'s producing earth ψ 90^{2} (יֻלָּדוּ ‖); of his bringing forth Isr. (with difficulty, v. Di) Dt 32^{18}; of north wind bringing forth rain Pr 25^{23}; רַב מְחוֹלֵל כֹּל 26^{10} *a master produceth everything* (on trans. see VB; Ew. al. derive fr. חלל *wound*). **3.** *wait anxiously* (cf. **Qal 2 d**), sq. לְ Jb 35^{14} (Elihu). **Po'lal.** *Pf.* חוֹלָלְתִּי ψ 51^{7} + 2 t.; חוֹלָלְתָּ Jb 15^{7}; *Impf.* יְחוֹלָלוּ Jb 26^{5};—**1.** *be made to writhe* Jb 26^{5} (הָרְפָאִים). **2.** *be brought forth* Jb 15^{7} (תִּוָּלֵד ‖), ψ 51^{7} (יחם ‖), metaph. of wisdom Pr $8^{24.25}$. **Hiph.** *Impf.* יָחִיל ψ $29^{8.8}$ *cause to be in anguish,* c. acc. מִדְבָּר, subj. י׳. **Hoph.** *Impf.* יוּחַל Is 66^{8} *be born* (= travailed with, Che), subj. אֶרֶץ (יִוָּלֵד גוי ‖). **Hithpol.** **1.** *Pt.* מִתְחוֹלֵל *whirling* סַעַר מתח׳ Je 23^{19} (= סער מִתְגּוֹרֵר 30^{23}). **2.** *writhing, suffering torture* Jb 15^{20} (of life of wicked). **3.** *Imv.* הִתְחוֹלֵל ψ 37^{7} *wait longingly* sq. לְ *for,* ‖ דּוֹם. **Hithpalp.** *Impf.* 3 fs. וַתִּתְחַלְחַל Est 4^{4} *and she writhed* in anxiety.

† חוֹל **n.m.**$^{Ho 2, 1}$ **sand** (perh. as turning or 2344
whirling; otherwise explained by Sta, vid. sub חֲוִילָה; NH *id.*, Aram. חָלָא, ܚܠܐ)—ח׳ abs. Gn 22^{17} + 15 t.; cstr. Gn 32^{13} + 6t.;—*sand* Ex 2^{12} (E); set as bound for sea Je 5^{22}; שְׂפֻנֵי טמוני ח׳ Dt 33^{19} *hidden treasures of sand,* poet. for *glass* (regarded as mysteriously produced out of sand, v. Di and reff.); **a.** usu. sand of seashore, sim. of numberlessness, vastness, so of Abraham's seed Gn 22^{17} (J; cf. 15^{5}); Jacob's 32^{13} (E); of a host Jos 11^{4} (JE), Ju 7^{12} 1 S 13^{5} 2 S 17^{11}; a people 1 K 4^{20} Ho 2^{1} Is 10^{22} 48^{19} (וְצֶאֱצָאֵי מֵעֶיךָ כִּמְעֹתָיו ‖), Je 33^{22} Hb 1^{9}; of corn gathered by Joseph Gn 41^{49}; of days of Job Jb 29^{18} (on interpr. = *phœnix,* vid. Di); of birds עוף כנף (i.e. quails) ψ 78^{27} (כֶּעָפָר ‖); of vast extent of Sol.'s wisdom 1 K 5^{9}. **b.** in comp., *more than the sand* Je 15^{8} (widows of Judah); thoughts of God ψ 139^{18}. **c.** of weight (in balances), metaph. of Job's vexation (כַּעַשׂ) Jb 6^{3} *heavier than the* sand, cf. כֹּבֶד ‖ וְנֵטֶל הַחוֹל Pr 27^{3} (אֶבֶן ‖), said of כַּעַס אֱוִיל.—Combinations are: כח׳ אשר על שפת הים Gn 22^{17} Jos 11^{4} 1 S 13^{5} 1 K 5^{9}; כח׳ הַיָּם אשר לא יִמַּד Gn 32^{13} 41^{49} Is 10^{22} Ho 2^{1} (+ ולא יִסָּפֵר); ח׳ הַיָּם Je 33^{22}; כח׳ שֶׁעַל־שְׂפַת הים לרב Ju 7^{12}; כח׳ אשר־על־הים לרב 2 S 17^{11} 1 K 4^{20}; (מ)חול יַמִּים Jb 6^{3} ψ 78^{27} Je 15^{8}.

† חִיל **n.m.**$^{Ex 15, 14}$ **a writhing, anguish**;— 2427
ח׳ abs. Ex 15^{14} + 5 t.—**1.** *writhing* (contortions of fear) Ex 15^{14} (‖ vb. רָגַז). **2.** *anguish,* always in sim. כַּיּוֹלֵדָה ψ 48^{7} (allied kings against Jerus.); Zion, before Assyrians Mi 4^{9}; before Scythians or Chaldeans Je 6^{24} (צָרָה ‖), = 50^{43} (of king of Babylon; צָרָה ‖); 22^{23} (חבלים ‖ q.v.)

† חִילָה **n.f. anguish,** Jb 6^{10}. 2427

2426 †חֵיל, חֵל **n.m.** $^{Ob\ 20}$ **rampart, fortress** (perh. orig. *surrounding wall*, cf. Sab. Denkm. $^{91\ n.\ 2}$)—abs. חֵיל Na 3^{8}, חֵל La 2^{8} + 3 t. (+ ψ 10^{10} Qr v. חלכה); cstr. חֵל 1 K 21^{23}; sf. חֵילֵךְ ψ 122^{7},
2430 חֵילָהּ Zc 9^{4}; חֵילָה = חֵילָהּ ψ 48^{14}, Ol $^{§\ 40\ c.\ 75\ g.\ 96\ e}$ Sta $^{§\ 347\ c}$;—**1.** *rampart* (defined by Jews as בֵּן חוֹמָה, i.e. a little wall, cf. Ki s.v.), of an outer fortification 2 S 20^{15} (others, by meton., of space between outer and inner fortif., incl. moat, v. Dr Kit); Is 26^{1} La 2^{8} (both ‖ חומות); in gen. of defences, or sea-power of Tyre וְהִכָּה בַיָּם חֵילָהּ Zc 9^{4} (v. Sta $^{ZAW\ i.\ 1881,\ 15}$), of No-Amon (Thebes) אֲשֶׁר חֵיל יָם מִיָּם חוֹמָתָהּ Na 3^{8}; of Zion ψ 122^{7}, also 48^{14} (חֵילָהּ = חילה, cf. supr.; both ‖ ארמנותיך).—For חֵל 1 K 21^{23} rd. prob. חֵלֶק, q. v. **2.** *fortress* גָּלֻת הַחֵל הַזֶּה Ob ^{20} *the exiles of this fortress* (Hi-St; Or AVRV *this army*, חֵל = חַיִל).

2430 †חֵילָה ψ 48^{14}, v. חֵל supr.

2431 †חֵילָם **n.pr.loc.** E. of Jordan 2 S 10^{16} (Th *their army*, but 𝔊 𝔖 𝔗 Ew $^{Gesch.\ iii.\ 211\ Anm.\ 1=H\ iii.\ 155\ n.\ 2}$ We Dr) = חֵלָאמָה v^{17} (𝔊 Αιλαμ); + חילם Ez 47^{16} (𝔊 Ηλιαμ) Co; acc. to this it lay on the border between Damascus and Hamath.

2432 †חִילֵן **n.pr.loc.** in Judah 1 Ch 6^{43} = חֹלֹן **2.**

2473 †חֹלֹן, חֹלוֹן **n.pr.loc.** **1.** in Moab חֹלוֹן Je 48^{21} (𝔊 Χελων, Χαιλων). **2.** in Judah חֹלֹן Jos 15^{51} (𝔊 Χαλου, 𝔊L Χειλου); priestly city 21^{15} (𝔊 Γελλα, 𝔊L Ιλων) = חִילֵן 1 Ch 6^{43} (𝔊L Χελων).

2497 †חֵלֹן **n.pr.m.** a man of Zebulon Nu 1^{9} 2^{7} $7^{24.29}$ 10^{16} (𝔊 Χαιλων, 𝔊L Χελων).

2479 †חַלְחָלָה **n.f. anguish,** מָלְאוּ מָתְנַי ח׳ Is 21^{3}, ח׳ בכל מתנים Na 2^{11}; Ez $30^{4.9}$ (‖ החריד).

4234 †מָחוֹל **n.m.** $^{La\ 5,\ 15}$ **dance**;—abs. מ׳ ψ 30^{12} + 3 t.; cstr. מְחוֹל Je 31^{4}; מְחוֹלֵנוּ La 5^{15};—*dance*, token of joyousness ψ 30^{12} (opp. מספד), Je $31^{4.13}$ (cf. v^{b}), La 5^{15} (opp. אֵבֶל); act of praise to י׳ ψ 149^{3} 150^{4}; accompanied by timbrel (תֹּף) and sometimes other instruments ψ $149^{3.4}$ Je 31^{13}.

4246 †[מְחוֹלָה] **n.f. id.**;—cstr. מְחֹלַת Ct 7^{1}; pl. מְחֹלֹת Ex 32^{19}; מְחֹלוֹת Ex 15^{20} + 5 t.; *dancing*, token of joyousness after victory, Ju 11^{34} 1 S 18^{16} 21^{12} 29^{5}; in worship, at feast Ju 21^{21}; act of praise to י׳ Ex 15^{20} (song); in idolatrous worship Ex 32^{19} (E); as graceful and beautiful Ct 7^{1}; accomp. by timbrel Ex 15^{20} Ju 11^{34}, and by singing Ex 15^{20} 1 S 18^{6} (where however rd. prob. Po'lel Pt. הַמְּחֹלְלוֹת, cf. vb. חול supr.; so 𝔊 We Dr), 21^{12} 29^{5}.

†II. [חִיל, חוּל] **vb. be firm, strong** (Aram. 2342
Pa. *strengthen*, חֵילָא, ܚܝܠܐ *strength*; Palm. רב חילא *general-in-chief* Vog $^{No.\ 28}$ al.; Sab. חיל Sab. Denkm.^{91} (on חל in Sab. n.pr. v. Hal $^{JAS\ Juin,\ 1872,\ 533}$); Eth. ኀለ: ኀየለ: *be strong*, ኀይል: *strength, army*, ኀያል: *strong*; As. *ḫâ(i)ltu, army* Flood Tabl. $^{iii.\ 22}$ (*ḫaiialtu* Jäger $^{BAS\ i.\ 461}$); poss. comp. Ar. خَيْلٌ *horses* (as *strong ones*? cf. ψ 33^{17}))—only **Qal** *Impf.* in לֹא יָחִיל טוּבוֹ Jb 20^{21} *his prosperity is not firm* (does not endure); יָחִילוּ דְרָכָו בְּכָל־עֵת ψ 10^{5} *his ways are always firm* (stable, prosperous), so Ol De Pe Che al.

חַיִל ^{244} **n.m.** $^{2\ K\ 10,\ 2}$ **strength, efficiency,** 2428
wealth, army;—abs. ח׳ Gn 47^{6} +, חָיִל ψ 60^{14} +, חָיִל ψ 60^{14} +, חֵיל Is 36^{2} 2 K 18^{17}; cstr. חֵיל Ex 14^{28} + (on ψ 10^{10} v. חלכה); sf. חֵילִי Jb 31^{25} + 2 t.; חֵילֵךְ Je 15^{13} +; חֵילוֹ Ex 14^{4} +, etc.; pl. חֲיָלִים 1 Ch 7^{5} + 19 t.; sf. חֵילֵיהֶם Is 30^{6};—**1.** *strength*, usu. physical: **a.** seld. alone (chiefly poet.) 1 S 2^{4} ψ $18^{33.40}$ = 2 S $22^{33.40}$; also גָּבְרוּ ח׳ Jb 21^{7}, cf. Ec 10^{10}; בְּכֹחַ ח׳ ψ 84^{8}; מֵחַיִל אֶל־חָיִל 2 Ch 26^{13}; of virility Pr 31^{3}; of י׳'s power ψ 59^{12} 110^{3}, cf. Hb 3^{19}; strength of horse ψ 33^{17}; fig. of product of vine and fig-tree Jo 2^{22} (‖ פְּרִי). **b.** of result or display of strength עשׂה ח׳ *achieve might* = *do valiantly* Nu 24^{18} (JE), 1 S 14^{48} ψ 60^{14} = 108^{14}, $118^{15.16}$. **c.** oft. in phrases גִּבּוֹר(הַ)ח׳, גִּבּוֹרֵי(הַ)ח׳, *hero(es) of strength, mighty man (men) of valour* Jos 1^{14} (D), 6^{2} 8^{3} 10^{7} (all JE), Ju 6^{12} 11^{1} 1 S 9^{1} 16^{18} 1 K 11^{28} 2 K 5^{1} 15^{20} $24^{14.16}$ 1 Ch 5^{24} $7^{2.9}$ 8^{40} + (very freq. in Ch), note esp. הַגִּבּוֹרִים וכל גבורי ח׳ 28^{1}; also ג׳ ח׳ 2 Ch 13^{3} (‖ ג׳ מלחמה); ג׳ (הַ)חֲיָלִים 1 Ch $7^{5.7.11.40}$ 11^{26} (v. also גִּבּוֹר, p. 150); בֶּן־(הַ)ח׳, בְּנֵי(הַ)ח׳ Dt 3^{18} Ju 18^{2} + (v. בֵּן **8**, p. 121); אִישׁ ח׳, אַנְשֵׁי ח׳ Ju 3^{29} $20^{44.46}$ 1 S 31^{12} 11^{16} 2 S 23^{20} (Qr; Kt חי, on phr. בן־איש חיל cf. Dr) = 1 Ch 11^{22} (Kt חיל), 2 S 24^{9} Na 2^{4} Je 48^{15} 1 Ch 10^{12} Ne 11^{6} ψ 76^{6}; ironical אַ׳ ח׳ לִמְסֹךְ שֵׁכָר Is 5^{22} (‖ גבורים לשתות יין); Ec 12^{3} metaph. of legs. **2.** *ability, efficiency*, often involving moral worth אַנְשֵׁי ח׳ Gn 47^{6} (J), Ex $18^{21.25}$ (both E); of a woman אֵשֶׁת ח׳ Pr 12^{4} 31^{10} Ru 3^{11}; cf. 1 K $1^{42.52}$ (opp. רעה), and esp. אַנְשֵׁי ח׳ יִרְאֵי אלהים אַנְשֵׁי אֱמֶת שֹׂנְאֵי בָצַע Ex 18^{21} (E); עָשָׂה חיל Pr 31^{29} *do worthily, efficiently*, perh. also Ru 4^{11}; late (with weakened mng. of גִּבּוֹר) גִּבּוֹרֵי חֵיל מְלֶאכֶת עֲבוֹדַת בֵּית הָאֱלֹהִים 1 Ch 9^{13}, cf. אִישׁ ח׳ בַּכֹּחַ לַעֲבֹדָה 26^{8}. So also 1 S 10^{26} (rd. בְּנֵי ח׳, v. 𝔊 We Dr, *men of worth*, opp. בני בליעל

v^{27}) for MT ח׳ *force, band.* **3.** *wealth* Gn 34^{29} Nu 31^{9} (both P), Dt 8$^{17.18}$ 33^{11} Is 8^{4} 10^{14} 30^{6} (‖ אוֹצְרֹתָם), 60^{5} (‖ הֲמוֹן יָם), v^{11} 61^{6} Mi 4^{13} Je 15^{13} 17^{3} (both ‖ אצרות), Zp 1^{13} Ez 26^{12} 28$^{4.5.5}$ Zc 14^{14} Jb 5^{5} 15^{29} 20$^{15.18}$ 31^{25} ψ 49$^{7.11}$ 62^{11} 73^{12} Pr 13^{22}. **4.** *force, army,* very oft. Ex 14$^{4.9.17.28}$ (all P), 15^{4} (song), 1 S 17^{20} 2 S 8^{9} 2 K 6$^{4.15}$ 25$^{1.5.5.10}$ 2 Ch 13^{3} (בְּחַיִל גִּבּוֹרֵי מלחמה), 14^{7} 16^{7} 23^{14}+; so usu. Jer.: Je 32^{2} 34^{1}+; freq. Ezek.: Ez 17^{17} 27^{10}+; Dn 11$^{7.13.25.25.26}$; = *a band* 1 S 10^{26} (MT, but v. **2,** *ad fin.*); of train of Queen of Sheba ח׳ גדול 1 K 10^{2} = 2 Ch 9^{1}; חַיִל כָּבֵד Is 36^{1} = 2 K 18^{17} *a powerful army* (on form cf. Sta$^{§ 194 c}$); also (late) חֵיל הַצָּבָא 1 Ch 20^{1} 2 Ch 26^{13}, חֵיל עָם Est 8^{11}; הֲמוֹן חֲיָלִים Dn 11^{10}; שַׂר־הח׳ 2 S 24^{2} *captain of the host,* שָׂרֵי הח׳ v$^{4.4}$; שָׂרֵי הַחֲיָלִים *captains of armies* (bands, divisions) 1 K 15^{20} = 2 Ch 16^{4}, 2 K 25^{23} Je 40$^{7.13}$ 41$^{11.13.16}$ 42$^{1.8}$ 43$^{4.5}$; פְּקוּדֵי החיל Nu 31^{14} (P).—חֵילוֹ Ez 32^{31} om. B Hi Co; for חֵילֵךְ Ez 27^{11} rd. prob. a n.pr.loc., cf. Da; Co prop. חתלון (cf. 47^{15} 48^{1}), Hal$^{Mél. Epigr. 1874, 69}$ חלך = *Cilicia,* v. Lag$^{M i, 211}$.

2343 †חוּל **n.pr.m.** a 'son' of Aram Gn 10^{23} = 1 Ch 1^{17}, named between עוּץ and גֶּתֶר 𝔊 Ουλ.

חום (√of foll.; meaning dub.; NH חוּם = *be warm*).

2345 †חוּם **adj.** darkened, dark brown or black, only of colour of sheep (in Gn 30, J);—וכל־שֶׂה־חוּם בכשׂבים Gn 30^{32}, וְחוּם בכ׳ Gn 30$^{33.35}$, וכל־חוּם בְּצאֹן Gn 30^{40} (cl. prob. interpol. Ol Hup De We Di).

2346 חוֹמָה v. sub חמה. p. 327

2347 †[חוּס] **vb.** pity, look upon with compassion (Aram. ܚܣ, חוּס *pity, spare;* As. *ḫûs,* in n.pr. cf. Dl$^{Pr 181}$)—**Qal** *Pf.* 3 fs. חָסָה Ez 16^{5}, 2 ms. חַסְתָּ Jon 4^{10}; *Impf.* 3 ms. יָחוּס Je 21^{7}; יָחֹס ψ 72^{13}; 3 fs. תָּחוּס Is 13^{18}; תָּחוֹס Dt 7^{16}+9 t. (Ges$^{§ 72 R 4}$ Bö$^{§ 1133 (2)}$); תָּחֹס Gn 45^{20} Ez 9^{5}; וַתָּחָס 1 S 24^{11} Ez 20^{17}; 1 s. אָחוּס Je 13^{14}+2 t.; *Imv.* חוּסָה Jo 2^{17} Ne 13^{22}:—**a.** of the eye, עין, (לא) תח(ו)ס על the eye *shall (not) look with compassion, pity, upon* Dt 7^{16} 13^{9} 19^{13} Is 13^{18} Ez 7^{4} 20^{17}; לא חסה עָלַיִךְ עין Ez 16^{5}; עֵינְכֶם אַל־תָּחֹס עַל־כְּלֵיכֶם Gn 45^{20} (R^{JE}) *let not your eye look with regret upon your stuff;* with ellipsis of עַיִן 1 S 24^{11} (but rd. וָאָחֹס for וַתָּחָס 𝔊 𝔖 𝔗 We Klo Dr); with ellipsis of על Dt 19^{21} 25^{12} Ez 5^{11} 7^{9} 8^{18} 9^{10}; (אל) עַל תחס עינכם Ez 9^{5}. **b.** of God חוסה על Ne 13^{22} Jo 2^{17}; לא אחוס על נינוה Jon 4^{11}; ellipsis of עַל Je 13^{14} Ez 24^{14}. **c.** of man: the Messianic king עַל־דַּל וְאֶבְיוֹן ψ 72^{13} *he shall have pity on poor and needy,* Nebuchadrezzar עליהם (i.e. on Zedekiah and the people) Je 21^{7}; Jonah, על הקיקיון Jon 4^{10}.—Vid. also חמל.

חוּף v. sub II. חפף. p. 342 2348

†חוּפָּם **n.pr.m.** head of a Benjamite family 2349
Nu 26^{39}, not in 𝔊; (= חֻפִּים Gn 46^{21}, cf. also 1 Ch 7$^{12.15}$).

†חוּפָמִי **adj. gent.** of foregoing, c. art. = 2350
n. coll. הַח׳ Nu 26^{39}.

I. **חוץ** (√of foll., meaning unknown).

חוּץ **n.[m.]** the outside, sts., esp. in pl., 2351
spec. a street, never with sf. in sg., with ־ָה *loc.* חוּצָה, חֻצָה, pl. חוּצוֹת, חֻצוֹת, with sf. חוּצֹתָיו etc., Is 15^{3} etc.;—**1.** *the outside,* of a house, tent, city, camp, etc., oft. used, esp. with preps., to express the adv. idea of *outside, abroad* (Aram. syn., exc. in sense **2 a**, is בַּר, ܒܪ): **a.** as accus. after vb. of motion Dt 23^{13} יָצָא חוּץ to go forth outside (sc. a camp), v^{14} (as adv. accus.) בְּשִׁבְתְּךָ חוּץ *outside,* הוֹצִיא הַחוּץ to bring forth *outside* (a house or chamber) Ju 19^{25} 2 S 13^{18} cf. Ne 13^{8}, Ju 12^{9b} בָּנוֹת הֵבִיא לְבָנָיו מִן־הַחוּץ from *outside,* from *abroad,* 2 K 4^{3} שַׁאֲלִי־לָךְ כֵּלִים מִן־הַחוּץ from *outside* (opp. בַּבַּיִת v^{2}); as genit. Lv 18^{9} מוֹלֶדֶת חוּץ one born *abroad* (i.e. by another father or mother, of a half-sister: opp. מוֹלֶדֶת בַּיִת) Ez 47$^{2.2}$. With ־ָה *loc.* חוּצָה, after a vb. of motion Ex 12^{46} מִן־הַבַּיִת . . . חוּצָה, Pr 5^{16} 2 Ch 29^{16}, 33^{15} מִקִּיר הָעִיר חוּצָה לָעִיר *outside of* the city, Nu 35^{4} וָחוּצָה from the wall of the city *and outwards;* = *on the outside, without* 1 K 6^{6} Is 33^{7} צָעֲקוּ חוּצָה cry *without,* 2 Ch 24^{8}: so הַחוּצָה Gn 15^{5} וַיּוֹצֵא אֹתוֹ הח׳ and brought him *outside,* 19^{17} 24^{29} Jos 2^{19}+, 1 K 8^{8} לֹא יֵרָאוּ הַחוּצָה were not seen *towards the outside,* Dt 25^{5} לֹא תִהְיֶה אֵשֶׁת הַמֵּת הַחוּצָה לְאִישׁ זָר i.e. shall not be married into another family, cf. Ju 12^{9a}. **b.** with preps.: *a.* †אל־החוץ *towards the outside* Ez 41^{9}, †34^{21} pleon. אל־החוצה. *b.* בחוץ Gn 9^{22} *outside* (opp. בְּתוֹךְ אָהֳלֹה v^{21}), 24^{31} לָמָּה תַעֲמֹד בַּחוּץ, Dt 24^{11} Ex 21^{19} אם יקום והתהלך בחוץ (after leaving a sick couch), 2 K 10^{24} ψ 31^{12} Ez 7^{15} (opp. מִבַּיִת), Ho 7^{1}+. *c.* †לחוץ ψ 41^{7} יצא לחוץ; = *on the outside* Ez 41^{17} 42^{7}, †לַחוּצָה 2 Ch 32^{5} *towards the outside.* *d.* מִחוּץ *on* (מִן **3 c**) *the outside* Ez 40^{19} 46^{2}, מִבַּיִת וּמִחוּץ within and *without* (of an ark, building, etc.) Gn 6^{14} Ex 25^{11} = 37^{2} 1 K 7^{9}, Dt 32^{25} מחוץ תְּשַׁכֶּל־חֶרֶב (opp. וּמֵחֲדָרִים

אִימָה), La 1[20] (cf. Ez 7[15] supr. *b*); so מֵהַחוּץ †Ez 41[25]. מִחוּץ לְ *on the outside of*, Gn 19[16] וַיַּנִּחֻהוּ מִחוּץ לָעִיר, 24[11] Ex 26[35] 37[7.7] Lv 8[17] 14[3] Nu 35[5] Jos 6[23] Je 21[4]+, even after a vb. of motion 1 K 21[13] וַיֹּצִיאֻהוּ מִחוּץ לָעִיר, 2 K 23[6], though in this case אל מחוץ ל is more common, Lv 4[12.21] אל מחוץ למחנה, 6[4] 10[4] 14[40.41]+oft. P, Dt 23[11]. *e.* †מחוּצָה Ez 40[40] *on the outside*, מִחוּצָה לְ v[44]. *f.* (late) †חוּץ מִן *outside of*, Ec 2[25] who can eat, and who enjoy, חוּץ מִמֶּנִּי *outside of* me, i.e. *except* me? (but rd. rather, with 𝔊 𝔖 De Now al., חוּץ מִמֶּנּוּ *apart from, without* him, i.e. God). (So NH חוּץ מִן *except, without*, v. De[Ec 2, 25]. Cf. the Aram. syn. בַּר מִן *except* Ex 20[3] 𝔗, *apart from, without* Is 36[10] 𝔗; Syr. ܒܪ ܡܢ *id.*)

2. Of a definite locality, viz. **a.** that which is outside the houses of a town, i.e. *a street* Is 51[23] כַּחוּץ לַעֹבְרִים, Je 37[21] חוּץ הָאֹפִים the Bakers' *street*, Pr 1[20] בַּחוּץ ‖ בָּרְחֹבוֹת: so 7[12] 22[13] Je 9[20]); oft. in pl., as חוצת אַשְׁקְלוֹן the *streets* of Ashkelon 2 S 1[20], ח׳ ירושלם Je 5[1] 7[17.34]+oft. Jer., 1 K 20[34] וְחֻצוֹת תָּשִׂים־לְךָ בְדַמֶּשֶׂק and *streets* (i.e. bazaars) shalt thou make thee in D., as my father made in Samaria (a concession involving the right of trading), Am 5[16] Is 15[3] 24[11] (as scene of mourning), Is 5[25] Je 51[4] Ez 11[6] 28[23] (as filled with corpses of slain), בְּרֹאשׁ כָּל־חוצות i.e. in conspicuous places, Na 3[10] La 2[19] 4[1] Is 51[20], טִיט חוצות mire of *streets* Zc 10[5] (trampled on by warriors), in simile, of foes trodden under foot, ψ 18[43] Mi 7[10] (so כְּחֹמֶר ח׳ Is 10[6]), metaph. of cheapness and abundance Zc 9[3]. **b.** more gen., that which is outside enclosed cities, the *open country*, Jb 18[17] וְלֹא שֵׁם לוֹ עַל־פְּנֵי־חוּץ (v. De), cf. Pr 24[27]; in the pl. Jb 5[10] וְשֹׁלֵחַ מַיִם עַל פְּנֵי חוצות, Pr 8[26] ψ 144[13] (as place where flocks abound).

2435 †חִיצוֹן **adj.** outer, external (opp. פְּנִימִי) f. חִיצוֹנָה (for חוצון, by dissim., Ba[NB xxix] Phil BAS ii. 2. 362 Ges[§ 27. 3 R 6])—**1.** 2 K 16[18] מְבוֹא הַמֶּלֶךְ הַחִיצוֹנָה the *outer* entry of the king (viz. to the Temple), Ez 44[1] the *outer* gate of the sanctuary, החצר החיצונה the *outer* court (of the Temple) Ez 10[5] 40[17.20.31.34.37] 42[1.3.7.8.9.14] 44[19.1] 46[9.20.21], cf. Est 6[4] (of Ahasuerus' palace), 2 Ch 33[14] חוֹמָה ח׳ an *outer* wall (built by Manasseh for the עִיר דָּוִיד); הַחִיצוֹן absol., in לַחִיצוֹן 1 K 6[29.30], בַּחִיצוֹן Ez 41[17] (הַבַּיִת being understood) of the *outer* (part of the Temple), i.e. the Holy Place (cf. פְּנִימִי, פְּנִימָה, of the Holy of holies). **2.** fig. *outward, external* הַמְּלָאכָה הַחִיצוֹנָה Ne 11[16] 1 Ch 26[29], of business not distinctively sacred, in which Levites were engaged (cf. the NH use of ח׳ to denote *extra-canonical*, as *Sanh.* 10[1] [Jost, 11[1] Surenh.] ספרים החיצונים).

II. חוץ (√of foll.; cf. Ar. خَاصَ *sew together*, Aram. ܚܳܨ *bind, compress*, σφίγγειν, ܚܨܳܐ *bandage:* خاط iv. *encompass*, حَائِط *wall*, which is oft. compared, does not correspond phonetically).

†חַיִץ **n.[m.]** party-wall (NH *id.*, prob. from Ez *l. c.*)—Ez 13[10], acc. to Ki מחיצה גרועה i.e. a thin or party-wall. 2434

חִיק, חוק (√of foll.; As. *ḫîḳu*, *embrace*, Creation Tabl.[a. 1. 5]; Ar. حَوْقٌ *ring*, حَوَقٌ *width* of desert, of well, of vulva, أَحْوَقُ *wide;* Di comp. also Eth. ሐይቅ: *shore* of sea, fr. *surrounding*, cf. As. supr.)

†[חוֹק] **n.[m.]** bosom, ψ 74[11] Kt חוקך (but rd. Qr חֵיקְךָ, v. following). 2436

†חֵיק, חֵק **n.[m.]** bosom (NH *id.*)—abs. חֵיק Ez 43[17] Pr 16[33]+Ez 43[13] (Co חיקו, cf. ZKW 1883, pp. 67 ff.; חֵיקָה Dr[Sm xxxi]), חֵק Pr 21[14]; cstr. חֵיק 1 K 22[35]+3 t.+Ez 43[14] (Co חיקו) חֵק Pr 5[20] (om. by accident in Baer, cf. Str[ad loc.]) 17[23]; sf. חֵיקִי 1 K 3[20] ψ 89[51]; חֵקִי Jb 19[27] etc.; elsewh. alw. plene c. sf.; חוקך Kt ψ 74[11] (Qr חֵיקְךָ);—*bosom*, specif. **1.** of fold of garment, at breast Ex 4[6.6.7.7.7] (all J), Pr 6[27] 16[33], metaph. of י׳ ψ 74[11]; שֹׁחַד בח׳ Pr 21[14] is a *hidden reward* (concealed in bosom; ‖ מַתָּן בַּסֵּתֶר); שֹׁחַד מֵחֵק 17[23] is a *gift secretly given;* fig., *requite into bosom* Is 65[6.7] ψ 35[13] 79[12] Je 32[18]. **2.** *carry* (נָשָׂא) *in bosom*, Moses the people Nu 11[12] (JE); Naomi, Ruth's child Ru 4[16], cf. 1 K 3[20.20] 17[19]; ewe lamb 2 S 12[3] Is 40[11] (metaph.); La 2[12] of infants dying in their mothers' arms; fig. of carrying insults in one's bosom ψ 89[51] (rd. prob. כְּלִמַּת for כֹּל, v. Bi Che). **3.** *bosom* as part of body: **a.** external, *lie in bosom*, of wife שֹׁכֶבֶת Mi 7[5], cf. 2 S 12[8]; concubine Gn 16[5] (J) cf. 1 K 1[2]; אֵשֶׁת חיק(ך) Dt 13[7] 28[54], cf. also Pr 5[20] אִישׁ חֵיקָהּ; תְּחַבֵּק חֵק נָכְרִיָּה Dt 28[56]. **b.** internal, anger resteth בח׳ כסילים Ec 7[9]; כָּלוּ כִלְיֹתַי בְּחֵקִי Jb 19[27] *my reins are consumed within me;* Jb 23[12] (rd. בְּחֵקִי for מֵחֻקִּי, so 𝔊 𝔙 Ol Me Stu Di) *in my breast have I hidden the words of his mouth* (cf. בְּלִבִּי ψ 119[11]); fig. of interior of chariot 1 K 22[35] ח׳ הרכב; of hollow bottom

of altar Ez 43^{13.14.17} (Sm *Rinne;* Co *Grundeinfassung*).

2712 †חוּקֹק **n.pr.loc.** city in Asher 1 Ch 6^{60} 𝔊 Ικακ, 𝔊L Ακωκ; but rd. prob. חֶלְקַת (as Jos 19^{25}) q. v.—חֶלְקָה Jos 19^{34} v. sub חקק. p. 324, 350

2357 †I. [חָוַר] **vb.** **be** or **grow white, pale** (Ar. حَوِرَ *be white,* حَوَرٌ *whiteness,* Aram. ܚܘܰܪ, חֲוַר *be white*)—only **Qal** *Impf.* 3 mpl. וְלֹא עַתָּה פָּנָיו יֶחֱוָרוּ Is 29^{22} (‖ לֹא עַתָּה יֵבוֹשׁ יַעֲקֹב).

2353 †I. חוּר **n.**[**m.**] **white stuff** (dub. whether cotton or linen, cf. כַּרְפַּס), ‖ תְּכֵלֶת:—of Mordecai's garments בִּלְבוּשׁ מַלְכוּת תְּכֵלֶת וָחוּר Est 8^{15a} *in a royal garment of violet and white stuff* (cf. וְתַכְרִיךְ בּוּץ וְאַרְגָּמָן v^{b}); of furnishings of royal palace of Susa ח׳ כַּרְפַּס וּתְכֵלֶת אָחוּז בְּחַבְלֵי־בוּץ וְאַרְגָּמָן 1^{6} *white stuff of fine linen*(?) *held fast by cords of byssus and purple.*

2355 †חוֹרִי **n.m. white stuff**, cf. I. חור; וְאֹרְגִים חוֹרָי Is 19^{9} *and* (those) *weaving white stuff.*

2751 †I. חֹרִי **n.**[**m.**] **white bread or cake** שְׁלֹשָׁה סַלֵּי חֹרִי Gn 40^{16} *three baskets of white bread.*—
II. חֹרִי v. III. חרר. p. 359

2354 †II. חוּר **n.pr.m.** (mng. dub.; cf. Nab. n.pr. חורו Nö in Eut^{p. 45})—**1.** 𝔊 Ωρ, named with Aaron as compan. of Moses Ex 17^{10.12} 24^{14} (all E). **2.** 𝔊 Ωρ, a Judahite Ex 31^{2}=35^{30}, cf. 38^{22} (all P) 1 Ch 2^{19.20.50} (on div. of verse v. Be VB); also 4^{1.4} 2 Ch 1^{5}. **3.** 𝔊 Ουρ, a king of Midian Nu 31^{8} Jos 13^{21} (both P). **4.** 𝔊L Σουρ (B om.) head of fam. of returned exiles Ne 3^{9}.
1133 **5.** בֶּן־חוּר officer of Sol. 1 K 4^{8}, v. sub בֵּן p. 122.
2352 III. חוּר = חֹר v. sub III. חרר. p. 359

2360 †חוּרַי **n.pr.m.** a hero of David ח׳ מִנַּחֲלֵי
1914 גָעַשׁ 1 Ch 11^{32} 𝔊 Ουρ(ε)ι, 𝔊L Ουρια; = הִדַּי 2 S 23^{30} (om. B; A Αθθαι, 𝔊L Αδδαι). p. 213

2359 †חוּרִי **n.pr.m.** a Gileadite (of Gad) 1 Ch 5^{14} (𝔊 Ουρ(ε)ι).

2437 †חִירָה **n.pr.m.** (√חור but mng. dub.) an Adullamite, friend of Judah Gn 38^{1.12} (both J), 𝔊 Ειρας.

2361 חוּרָם v. חִירָם sub אָח, אחה supr. p. 27 b.

II. חור (√of foll.; cf. Ar. خَارَ *bend, turn, incline,* of man *be weak,* Lane^{820 c}, خَوْرٌ *hollow, depressed ground between hills*).

2735 †I. חֹר **n.**[**m.**] **hollow,** only in חֹר הַגִּדְגָּד Nu 33^{32} *hollow of Gidgad* (v. Di).

2715 II., III. חֹר, חוֹר, (חוֹרִים) v. sub II., III. חרר. p. 359

2362 †חַוְרָן **n.pr.terr.** (meaning unknown; conjectures are:—*black-land* (as basaltic region), supported by حَوْر *black,* dial. of Yemen, Maltzan ZMG 1874, 230, and tokens of immigration from Yemen into Ḥaurân, Wetzst in De^{Job 2, 598; ZKW 1884, 120}; *land of caves,* Thes Hi-Sm, Porter^{Dict. Bib.}, and *hollow,* GASm^{Geogr. 552}, who comp. Heb. חור *hole;* but this prob. fr. III. חרר, and Ar. حَوْر, *hollow,* diff. fr. حَوْرَان)—district SE. fr. Mt. Hermon, extending between Jaulan and Lejah, toward Syr. desert; only גְּבוּל חַוְרָן Ez 47^{16} cf. מִבֵּין חַוְרָן וּמִבֵּין דַּמֶּשֶׂק v^{18}; = As. *Ḥaurani* Dl^{Pa 294}; 𝔊 Αυρανιτις, and so Jos^{Ant. xv. 10, 1 etc.}, Ar. حَوْرَان. On this district v. Wetzst^{Hauran, (1860)} and in De^{Job 2. 597 ff.} Bd^{Pal 195 ff.} Schumacher^{Across the Jordan, 1889; ZPV xii. 1889, 225 ff. (with map)} GASm^{Geogr. 552 f. 609 ff.}

2363, 2439 †I. חוּשׁ **vb. haste, make haste** (As. *ḫâšu,* Dl^{Pr 180}, Eth. ሖሰ:; on this vb. v. Nö^{ZMG 1883, 538})—**Qal** *Pf.* 3 ms. חָשׁ Dt 32^{35} (or *Pt.*, but v. Di), 1 s. חַשְׁתִּי ψ 119^{60}; *Impf.* 3 fs. וַתָּחַשׁ (sic!) Jb 31^{5} Ges^{§ 72 R. 9}; *Imv.* חוּשָׁה 1 S 20^{38} + 6 t. ψ, + ψ 71^{12} Qr (Kt חישה); *Inf.* sf. חוּשִׁי Jb 20^{2}; *Pt. act.* חָשׁ Hb 1^{8} + Is 8^{1.3} in n.pr.; *pass.* חָשִׁים Nu 32^{17}; but v. infr.:—*make haste* Dt 32^{35} (‖ קרוב), ψ 119^{60}; in prophetic n.pr. מַהֵר שָׁלָל חָשׁ בַּז Is 8^{1.3}; of eagle (in sim. of Chald. army) נשר חש לאכול Hb 1^{8}; Jb 31^{5} subj. רגל, sq. על־מרמה; חוּשִׁי בִי Jb 20^{2} *my haste in me,* i.e. my inward excitement—esp. *Imv.* 1 S 20^{38} (‖ מהרה), and in ψψ: sq. לְעֶזְרָתִי 22^{20} 38^{23} 40^{14} 70^{2} 71^{12} (Qr); sq. לִי 70^{6} 141^{1}; *pt. pass.* נֵחָלֵץ חֲשִׁים Nu 32^{17}, but prob. for חֲמֻשִׁים (Kn Di comp. Ex 13^{18} etc.); Ba^{NB 180} retains חוּשִׁים and regards it as act. (intrans.) = *hastening.* **Hiph.** *Pf.* הֶחִישׁוּ Ju 20^{37}; *Impf.* יָחִישׁ Is 28^{16}; יָחִישָׁה coh. 5^{19} (Ges^{§ 48. 3}); אָחִישָׁה coh. ψ 55^{9}; *sf.* אֲחִישֶׁנָּה Is 60^{22};—**1.** *shew haste, act quickly* Ju 20^{37}; *hasten, come quickly* Is 5^{19} (subj. מַעֲשֵׂהוּ ‖ יְמַהֵר); others: *let him hasten on his work*), יָחִישׁ Is 28^{16} *hasten away* (flee), or *hasten about* distractedly (si vera l.; Che Guthe rd. ימיש *yield, give way*). **2.** transit. c. sf. Is 60^{22} *I will hasten it;* c. acc. ψ 55^{9} *I would hasten* (=secure quickly) *my escape.*

2440 †חִישׁ **adv. quickly,** כי גז חיש ψ 90^{10} of passing away of human life.

2363 †II. [חוּשׁ] **vb. feel, enjoy** (with the senses) (Now comp. Ar. حَسَّ *feel, perceive* by senses; NH חוּשׁ *feel pain;* Aram. ܚܫ, חוּשׁ, *feel pain;*

Eth. ሕዋስ: *perception*)—only **Qal** *Impf.* 3 ms. מִי יֹאכַל וּמִי יָחוּשׁ Ec 2^{25} *who can eat and who can feel* (i.e. *enjoy pleasure*)?

2364 †**חוּשָׁה n.pr.m.** a 'son' of חוּר = place in Judah 1 Ch 4^{4}.

2843 †**חֻשָׁתִי adj.gent.** of foregoing:—**1.** of individ., c. art. הַח׳ 2 S 21^{18} = 1 Ch 20^{4}, 2 S 23^{27} = 1 Ch 11^{29}, v. also 1 Ch 27^{11}.

2365 †**חוּשַׁי n.pr.m. 1.** ח׳ הָאַרְכִּי 2 S 15^{32} so $17^{5.14}$, called רֵעֶה דוד 15^{37} *friend of David*, so $16^{16\,a}$; cf. $16^{16\,b.17.18}$ 1 Ch 27^{33}; also 1 S $17^{6.7.8.15}$. **2.** 1 K 4^{16} father of one of Solomon's officers.

2366 †I. **חוּשִׁים, חֻשִׁים n.pr.f.** wife of Shaharaim of Benjamin, חוּשִׁים 1 Ch 8^{8}, חֻשִׁים v^{11}.

2366 †II. **חֻשִׁים n.pr.m.** of Dan, וּבְנֵי דָן ח׳ Gn 46^{23} cf. חֻשִׁם בְּנֵי אַחֵר 1 Ch 7^{12} (v. Be VB); = שׁוּחָם (q.v.) Nu 26^{42} cf. שׁוּחָמִי $v^{42.43}$.

2367 †**חֻשָׁם, חוּשָׁם n.pr.m.** a king of Edom: חֻשָׁם Gn $36^{34.35}$ = חוּשָׁם 1 Ch $1^{45.46}$.

2368-69 **חוֹתָם** v. sub חתם. p. 368

2371 **חֲזָאֵל** v. **חֲזָהאֵל** sub I. חזה. p. 303

2372 †I. **חָזָה vb.** (almost wholly poet.) **see, behold** (Aram. ܚܙܐ, חֲזָא, *see, perceive with the eyes*; Palm. Ethp. אתחזי = ἔδοξεν Reckendorf ZMG, 1888, 397; Ar. حَزَى, *perceive with the inner vision*, only; حَازٍ *astronomer, astrologer*)—**Qal** *Pf.* ח׳ ψ 58^{11} + 6 t.; חָזִיתָ Pr 22^{29} 29^{20}; חָזִית Is 57^{8}; חָזִיתִי Jb 15^{17}; חֲזִיתִךָ ψ 63^{3}; חָזוּ Jb 24^{1} + 5 t.; חֲזִיתֶם Jb 27^{12} Ez $13^{7.8}$; *Impf.* יֶחֱזֶה Nu 24^{4} + 2 t.; 3 fs. וְתַחַז Mi 4^{11}; 2 ms. תֶּחֱזֶה Ex 18^{21}; 1 s. אֶחֱזֶה ψ 17^{15} + 4 t.; אֶחַז Jb 23^{9}; pl. יֶחֱזוּ Is 26^{11} + 4 t.; יֶחֱזָיוּן Is 26^{11}; תֶּחֱזֶינָה Is 33^{17} + 2 t.; תֶּחֱזוּ Is 30^{10} Ct 7^{1}; 1 pl. וְנֶחֱזֶה Ct 7^{1}; *Imv.* חֲזֵה Is 33^{20} 48^{6}; חֲזוּ ψ 46^{9} Is 30^{10}; *Inf. cstr.* חֲזוֹת ψ 27^{4} Ez 21^{34}; *Pt.* חֹזֶה Ez 12^{27}; pl. חֹזִים Is 47^{13} Ez $13^{9.16}$ 22^{28}. (All other ptc. forms are used as nouns, v. חֹזֶה.) **1.** *see, behold*: **a.** *with the eye*, acc. rei ψ $58^{9.11}$ Pr 22^{29} 29^{20} Is 33^{20} 57^{8}; God in theophany Ex 24^{11} (JE); God, after death, apart from the flesh Jb $19^{26.27}$; the face of God ψ 11^{7} 17^{15} (after death). **b.** subj. *the eyes themselves;* man's eyes: תֶּחֱזֶינָה עֵינֶיךָ *thine eyes will behold* Is 33^{17}; also of God's eyes: ψ 11^{4} 17^{2}. **c.** with בְּ *look on* (intensely, with gratification); a damsel Ct $7^{1.1}$; Zion Mi 4^{11}; נֹעַם י׳ in the temple ψ 27^{4}; the work of God Jb 36^{25}; with investigation בַּכּוֹכָבִים on the stars, as stargazers, in astrology Is 47^{13}. **2.** *see as a seer in the ecstatic state*, with acc. of the vision seen: חזון Is 1^{1} Ez 12^{27} 13^{16}; מחזה Nu $24^{4.16}$ (JE; poet., Balaam); מחזה שׁוא Ez 13^{7}; משׂא Is 13^{1} Hb 1^{1}; משׂאות שׁוא La 2^{14}; שׁוא Ez $13^{6.9.23}$ 21^{34} 22^{28} La 2^{14}; כזב Ez 13^{8}; שֶׁקֶר Zc 10^{2}; obj. *deceitful things* Is 30^{10}; דבר(ים) Is 2^{1} Am 1^{1} Mi 1^{1}; with לְ, *be a seer, for* any one Is 30^{10}; *see a vision for* one La $2^{14.14}$. **3.** *see, perceive:* **a.** with the intelligence, abs. Jb 34^{32} Pr 24^{32}; acc. rei Is 48^{6}; Yahweh in his temple ψ 63^{3}; in his providential workings Jb 23^{9} ψ 46^{9} Is $26^{11.11}$. **b.** *see*, by experience abs. Jb 27^{12}; acc. rei Jb 15^{17} 24^{1}. **c.** *provide*, תחזה מכל העם אנשׁי חיל Ex 18^{21} *provide from all the people men of ability* (E).

Note.—בֵּית אֲבָנִים יֶחֱזֶה Jb 8^{17} is difficult: RV renders *he* (*it*) *beholdeth the place of stones* (the root of the plant personified) Hengst, cf. Reuss al. after 𝔖 𝔗. Other renderings are: *pierceth* (cf. חָזָז) Bö Ew Hi (יְחַזֶּה), Di De MV; *between* (v. p. 108) *the stones it liveth* (יִחְיֶה) 𝔊 Siegf.

חוֹזָי 2 Ch 33^{19}, v. following. 2335

†**חֹזֶה n.m. seer**;—abs. ח׳ Am 7^{12} + 7 t.; 2374
cstr. חֹזֵה 1 Ch 21^{9} + 3 t.; חֹזֵה 2 Ch 35^{15}; pl. חֹזִים Is 29^{10} + 4 t.; חוֹזִים 2 Ch 33^{19} (so rd. with 𝔊; חוֹזָי MT scribal error)—**1.** *seer:* **a.** of unnamed 2335
persons, syn. נבא(ים) 2 K 17^{13} Is 29^{10}; רֹאִים Is 30^{10}; קֹסְמִים Mi 3^{7}; historical writers דִּבְרֵי הַחֹזִים 2 Ch 33^{18}, דברי חוזים (𝔊) 2 Ch 33^{19} (MT appar. n.pr.) **b.** named prophets; Gad 2 S 24^{11} = 1 Ch 21^{9}, 1 Ch 29^{29} 2 Ch 29^{25}; Amos Am 7^{12}; Iddo 2 Ch 9^{29} 12^{15}; Jehu 2 Ch 19^{2}. **c.** the singers: Heman 1 Ch 25^{5}; Asaph 2 Ch 29^{30}; Jeduthun 2 Ch 35^{15}. *Note*—It seems best to add **2.** *vision* (cf. רֹאֶה Is 28^{7}) עִם שְׁאוֹל עָשִׂינוּ חֹזֶה Is 28^{15} *with She'ôl we made a vision* (had a vision, in connexion with She'ôl—i.e. by necromancy, v. Du—which makes us secure; ‖ כרת ברית אֶת־מָוֶת); Ew § 156 e trans. *oracle* here and 2 K 17^{13}; Hoffm ZAW iii. 95 puts this under **1**: 'we have appointed a prophet with She'ôl (SS "Ein bei der Scheol bestellter Seher"), who is answerable to us for it;' 𝔊 𝔙 𝔗 AV RV Che Di al., *are at* (or *have made an*) *agreement* (prophetic advice of seers being taken at time of making treaties; v. חָזוּת **1**). —Vid. also כָּל־חֹזֶה **n.pr.m.** sub כל.

†**חָזוֹן n.m.** Dn 8, 1 **vision** (on format. cf. Lg 2377
BN 204)—abs. ח׳ Ho 12^{11} + 25 t.; cstr. חֲזוֹן Is 1^{1} + 8 t. **1.** *vision*, as seen in the ecstatic state

|| קסם Mi 3^{6}; || מקסם Ez 12^{24}; || חלמות Dn 1^{17}; || נביא Dn 9^{24}; חזה ח׳ Ez 12^{27} 13^{16}; ראה ח׳ Dn 8^{15}; ראה בח׳ Dn 8$^{2.2}$ 9^{21}; דבר בח׳ ψ 89^{20}; חזון נראה אל Dn 8^{1} *vision appeared unto;* מצא ח׳ מיהוה La 2^{9} *find a vision from Yahweh;* also Ez 12$^{22.23}$ Dn 8$^{13.17.26}$ 10^{14} 11^{14}. **2.** *vision,* in the night חֲזוֹן לַיְלָה Is 29^{7}. **3.** *divine communication in a vision, oracle, prophecy* בקש ח׳ מנביא *seek a vision* (*prophecy*) *from prophet* Ez 7^{26}; || דבר(ים) 1 S 3^{1} 1 Ch 17^{15}; חֲזוֹן לִבָּם יְדַבֵּרוּ Je 23^{16} *a prophecy of their own hearts* (*minds*) they speak; חֲזוֹן שֶׁקֶר וְקֶסֶם אֱלִיל וְתַרְמִית לִבָּם הֵמָּה מִתְנַבְּאִים Je 14^{14} *false vision and* (v. אֱלִיל) *worthless divination & deceit of their own hearts they are prophesying;* כתב ח׳ *write the vision* Hb 2^{2}; also Ho 12^{11} Hb 2^{3} Pr 29^{18} Ez 7^{13} (del. Co). **4.** *vision,* as title of book of prophecy, ספר חזון נחום Na 1^{1}; ח׳ ישעיהו Is 1^{1}; ח׳ עבדיה Ob^{1}; of other writings of prophets 2 Ch 32^{32}.

2378 † [חָזוּת] **n.[f.]**, only cstr. בַּחֲזוֹת יֶעְדוֹ *in the visions* (prophecies) *of Iddo* 2 Ch 9^{29}, the title of a collection of prophetic history, v. חָזוֹן **4.**

2380 † חָזוּת **n.f. vision, conspicuousness** (on format. cf. Lg$^{BN\ 202}$)—abs. ח׳ Is 21^{2} Dn 8$^{5.8}$; cstr. חָזוּת Is 29^{11}; sf. חָזוּתְכֶם Is 28^{18};—**1.** *vision, oracle of a prophet* חָזוּת קָשָׁה הֻגַּד־לִי Is 21^{2} *a hard vision is declared to me;* וַתְּהִי לָכֶם חָזוּת הַכֹּל כְּדִבְרֵי הַסֵּפֶר הֶחָתוּם Is 29^{11} *the vision* (prophecy) *of the whole is become to you as the words of a sealed writing;* חָזוּתְכֶם אֶת־שְׁאוֹל לֹא תָקוּם Is 28^{18} *your agreement with Sheol will not stand,* so Thes MV De Che Di al. after Vrss, but Ew ^{§156e} renders *oracle,* and Siegf. *Hellseherei,* v. חֹזֶה **2.** **2.** *conspicuousness in appearance:* קֶרֶן חָזוּת *a conspicuous horn* Dn 8^{5} = the great horn v$^{8.21}$; so חָזוּת אַרְבַּע Dn 8^{8}, but < rd. אֲחֵרוֹת *others,* as 𝔊 Gr Bev.

2384 חִזָּיוֹן **n.m.** $^{2\ S\ 7,17}$ **vision** (on format. cf. Lg$^{BN\ 200}$)—abs. ח׳ 2 S 7^{17} Is 22$^{1.5}$; cstr. חֶזְיוֹן Jb 20^{8} 33^{15}; sf. חֶזְיֹנוֹ Zc 13^{4}; pl. abs. חֶזְיֹנוֹת Jb 7^{14} Jo 3^{1}, cstr. *id.* Jb 4^{13};—**1.** *vision,* in the ecstatic state ראה ח׳ Jo 3^{1}; גי(א) ח׳ *valley of vision* Is 22$^{1.5}$. **2.** *vision,* in the night חֶזְיוֹנ(וֹת) לַיְלָה Jb 4^{13} 20^{8} 33^{15}; || חֲלֹמוֹת Jb 7^{14}. **3.** *divine communication in a vision, oracle, prophecy:* || דברים 2 S 7^{17} (= חזון 1 Ch 17^{15}); יֵבֹשׁוּ אִישׁ מֵחֶזְיֹנוֹ בְּהִנָּבְאֹתוֹ Zc 13^{4} *they will be ashamed, every one of his vision when he prophesieth.*

† חֶזְיוֹן **n.pr.m.** (*vision*) ancestor of Benha- 2383
dad king of Aram 1 K 15^{18} (Klo prop. חֶזְרוֹן and comp. 𝔊 1 K 11$^{23\ f.}$).

† חֲזָהאֵל **n.pr.m.** (*Ēl sees; As. Ḫaza'ilu* 2371
COT^{Gloss}) king of Aram 2 K 8$^{8.13.15}$, v^{29} = 2 Ch 22^{6}; contr. חֲזָאֵל 1 K 19$^{15.17}$ 2 K 8$^{9.12}$, v^{28} = 2 Ch 22^{5}, 2 K 9$^{14.15}$ 10^{32} 12$^{18.18.19}$ 13$^{3.3.22.24.25}$; בֵּית חֲזָאֵל Am 1^{4}.

† חֲזִיאֵל **n.pr.m.** (*vision of Ēl*) Levite of 2381
the line of Gershon, of the time of Solomon 1 Ch 23^{9}.

† חֲזָיָה **n.pr.m.** (*Yah hath seen*) one of the 2382
chiefs of the בְּנֵי יְהוּדָה Ne 11^{5}.

† יַחֲזִיאֵל **n.pr.m.** (*Ēl sees*)—**1.** Benja- 3166
mite warrior of David 1 Ch 12^{4}. **2.** priest of David 1 Ch 16^{6}. **3.** a Levite 1 Ch 23^{19} 24^{23}. **4.** a Levite of the sons of Asaph 2 Ch 20^{14}. **5.** ancestor of one of the families of the restoration Ezr 8^{5}.

† יַחְזְיָה **n.pr.m.** (*Yah sees*) a prince of the 3167
restoration Ez 10^{15}.

† מַחֲזֶה **n.[m.] vision**—abs. מ׳ Gn 15^{1}; cstr. 4236
מַחֲזֵה Nu 24$^{4.16}$ Ez 13^{7};—*vision, in the ecstatic state* מַחֲזֵה שָׁוְא (|| מִקְסַם כָּזָב) Ez 13^{7} of the false prophets; מַחֲזֵה שַׁדַּי Nu 24$^{4.16}$ (JE; poems of Balaam); הָיָה דְבַר י׳ אֶל־אַבְרָם בַּמַּחֲזֶה Gn 15^{1}(R) *the word of* י׳ *came unto Abram in a vision.*

† מֶחֱזָה **n.f. light, place of seeing, win-** 4237
dow, מֶחֱזָה אֶל־מֶחֱזָה *light over against light* 1 K 7$^{4.5}$.

† מַחֲזִיאוֹת **n.pr.m.** (*visions*) 1 Ch 25^{4} (but 4238
on this list cf. RS$^{OTJC\ 422;\ ed.\ 2,\ 143}$), = מַחֲזִיאוֹת 1 Ch 25^{30} a Hemanite chief of a course of singers.

II. חזה (√ of foll.; Ar. حَذَا III., حِذَآءٌ *be opposite,* حِذَآءَ *front,* Lane$^{537\ b}$; v. Lg$^{BN\ 50}$ Dr^{§178}, cf. Sab. חדית prep. *opposite* DHM in MV).

† חָזֶה **n.m.** $^{Lv\ 7,31}$ **breast of animals** (Aram. 2373
חַדְיָא, ܚܕܝܐ)—abs. ח׳ Ex 29^{26} + 4 t.; cstr. חֲזֵה Ex 29^{27} + 5 t.; pl. חָזוֹת Lv 9$^{20.21}$—*breast,* only P, and only of sacrificial animals; always as wave-offering; of ram of installation Ex 29$^{26.27}$ Lv 8^{29}, of peace-offering Lv 7$^{30.30}$ 9$^{20.21}$, of Nazirite sacrif. Nu 6^{20}; perquisite of Aaron and his sons Lv 7$^{31.34}$ 10$^{14.15}$, cf. Nu 18^{18}.

† חֲזוֹ **n.pr.m.** son of Nahor Gn 22^{22}, 𝔊 Αζαυ 2375
(cf. As. n.pr.loc. *Hazû,* mentioned with *Bazû*

(v. III. בּוּז) by Esar. Dl$^{Pa\ 307;\ ZK\ 1885,\ 93\ f.}$ COT on Gn 22^{21}; also Di).

חזז (√of foll.; Ar. حَزَّ *cut* or *notch;* حَزَّ *pierce* (Frey)).

2385 †[**חָזִיז**] **n.[m.]** **thunder-bolt, lightning-flash** (NH חָזִיז; Aram. חֲזִיזָא *shining cloud*)—only cstr. חֲזִיז and pl. חֲזִיזִים; וְדֶרֶךְ לַחֲזִיז קֹלוֹת Jb 28^{26} *and a way for thunder-bolts* = 38^{25}; י׳ עֹשֶׂה חֲזִיזִים Zc 10^{1} (‖ מְטַר־גֶּשֶׁם).

2388 **חָזַק** $_{291}$ **vb. be** or **grow firm, strong, strengthen** (NH *id.;* Aram. ܚܙܩ, חֲזַק *bind on* or *about, gird on,* cf. Ar. حَزَقَ *bind, squeeze*)—†**Qal** *Pf.* ח׳ Gn 41^{57} + 4 t.; חָזָ֑ק 2 Ch 26^{15}; sf. חֲזָקוֹ 2 Ch 28^{20}, etc.; *Impf.* יֶחֱזַק 2 Ch 28^{7} (Baer) + 2 t.; וַיֶּחֱזַק Gn 41^{56} +; יֶחֶזְקוּ 2 S 10^{11} + 2 t.; יֶחְזְקוּ Is 28^{22}; *Imv.* חֲזַק Dt 12^{23} +; חִזְקוּ Dt 31^{6} +; *Inf. cstr.* לְחָזְקָה 2 K 12^{13}; sf. לְחָזְקָהּ Ez
2390 30^{21}; *Pt.* חָזֵק Ex 19^{19} 2 S 3^{1}, etc.;—**I.** intrans. *be* or *grow strong:*—**1. a.** of physical strength of hands Ju 7^{11} 2 S 2^{7} 16^{21} Ez 22^{14} Zc 8$^{9.13}$ (on Ez 3^{14} v. infr.); of arm, sq. inf. Ez 30^{21}; used of recovery fr. illness Is 39^{1}; sq. מִן compar. *over-power* 1 S 17^{50} (c. בְּ instr.), 2 S 13^{14}. **b.** of people, army Dt 11^{8} Jos 17^{13} (JE), = Ju 1^{28}, Ezr 9^{12}; sq. מִן compar. *be stronger than, too strong for, prevail against* 2 S 10$^{11.11}$ = 1 Ch 19$^{12.12}$ 1 K 20$^{23.25}$; *id.,* sq. acc. 1 K 16^{22}, cf. of י׳ as prevailing over man Je 20^{7} (‖ יָכֹל); sq. עַל 2 Ch 8^{3} 27^{5}. **c.** of royal power וְדָוִד הֹלֵךְ וְחָזֵק 2 S 3^{1} (opp. הֹלְכִים וְדַלִּים); cf. 2 Ch 26^{15} (‖ חֶזְקָה v^{16}), Dn 11^{5a}. **d.** *prevail over, upon,* of word of king 2 S 24^{4} (sq. אֶל־) = 1 Ch 21^{4} (sq. עַל). **e.** of bonds Is 28^{22}. **f.** of sound of trumpet הוֹלֵךְ וְחָזֵק מְאֹד Ex 19^{19} (E, cf. חָזָק v^{16}) *it grew much louder and louder.* **2.** *be firm, fast:*—**a.** lit. *be caught fast,* of Absalom's head 2 S 18^{9} (sq. בְּ). **b.** *be firm, secure,* of a kingdom 2 K 14^{5} (+ בְּיָדוֹ) = 2 Ch 25^{3} (+ עָלָיו). Oftener **c.** *be firm* = courageous, confident, esp. Imv., usually ‖ אמץ (q.v.), Dt 31$^{6.7.23}$ Jos 1$^{6.7.9.18}$ 10^{25} 23^{6} (all D), 2 S 10^{12} 13^{28} 1 K 2^{2} 1 Ch 19^{13} (‖ התחזק), 22^{13} 28$^{10.20}$ 2 Ch 15^{7} 19^{11} 32^{7} Ezr 10^{4} ψ 27^{14} 31^{25} Is 35^{4} 41^{6} Hg 2$^{4.4.4}$ Dn 10$^{19.19}$; sq. לַמִּלְחָמָה 2 Ch 25^{8}. **d.** *hold firmly to, devote oneself to,* sq. בְּ 2 Ch 31^{4}. **e.** sq. Inf. *be firm* not to eat blood, i.e. *firmly refrain* from it Dt 12^{23}, cf. 1 Ch 28^{7}. **3.** *press, be urgent,* sq. עַל + Inf. Ex 12^{33} (E); sq. עַל of hand of י׳ in prophetic ecstasy Ez 3^{14} (𝔊 Co rd. חֲזָקָה, adj., v. חָזָק). **4.** in bad sense: **a.** *grow stout, rigid, hard,* with idea of perversity, of Pharaoh's heart Ex 7$^{13.22}$ 8^{15} (all P), 9^{35} (R); cf. חזקו עָלַי דבריכם Mal 3^{13}. **b.** *be severe, grievous,* of battle 2 K 3^{26}; of famine Gn 41$^{56.57}$ (E), 47^{20} (J; sq. עַל), 2 K 25^{3} = Je 52^{6}. **II.** transit. only לֹא חֲזָקוֹ 2 Ch 28^{20} *strengthened him not,* but txt. very dub. (‖ וַיָּצַר לוֹ). †**Pi.** *Pf.* חִזַּק ψ 147^{13} +, etc.; *Impf.* וַיְחַזֵּק Ex 9^{12} + 10 t., etc.; *Imv.* חַזֵּק Ne 6^{9} + 2 t.; fs. חַזְּקִי Na 3^{14}; חַזֵּקִי Is 54^{2} etc.; *Inf. cstr.* חַזֵּק 2 K 12^{9} + 12 t.; *Pt.* מְחַזֵּק Ex 14^{17}; מְחַזְּקִים 2 K 12^{9};—**1.** *make strong* (physically): **a.** sq. acc. pers. Ju 16^{28}; sq. עַל 3^{12}; sq. מָתְנַיִם Na 2^{2} (‖ אַמֵּץ כֹּחַ; of personif. people). **b.** = *restore to strength* Dn 10$^{18.19}$; *to health* Ez 34$^{4.16}$; c. לְ *give strength to* 1 Ch 29^{12}; so, sq. זְרוֹעֹתָם, Ho 7^{15} Ez 30^{24} (and v^{25} Co, v. **Hiph.**) **c.** sq. acc. rei Is 41^{7} Je 10^{4} (both c. בְּ instr.; of manufacture of idols); of strengthening tent-pegs, in metaph. Is 54^{4}, cf. 33^{23}; sq. bars of gates ψ 147^{13}; oft. of *making strong, fortifying* a town, etc. Na 3^{14} 2 Ch 11$^{11.12}$ 26^{9} 32^{5}; = *repair* (wall, obj. not expr.) Ne 3^{19} v. Hiph.; c. acc. of temple 2 K 12$^{6.7.15}$ 22^{6} 2 Ch 24$^{5.12}$ 29^{3} 34^{8}, cf. v^{10} (‖ לִבְדּוֹק); sq. לְבֵית י׳ 1 Ch 26^{27}; obj. breaches (acc.) 2 K 12$^{8.9.13}$ 22^{5}. **d.** of establishing kingdom 2 Ch 11^{17}. **2.** *strengthen* the hands (acc.) of any one, i.e. *sustain, encourage* (opp. רִפָּה) Ju 9^{24} Je 23^{14} Ez 13^{22} Is 35^{3} Jb 4^{3} Ezr 6^{22} Ne 2^{18} 6^{9} 2 Ch 29^{34}; וַיְח׳ ידו בֵּאלהים 1 S 23^{16}; sq. בְּ Ezr 1^{6} (+ בְּ instr.) **3.** *make strong* = *bold, encourage,* c. acc. Dt 1^{38} 3^{28} 2 S 11^{5} Is 41^{7}; c. acc. pers. + לַעֲבֹדַת בֵּית י׳ 2 Ch 35^{2}. **4.** *make firm:*—**a.** c. 2 acc. וְאַבְנֵטְךָ אֲחַזְּקֶנּוּ Is 22^{21} *and with thy sash* (of office) *will I make him firm,* i.e. bind it firmly about him (‖ הלביש). **b.** *make firm* or *fixed,* = *definitely adopt* יח׳־ לָמוֹ דָּבָר רָע ψ 64^{6}. **5.** *make rigid, hard,* i.e. perverse, obstinate, *harden* (the heart of any one) Ex 4^{21} 10$^{20.27}$ (all E), 9^{12} 11^{10} 14$^{4.8.17}$ (all P), Jos 11^{20} (D); v. also ח׳ פניהם מִסֶּלַע Je 5^{3}†. **Hiph.** $_{118}$ *Pf.* הֶחֱזִיק Ju 7^{8} +; 3 fs. הֶחֱזִיקָה Je 49^{24} +; sf. הֶחֱזַקְתַּנִי Je 8^{21}; הֶחֱזַקְתִּי Ne 5^{16} + 3 t.; וְהַחֲזַקְתִּי Ez 30^{25}, etc.; *Impf.* יַחֲזִיק Jb 8^{15} + 2 t.; 1 s. וָאַחֲזִק Is 42^{6}; יַחֲזִיקוּ Je 6^{23} + 2 t.; יַחֲזִקוּ Dn 11^{32}, etc.; *Imv.* הַחֲזֵק 2 S 11^{25} + 2 t., etc.; *Inf. cstr.* הַחֲזִיק 2 K 15^{19} Is 64^{6}; sf. הַחֲזִיקִי Je 31^{32} (הַח׳ Cod. Petrop. v. RS$^{JPh\ xvi,\ 1888,\ 73}$); *Pt.* מַחֲזִיק Ex 9^{2} + 9 t.; sf. מַחֲזִקוֹ Dn 11^{6}; fs. מַחֲזֶקֶת Ne 4^{11}; pl. מַחֲזִיקִים Ne 4^{10} + 5 t.; cstr. מַחֲזִיקֵי Ez 27$^{9.27}$;—†**1. a.** *make strong, strengthen* Je 51^{12}. **b.** *make firm,* the kingdom 2 K 15^{19} (+ בְּיָדוֹ). **c.** *display strength* (late) 2 Ch 26^{8}

(‖ וְיֵלֵךְ שְׁמוֹ עַד וגו׳), Dn 11^{32} (‖ וְעָשׂוּ). †**2.** *make severe,* of battle 2 S 11^{25}. †**3.** sq. יד = *support* Ez 16^{49}; sq. זְרוֹעוֹת 30^{25} (subj. י׳; but Co rds. **Pi.** as v^{24})†. **4.** = *repair,* walls of Jerus., Ne 3$^{4.4.4}$ + 31 t. Ne 3; cf. (in gen.) pt. used substant. מחזיקי בדקך Ez 27$^{9.27}$ of Tyre and her ships (‖ מַלָּחִים, etc.) †**5.** *prevail,* abs. Dn 11^{7}; sq. עַל Jb 18^{9}; *prevail upon to* הח׳ בּוֹ לֶאֱכָל 2 K 4^{8}. **6.** esp. *take* or *keep hold* of, *seize, grasp:* **a.** *take hold* of, *seize, catch,* sq. בְּ Gn 19^{4}(J), 21^{18}(E), Ex 4^{4} (J; ‖ אחז), Ju 7^{20} 1 S 15^{27} 2 S 1^{11} 1 K 1^{50} 2^{28} 2 K 2^{12} 4^{27} Is 4^{1} Zc 8$^{23.23}$ Pr 7^{13} 26^{17}, cf. also Ju 19$^{25.29}$ 2 Ch 28^{15}; with violence Dt 22^{25} 25^{11} 1 S 17^{35} (perh. pf. consec. freq., v. Dr), 2 S 2^{16} 13^{11}; sq. לְ 2 S 15^{5}; fig. *take hold* in order to lead one (subj. י׳) sq. בְּ Je 31^{32}, c. acc. Is 41$^{9.13}$; cf. Is 51^{18} (בְּ; ‖ נֵהֵל); sq. acc. Na 3^{14} *take hold of the brick-mould,* Je 6^{23} = 50^{42}, Zc 14^{13} (with violence), ψ 35^{2} Ne 4$^{10.11}$, seize the kingdom Dn 11^{21}; in metaph. Mi 4^{9} (הֶחֱזִיקֵךְ חִיל), Je 6^{24} 8^{21} 49^{24} (v. Gie), 50^{43}; of pious laying hold of י׳, sq. בְּ Is 64^{6}, cf. 27^{5} 56$^{2.4.6}$; of other gods 1 K 9^{9} = 2 Ch 7^{22}; laying hold of wisdom Pr 3^{18}, cf. 4^{13} Jb 2$^{3.9}$ 27^{6} Je 8^{5}. **b.** *have* or *keep hold of,* sq. בְּ Ju 16^{26} 2 S 3^{29} Je 50^{33} Ne 4^{15}. **c.** *hold up,* sq. בְּ, fig. = *sustain, support* Lv 25^{35}; of י׳ holding his servants Is 42^{6} 45^{1}, cf. Jb 8^{20}; v. also pt. used substantively Dn 11^{1} (‖ מָעוֹז), v^{6} (‖ מֵבִיא, יֹלֵד); of Ne. holding fast to (בְּ) his work Ne 5^{16}; cf. of wicked, holding to his house Jb 8^{15}; *cleave* or *cling to* (על) one's brethren Ne 10^{30}. hence **c.** *keep, retain,* sq. בְּ Ex 9^{2} (J), Ju 7^{8} 19^{4}; so Ez 7^{13} Sm Co (MT Hithp.); sq. anger (acc.) Mi 7^{18}. **d.** hence also *hold, contain,* sq. acc. 2 Ch 4^{5}. †**Hithp.** (esp. Ch) *Pf.* הִתְחַזֵּק 2 Ch 13^{7} + 3 t., etc.; *Impf.* וַיִּתְחַזֵּק Gn 48^{2} + 7 t.; וַיִּתְחַזֵּק 2 Ch 21^{4} 32^{5}; יִתְחַזָּקוּ Ez 7^{13} (but Sm Co rd. Hiph.), etc.; *Imv.* הִתְחַזֵּק 1 K 20^{22}; הִתְחַזְּקוּ 1 S 4^{9}; *Inf. cstr.* לְהִתְחַזֵּק 2 Ch 13^{8} 16^{9}; *Pt.* מִתְחַזֵּק 2 S 3^{6} Dn 10^{21}; pl. מִתְחַזְּקִים 1 Ch 11^{10};—**1.** *strengthen oneself* 2 S 3^{6} 1 K 20^{22} 2 Ch 1^{1} 12^{13} 13^{21} 21^{4} 23^{1} 25^{11} 27^{6}; sq. עַל *against* 2 Ch 17^{1}; *gain strength* Ezr 7^{28} Dn 10^{19}, cf. הִתְח׳ ביהוה 1 S 30^{6}; fig. = *take courage* 2 Ch 15^{8}. **2.** *put forth strength, use one's strength* Gn 48^{2} (i.e. he exerted himself, he sat up by a great effort), Nu 13^{20} Ju 20^{22} 1 S 4^{9} 2 S 10^{12} 1 Ch 19^{13} 2 Ch 32^{5}. **3.** sq. לִפְנֵי *withstand* 2 Ch 13$^{7.8}$. **4.** sq. עִם *hold strongly with* 1 Ch 11^{10} Dn 10^{21}, cf. of י׳ להתח׳ עִם לְבָבָם שָׁלֵם אֵלָיו 2 Ch 16^{9}.—For יִתְחַזָּקוּ Ez 7^{13} rd. Hiph., v. Sm Co Da.

†חָזָק **adj.** strong, stout, mighty;—ח׳ 2389
Ex 10^{19} + 18 t.; f. חֲזָקָה Ex 3^{19} + 31 t. + Ez 3^{14} (Co for MT vb. 3 fs.); pl. חֲזָקִים Ju 18^{25} + 2 t.; cstr. חִזְקֵי Ez 2^{4} (del. Co v. infr.) 3^{7};—**1.** *strong:* **a.** of men, rarely pred. Nu 13^{18} (opp. רָפֶה), v^{31} (compar. c. מִן), Jos 14^{11} 17^{18} (all JE), Ju 18^{26} (compar. c. מִן); also of גֹּאֲלָם Je 50^{34} Pr 23^{11}; of hand of י׳ Jos 4^{24} (D), so Ez 3^{14} 𝔊 Co (v. supr. and חָזַק **Qal 3**); cf. of Tyre הָיְתָה חֲזָקָה בַּיָּם Ez 26^{17} (del. B Co). **b.** usu. attrib.; of arm of Pharaoh Ez 30^{22} (opp. נִשְׁבָּרֶת); esp. of hand of י׳ in delivering Isr. from Egypt, Ex 3^{19} (gloss? v. Di), 6$^{1.1}$ 13^{9} (all J), Dt 6^{21} 7^{8} 9^{26} Dn 9^{15}; in wonders done by agency of Moses Dt 34^{12}; also בְּכֹחַ גָּדוֹל וּבְיָד חֲזָקָה Ex 32^{11} (JE), cf. Ne 1^{10}, but oftener ביד חזקה וּבִזְרוֹעַ נְטוּיָה Dt 4^{34} 5^{15} 7^{19} 11^{2} 26^{8} Je 32^{21} ψ 136^{12}; of control of enemies and deliverance from exile Ez 20$^{33.34}$; more gen. Dt 3^{24} (‖ גָּדְלְךָ), 1 K 8^{42} = 2 Ch 6^{32}; of י׳'s opposition to Zedekiah Je 21^{5}; once of Edom, opp. Isr. בעם כבד וביד חזקה Nu 20^{20} (JE). **c.** of sword of י׳ Is 27^{1} (‖ הַקָּשָׁה וְהַגְּדוֹלָה), of wind Ex 10^{19} (J), 1 K 19^{11}; sound of trumpet (= *loud*) Ex 19^{16} (E). **d.** *severe, sharp, hot,* of war 1 S 14^{52} (pred.), battle 2 S 11^{15}, sickness 1 K 17^{17} (pred.), famine 18^{2}. **e.** *firm, hard,* of face, פנים Ez 3^{8}, forehead, מֵצַח v^{8}; adamant, sim. of forehead v^{9} (compar., c. מִן); of sky Jb 37^{18} (pred.) In pl. cstr. ח׳ לֵב Ez 2^{4} *hard of heart* (‖ קְשֵׁי פָנִים) but om. B Co, ח׳־מֵצַח 3^{7} *hard* (= impudent) *of forehead* (‖ קְשֵׁי־לֵב). **2.** as subst., *a strong one,* of י׳ (בְּחָזָק, *as, in the character of, a strong one*) Is 40^{10}; of י׳'s agent Is 28^{2} (‖ אַמִּיץ); v. also וְחָזָק לֹא יְאַמֵּץ כֹּחוֹ Am 2^{14}; c. מִן comp. = *one too strong for* Je 31^{11} ψ 35^{10}. In Ez 34^{16} MT uses הח׳ in bad sense (‖ הַשְּׁמֵנָה), 𝔊 Co, with diff. text, in good sense (v. VB).

חָזֵק **adj.verb.** v. חָזַק **Qal** *Pt.* p. 304 2390

†[חֵזֶק] **n.[m.]** strength, only חִזְקִי י׳ ψ 18^{2} 2391
(om. by error ‖ 2 S 22^{2} where 𝔊L ἰσχύς μου). (De al. der. fr. חֹזֶק, but [חֶזְקָה] favours חֵזֶק).

†[חֶזְקָה] **n.f. strength, force** (strictly Inf. 2393
form fr. חזק v. Ges§45.1b)—**1.** of urgency of י׳'s hand in prophetic inspiration בְּחֶזְקַת הַיָּד Is 8^{11} (cf. חָזַק Ez 3^{14}). **2.** of royal power כְּחֶזְקָתוֹ 2 Ch 12^{1} 26^{16} (‖ חָזַק v^{15}), Dn 11^{2}.

†חֹזֶק **n.m.** strength;—ח׳ cstr. Ex 13^{3} + 2392
3 t.; חָזְקֵנוּ Am 6^{13};—**1.** of י׳, ח׳ יָד Ex 13$^{3.14.16}$ (all JE). **2.** national strength Am 6^{13} Hg 2^{22}.

2394 †חָזְקָה **n.f.** strength, force, violence, alw. בְּחָזְקָה, *with strength, force*, etc.;—**1.** of oppression Ju 4^{3} *forcibly, violently;* capture *by force* 1 S 2^{16}; Ez 34^{4} of ruling בְּח׳ וּבְפָרֶךְ *with force and with rigour.* **2.** rebuke *severely, sharply* Ju 8^{1}; cry *mightily,* insistently Jon 3^{8}.—לְחָזְקָה 2 K 12^{13} v. חָזַק **Qal** *Inf.*

2395 †חִזְקִי **n.pr.m.** a Benjamite 1 Ch 8^{17}, 𝔊 Αζακ(ε)ι; 𝔊L Εζεκια.

2396, 3169 חִזְקִיָּהוּ, חִזְקִיָּה, יְחִזְקִיָּהוּ, יְחִזְקִיָּה **n.pr.m.** (*י׳ hath strengthened, י׳ strengtheneth;* = As. *Ḫazaki(i)au,* Schr^{COT} on 2 K $18^{1\,ff.}$, Jäger$^{BAS\ i.\ 469}$; cf. n.pr. יחזק on seal Gann$^{JAs\ 1883\ Feb.—Mar.,\ 134\ No.\ 7}$;—on format. v. Lag$^{BN\ 134}$)—**1.** 𝔊 Εζεκιας, *son of Ahaz,* King of Judah, seldom †חִזְקִיָּה 2 K $18^{1.10.14.14.15.16.16}$, also אַנְשֵׁי ח׳ Pr 25^{1}†; elsewh. in 2 K (exc. 20^{10}) חִזְקִיָּהוּ: 16^{20} 18^{9} + 34 t., 2 K 18–21 ‖ Is 36^{1} + 31 t., Is 36–39; also †Je $26^{18.19}$ 1 Ch 3^{13} 2 Ch $29^{18.27}$ 30^{24} 32^{15}; in Ch usu. יְחִזְקִיָּהוּ 1 Ch 4^{41} 2 Ch 28^{27} + 35 t. 2 Ch 29–33; also 2 K 20^{10} Je 15^{4}, and in title Is 1^{1}; †יְחִזְקִיָּה Ho 1^{1} Mi 1^{1} †(if י in these three be not txt. err. for ו). †**2.** חִזְקִיָּה great-great-grandfather of proph. Zephaniah Zp 1^{1}, 𝔊 τοῦ Εζεκιου, perh. = **1.** †**3.** 𝔊 Εζεκια(ς), חִזְקִיָּה man of royal Davidic line 1 Ch 3^{23} prob. near time of Chr. †**4.** יְחִזְקִיָּה, 𝔊 Εζεκια(ς), head of a family of returned exiles Ezr 2^{16} = חִזְקִיָּה Ne 7^{21}, cf. also ח׳ Ne 10^{18}. †**5.** יְחִזְקִיָּהוּ 𝔊 Εζεκιας, an Ephraimite, Ahaz's time 2 Ch 28^{12}.

3168 †יְחֶזְקֵאל **n.pr.m.** (*God strengtheneth,* cf. foreg.; v. Lag$^{BN\ 134}$)—**1.** the well-known priest and prophet, son of Buzi, 𝔊 Ιεζεκιηλ, Ez 1^{3} 24^{24}. **2.** priest of 19th course (assigned to David's time) 1 Ch 24^{16}, 𝔊 Εζεκηλ, 𝔊L (20th course, cf. A) Ιεζεκιηλ.

3169 יְחִזְקִיָּהוּ, יְחִזְקִיָּה v. חִזְקִיָּהוּ supr.

חזר (√ of foll.; meaning dub.; perh. cf. Ar. خَزِرَ *the eye was* or *became narrow, small,* Lane $^{731\ c}$; hence *narrow-eyed* animal).

2386 †חֲזִיר **n.m.**$^{ψ\ 80,\ 14}$ swine, boar (NH *id.;* Aram. חֲזִירָא, ܚܙܝܪܐ; Ar. خِنْزِيرٌ (Aram. loan-wd. acc. to Frä^{110}, yet v. Lag$^{BN\ 113}$); Eth. ሐንዚር: (only once; = wild boar), v. Hom$^{NS\ 319\ f.\ 358,\ 385}$)—alw. st. abs., 4 t. c. art. הַח׳;—**1.** *swine,* forbidden as food Lv 11^{7} (P), Dt 14^{8}, cf. בְּשַׂר הַח׳ Is 65^{4} 66^{17}, and דַּם־ח׳ 66^{3} as heathen offering (RS$^{Sem.\ i,\ 272.325.338.392}$); with implication of repulsiveness נֶזֶם זָהָב בְּאַף ח׳ Pr 11^{22} sim. of fair woman with dub. character. **2.** *wild boar* ח׳ מִיָּעַר ψ 80^{14} fig. of foes of Isr. (in fig. of vineyard).

†חֵזִיר **n.pr.m.** (cf. inscr. in RA$^{1867,\ pl.\ 7}$, 2387
Dr$^{Sm\ xxiii}$; Nö$^{ZMG\ 1886,\ 162}$ 'pointing ֵ to avoid offence;' but Nbr$^{Acad.\ 1887,\ Dec.\ 17}$ comp. Talm. & 𝔗 (חֵיזוּרָא, חֵיזוּר, חֲזוּרָא etc.) *pomegranate* (and *apple;* Syr. ܚܙܘܪܐ, ܚܙܘܪܐ), cf. בְּנֵי רִמּוֹן 2 S $4^{2.5.9}$)—**1.** a priest of 17th course (assigned to David's time) 1 Ch 24^{15}; 𝔊 Χηζειν (16th, v^{14}), but A Ιεζειρ, 𝔊L Χηζειρ. **2.** one of those sealed Ne 10^{21}; 𝔊 Ηζειρ, 𝔊L Αζηρ.

†יַחְזֵרָה **n.pr.m.** 1 Ch 9^{12} cf. אַחְזַי p. 28 b. 274, 3170
p. 403

חַח, חָח v. sub חוח. p. 296 2397

†חָטָא $_{238}$ **vb.** miss (a goal or way), **go** 2398
wrong, sin (NH *id.;* Aram. חֲטָא, ܚܛܐ; As. *ḫaṭû,* Zim$^{BP\ 46}$; Sab. חטא, החטא, *id.,* DHM in MV; Ar. خَطِئَ *do wrong, commit a mistake* or *an error;* II. *make to miss the mark;* IV. *miss the mark, miss the way;* Eth. ኀጥአ: *fail to find* or *have;* sts. *sin,* esp. in deriv.)—**Qal** *Pf.* ח׳ Ex 32^{31} + 29 t., 3 fs. חָטְאָה Lv 5^{15} La 1^{8}, חָטָאָה Je 50^{14} Ez 16^{15}, חָטָאת Ex 5^{16}, etc., + 82 t. Pf.; *Impf.* יֶחֱטָא Lv 4^{3} + 12 t., תֶּחֱטָאוּ Ex 20^{20} ψ 4^{5}, etc. + 20 t. Impf.; *Inf.* חֲטֹא Ez 3^{21} + 8 t., מֵחֲטוֹא ψ 39^{2}, מֵחֲטוֹ (txt. err. for מחטא) Gn 20^{6}, בְּחֶטְאָה Nu 15^{28}, חֲטֹאתוֹ Ez 33^{12} (del. Co); *Pt.* חוֹטֵא Pr 13^{22} + 6 t., חֹטֵא Is 1^{4} Ec 9^{2}, חוֹטֶא Is 65^{20} + 2 t., חֹטֶא Ec 8^{12}, sf. חֹטְאִי Pr 8^{36}, pl. חֹטְאִים 1 S 14^{33}, sf. חֹטֵאת Ez $18^{4.20}$;—**1.** *miss:* לא תחטא *thou shalt not miss anything* Jb 5^{24}, אָץ בְּרַגְלַיִם חוֹטֵא Pr 19^{2} *one hastening with his feet misseth* (the way or the goal); חֹטְאִי חֹמֵס נַפְשׁוֹ Pr 8^{36} *the one missing me* (Wisdom) *is one wronging himself* (opp. מֹצְאִי); *miss,* i.e. *endanger,* one's life Pr 20^{2} Hb 2^{10} acc. to De VB (others sub **3** q. v.) **2.** *sin, miss the goal* or *path of right and duty:* **a.** *against man,* abs. Ex 5^{16} (E), 1 S 26^{21} 2 S 19^{21} 1 K 18^{9} 2 K 18^{14}; with לְ of the person against whom or towards whom one sins, Gn 40^{1} (E), Ju 11^{27} 1 S 2^{25} 19^{4} 24^{12}, 1 K 8^{31} = 2 Ch 6^{22}; מה חטאתי לך *wherein have I sinned against thee?* Gn 20^{9} (E) Je 37^{18}; with בְּ, אל תחטאו בילד Gn 42^{22} (E) *do not sin against* the lad, against David 1 S $19^{4.5}$. **b.** elsewhere always *against God,* abs. Ex 20^{20} (E), 9^{34} (J) Jos 7^{11} (D) Lv 4^{3} $5^{1.11.17.21.23}$ Nu 16^{22} (P), Ne 6^{13} Jb $1^{5.22}$ 7^{20} 10^{14} 24^{19} 35^{6} ψ 4^{5} 78^{32} Is 43^{27} 64^{4} Je 2^{35} La 5^{7} Ez $3^{21.21}$ 16^{51} 28^{16} 33^{12} Ho 8^{11}

(del. We[Kl. Proph.]), v[11] 10[9] 13[2]; לא נתתי לחטא חכי *I have not permitted my palate to sin* Jb 31[30]; *Pt.* חֹטֵא, used as adj., sinful nation Is 1[4], sinful person Ez 18[4.20]; but usually as noun, *sinner* Pr 11[31] 13[22] 14[21] Ec 2[26] 7[26] 8[12] 9[2.18] Is 65[20]. Sin is confessed: חָטָאנוּ *we have sinned* Nu 14[40] 21[7] (E) Ju 10[15] 1 S 12[10], 1 K 8[47] = 2 Ch 6[37], Ne 1[6] ψ 106[6] La 5[16] Dn 9[5.15]; חטאתי *I have sinned* Ex 9[27] Nu 22[34] (J) 1 S 15[24.30] 2 S 24[10.17] 1 Ch 21[8.17] Jb 33[27]. Sin is universal: אין אדם אשר לא יחטא *there is no man who sinneth not* 1 K 8[46] = 2 Ch 6[36], כי אדם אין צדיק בארץ אשר יעשה טוב ולא יחטא Ec 7[20] *for man there is none righteous in the earth who doeth good and sinneth not;* with לְ, against God Gn 20[6](E), 39[9](J), Ex 32[33] Nu 32[23](both JE), Dt 9[16] 20[18] 1 S 2[25] 12[23] 14[33.34], 1 K 8[33.35.46.50] = 2 Ch 6[24.26.36.39], 2 K 17[7] Ho 4[7] Mi 7[9] Zp 1[17] Je 40[3] 44[23] 50[7.14] Ez 14[13] Is 42[24] Jb 8[4] ψ 78[17] 119[11] Ne 1[6]; in confession חטאתי ל Ex 10[16] Jos 7[20] (J), 2 S 12[13] ψ 41[5] 51[6]; חטאנו ל Dt 1[41] Ju 10[10] 1 S 7[6] Je 3[25] 8[14] 14[7.20] Dn 9[8.11]; with בְּ of instr., lips Jb 2[10], tongue ψ 39[2]; wherein Ez 37[23] Lv 4[23] (P), therein Lv 5[22] (P); ellipsis of בְּ in phrase עונם אשר ח׳ לי *(their) iniquity wherein they sinned against me* Je 33[8.8]; בשגגה *by error, unwittingly* Lv 4[2.22.27] 5[15] Nu 15[27.28] (all P); *against* thy judgments Ne 9[29]; with עַל, *with regard to* Lv 5[5] Nu 6[11](P) Ne 13[26]; with cognate acc. ח׳ חֲטָאָה Ex 32[30.31](JE); חַטָּאת אשר ח׳ Nu 12[11] (J) Lv 4[3.28.28.35] 5[6.10.13] (all P) 19[22.22] (H), Dt 9[18] 1 K 14[16.22] 15[30] 16[13.19] 2 K 21[17] Ez 18[24] 33[16]; חטאת אשר ח׳ ל Je 16[10] Ne 1[6]; חטאת אשר ח׳ על Lv 4[14](P); חֵטְא ח׳ La 1[8]; חֵטְא אשר ח׳ Dt 19[15]. **3.** *incur guilt, penalty by sin, forfeit:* וחטאתי לך כל הימים Gn 43[9] *I shall incur the blame of sinning against thee all my days,* cf. 44[32](J); c. acc. חוֹטֵא נפשׁ *forfeiting oneself, one's life* Pr 20[2] Hb 2[10] acc. to most, yet v. sub **1.**—והביא אשמו אשר ח׳ Lv 5[7] *he shall bring his trespass-offering which he has incurred by sin;* קרבנו אשר ח׳ Lv 5[11]; את אשר ח׳ מן־הקדשׁ ישׁלם v[16] *what he hath incurred by taking of the holy thing he shall pay.* **Pi.** *Pf.* חִטֵּא Lv 14[52]; sf. חִטְּאוֹ Nu 19[19], חִטֵּאתָ Ex 29[36] + 2 t.; 3 pl. חִטְּאוּ Ez 43[22.22]; *Impf.* וַיְחַטֵּא Lv 8[15]; sf. וַיְחַטְּאֵהוּ Lv 9[15], תְּחַטְּאֵנִי ψ 51[9], אֲחַטֶּנָּה Gn 31[39], וַיְחַטְּאוּ 2 Ch 29[24]; *Inf.* חַטֵּא Lv 14[49] Ez 43[23]; *Pt.* הַמְחַטֵּא Lv 6[19];—**1.** *bear loss:* אָנֹכִי אֲחַטֶּנָּה *I bare the loss of it* Gn 31[39] (E; lit. *I let it be missing?* poss. rd. אֲחֻטֶּנָּה *I was made to miss it?*). **2.** *make a sin-offering:* c. sf. referring to שׂעיר Lv 9[15] (P); to sin-offering Lv 6[19] (P); על המזבח *upon the altar* Ex 29[36] (P; not *cleanse the altar* RV); ח׳ את דמם המזבחה 2 Ch 29[24] *made a sin-offering with their blood on the altar.* **3.** *purify from sin:* the altar, by putting the blood of the sin-offering on its horns, Lv 8[15](P), Ez 43[20.22.22.23]; the sanctuary, by applying to it the blood of the sin-offering Ez 45[18]. **4.** *purify from uncleanness:* the house of the leper by application of the mixture of living water and blood of the bird Lv 14[49.52] (P); a person, by application of the mixture of living water and ashes of the red heifer Nu 19[19] (P), by sprinkling with a hyssop sprig ψ 51[9]. **Hiph.** *Pf.* הֶחֱטִיא 1 K 14[16] + 17 t., הֶחֱטִי (Kt err. for החטיא) 2 K 13[6]; sf. הֶחֱטִיאָם 2 K 17[21]; pl. הֶחֱטִיאוּ 1 K 16[13] Ne 13[26]; *Impf.* יַחֲטִא Ju 20[16] 2 K 21[11]; תַּחֲטִיא Dt 24[4]; וַתַּחֲטִא 1 K 16[2] 21[22]; pl. יַחֲטִיאוּ Ex 23[33]; *Inf.* הַחֲטִיא Ec 5[5] 1 K 16[19] Je 32[35] (Qr), הַחֲטִי Je 32[35] (Kt err.); *Pt.* pl. cstr. מַחֲטִיאֵי Is 29[21];—**1.** *miss the mark:* קֹלֵעַ בָּאֶבֶן אֶל־הַשַּׂעֲרָה וְלֹא יַחֲטִא Ju 20[16] *slinging with stones at an hair and would not miss.* **2.** *induce* or *cause to sin:* with acc. Ex 23[33] (JE), Ne 13[26]; elsewh. in the phrase החטיא את ישׂראל *(he) caused Israel to sin* 1 K 14[16] 15[26.30.34] 16[2.13.19.26] 21[22] 22[53] 2 K 3[3] 10[29.31] 13[2.6.11] 14[24] 15[9.18.24.28] 23[15]; c. sf. ref. to Isr. 2 K 17[21]; את יהודה 2 K 21[11.16] Je 32[35] (sts. c. 2nd acc.—חטאת, or אשׁר ref. to חטאת:—1 K 15[26.34] 16[26] 2 K 17[21] 21[16]; prob. also 1 K 14[16] 15[30] 16[13]; no 2nd acc. 1 K 16[2.19] 21[22] 22[53] 2 K 21[11] 23[15] Je 32[35]; the rest are ambiguous). **3.** *bring into guilt, condemnation, punishment:* מחטיאי אדם Is 29[21] *who bring a man into condemnation;* לא תחטיא את הארץ Dt 24[4] *thou shalt not bring the land into guilt;* אל תתן את־פיך לחטיא את־בשׂרך Ec 5[5] *do not permit thy mouth to bring thy flesh into punishment.* **Hithp.** *Impf.* יִתְחַטָּא Nu 19[12] + 4 t., יִתְחַטְּאוּ Nu 8[21], יִתְחַטָּאוּ Jb 41[17], תִּתְחַטְּאוּ Nu 31[19], תִּתְחַטָּאוּ Nu 31[20];—**1.** *miss oneself, lose oneself,* fig. for *be bewildered, beside oneself,* מִשְּׁבָרִים יִתְחַטָּאוּ Jb 41[17] *by reason of consternation they are beside themselves* (‖ יגורו *are afraid*). **2.** *purify oneself from uncleanness,* only in P: **a.** Levites Nu 8[21]. **b.** those in contact with the dead Nu 19[12.13.20] 31[19.20]; with בְּ, בְּמֵי נִדָּה Nu 31[23]; by a mixture of ashes of the red heifer with fresh water Nu 19[12].

†חֵטְא **n.m.**[Dt 15, 9] sin (on format. v. Lag[BN] 2399
142)—ח׳ Lv 19[17] + 15 t.; sf. חֶטְאוֹ Lv 24[15] + 5 t., חֲטָאוֹ La 3[39], חֶטְאָם Lv 20[20]; pl. חֲטָאִים Ec 10[4]; cstr. חֲטָאֵי 2 K 10[29] Ez 23[49]; sf. חֲטָאַי Gn 41[9],

חֲטָאַי Is 38[17] ψ 51[11], חֲטָאֵינוּ Dn 9[16] ψ 103[10], חֲטָאֵיכֶם Is 1[18];—**1.** *sin:* **a.** against man Gn 41[9](E) Ec 10[4]. **b.** elsewh. ag. God, abs. Is 31[7] Ho 12[9]; ח׳ חֵטְא La 1[8] cf. Dt 19[15] 2 K 10[29]; ח׳ משפט מות *sin* worthy of death Dt 21[22]=ח׳ מות 22[26]; with בְּ, *because of,* Dn 9[16]; God is entreated: *hide thy face from my sins* ψ 51[11]; and it is said in faith, *thou wilt cast behind thy back all my sins* Is 38[17]. **2.** *guilt of sin:* היה חטא ב *sin* (the guilt of sin) *come on one* Dt 15[9] 21[22] 23[22.23] 24[15]; בחטאו מת *in his sin* (guilt) *die* Nu 27[3] (P); איש בחטאו *each for his own sin* Dt 24[16]=2 K 14[16]=2 Ch 25[4]; בחטא יחמתני אמי ψ 51[7] *in sin* (condition of sin and guilt) *my mother conceived me;* אם חטאיכם כשנים Is 1[18] *though your sins be like scarlet* (in guilt); לא כחטאינו עשה לנו ψ 103[10] *not according to our sins* (their guilt) *hath he done to us.* **3.** *punishment for sin:* נשׂא ח׳ *bear sin* (its punishment) Lv 20[20] 24[15] (H), Nu 9[13] 18[22] (P); with עַל, *bear sin because of* Lv 19[17] 22[9] (H) Nu 18[32] (P); bear sins of idols (in worshipping idols) Ez 23[49]; the ideal servant of Yahweh *bore the sins of many* Is 53[12]; without נשׂא, only La 3[39] גבר על חטאו (wherefore doth) *a man* (complain) *for the punishment of his sin?*

2400 †[חַטָּא] **adj.** and **n.m. 1.** sinful, **2.** sinners—as adj.f. חַטָּאָה Am 9[8], elsewhere only pl. חַטָּאִים Nu 32[14]+15 t.; cstr. חַטָּאֵי Am 9[10]; sf. חַטָּאֶיהָ Is 13[9];—**1. adj. a.** *sinful* men Nu 32[14] (J), kingdom Am 9[8]. **b.** *exposed to condemnation, reckoned as offenders* 1 K 1[21] (cf. Hiph. Pt. Is 29[21]). Elsewh. **2. n.m.** *sinners* Nu 17[3](P), 1 S 15[18] Am 9[10] Is 1[28] 13[9] 33[14] ψ 1[1.5] 25[8] 26[9] 51[15] 104[35] Pr 1[10] 13[21] 23[17]; ח׳ ליהוה *sinners against* י׳ Gn 13[13] (J).

2402 †חַטָּאָה **n.f.** sinful thing, sin, Ex 34[7] (JE) Is 5[18].

2401 †חֲטָאָה **n.f.** sin, sin-offering (?)—**1.** *sin,* chiefly in the phrase ח׳ גְּדֹלָה *great sin* Gn 20[9](E) Ex 32[21.30.31] (JE), 2 K 17[21]; כְּסוּי ח׳ ψ 32[1] *he whose sin is covered* is blessed; but the *prayer* of the wicked *becomes sin when he is judged* ψ 109[7]. **2.** *sin-offering* (acc. to most) עולה וחטאה ψ 40[7] *whole burnt-offering and sin-offering* (so Vrss Thes MV SS al., but < *whole burnt-offering with sin* v. Br [MP 329]).

2403 †חַטָּאת **n.f.**[1 S 14,38] (Gn 4[7] no exception for רֹבֵץ is noun=crouching beast) **sin, sin-offering,** ח׳ Gn 4[7]+124 t.; לַחַטָּת Nu 15[24] (txt. err. for לחטאת), לְחַטָּאת Zc 13[1] (but rd. לְחַטָּאָה Sta [ZAW i. 35]); cstr. חַטַּאת Ex 30[10]+19 t.; sf. חַטָּאתִי Gn 31[36]+16 t.; חַטָּאתוֹ 1 K 16[26], חַטַּאתְכֶם Ex 32[30]+3 t., etc., +52 t. sf.; pl. חַטָּאוֹת 2 K 12[17]+3 t.; cstr. חַטֹּאות ψ 25[7]+17 t.; חַטֹּאת Nu 5[6]+6 t.; sf. חַטֹּאותַי ψ 25[18]; חַטֹּאתָו Ez 18[21] 33[16], etc., +40 t. sf.;—**1.** *sin:* **a.** *against man* Gn 31[36] 50[17] (E), Nu 12[11] (J) 1 S 20[1]; ח׳ אדם *sins against man* Nu 5[6] (P). Elsewhere **b.** *against God* Lv 4[14.23.28] (P), 1 S 2[17] 14[38] 1 K 16[13.13] 2 K 21[16.17] 2 Ch 33[19] Is 3[9] 30[1] 58[1] 59[2.12] Je 5[25] 16[10.18] 30[14.15] 50[20] La 4[6.22] Ez 16[51] 18[14] 21[29] 33[10.16] Am 5[12] (We [Kl. Proph.] rds. חטאיכם, as Is 1[18]—v. חֵטְא—on acc. of masc. עצומים), Mi 1[13] 3[8] ψ 32[5] 51[5] 59[4] Pr 5[22] 13[6] 14[34] 21[4] 24[9] Jb 13[23.23] Dn 9[20.20]; ח׳ נעורי *sins of my youth* ψ 25[7]; פרי בטני ח׳ נפשי Mi 6[7] *fruit of my body* (my child as an offering) for the *sin of myself;* sin of divination 1 S 15[23]; of the mouth ψ 59[13]; ח׳ עמי יאכלו Ho 4[8] *the sin of my people they eat* (gain their daily food by means of it, cf. We; 𝔗 Hi Or al. *sin-offering,* but this not elsewhere in early proph., and ‖ עָוֹן against it, v. We [Prol. 3. 76]); לפתח חטאת רבץ Gn 4[7] (J) *at the door* (of Cain) *sin is a crouching beast;* sin of the people is embodied in the golden calf Dt 9[21]; and the high places of Beth Aven Ho 10[8]; c. בְּ *on the ground of sin* Ne 9[37]; *for sin* Mi 1[5] 2 K 24[3] Is 40[2] Je 15[13] 17[3] Ez 16[52]; *with* or *by sin* 1 K 14[22] 16[2] Is 43[24]; הלך בח׳ *walk in sin* 1 K 15[3.26.34] 16[19.26.31] 2 K 17[22]; דבק בח׳ *cleave unto sin* 2 K 3[3]; c. עַל, *on account of sin* Dt 9[18] 1 K 15[30] 16[19] Mi 6[13]; *for sin* Lv 4[3.28.35] 5[6.13] (P) 19[22] 26[18.24.28] (H); יסף על ח׳ *add unto sin* 1 S 12[19] 2 Ch 28[13] Is 30[1] Jb 34[37]; c. כְּ *according to sin* Lv 26[21]; c. לְ *to* or *for sin* Lv 16[16.21] Dt 19[15] 1 K 12[30] 13[34] Pr 10[16] Zc 13[1]; c. מִן *because of sin* Lv 4[26] 5[6.10] 16[34] (P), 19[22] (H), La 4[13]; *more than sin* Jb 35[3]; טָהַרְתִּי מֵחַטָּאתִי *I am clean from my sin* Pr 20[9]; מפני ח׳ *because of sin* ψ 38[4]; בגלל ח׳ *because of sin* 1 K 14[16]; הלך אחר ח׳ *walk after sin* 2 K 13[2]. **c.** men should *return from sin* שׁוּב מִן 1 K 8[35]=2 Ch 6[26], Ez 18[21] 33[14]; *depart from it* סוּר מֵעַל 2 K 10[31] 15[18]; סור מן 2 K 13[6.11] 14[24] 15[9.24.28]; *be concerned about* דאג מן ψ 38[19]; *confess* הִתְוַדָּה ח׳ Nu 5[7](P); התודה על ח׳ Ne 1[6] 9[2]. **d.** God deals with sin: (1) he *visits punishment* upon it פקד (על) Ex 32[34] (JE) Ho 8[13] 9[9] Je 14[10]; *inquires after it* דרשׁ ל Jb 10[6]; *watches over it* שׁמר על Jb 14[16]; *hoards it up* Ho 13[12]; (2) *by forgiveness:* נשׂא ח׳ Ex 10[17] 32[32] (JE), 1 S 15[25]; נשׂא עון ח׳ ψ 32[5]; נשׂא לח׳

Jos 24^{19}(E), ψ 25^{18}; *pardon* סלח לח׳ Ex 34^{9}(JE) 1 K $8^{34.36}$ 2 Ch $6^{25.27}$ 7^{14} Je 36^{3}; *removal* הסר Is 27^{9}; העביר 2 S 12^{13}; *casting into the depths of the sea* Mi 7^{19}; (3) *by covering over, making atonement for* חַטָּאתְךָ תְּכֻפָּר Is 6^{7} *thy sin shall be covered over;* actively, כפר עַל ח׳ ψ 79^{9}; כסה ח׳ ψ 85^{3} (cf. כְּסוּי חֲטָאָה ψ 32^{1}); לְהָתֵם ח׳ (Qr) *make an end of sins* Dn 9^{24}; (4) *by blotting out* מחה ח׳ Is 44^{22} Je 18^{23} ψ 109^{14} Ne 3^{37}; *cleanse from sin* טַהֲרֵנִי מח׳ ψ 51^{4}; מקור לח׳ *a fountain for sin* Zc 13^{1}; (5) *by not remembering it* לֹא זכר ח׳ Is 43^{25}; לח׳ לֹא זכר Je 31^{34}; אַל־תֵּפֶן אֶל־חַטָּאתוֹ Dt 9^{27} *look not unto his sin.* **e.** atonement may be secured for, כפר בעד ח׳ Ex 32^{30} (JE; Moses, by his intercession). **f.** acc. to P (H) the priest is to make atonement for a person (כפר על) by sin-offering or trespass-offering, מח׳ *because of sin* Lv 4^{26} $5^{6.10}$ 16^{34}; על ח׳ 4^{35} 5^{13} (all P), 19^{22} (H; v. We $^{\text{Comp., 59 = JBTh xxii, 427}}$), so that the man is *clean from sin* טהר מח׳ Lv 16^{30}. **2.** *condition of sin, guilt of sin* Gn 18^{20} Nu 16^{26} 32^{23} (J), Ez 3^{20} 18^{24}, ח׳ יְהוּדָה חֲרוּשָׁה עַל־לוּחַ לִבָּם וּלְקַרְנוֹת מִזְבְּחוֹתֵיכֶם *the sin* (guilt) *of Judah is graven upon the table of their heart, and upon the horns of your altars* Je 17^{1}. **3.** *punishment for sin:* זֹאת תִּהְיֶה ח׳ מִצְרָיִם וח׳ כָּל־הַגּוֹיִם Zc 14^{19} *this will be the punishment for sin of Egypt and the punishment for sin of all nations* (the plague with which Yahweh will smite them). **4.** *sin-offering:* one of the kinds of offering of P, Lv 7^{37}; first in the history 2 K 12^{17} (reign of Jehoash), where חטאת of money given to priests; elsewh. only in Chr.; 2 Ch $29^{21.23.24}$ Hezekiah had made a ח׳ of 7 צְפִירֵי עִזִּים at purification of temple; Ezr 8^{35} 12 צְפִירֵי ח׳ were offered; Ne 10^{34} ח׳ ‖ עולות;—in these no evidence of special ritual. Sin-offering elsewh. only in codes of H Ez and P.—On Ho 4^{8} v. **1** supr. In H, Lv 23^{19} a שְׂעִיר עִזִּים, for feast of weeks. In Ez ח׳ in gen. ‖ other sacrifices, Ez 40^{39} $45^{17.25}$ 46^{20}; and priests eat them Ez 42^{13} 44^{29}. At dedication of altar, the blood of a young bullock was to be applied to horns of altar, the corners of its settle and its border, the bullock itself burnt without the sanctuary; for each of the 7 days following a שְׂעִיר עִזִּים was to be offered Ez $43^{19.21.22.25}$. On first day of first month a young bullock was to be offered to cleanse the sanctuary: its blood put on the door posts of the house and of the gate of the inner court and on the four corners of the settle of the altar; also on the seventh day (𝔊 first day of seventh month) Ez $45^{17.19}$ (cf. $v^{18.20}$). On 14th day of first month the prince was to offer a bullock for himself and the people and on each of the 7 days of the Passover week a שְׂעִיר עִזִּים Ez $45^{22.23}$. When a priest entered the sanctuary to minister after his cleansing he was to offer his sin-offering Ez 44^{27}. P gives several grades: **a.** a ruler should offer a he-goat Lv $4^{24.25}$ Nu $7^{16.22.28.34.40.46.52.58.64.70.76.82.87}$; an ordinary person a she-goat Lv 4^{29} (cf. v^{28}) 5^{6} Nu 15^{27}, ewe lamb Lv $4^{32.33.33.34}$ 14^{19} Nu $6^{14.16}$, a turtle dove or young pigeon Lv $5^{7.8.9.9}$ $12^{6.8}$ $14^{22.31}$ $15^{15.30}$ Nu 6^{11}, or one-tenth of an ephah of fine flour Lv $5^{11.11.12}$; according to ability of the person, and nature of offence. The victim was brought unto the tent of meeting, the hands of the offerer laid on its head, it was slaughtered by the offerer, the priest took some of the blood and put it on horns of altar of burnt-offering and the rest of the blood he poured out at the base of it, to cover over the sin, or cleanse the altar from the sin defiling it. All the fat pieces (cf. Lv 4^{22-35}) and a handful of the flour (cf. Lv 5^{12}) were burned on altar. The rest of the flesh and the flour were eaten by priests in court of Holy place Lv 5^{13} $6^{10.18.18.23}$ (cf. $v^{11.19}$), 7^{7} $10^{16.17.19.19}$ 14^{13} Nu 18^{9}. **b.** a bullock was offered for priests Ex $29^{14.36}$ Lv $4^{3.8.20}$ $8^{2.14.14}$ $9^{2.7.8.10}$; for Levites at their installation Nu $8^{8.12}$ and for whole congregation Lv $4^{14.21}$; but usu. offering for congregation was he-goat Nu $15^{24.25}$, esp. at dedication of altar Lv $9^{3.15.22}$, and in ritual of feasts Nu $28^{15.22.30}$ $29^{5.11.16.19.22.25.28.31.34.38}$. Before consecr. of tabernacle the blood went to altar of burnt-offering (Lv 9^{9}), but subsequ. some of it was sprinkled seven times before the vail and some of it put on horns of altar of incense to cleanse this higher altar; the fat pieces were burned on altar of burnt-offering, and the rest of the victim burned without the camp (Lv 4^{3-21} 6^{23} $8^{16.17}$ $9^{10.11}$). **c.** on day of atonement, sin-offering for high priest was a bullock Lv $16^{3.6}$; and for congregation two he-goats, one לַעֲזָאזֵל (v. עזאזל) Lv 16^{5} (cf. $v^{8.10.20-22}$), the other for sacrifice ליהוה Lv 16^{9} (cf. v^{8}). Some of the blood of Aaron's bullock was first taken into innermost sanctuary and sprinkled on the כפרת and seven times before it; so also blood of the he-goat Lv $16^{11.11.15}$ (cf. $v^{12-14.16.17}$) to cleanse highest altar: then the blood of the two victims was applied to lower altars as in **a** and **b** and so sin was covered over at the three altars Ex 30^{10} (cf. Lv 16^{16-19}). The fat pieces went to altar of burnt-offering and the rest of the victims was burnt without the camp Lv $16^{25.27.27}$. (Sins which might be covered over were limited to those committed בשגגה Lv $4^{2.22.27}$ Nu 15^{27}, לשגגה Nu 15^{24}, minor offences Lv 5^{1-6}; and ceremonial uncleanness Lv $12^{6.8}$ 14^{13} 15^{15} Nu $6^{11.14}$.) —Phrases for sacrificing are: עשה ח׳ Lv $9^{7.22}$

14[19] Nu 6[16] Ez 45[17], הקריב ח׳ Lv 10[19] Ez 44[27], שחט ח׳ Lv 14[13] Ez 40[39]. **5.** *purification* from sins of ceremonial uncleanness, all P: מֵי ח׳ Nu 8[7] *water of purification from sin;* מֵי נִדָּה ח׳ הוא *water of (cleansing from) impurity, it is a purification from sin* Nu 19[9]; עֲפַר שְׂרֵפַת הח׳ Nu 19[17] *ashes of the burning of the purification from sin* (RV renders *sin-offering;* but there was no offering made, only water of purification was used).

2404 †I. [חָטַב] **vb. cut or gather wood**, usu. *firewood* (NH *id.*; Ar. حَطَبٌ *firewood*, حَطَبَ *collect firewood* (v. Wetzst in De[ψ 144, 12]); Eth. ሐጠበ: *cut* (or gather) *firewood*)—**Qal** *Impf.* יַחְטְבוּ Ez 39[10]; *Inf.* לַחְטֹב Dt 19[5]; *Pt.* חֹטֵב Dt 29[10]; pl. חֹטְבִים 2 Ch 2[9]; cstr. חֹטְבֵי Jos 9[21] + 3 t.; pass. pl. f. חֲטֻבוֹת Pr 7[16]—*cut or gather* wood, sq. acc. Dt 19[5] 29[10] (|| שׁאב מים); cf. Ez 39[10] מן־היערים (obj. in preceding cl.); 2 Ch 2[9] (|| כֹּרְתֵי הָעֵצִים); *Pt.* cstr. ח׳ עצים Je 46[22], and (|| שֹׁאֲבֵי מָיִם) Jos 9[21.23.27]. **Pu.** *Pt.* מְחֻטָּבוֹת ψ 144[12] meaning dub.; perhaps *hewn* (so, in substance, Thes MV SS Ew Che Bae; v. however II. חטב), of corner-pillars (זָוִיּוֹת v. זָוִית p. 265 supr.), sim. of beautiful, stately daughters.

II. חטב (√of foll.; cf. Ar. حَطِبَ be of the colour حُطْبَةٌ, i.e. *turbid, dusky, mixed with yellowish red*, etc.; Aram. *Pt.* ܡܚܛܒܐ *variegated* 𝔖 2 S 13[19]).

2405 †חֲטֻבוֹת **n.f.pl. dark-hued stuffs**, only in חֲטֻבוֹת אֵטוּן מִצְרָיִם Pr 7[16] *dark-hued stuffs* (of) *yarn of Egypt* (|| מַרְבַדִּים), v. De Now; מְחֻטָּבוֹת ψ 144[12] der. fr. this √by De (q.v., and Wetzt.'s n.), but v. I. חטב.

2406 חִטָּה *wheat*, v. sub חנט. p. 334

חטט (√of foll.; cf. Ar. خَطَّ *make lines, marks*, خَطٌّ *line, streak, stripe*; Aram. חֲטַט, ܚܛ *dig*, ܚܛܘܛܐ *furrow, trench*).

2410 †חֲטִיטָא **n.pr.m.** head of a Levit. family, returned exiles Ezr 2[42] 𝔊 Ατητα, = Ne 7[45] 𝔊 Ατειτα; in both A Ατιτα, 𝔊L Αζιζα.

חטל (√of foll.; Ar. خَطِلَ = *be flabby* (of ear), *be tall, long, quivering, be light, quick*).

2411 †חֲטִיל **n.pr.m.** head of a family of 'the children of Sol.'s servants' Ezr 2[57] 𝔊 Αττεια, A Αττιλ = Ne 7[59] 𝔊 Εγηλ, A Εττηλ, 𝔊L Αττιλ in both.

†חָטַם **vb. hold in, restrain** (Ar. خَطَمَ 2413
strike the nose, attach the خِطَامٌ = *camel-halter*, خَطْمٌ n. *muzzle, nose of beast*; NH חֲטָם *nose-ring of camel*, חוֹטָם; Aram. חוּטְמָא *nose*; cf. חטם, Inscr. Zinj.; acc. to DHM[Sendsch. 34], of taming wild beasts)—**Qal** *Impf.* אֶחֱטָם־לָךְ לְבִלְתִּי הַכְרִיתֶךָ׃ Is 48[9] *I will restrain for thee* (mine anger), *not to cut thee off* (|| אַאֲרִיךְ אַפִּי).

†חָטַף **vb. catch, seize** (Ar. خَطِفَ; cf. 2414
As. *taḫtîpu, oppression*, Dl[Pr 181]; NH חָטַף, Aram. ܚܛܦ *seize*, חֲטַף *do hurriedly*)—**Qal** *Pf.* וַחֲטַפְתֶּם consec. Ju 21[21] lit., *seize* wives; *Impf.* יַחְטֹף עָנִי ψ 10[9]; *Inf.* לַחֲטוֹף עָנִי ψ 10[9] both fig. of oppressor *catching* the distressed; all sq. acc.

†חֲטִיפָא **n.pr.m.** head of a family of 2412
Nethinim, post-exil., Ezr 2[54] 𝔊 Ατουφα, A Ατιφα = Ne 7[56] 𝔊 Ατειφα; 𝔊L both Ατουφα.

חטר (√of foll.; cf. Ar. خَطَرَ *lash with the tail, move spear up and down, shake, quiver* (said of spear), etc.; Aram. ܚܘܛܪܐ, חוּטְרָא, As. *ḫutartu*, all = *staff*, Schr[COT Gloss] and on 2 K 9[2]; חטר *sceptre*, Inscr. Zinj. DHM[Sendsch. 57]; on format. v. Lag[BN 144]).

†חֹטֶר **n.m. branch** or **twig, rod**—metaph. 2415
abs. ח׳ *branch, twig*, Is 11[1] ויצא ח׳ מִגֵּזַע יִשָׁי (|| נֵצֶר); cstr. *rod*, בְּפִי־אֱוִיל חֹטֶר גַּאֲוָה Pr 14[3].

חַטָּת v. חַטָּאת sub חטא. p. 308 2403

חטשׁ (√of foll.; meaning unknown).

†חַטּוּשׁ **n.pr.m. 1.** man of Davidic line, 2407
post-exil., 1 Ch 3[22] 𝔊 Χαττους 𝔊L Ατους, Ezr 8[2] 𝔊 Τους, A𝔊L Αττους. **2.** a builder at the wall of Jerus. Ne 3[10], 𝔊 Ατουθ, 𝔊L Αττους. **3.** head of a priestly house, post-exil., Ne 10[5] 𝔊 Τους, 𝔊L Αττους, 12[2] 𝔊L Αττους (B om.); relation to **2** dubious.

חַי, חִיאֵל v. sub חיה infr. p. 27, 311, 313 2416, 2419

חִידָה v. sub חוד. p. 295 2420

חָיָה[283] **vb. live** (NH Ph. *id.*; Ar. حَيِيَ, حَيَّ; 2421,
Sab. חיו Mordt[ZMG 1876, 28]; Eth. ሐይወ: Aram. ܚܝܐ, 2425
חֲיָא; Palm. חיי *life, life-time*, Vog[32, 74])—**Qal**[203] *Pf.* חָיָה Ec 6[6] + 4 t.; וְחָיָה Je 21[9] 38[2]; חַי Gn 5[5] + 23 t. (this and the following form are treated as ע״ע, the original weakness of the stem final י admitting of either ל״ה or ע״ע, Ges[§76 (2) g]);

וְחַי Lv 25^{36} (Bö ^{§1181}); 3 fs. חָיְתָה Gn 12^{13} Je 38^{17}; וְחָיָת Ex 1^{16} (for חָיָה Bö $^{§1123(3)}$, Sam. חיתה); 2 ms. חָיִיתָ Dt 30^{16}, חָיִתָה Je 38^{17}; 3 m. pl. חָיוּ Nu 14^{38}, וְחָיוּ consec. Nu 4^{19} + Zc 10^{9} (where rd. Pi. וְחִיּוּ Sta $^{ZAW\ i.\ 1881,\ 22}$ so 𝔊), וִחְיִיתֶם Ez 37^{5} + 2 t.; *Impf.* יִחְיֶה Gn 17^{18} + 27 t.; יְחִי Dt 33^{6} + 10 t.; וִיחִי ψ 49^{10} + 2 t.; וַיֶּחִי Is 38^{21}, וַיְחִי Gn 5^{3} + 37 t.; וַיֶּחִי Dt 4^{33} + 4 t.; 3 fs. תִּחְיֶה Jos 6^{17}, תְּחִי Gn 19^{20} + 5 t.; 2 ms. תִּחְיֶה Gn 27^{40} + 7 t.; 2 fs. תִּחְיִי 2 K 4^{7}; 1 s. אֶחְיֶה 2 K 1^{2} + 8 t.; 3 mpl. יִחְיוּ Jos 9^{21} + 8 t.; 3 fpl. תִּחְיֶינָה Ez 13^{19} 37^{3}; 2 mpl. תִּחְיוּ Dt 4^{1} + 2 t.; תִּחְיוּן Dt 5^{30} 8^{1}; 1 pl. נִחְיֶה 2 K 7^{4} + 7 t.; *Imv.* וֶחְיֵה Gn 20^{7} Pr 4^{4}, וֶחְיֵה Pr 7^{2}; fs. חֲיִי Ez $16^{6.6}$; mpl. וִחְיוּ Gn 42^{18} + 7 t.; *Inf. abs.* חָיֹה 2 K 8^{10} + 6 t.; חָיוֹ Ez 3^{21} + 3 t.; *cstr.* לִחְיוֹת Ez 33^{12}, sf. חֲיוֹתָם Jos 5^{8};—**1.** *live:* **a.** *have life,* Gn 31^{32} (E), Ex 33^{20} (J), Nu 4^{19} (P), Dt 30^{16} +; also in phrase וַיְחִי *and he lived* (so many years) with acc. of time, Gn 5^{3-30} (16 t.) 9^{28} 11^{11-26} (14 t.) 47^{28} (all P), 50^{22} (E), 2 K 14^{17} = 2 Ch 25^{25} Jb 42^{16}. **b.** *continue in life, remain alive* Gn 20^{7} (E), Lv 25^{36} 2 S 12^{22} +; also † ח׳ נפשׁ *live, of the soul* or *the self* Gn 12^{13} 19^{20} (J), 1 K 20^{32} ψ 119^{175} Je $38^{2.17.20}$ Is 55^{3}; וְחַי הַיָּלֶד *and the boy may live* 2 S 12^{22}; † ח׳ לִפְנֵי *live in the presence of* Gn 17^{18} (P) Ho 6^{2}; † ח׳ ב׳ *live among* La 4^{20}. † **c.** *sustain life, live on* or *upon* (על), of the animal life, by the sword Gn 27^{40} (J), by bread Dt 8^{3}; elsewh. in pregnant sense of fulness of life in divine favour, sustained by (על) everything that issueth out of the mouth of י׳ Dt 8^{3}; his promises (?) Is 38^{16}; of wicked man, by repentance Ez 33^{19}; c. בְּ by the statutes and judgments of י׳ if a man do them, Lv 18^{5} (H) Ez $20^{11.13.21.25}$ Ne 9^{29}; צַדִּיק בֶּאֱמוּנָתוֹ יִחְיֶה *a righteous man by his faithfulness shall live* Hb 2^{4}. † **d.** *live* (prosperously) יְחִי הַמֶּלֶךְ *may the king live* 1 S 10^{24} 2 S $16^{16.16}$ 1 K $1^{25.31.34.39}$ 2 K 11^{12} 2 Ch 23^{11}; יְחִי לְבַבְכֶם ψ 22^{27} 69^{33}; המלך לעולם יחיה Ne 2^{3}. † **2.** *be quickened, revive:* **a.** *from sickness* Nu $21^{8.9}$ Jos 5^{8} (E) 2 K 1^{2} $8^{8.9.10.14}$; 2 K $20^{1.7}$ = Is $38^{1.9.21}$. **b.** *fr. discouragement* of the spirit Gn 45^{27} (E). **c.** *fr. faintness* Ju 15^{19}. **d.** *fr. death* 2 K 13^{21} Jb 14^{14} Is $26^{14.19}$; by return of נפשׁ 1 K 17^{22}, of רוּחַ Ez $37^{3.5.6.9.10.14}$ (and so Ju 15^{19} **c**). † **Pi.** *Pf.* 3 ms. חִיָּה ψ 22^{30}; 3 fs. sf. חִיָּתְנִי ψ 119^{50}; 2 ms. sf. חִיִּתַנִי ψ 30^{4}; חִיִּיתַנִי ψ 119^{93}; 3 pl. חִיּוּ Ju 21^{14}, הַחִיִּיתֶם Nu 31^{15}; *Impf.* יְחַיֶּה 1 S 27^{9} +, etc.; *Imv.* sf. חַיֵּנִי ψ 119^{25} + 8 t., חַיֵּיהוּ Hb 3^{2}; *Inf. cstr.* חַיּוֹת Gn 7^{3} Ez 13^{19}; sf. חַיֹּתֵנוּ Dt 6^{24} +, etc.; *Pt.* מְחַיֶּה Ne 9^{6} 1 S 2^{6};—**1.** *preserve alive, let live* Ex $1^{17.18.22}$ 22^{17} Jos 9^{15} (JE), Gn 12^{12} (J), Nu 31^{15} (P), Dt 6^{24} 20^{16} Ju 21^{14} 1 S $27^{9.11}$ 1 K 18^{5} 2 K 7^{4} Je 49^{11} Ez 3^{18} Hb 3^{2} Jb 36^{6} ψ 30^{4} 33^{19} 41^{3} 138^{7}; ח׳ נפשׁ *preserve oneself alive* ψ 22^{30} Ez 18^{27}, or *preserve persons alive* Ez $13^{18.19}$, or *preserve life* 1 K 20^{31}; ח׳ זרע *preserve seed alive* Gn 7^{3} $19^{32.34}$ (J); *keep in existence* heaven and earth Ne 9^{6}; *nourish,* young cow Is 7^{21}, lamb 2 S 12^{3}. **2.** *give life,* to man when created Jb 33^{4}. **3.** *quicken, revive, refresh:* **a.** *restore to life,* the dead 1 S 2^{6} Dt 32^{39} Ho 6^{2}; the dying ψ 71^{20}. **b.** *cause to grow,* grain Ho 14^{8}. **c.** *restore,* a ruined city 1 Ch 11^{8}, stones destroyed by fire Ne 3^{34}. **d.** *revive,* the people of י׳ by י׳ himself with fulness of life in his favour ψ 80^{19} 85^{7} $119^{25.37.40.50.88.93.107.149.154.156.159}$ 143^{11} Ec 7^{12}. † **Hiph.** *Pf.* הֶחֱיָה Jos 6^{25} + 5 t.; 2 ms. sf. הֶחֱיִתָנוּ Gn 47^{25}; 1 s. הֶחֱיֵיתִי Nu 22^{33}, הַחֲיִתֶם Jos 2^{13} Ju 8^{19}; *Imv.* sf. הַחֲיֵינִי Is 38^{16}; הַחֲיוּ Nu 31^{18}; *Inf. abs.* הַחֲיָה Jos 9^{20}; *cstr.* הַחֲיוֹת Gn 6^{20} + 6 t.; הַחֲיֹת Gn 6^{19} 50^{20}; sf. הַחֲיֹתוֹ Ez 13^{22};—**1.** *preserve alive, let live* Gn 45^{7} 50^{20} (E), 47^{25} Nu 22^{33} Jos 2^{13} 6^{25} (all J), 14^{10} (D); Gn $6^{19.20}$ Nu 31^{18} Jos 9^{20} (P), Ju 8^{19} 2 S 8^{2} Ez 13^{22}; with נפשׁ Gn 19^{19} (J). **2.** *quicken, revive:* **a.** *restore* to health, a leper 2 K 5^{7}, Hezekiah Is 38^{16}. **b.** *revive* the לֵב and רוּחַ Is $57^{15.15}$. **c.** *restore to life,* the dead 2 K $8^{1.5.5.5}$.

† I. חַי **adj. alive, living;**—ח׳ Gn 25^{6} +; חָי 2416
Gn 3^{20} +, חֵי Am 8^{14} + 15 t. (Ew ^{§329} explains as cstr., but Ges $^{§93,\ R\ 7\ n}$ al. as contracted abs.); f. חַיָּה Gn 1^{20} +; pl. חַיִּים ψ 116^{9} +;—**1. a.** *of God,* as the *living one,* the fountain of life אֵל חַי Jos 3^{10} (J), Ho 2^{1} ψ 42^{3} 84^{3}; אלהים חי 2 K $19^{4.16}$ = Is $37^{4.17}$; אלהים חיים Dt 5^{23} 1 S $17^{26.36}$ Je 10^{10} 23^{36}; חי יהוה *Yahweh is living* ψ 18^{47} = 2 S 22^{47}; גאלי חי *my avenger is living* Jb 19^{25}; the formula of the oath is חַי י׳ Ju 8^{19} Ru 3^{13} 1 S $14^{39.45}$ 19^{6} 20^{21} 25^{34} $26^{10.16}$ 28^{10} 29^{6} 2 S 4^{9} 12^{5} 14^{11} 15^{21} 1 K 1^{29} 2^{24} $17^{1.12}$ 18^{10} 22^{14} = 2 Ch 18^{13}, 2 K $5^{16.20}$ Ho 4^{15} Je 4^{2} 5^{2} 12^{16} $16^{14.15}$ $23^{7.8}$ 38^{16}; חי אל Jb 27^{2}; חי האלהים 2 S 2^{27}; חי אדני י׳ Je 44^{26}; חי י׳ צבאות 1 K 18^{15} 2 K 3^{14}; as used by God Himself it is חי אנכי Dt 32^{40}, elsewhere חי אני Nu $14^{21.28}$ (P) Is 49^{18} Je 22^{24} 46^{18} Ez 5^{11} $14^{16.18.20}$ 16^{48} $17^{16.19}$ 18^{3} $20^{3.31.33}$ $33^{11.27}$ 34^{8} $35^{6.11}$ Zp 2^{9}, cf. also חֵי דרך באר שבע, חֵי אלהיך דן Am 8^{14}; with the exception of בְּחֵי הָעוֹלָם *by him who liveth for ever* Dn 12^{7}, חֵי is always (as an artificial distinction of scribes) used of non-sacred oaths, v. **b.** **b.** *of*

man: אָדָם חַי *a living man* La 3^{39}, in antith. מֵת: חי חי Is 38^{19}; הַחַי collective Ec 7^{2}; Absalom 2 S 19^{7}; Naboth 1 K 21^{15}; a son or lad 2 S 12^{21} 1 K $3^{22.22.23.23.25.26.26.27}$ 17^{23}; usually pl. חיים *alive, living* Nu $16^{30.33}$ (J), 17^{13} (P), Dt 4^{4} 5^{3} Is 8^{19} ψ 55^{16} 124^{3} Pr 1^{12} Ec $4^{2.2.15}$ 6^{8} $9^{4.5}$ Ru 2^{20}; taking prisoners *alive* Jos 8^{23} (J) 1 S 15^{8} 1 K $20^{18.18}$ 2 K 7^{12} $10^{14.14}$ 2 Ch 25^{12}; *living* (prosperously) 1 S 25^{6} (We rds. לְאָחִי=לָחִי (v. Klo Dr) *to my brother*, after 𝔙 *fratribus meis*); elsewh. in phrase כל־הימים אשר הֵם (אַתֶּם) חיים על (פני) האדמה *all the days that they (ye) live upon (the face of) the land* Dt 4^{10} 12^{1} 31^{13} 1 K 8^{40} = 2 Ch 6^{31}. Note phrases: עוֹד חַי (ים) *yet alive* Gn 25^{6} $43^{7.27.28}$ 45^{28} 46^{30} (J), $45^{3.26}$ Ex 4^{18} (E), Dt 31^{27} 1 S 20^{14} 2 S 12^{22} 18^{14} 1 K 20^{32}; בהיות חי 2 S 12^{18} 1 K 12^{6} 2 Ch 10^{6}; אֶרֶץ (ה)חַיִּים *land of the living* Is 38^{11} 53^{8} Je 11^{19} Ez 26^{20} $32^{23.24.25.26.27.32}$ ψ 27^{13} 52^{7} 142^{6} Jb 28^{13}; ארצות הח׳ ψ 116^{9}; ספר ח׳ ψ 69^{29}; צרור הח׳ *bundle of the living* 1 S 25^{29}; אור הח׳ *light of the living* Jb 33^{30} ψ 56^{14}. In the oath by life of men חי is pointed always חֵי: חֵי אדני המלך *as my lord the king liveth* 2 S 15^{21}; חֵי פרעה Gn $42^{15.16}$ (E); חֵי נַפְשְׁךָ 1 S 1^{26} 17^{55} 2 S 14^{19}; חַי י׳ וְחֵי נַפְשְׁךָ *as Yahweh liveth and as thy soul* (or thyself) *liveth* 1 S 20^{3} 25^{26} 2 K $2^{2.4.6}$ 4^{30} חַיֶּךָ וְחֵי נ׳ 2 S 11^{11} (but on txt. v. We Dr). **c.** of animals, *alive, living:* ox Ex 21^{35} 22^{3} (E); goat Lv $16^{10.20.21}$ (P); bird Lv $14^{4.6.6.7.51.53}$; dog, לְכֶלֶב חַי הוּא טוֹב מִן־הָאַרְיֵה הַמֵּת Ec 9^{4} (comp. Ar. prov. *Kelb ḥei wa-lâ meijit, a living dog and no dead lion* Wetzst Verhand. Berl. Anthrop. Ges. 1878, 388); reptiles Gn 1^{28} (P); animals in general Gn 9^{3} (P); בשׂר חי *living, raw flesh* Lv $13^{10.14.15.15.16}$ (P) 1 S 2^{15}. **d.** *animals* and *man*, phrases for either or both: כל חי Gn 3^{20} 8^{21} (J) Jb 12^{10} 28^{21} 30^{23} ψ 143^{2} 145^{16}; כל החי Gn 6^{19} (P); נֶפֶשׁ חַיָּה Gn $1^{20.24.30}$ (P) $2^{7.19}$ (J); כל נֶפֶשׁ חַיָּה Gn $9^{12.15.16}$ (P) Ez 47^{9}; כל נפשׁ החיה Gn 1^{21} 9^{10} Lv $11^{10.46}$ (P). **e.** (dub.) of vegetation, as thorns, *green*, ψ 58^{10} (Ges Ew Ol Pe, but De Ri Che Bae *raw flesh*, v. **c** supr. ad fin.) **f.** of water, *flowing, fresh* מים חיים Gn 26^{19} (J), Lv $14^{5.6.50.51.52}$ 15^{13} Nu 19^{17} (P), Je 2^{13} 17^{13} Zc 14^{8} Ct 4^{15}. **2.** (dub.) *lively, active:* אִישׁ חַי *an active man* 2 S 23^{20} (but Qr אִישׁ חַיִל is to be preferred); איבי חיים mine enemies *are lively* ψ 38^{20} (RV, but Houb Ol Ew Hu Che al. rd. חִנָּם, ‖ שׁקר). **3.** *reviving:* כָּעֵת חַיָּה *at the time* (when it is) *reviving*, the spring Gn $18^{10.14}$ (J), 2 K $4^{16.17}$.

† II. [חַי] **n.[m.] kinsfolk** (Ar. حَيّ a group 2416
of families united by vital ties RS K 36-40 Dr Sm 119), pl. sf. חַיַּי 1 S 18^{18}, incorrectly pointed with the interpretation *my life* RV, but rd. חַיַּי *my kinsfolk*, We Ki Dr RS SS RVm VB. It is explained by the gloss משפחת אבי We (Klo rds. אַחַי ו).

† I. חַיָּה **n.f. living thing, animal** (Zinj. 2416
wild beast DHM Sendsch. 34)—ח׳ Gn 8^{17}+; cstr. חַיַּת Is 57^{10}+; old case ending (poetic) חַיְתוֹ Gn 1^{24} ψ 50^{10} 79^{2} $104^{11.20}$ Is $56^{9.9}$ Zp 2^{14}; sf. חַיָּתִי ψ 143^{3}, etc.; pl. חַיּוֹת Lv 14^{4} + 12 t.—**1.** *animal*, as a living, active being: **a.** *in general*, Gn 8^{17} Lv $11^{2.27.47.47}$ Nu 35^{3} (P) ψ 104^{25} Is 46^{1} Dn 8^{4}. **b.** *wild animals*, on account of their vital energy and activity Gn $7^{14.21}$ $8^{1.19}$ 9^{5} (P) Lv 17^{13} 25^{7} (H) Jb 37^{8} ψ 148^{10} Is 40^{16} Ez 14^{15} 33^{27} Zp $2^{14.15}$; ח׳ קנה ψ 68^{31} *wild animal of the reeds*; ח׳ רעה *evil beast* Gn $37^{20.33}$ (JE) Lv 26^{6} (H) Ez 5^{17} $14^{15.21}$ 34^{25}; ח׳ טמאה Lv 5^{2} (P) *unclean beast;* ח׳ הארץ Gn $1^{25.30}$ $9^{2.10.10}$ (P) 1 S 17^{46} Ez 29^{5} 32^{4} 34^{28} Jb 5^{22}; חיתו ארץ Gn 1^{24} (P) ψ 79^{2}; ח׳ השׂדה Ex $23^{11.29}$ (covt. code) Lv 26^{22} (H) Dt 7^{22} 2 S 21^{10}, 2 K 14^{9} = 2 Ch 25^{18}, Ho $2^{14.20}$ 4^{3} 13^{8} Is 43^{20} Je 27^{6} 28^{14} Ez 38^{20} 39^{4} Jb 5^{23} 39^{15}; כל ח׳ השׂדה Gn $2^{19.20}$ $3^{1.14}$ (J) Jb 40^{20} Je 12^{9} Ez $31^{6.13}$ $34^{5.8}$ 39^{17}; חיתו שׂדי Is 56^{9} ψ 104^{11}; חיתו (ב)יער Is 56^{9} ψ 50^{10} 104^{20}; פְּרִיץ חיות Is 35^{9} *destroyer among beasts*. **c.** *living beings*, of the cherubic chariot Ez $1^{5.13.13.14.15.15.19.19.20.21.22}$ 3^{13} $10^{15.17.20}$. **2.** *life*, only in late poetry, ψ 143^{3} Jb $33^{18.20.22.28}$ 36^{14} Ez $7^{13.13}$, and (dub.) ψ 74^{19} 78^{50}. **3.** *appetite*, activity of hunger: חית כפרים *appetite of young lions* Jb 38^{39}. **4.** *revival, renewal:* חַיַּת יָדֵךְ מָצָאתְ *thou didst find renewal of thy strength* (re-invigoration) Is 57^{10}; v. חָיָה **2.**

† II. חַיָּה **n.f.** (si vera l.) **community** (=fem. 2416
of II. חַי acc. to Nö ZMG, 1886, 176)—וְחַיַּת פְּלִשְׁתִּים חֹנָה *and a community of Philistines* (i.e. a group of allied families, making a raid together) *was encamping* 2 S 23^{13} (= מַחֲנֵה 1 Ch 11^{15}); perh. also ψ 68^{11} (cf. infr.)

Note.—Several other passages are dub.: וַיֵּאָסְפוּ פְלִשְׁתִּים לַחַיָּה 2 S 23^{11} *assembled into a troop*, or *by bands* (RV, but neither rend. justif.: Bö Ew We Klo Dr rightly rd. לֶחְיָה to *Lehi*, cf. Ju 15^{9}; wd. om. by accident in ‖ 1 Ch 11^{13} Dr); חַיָּתְךָ יָשְׁבוּ־בָהּ ψ 68^{11} *thy troop dwelt in it* (Thes SS RVm Hi Ri Che, but 𝔊 𝔖 Jer Pe *thy* (*living*) *creatures*, of the people; Hup *id.*, ref. to quails; improb.); אַל־תִּתֵּן לְחַיַּת נֶפֶשׁ תּוֹרֶךָ חַיַּת עֲנִיֶּיךָ אַל־תִּשְׁכַּח לָנֶצַח ψ 74^{19} *give not the soul of thy turtle-dove to the wild beasts, the life of thine afflicted do not forget for ever:* RV Hi Pe Bae Sch render thus, giving חית diff. meanings in the two clauses, the former being archaic fem. abs. Ges$^{§ 80, 2. R. 2}$; text doubtless corrupt, rd. poss. למות Schr Ri, for לחית, or לשחת Kroch; Gr either of these; Che either, or better לחרב.

2422 †[חָיֶה] **adj. having the vigour of life, lively** (on format. v. Lag$^{BN 49}$)—fpl. חָיוֹת Ex 1^{19}(E), of Hebrew women in childbirth, bearing quickly, easily.

2416 †חַיִּים **n.m.** $^{Dt 28, 66}$ **pl. abstr. emph. life**, ח׳ Gn 2^{7}+; חַיִּין Jb 24^{22} (Aramaism Ges$^{§ 87 (1) a}$); חַיֵּי Gn 23^{1}+; sf. חַיַּי Gn 47^{9}+; חַיָּיְכִי ψ 103^{4}; (Ges$^{§ 91 (2) R. 2}$), etc.;—**1.** *life:* physical Gn 27^{46} Ex 1^{14} (P), Dt 28$^{66.66}$ 2 S 11^{11} 15^{21} Is 38^{12} Je 8^{23} La 3$^{53.58}$ Ez 7^{13} Jb 3^{20} 7^{7} 9^{21} 10^{12} 24^{22} ψ 7^{6} 17^{14} 21^{5} 26^{9} 31^{11} 34^{13} 63^{4} 64^{2} 66^{9} 88^{4} 103^{4} Pr 18^{21} Ec 2^{17} 6^{12} 7^{13} 9$^{9.9}$ 10^{19} Jon 2^{7} 4$^{3.8}$; חַיֵּי שׂרה *life of Sarah* Gn 23^{1} (P); שְׁנֵי ח׳ *years of the life of* 2 S 19^{35} Gn 23^{1} 25$^{7.17}$ 47$^{8.9.9.28}$ Ex 6$^{16.18.20}$ (P); שְׁנָה לח׳ Gn 7^{11} (P); שְׁנוֹת חַיִּים Pr 3^{2} 4^{10} 9^{11}; יְמֵי ח׳ *days of the life of* Ec 2^{3} 5$^{17.19}$ 6^{12} 8^{15} 9^{9}; כֹּל יְמֵי ח׳ Gn 3$^{14.17}$(J) Dt 4^{9} 6^{2} 16^{3} 17^{19} Jos 1^{5} 4^{14}(D) 1 S 1^{11} 7^{15} 1 K 5^{1} 11^{34} 15$^{5.6}$, 2 K 25$^{29.30}$=Je 52$^{33.34}$, Is 38^{20} (poem of Hez.) ψ 23^{6} 27^{4} 128^{5} Pr 31^{12}; בח׳ *in* or *during one's life* Gn 27^{46}(P) Lv 18^{18}(H) Ju 16^{30} 2 S 1^{23} 18^{18} ψ 49^{19} 63^{5} 104^{33} 146^{2} Jb 10^{1} Ec 3^{12} 9^{3}; רוּחַ ח׳ Gn 6^{17} 7^{15} (P); ח׳ רוּחִי Is 38^{16} (poem of Hez.); ח׳ בשׂרים Pr 14^{30}; נִשְׁמַת (רוּחַ) ח׳ Gn 2^{7} 7^{22}(J). **2.** *life:* as welfare and happiness in king's presence Pr 16^{15}; as consisting of earthly felicity combined (often) with spiritual blessedness Dt 30$^{6.15.19.19.20}$ 32^{47} ψ 30^{6} 133^{3} Pr 3^{22} 4$^{13.22}$ 8^{35} 10^{16} 11^{19} 12^{28} 19^{23} 21^{21} 22^{4} Mal 2^{5}; used only once distinctly of eternal life (late) ח׳ עולם Dn 12^{2}; אֵל חַיַּי ψ 42^{9} *God of my life;* מעוז ח׳ ψ 27^{1}; מקור ח׳ ψ 36^{10} Pr 10^{11} 13^{14} 14^{27} 16^{22}; עֵץ (ה)חַיִּים Gn 2^{9} 3$^{22.24}$ (J) Pr 3^{18} 11^{30} 13^{12} 15^{4}; ארח ח׳ ψ 16^{11} Pr 5^{6} 15^{24}; ארח לח׳ Pr 10^{17}; ארחות ח׳ Pr 2^{19}; דֶּרֶךְ (ה)חַיִּים Pr 6^{23} Je 21^{8}; חקות ח׳ Ez 33^{15}; תוצאות ח׳ Pr 4^{23} *sources* (origin and direction) *of life;* תוכחת ח׳ Pr 15^{31}; כָּתוּב לַחַיִּים Is 4^{3} *written unto life.* **3.** *sustenance, maintenance:* חַיִּים לְנַעֲרוֹתֶיךָ Pr 27^{27} *maintenance for thy maidens*, v. מִחְיָה infr.

†חַיּוּת **n.f. abstr.** אַלְמְנוּת חַיּוּת 2 S 20^{3}, lit. 2424
'widowhood of livingness,' Dr; We rds. אַלְמָנוֹת חַיּוֹת *living widows* ('grass-widows,' who were separated from their husbands), after 𝔊 χῆραι ζῶσαι, so SS.

†מִחְיָה **n.f. preservation of life, susten-** 4241
ance, מ׳ Gn 45^{5}+4 t.; cstr. מִחְיַת Lv 13$^{10.24}$; sf. מִחְיָתֶךָ Ju 17^{10};—**1.** *preservation of life* Gn 45^{5} (E), 2 Ch 14^{12}. **2.** *sustenance* Ju 6^{4} 17^{10}. **3.** *reviving*, Ezr 9$^{8.9}$. **4.** *the quick* (בָּשָׂר) מִחְיַת *the quick* (or raw spot) *of the flesh* Lv 13$^{10.24}$ (P).

†חִיאֵל **n.pr.m.** (*Ēl lives* (or abbrev. for 2419
יחיאל); Sab. חיאל, name of coin, after n.pr. of king DHM$^{ZMG 1875, 613, 1883, 15}$; cp. also foll., and Ph. (כמשיחי, מריחי)—name of the rebuilder of Jericho 1 K 16^{34}; 𝔊 Αχ(ε)ιηλ, om. 𝔊L. p. 27

†יְחִיאֵל **n.pr.m.** (*may Ēl live;* Ph. יחואלן, 3171
יחומלך v. Eut$^{ZMG 1876, 136}$)—𝔊 usu. Ιειηλ, Ιαιηλ;—**1.** one of David's chief musicians 1 Ch 15^{18} (𝔊 Ιειηλ, 𝔊L Ιαιηλ), v^{20} (𝔊 Ειθηλ, 𝔊L Ιειηλ), 16^{5} (𝔊 Ειειηλ, 𝔊L Ιαιηλ). **2.** one of David's chiefs of the Levites 1 Ch 23^{8} (𝔊 Ι(ει)ηλ), 29^{8} (𝔊 Βεσιηλ, A 𝔊L Ιειηλ). **3.** tutor of David's sons 1 Ch 27^{32} (𝔊 Ιε(ρι)ηλ, 𝔊L Ιωηλ). **4.** son of Jehoshaphat 2 Ch 21^{2}. **5.** יְחוּאֵל Hemanite of Hezekiah's reign 2 Ch 29^{14}. **6.** overseer in Hezekiah's reign 2 Ch 31^{13}. **7.** ruler of the temple in Josiah's reign 2 Ch 35^{8}. **8.** contemporaries of Ezra, Ezr 8^{9} (𝔊 Ιεμα, A Ιεειηλ, 𝔊L Ιειηλ), 10$^{2.21.6}$.

†יְחִיאֵלִי **n.pr.m.** (patronym.), 1 Ch 26$^{21.22}$ 3172
(𝔊 Ιειηλ; 𝔊L om. in v^{22}).

†יְחִיָּה **n.pr.m.** (*may Yah live*) keeper of 3174
the ark 1 Ch 15^{24} (𝔊 Ιε(α)ια, 𝔊L Ιειηλ).

חִיל v. I. II. חול supr. p. 296, 298 2342

חֵילָן, חֵילָם, חִילָה, חִיל, חֵיל, חֲיִל 2426, 2428
v. sub I. II. חול supr. p. 297f 2427, 2431

חִין v. sub חנן. p. 336 2433

חִיצוֹן, חַיִץ v. sub I. II. חוץ. p. 300 2434-35

חֵיק v. sub חוק. p. 300 2436

חִירָה v. sub I. חור. p. 301 2437

חִירָם, חִירוֹם v. sub אח, אחה supr. p. 27^{b}. 2438

חֵךְ v. sub חנך. p. 335 2441

2442 †[חָכָה] **vb. wait, await**—**Qal** *Pt.* pl. cstr. חוֹכֵי Is 30^{18}, with לְ *waiting for him* (ל׳). **Pi.** חִכָּה Jb 32^{4}; חִכְּתָה ψ 33^{20}; חִכִּיתִי Is 8^{17}; חִכּוּ ψ 106^{13}; חִכִּינוּ 2 K 7^{9}; *Impf.* יְחַכֶּה Is 30^{18}; תְּחַכֶּה 2 K 9^{3}; *Imv.* חַכֵּה־ Hb 2^{3}; חַכּוּ Zp 3^{8}; *Inf. cstr.* כְּחַכֵּי Ho 6^{9} (Ephraimit. for חַכֵּה ?); *Pt.* מְחַכֶּה Dn 12^{12}; cstr. מְחַכֵּה Is 64^{3}; pl. מְחַכִּים Jb 3^{21};—**1.** *wait, tarry*, abs. 2 K 9^{3} *tarry not;* with עַד till morning light 2 K 7^{9}; c. acc. את איוב בדברים Jb 32^{4} *tarry for Job with words.* **2.** *wait* (in ambush), כְּחַכֵּי אִישׁ גְּדוּדִים Ho 6^{9} *as marauding bands wait for a man* AV RV De, or *as marauders lie in wait* Hi Ew (taking איש as cstr.) **3.** *wait for, long for*, with לְ for י׳ Is 8^{17} 64^{3} Zp 3^{8} ψ 33^{20}; for his counsel ψ 106^{13}; for his vision Hb 2^{3}; for death Jb 3^{21}; יחכה יהוה לחננכם *Yahweh waiteth to be gracious unto you* Is 30^{18} (Di regards this as threatening and refers it to **1**); abs. *waiteth* (and cometh to the days of blessedness) Dn 12^{12}.

2443 חַכָּה v. sub חנך. p. 335

חכל (√of foll.; cf. Ar. حَكَلَ iv. *be confused, vague;* حُكْلَةٌ *barbarousness,* or *impediment in speech;* As. *akâlu, be gloomy, êklu, dark, eklitu, darkness,* Dl in Zim[BP 115, W. 385 ff.], cf. Jäger[BAS ii, 282]).

2444 †חֲכִילָה **n.pr.loc.** (*dark*) a hill in southern Judah, on edge of wilderness of Ziph 1 S 23^{19} $26^{1.3}$ (Glaser[Skizze ii, 326] rds. also for חוילה, q.v., in 1 S 15^{7}); 𝔊 Εχελα (26^{1} B Χελμαθ, A Αχιλα).

2447 †חַכְלִילִי **adj. (dark) dull,** from wine, ח׳ עינים מִיָּיִן Gn 49^{12}.

2448 †חַכְלִלוּת **n.f. dulness,** of eyes in drunkenness, לְמִי חַכ׳ עֵינָיִם׃ Pr 23^{29} (v^{30} לַמְאַחֲרִים עַל־הַיָּיִן).

2446 †חֲכַלְיָה **n.pr.m.** (mng. dub.; perhaps חַכֵּה לְיָהּ *wait for Yahweh,* √חכה, so We ?)—father of Nehemiah Ne 1^{1}, 𝔊 Χελκ(ε)ια, 𝔊L Χελκιας(ου), א A Αχαλια; 10^{2} 𝔊 Αχελια, A 𝔊L Αχαλια.

2449 †חָכַם **vb. be wise** (NH *id.;* Aram. ܚܟܡ, חֲכַם *id.;* Zinj. חכמה *wisdom,* DHM[Sendsch. 57]; As. *ḫakâmu, know* (with exceptional ח v. Dl[Pr 178 f.]); Ar. حَكَمَ *restrain from acting in an evil manner, judge, govern;* iv. *make firm, sound, free from defect* by the exercise of skill)—**Qal** *Pf.* ח׳ Pr 23^{15}; 3 fs. חָכְמָה Zc 9^{2}; חָכַמְתָּ Pr $9^{12.12}$, etc. + 3 t. Pf.; *Impf.* יֶחְכַּם Pr 9^{9} 21^{11}; וַיֶּחְכַּם 1 K 5^{11}; יֶחְכָּם Pr 20^{1} +; וֶחְכָּם Pr 13^{20}; תֶּחְכַּם Pr 19^{20}; אֶחְכָּמָה Ec 7^{23}; pl. יֶחְכָּמוּ Jb 32^{9}; *Imv.* חֲכַם Pr 27^{11}; חֲכָם Pr 6^{6} 23^{19} + 13^{20} Kt; חֲכָמוּ Pr 8^{33};—*be* or *become wise, act wisely* Dt 32^{29} (poet.) 1 K 5^{11} Jb 32^{9} Pr 6^{6} 8^{33} $9^{9.12.12}$ 13^{20} 19^{20} 20^{1} 21^{11} 23^{19} 27^{11} Ec 2^{15} 7^{23} Zc 9^{2}; אם חכם לבך *if thy mind be wise* Pr 23^{15}; c. acc. שחכמתי Ec 2^{19} *wherein I have acted wisely.* **Pi.** *Impf.* יְחַכֵּם ψ 105^{22}; sf. יְחַכְּמֵנוּ Jb 35^{11}; תְּחַכְּמֵנִי ψ 119^{98}; all *make wise, teach wisdom,* c. acc. **Pu.** *Pt. made wise,* intensive, as it were the embodiment of wisdom חוֹבֵר חֲבָרִים מְחֻכָּם ψ 58^{6}, pl. הֵמָּה חֲכָמִים מְחֻכָּמִים Pr 30^{24} (of intelligent animals). **Hiph.** *Pt.* cstr. מַחְכִּימַת פֶּתִי ψ 19^{8} *making wise the simple.* **Hithp.** *Impf.* נִתְחַכְּמָה לוֹ Ex 1^{10} (E) *let us deal wisely* (*shrewdly*) *toward it* (the people); 2 ms. תִּתְחַכַּם Ec 7^{16} *make or shew thyself wise.*

†חָכָם **adj. wise,** ח׳ Dt 4^{6} + 67 t.; cstr. 2450
חֲכַם Is 3^{3} + 9 t.; pl. חֲכָמִים Dt 1^{13} + 39 t.; cstr. חַכְמֵי Ex 28^{3} + 4 t.; sf. חֲכָמֶיךָ Is 19^{12} etc. + 8 t.; f. חֲכָמָה 2 S 14^{2} 20^{16}; cstr. חַכְמַת Ex 35^{25}; pl. חֲכָמוֹת Je 9^{16}; cstr. חַכְמוֹת Ju 5^{29} Pr 14^{1} (but rd. חָכְמוֹת De);—**1.** *skilful* in technical work; artificers Is 3^{3}; sailors Ez 27^{8}, so (prob.) v^{9}; mourning women Je 9^{16}; artisans of tabern. and temple and their furniture Ex 28^{3} 31^{6} 35^{10} $36^{1.2.4.8}$ (P), 1 Ch 22^{15} 2 Ch $2^{6.12.13.13}$; women in spinning Ex 35^{25} (P); goldsmiths and other artisans Je 10^{9}; makers of idol-images Is 40^{20}. **2.** *wise in the administration of affairs:* Joseph in Egypt Gn $41^{33.39}$ (E); heads of tribes Dt $1^{13.15}$, judges 16^{19}; of David 2 S 14^{20}, of Solomon 1 K 2^{9} 3^{12} 5^{21} = 2 Ch 2^{11}; the prince of Tyre, in satire Ez 28^{3}; of kings in general Pr 20^{26}; class of political advisers of Judah Is 29^{14} Je 18^{18}, appar. also Is 5^{21}; of Egypt Is $19^{11.11.12}$, Edom Ob^{8}, the nations Je 10^{7}; so of God Is 31^{2}. **3.** *shrewd, crafty, cunning:* Jonadab 2 S 13^{3}; the princesses Ju 5^{29}; אשה חכמה *wise woman* 2 S 14^{2} 20^{16}; gen., Je 9^{22}; intelligent animals Pr 30^{24}; לכד ח׳ בערמם *taking the cunning in their craft* Jb 5^{13}; חכם בעיני *wise in one's own eyes* Pr 3^{7} $26^{5.12.16}$ 28^{11}; חכמי לב *wise of mind* (in their own mind) Jb 37^{24}. **4.** pl. class of *learned* and *shrewd* men, incl. astrologers, magicians and the like, of Egypt Gn 41^{8} (E), Ex 7^{11} (P; cf. Is $19^{11.11.12}$); Babylon Is 44^{25} Je 50^{35} 51^{57}; Persia Est 1^{13} 6^{13}. **5.** *prudent,* towards king Pr 16^{14}; in controversies Pr 11^{29} $29^{8.9.11}$; religious affairs Ho 13^{13} 14^{10} Je 4^{22} $8^{8.9}$ Dt 4^{6} 32^{6} ψ 107^{43}; איש ח׳ Je 9^{11}. **6.** *wise,* ethically and religiously, in WisdLt: **a.** as adj., חֲכַם לֵב *wise of mind* Pr

10[8] 16[21]; לב חָכָם Ec 8[5]; of the son Pr 10[1]=15[20], 13[1] 23[24] Ec 2[19]; ילד ח׳ Ec 4[13] *wise boy;* גבר ח׳ Jb 34[34] *wise man;* מוכיח ח׳ *wise reprover* Pr 25[12]. **b.** = subst.: (1) as a *wise learner* in school of wisdom, he fears God and departs from evil Pr 14[16]; is silent Pr 17[28]; hearkens to counsel Pr 12[15]; hears and increases in learning Pr 1[5]; his ear seeketh knowledge Pr 18[15]; he receives it Pr 21[11]; and stores it up Pr 10[14]; his ears hearken to the reproof which giveth life Pr 15[31]; and he becomes wiser through it Pr 9[8.9]. (2) as a *wise teacher, a sage,* he does not answer with windy knowledge Jb 15[2]; he tells the experience of the past Jb 15[18]; has knowledge Jb 34[2]; teaches it Ec 12[9]; disperses it Pr 15[7]; his tongue is health Pr 12[18]; it utters knowledge aright Pr 15[2]; his mind instructs his mouth and adds learning to his lips Pr 16[23]; his words are gracious Ec 10[12]; it is good to hear his rebuke Ec 7[5]; his instruction is a fountain of life Pr 13[14]; one walking with him becomes wiser Pr 13[20]. The חכמים recall the Gk. σόφοι, having their schools, pupils (בֵּן), discipline (מוּסָר), principles and collections of wisdom, דברי חכמים Pr 1[6] 22[17] (cf. 24[23]), Ec 9[17] 12[11]; God himself is חכם לבב Jb 9[4]. (3) *the wise* are prosperous: true, in sceptical view of Ec., they have no advantage over the fool Ec 6[8]; but die as the fool Ec 2[16.16] ψ 49[11]; they will not be able to find the works of God Ec 8[17]; like others are in the hands of God Ec 9[1]; they do not secure bread Ec 9[11]; but elsewhere reverse is true: precious treasure is in his dwelling Pr 21[20]; his lips preserve him Pr 14[3]; they inherit glory Pr 3[35]; wealth is their crown Pr 14[24]; the wise man is strong Pr 24[5] Ec 7[19]; his eyes are in his head Ec 2[14]; his mind is at his right hand Ec 10[2]; he interprets things Ec 8[1]. (4) the *wise* man is a blessing to others: he wins men Pr 11[30]; scales the city of the mighty Pr 21[22]; though poor he delivers the city Ec 9[15]; is a reproof to scorners Pr 15[12]; his mind is in the house of mourning Ec 7[4]; injustice makes him foolish Ec 7[7]; Job finds no wise men among his cruel friends Jb 17[10].

2451 †חָכְמָה **n.f. wisdom,** ח׳ Ex 28[3] + 106 t.; cstr. חָכְמַת Ex 35[35] + 15 t.; sf. חָכְמָתִי Ec 2[9], etc.
2454 + 25 t. sf.; pl. abst. emph. חָכְמוֹת ψ 49[4] Pr 1[20] 9[1] 24[7]; חַכְמוֹת Pr 14[1] (incorrectly pointed as adj. cstr. f.; rd. חָכְמוֹת De);—**1.** *skill* in war Is 10[13]; in technical work Ex 28[3] 31[3.6] 35[26.31.35] 36[1.2] (P), cf. 1 K 7[14], 1 Ch 28[21]; of sailors ψ 107[27]. **2.** *wisdom,* in administration Dt 34[9] Is 29[14] Je 49[7.7] 2 S 14[20]; of prince of Tyre Ez 28[4.5.7.12.17]; Sol.'s wisdom included this with other forms of cleverness and shrewdness 1 K 2[6] 3[28] 5[9.10.14.14.26] 10[4.6.7.8.23.24] = 2 Ch 9[3.5.6.7.22.23], 1 K 11[41] 2 Ch 1[10.11.12]; the Messiah is to have רוּחַ חָכְמָה וּבִינָה Is 11[2]. **3.** *shrewdness, wisdom,* 2 S 20[22] 1 K 5[10.10] Je 9[22]; withheld by God from the ostrich Jb 39[17]; of magicians and prophets Is 47[10] Dn 1[4.17.20]. **4.** *wisdom, prudence* in religious affairs Dt 4[6] ψ 37[30] 51[8] 90[12] Pr 10[31] Is 33[6] Je 8[9]. **5.** *wisdom,* ethical and religious: **a.** of God, as a divine attribute or energy; his wisdom is in the skies Jb 38[36]; by it he numbers the clouds Jb 38[37]; founded the earth Pr 3[19]; and made all things Je 10[12] = 51[15], ψ 104[24]; it is with him Jb 12[13]; not to be found by the most persevering human search Jb 28[12.20]; he alone knows it Jb 28[23]; gives it Pr 2[6]; and shews its secrets Jb 11[6]. **b.** the divine wisdom is personified: she was begotten before all things to be the architect and counsellor of God in the creation (Pr 8[22-31]); she builds a palace and spreads a feast for those who will receive her instruction 9[1] (cf. v[2-5]); she teaches in public places 1[20] 8[1.5.11.12] (v. context); gives her pupils the divine spirit 1[23]; by her discipline simple become wise, rulers rule wisely, and those seeking her are richly rewarded 8[14] (cf. v[1-21]). **c.** of man: to get wisdom is principal thing Pr 4[7.7]; its fundamental principle is to fear God ψ 111[10] Pr 15[33] Jb 28[28] (|| סוּר מֵרָע בִּינָה); and know י׳, the All Holy Pr 9[10] 30[3]; it is of inestimable worth Jb 28[18] Pr 8[11] 16[16] 17[16] 23[23] 24[7]; beyond the reach of scorners Pr 14[6]; God giveth it to the good Ec 2[26]; men are to incline the ear Pr 2[2]; attend unto wisdom Pr 5[1]; seek Ec 7[25]; know Pr 24[14] Ec 1[17] 8[16]; behold Ec 2[12] 9[13]; get her Pr 4[5.7]; treat her as sister Pr 7[4]; happy the man who finds her Pr 3[13]; he who has wisdom is אִישׁ תְּבוּנָה Pr 10[23]; נָבוֹן Pr 10[13] 14[33]; מֵבִין Pr 17[24]; cf. also ψ 49[4] Jb 4[21] 12[2.12] 13[5] 15[8] 26[3] 32[7.13] 33[33] Pr 1[2.7] 2[10] 4[11] 11[2] 13[10] 14[1.8] 18[4] 21[30] 24[3] 28[26] 29[3.15] 31[26] Ec 1[13.16.16.18] 2[3.9.13.21] 7[10.11.12.12.19.23] 8[1] 9[10.15.16.16.18] 10[1.10];—on Solomon's wisdom v. supr.

†חַכְמוֹנִי **n.pr.m.** (*wise*)—**1.** father of one 2453
of David's warriors 1 Ch 11[11]. **2.** father of the tutor of David's sons 1 Ch 27[32].

†תַּחְכְּמֹנִי **adj.gent.** 2 S 23[8] = בן חכמוני 8461
1 Ch 11[11]; rd. הַחַכְמֹנִי We Klo Dr VB.

חֵל v. חַיִל sub I. חול. p. 298 2426

חֵל v. sub III. חלל. p. 320 2455

2456 †I. [חָלָא] **vb. be sick, diseased** (=חלה, v. Ges^{§75,22})—**Qal** *Impf.* וַיֶּחֱלֶא אָסָא ... בְּרַגְלָיו 2 Ch 16^{12} (=חלה 1 K 15^{23}).

8463 †תַּחֲלֻאִים† **n.pl.m.**$^{2 Ch 21,19}$ **diseases**, abs. ת׳ Je 16^{4} 2 Ch 21^{19}; cstr. תַּחֲלוּאֵי Je 14^{18}; תַּחֲלוּאָיְכִי ψ 103^{3}; תַּחֲלֻאֶיהָ Dt 29^{21};—*diseases* Dt 29^{21} 2 Ch 21^{19} ψ 103^{3}; מְמוֹתֵי תחלאים יָמֻתוּ Je 16^{4}; תחלואי רעב Je 14^{18} *diseases of famine* (‖ חַלְלֵי־חֶרֶב).

II. חלא (√of foll.; DHM in MV comp. Sab. פחטאת ותחלאן *she sinned and defiled herself*).

2457 †I. [חֶלְאָה] **n.f. rust** (perh. as *filth* v. supr.)—חֶלְאָתָהּ Ez $24^{6.12}$ + v$^{11.12}$ (del. Co intern. grounds) + v^{6} חֶלְאָתָה (cf. Ges$^{§91,1; R.2}$) *rust* on metal pot, symbol of impurity of Jerusalem.

2458 †II. חֶלְאָה **n.pr.f.** (meaning dub.)—wife of Ashḥur (of Judah) 'father' of Tekoah 1 Ch $4^{5.7}$ 𝔊 Αωδα, Αοαδα, Αλαα, Ελαα, Ελεα.

2481 חֲלָאִים v. חֳלִי sub III. חלה. p. 318

2431 חֶלְאמָה v. חֵילָם sub I. חול. p. 298

I. חלב (√of foll.; meaning unknown).

2461 †חָלָב **n.m. milk** (NH *id.* (and vb. denom.); Aram. חֲלָבָא, ܚܠܒܐ, Ph. חלב; Ar. حَلِيبٌ n. *fresh milk*, حَلَبَ vb. *milk*; As. *alibu, milk*, v. Dl$^{Pr 174}$; Eth. ሐሊብ:)—ח׳ abs. Gn 18^{18} + 35 t. + Ez 34^{3} (v. infr.); cstr. חֲלֵב Ex 23^{19} + 5 t.; sf. חֲלָבִי Ct 5^{1}, חֲלָבֵךְ Ez 25^{4};—*milk*: **a.** as common food Gn 18^{8} (J; distinct from חֶמְאָה *curd*, q.v.), חֲלֵב צֹאן Dt 32^{14} (poet.; distinct fr. חֶמְאַת בָּקָר); in Ju 5^{25} חָלָב is used parallel with חֶמְאָה; elsewhere חֶמְאָה seems to be produced fr. חָלָב:—מִיץ חָלָב יוֹצִיא חֶמְאָה Pr 30^{33} *a pressing (squeezing) of milk produces curd;* מֵרֹב עֲשׂוֹת חָלָב יֹאכַל חֶמְאָה Is 7^{22} *because of abundant yield of milk he shall eat curd;* cf. also חֲרִצֵי הֶחָלָב 1 S 17^{18} *cuts of milk*, i.e. *cheeses*; it was received in buckets or pails (עֲטִינָיו) Jb 21^{24} (v. Ew De Di VB), and kept in skins (נֹאוד ח׳) Ju 4^{19}; men drank it (שׁתה) Ez 25^{4} (cf. השׁקה Ju 4^{19}), but also ate it (אכל), if emend. הֶחָלָב Ez 34^{3} (for הַחֵלֶב) is right, 𝔊 𝔙 Bo Hi-Sm Co, al.; it was poured out, v. sim. of formation of the embryo הֲלֹא כֶּח׳ תַּתִּיכֵנִי Jb 10^{10} *hast thou not poured me out like milk?* specif. (1) חֲלֵב עִזִּים לְלַחְמְךָ Pr 27^{27} *milk of goats for thy food* (RS$^{Sem. i. 204}$). (2) c. אֵם *mother's milk*: of kid לֹא־תְבַשֵּׁל גְּדִי בַּחֲלֵב אִמּוֹ Ex 23^{19} = 34^{26} (JE) = Dt 14^{21}, cf. טְלֵה ח׳ 1 S 7^{9} *sucking lamb* (for sacrif.); but also of human beings גְּמוּלֵי מֵח׳ Is 28^{9} *weaned from milk* (‖ עַתִּיקֵי מִשָּׁדָיִם); fig. in promise to Zion וְיָנַקְתְּ חֲלֵב גּוֹיִם Is 60^{16} *and thou shalt suck the milk of nations* (‖ וְשֹׁד מְלָכִים תִּינָקִי). (3) ח׳ with wine, as esp. delicacy Ct 5^{1} (v. De), fig. of י׳'s choicest blessings Is 55^{1}. (4) oft. in phr. of productiveness of land of Canaan (זָבַת חָלָב וּדְבָשׁ (דְּבַשׁ *flowing with milk and honey* Ex $3^{8.17}$ 13^{5} 33^{3} Nu 13^{27} 14^{8} $16^{13.14}$ (all JE), Lv 20^{24} (H), Dt 6^{3} 11^{9} $26^{9.15}$ 27^{3} 31^{20} Jos 5^{6} Je 11^{5} 32^{22} Ez $20^{6.15}$; in Messian. time the hills תֵּלַכְנָה ח׳ Jo 4^{18} (‖ יִטְּפוּ הֶהָרִים עָסִיס); fig. of charms of loved one דְּבַשׁ וְח׳ תַּחַת לְשׁוֹנֵךְ Ct 4^{12} *honey and milk are under thy tongue.* **b.** *milk* as white לְבֶן־שִׁנַּיִם מֵח׳ Gn 49^{12} *white of teeth, from milk;* צַחוּ מֵח׳ La 4^{7} *they were whiter than milk* (‖ זַכּוּ מִשֶּׁלֶג); so also prob. of eyes (iris) רֹחֲצוֹת בֶּח׳ Ct 5^{12} *bathed in milk*, i.e. the white of the eye.—On milk as not used by Israel in sacrifice v. RS$^{Sem. 204}$.

II. חלב (√of foll.; perh. cf. As. *ḫalâbu, be covered*, VR 8^{83} Lyon$^{Manual, Gloss}$, *ḫallibu, cover, clothe*, IR$^{18, 68}$ *ḫallubtu, clothing*, Lyon$^{Sargontexte 14}$, *ḫitlupatu, naḫlapu* (rd. *b* for *p*) Schr$^{COT Gloss}$).

I. חֵלֶב **n.m.**$^{Ex 29, 13}$ **fat** (NH *id.*, *fat*, so Ph. 2459
חלב (prob.); Aram. ܚܠܒܐ (also *diaphragm* in Lexx., v. PS^{1274}) orig. *diaphragm, midriff;* Ar. خِلْبٌ, incl. *midriff-fat*, RS$^{Sem. i. 360}$);—ח׳ abs. Lv 3^{16} + 40 t.; cstr. Gn 45^{18} + 21 t.; sf. חֶלְבּוֹ Lv 3^{9} + 6 t.; חֶלְבָּהּ Lv $4^{31.35}$, חֶלְבָּם Nu 18^{17}, חֶלְבֵּהֶן Lv $8^{16.25}$ (rd. n.pl. חלביהן Sam. Di); pl. הַחֲלָבִים Lv 8^{26} + 7 t.; cstr. חֶלְבֵי Lv 6^{5} + 4 t.; sf. חֶלְבֵּהֶן Gn 4^{4} (חלביהן Sam. Di, cf. Lv $8^{16.25}$ supr.);—**1.** *fat* of human body Ju 3^{22} (covering intestines); ח׳ גִּבּוֹרִים 2 S 1^{22} as smearing warrior's shield; of grossness of wicked כִּסָּה פָנָיו בְּחֶלְבּוֹ Jb 15^{27}; *fat* (of midriff) fig. of unreceptive heart ח׳ סָגְרוּ ψ 17^{10}, v. also 73^{7} (rd. מֵחֵלֶב עֲוֺנָמוֹ for מחלב עֵינֵמוֹ 𝔊 𝔖 Hi Ew Ol De Che Bae al.); טָפַשׁ כַּח׳ לִבָּם ψ 119^{70} i.e. their heart is as unresponsive as the midriff-fat near it. **2.** *fat* of beasts: **a.** as rich food (poet.) Dt 32^{14} and in sim. ψ 63^{6} (‖ דֶּשֶׁן); so MT Ez 34^{3} (but rd. הֶחָלָב, v. חָלָב), 39^{19} (𝔖 Co בשׂר). **b.** esp. as offered in sacrifice, sg., to י׳ Ex 23^{18} (JE), 1 S $2^{15.16}$ Ex $29^{13.13.22.22.22}$

Lv 3[3.3.4.9.9.9.10.14.14.15] + 23 t. Lv, Nu 18[17] (all P), Lv 17[6] (H), 1 S 15[22] Is 1[11] 43[24] Ez 44[7.15]; v. Is 34[6.6.7] of fat of Edomites slaughtered by ׳י's sword (under fig. of lambs, rams, and bulls); as eaten by (strange) gods Dt 32[38] (poet.), not to be eaten by men Lv 3[17] 7[23.24.24.25] (all P); also pl., *fat parts* or *pieces* Gn 4[4] (J) Lv 6[5] + 8 t. Lv, 1 K 8[64.64] 2 Ch 7[7.7] 29[35] 35[14]. **3.** *choicest, best part* of products of land Gn 45[18] (E), specif. of oil Nu 18[12] and wine v[12]; of corn and oil v[29.30.32]; also (poet.) ח׳ כִּלְיוֹת חִטָּה Dt 32[14] *kidney-fat of wheat* (i.e. the very choicest, cf. Is 34[6]), ח׳ חִטָּה ψ 81[17], ח׳ חִטִּים 147[14].

2460 †II. חֵלֶב **n.pr.m.** (Sab. n.pr.m. חלבן = *the crafty one* Sab.Denkm. [27.28])—one of David's heroes 2 S 23[29] (but rd. חלד(י), v. Dr), 𝔊 Εσθαει, A Αλαφ, 𝔊L Αλλαν (= חֵלֶד 1 Ch 11[30] = חֶלְדַּי 27[15]).

2462 †חֶלְבָּה **n.pr.loc.** town assigned to Asher Ju 1[31], site unknown, 𝔊 Χεβδα, 𝔊L Ελβα; (comp. As. *Maḫalliba* Schr Dl, but v. אַחְלָב infr.)

2463 †חֶלְבּוֹן **n.pr.loc.** place whence wine came (to Tyre) יֵין ח׳ Ez 27[18]; so also As. n.pr.terr. *Ḫilbunim* or *Hilbunu*, v. Schr[COT] and Dl in Co. Mod. *Ḫalbûn*, NW. fr. Damascus, Wetzst [ZMG xi. 1857, 490 f.] Bd [Pal 341].

2464 †חֶלְבְּנָה **n.f.** (Aram. חֶלְבְּנִיתָא, ܚܠܒܢܝܬܐ, 𝔊 χαλβάνη, 𝔙 *galbanum*)—a kind of gum Ex 30[34], ingredient of the holy incense, v. Di Löw[115].

303 †אַחְלָב **n.pr.loc.** town assigned to Asher Ju 1[31], site unknown, 𝔊 Δαλαφ (= Αλαφ) (WMaxMüller[Asien u. Europa 194] thinks corrupt. for מחלב, As. *Maḫalliba* (which Schr[COT] Ju 1[37] Dl[Pa 283] comp. with אחלב and חֶלְבָּה); he rds. n.pr.loc. מחלב for מֵחֶבֶל Jos 19[29], 𝔊 καὶ ἀπὸ Λεβ = וּמֵחֹלֶב; this would be on coast, N. of Achzib).

I. חלד (√ of foll.; Ar. خَلَدَ *abide, continue*, often in Qor of righteous in Paradise).

2465 †חֶלֶד **n.[m.]**[Jb 11, 17] **duration, world** (= αἰών) (Ar. خُلْدٌ *perpetual duration, eternity*)—abs. ח׳ ψ 17[14]; חָ֑לֶד Jb 11[17] + 2 t. + Is 38[11] Che De, sq. Cod. Bab. etc. (Baer חָדֶל); sf. חֶלְדִּי ψ 39[6]; = *duration of life* Jb 11[17] ψ 39[6] (|| יָמַי), זְכָר אֲנִי מֶה־חָ֑לֶד 89[48] *of what duration I am* Dr [§ 189. 2], or (אדני for אני) *what is life*(?) Hi Ew Now al.; *world* (= αἰών, not κόσμος) ψ 17[14] 49[2] (יֹשְׁבֵי ח׳ || כל־עמים), cf. Is 38[11] (v. supr.; || אֶרֶץ הַחַיִּים).

II. חלד (√ of foll.; cf. NH חלד *dig*, or *hollow out*, Aram. ܚܠܕ *creep, crawl*).

†חֵלֶד **n.pr.m.** (Sab. n.pr. חלד DHM[Epigr. 2466
Denkm. 35]) one of David's heroes, son of בַּעֲנָה 1 Ch 11[30] A 𝔊L Αλαδ (= חֶלְדַּי 27[15] = חֵלֶב 2 S 23[29]).

†חֹלֶד **n.[m.] weasel** (NH חוּלְדָּא; Ar. خُلْدٌ 2467
mole or *blind-rat*, or *a species of rat*; on format. v. Lag[BN 144])—*weasel* Lv 11[29] (Vrss Ki Thes al. v. esp. Di; > Saad Bo MV SS Lag[l.c.] *mole*).

†חֻלְדָּה **n.pr.f.** prophetess, Josiah's time, 2468
2 K 22[14] = 2 Ch 34[22], 𝔊 Ολδα.

†חֶלְדַּי **n.pr.m.** **1.** one of David's heroes 2469
1 Ch 27[15] (= חֵלֶד 11[30] = חֵלֶב 2 S 23[29]) 𝔊 Χολδεια (-δαι), 𝔊L Ολδια. **2.** a returned exile Zc 6[10] (om. 𝔊) = חֵלֶם v[14].

†I. חָלָה **vb. be weak, sick** (NH *id.*; 2470
Aram. חֲלָא *suffer* (rare); As. *ḫalû, sickness, grief,* Dl[Pr 181])—**Qal** *Pf.* ח׳ 1 K 14[1] + 8 t.; 2 fs. חָלִית Is 57[10]; 1 s. חָלִיתִי 1 S 30[13] + 2 t.; וְחָלִיתִי consec. Ju 16[7.11.17], חָלוּ Je 5[3] (so rd., v. infr.); *Impf.* וַיָּחַל 2 K 1[2]; *Inf.* sf. חֲלֹתוֹ Is 38[9]; חַלּוֹתִי ψ 77[11] cf. sub **Pi.**; חֲלוֹתָם ψ 35[13]; *Pt.* חֹלֶה Gn 48[1] + 6 t. + 1 S 22[8] (v. infr.); חולה Ne 2[2] Mal 1[13]; f. חולה Ec 5[12] + 3 t. (for Je 4[31] v. I. חול), cstr. חוֹלַת Ct 2[5] 5[8];—**1.** *be* or *become weak*, Samson Ju 16[7.11.17]; *feel weak* Is 57[10] (Che) Ez 34[4.16]. **2.** *become sick, ill* Gn 48[1] (E) 1 S 19[14] 30[13] 1 K 14[1.5] 15[23] (of Asa, = חלא 2 Ch 16[2]) 17[17] 2 K 1[2] 8[7] 13[14] (c. acc. cogn.) 20[12] = Is 39[1], Is 33[24] 38[9] Pr 23[35] ψ 35[13] Ne 2[2], cf. ψ 77[11] חַלּוֹתִי for חֲלוֹתִי Che after Bi; *lame and sick*—i.e. imperfect for sacrifice—of animals Mal 1[8.13]; *sick* from effect of wounds 2 K 8[29] = 2 Ch 22[6], cf. Pr 23[35], מַכָּה with חֳלִי Dt 28[59.61] Je 6[7] 10[19]; hyperbol. *sick* from love חולת אַהֲבָה אני Ct 2[5] 5[8]; *be sick unto dying* ח׳ עד־למות 2 K 20[1] = Is 38[1], חלה לָמוּת (late) 2 Ch 32[24]; Je 5[3] rd. prob. לֹא חָלוּ (for MT חָלוּ, v. I. חול) of the people, unmoved by ׳י's chastisements; *thou hast smitten them, but they are not sick* (cf. **Niph.** Am 6[6]); of sickness of the mind in MT 1 S 22[8] sq. עַל (but rd. rather חֹמֵל 𝔊 Gr Klo Dr); *pt.* as adj. *severe, sore* רָעָה חוֹלָה Ec 5[12.15];—on Je 4[31] v. I. חול. **Niph.** *Pf.* 1 s. נֶחֱלֵיתִי Dn 8[27]; 3 pl. נֶחְלוּ Am 6[6] Je 12[13]; *Pt.* f. נַחֲלָה Is 17[11] + 4 t.; pl. נַחֲלוֹת Ez 34[4] (del. Co) v[21];—**1.** *make oneself sick*, fig. for *strain oneself* Je 12[13] (but Gr נִלְאוּ). **2.** *be made sick* Dn 8[27]; לֹא נֶח׳ of indifference, apathy Am 6[6] sq. עַל (cf. **Qal** Je 5[3]);

pt. *diseased*, as subst. c. art. Ez 34^{4} (del. Co) v^{21}; =*severe, sore* (pred. of מַכָּה) Na 3^{19} Je 10^{19} 14^{17} 30^{12}; also (מַכָּה om.) Is 17^{11}. **Pi.** *Pf.* חִלָּה *make sick*, c. acc. cogn. + בְּ of land Dt 29^{21}; *Inf. cstr.* חַלּוֹתִי הִיא ψ 77^{11} rd. prob. חֲלוֹתִי, Inf. Qal; *my sickness*, so Bi Che (others der. fr. חלל *my wounding*, v. De).—For other forms of Pi. v. II. חלה. **Pu.** *Pf. be made weak*, 2 ms. חֻלֵּיתָ Is 14^{10}. **Hithp.** *Impf.* וַיִּתְחָל 2 S 13^{6}; *Imv.* הִתְחָל 2 S 13^{5}; *Inf.* הִתְחַלּוֹת 2 S 13^{2};—*make oneself sick*, of Ammon's morbid passion for his sister 2 S 13^{2}, sq. בַּעֲבוּר; of his pretended sickness of body 2 S $13^{5.6}$. **Hiph.** *Pf.* 3 ms. הֶחֱלִי Is 53^{10}; 1 s. הֶחֱלֵתִי Mi 6^{13}; pl. הֶחֱלוּ Ho 7^{5} (on txt. v. infr.); *Pt.* מַחֲלָה Pr 13^{12};—**1.** *make* (*sick*, i.e.) *sore thy smiting* הַכּוֹתֶךָ Mi 6^{13} (cf. Na 3^{19}, Niph.); obj. (implic.) a person, וי׳ חָפֵץ דַּכְּאוֹ הֶחֱלִי Is 53^{10} *it pleased* ׳י *to bruise him, making him sick* = to bruise him *sorely*, v. further Di. **2.** *make sick*, obj. לֵב (of hope deferred) Pr 13^{12}. **3.** *shew* (signs of) *sickness, become sick*, only הֶח׳ שָׂרִים חֲמַת מִיָּיִן Ho 7^{5} *princes are become sick with fever of wine* (Now Che VB; > Vrss Hi-St who rd. הֶחֵלּוּ *they begin* the day with wine-fever). **Hoph.** *Pf. be made sick* = *wounded* הָחֳלֵיתִי 1 K 22^{34} = 2 Ch 18^{33}, 2 Ch 35^{23}.

2483 †חֳלִי **n.m.** $^{Dt\ 28,59}$ sickness, חֳלִי Dt 28^{61} + 8 t.; חֹלִי Dt 7^{15} + 2 t.; sf. חָלְיוֹ Is 38^{9} + 7 t. + Ec 5^{16} (where del. sf., cf. Vrss Now); pl. חֳלָיִם Dt 28^{59}, חֳלָיִים 2 Ch 21^{15}, חֳלָיֵנוּ Is 53^{4};—*sickness, disease* Dt 7^{15} $28^{59.61}$ 1 K 17^{17} 2 K 1^{2} $8^{8.9}$ 13^{14} Is 38^{9} 2 Ch $16^{12.12}$ $21^{15.15.19}$ ψ 41^{4} Ec 6^{2}; of the suffering servant of ׳י Is $53^{3.4}$ (in both ‖ מַכְאֹב); of rich man Ec 5^{16} (rd. וָחֳלִי, v. supr.); *incurable disease* ח׳ לְאֵין מַרְפֵּא 2 Ch 21^{18}; *recover from sickness* חיה מֵחלי Is 38^{9}; metaph. of distress of land Ho 5^{13} (‖ מָזוֹר), Is 1^{5} Je 10^{19}; = *wound*, of violence in Jerusalem Je 6^{7} (‖ מַכָּה).

4245 †[מַחֲלֶה] **n.[m.]** sickness, disease—sf. מַחֲלֵהוּ Pr 18^{14} *his sickness* (=any sickness of his); of specif. disease, cstr. מַחֲלֵה מֵעֶיךָ 2 Ch 21^{15} (+ מֵחֳלִי, בָּחֳלָיִים רַבִּים).

4245 †מַחֲלָה **n.f.** sickness, disease, מַחֲלָה Ex 15^{26} + 3 t.—*sickness, disease* (in gen.) Ex 23^{25} (JE); so c. כל, 1 K 8^{37} = 2 Ch 6^{28} (‖ כָּל־נֶגַע), Ex 15^{26} (JE; cf. אני יהוה רֹפְאֶךָ *ad fin.*)

†[מַחֲלוּי] **n.m. sickness, suffering** (caused 4251
by wounds, cf. חלה 2 K 8^{29})—only pl. intens. מַחֲלֻיִים 2 Ch 24^{25}.

†II. [חָלָה] **vb.** only **Pi.** sq. פְּנֵי, פָּנֶיךָ, פָּנַיִךְ 2470
=**mollify, appease, entreat the favour of**, lit. *make the face* of any one *sweet* or *pleasant* (cf. Ar. حَلَا, حَلِىَ *be sweet, pleasant*, Aram. ܚܠܐ, חֲלֵי, *id.*, adj. חָלֵי *sweet*);—**Pi.** *Pf.* חִלָּה 2 Ch 33^{12}, חִלֵּיתִי 1 S 13^{12} ψ 119^{58}, וְחִלּוּ consec. Jb 11^{19}, חִלִּינוּ Dn 9^{13}; *Impf.* וַיְחַל Ex 32^{11} + 3 t., יְחַלּוּ ψ 45^{13} Pr 19^{6}; *Imv.* חַל־נָא 1 K 13^{6}, חַלּוּ־נָא Mal 1^{9}; *Inf. cstr.* לְחַלּוֹת Zc 7^{2} + 2 t.;—**1.** ח׳ את־פני־י׳: **a.** *mollify, pacify, appease* ׳י, i.e. induce him to shew favour in place of wrath and chastisement Ex 32^{11} (JE), 1 K 13^{6} (+ הִתְפַּלֵּל), v^{6} 2 K 13^{4} Je 26^{19} (+ וַיִּנָּחֶם), 2 Ch 33^{12} (‖ וַיִּכָּנַע מאד מִלִּפְנֵי), Dn 9^{13}; also ח׳ פני־אֵל Mal 1^{9} (sq. וִיחָנֵּנוּ *that he may be gracious to us*). **b.** *entreat the favour of* ׳י, i.e. aim at success, prosperity, etc., through his favour, 1 S 13^{12} (in anticipation of war), Zc $8^{21.22}$ (‖ לְבַקֵּשׁ אֶת־י׳; of cities and nations assembling at Jerusalem for worship), Zc 7^{2} (‖ לְבַקֵּשׁ אֶת־י׳) of worship at Jerusalem; quite gen., as habit of God-fearing man, ψ 119^{58} (+ בְּכָל־לֵב). **2.** *entreat favour* of men (in sense of **1 b**)—רַבִּים יְח׳ פְּנֵי־נָדִיב Pr 19^{6} *many entreat a prince's favour* (‖ וְכָל־הָרֵעַ לְאִישׁ מַתָּן); יְח׳ פָּנַיִךְ ψ 45^{13} of favour of king's bride; וְח׳ פָּנֶיךָ רַבִּים Jb 11^{19} favour of Job when absolved and restored.

†מַחֲלַת **n.f.** only in ψ titles עַל־מ׳ ψ 53^{1} 4257
88^{1}; appar. a catchword in a song, giving name to tune; mng. dub.; Aq. Symm. 𝔊 מְחֹלַת *dance*; v. Ol $^{Psalmen,\ p.\ 27}$ Bae $^{Psalmen,\ p.\ xviii}$.

III. חלה (*adorn*; cf. Ar. حَلَى *adorn*, حَلْىٌ (neck-)*ornament*).

†I. חֲלִי **n.m. ornament**, נֶזֶם זָהָב וַחֲלִי־כָתֶם 2481
Pr 25^{12} *a* (nose- or ear-) *ring of gold and* (neck- or breast-) *ornament of fine gold*; pl. חֲלָאִים Ct 7^{2}, in sim. of grace and beauty.

†II. חֲלִי **n.pr.loc.** in Asher Jos 19^{25}, site 2482
unknown (v. conject. in Di).

†[חֶלְיָה] **n.f.** jewelry, נִזְמָהּ וְחֶלְיָתָהּ Ho 2^{15} 2484
(v. Now Che).

†חֲלַח **n.pr.loc.** a city or district under 2477
Assyr. control, whither Isr. captives were taken 2 K 17^{6} = 18^{11}, 1 Ch 5^{26}, cf. *Ḥalaḫḫu* in Meso-

potamia, Schr [COT] on 2 K 17[6]; > Hal [Mél. Epigr. 1874, 70] *Cilicia* (=Ph. חלך, Lag [M. i. 211], As. *Ḫilakku*, Lyon [Sargontexte]) Lag [BN 57].

2478 † חַלְחוּל **n.pr.loc.** town in Judah, Jos 15[58] Lag [Onom. 119. 7, 2nd ed. 152] Elul in tribu Iuda, cf. Alula juxta Chebron; mod. Ḥalḥûl, 1½ hour (3½ miles) N. fr. Hebron, v. Di (and reff.) Bla Rob [BR iii. 281 f.] Guérin [Judée iii. 284 ff.]

2479 חַלְחָלָה **n.f.** v. I. חול. p. 298

2480 †[חָלַט] **vb.** only וַיַּחְלְטוּ הֲמִמֶּנּוּ 1 K 20[33], rd. prob. וַיַּחְלְטוּהָ מִמֶּנּוּ (cf. 𝔊 ἀνέλεξαν τὸν λόγον ἀπὸ τοῦ στόματος αὐτοῦ and Sta [G i. 445 f.]) *and they snatched it from him*, caught the word fr. his lips; Sta [§ 529a] as **Qal**; Kö [i. 251] Ges [§ 53. 3 R 4] and most as **Hiph.**, with ـَ om.

חלך (√ of foll.; poss. (si vera l.) cf. Ar. حَلِكَ *be black* (passing into fig. sense, *unfortunate*, in Heb.), v. Bae [ψ 10, 8]; cf. Aram. חֲשׁוֹךְ).

2489 † חֵלְכָה rd. חֶלְכָּה, חַלְכָּה, or חָלְכָה, **adj. hapless, unfortunate**, only as subst. *hapless, luckless one(s)*—לְחֵלְכָה ψ 10[8], 𝔊 εἰς τὸν πένητα, 𝔖 𝔗; חֵלְכָה 10[14] 𝔊 ὁ πτωχός; חלכאים 10[10] Kt, rd. pl. חַלְכָּאִים (חֳלִי, חֵלְ׳); Qr חֵל כָּאִים, 𝔊 τῶν πενήτων. In all txt. and mng. dub. (MT rds. חֵילְךָ=חֵלְכָה *thine army*; and חֵל כָּאִים v[10] *army of dejected ones*, but this against usage of חֵל, and no such fig. sense of חַיִל, v. Ol Hup De Bae Che, and crit. n.)

2490 † I. חָלַל **vb. bore, pierce** (Ar. خَلَّ *perforate, pierce through, transfix*, Eth. ኀለት: (hollow) *reed*; Aram. חֲלַל *hollow out*, חֲלִילָא *pipe*; ܚܠܝܠܐ adj. *hollow*, ܡܚܠܠܐ *cave*, ܬܚܠܐ *sheath*, etc.; NH in deriv. חָלָל n. *hollow*, adj. *slain*, חָלִיל *pipe*);—**Qal** *Pf.* לִבִּי חָלַל בְּקִרְבִּי *my heart is pierced* (wounded) *within me* ψ 109[22] (? lit. *one has pierced my heart*; or rd. **Pu.** חֻלַּל?); *Inf. cstr.* חַלּוֹתִי הִיא ψ 77[11] *it is my piercing, my wound* (my woe, my cross; so Ew Hi De Bae MV SS Kö [i. 341], but Hu Pe Bi Che rd. חֲלוֹתִי *my sickness*). **Pi.** *Pt.* pl. (Baer) בְּיַד מְחַלְלֶיךָ Ez 28[9] *in the hand of the ones wounding thee* (Sm Co rd. מְחוֹלְלֶךָ). **Pu.** *Pt.* מְחֻלְּלֵי חֶרֶב *pierced by the sword* Ez 32[26]. **Po'el** *Pf.* 3 fs. חֹלְלָה יָדוֹ נָחָשׁ בָּרִחַ Jb 26[13] *his hand pierced the fleeing serpent*; *Pt.* f. מְחוֹלֶלֶת תַּנִּין Is 51[9] *who pierced the dragon*. **Po'al** *Pt.* מְחֹלָל מִפְּשָׁעֵנוּ Is 53[5] *pierced, wounded because of our transgressions* (of the servant of י׳, ‖ מְדֻכָּא מֵעֲוֹנֹתֵינוּ).

I. חָלָל [90] **n.m. pierced**, ח׳ abs. Dt 21[1] + 25 t.; 2491
cstr. חֲלַל Nu 19[16]; pl. חֲלָלִים Nu 23[24] + 28 t.; cstr. חַלְלֵי Is 22[2] + 21 t.; sf. חֲלָלֶיךָ ψ 69[27], etc. + 11 t. sfs.;—**1.** *pierced, fatally wounded* ψ 69[27] Je 51[52] Ez 26[15] 30[24] La 2[12]. Elsewhere **2.** *slain* Nu 19[18] 31[8. 19] (P), etc.; sg. coll. 2 S 23[8. 18] = 1 Ch 11[11. 20] Ez 6[7] 30[11], etc., but usu. pl. 1 S 17[52] (RV *wounded*) Je 51[49], etc.; † חַלְלֵי חֶרֶב Is 22[2] Je 14[18] Ez 31[17. 18] 32[20. 21. 25. 28. 29. 30. 31. 32] Zp 2[12] La 4[9]; חַלְלֵי רעב La 4[9]; חַלְלֵי יהוה Is 66[16] Je 25[33].

† חַלָּה **n.f.** a kind of cake (prob. as *perforated*, v. Di Lv 2[4])—ח׳ abs. Nu 15[20] Lv 24[5]; 2471
cstr. חַלַּת Ex 29[23] + 4 t.; pl. חַלּוֹת Lv 2[4] + 2 t.; חַלֹּת Ex 29[2] + 3 t.—used in offerings: **1.** at the sacrif. of David on removal of ark, given to each person as part of peace-offering 2 S 6[19]. **2.** elsewh. only P (H Lv 24[5. 5]): **a.** of the 12 cakes of the table of the holy place, made of סלת Lv 24[5. 5]. **b.** made of ראשית ערסת as an offering of first-fruits Nu 15[20]. **c.** of לחם שמן, to be burnt with the עֹלָה Ex 29[23] = Lv 8[26]. **d.** of מַצָּה burnt on the altar with **c** Lv 8[26], but usu. to be eaten by participants in the several forms of peace-offering Nu 6[19], and as such mingled with oil Ex 29[2] Lv 2[4] 7[12. 12] Nu 6[15]. **e.** ח׳ לחם חמץ to be used by the offerer in connexion with the unleavened cakes of **d** Lv 7[13].

† חַלּוֹן **n.m.** [Jos 2, 18] and **f.** [Ez 40, 16] **window**, abs. 2474
הַחַלּוֹן Gn 26[8] + 12 t.; cstr. חַלּוֹן Gn 8[6] Pr 7[6]; sf. חַלּוֹנוֹ Ez 40[22]; mpl. חַלּוֹנִים Ez 40[25] + 3 t.; cstr. חַלּוֹנֵי 1 K 6[4]; sf. חַלּוֹנָי Je 22[14] (defective pl. Ges [§ 87 (1) c], dual Ew [§ 177 a], but rd. ـָיו סְפֻון Mich Hi Gf Or Gie); חַלּוֹנֵינוּ Je 9[20]; f. חַלּוֹנוֹת Ez 40[16] + 4 t.; חַלֹּנוֹת Ct 2[9] + 3 t.; *window* פָּתַח ח׳ *open the window* Gn 8[6] (P) 2 K 13[17]; עלה בח׳ Je 9[20]; בעד הח׳ *through the window* Gn 26[8] Jos 2[15] (J) Ju 5[28] 1 S 19[12] 2 S 6[16] = 1 Ch 15[29], 2 K 9[30] Jo 2[9]; *latticed windows* 1 K 6[4] Ez 40[16] 41[16. 26]; בח׳ Jos 2[18. 21] (J) Pr 7[6] Zp 2[14]; אֶל־הח׳ 2 K 9[32]; מִן־הח׳ Ct 2[9]; *windows* of palace, קָרַע לוֹ חַלּוֹנָי(ו) Je 22[14] *cutteth him out his windows*; of the gates of Ezek.'s temple Ez 40[16. 22. 25. 25. 29. 33. 36], of the temple itself Ez 41[16. 16].

† חָלִיל **n.m. flute, pipe**, ח׳ 1 S 10[5] Is 5[12] 2485
30[29]; pl. חֲלִלִים 1 K 1[40] Je 48[36. 36].

2490 †II. [חלל] **vb. denom.** **play the pipe, pipe**—**Qal** *Pt.* pl. וְשָׁרִים כְּחֹלְלִים ψ 87^{7} *as well the singers as the pipe-players*, cf. AV; < RV Pe De Che Bae al. **Polel** *Pt.* fr. I. חול *dancers*. **Pi.** *Pt.* וְהָעָם מְחַלְּלִים בַּחֲלִלִים 1 K 1^{40} *and the people piped with pipes* (cf. As. *ḫâlalu*, acc. to Dl in Zim$^{BP\ 117}$).

4247 †[מְחִלָּה] **n.f.** hole, מְחִלּוֹת עָפָר *holes of the dust* Is 2^{19} (‖ מְעָרוֹת צֻרִים *caves of the rocks*).

2490 †III. [חָלַל] **vb.** **pollute, defile, profane**; **Hiph.** also **begin** (lit. *untie, loosen, open*, v. Arab.) (Ar. حَلَّ *untie, undo, become free, lawful, free from obligation* or *tie*; IV. *make lawful*; X. *esteem lawful* or *free, profane, desecrate, violate*; NH חלל *be profane, desecrated* (also Pi. Hiph. transit.), cf. Aram. חֲלַל; ܚܰܠܶܠ Pa. is *purify*, ܐܰܚܶܠ Aph. is *profane*)—**Niph.** *Pf.* נִחַל Ez 25^{3}, נִחַלְתְּ (-תִּי Co) Ez 22^{16}, נִחֲלוּ Ez 7^{24}; *Impf.* יֵחַל Is 48^{11}, תֵּחֵל Lv 21^{9}, וָאֵחַל Ez 22^{26}; *Inf.* הֵחֵל Ez 20$^{9.14.22}$, sf. לְהֵחַלּוֹ Lv 21^{4}.—**1.** reflex. *pollute, defile oneself* **a.** ritually, by contact with dead ‖ טמא, Lv 21^{4} (H). **b.** *sexually* ‖ זנה Lv 21^{9} (H). **2.** Pass., *be polluted, defiled*, of holy places Ez 7^{24} 25^{3}, name of God Ez 20$^{9.14.22}$ Is 48^{11} and even God himself Ez 22$^{16.26}$. **Pi.** *Pf.* חִלֵּל Lv 19^{8} + 3 t.; sf. חִלְּלוֹ Dt 20^{6}; 2 ms. חִלַּלְתָּ Gn 49^{4} + 3 t.; 2 fs. חִלַּלְתְּ Ez 22^{8}; 3 pl. sf. חִלְּלוּהָ Ez 7^{21} etc., + 16 t. Pf.; *Impf.* יְחַלֵּל Lv 21$^{12.15.23}$; sf. יְחַלְּלֶנּוּ Dt 20^{6}; pl. יְחַלְּלוּ Lv 21^{6} + 4 t., יְחַלֵּלוּ ψ 89^{32} etc., + 13 t. Impf.; *Inf.* חַלֵּל Am 2^{7} + 4 t.; חַלְּלוֹ Ez 23^{39} + 4 t.; חַלְּלָם Je 16^{18}; *Pt.* מְחַלֵּל Ez 24^{21} pl. מְחַלְּלִים Mal 1^{12} Ne 13^{17}; sf. מְחַלְלֶיהָ Ex 31^{14}; f. מְחַלֶּלֶת Lv 21^{9};—**1.** *defile, pollute*: **a.** sexually, Gn 49^{4} (poem) = 1 Ch 5^{1} (the father's bed); a woman = זנה Lv 19^{29} 21^{9} (H); זַרְעוֹ Lv 21^{15} (H). **b.** ceremonially, *profane*, the altar by a tool Ex 20^{25} (JE); sacred places Lv 21$^{12.23}$ (H), Ez 7$^{21.22.22}$ 23^{39} 24^{21} 44^{7} Zp 3^{4} Mal 2^{11} ψ 74^{7} Dn 11^{31}; the holy land Je 16^{18}; sacred things Lv 19^{8} 22$^{9.15}$ (H) Nu 18^{32} (P) Ez 22^{26}; the sabbath Ex 31^{14} (P), Is 56$^{2.6}$ Ez 20$^{13.16.21.24}$ 22^{8} 23^{38} Ne 13$^{17.18}$; and so the sanctity of the prince of Tyre who made himself God, and his holy places, Ez 28$^{7.16.18}$. **c.** the name of God Lv 18^{21} 19^{12} 20^{3} 21^{6} 22$^{2.32}$ (all H), Am 2^{7} Je 34^{16} Ez 20^{39} 36$^{20.21.22.23}$ Mal 1^{12}, God himself Ez 13^{19}. **d.** ׳י *defiles* or *profanes* his inheritance by giving it over to Babylon Is 47^{6}; the princes of the sanctuary by giving them to Chaldeans Is 43^{28}. **2.** *violate the honour of, dishonour*, ׳י subj., crown of Davidic kingdom ψ 89^{40} (sq. לארץ pregn.), kingdom of Judah La 2^{2}; the גאון כל צבי Is 23^{9}. **3.** *violate* a covenant ψ 55^{21} 89^{35} Mal 2^{10}, the חקות of God ψ 89^{32}. **4.** *treat* a vineyard *as common* (v. חֹל) *by beginning to use its fruit* Dt 20$^{6.6}$ 28^{30} Je 31^{5} (v. the law Lv 19$^{23-25}$, H). **Pu.** *Pt.* שְׁמִי הַגָּדוֹל הַמְחֻלָּל בַּגּוֹיִם Ez 36^{23} *my great name which is profaned among the nations*. **Hiph. 1. a.** *Impf.* לֹא אַחֵל אֶת־שֵׁם־קָדְשִׁי עוֹד Ez 39^{7} *I will not let my holy name be profaned any more*. **b.** לֹא יַחֵל דְּבָרוֹ *he shall not violate his word* Nu 30^{3} (P). **2.** *begin*, *Pf.* הֵחֵל Gn 6^{1} + 15 t., הֵחֵלָּה Ju 20^{40}, הַחִלּוֹתָ Dt 3^{24} Est 6^{13}, הַחִלֹּתִי Dt 2^{31} 1 S 22^{15}, הֵחֵלּוּ Ezr 3^{6} + 6 t.; *Impf.* יָחֵל Ju 10^{18} 13^{5}, וַיָּחֶל Gn 9^{20} + 5 t., 3 fs. וַתָּחֶל Ju 13^{25} 16^{19}, 2 ms. תָּחֵל Dt 16^{9}, וַתְּחִלֶּינָה Gn 41^{54}, תָּחֵלּוּ Ez 9^{6}; *Imv.* הָחֵל Dt 2$^{24.31}$; *Inf. cstr.* הָחֵל 1 S 3^{12} + 2 t.; sf. הַחִלָּם Gn 11^{6}; *Pt.* מֵחֵל Je 25^{29};—*begin*, Nu 17$^{11.12}$ (P) Dt 16^{9} 2 Ch 29$^{27.27}$; so 2 S 24^{15} 𝔊 We Dr (𝔊 inserts וְהַמַּגֵּפָה הֵחֵלָּה בָּעָם bef. וַיָּמָת); c. Inf. (ל) *begin to* Gn 41^{54} (E), Gn 6^{1} 10^{8} = 1 Ch 1^{10}, Gn 11^{6} Nu 25^{1} (all J), Dt 2$^{25.31}$ 3^{24} 16^{9} Jos 3^{7} (D), Ju 10^{18} 13$^{5.25}$ 16$^{19.22}$ 20$^{31.39.40}$ 1 S 3^{2} 14^{35} 22^{15} 2 K 10^{32} 15^{37} 1 Ch 27^{24} 2 Ch 3$^{1.2}$ 29^{17} 31$^{7.10.21}$ 34$^{3.3}$ Ezr 3^{6} Ne 4^{1} Est 6^{13} 9^{23} Je 25^{29} Jon 3^{4}; c. ו consec. Gn 9^{20} (J), Ezr 3^{8}; c. בְּ *begin with* Gn 44^{12} (J), Ez 9^{6}, 2 Ch 20^{22}; so 2 S 24^{5}, rd. וַיָּחֵלּוּ for וַיַּחֲנוּ 𝔊L We Dr.; c. מן *begin from* Ez 9^{6}; הָחֵל רָשׁ *begin! possess!* Dt 2$^{24.31}$; הָחֵל וְכַלֵּה *beginning and ending* 1 S 3^{12} (i.e. accomplishing my full purpose, v. Dr). **Hoph.** *Pf.* אָז הוּחַל לִקְרֹא בְּשֵׁם ׳י *then it was begun* (= men began) *to call on the name of* ׳י Gn 4^{26} (J).

Note.—וַיָּחֵלּוּ מְעַט מִמַּשָּׂא Ho 8^{10} *begin to be minished by reason of the burden* RV Hi al.; Wü Now rd. וְיָחִילוּ (I. חול, חיל)—for om. of dagh. v. also וְיָחֵלוּ of Cod. Bab.—*shall be in anguish a little for the burden*, so Ra AV; Ew וְיָחִלוּ *that they may wait* (?) *a little*; 𝔊 וחדלו מעט ממשח *cease a little from anointing*, so Che We, this probably best.

†חֹל **n.[m.]** **profaneness, commonness**;— 2455
לֶחֶם חֹל 1 S 21^{5}, דֶּרֶךְ חֹל v^{6}; in concrete sense, opp. קֹדֶשׁ Lv 10^{10} (P), Ez 22^{26} 42^{20} 44^{23} 48^{15}.

2491 II. †חָלָל **adj. profaned**;—חָלָל רָשָׁע (rd. cstr. חֲלַל SS) *profaned, dishonoured wicked one* Ez 21^{30} (so AV Thes MV SS Co Or; but RV Hä *deadly wounded*, Ew Sm *fallen, slain*); pl. cstr. חַלְלֵי רְשָׁעִים Ez 21^{34}; fs. חֲלָלָה of woman sexually dishonoured Lv 21$^{7.14}$ (H; || זֹנָה).

2486 †חָלִ֫ילָה **subst.** c. ה loc., used as exclam. lit. *ad profanum!* i.e. **far be it** (for me, thee, etc.)! (v. Ba$^{NB\ 136}$)—ח׳ Gn 44^{7} + 17 t., חָלִלָה Gn 18^{25} + 2 t.—alone, 1 S 14^{45} 20^{2}; elsewh. c. לְ pers.: Gn 18$^{25\,b}$ (J), 1 S 2^{30} 20^{9} 22^{15}; + מִן and inf. of act deprecated Gn 18$^{25\,a}$ 44$^{7.17}$ (all J), Jos 24^{16} (E), 1 S 12^{23} 2 S 23^{17}; + לְ + מִמֶּנּוּ (peculiarly) Jos 22^{29} (P; = *from it, even to rebel*); + אִם (= *surely not*) 2 S 20^{20} (ח׳ ח׳), Jb 27^{5}; strengthened idiom. by מיהוה, ח׳ לִי מִי׳ sq. מִן and inf. 1 S 26^{11} 1 K 21^{3} + 2 S 23^{17} (rd. מיהוה, 𝔊L 𝔖 𝔗) = 1 Ch 11^{19} (מאלהי) sq. אִם 1 S 24^{7}; ח׳ לָאֵל מֵרֶשַׁע Jb 34^{10}.

8462 †תְּחִלָּה **n.f. beginning**, הַתְּחִלָּה Ne 11^{17} (rd. הַתְּהִלָּה 𝔊 𝔙 SS Öt), בַּתְּחִלָּה Gn 13^{3} + 10 t.; cstr. תְּחִלַּת Ho 1^{2} Pr 9^{10} Ec 10^{13}, בִּתְחִלַּת 2 K 17^{25} + 4 t., תְּחִלַּת° 2 S 21^{9}, מִתְּחִלַּת 2 S 21^{10}:—cstr. with nouns ת׳ חָכְמָה Pr 9^{10} *the beginning, first principle* of wisdom ת׳ דִּבְרֵי Ec 10^{13} *the first word*, sq. rel. clause ת׳ דִּבֶּר י׳ *at the beginning of, Yahweh spake* (= when Yahweh first spake) Ho 1^{2}; preceded by prep. מִן 2 S 21^{10}, elsewhere by בְּ *in the beginning*, of the harvest Ru 1^{22} 2 S 21^{9} (Qr), of the kingdom Ezr 4^{6}, of their dwelling there 2 K 17^{25}, of supplications Dn 9^{23}, of the shooting up of vegetation Am 7^{1}, כְּבַתְּ׳ as in the beginning Is 1^{26}; בַּתְּ׳ *at first, first* in order Ju 1^{1} 20$^{18.18}$ 2 S 17^{9}; *at the first, first* (or *former*) *time*, i.e. first in a series of occurrences, Gn 13^{3} (J), 41^{21} (E), 43$^{18.20}$ (J), Dn 8^{1} 9^{21}.

2492 †I. [חָלַם] **vb. be healthy, strong** (NH *id.*; Aram. ܚܠܡ Ethp. *be made healthy, strong*, Aph. causat., also deriv.; חֲלַם *press firmly together*)—**Qal** *Impf.* יַחְלְמוּ בְנֵיהֶם Jb 39^{4} *their young are healthy*. **Hiph.** *Impf.* 2 ms. וְתַחֲלִימֵנִי Is 38^{16} *and restore me to health* (|| וְהַחֲיֵנִי).

2494 †חֵ֫לֶם **n.pr.m.** (*strength*)—a returned exile Zc 6^{14} = חֶלְדַּי v^{10}.

2492 †II. חָלַם **vb. dream** (NH *id.*; Aram. חֲלַם, ܚܠܡ; Eth. ሐለመ: Ar. حَلَمَ, *dream, experience an emission of the seminal fluid, attain to puberty*)—**Qal** *Pf.* ח׳ Gn 42^{9} Dn 2^{1}, חָלַמְתִּי Gn 37^{9} + 3 t., חָלָמְתִּי Gn 37^{6} + 2 t., etc., + 3 t. Pf.; *Impf.* יַחֲלֹם Is 29^{8} + 5 t., יַחְלְמוּ Jb 39^{4}, וַיַּחַלְמוּ Gn 40^{5}, יַחֲלֹמוּן Jo 3^{1}, נַחֲלְמָה Gn 41^{11}; *Pt.* חֹלֵם חולם Dt 13^{4}, חֹלֵם Gn 41^{1} Dt 13$^{2.6}$, חֹלְמִים ψ 126^{1};—*dream*: **a.** of ordinary dreams of sleep Is 29$^{8.8}$ ψ 126^{1}. **b.** of dreams with prophetic meaning: of Jacob Gn 28^{12}, Joseph Gn 37$^{5.6.9.9.10}$ 42^{9}, of Pharaoh and his servants Gn 40$^{5.8}$ 41$^{1.5.11.11.15}$ (all E, not elsewh. in Hex.); of Midianite Ju 7^{13}, Nebuchad. Dn 2$^{1.3}$, old men in latter days Jo 3^{1}. **c.** of dreams of false prophets Dt 13$^{2.4.6}$ Je 23$^{25.25}$. **Hiph.** *Pt.* מַחְלְמִים *dream* (of false prophets, c. acc. cogn.) Je 29^{8} (but rd. חֹלְמִים [מ by dittogr. fr. אַתֶּם], Hi Gf Gie Gr).

†חֲלוֹם **n.m.**$^{Gn\ 37,10}$ **dream**;—ח׳ abs. Gn 2472
37^{5} +, cstr. Gn 20^{3}, חֲלֹם abs. Gn 20^{6}, cstr. 31^{24}; sf. חֲלוֹמִי Gn 40$^{9.16}$, חֲלֹמִי Gn 41$^{17.22}$, חֲלֹמוֹ Gn 40^{5} + 5 t.; pl. חֲלֹמוֹת Je 23^{32} + 10 t. etc., + 7 t. sf.—*dream* **1.** ordinary dream of sleep Jb 7^{14} 20^{8} ψ 73^{20} Ec 5$^{2.6}$ Is 29^{7}. **2.** dreams with prophetic meaning, the lowest grade of prophecy (v. Br$^{MP\ 6}$): **a.** dream of Abimelek Gn 20$^{3.6}$, of Jacob 31$^{10.11}$, Laban 31^{24}, Joseph 37$^{5.6.8.9.9.10.19.20}$ 42^{9}, Pharaoh and his servants 40$^{5.5.5.8.9.9.16}$ 41$^{7.8.11.11.12.12.15.15.17.22.25.26.32}$; of a lower order of prophets than Moses Nu 12^{6}, (all E, not elsewh. in Hex.), Jb 33^{15}, of Midianite Ju 7$^{13.13.15}$, desired by Saul 1 S 28$^{6.15}$; of Sol. 1 K 3$^{5.15}$; of old men in latter days Jo 3^{1}, of Nebuchad. Dn 2$^{1.2.3.3}$; Daniel הֵבִין בְּכָל־חָזוֹן וַחֲלֹמוֹת Dn 1^{17} *had understanding* in all visions and *dreams*. **b.** of false prophets Dt 13$^{2.4.6}$ Je 23$^{27.28.28.32}$ 27^{9} 29^{8} Zc 10^{2}.

חַלָּמוּת **n.f.** name of a plant, with thick, 2495
slimy juice, *purslain*, Jb 6^{6} RVm, so Thes Rob Ges al.; 𝔖 ܚܠܡܘܬܐ, *anchusa* PS$^{i.\ 1284}$; on this, and later interpr. v. Bö Di Löw$^{pp.\ 165,\ 361}$; only אִם־יֶשׁ־טַעַם בְּרִיר חַלָּמוּת Jb 6^{6} *is there any taste in the juice of* ח׳ (fig. of insipid and dull discourse); > AV RV Ew Hi SS after 𝔗 Saad Rabb. *in the white of an egg*.

חלמיש (quadrilit. √of following; meaning unknown).

†חַלָּמִישׁ **n.m. flint**;—חַלָּמִישׁ Dt 8^{15} + 3 t.; 2496
cstr. חַלְמִישׁ Dt 32^{13};—*flint* צוּר הַח׳ *rock of flint* = flinty rock, whence water flowed for Isr. in desert Dt 8^{15}, and (no צוּר) ψ 114^{8}; worked by miners Jb 28^{9}; hyperb. *oil out of* ח׳ צוּר Dt 32^{13} *flint of rock* = rocky flint (poet.);—in sim. of firmness עַל־כֵּן שַׂמְתִּי פָּנַי כַּחַלָּמִישׁ Is 50^{7}.

2473, 2497 חֲלוֹן, חִלֹּן v. sub I. and II. חול.

2498 †חָלַף **vb. pass on or away, pass through** (mostly poet.) (NH *id., pass by* or *away, change;* Ph. חלפת *equivalent*, Reinach RÉJ 1888, 276; Hoffm G. G. Abh. xxxvi. 1890, 20; Aram. חֲלַף *pass away, change;* ܚܠܦ *change, substitute;* Nab. חלף *change* (?) Eut p. 53; Ar. خَلَفَ *come after, succeed, replace* [cf. 'Caliph' i.e. *successor* (of Mohammed)] and many deriv. Lane 792–799; so also ויחלפה MI ^{6} *and his son succeeded him;* Eth. ኀለፈ: *pass by, across, through*)—**Qal** *Pf.* חָלַף Ct 2^{11} Hb 1^{11} etc.; *Impf.* יַחֲלֹף Jb 4^{15} + 4 t.; 3 fs. sf. תַּחְלְפֵהוּ Jb 20^{24}; יַחֲלֹפוּ ψ 102^{27}; *Inf. cstr.* לַחֲלוֹף Is 21^{1}; —**1. a.** *pass on quickly* 1 S 10^{3}; elsewh. only poet., *move* or *sweep on*, of a flood Is 8^{8}, or wind 21^{1} Jb 4^{15} Hb 1^{11}, of God Jb 9^{11} 11^{10}. **b.** *pass away* (*vanish*) Jb 9^{26} (of days); Ct 2^{11} (of rain ‖ עבר), of the heavens ψ 102^{27}, of idols Is 2^{18}, (but perhaps gloss JBL ix. 1890, 86). **2.** of grass, *come on anew*, i.e. *sprout again* (cf. **Hiph. 2**) ψ $90^{5.6}$, so Thes AV De Hi Che Bae al.; less suitably in context, 𝔊 𝔙 Ew *pass away*, supr. **1 b. 3.** trans. **a.** *pass through*, i.e. pierce, sq. acc. Ju 5^{26} Jb 20^{24}. **b.** *overstep, transgress* Is 24^{5} (‖ עבר), (cf. Ar. IV. to *break* a promise). **Pi.** *Impf.* וַיְחַלֵּף (*cause to pass*) *change*, sq. acc. garment Gn 41^{14} (E) 2 S 12^{20}. **Hiph.** *Pf.* הֶחֱלִף Gn 31^{7}; *Impf.* יַחֲלִיף Jb 14^{7}; sf. יַחֲלִיפֶנּוּ Lv 27^{10}; 3 fs. תַּחֲלִיף Jb 29^{20}; 2 ms. וַתַּחֲלֵף Gn 31^{41}; sf. תַּחֲלִיפֵם; יַחֲלִיפוּ Is 40^{31} 41^{1}; נַחֲלִיף Is 9^{9};—**1.** *change* (trans.) garments Gn 35^{2} (E) ψ 102^{27}, wages Gn $31^{7.41}$ (both E); no obj. expr. Lv 27^{10} (H); *substitute* i.e. *cause to succeed* Is 9^{9}; *change* for better, *renew*, obj. כֹּחַ Is 40^{31} 41^{1}. **2.** *shew newness*, of tree, putting forth fresh shoots Jb 14^{7}, of bow 29^{20}.

2500 †I. חֵלֶף **n.[m.] exchange**, only cstr., as prep. *in return for* (so חֲלַף, ܚܠܦ, common in Aram. e.g. Gn 4^{23} 𝔗𝔖 for Heb. תַּחַת)—ח׳ עֲבֹדָתָם (עֲבֹדַתְכֶם) Nu $18^{21.31}$ (both P).

2501 †II. חֵלֶף **n.pr.loc.** in Naphtali, site unknown Jos 19^{33}.

2475 †חֲלוֹף **n.m. a passing away, vanishing** (properly Inf. of חלף)—בְּנֵי ח׳ Pr 31^{8} i.e. those who are passing away, transitory (cf. **Qal 1 b**).

2487 †[חֲלִיפָה] **n.f. a change** (from idea of *replacing, changing, substituting*, cf. Ar., Aram.)—sf. חֲלִיפָתִי Jb 14^{14}; pl. abs. חֲלִיפוֹת Ju 14^{19} + 3 t.; cstr. *id.* Ju 14^{13} 2 K 5^{5}; חֲלִפוֹת Gn 45^{22} + 2 t.; חֲלִפֹת Gn 45^{22} Ju 14^{12};—**1.** *change* of raiment ח׳ שׂמלת Gn $45^{22.22}$, elsewhere ח׳ בגדים Ju $14^{12.13}$ 2 K $5^{5.22.23}$; so without בגדים Ju 14^{19}. **2.** *relays* 1 K 5^{28}; cf. ח׳ וצבא Jb 10^{17} (Di). **3.** revival after death, under fig. of *relief* from milit. service Jb 14^{14}. **4.** *changing, varying*, of course of life אֲשֶׁר אֵין חֲלִיפוֹת לָמוֹ ψ 55^{20} of the wicked, *with whom are no changings*, i.e. they do evil incessantly, steadily (‖ ולא יָרְאוּ אלהים) so Kmp Hu De Sch al.; but the expression is peculiar and obscure; Calv *vicissitudes;* Hengst *discharges;* text perhaps corrupt.

†[מַחֲלָף] **n.m. knife**, so 𝔙 (cf. Syr. ܚܠܦ 4252
totondit (in Lex.), ܡܚܠܦܐ, ܚܘܠܦܐ, *knife*, Talm. חליפות *knives*, acc. to Levy, Jastr; Thes as *passing through* (cf. vb. **3 a**)); but √ and meaning not certain, only Pl. מַחֲלָפִים Ezr 1^{9}, among temple utensils (v. BeRy Ryle).

†[מַחְלָפָה] **n.f. plait** (of hair; so called fr. 4253
intertwining, passing through each other, of the strands)—Pl. cstr. מַחְלְפוֹת ראשׁי Ju 16^{13}, cf. v^{19}.

†I. חָלַץ **vb. draw off** or **out, withdraw** 2502
(NH *id.;* Aram. חֲלַץ; ܚܠܨ *despoil*, usu. Pa. etc.; Ph. n.pr. חלצבעל *Baal has rescued*, and חלץ alone; Ar. خَلَصَ *withdraw, retire*)—**Qal** *Pf.* Ho 5^{6}; וְחָלְצָה consec. Dt 25^{9}; חָלְצוּ La 4^{3}; *Impf.* 2 ms. תַּחֲלֹץ; *Pt. pass.* cstr. חֲלוּץ Dt 25^{10};—**1.** *draw, draw off*, c. acc. of sandal Dt 25^{9} Is 20^{2} (both sq. מִן c. רֶגֶל), cf. בֵּית חֲלוּץ הַנָּעַל Dt 25^{10}; *draw out, present* the breast, of animal giving suck La 4^{3}. **2.** intrans. *withdraw* (himself) sq. מִן Ho 5^{6}. **Niph.** *Pf. be delivered* נֶחֱלָץ Pr 11^{8} (sq. מִן); *Impf.* יֵחָלֵצוּ Pr 11^{9}; יֵחָלְצוּן ψ 60^{7} = 108^{7} (Ges § 51. 2. R. 2). **Pi.** *Pf.* חִלֵּץ Lv 14^{43} etc.; *Impf.* יְחַלֵּץ Jb 36^{15}; וָאֲחַלְּצָה ψ 7^{5} (but on text vid. infr. ad fin.); sf. אֲחַלֶּצְךָ ψ 50^{15}; אֲחַלֶּצְךָ ψ 81^{8}, etc.; *Imv.* חַלְּצָה ψ 6^{5}; חַלְּצֵנִי ψ 119^{153} 140^{2};—**1.** *pull out, tear out* Lv $14^{40.43}$ (P; stones fr. infested house). **2.** *rescue, deliver*, c. obj. pers., but only poet.;—sq. נפשׁי ψ 6^{5} 116^{8} (מִמָּוֶת); cf. 140^{2} (sq. מִן); abs. c. acc. ψ 18^{20} = 2 S 22^{20}, ψ 34^{8} 50^{15} 81^{8} 91^{15} 119^{153} Jb 36^{15}; וָאֲחַלְּצָה ψ 7^{5}; sq. acc., *but I delivered* AV Hup Ri, cf. Ew; *and spoiled, despoiled* Ges Hi De Bae (but this only in Aram.); < *and oppressed* (rd. וָאֶלְחֲצָה) Krochm Dy Gr Che; (‖ וְגָמַלְתִּי רָע).

†[חֲלִיצָה] **n.f. what is stripped off a** 2488
person, as plunder, in war;—only sf. חֲלִצָתוֹ 2 S 2^{21}; חֲלִיצוֹתָם Ju 14^{19}.

4254 †[מַחֲלָצָה] **n.f.** **robe of state** (*taken off* in ordinary life);—only pl. abs. מַחֲלָצוֹת Is 3^{22} robes of ladies of Jerusalem; Zc 3^{4} of high priest.

2502 † II. [חָלַץ] **vb.** **equip** for war (primary idea of *strength, vigour*, v. Hiph., n. חֲלָצַיִם, and As. *ḫalṣu, fortification* (Schr COT Gloss Asrb Annals ii. 52), cf. *ḫilṣu, belt*, Zehnpfund BAS i. 499; Aram. ܚܠܝܨ *accinctus ad opus, strenuus*, ܚܠܝܨܘܬܐ *fortitudo, strenuitas*, Gk. ἀνδρεία, > Thes Rob Ges SS who regard as = I. חלץ in sense *strip* for battle, *expeditus*)—**Qal** only *Pt. pass.* חָלוּץ Nu 32^{21} + 7 t., cstr. חֲלוּץ Nu 32^{27}; pl. חֲלוּצִים Nu 32^{30} + 2 t., cstr. חֲלוּצֵי 1 Ch 12^{24} + 3 t.; חֲלֻצֵי Is 15^{4};—*equipped:* **1.** as adj. Nu $32^{30.32}$ Dt 3^{18}. **2.** as subst. sg. coll. Nu 32^{21} (JE; v. Niph. v^{20}) 2 Ch 20^{21} 28^{14}, c. art. הֶח׳ Jos $6^{7.9.13}$ (JE); חֲלוּץ צָבָא Nu 32^{27} *men equipped for war* (JE), so ח׳ הַמִּלְחָמָה 32^{29} (P); הֶחָ׳ לַצָּבָא 1 Ch 12^{24} (v^{23} van d. H); pl. חֲלוּצֵי צָבָא Nu 31^{5} (P) 1 Ch 12^{25} (v^{24} van d. H) 2 Ch 17^{18}; ח׳ הַצ׳ Jos 4^{13} (P); note חֲלֻצֵי מוֹאָב Is 15^{4} *warriors* (*equipped ones*, Che *men-at-arms*) *of Moab.* **Niph.** *Impf.* 2 mpl. תֵּחָלְצוּ Nu 32^{20}, 1 pl. נֵחָלֵץ Nu 32^{17}; *Imv.* הֵחָלְצוּ Nu 31^{3}; *be*, or *go equipped*, sq. לִפְנֵי Nu $32^{17.20}$ (both JE; v. Qal Pt. v^{21}); sq. לַצָּבָא 31^{3} (P; Niph. Imv. here surprising with מֵאִתְּכֶם, v. Di). **Hiph.** *Impf.* עַצְמֹתֶיךָ יַחֲלִיץ Is 58^{11} *he* (י׳) *will brace up, invigorate, thy bones* (MV De Di; Hup Che crit. n. Du al. rd. יַחֲלִיף *renew, rejuvenate*).

2504 †[חָלָץ] **n.[f.]** only dual, **loins** (as seat of strength, vigour; cf. Aram. חַרְצָא *hip, loin*, Syr. ܚܨܐ, Nö ZMG 1886, 741)—חֲלָצַיִם Is 32^{11}; sf. חֲלָצֶיךָ Gn 35^{11} + 4 t.; חֲלָצָיו Is 5^{27} + 2 t.; + חלצו Kt Jb 31^{20}, Qr חֲלָצָיו;—*loins:* **1.** as seat of virility יצא מן ח׳ Gn 35^{11} (P), 1 K 8^{19} 2 Ch 6^{9}. **2.** as girded אֱזָר־נָא כְגֶבֶר ח׳ Jb 38^{3} 40^{7}; אֵזוֹר חֲלָצָיו Is 5^{27} (v. אֵזוֹר), וַחֲגוֹרָה עַל חֲלָצָיִם 32^{11}, cf. Jb 31^{20} where the clothed loins are conceived as blessing charitable giver; metaph. Is 11^{5} faithfulness waist-cloth of his loins (‖ מתניו). **3.** as seat of pains, like a woman's in travail, Je 30^{6}.

2503 †חֶלֶץ **n.pr.m.** (*vigour*). **1.** one of David's heroes 2 S 23^{26}, 𝔊 Σελλης, A Ελλης, 𝔊L Χαλλης; = 1 Ch 11^{27} 𝔊 Χελλης, 𝔊L Ελλης; also 1 Ch 27^{10} 𝔊 Χεσλης, A 𝔊L Χελλης (in both, Baer חֶלֶץ, van d. H. חֵלֶץ). **2.** man of Judah 1 Ch 2^{39} = חָלֶץ v^{39} 𝔊 Χελλης, 𝔊L Αλλαν.

חָלֶץ **n.pr.m.** v. חֶלֶץ supr.

† I. חָלַק **vb.** **divide, share** (NH *id.*; Aram. חֲלַק *field*, חוּלָקָא *portion*, ܚܠܩ *divide, determine, decree*; Ar. خَلَقَ *measure, measure off*; As. *eḳlu, possession, field*, Jäger BAS ii. 296; Eth. ኈለቈ: I. 2, is *enumerate*, ኈልቍ: ኍለቄ: *enumeration, number*) 2505
—**Qal** *Pf.* ח׳ Dt 4^{19} + 5 t.; חָלְקוּ Jos 18^{2}; *Impf.* יַחֲלֹק Jb 27^{17} Pr 17^{2}; 2 ms. sf. וַתַּחְלְקֵם Ne 9^{22}; 3 pl. וַיַּחְלְקוּ Jos 14^{5}; יַחֲלֹקוּ 1 S 30^{24}; וַיַּחְלְקוּם 1 Ch $24^{4.5}$; תַּחְלְקוּ 2 S 19^{30}; *Imv.* חִלְקוּ Jos 22^{8}; *Inf.* לַחֲלֹק Ne 13^{13}; *Pt.* חוֹלֵק Pr 29^{24};—**1.** *divide, apportion*, sq. acc. (of gods) and לְ pers. Dt 4^{19} 29^{25}; acc. not expressed Ne 13^{13} (ref. to offerings and tithes); c. acc. (of land) Jos 14^{5} (P), 18^{2} (JE), 2 S 19^{30}: obj. people Ne 9^{22}; ח׳ עִם *divide with* others Jos 22^{8} (D ?). **2.** *assign, distribute:* Levites over (על) temple 2 Ch 23^{18}, cf. 1 Ch $24^{4.5}$. **3.** *assign, impart*, sq. בִּינָה & לְ Jb 39^{17}. **4.** *share* (in), sq. acc. silver Jb 27^{17}; inheritance Pr 17^{2}; spoil 1 S 30^{24} (obj. om.); sq. עם *have shares with* ח׳ עם גַּנָּב Pr 29^{24}. **5.** *divide up* = *plunder* the temple, sq. acc. 2 Ch 28^{21} (v. Be). **Niph.** *Impf.* יֵחָלֵק Nu 26^{55} 1 K 16^{21}; יֵחָלֶק Jb 38^{24}; וַיֵּחָלֵק Gn 14^{15}; 3 fs. תֵּחָלֵק Nu 26^{53} 26^{56}; וַיֵּחָלְקֵם (Baer) 1 Ch 23^{6} 24^{3} cf. Be & infr. sub **Pi.**;—**1.** reflex., *divide oneself* Gn 14^{15} (i.e. one's men). **2.** pass. *be divided:* **a.** *apportioned*, the land Nu $26^{53.55}$ (by lot) v^{56} (*id.*); all P. **b.** of people, *divided into* two factions 1 K 16^{21}. **c.** of light, *parted, spread abroad* Jb 38^{24}. **3.** trans. *assign, distribute* 1 Ch 23^{6} 24^{3}, but trans. Niph. is unlikely, v. infr. **Pi.** *Pf.* 3 pl. חִלְּקוּ Jo 4^{2}; וְחִלַּקְתֶּם consec. Ez 47^{21}; sf. חִלְּקָם La 4^{16}; 3 fs. sf. חִלְּקַתָּה Is 34^{17}; 2 ms. sf. וְחִלַּקְתָּם Ez 5^{1};—*Impf.* יְחַלֵּק Gn 49^{27} + 4 t., etc.; prob. rd. יְחַלְּקֵם 1 Ch 23^{6} 24^{3} (v. supr. **Niph.**), etc.; *Imv.* חַלֵּק Jos 13^{7}; *Inf.* חַלֵּק Jos 19^{51} Pr 16^{19}; sf. חַלְּקָם Is 9^{2};—**1.** *divide, apportion:* food, at festival 2 S 6^{19}, sq. acc. & לְ = 1 Ch 16^{3}, garments ψ 22^{19}, sorrows Jb 21^{17} (no לְ); *give a portion to*, sq. לְ (no acc. expr.) Is 53^{12}; a land Jo 4^{2} (no ind. obj.) Jos 19^{51} (P), also Mi 2^{4}, ψ 60^{8} = 108^{8}, Dn 11^{39}; sq. acc. & לְ Jos 13^{7} 18^{10} 1 K 18^{6} Is 34^{17} Ez 47^{21}; *divide* hair (symbol.) Ez 5^{1}; *divide* spoil (שָׁלָל) Is 9^{2} Pr 16^{19} Gn 49^{27} (poem), Ex 15^{9} (song); Ju 5^{30} ψ 68^{13} Is 53^{12}. **2.** *assign, distribute:* Levites to their service, prob. 1 Ch 23^{6} 24^{3} (v. supr.) **3.** *scatter*, sq. acc. Gn 49^{7} (poem) (‖ הפיץ), La 4^{16}. **Pu.** *Pf.* חֻלַּק Is 33^{23};

וְחָלַק consec. Zc 14^{1}; *Impf.* 3 fs. תֵּחָלֵק Am 7^{17}; *be divided*, of land Am 7^{17}; spoil Is 33^{23} Zc 14^{1}. **Hithp.** *Pf.* וְהִתְחַלְּקוּ consec. Jos 18^{5} *divide* (land) *among themselves.* **Hiph.** *Inf.* לַחֲלֹק Je 37^{12}; *to receive a portion* (denom. fr. חֵלֶק), but dub.

2506 †I. חֵ֫לֶק **n.m.** Jos 18, 5 **portion, tract, territory** —ח׳ abs. Gn 31^{14}+; cstr. Gn 14^{24}+; sf. חֶלְקִי ψ 16^{5}+6 t.; חֶלְקְךָ Nu 18^{20} Ec 9^{9}; חֶלְקֶ֑ךָ ψ 50^{18}; חֶלְקֵךְ Is 57^{6}; חֶלְקוֹ Hb 1^{16}+5 t.; חֶלְקָם Gn 14^{24} +3 t.; pl. חֲלָקִים Jos 18^{5}+5 t.; sf. חֶלְקֵיהֶם Ho 5^{7};—**1.** *portion, share:* **a.** of booty Gn 14$^{24.24}$ Nu 31^{36} (P) 1 S 30$^{24.24}$. **b.** of food Lv 6^{10} (P); ח׳ כח׳ יאכלו Dt 18^{8};=food Hb 1^{16} (‖ מַאֲכָל); so (of unrestricted charity) Ec 11^{2} v. Now. **c.** sq. בְּ, *share* or *interest in* Ec 9^{6}, with idea of *obligation to* Gn 31^{14} (E; in father's house), 2 S 20^{1}=1 K 12^{16}=2 Ch 10^{16} (in royal line; all ‖ נַחֲלָה); of *right* (*privilege*) *in* ח׳ ביהוה Jos 22$^{25.27}$ (P); Ne 2^{20} (in Jerus.; + צְדָקָה וְזִכָּרוֹן). **d.** proper *share* or *part* אַעֲנֶה חֶלְקִי Jb 32^{17} i.e. I will do my part in replying. Esp. **2.** *portion, tract,* of land: **a.** as distrib. at conquest Jos 19^{9}, seven *portions* 18$^{5.6.9}$ (all JE) v^{7} (JE; + נחלה in ‖ cl.), 15^{13} 19^{9} (both P); none for tribe of Levi Dt 10^{9} 12^{12} 14$^{27.29}$ 18^{1} Jos 18^{7} (all D; ‖ נחלה), Jos 14^{4} (P), none for priests Nu 18^{20} (P; ‖ vb. נחל). **b.** of land possessed by people Ho 5^{7} Mi 2^{4}. **c.** portion to be assigned after exile Is 61^{7} Ez 45^{7} 48$^{8.21}$, חֶלְקוֹ עַל־אַדְמַת הַקֹּדֶשׁ Zc 2^{16}. **d.** specif. of *town-land,* district about a town, ח׳ יִזְרְעֶאל 2 K 9$^{10.36}$ +1 K 21^{23} (MT חֵל), הַשָּׂדֶה בְּח׳ יִז׳ v^{37}. **e.** הַחֵלֶק Am 7^{4} (opp. תְּהוֹם) appar. of *land* of Isr. **3.** hence *portion,* i.e. (acquired) *possession:* **a.** of people as י׳'s possession Dt 32^{9} (‖ חֶבֶל נחלתו); but esp. **b.** of י׳ as possession of his servants: of priests, as enjoying perquisites of altar Nu 18^{20} (P; ‖ נחלה), in spiritual sense ψ 73^{26} 119^{57} La 3^{24}; ח׳ בְּאֶרֶץ הַחַיִּים ψ 142^{6}; י׳ מְנָת חֶלְקִי ψ 16^{5}; hence ח׳ יעקב of י׳ Je 10^{16}=51^{19} (שֵׁבֶט נַחֲלָתוֹ in ‖ cl.) **4.** chosen *portion,* habitual mode of life עִם־מְנָאֲפִים ח׳ ψ 50^{18} *with adulterers is thy chosen life* (companionship, shewing character); בְּחַלְּקֵי־נַחַל חֶלְקֵךְ Is 57^{6} *among smooth* (things i.e. stones) *of a brook-bed is thy chosen life* (of idolatrous habit; v. חָלָק); חֶלְקָם בַּחַיִּים ψ 17^{14}. **5.** *portion, award,* from God ח׳ אֱלוֹהַּ Jb 31^{2} (‖ נחלה); specif. of punishment of wicked Is 17^{14} (‖ גּוֹרָל), עִם־אֵל Jb 27^{13}, מֵאֱלֹהִים 20^{29} (‖ נחלה);= *profit, reward* חֶלְקִי מִכָּל־עֲמָלִי Ec 2^{10}, cf. v^{21} 3^{22} 5$^{17.18}$ 9^{9}.—לְחֵלֶק Jb 17^{5} is dub.: *a share* of feast, or of booty, Kmp Hi; *a prey, spoil,* Ew Di Da; AV *flattery* does not suit context.

†II. חֵ֫לֶק **n.pr.m.** (**portion**) a Gileadite 2507
Nu 26^{30} Jos 17^{2}. 𝔊 Χελεγ, (κ), Κελεζ, etc.; 𝔊L Jos 17^{2} Ελεκ.

†חֶלְקִי **adj.gent.** of foreg.; only c. art. as 2516
subst. coll. after מִשְׁפַּחַת Nu 26^{30}.

†I. חֶלְקָה **n.f.** portion of ground;—abs. ח׳ 2513
Am 4$^{7.7}$+8 t.; cstr. חֶלְקַת Gn 33^{19}+12 t.; sf. חֶלְקָתִי Je 12^{10}; חֶלְקָתָם Jb 24^{18}; *portion* of ground, **1.** esp. **a.** ח׳ הַשָּׂדֶה=the clearly divided *field* Gn 33^{19} Jos 24^{32} (both E), 2 S 23^{11} Ru 2^{3} 4^{3} 2 K 9^{25} 1 Ch 11^{13}. Also **b.** without השדה Am 4$^{7.7}$ 2 S 14$^{30.30.31}$ 23^{12} 2 K 3$^{19.25}$ 9$^{21.26.26}$ 1 Ch 11^{14} Jb 24^{18}; of י׳'s land Je 12$^{10.10}$ (‖ כַּרְמִי); cf. also n.pr.loc. חלקת הַצֻּרִים 2 S 2^{16} *field of sword-edges* (Dr), 𝔊 Ew G iii. 156, Eng. tr. 114 We rd. ח׳ הַצֹּדִים *field of plotters* or *liers-in-wait* (v. Dr). **2.** *portion* of ground assigned to one, ח׳ מחקק Dt 33^{21} *commander's portion.*

†[חֲלֻקָּה] **n.f.** part, portion, חֲלֻקַּת בֵּית־אָב 2515
לַלְוִיִּם 2 Ch 35^{5}.

†חֶלְקַי **n.pr.m.** priest, time of Joiakim son 2517
of Jeshua, Ne 12^{15} (perh. abbrev. for חלקיהו, (q.v.), 𝔊L Χελκιας (B om.)

†חֶלְקָת **n.pr.loc.** (*portion, possession*) city 2520
in Asher Jos 21^{31}, 𝔊 Χελκατ, A Θελκαθ, 𝔊L Χαλκαθ,
= חֶלְקַת 19^{25} 𝔊 Ελεκεθ, A Χελκαθ, 𝔊L Ελκαθ. 2520

†חֶלְקַת הַצֻּרִים **n.pr.loc.** a place near 2521
pool of Gibeon where Ishbosheth's men were killed by Dvd.'s men under Joab 2 S 2^{16}, 𝔊 Μέρις τῶν ἐπιβούλων; on mng. of name v. I. חֶלְקָה supr.

†חִלְקִיָּה, חִלְקִיָּהוּ **n.pr.m.** (*my portion* 2518
is י׳) 𝔊 usu. Χελκ(ε)ιας, Χελχιας;—**1.** father of Eliakim, Hezekiah's officer, חלקיהו 2 K 18$^{18.26}$ Is 22^{20} 36$^{3.22}$; חלקיה 2 K 18^{37}. **2.** high priest, Josiah's time, חלקיהו 2 K 22$^{4.8.14}$ 23$^{4.24}$ 2 Ch 34$^{9.14.15.15.18.20.22}$; חלקיה 2 K 22$^{8.10.12}$ 1 Ch 5$^{39.39}$ 9^{11} 2 Ch 35^{8} Ezr 7^{1}, cf. also Ne 11^{11}. **3.** חלקיהו father of Jerem. Je 1^{1}.—The foll. are all חלקיה: **4.** Levites: **a.** 1 Ch 6^{30}. **b.** 1 Ch 26^{11}. **5.** a priest, contemp. of Ezra Ne 8^{4} 12$^{7.21}$. **6.** father of Gemariah, an ambassador of Zedekiah to Nebuchadrezzar Je 29^{3}.

מַחֲלֹ֫קֶת **n.f.** division, course (almost 4256

wholly Chr.)—מ׳ abs. 1 Ch $27^{1.2}$; cstr. 1 Ch 27^{4}; sf. מַחְלֻקְתּוֹ 1 Ch 27^{2} + 14 t. 1 Ch 27; abs. מַחְלְקוֹת 1 Ch 23^{6} + 6 t. Ch + 1 S 23^{28} (v. infr.); cstr. *id.* 1 Ch 26^{12} + 5 t. Ch + Ne 11^{36}; sf. מַחְלְקוֹתֵיכֶם 2 Ch 35^{4}; מַחְלְקוֹתֵיהֶם 2 Ch $31^{16.17}$; מַחְלְקוֹתָם 1 Ch 24^{1} + 3 t. in Ch; מַחְלְקֹתָם Jos 11^{23} 12^{7} 18^{10} Ez 48^{29};—**1.** *division, part,* of land assigned to the several tribes of Isr. Jos 11^{23} 12^{7} (both D) 18^{10} (JE; others, divisions of Isr., but v.) Ez 48^{29}. **2.** techn. term of organization of priests and Levites (late), 1 Ch 23^{6} 24^{1} $26^{1.12.19}$ 2 Ch $8^{14.14}$ $31^{2.2}$ $35^{4.10}$ Ne 11^{36} + 26 t. in Ch.—סֶלַע הַמַּחְלְקוֹת n.pr. 1 S 23^{28} was popularly connected with this √, = *rock of divisions,* where Saul and David parted from neighbourhood of each other (Dr) so Vrss Th al.; Bö Klo, where their forces lay divided from each other; orig. connex. was perh. with II. חלק, *smooth, slippery;* Ges De W Ke al. expl. here as *rock of escapes,* but this meaning for חלק dubious.

2505 II. חָלַק **vb. be smooth, slippery** (NH adj. חָלָק *smooth, empty,* Ar. خَلَقَ *make smooth, lie, forge, fabricate*)—**Qal** *Pf.* ח׳ Ho 10^{2}; 3 mpl. חָלְקוּ ψ 55^{22};—*smooth, slippery,* only fig.: Ho 10^{2} of heart of faithless Isr. (so Ew Ke Wü Now RVm), We *false;* > Vrss (not 𝔊) Hi St who rd. חֻלַּק, *divided* is their heart; 𝔊 ἐμέρισαν; of words, *smooth* ψ 55^{22} i.e. deceptive (‖ רַכּוּ דְבָרָיו מִשֶּׁמֶן). **Hiph.** *Pf.* הֶחֱלִיק ψ 36^{3}, הֶחֱלִיקָה Pr 2^{16} 7^{5}; *Impf.* יַחֲלִיקוּן ψ 5^{10}; *Pt.* מַחֲלִיק Pr 28^{23} + 2 t.; *make smooth:* **1.** lit. of idol-maker Is 41^{7} c. acc. instr. פַּטִּישׁ *hammer.* **2.** fig. *the tongue,* i.e. flatter with it ψ 5^{10} Pr 28^{23}, words Pr 2^{16} 7^{5} אֲמָרֶיהָ הֶחֱלִיקָה; abs. *deal smoothly,* sq. אֶל־ ψ 36^{3}, עַל Pr 29^{5}.

2506 †III. חֵלֶק **n.[m.] smoothness, seductiveness** of speech, only sg. cstr. בְּחֵלֶק שְׂפָתֶיהָ תַּדִּיחֶנּוּ Pr 7^{21} *with the seductiveness of her lips she impelleth him* (‖ הִטַּתּוּ בְּרֹב לִקְחָהּ).—I. and II. חֵלֶק v. sub I. חלק.

2509-10 †חָלָק **adj. smooth**—**1.** lit. אִישׁ חָלָק Gn 27^{11} (J), *smooth man* (opp. אִישׁ שָׂעִר); הָהָר הֶחָלָק Jos 11^{17} 12^{7} *the bald mt.* (both D); southern limit of Jos.'s conquest, identif. dub.; (1) white cliffs 8 m. S. of Dead Sea, and (2) Mt. Mâdara SW. fr. Pass es-Ṣafâ are proposed, v. Di.; as subst.
2511 חַלְּקֵי־נַחַל Is 57^{6} (v. I. חֵלֶק, **4**) *smooth* (stones) of a brook-bed (ravine, wady), i.e. thou worshippest common round stones (contempt., v. Che Di). **2.** fig. of mouth uttering smooth words וְחָלָק מִשֶּׁמֶן חִכָּהּ Pr 5^{3} cf. 26^{28}. **3.** as subst. = *flattery* מִקְסַם חָלָק Ez 12^{24} *divination of flattery.*

†II. [חֶלְקָה] **n.f. smooth part, smooth-** 2513
ness, flattery;—cstr. חֶלְקַת Gn 27^{16} Pr 6^{24}; pl. חֲלָקוֹת ψ 12^{3} + 3 t.;—**1.** *smoothness, smooth part* חֶלְקַת צַוָּארָיו Gn 27^{16}. **2.** pl. *slippery places* ψ 73^{18} fig. of situation of wicked. **3.** *smoothness = flattery* שְׂפַת ח׳ ψ 12^{3}, cf. v^{4}; חֶלְקַת לָשׁוֹן Pr 6^{24}; = subst. pl. *smooth things,* i.e. *agreeable, flattering things* Is 30^{10}.—I. חֶלְקָה v. sub I. חלק.

†[חָלָק] **adj. smooth,** only pl. cstr. חַלֻּקֵי 2512
אֲבָנִים 1 S 17^{40} *smooth ones of (among) stones = smooth (or smoothest?) stones* Ges$^{§§ 132 R 2, 133,3}$ Dr^{Sm}.

†[חֲלַקָּה] **n.f. smoothness, flattery,** only 2514
pl. abs.: **fine promises,** יַחֲנִיף בַּחֲלַקּוֹת Dn 11^{32} (perhaps directly from חָלָק, exceptional pl., cf. קְטַנּוֹת, קְטַנִּים, קְטַנָּה, גְּמַלִּים).

†חֲלַקְלַקּוֹת **n.pl.f.abstr. smoothness,** 2519
slipperiness, flattery, fine promises; **1.** *slipperiness* יְהִי־דרכם חשך וַחֲלַקְלַקֹּת ψ 35^{6}; יהיה דרכם להם כַּחֲלַקְלַקּוֹת Je 23^{12}. **2.** *fine promises* והחזיק מלכות בַּחֲלַקְלַקּוֹת Dn 11^{21}; cf. 11^{34}.

†II. מַחְלְקוֹת **n.f.pl. smoothness,** סֶלַע הַמ׳ 5555
1 S 23^{28} *rock of smoothness,* i.e. *slippery rock,* perhaps original meaning of this n.pr., v. further I. מחלקות sub I. חלק.

†[חָלַשׁ] **vb. 1. be weak, prostrate. 2.** 2522
(si vera l.) **weaken, disable, prostrate** (Aram. חֲלַשׁ *be weak;* ܚܠܫ, חַלָּשׁ *weak,* as in Heb.; Ar. مُخْلِس *poor* (Frey))—**Qal** *Impf.* וַיַּחֲלֹשׁ Ex 17^{13}, וַיֶּחֱלָשׁ Jb 14^{10}; *Pt.* חוֹלֵשׁ Is 14^{12}; **1.** וגבר ימות ויח׳ Jb 14^{10} *but man dieth and is prostrate.* **2.** *disable, prostrate,* sq. acc. pers. Ex 17^{13} (E; point as **Hiph.**?); sq. עַל pers. (strangely) Is 14^{12}.

†חַלָּשׁ **adj. weak,** only c. art. as subst., 2523
הַחַלָּשׁ יאמר גבור אני Jo 4^{10} *the weak, let him say, I am a mighty man.*

†חֲלוּשָׁה **n.f. weakness, prostration,** אֵין 2476
קוֹל עֲנוֹת ח׳ Ex 32^{18} *it is not the sound of the answering of weakness* (JE; opp. גְּבוּרָה).

†I. חָם **n.pr.pers. m.** and **loc.** (cf. Sab. חם 2526
Hal^{243})—𝔊 Χαμ:—**1. Ham,** 2nd son of Noah Gn 5^{32} 6^{10} 7^{13} $9^{18.18}$ 1 Ch 1^{4}; called father of

Canaan Gn 9^{22} and of various peoples 10$^{1.6.20}$ 1 Ch 1^{8}, cf. מִן־חָם הַיֹּשְׁבִים שָׁם 4^{40}; these peoples were inhabitants of southern lands, or related historically or politically to such inhabitants; v. כּוּשׁ, כְּנַעַן, מִצְרַיִם, פּוּט, etc. **2.** in late ψψ a name (coll.) for Egyptians:—אָהֳלֵי־ח׳ ψ 78^{51}; אֶרֶץ־ח׳ 105$^{23.27}$ 106^{22} (all ‖ מִצְרַיִם, exc. 105^{27}).—On historical significance, and attempts at etymol. v. Di$^{\text{Gen. ed. 6, chap. 10, esp. pp. 165, 168 f.}}$, Hom$^{\text{SV i. 427}}$ Bu$^{\text{Urg. 323}}$ Wiedemann$^{\text{Ägypt. Gesch. i. 22}}$.

2524 II. חָם *husband's father*, v. חמה. p. 327

2525 III. חָם **adj.** *warm, hot*, v. sub חמם. p. 328

2527 חֹם v. sub חמם. p. 328

חמא (√ of foll.; cf. Ar. خَمَا *be hard*, used of curdled milk, Frey).

2529 †חֶמְאָה **n.f. curd**;—ח׳ Gn 18^{8}+6 t.; = חֵמָה Jb 29^{6}; cstr. חֶמְאַת Dt 32^{14}; *curd, curdled milk*, mod. *lebben* מִיץ חָלָב יוֹצִיא ח׳ Pr 30^{33}, elsewhere joined with חָלָב Gn 18^{8} (J) Dt 32^{14} (poem; חֶמְאַת בָּקָר וַחֲלֵב צֹאן), Ju 5^{25} (where served בְּסֵפֶל אַדִּירִים, v. ספל); with דְּבַשׁ 2 S 17^{29} Is 7$^{15.22.22}$; cf. נַחֲלֵי דבשׁ וח׳ fig. of abundance Jb 20^{17}; בִּרְחֹץ הֲלִיכַי בְּחֵמָה Jb 29^{6} (‖ צוּר יָצוּק : פַּלְגֵי־שָׁמֶן).

2534 †חֵמָא v. חֵמָה sub יחם. p. 404

2530 †חָמַד **vb. desire, take pleasure in** (Aram. חֲמַד (not in Syr.); Ar. حَمِدَ *praise, eulogize, approve of*; Sab. חמדם *in gratitude* [praise] *there-for* DHM$^{\text{ZMG 1875, 595; 1876, 686}}$)—**Qal** *Pf.* ח׳ ψ 68^{17} Pr 12^{12}; חָמָדוּ Pr 1^{22}; וְחָמְדוּ consec. Mi 2^{2}; חֲמַדְתֶּם Is 1^{29}; *Impf.* יַחְמֹד Ex 34^{24}; 2 ms. תַּחְמֹד Ex 20$^{16.16}$+3 t. (incl. Pr 6^{25} juss.); sf. וָאֶחְמְדֵם Jos 7^{21}; וְנֶחְמְדֵהוּ Is 53^{2}; *Pt. pass.* חֲמוּדוֹ ψ 39^{12} Jb 20^{20}, חֲמוּדֵיהֶם Is 44^{9};—*desire*: **a.** in bad sense of inordinate, ungoverned, selfish desire, sq. acc. Ex 20$^{17.17}$ (E) = Dt 5^{18} (v^{18b} has תִתְאַוֶּה), Ex 34^{24} (JE) Dt 7^{25} Jos 7^{21} (JE) Mi 2^{2} Pr 12^{12}; of lustful desire Pr 6^{25}. **b.** = *take pleasure in*, of idolatrous tendency Is 1^{29}, so pt. pl. חֲמוּדֵיהֶם Is 44^{9} *their delightful things* (things in which they delight, v. also v^{11} and Bev$^{\text{JPh. xvii. 1888, p. 126}}$); לֵצִים לָצוֹן חָמְדוּ Pr 1^{22} how long do *scorners delight in scorning*. **c.** less often in good sense, said of God הָהָר חָמַד א׳ לְשִׁבְתּוֹ, poet. ψ 68^{17}; obj. the suffering servant of י׳, Is 53^{2} no beauty in him, *that we should desire him* (choose him, be drawn toward him); pt. pass. coll. חֲמוּדוֹ ψ 39^{12} *his desired* things, i.e. chosen, choice, desirable (v. Niph.); so prob. Jb 20^{20}. **Niph.** *Pt.* נֶחְמָד Gn 2^{9}+2 t.; הַנֶּחֱמָדִים ψ 19^{11};—*desirable*: עֵץ נ׳ לְמַרְאֶה Gn 2^{9}, נ׳ לְהַשְׂכִּיל 3^{6}, הַנּ׳ מִזָּהָב ψ 19^{11} which are *more desirable than gold*; אוֹצָר נֶחְמָד Pr 21^{20} *desirable*, i.e. costly *treasure*. **Pi.** *Pf.* 1 s. *delight greatly* בְּצִלּוֹ ח׳ וְיָשַׁבְתִּי Ct 2^{3} *in his shadow I greatly delighted and sate*, i.e. sate with great delight.

†חֶמֶד **n.[m.] desire, delight**—abs. ח׳ Am 2531
5^{11}+4 t.; only after a cstr.; כַּרְמֵי־ח׳ נְטַעְתֶּם Am 5^{11} *vineyards of desire* (i.e. delightful vineyards) *have ye planted*; so rd. also Is 27^{2} (for MT כֶּרֶם חֶמֶר) Codd. ℌ 𝔊 van d. H Lo Hi Ew De Di Che Du; so of fields שְׂדֵי ח׳ Is 32^{12}; elsewh. of young men בַּחוּרֵי ח׳ Ez 23$^{6.12.23}$ *desirable young men* = *fine, attractive, young men*.

†חֶמְדָּה **n.f.** id.—ח׳ Ho 13^{15}+8 t.; cstr. 2532
חֶמְדַּת 1 S 9^{20}+3 t.; sf. חֶמְדָּתִי Je 12^{10}; חֶמְדָּתֵךְ Ez 26^{12}; חֶמְדָּתָם Dn 11^{8};—*desire* of Israel 1 S 9^{20} sq. לְ before obj. of desire; בְּלֹא ח׳ = *without desire* 2 Ch 21^{20} (i.e. he lived as no one desired), v. Öt 𝔊 (not 𝔊L) 𝔙; concrete: כל־ח׳ ישׂראל 1 S 9^{20} and for whom is *all that is desirable in Isr.?* so 𝔊 𝔙 RV Dr; (> AV and on whom is *all the desire of Isr.?*); cf. ובאו ח׳ כל־הגוים Hg 2^{7} (i.e. the desirable, precious things of all nations); elsewh. after cstr. as חֶמֶד; esp. כלי ח׳ Ho 13^{15} Na 2^{10} Je 25^{34} 2 Ch 32^{27} 36^{10} Dn 11^{8}; שְׂכִיּוֹת ח׳ Is 2^{16}, אֶרֶץ ח׳ ψ 106^{24} Je 3^{19} Zc 7^{14}, cf. חֶלְקַת ח׳ Je 12^{10}; בתי ח׳ Ez 26^{12}; ח׳ נשׁים Dn 11^{37}, appar. ref. to some obj. of idolatrous worship, perhaps *Adonis* = *Tammuz* Ew Bev (*Astarte*, Meinh).

†[חֲמוּדָה] **n.f. desirableness, precious-** 2530
ness—*Pl.* abs. חֲמוּדוֹת Dn 9^{23}; חֲמוּדֹת Ezr 8^{27}; חֲמֻדוֹת 2 Ch 20^{25}+4 t.; חֲמֻדֹת Gn 27^{15}; cstr. חֲמֻדוֹת Dn 11^{43};—*desirable, choice things* i.e. garments Gn 27^{15} (‖ בגדים); cf. Dn 11^{38} (‖ אבן יקרה), 11^{43} (חֲמֻדוֹת מִצְרָיִם); = *precious things* Ezr 8^{27} (as gold); כלי ח׳ 2 Ch 20^{25}; לֶחֶם ח׳ Dn 10^{3}; of man only אִישׁ־ח׳ Dn 10$^{11.19}$, and, without אִישׁ, ח׳ אָתָּה Dn 9^{23} *thou art a precious treasure* (on construction v. Dr$^{\text{§ 189, 2}}$; v. Bev and cf. neg. חמד Is 53^{2}).

†חֶמְדָּן **n.pr.m.** an Edomite Gn 36^{26} 𝔊 2533
Αμαδα = חַמְרָן 1 Ch 1^{41} (𝔊 Εμερων, 𝔊L Αμαδαμ).

†מַחְמָד **n.m. desire, desirable thing**— 4261
abs. מַחְמָד Ho 9^{6}; cstr. *id.* 1 K 20^{6}+3 t. Ez; pl. מַחֲמַדִּים Ct 5^{16}; cstr. מַחֲמַדֵּי La 2^{4} Ho 9^{16};

sf. מַחֲמַדֵּי Jo 4^{5}; מַחֲמַדֵּינוּ Is 64^{10}; מַחֲמַדֶּיהָ 2 Ch 36^{19} La 1^{10}; מַחֲמַדֵּיהֶם La 1^{11} Qr (v. also מַחְמֹד);—*desirable, precious things* כלי־מ׳ 2 Ch 36^{19}; sg. coll. Ho 9^{6}; pl. Jo 4^{5} Is 64^{10} La $1^{10.11\,(Qr)}$, מ׳ בִּטְנָם Ho 9^{16}; v. esp. pl. intens. כֻּלּוֹ מַחֲמַדִּים Ct 5^{16} *all of him is delightfulnesses* (‖מַמְתַקִּים); elsewh. מַחְמַד עינים *desire of the eyes*, i.e. that in which the eyes take delight 1 K 20^{6} Ez 24^{16} (of proph.'s wife), $v^{21.25}$; pl. La 2^{4}.

4262 †[מַחְמֹד] **n.[m.] desirable, precious thing**;—מַחֲמֹדֶיהָ La 1^{7}, מַחֲמוֹדֵיהֶם La 1^{11} Kt (Qr מַחֲמַדֵּיהֶם). Perh. מַחֲמַד׳ to be read in both; cf. Sta$^{§\,273\,a}$.

I. **חמה** (√of foll.; cf. Ar. حَمَى *protect, guard*, RS$^{K\,136}$ Lag$^{BN\,156}$; Dl$^{Pr\,91;\,BAS\,ii.\,43}$ comp. an As. *êmû, surround, guard*, cf. Mod. Syr. ܣܥܠ *id.*; Eth. ሐመወ: III. 1 means *contract affinity, be joined by affinity*, prob. denom.)

2524 †II. [חָם] **n.m. husband's father** (NH *id.*, of husband's or wife's father, so Aram. חֲמָא; Ar. حَمْ *husband's male relation* (father, brother, paternal uncle), but also *wife's father*, etc.; Eth. ሐም: As. *êmû*, Zim$^{BP\,48}$);—only sf. חָמִיךְ Gn $38^{13.25}$, of Judah as Tamar's father-in-law; חָמִיהָ 1 S $4^{19.21}$ of Eli, father-in-law of Phinehas' wife.

2545 †[חָמוֹת] **n.f. husband's mother** (NH חָמוֹת, Aram. חֲמָתָא; Ar. حَمَاةٌ *husband's mother*; As. *êmêtu*, Zim$^{BP\,48}$; Eth. ሐማት:)—only sf. חֲמוֹתֵךְ Ru 2^{11} 3^{17}; חֲמוֹתָהּ Ru 1^{14}+7 t.; חֲמֹתָהּ Mi 7^{6};—of Naomi Ru 1^{14} $2^{11.18.19.19.23}$ $3^{1.6.16.17}$; בַּת קָמָה בְאִמָּהּ כַּלָּה בַּחֲמֹתָהּ Mi 7^{6}.

2346 **חוֹמָה** $_{133}$ **n.f. wall** (as *protection*; cstr. חמת MI$^{21.21}$)—abs. ח׳ Lv 25^{29}+59 t. (incl. לְהַחוֹמָה Ne 12^{38}); חֹמָה Ex 14^{29}+8 t.; cstr. חוֹמַת Jos 6^{5} +28 t.; sf. חוֹמָתָהּ Na 2^{6} 3^{8}; pl. abs. חוֹמוֹת 2 Ch 8^{5} Is 26^{1}; חֹמוֹת Ct 5^{7}; cstr. חוֹמוֹת ψ 51^{20}; חוֹמֹת 2 K 25^{10}+9 t.; sf. חוֹמֹתַי Is 56^{5}; חֹמֹתַיִךְ Dt 28^{52} Is 25^{12}; חוֹמוֹתַיִךְ Ez $26^{10.12}$ $27^{11.11}$; חוֹמֹתַיִךְ Is 49^{16} +2 t.; חֹמֹתַיִךְ Is 60^{10}; חוֹמֹתַיִךְ Ez 26^{9}; חוֹמֹתֶיהָ Je 50^{15}; חוֹמֹתֶיהָ ψ 55^{11} Je 1^{15}; du. חוֹמֹתַיִם Is 22^{11}; הַחֹמֹתַיִם 2 K 25^{4}=Je 52^{7}; הַחֹמֹתַיִם Je 39^{4} (on form v. Ol$^{§\,113\,a}$);—**1.** usu. term for *wall* of city Dt 28^{52} Jos 2^{15} $6^{5.20}$ (all JE), 1 S $31^{10.12}$ 2 S $11^{20.21.21}$ 2 K $18^{26.27}$=Is $36^{11.12}$, Am $1^{7.10.14}$ Is 2^{15} $20^{10.11}$ 25^{12} Na 2^{6} 3^{8} Ez 26^{9}+, Je 1^{15}+, Jo $2^{7.9}$; בֵּין הַחֹמֹתַיִם (of Jerus.) i.e. *between the two walls* of the Ophel and the SW. hill respectively, of a reservoir Is 22^{11}, a gate 2 K 25^{4}=Je 34^{4} =52^{7}; symbol of Isr., Am 7^{7}; 2 Ch 8^{5} 14^{6} 25^{23} $26^{6.6.6}$ ψ 51^{20} Ne 1^{3}+31 t. in Ne; חוֹמַת אֲנָךְ Am 7^{7} (lit. *wall of a plummet*) is of doubtful mng.: *a wall built plumb*, or *by means of a plumb-line*? We thinks unintelligible; עִיר חוֹמָה=*walled city*, Lv 25^{29}, עיר אשר לא ח׳ v^{30} (לוֹ=לֹא), opp. הַחֲצֵרִים אשר אין להם ח׳ v^{31} (all H); more elaborately עָרִים בְּצֻרֹת ח׳ גְּבֹהָה דְּלָתַיִם וּבְרִיחַ Dt 3^{5}, cf. 2 Ch 8^{5}; ע׳ גְּדֹלוֹת חוֹמָה וּבְרִיחַ נְחֹשֶׁת 1 K 4^{13}; ח׳ בְּצוּרָה Is 2^{15}; ח׳ sg. of wall of Jerus. 1 K 3^{1}+ oft.; contempt. חוֹמַת אֲבָנֵיהֶם Ne 3^{35}; less oft. pl. Ne 2^{13}+; of specific portions of wall ח׳ הָעֹפֶל 2 Ch 27^{3} Ne 3^{27}; ח׳ בְּרֵכַת הַשֶּׁלַח Ne 3^{15}; הַח׳ הָרְחָבָה 3^{8} 12^{38}; also (generally) of Babylon Je 51^{58}.—Men *build*, בנה, the ח׳ 1 K 9^{15}+, esp. (of rebuilding), Ne 2^{17}+; fortify it בִּצֵּר Is 22^{10}; it is *joined together* קשׁר Ne 3^{38}; is *repaired* עָלְתָה אֲרוּכָה לַח׳ Ne 4^{1}; it *falls* נפל Jos $6^{5.20}$ 1 K 20^{30} Ez 38^{20}; the enemy *makes it fall* הִפִּיל 2 S 20^{15} (preceded by מַשְׁחִית si vera l., v. Dr); *destroys* it הִשְׁחִית La 2^{8}; שִׁחֵת Ez 26^{4}; *makes a breach in it* פָּרַץ בְּ׳ 2 K 14^{13}=2 Ch 25^{23}, cf. פרץ c. acc. 2 Ch 26^{6} Ne 3^{35}, and וַיִּבֶן אֶת־כָּל־הַח׳ הַפְּרוּצָה 2 Ch 32^{5}; also (in sim.) עִיר פְּרוּצָה ואין ח׳ Pr 25^{28}; and Pu. pt. מְפֹרָצֶת Ne 1^{3}; one *breaks it down* נָתַץ 2 K 25^{10} 2 Ch 36^{19} Je 39^{8} 52^{14}; *tears it down* הָרַס Ez 26^{12}, cf. pass. Je 50^{15}; Amos predicts that י׳ will *send fire* into wall (of Gaza, etc.): וְשִׁלַּחְתִּי אֵשׁ בְּח׳ Am $1^{7.10}$; or *kindle fire in* וְהִצַּתִּי אֵשׁ בְּח׳ v^{14}, so Je 49^{27}. **2.** *wall* of a building: **a.** citadel, fortress ח׳ ארמנותיה La 2^{7}. **b.** surrounding new temple Ez 40^{5} 42^{20}. **3.** fig. of waters of Red Sea Ex $14^{22.29}$ (P), cf. Na 3^{8}; of David's men as protectors of Nabal's shepherds 1 S 25^{16}; of prophet as object of assault חוֹמַת נְחֹשֶׁת בְּצוּרָה Je 1^{18}; ח׳ נחשת Je 15^{20}; of strong, virtuous woman Ct $8^{9.10}$; of salvation, יְשׁוּעָה, as defence Is 26^{1} (‖חֵל); of י׳ himself ח׳ אֵשׁ Zc 2^{9}; a dangerous polit. scheme is called breach in ח׳ נִשְׂגָּבָה Is 30^{13}; ח׳ נִשְׂגָּבָה in sim. of wealth Pr 18^{11} (‖קִרְיַת עֻזּוֹ); a reckless man is עִיר פְּרוּצָה אֵין ח׳ Pr 25^{28}.

†**יַחְמַי** **n.pr.m.** (perh.=יַחְמְיָה *may* י׳ *protect!* cf. Sab. יחמאל Hal^{187})—a man of Issachar 1 Ch 7^{2}, 𝔊 Εικαν, A Ιεμου, 𝔊L Ιαμιν. 3181

†**חֲמוּטַל** Qr, **חמיטל** Kt, **n.pr.f.** (meaning dub.; perh., if Kt right, *my husband's father is the dew*, cf. אֲבִיטַל)—𝔊 Αμειται, Μιτατ; A Αμιταλ, Αμιταθ; 𝔊L Αμιταλ;—mother of the kings Jehoahaz and Zedekiah, sons of Josiah 2 K 23^{31} 24^{18} Qr (Kt חמיטל)=Je 52^{1} Qr (Kt *id.*) 2537

2534 חֵמָה *wrath*, v. sub יחם; חֵמָה Jb 29[6], v.
2529, 2552 חֶמְאָה; חַמָּה, חַמָּן, חַמּוֹן, חַמַּת v. sub חמם. below

2536 חַמּוּאֵל **n.pr.m.** v. sub חמם. p. 329

2545 חָמוֹת v. sub חמה supr. p. 327

חמט (√ of foll.; cf. As. *ḫamâṭu*, *hasten*, Prä[ZMG 1874, 88 ff.], *ḫamṭu*, swift, Zim[BP 84 n.]; Aram. חֲמַט, חֲמֵיט is *sink* or *fall to the ground*, *kneel*).

2546 †חֹמֶט **n.[m.]** a kind of lizard, only in list of unclean creeping animals Lv 11[30] וְהָאֲנָקָה וְהַכֹּחַ וְהַלְּטָאָה וְהַחֹמֶט וְהַתִּנְשָׁמֶת׃ (Aram. ܚܘܡܛܐ is *chameleon*).

2547 †חֻמְטָה **n.pr.loc.** city in Judah Jos 15[54], 𝔊 Εὔμα, 𝔊L Αμματα; site unknown.

2537 חֲמִיטַל v. חמוטל supr. p. 327

2550 †חָמַל **vb. spare** (Ar. حَمَلَ is *bear*, *become responsible*; Aram. ܚܡܠ *comportavit*, *congessit*);—**Qal** *Pf.* ח׳ 1 S 15[15]+3 t.; חָמַל 2 S 12[6] La 2[17]; חָמַלְתָּ La 2[21] 3[43]; וְחָמַלְתִּי Mal 3[17]; *Impf.* יַחְמֹל Jb 16[13]+6 t.; יַחְמוֹל Jb 6[10]+3 t.; וַיַּחְמֹל 1 S 15[9]+3 t.; 3 fs. וַתַּחְמֹל Ex 2[6]; 2 ms. תַּחְמֹל Dt 13[9] 1 S 15[3]; אֶחְמֹל Ez 8[18] 9[10]; אֶחְמוֹל Je 13[14]+4 t.; וְאֶחְמֹל Ez 36[21]; יַחְמֹלוּ Is 9[18]; תַּחְמְלוּ Je 50[14] 51[3]; תַּחְמֹלוּ Ez 9[5]; *Inf. cstr.* חֶמְלָה Ez 16[5] (Ges[§ 45. 1. b]);—*spare, have compassion*, c. על Ex 2[6] (E), 1 S 15[3.9.15] 23[21] 2 S 21[7] 2 Ch 36[15.17] Je 15[5] Ez 16[5] 36[21] Jb 20[13] Zc 11[5.6] Mal 3[17.17] Jo 2[18]; Dt 13[9] (|| חוס sq. על), Je 21[7] (|| חוס sq. על + רחם), Ez 9[10] (|| חוס sq. על acc. to 𝔖 𝔗 Co); sq. אֶל־ Je 51[3] Is 9[18]; note poet. אַל־תַּח׳ אֶל־חֵץ = *spare no arrow* Je 50[14]; sq. *Inf.* 2 S 12[4]; abs. 2 S 12[6] Is 30[14] La 2[17.21], also v[2] where appar. sq. acc., 3[43] Jb 6[10] 16[13] 27[22] Pr 6[34] Hb 1[17]; || חוס Ez 5[11] 7[4] (del. Co as doubl. of v[9]), 7[9] 8[18] 9[5]; Jer 13[14] (|| חוס אחוס and ארחם).

2538 †חָמוּל **n.pr.m.** (*spared*);—grandson of Judah Gn 46[12] = 1 Ch 2[5], Nu 26[1]; 𝔊 Ιεμουηλ, [Ι]αμουηλ.

2539 †חָמוּלִי **adj. gent.** of foreg.; only c. art. הֶחָ׳, as subst. coll. Nu 26[21].

2551 †[חֶמְלָה] **n.f. compassion, mercy**, of י׳ (strictly Inf. form from חמל, v. Ges[§ 45, 1 b])—cstr. בְּחֶמְלַת י׳ עָלָיו Gn 19[16] (J), בְּאַהֲבָתוֹ וּבְחֶמְלָתוֹ גְּאָלָם Is 63[9].

2550 חֶמְלָה v. חמל *Inf.* above

†[מַחְמָל] **n.[m.] thing pitied, object of** 4263
compassion, only cstr. מַחְמַד עיניכם וּמַחְמַל נַפְשְׁכֶם Ez 24[21] *object of your eyes' desire, and of your soul's compassion.*

†[חָמַם] **vb. be** or **become warm** (NH 2552
id., Pi., *make warm*, Aram. ܚܡ, חֲמַם *be warm*; Ar. حَمَّ *become hot*, of water; also *heat*, *kindle fire in*)—**Qal** *Pf.* חַם ψ 39[4] Ex 16[21]; וְחַם consec. 1 K 1[2] Ec 4[11]; חַמּוֹתִי Is 44[16]; *Impf.* יָחֹם Is 44[16]; וַיָּחָם 2 K 4[34] Is 44[15]; also יֵחַם 1 K 1[1]; יֵחַם Dt 19[6]; יֵחָם Ec 4[11]; 3 fs. תֵּחַם Ez 24[11]; יֵחַמּוּ Ho 7[7]; וַיֶּחֱמוּ Gn 30[39]; וַיֵּחַמְנָה v[38] (last seven forms could be also from יחם q.v.; but no decisive evidence that this √ is used in Qal; they are placed under חמם by Thes Ew[§ 193 a] Ol[§ 243 b]; v. also Kö[i. 365, 417 ff.], who on account of יחם Pi. Inf. Gn 30[41] 31[10], der. last two, needlessly, fr. יחם); *Inf.* לַחְמָם Is 47[14], cf. Jb 30[4] (where, however, ל׳ is fr. לֶחֶם Mich Di unless (Luzz Che) we read לְחַמֵּם Pi. Inf. in both); חֹם 1 S 11[9] Hg 1[6] Ne 7[3]; sf. חֻמּוֹ Jb 6[17]; חֻמָּם Je 51[39];—**1.** lit., *be* or *grow warm* Ex 16[21] (P; subj. שֶׁמֶשׁ), cf. 1 S 11[9] Ne 7[3] and Jb 6[17] (sf. of impers. subj.); from fire Is 44[15.16.16] 47[14] (cf. supr.); natural heat 1 K 1[1.2] (by personal contact), so 2 K 4[34] Ec 4[11.11], fr. clothing Hg 1[6]; of Jerusalem under fig. of pot or caldron Ez 24[11]. **2.** fig., subj. לִבִּי ψ 39[4] (|| בַּהֲגִיגִי תִבְעַר־אֵשׁ), cf. Dt 19[6]; of conspirators Ho 7[7]; Chaldeans Je 51[39]. **3.** of heat in conception (animals) Gn 30[38.39] (cf. יחם). **Niph.** *Pt.* נֵחָמִים באלים Is 57[5] (Kö[i. 371]), *inflame oneself with*, of idolatry. **Pi.** *Impf.* 3 fs. תְּחַמֵּם Jb 39[14] *keep* eggs *warm* (of ostrich). **Hithp.** *Impf.* יִתְחַמָּם *warm oneself* Jb 31[20] מִגֵּז כְּבָשַׂי *by means of fleece of sheep.*

†חֹם **n.m.** Je 17[8] **heat**;—חֹם abs. Gn 8[22]+ 2527
3 t.+1 S 21[7] (v. infr.); cstr. Gn 18[1]+3 t.; of heat of (mid-)day חֹם היום Gn 18[1] (J), 1 S 11[11] 2 S 4[5]; in promise of regular seasons Gn 8[22] (opp. קֹר); cf. Is 18[4.4] (ח׳ קָצִיר); but as dangerous to plant-life Je 17[8]; it melts snow Jb 24[19]; לֶחֶם חֹם 1 S 21[7] *bread of heat = hot bread*, rd. perhaps לֶ׳ חָם (as Jos 9[12]).

†III. חָם **adj. hot**;—לחם ח׳ Jos 9[12] *hot bread* 2525
(JE), i.e. freshly baked; בגדים חַמִּים Jb 37[17] of
garments heated by south wind.—I. חָם v. supr. 2526
p. 325. II. חָם v. sub חמה. p. 327 2524

†חַמָּה **n.f. heat, sun** (poet.)—חַמָּה Is 24[23]+ 2535
4 t.; חַמָּתוֹ ψ 19[7];—**1.** *heat* of sun ψ 19[7]. **2.**

= *sun* Jb 30^{28}; ‖ לְבָנָה *moon* Is 24^{23} $30^{26.26}$ Ct 6^{10}.

2553 †[חַמָּן] **n.m.** sun-pillar, used in idolatrous worship (v. Thes[489 ff.] RS[Sem. i, 469] Lag[M i, 228] Now[Arch. ii, 302]; = Palm. חמנא Vog[No. 123 a]; Ph. לבעל חמן oft. as epithet of solar Baal);—only pl. abs. חַמָּנִים Is 27^{9} + 4 t.; sf. חַמָּנֵיכֶם Lv 26^{30} + 2 t.; ‖ בָּמוֹת Lv 26^{30} (H), 2 Ch 14^{4}, cf. Ez $6^{4.6}$; ‖ מזבחות הבעלים 2 Ch 34^{4}; ‖ אשרים Is 17^{8} 27^{9}; ‖ אשרים and פְּסִלִים 2 Ch 34^{7}.

2540 †חַמּוֹן **n.pr.loc.** (*hot* spring?)—**1.** town in Asher Jos 19^{28}. **2.** in Naphtali 1 Ch 6^{61} (perh. = 1. חַמַּת, חַמֹּת דֹּאר, v. Be and Di Jos 19^{35}).

2575 †I. חַמַּת **n.pr.loc.** (*hot* spring)—town in Naphtali Jos 19^{35} (perh. = חַמּוֹן **2** v. Di); 𝔊 Ωμαθαδακεθ (= חַמַּת רַקַּת), A Αμαθ, 𝔊L Αμμαθ; Jos[Ant. xviii, 2. 3] Αμμαθους (ed. Niese), cf. Id.[BJ. iv, 1. 3] Guthe[ZPV 1891, xiii, 284]; prob. = Talm. *Ḥamata* Nbr[Géogr. du Talm. 207] (with hot springs), 35 minutes south of Tiberias, v. Rob[BR ii, 385] Buhl[ZPV xiii, 1890, 39 f.] Guthe[l. c.] GASm[Geogr. 450] (Furrer[ZPV ii, 1878, 55; xiii, 1890, 194 ff.] al. say north of Tiberias);
2576, 2540 v. חַמֹּת דֹּאר, חַמּוֹן. below & above

2575 †II. חַמַּת **n.pr.m.** father of the house of Rechab 1 Ch 2^{55}.

2576 †חַמֹּת דֹּאר **n.pr.loc.** in Naphtali, Levitical city Jos 21^{32} (perh. = 1. חַמַּת, חַמּוֹן **2** v. Di), 𝔊 Νεμμαθ, A Εμαθδωρ, 𝔊L Αμαθδωρ.

2536 †חֲמוּאֵל **n.pr.m.** (mng.? comp. Sab. [חמא[ל Hal[215])—a Simeonite 1 Ch 4^{26} 𝔊L Αμουηλ.

2554 †[חָמַס] **vb. treat violently, wrong** (NH *id., act violently, treat violently;* Aram. חֲמַס (rare) *violently seize;* Ar. حَمِسَ is *be hard, strict, rigorous*)—**Qal** *Pf.* 3 pl. חָמְסוּ Ez 22^{26} Zp 3^{4}; *Impf.* יַחְמֹס Jb 15^{33}, וַיַּחְמֹס La 2^{6}; תַּחְמֹסוּ Jb 21^{27} Je 22^{3}; *Pt.* חֹמֵס Pr 8^{36};—*treat violently, wrong;*—**1.** of physical wrong: תַּח׳ Je 22^{3} (‖ תֹּנוּ) of wrong to widows and orphans; וַיַּח׳ כַּגַּן שֻׂכּוֹ La 2^{6} *and hath done violence to his pavilion as to a garden* (‖ שִׁחֵת מֹעֲדוֹ); so, fig., of vine, *wrong,* i.e. fail to nourish, kill יַח׳ כַּגֶּפֶן בִּסְרוֹ Jb 15^{33}. **2.** of ethical wrong, obj. תּוֹרָה Zp 3^{4} Ez 22^{26} (both ‖ חִלֵּל קֹדֶשׁ); cf. מְזִמּוֹת עָלַי תַּחְמֹסוּ Jb 21^{27} *the devices* (wherewith) *ye do me violence.* **3.** both physical and ethical חֹטְאִי חֹמֵס נַפְשׁוֹ Pr 8^{36}. **Niph.** *Pf.* 3 pl. נֶחְמְסוּ Je 13^{22} thy heels *suffer violence* (‖ נִגְלוּ שׁוּלַיִךְ).

†חָמָס **n.m.** [ψ 7, 17] **violence, wrong** — abs. 2555
ח׳ Gn 6^{11} + 44 t.; cstr. חֲמַס Ju 9^{24} + 7 t.; sf. חֲמָסִי Gn 16^{5} Je 51^{35} (in both = wrong *done to me*); חֲמָסוֹ ψ 7^{17}; pl. חֲמָסִים 2 S 22^{49} + 3 t.;—*violence,* specif. of physical violence Ju 9^{24} 2 S 22^{3} (not ‖ ψ 18^{3}), Ob ^{10}, Hb 1^{9} Je 51^{35} (of Chaldeans), Hb $2^{8.17.17}$ Jo 4^{19} ψ 72^{14}; but also *wrong,* incl. injurious language, harsh treatment, etc. Gn 16^{5} (J, of wrong done to Sarah by Hagar), Jb 19^{7} Mal 2^{16}; in gen. of rude wickedness of men, their noisy, wild, ruthlessness Mi 6^{12} Hb 1^{2} Zp 1^{9} Pr $10^{6.11}$ 13^{2} 26^{6} + Ez 7^{11} (si vera l., v. Co), ‖ שֹׁד Am 3^{10} Hb 1^{3} Je 6^{7} 20^{8} Ez 45^{9} Is 60^{18}, ‖ רִיב ψ 55^{10}, ‖ עָמָל 7^{17}, ‖ גַּאֲוָה 73^{6}, אֹהֵב ח׳ 11^{5} (‖ רָשָׁע), denied, of servant of י׳ Is 53^{9}, ח׳ בארץ Je 51^{46}, cf. Gn $6^{11.13}$ (P), Ez 8^{17} 12^{19}; מָלְאוּ הָעִיר מָלְאָה ח׳ Ez 7^{23} 28^{16}, מַחֲשַׁכֵּי־אֶרֶץ נְאוֹת ח׳ ψ 74^{20}, שֶׁבֶת ח׳ Am 6^{3} is (prob.) *enthronement of violence;* כְּלֵי ח׳ Gn 49^{5} (poem) *instruments, weapons, of violence;*—other phrases are: ח׳ בְּיָדַיִם Jon 3^{8} 1 Ch 12^{17}, cf. Jb 16^{17}, ח׳ יְדֵיכֶם ψ 58^{3} and פֹּעַל ח׳ בְּכַפֵּיהֶם Is 59^{6}; עֵד ח׳ i.e. a witness that promotes violence and wrong Ex 23^{1} (JE), Dt 19^{16}, עֲדֵי ח׳ ψ 35^{11}; עֲדֵי שֶׁקֶר וִיפֵחַ חָמָס ψ 27^{12}; שִׂנְאַת ח׳ ψ 25^{19} = hatred characterized by violence; אִישׁ חָמָס = *violent man* ψ 18^{49} (2 S 22^{49} has the later א׳ חמסים, cf. infr.) 140^{12} Pr 3^{31} 16^{29}; איש חמסים (later) ψ $140^{2.5}$ 2 S 22^{49}; יֵין חֲמָסִים Pr 4^{17} i.e. wine gained by violence (‖ לֶחֶם רֶשַׁע).

†תַּחְמָס **n.[m.]** name of **male ostrich,** acc. 8464
to Bo[ii. 830] Thes (Thes der. fr. *violence* of this bird, cf. Ar. ظَلِيمٌ *violence,* also *ostrich;* other conject. are: *owl* 𝔊𝔙; *swallow,* Saad: v. also Kn in Di)—mentioned as unclean Lv 11^{16} (P) Dt 14^{15}.

†I. חָמֵץ **vb. be sour, leavened** (NH *id.,* 2556
Pi. Hiph. *make sour, leaven;* Ar. حَمُضَ *be sour;* Aram. חֲמַע *be sour, leavened,* ܚܡܥ, *be leavened*)—**Qal** *Pf.* חָמֵץ Ex 12^{39}; *Impf.* יֶחְמָץ Ex 12^{34}; *Inf.* sf. חֻמְצָתוֹ Ho 7^{4};—*be leavened,* of dough (בָּצֵק), Ex $12^{34.39}$ (E), cf. Ho 7^{4}. **Hithp.** *be soured, embittered,* ψ 73^{21} (‖ כִּלְיוֹתַי אֶשְׁתּוֹנָן).

†חָמֵץ **n.m.** [Ex 13, 3] **that which is leavened** 2557
—ח׳ Ex 12^{15} + 10 t.—forbidden at Passover Ex 12^{15} (P), $13^{3.7}$ (JE), Dt 16^{3}, in all sacrifices Ex 23^{18} 34^{25} (both JE); cf. Am 4^{5}; Lv 2^{11} 6^{10} (P; appos.); exceptions are לֶחֶם ח׳ of peace-offering Lv 7^{13} (P), and the wave-loaves (ח׳ appos.) Lv 23^{17} (H).—v. RS[Sem 203 OTJC 2, 345].

2558 †חֹמֶץ **n.m. vinegar**—ח׳ abs. Pr 10^{26} + 3 t.; cstr. Nu $6^{3.3}$;—a common condiment Ru 2^{14}, forbidden to Nazirite (ח׳ יין and ח׳ שֵׁכָר) Nu $6^{3.3}$ (P), offered (in cruelty) to a thirsty man ψ 69^{22} (fig. for harshness, lack of sympathy); in sim. of sluggard כַּחֹמֶץ לַשִּׁנַּיִם Pr 10^{26}, ח׳ עַל־נָתֶר Pr 25^{20} *vinegar on nitre* (sim. of merry songs for the heavy-hearted).

2548 †חָמִיץ **adj. seasoned** (viz. with salt, or a salt herb—Ar. حَمْض, Pun. 'Αμουτ [=*חמוץ] Blau ZMG 1873, 522; v. Thes—rendering it more tasty), of provender for cattle בְּלִיל חָמִיץ יֹאכֵלוּ Is 30^{24}.

2556 חֲמִצָה v. I. חמץ Inf. p. 329

2557 †מַחְמֶצֶת **n.f. anything leavened**, only Ex $12^{19.20}$ (P).

2556 †II. [חָמֵץ] **vb. be red** (? cf. Aram. ܚܡܰܨ Ethpa. *blush, be ashamed*, poss. orig. *be red*);—**Qal** *Pt. pass.* cstr. חֲמוּץ בְּגָדִים *red of garments* Is 63^1; poss. also *Impf.* 3 fs. תֶּחְמַץ ψ 68^{24} *that thy foot may be red with blood* (for MT תמחץ; so Krochm Hi Gr; most, however, rd. תרחץ v. רחץ).

2556 †III. [חָמַץ] **vb. be ruthless** (dub. √; perh. by-form of חמס; perh. err. for it; identif. by most with I. חמץ, *be sour*, hence *sharp, violent*, but connexion improb.)—only **Qal** *Pt. act.* מִכַּף מְעַוֵּל וְחוֹמֵץ ψ 71^4 *from the hand of the unjust and ruthless* (‖ מִיַּד רָשָׁע).

2541 †חָמוֹץ **n.[m.]** coll. **the ruthless**—only אַשְּׁרוּ ח׳ Is 1^{17} *set right the ruthless*, so Hi Ew Kn De Che Di; Vrss give passive (perh. חָמוּץ) hence AV *relieve the oppressed;* but on form חָמוֹץ = doer of action v. Ew § 152 b.

2559 †חָמַק **vb. turn away** (intr.)—**Qal** *Pf.* 3 ms. וְדוֹדִי ח׳ עָבָר Ct 5^6 *and my beloved had turned away, passed on.* **Hithp.** *Impf.* 2 fs. עַד־מָתַי תִּתְחַמָּקִין הַבַּת הַשּׁוֹבֵבָה Je 31^{22} *turn hither and thither*, v. Gf VB.

2542 †[חַמּוּק] **n.m. curving, curve,** חַמּוּקֵי יְרֵכַיִךְ Ct 7^2 *the curvings* (curved lines, curves) *of thy thighs.*

2560 †I. חָמַר **vb. ferment, boil** or **foam up** (Ar. خَمَرَ *ferment, leaven*, خُمْرَةٌ, خَمِيرَةٌ n. *leaven;* v. Lag BN 207);—**Qal** *Pf.* 3 ms. וְיַיִן ח׳ ψ 75^9 *and wine which foams*, (others fr. IV. חמר *be red*); 3 pl. חָמְרוּ is suggested by We as poss. Hb 3^{15} (for MT חֹמֶר q.v.) the *great waters foamed; Impf.* 3 mpl. יֶהֱמוּ יֶחְמְרוּ מֵימָיו ψ 46^4 *let its water roar and foam.* **Peʿalʿal** *Pf. pass.* 3 pl. מֵעַי חֳמַרְמָרוּ La 1^{20} *my bowels are in a ferment* (‖ נֶהְפַּךְ לִבִּי), of distress at calamities of Jerus.; so מֵעַי חֳמַרְמְרוּ La 2^{11}.—Jb 16^{16} v. IV. חמר.

†חֶמֶר **n.[m.] wine** (poet.) (Aram. ܚܰܡܪܳܐ, חַמְרָא; Ar. خَمْر, v. Lag BN 207)—וְדַם־עֵנָב תִּשְׁתֶּה־חָמֶר Dt 32^{14}; כֶּרֶם חֶמֶר Is 27^2, but rd. here כֶּרֶם חֶמֶד (v. חֶמֶד). 2561

†חֵמָר **n.[m.] bitumen, asphalt** (fr. I. חמר acc. to OBlau ZMG 1869, 279, bitumen as *seething, swelling up;* Thes MV, fr. IV. חמר, with ref. to reddish-brown colour)—חֵמָר Gn 11^3 + 2 t.; used for cement in building Babel Gn 11^3 (J); abounding in vale of Siddim בֶּאֱרֹת בֶּאֱרֹת ח׳ Gn 14^{10}; used in coating Moses' 'ark' of bulrushes Ex 2^3 (E; ‖ זָפֶת). 2564

†I. חֹמֶר **n.m. cement, mortar, clay**;—ח׳ abs. Gn 11^3 + 13 t.; cstr. Is 10^6 + 2 t.;—**1.** *mortar, cement* for holding building-stones (brick) together Gn 11^3 (J), Ex 1^{14} (P; both ‖ לְבֵנִים); Na 3^{14} (‖ טיט). **2.** *clay:* **a.** as material of vessels Je $18^{4.6}$, ח׳ היצר Is 29^{16}, in sim. of God's fashioning man Is 45^9 64^7 Jb 10^9; as material of human bodies בָּתֵּי ח׳ Jb 4^{19} cf. 33^6; as material of bulwarks (disparagingly) Jb 13^{12}; ח׳ חותם = *seal-clay* i.e. clay upon which seal is pressed. **b.** = *mire* ח׳ חוצות Is 10^6; הֹרָנִי לַח׳ Jb 30^{19} *he hath cast me into the mire*, i.e. deeply humiliated me (עָפָר and אֵפֶר in ‖ cl.); as sim. of commonness, abundance Jb 27^{16} (‖ עָפָר). 2563

†II. [חָמַר] **vb. denom. cover** or **smear with asphalt**, only **Qal** *Impf.* 3 fs. sf. וַתַּחְמְרָה Ex 2^3 (E); on form of sf. v. Ges § 58, 3, R. 1. 2560

III. חמר (√ of foll.; NH חָמַר *heap up;* Aram. חֲמַר *make a ruin-heap;* Ar. جَمَارَةٌ *great mass of stone, heap of stones*).

II. חֹמֶר **n.[m.] heap** (cf. I. חֲמוֹר)—ח׳ cstr. ח׳ מַיִם רַבִּים Hb 3^{15} *a heap of great waters* (‖ יָם) —but txt. dub., v. I. חמר; pl. חֳמָרִים חֳמָרִים Ex 8^{10} (J), of dead frogs gathered in *heaps*. 2563

†III. חֹמֶר **n.m. homer,** a dry measure (perh. fr. above √, but dub.; cf. As. *amâru, surround, contain*, II. R $36^{19\,a.\,b}$ Strm 4760, *imêru, a measure* Zim BP 6 n)—ח׳ abs. Is 5^{10} + 5 t. Ez; cstr. Ho 3^2 + 3 t.; pl. חֳמָרִים Nu 11^{32};—ח׳ of barley Ho 3^2 Ez 45^{13}, cf. זֶרַע ח׳ שְׂעֹרִים Lv 27^{16} 2563

i.e. land on which a ׳ח of barley seed was sown (taxed at 50 shekels); ׳ח of wheat Ez 45^{13}; in gen. ׳זֶרַע ח Is 5^{10}; = 10 ephahs (or baths, v. בַּת sub בתת) Ez 45$^{11.11.11.14.14}$ (in v^{14} del. Co); on actual size of ׳ח, = 393·9 litres, v. Hultzsch $^{\text{Metrol. 2nd ed. 448, 452 f.}}$ See further II. בַּת and reff., Benz$^{\text{Arch. 183 f.}}$ Now$^{\text{Arch. i, 203 f.}}$

2543 †I. חֲמוֹר **n.[m.]** heap, abs. ׳ח with du.
2565 חֲמֹרָתָיִם (Baer ׳חֲמֹרֹת), as if fr. חֲמֹרָה;— בִּלְחִי הַחֲמוֹר חֲמוֹר חֲמֹרָתָיִם Ju 15^{16} *with the ass's jawbone, a heap, two heaps,* i.e. so many slain.

2543 חֲמֹרָתָיִם v. I. חֲמוֹר. above

2560 †IV. [חמר] **vb. be red** (Ar. حَمَرَ II. *dye red,* حُمْرَةٌ *redness, reddish brown* (appar. *skin-colour*) so Thes MV Ba$^{\text{NB 192}}$al.)—only **Peʿalʿal** *Pf.* pass. פָּנַי חֳמַרְמְרָה Jb 16^{16} *my face is reddened* from weeping.—La 1^{20} 2^{11} v. I. חמר.

2543 †II. חֲמוֹר **n.m.**$^{\text{Gn 45, 23}}$ (he)-ass (NH *id.* (sts. female, but this regularly חֲמוֹרָה); Aram. חֲמָרָא, ܚܡܳܪܳܐ; Ar. حِمَارٌ, Palm. חמרא Reckendorf $^{\text{ZMG 1888, 404}}$; As. *imêru,* Schr$^{\text{COT Gloss}}$;— name fr. *reddish* colour) — abs. חֲמוֹר Gn 22^{5} + 43 t.; חֲמֹר Ex 13^{13} Dt 22^{10}; cstr. חֲמוֹר Ex 23^{5} + 4 t.; חֲמֹר Gn 49^{14}; sf. חֲמֹרְךָ Dt 5^{14} 28^{31}; חֲמֹרֶךָ Ex 23^{12}; חֲמֹרוֹ Gn 22^{3} + 8 t.; pl. חֲמוֹרִים Ju 19^{10} + 9 t.; חֲמֹרִים Gn 12^{16} + 16 t.; sf. חֲמוֹרֵינוּ Ju 19^{19}; חֲמֹרֵינוּ Gn 43^{18}; חֲמוֹרֵיכֶם 1 S 8^{16}; חֲמֹרֵיהֶם Gn 34^{28} + 4 t.; חֲמוֹרֵיהֶם Jos 9^{4};—*ass* (*he-ass;* אתון = *she-ass*) found in all periods (coll. only Gn 32^{6} Is 21^{7});—**1.** as (valuable) property, with oxen, sheep, camels, slaves, etc. Gn 12^{16} 24^{35} 30^{43} 47^{17} Ex 9^{3} (all J) Ex 20^{17} (E), 21^{33} 22$^{3.8.9}$ 23$^{4.5.12}$ Nu 16^{15} Jos 6^{21} 7^{24} (all JE); note also Ex 13^{13} = 34^{20} (JE; firstlings belong to ׳י); Gn 36^{24} Nu 31$^{28.30.34.39.45}$ (all P); Dt 5$^{14.18}$ 22$^{3.4}$ Ju 6^{4} 1 S 8^{16} 12^{3} 15^{3} 22^{19} 27^{9} 1 Ch 5^{21} Ezr 2^{67} = Ne 7^{68} (Baer), Zc 14^{15}; coll. Gn 32^{5} (J; ‖ שׁוֹר, צֹאן, עֶבֶד, שִׁפְחָה), but pl. (similar ‖) Gn 34^{28} (P), 47^{17} (J); cf. also ׳ח יְתוֹמִים Jb 24^{3} *the orphans' ass* (‖ שׁוֹר אַלְמָנָה); as knowing its master's crib Is 1^{3} (‖ שׁוֹר); found in camp 2 K 7$^{7.10}$ (both ‖ סוּסִים); as harnessed ׳מֶתֶג לַח Pr 26^{3} (‖ סוּס). **2.** used for riding: **a.** by women Ex 4^{20} (J), Jos 15^{18} (JE) = Ju 1^{14} 1 S 25$^{20.23.42}$, cf. 2 Ch 28^{15}. **b.** by men 2 S 16^{2} 17^{23} 19^{27} 1 K 2^{40} 13$^{13.13.23.24.27.28.28}$ Is 21^{7} Zc 9^{9}. **c.** צֶמֶד חמורים *a pair of asses* 2 S 16^{1} (for burdens and for riding); for man and woman Ju 19$^{3.10.19.21}$; carrying dead body v^{28}, cf. ׳ח 1 K 13^{29}. **3.** beast of burden Gn 22$^{3.5}$ (cf. v^{6}), 42$^{26.27}$ 45^{23} (all E) 43$^{18.24}$ 44$^{3.13}$ (all J), Jos 9^{4} (JE), 1 S 25^{18} 1 Ch 12^{41} Ne 13^{15} (cf. also ׳צֶמֶד ח 2 S 16^{1} supr.); metaph. of Issachar ׳ח גָּרֶם Gn 49^{11} (poem), *an ass of* (strong) *bones.*—׳ח לֶחֶם 1 S 16^{20} rd. prob. חֲמִשָּׁה *five,* or better עֲשָׂרָה *ten,* v. We Dr. **4.** used in tillage Is 32^{20}; not to be used in ploughing with an ox (שׁוֹר) Dt 22^{10}. **5.** parts of body of ass mentioned are: ׳לְחִי ח Ju 15$^{15.16}$ jawbone, Samson's weapon; ׳ראשׁ ח 2 K 6^{25} eaten in famine; ׳בְּשַׂר ח Ez 23^{20} genital organ of ass (contempt. sim.) **6.** ׳קְבוּרַת ח Je 22^{19} *burial of an ass,* in fig. of ignominious treatment of a corpse.

†III. חֲמוֹר **n.pr.m.** father of Shechem (*he-ass;* v. RS$^{\text{K 220; Sem i. 449}}$)—Gn 33^{19} 34$^{2.4.6.8.13.18.18.20.24.26}$ Jos 24^{32} Ju 9^{28}. 2544

†חַמְרָן **n.pr.m.** 1 Ch 1^{41} (= חֶמְדָּן Gn 36^{26} q.v.) 2566

†יַחְמוּר **n.[m.]** roebuck (Sam. יחמור, Syr. ܝܰܚܡܽܘܪܳܐ, ܣ יַחְמוּרָא v. Hom$^{\text{NS 392 (and 333)}}$, Lag$^{\text{BN 127}}$; name from *reddish* colour?)—as edible Dt 14^{5} 1 K 5^{3};—on identif. with roebuck, v. Tristr $^{\text{Proc. Zool. Soc. London, May 2, 1876}}$ Conder$^{\text{Tent Work, 1887, p. 91}}$. 3180

I. חמשׁ (√ of foll.; meaning unknown).

חָמֵשׁ, חֲמִשָּׁה$_{342}$ **n.m.** and **f. five** (NH *id.,* 2568
id.; Aram. חֲמֵשׁ, חַמְשָׁא, ܚܰܡܫܳܐ, ܚܡܶܫ; Ph. חמשת; Palm. חמשא, c. n. masc., Reckendorf $^{\text{ZMG 1888, 408}}$; As. *ḫamšu, ḫamiltu* Dl$^{\text{§75}}$; Eth. ኃምስ: ኃምስቱ: Ar. خَمْسٌ, خَمْسَةٌ; Sab. & Liḥyân. חמס DHM$^{\text{ZMG xxix. 613; Epigr. Denkm. 71, 73}}$); — **m.** (c. **n.f.**) abs. חָמֵשׁ Gn 5^{6} + 94 t. + Ez 40^{30} (del. 𝔊B Hi-Sm Co; Co del. also in v$^{25.29.33.36}$) + Ez 45^{3} Kt (where rd. **f.** with Qr); cstr. חֲמֵשׁ Gn 5^{10} + 67 t. + Ez 48^{16} Kt; **f.** (c. **n.m.**) abs. חֲמִשָּׁה v. Lag$^{\text{BN 80}}$ Gn 18^{28} + 139 t. (incl. Ez 8^{16} del. B Co al.); cstr. חֲמֵשֶׁת Nu 3$^{47.47}$ + 26 t.;—on pl. חֲמִשִּׁים *fifty,* see below;—*five,* in Hex. chiefly P;—**1.** without other numeral: **a.** חָמֵשׁ, before fpl. noun Gn 43^{34} + 35 t.; before n. coll. ׳ח צֹאן 1 S 25^{18}; v. also ׳ח בָּאַמָּה *five in cubit(s)* = five cubits 1 K 7^{23} 1 Ch 11^{23} 2 Ch 4^{2}; after noun (late) 2 K 8^{16} (בִּשְׁנַת חָמֵשׁ לְיוֹרָם = *in the fifth year*) + 6 t. Ch; no noun expr. 1 K 7$^{39.39.49.49}$ 1 Ch 3^{20} 2 Ch 4$^{7.7}$. **b.** חֲמִשָּׁה before mpl. noun Gn 47^{2} + 18 t.; after noun Ex 36^{38} + 36 t. Nu (all P); no noun expr. Gn 14^{9} (only here c. art.) + 20 t. **c.** חֲמֵשׁ before noun (usu. defined; exc. אֲלָפִים, מֵאוֹת, v. **3, 4**) Ex 26$^{3.9}$ 36$^{10.16}$ + Ez 42^{16} ׳ח אַמּוֹת Kt, but Qr ׳ח מאות, v. infr. **d.** חֲמֵשֶׁת הַמְּלָכִים Jos 10^{5} + 5 t.; ׳ח הָאֲנָשִׁים Ju 18$^{7.14.17}$; ׳ח שקלים Nu 18^{16}; also, distrib., ׳ח ׳ח שְׁקָלִים 3^{47}; ׳ח הַסְּרָנִים Jos 13^{3} Ju 3^{3} 1 S 6^{18}; ׳ח בני מ׳ 2 S 21^{8}. **e.** = ordinal, בִּשְׁנַת חָמֵשׁ ליורם 2 K 8^{16} *the fifth* (year) *of Joram;*

בַּחֲמִשָּׁה לַחֹדֶשׁ *on the fifth* (day) *of the month* Ez $1^{1.2}$ 8^{1} 33^{21}; (so also 15th, 25th, etc.) **2.** ח׳ combined with עָשָׂר, עשׂרה *ten* = *fifteen*: **a.** חֲמֵשׁ עֶשְׂרֵה (c. **n.f.**) Gn 5^{10} 7^{20} Ex $27^{14.15}$ $38^{14.15}$ 2 K $14^{17.23}$ 20^{6} 2 Ch 15^{10} 25^{25} Is 38^{5}. **b.** חֲמִשָּׁה עָשָׂר (c. **n.m.**), (1) after noun Est 9^{21}; (2) before noun Ex 16^{1} (= ordinal *fifteenth*, so Lv 23^{6}+) Ho 3^{2}+. **c.** חֲמֵשֶׁת עָשָׂר before n. 2 S 19^{18}+. **d.** חֲמֵשֶׁת עָשָׂר, without n. = ordinal *fifteenth* 1 Ch 24^{14}+4 t.+Ez 45^{12} (rd. חֲמִשִּׁים A Hi Co). **3.** חֲמֵשׁ מֵאוֹת = 500 Gn $5^{30.32}$+49 t.+Ez 42^{16} Qr. **4.** חֲמֵשֶׁת אֲלָפִים = 5000 Nu 31^{32} Jos 8^{12} Ju 20^{45} 1 S 17^{5} Ez 45^{6} 48^{15} 1 Ch 29^{7} 2 Ch 35^{9} Ezr 1^{11} 2^{69};—in 25,000, 35,000 etc. חֲמִשָּׁה (usu. without א׳) precedes the 20,000, 30,000, etc. **5.** with other numerals: **a.** חָמֵשׁ before larger numeral: (1) noun repeated Gn 5^{6}+4 t.; (2) noun with 2nd num. only, Gn 5^{17}+8 t.+Ez 45^{3} Kt; (3) noun c. בְּ with 2nd num. Ez 40^{21}+2 t. **b.** חָמֵשׁ after larger num.: (1) noun repeated Gn 25^{7}; (2) noun foll. ח׳ (only) Ju 14^{10}+ (esp. in expressions of age and duration); (3) noun before both num., st. abs., 2 Ch 3^{15}; st. cstr. 2 Ch 15^{19}. **c.** no noun expr., ח׳ between other num., e.g. שֵׁשׁ מאות ח׳ ושבעים Nu 31^{37}. **d.** חֲמִשָּׁה before larger num., noun foll. larger num. Nu 1^{25}+22 t. **e.** ח׳ follows, and (1) is foll. by noun Ju 20^{35}+7 t.; (2) noun precedes both 1 K 7^{3} Je 52^{30}. **f.** ח׳ precedes, no noun expr. 1 K 5^{12}. **g.** ח׳ follows, no noun expr. Gn 18^{28}+. **h.** no noun expr. ח׳ between other num. Ex 38^{28} Ezr 2^{5}.

2569 †I. חֹמֶשׁ **n.[m.] fifth part**—only לְפַרְעֹה לַחֹמֶשׁ Gn 47^{26}, but connex. with preceding awkward; rd. perh. הַחֹמֶשׁ (𝔖), or לְחַמֵּשׁ 𝔊, v. Di.

2567 †II. [חָמַשׁ] **vb. denom.** only **Pi.** וְחִמֵּשׁ אֶת־אֶרֶץ מִצְרָיִם Gn 41^{34} (E) *and he shall fifth* (take the fifth part of) *the land of Egypt*, i.e. the fifth part of the produce (cf. Ar. خَمَسَ *take a fifth part*; Eth. ኀመሰ: I. 2 *quinque facere*).

2572 חֲמִשִּׁים $_{164}$ **n.pl.** (a) **fifty** (Ar. خَمْسُونَ, Aram. ܚܡܫܝܢ, Ph. חמשם; MI[28] חמשן; As. *ḫamšâti* Dl in Lotz[TP 80])—חֲמִשִּׁים Gn 6^{15}+154 t. (incl. Ez $40^{25.29.33}$, del. Co)+Ez 45^{12} (so rd. A Hi Co for חמשה); sf. חֲמִשֶּׁיךָ 2 K $1^{10.12}$, חֲמִשָּׁיו 2 K 1^{9}+4 t., חֲמִשֵּׁיהֶם 2 K 1^{14};—**1.** abs. **a.** *a fifty*, a company of fifty Ex $18^{21.25}$ Dt 1^{15} 1 S 8^{12} 2 K $1^{9.9}$+13 t. 2 K 1 (in v^{14} = *fifties*), Is 3^{3}. **b.** elsewhere, without noun expr., (1) without other numeral Nu $31^{30.47}$ Ez $27^{18.18}$ Hg 2^{16}; (2) with other num. ח׳ preceding Ex $30^{23.23}$+11 t.;+1 Ch 12^{34} Baer, van d. H. v^{33} (sq. אֶלֶף); (3) ח׳ following Ex 38^{26}+10 t.; (4) ח׳ between other num. Nu 1^{23}+23 t. **2.** חֲמִשִּׁים without other num.: **a.** before noun Gn 6^{15}+58 t.+ח׳ בָּאַמָּה Ex 38^{12}. **b.** after noun 2 S 24^{24} Ex 26^{11}+4 t. Chr. **3.** ח׳ before other num.: **a.** foll. by noun Gn 7^{24}+. **b.** preceded by noun 1 Ch 5^{21}. **4.** ח׳ after other num., and **a.** this after noun 1 Ch 8^{40} Ezr $8^{3.26}$. **b.** noun repeated e.g. Gn $9^{28.29}$. **5.** ח׳ preceded by cstr. e.g. בִּשְׁנַת ח׳ שָׁנָה 2 K $15^{23.27}$ Lv $15^{10.11}$. **6.** ח׳ = ordinal, *fiftieth* Lv $25^{10.11}$ 2 K 15^{23}, cf. v^{27}.

†חֲמִישִׁי **m.**, חֲמִישִׁית **f. adj. num. ordin.** 2549
fifth;—**m.** חֲמִשִׁי Gn 1^{23}+22 t.; חֲמִשִׁי Zc 7^{3}+3 t.; **f.** חֲמִישִׁית abs. 1 K 14^{25}+4 t.; חֲמִשִׁית Lv 19^{25} Je 36^{9}; חֲמִשִּׁית 1 K 6^{31}; cstr. חֲמִישִׁית Lv $27^{15.19}$; sf. חֲמִישִׁתוֹ Lv 5^{16}+2 t.; חֲמִשִׁיתוֹ Lv 22^{14} 27^{31}; חֲמִשְׁתוֹ Lv 27^{27}, cf. חֲמִשְׁתָיו Lv 5^{24}, rd. ־תוֹ Sam. Di (q.v.);—*fifth*, usu. in enum. days, months, years, sons, etc.; definite, exc. *masc.* Gn 1^{23} 30^{17}, *fem.* Gn 47^{24} 1 K 6^{31} Ne 6^{5};—**1. m.** Gn 1^{23} Nu 7^{36} 29^{26} 33^{38} Jos 19^{24} (all P), Gn 30^{17} (E), Ju 19^{8} 2 K 25^{8} Je 1^{3} 28^{1} 52^{12} Zc 7^{3} 1 Ch 27^{8} Ezr $7^{8.9}$; noun om. 2 S 3^{4} 1 Ch 2^{14} 3^{3} 8^{2} $26^{3.4}$ (all of בֵּן), 1 Ch 24^{9} 25^{12} (גּוֹרָל), Zc 8^{19} (חֹדֶשׁ), 1 Ch 27^{8} (יוֹם). **2. f.** Lv 19^{25} 1 K 14^{25} Je 36^{9} Ez 1^{2} 2 Ch 12^{2}; פַּעַם ח׳ Ne 6^{5}. **3.** חֲמִשִׁית 1 K 6^{31} as subst. *a fifth part*, so חֲמִישִׁית Gn 47^{24} Lv $5^{6.24}$ 22^{14} $27^{13.27.31}$ Nu 5^{7}; cstr. חמישית כֶּסֶף Lv $27^{15.19}$.

III. חמשׁ (√ of foll.; meaning dubious).

†II. חֹמֶשׁ **n.m. belly** (Aram. ܚܘܡܫܐ—הַחֹמֶשׁ— 2570
2 S 2^{23}+3 t.; וַיַּכֵּהוּ . . . אל־הח׳ 2 S 2^{23} *and he smote him in the belly*; 2 S 20^{10}+4^{6}, rd. וַתָּנָם וַתִּישַׁן *and she slumbered and slept* 𝔊 We Dr.; yet corruption difficult to explain, v. Klo; וַיַּכֵּהוּ שָׁם הח׳ 2 S 3^{27} (where prob. ins. אל־ cf. Dr).

IV. חמשׁ (√ of foll.; mng. dub.; perh. cf. Ar. خَمِيسٌ *army*, Sab. חמס men of a tribe who can bear arms; √ then poss. = I. חמשׁ (e.g. army as composed of *five parts*) v. Lane Frey; also Sab. Denkm.[24], which cites *tribus* (fr. *tres*), *quartier* (fr. *quartus*, *quatuor*); > Thes MV al. who comp. Ar. حَمَسَ *be firm strong*, حَمِسَ *be courageous*, etc.)

†חֲמֻשִׁים **adj. pl. in battle array**, alw. this 2571
form, Ex 13^{18} (E), Jos 1^{14} 4^{12} (both D), Ju 7^{11}+Nu 32^{17} (JE), v. חושׁ.

חמת (√ of foll.; mng. unknown; MV al., very improbably, fr. Ar. حَمِتَ *grow rancid, putrid*; see on formation, Lag[BN 154]).

†חֵמֶת, חֵמֶת, חֵמֶת **n.[m.] waterskin** (NH *id.*) 2573

—הַחֵמֶת Gn 21^{15}; הַחֵ֫מֶת Gn 21^{19}; וְחֵ֫מֶת מַ֫יִם Gn 21^{14} (v. Di), [Hb 2^{5} חֲמָתְךָ v. חֵמָה].

2574 †חֲמָת, חֲמַת **n.pr.loc.** (√dub.; Thes MV al. der. fr. חָמָה, חֹמָה, חֹמַת=*fortress*, or (v. RS$^{Sem. i, 140}$), *sacred enclosure, temenos, ḥimā*, cf. Hal$^{JAS\ 7ème\ Sér.\ x,\ 392}$ Lag$^{BN\ 82,\ 156}$; but no certainty that name is Shemitic; Ar. حَمَاةُ, As. *Amattu*, Dl$^{PA\ 275\ ff.\ Pr\ 174}$); —mod. Ḥamâ, on *el-'Âṣi* (Orontes), 38 h. (c. 115 m.) N. of Damascus, v. Bd$^{Pal\ 398\ f.}$ It had a king, תֹּעִי, in David's time 2 S 8^{9}=1 Ch 18^{9}, and in 8th cent. B.C. 2 K 19^{13}=Is 37^{13}; gods of its own 2 K 17^{30} 18^{34}=Is 36^{19}; gave its name to land (limits unknown) רִבְלָה בְּאֶרֶץ ח׳ 2 K 23^{33} 25^{21} Je 39^{5} $52^{9.27}$, cf. 2 Ch 8^{4}; contained Isr. exiles Is 11^{11}; furnished colonists for Samaria 2 K 17^{24} (cf. v^{30} supr.) after being conquered by Sargon, (COT 2 K 17^{24} 18^{34} cf. Is 10^{9}). It is called
2579 *great Hamath* by Am 6^{2} (חֲמַת רַבָּה,—חֲמַת only here). ח׳ is mentioned with צִידוֹן, צֹר, דַּמֶּשֶׂק in prophecy against land Hadrach (חַדְרָךְ) Zc 9^{2}, cf. Je 49^{23}. Often in phr. לְבֹא ח׳ (עַד־)=*the entrance to H.*, i.e. *the approach to H.*, as territorial limit Ju 3^{3}; usu. as denoting (ideal) northern limit of Isr. territory Jos 13^{5} Nu 13^{21} 34^{8} Am 6^{14} 1 K 8^{65}=2 Ch 7^{8}, 2 K 14^{25} 1 Ch 13^{5};
2578 חֲמָ֫תָה 1 Ch 18^{3}; ח׳ צוֹבָה 2 Ch 8^{3}, and הֵשִׁיב אֶת־דַּמֶּשֶׂק וְאֶת־ח׳ לִיהוּדָה 2 K 14^{28}; so also Ez 47, 48: גְּבוּל ח׳ Ez 47^{17}, cf. v^{16b}+v^{16a} (del. Co); לְבוֹא ח׳ 48^{1}, cf. 47^{20}; אֶל־יַד ח׳ 48^{1}.

2577 †חֲמָתִי **adj.gent.** c.art.=subst. הַחֲמָתִי, as descendants of Canaan Gn 10^{18}=1 Ch 1^{16}.

2575 חַמַּת **n.pr.loc.** v. sub חמם. p. 329

2580-82, 2584 חֵן, חֵנָדָד, חַנָּה v. sub חנן. p. 336-37

2583 חָנָה$_{143}$ **vb. decline, bend down, encamp** (Aram. ܚܢܳܐ *to aim at, incline towards, reach*; Zinj. מחנת cstr. *camp*, Inscr. Panammu$^{13.16.17}$; Ar. حَنَا *bend, curve, bend down*; As. *mûnu, mênu* and *tênû, couch, mânîtu, house*, Zim$^{BP\ 44,\ 45}$ Dl in Zim^{117})—**Qal** *Pf.* חָנָה 1 S 26^{5} Is 29^{1}; וְחָנִ֫יתִי consec. Is 29^{3} Zc 9^{8}; חָנוּ Nu 2^{34}+2 t.; וְחָנוּ consec. Nu 1^{52}; *Impf.* וַיִּחַן Gn 26^{17}+9 t.; 3 fs. תַּחֲנֶה ψ 27^{3}; יַחֲנוּ Nu 1^{50}+13 t. Nu+Ex 14^{2}: וַיַּחֲנוּ Ex 13^{20}+79 t. (of which 42 in Nu 33); וַיַּחֲנוּן Ju 11^{18}; 2 mpl. תַּחֲנוּ Ex 14^{2}; 1 pl. וַנַּחֲנֶה Ezr 8^{15}; *Imv.* חֲנֵה 2 S 12^{28}; חֲנוּ Nu 31^{19} Je 50^{29}; *Inf.* חֲנוֹת Ju 19^{9}; חֲנֹת Nu 1^{51}; sf. חֲנֹתֵנוּ Nu 10^{31}; חֲנֹתְכֶם Dt 1^{33}; *Pt.* חֹנֶה Ex 18^{5} ψ 34^{8}; f. חֹנָה 2 S 23^{13} 1 Ch 11^{15}; חֹנָךְ ψ 53^{6}; pl. חֹנִים Ex 14^{9}+11 t.; חוֹנִים Nu 2^{2} Na 3^{17};—**1.** *decline*, of day drawing to its close חֲנוֹת הַיּוֹם Ju 19^{9} (‖ רָפָה הַיּ׳); also נְטוֹת הַיּ׳ v^{8}; הַיּוֹם רַד מְאֹד לַעֲרוֹב v^{11}). **2.** *encamp* (prop. *verge toward, incline to, settle at*, of goal of day's march):—**a.** of single nomad Gn 26^{17} (J; sq. ב), 33^{18} (E; sq. אֶת־פְּנֵי). **b.** of Israel at Exod. and in wilderness Ex 13^{20} (ב) 14^{2} (לִפְנֵי), v^{2} (עַל), + c. 80 t. (Hex. chiefly P); also (abs.) Nu $9^{18.20.22.23}$ cf. Ezr 8^{15}; Ne 11^{30} *so they encamped* (i.e. *settled*, or *were settled*) from Beersheba to the valley of Hinnom (‖ ישבו v^{25}). **c.** of armies: (1) Israel (conquering Canaan, etc.) Jos 4^{19} 5^{10}+oft.; (2) Philistines 1 S 4^{1} 13^{16} 2 S 23^{23}+; usu. sq. ב loc. Nu 10^{31} 1 S 4^{1} 13^{16} Jos 4^{19} 1 S 13^{5}+63 t. (וַיַּחֲנוּ בְ 2 S 24^{5} rd. וַיָּחֵלּוּ מִן 𝔊L We Dr v. חלל); so of locusts in hedges (in sim.) Na 3^{17}; also sq. עַל=*by, near* Ex $14^{2.9}$ 15^{27} Nu 1^{52} $2^{2.5.12.27}$ $3^{29.35}$ (על ירך), 33^{10} Ju 7^{1} 1 S 4^{1}; על־פני השדה (על in diff. sense) 2 S 11^{11}; sq. עַל also=*against, encamp* with hostile purpose Jos $10^{5.31.34}$ Ju 6^{4} 20^{19} 1 S 11^{1} 2 S 12^{28} 1 K 16^{15} 2 K 25^{1} 2 Ch 32^{1} Je 50^{29} 52^{4} ψ 27^{3}; sq. אֶל־ in same sense Jos 11^{5}; metaph. of God's hostility to apostate Jerusalem (עַל) Is 29^{3}; sq. also לְ=*at, by* Nu 2^{34} Zc 9^{8}; אשר . . . שָׁם Ex 18^{5} 1 S 26^{5}; sq. סביב לְ for protection Nu $1^{50.53}$, cf. metaph. ψ 34^{8}, but also hostility Jb 19^{12}; also sq. other prep. and prep. phrases, e.g. מֵעֵבֶר Nu 21^{13}; מחוץ Nu 31^{19}; בין 1 S 17^{1}; נגד 1 K 20^{27} etc.; sq. acc. loc. 2 S 17^{26}; sq. sf. acc. with hostile sense חֹנָךְ ψ 53^{6}; without prep. or noun foll., in sense of *encamp, be* or *abide in encampment* Nu $9^{18.20.22.23}$ Ezr 8^{15} 2 S 11^{11}+; poet. of David in Jerusalem, Is 29^{1} *city in which David fixed his camp*.

2588 †[חָנוּת] **n.f. cell** (as having *curved* or *vaulted roof, arched*; v. Thes Gf, and cf. Aram. ܚܢܘܬܐ *vaulted room*)—הַחֲנֻיּוֹת Je 37^{16} (‖ בֵּית הַבּוֹר).

2595 †חֲנִית **n.f. spear** (as *flexible*? v. Thes);—*abs.* חֲנִית 2 S 13^{19}+26 t.; cstr. *id.* 1 S 26^{16} (so v^{22} Qr, where Kt has art.); sf. חֲנִיתֶךָ Hb 3^{11}; חֲנִיתוֹ 1 S $17^{7.7}$+11 t.+2 S 23^{8}, v. infr.; pl. חֲנִיתִים 2 Ch 23^{9}; חֲנִיתוֹתֵיהֶם Is 2^{4}=חֲנִיתֹתֵיהֶם Mi 4^{3};—**1.** *spear*, as hurled 1 S $18^{10.11}$ $19^{9.10.10}$ 20^{33}; held by king 22^{6}; sign of king's presence $26^{7.8.11.12.16.22}$ (v. RS$^{K\ 171}$); also 2 S 1^{6} 2^{23} 21^{19} $23^{18.21.21.21}$ 1 Ch 11^{11}=2 S 23^{8}, where rd. הוּא עוֹרֵר אֶת־חֲנִיתוֹ (for הוּא עֲדִינוֹ הָעֶצְנוֹ) acc. to Ew Th Ke Klo Dr (not We), 1 Ch $11^{20.23.23.23}$; pl. 2 Ch 23^{9}; oft. ‖ חֶרֶב 1 S $13^{19.22}$ $17^{45.47}$ 21^{9} Is 2^{4}=Mi 4^{3}, Na 3^{3}; ‖ שְׁלָטִים 2 K 11^{10}; ‖ צִנָּה 1 Ch 12^{35} (Baer); מַסָּע

Jb 41^{18}; סִגְר ‖ ψ 35^{3}; ‖ קֶשֶׁת ψ 46^{10}. **2. a.** *shaft of spear* is עֵץ ח׳ 2 S 23^{7} 1 Ch 20^{5} + 1 S 17^{7} Qr (doubtless right; Kt חץ). **b.** *spear-head* לַהֶבֶת ח׳ 1 S 17^{7}, cf. לַהַב ח׳ Jb 39^{23}; בְּרַק ח׳ Na 3^{3} Hb 3^{11}. **c.** *butt of spear* אַחֲרֵי ח׳ 2 S 2^{23}. **3.** metaph. of teeth of lions ψ 57^{5} (‖ חצים; fig. of Psalmist's enemies).

4264 מַחֲנֶה $_{214}$ **n.m.** $^{Gn\,33,8+16\,t.}$ and **f.** $^{\psi\,27,3;\,1\,Ch\,11,15}$ (on Gn 32$^{9\,a}$ v. Di) **encampment, camp**—abs. מ׳ Gn 32$^{9.9}$ + 126 t. (incl. Ez 1^{24}, del. Co); cstr. מַחֲנֵה Gn 32^{3} + 56 t.; sf. מַחֲנֵהוּ Nu 1^{52} + 5 t.; מַחֲנֶיךָ Dt 23^{15} 29^{10}, מַחֲנֶךָ Dt 23^{15}, מַחֲנֵיכֶם Am 4^{10}, מַחֲנֵיהֶם Nu 5^{3} Ju 8^{10} (cf. infr., and on form of noun c. sf. vid. Ges$^{§\,93.3,\,R\,3}$); pl. abs. מַחֲנוֹת Gn 32^{8} + 9 t.; cstr. 1 Ch 9^{18} + 2 t., מַחֲנִים Nu 13^{19}; sf. (appar. pl. n.) מַחֲנֵיהֶם Jos 10^{4} + 5 t.;—on du. v. מ׳ **n.pr.** infr. **1.** *camp, place of encampment:* **a.** of caravan of travellers Gn 32^{22} (J), esp. of Isr. at Exod. and in wildern. Ex 16$^{13.13}$ 19$^{16.17}$ (all P; disting. fr. עַם); שַׁעַר מ׳ Ex 32^{26} (JE); esp. מִחוּץ הַמּ׳ in connexion with uncleanness, etc., Ex 29^{14} Lv 4^{12} (P) + oft., of position of tent of meeting Ex 33$^{7.7}$ (JE), contr. Nu 2^{17} (P), where of encampments of several tribes, cf. 1^{52} 2^{3} 10$^{2.5.6.25}$ etc., (all P), already passing over to **3** (cf. הַחֹנִים 10$^{5.6}$); specif. of *camp of Levites*, surrounding tabernacle, so that P can say אֹהֶל־מוֹעֵד מַחֲנֵה הַלְוִיִּם Nu 2^{17}; and so (late) of temple הַשֹּׁעֲרִים לְמַחֲנוֹת בְּנֵי לֵוִי 1 Ch 9^{18}, as well as שַׁעֲרֵי מַחֲנוֹת י׳ 2 Ch 31^{2}; pl. (opp. מִבְצָרִים = *fortresses*) Nu 13^{19}. **2.** *camp of armed host* Jos 6$^{11.11.14}$ (JE), 1 S 4$^{3.5.6.6.7}$ 17^{53} 2 K 7^{16} etc. **3. a.** *those who encamp* Nu 10$^{5.6}$ 1 Ch 11^{15} ψ 27^{3} (all c. vb. חנה), cf. (prob.) Is 37^{36} = 2 K 19^{35}, etc. **b.** *company, body of people;* people and beasts Gn 32$^{8.9.9.11}$ 33^{8}, funeral company of Jacob Gn 50^{9}; of Isr. on march Ex 14$^{19.20}$ cf. Nu 10$^{5.6}$. **c.** *army, host* Jos 8^{13} 10^{5} 11^{4} Ju 4$^{15.16.16}$ 7$^{1.8}$ 8$^{10.10.11.11.12}$ 1 S 17$^{1.46}$ 2 K 3^{9} even while in the thick of the fight; 1 K 22^{34} = 2 Ch 18^{33} etc.

4265 †מַחֲנֵה־דָן **n.pr.loc.** = *camp of Dan*, name given, Ju 13^{25} 18^{12}, to place where Danites encamped (v. Bla).

4266 †מַחֲנַיִם **n.pr.loc.** (*two camps*)—E. of Jordan; name from Jacob's meeting angels acc. to Gn 32^{3} (J), place on border of Gad Jos 13^{26}, of Manasseh v^{30} (P); Levit. city in Gad 21^{36} (P) = 1 Ch 6^{65}; named also 2 S 2^{8} (מַחֲנָיִם), v$^{12.29}$ (־נָיִם), 19^{33} 1 K 2^{8} (־נָיִם); מַחֲנַיְמָה 2 S 17$^{24.27}$ 1 K 4^{14}; site unknown, v. Di^{Gn}; כִּמְחֹלַת הַמַּחֲנָיִם Ct 7^{1} is put here by Ew Hi Öt al.: *as at a* (the) *dance of Mahanaim; dance of a double choir* Gi Stickel RV.

†תַּחַן **n.pr.m.** (perh. abbrev. fr. תַּחֲנָה)—an Ephraimite Nu 26^{35} 𝔊 Ταναχ, 1 Ch 7^{25} 𝔊 Θαεν, 𝔊L Θααν. 8465

†תַּחֲנִי **adj.gent.** only c. art. as subst. coll., הַתּ׳ Nu 26^{35}. 8470

†[תַּחֲנָה] **n.f. encamping,** or **encampment;**—pl. sf. תַּחֲנֹתִי (si vera l.) אֶל־מְקוֹם פְּלֹנִי אַלְמֹנִי 2 K 6^{8}, *unto such and such a place is my encamping;* but form very strange. Rd. prob. תֵּחָבְאוּ *ye shall hide yourselves*, so 𝔖 Th Klo. 8466

†חָנַט **vb. spice, make spicy, embalm** (NH *id., bud, blossom;* Ar. حَنَطَ *become mature*, II. *prepare for burial*, حَنُوطٌ *spices* for a corpse; حَنَّاطٌ *embalmer*, Dozy$^{I,\,322}$ after PS^{1320}; Aram. חֲנַט, ܚܢܰܛ *embalm;* so Eth. ሐነጠ: (loan-word Di^{110}));—**Qal** *Pf.* 3 fs. חָנְטָה Ct 2^{13}; *Impf.* 3 mpl. וַיַּחַנְטוּ Gn 50$^{2.26}$; *Inf. cstr.* לַחֲנֹט Gn 50^{2};—**1.** *spice, make spicy* הַתְּאֵנָה ח׳ פַּגֶּיהָ Ct 2^{13} *the fig-tree spiceth its figs*, so VB De in transl. (Ew De in notes Öt al. prefer *reddeneth*, on account of spring season, cf. the less common and perhaps secondary sense in Ar. *become red* (of leather) Lane$^{657\,a}$). **2.** *embalm*, sq. acc. pers. Gn 50$^{2.2}$ (performed by הָרֹפְאִים), v^{26}. 2590

†חֲנֻטִים **n.[m.]pl.abstr. embalming,** only יְמֵי הַח׳ Gn 50^{3} i.e. the days consumed in the embalming process = אַרְבָּעִים יוֹם v. Di. 2590

†חִטָּה **n.f. wheat** (NH *id.*, Aram. חִנְטִין, חִיטְּתָא, ܚܶܛܳܐ; Ar. حِنْطَةٌ);—abs. ח׳ Ex 9^{32} + 6 t.; pl. חִטִּים Gn 30^{14} + 20 t.; חִטִּין Ez 4^{9}; cstr. חִטֵּי Ez 27^{17};—*wheat*, sg. chiefly poet., of growing wheat Ex 9^{32} (E), Dt 8^{8} Jb 31^{40} Jo 1^{11}; sown Is 28^{25}; food-product Dt 32^{14} (חֵלֶב כִּלְיוֹת ח׳ *kidney-fat of wheat*, i.e. the choicest, v. חֵלֶב), חֵלֶב ח׳ ψ 81^{17} (cf. 147^{14} infr.); elsewh. pl.; wheat as sown Je 12^{13}; *wheat-harvest* קְצִיר ח׳ Gn 30^{14} (J), Ex 34^{22} (JE), Ju 15^{1} 1 S 6^{13} 12^{17} Ru 2^{23}, + 2 S 24^{15} where insert acc. to 𝔊 We Dr; wheat threshed Ju 6^{11} 1 Ch 20^{21} cf. v^{23}; measured 1 K 5^{25} = 2 Ch 2^{9} (חטים מַכּוֹת, rd. ח׳ מַכֹּלֶת as 1 K 5^{25} = *wheat for food* Th Be Ke after Vrss), v^{14} 27^{5} Ez 45^{13}; stored (with barley, oil and honey) Je 41^{8}; for food 2 S 17^{28}, חֵלֶב חִטִּים ψ 147^{14} (cf. 81^{14} supr.); לֹקְחֵי חִטִּים 2 S 4^{6} (rd. סֹקֶלֶת ח׳ 𝔊 We Dr); סֹלֶת ח׳ *fine wheaten flour* 2406

Ex 29^{2} (P); Ez 4^{9} (חִטִּין, Aram. pl.) mixed with barley, beans, lentils, etc., and made into bread.

2592 חֲנִיאֵל **n.pr.**, and חֲנִינָה v. sub חנן. p. 337

2595 חֲנִית v. sub חנה. p. 333

I. חנך (√of foll. (see Ar. Syr.); meaning unknown).

2441 †חֵךְ **n.m. palate, roof of mouth, gums** (NH *id.*; Aram. ܚܶܟܳܐ, חִכָּא; Ar. حَنَكٌ *palate, roof of mouth, jaws, lower part of mouth, lower jaw* of horse, *mouth*, etc. Lane^{659} Dozy$^{i. 332}$);—abs. ח׳ Jb 12^{11} 34^{3}; sf. חִכִּי Pr 8^{7} + 6 t., חִכְּךָ Ho 8^{1}, חִכֵּךְ Ez 3^{26} Pr 24^{13}; chiefly poet., esp. WisdLt:—חִכֵּךְ Ct 7^{10}, חִכּוֹ La 4^{4} + 2 t., חִכָּהּ Pr 5^{3}, חִכָּם Jb 29^{10};—*palate, roof of mouth*: **a.** אֶל־חִכְּךָ שֹׁפָר Ho 8^{1} *a trumpet to thy palate!* (or *gums*; as in Eng., *to thy lips*); oft. c. לָשׁוֹן, *tongue clings* (דבק) *to* חך, expression for speechlessness Ez 3^{26} Jb 29^{10}, as imprecation ψ 137^{6}; for the parching of extreme thirst La 4^{4} (בַּצָּמָא), cf. ψ 22^{16} MT יָבֵשׁ כַּחֶרֶשׂ כֹּחִי, rd. חִכִּי for כחי v. Che$^{crit. n.}$ (לְשׁוֹנִי מֻדְבָּק מַלְקוֹחָי‖). **b.** as organ of speech Pr 5^{3} 8^{7} (both ‖ שְׂפָתַיִם), Jb 31^{30} 33^{2} (‖ פָּתַחְתִּי פִי) דִּבְּרָה לְשׁוֹנִי בְחִכִּי. **c.** as organ of taste Jb 12^{11} 34^{3}, פִּרְיוֹ מָתוֹק לְחִכִּי Ct 2^{3} *his fruit was sweet to my palate*, Pr 24^{13} (implied sim. of wisdom as sweet to the soul); fig. of God's words as sweet לְח׳ ψ 119^{103} (‖ פִּי); of taste as distinguishing misfortunes Jb 6^{30} (‖ לָשׁוֹן; > others of speech); of keeping wickedness בְּתוֹךְ ח׳ Jb 20^{13} (‖ תַּחַת לְשׁוֹנוֹ), i.e. delighting in and prolonging the taste of it. **d.** nearly = *mouth*, as an element in personal sweetness and beauty Ct 5^{16} 7^{10}.

2596 †II. חָנַךְ **vb. train up, dedicate** (cf. Ar. حَنَكَ appar. denom. fr. حَنَكٌ, *rub palate* of child with chewed dates, Lane$^{659 a}$, of midwife *rub palate* of new-born child with oil, etc., before it begins to suck, Dozy$^{ii. 332}$; also *make experienced, submissive*, etc. (as one does a horse by a rope in its mouth) Lane; v. also We$^{Skizzen iii, 154}$; NH חָנַךְ *accustom*; Aram. חֲנַךְ *dedicate*, חַנֵּיךְ as NH; Eth. II. ሐነከ: *perceive, understand* (Di^{108}, ሐንከ: *initiatio* is loan-word Id.$^{ib.}$))—**Qal** *Pf.* 3 ms. sf. חֲנָכוֹ Dt 20^{5}; *Impf.* 3 ms. sf. יַחְנְכֶנּוּ Dt 20^{5}, 3 mpl. וַיַּחְנְכוּ 1 K 8^{63} 2 Ch 7^{5}; *Imv.* חֲנֹךְ Pr 22^{6};—**1.** *train, train up* a (the) youth (לַנַּעַר) Pr 22^{6} (cf. NH חִנּוּךְ). **2.** *dedicate*, of formal opening of a new house Dt 20$^{5.5}$; *dedicate, consecrate* temple 1 K 8^{63} = 2 Ch 7^{5} (all sq. acc.)

†חֲנוֹךְ **n.pr.m. 1.** son of Cain Gn 4$^{17.17.18}$ 2585
𝔊 Ενωχ, 𝔊L Ενως. **2.** son of Jered (line of Seth), the pious Enoch, who walked with God and was taken by him Gn 5$^{18.19.21.22.23.24}$ 1 Ch 1^{3} 𝔊 Ενωχ. **3.** חֲנֹךְ a son of Midian Gn 25^{4} 1 Ch 1^{33}, 𝔊 Ενωχ. **4.** חֲנוֹךְ a son of Reuben Gn 46^{9} Ex 6^{14} Nu 26^{5} 1 Ch 5^{3}, 𝔊 Ενωχ.

†חֲנֹכִי **adj.gent.** of חֲנוֹךְ **4,** only c. art. הַח׳ 2599
= subst. coll. Nu 26^{5}.

†[חָנִיךְ] **adj. trained, tried, experienced,** 2593
only pl. sf. חֲנִיכָיו יְלִידֵי בֵיתוֹ, Gn 14^{14} i.e. his tried and trusty men, born in his house.

†חֲנֻכָּה **n.f. dedication, consecration,** as 2598
a matter of usage only P and late (NH חֲנוּכָּה Feast of Dedication; so Aram. חֲנֻכְּתָא)—abs. ח׳ Ne 12^{27}; cstr. חֲנֻכַּת Nu 7^{10} + 6 t.; dedication of wall of Jerus. Ne 12$^{27.27}$, by sacrifices and processions, with music; of altar in temple 2 Ch 7^{9}; of 'the house' ψ 30^{1} (title), i.e. the temple (re-dedication by Judas Maccab., 1 Macc. 4$^{52 ff.}$), v. Ol Bae al. (opp. De), and esp. Che$^{OP 234, 247}$; = *dedication-offering* for altar in tabernacle Nu 7^{10} (acc. c. וַיַּקְרִיבוּ), cf. יַקְרִיבוּ אֶת־קָרְבָּנָם לַחֲנֻכַּת הַמִּזְבֵּחַ v^{11}, also v$^{84.88}$ (all P; v Di Nu 7^{20}).

†חַכָּה **n.f. hook** fastened in jaw, **fish-hook** 2443
(NH *id.*, Aram. חַכְּתָא)—abs. ח׳ Jb 40^{25} + 2 t.; כָּל־מַשְׁלִיכֵי בַיְאוֹר חַכָּה Is 19^{8} (‖ הַדַּיָּגִים), כֻּלֹּה בְּחַכָּה הֵעֲלָה Hb 1^{15} (of אדם, who, v^{14}, is comp. to דְּגֵי הַיָּם, and רֶמֶשׂ), cf. תִּמְשֹׁךְ לִוְיָתָן בְּחַכָּה Jb 40^{25}.

חִנָּם v. sub חנן. p. 336 2600

†חֲנַמְאֵל **n.pr.m.** (perh. = חנן־אל)—Jere- 2601
miah's cousin, son of his uncle Je 32$^{7.8.9}$, cf. ח׳ דֹּדִי v^{12}; 𝔊 Αναμεηλ.

†[חֲנָמַל] **n.[m.]** only בַּחֲנָמַל ψ 78^{47} (on 2602
form v. Dr$^{Sm p. 98}$) as instr. of destroying sycomores (‖ בָּרָד); meaning conject.; 𝔊 𝔙 *frost*.

†I. חָנַן **vb. shew favour, be gracious** (NH 2603, 2589
id., Aram. חֲנַן, ܚܰܢ; Ar. حَنَّ *yearn towards, long for, be merciful, compassionate, favourable, inclined towards*; Sab. חן in n.pr. חן מסבררהם DHM$^{Epigr. Denkm. 40}$; Ph. חנן in חן *favour*, and n.pr. as אלחנן, חננבעל; As. in deriv. *annu, grace, favour, unninu, têninu nannu, id.*, Lotz^{TP} Zim$^{BP 23, 66}$)—**Qal** *Pf.* חָנַן Gn 33^{5}; sf. חַנַּנִי Gn 33^{11}; יְחָנַּנִי 2 S 12^{22}; חַנֹּתִי Ex 33^{19}; חֲנָנוּ La 4^{16}; *Impf.* יֶחֱנַן Am 5^{15}; יָחֹן Dt 28^{50}; וַיָּחָן 2 K 13^{23}; sf. יְחָנְךָ Gn 43^{29} Is 30^{19}; וִיחֻנֶּךָּ Nu 6^{25};

יְחָנֶּנּוּ Is 27^{11} Jb 33^{24}; יְחָנֵּנוּ ψ 67^{2} 123^{2} Mal 1^{9}; תָּחֹן ψ 59^{6}; sf. תְּחָנֵּם Dt 7^{2}; אָחֹן Ex 33^{19}; *Imv.* sf. חָנֵּנִי ψ 4^{2} + 17 t. ψψ; חָנְנֵנִי ψ 9^{14} (Baer pts. חַנְנֵנִי); חָנֵּנוּ Is 33^{2} ψ 123$^{3.3}$; חָנּוּנוּ Ju 21^{22}; חָנֻּנִי Jb 19$^{21.21}$; *Inf. abs.* חָנוֹן Is 30^{19}; *cstr.* חַנּוֹת ψ 77^{10}; חֶנְנָהּ ψ 102^{14}; חֲנַנְכֶם Is 30^{18}; *Pt.* חוֹנֵן Pr 14^{31}; חוֹנֵן ψ 37^{21} + 5 t. ψψ Pr.—*favour, shew favour;* **1.** of man: **a.** Ju 21^{22} *favour us with them* (2 acc.; i.e. by giving them to us). **b.** in *dealing with the poor, needy, and orphans,* abs. ψ 37$^{21.26}$ = 112^{5}; c. acc. Pr 14^{31} 19^{17} 28^{8}; c. לְ ψ 109^{12}. **c.** by *considering and sparing,* c. acc. Dt 7^{2} 28^{50} La 4^{16} Jb 19$^{21.21}$. **2.** of God, **a.** in the bestowal of favours, with acc. Gn 33^{11} (E), 43^{29} (J), Nu 6^{25} (P), 2 S 12^{22}; double acc. Gn 33^{5} (E), תּוֹרָתְךָ חָנֵּנִי *be gracious unto me* (in giving) *thy law* ψ 119^{29}. **b.** usually in the bestowal of redemption from enemies, evils, and sins; abs. ψ 77^{10}, elsewhere c. acc. Ex 33$^{19.19}$ (JE), Am 5^{15} 2 K 13^{23} Is 27^{11} 30$^{18.19.19}$ 33^{2} Mal 1^{9} ψ 4^{2} 6^{3} 9^{14} 25^{16} 26^{11} 27^{7} 30^{11} 31^{10} 41$^{5.11}$ 51^{3} 56^{2} 57$^{2.2}$ 59^{6} 67^{2} 86$^{3.16}$ 102^{14} 119$^{58.132}$ 123$^{2.3.3}$ Jb 33^{24}.—Jb 19^{17} v. II. חנן. **Niph.** *Pf.* 2 fs. נֵחַנְתְּ Je 22^{23} *be pitied* (cf. נֵאַר √ארר) but 𝔊 𝔖 𝔙 express *groan* (i.e. נֶאֱנַחְתְּ), which is favoured by context, and adopted by Hi Ew Gf Gie al. **Pi.** *Impf.* 3 ms. *make gracious, favourable* כִּי־יְחַנֵּן קוֹלוֹ Pr 26^{25}. **Poʿel** *Impf.* 3 ms. *direct favour to* (Ges $^{§ 55, 1}$) וְאֶת־עֲפָרָהּ יְחֹנֵנוּ ψ 102^{15}; *Pt.* מְחוֹנֵן עֲנָוִים Pr 14^{21}. **Hoph.** *Impf.* יֻחַן *be shewn favour, consideration* Is 26^{10} Pr 21^{10}. **Hithp.** *Pf.* 2 ms. הִתְחַנַּנְתָּה 1 K 9^{3} + 5 t. Pf.; *Impf.* וַיִּתְחַנֵּן 2 K 1^{13}; וַתִּתְחַנֶּן־ Est 8^{3}; אֶתְחַנָּן ψ 30^{9} + etc. + 6 t. Impf.; *Inf.* לְהִתְחַנֶּן־ Est 4^{8}; בְּהִתְחַנְנוֹ Gn 42^{21}—*seek or implore favour:* **1.** *of man,* with אֶל Gn 42^{21} (E) 2 K 1^{13}; with לְ Jb 19^{16} Est 4^{8} 8^{3}. **2.** of *God,* with אֶל־ Dt 3^{23} 1 K 8$^{33.47}$ = 2 Ch 6^{37}, Jb 8^{5} ψ 30^{9} 142^{2}; with לְ Ho 12^{5} Jb 9^{15}; with לפני 1 K 8^{59} 9^{3} 2 Ch 6^{24}.

2580 †I. חֵן **n.m.** $^{ψ 45, 3}$ **favour, grace;**—ח׳ Gn 6^{8} + 67 t.; sf. חִנּוֹ Gn 39^{21};—**1.** *favour, grace, elegance:* **a.** of *form and appearance,* of a woman ‖ יֹפִי Pr 31^{30}; אֵשֶׁת חֵן Pr 11^{16}; זונה טובת חן Na 3^{4}; of a doe Pr 5^{19}; precious stone אבן חן Pr 17^{8}; of ornaments Pr 1^{9} = 4^{9}, 3^{22}. **b.** of *speech,* lips ψ 45^{3} Pr 22^{11}; words Ec 10^{12}. **2.** *favour, acceptance:* **a.** *with men* Pr 13^{15} 22^{1} Ec 9^{11}. **b.** *with God* Zc 4$^{7.7}$ 12^{10}; chiefly in phrases: מצא חן בעיני *find favour in the eyes of:* (1) *men* Gn 30^{27} 32^{6} 33$^{8.10.15}$ 34^{11} 39^{4} 47$^{25.29}$ 50^{4} Nu 32^{5} (all J); Dt 24^{1} Ru 2$^{2.10.13}$ 1 S 1^{18} 16^{22} 20$^{3.29}$ 25^{8} 27^{5} 2 S 14^{22} 16^{4} 1 K 11^{19} Est 5^{8} 7^{3}; (2) *of God* Gn 6^{8} 18^{3} 19^{19} Ex 33$^{12.13.13.16.17}$ 34^{9} Nu 11$^{11.15}$ (all J); Ju 6^{17} 2 S 15^{25} Pr 3^{4}; abs. מצא חן (with man) Pr 28^{23}; (with God) Je 31^{2}; מצא חן לפניו Est 8^{5} (i.e. of the king); נתן חן בעיני *give favour in the eyes of* (1) man Gn 39^{21} Ex 3^{21} 11^{3} 12^{36} (J); abs. נתן חן of man ψ 84^{12}; (2) of God Pr 3^{34}; נשׂא חֵן בְּעֵינֵי *obtain favour in the eyes of* Est 2^{15}; of the king 5^{2}; so וַתִּשָּׂא־חֵן וָחֶסֶד לְפָנָיו Est 2^{17}.

חִנָּם **subst.,** used chiefly in the accus. as **adv.** (cf. As. *annâma, in vain,* Dl$^{K 7, Pr 44}$; from חֵן, with aff. ־ָם, which is sometimes found in substantives proper, as סֻלָּם, and pr. names, but is more partic. used with substs. applied adverbially, as רֵיקָם, דּוּמָם, אָמְנָם, יוֹמָם: Sta$^{§ 293}$ Ba$^{NB § 216}$)—lit. **out of favour**; i. e. **a.** *gratis, gratuitously, for nothing,* עָבַד חִנָּם to serve *for nought* Gn 29^{15} Jb 1^{9}, Is 52^{3} to be sold (fig.) *for nought* v^{5}; Ex 21$^{2.11}$ יָצָא חִנָּם to go out (from slavery) *freely, for nothing,* Nu 11^{5} which we used to eat in Eg. *for nought,* Je 22^{13} 1 Ch 21^{24}; in the genitive 2 S 24^{24} עלות חִנָּם i.e. burnt-offerings *which cost nothing* (in the ‖ 1 Ch 21^{24} the constr. is changed). **b.** *for no purpose, in vain* Pr 1^{17} Mal 1^{10}: once אֶל חִנָּם (cf. אֶל **7**) Ez 6^{10}. **c.** *gratuitously, without cause, undeservedly,* esp. of groundless hostility or attack 1 S 19^{5} לְהָמִית חִנָּם to slay David *without cause,* 25^{31} ψ 35$^{7.7}$ 109^{3} 119^{161} רְדָפוּנִי חִנָּם, Pr 1^{11} 3^{30} 23^{29} Jb 2^{3} לְבַלְּעוֹ ח׳, 9^{17} 22^{6} Ez 14^{23}, ψ 35^{19} and 69^{5} שֹׂנְאַי חִנָּם my haters *without cause,* La 3^{52} אֹיְבַי חִנָּם; in the genitive 1 K 2^{31} דְּמֵי חִנָּם blood shed *without cause* (cf. 1 S 25^{31}), Pr 24^{28} אַל־תְּהִי עֵד ח׳ בְּרֵעֶךָ, 26^{2} קִלְלַת ח׳ the *causeless* curse. 2600

†II. חֵן **n.pr.m.** (*favour*) — contemp. of 2581
Zerubbabel Zc 6^{14}, so RV SS We, but RVm Ew Hi Ke Or *grace, favour, kindness.*

†חִין **n.**[**m.**] חִין עֶרְכּוֹ Jb 41^{4} the *grace* of 2433
his proportions (= חֵן Aram. חִנָּא) so AV RV Thes De Volck Da al.; meaning not very appropr. in context (description of crocodile); but nothing better has been proposed; v. suggestions in Di.

†חַנָּה **n.pr.f.** 𝔊 Ἄννα (cf. Nab. חנה Eut$^{No. 20}$), 2584
mother of Samuel 1 S 1$^{2.2.5.5.8.9.13.15.19.20.22}$ 2$^{1.21}$.

†חָנָן **n.pr.m.** (*gracious;* cf. Sab. חנן, Ph. 2605
חנא)—**1.** one of the warriors of David 1 Ch 11^{43}. **2.** one of the heads of families of Nethinim Ezr 2^{46} = Ne 7^{49}. **3.** names of Levites Ne 8^{7} 10^{11} 13^{3}. **4.** chiefs of the people: **a.** Ne 10^{23}. **b.** Ne 10^{27}. **5.** Benjamite name 1 Ch 8$^{23.38}$ 9^{44} (cf. n.pr.loc. בֵּית חָנָן,

Mish. (כְּפַר חָנָן). **6.** אִישׁ הָאֱלֹהִים head of a prophetic guild, בְּנֵי חָנָן Je 35^{4}.

2586 †חָנוּן **n.pr.m.** (*favoured;* cf. As. *Ḫanunu,* king of Gaza COT on 2 K 15^{29});—**1.** an Ammonite king 2 S 10$^{1.2.3.4}$ 1 Ch 19$^{2.2.3.4.6}$. **2.** Jewish chiefs, contemporaries of Nehemiah: **a.** Ne 3^{13}. **b.** Ne 3^{30}.

2587 †חַנּוּן **adj. gracious,** only used as an attribute of God, as hearing the cry of the vexed debtor Ex 22^{26} (covt. code), ‖ מְרַחֵם ψ 116^{5}; elsewhere in the earlier phrase רַחוּם וְחַנּוּן Ex 34^{6} (JE) = ψ 86^{15} 103^{8}, or the later חַנּוּן וְרַחוּם 2 Ch 30^{9} Ne 9$^{17.31}$ ψ 111^{4} 112^{4} 145^{8} Jo 2^{13} Jon 4^{2}.

2594 †חֲנִינָה **n.f. favour** לֹא־אֶתֵּן לָכֶם חֲנִינָה *I will shew you no favour* Je 16^{13} (v. on form Ba$^{NB\ 136}$).

2592 †חַנִּיאֵל **n.pr.m.** (*favour of Ēl;* cf. Ph. חנבעל, חנמלקרת (Hamilcar) *favour of Melqart;* Nab. חנאל Vog$^{No.10}$)—**1.** prince of tribe of Manasseh Nu 34^{23}. **2.** a chief of the tribe of Asher 1 Ch 7^{39}.

2606 †חֲנַנְאֵל **n.pr.m.** (*Ēl is gracious;* cf. Ph. חננבעל, אלחנן, etc.)—name of a tower at Jerusalem Je 31^{38} Zc 14^{10} Ne 3^{1} 12^{39}.

2582 †חֵנָדָד **n.pr.m.** (חֵן+הֲדַד *favour of Hadad*)—Levite chief Ezr 3^{9} Ne 3$^{18.24}$ 10^{10}.

2607 †חֲנָנִי **n.pr.m.** (perh. abbrev. from foll.);—**1.** father of the prophet Jehu 1 K 16$^{1.7}$ 2 Ch 16^{7} 19^{2} 20^{34}. **2.** brother of Nehemiah Ne 1^{2} 7^{2}. **3.** a chief musician of David 1 Ch 25$^{4.25}$. **4.** a chief musician in time of Nehemiah Ne 12^{36}. **5.** a priest of Ezra's time Ezr 10^{20}.

2608 †חֲנַנְיָה, חֲנַנְיָהוּ **n.pr.m.** (י׳ *hath been gracious*)—𝔊 Ἀνανίας; חֲנַנְיָהוּ: (cf. חנניהו on Israel. seal, Ganneau$^{JAs\ Fev.-Mars\ 1883,\ 128,\ No.\ 1}$)—**1.** father of a prince under Jehoiakim Je 36^{12}. **2.** captain of Uzziah's army 2 Ch 26^{11}. **3.** chief of one of the divisions of musicians of David 1 Ch 25^{23} = חֲנַנְיָה v^{4}.—חֲנַנְיָה: **4.** a false prophet of Jeremiah's time Je 28$^{1.5.10.11.12.13.15.15.17}$. **5.** one of the three companions of Daniel Dn 1$^{6.7.11.19}$. **6.** grandfather of an officer of the guard in Jeremiah's time Je 37^{13}. **7.** a son of Zerubbabel 1 Ch 3$^{19.21}$. **8.** a Benjamite 1 Ch 8^{24}. **9.** various postexilic persons. **a.** Ezr 10^{28}. **b.** Ne 3^{8}. **c.** Ne 3^{30}. **d.** Ne 7^{2}. **e.** Ne 10^{24}. **f.** Ne 12$^{12.41}$.

2615 †חַנָּתֹן **n.pr.loc.** place in the tribe of Zebulun Jos 19^{14}; 𝔊 Αμωθ, A Εvvαθωθ, 𝔊L Αvαθωθ; site unknown; acc. to Conder = Talm. Caphar Hanania (Nbr$^{Géogr.\ 176.226}$) on the border of Upper and Lower Galilee, mod. Kefr' Anân, Survey$^{WP\ i.\ 205.207}$.

†I. תְּחִנָּה **n.f. favour, supplication for** 8467
favour;—ת׳ Jos 11^{20}+4 t.; cstr. תְּחִנַּת 1 K 8$^{30.52.52}$; תְּחִנָּתִי Je 37^{20}+5 t.; תְּחִנֹּתֵיהֶם 2 Ch 6^{39} etc. + 10 t. sf.;—**1.** *favour,* shewn by Israel Jos 11^{20} (D); מאת יהוה Ezr 9^{8}. **2.** *supplication for favour,* from God 1 K 8$^{52.52}$ 2 Ch 33^{13} ψ 119^{170}; ‖ תְּפִלָּה 1 K 8^{28} = 2 Ch 6^{19}, ψ 6^{10} 55^{2}; תפלה (ו)תחנה 1 K 8$^{38.45.49.54}$ = 2 Ch 6$^{29.35.39}$ 1 K 9^{3}; ת׳ אשר התפלל 1 K 8^{30} (= תְּחִנּוּן 2 Ch 6^{21}); תִּפֹּל ת׳ לִפְנֵי *let the supplication fall before,* Yahweh Je 36^{7}, the king Je 37^{20}, Jeremiah Je 42^{2}; הִפִּיל ת׳ לִפְנֵי *present supplication before,* Yahweh Je 42^{9} Dn 9^{20}, the king Je 38^{26}.

†II. תְּחִנָּה **n.pr.m.** one in the line of Judah 8468
1 Ch 4^{12}.

†[תַּחֲנוּן] **n.[m.]** only **pl.abstr. supplica-** 8469
tion for favour;—abs. תַּחֲנוּנִים Pr 18^{23}+4 t.; cstr. תַּחֲנוּנֵי Je 3^{21} 2 Ch 6^{21}; sf. 1 s. תַּחֲנוּנַי ψ 28^{2} etc., +9 t. sf.; also תַּחֲנוּנוֹתָי ψ 86^{6};—**1.** made to men: דִּבֶּר ת׳ (a poor man to the rich) Pr 18^{23}; ת׳ אֶל *supplication unto* (crocodile to man) Jb 40^{27}; elsewhere **2.** to God: ‖ תפלה ψ 143^{1} Dn 9$^{3.17}$; ת׳ אשר התפלל 2 Ch 6^{21} (= תחנה 1 K 8^{30}); קוֹל ת׳ *voice of supplication* ψ 28$^{2.6}$ 31^{23} 86^{6} 130^{2} 140^{7}, also 116^{2} (for קוֹלִי is old case-ending, and cstr. as 𝔊 𝔙 Che Bae al.); ‖ בְּבִי Je 31^{9}; בְּכִי ת׳ Je 3^{21}; רוח חן ות׳ Zc 12^{10}; אֲנַחְנוּ מַפִּילִים ת׳ לְפָנֶיךָ Dn 9^{18} *we are presenting our supplications before thee;* בִּתְחִלַּת ת׳ Dn 9^{23} *at the beginning of thy supplication.*

†II. [חָנַן] **be loathsome** (cf. Ar. خَنَّ x. 2603
foetorem emisit (puteus); Syr. ܡܚܝܢܐ *rancid*);—only וְחַנֹּתִי לִבְנֵי בִטְנִי Jb 19^{17} *and I am loathsome* to the sons of my womb (‖ זָרָה v. II. זור), so RVm Ew De Di al. (On the tone v. De.)

†חָנֵס **n.pr.loc.** Is 30^{4} in Lower Egypt, on 2609
island in Nile, S. of Memphis (‖ צֹעַן) = Egypt. *Ḥnnstn* [**Ḥnēnsě*], As. *Ḫininši;* Herodot.$^{ii.\ 137}$ Ἄνυσις, afterward *Heracleopolis magna,* now *Ahnâs;* v. Steindorff$^{BAS\ i.\ 602}$.

†[חָנֵף] **vb. be polluted, profane** (Ar. 2610
حَنَفَ *incline, decline,* hence حَنِيفٌ *inclining to a right state,* but in Heb. of *inclining away from right, irreligion, profaneness,* cf. حَنِفَ *have a* حَنَفٌ i.e. *distortion of foot;* Syr. in deriv.

be profane, etc.; NH Hiph., Aram. Aph. *act falsely toward, flatter,* חֲנוּפָּה *hypocrisy;* As. *ḫanpu, ruthlessness; hanâpu, exercise ruthlessness toward,* Tel Amarna Zim ZA vi, 1891, 256)—**Qal** *Pf.* 3 fs. חָֽנְפָה Is 24^{5}; 3 pl. חָנֵ֫פוּ Je 23^{11}; *Impf.* 3 fs. תֶּחֱנַף Je 3^{1}; תֶּחֱנָף Mi 4^{11}; וַתֶּחֱנַף Je 3^{9} ψ 106^{38}; *Inf. abs.* חָנוֹף Je 3^{1};—**1.** *be polluted:* of land Is 24^{5} Je 3$^{1.1}$ ψ 106^{38}; of Zion Mi 4^{11}. **2.** of prophet and priest = be חָנֵף (cf. infr.) i.e. *profane, godless* Je 23^{11}.—Je 3^{9} appar. trans. וַתֶּחֱנַף את הארץ, Gf del. את, Gie cites Ges § 121, 1, but rd. rather Hiph. וַתַּחֲנִף with Codd. 𝔊 Ew al. (v. also Gf Gie). **Hiph.** *Impf.* יַחֲנִיף Nu 35^{33} Dn 11^{33}; 2 fs. וַתַּחֲנִ֫יפִי Je 3^{2}; 2 mpl. תַּחֲנִ֫יפוּ;—**1.** *pollute:* the land Nu 35$^{33.33}$ (by blood; P), Je 3^{2} (by idolatry, etc.) + Je 3^{9} (v. supr.) **2.** *make profane, godless* Dn 11^{32} c. acc. pers.

2612 † חֹ֫נֶף **n.[m.] profaneness**—לַעֲשׂוֹת ח׳ Is 32^{6} *to practise profaneness* (+ תּוֹעָה, אָוֶן, נְבָלָה).

2611 † חָנֵף **adj. profane, irreligious** (Syr. ܚܢܦܐ *profane*, hence oft. *heathen, apostate;* Ar. حَنِيفٌ *inclining to a right state*, esp. *the true religion, a Muslim*)—abs. ח׳ Jb 8^{13} + 10 t.; pl. חֲנֵפִים Is 33^{14}; חַנְפֵי Jb 36^{13} ψ 35^{16};—*profane, godless:* of persons, אָדָם ח׳ Jb 34^{30}; גּוֹי ח׳ Is 10^{6}; as subst. *godless man* Is 9^{16} (‖ מרע) Jb 8^{13} 13^{16} 17^{8} 20^{5} 27^{8} Pr 11^{9}; coll. עֲדַת ח׳ Jb 15^{34}; pl. Is 33^{14}; חַנְפֵי־לֵב Jb 36^{13}; בְּחַנְפֵי לַעֲגֵי מָעוֹג ψ 35^{16} *as profane men, mockers for cake* (i.e. table-jesters; on cstr. v. Ges § 130.5), but txt. dub. (v. Che crit. n. Bae).

2613 † חֲנֻפָּה (so Baer; van d. H חֲנֻפָּה) **n.f. profaneness, pollution,** Je 23^{15}.

2614 † [חָנַק] **vb. strangle** (NH *id.*, Aram. חֲנַק, ܚܢܩ; Ar. خَنَقَ);—**Niph.** *Impf.* וַיֵּחָנַק 2 S 17^{23} *strangled himself* (+ וַיָּמֹת). **Pi.** *Pt.* מְחַנֵּק Na 2^{13} *strangle*, of lion strangling prey, fig. of Ninevitish king (object not expressed).

4267 † מַחֲנָק **n.[m.] strangling, suffocation,** as a mode of death, וַתִּבְחַר מַחֲנָק נַפְשִׁי Jb 7^{15} *and my soul chooseth strangling* (‖ מָוֶת).

2615 חֲנָתֹן v. sub חנן. p. 337

2616 † I. [חָסַד] **vb. 1. be good, kind** (NH חָסַד in deriv. חָסִיד *pious;* Aram. חֲסַד *be kind, mild* (then *beg*), chiefly in deriv. חִסְדָּא etc.; cf. perh. Ar. حَشَدَ usu. pl. *they assembled*, sq. لَهُ *they combined for him, and took pains to shew him courtesy* Lane 574 c, v. also RS Proph. iv. n. 9 (and Schu AE v. in Thes); > Thes al. who find primary meaning in *eager zeal* or *desire* (‖ קנא), whence develop *kindness* (as above), and *envy*, Ar. حَسَدَ, حَسَدٌ *envy* (vb. & n.), Aram. חֲסַד *be put to shame*, ܚܣܕ, חַסֵּד *reproach, revile*, v. II. חסד)—only **Hithp.** *Impf.* עִם־חָסִיד תִּתְחַסָּד *thou shewest thyself kind* 2 S 22^{26} = ψ 18^{26}.—On **Pi.** Pr 25^{10} v. II. חסד.

† I. חֶ֫סֶד 247 **n.m.** 2 S 16, 17 **goodness, kindness;** 2617
—abs. ח׳ Gn 24^{12} + 85 t.; חָ֫סֶד Gn 39^{21} + 12 t.; cstr. חֶסֶד 1 S 20^{14} + 8 t.; sf. חַסְדִּי ψ 59^{18} + 120 t. sfs.; pl. חֲסָדִים Gn 32^{11}; cstr. חַסְדֵי Is 55^{3} + 5 t. (Baer Jes p. 79 Ges § 93, R. 1 F.); sf. חֲסָדַי Ne 13^{14} + 10 t. sfs.; (not in H or P). **I.** *of man:* **1.** *kindness* of men towards men, in doing favours and benefits 1 S 20^{15} 2 S 16^{17} ψ 141^{5} Pr 19^{22} 20^{6}; ח׳ יהוה 1 S 20^{14} *the kindness of* י׳ (such as he shews, Thes MV; that sworn to by oath to Yahweh Mich Dathe; shewn out of reverence to Yahweh Th Ke), cf. ח׳ אלהים 2 S 9^{3}; תּוֹרַת־ח׳ Pr 31^{26} *instruction in kindness, kindly instruction* עָשָׂה חֶסֶד עִמָּדִי *do or shew kindness* (in dealing) *with me* Gn 20^{13} 40^{14} (E), 1 S 20^{14} 2 S 10^{2} (עִמִּי in ‖ 1 Ch 19^{2}); c. עִם Gn 21^{23} (E), 24$^{12.14}$ Jos 2$^{12.12}$ Ju 1^{24} (J), 8^{35} 1 S 15^{6} 2 S 2^{5} 3^{8} 9$^{1.3.7}$, 10^{2a} = 1 Ch 19^{2a}, 1 Ch 19^{2b} 2 Ch 24^{22}; c. עַל 1 S 20^{8}; c. לְ 1 K 2^{7}; נשׂא ח׳ לפני *obtain kindness before* Est 2$^{9.17}$; היטיב ח׳ Ru 3^{10}. **2.** *kindness* (especially as extended to the lowly, needy and miserable), *mercy* Pr 20^{28} Jb 6^{14}; איש חסד *merciful man* Pr 11^{17} (opp. אַכְזָרִי); מַלְכֵי ח׳ *merciful kings* 1 K 20^{31}; עשׂה ח׳ ψ 109^{16}; in this sense usu. with other attributes (v. also infr. II. **2**); ‖ אמת Ho 4^{1} Is 16^{5}; ח׳ ואמת Pr 3^{3} 14^{22} 16^{6} 20^{28}; עשׂה ח׳ ואמת Gn 24^{49} 47^{29} Jos 2^{14} (J; RV gives these under **1**); ‖ צדקה Ho 10^{12}; צדקה וח׳ Pr 21^{21}; ‖ משׁפט Mi 6^{8}; ח׳ ומשׁפט Ho 12^{7}; ‖ חוֹנֵן ψ 109^{12}; ח׳ ורחמים Zc 7^{9} Dn 1^{9}.—(On Ho 6$^{4.6}$ v. **3** infr.) **3.** (rarely) *affection* of Isr. to י׳, *love to God, piety:* ח׳ נְעוּרַיִךְ Je 2^{2} *piety of thy youth* (‖ *love of thine espousals* to Yahweh); poss. also חַסְדְּכֶם כַּעֲנַן־בֹּקֶר Ho 6^{4} *your piety is like a morning cloud* (fleeting), and כִּי חֶסֶד חָפַצְתִּי וְלֹא־זָבַח Ho 6^{6} *for piety I delight in and not in peace-offering* (‖ דעת אלהים, cf. 1 S 15^{22}); —so Wü Now Hi (v^{4}) Che; Ke Hi (v^{6}) al. sub **2** (or **1**);—אַנְשֵׁי חֶסֶד *men of piety* Is 57^{1} (‖ צַדִּיק); pl. *pious acts* 2 Ch 32^{32} 35^{26} Ne 13^{14}. **4.** *lovely appearance:* כָּל־חַסְדּוֹ כְּצִיץ הַשָּׂדֶה Is 40^{6} *all its loveliness as the flower of the field* (so Thes Hi De Che Di al.; but δόξα 𝔊 1 Pet 1^{24} & *gloria* 𝔙 favour an original reading הודו Lo or כְּבוֹדוֹ Ew, see

Br$^{MP 375}$; Du הָדְרוֹ). **II.** *of God: kindness, lovingkindness* in condescending to the needs of his creatures. He is חַסְדָּם *their goodness, favour* Jon 2^{9}; חַסְדִּי ψ 144^{2}; אֱלֹהֵי חַסְדִּי *God of my kindness* ψ 59^{18}; in v^{11} rd. אֱלֹהֵי חַסְדּוֹ *my God with his kindness* 𝔊 𝔙 Ew Hup De Pe Che Bae; his is the kindness ψ 62^{13}; it is with him ψ 130^{7}; he delights in it Mi 7^{18}. **1.** specif. lovingkindness: **a.** *in redemption from enemies and troubles* Gn 19^{19} 39^{21} (J), Ex 15^{13}(song), Je 31^{3} Ezr 7^{28} 9^{9} ψ 21^{8} $31^{17.22}$ 32^{10} 33^{22} $36^{8.11}$ 42^{9} 44^{27} 48^{10} 59^{17} 66^{20} 85^{8} 90^{14} 94^{18} $107^{8.15.21.31}$ $143^{8.12}$ Jb 37^{13} Ru 1^{8} 2^{20}; men should trust in it ψ 13^{6} 52^{10}; rejoice in it ψ 31^{8}; hope in it ψ 33^{18} 147^{11}. **b.** *in preservation of life from death* ψ 6^{5} 86^{13} Jb 10^{12}. **c.** *in quickening of spiritual life* ψ 109^{26} $119^{41.76.88.124.149.159}$. **d.** *in redemption from sin* ψ 25^{7} 51^{3}. **e.** *in keeping the covenants,* with Abraham Mi 7^{20}; with Moses and Israel שֹׁמֵר הַבְּרִית וְ(הַ)חֶסֶד *keepeth the covenant and the lovingkindness* Dt $7^{9.12}$ 1 K 8^{23}=2 Ch 6^{14}, Ne 1^{5} 9^{32} Dn 9^{4}; with David and his dynasty 2 S 7^{15}=1 Ch 17^{13}, 2 S 22^{51}=ψ 18^{51}, 1 K $3^{6.6}$=2 Ch 1^{8}, ψ $89^{29.34}$; with the wife Zion Is 54^{10}. **2.** חֶסֶד is grouped with other divine attributes: חסד ואמת *kindness (lovingkindness) and fidelity* Gn 24^{27} (J), ψ 25^{10} $40^{11.12}$ 57^{4} 61^{8} 85^{11} 89^{15} 115^{1} 138^{2}; עשׂה ח׳ ואמת עם 2 S 2^{6} 15^{20} (𝔊, v. Dr); רַב ח׳ ואמת Ex 34^{6} (JE), ψ 86^{15}; also ‖ אמת Mi 7^{20} ψ 26^{3} 117^{2}; ‖ אֱמוּנָה ψ 88^{12} 89^{3} 92^{3}; ח׳ ואמונה ψ 89^{25}; אמונה וח׳ ψ 98^{3}; ‖ רחמים ψ 77^{9}; ח׳ ורחמים Je 16^{5} Ho 2^{21} ψ 103^{4}; ח׳ ומשפט Je 9^{23} ψ 101^{1}; ‖ צדקה ψ 36^{11}; טוב וח׳ ψ 23^{6}. **3.** the *kindness* of God is **a.** *abundant:* רַב־חֶסֶד *abundant, plenteous in kindness (goodness)* Nu 14^{18} (J), Ne 9^{17} (Qr), Jo 2^{13} Jon 4^{2} ψ 86^{5} 103^{8} (cf. Ex 34^{6} JE; ψ 86^{15}); רֹב חַסְדְּךָ Ne 13^{22} ψ 5^{8} 69^{14} 106^{7} (𝔊 𝔙 Aq 𝔗, to be preferred to MT חֲסָדֶיךָ); רֹב חֲסָדָו La 3^{32} ψ 106^{45}(Kt 𝔊 in both to be preferred). **b.** *great in extent:* גֹּדֶל ח׳ *greatness of thy mercy* Nu 14^{19} (J); גְּדָוֹל־ח׳ ψ 145^{8}; it is kept for thousands Ex 34^{7}(JE), Je 32^{18}, esp. of those connected with lovers of י׳, Ex 20^{6}=Dt 5^{10}; for 1000 generations Dt 7^{9}; it is great as the heavens ψ 57^{11} 103^{11}, cf. 36^{6} 108^{5}; the earth is full of it ψ 33^{5} 119^{64}. **c.** *everlasting:* לעולם חסדו Je 33^{11} 1 Ch $16^{34.41}$ 2 Ch 5^{13} $7^{3.6}$ 20^{21} Ezr 3^{11} ψ 100^{5} 106^{1} 107^{1} $118^{1.2.3.4.29}$ $136^{1-26 (26 t.)}$; חסדך לעולם ψ 138^{8}; ח׳ מעולם ועד עולם ψ 103^{17}; ח׳ עולם Is 54^{8}; ח׳ אל כל היום ψ 52^{3}. **d.** *good:* כִּי־טוֹב חַסְדְּךָ ψ 69^{17} 109^{21}; כי טוב חסדך מחיים ψ 63^{4}. **4.** pl. *mercies, deeds of kindness,* the historic displays of lovingkindness to Israel: shewn to Jacob Gn 32^{11}(R); but mostly late Is 63^{7} ψ 25^{6} 89^{2}; כְּרֹב חסדיו Is 63^{7}, see **3 a**; promised in the Davidic covenant ψ 89^{50}; חַסְדֵי דָוִיד *mercies to David* Is 55^{3} 2 Ch 6^{42}; *mercies* in general La 3^{22} ψ 17^{7} $107^{43 f.}$—חֶסֶד in n.pr.m. בן־ח׳ v. sub בֵּן. On Lv 20^{17} Pr 14^{34} v. II. חֶסֶד sub II. חסד.

†חָסִיד **adj.m.** kind, pious (so, as denoting 2623
active practice of חֶסֶד, kindness, Thes MV De and most, cf. קָצִיר, פָּקִיד etc.; >Hup on ψ 4^{4} RVm who expl. as passive *reception* of י׳'s חֶסֶד, cf. אָסִיר, שָׂכִיר etc.; its use as attribute of God Je 3^{12} ψ 145^{17}, and the context ψ 12^{1} Mi 7^{2} etc., favour active sense)—ח׳ ψ 4^{4}+9 t.; חֲסִידְךָ Dt 33^{8} ψ 89^{20}; חֲסִידֶיךָ ψ 16^{10}; pl. חֲסִידִים ψ $149^{1.5}$; sf. חֲסִידַי ψ 50^{5}; חֲסִידָו 1 S 2^{9}+15 t. sfs.;—**1.** *kind:* **a.** of man עם ח׳ תתחסד *with the kind thou shewest thyself kind* 2 S 22^{26}=ψ 18^{26}. **b.** of wing of ostrich אִם אֶבְרָה חֲסִידָה Jb 39^{13} *is it a kindly pinion?* poss. with play on חֲסִידָה n.f. *stork* (is the ostrich kind like the stork?). **c.** of God, only Je 3^{12} ψ 145^{17}. **2.** *pious, godly,* either as exhibition of 'duteous love' toward God (Che$^{OP 378}$), or (in view of rarity of such passages as Ho $6^{4.6}$ Je 2^{2}, and their possible ambiguity) because *kindness,* as prominent in the godly, comes to imply other attributes, and to be a designation of the godly character, *piety:* **a.** as adj.—גּוֹי לא חסיד *a nation, not pious,=ungodly* ψ 43^{1}. **b.** elsewh. as subst.: sing., *a pious man, the godly* ψ 4^{4} 12^{2} 32^{6} 86^{2}, ‖ יָשָׁר Mi 7^{2}; *(thy) pious one(s)* ψ 16^{10} (Kt pl.), 1 S 2^{9}(Qr pl.) Pr 2^{8}, אִישׁ חֲסִידֶךָ *men of thy pious one* Dt 33^{8} (Moses, v. Di; others, *the man, thy godly one,* i.e. Levi); pl. *the pious, godly,* those of the people who were faithful, devoted to God's service, only in Psalter and chiefly, if not entirely, in late Psalms ψ $149^{1.5}$; *his pious ones* ψ 30^{5} 31^{24} 37^{28} 85^{9} 97^{10} 116^{15} 148^{14} 149^{9}; *thy pious ones* ψ 52^{11} 79^{2} 89^{20} 132^{9} = 2 Ch 6^{41}, ψ 145^{10}; *my pious ones* ψ 50^{5}, *her* (Zion's) *pious* ψ 132^{16}.—(In Maccab. age, συναγωγὴ Ἀσιδαίων denoted, technically, the party of *the pious,* who opposed the Hellenization of Judaea, v. 1 Macc 2^{42} 7^{13} 2 Macc 14^{6} and Che$^{OP 48, 56}$; so perhaps ψ 116^{15} $149^{1.5.9}$.)

†I. חֲסִידָה **n.f.** stork (so called as kind 2624
and affectionate to its young)—Lv 11^{19}=Dt 14^{18}, ψ 104^{17} Je 8^{7} Zc 5^{9}.

†חֲסַדְיָה **n.pr.m.** (*Yah is kind*) son of 2619
Zerubbabel 1 Ch 3^{20}.

2616 †II. [חָסַד] **vb. be reproached, ashamed** (Aramaism, v. RS [Proph. iv, n. 9]; Aram. חֲסַד *be put to shame*, ܚܣܕ, חַסֵּד *reproach, revile*; חִסּוּדָא, ܚܘܣܕܐ *shame, reproach*, oft. in 𝔗 𝔖 for חֶרְפָּה);—only **Pi.** *Impf.* פֶּן־יְחַסֶּדְךָ Pr 25^{10} *lest he reproach thee, expose thee to shame.*

2617 †II. חֶסֶד **n.m. shame, reproach,** only abs.:—חֶ׳ הוּא Lv 20^{17} (H) *it is a shame* (shameful thing); חֶ׳ לְאֻמִּים חַטָּאת Pr 14^{34} *sin is a reproach to peoples.*

2620 †חָסָה **vb.** (mostly poet. and fig.) **seek refuge** (Ar. خَشِيَ III. is *set aside*; v. *go aside, apart*; خَشًى *shelter, protection*; but ? ش=ס)—**Qal** *Pf.* חָ׳ ψ 64^{11}; 3 fs. חָסָ֫יָה ψ 57^{2}, חָסִ֫יתִי ψ 7^{2} + 7 t.; pl. חָסוּ ψ 37^{40} Zp 3^{12}, חָסָ֫יוּ Dt 32^{37}; *Impf.* יֶחְסֶה ψ 34^{9}, תֶּחְסֶה ψ 91^{4}, אֶחְסֶה ψ 57^{2} (see Baer ψ 34^{9}), אֶֽחֱסֶה ψ 18^{3} + 2 t.; pl. יֶחֱסוּ Is 14^{32}, יֶֽחֱסָיוּן ψ 36^{8}; *Imv.* חֲסוּ Ju 9^{15}; *Inf.* חֲסוֹת ψ 118^{8} + 3 t.; *pt.* חוֹסֶה Is 57^{13}, חֹסֶה Pr 14^{32}, חוֹסִים ψ 17^{7} + 3 t.; חֹסִים Pr 30^{5} 2 S 22^{31} (see Baer Pr 30^{5}), חוֹסֵי ψ 2^{12} 5^{12}, חֹסֵי Na 1^{7};—*seek refuge*, c. בְּ: בְּצֵל in the shadow of a tree Ju 9^{15}, בְּצֵל מצרים Is 30^{2}; בָּהּ Is 14^{32} in Zion, in gods Dt 32^{37} (poem), elsewhere *in God* 2 S 22^{3} = ψ 18^{3}; Na 1^{7} ψ 2^{12} 5^{12} 7^{2} 11^{1} 16^{1} 25^{20} $31^{2.20}$ $34^{9.23}$ 37^{40} 57^{2} 64^{11} 71^{1} $118^{8.9}$ 141^{8} 144^{2}, Is 57^{13}; מגן הוא ל(כל ה)חוסים בו *a shield is he to (all) who seek refuge in him* 2 S 22^{31} = ψ 18^{31}, Pr 30^{5}; בְּ׳ is probably to be supplied in thought at least: מושיע חוסים ψ 17^{7} *saviour of those seeking refuge* (in thee); צדיק חסה במותו Pr 14^{32} *a righteous man in his death seeketh refuge* (in Yahweh), בשם י׳ Zp 3^{12}, בצל כנפיך *in the shadow of thy wings* ψ 36^{8} 57^{2}; בסתר כנפיך ψ 61^{5}, תחת כנפיו *under his wings* ψ 91^{4} = Ru 2^{12}.

2621 †חֹסָה **1. n.pr.m.** (refuge)—name of one of the Levitical doorkeepers of the temple 1 Ch 16^{38} $26^{10.11.16}$. **2. n.pr.loc.** place in the tribe of Asher Jos 19^{29}; site unknown; 𝔊 Ιασιφ, A Σουσα, 𝔊L Ωσα.

2622 †חָסוּת **n.f. refuge**;—וְהֶחָסוּת בְּצֵל מִצְרַיִם Is 30^{3} (|| מָעוֹז פַּרְעֹה).

4268 †מַחְסֶה **n.m.** [Pr 14, 26] **refuge, shelter**;—abs. מַ׳ Jb 24^{8} + 5 t.; מַחֲסֶה ψ 46^{2} + 2 t.; cstr. מַחְסֵה Is 28^{17}; sf. מַחְסִי ψ 62^{8} + 5 t.; מַחֲסִי ψ 71^{7} Je 17^{17}, מַחְסֵהוּ ψ 14^{6}, מַחְסֵנוּ Is 28^{15};—*shelter*: **a.** from rain and storm Is 4^{6} 25^{4} Jb 24^{8}. **b.** from danger סְלָעִים מַחְסֶה לַשְׁפַנִּים *rocks a refuge for conies* ψ 104^{18}; מחסה כזב *refuge of falsehood* Is 28^{17}; כזב מחסנו *falsehood our refuge* Is 28^{15}; elsewhere of God as the refuge of his people ψ 14^{6} 46^{2} 61^{4} $62^{8.9}$ 71^{7} 73^{28} $91^{2.9}$ 94^{22} 142^{6} Pr 14^{26} Je 17^{17} Jo 4^{16}.

†מַחְסֵיָה **n.pr.m.** (י׳ *is a refuge*) ancestor 4271
of Baruch and Seraiah Je 32^{12} (Baer מַחְסֵ׳) 51^{59}.

†[חָסַל] **vb. finish off, consume** (Aram. 2628
חֲסַל *come to an end*, Aph. *bring to an end*)—**Qal** *Impf.* יַחְסְלֶנּוּ הָאַרְבֶּה Dt 28^{38} of locusts destroying crops.

†חָסִיל **n.m.** a kind of **locust** (sg. coll.), 2625
alw. abs. חָ׳, and alw. as destructive; 1 K 8^{37} = 2 Ch 6^{28} ψ 78^{46} (all || אַרְבֶּה), Jo 1^{4} 2^{25} (|| יֶלֶק, גָּזָם, אַרְבֶּה); cf. אֹסֶף הֶחָ׳ Is 33^{4} *the gathering of the locust*, in sim. of despoiling of Assyria (|| גֵּבִים).

†[חָסַם] **vb. stop up, muzzle** (NH *id.*, 2629
חסום *muzzle*; Aram. חֲסַם *bind up fast*)—**Qal** *Impf.* לֹא תַחְסֹם שׁוֹר בְּדִישׁוֹ Dt 25^{4} *thou shalt not muzzle an ox when it is treading* (i.e. threshing); *Pt.* וְחֹסֶמֶת הִיא Ez 39^{11} *and it shall stop* (the way of) the passers-by; but rd. וְחָסְמוּ אֶת־הַגַּיְא *and they shall stop up the valley*, Co v. 𝔊 𝔖 Hi.

†מַחְסוֹם **n.m. muzzle,** אֶשְׁמְרָה־לְפִי מ׳ ψ 39^{2} 4269
let me keep a muzzle for my mouth, to avoid (hasty and) erring speech.

חסן (√of foll.; Aram. חֲסַן, ܚܣܢ, ܚܣܢ, 2630
be strong, also *take possession of*, חֲסִין, ܚܣܝܢ *strong*, etc.; Ar. خَشُنَ *be rough, hard, coarse*).

†חֹסֶן **n.m.** [Pr 15, 6] **wealth, treasure** (on 2633
relation to √mng. cf. חַיִל)—חֹ׳ abs. Pr 15^{6} + 2 t.; cstr. Is 33^{6} Je 20^{5};—*wealth, treasure*, of individuals Pr 15^{6} (חֹ׳ רָב, opp. נֶעְכָּרֶת), Pr 27^{24} (|| נֵזֶר), Ez 22^{25} (|| יְקָר); of city חֹ׳ הָעִיר הַזֹּאת Je 20^{5} (|| אוֹצְרוֹת, יְקָר, יְגִיעַ); in transf. sense חֹ׳ יְשׁוּעֹת, *wealth* (or *abundance* VB) *of salvations*, חֹ׳ יְשׁ׳ חָכְמַת וָדָעַת יִרְאַת י׳ הִיא אוֹצָרוֹ Is 33^{6} and stability of thy times shall be *abundance of salvations* (helps, deliverances), etc.

†חָסֹן **adj. strong,** of the Amorite Am 2^{9} 2634
(חָ׳ כָּאַלּוֹנִים, *strong as the oaks*); הֶחָסוֹן as subst. *the strong one* Is 1^{31}.

†חֲסִין **adj. strong, mighty** (Aramaism);— 2626
only מִי־כָמוֹךָ חֲסִין יָהּ ψ 89^{9}.

2636 †[חֲסַפְסַ] **vb.** only *Pt. pass.* **(scaled off) scale-like** (appar. redupl. fr. *חסף for חספסף, v. Ew $^{§ 158 c}$ Ol $^{§§ 214, 276}$ Ges $^{§ 55, 6}$ Sta$^{§ 291}$; Kö$^{1, 250}$ thinks euphon. for מְחֻסְפָּף; to be comp. are Ar. خَشِفَ, *have scab, itch* (Frey; but ش=ס?); Aram. חַסְפָּא *potsherd*, חַסְפִּנִיתָא *scale* (of fish), *scurf;* Eth. ኀሠፈ: *scabiosus fuit* Di^{587} and Ex 16^{14})—hence מְחֻסְפָּס *scaled off, scale-like*, as 𝔊 𝔗 Thes RobGes MV SS VB;—of the manna דַּק מְחֻסְפָּס דַּק כַּכְּפֹר Ex 16^{14} *a fine, scale-like thing, fine as the hoar-frost.*

2637 † חָסֵר **vb. lack, need, be lacking, decrease** (v. Lag$^{BN 143}$; NH חִסֵּר *cause to lack* or *fail, diminish* (act.), and deriv.; Aram. חֲסַר, ܚܣܰܪ, *want, lack*, and deriv., cf. Ph. מחסר, v. מחסור infr.; Ar. حَسَرَ *remove, strip off; disappear, retire* (of water), *fail* (of sight), etc.; perh. also Eth. ኀሰረ: *be inferior, worthless, diminished* Di^{590} and deriv.)—**Qal** *Pf.* 3 ms. ח׳ 1 K 17^{16}; 2 ms. חָסַרְתָּ Dt 2^{7}; 3 pl. חָסֵרוּ Ne 9^{21}; 1 pl. חָסַרְנוּ Je 44^{18}; *Impf.* יֶחְסַר Dt 15^{8} + 2 t.; יֶחְסָר Pr 31^{11} Ec 9^{8}; 3 fs. תֶּחְסָר 1 K 17^{14} Pr 13^{25}; 2 ms. תֶּחְסַר Dt 8^{9}; 1 s. אֶחְסָר ψ 23^{1}; pl. יַחְסְרוּ ψ 34^{11} Ez 4^{17}; וַיַּחְסְרוּ Gn 8^{3}; יַחְסְרוּן Gn 18^{28}; *Inf. cstr.* חֲסַר Pr 10^{21} Ew$^{§ 238 a}$, cf. Ges$^{§ 45. 1 a}$; *abs.* חָסוֹר Gn 8^{5}; *Pt.* חָסֵר 1 K 11^{22} Ec 10^{3} (v. חָסֵר infr.);—**1. lack: a.** c. acc. Gn 18^{28} (J) *perchance the fifty righteous lack five*, Dt 2^{7} *thou hast not lacked anything*, 8^{9} Je 44^{18} 1 K 11^{22} Ez 4^{17} ψ 34^{11} Pr 31^{11}, cf. also בַּחֲסַר־לֵב Pr 10^{21} *by lacking intelligence* (*sense*), (Di puts here Dt 15^{8}, v. infr.) **b.** abs. *be in want, want* ψ 23^{1} Pr 13^{25} Ne 9^{21}. **2.** *be lacking*, מַחְסֹרוֹ אֲשֶׁר יֶח׳ לוֹ Dt 15^{8} *his lack* (i.e. thing needed), *which is lacking to him* (possible also is, *which he lacks for himself*, so Di, v. supr.); שֶׁמֶן עַל־רֹאשְׁךָ אַל־יֶח׳ Ec 9^{8} *oil on thy head let it not be lacking;* v. also abs. Is 51^{14} Ct 7^{3}, and לִבּוֹ חָסֵר Ec 10^{3} *his sense is lacking;* of jar of oil 1 K 17$^{14.16}$ (abs.) by meton. for the oil itself (cf. || כלה *be consumed, exhausted*). **3.** *diminish, decrease*, of waters Gn 8^{3} (P), cf. הָלוֹךְ וְחָסוֹר v^{5} (P), waters *continually diminished* (v. הלך supr. p. 233^{b}). **Pi.** *cause to lack*, c. acc. pers., *Impf.* 2 ms. sf. וַתְּחַסְּרֵהוּ מעט מֵאֱלֹהִים ψ 8^{6} *and thou didst make him lack little of God; Pt.* וּמְחַסֵּר את־נפשי מטּוֹבָה Ec 4^{8} for whom am I labouring *and depriving myself of good things?* **Hiph.** *Pf.* הֶחְסִיר Ex 16^{18}; *Impf.* יַחְסִיר Is 32^{6};—*cause to be lacking, fail*, c. acc. rei מַשְׁקֵה צָמֵא יַח׳ Is 32^{6}; *the drink of the thirsty he causeth to fail* (|| לְהָרִיק נפש רָעֵב); abs. Ex 16^{18} (P), *he that gathered little caused no lack.*

2639 † חֶסֶר **n.m.**$^{Pr 28, 22}$ **want, poverty**—alw. abs.; ח׳ יְבֹאֶנּוּ Pr 28^{22} *want shall come to him;* || כָּפָן *hunger* Jb 30^{3}.

2640 † חֹסֶר **n.[m.] want, lack** (Lag$^{BN 144}$)—only cstr. ח׳ לֶחֶם Am 4^{6}; ח׳ כֹּל Dt 28$^{48.57}$.

2638 † חָסֵר **adj.** needy, lacking, in want of—ח׳ abs. Ec 6^{2}; cstr. חֲסַר 1 S 21^{16} + 13 t.;—*needy, in want of* ח׳ משגעים אני 1 S 21^{16} *am I in want of madmen?* 2 S 3^{29} *in need of bread*, so Pr 12^{9}; usu. חֲסַר־לֵב *lacking understanding, sense* Pr 6^{32} 7^{7} 9$^{4.16}$ 10^{13} 11^{12} 12^{11} 15^{21}; אָדָם ח׳־לֵב Pr 17^{18} 24^{30}; נָגִיד ח׳ תְּבוּנוֹת Pr 28^{16}; אֵינֶנּוּ חָסֵר לְנַפְשׁוֹ מִכֹּל וג׳ Ec 6^{2} *neither is he lacking for his soul in aught of* (מן *part.*) *all that he desireth.*

2641 † חַסְרָה **n.pr.m.** grandfather of Shallum who was husband of Huldah the prophetess (𝔊A Εσσερη, 𝔊L Ασερ)=חַרְחַס 2 K 22^{14} (𝔊 Αρααs, 𝔊L Αδρα).

2642 † חֶסְרוֹן **n.m.** thing lacking, deficiency (Lag$^{BN 198}$)—only ח׳ לֹא־יוּכַל לְהִמָּנוֹת Ec 1^{15} *what is lacking cannot be counted.*

4270 † מַחְסוֹר, מַחְסֹר **n.[m.] need, thing needed, poverty;**—מ׳ abs. Pr 11^{24} + 6 t.; cstr. Ju 18^{10} 19^{19}; sf. מַחְסוֹרְךָ Ju 19^{20}; מַחְסֹרְךָ Pr 6^{11}; מַחְסֹרוֹ Dt 15^{8}; pl. sf. מַחְסֹרֶיךָ Pr 24^{34};—**1.** *need=thing needed* דֵּי מַחְסֹרוֹ Dt 15^{8} *enough for his need* (sq. אשר יֶחְסַר לוֹ, cf. חָסֵר vb.); כָּל־מ׳ עָלָי Ju 19^{20} *all thy need* be *upon me* (for me to provide). **2.** *lack, want* אֵין מ׳ כָּל־דָּבָר Ju 18^{10} *no lack of anything*, 19^{19} ψ 34^{10}. **3.** in gen., *need, poverty* Pr 6^{11} (|| רֵאשׁ)=24^{34} (|| רֵישׁ), 11^{24} 14^{23} 21^{5} 22^{16} 28^{27}; אִישׁ מ׳ 21^{17} *a man of poverty.*

2643 חַף v. II. חפף. p. 342

2644 †[חָפָא] **vb. do secretly** (prop. cover, =חפה, q.v.);—only **Pi.** *Impf.* וַיְחַפְּאוּ . . . דברים *and they did things secretly* 2 K 17^{9}.

2645 †[חָפָה] **vb. cover** (NH *id.*, esp. Pi.; Aram. חֲפָא, ܚܦܳܐ (esp. Pa.); Ar. خَفِيَ *be hidden*, خَفَّى *hide*)—**Qal** *Pf.* חָפוּ 2 S 15^{30} + 3 t.; *Pt.* חָפוּי 2 S 15^{30}; cstr. חֲפוּי Est 6^{12};—*cover* the head (רֹאשׁ), in token of grief 2 S 15^{30} Je 14$^{3.4}$; *pt.* agrees with ר׳ 2 S 15^{30}; אָבֵל || חֲפוּי ראשׁ Est 6^{12}; in token of sentence of death Est 7^{8}. **Niph.** *Pt.* f. נֶחְפָּה ψ 68^{13} (כנפי יונה נ׳), c. בְּ

of material. **Pi.** *Pf.* (late) חִפָּה 2 Ch 3$^{8.9}$; *Impf.* וַיְחַף 2 Ch 3^{7}; sf. וַיְחַפֵּהוּ 2 Ch 3$^{5.8}$; *overlay* sq. 2 acc. (one of material) 2 Ch 3$^{5.5.7.8.9}$.

2646-47 I. חָפָה, II. חָפָה v. sub חפף. below

2648 †[חָפַז] **vb. be in trepidation, hurry, or alarm** (Ar. حَفَزَ *hasten, incite, urge*);—**Qal** *Impf.* יַחְפּוֹז Jb 40^{23}; תַּחְפְּזוּ Dt 20^{3}; *Inf. cstr.* sf. בְּחָפְזִי ψ 31^{23} 116^{11}; בְּחָפְזָהּ 2 S 4^{4}; בְּחָפְזָם 2 K 7^{15} Qr (Kt הֵחָפְזָם);—**1.** *be in a hurry* or *alarm*, of hurried flight 2 S 4^{4} 2 K 7^{15}; *Inf.* c. ב = noun, *in my alarm* ψ 31^{23} 116^{11}; *be alarmed* Dt 20^{3} (‖תיראו), Jb 40^{23} (of hippopot.) **Niph.** *Pf.* נֶחְפָּזוּ ψ 48^{6} (‖נִבְהֲלוּ) *hurry away in alarm;* so *Impf.* יֵחָפֵזוּן ψ 104^{7} (‖יְנוּסוּן); *Inf.* הֵחָפְזָם 2 K 7^{15} Kt v. *supr.*; *Pt.* נֶחְפָּז 1 S 23^{26} *hurried* ויהי דוד נ׳ ללכת *and David became hurried to go.*

2649 †חִפָּזוֹן **n.[m.] trepidation, hurried flight** (Lag$^{BN\ 200}$)—always בח׳ Ex 12^{11} (P), Dt 16^{3} Is 52^{12} (‖ מְנוּסָה).

2650 חֻפִּים v. sub חפף. below

חפן (√of foll.; Ar. حَفَنَ *take with both hands*, حُفْنَةٌ *handful;* NH חָפַן, Aram. חֲפַן *fill the hands* with).

2651 †[חֹפֶן] **n.[m.] hollow of hand** (NH חוֹפֶן, Aram. חוּפְנָא, חָפְנֵי, ܚܘܦܢܐ; Eth. ሕፍን:—also Ar. حُفْنَةٌ *hollow in the ground;* and, acc. to Zehnpfund$^{BAS\ i.\ 635}$, As. *ḫupunnu, bowl,* but ḫ = ح ?)—only du. חָפְנַיִם Ec 4^{6}; cstr. חָפְנֵי Ez 10^{7} (del. Co intern. grounds); sf. חָפְנֶיךָ Ez 10^{2}; חָפְנָיו Lv 16^{2} Pr 30^{4}; חָפְנֵיכֶם Ex 9^{8}; מְלֹא ח׳ Ez 10^{2} + v^{7} (del. Co cf. supr.);—מְלֹא ח׳ = *handful* Ex 9^{8} Lv 16^{12} (both P), Ec 4^{6}, material follows in implic. acc.; מי־אסף רוח בח׳ Pr 30^{4}.

2652 †חָפְנִי **n.pr.m.** (Sab. n.pr. חפן Hal$^{No\ 14}$)—one of Eli's two sons 1 S 1^{3} 2^{34} 4$^{4.11.17}$.

2653 †I. [חָפַף] **vb. enclose, surround, cover** (Ar. حَفَّ, *surround,* حِفَافٌ *side,* or *border* of a thing)—only **Qal** *Pt.* חֹפֵף עָלָיו Dt 33^{12} (poem) he (י׳) *is covering him over,* fig. of י׳'s sheltering Benj. (in temple; on omission of subj. v. Ges$^{§\ 116.\ 5.\ R.\ 3}$).

2348 †חוֹף **n.[m.] shore, coast** (as *surrounding, enclosing*)—ח׳ only cstr. Gn 49$^{13.13}$ + 5 t.:—*shore of sea* ח׳ הַיָּם Dt 1^{7} Jos 9^{1} (both D), Ju 5^{17} Je 47^{7} Ez 25^{16}; ח׳ יַמִּים Gn 49^{13} (poem); ח׳ אֳנִיּוֹת v^{13} *the shore of ships,* i.e. to which ships come.

†I. חֻפָּה **n.f. canopy, chamber** (as *cover-* 2646
ing, enclosing)—abs. ח׳ Is 4^{5}; sf. חֻפָּתוֹ ψ 19^{6}; חֻפָּתָהּ Jo 2^{16};—**1.** *canopy,* על־כל־כבוד ח׳ Is 4^{5} *over all glory a canopy* (for protection). **2.** *chamber,* of bridegroom ψ 19^{6} (metaph. of sun rising); of bride Jo 2^{16} (‖ חֶדֶר of bridegroom).

†II. חֻפָּה **n.pr.m.** 1 Ch 24^{13} priest of 13th 2647
course, 𝔊 Οφφα.

†חֻפִּים **n.pr.m.** a son of Benjamin Gn 46^{21} 2650
(𝔊 Οφιμ(ε)ιν, Οφμειν), descendant of Benjamin 1 Ch 7^{15} (𝔊 Αμφειν, Αφφειν, 𝔊L Οφερ), and so חֻפִּם v^{15}; v. חוּפָם.

II. חפף (NH חָפַף; Aram. חֲפַף, ܚܦ, ܚܘܦ, all *rub, cleanse,* esp. the head).

†חַף **adj.** clean—only זַךְ אֲנִי בְּלִי פָשַׁע חַף 2643
אָנֹכִי Jb 33^{9} *I am pure, without transgression, I am clean* (in speech of Elihu).

†חָפֵץ **vb. delight in** (cf. Ar. حَفِظَ *be* 2654
mindful of, attentive to, keep, protect, Aram. ܚܦܛ whence ܚܦܝܛ *eager, zealous,* Ar. حَفِيظَةٌ *anger* (excitement), اِحْفَظَ *enrage* (Aram. and Ar. of *excited* attention, Heb. of *delighted* attention), Dl$^{Pr\ 168}$ Nö$^{ZMG\ 1886,\ 742}$; NH חָפֵץ weakened to *thing,* v. De$^{Ec.Gloss.}$, Ph. in n.pr. חפצבעל);—**Qal** *Pf.* ח׳ Gn 34^{19} + 28 t.; f. חָפֵצָה Is 66^{3}; 2 m. חָפַצְתָּ Dt 21^{14} + 4 t.; חָפַצְנוּ Jb 21^{14}, etc., + 14 t. Pf.; *Impf.* יַחְפֹּץ Dt 25^{7} + 7 t.; יֶחְפָּץ ψ 37^{23} 147^{10}; pl. יַחְפְּצוּ Is 13^{17} Je 6^{10}; יֶחְפָּצוּ ψ 68^{31}; יֶחְפָּצוּן Is 58$^{2.2}$ etc. + 9 t. Impf.; *Inf. abs.* חָפֹץ Ez 18^{23}; on *Pt.* חָפֵץ = adj. verb., v. infr.;—**1.** of *men:* **a.** *take pleasure in, delight in,* c. בְּ, a woman Gn 34^{19} (J), Dt 21^{14} Est 2^{14}; a man 1 S 18^{22} 19^{1} 2 S 20^{11}; in matters and things 2 S 24^{3} Is 13^{17} 66^{3} Je 6^{10} ψ 109^{17} 112^{1} 119^{35} Pr 18^{2} Est 6$^{6.7.9.9.11}$; c. acc. ψ 68^{31} Is 58^{2} Ec 8^{3}; implic. obj. ψ 73^{25}. **b.** *delight, desire, be pleased* to do a thing, *would* do it Dt 25$^{7.8}$ 1 K 9^{1} Est 6^{6} Ru 3^{13} ψ 40^{9} Jb 9^{3} 13^{3} 21^{14} 33^{32} Is 58^{2} Je 42^{22}. **c.** abs. עַד שֶׁתֶּחְפָּץ *until it please* (of love) Ct 2^{7} 3^{5} 8^{4}. **2.** *of God:* **a.** *delight in, have pleasure in,* c. בְּ, persons Nu 14^{8} (J), 2 S 15^{26} 22^{20} = ψ 18^{20}, 1 K 10^{9} = 2 Ch 9^{8}, ψ 22^{9} 41^{12} Is 62^{4}; not in the strength of a horse ψ 147^{10}; in doing evil Mal 2^{17}; in the death of the sinner Ez 18^{32} 33^{11}; but in mercy, justice, and righteousness Je 9^{23}; בחר באשר (לא) חפצתי Is 56^{4} 65^{12} 66^{4}; not with (acc.) the blood of bullocks Is 1^{11}; זבח(ים) ψ 40^{7} 51$^{18.21}$, or the death of the sinner Ez 18$^{23.23}$; but with חסד Ho 6^{6} Mi 7^{18}, אמת

ψ 51^{8}; with the way of a man ψ 37^{23}; כל אשר חפץ ψ 115^{3} 135^{6} Pr 21^{1}; אשר חפץ Is 55^{11} Jon 1^{14}. **b.** *pleased* to do a thing c. inf. Ju 13^{23} 1 S 2^{25} Is 53^{10}. **c.** with impf. subj. (Ges $^{§142(3)c}$) י׳ חָפֵץ יגדיל תורה *Yahweh was pleased to magnify teaching* Is 42^{21}.—On Jb 40^{17} v. חָפַץ.

2655 †**חָפֵץ adj. verb. delighting in, having pleasure in**;—ח׳ ψ 5^{5}+4 t.; pl. חֲפֵצִים Mal 3^{1} Ne 1^{11}; cstr. חֲפֵצֵי ψ 35^{27}+2 t.; sf. חֲפֵצֵיהֶם ψ 111^{2}; f. חֲפֵצָה 1 Ch 28^{9};—**1.** *of man*, c. acc. ψ 34^{13} 35^{27} Mal 3^{1}; c. inf. Ne 1^{11}; abs. הֶחָפֵץ *whosoever would* 1 K 13^{33}; אם חפץ אתה *if thou pleasest* 1 K 21^{6}; נֶפֶשׁ חֲפֵצָה *willing soul* 1 Ch 28^{9}; pl. cstr. before nouns abs. ψ 35^{22} 40^{15} = 70^{3}; דְּרוּשִׁים לְכָל־חֶפְצֵיהֶם *studied of all who take pleasure in them* ψ 111^{2}. **2.** *of God*, לֹא אֵל־חָפֵץ רֶשַׁע אָתָּה *thou art not a God taking pleasure in wickedness* ψ 5^{5}.

2656 †**חֵפֶץ n.m.**$^{Pr 3, 15}$ **delight, pleasure**;—ח׳ Is 54^{12}+20 t.; sf. חֶפְצְךָ Is 58^{13} etc.+13 t. sfs.; pl. חֲפָצִים Pr 8^{11}; sf. חֲפָצֶיךָ Pr 3^{15}; חֲפָצֶךָ Is 58^{13}—**1.** *delight* אבני ח׳ Is 54^{12} *delightful stones;* אֶרֶץ ח׳ Mal 3^{12} *delightsome land;* דִּבְרֵי ח׳ Ec 12^{10}; so perhaps also בִּגְדֵי ח׳ Ez 27^{20} *garments of delight*, i.e. of beauty and luxury (Gr; MT חֹפֶשׁ q. v.); c. בְּ of persons ψ 16^{3} Ec 5^{3} Mal 1^{10}; of things 1 S 15^{22} 18^{25} ψ 1^{2} Jb 21^{21} Ec 12^{1}; כְּלִי אֵין חֵפֶץ בּוֹ *vessel wherein is no pleasure* Je 22^{28} 48^{38} Ho 8^{8}; הַחֵפֶץ לְשַׁדַּי כִּי Jb 22^{3} *is it a pleasure to Shadday that?* **2.** *desire, longing* מנע מח׳ דלים Jb 31^{16} *withhold the poor from (their) desire;* מְחוֹז חֶפְצָם *the city of their desire* ψ 107^{30}; כל חפץ *all (one's) desire* 2 S 23^{5} 1 K 5$^{22.23.24}$ 9^{11}, 10^{13} = 2 Ch 9^{12}; כל חפצים *all things to be desired* Pr 3^{15} 8^{11}. **3.** *the good pleasure, will, purpose*, of Yahweh Is 44^{28} 46^{10} 48^{14}. **4.** *that in* which one takes delight, his *business* (late), or *matter* (very late, cf. in Mish. = *thing*) חֵפֶץ י׳ בְּיָדוֹ יִצְלָח *the good pleasure (cause, business) of Yahweh will prosper in his hands* Is 53^{10}; מצא ח׳ Is 58$^{3.13}$; עֲשׂוֹת חֲפָצֶךָ *doing thy affairs* Is 58^{13} (see De in loco); בְּחֵפֶץ כַּפֶּיהָ *in the business of her hands* Pr 31^{13}; עֵת לְכָל־חֵפֶץ *time for every matter, affair* Ec 3$^{1.17}$ 8^{6}; אַל־תִּתְמַהּ עַל־הַחֵפֶץ *marvel not at the matter* Ec 5^{7}.

Note.—חפץ is not used in any of its forms in E D^{2} H P of the Hexateuch.

2657 †**חֶפְצִי־בָהּ n.pr.f.** (*my delight is in her;* cf. Ph. חפצבעל)—**1.** mother of king Manasseh 2 K 21^{1}. **2.** fig. name of Zion Is 62^{4}, here expl. by כִּי חפץ יהוה בָּךְ *for Yahweh delighteth in thee.*

†[**חָפַץ**] **vb.** bend down (Ar. خَفَضَ *lower, depress*, as wings Qor 15^{88})—only **Qal** *Impf.* יַחְפֹּץ זְנָבוֹ כְמוֹ־אָרֶז Jb 40^{17}; *he bendeth down (extendeth down stiffly) his tail like a cedar*, v. Wetzst in De$^{Job 526}$ Hi$^{Hiob 299}$. 2654

†I. **חָפַר vb.** dig, search for (Ar. حَفَرَ *id.;* Aram. חֲפַר, ܚܦܰܪ, *id.;* NH חֲפִר *act of digging*)—**Qal** *Pf.* ח׳ Jb 39^{29}; וְחָפַרְתָּ Jb 11^{18}; וְחָפַרְתָּה Dt 23^{14}; חָפַרְתִּי Gn 21^{30}; חָפְרוּ Gn 26^{18}+2 t.; חָפְרוּ Gn 26^{32}; חֲפָרוּהָ Nu 21^{18}; *Impf.* וַיַּחְפֹּר Gn 26$^{18.22}$; וַיַּחְפְּרֵהוּ ψ 7^{16}; וָאֶחְפֹּר Je 13^{7}; יַחְפְּרוּ Jb Jb 39^{21} (but rd. יַחְפֹּר so 𝔊 𝔙 𝔖 Di) Dt 1^{22}; וַיַּחְפְּרוּ Gn 26^{19}+2 t.; וַיַּחְפְּרֻהוּ Jb 3^{21}; *Inf. cstr.* לַחְפֹּר Jos 2$^{2.3}$+Is 2^{20} (cf. infr.); *Pt.* חֹפֵר Ec 10^{8};—**1.** *dig:* **a.** a well, c. acc. בְּאֵר Gn 21^{30} (E), 26$^{15.18.18.19.21.22.32}$ (J), Nu 21^{18} (E); cf. Ex 7^{24} (E); *dig* (a hole, implied as obj.) Dt 23^{14}; a pit, with hostile purpose, as snare or trap, fig. of malicious plan, c. acc. בּוֹר ψ 7^{16} (|| כָּרָה); so c. acc. גומץ Ec 10^{8}, cf. [שַׁחַת] ח׳ לְנַפְשִׁי ψ 35^{7}; of horse, *dig*, i. e. *paw* the ground, יַחְפֹּר בָּעֵמֶק Jb 39^{21} (so rd., v. supr.) *he paweth in the valley* (cf. Ar. حَافِرٌ *hoof*). **b.** *dig* for something hidden, c. acc. Jb 3^{21} (fig. of longing for death), Je 13^{7} (no obj. expr.) **2.** *search, search out, explore*, c. acc. הָאָרֶץ Jos 2$^{3.3}$ (JE), Dt 1^{22}; of eagle, *search for* food, c. acc. ח׳ אֹכֶל Jb 39^{29}, with esp. reference to keen vision (|| מֵרָחוֹק עֵינָיו יַבִּיטוּ); so = *search* or *look carefully about* before going to rest Jb 11^{18} (no obj.).—לַחְפֹּר Is 2^{20} v. חֲפַרְפָּרָה infr. 2658

† I. **חֵפֶר n.pr.m.** **1.** a Manassite Nu 26$^{32.33}$ 27^{1} Jos 17$^{2.3}$, 𝔊 Οφερ. **2.** a man of Judah 1 Ch 4^{6}; 𝔊 Ηφαλ, 𝔊L Αφερ. **3.** one of David's heroes, acc. to 1 Ch 11^{36} (but on txt. v. Be VB and Dr 2 S 23^{36}). 2660

†**חֶפְרִי adj.gent.** of I. חֵפֶר **a**; only c. art. as n.pr. coll. הַח׳ Nu 26^{32}. 2662

†II. **חֵפֶר n.pr.loc.** **1.** Canaanitish town, with a king, named just before Aphek Jos 12^{17}, exact site unknown. **2.** 1 K 4^{10} in Judah (ארץ ח׳);—on גַּתָּה ח׳ Jos 19^{13}, גַּת הַח׳ 2 K 14^{25}, v. גַּת sub גנן. 2660

†**חֲפָרַיִם n.pr.loc.** in Issachar Jos 19^{19}, 𝔊 Αγειν, A Αφεραειμ, 𝔊L Αμφαραιμ; = Egypt. Ḥa-pu-ru-m-â WMM$^{Asien. 170}$; site dub.; 6 m. N. of *Legio* acc. to Lag$^{Onom. 223, 2nd ed. 241}$. 2663

2661 †[חֲפַרְפָּרָה] **n.f. mole** (as *digger*)—only
6512 Is 2^{20}, rd. לַחֲפַרְפָּרוֹת (MT לַחְפֹּר פֵּרוֹת, meaning obscure, v. conject. in Thes Ges[Comm.] Di).

2659 †II. [חָפֵר] **vb. be abashed, ashamed** (𝔗 חֲפַר Pr 13^5, מַחְפְּרָנָא *one causing shame* Pr 19^{26}; Syr. ܚܦܪ, esp. Aph. *be ashamed, put to shame;* Ar. خَفَرَ *be bashful,* خَفِرٌ *shy, bashful;* Eth. ኀፈረ: *be ashamed, blush*)—**Qal** *Pf.* 3 fs. חָֽפְרָה Je 50^{12}; וְחָֽפְרָה consec. Is 24^{23}; וְחָֽפְרָה Je 15^9; חָפְרוּ ψ 71^{24}; וְחָפְרוּ consec. Mi 3^7; *Impf.* יַחְפְּרוּ ψ 35^4 + 4 t.; יֶחְפָּרוּ ψ 34^6; וַיֶּחְפָּרוּ Jb 6^{20}; תַּחְפְּרוּ Is 1^{29};—*be abashed, ashamed,* said of face ψ 34^6 (avoided by looking to י׳); elsewhere always ‖ בּוֹשׁ, of enemies of righteousness ψ 71^{24} $35^{4.26}$ 40^{15} = 70^3 83^{18}; of idolaters Is 1^{29}; diviners Mi 3^7; of distressed Jerusalem Je 15^9; so of Babylon 50^{12}; of moon Is 24^{23}; *be put to shame* (disappointment), of caravans looking for water Jb 6^{20}. **Hiph.** *Pf.* הֶחְפִּיר Is 33^9; *Impf.* יַחְפִּיר Pr 13^5; תַּחְפִּירִי Is 54^4; *Pt.* מַחְפִּיר Pr 19^{26};—*display shame,* fig. of Lebanon Is 33^9 (‖ קָמַל 'dried up' Che); of Israel Is 54^4 (‖ בּוֹשׁ Qal); of an unfilial son, *cause shame* Pr 19^{26} (‖ מֵבִישׁ); cf. Pr 13^5 of wicked (‖ יבאישׁ: v. באשׁ **Hiph.** supr. p. 93).

6548 †חָפְרַע **n.pr.m. Apries,** reigned in Egypt alone, B.C. 589–570 and with Amasis 570–564;
6548 named as פַּרְעֹה ח׳ מֶלֶךְ־מִצְרַיִם Je 44^{30} *Pharaoh Hophraʿ king of Egypt* (v. פַּרְעֹה); 4th king of 26th dynasty; 𝔊 Οὐαφρη; Manetho Οὔαφρις; Egypt. Monum. *Uaḥ-âbra,* Wiedemann[Ägypt. Gesch. 602, 636 ff.; Gesch. Ägypt. 163 ff.]; Gk. Ἀπρίης Herodot. ii. 161 etc. (v. Wied[Herodot's 2tes Buch, 569]), Diodor[i. 68]; Ἀπρίας Ctesias (Athen. 13^{560}).

2661 חֲפַרְפָּרָה v. sub I. חפר. above

2664 †[חָפַשׂ] **vb. search** (𝔗[Jer] חֲפַס *dig, seek;* Pal. Syr. *dig* (Schw); perh. As. *êppêšu, êtpêšu, sensible,* Lyon[Sargontexte 65])—**Qal** *Impf.* 2 ms. sf. תַּחְפְּשֶׂנָּה Pr 2^4; יַחְפְּשׂוּ ψ 64^7; נַחְפְּשָׂה La 3^{40}; *Pt.* חֹפֵשׂ Pr 20^{27};—*search, search out,* fig.; **1.** *search for,* obj. בִּינָה etc. Pr 2^4 (‖ בקשׁ). **2.** =*think out, devise,* c. acc. עולות unjust acts ψ 64^7 (cf. also sub **Pu.**) **3.** *search = test,* La 3^{40} (obj. דרכינו; ‖ חקר), Pr 20^{27}. **Niph.** *Pf.* נֶחְפְּשׂוּ Ob ^{6} subj. עֵשָׂו coll.; *searched out* = exposed and plundered (‖ נִבְעוּ מַצְפֻּנָיו). **Pi.** *Pf.* וְחִפַּשְׂתִּי 1 S 23^{23}; וְחִפְּשׂוּ 1 K 20^6; *Impf.* וַיְחַפֵּשׂ Gn 31^{35} + 2 t.; אֲחַפֵּשׂ Am 9^3 Zp 1^{12}; *Imv.* חַפְּשׂוּ 2 K 10^{23};—**1.** *search through,* c. acc., a house 1 K 20^6, Jerusalem (metaph.) Zp 1^{12}; no obj. expr. 2 K 10^{23}. **2.** *search for:* **a.** a person c. acc. 1 S 23^{23}. **b.** a thing, c. acc. Gn 44^{12} (J; Joseph searching for his cup); Gn 31^{35} (E; no obj. expr., Laban looking for his teraphim); Am 9^3 (י׳ searching for evildoers), ψ 77^7 (soul searching to understand י׳'s dealings with his servants). **Pu.** *Impf.* יְחֻפָּשׂ Pr 28^{12} *be searched for* = be hidden; *Pt.* מְחֻפָּשׂ ψ 64^7 in חֵפֶשׂ מ׳ = *a searched out search,* i.e. a device well thought out (cf. Che; ‖ **Qal** q. v.); v. also חֵ֫פֶשׂ. **Hithp.** *Pf.* הִתְחַפֵּשׂ 2 Ch 35^{22} (but 𝔊 הִתְחַזֵּק, cf. also 𝔙 𝔖 3 Esdr 1^{26}, so Be Öt); *Impf.* יִתְחַפֵּשׂ Jb 30^{18}; וַיִּתְחַפֵּשׂ 1 S 28^8 + 3 t.; *Inf. abs.* הִתְחַפֵּשׂ 1 K 22^{30} = 2 Ch 18^{29};—*disguise oneself* (lit. *let oneself be searched for*) 1 S 28^8 1 K $22^{30.30}$ = 2 Ch $18^{29.29}$, 2 Ch 35^{22} (but v. supr.), all of disguise by change of garments; 1 K 20^{38} באפר i.e. with headgear over eyes; subj. לבושׁ Jb 30^{18}, i.e. his garment is disguised, no longer looks like the mantle it is.

†חֵ֫פֶשׂ **n.[m.] a (shrewd) device, plot,** 2665
only in תָּמְנוּ ח׳ מְחֻפָּשׂ ψ 64^7 (cf. חָפַשׂ supr.)

†[חָפַשׁ] **vb. be free**—only **Pu.** *Pf.* 3 fs. 2666
כִּי לֹא חֻפָּ֑שָׁה Lv 19^{20} (H), *because she was not freed* (a freed-woman).

†חֹ֫פֶשׁ **n.[m.]** very dub.; only בִּגְדֵי־חֹ֫פֶשׁ 2667
לְרִכְבָּה Ez 27^{20} *wide-spread* (?) *garments for riding,* i.e. saddle-cloths, acc. to Thes Sm Co Da al.; but mng. *spread* for √ purely conject.; Gr suggests, plausibly, חֵ֫פֶן (q. v.)

†חֻפְשָׁה **n.f. freedom,** only ח׳ לֹא נִתַּן־לָהּ 2668
Lv 19^{20} (H) *freedom had not been given to her.*

†חָפְשִׁי **adj. free** (NH *id.*)—ח׳ Ex 21^5 + 2670
10 t. + ψ 88^6; pl. חָפְשִׁים Is 58^6 + 4 t.—**1.** *free* from slavery: of Hebrew bondslave (male or female) set free in 7th year Ex $21^{2.5}$ (JE), Dt $15^{12.13.18}$, cf. Je $34^{9.10.11.14.16}$; of slave (male or female) set free on account of injury done Ex $21^{26.27}$ (JE); עֶבֶד ח׳ מֵאֲדֹנָיו Jb 3^{19} *a slave is free from his master* (i.e. in She'ôl); but בַּמֵּתִים חָפְשִׁי ψ 88^6 *among the dead* I am *free* (i.e. adrift, cut off from Yahweh's remembrance); more gen., שַׁלַּח רְצוּצִים חָפְשִׁים Is 58^6 *to let oppressed ones go free.* **2.** *free* from taxes, obligations, etc. אֵת בֵּית אָבִיו יַעֲשֶׂה חָפְשִׁי בְּיִשְׂרָאֵל 1 S 17^{25} *his father's house will he make free in Israel.*

2669 †חָפְשִׁית, חפשות **n.f.** freedom, separateness, only בֵּית הַחָפְשִׁית 2 K 15^{5} = 2 Ch 26^{21} Qr (Kt החפשות) i.e. (si vera l.) a separate house—a house apart (on account of his disease).

2671 חֵץ v. sub חצץ. p. 346

2672 †[חָצַב] חָצֵב **vb.** hew, hew out, cleave (NH *id.*, Aram. חֲצַב; SI$^{4.6}$ pt. pl. החצבם; cf. Ph. מחצב = Heb. *id.*)—**Qal** *Pf.* חָצַב Is 5^{2}; חָצְבָה Pr 9^{1}; חָצַבְתִּי Ho 6^{5}, etc.; *Impf.* וַיַּחְצֹב 2 Ch 26^{10}; 2 ms. תַּחְצֹב Dt 8^{9}; *Inf. cstr.* לַחְצֹב Je 2^{13}; לַחְצוֹב 1 Ch 22^{2}; *Pt. act.* חֹצֵב Is 10^{15} + 4 t.; cstr. חֹצְבִי Is 22^{16}; חֹצְבִים 1 Ch 22^{2} + 3 t.; חֹצְבֵי 2 K 12^{13}; pass. חֲצוּבִים Dt 6^{11} Ne 9^{25};—**1.** *hew out, (dig)*, wine-vat יֶקֶב Is 5^{2}; sepulchre (קֶבֶר) Is 22$^{16.16}$; cisterns בֹּרוֹת Dt 6$^{11.11}$ 2 Ch 26^{10} Ne 9^{25}, cf. Je 2^{13}; of mining מהרריה תַּח׳ נחשת Dt 8^{9} *out of its mountains thou mayst hew out copper.* **2. a.** *hew* stone 1 Ch 22^{2}; metaph. of pillars Pr 9^{1} (subj. wisdom); elsewhere pt., *hewer* of stone 2 K 12^{13} 1 Ch 22$^{2.15}$ (v. SI$^{4.6}$ supr.); prob. 1 K 5^{29} 2 Ch 2$^{1.17}$ (ח׳ בָּהָר v. Be), cf. 24^{12} Ezr 3^{7}. **b.** appar. *hew wood* Is 10^{15} ח׳ בּוֹ (i.e. בַּגַּרְזֶן). **3.** metaph. *hew in pieces* Ho 6^{5} fig. of י׳ attacking people by agency of prophets (‖ הֲרַגְתִּים); *divide, cleave* subj. י׳'s voice ψ 29^{7} obj. להבות אש, i.e. the thunder of his voice sends forked lightnings (but on txt. cf. Che and crit. n.) **Niph.** *Impf.* יֵחָצְבוּן *be cut, hewn, graven* (words on rock) Jb 19^{24}. **Pu.** *Pf.* חֻצַּבְתֶּם Is 51^{1} fig., *hewn* out of rock (of Isr.'s origin; ‖ נֻקַּר). **Hiph.** *Pt.* מַחְצֶבֶת Is 51^{9} *hew in pieces* = **Qal 3**, fig. of destroying רהב = Egypt (cf. ψ 89^{11}).

4274 †מַחְצֵב **n.[m.]** hewing, alw. אַבְנֵי מ׳ = *hewn stones* 2 K 12^{13} 22^{6} = 2 Ch 34^{11} (in all ‖ עֵצִים).

2673 †חָצָה **vb.** divide (NH *id.*; Ar. حَظِيَ is *be fortunate, happy* with one's husband or wife, etc., i.e. have a *share* in happiness; حُظْوَةٌ *a small arrow;* Di^{134} puts here Eth. ሐጽ: *arrow*, cf. חֵצִי)—**Qal** *Pf.* חָצָה Nu 31^{42}; וְחָצִית consec. Nu 31^{27}; וְחָצוּ consec. Ex 21^{35}; *Impf.* יֶחֱצֶה Is 30^{28}; וַיַּחַץ Gn 32^{8} + 2 t.; וַיֶּחֱצֵם Ju 9^{43}; יֶחֱצוּ ψ 55^{24}; יֶחֱצוּן Ex 21^{35}; יֶחֱצוּהוּ Jb 40^{30};—**1.** *divide*, sq. כסף Ex 21^{35}; שור v^{35} (both JE), לִוְיָתָן crocodile Jb 40^{30}; prey, מלקוח, Nu 31^{27} (P; c. לְ before parts); a company of people Gn 32^{8} (sq. לְ as foreg.), 33^{1} (both J) Ju 9^{43} (לְ as foreg.) but cf. 7^{16}. **2.** (appar. denom. fr. חֵצִי) ψ 55^{24} לא יח׳ ימיהם *shall not halve their days*, i.e. enjoy even half of the normal number; Is 30^{28} עד צואר יח׳ *shall halve unto the neck* = shall reach to the neck and so divide the man in half. **Niph.** *Impf.* 3 fs. apoc. תֵּחָץ Dn 11^{4} *be divided* (of kingdom), sq. לְ; ולא יֵחָצוּ עוד לשני גוים Ez 37^{22} (Judah and Isr.); waters of Jordan 2 K 2$^{8.14}$.

†[חֲצוֹת] **n.f.** (Inf. form.) division, middle 2676
—only cstr. חֲצֹת הַלַּיְלָה Ex 11^{4} (J) = *midnight;* חֲצוֹת לַיְלָה Jb 34^{20} ψ 119^{62}; in all = adverb. phr. of time (בְּ om.)

חֵצִי$_{123}$ **n.m.**$^{Nu\,12,12}$ half (NH *id.;* Ph. חצי; 2677
on format. v. Lag$^{BN\,113}$)—abs. חֵצִי 1 K 3$^{25.25}$ + 3 t.; הַחֵצִי 1 K 10^{7}, cf. 16^{21}; וְחֵצִי Ez 40^{42}; וְחֵצִי Dn 12^{7} + 13 t. (usu. c. Pashta or Tiphcha), cf. בַּחֲצִי 2 S 10^{4} 1 Ch 19^{4}; cstr. חֲצִי Ex 12^{29} + 84 t.; sf. חֶצְיוֹ Ex 38^{4} + 7 t. + Jos 8^{33} וְהֶחֶצְיוֹ (but art. suspicious. v. Ges$^{§\,127\,R3,\,4}$); חֶצְיָהּ Ne 3^{38}; חֶצְיֵנוּ 2 S 18^{3}; חֲצָיִם Zc 14$^{8.8}$ + 2 t. — **1.** *half* of anything:—blood of offering Ex 24$^{6.6}$ (JE), beard 2 S 10^{4}, a hin Nu 15$^{9.10}$ 28^{14} (P); curtain Ex 26^{12} (P); week ח׳ השבוע Dn 9^{27} etc.; ח׳ אַמָּה *half a cubit* Ex 26^{16} 36^{21} (P) +; esp. ח׳ שבט *half a tribe* Nu 32^{33} 34$^{13.14.15}$ (P) +; half of people 2 S 18^{3} 19^{41} 1 K 16$^{21.21.21}$ +, etc. so ח׳ הַמְּנֻחוֹת 1 Ch 2^{52} and ח׳ הַמָּנַחְתִּי v^{54} (v. Be and מָנַחַת sub נוח).—On כבחצי 1 S 14^{4} v. We Dr. **2.** *middle* ח׳ הלילה Ex 12^{29} (J) *midnight*, so Ju 16$^{3.3}$ Ru 3^{8}; of garments 2 S 10^{4} 1 Ch 19^{4}; altar Ex 27^{5}; of the Mt. of Olives Zc 14^{4}; ח׳ יָמַי ψ 102^{25} *the midst of my days* (when they are but half done), Je 17^{11}.

חֲצִי הַמְּנֻחוֹת 1 Ch 2^{52}, and חֲצִי הַמָּנַחְתִּי 2679-80
v^{54}, v. מָנַחַת sub נוח. p. 630

†חֵצִי **n.m.**$^{2\,K\,9,\,24}$ arrow (cf. Ar. حُظْوَةٌ, Eth. 2678
ሐጽ: *id.*, Di^{134}, and v. Dr on 1 S 20^{36})—abs. הַחֵצִי 1 S 20$^{36.37.37}$ + v^{38} Kt (Qr הַחִצִּים), perh. also v$^{21.22}$ (so 𝔊 We, for MT pl. הַחִצִּים), 2 K 9^{24}; the usual form is חֵץ; v. infr.

†יַחְצְאֵל, יַחְצִיאֵל **n.pr.m.** (*God divideth,* 3183, 3185
apportioneth)—son of Naphtali; יַחְצְ׳ Gn 46^{24} (𝔊 Ασιηλ, 𝔊L Ιασβηλ), Nu 26^{48} (Σαηλ, Ασιηλ) = יַחְצִי׳ 1 Ch 7^{13} (Ιεσιηλ, 𝔊L Ιασσιηλ).

†יַחְצְאֵלִי **adj.gent.** of foregoing; only c. 3184
art. as n.pr.coll., Nu 26^{48}.

†מֶחֱצָה **n.f.** half, of spoils;—abs. מֶחֱצָה 4275
Nu 31^{36}; cstr. מֶחֱצַת Nu 31^{43} (both P).

†מַחֲצִית **n.f.** half, middle—cstr. מַחֲצִית 4276

Ex 30$^{13.13}$ + 8 t.; מַחֲצִת Nu 31$^{30.47}$; sf. מַחֲצִיתוֹ Ex 30^{23}, מַחֲצִיתָהּ Lv 6$^{13.13}$, מַחֲצִיתָם Nu 31^{29}—**1.** *half* of a shekel Ex 30$^{13.13.15}$ cf. v^{23} 38^{26}; the flour for offering Lv 6$^{13.13}$, of spoils Nu 31$^{29.30.42.47}$; of tribe Jos 21^{25} (all P), 1 Ch 6$^{46.55}$; of chariots 1 K 16^{9}. **2.** *middle* מ׳ היום = *midday, noon*
2676-77 Ne 8^{3} (cf. *midnight*, חָצוֹת, חֲצִי **2**). p. 345

חצן (√ of foll.; meaning dub.; denom. seem to be Ar. حَضَنَ, Eth. ሐፀነ: *carry in the arms* or *bosom, rear, foster*; perhaps also As. *êṣênu, bring together*, also *drink* or *draw in* sweet odours Flood Tablet $^{iii, 49}$ Hpt in KAT$^{2\ Gloss\ i}$).

2683 †[**חֹצֶן**] **n.m.** bosom of a garment (Ar. حِضْنٌ, Eth. ሐፅን: also Syr. ܚܶܨܢܳܐ *bosom* (= ܚܘܕܢܐ*), v. Hoffm$^{ZMG\ 1878,\ 753}$ Lag$^{M\ ii.\ 361\ ff.;\ BN\ 46\ f.}$; on this word and foll. v. Ba$^{NB\ 120;\ ZMG\ 1889,\ 183}$)—שֶׁלֹּא מִלֵּא כַפּוֹ קוֹצֵר וְחִצְנוֹ מְעַמֵּר ψ 129^{7} (grass) *with which a reaper filleth not his hand, nor a binder his bosom.*

2684 †**חֹצֶן** **n.m.** bosom;—חָצְנִי נָעַרְתִּי Ne 5^{13} *I shook out my bosom* (the bosom of my garment); וְהֵבִיאוּ בָנַיִךְ בְּחֹצֶן Is 49^{22} *and they shall bring thy sons in the bosom* (i.e. in the arms, clasped to the bosom, like infants; ‖ עַל־כָּתֵף).

2686 †I. [**חָצַץ**] **vb. divide** (NH *make a partition;* As. *ḫaṣâṣu, cut in two*, Zim$^{BP\ 24\ n.}$; Eth. ሐጸጸ: *curtail, diminish*)—**Qal** *Pt.* חֹצֵץ intr. Pr 30^{27} of locusts ויצא ח׳ כלו; i.e. dividing (themselves) into companies or swarms. **Pi.** *Pt.* מְחַצְצִים v. II. חצץ. **Pu.** *Pf.* מספר חדשיו חֻצָּצוּ Jb 21^{21} *the number of his months, they have been cut in two* (fig. for *curtailed*).

2687 †**חָצָץ** **n.[m.] gravel** (as *divided, comminuted;* Aram. חֲצָצָא, ܚܨܨܐ)—only abs. ח׳ Pr 20^{17} La 3^{16} [חֲצָצֶיךָ ψ 77^{18} v. חֵץ].—יִמָּלֵא־פִיהוּ ח׳ Pr 20^{17} fig. of a liar; וַיַּגְרֵס בח׳ שִׁנָּי La 3^{16} *and he hath crushed my teeth with gravel-stones*, fig. of י׳'s dealings with sufferer.

2671 †**חֵץ** **n.m.**$^{1\ S\ 20,\ 20}$ **arrow**, mostly poet. and proph. (cf. חֵצִי supr. sub חצה)—abs. ח׳ ψ 91^{5} + 9 t. + 1 S 17^{7} Kt (Qr עֵץ q.v.); cstr. *id.* 2 K 13$^{17.17}$; sf. חִצִּי Jb 34^{6}, חִצּוֹ ψ 58^{8} Zc 9^{14}, חִצָּם ψ 11^{2} 64^{4}; *Pl.* חִצִּים Gn 49^{23} + 17 t. + 1 S 20^{38} Qr (Kt חֵצִי q.v.) + 2 S 22^{15} (< חִצָּיו ‖ ψ 18^{15}); cstr. חִצֵּי Jb 6^{4} ψ 120^{4} + Ez 5^{16} (Co חִצֵּי cf. 𝔊 𝔖 Hi); חִצַּי Dt 32$^{23.42}$ (Ez 5^{16} v. supr.), חִצֶּיךָ ψ 38^{3} + 4 t.; חִצָּיו Is 5^{28} + 5 t.;—*arrow:* **1.** lit., shot from bow by hand 1 S 20$^{20.21.21.22}$ (𝔊 We sg., i.e. הַחֵצִי, in v$^{21.22}$, see also Dr) v$^{36.38\ Qr}$ 2 K 19^{32} = Is 37^{33}, Is 5^{28} 7^{24} Je 50$^{9.14}$ 51^{11} Ez 39$^{3.9}$ 1 Ch 12^{2}; shot from engine of war 2 Ch 26^{15}; used in divination Ez 21^{26} cf. 2 K 13$^{15.15.17.17.18}$; בַּעֲלֵי חִצִּים = archers Gn 49^{23}. **2.** fig. of Israel's weapons Nu 24^{8}, of the (Messianic) king ψ 45^{6}, of Yahweh's judgments Dt 32$^{23.42}$ Jb 6^{4} (cf. חִצִּי = *my wound* 34^{6}), ψ 7^{14} 38^{3} 58^{8} (but on text cf. Che$^{crit.\ n.}$) 64^{8} 120^{4} (? cf. Che); further Pr 7^{23} La 3^{12} Ez 5^{16}; in theoph. ψ 18^{15} = 2 S 22^{15}, cf. Hb 3^{11} Zc 9^{14} ψ 144^{6}; of wicked men's violence ψ 11^{2} cf. 91^{5}, under fig. of lion's teeth ψ 57^{5}; their words ψ 64^{4} cf. Pr 25^{18} Je 9^{8}; simile, of strength and efficiency derived from one's children, ψ 127^{4}; of a deceiver's words Pr 26^{18}; metaph. of servant of י׳ ח׳ בָּרוּר Is 49^{2}.—In 1 S 17^{7} rd. עֵץ (for חֵץ) as Qr and ‖ 2 S 21^{19} = *the shaft;* v. עֵץ; so Klo Dr.

†**חַצְצֹן תָּמָר** **n.pr.loc.** (ח׳ *of the palm*);— 2688
abode of Amorites Gn 14^{7}, 𝔊 Ασασαν Θαμαρ; חַצְצוֹן תָּמָר הִיא עֵין גֶּדִי 2 Ch 20^{2} base of operations for אֲרָם (rd. אֱדוֹם) ag. Judah (vid. Jos$^{Ant.\ ix,\ 1.2}$); it was on W. side of Dead Sea (v. עֵין גֶּדִי); see Rob$^{BR\ i,\ 500\text{-}509}$ Bd$^{Pal\ 143}$ GASm$^{Geogr.\ 269\ ff.}$; Wady *Ḥuṣāṣā* (= חצצן?) lies NW. fr. Engedi GASm$^{l.\ c.}$ cf. Rob$^{BR\ i,\ 506}$ Bd$^{Pal\ 14\ (map)}$; GASm suggests also possibility of finding here תָּמָר 1 K 9^{18} Kt (= תַּדְמֹר Qr and 2 Ch 8^{4}), Ez 47^{19} 48^{28} (v. תָּמָר n.pr.loc.)

†II. [**חצץ**] **vb.denom.** only **Pi.** *Pt.* מְחַצְצִים 2686
Ju 5^{11} *archers* (> *those dividing* spoil, since no obj. expr. and חלק more suitable for such mng.)

חצצר, חֲצֹצְרָה v. IV. חצר. p. 348 2689

I. **חצר** (√ of foll.; cf. Ar. حَصَرَ *encompass, surround;* Eth. ሐጸረ: *surround, enclose* by wall, etc.; ሐጹር: *enclosure;* NH חָצֵר *court*, Ph. חצר *id.*, Syr. ܚܨܪܐ, *id.*)

I. **חָצֵר**$_{145}$ **n.m.**$^{Ez\ 40,\ 23}$ and (oftener) **f.**$^{1\ K\ 6,\ 36}$ 2691, 2699
enclosure, court—abs. ח׳ 1 K 7^{8} +, חֲצֵרָה Je 36^{20}; cstr. חֲצַר Ex 27^{9} +; sf. חֲצֵרוֹ 2 S 17^{18}; חֲצֵרוֹת Ex 8^{9} + 4 t.; cstr. חַצְרֵי Ne 13^{7}, חַצְרוֹת 2 K 21^{5} + 10 t.; sf. חֲצֵרָיו Is 1^{12} Zc 3^{7}; חֲצֵרֶיךָ ψ 65^{5} 84^{11}; חֲצֵרֹתַי 1 Ch 28^{6}; חֲצֵרֹתָיו ψ 100^{4}, לַחֲצֵרוֹתָיו ψ 96^{8}, וּבְחַצְרֹתֵיהֶם Ne 8^{16};—**1.** *enclosures* (in Egypt), perhaps court-yards, or cattle-yards, distinct from houses and from fields Ex 8^{9} (J). **2.** *court* of private house 2 S 17^{18} (containing well), cf. Ne 8^{16}; of a palace, חָצֵר הָאַחֶרֶת 1 K 7^{8} *the other court*, immediately surrounding palace, so called in distinct. from (הֶ)ח׳ הַגְּדוֹלָה v$^{9.12}$ *the great court*, including ח׳ הא׳ and הֶח׳ הַפְּנִימִית of temple (v. **3 b**) in one great enclosure (v.

Sta $^{\text{Salomos Bauten, ZAW 1883, 152 f.}}$); 2 K 20^{4} (Qr Vrss The Kmp Klo al.; Kt Ke al. הָעִיר), Je 36^{20} Est 1^{5} 2^{11} 4^{11} $5^{1.2}$ $6^{4.4.5}$; ח׳ מַטָּרָה *court of guard*, place of (honourable) confinement Je 32^{2} (in king's house), $v^{8.12}$ 33^{1} $37^{21.21}$ $38^{6.13.28}$ $39^{14.15}$. Esp. **3. a.** *court* of tabernacle חֲצַר הַמִּשְׁכָּן Ex 27^{9}, cf. $v^{9.12.13}$ + 24 t. Ex (all P; שַׁעַר הֶח׳ *gate of the court* Ex 35^{17} $38^{15.18.31}$ 39^{40} $40^{8.33}$); Lv $6^{9.19}$ Nu $3^{26.26}$ (פֶּתַח הֶח׳), v^{37} $4^{26.26}$ (פֶּתַח שַׁעַר הֶח׳), v^{32}; *courts* of house of י׳ 1 Ch 23^{28}. **b.** *court(s)* of Sol.'s temple, *inner c.* הֶח׳ הַפְּנִימִית 1 K 6^{36} 7^{12} (but on txt. v. Sta$^{\text{l. c.}}$) Ez 8^{16} 10^{3} cf. v^{4}; = *upper c.* הֶח׳ הָעֶלְיוֹן Je 36^{10} (v. Gf), and ח׳ הַכֹּהֲנִים 2 Ch 4^{9} (where also הָעֲזָרָה הַגְּדוֹלָה, as oft. Ezek., also דַּלְתוֹת לָעֲזָרָה); *outer* court הֶח׳ הַחִיצֹנָה Ez 10^{5} = הֶח׳ הַחֲדָשָׁה 2 Ch 20^{5}; v. further 1 K 8^{64} = 2 Ch 7^{7}, 2 Ch 24^{21} 29^{16} Je 19^{14} 26^{2} Ez 8^{7}; *two courts* 2 K 21^{5} = 2 Ch 33^{5}, 2 K 23^{12}; *courts* Ez 9^{7} 1 Ch 28^{12} 2 Ch 23^{5} Ne 8^{16} 13^{7}; oft. poet., *courts* of י׳ Is 1^{12} 62^{9} (ח׳ קדשׁי), Zc 3^{7} ψ 65^{5} $84^{3.11}$ 96^{8} 100^{4} 116^{19} 135^{2}. **c.** *courts* of Ezek.'s temple Ez 40^{14} + 38 t. Ez 40–46 (of these rd. הַשַּׁעַר for החצר $40^{19.32}$ with 𝔊 Hi Co; and החיצון for החצר 41^{15} with 𝔊 Ew Co).

II. חצר (√ of foll.; cf. Ar. حَضَرَ *be present, settle* or *dwell*, v. Lag$^{\text{BN 47 f.}}$; Sab. חצר *fixed abode* Os (Levy)$^{\text{ZMG 1865, 185}}$ CIS$^{\text{iv, 1. 2, No. 79. 82}}$).

2691, 2699 II. [חָצֵר]$_{46}$ **n.m.**$^{\text{Ne 11, 25}}$ **settled abode, settlement, village** (Lag$^{\text{l. c.}}$)—always pl., abs. חֲצֵרִים Jos 19^{8} + 5 t.; cstr. חַצְרֵי 1 Ch 9^{16} Ne 12^{28}; sf. חֲצֵרֶיהָ Jos 21^{12} + 4 t.; חַצְרֵיהֶם 1 Ch 4^{33} + 6 t.; חַצְרֵיהֶן Jos 13^{23} + 24 t. Jos;—**a.** settlements of Ishmaelites Gn 25^{16} (P; ‖ טִירוֹת *circles* of tents); of עַוִּים Dt 2^{23}; of Kedar Is 42^{11} (‖ עָרִים); בָּתֵּי הַחֲצֵרִים אֲשֶׁר אֵין־לָהֶם חֹמָה סָבִיב Lv 25^{31} (H), *houses of the villages which have no wall about them;* מַאֲרַב חֲצֵרִים ψ 10^{8} *lurking-place(s) of villages* (i.e. where oppressor, as a wild beast, watches his opportunity to attack the defenceless). Usu. **b.** as dependencies of cities Jos 15^{46}, with בְּנֹתֶיהָ (v. supr. בַּת **4** p. 123) Jos $15^{45.47.47}$ (all JE?); וְכָל־הַח׳ אֲשֶׁר סְבִיבוֹת הֶעָרִים 19^{8} (P), also 21^{12} (P) = 1 Ch 6^{41}, Ne 12^{29}; also Jos $13^{23.28}$ 15^{32} + 23 t. Jos (all P), Ne $11^{25.30}$ (‖ בָּנוֹת $v^{25.27}$ etc.), 12^{28}. **c.** villages, not contrasted with cities (cf. Is 42^{11} supr.) 1 Ch $9^{16.22.25}$ (all of Levites). **d.** ח׳ appar. incl. all settlements outside of Jerusalem הַח׳ בִּשְׂדֹתָם Ne 11^{25}.—ח׳ in n.pr.loc. v. infr. (and see Bla on Jos 15^{20-32}).

2692 † חֲצַר־אַדָּר **n.pr.loc.** place on southern border of Canaan (Judah) Nu 34^{4} 𝔊 ἔπαυλις Αραδ; = חֶצְרוֹן (q.v.) Jos 15^{3} (+ אַדָּרָה) 𝔊 Σαραδα, A 𝔊L Αδδαρα.

† חֲצַר גַּדָּה **n.pr.loc.** in southern Judah 2693
Jos 15^{27} 𝔊 Σερει, A 𝔊L Ασεργαδδα.

† חֲצַר סוּסָה, ח׳ סוּסִים **n.pr.loc.** (cf. *Kefr* 2701-02
Susê, 'Rossdorf,' close to Damascus on the south, Nö$^{\text{ZMG, 1875, xxix. 476}}$)—in Simeon ח׳ סוסה Jos 19^{5} 𝔊 Σαρσουσειμ, 𝔊L Ασαρσουσιν = ח׳ סוסים 1 Ch 4^{31}, 𝔊 Ἡμισυσεσοραμ, 𝔊L Ασερσουσι.

† חֲצַר עֵינוֹן, ח׳ עֵינָן **n.pr.loc.** on NE. 2703-04
border of Canaan Ez 47^{17}; חֲצַר עֵינָן 48^{1} (Co in both חֲצַרָה עינון); ח׳ עֵינָן Nu $34^{9.10}$; where it is said (v^{9}) זֶה יִהְיֶה לָכֶם גְּבוּל צָפוֹן; 𝔊 Αρσεναιειμ, 𝔊L Ασερναιν;—v. also חֲצַר הַתִּיכוֹן infr.

† חֲצַר שׁוּעָל **n.pr.loc. 1.** place in southern 2705
Judah Jos 15^{28} = 1 Ch 4^{28}, Ne 11^{27}. **2.** place in Simeon Jos 19^{3}.—𝔊 Αρσωλα, Χολασεωλα, Ασαρσουλα, Ασαρσουαρ, etc.

† חֲצַר הַתִּיכוֹן **n.pr.loc.** Ez 47^{16} 𝔊 Sm Co 2694
חֲצַרָה עינון (q.v.); it is described as אֲשֶׁר אֶל־גְּבוּל חַוְרָן; Wetzst$^{\text{ZKW, 1884, v. 114}}$ identif. with *Ḥaḍar* (حضر) 'at the foot of the eastern corner of Hermon.'

† חָצוֹר, חָצֹר **n.pr.loc.** (Lag$^{\text{BN 47 f.}}$)—𝔊 Ασωρ, 2674
etc.; **1.** a royal city of northern Canaan Jos 11^{1} יָבִין מֶלֶךְ־ח׳, cf. 12^{19}, and Ju $4^{2.17}$ 1 S 12^{9}; Jos $11^{10.10.11.13}$ 19^{36} 2 K 15^{29}; חָצֹר 1 K 9^{15}. **2.** places in the Negeb: **a.** Jos 15^{23}. **b. c.** Jos 15^{25} וְחָצוֹר חֲדַתָּה וּקְרִיּוֹת חֶצְרוֹן הִיא חָצוֹר. **3.** חָצוֹר Ne 11^{33} a Benjamite town, prob. = בַּעַל חָצוֹר q.v. **4.** מַמְלְכוֹת חָצוֹר אֲשֶׁר הִכָּה נְבוּכַדְרֶאצּוֹר Je 49^{28}, cf. $v^{30.33}$, an Arabian locality, v. Winer$^{\text{RW Hazor}}$ Gf Gie.—ח׳ עֵין Jos 19^{37}, v. sub עַיִן.

† חָצוֹר חֲדַתָּה **n.pr.loc.** (si vera l. perhaps 2675
new Ḥaṣôr, with Aram. ת in adj.)—Jos 15^{25}, v. חָצוֹר; in *Negeb* of Judah, site unknown.

† I. חָצִיר **n.[m.] settled abode or haunt** 2681
(‖ form of חָצֵר *supr.*, or txt. err. for it);—נְוֵה תַנִּים חָצִיר לִבְנוֹת יַעֲנָה Is 34^{13} *a dwelling of jackals (and) a haunt for ostriches;* also בִּנְוֵה תַנִּים רִבְצָהּ חָצִיר לְקָנֶה וָגֹמֶא 35^{7} *an abode, home, of reeds and rushes* (so Che Di Du al.; others put this under II. חָצִיר); Che Du think the v. mutilated, and would emend this line acc. to 34^{13}.

† חֶצְרוֹ, חֶצְרַי (**n.pr.m.** cf. Sab. n.pr.m. חצר 2695
DHM$^{\text{Epigr. Denkm. 56}}$)—one of David's heroes, called

the Carmelite, חצרו 2 S 23^{35} Kt (חֶצְרַי Qr; 𝔊 Ασαραι)=חֶצְרוֹ 1 Ch 11^{37} 𝔊 Ησεραι, Ασαραι, Εσρει.

2696 †חֶצְרוֹן, חֶצְרֹן **n.pr.loc.** et **pers.** (cf. Sab. חצֿרן n.pr.loc. vel. trib. Hal [No. 661] DHM [ZMG 1883, 15])—**1. n.pr.loc.** 𝔊 Ασωρων, Ασερων, Εσρωμ: **a.** חֶצְרוֹן Jos 15^3 place in extreme south of Judah, + אַדָּרָה=חֲצַר־אַדָּר (q.v.) Nu 34^4. **b.** קְרִיּוֹת חֶצְרוֹן הִיא חָצוֹר Jos 15^{25} another town of Judah in south. **2. n.pr.m.** 𝔊 Ασρωμ(ν), Εσρων, etc.: **a.** חֶצְרֹן son of Reuben Gn 46^9 Ex 6^{14} Nu 26^6 =חֶצְרוֹן 1 Ch 5^3. **b.** son of Pereṣ and grandson of Judah Gn 46^{12} Nu 26^{21}=חֶצְרוֹן Ru $4^{18.19}$ 1 Ch $2^{5.9.18.21.24.24.25}$ 4^1.

2697 †חֶצְרֹנִי, חֶצְרוֹנִי **adj.gent.** only c. art. as n. coll. **1.** הַחֶצְרוֹנִי Nu 26^6, of **2 a** supr. **2.** החצרני v^{21}, of **2 b** supr.

2698 †חֲצֵרוֹת, חֲצֵרֹת **n.pr.loc.** 𝔊 Ασηρωθ, a station of Isr. in wilderness: חֲצֵרוֹת Nu $11^{35.35}$ 12^{16}=חֲצֵרֹת $33^{17.18}$ Dt 1^1.

2700 †חֲצַרְמָוֶת **n.pr.m.** (Ar. حَضْرَمَوْت, Sab. חצֿרמות, חצֿרמת, Os [ZMG 1865, 239 ff.] DHM [ZMG 1883, 18. 412])—a 'son' of יָקְטָן, 5th in order from Shem (שֵׁם, 1. אַרְפַּכְשַׁד; 2. שֶׁלַח; 3. עֵבֶר; 4. יָקְטָן; 5. ח׳) Gn 10^{26}=1 Ch 1^{20}, 𝔊 Ασαρ(α)μωθ;=**n.pr.terr.** a district in southern Arabia, where dwelt the Χατραμωτῖται (Strabo [xvi. 4. 2]); mod. *Ḥaḍramaut* (or *Ḥaḍramût*, see Maltzan [ZMG 1871, 493] Mordt [ZMG 1876, 323], van d. Berg [p. 9], v. infr.) is same land, but not quite co-extensive; v. Di Gn 10^{26}, Ritter [Erdkunde xii (Arabien i) 609 ff.], de Goeje [Hadhr. 1886], van den Berg [Hadhramout, 1886], Glaser [Skizze ii. 20, 423 ff. etc.]; on its precise limits see esp. Ritter [611 ff.], de Goeje [l. c.] van d. Berg [ch. 1].

III. חצר (√of foll.; Ar. خَضِرَ *be green*).

2682 † II. חָצִיר **n.m.** [Is 15, 6] **green grass, herbage**, abs. חָצִיר Nu 11^5 + 16 t.; cstr. חֲצִיר Is 37^{27}=2 K 19^{26}, ψ 129^6;—**1.** *grass*, as food for animals 1 K 18^5 Jb 40^{15} ψ 104^{14} 147^8 Pr 27^{25} (‖ דֶּשֶׁא and עֵשֶׂב), Is 15^6 (‖ דֶּשֶׁא and יֶרֶק); spec. of *leeks* (as still sometimes in Aram., v. Löw [pp. 226, 228]) Nu 11^5 (v. Di); in sim. of abundant growth Is 44^4 (v. 𝔊 Ew Che); on Is 35^7 v. I. חָצִיר *supr.* **2.** as type of what is quickly perishing Jb 8^{12}, hence fig. of perishing enemies חֲצִיר גַּגּוֹת Is 37^{27}=2 K 19^{26} (‖ עֵשֶׂב, דֶּשֶׁא), ψ 129^6, i.e. having no depth of root; of wicked, soon to be cut down ψ 37^2; with special reference to Israel's oppressors Is 40^6 (‖ צִיץ [השׂדה]), v^7 (‖ *id.*), $v^{7.8}$ (‖ *id.*), 51^{12}; in sim. of frail man ψ 90^5; man's days ψ 103^{15} (‖ צִיץ השׂדה).

IV. חצר (assumed as √ for redupl. חצֹצר whence foll.; mng. unknown; perh. onomatop., v. Thes Ol [§§ 82 c. 188 a] Sta [§ 124 b]; see also Lag [Or ii. 18]).

†חֲצֹצְרָה **n.f. clarion** (NH חֲצוֹצֶרֶת, Aram. 2689
חֲצוֹצַרְתָּא)—mostly P and late;—abs. ח׳ Ho 5^8; pl. abs. חֲצֹצְרוֹת Nu 10^8+22 t.; חֲצֹצְרֹת Nu $10^{9.10}$; cstr. *id.* Nu 31^6 2 Ch 13^{12}; חֲצוֹצְרֹת Nu 10^2; *clarion*: **1.** as secular instr. Ho 5^8 (‖ שׁוֹפָר) 2 K $11^{14.14}$=2 Ch $23^{13.13}$. **2.** as sacred instr. 2 K 12^{14}, esp. for use by priests (only P, ψ 98 and Chr). **a.** תקע בח׳ (of blowing a single long blast) Nu $10^{3.4.7.8}$, to gather congreg. or נשׂיא׳ together, and, on festivals, over sacrif., 'to be remembered before י׳,' v^{10}. **b.** תקע תרועה בח׳, or הריע בח׳ (of sounding alarm,—a series of quick blasts) for camps to move Nu $10^{5.6}$, also in battle, v^9, 'to be remembered before י׳;' so Nu 31^6 2 Ch 13^{12} (cf. v^{14}), both ח׳ התרועה. **c.** esp. in Chr's descriptions of ceremonies at festivals, to express rejoicing: 1 Ch 13^8 15^{28} (‖ קוֹל שׁוֹפָר), $16^{6.42}$ 2 Ch 15^{14} (‖ שׁוֹפָר), 20^{28} $29^{26.27}$ Ezr 3^{10} Ne $12^{35.41}$, ψ 98^6 (‖ קוֹל שׁוֹפָר); הֵרִים קוֹל בח׳ 2 Ch 5^{13}; מחצצרים בח׳ 1 Ch 15^{24} 2 Ch $5^{12.13}$ 13^{14}; in 2 Ch 29^{28} this pt. agrees with noun in *sense*, and is masc.; *and the clarions* (=players on the clarions) *sounded*.—The חֲצֹצְרָה, or (sacred) clarion, was a long, straight, slender metal tube, with flaring end, v. Benz [Archäol. 277]; distinguished thus from the שׁוֹפָר which was originally a ram's horn, and prob. always retained the horn-shape; the שׁוֹפָר is mentioned constantly in the earlier lit., and was used by watchmen, warriors, etc., as well as priests (v. Benz [ib. 276] and שׁוֹפָר).

† [חִצְצֵר] **vb.** Kt, [חִצֵּר] Qr, denominat. 2690
from חצצרה=*sound a clarion*—**Pi.** *Pt.* מְחַצְּצְרִים 2 Ch 5^{13} (Qr מְחַצְּרִים)=*players on clarions*. **Hiph.** *Pt.* מַחְצְצְרִים (Qr מַחְצְרִים as Hiph. v. Kö [ii, 252]) 1 Ch 15^{24}+3 t.+2 Ch 5^{12} Baer, (van d. H מחצררים); *sound with clarions* מח׳ בחצצרות 1 Ch 15^{24} 2 Ch 5^{12} 13^{14}; abs. *sounded* (*sounding*) 2 Ch 7^6 29^{28}, cf. חצצרה *ad fin.* (Kt in all to be pronounced (prob.) מְחַצְצְרִים).

חֵק v. חֵיק sub חוק; חֹק v. sub חקק. p. 300, 349 2436, 2706

† חָקָה **vb.** only **Pu.** cut in, carve (NH 2707
represent, imitate; ‖ חקק)—**Pu.** *Pt.* מְחֻקֶּה 1 K 6^{35} Ez 8^{10} + 23^{14} (Co מְחֻקִּים, after 𝔊 𝔖 𝔗 𝔙), *carved* figure on wall Ez 8^{10} 23^{14} (where rd. אנשים מחקים, v. supr.)=subst. *carved work* 1 K 6^{35} (on doors of temple). **Hithp.** *Impf.* 2 ms. עַל־שָׁרְשֵׁי רַגְלַי תִּתְחַקֶּה Jb 13^{27} *thou gravest thee a*

graving (=markest a line) *for* (i.e. about) *the soles of my feet*, fixest limits for them (v. Di).

2708 חֻקָּה v. sub חקק. below

2709 †**חֲקוּפָא n.pr.m.** head of a family of returning exiles Ezr 2^{51} = Ne 7^{53}, 𝔊 Αφεικα, Αχειφα, Ακουφα, etc.

2710 †**[חָקַק] vb. cut in, inscribe, decree** (NH *id.*, Aram. חֲקַק, Zinj. חקק; Ph. *id. Pt.* Hiph.; Ar. حَقَّ *be just, right, obligatory*, also *make* or *decide to be just*, etc.; حَقٌّ *justness, truth, necessity, obligation;* Eth. ሐቅ: adj. *moderate, sufficient;* cf. also חקה)—**Qal** וְחַקּוֹתָ Ez 4^{1}; sf. חַקֹּתִיךְ Is 49^{16}; *Inf.* sf. בְּחֻקוֹ Pr 8^{27}; בְּחוּקוֹ Pr 8^{29} (assim. to בְּשׂוּמוֹ); חֻקָּהּ Is 30^{8}; *Pt.* חֹקְקִי Is 22^{16} (archaic case ending Ges §90.3a); pl. חֹקְקִים Is 10^{1}; cstr. חוֹקְקֵי Ju 5^{9} (poss. Poʿel=מחוקקי with מְ omitted, v. Ges §52(2), note 6); *Pt. pass.* pl. חֲקֻקִים Ez 23^{14} (Co חקוקים);—**1.** *cut in*, with בְּ, Is 22^{16}, of a dwelling-place=tomb, in a rock. **2.** *cut in* or *on, upon, engrave, inscribe*, c. על on roll of a book Is 30^{8}; representation of city on brick (as in Babylonia) Ez 4^{1}; images on a wall Ez 23^{14}; fig. of Zion's walls on palms of י׳ Is 49^{16}. **3.** *trace, mark out*, a circle, c. על over the face of deep Pr 8^{27}; c. acc., foundations of earth v^{29}. **4.** of a law, *engrave, inscribe* (on a tablet), fig. for *enact, decree* חקקים חקקי און Is 10^{1}(|| כתב עמל); חוקקי ישׂראל poet.=*commanders* (v. **Poʿel**) Ju 5^{9} (|| מחקקים v^{14}). **Poʿel** *Impf.* יְחוֹקְקוּ Pr 8^{15}; *Pt.* מְחֹקֵק Gn 49^{10} Nu 21^{18} Dt 33^{21}; sf. מְחֹקְקִי ψ 60^{9} 108^{9}; מְחֹקְקֵנוּ Is 33^{22}; pl. מְחֹקְקִים Ju 5^{14};—*inscribe* (as a law), *enact* (poet.): c. acc. צֶדֶק Pr 8^{15} elsewh. pt. **a.** *prescriber* of laws, hence (as sovereign authority in a warlike clan) *commander* Dt 33^{21} (of warlike tribe of Gad), Ju 5^{14} Is 33^{22} (of י׳; || מַלְכֵּנוּ, שֹׁפְטֵנוּ). **b.** *commander's staff* Gn 49^{10} (|| שֵׁבֶט), Nu 21^{18} (both poet.), ψ 60^{9}=108^{9}. **Pu.** *Pt.* מְחֻקָּק *that which is decreed* Pr 31^{5} (late). **Hoph.** *Impf.* יֻחָקוּ Jb 19^{23} *inscribed* in (בְּ) a book.

2706 חֹק 127 **n.m.** Mi 7,11 **something prescribed, a statute or due;**—ח׳ Gn 47^{22} + 22 t.; חָק־ Ex 30^{21} + 14 t.; sf. חֻקִּי Pr 30^{8} + 3 t.; חָקְךָ Lv $10^{13.14}$ etc. + 4 t. sfs.; pl. חֻקִּים Dt 4^{5} + 31 t.; cstr. חֻקֵּי
2711 Ex 18^{16}; חוּקֵּי Ez 20^{18}; also חִקְקֵי Ju 5^{15} Is 10^{1} (Ges §93.1 R 7); חֻקּוֹ Jb 14^{5} etc. + 44 t. sfs.—**1.** *prescribed task*, assigned to Isr. in Egypt Ex 5^{14} (E). **2.** *prescribed portion*, or allowance of food Gn $47^{22.22}$ (J); Pr 30^{8} 31^{15} Ez 16^{27}; מחקי Jb 23^{12} (RV; < 𝔊 𝔙 Ol Me Di SS בְּחֵקִי *in my bosom*). **3.** *action prescribed* for oneself, *resolve:* חִקְקֵי לֵב Ju 5^{15} *resolves of mind* || חִקְרֵי לֵב v^{16}. **4.** *prescribed due* of the priests from offerings Lv 6^{11} $10^{13.13.14.14}$ (P); *due* of י׳ Lv 6^{15} (P); לח׳ עולם Ex 29^{28} Lv 7^{34} 10^{15} Nu $18^{8.11.19}$ (all P), Lv 24^{9} (H); portion of oil for the תרומה Ez 45^{14}. **5.** *prescribed limit, boundary:* of sea Je 5^{22} Pr 8^{29} Jb 26^{10} 38^{10}; of heavens ψ 148^{6}; of land of Israel Mi 7^{11}; of time Jb $14^{5.13}$; so פָּעֲרָה פִיהָ לִבְלִי חֹק Is 5^{14} Sheʾôl *openeth wide her mouth, without limit.* **6.** *enactment, decree, ordinance* of either God or man: **a.** *specific decree:* law of fifth in Egypt Gn 47^{26} (J); of passover Ex 12^{24} (J); lament for Jephthah's daughter Ju 11^{39}; for Josiah 2 Ch 35^{25}; חק ומשפט Ex 15^{25} Jos 24^{25} (both E), 1 S 30^{25}; חק עולם Ex 30^{21}; || מִשְׁפָּט, עֵדוּת ψ $81^{5.6}$ (law of a festival). **b.** of י׳ in nature Jb 28^{26}. **c.** respecting Mess. king ψ 2^{7}; day of י׳ Zp 2^{2} MT, but on txt. v. We and טֶרֶם, infr.; covenant with Jacob ψ 105^{10}=1 Ch 16^{17}; destiny of man Jb 23^{14}. **d.** *law in general* עלי חק *according to law, right* ψ 94^{20} (others *against law*); לַמֵּד ח׳ ומשפט Ezr 7^{10}; || ברית and תורות Is 24^{5}; || עדות ψ 99^{7}. **7.** pl. חֻקִּים *enactments, statutes* of a law: **a.** of י׳ in nature Je 31^{36}. **b.** of the prophets Zc 1^{6}. **c.** *conditions* of deed of purchase Je 32^{11}. **d.** *enactments* || מִשְׁפָּטִים: ancestral Ez 20^{18}; given by God as punishment for disobedience 20^{25}. **e.** *decrees* of unjust judges חִקְקֵי־אָוֶן Is 10^{1}. **f.** *civil enactments prescribed by God:* חֻקֵּי האלהים Ex 18^{16} (E; || תּוֹרֹתָיו), v^{20} (E; || *id.*) **g.** elsewh. of prescriptions of the several codes of Hex: Lv 10^{11} Nu 30^{17} (P), Dt 4^{6} 6^{24} 16^{12} ψ 119^{5} + 20 t., Mal 3^{7}; || תּוֹרַת י׳ Am 2^{4}; ח׳ ותורות ψ 105^{45}; דברי הת׳ והח׳ Dt 17^{19}; || ברית ψ 50^{16}; ח׳ וברית ועדות 2 K 17^{15}; usu. either || משפטים Dt $4^{1.5.8.14}$ 5^{1} 11^{32} 12^{1} 26^{16}, 1 K 9^{4}=2 Ch 7^{17}, 1 Ch 22^{13} Ez 11^{12} 36^{27}, or else ח׳ ומשפטים combined with other synon. (usu. preceding): e.g. דבר(ים) ψ 147^{19}; תורה 2 Ch 33^{8} Mal 3^{22}; מצוה Dt 5^{28} 6^{1} 7^{11}; מצות Ne 1^{7} 1 K 8^{58}; תורה, מצוה 2 Ch 19^{10}; עֵדֹת Dt 4^{45} 6^{20}; sts. foll.: e.g. תורות Lv 26^{46}; מצוה, תורה 2 K 17^{37}; or in different order, e.g. מ׳ ותורות ח׳ ומצות Ne 9^{13}; מצות ומ׳ וח׳ Ne 10^{30}; ח׳ ומצות ומ׳ Dt 26^{17}. Apart from משפטים it is combined with מצות, e.g. מ׳ וח׳ Ex 15^{26} (R), Dt 27^{10}; ח׳ ומ׳ Dt 4^{40} 1 K 3^{14} 8^{61}; מ׳ וח׳ ותורה Ne 9^{14}; מ׳ ועדות וח׳ Dt 6^{17} 1 Ch 29^{19} 2 Ch 34^{31}; דברי מ׳ וח׳ Ezr 7^{11}; it is used c. vbs.: נתן Lv 26^{46} + 3 t.; צוּה Nu 30^{17} + 9 t.; למד Dt 4^{1} + 10 t.; שמר Dt 26^{17} + 16 t.; עשׂה Dt 6^{24} + 5 t.; שמר לעשות Dt 11^{32} + 4 t.; הלך בְּ 1 K 8^{61} + 3 t.—[On usage of חק v. חֻקָּה ad fin.]

†חֻקָּה 104 **n.f.** Ex 13,10 **something prescribed, enactment, statute;**—ח׳ Nu 9^{14} + 2 t.; cstr. חֻקַּת 2708

Ex 12^{14} + 28 t.; pl. חֻקּוֹת Je 5^{24} + 12 t.; חֻקֹּת Lv 20^{23} Je 31^{35}; sf. חֻקֹּתַי Gn 26^{5} + 14 t.; חֻקֹּתַי Lv 18^{4} + 21 t. etc.;—**1.** sg. *statute*, of special ritual laws: of passover Ex 13^{10} (J); elsewhere only in P (and H), חקת הפסח Ex 12^{43} Nu 9$^{12.14}$; ח׳ התורה Nu 19^{2} 31^{21}; ח׳ משפט Nu 27^{11} 35^{29}; ח׳ עולם Ex 12$^{14.17}$ 27^{21} 28^{43} 29^{9} Lv 3^{17} 7^{36} 10^{9} 16$^{29.31.34}$ 23$^{21.31}$ 24^{3} Nu 10^{8} 15^{15} 18^{23} 19$^{10.21}$ (all P), Lv 17^{7} 23$^{14.41}$ (H); חֻקָּה אַחַת לַגֵּר ולאזרח Nu 9^{14} 15^{15}. **2.** pl. *statutes:* **a.** of nature ח׳ שמים Jb 38^{33} Je 33^{25}; of moon and stars Je 31^{35}; of weeks of harvest Je 5^{24}. **b.** fig. of a firmly established custom ח׳ הגוי(ם) Lv 20^{23} (H) 2 K 17^{8}; ח׳ העמים Je 10^{3} ח׳ עמרי Mi 6^{16}; idolatry ח׳ ישׂראל 2 K 17^{19}; sexual offences Lv 18^{30} (H). **c.** ח׳ דוד statutes of David 1 K 3^{3}. **d.** ‖ משפטים 2 S 22^{23} = ψ 18^{23} (of the law known to David); ‖ מצות ψ 89^{32}; ברית וח׳ 1 K 11^{11}; elsewhere of the prescriptions of the codes of D, H, P, Ez: usu. חקות ומשפטים Lv 18$^{5.26}$ 19^{37} 20^{22} (H), 25^{18} Nu 9^{3} (P), 1 K 11^{33} Ez 5^{7} 11^{20} 18^{9} 20$^{11.13.19.21}$; preceded by מצות Dt 30^{16}; followed by מצות Lv 26^{15} (H), Dt 11^{1} 1 K 6^{12}; תורה ומצוה 2 K 17^{34}; or else משפטים וחקות Lv 18^{4} 26^{43} (H), Ez 5$^{6.6}$ 18^{17} 20$^{16.24}$ 37^{24}; preceded by מצות Dt 8^{11}; in diff. order, ח׳ מצות ומ׳ ועדות 1 K 2^{3}; frequently also ח׳ ומצות Lv 26^{3} (H), Dt 6^{2} 1 K 11^{38} 2 Ch 7^{19}; or מצות (ו)ח׳ Dt 10^{13} 28$^{15.45}$ 30^{10} 1 K 9^{6} 11^{34} Ez 43^{11} (Co), 2 K 17^{13}; foll. by תורות Gn 26^{5} (R); מצות ועדות וח׳ 2 K 23^{3}; תורה וח׳ Je 44^{10}; ותורה וח׳ 44^{23}; ח׳ ותורות Ez 44^{5} 43^{11} (Co); תורות יח׳ ועדות 44^{24}; special ordinances are ח׳ המזבח Ez 43^{18}; ח׳ בית י׳ Ez 44^{5}; ח׳ חיים Ez 33^{15} (which are life to those who keep them); ח׳ עולם תמיד (𝔊 𝔖 𝔙 Talm Co del. עולם) Ez 46^{14}. **e.** phrases of obedience are הלך ב׳ Lv 18^{3} 20^{23} 26^{3} (H), 1 K 3^{3} 6^{12} 2 K 17$^{8.19}$ Je 44$^{10.23}$ Ez 5$^{6.7}$ 11^{20} 18$^{9.17}$ 20$^{13.16.19.21}$ 33^{15}; שׁמר Lv 18$^{4.5.26}$ 19$^{19.37}$ 20$^{8.22}$ (H), Gn 26^{5} (R), Dt 6^{2} 8^{11} 10^{13} 11^{1} 28^{45} 30$^{10.16}$ 1 K 2^{3} 9^{6} 11$^{11.34.38}$ 2 K 17^{13} 23^{3} Ez 18$^{19.21}$ 37^{24} 43^{11} 44^{24}; עשׂה Lv 25^{18} (P), Dt 28^{15} 1 K 11^{33}; עשׂה כח׳ 2 K 17^{34}; בח׳ אֶשְׁתַּעֲשָׁע ψ 119^{16}; phrases of disobedience are מאס ח׳ Ez 20^{24} מאס בח׳ Lv 26^{15} (H); געל Lv 26^{43} (H); עזב 2 Ch 7^{19}; חלל ψ 89^{32}.—חֹק and חֻקָּה differ somewhat in shade of meaning and frequency in various writings: e.g. חק oftener in Jb ψ Pr (חֻקָּה not at all Pr, once Jb), and in Chr (חֻקָּה only 2 Ch 7^{19}); חֻקָּה oft. in K, rarely in Hex. except in P (H); in proph., חק occurs Am 2^{4} Is 5^{14} 24^{5} Mi 7^{11} Je 3 t., Ez 6 t., חֻקָּה only Ez, Je (6 t.) and Mi 6^{16}; חֻקִּים esp. in Dt and ψ 119, חֻקּוֹת esp. in H, Ez and sometimes (8 t.) Dt; חק עוֹלָם usu. = *due*, חֻקַּת ע׳ much more often *statute, ordinance*, etc.]

† [חֲקֹק] **n.pr.loc.** in tribe of Naphtali, only c. ה loc. חֲקֹקָה Jos 19^{34}; identif. with *Yakûk* c. 4 m. NW. of Lake Tiberias by Rob $^{BR iii. 81}$ Survey $^{WP i. 365}$. 2712

חוּקֹק† **n.pr.loc.** only 1 Ch 6^{60}, prob. err. for חֶלְקַת (q.v.) Jos 19^{25} 21^{31}. p. 324 2712

חֹקְקֵי v. חק supr. p. 349 2706

† [חָקַר] **vb. search** (NH *id.*, Niph. pass., Aram. חֲקַר)—**Qal** *Pf.* 3 ms. sf. וַחֲקָרוֹ consec. Pr 18^{17}; חֲקָרָהּ Jb 28^{27}; וְחָקַרְתָּ Dt 13^{15} etc.; *Impf.* יַחְקֹר Jb 13^{19}; יַחֲקָר־ ψ 44^{22}; יַחְקְרֶנּוּ Pr 28^{11}; אֶחְקֹר 1 S 20^{12}; תַּחְקְרוּן Jb 32^{11}; נַחְקְרָה La 3^{40} etc.; *Imv.* חָקְרֵנִי ψ 139^{23}; חִקְרוּ Ju 18^{2}; *Inf.* חֲקֹר 2 S 10^{3} + 2 t.; לַחְקוֹר Pr 23^{30}; לְחָקְרָהּ Ju 18^{2};—**1.** *search (for)*, sq. acc. Pr 23^{30} Jb 32^{11}; abs. וְדָרַשְׁתָּ וְחָקַרְתָּ וְשָׁאַלְתָּ הֵיטֵב Dt 13^{15}; lit. Ez 39^{14} (i.e. for bones unburied). **2. a.** *search through, explore*, lit., obj. הארץ Ju 18^{2} (‖ רַגֵּל) v^{2}, 1 Ch 19^{3} (‖ *id.*); city העיר 2 S 10^{3} (‖ *id.*), of mining Jb 28^{3}; *search out* a subject or matter Jb 5^{27} 28^{27} Pr 25^{2} ψ 44^{22}. **b.** *search* a man, find out his sentiments (AV *sound* him) 1 S 20^{12}. **c.** of י׳ *searching* man, c. acc. ψ 139^{1} (‖ ידע), v^{23} (‖ *id.*) Jb 13^{9}, cf. Je 17^{10} (obj. לֵב). **d.** of *examining thoroughly*, so as to expose weakness in a case Jb 29^{16} Pr 18^{17}, cf. 28^{11}; so of self-examination ח׳ דרכים La 3^{40} (‖ חפשׂ). **Niph.** *Pf.* נֶחְקַר 1 K 7^{47} 2 Ch 4^{18}; *Impf.* יֵחָקֵר Je 46^{23}; יֵחָקְרוּ Je 31^{37} *be searched out, found out, ascertained*, 1 K 7^{47} 2 Ch 4^{18} (weight of the bronze used in temple utensils), of forest Je 46^{23}; *searched out*, Je 31^{37} subj. מוסדי ארץ. **Pi.** *Pf.* חִקֵּר Ec 12^{9} *he sought out* many proverbs (מְשָׁלִים; ‖ אִזֵּן). 2713

†חֵקֶר **n.m.** $^{Ju 5,16}$ **searching, thing (to be) searched out**;—abs. חֵקֶר Jb 5^{9} + 8 t.; cstr. *id.* Jb 8^{8} + 2 t.; pl. cstr. חִקְרֵי Ju 5^{16};—חִקְרֵי לֵב Ju 5^{16} *searchings, questionings of heart;* Jb 11^{7} canst thou reach ח׳ אֱלוֹהַּ i.e. what is to be explored in him, the whole range of his nature, so ח׳ תהום 38^{16} the range of the deep; esp. אֵין ח׳ i.e. *it is unsearchable* Jb 5^{9} 9^{10} ψ 145^{3} Pr 25^{3} Is 40^{28}, cf. לא ח׳ Jb 34^{24} 36^{26}; ח׳ אבותם 8^{8} i.e. thing searched out by their fathers. 2714

† [מֶחְקָר] **n.m. range** (as place to be explored), מֶחְקְרֵי־אָרֶץ ψ 95^{4} (cf. חֵקֶר Jb 38^{16}). 4278

2352, 2356, חֹר *noble*, חוֹר, חֹר, חֻר *hole*, v. sub II. חרר; חֹר
2715, 2735 הַגִּדְגָּד v. sub II. חור. p. 301, 359

חרא, or **חרה** (√of following; meaning unknown).

2716 †[חֲרָא, or חֲרִי] **n.[m.]** dung (NH חרא (‐ֵי), *id.*; Aram. ܚܪܳܐ *id.*; Mand. חרא (on this and cogn. lang. in gen. v. Nö[M 56]); Ar. خُرْءٌ *id.*, whence vb. خَرِئَ of act, and n. مَخْرَأَةٌ of place; Amh. ሐሩ: (Di[Lex. Aeth. 88]))—pl. sf. חֲרָאֵיהֶם Is 36[12] Kt (Qr צוֹאָתָם); ‖ 2 K 18[27] has חֲרֵיהֶם (v. sg. חרי
2755, 6[25]; Qr as above); חֲרֵי יוֹנִים *dove's dung* 2 K
3123 6[25] Kt (Qr דִּבְיוֹנִים); v., further, Gei[Urschrift, 409].

4280 †[מַחֲרָאָה] **n.f.** pl. draught house, 2 K 10[27].

2717 †I. [חָרֵב] **vb. be dry, dried up** (cf. יָבֵשׁ) (Aram. חֲרוֹב *be dry*, חוּרְבָּא *drought*);—**Qal** *Pf.* 3 pl. חָרְבוּ Gn 8[13.13], Is 19[6]; *Impf.* 3 ms. יֶחֱרַב Ho 13[15] + 2 t., וַיֶּחֱרָב ψ 106[9]; *Imv.* fs. חֳרָבִי Is 44[27];—*be dry, dried up*: **1.** of ground, be freed from waters of flood ח׳ פְּנֵי הָאֲדָמָה Gn 8[13b] (J). **2.** of waters, *be dried up*, taken away; of waters of flood Gn 8[13a] (P); of Nile וְנָהָר יֶחֱרַב וְיָבֵשׁ Is 19[5] (‖ וְנִשְּׁתוּ־מַיִם מֵהַיָּם), v. same combination Jb 14[11] (‖ אָזְלוּ מַיִם מִנִּי־יָם); Is 19[6] (‖ דָּלְלוּ) 44[27] (‖ הוֹבִישׁ); of Red Sea ψ 106[9]; fig. of Ephraim's freshness and vigour Ho 13[15]. **Pu.** *Pf.* 3 pl. לֹא חֹרָבוּ Ju 16[7.8], of fresh bow-strings (of gut, v. Bla). **Hiph.** *Pf.* הֶחֱרִיב Na 1[4], of י׳'s *drying up* rivers (‖ וַיַּבְּשֵׁהוּ), perh. also Is 11[15] (for MT החרים) v. 𝔊 𝔖 𝔙 𝔗; וְהַחֲרַבְתִּי the Euphrates Je 51[36] (‖ הוֹבַשְׁתִּי); *Impf.* אַחֲרִיב יָם Is 50[2], subj. י׳, *I dry up a sea* (‖ אָשִׂים נְהָרוֹת מִדְבָּר); אַחְרִב Is 37[25] = אַחֲרִב 2 K 19[24], of king of Assyria *drying up* rivers of Egypt; *Pt.* fs. הַמַּחֲרֶבֶת Is 51[10] of י׳'s arm *drying up* (Red) Sea.

2720 †I. [חָרֵב] **adj. dry**, only fs. חֲרֵבָה Lv 7[10] of meal-offering not moistened (with oil; P); פַּת־חֲרֵבָה Pr 17[1] *a dry morsel.*

2721 †I. חֹרֶב **n.m.**[Gn 31, 40] **dryness, drought, heat,** abs. ח׳ Gn 31[40] + 11 t. + Dt 28[22] (for MT חֶרֶב; v. Di, sq. 𝔙; 𝔊 and 𝔊L om.);—**1.** *dryness* Ju 6[37.39.40] (all of absence of dew); Je 50[38] (‖ יָבֵשׁ); so rd. also Zc 11[17] (for MT חֶרֶב, see v[b] and Sta ZAW i. 1881, 29), *a drying up upon his arm* (i. e. a *withering*) *and upon his right eye.* **2.** *drought* Hg 1[11] + Dt 28[22] v. supr. **3.** *parching heat* (of sun) Gn 31[40] (opp. קֶרַח), Je 36[30] (opp. *id.*); Is 4[6] 25[4.5.5]; of fever Jb 30[30].

†חָרָבָה **n.f.** dry ground;—abs. ח׳ Gn 7[22] + 2724
7 t.; opp. הַיָּם Ex 14[21] (J), Hg 2[6]; cf. Gn 7[22] (J); opp. water of Jordan Jos 3[17.17] (J), 4[18] (E), 2 K 2[8]; of Nile-arms וְנָתַתִּי יְאֹרִים ח׳ Ez 30[12].

†[חֲרָבוֹן] **n.m.** drought, only pl. cstr. 2725
בְּחַרְבֹנֵי קַיִץ ψ 32[4] metaph. of fever heat.

†II. [חָרֵב] **be waste, desolate** (NH חָרֵב 2717
id.; Aram. חֲרוֹב, ܚܪܶܒ *be laid waste*; Zinj. חרב adj.; Ar. خَرِبَ *be in ruins, waste, depopulated*; As. *ḫarâbu*, *be waste*, Dl[Pr 175], *ḫuribtu*, *desert*, Lotz[TP]);—**Qal** *Impf.* 3 fs. תֶּחֱרַב Je 26[9], תֶּחֱרָב Is 34[10]; 3 mpl. יֶחֱרָבוּ Ez 6[6], יֶחֱרָבוּ Am 7[9] Is 60[12]; 3 fpl. תֶּחֱרַבְנָה Ez 6[6] 12[20]; *Imv.* חִרְבוּ (so, not חֹרְבוּ—Theile—see van d. H Hahn Kö[i. 244]) Je 2[12]; *Inf. abs.* חָרֹב Is 60[12];—*be waste, desolate;* of sanctuaries of Isr. Am 7[9] (‖ נָשַׁמּוּ), of altars Ez 6[6]; of cities Je 26[9] Ez 6[6] 12[20] (‖ שׁמם); of nations Is 34[10], 60[12] חָרֹב יֶחֱרָבוּ (‖ יֹאבֵדוּ); fig., in address to the heavens חִרְבוּ מְאֹד Je 2[12]—(‖ שֹׁמּוּ, וְשַׂעֲרוּ), *be very desolate* (at sins of Isr.); others, *be amazed, astounded* (on relation of meanings v. שׁמם). **Niph.** *Pt.* f. נֶחֱרֶבֶת Ez 26[19] as adj., *desolate* city, i.e. uninhabited, v. context; נַחֲרָבוֹת 30[17] of *desolate* countries (‖ נְשַׁמּוּ). **Hiph.** *Pf.* הֶחֱרִיב Ez 19[17]; 1 s. הֶחֱרַבְתִּי Zp 3[6]; 3 pl. הֶחֱרִיבוּ Is 37[18] 2 K 19[17]; *Impf.* 1 s. אַחֲרִיב Is 42[15]; *Pt.* מַחֲרִיב Ju 16[24]; pl. c. sf. מַחֲרִיבַיִךְ Is 49[17];—*lay waste, make desolate*, human subj.; nations and lands Is 37[18] = 2 K 19[17], Is 42[15], cf. pt. Is 49[17] (‖ מְהָרְסַיִךְ); add prob. with We Am 4[9] (הֶחֱרַבְתִּי) for the untranslateable הַרְבּוֹת) *I have devastated your gardens and vineyards;* pt. Ju 16[24] *desolater of our country* (‖ הִרְבָּה אֶת־חֲלָלֵינוּ); obj. cities Ez 19[7]; streets Zp 3[6] (‖ נִשְׁמוּ). **Hoph.** *Pf.* 3 fs. הָחֳרָבָה Ez 26[2] *she is laid waste*, of a city; *Pt.* מָחֳרָבוֹת Ez 29[12] *laid waste*, of cities (‖ שׁמם).

†II. חָרֵב **adj.** waste, desolate;—ms. abs. ח׳ 2720
Je 33[10] + 3 t.; fs. חֲרֵבָה Ne 2[3] + 2 t.; fpl. הֶחֳרֵבוֹת Ez 36[35.38] (v. Kö[i. 241]);—of a city, defined מֵאֵין אָדָם וּמֵאֵין בְּהֵמָה Je 33[10], cf. v[12]; also Ne 2[3.17]; הֶעָרִים הֶחֳרֵבוֹת Ez 36[35] (+ הַנְּשַׁמּוֹת, הַנֶּהֱרָסוֹת; opp. בְּצוּרוֹת יָשָׁבוּ).

†II. חֹרֶב **n.[m.]** desolation;—עָרֵי ח׳ Is 61[4] 2721
cities of desolation (‖ שֹׁמֵמוֹת, and, in v[a], חָרְבוֹת); cf. Zp 2[14] Je 49[13], and מִצְרַיִם חָרְבוֹת ח׳ Ez 29[10] Egypt shall be *wastes of desolation* (but 𝔊 𝔙 Co *wastes of the sword*, חֶרֶב for חֹרֶב); + Ez 38[8] Co, who rds. מֵחֶרֶב (or מְחָרָבָה).

2722 **†חֹרֵב, חוֹרֵב n.pr.mont.** Horeb (*waste, desert*)—𝔊 Χωρηβ (v. Lag$^{BN\ 85}$); אֱלֹהִים הָאֱלֹהִים חֹרֵבָה Ex 3^{1} (E), cf. עַד הַר הָאֱלֹהִים חֹרֵב 1 K 19^{8}; הַצּוּר בְּחֹרֵב Ex 17^{6}, מֵהַר חוֹרֵב 33^{6} (both E); בְּחֹרֵב Dt 1$^{2.6.19}$ 4$^{10.15}$ 5^{2} 9^{8} 18^{16} 28^{69}; 1 K 8^{9} 2 Ch 5^{10} ψ 106^{19} Mal 3^{22}; the sacred mountain of the wilderness, no geograph. diff. from סִינַי discoverable, but synonym of it in E and (esp.) D (except poem Dt 33^{2}; vid. סִינַי P).

2723 **†חָרְבָּה n.f. waste, desolation, ruin**;—abs. ח׳ Lv 26^{31} + 15 t. + Ez 38^{8} (del. 𝔊 Co) + Ez 38^{12} חרבה 𝔊 Co for חרבות; pl. חֳרָבוֹת ψ 9^{7} + 11 t. (Ez 38^{12}, cf. supr.); cstr. חָרְבוֹת Is 5^{17} + 7 t.; sf. חָרְבֹתַיִךְ Is 49^{19}; חָרְבֹתָיו Ezr 9^{9}; חָרְבֹתֶיהָ Is 51^{3}; חָרְבוֹתֶיהָ Is 44^{26}; חָרְבוֹתֵיהֶם ψ 109^{10} + 2 Ch 34^{6} (cf. חֶרֶב and infr.); (chiefly mid. and late Heb. Is^{2} 8 t.; Je 10 t. Ez 14 t.—incl. 38^{8}, q. del. Co);—**1.** *waste, ruin*, of cities of Israel Lv 26$^{31.33}$(H); Judah Is 44^{26} 49^{19} (‖ שֹׁמֵמוֹת), 58^{12} (בנה), Je 25^{18} 27^{17} 44$^{2.6}$ Ez 5^{14}; ruins of Jerusalem Is 52^{9} Dn 9^{2}; also Ez 35^{4}; cf. Mal 1^{4} (c. בנה), Ez 36^{10} (c. בנה) v^{33} (*id.*); Egypt Ez 29$^{9.10}$ (in both ‖ שְׁמָמָה; חרבות חֹרֶב in v^{10}); ruin of temple Ezr 9^{9}; =ruined dwellings ψ 109^{10}; cf. 2 Ch 34^{6}, where rd. perh. בְּחָרְבֹתֵיהֶם for בחר בתיהם (v. חֶרֶב sub III. חרב); Je 22^{5}; in gen. *ruins* (si vera l., v. Di; obj. of בנה) Jb 3^{14}; כּוֹס ח׳ ψ 102^{7} *an owl of a ruin*. **2.** of land: waste place amid ruins Is 5^{17}, cf. 51^{3} (‖ עֲרָבָה, מִדְבָּר); land a desolation Je 7^{34} 44^{22} Ez 25^{13} (Edom) Je 25^{11} Is 64^{10} and Ez 33$^{24.27}$ (of Judah), cf. Ez 13^{4}, כְּשֻׁעָלִים בח׳ sim. of the prophets; הַשֹּׁמֵמוֹת הח׳ Ez 36^{4} (of Israel); of desolation of enemies of Isr. ψ 9^{7} (ח׳ לָנֶצַח); ח׳ עולם = old ruins Is 61^{4} (c. בנה); elsewhere perpetual ruin, desolation Je 25^{9} 49^{13} (cities of Bosra); ח׳ מעולם Ez 26^{20} (sim. of Tyre).

2717 **†III. [חָרַב] vb.** (Aram. and rare) **attack, smite down** (cf. Ar. حَرَبَ *plunder*, III. *wage war with*, VI. *fight together*, حَرْبٌ *war, battle;* Syr. ܚܪܒ *smite, slay*)—**Qal** *Imv.* ms. חֲרֹב Je 50^{21} *attack* (+ וְהַחֲרֵם אַחֲרֵיהֶם); mpl. חִרְבוּ v^{27} obj. כָּל־פָּרֶיהָ, fig. of men of Babylon. **Niph.** *Pf.* 3 pl. נֶחֶרְבוּ המלכים (v. **Hoph.**) הָחֳרֵב 2 K 3^{23} *the kings have attacked one another, fought together* (‖ וַיַּכּוּ אִישׁ אֶת־רֵעֵהוּ). **Hoph.** *Inf. abs.* 2 K 3^{23}, v. **Niph.**, but rd. perhaps הֶחֳרֵב, cf. Dr Lv 19^{20}, note.

2719 **חֶרֶב$_{411}$ n.f.**$^{Is\ 21,\ 15}$ **sword** (as weapon; Aram. חַרְבָּא, ܚܰܪܒܳܐ, Zinj. חרב; Ar. حَرْبَةٌ *dart, javelin*)—abs. חֶרֶב Gn 3^{24} +; חָרֶב Ex 17^{13} +; cstr. חֶרֶב Dt 33^{29} +; sf. חַרְבִּי Ex 15^{9} + 13 t.; חַרְבְּךָ Gn 27^{40} + 7 t.; חַרְבֶּךָ 1 S 17^{33} ψ 17^{13}; חַרְבּוֹ Nu 22^{23} + 24 t.; חַרְבְּכֶם Je 2^{30} Ez 33^{26}; חַרְבָּם ψ 37^{15} 44^{4}; pl. חֲרָבוֹת Is 21^{15} + 5 t.; cstr. חַרְבוֹת Jos 5^{2} + 2 t.; sf. חַרְבוֹתָיו Ez 26^{9}; חַרְבוֹתָם Is 2^{4} + 5 t.; חַרְבֹתֵיהֶם Mi 4^{3} + 2 t.;—**1. a.** *sword*, as weapon of war Gn 48^{22} (E), Ju 7$^{14.20}$ 1 S 21^{9}, and so in all periods; *two-edged* (short) *sword* ח׳ וְלָהּ שְׁנֵי פֵיוֹת גֹּמֶד אָרְכָּהּ Ju 3^{16}, cf. ח׳ פִּיּוֹת Pr 5^{4} (in sim.), ח׳ פִּיפִיּוֹת ψ 149^{6}; v. also צוּר ח׳ *edge of sword* ψ 89^{44}. **b.** *gird on sword* = חָגַר הח׳ 1 S 17^{39} 25$^{13.13.13}$ ψ 45^{4} (הח׳ (עַל יָרֵךְ), שִׂים על ירך Ex 32^{27}, cf. esp. 2 S 20^{8}. **c.** *draw the sword* הֵרִיק הח׳ Ex 15^{9} Lv 26^{33} Ez 5$^{2.12}$ 12^{14} 28^{7}, הוציא הח׳ Ez 21$^{8.10}$, פתח הח׳ ψ 37^{14} Ez 21^{33}, נטש Is 21^{15} (Gr Che לטש v. infr.); usu. שָׁלַף הח׳ Nu 22$^{23.31}$ Jos 5^{13} Ju 3^{22} 8$^{10.20}$ 9^{54} 1 S 17^{51} 31^{4} = 1 Ch 10^{4} 21^{16}, and as characteristic of warriors שֹׁלֵף ח׳ Ju 20$^{2.15.17.25.35.46}$ 2 S 24^{9} 2 K 3^{26}, 1 Ch 21$^{5.5}$; וַתִּדְבַּק יָדוֹ אֶל־הַח׳ 2 S 23^{10}, ins. also in ‖ 1 Ch 11^{13} (Dr). **d.** *whet, sharpen the sword* לטש הח׳ ψ 7^{13} (cf. Is 21^{15} supr.), but also שנן Dt 32^{41} cf. ψ 64^{4}, הוּחַדָּה Ez 21$^{14.16}$. **e.** put up the sword into the sheath הֵשִׁיב הח׳ אֶל־נְדָנָהּ 1 Ch 21^{27} (*sheath* of sword is elsewhere תַּעַר 1 S 7^{51} 2 S 20^{8} Je 47^{6} Ez 21^{8}). **f.** *slay with sword* הרג בח׳ Jos 10^{11} 13^{22} +; in ימותו אנשים 1 S 2^{33}, insert בְּחֶרֶב before אנשים 𝔊 We Dr; rarely הכה בח׳ Jos 11^{10} 2 K 19^{37} = Is 37^{38}; very oft. הִכָּה לְפִי־ח׳ *smite acc. to the mouth of the sword* i.e as the sword can devour (2 S 2^{26} 11^{25}) = *without quarter* Nu 21^{24} (E) Dt 13^{16a} 20^{13} Jos 11$^{11.12.14}$ (all D) Ju 18^{27} 21^{10} 1 K 10^{25} Jb 1$^{15.17}$; also c. העיר as sole obj. Jos 8^{24} 10$^{28.30.32.35.37}$, cf. v^{39} 19^{47} Ju 1$^{8.25}$ 20^{37} 1 S 22$^{19.19}$ 2 S 15^{14}; הרג לפי־ח׳ + Gn 34^{26} (J); החרים לפי־ח׳ Dt 13^{16b} (incl. הָעִיר in obj.), Jos 6^{21} 1 S 15^{8}, חלשׁ לפי־ח׳ + Ex 17^{13} (E); נפל לפי־ח׳ Jos 8^{24} Ju 4^{16}; וַיָּהָם י׳ ... לפי־ח׳ Ju 4^{15};—(לפי־ח׳) is chiefly in Jos and Ju (21 t.), in Hexat. only JED; but Jb post-ex.). **g.** אכלה הח׳ etc., of the sword as *devouring*:—תֹּאכַל חַרְבִּי בָשָׂר Dt 32^{42} (poet.), 2 S 2^{26} 11^{25} 18^{8} Is 1^{10} Je 2^{30} Je 46$^{10.14}$ Na 2^{14}. **h.** *slain by sword* is חַלְלֵי־ח׳ Nu 19^{16} (P) and frequently Ez, חַלְלֵי־ח׳ 31$^{17.18}$ 32$^{21.25.28.29.30.32}$ 35^{8} מְחֻלְּלֵי ח׳ v^{26} < Co חללי־ח׳ (on text of 32$^{20.22.31}$ v. Co). **i.** שְׁבֻיוֹת ח׳ Gn 31^{26} are *captives of* (taken by) *sword*. **j.** sword frequently agent of י׳ Ju 7^{20} Is 34^{6} Je 12^{12} 47^{6} etc.,—so Dt 28^{22}, but rd. חֹרֶב v. sub I. חרב (cf. on other hand 1 S 17^{47}); note esp. Gn 3^{24} לַהַט הח׳ הַמִּתְהַפֶּכֶת; poet. לַהַב ח׳ Na 3^{3}, בְּרַק ח׳ Dt 32^{41}.

k. ח׳ fig. of tongue ψ 57[5] cf. 59[8]; fig. of violence, war, etc., Gn 27[40]; in sim. Pr 5[4] (of grievous end of dealings with strange women). **2.** *knife* ח׳ צֻרִים flint knives for use in circumcision Jos 5[2.3] (v. We[Skizzen iii, 166]); Ez 5[1.2] ח׳ חַדָּה תַּעַר הַגַּלָּבִים (acc. to Co use of *sword* as razor is significant). **3.** of tools used in hewing stone חַרְבְּךָ הֵנַפְתָּ עליה Ex 20[25]; יִתֵּן בח׳ Ez 26[9], acc. to most=*tools*, axes, 'steel' (Co '*Eisen*'), but poss. *swords* as implement ready to hand; 2 Ch 34[6] Qr בְּחַרְבֹתֵיהֶם *with their tools;* rd. perh. בְּחָרְבֹתֵיהֶם *in their ruins*, Be, who comp. ψ 109[10]; v. חָרְבָּה sub II. חרב (𝔊 𝔙 om. חרב).

2726 †חַרְבוֹנָא **n.pr.m.** eunuch of Ahasuerus Est 1[10]=חַרְבוֹנָה 7[9] (Pers. خربان=*donkey driver*, Vullers[i, 668 b]).

2726 חַרְבוֹנָה **n.pr.m.** v. foregoing.

2727 †[חָרַג] **vb.** quake (cf. (si vera l.) Ar. حَرِجَ *be straitened, unable to move for fear and rage* (Lane), also *put oneself in a rage* (Dozy); 𝔗 חַרְגַת מוֹתָא Dt 32[25] *terror of death*)—only **Qal** *Impf.* 3 mpl. וְיַחְרְגוּ מִמִּסְגְּרוֹתֵיהֶם ψ 18[46] pregn. *and come quaking out of their fortresses* (cf. יִרְגְּזוּ in like connex. Mi 7[17]); rd. the same also in ‖ 2 S 22[46] (for MT וְיַחְגְּרוּ, v. חגר; possible would be also ויחרדו in both, as Ho 11[10.11] etc.)

חרגל (quadril. √of foll.; cf. Ar. حَرْجَلَ *run right and left, run swiftly* (Frey)).

2728 חַרְגֹּל **n.[m.]** a kind of **locust** (NH *id.;* Aram. ܚܰܪܓܽܘܠܳܐ, חַרְגּוֹלָא; حَرْجَلٌ (Dozy), all = *locust;* حَرْجَلَةٌ *swarm of locusts* (Frey))—only Lv 11[22] (P) in list of edible insects, ‖ אַרְבֶּה, חָגָב, סָלְעָם.

2729 †חָרֵד **vb.** tremble, be terrified (As. *ḫarâdu*, *id.*, acc. to Dl[HA 20, Pr 46]; Ar. خَرِدَ *be bashful, shamefaced;* NH חֲרָדָה *a trembling*)—**Qal** *Pf.* וְחָרַד consec. Is 19[16], חָרְדָה Is 10[29], חָרַדְתְּ 2 K 4[13], חָרְדוּ 1 S 13[7] 14[15], וְחָרְדוּ consec. Ez 26[16] 32[10]; *Impf.* יֶחֱרַד Jb 37[1], וַיֶּחֱרַד Gn 27[33] +5 t.; יֶחֶרְדוּ Ho 11[10] Ez 26[18], יֶחֶרְדוּ Ho 11[11], יֶחֱרָ֑דוּ Am 3[6] Is 41[6], וַיֶּחֶרְדוּ Gn 42[28]+2 t.; *Imv.* חִרְדוּ Is 32[11];—**1.** *tremble, quake,* of a mountain Ex 19[18]—so 𝔐, but rd. הָעָם, 𝔊 v. Di (E); of isles Ez 26[18] (metaph., in fear); so Is 41[5] (קְצוֹת הארץ, ‖ איים יראו). **2.** *tremble,* of persons under supernat. infl. 1 S 14[15] (‖ וַתִּרְגַּז הָאָרֶץ, חֲרָדָה); *start, start up* (out of sleep) Ru 3[8]; in mental disturbance Gn 27[33] (J; c. acc. cogn.) *tremble,* in terror Ex 19[16] (E), Is 32[11] (‖ רגז), *be startled* (at sound of trumpet) Am 3[6] cf. 1 K 1[49] (+קום, ירא, הלך); *tremble* Ez 26[16] 32[10] sq. לְ=*at*, Jb 37[1] (לִבִּי), *be terrified,* of Egypt (personif.) Is 19[16] (‖ פָּחַד), Ramah 10[29], of Saul 1 S 28[5] subj. לִבּוֹ, ‖ ירא). **3.** *be anxiously careful* חָרַדְתְּ אֵלֵינוּ אֶת־כָּל הַחֲרָדָה הַזֹּאת 2 K 4[13]. **4.** with preps. pregn. = *go* or *come trembling* 1 S 13[7] (sq. מֵאחריו 𝔊L We Dr) Gn 42[28] (E; sq. אֶל־) 1 S 16[4] (sq. לִקְרָאתוֹ) so 21[2], Ho 11[10] (מִיָּם) v[11] (מִמִּצְרַיִם).
Hiph. *Pf.* הֶחֱרִיד Ju 8[12], וְהַחֲרַדְתִּי 2 S 17[2]; *Pt.* מַחֲרִיד Lv 6[26]+11 t.; *Inf. cstr.* הַחֲרִיד Ez 30[9] Zc 2[4];—*drive in terror, rout* an army, sq. acc. Ju 8[12] Ez 30[9] Zc 2[4] cf. 2 S 17[2]; (We prop. החרידו Ho 5[8] '*setzt Benj. in Schrecken,*' for MT אַחֲרֶיךָ); in *Pt.* abs., only in וְאֵין מ׳; *and none shall terrify,* i.e. disturb the peace of those reposing—שׁכב, ישׁב לָבֶטַח, ישׁב, רבץ, שׁקט—in the promised land Lv 26[6], so after captivity Je 30[10]=46[27], also Ez 34[28] 39[26] Mi 4[4] Zp 3[13]; of undisturbed peace of the righteous Jb 11[19]; peace of flocks in forsaken cities Is 17[2]; undisturbed feeding on carrion by fowl and beast Dt 28[26] Je 7[33], undisturbed prowling of lions Na 2[12] (metaph. of Assyrians).

†חָרֵד **adj.verb.** of foregoing, trembling;— 2730
חָרֵד Ju 7[3]+3 t.; חֲרֵדִים Is 66[5] Ezr 10[3]—*trembling* (from fear), abs. Ju 7[3] (‖ ירא), 1 S 4[13] (subj. לִבּוֹ, sq. עַל, *for*, in behalf of); in awe and reverence, at word of God, sq. בְּ Ezr 9[4] Is 66[2] (sq. עַל), v[5] (sq. אֶל); cf. ח׳ בְּמִצְוַת אל׳ Ezr 10[3].

†חֲרֹד **n.pr.loc.** only עֵין ח׳ (v. sub עַיִן), 5878
a camping-place of Gideon and Israel. Ju 7[1]. p. 745

†חֲרֹדִי **adj.loc.** only c. art. הַח׳, of Harod 2733
2 S 23[25a] (v. Dr and Ju 7[1]);=הַהֲרוֹרִי 1 Ch 11[27] 2033
(rd. הַחֲרוֹדִי); also 1 S 23[25b] but prob. not genuine; not in 𝔊 or 1 Ch 11, 27 (v. Dr and אֱלִיקָא supr. p. 45[b]).

†I. חֲרָדָה **n.f.** trembling, fear, anxiety— 2731
חֲרָדָה Gn 27[33]+5 t.+Ez 38[21] (rd. for הָרַי, B Co cf. Dr 1 S 14[15]); cstr. חֶרְדַּת 1 S 14[15] Pr 29[25] (v. Lag[BN 113]); pl. חֲרָדוֹת Ez 26[16];—**1.** *trembling, quaking* (of terror ascribed to supernat. cause) 1 S 14[15.15] (hence ח׳ אלהים v. Dr; ‖ וַתִּרְגַּז הארץ) cf. Ez 38[21] (v. supr.); Dn 10[7]; קוֹל ח׳ Je 30[5] *voice of trembling;* sq. gen. obj. ח׳ אָדָם Pr 29[25] *trembling before man;* opp. pleasure Is 21[4]; *tremblings* (pl.) Ez 26[16] under fig. of garment (ח׳ ילבשׁו), of effect on coast-princes of fall of Tyre. **2.** *anxious care* 2 K 4[13], acc. cogn. c. חָרַד.

2732 †II. חֲרָדָה **n.pr.loc.** a station of Isr. in wilderness Nu 33$^{24.25}$, site unknown.

2734, 8474 †חָרָה **vb.** **burn, be kindled, of anger** (Aram. חרי Pa. *cause fire to burn* (rare); Zinj. חרא *anger*, Nö ZMG 1893, 98. 103; Ar. حَرْوَةٌ *burning sensation, in throat,* etc., *fr. rage and pain*)—**Qal** *Pf.* ח׳ Gn 4^{6} + 20 t.; *Impf.* יֶחֱרֶה Ex 32^{11} + 2 t.; יִחַר Gn 18^{30} + 7 t.; וַיִּחַר Gn 4^{5} + 46 t.; *Inf. abs.* חָרֹה 1 S 20^{7}; cstr. חֲרוֹת 2 S 24^{1} ψ 124^{3};— **1.** of man: **a.** חרה אף (one's) *anger was kindled, burned* Gn 39^{19} Nu 22^{27} (J), Ex 32$^{19.22}$ (JE), Ju 9^{30} 14^{19} 1 S 11^{6} Jb 32$^{2.5}$; c. בְּ *against* Gn 30^{2} (E), 44^{18} (J), 1 S 17^{28} 20^{30} 2 S 12^{5} 2 Ch 25^{10} ψ 124^{3} Jb 32$^{2.3}$; c. אֶל Nu 24^{10} (E). **b.** impers., אף omitted; חרה לְ *it was kindled for* (him) *he burned with anger* Gn 31^{36} (E), 4$^{5.6}$ 34^{7} Nu 16^{15} (J), 1 S 15^{11} (rd. perh. וַיֵּצֶר, Weir in Dr), 18^{8} 20$^{7.7}$ 2 S 3^{8} 6^{8} = 1 Ch 13^{11}, 2 S 13^{21} 19^{43} Ne 3^{33} 4^{1} 5^{6} Jon 4$^{1.4.9.9}$; ins. ויחר לדוד 2 S 11^{22} 𝔊 We Dr; ח׳ בְּעֵינֵי Gn 31^{35} 45^{5} (E). **2.** of God: **a.** ח׳ אף Ex 22^{23} Nu 22^{22} (E), Nu 11$^{1.10}$ 32^{10} (J); c. בְּ Ex 4^{14} 32^{10} Nu 12^{9} Dt 31^{17} (J), 6^{15} 7^{4} 11^{17} 29^{26} Jos 23^{16} (D), Ju 6^{39} 2 S 6^{7} = 1 Ch 13^{10}, Ho 8^{5} 2 K 23^{26} 2 Ch 25^{15} Jb 42^{7}; בְּעַם Ex 32^{11} Nu 11^{33} (J), Is 5^{25} ψ 106^{40}; בישׂראל Nu 25^{3} 32^{13} (JE); Ju 2$^{14.20}$ 3^{8} 10^{7} 2 S 24^{1} 2 K 13^{3}; בבני ישׂראל Jos 7^{1} (R); בנהרים, אף omitted, Hb 3^{8}; c. עַל Zc 10^{3}. **b.** חרה לְ Gn 18$^{30.32}$ (J) 2 S 22^{8} = ψ 18^{8}.—*Note:* חרה not in H P (who use קצף); nor in Je Ez Is^{2} Pr or poetry of Jb. **Niph.** *Pf.* נִחֲרוּ sq. בְּ Ct 1^{6} (acc. to Bö ii. 379 De Kö i. 551) *be angry* with; *Pt.* כֹּל הַנֶּחֱרִים בְּ׳ *all that are incensed against* (*thee*) Is 41^{11}, so 45^{24}. **Hiph.** *Pf.* הֶחֱרָה הֶחֱזִיק Ne 3^{20} *burned with zeal* (?) *in repairing*, but 𝔊 om. החרה; prob. dittogr.; *Impf.* וַיִּחַר עָלַי אַפּוֹ Jb 19^{11} *and kindled his anger against me.* **Hithp.** *Impf.* אַל תִּתְחַר ψ 37$^{1.7.8}$ Pr 24^{19} *heat oneself in vexation.*—The foll. forms are somewhat dub.: *Impf.* 2 ms. אֵיךְ תְּתַחֲרֶה אֶת־הַסּוּסִים Je 12^{5} *how canst thou hotly contend* (in a race) *with the horses? Pt.* כִּי אַתָּה מְתַחֲרֶה בָאֶרֶז Je 22^{15} *because thou strivest eagerly* (to excel) *in cedar;* expl. as *Tiphʿēl* by Thes Ges § 55, 5 Ew § 122 a Ol § 255 a Sta § 159 b Kö i. p. 557 al., and regarded by most as a rare *causative* stem; but ag. existence of *Tiphʿēl* v. Ba NB § 180 a; ZMG 1894, 20; Ba regards the form as denom. (fr. a noun formed by ת preform., cf. Aram. ܬܚܪܝܢܐ *contention*); SS would point as Hithp. [cf. Syr. ܐܬܚܪܝ *contend with,* ܚܪܝܢܐ *contention*], although meaning of Hithp. is diff., v. supr.

†חָרוֹן **n.m.** (burning of) anger (cf. Lag BN 2740
204 Anm. **)—ח׳ Ez 7^{12} + 2 t.; cstr. חֲרוֹן Nu 25^{4} + 33 t.; sf. חֲרוֹנִי Ez 7^{14} (Co חרון), חֲרוֹנוֹ ψ 2^{5}; חֲרֹנְךָ Ex 15^{7}; pl. sf. חֲרוֹנֶיךָ ψ 88^{17};—alw. of God's anger (v. note, infr.), חֲרוֹן אַף Ex 32^{12} Nu 25^{4} 32^{14} Jos 7^{26} (J), Dt 13^{18} 1 S 28^{18} 2 K 23^{26} 2 Ch 28$^{11.13}$ 29^{10} 30^{8} Ezr 10^{14} Ho 11^{9} Na 1^{6} Zp 2^{2} 3^{8} Is 13$^{9.13}$ Je 4$^{8.26}$ 12^{13} 25$^{37.38}$ 30^{24} 49^{37} 51^{45} Jon 3^{9} ψ 69^{25} 78^{49} 85^{4} Jb 20^{23} La 1^{12} 4^{11}; אף om., Ex 15^{7} (song), Ne 13^{18} ψ 2^{5} Ez 7^{12} (del. Co), v^{14}; pl. *bursts of burning anger* ψ 88^{17}.—*Note:* כְּמוֹ־חָרוֹן ψ 58^{10} *burning anger* 𝔊 𝔙 Jer AV Bae Che; but Thes MV SS DeW Ew Ol Pe, something burning, e.g. thorns, antith. *green* thorns; Hengst De *cooked* flesh, antith. *raw;* Je 25^{38} מפני ח׳ הַיּוֹנָה because of the *fierceness of the oppressor* (? AV) would then be the only use of the word of other than God's anger; here 𝔊 𝔗 Ew Hi Gf Ke Che Gie RV rightly rd. חרב *oppressing sword* (as 46^{16} 50^{16}). חרון is not used in H P D^{2} or E (except song, Ex 15^{7}) of the Hex; nor in Ez except 7^{12} (del. Co), v^{14}.

†חֳרִי **n.m.** burning, alw. חֳרִי (הָ)אַף of Moses 2750
Ex 11^{8} (J); Jonathan 1 S 20^{34}; army of Ephraim 2 Ch 25^{10}; Rezin Is 7^{4}; of God Dt 29^{23} La 2^{3}.

חַרְהֲיָה v. חרחיה. below 2736

†חֲרוּמַף **n.pr.m.** father of one of the 2739
builders of the wall Ne 3^{10}.

חרז (√ of foll.; NH חָרַז *string together,* esp. jewels or pearls; Aram. חֲרַז *id.;* ܚܪܙ *id.;* Ar. خَرَزَ *sew* or *stitch,* خَرَزٌ *beads strung together, neck-ornament*).

†[חָרוּז] **n.[m.]** **string of beads,** only pl. 2737
צַוָּארֵךְ בַּחֲרוּזִים Ct 1^{10} *thy neck* (is comely) *with strings of beads.*

†חַרְהֲיָה (van d. H חרחיה), **n.pr.m.** (√ and 2736
mng. unknown)—father of one of the builders of the wall, Neh.'s time Ne 3^{8}.

חַרְחֻר, חַרְחוּר v. sub I. חרר. p. 359 2744, 2746

†חַרְחַס **n.pr.m.** grandfather of Shallum, 2745
who was husband of Huldah the prophetess 2 K 22^{14}.

I. חרט (√ of foll.; Aram. ܚܪܛ *cut, scratch, tear;* cf. Ar. خَرَطَ *peel off bark, strip off leaves* (mod. Ar. *turn* wood), مِخْرَطٌ *iron instrument for doing this*).

†חֶרֶט **n.[m.]** **graving-tool, stylus—1.** 2747
graving-tool, with which Aaron fashioned (וַיָּצַר)

the molten calf Ex 32^{4} (E). **2.** *stylus*, for writing on tablet (גִּלָּיוֹן): כְּתֹב עָלָיו בְּחֶרֶט אֱנוֹשׁ Is 8^{1} *write on it with a man's* (i.e. an ordinary) *stylus*=in common characters, intelligible to all (v. Benz $^{Arch. 290}$).

2748 †[חַרְטֹם] **n.m.** $^{Ex\ 7, 22}$**engraver, writer,** only in deriv. sense of one possessed of occult knowledge, *diviner, astrologer, magician* (prob.= חֶרֶט+ם, v. Di Ol $^{§216, 5}$ Sta $^{§§295, 327\ a}$)—only pl. abs. חַרְטֻמִּים Gn 41^{24}+4 t.; חַרְטֻמִּם Ex 8^{15} 9^{11}; cstr. חַרְטֻמֵּי Gn 41^{8}+2 t.;—**1.** *magicians* of Egypt Gn 41^{8} (E; ‖ חֲכָמִים), v^{24} (E), Ex $8^{3.14.15}$ 7^{11} (‖ מְכַשְּׁפִים, חֲכָמִים), v^{22} $9^{11.11}$ (all P). **2.** *magicians* of Babylon Dn 2^{2} (‖ מְכַשְּׁפִים, אַשָּׁפִים, כַּשְׂדִּים).

II. **חרט** (√of foll.; relation to I. חרט obscure).

2754 †[חָרִיט] **n.m.** $^{1K\ 5, 23}$**bag, purse** (cf. Ar. خَرِيطَةٌ *bag* or *purse* made of skin or other material)—only pl. abs. שְׁנֵי חֲרִטִים 2 K 5^{23}, containing each a talent of silver; הַחֲרִיטִים Is 3^{22} in list of ladies' finery.

2751 I. חֹרִי *white bread* v. sub I. חור. p. 301

2752-53 II. חֹרִי, חוֹרִי **n.pr.gent.** v. sub III. חרר. p. 360

2755 חֲרִיהֶם, חֲרֵי יוֹנִים v. [חרי, חרא]. p. 351

2760 †I. [חָרַךְ] **vb. set in motion, start** (cf. Ar. حَرَّكَ *move, be agitated*, II. *set in motion*)—only **Qal** *Impf.* 3 ms. לֹא־יַחֲרֹךְ רְמִיָּה צֵידוֹ Pr 12^{27} *slackness* (i.e. a slack or slothful man) *doth not start its game* De RVm, cf. Now (>Be Ew after Jewish trad., *doth not roast*, Aram. חֲרַךְ, ܚܪܟ *scorch, parch*).

II. **חרך** (√of foll.; meaning unknown).

2762 †חֲרַכִּים **n.[m.]pl. lattice** or other opening through which one may look (Aram. חֲרַכָּא 𝔗 Jos 2^{15} al.=Heb. חַלּוֹן; but NH חֲרַךְ is an opening smaller than a window)—only מֵצִיץ מִן־הַח׳ Ct 2^{9} *peeping in at the lattice* (‖ מַשְׁגִּיחַ מִן־הַחַלֹּנוֹת).

חרל (√of foll.; meaning unknown).

2738 †חָרוּל **n.[m.]** a kind of weed, perh. **chick-pea** (*cicercula*), v. Löw $^{p. 153}$ (Syr. ܚܘܪܠܐ *fodder for horses;* 𝔗 Pr 24^{31} gives חוּרְלָא)—abs. ח׳ Jb 30^{6} Zp 2^{9}; pl. חֲרֻלִּים Pr 24^{31};—as growing in devastated land, coll. Zp 2^{9}; in vineyard of slothful, pl. כָּסּוּ פָנָיו ח׳ Pr 24^{31} (‖ קִמְּשֹׂנִים); as sole shelter of certain outcast peoples Jb 30^{7} (שִׂיחִים).

†I. [חָרַם] **vb. Hiph.** ban, devote, exter- 2763
minate (MI ^{17} החרמתה of *devoting, dedicating* a city to Chemosh, in cl. with כי explaining massacre of all inhabitants; the altar-hearth of י׳ there was dragged before Chemosh; حَرُمَ *be prohibited, forbidden, unlawful, become sacred;* II. *make, pronounce sacred, inviolable;* Eth. **ሐረመ፡** *prohibit from common use, consecrate to God, esteem unlawful;* Palm. חרם=*consacré* Vog $^{No\ 35}$; Nab. *id.*, Eut $^{p. 28}$; Sab. מחרם *sanctuary, temple,* Os $^{ZMG\ 1865,\ 176.\ 252}$, חרמתן DHM $^{ZMG\ 1875,\ 594}$; Aram. אַחֲרֵים, and esp. ܐܚܪܡ *anathematize, excommunicate;* v. also We $^{Skizzen\ iii,\ 165}$, Dr $^{Sm\ 100\ ff.}$, RS $^{Sem.\ i.\ 140\ (150)}$)—**Hiph.** *Pf.* הֶחֱרִים Jos 8^{26}+5 t.; הֶחֱרִם Jos 10^{28}; 2 ms. וְהַחֲרַמְתָּה 1 S 15^{18}; 1 s. וְהַחֲרַמְתִּי 1 S 15^{20}; וְהַחֲרַמְתִּי Nu 21^{2}; 2 fs. וְהַחֲרַמְתְּ(י) consec. Mi 4^{13} (so 𝔊 𝔙 𝔖 𝔗 RV most; MT 1 s.), v. Ges $^{§44,\ R.\ 4}$; pl. הֶחֱרִימוּ 1 S 15^{9} 2 Ch 32^{14} etc.; (1 S 15^{3} rd. והחרמתו 𝔊 We Dr); *Impf.* יַחֲרִם Lv 27^{28}; וַיַּחֲרֵם Nu 21^{3} Jos 10^{37}; sf. וַיַּחֲרִימָהּ Jos 10^{1}; 1 pl. וַנַּחֲרֵם Dt 2^{34} 3^{6} etc.; *Imv.* הַחֲרֵם Dt 13^{16}; pl. הַחֲרִימוּ Je 51^{3}; sf. הַחֲרִימוּהָ Je 50^{26}; *Inf. abs.* הַחֲרֵם Dt 3^{6}+4 t.; cstr. הַחֲרִים 2 Ch 20^{23} Dn 11^{44}; sf. הַחֲרִימָם Jos 11^{20}+4 t.;—*ban, devote* (esp. religiously, sq. objects hostile to the theocracy [v. esp. Ex 22^{19} Hoph.]; this involved gen. their destruction; when a city was 'devoted' the inhab. were put to death, the spoil being destroyed or not acc. to the gravity of the occasion [contrast Jos $6^{17.21}$ 1 S 15^{3} with Dt $2^{34f.}$ $3^{6.7}$], cf. MI ^{17} לעשתר כמש החרמתה *to Ashtar-Chemosh I devoted it*, i.e. the city Nebo);—**1.** most oft. of devoting to destruction cities of Canaanites and other neighbours of Isr., *exterminating* inhabitants, and destroying or appropriating their possessions: **a.** Isr. and her leaders subj. Nu $21^{2.3}$ (destruction acc. to vow), Jos 6^{21} (cf. חֵרֶם ליהוה v^{17}; all J); in v^{18} rd. תַּחְמְדוּ (for MT תַּחֲרִימוּ, v. Di VB); 8^{26} (𝔊, not 𝔊L, om. v.), 10^{1} (JE), Dt 2^{34} $3^{6.6}$ $7^{2.2}$ (commanded through Moses, cf. for underlying thought $v^{4.5.6}$), $20^{17.17}$ (commanded by י׳), Jos 2^{10} $10^{28.35.37.39.40}$ (divine command), $11^{11.12.20.21}$ (divine command $v^{12.20}$; all D), 1 S $15^{3.8.9.9.15.18.20}$ (divine command $v^{3.18.20}$, cf. $v^{11.22.23}$); quite secondary is simple *exterminate* 1 K 9^{21}, 1 Ch 4^{41}. **b.** secondary mng. *destroy, exterminate*, also with other nations subj.:—2 K 19^{11}=Is 37^{11}=2 Ch 32^{14}, 2 Ch 20^{23}, Je $50^{21.26}$ (both by divine command), 51^{3} Dn 11^{44}. **c.** *God as subj.*, fig. all nations and their armies Is 34^{2}; the nations of Western Asia Je 25^{9}; the tongue of the Egyptian sea (by drying it up)

Is 11^{15} (but rd. perh. החריב with 𝔊 𝔖 𝔙 𝔗). **d.** so also of *devoting* even Israelites: a city of Isr. for worshipping other gods Dt 13^{16}; residents of Jabesh-Gilead for not joining in campaign against Benj. Ju 21^{11}. **2.** *devote to* 'י: for sacred uses החרים ליהוה the spoil of the nations Mi 4^{13}; private possessions, whether a man, animal, or field Lv 27^{28} (P). **Hoph.** *Impf.* יָחֳרַם Lv 27^{29} Ezr 10^{8}; יָחֳרָם Ex 22^{19};—**1.** *be put under the ban, devoted* (to death), for worshipping other gods than 'י Ex 22^{19} (JE; earliest use of word in OT); for some other theocratic offence Lv 27^{29} (P; v. Di). **2.** *devoted*, i.e. *forfeited*, to the temple treasures Ezr 10^{8}.—On חרם v. esp. Di (Kn) Lv 27^{28}; Ew $^{Antiq. 75.78}$, Dr 1 S 15^{33}.

2764 †I. חֵ֫רֶם **n.m.** $^{Lv 27, 28}$ **1. devoted thing. 2.**
devotion, ban;—ח' abs. Jos 6^{17} + 24 t. (most rd. חֵרֶם Zc 14^{11}, Baer חֵרֶם); חֵרֶם Jos 7^{1}; sf. חֶרְמִי 1 K 20^{42} Is 34^{5};—*thing devoted* to 'י: **1.** thing hostile to theocracy, and therefore (in the strictest application) to be either destroyed, or, in the case of certain objects (e.g. silver and gold, vessels of brass and iron Jos 6$^{19.24}$), set apart to sacred uses; esp. **a.** of a Canaan. city, as Jericho, incl. all inhab. (exc. Rahab's family) and spoil Jos 6$^{17.18.18}$ 7$^{1.11.15}$; Achan by taking מִן־הַחֵרֶם made (camp of) Isr. ח' 7^{12} cf. 6^{18}, and became himself ח', and was stoned and, with his family and possessions, incl. the spoil, was burnt 7$^{1.11.12.13.13}$ (all JE exc. 7^{1} P; cf. v$^{15.24.25}$); מָעַל מַעַל בַּח' *committed unfaithfulness in the* matter of the *devoted thing* is term for the sin Jos 7^{1} 22^{20} (both P), cf. מָעַל בַּח' 1 Ch 2^{7}; Saul and Isr. spared Agag king of Amalek and רֵאשִׁית הַח' i.e. of the spoil (sheep and oxen), wh. should have been utterly destroyed 1 S 15^{21} (cf. v$^{3.8}$; Saul rejected by 'י for this v$^{11.26}$); so an idolatr. city in Isr. should become ח', with all its contents, and be utterly destroyed Dt 13^{17} (cf. v$^{13.15.16}$). **b.** of individuals, one having relic of Canaanit. god in his house should become ח', the relic being ח' Dt 7$^{26.26}$; every human being who became ח' should be killed Lv 27$^{29.29}$ (P; v. Di). **2.** appar. (so Di) anything *devoted* to sanctuary under specially stringent conditions Lv 27^{28} (v. Di; and cf. Ezr 10^{8}); a field consecrated to 'י becomes under certain conditions כִּשְׂדֵה הַח' Lv 27^{21}; every ח' is קֹדֶשׁ קָדָשִׁים ליהוה v^{28}, and no ח' that a man may devote, whether man, beast or field, may be sold or redeemed v^{28}; every such ח' (as in case of metals and metal objects Jos 6$^{17.19}$) went to Aaron and his sons Nu 18^{14} (P), to Zadokite priests Ez 44^{29}. **3.** *devotion, ban,* involving destruction; אִישׁ חֶרְמִי 1 K 20^{42} *man under my* ('י's) *ban* (of Benhadad); עַם חֶרְמִי Is 34^{5} (of Edom); נתן לַח' Is 43^{28} fig. of 'י's giving over Jud. to Chald.; ח' not to be in future Zc 14^{11}; פֶּן־אָבוֹא וְהִכֵּיתִי אֶת־הָאָרֶץ ח' Mal 3^{24} *smite the land with a ban,* i.e. utterly destroy it.

†חֳרֵם **n.pr.loc.** (*sacred*; cf. Sab. n.pr.loc. 2765
אחרם DHM $^{Epigr. Denkm. 43}$)—a place in tribe of Naphtali Jos 19^{38} (P); not identified.

†חָרִם **n.pr.m.** (*consecrated*; cf. Sab. n.pr.m. 2766
חרם, יחרמאל Hal $^{411. 504}$ DHM $^{l.c.}$)—**1.** priest of the third course, David's time, acc. to 1 Ch 24^{8}. **2.** priest of time of Nehemiah Ne 10^{6}. **3.** heads of families of returning exiles: **a.** Ezr 2^{39} = Ne 7^{42}, Ezr 10^{21} Ne 12^{15}. **b.** Ezr 2^{32} = Ne 7^{35}, Ezr 10^{31} Ne 3^{11}. **4.** a prince Ne 10^{28}.

†חָרְמָה **n.pr.loc.** (*asylum*, cf. Ar. *id.*, 2767
Wetzst $^{ZKW v. 1884, 115}$)—a royal city of Canaanites, in the South, in tribe of Simeon Nu 14^{45} (JE; art. only here v. Di), 21^{3} (J) where name expl. from Israel's *devoting* Canaanites of Arad to destruction; Jos 15^{30} 19^{4} (P), Dt 1^{44} Jos 12^{14} (D), 1 S 30^{30} 1 Ch 4^{30}; originally called צְפַת Ju 1^{17}, where name is said to have been changed to Ḥormah because Judah and Simeon (after death of Joshua) *devoted* its inhabitants to destruction, v. Di Nu 21^{3}.—On site v. צְפַת.

†חֶרְמוֹן **n. pr. mont.** Hermon (*sacred* 2768
mountain, cf. Sab. מחרם, etc., *temple*, Ar. حَرَامٌ *interior of mosque*, حُرْمَةٌ *asylum*, Wetzst $^{ZKW v. 1884, 115}$ RS $^{Sem. i, 93; 2nd ed., 94}$)—the highest peak of Anti-Lebanon range, usually snow-capped, commanding southern Syria & northern Palestine; it is called שִׂיאֹן by the author of Dt 4^{48}; by the Amorites שְׂנִיר, by the Sidonians שִׂרְיֹן Dt 3^{9}. It has three peaks; and the names חרמון and שׂניר, distinguished in 1 Ch 5^{23} Ct 4^{8}, may refer
to two of these peaks; חֶרְמוֹנִים ψ 42^{7} prob. 2769
refers to these different peaks (see Rob $^{BR iii, 357}$ Bäd $^{Pal 301}$). It is a northern boundary עד הר ח' Dt 3^{8} Jos 12^{1}; הר חרמון *mount Hermon* is used also Jos 11^{17} 12^{5} 13$^{5.11}$ 1 Ch 5^{23}; but חרמון Jos 11^{3} ψ 89^{13} 133^{3} Ct 4^{8}. Vid. בַּעַל חֶרְמוֹן Ju 3^{3} 1 Ch 5^{23} (see Wetzst $^{ib. 115}$).

חֶרְמוֹנִים v. foregoing. 2769

†II. [חָרַם] **vb. slit** (nose, lip, ear, etc.), 2763
mutilate, esp. face (Ar. خَرَمَ *perforate, pierce, slit the partition between the nostrils, or the lip, or the lobe of the ear*)—**Qal** *Pt. pass.* אִישׁ עִוֵּר אוֹ פִסֵּחַ אוֹ חָרֻם אוֹ שָׂרוּעַ *a man blind or lame or*

mutilated in the face (in nose, lip, ear, etc.), *or too long in a limb* Lv 21^{18} (H), v. Di (Kn).

2764 †II. חֵ֫רֶם **n.m. net** (as something perforated; cf. Ar. مُخَرَّمٌ *perforated work*, Fl in NHWB $^{ii, 208}$; NH חֵרֶם *net;* Ph. חרם *maker of nets*)—abs. ׳ח Mi 7^{2}; sf. חֶרְמִי Ez 32^{3}, חֶרְמוֹ Hb $1^{15.16.17}$; pl. חֲרָמִים Ec 7^{26} Ez $26^{5.14}$ 47^{10};—*hunter's net* Mi 7^{2} Ec 7^{26}; *fisherman's net* Ez $26^{5.14}$ 32^{3} 47^{10} Hb $1^{15.16.17}$.

2770 †חֶרְמֵשׁ **n.[m.] sickle** (on form v. Ges $^{§ 85 xii. 55}$)—Dt 16^{9} 23^{26}.

2771 †I. חָרָן **n.pr.loc.** city in northern Mesopotamia (As. *ḫarrânu=road, path* COT^{Gloss}; cf. Dl$^{Pa 185}$; Jensen$^{Kosmologie 28}$ '*junction of trading-routes*'=*cross-roads*)—mentioned as city of Abram's sojourn Gn 11^{31}, where his father Teraḥ died v^{32}, and whence he departed for Canaan $12^{4.5}$; where Laban, Jacob's uncle, lived, and whither Jacob fled 27^{43} 28^{10} (both חָרָ֫נָה), 29^{4}; as conquered by fathers of Sennacherib 2 K 19^{12}=Is 37^{12}; as place of trade Ez 27^{23}; As. *Ḫarrana (-ni)*, Schr^{COT} on Gn 11^{31} 27^{43} 𝔊 Χαρραν. It was an ancient seat of worship of moon-god (Sin), v. Schr$^{KG 355, 536}$; see further Chwolsohn$^{Ssabier i, 303 ff.}$ Wüstenfeld$^{ZMG 1864, 443 f.}$ Schr$^{KG 355, 536}$ Sachau$^{Reise 217 ff.}$ Mez$^{Gesch. d. Stadt Harran, 1892}$.

2771 †II. חָרָן **n.pr.m.** son of Caleb of Judah 1 Ch $2^{46.46}$; 𝔊 Αρραν, 𝔊L Ωρων (Sab. n.pr. חרן DHM$^{Epigr. Dakm. 56}$).

1032 חֹרֹן, חוֹרֹן v. בֵּית חוֹרֹן p. 111 supr.

2772 חֹרֹנִי **adj.gent.** v. *id.*

2773 †חֹרֹנַיִם, חֹרֹנַיִם **n.pr.loc.** (poss. *two hollows, caves, ravines*, v. בֵּית חוֹרֹן)—דֶּרֶךְ חרונים Is 15^{5} Je 48^{3}, מוֹרַד חֹרֹנַיִם Je 48^{5}, חֹרֹנַיִם 48^{34}, city of Moab; = MI$^{31.32}$ חורנן (i.e. prob. חוֹרֹנֵן); 𝔊 Αρωνιειμ, Ωρωναιμ.—On חֹרֹנַיִם 𝔊 Jos $13^{10.11}$ 2 S 13^{34} v. We Dr and בֵּית חוֹרֹן.

2774 †חַרְנֶ֫פֶר **n.pr.m.** name in tribe of Asher 1 Ch 7^{36}=**n.pr.loc.** v. Be.—𝔊 Αναρφαρ, A Αρναφαρ, 𝔊L Αριαφερ.

חרם (√ of foll.; meaning dubious).

2775 †I. חֶ֫רֶס **n.m.**$^{Ju 14, 18}$ **sun** (NH *id.*)—abs. ׳ח Jb 9^{7} (‖כּוֹכָבִים); c. ה epenth. בְּטֶרֶם יָבֹא הַחַ֫רְסָה Ju 14^{18} (cf. לַיְלָה, לַיִל) before the *sun* could go down (but rd. perh. הַחַ֫דְרָה *into the* (bridal) *chamber* Sta$^{ZAW 1884, 253 ff.}$).

2776 †II. [חֶ֫רֶס] **n.pr.loc. 1.** abode of Amorites, בְּהַר־חֶרֶס בְּאַיָּלוֹן וּבְשַׁעַלְבִים Ju 1^{35}, since חֶרֶס *sun*=שֶׁמֶשׁ, perh.=בֵּית שֶׁמֶשׁ **1.** (q. v.), so Stu (who prop. עִיר חֶרֶס=עָר), Ke Be Bu$^{RS 17}$ Öt Bla; 𝔊 ἐν τῷ [ὄρει τοῦ] Μυρσινῶνι(-ος)=הַר הֲדַס. **2.** place E. of Jordan מִלְמַעֲלֵה הֶחָרֶס Ju 8^{13} *from the ascent of Ḥeres*, 𝔊 Αρες; the point whence Gideon turned back from pursuing Midian; Aq Symm rd. הֶהָרִים (v. Lag$^{Onom. 96, 2nd ed. 131}$) so SS.—תִּמְנַת־חֶרֶס Ju 2^{9} v. sub תִּמְנַת, √מנה.

III. חֶרֶס, חַרְסִית, חרסות v. sub חרשׁ p. 360 2775, 2777

חרע (√ of foll.; perh. cf. Aram. ܐܬܚܪܥ Ethpa. *be clever*, ܚܪܝܥܐ *shrewd*, esp. in bad sense; Ar. خَرَعَ *split*, VIII. *originate, invent*).

8475 †תַּחְרֵעַ **n.pr.m.** a great-great-grandson of
8390 Saul 1 Ch 9^{41} 𝔊 Θαρα(χ)=תַּאְרֵעַ 8^{35} 𝔊 Θερεε, A Θαρεε; 𝔊L in both Θαραα.

2778 †I. [חָרַף] **vb. reproach** (NH Pi. *id.*; Aram. חֲרַף *id.*, ܚܪܦ *sharpen*, ܚܪܝܦ *sharp, keen, acute*);—**Qal** *Impf.* לֹא־יֶחֱרַף לְבָבִי מִיָּמָי Jb 27^{6}; *Pt. sf.* חֹרְפִי ψ 119^{42} Pr 27^{11}; חוֹרְפֶיךָ ψ 69^{10}. **Piel.** *Pf.* חֵרֵף Ju 5^{18}+6 t.; חֵרַפְתָּ Is 37^{23}+4 t. etc.+10 t. pf.; *Impf.* יְחָרֵף 2 S 21^{21} 1 Ch 20^{7}; יְחָרֶף ψ 74^{10}+2 t. sf.; *Inf.* לְחָרֵף Is 37^{4}+5 t.; בְּחָרְפָם 2 S 23^{9} (but v. infr.); *Pt.* מְחָרֵף ψ 44^{17};—*reproach*,—prop. *say sharp things against*,—*taunt*, c. acc. Ju 8^{15} 1 S $17^{10.25.26.36.45}$ 2 S 21^{21} + 1 Ch 20^{7}; God, by injustice to the poor Pr 14^{31} 17^{5}; Yahweh, by idolatry Is 65^{7}; Yahweh as the God of Israel 2 K $19^{4.16.22.23}$=Is $37^{4.17.23.24}$ = 2 Ch 32^{17} (c. לְ); c. בְּ, Philistines 2 S 23^{9} MT (but rd. בְּפַס דַּמִּים *at Pas-dammîm*, n.pr.loc., as 1 Ch 11^{12} We Dr); *reproach*, Ne 6^{13} ψ 42^{11} 44^{17} 55^{13} 57^{4} $74^{10.18}$ 79^{12} $89^{52.52}$ 102^{9} Zp $2^{8.10}$; poet. and fig., *despise, scorn*, ח׳ נפשׁ למות Ju 5^{18}.

2781 †חֶרְפָּה **n.f. reproach**—׳ח Gn 34^{14}+35 t.; cstr. חֶרְפַּת Jos 5^{9}+15 t.; sf. חֶרְפָּתְךָ ψ 74^{22} etc. +17 t. sfs.; pl. חֲרָפוֹת ψ 69^{11} Dn 12^{2}; cstr. חֶרְפּוֹת ψ 69^{10}.—**1.** *taunt* of enemy 1 S 17^{26}; so also 1 S 25^{39}; *reproach* cast upon another, *scorn, contumely* Ne 3^{36} 5^{9} ψ $69^{20.21}$ 71^{13} 89^{51} 119^{22} Pr 18^{3} Is 51^{7} Ez 21^{33}; ׳שׁמע ח Je 51^{51} Zp 2^{8} La 3^{61}; נתן ח׳ על Je 23^{40}; נשׂא ח׳ על ψ 15^{3} (slander); נשׂא ח׳ Je 31^{19} Ez 36^{15} Mi 6^{16} (reproach); נשׂא ח׳ על *bear reproach for* ψ 69^{8} Je 15^{15} Zp 3^{18}; השׁיב ח׳ Ho 12^{15} Ne 3^{36}; ׳חרף ח ψ 69^{10} 79^{12} 89^{51}; ׳העביר ח ψ 119^{39}; הסיר ח׳ מעל 1 S 17^{26} Is 25^{8}; *reproaches against* God ψ 69^{10} (חֶרְפּוֹת חוֹרְפֶיךָ).

74[22] 79[12]. **2.** *reproach* which rests upon one, condition of *shame, disgrace*: **a.** sexual 2 S 13[13] Is 47[3] Ez 16[57] Pr 6[33]. **b.** barrenness of womb Gn 30[23] (E) Is 4[1]; widowhood Is 54[4]. **c.** hunger Ez 36[30]; disease Jb 19[5]. **d.** ritual, uncircumcision Gn 34[14] (P) Jos 5[9] (JE). **e.** injuries from enemies La 3[30] 5[1] Ne 1[3] 2[7] Jb 16[10] Dn 11[18.18]. **3.** *a reproach*, the object of reproach, the person or thing reproached חֶרְפַּת אָדָם *a reproach of man* ψ 22[7]; היה ח׳ ל׳ 39[9]; ח׳ נבל *become an object of reproach to* 31[12] 79[4] 89[42] 109[25] Ez 5[15]; (היה) לח (ל׳) Is 30[5] Je 6[10] 20[8] 42[18] 44[8.12] 49[13] ψ 69[11] Dn 9[16] 12[2]; נתן ח׳ (ל׳) Ez 22[4] Jo 2[19] ψ 78[66]; נתן לח׳ Je 24[9] 29[18] Ez 5[14] Jo 2[17]; שׂים ח׳ ל׳ ψ 44[14]; שׂים ח׳ על 1 S 11[2].

† II. חרף (√of foll.; cf. Ar. خَرَفَ *gather fruit, pluck*).

2779 † חֹ֫רֶף **n.m.** **harvest-time, autumn** (Ar. خَرِيفٌ *freshly gathered fruit, autumn* (also *rain of autumn* or *beginning of winter*) = Sab. (ן)חרפ DHM [ZMG 1875, xxix. 597]; Sab. חרף, חרפם = *year*, cf. Eth. ኀረፍ: *annus currens* Os (Levy) [ZMG 1865, 168, 174] DHM [ZMG 1883, 369]; As. *ḫarpu*, Schr [JPTh 1875, 341] KAT[2 53 n.] = COT[i. 54 n.])—abs. ח׳ Zc 14[8] + 5 t.; sf. חָרְפִּי Jb 29[4];—קַיִץ וָחֹרֶף Gn 8[22] (J), ψ 74[17] Zc 14[8]; בֵּית הַח׳ *autumn-house* or *palace* Am 3[15] Je 36[22] (+ בַּחֹדֶשׁ הַתְּשִׁיעִי *in the 9th month*, i.e. Nov.–Dec.); מח׳ עָצֵל לֹא יַחֲרֹשׁ Pr 20[4] *a sluggard ploughs not after harvest*; as implying maturity, בִּימֵי חָרְפִּי Jb 29[4] *in the days of my autumn* (prime).

2778 III. [חָרַף] **vb.denom.** **remain in harvest-time** (so Ar. خَرَفَ; Eng. *to winter*)—only **Qal** *Impf.* 3 fs. כָּל־בֶּהֱמַת הָאָרֶץ עָלָיו תֶּחֱרָ֑ף Is 18[6] *all the beasts of the earth shall spend the harvest-time upon it*.

2780 † חָרֵף (dub. whether from I. or II.) **n.pr.m.** a chief of the line of Judah 1 Ch 2[51].

2756 † חָרִיף, חָרִף **n.pr.m.** (cf. Ar. خَرِيفٌ *autumn*, v. חֹרֶף supr.)—**1.** חָרִף head of a family of returned exiles Ne 7[24] (𝔊 Αρειφ, 𝔊L Ιωρηε) = יוֹרָה (cf. יוֹרֶה *early rain*) Ezr 2[18] (𝔊 Ουρα, A Ιωρα, 𝔊L Ωραι). **2.** חָרִיף one of those sealed Ne 10[20] 𝔊 Αρειφ(α), 𝔊L Αρηφ.

2741 † חֲרִיפִי Qr, חרופי Kt, **adj.gent.** c. art.; שְׁפַטְיָהוּ הַח׳ 1 Ch 12[6] (Baer, v[5] van d. H), 𝔊 Χαρα(ι)φ(ε)ι, A Αρουφι; perh., if Qr right, connected with חָרִף Ne 7[24].

2778 † IV. [חָרַף] **vb.** **acquire** (cf. Ar. حَرَفَ *turn a thing from its proper way or manner*, but also *gain, acquire* [subsistence] for one's family)—only **Niph.** *Pt. f.* שִׁפְחָה נֶחֱרֶפֶת לְאִישׁ *a maidservant acquired for a man* (viz. as his concubine) Lv 19[20] (H; cf. NH חֲרוּפָה of woman *designated* for a man).

† I. חָרַץ **vb.** **cut, sharpen, decide** (NH 2782 *id.*, *cut in, decide*, Aram. in deriv.; As. *ḫarâṣu*, *dig, decide*, *ḫariṣu*, *trench*, Zehnpfund [BAS i. 502]; Ph. חרץ *decision*, Hoffm [AGG xxxvi. May 1889, 11])—**Qal** *Pf.* 3 ms. ח׳ Jos 10[21]; חָרָ֑צְתָּ 1 K 20[40]; *Impf.* יֶחֱרַץ Ex 11[7]; 2 ms. תֶּחֱרָ֑ץ 2 S 5[24]; *Pt. pass.* חָרוּץ 2742 Is 10[22] Lv 22[22]; pl. חֲרוּצִים Jb 14[5] (v. also חָרוּץ infr.)—**1.** *cut, mutilate* Lv 22[22] (עַוֶּרֶת אוֹ שָׁבוּר אוֹ־חָרוּץ אוֹ יַבֶּלֶת). **2.** *sharpen*, fig. the tongue, לֹא יֶחֱ׳־כֶּלֶב לְשֹׁנוֹ לְ Ex 11[7] (J), i.e. utter no sound against Isr., Jos 10[21]. **3.** *decide* 1 K 20[40] (abs.); so pt. pass. חרוצים ימיו Jb 14[5] *his days are determined, fixed* (|| מִסְפַּר חדשׁיו), Is 10[22] כִּלָּיוֹן ח׳; *act with decision* 2 S 5[24]. **Niph.** *Pt.* נֶחֱרָצָה Is 10[23] + 3 t.; נֶחֱרֶצֶת Dn 9[26] (both these forms inf. cstr. acc. to Ba [NB 90]); *decisive* כָּלָה וְנֶחֱ׳ Is 10[23] 28[22] Dn 9[27] a consumption and *strict decision* (i.e. that which is strictly determined), כי נ׳ נֶעֱשָׂתָה Dn 11[36]; נח׳ שֹׁמֵמוֹת Dn 9[26] *strict determining of desolation*.

† I. חָרוּץ **adj.** **sharp, diligent** (on this and 2742 foll. v. Ba [NB 173])—חָרוּץ Is 28[27] + 11 t.; pl. חֲרוּצִים Pr 10[4] 12[24]; חֲרֻצִים Pr 13[4]; חֲרֻצוֹת Am 1[3];—**1.** *sharp*: of threshing instrument מוֹרַג ח׳ חָדָשׁ Is 41[15]; without מ׳, as subst., 28[27] (where יוּדַשׁ); ח׳ הַבַּרְזֶל Am 1[3]; Jb 41[22] (fig. of crocodile). **2.** fig. *diligent*: as subst. Pr 21[5]; opp. רְמִיָּה Pr 10[4] 12[24.27]; opp. עָצֵל Pr 13[4].—Dn 9[25] v. IV. חרוץ.

† II. חָרוּץ **n.[m.]** **strict decision**, only עֵמֶק 2742 הֶחָרוּץ Jo 4[14.14] *valley of strict decision* (v. Ba[l. c.]).

† III. חָרוּץ **n.[m.]** **trench, moat** (Aram. חֲרִיצָא; As. *ḫariṣu*, *ḫiriṣu*, *id.*, Dl[HWB])—only in רְחוֹב וְח׳ Dn 9[25], si vera l.; as above Ges Herzf Ew Zö Meinh (q.v.); Gr רְחוֹב וחיץ; < 𝔖 Bev רְחוֹב וָחוּץ *with public places and streets*.

† IV. חָרוּץ **n.pr.m.** father of king Amon's 2743 mother 2 K 21[19], 𝔊 Αρους.

† [חָרִיץ] **n.m.** [1 S 17, 18] **a cut, thing cut, sharp** 2757 **instrument**;—pl. cstr. חֲרִיצֵי 1 S 17[18] 1 Ch 20[3]; חֲרִצֵי 2 S 12[31];—**1.** ח׳ הֶחָלָב 1 S 17[18] *cuts of milk* i. e. cheeses. **2.** *sharp instr.* of iron, 2 S 12[31] =

1 Ch 20^{3} בַּמְּגֵרָה ובח׳ הַבַּרְזֶל וּבַמְּגֵרוֹת (cf. Am 1^{3} sub חרוץ **1**, and Dr^{Sm}).

2785 †חַרְצַנִּים **n.m.pl.** some insignificant vine-product, usu. taken as **grape-kernels, grape-stones**, fr. acrid taste, so Thes (after Onk Mishn), v. also זָג p. 260 supr.: מִגֶּפֶן הַיַּיִן מֵח׳ וְעַד־זָג Nu 6^{4} *of the wine-vine, including both* חרצנים *and* זג, he shall not eat.

II. **חרץ** *be yellow* (prob. ✓ of foll.: Syr. ܚܪܨ *id.* (rare), ܚܘܪܨܐ *yellow;* cf. Aram. חריע *safflower*, Ar. إِحْرِيضٌ *id.:* v. Nö $^{ZMG\ 1886,\ 728}$, Löw $^{Aram.\ Pflanzenn.\ 218}$ Kö$^{ii.\ 1,\ 137}$).

2742 †v. **חָרוּץ** **n.m.**$^{Pr\ 8,\ 10}$ **gold**, poet. (Ph. חרץ, v. Dr$^{Sm\ xxviii}$; As. *ḫurâṣu*)—חָרוּץ ψ 68^{14} + 5 t.; *gold*, always ‖ כֶּסֶף; Zc 9^{3}, of dove's wings ψ 68^{14} בִּירַקְרַק ח׳; elsewh. in comparison with value of wisdom, etc. Pr 3^{14} 8^{10} (ח׳ נִבְחָר) v^{19} 16^{16}.

חרצב (quadrilit. ✓ of foll.; cf. Ar. حَضْرَبَ *bind* or *twist powerfully*, Frey).

2784 †[**חַרְצֻבָּה**] **n.[f.]** **bond, fetter, pang,** only pl. חַרְצֻבּוֹת; — **1.** cstr. ח׳ רֶשַׁע Is 58^{6} *bonds of wickedness* i.e. imposed by wicked men (‖ אֲגֻדּוֹת מוֹטָה). **2.** *pangs* (cf. חֵבֶל, חֶבֶל), abs. אֵין ח׳ לְמוֹתָם ψ 73^{4} *they have no pangs* (rd. לָמוֹ תָּם וגו׳).

2785 חַרְצַנִּים v. sub I. חרץ. above

2786 †**חָרַק** **vb.** **gnash** or **grind** the teeth, only poet. (NH *id.;* Ar. حَرَقَ *file, rub together, grate* or *grind* (teeth); Aram. ܚܪܩ *id.*) — **Qal** *Pf.* 3 ms. ח׳ Jb 16^{9}; *Impf.* יַחֲרֹק ψ 112^{10}; וַיַּחַרְקוּ־ La 2^{16}; *Inf. abs.* חָרֹק ψ 35^{16}; *Pt.* חֹרֵק ψ 37^{12};— *grind* the teeth in rage against: ח׳ שִׁנָּיו על ψ 37^{12} 35^{16}; abs. without על 112^{10} La 2^{16} (only here c. שֵׁן sing.); c. בְּ instr. (Ges$^{§\ 119.\ 3\ b.\ R.}$ Da$^{Synt.\ §\ 73\ R.\ 6}$) ח׳ בשניו על־ Jb 16^{9}.

2787 †I. [**חָרַר**] **vb.** **be hot, scorched, burn,** poet. & late (Ar. حَرَّ *be hot, burn, thirst;* Eth. ሐረረ: Aram. חַר; cf. As. *arâru, glow*, SASm $^{Asrb.\ i,\ p.\ 97}$ Belser$^{BAS\ ii,\ 155}$)—**Qal** *Pf.* 3 fs. חָרָה Jb 30^{30}, וְחָרָה consec. Ez 24^{11}, חָרוּ Is 24^{6};—**1.** *be hot, scorched*, Jerus., under fig. of caldron Ez 24^{11}. **2.** *burn* = *be burned*, fig. of men, in י׳'s judgment, Is 24^{6}. **3.** *burn*, of bones of sick men in fever ח׳ מִנִּי־חֹרֶב Jb 30^{30}. **Niph.** *Pf.* נָחַר Je 6^{29}, נָחָר Ez 15^{4}, נִחַר ψ 69^{4}; 3 pl. נִחָרוּ ψ 102^{4} (Kö$^{i.\ 368}$); *Impf.* יֵחָר Ez 15^{5} יֵחָרוּ Ez 24^{10} (del. Co B al.) **1.** *be scorched*, of bellows מַפֻּחַ in fierce fire Je 6^{29} (fig.); *scorched, charred*, of the vine (as fuel) Ez 15^{4,5} middle part charred, the ends devoured (אכל) by fire (sim. of inhab. of Jerus.); bones (sim. *id.*) Ez 24^{10} (v. supr.). **2.** *burn*, of bones in fever ψ 102^{4} (כְּמוֹקֵד, cf. **Qal** Jb 30^{30}); *be parched*, of throat נח׳ גרוני 69^{4}. —Is 41^{11} 45^{24} Ct 1^{6} v. חרה. **Pilp.** *Inf.* לְחַרְחַר־רִיב Pr 26^{21} *to kindle strife.*

†[**חָרֵר**] **n.[m.]** **parched place** (Ar. حَرَّاتٌ, Bd $^{Pal\ 196}$), only pl. abs. חֲרֵרִים; ח׳ במדבר Je 17^{6} (‖ עֲרָבָה) fig. of life of godless. 2788

†**חַרְחֻר** **n.m.** **violent heat, fever** (v. Ba 2746
$^{NB\ 206}$)—בַּשַּׁחֶפֶת וּבַקַּדַּחַת וּבַדַּלֶּקֶת וּבח׳ ובחרב וגו׳ Dt 28^{22}.

†**חַרְחוּר** **n.pr.m.** head of a family of 2744
returning exiles Ezr 2^{51} = Ne 7^{53}; 𝔊 Αρου(α)ρ (meaning as above? or fr. II. חרר?).

II. **חרר** (✓ of foll.; Ar. حَرَّ *be* or *become free*, حُرٌّ *free, freeborn;* NH חרר Pi. *set free*, חוֹר *freeman;* Aram. חֲרַר, ܚܪܪ Pa. *set free*, חֹרָא, חֹרְתָּא *freed-man, -woman;* Sab. חר *freeman, noble* (?) DHM$^{Epigr.\ Denkm.\ 57}$; Eth. ሐራ: coll. *army, troops* (in Amhar. *free, noble*, acc. to Di^{85}), ሐራዊ: *free, noble*, etc.)

† II. [**חֹר**] **n.m.**$^{1\ K\ 21,\ 8}$ **noble**, late, esp. Neh., 2715
v. Dr$^{Intr\ 519\ n.}$ (v. Lag$^{BN\ 32}$)—only pl. חֹרִים 1 K 21^{8} + 6 t., חוֹרִים Ec 10^{17}, Ne 6^{17} + 3 t.; sf. חֹרֶיהָ Is 34^{12};—*nobles* in Naboth's city 1 K 21$^{8.11}$; nobles of Judah, חֹרֵי יְהוּדָה 6^{17} 13^{17} Je 27^{20} 39^{6} Ne 6^{17} 13^{17}, הח׳ והסגנים (in Jerusalem) Ne 2^{16} 4$^{8.13}$ 5^{7} 7^{5}, Ec 10^{17}, of Edom Is 34^{12}.—I. חֹר, v. II. חור.

III. **חרר** (✓ of foll.; v. As. *ḫarâru, bore, pierce, ḫurru, hole, ravine* Dl$^{Pr\ 150,\ 182}$; Ar. خُرٌّ *hole* or *mouth* of millstone; NH חִרְחֵר *bore, pierce*).

† III. **חֹר, חוֹר** **n.[m.]** **hole**;—abs. חֹר 2 K 12^{10} 2356
Ez 8^{7} (del. Co B etc.), חוֹר Ct 5^{4}, חֹרִים 1 S 14^{11}; cstr. חֹרֵי Jb 30^{6}; sf. חֹרָיו Na 2^{13}, חֹרֵיהֶן Zc 14^{12}; —*hole* in lid of chest 2 K 12^{10} (made by boring, נקב), in door Ct 5^{4}; in wall Ez 8^{7} (v. supra); = eye-*socket* עיניו תִּמַּקְנָה בְּח׳ Zc 14^{12} (plague of enemies of Jerusalem); *holes* as hiding-places for men 1 S 14^{11}, so also 13^{6} Ew We Dr (for MT חוחים), dwelling of outcast people חרי עָפָר Jb 30^{6}; of *dens* of lions Na 2^{13}.—I. חֹר, v. II. חור.
p. 301

†**חֻר, חוּר** **n.[m.]** id. — coll. חוּר Is 42^{22} 2352
as hiding-places of men; cstr. חֻר Is 11^{8} hole of asp (פֶּתֶן).

2752-53 †II. חֹרִי, חוֹרִי **adj.**, usu. **n.pr.gent.** et
pers. (prob. = *cave-dweller*, so Thes RobGes MV
VB; v. also W Max Müll $^{\text{Asien u. Europa 136, 155, 156}}$)—**1.**
2752 **adj. gent.** שֵׂעִיר הַח׳ Gn 36^{20} *Seir the Horite* (P);
2752 rd. הַח׳ also v^{2} for MT הַחִוִּי. **2. n.pr.gent.** alw.
c. art.; usu. sg. coll. הַחֹרִי, ancient inhabitants
of land of Edom Gn 14^{6} (בְּהַרְרָם שֵׂעִיר); in P
called בְּנֵי שֵׂעִיר בְּאֶרֶץ אֱדוֹם 36^{21} (vid. v^{20}); cf.
v$^{29.30}$; acc. to Dt 2^{12} (where alone הַחֹרִים), v^{22}
they were driven out by sons of Esau (yet v.
Gn 36$^{1.c.}$ and Di); 𝔊 ὁ Χορραιος, οἱ Χορραιοι,
2753 (Gn 36$^{29.30}$ Χορρ(ε)ι). **3. n.pr.pers.m. a.** חֹרִי
an Edomite Gn 36^{22} = 1 Ch 1^{39}; 𝔊 Χορρ(ε)ι.
2753 **b.** חוֹרִי a Simeonite Nu 13^{5}, but 𝔊 Σουρ(ε)ι, 𝔊L
Σουδρι.—I. חֹרִי v. sub I. חור.

חרשׁ (√ of foll.; cf. Ar. خَرَشَ vb. *scratch,
lacerate*, خِرَاشٌ *irritation*, etc.)

2789 †**חֶרֶשׂ n.[m.] earthenware, earthen vessel, sherd, potsherd,** P and late (NH חֶרֶס,
Aram. חֲרַס)—abs. ח׳ Lv 6^{21} + 9 t., חָ֫רֶשׂ Nu 5^{17}
+ 4 t.; pl. cstr. חַרְשֵׂי Is 45^{9}; sf. חַרְשָׂהּ Ez 23^{34}.
—**1.** *earthenware:* כְּלִי־ח׳ *earthen vessel* Je 32^{14};
esp. P Lv 6^{21} 11^{33} 14$^{5.50}$ 15^{12} Nu 5^{17}; without
כְּלִי Pr 26^{23}; cf. בַּקְבֻּק יוֹצֵר ח׳ Je 19^{1}; לְנִבְלֵי ח׳
La 4^{2} they are reckoned *as earthen vessels*, sim.
of sons of Zion; חֶרֶשׂ אֶת־חַרְשֵׂי אֲדָמָה Is 45^{9}
a potsherd (perh. = *earthen vessel*, v. Pr 26^{23}
supr.) *among earthen potsherds* (of men, over
against י׳ their potter); sim. of dryness ψ 22^{16}.
2. *a fragment of earthenware, sherd* Is 30^{14}
Ez 23^{34}; ח׳ לְהִתְגָּרֵד Jb 2^{8} *a sherd to scrape
himself;* חַדּוּדֵי ח׳ Jb 41^{22} *sharpest potsherds*,
fig. of sharp scales on belly of crocodile.

חֲרֶשֶׂת v. קִיר־חֲרֶשֶׂת.

2775 †III. [**חֶרֶס**] **n.[m.]** an eruptive disease, **itch**
(Aram. חַרְסָא, ܚܰܪܣܳܐ; also ܚܰܪܘܣܳܐ *rough*, etc.)
—חֶרֶס וּבְחָ֑רֶס Dt 28^{27} (|| עפלים Kt, גָּרָב).—I, II. חרס
v. sub חרם. p. 357

2777 †**חרסות** Kt, **חַרְסִית** Qr **n.f.coll. potsherd**—פֶּתַח שַׁעַר הַחַרְסוּת Je 19^{2}, designation of a
gate in Jerus.; opening of the *gate of potsherds*,
i.e. where they were thrown (vid. v$^{10.11}$ and Gf);
it led into the valley of Hinnom; 𝔊 χαρσ(ε)ιθ
favours Qr.

2790 †I. [**חָרַשׁ**] **vb. cut in, engrave, plough,
devise** (NH *id.*, *plough*, so Eth. ሐረሰ: Ph. חרש,
Aram. (rare) חֲרַת *engrave*, ܚܪܰܫ *cleave, plough*, Ar.
حَرَثَ *plough*)—**Qal** *Pf.* חָרְשׁוּ ψ 129^{3}, חֲרַשְׁתֶּם Ju
14^{18} Ho 10^{13}; *Impf.* יַחֲרֹשׁ Is 28^{24} Pr 20^{4}; יַחֲרוֹשׁ
Ho 10^{11} + Am 6^{12} (v. infr.); 2 ms. תַּחֲרֹשׁ Dt 22^{10}
Pr 3^{29}; *Inf. cstr.* חֲרֹשׁ 1 S 8^{12}; *Pt.* חֹרֵשׁ Gn 4^{22} 2794
+ 5 t.; חוֹרֵשׁ Am 9^{13}; pl. חֹרְשִׁים ψ 129^{3}, חֹרְשֵׁי
Jb 4^{8} + 3 t., fpl. abs. חֹרְשׁוֹת Jb 1^{14}; *pass.* חֲרוּשָׁה
Je 17^{1}:—**1.** *cut in, engrave*, of worker in
metals ח׳ נְחֹשֶׁת וּבַרְזֶל Gn 4^{22}(J), ח׳ נחשת 1 K 7^{14};
fig. ח׳ עַל־לוּחַ לִבָּם Je 17^{1} *engraved on the tablet
of their heart.* **2.** *plough*, lit., human subj.
(animal usu. c. בְּ), no obj. expr. 1 K 19^{19} Dt 22^{10}
Is 28^{24}, so יַחֲרוֹשׁ בבקרים Am 6^{12} (but rd. prob.
יֵחָרֵשׁ בבקר יָם, v. We al.); c. acc. cogn. ח׳ חֲרִישׁוֹ
1 S 8^{12} *plough his ploughing* (= *do his ploughing*), Pr 20^{4}; fig. of Judah Ho 10^{11}; with ethical
ref. ח׳ רֶשַׁע v^{13} (||קצר), ח׳ אָוֶן Jb 4^{8} (||זרע,
קצר); עַל־גַּבִּי חָרְשׁוּ חֹרְשִׁים ψ 129^{3} *upon my back
have ploughmen ploughed* (fig. of oppression by
wicked); חֹרֵשׁ = *ploughman* Is 28^{24}, Am 9^{13}
(||קוֹצֵר); ח׳ with oxen subj. only Jb 1^{14}. **3.**
devise (as one who *works in, practises*), usu.
bad sense, obj. רָעָה Pr 3^{29}, רַע 6^{14}; מַחְשְׁבוֹת אָוֶן
v^{18}, חֹרְשֵׁי רַע Pr 12^{20} 14^{22}; but also חֹרְשֵׁי טוֹב v^{22}.
Niph. *Impf.* 3 fs. צִיּוֹן שָׂדֶה תֵּחָרֵשׁ Mi 3^{12} Zion,
as a field she *shall be ploughed* = Je 26^{18}.
Hiph. *Pt.* מַחֲרִישׁ רָעָה עַל־ 1 S 23^{9} *fabricating
mischief against* (v. Dr, and cf. We).

†**חָרָשׁ n.m.** $^{\text{Ex 38, 23}}$ **graver, artificer** (Ph. 2796
חרש)—abs. ח׳ (= *חַרָּשׁ) Ex 35^{35} + 14 t.; cstr. חָרַשׁ
Ex 28^{11} + 2 t.; pl. חָרָשִׁים Ho 13^{2} + 7 t.; חֲרָשִׁים
1 Ch 4$^{14.14}$ Ne 11^{35} (v. infr.); cstr. חָרָשֵׁי 2 S 5^{11}
+ 6 t.;—**1.** *graver, artificer:* **a.** worker in
metal 1 S 13^{19} Ho 8^{6} 13^{2} Dt 27^{15} Je 10^{9} (|| צֹרֵף), Is
40^{19} (|| *id.*), 54^{16} 1 Ch 29^{5}; ח׳ בַּרְזֶל Is 44^{12} 2 Ch
24^{12}; perh. also Is 41^{7} (+ צֹרֵף); appar. = hammerer Zc 2^{3} (symbol.). **b.** worker in wood ח׳ עֵץ
2 S 5^{11} = 1 Ch 14^{1} (עֵצִים), 2 K 12^{12} 22^{6} = 2 Ch 34^{11},
Je 10^{3} Is 40^{20} 44^{13} (v. also 1 Ch 22^{15} infr.); perh.
also Ezr 3^{7} 2 Ch 24^{12} (both || חצב). **c.** worker
in stone ח׳ אֶבֶן קִיר 2 S 5^{11} = 1 Ch 14^{1} (om. אבן);
also of engraving on gems ח׳ אבן Ex 28^{11} (P;
|| פִּתּוּחֵי חֹתָם); see also foll. **d.** in gen. ח׳ אֶבֶן וָעֵץ
1 Ch 22^{15}; *idol-maker* ח׳ צִירִים Is 45^{16}, cf. 44^{11}
(also v$^{12.13}$ supr.), 2 K 24$^{14.16}$ Je 24^{1} 29^{2} (all
|| מַסְגֵּר), Ex 35^{35} 38^{23} (both P; both || חֹשֵׁב). In
גֵּי הַח׳ 1 Ch 4^{14}, גֵּיא חֲרָשִׁים Ne 11^{35} *valley of (the)* 1516,
artificers, and חֲרָשִׁים *artificers* 1 Ch 4^{14}, ח has ֲ 2798
exceptionally, v. Ol $^{§ 183 a}$ Kö $^{\text{ii, § 60. 5}}$; rd. חָרָשִׁים?
2. fig. ח׳ מַשְׁחִית Ez 21^{36} *men skilled to destroy.*

†I. **חֲרֹשֶׁת n.f. carving, skilful working,** 2799
only cstr. חֲרֹשֶׁת עֵץ Ex 31^{5} 35^{33}; ח׳ אֶבֶן 31^{5} 35^{33}.
—II. חֲרֹשֶׁת v. p. 361 infr. 2800

2758 †חָרִישׁ n.m. ploughing, ploughing-time—abs. ח׳ וְקָצִיר Gn 45^{6} (E) *ploughing and harvesting;* also (=*time of ploughing and harvest*) Ex 34^{21} (JE); c. sf. as acc. cogn. חָרַשׁ חֲרִישׁוֹ 1 S 8^{12} (v. supr. חָרַשׁ **2**).

4281-82 †[מַחֲרֵשָׁה, מַחֲרֶשֶׁת] **n.f.** ploughshare—sg. sf. לִלְטוֹשׁ אִישׁ מַחֲרַשְׁתּוֹ v^{20} *to sharpen each man his ploughshare* 1 S 13^{20} (+ אֵתוֹ, קַרְדֻּמּוֹ) + מַחֲרֵשָׁתוֹ v^{20}, rd. prob. דָּרְבָנוֹ *his goad* (so 𝔊 𝔖 We Dr, see v^{21}); pl. abs. מַחֲרֵשֹׁת v^{21} (+ similar list; on txt. of both vv. see Dr).

2790 † II. [חָרֵשׁ] **vb. 1.** be silent, dumb, speechless; **2.** be deaf; chiefly poet. (NH Pi. *make deaf;* Aram. ܚܪܫ, ܚܪܶܫ *be dumb, deaf;* Ar. خَرِسَ *be dumb, speechless,* cf. As. *ḫarâšu, restrain,* acc. to Dl $^{Pr\ 100}$; v. Lag $^{BN\ 120}$)—**Qal** *Impf.* יֶחֱרַשׁ ψ 50^{3}; 2 ms. תֶּחֱרַשׁ ψ 28^{1} 83^{2}; תֶּחֱרַשׁ ψ 35^{22} 109^{1}; תֶּחֱרַשׁ ψ 39^{13}; 3 fpl. תֶּחֱרַשְׁנָה Mi 7^{16};—**1.** *be silent,* alw. of God's keeping silence when men pray ψ 35^{22} 50^{3} 83^{2} 109^{1}; sq. אֶל־ 39^{13}. **2.** *be deaf,* subj. י׳, sq. מִמֶּנִּי ψ 28^{1}; subj. אָזְנֵיהֶם Mi 7^{16}. **Hiph.** *Pf.* הֶחֱרִשׁ Nu 30^{15} Gn 34^{5}; וְהֶחֱרִישׁ consec. Nu 30$^{5.8}$; וְהֶחֱרִשׁ consec. Nu 30^{12}; הֶחֱרַשְׁתִּי Est 7^{4} + 2 t. etc.; *Impf.* יַחֲרִישׁ Nu 30^{15} + 2 t. (incl. Zp 3^{17} v. infr.); 2 ms. תַּחֲרִישׁ Hb 1^{13}; juss. תַּחֲרֵשׁ 1 S 7^{8}; 2 mpl. תַּחֲרִישׁוּן Jb 13^{5}; תַּחֲרִשׁוּן Ex 14^{14}, etc.; *Imv.* הַחֲרֵשׁ Ju 18^{19} + 2 t.; הַחֲרִישִׁי 2 S 13^{20}; הַחֲרִישׁוּ Jb 13^{13} Is 41^{1}; *Inf. abs.* הַחֲרֵשׁ Nu 30^{15} + 2 t.; *Pt.* מַחֲרִישׁ Gn 24^{21} + 2 t. (incl. 1 S 10^{27} v. infr.); מַחֲרִישִׁים 2 S 19^{11};—**1.** *be silent* (=*exhibit silence*) **a.** almost alw. of men Gn 24^{21} 34^{5} Ex 14^{14} (all J), Ju 18^{19} 2 S 13^{20} 19^{11} 2 K 18^{36}=Is 36^{21}, Je 4^{19} Jb 6^{24} 13$^{5.5.19}$ 33$^{31.33}$ Pr 11^{12} 17^{28} ψ 32^{3} Ne 5^{8} Est 4$^{14.14}$ 7^{4}; also וַיְהִי כְּמַחֲרִישׁ 1 S 10^{27} (but rd. rather ויהי כְּמֵחֹדֶשׁ *and it came to pass after about a month,* 𝔊 Dr); יחריש באהבתו Zp 3^{17} (𝔊 𝔖 יְחַדֵּשׁ *he will renew* his love, v. esp. Buhl $^{ZAW\ v.\ 1885,\ 183}$); ח׳ c. לְ pers. *keep silence at* one, i.e. fail to make objection at proper time Nu 30$^{5.8.12.15.15.15}$ (all P); הח׳ אלי Is 41^{1} pregn.=*come silently unto me;* sq. מִן pers. *cease to speak with* Je 38^{27}; *be silent about, pass by in silence,* sq. acc. אח׳ בַּדָּיו Jb 41^{4}. **b.** rarely of God, permitting evil in silence Hb 1^{13} Is 42^{14} ψ 50^{21}. **2.** once causat. *make silent,* c. acc. Jb 11^{3}. **3.** *be deaf, shew deafness:* אַל־ תַּחֲרֵשׁ מִמֶּנּוּ מִזְּעֹק 1 S 7^{8} *be not deaf* (turning) *from us, so as not to cry.*

2795 †חֵרֵשׁ **adj.** deaf—חֵרֵשׁ (=*חִרֵּשׁ) Ex 4^{11} + 4 t.; pl. חֵרְשִׁים Is 29^{18} + 3 t.;—*deaf,* Ex 4^{11} (J; ‖ אִלֵּם), ψ 38^{14} (‖ *id.*); also Lv 19^{14} (H), Is 29^{18} 35^{5} 42$^{18.19}$ + v$^{19\,b}$ (for last עִוֵּר, cf. 43^{8}; Gr $^{JQ\ 1891,\ Oct.\ p.\ 2}$ v. Che $^{Comm.,\ JQ\ Jan.\ 1892,\ 332}$), 43^{8}; פֶּתֶן ח׳ ψ 58^{5} *a deaf adder.*

† I. חֶרֶשׁ **n.[m.]** as **adv. silently, secretly**—מְרַגְּלִים ח׳ Jos 2^{1} (JE) *exploring secretly.* 2791

III. חרשׁ (√of foll.; meaning unknown).

†חֹרֶשׁ **n.m.** $^{Ez\ 31,3}$ **wood, wooded height** (As. *ḫuršu, wooded height* COT ^{Gloss} Lyon $^{Sargontexte,\ Gloss}$ (v. also Dl $^{Pr\ 180}$ Che $^{crit.\ n.\ on\ Is\ 17,\ 9}$); NH חוֹרֶשׁ *wood, forest;* Aram. חוּרְשָׁא *id.*)—abs. ח׳ Is 17^{9} Ez 31^{3} (but on both v. infr.); חֹרְשָׁה 1 S 23^{16} (v. Dr); בַּחֹרְשָׁה 1 S 23$^{15.18.19}$; pl. חֳרָשִׁים 2 Ch 27^{4};—*wooded height* 1 S 23^{15} (‖ בָּהָר v^{14}), v$^{16.18}$, so בַּמְּצָדוֹת בַּח׳ v^{19}; וּבֶח׳ בנה בִּירָנִיּוֹת וּמִגְדָּלִים 2 Ch 27^{4} *and on the wooded heights he built fortresses and towers* (‖ בְּהַר יְהוּדָה); עֲזוּבַת הַחֹרֶשׁ וְהָאָמִיר Is 17^{9} *the forsaken places of the wooded heights and summits* Ges Ew De Di RV; but rd. prob. ע׳ החוי והאמרי *forsaken places of the Hivites and the Amorites,* so 𝔊 Lag Che Or Brd Du; ח׳ מֵצַל Ez 31^{3} *shade-giving wood* or *thicket,* of close branches of cedar (but sense hardly legitimate; del. 𝔊 Co).

IV. חרשׁ (√ of foll.; meaning unknown; suggestions on etym. v. infr.)

† II. [חֶרֶשׁ] **n.[m.]** **magic art,** or perh. **magic drug** (Aram. ܚܪܰܫ *practise magic,* חָרָשׁ, ܚܰܪܳܫܳܐ *magician,* ܚܶܪܫܳܐ *incantation, magic art, preparation of magic potion,* so Eth. ሐረሰ: *one using incantations;* ሐረስ: ሐርስ: ሐረስ: *incantation, magic;* comp. perh. Ar. خُرْسٌ, خُرْسَةٌ a medicinal broth given to women in childbed; חֶרֶשׁ perh. magical drug, v. RS $^{JPh\ xiv.\ 1885,\ 125}$)—only חֲכַם חֲרָשִׁים Is 3^{3} *skilled in magic arts,* or *drugs* (‖ נְבוֹן לָחַשׁ), (> others gen.=*handicraft*). 2791

† III. חֶרֶשׁ **n.pr.m.** a Levite 1 Ch 9^{15} 𝔊 Ραραιηλ, A Αρες, 𝔊L Αρης. 2792

†חַרְשָׁא **n.pr.m.** head of a family of returning exiles Ezr 2^{52} 𝔊 Αρησα, 𝔊L Βαασα, = Ne 7^{54} 𝔊 Αδασα. 2797

† II. חֲרֹשֶׁת **n.pr.loc.** only in combin. ח׳ 2800
הַגּוֹיִם, *Ḥarosheth of the nations* (v. גּוֹי), Ju 4$^{2.13.16}$; 1471
perh. mod. *el-Ḥaritiye,* on right bank of lower Kishon, v. Thomson $^{Land\ and\ Book;\ Central\ Palestine,\ 1883,\ 215\ ff.}$ Bd $^{Pal\ 241}$ Be Bla Cooke $^{Hist.\ Deb.\ 3}$ GASm $^{Geog.\ 393}$.

חֲרָשִׁים v. חָרָשׁ and גַּיְא; also II. חֶרֶשׁ. 1516, 2791, above & p. 360 2796, 2798

2759 †[חֲרִישִׁי] **adj.** meaning wholly dub.; only רוּחַ קָדִים חֲרִישִׁית Jon 4[8]; *a silent east wind* is not suitable in context; *still=sultry* is mere conject.; Hi *autumnal* (√ I. חרשׁ); St prop. חרישׁית=חריסית, fr. חֶרֶס *sun* (or √whence חֶרֶס comes) *hot east wind;* We makes no attempt to explain.

2801 †[חָרַת] **vb. grave, engrave,** only **Qal** *Pt. pass.* חָרוּת עַל הַלֻּחֹת Ex 32[16] (E), *engraved upon the tablets* (by finger of God), but fr. absence of ‖ in cogn. lang. (Ar. حَرَتَ is *perforate, bore, slit*) prob. error for חָרוּשׁ (Je 17[1]).

2802 †[חֲרֶת] **n.pr.loc.,** only in יַעַר חֲרֶת 1 S 22[5].

2820 †חָשַׂךְ **vb. withhold, refrain** (NH חָשַׂךְ, Aram. חֲשַׂךְ, ܚܣܟ; Palm. חסך *remit, spare,* Vog[Nos. 6, 15]; Sab. משחכן *weaned* (child) DHM[ZMG 1875, 608])—**Qal** *Pf.* חָשַׂךְ Gn 39[9] + 4 t. (+ Ez 30[18] Ba; v. חשׁך; Is 38[17] v. infr.), חָשָׂךְ Is 14[6], חָשָׂכוּ Jb 30[10], חָשָׂכוּ Je 14[10], etc.; *Impf.* יַחְשֹׂךְ Jb 16[5] + 2 t.; 2 ms. תַּחְשֹׂךְ Is 58[1], תַּחְשׂוֹךְ Pr 24[11]; 2 fs. תַּחְשְׂכִי Is 54[2], etc.; *Imv.* חֲשֹׂךְ ψ 19[14]; *Pt.* חֹשֵׂךְ Pr 10[19] 11[24]; חוֹשֵׂךְ Pr 13[24] 17[27]; sq.—**1. a.** *withhold, keep back, keep for oneself,* acc., Gn 22[12] (E), v[16] 39[9] (sq. מִמֶּנִּי; both J); abs. Pr 21[26] (opp. נָתַן); *withhold the rod* (שׁבט) in discipline, Pr 13[24]; no obj. expr. 11[24] 24[11]. **b.** *keep* one from evil, calamity, She'ôl, etc., c. acc. and מִן Gn 20[6] (E), 1 S 25[39] ψ 19[14]; ח׳ מִמָּוֶת נַפְשָׁם ψ 78[50] cf. Jb 33[18] Is 38[7] (rd. חָשַׂכְתָּ or חֲשֹׂךְ for MT חָשַׁקְתָּ, v. חשׁק); abs. *hinder* (i.e. calamities fr. coming) Is 14[6]; ח׳ לְמַטָּה מֵעֲוֺנֵנוּ Ezr 9[13] thou hast *kept back, downward* (=and kept down), *part of our iniquity,* i.e. hast not punished us according to our full desert. **c.** *hold in check* c. acc. 2 S 18[16] (or *spare* v. infr.); obj. רַגְלֵיהֶם Je 14[10]; esp. of keeping silence, obj. פִּי Jb 7[11] *restrain my mouth,* שׂפתים Pr 10[19], אמרים 17[27]; מִפָּנַי לֹא ח׳ רֹק Jb 30[10] *from my face they have not withheld spittle* (=they have spit in my face). **d.** *refrain* (fr. doing what is mentioned in the context), abs. Is 54[2] 58[1]. **e.** *spare,* c. acc. pers. 2 K 5[20] *he hath spared* Naaman מִקַּחַת *so as not to take* (=and hath not taken anything) out of his hand; perh. also 2 S 18[16] Joab *spared* the people (v. supr.). **f.** *reserve* for, c. acc. + לְ Jb 38[23]. **2.** (abs.) *restrain, check* (pain) i.e. *assuage,* so appar. MT Jb 16[5] (v. Di Kau; *I would not restrain condolence of my lips,* 𝔊 𝔖 Me, rdg. לא אחשׂך for יחשׂך).—Ez 30[18] v. חשׁך.

Niph. *Impf.* לְיוֹם אֵיד יֵחָשֶׂךְ רָע Jb 21[30] *at the day of calamity the wicked is spared* (pass. of **Qal 1 e**); יֵחָשֵׂךְ Jb 16[6] *be assuaged,* of pain (pass. of **Qal 2**).

†חָשַׂף **vb. strip off, strip, make bare**— 2834
Qal *Pf.* חָשַׂף Is 52[10], חֲשָׂפָהּ Jo 1[7], חָשַׂפְתִּי Je 13[26] 49[10]; *Impf.* וַיֶּחֱשֹׂף ψ 29[9]; *Imv.* fs. חֶשְׂפִּי־ Is 47[2]; *Inf. abs.* חָשֹׂף Jo 1[7]; *cstr.* לַחְשֹׂף Is 30[14] Hg 2[16]; *Pt. pass.* חֲשׂוּפָה Ez 4[7], חֲשׂוּפַי Is 20[4] (pl. cstr.? cf. *infr.*).—**1.** *strip off,* expose oneself by removing (obj. שֹׁבֶל, flowing skirt, train) Is 47[2] of Babylon, personified as queen (‖ גַּלִּי שׁוֹק), ח׳ שׁוּלַיִךְ עַל־פָּנָיִךְ Je 13[26]. **2.** *strip, lay bare,* fig. of י׳ Is 52[10] obj. זְרוֹעַ קדשׁו; of prophet, Ez 4[7] (but Co del. v. as interpol.); obj. pers. Je 49[10] (‖ גִּלֵּיתִי); חָשֹׂף חשׂפהּ Jo 1[7] of locusts stripping fig-tree; חֲשׂוּפַי שֵׁת Is 20[4] (pt. either sg. coll., with formative ending ־ַי, De Lag[Se i. 19 (cf. 69); BN 192]; or pl. cstr., v. Ges[§ 87, 1 c.]); ח׳ יְעָרוֹת ψ 29[9] of voice of י׳ (i.e. a storm) stripping forests. **3.** *draw* (water) Is 30[14]; (wine) Hg 2[16]; properly *take from the surface, skim.*

†[חָשִׂיף] **n.m.** only pl. cstr. כִּשְׁנֵי חֲשִׂפֵי 2835
עִזִּים 1 K 20[27] 𝔊 𝔙 𝔗 and most, *two little flocks of goats* (חשׂיף=*segregatum,* strictly *what is stripped off*), but this without other evidence than authority of the Vrss; Klo proposes בַּשְּׁפִי מִשְׁפַּט עִזִּים *on the bare height, after the manner of goats.*

†חֲשׂוּפָא, חֲשֻׂפָא **n.pr.m.** head of a 2817
family of Nethinim among the returning exiles חֲשׂוּפָא Ezr 2[43]=חֲשֻׂפָא Ne 7[46].

חֲשׂוּפַי Is 20[4] v. חשׂף. above 2834

†מַחְשֹׂף **n.m. a laying bare, stripping**— 4286
only cstr. מַחְשֹׂף הַלָּבָן Gn 30[37] (J) *a stripping of the white,* i.e. so as to shew wood under the bark.

†חָשַׁב **vb. think, account** (NH *id.;* 2803
Aram. חֲשַׁב, ܚܫܒ; Ar. حَسَبَ; Eth. ሐሰበ: *id.;* Ph. n. חשׁב mng. dub. v. CIS[i. 86])—**Qal** *Pf.* ח׳ Is 33[8] + 9 t.; חָשַׁבְתָּה 2 S 14[13] etc.; *Impf.* יַחְשֹׁב Is 10[7] + 4 t.; יַחֲשָׁב־ 2 S 19[20] ψ 40[18]; sf. יַחְשְׁבֵנִי Jb 19[11] 33[10]; pl. יַחְשְׁבוּ ψ 41[8] Dn 11[25]; יַחְשֹׁבוּ Is 13[17]; יַחְשְׁבוּן ψ 35[20]; נַחְשְׁבָה Je 18[18], etc. + 9 t. *Impf.; Inf. cstr.* לַחְשֹׁב Ex 31[4] + 3 t.; *Pt.* חֹשֵׁב Ex 26[1] + 15 t., חוֹשֵׁב 2 Ch 26[15]; חֹשְׁבִים Ne 6[2] + 3 t., חֹשְׁבֵי Mi 2[1] + 3 t.;—**I.** of man: **1.** *think,*

account לבבו לא כן יחשב Is 10^{7} *not so thinketh his mind;* חשבי שמו Mal 3^{16} those *thinking of his name;* sq. 2 acc. חשבנהו נגוע Is 53^{4} *we thought him stricken;* elsewhere c. acc. + לְ Gn 38^{15} (J), 1 S 1^{13} Jb 19^{15} 35^{2} 41^{24}; so, fig., of crocodile Jb 41^{19} *he reckoneth iron as straw.* **2.** *devise, plan, mean,* c. acc. מַחֲשֶׁבֶת רָעָה Ez 38^{10}, מְזִמּוֹת ψ 35^{4} 140^{3} Zc 7^{10} 8^{17}, תַּהְפֻּכוֹת Pr 16^{30}, רעה ψ 10^{2} 21^{12}, דִּבְרֵי מִרְמוֹת ψ 35^{20}, אָוֶן Mi 2^{1} Ez 11^{2} ψ 36^{5}, הַוּוֹת ψ 52^{4}; ח׳ רע(ה) על *devise evil against* Gn 50^{20} (E), Je 48^{2} Na 1^{11}, ח׳ רעה לְ ψ 41^{8}, ח׳ מַחֲשֶׁבֶת על Je 11^{19} 18^{18} 49^{30} Dn 11^{25} Est 8^{3} 9^{25}, ח׳ כזאת על 2 S 14^{13}; c. inf. 1 S 18^{25} Je 18^{8} 23^{27} Jb 6^{26} Ne $6^{2.6}$ Est 9^{24} ψ 140^{5}; c. לבלתי + Impf. 2 S 14^{14} (where, however, Ew rds. חוֹשֵׁב for וחשב cf. We Dr; in this case לבלתי carries on לֹא יִשָּׂא). **3.** *charge, impute* ח׳ עון לְ, 2 S 19^{20} *impute iniquity to.* **4.** *esteem, value, regard,* silver Is 13^{17}, a man Is 33^{8}, the servant of י׳ Is 53^{3}. **5.** *invent* ingenious and artistic things, ח׳ להם כלי שיר Am 6^{5} *invent* for themselves instruments of music; ח׳ (כל) מחשבת *invent cunning work* (of artistic devices in constr. of tabern.) Ex 31^{4} $35^{32.35}$ (all P), so 2 Ch 2^{13}; מַעֲשֵׂה חֹשֵׁב *work of the cunning* (ingenious, inventive) *workman* (of artistic devices in weaving; see esp. VB and Di) Ex $26^{1.31}$ $28^{6.15}$ $36^{8.35}$ $39^{3.8}$ (all P); מַחֲשְׁבֹת חוֹשֵׁב 2 Ch 26^{15} *inventions of inventive men* (of engines of war); חָרָשׁ וְחֹשֵׁב *craftsman and inventive workman* (in constr. of tabern., vid. supr.) Ex 35^{35} 38^{23} (P). **II.** of God: **1.** *think,* c. acc. pers + לְ indirect obj. *account one* לאויב, *for an enemy* Jb 13^{24} 33^{10}; ח׳ לו כצריו Jb 19^{11} *he accounted me unto him as his adversaries.* **2.** *devise, plan, mean,* c. acc. + ל indirect obj. לטבה *for good* Gn 50^{20} (E); c. ל pers. לִי *devise for me* ψ 40^{18}; acc. rei + עַל, *devise something against a person* Mi 2^{3} Je 18^{11}; *towards* one Je 29^{11}, c. אל against Je 49^{20} 50^{45}; sq. inf. Je 26^{3} 36^{3} La 2^{8}. **3.** *impute, reckon,* c. acc. rei + ל pers., the habit of believing in י׳ *he reckoned* to Abram as righteousness Gn 15^{6} (JE; cf. **Niph. 3**); not *impute iniquity to* one ψ 32^{2}. **Niph.** *Pf.* נֶחְשַׁב Nu $18^{27.30}$, נֶחְשַׁבְתִּי ψ 88^{5} etc. + 10 t. *Pf.; Impf.* יֵחָשֵׁב Lv 7^{18} + 7 t., etc., + 6 t. *Impf.; Pt.* נֶחְשָׁב Is 2^{22} 1 K 10^{21} 2 Ch 9^{20}:—**1.** *be accounted, thought, esteemed,* c. כְּ *as* Ho 8^{12} Is 5^{28} 29^{16} 40^{15} ψ 44^{23} Jb 18^{3} 41^{21}; c. לְ Is 29^{17} = 32^{15}, La 4^{2}; עִם *with, among* ψ 88^{5}, בַּמֶּה Is 2^{22} *at what* (value)? (v. prob. interpol.; om. 𝔊); c. acc. Dt $2^{11.20}$ Pr 17^{28} Ne 13^{13}; נָכְרִיּוֹת נֶחְשַׁבְנוּ לוֹ Gn 31^{15} (E; 𝔊 Sam כְּנֶח׳) Is 40^{17}. **2.** *be computed, reckoned,* c. לְ Jos 13^{3} (D), עַל Lv 25^{31} (P), 2 S 4^{2}: abs. כסף *was not counted* (so plentiful was it) 1 K 10^{21} = 2 Ch 9^{20} 2 K 22^{7}. **3.** *be imputed to any one,* c. לְ Lv 7^{18} Nu $18^{27.30}$ (all P), Lv 17^{4} (H) Pr 27^{14}; the interposition of Phinehas נח׳ לו לצדקה ψ 106^{31} *was imputed to him for righteousness* (cf. **Qal II 3**). **Pi.** *Pf.* 3 ms. חִשַּׁב Lv 25^{27} + 4 t.; f. חִשְּׁבָה Jon 1^{4}; 1 s. חִשַּׁבְתִּי ψ 77^{6} 119^{59}; *Impf.* יְחַשֵּׁב Pr 16^{9} Dn 11^{24}, תְּחַשְּׁבוּן Na 1^{9}, etc., + 4 t. *Impf.; Pt.* מְחַשֵּׁב Pr 24^{8}:—**1.** *think upon, consider, be mindful of,* c. acc. ψ 77^{6} 119^{59}, (מה) בֶּן־אֱנוֹשׁ וַתְּחַשְּׁבֵהוּ ψ 144^{3} *what* (is) *man's son, and thou thinkest upon him* (|| תֵּדָעֵהוּ). **2.** *think* to do, *devise, plan,* c. acc. Pr 16^{9}, אֶל of persons against whom Ho 7^{15} Na 1^{9}, עַל Dn 11^{24}; c. inf. ψ 73^{16} Pr 24^{8}; so of inanim. object הָאֳנִיָּה חִשְּׁבָה לְהִשָּׁבֵר Jon 1^{4} *the ship was about to* (minded to) *be broken up.* **3.** *count, reckon,* the years since a sale of land Lv 25^{27} (H); c. לְ pers. Lv 25^{52} (H), $27^{18.23}$ (P); c. עִם Lv 25^{50} (P); c. אֶת 2 K 12^{16}. **Hithp.** *Impf.* בַּגּוֹיִם לֹא יִתְחַשָּׁב Nu 23^{9} (JE) *among the nations it shall not reckon itself.*

†חֵשֶׁב **n.m. ingenious work,** name of the 2805
girdle or *band* of the ephod (*cunningly woven band,* RV), only P; alw. in combin., ח׳ האפ(ו)ד Ex $28^{27.28}$ 29^{5} $39^{20.21}$ Lv 8^{7}; ח׳ אֲפֻדָּתוֹ Ex 28^{8} 39^{5}.

†חֲשֻׁבָה **n.pr.m.** (*consideration*)—son of 2807
Zerubbabel 1 Ch 3^{20}; 𝔊 Ασουβε, 𝔊L Λασαβαθ.

†חַשּׁוּב **n.pr.m.** (*considerate*)—**1.** a Levite 2815
chief 1 Ch 9^{14} Ne 11^{15}, 𝔊 Ασουβ. **2.** builders at the wall: **a.** Ne 3^{11} 10^{24}, 𝔊 Ασουβ, Ασουθ. **b.** Ne 3^{23}, 𝔊 Ασουβ.

†I. חֶשְׁבּוֹן **n.m. reckoning, account** (NH 2808
Aram. *id.*) Ec 9^{10}, בקש ח׳ Ec 7^{25}, מצא ח׳ Ec 7^{27}.

†II. חֶשְׁבּוֹן **n.pr.loc.** of the city of Sihon 2809
king of the Amorites Nu $21^{26.27.28.30.34}$ 32^{3} (all E); Dt 1^{4} $2^{24.26.30}$ $3^{2.6}$ 4^{46} 29^{6} Jos 9^{10} $12^{2.5}$ $13^{10.21.27}$ (all D) Ju 11^{19} Je 48^{45} Ne 9^{22}; captured by Israel who dwelt in it Nu 21^{25} (E) Ju 11^{26}; rebuilt by Reuben Nu 32^{37} (E), given to Reuben at the division of the land Jos 13^{17} (P); on the border of Gad, Jos 13^{26} (P), it subsequently fell to Gad and was assigned to Levites out of that tribe Jos 21^{39} (P) 1 Ch 6^{66}; the Moabites gained possession of it Is 15^{4} $16^{8.9}$ and subsequently

the Ammonites Je 48$^{2.34.45}$ 49^{3}; it was celebrated for its fish ponds Ct 7^{5}.—Mod. *Ḥusbân*, Seetzen Reisen i. 407 Rob$^{BR\ i.\ 551}$ Bd$^{Pal\ 191}$ Survey$^{EP\ 8}$.

2810 †[חִשָּׁבוֹן] **n.m. device, invention** (cf. Lag BN 200)—only pl. abs. חִשְּׁבֹנוֹת; עָשָׂה הָאֱלֹהִים אֶת־הָאָדָם יָשָׁר וְהֵמָּה בִקְשׁוּ חִשְּׁבֹנוֹת רַבִּים Ec 7^{29} *God made mankind upright but they sought out many devices;* וַיַּעַשׂ חִשְּׁבֹנוֹת מַחֲשֶׁבֶת חוֹשֵׁב 2 Ch 26^{15} *and he made contrivances* (i.e. engines of war for hurling stones and arrows, see v^{b}) *the invention of inventive men.*

2811 †חֲשַׁבְיָה, חֲשַׁבְיָהוּ **n.pr.m.** (*Yah(u) has taken account*)—**1.** חֲשַׁבְיָהוּ a temple musician 1 Ch 25^{3}=חֲשַׁבְיָה v^{19}; 𝔊 in both Ασαβια. **2.** חֲשַׁבְיָה a Levite, David's time 1 Ch 27^{17}; perh. =חֲשַׁבְיָהוּ, officer of David in Hebron 1 Ch 26^{30}; in both 𝔊 Ασαβιας. **3.** חֲשַׁבְיָהוּ a Levite, Josiah's time 2 Ch 35^{9}; 𝔊 Ασαβια. Elsewhere חשביה: **4.** Levite in line of Merari 1 Ch 6^{30} 𝔊 Ασεβ(ε)ι, Ασαβια. **5.** Levite 1 Ch 9^{14}, 𝔊 Ασαβια=Ne 11^{15}, A 𝔊L Ασαβιου[ας]. **6.** Levite, Ezra's time Ezr 8$^{19.24}$ Ne 10^{12} 11^{22} 12^{24} (𝔊 Ασαβιας etc.)=חֲשַׁבְנְיָה **2,** q.v. **7.** head of a family of priests Ne 12^{21}, 𝔊 Ασαβιας. **8.** a builder at the wall Ne 3^{17}, 𝔊 Ασαβια(ς).

2812 †חֲשַׁבְנָה **n.pr.m.** (this and foll. perh. txt. err. for חשביה(ו); yet 𝔊 Εσαβανα, 𝔊L Ασβανα) —a chief of the people, Nehemiah's time Ne 10^{26}. Vid. also following.

2813 חֲשַׁבְנְיָה **n.pr.m.** (v. foregoing);—**1.** father of a builder at the wall Ne 3^{10}, 𝔊 Ασβαναμ; 𝔊L Σαβανιου[-ας]. **2.** a Levite Ne 9^{5} (om. 𝔊) =חֲשַׁבְיָה **6.**

4284 †מַחֲשָׁבָה **n.f. thought, device** (chiefly poet. and late)—abs. מ׳ Je 18^{11} 49^{30}; מַחֲשֶׁבֶת Ez 38^{10}; מַחֲשָׁבֶת Ex 35^{33} 2 Ch 2^{13}; cstr. מַחֲשֶׁבֶת Est 8^{5} 2 Ch 26^{15}; sf. מַחֲשַׁבְתּוֹ Est 8^{3} 9^{25}; pl. מַחֲשָׁבוֹת Je 11^{19}+7 t.; מַחֲשָׁבֹת Ex 31^{4}+3 t.; cstr. מַחְשְׁבוֹת Is 59^{7}+13 t.; מַחְשְׁבֹת Gn 6^{5}; sf. מַחְשְׁבוֹתַי Is 55^{8} etc.+19 t. sfs.;—**1.** *thought*: **a.** of man מ׳ אדם ψ 94^{11}; מ׳ לֵב ψ 33^{11} *thoughts of the mind;* (כל) יצר מ׳ (לב) Gn 6^{5} (J), 1 Ch 28^{9} 29^{18}. **b.** of God מ׳ יהוה Mi 4^{12}; c. אֶל־ ψ 40^{6}; עַל־ Je 51^{29}; the thoughts of God are exceeding deep ψ 92^{6}; higher than man's thoughts Is 55$^{8.8.9.9}$. **2.** *device, plan, purpose* Is 55^{7} 59^{7} 65^{2} 66^{18} Je 6^{19} 18^{12} ψ 56^{6} Pr 19^{21} Jb 21^{27} La 3$^{60.61}$ Est 8^{5}; מ׳ חָרוּץ Pr 21^{5}; מ׳ עֲרוּמִים Jb 5^{12}; מ׳ צדיקים Pr 12^{5}; מ׳ עמים ψ 33^{10}; מ׳ אָוֶן Is 59^{7} Je 4^{14} Pr 6^{18}; מ׳ רע Pr 15^{26}; מ׳ שָׁלוֹם Je 21^{11}; חשב מ׳ *devise devices* 2 S 14^{14} Je 11^{19} 18$^{11.18}$ 29^{11} 49$^{20.30}$ 50^{45} Ez 38^{10} Dn 11$^{24.25}$ Est 8^{3} 9^{25}; מ׳ as subj. of נָכוֹן *be established* Pr 16^{3} 20^{18}; הפר מ׳ *break plans* Pr 15^{22}. **3.** *invention* Ex 31^{4} 35$^{32.33.35}$ (all P), 2 Ch 2^{13} 26^{15} (v. חָשַׁב **I 5**).

†חֲשַׁבַּדָּנָה **n.pr.m.** (etym. dub.)—one of 2806
those who stood with Ezra at the reading of the law Ne 8^{4}; B om.; A Ασαβααμα, 𝔊L Αβααvας.

†[חָשָׁה] **vb. be silent, inactive, still** 2814
(chiefly poet. and late) (NH *id.*, Aram. in deriv.)—**Qal** *Impf.* 2 ms. תֶּחֱשֶׁה ψ 28^{1} Is 64^{11}; אֶחֱשֶׁה Is 62^{1} 65^{6}; יֶחֱשׁוּ Is 62^{6}; וַיֶּחֱשׁוּ ψ 107^{29}; —*be silent* Ec 3^{7} (opp. לְדַבֵּר); Is 62$^{1.6}$ (= neglect to speak); of י׳ i.e. be unresponsive ψ 28^{1} (‖חרש); Is 64^{11} (‖הִתְאַפֵּק); but 65^{6} of י׳'s keeping silence at iniquity, i.e. overlooking it (cf. 57^{11} Hiph.); of waves, *be still* ψ 107^{29} (subj. גַּלֵּיהֶם). **Hiph.** *Pf.* הֶחֱשֵׁיתִי ψ 39^{3} Is 42^{14}; *Imv.* הֶחֱשׁוּ 2 K 2$^{3.5}$; *Pt.* מַחְשֶׁה Is 57^{11}; pl. מַחְשִׁים Ju 18^{9}+3 t.;—**1.** *exhibit silence, be silent* 2 K 2$^{3.5}$ 7^{9} ψ 39^{3} (sq. מִטּוֹב ‖ נֶאֱלַמְתִּי), fig. Is 42^{14} (‖אחריש); of י׳'s *being silent* at iniquity Is 57^{11} (i.e. overlooking it, cf. Qal 65^{5}), poss. also is *be silent*, opp. *rescue*, Ges Che Di Du. **2.** *shew inactivity* Ju 18^{9}, הח׳ מִקַּחַת 1 K 22^{3} Gilead is ours, and we *shew inactivity so as not to take it.* **3.** causat. *make still, quiet*, sq. לְ, of direct obj. Ne 8^{11} (v^{b} הַסּוּ q. v.)

חֻשָׁם, חֻשִׁים v. supr. p. 302 a. 2366-67

†חָשַׁךְ **vb. be, grow dark** (NH *id.;* Aram. 2821
חֲשַׁךְ, ܚܫܟ; Ar. حَسِكَ *bear rancour*, v. Lag BN 30) —**Qal** *Pf.* ח׳ Is 5^{30}+4 t.; וְחָֽשְׁכָה consec. Mi 3^{6} (but v. infr.); חָשְׁכוּ La 5^{17}; וְחָֽשְׁכוּ consec. Ec 12^{3}; *Impf.* 3 fs. תֶּחְשַׁךְ Ec 12^{2}; וַתֶּחְשַׁךְ Ex 10^{15}; 3 mpl. יֶחְשְׁכוּ Jb 3^{9}; 3 fpl. תֶּחְשַׁכְנָה ψ 69^{24};—**1.** *be, grow dark,* אור Is 5^{30}, cf. (fig.) Jb 18^{6}; הַשֶּׁמֶשׁ Is 13^{10} (fig.); היום Ez 30^{18} (where rd. חשך, for MT Baer חשך); Jb 3^{9} (subj. כוכבים), cf. Ec 12^{2} (subj. השמש, הכוכבים, הירח, האור); impers. Mi 3^{6} (si vera l.; but rd. prob. וַחֲשֵׁכָה, corresponding with לַיְלָה preceding). **2.** *have a dark colour:* ח׳ מִשְּׁחוֹר תָּאֳרָם La 4^{8} *darker than blackness is their visage;* of the earth הָאָרֶץ Ex 10^{15}. **3.** *grow dim* La 5^{17} (subj. עינינו), cf. ψ 69^{24} (fig.), Ec 12^{3} subj. הָרֹאוֹת i.e. the eyes. **Hiph.** *Pf.* הֶחְשִׁיךְ Am 5^{8}, וְהַחֲשַׁכְתִּי Am 8^{9}; *Impf.* יַחְשִׁיךְ ψ 139^{12}; יַחְשִׁךְ Je 13^{16}; וַיַּחְשִׁךְ ψ 105^{28}; *Pt.* מַחְשִׁיךְ Jb 38^{2};—**1.**

make dark, יום לילה הח׳ Am 5^{8}; abs. *cause darkness* Je 13^{16} ψ 105^{28}, cf. Am 8^{9} (לארץ). **2.** =*hide, conceal*, sq. מִמְּךָ ψ 139^{12}. **3.** fig. *obscure, confuse* Jb 38^{2} (obj. עֵצָה).

2822 †חֹשֶׁךְ **n.m.**$^{\text{Ex 10, 21}}$ **darkness, obscurity**;—abs. חֹשֶׁךְ Gn 1^{2} + 75 t. (+ Ez 8^{12} del. Co A B etc.); cstr. *id.* Ex 10^{22}; sf. חָשְׁכִּי ψ 18^{29} = 2 S 22^{29};—**1.** *darkness* (opp. אור) lit. Gn $1^{2.4}$ (P), Is 45^{7} Jb 26^{10} Ec 2^{13}, cf. in imprecation Jb $3^{4.5}$ (ח׳ וצלמות) = לילה Gn $1^{5.18}$ (P), cf. Jos 2^{5} (JE), Is 45^{19} Jb 17^{12} 24^{16} 38^{19} ψ 104^{20}; *darkness* in mines Jb 28^{3}; of *extraordinary darkness*, in Egypt Ex $10^{21.21}$(E); ח׳־אֲפֵלָה Ex 10^{22}(E), ψ 105^{28}, from pillar of cloud Ex 14^{20} (J); at Mt. Sinai Dt 4^{11} 5^{20}; of clouds of theophany 2 S 22^{12} = ψ 18^{12}; of darkness in death, or She'ôl, 1 S 2^{9} Jb 10^{21} (אֶרֶץ ח׳ וצלמות), 17^{13} 18^{18} ψ 88^{13} Pr 20^{20} (אִישׁוֹן ח׳ = *extreme of darkness*). **2.** =*secret place(s)* Is 45^{3} Jb 12^{22} (‖ צלמות); =*hiding-place* Jb 34^{22} (‖ *id.*), cf. ψ $139^{11.12}$;—on Ez 8^{12}, v. supr. **3.** fig., **a.** =distress Is 5^{30} 9^{1} 29^{18} (fig. of blindness), 42^{7} 49^{9} 58^{10} 59^{9} 60^{2} La 3^{2} Mi 7^{8} ψ 18^{29} = 2 S 22^{29}, Jb $15^{22.23.30}$ 20^{26} 22^{11} 23^{17} 29^{3} ψ $107^{10.14}$ (in both ‖ צלמות), 112^{4} Ec 5^{16} 11^{8}. **b.** =dread, terror, symbol. of judgment Am $5^{18.20}$ Zp 1^{15} Na 1^{8} Ez 32^{8} Jo 2^{4} 3^{4}. **c.** =mourning Is 47^{5}. **d.** =perplexity Jb 5^{14} 12^{25} 19^{8}; confusion ψ 35^{6}. **e.** =ignorance Jb 37^{19} Ec 2^{14}. **f.** =evil, sin Is $5^{20.20}$ Pr 2^{13}. **g.** =obscurity Ec $6^{4.4}$.

2823 †[חָשֹׁךְ] **adj. obscure, low**, only mpl. as subst.; בַּל־יִתְיַצֵּב לִפְנֵי חֲשֻׁכִּים Pr 22^{29} *he shall not stand before obscure men* (opp. לפני־מלכים).

2825 †חֲשֵׁכָה **n.f. darkness** (chiefly poet.)—ח׳ Gn 15^{12} + 2 t., so rd. also prob. Mi 3^{6} (for MT
2824 חָשְׁכָה); חֲשֵׁיכָה ψ 139^{12}; cstr. חֶשְׁכַת ψ 18^{12}; pl. חֲשֵׁכִים Is 50^{10};—*darkness*, opp. light (אורה) ψ 139^{12}; supernat., ח׳ גדולה Gn 15^{12} (JE); חֶשְׁכַת־מַיִם ψ 18^{12} in theoph. (but ‖ 2 S 22^{12} חַשְׁרַת־מים *a mass of water*); fig. = lack of understanding ψ 82^{5}; =distress Is 8^{22} (‖ צָרָה), 50^{10}.

4285 †מַחְשָׁךְ **n.m. dark place** (poet.)—abs. מ׳ Is 29^{15} 42^{16}; מַחְשָׁךְ ψ 88^{19}; pl. מַחֲשַׁכִּים 88^{7} 143^{3} = La 3^{6}; cstr. מַחֲשַׁכֵּי ψ 74^{20};—*dark place*: **a.** =*hiding-place* מח׳־ארץ 74^{20}. **b.** *dark region*, in which men may lose their way Is 42^{16}. **c.** = *grave*, or שׁאול ψ 88^{19} (v. Che); of dark place of God's wrath (like She'ôl) 88^{7}; cf. 143^{3} = La 3^{6}. **d.** =*secret place, secrecy* (of plots) Is 29^{15}.

2826 †[חָשַׁל] **vb. shatter** (BAram. חֲשַׁל *shatter*; NH Pi., ‖ משבר; Syr. ܚܫܠ *forge* a metal, Ar. حَسَلَ *drive* cattle *violently*; As. *ḫašâlu, shatter, destroy* Zim$^{\text{BP 12}}$ Dl$^{\text{Pr 42}}$)—**Niph.** *Pt.* fig. כָּל־הַנֶּחֱשָׁלִים Dt 25^{18} *all the shattered ones*, i.e. those broken down, worn out, sq. וְאַתָּה עָיֵף וְיָגֵעַ; others think = חלשׁ.

†חָשֻׁם **n.pr.m.** head of a family of returned exiles Ezr 2^{19} = Ne 7^{22}, Ezr 10^{33} cf. Ne 8^{4} 10^{19}. 2828

†חַשְׁמַל **n.[m.]** etym. and exact mng. dub.; evidently some *shining* substance; AV **amber**; supposed by Thes (q. v.) and most to be a brilliant amalgam of gold and silver, 𝔊 ἤλεκτρον (v. Liddell & Scott s. v. **2**), 𝔙 *electrum*; v. also Dl in Baer$^{\text{Ezech. xii}}$; only in the combination כְּעֵין ח׳ *like the appearance of* ח׳ Ez $1^{4.27}$; כְּעֵין הַחַשְׁמַלָה Ez 8^{2} (on ending ־ָה v. Ges$^{\text{§ 90, 2 R a}}$; Co del.) 2830

†[חַשְׁמַן] **n.m.** only pl. חַשְׁמַנִּים ψ 68^{32}; mng. unknown, 𝔊 𝔖 𝔙 *ambassadors*, Rabb. *nobles*, conject. from context; doubtless txt. err.; Nes$^{\text{JBL 1891, 152}}$ prop. בשמנים they shall come *with oils, ointments*, Hilg Che (after Aq Jer) חָשִׁים *hasting*. 2831

†חֶשְׁמוֹן **n.pr.loc.** town in southern Judah, site unknown Jos 15^{27}. 2829

†חַשְׁמֹנָה **n.pr.loc.** a station of Isr. in wilderness Nu $33^{29.30}$, site unknown. 2832

חשן (√ of foll.; meaning not certain; Ar. حَسُنَ is *be excellent, beautiful*; حُسْنٌ *beauty, all excellence*; hence poss. חֹשֶׁן either as chief ornament of ephod, or as the most excellent, precious article of high priest's attire).

†חֹשֶׁן **n.m. the breast-piece** or **sacred pouch**, containing the אורים ותמים, worn on the breast of the high priest when he ministered in the Holy Place to bring the tribes for memorial before י׳. It was made of the same material as the ephod (v. אֵפוֹד), a span square; set in front with twelve jewels in four rows, engraved with the names of the twelve tribes. It was firmly fastened to the shoulders of the ephod by gold chains passing through gold rings, and to the lower part of the ephod just above the girdle by a blue ribbon passing through other gold rings. It was חֹשֶׁן (ה)מִּשְׁפָּט (Ex $28^{15.29.30}$) *pouch of judgment*, because of the decision given by the אוּרִים וְתֻמִּים. The name occurs only in P, Ex 25^{7} $28^{4.15.22.23.23.24.26.28.28.29.30}$ 29^{5} $35^{9.27}$ $39^{8.9.15.16.17.19.21.21}$ Lv $8^{8.8}$.—Vid. Now$^{\text{Arch. ii. 119}}$. 2833

†I. חָשַׁק **vb. be attached to, love** (NH *press together, desire* (rare); Aram. חֲשַׁק *bind,* 2836

saddle (an ass))—**Qal** *Pf.* ח׳ Dt 7^{7} + 4 t.; חָֽשְׁקָה Gn 34^{8}; וְחָשַׁקְתָּ Is 38^{17} (but v. infr.); וְחָשַׁקְתָּ Dt 21^{11};—*be attached to*, only fig.=*love*, a woman sq. בְּ Gn 34^{8} (P) Dt 21^{11}; elsewh. of י׳'s love for Israel Dt 7^{7} 10^{15}, and of love to י׳ ψ 91^{14}; sq. acc. cogn. + לְ and inf. כל־חֵשֶׁק שְׁלֹמֹה אשר ח׳ לִבְנוֹת 1 K 9^{19} = 2 Ch 8^{6}; חָשַׁקְתָּ נַפְשִׁי מִשַּׁחַת Is 38^{17} lit. *thou hast loved my soul out of the pit*, i.e. lovingly delivered it; but rd. חָשַׂכְתָּ *thou hast held back, kept*, from 𝔊 𝔙 Lo Ew Che Di, or חֲשֹׂךְ *hold back* (Imv.), so Du.

2837 † חֵשֶׁק **n.m.** desire = thing desired—cstr. חֵשֶׁק שְׁלֹמֹה 1 K 9^{19} = 2 Ch 8^{6}, 1 K 9^{1}; sf. נֶשֶׁף חִשְׁקִי Is 21^{4} *the twilight of my pleasure.*

2838 † [חָשׁוּק] **n.[m.]** **fillet** or **ring** clasping (*binding*) a pillar of the tabernacle, only pl. sf. חֲשֻׁקֵיהֶם Ex 27^{10} + 5 t.; חֲשׁוּקֵיהֶם Ex $38^{12.17}$; those of the pillars at door of tabernacle (הָאֹהֶל) were overlaid with gold Ex 36^{38}; those of the pillars of the court with silver $27^{10.11}$ $38^{10.11.12.17.19}$ (all P), v. Di on Ex 27^{10}; > Thes and most who understand of *connecting-rods,* joining tops of pillars, from which curtains were hung.

2836 † II. [חשק] **vb. denom.** only **Pi.** **furnish with fillets or rings,** and **Pu.** pass.; **Pi.** *Pf.* 3 ms. חִשַּׁק Ex 38^{28} (P), subj. Bezaleel. **Pu.** *Pt.* מְחֻשָּׁקִים כֶּסֶף Ex 27^{17} 38^{17} *furnished with silver fillets,* in agreement with הָעַמּוּדִים (both P).

2839 † [חִשּׁוּק] **n.[m.]** **spoke** of a wheel (as *binding* felloe to nave)—pl. sf. חִשֻּׁקֵיהֶם 1 K 7^{33}.

חשר (√ of foll.; cf. As. *ašâru, collect, gather* Zim[BP 39]. In Ar., *collect* is حَشَرَ, but ش not usu. = שׂ).

2841 † [חַשְׁרָה] **n.f.** **collection, mass,** only (si vera l.) חַשְׁרַת־מַיִם 2 S 22^{12} (חֶשְׁכַת in ∥ ψ 18^{12}).

2840 † [חִשּׁוּר] **n.[m.]** **nave, hub** of a wheel (which *gathers in* the spokes)—pl. sf. חִשֻּׁרֵיהֶם 1 K 7^{33}.

חשׁשׁ (√ of foll.; cf. Ar. حَثَّ *hasten, hurry* (trans.), حُثٌّ *particles of straw, sand, dust,* as flying quickly about; v. Lag[BN 40]).

2842 † חֲשַׁשׁ **n.m.**[Is 59, 24] **chaff**;—abs. תַּהֲרוּ ח׳ תֵּלְדוּ קַשׁ Is 33^{11} *ye conceive chaff, ye bring forth stubble* (fig. of vain attempt of Assyr.); cstr. ח׳ לֶהָבָה יִרְפֶּה Is 5^{24} (∥ קַשׁ) *as flaming chaff sinketh down* (sim. of perishing of heedless Judahites).

חָשְׁתִּי v. חוּשׁ. p. 302 2843

חַת, חִתָּה v. חתת. p. 369 2844, 2847

† חֵת **n.pr.m.** appar. represented as ancestor of the Hittites (etym. and mng. unknown; pronounced as fr. √ ע״ע in Heb. & As., but not Egypt.; v. חִתִּי infr.)—'begotten' by Canaan Gn 10^{15} (J) = 1 Ch 1^{13}; elsewh. only in combin. with בְּנֵי, בְּנוֹת; **a.** בְּנֵי־חֵת acc. to P lived at Mamre (Hebron), and one of them sold Abraham the cave of Machpelah for a sepulchre Gn $23^{3.5.10.10.16.18.20}$ 25^{10} 49^{32}. **b.** בְּנוֹת(־)חֵת only of wives of Esau Gn $27^{46.46}$ (P; 𝔊 om. v^{b}; ∥ בְּנוֹת הָאָרֶץ = בְּנוֹת כְּנָעַן 28^{1}). 2845

2850 † חִתִּי **adj.** et **n.gent. Hittite(s)** (Egypt. *Ḥ-tá, Ḥetá,* W Max Müll[Asien u. Europa, 319 ff.]; As. *Ḫatti,* Schr[KG 192 ff.] COT on Gn 10^{19} Dl[Pa, 269 ff.]; Tel-el-Amarna *Ḫatti, Ḫatta* Bez[Tel el Amarn. Brit. Mus. 150])—m. alw. c. art. הַחִתִּי Gn 23^{10} Ex 3^{8} +; f. חִתִּית Ez $16^{3.45}$; mpl. הַחִתִּים Jos 1^{4} + 3 t.; fpl. חִתִּיֹּת 1 K 11^{1};—**1. adj.,** of seller of Machpelah to Abr., עֶפְרוֹן הַחִתִּי Gn 23^{10} $49^{29.30}$ 50^{13}; עֶפְרֹן בֶּן־צֹחַר הַח׳ 25^{9} (all P); of fathers of Esau's wives בְּאֵרִי הַח׳ Gn 26^{34}; אֵילוֹן הַח׳ v^{34} 36^{2} (all P); also of warriors of David, אֲחִימֶלֶךְ הַח׳ 1 S 26^{6}, and esp. אוּרִיָּה הַח׳ 2 S $11^{3.6.17.21.24}$ $12^{9.10}$ 23^{39} 1 K 15^{5} 1 Ch 11^{41}; fs. = subst., only of (religious) ancestry of Jerus. Ez 16^{3} *thy father was the Amorite, and thy mother was a Hittite woman* חִתִּית, similarly v^{45}; fpl. = subst. of Sol.'s foreign wives, חִתִּיֹּת 1 K 11^{1} *Hittite women* (+ מוֹאֲבִיּוֹת, עַמֳּנִיּוֹת, צֵדְנִיֹּת, אֲדֹמִיֹּת). **2. n.** usu. **a.** coll. הַחִתִּי *the Hittites:* in lists of Canaanitish peoples Gn 15^{20} (JE), Ex $3^{8.17}$ (both J), 13^{5} $23^{23.28}$ 33^{2} 34^{11} Nu 13^{29} Jos 3^{10} (all JE), Dt 7^{1} 20^{17} Jos 9^{1} 12^{8} 24^{11} (all D); rd. also for הַחִוִּי Ju 3^{3} (so We Mey Bu[Urg 350]); in Jos 11^{3} (D) del. הַחִתִּי We Mey Bu[l. c.], and rd. then הַחִתִּי for הַחִוִּי v^{b} (so 𝔊, not 𝔊L); further 1 K 9^{20} = 2 Ch 8^{7}, Ezr 9^{1} Ne 9^{8}. **b.** pl. הַחִתִּים: כֹּל אֶרֶץ הַחִתִּים Jos 1^{4} (D) nearly = land of Canaanites; ארץ הח׳ specif. of northern home of Hittites Ju 1^{26}; so also 2 S 24^{6} where rd. אֶרֶץ הַחִתִּים קָדֵשָׁה (for MT תחתים חָדְשִׁי, v. קָדֵשׁ, חָדְשִׁי); מַלְכֵי הַחִתִּים 1 K 10^{29} = 2 Ch 1^{17} (both + מַלְכֵי אֲרָם), 2 K 7^{6} (+ מַלְכֵי מִצְרַיִם, both feared by אֲרָם). Hence it appears that (הַחִתִּי(ם had their proper seat in the north—where also they were encountered by Assyrians from time of TP I (v. Schr Dl[l. c.]), and by Egyptians from time of Tutmes III (v. WMaxMüll.[l. c.])—(cf. also Ju 3^{3} Jos 11^{3} supr.), but that individual Hittites were known in Isr.

(cf., besides 1 S 2^{6} 2 S 11^{3} etc., 1 K 9^{20} supr.); that the Hittites were regarded (by JED) as one of the peoples of Canaan, and that the name even came to be used in more gen. sense for Canaanites. Only in P do they appear as having a definite settlement in the south, and are designated by בְּנֵי־חֵת (v. חֵת), as well as by the adj. הַחִתִּי.

2846 †[**חָתָה**] **vb. snatch up,** usu. fire, coals (NH *id.*; 𝔗 חֲתָא, *id.* (rare); As. *ḫatû* is *destroy* (i.e. *snatch away*?) v. SASmith$^{Asrb\ i.\ 90}$)—**Qal** *Impf.* יַחְתֶּה Pr 6^{27}; sf. יַחְתְּךָ ψ 52^{7}; *Inf. cstr.* לַחְתּוֹת Is 30^{14}; *Pt.* חֹתֶה Pr 25^{22};—*snatch up,* c.acc. אֵשׁ מִיָּקוּד Is 30^{14} *to snatch up fire from a hearth* (|| לַחְשֹׂף מַיִם מִגֶּבֶא); אֵשׁ בְּחֵיקוֹ Pr 6^{27} shall a man *snatch up fire in his bosom* and his garments not be burned? (in sim. of adulterer); pregn. *seize* (and put) *upon* גֶּחָלִים אַתָּה ח׳ עַל־רֹאשׁוֹ Pr 25^{22}; יַחְתְּךָ וְיִסָּחֲךָ מֵאֹהֶל ψ 52^{7} God . . . *shall snatch thee away,* and pluck thee up tent-less.

3189 †**יַחַת** **n.pr.m.** (perh. for יַחְתֶּה, *he* (God) *will snatch up*)—**1.** grandson of Judah 1 Ch 4$^{2.2}$, 𝔊 Ιεθ, 𝔊L Ιαωθ. **2.** Levites: **a.** 1 Ch 6$^{5.28}$, 𝔊 Ιεεθ, 𝔊L Ιααθ. **b.** 1 Ch 23$^{10.11}$, 𝔊 Ιεθ, 𝔊L Ιειηλ. **c.** 1 Ch 24^{22}, 𝔊 Ιναθ, 𝔊L Ιααθ. **d.** 2 Ch 34^{12}, 𝔊 Ιε(θ), 𝔊L Ιαεθ.

4287 †**מַחַת** **n.pr.m.** (perh. from מַחְתָּה *thing seized*)—Levites: **a.** 1 Ch 6^{20}, 𝔊 Μεθ, A Μααθ, 𝔊L Αμιωθ. **b.** 2 Ch 29^{12} 31^{13}, 𝔊 Μααθ, Μαεθ, 𝔊L Μααθ, Ααθ.

4289 †**מַחְתָּה** **n.f. fire-holder, censer, snuff-dish;**—abs. מ׳ Lv 16^{12} Nu 17^{11}; sf. מַחְתָּתוֹ Lv 10^{1} + 4 t.; pl. abs. מַחְתּוֹת Nu 16^{6} + 4 t.; מַחְתֹּת Nu 16^{17} + 3 t.; cstr. מַחְתּוֹת Nu 17$^{3.4}$; sf. מַחְתֹּתָיו Ex 27^{3}; מַחְתֹּתֶיהָ Ex 25^{38} + 2 t.;—**1.** *snuff-holder,* snuff-dish (Now$^{Archäol.\ ii,\ 63.\ 65}$) of gold Ex 25^{38} 37^{23} Nu 4^{9} (all P). **2.** bronze utensils, *fire-pans,* belonging to altar of burnt-offerings Ex 27^{3} 38^{3}, cf. Nu 4^{14} (all P); *fire-pans* of gold 1 K 7^{50} = 2 Ch 4^{22}, 2 K 25^{15} = Je 52^{19}. **3.** *censer,* Lv 10^{1} 16^{12} Nu 16$^{6.17.17.17.17.18}$ 17$^{2.3.4}$ (of bronze), v^{11} (all P).

2847, 2879 **חַתְחַת, חִתָּה** v. sub חתת. p. 369

2852 †[**חָתַךְ**] **vb. divide, determine** (NH *id., cut, cut off, decide,* so Aram. חתך Pa. Ethpa.)—only **Niph.** *Pf.* שָׁבֻעִים שִׁבְעִים נֶחְתַּךְ עַל־עַמְּךָ Dn 9^{24} seventy weeks *are determined* upon thy people.

†[**חָתַל**] **vb.** perh. **entwine, enwrap** 2853
(poss. denom., so MV al.; yet cf. NH חוֹתָל *woven date-basket*)—**Pu.** *Pf.* 2 fs. חֻתָּלְתְּ and **Hoph.** *Inf. abs.* הָחְתֵּל *be swathed, swaddled;*—וְהָמְלֵחַ לֹא הֻמְלַחַתְּ וְהָחְתֵּל לֹא חֻתָּלְתְּ Ez 16^{4} *and not at all wast thou rubbed with salt, and not at all wast thou swaddled,* of Jerusalem under fig. of infant.

†[**חֲתֻלָּה**] **n.f. swaddling-band** (v. Ba 2854
NB 146)—only בְּשׂוּמִי עָנָן לְבֻשׁוֹ וַעֲרָפֶל חֲתֻלָּתוֹ Jb 38^{9} *when I made cloud its garment, and thick darkness its swaddling-band,* fig. of dark clouds enveloping the sea.

†**חִתּוּל** **n.[m.] bandage**—ח׳ Ez 30^{21}, for 2848
broken arm (in fig. of Pharaoh's broken arm).

†**חֶתְלֹן** **n.pr.loc.,** on the extreme northern 2855
boundary of Isr. territory (in Ezek.'s conception), only דֶּרֶךְ(־)ח׳ Ez 47^{15} 48^{1}; mod. *Ḥeitela* nearly two hours from sea-coast, acc. to Furrer ZPV viii, 27.

†**חָתַם** **vb. seal, affix seal, seal up** (NH 2856
id.; Aram. חֲתַם, ܚܬܡ; Eth. ኀተመ: Ar. خَتَمَ (whence خَاتَمٌ is loan-word acc. to Frä^{252})—**Qal** *Impf.* 3 ms. יַחְתֹּם Jb 9^{7} 33^{6}, יַחְתּוֹם Jb 37^{7}, וַיַּחְתֹּם Est 8^{10}, etc.; *Imv.* חֲתֹם Dn 12^{4}, חֲתוֹם Is 8^{16}, חִתְמוּ Est 8^{8}; *Inf. abs.* חָתוֹם Je 32^{44}; *cstr.* לַחְתֹּם Dn 9^{24}, + v^{24} Kt (Qr לְהָתֵם); *Pt. act.* חוֹתֵם Ez 28^{12}; *pass.* חָתוּם Dt 32^{34} + 2 t., etc.;—**1.** *seal, affix one's seal,* in attestation; seal with king's seal (בְּחֹתָמוֹ) 1 K 21^{8}, בְּטַבַּעַת המלך Est 8$^{8.10}$; of covenant with י׳, *attested by seal* (pass.) Ne 10$^{1.2}$; fig., of י׳ putting his seal upon (בְּ) discipline, i.e. ratifying it, Jb 33^{16}; perh. also upon hand of man (that man may know י׳'s ways) 37^{7} v. De; Di sub **2.** *seal up* hand of man, so that he cannot work with it (in winter). **2.** *seal up, fasten up by sealing,* a deed of sale Je 32$^{10.11}$ (opp. הַגָּלוּי *that which was left open*), v$^{14.44}$, a book of prophecy Dn 12^{4} (|| סְתֹם הַדְּבָרִים), cf. v^{9} (|| *id.*), 9$^{24\ b}$; so in sim. of unintelligible prophecy Is 29$^{11.11}$; חֲתוֹם תּוֹרָה בְּלִמֻּדָי Is 8^{16} *seal up the teaching among my disciples,* i.e. keep it securely (|| צוֹר); of י׳'s remembrance of offences חָתֻם בְּאוֹצְרֹתָי Dt 32^{34} (|| כָּמֻס עִמָּדִי), so חָתֻם בִּצְרוֹר פִּשְׁעִי Jb 14^{17} (|| וַתִּטְפֹּל עַל־עֲוֹנִי); מַעְיָן חָתוּם Ct 4^{12} *a fountain sealed up,* metaph. of chaste woman (|| גַּן (גַּל) נָעוּל); וּבְעַד כּוֹכָבִים יַח׳ Jb 9^{7} *and about the stars he putteth a seal* (|| of forbidding sun

to rise).—אַתָּה חוֹתֵם תָּכְנִית Ez 28^{12} is obscure: *thou* wast one *sealing proportion*, i.e. *perfection*, —wast complete perfection, Ges Sm.; wast *a sealer of symmetry* v. Da; wast a *seal* (*ring*) —i.e. חוֹתַם cstr.—of proportion Codd. 𝔊 𝔙 Hi cf. Ew; txt. perh. corrupt, v. suggestions in Co.—Dn 9^{24a} rd. Qr לְהָתֵם (v. תמם). Jb 33^{16} 37^{7} v. sub **1.** **Niph.** *Pf.* 3 ms. [or *Pt.*?] נִכְתָּב וְנֶחְתָּם Est 3^{12} (it was) *written and sealed* בְּטַבַּעַת הַמֶּלֶךְ; *Inf. abs.* וְנַחְתּוֹם Est 8^{8} (continuing pt. נִכְתָּב) also + בְּטַבַּעַת הַמּ׳; both pass. of **Qal 1.** **Pi.** *Pf.* 3 pl. יוֹמָם חִתְּמוּ־לָמוֹ Jb 24^{16} lit. *by day they seal up for themselves*, i.e. acc. to most, they shut themselves up, do not shew themselves (|| לֹא יָדְעוּ אוֹר); 𝔊 C has ἡμέρας ἐσφράγισαν ἑαυτοῖς (B al. ἑαυτους), whence Siegf conj. plausibly יָמִים ח׳ ל׳ *they seal up the days unto themselves*, i.e. daytime is for them sealed up and unused. **Hiph.** *Pf.* 3 ms. אוֹ־הֶחְתִּים בְּשָׂרוֹ מִזּוֹבוֹ Lv 15^{3} *or hath his flesh* (genital organ) *shewn stoppage by reason of his flux.*

2368 †I. חֹתָם, חוֹתָם **n.m.**$^{Jb\ 41,7}$ **seal, signet-ring** (Aram. ܚܬܡܐ; Eth. ማኅተም:—v. Lag$^{BN\ 116}$)—abs. חֹתָם Ex 28^{11} + 2 t.; חוֹתָם Je 22^{24} + 8 t.; sf. חֹתָמְךָ Gn 38^{18}, חֹתָמוֹ 1 K 21^{8};—on supposed cstr. חוֹתַם v. foregoing;—*seal, signet-ring*, hung by a cord (פָּתִיל) about the neck Gn 38^{18} (J; = חֹתֶמֶת v^{25}), or (later?) worn on (finger of) right hand Je 22^{24}, (Benz$^{Archäol.\ 106}$); the two customs appar. combined Ct 8^{6} (עַל־לִבֶּךָ, עַל־זְרוֹעֶךָ); used to attest a royal missive 1 K 21^{8} (instr. of vb. חתם); a precious article Hg 2^{23} (sim. of Zerubbabel); פִּתּוּחֵי ח׳ *engravings of a seal*, as model for cutting names and inscr. on precious stones and gold plate Ex 28$^{11.21.26}$ 39$^{6.14.30}$ (all P; v. Benz$^{258\ ff.}$); חֹמֶר ח׳ Jb 38^{14} = *clay of* (under) *a signet*; ח׳ צָר 41^{7} *a close signet*, i.e. one that is closely pressed down, sim. of closely joined (סָגוּר) scales of crocodile.

2369 †II. חוֹתָם **n.pr.m. 1.** man of Asher 1 Ch 7^{32} 𝔊 Χωθαν(μ) (= הֵלֶם v^{35}; A Ελαμ, 𝔊L Ιασουλ). **2.** father of two of David's heroes 1 Ch 11^{44}, 𝔊 Κωθαν, 𝔊L Χωθαν.

2858 חֹתֶמֶת **n.f. signet-ring**—only הַח׳ Gn 38^{25} (J; for I. חֹתָם v^{18}) *the signet-ring* (acc. to Bö$^{NÄ\ i,\ 23}$ fem. coll. *the sealing-apparatus*).

I. חתן (√of foll.; prob. *circumcise;* cf. Ar. خَتَنَ *circumcise*, خِتَانٌ *circumcision, circumcision-feast*).

†חֹתֵן **n.verb. 1. m. wife's father** (Ar. 2859
خَاتِنٌ *a circumciser*, hence father-in-law, with ref. to circumcision performed on young men just before marriage; خَتَنٌ *relation on wife's side;* v. We$^{Prol.\ 1886,\ 355\ Anm.\ 1;\ Skizzen\ iii,\ 154}$ Sta$^{ZAW\ 1886,\ 143\ Anm.}$ Nö$^{ZMG\ 1886,\ 187}$; otherwise Dl$^{Pr\ 91}$ Lag$^{BN\ 116}$)—cstr. חֹתֵן Ex 18^{1} + 9 t., חֹתֶנְךָ Ex 18^{6}, חֹתְנוֹ Ex 3^{1} + 9 t.; —usu. of Moses' *wife's father* Ex 3^{1} 4^{18} 18$^{1.2.5.6.7.8.12.12.14.15.17.24.27}$ (all E), Nu 10^{29} (J), Ju 1^{16} 4^{11}; of a Levite Ju 19$^{4.7.9}$. **2. f.** *wife's mother*, only sf. חֹתַנְתּוֹ Dt 27^{23}.

†חָתָן **n.m. daughter's husband, bride-** 2860
groom (as one who undergoes circumcision, v. supr.; NH *id.;* Aram. חַתְנָא, and ܚܬܢܐ (also sister's husband, etc.); vulg. Ar. خَتَنٌ *daughter's husband*, then more gen. wife's and husband's relations; Sab. (Liḥyân) חתן *daughter's husband* DHM$^{Epigr.\ Denkm.\ 87}$; As. *ḫatanu, daughter's husband* COT^{Gloss})—abs. ח׳ 1 S 18^{18} + 10 t. + Gn 19^{12} (where rd. חֲתָנֶיךָ 𝔊 Ol Di); cstr. חֲתַן Ex 4^{25} + 4 t.; sf. חֲתָנוֹ Ju 19^{5}; חֲתָנָיו Gn 19$^{14.14}$;—**1.** in relation to a father, *daughter's husband, or bridegroom* Gn 19$^{12.14}$ (ח׳ לֹקְחֵי בְנֹתָיו), v^{14} (all J), Ju 15^{6} 19^{5} 1 S 18^{18} 22^{14} Ne 6^{18} 13^{28}; v. also חֲתַן בֵּית אַחְאָב 2 K 8^{27} *son-in-law of the house of Ahab*, said of Ahaziah, whose mother Athaliah was the daughter of Ahab. **2.** in relation to the bride, *bridegroom* ח׳ דָּמִים אַתָּה לִי Ex 4^{25} *a bloody bridegroom art thou to me*, cf. v^{26} (J; on this v. We$^{Prol.\ 1886,\ 355}$); || כַּלָּה Je 7^{34} 16^{9} 25^{10} 33^{11} Jo 2^{16}; in sim. of י׳'s work for and delight in his people Is 61^{10} 62^{5}; of sun ψ 19^{6}.

†II. [חתן] **vb. denom.** only **Hithp. make** 2859
oneself a daughter's husband (NH Hithp. *id.*, Aram. Ithpa. *id.*)—*Pf.* 2 mpl. וְהִתְחַתַּנְתֶּם consec. Jos 23^{12}; *Impf.* וַיִּתְחַתֵּן 1 K 3^{1} 2 Ch 18^{1}; 2 m. תִּתְחַתֵּן Dt 7^{3} 1 S 18^{21}; *Imv.* הִתְחַתֵּן 1 S 18^{22}, הִתְחַתְּנוּ Gn 34^{9}; *Inf.* הִתְחַתֵּן 1 S 18^{23} + 3 t.;—**1.** *make oneself daughter's husband* (son-in-law) *to*, c. בְּ 1 S 18$^{21.22.23.26.27}$; c. אֶת 1 K 3^{1}, Gn 34^{9} (P); c. לְ 2 Ch 18^{1}, of marriage of Jehoshaphat's son and Ahab's daughter (cf. 2 K 8^{18} = 2 Ch 21^{6}). **2.** in gen. *form marriage-alliance with*, c. בְּ Dt 7^{3} Jos 23^{12} (D), Ezr 9^{14}.

†[חֲתֻנָּה] **n.f. marriage, wedding** (NH 2861
חִיתּוּן *id.;* Aram. חִיתּוּנָא *id.;* Ar. خُتُونَةٌ *marriage-alliance, marriage*)—only בְּיוֹם חֲתֻנָּתוֹ Ct 3^{11} *on the day of his marriage.*

†[חָתַף] **vb. seize, snatch away** (cf. Aram. 2862

ܚܬܦ Pa. *break in pieces;* Ar. حَتْفٌ *death*)—**Qal** *Impf.* no obj. expr. הֵן יַחְתֹּף וּמִי יְשִׁיבֶנּוּ Jb 9^{12} *lo! he seizeth, and who shall turn him back?*

2863 †חֶתֶף† **n.[m.]** prey—only אַף־הִיא כְּחֶ׳ תֶּאֱרֹב Pr 23^{28} *she also lieth in wait as* for *prey* (said of strange woman).

2864 †חָתַר† **vb.** dig, row (NH *id.*, bore (through), so Aram. חֲתַר 𝔗 (rare))—**Qal** *Pf.* ח׳ Jb 24^{16}, חָתַרְתִּי Ez 12^{7}; *Impf.* וָאֶחְתֹּר Ez 8^{8}, יַחְתְּרוּ Ez 12^{12} Am 9^{2}, וַיַּחְתְּרוּ Jon 1^{13}; *Imv.* חֲתָר־ Ez 8^{8} 12^{5};—**1.** *dig into* houses, c. acc. בָּתִּים Jb 24^{16} (of burglary); sq. בְּ into or through a wall Ez 8$^{8.8}$ (Co del. on intern. grounds), 12$^{5.7.12}$; metaph. sq. בשאול Am 9^{2} *dig into Sheʼôl,* i.e. as a refuge. **2.** *row* (as *digging* into the water) Jon 1^{13}.

4290 †מַחְתֶּרֶת† **n.m.** breaking in, burglary—אִם־בַּמּ׳ יִמָּצֵא הַגַּנָּב Ex 22^{1} i.e. caught in the act (JE); so לֹא בַמּ׳ מְצָאתִים Je 2^{34}, *not in the act of breaking in didst thou find them* (2 fs. sf. Ges^{§44,2,R4}), i.e. those whom thou hast slain were not detected in crime.

2865 †[חָתַת] **vb.** be shattered, dismayed (As. *ḫattu, terror,* Dl$^{HWB\,296}$; Talm. חִתִּית *id.;* Eth. **ሐተተ:** is *scrutari, examinare,* v. Di$^{Lex.\,105}$)—**Qal** *Pf.* 3 ms. חַת Je 50^{2}; 3 fs. חַתָּה Je 14^{4} + 2 t., וְחַתָּה Je 48^{1}; 3 pl. חַתּוּ Is 37^{27} + 4 t., וְחַתּוּ consec. Is 20^{5} + 2 t., וְחַתּוּ consec. Je 50^{36}; *Impf.* (Kö$^{i.\,366}$) אֵחַתָּה Is 7^{8} 30^{31}, יֵחַת Jb 39^{22}, יֵחַת Is 31^{4}, Je 17^{18}, יֵחַתּוּ 1 S 2^{10} + 3 t.—On יֵחָתּוּ Jb 21^{13} v. נָחַת;—תֵּחָתּוּ Jos 10^{25} + 2 t., etc.; *Imv.* וָחֹתּוּ Is 8$^{9.9.9}$;—**1.** *be shattered, broken,* fig. of nations under divine judgment Is 7^{8} 30^{31}; so prob. also Is 8$^{9.9.9}$ (but del. in v^{a}), and perh. (of י׳'s foes in gen.) 1 S 2^{10} (song;—others render *dismayed* in all exc. Is 7^{8}); fig. of י׳'s righteousness Is 51^{6} (= be abolished, annihilated); lit. of bows Je 51^{56}, acc. to Gie's rdg. חִתְּתָה, v. **Pi.** **2.** *be dismayed,* usu. **a.** abs.: ‖ יָרֵא Dt 1^{21} 31^{8} Jos 8^{1} 10^{25} (all D), 1 S 17^{11} Je 23^{4} 30^{10} 46^{27} Ez 2^{6} 3^{9} 1 Ch 22^{13} 28^{20} 2 Ch 20$^{15.17}$ 32^{7}; ‖ בּוֹשׁ Is 20^{5} 37^{27} = 2 K 19^{26} Je 8^{9} 17$^{18.18}$ 48$^{1.20.39}$ 50$^{2.2}$ (others assign 48$^{20.39}$ 50$^{2.2}$ to **1**); fig. of the ground הָאֲדָמָה, *dismayed* for lack of rain Je 14^{4} (‖ בּוֹשׁ of the husbandmen); no ‖ Je 50^{36} Ob^{9} Jb 39^{22}. **b.** *be dismayed at, by reason of,* sq. מִן Is 31$^{4.9}$ 51^{7} (‖ יָרֵא) Je 1^{17} 10$^{2.2}$. **Niph.** *Pf.* only 3 ms. וּמִפְּנֵי שְׁמִי נִחַת Mal 2^{5} and at my name *he is put in awe* (‖ יָרֵא). **Pi.** *Pf.* *dismay, scare,* 2 ms. sf. וְחִתַּתַּנִי בַחֲלֹמוֹת (Kö$^{i.\,372}$) consec. Jb 7^{14} *and thou scarest me with dreams* (‖ בִּעֵת); 3 fs. חִתְּתָה Je 51^{56} (of bows) is intrans. [inchoat. Ew$^{§120,\,2\,d}$], Gf. al., *be shattered,* but txt. prob. erron. Gie חַתָּה (v. **Qal 1**). **Hiph.** *Pf.* 2 ms. הַחִתֹּתָ Is 9^{3}; 1 s. וְהַחִתֹּתִי Je 49^{37} (Kö$^{i.\,372}$); *Impf.* 3 ms. sf. יְחִתֵּנִי Jb 31^{34}, sf. 3 fpl. יְחִיתַן Hb 2^{17} (Kö$^{i.\,374}$; but 𝔊 𝔗 𝔖 Ew Ol Sta We יְחִתֶּךָ); 1 s. sf. אֲחִתְּךָ Je 1^{17} (sq. לפניהם).—**1.** *shatter* c. acc. Is 9^{3}. **2. a.** *cause to be dismayed* Je 49^{37} sq. לִפְנֵי. **b.** *dismay, terrify,* sq. sf. Jb 31^{34} Hb 2^{17}.

†I. [חַת] **n.m.**$^{Gn\,9,\,2}$ terror, fear—חָת Jb 41^{25}, 2844
חִתְּכֶם Gn 9^{2};—c. sf. as obj. gen., Gn 9^{2} *terror of you* (‖ מוֹרַאֲכֶם); in description of crocodile c. neg., הֶעָשׂוּ לִבְלִי־חָת Jb 41^{25} *one made for fearlessness.*

†II. [חַת] **adj.** shattered, dismayed—mpl. 2844
חַתִּים:—**1.** *shattered* קֶשֶׁת גִּבֹּרִים ח׳ 1 S 2^{4} (song; on pl. חַתִּים v. Dr); so fig. Ez 32^{30} acc. to 𝔊 Codd. Co (חַתִּים for MT חִתִּיתָם) *broken in their might,* of Sidonians in Sheʼôl. **2.** *dismayed* Je 46^{5} of Egyptians defeated by Nebuchadrezzar.

†I. חֲתַת **n.[m.]** terror—only תִּרְאוּ ח׳ וַתִּירָאוּ 2866
Jb 6^{21} (> Baer תִּירְאוּ for תִּרְאוּ) *ye see a terror, and fear* (note paronomasia in Heb.; v. Di).

†[חִתָּה] **n.f.** terror—חִתַּת אלהים עַל־הֶעָרִים 2847
Gn 35^{5} *a terror of* (=from) *God was upon the cities.*

†II. חֲתַת **n.pr.m.** son of Othniel and 2867
grandson of Kenaz (brother of Caleb), חֲתָת 1 Ch 4^{13}.

†[חַתְחַת] **n.[m.]** terror, only pl. חַתְחַתִּים 2849
בַּדֶּרֶךְ Ec 12^{5} *terrors* are *in the way* (‖ יירא).

חִתִּית **n.f.** terror, only Ezek.; abs. ח׳ Ez 32^{23}, 2851
but Co rds. חִתִּיתָם (with 𝔊 and v$^{24.26}$); cstr. *id.* 32^{27}; sf. חתיתו 32^{32} Kt (> חִתִּיתִי Qr); חִתִּיתָם 32^{24} + 2 t. + 26^{17} (rd. חִתִּיתָהּ, with 𝔊 Ew Co, see VB), 32^{30} (rd. חַתִּים, v. II. חת);—*terror,* caused by powerful cities, nations, kings, etc.: usu. c. sf. as obj. genit. Ez 26^{17} (of Tyre); elsewh. only Ez 32: v^{27} (ח׳ גִּבּוֹרִים, 𝔖 Co ח׳ גבור תם), v^{30} (חִתִּיתָם, but rd. חַתִּים, v. supr.); esp. in phr. נָתַן ח׳ בארץ חַיִּים *cause one's terror* (terror of oneself) *in the land of the living* v$^{23.24.25}$ (del. 𝔊 Co), v$^{26.32}$.—חִתִּית Ez 16$^{3.45}$ v. חִתִּי sub חֵת supr. p. 366.

†מְחִתָּה† **n.f.** terror, destruction, ruin, 4288

poet. (esp. Pr)—abs. מ׳ Pr 10^{14} + 8 t.; cstr. מְחִתַּת Pr 10^{15} 14^{28};—**1. a.** *terror*, Is 54^{14} (|| עֹשֶׁק), Je 17^{17}; =obj. of terror, 48^{39} (|| שְׂחֹק). **b.** *dismay*, Pr 21^{15} (opp. שִׂמְחָה). **2.** *ruin*, of strongholds ψ 89^{41}; בְּאֶפֶס לְאֹם מ׳ רָזוֹן Pr 14^{28} *without people is ruin to a prince* (opp. הַדְרַת־מֶלֶךְ); מ׳ דַּלִּים רֵישָׁם 10^{15} *the ruin of the poor* (is) *their poverty;* as consequence of evil-doing מ׳ לְפֹעֲלֵי אָוֶן Pr 10^{29} (opp. מָעוֹז); of fools פִּי כְסִיל מ׳־לוֹ 18^{7}, cf. 13^{3} (opp. שֹׁמֵר נַפְשׁוֹ); פִּי אֱוִיל מ׳ קְרֹבָה 10^{14} *the mouth of a fool is imminent ruin.*

חַת, חִתִּי v. supr. p. 366. 2845, 2850

ט

ט, *Têth*, ninth letter; =numeral 9 in postB Heb.; ט״ו = 15 (9 + 6), ט״ז = 16 (9 + 7), to avoid י״ה and י״ו, v. י, Ges $^{§ 5. 4, R 3}$ Nes $^{ZAW 1884, 249}$.

2894 † **[טֵאטֵא]** vb. **Pilpēl**, only *Pf.* 1 s. sf. וְטֵאטֵאתִיהָ בְּמַטְאֲטֵא הַשְׁמֵד Is 14^{23} *and I will sweep it with the besom of destruction*, of י׳'s laying Babylon waste. (Form of √dub.; ע״ו Ol $^{§ 253}$; ע״ע Sta $^{§ 464}$; undecided Kö $^{i. 652 ff.}$ (q. v.), cf. Ew $^{§ 121 b}$.)

4292 † **מַטְאֲטֵא** **n.[m.]** broom, besom, only Is 14^{23}, v. foregoing.

2870 † **טָֽבְאֵל** **n.pr.m.** (Aram.; =*God is good*, v. טוֹב; acc. to Wkl (v. infr.) *God is wise*, cf. Aram. ܛܒ, Eth. ጠበበ: *be wise;* Ar. طَبَّ *act as physician*, طَبٌّ *expert*)—Persian officer in Samaria Ezr 4^{7}, 𝔊 Ταβεηλ.

2870 † **טָֽבְאַל** **n.pr.m.** (appar. pointed to mean *good-for-nothing* (אַל as neg.) v. De Di Du Sta $^{Gesch i. 590}$, orig. טָֽבְאֵל; Ol $^{§ 91 d}$ Kö $^{ii. 537}$ al. think אָל- simply pausal form)—Aramean, whose son Pekaḥ and Reṣin proposed to make king of Jerus. in place of Ahaz; only בֶּן־טָֽבְאַל Is 7^{6} (Wkl $^{Alttest. Untersuch. 1892, 74}$ identif. with Reṣin, comparing טַבְרִמֹּן father of Benhadad).

2873 † **[טָבַח]** vb. **slaughter, butcher, slay** (NH *id.* (rare) and deriv.; Ph. טבח pt.; As. *ṭabâḫu* Asrb $^{Annals iii. 56}$; Aram. ܛܒܚ, טְבַח (rare) and deriv.; Ar. طَبَخَ *cook* meat, also *bake* bread; Eth. ጠብሐ: *slay*)—**Qal** *Pf.* 3 ms. sf. וּטְבָחוֹ consec. Ex 21^{37}; 3 fs. טָֽבְחָה Pr 9^{2}; 2 ms. טָבַחְתָּ La 2^{21}; 1 s. טָבַחְתִּי 1 S 25^{11}; *Imv.* וּטְבֹחַ Gn 43^{16}; *Inf. cstr.* טְבֹחַ Ez 21^{15}; לִטְבוֹחַ ψ 37^{14} + 3 t. (so Baer; van d. H לִטְבּוֹחַ, exc. לִטְבֹוחַ Je 51^{40}); *Pt. pass.* טָבוּחַ Dt 28^{31};—**1.** *slaughter, butcher* animals for food Ex 21^{37} (E), Pr 9^{2} (fig. of Wisdom's furnishing her table); so c. acc. cogn. ט׳ טֶבַח Gn 43^{16} (J), ט׳ טִבְחָה 1 S 25^{11}; cf. also Dt 28^{31}, where punishment lies in fact that the owner does not eat of the slain ox; כְּכֶבֶשׂ אַלּוּף יוּבַל לִטְבוֹחַ Je 11^{19} *like a mild lamb that is led to slaughter*, sim. of the prophet exposed to his enemies, 51^{40} sim. of י׳'s vengeance upon Babylon (v. also טִבְחָה, טֶבַח), 25^{34} of kings and rulers, under fig. of shepherds & choice sheep. **2.** poet. & fig., *slay, kill ruthlessly*, c. acc. pers. ψ 37^{14}; abs. La 2^{21} (|| הָרַג; opp. חמל); c. acc. cogn. ט׳ טֶבַח Ez 21^{15} of a sword sharpened for the *slaughter* of Isr. in judgment.

† I. **טֶ֫בַח** **n.m.** $^{Is 34, 6}$ **slaughtering, slaughter**—abs. ט׳ Gn 43^{16} + 6 t.; טָבַח Ez 21^{20} + 3 t.; 2874
sf. טִבְחָהּ Pr 9^{2};—**1.** *slaughtering, slaughter*, of animals for food; as acc. cogn. after טָבַח (q. v.) Gn 43^{16} (J), Pr 9^{2}; כַּשֶּׂה לַטֶּ׳ יוּבָל Is 53^{7}, sim. of suffering servant of י׳; also Pr 7^{22} sim. of fatuousness of one following a strange woman, thoughtless of consequences; יֵרְדוּ לַטֶּ׳ Je 50^{27} metaph. of Babylonian leaders, under fig. of bullocks; so prob. 48^{15}, and perh. לַטֶּ׳ תִּכְרָעוּ Is 65^{12}. **2.** in poet. fig. *slaughter*, to which the nations are given over by י׳ Is 34^{2}, specif. of Edom v^{6} (|| זֶבַח; v. ז׳ **6**, p. 258^{a}); of Isr. Ez 21^{20}, as acc. cogn. after טָבַח v^{15}; of Ammon v^{33}.

† II. **טֶ֫בַח** **n.pr.m.** son of Nahor by his con- 2875
cubine Gn 22^{24}, 𝔊 Ταβεκ(χ).

† **טִבְחָה** **n.f. thing slaughtered, slaugh-** 2878
tered meat, slaughter—**1.** sf. טִבְחָתִי as acc. cogn. after טָבַח 1 S 25^{11} of meat killed for food: **2.** *slaughter for food* (=I. טֶבַח **1**): כְּצֹאן ט׳

ψ 44[23] *like a flock for slaughter*, sim. of the harassed godly; כְּצֹאן לְטִבְחָה Je 12[3] sim. of judgment of wicked (|| לְיוֹם הֲרֵגָה).

2876 **טַבָּח n.m.**[1 8 9, 23] **1. cook, 2. guardsman;**—†**1.** *cook* (who also killed the animal for food and served it) טַבָּח abs. 1 S 9[23.24]†. **2.** elsewh. only pl. טַבָּחִים *guardsmen, bodyguard* (orig. royal *slaughterers;* v. RS [OTJC 426 (262); Sem. i. 1st ed., 396]); alw. in the foll. combinations: שַׂר הַטּ׳ *captain of* Pharaoh's *bodyguard* Gn 37[36] 39[1] (both J), 40[3.4] 41[10.12] (all E); רַב־ט׳ *chief of* Nebuchadr.'s *bodyguard* 2 K 25[8.10.11.12.15.18.20] Je 39[9] + 16 t. Je (hence Aram. רַב טַבָּחַיָּא Dn 2[14]).

2879 †[טַבָּחָה] **n.f. female cook;**—only pl. abs. טַבָּחוֹת 1 S 8[13] (+ רַקָּחוֹת *perfumers* and אֹפוֹת *bakers*, all as menials).

4293 †מַטְבֵּחַ **n.[m.] slaughtering-place** (Ph. מטבח *id.* CIS [i. 175]), Is 14[21], for Babylonians (under implicit fig. of animals).

2880 †טִבְחַת **n.pr.loc.** a Syrian city; מִטִּבְחַת 1 Ch 18[8] (𝔊 Μεταβηχα(ς), 𝔊L ταβααθ); so rd. also for II. בֶּטַח 2 S 8[8] (v. p. 105[b] supr.)

2881 †I. טָבַל **vb. dip** (NH *id.;* Aram. טְבַל *dip, bathe;* cf. perh. Ar. طَبَلَ *saturavit tinctura vestem*, Frey)—**Qal** *Pf.* וְטָבַל consec. Lv 4[6] + 5 t.; וְטָבַלְתְּ consec. Ru 2[14]; וּטְבַלְתֶּם consec. Ex 12[22]; *Impf.* וַיִּטְבֹּל Lv 9[9] + 3 t.; 2 ms. sf. תִּטְבְּלֵנִי Jb 9[31]; וַיִּטְבְּלוּ Gn 37[31];—*dip:* **1.** trans., *dip* a thing *in*, c. acc. rei + בְּ: in blood Gn 37[31] (J), so esp. in connexion with sacrifices Lv 4[6] 9[9] 14[6.51] (also in fresh water); in water, for purification Nu 19[18] (all P); of dipping rod in honey 1 S 14[27], bread in vinegar Ru 2[14], foot in oil Dt 33[24] (poem); בַּשַּׁחַת תִּטְבְּלֵנִי Jb 9[31] *in the ditch dost thou dip me;* acc. omitted Ex 12[22] (JE; in blood), 2 K 8[15] (in water); but also + מִן = *moisten with, with some of* Lv 4[17] (blood), 14[16] (oil). **2.** intrans., *dip (oneself)*, sq. בְּ, 2 K 5[14] in Jordan (|| רָחַץ בְּ v[10.12]).

2882 †טְבַלְיָהוּ **n.pr.m.** (*י׳ hath dipped*, i.e. *purified*)—name of one of the porters, line of Merari 1 Ch 26[11] (𝔊L Ταβεηλ).

II. טבל (perh. to be assumed as √ of foll.; cf. Eth. ጠብለለ: *wind about, wrap up;* As. *tublu, turban*, Dl in Baer's Ezech [xii]).

2871 †[טְבוּל] **n.m. turban** (v. Sim in Thes Rob Ges Dl [l. c.])—only סְרוּחֵי טְבוּלִים בְּרָאשֵׁיהֶם Ez 23[15] extended in respect to *turbans on their heads* = *with pendant turbans* (Dl SS, cf. Da) > Hi-Sm who comp. Ar. طَمَلَ *dye* (v. I. טבל).

†טָבַע **vb. sink, sink down** (NH. *id.;* Aram. ܛܒܰܥ, טְבַע; Ph. טבע *coin;* As. *têbû, sink in, ṭabbî'u, diver* (water-fowl) etc., v. Muss-Arnolt [JBL xi, 1892, 170] Dl [HWB]; Ar. طَبَعَ *seal, stamp, imprint;* Eth. ጠምዐ: *dip*)—**Qal** *Pf.* טָבַעְתִּי ψ 69[3]; טָבְעוּ ψ 9[16] La 2[9]; *Impf.* וַיִּטְבַּע Je 38[6]; וַתִּטְבַּע 1 S 17[49]; אֶטְבָּעָה ψ 69[15];—*sink, sink down,* intrans., c. בְּ; 1 S 17[49] (stone into Goliath's forehead); Je 38[6] (Jerem. in mire of dungeon); La 2[9] (gates of Jerus. into ground); metaph. of distress; ψ 69[3] ט׳ בִּיוֵן מְצוּלָה; 69[15] (|| הצילני מִטִּיט); nations into the pit (בַּשַּׁחַת) 9[16]. **Pu.** *Pf.* טֻבְּעוּ *be sunk* Ex 15[4] (poem) of Egyptians drowned בְּיַם־סוּף. **Hiph.** *Pf.* הָטְבְּעוּ *be sunk* בַּבֹּץ *in the mire*, of feet, metaph. of entanglements and difficulties Je 38[22]; הָטְבָּעוּ, of pedestals (אֲדָנִים) of the earth, as *settled, planted* עַל Jb 38[6] (|| ירה פִּנָּה); abs. of mountains Pr 8[25]. 2883

טַבַּעַת **n.f. signet, signet-ring, ring** (on format. v. Lag [BN 88]; As. *ṭimbu'u, seal-ring*, Muss-Arnolt [l. c.])—abs. טַבַּעַת Ex 26[24] + 3 t.; cstr. *id.* Est 3[12] + 3 t.; טַבַּעְתּוֹ Gn 41[42] + 2 t.; pl. abs. טַבָּעוֹת Is 3[1] Ex 28[23]; טַבְּעֹת Ex 25[12.12] + 14 t.; cstr. טַבְּעוֹת Ex 28[23] + 2 t.; טַבְּעֹת Ex 25[12] + 12 t.; sf. טַבְּעֹתָו Ex 28[28] 39[21]; טַבְּעֹתֵיהֶם Ex 26[29]; טַבְּעֹתָם 36[34];—**1.** *signet-ring*, of king, taken from his hand and given as token of authority Gn 41[42] (E), Est 3[10] 8[2]; used in sealing official missives Est 3[12] 8[8.8.10] (vb. חָתַם). **2.** *ring*, as ornament Is 3[21]; as gift for sacred purposes Ex 35[22] Nu 31[50] (both P). **3.** most often (only in Ex.) of rings for staves of ark, for curtains, for ephod, and other sacred furniture Ex 25[12.12.12] + 35 t. in Ex (all P). 2885

†טַבָּעוֹת **n.pr.m.** a family name among the Nethinim Ezr 2[43] = Ne 7[46]. 2884

טבר (√ of foll.; meaning dubious).

†טַבּוּר **n.[m.] highest part, centre** (acc. to 𝔊 𝔙 *navel*, so NH *id.*, and טִיבּוּר, Aram. טִיבּוּרָא, טִיבּוּרְיָא)—הִנֵּה עָם יֹרְדִים מֵעִם טַבּוּר הארץ Ju 9[37] *behold people descending from the highest part of the land;* יֹשְׁבֵי עַל־טַבּוּר הארץ Ez 38[12] those *dwelling upon the navel of the earth*, i.e. upon the mountainous country of Israel, central and prominent in the earth. 2872

2886 †טַבְרִמּוֹן **n.pr.m.** (Aram.;=*Ramman is good*, or *is wise*, v. Wkl on טבאל supr.)—father of Benhadad king of Aram 1 K 15^{18}.

2887 †טֵבֵת **n.pr.** 10th month=Dec.–Jan., Est 2^{16} (Nab. טבת Eut$^{No. 3}$ Palm. *id.*, Vog$^{No. 66}$; loan-word from As. *Têbêtum*, Schr^{COT} on Ne 1^{1}, Hpt$^{E\text{-}Vowel\ 10}$, Jen$^{ZA\ iv\ (1889)\ 272\ f.}$, √ perh. *ṭebû*=טבע v. esp. Hpt$^{l.c.}$, Muss-Arnolt$^{JBL\ xi,\ 1892,\ 170}$, month of *sinking in*=muddy month).

2888 †טַבַּת **n.pr.loc.** Ju 7^{22}, spot near which Gideon's pursuit of Midianites ended, site unknown.

2891 †טָהֵר **vb. be clean, pure** (Ar. طَهَرَ, طَهُرَ *id.*; NH *id.*, Pi. *make* or *declare ceremonially clean*; Aram. טְהַר *emptiness*, טִיהֲרָא *brightness*; Sab. טהר Hal^{682}; Eth. አጥሀረ: ተጠሀረ: *purify, wash oneself with water*)—**Qal** *Pf.* ט׳ Lv 11^{32} +12 t.; 3 fs. טָהֲרָה Lv 12^{7} 15^{28}; טָהֵרָה Lv 12^{8} etc., +5 t. *Pf.*; *Impf.* יִטְהַר Lv 15^{13} Jb 4^{17} etc., +9 t. *Impf.*; *Imv.* טְהָר 2 K 5$^{10.13}$;—**1.** *be clean*, i.e. (miraculously) freed from leprosy by washing in the Jordan 2 K 5$^{10.12.13.14}$. **2.** *be clean ceremonially* (only H P), Lv 15$^{13.28.28}$ (P), 22^{4} (H); by washing with water, the flesh Lv 22^{7} (H); garments Lv 13$^{6.34.58}$ Nu 31^{24} (all P); both flesh and garments Lv 17^{5} (H), 14$^{8.9}$ 15^{13} Nu 19^{19} (all P); other articles Lv 11^{32} (P); passing things through the fire Nu 31^{23} (P); offering sin-offerings Lv 12$^{7.8}$ 14^{20} (P); by the ceremony of the two birds Lv 14^{53} (P); by ashes of red heifer Nu 19$^{12.12}$ (P). **3.** *be clean morally*, of people, made clean by י׳'s scattering clean water upon them Ez 36^{25}; of Jerus., specif. made clean from idolatry, under fig. of adultery Je 13^{27}; also sq. מִן Ez 24$^{13.13}$ (purification by י׳); *made clean* מִכֹּל־חַטֹּאתֵיכֶם Lv 16^{30} (P; by the sin-offering of the atonement day); also of the individual, *be clean* מֵחַטָּאוֹת Pr 20^{9} (‖ זכה); *become clean* by use of hyssop ψ 51^{9} (‖ אַלְבִּין); more generally אִם־מֵעֹשֵׂהוּ יִטְהַר־גָּבֶר Jb 4^{17} *shall a man be more pure than his maker?* (‖ יִצְדַּק). **Pi.** *Pf.* טִהַר Lv 13^{3}+4 t.; sf. טִהֲרוֹ Lv 13^{6}+5 t.; 2 ms. טִהַרְתָּ Nu 8$^{6.15}$ etc.+7 t. *Pf.*; *Impf.* יְטַהֵר 2 Ch 34^{5} etc.+4 t. *Impf.*; *Imv.* sf. טַהֲרֵנִי ψ 51^{4}; *Inf. cstr.* טַהֵר Ez 39^{12}+5 t.; sf. טַהֲרִי Ez 36^{33} etc. +4 t. *Inf.*; *Pt.* מְטַהֵר Lv 14^{11} Mal 3^{3};—chiefly P; **1.** *cleanse, purify*: **a.** *physically*, metals from dross Mal 3^{3}; land from corpses Ez 39$^{12.14.16}$; heavens from clouds Jb 37^{21}; temple from unclean things 2 Ch 29$^{15.16.18}$; land and city from Asherim and images 2 Ch 34$^{3.5.8}$; store-chambers of temple from household stuff Ne 13^{9}; priesthood by exclusion of alien blood Ne 13^{30}. **b.** *ceremonially*, the altar of incense by the blood of the annual sin-offering Lv 16^{19} (P); the people, gates, and wall (by some undefined ceremony) Ne 12^{30}; the altar of the court by the blood of sin-offerings Ez 43^{26}; of consecration of Levites by מֵי חטאת Nu 8$^{6.7}$ (P), and חטאת Nu 8$^{15.21}$ (P). **c.** *morally* Lv 16^{30} (P), Ez 37^{23} Mal 3^{3}; מֵחַטָּאת ψ 51^{4}; מֵעוֹנ(ות) Je 33^{8} Ez 36^{33}; מִטֻּמְאָ(וֹ)ת Ez 24^{13} 36^{25}. **2.** *pronounce clean*, ceremonially Lv 13$^{6.13.17.23.28.34.37.59}$ 14$^{7.48}$ (all P). **3.** *perform the ceremony of cleansing* Lv 14^{11} (P). **Pu.** *Pf.* 3 ms. טֹהַר 1 S 20^{26} (so rd. for MT טהור 𝔊 We Dr, he is not clean, because *he hath not been cleansed*); *Pt.* אֶרֶץ לֹא מְטֹהָרָה *a land not cleansed* Ez 22^{24} (but 𝔊 Hi Ew Co SS rd. *a land not rained upon*, v. מטר). **Hithp.** *Pf.* 3 pl. הִטֶּהָרוּ Ezr 6^{20}; הִטֶּהָרוּ (Kö$^{i.\ 271}$) 2 Ch 30^{18} Nu 8^{7}; 1 pl. הִטַּהַרְנוּ Jos 22^{17}; *Impf.* יִטַּהֲרוּ Ne 12^{30}; *Imv.* הִטַּהֲרוּ Gn 35^{2}; *Pt.* מִטַּהֵר Lv 14^{7}+11 t.; *pl.* מִטַּהֲרִים Ne 13^{22} Is 66^{17};—reflexive: **1.** *purify oneself*: **a.** ceremonially, esp. in preparation for sacred duties Gn 35^{2} (R), Nu 8^{7} 2 Ch 30^{18} Ezr 6^{20} Ne 13^{22}; also for heathen mysteries Is 66^{17}; of purifying priests, people, and wall Ne 12^{30} (cf. **Pi. 1 b**). **b.** morally Jos 22^{17} (P). **2.** *present oneself for purification*, only pt. הַמִּטַּהֵר *the candidate for purification* Lv 14$^{4.7.8.11.14.17.18.19.25.28.29.31}$ (P).

†טֹהַר **n.[m.] purity, purifying**—**1.** *purity*, כְּעֶצֶם הַשָּׁמַיִם לָטֹהַר Ex 24^{10} (JE), *as the body of the heavens for purity*. **2.** sf. יְמֵי טָהֳרָהּ Lv 12$^{4.6}$ *the days of her purifying* (menstruation). 2892

†[טְהָר] (v. Ges$^{§\ 10.\ 2.\ B}$), or [טֳהָר] (Ol$^{§\ 173\ b}$ Bö$^{§\ 386}$) **n.[m.] clearness, lustre** (dub. word; sub טהר Hup Pe SS; so Thes, reading מִטְּהָרוֹ) —only הִשְׁבַּתָּ מִטְּהָרוֹ ψ 89^{45}; De Hup Pe Sch *thou hast made* (him) *to cease from his lustre*; 𝔖 𝔙 *made his lustre to cease*, so AE Ki al. reading n. מִטְהָרוֹ or מְטֻהָרוֹ (D. f. acc. to Ges$^{§\ 20.\ 2.\ 2\ b}$), and Schr$^{SK\ 1868,\ 642}$ who reads הִשְׁבַּתָּה מַטֵּה הוֹדוֹ; Gr prop. מַטֶּה מִיָּדוֹ עֲטָרְתוֹ *his crown*; Bae *sceptre from his hand*. 2892

†טָהֳרָה **n.f. purifying, cleansing**;—abs. ט׳ Lv 12^{4}+2 t.; cstr. טָהֳרַת 1 Ch 23^{28} 2 Ch 30^{19}; sf. טָהֳרָתוֹ Lv 13^{7}+7 t.;—**1.** *purifying, menstruation* Lv 12$^{4.5}$. **2.** *cleansing, purification*, of leper Lv 13$^{7.35}$ 14$^{2.23.32}$; of Nazirite Nu 6^{9}; from an issue Lv 15^{13} (all P); from contact with the dead Ez 44^{26}; of sacred things in gen. 1 Ch 23^{28}; of persons for the passover 2 Ch 30^{19}; 2893

מִשְׁמֶרֶת הַטָּהֳרָה Ne 12^{45} *the charge, requirement of purification.*

2889-90 †טָהוֹר **adj.** clean, pure;—m. abs. ט׳ Ex 25^{11} + 68 t.; טָהֹר Lv 11^{47} + 4 t.; cstr. טְהוֹר Hab 1^{13}; טְהָוֹר Pr 22^{11}; טְהָר־ Jb 17^{9}; f. טְהוֹרָה Mal 1^{11} + 3 t.; טְהֹרָה Gn 7^{2} + 8 t.; mpl. טְהוֹרִים Ez 36^{25} Ezr 6^{20}; טְהֹרִים Pr 15^{26}; fpl. טְהוֹרוֹת Lv 14^{4} ψ 12^{7};—**1.** ceremonially *clean*, of animals Gn $7^{2.2.8.8}$ $8^{20.20}$ (all J), Lv 14^{4} (P), $20^{25.25}$ (H), Dt $14^{11.20}$; places Lv 4^{12} 6^{4} 10^{14} 11^{36} Nu 19^{9} (all P); things Lv 10^{10} $11^{37.47}$ 14^{57} (P), Ez 22^{26} 44^{23} Is 66^{20} Mal 1^{11}; persons Lv 7^{19} $13^{13.17.37.39.40.41}$ 15^{8} Nu 5^{28} 9^{13} $18^{11.13}$ $19^{9.18.19}$ (all P), Dt $12^{15.22}$ 15^{22} 23^{11} 1 S 20^{26a} + v.^{26b} MT but rd. טֹהַר Pu., see טָהֵר, 2 Ch 30^{17} Ezr 6^{20}. **2.** physically *pure:* of gold זָהָב Ex $25^{11.17.24.29.31.36.38.39}$ $28^{14.22.36}$ 30^{3} $37^{2.6.11.16.17.22.23.24.26}$ $39^{15.25.30}$ (all P), 1 Ch 28^{17} 2 Ch 3^{4} 9^{17}; כֶּתֶם Jb 28^{19}; of water מַיִם Ez 36^{25}; of incense קְטֹרֶת Ex 30^{35} 37^{29} (P); of lamp stand מְנֹרָה Ex 31^{8} 39^{37} (P), Lv 24^{4} (H); of the table שֻׁלְחָן Lv 24^{6} (H), 2 Ch 13^{11}; *clean*, of turban Zc $3^{5.5}$. **3.** ethically *pure, clean* Pr 30^{12} Ec 9^{2} Jb 14^{4}; of heart ψ 51^{12} Pr 22^{11}; hands Jb 17^{9}; eyes Hab 1^{13} (of God); words of men Pr 15^{26}; words of God ψ 12^{7}; law of י׳ as object of reverential fear ψ 19^{10}.

2895 †I. טוב **vb.** pleasing, good (NH *id.*, Hiph.; also deriv.; Ar. طَابَ, med. ى, *be pleasant, delightful, delicious, sweet* or *savoury* in taste or odour, *be pure and clean, cheerful, happy* (Lane); Aram. טִיב, טַב, טְאֵב, [Syriac] and esp. deriv. *glad, joyful;* As. *ṭâbu, be good, kind, acceptable, joyful, vigorous* Dl$^{\text{HWB 299}}$)—**Qal** *Pf.* טוֹב Nu 11^{18} + 32 t.; pl. טֹבוּ Nu 24^{5} Ct 4^{10}; (*Impf.* יִיטַב from יָטַב); *Inf. abs.* טוֹב Ju 11^{25}; *cstr.* טוֹב Je 32^{39} + 6 t., בְּטוֹב Ju 16^{25} Qr (Kt כי טוב); *Pt.* טוֹב Ju 11^{25} 1 S 2^{26}; (for these forms v. Bö$^{\S 1133,4}$ SS s.v.; Ges recognises only *Pfs.* and fewer of them than above. It is often difficult to decide between vb. and adj.);—**1.** *be pleasant, delightful*, of tents of Jacob Nu 24^{5} (JE; poet.); of caresses Ct 4^{10} (sq. מִיַּיִן comp.) **2.** *be glad, joyful* טוֹב לֵב Ju 16^{25} (Qr), 1 S 25^{36} 2 S 13^{28} Est 1^{10} (v. טוב **2 c**). **3.** of rank, position, claim: הֲטוֹב טוֹב אתה מבלק Ju 11^{25} *art thou really better than Balak?* **4.** טוֹב לְ *be well with, good for* Nu 11^{18} (J), Dt 5^{30} 15^{16} 19^{13} 1 S $16^{16.23}$ 2 S 14^{32} ψ 119^{71} 128^{2} Je 22^{15}; so (sc. לוֹ) Is 3^{10} it is *well* (with him); אז טוב Je 22^{16} (cf. v^{15}); טוֹב אֶל־ 1 S 20^{12} *there is good toward* David. **5.** *be pleasing* טוֹב בְּעֵינֵי (v. II. טוב **2 b c f**) Nu 24^{1} (J) 2 S $3^{19.36}$ 15^{26} 19^{38}; אִם טוֹב בְּעֵינֵי 1 K 21^{2} Je 40^{4} Zc 11^{12}; later usage is אִם טוֹב עַל *if it seem good unto* (so As. *ṭâbu eli, be pleasing unto,* Dl$^{\text{HWB 300a}}$), 1 Ch 13^{2} Ne $2^{5.7}$ Est 1^{19} 3^{9} $5^{4.8}$ 7^{3} 8^{5} 9^{13} (cf. טוב adj.). **Hiph.** *Pf.* 2 ms. הֱטִיבוֹתָ, 2 Ch 6^{8}, הֱטִיבֹתָ 1 K 8^{18} 2 K 10^{30};—*do well, act right*, sq. כִּי *that* 1 K 8^{18} *thou didst well, that it was in thine heart* = 2 Ch 6^{8}; sq. inf. c. לְ 2 K 10^{30} *thou hast done well in performing what was right in mine eyes.*

2896 †II. טוֹב **adj.** pleasant, agreeable, good (v. Lag$^{\text{BN 26}}$; Aram. טָב, Palm. טב Vog$^{\text{No. 81}}$, טבא Vog$^{\text{No. 75}}$)—m. ט׳ Gn 2^{12} + 22 t., טוֹבָם Mi 7^{4}; f. טוֹבָה Est 8^{5} + 50 t., טֹבָה Dt 6^{18} + 2 t.; cstr. טוֹבַת Gn 26^{7} + 6 t., טֹבַת Gn 24^{16}; pl. טוֹבִים Je 44^{17} + 28 t.; טֹבִים Gn 27^{9} + 4 t.; cstr. טוֹבֵי Dn 1^{4} + 2 t.; pl. טוֹבוֹת Est 2^{2}, טֹבוֹת Je 24^{2} + 6 t., טֹבֹת Gn 6^{2} + 4 t.;—**1.** *pleasant, agreeable* to the senses: **a.** to the sight, *fair*, of daughters of men Gn 6^{2} (J); of a son Ex 2^{2} (E), 1 S 9^{2} 1 K 20^{3}, young men (but rd. *herds* 𝔊 Th We Klo Dr Bu) 1 S 8^{16}; טֹבַת מראיהם *their appearance* Dn 1^{15}, טֹבַת מראה Gn 24^{16} 26^{7} (both J), 2 S 11^{2} Est 1^{11} $2^{3.7}$; טוב ראי 1 S 16^{12}; טוב תאר 1 K 1^{6}; טוֹבַת חן Na 3^{4}; טוֹבוֹת מראה Est 2^{2}; טוֹבֵי מראה Dn 1^{4}; טוב לעינים Ec 11^{7}; טובה בעיניו *fair in his eyes* Est 8^{5}; of mantle Jos 7^{21} (J); goodly houses Is 5^{9} Dt 8^{12}; cities Dt 6^{10}; situation of city 2 K 2^{19}. **b.** to the taste, *good, sweet, agreeable for eating* למאכל Gn 2^{9} 3^{6} (both J); ears of grain Gn $41^{5.22.24.26}$ (E); figs Je $24^{2.3.3.5}$; honey Pr 24^{13}; כְּיֵין הטוב Ct 7^{10} *as wine of the best sort* (Hi rds. כַּיַּיִן); תְּנוּבָתִי הַטּוֹבָה Ju 9^{11} *my sweet fruit* (‖ מָתְקִי). **c.** to the smell, *sweet-scented*, of ointment Ct 1^{3}; קנה הטוב Je 6^{20} *the fragrant cane.* **d.** of *pleasant* shadow of tree Ho 4^{13}. **2.** *pleasant* to the higher nature, giving pleasure, happiness, prosperity, and so *agreeable, pleasing, well:* **a.** of time: יום טוב *good day*, festal day 1 S 25^{8} Est 8^{17} $9^{19.22}$; of feasts Zc 8^{19}; prosperous years Gn 41^{35} (E). **b.** of place, טוב בית הנשים Est 2^{9} *the best part of the women's house;* בַּטּ׳ לוֹ Dt 23^{17}, בַּטּ׳ בְּעֵינֵי Gn 20^{15} (v. **c f** infr.) **c.** of persons, טוב בעיני (אתה) *pleasing in the eyes of* 1 S $29^{6.6.9}$ טוב בעיני י׳ Mal 2^{17} (cf. **vb. 4**, and **f** infr.); later לִפְנֵי Ec $2^{26.26}$ 7^{26}; inserted in 1 S 29^{10} 𝔊 We Dr; cf. ט׳ עם 1 S 2^{26}. **d.** of word or message, בְּשׂוֹרָה טוֹבָה 2 S 18^{27} *good tidings;* שְׁמוּעָה ט׳ *good report* 1 S 2^{24} Pr 15^{30} 25^{25}; דבר בעתו Pr 15^{23} *a word in its season;* דבר טוב Pr 12^{25} *an agreeable word* (maketh the heart glad); דבר טוב ψ 45^{2} *a good theme.* **e.** of other things, דֶּרֶךְ טובה 1 S 24^{20} *a pleasant, prosperous journey;*

מנחה כי טוב Gn 49^{15} (poem); of unity of brethren מה טוב ומה נעים ψ 133^{1} *how good and how pleasant it is!* (יהיה) טוב לְ *it shall be well for* Ec 2^{3} 6^{12} 8$^{12.13}$ (cf. **vb. 3**); הֲטוב כִּי Jb 13^{9} *will it be advantageous that* (v. **5**). **f.** עשה הטוב בעיני *do what is pleasing in the eyes of* Gn 16^{6} (J), Ju 19^{24} 1 S 1^{23} 3^{18} 14^{40} 2 S 10^{12} = 1 Ch 19^{13}, 2 S 19$^{19.28.39}$ 2 K 10^{5} 20^{3} = Is 38^{3}, 1 Ch 21^{23} = 2 S 24^{22} where obj. of העלה; עשה (כ)(כל)(ה)טוב בע׳ Gn 19^{8} (J), Ju 10^{15} 1 S 11^{10} 14^{36} Est 3^{11}; עשה (כ)הטוב ו(כ)הישר בע׳ Dt 12^{28} Jos 9^{25} (D), 2 Ch 14^{1} Je 26^{14}, cf. Est 8^{8}; nouns reversed Dt 6^{18}; עשה הטוב והישר לפני 2 Ch 31^{20}; טוב בע׳ in other combinations Nu 36^{6} (P), Je 40^{4}; ראה הטוב והישר 2 K 10^{3}; דבר ט׳ 1 K 22^{13} = 2 Ch 18^{12}, Nu 10^{29} (J), 1 S 19^{4} Est 7^{9}; דבר מטוב עד־רע *speak either good or bad* Gn 31$^{24.29}$ (E); למרע ועד טוב 2 S 13^{22}; רע או טוב Gn 24^{50} (J); התנבא ט׳ 1 K 22$^{8.18}$ = 2 Ch 18^{17}; cf. 1 K 22^{13} = 2 Ch 18^{12}. **3.** *good, excellent* of its kind: **a.** of the several creations, וירא אלהים כי טוב *and God saw that it was good, excellent* Gn 1$^{4.10.12.18.21.25}$ (P); כל אשר עשה והנה טוב מאד 1^{31} (P) God saw *all that he had made, and behold it was very excellent.* So **b.** of land, soil, *fruitful, fertile:* ארץ Ex 3^{8} Nu 13^{19} (both J), 14^{7} (P), Dt 1$^{25.35}$ 3^{25} 4$^{21.22}$ 6^{18} 8$^{7.10}$ 9^{6} 11^{17} Jos 23^{16} (D), Ju 18^{9} 1 Ch 28^{8}; אדמה 1 K 14^{15} Jos 23$^{13.15}$ (D); הר Dt 3^{25}; חלקה 2 K 3$^{19.25}$; שׂדה Ez 17^{8}; נָוֶה Ez 34^{14}; מרעה 1 Ch 4^{40} Ez 34$^{14.18}$. **c.** of vegetation, *choice, fruitful* זֵיתִים 1 S 8^{14}; עץ 2 K 3$^{19.25}$ Ez 31^{16}; שמן טוב 2 K 20^{13} *precious oil* = Is 39^{2}, ψ 133^{2} Ec 7^{1}; of seed, אם שניהם טובים Ec 11^{6} *whether both of them will be fruitful.* **d.** of animals, *fat* בקר Gn 18^{7} (J); עזים Gn 27^{9} (J); פרות Gn 41^{26} (E); יָרֵךְ Ez 24^{4}. **e.** of minerals, *fine, pure* זהב Gn 2^{12} (J), 2 Ch 3$^{5.8}$; כֶּתֶם La 4^{1}; brass Ezr 8^{27}, soldering Is 41^{7}. **4.** *good, rich, valuable in estimation:* **a.** in quantity, שיבה טובה *good old age* Gn 15^{15} (R), 25^{8} (P), Ju 8^{32} 1 Ch 29^{28}; dowry Gn 30^{20} (E; many sons); treasury Dt 28^{12} (from which י׳ sends blessings). **b.** in price, *goodly, valuable:* of the estimation put upon house, beast, and tithe Lv 27$^{10.10.12.14.33}$ (H); profit Pr 31^{18}; hire Ec 4^{9}; מחמדי הטבים Jo 4^{5} *my goodly precious things.* **5.** *good, appropriate, becoming,* טוב אשר Ec 7^{18} (cf. 5^{4} infr.); טובה חכמה עם נחלה Ec 7^{11} *wisdom is good with an inheritance* (other trans. see in VB); ‖ יָפֶה Ec 5^{17}; c. עֵצָה 2 S 17$^{7.14}$ *good advice;* טוב פתר Gn 40^{16} (E) that *he interpreted well;* (לא) טוב הדבר Ex 18^{17} (E) *the thing is* (not) *good, wise,* so Dt 1^{14} 1 S 26^{16}; טוב (ה)דבר *the word is good, is well said* 1 S 9^{10} 1 K 2$^{38.42}$ 18^{24} 2 K 20^{19}

= Is 39^{8}, for which abbreviated טוב *well! good!* exclamation Ru 3^{13} 1 S 20^{7} 2 S 3^{13} 1 K 2^{18}; followed by כִּי *it is good that* 2 S 18^{3} Ru 2^{22} La 3^{27} Jb 10^{3} (cf. 13^{9} **2 e**); c. inf. Gn 2^{18} (J), ψ 73^{28} 92^{2} 147^{1} Pr 25^{27} (cf. sub **10**); with וְ (strangely) טוב וְיָחִיל וגו׳ La 3^{26} *it is good that one wait* (v. יָחִיל, דּוּמָם); בלא דעת נֶפֶשׁ לא טוב Pr 19^{2} *that a soul be without knowledge is not good.* **6.** c. מִן compar. = *better,* sq. inf. Gn 29^{19} (E), Ex 14^{12} (J), ψ 118$^{8.9}$ Pr 16^{19} 25^{7} Ec 6^{9} 7^{2}; inf. om. Pr 21$^{9.19}$ 25^{24}; מן om. Nu 14^{3} (J; compar. only implied); c. מן pers. Ju 15^{2} Ru 4^{15} 1 S 1^{8} 9^{2} 15^{28} 1 K 2^{32} 19^{4} 2 Ch 21^{13} Pr 12^{9} 16^{32} 19$^{1.22}$ 27^{10} 28^{6} La 4^{9} Est 1^{19} Ec 4$^{3.9.13}$ 6^{3} 7$^{5.8}$; c. מן rei Ju 8^{2} 1 S 15^{22} 2 S 17^{14} 1 K 21^{2} 2 K 5^{12} Ho 2^{9} Am 6^{2} Is 56^{5} Jon 4$^{3.8}$ ψ 37^{16} 63^{4} 84^{11} 119^{72} Pr 3^{14} 8$^{11.19}$ 15$^{16.17}$ 16$^{8.16}$ 17^{1} 22^{1} 27^{5} Ct 1^{2} Ec 4^{6} 7$^{1.3.8.10}$ 9$^{4.16.18}$; sq. מִשְּׁ- Ec 5^{4}; מַה־טּוֹב . . . הֲ . . . אִם *is it better . . . or?* Ju 9^{2}; אין הַטּוב . . . אוֹ 18^{19}; אין טוב מאשר Ec 2^{24} (rd. מִשְּׁ- v. Comm.); טוב שֶׁ- Ec 3^{22}; אין טוב כִּי אִם Ec 3^{12} 8^{15}; so 1 S 27^{1} 𝔊 We Dr Klo Kit Bu (MT only כי c. Impf.) **7.** of man's sensuous nature, *glad, happy, prosperous:* טוב לב *merry, glad heart* Pr 15^{15} Est 5^{9} Ec 9^{7}; טוֹבֵי לב 1 K 8^{66} = 2 Ch 7^{10}; וַנִּהיה טובים Je 44^{17} *we were prosperous;* similarly ψ 112^{5}. **8.** of man's intellectual nature, שֵׂכֶל טוב *good understanding* 2 Ch 30^{22} ψ 111^{10} Pr 3^{4} 13^{15}; טוֹבַת שֶׂכֶל 1 S 25^{3}. **9.** *good, kind, benign:* **a.** of men, themselves 1 S 25^{15} 2 S 18^{27} 2 Ch 10^{7}; the eye Pr 22^{9}; דברים טובים *kind words* 1 K 12^{7} = 2 Ch 10^{7}. **b.** of God, himself Na 1^{7} 2 Ch 30^{18} ψ 86^{5}; כי טוב for *he is good, kind* ψ 34^{9} 100^{5} 135^{3} Je 33^{11}; כי טוב כי לעולם חסדו 1 Ch 16^{34} 2 Ch 5^{13} 7^{3} Ezr 3^{11} ψ 106^{1} 107^{1} 118$^{1.29}$ 136^{1}; טוב לְ *kind to* 73^{1} 145^{9} La 3^{25}; יד (ה)טובה על Ezr 7^{9} 8^{18} Ne 2$^{8.18}$; רוחך (ה)טובה 9^{20} ψ 143^{10}; שמך כי טוב 52^{11} 54^{8}; כי טוב חסדך 69^{17} 109^{21}; הדבר(ים) הטוב(ים) *the good, kind word(s)* spoken in promise Jos 21^{43} 23$^{14.15}$ (D), 1 K 8^{56} Je 29^{10} 33^{14} Zc 1^{13}. **10.** *good* (ethical), *right:* מה טוב ‖ what Yahweh requires Mi 6^{8}, ‖ משפט Jb 34^{4}: **a.** of man himself ‖ ישר Mi 7^{4}; איש טוב Pr 14^{14}; (ה)טוב(ים) = (*the*) *good* 2 Ch 19^{11} ψ 125^{4} Pr 2^{20} 12^{2} 13^{22} 14^{19} 15^{3} Ec 9$^{2.2}$; man's deeds דברים 2 Ch 2^{12} 19^{3}; מעשׂה 1 S 19^{4} Ec 12^{14}; מעללים Ez 36^{31}; דֶּרֶךְ הטובה והישרה 1 S 12^{23} *the good and right way;* (הַ)דֶּרֶךְ (ה)טוב(ה) (*the*) *good way* 1 K 8^{36} = 2 Ch 6^{27}, Is 65^{2} Je 6^{16} ψ 36^{5} Pr 16^{29}; דבריך טובים ונכחים 2 S 15^{3} *good and right is thy case;* דבר טוב *good thing* 1 K 14^{13}; לא טוב

הדבר Ne 5^{9}; אשר לא טוב עשה Ez 18^{18}; so of מאזני מרמה etc., Pr 20^{23}; לא טוב c. inf. (v. **5**) *it is not good or right to:* ענוש לצדיק Pr 17^{26}; שאת פני רשע 18^{5}; הכר פנים 28^{21} 24^{23} (בל טוב). **b.** of God טוב אתה ומטיב ψ 119^{68}; טוב וישר יהוה 25^{8}; משפטיך טובים 119^{39}; his commands מצות Ne 9^{13}; חקים Ez 20^{25} (לא טובים); לקח טוב Pr 4^{2}; מפי עליון לא תצא הרעות והטוב La 3^{38}.

2896 † III. טוֹב n.m.$^{Je 17, 6}$ (cf. טוֹבָה n.f.) **a good thing, benefit, welfare**;—ט׳ Gn 26^{29} + 134 t.;—**1.** *welfare, prosperity, happiness:* ‖ שָׁלוֹם Is 52^{7} Je 8^{15} 14^{19}; אם טוב ואם רע 42^{6} *whether prosperity or adversity;* יבוא טוב 17^{6} *prosperity cometh;* שׂמח בט׳ Dt 26^{11} 2 Ch 6^{41}; ראה בט׳ Ec 2^{1} Je 29^{32}; obj. of ראה ψ 4^{7} 34^{13} Ec 2^{24} 3^{13} Jb 7^{7}; of דרשׁ Est 10^{3}; of בקשׁ ψ 122^{9}; מנע 84^{12} Je 5^{25}; נתן ψ 85^{13}; קוה Jb 30^{26}; מצא Pr 16^{20} 17^{20} 18^{22} 19^{8}; נחל Pr 28^{10}; חסר ψ 34^{11}; בשׂר 1 K 1^{42} Is 52^{7}; חול לט׳ Mi 1^{12}; חכמה וט׳ 1 K 10^{7}; טוב וחסד ψ 23^{6}; בטוב *in prosperity* 25^{13} Jb 21^{13} 36^{11} Ec 7^{14}; מטוב *because of prosperity* Zc 1^{17}; *afar from happiness* ψ 39^{3}; כטוב Ho 10^{1}; לטוב Dt 30^{9} Je 15^{11}; לטוב לָנוּ Dt 6^{24} *for good to us,*= *for our good,* 10^{13} (לְךָ), Je 32^{39} (לָהֶם); cf. לרע ל Je 7^{6} 25^{7}). **2.** *good things,* (coll.) ברכ(ו)ת ט׳ *blessing of good things* ψ 21^{4} Pr 24^{25}; מִלֵּא בָתֵּיהֶם ט׳ Jb 22^{18} *filled their houses with good things;* obj. of שׂבע ψ 104^{28} Pr 12^{14}; מלא ψ 107^{9}; השׂביע בט׳ ψ 103^{5}; לקח Ho 14^{3}; אכל Pr 13^{2} Is 55^{2}; *goods, possessions* 1 S 15^{9}. **3.** *good=benefit:* גְּמָלַתְהוּ טוֹב וְלֹא־רָע Pr 31^{12} *she doeth him good and not evil;* תַּאֲוַת צַדִּיקִים אַךְ־טוֹב Pr 11^{23} *the desire of the righteous is only good;* obj. of קבל Jb 2^{10}; מנע Pr 3^{27}; שׁחר 11^{27}; שׁלּם 13^{21}; עשׂה Gn 26^{29} (J), ψ 119^{65}; היטיב Nu 10^{32} (J); ערב לט׳ ψ 119^{122}; חֹרְשֵׁי ט׳ Pr 14^{22} *who devise good.* **4.** *moral good,* ידע טוב ורע Gn 2$^{9.17}$ 3$^{5.22}$ (J), Dt 1^{39}; בין טוב לרע 2 S 19^{36}; in antithesis with רע elsewh. Dt 30^{15} 2 S 14^{17} 1 K 3^{9} Is 5$^{20.20}$ 7$^{15.16}$ Am 5$^{14.15}$ Mi 3^{2} ψ 34^{15} 37^{27} 52^{5}; זנח ט׳ Ho 8^{3} *cast off good;* עשׂה טוב *do good* ψ 14$^{1.3}$=53$^{2.4}$, 37^{3} Ec 7^{20}, in 3^{12} this mng. seems less fitting; rd. perh. לִרְאוֹת ט׳ (Gr, v. also De) and tr. to **1**; רדף ט׳ ψ 38^{21} *pursue good;* מַעְגַּל־ט׳ Pr 2^{9} *path of good.*

2899 † טוֹב אֲדוֹנִיָּה n.pr.m. (*good is my Lord,* ׳י)—וַאֲדֹנִיָּהוּ וְטוֹבִיָּהוּ וְטוֹב אֲדוֹנִיָּה in list of Levites assigned to reign of Jehoshaphat 2 Ch 17^{8}, but txt. suspicious; 𝔊L Τωβαδωνια, but 𝔊 only Τωβαδωβεια for all three names.

† טוּב n.m.$^{Jb 20, 21}$ **good things, goods, goodness**;—ט׳ Gn 24^{10} + 17 t.; sf. טוּבִי Ex 33^{19} Je 31^{14}; 2898
טוּבְךָ ψ 25^{7} + 4 t.; טוּבוֹ Ho 3^{5} + 2 t.; טוּבָהּ Ne 9^{36} Je 2^{7}; טוּבָם Jb 21^{16};—not in H P Chr Ez or post-ex. proph.—**1.** *good things,* coll., produce of the land to be eaten Gn 45$^{18.20.23}$ (E), Is 1^{19} Je 2^{7} Ezr 9^{12} Ne 9$^{35.36}$, to be enjoyed; good things of ׳י as given by him Ho 3^{5} Je 31$^{12.14}$ ψ 27^{13}; of house of ׳י ψ 65^{5}, fig. of spiritual blessings. **2.** *goods, property* Gn 24^{10} (J), Dt 6^{11} 2 K 8^{9} Ne 9^{25}. **3.** abstr.: **a.** *fairness, beauty,* of neck of heifer Ho 10^{11}; of people of ׳י Zc 9^{17}; of ׳י himself Ex 33^{19} (JE). **b.** טוּב לב(ב) *joy* of heart Dt 28^{47} Is 65^{14} (v. I. טוֹב **2**, II. ט׳ **7**). **c.** *prosperity* Jb 20^{21} 21^{16}; of Jerusalem ψ 128^{5}; בְּטוּב צַדִּיקִים Pr 11^{10} *in the prosperity of the righteous* the city rejoiceth. **d.** *goodness* of taste, discernment ψ 119^{66}. **4.** abstr., *goodness* of God: **a.** in bestowing good things Ne 9^{25}. **b.** in the salvation of his people Is 63^{7} ψ 25^{7} 145^{7}. **c.** stored up for his saints ψ 31^{20}.

† טוֹבָה n.f. **welfare, benefit, good things,** 2896
good;—abs. ט׳ Dt 28^{11} + 54 t.; cstr. טוֹבַת ψ 106^{5}; sf. טוֹבָתִי ψ 16^{2} etc. + 4 t. sfs.; pl. טוֹבוֹת Je 12^{6}; טֹבוֹת 2 K 25^{28} Je 52^{32}; sf. טוֹבֹתָיו Ne 6^{19};—**1.** *welfare, prosperity, happiness:* ‖ שׁלום Dt 23^{7} Je 33^{9} Ezr 9^{12} La 3^{17}; יום טובה Ec 7^{14} *day of prosperity;* טוֹבָתִי בַּל־עָלֶיךָ ψ 16^{2} *is not my welfare dependent upon thee?* תְּבוֹאֲתְךָ ט׳ Jb 22^{21} *prosperity shall come to thee;* לטובה Gn 50^{20} (E), Dt 28^{11} 30^{9} 2 Ch 18^{7} Je 14^{11}; לרעה ולא לטובה Am 9^{4} Je 21^{10} 39^{16} 44^{27}; obj. of vb. בקשׁ Ne 2^{10}; הביא Je 32^{42}; ראה Jb 9^{25} Ec 5^{17} 6^{6}; אבד Ec 9^{18}; ראה בט׳ ψ 106^{5}; חסר מט׳ Ec 4^{8}; obj. of אכל fig. Jb 21^{25}=*taste happiness;* of שׂבע Ec 6^{3}; after נחם על Je 18^{10}. **2.** *good things* (coll.): **a.** of good words, obj. of דבר 1 S 25^{30} 2 S 7^{28}= 1 Ch 17^{26}, Je 18^{20}; pl. דבר טובות Je 12^{6} 52^{32}= 2 K 25^{28}. **b.** of material possessions ברבות הט׳ Ec 5^{10} *when good things increase.* **3.** *bounty, good* שְׁנַת טוֹבָתֶךָ ψ 65^{12} *year of thy bounty* (harvest bestowed by God), so also טובתך ψ 68^{11}; עשׂה (ה)ט׳ Ex 18^{9} (E), Nu 24^{13} (JE), Ju 8^{35} 9^{16} 1 S 24^{19} 2 S 2^{6} 1 K 8^{66}=2 Ch 7^{10}, 2 Ch 24^{16} Je 33^{9}; obj. of גמל 1 S 24^{18}; שׁלּם 1 S 24^{20}; רעה תחת טובה Gn 44^{4} (J), 1 S 25^{21} ψ 35^{12} 38^{21} 109^{5} Pr 17^{13} Je 18^{20}; ט׳ תחת קללה 2 S 16^{12}; זכר לי לט׳ *remember it for me for good* Ne 5^{19} 13^{31}; לטובה Ezr 8^{22} Ne 2^{18} Je 24$^{5.6}$ ψ 86^{17}; pl. טוֹבֹתָיו Ne 6^{19} *his benefits* (i.e. good deeds of Tobiah).

† טוֹבִיָּה, טוֹבִיָּ֫הוּ n.pr.m. (*Yah(u) is my* 2900

good)—**1.** טוֹבִיָּהוּ a Levite, assigned to reign of Jehoshaphat 2 Ch 17[8], not 𝔊; 𝔊 L Τωβιας, elsewhere טוֹבִיָּה 𝔊 Τωβια(ς). **2.** Ammonite adversary of Nehem. Ne 2[10.19] 3[35] 4[1] 6[1.12.14.17.17.19] 13[4.7.8]. **3.** head of a family of returning exiles of doubtful lineage Ezr 2[60]=Ne 7[62]. **4.** a chief of returning exiles Zc 6[10.14], 𝔊 χρησίμων (-μοις) αὐτῆς, i.e. טוֹבֶיהָ.

2897 †IV. טוֹב **n.pr.loc.** (perh. fr. above √)—a region beyond Jordan, N. or NE. of Gilead, prob. Aramean; אֶרֶץ טוֹב Ju 11[3.5], 𝔊 Τωβ; אִישׁ טוֹב 2 S 10[6.8] *men of Ṭôb*, 𝔊 (Ε)ιστωβ; =Τούβιον, Τώβιον 1 Macc 5[13]; identif. by Conder[Handb. 295] with southern Bashan, where is still *Taiyibeh*, 12 m. SE. from Sea of Galilee.

2901 †[טָוָה] **vb. spin** (NH *id.*; Aram. מַטְווָיְתָא *spider* Jb 8[14] 𝔗 (but Syr. ܛܘܐ =*roast, broil*, v. Dr[JPh xi, 1882, 207]); As. *ṭâmû* (*ṭâvû*), *spin*, Hpt[ZA, 1887, 274] Dl[HWB 302]; Ar. طَوَى *fold, wind*; Eth. ጠወየ: *be twisted*)—**Qal** *Pf.* 3 pl. טָווּ work of women of Isr. Ex 35[25] abs., v[26] sq. acc. אֶת־הָעִזִּים *goats*, i.e. goats' hair (P).

4299 †מַטְוֶה **n.[m.]** that which is spun, yarn, Ex 35[25] (P).

2902 †[טוּחַ] **vb. over-spread, over-lay, coat, besmear** (NH *id.*; Aram. *id.*; cf. Ar. طَاخَ *re foeda contaminatus fuit*, or *contaminavit*; مُطَيَّخ camel *smeared with tar*);—**Qal** *Pf.* 3 ms. וְטָח consec. Lv 14[42] (on טַח Is 44[18] v. טחח); 3 pl. טָחוּ Ez 22[28]; טַחְתֶּם Ez 13[12.14]; *Inf. cstr.* לָטוּחַ 1 Ch 29[4]; *Pt.* pl. טָחִים Ez 13[10]+2 t.; cstr. טָחֵי Ez 13[11]; only P Ez Ch;—*over-spread, coat* (c. acc. of house) with earth (clay, עָפָר) Lv 14[42]; *over-lay* (walls with gold and silver) c. acc. of wall 1 Ch 29[4]; metaph. of coating over Jerusalem, under fig. of a wall, with a superficial coating, to hide its real weakness Ez 13[15] (acc. of wall), v[12] c. acc. of coating (טִיחַ); with תָּפֵל (q.v.) v[11]; c. 2 acc. v[10.14.15]; cf. וּנְבִיאֶיהָ טָחוּ להם תָּפֵל Ez 22[28] where sf. ref. to oppressive nobles, i.e. the prophets 'whitewash' for them (their evil deeds). **Niph.** *Inf. cstr.* הִטּוֹחַ *be coated* (with עפר) Lv 14[43]; and, fully, הִטּוֹחַ את־הבית 14[48] (both P).

2915 †טִיחַ **n.[m.]** a coating, only אַיֵּה הַטִּיחַ אֲשֶׁר טַחְתֶּם Ez 13[12].

2910 †טֻחוֹת **n.f.pl. inward parts** (as *covered over*, concealed)—טֻחוֹת of seat of faithfulness, אֱמֶת חָפַצְתָּ בַטּ׳ ψ 51[8] *faithfulness thou desirest in the inward parts*, i.e. in the heart (|| סָתֻם); of seat of wisdom מִי שָׁת בַּטּ׳ חָכְמָה Jb 38[36] (|| שֶׂכְוִי q.v.); fr. context this can hardly=heart of man (kidneys, 'reins,' 𝔗, Jewish interpr., v. NHWB ii, 144 al.), but is rather *cloud-layers* (as dark, *hidden* spaces, v. Di VB); their 'wisdom' appears in their obedience to natural law.

טוט, טיט (√ of foll.; meaning unknown).

†טִיט **n.m. mud, mire, clay** (NH *id.*; As. *ṭîṭu*, *id.*, Flood Tabl.[iii, 10. 25])—abs. טִיט Jb 41[22] +6 t.; cstr. *id.* Mi 7[10]+5 t.;—**1.** *mud, mire* of streets (always in sim. of contempt, ignominious treatment) ט׳ חוּצוֹת Mi 7[10] ψ 18[43]=2 S 22[43], Zc 9[3] 10[5]; of Jeremiah's dungeon Je 38[6.6]; of mire in which crocodile lies Jb 41[22]; cast up by sea Is 57[20] (|| רֶפֶשׁ); of a bog (fig. of distress) ψ 69[15] and ט׳ הַיָּוֵן ψ 40[30]. **2.** poet. of potter's *clay* (|| חֹמֶר) Is 41[25], brick-*clay* (|| *id.*) Na 3[14]. 2916

טֹטָפֹת, טוֹטָפֹת v. טטף. p. 377 2903

[טוּל] **vb. Pilp.** etc., **hurl, cast** (Ar. طَالَ *be extended, elongated*; v. Hom[NS 87] who comp. As. *tâlu*, Aram. ܛܐܠ, טַיֵּל all *walk about* (cf. *spatiari*, fr. *spatium*); Eth. አጠሰለ: *hang loosely*, አጠለለ: *expand*)—**Pilp.** *Pt.* מְטַלְטֶלְךָ טַלְטֵלָה גָּבֶר Is 22[17] *hurleth thee* violently. **Hiph.** *Pf.* הֵטִיל Jon 1[4]; וְהֵטַלְתִּי Je 16[13] 22[26]; *Impf.* וַיָּטֶל 1 S 18[11] (but v. infr.), 20[33]; אֲטִילְךָ Ez 32[4] (𝔊 Co om.) וַיָּטִלוּ Jon 1[5]; וַיְטִלֻהוּ Jon 1[15]; *cast, cast out*, of casting a javelin (חֲנִית) 1 S 18[11] (but rd. here וַיִּטֹּל, √ נטל, *and took up*, so 𝔊 𝔗 Th We Kp Kit, v. also Dr); 20[33] sq. על pers. aimed at; Jonah אֶל־הַיָּם Jon 1[12.15]; also the cargo כֵּלִים 1[5]; fig. of י׳ casting Pharaoh על־פני השדה Ez 32[4] (Co del. v. supr.; || וּנְטַשְׁתִּיךָ בָאָרֶץ); *hurl* (send violently), of י׳ sending furious wind Jon 1[4]; fig. of hurling king of Judah, etc. into exile Je 16[3] sq. acc. + מעל of land from which, and על of that to which; Je 22[26] c. acc. + על of land to which. **Hoph.** *Pf.* הוּטְלוּ Je 22[28]; *Impf.* יוּטַל Pr 16[33]; יוּטָל ψ 37[24]; יֻטָל Jb 41[1];—**1.** *be hurled*, e.g. into exile Je 22[28] (|| הֻשְׁלְכוּ); *hurled down, headlong*, כִּי יִפֹּל לֹא יוּטָל ψ 37[24] *when he falls he shall not be hurled headlong* (fig. of a good man); יֻטָל Jb 41[1] *be overwhelmed*, at sight of the crocodile. **2.** of inanimate thing, *be cast, thrown*, the lot בַּחֵיק יוּטַל אֶת־הַגּוֹרָל Pr 16[33]. 2904

†טַלְטֵלָה **n.f.** a hurling, Is 22[17], v. supr. **Pilp.**, lit. *hurleth thee with a hurling*, O man; 2925

rd. perh. (Du), with a diff. word-division, טַלְטֵל הַגֶּבֶר (inf. abs.)

טור (√ of foll.; cf. Ar. طَارَ *go* or *hover about, approach,* طَوْرٌ *limit, border*).

2905 †**טוּר n.m.**$^{Ex\ 28,17}$ **row**—abs. ט׳ Ex 28^{17} + 9 t.; cstr. *id.* 28^{17} + 3 t.; pl. טוּרִים 28^{17} + 7 t.; טֻרִים 1 K 7^{20}; cstr. טוּרֵי Ex 39^{10} + 2 t.;— **1.** *row, course* of building-stones, in temple and in Solomon's house 1 K 6^{36} 7^{12}; forming enclosures in corner of court Ez 46^{23a}; of beams 6^{36} 7^{12}, v. also 7^{4} (Th Klo, v. שֶׁקֶף, שְׁקֻפִים); of pillars 7$^{2.3}$. **2.** *row* of jewels, on high priest's breast-piece Ex 28$^{17.17.17.18.19.20}$ 39$^{10.10.10.11.12.13}$ (all P); of pomegranates on capitals of pillars in temple 1 K 7$^{20.42}$ 2 Ch 4^{13}, so also prob. 1 K 7^{18}, v. Th Klo, after 𝔊; of knops round the molten sea 7^{24}, cf. 2 Ch 4^{3} (oxen הַבָּקָר, erron. for הַפְּקָעִים 1 K 7^{24}).

2918 †[**טִירָה**] **n.f. encampment, battlement** (fr. idea of *surrounding,* enclosure; Syr. ܛܝܪܐ *sheepfold,* ἔπαυλις)—cstr. טִירַת Ct 8^{9}; טִירָתָם ψ 69^{26}; pl. טִירוֹת Ez 46^{23}; sf. טִירֹתָם Nu 31^{10} Gn 25^{16}; טִירוֹתָם 1 Ch 6^{39}; טִירוֹתֵיהֶם Ez 25^{4};— **1.** *encampment,* esp. of circular encampment of nomad tribes, mentioned with חצר Gn 25^{16}; with ערים Nu 31^{10}, Ez 25^{4}(‖ מִשׁכניהם); *encampment* (poet.) = habitation ψ 69^{26} (‖ אהליהם); more gen., 1 Ch 6^{39}(‖ מושבות). **2.** in metaph. ט׳ כָּסֶף Ct 8^{9} *a battlement of silver.* **3.** *row* of stones, only pl. טִירוֹת Ez 46^{23}, virtually pl. of טוּר **1,** q.v.

3195 †**יְטוּר n.pr.m.** and **gent.** (perh. connected etymolog. with טִירָה, v. Gn 25^{16})—a 'son' of Ishmael Gn 25^{15} = 1 Ch 1^{31} = tribe with which Reuben, Gad, and half Manasseh made war 1 Ch 5^{19}; Ἰτουραῖοί τε καὶ Ἄραβες Strabo$^{xvi.\ 2,\ 18}$, Ἰτουραίους Joseph$^{Ant.\ xiii.\ 11.\ 3}$ ed. Niese; they gave name to their region, which was, substantially, Anti-Lebanon, cf. τῆς Ἰτουραίας καὶ Τραχωνίτιδος χώρας Luke 3^{1}; on יְטוּר and (later) n.pr.terr. *Ituraea,* v. esp. GASm$^{Geogr.\ 544\ ff.}$ and reff.

2907 †[**טוּשׂ**] **vb. rush, dart** (Aram. ܛܳܣ, טוּס *fly*)—only **Qal** *Impf.* כְּנֶשֶׁר יָטוּשׂ עֲלֵי אֹכֶל Jb 9^{26} *like a vulture, which rusheth upon its food* (sim. of swiftly passing days of Job's life).

2909 †[**טָחָה**] **vb. hurl, shoot** (NH *id.;* Ar. طَحَى *spread, extend, carry far with,* e. g. a ball Lane^{1832c})—only **Pil.** *Pt.* (Ges$^{§\ 75\ R\ 18}$) pl. cstr. הַרְחֵק כִּמְטַחֲוֵי קֶשֶׁת Gn 21^{16} (E), lit. *making distant like shooters of a bow = about a bowshot off.*

†[**טָחַח**] **vb. be besmeared**—only **Qal** *Pf.* 3 ms. טַח מֵרְאוֹת עֵינֵיהֶם Is 44^{18} *their eyes have been besmeared so that they do not see,* v. Di Du, and on sg. c. subj. pl. Ges$^{§\ 145,\ 7\ a}$; others regard טַח as metaplastic pointing for טָח, fr. טוח, v. Sta$^{§\ 385\ d}$. 2902

†[**טָחַן**] **vb. grind** (NH *crush,* olives, etc.; Aram. ܛܚܶܢ, טְחַן *grind;* Ar. طَحَنَ *grind;* Eth. ጥሕን: *polenta, farina hordacea*)—**Qal** *Pf.* וְטָחֲנוּ Nu 11^{8}; *Impf.* וַיִּטְחַן Ex 32^{20}; 3 fs. תִּטְחַן Jb 31^{10}; 2 mpl. תִּטְחָנוּ Is 3^{15}; *Inf. abs.* טָחוֹן Dt 9^{21}; *Imv.* fs. טַחֲנִי Is 47^{2}; *Pt.* טוֹחֵן Ju 16^{21}; טֹחֲנוֹת Ec 12^{3};—*grind,* the work of women, c. acc., with millstones רֵחַיִם Nu 11^{8} (JE; obj. the manna), Is 47^{2} (obj. קֶמַח), this fig. of humiliation of Babylon; abs. Ju 16^{21}; תטחן לאחר אשתי Jb 31^{10}, i.e. serve him as his slave; no obj. expr. Ex 32^{20} (E), Dt 9^{21} (of golden calf); הַטֹּחֲנוֹת Ec 12^{3} = the teeth (cf. Ar. طَوَاحِنُ *molar teeth;* so in Lexx Syr. ܛܳܚܢܳܬܳܐ, ܛܚܽܘܢܳܐ); פְּנֵי עֲנִיִּים ט׳ Is 3^{15} *the face of the poor ye grind,* fig. of extreme oppression. 2912

†**טְחוֹן n.**[**m.**] **grinding-mill, hand-mill;** only בַּחוּרִים ט׳ נָשָׂאוּ La 5^{13} *the young men have borne the mill* (i.e. been compelled to bear it). 2911

†**טַחֲנָה n.f. mill** = foregoing, בִּשְׁפַל קוֹל הַט׳ Ec 12^{4} *when the sound of the mill is low* (cf. v^{3}, sub vb. supr.) 2913

טחר (√ of foll.; cf. Ar. طَحَرَ *eject;* Aram. טְחַר, ܛܚܰܪ *strain at stool,* ܛܰܚܪܳܐ *dysentery*).

†[**טְחוֹר**] **n.m.**$^{1\ S\ 6,\ 4}$ only pl. **tumours,** result of dysentery (v. Aram. √) (so Aram. טְחוֹרַיָּא, ܛܰܚܘܪܶܐ)—chiefly Qr for Kt עפלים, עֳפָלַי, *hemorrhoids:* viz. טְחֹרִים Dt 28^{27} 1 S 5$^{6.9.12}$; טְחֹרֵי זָהָב 6^{4}; צַלְמֵי טְחֹרֵיכֶם 6^{5}; twice it has found its way into the Kt טְחֹרֵיהֶם 6^{17}, צַלְמֵי טְחֹרֵי הַזָּהָב 6^{11}; We$^{Sam.\ 27\ n.}$, cf. Gei$^{Urschrift\ 408\ f.}$ 2914

טטף (perh. √ of foll.; meaning dub.; Dl$^{Pr\ 46}$ comp. As. *ṭatâpu, surround, encircle;* Thes Di prop. √ טוף (cf. Ar. طَافَ *go around*), whence טפטפות = טוטפות; Kn., foll. by Klein$^{JPTh\ 1881,\ 673}$ al., assumes √ טפף *tap, strike,* comp. στίγμα, and thinks of actual sign or mark in the flesh as orig. meant).

†**טוֹטָפוֹת n.f.pl. bands** (NH טוֹטֶפֶת; Aram. טוֹטֶפְתָּא, and esp. pl. טוטפין *id.*)—alw. *bands, frontlet-bands, between the eyes* (‖ אות על יד; cf. זִכָּרוֹן בֵּין עֵינֶיךָ Ex 13^{9} ‖id.); fig. of dedication 2903

of firstborn וְהָיָה . . . לְטוֹטָפֹת בין עיניך Ex 13[16] (JE); of commandments of י׳, וְהָיוּ לְטוֹ׳ Dt 11[18] and וְהָיוּ לְטֹטָפֹת Dt 6[8].—This injunction, orig. fig. for *perpetual remembrance* (otherwise Kn, and Klein[l. c. 666 ff.], vid. supr., Benz[Arch. 111] Now[Arch. i. 134]), was taken literally by later Jews, and hence the custom of wearing *phylacteries;* v. Di (on Ex 13[16]) Winer[RE] Ri[HWB] (art. *Denkzettel*) Smith[Dict. Bib.] (art. *Frontlets*) Sta[ZAW 1894, 312 f., 317].

2915 טִיחַ v. sub טוח. p. 376

2916 טִיט v. sub טוט. p. 376

2918 טִירָה v. sub טור. p. 377

2919 טַל v. sub I. טלל. below

2921 †[טָלָא] **vb. patch, spot** (NH *id., patch*)—**Qal** *Pt. pass.* טָלוּא Gn 30[32.32.33]; pl. טְלֻאִים v[35.39]; טְלֻאוֹת Ez 16[16]; טְלֻאֹת Gn 30[35]; chiefly of *spotted, variegated* sheep and goats (Jacob & Laban); || נָקֹד, נְקֻדִּים Gn 30[32.32.33.35]; || עקדים Gn 30[35]; || both, v[39] (all J); of high places, *variegated* (gaily-coloured shrines) Ez 16[16]. **Pu.** *Pt.* מְטֻלָּאוֹת *patched,* of sandals Jos 9[5] (JE).

2923 †I. טְלָאִים **n.pr.loc.** c. art. הַטְּלָ׳, place where Saul mustered his forces 1 S 15[4], prob. = טֶלֶם q.v.

2923 II. טְלָאִים v. following.

טלה (√ of foll.; mng. dub.; Ar. طلى, طلو is *tie a lamb* to a stake, *confine;* Syr. ܛܠܐ is *make young,* both appar. denom.; Lag[Armen. Stud. § 2229] finds earlier form of טָלֶה in Armenian).

2922, †טָלֶה **n.m.**[1 S 7, 9] **lamb** (NH *id., lamb;* Aram.
2924 טַלְיָא *lamb, youth,* טַלְיְתָא *girl,* ܛܠܝܐ *boy, youth,* ܛܠܝܬܐ *girl* (cf. Mk 5[41] 𝔖); Ar. طَلًا *young* of cloven-footed animals, esp. *young gazelle* Hom[NS 235], Nedj. *tully, male lamb,* Doughty[Arab. Desert. i. 429, ii. 269]; Eth. ጠሊ: *flock of goats, goat, kid*)—טְלֵה חָלָב 1 S 7[9] *sucking lamb* (for burnt-offering); in prediction זְאֵב וְטָלֶה יִרְעוּ Is 65[25] *wolf & lamb*
2923 *shall feed;* טְלָאִים pl. of foregoing, only Is 40[11] in metaph. of י׳ shepherding his people.

טלטלה v. sub טול.

I. **טלל** (√ of foll.; mng. dub.; perh. denom. are Ar. طَلَّ (the sky) *rained fine rain;* Eth. ጠለለ: *be (moist), fat,* II. *fertilize*).

2919 †טַל **n.m.**[Ju 6, 37] **night-mist, dew** (NH טַל *dew;* Aram. ܛܠܐ, טַלָּא *dew;* Ar. طَلّ *light rain, dew;* Eth. ጠል: *dew*)—ט׳ abs. 1 S 1[21] + 12 t.; טָל Ju 6[13] + 9 t.; cstr. טַל Gn 27[28] + 4 t.; sf. טַלֶּךָ Is 26[19], טַלָּם Zc 8[12];—*night-mist,* taking place of our *dew* (v. Che Is 18[4] & ψ 110[3]; Lane[1862], Neil[Pal. Explored 129]); as coming from the sky and bringing fertility, טַל הַשָּׁמַיִם Gn 27[28] (God gives it, נתן), & v[39] (+ מֵעָל), cf. Dt 33[28] (heavens distil it, ערף), Hg 1[10] Zc 8[12] (heavens give it, נתן); in Dt 33[13] rd. perh. מֵעָל for מִטַּל (v. || Gn 49[25] and Di); clouds distil it (רעף) Pr 3[20]; sq. עַל, it descends (ירד) upon the camp Nu 11[9] (JE); it is upon the ground Ju 6[39.40], cf. 2 S 1[21] (+ מָטָר); upon the fleece Ju 6[37]; is wrung out (מוץ) of the fleece v[38]; remains through the night (לון) Jb 29[19], cf. שִׁכְבַת הַטּ׳ *the lying of dew* = the dew lying Ex 16[13.14] (P; it goes up (עלה) in morning); it is in drops מִי הוֹלִיד אֶגְלֵי טָל Jb 38[28]; covers the head of one out at night Ct 5[2]; it comes (היה) by word of prophet 1 K 17[1] (+ מָטָר); sim. of stealthy approach כַּאֲשֶׁר יִפֹּל הַטַּל עַל־הָאֲדָמָה 2 S 17[12]; sim. denoting welcome and gentle refreshment, of speech, which distils (נזל) like it Dt 32[2] (poem; || שְׂעִירִים, רְבִיבִים); of fraternal unity כְּטַל חֶרְמוֹן ψ 133[3] (ירד על); of king's favour Pr 19[12] (על); of י׳'s kindness Ho 14[6]; כְּעָב טַל Is 18[4] like a *mist-cloud,* of י׳'s quiet watching; of Jacob's influence among nations Mi 5[6] (ט׳ מֵאֵת י׳ || רְבִיבִים); טַל אוֹרֹת טַלֶּךָ Is 26[19] *a dew of light is thy dew* (v. I. אוֹרָה, p. 21[b] supr. and Baud[Stud. Sem. Rel. ii. 264 f.]); as transitory, כַּטַּל מַשְׁכִּים הֹלֵךְ Ho 6[4] *like the dew early departing,* so 13[3] (both || עֲנַן־בֹּקֶר); fig. of young warriors of king established by י׳, with flashing weapons, like dewdrops טַל יַלְדֻתֶךָ ψ 110[3].

†II. [טָלַל] **vb. cover over, roof,** Aram. 2926
loan-word, v. צלל (ܛܠܠ *cover over,* esp. *put on roof,* ܛܛܠܠܐ *roof,* στέγη: so Palm. v. Eut[SBAk. 1885, 669])—only **Pi.** *Impf.* 3 ms. sf. וַיְטַלְלֶנּוּ Ne 3[15] he built it (kept on building it, i.e. a city-gate) and *covered it over* (laid timbers to cover it, cf. קֵרוּהוּ *they laid its timbers* v[3.6]; v. also בְּצֵל קֹרָתִי Gn 19[8] *in the shadow of my roof*).

טלם (√ of foll.; perh. cf. Ar. ظَلَمَ; Aram. טְלַם, ܛܠܡ; Eth. ጠለመ: all *oppress, injure;* in this case טַלְמוֹן, טֶלֶם will be Aramaic names, since ظ = Heb. צ).

†טֶלֶם **n.pr.loc.** et **pers.** **1. n.pr.loc.** in 2928

the Negeb of Judah, Jos 15^{24}=טלאים 1 S 15^{4}, rd. perh. טְלָאִם We Dr. We rds. טֶלֶם also for חוילה 1 S 15^{7}, cf. Dr. **2. n.pr.m.** one of the porters Ezr 10^{24}.

2929 †טַלְמֹן, once טַלְמוֹן **n.pr.m.** name of porters. **1.** 1 Ch 9^{17} Ezr 2^{42}=Ne 7^{45}. **2.** Ne 11^{19} 12^{25} (טַלְמוֹן).

2930 †I. טָמֵא **vb. be or become unclean** (NH Pi. *pollute* (ceremonially); Aram. טְמָא and esp. deriv., ܛܰܡܶܐ Pa. *pollute;* v. RS$^{K\ 307\ ff.}$)—**Qal** *Pf.* 3 ms. ט׳ Lv 11^{25}+22 t.; 3 fs. טָמְאָה 12^{2}+2 t.; 2 fs. טָמֵאת Ez 22^{4}; pl. טָמְאוּ Lv 15^{18}; *Impf.* יִטְמָא Lv 5^{3}+34 t.; 3 fs. תִּטְמָא 12^{2}+4 t.; pl. יִטְמְאוּ ψ 106^{39}; *Inf.* טָמְאָה Lv 15^{32}+6 t.;—*be* or *become unclean:* **1.** sexually, c. בְּ Lv $18^{20.23}$ (H), Ez 23^{17}; the land Lv $18^{25.27}$(H). **2.** religiously, with idols Ez 22^{3}; c. בְּ v^{4}; with necromancers Lv 19^{31} (H); by sacrificing children to idols ψ 106^{39}. **3.** ceremonially, by contact with carcasses of unclean animals Lv $11^{24.27.28.31.32.33.34.34.35.36.40}$(P); any carcass 17^{15}(H); eating of a carcass 22^{8}(H); by issues $15^{4.9.20.20.24.27.32}$(P); by contact with an unclean man 5^{3} 15^{4}(P), 22^{5}(H), or thing 22^{6}(H); by leprosy $13^{14.46}$ $14^{36.46}$(P); by contact with the dead Nu 6^{12} 19^{20}(P), Ez 44^{25}, or with one unclean by such contact Nu 19^{22}(P), Hg $2^{13.13}$; by contact with creeping things Lv 22^{5}(H); certain animals were alw. unclean $11^{26.27}$(P). In ordinary cases of uncleanness טמא עד הערב *unclean till even* Lv $11^{24.25.27.28.31.32.39.40.40}$ 14^{46} $15^{5.6.7.8.10.10.11.16.17.18.19.21.22.23.27}$ Nu $19^{7.8.10.21.22}$ (all P), Lv 17^{15} 22^{6}(H); but uncleanness lasted 7 days for woman bearing a son Lv $12^{2.2}$(P), for man lying with woman having an issue 15^{24}(P), or one coming in contact with the dead Nu $19^{11.14.16}$(P); it lasted 14 days for a woman bearing a daughter Lv 12^{5}(P). **Niph.** *Pf.* 3 ms. נִטְמָא Ho 5^{3} 6^{10}; 3 fs. נִטְמְאָה Nu $5^{27.28}$; נִטְמָאָה 5^{13}+5 t.; 1 s. נִטְמֵאתִי Je 2^{23}; 2 m.pl. נִטְמֵתֶם Lv 11^{43} (א omitted by scribal error; but Ges al. derive from טמה), etc.+4 t. pf.; *Pt.* pl. נִטְמְאִים Ez $20^{30.31}$;—*defile oneself, be defiled:* **1.** sexually, Lv 18^{24}(H), Nu $5^{13.14.14.20.27.28.29}$(P). **2.** by idolatry conceived as whoredom Ho 5^{3} 6^{10} Je 2^{23} Ez $20^{30.31.43}$ $23^{7.13.30}$. **3.** ceremonially, by eating creeping things Lv 11^{43}. **4.** *be regarded as unclean* (cf. **Pi. 4**), prob. נִטְמִינוּ Jb 18^{3} *we are accounted as unclean;* metapl. form; on another view v. טמה. **Pi.** *Pf.* טִמֵּא Gn 34^{5}+15 t.; sf. טִמְּאוֹ Lv 13^{8}+3 t.; 2 fs. טִמֵּאת Ez 5^{11}, etc.+7 t. Pf.; *Impf.* יְטַמֵּא 2 K 23^{8}, etc.+12 t. Impf.; *Imv.* pl. טַמְּאוּ Ez 9^{7}; *Inf.* טַמֵּא Lv 13^{44}+2 t.; sf. טַמְּאָם 15^{31}, etc.+4 t. Inf.;—*defile:* **1.** sexually Gn $34^{5.13.27}$(R), Ez $18^{6.11.15}$ 22^{11} 33^{26}; the land by sexual impurities of the people Lv 18^{28}(H); Isr. by spiritual whoredom Ez 23^{17}. **2.** religiously: the land, by bloodshed Nu 35^{34}(P); by allowing the dead body of the murderer to hang on the tree over night Dt 21^{23}; by idolatry Je 2^{7} Ez $36^{17.18}$; Isr. defiled the *sacred places* by the sacrifice of children Lv 20^{3}(H), Ez 23^{38}, and God defiled him thereby 20^{26}; he defileth the sacred places by idolatry 2 Ch 36^{14} Je 7^{30}=32^{34}, Ez 5^{11}; the holy name of י׳ $43^{7.8}$; Josiah defiled the idolatrous places of worship by destroying them and making them unfit for use 2 K $23^{8.10.13.16}$; of Isr. defiling idolatrous images Is 30^{22}, and the nations the temple of God ψ 79^{1}. **3.** ceremonially: by ceremonial uncleanness, the sacred places Lv 15^{31} Nu $19^{13.20}$(P); the camp Nu 5^{3}(P); the temple by dead bodies Ez 9^{7}; the Nazirite's head of separation by a death occurring in his presence Nu 6^{9}(P); the people defile themselves (נפשתיכם) by creeping things Lv 11^{44}(P). **4.** *pronounce or declare* ceremonially *unclean:* the leper Lv $13^{3.8.11.15.20.22.25.27.30.44.44.59}$(P); unclean animals 20^{25}(H). **Pu.** *Pt.* נַפְשִׁי לֹא מְטֻמָּאָה Ez 4^{14} *myself is not polluted.* **Hithp.** *Impf.* יִטַּמָּא Lv 21^{1}+4 t.; pl. יִטַּמְּאוּ Ez 14^{11} 37^{23}; יִטַּמָּאוּ Ho 9^{4} Ez 44^{25}, etc.+6 t. Impf.;—reflexive, *defile oneself:* by eating of an unaccepted peace-offering Ho 9^{4}; c. בְּ Lv $18^{24.30}$(H), 11^{43}(P), Ez 14^{11} $20^{7.18}$ 37^{23}; c. לְ *for* a dead person Lv $21^{1.3.11}$(H), Nu 6^{7}(P); *by* Lv 11^{24}(P); without prep. 21^{4}(H), Ez 44^{25}. **Hothp.** *Pf.* אַחֲרֵי אֲשֶׁר הֻטַּמָּאָה Dt 24^{4} *after that she has been defiled* (sexually); on form v. Ges$^{§\ 54.\ 3}$.

†II. טָמֵא **adj. unclean**;—ט׳ Lv 5^{2}+58 t.; 2931
cstr. טְמֵא 22^{4}+3 t.; f. טְמֵאָה 5^{2}+11 t.; cstr. טְמֵאַת Ez $22^{5.10}$; pl. טְמֵאִים Lv 11^{8}+10 t.;—*unclean,* **1.** ethically and religiously ט׳ שפתים Is $6^{5.5}$ *unclean of lips;* ט׳ השם Ez 22^{5} *defiled of name, infamous;* טהור מט׳ Jb 14^{4}. **2.** ritually: **a.** of persons, ‖ טהור Dt $12^{15.22}$ 15^{22} Ec 9^{2}; ט׳ נפש Lv 22^{4}(H); ט׳ לנפש (אדם) *unclean for a (dead) person* Nu 5^{2} $9^{6.7.10}$ (P)=ט׳ נפש Hg 2^{13}; elsewh. for various reasons Dt 26^{14}; Lv 5^{2} $13^{11.36.44.45.45.46}$ $15^{2.25.33}$ Nu $19^{13.17.19.20.22}$ (all P), 2 Ch 23^{19} Is 64^{5} Ez 4^{13} 22^{10} La 4^{15}. **b.** of animals Lv $5^{2.2.2.2}$ $7^{21.21}$ $11^{4.5.6.7.8.26.27.28.29.31}$ $27^{11.27}$ Nu 18^{15}(all P), Lv $20^{25.25}$(H), Dt $14^{7.8.10.19}$. **c.** of things in gen. Lv $11^{35.35.38}$ 15^{26} Nu 19^{15} (all P), Is 52^{11}; food Ju 13^{4} Ho 9^{3}; houses Je 19^{13}; leprosy Lv $13^{15.51.55}$ $14^{44.57}$(P); offering Hg 2^{14}. **d.** persons and things in general כל טמא Lv $7^{19.21}$(P); הבדיל בין הט׳ ובין הטהור Lv 10^{10}

11^{47}; הודיע בין (ה)ט׳ לטהור Ez 22^{26} 44^{23}; of aliens Is 52^{1} (‖ עָרֵל), perhaps also 35^{8}. **3.** specif. of places: מקום ט׳ *unclean place* (place of refuse away from holy place and human habitation) Lv 14$^{40.41.45}$ (P); טמאה ארץ land on the east of the Jordan separated from the land of the tabernacle of י׳ Jos 22^{19} (P); so אדמה ט׳ a foreign land Am 7^{17}.

2932 †טֻמְאָה **n.f. uncleanness**;—abs. ט׳ Nu 5^{19}
+ 4 t.; cstr. טֻמְאַת Lv 5^{3} + 4 t.; sf. טֻמְאָתֵךְ Ez 22^{15} + 2 t. etc., + 18 t. sfs.; pl. טֻמְאֹת Lv 16$^{16.19}$; sf. טֻמְאוֹתֵיכֶם Ez 36$^{25.29}$; טֻמְאֹתָם Lv 16^{16};—**1.** sexual Nu 5^{19} (P), La 1^{9}. **2.** of a foul or filthy mass Ez 24^{11} (in a caldron), 2 Ch 29^{16} (in the temple). **3.** ethical and religious Lv 16^{16} (P), Ez 22^{15} 24^{13} 39^{24}; כפר על הקדש מט׳ Lv 16^{16} (P); קדש מט׳ Lv 16^{19} (P); טהר מט׳ Ez 24^{13} 36^{25}; הושיע מכל ט׳ 36^{29}; רוּחַ הט׳ *unclean spirit,* which inspired the prophets to lie Zc 13^{2}. **4.** ritual, of men Lv 5$^{3.3}$ 7$^{20.21}$ 14^{19} 15$^{3.3.31.31}$ Nu 19^{13} (all P), Lv 22$^{3.5}$ (H); of women 2 S 11^{4}; וַיִּשְׁכַּב עִמָּהּ וְהִיא מִתְקַדֶּשֶׁת מִטֻּמְאָתָהּ v. Dr; a time favourable to conception RS$^{K\ 276}$; Lv 15$^{25.26.30}$ (P), 18^{19} (H), Ez 36^{17}; of meats Ju 13$^{7.14}$. **5.** local, of the nations Ezr 6^{21} 9^{11}.

2930, †טְמֵאָה **n.f.** uncleanness (טֻמְאָה, Baer,
2932 seems to rest upon a misinterpretation of the form) Mi 2^{10} (so Thes MV SS); of ethical uncleanness, from wrong-doing.

2933 †[טָמָה] **vb.** only **Niph.** *Pf.* נִטְמִינוּ *we*
are stopped up, stupid Jb 18^{3} so Thes MV Di De Zö (Aram. טַמְטֵם, טַמֵּם *stop up* (e.g. of ear or heart), ܛܰܡܶܡ, etc., and deriv.; Ar. طَمَّ *fill* or *choke up*); 𝔙 Ew Hgst AV RV Da SS take it as metaplastic for נִטְמֵאנוּ *we are regarded as unclean,* see Ew$^{§\ 198\ b}$ Kö$^{i,\ 614}$; 𝔊 rds. נִדְמִינוּ σεσιωπήκαμεν; 𝔗 טְמַעֲנָא.

2934 †טָמַן **vb. hide, conceal,** esp. in *earth* (NH
id.; whence perh. Aram. טְמַן *keep, preserve;* cf. Ar. طَمَرَ *bury, hide* (loan-word Frä^{137}); Aram. טְמַר, ܛܡܰܪ *id.*);—**Qal** *Pf.* טָמַן ψ 35^{8} + 2 t. etc.; *Impf.* וַיִּטְמֹן Gn 35^{4}, etc.; *Imv.* sf. טָמְנֵהוּ Je 13^{4}; טָמְנֵם Jb 40^{13}; *Inf. cstr.* לִטְמוֹן Jb 31^{33} ψ 64^{6}; *Pt. pass.* טָמוּן Jb 3^{16} + 3 t.; טְמוּנָה Jos 7^{22}; pl. טְמֻנִים Jos 7^{21}; cstr. טְמוּנֵי Dt 33^{19};—**1.** *hide,* c. acc. Gn 35^{4}(E), Ex 2^{12}(E; dead body in sand), Jos 2^{6} (JE; spies under flax-stalks), Jos 7$^{21.22}$ (JE; Achan's theft), Je 13$^{4.5.6.7}$ (Jer.'s girdle), 43$^{9.10}$ (stones at Tahpanhes); *hide, bury* hand in dish (צַלַּחַת) Pr 19^{24} 26^{15} (of עָצֵל the sluggard); נֵפֶל טָמוּן Jb 3^{16} *hidden abortion,* i.e. a lifeless child at once buried; שְׂפֻנֵי טְמוּנֵי חוֹל Dt 33^{19} (poem); of hiding iniquity עון Jb 31^{33}; hiding the wicked in the dust עפר Jb 40^{13}. **2.** often of *hiding, concealing, secretly laying* a snare רֶשֶׁת ψ 9^{16} 35^{8}, sq. לִי 31^{5}; שַׁחַת רִשְׁתָּם 35^{7}; פַּח sq. לִי 140^{6} 142^{4}; sq. לרגלי Je 18^{22}; חבל Jb 18^{10}; מוקשים ψ 64^{5}. **3.** טָמוּן *that which is darkened = darkness,* Jb 40^{13} nearly = שְׁאוֹל: פניהם חֲבֹשׁ בט׳ *bind their faces in darkness* (i.e. the wicked); *hide = reserve* Jb 20^{26} *all darkness is held in reserve for his treasures,* i.e. all calamities are stored up for them. **Niph.** *Imv.* הִטָּמֵן בֶּעָפָר מִפְּנֵי פַּחַד י׳ Is 2^{10} *hide thyself in the dust, from before the terror of* י׳. **Hiph.** (or **Qal**? Ba ZMG 1889, 180) *Impf.* וַיֵּלְכוּ וַיַּטְמִנוּ 2 K 7$^{8.8}$ *and they went and hid* (it), i.e. plunder fr. Aram. camp.

†מַטְמוֹן **n.m. hidden treasure, treasure**;— 4301
abs. מַטְמוֹן Gn 43^{23}; pl. מַטְמֹנִים Je 41^{8} Pr 2^{4}; מטמונים Jb 3^{21}; cstr. מַטְמֻנֵי Is 45^{3}; (*hidden*) *treasure* Gn 43^{23} (of money in sacks); מַטְמֻנֵי מִסְתָּרִים Is 45^{3} (i.e. treasures now hidden in secret places, shall become spoil of Cyrus; ‖ אוצרות חשך), Je 41^{8}, appos. חִטִּים שְׂעֹרִים שֶׁמֶן דבשׁ; in compar. Jb 3^{21} (longing for death more than for treasure), Pr 2^{4} (wisdom sought for like treasure).

טנא (√ of foll.; Ph. טנא is *set up, erect,* also *offer, present,* acc. to DHM in MV^{10}, 983).

†טֶנֶא **n.m.**$^{Dt\ 28,\ 5}$ **basket** (NH טְנִי is a large 2935
metal vessel)—abs. טַנְאֲ Dt 26^{4}, טֶנֶא v^{2}; sf. טַנְאֲךָ 28$^{5.17}$; in all a receptacle for products of soil (in last two ‖ מִשְׁאֶרֶת).

†[טָנַף] **vb. soil, defile** (NH Pi. *id.;* Aram. 2936
Pa. טַנֵּף, ܛܰܢܶܦ; As. *ṭanâpu* II, 1, Dl$^{Pr\ 33;\ HWB\ 302}$; Ar. طَنِفَ is *be suspicious, be intrinsically corrupt*)—**Pi.** *Impf.* אֲטַנְּפֵם Ct 5^{3} *how should I soil them,* i.e. my feet (poet. Aramaism).

†[טָעָה] **vb. wander, stray** (NH *id., err;* 2937
Aram. טְעָא, ܛܥܳܐ; Ar. طَغَى *exceed just limit, be immoderate, extravagant,* طَاغِيَةٌ *one who deviates from right way;* Eth. ጣዖት: *apostasy, superstition, idolatry*)—**Qal** *Pt.* f. (כְּ)טֹעִיָּה Ct 1^{7} *like a wandering* (vagrant) *woman,* for MT כְּעֹטְיָה acc. to 𝔖 Sym. 𝔗 𝔙 Bö Hi Gr al. **Hiph.** *Pf.* הִטְעוּ אֶת־עַמִּי Ez 13^{10} fig., *they have led astray my people.*

†טָעַם **vb. taste, perceive** (NH *id.;* Aram. 2938
טְעֵים, ܛܥܶܡ *taste;* As. n. *ṭêmu, sense, command,*

Zim[BP 92] Lyon[Sargontexte 67] Asrb[Annals iii, 95]; Ar. طَعِمَ *eat, taste, examine by tasting;* Eth. ጥዕመ: ጠዐመ: *taste, examine by tasting,* etc.)—**Qal** *Pf.* 3 ms. ט׳ 1 S 14^{24}; 3 fs. טָֽעֲמָה Pr 31^{18}; 1 s. טָעַמְתִּי 1 S $14^{29.43}$; *Impf.* 3 ms. יִטְעַם 1 S 19^{36} + 2 t.; 1 s. אֶטְעַם 2 S 3^{35}; 3 mpl. יִטְעֲמוּ Jon 3^{7}; *Imv.* mpl. טַעֲמוּ ψ 34^{9}; *Inf. abs.* טָעֹם 1 S 14^{43};—**1.** *taste,* of eating in small quantity, sq. acc. לֶחֶם 1 S 14^{24}, מְעַט דְּבַשׁ v^{29}, so v^{43} (טָעֹם טָעַמְתִּי); לֶחֶם אוֹ כָל־מְאוּמָה 2 S 3^{35}; מְאוּמָה Jon 3^{7}. **2.** of sense of taste, obj. אֶת־אֲשֶׁר אֹכַל וְאֶת־אֲשֶׁר אֶשְׁתֶּה 2 S 19^{36}; so חֵךְ אֹכֶל יִטְעַם־לוֹ Jb 12^{11}; חֵךְ יִטְעַם לֶאֱכֹל 34^{3}. **3.** fig. Pr 31^{18} *she tasteth that her gain is good* (obj. cl. c. כִּי), i.e. she experiences that her trade is profitable; so טַעֲמוּ וּרְאוּ כִּי־טוֹב יהוה ψ 34^{9} *taste ye and see that* י׳ *is good.*

2940 † טַ֫עַם **n.m.**[Je 48, 11] **taste, judgment**—ט׳ abs. Jb 6^{6} ψ 119^{66}; טָ֑עַם Pr 11^{22} 26^{16}; cstr. טַעַם Nu 11^{8} + 2 t.; sf. טַעְמוֹ Ex 16^{31} + 4 t.; טַעְמֵךְ 1 S 25^{33};—**1.** *taste* of manna Ex 16^{31} (P), Nu 11^{8} (JE), cf. v^{8}; in juice of purslain Jb 6^{6}; of Moab under fig. of wine Je 48^{11} (‖ רֵיחַ). **2.** fig. *judgment, discretion, discernment,* 1 S 25^{33} Pr 11^{22} Jb 12^{20}, so טוּב טַעַם וָדַעַת לַמְּדֵנִי ψ 119^{66}; מְשִׁיבֵי ט׳ Pr 26^{16} *those answering discretion,* i.e. discreetly; שׁנה טעם *change, disguise one's judgment, sense* 1 S 21^{13} ψ 34^{1}, of David feigning madness. **3.** (late Aramaism, cf. Dn 3^{10} etc.) *decision, decree* טַעַם מֶלֶךְ וּגְדֹלָיו Jon 3^{7}.

4303 † [מַטְעָם] **n.m.** only pl. **tasty** or **savoury food, dainties**—מַטְעַמִּים Gn $27^{4.7.9.14.17.31}$ (all J); sf. מַטְעַמֹּתָיו Pr 23^{3}; מַטְעַמּוֹתָיו v^{6}.

2943 † I. [טָעַן] **vb. load** (NH *id.*; Aram. ܛܥܰܢ, טְעַן, טְעֵין *carry,* also *load*)—**Qal** *Imv.* טַעֲנוּ אֶת־בְּעִירְכֶם Gn 45^{17} (E) *load your beasts.*

2944 † II. [טָעַן] **vb. pierce** (Aram. Pa. טָעֵין *pierce*; Ar. طَعَنَ *pierce, wound, goad*)—only **Pu.** *Pt.* מְטֹעֲנֵי חָ֑רֶב Is 14^{19} *those pierced with a sword.*

2945 טַף v. sub טפף. below

2946 † [טָפַח] **vb. extend, spread** (Ar. طَفَحَ *be full to overflowing, abound*; Aram. ܛܦܰܚ *extend, spread*; טְפוּחָא *a step, foot-length*; NH טֶפַח *a span* (cf. טֶפַח infr.))—**Pi.** *Pf.* טִפְּחָה Is 48^{13}; טִפַּחְתִּי La 2^{22};—**1.** *spread out* the heavens Is 48^{13} (‖ יָסְדָה ארץ). **2.** denom. fr. טֶפַח *carry on the palms, dandle* La 2^{22} (‖ רִבִּיתִי *I have brought up, reared*).

† טִפֻּחִים **n.[m.]** **pl. abstr. dandling,** עֹלְלֵי 2949
ט׳ La 2^{20}.

† טֶ֫פַח **n.[m.]** **1. a span, hand-breadth;** 2947
2. coping (?);—**1.** *a span, hand-breadth,* טֶפַח 1 K 7^{26} = 2 Ch 4^{5} of thickness of the molten sea; pl. טְפָחוֹת ψ 39^{6} (a few) *hand-breadths* are my days. **2.** architectural term, perh. *coping,* וּמִמַּסַּד עַד־הַטְּפָחוֹת 1 K 7^{9}.

† טֹ֫פַח **n.m.**[Ez 40, 43] **span, hand-breadth**— 2948
alw. abs. טֹפַח Ex 25^{25} 37^{12} (both P), width of border of table in tabernacle; Ez 40^{5} 43^{13} addit. to common cubit; Ez 40^{43} width of border (ledge) of four tables in new temple (Sm Co).

† מִטְפַּ֫חַת **n.f. cloak,** abs. הַמִּטְפַּחַת אֲשֶׁר־ 4304
עָלַיִךְ Ru 3^{15}; pl. הַמִּטְפָּחוֹת Is 3^{22}.

† [טָפַל] **vb. smear** or **plaster** (over), **stick,** 2950
glue (NH *id., besmear, plaster*; Aram. טְפַל *id.,* fig. *attack*; טְפִילָא *mortar*; ܛܦܰܠ *defile*; As. *ṭapâlu, besmear* (?), Dl[Pr 48; HWB])—**Qal** *Pf.* 3 pl. טָֽפְלוּ ψ 119^{69}; *Impf.* 2 ms. וַתִּטְפֹּל Jb 14^{17}; *Pt.* pl. cstr. טֹפְלֵי Jb 13^{4};—טָֽפְלוּ עָלַי שֶׁקֶר זֵדִים ψ 119^{69} *insolent men have plastered falsehood over me,* 'making his real character unrecognisable' (De); טֹפְלֵי שָׁ֑קֶר Jb 13^{4} ye are *falsehood-plasterers* (‖ רֹפְאֵי אֱלִל); cf. As. *amât taškirti ṭâpilti Ullusum, a speech of falsehood besmearing Ullusum,* Dl[Pr 48]; וַתִּטְפֹּל עַל־עֲוֺנִי Jb 14^{17} *and thou hast glued over mine iniquity,* i.e. glued it up, for safe keeping against the day of reckoning (‖ חָתֻם בִּצְרוֹר פִּשְׁעִי).

† טִפְסָר **n.[m.]** **scribe, marshal** (if meaning 2951
correct, then As. loan-word, fr. *dupsarru, tablet-writer, scribe,* v. Len[Langue Primit. de la Chaldée, 365] Schr[COT] on Je 51^{27}, Lotz[TP 180]; *dupšarru,* acc. to Dl[HWB 227])—pl. sf. טַפְסְרַיִךְ Na 3^{17} (as if fr. טַפְסֵר) *thy scribes, marshals,* of high officials of Nineveh; abs. sg. פִּקְדוּ עָלֶיהָ טִפְסָר Je 51^{27} *appoint a marshal against her,* i.e. against Babylon.—On military function of those skilled in writing cf. שֹׁטֵר.

† [טָפַף] **vb. trip, take quick little steps** 2952
(cf. Ar. طَفَّ *pass by quickly,* طَفَّافٌ *light, brisk, quick,* of horse; poss. cf. Syr. ܛܦܛܦ *flicker*)—**Qal** *Inf. abs.* טָפֹף Is 3^{16} הָלוֹךְ וְטָפֹף תֵּלַכְנָה, of women of Jerusalem.

טַף[42] **n.m.** coll. **children** (as going with 2945
quick, tripping steps; Eth. ጠፍ: Di[1251])—טַף Je 41^{16} + 11 t.; טָ֑ף Je 40^{7} + 5 t.; sf. טַפֵּנוּ Gn 43^{8}

+ 5 t.; טַפְּכֶם Gn 45^{19} + 10 t.; טַפָּם Gn 34^{29} + 6 t.; never cstr. and never pl. (in Gn 47^{24} om. 𝔊, cf. Di);—*children, little ones*, Gn 34^{29} (E) + 18 t. JE (Gn Ex Nu), also Dt 1^{39} + 8 t. D (incl. Jos 1^{14} 8^{35}); P only Nu $31^{9.17.18}$, where note זָכָר בַּטָּף v^{17} = *young boys*, and הַטַּף בַּנָּשִׁים v^{18} = *young girls;* also Ju 18^{21} 21^{10} 2 S 15^{22} Je 40^{7} 41^{16} 43^{6} Ez 9^{6} 2 Ch 20^{13} 31^{18} Ezr 8^{21} Est 3^{13} 8^{11}; the words מְתִים וְנָשִׁים וְהַטָּף Dt 2^{34} 3^{6} incl. all inhabitants; so אֲנָשִׁים וְהַנָּשִׁים וְהַטָּף Dt 31^{12} Je 40^{7} 43^{6}; טַף distinguished from בָּחוּר וּבְתוּלָה Ez 9^{6}; also from בְּנֵיהֶם 2 Ch 20^{13}, and from בְּנֵיהֶם וּבְנוֹתֵיהֶם 2 Ch 31^{18}.

2954 †**טָפַשׁ vb. be gross** (NH Hithp. *grow stupid*, and deriv.; Aram. טְפֵשׁ, for Heb. שׁמן Is 6^{11}, Ithp. *be stupid;* cf. As. *ṭapâšu, be abundant, large*, Guy$^{JAS\ 1883,\ Août\text{-}Sept.\ 189}$)—metaph. טָפַשׁ כַּחֵלֶב לִבָּם ψ 119^{70} *their heart is gross, like fat*.

2955 †**טָפַת n.pr.f.** daughter of Solomon, & wife of בֶּן־אֲבִינָדָב 1 K 4^{11}.

2956 †**[טָרַד] vb. pursue, chase, be continuous** (Ar. طَرَدَ *pursue;* II. *prolong* one's voice; VIII. *continue uninterruptedly;* As. *ṭarâdu, drive away* COT^{Gloss}, so Aram. ܛܪܕ, טְרַד)—only **Qal** *Pt. act.* וְדֶלֶף טֹרֵד Pr 19^{13} *a continuous dripping, dropping*, i.e. one in which one drop *pursues* another; so ד׳ טוֹרֵד 27^{15}; in both sim. of a contentious woman.

4308 †**מַטְרֵד n.pr.f.** mother-in-law of Hadar (Hadad) Gn 36^{39} 𝔊 Ματρ(α)ε(ι)θ (𝔊 here, not in Ch, makes מ׳ *son* of Mezahab, i.e. n.pr.m.) = 1 Ch 1^{50}, 𝔊 Ματραδ, Ματρηθ.

טרה (√of foll.; cf. Ar. طَرِىَ, طَرُوَ *be fresh, juicy, moist;* Eth. ጥሬይ: *raw*).

2961 †**[טָרִי] adj. fresh**, only fs. טְרִיָּה *fresh*, לְחִי־חֲמוֹר טְרִיָּה Ju 15^{15} *the fresh jawbone of an ass*, i.e. not yet dry and brittle; מַכָּה ט׳ Is 1^{6} *fresh, raw wound*, not yet healed or even treated (so Ges Ew Brd Di Du; *festering* De Che).

2959 †**[טָרַח] vb. toil, be burdened** (NH *id.*, *toil*, Hiph. *weary, importune;* Aram. טְרַח *toil*, etc.; Ar. طَرَحَ is *cast, throw, remove*)—**Hiph.** *Impf.* אַף־בְּרִי יַטְרִיחַ עָב Jb 37^{11} *he burdeneth* with moisture the cloud(s).

2960 †**טֹרַח n.m. burden**, fig., הָיוּ עָלַי לָטֹרַח נִלְאֵיתִי נְשֹׂא׃ Is 1^{14} *they are become a burden on me, I am weary of bearing;* אֵיכָה אֶשָּׂא טָרְחֲכֶם Dt 1^{12} (+ מַשַּׂאֲכֶם וְרִיבְכֶם) *how can I bear the burden of you?*

טֶרֶם$_{54}$, once (Ru 3^{14} Kt) **טרום, adv. of** 2958, 2962
time, not yet, ere, before that (deriv. unknown: not found in cogn. languages)—construed mostly with the impf. (with the pf. only Gn 24^{15} (v^{45} impf.), 1 S 3^{7a} (v^{b} impf.), and בְּטֶרֶם ψ 90^{2} Pr 8^{25}):—**1.** †טֶרֶם in an independent sentence, *not yet*, Gn 2^{5} and all the plants of the field טרם יהיה בארץ were *not yet* in the earth, etc., 19^{4} טרם ישכבו *not yet* had they lain down, when etc., $24^{15.45}$ Nu 11^{33} Jos 2^{8} 1 S $3^{3.7.7}$; of present time, Ex 9^{30} 10^{7} הֲטֶרֶם תֵּדַע dost thou *not yet* know, etc.?; in a subord. clause, *ere, before that*, Ex 12^{34} they took their dough טרם יחמץ *before* it was leavened, Jos 3^{1} ψ 119^{67}; of future time Is 65^{24}. More frequently **2.** בְּטֶרֶם$_{39}$, with the same force: of past time, Gn 27^{33} I ate of all בטרם תבא *before* thou camest, 37^{18} 41^{50} Ju 14^{18} 1 S 2^{15} Je 1^{5} 47^{1} Ez 16^{57}; ψ 90^{2} Pr 8^{25} (both with pf.); more oft. of pres. or fut., as Gn 27^{4} בטרם אמות *before* I die (so 45^{28}, cf. ψ 39^{14} Jb 10^{21}), Lv 14^{36} Dt 31^{21} 1 S 9^{13} 2 K 2^{9} Is 7^{16} 42^{9} 48^{5} Je 13^{16}; the impf. with a freq. force, Ex 1^{19} *before* the midwife *cometh*, they are wont to bear, Ru 3^{14} Pr 18^{13}. Pleon. בְּטֶרֶם לֹא Zp $2^{2.2}$. Construed with a subst. in the gen., †Is 17^{14} בְּטֶרֶם בֹּקֶר = *ere* morning, 28^{4} בְּטֶרֶם קַיִץ; with an inf. †Zp 2^{2a} (but rd. here with 𝔊 We בְּטֶרֶם לֹא תִהְיוּ כְּמוֹץ עֹבֵר, without יוֹם, 'before ye become as chaff passing away'). **3.** †מִטֶּרֶם Hg 2^{15} (sq. inf.) מִטֶּרֶם שׂוּם אֶבֶן *from before* the laying of one stone upon another, etc.

†**טָרַף vb. tear, rend, pluck** (NH *id.*, esp. 2963
of wild beasts; Aram. טְרַף *tear, seize*, esp. of creditors; טְרֵיפָא *torn flesh* or *animal;* Ar. طَرَفَ *depasture*, said of camel)—**Qal** *Pf.* טָרַף Jb 16^{9}; טָרָף Ho 6^{1}, etc.; *Impf.* יִטְרֹף ψ 7^{3}; וַיִּטְרֹף Am 1^{11} (but v. infr.); יִטְרָף Gn 49^{27}; אֶטְרֹף Ho 5^{14} ψ 50^{22}; *Inf.* לִטְרֹף ψ 17^{12}; *Pt. act.* טֹרֵף Jb 18^{4}, etc.;—*tear rend*, of wild beasts, Gn 37^{33} (J), 44^{28} (J; inf. abs. c. Pu. q. v.), Ex 22^{12} (JE; inf. abs. c. **Niph.** q.v.) Elsewh. only in sim. and metaph.; sim. of Gad's fierceness Dt 33^{20} (like a lioness, poem); so of Benjamin Gn 49^{27} (as a wolf, poem); of the remnant of Jacob, like a young lion among sheep, רָמַס וְטָרַף Mi 5^{7}; of the wicked, ψ 17^{12} (lion), 7^{3} obj. נַפְשִׁי (like a lion); 22^{14} psalmist's foes like lion (|| שֹׁאֵג); Ez 22^{25} (טֹרֵף טָרֶף), princes like wolves v^{27} (*id.*); metaph. of Israel's princes, like young lion $19^{3.6}$ (c. טֶרֶף

acc. cogn.); of Nineveh's king Na 2^{14} (as lion); of God's treatment of the wicked Ho 5^{14} (like a lion), ψ 50^{22}; subj. wrath of God (אַף) conceived as assailing Job, Jb 16^{9} *his wrath teareth* and persecuteth me; cf. טָרָף וְיִרְפָּאֵנוּ Ho 6^{1} subj. י׳ (|| יַךְ וְיַחְבְּשֵׁנוּ); on tenses v. Dr $^{§ 84 β; 171, 174 n. 1}$); subj. anger of Edom (abs.) Am 1^{11}, but rd. perh. וַיִּטֹּר for וַיִּטְרֹף *and he kept his anger perpetually*, so Ol on ψ 103^{9} We; טֹרֵף נַפְשׁוֹ בְּאַפּוֹ, said of Job by Bildad Jb 18^{4}. **Niph.** *Impf.* of animal *torn* (by wild beasts) טָרֹף יִטָּרֵף Ex 22^{12} (JE); יִטָּרֵף also in prediction of judgment on people of Jerusalem Je 5^{6}. **Pu.** *Pf.* טֹרַף טֹרַף יוֹסֵף Gn 37^{33} (J) *Joseph has certainly been torn in pieces*; cf. ט׳ טֹרָף 44^{28} (J). **Hiph.** *Imv.* ms. sf., note esp. 2nd acc. לֶחֶם, הַטְרִיפֵנִי לֶחֶם חֻקִּי Pr 30^{8} *let me devour my appointed bread* (of men, late; cf. טֶרֶף 31^{15}, and ψ 111^{5} Mal 3^{10}).

2965 † **טָרָף adj. fresh-plucked** (Aram. ܛܪܳܦܳܐ, טַרְפָּא *fresh leaf*)—עֲלֵה זַיִת טָרָף Gn 8^{11} (J) *a fresh-plucked olive leaf.*

2964 † **טֶ֫רֶף n.m.** $^{Na\ 3,1}$ **prey, food; leaf**;—טֶרֶף Gn 49^{9}+; טָ֑רֶף Jb 4^{11}+; sf. טַרְפֵּךְ Na 2^{14}; טַרְפּוֹ Is 31^{4}; pl. cstr. טַרְפֵּי Ez 17^{9};—**1.** *prey* of lion Am 3^{4} Jb 4^{11} 38^{39} ψ 104^{21}; metaph. of Judah's conquests Gn 49^{9}, Israel like lion Nu 23^{24} (both poems in JE); of Assyrians Is 5^{29}; of Nineveh and its king Na $2^{13.14}$ 3^{1}; Israel's princes (as young lion) Ez $19^{3.6}$; sim. of false prophet (like lion) 22^{25}; of princes of Judah v^{27}; sim. of י׳'s descending to battle, like lion Is 31^{4}; cf. ψ 76^{5} coming down from *mountains of prey* (the lion's lair), but rd. perh. עַד, cf. 𝔊 Bi Che $^{crit.\ n.}$; fig. of spoil of wicked Jb 29^{17}, cf. ψ 124^{6}. **2.** *food*, of outcasts, under fig. of wild ass פֶּרֶא Jb 24^{5}; of human food (late): for those who fear God ψ 111^{5}; for household Pr 31^{15}; in י׳'s house Mal 3^{10}. **3.** *leaf*, (cf. Gn 8^{11}) טַרְפֵּי צִמְחָהּ Ez 17^{9} metaph. of Judah.

† **טְרֵפָה n.f. animal torn** (by wild beasts); 2966
torn flesh;—abs. ט׳ Gn 31^{39} + 8 t. **1.** *animal torn* (by wild beasts), of sheep and goats Gn 31^{39} (E); ox, ass or sheep Ex 22^{12} (JE; del. We ^{KlPr} on Am 3^{12}, as gloss fr. Gn 31^{39}); indef. v^{31} (JE; forbidden as food); commonly c. נְבֵלָה (i.e. what dies naturally) as forbidden food, Lv 7^{24} (P), 17^{15} 22^{8} (both H), Ez 4^{14} 44^{31}; *torn flesh*, in metaph. of Nineveh's king as lion Na 2^{13} (|| טֶ֫רֶף).

י

י, *Yôdh*, tenth letter; used as numeral 10 in postBHeb.; יא or י״א = 11; יב, י״ב = 12, etc.; 14 and 15, however, are not י״ד, י״ה, which might stand for abbrev. of יהוה, but ט״ו, ט״ז, v. ט, and Ges $^{§ 5. 4. R. 3a}$.

2968 † **[יָאַב] vb. long, desire** (Aram. ܝܐܒ, and esp. Ethpa. and deriv.)—**Qal** *Pf.* 1 s. יָאַבְתִּי לְמִצְוֺתֶיךָ ψ 119^{131}, late Aramaism.

2969 † **[יָאָה] vb. befit, be befitting** (NH 𝔗 יָאֵי, יָאֶה adj. *worthy, fitting, fine*; יָאוּת adv. *right, well*; Ph. יא *fair*; Syr. ܝܳܐܶܐ adj. for נאוה ψ 33^{1}, πρέπει Mt 3^{15})—**Qal** *Pf.* לְךָ יָאָתָה Je 10^{7}, *for thee it* (i. e. fear) *is befitting*, late Aramaism.

2975 יאור v. יְאֹר. p. 384

2970 יַאֲזַנְיָה, יַאֲזַנְיָהוּ v. sub אזן p. 24ᵇ supr.

2971-72 יָאִיר, יָאִירִי v. sub אור p. 22ᵇ supr.

2973 †I. **[יָאַל] vb. be foolish** (cf. I. אול)—**Niph.** *Pf.* 3 mpl. נוֹאֲלוּ Is 19^{13} Je 5^{4}; וְנֹאָלוּ Je 50^{36}; 1 pl. נוֹאַלְנוּ Nu 12^{11};—*do* or *act foolishly*:—**1.** *shew wicked folly* = sin חַטָּאת אֲשֶׁר נוֹאַלְנוּ וַאֲשֶׁר חָטָאנוּ Nu 12^{11} (J); in Je 5^{4} an exhibition of this folly is ascribed to ignorance. **2.** *become fools*, lacking insight and judgment: נוֹאֲלוּ שָׂרֵי צֹעַן Is 19^{13} *the princes of Zoan have become fools* (|| נִשְּׁאוּ שָׂרֵי נֹף, and, in v^{11} אֱוִלִים שָׂרֵי צֹעַן, etc.); חֶרֶב אֶל־הַבַּדִּים וְנֹאָלוּ Je 50^{36} *a sword is against the praters, and they shall become fools*—be shewn up as such (|| חָתּוּ).

†II. **[יָאַל] vb.** only **Hiph. shew willing-** 2974
ness, be pleased, determine, undertake to do anything (and do it) (v. Ki Thes; Ar. وَأَلَ is *take refuge with, escape, hasten to* a place; cf. II. אול *be in front of*, Nö $^{MBAk\ 1880,\ 775}$; Sab. ואל in n.pr. מואלת DHM $^{Epigr.\ Denkm.\ 53}$; perh. As. *âlû, accept*, Lyon $^{Sargontexte\ 72}$)—**Hiph.** *Pf.* 3 ms. הוֹאִיל Ho 5^{11} + 2 t.; 2 ms. הוֹאַלְתָּ 1 Ch 17^{27}; 1 s. הוֹאַלְתִּי Gn $18^{27.31}$; 1 pl. הוֹאַלְנוּ Jos 7^{7}; *Impf.* וַיֹּאֶל Jb 6^{9}

(juss.); וַיּוֹאֶל Ex 2^{21} + 4 t.; וַיֹּאֶל 1 S 17^{39} (but v. infr.); *Imv.* הוֹאֶל 2 S 7^{29} 2 K 5^{23}; הוֹאֶל־נָא Ju 19^{6}; הֹוֹאֶל נָא 2 K 6^{3}; הוֹאִילוּ Jb 6^{28};—**1.** *shew willingness* to do anything, *accept an invitation, acquiesce*, sq. inf. וַיּוֹאֶל משֶׁה לָשֶׁבֶת אֶת־הָאִישׁ Ex 2^{21} (JE) *and Moses was willing to dwell with the man* (and did so), = Ju 17^{11} (of Levite); elsewh. foll. by vb. fin.; וְלוּ הוֹאַלְנוּ וַנֵּשֶׁב Jos 7^{7} *and would that we had been willing and had stayed;* esp. imv., sq. imv.: הוֹאֶל־נָא וְלִין Ju 19^{6} *be willing and spend the night* (kindly accept my invitation) v. Ges § 110. 2 a, R 2; 120. 2 a, 2 K 6^{3} and (no וְ) 5^{23}; הוֹאִילוּ פְּנוּ־בִי Jb 6^{28} i.e. be good enough to look upon me. **2.** more actively, voluntarily *undertake* to do anything (and do it), sq. inf.: Gn 18^{27} *I have undertaken to speak* = v ^{31} (both J); so 1 S 17^{39} MT, but rd. וַיִּלֶא, *and he laboured vainly*, for וַיֹּאֶל, so 𝔊, Gei Urschrift, 377 We Dr (cf. also v ^{b} לֹא אוּכַל לָלֶכֶת בָּאֵלֶּה); sq. vb. fin. הוֹאִיל משֶׁה בֵּאֵר Dt 1^{5} i.e. Moses *took upon himself* to expound the law. **3.** more actively still, *be pleased, determine* on one's own responsibility, *resolve*, sq. inf.: Jos 17^{12} (JE) = Ju 1^{27} but the Canaanites *were determined* (shewed a determination) to remain in this territory (= *persisted in dwelling there*); Ju 1^{35} *the Amorites persisted in dwelling* in Har-Ḥeres, etc.; sq. vb. fin., of irreligious action, הוֹאִיל הָלַךְ Ho 5^{11} Ephraim *persisted, he walked* after vanity (rd. שׁוא for צו, v. Che); elsewh. only of the divine *good pleasure:* sq. inf. 1 S 12^{22} י׳ *hath been pleased to make you a people for himself;* 1 Ch 17^{27}; sq. vb. fin. הוֹאֵל וּבָרֵךְ 2 S 7^{29} *be pleased and bless* the house of thy servant; וְיֹאֵל אֱלוֹהַּ וִידַכְּאֵנִי Jb 6^{9} *and that Eloah would be pleased and crush me!* (v. Ges § 120, 2 a Da Synt. § 83 b).

2975 †יְאֹר, יְאוֹר **n.m.** Ex 7, 21 **stream** of the Nile, **stream, canal** (Egypt. loan-word = Egypt. *'iotr, 'io'r, watercourse*, Copt. *eioor, ior;* also *'iotr'o, 'io'r'o*, Copt. *eiero, iaro, Nile*, Steindorff BAs i. 612; in As. *ia'uru, stream, 'Iaru'û, river Nile*, Id ib., Hpt ib. 171 Jäger ib 466)—abs. הַיְאֹר Gn 41^{1} + 37 t.; הַיְאוֹר Is 19^{8}; הַיְאֹרָה Ex 1^{22}; יְאוֹר Is $19^{7.7.7}$ + 2 t.; כָּאֹר (err. for כַּיְאֹר) Am 8^{8}; cstr. כִּיאֹר Am 9^{5}; כִּיאוֹר Am 8^{8}; sf. יְאֹרִי Ez 29^{3b} (Co יאר, cf. v ^{9} and 𝔖 𝔗); pl. יְאֹרִים Ex 8^{1} + 4 t.; cstr. יְאֹרֵי Is 7^{18} + 2 t.; יְאֹרֵי 2 K 19^{24}; sf. יְאֹרֶיךָ Ez $29^{4.4.5}$ + v ^{4} (del. 𝔊 Co) + 29^{10} (Co יְאֹרְךָ); יְאֹרָיו Ez 29^{3}; יְאֹרֵיהֶם Ex 7^{19} ψ 78^{44};—**1.** *stream* of the Nile, *river Nile*, usu. c. art. Gn $41^{1.2.3.3.18}$ Ex 1^{22} $2^{3.5.5}$ $4^{9.9}$ $7^{15.17.18.18.18.20.20.21.21.21.24.24.28}$ $8^{5.7}$ 17^{5} (all JE), Am 8^{8} 9^{5} Is $19^{7.7.7.8}$ 23^{3} (‖ שִׁחֹר), v ^{10} Je $46^{7.8}$ (sim. of Egypt. invasion), Ez 29^{3b} (rd. יאר, v. supr.), v ^{9} Zc 10^{11}; more fully יְאֹר מִצְרַיִם Am 8^{8} 9^{5}. **2.** pl.: **a.** *Nile-arms, Nile-canals,* יְאֹרֵי מִצְרַיִם Is 7^{18}; יְאֹרֵי מָצוֹר 19^{6} (‖ נְהָרוֹת), 37^{25} = 2 K 19^{24}; v. also Na 3^{8} Ex 7^{19} 8^{1} (both P; ‖ נְהָרֹת, אֲגַמִּים, etc.), ψ 78^{44} (‖ נֹזְלִים), Ez $29^{3.4.4.5.10}$ + v ^{4} MT (but del. 𝔊 Co), 30^{12}. **b.** *watercourses* in gen., יְאֹרִים רַחֲבֵי יָדַיִם Is 33^{21} (‖ נְהָרִים; cf. NH יְאוֹר, late Aram. יְאוֹרָא). **3.** *shafts*, made in mining Jb 28^{10} (בְּצוּרוֹת). **4.** יְאֹר, sg., of *Tigris*, Dn $12^{5.5.6.7}$ (cf. 10^{4}).

†[יָאַשׁ] **vb. despair** (not in **Qal**) (NH 2976
Hithp. *despair of,* יֵאוּשׁ *desperation;* Aram. Pa. יָאֵשׁ, etc., *make despair* (so 𝔗 Ec 2^{20}); Ar. يَئِسَ *despair*) — **Niph.** *Pf.* וְנוֹאַשׁ consec. 1 S 27^{1}; *Pt.* נוֹאָשׁ Je 2^{25} + 3 t.;—*despair,* וְנ׳ מִמֶּנִּי שָׁאוּל לְבַקְשֵׁנִי 1 S 27^{1} *and Saul shall despair of me, to seek me;* pt. *desperate, despairing,* of Job, Jb 6^{26}; elsewh. נוֹאָשׁ (foll. אמר) *desperate! = there is no hope!* Je 2^{25} 18^{12} Is 57^{10}. **Pi.** *Inf.* לְיַאֵשׁ אֶת־לִבִּי עַל כָּל־הֶעָמָל Ec 2^{20} *to make my heart despair, concerning all the toil.*

יֹאשִׁיָּה, יֹאשִׁיָּהוּ v. sub אשׁה p. 78^{b} supr. 2977

†יְאַתְרַי **n.pr.m.** an ancestor of Asaph 1 Ch 2979
6^{6} appar. = אֶתְנִי v ^{26}.

†[יָבַב] **vb.** only **Pi. cry shrilly** (NH 2980
Pi. *lament;* Aram. ܝܰܒܶܒ, יַבֵּב *sound* clarions, *exult;* Eth. የበበ: esp. I. 2)—**Pi.** *Impf.* 3 fs. וַתְּיַבֵּב Ju 5^{28} through the windows she looked and *shrilly cried.*

†יוֹבָב **n.pr.m.** (Sab. n.pr. יהיבב Glaser Skizze 3103
ii. 303 ff.)—**1.** 'son' of Yoḳtân Gn 10^{29} = 1 Ch 1^{23}, 𝔊 Ιωβαβ. **2.** a king in Edom Gn $36^{33.34}$ = 1 Ch $1^{44.45}$, 𝔊 Ιω(α)βαβ. **3.** king of Madon (Northern Canaan) Jos 11^{1}, 𝔊 Ιω(β)αβ. **4.** Benjamites: **a.** 1 Ch 8^{9}, 𝔊 Ιωβαβ. **b.** 1 Ch 8^{18}, 𝔊 Ιω(β)αβ.

יְבֻסִי, יְבוּסִי, יְבוּס v. sub בוס p. 101^{a} supr. 2982-83

יִבְחָר v. sub בחר p. 104^{b} supr. 2984

יָבִין v. sub בין p. 108^{a} supr. 2985

†[יָבַל] **vb. Hiph.** conduct, bear along, 2986
esp. in *procession* (Aram. יְבַל, אוֹבִיל *id.*, ܝܰܒܶܠ, Pa. *lead along*, also Ethpa.; Aph. *lead, conduct;* Zinj. יבל *id.*, DHM Sendsch. Gloss.; As. *abâlu* (ובל), *bring, conduct*, COT Gloss. Dl Pr 122 ff.; Ar. وَبَلَ is *run vehemently* (of horse), *pursue sharply, pour*

down rain, وَبْلٌ violent rain)—**Hiph.** *Impf.* 3 ms. sf. יוֹבִלֵנִי ψ 60^{11} 108^{11}; 1 s. sf. אוֹבִילֵם Je 31^{9}; 3 mpl. יוֹבִילוּ ψ 68^{30}; יֹבִילוּ 76^{12} (juss.); יוֹבִלוּן Zp 3^{10}; sf. יֹבִלוּהָ Is 23^{7};—**1.** *bear along* offerings, c. acc. rei, Zp 3^{10}; c. לְ pers. ψ 68^{30} 76^{12}. **2.** *carry away*, only יֹ׳ רַגְלֶיהָ מֵרָחוֹק לָגוּר Is 23^{7} *her feet used to carry her far away to sojourn* (of Tyre as colonizing and trading city). **3.** *lead, conduct*, c. obj. as sf., of returning exiles Je 31^{9}; triumphant army, sq. acc. loc., ψ 60^{11}= 108^{11}. **Hoph.** *Impf.* 3 ms. יוּבַל(־) Is 18^{7} Je 11^{19}; יוּבָל Ho 12^{2}+3 t.; 3 fs. תּוּבַל ψ 45^{15}; 1 s. אוּבָל Jb 10^{19}; 3 mpl. יוּבָלוּ Jb 21^{30}; 3 fpl. תּוּבַלְנָה ψ 45^{16}; 2 mpl. תּוּבָלוּן Is 55^{12};—**1.** *be borne along:* of things, sq. לְ, a gift Is 18^{7}; idol Ho 10^{6}; oil 12^{2}. **2.** *be borne* to the grave: מִבֶּטֶן לַקֶּבֶר אוּבָל Jb 10^{19}; לִקְבָרוֹת יוּבָל 21^{32}. **3.** *be led, conducted*, sq. לְ, ψ 45^{15} Je 11^{19} Is 53^{7}; abs. ψ 45^{16}; *be led* forth (from captivity in Babylon) Is 55^{12}, abs. (‖ יצא); the wicked (for judgment) abs. Jb 21^{30}.

2988 †I. [יָבָל] **n. [m.]** **watercourse, stream** (prop. *conduit*), as irrigating;—only pl. cstr. יִבְלֵי(־)מַיִם Is 30^{25} (‖ פְּלָגִים), 44^{4}.

2989 †II. יָבָל **n.pr.m.** son of Lamech by Adah, and founder of pastoral life acc. to Gn 4^{20} (J); 𝔊 Ιωβελ, 𝔊L Ιωβηλ.

3105 †I. יוּבַל **n.[m.]** **stream**, Je 17^{8} (‖ מַיִם).

3106 †II. יוּבָל **n.pr.m.** son of Lamech by Adah, and inventor of musical instr. Gn 4^{21} (J); 𝔊 Ιωβαλ.

2981 †יְבוּל **n.m.**$^{Jb 20, 28}$ **produce** of soil;—abs. י׳ Hb 3^{17}; cstr. *id.* Ju 6^{4} Jb 20^{28}; sf. יְבוּלָהּ Dt 11^{17} +7 t.; יְבֻלָהּ Dt 32^{22}; יְבוּלָם ψ 78^{46};—*produce:* יְ׳ הָאָרֶץ Ju 6^{4}; אֶרֶץ וִיבֻלָהּ Dt 32^{22}; וְהָאָרֶץ כָּלְאָה יְבוּלָהּ Hg 1^{10}; sf. ψ 78^{46} (‖ יְגִיעַ); esp. וְנָתְנָה הָאָרֶץ יְבוּלָהּ Lv 26^{4} *the land shall yield its produce*, so v^{20} Ez 34^{27} Zc 8^{2} (all ‖ פְּרִי), ψ 67^{7} 85^{13}; also, subj. הָאֲדָמָה Dt 11^{17}; of grapes only וְאֵין יְבוּל בַּגְּפָנִים Hb 3^{17} (‖ תְּאֵנָה לֹא־תִפְרָח and כִּחֵשׁ מַעֲשֵׂה־זַיִת); more generally יְבוּל בֵּיתוֹ Jb 20^{28} *the produce* (acquired possessions) *of his house.*

944 †בּוּל **n.[m.]** **produce, outgrowth** (abbrev. or scribal err. for foregoing)—only sg. cstr. בּ׳ הָרִים Jb 40^{20}; also בּ׳ עֵץ Is 44^{19} *the produce of a tree*, i.e. a block of wood.

†יוֹבֵל, יֹבֵל **n.m.**$^{Nu 36, 4}$ **ram, ram's horn,** 3104
cornet (Ph. יבל *ram;* cf. Di Lv 25^{10} Dl$^{Pr 124}$)—abs. יוֹבֵל Jos 6^{5}+7 t.; יֹבֵל Ex 19^{13}+13 t.; pl. יוֹבְלִים Jos 6^{4}+2 t.; יֹבְלִים Jos 6^{13};—**1.** *ram*, only in combin.: בִּמְשֹׁךְ בְּקֶרֶן הַיּ׳ Jos 6^{5} *the ram's horn*, as wind-instrument; so שׁוֹפְרוֹת (ה)י(ו)בלים Jos 6$^{4.6.8.13}$ *rams' horns* (v. Benz$^{Archäol. 276}$); יֹבֵל alone, בִּמְשֹׁךְ הַיֹּבֵל Ex 19^{13} *at the sounding of the ram*('s horn). **2.** designation of 50th year, marked by blowing of cornets, AV 'jubile' (so NH יוֹבֵל, 𝔗 יוֹבֵילָא, as loan-word); orig. no doubt שְׁנַת הַיּוֹבֵל *year of the ram*('s horn), as Lv 25$^{13.28.40.50.52.54}$ (all H), 27$^{17.18.23.24}$(all P), but then, without שׁנת, as יוֹבֵל הִוא תִּהְיֶה לָכֶם 25^{10} *a ram*('s horn blowing) *shall it be to you;* so v$^{11.12.15.28.30.31.33}$(all H), 27^{18} Nu 36^{4} (both P).

†[יַבָּל] **adj.** **running, suppurating**—only 2990
fs. as subst., יַבֶּלֶת *a running sore* or *ulcer* Lv 22^{22} (+ עַוֶּרֶת, שָׁבוּר, חָרוּץ, גָּרָב, יַלֶּפֶת).

†אוּבַל **n.[m.]** **stream, river** (=יוּבַל)— 180
only אוּבַל אוּלָי Dn 8^{2} *the river Ulai.*

†תֵּבֵל **n.f.**$^{Na 1, 5}$ (appar. **m.** Is 14^{17}) **world,** 8398
poet. synon. of אֶרֶץ (perh. orig. as *productive*, cf. יְבוּל, בּוּל, but this sense not clearly maintained; cf. also As. *tabalu* in *êlî tabali, by land*, ‖ *êlî nâru, by water* (*river*) Meissner$^{ZA 1889, iv. 3, 261, 263, 265 f.}$ SASm$^{As. Letters iv. pl. viii. ix, l. 33}$)—usu. abs. תּ׳ (no art.), cstr. Jb 37^{12} Pr 8^{31}; *world*, usu. ‖ אֶרֶץ: 1 S 2^{8} (י׳ set תּ׳ on מְצֻקֵי אֶרֶץ), Is 14^{21} 24^{4} 34^{1} Je 10^{12} =51^{15}, 1 Ch 16^{30} (=ψ 96^{10} infr.) Jb 34^{13} ψ 19^{5} 77^{19}=97^{4}, 90^{2} 96^{13} (+ עַמִּים), 98^{9} (+ *id.*); תּ׳ וְיֹשְׁבֵי בָהּ Na 1^{5} ψ 24^{1}; יֹשְׁבֵי תּ׳ 33^{8} Is 18^{3} (‖ שֹׁכְנֵי ארץ), 26$^{9.18}$ La 4^{12}; תּ׳ וּמְלֹאָהּ ψ 89^{12} (+ שָׁמַיִם, cf. ארץ ומלאה 24^{1}); עַל־פְּנֵי תֵ׳ אַרְצָה Jb 37^{12} *upon the face of the world of earth* (earthly world, the whole expanse of earth); בְּתֵ׳ אַרְצוֹ Pr 8^{31}; on the other hand עַפְרוֹת תּ׳ v^{26}; תּ׳ alone Jb 18^{18}; other combin. תּ׳ וּמְלֹאָהּ ψ 50^{12} (cf. 89^{12} supr.); פְּנֵי־תּ׳ Is 27^{6} (cf. Jb 37^{12} supr.); מֹסְדוֹת תּ׳ 2 S 22^{16} *foundations of the world* = ψ 18^{16}, cf. תִּכּוֹן תּ׳ ψ 93^{1} 96^{10} (=1 Ch 16^{30}); world as object of י׳'s judgment 9^{9} (‖ לְאֻמִּים; v. also 96^{13} supr.), cf. תּ׳ וישבי בה 98^{7} (‖ יָם), Is 13^{11} (‖ רשעים); as devastated by Babylonian conqueror Is 14^{17} (‖ עָרָיו).

†יִבְלְעָם **n.pr.loc.** a city of Manasseh in 2991
West-Jordan land Jos 17^{11} (JE; but יִבְ׳ here dub., v. Bu$^{RS 13 f.}$), Ju 1^{27} 2 K 9^{27}; so rd. also 2 K 15^{10} for MT קָבָל־עָם (𝔊L ἐν Ιεβλααμ; v. Klo);

=בִּלְעָם 1 Ch 6[55], q.v.; rd. יִבְלְעָם also in Jos 21[25] (∥ 1 Ch 6[55]), for MT גַּת רִמּוֹן, 𝔊 Ιεβαθα (𝔊L after MT Γεθρεμμων), v. Di; it lay about 13 m. E. of N.fr. Samaria, three-fifths of the way to Jezreel; mod. ruin *Belʿame* Bd [Pal 228], cf. Schultz [ZMG iii. 49]; (Old Egypt. *Y-b-ra-ʿa-mụ* WMM[195]).

2990 יַבֶּ֫לֶת v. יַבָּל. p. 385

יבם (appar. √ of foll.; meaning dubious).

2993 †[יָבָם] **n.m. husband's brother** (NH *id.*; 𝔗 יַבְמָא; v. Lag [M ii. 78]) — only sf. יְבָמִי Dt 25[7], יְבָמָהּ 25[5], in law of levirate marriage (cf. Gn 38[8]; v. also Dr [Dt 25. 5-10]).

2994 †[יְבֵ֫מֶת] **n.f. sister-in-law** (NH יְבָמָה, 𝔗 יְבִימְתָּא, יַבִמְתָּא; Syr. ܝܒܡܬܐ)—only sf. יְבִמְתּוֹ Dt 25[7.7.9] *his brother's wife (widow)*, (cf. Gn 38[8]) in levirate law; יְבִמְתֵּךְ Ru 1[15.15] *thy husband's brother's wife.*

2992 †[יָבַם] **vb.denom.**, only **Pi.** *do the duty of* יָבָם *to* a brother's widow; *Pf.* וְיִבְּמָהּ consec. Dt 25[5] *and shall do a brother-in-law's office to her; Imv.* יַבֵּם אֹתָהּ Gn 38[8] (i.e. אֵשֶׁת אָחִיךָ v[a]); *Inf. sf.* לֹא אָבָה יַבְּמִי Dt 25[7] (on nominal sf. as obj. of inf., v. Ges [§ 115 R. 2 ad fin.]).

2995-98 יִבְנְיָה, יַבְנִיָּה, יַבְנֶה, יַבְנְאֵל v. sub בנה. p. 125

2999 יַבֹּק v. sub בקק p. 132[b] supr.

3000 יְבֶרֶכְיָ֫הוּ v. sub ברך p. 140[a] supr.

3005 יִבְשָׂם v. sub בשׂם p. 142[a] supr.

3001 †I. יָבֵשׁ **vb. be dry, dried up, withered** (NH *id.* (rare), 𝔗 יְבֵישׁ, chiefly Pa. Ithp., Syr. ܝܒܫ; Sab. Palm. deriv.; Ar. يَبِسَ; Eth. የብሰ:) —**Qal** *Pf.* 3 ms. יָבֵשׁ Jos 9[5] + 8 t.; וְיָבֵשׁ consec. Is 19[5] + 4 t.; 3 fs. יָֽבְשָׁה Gn 8[14]; 3 pl. יָֽבְשׁוּ Je 23[10] + 2 t.; יָבֵ֑שׁוּ 50[38] + 2 t.; *Impf.* 3 ms. יִבַשׁ Is 19[7]; יִיבָ֑שׁ Je 12[4] Jb 8[12]; וַיִּיבַשׁ 1 K 17[7]; וַיִּיבָ֑שׁ Jon 4[7]; 3 fs. תִּיבַשׁ Ez 17[10]; תִּיבָ֑שׁ v[10] + 3 t., etc.; *Inf. cstr.* (בִּ)יבֹשׁ Is 27[11]; יְבֹשֶׁת Gn 8[7]; *abs.* יָבוֹשׁ Zc 11[17]; יָבֹשׁ Ec 17[10];—**1.** *be dry, dried up without moisture:* **a.** of bread Jos 9[5.12] (JE). **b.** of ground lacking rain Am 4[7], cf. Am 1[2] (of Carmel at utterance of י׳'s voice), Je 23[10]. **c.** of earth after the flood Gn 8[14] (P), cf. חָרֵב. **d.** of grass, herbage, trees and crops (already implied in **b**)=*wither* Is 15[6] 19[7] 27[11] Je 12[4] Jb 8[12] Jo 1[12] Jon 4[7]; in sim. of shortness of life ψ 90[6] 102[12] 129[6], v. also Is 40[7.8] (in these two ∥ נָבֵל); of heart under fig. of grass ψ 102[5]; of Judah under fig. of vine Ez 17[9.9.10.10.10], cf. 19[12]; of princes under fig. of tree Is 40[24]; of roots of Ephr. under fig. of tree Ho 9[16], so of roots of wicked Jb 18[16]. **e.** of hand, arm, *dry up, wither,* as judgment from י׳, 1 K 13[4] Zc 11[17.17]; in distress יָבֵשׁ כַּחֶרֶשׂ כֹּחִי ψ 22[16] *my strength is dried up like the potsherd;* of skin La 4[8], and (fig.) of bones Ez 37[11]. **2.** *be dried up:* of water Gn 8[7] (J), Is 19[5] 1 K 17[7] Je 50[38] Jo 1[20] Jb 12[15] 14[11]. **Pi.** *make dry, dry up,* only *Impf.* 3 ms. sf. וַיַּבְּשֵׁהוּ Na 1[4] *and hath made it dry* (י׳, the sea); 3 fs. תְּיַבֵּשׁ Jb 15[30] the flame *shall dry up* his branches (fig. of wicked); fig. תְּיַבֶּשׁ־גָּ֑רֶם Pr 17[22] a broken spirit *maketh dry (the) bones.* **Hiph.** *Pf.* 3 ms. הוֹבִישׁ Jos 2[10] + 3 t. + Jo 1[10] (v. infr.); הֹבִישׁ Ez 19[12] + 2 t. Jo (v. infr.); 3 fs. הוֹבִישָׁה Jo 1[12] (v. infr.); 2 ms. הוֹבַשְׁתָּ ψ 74[15]; 1 s. הוֹבַשְׁתִּי Ez 17[24]; וְהוֹבַשְׁתִּי Je 51[36]; 3 pl. וְהֹבִישׁוּ consec. Zc 10[11]; *Impf.* 1 s. אוֹבִישׁ Is 42[15.15] 44[27];—*dry up, make dry:* **1.** *dry up water,* י׳ subj., Jos 2[10] 4[23.23] 5[1] (all D), Je 51[36] (∥ הֶחֱרִיב), Is 42[15] 44[27] (∥ חָרְבִי in ∥ cl.), ψ 74[15]. **2.** *make dry, wither:* herbage, trees, crops, etc., of י׳, Is 42[15] (∥ החריב); obj. Babylon under fig. of tree Ez 17[24]; of east wind's drying up Judah's fruit Ez 19[12]. **3.** *exhibit dryness:* of river-deeps laid bare Zc 10[11].—In like manner might be taken Jo 1[10.12.12.17], if fr. יבשׁ; but the sense would be difficult, esp. in v[10.12], and הֹבִישׁ v[11] must be fr. בּוֹשׁ, to which all these cases in Jo may be consistently assigned; v. בּוֹשׁ.

†II. יָבֵשׁ **adj. verb.** or **pt. dry, dried,** so, ms. 3002
abs. Na 1[10] + 4 t.; fs. יְבֵשָׁה Nu 11[6]; mpl. (וִ)יבֵשִׁים Nu 6[3]; fpl. יְבֵשׁוֹת Ez 37[2.4];—**1.** *dried,* lit. only עֲנָבִים יְבֵשִׁים Nu 6[3] *dried grapes* (P; opp. ע׳ לַחִים); fig. נַפְשֵׁנוּ יְבֵשָׁה 11[6] (JE) *our soul* (i.e. our appetite) *is dried up,* viz. for want of fresh, juicy meat. **2.** *dry,* of chaff, קַשׁ Na 1[10] in sim. of Ninevites under impending judgment; cf. in fig. of Job, Jb 13[25]; of tree Ez 17[24] (fig. of Davidic house; opp. עֵץ לַח), 21[3] (in prediction of Judah's devastation by Babylon, opp. *id.*); Is 56[3] fig. of eunuch; of the bones in Ezek.'s vision Ez 37[2.4].

†III. יָבֵשׁ, יָבִישׁ **n.pr.loc.** et **pers. 1. n.** 3003
pr.loc. יָבֵשׁ גִּלְעָד *Jabesh of Gilead,* 𝔊 Ιαβ(ε)ις Γαλααδ, exact site unknown, Ju 21[8.9.10.12.14] 2 S 21[12]; 1 Ch 10[11] (𝔊L Ιαβις τῆς Γαλααδ); יָבֵישׁ גִּלְעָד 1 S 11[1.9] 31[11] 2 S 2[4.5] (in these three 𝔊L Ιαβις τῆς Γαλααττιδιτος); יָבֵישׁ 1 S 11[1.3.5.9.10]; יָבֵשׁ 1 Ch 10[12]; יָבֵ֫שָׁה v[12]; ∥ יָבֵ֫שָׁה 1 S 31[12.13]. **2. n.pr.m.** יָבֵשׁ father of Shallum 2 K 15[10.13.14].

3004 †יַבָּשָׁה **n.f.** dry land, dry ground (Sab. יבסם, opp. בחרם *sea*, DHM in MV; Palm. יבשא (*dry*) *land* Vog[No.79])—alw. abs. sg. יַבָּשָׁה: Ex 4^9 (J); of dry ground as path of Isr. through Red Sea Ex $14^{16.22.29}$ 15^{19} (all P), Ne 9^{11} ψ 66^6; through Jordan Jos 4^{22} (D); of dry land, opp. sea, at creation Gn $1^{9.10}$ (P); cf. Jon 1^9; specif. of shore of sea Jon 1^{13} 2^{11}; fig. of needy Israel, to be refreshed by י׳'s spirit Is 44^3 (|| צָמֵא).

3006 †יַבֶּשֶׁת **n.f.** id., made by God's hands ψ 95^5; water shall become blood בַּיַּבָּשֶׁת Ex 4^9 (J).

3008 יִגְאָל v. sub I. גאל p. 145[b] supr.

3009 †[יָגַב] **vb.** till, be husbandman, only **Qal** *Pt.* pl. לְכֹרְמִים וּלְיֹגְבִים Je 52^{16} 2 K 25^{12} Qr (Kt גבים); v. גוב p. 155[b] supr.

3010 †[יָגֵב] **n.m.** field, כְּרָמִים וִיגֵבִים Je 39^{10}, but text dub., v. 52^{16} = 2 K 25^{12}; also גּוֹב, II. גֵּב p. 155[b] supr.

3011 יָגְבְּהָה v. sub גבה p. 147[a] supr.

3012 יִגְדַּלְיָהוּ v. sub גדל p. 153[b] supr.

3013 †I. [יָגָה] **vb.** suffer, not in **Qal** (cf. Ar. وَجَى *castravit*, وَجِيَ *be abraded* (of the foot); of horse, *have pain in the hoof*)—**Niph.** *Pt.* fpl. נוּגוֹת (on form v. Kö[i.582]) La 1^4 (|| מַר, נֶאֱנָחִים) *grieved*, mpl. cstr. נוּגֵי (v. Kö[l.c.]) Zp 3^{18} (sq. prep., cf. Ges[§130.1]); of virgins of Zion La 1^4; of exiles Zp 3^{18}. **Pi.** *Impf.* וַיַּגֶּה (for וַיְיַגֶּה, v. Kö[i.582.412]) *grieve*, sq. acc. La 3^{33} (|| עִנָּה). **Hiph.** *Pf.* 3 ms. הוֹגָה La 1^{12} 3^{32}; sf. הוֹגָהּ La 1^5; *Impf.* 2 mpl. תּוֹגְיוּן Jb 19^2; *Pt.* pl. sf. מוֹגַיִךְ Is 51^{23};—*cause grief* or *sorrow*, abs. La 3^{32} (opp. רִחַם); sq. acc. (Zion) La 1^5, cf. Is 51^{23}, also La 1^{12} (obj. om., but אשׁר of grief = *wherewith*); sq. נַפְשִׁי Jb 19^2.—On 2 S 20^{13} v. II. יגה.

3015 †יָגוֹן **n.[m.]** grief, sorrow;—abs. יָגוֹן Gn 42^{38} + 12 t.; sf. (מִ)יְּגוֹנָם Je 31^{13};—*sorrow*, Gn 42^{38} 44^{31} (J), ψ 13^3 Je 8^{18}; || אֲנָחָה ψ 31^{11} Is 35^{10} 51^{11}; cf. ψ 107^{39} (|| רָעָה, עֹצֶר), 116^3 (|| צָרָה), Je 20^{18} (|| עָמָל), 31^{13} (|| אֵבֶל, opp. שִׂמַּחְתִּים), 45^3 (|| מַכְאֹבִי), Ez 23^{33} (|| שִׁכָּרוֹן, but Co.; שברון with Codd.; cf. 21^{11}); Est 9^{22} (opp. שִׂמְחָה).

8424 †תּוּגָה **n.f.** grief (poet.)—abs. ת׳ ψ 119^{28} Pr 14^{13} 17^{21}; cstr. תּוּגַת 10^1;—*grief* ψ 119^{28}; Pr 10^1 (opp. יְשַׂמַּח), 14^{13} (opp. שִׂמְחָה), 17^{21} (|| לֹא יִשְׂמַח).

†II. [יָגָה] **vb.** only **Hiph.** *Pf.* 3 ms. הֹגָה 3014
(Kö[i.584]) thrust away (Syr. ܐܘܓܝ *remove, repel*; Ar. وَجَا IV. *repel*)—כַּאֲשֶׁר הֹגָה מִן־הַמְּסִלָּה 2 S 20^{13} *when he had thrust* (him, the murdered Amasa) *out of the highway* (|| וַיַּסֵּב אֶת־עֲמָשָׂא מִן־הַמְּסִלָּה הַשָּׂדֶה v[12]).

יָגוּר v. sub I. גור p. 158[b] supr. 3017

יָגְלִי v. sub גלה p. 163[b] supr. 3020

יגן (√of foll.; cf. Ar. وَجَنَ *beat* cloth (said of a fuller); in Heb. only in deriv. *wine-press*).

†I. גַּת **n.f.** wine-press (contracted from 1660
*גַּנְתְּ = *יְגַנְתְּ)—abs. גַּת Ju 6^{11} + 3 t.; גִּתּוֹת Ne 13^{15};—*wine-press*, lit. חֹבֵט חִטִּים בַּגַּת Ju 6^{11} *beating out wheat in the wine-press*, to hide it from Midian; the juice of the grapes was pressed out by treading, דֹּרֵךְ בְּגַת Is 63^2 (in sim.), but also as acc. דֹּרְכִים גִּתּוֹת Ne 13^{15}; in fig. of judgment, גַּת דָּרַךְ אֲדֹנָי לִבְתוּלַת וגו׳ La 1^{15} *a wine-press hath Adonay trodden for the virgin daughter of Judah*; also רְדוּ כִּי מָלְאָה גַּת Jo 4^{13} (רדה only here with גַּת).—On the form and use of wine-press, and Heb. synonyms, v. Smith[DB] (art. *wine-press*) Benz[Arch. 212 f.] Rob[BR iii, 137] Schick[ZPV x, 1887, 146, 150, and Pl. v. vii.] Anderlind[ZPV xi, 1888, 166 f.]

†II. גַּת **n.pr.loc.** (*wine-press*)—Philistine 1661
city 𝔊 Γεθ, 𝔙 *Geth*, Jos[Ant. vi. 12, 2] etc., Γιττα (ed. Niese), exact site unknown (v. GASm[Geog. 194 ff.]), named with Gaza and Ashdod Jos 11^{22} as home of remaining ʿAnaḳim; named with Ashdod, Gaza, Ashḳelon and ʿEḳron 1 S 6^{17}; with Ashḳelon 1 S 1^{20}; with Ashḳelon, Yabne and Ashdod 2 Ch 26^6; מֵעֶקְרוֹן וְעַד־גַּת 1 S 7^{14}, cf. 17^{52b} and also v[52a] (rd. גַּת for גַּיְא 𝔊 We Dr); called גַּת פְּלִשְׁתִּים Am 6^2; built up by Rehoboam, acc. to 2 Ch 11^8; taken by Hazael 2 K 12^{18}; also 1 S 5^8 $17^{4.23}$ (of Goliath), cf. 2 S $21^{20.22}$ = 1 Ch $20^{6.8}$; 1 S $21^{11.13}$ $27^{2.3.4.11}$ 2 S 15^{18} 1 K $2^{39.39.40.41}$ ψ 56^1 Mi $1^{10.14}$ 1 Ch 7^{21} 8^{13}, also 18^1 (but || מֶתֶג הָאַמָּה 2 S 8^1; on change of this into reading in Ch v. We); c. ה loc., גִּתָּה 1 K 2^{40}.

†גַּת הַחֵפֶר 2 K 14^{25} (*wine-press of digging*) 1662
home of Jonah, proph.; גִּתָּה חֵפֶר Jos 19^{13}, perh. mod. *El-Meshhed*, c. 3 m. E. of N. fr. Nazareth, Rob[BR ii. 350] Bd[Pal 252].

†גַּת־רִמּוֹן **n.pr.loc.** in Dan Jos 19^{45}; Levi- 1667
tical city 21^{24} = 1 Ch 6^{54}; site unknown.—גַּת רִמּוֹן in Manasseh Jos 21^{25} is scribal error; rd. יִבְלְעָם, q. v.

1663 †גִּתִּי **adj.gent.** of II. גַּת **1**; of Obed-edom 2 S 6$^{10.11}$ = 1 Ch 13^{13}; Ittai 2 S 15$^{19.22}$ 18^{2}; Goliath 21^{19} 1 Ch 20^{5}; pl. c. art. as subst., הַגִּתִּים 1 S 15^{18} *the Gittites* (but read אִתַּי הַגִּתִּי We Klo Kit Bu Now$^{\text{Arch.i.308 n.}}$); sg. c. art. as n.pr.coll. הַגִּתִּי Jos 13^{3} (with men of Gaza, Ashdod, Ashkelon, Ekron, and the Awwim).

1665 †גִּתִּית **f.** of foregoing (si vera l.) only in phr. עַל־הַגִּתִּית in three ψ-titles: ψ 8^{1} 81^{1} 84^{1}; *upon the Gittite (lyre)* so 𝔗, *to the Gittite (melody)* Ew Ol De, or either of these Hup Pe; 𝔊 𝔙 הַגִּתּוֹת *wine-presses*, whence Bae al. *at the wine-presses*, i.e. (Bae) a song for the feast of booths.

1664 †גִּתַּיִם **n.pr.loc.** in Judah;—ג׳ Ne 11^{33}; גִּתַּיְמָה 2 S 4^{3}; site unknown.

3021 †[יָגַע, יָגֵעַ] **vb. toil, grow** or **be weary** (NH *id.*; As. *êgû*, *grow weary* Dl$^{\text{Pr 140}}$; Ar. وَجِعَ *have pain, suffer*)—**Qal** *Pf.* יָגְעָה 2 S 23^{10}; יָגַעְתָּ Jos 24^{13} Is 43^{22}; יָגַעַתְּ 47^{12} + 2 t.; יָגָעַתְּ Is 47^{15}; יָגַעְתִּי ψ 6^{7} + 3 t.; יָגַעְנוּ La 5^{5}; *Impf.* יִיגַע Is 40^{28}; 2 ms. תִּיגַע Pr 23^{4}; אִיגָע Jb 9^{29}; יִיגְעוּ Hb 2^{13}; יִגְעוּ Je 51^{58} Is 65^{23}; יִיגָעוּ Is 40^{31}; יִגְעוּ v^{30};—**1.** *toil, labour* for (בְּ), Jos 24^{13} (D), Is 62^{8}; sq. acc. (אשׁר) 47^{15}; sq. בְּ instr. v^{12}; abs. 49^{4} (לְרִיק, וְהֶבֶל כֹּחִי כִלֵּיתִי ||), cf. 65^{23} Je 51^{58} (|| יעף), Hb 2^{13} (|| *id.*), La 5^{5} (|| לֹא־הוּנַח־לָנוּ), Jb 9^{29}, sq. inf. Pr 23^{4}. **2.** *grow* or *be weary*, from toil, exertion, endurance, 2 S 23^{10} (om. by accident in || 1 Ch 11^{13} v. Dr); *weary of*, sq. בְּ, ψ 6^{7} 69^{4} Is 43^{22} 57^{10} Je 45^{3}; abs. Is 40$^{28.30.31}$ (in all || יעף). **Pi.** *Impf.* 3 fs. sf. 3 ms. תְּיַגְּעֶנּוּ Ec 10^{15} *weary, make weary*, subj. עֲמַל הכסילים; 2 ms. תְּיַגַּע *cause to go toilsomely* Jos 7^{3}, sq. acc. **Hiph.** *Pf.* 2 ms. sf. הוֹגַעְתַּנִי Is 43^{24}; הוֹגַעְתִּיךָ v^{23}; pl. הוֹגַעְתֶּם Mal 2^{17}; הוֹגַעֲנוּ v^{17};—*make to toil* (alw. c. בְּ instr.), c. acc. pers. *make to toil, weary* Is 43^{23} (|| העביד), obj. י׳ v^{24} (*weary*, fig.), and so Mal 2$^{17.17}$.

3022 †יְגָע **n.[m.] gain** (=product of *labour*)—יְגָע Jb 20^{18} (|| תְּמוּרָה).

3023 †יָגֵעַ **adj. weary, wearisome**;—יָגֵעַ Dt 25^{18} *weary* (|| עָיֵף); 2 S 17^{2} (|| רְפֵה יָדַיִם); כָּל־הַדְּבָרִים יְגֵעִים Ec 1^{8} *all things are wearisome* ('full of labour').

3024 †[יְגִעָה] **n.f. wearying** (late format., Dr Intr.^{455} Siegf$^{\text{NH Gram. § 47 b}}$) וְלַהַג הַרְבֵּה יְגִעַת בָּשָׂר Ec 12^{12} *and studying much is a wearying of flesh.*

†[יָגִיעַ] **adj. weary**;—pl. cstr. וְשָׁם יָנוּחוּ 3019
יְגִיעֵי כֹחַ Jb 3^{17} *and there are resting the weary in strength*, the toil-worn.

†[יְגִיעַ] **n.m. toil, product**;—cstr. יְגִיעַ Gn 3018
31^{42} + 5 t.; sf. יְגִיעֲךָ Dt 28^{33}; יְגִיעֶךָ Jb 39^{11}; יְגִיעֵךְ Ez 23^{29}; יְגִיעוֹ ψ 109^{11} Ne 5^{13}; יְגִיעָהּ Jb 39^{16} Je 20^{5}; וִיגִיעֲכֶם Is 55^{2}; וִיגִיעָם ψ 78^{46}; pl. sf. יְגִיעַי Ho 12^{9} (but יְגִיעָיו 𝔊 Che);—**1.** *toil*, יְג׳ כַּפַּיִם Gn 31^{42} (E; || עָנְיִי), Jb 39^{11} (=husbandry), laying of eggs 39^{16}. **2.** result of toil, *product, produce, acquired property*: יְגִיעַי Ho 12^{9} (|| אוֹן, on text v. supr.), Dt 28^{33} (|| פְּרִי אדמתך), ψ 78^{46} (|| יְבוּל); יְגִיעַ כַּפֶּיךָ 128^{2}, Hg 1^{11} (|| דָּגָן, תִּירוֹשׁ, יִצְהָר, בְּהֵמָה, אָדָם, אֲשֶׁר תּוֹצִיא הָאֲדָמָה); Ne 5^{13} (|| בית), ψ 109^{11} (|| כל־אשׁר־לוֹ), Is 45^{14} (יגיע מצרים || סחר־כושׁ), 55^{2} (|| כֶּסֶף), Je 3^{24} (|| צֹאן, בָּקָר, בָּנִים, בָּנוֹת), 20^{5} (|| חֹסֶן, יְקָר, of city), Ez 23^{29}; of Job as product of God's hands (יְג׳ כַּפֶּיךָ) Jb 10^{3}.

†[יָגֹר] **vb. be afraid, fear** (Ph. in n.pr. 3025
יגר אשמן = *he feareth Eshmun*; Ar. وَجِرَ *metuens cavit*, Frey; Lag$^{\text{BN 26. 30}}$; cf. III. גּוּר)—**Qal** *Pf.* 2 ms. יָגֹרְתָּ Dt 28^{60}; יָגֹרְתִּי 9^{19} + 3 t.;—*be afraid*, sq. מִפְּנֵי *before, of*; of wrath of י׳ Dt 9^{19}; of diseases of Egypt 28^{60}; *fear*, sq. acc. Jb 3^{25} 9^{28} ψ 119^{39}.

†יָגוֹר **adj. vb. fearing**, men אֲשֶׁר אַתָּה יָגוֹר 3016
מִפְּנֵיהֶם Je 22^{25} 39^{17}.

יָד 1604 **n.f.** $^{\text{Gn 25, 26 + oft.}}$ (**m.** †Ex 17^{12}† v. Di; on 3027
יִרְפּוּ יָדַיִם 2 S 4^{1} Zp 3^{16} 2 Ch 15^{7} Ne 6^{9}, v. Ges $^{\text{§ 145. 7 a, R. 1}}$) **hand** (NH *id.*; Aram. יְדָא, ܐܝܕܐ; Zinj. יד DHM$^{\text{Sendsch. Gloss}}$; Ar. يَدٌ; Sab. יד DHM $^{\text{ZMG 1883, 343}}$ Mordt $^{\text{Ib. 1879, 492}}$; Eth. እድ፡ (v. Lag$^{\text{BN 22}}$); Sam. ࠉࠃ; As. *îdu*, *strength* COT^{Gloss};—der. by most fr. √ ל״י, on ground of pl. and sf. forms in cogn. lang., v. esp. Philippi $^{\text{ZMG 1878, 74}}$ Ba $^{\text{ZMG 1887, 637}}$, but no trace of final י or ו in Heb., and meaning of such √ ל״י not clear; Thes al. fr. ידה *extend, throw*, but this in Ar. Eth. פ״ו, not פ״י, cf. Heb. Hiph.; Philippi comp. Ar. يَدَى IV. *strengthen*;—Sta $^{\text{§ 182, 183}}$ regards יד as bilit.)—abs. יָד Gn 38^{28}+; cstr. יַד 41^{35}+; sf. יָדִי 14^{22}+; יָדְךָ 22^{12}+; יָדְכָה Ex 13^{16}; יֶדְכֶם Gn 9^{2}+; יֶדְכֶן Ez 13$^{21.21.23}$, etc.; du. יָדַיִם Gn 34^{21}+; cstr. יְדֵי 24^{30}+; וִידֵי Ex 15^{17}+, etc.; fpl. (in fig. senses) abs. יָדוֹת Gn 43^{24} + 8 t.; יָדֹת 47^{24} + 2 t.; cstr. יְדוֹת 1 K 7^{32}; sf. יְדֹתָיו Ex 26$^{19.19}$ + 2 t.; יְדֹתֶיהָ 1 K 7$^{35.36}$; וִידוֹתָם 1 K 7^{33};—**1.** *hand* of man Gn 3^{22} 4^{11} 8^{9} + oft.; תַּבְנִית יָד Ez 8^{3} *the shape of a hand* (of God in Ezek.'s vision); of cherubim

ת׳ יַד אָדָם 10^{8}, דְּמוּת יְדֵי אָדָם v^{21}: **a.** *right hand* יַד־יְמִינ(וֹ) Gn 48^{17} (JE), Ju 7^{20} 2 S 20^{9} Je 22^{24} Ez 39^{3} ψ 73^{23} 121^{5}; יד[ם] הַיְמָנִית Ex 29^{20} Lv $8^{23.24}$ $14^{14.17.25.28}$ (all P); a left-handed man is אִטֵּר יַד־יְמִינוֹ Ju 3^{15} 20^{16} (v. אטר); *left hand* יַד שְׂמֹאל(וֹ) 3^{21} 7^{20} Ez 39^{3}; both hands of one pers. are denoted by du., יָדַיִם Gn 27^{22} 2 K 3^{11} + oft.; occasionally + numeral, שְׁתֵּי יָדָי Dt $9^{15.17}$, so Lv 16^{21} (P); du. also of hands of several persons Gn 5^{29} Ex $29^{10.15.19}$ Dt 31^{29} 2 K 11^{16} = 2 Ch 23^{15}, Ez 21^{12} +; yet sts. sg. of hand of several persons Gn 19^{16} Ex 29^{9} Lv 8^{24} Dt 1^{25} $17^{7.7}$ Ju $7^{20.20}$ +. **b.** שְׁתֵּי כַּפּוֹת ידיו 1 S 5^{4} *the two palms of his hands;* כַּפּוֹת הידים 2 K 9^{35} Dn 10^{10}; אַצִּילוֹת יָדֶיךָ *armpits* Je 38^{12} Ez 13^{18}; בֹּהֶן יָדָיו Ex 29^{20} (P) = *his thumbs* (opp. בֹּהֶן רַגְלָם); בְּהֹנוֹת יד(יו) ורגל(יו) Ju $1^{6.7}$; bracelets were worn on *hands*, i.e. wrists Gn $24^{22.30.47}$ (J), cf. thread bound on *hand* of Zerach $38^{28.28.29.30}$ (J), and cords on *hands* of Samson Ju 15^{14}; the ring was worn on *hand*, i.e. finger Gn 41^{42} (E), Est 3^{10}. **c.** as to *hands* in use, note זְרֹעֵי ידיו Gn 49^{24} *arms of his hands*, i.e. arms which make his hands serviceable; מִלֵּא יָדוֹ בַּקֶּשֶׁת 2 K 9^{24} *he filled his hand with the bow*, i.e. caused his hand to grasp it, seized it; הַרְכֵּב יָדְךָ עַל־הַקֶּשֶׁת 2 K $13^{16.16}$; esp. fig. of consecrating or installing (as priest), מִלֵּא יַד *he filled the hand* of any one (perh. orig. gave the selected portions of animal-sacrifices to, v. Lv $8^{25 ff.}$, so Di), *installed* as priest Ju $17^{5.12}$ 1 K 13^{33} (sq. וְ subord.); elsewhere only P and late: Ex 28^{41} (‖ קִדֵּשׁ), 29^{9} also v^{29} (‖ משׁח), v^{33} (קדשׁ), v^{35} Lv 8^{33} 2 Ch 13^{9} 16^{33}, sq. inf. Lv 16^{33} (‖ משׁח), 21^{10} (‖ יוּצַק שֶׁמֶן), Nu 3^{3} (‖ משׁח); מִלֵּאתֶם יֶדְכֶם ליהוה 2 Ch 29^{31} = ye have consecrated yourselves to י׳, is addressed appar. to the whole congregation (otherwise Be Öt and Di Ex 32^{29}); so the same expression Ex 32^{29} (poss.) and 1 Ch 29^{5} (certainly) of offering gifts to י׳; מִלְאוּ יָדוֹ Ez 43^{26} of consecrating the altar (‖ טִהַר, כִּפֶּר); שָׁלַח יַד לְ Ju 5^{26} *stretch out hand to*, so ישׁלח אֶל־ 2 S 6^{6} (insert ידו Vrss Dr); hence מִשְׁלַח יד(כ)ם *that to which one puts the hand*, fig., = undertaking, †Dt $12^{7.18}$ 15^{10} 23^{21} $28^{8.20}$†; שׁלח יד also in hostile sense, c. בְּ, Ex 22^{7} 1 S $24^{7.11}$ 26^{11} ψ 55^{21} +; cf. מוֹאָב מִשְׁלוֹחַ יָדָם Is 11^{14}; אֶבֶן־יַד Nu 35^{17} (P) *a stone (thrown from) the hand;* כְּלִי עֵץ־יָד v^{18} *a weapon in the hand;* מַקֵּל יָד Ez 39^{9} *a staff in the hand;* idols are מַעֲשֵׂה יְדֵי וגו׳ Is 2^{8} + oft. v. מַעֲשֶׂה; man is work of God's hand Jb 14^{15}. **d.** special phrases: kissing with the hand וַתִּשַּׁק יָדִי לְפִי Jb 31^{27}; (in silence) יָדִי שַׂמְתִּי לְמוֹ פִי 40^{4} Mi 7^{16} (עַל־פֶּה); the creditor is בַּעַל מַשֵּׁה יָדוֹ Dt 15^{2}; the debt מַשָּׁא כָל־יָד Ne 10^{32}; תְּרוּמַת יֶדְכֶם Dt $12^{6.11.17}$ *heave-offering of your hand;* the hand is placed תחת יְרֵכְךָ in taking an oath Gn 24^{2} (J); lifted (הרים) to י׳ 14^{22}; so perhaps יָד עַל־כֵּס יָהּ Ex 17^{16} (E) *hand on the throne of Yah!* (but difficult, v. Di VB); oft. c. נשׂא: the hand is lifted (נשׂא) to heaven Dt 32^{40} (of י׳'s oath, poem); elsewh. chiefly Ez and P: simply *lift* (נשׂא) *the hand* (= נשׁבע), sq. inf. Ex 6^{8} Nu 14^{30} (both P), Ez $20^{28.42}$ 47^{14}; sq. לְ pers. Ez $20^{5.5}$ (del. Co as gloss); sq. לְ pers. + inf. Ez $20^{6.15.23}$; abs. 36^{7}; hence (citations) Ne 9^{15} ψ 106^{26}; cf. Ne 8^{6} the people answered אָמֵן אָמֵן בְּמֹעַל יְדֵיהֶם; נשׂא יד(ים) elsewh. (of men) in prayer ψ 28^{2}; cf. 68^{32}, and יָדִי לַיְלָה נִגְּרָה 77^{3}. Also of God, to give a signal Is 49^{29}; to rescue ψ 10^{12}. יְנֹפֵף יָדוֹ Is 10^{32} *he brandisheth his hand* (Assyrian, in defiance); הֵנִיף יָדוֹ Is 11^{15} (of י׳ in judgment), cf. 19^{16} Zc 2^{13} (sq. עַל); הֵנִיעַ יָדוֹ Zp 2^{15} (in derision); הוֹשִׁיעַ יד לְ one's *hand bringing deliverance to, gaining success, by force, for* 1 S 25^{26} + (v. Dr), ins. also v^{31} (𝔊 We Dr); the hand is weary יָגְעָה 2 S 23^{10}, it cleaves (דבק) to the sword (אֶל־הַחֶרֶב) v^{10} (both om. by accident in ‖ 1 Ch 11^{13}, see VB); שֶׁבֶר יָד Lv 21^{19} (H) *fracture of hand* = arm (‖ שֶׁבֶר רגל); after נָתַן: *give a pledge* וַיִּתְּנוּ יָדָם לְהוֹצִיא נְשֵׁיהֶם Ezr 10^{19}; *submit* נָתַן יַד תַּחַת שְׁלֹמֹה 1 Ch 29^{24}, i.e. they acknowledged him as their lord; תְּנוּ־יָד ליהוה 2 Ch 30^{8}; other phr. c. prep. v. infr. **e.** of hand as strong, helpful, etc.:—(1) of man: עֹצֶם יָדִי Dt 8^{17} (‖ כֹּחִי); of fighting power of Edom בְּיָד חֲזָקָה Nu 20^{20} (JE; ‖ בְּעַם כָּבֵד; cf. infr. of God); קִצְרֵי־יָד *small in power* 2 K 19^{26} = Is 37^{27} (cf. infr. of God); Isr. went out of Egypt בְּיָד רָמָה acc. to P, Ex 14^{8} Nu 33^{3} i.e. boldly, defiantly; same phr. of presumptuousness (against י׳) Nu 15^{30} (P, cf. יָדֵנוּ רָמָה Dt 32^{27}). Phrases of *strengthening* are: חִזֵּק יָדָיו Ju 9^{24} Ne 6^{9}; חִזֵּק בִּידֵיהֶם Ezr 1^{6}; החזיק בְּיַד־ Jb 8^{20} (v. חזק); לִהְיוֹת יָדָיו אִתּוֹ 2 K 15^{19} *that his hands might be with him*, to confirm the kingdom in his hand; note also מִי־הוּא לְיָדִי יִתָּקֵעַ Jb 17^{3} *who is he (that) will strike his hand into mine*, i.e. give me a pledge (v. sub תקע); strength fails when hands drop: וַיִּרְפּוּ יָדָיו 2 S 4^{1} *then his hands dropped down*, he grew feeble, spiritless (v. רפה); רְפֵה יָדַיִם 17^{2} *weak-handed, weak* (‖ יָגֵעַ). (2) of (mighty) hand of God, pointing to earlier anthropomorphism; as strengthening Joseph Gn 49[24] (poem in J); as stretched out (שׁלח) to smite Ex 9[15] (J); so of מַלְאַךְ י׳ 2 S 24[16], sq. acc. + לְ inf., opp. הֶרֶף יָדֶךָ v[16]; as smiting (נְגַעָה בְּ) 1 S 6[9] Jb 19[21]; as against (בְּ *among, in*) cattle, etc., v[3] (J); city 1 S 5[9]; the murrain v[3] (J); יַד־יהוה as heavy against (כבדה אֶל) 1 S 5[6]; כָּבְדָה שָׁם v[11]; קָשְׁתָה עַל v[7]; of withdrawal of י׳'s chastising hand תָּסוּר יָדוֹ מִכֶּם 1 S 6[3]; and (י׳ subj.) יָקֵל אֶת־יָדוֹ מֵעֲלֵיכֶם v[5]; of י׳'s power to deliver his people:—†חֹזֶק יָד Ex 13[3.14.16] (all JE)†; יָד חֲזָקָה 6[1.1] (JE), 13[9] (JE), Dt 6[21] 7[8] Jos 4[24] (D); esp. in phr. (בְּ)יָד חֲזָקָה וּ(ב)זְרוֹעַ נְטוּיָה Dt 4[34] + (v. זְרוֹעַ p. 284); יד חזקה + כֹּחַ גָּדוֹל Ex 32[11] (JE), Ne 1[10]; הֲיַד י׳ תִּקְצָר Nu 11[23] (JE) *is the hand of* י׳ *shortened?* Is 50[2] 59[1] (both sq. מִן); יָד נְטוּיָה in judgment Is 9[11.16.20] 10[4]; הָיְתָה יַד־י׳ עלי(ו) of grasp of י׳'s hand in prophetic inspiration Ez 1[3] 3[22] 37[1] 40[1] 2 K 3[15]; יַד־י׳ עָלַי חזקה Ez 3[14]; so בְּחֶזְקַת הַיָּד Is 8[11]; of God's (י׳'s) *good hand* = favour, (late) יַד אלה(יו) טובה על(יו) Ezr 7[9] 8[18] Ne 2[8.18]; without טוֹבָה Ezr 7[6.28] 8[22.31]; sq. inf. יַד האלהים לָתֵת לָהֶם 2 Ch 30[12]; בְּיָדְךָ לְגַדֵּל 1 Ch 29[12]; in gen. בְּיָדְךָ כֹּחַ וּגְבוּרָה v[12]; of protection בְּצֵל יָדוֹ Is 49[2] *in the shadow of his* (י׳'s) *hand.*

2. Fig. = *strength, power*:—לֹא הָיָה בָהֶם יָדַיִם לָנוּס Jos 8[20] (JE) *there was not in them strength to flee;* לֹא מָצְאוּ כָל־אַנְשֵׁי־חַיִל יְדֵיהֶם ψ 76[6] *none of the men of might have found their hands*, i.e. their powers are paralyzed in death (‖ נָמוּ שְׁנָתָם); with ref. to pecuniary *ability*: תַּגִּיעַ יָדוֹ דֵּי שֶׂה Lv 5[7] (on this and others c. דֵּי v. דַּי p. 191); תַּגִּיעַ יָדוֹ לִשְׁתֵּי תוֹרִים v[11] if *his hand* do not *reach to two turtledoves;* אֵין יָדוֹ מַשֶּׂגֶת 14[21] if *his hand be unable to reach;* so combinations with נשׂג Hiph.: v[22.30.31.32] Nu 6[21] (all foregoing P), Lv 25[26.47.49] 27[8] (all H), Ez 46[7]; כְּמַתְּנַת יָדוֹ Dt 16[17] *according to the giving of his hand*, i.e. his ability; similarly מַתַּת יָדוֹ Ez 46[5.11]; on יֶשׁ־לְאֵל יָדִי Gn 31[29], etc., v. II. אֵל p. 43[a] supr.; other phr. c. prep. v. infr.; of *dominion* of king לְהָשִׁיב יָדוֹ בְּ 2 S 8[3] rd. prob. as ‖ 1 Ch 18[3] לְהַצִּיב יָדוֹ בְּ *to establish his dominion at; hand* = *display of strength, action* of י׳ ψ 78[42] Jb 27[11] Dt 34[12]; esp. הַיָּד הַגְּדֹלָה אֲשֶׁר עָשָׂה י׳ Ex 14[31] (J) = *the great achievement which* י׳ *did.*

3. Fig. = *side*: **a.** of way יַד דֶּרֶךְ 1 S 4[13] Qr (Kt יך; but rd. prob. לְיַד השׁער v. Dr). **b.** of gate בְּעַד יַד־הַשַּׁעַר 1 S 4[18] (txt. dub., v. Dr). **c.** of stream or wady כָּל־יַד נַחַל יַבֹּק Dt 2[37]. Esp. du.: **d.** of land, ארץ רַחֲבַת יָדַיִם Gn 34[21] (P) *the land is wide of* (*on*) *both hands*, i.e. in both directions, Ju 18[10] Is 22[18] 1 Ch 4[40]; of city Ne 7[4]; of sea ψ 104[25]; of streams רַחֲבֵי יָדַיִם Is 33[21]; מִיַּד כִּתִּים Nu 24[24] (JE) *from the direction of Kittim.*—Other phr. c. prep. v. infr. **e.** *side* = *place*, properly *place at one side* וְיָד תִּהְיֶה לְךָ מִחוּץ לַמַּחֲנֶה Dt 23[13]; אִישׁ אֶת־יָדוֹ Je 6[3] *each* (*in*) *his place;* so כָּל־אִישׁ עַל־יָדוֹ Nu 2[17] (P);—v. other phrases c. prep. infr.

4. יָד is used in various special, technical senses:—**a.** *sign, monument* 1 S 15[12] 2 S 18[18]. †**b.** *part, fractional part* or *share*: of seed Gn 47[24] (J); share in king 2 S 19[44]; of fighting men 2 K 11[7]; of people Ne 11[1]. †**c.** *time, repetition* Gn 43[34] (J), Dn 1[20]. Also f. pl. (only in fig. senses):—†**d.** *axle-trees* 1 K 7[32.33] (𝔖 ܩܘܛܒܐ). †**e.** *stays, supports* for laver 1 K 7[35.36]; *stays* at sides of throne 1 K 10[19.19] = 2 Ch 9[18.18]. †**f.** *tenons* on sides of boards of tabernacle שְׁתֵּי יָדוֹת Ex 26[17] (P), also v[19.19] 36[22.24.24]. **g.** יָד חָזִית Is 57[8] acc. to Hi De Che Or Brd Du and most = *a phallus thou beholdest;* this favoured by context but without support in Heb. usage; Di *a* (beckoning) *hand.*

5. יַד with prep.:—**a.** אֶל־יַד:—(1) after vb. of motion, *into the charge, custody, of* Est 2[3.8.8.14]; (2) אֶל־יַד *by the side of* gate 2 S 18[4]; אֶל־יָדִי *by my side, next to me* 14[30]; אֶל־יַד דֶּרֶךְ Ez 48[1a]; אֶל־יַד חֲמָת v[b] (but on txt. v. Co); cf. also לְיַד, עַל־יַד. **b.** בְּיַד *into the hand*: (1) נָתַן בְּיַד *give into the hand of*, lit., Gn 27[17]; (2) *into the possession of* נָתַן בְּיַד Ex 10[25] (JE); esp. (3) נתן ביד = *give into the power of, deliver over to* Jos 6[2] 7[7] (both JE), Dt 1[27] Ju 2[14a] 13[1] 15[12] 1 K 22[6] 2 K 18[30] 19[10]; מָכַר בְּיַד *sell into the hand of* Ju 2[14b] 3[8] 4[2.9] 10[7]; נפל בְּיַד *fall into the hand of* 15[18] 2 S 24[14]; וַיְשַׁלְּחֵם בְּיַד פִּשְׁעָם Jb 8[4] *and he delivered them into the power of their transgression*, gave them over to it; also Is 64[6], which read וַתְּמַגְּנֵנוּ for MT וַתְּמוּגֵנוּ; (4) נתן בְּיַד = *entrust to* Gn 30[35] 32[17]. **c.** בְּיַד *in the hand of*: (1) lit. מַטְּךָ אֲשֶׁר בְּיָדֶךָ Gn 38[18] (J) *thy staff which is in thy hand*, Ex 7[17] (J), 17[9] (E), 32[15] Nu 22[23.31] Jos 5[13] 8[18] (all JE), 1 S 13[22] 14[27] 17[50] 18[10] 20[10] 2 K 11[8.11] = 2 Ch 23[7], Am 7[7] Is 6[6] Ez 40[3.5] 47[3] Zc 2[5] 8[4]; אֵין בְּיָדִי רָעָה וָפֶשַׁע 1 S 14[12] *there is not in my hand evil or transgression* (orig. prob. of stains of blood, or other evidences of crime); מַה־בְּיָדִי רָעָה 26[18]; (2) fig. *in the possession of*, Ex 21[16] (JE); נִמְצָא בְּיָדִי 1 S 9[8] *there is found* *in my hand*, i.e. I happen to have ($\frac{1}{4}$ shekel); (3) *in the (physical) power of* Gn 16^{6} (J; cf. תִּתְעַנִּי תַּחַת יָדֶיהָ v^{9}), Jb 1^{12}; בְּיַד לָשׁוֹן Pr 18^{21} *in the power of a tongue; in the care* or *charge of, entrusted to,* Gn 39^{23} (J); *under the authority of* 2 S 18$^{2.2.2}$ Nu 31^{49} (P);—in Je 41^{9} (AV *because of Gedaliah*), rd. בּוֹר גָּדוֹל הוּא for ביד גדליהו הוא 𝔊 Hi Kue Gf Che Gie Dr$^{Sm 291}$; (4) בְּיַד also with vbs. of *taking*, וַיִּקַּח בְּיָדוֹ אֶת־הָאֵשׁ Gn 22^{6} *and he took the fire in his hand*, Ex 4$^{17.20.21}$ (all E), 1 S 17^{40} 2 K 9^{1}; thence to denote accompaniment, taking or being *with* one Jos 9^{11} (JE), 2 S 8^{10} 1 K 14^{3} 2 K 5^{5}; אִישׁ שׁוֹרוֹ בְּיָדוֹ 1 S 14^{34} cf. 16^{2}; קַח בְּיָדְךָ שְׁלֹשִׁים אֲנָשִׁים Je 38^{10}. **d.** בְּיַד *by the agency* or *instrumentality of* Gn 38^{20} (J), Ju 6^{36} 1 S 11^{7} 16^{20} 2 S 3^{18} 10^{2} 11^{14} 12^{25} 2 K 14^{27} (the orig. lit. sense is discernible in some of these); esp. of י׳'s speaking *by the agency* of prophets Ex 9^{35} (R), Lv 8^{36} 10^{11} Nu 4$^{37.45}$ 9^{23} 10^{13} 17^{5} Jos 14^{2} 20^{2} 21$^{2.8}$ (all P), 1 S 28$^{15.17}$ 1 K 16$^{7.12.34}$ 2 K 9^{36} 17$^{13.23}$ 2 Ch 1^{17} 7^{6} 10^{15} 33^{8} 34^{14} 35^{6} Ne 8^{14} 9$^{14.30}$; מוּת בְּיַד י׳ Ex 16^{3} (P) *die by the hand of* י׳; בְּיַד *by* or *at the side of* (very rare) Zc 4^{12} olive-branches *beside* the two golden pipes; =*near to*, in time, נָכוֹן בְּיָדוֹ יוֹם חֹשֶׁךְ Jb 15^{23} *ready at his hand is a day of darkness* (i.e. near *at hand*). **e.** כְּיַד הַמֶּלֶךְ 1 K 10^{13} *acc. to the hand of the king*, i.e. his royal munificence, so Est 2^{18} cf. 1^{7}. **f.** לְיַד *by the side of* 1 S 19^{3} 1 Ch 18^{17} 23^{28} Ne 11^{24} Pr 8^{3} ψ 140^{6}. **g.** מִיַּד *out of the hand*:—(1) *out of the power of*, often nearly = מִן, used idiomat. c. many vbs.: c. הִצִּיל Gn 32$^{12.12}$ (J), Ex 2^{19} 18$^{9.10.10}$ (all JE), 1 S 17^{37}; מִתַּחַת יַד Ex 18^{10} (JE; so c. פשׁע 2 Ch 21$^{8.10.10}$; cf. **i.** infr.); of animals מִיַּד 1 S 17$^{37.37}$, מִיַּד־כֶּלֶב ψ 22^{21}; even of inanimate things הִצִּיל מִיַּד לֶהָבָה Is 47^{14}; c. לָקַח Nu 21^{26} (JE), 1 K 11$^{34.35}$; c. קָרַע v$^{12.31}$; c. מִלֵּט מ׳ מִיַּד שְׁאוֹל, ψ 89^{49}; c. פָּדָה פ׳ מִיַּד שְׁאוֹל Ho 13^{14} (|| מִמָּוֶת), ψ 49^{16}; פ׳ מִידֵי חָרֶב Jb 5^{20}; pregn. יִשְׁפְּטֵנִי מִיָּדֶךָ 1 S 24^{16} *may he* (י׳) *judge* (and save) *me out of thy hand;* so 2 S 18^{19} and (with רִיב for שׁפט) 1 S 25^{39}; (2) מִיַּד of separation, מִיָּדְךָ נִגְזָרוּ ψ 88^{6} of wicked, cut off from nearness to God; (3) דָּרַשׁ מִיַּד *exact (at the hand) of* 2 S 4^{11} Gn 9$^{5.5}$ (P), Ez 33^{6} 34^{10} (= דָּרַשׁ מֵעִם Dt 18^{19}), also of animals Gn 9^{5}; בִּקֵּשׁ מִיַּד Ez 33^{8}; קָנָה מִיַּד Ru 4$^{5.9}$ *acquire at the hand of;* with ref. to offerings הִקְרִיב מִיַּד Lv 22^{25} (H), רָצָה מִיַּד (י׳ subj.) Mal 1$^{10.13}$; לָקַח רָצוֹן מִיַּד 2^{13}. **h.** עַל־יַד (י׳):—(1) *upon the hand(s) of* תְּנָה אֹתוֹ עַל־יָדִי Gn 42^{37} = *entrust him to me* (E; lit. *put him upon my hand*); יַגִּירֵהוּ עַל־יְדֵי־חָרֶב ψ 63^{11} *they shall pour him out upon the hands of the sword* = *deliver him up to the sword;* so Je 18^{21} Ez 35^{5}; (2) עַל־יַד, עַל־יְדֵי *acc. to the hand(s) of* = at the guidance, direction of: עַל־יַד 1 Ch 25^{2a} 2 Ch 26^{13}; עַל־יְדֵי Je 5^{31} 33^{13}, and esp. Chr: 1 Ch 25$^{2b.3.6.6}$; עַל־יְדֵי דָוִיד 2 Ch 23^{18} Ezr 3^{10}; עַל־יְדֵי כְּלֵי דָוִיד 2 Ch 29^{27} *acc. to the guidance of the instruments of David;* (3) *by the side of*, way עַל־יַד דֶּרֶךְ הַשַּׁעַר 2 S 15^{2}; river (היאר) עַל־יַד Ex 2^{5} (E), Nu 13^{29} (JE; || עַל־הַיָּם), Je 46^{6} Dn 10^{4}; city Jos 15^{46} (JE); person (=*in the company of*) 2 S 15^{18}; people 2 Ch 21^{16}; esp. late עַל־יַד *next to* (in a series) 17$^{15.16.18}$ 31^{15} Ne 3$^{2.2}$ + 13 t. Ne 3, 13^{13}; עַל־יְדֵי *by the side of* Ju 11^{26}; people (אדום) Nu 34^{3} (P), 1 Ch 7^{29}; cattle Jb 1^{14}; הֶעֱמִיד עַל־יְדֵי שִׁיר 1 Ch 6^{16} *he stationed them by the side of song*, i.e. to watch over the singing. **i.** תַּחַת יַד *under the hand* = in the possession, at the disposal of; וְאֵין יֶשׁ־פֹּה תַּחַת־יָדְךָ חֲנִית וגו׳ 1 S 21^{9}; = in the power of, subject to Is 3^{6} come, thou shalt be our ruler and this ruin *under thy hand;* pl. sq. vb., וְהִתְעַנִּי תַּחַת יָדֶיהָ Gn 16^{9} (J) *and submit thyself under her hands*, her authority, Is 3^{6}.—מִתַּחַת יַד v. **g.** (1) supr., and sub תַּחַת.

†יִדְאֲלָה **n.pr.loc.** in Zebulun Jos 19^{15}, 𝔊 3030
Ιερειχω, 𝔊L Ιεδαλα; 𝔖 ܝܕܐܠܐ; site unknown.

יִדְבָּשׁ v. sub דְּבַשׁ p. 185^{b} supr. 3031

†I. [יָדַד] **vb.** cast a lot (cf. Eth. ወደየ: 3032
immittere, etc., Di 935)—only **Qal** *Pf.* 3 mpl. יַדּוּ גוֹרָל עַל Na 3^{10} Ob^{11}; יַדּוּ גוֹרָל אֶל־ Jo 4^{3}. (Poss. wrongly pointed pfs. of ידה **Pi.** q. v.)

II. ידד (√of foll.; *love*, cf. Ar. وَدَّ *love;* Aram. Pa. ܝܰܕܶܕ *love*, also deriv.; Sab. epith. f. ודת *loving-one, friend, amie*, DHM$^{ZMG 1883, 391}$; v. also דוד).

†[יָדִיד] **adj.** (poet.) beloved (NH *id.*, 3039
Aram. ܝܕܝܕܐ)—cstr. יְדִיד Dt 33^{12}; sf. לִידִידִי Is 5$^{1.1}$ Je 11^{15}; לִידִידוֹ ψ 127^{2}; pl. sf. יְדִידֶיךָ 60^{7} 108^{7}; f. יְדִידֹת 45^{1}; יְדִידוֹת 84^{2};—**1.** *my beloved*, used by proph. of י׳ under fig. of husbandman Is 5$^{1.1}$; so *my* (thy, his) *beloved* Je 11^{15} ψ 60^{7} = 108^{7}, 127^{2}; *beloved*, of Benj. as beloved by י׳ Dt 33^{12}. **2.** *lovely*, מַה־יְּדִידוֹת מִשְׁכְּנוֹתֶיךָ ψ 84^{2} *how lovely are thy habitations!* **3.** fpl. as abstr. subst. שִׁיר יְדִידֹת ψ 45^{1} = *a song of love*.

3033 †יְדִדוּת n.f. love=obj. of love;—only cstr. יְדִדוּת נַפְשִׁי Je 12^{7} (′י speaks) *love* (i.e. beloved) *of my soul.*

3040 †יְדִידָה n.pr.f. (*beloved*) mother of Josiah 2 K 22^{1}; 𝔊 Ιεδεια, 𝔊L Ιεδιδα.

3041 †יְדִידְיָה n.pr.m. (*beloved of Yah;* cf. Sab. ודדאל DHM$^{ZMG 1875, 604; 1883, 15}$)—name given to Solomon by Nathan; וַיִּקְרָא אֶת־שְׁמוֹ יְדִידְיָהּ בַּעֲבוּר יהוה 2 S 12^{25}; 𝔊 Ιδεδει, 𝔊L Ιεδδιδια.

3035 †יִדּוֹ n.pr.m. **1.** a Manassite, 1 Ch 27^{21}, 𝔊 Ιαδδαι. **2.** one of those who took foreign wives Ezr 10^{43} Kt (Qr יַדַּי; cf. Palm. ידי=*dilectus* Vog$^{No. 5}$), 𝔊 Δια, A Ιαδει, 𝔊L Ιαδιαι.

3035 יַדַּי n.pr.m. v. יִדּוֹ. above

4312 †מֵידָד n.pr.m. one who (with אֶלְדָּד) prophesied in the camp of Isr. Nu $11^{26.27}$ (JE), 𝔊 Μωδαδ.

3034 †[יָדָה] vb. throw, cast (Ar. وَدَى *exeruit, emisit,* II. IV. *emisit* (all now in special senses); Eth. ወደየ: *throw, cast* on or in (very oft.; cf. ወደደ:); whence **Hiph.** *give thanks, confess* (orig. *acknowledge?*) is commonly derived, perhaps from gestures accompanying the act, v. Thes Lag$^{Or. ii. 22}$, yet connexion uncertain; Aram. Pa. וַדִּי, Aph. אוֹדִי *confess,* ܐܘܕܝ, ܐܬܘܕܝ *id.;* but Eth. አስተዋደየ: *accuse,* perh. also fr. gesture; Palm. מודא *render thanks,* oft. in votive inscrr., see Vog on No. 79; עבד ומודא Vog$^{No. 101}$=εὐχαρίστως ἀνέθηκε; מודן כל יום Vog$^{No. 93. 1}$; ידתא *pious* Vog$^{No. 29}$)—**Qal** *Imv.* יְדוּ אֶל־ *shoot* (arrows) *at* Je 50^{14} (rd. prob., with some Codd. יְרוּ). **Pi.** *Impf.* וַיַּדּוּ בִי La 3^{53} *and they cast* (stones) *on me;* *Inf.* יַדּוֹת Zc 2^{4} *to cast down* (the horns of the nations).

Hiph. (connex. with ידה *throw,* obscure, yet v. supr.) *Pf.* הוֹדוּ 1 K 8^{33} + 3 t.; הוֹדִינוּ ψ $75^{2.2}$; *Impf.* יְהוֹדֶה Ne 11^{17} (on form v. Ges$^{§ 53, R. 7}$); יוֹדֶה ψ 6^{6}; 1 s. sf. אֲהוֹדֶנּוּ 28^{7} (Ges$^{l.c.}$); אוֹדֶנּוּ $42^{6.12}$ 43^{5}; pl. יוֹדוּ 99^{3} + 6 t.; sf. יְהוֹדוּךָ 45^{18} (Ges$^{l.c.}$); יוֹדֻךָ 49^{19}, etc. + 41 t. Impf.; *Imv.* הוֹדוּ Is 12^{4} + 16 t.; הֹדוּ ψ 107^{1}; *Inf.* הוֹדוֹת 1 Ch 25^{3} + 11 t.; הוֹדֹת Ezr 3^{11}; הֹדוֹת 1 Ch 16^{7} + 4 t. (see Baer ψ 92^{2}); *Pt.* מוֹדֶה Pr 28^{13}; pl. מוֹדִים 1 Ch 29^{13};—**1.** *give thanks, laud, praise;* **a.** c. acc. (1) of men, Judah Gn 49^{8} (poetic play on name); Job (ironical) Jb 40^{14}; the king ψ 45^{18}; the rich 49^{19}; (2) of ′י, Gn 29^{35} (J expl. name יהודה); elsewhere (mostly ψψ and Ch) of *ritual* worship (v. Lag $^{Or. ii. 22 f.}$); obj. שֵׁם ′י Is 25^{1} ψ 44^{9} 54^{8} 99^{3} 138^{2} 142^{8}; פֶּלֶא ′י 89^{6}; יהוה 7^{18} 9^{2} 109^{30} 111^{1}; יָהּ 118^{19}; sf. ךָ- referring to God $30^{10.13}$ 35^{18} 43^{4} 52^{11} $67^{4.4.6.6}$ 71^{22} 76^{11} 88^{11} $118^{21.28}$ 119^{7} 138^{1} 139^{14} Is $38^{18.19}$ (song of Hez.); ־ֶנּוּ ψ $42^{6.12}$ 43^{5}; מִשִּׁירִי אֲהוֹדֶנּוּ 28^{7} *with my song will I praise him;* אוֹדְךָ ′י *I will praise thee* ′י 2 S 22^{50}=ψ 18^{50}=108^{4}, Is 12^{1} (exilic hymn); אדני ψ 57^{10} 86^{12}, cf. 138^{4} 145^{10}. **b.** sq. לְ, only of the ritual worship: לְשֵׁם ′י ψ 106^{47}=1 Ch 16^{35}, ψ 122^{4} 140^{14}; לְזֵכֶר קָדְשׁוֹ 30^{5} 97^{12}; לי′ 1 Ch $16^{4.7.41}$ 23^{30} 25^{3} 2 Ch 5^{13} 7^{6} 20^{22} ψ 33^{2} 92^{2} 105^{1}=1 Ch 16^{8}=Is 12^{4}; הודו לי′ כי טוב *give thanks to* ′י *for he is good* ψ 106^{1} 107^{1} $118^{1.29}$ 136^{1} 1 Ch 16^{34}; so Je 33^{11} (sq. אֶת־י′); cf. הוד(ו)ת לאלהים 2 Ch 7^{3} Ezr 3^{11}; יודו לי′ חסדו ψ $107^{8.15.21.31}$; Ne 12^{46} ψ 136^{1}; לאדני v^{3}; לאל v^{26}; sfs. referring to God: לְךָ 6^{6} 79^{13} 119^{62}; לוֹ 100^{4}; אלהים+לך $75^{2.2}$ 1 Ch 29^{13}; abs. 2 Ch 31^{2} Ne 11^{17} 12^{24} all of the ritual worship. **2.** *confess,* **a.** the name of God, ||התפלל, התחנן, שׁוּב, 1 K $8^{33.35}$=2 Ch $6^{24.26}$. **b.** עֲלֵי פשׁע ψ 32^{5} (|| לֹא כִסִּיתִי); מוֹדֶה וְעֹזֵב (פשׁעיו) Pr 28^{13} *confessing and forsaking* (his transgressions; opp. מְכַסֶּה).

Hithp. *Pf.* הִתְוַדָּה Lv 5^{5} 16^{21}; הִתְוַדּוּ 26^{40} Nu 5^{7}; *Impf.* 1 s. אֶתְוַדֶּה Dn 9^{4}; pl. יִתְוַדּוּ Ne 9^{2}; *Inf.* sf. הִתְוַדֹּתוֹ Ezr 10^{1}; *Pt.* מִתְוַדֶּה Ne 1^{6} Dn 9^{20}; pl. מִתְוַדִּים 2 Ch 30^{22} Ne 9^{3};—**1.** *confess,* abs. Ezr 10^{1} Ne 9^{3} Dn 9^{4}; c. acc. עָוֹן Lv 16^{21} (P), 26^{40} (H); חטאת Nu 5^{7} (P), Dn 9^{20}; אֲשֶׁר חָטָא Lv 5^{5} (P); על חטאות Ne 1^{6} 9^{2}. **2.** *give thanks,* ליהוה, in the ritual worship 2 Ch 30^{22}.

†הֻיְּדוֹת n.f.pl. songs of praise;—Ne 12^{8}; 1960
so Thes MV, but form strange and dub.; acc. to Ew$^{§ 165 b}$ abstr. הֻיְּדוֹת (many MSS.) *praising;* so Be Ke Öt; Ol$^{§ 220}$ rds. inf. הוֹדוֹת, so SS.

†תּוֹדָה n.f. thanksgiving, ת′ Lv 7^{12} + 23 t.; 8426
cstr. תּוֹדַת Lv $7^{13.15}$; pl. תּוֹדוֹת ψ 56^{13} + 3 t.; תּוֹדֹת Ne $12^{31.40}$;—**1.** *give praise to* ′י Jos 7^{19} (JE; || שִׂים כָּבוֹד לְי′), Ezr 10^{11}, in both of praise rendered by acknowledging and abandoning sin; v. Di on Jos, and on Ezr. Öt and esp. Ryle; cf. vb. ידה c. לְ; so RVm; >Thes MV SS Be RV al. *confession.* **2.** *thanksgiving in songs of liturgical worship* קול ת′ ψ 26^{7} 42^{5} Jon 2^{10}; || שִׁיר ψ 69^{31} Ne 12^{27}; || זְמִרוֹת ψ 95^{2}; || קוֹל זִמְרָה Is 51^{3}; || תְּהִלָּה ψ 100^{4}; || כִּנּוֹר 147^{7}. **3.** *thanksgiving choir, procession, line, company* Ne $12^{31.38.40}$, prob. also Je 30^{19} (|| קוֹל מְשַׂחֲקִים). **4.** *thank-offering* קטר ת′ Am 4^{5} (|| נְדָבוֹת); a division of זֶבַח הַשְּׁלָמִים Lv 7^{12a}; זבח ת′ שׁלמיו v$^{13.15}$;

ת׳(ה) זבח v$^{12\,b}$ (all P), 22^{29} (H); זבחים ותודות 2 Ch 29$^{31.31}$; זבח זבח(י) ת׳ 33^{16}; זבחי שְׁלָמִים ות׳ ψ 107^{22} 116^{17}; מבאי(ם) ת׳ Je 17^{26} 33^{11}; לתודה ψ 100^{1} (title); in ψψ ‖ נדרים: זָבַח ת׳ *offer a thank-offering* 50$^{14.23}$ (see Br$^{MP. 239}$); שִׁלֵּם ת׳ 56^{13}.

3038 † **יְדוּתוּן, יְדֻתוּן** **n.pr.m.** usu. יְדוּתוּן; יְדֻתוּן 2 Ch 5^{12} 35^{15}; יְדִיתוּן ψ 39^{1} 77^{1} Ne 11^{17} 1 Ch 16^{38}; chief of one of the three choirs of the temple (only Chr & ψ-titles) 1 Ch 9^{16} 16$^{38.41.42}$ 25$^{3.3.6}$ 2 Ch 5^{12}; the king's seer 35^{15}; his descendants formed one of the perpetual temple choirs בְּנֵי יְדוּתוּן 1 Ch 16^{42} 25$^{1.3}$ 2 Ch 29^{14}; בֶּן־יְדִיתוּן Ne 11^{17}. In ψ-titles על ידותון ψ 62^{1}, 77^{1} (Qr); לִידִיתוּן 39^{1} (לְ error for עַל־), all = *after the manner of* (the choir of) *Yeduthun* (musical term acc. to RS$^{OTJC\ 422,\ 2nd\ ed.\ 143}$).—v. also Lag$^{Or\ ii.\ 16\,ff.}$ and n.pr. הֵימָן, אָסָף (sub אמן), אֵיתָן (sub יתן).

3042 † **יְדָיָה** **n.pr.m.** **1.** a Simeonite chief 1 Ch 4^{37}, 𝔊 Ιδια, 𝔊L Ιεδδαα. **2.** a builder at the wall Ne 3^{10}, 𝔊 Ιεδαια, 𝔊L Ιεδδεια.

3041 **יְדִידְיָה** v. sub ידד supr. p. 392

3042 **יְדָיָה** v. sub ידה supr.

3043 **יְדִיעֲאֵל** v. sub ידע infr. p. 396

3038 **ידיתון** = ידותון v. sub ידה. above

3044 † **יִדְלָף** **n.pr.m.** son of Nahor Gn 22^{22} (J) (√ דלף ? = *he weepeth* ?) 𝔊 Ιελδαφ, 𝔊L Ιεδλαφ.

3045 **יָדַע** ^{943} **vb. know** (NH *id.*; Aram. יְדַע, ܝܕܰܥ; Ph. ידע; Eth. አእመረ: II. 1. *indicate, announce, narrate*; As. *idû, know*, COT^{Gloss}; Sab. ידע, esp. in cpd. n.pr. DHM$^{ZMG\ 1875,\ 612}$)—**Qal** *Pf.* יָדַע Gn 4^{1} +; יָדָ֑ע Lv 5^{1} +; sf. יְדָעוֹ Dt 34^{10} Jb 28^{7}; יְדָעָהּ Gn 24^{16} 1 K 1^{4}; יְדָעָ֫נוּ Is 63^{16}; 3 fs. יָֽדְעָה Ju 11^{39} + 4 t.; 2 ms. יָדַעְתָּ Gn 30^{26} +; יָדַ֫עְתָּה 2 S 2^{26}; יָדַעַתְּ Ru 2^{11} 1 K 2^{15}; יָדָ֑עַתְּ Je 50^{24}; וְיָדַעַתְּ consec. Ru 3^{4} + 6 t. (incl. Ez 22^{16}, Co וִידַעְתֶּם, so 𝔊 𝔗) + Ez 28^{22} Co (for וְיָֽדְעוּ), so 𝔊; יָדַ֫עְתִּי Gn 4^{9} +; sf. יְדַעְתִּ֫יךָ Ex 33^{12} + 2 t.; יְדַעְתִּיו Gn 18^{19}; יְדַעְתִּים Pr 30^{18}; יְדַעְתִּין Is 48^{7}; יָֽדְעוּ Gn 19^{8} +; יָדָ֑עוּ 2 K 4^{39} +; יָֽדְעוּן Dt 8$^{3.16}$ (Dr$^{§\ 6\ n.}$); 2 mpl. יְדַעְתֶּם Gn 44^{15} +; 2 fpl. יְדַעְתֶּן Gn 31^{6}; וִידַעְתֶּן consec. Ez 13$^{21.23}$, etc.; *Impf.* יֵדַע Is 7^{16} +; יֵדָ֑ע Jos 22^{22} + 5 t.; יֵידָ֑ע ψ 138^{6} (rd. prob. יֵדָ֑ע v. Ges$^{§\ 69.\ 2\ R.\ 3}$); וַיֵּדַע Gn 4^{17} +; sf. יֵדָעֶ֫נּוּ Je 17^{9}; וְיֵדָעֵם Ho 14^{10}; *Imv.* דַּע Gn 20^{7} + 10 t.; דְּעֵה Pr 24^{14}; דָּ֑ע Ec 11^{19}; sf. דָּעֵ֫הוּ Pr 3^{6}; דְּעִי Je 2^{19} + 4 t.; דְּעוּ Nu 32^{23} + 15 t.; *Inf. cstr.* דֵּעָה Ex 2^{4}; דַּ֫עַת Gn 3^{22} +; דַּעְתִּי Dt 9^{24}, etc.; *Inf. abs.* יָדוֹעַ Gn 43^{7} Jos 23^{13}; יָדֹעַ Gn 15^{3} + 11 t.; *Pt. act.* יֹדֵעַ Gn 3^{5} +; f. יֹדַ֫עַת Nu 31^{17} + 2 t.; יֹדְעִים 2 K 17^{26} +; *pass.* וִידוּעַ cstr. Is 53^{3}; pl. וִידֻעִים Dt 1$^{13.15}$;—**1. a.** *know, learn to know*, good and evil Gn 3^{22} (J), sq. אֶת־אֲשֶׁר 1 S 28^{9}; מִסְפַּר הָעָם 2 S 24^{2}; *anything* מְאוּמָה 1 S 20^{39}; לֹא יָדַע אִתּוֹ מְאוּמָה Gn 36^{6} (v. II. אֵת **1 b**), so v^{8}; כָּל־דָּבָר 2 S 15^{11}; subj. God, knowing fowls ψ 50^{11}; way to wisdom Jb 28^{23}, etc.; of bird of prey נָתִיב לֹא יְדָעוֹ עָיִט Jb 28^{7}; the price of wisdom Jb 28^{13}; something future יוֹם מוֹתִי Gn 27^{2} (J); esp. sq. cl. Gn 12^{11} (J) *I know that thou art a woman of fair appearance*, 22^{12} (E), Ec 1^{17}; לֹא ידעתי Gn 28^{16}; answering qu. Where? without other obj., 4^{9} (both J); sq. acc. + בְּ, *in, in the matter of* (v. בְּ **I 2 b**) לֹא יָדַע עַבְדְּךָ בְּכָל־זֹאת דָּבָר קָטֹן אוֹ גדול 1 S 22^{15} *thy servant knoweth not of all this anything, little or much*; sq. בְּ (rare), *gain knowledge of, learn of* or *about*, c. inf., הֲתֵדַע בְּשׂוּם־אֱלוֹהַּ עֲלֵיהֶם Jb 37^{15} *dost thou know about God's enjoining upon them?* also c. subst. אִישׁ אַל־יֵדַע בַּדְּבָרִים הָאֵלֶּה Je 38^{24} *let not a man know of these words*; similarly sq. עַל, only הֲתֵדַע עַל־מִפְלְשֵׂי־עָב Jb 37^{16} *dost thou know concerning the balancings of clouds?* (in Jb 12^{9} בְּ is instr., as Gn 15^{8} ψ 41^{12}); sq. מִן, רְאוּ וּדְעוּ מִכֹּל־הַמַּחֲבֹאִים 1 S 23^{23} *observe and get knowledge of all the hiding-places*; but sq. obj. cl. + מִן of source, קֶדֶם יָדַעְתִּי מֵעֵדֹתֶיךָ כִּי ψ 119^{152} *long ago I gained knowledge out of thy testimonies that* etc.; sq. לְ, *have knowledge of*, + יָדַעְתָּ לְאִוַּלְתִּי ψ 69^{6} *thou knowest my foolishness*; esp. וידע כי אני יהוה *and he shall* (*thou shalt*, etc.) *know that I am Yahweh* Ex 10^{2} (R), 6^{7} 14^{4} 16^{12} 29^{46} (all P), Ez 6$^{7.10.13}$ + oft. in Ezek., 1 K 20$^{13.28}$; sq. acc., which is really subj. of foll. cl., Gn 18^{19} (J) *I know him that he will*, etc. 2 S 3^{25} (Ges$^{§\ 117.\ 1,\ R.\ 6}$). **b.** *perceive* Gn 19$^{33.35}$ (J; obj. cl., inf. c. בְּ); with added idea of *observing, taking note of*, a place, acc. Ru 3^{4}; c. בְּ, יָדַעְתָּ בְּצָרוֹת נַפְשִׁי ψ 31^{8} (‖ רָאָה אֶת־). **c.** ‖ ראה, imv. דע וראה *perceive and see* 1 S 12^{17} 24^{12}; *find out and discern* 14^{38} 23^{22}; in reverse order, ראו ודעו only 23^{23} (v. **a** supr.), Je 5^{1} (v. Dr^{Sm}).—Vid. also **g** infr. **d.** *discriminate, distinguish* הַאֵדַע בֵּין־טוֹב לְרָע 2 S 19^{36}, cf. Dt 1^{39} (no בֵּין); לֹא יָֽדְעוּ בֵּין־יְמִינוֹ לִשְׂמֹאלוֹ Jon 4^{11} *they cannot distinguish between their right hand and their left.* **e.** *know by experience*, וִידַעְתֶּם בְּכָל־לְבַבְכֶם וּבְכָל־נַפְשְׁכֶם כִּי Jos 23^{14} (D) *and know in all your hearts, and all your souls, that*, etc.;

learn to know ׳י Ho 13^{14}; *learn* (a bitter lesson) Ho 9^{7} Is 9^{8} ψ 14^{4}; *experience* ׳י's vengeance Ez 25^{14} ψ 14^{4}(abs.); quietness Jb 20^{20}. **f.** *recognise, admit, acknowledge, confess* Je 3^{13} 14^{20} Is 59^{12} ψ 51^{5}. **g.** *consider* דְּעוּ מַה־תַּעֲשׂוּ Ju 18^{14}; ‖ ראה, imv. דע וראה, דעו וראו, 2 S 24^{13} 1 K 20$^{7.22}$; also וְיָדַעְתָּ עִם־לְבָבֶךָ כִּי Dt 8^{5} *and thou shalt consider with (in) thy heart, that,* 4^{39}. **h.** לֹא ידע *not know = not expect* Is 47^{11} ψ 35^{8}. **2.** *know* a person, *be acquainted with* Gn 29^{5} (J), Ex 1^{8} (E), Jb 42^{11}, *know* ׳י 24^{1}; c. לֹא, obj. esp. other gods, strange land, etc. = have no knowledge of, or acquaintance with, have not heard of, esp. Dt Je:—Dt 11^{28} 13$^{3.7.14}$ 28^{64} 29^{25} 32^{17} (poem), Je 7^{9} 9^{15} 14^{18} 16^{13} 17^{4} 19^{4} 22^{28} 44^{3}; pt. act. *acquaintance* Jb 19^{13}; †pt. pass. *acquainted with* אִישׁ מַכְאֹבוֹת וִידוּעַ חֹלִי Is 53^{3} (lit. *known of sickness*, v. Thes Ew Che Di Du); *well-known* (with implied trustworthiness) Dt 1$^{13.15}$+; of beasts *knowing* owner and master's crib Is 1^{3} (cf. Je 8^{7}); esp. of knowing God (׳י) לֹא יָדַעְתִּי אֶת־׳י Ex 5^{2} (J); involving intelligent worship, obedience, etc. Ju 2^{10} 1 S 2^{12} (rd. יָדֵעַ for MT יָדַע, Dr), 3^{7} Ho 2^{22} 8^{2} 5^{4} Jb 18^{21} ψ 79^{6} (v. also דַּעַת **2 b**); of God's *knowing* persons, etc., thoroughly Ho 5^{3} Jb 11^{11}; knowing the heart 1 K 8^{39} 2 Ch 6^{30} ψ 139^{4}; *knowing* his true servants, *recognising* and *acknowledging* them 2 S 7^{20} Na 1^{7} 1 Ch 17^{18}+; יְדַעְתִּיךָ בְשֵׁם Ex 33^{12} (JE); = *take notice of, regard* ψ 1^{6} 31^{7} 37^{18}; so of Isr. as chosen people Am 3^{2} Ho 13^{5} (As. *ilu idûšu, God regardeth him,* Hpt$^{BAS\ i.\ 15}$) cf. Gn. 18^{19}(J). **3.** *know a person* carnally, of sexual intercourse, sq. acc.: man subj. Gn 4$^{1.17.25}$ 24^{16} 38^{26} (all J), 1 S 1^{19} Ju 19^{25} 1 K 1^{4}; woman subj. Gn 19^{8} (J), Nu 31$^{17.18.35}$ (all P), Ju 11^{39}; יָדְעַת מִשְׁכַּב זָכָר Ju 21^{11}; לֹא יָדְעָה אִישׁ לְמִשְׁכַּב זָכָר v^{12}; man subj. and obj. (of sodomy) Gn 19^{5} (J), Ju 19^{22}. **4. a.** *know how* to do a thing, be able to do it, oft. c. לֹא and sq. inf.: לֹא יָדְעוּ עֲשׂוֹת־נְכֹחָה Am 3^{10} *they know not how to do right;* לֹא יָדַעְתִּי דַּבֵּר Je 1^{6} 6^{15} 1 K 3^{7} Is 56$^{11.11}$, c. לְ 50^{4} Ec 10^{15}; לֹא יָדַע לְהִזָּהֵר Ec 4^{13} *know not how to be admonished* (v^{17} know *that*); inf. abs. ידע מָאוֹס בָּרָע וּבָחוֹר בַּטּוֹב Is 7$^{15.16}$. **b.** *be skilful in*, esp. pt., sq. acc. יֹדֵעַ צַיִד Gn 25^{27} (J) *skilled in hunting;* ידע סֵפֶר *skilled in a book, learned* Is 29$^{11.12.12}$; as pl. cstr. יוֹדְעֵי נֶהִי Am 5^{16} *knowers of lamentation*, professional mourners; יֹדְעֵי הַיָּם 1 K 9^{27} *skilled in the sea*, 2 Ch 8^{18}; esp. sq. inf. יֹדֵעַ נַגֵּן 1 S 16^{18} *skilled in playing*, 1 K 5^{20} 2 Ch 2$^{6.7.13}$: יֹדֵעַ מְנַגֵּן בַּכִּנּוֹר 1 S 16^{16} *knowing*, (as) *a player on the lyre* (v. Dr). **5.** abs. *have knowledge, be wise:* לְיֹדְעִים Ec 9^{11} (‖ נְבֹנִים, חֲכָמִים); esp. have knowledge of God and duty, or in practical affairs Is 1^{3} (‖ בין), 56^{10}; oft. c. acc. cogn.: דַּעַת Pr 17^{27} 30^{3}; בִּינָה Is 29^{24} Pr 4^{1} 2 Ch 2^{12}, cf. יוֹדְעֵי בִינָה לָעִתִּים 1 Ch 12^{33} (Baer), Est 1^{13}; also יֹדְעֵי דַעַת וּמְבִינֵי מַדָּע Dn 1^{4}; obj. יֹדְעֵי דָּת וָדִין v^{13}; חָכְמָה וּמוּסָר Pr 1^{2} (‖ בֵּן חָכָם); שֶׂכֶל וּבִינָה 2 Ch 2^{11} (‖ הבין אִמְרֵי בִינָה); חָכְמָה Pr 24^{14} Ec 8^{16}.

†**Niph.** *Pf.* נוֹדַע Gn 41^{21} + 10 t.; וְנוֹדַע consec. 1 S 6^{3} + 2 t.; 3 fs. וְנוֹדְעָה Lv 4^{14} Is 66^{14}, etc.; *Impf.* יִוָּדַע Gn 41^{31} + 10 t.; יִוָּדֵעַ Pr 10^{9}; וַיִּוָּדַע Est 2^{22}; 3 fs. תִּוָּדֵעַ Pr 14^{33}; 2 fs. תִּוָּדְעִי Ru 3^{3}; וָאִוָּדַע Ez 20^{5}; *Inf.* sf. הִוָּדְעִי Je 31^{19}; *Pt.* נוֹדָע ψ 76^{2} + 2 t.;—**1.** *be made known, be* or *become known*, of things Gn 41^{31} (sq. בְּ), Ex 2^{14} (both E), Lv 4^{14} (P), Ju 16^{9} 2 S 17^{19} Na 3^{17} Zc 14^{7} (sq. לְ), ψ 77^{20} 79^{10} (sq. בְּ), 88^{13} (sq. בְּ); of hand of ׳י Is 66^{14} (sq. אֶת); c. subj. cl. Ex 21^{36} 33^{16} (both JE), Dt 21^{1} 1 S 6^{3}(sq. לְ), 1 K 18^{36} Ez 36^{32}(sq. לְ), Ru 3^{14} Ec 6^{10} Est 2^{22} (sq. לְ); of pers., Pr 31^{23} (sq. בְּ) Is 61^{9} (sq. בְּ and בְּתוֹךְ); of ׳י ψ 76^{2} (sq. בְּ); = *be revealed, discovered*, of pers. 1 S 22^{6} Je 28^{9} Pr 10^{9}; of things Ne 4^{9} Pr 12^{16} 14^{33}. **2.** *make oneself known*, of pers., sq. לְ Ru 3^{3}, usu. of God (׳י) Ex 6^{3} (P; ‖ וָאֵרָא אֶל־), Is 19^{21} Ez 20^{5}, sq. לְעֵינֵי 38^{23}; sq. אֶל־ 20^{9}; sq. בְּ 35^{11} ψ 48^{4}; without prep. 9^{17}. **3.** *be perceived* (pass. of **Qal**), of perception by the eye Gn 41^{21} (E), ψ 74^{5}. **4.** *be instructed* (pass. of **Hiph.**) Je 31^{19}, in spiritual sense, through chastisement.

†**Pi.** *Pf.* 2 ms. יִדַּעְתָּ, only ידעתה שַׁחַר מְקֹמוֹ Jb 38^{12} Kt; rd. with Qr יִדַּעְתָּ הַשַּׁחַר *cause to know*, sq. 2 acc.; so ψ 104^{19} acc. to Bae, who rds. יִדַּע, after Aq Symm.

†**Po.** *Pf.* 1 s. יוֹדַעְתִּי 1 S 21^{3} *I have caused to know*, i.e. directed, sq. acc., but rd. יוֹעַדְתִּי or יָעַדְתִּי, fr. יעד, so 𝔊 We Dr.

†**Pu.** *Pt. known* מידעת Is 12^{5} Kt (Qr מוּדַעַת v. **Hoph.**); elsewhere as subst. = *acquaintance* מְיֻדָּעַי ψ 88^{9} מְיֻדָּעָיו 2 K 10^{11}; מְיֻדָּעַי ψ 55^{14}; Jb 19^{14} (‖ קְרוֹבַי), ψ 88^{19}(‖ אֹהֵב and רֵעַ); מְיֻדָּעַי ψ 31^{12}, Kt מידע Ru 2^{1} (Qr מוֹדַע q.v. infr.)

†**Hiph.** *Pf.* הוֹדִיעַ ψ 98^{2}; הוֹדִיעֲנִי Je 11^{18}; הוֹדַעְתָּ 1 K 1^{27} + 2 t.; הוֹדַעְתָּ Jb 26^{3}, etc.; *Impf.* יוֹדִיעַ ψ 103^{7} Is 38^{19}; *juss.* יֹדַע Nu 16^{5}; וַיֹּדַע Ju 8^{16}; יוֹדִיעֶנּוּ Is 40$^{13.14}$; 2 ms. תּוֹדִיעַ Hb 3^{2}; תּוֹדִיעֵנִי ψ 16^{11} 51^{8}; 1 s. אוֹדִיעַ ψ 89^{2} Ez 39^{7}; אוֹדִיעָה Pr 1^{23} Is 5^{5}; יוֹדִיעוּ Jb 32^{7}; יוֹדִעֻם Ez 44^{23}; נוֹדִיעָה 1 S 14^{12}; *Imv.* הוֹדַע Pr 9^{9} + 3 t. (הוֹדַע ψ 90^{12}); sf. הוֹדִיעֵנִי Jb 10^{2} + 6 t., etc.; *Inf. cstr.* הוֹדִיעַ 2 S 7^{21} + 3 t.;

הוֹדִיעַ 1 Ch 17^{10}; הוֹדִיעֲנִי 1 S 28^{15}, etc.; *Pt.* מוֹדִיעֲךָ Dn 8^{19}; מוֹדִיעָם Je 16^{21}; מוֹדִיעִים Is 47^{13} 2 Ch 23^{13};—*make known, declare*, c. acc. rei Nu 16^{5} (P), Ez 39^{7} 1 Ch 17^{19} Jb 26^{3} ψ 89^{2} 98^{2} 106^{8}; obj. om. Hb 3^{2}; *teach*, c. acc. rei Jb 32^{7}; sq. inf. ψ 90^{12} and (peculiarly) מ׳ לְהַלֵּל 2 Ch 23^{13} i.e. *led in praising;* c. לְ pers. Pr 9^{9}; c. acc. pers. Is 40^{13} Ju 8^{16} (but rd. וַיָּדָשׁ, v. דושׁ); *make known, declare*, c. acc. rei, + לְ pers. Ex 18^{20} Dt 4^{9} Ne 8^{12} 9^{14} ψ 78^{5} 103^{7} 145^{12} Is 38^{19} 64^{1}; c. cl. of thing, + לְ pers. 1 S 10^{8}; *make* one *know*, c. cl. of thing and acc. (sf.) pers. Ex 33^{12} Dt 8^{3} 1 S 6^{2} 16^{3} 28^{15} Jb 10^{2} 37^{19}; c. acc. rei + sf. pers. הוֹדִעֵנִי נָא אֶת־דְּרָכֶךָ וְאֵדָעֲךָ Ex 33^{13} (JE) *make me, I pray, to know thy ways, that I may know thee;* Je 16^{21} Ez 20^{4} 22^{2} 43^{11} Is 40^{14} (‖ וַיְלַמְּדֵהוּ דַּעַת), also v^{a} (וַיְבִינֵהוּ), Pr 22^{21} Jb 13^{23} ψ 16^{11} 25^{4} (‖ לַמְּדֵנִי), v^{14} (on inf. c. לְ v. Ges$^{§ 114. 2, R. 2, Exx.}$), 39^{5} 51^{8} 143^{8} (‖ הַשְׁמִיעֵנִי) 32^{5} חַטָּאתִי אוֹדִיעֲךָ (‖ עֲוֺנִי לֹא־כִסִּיתִי); sq. 2 separate acc. Gn 41^{39} (E), 1 S 14^{12} Is 5^{5} Ez 20^{11} 16^{2} Pr 1^{23} Dn 8^{19}; acc. pers. om. Ex 18^{16} (E); acc. rei om. Jos 4^{22} = *teach* one (D), so Is 40^{13}, 2 S 7^{21} 1 K 1^{27}; = *answer* Jb 38^{2} 40^{7} 42^{4}; c. sf. pers., acc. rei om. Je 11^{18} 16^{21} Pr 22^{19}; sq. acc. rei + בְּ ψ 77^{15} *thou hast made known thy might among the peoples*, Is 12^{4} 1 Ch 18^{8} = ψ 105^{1}; sq. cl. + בְּ pers. Ho 5^{9}; sq. בֵּין, *teach the difference between, to discriminate between* בֵּין הַטָּמֵא לְטָהוֹר Ez 22^{26}; + sf. pers. 44^{23} (cf. **Qal 1 d**); sq. מִן partit. מוֹדִעִים לֶחֳדָשִׁים מֵאֲשֶׁר יָבֹאוּ Is 47^{13} *who declare, at the new moons, of* (*the things*) *which are to come.*

†**Hoph.** *Pf.* הוֹדַע Lv 4$^{23.28}$ (v. Kö$^{i, 427}$); *Pt.* מוּדַעַת Qr Is 12^{5} (> Kt מְיֻדַּעַת);—*made known* (Pt.) Qr Is 12^{5} let this *be made known* in (בְּ) all the earth (> Kt Pu. Pt. which is not elsewhere in this sense); sq. אֵלָיו if his sin be *made known unto himself* Lv 4$^{23.28}$ (P).

†**Hithp.** *Impf.* אֶתְוַדָּע Nu 12^{6} (E); sq. אֶל־ *make oneself known to*, of י׳; *Inf.* הִתְוַדַּע אֶל־ Gn 45^{1} (E), of Joseph.

3047 †יָדָע† **n.pr.m.** (Sab. ידע, epith. of king, *the knowing, shrewd one* Mordt$^{ZMG 1876, 37}$)—a man of Judah 1 Ch 2^{28} (יָדָע), v^{32}.

1843 †[דֵּעַ] **n.[m.] knowledge, opinion** (late)—only sf. דֵּעִי Jb 32^{6} + 3 t., and pl. דֵּעִים 37^{16}; all in speech of Elihu. **1.** *knowledge*, תְּמִים ד׳ Jb 37^{16} *one perfect in knowledge* (of God). **2.** *judgment, opinion* Jb 36^{3}; חַוֺּת דֵּעִי 32^{6} *to declare my opinion*, so v$^{10.17}$.

†דֵּעָה† **n.f. knowledge** (strictly Inf. of ידע) 1844 —דֵּעָה ψ 73^{11} + 3 t.; pl. דֵּעוֹת 1 S 2^{3} Jb 36^{4};—תְּמִים ד׳ Jb 36^{4} (of Elihu); of God's knowledge, אֵל ד׳ י׳ 1 S 2^{3} *a God of knowledge is* י׳ (on pl. v. Dr); יֵשׁ דֵּעָה בְעֶלְיוֹן ψ 73^{11} (‖ אֵיכָה יָדַע־אֵל); *knowledge*, with י׳ as obj. Is 11^{9} (where verbal force of noun appears); as taught by proph. Is 28^{9}; וְרָעוּ אֶתְכֶם דֵּעָה וְהַשְׂכֵּיל Je 3^{15} of י׳'s shepherds (i.e. future ideal rulers). Gr prop. (plausibly) רָעָה, after 𝔊, v. also Gie.

†דַּעַת† **n.f.** $^{ψ 139, 6\ Dn 12, 4}$ (**m.** Pr 2^{10} 14^{6}, poss. Jb 1847 33^{3} Ew$^{§ 174 g}$) **knowledge** (prop. Inf., which appears clearly Gn 2$^{9.17}$ Je 22^{16})—abs. דַּעַת Gn 2^{9} + 35 t.; דָּעַת Jos 20^{3} + 35 t.; cstr. דַּעַת Nu 24^{16} + 10 t.; sf. דַּעְתִּי Pr 22^{17}; דַּעְתְּךָ Jb 10^{7}; דַּעְתֵּךְ Is 47^{10}; דַּעְתּוֹ Pr 3^{20} Is 53^{11}; דַּעְתְּכֶם Jb 13^{2}; דַּעְתָּם Is 44^{25};—**1. a.** *knowledge, perception* in phrase בִּבְלִי ד׳ Dt 4^{42} = *unintentionally*, 19^{4} Jos 20^{3} (where P's synonym is בִּשְׁגָגָה v$^{3.9}$, cf. Nu 35$^{11.15}$), v^{5}; *without knowing* מִבְּלִי ד׳ Is 5^{13} (= before they knew it, suddenly). **b.** = *skill* (in workmanship) Ex 31^{3} 35^{31} (both P; both ‖ תְּבוּנָה and חָכְמָה), 1 K 7^{14} (sq. inf.); creative skill Is 40^{14} (‖ דֶּרֶךְ תְּבוּנוֹת, אֹרַח מִשְׁפָּט). **c.** of proph. knowledge יֹדֵעַ ד׳ עליון Nu 24^{16} (JE), cf. ψ 19^{3}. **d.** esp. knowledge with moral quality Gn 2$^{9.17}$ (J; in both verbal force, הַדּ׳ טוֹב וָרָע *the knowing good and evil*). **e.** *knowledge* possessed by God Jb 10^{7} ψ 139^{6} Pr 3^{20} (‖ חָכְמָה and תְּבוּנָה), 21^{12}; taught by God to men ψ 94^{10} 119^{66} (‖ טוּב טַעַם), Pr 2^{6} (‖ חָכְמָה and תְּבוּנָה). **f.** דַּעַת־רוּחַ = *windy* (unreal) *knowledge* Jb 15^{2}. **2.** esp. in WisdLt = *discernment, understanding, wisdom:* **a.** Jb 13^{2} 33^{3} (ד׳ שְׂפָתַי), לֹא בְדַעַת Jb 34^{35} (‖ חכמה), Pr 8$^{9.10}$ (‖ מוסר), 10^{14} 11^{9} 18$^{15.15}$ 22^{12} 29^{7}, cf. Is 32^{4} 53^{11} Je 10^{14} = 51^{17}; בבלי דעת Jb 35^{16} 36^{12}; בלי ד׳ 38^{2} 42^{3}, בְּלֹא ד׳ Pr 19^{2}; ‖ תְּבוּנָה Pr 17^{27} Is 44^{19}; ד׳ מְזִמּוֹת 8^{12}; ‖ מְזִמָּה Pr 1^{4} 5^{2}; חכמה + ת׳ Pr 24^{4}, ‖ vb. עָרַם 19^{25}; ‖ מִצְוֺת 22^{20}; ‖ מוּסָר 12^{1} 19^{27} 23^{12}; ‖ תּוֹרָה Mal 2^{7}; ‖ חכמה Pr 14^{6} Ec 1$^{16.18}$ 2$^{21.26}$ 7^{12} 9^{10}; connected with חָכָם Pr 21^{11} Ec 12^{9}; דברי חכמים Pr 22^{17}; Is 33^{6} (חכמת) Is 44^{25} (חכמים); wisdom of magicians 47^{10} Dn 1^{4} (‖ חָכְמָה and מַדָּע). **b.** in highest sense, *knowledge* of God (incl. obedience) Ho 4$^{1.6}$ (מִבְּלִי הַדַּעַת), v^{6} 6^{6} Jb 21^{14} Pr 2^{5} (‖ יראת י׳), so Is 11^{2} 58^{2} Je 22^{16} (verbal force, c. acc.), Pr 9^{10} (‖ חָכְמָה, ד׳ קדשים ‖ יראת י׳), 30^{3} (*id.*, ‖ חָכְמָה); v. also 1^{7} יִרְאַת י׳ ראשית ד׳ (‖ חָכְמָה מוּסָר), v$^{22.29}$ (‖ יִרְאַת י׳), 2^{10} (‖ חָכְמָה). **c.** opp. אִוֶּלֶת Pr 12^{23} 13^{16} 14^{18} 15^{2}

cf. v^{7}, also v^{14}. **d.** איש ד׳ שְׂפָתֵי־ד׳ Pr 14^{7} 20^{15}; 24^{5} (|| גֶּבֶר חָכָם).—Dn 12^{4} is dub.; 𝔊 Bev rd. ותרבה הָרָעָה.

3048 †יְדַעְיָה **n.pr.m.** (Sab. n.pr. ידעאל DHM $^{ZMG\ 1875,\ 605}$) priestly name;—**1.** 1 Ch 9^{10} 𝔊 Ιωαδε, 24^{7} 𝔊 (Ανε)ιδεια. **2.** Ezr 2^{36} Ne 7^{39} 𝔊 Ιεουδα, (Ι)εδδουα, Ιωαδε. **3.** Ne 11^{10} 12$^{6.19}$ 𝔊 Δαδεια, Ιαδιας, Ιδειας, etc. **4.** Ne 12$^{7.21}$ 𝔊L Ωδουιας. **5.** Zc 6$^{10.14}$ 𝔊 (παρὰ) τῶν ἐπεγνωκότων αὐτήν.

3037 †יַדּוּעַ **n.pr.m.** **1.** a chief of the people, one of those sealed Ne 10^{22} 𝔊L Ιεδδουα. **2.** a priest, prob. the high priest in time of Alexander the Great Ne 12$^{11.22}$ 𝔊 Ιαδου, 𝔊L Ιεδδου (whence Lag$^{BN\ 113}$ rds. יִדּוּעַ).

3043 †יְדִיעֲאֵל **n.pr.m.** (Palm. ידיבעל DHM in MV$^{10,\ 983}$ cf. Sab. n.pr. with ידע DHM$^{ZMG\ 1875,612}$)—**1.** a Benjamite 1 Ch 7$^{6.10.11}$, 𝔊 Αδειηλ, Ιεδιηλ, etc. **2.** one of David's heroes acc. to 1 Ch 11^{45} appar. = the Manassite captain of 12^{21} (Baer; van d. H v^{20}), 𝔊 Ελθειηλ, Ιεδιηλ. **3.** a Korahite porter 1 Ch 26^{2} 𝔊 Ιδερηλ, Ιεδιηλ.

1845 †דְּעוּאֵל **n.pr.m.** a Gadite, Nu 1^{14} 7$^{42.47}$ 10^{20}, but 𝔊 in all Ραγουηλ, so Sam 𝔖; = רְעוּאֵל Nu 2^{14}, where, however, 𝔙 and Heb. Codd. ד׳ (all P); v. further sub רעה. p. 944ff

3049 †יִדְּעֹנִי **n.m.** **familiar spirit** (prop. either as *knowing, wise* (acquainted with secrets of unseen world), Ew *vielwisserisch;* or as *intimate acquaintance* of soothsayer, v. RS $^{JPh\ xiv.\ 1885.\ 127}$)—abs. יִדְּעֹנִי Dt 18^{11} + 2 t.; pl. יִדְּעֹנִים 1 S 28^{3} + 6 t.; הַיִּדְּעֹנִי מִן 1 S 28^{9}, rd. הַיִּדְּעֹנִים מִן (v. 𝔊 Th We Klo Dr); *familiar spirit,* always || אוֹב, אֹבוֹת 1 S 28$^{3.9}$ Is 8^{19} 19^{3} 2 K 21^{6} (עשׂה אוֹב || עוֹנֵן, נִחֵשׁ) = 2 Ch 33^{6}, 2 K 23^{24} Lv 19^{31} 20$^{6.27}$ (all H; on last two cf. Acts 16^{16} and Dr $^{Dt\ 18,\ 11}$), Dt 18^{11} (|| אוֹב + דֹּרֵשׁ אֶל־הַמֵּתִים).

4129 †מוֹדַע, מֹדָע **n.m.** **kinsman,** מידע לְ Ru 2^{1} Kt, but Qr מוֹדַע *a kinsman* of her husband; fig. מֹדָע לַבִּינָה תִקְרָא Pr 7^{4} *a kinsman shalt thou call understanding* (|| אֱמֹר לַחָכְמָה אֲחֹתִי אָתְּ).

4130 †[מֹדַעַת] **n.f.** **kindred, kinship**—sg. sf. מֹדַעְתָּנוּ Ru 3^{2} is not Boaz (of) *our kindred?*

4093 †מַדָּע **n.m.** $^{2\ Ch\ 1,\ 12}$ **knowledge, thought** (late); מַדָּע 2 Ch 1^{10} + 4 t.; מַדָּעֲךָ Ec 10^{20};—**1.** *knowledge* (|| חָכְמָה) of Solomon, 2 Ch 1$^{10.11.12}$ Dn 1^{4} (|| חָכְמָה and דַּעַת), v^{7} (|| הַשְׂכֵּל). **2.** *place of knowledge, mind,* (in our idiom also) *thought* Ec 10^{20}.

מַדּוּעַ $_{61}$ and $^{(Ez\ 18,\ 19)}$ מַדֻּעַ **adv.** **wherefore?** 4069
(prob. contr. from מַה־יָּדוּעַ *what being known?* i.e. from what motive? so Ges Ew$^{§\ 325\ c}$ Ol$^{§\ 222\ f}$, cf. in Gk. τί μαθών;)—*wherefore? on what account?* Gn 26^{27} מַדּוּעַ בָּאתֶם אֵלָי, 40^{7} Ex 1^{18} 2^{18} 3^{3} (in an indirect question), 5^{14} 18^{14} Lv 10^{17} Jos 17^{14} (all in Hex), Ju 5$^{28.28}$ 2 S 3^{7} 11^{10} etc., Is 5^{4} 50^{2} 63^{2} (all in Is.); in Jer. 16 t., oft. rhetorically, after a double question introduced by הֲ . . . אִם, expressing affected surprise: † 2^{14} (v. Gf) is Israel a slave (unable to defend himself)? *wherefore,* then, is he become a prey? (some other cause must therefore be found for Israel's misfortune), v^{31} 8$^{5.19.22}$ 14^{19} 22^{28} 49^{1}, cf. 30^{6}; Jb 3^{12} 18^{3} (never in ψ).

יָהּ **n.pr.dei,** v. sub הוה p. 219^{b} supr. 3050

†[יָהַב] **vb.** **give** (Aram. יְהַב, ܝܗܒ; Ar. 3051
وَهَبَ; Eth. ወሀበ: Sab. והב DHM$^{ZMG\ xxix.\ 1875,\ 614\ f.}$ ול יהב Id$^{ib.\ 603}$)—only **Qal** *Imv.* הַב Pr 30$^{15.15}$; emph. הָבָה Gn 11^{3} + 10 t. (6 t. sq. monosyll.); הָבָה Gn 29^{21} before gutt. (Di on Gn 28^{2} Kö$^{i.\ 418}$), fs. הָבִי Ru 3^{15}; mpl. הָבוּ Gn 47^{16} + 16 t.; הָבוּ לִי, Jb 6^{22} (on these forms v. also Sta$^{§\ 606\ a}$ Bö$^{i.\ 225}$ Ges$^{§\ 69.\ 2,\ R.\ 2}$);—**1.** *give,* sq. acc. Gn 29^{21} (E) *give* (me) *my wife,* 47^{16} (J), Ru 3^{15} Zc 11^{12} (*price*); of *giving* (i.e. causing to come forth, in deciding by lot) Urim and Thummim 1 S 14$^{41.41}$ (𝔊 We Dr, v. אוּרִים); sq. acc. rei + לִי Gn 30^{1} (E), Ju 1^{15}; acc. rei + לָנוּ Gn 47^{15} (J), ψ 60^{13} = 108^{13}; הָבוּ לִי Jb 6^{22} (no acc. expr.); abs. הַב ׀ הַב Pr 30^{15}. **2.** = *set,* sq. acc. (Uriah) + אֶל־מוּל פְּנֵי הַמִּלְחָמָה 2 S 11^{15} *set Uriah in the fore-front of the battle.* **3.** with reflex. לְ (v. לְ, **5 h**) = *provide,* c. acc. הָבוּ לָכֶם אֲנָשִׁים חֲכָמִים Dt 1^{13}; Jos 18^{4} (JE), Ju 20^{7} 2 S 16^{20}. **4.** *ascribe* glory, etc., to י׳ (God): c. כבוד לְ ψ 29$^{1.1.2}$ = 96$^{7.7.8}$ = 1 Ch 16$^{28.28.29}$; הָבוּ גֹדֶל לאלהינו Dt 32^{3} (poem) *ascribe greatness to our God.* **5.** = *come now* (orig. *grant, permit*), before voluntat.: Gn 11$^{3.4.7}$ 38^{16} (all J), Ex 1^{10} (E).

†[יְהָב] **n.[m.]** **lot** (as that which is *given*)— 3053
הַשְׁלֵךְ עַל י׳ יְהָבְךָ ψ 55^{23} *cast on* י׳ *thy lot* (the care, anxiety, etc. which are thy portion; cf. גּוֹל עַל־י׳ דרכך ψ 37^{5}).

†[הַבְהָב] **n.m.** **gift** (? on form, then comp. 1890
צאצא Ges$^{§\ 84\ b\ viii}$; but mng. (and √) dub.; poss. fr. NH הִבְהֵב *roast,* Levy$^{NHWB\ i.\ 447\ b}$)—only pl. sf.: זִבְחֵי הַבְהָבַי יִזְבְּחוּ Ho 8^{13} *as the sacrifices of my*

gifts (=*my sacrificial gifts*, so Che) *they sacrifice flesh.*

3054 [יהד] **vb.** v. sub יְהוּדָה infr.

3056 יֶהְדַּי, יָהְדַּי **n.pr.m.** v. sub הדה p. 213^{a} supr.

3055 †יְהֻד **n.pr.loc.** in Dan, Jos 19^{45};=mod. *Yehûdîyeh*, 8 m. E. of Joppa, and 1½ h. [5½ m.] W. of N. fr. Lydda, Survey$^{ii. 258}$ Guérin$^{Judée\ i. 322}$; 𝔊 Ιουθ, 𝔊L [Ι]ουδ (on form of name Jastr$^{JBL\ xii, 1893, 61\ ff.}$ comp. *Ia-u-du*, Tel el-Amarna$^{No. 39}$).

3068 יְהוֹ, **n.pr.** cpd. with, v. sub יהוה supr. pp. 219 ff.

3058 יֵהוּא **n.pr.m.** v. sub יהוה supr. p. 219.

3063 יְהוּדָה $_{820}$ **n.pr.m.** et **terr. Judah** (treated Gn 29^{35} 49^{8} (q. v. infr.) as if der. fr. Hoph. of ידה=*praised, object of praise* (on ה cf. Hiph. אֲהוֹדֶנּוּ ψ 28^{7}, יְהוֹדֶה Ne 11^{17}), but this dubious; relation to יְהֻד, II. יְהוּדִית unexpl.; v. further Jastr$^{JBL\ xii, 1893, 61\ ff.}$; As. *Ia-u-du*, of land; *Ia-u-da-ai, Judaean* COT^{Gloss})—**I. n.pr.m. 1.** *son of Jacob and Leah*, expl. by Leah's words *I will praise* י׳ Gn 29^{35} (J); cf. Jacob's prediction, *thy brethren shall praise thee* Gn 49^{8} (poem in JE), see also v$^{9.10}$; elsewh. Gn 37^{26} 38^{1} + 14 t. Gn 38, $43^{3.8}$ $44^{14.16.18}$ 46^{28} (all J), 35^{23} (P), 1 Ch $2^{1.3}$ Ru 4^{12}; בְּנֵי יְהוּדָה *sons of Judah* Gn 46^{12} Nu 26^{19} (P), 1 Ch $2^{3.4}$ 4^{1}. **2.** *tribe* descended from Judah Dt 33^{7} (poem), Nu 1^{7} (P), Dt 27^{12}+; בְּנֵי יהודה Nu 1^{26} (P), Jos 14^{6} (D), Ju 1^{8}+; שֵׁבֶט יהודה Jos 7^{16} (J), 1 K 12^{20} 2 K 17^{18} ψ 78^{68}; מַטֵּה בְנֵי יהודה Jos $15^{1.20.21}$ 21^{9} (all P), 1 Ch 6^{50}; elsewhere מַטֵּה יהודה Ex 31^{2} 35^{30} 38^{22} Nu 1^{27} 7^{12} 13^{6} 34^{19} Jos $7^{1.18}$ 21^{4} (all P); איש יהודה Ju 15^{10}+; אנשי יהודה 2 S 2^{4}+, (cf. *amelûti* [*sabê*] *Ia-u-du* Tel el-Amarna No. 39 Jastr$^{JBL\ xii, 1893, 64}$). **3.** *nation*, of southern kingdom under dynasty of David, as distinguished from northern kingdom of Ephraim or Israel: Ho 4^{15} Je 2^{28} 2 Ch 12^{12}+; of the returned exiles Ne 4^{4}; עַם יהודה 2 K 14^{21}=2 Ch 26^{1}, Je $25^{1.2}$ Ezr 4^{4}; בְּנֵי יהודה Ho 2^{2} Je 7^{30} 2 Ch 13^{18} 25^{12} 28^{10}; בֵּית יהודה Ho 1^{7} Je 3^{18} Ez 4^{6}+; מַלְכוּת יהודה 2 Ch 11^{17}; personified, בַּת י׳ La 1^{15} $2^{2.5}$. **4.** Levite, Ezra's time, Ezr 10^{23}. **5.** an overseer of Jerus. Ne 11^{9}. **6.** Levite musician Ne 12^{8}. **7.** priest Ne 12^{36}.

II. n.pr.terr. *land of Judah*, **f.** Is 7^{6} Je 23^{6}=33^{16}, Jo 4^{30} ψ 114^{2}+; ארץ יְהוּדָה 1 S 22^{5} 2 K 23^{24}+; אדמת יהודה Is 19^{17}; עָרֵי יהודה 2 S 2^{1} 1 K 12^{17} 2 K 18^{13} $23^{5.8}$ Is 40^{9} 44^{26} Zc 1^{12} ψ 69^{36} La 5^{11}; elsewhere 15 t. Chr., 23 t. Jer.; בִּיהודה Ju 15^{9}+; מיהודה 1 K 13^{1}+; הר יהודה *the hill-country of Judah* Jos 11^{21} (D), 20^{7} 21^{11} (P), 2 Ch 27^{4}; נֶגֶב יהודה *the south* (*country*) *of Judah* 1 S 27^{10} 2 S 24^{7}; מדבר יהודה Ju 1^{16} ψ 63^{1} (title).

†I. יְהוּדִי **adj.gent. Jewish,** as subst. a **Jew**;—**adj.m.** אִישׁ יְהוּדִי Zc 8^{23}; pl. אֲנָשִׁים יְהוּדִים *Jewish men* Je 43^{9} Est 2^{5}; as subst. Je 34^{9} Est 3^{4}; 3064
הַיְּהוּדִי *the Jew* Est 5^{13} 6^{10} 8^{7} $9^{29.31}$ 10^{3}; *f.* הַיְהֻדִיָּה 3057
the Jewess 1 Ch 4^{18}; pl. *Jews* יְהוּדִים Je $52^{28.30}$; הַיְּהוּדִים *the Jews* 2 K 16^{6} 25^{25} Je 32^{12} 38^{19} $40^{11.12}$ 41^{3} 44^{1} Ne 1^{2} 2^{16} $3^{33.34}$ 4^{6} $5^{1.8.17}$ 6^{6} 13^{23} Est $3^{6.10.13}$ $4^{3.13.14.16}$ 6^{13} $8^{3.5.8.9.9.11.16.17.17}$ $9^{1.1.2.3.5.6.10.12.13.16.19.20.22.23.24.24.25.27.28.30}$ 10^{3}; הַיְּהוּדִיִּים Est 4^{7} $8^{1.7.13}$ $9^{15.18}$

†I. יְהוּדִית **adj.gent., f.** of foregoing, but only as **adv. in Jewish**=*in the Jewish language* 2 K $18^{26.28}$=Is $36^{11.13}$=2 Ch 32^{18}; Ne 13^{24}. 3066

†II. יְהוּדִי **n.pr.m.** officer of Jehoiakim Je $36^{14.21.21.23}$, 𝔊 Ιουδιν (perh. orig. appell. *Jewish*, of one not so by ancestry, v. Gf Gie). 3065

†II. יְהוּדִית **n.pr.f.** (relation to foregoing names obscure)—wife of Esau Gn 26^{34}, daughter of בְּאֵרִי the Hittite (not named Gn 36^{1}); 𝔊 Ιουδιν. 3067

†[יהד] **vb.denom. Hithp. become a Jew** —only pt. מִתְיַהֲדִים Est 8^{17} many of the people of the land *were becoming Jews.* 3054

יהוה **n.pr.dei,** v. sub הוה p. 217 ff. 3068-69

יְהוּכַל **n.pr.m.** v. sub יהוה p. 220 supr. 3081

יְהַלֶּלְאֵל v. sub II. הלל p. 239^{b} supr. 3094

יַהֲלֹם v. sub הלם p. 240^{b} supr. 3095

יהץ (√ of foll.; Ar. وَهَصَ *break, split; valide calcavit;* وَهْصَةٌ *terra depressa* et *rotunda*).

†יַהַץ, יַ֫הְצָה **n.pr.loc.** in Moab, site unknown (MI$^{19.20}$ יהץ)—יהץ Is 15^{4} Je 48^{34}; c. ה loc. יַ֫הְצָה, on border of territory of Amorites (under Sihon) Nu 21^{23} Dt 2^{32}; also בְּיַ֫הְצָה Ju 11^{20}; called יַ֫הְצָה Jos 13^{18} (assigned to Reuben); יַ֫הְצָה 1 Ch 6^{63} (Levit. city in Reuben), Je 48^{21}. 3096

יהר (√ of foll.; cf. NH יָהַר Hithp. *shew oneself haughty,* adj. יָהִיר; Aram. יְהַר Pa. *be haughty,* adj. יְהִירָא; cf. Ar. اِسْتَيْهَرَ *be insane*).

†יָהִיר **adj. proud, haughty,** זֵד יָהִיר לֵץ שְׁמוֹ Pr 21^{24} *a presumptuous man,* (who is) *haughty, scoffer is his name* (+ עוֹשֶׂה בְּעֶבְרַת זָדוֹן); גֶּבֶר יָהִיר וְלֹא יִנְוֶה Hb 2^{5}. 3093

3068 יוֹ = יְהוֹ **n.pr.** cpd. with, v. sub יהוה supr.
3097, etc. p. 222 :—viz. יוֹאָב ,יוֹאָח ,יוֹאָחָז ,יוֹאֵל ,יוֹאָשׁ ,יוֹיָכִין, יוֹיָקִים ,יוֹיָרִיב ,יוֹעֵד ,יוֹעָשׁ ,יוֹקִים ,יוֹרָם ,יוֹתָם, etc. p. 219-22

3102 †יוֹב **n.pr.m.** son of Issachar Gn 46^{13}, but rd. rather יָשׁוּב as Sam. Nu 26^{24} 1 Ch 7^{1} (Qr) 𝔊 Ol al.; 𝔊 Ιασουφ, 𝔊L Ιασουβ.

3103-05 יוֹבָב **n.pr.** v. יבב ; יוֹבֵל ,יוּבַל v. יבל. p. 384-85

3109 †יוֹחָא **n.pr.m.** (√ & mng. dub.; ?=יוֹאָח)—**1.** a Benjamite 1 Ch 8^{16}. **2.** one of David's heroes 1 Ch 11^{45}.

3194 יוּטָּה = יֻטָּה q.v. sub נטה. p. 641

3116 יוּכַל **n.pr.m.** v. יְהוּכַל sub יהוה supr. p. 220.

3117 יוֹם$_{2285}$ **n.m.** $^{Gn\ 1,5}$ day (NH *id.*; Aram. יוֹמָא, ܝܰܘܡܳܐ; Ph. ים; MI^{5} ימן, sf. ימי l.$^{6.9.33}$, pl. cstr. ימי l.^{8}, sf. 3 ms. ימה l.^{8}; SI^{3} ים; Zinj. יום DHM$^{Sendsch.\ Gloss}$; Palm. יום ים Vog$^{No.\ 123\ a,\ Oxon.\ iii}$; Ar. يَوْمٌ; Eth. **ዕለት**: Sab. יום, ים Mordt$^{ZMG\ 1876,\ 29}$, יומה DHM$^{ZMG\ 1883,\ 328}$ SabDenkm^{61}; As. *ummu, ûmu* COT^{Gloss}; deriv. unknown; on √ and relation of יום to Ph. ימם, Aram. ימם, ܝܰܘܡܳܬܳܐ, v. Nö$^{ZMG\ 1886,\ 721}$ Ba$^{ZMG\ 1887,\ 632\ f.}$) —יוֹם abs. Gn 1^{5}+; cstr. Gn 2^{4}+; sf. יוֹמְךָ Je 50^{31}; יוֹמוֹ Ex 5^{13}+22 t.; יוֹמָם Je 50^{27} Ez 21^{34}; du. †יוֹמַיִם Ex 21^{21}; יוֹמַיִם Ex 16^{29} Nu 11^{19}; יֹמַיִם 9^{22}; יָמִין ;יֹמָיִם Ho 6^{2}†; pl. יָמִים Gn 4^{3}+; יָמִם Nu 6^{5}; מִיָּמִים יָמִימָה (Aram. form; Ges$^{§87,1\,a}$) Dn 12^{13}; Ex 13^{10}+4 t.; cstr. יְמֵי Gn 3^{14}+; †יְמוֹת Dt 32^{7} ψ 90^{15}†; sf. יָמַי Jb 7^{6}+9 t.; יָמָי Gn 29^{21}+8 t.; יָמֵינוּ Je 35^{8}+7 t., etc.;—**1.** *day*, opp. night, Gn 7$^{4.12}$ 8^{22} (all J), 31$^{39.40}$ (E), Ex 24^{18} 34^{28} Nu 11$^{32.32}$ Jos 10^{13} (all JE), Dt 9$^{9.11.18.25}$ 10^{10} (D), Gn 1$^{5.14.16.18}$ (P), 1 S 30^{12} Ju 19$^{8.9.9.11}$ Am 5^{8} 1 K 8^{29} 19^{8} Ne 4^{16} Ec 8^{16}; ‖ לִפְנֵי בוֹא־הַשֶּׁמֶשׁ 2 S 3^{35}; חֹם הַיּ׳ Gn 18^{1} (J) *the heat of the day* 1 S 11^{11} 2 S 4^{5}; עוֹד הַיּ׳ גָּדוֹל Gn 29^{7} (J) *the day is still high*, not near its end; רוּחַ הַיּ׳ 3^{8} *cool of the day;* מִן־הָאוֹר עַד־מַחֲצִית הַיּ׳ Ne 8^{3} *from dawn until mid-day;* so also prob. of mid-day הוֹלֵךְ וָאוֹר עַד־נְכוֹן הַיּוֹם Pr 4^{18} *growing lighter and lighter until the full day;* note phr. in Ju 19, עַד־נְטוֹת הַיּ׳ Ju 19^{8} *until the declining of the day;* רָפָה הַיּ׳ לַעֲרוֹב v^{9} *the day hath sunk down to become evening;* חֲנוֹת הַיּ׳ v^{9} *the declining of the day;* הַיּ׳ רַד מְאֹד v^{11} *the day has gone down exceedingly* (is far spent).

2. *Day* as division of time: **a.** *working-day* Ex 20$^{9.10}$ (E)=Dt 5^{13}, Ex 16$^{26.30.30}$ (J), 23^{12} (JE), 31^{15} (P), Lv 23^{3} (H); יְמֵי הַמַּעֲשֶׂה Ez 46^{1}. **b.** דֶּרֶךְ יוֹם *a day's journey* Nu 11$^{31.31}$ (JE), 1 K 19^{4}; מַהֲלַךְ יוֹם אֶחָד Jon 3^{4}; דֶּרֶךְ שְׁלֹשֶׁת יָמִים *a three days' journey* Gn 30^{36} Ex 3^{18} 5^{3} 8^{23} (all J), Nu 10$^{33.33}$ (JE), 33^{8} (P); מַהֲלַךְ שְׁלֹשֶׁת יָמִים Jon 3^{3}; so *seven days' journey* Gn 31^{23} (E), 2 K 3^{9}; without דֶּרֶךְ etc., שְׁלֹשֶׁת יָמִים Ex 15^{22} (E) they went *three days*, etc. **c.** to denote duration of various other acts or states: *seven days* Gn 7$^{4.10}$ 8$^{10.12}$; *forty days* 7^{17} 8^{6} (all J); 150 *days* 7^{24} 8^{3} (both P), 1 S 25^{38} 1 K 8$^{65.65}$ Je 42^{7} Ez 4$^{5.6}$ 1 Ch 9^{25} Ezr 6^{22} Est 1^{4} etc. In Est 4^{16} **1** & **2** are combined: וְאַל־תִּשְׁתּוּ שְׁלֹשֶׁת יָמִים לַיְלָה וָיוֹם *do not eat and do not drink for three days, night or day* (v. Zc 14^{7} sub **3** infr.) **d.** day as defined by *evening and morning* Gn 1$^{5.8.13.19.23.31}$ (all P; cf. further בֹּקֶר, עֶרֶב); v. also 2$^{2.2.3}$ (P), Ex 20$^{11.11}$ (E), 32$^{17.17}$ (P). **e.** *day* of month (c. num. ordin.), chiefly P and late: Gn 7^{11} 8$^{4.14}$ Ex 12$^{6.18.18}$+, 1 K 12$^{32.33}$ Ez 45$^{21.25}$ Zc 1^{7} Hg 1$^{1.15.18}$ 2 Ch 29$^{17.17}$ Ezr 3^{6} Ne 8^{2} 9^{1} Dn 10^{4} Est 3^{12} 9^{1}+; (יוֹם oft. om. e.g. Gn 8$^{5.13}$ Ex 12^{10} 2 K 25$^{1.3}$ Ez 1$^{1.2}$ Hg 2$^{1.20}$ Zc 7^{1} 2 Ch 3^{2} Ezr 6^{19} Est 3^{13}, etc.) **f.** יוֹם defined by subst., inf., or other cl.: (1) cstr. יוֹם הַשֶּׁלֶג = *the snowy day* 2 S 23^{20}=1 Ch 11^{22}; יוֹם סַגְרִיר Pr 27^{15}=*rainy d.;* יוֹם קָרָה 25^{20}=*cold d.;* (so,=*time* יוֹם צָרָתִי Gn 35^{3} (E) *d. of my distress;* Je 18^{17} La 1^{7} Pr 24^{10} 25^{19} 27^{10}); יוֹם מוֹתוֹ etc. Ju 13^{7} 2 S 6^{23} 2 K 15^{5} +oft.; cf. יוֹם הֻלֶּדֶת אֶת־פַּרְעֹה Gn 40^{20} (E) = *Pharaoh's birthday;* כְּיוֹם הִוָּלְדָהּ Ho 2^{5} cf. Ec 7^{1} (v. also **7 d** infr.; cf. יוֹמוֹ Jb 3^{1}), יוֹם חֲתֻנָּתוֹ Ct 3^{11}; of day emphat. characterized by proph. and others יוֹם מְהוּמָה וּמְבוּסָה וּמְבוּכָה Is 22^{5} (v. מְהוּמָה sub הום); יוֹם צָרָה וְתוֹכֵחָה וּנְאָצָה 37^{3}=2 K 19^{3}; on the other hand יוֹם רָצוֹן לי׳ Is 58^{5} *a day of acceptableness to* י׳; pl. sq. subst. יְמֵי שָׂכִיר Lv 25^{50} (H) *the days of an hireling;* יְמֵי (מִלֻּאֵיכֶם) Lv 8^{33} Nu 6^{13}; sq. rel. cl. אָרוּר הַיּוֹם אֲשֶׁר יֻלַּדְתִּי בּוֹ יוֹם אֲשֶׁר־יְלָדַתְנִי אִמִּי וגו׳ Je 20^{14} cf. Jb 3^{3}; also ψ 118^{24} (v. **i**). **g.** particular days defined by n.pr.loc.: יוֹם יִזְרְעֶאל Ho 2^{2} i.e. of judgment, with implied restoration; v. also Is 9^{3} Ez 30^{9}; יְמֵי הַגִּבְעָה Ho 9^{9} 10^{9}, i.e. of the outrage at Gibeah (Ju 19$^{22\,ff.}$); יוֹם ירושלם ψ 137^{7} i.e. of Jerusalem's calamity, cf. Je 50$^{27.31}$. **h.** c. sf., *thy, his,* or *their day*, in sense of (1) day of disaster or death: †בָּא יוֹמְךָ Je 50^{31} *thy day has come;* אוֹ יוֹמוֹ יָבוֹא וָמֵת 1 S 26^{10}; יוֹמוֹ in this sense also Ez 21^{30} ψ 37^{13} Jb 18^{20}; †בָּא יוֹמָם Je 50^{27} Ez 21^{34}. **i.** specif. a holy day: יוֹם הַשַּׁבָּת *the sabbath day* (v. also שַׁבָּת), Ex 20$^{8.11}$ (E) =Dt 5$^{12.15}$, Ex 31^{15} 35^{3}+; = יוֹם קָדְשִׁי Is 58^{13}; repetition בְּיוֹם הַשַּׁבָּת בְּיוֹם הַשַּׁבָּת Lv 24^{8} *every sabbath day;* also †יוֹם הַכִּפֻּרִים Lv 23^{27} 25^{9}; יוֹם כִּפֻּרִים 23^{28}; יוֹם הַבִּכּוּרִים Nu 28^{26}; יוֹם חַגֵּנוּ ψ 81^{4}; יוֹם מַלְכֵּנוּ Ho 7^{5}; also of false gods, יְמֵי הַבְּעָלִים 2^{11}.

3. יוֹם י׳ *day of Yahweh*, chiefly as time of his coming in judgment, involving often blessedness for righteous (v. RS$^{Proph. 396 f.}$Dr$^{Is 28}$); Am $5^{18.18.20}$ Is 2^{12} $13^{6.9}$ Zp 1^{7} (cf. v^{8}), v$^{14.14}$ (cf. v$^{15.16}$), Je 46^{10} Ez 13^{5} 30^{3} (cf. 36^{33} $39^{8.11.13}$), Ob ^{15} Zc 14^{1} Mal 3^{23} (cf. Zc 14^{7} Mal $3^{2.17.19.19.21}$), Jo 1^{15} $2^{1.11}$ (cf. v$^{2.2}$), 3^{4} 4^{14}; יוֹם עֶבְרַת י׳ Zp 1^{18}; יוֹם עֶבְרָה Pr 11^{4}; יוֹם חֲרוֹן אַפּוֹ Is 13^{13} La 1^{12}; יוֹם נָקָם Is 34^{8} 61^{2} 63^{4}; יוֹם אַפּוֹ Je 46^{10}; יוֹם אַף י׳ Zp $2^{2.3}$ La 2^{22}; יוֹם נְקָמָה La 2^{1}; cf. also Zc 14^{7} (where senses of **1** and **2** are combined, cf. Est 4^{16} **2 c** supr.); וְהָיָה יוֹם־ אֶחָד הוּא יִוָּדַע לי׳ לֹא יוֹם וְלֹא לָיְלָה *but there shall be one day, known shall it be of* י׳, *not day and not night;* cf. also ביום ההוא **7 g** infr.

4. Pl. *days* of any one: **a.** = his life, his age Gn 6^{3} (J), Dt $22^{19.29}$ 23^{7} Jos $24^{31.31}$ (D), Ju $2^{7.7.18}$ 1 S 25^{28}, etc.; Gn $5^{4.8.11}$ 9^{29} 11^{32} (all P), Jb $7^{1.1.6.16}$ 8^{9} ψ $39^{5.6}$ $90^{9.10.12.14}$ 103^{15}; כָּל־יְמֵי חַיֶּיךָ Gn $3^{14.17}$ (J), ψ 23^{6}, so Pr 31^{12}; יְמֵי שְׁנֵי חַיִּים 2 S 19^{35} Gn 25^{7} $47^{8.9}$ (all P); יְמֵי חַיָּיו Ec $5^{17.19}$; יְמֵי שָׁנָיו 6^{3}; מִסְפַּר יְמֵי חַיֵּיהֶם Ec 2^{3}; יְמֵי שְׁנוֹתֵינוּ ψ 90^{10}; מִסְפַּר יְמֵי חַיֵּי הֶבְלוֹ 6^{12} *the number of the days of the years of his vanity*, i.e. his empty, fleeting years; כָּל־הַיָּמִים אֲשֶׁר־הֵם חַיִּים עַל־פְּנֵי הָאֲדָמָה 1 K 8^{40}; יָמִים רַבִּים *long life* 1 K 3^{11} = 2 Ch 1^{11}; בָּא בַּיָּמִים *advanced in days* = of advanced age Gn 18^{11} 24^{1} (both J), Jos $13^{1.1}$ (JE), $23^{1.2}$ (D), 1 K 1^{1}; מִיָּמָיו 1 K 1^{6} *from his* (earliest) *days*, so מִיָּמֶיךָ 1 S 25^{28} (v. Dr), Jb 38^{12}; שְׂבַע יָמִים Jb 42^{17} 1 K 8^{40}; יַאֲרִכוּן יָמֶיךָ Ex 20^{12} (JE) *that thy days may be long* = Dt 5^{16}, v. further ארך; יָמִים עַל־יְמֵי־מֶלֶךְ תּוֹסִיף ψ 61^{7} i.e. prolong the king's life; *outlive* is הֶאֱרִיךְ יָמִים אַחֲרֵי Jos 24^{31} (D), Ju 2^{7}; אֹרֶךְ יָמִים וּשְׁנוֹת חַיִּים Pr 3^{2} *length of days and years of life;* אֹרֶךְ יָמִים v^{16}; כְּיָמֶיךָ דבאך Dt 33^{25} *according to* (the length of) *thy life shall be* [*thy strength*? rd. רבאך?] v. Di VB; rarely sg. e.g. קְשֵׁה־ יוֹם Jb 30^{25} *one hard of day*, i.e. whose day (= *life*) was hard; of life as approaching its end, וַיִּקְרְבוּ יְמֵי ישראל לָמוּת Gn 47^{29} (J) *and the days of Israel drew near for dying*, so Dt 31^{14} 1 K 2^{1} (cf. Jb $7^{6.16}$ 8^{9} Ec 2^{3} supr.) **b.** (*in*) *the days of* (i.e. life-time, reign, or activity of) Gn 10^{25} (J), 14^{1} Ju $5^{6.6}$ 8^{28} 2 S 21^{1} 1 K 16^{34} $21^{29.29}$ 22^{47} 2 K 20^{19} 2 Ch 13^{20} 35^{18} + oft. (so MI$^{6.8.8.9.33}$). **c.** hence in phr. סֵפֶר דִּבְרֵי הַיָּמִים לְ 1 K $14^{19.29}$ + 31 t. K, Ne 12^{23} Est 2^{23} 10^{2}; מִסְפַּר דִּבְרֵי הַיָּמִים 1 Ch 27^{24}; סֵפֶר הַזִּכְרֹנוֹת דִּבְרֵי הַיָּמִים Est 6^{1}.

5. *Days:* **a.** indef.: יָמִים אֲחָדִים *some days, a few days* †Gn 27^{44} (J), 29^{20} (E), Dn 11^{20}; יָמִים alone 40^{4} (E) they were *days* (a certain time) in the prison 1 K 17^{15} Ne 1^{4}; עוּל יָמִים Is 65^{20} *a suckling of* (a few) *days;* מִיָּמִים Ju 11^{4} *after a time*, 15^{1}; so מִקֵּץ יָמִים Gn 4^{3} (J) *after the end of days*, 1 K 17^{7}; יוֹם אוֹ יוֹמַיִם Ex 21^{21} (JE) *a day or two.* יָמִים אוֹ עָשׂוֹר Gn 24^{55} (J) *some days, or ten* (days or a dekad; on question of txt. v. Di). **b.** of long time, זֶה יָמִים אוֹ זֶה שָׁנִים 1 S 29^{3} *these days or these years;* אוֹ יֹמַיִם אוֹ חֹדֶשׁ אוֹ יָמִים Nu 9^{22} (P) *whether two days or a month or days* (an indefinitely long period); יָמִים רַבִּים *many days* Gn 21^{34} (JE) 37^{34} (J) +; וַיִּרְבּוּ הַיָּמִים וגו׳ Gn 38^{12} (J) *and the days were multiplied* (= time passed) and Judah's wife died, 1 S 7^{2}; אָֽרְכוּ לוֹ שָׁם הַיָּמִים Gn 26^{8} (J) *the days were long to him there* = *he had been there a long time;* בְּהַאֲרִיךְ הֶעָנָן... יָמִים רַבִּים Nu 9^{19} (P) *when the cloud prolonged many days* (remained a long time) upon the tabern.—Vid. also **6** infr. **c.** *days of old, former* or *ancient times* (esp. of early period of Isr. hist.): יְמוֹת עוֹלָם Dt 32^{7} (poem); יְמֵי עולם Mi 5^{1} 7^{14} Is $63^{9.11}$; יְמֵי קֶדֶם Mi 7^{20}; יָמִים מִקֶּדֶם ψ 77^{6} 143^{5}; cf. הַיָּמִים הָרִאשֹׁנִים Ec 7^{10}; *coming days* הַיָּמִים הַבָּאִים Ec 2^{16}; *coming time* יוֹם אַחֲרוֹן Pr 31^{25}; esp. (ב)אַחֲרִית הַיָּמִים v. p. 31 supr.; לְקֵץ הַיָּמִין Dn 12^{13}.

6. יוֹם = *time;* **a.** vividly in gen. sense (v. also **5** supr.): *time* of harvest Pr 25^{13}; usu. יְמֵי Gn 30^{14} (J), Jos 3^{15} Nu $13^{20.20}$ (all JE), Ju 15^{1} 2 S 21^{9}; *proper time* for paying wages Dt 24^{15} cf. Jb 14^{6}; time of parturition וַיִּמְלְאוּ יָמֶיהָ לָלֶדֶת Gn 25^{24}. **b.** appos. to other expr. of time (Dr$^{§192(1)}$Da$^{Synt. §29.d}$): חֹדֶשׁ יָמִים *a month of time* Gn 29^{14} (J; lit. *a month, time*), Nu $11^{20.21}$ (JE); = יֶרַח יָמִים Dt 21^{13} 2 K 15^{13}; יָמִים ארבעה חדשים Ju 19^{2} *time, four months* (si vera l., v. 1 S 27^{7}); †(מִקֵּץ) שְׁנָתַיִם יָמִים Gn 41^{1} (E) *two years* (*of*) *time*, 2 S 13^{23} 14^{28} Je $28^{3.11}$; שְׁלֹשָׁה שָׁבֻעִים יָמִים Dn $10^{2.3}$ *three weeks* (*of*) *time.* **c.** pl. in specific sense, appar. = *year*, lit. יָמִים 1 S 27^{7} Lv 25^{29} (H); לַיָּמִים Ju 17^{10}; זֶבַח הַיָּמִים 1 S 1^{21} 2^{19} 20^{6}; יָמִים וארבעה חדשים 27^{7} = *a year and four months* (cf. Ju 19^{2} supr. **b**); מִיָּמִים יָמִ֫ימָה = *from year to year, yearly* Ex 13^{10} (JE), Ju 11^{40} (cf. v^{b}), 21^{19} 1 S 1^{3} 2^{19}; מִקֵּץ יָמִים לַיָּמִים 2 S 14^{26}; יֹמַיִם אוֹ חֹדֶשׁ אוֹ־יָמִים Nu 9^{22} (P); distrib. Nu $14^{34.34}$ (P), Ez $4^{6.6}$; וַיְהִי לְיָמִים מִיָּמִים וּכְעֵת צֵאת הַקֵּץ לְיָמִים שְׁנַיִם 2 Ch 21^{19} *and it came to pass at days from days* (= after some days) *even about the time of the outgoing of the end of two* (series of) *days* (i.e. prob. *years*, v. Be).

7. Phrases, without prep. and with, are: **a.** (1) הַיּוֹם = *to-day* Gn 4^{14} $31^{43.48}$ Ex 13^{4} (JE) + oft.; opp. תְּמוֹל *yesterday* Ex 5^{14} 1 S 20^{27}; opp. מָחָר

Ex 19^{10}; (2) †(בְּ)יוֹם מָחָר = *to-morrow* Gn 30^{33} Is 56^{12} Pr 27^{1}; (3) יוֹם אֶתְמוֹל ψ 90^{4}; (4) הַיּוֹם שְׁלֹשֶׁת הַיָּמִים 1 S 9^{20} *three days ago* (v. Dr); = הַיּוֹם שְׁלֹשָׁה 1 S 30^{13}; †(5) כַּיּוֹם Ju 13^{10} appar. = *the other day* (v. Be); (6) יוֹם אֶחָד no prep., emphat. = *in one day*, Gn 27^{45} Is 9^{13}; c. בְּ 10^{17} 47^{9}; *for, during, one day* Gn 33^{13} Nu 11^{19}; unemphat., *one day* (= *some day*) 1 S 27^{1}; יוֹם אֶחָד לִפְנֵי 9^{15} *one day, before* Saul came. †**b.** וַיְהִי הַיּוֹם וַ־ *and the day came, that* (or *when*) 1 S 1^{4} (v. Dr), 2 K 4$^{8.11.18}$ Jb 1$^{6.13}$ 2^{1}. **c.** הִנֵּה יָמִים בָּאִים *lo! days are coming*, when, etc.; esp. in Am Je: 1 S 2^{31} Am 4^{2} 8^{11} 9^{13} Is 39^{6} = 2 K 20^{17}, Je 7^{32} + 13 t. Je. **d.** יוֹם in cstr. bef. vbs., both literally, *the day of*, and (oft.) in gen. sense = *the time of* (forcible and pregn., representing the act vividly as that of a single day): (1) bef. inf., †(*a*) sg. without prep. אֶת־יוֹם צֵאתְךָ Dt 16^{3} and thou shalt remember *the day of thy going out* from the land of Egypt, Is 58^{5} Ez 39^{13} Mal 3^{2} cf. Ec 7^{1} (מִן compar.); (β) עַד־יוֹם Jos 6^{10} Ju 18^{30} + 5 t.; (γ) בְּיוֹם Gn 2$^{4.17}$ 3^{5} + 53 t.; †(δ) כְּיוֹם Ho 2$^{5.17}$ Zp 3^{8} Zc 14^{3}; †(ε) מִיּוֹם 1 S 7^{2} 8^{8} 29^{6} 2 S 13^{32} 2 K 8^{6} Dt 9^{24} Lv 23^{15} Ez 28^{15}; †(ζ) לְמִיּוֹם Ju 19^{30} 2 S 7^{6} Is 7^{17}; †(2) pl. cstr. bef. inf.: (*a*) כָּל־יְמֵי Ju 18^{31} 1 S 22^{4} 25$^{7.16}$ Lv 26$^{34.35}$ Nu 6^{6} 2 Ch 36^{21}; (β) בִּימֵי Ru 1^{1} 2 Ch 26^{5}; (γ) כִּימֵי Mi 7^{15}; †(3) sg. cstr. c. prep. bef. finite vb. in pf.: (*a*) cf. בְּ, בְּיוֹם דִּבֶּר י׳ Ex 6^{28} *in the day* (*when*) י׳ *spoke*, so Nu 3^{1} Dt 4^{15}; also Lv 7^{35} 2 S 22^{1} = ψ 18^{1}, ψ 138^{3} Zc 8^{9}; (β) מִיּוֹם Je 36^{2}; †(4) sg. cstr. bef. impf.: בְּיוֹם אֶקְרָא ψ 56^{10} *in the day* (*when*) *I cry*, 103^{3} La 5^{7}; also without בְּ, יוֹם אִירָא ψ 56^{4} (*at the*) *time* (*when*) *I am afraid*; †(5) pl. cstr. bef. pf.: כָּל־יְמֵי הִתְהַלַּכְנוּ אִתָּם 1 S 25^{15}, so Lv 14^{46} (prob., v. Di); כִּימוֹת ψ 90^{15}; †(6) pl. cstr. bef. impf.: כִּימֵי אֱלוֹהַּ יִשְׁמְרֵנִי Jb 29^{2}; †(7) מִיּוֹם cstr. bef. rel. cl.: מִיּוֹם אֲשֶׁר הָיִיתִי לְפָנֶיךָ 1 S 29^{8} *since the day when* (= *as long as*) *I have been before thee*, Ne 5^{14}; †(8) pl. cstr. bef. rel. cl. כָּל־יְמֵי אֲשֶׁר יִשְׁכֹּן Nu 9^{18} *as long as the cloud remained*, etc. **e.** (1) יוֹם יוֹם *day by day* Gn 39^{10} (J), Ex 16^{5} (P), Pr 8$^{30.34}$ ψ 61^{9} 68^{20} (+ Je 7^{25} ψ 13^{3} Lag, v. יוֹמָם); so (late) †לְיוֹם בְּיוֹם 2 Ch 24^{11}; †יוֹם בְּיוֹם 30^{21} Ne 8^{18}; †לְעֶת־יוֹם בְּיוֹם 1 Ch 12^{22}; עֹלַת יוֹם בְּיוֹם Ezr 3^{4}; †בִּדְבַר יוֹם בְּיוֹם 2 Ch 8^{13}; מִיּוֹם אֶל־יוֹם *from day to day* 1 Ch 16^{23} = מִיּוֹם לְיוֹם ψ 96^{2} (Est 3^{7} v. infr.); †יוֹם וָיוֹם Est 3^{4} (very late, v. וְ **1 i** (*b*), p. 253 supr. and Dr$^{\text{Intr. 505}}$); †בְּכָל־יוֹם וָיוֹם 2^{11}; †כְּיוֹם בְּיוֹם 1 S 18^{10} *as daily* = *according to daily habit*; (2) מִיּוֹם לְיוֹם Est 3^{7}, is in phr. of casting lots for *one day after another*; (מִיָּמִים יָמִ֫ימָה v. **6 c**); (3) of daily duties, observances, etc.: †דְּבַר יוֹם בְּיוֹמוֹ *each day's affair in its day* Ex 5$^{13.19}$ 16^{4} (all J), Lv 23^{37} (H), 1 K 8^{59} 2 K 25^{30} = Je 52^{34}, Ezr 3^{4} Ne 11^{23} 12^{47} Dn 1^{5}; לִדְבַר יוֹם בְּיוֹמוֹ 1 Ch 16^{37} 2 Ch 8^{14} 31^{16}. **f.** †כָּל־הַיָּמִים† = *always, continually*, Gn 43^{9} 44^{32} (both J), Dt 4^{40} 5^{26} 6^{24} 11^{1} 14^{23} 18^{5} 19^{9} 28$^{29.33}$ Jos 4^{24} (D), Ju 16^{16} 1 S 2$^{32.35}$ 18^{29} 23^{14} 28^{2} 2 S 13^{37} 19^{14} Je 31^{36} 32^{39} 33^{18} 35^{19} 1 K 5^{15} 9^{3} 11$^{36.39}$ 12^{7} 14^{30} 2 K 8^{19} 13^{3} 17^{37} 2 Ch 7^{16} 10^{7} 12^{15} 21^{7} Jb 1^{5}; also (only in proph. writers and in poetry) †כָּל־הַיּוֹם Gn 6^{5} (J), Ho 12^{2} Dt 28^{32} 33^{12} Je 20$^{7.8}$ Is 28^{24}, 51^{13} 52^{5} (both תָּמִיד כל־היום), 65$^{2.5}$ La 1^{13} 3$^{3.14.62}$ ψ 25^{5} 32^{3} 35^{28} 37^{26} 38$^{7.13}$ 42$^{4.11}$ 44$^{9.16.23}$ 52^{3} 56$^{2.3.6}$ 71$^{8.15.24}$ 72^{15} 73^{14} 74^{22} 86^{3} 88^{18} 89^{17} 102^{9} 119^{97} Pr 21^{26} 23^{17}. **g.** additional phr. c. בְּ = *on* a particular day: בַּיּוֹם הַחֲמִישִׁי Ju 19^{18}, so Gn 2$^{2.2}$ + oft.; בְּכָל־יוֹם *every day* ψ 7^{12} 88^{10} 145^{2}; בַּיּוֹם הַהוּא of definite time in past Gn 15^{18} 33^{16} + (v. also **3** supr.); cf. הַיּוֹם הַזֶּה (no prep.) Ex 13^{3} (JE); בַּיּוֹם הַהוּא of time defined in subsequent context, 1 S 3^{2} *at that time* when Eli was laid down, i.e. at the particular time of the foll. incident (= *at a certain time, on one particular day*; cf. Gn 39^{11} sub **h**; see Da$^{\text{Synt. §21. e. R. 1, 2}}$ and esp. Dr 1 S 1^{4} 19^{3}); בַּיּוֹם הַזֶּה Gn 7^{11} +; בְּעֶצֶם הַיּוֹם הַזֶּה *on this selfsame day* Gn 7^{13} + (v. עֶצֶם); בַּיּוֹם הַהוּא also of future 1 S 3^{12} Dt 31$^{17.17.18}$; and very oft. in proph., as formula in describing what is to come at time of future blessing, retribution, etc., Am 8$^{3.9}$ Ho 2$^{18.20.23}$ etc., esp. Is 2$^{11.17.20}$ 3$^{7.18}$ 4$^{1.2}$ + oft.; pl. בַּיָּמִים הָהֵם of past Gn 6^{4} (J), Ju 18$^{1.1}$ 19^{1} 21^{25} 1 S 3^{1} + oft.; of future Dt 17^{9} 19^{17} 26^{3}. **h.** c. כְּ: כַּיּוֹם *as* or *like the day* ψ 139^{12}; כַּיּוֹם הַהוּא Jos 10^{14}; כְּיוֹם Ho 2^{5} *as at the day of*; כְּיוֹם תָּמִים Jos 10^{13} *about a whole day*; †כַּיּוֹם lit. *at* (*about*) *to-day* = *now* (v. כְּ) 1 S 9^{27} 1 K 22^{5} = 2 Ch 18^{4} Is 58^{4}; so †כְּהַיּוֹם 1 S 9^{13} + v^{12} We Dr (for MT כי היום), Ne 5^{11}; †כַּיּוֹם = *at once, first of all* Gn 25$^{31.33}$ 1 S 2^{16} 1 K 1^{51}; oft. c. adj. pron. to point out agreement of result with promise or prediction, †כַּיּוֹם הַזֶּה *as* it is *at this day* Gn 50^{20} (E), 1 S 22$^{8.13}$, and esp. Dt Je and subseq. writings: Dt 2^{30} 4$^{20.38}$ 8^{18} 10^{15} 29^{27} Je 11^{5} 25^{18} (gloss, om. 𝔊, cf. esp. Kue$^{\text{Einl. §56. 1}}$), 32^{20} 44$^{6.23}$ 1 K 3^{6} 8$^{24.61}$ 1 Ch 28^{7} 2 Ch 6^{15} Dn 9$^{7.15}$; so †כְּהַיּוֹם הַזֶּה Dt 6^{24} Je 44^{22} Ezr 9$^{7.15}$ Ne 9^{10}; in Gn 39^{11} (J) this phr. = *on this particular day* (when the incident to be narrated occurred; cf. ביום ההוא **g** supr.) **i.** c. לְ: לְיוֹם *on, at* (lit. *with reference to*) †Ho 9$^{5.5}$ *what will ye do on the day of assembly*, etc., Is 10^{3}; לְיוֹם אֶחָד 1 K 5^{2}

bread *for one day;* הַמְּלָאכָה לֹא לְיוֹם אֶחָד וְלֹא לִשְׁנַיִם Ezr 10^{13}; distrib. phr. נָשִׂיא אֶחָד לַיּוֹם נָשִׂיא אֶחָד לַיּוֹם Nu 7^{11} (P), Jb 21$^{30.30}$; cf. לַיּוֹם Mal 1^{17}; לַיּוֹם *against*, i.e. in expectation of Ex 19^{11}, so לְיוֹם קְרָב Jb 38^{23} Pr 21^{31}; לְיוֹם קוּמִי alm.=*until* Zp 3^{8}; לִפְנֵי יוֹם Is 48^{7} *before to-day;* late phr. are †לְיָמִים מִיָּמִים 2 Ch 21^{19}=*in the course of time;* לְיָמִים רַבִּים Dn 8^{26} *at* (the end of) *many days;* לַיּוֹם=*for every day, daily,* †Ex 29$^{36.38}$ Nu 7$^{11.11}$ 28$^{3.24}$ 1 Ch 26$^{17.17}$ Je 37^{21} Ez 4^{10} 43^{25} 45$^{23.23}$ 46^{13}; לַיּוֹם in exclam. הָהּ לַיּ׳ Ez 30^{2} *alas for the day!* אֲהָהּ לַיּ׳ Jo 1^{15}. **j.** c. מִן: מִיּוֹם *since the day (time) of* (or *when*), Ex 10^{6} Lv 23^{15} Dt 9^{24} 1 S 7^{2} etc.; מִיּוֹם הראשון Ex 12^{15} *from the first day* (on om. of art. v. Dr$^{§ 209 (1)}$); מִימֵי השפטים 2 K 23^{22}, etc.; מִיּוֹם=*from to-day, from this day forth* Is 43^{13} Ez 48^{35}; מֵהַיּוֹם הַהוּא וָמָ֫עְלָה 1 S 16^{13} 30^{25} *from that day forward;* so מֵהַיּ׳ הַה׳ וְהָלְאָה 1 S 18^{9}; מִן־הַיּוֹם הַזֶּה וָמָ֫עְלָה Hg 2$^{15.18}$ *from this day onward* (v. Add. on p. 751^{b}); עַד־הַיּוֹם הַזֶּה Gn 47^{26} *until now;* מִיָּמִים רַבִּים *after many days* Jos 23^{1} Ez 38^{8}; מִיָּמִים *after a time* Ju 11^{4} 14^{8} 15^{1}; but usu. מִקֵּץ י׳, v. קֵץ; מִיֹּמָיִם Ho 6^{2} *after two days;*—מִיָּמִים יָמִ֫ימָה v. **e** (4) supr. †**k.** c. לְמִן (v. לְ *ad fin.*): לְמִן הַיּוֹם אֲשֶׁר Dt 4^{32} 9^{7} 2 S 7^{11} Je 7^{25} 32^{31} Hg 2^{18}; twice sq. inf. appos. Ex 9^{18} 2 S 19^{25} (cf. also 2 Ch 8^{16}; v. Dr$^{Sm. \& § 190, Obs.}$); לְמִימֵי קֶדֶם: לְמִ׳ 2 K 19^{25} *since days of old=long ago,* cf. Mal 3^{7} *since the days of your fathers.*† **l.** עַד (ה)יום: עַד יוֹם הָאֶחָד וגו׳ Ex 12^{18} *until the 21st day,* Lv 19^{6}+; עַד־יוֹם מוֹתוֹ Ju 13^{7} 1 S 15^{35} 2 S 6^{23}+, etc., v. also (sq. inf.) **c** supr.; עַד־הַיּוֹם *until to-day,* denoting esp. permanence of a name or situation, or of result of an event, †Gn 19$^{37.38}$ (J), 35^{20} (E), 2 K 10^{27} Ez 20^{31}†; more often עַד־הַיּוֹם הַזֶּה *until this day* Gn 26^{33} (J), 32^{33} (P or R), 47^{26} (J), 48^{15} (E), Ex 10^{6} Nu 22^{30} (both J), Dt 2^{22} 3^{14} 10^{8} 11^{4} 29^{3} 34^{6} Jos 4^{9} 5^{9} 6^{25} 7$^{26.26}$ 8$^{28.29}$ 9^{27} 13^{13} 14^{14} 15^{63} 16^{10} (all JE), 22^{3} (D), v^{17} (P), 23$^{8.9}$ (D), Ju 1$^{21.26}$ 6^{24} 10^{4} 15^{19} 18^{12} 19^{30} 1 S 5^{5} 6^{18} 8^{8} 12^{2} 27^{6} 29$^{3.6.8}$ 30^{25} 2 S 4^{3} 6^{8} = 1 Ch 13^{11}, 2 S 7^{6}=1 Ch 17^{5}, 2 S 18^{18}+oft.; עַד־עֶצֶם הַיּוֹם הַזֶּה †Jos 10^{27} (JE), Ez 2^{3} (cf. Lv 23^{14} H); עַד־הַיּוֹם הַהוּא †Ju 18^{1} Ne 8^{17}. **m.** once עַל־יוֹם טוֹב 1 S 25^{8} *upon a good day,* i.e. a day of social cheerfulness, feasting, rejoicing (c. rare עַל temp. cf. Dr; יוֹם טוֹב also Est 8^{17} 9$^{19.22}$, v. טוֹב **adj.**)

3119 יוֹמָם $_{51}$ **subst.** and **adv.** daytime, by day (cf. Aram. יְמָמָא, ܐܺܝܡܳܡܳܐ *day* (as opp. to *night*); 𝔗 יְמָם *by day;* perh. Ph. יממ (in dates, before num.), CIS$^{I. i. 10. 1 (see note)}$; so Nö$^{ZDMG 1886, 721}$: on ־ָם, v. sub חִנָּם)—**1. subst.** *daytime* (rare) Je 15^{9} בעוד יומם while it is yet *daytime,* 33^{20b} לְבִלְתִּי הֱיוֹת יומם ולילה *daytime* and night, v^{25} בְּרִיתִי י׳ ולילה (? rd. יום as v^{20a}); Ez 30^{16} צָרֵי יוֹמָם foes of *daytime,* i.e. coming by day (cf. Je 15^{8}; but text appar. defective, v. 𝔊 Sm); once (late) בְּיוֹמָם (cf. 𝔗 בִּימָם 1 S 25^{16} Jb 5^{14}), Ne 9^{19} (varied from Ex 13^{21} Dt 1^{33} יומם).—Nu 9^{21} the sense required is (during) *a day* and a night; rd. prob. יוֹם. **2. adv.** *in the daytime, by day,* Nu 10^{34} Jb 24^{16} (but v. חִתֵּם), Is 4^{6} Ez 12$^{3.4.7}$; mostly c. לַיְלָה, and then oft. poet.=*continually:* so יוֹמָם וָלַיְלָה Ex 13^{21} Jos 1^{8} 1 K 8^{59} ψ 1^{2} 32^{4}+, לַיְלָה וְיוֹמָם †Dt 28^{66} Is 34^{10} Je 14^{17}, in parallel clauses (esp. in poetry) 2 S 21^{10} Is 21^{8} Je 31^{35} ψ 22^{3} 42^{9} 91^{5} 121^{6}+. ψ 13^{3} *by day* yields a lame sense: either add וָלַיְלָה (𝔊 Del Gr Ch), or rd. יֹם יֹם (יום יום) Lag$^{Nov. Psalt. Gr. Ed. Spec. 13}$ Now.

I. יון (√ of foll.; meaning unknown).

†[יָוֵן] **n.[m.]** mire;—abs. מִטִּיט הַיָּוֵן ψ 40^{3}; 3121
cstr. טָבַעְתִּי בִּיוֵן מְצוּלָה 69^{3}.

II. [יון] (√ of foll., mng. unknown; יוֹנָה acc. to Lag$^{Armen. Stud. 7. 53; M. i. 228}$=Pers. *wanâ*, but improb.; Sta$^{§ 259 a}$ conject. יוֹנָה to be fr. אָנָה *mourn,* so Dl$^{Pa 157}$).

†I. יוֹנָה **n.f.** dove (NH *id.;* Aram. *id.,* 3123
ܝܰܘܢܳܐ)—abs. יוֹנָה Gn 8^{8}+20 t.; cstr. יוֹנַת ψ 56^{1}; sf. יוֹנָתִי Ct 2^{14}+2 t.; pl. יוֹנִים Na 2^{8}+6 t.; cstr. יוֹנֵי Ez 7^{16} (v. infr.);—*dove* Gn 8$^{8.9.10.11.12}$ (all J); oft. of offerings, בֶּן־יוֹנָה Lv 12^{6} (P; an individual of the species; || תֹּר); (תֹּרִים ||) בְּנֵי (ה)יוֹנִים 1^{14} 5$^{7.11}$ 12^{8} 14$^{22.30}$ 15$^{14.29}$ Nu 6^{10} (all P); חֲרֵי יוֹנִים *dove's dung* 2 K 6^{25} (Kt, yet v. Gei$^{Urschrift 409}$); in various similes: Ephr. is כְּיוֹנָה פוֹתָה *like a silly dove* Ho 7^{11} (allowing itself to be snared); sim. of return of exiles, like eager flight of doves 11^{11}, of ships with white outspread sails Is 60^{8}; אֵבֶר כַּיּוֹנָה ψ 55^{7}; v. also כַּנְפֵי יוֹנָה 68^{14}; sim. of fugitive Moab Je 48^{28}; also כְּיוֹנֵי הַגֵּאָיוֹת Ez 7^{16} *like the doves of the valleys* (but on txt. v. Co, who emends כיונים הוגיות, but regards phr. as gloss); sim. of mourning כְּקוֹל יוֹנִים Na 2^{8}; without קוֹל, הגה כיונים Is 38^{14} 59^{11} (from mournful note); fig. of beauty (only Ct): עֵינַיִךְ יוֹנִים *thine eyes are* (those of) *doves* Ct 1^{15} 4^{1}, v. also v^{12}; term of endearment, יוֹנָתִי *my dove* Ct 2^{14} 5^{2} 6^{9}.
Elsewh. only ψ 56^{1} (title) (עַל) יוֹנַת אֵלֶם רְחֹקִים 3128
prob. name of melody: *To 'the dove of distant*

terebinths' (rd. אֵלִים for אֵלָם; v. אֵלָם supr. p. 48, and Bae$^{\psi\psi, p. xvii}$).—On sanctity of dove among Shemites, v. RS$^{Sem. i. 202, 275}$.

3124 †II. יוֹנָה **n.pr.m.** prophet, acc. to 2 K 14^{25} he was הַנָּבִיא, son of אֲמִתַּי, fr. גַּת הַחֵפֶר, and predicted the recovery of Isr.'s territory which Jerob. II effected; he is also the principal figure of the Book of Jonah: 1^{1} (בֶּן־אֲמִתַּי), v$^{3.5.7.15}$ 2$^{1.1.2.11}$ 3$^{1.3.4}$ 4$^{1.5.6.6.8.9}$.

3238 III. הַיּוֹנָה v. יָנָה Pt. p. 413

3120 †יָוָן **n.pr.gent. Ionia(ns), Greece** (Gk. Ἰάονες (i.e. orig. Ἰάϝονες), v. also 𝔊 infr.; OPers. *Yauna* Spieg$^{APK 237}$; As. *Iamanu* (*Iavanu*) Dl$^{Pa 248 ff.}$ COT^{Gloss}; Egypt. *Y^{e}-v^{a}n-(n)a*, v. WMM$^{369 f. cf. also 24 ff.}$; v. esp. on this word Sta$^{De Populo Javan 1880}$)—*Ionians*, as traders Ez 27^{13}, 𝔊 Ἑλλάς (named with תֻּבַל, מֶשֶׁךְ; in v^{12} תַּרְשִׁישׁ, in v^{14} תּוֹגַרְמָה); cf. יְוָנִי (adj. gent.) infr.; as distant, Is 66^{19}, 𝔊 Ἑλλάς (with תַּרְשִׁישׁ, פּוּל, לוּד, תֻּבַל, and הָאִיִּים הָרְחֹקִים; list to be emended fr. 𝔊 Sta$^{ib. 5 ff.}$); called 'son' of Japhet Gn 10^{2}(P) = 1 Ch 1^{5}, and 'father' of אֱלִישָׁה, תַּרְשִׁישׁ, כִּתִּים and רֹדָנִים (so rd. for דֹּדָנִים) Gn 10^{4}(P) = 1 Ch 1^{7} (in these 𝔊 Ιωυναν, v. Lag$^{BN 84 Anm. **}$); addressed (personif.) בָּנַיִךְ יָוָן Zc 9^{13} (opp. בניך ציון) (𝔊 Ἕλληνες, and so in foll.; מֶלֶךְ יָוָן Dn 8^{21} (v. מַלְכֵי מָדַי וּפָרָס v^{20})=*king of Greece* i.e. kingdom over which Alexander ruled, whose dominion was afterward divided (see v$^{22 ff.}$); שַׂר־יָוָן 10^{20} of the guardian-angel of Greece (v. שַׂר פָּרָס v^{a}); מַלְכוּת יָוָן 11^{2} (v^{b} פָּרָס).—Ez 27^{19} וְיָוָן is text. err., v. וְדָן supr. p. 255^{a}.

3125 †[יְוָנִי] **adj.gent.** only c. art. as n.pr.gent.: וּבְנֵי יְרוּשָׁלַםִ מְכַרְתֶּם לִבְנֵי הַיְּוָנִים Jo 4^{6} (𝔊 Ἕλληνες) *and the sons of Jerusalem ye have sold to the sons of the Ionians* (cf. יָוָן Ez 27^{13}).—Vid. Sta$^{ib.}$

3130-31 יוֹסִפְיָה, יוֹסֵף v. sub יסף. p. 415

3132 יוֹעֵאלָה v. sub יעל. p. 418

3139 יוֹרָה v. sub ירה. p. 435

3142 יוּשַׁב חֶסֶד v. sub שׁוב. p. 1000

3144-45 יְשַׁוְיָה, יוֹשָׁה v. sub ישה. p. 444

יזה (√ whence first element of foll.; perh. cf. Ar. وَزَى *congregatus, conglomeratus fuit,* Frey).

3149 †[יַזִּיאֵל, יזואל] **n.pr.m.** one of David's heroes וְיִזוֹאֵל 1 Ch 12^{3}.

יְזִיָּה v. sub נזה. p. 633 3150

[יזן] **vb.** only **Pu.** *Pt.* pl. מְיֻזָּנִים Je 5^{8} Qr 2109
(< Kt מוּזָנִים v. זון); mng. dub. (comp. by Schu al. with Ar. وَزَنَ *weigh*, whence *furnished with weights*, i.e. testicles, but sense remote and very uncertain).

יָזִיז v. sub I. זוז p. 265^{b} supr. 3151

יִזְלִיאָה v. sub זלא p. 272^{b} supr. 3152

יְזַנְיָה, יְזַנְיָהוּ v. sub I. אזן p. 24^{b} supr. 3153

יזע (√ of foll.; cf. Ar. وَذَعَ *fluxit aqua* (Frey); NH and Aram. in deriv., v. infr.)

†[יֶזַע] **n.[m.] sweat** (v. זֵעָה infr.)—לֹא יַחְגְּרוּ 3154
בַּיָּזַע Ez 44^{18} del. Co, q.v.

†[זֵעָה] **n.f. sweat** (NH זֵיעָה (Levy), better 2188
זֵיעָה (Jastr); Aram. דֵּיעֲתָא, ܕܘܥܬܐ)—בְּזֵעַת אַפֶּיךָ תֹּאכַל לֶחֶם Gn 3^{19} (J).

יִזְרַחְיָה, יִזְרָח v. sub זרח p. 280^{b} supr. 3155-56

יִזְרְעֶאל v. sub זרע p. 283^{a} supr. 3157

יחבה v. חֻבָּה sub חבב. p. 285 3160

†[יָחַד] **vb. be united** (Ar. وَحَدَ *be alone*, 3161
II. *make one;* NH Pi. יִחֵד *make* or *declare one;* Aram. יַחֵד *unite*, ܐܬܝܚܕ *set alone*)—**Qal** *Impf.* 3 fs. Gn 49^{6} בִּקְהָלָם אַל־תֵּחַד כְּבֹדִי in their assembly let my glory *not be united* (‖ בְּסֹדָם אַל־תָּבֹא נַפְשִׁי); 2 fs. Is 14^{20} לֹא תֵחַד אִתָּם בִּקְבוּרָה. **Pi.** *Imv.* ψ 86^{11} יַחֵד לְבָבִי לְיִרְאָה שְׁמֶךָ *unite* my heart (i.e. concentrate its affections, cf. Je 32^{39}) to fear thy name (but 𝔊 𝔖 𝔙 Gr Bi Ch יִחַד (from חָדָה) *let* my heart *rejoice*, etc.)

†יָחִיד **adj.** and **subst.** only, only one, 3173
solitary (NH *id.;* Aram. יְחִידַי, יְחִיד, ܝܚܝܕܝܐ, ܝܚܝܕܐ *id.;* Arab. وَحِيدٌ *solitary*)—**1.** *only one*, esp. of an only son, Gn 22$^{2.12.16}$ את בנך את יְחִידְךָ thy son, thine *only one*, אֵבֶל יָחִיד Am 8^{10} Je 6^{26} mourning for *an only son*, כמספד על היחיד Zc 12^{10}, Pr 4^{3} רַךְ וְיָחִיד לִפְנֵי אמי; so fem. יְחִידָה Ju 11^{34}. **2.** fem. יְחִידָה as subst. ψ 22^{21} 35^{17} יְחִידָתִי my *only one*, poet. for *my life*, as the one unique and priceless possession which can never be replaced (in each ‖ נַפְשִׁי). **3.** *solitary*, ψ 25^{16} כי יחיד ועני אני; 68^{7} מוֹשִׁיב יְחִידִים בַּיְתָה causing *solitary, isolated* ones (i.e. friendless wanderers or exiles; ‖ אֲסִירִים) to dwell at home (Lag Ch al. מֵשִׁיב *bringing back* home).

3162 †יַחַד $_{45}$ **n.[m.]** unitedness. **1.** as **subst.** only 1 Ch 12[17] (peculiar) יִהְיֶה־לִּי עֲלֵיכֶם לֵבָב לְיָחַד I will have a heart toward you *for unitedness*, i.e. my heart shall be ready to become one with yours (cf. v[38] לב אחד). **2.** elsewhere always in acc. as **adv.** *in union, together* (cf. Ar. وَحْدَ in acc. with sf. *in his solitariness=alone*)—**a.** *together*, of community in action, place, or time (oft. combined, but one usu. more prominent than the others); (1) in action, Jb 38[7] בְּרָן־יַחַד כּוֹכְבֵי אֵל when the stars of God shouted *together;* Ezr 4[3] we *together* will build (opp. to *you*), with נִלָּחֵם 1 S 17[10], נִשָּׁפְטָה Is 43[26]; (2) in place 1 S 11[11] וְלֹא נִשְׁאֲרוּ בָם שְׁנַיִם יָחַד; 2 S 10[15] וַיֵּאָסְפוּ יָחַד ψ 2[2] 31[14] 88[18], 133[1] שֶׁבֶת יַחַד, Is 50[8], as pred. Mi 2[12] יַחַד אֲשִׂימֶנּוּ; (3) in place and time at once, 2 S 21[9] וַיִּפְּלוּ יָחַד and they perished *together*, 14[16] to destroy אתי ואת בני יחד; (4) of time alone (poet.) Is 42[14] אֶשֹּׁם וְאֶשְׁאַף יחד I will gasp and pant *together*, 45[8] Jb 6[2] 17[16] ψ 141[10] יחד אנכי עד אעבור while *I* at the same time pass on. **b.** *all together, altogether* (poet. syn. of כֻּלָּם, but more forcible, suggesting oft., esp. with כל, *all at once*, as well as *altogether*), Is 44[11] יפחדו יבשו יחד (cf. ψ 40[15]), ψ 62[10] הֵמָּה מֵהֶבֶל יָחַד they are *all together* (made) of vanity, Is 22[3] כל קציניך נדדו יחד (with כל also ψ 41[8] Jb 34[15]): oft. in poet. beginning a clause with emph., Dt 33[5] Jb 3[18] יחד אסירים שאננו, 16[10] 19[12] יחד יבאו גדודיו, 24[4] 31[38] ψ 41[8] 98[8] Ho 11[7] (with a neg.), v[8]; in connexion with a sf., or obj. of a vb., Is 27[4] אציתנה יָחַד I will burn it *altogether*, ψ 33[15] הַיֹּצֵר יַחַד לִבָּם who formeth the hearts of them *all together*, 74[6.8] Jb 10[8] יַחַד סָבִיב *altogether* round about (but rd. perh. with 𝔊 𝔖 Del Di אַחַר תְּסוֹב), 40[13]. **c.** *together*, in the sense of *alike*, the one as well as the other, ψ 49[3.11] יחד כסיל ובער יאבדו, Jb 21[26] 34[29]. More frequent is

3162 יַחְדָּו $_{92}$ (Je 46[12.21] 49[3] יַחְדָּיו), **adv.** together (prop. (in) *his* or *its unitednesses* (cf. Ar. وَحْدَهُ *alone;* and for the form אַשְׁרָיו), but, the orig. of the term. being forgotten, applied gen. as an adv., without regard to number, gender, or person: so Ges Ol [§ 135 c] Sta [§ 370 a])—*together:* **a.** of community in action, ψ 34[4] ונרוממה שמו יחדו let us exalt his name *together*, Is 52[9], with נוֹעַץ *take counsel*, 45[21] ψ 71[10] 83[6] Ne 6[7]; נִצָּה to *struggle* Dt 25[11]; in place, as with ישב Gn 13[6] Dt 25[5], הלך Gn 22[6.8] Am 3[3], בוא Je 3[18] Jb 9[32], קרב Is 41[1], נפל 2 S 2[16], אכל Ju 19[6] Je 41[1], התקבץ Jos 9[2], נאסף Ju 6[33], etc.; Dt 22[10] בשור ובחמור יחדו; coupling pairs, and so strengthening וְ (mostly poet.), v[11] Am 1[15] הוא ושׂריו יחדו (cf. Je 48[7] Qr [Kt יחד], 49[3]) Je 6[11.12] שׂדות ונשים י׳, v[21] (accents), 13[14] 31[8.13] 50[4.33] Is 41[19], cf. 65[7]; in time (rare: but v. infr.), ψ 4[9] in peace יחדו אשכבה ואישן will I *at once* lie down and sleep (i.e. lie down and fall asleep immediately). **b.** emph. (esp. poet.) =*all together* 1 S 31[6], Is 10[8] הלא שׂרי יחדו מלכים are not my princes *all together*, all alike, kings? 18[6] 40[5] 41[20.23] 45[16] (|| כֻּלָּם), 46[2] קרסו כרעו יחדו, 48[13] 66[17] ψ 14[3] (|| הַכֹּל), 19[10] צדקו יחדו (of J.'s ordinances), 35[26] 37[38]; sts. (like יַחַד **b**) suggesting *all at once*, as well as *all together*, Ex 19[8] ויענו כל העם יחדו (so, with כל, Is 22[3] 31[3] Zc 10[4]), Is 1[28.31] ובערו שניהם יחדו. Prefixed to a clause (like יחד), Dt 33[17] (cf. יחד v[5]), Is 9[20] 11[7.14] 31[3] 43[17] 45[16] 52[8] Je 46[12] 51[38] La 2[8] Jb 24[17] (strengthening לָמוֹ). **c.** *alike*, the one as well as the other, Dt 12[22] (=15[22]) the unclean and the clean *alike* may eat it, 1 S 30[24] יַחְדָּו יַחֲלֹקוּ׃ they shall share *together*, i.e. *alike*.

†יַחְדִּי Baer, יַחְדּוֹ van d. H, **n.pr.m.** a Gileadite, 1 Ch 5[14], 𝔊 Ιουραι, A Ιεδδαι, 𝔊L Ιεδδω. 3163

יֶחְדְּיָהוּ, יַחְדִּיאֵל v. sub חדה. p. 292 3164

יַחֲוָאֵל v. sub חיה. p. 313 3171

יַחְזִיאֵל, יַחְזְיָה v. sub חזה. p. 303 3166-67

יְחֶזְקֵאל, יְחִזְקִיָּה(וּ) v. sub חזק. p. 306 3168-69

†יַחְזֵרָה **n.pr.m.** a priest 1 Ch 9[12] (for 3170
which אַחְזַי (q.v.) Ne 11[13]), v. now also Ryle 273
on Ne 11[13]. p. 28, 306

יְחִיאֵל, יְחִיאֵלִי, יְחִיָּה v. sub חיה. p. 313 3171-72, 3174

†[יָחַל] **vb. Niph.** wait; **Pi.** await (cf. NH 3176
יִחוּל *expectation*);—**Niph.** *Pf.* 3 fs. נוֹחֲלָה Ez 19[5] (yet v. infr.); *Impf.* וַיִּיָּחֶל Gn 8[12] + 1 S 13[18] Kt (v. Dr; Qr Hiph. וַיּוֹחֶל);—*wait:* Gn 8[12] *and he waited* yet seven days; so 1 S 13[18] Kt; of Isr. under fig. of lioness, וַתֵּרֶא כִּי נוֹחֲלָה אָבְדָה תִּקְוָתָהּ Ez 19[5] *when she saw that her hope tarried, was lost* (but dub.; Sm comp. Aram. ܐܬܚܠ *be weak*, whence perh. *sink down;* Hi (perh. after 𝔊) כִּי נִדַּח לָהּ *that he was thrust away from her;* Co plausibly נוֹאֲלָה that *she had acted foolishly*). **Pi.** *Pf.* 2 ms. sf. יִחַלְתָּנִי ψ 119[49]; 1 s. יִחַלְתִּי v[43] + 4 t. ψ 119; 3 mpl. יִחֲלוּ Jb 29[23] Ez 13[6]; יִחֵלוּ Jb 29[21]; 1 pl. יִחַלְנוּ ψ 33[22]; *Impf.* יְיַחֵל Mi 5[6];

אֵיחַל Jb 6^{11}+3 t.; אֲיַחֵלָה 30^{26}; יְיַחֵלוּ Is 42^4; יְיַחֵלוּן 51^5; *Imv.* יַחֵל ψ 130^7 131^3; *Pt.* מְיַחֵל 69^4; מְיַחֲלִים 31^{25}+2 t.;—**1.** *wait, tarry* for, sq. לְ Mi 5^6 (of rain, ‖ יְקַוֶּה); so 1^{12} acc. to We, who reads יִחֲלָה (Pf.) for חָלָה; abs. *wait* Jb 14^{14}. **2.** *wait for=hope for*, sq. לְ Is 42^4 Jb $29^{21.23}$ 30^{26} (‖ קִוִּיתִי), ψ 31^{25} $33^{18.22}$ 69^4 $119^{43.49.74.81.114.147}$; sq. לְ inf. יח׳ לְקַיֵּם דָּבָר Ez 13^6; sq. אֶל Is 51^5 ψ 130^7 131^3; abs. *hope*, Jb 6^{11} 13^{15} ψ 71^{14}. **Hiph.** *Pf.* הוֹחַלְתִּי Jb 32^{11}, etc.; וְהוֹחַלְתִּי (consec., v. Hi De² Dr §§ 106, 119 γ) Jb 32^{16}; *Impf.* וַיּוֹחֶל 1 S 13^8 Qr; 2 ms. תּוֹחֵל 10^8; אוֹחִיל 2 K 6^{33} La $3^{21.24}$; אוֹחִילָה Je 4^{19} Qr (Kt אָחוּלָה), Mi 7^7; אֹחִילָה 2 S 18^{14};—*wait, tarry*, abs. (prop. *shew a waiting* attitude): 1 S 10^8 (sq. עַד בּוֹאִי), 13^8 (Qr; cf. Niph.); 2 S 18^{14} Jb 32^{16} Je 4^{19} (but v. חול); *wait for, hope for* (as **Pi.**), sq. לְ 2 K 6^{33} Mi 7^7 La 3^{24} Jb 32^{11} ψ 38^{16} $42^{6.12}$ 43^5 130^5 (‖ קִוִּיתִי); abs. *hope*, La 3^{21}.

3175 †יָחִיל **adj.verb. waiting,** so Thes SS Buhl, but very dub.,—only טוֹב וְיָחִיל וְדוּמָם לְ La 3^{26} *good* is it that one be *waiting and that silently* (but v. דוּמָם) *for* the salvation of י׳; construct. with ו and adj. hardly poss.; Ew Ke Löhr Kö ii. 407 al. regard as vb. (fr. חול); rd. perh. וְיֹחִיל Hiph. Impf. fr. יחל (cf. v^{24}).

8431 †תּוֹחֶלֶת **n.f.** hope, abs. ת׳ Pr 13^{12}; cstr. *id.* Pr 10^{28} 11^7; sf. תּוֹחַלְתִּי ψ 39^8 La 3^{18}; תֹּחַלְתּוֹ Jb 41^1;—*hope*, sq. subj. gen. Jb 41^1 Pr 10^{28} 11^7 La 3^{18}; sq. subj. gen.+ לְ ψ 39^8 (תּוֹחַלְתִּי לָךְ); alone Pr 13^{12}.

3177 †יַחְלְאֵל **n.pr.m.** (*wait for God!*);—a Zebulunite Gn 46^{14} Nu 26^{26} (𝔊 Αλοηλ, Αιηλ, Αλληλ).

3178 †יַחְלְאֵלִי **adj.gent.** of foregoing: only c. art. as n.pr.coll. Nu 26^{26}.

3179 †[יָחַם] **vb. be hot, Pi. conceive** (Ar. وَحِمَ v. *incaluerunt* pecora, Frey; Aram. יְחַם *be hot*, usu. of sexual impulse of animals)—**Qal** v. חמם. **Pi.** *Pf.* 3 fs. sf. יֶחֱמַתְנִי ψ 51^7 in sin my mother *conceived me* (‖ חוֹלָלְתִּי); *Inf. cstr.* of heat of cattle in breeding, conception; בְּכָל־יַחֵם Gn 30^{41} *at every breeding-heat* of the flock (J); בְּעֵת יַחֵם 31^{10} *at the time of* the flock's *being hot in breeding* (E); sf. 3 fpl. לְיַחְמֵנָּה 30^{41} *in order that they might have breeding-heat* (J).

2534 חֵמָה (once חֵמָא) $_{121}$ **n.f. heat, rage** (for *יַחְמָה; NH *id.*; Aram. יַחְמָא *poison*, ܚܡܬܐ *heat, wrath, poison*, Brock Lex. 116, also Nö § 105; Ar. حُمَةٌ *poison*, Lane 651; As. *imtu, spittle, breath, poison*, Dl HWB 78 Muss-Arnolt CD 62)—abs. חֵמָה Na 1^2+39 t.; חֵמָא + Dn 11^{44}; cstr. חֲמַת Gn 27^{44} + 25 t.; sf. חֲמָתִי Je 4^4 + 36 t.; חֲמָתְךָ Je 10^{25} + 8 t.; חֲמָתֶךָ ψ 88^8 89^{47}; חֲמָתוֹ Is 51^{17} + 8 t.; חֲמָתָם Jb 6^4; pl. חֵמוֹת Pr 22^{24}, חֵמֹת ψ 76^{11};—**1.** *heat*: **a.** *fever*, חֲמַת מִיָּיִן Ho 7^5 *fever from wine, wine-fever* (on st. cstr. v. Ges § 130, 1). **b.** *venom, poison* (fig.): חֲמַת זֹחֲלֵי עָפָר Dt 32^{24}; ח׳ תַּנִּינִם v^{33}; ח׳ נָחָשׁ ψ 58^5 cf. v^5; ח׳ עַכְשׁוּב ψ 140^4; *poison* of arrows (of י׳) Jb 6^4. **2.** *burning anger, rage*: **a.** of man: Gn 27^{44} (J), 2 S 11^{20} 2 K 5^{12} Est 1^{12} 2^1 3^5 5^9 (against, עַל), $7^{7.10}$ ψ 37^8 (‖ אַף), 76^{11} (yet on txt. v. Che), Pr 6^{34} $15^{1.18}$ (אִישׁ חֵמָה *man of rage*=raging or wrathful man), 16^4 19^{19} (גְּדָל־ח׳) Qr =*one great in rage*, v. De Now), 27^4 (‖ אַף), Is $51^{13.13}$ Ez 23^{25}; אִישׁ חֵמוֹת Pr 22^{24} (‖ בַּעַל אַף); בַּעַל חֵמָה 29^{22} (‖ אִישׁ אַף); חֵמָה עַזָּה *strong rage* Pr 21^{14} (‖ אַף); חֲמַת רוּחִי Ez 3^{14} *the rage of my spirit*. **b.** of the he-goat in Daniel's vision, בַּחֲמַת כֹּחוֹ Dn 8^6 *in the fury of his power*. **c.** of God (י׳), oft. Je Is² Ez ψ: Je 4^4+16 t. Je; 2 K $22^{13.17}$ Is 27^4 (Hi Ew Di Du; on other interpr., and on txt. v. Di), 63^5 La 2^4 Ez 5^{13}+29 t. Ez; Nu 25^{11} (P), 2 Ch 12^7 $34^{21.25}$ 36^{16} ψ 59^{14} 79^6 88^8 89^{47} 106^{23} Jb 21^{20}; appar. also 19^{29} 36^{18} v. Di; oft. ‖ אַף, Mi 5^{14} Dt 9^{19} 29^{22} Is 42^{25} (אַפּוֹ as appos., עֱזוּז מִלְחָמָה), $63^{3.6}$ Dn 9^{16} ψ 6^2 78^{38} 90^7; לְהָשִׁיב + בְּחֵמָה אַפּוֹ 66^{15} (‖ וְגַעֲרָתוֹ בְּלַהֲבֵי־אֵשׁ), + Je 23^{19} 30^{23} of the whirlwind of י׳; ‖ קֶצֶף גָּדוֹל + אַף Dt 29^{27} Je 21^5 32^{37}; ‖ תֹּכְחוֹת חֵמָה + אַף Ez 5^{15}, cf. תּוֹכְחוֹת חֵמָה alone 25^{17}; ‖ חֲרוֹן אַפּוֹ Na 1^6 La 4^{11}; ‖ קֶצֶף Is 34^2 (of fury *against*, עַל), ψ 38^2; ‖ גְּעָרָה Is 51^{20}; ‖ גְּמוּל 59^{18}; ‖ קִנְאָה Ez 36^6, cf. חֵמָה גְדוֹלָה קִנֵּאתִי Zc 8^2 (‖ קִנְאָה גדולה); דַּם חֵמָה וְקִנְאָה Ez 16^{38} (on txt. v. Co); חֲמַת קֶרִי Lv 26^{28} *rage of meeting*, i.e. *encountering* them *in rage*; כּוֹס חֲמָתוֹ(-תִי) Is $51^{17.22}$ *the cup of his* (*my*) *fury*; כּוֹס הַיַּיִן הַחֵמָה הַזֹּאת Je 25^{15}; בַּעַל חֵמָה *a possessor of fury*=*furious* Na 1^2 (‖ אֵל קַנּוֹא, נֹקֵם). [חֵמָה עַל=*rage against* one: Is 34^2 2 Ch 28^9.—Vbs. used with חֵמָה are: **2. a.**: שׁוּב Gn 27^{44}, הֵשִׁיב Pr 15^1, עָלָה 2 S 11^{20}, בָּעַר Est 1^{12}, שָׁכַךְ 2^1 7^{10}; **2. c.**: הֵשִׁיב *turn away* wrath of י׳ Nu 25^{11} ψ 106^{23} Je 18^{20} (but הָשִׁיב בְּחֵמָה אַפּוֹ Is 66^{15} *to recompense his anger in fury*, give it as requital); ח׳ י׳ *is kindled against* one יצת ב Niph. 2 K $22^{13.17}$; it *burns* בָּעֲרָה Je 4^4 21^{12} 44^6 ψ 89^{47}; *arises* עלה 2 Ch 36^{16}, cf. as obj. of עלה Hiph. Ez 24^8; *is* *poured out* נִתְּכָה בְּ 2 Ch 12^{7} 34$^{21.25}$ Je 7^{20}; נִתְּכָה עַל 42$^{18.18}$ 44^{6}; נִתְּכָה כָאֵשׁ Na 1^{6}; ׳י *pours it out* שָׁפַךְ עַל ψ 79^{6}; שָׁפַךְ אֶל Is 42^{25} Je 10^{25} Ez 7^{8} 9^{8} 14^{19} 16^{38} (acc. to Co's conject.), 20$^{8.13.21}$ 22^{22} 30^{15} 36^{18}; שָׁפַךְ כָּאֵשׁ La 2^{4}; חֵמָה שְׁפוּכָה Ez 20$^{33.34}$; הֵנִיחַ ח׳ בְּ *bring to rest* (i.e. satisfy) *one's fury upon* Ez 5^{13} 16^{42} 24^{13}; כִּלָּה ח׳ La 4^{11}; + בְּ Ez 5^{13} *I have accomplished my fury upon them* (in their case), 6^{12} 13^{15}.]

3180 יַחְמוּר v. sub IV. חמר. p. 331

3181 יַחְמַי v. sub חמה. p. 327

יחף (√of foll.; orig. mng. unknown; NH Aram. יָחֵף adj. as Heb.; Syr. Aph. ܚܦܝ *discalceatus fuit*; cf. perh. Ar. حَفِيَ (transp.) *walk barefoot*, also *become chafed*, of foot or hoof).

3182 † יָחֵף **adj. barefoot**, alw. abs. יָחֵף Is 20^{2} + 4 t.;—הלך עָרוֹם וְיָחֵף Is 20^{2} (נַעַלְךָ תַחֲלֹץ מֵעַל רַגְלֶךָ in preceding cl.), v^{3}; הֹלֵךְ יָחֵף 2 S 15^{30}; נָהַג יָחֵף Is 20^{3}; appar. = subst., מִנְעִי רַגְלֵךְ מִיָּחֵף Je 2^{25} *withhold thy foot from bareness* (Syr. ܚܦܝܘܬܐ *discalceatio*).

3183-85 יַחְצְאֵל, יַחֲצִיאֵל, יַחְצְאֵלִי v. sub חצה. p. 345

310, 3186 (ו)ייחר Kt 2 S 20^{5} (Qr וַיּוֹחֶר), v. אחר supr. p. 29^{b} and Dr^{Sm}.

יחשׂ (√of foll.; meaning unknown; deriv. common in NH and Aram.)

3188 † יַחַשׂ **n.[m.] genealogy** (NH יַחַס, יִחוּס, Aram. יִחוּס)—סֵפֶר הַיַּחַשׂ Ne 7^{5} *book of genealogy*.

3187 † [הִתְיַחֵשׂ] **vb. Hithp. denom. enrol oneself or be enrolled by genealogy** (NH oft. in Pi. (also Hithp.), Aram. Pa. (Ithpa.))—*Pf.* 3 mpl. הִתְיַחְשׂוּ 1 Ch 5^{17} 9^{1}; *Inf. cstr.* הִתְיַחֵשׂ 5^{1} + 5 t.; sf. הִתְיַחְשָׂם 1 Ch 4^{33} + 7 t.; *Pt.* pl. הַמִּתְיַחְשִׂים Ezr 2^{62} Ne 7^{64};—*be enrolled by genealogy* 1 Ch 5^{17} 9^{1} Ne 7^{5}; perh. also לְהִתְי׳ 2 Ch 12^{15} (tr. to 11^{16} acc. to Hi Be, v. VB); וְלֹא לְהִתְי׳ לַבְּכֹרָה 1 Ch 5^{1} *but he is not to be enrolled in the place of first-born*; sq. בְּ (*among, of, consisting in*) 7^{40}, without לְ 7^{7} Ezr 8^{1}; הִתְי׳ הַכֹּהֲנִים 2 Ch 31^{17}; *Inf.* = *genealogical enrolment* 1 Ch 4^{33} these were their dwellings and they had (לָהֶם) *genealogical enrolment*, cf. 7$^{5.9}$; בְּהִתְי׳ 5^{7} *at the enrolment* of (לְ) their generations; הֵמָּה בְּחַצְרֵיהֶם הִתְיַחְשָׂם 1 Ch 9^{22} *as for them, in their villages was their enrolment*; nearly = *genealogical list* 2 Ch 31^{16} (לִזְכָרִים; i.e. the males whose names were in the list), so Ezr 8^{3}, cf. 2 Ch 31$^{18.19}$ (all sq. בְּ *among, of*); *Pt.* pl. c. art. בִּקְשׁוּ כְתָבָם הַמִּתְיַחְשִׂים Ezr 2^{62} = Ne 7^{64} *they sought their writing* (their book), namely *the enrolled*, i.e. their genealogical record.

יַחַת v. sub חתה. p. 367 3189

†[יָטַב] **vb. be good, well, glad, pleasing** 3190
(Aram. יְטַב; Zinj. יטב DHM Sendsch. 57)—**Qal** (*Pf.*
not in use, v. טוב **vb.**) *Impf.* יִיטַב Gn 12^{13} + 34 t., 2895
יִטַב 1 S 24^{5} + 3 t.; תִּיטַב Est 2^{4} + 2 t.; תֵּיטְבִי (incorrect for תִּיטְבִי Ges §70R) Na 3^{8}; pl. יִיטְבוּ Gn 34^{18}; for *Inf.* and *Pt.* v. טוֹב.—**1.** *be glad, joyful*, לֵב Ju 18^{20} 19$^{6.9}$ 1 K 21^{7} Ru 3^{7} Ec 7^{3}. **2.** *be well placed*, הֲתֵיטְבִי מִנֹּא אָמוֹן Na 3^{8} *art thou better placed than No of Amon?* **3.** impers. c. לְ, *be well for* or *with, go well with* Gn 12^{13}(J), 40^{14}(E), Dt 4^{40} 5$^{16.26}$ 6$^{3.18}$ 12$^{25.28}$ 22^{7} 2 K 25^{24} Ru 3^{1} Je 7^{23} 38^{20} 40^{9} 42^{6}. **4.** *be pleasing* בְּעֵינֵי Gn 34^{18}(J), 41^{37} 45^{16} (E), Dt 1^{23} Lv 10$^{19.20}$ Jos 22$^{30.33}$ (P), 1 S 18^{5} 24^{5} 2 S 3^{36} 18^{4} 1 K 3^{10} Est 1^{21} 2$^{4.4.9}$; c. לְ, *be pleasing to*, ψ 69^{32}; c. לִפְנֵי (late) Ne 2$^{5.6}$ Est 5^{14}. **Hiph.** *Pf.* הֵיטִיב Gn 12^{16} Jos 24^{20}; הֵיטֵב 1 S 25^{31}; sf. הֵיטִבְךָ Dt 30^{5}; הֵיטַבְתָּ Je 1^{12}; הֵיטַבְתְּ Ru 3^{10}, etc.; וְהֵטִבֹתִי Ez 36^{11} (for הֵיטַבְתִּי as if from טוב Ges §70R); *Impf.* יֵיטִיב Nu 10^{32} + 3 t.; יֵיטֵב Pr 15^{13} + 2 t.; יֵיטִב Jb 24^{21} (Ges §70R); יֵיטִיב 1 K 1^{47} (Ges §70R); וַיֵּיטֶב Ex 1^{20}; sf. וִיטִבְךָ Ec 11^{9}, etc.; *Imv.* הֵיטִיבָה ψ 51^{20}; הֵיטִיבִי Is 23^{16}, etc.; *Inf. abs.* הֵיטֵב Je 7^{5} 10^{5}; הֵיטֵב Gn 32^{13} + 10 t.; *Inf. cstr.* הֵיטִיב Lv 5^{4} + 7 t.; הֵטִיב Je 32^{41}; sf. הֵיטִיבִי Je 32^{40}, etc.; *Pt.* מֵיטִיב 1 S 16^{17}; מֵטִיב ψ 119^{68}; מֵטִב Ez 33^{32}, etc.;—**1.** *make glad, rejoice* לֵב Ju 19^{22}; פנים Pr 15^{13}; the person Ec 11^{9}. **2.** *do good* to, *deal well* with, a person, usu. c. prep.: c. לְ, Ex 1^{20} Jos 24^{20} (both E), Gn 12^{16} Nu 10$^{29.32}$ (all J), Ju 17^{13} 1 S 25^{31} ψ 49^{19} 125^{4}; c. עִם, Gn 32$^{10.13.13}$ Nu 10^{32} (all J), Mi 2^{7}; c. acc. Dt 8^{16} 28^{63} 30^{5} 1 S 2^{32} Je 18^{10} 32$^{40.41}$ Zc 8^{15} Jb 24^{21} ψ 51^{20}; abs. Ez 36^{11}; opp. הֵרַע (in prov. phr., cannot *do good or ill*, = cannot do anything at all; test of deity) Zp 1^{12} Is 41^{23} Je 10^{5}. **3.** *do well* or *thoroughly*: הֵטִיבוּ (כל)אשׁר דברו *they have done well* (all) *that they have spoken* Dt 5^{25} 18^{17}; על הרע כפים להיטיב Mi 7^{3} *their hands are upon the evil to do it well*, i.e. *diligently, thoroughly*, lit. *make* (*it*) *good*, with play on הרע; esp. as auxil. sq. inf.; היט׳ דעת Pr 15^{2} = *know well*; לראות Je 1^{12} *see well*; (לְ)נַגֵּן *play well, skilfully* 1 S 16^{17} Is 23^{16} Ez 33^{32}; cf. pt. cstr. sq. subst. מֵטִבֵי צָעַד Pr 30^{29} *marching well*,

in a stately manner, so מֵיטִבֵי לָכֶת v[29]; inf. abs. הֵיטֵב as adv.=*thoroughly*, c. vbs.: כתת Dt 9[21], שאל 13[15], דרש 17[4] 19[18], באר 27[8], שׁבר 2 K 11[18]. **4.** *make a thing good, right, beautiful:* c. acc. rei: the head 2 K 9[30]; *dress, trim:* a lamp Ex 30[7] (P); מַצֵּבוֹת Ho 10[1]; גֵּהָה Pr 17[22] a glad heart *maketh a good cure;* sq. מִן compar., obj. שֵׁם 1 K 1[47] (= *make it more glorious than*); חֶסֶד Ru 3[10]; sq. דֶּרֶךְ=*course of life* or *action* Je 2[33] (in order to win love); *amend* one's ways and doings Je 7[3] 18[11] 26[13] 35[15]; הֵיטֵב תֵּיטִיבוּ את־ד׳ 7[5]. **5.** *do well, right,* ethically, abs.: **a.** of men, Gn 4[7.7] (J), Lv 5[4] (P), ψ 36[4] Is 1[17] Je 4[22] 13[23]. **b.** of God, טוֹב מֵטִיב *good and doing good* ψ 119[68]; so inf. abs. as adv. הַהֵיטֵב חָרָה לךְ Jon 4[4.9] *art thou rightly angry?* sq. לי v[9]. In כִּי־יֵיטִב אֶל־אָבִי 1 S 20[13] vb. is appar. intrans., =**Qal**, *if it be pleasing unto my father,* but **Hiph.** not elsewh. in this sense; point rather יִיטַב; on this and on foll. אֶת־ v. We Dr.

3192 †יָטְבָה **n.pr.loc.** (*pleasantness*) city prob. in Judah 2 K 21[19], site unknown.

3193 †יָטְבָ֫תָה **n.pr.loc.** (*pleasantness*) station of Isr. in wilderness Nu 33[33.34] (P), Dt 10[7], site unknown.

4105 †מְהֵיטַבְאֵל **n.pr.pers.** (=מֵיטִיב אֵל *God benefits*)—**1. f.** an Edomite princess Gn 36[39] (P), 1 Ch 1[50]. **2. m.** ancestor of the false prophet Shemaiah Ne 6[10].

4315 †(מֵיטָב) **n.**[**m.**] **the best,** only cstr. מֵיטַב and as superl.; *the best* of a thing: מ׳ שָׂדֵהוּ ומ׳ כַּרְמוֹ Ex 22[4] (JE) *the best* of his field and *the best* of his vineyard (choicest fruit); מ׳ הַצֹּאן *the best of the sheep* 1 S 15[9.15]; בְּמ׳ הָאָרֶץ *in the best of the land* Gn 47[6.11] (P).

3194 יוּטָּה, יֻטָּה v. sub נטה. p. 641

3195 יְטוּר v. sub טור. p. 377

יין (√of foll.; meaning unknown; regarded as loan-word by Lag[Armen. Stud. § 484] al.; Hom[ZMG 1889, 653 ff.; Aufsätze, 1892, 102] comp. Georgian *g'wino, wine,* whence also (acc. to him) Armen. *gini,* Gk. Ϝοῖνος, Lat. *vinum;* cf. on the other hand Jen[l. c. infr.])

3196 יַ֫יִן[141] **n.m.**[ψ 75, 9] **wine** (NH *id.;* Eth. ወይን: *vitis, vinea, vinum;* Ar. وَيْنٌ (*black*) *grapes,* v. Hom[ZMG 1889, 654]; Sab. וין *vineyard,* Mordt[ZMG 1887, 364] Hom[l. c. 659] (both after Glaser); As. *inu* in vocabularies, but this loan-word from western Shemites, acc. to Hom[Aufsätze 102]; Jen[ZA i. 186 f., ZMG 1890, 705] argues to the contrary)—abs. יָ֫יִן Gn 9[21] + 84 t.; יָיִן Gn 14[18] + 33 t.; cstr. יֵין ψ 60[5] Ct 8[2]; יֵין Dt 32[18] + 9 t.; sf. יֵינִי Ct 5[1], etc.;—*wine:* **a.** common drink, for refreshment Gn 14[18] (E?) 27[25] (J), Ju 19[19] 2 S 16[2] Am 5[11] 9[14] Ho 14[8] Jb 1[13.18] Dn 1[5] +, tonic Pr 31[6]; art. of commerce Ez 27[18] Ne 13[15]; among supplies in strongholds 2 Ch 11[11]; as making merry 2 S 13[28] Zc 9[15] 10[7] Est 1[10] Ec 9[7] 10[19] ψ 104[15]. †**b.** used for rejoicing before י׳ Dt 14[26], cf. Ho 9[4]; as drink-offering in prescribed ritual Ex 29[40] Lv 23[13] Nu 15[5.7.10] 28[14]; among temple stores 1 Ch 9[29]; used also in heathen ceremonial, v. Dt 32[33]. **c.** intoxicating 1 S 1[14] 25[37] Gn 9[21.24] 19[32.33.34.35] (all J), Is 5[11.22] Pr 21[17] 23[30.31] +; ‖ תִּירוֹשׁ Ho 4[11]; ‖ שֵׁכָר 1 S 1[15] Mi 2[11] Is 24[9] 28[7.7] 56[12] + 12 t.; forbidden to Nazirites †Nu 6[3.3] (חֹמֶץ יַיִן וְחֹמֶץ שֵׁכָר), v[4.20], cf. Am 2[12]; to Rechabites †Je 35[2.5 f.]; to mother of Samson †Ju 13[4.7.14]; to priests entering sanctuary †Lv 10[9] (P), Ez 44[21]; unfitting for kings Pr 31[4]. †**d.** combinations are: יֵין הַטּוֹב Ct 7[10]=*the best wine* (rd. כַּיַּיִן?) Ges[§ 133. 3, R. 1]; יֵין מַלְכוּת Est 1[7] *royal wine;* אֹצְרוֹת הַיַּיִן 1 Ch 27[27] *stores of wine, wine-supply;* יֵין הָרֶקַח Ct 8[2] *spiced wine;* מִשְׁתֵּה הַיַּיִן *wine-feast* Est 5[6] 7[2.7.8]; סֹבְאֵי יַיִן Pr 23[20] *wine-bibbers;* נאד יין *wine-skin* Jos 9[4.13] 1 S 16[20]; נֵבֶל יין *id.* 1 S 1[24] 10[3] 25[18] 2 S 16[1] Je 13[12.12]; בֵּית הַיָּיִן Ct 2[4] either *wine-house,* where wine is drunk, feasting-house (De al.), or *place of wine*=vineyard (Ew al.; cf. גֶּפֶן יַיִן Nu 6[4]). †**e.** metaph. of wisdom's drink Pr 9[2.5], cf. Is 55[1]; of י׳'s wrath Je 25[15] (כּוֹס היין); of confusion sent by י׳, יֵין תַּרְעֵלָה *wine of reeling* ψ 60[5], cf. 75[9]; of י׳'s awaking for vengeance, like a wine-shouter ψ 78[65]; of Babylon's fierce power Je 51[7]; of love Ct 5[1]; יֵין חֲמָסִים Pr 4[17]; in sim. of one bursting with words Jb 32[19]; of disheartened proph. Je 23[9] (כְּגֶבֶר עֲבָרוֹ יָיִן); of lover's mouth Ct 7[10] (v. supr.); love is better than wine Ct 1[2] 4[10].

יך 1 S 4[13] Kt; err. for יד Qr. p. 388 3027, 3197

†[יָכַח] **vb. Hiph. decide, adjudge, prove,** 3198 (NH Pi. וִכַּח *argue with* (עם), cf. Hithp., Hiph. *prove, correct;* Aram. Pa וַכַּח, Aph. אוֹכַח, *id.*)—**Hiph.** *Pf.* הוֹכִיחַ Is 2[4] + 5 t.; הֹכִיחַ Gn 24[44]; הוֹכַח Gn 21[25]; 2 ms. הֹכַחְתָּ Gn 24[14]; 1 s. sf. הוֹכַחְתִּיו 2 S 7[14]; *Impf.* יוֹכִיחַ Is 11[3] + 5 t.; יוֹכַח Ho 4[4] + 4 t.; יוֹכַח 1 Ch 12[17]; sf. יוֹכִיחֵנִי ψ 141[5] + 12 t. Impf.; *Imv.* הוֹכַח Pr 9[8]; *Inf. abs.* הוֹכֵחַ Lv 19[17] + 5 t.; cstr. הוֹכִיחַ Hb 1[12]; הַלְהוֹכַח Jb 6[26]; *Pt.* מוֹכִיחַ Ez 3[26] + 8 t.; pl. מוֹכִיחִים Pr 24[25];—**1.** *decide, judge,* abs. Gn 31[42] (E), 1 Ch 12[17] Is 11[3] ψ 94[10]; c. לְ, *decide for*

Is 2^{4}=Mi 4^{3}, Is 11^{4}; c. בֵּין, Gn 31^{37} (E), Jb 9^{33}; לְגֶבֶר עִם אֱלוֹהַּ Jb 16^{21}. **2.** *adjudge, appoint,* c. לְ, Gn $24^{14.44}$ (J). **3.** *shew to be right, prove,* c. acc. rei and עַל pers. *against* Jb 19^{5}; c. אֶל pers. *unto* Jb 13^{15}; so *argue* before v^{3}, and (abs.) 15^{3}. **4.** *convince, convict,* c. acc. pers. ψ 50^{21} בְּ pers. Pr 30^{6}; c. לְ pers. Jb 32^{12}. **5.** *reprove, chide:* **a.** of God, c. acc. pers. Jb 22^{4} ψ 50^{8} 105^{14} =1 Ch 16^{21}; c. בְּ obj. 2 K 19^{4}=Is 37^{4}. **b.** of man, abs. Ho 4^{4} Ez 3^{26} Jb $6^{25.25}$ Pr 24^{25} 25^{12}; מוֹכִיחַ בַּשַּׁעַר Am 5^{10} Is 29^{21}; c. acc. pers. Gn 21^{25} (E), Lv $19^{17.17}$ (H), Pr 9^{8} 28^{23} Je 2^{19}; מוֹכִיחַ אֱלוֹהַּ Jb 40^{2}; acc. rei Jb 6^{26}; c. לְ, Pr $9^{7.8}$ 15^{12} 19^{25}. **6.** *correct, rebuke,* of God, abs. Hb 1^{12}; c. acc. pers. ψ 141^{5} Jb $13^{10.10}$; בְּשֵׁבֶט 2 S 7^{14}; happy the man whom God corrects Jb 5^{17}; for God loves him Pr 3^{12}; God is entreated not to correct in anger ψ 6^{2} 38^{2}. **Hoph.** *Pf.* וְהוּכַח בְּמַכְאוֹב *he is chastened also with pain* Jb 33^{19}. **Niph.** *Impf.* לְכוּ־נָא וְנִוָּכְחָה Is 1^{18} *come now and let us reason together;* *Pt.* שָׁם יָשָׁר נוֹכָח עִמּוֹ Jb 23^{7} *there an upright man might reason with him;* f. (pass.) וְנֹכַחַת Gn 20^{16} (E), but Di SS rd. וְנֹכַחַתְּ 2 fs. *Pf. and thou art set right, righted, justified.* **Hithp.** *Impf.* עִם־יִשְׂרָאֵל יִתְוַכָּח Mi 6^{2} *with Israel he will argue* (‖ רִיב לי׳ עִם).

8433 †תּוֹכֵחָה **n.f.** rebuke, correction;—יוֹם ת׳ Ho 5^{9}; יום צרה ות׳ 2 K 19^{3}=Is 37^{3}; pl. תּוֹכֵחוֹת ψ 149^{7} (‖ נקמה).

8433 †תּוֹכַחַת **n.f.** argument, reproof;—ת׳ Pr 10^{17}+9 t.; sf. תּוֹכַחְתִּי Hb 2^{1}+5 t.; תּוֹכַחְתּוֹ Pr 3^{11}; pl. תּוֹכָחוֹת ψ 38^{15}+3 t.; cstr. תּוֹכְחוֹת Pr 6^{23} Ez 25^{17}; תֹּכְחוֹת 5^{15} (but latter del. Co; given by SS under תּוֹכֵחָה);—**1.** *argument, impeachment,* spoken by lips and mouth ψ 38^{15} Jb 13^{6} 23^{4} Hb 2^{1}. **2.** *reproof, chiding* Pr 1^{23} 27^{5}; ‖ עצה $1^{25.30}$; ‖ מוסר 3^{11} 5^{12} 10^{17} 12^{1} 13^{18} $15^{5.10.32}$; ת׳ מוסר 6^{23} *reproofs for discipline;* ת׳ חיים 15^{31} *reproof that giveth life;* איש תוכחות 29^{1} *man of reproofs* (who deserves them). **3.** *correction, rebuke* ψ 39^{12} 73^{14}; שֵׁבֶט ות׳ Pr 29^{15}; ת׳ חֵמָה Ez 5^{15} 25^{17}.

3201 יָכֹל, יָכוֹל T 193 **vb.** be able, have power, prevail, endure (NH *id.*; Aram. יְכֵיל; As. *akâlu*, Hpt in KAT^{2} Gloss 1.)—**Qal** *Pf.* יָכֹל Gn 32^{26} +8 t.; יָכוֹל 1 S 4^{15}+2 t.; 3 fs. יָֽכְלָה Gn 36^{7} Ex 2^{3}; 2 ms. וְיָכָלְתָּ Ex 18^{23}; 1 s. יָכֹלְתִּי Gn 30^{8}+2 t.; sf. יְכָלְתִּיו ψ 13^{5}; 3 pl. יָֽכְלוּ Gn 13^{6}+27 t.+Jos 15^{63} Qr; יָכֹלוּ Ex 8^{14}+2 t.; *Impf.* 3 ms. יוּכַל Gn 13^{16}+34 t.; יוּכָל Jb 4^{2}+4 t.; וַיּוּכַל Ho 12^{5}; 3 fs. תּוּכַל Am 7^{10}+2 t.; 2 ms. תּוּכַל Gn 15^{5}+16 t.; 1 s. אוּכַל Gn 19^{19}+30 t., etc. (on these Impf. forms as irreg. Qal, v. Ges §69.2, R.3 Kö I. 407 W SG 237; others **Hoph.**); *Inf. cstr.* יְכֹ֫לֶת Nu 14^{16} Dt 9^{28}; *Inf. abs.* יָכוֹל Nu 13^{30} 2 Ch 32^{13}; יָכֹל Nu 22^{38} 1 S 26^{25}; P 8 t. (not Lv), Ez 3 t.; oft. JED Je Is², not seld. SK Ch;—**1.** *be able,* to do a thing, whether ability be physical, moral, constitutional, or dependent on external authority; usu. of man Gn 13^{16} (J)+, but also of gods 2 Ch $32^{13.15}$, and of י׳ Nu 14^{16} (JE), Dt 9^{28} Je 44^{22}; occasionally of inanimate things Am 7^{10} Gn 36^{7} (P), Ct 8^{7} Ec $1^{15.15}$, etc.: **a.** usu. sq. inf. c. לְ (122 t.), Gn 31^{35} *I am not able to rise up;* 45^{1} *Joseph was not able to restrain himself,* v^{3} 48^{10}; Ex $7^{21.24}$ *were not able to drink,* 12^{39} Jos 24^{19} (all E); Gn 13^{16} *if a man can number the dust,* $19^{19.22}$ 43^{32} $44^{22.26.26}$ Ex 10^{5} 19^{23} (all J), Gn 15^{5} Ex 15^{23} Nu 11^{14} (all JE)+10 t. JE; Dt 7^{17}+10 t. D; Gn 13^{6} *they could not dwell together,* 34^{14} 36^{7} Ex 9^{11} 40^{35} Nu 9^{6} Jos 9^{19} (all P); 1 S 3^{2} 6^{20} 1 K 9^{21} (on ‖ 2 Ch 8^{8} and text of Ju 1^{19} v. Bu RS 8), Am 7^{10} Ho 5^{13} Zp 1^{18} Je 6^{10} 11^{11} 13^{23} 18^{6} 19^{11}+. †**b.** sq. inf. without לְ (27 t.; not P): Gn 37^{4} Ex 2^{3} $18^{18.23}$ (all E), Gn 24^{50} 44^{1} (J), Nu $22^{37.38}$ (JE), Dt 1^{9} 7^{22} 14^{24} 22^{29} Ju 8^{3} Je $49^{10.23}$ Hb 1^{13} Is 46^{2} $47^{11.12}$ 57^{20} La 1^{14} ψ 18^{39} 36^{13} 78^{20} Pr 30^{21} Jb 4^{2} 33^{5}. †**c.** c. inf. implic., alw. neg., Gn 29^{8} go and feed them; and they said, *We are not able, cannot* (J), Ex 8^{14} (P), Is 29^{11} Je 20^{9} ψ 21^{12} Jon 1^{13}. **d.** c. neg.=*may not* (of moral inability): Gn 43^{32} (J) the Egyptians *might not eat* bread with the Hebrews; Ju 21^{18} *we may not give* them wives; esp. D, Dt 7^{22} 12^{17} 14^{24} 16^{5} 17^{15} 22^{3} $28^{27.35}$. †**e.** *be able,* sq. impf.: אוּלַי אוּכַל נַכֶּה Nu 22^{6} (JE) *perchance I am able* (so that) *we smite* (v. Di; rd. perh. נוּכַל for אוּכַל Ges §120.1 b); לֹא יוּכְלוּ יִגְּעוּ La 4^{14} *they are unable, they touch=are unable to touch* (Dr §163, Obs.) †**f.** *be able,* sq. pf. consec., only very late, אוּכַל וְרָאִיתִי Est $8^{6.6}$, lit. how *shall I be able and see?*—Also in various combinations where English idiom would make it an auxiliary to another verb: †**g.** *able to gain, accomplish:* sq. acc. לֹא יוּכְלוּ נִקָּיֹן Ho 8^{5} how long *will they be unable* (to gain) *innocence?* יָדַעְתָּ כִּי־כֹל תּוּכָל Jb 42^{2} *I know that thou art able* (to do) *all things;* אֵין הַמֶּלֶךְ יוּכַל אֶתְכֶם דָּבָר Je 38^{5} *the king is not* (one who is) *able* (to do) *anything with* (אֶתְכֶם for אִתְּכֶם v. Gf, i.e. *against*) *you.* †**h.** *able to endure:* לֹא אוּכַל אָוֶן וַעֲצָרָה Is 1^{13} *I cannot endure iniquity and* (with) *a solemn assembly,* ψ 101^{5}. †**i.** *able to reach,* sq. לְ, ψ 139^{6} it is high, לֹא אוּכַל לָהּ *I cannot* (reach) *to it.*

†**2.** *prevail:* **a.** abs. *prevail, overcome, be victor* Gn 30^{8} (E), 32^{29} (J), Ho 12^{5} 1 S 26^{25} 1 K 22^{22} = 2 Ch 18^{21} Je 20$^{7.11}$; of waves 5^{22}; *succeed* Is 16^{12}, Je 3^{5} (VB *hast had thy way*). **b.** sq. לְ pers., *prevail against, over* Gn 32^{26} (J), Nu 13^{30} (JE), Ju 16^{5} 1 S 17^{9} Je 1^{19} 15^{20} 20^{10} 38^{22} Ob^{7} ψ 129^{2} Est 6^{13}. **c.** once c. sf., יְכָלְתִּיו ψ 13^{5} *I have prevailed over him*, + Zc 9^{15} (where rd. וְיָכְלוּם for וְאָכְלוּ with 𝔊 𝔗 Klo$^{Th LZ 1879. 564}$ Sta$^{ZAW 1881, 18}$). †**3.** abs. *have ability, strength*, only neg. מִשְּׂאֵתוֹ לֹא אוּכָל Jb 31^{23} *because of his loftiness I have no ability*, am inadequate (to anything).

3081 יוּכַל **n.pr.m.** v. יְהוּכַל supr. p. 220^{b}.

3203 †יְכָלְיָה, יְכָלְיָהוּ **n.pr.f.** (*'י hath been able*; cf. Sab. יכלאל Hal^{465}) mother of king Azariah: יכליהו 2 K 15^{2}, 𝔊 Χαλεια, 𝔊L Ιεχελια; יכליה 2 Ch 26^{3} (Qr; Kt יכיליה), 𝔊 Χααια, A 𝔊L Ιεχελια.

3078,3204 יְכָנְיָה(וּ), יְכוֹנְיָה v. יְהוֹיָכִין p. 220^{b}.

3205 **יָלַד**$^{T 497}$ **vb.** bear, bring forth, beget (NH *id.*; Aram. יְלִיד, יְלֵד, ܝܠܕ; Ar. وَلَدَ *bear, bring forth*, so Eth. ወለደ: As. *alâdu*, COT^{Gloss})—**Qal** *Pf.* יָלַד Gn 4$^{18.18.18}$ + 16 t.; יָלָ֑דָה Je 17^{11}; וְיָלַד consec. ψ 7^{15}; sf. יְלָֽדֶךָ Dt 32^{18}; 2 ms. sf. ילדתני Je 2^{27} Kt; Qr יְלִדְתָּנוּ (Kö$^{i. 410}$ Ges$^{§ 70. 2. R. 4}$); 1 s. sf. יְלִדְתִּיךָ ψ 2^{7}; יְלִדְתִּיהוּ Nu 11^{12}, etc.; *Impf.* יֵלֶד(יוֹם) Pr 27^{1}; 3 fs. תֵּלֵד Gn 17^{17} + 6 t.; וַתֵּ֫לֶד 4^{1} + 61 t.; 2 fs. תֵּלְדִי 3^{16}; אֵלֵד 18^{13}; וָאֵלֵד 1 K 3^{17}; יֵלֵדוּ Is 65^{23}; 3 fpl. תֵּלַדְנָה Je 29^{6}; וַתֵּלַדְנָה Ez 23^{4}; וַתֵּלַדְןָ Gn 30^{39}, etc.; *Inf. abs.* יָלֹד Jb 15^{35}; cstr. לֵדָה Ho 9^{11} + 3 t.; לֶ֫דֶת Gn 4^{2} + 10 t.; לָלַת 1 S 4^{19} (Kö$^{i. 402}$, but prob. txt. err. Dr); sf. לִדְתִּי 1 K 3^{18}, etc.; *Pt. act.* יֹלֵד Pr 17^{21} Je 30^{6}, etc.; f. יוֹלֵדָה Ho 13^{13} + 12 t.; יֹלֶ֫דֶת Gn 17^{19} + 4 t.; יֹלַדְתְּ 16^{11} + 2 t. (Kö$^{i. 404 f.}$; perh. יֹלֶ֫דֶת intended by Kt, cf. Sta$^{§ 213 b}$); sf. Pr 23^{25}; יוֹלַדְתּוֹ Pr 17^{25}, etc.; pl. יֹלְדוֹת Je 16^{3}; *Pt. pass.* יָלוּד 1 K 3$^{26.27}$; cstr. יְלוּד Jb 14^{1} + 2 t.; pl. יְלוּדִים 1 Ch 14^{4};—**1.** *bear, bring forth:* **a.** (a mother a child,) so commonly, c. 208 t.; sq. acc. Gn 3^{16} 4^{1} & constantly; acc. om. 6^{2} etc. = *be delivered of a child*, 1 K 3$^{17.18}$ 2 K 19^{3} = Is 37^{3} (in proverb c. neg., i.e. human power exhausted); of animals Gn 30^{39} 31$^{8.8}$ Je 14^{5} 17^{11} (bird laying eggs, or hatching out young), Ez 31^{6} Jb 39$^{1.2}$; but also of whole process of labour (cf. חול) וַתְּקַשׁ בְּלִדְתָּהּ Gn 35^{16} cf. v^{17}, 38$^{27.28}$, cf. 1 S 14^{19} Je 31^{18} Mi 5^{2} (of a man, as preposterous, Je 30^{6}, cf. Moses as mother of Israel Nu 11^{12}). **b.** hence in simile of distress Mi 4$^{9.10}$ Is 13^{8} 21^{3} 42^{14} Je 6^{24} 13^{21} 22^{23} 30^{6} 49^{24} 50^{43} ψ 48^{7}, cf. Ho 13^{13}; ילד על־ברכים (Sta$^{ZAW 1886, 143 ff.}$) Gn 30^{3} 50^{23} (cf. Jb 3^{12}). **c.** fig. of wicked וְהָרָה עָמָל וְיָלַד שָׁ֑קֶר ψ 7^{15} cf. Jb 15^{35} also Is 33^{11}; of Israelites, bringing forth wind (of vain efforts for deliverance) 26^{18}; כְּפֹר שָׁמַיִם מִי יְלָדוֹ Jb 38^{29}; of Tyre as mother of her inhabitants Is 23^{4}; of Jerus. Is 51^{18} 54^{1} 66$^{7.8}$ Ez 16^{20}, Isr. *bearing* disloyal children Ho 5^{7}; Jerus. and Sam., as Oholibah and Oholah Ez 23^{37}; of Babylon Je 50^{12}; of a day, as producing events לֹא־תֵדַע מַה יֵּ֫לֶד יוֹם Pr 27^{1}; perh. of God (fig. of rock צור), as mother of Isr. bringing forth with labour Dt 32^{18} yet v. **2**. **2.** less often *beget:* **a.** lit., c. 22 t., alw. c. acc.; in Hex a mark of J; Gn 4$^{18.18.18}$ 10$^{8.13.15.24.24.26}$ = 1 Ch 1$^{10.11.13.18.18.20}$, Gn 22^{23} 25^{3} (Dt 32^{18} & Nu 11^{12} E are dub.; P uses **Hiph.**), elsewh. Pr 17^{21} 23$^{22.24}$ Dn 11^{6}. **b.** *beget*, fig. ψ 2^{7} of 'י's formally installing king into theocratic rights. **3.** Zc 13$^{3.3}$, of both parents (lit.); Pt. pass. 3 t. = *child* 1 K 3$^{26.27}$ where mother is named, 1 Ch 14^{4} where father named. †**Niph.** *Pf.* נוֹלַד 1 Ch 2^{3} + 6 t. + הִנּוֹלֶד־ Gn 21^{3} acc. to points, but rd. Pt. (v. Di); נוֹלְדוּ 3^{5} 20^{8} (cf. Ol$^{§ 263 b}$ Ges$^{§ 70. 2. R. 5}$); *Impf.* יִוָּלֵד Gn 17^{17} + 4 t.; יִוָּ֫לֵד Is 66^{8}; וַיִּוָּלֵד Gn 4^{18} + 2 t., etc.; *Inf.* הִוָּלֶד Gn 21^{5}; הִוָּלְדוֹ Ec 7^{1}; הִוָּלְדָהּ Ho 2^{5}; *Pt.* נוֹלָד 1 K 13^{2} + 3 t. (Gn 21^{3} v. supr.); נוֹלָדִים 48^{5} 1 Ch 7^{21};—*be born:* of human beings, sq. לְ (born to such and such a man), Gn 4^{18} 10^{1} 17^{17} 21$^{3.5}$ 46^{20} 48^{5} Nu 26^{60} Dt 23^{9} 2 S 3^{2} (Qr), 5^{13} 14^{27} 1 Ch 2$^{3.9}$ 3$^{1.4.5}$ 20$^{6.8}$ 22^{9} 26^{6} Jb 1^{2} cf. 1 K 13^{2}; without לְ, Jb 3^{3} 38^{21} ψ 78^{6} 1 Ch 7^{21} Ec 7^{1} (טוֹב שֵׁם מִשֶּׁמֶן טוֹב וְיוֹם הַמָּוֶת מִיּוֹם הִוָּלְדוֹ׃); metaph. of Israel (under fig. of unfaithful wife) Ho 2^{5}; of nation, גּוֹי, Is 66^{8}, people, עַם, ψ 22^{32}; of animals Lv 22^{27} Dt 15^{19}; *Pt.* כָּל־נָשִׁים וְהַנּוֹלָד מֵהֶם Ezr 10^{3}; c. pred. or appos. on which emph. rests, נ׳ רָשׁ Ec 4^{14} *he was born poor;* אֹהֵב הָרֵעַ וְאָח לְצָרָה יִוָּלֵד Pr 17^{17}; עִיר פרא אדם יִוָּלֵד Jb 11^{12} 15^{7}. †**Pi.** *Inf.* בְּיַלֶּדְכֶן Ex 1^{16}; *Pt. abs.* מְיַלֶּ֫דֶת Gn 35^{17} + 2 t.; *pl. abs.* מְיַלְּדוֹת Ex 1^{15} + 5 t. in Ex 1;—*cause* (or *help*) *to bring forth*, viz., *assist* or *tend as midwife* Ex 1^{16} sq. acc.; elsewh. only *Pt. f.* as subst. = *midwife;* Gn 35^{17} (E), 38^{28} (J), Ex 1$^{15.17.18.19.19.20.21}$ (E). †**Pu.** *Pf.* יֻלַּד Gn 4^{26} + 13 t.; יוּלַּד Ju 18^{29}; יֻלַּד Gn 41^{50}; יוּלָּ֑ד Jb 5^{7}; יֻלְּדוּ Gn 6^{1} + 4 t. + 2 S 3^{2} Kt (Qr וַיִּוָּלְדוּ); יֻלָּ֑דוּ ψ 90^{2}, etc.; *Pt.* (? cf. Kö$^{i. 433}$; Ges$^{§ 52. 2. R. 6}$) הַיּוּלָּד Ju 13^{8} (Bö$^{ii. p. 244}$ pass. Qal); i. q. Niph. *be born*, sq. לְ of father Gn 4^{26} 6^{1} 10$^{21.25}$ 24^{15} (all J), 41^{50} (E), 35^{26} 36^{5} 46$^{22.27}$ (all P),

Ju 18[29] 2 S 3[2.5] 21[20.22] 1 Ch 1[19] Je 20[15]; sq. לְ before grandmother's name Ru 4[17] cf. לָנוּ Is 9[5]; sq. לְ of purpose, destiny, אדם לעמל יוּלָּד Jb 5[7]; יֻלְּדוּ עַל־בִּרְכֵּי יוֹסֵף Gn 50[23] (E; Sam. בִּימֵי יו׳, cit. Di) denoting recognition of children as his; no prep. Je 20[14] 22[26], cf. Ju 13[8] (v. supr.); fig. of foreigners incorporated in spiritual Zion ψ 87[4.5.6]; of production of mountains ψ 90[2]. **Hiph.** *Pf.* הוֹלִיד Gn 11[27]+; הוֹלִד Nu 26[58]; הֹלִיד 1 Ch 2[36]+; sf. וְהוֹלִידָהּ consec. Is 55[10]; הוֹלַדְתָּ Gn 48[6], etc.; *Impf.* יוֹלִיד Gn 17[20] Ec 6[3]; וַיּוֹלֶד Gn 5[3]+; 2 ms. תּוֹלִיד Dt 4[25]+4 t.; אוֹלִיד Is 66[9]; *Imv.* הוֹלִידוּ Je 29[6]; *Inf. abs.* הוֹלֵיד Is 59[4]; *cstr.* sf. הוֹלִידוֹ Gn 5[4]+16 t.; *Pt.* מוֹלִיד Is 66[9]; מוֹלִדִים Je 16[3];—**1.** *beget* (a father a child) Gn 5[3.4.4]+56 t. in Gn., Lv 25[45] Nu 26[29.58] (all these P, v. sub **Qal**)+Dt 4[25] 28[41] (v. Di), 1 Ch 2[10.10.11.11]+84 t. Chr.; Ru 4[18]+8 t., Ju 11[1] 2 K 20[18]=Is 39[7], Je 29[6] Ez 18[10.14] 47[22] Ec 5[13] 6[3], cf. Is 45[10]; also Je 16[3] אֲבוֹתָם הַמּוֹלִדִים אוֹתָם, cf. freq. Assyr. *abu banûa*, e.g. VR 1[8]; fig. of producing dewdrops Jb 38[28]; of causing the earth to bear grain Is 55[10]; causing Zion to bring forth 66[9]. **2.** *bear*, only fig. 59[4] (‖ הָרוֹ), of wicked, bringing forth iniquity (this favoured by context; others, *beget*). †**Hoph.** *Inf.* הֻלֶּדֶת Gn 40[20] Ez 16[5]; הוּלֶּדֶת Ez 16[4] (Co as foregoing); only יוֹם ה׳ אֶת־ Gn 40[20] Ez 16[4.5] *day of one's being born* = birthday. †**Hithp.** *Impf.* וַיִּתְיַלְדוּ Nu 1[18] denom. fr. תולדת *declared their pedigree* (v. Di).

2056 †וָלָד **n.m. offspring, child,** only אֵין לָהּ וָלָד Gn 11[30] (J); si vera l.=Ar. وَلَدٌ; Eth. ወልድ፡ (with orig. ו);—in 2 S 6[23], where some edd. have ולד Kt, יֶלֶד Qr, Baer and van d. H give יָלֶד Kt.

3206 †יֶלֶד[89] **n.m.**[Gn 21, 8] **child, son, boy, youth**;—יֶלֶד abs. Gn 4[23]+; cstr. Je 31[20]; יָלֶד Gn 21[16]+; pl. יְלָדִים 33[1]+; cstr. יַלְדֵי Ex 2[6]+2 t.; יַלְדֵי־ Is 57[4]; sf. יְלָדַי Gn 30[26] 2 K 4[1]; יַלְדֵיהֶם Jb 21[11]; יַלְדֵיהֶן Gn 33[2]+4 t., etc.;—**a.** *child=son, boy,* Gn 21[8.14.15.16] 37[30] 42[22] (all E), 32[23] (Dinah not included), cf. 30[26] 33[1.2.2.5.5.6.7.13.14] 44[20] (all J); Ex 1[17.18] (‖ בֵּן v[16]), 2[3.6.6.7.8.9.9.10] (all E), 21[4] (E; app. =sons+daughters, but ‖ בָּנָיו v[5]); pl.=offspring 21[24] (E; Hex, only Gn & Ex, JE); also Ru 1[5] 4[16] 2 S 12[15.18.18.18.18.19.19.21.21.22.22] 1 K 3[25] (cf. v[20]), 14[12] 17[21.21.22.23] 2 K 4[1] (cf. v[5]) v[18.26.34.34] Is 8[18] 9[5] (‖ בֵּן), Jo 4[3] (opp. יַלְדָּה), Zc 8[5] (*id.*); of *young* of raven Jb 38[41]; of wild goats and hinds 39[3]; of cow and bear Is 11[7]. **b.** (little) *child, children* 1 S 1[2.2] 2 S 6[23] Ezr 10[1] Ne 12[43] Jb 21[11] (‖ עֲוִילִים), Ho 1[2] La 4[10] Is 57[5]. **c.** *descendants* Is 29[23], יַלְדֵי נכרים (cf. בֵּן 2[6]. **d.** *youth* Gn 4[23] (J), 1 K 12[8.10.14] = 2 Ch 10[8.10.14], Dn 1[4.10.13.15.17] cf. 2 K 2[24] (‖ נְעָרִים קְטַנִּים v[23]), Ec 4[13.15]. **e.** fig. of apostate Israelites יַלְדֵי־פֶשַׁע Is 57[4] (‖ זֶרַע שָׁקֶר); cf., in good sense, ילד שַׁעֲשֻׁעִים Je 31[20] of Ephraim (‖ בֵּן יַקִּיר).

†יַלְדָּה **n.f. girl, damsel**;—abs. יַלְדָּה Gn 34[4] 3207
Jo 4[3]; וִילָדוֹת Zc 8[5];—*marriageable girl*: of Dinah, daughter of Jacob Gn 34[4]; opp. יֶלֶד Zc 8[5] Jo 4[3].

†יַלְדוּת **n.f. childhood, youth**;—abs. יַלְדוּת 3208
Ec 11[10] (‖ שַׁחֲרוּת); יַלְדוּתֶךָ 11[9]; =young men טַל יַלְדֻתֶךָ ψ 110[3].

†יִלּוֹד **adj. born** (irreg. punctuation for 3209
יָלוּד, Dr 2 S 5[14])—יִלּוֹד Ex 1[22] 2 S 12[14]; יִלֹּדִים Jos 5[5] 2 S 5[14]; יִלּוֹדִים Je 16[3]; הַבֵּן הַיִּל׳ Ex 1[22] (E), 2 S 12[14] (+לְךָ); הָעָם הַיִּל׳ בַּמִּדְבָּר Jos 5[5] (D); עַל־הַבָּנִים וְעַל־הַבָּנוֹת הַיִּלּוֹדִים בַּמָּקוֹם הַזֶּה Je 16[3]; הַיִּלּוֹדִים לוֹ 2 S 5[14].

†[יָלִיד] **adj. born,** only *cstr.* יְלִיד Gn 17[12] 3211
+4 t.; pl. יְלִידֵי 14[14]+6 t.; בִּילִדֵי 2 S 21[18];—*born*, esp. of slave יְלִיד בַּיִת born in (one's) house (opp. purchased by money) Gn 17[12.13.27] Lv 22[11] (all P), cf. Je 2[14] where denied of Israel; יְלִידֵי בַיִת *id.* Gn 14[14]; pl. elsewh. subst. = *children, sons* יל׳ הָרָפָה 2 S 21[16.18] cf. יל׳ הָרְפָאִים 1 Ch 20[4]; יל׳ הענק Nu 13[22.28] Jos 15[14] (all JE).

†מוֹלֶדֶת **n.f. kindred, birth, offspring**;— 4038
מ׳ cstr. Lv 18[9.11]; sf. מוֹלַדְתִּי Gn 24[4]+3 t., etc.; pl. sf. מוֹלְדוֹתַיִךְ Ez 16[4]; מְלֹדֹתַיִךְ v[3];—**1.** *kindred* Gn 12[1] (‖ ארצך, בית אביך), 24[4] (‖ ארץ), Nu 10[30] (‖ *id.*), Gn 31[3] (‖ ארץ אבותיך), 43[7] (all J); ‖ עַם Est 2[10.20] 8[6]; esp. אֶרֶץ מ׳ *land of one's kindred* Gn 11[28] 24[7] (both J), 31[13] (E), Je 22[10] 46[16] Ez 23[15] Ru 2[11]. **2.** pl. *circumstances of birth, birth* (fig. of origin of Jerus.) מְכֹרֹתַיִךְ וּמ׳ מֵאֶרֶץ הַכְּנַעֲנִי Ez 16[3], cf. v[4]. **3.** (female) *offspring, one born* Lv 18[9.9], *begotten* v[11] (all H); coll.=*issue, offspring* מוֹלַדְתְּךָ אֲשֶׁר הוֹלַדְתָּ Gn 48[6] (P).

†מוֹלָדָה, מֹלָדָה **n.pr.loc.** town in Simeon 4137
מוֹל׳ Jos 19[2]=1 Ch 4[28]; inhabited after exile Ne 11[26]; name occurs also Jos 15[26] (where prob. interpol. from Ne 11[26] v. Di); 𝔊 Μωλαδα, etc.; identified by Rob[BR ii, 201] Guérin[Judée iii, 184 ff.] with Tel *Milḥ*, 4 hours E. from Beersheba=Μάλαθα Jos[Ant. xviii. 6, 2]; Μαλα(α)θων, *Malatha* Lag[Onom. 214. 266. 87. 119], v. also Di.

4140 † מוֹלִיד **n.pr.m.** a Judahite 1 Ch 2[29].

8435 [תּוֹלֵדוֹת] [39] **n.f.pl. generations**, esp. in genealogies=**account of a man and his descendants**;—cstr. תּוֹלְדוֹת Gn 2[4] Ru 4[18]; תּוֹלְדֹת Gn 5[1]+6 t.; תֹּלְדוֹת 36[1]+2 t.; תֹּלְדֹת 25[12]; sf. תֹּלְדֹתָיו 1 Ch 26[31]; תּוֹלְדֹתָם Ex 28[10]+16 t.; תֹּלְדוֹתָם 1 Ch 5[7]+5 t.; תֹּלְדֹתָם Ex 6[16.19];—**a.** *account of men and their descendants* Gn 5[1] 6[9] 10[1] 11[10.27] 25[12.19] 36[1.9] 37[2] Nu 3[1] Ru 4[18] 1 Ch 1[29]; *successive generations* (in) of families (מִשְׁפָּחֹת) Gn 10[32] cf. 25[13], Ex 6[16.19] 28[10]; *genealogical divisions*, by parentage Nu 1[20] (ת׳ לְמִשְׁפְּחֹתָם)+11 t. Nu 1; וְאֶחָיו לְמִשְׁפְּחֹתָיו בְּהִתְיַחֵשׂ לתולדותם 1 Ch 5[7] cf. 7[9] and prob. also 7[2] v. Be, 7[4] 8[28] 9[9.34] 26[31]. **b.** metaph. תּוֹלְדוֹת הַשָּׁמַיִם וְהָאָרֶץ Gn 2[4] lit. *begettings of heaven and earth*, i.e. ***account of heaven and earth and that which proceeded from them*** (cf. Dr[Intr. 5 n.]) In Hex always P.

8434 † תּוֹלָד **n.pr.loc.** in Simeon 1 Ch 4[29], 𝔊 Θουλαεμ, A Θωλαδ, 𝔊L Θολαθ; appar.=אֶלְתּוֹלַד q. v. supr. p. 39.

3213 † [יָלַל] **vb. Hiph.** howl, make a howling (onomatop.)—**Hiph.** *Pf.* וְהֵילִל consec. Je 47[2]; וְהֵילִילוּ consec. Am 8[3]; *Impf.* יְיֵלִיל Is 15[2]+3 t. (Ges [§ 70. 2, R. 2] Kö [i. 437, 421]); אֵילִיל Je 48[31]; וְאֵילִילָה Mi 1[8]; יְיֵלִילוּ Ho 7[14] (Kö[i. 421]); יְהֵילִילוּ Is 52[5]; תְּיֵלִילוּ Is 65[14]; *Imv.* הֵילֵל Ez 21[17] Zc 11[2]; הֵילִילִי Is 14[31] 49[3]+Je 48[20] Kt; הֵילִילוּ Is 13[6]+13 t.+ Je 48[20] Qr, +Ez 30[2] (del. 𝔊 Co);—*utter* or *make a howling, give a howl*, in distress, ‖ זעק Ho 7[14] Je 47[2] Is 14[31] Je 25[34] 48[20.31] (sq. עַל), Ez 21[17]; ‖ צעק Is 65[14] (sq. מִן of occasion, source); ‖ ספד Mi 1[8] Je 4[8] Jo 1[13]; ‖ הֹבִישׁ Jo 1[11]; ‖ בכה 1[5] (cf. Is 15[2.3]+בֶּכִי); sq. עַל Je 51[8] Is 15[2.3]; We prop. ילילו for יגילו Ho 10[5] (others יחילו, v. גיל supr. p. 162); sq. לְ Is 16[7]; abs. והילילו שירות היכל Am 8[3] *and palace-songs shall become howlings*, Is 13[6] 16[7] 23[1.6.14] Je 48[39] 49[3] (Ez 30[2] v. supr.), Zp 1[11] Zc 11[2.2]; in cruel exultation Is 52[5] cf. De Che Di.—On הֵילֵל בֶּן־שָׁחַר Is 14[12] cf. sub I. הלל supr. p. 237.

3214 † יְלֵל **n.[m.]** **howling** (of beasts);—וּבְתֹהוּ יְלֵל יְשִׁמֹן Dt 32[10] *in a waste of howling of a desert* (=*in the howling waste of a desert;* v. Dr).

3215 † יְלָלָה **n.f. howling**;—וִילָלָה Zp 1[10]; cstr. יִלְלַת Je 25[36] Zc 11[3]; יִלְלָתָהּ Is 15[8.8];—*howling* in distress Is 15[8.8] (‖ זְעָקָה), Je 25[36] (of leaders of flock, metaph. for princes; ‖ קול צעקה), Zp 1[10] (‖ *id.*); קול יִלְלַת הָרֹעִים Zc 11[3] (רעים metaph. for princes).

יַלַע Pr 20[25] v. לעע. p. 534 3216

יָלַף (√of foll.; mng. dub.; Ar. وَلَفَ III. is *conjunctus fuit* cum aliquo, etc., Frey; whence ילפת as an *accretion?* so Thes 'ab adhaerendo').

† יַלֶּפֶת **n.f. scab, scurf,** an eruptive disease, 3217
Lv 21[20] 22[22] (in both ‖ גָּרָב).

ילק (√of following; meaning dubious; Thes al. comp. לקק *lick;* Ar. وَلَقَ is *hasten*, etc.)

† יֶלֶק **n.m.** [Na 3. 16] a kind of **locust**, abs. יֶלֶק 3218
Na 3[16]+5 t.; יָלֶק Jo 1[4]+2 t.;—alw. coll.: **a.** as devouring ‖ אַרְבֶּה, חָסִיל, גָּזָם, Jo 1[4.4] 2[25]; ‖ אַרְבֶּה ψ 105[34] (of Egyptian plague), cf. Na 3[15a] (but del. We). **b.** in sim. of multitude of men Na 3[15b] Je 51[14]; of horses v[27] (יֶלֶק סָמָר). **c.** in sim. of scattering and disappearing Na 3[16].

יַלְקוּט v. לקט. p. 545 3219

† יְמוּאֵל **n.pr.m.** son of Simeon Gn 46[10] Ex 3223
6[15] (𝔊 Ιεμουηλ)=נְמוּאֵל (q.v.) Nu 26[12] 1 Ch 4[24].

† יְמִימָה **n.pr.f.** (cf. perh. Ar. يَمَامَةٌ *dove*, 3224
nom. unit. of يَمَامٌ Frey)—daughter of Job Jb 42[14].

יִמְלָה **n.pr.** v. יִמְלָא sub מלא. p. 571 3229

ימם (√assumed for foll.; actual existence and meaning dubious, v. infr.)

יָם [390] **n.m.** [Ex 14, 27] **sea** (Ph. ים; Ar. يَمٌّ; Palm. 3220
בימא *on the sea*, Vog[No. 79]; on As. *idmu*, (*āmu*), *sea*, v. Dl[HWB 307] M-A[CD 52] Hpt[BAS i. 171 n.])—abs. יָם 1 S 13[5]+; יָמָּה Gn 28[14]+; cstr. יָם Gn 14[3]+23 t., also יָמָּה סוּף Ex 10[19], but alw. יַם־סוּף Ex 13[18]+22 t.; sf. יַמָּהּ Je 51[36]; pl. יַמִּים Ju 5[17]+29 t.;—*sea*: esp. **1.** *Mediterranean* Nu 13[29] (E), 34[5] (P), Dt 1[7] Jos 5[1] 1 K 5[23.23] Jon 1[4.4]+oft.; the Mediterr. is called also הַיָּם הַגָּדוֹל Nu 34[6.7] Jos 15[12.47] Ez 48[28]+, cf. הַיָּם הַגּ׳ מְבוֹא ψ 104[25]; הַיּ׳ גּ׳ וּרְחַב יָדַיִם הַשֶּׁמֶשׁ Jos 1[4] 23[4] (v. As. name of Mediterr. *tiamtu rabitu ša sulmu šamši*, etc., Schr[Namen der Meere, 171 ff.]); הַיּ׳ הַגּ׳ אֶל־מוּל הַלְּבָנוֹן Jos 9[1]; הַיּ׳ הָאַחֲרוֹן *the hinder sea* Dt 11[24] 34[2] Zc 14[8] Jo 2[20] (in the last two opp. הַיּ׳ הַקַּדְמֹנִי, v. infr.); of Mediterr. in particular part יָם פְּלִשְׁתִּים Ex 23[31] (JE); יָם יָפוֹ 2 Ch 2[15]= יָם יָפוֹא Ezr 3[7]. **2.** יַם־סוּף '*Red Sea*' (v. סוּף) Ex 13[18] (cf. 10[19]), 15[4] Nu 14[25] Dt 1[40] Jos 2[10] Ju

11^{16}+oft.; also הַיָּם Ex 14$^{2.2.9}$ Is 51$^{10.10}$ 63^{11}+; prob. also יַם־מִצְרַיִם 11^{15}; 'Red Sea' named or referred to c. 66 t.; יַם־סוּף clearly of Ælanitic Gulf 1 K 9^{26} (cf. 2 Ch 8^{17}). **3.** *Dead Sea,* יָם מֶלַח *sea of salt* Gn 14^{3} Nu 34$^{3.12}$ Dt 3^{17} Jos 3^{16} 12^{3} 15$^{2.5}$ 18^{19}; יָם הָעֲרָבָה Dt 3^{17} 4^{49} Jos 3^{16} 12^{3} 2 K 14^{25}; הַיָּ׳ הַקַּדְמֹנִי Ez 47^{18} Zc 14^{8} Jo 2^{20} (v. supr.); simply יָם Is 16^{8} Je 48^{32};—in יָם יַעְזֵר Je 48^{32} יָם is text. error, del. c. Gf Gr Che Gie. **4.** *Sea of Galilee* יָם כִּנֶּרֶת Nu 34^{11} Jos 13^{27}; יָם כִּנְּרוֹת 12^{3}; simply יָם Dt 33^{23}. **5.** more gen. *sea,* opp. earth and (or) sky Gn 1$^{26.28}$ 9^{2} (P), Ex 20^{11} (E), Hg 2^{6}+oft. Jb ψ Is^{2} etc.; Am 6^{12} rd. בַּבָּקָר יָם for בבקרים (v. בָּקָר); *sea* as under earth ψ 24^{2} (cf. Gn 1^{10} 6^{11} Ex 20^{5}=Dt 5^{3}); fig. of *flood* of invaders, עָלָה עַל־בָּבֶל הַיָּם Je 51^{42}. **6.** of a *mighty river,* the Nile Na 3$^{8.8}$ Is 19^{5} (‖ נָהָר); cf. הַתַּנִּין אֲשֶׁר בַּיָּם 27^{1} and כַּתַּנִּים בַּיַּמִּים Ez 32^{2} (sim. of Pharaoh); of Euphrates Is 21^{1} Je 51^{36} (acc. to Che Gf al.; Is 21^{1} perhaps better of Persian Gulf, v. Di). **7.** the great basin in temple-court, called *the sea:* וַיַּעַשׂ אֶת־הַיָּם מוּצָק 1 K 7^{23} =2 Ch 4^{2}; יָם הַנְּחֹשֶׁת 2 K 25^{13} 1 Ch 18^{8} Je 52^{17}; הַיָּם alone 1 K 7$^{24.25}$+10 t. K Ch+Je 52^{20}. **8.** combinations are: **a.** *shore of sea, sea-shore* שְׂפַת הַיָּם Jos 11^{4} 1 K 5^{9}, and in sim. Gn 22^{17} Ju 7^{12} 1 S 13^{5}; חוֹף הַיָּ׳ Jos 9^{1} Ez 25^{16}; חוֹף יַמִּים Gn 49^{13} Ju 5^{17}; cf. חֶבֶל הַיָּם Zp 2^{5} *region by the sea;* so v^{6} but dub., v. I. חֶבֶל **3.** **b.** *sand of the sea* (*shore*) חוֹל הַיָּם (in sim.) Gn 32^{13} 41^{49} Ho 2^{1} Is 10^{22}+oft. (v. חוֹל); חוֹל גְּבוּל לַיָּם Je 5^{22}. **c.** לְשׁוֹן הַיָּם *tongue* (*arm* or *gulf*) *of sea* Jos 15^{5} 18^{19} Is 11^{15}. **d.** מִיָּם עַד־יָם Am 8^{12} Zc 9^{10} ψ 72^{8}, cf. Mi 7^{12} Zc 14$^{8.8}$ Jo 2$^{20.20}$ Dn 11^{45}. **9.** =*west, westward* (orig. *sea-ward,* fr. position of Mediterr. with ref. to Palestine, and this sense still often perceptible): with other three points of compass Gn 13^{14} 28^{14} (J), Nu 2^{18} 35^{5} (P), Dt 3^{27} 1 K 7^{25} 1 Ch 9^{24} 2 Ch 4^{4} Ez 42^{19}+6 t. Ez, Zc 14^{4} Dn 8^{4} ψ 107^{3} (מִמִּזְרָח וּמִמַּעֲרָב מִצָּפוֹן וּמִיָּם); but rd. perh. וּמִיָּמִין *from the south,* Hu Pe Bi Che); opp. east Jos 11^{2} 16^{6}+16 t. Ez 48; *west* alone Gn 12^{8} (J); רוּחַ יָם Ez 10^{19} (J) *west wind;* מִיָּם לְ *westward* Jos 8$^{9.12.13}$+; יָ֫מָּה *westward,* oft. of tabernacle Ex 26$^{22.27}$ Nu 3^{23}+(all P), and of land Jos 5^{1} 15$^{8.10}$ etc., +oft. Ez; דֶּרֶךְ הַיָּם=*westward* Ez 41^{12}; פְּאַת־יָם גְּבוּל יָם *western border* Nu 34$^{6.6}$ Jos 15^{2}; *west side* Ex 27^{12} 38^{12} Nu 35^{5} Jos 18^{14}; פְּאַת דרך הים Ez 41^{12} (v. further פאה).

3222 †יֵמִם **n.[m.]** appar. pl., meaning dub.; only in הוּא עֲנָה אֲשֶׁר מָצָא אֶת־הַיֵּמִם בַּמִּדְבָּר Gn 36^{24} *that is the 'Ana that found the* יֵמִם *in the wilderness* when he was pasturing the asses of Ṣib'ōn his father; perh. *hot springs,* 𝔙 *aquae calidae;* so Thes MV Dechent$^{ZPV\ vii.\ 1884,\ 172}$ al.; yet no suitable √ ימה (or ימם) known; v. further Di Buhl$^{Edomiter\ 46}$.

ימן (√of foll.; found in deriv. in all cogn., 541
but orig. mng. dubious; Thes al. comp. אמן *confirm,* whence *right hand* as the *stronger;* others fr. use of right hand in *confirming* by an oath).

I. יָמִין$_{137}$ **n.f.** $^{Ex\ 15,6}$ (Pr 27^{16} no exc., v. Now 3225
Str) **right hand** (NH *id.;* SI^{3} מִימִן *on the right;* Aram. יַמִּינָא, ܝܰܡܺܝܢܳܐ; Ar. يَمِينٌ *right, right side, right hand, south;* Eth. የማን፡ *right hand,* ደማን፡ *right side;* Sab. ימן *right hand,* ימנת *south,* are also quoted; As. *imnu, right, right side, on the right,* Dl$^{HWB\ 307}$)—abs. יָמִין Gn 13^{9} +40 t.; cstr. יְמִין 1 S 23^{24}+19 t.; sf. יְמִינִי Je 22^{24}+6 t., etc.; always sg.:—**1.** *right hand:* **a.** lit. of man, oft. opp. שְׂמֹאול Gn 48$^{13.14}$ (cf. v^{18}), Dn 12^{7}; יָדַע בֵּין־יְמִינוֹ לִשְׂמֹאלוֹ Jon 4^{11} *distinguish between one's right hand and one's left;* שלח ימין Ju 5^{26} (‖ יד); as holding the lot Ez 21^{27}; also of right hand as skilful ψ 137^{5}; as receiving bribes 26^{10} (‖ יָדַיִם); used in false swearing יְמִינָם יְמִין שָׁקֶר 144$^{8.11}$ *their right hand is a right hand of falsehood;* oft. also c. יַד, יַד־יְמִינוֹ Gn 48^{17} (E) *hand of his right=his right hand* Ju 7^{20} 2 S 20^{9}; אִטֵּר יַד־יְמִינוֹ Ju 3^{15} 20^{16} *bound as to one's right hand,* i.e. left-handed. **b.** fig., of right hand as held by ′י Is 41^{13} 45^{1}; so יַד־ימיני ψ 73^{23}. **c.** *right hand of* ′י, as instr. of delivering Israel Ex 15$^{6.6.12}$+, cf. בִּגְבוּרוֹת יֵשַׁע יְמִינוֹ ψ 20^{7}; שְׁנוֹת יְמִין עֶלְיוֹן 77^{11}, ‖ זְרוֹעַ 98^{1}; as acquiring the temple-site 78^{54}; as holding his servant 18^{36} (line om. in ‖ 2 S 22^{36}), cf. 63^{9} & בִּימִין צִדְקִי Is 41^{10}; as finding, lighting upon (מצא) his enemies ψ 21^{9} (‖ יד); as full of צֶדֶק 48^{11}; as dispensing blessings 16^{11} נעימות בימינך (cf. Pr 3^{16} of wisdom, personified); used in divine oath Is 62^{8} (‖ זְרוֹעַ). **2.** of situation on, or direction toward, *the right:* **a.** of situation, c. מִן, מִימִינָם וּמִשְּׂמֹאלָם Ex 14$^{22.29}$ a wall *on their right hand and on their left hand;* similarly 2 S 16^{6} 1 K 7$^{39.49}$=2 Ch 3^{17} 4^{6}, 1 K 22^{19} (=2 Ch 18^{18} c. עַל), 2 Ch 4$^{7.8}$ ψ 91^{7} (‖ מִצִּדְּךָ); for protection 16^{8}; מימין ל 2 K 23^{13} Ez 10^{3}; c. לְ, וַתֵּשֶׁב לִימִינוֹ 1 K 2^{19}, so ψ 110^{1} 45^{10} 109^{31}; c. עַל־ Zc 3^{1} 1 Ch 6^{24} 2 Ch 18^{18} (=1 K 22^{19} c. מִן), Ne 8^{4} Jb 30^{12} ψ 109^{6} cf. 110^{5}; without prep. יְמִין הָעִיר 2 S 24^{5} Jb 23^{9}. **b.** of direction toward, lit. נָטָה ימין Nu 20^{17} 22^{26} (both

JE); סור ימין Dt 2[27] 1 S 6[12]; פָּרַץ ימין ושׂ׳ Is 54[3]; also (vb. הַפְרֵד in prev. cl.) Gn 13[9]; הַבֵּיט ימין ψ 142[5], and *looking* is implied also in Ez 1[10] (c. על, נטה (לָלֶכֶת) על הַיָּמִין; opp. (מֵהַשְּׂמֹאול); c. אֶל־ 2 S 2[19.21]; פנה על־ימין Gn 24[49]; sq. אֶל, of course (הלך) of boundary Jos 17[1]; c. לְ, לַיָּמִין מֵעַל לַחוֹמָה Ne 12[31] (vb. om., *went*) *to the right above the wall;* fig. of moral deviation, סוּר מִן־הַדָּבָר . . . יָמִין וּשְׂמֹאול Dt 17[11], so 5[29] 17[20] 28[14] Jos 1[7] 23[6] 2 K 22[2] = 2 Ch 34[2]; נטה ימין ושׂ׳ Pr 4[27]; also (very late) of *the right* as morally good, לֵב חָכָם לִימִינוֹ (opp. שְׂמֹאל) Ec 10[2] De Reuss Now. †**3.** of other parts of the body, besides hand (v. יַד־ימינו etc. supr.): *right* thigh יֶרֶךְ יְמִינוֹ Ju 3[16.24]; eye עֵין יָמִין 1 S 11[2]; עין ימינו Zc 11[17.17]; esp. שׁוֹק הַיָּמִין i.e. *the right* (upper) *leg* of sacrificial animal Ex 29[22] Lv 7[32.33] 8[25.26] 9[21] Nu 18[18]. †**4.** = *south*, because when facing east the right hand is toward the south: ישׁב מִימִין הַיְשִׁימוֹן 1 S 23[19]; אֶל־יְמִין v[24]; מִימִינֵךְ Ez 16[46] (|| עַל־שְׂמאולך); צָפוֹן וְיָמִין ψ 89[13]; perh. also 107[3], v. יָם **9.**

3227 †I. יְמִינִי **adj.** Kt *right hand, on the right:* שֵׁם הימיני יָכִין 2 Ch 3[17] the name of *the one on the right* was Yakin; צִדְּךָ הימיני Ez 4[6] *thy right side* (Qr in both הַיְמָנִי, v. infr.)

3228 †II. יְמִינִי **adj.gent.** fr. בִּנְיָמִן, abbrev. for
1145 בֶּן־יְמִינִי (q. v.);—אֶרֶץ יְמִינִי 1 S 9[4]; אִישׁ יְמִינִי 2 S
20[1] Est 2[5]; בֶּן־אִישׁ יְמִינִי 1 S 9[1].

541, 3231 †II. [יָמַן] **vb. denom. Hiph.** go to or choose the right, use the right hand;—*Impf.* 1 s. coh. וְאֵימְנָה Gn 13[10] (J) *then I will go to the right* (opp. וְאַשְׂמְאִלָה); 2 mpl. תַּאֲמִינוּ Is 30[21], fig. of turning aside from right course of life (|| תַשְׂמְאִילוּ); *Inf. cstr.* in phr. אִם־אִשׁ לְהֵמִין וּלְהַשְׂמִיל מִכֹּל אֲשֶׁר דִּבֶּר אֲדֹנִי הַמֶּלֶךְ 2 S 14[19] it is surely impossible *to turn to the right or to the left,* etc.; *Imv.* fs. הֵימִינִי Ez 21[21] *go to the right!* (opp. הַשְׂמִילִי); *Pt.* pl. *use the right hand:* מַיְמִינִים וּמַשְׂמְאִלִים בָּאֲבָנִים וּבַחִצִּים בַּקָּשֶׁת 1 Ch 12[2] *using the right hand and the left hand with stones and with arrows in the bow* (i.e. in throwing and shooting).

3233 †יְמָנִי **adj.** right hand, right—m. of pillar הָעַמּוּד הַיְמָנִי 1 K 7[21] = הַיְמָנִי in || 2 Ch 3[17] Qr (Kt הימיני); f. of side of house (temple): כֶּתֶף הַבַּיִת הַיְמָנִית 1 K 6[8] 7[39] (|| כֶּתֶף הבית מִיָּמִין), 2 K 11[11] (opp. הַשְּׂמָאלִית), Ez 47[1], cf. v[2] 2 Ch 4[10] 23[10] (opp. הַשְּׂמָאלִית); elsewhere of parts of body (P): *right ear, hand and foot* [ה]אזן הַיְמָנִית + יד(ם) הַי׳ + רגל(ם) הַי׳ Ex 29[20] Lv 8[23.24] 14[14.17.25.28]; *right finger* אֶצְבָּעוֹ הַי׳ 14[16.27]; cf. also *right side,* m. צִדְּךָ הַיְמָנִי Ez 4[6] Qr (Kt הימיני).

†II. יָמִין **n.pr.m. 1.** son of Simeon Gn 3226
46[10] Ex 6[15] Nu 26[12] 1 Ch 4[24]. **2.** man of Judah 1 Ch 2[27]. **3.** Levite (?) name, time of Ezra Ne 8[7].

†יָמִינִי **adj.gent.** of II. ימין **1**; only c. art. 3228
as subst. coll. Nu 26[12].

†יִמְנָה **n.pr.m.** (cf. perh. Ar. يُمْنٌ *good* 3232
fortune, يَمْنَةٌ *right side*)—**1.** a son of Asher Gn 46[17] Nu 26[44], also (for adj.gent.) הַיִּמְנָה v[44] = the family of *the Yimnites* 1 Ch 7[30]. **2.** a Levite 2 Ch 31[14].

†I. תֵּימָן **n.f.** [Is 43, 6] **south, south wind,** chiefly 8486
poet., P & Ez (lit. *what is on the right* (hand), i.e. as one faces east; v. Wetzst [Verhandl. d. Berl. Anthrop. Ges. 1878, 390])—abs. ת׳ Zc 9[14] + 6 t. (הַתּ׳ only Zc 6[6]); תֵּמָן Jb 9[9]; c. ה loc. תֵּימָ֫נָה Ex 26[18] + 12 t.; —**1. a.** *south, southern quarter* of sky, לְתֵימָן Jb 39[26] (of flight of bird); of constellations חַדְרֵי ת׳ 9[9]; סַעֲרוֹת ת׳ Zc 9[14] *whirlwinds of the south;* of territory, *the south* Is 43[6] (opp. צָפוֹן), also אֶרֶץ הַתּ׳ Zc 6[6] (opp. אֶרֶץ צָפוֹן); נֶגְבָּה מִקְצֵה ת׳ Jos 15[1] *southward at the end of the south,* i.e. in the remotest south (of the land);—see also II. ת׳. **b.** c. ה loc. *toward the south,* esp. in topograph. description (oft. with other points of compass), פְּאַת נֶ֫גְבָּה תֵימָ֫נָה Ex 26[18] (P), פ׳ ת׳ נ׳, פ׳ נֶגֶב ת׳ Ez 47[19], Ex 27[9] 36[23] 38[9] (all P), Ez 47[19] 48[28]; + צלע *side* Ex 26[35], ירך Nu 3[29] (both P); also Nu 2[10] 10[6] (P); יָמָּה וְצָפֹנָה וְת׳ וּמִזְרָחָה Dt 3[27]; ה loc. is redundant in דֶּרֶךְ תֵּימָנָה Ez 21[2] turn thy face *southward* (|| דָּרוֹם and נֶגֶב). **2.** *south wind* ψ 78[26] (קָדִים in || cl.), Ct 4[16] (צָפוֹן in || cl.)

†II. תֵּימָן **n.pr. (m. et) loc.** a N. district 8487
of Edom, poet. often = Edom Am 1[12] (|| אֱדוֹם v[11], and בָּצְרָה), Ob[9] (|| הַר־עֵשָׂו), Je 49[7.20] Ez 25[13] (all || אֱדוֹם); Hb 3[3] (|| הַר־פָּארָן); prob. also Jos 12[3] 13[4] (both D); in Gn 36 (P) as name of an Edomite chief, son of אֱלִיפַז and grandson of Esau v[11] = 1 Ch 1[36]; v[42] = 1 Ch 1[53]; so תֵּימָן Gn 36[15].—Vid. further Buhl [Edomiter 30].

†תֵּימָנִי **adj.gent.** alw. c. art. אֱלִיפַז הַתֵּימָנִי 8489
(v. supr.) Jb 2[11] 4[1] 15[1] 42[7.9] = אֱלִ׳ הַתֵּימָנִי 22[1]; = n.pr.coll. אֶרֶץ הַתּ׳ Gn 36[34] *the land of the Temanites* = 1 Ch 1[45].

†תֵּימְנִי appar. **n.pr.m.** in Judah 1 Ch 4[6]. 8488

3234 יִמְנַע v. sub מנע p. 586

3235 ימר vb. assumed in Thes to expl. **Hiph.** הֵמִיר=הֵימִיר Je 2^{11}, and **Hithp.** תִּתְיַמָּרוּ Is 61^{6}; but on הימיר v. מור (Kö[I. 457]), and תִּתְיַמָּרוּ is prob. from אמר q. v. supr. p. 56^{b}.

3236 יִמְרָה v. sub מרה. p. 598

3237 † יָמַשׁ **vb.** (si vera l.) touch, **Hiph.** *Imv.* sf. והימשני Kt (i.e. וַהֲיִמִשֵׁנִי) Ju 16^{26} (וַהֲמִישֵׁנִי Qr) *and let me touch* (no doubt txt. error for הֲמִשֵּׁנִי from משׁשׁ, q. v.)

3238 †[יָנָה] **vb. suppress** (?), **oppress, maltreat** (NH Hiph. *vex* with words; so Aram. Aph. אוֹנִי, but also 𝔗 for Heb. הוֹנָה *maltreat;* Ar. وَنَى is *laxus, debilis fuit,* IV. *debilitavit, defatigavit,* but connex. dub.)—**Qal** *Impf.* 1 pl. sf. נִינָם ψ 74^{8}; *Pt.* יוֹנָה Je 25^{38} + 3 t. + ψ 123^{4} (v. infr.);—*suppress* (?), sq. acc. ψ 74^{8} (text dub.); elsewhere *oppress; Pt.* abs. as adj. הָעִיר הַיּוֹנָה Zp 3^{1}; subst. f. coll. הַיּוֹנָה *oppressors* Je 25^{38} (but rd. חֶרֶב for חֲרוֹן, with 𝔊 Ew Hi Gf Ke etc., as 46^{16} 50^{16}); ψ 123^{4} Qr לִגְאֵי יוֹנִים *proudest oppressors* (st. cstr. in superlat., cf. Ges[§133, 3, R. 1]; yet most follow Kt לגאייונים, and der. from גַּאֲיוֹן q. v. p. 145 supr.) **Hiph.** *Pf.* הוֹנָה Ez $18^{12.16}$; הוֹנוּ $22^{7.29}$; *Impf.* יוֹנֶה 18^{7}; 2 ms. תּוֹנֶה Ex 22^{20}; תּוֹנֶנּוּ Dt 23^{17}; יוֹנוּ Ez 45^{8}; תּוֹנוּ Lv 19^{33} + 2 t.; תֹּנוּ Je 22^{3}; *Inf.* sf. הוֹנֹתָם Ez 46^{18}; *Pt.* מוֹנַיִךְ Is 49^{26};—*oppress, maltreat,* sq. acc., esp. of ill-treatment of poor and weak, partic. of the גֵּר, the 'stranger,' sojourner, by the rich and powerful, Ex 22^{20} (JE), Lv 19^{33} $25^{14.17}$ (H), Dt 23^{17} Je 22^{3} Ez $18^{7.12.16}$ $22^{7.29}$ 45^{8} 46^{18}; of a foreign oppressor only Is 49^{26}.

3239, 3241 יָנוֹחַ v. נוח; יָנוּם v. נום. p. 629-30

3243, 5143 †[יָנַק] **vb. suck** (NH *id.;* Aram. יְנַק, ܝܢܩ, and deriv.; As. *êniḳu, suck,* SASm[Asrb. i, Gloss], *mušeniḳtu, nurse,* Jen[ZA, 1886, 402])—**Qal** *Pf.* וְיָנַקְתְּ consec. Is 60^{16}; וִינַקְתֶּם 66^{12}; *Impf.* יִינָק Jb 20^{16}; אִינָק 3^{12}; תִּינְקִי Is 60^{16}; יִינְקוּ Dt 33^{19}; תִּינְקוּ Is 66^{11}; *Pt.* יוֹנֵק Dt 32^{25} + 7 t.; יֹנֵק Nu 11^{12}; יוֹנְקִים ψ 8^{3}; יוֹנְקֵי Jo 2^{16};—*suck,* of infant at mother's breast, abs. Jb 3^{12}; metaph. of abundance and honour of Jerusalem in future, Is 66^{11} abs.; sq. acc. of breast 60^{16}, acc. of milk v^{16} 66^{12}; sq. acc. ראשׁ פְּתָנִים Jb 20^{16} of punishment of wicked; pt. sq. acc. יוֹנֵק שְׁדֵי אִמִּי Ct 8^{1}; cstr. יוֹנְקֵי־שָׁדָיִם Jo 2^{16}; elsewh. as subst., *suckling, babe* Nu 11^{12} Dt 32^{25} (opp. אִישׁ שֵׂיבָה); || עוֹלֵל 1 S 15^{3} 22^{19} ψ 8^{3} Je 44^{7} La 2^{11}; || עוֹלָל 4^{4}, cf. Jo 2^{16}; || גָּמוּל Is 11^{8};—on Is 53^{2} v. יוֹנֵק infr. **Hiph.** *Pf.* הֵינִקָה Gn 21^{7}; הֵינִיקוּ La 4^{3}; *Impf.* sf. וַיֵּנִקֵהוּ Dt 32^{13}; 3 fs. תֵּינִק Ex 2^{7}; וַתֵּינֶק 1 S 1^{23}; וַתְּנִיקֵהוּ Ex 2^{9}; *Imv.* fs. sf. הֵינִקֵהוּ v^{9}; *Inf.* לְהֵינִיק 1 K 3^{21}; *Pt.* מֵינֶקֶת Ex 2^{7}; cstr. *id.* Gn 35^{8}; מֵנִקְתּוֹ 2 K 11^{2}; מֵינִקְתּוֹ 2 Ch 22^{11}; מֵנִקְתָּהּ Gn 24^{59}; מֵינִיקוֹת 32^{16}; מֵינִיקֹתַיִךְ Is 49^{23};—*give suck to, nurse,* sq. acc. Gn 21^{7} 1 K 3^{21} Ex $2^{7.9}$ 1 S 1^{23}; cause to suck honey, fig. Dt 32^{13} (2 acc.); of animals La 4^{3} sq. acc.; pt. fem.=*nursing,* אִשָּׁה מֵינֶקֶת Ex 2^{7} lit. *a nursing woman, a nurse;* מ׳ alone as subst.=*nurse* Gn 24^{59} (J), 35^{8} (E; דְּבֹרָה), 2 K 11^{2} 2 Ch 22^{11}; metaph. Is 49^{23}; of camels גְּמַלִּים מֵינִיקוֹת Gn 32^{16}.

†יוֹנֵק **n.m. young plant, sapling** (*sucker*) 3126
—Is 53^{2} (|| שֹׁרֶשׁ) in sim. of the suffering servant of י׳.

†[יוֹנֶקֶת] **n.f. young shoot, twig** (=foregoing)—יוֹנַקְתּוֹ Jb 8^{16} + 2 t.; יוֹנְקוֹתָיו Ho 14^{7}; יְנִקוֹתָיו Ez 17^{22}; יוֹנְקוֹתֶיהָ ψ 80^{12};—*shoot, twig,* of tree Jb 14^{7}; cf wicked under fig. of tree Jb 8^{16} 15^{30}; Israel under fig. of olive-tree Ho 14^{7}, of cedar Ez 17^{22}, of vine ψ 80^{12}. 3127

†[יְנִיקָה] **n.f.** id., only pl. sf. יְנִיקוֹתָיו Ez 17^{4} of Israel under figure of cedar. 3242

יַנְשׁוּף, יַנְשׁוֹף v. sub נשׁף. p. 676 3244

†יָסַד **vb. establish, found, fix** (NH *id.*, esp. Pi.; Aram. יְסַד; perh. orig. *fix firm* or *close;* Ar. وِسَادٌ *pillow;* vb. denom. II. *fix as a pillow against one;* V. *lean against, recline,* Lane[2940] Saad Gn 28^{11}; in Heb. usu. *fix firm* so as to *found*)—**Qal** *Pf.* יָסַד ψ 104^{5} Pr 3^{19}; sf. יְסָדָהּ ψ 24^{2} + 3 t.; 3 fs. יָסְדָה Is 48^{13}; יָסַדְתָּ ψ 104^{8}; יָסַדְתָּ 102^{26}; sf. יְסַדְתּוֹ Hab 1^{12}; יְסַדְתָּם ψ 89^{12} 119^{152}; וִיסַדְתִּיךְ consec. Is 54^{11}; *Inf.* יְסוֹד 2 Ch 24^{27}; לִיסּוֹד 31^{7} (v. Ges[§69, 2, R. 1]; Baer לְיַסֹּד); לִיסֹד Is 51^{16}; יָסְדִי Jb 38^{4}; יָסְדוֹ Ezr 3^{12}; *Pt.* יֹסֵד Is 51^{13} Zc 12^{1} + Is 28^{16} (Che[crit. n.], MT יִסַּד);—*found, establish,* c. acc., the earth ψ 24^{2} (|| כונן), cf. 78^{69} (obj. om.), 89^{12} 102^{26} 104^{5} cf. v^{8} (sq. לְ), Pr 3^{19} Is 48^{13} Jb 38^{4} Is $51^{13.16}$ Zc 12^{1}, vault of heaven Am 9^{6}; of *founding* the second temple Ezr 3^{12}, of restoration under Joash, Inf. יְסוֹד 2 Ch 24^{27}; metaph. of future Israel Is 54^{11}; of י׳, *establish* the Chaldaean (as his instrument) להוכיח for correction Hb 1^{12} (|| שִׂים), his commandments ψ 119^{152}; in weakened sense (si vera l.) יָסַד לְצִיִּים Is 23^{13} *appoint* a city for desert-creatures (on meaning in context, v. Di); *appoint, fix* Ezr 7^{9} 3245

emend. (v. יָסַד); *found, begin*, heaps of offerings in י׳'s house 2 Ch 31^7. **Niph.** *Pf.* 3 pl. נוֹסְדוּ ψ 2^2; *Impf.* 2 ms. תִּוָּסֵד Is 44^{28}; *Inf.* הִוָּסְדָהּ Ex 9^{18}; הִיָּסְדָם ψ 31^{14};—**1.** *fix* or *seat themselves close together, sit in conclave* ψ 2^2 31^{14} (> Bae from ܐܬܘܥܕ, ὁμιλία), but Lag's emend. נוֹעֲדוּ is prob. (cf. Ne 6^2). **2.** *be founded*, Is 44^{28} (temple), Ex 9^{18} (Egypt). **Pi.** *Pf.* יִסַּד Is 14^{32} + 3 t.; יִסְּדָהּ 1 K 16^{34}; יִסַּדְתָּ ψ 8^3; יִסְּדוּ Zc 4^9 Ezr 3^{10}; *Impf.* יְיַסְּדֶנָּה Jos 6^{26}; *Inf.* לְיַסֵּד 1 K 5^{31};—**1.** *found* (= **Qal**), sq. acc., city Jos 6^{26} (JE), 1 K 16^{34}, temple 1 K 5^{31} Zc 4^9 Ezr 3^{10}; Zion Is 14^{32} 28^{16} הִנְנִי יִסַּד (rd. יֹסֵד; v. supr.) **2.** *establish* ψ 8^3 sq. עֹז; *appoint, ordain* (late) 1 Ch 9^{22} (sq. acc.), Est 1^8 (abs.) **Pu.** *Pf.* יֻסַּד 1 K 6^{37} + 2 t.; יֻסָּד Ezr 3^6; *Pt.* מְיֻסָּד 1 K 7^{10}; מְיֻסָּדִים Ct 5^{15}; *be founded, be laid*, of a foundation 1 K 6^{37} Ezr 3^6 Hg 2^{18} Zc 8^9; *Pt.* = subst. foundation 1 K 7^{10}, cf. מוסד infr.; pillars set on bases, sim. of legs Ct 5^{15}. **Hoph.** *be founded*: *Inf.* הוּסַד 2 Ch 3^3 Ezr 3^{11}; *Pt.* מוּסָּד Is 28^{16};—*the being founded, founding*, עַל הוּסַד בֵּית י׳ Ezr 3^{11} *because of the founding* (*laying the foundation*) *of the house of* י׳; וְאֵלֶּה הוּסַד שְׁלֹמֹה לִבְנוֹת וגו׳ 2 Ch 3^3 and *this is* (lit. these are) *the founding of Solomon to build* the house of God, i.e. *this is the foundation which Solomon laid for building*, etc.; *Pt.* מוּסָד מוּסָּד Is 28^{16} *a foundation founded*, i.e. *well laid* (cf. חָכָם מְחֻכָּם, חֵפֶשׂ מְחֻפָּשׂ).

3246 †יְסֻד **n.[m.]** foundation, beginning, Ezr 7^9 יְסֻד הַמַּעֲלָה, but rd. rather, c. 𝔊, יִסַּד (הוּא = Ezra subj.), v. Ry.

3247 †יְסוֹד **n.f.** $^{Ezr 13,17}$ (**m.** $^{Jb 22,16}$) foundation, base, abs. יְסוֹד Hb 3^{13} + 2 t.; cstr. *id.* Ex 29^{12} + 9 t.; sf. יְסֹדוֹ Ez 13^{14}; יְסוֹדָם Jb 4^{19} 22^{16}; וִיסֹדֶיהָ Mi 1^6; יְסֹדֹתֶיהָ La 4^{11}; יְסוֹדוֹתֶיהָ Ez 30^4;—**1.** *foundation* of city (wall) Mi 1^6 ψ 137^7, cf. La 4^{11}; fig. of Egypt Ez 30^4; שַׁעַר הַיְסוֹד 2 Ch 23^5 one of gates of temple (but rd. ש׳ סוּר 2 K 11^6 or ש׳ סוּס [rather ש׳ הַסּוּסִים] Th Klo); fig. of men שֹׁכְנֵי || יְס׳ בֶּעָפָר בָּתֵּי חֹמֶר Jb 4^{19}, cf. 22^{16}; of righteous Pr 10^{25}; of hostile prince under fig. of house Hb 3^{13} (details obscure, v^b prob. corrupt, v. We); of false prophecies under fig. of wall of defence Ez 13^{14}. **2.** *base, bottom*, of altar Ex 29^{12} Lv 4$^{7.18.25.30.34}$ 5^9 8^{15} 9^9 (all P).

3248 †[יְסוּדָה] **n.f.** foundation = city founded; יְסוּדָתוֹ בְּהַרְרֵי־קֹדֶשׁ ψ 87^1 (|| אֹהֵב י׳ שַׁעֲרֵי צִיּוֹן).

4143 †מוּסָד **n.m.** $^{Is 28,16}$ foundation, foundation-laying;—מוּסָד Is 28^{16} (v. יסד Hoph.); עַד־הַיּוֹם מוּסַד בֵּית י׳ 2 Ch 8^{16} *until the day* (of) *the foundation-laying of the house of* י׳.

†מוּסָדָה **n.f.** foundation, appointment, 4145
מַטֵּה מוּסָדָה Is 30^{32} *rod of appointment* (cf. Hb 1^{12} יְסַדְתּוֹ), *appointed rod* (of punishment); pl. cstr. מוּסְדוֹת Ez 41^8 Qr, must mean *foundations* (si vera l.); Kt perhaps intends **Pu.** *Pt.* מְיֻסָּדוֹת 4328
founded, furnished with foundations (conject. emendation by Co).

†[מוֹסָד] **n.m.** $^{ψ 18,8}$ foundation;—pl. abs. 4144,
מֹסְדוֹת Je 51^{26}; cstr. מוֹסְדוֹת ψ 18^{16} + 2 t.; מֹסְדוֹת 4146
2 S 22^{16}; מוֹסְדֵי Dt 32^{22} + 6 t.; מֹסְדֵי Mi 6^2;—*foundations* אֶבֶן לְמ׳ Je 51^{26}; מוֹסְדֵי אֶרֶץ *foundations* of the earth Mi 6^2 Is 24^{18} Je 31^{37} ψ 82^5 Pr 8^{29}; מ׳ הא׳ Is 40^{21}; מ׳ תֵּבֵל ψ 18^{16} = 2 S 22^{16}; מ׳ הרים Dt 32^{22} ψ 18^8; 2 S 22^8 has (less well) מ׳ שמים; מ׳ דור־ודור Is 58^{12} (|| חָרְבוֹת עולם) i.e. ancient foundations, now ruined.

†מַסַּד **n.[m.]** foundation;—מַמַּסַּד 1 K 7^9 4527
|| עַד־הַטְּפָחוֹת; Co rds. מַסַּד also Ez 41^8 (for MT מיֻסְדוֹת).

†**יסך**, only in יִיסָךְ Ex 30^{32}, rd. יוּסָךְ, v. 3251
סוך (Kö $^{i. 436}$). p. 691 5480

†יִסְכָּה **n.pr.f.** (etym. dubious)—a daughter 3252
of הָרָן, and sister of מִלְכָּה Gn 11^{29}, 𝔊 Ιεσχα.

יִסְמַכְיָהוּ v. sub סמך. p. 702 3253

יסף $^{T 214}$ **vb. add** (NH *id.*, Hiph.; Aram. Aph. 3254
אוֹסִיף, ܐܘܣܦ; Ph. יסף; MI^{29} יספתי, l^{21} לספת; Sab. וסף Hom $^{ZMG 1892, 530}$; As. *esêpu* dub. (*eṣêpu* Dl))—
†**Qal** *Pf.* יָסַף Gn 38^{26} +; יָסְפָה Gn 8^{12}; וְיָסְפָה consec. 2 K 19^{30} = Is 37^{31}; יָסַפְתָּ Is 26^{15} 2 Ch 9^6; וְיָסַפְתָּ Dt 19^9, etc.; *Imv.* סְפוּ Is 29^1 Je 7^{21}; + *Inf. cstr.* לָסֶפֶת for MT לִסְפּוֹת Nu 32^{14} Is 30^1 (Ges $^{§ 69. 2. R}$); *Pt.* יוֹסֵף (rd. יוֹסִף) Is 29^{14} 38^5 (Kö $^{i. 403}$ adds Ec 1^{18} יוֹסִיף, fr. form and connexion less likely); pl. יֹסְפִים Dt 5^{22};—*add*, sq. acc. + עַל 1 S 12^{19} Je 7^{21} 45^3 Is 29^1 30^1 38^5 Dt 19^9 (+ עוד), Lv 22^{14} 26^{21} 27$^{13.15.19.27}$; sq. acc. 2 K 19^{30} = Is 37^{31}, Nu 32^{14} 2 Ch 9^6 sq. עַל (no acc.; יָסַפְתָּ עַל־הַשְּׁמוּעָה אֲשֶׁר שָׁמָעְתִּי); sq. לְ (no acc.) = *increase* Is 26$^{15.15}$ (יָסַפְתָּ לַגּוֹי); sq. acc. *increase, have more* 29^{19} (וְיָסְפוּ עֲנָוִים בּיהוה שִׂמְחָה); 14 t. sq. inf. Gn 8^{12} (לֹא יָסְפָה שׁוּב אֵלָיו עוֹד, i.e. it *did not again return unto him*), 38^{26} (+ עוד), Lv 26^{18} Nu 32^{15} (+ עוד), Dt 5^{22} (+ עוד), 20^8 Ju 8^{28} 13^{21} (+ עוד), 1 S 7^{13} (+ עוד), 15^{35} 27^4 (וְלֹא יוֹסֵף עוֹד), 2 S 2^{28} (+ עוד), 2 K 6^{23} (+ עוד), Is 29^{14}; cf. Nu 11^{25} Dt 5^{19}, where

inf. not expressed, but implied from context; both c. לא *and did not do it again.* †**Niph.** *Pf.* נוֹסַף Je 36^{32}; וְנ׳ consec. Ex 1^{10} Nu 36^{3}; 3 fs. וְנוֹסְפָה consec. Nu 36^{4}; *Pt.* וְנוֹסָף Pr 11^{24}; נוֹסָפוֹת Is 15^{9};—**1.** *join* (intr.), *join oneself to* (עַל) Ex 1^{10}. **2.** *be joined, added to* (עַל) Nu 36$^{3.4}$ Je 36^{32}; pt. abs. *is increased* Pr 11^{24}; pt. fem. pl.=*things added, additions* (i.e. additional calamities) Is 15^{9}. **Hiph.** $_{172}$ *Pf.* הֹסִיף 2 K 24^{7}; הוֹסַפְתָּ 1 K 10^{7}, etc.; *Impf.* $_{164}$ יוֹסִיף Jos 23^{13}+; *juss.* יוֹסֵף Gn 30^{24}+; יֹסֶף (bef. tone) Pr 1^{5} 9^{9}; וַיֹּסֶף Is 7^{10}+; וַיֹּאסֶף 1 S 18^{29}; 2 ms. תּוֹסִיף Am 7^{13}+; *juss.* תֹּסֵף Dt 13^{1}; תּוֹסַף Jb 40^{32}; תּוֹסְףְּ Pr 30^{6}; אוֹסִיף Ho 1^{6}+; volunt. אוֹסְפָה 9^{15}; אֹסֵף Dt 18^{16}+Ez 5^{16} (del. Co); אֹסְפָה 2 S 12^{8}+prob. Dt 32^{23} (for MT אַסְפֶּה); 3 mpl. יוֹסִפוּן 1 K 19^{2}; 2 mpl. תּוֹסִפוּ Is 1^{5}+; תֹּסִפוּן Gn 44^{23}+2 t.; תֹּאסִפוּן Ex 5^{7} (per contr. 2 S 6^{1} ψ 104^{29}, cf. sub אסף), etc.; *Pt.* pl. מוֹסִיפִים Ne 13^{18}; *Inf. cstr.* הוֹסִיף Lv 19^{25}+3 t.;—**1.** *add* (=**Qal**), sq. acc.+עַל 2 K 20^{6} Lv 5$^{16.24}$ 27^{31} Nu 5^{7} Jb 34^{37} (Elihu), ψ 61^{7} Pr 16^{23} Ez 5^{16} (v. supr.), Ne 13^{18}+Dt 32^{23}; sq. acc.+לְ Gn 30^{24} Pr 3^{2} 9^{11}; sq. acc.+אֶל 1 K 10^{7} (i.e. thou hast more wisdom and prosperity than is reported); sq. acc.+אִם Pr 10^{22}; cf. וְהוֹסַפְתִּי עַל־כָּל־תְּהִלָּתֶךָ ψ 71^{14} (i.e. increase); וְהוֹסַפְתִּי חכמה על כל־אשר־היה לְפָנַי Ec 1^{16} (|| וְהִגְדַּלְתִּי) (i.e. gain more); cf. 2^{9} (|| וְגָדַלְתִּי); וַיּוֹסֶף ה׳ לכם תבואתו Lv 19^{25} (i.e. yield more); אַחְאָב לַעֲשׂוֹת לְהַכְעִיס אֶת־יהוה . . . מִכֹּל וגו׳ 1 K 16^{33} (*did more to provoke*); *add to, increase* (sq. עַל), no obj. expr. ה׳ עַל־חַטֹּאתֵנוּ 2 Ch 28^{13}; עַל־אַשְׁמַת ישׂראל Ezr 10^{10}; עליו אֵין להוסיף Ec 3^{14} (opp. לִגְרֹעַ), cf. Dt 4^{2} 13^{1} 1 K 12$^{11.14}$ 1 Ch 22^{14} 2 Ch 10$^{11.14}$ Pr 30^{6} ψ 115^{14}; sq. אֶל (no other obj. expr.) Ez 23^{14}; =*give in addition* וְאֹסְפָה לךָ 2 S 12^{8}; מַה־יֹּסִיף לָךְ ψ 120^{4} (|| מַה־יִּתֵּן לְךָ); esp. in phr. כה יעשׂה אלהים (י׳) לך (לי) וכה יוסיף 1 S 3^{17} *so may God do to thee and more also,* 14^{44} 20^{13} 25^{22} 2 S 3^{9} (וכה יוסיף לו), v^{35} 19^{14} 1 K 2^{23} 2 K 6^{31} Ru 1^{17}; subj. heathen gods 1 K 19^{2} 20^{10}; c. acc. ה׳ אֹמֶץ *add strength*=grow stronger Jb 17^{9}, cf. Pr 1^{5} 9^{9} Ec 1$^{18.18}$, also Is 1^{5} Pr 16^{21}; also, where subj. different from indirect obj. Pr 10^{27} (יראת י׳ יוסיף ימים), 19^{4} 23^{28}; =*multiply* ה׳ עליכם כָּכֶם אלף פעמים Dt 1^{11} cf. 1 Ch 21^{3}; וְיוֹסֵף י׳ אלהיך אל־העם כָּהֵם וְכָהֵם וַיֹּסֶף י׳ את־כל־אשר לְאִיּוֹב מֵאָה פְּעָמִים 2 S 24^{3}; cf. לְמִשְׁנֶה Jb 42^{10}. **2. a.** sq. inf. (with or without לְ) *add to do*=*do again* or *more* (in Hex only JE & D); +עוֹד Gn 8$^{21.21}$ 18^{29} 37$^{5.8}$ Ex 10^{29} 14^{13} Nu 25^{15} Dt 3^{26} 17^{16} 19^{20} 28^{68} Ju 9^{37} 20^{28} 1 S 3^{6} 18^{29} (increase), 23^{4} 27^{4} (Kt), 2 S 2^{22} 5^{22} 7^{20} (inf. om. in || 1 Ch 17^{18}), 14^{10} 18^{22} 2 K 24^{7} Am 7$^{8.13}$ 8^{2} Is 8^{5} 10^{20} 23^{12} 51^{22} Na 2^{1} Zp 3^{11} Je 31^{12} Ez 36^{12} ψ 10^{18} 78^{17}; inf. om. Pr 19^{19} 1 Ch 17^{18}; עוֹד om. Gn 4$^{2.12}$ 8^{10} 44^{23} Ex 5^{7} 8^{25} 9$^{28.34}$ 10^{28} Nu 25$^{19.25}$ Dt 13^{12} 18^{16} 25^{3} Jos 7^{12} 23^{13} Ju 2^{21} 3^{12} 4^{1} 10$^{6.13}$ 13^{1} 20$^{22.23}$ 1 S 3$^{8.21}$ 9^{8} 19^{8} 20^{17} 2 S 3^{34} 7^{10} 24^{1} 2 K 21^{8} Is 1^{13} 7^{10} 24^{20} Ho 9^{15} 13^{2} Am 5^{2} 1 Ch 17^{9} 2 Ch 28^{22} 33^{8} Jb 27^{1} 29^{1} ψ 41^{9} 77^{8} La 4$^{15.16.22}$ Jon 2^{5}; inf. om. Ex 11^{6} Dt 25^{3} Jb 20^{9} 34^{32} (Elihu), 38^{11} 40$^{5.32}$ Jo 2^{2}; cf. also ה׳ עֲבוֹר Nu 22^{26} i.e. *went on further.* **b.** sq. Impf. c. וְ׳ (of past time) Gn 25^{1} 1 S 19^{21} Est 8^{3} Jb 36^{1} (Elihu), Dn 10^{18}; +עוֹד Gn 38^{5} Ju 11^{14} 1 Ch 14^{13}. **c.** sq. Impf. asynd. (Ges $^{§ 120, 1 b, 2 b}$) אוֹסִיף אֲבַקְשֶׁנּוּ עוֹד Pr 23^{35}; לא תוסיפי יקראו־לָךְ Is 47$^{1.5}$; לא אוסיף עוֹד אֲרַחֵם אֶת־בֵּית ישׂראל Ho 1^{6}; לא יוסיף יָבֹא־בָךְ עוד Is 52^{1}.

יוֹסֵף $_{212}$ and **יְהוֹסֵף** (+ψ 81^{6} v. Ges $^{§ 53, 3, R. 7}$). 3084, 3130
n.pr.m. (*he adds, increases,* v. יוספיה infr.;—on n.pr. loc. in Pal. *Yšap'ara* (Egypt. form,=יוסף אל) v. Mey$^{ZAW\ vi, 8}$ WMM $^{Asien\ u.\ Europa\ 162}$)—**1.** elder son of Jacob and Rachel; **a.** as an individual Gn 30^{24} (name expl. v^{23} (E) from אָסַף=*take away,* but v^{24} (J) from יָסַף *add*) +155 t. Gn, chiefly in narrative of JE, also poem 49$^{22.26}$ and, dependent on this, 1 Ch 5$^{1.2}$; P only 35^{24} 37^{2a} 41$^{46.46}$ 46$^{19.20.27}$ 47$^{5.7.11}$ 48^{3}; also Ex 1$^{5.6}$ (P), v^{8} 13^{19} Jos 24^{32} (all E), 1 Ch 2^{2} ψ 105^{17}. †**b.** as founder of a tribal division מַטֵּה י׳ (=Manasseh) Nu 13^{11}; usu. בְּנֵי־י׳ 1^{32} (=Ephraim), commonly =Ephraim and Manasseh 1^{10} 26$^{28.37}$ 34^{23} Jos 14^{4} 16$^{1.4}$ 17$^{14.16}$ 18^{11}, cf. 24^{32} 1 Ch 7^{29}, but also of E. Jordan Israel (where half Manasseh settled) Nu 36^{1}=מַטֵּה בני י׳ v^{5}; cf. חֲצִי שֵׁבֶט מנשׁה בֶּן־יוֹסֵף 32^{33} cf. 36^{12}, and Jos 17$^{1.2}$; בֵּית י׳ (Manasseh and Ephraim) 17^{17} (so orig. v^{14} acc. to Di), 18^{5} Ju 1$^{22.23.35}$, occupying the great central region of Palestine; 2 S 19^{21} 1 K 11^{28}; ultimately=**c.** the northern kingdom Am 5^{6} Zc 10^{6} (|| בֵּית יְהוּדָה); so יוֹסֵף alone Am 5^{15} 6^{6} Dt 27^{12} 33$^{13.16}$ Ob^{18} (|| בית יעקב), Ez 37$^{16.19}$ 47^{13} 48^{32}; בְּנֵי יַעֲקֹב ויוסף ψ 77^{16}; אֹהֶל יוֹסֵף ψ 78^{67} (|| שֵׁבֶט אֶפְרַיִם). **d.**=entire nation ψ 80^{2} (|| ישׂראל); so יְהוֹסֵף 81^{6} (|| *id.*) †**2.** a man of Issachar Nu 13^{7}. †**3.** a son of Asaph 1 Ch 25$^{2.9}$. †**4.** one of those who took strange wives Ezr 10^{42}. †**5.** a priest Ne 12^{14}.

†**יוֹסִפְיָה** **n.pr.m.** (*י׳ adds*)—father of one of Ezra's companions Ezr 8^{10}. 3131

†[**יָסַר**] **vb. discipline, chasten, admonish** 3256
(Talm. ᵀ (י)סּוּר *chastisement;* but Aram. יְסַר is *bind*)—**Qal** *Impf.* 3 m. sf. וְיִסְּרֵנִי Is 8^{11} (Di De SS

see Bo^{§1103} Ew^{§249d}, but Thes MV Che al. **Pi.** Pf.); 1 s. sf. וְאֶסֳּרֵם Ho 10^{10} (Ges^{§71}); *Inf. abs.* יָסֹר 1 Ch 15^{22} (noun Ke, point as pt. Öt); *Pt.* יֹסֵר Pr 9^{7} ψ 94^{10}; יסורי Je 17^{13} Kt v. סוּר;—**1.** *admonish* Is 8^{11} (sq. sf. + מִלֶּכֶת *away from walking*, i.e. not to walk), Pr 9^{7} (‖ מוֹכִיחַ). **2.** *instruct*, 1 Ch 15^{22}. **3.** *discipline*, of God Ho 10^{10} ψ 94^{10}. **Niph.** *Impf.* יִוָּסֶר עָבֶד Pr 29^{19}; אִוָּסֵר Je 31^{18}; תִּוָּסְרוּ Lv 26^{23}; *Imv.* f. הִוָּסְרִי Je 6^{8}; mpl. הִוָּסְרוּ ψ 2^{10};—(Niph. *tolerat.*, Ges$^{§51.2}$), *let oneself be corrected, admonished* by words of man ψ 2^{10} Pr 29^{19}; *let oneself be chastened* by discipline of God Je 6^{8} 31^{18} Lv 26^{23}. **Pi.** *Pf.* יִסַּר 1 K 12^{11} + 3 t.; sf. יִסְּרַנִּי ψ 118^{18}; יִסְּרוֹ Is 28^{26}; 3 f. sf. יִסְּרַתּוּ Pr 31^{1}; 2 m. יִסַּרְתָּ ψ 39^{12} Jb 4^{3}, etc. + 8 t. Pf.; *Impf.* יְיַסֵּר Dt 8^{5}; 2 m. sf. תְּיַסְּרֶנּוּ ψ 94^{12}, etc. + 5 t. Impf.; *Imv.* יַסֵּר Pr 19^{18} 29^{17}; sf. יַסְּרֵנִי Je 10^{24}; *Inf. abs.* יַסֹּר ψ 118^{18}; *cstr.* יַסְּרָה Lv 26^{18}; sf. יַסְּרֶךָּ Dt 4^{36}; *Pt.* מְיַסְּרֶךָּ Dt 8^{5};—**1.** *discipline, correct* (the moral nature, with more or less severity acc. to circumstances): **a.** of God, c. acc. Ho 7^{15} (of *training* arms), Dt 4^{36} (v. Dr), 8^{5} (Israel as son), Is 28^{26}, happy the man אשׁר תיסרנו יה ψ 94^{12}, 118$^{18.18}$. **b.** of man, c. acc. Dt 8^{5} Pr 19^{18} 29^{17} (all of a father his son), Jb 4^{3} Pr 31^{1}, ψ 16^{7} my reins (the emotions of my own heart) *correct, admonish* me. **2.** more severely, *chasten, chastise*: **a.** of God, sq. acc. pers., Je 31^{18}; אַל־בַּחֲמָתְךָ תְיַסְּרֵנִי ψ 6^{2} 38^{2}; בְּמִשְׁפָּט אל באף Je 10^{24}; למשׁפט 30^{11} = 46^{28}; על חטאת Lv 26$^{18.28}$; בתוכחות על עון ψ 39^{12}. **b.** of man, a father his son Dt 21^{18}; elders a man Dt 22^{18} (including, as perh. 21^{18}, bodily chastisement); a king his subjects בַּשּׁוֹטִים and בָּעַקְרַבִּים 1 K 12$^{11.14}$ = 2 Ch 10$^{11.14}$. **c.** תְּיַסְּרֵךְ רָעָתֵךְ Je 2^{19} *thy badness will chastise thee.* **Nithp.** *Pf.* נִוַּסְּרוּ Ez 23^{48} (for נִתְיַסְּרוּ Ges$^{§55R.7}$); *pass. be disciplined, corrected.* **Hiph.** *Impf.* 1 s. sf. אַיְסִירֵם (Ew^{§131c}, but error for אֲיַסְּרֵם Bö^{§437f} SS), c. acc. *chasten* Ho 7^{12}.

3250 †יִסּוֹר **n.m.** one who reproves, fault-finder, הֲרֹב עִם־שַׁדַּי יִסּוֹר Jb 40^{2} *shall a reprover contend with Shadday?*

4148 †מוּסָר **n.m.** Pr 15.10 **discipline** (of the moral nature), **chastening, correction**;—מ׳ Je 2^{30} + 31 t. (Ez 5^{15} del. Co); cstr. מוּסַר Dt 11^{2} + 14 t. (for Jb 12^{28} see אסר); sf. מוּסָרִי Pr 8^{10}; מוּסָרְךָ Is
4561 26^{16}; מֻסָּרָם Jb 33^{16} (for מֹסֵרָם Di SS);—*discipline, correction*, of God, Dt 11^{2} מוּסַר י׳ the *discipline* of י׳ (of Y.'s wonders, as exercising a disciplinary, educating influence upon Israel, cf. Dr); לקח מ׳ Je 17^{23} 32^{33} 35^{13} Zp 3$^{2.7}$; ψ 50^{17} Jb 33^{16} 36^{10}; מ׳ כְּלִמָּתִי the *correction* of (i.e. which leadeth to) my shame Jb 20^{3}. **b.** מ׳ הבלים עֵץ הוּא the *discipline* of unreal gods is wood (is like themselves, destitute of true moral force) Je 10^{8}; Ez 5^{15} = *warning example* (?) Ew Sm (‖ שַׁמָּה; del. 𝔊 Co). **c.** in Proverbs, *discipline* in the school of wisdom: חכמה ומ׳ 1$^{2.7}$ 23^{23}; מ׳ חכמה *discipline of wisdom* 15^{33}; מ׳ הַשְׂכֵּל 1^{3}; תוכחות מ׳ 6^{23}; הָבִיאָה לַמּ׳ לִבֶּךָ 23^{12} *apply thy mind to discipline;* קבל מ׳ 19^{20}; לקח מ׳ 1^{3} 8^{10} 24^{32} (cf. Je supr.); קנה מ׳ 23^{23}; אהב מ׳ 12^{1}; שׁמר מ׳ 10^{17}; שׁמע מ׳ 8^{33} 19^{27}; החזק במ׳ 4^{13}; the reverse פרע מ׳ 13^{18} 15^{32}; שׂנא מ׳ 5^{12}; בזה מ׳ 1^{7}; באין מ׳ *for lack of discipline* 5^{23} (‖ בְּרֹב אִוַּלְתּוֹ); מ׳ אֱוִלִים אִוֶּלֶת 16^{22} *the discipline of fools is folly;* of paternal discipline, correction, Pr. 1^{8} 4^{1} 13^{1}. **2.** more severely, *chastening, chastisement*: **a.** of God, מ׳ יהוה Pr 3^{11} *chastening of Yahweh;* מ׳ שַׁדַּי Jb 5^{17}; מוּסָרְךָ Is 26^{16}; מ׳ שְׁלוֹמֵנוּ עָלָיו Is 53^{5} *chastisement of* (i.e. leading to) *our peace was upon him;* לקח מ׳ Je 2^{30} 5^{3} 7^{28}; מ׳ אַכְזָרִי Je 30^{14} *chastisement of a cruel one*, MT, but rd. מוּסָר א׳ *cruel chastisement*, Gf and esp. Gie; אני מ׳ לְכֻלָּם Ho 5^{2} *I am a chastisement for them all.* **b.** of man, Pr 15^{5} 23^{13}; שֵׁבֶט מ׳ 22^{15}; שִׁחֲרוֹ מ׳ 13^{24}; מ׳ אויל 7^{22} *chastisement of a fool;* מוּסָר רָע 15^{10} *grievous chastisement.*

[מֹסֶר] v. מוּסָר. above 4561

יָעֵץ v. sub יעה; יַעְבֵּץ v. sub עבץ. p. 418, 716 3257-58

†יָעַד **vb. appoint** (NH *id., appoint, assign,* 3259
esp. of acquiring or designating as wife; Aram. *id.*; Ar. وَعَدَ *promise, threaten, predict*, III. *appoint a time* or *place*; perh. As. *âdu*, *decide*, M-A^{17} Dl$^{HWB\ 230}$; Ph. n. pr. אשמניעד)—**Qal** *Pf.* sf. יְעָדוֹ 2 S 20^{5}; יְעָדָהּ Ex 21^{8} + 2 t.; *Impf.* 3 m. sf. יִיעָדֶנָּה Ex 21^{9};—*appoint*, a time 2 S 20^{5}; place Je 47^{7}; a rod Mi 6^{9}; *assign* or *designate* as concubine Ex 21$^{8.9}$ (JE). **Niph.** *Pf.* נוֹעַדְתִּי Ex 25^{22}; נֹעַדְתִּי Ex 29^{43}; pl. נוֹעֲדוּ ψ 48^{5} Nu 10$^{3.4}$; נוֹעָדוּ Am 3^{3}; *Impf.* אִוָּעֵד Ex 29^{42} + 3 t.; 3 pl. וַיִּוָּעֲדוּ Jos 11^{5} Jb 2^{11}; 1 pl. נִוָּעֵד Ne 6^{10}; וְנִוָּעֲדָה v^{2}; *Pt.* pl. נוֹעָדִים Nu 14^{35} + 3 t.; נֹעָדִים 16^{11};—**1.** reflexive, *meet at an appointed place*, with לְ, of Yahweh *meeting* Moses at the Tent of 'Meeting' Ex 29$^{42.43}$ 30^{36} (P); at the throne of the Kapporeth 25^{22} 30^{6} Nu 17^{19} (P). **2.** *meet by appointment* Am 3^{3} Jb 2^{11}; with בְּ of place Ne 6^{2}; אֶל of place v^{10}. **3.** *gather, assemble by appointment*, kings for a campaign (abs.) Jos 11^{5} (D), ψ 48^{5};

with אֶל, unto Moses Nu 10^{4} (P); to the door of the tent of meeting v^{3} (P); with עַל, unto Solomon 1 K 8^{5} = 2 Ch 5^{6}; against Yahweh Nu 14^{35} 16^{11} 27^{3} (P). **Po'ēl** *Pf.* 1 s. יוֹעַדְתִּי (for MT יוֹדַעְתִּי) 1 S 21^{3} sq. acc. pers. + אֶל of place, acc. to 𝔊 We Dr Kit Bu. **Hiph.** *Impf.* מִי יוֹעִדֵנִי Je 50^{44} = מִי יְעִידֵנִי 49^{19} = מִי יוֹעִידֵנִי Jb 9^{19} *who will make me meet him at the appointed place* (of judgment)? i.e. *who will summon* or *arraign me?* **Hoph.** *Pt.* מוּעָדִים לִפְנֵי Je 24^{1} *be set, placed before;* אָנָה פָּנַיִךְ מֻעָדוֹת Ez 21^{21} *whither thy face is set.*

5712 **עֵדָה**$_{149}$ **n.f. congregation** (prop. *company assembled together by appointment,* or *acting concertedly*)—ע׳ Nu 16^{2} + 85 t.; cstr. עֲדַת Ex 12^{3} + 52 t.; sf. עֲדָתִי Jb 16^{7} + 9 t. sfs.;—**1.** עֲדַת־אֵל ψ 82^{1} *congregation of Ēl,* of company of angels (בקרב אלהים ‖); ע׳ לְאֻמִּים 7^{8} *congregation of peoples;* ע׳ צַדִּיקִים 1^{5} *congregation of the righteous;* ‖ סוֹד יְשָׁרִים 111^{1}; ‖ קהל Pr 5^{14}; כָּל־עֲדָתִי Jb 16^{7} (of Job's circle of dependents); in a bad sense, ע׳ מְרֵעִים *company of evil doers* ψ 22^{17}; ע׳ עריצים 86^{14}; ע׳ חנף Jb 15^{34}; ע׳ קֹרַח *company of Korah* Nu 26^{9} 27^{3} (P), so עֲדָתוֹ, עֲדָתְךָ 16$^{5.6.11.16}$ 17^{5} (P), and הָעֵדָה 26^{10} 27^{3} (P); ע׳ אֲבִירָם ψ 106^{17}, cf. v^{18}. **2.** of *animals* ע׳ אַבִּירִים ψ 68^{31} (fig. of nobles); ע׳ דְּבֹרִים Ju 14^{8} *a swarm of bees.* **3.** elsewhere of Israel Ho 7^{12} עֲדָתָם i.e. the whole assemblage of them; 1 K 8^{5} (= 2 Ch 5^{6}) כל עדת יש׳ of those gathered to Sol.; 12^{20} העדה of assembly at Shechem; Je 6^{18} (text very dub.); עֲדָתוֹ 30^{20} of restored people; עֲדָתְךָ ψ 74^{2} (שבט נחלתך ‖); elsewhere in P, except possibly Nu 20^{11} (R), in technical sense, of the *company* of Israel of the Exodus, the *congregation* (115 t.), esp. in the phrases †ע׳ יהוה Nu 27^{17} 31^{16} Jos 22$^{16.17}$; †ע׳ ישׂראל Ex 12$^{3.6.19.47}$ Lv 4^{13} Nu 16^{9} 32^{4} Jos 22$^{18.20}$; †ע׳ בני ישׂראל Ex 16$^{1.2.9.10}$ 17^{1} 35$^{1.4.20}$ Lv 16^{5} 19^{2} (H), Nu 1$^{2.53}$ 8$^{9.20}$ 13^{26} 14$^{5.7}$ 15$^{25.26}$ 17^{6} 19^{9} 25^{6} 26^{2} 27^{20} 31^{12} Jos 18^{1} 22^{12}; הָעֵדָה Lv 8^{4} + 29 t. (cf. Ju 20^{1} 21^{10}); כל־הע׳ Lv 8^{3} + 33 t. (cf. Ju 21^{13}); †נְשִׂיאֵי (ה)ע׳ *princes of the congregation* Ex 16^{22} Nu 4^{34} 16^{2} 31^{13} 32^{2} Jos 9$^{15.18}$ 22^{30}; כָּל־הַנְּשִׂאִים בָּעֵ׳ Ex 34^{31}; זִקְנֵי הע׳ *elders of the congregation* Lv 4^{15} (cf. Ju 21^{16}); ראשׁי אבות הע׳ Nu 31^{26}.

4150 **מוֹעֵד**$_{223}$ **n.m.**$^{\psi\ 102,\ 14}$ **appointed time, place, meeting;** מ׳ Ex 9^{5} + 183 t.; מֹעֵד Dt 31^{10}; מוֹעֲדוֹ Nu 9^{2} + 2 t.; מֹעֲדוֹ La 2^{6} + 3 t. + 5 t. sfs.; pl. מוֹעֲדִים Dn 12^{7} + 6 t.; מֹעֲדִים Zc 8^{19} 1 Ch 23^{31}; מוֹעֲדוֹת 2 Ch 8^{13}; cstr. מוֹעֲדֵי Lv 23^{2} + 6 t.; מֹעֲדֵי Lv 23^{44}; sfs. מוֹעֲדַי Ez 44^{24}; מֹעֲדֵיכֶם Nu 15^{3} + 6 t. sfs.;—†**1.** *appointed time:* **a.** in general with prefix לְ, *at an* or *the appointed time* Gn 18^{14} Ex 13^{10} (J), Ex 23^{15} 34^{18} Jos 8^{14} (all JE), Gn 17^{21} 21^{2} (P), 1 S 9^{24} 13^{8} (after אשׁר insert either אָמַר 𝔊 𝔗 or שָׂם Dr), v^{11} 2 K 4$^{16.17}$ Hb 2^{3} Dn 8^{19} 11$^{27.29.35}$; למ׳ דוד *at the time appointed* with David 1 S 20^{35} (Thes SS *place appointed*); c. prefix בְּ Ho 2^{11} Lv 23^{4} Nu 9$^{2.3.7.13}$ 28^{2} (P); c. מִן 2 S 20^{5}; עַד עֵת מ׳ 24^{15} *unto the time appointed* (but dub., v. Dr); c. vbs. בא מ׳ ψ 102^{14}; לקח מ׳ 75^{3}; שׂים מ׳ Ex 9^{5} (J); העביר המ׳ Je 46^{17}; the stork ידעה מ׳ Je 8^{7} *knows her appointed time;* מ׳ צאתך Dt 16^{6} *time of thy going forth* (from Egypt). **b.** in particular (cf. Ex 13^{10} 23^{15} 34^{18}), *sacred season,* RV usu. *set feast* or *appointed season* (wider than חַג, which was only a feast celebrated by a *pilgrimage*), יוֹם (ימי) מ׳ *day(s) of appointed season* (i.e. *festivals*) Ho 9^{5} 12^{10} La 2$^{7.22}$; sg. indef. 1^{4}; of the feast of booths Dt 31^{10}; ‖ חג חדשׁ שׁבת Ho 2^{13}; ‖ שׁבת La 2^{6}; usu. pl. מ׳ יהוה Lv 23$^{2.4.37.44}$ (P), 2 Ch 2^{3} Ezr 3^{5}; with sfs. referring to י׳ Lv 23^{2} (P); במ׳ Nu 15^{3} 29^{39} (P), Ez 36^{38} 46^{9}; קרית מ׳ *city of our solemnities* (sacred seasons) Is 33^{20}; למ׳ טובים Zc 8^{19}; ‖ שׁבתות Ez 44^{24}; ‖ חדשׁים Is 1^{14} 1 Ch 23^{31} 2 Ch 8^{13} 31^{3} Ne 10^{34}; ‖ חגים Ez 46^{11}; חגים חדשׁים Ez 45^{17}; ‖ ראשׁי חָדְשֵׁכֶם Nu 10^{10} (P).—*Notes.* It is most probable that in Gn 1^{14} (P), where מ׳ ‖ אֹתֹת, the reference is to the sacred seasons as fixed by the moon's appearance; and so also עשׂה ירח למ׳ *he made the moon for sacred seasons* ψ 104^{19}, although many Lexx. & Comm. refer these to the *seasons* of the year.—למועד מועדים וחצי Dn 12^{7} *for a set time, times, and a half* = 3½ appointed times = half the prophetic week of years, cf. Br$^{\text{MP 453 f.}}$—ויאכלו את המ׳ they ate throughout the *sacred season* (of Maṣṣoth) 2 Ch 30^{22} AV RV, but Thes SS Be Ke Öt they ate *the offerings of the sacred season;* 𝔊 וַיְכַלּוּ. **2.** *appointed meeting:* בֵּית מ׳ לְכָל־חַי Jb 30^{23} *house of meeting for every living* (of She'ol); קְרִאֵי מ׳ Nu 16^{2} (P) *called to the assembly* = קְרִאֵי הָעֵדָה; קרא עלי מ׳ La 1^{15} *called a festal meeting against me;* בקרב מ׳ ψ 74^{4} *in the midst of thine assembly;* הַר מוֹעֵד Is 14^{13} *mount of meeting* or *assembly* (of the gods; the mountain of the gods in the extreme north, the oriental Olympus, Persian *Alborg,* Hindu *Meru,* Babylon. *Aralli,* cf. Len$^{\text{Origines ii, ch. ix}}$). **3.** *appointed place:* **a.** the temple, ‖ שֻׂכּוֹ La 2^{6}, נוּגֵי ממ׳ *afflicted* (and driven) *from the place of assembly* Zp 3^{18} (cf. Br$^{\text{MP 225}}$). **b.** synagogues, כָּל־מוֹעֲדֵי־אֵל בָּאָרֶץ *all* *the appointed places of Ēl in the land* ψ 74^{8}= בֵּית וַעַד *Sota* 9^{15}. **4.** *appointed sign, signal,* Ju 20^{38}. **5.** אֹהֶל מוֹעֵד *tent of meeting* (of God with his people: see יָעַד Niph. **1**); the sacred tent of the Exodus (see אֹהֶל **3**) Ex $33^{7.7}$ Nu 12^{4} Dt $31^{14.14}$ (E), Nu 11^{16} (J); oft. in P, as Ex 27^{21} 29^{4} Lv $1^{1.3}$ Jos 18^{1} 19^{51}, etc. (131 t.); elsewhere only 1 S 2^{22b} (om. 𝔊), 1 K 8^{4}=2 Ch 5^{5}, 1 Ch 6^{17} 9^{21} 23^{32} 2 Ch $1^{3.6.13}$.

4151 †[מוֹעָד] **n.[m.]** **appointed place** (of soldier in army); pl. sf. מוֹעָדָיו i.e. *his ranks* Is 14^{31}, so Thes SS RVm Ew De Che Dr Du; *his places of assemblage* Di; *at his appointed times* RV.

4152 †מוּעָדָה **n.f.** עָרֵי הַמּ׳ *cities appointed* (for refuge) Jos 20^{9} (P).

5129 †נוֹעַדְיָה **n.pr.** (*meeting with Yah*)—**1. m.** Levite, cotemp. Ezra Ezr 8^{33}. **2. f.** a prophetess hostile to Nehemiah Ne 6^{14}.

3260,5714 יֶעְדּוֹ Qr, ידעי Kt **n.pr.m.** 2 Ch 9^{29} v. עִדּוֹ sub עדד. p. 723

3261 †יָעָה **vb.** **sweep together** (with collat. idea of *carrying away*) (Ar. وَعَى is *collect, gather*)—**Qal** *Pf.* וְיָעָה consec. Is 28^{17} subj. בָּרָד c. acc. (ויעה ב׳ מַחְסֵה כָזָב).

3257 †[יָע] **n.[m.]** **shovel** (𝔗^{Jer} יָעֵי Ex 27^{3})—pl. הַיָּעִים Ex 38^{3}+7 t.; יָעָיו 27^{3};—utensils for cleaning altar, *shovels* Ex 27^{3} 38^{3} Nu 4^{14} (all P), 1 K $7^{40.45}$ 2 K 25^{14} 2 Ch $4^{11.16}$ Je 52^{18} (only in lists of utensils).

3262, 3273 †יְעוּאֵל, יְעִיאֵל, יְעוֹאֵל **n.pr.m.** **1.** יְעוּאֵל son of Zerah 1 Ch 9^{6}, 𝔊 Επειηλ, A 𝔊L Ιεηλ. **2.** יְעִיאֵל: **a.** a companion of Ezra Ezr 8^{13}, 𝔊L Ιειηλ. **b.** a chief of the Reubenites 1 Ch 5^{7}, 𝔊 Ιωηλ. **c.** Levites, 𝔊 Ιωηλ, Ιειηλ, etc.: (1) 1 Ch $15^{18.21}$ $16^{5.5}$ 2 Ch 20^{14}; (2) 2 Ch 35^{9}. **d.** one of those who took strange wives Ezr 10^{43}, 𝔊 Ιαηλ, Ιειηλ, etc. **3.** יעואל Kt, יְעִיאֵל Qr: **a.** man of Gibeon, ancestor of Saul 1 Ch 9^{35}, 𝔊 Ιηλ, Ιε(ι)ηλ. **b.** one of David's heroes 11^{44}, 𝔊 (Ι)εια, A 𝔊L Ιειηλ. **c.** the סוֹפֵר (q.v.) of King Uzziah 2 Ch 26^{11}, 𝔊 Ιειηλ. **d.** a Levite 29^{13} A 𝔊L Ιειηλ.

3263-65 יעוץ v. sub עוץ; יעור v. sub עור. p. 420, 734-35

3264 יְעוֹרִים v. יַעַר. p. 420

3266 יְעוּשׁ v. sub עוּשׁ. p. 736

3267 †[יָעַז] **vb.** only **Niph.** *Pt.* as adj. (precise mng. dub.; Ar. وَعَزَ is *give a nod* or *sign,* then *command,* whence Heb. might have meaning *nodding, making signs* (not intelligibly speaking), so Hi—Che *barbarous,* De *'ungeberdig'*—which context favours, or *arrogant;* Thes prop. *durus, saevus,* and comp. עזז)—in phr. עַם נוֹעָז Is 33^{19} *a barbarous*(?) *people,* of foreign invader.

יעזיאל, יעזיהו v. sub עזה. p. 739 3268-69

יַעְזֵר v. sub עזר. p. 741 3270

†[יָעַט] **vb.** **cover**;—only **Qal** *Pf.* 3 ms. 3271
sf. מְעִיל צְדָקָה יְעָטָנִי Is 61^{10} (הִלְבִּישַׁנִי בִּגְדֵי־יֶשַׁע ‖), but cf. עָטָה.

יָעִיר v. sub עור. p. 735 3265

יְעִישׁ v. sub עושׁ. p. 736 3274

יַעְכָּן v. sub עכן. p. 747 3275

† I. [יָעַל] **vb.** only **Hiph.** **profit, avail,** 3276
benefit;—**Hiph.** *Pf.* הוֹעִיל Hb 2^{18}; *Impf.* יוֹעִיל Je 2^{11}+2 t.; אוֹעִיל Jb 35^{3}; יוֹעִילוּ 1 S 12^{21}+6 t.; יוֹעִלוּ Je 2^{8} 12^{13}; יוֹעִילֻךְ Is 57^{12}; נוֹעִיל Jb 21^{15}; *Inf. abs.* הוֹעִיל Je 23^{22}; cstr. הוֹעִיל 7^{8}+4 t.; *Pt.* מוֹעִיל 16^{19};—*profit, avail, benefit,* always (exc. Jb 30^{13} where in bad sense, Is 47^{12}) c. neg., or in question implying neg.; esp. of idols or false gods (as *unprofitable*), so Hb 2^{18} Is $44^{9.10}$ 57^{12} Je 2^{8} v^{11} אחרי לא יועילו הלכו, המיר כבודו בלוא יועיל 16^{19} ואין בם מועיל, 1 S 12^{21}, of vain confidences Je 7^{8}, or promises $23^{32.32}$ (sq. לְ); of Egypt as ally Is 30^{5} (sq. לְ), $v^{5.6}$; of *wickedness* Pr 10^{2}; *wealth* 11^{4}; *worthless* men Jb 30^{13} (לְהַוָּתִי יוֹעִילוּ i.e. promote it); of words Jb 15^{3} (‖ דָּבָר לֹא יִסְכּוֹן); in gen. *gain profit* Is 47^{12} 48^{17} Je 12^{13} Jb 21^{15} 35^{3}.

†יוֹעֵאלָה **n.pr.m.** (perh. from *יוֹעֲלָה *may* 3132
he avail!)—one of David's heroes 1 Ch 12^{8} (Baer; v^{7} van d. H).

II. יעל (√of foll.; Ar. وَعَلَ *eminuit, prominuit;* v. *ascend,* Kam Frey).

† I. [יָעֵל] **n.[m.]** **mountain-goat** (NH *id.;* 3277
𝔗 יַעְלָא, Syr. ܝܥܠܐ; Ar. وَعْلٌ, وَعِلٌ; As. *ia'ilu* Dl $^{S\,53}$ (but Hpt $^{BAS\,i.\,170}$, Jäger $^{ib.\,465}$); Eth. ወዕል: v. Hom $^{NS\,280}$)—*Pl.* יְעֵלִים ψ 104^{18} (‖ שְׁפַנִּים); צוּרֵי יַעֲלֵי־סֶלַע 1 S 24^{3}; הַיּ׳ Jb 39^{1} (‖ אַיָּלוֹת; cf. 1. יַעֲלָה).

† II. יָעֵל **n.pr.f.** wife of Heber the Kenite, 3278
slayer of Sisera Ju $4^{17.18.21.22}$ 5^{24}, prob. also v^{6} (others find here name of a man, a 'judge').

† I. [יַעֲלָה] **n.f.** = I. יָעֵל (female);—אַיֶּלֶת 3280
אֲהָבִים וְיַעֲלַת חֵן Pr 5^{19} fig. of wife.

3279 †II. יַעְלָא, יַעֲלָה **n.pr.m.** *head of a family of returning exiles*, יַעְלָא Ne 7^{58} = יַעֲלָה Ezr 2^{56}.

3281 יַעְלָם v. sub עלם. p. 761

3282 I. יַ֫עַן **prep. and conj.** v. sub I. ענה. p. 774

1842 II. יַעַן in דַּנָּה יַעַן 2 S 24^{6} v. supr. p. 193.

יען (√of foll.; acc. to Ges Ew GGA 1864, No. 27 Aram. ܡܚܢܡ, ܡܚܢܐ *avidus, cupidus;* hence בַּת־יַעֲנָה = *daughter of greed*, of *ostrich* as *voracious* bird; but Wetzst Del Jb 31, 39 = *daughter of the desert* or *steppe*, from وَعْنَةٌ *hard, unproductive soil;* cf. the Arab. name أَبُو ٱلصَّحَارَى *father of the plains.*)

3283 †[יָעֵן] **n.[m.] ostrich** (i.e. *voracious* one?);—only pl. abs. כי ענים בַּמִּדְבָּר La 4^{3} Kt; Qr כַּיְעֵנִים.

3284 †יַעֲנָה **n.f. greed**(?);—only in בַּת־הַיַּעֲנָה Lv 11^{16} Dt 14^{15}; בְּנוֹת־יַעֲנָה Mi 1^{8} + 5 t.;—*ostrich*, (vid. √יען supra); as wailing (sim. of mourning) Mi 1^{8} (‖ תַּנִּים); symbol. of loneliness Jb 30^{29} (אָח הָיִיתִי לְתַנִּים וְרֵעַ לב׳ יַעֲ׳); of desolation, as dwelling among ruins Is 13^{21} 34^{13} (‖ תַּנִּים), Je 50^{39}; dwelling in desert Is 43^{20} (‖ תַּנִּים); unclean fowl Lv 11^{16} Dt 14^{15}.

3285 יַעְנַי **n.pr.** v. sub ענה. p. 774ff

3286 †I. [יָעֵף] **vb. be weary, faint** (Ar. وَغَفَ *run* and *shew weariness*)—**Qal** *Pf.* וְיָעֵפוּ consec. Je 51$^{58.64}$; *Impf.* יִיעַף Is 40^{28}; וַיִּיעָף 44^{12}; יִעֲפוּ 40^{30}; יִיעָפוּ v^{31} Je 2^{24}; יִעָפוּ Hb 2^{13};—*be* or *grow weary* Je 2^{24} (in seeking); = exhaust oneself fruitlessly Hb 2^{13} (‖ יגע), hence Je 51$^{58.64}$ (repeated by error from v^{58}); of י׳ (neg.) Is 40^{28} (‖ יגע); youth 40^{30} (‖ *id.*); the god-fearing v^{31} (‖ *id.*); *be faint* from lack of water 44^{12} (‖ אֵין כֹּחַ from hunger). **Hoph.** *Pt. wearied* Dn 9^{21} מֻעָף בִּיעָף (v. יְעָף).

3287 †יָעֵף **adj. weary, faint;**—always as subst., exc. Ju 8^{15} אנשיך הַיְּעֵפִים (of physical fatigue from lack of bread); הַיָּעֵף 2 S 16^{2} (from lack of drink); of mind and spirit Is 40^{29} (‖ אֵין אוֹנִים), 50^{4}.

3288 †יְעָף **n.[m.] weariness, faintness** (Aramaism, acc. to Lag BN 175);—מֻעָף בִּיעָף *weary with weariness*, utterly weary Dn 9^{21} (from winged flight, said of Gabriel).

II. **יעף** (√of following; cf. Ar. يَفَعَ *ascend a mountain*, يَفَعٌ *hill*).

8443 †[תּוֹעָפָה] **n.f. eminence**; of *towering* horns (? v. Di) כְּתוֹעֲפֹת רְאֵם לוֹ Nu 23^{22} 24^{8}, sim. of strength of Israel; of peaks תּוֹעֲפוֹת הָרִים לוֹ ψ 95^{4} (‖ מֶחְקְרֵי־אָרֶץ); of silver Jb 22^{25} כֶּסֶף תּוֹעָפוֹת לָךְ, very dubious, perhaps *heaps* or *bars* (ingots).

†יָעַץ **vb. advise, counsel** (only twice in 3289
Hex) (Aram. יְעַט; Ar. وَعَظَ *exhort, admonish*)—**Qal** *Pf.* 3 ms. יָעַץ Is 7^{5} + 11 t.; יָעָץ 14^{27} + 2 t.; sf. יְעָצַנִי ψ 16^{7}; יְעָצָהּ Is 23^{9} + יְעָצֻהוּ Baer 2 Ch 10^{8}; 3 pl. יָעֲצוּ ψ 62^{5}; sf. יְעָצֻהוּ 1 K 12^{8} + 2 t. (incl. 2 Ch 10^{8}, Baer יְעָצֻהוּ), etc.; *Impf.* אִיעֲצָה ψ 32^{8} (Ol Che אִיעָצְךָ); אִיעָצְךָ Ex 18^{19} Nu 24^{14} (not elsewhere Hex), Je 38^{15}, cf. also foregoing; אִיעָצְךָ 1 K 1^{12}; *Pt. act.* יוֹעֵץ Is 3^{3} + 9 t.; cstr. יֹעֵץ Na 1^{11}, יוֹעֵץ 2 S 15^{12}; יוֹעֲצֵךְ Mi 4^{9}; pl. יוֹעֲצִים Jb 12^{17} + 3 t.; יֹעֲצִים Ez 11^{2}; cstr. יֹעֲצֵי Is 19^{11} + 2 t., etc.; fs. sf. יוֹעַצְתּוֹ 2 Ch 22^{3}; *Pt. pass.* f. יְעוּצָה Is 14^{26};—*advise, counsel*, c. acc. Is 32$^{7.8}$ 23^{9} (subj. י׳) Mi 6^{5}; sq. בְּלִיַּעַל Na 1^{11} 7^{5} (sq. עַל = *against*), 19^{12} (sq. *id.*), 23^{8} (sq. *id.*), Hb 2^{10} (sq. לְ); oft. c. acc. cogn. 2 S 16^{23} 17^{7} Ez 11^{2}; sq. אֶל *against* Je 49^{20} 50^{45} (in both of י׳); sq. עַל *against* 49^{30} Is 19^{17} (of י׳); cf. pass. pt. Is 14^{26}; c. acc. cogn. + sf. pers. 1 K 12$^{8.12.13}$ 2 Ch 10^{8}; c. acc. pers. 2 S 17^{15} ψ 16^{7} Ex 18^{19} Nu 24^{14} (+ rel. cl.) Je 38^{15}; abs. (of י׳) Is 14^{24} (c. adv. כאשר), v^{27}; of man 2 S 17^{15} (כזאת וכזאת), v^{21} (על + ככה); sq. inf. ψ 62^{5} 2 Ch 25^{16} (of אלהים); sq. cl. without connective 2 S 17^{11}; sq. לְלֹא חָכְמָה Jb 26^{3};—אִיעֲצָה עליך עיני ψ 32^{8} (v. supr.).—*Pt. act.* as subst. = *counsellor*, king's adviser 2 S 15^{12} 1 Ch 27^{33} 2 Ch 22^{4} 25^{16} Ezr 7^{28} 8^{25} Is 19^{11}; so fem. 2 Ch 22^{3}; prob. also 1 Ch 27^{32} (‖ אִישׁ מֵבִין וְסוֹפֵר); cf. Mi 4^{9}, also Is 1^{26} (‖ שֹׁפְטִים), Jb 12^{17} (‖ *id.*);—in these three, of importance for people; so also Is 3^{3} Pr 11^{4} = 24^{6}; cf. Jb 3^{14}, and particularly פֶּלֶא יוֹעֵץ Is 9^{5} *wonder of a counsellor*, of the ideal ruler predicted. More generally, *counsellor, adviser* Pr 15^{22}; יוֹ׳ בְּשֶׂכֶל 1 Ch 26^{14} (specific reason for title unknown); יֹעֲ׳ שָׁלוֹם Pr 12^{20}; = *prophet* Is 41^{28}, nearly = *agents* (hired by adversaries of Judah) Ezr 4^{5}. **Niph.** (reflex. or recipr.) *Pf.* נוֹעַץ Is 40^{14}; נוֹעֲצוּ ψ 71^{10} 83^{6}; *Impf.* וַיִּוָּעַץ 1 K 12^{6} + 10 t.; יִוָּעֲצוּ Is 45^{21}; וַיִּוָּעֲצוּ 2 Ch 30^{23}; נִוָּעֲצָה Ne 6^{7}; *Pt.* pl. נוֹעָצִים 1 K 12^{6} + 4 t.;—*consult together, exchange counsel*, of king with advisers, sq. אֶת־ 1 K 12$^{6.8}$ = 2 Ch 10$^{6.8}$; and so of י׳ Is 40^{14}; sq. אֶל־ 2 K 6^{8} 2 Ch 20^{21}; sq. עִם 1 Ch 13^{1} 2 Ch 32^{3}; abs. *consider* 1 K 12^{28} 2 Ch 25^{17} 30^{2}; cf. 1 K 12^{6} (sq. inf.) = 2 Ch 10^{6}, 1 K 12^{9} (sq. Impf. + ו subord.) = 2 Ch

10^{9}; in gen. *consult, take counsel*, abs. Pr 13^{10}; יַחְדָּו ψ 71^{10} Ne 6^{7} Is 45^{21}; sq. לֵב יַחְדָּו (with heart together) ψ 83^{6} nearly=*determine*, sq. inf. 2 Ch 30^{23}. † **Hithp.** *Impf.* יִתְיָעֲצוּ ψ 83^{4} *conspire against*, sq. עַל (|| יַעֲרִימוּ סוֹד עַל).

6098 †עֵצָה **n.f. counsel, advice** (=(יְ)עֵצָה)—ע׳ Ju 20^{7}+28 t.; cstr. עֲצַת Is 5^{19}+33 t.; sf. עֲצָתִי Pr 1^{25}+5 t. (+Is 46^{11} Qr; Kt עצתו better); עֲצָתְךָ ψ 20^{5} 73^{24}; עֲצָתוֹ Ho 10^{6}+7 t. (incl. Is 46^{10} Kt v. supr.); עֲצָתָם Je 18^{23}+4 t.; pl. עֵצוֹת Dt 32^{28}+2 t.; עֲצָתָיִךְ Is 47^{13};—*counsel, advice* 2 S $15^{31.34}$ $16^{23.23}$ $17^{14.14.14.23}$ 1 K $12^{8.13.14}$ =2 Ch $10^{8.13.14}$, 2 Ch 22^{5} 25^{16} Ezr 10^{3} (where rd. ע׳ אֲדֹנָי Reuss Ry), v^{8} Jb 29^{21}; political *consultation* Is 47^{13}; as acc. cogn. 2 S 17^{7} 1 K 1^{12} Is 8^{10} Ez 11^{2} (עצת־רָע, || אָוֶן); c. הָבוּ ע׳ *give counsel* Ju 20^{7} 2 S 16^{20}; הֵבִיא ע׳ Is 16^{3}; עשׂה ע׳ 30^{1}; אָשִׁית עֵצוֹת בְּנַפְשִׁי ψ 13^{3};=*design, purpose* Ezr 4^{5} Ne 4^{9} 1 Ch 12^{20} (Baer), ψ 14^{6} 20^{5} Je 18^{23} (sq. עַל = *against*), 49^{30} (|| מַחֲשָׁבָה); עֲצַת־גּוֹיִם ψ 33^{10}; suitable *counsel* for war (=generalship) 2 K 18^{20}=Is 36^{5} (cf. Pr 20^{18} infr.); also עֲצַת שָׁלוֹם Zc 6^{13} *counsel of peace;* practical wisdom, *sagacity* Is 19^{3}, cf. v^{11}, Je 19^{7} Dt 32^{28} (|| תְּבוּנָה), Ho 10^{6}. Esp. in WisdLt and proph.; *counsel*=*good counsel, wisdom* Jb 38^{2} 42^{3} Pr 12^{15} 20^{5} (its seat בְּלֶב־אִישׁ); || תּוּשִׁיָּה Pr 8^{14} Is 28^{29} (of י׳); || חָכְמָה Je 49^{7}; || חָכְמָה and תְּבוּנָה Jb 12^{13} Pr 21^{30}; || מוּסָר 19^{20}; || תַּחְבֻּלוֹת 20^{18} (cf. Is 36^{5} supr.); ע׳ נִפְתָּלִים Jb 5^{13}; רוּחַ ע׳ וּגְבוּרָה Is 11^{2} (|| ר׳ חָכְמָה וּבִינָה); *hearty counsel* ע׳ נֶפֶשׁ Pr 27^{9}; *counsel of wisdom*, when wisdom is personif. Pr $1^{25.30}$ (|| תּוֹכַחַת); in bad sense ע׳ רשׁעים Jb 10^{3} 21^{16} 22^{18} ψ 1^{1}, cf. Jb 18^{7} ψ 106^{43} Is 29^{15}; of plan of י׳; ע׳ י׳ ψ 33^{11} Pr 19^{21} Is 19^{17} 14^{26} (הע׳ הַיְּעוּצָה), 25^{1} $46^{10.11}$; ע׳ קדושׁ ישׂראל 5^{19}; also Mi 4^{12} Je 32^{19} (גְּדֹל הָעֵצָה), 49^{20} 50^{45} ψ 106^{13}; ע׳ עֶלְיוֹן ψ 107^{11}; instruction, guiding wisdom of י׳ ψ 73^{24}; אִישׁ־עֲצָתוֹ i.e. counsellor of י׳ Is 40^{13}; in fig. אַנְשֵׁי עֲצָתִי ψ 119^{24}=*my counsellors*, said of testimonies of God;=*prophecy*, ע׳ מלאכיו Is 44^{26} (|| דְּבַר עַבְדּוֹ); תֹּאבַד ע׳ מִזְּקֵנִים Ez 7^{26} (cf. 1 K 12^{8}; || תּוֹרָה, חָזוֹן), מֵחָכָם Je 18^{18} (|| תּוֹרָה, דָּבָר).

4156 †[מוֹעֵצָה] **n.f. counsel, plan, principle, device**;—pl. abs. מֹעֵצוֹת Pr 22^{20} (|| דַּעַת) in good sense; in bad sense מוֹעֵצוֹת Je 7^{24} (|| שְׁרִרוּת לִבָּם הָרָע); מֹעֲצוֹתֵיהֶם Ho 11^{6} ψ 5^{11}; מוֹעֲצוֹתֵיהֶם ψ 81^{13}; מֹעֲצֹתֵיהֶם Pr 1^{31}; מֹעֲצוֹתָם Mi 6^{16}.

3290-91 יַעֲקֹב, יַעֲקֹ֫בָה v. sub עקב. p. 784-85

יַעְקָן v. עֲקָן. p. 122, 785 3292

I. יער (√ of foll.; Ar. وَعُرَ is *be rugged*, of mountain, etc., *be difficult;* وَعْرٌ *rough* or *difficult place, mountain*).

†I. יַ֫עַר **n.m.** [2 S 18,8] **wood, forest, thicket** 3264, 3293
(MI[21] pl. היערן (=n.pr.loc.?); Ph. יער and יר, cf. DHM in MV[(10) 983]; Aram. יַעֲרָא, ܥܒܐ *wood, thicket;* As. *âru* Dl[HWB 230], cf. Jäger[BAS i. 476])—abs. יַ֫עַר Is 7^{2}+; יָ֑עַר Mi 3^{12}+; c. ה loc. יַ֫עְרָה Jos 17^{15}; cstr. יַ֫עַר 2 S 18^{6}; יַעְרָהּ Je 46^{23}, etc.; pl. יְעָרִים Ezr 2^{25}+4 t. (incl. Ez 34^{25} Qr, so Co); יְעָרוֹת ψ 29^{9};—**a.** *wood, forest, wooded height*, with trees to be felled Jos 17^{15} (c. עלה *go up* to), v^{18} (J), Dt 19^{5} (not elsewhere Hex); עֵץ מִיַּעַר כְּרָתוֹ Je 10^{13} *as wood out of a forest he hath cut it;* יחטבו מן־היערים Ez 39^{10} (עצים מן־השׂדה in || cl.); as producing trees יער צוֹמֵחַ עֵצִים Ec 2^{6}; in designation of Solomon's palace בֵּית יַעַר הַלְּבָנוֹן 1 K 7^{2} (on structure of this house v. Sta [Salomos Bauten, ZAW 1883, 150]), $10^{17.21}$=2 Ch $9^{16.20}$; cf. בֵּית הַיָּ֑עַר Is 22^{8}; fig. of foes to be cut down and destroyed נִקַּף סִבְכֵי היער Is 10^{34}; כָּרְתוּ יַעְרָהּ Je 46^{23}; so Is 32^{19} and יער הַבָּצִוֹר Zc 11^{2} (rd. Kt הַבָּצוּר *inaccessible forest*). **b.** as hiding-place for fugitive 1 S 22^{5}; lurking-place of wild beasts Am 3^{4} Mi 5^{7} 2 K 2^{24} Je 5^{6} 12^{8} Is 56^{9} ψ 50^{10} 80^{14} 104^{20}, cf. Ez 34^{25} (rd. Qr, v. supr.) **c.** stripped by voice of י׳ ψ 29^{9}; devoured by fire Is 9^{17} (סִבְכֵי הַיּ׳; fig. of the people); so in metaph. or sim. of י׳'s judgments Is 10^{18} (כְּבוֹד יַעְרוֹ; fig. of Assyr.), Je 21^{14} Ez $21^{2.3}$ (v. infr.) ψ 83^{15}. **d.** opp. כַּרְמֶל (*garden-land*) Is 29^{17} 32^{15}; but also יַעַר כַּרְמִלּוֹ *his garden woodland* 2 K 19^{23} =Is 37^{24}, and יַעַר בְּתוֹךְ כַּרְמֶל Mi 7^{14} (secluded and fertile abode for flock, fig. of people, v. Che; Hi-St thinks of *sacred grove*). **e.** =*thicket*, esp. as symbol of desolation Ho 2^{14}; בָּמוֹת יער *thicket-covered heights* (overgrown with bushes and trees) Mi 3^{12}=Je 26^{18}; also בַּיַּעַר בַּעְרַב Is 21^{13} *in the thicket* (or *bushes*, so VB) *in Arabia* must ye lodge, caravans of Dedanites. **f.** עֲצֵי (ה)יער *trees of the forest* Is 7^{2} (in sim.), 10^{19} (שְׁאָר עֵץ יַעְרוֹ, fig.), 44^{14} Ez 15^{2}, also v^{6} (עֵץ היער), Ct 2^{3} (in sim.); fig., as singing before י׳ ψ 96^{12}=1 Ch 16^{33}, Is 44^{23} (יער וְכָל־עֵץ בּוֹ). **g.** particular forests are: יער אפרים 2 S 18^{6}, see אֶפְרַיִם p. 68 supr.; cf. $v^{18.17}$ (v. also Jos $17^{15.18}$); יַעַר חָ֑רֶת 1 S 22^{5} (v. supr.); יַעַר לְבָנוֹן (v. supr.); יַעַר הַשָּׂדֶה נֶגֶב and יַעַר הַנָּ֑גֶב Ez $21^{2.3}$ (v. supr.) fig. of Judah

(land and people); v. also יְעָרִים infr.—שְׂדֵי־יָ֑עַר
ψ 132^{6} is a n.pr.loc. (but Bae thinks appellat.
'auf waldigem Gefilde'), v. קִרְיַת יְעָרִים. On
1 S 14$^{25.26}$, v. II. יער.— יעורים Ez 34^{25} Kt, rd.
יְעָרִים Qr, v. supr.

II. יער (√of following; meaning dubious;
MV identif. with I, from roughness and porous-
ness (?) of honeycomb, cf. Buhl.

3293 † II. יַ֫עַר **n.[m.] honeycomb,**—abs. יַעַר 1 S
14$^{25.26}$; sf. יַעְרִי Ct 5^{1};—*honeycomb*, containing
honey 1 S 14^{25} (where rd. וְיַעַר הָיָה עַל־פְּנֵי הַשָּׂדֶה
with 𝔊 We Dr Kit in Kau^{AT}, instead of v. as
in MT); וַיָּבֹא העם אֶל־הַיַּעַר 1 S 14^{26} (‖ דבשׁ v^{25})
and when the people came to the honeycomb
behold its bees had departed (v. 𝔊 We Dr Kit
VB); אָכַלְתִּי יַעְרִי עִם־דִּבְשִׁי Ct 5^{1}; v. also I. יַעְרָה.

3295 † I. [יַעְרָה] **n.f. honeycomb,** only cstr. יַעְרַת
הַדְּבָשׁ 1 S 14^{27} (v. II. יער).—יְעָרוֹת v. I. יַעַר.

3294 † II. יַעְרָה **n.pr.m.** a descendant of Saul
1 Ch 9$^{42.42}$, prob. corrupt, v. יְהוֹעַדָּה p. 221 supr.

3296 † יַעְרֵי אֹרְגִים **n.pr.m.** father of Elḥanan
2 S 21^{19} (=יָעוּר 1 Ch 20^{5}); א׳ prob. scribal err.
anticipating א׳ in foll. line (We Dr), and יַעְרֵי
error for יָעִיר (We) q. v. sub עור.

3297 † יְעָרִים **n.pr.mont.** only הַר־יְעָרִים Jos 15^{10}
(𝔊 πόλιν Ιαρειν), where explained as=כְּסָלוֹן (𝔊
Χασ(α)λων), mod. *Kesla*, NE. of Beth Shemesh,
cf. Rob$^{BR\ ii.\ 30\ n.;\ iii.\ 154}$.—קִרְיַת יְעָרִים v. sub קִרְיָה.

3298 יַעְרֶשְׁיָה v. sub ערשׁ. p. 793

3299-300 יַעֲשַׂי, יעשׂו, יַעֲשִׂיאֵל v. עשׂה. p. 795

3301 יִפְדְיָה v. sub פדה. p. 804

3302 † [יָפָה] **vb. be fair, beautiful** (NH *id.* Pi.
and deriv.; Aram. Aph. ܐܘܦܝ is *suffice, finish,*
fail; cf. Aram. ܦܐܝܐ (PS^{3015}) *beautiful, fit,* Nö^{§172}
C. Anm. G H[offmann]$^{LCB\ 1882,\ 321}$; Ar. وَفَى *fulfil,*
perform; Eth. አወፈየ: II. **2**, *give* (entirely)
over to, into power of, Di^{949})—**Qal** *Pf.* יָפִית
Ct 7^{7}; יָפוּ 4^{10} 7^{2}; *Impf.* 2 fs. וַתִּיפִי (Kö$^{Lgb.\ i.\ 581}$)
Ez 16^{13}; 3 ms. apoc. וַיִּיף 31^{7};—*be beautiful,* subj.
pers. Ct 4^{10} 7^{7}; of feet v^{2}; of Jerus. under fig.
of woman Ez 16^{13}; Egypt under fig. of tree
31^{7}. **Pi.** *Impf.* 3 ms. sf. יְיַפֵּהוּ Je 10^{4} *beautify*
an idol. The (**Peʿal ʿal** ?) *Pf.* form יָפְיָפִיתָ מִבְּנֵי
אָדָם ψ 45^{3} is contrary to all anal.: rd. either
יָפִיתָ or יְפִיפִיתָ Ges$^{§55.\ 3}$ Sta$^{§156\ R}$ Now (Kö$^{i.\ 583\ f.}$
defence is artificial): *thou art more beautiful*
than, etc. **Hithp.** *Impf.* 2 fs. תִּתְיַפִּי *beautify*
thyself Je 4^{30}.

† יָפֶה **adj. fair, beautiful**;—m. abs. יָפֶה 2 S 3303
14^{25} + 4 t.; cstr. יְפֵה Gn 39$^{6.6}$ + 6 t.; f. יָפָה 12^{14}
+ 14 t.; cstr. יְפַת 2^{11} + 6 t.; sf. יָפָתִי Ct 2$^{10.13}$;
pl. יָפוֹת Jb 42^{15} Am 8^{13}; cstr. יְפוֹת Gn 41^{2}; יָפֹת
v$^{4.18}$;—*fair, beautiful,* as attribute of woman
2 S 13^{1} 1 K 1^{3} Am 8^{13} Pr 11^{22}; cf. Jb 42^{15} Ct 6^{10}
(י׳ כלבנה); pred. Gn 12^{14} 1 K 1^{4} Ct 1$^{15.15}$ 4$^{1.1.7}$ 6^{4};
=subst. *fair one* 1^{8} 2$^{10.13}$ 5^{9} 6^{1}; oft. cstr. יְפַת־
מַרְאֶה Gn 12^{11} 29^{17} 2 S 14^{27}; יְפַת־תֹּאַר Gn 29^{17}
1 S 25^{3} Dt 21^{11} Est 2^{7}: of kine יְפוֹת־מַרְאֶה Gn
41^{2}, cf. v^{4}; יְפוֹת־תֹּאַר v^{18}; less oft. of boy, young
man אִישׁ יָפֶה 2 S 14^{25}; pred. Ct 1^{16}; יְפֵה תֹאַר
Gn 39^{6}; וִיפֵה מַרְאֶה v^{6} (of Joseph); of Jerusalem
יְפֵה נוֹף ψ 48^{3}; of a singer יְפֵה קוֹל Ez 33^{32}; of
trees: olive יְפֵה פְרִי־תֹאַר Je 11^{16}; cedar (fig. of
Egypt) יְפֵה עָנָף Ez 31^{3}, cf. v^{9}; יָפֶה of everything
in its time Ec 3^{11}; of various acts 5^{17}.—In עִם
יְפֵה עֵינַיִם 1 S 16^{12}, עִם יְפֵה מַרְאֶה 17^{42}, either יפה
=subst. abstr. *with beauty of eyes,* or עם is
textual error (Gr Krenkel$^{ZAW,\ 1882,\ 309}$ Bu עֶלֶם
youth), v. Dr.

† יְפֵה־פִיָּה, rd. יְפֵהפִיָּה, or better יְפֵיפִיָּה (Ol 3304
§188 a Gr Gie; reduplicated, with the force of a
diminutive, Sta^{§156}; cf. אֲדַמְדָּם, יְרַקְרַק), **adj. f.**
pretty, עֶגְלָה יְפֵה־פִיָּה מִצְרַיִם Je 46^{20} Egypt is a
pretty heifer (𝔊 κεκαλλωπισμένη).

יְפִי v. יֳפִי. below 3308

† [יֳפִי] **n.m. beauty**;—abs. יֹ֫פִי Is 3^{24} + 5 t.; 3308
cstr. יְפִי Ez 28^{7}; sf. יָפְיֵךְ v^{17}; יָפְיֵךְ ψ 45^{12} + 5 t.;
יָפְיוֹ Is 33^{17} + 2 t.; יָפְיָהּ Pr 6^{25} Est 1^{11}; *beauty* of
a woman Is 3^{24} ψ 45^{12} Est 1^{11} Pr 6^{25}, cf. Pr 31^{30};
of Jerus. under fig. of woman Ez 16$^{14.15.25}$; Tyre
27^{3} (כְּלִ֫ילַת יֹ֫פִי), cf. v$^{4.11}$; prince of Tyre, *beauty*
of (his) wisdom 28^{7}; king of Tyre v^{12} (כְּלִיל יפי),
v^{17}; ideal beauty of king of Judah Is 33^{17}, Zion
(מִכְלַל־יֹפִי) ψ 50^{2}, cf. La 2^{15} (כְּלִילַת יֹפִי); of Egypt
under fig. of tree Ez 31^{8}; of ransomed people
of י׳ Zc 9^{17}.

† יָפוֹ, יָפוֹא **n.pr.loc. Joppa** (Ph. יפי; As. 3305
Ja(p)pu COT^{Gloss} Bez$^{Tel-el-Amarna\ Tabl.\ in\ Brit.\ Mus.\ 146}$;
Egypt. *Ye-pu* WMM^{159})—seaport town of
Palestine (Jerusalem), יָפוֹ Jos 19^{46} Jon 1^{3} 2 Ch
2^{15}=יָפוֹא Ezr 3^{7}; 𝔊 Ιοππα, mod. *Jaffa*.

3306 **[יָפַח] vb.** breathe, puff (by-form of פּוּחַ, q.v.; see Ba[NB 189]; cf. Talm. יפח *breath*)—only **Hithp.** *Impf.* 3 fs. תִּתְיַפֵּחַ Je 4[31] she *gaspeth for breath.*

3307 †**[יָפֵחַ] adj.** breathing or puffing out, cstr. וִיפֵחַ חָמָס ψ 27[12] *puffing out violence* (cf. Che).

3310 יַפְלֵט v. sub פלט. p. 812

3312 יְפֻנֶּה v. sub פנה. p. 819

3313 †**[יָפַע] vb.** only **Hiph.** shine out or forth, send out beams, cause to shine (NH *id.*, in fig. senses; 𝔗 יְפַע; As. Shaph. *šûpu, shine, cause to shine, glorify,* Lotz[TP Col. vii. 93] Zim[BP 97, 105] SAS[Asrb. ii. 18]; cf. Ar. وَقْعٌ *aedificium elatum;* kindred seem to be يَفَعَ *ascendit* montem, *adultus fuit;* Sab. יפע *raise, heighten* Os[ZMG 1865, 210f.], יפע name of a temple DHM[ZMG 1883, 350])—**Hiph.** *Pf.* הוֹפִיעַ Dt 33[2] ψ 50[2]; וְהוֹפִיעַ consec. Jb 37[15]; 2 ms. הוֹפַעְתָּ 10[3]; *Impf.* 3 fs. תּוֹפַע 3[4]; וַתֹּפַע 10[22]; *Imv.* הוֹפִיעַ ψ 94[1]; הוֹפִיעָה 80[2];—**1.** *shine out, forth, display beams:* of י׳ Dt 33[2] ψ 50[2] 80[2] 94[1] Jb 10[3] (sq. עַל); subj. נְהָרָה *light* Jb 3[4]; 10[22] וַתֹּפַע כְּמוֹ אֹפֶל (of She'ôl). **2.** *cause to shine* וְהוֹפִיעַ אוֹר עֲנָנוֹ Jb 37[15], subj. י׳.

3314 †**[יִפְעָה] n.f.** brightness, splendour, יִפְעָתֶךָ Ez 28[7.17] of prince and king of Tyre.

3309 †**יָפִיעַ n.pr.pers.** et **loc. 1. n.pr.m.** (cf. Sab. יפעאל Hal[150])—**a.** a king of Lachish Jos 10[3], 𝔊 Ιεφθα, A 𝔊L Ιαφ(α)ιε. **b.** a son of David 2 S 5[15] (𝔊 Ιεφιες, 𝔊L Ναφεθ) = 1 Ch 3[7] (𝔊 Ιανουε, A Ιαφιε, 𝔊L Αχικαμ) = 14[6] (𝔊 Ιανουου, A Ιαφιε, 𝔊L Ιαβεγ). **2. n.pr.loc.** on border of Zebulun Jos 19[12], perh. = mod. *Yâfa*, ½ hour fr. Nazareth, Rob[BR ii. 343f], but 𝔊 Φαγγαι, A Ιαφαγαι; 𝔊L Ιαφφιε.

4158 †**מֵיפַעַת n.pr.loc.** (Sab. n.pr.loc. מיפעת, מיפע DHM[ZMG 1876, 679; 1883, 362])—1 Ch 6[64] Levitical city in Reuben; in Reuben מֵפָעַת Jos 13[18]; מוֹפָעַת Je 48[21] in Moab.

3315 יֶפֶת v. sub פתה. p. 834

3316-17 יִפְתָּח, יִפְתַּח־אֵל v. sub פתח. p. 836

3318 **יָצָא** [1068] **vb.** go or come out (NH *id.*; Aram. יְצָא; Eth. ወፅአ:, ወጽአ:; As. *âṣû* Dl[HWB 237], all = *go out, forth;* Syr. ܝܼܨܵܐ *go forth* (in sense of *germinate*), *grow;* Ph. יצא *march out;* cf. SI[5] המוצא *the source* (of water); Sab. וצא *go out,* DHM in MV; Ar. وَضُؤَ is *be* or *become fair, beautiful, neat, clean,* cf. Nö[ZMG 1886, 725])—**Qal** *Pf.* יָצָא Gn 10[11] + 92 t.; 3 fs. יָצְאָה Nu 16[35] + 13 t.; יָצָאָה Is 28[29]; 2 ms. יָצָאתָ Gn 24[5] + 7 t.; 2 fs. וְיָצָאת Je 31[4]; 2 mpl. יְצָאתֶם Ex 13[3] Dt 11[10]; וִיצָאתֶם Ju 21[21] Mal 3[20]; 3 pl. sf. יְצָאֻנִי Je 10[20], etc.; *Impf.* יֵצֵא Gn 15[4] + 64 t.; וַיֵּצֵא 4[16] + 132 t.; 3 fs. תֵּצֵא Ex 21[7] + 22 t.; וַתֵּצֵא Gn 30[16] + 14 t.; 2 ms. תֵּצֵא Dt 20[1] + 16 t.; 3 pl. יֵצְאוּ Gn 15[14] +; וַתֵּצֶאןָ 17[6] +; 3 fpl. וַתֵּצֶאנָה 1 S 18[6] 2 K 2[24]; וַתֵּצֶאןָ Ex 15[20]; 2 fpl. תֵּצֶאנָה Am 4[3], etc.; *Imv.* צֵא Gn 8[16] + 15 t.; וָצְאָה Ju 9[29]; fs. צְאִי Ct 1[8]; mpl. צְאוּ Gn 19[14] + 11 t.; צֵאוּ Is 49[9] Ez 9[7] + Je 58[8] Qr (Kt וּצְאוּ) צְאֶינָה Ct 3[11]; *Inf. abs.* יָצוֹא Gn 8[7] + 2 t.; יָצֹא 27[30] + 3 t.; *Inf. cstr.* צֵאת 24[11] + 31 t.; sf. צֵאתִי Ex 9[29] + 3 t.; צֵאתֵנוּ Jo 9[12]; צֵאתְךָ Dt 16[3] + 10 t., etc.; *Pt.* יֹצֵא (יוֹצֵא) Gn 2[10] + 62 t.; fs. יֹצֵאת Ec 10[5]; יֹצֵאת (יו׳) Gn 24[15] + 11 t.; יֹצֵת Dt 28[57], etc.;—**1.** *go* or *come out* or *forth:* **a.** from (מִן) a place, e.g. a tent Gn 31[33] (E; opp. בּוֹא בְּ), מִפֶּתַח אֹהֶל מוֹעֵד Lv 8[33] 10[7] (P), cf. מִן־הַמִּקְדָּשׁ 21[12] (H); from a house 2 S 11[8], the doors (דלתי) of a house Jos 2[19] (JE), Ju 11[31]; מִפֶּתַח ביתו Ex 12[22] (JE), from a camp 1 S 13[17] 2 K 7[12], a city Gn 19[14] (J), 12[4] (P), 1 K 11[29] 20[17] Mi 4[10], a cave 1 S 24[9], the ark Gn 9[18] (J), 8[16.19] (both P); out of vineyards Ju 21[21]; sq. acc. אֶת־הָעִיר Gn 44[4] (E), Ex 9[29] (J); c. בְּ also, of gate Je 17[19] Ne 2[13]; sq. acc. local. לֹא אֵצֵא פָתַח Jb 31[34]; pt. cstr. יֹצְאֵי הַתֵּבָה Gn 9[10] (P), יֹצְאֵי שַׁעַר עִירוֹ 34[24] (P); abs. Jos 2[5] (JE), Ju 3[24] Ex 34[34] (P), Nu 33[3] (P; Israel going out [from Egypt]), 2 Ch 26[20] +; specif., of going out (מִן) from a land (of emigration) Gn 10[11.14] 24[5] (all J); partic. of *coming forth* from (the land of) Egypt (the Exodus) Ex 12[41] (J), 13[3.8] 23[15] 34[18] Nu 11[20] 22[5] (all JE), and esp. D, Dt 4[45.46] 9[7] 11[10] 16[3.3.6] 23[5] 24[9] 25[17] Jos 2[10] 5[4.5.6] (all D), Nu 33[1] (P), 1 K 6[1] 8[9] = 2 Ch 5[10], 2 K 21[15] Je 7[25] Hg 2[5] ψ 114[1]. **b.** *go forth* from (the presence of) a person: Ex 8[26] 9[33] 10[6] (all sq. מֵעִם), Gn 44[28] Ex 5[20] Jer 2[37] (מֵאֵת), Ju 3[19] (מֵעָלָיו); sq. מִלִּפְנֵי Gn 4[16] (J), 41[46] 47[10] Est 8[15] Ec 10[5]; sq. מֵעִם פְּנֵי Jb 1[12], מֵאֵת פְּנֵי 2[7]; sq. sf. יְצָאֻנִי Je 10[20] (v. De Ec 7[18]). **c.** in technical senses: abs. *go forth,* of emancipation Ex 21[2.3.3.4.5.7.7.7.11] (all JE), cf. יצא מִתַּחַת יַד־אֲרָם 2 K 13[5]; of release in the year of jubilee, land, etc. Lv 25[28.30.31.33] (all H), 27[21] (P); also of a debtor-slave 25[54] (H); of divorce וְיָצְאָה מִבֵּיתוֹ Dt 24[2]; of condemnation בְּהִשָּׁפְטוֹ יֵצֵא רָשָׁע ψ 109[7] *when he is judged let him go out as a criminal,* i.e. be condemned;

of bowels (מֵעִים) falling out by reason of disease 2 Ch $21^{15.19}$. **d.** of flight, involving escape: sq. כִּי נָצֹא תֵּצֵא ,הַחוּצָה || נוּס, *flee* Gn $39^{12.15}$ (J), רָעָה אֲשֶׁר Je 48^{9}; opp. taken (by lot) 1 S 14^{41}; לֹא־יוּכְלוּ לָצֵאת מִמֶּנָּה Je 11^{11} *calamity from which they shall not be able to escape;* perh. also יְרֵא אֱלֹהִים יֵצֵא אֶת־כֻּלָּם Ec 7^{18} *he that feareth God shall escape* (or *be freed from*, v. De Hi-Now Mishn) *all of them* (see VB),—on acc. with יצא v. De. **e.** *depart* בְּצֵאת נַפְשָׁהּ Gn 35^{18} i.e. *when she was expiring;* so תֵּצֵא רוּחוֹ ψ 146^{4}; בְּצֵאת הַיַּיִן מִנָּבָל 1 S 25^{37} i.e. *when Nabal became sober;* also fig. וַיֵּצֵא לִבָּם Gn 42^{28} (E) i.e. *their heart failed* (|| וַיֶּחֶרְדוּ); rust from (מִן) caldron Ez 24^{16} (v. Co Ez 12^{5}); of glory of ׳י 10^{18}; וַיֵּצֵא מִן בַּת־צִיּוֹן כָּל־הֲדָרָהּ La 1^{6}; hence inf.=*exit, end* בְּצֵאת הַשָּׁנָה Ex 23^{16} (JE), and, redundantly, כְּעֵת צֵאת הַקֵּץ לְיָמִים שְׁנַיִם 2 Ch 21^{19} i.e. *at the end of two years.* **f.** of inanimate things: river out of Eden Gn 2^{10} (J), water out of rock Ex 17^{6} (E), Nu 20^{11} (JE), from Leḥi Ju 15^{19}; of molten calf out of fire Ex 32^{24} (E); of gold (after refining) Jb 23^{10} (abs., in sim.); in prophecy of fountain from house of ׳י Ez $47^{1.8.12}$ Zc 14^{8} Jo 4^{18}; of seed (semen virile) from man Lv $15^{16.32}$ (P), 22^{4} (H); of weapon which has pierced body 2 S 2^{23} (מֵאַחֲרָיו), 2 K 9^{24} (מִלִּבּוֹ), Jb 20^{25} (מִגֵּוָה); וַתֵּצֵא אַחֲרָיו מַשְׂאַת הַמֶּלֶךְ 2 S 11^{8} *and there went out* (=was sent out) *after him the king's portion* (i.e. the food given by the king); idiomatically of expenditure of money 2 K 12^{13} (abs., cf. Hiph. v^{12}); of swift movement of arrow from bow Zc 9^{14} (like lightning), of lightning out of fire Ez 1^{13}; abs. of *sunrise* (subj. שֶׁמֶשׁ) Ju 5^{31} (in sim.), Gn 19^{23}, cf. Is 13^{10} (so As., e.g. *ultu ṣît šanši adi êrib šanši* COT Gn 19^{23}); of rising of stars (כּוֹכָבִים) Ne 4^{15}; of sentence of judge Hb $1^{4.4}$ ψ 17^{2}; of judgment, or right appearing (with sim. of light) Hos 6^{5} (rd. וּמִשְׁפָּטִי כָאוֹר יֵצֵא), Is 62^{1}; of a lot וַיֵּצֵא הַגּוֹרָל לִבְנֵי יוֹסֵף Jos 16^{1} (JE), and esp. P, Nu 33^{54} Jos $19^{1.17.24.32.40}$ 21^{4}, cf. also ויצא גְּבוּל גּוֹרָלָם 18^{11} (P). **g.** with especial emphasis on idea of origin, source: hyssop out of the wall 1 K 5^{13}; מיהוה יצא הדבר Gn 24^{50} (J) *from* ׳י *has the thing proceeded,* of a providential arrangement, so מֵעִם ׳י Is 28^{29}; מֵרְשָׁעִים יֵצֵא רֶשַׁע 1 S 24^{14} (an ancient proverb); of pollution proceeding from (מֵאֵת) prophets Je 23^{15}; of fire from Heshbon Nu 21^{28} (JE), Je 48^{45}, cf. Ju $9^{15.20.20}$; of fire מִלִּפְנֵי ׳י Lv 9^{24} 10^{2}, מֵאֵת ׳י Nu 16^{35} (all P); in theophany יצא רֶשֶׁף לְרַגְלָיו Hb 3^{5}; iniquity from unreceptive heart ψ 73^{7} (v.I. לֵבָב **1**); wrath מִלִּפְנֵי ׳י Nu 17^{11} (P); abs. Je 4^{4}=21^{12}, 23^{19}=30^{23}; so salvation Is 51^{5}; וְנִשְׁמַת־מִי יָצְאָה מִמֶּךָּ Jb 26^{4}; of words *going forth* from mouth of speaker (of solemn or formal speech) לֹא יֵצֵא מִפִּיכֶם דָּבָר Jos 6^{10} (JE), Ju 11^{36} 1 S 2^{3} Je 44^{17} Jb 37^{2} Est 7^{8}, also Nu 30^{3} 32^{24} (both P); of ׳י's words going forth from his mouth, or from him Is 45^{23} 48^{3} 51^{4} 55^{11} Ez 33^{30}; of ׳י's words, instruction, command, etc., going forth Is 2^{3}=Mi 4^{2} (from Jerusalem), Dn 9^{23}; of human commandment Est 1^{19}, cf. v^{17}. **h.** of children as *going forth* from loins (of father) מִמֵּעִים 2 S 7^{12} 16^{11}; מֵחֲלָצִים Gn 35^{11} (P), 1 K 8^{19}=2 Ch 6^{9}; sq. מִן alone 2 K 20^{18}=Is 39^{7}; also יֹצְאֵי יְרֵכוֹ Ju 8^{30} Gn 46^{26} Ex 1^{5} (both P); also of birth מֵרֶחֶם (אִמּוֹ) Nu 12^{12} (JE), Je 1^{5} 20^{18} Jb 3^{11}; fig. of sea 38^{8}, of ice v^{29}; מִבֶּטֶן אִמּוֹ Jb 1^{21} Ec 5^{14}; lit., source not expr., Gn $25^{25.26}$ $38^{28.29.30}$ (all J); of untimely birth Ex 21^{22} (JE); cf. הַיּוֹצֵת מִבֵּין רַגְלֶיהָ Dt 28^{57} (|| תֵּלֵד); of family or race connexion (sq. מִן) Na 1^{11} Is 48^{1} 1 Ch 1^{12} 2^{53}; יצא also of produce of vine (מִגֶּפֶן) Ju 13^{14}, cf. הַיֹּצֵא הַשָּׂדֶה Dt 14^{22} (rd. יצא Sam., v. Di); אֶרֶץ מִמֶּנָּה יצא לֶחֶם Jb 28^{5}; of viper proceeding from serpent's root Is 14^{29}; further, with idea of unfolding, growth Jb 8^{16} 14^{2} 31^{40}; וְיָצָא חֹטֶר מִגֵּזַע יִשָׁי Is 11^{1}; of the little horn Dn 8^{9}; so of branches of candlestick in tabernacle Ex $25^{32.33.35}$ $37^{18.19.21}$ (all P); then simply *project* (tower from wall) Ne $3^{25.26.27}$; of measuring-line *going forth* (abs.) in a particular direction Je 31^{39}; of a boundary(-line) *going out* (abs.) so as then to turn and make an angle Nu $34^{4.9}$ Jos $15^{3.4.9.11.11}$ $16^{2.6.7}$ $18^{15.15.17.17}$ $19^{12.13.27.34.47}$. **2. a.** *go forth* to a place Gn 27^{3} (J), Je 14^{18} Ez 3^{22} Zc $6^{6.6.7}$+; so וַיֵּצֵא הַפַּרְשְׁדֹנָה Ju 3^{22} (see VB); go forth in surrender 1 S 11^{3} (sq. אֶל pers.), 2 K 18^{31}=Is 36^{16}, Je $38^{17.21}$; אֵין פֶּרֶץ וְאֵין יוֹצֵאת ψ 144^{14}; into captivity לֹא יֵצְאוּ אִתְּכֶם יָצָא מִן־הַמָּקוֹם בַּגּוֹלָה Je 29^{16}, cf. 48^{7} Zc 14^{2}; also הַזֶּה Je 22^{11}, cf. בְּנֵי יְצָאֻנִי 10^{20}. **b.** *go forward, proceed* to or toward something, fig., מֵרָעָה אֶל־רָעָה יָצָאוּ Je 9^{2} *from evil to evil they go on;* in like manner 2 S 20^{8} si vera l., but read rather וְהִיא יָצְאָה *and it* (i.e. the sword) *came out* (of the sheath) *and fell* 𝔊 We Dr Kit Bu. **c.** *come* or *go forth,* with esp. ref. to purpose or result: יָצָא שָׁאוּל וְיָצָאתִי אַחֲרָיו וְהִכִּתִיו 1 S 17^{35}, cf. 24^{15}; לְבַקֵּשׁ נַפְשׁוֹ 23^{15}, cf. 26^{20}, further 2 S 2^{13} 18^{4} 1 K $20^{18.18.19.39}$ 2 K 5^{2} Mi 1^{11} Je 37^{5} Zc 14^{3} Dn $11^{11.44}$+; of an adulteress Pr 7^{15}; of an angel Nu 22^{32} (JE),

Dn 9[22]; for יֵצֵא ... אִתְּכֶם 1 S 22[3] (*let* my father etc. *go forth* [to be] *with you*, cf. Klo) rd. perh. יֵשְׁבוּ as 𝔖 𝔙 Kit, v. also Dr; of army marching out to form battle line יֹצֵא אֶל־הַמַּעֲרָכָה 1 S 17[20] (c.art., MT, < om. We Dr Kit Bu); בְּכֹל אֲשֶׁר יָצְאוּ Ju 2[15] *in all to which they went forth*, יָצָא לפני 1 S 8[20] of king going out at the head of his soldiers; so of י׳ before his people Ju 4[14] 2 S 5[24] ψ 68[8], cf. 108[12] 1 Ch 14[15]; of י׳ going out from Seir Ju 5[4], cf. Hb 3[13]; of the hand of י׳, in hostility יָצְאָה בִי יַד־י׳ Ru 1[13]; abs. of fire *breaking out* Ex 22[5] (JE). **3.** of combinations, note esp.: יָצוֹא וָשׁוֹב (inf. abs.) Gn 8[7] *going out and returning*, nearly = *to and fro;* אִישׁ יוֹצֵא ... יָצוֹא יָצָא וּמְקַלֵּל 2 S 16[5] = *coming forth, cursing as he came;* יצא ובא, lit. אֵין יוֹצֵא וְאֵין בָּא Jos 6[1] *none went out and none came in*, i.e. there was no free egress or ingress (of besieged city), cf. 1 K 15[17] = 2 Ch 16[1], 2 Ch 15[5]; to *go out* and *come in* before, of leader in war Nu 27[17] 1 S 18[16], cf. 29[6]; fig. Dt 28[6] blessed shalt thou be בבואך ובצאתך, i.e. when thou completest and beginnest any undertaking, so v[19] 31[2] לא אוכל לצאת ולבוא, i.e. I can no more engage in active undertakings; similarly Jos 14[11] 1 K 3[7] Is 37[28] (+ שִׁבְתְּךָ) = 2 K 19[27], ψ 121[8].

† **Hiph.** 278 *Pf.* הוֹצִיא Gn 14[18] +; וְהוֹצֵא consec. Dt 22[14]; הוֹצֵאתָ Ex 32[11] + 7 t.; וְהוֹצֵאתָ Nu 20[8] + 3 t.; 2 fs. וְהוֹצֵאת 1 K 17[13]; sf. הוֹצִיאַנִי Ez 42[15]; הוֹצִיאָנוּ Ex 13[14] + 2 t.; הוֹצִיאֲךָ Dt 6[12] 16[1], הוֹצִאֲךָ Ex 13[9] Dt 7[19]; הוֹצִיאָם Ex 32[12] + 2 t., etc.; *Impf.* יוֹצִיא (יֹצִא) Lv 16[27] + 9 t.; וַיּוֹצֵא (וַיֹּצֵא) Gn 15[5] + 23 t.; וַיּוֹצֵא (וַיֹּצֵא) Dt 4[20] + 4 t.; sf. יוֹצִיאֵנִי Mi 7[9]; וַיּוֹצִאֲךָ Dt 4[37] 5[15]; וַיּוֹצִאָהּ Ex 4[6.7]; 3 fs. תּוֹצִיא Is 61[11] Hg 1[11]; juss. תּוֹצֵא Gn 1[24]; וַתּוֹצֵא v[12] Ru 2[18]; 2 ms. תּוֹצִיא Ex 12[46] + 5 t.; הֲתֹצִיא Jb 38[32]; וַתֹּצֵא Je 32[21]; וַיּוֹצִיאוּ (וַיֹּצְאוּ) Lv 24[23] +; sf. וַיּוֹצִיאֻהוּ 2 K 12[12]; וַיֹּצִאֻהוּ Gn 19[16]; וַיֹּצִיאֻהוּ 1 K 21[13]; יוֹצִיאוּם 1 Ch 9[28], etc.; *Imv.* הוֹצֵא Gn 19[12] + 5 t. + 8[17] Kt (Qr הַיְצֵא); הוֹצִיא Is 43[8]; הוֹצִיאָה ψ 142[8]; sf. הוֹצִיאֵנִי 25[17] 1 K 22[34], etc.; *Inf.cstr.* הוֹצִיא Ex 6[13] +; sf. הוֹצִיאִי (הוֹצְאִי) Ex 16[32] +; לְהוֹצִאֲהוּ Je 39[14], anom. (Kö[i. 642]), etc.; *Pt.* מוֹצִיא Ex 6[7] + 11 t.; מוֹצֵא ψ 135[7]; sf. מוֹצִיאִי 2 S 22[49], מוֹצִיאֲךָ Dt 8[14] 13[11], etc.;—**1.** *cause to go* or *come out, bring out, lead out:* **a.** a person from a place, + מִן loc., out of prison, etc. Gn 40[14] (E), Je 20[3], 52[31] (not ‖ 2 K 25[27]); so with the servant of י׳ subj. Is 42[7]; out of house Jos 6[22] (JE), a city Gn 19[12] (J), Ez 14[22] (so 𝔊 𝔖 𝔙 Co VB; MT Hoph.); of י׳ bringing people of Jerusalem out of city to deliver them to enemy Ez 11[7] (MT (*one*) *shall bring*, but rd. 1 s., see VB), v[9]; fr. a land Je 26[33]; esp. of Moses bringing Israelites out of Egypt Ex 3[10.11.12] (E), 14[11] (J); of Moses and Aaron 6[13.26.27] (P); of י׳ bringing Israelites out of (מִן) Egypt Ex 18[1] 20[2] Jos 24[6] (all E), Ex 13[3.9.14.16] 32[11] Nu 20[16] 23[22] 24[8] (all JE), Dt 1[27] 4[20.37] 5[6.15] 6[12.21.23] 8[14] 9[12.26.28] 13[6.11] 16[1] 26[8] (all D), Lv 19[36] 22[33] 23[43] 25[38.44.55] 26[13.45] (all H), Ex 6[6.7] (מִתַּחַת סִבְלֹת מצרים), 7[4.5] 12[17.42.51] 16[6.32] 29[46] Nu 15[41] (all P), Ju 2[12] 6[8] 1 S 12[8] 1 K 8[16] = 2 Ch 6[5], 1 K 8[21.51.53] 9[9] Je 7[22] 11[4] 31[32] 32[21] 34[13] Ez 20[6.10], cf. v[9] (del. Co), 2 Ch 7[22] ψ 136[11] Dn 9[15]; abs., same sense, Jos 24[5] (E), Dt 7[8.19] Ez 20[14.22] ψ 105[37.43]; of י׳ bringing Israelites out of exile (sq. מִן) Ez 20[34.41] 34[13]; obj. rebels (out of, מִן, land) Ez 20[38]; of charioteer bringing Ahab out of battle 1 K 22[34] = 2 Ch 18[33]; of Joseph's bringing out his sons from between Jacob's knees Gn 48[12] (E). **b.** of bringing *from* a place *for a particular purpose* (human subj.) Ex 19[17] (מִן); also (point of departure not expr., and purpose sometimes only implied) Gn 38[24] (J), Jos 2[3] 6[23.23] Ju 6[30] 2 S 12[31] = 1 Ch 20[3], 2 K 11[12] = 2 Ch 23[11], 2 Ch 23[14] Is 43[8]; י׳ subj., of bringing Israelites out of Egypt to slay them Ex 32[12] (JE), Dt 9[28.29]; obj. Gog Ez 38[4]; subj. יַד י׳ Ez 37[1]. **c.** *lead out* as an army 2 S 10[16] = 1 Ch 19[16], so of י׳ Is 43[17]; hence with הֵבִיא, of a ruler's function to *lead people out and in* 2 S 5[2] = 1 Ch 11[2], Nu 27[17] (P). **d.** הוֹצִיא מֵרֶחֶם of God's agency in birth Jb 10[18]. **e.** = *remove* (from a person's presence) הוֹצִיאוּ כָל־אִישׁ מֵעָלָי Gn 45[1] 2 S 13[9]; without ‖ מעל v[18]. **f.** of *putting away* wives and children Ezr 10[3.19] (opp. הוֹשִׁיב v[2], cf. יצאה מביתו Dt 24[2]). **g.** *bring out* person unto (אֶל) a place (human subj.) Jos 10[22.23] (JE), Dt 17[5] 22[21.24] (all D), Lv 24[14.23] (H), Nu 15[36] (P; all אֶל־מִחוּץ), 1 K 21[10.13] (מִחוּץ of motion to), 2 K 11[15] = 2 Ch 23[14]; לְהוֹצִאֵהוּ אֶל־הַבָּיִת Je 39[14]; subj. angels in form of men Gn 19[16.17] (J), Ez 42[1.15] 46[21] 47[2]; also Gn 15[5] (JE; י׳ subj.); for a specific purpose Ex 16[3] (P). **h.** unto a person Gn 43[23] (J), with purpose expressed or implied Ho 9[13] Gn 19[5.8] (J), Ju 19[22.24]; Jos 10[24] (JE), Je 38[23] Ezr 8[7] (c. על) Kt (but read Qr אֲצַוֶּה). **i.** unto a place and a person Jos 10[22.23] (JE), Dt 21[19] Ju 19[25]. **2.** fig., obj. persons, *bring out of* (מִן) distress, etc. ψ 25[17] 68[7] 107[14.28] 142[8] 143[11]; deliver from enemies 2 S 22[49] (but ‖ ψ 18[49] מְפַלְּטִי); one's feet out of net ψ 25[15] 31[5]; bring out into a large place 2 S 22[20] = ψ 18[20], cf. ψ 66[12]. **3.** *bring out* animals: horses out of Egypt 1 K 10[29] = 2 Ch 1[17] (but read **Qal** יֵצְאוּ 𝔊 Klo Kmp in Kau[AT]), 2 Ch 1[17] 9[28]; animals

(from ark, no מִן) Gn 8^{17} (P); for sacrifice, to a place Nu 19^{8}. **4.** inanimate obj.: **a.** *carry* or *bring out* (with and without מִן) Ex 12^{39} (E) Am 6^{10} 2 S 12^{30}=1 Ch 20^{2}, 2 K 10^{26} 23$^{4.6}$ 24^{13} 1 Ch 9^{28} 2 Ch 29$^{5.16.16}$ 34^{14} Je 8^{1} 17^{22} 50^{25} (subj. ׳י), Ez 12$^{4.7}$ (in v$^{5.6.7b.12}$ read **Qal**, cf. v^{4b}, so Co), also 24^{6} (Co 24^{10}); obj. הָאֶבֶן הָרֹאשָׁה Zc 4^{7}; Lv 26^{10} (H), Ezr 1$^{7.7.8}$. **b.** *take* or *draw out* (from one's person or luggage) Gn 24^{53} (J); draw out hand from one's bosom Ex 4$^{6.7}$ (J), cf. Ru 2^{18} (food from one's cupboard). **c.**=*draw* חַרְבִּי מִתַּעְרָהּ Ez 21$^{8.10}$ (subj. ׳י). **d.** *bring out to* a place Dt 28^{38} Lv 4$^{12.21}$ 6^{4} 14^{45} 16^{27} Ez 46^{20}, cf. Dt 14^{28}. **e.** *bring out* to (or for) a person Gn 14^{18} Ju 6^{19} cf. v^{18}, 1 K 17^{13} 2 K 10$^{22.22}$. **f.** *bring out* from (מִן) a place to people Nu 17^{24} (P). **g.** *bring out* in payment, *pay* (money, tribute, etc.) 2 K 12^{12} 15^{20} (עַל=in behalf of: or *put it forth, imposed it, on* Israel). **h.** *bring forth* (=cause to rise or appear) the heavenly bodies Is 40^{26} Jb 38^{32}; see also וְתַעֲלֻמָה יֹצִא אוֹר 28^{11} *and hidden things he* (the miner) *bringeth forth to light*. **i.** *bring forth* by miracle: Moses, water out of rock Nu 20$^{8.10}$ (JE); ׳י, id. Dt 8^{15} Ne 9^{15} ψ 78^{16}. **j.** =*produce, generate, bring into being*: of magicians trying to produce lice Ex 8^{14} (P); a smith producing weapon Is 54^{16}; see the threefold הוציא Pr 30$^{33.33.33}$; of ׳י causing לֶחֶם to proceed out of (מִן) earth ψ 104^{14}; elsewhere of earth as producing Gn 1$^{12.24}$ (both P), Is 61^{11} Hg 1^{11}; of Aaron's rod bringing forth blossoms Nu 17^{23} (P). **k.** *bring forth* words (out of mouth, etc.), i.e. *speak* Jb 8^{10} 15^{3} Pr 10^{18} 29^{11} Ne 6^{19} Is 48^{20} (|| השמיע, הגיד); abs. Ec 5^{1}; of *publishing* a report הו׳ עָלֶיהָ שֵׁם רָע Dt 22^{14} (|| שָׂם לָהּ עֲלִילֹת דְּבָרִים), cf. v^{19}; הו׳ דִּבַּת הָאָרֶץ (רָעָה) Nu 13^{32} 14^{37}; so 14^{36} (דִּבָּה עַל־הָאָרֶץ). **5.** fig., subj. ׳י, *bring forth* from (מִן) Bel's mouth what he has swallowed Je 5^{44}; wind, out of treasuries 10^{13} 51^{16} ψ 135^{7}; fire, out of Tyre Ez 28^{18}; curse, over the land Zc 5^{4}; of Jeremiah, אִם תּוֹצִיא יָקָר מִזּוֹלֵל Je 15^{19} *if thou bring forth the precious from* (Gie *without*) *the base*, i.e. if thou free that which is pure in thee from base admixture (Gf; Gie *if thou produce the noble without the base*); bring forth, i.e. *exhibit*, righteousness (innocence Che) ψ 37^{6} Je 51^{10} (cf. **Qal 1 f** end); וַיֹּצֵא לָאוֹר צַלְמָוֶת Jb 12^{22}, cf. Mi 7^{9}; subj. servant of ׳י, of publishing מִשְׁפָּט (i.e. religion) to the world Is 42$^{1.3}$.

† **Hoph.** *Pf.* 3 fs. הוּצָאָה Ez 38^{8} (del. Co); *Pt.* fs. מוּצֵאת Gn 38^{25}; m.pl. מוּצָאִים Ez 14^{22} 47^{8} (but v. infr.); f.pl. מוּצָאוֹת Je 38^{22};—*be brought forth* Gn 38^{25} (J; of Tamar); of women as captives Je 38^{22}; remnant out of Jerusalem Ez 14^{22} MT (but rd. Hiph., v. supr.); exiles, from among the peoples 38^{8} (om. 𝔖 Co); of waters, אֶל־הַיָּמָּה הַמּוּצָאִים Ez 47^{8} *which are caused to flow into the sea* (but 𝔖 Co אֶל־הַמַּיִם הַחֲמוּצִים *into the sour* (*bitter, salt*) *waters*, see Field VB).

† [יָצִיא] **adj. coming forth**; only c. מִן and 3329
sf., ומיציאו מֵעָיו 2 Ch 32^{21} Kt (וּמִיצִיאֵי Qr), *and some of those who came forth from his loins* (בניו in || Is 37^{38}).

† [צֶאֱצָא] **n.m.** $^{Jb\ 27,\ 14}$ only pl., **issue, off-** 6631
spring, produce (Nö$^{ZMG\ 1886,\ 725}$ comps. ضِئْضِئٌ *origin, root, stock*)—**1.** *offspring* of men, abs. הַצֶּאֱצָאִים וְהַצְּפִעוֹת Is 22^{24}; elsewhere only Is$^{2.3}$ and Job: cstr. צֶאֱצָאֵי מֵעֶיךָ Is 48^{19} (|| זַרְעֶךָ); sf. צֶאֱצָאַי Jb 31^{8}, צֶאֱצָאֶיךָ 5^{25} (|| זַרְעֶךָ), Is 44^{3} (|| *id.*); צֶאֱצָאָיו Jb 27^{14} (|| בָּנָיו); צֶאֱצָאֵיהֶם 21^{8} (|| זַרְעָם), Is 61^{9} (|| *id.*), 65^{23}. **2.** *produce* of earth, sf. תֵּבֵל וְכָל־צֶאֱצָאֶיהָ Is 34^{1}; הָאָרֶץ וְצ׳ 42^{5}.

† I. מוֹצָא **n.m.** $^{Ho\ 6,\ 3}$ **place** or **act of going** 4161
forth, issue, export, source, spring;—abs. מ׳ Jb 28^{1} ψ 75^{7}; cstr. מ׳ Nu 30^{13}+9 t.; מֹצָא Jb 38^{27} Dn 9^{25}; sf. מוֹצָאֲךָ 2 S 3^{25}; מֹצָאוֹ Ho 6^{3}; מוֹצָאוֹ ψ 19^{7}; pl. cstr. מוֹצָאֵי Is 41^{18}+5 t.; sf. מוֹצָאָיו Ez 43^{11}; מוֹצָאֵיהֶם Nu 33$^{2.2}$; מוֹצָאֶיהָ Ez 42^{11};—**1.** *a going forth*: **a.** the act, of ׳י Ho 6^{3}; of the sun=*rising* ψ 19^{7} (v. יצא **1 f**); of a man 2 S 3^{25} (opp. מָבוֹא Kt); מ׳ דָּבָר Dn 9^{25} *going forth of a command*. **b.** concrete, מוֹצָאֵי גוֹלָה Ez 12^{4} *goings forth of* exile, i.e. *those going forth into* exile (in sim.). **c.** *way out, exit*: concrete, of chambers in temple Ez 42^{11} 43^{11} (opp. מוֹבָאָיו); מוֹצָאֵי הַמִּקְדָּשׁ Ez 44^{5} (opp. מְבוֹא הַבַּיִת). **2.** *that which goes forth*: **a.** *utterance* of mouth or lips (esp. of solemn or formal speech), מוֹצָא פִי־י׳ Dt 8^{3}; מ׳ שְׂפָתַי Je 17^{16} ψ 89^{35}; so Dt 23^{24} Nu 30^{13} (P). **b.** *export* of horses 1 K 10^{28}=2 Ch 1^{16}. **3.** *place of going forth*: **a.** *source* or *spring* of water 2 K 2^{21} Is 58^{11} (in sim.), ψ 107^{33} (|| נְהָרוֹת), v^{35} (|| אֲגַם־מַיִם)=Is 41^{18} (|| *id.*); מוֹצָא מֵימֵי גִיחוֹן הָעֶלְיוֹן 2 Ch 32^{30}. **b.** *place of departure* of Israel on march Nu 33$^{2.2}$ (P). **c.** מוֹצָא=*east* (place of sun's going forth) ψ 75^{7} (opp. מַעֲרָב); zeugmatically, 65^{9} מוֹצָאֵי בֹקֶר וָעֶרֶב i.e. *the east and the west* (cf. *the two Orients*, Qor 43^{37}). **d.** place whence silver comes=*mine* Jb 28^{1}; וּלְהַצְמִיחַ מֹצָא דֶשֶׁא 38^{27} and to cause the *growing-place* (others, *the growth*) of young grass to sprout.

4162 †II. מוֹצָא **n.pr.m.** **1.** son of Caleb by Ephah his concubine 1 Ch 2^{46}, 𝔊 Ιωσα(ν), 𝔊L Μουσα. **2.** a descendant of Saul 1 Ch 8$^{36.37}$ (𝔊 Μαισα)= 9$^{42.43}$ (𝔊 Μασσα; 𝔊L in both Μωσα).

4163 † [מוֹצָאָה] **n.f.** only pl.: **a.** Mi 5^{1} מוֹצָאֹתָיו (of future ruler out of Bethlehem), *his origin.* **b.** 2 K 10^{27} Qr מוֹצָאוֹת *places of going out to,* i.e. *a privy* (cf. Ar. مَخْرَجٌ; Germ. *Abtritt*), euphemistically for Kt מַחֲרָאוֹת.

8444 † [תּוֹצָאָה] **n.f. outgoing, extremity, source** (?), **escape**; only pl.; chiefly P and late;—abs. תּוֹצָאוֹת ψ 68^{21}; cstr. תּוֹצְאוֹת Pr 4^{23} + Jos 18^{19} Qr (Kt תוצאותיו); תּוֹצְאֹת Nu 34^{8} Ez 48^{30}; תֹּצְאוֹת Jos 15^{4} + 2 t.; sf. תּוֹצְאֹתָיו Nu 34^{4} + 3 t.; תֹּצְאֹתָיו Jos 15^{7} + 8 t. + 16^{3} Qr (Kt תצאתו); תּוֹצְאֹתָם 1 Ch 5^{16};—**1.** *outgoing, extremity* of border of territory Jos 16^{3} 17^{18} (both JE), elsewhere P: Nu 34$^{4.5.8.9.12}$ Jos 15$^{4.7.11}$ 16^{8} 17^{9} 18$^{12.14.19}$ 19$^{14.22.29.33}$; *outskirts* of city Ez 48^{30}, cf. 1 Ch 5^{16}. **2.** ת׳ חַיִּים Pr 4^{23} (? read מוֹצָאוֹת) *sources of life.* **3.** לַמָּוֶת ת׳ ψ 68^{21} *escapes from* (lit. *for,* i.e. *in view of*) *death.*

3320 † [יָצַב] **vb.** only **Hithp. set** or **station oneself, take one's stand** (𝔗 יצב Pa. & deriv.; Ar. وَصَبَ *be constant, firm*)—**Hithp.** *Pf.* 3 pl. הִתְיַצְּבוּ 2 Ch 11^{13}; וְהִת׳ consec. Nu 11^{16}; *Impf.* יִתְיַצֵּב Dt 7^{24} + 6 t.; יִתְיַצָּב Jb 41^{2}; יִתְיַצֵּב Pr 22^{29}; וַיִּתְיַצֵּב 1 S 3^{10} + 5 t.; 3 fs. וַתֵּתַצַּב Ex 2^{4} (but read וַתִּתְיַצֵּב, cf. Sam Ges^{§71} Kö$^{i.430}$); 2 ms. תִּתְיַצֵּב 2 S 18^{13}; וְאֶתְיַצְּבָה Hb 2^{1}; יִתְיַצְּבוּ ψ 2^{2} + 2 t.; וַיִּתְיַצְּבוּ Ex 19^{17} + 4 t.; *Imv.* הִתְיַצֵּב 8^{16} + 5 t.; הִתְיַצְּבוּ 1 S 10^{19} + 6 t.; *Inf. cstr.* (מֵ)הִתְיַצֵּב 2 S 21^{5} + 4 t.;—*station oneself, take one's stand, stand:* **a.** c. phr. of place, Ex 2^{4} (E, c. מֵרָחוֹק), 2 S 18^{13} (c. מִנֶּגֶד), fig.= *stand aloof* (VB Dr); v^{30} (c. כֹּה, || עֲמֹד); c. ב loc. Ex 19^{17} Nu 22^{22} (both E), Ju 20^{2} Dt 31$^{14.14}$, also (in sense of *having a place* or *position*) נִשְׁמַדְנוּ מֵהִתְיַצֵּב בְּכָל־גְּבֻל יִשְׂרָאֵל 2 S 21^{5}; c. בְּתוֹךְ pers. 1 S 10^{23}, loc. 2 S 23^{12}= 2 Ch 11^{14}; c. עַל loc., *at, by* Nu 23$^{3.15}$ (JE), *upon* Hb 2^{1} (|| עמד), ψ 36^{5} (fig.); c. עַל pers. v. infr.; c. שָׁם and עִם pers. Ex 34^{5} (subj. י׳), Nu 11^{16} (both JE). **b.** abs. 1 S 3^{10} (י׳ subj.); esp. of standing quiet and passive, to see the mighty deliverance of י׳ Ex 14^{13} (J), 1 S 12$^{7.16}$ 2 Ch 20^{17} (|| עמד); of taking a stand to fight 1 S 17^{16} ψ 2^{2}; in military array Je 46^{4} (c. ב accomp.), v^{14} (|| הִכֹּן לָךְ); to answer a charge Jb 33^{5}; וְיִתְיַצְּבוּ כְּמוֹ לְבוּשׁ 38^{14} *and they* (terrestrial things) *stand forth* (in the light) *like a garment.* **c.** c. לִפְנֵי pers. =*present oneself before* Ex 8^{16} 9^{13} (both J), Pr 22$^{29.29}$; לִפְנֵי י׳ Jos 24^{1} (E), 1 S 10^{19} (v. also **d**); so as servants or courtiers (v. על **6 c**), with implication of readiness for service, עַל־אֲדֹנֵי Zc 6^{5}; על י׳ Jb 1^{6} 2$^{1.1}$. **d.** c. עַל pers. *take one's stand on the side of* 2 Ch 11^{13}; c. ל, עִם מִי־יִתְיַצֵּב לִי עִם ψ 94^{16} *who will take a stand for me against* the workers of iniquity (|| מִי יָקוּם לִי עִם); of *holding one's ground,* maintaining one's position before י׳ (לְנֶגֶד עֵינֶיךָ) ψ 5^{6}; so c. לִפְנֵי Jos 1^{5} (D), Dt 9^{2} Jb 41^{2}; c. בְּפָנֶיךָ Dt 7^{24} 11^{25}; abs. וְאֵין עֹמֵד לְהִתְיַצֵּב 2 Ch 20^{6}.

† [יָצַג] **vb. Hiph. set, place,** a vivid and 3322
forcible syn. of שִׂים (Kö$^{i.430}$ Ges^{§71})—**Hiph.** *Pf.* sf. הִצִּיגַנִי Je 51^{34} Qr (Kt הציגנו), Jb 17^{6}; 1 s. sf. הִצַּגְתִּיו Gn 43^{9}; וְהִצַּגְתִּיהָ consec. Ho 2^{5}; *Impf.* וַיַּצֵּג Gn 30^{38} Ju 8^{27}; sf. וַיַּצִּגֵם Gn 47^{2}; 2 ms. תַּצִּיג Ju 7^{5}, etc.; *Imv.* הַצִּיגוּ Am 5^{15}; *Inf. cstr.* הַצֵּג Dt 28^{56} (Ges$^{§53,3,R.2}$ Kö$^{l.c.}$); *Pt.* מַצִּיג Ju 6^{37};—*set, place,* c. acc.: + ב loc. Gn 30^{38} (J; + לְנֹכַח צֹאן), Ju 6^{37} 8^{27} 2 S 6^{17} (+ בְּתוֹךְ), c. בְּתוֹךְ in || 1 Ch 16^{1}; + אֵצֶל 1 S 5^{2}; of setting foot on (על) ground Dt 28^{56}; Gn 33^{15} (J; sq. עִם)=*station with* thee some of my retinue; + לִפְנֵי Gn 43^{9} (J); so with idea of *presenting, introducing to* Gn 47^{2} (J); *set* (so that all may see) + לְ Jb 17^{6}; sq. 2 acc. (=*set as*) Je 51^{34}; וְהִצַּגְתִּיהָ כְּיוֹם הִוָּלְדָהּ Ho 2^{5} *and* (lest) *I set* (=*exhibit*) *her as in the day when she was born* (|| אַפְשִׁיטֶנָּה עֲרֻמָּה); fig. *set up, establish,* הציגו בשער משפט Am 5^{15} (opp. v^{7} לארץ הניחו). **Hoph.** *Impf.* יֻצָּג Ex 10^{24} (E) *be stayed, stopped, detained* (of herds, etc.)

יִצְהָר, יִצְחָק, יִצְחָר v. sub צהר, צחק, צחר. 3323, 3327-28
p. 844, 850

† [יָצַע] **vb. Hiph. lay, spread,** late (Ges 3331
§71; Aram. יְצַע Pa. Aph. *id.,* also *expound,* '*auslegen;*' Ar. وَضَعَ is *put* or *lay* (down, on a place, etc.), but ض=Aram. ע)—**Hiph.** *Impf.* יַצִּיעַ Is 58^{5}; אַצִּיעָה ψ 139^{8}; *lay, spread out,* sq. acc. שַׂק וָאֵפֶר Is 58^{5}; שְׁאוֹל ψ 139^{8} *if I spread out She'ôl* (as my couch). **Hoph.** *Impf.* יֻצַּע (**Pu.** *Pf.* De Di al.) *be laid, spread;* subj. שק ואפר Est 4^{3}; subj. רִמָּה worm, as couch for king of Babylon Is 14^{11}.

† [יָצוּעַ] **n.[m.] couch, bed** (poet.);—sf. 3326
יְצוּעִי Gn 49^{4}; pl. cstr. יְצוּעֵי 1 Ch 5^{1}; sf. יְצוּעָי Jb 17^{13} + 2 t. (+ 1 K 6$^{5.6.10}$ Kt, v. יָצִיעַ); *couch, bed,*

of wedlock or concubinage, Gn 49^{4} (J), hence 1 Ch 5^{1}; in gen. ψ 63^{7}, עֶרֶשׂ יְצוּעָי 132^{3}; בַּחֹשֶׁךְ רִפַּדְתִּי יְצוּעָי Jb 17^{13} (|| אִם־אֲקַוֶּה שְׁאוֹל בֵּיתִי); cf. ψ 139^{8}).

3326 †[יָצִיעַ] **n.m.**$^{1 K 6.10}$ only Qr, properly *flat surface*, only of lower projecting story of temple, יָצוּעַ 1 K 6$^{5.10}$; v^{6} rd. הַצֵּלָע *the side-chamber*, as 𝔊 Bö$^{§ 658}$ Sta$^{ZAW 1883, 136}$, v. also v$^{5.8}$ Ez 41$^{5.6}$.

4702 †מַצָּע **n.m. couch, bed**; קָצַר הַמּ׳ מֵהִשְׂתָּרֵעַ Is 28^{20} *the bed is too short for one to stretch oneself* (מַסֵּכָה *coverlet* in || cl.)

3332 †יָצַק **vb. pour, cast, flow** (Talm. *id.*)—**Qal** *Pf.* יָצַק Lv 8^{15} + 2 t.; וְיָצַק consec. 2^{1} 14^{15}; sf. יְצָקָם 1 K 7^{46} 2 Ch 4^{17}, etc.; *Impf.* יִצֹק Lv 14^{26} Nu 5^{15}; וַיִּצֹק Gn 28^{18} + 8 t.; וַיִּצֶק 1 K 22^{35} (intrans. sense); 3 fs. וַתִּצֹק 2 S 13^{9}; אֶצָּק Is 44^{3}; אֶצָּק־ v^{3}; וַיִּצְקוּ 2 K 4^{40}; *Imv.* יְצֹק Ez 24^{3}; צַק 2 K 4^{41}; יִצְקוּ 1 K 18^{34}; *Inf.* צֶקֶת Ex 38^{27} Jb 38^{38}; *Pt. pass.* יָצוּק Jb 28^{2} + 5 t.; pl. יְצוּקִים 2 Ch 4^{3}; יְצֻקִים 1 K 7^{24}; יְצֻקוֹת v^{30};—**1.** *pour, pour out*, oil, in anointing, sq. acc. (שמן) + על Gn 28^{18} (E), 35^{14} (J); sq. מִשֶּׁמֶן + על Lv 8^{12} (P); sq. על (שמן implied from context) Ex 29^{7} (P), 1 S 10^{1} 2 K 9^{3}; sq. אֶל־ + שֶׁמֶן v^{6}; fig., c. רוּחִי + על Is 44^{3}; oil in sacrifice, + על Lv 2$^{1.6}$ Nu 5^{15}; in cleansing, + על Lv 14$^{15.26}$ (upon his palm; all P); oil into (אֶל) vessels 2 K 4^{4}; water, for washing, + על 3^{11}; for drenching, + על 1 K 18^{34}; for boiling (into (בְּ) the caldron), symbol., Ez 24^{3}; for satisfying thirst (fig.) + על Is 44^{3}; blood (of sacrifice) + אֶל־יְסוֹד Lv 8^{15} 9^{9} (P); pottage, for eating, 2 K 4$^{40.41}$; cakes (לְבִבוֹת) 2 S 13^{9}; fig. of disease יָצוּק בּוֹ ψ 41^{9} *infused into him* (al. less prob. as **3** *molten*, i. e. *fixed upon*). **2.** *cast* (objects of metal) Ex 25^{12} 26^{37} 36^{36} 37$^{3.13}$ 38$^{5.27}$ (all P), 1 K 7^{46} = 2 Ch 4^{17}, 1 K 7$^{24.30}$ 2 Ch 4^{3}. **3.** *Pt. pass.* as adj. fig. *cast, hard*, of crocodile's scales Jb 41^{15}; of crocodile's heart v$^{16.16}$ (as stone). **4.** intrans. *flow, pour*, only וַיִּצֶק 1 K 22^{35} (of blood), Jb 38^{38} בְּצֶקֶת עָפָר לַמּוּצָק. **Hiph.** *Impf.* וַיַּצִּקוּ 2 S 15^{24}; וַיַּצִּקֻם Jos 7^{23}; *Pt. f.* מוֹצָקֶת 2 K 4^{5};—*pour* (oil) 2 K 4^{5}, fig. of shekels of silver, etc., *pour out* Jos 7^{23}; of the ark, 2 S 15^{24} *set down* (?); but read וַיַּצִּגוּ (Dr Gr). **Hoph.** *Pf.* הוּצַק ψ 45^{3}; *Impf.* יוּצַק Lv 21^{10} Jb 22^{16}; *Pt.* מוּצָק 1 K 7$^{23.33}$ 2 Ch 4^{2} Jb 37^{18}; מֻצָק 11^{15}; cstr. מֻצַק 1 K 7^{16};—**1.** *be poured*, subj. שֶׁמֶן, sq. על (in anointing), Lv 21^{10} (H); fig. of foundation of wicked Jb 22^{16}, v. Di; of grace חֵן, on lips, ψ 45^{3} (sq. בְּ), v. Che. **2.** *Pt.* = *cast, molten* הים המ׳ 1 K 7^{23} = 2 Ch 4^{2}; as predicate 1 K 7^{33}; cstr. as subst. מֻצַק נְחֹשֶׁת 1 K 7^{16}. **3.** *Pt.*, fig. *firmly established*, pred. of pers., וְהָיִיתָ מ׳ Jb 11^{15} *and thou shalt be established* (|| לֹא תִירָא).

†[יְצֻקָה] **n.f. a casting** (of metal);—יְצֻקִים 3333
בְּיִצֻקָתוֹ 1 K 7^{24} *cast at its casting* (בְּמֻצַקְתּוֹ in || 2 Ch 4^{3}).

†I. מוּצָק **n.m. a casting**; מ׳ אֶחָד 1 K 7^{37} 4165
(of metal); of dust compacted into clod בְּצֶקֶת עָפָר לַמּוּצָק Jb 38^{38}.—II. מוצק v. sub צוק. p. 848

†[מוּצֶקֶת] **n.f. 1. pipe** (through which oil 4166
is *poured*) מוּצָקוֹת Zc 4^{2}. **2. a casting** (cf. יְצֻקָה), יְצוּקִים בְּמֻצַקְתּוֹ 2 Ch 4^{3}.

†יָצַר **vb. form, fashion** (NH in pt. יוֹצֵר 3335
potter, creator, and deriv.; Ph. יצר *potter*; 𝔗 יצר; Syr. [illegible] = יְצַר, etc.; Ar. وَصَرَ *covenant, contract*; As. *êṣêru*, as Heb., Dl$^{HWB 309}$)—**Qal** *Pf.* י׳ Is 44^{10}; יָצַר Gn 2^{8}; sf. יְצָרָהּ Is 45^{18}; 2 m. יָצַרְתָּ ψ 104^{26} + 8 t. Pf.; *Impf.* 3 m. וַיִּיצֶר Gn 2^{7}; וַיִּצֶר v^{19}; sf. יִצְּרֵהוּ Is 44^{12}; 1 s. sf. אֶצָּרְךָ Je 1^{5}; *Pt.* יוֹצֵר Is 41^{25} + 20 t.; יֹצֵר 45^{18} + 6 t.; sf. יֹצְרִי 49^{5} + 11 t. sf.; pl. יוֹצְרִים 30^{14} 1 Ch 4^{23}; cstr. יֹצְרֵי Is 44^{9};—**1.** of *human activity*: **a.** of a potter who forms out of clay a vessel Is 29^{16} 41^{25} Je 18$^{4.4.6.6}$ 1 Ch 4^{23} La 4^{2} Zc 11$^{13.13}$ (these last two acc. to Thes SS et al. error for אוֹצָר); כְּלִי (ה)י׳ *potter's vessel* 2 S 17^{28} ψ 2^{9} Je 19^{11}; חֹמֶר הי׳ *potter's clay* Is 29^{16}; נֵבֶל י׳ 30^{14}; בַּקְבֻּק י׳ Je 19^{1}; בית הי׳ 18$^{2.3}$. **b.** of a carver of wood, graven images Is 44$^{9.10.12}$ Hb 2$^{18.18}$. **c.** *frame, devise* in the mind י׳ עָמָל ψ 94^{20}. **2.** of *divine activity*: **a.** (as a potter) forming Adam out of עפר from אדמה Gn 2$^{7.8}$ (J), beasts and birds, also from אדמה v^{19} (J); Israel as a people Is 27^{11} 43$^{1.21}$ 44^{21} 45$^{9.9.11}$ 64^{7}, even from the womb 44$^{2.24}$; the servant of Yahweh from the womb 49^{5}; of the formation of the individual man 43^{7}; Jeremiah in the womb Je 1^{5}; the eye of man ψ 94^{9}; the locust Am 7^{1}; Leviathan ψ 104^{26}; the dry land 95^{5}; the earth Is 45$^{18.18}$; the mountains Am 4^{13}; הַכֹּל Je 10^{16} = 51^{19}. Fig. perh. lost sight of in some of the above, and quite certainly in the forming of light Is 45^{7}, of summer and winter ψ 74^{17}, the רוּחַ of man Zc 12^{1}, and the לב of men ψ 33^{15}. **b.** fig. for *frame, pre-ordain, plan* (in divine purpose), of a situation מֵרָחוֹק Is 22^{11}; of an

occurrence מִימֵי קֶדֶם 37[26]=2 K 19[25]; יְצַרְתִּי אַף אֶעֱשֶׂנָּה *I have planned, I will also do it* 46[11]; רעה על ׳י Je 18[11]; ׳י לַהֲכִינָהּ *devised it to establish it* 33[2]. **Niph.** *Pf.* לְפָנַי לֹא־נוֹצַר אֵל Is 43[10] *before me a god was not formed* (created). **Pu.** *Pf.* יָמִים יֻצָּרוּ *days* (that) *were pre-ordained* (in the divine purpose) ψ 139[16] (cf. **Qal, 2 b**). **Hoph.** *Impf.* כָּל־כְּלִי יוּצַר עָלַיִךְ לֹא יִצְלָח Is 54[17] *any weapon that is formed against thee will not prosper.*

3336 †I. יֵ֫צֶר **n.m.**[Is 26, 3] **form, framing, purpose;**—׳י Gn 6[5] + 5 t.; יִצְרוֹ Dt 31[21] Hb 2[18]; יִצְרֵנוּ ψ 103[14];—**1.** *pottery*, formed by the potter Is 29[16]. **2.** form of a graven image Hb 2[18]. **3.** form of man as made of the dust ψ 103[14]. **4.** of what is framed in the mind (cf. יָצַר **1 c, 2 b**), *imagination, device, purpose:* יצר מחשב(ו)ת לב(ב) Gn 6[5] (J), 1 Ch 29[18]; ׳י מחשבות 28[9]; ׳י לב Gn 8[21] (J); יֵצֶר alone Dt 31[21] (J); יֵצֶר סָמוּךְ Is 26[3] a *stedfast purpose* (or *frame* of mind). (In NH יֵצֶר is common in sense of *impulse:* יצר הטוב and יצר הרע of good and bad tendency in man.)

3337 †II. יֵ֫צֶר **n.pr.m.** son of Naphtali Gn 46[24] = 1 Ch 7[13], Nu 26[49] (P).

3339 †יִצְרִי **n.pr.m.** **a.** chief of one of the Levitical choirs of singers 1 Ch 25[11]. **b. adj.**
3340 **gent.** of II. יֵצֶר, c. art. = subst. coll. Nu 26[49] (P).

3338 †[יְצֻרִים] **n.m.pl.** sf. יְצֻרַי my *forms, members* of my body Jb 17[7].

3341 †[יָצַת] **vb. kindle, burn** (intr.) (NH *id.* (rare))—**Qal** *Impf.* 3 fs. וַתִּצַּת Is 9[17]; יִצַּתּוּ 33[12] Je 51[58] (Kö[i. 431]); 3 fpl. תִּצַּתְנָה Je 49[2];—*kindle*, intr., fig. of wickedness, Is 9[17]; sq. בָּאֵשׁ *be kindled with fire* (=set on fire), of thorns (in sim.) 33[12], Je 49[2] (of dependent towns and villages of Rabbah, under fig. of daughters), 51[58] (of gates of Babylon). **Niph.** *Pf.* נִצְּתָה 2 K 22[13] Je 9[11] + 2[15] Kt (Qr נִצְּתוּ); וְנִצְּתָה consec. 2 K 22[17] Je 46[19]; נִצְּתוּ Ne 1[3] + 2 t. + Je 2[15] Qr (cf. supr.);—*be kindled*, fig. of wrath of ׳י, 2 K 22[13.17]; *be burned*, of gates of Jerusalem, sq. בָּאֵשׁ, Ne 1[3] 2[17]; =*desolated* Je 2[15] (of cities of Israel), cf. 46[19], 9[9] (of mountains and pastures); of land 9[11] (‖ אָבְדָה). **Hiph.** *Pf.* הִצִּית Je 11[16]; 1 s. וְהִצַּתִּי consec. Je 17[27] + 5 t.; והוציתיה 2 S 14[30] Kt; (< Qr וְהַצִּיתוּהָ *Imv.*, Ges[§ 71] Kö[i. 431]); הִצִּיתוּ v[31] Je 51[30]; וְהִצִּיתוּ consec. 32[29]; *Impf.* וַיַּצֶּת־ La 4[11]; אַצִּיתֶנָּה Is 27[4] (rd. אַצִּיתֶנָּה Kö[l. c.] Ges[l. c.]); וַיַּצִּיתוּ Jos 8[19] + 2 t.; תַּצִּיתוּ v[8]; *Imv.* 2 S 14[30] Qr, cf. supr.; *Pt.* מַצִּית Ez 21[3];—*kindle, set on fire*, sq. acc., עִיר + בָּאֵשׁ Jos 8[8.19] (JE), Je 32[29] (+שׂרף); field of corn, + בָּאֵשׁ 2 S 14[30.30.31]; dwellings (no באשׁ) Je 51[30], cf. also Ju 9[49]; also sq. acc. אֵשׁ + prep. על, Je 11[16] (of Jerusalem under fig. of olive-tree); elsewh. + בְּ, Am 1[14], והצתי אשׁ ב׳ (hence Je 17[27] 21[14] 43[12] 49[27] 50[32]) La 4[11] Ez 21[3].

יקב (√of foll.; comp. Ar. وَقَبَ *be sunk, depressed;* وَقْبٌ *hollow, cavity*).

†יֶ֫קֶב **n.m.**[Pr 3, 10] **wine-vat** (a trough or hol- 3342
low excavated (חצב Is 5[2]) in the rock for receiving the juice trodden out in the גַּת: Benz[212 f.]), sometimes also **wine-press** (the trough in which the grapes were trodden out);—abs. יֶ֫קֶב Is 5[2] + 4 t.; יָ֑קֶב Nu 18[30]; cstr. יֶ֫קֶב Ju 7[25]; sf. יִקְבֶךָ Dt 15[14] 16[13]; pl. יְקָבִים Jb 24[11] + 4 t.; יִקְבֵי Zc 14[10]; יְקָבֶיךָ Pr 3[10];—wine-*vat*, Is 5[2] Hg 2[16] Jo 4[13] (‖ גַּת), Pr 3[10]; oft. ‖ גֹּרֶן, Nu 18[27.30] Dt 15[14] 16[13] 2 K 6[27] Ho 9[2] Jo 2[24]; appar. of the *wine-press* Jb 24[11] יְקָבִים דָּרְכוּ, Is 16[10] (hence Je 48[33]). Designating particular localities, Ju 7[25] יֶקֶב זְאֵב, Zc 14[10] יִקְבֵי הַמֶּלֶךְ (near Jerusalem).

יְקַבְצְאֵל v. sub קבץ. p. 868 3343

†[יָקַד] **vb. be kindled, burn** (Aram. יְקַד, 3344
ܝܩܕ, *burn*, intrans.; Ar. وَقَدَ, *id.*)—**Qal** *Impf.* 3 ms. יֵקַד Is 10[16]; 3 fs. וַתִּיקַד Dt 32[22]; *Pt. act.* f. יֹקֶ֫דֶת Is 65[5]; *pass.* יָקוּד 30[14];—*be kindled*, fig. of judgment, יֵקַד יְקֹד כִּיקוֹד אֵשׁ Is 10[16]; so *burn*, Dt 32[22] *a fire hath been kindled* (קָדְחָה) *in my wrath*, וַתִּיקַד עַד־שְׁאוֹל *and it burneth unto She'ôl;* fig. of people displeasing to ׳י, אֵלֶּה עָשָׁן בְּאַפִּי אֵשׁ יֹקֶדֶת כָּל־הַיּוֹם Is 65[5]; pt. יָקוּד *kindled*, as subst. לַחְתּוֹת אֵשׁ מִיָּקוּד 30[14] *to take fire from that which is kindled*, i.e. from the hearth (Lg[BN 60]). **Hoph.** *Impf.* 3 fs. תּוּקַד Lv 6[2.5.6]; תּוּקָ֑ד Je 15[14] 17[4];—*be burning, burn*, of (perpetual) altar-fire Lv 6[2.5.6] (P); fig. of ׳י's judgment, אֵשׁ קָדְחָה בְאַפִּי עֲלֵיכֶם תּוּקָד Je 15[14], similarly 17[4] (cf. Dt 32[22] supr., as prob. source of both).

†יְקוֹד **n.[m.] a burning** (properly *Inf. cstr.* 3350
of יָקַד)—only Is 10[16], abs. and cstr., fig. of ׳י's judgment, v. [יָקַד] supr.

†מוֹקֵד **n.[m.] a burning mass;**—abs. 4168
עַצְמוֹתַי כְּמוֹקֵד נִחָרוּ ψ 102[4] my bones are scorched through like a *burning mass;* pl. cstr., fig. of ׳י's judgment, מוֹקְדֵי עוֹלָם Is 33[14] (‖ אֵשׁ אוֹכֵלָה).

4169 **†מוֹקְדָה n.f. hearth** (=*place of burning*), only of *altar-hearth*, the plate or top of altar, on which burnt-offering was laid and consumed, הִוא הָעוֹלָה עַל מ׳ עַל הַמִּזְבֵּחַ Lv 6² (sq. וְאֵשׁ הַמִּזְבֵּחַ תּוּקַד בּוֹ).

3347 **†יָקְדְעָם n.pr.loc.** a city of Judah Jos 15⁵⁶; site unknown. 𝔊 Ιαρεικαμ, A Ιεκδααμ, 𝔊L Ιεκνααμ.

יקה (√of following; cf. Ar. وَقَى *preserve* (from evil, or fear); VIII. *be pious, careful of one's religious duties* (Lane³⁰⁵⁹)).

3348 **†יָקֶה n.pr.m.** father of Agur, אָגוּר בִּן־יָקֶה הַמַּשָּׂא Pr 30¹ (read probably הַמַּשָּׂאִי or מִמַּשָּׂא: v. Be-Now^xvi ff.)

3354 **†יְקוּתִיאֵל n.pr.m.** (Impf. from √ע״ו + אֵל acc. to Ol^§ 277 h 2, meaning dubious; perhaps better regard יקות as n. abstr. from יקה, and render *Preservation of God*) a man of Judah 1 Ch 4¹⁸; 𝔊 Χετιηλ, A* Ιεκθυηλ, 𝔊L Ιεφθιηλ.—Vid. יָקְתְאֵל.

יקה (√of following; cf. Ar. وَقِهَ *be obedient;* so As. *âḳû* (וקה?) Dl^HWB 123; Sab. וקה *hear* (favourably), *hear* (and answer), also in n.pr. יקהמלך, יקהאל, וקהאל, DHM in MV).

3349 **†[יְקָהָה] n.f. obedience**;—cstr. יִקְּהַת עַמִּים Gn 49¹⁰ c. subject. genit. (Daghesh forte dirim. Ges^§ 20, 2b Lag^BN 82), לִיקְּהַת אֵם Pr 30¹⁷ c. object. genit.

יָקוֹט Jb 8¹⁴ v. קוט. p. 876

3351, 3359-61, 3365 יָקוּם, יָקִים, יְקַמְיָה, יְקַמְעָם, יָקְמְעָם v. sub קום. p. 879-80

3354 יְקוּתִיאֵל v. sub יקה. above

3355 **†יָקְטָן n.pr.m.** son of Eber, descendant of Shem (DHM in MV comp. his name in Arab. tradition, viz. *Ḳaḥṭân;* the √√ قحط and وقط being both expl. in *Muḥîṭ* by ضرب *strike, beat;* v. Lane^1777 ff.)—Gn 10²⁵·²⁶·²⁹ = 1 Ch 1¹⁹·²⁰·²³, 'father' of various tribes of Yemen; 𝔊 Ιεκταν.

3362 **†יָקְנְעָם n.pr.loc.** Canaanitish city, with a king, defined by לַכַּרְמֶל Jos 12²²; in Zebulun 19¹¹; Levitical city 21³⁴.

3363 **†יָקַע vb. be dislocated, alienated** (Ar. وَقَعَ is *fall, fall down, fall upon, befal, happen*) —**Qal** *Impf.* 3 fs. תֵּקַע Je 6⁸; וַתֵּקַע Gn 32²⁶ + 2 t.; *dislocated* Gn 32²⁶ (Jacob's thigh); elsewhere fig. of נפשׁ; *torn away, alienated* from any one, sq. מִן Je 6⁸ Ez 23¹⁷; sq. מֵעַל v¹⁸. **Hiph.** *Pf.* וְהוֹקַעֲנוּם consec. 2 S 21⁶; *Impf.* וַיֹּקִיעֻם v⁹; *Imv.* הוֹקַע Nu 25⁴; of some solemn form of execution, but mng. uncertain: Aq Ges *impale;* 𝔊𝔖 *expose* (ἐξηλιάζειν, παραδειγματίζειν); 𝔗𝔙ₛ *crucify;* RS^Rel. Sem. 398 (419) *throw down* (Ar. اَوْقَعَ) a rock (cf. 2 Ch 25¹²): + ליהוה 2 S 21⁶ (לִפְנֵי י׳ v⁹), Nu 25⁴. **Hoph.** *Pt.* הַמּוּקָעִים 2 S 21¹³; pass. of Hiph.

†[יָקַץ] vb. awake (Ar. يَقِظَ *wake, be awake*)—**Qal** *Impf.* יִקַץ 1 K 18²⁷; וַיִּיקַץ Gn 28¹⁶ + 3 t.; וַיִּקַץ Ju 16²⁰ ψ 78⁶⁵ 1 K 3¹⁵ (v. Baer); וָאִיקָץ Gn 41²¹; יִקְצוּ Hb 2⁷;—*awake*, Gn 41⁴·⁷·²¹ (E), 1 K 3¹⁵; of Baal 18²⁷; sq. מִשְּׁנָתוֹ Gn 28¹⁶ (J), Ju 16¹⁴·²⁰; of Noah, מִיֵּינוֹ Gn 9²⁴ (J), i.e. from drunken sleep; fig. of י׳ ψ 78⁶⁵, i.e. *become suddenly active;* of enemies Hb 2⁷.—Vid. also קיץ **Hiph.** 3364

†[יָקַר] vb. be precious, prized, appraised (NH *id.*, Pi., Hiph.; Aram. יְקַר, ܝܩܰܪ, *be heavy, precious;* Pa. *honour;* יַקִּיר, ܝܰܩܺܝܪ, *weighty, precious, honoured;* cf. As. *akâru, be precious, costly*, and deriv., Dl^HWB 240; Ar. وَقُرَ *be heavy*, II. *honour;* وَقَارٌ *dignity;* Sab. n. וקר *honour* DHM^ZMG 1883, 402)—**Qal** *Pf.* 3 fs. יָקְרָה 1 S 16²¹; 2 ms. יָקַרְתָּ Is 43⁴; 1 s. יָקַרְתִּי Zc 11¹³; 3 pl. יָקְרוּ ψ 139¹⁷; *Impf.* וַיִּיקַר 1 S 18³⁰; וְיֵקַר ψ 49⁹; וְיֵיקַר 72¹⁴; juss. (תִּיקַר(־נָא 2 K 1¹³·¹⁴;—**1.** *be precious:* **a.** = *highly valued, esteemed*, David's name, וַיִּיקַר שְׁמוֹ מְאֹד 1 S 18³⁰; of Israel, יָקַרְתָּ בְעֵינַי Is 43⁴ (+ אֲהַבְתִּיךָ, נִכְבַּדְתָּ); of God's thoughts וְלִי מַה־יָּקְרוּ רֵעֶיךָ ψ 139¹⁷ (Ew Hi Hup render *hard, difficult:* cf. יַקִּירָה Dn 2¹¹). **b.** esp. of life (נֶפֶשׁ), in phr. יָקְרָה נַפְשִׁי בְּעֵינֶיךָ 1 S 26²¹, i.e. thou hast spared it; so (juss.) 2 K 1¹³·¹⁴; similarly יֵיקַר דָּמָם בְּעֵינָיו ψ 72¹⁴ (|| מִתּוֹךְ וּמֵחָמָס יִגְאַל נַפְשָׁם). **c.** *be costly*, וְיֵקַר פִּדְיוֹן נַפְשָׁם ψ 49⁹. **2.** *be appraised, valued*, אֶדֶר הַיְקָר אֲשֶׁר יָקַרְתִּי מֵעֲלֵיהֶם Zc 11¹³ *the magnificence of the price at which I was appraised* (and dismissed) *from them!* **Hiph.** *Impf.* 1 s. אוֹקִיר אֱנוֹשׁ מִפָּז Is 13¹² *I will make men more rare* (lit. *precious*) *than fine gold. Imv.* הֹקַר Pr 25¹⁷ *make rare* (i.e. *withhold*) thy foot from the house of thy friend. 3365

†יָקָר adj. precious, rare, splendid, weighty;—abs. יָקָר 1 S 3¹ + 9 t.; cstr. יְקַר־ Pr 17²⁷ Qr (Kt וקר; v. infr.); כִּיקַר ψ 37²⁰; f. יְקָרָה 2 S 12³⁰ + 14 t.; cstr. יִקְרַת Is 28¹⁶; mpl. יְקָרִים La 4²; fpl. יְקָרוֹת 1 K 5³¹ + 2 t. + Zc 14⁶ (v. infr.); יְקָרֹת 1 K 7⁹; sf. בְּיִקְּרוֹתֶיךָ ψ 45¹⁰ (so Baer; van d. H בִּיקְ׳);—**1.** *precious:* **a.** *costly*, אֲבָנִים יְקָרוֹת 3368

of costly building-stones 1 K 5^{31} $7^{9.10.11}$ cf. פִּנַּת יִקְרַת מוּסָד מוּסָּד Is 28^{16} *a costly corner*(-stone) of a foundation,—on cstr. v. Da Synt. § 28, R. 3, 6; הוֹן יָקָר *costly wealth* Pr 1^{13} 12^{27}; הוֹן יָקָר וְנָעִים 24^{4}. **b.** *precious, highly valued:* נֶפֶשׁ יְקָרָה Pr 6^{26} *precious life;* opp. זוֹלֵל Je 15^{19} (of choice elements of character); יָקָר בְּעֵינֵי י׳ הַמָּוְתָה לַחֲסִידָיו ψ 116^{15}; יְקָרָה הִיא מפניים Pr 3^{15} *she* (wisdom) *is more precious than rubies* (v. also **c**); *prized*, of חסד י׳ ψ 36^{8}; = subst. בְּנוֹת מְלָכִים בְּיִקְּרוֹתֶיךָ ψ 45^{10} *king's daughters are among thy precious* (=*dear*) *ones.* **c.** אֶבֶן יְקָרָה coll. *precious stones, jewels* 2 S 12^{30} = 1 Ch 20^{2}, 1 K $10^{2.10.11}$ = 2 Ch $9^{1.9.10}$, 1 Ch 29^{2} 2 Ch 3^{6} 32^{27} Ez 27^{22} 28^{13} (list of precious stones follows), Dn 11^{38}; so also La 4^{2}, read אַבְנֵי צִיּוֹן הַיְקָרִים (for MT בְּנֵי וגו׳), see VB; שֹׁהַם יָקָר Jb 28^{16} (v. also Pr 3^{15} sub **b**). **2.** *rare,* 1 S 3^{1} (cf. √ Hiph. Is 13^{12}). **3.** *glorious, splendid* (cf. Aram.), of the moon Jb 31^{26}; as subst. = *glory,* the wicked perish, כִּיקַר כָּרִים ψ 37^{20} *like the glory of the pastures* (i.e. like gay, but short-lived, flowers). **4.** (late and Aram.) *weighty, influential,* יָקָר מֵחָכְמָה Ec 10^{1} *weightier than wisdom* and honour is a little folly.—In Pr 17^{27} read Kt וְקַר־רוּחַ *and one cool of spirit* (see VB); in Zc 14^{6} read לֹא יִהְיֶה אוֹר וְקָרוֹת וְקִפָּאוֹן *there shall not be light but cold and congelation* (see *id.* and Vrss.); v., however, also Addenda.

3366 † יְקָר **n.m. preciousness, price, honour** (late: cf. BA 𝔗 יְקָר, ܝܩܪܐ *glory*);—abs. יְקָר Zc 11^{13} + 5 t.; בִּיקָר etc. ψ 49^{13} + 3 t.; cstr. יְקַר Est 1^{4}; sf. בִּיקָרוֹ 6^{6} + 4 t.; יְקָרָהּ Je 20^{5};—**1.** *preciousness:* **a.** = *precious (costly) things* (coll.) Je 20^{5} (om. 𝔊), חֹסֶן וִיקָר Ez 22^{25}; כָּל־יְקָר Jb 28^{10}. **b.** כְּלִי יְקָר Pr 20^{15} *a jewel of preciousness = precious jewel* (|| פְּנִינִים, זָהָב). **2.** *price* Zc 11^{13}, v. יָקַר **2.** **3.** *honour,* ψ $49^{13.21}$; elsewhere only Est.: יְקָר תִּפְאֶרֶת גְּדוּלָּתוֹ Est 1^{4} (|| כְּבוֹד מַלְכוּתוֹ); יִתְּנוּ יְקָר לְ v^{20} all wives *give honour to* their lords; מַה־נַּעֲשָׂה יְקָר וּגְדוּלָּה לְמָרְדֳּכַי 6^{3}, c. עשׂה לְ also v^{6}; לַיְּהוּדִים הָיְתָה אוֹרָה וְשִׂמְחָה וְשָׂשֹׂן וִיקָר 8^{16}; (הָ)אִישׁ אֲשֶׁר הַמֶּלֶךְ חָפֵץ בִּיקָרוֹ *the man in whose honour the king delighteth* $6^{6.7.9.9.11}$.

3357 † יַקִּיר **adj.** intrans. **very precious, dear;** only הֲבֵן יַקִּיר לִי אֶפְרַיִם Je 31^{20} *is Ephraim a very precious son unto me?* (|| יֶלֶד שַׁעֲשֻׁעִים).

3369 † [יָקֹשׁ] **vb. lay a bait or lure** (v. מוֹקֵשׁ), then gen. **lay snares** (v. also קוש, נקשׁ)—**Qal** *Pf.* יָקֹשְׁתִּי Je 50^{24}; יָקְשׁוּ ψ 141^{9}; *Pt.* pl. יוֹקְשִׁים 124^{7};—*lay snares,* fig. of devices of wicked 141^{9} (c. acc. cogn.); of י׳'s plan to destroy Babylon Je 50^{24} יקשתי לך וגם נלכדת; *Pt.* as subst. *bait-layers, fowlers* ψ 124^{7} (cf. 141^{9}) sim. **Niph.** *Pf.* נוֹקַשְׁתָּ Pr 6^{2}; וְנוֹקְשׁוּ consec. Is 8^{15} 28^{13}; *Impf.* 2 ms. תִּוָּקֵשׁ Dt 7^{25}; *be caught by a bait, ensnared,* in business entanglements Pr 6^{2}; in disastrous consequences of idolatry Dt 7^{25} (|| נלכד); of those ensnared by י׳'s plans (sq. ונלכדו) Is 8^{15} 28^{13}. **Pu.** *Pt.* יוּקָשִׁים (for מְיוּקָּשִׁים, unless this should be read: Ges § 52. R. 6; Sta § 220): *entrapped,* in circumstances of life Ec 9^{12}.

† יָקוֹשׁ **n.[m.]** bait-layer, fowler, פַּח יָקוּשׁ 3352
Ho 9^{8} *the snare of a fowler.*

† יָקוּשׁ **n.[m.]** id.; פַּח יָקוּשׁ ψ 91^{3}; כְּצִפּוֹר 3353
מִיַּד יָקוּשׁ Pr 6^{5}; pl. יְקוּשִׁים Je 5^{26} (in sim.)

† מוֹקֵשׁ **n.m.** Pr 12, 13 prop. **a bait or lure** in 4170
a fowler's net; then fig. **snare**—abs. מוֹקֵשׁ Ex 10^{7} + 15 t.; cstr. Pr 18^{7} 20^{25}; pl. מוֹקְשִׁים ψ 64^{6} Jb 40^{24}; מֹקְשִׁים ψ 140^{6}; cstr. מוֹקְשֵׁי 18^{6} + 3 t.; מֹקְשֵׁי 2 S 22^{6}; *f.* מֹקְשׁוֹת ψ 141^{9}; *bait* or *lure,* in a net for birds Am 3^{5}; will not pierce nostril of hippopotamus Jb 40^{24}; elsewhere fig. of what allures and entraps any one to disaster or ruin; Moses a *snare* to Egyptians Ex 10^{7} (J); מוֹקְשֵׁי עָם Jb 34^{30}, of men who are the ruin of their people; idols and idol-worship a pernicious *lure* to Israel Ex 23^{33} (JE), Dt 7^{16} Ju 2^{3} 8^{27} ψ 106^{36}; so alliances with Canaanites Ex 34^{12} (JE), Jos 23^{13} (D); Michal, to David 1 S 18^{21}; of י׳ as cause of ruin to evildoers Is 8^{14}; of plots of wicked ψ 64^{6} 140^{6} (vb. שִׁית; || פַּח, חֲבָלִים, רֶשֶׁת), 141^{9} (|| פַּח); a *lure* or *snare* for wicked in their transgressions Pr 29^{6} ψ 69^{23} (|| פַּח); consisting in transgressions of lips Pr 12^{13}, cf. 18^{7} 20^{25}; in wrathfulness 22^{25}; in fear of man 29^{25}; מ׳ מָוֶת ψ 18^{6} = 2 S 22^{6} (|| חֶבְלֵי שְׁאוֹל), Pr 13^{14} 14^{27}.

† יָקְשָׁן **n.pr.m.** son of Abraham and Keturah 3370
Gn $25^{2.3}$ = 1 Ch $1^{32.32}$; 𝔊 Ιεξαν; 𝔊L Gn $25^{2.3}$ Ιεκταν.

† יָקְתְאֵל **n.pr.loc.** (acc. to Ol § 277 k. 3 יקת is 3371
Impf. from a √קות, meaning dubious; poss. = יְקוּתִיאֵל q. v.; see Wetzst in De Is 3, 703 f.)—**1.** in the *Shephelah* of Judah Jos 15^{38}, site unknown; 𝔊 Ιακαρεηλ A Ιεκθαηλ, 𝔊L Ιεχθαηλ. **2.** name given to סֶלַע (=Petra) by King Amaziah, its captor 2 K 14^{7}; 𝔊 Καθοηλ; A Ιεκθοηλ.

3372 †יָרֵא vb. fear (NH *id.*; As. *irû*, *id.*; Hpt
KAT$^{2, Gloss i}$, COT^{Gloss})—**Qal**$_{328}$ *Pf.* יר׳ Gn 19^{30}+
14 t.; 3 f. יָֽרְאָה Je 3^{8} ψ 76^{9}; יָרֵאָה Gn 18^{15}; pl.
2 m. יְרֵאתֶם Nu 12^{8}+2 t.; +23 t. Pf.; *Impf.*
יִירָא Am 3^{8}+3 t.; וַיִּירָא Gn 28^{17}+5 t.; וַיִּרָא Je
26^{21}+5 t.; pl. יִירְאוּ (יִרְאוּ) 23^{4}+; יִרְאוּן Dt 13^{12},
+, etc.; 136 t. Impf.; *Imv.* יְרָא Pr 3^{7}+3 t.; יִרְאוּ
Jos 24^{14}+2 t.; *Inf. cstr.* יְרֹא Jos 22^{25}; לְרָא 1 S
18^{29} (Ges $^{§ 69, R. 1}$); לְיִרְאָה Dt 4^{10}+13 t.; sf. יִרְאָתוֹ
2 S 3^{11}; יִרְאָתָם Is 29^{13}; יְרָאתֶם Jos 4^{24} (rd. יִרְאָתָם
3373 Bö $^{§ 1081 a}$ Ew $^{337 b}$ Di etc.); *Pt.* יָרֵא Gn 32^{12}+15 t.;
cstr. יְרֵא 22^{12}+10 t.; pl. יְרֵאִים Je 42^{11}+6 t.;
cstr. יִרְאֵי Ex 18^{21}+12 t.; f. cstr. יִרְאַת Pr 31^{30};—
1. *fear, be afraid* (not in P): **a.** abs. Gn 3^{10}
18^{15} 32^{8} 43^{18} Ex 14^{10} (J), Gn 20^{8} 28^{17} 42^{35} Ex 2^{14}
Jos 10^{2} (E), Dt 20^{8} 31^{8} Ju 7^{3} 8^{20} 1 S 4^{7} 17$^{11.24}$
23^{3} 28^{5} 31^{4}=1 Ch 10^{4}, 2 K 10^{4} 2 Ch 20^{3} Ne 2^{2}
6^{13} Is 54^{14} Je 3^{8} 23^{4} 26^{21} Am 3^{8} Jon 1$^{5.10}$ ψ 27^{3}
46^{3} 49^{6} (but Bae reads ראה) 56$^{4.5.12}$ 64$^{5.10}$ 76^{9} 112^{8}
118^{6} Pr 14^{16} Jb 6^{21} 11^{15}; אַל־תִּירָא(י, וּ) *fear not*
Gn 15^{1} 21^{17} 35^{17} 50$^{19.21}$ Ex 20^{20} Jos 10^{25} (E), Gn
26^{24} 43^{23} Ex 14^{13} Jos 8^{1} (J), Dt 1^{21} 20^{3} 31^{6} Ju 4^{18}
6^{23} 1 S 4^{20} 12^{20} 22^{23} 23^{17} 28^{13} 2 S 9^{7} 13^{28} 1 K 17^{13}
2 K 6^{16} 1 Ch 22^{13} 28^{20} 2 Ch 20^{17} Is 7^{4} 35^{4} 40^{9}
41$^{10.13.14}$ 43$^{1.5}$ 44^{2} 54^{4} Je 30^{10} 46$^{27.28}$ Jo 2$^{21.22}$ Zp 3^{16}
Hg 2^{5} Zc 8$^{13.15}$ ψ 49^{17} La 3^{57} Dn 10$^{12.19}$ Ru 3^{11};
יִשְׁמְעוּ וי׳ *hear and fear* Dt 13^{12} 17^{13} 19^{20} 21^{21};
(י)ראו וי׳ *see and fear* ψ 40^{4} 52^{8} Is 41^{5} Zc 9^{5}. †**b.**
c. acc. rei or pers. Nu 14$^{9.9}$ (J), 21^{34} (E), Dt 3$^{2.22}$
Ju 6^{27} 1 S 15^{24} 2 S 3^{11} 1 K 1^{51} Is 8^{12} 51^{7} 57^{11} Ez 3^{9}
11^{8} Hb 3^{2} (acc. פעלך in corrected rhythm), ψ 23^{4}
Dn 1^{10}; acc. of God (י׳) 1 S 12^{18} 2 S 6^{9}=1 Ch 13^{12}
Is 57^{11} Je 5^{22} Jon 1^{16} Jb 9^{35} 37^{24}. **c.** with מִן *be*
afraid of, Dt 1^{29} 2^{4} 7^{18} 20^{1} 28^{10} Jos 10^{8} (D) 1 S
28^{20} 2 K 25^{24} Is 10^{24} 51^{12} Je 10^{5} 42$^{11.16}$ Ez 2$^{6.6.6}$
Mi 7^{17} ψ 3^{7} 27^{1} 65^{9} 91^{5} 112^{7} 119^{120} Pr 3^{25} 31^{21}
Jb 5$^{21.22}$ Ec 12^{5}; with מִפְּנֵי Dt 5^{5} 7^{19} Jos 9^{24} 11^{6}
(D), 1 S 7^{7} 18^{29} 21^{23} 1 K 1^{50} 2 K 1^{15} 19^{6} (=Is 37^{6})
25^{26} 2 Ch 20^{15} 32^{7} Ne 4^{8} Je 1^{8} 41^{18} 42$^{11.11}$; מִלִּפְנֵי
1 S 18^{12}, with בְּ *because of, for* Je 51^{46}. **d.** with
inf. and לְ *fear to do* a thing Gn 19^{30} 26^{7} (J),
Nu 12^{8} (E), Ju 7^{10} 2 S 1^{14} 10^{19} 12^{18}; with infin.
and מִן, *afraid of doing* Gn 46^{3} Ex 3^{6} (E), 1 S 3^{15}
Je 40^{9} Jb 32^{6}. **e.** with פֶּן *fear lest* Gn 31^{31} (E)
32^{12} (J). **2.** *stand in awe of*, with מן and
inf. וַיִּירְאוּ מִגֶּשֶׁת אֵלָיו Ex 34^{30} (P) *and they stood*
in awe of drawing nigh unto him; יִירְאוּ מֵיהוה
וגו׳ ψ 33^{8} let all the earth *stand in awe of*
Yahweh; וְיָרֵאתָ מֵאֱלֹהֶיךָ *and thou shalt stand*
in awe of thy God Lv 19$^{14.32}$ 25$^{17.36.43}$ (all H);
with מִפְּנֵי, of the king Solomon 1 K 3^{28}; מִפְּנֵי י׳
אלהים Ex 9^{30} (J?); מפני י׳ Hg 1^{12}; י׳ מלפני (אלהים)
stand in awe before (God) Ec 3^{14} 8$^{12.13}$. **3.**
fear, reverence, honour, e.g. parents Lv 19^{3} (H),
Moses and Joshua Jos 4$^{14.14}$, the oath 1 S 14^{26}
Ec 9^{2}, commandment Pr 13^{13}, the sanctuary Lv
19^{30} 26^{2} (H), other gods Ju 6^{10} 2 K 17$^{7.35.37.38}$;
elsewhere of God: **a.** abs. Je 44^{10}. **b.** with acc.
(ה)אלהים Gn 22^{12} 42^{18} Ex 1$^{17.21}$ 18^{21} (E), Dt 25^{18}
ψ 55^{20} 66^{16} Jb 1$^{1.8.9}$ 2^{3} Ec 5^{6} 7^{18} 8^{12} 12^{13} Ne 7^{2};
יר׳ יהוה Ex 14^{31} (J), Jos 22^{25} (P), 24^{14} (E), 1 S
12$^{14.24}$ 1 K 18$^{3.12}$ 2 K 4^{1} 17$^{25.28.32.33.34.41}$ Is 50^{10} Je
5^{24} 26^{19} Ho 10^{3} Jon 1^{9} Mal 3$^{16.16}$ ψ 15^{4} 22^{24} 25^{12}
34^{10} 112^{1} 115$^{11.13}$ 118^{4} 128$^{1.4}$ 135^{20} Pr 3^{7} 14^{2} 24^{21}
31^{30}; יר׳ י׳ אֱלֹהֶיךָ (and other sfs.) Dt 6$^{2.13.24}$ 10$^{12.20}$
14^{23} 17^{19} 31$^{12.13}$ Jos 4^{24} (D), 2 K 17^{39}; with sfs.
referring to Yahweh or Elohim Dt 4^{10} 5^{26} 8^{6} 13^{5}
1 K 8$^{40.43}$ = 2 Ch 6$^{31.33}$, 2 K 17^{36} Is 25^{3} 29^{13} Je
10^{7} 32^{39} Mal 2^{5} 3^{5} Zp 3^{7} ψ 22^{26} 25^{14} 31^{20} 33^{18} 34$^{8.10}$
60^{6} 67^{8} 72^{5} 85^{10} 103$^{11.13.17}$ 111^{5} 119$^{63.74.79}$ 145^{19}
147^{11}; הַיָּרֵא אֶת־דְּבַר י׳ Ex 9^{20} *he that feared the*
word of Yahweh (J); *the name* (*of Yahweh*) Dt
28^{58} Is 59^{19} Mal 3^{20} ψ 61^{6} 86^{11} 102^{16} Ne 1^{11}.

Niph.$_{45}$ *Impf.* 2 m. תִּוָּרֵא ψ 130^{4}; *Pt.* נוֹרָא
Gn 28^{17}+33 t.; f. נוֹרָאָה Is 21^{1}; pl. נוֹרָאוֹת 64^{2}
+5 t.; נוֹרָאֹת Dt 10^{21}; נֹרָאוֹת 2 S 7^{23}; sf. נוֹרְאוֹתֶיךָ
ψ 145^{6};—**1.** *be fearful, dreadful*, e.g. wilderness
Dt 1^{19} 8^{15}, land Is 21^{1}, people 18$^{2.7}$ Hb 1^{7}, ice (in
sim.) כְּעֵין הַקֶּרַח הנ׳ Ez 1^{22} (del. 𝔊 Co). **2.**
cause astonishment and awe: of Yahweh himself
ψ 47^{3} 68^{36} 76^{8}; נוֹרָא תְהִלֹּת *awe-inspiring in*
praises Ex 15^{11} (song); עַל־אֱלוֹהַּ נוֹרָא הוֹד *awe-*
inspiring majesty (is) upon Eloah Jb 37^{22}; c. לְ, to
kings of the earth ψ 76^{13}; c. עַל of hostile nations
Zp 2^{11}; of י׳'s doings Ex 34^{10} (J) ψ 66$^{3.5}$; (ה)נוראות
wonderful, glorious things, of Messianic king
45^{5}; of Yahweh himself Dt 10^{21} 2 S 7^{23}=1 Ch
17^{21} Is 64^{2} ψ 106^{22} 145^{6}; נו׳ adverbially in ψ 65^{6}
139^{14} Ges$^{§ 118.5.b}$ Da$^{Synt. § 70(b)}$; יום י׳ הגדול והנורא *the*
great and awful day of Yahweh Jo 3^{4} Mal 3^{23}
cf. Jo 2^{11}. **3.** *inspire reverence, godly fear,*
and awe: **a.** as attribute of God, לְמַעַן תִּוָּרֵא
that thou mightest be revered ψ 130^{4}; (ה)גָּדוֹל
ו(ה)נוֹרָא (the) *great and awful* (God) Dt 7^{21} 10^{17}
Ne 1^{5} 4^{8} 9^{32} Dn 9^{4}; with עַל, *above* all gods ψ 96^{4}
=1 Ch 16^{25}; above the angels round about him
ψ 89^{8}. **b.** of the name of Yahweh Dt 28^{58}
ψ 99^{3} 111^{9} Mal 1^{14}. **c.** of sacred things: מלאך
האלהים Ju 13^{6}; place of theophany Gn 28^{17} (E).

Piel.$_{5}$ *Pf.* 3 m. sf. יֵרְאֻנִי 2 S 14^{15}; *Inf. sf.*
לְיָֽרְאֵנִי Ne 6^{19}; לְיָֽרְאָם 2 Ch 32^{18}; *Pt.* pl. מְיָֽרְאִים
Ne 6$^{9.14}$ *make afraid, terrify*, with acc.

יָרֵא **adj. verb.** v. supr. *Pt.* 3373

3374 †יִרְאָה **n.f.** fear;—יר׳ Ez 30^{13} + 6 t.; cstr. יִרְאַת Gn 20^{11} + 27 t.; sf. יִרְאָתִי Je 32^{40}; יִרְאָתוֹ Ex 20^{20}; יִרְאָתְךָ Jb 4^{6} + 3 t.; יִרְאָתֶךָ ψ 5^{8} + 2 t.;—**1.** *fear, terror* Is 7^{25} Ez 30^{13}; י׳ גְדוֹלָה *great fear* Jon $1^{10.16}$; ‖ פַּחַד Dt 2^{25}; ‖ רעד(ה) ψ 2^{11} 55^{6}. **2.** *a terror = obj. of terror*, ‖ גֹּבַהּ Ez 1^{18} (del. Co). **3.** *fear of God, reverence, piety* יִרְאַת אֱלֹהִים Gn 20^{11} (E), 2 S 23^{3} Ne 5^{15}; יר׳ שַׁדַּי Jb 6^{14}; יר׳ אֱלֹהֵינוּ Ne 5^{9}; יר׳ יהוה 2 Ch 19^{9} Is 11^{3} 33^{6} ψ 34^{12} Pr 10^{27} $14^{26.27}$ 15^{16} 19^{23} 22^{4} 23^{17}; ‖ the knowledge (of God) Pr 1^{29} 2^{5} Is 11^{2}; is the beginning of wisdom ψ 111^{10} Pr 9^{10}, and knowledge 1^{7}; the instruction of wisdom 15^{33}, is to hate evil 8^{13}, and it involves departing from evil 16^{6}; י׳ אֲדֹנָי is wisdom Jb 28^{28}; יִרְאָה is defined by context 15^{4}; with sfs. these are usually obj., *fear of him* Ex 20^{20} (E), *of thee* ψ 5^{8} 90^{11} 119^{38} Is 63^{17}, *of me* Je 32^{40}, but subj., *thy fear* (i.e. thy religion) Jb 4^{6} 22^{4}. **4.** יִרְאַת יהוה ψ 19^{10} the *fear* of י׳ = the law as *revered*.

3375 †יִרְאוֹן **n.pr.loc.** city in Naphtali Jos 19^{38}; prob. *Jarûn* Bd^Pal 261 Survey^i. 204.

4172 †מוֹרָא **n.m.** ^Dt 4, 34 fear, מ׳ Mal 2^{5} + 3 t.; מֹרָא Dt 26^{8}; sfs. מוֹרָאִי Mal 1^{6}; מוֹרָאוֹ Is 8^{12}; מוֹרַאֲכֶם v^{13} + 2 t.; pl. מוֹרָאִים Dt 4^{34};—**1.** *fear, terror*, ‖ חַת Gn 9^{2} (P); ‖ פַּחַד Dt 11^{25}. **2.** *reverence:* אַיֵּה מוֹרָאִי *where is the reverence due to me* Mal 1^{6}. **3.** *object of reverence*, esp. God Is $8^{12.13}$ ψ 76^{12}; ‖ בְּרִית Mal 2^{5}. **4.** *awe-inspiring spectacle* or *deed* (ה)מ׳ (ה)גדול(ים) Dt 4^{34} 26^{8} 34^{12} Je 32^{21}.

4172 †מוֹרָה **n.**[**m.**] שִׁיתָה מוֹרָה לָהֶם ψ 9^{21}, prob. *appoint* (Hos 6^{11}) *terror* (i.e. some awe-inspiring exhibition of power) *for them* Thes SS RV Ew De Hu Pe Che after Mas 𝔗 Aq Jer (מוֹרָה a variation of or prob. error for מוֹרָא); poss. *set them a teacher, master* Bae after 𝔊 𝔙 𝔖 מוֹרֶה, νομοθέτην; neither altogether satisfactory.

8493 תִּירְיָא **n.pr.m.** (in Judah) 1 Ch 4^{16} van d. H, appar. der. fr. √ירא, cf. MV Buhl; but Baer תִּרְיָא (𝔊B om.; A Θηρια, 𝔊L Εθρια).

3384 †[יָרָא] **vb.** shoot, pour (Aram. orthogr. of יָרָה q.v.)—**Qal** *Inf. cstr.* לִירוֹא בַּחִצִּים 2 Ch 26^{15} *shoot with arrows.* **Hiph.** *Impf.* וַיֹּרְאוּ 2 S 11^{24} *and they shot at* (אֶל־); *Pt.* pl. הַמּוֹרְאִים v^{24} *the shooters, archers;* Kt to be read הַמֹּרְאִים, וַיֹּרְאוּ; but Mas. noting א as superfluous, would read וַיֹּרוּ, הַמּוֹרִים from יָרָה (Bö^§ 1088 (8), (9)). **Hoph.** *Impf.* only in וּמַרְוֶה גַּם הוּא יוֹרֶא Pr 11^{25} he that watereth *shall* himself also *be watered* (Fl De MV al. derive—'non bene,' Thes—from √רוה, q.v., יוֹרֶא for *יָרְוֶה; but v. Thes Ew^§ 131 f. Bö^§ 161 (4) SS Buhl Kö^i. 585; cf. ירה **4**).

יִרְאִיָּה **n.pr.m.** v. sub ראה. p. 909 3376

יְרֻבַּעַל, יָרָבְעָם, יְרֻבֶּשֶׁת, יָרֵב v. sub ריב. p. 914, 937 3377-80

יָרַד **vb.** come or go down, descend 3381
(NH *id.*; MI ^{32} וארד and רד; As. *arâdu*, Dl^HWB 240; Ar. وَرَدَ *come to, arrive at*, also *descend;* Eth. ወረደ: *descend;* Sab. ורד and הורד *id.*, DHM in MV)—**Qal** $_{306}$ *Pf.* יָרַד Ex 19^{18} +; יָרַד Ju $5^{13.13}$ (but read יָרַד or יֵרֵד); רַד 19^{11} (read יָרַד), etc.; *Impf.* יֵרֵד Gn 42^{38} +; וַיֵּרֶד Gn 11^{5} +; תֵּרֵד 2 S 22^{10} + 2 t.; 3 fs. (אֵשׁ) תֵּרֶד 2 K $1^{10.12}$; וַיֵּרֶד Je 13^{17} La 3^{48}; תֵּרֵד Is 34^{5} 63^{14}; תֵּרֵד Ez 26^{11} (יוֹרִיד Vrss Co); וַתֵּרֶד Gn 24^{16} + 7 t.; 2 ms. תֵּרֵד Gn 26^{2} + 5 t. + 1 S 20^{19}, where rd. תִּפָּקֵד We Dr., cf. 𝔊 𝔖 𝔗; 1 s. אֵרֵד Gn 37^{35} + 3 t.; וָאֵרֵד Ex 3^{8} + 3 t.; cohort. אֵרְדָה־נָּא Gn 18^{21}; יֵרְדוּ 1 S 13^{12} + 4 t.; וַיֵּרְדוּ Gn 42^{3} + 19 t.; 3 f. pl. תֵּרַדְנָה Je 14^{17} + 2 t.; 1 pl. נֵרֵד Gn 43^{5}; cohort. נֵרְדָה Gn 11^{7} + 2 t.; וַנֵּרֶד 2 K 10^{13}; *Imv.* רֵד Ex 19^{21} +; רְדָה Gn 45^{9} Ez 32^{19}; רְדָה 2 K $1^{9.11}$; fs. רְדִי Je 48^{18} Is 47^{1}; mpl. רְדוּ Gn 42^{2} + 5 t.; *Inf. abs.* יָרֹד Gn 43^{20}; *cstr.* רֶדֶת Gn 44^{26} +; (מֵ)רְדָה Gn 46^{3} (v. Kö^i. 402); sf. רִדְתִּי ψ 30^{10}, etc. (in ψ 30^{4} rd. Kt מִיּוֹרְדֵי, so 𝔊 𝔖 Che Bae, v. Ol^§§ 160 b, 245 d); *Pt.* יוֹרֵד Ju 9^{36} +; fs. יֹרְדָה La 1^{16}; (הַ)יֹּרֶדֶת Ec 3^{21} 1 S 25^{30}, etc.;—**1. a.** *come* or *go down:* from (מִן) a mountain Ex 19^{14} $32^{1.15}$ (all E), $34^{29.29}$ (JE), Dt 9^{15} 10^{5} Nu 20^{28} (P) +; abs. Ex $19^{21.24}$ (J), v^{25} (J; c. אֶל pers.); from the air, of birds, sq. עַל Gn 15^{11} (JE). **b.** *go down* (usu. from mountain or hill-country into plain), to battle, abs. Ju 5^{14}; sq. לָעֵמֶק Ju 1^{34}; sq. לַשְּׁעָרִים Ju 5^{11}; sq. אֶל $v^{10.11}$, cf. 1 S 17^{8} (sq. אֶל pers.); sq. לִקְרַאת Ju 7^{24}; sq. אַחֲרֵי pers. 1 S 14^{36}; sq. בְּ loc. Ju 7^{9}; בַּמִּלְחָמָה יֵרֵד וְנִסְפָּה 1 S 26^{10}, cf. 29^{4} 30^{24}; of single combat, וַיֵּרֶד אֵלָיו בַּשָּׁבֶט 2 S 23^{21} = 1 Ch 11^{23}. **c.** *go down* to (acc.) threshing-floor, Ru $3^{3.5}$; (from David's palace) to Uriah's house (אֶל) 2 S $11^{9.10.10.13}$; from temple to (acc.) king's house Je 36^{12} (+ עַל־לִשְׁכַּת הַסֹּפֵר); רֵד בֵּית־מֶלֶךְ יְהוּדָה 22^{1}, etc. **d.** *go down* (abs.) from Palestine to Egypt Gn 42^{3} (E), v^{38} (J) + 6 t. JE; †sq. אֵלַי Gn 45^{9} (E); sq. מִצְרַיְמָה Gn $46^{3.4}$ (E), 12^{10} 26^{2}

(both J), Nu 20[15] (JE); sq. מִצְרַיִם Jos 24[4] (E), Gn 43[15] (J), Is 30[2] 31[1] 52[4]; sq. שָׁמָּה Gn 42[2] (E)†; so to Philistine cities Ju 14[19] 16[31] 1 S 13[20] Am 6[2]. **e.** from Jerusalem, abs. Ju 1[9] 1 K 1[25] Ne 6[3] 2 Ch 20[16] (to battle); to Jezreel 2 K 8[21] =9[26]=2 Ch 22[6]; to Samaria 1 K 22[2]=2 Ch 18[2]; (to Gihon) 1 S 1[38], etc. †**f.** from altar ירד מֵעֲשׂוֹת הַחַטָּאת Lv 9[22] (P); from chariot, c. מֵעַל Ju 4[15]; from ass, c. מֵעַל 1 S 25[23]; from throne, c. מֵעַל Ez 26[16], abs. Is 47[1], cf. רְדִי מִכָּבוֹד Je 48[18]; from ships, c. מִן Ez 27[29]; from bed, c. מִן 2 K 1[4.6.16] (all opp. עלה). †**g.** *go down* הָעַיְנָה Gn 24[16.45] (J); sq. לִרְחֹץ עַל הַיְאֹר Ex 2[5] (E), cf. (abs.) 2 K 5[14]; sq. acc. הַסֶּלַע 1 S 23[25]; יוֹרְדֵי הַיָּם Is 42[10]; יוֹרְדֵי הַיָּם בָּאֳנִיּוֹת ψ 107[23]; abs. (into pit or well) 2 S 23[30]=1 Ch 11[22], sq. שָׁם (i.e. בְּאֵר) 2 S 17[18]. —וַיָּרַדְתִּי Ju 11[37], rd. וְרַדְתִּי (√רוד, *wander about*), RS in Bla. †**h.** =*sink*, in water יָרְדוּ בִמְצוֹלֹת כְּמוֹ־אָבֶן Ex 15[5] (song in E); לְקִצְבֵי הָרִים יָרַדְתִּי Jon 2[7]; more gen., opp. rising, יַעֲלוּ הָרִים יֵרְדוּ בְקָעוֹת ψ 104[8] *mountains rise, valleys sink*; יַעֲלוּ שָׁמַיִם יֵרְדוּ תְהוֹמוֹת 107[26]. **i.** *go down* to She'ôl: †sq. שְׁאוֹלָה Gn 37[35] (J; + אֶל־בְּנִי), Nu 16[30.33] (JE), Ez 31[15.17]; sq. שְׁאוֹל Ez 32[27] ψ 55[16] Jb 7[9] (opp. עלה); בַּדֵּי שְׁאֹל תֵּרַדְנָה Jb 17[16]; abs. Is 5[14] Ez 32[19] (|| הָשְׁכְּבָה), v[21.30], ψ 49[15] (sq. אַחֲרָיו); אֶל־שַׁחַת יָרְדוּ עֲרֵלִים Ez 32[24]; sq. שַׁחַת Jb 33[24], ψ 30[10]; sq. בּוֹר ψ 30[4] Qr (Kt יורדי) יוֹרְדֵי); אֶל־אַבְנֵי־בוֹר Is 14[19]†; יוֹרְדֵי בוֹר ψ 28[1] Ez 26[20.20] (|| אֶרֶץ תַּחְתִּיּוֹת) + 11 t. (v. בּוֹר); יוֹרְדֵי עָפָר† ψ 22[30]; יוֹרְדֵי דוּמָה 115[17] (|| הַמֵּתִים); רַגְלֶיהָ יֹרְדוֹת מָוֶת Pr 5[5], cf. 7[27] (|| דַּרְכֵי שְׁאוֹל); note also מִי יוֹדֵעַ . . . רוּחַ הַבְּהֵמָה הַיֹּרֶדֶת הִיא לְמַטָּה לָאָרֶץ Ec 3[21] (opp. הָעֹלָה הִיא לְמָעְלָה; rd. הָעֹלָה, הַיֹּרֶדֶת, with Vrss, see VB). **j.** fig. יֹרֵד בַּבֶּכִי Is 15[3] *going down* (dissolving) *in tears* (|| יְיֵלִיל; cf. **3 c**). †**k.** =*be prostrated*, abs., of horses and riders Hg 2[22], cf. Is 34[7], perh. also Je 48[15] 50[27] (+ לַטָּבַח); forest Is 32[19] Zc 11[2]; city Dt 20[20] La 1[9]; wall Dt 28[52]; nation תֵּרֵד מַטָּה מָּטָּה Dt 28[43] (opp. עלה); מַצֵּבוֹת Ez 26[11] + לָאָרֶץ (where Co ויחרדו). †**2.** of divine manifestations: *descend*, of י׳ in theoph. יָרַד עָלָיו [=על ההר] י׳ בָּאֵשׁ Ex 19[11.18] (E), v[20] (J; אֶל־רֹאשׁ הָהָר), cf. Ne 9[13]; יֵרֵד י׳ צְבָאוֹת לִצְבֹּא עַל־הַר־צִיּוֹן Is 31[4]; abs. Gn 11[5.7] 18[21] Ex 3[8] (all J), Nu 11[17] (JE), 2 S 22[10]=ψ 18[10] (cf. 144[5]), Mi 1[3] Is 63[19] 64[2]; וַיֵּרֶד י׳ בֶּעָנָן Ex 34[5] Nu 11[25], cf. 12[5] (all JE); of pillar of cloud Ex 33[9] (JE); מִי עָלָה־שָׁמַיִם וַיֵּרַד Pr 30[4]; of angels on סֻלָּם; עֹלִים וְיֹרְדִים בּוֹ Gn 28[12] (E). **3.** of inanimate things: **a.** hail c. עַל pers. Ex 9[19] (J); dew c. עַל loc. Nu 11[9] (JE), ψ 133[3]; rain (as אָבָק and עָפָר), sq. עַל + מִן הַשָּׁמַיִם pers. Dt 28[24], so in sim. of future king יֵרֵד כְּמָטָר עַל־גֵּז ψ 72[6]; of גֶּשֶׁם and שֶׁלֶג, c. מִן הַשָּׁמַיִם Is 55[10]; manna (c. עַל loc.) Nu 11[9] (JE); fire from (מִן) heaven 2 K 1[10.10.12.12.14] 2 Ch 7[1], abs. 2 Ch 7[3]. **b.** waters, flowing down הַנַּחַל הַיֹּרֵד מִן־הָהָר Dt 9[21], cf. Jos 3[13] (sq. מִלְמָעְלָה), v[16]; sq. עַל־יָם הָעֲרָבָה v[16]; עַל־הָעֲרָבָה Ez 47[8]; sq. מִן 47[1]. **c.** tears, פַּלְגֵי־מַיִם יָרְדוּ עֵינָי ψ 119[136], and so La 3[48]; also עֵינִי יֹרְדָה מַּיִם La 1[16], and so Je 9[17] 13[17] 14[17] (cf. also Is 15[3], **1 j**). **d.** of oil descending upon (עַל) beard, etc. ψ 133[2.2]. **e.** of shadow on dial 2 K 20[11]= Is 38[8.8]. **f.** of boundary *going down* (from or to a place) Jos 16[3] (JE), elsewhere P, Nu 34[11.11.12] Jos 15[10] 16[7] 17[9] 18[13.16]. **g.** *come down*, abs. of headdresses, in sign of humiliation Je 13[18]. **h.** pride of power Ez 30[6]. **i.** of calamity מֵאֵת י׳ Mi 1[12]; עַל־קָדְקֳדוֹ חֲמָסוֹ יֵרֵד ψ 7[17]; of sword descending on (עַל) Edom Is 34[5]. **j.** fig. of words of talebearer; יָרְדוּ חַדְרֵי־בָטֶן Pr 18[8]=26[22].—Vid. also supr. **1 k.**

†**Hiph.** *Pf.* 3 ms. הוֹרִד 2 K 16[17]; וְהוֹרִיד consec. Am 3[11] (We וְהוּרַד); 2 ms. וְהוֹרַדְתָּ 1 K 2[9]; 2 fs. sf. הוֹרַדְתִּנִי Jos 2[18] (v. Baer[n.] and Kö[i. 412]); הוֹרִידוּ 1 S 6[15] La 2[10] etc.; *Impf.* 3 ms. וַיּוֹרֶד Ju 7[5] + 5 t. (+ 1 K 6[32] Klo, who rds. וַיֹּרֶד for וַיָּרֶד, v. רדד); sf. יוֹרִידֵנִי Ob[3]; יוֹרִדֵהוּ 1 S 30[16] 1 K 17[23]; וַיֹּרִדֵם 1 K 18[40]; 2 ms. וְלֹא תוֹרִד 1 K 2[6]; sf. (הֲ)תוֹרִדֵנִי 1 S 30[15], תּוֹרִדֵם ψ 55[24] etc.; *Imv.* ms. הוֹרֵד Ex 33[5] + 2 t.; sf. הוֹרִדֵהוּ Ez 32[18]; הוֹרִידֵמוֹ ψ 59[12]; fs. הוֹרִידִי La 2[18]; mpl. הוֹרִידוּ Gn 43[7.11]; sf. הוֹרִדֻהוּ Gn 44[21]; *Inf. cstr.* לְהוֹרִיד Gn 37[25]; sf. הוֹרִדִי Ez 31[16]; *Pt.* מוֹרִיד 1 S 2[6]; מֹרִיד 2 S 22[48];—*cause to come* or *go down*: **1. a.** *bring down* (to Egypt), c. acc. pers. + שָׁמָּה Gn 39[1] (J); + הֵנָּה 45[13] (E); + אֵלַי 44[21]; abs. 43[7]; c. acc. rei 43[11]; + מִצְרַיְמָה 37[25]; abs. 43[22] (all J); from Canaan to desert Dt 1[25] (sq. אֵלֵינוּ); to (אֶל) Amalekites 1 S 30[15.15]; abs. v[16]; *bring down* (obj. pers. vel rei) אֶל־הַמַּיִם Ju 7[4.5]; אֶל־נַחַל Dt 21[4] 1 K 18[40]; יָמָּה 1 K 5[23]; to Gaza (עַזָּתָה) Ju 16[21]; from Jerusalem to Gihon, c. עַל (Qr אֶל) 1 K 1[38]; to valley of Jehosh. (אֶל) Jo 4[2]; from (מִן) temple (to king's house) 2 K 11[19]=2 Ch 23[20]; from (מֵעַל) altar 1 K 1[53]; from (מִן) upper chamber, sq. הַבַּיְתָה 1 K 17[23]; from

(מִן) the heavens Am 9[2]; Edom, from (מִן) nest in rocks Je 49[16] Ob[4]; cf. of Isr. כְּעוֹף הַשָּׁמַיִם Ho 7[12]; c. acc. of limit (אֶרֶץ) Ob[3]; *bring down* (from Babylon) into (בְּ) ships Is 43[14] (v. VB). **b.** *send down* rain (הַגֶּשֶׁם) Ez 34[26], cf. Jo 2[23]; =*cause to flow down*, obj. spittle, וַיּוֹרֶד רִירוֹ אֶל־זְקָנוֹ 1 S 21[14]; tears הוֹרִידִי כַנַּחַל דִּמְעָה La 2[18]; water-streams וַיּוֹרֶד כַּנְּהָרוֹת מָיִם ψ 78[16]. **c.** =*lay prostrate*, *prostrate* הוֹרִיד מִמֵּךְ עֻזֵּךְ Am 3[11] (where however We rds. וְהוּרַד), cf. Pr 21[22]; וְאוֹרִיד כַּאבִּיר יוֹשְׁבִים Is 10[13]; of God's casting down peoples ψ 56[8] Is 63[6] (sq. לָאָרֶץ); מוֹרִיד עַמִּים תַּחְתֵּנִי 2 S 22[48] (וַיַּדְבֵּר in ‖ ψ 18[48]); so perhaps Babylonians, like lambs, אוֹרִידֵם כְּכָרִים לִטְבוֹחַ Je 51[40]; so ψ 59[12] (si veral.; 𝔊 וְהַנִידֵמוֹ *make them vagabonds*, v. Lag[Proph. Chald. (1872), xlviii.] VB Hup Now Che Bae Dr[2 S 15, 20]). **d.** *bring down* to She'ôl: יי׳ מֵמִית וּמְחַיֶּה מוֹרִיד שְׁאוֹל וַיָּעַל 1 S 2[6]; sq. שְׁאוֹל also 1 K 2[6.9]; sq. שְׁאוֹלָה (obj. grey hair) Gn 42[38] 44[29.31] (all J); cf. Ez 26[30] 31[16] 32[18]; sq. לִבְאֵר שַׁחַת ψ 55[24]; לַשַּׁחַת Ez 28[8]. **2.** *take down* (from cart) 1 S 6[15]; the sea from upon (מֵעַל) the brazen oxen 2 K 16[17]; corpse from (מִן) tree Jos 8[29], and (מֵעַל) 10[27] (both JE); the מִשְׁכָּן Nu 1[51] (P); the פָּרֹכֶת Nu 4[5] (P); *take off* ornaments וְעַתָּה הוֹרֵד עֶדְיְךָ מֵעָלֶיךָ Ex 33[5] (JE). **3.** *let down* וַתֹּרֶד כַּדָּהּ עַל־יָדָהּ Gn 24[18], so, with מֵעָלֶיהָ v[46], to give one a drink; וַיּוֹרִדוּ אִישׁ אֶת־אַמְתַּחְתּוֹ אָרְצָה Gn 44[11] (all J); obj. pers. Jos 2[18], בַּחֶבֶל בְּעַד הַחַלּוֹן v[15] (both JE); הוֹרִידוּ בְּעַד הַחַלּוֹן 1 S 19[12]; cf. also הוֹרִידוּ לָאָרֶץ רֹאשָׁן בְּתוּלֹת יְרוּשָׁלָםִ La 2[10] *the virgins of Jerusalem have bowed down their heads to the ground.*

†**Hoph.** *Pf.* הוּרַד Gn 39[1] + 2 t. + 1 S 30[34] Kt (Qr **Qal** *Pt.*); וְהוּרַד consec. Zc 10[11]; 2 ms. וְהוּרַדְתָּ Ez 31[18]; *Impf.* 2 ms. תּוּרַד Is 14[15];—**1.** *be brought down* מִצְרָיְמָה Gn 39[1] (J); בַּמִּלְחָמָה 1 S 30[24] Kt (v. supr.); to She'ôl הוּרַד שְׁאוֹל גְּאוֹנֶךָ Is 14[11] (of king of Babylon); אֶל־שְׁאוֹל תּוּרַד v[15]; וְהוּרַדְתָּ אֶל־אֶרֶץ תַּחְתִּית Ez 31[18]; אֶל־יַרְכְּתֵי־בוֹר v[15]; וְהוּרַד גְּאוֹן אַשּׁוּר Zc 10[11].—In Am 3[11] We rds. וְהוּרַד מִמֵּךְ (v. **Hiph.** supr.) **2.** *be taken down*, of the מִשְׁכָּן Nu 10[17] (P).

3382 †יֶרֶד **n.pr.m. 1.** son of Mehall'ēl, fourth generation from Seth Gn 5[16.18.19.20]; יָרֶד v[15] 1 Ch 1[2]; 𝔊 Ιαρεδ (v. Lag[BN 77]). **2.** יֶרֶד man of Judah 1 Ch 4[18]; 𝔊 *id.*

4174 †מוֹרָד **n.[m.] descent, slope**; abs. מוֹ׳ Mi 1[4] + 2 t.; cstr. מוֹרַד Jos 10[11] Je 48[5];—**1.** *descent*, *slope*, as designation of locality Jos 7[5] 10[11] (בְּמ׳ בֵּית־חוֹרֹן; both JE); בְּמ׳ חֹרֹנַיִם Je 48[5]; + בְּמוֹרָד ins. in 2 S 13[34] 𝔊 We Dr; in gen. כְּמַיִם מֻגָּרִים בְּמוֹרָד Mi 1[4]. **2.** מַעֲשֵׂה מוֹרָד 1 K 7[29] *work of descent*, i.e. *hanging-work* (VB).

†יַרְדֵּן[:–182] **n.pr.fl. Jordan** (acc. to Rel Ol[§ 215 c], 3383
fr. ירד with ן— for orig. ןָ—, cf. 𝔊 ὁ Ιορδανης; =river as flowing *downward*, *descending*, then of particular stream as river κατ' ἐξοχήν. See also Sta[§ 294 e] (ןֵ— for ןָ—, but name acc. to Sta non-Hebr.))—abs. alw. הַיַּר׳ in prose Gn 13[10] + 162 t.; c. ה loc. הַיַּרְדֵּנָה Ju 8[4] + 3 t.; יַרְדֵּן only ψ 42[7] Jb 40[23]; cstr. יַרְדֵּן Nu 26[3] + 11 t. Nu Jos + 1 Ch 6[63];—the river of Palestine: in all periods, chiefly Hex (122 t.: Gn 5 t. J; Nu 20 t. P, 1 t. JE; Dt 26 t.; Jos 34 t. JE, 20 t. D, 16 t. P), Ju (12 t.), and S (18 t.); in K 13 t.; Ch 7 t.; elsewh. 10 t.;—הַיַּרְדֵּן הַזֶּה Gn 32[11] (J), Dt 3[27] 31[2] Jos 1[2.11] 4[22] (all D); בְּעֵבֶר הַיַּרְדֵּן Gn 50[10.11] (J), Jos 7[7] 24[8] (both JE), + 20 t. D + Ju 5[17] 10[8] 1 S 31[7]; P has also מֵעֵבֶר הַיַּרְדֵּן Nu 32[19], and מֵע׳ לְיַרְדֵּן v[19.32] 35[14] Jos 14[3], also Jos 17[5] (JE), 18[7] (D), Ju 7[25] 1 Ch 12[37] 26[30]; in P peculiarly יַרְדֵּן יְרֵחוֹ *the Jordan of* (at) *Jericho*, with עַל Nu 26[3.63] 31[12] 33[48.50] 35[1] 36[13], with לְ מֵעֵבֶר Nu 22[1] 34[15] Jos 13[32] 20[8] (= 1 Ch 6[63]), with מִן Jos 16[1] (E ?); עֵבֶר הַיַּרְדֵּן Is 8[23] Dt 4[49] Jos 13[27] (P); see sub עבר; מֵי הַיַּרְדֵּן Jos 3[13.13] 4[18.23] (all JE), 3[8] 5[1] (both D); מֵימֵי הַיַּרְדֵּן 4[7] (JE); גְּאוֹן הַיַּר׳ Je 12[5] 49[19] 50[44] Zc 11[3] (v. גאון p. 145 a, supr.); שְׂפַת הַיַּר׳ 2 K 2[13]; יֹשֵׁב עַל־הַיָּם וְעַל יַד הַיַּרְדֵּן Nu 13[29] (JE; elsewh. in Nu, P); כִּכַּר הַיַּרְדֵּן *the circle of Jordan*, i.e. the plain about Jericho Gn 13[10.11] (J), 1 K 7[46] 2 Ch 4[17]; מַעְבְּרוֹת הַיַּר׳ Ju 3[28] 12[5.6] *fords of the Jordan*; אֶל־גְּלִילוֹת הַיַּרְדֵּן אֶל־עֵבֶר בְּנֵי יִשְׂרָאֵל Jos 22[11], cf. v[10] (both P; v. גלילות supr. p. 165); אֶרֶץ יַרְדֵּן ψ 42[7] (without art. only here and in foll.); יָגִיחַ יַרְדֵּן אֶל־פִּיהוּ Jb 40[23] *a Jordan bursteth forth into his mouth.*

†יָרָה **vb. throw, shoot** (NH *shoot*, Hiph. 3384
teach; Aram. Aph. אוֹרִי *teach*; Eth. ወረወ: *jecit*; Amh. *warê* is *information*, *news*, v. Nö[ZMG 1886, 724]; As. *ârû*, *lead*, *guide*, Dl[HWB 241]; *têrtu*, *law*, Dl[HA 49]; Zinj. ירי *set*, *found*, DHM[Sendsch. 57], cf. **2** infr. — Buhl distinguishes **3** √ √ ירה: I. = *throw*, cf. mod. Ar. *warra*; II. Hiph. = *moisten*, cf. רוה; III. Hiph. = *teach*, cf. ראה, Ar. رأى, روى; but evidence for this division hardly sufficient) —**Qal** *Pf.* יר׳ Ex 15[4] + 3 t.; 1 s. יָרִיתִי Gn 31[51] Jos 18[6]; *Impf.* 1 pl. sf. וַנִּירָם Nu 21[30] (SS after

𝔊 וְנִינָם, see Ges $^{§76\ (2)\ e}$); *Imv.* יְרֵה 2 K 13^{17}; *Inf. abs.* יָרֹה Ex 19^{13}; cstr. לִיר(וֹ)ת ψ 11^{2} 64^{5}; *Pt.* יֹרֶה Pr 26^{18}; pl. יוֹרִים 1 Ch 10^{3}; יֹרִים 2 Ch 35^{23};—**1.** *throw, cast,* with acc.: cast lots Jos 18^{6} (E); army into (בְּ) the sea Ex 15^{4} (song). **2.** *cast* (=*lay, set*), corner-stone Jb 38^{6}; pillar Gn 31^{51} (E; v. Zinj. supr.) **3.** *shoot arrows,* abs. Ex 19^{13}(E) 2 K 13^{17}; acc. of arrows 1 S 20$^{36.37}$ Pr 26^{18}; acc. pers. Nu 21^{30} (song, E) ψ 64^{5}; with לְ pers. 11^{2}; יוֹ(וֹ)רִים *archers* 1 Ch 10^{3} 2 Ch 35^{23}. **4.** *throw water, rain:* Ho 6^{3}, but v. יוֹרֶה *early rain* (cf. **Hiph. 3**). **Niph.** *Impf.* יִיָּרֶה *shot through* (with arrows) Ex 19^{13} (E). **Hiph.** *Pf.* 3 ms. sf. הֹרַנִי Jb 30^{19} (הֹרָנִי Baer); הוֹרָהוּ 2 K 12^{3}; הוֹרֵתָנִי ψ 119^{102}; 1 s. וְהוֹרֵיתִי Ex 4^{15} 1 S 12^{23}; sf. הֹרֵיתִיךָ Pr 4^{11}; הוֹרֵיתִיךָ Ex 4^{12}; *Impf.* יוֹרֶה ψ 25^{8} + 5 t.; וַיּוֹר 2 K 13^{17} (for this and other forms see Ges $^{§76\ (2)\ e}$); וַיֹּרֵנִי Pr 4^{4}; יוֹרֵנוּ Ju 13^{8} + 2 t.; יוֹרֶנּוּ ψ 25^{12} Is 28^{26}; וַיּוֹרֵהוּ Ex 15^{25}; יֹרֵם 2 K 17^{27} ψ 64^{8}; 2 f. sf. תּוֹרְךָ ψ 45^{5}; תֹּרֶךָּ Jb 12$^{7.8}$; 2 m. sf. תּוֹרֵם 1 K 8^{36} = 2 Ch 6^{27}; 1 s. אוֹרֶה 1 S 20^{20} Jb 27^{11}; sf. אוֹרְךָ ψ 32^{8}; 3 mpl. יוֹרוּ Dt 24^{8} + 3 t.; יֹרוּ 2 S 11^{20} 2 Ch 35^{23}; יֹרֻהוּ ψ 64^{5}; יוֹרוּךָ Dt 17^{10} + 2 t.; *Imv.* sf. הֹרֵנִי Jb 34^{32}; הוֹרֵנִי ψ 27^{11} + 2 t.; pl. sf. הוֹרוּנִי Jb 6^{24}; *Inf. cstr.* הוֹרֹת Gn 46^{28} + 3 t.;
4175 הוֹרֹתָם Ex 24^{12}; *Pt.* מוֹרֶה 1 S 20^{36} + 5 t.; מֹרֶה Pr 6^{13}; pl. מוֹרִים 1 S 31^{3} + 2 t.; sf. מוֹרָי Pr 5^{13}; מוֹרֶיךָ Is 30$^{20.20}$;—**1.** *throw, cast,* with לְ, into the mire Jb 30^{19}. **2.** *shoot* (arrows) 1 S 20$^{20.36}$ 2 S 11^{20} 2 K 13^{17} 19^{32} = Is 37^{33}; with לְ, of pers. 2 Ch 35^{23}; acc. pers. ψ 64$^{5.8}$; מוֹרִים *archers* 1 S 31$^{3.3}$ 1 Ch 10^{3}. **3.** *throw water, rain:* וְיוֹרֶה צֶדֶק לָכֶם Ho 10^{12} *and rain righteousness for you* (Thes al. under **5**); hence מוֹרֶה *early rain* (cf. **Qal 4**). **4.** *point out, shew:* לְהוֹרֹת לְפָנָיו גֹּשְׁנָה Gn 46^{28} (J) *to point out before him* (the way) *to Goshen;* מֹרֶה בְּאֶצְבְּעֹתָיו Pr 6^{13} *pointing out with his fingers;* acc. pers. et rei Ex 15^{25} (JE) ψ 45^{5} Jb 6^{24}. **5.** *direct, teach, instruct:* **a.** of men, abs. Bezalel in handicraft Ex 35^{34} (P); c. acc. pers., a father his son Pr 4^{4}; the ancients Job Jb 8^{10}; the animals and the earth, the friends of Job 12$^{7.8}$; c. 2 acc. Is 28^{9}; בְּדֶרֶךְ in the way 1 S 12^{23} ψ 25^{8} 32^{8} Pr 4^{11}; בְּיַד־אֵל *concerning the hand of Ēl* Jb 27^{11}.—מוֹרֶה שֶּׁקֶר *teaching lies* is used of prophet Is 9^{14}. **b.** specially of the authoritative *direction* (v. תּוֹרָה) given by priests on matters of ceremonial observance, with acc. rei and לְ pers. Dt 33^{10} (song), they *teach* thy judgments to Jacob, and thy direction (law) to Israel; double acc. 17$^{10.11}$ according to the direction, wherewith they *direct* thee; 24^{8} (on leprosy), Lv 10^{11} (P), abs. 14^{57} (P), 2 Ch 15^{3} כֹּהֵן מוֹרֶה, Ez 44^{23} the Zadokite priests את־עמי יֹרוּ בֵּין קֹדֶשׁ לְחֹל; Mi 3^{11} the priests give such 'direction' for hire; less technically, of Moses Ex 24^{12} (E), of Jehoiada 2 K 12^{3}, of the Samaritan priests 2 K 17$^{27.28}$. **c.** of God: c. acc. pers. Is 28^{26} ψ 119^{102}; double acc. Ex 4$^{12.15}$ (J), Ju 13^{8} Jb 34^{32} 1 K 8^{36} (= אֶל הַדֶּרֶךְ 2 Ch 6^{27}), ψ 27^{11} 86^{11} 119^{33}; acc. pers. בְּדֶרֶךְ ψ 25^{12}; מִדְּרָכָיו *of his ways* Is 2^{3} = Mi 4^{2}. **d.** of idol-image Hb 2^{18} (מוֹרֶה שָׁקֶר), v^{19}.

†יוֹרָה **n.pr.m.** בְּנֵי י׳ one of the families of 3139
the restoration Ezr 2^{18} (𝔊 Ουρα, Ιωρα) = חָרִיף Ne 7^{24} (𝔊 Αρειφ).

†יוֹרֶה **n.[m.]** **early rain**, which falls in 3138
Palestine from the last of October until the first of December, opp. מַלְקוֹשׁ: Dt 11^{14} Je 5^{24} Ho 6^{3} (where MT makes יו׳ Pt., or Hiph. Impf., but v. We); cf. also I. מוֹרֶה. Vid. further Rob $^{BR\ i,\ 429\ f.}$ Chaplin $^{PEF\ 1883,\ 8\ ff.}$ Klein $^{ZPV\ iv,\ 72\ f.}$

†I. מוֹרֶה **n.m.** $^{ψ\ 84.7}$ **(early) rain** (cf. יוֹרֶה);— 4175
Jo 2^{23} (|| מַלְקוֹשׁ, גֶּשֶׁם) v^{23} (del. We), ψ 84^{7}.

†II. מוֹרֶה **n.m.** $^{Is\ 30.20}$ **teacher**;—abs. in 4175
אֵלוֹן מוֹרֶה Gn 12^{6} (J) = אֵלוֹנֵי מֹרֶה Dt 11^{30} (Sam 𝔊 אֵלוֹן), *the teacher's terebinth* (see אֵלוֹן) near
Shechem; cf. גִּבְעַת הַמּוֹרֶה Ju 7^{1} *teacher's hill* 4176
near the plain of Jezreel, prob. Little Hermon, *Nebî Daḥî* Bd $^{Pal\ 244}$; the terebinth being a holy tree from which divine teaching was given, and the hill of the teacher the seat of a holy place whence divine teaching was given; see also (of God) Jb 36^{22}; here belong prob. likewise מוֹרָי Pr 5^{13}, and מוֹרֶיךָ Is 30$^{20.20}$.

†תּוֹרָה **n.f.** $^{Dt\ 1.5}$ **direction, instruction,** 8451-52
law (poss. in first instance from *casting* lots, We $^{G\ i,\ 410;\ H\ 394}$ (less confidently We $^{Skizzen\ iii,\ 167}$), SS Sm $^{AT\ Rel.\ Gesch.\ 36}$ Benz $^{Arch.\ 408}$ Now $^{Arch.\ ii,\ 97}$, opp. by Kö $^{Offenb.\ ii,\ 347}$ Baud $^{Priesterthum\ 207}$);—ת׳, Ex 12^{49} + 88 t.; cstr. תּוֹרַת Ex 13^{9} + 65 t.; sfs. תּוֹרָתִי ψ 78^{1} + 16 t.; תּוֹרָתְךָ Je 32^{23}; תֹּרָתוֹ 44^{23} + 34 t. sfs.; pl. תּוֹרוֹת Ne 9^{13}; תּוֹרֹת Is 24^{5} + 2 t.; sf. תּוֹרֹתַי Ez 44^{24}; תּוֹרֹתָו 43^{11} 44^{5} + 5 t. sfs.;—**1.** *instruction:* **a.** human: of a mother Pr 1^{8} 6$^{20.23}$; of a father 3^{1} 4^{2} 7^{2}; of sages 13^{14} 28$^{4.4.7.9}$ 29^{18}; of a poet ψ 78^{1}; תּוֹרַת חֶסֶד *kind instruction* (of a wise wife) Pr 31^{26}. **b.** divine || אֲמָרִים Jb 22^{22}; through his servants Is 30^{9} Je 8^{8}; || אִמְרָה Is 5^{24}; || דָּבָר Is 1^{10}; || תְּעוּדָה 8$^{16.20}$; || חָזוֹן La 2^{9}; pl. תורות Dn 9^{10}. **c.** *a body of prophetic* (or sometimes perh. priestly) *teaching* Is 42$^{21.24}$ Je 9^{12} 16^{11}; in the heart Is 51^{7}

ψ 37^{31} 40^{9}; ‖ משפט Hb 1^{4}; ‖ משפטים ψ 89^{31}; ‖ דְּבָרִים Je 6^{19} 26^{4} Zc 7^{12}; ‖ חקים Am 2^{4}; ‖ חקות Je 44$^{10.23}$; myriads of precepts Ho 8^{12}. **d.** *instruction in Messianic age* Is 2^{3} = Mi 4^{4}, Is 42^{4} 51^{4} Je 31^{33}. **e.** *a body of priestly direction* or *instruction* relating to sacred things Ho 4^{6} Je 2^{8} 18^{18} Ez 7^{26} Hag 2^{11} Mal 2$^{6.7.8.9}$ Zp 3^{4} Ez 22^{26}; ‖ לֹא תוֹרָה לֹא כֹּהֵן מוֹרֶה 2 Ch 15^{3}. **2.** *law* (prop. *direction*): viz. **a.** of *special laws*, sg. of Feast of Maṣṣoth Ex 13^{9} (J), sabbath 16^{4} (J); of direction given by priests in partic. case Dt 17^{11}; of statutes of priest's code Ex 12^{49} (P), Lv 6$^{2.7.18}$ 7$^{1.7.11.37}$ 11^{46} 12^{7} 13^{59} 14$^{2.32.54.57}$ 15^{32} Nu 5$^{29.30}$ 6$^{13.21.21}$ 15$^{16.29}$ 19$^{2.14}$ 31^{21} (P); תּוֹרַת הַבַּיִת Ez 43$^{12.12}$; בֵּין ת׳ לְמִצְוָה 2 Ch 19^{10}; pl. תּוֹרוֹת *laws*, ‖ חקים Ex 18$^{16.20}$ (E; of decisions in civil cases given by Moses), ψ 105^{45}; ‖ מצות Ex 16^{28} (J); ‖ מצות, חקות Gn 26^{5} (J); ‖ חקים משפטים Lv 26^{46} (H); ‖ חק, ברית Is 24^{5}; ‖ משפטים חקים, מצות Ne 9^{13}; the laws of the new temple Ez 43^{11} 44$^{5.24}$; those laws in which men should walk Je 32^{23} (Kt). **b.** of *codes of law*, (1) הַתּוֹרָה as *written in the code of the covenant*, ‖ הַמִּצְוָה Ex 24^{12} (E); ספר תּוֹרַת אלהים Jos 24^{26} (E); prob. also Dt 33^{4}, ‖ משפטים v^{10}, ‖ בְּרִית Ho 8^{1} ψ 78^{10}, ‖ עֵדוֹת v^{5}; (2) *the law of the Deuteronomic code*, in D and Deuteronomic sections of Kings and sources of Chr., הַתּוֹרָה הַזֹּאת Dt 1^{5} 4$^{8.44}$ 17^{18} 31$^{9.11}$; דִּבְרֵי הַתּ׳ הזאת 27^{26} 31^{24}, + כל 17^{19} 27$^{3.8}$ 28^{58} 29^{28} 31^{12} 32^{46}; סֵפֶר הַתּ׳ הזאת 28^{61}; ספר התורה הזה 29^{20} 30^{10} 31^{26} Jos 1^{8}; ספר התורה 8^{34} 2 K 22^{8} = 2 Ch 34^{15}; דברי התורה Jos 8^{34} 2 K 23^{24}; so התורה אשר צוך משה Jos 1^{7}, similarly 22^{5} 2 K 17$^{13.34.37}$ 21^{8}; (ספר) תּוֹרַת משה Jos 8$^{31.32}$ 23^{6} 1 K 2^{3} 2 K 14^{6} = דִּבְרֵי סֵפֶר הַתּ׳ 2 Ch 25^{4}, 2 K 23^{25}; הַתּ׳ בספר מ׳ = 2 K 22^{11} = דברי הַתּ׳ 2 Ch 34^{19}; תּוֹרַת יהוה 2 K 10^{31}. It is probable that ת׳ in ψ 1$^{2.2}$ 94^{12} and some other parts of Chr., e.g. 1 Ch 22^{12} 2 Ch 6^{16} (= 1 K 8^{25} without ת׳), refers to Deuteronomic code. (3) other passages of Chr. may refer to code of D, but most of them certainly refer to *the law of the Priests' code*. The same is true of Mal Dn and late ψψ. The phrases are: (ספר) תורת משה 2 Ch 23^{18} 30^{16} Ezr 3^{2} 7^{6} Ne 8^{1} Mal 3^{22} Dn 9$^{11.13}$; (ספר) תורת יהוה Ezr 7^{10} Ne 9^{3} 1 Ch 16^{40} 2 Ch 12^{1} 17^{9} 31$^{3.4}$ 34^{14} 35^{26} ψ 19^{8} 119^{1}; (ספר) תורת האלהים Ne$^{8.18}$ 10$^{29.30}$; ספר הַתּ׳ 8^{3}; דִּבְרֵי הַתּ׳ v$^{9.13}$; הַתּוֹרָה 2 Ch 14^{3} 31^{21} 33^{8} Ezr 10^{3} Ne 8$^{2.7.14}$ 10$^{35.37}$ 12^{44} 13^{3}; תּ׳ פִּיךָ ψ 119^{72}; תורתך Ne 9$^{26.29.34}$ Dn 9^{11} ψ 119$^{18.29.34.44.51.53.55.61.70.77.85.92.97.109.113.126.136.142.150.153.163.165.174}$; תּוֹרָה (indef.) ‖ חקים, מצוות Ne 9^{14}. **3.** *custom, manner*: תּוֹרַת הָאָדָם 2 S 7^{19} *the manner of man*, not of God, i.e. deal with me as man with man, Thes, *law for man* RV, but Ew

[Gesch. iii. 180] reads (וַתַּרְאֵנִי) דּוֹרֹת hast shewed me *generations of men*; so We Dr.—On ת׳ v. further Dr on Dt 1^{10} 24^{8} 33^{10} and reff.

† יוֹרַי (= יוֹרָיָה whom *Yah teacheth*) **n.pr.m.** 3140
chief of the tribe of Gad 1 Ch 5^{13}, 𝔊 Ιωρεε.

† יְרוּאֵל (*founded of Ēl*) **n.pr.loc.** מִדְבַּר י׳ 3385
2 Ch 20^{16}, 𝔊 Ιεριηλ, not identified, prob. part of wilderness of Judah, near Ziz (*Wady Hŭṣâṣah*).

† יְרִיאֵל (= יְרוּאֵל) **n.pr.m.** chief of tribe 3400
of Issachar, 1 Ch 7^{2}, 𝔊 Ρειηλ, Ιερεηλ; 𝔊L Ιαρουηλ.

יְרִיָּהוּ 1 Ch 23^{19} 24^{23}, יְרִיָּה 26^{31} **n.pr.m.** 3404
(cf. יְרִיאֵל) chief of one of the Levitical courses, 𝔊 Ιδουδ, Ιερια, Ιεδδι, Ιεδειμος, etc.

† [יָרָה] **vb.** only **Qal** *Impf.* 3 mpl. תִּירְהוּ 7297
Is 44^{8} (van d. H Baer, but prob. תִּרְהוּ si vera l., so Thes); ? *be stupefied* (cf. Ar. وَرِهَ, Thes al.), but Frey *fatuus et stolidus fuit*; < Ew al. who rd. תִּירְאוּ fr. ירא (‖ פחד).

יְרוּשָׁלַםִ, יְרוּשָׁלַיִם $_{644}$ **n.pr.loc. Jerusalem** 3389
(in As. *Urusalim*, Tel Amarna, Zim[ZA, 1891, 252, 254]; *Ursalimmu*, COT[Gloss.]; 𝔊 Ιερουσαλημ; √ and mng. dub.; Rel Ew al. der. fr. יְרוּשׁ שלם *possession of peace* (or *Salem's possession*); Thes al. fr. יָרָה, i.e. יְרוּ + שָׁלֵם *a foundation of peace*; Grill [ZAW, 1884, 134 ff.] *foundation of Shalem* (Sh. = God of peace, = י׳); but name not certainly Hebr.; acc. to Sayce[Acad. Feb. 7, 1891, 138; Higher Crit. 176] (opposed by Zim[ZA. 1891, 263]), Jastr[JBL xi, 1892, 105] = *Uru* (*city*) + *Salim*, n.pr.div.);—usu. יְרוּשָׁלַםִ (*Qr perpetuum*), Jos 10^{10} +; יְרוּשָׁלָםִ 1 S 17^{54} +; -לַיִם 5 t. acc. to Mas. (vid. Frensdorff[Mass. Magna, 293]), viz. Je 26^{18} 1 Ch 3^{5} 2 Ch 25^{1} 32^{9} (c. ה loc.), Est 2^{6}, (but -לָםִ 1 Ch 3^{5} van d. H Baer), so Maccab. coins, Levy[Gesch. d. jüd. Münz. 42 f.]; c. ה loc. יְרוּשָׁלַמָה 1 K 10^{2} Is 36^{2} Ez 8^{3}; (-לַיְמָה 2 Ch 32^{9} supr.); -לָמָה 2 K 9^{28}; with prefixes: בִּירו׳ 2 S 9^{13} +; לִירו׳ 2 K 18^{22} +; מִירו׳ 2 S 15^{11} +; וִירו׳ 1 K 23^{1} +;—*Jerusalem*, renowned as capital of all Israel, afterwards of southern kingdom, seat of central worship in temple, first named as city of Canaanite Adoni-Ṣedeḳ †Jos 10$^{1.3.5.23}$ (all JE), cf. 12^{10} (D); inhabited by Jebusites Jos 15$^{63.63}$ (P), Ju 1$^{21.21}$, cf. v^{7} (Adoni-Bezeḳ); identif. with יְבוּס Ju 19^{10}, and הַיְבוּסִי (q.v.) Jos 15^{8} 18^{28} (both P); captured by Judah Ju 1^{8}; first named in connexion with David 1 S 17^{54} †; taken pos-

session of by David as king 2 S 5^{6}; David's royal seat v$^{5.13.14}$ 8^{7} 11^{1}+; it remained the capital until taken by Nebuchadrezzar, B.C. 588, 2 K 25^{1}+; it became the chief home of the returned exiles Ezr 1^{11} 2^{11} Ne 2$^{11.17}$+; mentioned S 31 t., K 92 t., Ch 151 t., Ezr 25 t., Ne 38 t., Is^{1} 27 t., Is$^{2.3}$ 22 t., Je 107 t., Ez 26 t., Zc 41 t., etc.—Vid. also n.pr.loc. יְבוּס, שָׁלֵם.

ירח (√of foll.; meaning dub.; acc. to MV Buhl=ארח, of moon as *wanderer*, so Lag$^{BN 46}$).

3394 †**יָרֵחַ n.m.**$^{Jos 10, 13}$ **moon**, esp. poet. (NH *id.*; Ph. ירח; As. *iriḫu*, acc. to Pinches$^{BOR Aug. 1888, 207}$; Eth. **ወርኅ:** *moon, month;* cf. sub יֶרַח)—abs. יָרֵחַ Gn 37^{9} + 25 t.; sf. וִירֵחֵךְ Is 60^{20}:—*moon*, usually named with sun Jos 10$^{12.13}$ (poem in JE), ψ 72^{5} (עִם־שָׁמֶשׁ וְלִפְנֵי יָרֵחַ), 89^{38} (in these two, a symbol of permanence), 121^{6} Is 60^{19} Hb 3^{11} Jo 3^{4}; obj. of idolatrous worship Jb 31^{26} (+sun); in same sense also+sun and stars Dt 4^{19} 17^{3} 2 K 23^{5} Je 8^{2}; as determiner of feast-times ψ 104^{19} (‖ sun); +stars, as shining by night ψ 136^{9} (‖ sun, by day), so חֻקֹּת יָרֵחַ Je 31^{35} (‖ *id.*); elsewh. + sun and stars Gn 37^{9} (E), Is 13^{10} Ez 32^{7} Jo 2^{10} 4^{15} ψ 148^{3} Ec 12^{2}; +stars ψ 8^{4} Jb 25^{5}; with neither sun nor stars only עַד־בְּלִי יָרֵחַ ψ 72^{7}.

3391 †I. **יֶרַח n.m.**$^{Zc 11, 8}$ **month** (Aram. יַרְחָא, ܝܰܪܚܳܐ *new moon, month;* Palm. ירח Vog$^{No. 1}$; As. *arḫu* COT$^{Gloss.}$ Muss-Arnolt$^{JBL xi. 1892, 73, 163}$; cf. Ph. Eth. sub יָרֵחַ; Sab. ורח *month*, DHM$^{ZMG 1876, 603; 1883, 369}$ Hal$^{JAS vii, 1, 516}$)—abs. יֶרַח 1 K 6^{37} + 3 t.; cstr. *id.* Dt 21^{13} 2 K 15^{13}; pl. יְרָחִים Ex 2^{2} + 3 t.; cstr. יַרְחֵי Jb 7^{3} 29^{2};—**1.** *month*, as measure of time, during, or in which Ex 2^{2} (E), Zc 11^{8} Jb 39^{2}; יַרְחֵי שָׁוְא Jb 7^{3}; יַרְחֵי קֶדֶם 29^{2}; pleon. יֶרַח יָמִים *a month (of) days=a month of time* Dt 21^{13} 2 K 15^{13}. **2.** *calendar month*, with name יֶרַח זִו 1 K 6^{37} (2nd mo., cf. v^{1}); יֶרַח בּוּל v^{38} (8th mo.); יֶרַח הָאֵתָנִים 1 K 8^{2} (7th mo.); cf. בְּמִסְפַּר יְרָחִים אַל־יָבֹא Jb 3^{6}; גֶּרֶשׁ יְרָחִים Dt 33^{4} *produce of months*, i.e. of various seasons of year.—Cf. synon. חֹדֶשׁ.

3392 †II. [**יֶרַח**] **n.pr.m.** 'son' of Joktan, only יָרַח Gn 10^{26} (𝔊 Ιαραδ, 𝔊L Ιεραχ)=1 Ch 1^{20} (𝔊L Ιαρε).

3386 †**יָרוֹחַ n.pr.m.** a Gadite, 1 Ch 5^{14}; 𝔊 Ιδαι, 𝔊L Αρουε.

3405 **יְרֵחוֹ** v. יְרִיחוֹ below

3395-96 **יְרַחְמְאֵל, יְרֹחָם** v. sub רחם. p. 934

†**יַרְחָע n.pr.m.** an Egyptian slave 1 Ch 2$^{34.35}$; 𝔊 Ιωχηλ, 𝔊L Ιερεε. 3398

†**יָרַט vb. be precipitate, precipitate** (trans.) (cf. Ar. وَرَّطَ *conjecit, praecipitem dedit in puteum, exitium*, Frey.)—**Qal** *Pf.* יָרַט Nu 22^{32}, app. c. subj. הַדֶּרֶךְ; the way *is precipitate*, (RV^{m} *headlong*) *before me*, but transit. עַל־יְדֵי רשעים ירטני Jb 16^{11} *into the hands of wicked men he precipitates me* (v. Di; יִרְטֵנִי=יִרְטֵנִי; Baer's text יִרְטֵנִי points to √רטה q. v.); hence perh. rd. יָרַטְתָּ Nu 22^{32}; *thou hast precipitated the journey* in front of me, i.e. rushed recklessly in front of me; v. Di; Kau^{AT} leaves untransl. 3399

יְרִיחוֹ, יְרִיחֹה, יְרֵחוֹ$_{57}$ **n.pr.loc. Jericho** (on form see Baer on Jos 2^{1} Je 39^{5} Kö$^{Einl. 49}$; √ and mng. dub.; acc. to Thes al. from רֵוַח, =*regio fragrans*, the district abounding in palms, rose-gardens, balsam, etc.);—יְרִיחוֹ Jos 2^{1} + 27 t. Jos. (19 t. JE, 3 t. D, 6 t. P), + 5 t. 2 K 2; יְרִחוֹ Jos 18^{21} 2 S 10^{5} Je 39^{5} 52^{8}; יְרִיחֹה 1 K 16^{34}; יְרֵחוֹ Dt 34^{1} (P), v^{3} (D), Nu 22^{1} (P) + 9 t. P, 2 K 25^{5} Ezr 2^{34} Ne 3^{2} 7^{36} + 3 t. Ch;—Canaanit. city taken by Josh. Jos 6^{1} (JE)+; having a king 2$^{2.3}$ 8^{2} 10^{1} (all JE), 10$^{28.30}$ 12^{9} (all D); near Jordan, whence (יְרִיחוֹ) יַרְדֵּן יְרֵחוֹ, v. יַרְדֵּן supr.; Mt. Nebo is described as עַל־פְּנֵי יְרֵחוֹ Dt 32^{49} 34^{1} (P); (called עִיר הַתְּמָרִים Jud 1^{16} 3^{13}; so in appos. Dt 34^{3} 2 Ch 28^{15}); the adjacent plain is called בִּקְעַת יְרֵחוֹ Dt 34^{3} (JE); עַרְבוֹת יְרֵחוֹ 2 K 25^{5}=Je 39^{5}=52^{8}; ע׳ יְרִיחוֹ Jos 4^{13} 5^{10} (both P); among returning exiles appear בְּנֵי יְרֵחוֹ Ezr 2^{34}=Ne 7^{36}, and among builders of wall אַנְשֵׁי יְרֵחוֹ Ne 3^{2} (BeRy Ryle *ad loc.* and Ezr 2^{34});—mod. *(E)rîḥâ;* see also GASm$^{Geogr. 266 ff.}$ 3405

ירך (√of foll.; meaning dubious).

†**יָרֵךְ n.f.**$^{Nu 5, 27}$ **thigh, loin, side, base** (NH *id.*; Aram. יַרְכָּא; Zinj. ירך *loin;* As. *arku, arkâtu, back, rear, hereafter* Dl$^{HWB 242}$; Ar. وَرِكٌ *hip*)—abs. יָרֵךְ Ju 15^{8} + 6 t.; cstr. יֶרֶךְ Gn 24^{9} + 11 t. + 2 S 3^{27} (v. infr.); sf. יְרֵכִי Gn 24^{2} 47^{29}; יְרֵכֵךְ Nu 5^{21}; יְרֵכוֹ Gn 32^{26} + 6 t.; יְרֵכָהּ Ex 25^{31} + 3 t.; du. יְרֵכַיִם Ex 28^{42}; sf. יְרֵכַיִךְ Ct 7^{2};—**1.** *thigh*, **a.** outside of thigh, where sword was worn, שִׂים חַרְבּוֹ עַל־יְרֵכוֹ Ex 32^{27} (E); וַיַּחְגֹּר אֹתָהּ עַל־יֶרֶךְ יְמִינוֹ Ju 3^{16} *and he girded it upon his right thigh*, v^{21} ψ 45^{4} Ct 3^{8}; כַּף הַיָּרֵךְ Gn 32^{33} *hollow of the thigh*, v$^{26.26.33}$ (all J); חַמּוּקֵי יְרֵכַיִךְ Ct 7^{2} *the roundings of thy thighs;* מִמָּתְנַיִם וְעַד־יְרֵכַיִם Ex 28^{42} (P); ‖ בֶּטֶן Nu 5$^{21.22.27}$ (P); צָלַע עַל־יְרֵכוֹ 3409

Gn 32^{32}(J), *limping upon his thigh;* סָפַק עַל־יָרֵךְ Je 31^{19} and (c. אֶל־) Ez 21^{17}, *smite upon thigh,* in token of consternation; וַיַּךְ אוֹתָם שׁוֹק עַל־יָרֵךְ Ju 15^{8} *and he smote them, hip upon thigh,* a great slaughter. **b.** *thigh=loins,* as seat of procreative power (RS$^{K. 34; Sem. i, 360 (380)}$) יֹצְאֵי ירך *those proceeding from the loins of* any one Gn 46^{26} Ex 1^{5} (both P), Ju 8^{30}; hence שִׂים יַד תַּחַת ירך *place the hand under thigh,* in taking oath Gn 24$^{2.9}$ (J), 47^{29}. **2.** *side* (flank) of altar 2 K 16^{14} Lv 1^{11} (P); of tabernacle Ex 40$^{22.24}$ Nu 3$^{29.35}$ (all P); also יֶרֶךְ הַשַּׁעַר (for MT תּוֹךְ הַשּׁ׳) 𝔊 Th We Dr Bu Kit. **3.** *base* (loins) of candlestick Ex 25^{31} 37^{17} Nu 8^{4} (all P).

3411 †[יַרְכָה], or יְרֵכָה Ol$^{§ 167. g}$] **flank, side,** du. **extreme parts, recesses**;—sf. יַרְכָתוֹ Gn 49^{13}; du. יַרְכָתַיִם Ex 26^{27} 36^{32} + Ez 46^{19} Qr (Kt ירכתם); יַרְכָתָיִם Ex 26^{23} 36^{28}; cstr. יַרְכְּתֵי Ju 19^{1} + 20 t. + 1 K 6^{16} Qr (Kt ירכותי);—**1.** *side,* i.e. *further side* of Zebulun, poet. for more distant border of his territory Gn 49^{13}. **2.** elsewhere always du. *the two thighs,* i.e. fig. *angle, recess, extreme parts:* as *recesses* of Mt. Ephr. Ju 19$^{1.18}$; of Lebanon 2 K 19^{23}=Is 37^{24}; of *recesses* or *innermost part* of a cave 1 S 24^{4}; a house Am 6^{10} ψ 128^{3}; the pit (בּוֹר) Is 14^{15} (‖ שְׁאוֹל), Ez 32^{23}; a ship Jon 1^{5}; יַרְכְּתֵי צָפוֹן *remote parts of the north* Is 14^{13} Ez 38$^{6.15}$ 39^{2} ψ 48^{3} (but here Lag. prop. יר׳ רצון); יַרְכְּתֵי אָרֶץ *remote parts of earth* Je 6^{22} 25^{32} 31^{8} 50^{41}; of a long building, *extreme* or *hinder part,* so of tabernacle Ex 26$^{22.23.27}$ 36$^{27.28.32}$ (all P); of temple 1 K 6^{16}; of Ezek.'s temple Ez 46^{19}.

3412 †יַרְמוּת **n.pr.loc. 1.** 𝔊 Ιερ(ε)ιμουθ, Canaanitish city, with a king, named between Hebron and Lachish Jos 10$^{3.5.23}$ (JE), 12^{11} (D); named with Adullam 15^{35} (P), cf. Ne 11^{29}. **2.** 𝔊 Ρεμμαθ, A 𝔊L Ιερμωθ, Levitical city in Issachar Jos 21^{29} (P).

3413 †יְרֵמַי **n.pr.m.** one of those who had strange wives Ezr 10^{33}; 𝔊 Ιεραμει(μ).

3406 †יְרִימוֹת, יְרֵמוֹת, יְרִמוֹת, יְרֵימוֹת **n.pr.m.** 𝔊 Αρειμωθ, Ιεριμουθ, etc.;—**1.** Benjamites: **a.** יְרִימוֹת 1 Ch 7^{7}. **b.** יְרֵימוֹת 1 Ch 7^{8}. **c.** יְרֵמוֹת 1 Ch 8^{14}. **2.** Levites: **a.** יְרֵמוֹת 1 Ch 23^{23}. **b.** *id.* 1 Ch 25^{22}=**c.** יְרִימוֹת 24^{30}. **d.** יְרִימוֹת 1 Ch 25^{4}. **e.** *id.* 2 Ch 31^{13}. **3.** *id.* Naphtalite 1 Ch 27^{19}. **4.** *id.* son of David and father of Rehoboam's wife 2 Ch 11^{18}. **5.** יְרֵמוֹת, men who had strange wives: **a.** Ezr 10^{26}, 𝔊 Ιερειμοιθ (-μωθ). **b.** Ezr 10^{27}, 𝔊 Αμων, א Αρμων, A Ιαρμωθ, 𝔊L Ιεριμωθ. **c.** Ezr 10^{29} Kt (Qr וְרָמוֹת), 𝔊 Μημων, A Ρημωθ, 𝔊L Αριμωθ.

יִרְמְיָהוּ ,יִרְמְיָה v. sub רמה. p. 941 3414

†[יָרַע] **vb. quiver** (cf. Ar. وَرِعَ *be timid, weak;* وَرَعٌ *pious fear;* 𝔗 יְרַע *be disheartened*) —**Qal** *Pf.* 3 fs. נַפְשׁוֹ יָרְעָה לוֹ Is 15^{4} *his soul quivereth* to him, i.e. is in terror and distress. 3415

יְרִיעָה$_{54}$ **n.f. curtain** (𝔗 יְרִיעֲתָא, Syr. ܝܪܝܥܬܐ) —abs. יְרִיעָה Ex 26^{2} + 24 t.; pl. abs. יְרִיעֹת Ex 26^{1} + 17 t.; יְרִיעוֹת 1 Ch 17^{1}; cstr. יְרִיעֹת Ex 26^{7} + 4 t.; יְרִיעוֹת Hb 3^{7} + 2 t.; sf. יְרִיעֹתַי Je 4^{20} 10^{20}; יְרִיעוֹתֵיהֶם Je 49^{29};—*curtain,* of tabern. Ex 26$^{1.2.2.2.8.8}$ + 38 t. Ex 26 and 36; Nu 4^{25} (all P); 2 S 7^{2}=1 Ch 17^{1};—in gen. (*tent-*) *curtains* Je 4^{20} 10^{20} 49^{29} Hb 3^{7} Ct 1^{5} (in all ‖ אֹהֶל); יְרִיעֹת . . . יַטּוּ Is 54^{2} (‖ הַרְחִיבִי מְקוֹם אָהֳלֵךְ), fig. of Jerusalem's prosperity; in sim. נוֹטֶה שָׁמַיִם כַּיְרִיעָה ψ 104^{2}. 3407

†יְרִיעוֹת **n.pr.m.**(?) only 1 Ch 2^{18}, where rd. perh. בַּת־יר׳ for MT וְאֶת־יר׳, see We VB; 𝔊 Ελιωθ, A 𝔊L Ιερ(ε)ιωθ. 3408

יִרְפְּאֵל v. sub רפא. p. 951 3416

I. ירק (√ of foll.; NH Hiph.; Aram. Aph. אוֹרִיק *grow green;* ܝܪܩ *be pale,* and deriv.; As. *arâku, grow pale* (of face), *arḳu,* yellow, green, etc., Dl$^{HWB 243}$; Ar. وَرَقٌ *leaf,* وَرَّقَ *put forth leaves,* cf. وُرْقَةٌ *ash-colour,* أَوْرَقُ *dusky-white,* of camel, وَرِقٌ *silver coin* Lag$^{BN 30}$; Sab. ורק *gold* (כתם וורק), Hal$^{ÉS, JAs. Déc. 1874, Nos. 47, 97}$ DHM$^{VOJ i. 26 f.}$, and Eth. ወርቅ: *gold,* both from *colour* acc. to DHM Di).

†יֶרֶק **n.m.**$^{Is 15, 6}$ **green, greenness** (on ܝܘܪܩܐ in gardens, v. Nö$^{ZMG 1876, 777}$ Löw$^{p. 236 f.}$)—abs. Ex 10^{15} Is 15^{6}; cstr. Gn 1^{30} + 3 t.;—יֶרֶק עֵשֶׂב Gn 1^{30} 9^{3} (both P); יֶרֶק דֶּשֶׁא ψ 37^{2}; יֶרֶק הַשָּׂדֶה Nu 22^{4} (E)=*green thing, grass;* alone Ex 10^{15} (J) *green thing,* incl. עֵץ and עֵשֶׂב, Is 15^{6}. 3418

†יָרָק **n.[m.] herbs** (coll.), **herbage** (green, greens)—abs. יָרָק Dt 11^{10} + 2 t.; cstr. יְרַק Is 37^{27} = 2 K 19^{26};—גַּן־יָרָק Dt 11^{10} 1 K 21^{2}; אֲרֻחַת יָרָק Pr 15^{17}; as subst., יְרַק דֶּשֶׁא Is 37^{27}=2 K 19^{26} *green shoots of grass* (‖ עֵשֶׂב שָׂדֶה, etc.) 3419

יַרְקוֹן only in מֵי הַיּ׳ Jos 19^{46} v. sub מַי. p. 566 4313

†יָרוֹק **n.[m.] green thing** (=יֶרֶק), only as food of wild ass Jb 39^{8}. 3387

3420 †יֵרָקוֹן **n.m. mildew, paleness, lividness;** **1.** *mildew* Am 4^{9} Dt 28^{22} 1 K 8^{37} Hg 2^{17} 2 Ch 6^{28} (all ‖ שִׁדָּפוֹן). **2.** *paleness* (of face) Je 30^{6}.

3422 †יְרַקְרַק (Sta$^{§ 156, 234}$) **adj. greenish, pale-green** (cf. As. *rakrakku*, Zim$^{BP 37}$)—Lv 13^{49} ψ 68^{14}; fpl. יְרַקְרַקּוֹת Lv 14^{37};—of plague spots Lv 13^{49} 14^{37}; as subst., ψ 68^{14} the *green-shimmering* (Che) of gold.

3421 †יָרְקְעָם **n.pr.m.** a name in Judah 1 Ch 2^{44}; 𝔊 Ιακλαν, A Ιερκααν, 𝔊L Ιερακαμ (and so for רֶקֶם v^{b}; otherwise רקם v^{43}).

3417 †II. יָרַק **vb. spit** (Eth. ወረቀ: *id.;* acc. to Lag$^{BN 200}$ II. ירק is not separate √; cf. יֵרָקוֹן, and Ar. يَرَقَانٌ *robigo*)—**Qal** *Pf.* and *Inf. abs.* יָרֹק יָרַק בְּפָנֶיהָ Nu 12^{14}; 3 fs. consec. וְיָרְקָה בְּפָנָיו Dt 25^{9}; both, as token of contempt. Cf. רקק, רֹק.

3423 יָרַשׁ$_{229}$ **vb. take possession of, inherit, dispossess** (MI^{7} וירש *take possession of;* Aram. יְרֵית, ܝܪܬ, *take possession of,* and *be heir to, inherit;* so Eth. ወረሰ: Ar. وَرِثَ *inherit;* v. also Sab. ורת *inherit,* CIS$^{iv, 37, 3}$), esp. D (62 t. Qal, 1 t. Pi, 7 t. Hiph. in Dt + 13 t. D in Jos);—**Qal** *Pf.* 3 ms. יָרַשׁ Je 49^{1}; וְיָרַשׁ consec. Je 49^{2} Nu 27^{11}; 2 ms. יָרַשְׁתָּ 1 K 21^{19}; וְיָרַשְׁתָּ Dt 6^{18} + 2 t.; sf. וִירִשְׁתָּהּ consec. Dt 17^{14} + 2 t. (on this and kindred forms v. Kö$^{i. 406, 411}$); וִירִשְׁתֶּם consec. Dt 19^{1} 31^{3}; 3 pl. יָרְשׁוּ Dt 3^{20} +; sf. וִירֵשׁוּךָ consec. Ez 36^{12} (Kö$^{l.c.}$); וִירֵשׁוּהָ consec. Is 34^{11} + 3 t.; 2 mpl. וִירִשְׁתֶּם consec. Dt 4^{1} + 7 t.; 1 pl. יָרַשְׁנוּ Dt 3^{12}, etc.; *Impf.* 3 ms. יִירַשׁ Gn 21^{10} ψ 25^{13}; 2 mpl. תִּירְשׁוּ Lv 20^{24} 1 Ch 28^{8}; תִּירָשׁוּ Ez 33$^{25.26}$; תִּירָשׁוּן Dt 5^{30}, etc.; *Imv.* ms. יְרָשׁ Dt 33^{23}; רֵשׁ Dt 1^{21} 1 K 21^{15}; רָשׁ Dt 2$^{24.31}$; mpl. רְשׁוּ Dt 1^{8} 9^{23}; *Inf. cstr.* לָרֶשֶׁת Dt 2^{31} + 17 t.; לָרֶשֶׁת Ne 9^{23}; sf. לְרִשְׁתְּךָ Gn 28^{4}; לְרִשְׁתּוֹ 1 K 21$^{16.18}$; לְרִשְׁתָּהּ Gn 15^{7} + 28 t.; *Pt.* יוֹרֵשׁ Gn 15^{3} + 6 t.; pl. יֹ(וֹ)רְשִׁים Dt 12^{2} Je 8^{10}; sf. יֹרְשָׁיו Je 49^{2};—**1.** *take possession of,* esp. by force, *have as a possession,* often with collat. idea of *taking in place of* others, *succeeding to, inheriting* (cf. **2**): **a.** land, sq. acc. Gn 15$^{7.8}$ Nu 13^{30} 21$^{24.35}$ Jos 18^{13} (all JE), 24$^{4.8}$ (E), Ju 2^{6} 11$^{21.22.23.24.24}$ 18^{9} Dt 1$^{8.21.39}$ + 25 t. Dt, + †Dt 11^{31} 17^{14} 26^{1} (all *possess* land *and dwell therein*), similarly Is 65$^{9.9}$ ψ 69^{36}; בְּאַרְצָם מִשְׁנֶה יִירָשׁוּ Is 61^{7} *in their land they shall possess the double;* הָחֵל רָשׁ Dt 2^{24}; הָחֵל רָשׁ לָרֶשֶׁת אֶת־אַרְצוֹ v^{31}; esp. phr. (הארץ) אֲשֶׁר אַתֶּם בָּאִים (עֹבְרִים etc.) שָׁמָּה לְרִשְׁתָּהּ Dt 4$^{5.14.26}$ + 12 t. Dt, also Ezr 9^{10}; v. Dt 30^{18} Jos 1$^{11.11.15.15}$ 12^{1} 13^{1} 21^{41} 23^{5} (all D); Am 2^{10} Ob$^{19.19}$ Hb 1^{6} Ez 33$^{24.25.26}$ Lv 20$^{24.24}$ (H), Gn 28^{4} Nu 33^{53} (both P), 1 Ch 28^{8} Ne 9$^{15.22.23.24}$; ψ 25^{13} 37$^{9.11.22.29.34}$; + ב instr. 44^{4}; also וַעֲמַל לְאֻמִּים יִירָשׁוּ 105^{44} (‖ וַיִּתֵּן לָהֶם אַרְצוֹת גּוֹיִם); †*take possession of* fields Je 8^{10} (obj. not expr.), 1 K 21$^{15.16.18.19}$ ψ 83^{13}; inheritance (in land) Nu 27^{11} 36$^{8.8}$ (all P); city (cities), Jos 19^{47} (JE), Ju 3^{13} Ob^{20}; so הַר־קָדְשִׁי Is 57^{13} (‖ נחל ארץ), 63^{18} where rd. prob. הַר־קָדְשֶׁךָ (for MT עַם־ק׳, see 𝔊 VB and ‖ cl.); *possess* city and dwell therein 2 K 17^{24} Is 34^{17}; Is 34^{11} yea the pelican and bittern shall *possess* it; so of nettles Ho 9^{6}; וְיִרַשׁ זַרְעֲךָ אֵת שַׁעַר אֹיְבָיו Gn 22^{17}, cf. 24^{60} (both J); *possess* houses Ez 7^{24} (del. Co), Ne 9^{25}; יוֹרֵשׁ עֶצֶר Ju 18^{7} *possessing wealth* (? see VB)†. †**b.** a *people* (with collat. idea of *being their heir* (**2**), and so *dispossessing them*), so esp. in Dt 2$^{12.21.22}$ 9^{1} (+ cities), 11^{23} 12$^{2.29.29}$ 18^{14} 19^{1} 31^{3}; Nu 21^{32} (Kt וַיִּירַשׁ; JE), Am 9^{12}; מַדּוּעַ יָרַשׁ מַלְכָּם אֶת־גָּד Je 49^{1} (on text see VB), v$^{2.2}$ (in these 3 perh. play on meaning *inherit,* cf. v^{1a}); Ez 36^{12} Ob^{17} Is 54^{3}; nations + countries Ez 35^{10}. †**2.** *inherit,* sq. acc. pers. = *be one's heir* Gn 15$^{3.4.4}$ (JE); שִׁפְחָה כִּי־תִירַשׁ גְּבִרְתָּהּ Pr 30^{23} (or, *dispossess* ?); abs. *be heir,* sq. עִם pers. = jointly with 21^{10} (E); (הַ)יּוֹרֵשׁ (*the*) *heir* 2 S 14^{7} Je 49^{1} (‖ בָּנִים); Mi 1^{15} (= possessor, captor), where paronom. with n. pr. loc. מָרֵשָׁה; *inherit* persons, as slaves לָרֶשֶׁת אֲחֻזָּה Lv 25^{46} (H). †**3.** = *impoverish,* הַלְיָרְשֵׁנוּ קְרָאתֶם Ju 14^{15} *to impoverish us did ye call* (us)?

†**Niph.** *Impf.* יִוָּרֵשׁ Pr 23^{21}; 2 ms. תִּוָּרֵשׁ Gn 45^{11} Pr 20^{13}; אִוָּרֵשׁ Pr 30^{9};—*be* (*dispossessed* =) *impoverished, come to poverty* Gn 45^{11} (E), Pr 20^{13} 23^{21} 30^{9} (opp. אֶשְׂבַּע).

†**Pi.** *Impf.* פְּרִי אַדְמָתְךָ יְיָרֵשׁ הַצְּלָצַל Dt 28^{42} *the fruit of thy ground shall the cricket get full possession of* (cf. Qal Ho 9^{6} Is 34^{11}), i.e. *devour.*

†**Hiph.** *Pf.* 3 ms. הוֹרִישׁ Ju 1^{27} +; 2 ms. הוֹרַשְׁתָּ 2 Ch 20^{7} ψ 44^{3}, etc.; *Impf.* 3 ms. יוֹרִישׁ Jos 3^{10}; וַיֹּ(וֹ)רֶשׁ Ju 1^{19} +; 3 fs. sf. 3 mpl. תּוֹרִישֵׁמוֹ Ex 15^{9}, etc.; *Inf. abs.* הוֹרֵשׁ Jos 3^{10} 17^{13}; הוֹרִישׁ Ju 1^{28}; *cstr.* לְהוֹרִישׁ Dt 4^{38} +, etc.; *Pt.* מוֹרִישׁ 1 S 2^{7} Dt 18^{12}; sf. מוֹרִישָׁם Dt 9$^{4.5}$;—**1.** *cause to possess,* or *inherit* Ju 11^{24}; מִירֻשָּׁתְךָ אֲשֶׁר הוֹרַשְׁתָּנוּ 2 Ch 20^{11}; sq. ל pers., וְהוֹרַשְׁתֶּם לִבְנֵיכֶם Ezr 9^{12} *and cause your sons to inherit* (it); fig. תּוֹרִישֵׁנִי עֲוֹנוֹת נְעוּרָי Jb 13^{26} *thou makest me to inherit* (the consequences of) *the iniquities of my youth.*

2. *cause* (others) *to possess* or *inherit*, then gen. *dispossess:* **a.** sq. acc. gent. vel pers., Jos 13^{13} 16^{10} (both JE), Ju $1^{29.30.31.32.33}$ (all opp. ישׁב בְּקֶרֶב), Jos 14^{12}(JE), 17^{13} (JE; הוֹרֵשׁ לֹא הוֹרִישׁוֹ), Ju 1^{28} (*id.*); opp. ישׁב אֶת Jos 15^{63}; opp. ישׁב בְּ Ju $1^{21.27}$; also Nu 21^{32} Qr, 32^{39} Jos 17^{18} (all JE), 13^{12} (D), Ju 1^{19b} 2^{23}; also וַיֹּרֶשׁ אֶת־הָהָר 1^{19a} (= וְהוֹרַשְׁתֶּם את־יושבי ההר see v^b), Dt 7^{17} ψ 44^3; וְהַאֲבַדְתָּם Dt 9^3; sq. acc. + מִפְּנֵי Ex 34^{24} Nu 32^{21} Jos 3^{10} (הוֹרֵשׁ יוֹרִישׁ; all these JE), Dt 4^{38} $9^{4.5}$ 18^{12} Jos 13^6 23^9 (both D), Nu $33^{52.55}$ (both P), Ju 2^{21} $11^{23.24}$ 1 K 14^{24} 21^{26} 2 K 16^3 17^8 21^2 (all D), 2 Ch 28^3 33^2; acc. + מִלִּפְנֵי Dt 11^{23} Jos $23^{5.13}$ (D; ‖ הָדַף), 2 Ch 20^7; acc. + מִשָּׁם Jos 15^{14} (JE) = Ju 1^{20}; of *cities* (i.e. their inhabitants) Jos 8^7 17^{12}; so of a *land* = Nu 33^{53} (P), see $v^{52.55}$ [𝔊 + יושבי]. **b.** sq. acc. rei, מִבִּטְנוֹ יֹרִשֶׁנּוּ אֵל Jb 20^{15} *God shall cast them out of his belly*, i.e. riches (‖ חַיִל בָּלַע וַיְקִאֶנּוּ). **3.** = *impoverish*, יהוה מוֹרִישׁ וּמַעֲשִׁיר 1 S 2^7 (song) י׳ *impoverisheth and maketh rich;* sq. acc. (of Tyre) אֲדֹנָי יוֹרִשֶׁנָּה Zc 9^4 (see v^3). **4.** nearly = *bring to ruin, destroy*, sq. acc. gent. אָרִיק חַרְבִּי תּוֹרִישֵׁמוֹ יָדִי Ex 15^9 (poem in E); so perh. also Nu 14^{12} (JE; AV *disinherit;* ‖ אַכֶּנּוּ בַדֶּבֶר). **5.** = **Qal** *take possession of* a land Nu 14^{24} (JE), but rd. prob. יְרֻשֶׁנָּה.

3424 †יְרֵשָׁה **n.f.** a possession, used of nation וְהָיָה אֱדוֹם יְרֵשָׁה וְהָיָה יְרֵשָׁה שֵׂעִיר אֹיְבָיו Nu 24^{18} (JE).

3388 †יְרוּשָׁא, יְרוּשָׁה **n.pr.f.** (*taken possession of*, i.e. *married?*) mother of king Jotham: יְרוּשָׁא 2 K 15^{33} = יְרוּשָׁה 2 Ch 27^1.

3425 †יְרֻשָּׁה **n.f.** (a) **possession, inheritance**;—abs. יר׳ Dt 2^5 + 7 t., cstr. יְרֻשַּׁת Ju 21^{17} ψ 61^6 (but on text v. infr.); sf. יְרֻשָּׁתְךָ 2 Ch 20^{11}; יְרֻשָּׁתוֹ Dt 2^{12} 3^{20}; יְרֻשַּׁתְכֶם Jos 1^{15};—used of land Dt $2^{5.9.9.19.19}$ 3^{20}; אֶרֶץ יְרֻשָּׁתוֹ 2^{12} *the land of his possession*, so Jos 1^{15}; further, $12^{6.7}$ Ju 21^{17} (but Bu[RS 152] נִשְׁאֲרָה), Je 32^8 ψ 61^6 (but < אֲרֶשֶׁת *request*, cf. Che[crit. n.]), 2 Ch 20^{11}.

7568 †רֶשֶׁת **n.f.**[Ex 27, 5] **net**;—abs. רֶשֶׁת Ho 5^1 + 11 t.; רָשֶׁת Pr 1^{17}; cstr. רֶשֶׁת Ex 27^4 38^4; sf. רִשְׁתִּי Ho 7^{12} + 2 t.; רִשְׁתּוֹ ψ 10^9 35^8; רִשְׁתָּם Ez 19^8 ψ 35^7;—**1.** *net:* **a.** for catching (birds, etc.) חִנָּם מְזֹרָה הָרָשֶׁת Pr 1^{17} *to no purpose is the net spread* in the eyes of any bird; elsewhere fig. (1) of judgment of י׳, all c. פרשׂ: Ho 7^{12} (‖ כְּעוֹף הַשָּׁמַיִם אוֹרִידֵם), Ez 12^{13} 17^{20} (both ‖ מְצוּדָתִי), 32^3 (of י׳ catching Pharaoh, under fig. of sea-monster; ‖ II. חֵרֶם); (2) of nations capturing king of Israel under fig. of lion 19^8 (c. פרשׂ; ‖ שַׁחְתָּם); (3) of priests and rulers (as entangling people in sin) Ho 5^1 (‖ פַּח). **b.** spread for feet of man (fig.): (1) by י׳ La 1^{13} (c. פָּרַשׂ); (2) by wicked (= *plot*) Pr 29^5 (c. פרשׂ), ψ 140^6 (c. *id.*; ‖ טָמַן פַּח), 10^9 25^{15}, שֻׁלַּח בְּרֶשֶׁת בְּרַגְלָיו Jb 18^8 (‖ שְׂבָכָה); elsewh. c. טמן ψ 9^{16} (‖ שַׁחַת), 31^5 35^7 (שַׁחַת רִשְׁתָּם), v^8; c. הֵכִין 57^7 (‖ שִׁיחָה). **2.** brazen *network* for altar of tabern. מִכְבַּר מַעֲשֵׂה ר׳ נְחֹשֶׁת Ex $27^{4.5}$; הָרֶשֶׁת 27^4 = 38^4 (all P).—On Inf. רֶשֶׁת, v. ירשׁ supr.

†[מוֹרָשׁ] **n.[m.] a possession**;—cstr. מוֹרַשׁ 4180
וְיָרְשׁוּ בֵּית קִפֹּד Is 14^{23} *a possession for bitterns;* יַעֲקֹב אֵת מוֹרָשֵׁיהֶם Ob[17] *and the house of Jacob shall possess their possessions* (but rd. perhaps מורישיהם *their dispossessors*, 𝔊 𝔙 𝔗 al.); fig. מוֹרָשֵׁי לְבָבִי Jb 17^{11}, i.e. *my cherished thoughts* (‖ זִמֹּתַי), but fig. is questionable, v. Di, who derives from ארשׁ *desire*, so Buhl.

†מוֹרָשָׁה **n.f. a possession**;—מ׳ Ex 6^8 + 4181
8 t.;—of land Dt 33^4 (poem), Ex 6^8 (P), Ez 11^{15} 25^{10} 33^{24} $36^{2.5}$; of people Ez 25^4 36^3.

†מוֹרֶשֶׁת **n.pr.loc.** apparently in neigh- 4182
bourhood of Gath Mi 1^{14} (גַּת vocative, acc. to 1661
We; > most, who render *M. of Gath*); prob. home of prophet Micah, v. foll.

†מ(ו)רַשְׁתִּי **adj. gent.** only מִיכָה הַמֹּרַשְׁתִּי 4183
Mi 1^1, מִיכָיָה הַמּ׳ Je 26^{18}; v. foregoing.

†תִּירוֹשׁ **n.m.**[Ju 9, 13] **must, fresh** or **new** 8492
wine;—abs. תִּירוֹשׁ Nu 18^{12} + 24 t.; תִּירשׁ Gn 27^{28} + 3 t.; sf. תִּירוֹשִׁי Ju 9^{13} Ho 2^{11}; תִּירשְׁךָ Dt 7^{13} + 4 t. Dt; תִּירוֹשֵׁךְ Is 62^8; תִּירוֹשָׁם ψ 4^8;—*must, new wine*, as enlivening ת׳ הַמְשַׂמֵּחַ אֱלֹהִים וַאֲנָשִׁים Ju 9^{13}; as injurious זְנוּת וְיַיִן וְת׳ יִקַּח־לֵב Ho 4^{11}; poet. regarded as contained in the grapes יִמָּצֵא הַתּ׳ בָּאֶשְׁכּוֹל Is 65^8, cf. 24^7 (‖ גֶּפֶן); as yielding wine (‖ יַיִן), תִּדְרֹךְ זַיִת וְלֹא תָסוּךְ שֶׁמֶן וְת׳ וְלֹא תִשְׁתֶּה יָּיִן Mi 6^{15}; usu. as a sign of fertility, or as valuable product: וְת׳ יְקָבֶיךָ יִפְרֹצוּ Pr 3^{10} *with must thy vats shall burst open;* + דָּגָן (q.v.) Gn $27^{28.37}$ (both J) Ho 2^{11} 7^{14} Zc 9^{17} ψ 4^8 Is 62^8; ת׳ Ho 9^2 (‖ יֶקֶב, גֹּרֶן, cf. v^1); אֶרֶץ ד׳ וְת׳ Dt 33^{28}; + יִצְהָר Jo 2^{24} Ne 10^{38} (+ פְּרִי כָל־עֵץ); + דָּגָן and יִצְהָר Ho 2^{10} 3^{24} Dt 7^{13} 11^{14} 12^{17} 14^{23} 18^4 28^{51} Je 31^{12} Hg 1^{11} Jo 1^{10} 2^{19} 2 Ch 32^{28} Ne 5^{11} 10^{40} $13^{5.12}$; חֵלֶב ת׳ Nu 18^{12} (v. ח׳; + *id.*); ת׳ 2 Ch 31^5 + דגן, יצהר, and דְּבַשׁ; אֶרֶץ דָּגָן וְת׳ אֶרֶץ לֶחֶם וּכְרָמִים Is 36^{17} = 2 K 18^{32} (+ ארץ זית יצהר ודבשׁ).

3455 [יָשַׁם] **vb.** *Impf.* וַיִּישֶׂם Gn 50^{26}, and so 24^{33} Kt, v. שׂוּם, שׂים.

3478 **יִשְׂרָאֵל n.pr.,** and deriv., v. sub I. שׂרה. p. 975

3480 **יְשַׂרְאֵלָה n.pr.m.** a son of Asaph 1 Ch. 25^{14} = אֲשַׂרְאֵלָה (q.v.) v^{2} (etym. dubious).

3485 †**יִשָּׂשכָר**$_{43}$ (so always MT, Qr perpet.; Ben Napht. יִשְׂשָׂכָר Baer$^{\text{Gn p. 84 f.}}$) **n.pr.m. Issachar** (etym. and mng. dub.; MT as if Niph. Impf. √שׂכר; Kt = יֵשׁ שָׂכָר *there is recompense* (cf. Gn 30^{18}), so Thes al.; this the true etym. acc. to Ol $^{\S\S 69c; 277f.}$ Kö$^{\text{i. 120}}$ v. יֵשׁ שָׂכָר Je 31^{16} 2 Ch 15^{7}; = אִישׁ שָׂכָר (a more prob. combination in n.pr.) We $^{\text{Sam 95}}$; > יִשָּׂשכָר (MT), or יִשָּׂא שׂכר; 𝔊 Ισσαχαρ, see esp. Gn 30^{18} Ισσαχαρ, ὅ ἐστιν μισθός) — **1.** fifth son of Jacob and Leah (appar. ninth son of Jacob) Gn 30^{18} 35^{23} 46^{13} 49^{14} Ex 1^{3} Nu 1^{8}; בְּנֵי יִשׂ׳ Nu 1^{28} 2^{5} 26^{23} Jos 19^{17} 1 Ch 7^{1} 12^{33} (v^{32} van d. H.); מִשְׁפְּחוֹת יִשׂ׳ Nu 26^{25} 1 Ch 7^{5}; מַטֵּה יִשׂ׳ Nu 1^{29} 2^{5} 13^{7} Jos 21$^{6.28}$ 1 Ch 6$^{47.57}$; מטה בני יִשׂ׳ Nu 10^{15} 34^{26} Jos 19^{23}; בֵּית יִשׂ׳ 1 K 15^{27}; hence יִשׂ׳ alone = *tribe* of Issachar, Nu 7^{18} Dt 27^{12} 33^{18} Jos 19^{17} Ju 5$^{15.15}$ 10^{1} Ez 48^{33} (שער יִשׂ׳), 1 Ch 27^{18} 2 Ch 30^{18}; = *territory* of the tribe Jos 17$^{10.11}$ 1 K 4^{17} 1 Ch 12^{41} (v^{40} van d. H.); transit. fr. *tribe* to *territory* Ez 48$^{25.26}$. **2.** 7th son of Obed-Edom 1 Ch 26^{5}.

3426 **יֵשׁ**$_{137}$ **subst. being, substance, existence** (on etym. v. **2**)—יֵשׁ Gn 18^{24} etc.; יֶשׁ־ 31^{29} + oft.; הֲיֵשׁ 24^{23} + 18 t. (so אִשׁ 2 S 14^{19}†, הַאִשׁ Mic 6^{10}†, v. p. 78), with sf. יֶשְׁךָ v^{42} + 2 t.; יֶשְׁכֶם v^{49}†; הֲיִשְׁכֶם Dt 13^{4}†; יֶשְׁנוֹ (Ol$^{\S 97b}$ Sta$^{\S 370b}$) 29^{14} 1 S 14^{39} (+ v^{41} 𝔊 We Dr), 23^{23} Est 3^{8}†;—**1.** *substance,* only Pr 8^{21} לְהַנְחִיל אֹהֲבַי יֵשׁ to cause them that love me to inherit *substance* (so Sir 42^{3}). **2.** elsewhere (prop. as a subst. in the *st. c.*), it asserts *existence,* and so corresponds to the *verb substantive,* **is (are, was, were, will be),** lit. *the being, presence of* . . . (so BA אִתַי; Aram. איתא, אית, ܐܝܬ [whence ܐܝܬܝܐ (self-)*existent,* ܐܝܬܘܬܐ *essence, substance*], with לָא contr. לֵית, לֵית, ܠܝܬ; Mand. עת, עית, לאיית; Ar. [with irreg. س] لَيْسَ (inflected as a verb, لَيْسَتْ, لَسْتَ, etc.; W$^{\text{AG i. §182, ii. §42}}$) *is not* (أَيْسَ is known only in two proverbial sayings, as a secondary form, Fl$^{\text{Kl. Schr. i. 146 f.}}$); As. *išû, be, have* Dl$^{\text{HWB 310}}$; with affix 1 s. *la-a i-ša-a-ku, I have not,* TP $^{\text{i. 57 f.}}$. On this word, see esp. Nö$^{\text{M. §213}}$, who exemplifies its different constructions in Semitic, and shews how it tends to pass into a verb;—(1) in BAram. Syr. Bab. 𝔗, with possessive sf.; (2) in later Pal. diall., Jer. 𝔗, Jer. Talm., sts. also in Bab. 𝔗 and Syr., with independent pers. pron. (as לית הוא, לית אנא); (3) in Mand. Bab. Talm., sometimes in Syr. and Ar., and in Heb. יֶשְׁנוֹ, with object. (verbal) sf.; (4) in Ar., as a true verb. In Eth. በ፡ lit. *therein,* Germ. *es gibt,* is similar in use (Di$^{\text{Gr. §167, 1}}$), though not of course in origin. In Heb. the corresponding neg. is אַיִן, q.v., the construction of which is quite similar)—**is, are, was, were,** etc., not, however, as a mere copula, but implying existence with emph. (hence in Engl. to be often represented by the subst. verb in italics): **a.** with a pred. following, Gn 28^{16} אכן יש י׳ במקום הזה surely Y. *is* (emph.) in this place! 44^{26} אִם יֵשׁ אָחִינוּ אִתָּנוּ; Ex 17^{7} הֲיֵשׁ יהוה בְּקִרְבֵּנוּ אִם אָיִן, Nu 22^{29} לו יש חרב בידי Oh that there *were* a sword in my hand! Dt 13^{4} הֲיִשְׁכֶם אֹהֲבִים whether you *do* love, 29^{17} פֶּן יֵשׁ בכם איש, v^{18} 1 S 9$^{11f.}$ and they said, *Is* the seer here? and they said יֵשׁ *He is,* 20^{8} 23^{23} Je 27^{18}. Alone, in answer to a question (asked with יֵשׁ), *He* (*it*) *is:* †1 S 9^{12} 2 K 10^{15} Je 37^{17}. But Je 23^{26} (where יש has no subst. or sf.) text must be corrupt: cf. Gie. **b.** absolutely, *there is* (*es gibt, il y a*), Gn 18^{24} אולי יש חמשים צדיקים בעיר perhaps there *are* fifty righteous in the city, 24^{23} היש בית אביך מקום לנו ללין, 42^{1} כי יש שבר במצ׳ that there *was* corn in Egypt, Ju 4^{20} היש פה איש, 2 S 9^{1} 2 K 5^{8} he shall know that there *is* (emph.) a prophet in Israel, Ru 3^{12} there *is* a kinsman nearer than I, ψ 58^{12} surely there *are* gods judging on the earth: so in aphorisms, asserting the existence of a partic. character, quality, etc., Pr 11^{24} יש מפזר ונוסף עוד, 12^{18} 13$^{7.23}$ 14^{12} 16^{25} 18^{24} 20^{15} Ec 2^{21} 4^{8} 5^{12} 6$^{1.11}$ 7$^{15.15}$ 8$^{14.14.14}$ 10^{5}. In questions, or protestations, יֵשׁ often implies a doubt whether what is asked about is to be found or exists: 1 K 18^{10} Je 5^{1} and see אם יש איש if there *is* (emph.) a man doing justice, etc. (cf. ψ 14^{2}), 14^{22} Is 44^{8} היש אלהים *is* there a god beside me? ψ 7^{4} אם יש עול בכפי if there *is* iniquity in my hands! 73^{11} *is* there knowledge in the Most High? Jb 5^{1} 6^{30} La 1^{12}. **c.** special phrases:—(*a*) after אִם and a ptcp., where an abiding *intention* is to be emphasized, †Gn 24^{42} אם־ישך־נא מצליח דרכי if thou *art* (really) prospering my way, v^{49} 43^{4} Ju 6^{36} (cf. II. אין **2 b**). (*b*) יֵשׁ לְ = *has* (*had*), esp. with prons. יֶשׁ לִי, יֶשׁ לְךָ; etc., Gn 33^{9} יֶשׁ־לִי רָב *I have* plenty, v^{11} 43^{7} היש לכם אח, 44^{20} יש לנו אב זקן, 1 S 17^{46} that they may know כי יש אלהים לישראל that Israel *has* (emph.) a god, 2 K 4^{2} מַה־יֶּשׁ־לָכִי what *hast* thou? Jb 14^{7} for a tree *has* (emph.) hope (cf. Ru 1^{12}), 25^{3} 28^{1} 38^{28} היש למטר אב: Gn 39$^{5.5.8}$

כל אשר יֶשׁ־לוֹ all that he had (v^4 without אשר, prob. error). (*c*) with inf. and לְ, *is it possible to . . .?* 2 K 4^{13} היש לדבר־לך *can* (I) *speak* for thee to the king? 2 Ch 25^9; so אִשׁ לְ 2 S 14^{19} (cf. אֵין לְ, sub II. אַיִן **5**). (*d*) . . . יֵשׁ אֲשֶׁר (if) *it was* that . . . †Nu $9^{20.21}$; there *were* some who . . . (with ptcp.) †Ne $5^{2.3.4}$ (cf. Syr. ܐܝܬ ܕ for ὁ μὲν . . . ὁ δὲ . . . Mt 13^8; ܐܝܬ ܕܡܐܐ PS ^{172}). (*e*) יֶשׁ־לְאֵל יָדִי Gn 31^{29} al.; v. II. אֵל **7**, p. 43. (*f*) 2 K 10^{15} וָיֵשׁ *and* (if) *it be* . . . (cf. וָלֹא 5^{17} 2 S 13^{26}); so Ju 6^{13} וְיֵשׁ י׳ אִתָּנוּ. (*g*) pleon. אֵין יֵשׁ †ψ 135^{17}. (*h*) לֹא יֵשׁ †Jb 9^{33} (cf. لَيْسَ, ܠܝܬ: but 𝔊 𝔖 Me al. לְאֹ).—As a rule, יֵשׁ precedes its subst. (from which, however, like אין, it may be separated: Gn 24^{23} 43^7 הֲיֵשׁ לָכֶם אָח, $44^{19.20}$ 1 S 20^8 etc.); but occasionally, for greater emphasis, this is prefixed: 1 S 21^5 כי אם לחם קדש יש but holy bread *there is!* Is 43^8 the blind people, ועינים יש though it *has* eyes, Ju 19^{19} לחם ויין יש לי (cf. אַיִן **2 c**).

3427 **יָשַׁב** $^{\dagger 1090}$ **vb.** sit, remain, dwell (NH *id.*; Aram. יְתֵיב, ܝܬܒ; MI$^{10.31}$ וישב, $1^{8.19}$ ישב, 1^{13} ואשב, *dwell*; Ph. ישב *dwell*; Zinj. ישב *sit* DHM$^{Sendsch. 58}$; As. *ašâbu, sit, dwell*, Dl$^{HWB 244}$; Ar. وَثَبَ *leap, jump*, Ḥimyer. dial. *sit*, Lane^{2919}; Eth. ኦውሰበ: II. 1 *secum cohabitare facere, marry, consummate marriage*, cf. **Hiph. 4)**—**Qal** *Pf.* 3 ms. יָשַׁב Gn 13^{12}+; 2 ms. יָשַׁבְתָּ Ju 5^{16}, וְיָשַׁבְתָּה בָּהּ consec. Dt 17^{14}; 2 mpl. יְשַׁבְתֶּם Dt 1^{46} Lv 18^3, וִישַׁבְתֶּם consec. Lv 25^{18} + 7 t., etc.; *Impf.* יֵשֵׁב 1 S 5^7+, יֵשֶׁב־ Gn 44^{33} Ez 44^3, יֵשָׁב before monosyll. 1 K 7^8 Jb 22^8; וַיֵּשֶׁב Gn 4^{16}+; וַיֵּשָׁב Ru 4^1; 1 s. אֵשֵׁב Ju 6^{18}+, וָאֵשֵׁב Dt 9^9 + 3 t. + Ez 3^{15b} (but Co אשר Kt); אֵשְׁבָה 1 S 27^5; אֵשֵׁבָה Is 49^{20}; וָאֵשְׁבָה Ez 9^3; 3 mpl. יֵשְׁבוּ Gn 47^4+; 3 fpl. תשבנה Ez 35^9 Kt (i.e. תֵּישַׁבְנָה Ol^{§242d} Kö$^{i. 401}$), Qr תָּשֹׁבְנָה (שׁוב √), Co prop. תִּוָּשַׁבְנָה; 1 pl. נֵשֵׁב Je $42^{13.14}$, וַנֵּשֶׁב Nu 20^{15} + 5 t.; *Imv.* ms. שֵׁב Gn 20^{15}+, שֶׁב־ Gn 35^1; שְׁבָה Gn 27^{19}+; fs. שְׁבִי Gn 38^{11}+; mpl. שְׁבוּ Gn 22^5+, etc.; *Inf. abs.* יָשֹׁב־ 1 S 20^5; *cstr.* שֶׁבֶת 1 S 7^2+; שָׁבֶת Is 40^{22}+; sf. שִׁבְתִּי 2 S 7^5+, etc.; *Pt.* m. י(ו)שֵׁב Gn 4^{20} 24^3+, etc.; f. יֹשְׁבָה Na 3^8; י(ו)שֶׁבֶת Ju 4^5+; יֹשַׁבְתִּי Je 22^{23}, י(ו)שֶׁבְתִּי Je 10^{17} La 4^{21} Ez 27^3 (Kt preferable in all these, v. Ol^{§123d} Ges$^{§90.3a}$); fpl. יֹשְׁבוֹת 1 S 27^8;—**1. a.** *sit* on (עַל) a seat 1 S 20^{25}, stone Ex 17^{12}, teraphim Gn 31^{34}, couch 48^2 (all E), Ez 23^{41}, knees 2 K 4^{20}, throne Ex 11^5 12^{29} (J), Dt 17^{18} 1 S 1^9 4^{13} 1 K $1^{13.17.20}$ +, v. abs. infr.; of י׳ הַיֹּשֵׁב עַל־חוּג הָאָרֶץ Is 40^{22}; dust Is 47^1, ground (אֶרֶץ) Ez 26^{16}, ashes Jon 3^6 (these in token of humiliation); *sit down* by (עַל) a well Ex 2^{15} or pool 2 S 2^{13}; c. אֶל 1 S 28^{23}; *sit* in (בְּ) house, street, doorway, assembly, etc. 2 S 7^1 Ju 19^{15} Gn 38^{14} (J), Je 15^{17} 26^{10} ψ 1^1 Ct 2^3 so Ez $31^{6.17}$ (fig.); of No of Amon (personif. city) הַיֹּשְׁבָה בַּיְאֹרִים Na 3^8 *she who sate amid the rivers;* c. לְ *sit on to* (pregn.) לָאָרֶץ Is 3^{26} 47^1 La 2^{10}, לְכִסֵּא ψ 9^5, *at*, לְפֶתַח בית Pr 9^{14}, לימינו(י) 1 K 2^{19}, ψ 110^1; לַמַּבּוּל ψ 29^{10}; c. לִפְנֵי Gn 43^{33} (J), + שָׁם Ju 20^{26} 21^2 2 S 7^{18} = 1 Ch 17^{16}; c. עִם 1 S 20^5 Pr 31^{23}; c. אֶת־ Je 16^8 Jb 2^{13}; c. תַּחַת Ju 6^{11} Mi 4^4, וַיֵּשֶׁב תַּחְתֶּיהָ בַּצֵּל Jon 4^5; c. מִנֶּגֶד Gn $21^{16.16}$ (E), נֶגֶד Is 47^{14}, מִקֶּדֶם לָעִיר Jon 4^5; מִצַּד 1 S 20^{25} Ru 2^{14}; c. acc. cogn. Ez 28^2; לִשְׁפֹּט Ex 18^{13} Jo 4^{12} (cf. ψ 9^5 Is 28^6); hence abs. of *sitting* as *king* or *judge* Ex 18^{14} ψ 61^8 Mal 3^3, יושבים Is 10^{13}, perh. Am $1^{5.8}$, esp. of י׳ *sitting* (enthroned), ψ 2^4 9^8 29^{10} 55^{20} 102^{13} La 5^{19}, so in יֹשֵׁב (הַ)כְּרוּבִים 1 S 4^4 2 S 6^2 = 1 Ch 13^6, 2 K 19^{15} ψ 99^1; יֹשֵׁב תְּהִלּוֹת יִשְׂרָאֵל ψ 22^4 (v. c. עַל, supr.); by meton. of thrones, for the judges sitting on them שָׁמָּה יָשְׁבוּ כִסְאוֹת לְמִשְׁפָּט ψ 122^5; הַיֹּשְׁבִים Ru 4^{14}, i.e. in the gate (cf. v^{11}), those in whose presence purchase of land took place. **b.** *sit, sit down*, abs., Ju 19^6 Ru $4^{1.2}$ Ne 1^4 Je 36^{15} (sq. cl. of purpose, *to eat*, etc.) Gn 37^{25} Est 3^{15}+; opp. קום Ex 32^6 (JE) ψ 139^2, מְאַחֲרֵי שֶׁבֶת ψ 127^2 (opp. מַשְׁכִּימֵי קוּם); so Is 37^{28} = 2 K 19^{27} (rd. לְפָנַי קֻמְךָ at end of v^{27} = 2 K 19^{26} We in Bl$^{Einl. 4, 257}$ RS$^{Proph. 351, and n. 9}$); but also קוּמִי שְׁבִי Is 52^2, expl. by (וַיָּקָם מֵהָאָרֶץ וַיֵּשֶׁב אֶל־הַמִּטָּה 1 S 28^{23} and) 2 S 19^9. †**c.** *sit down* outside (חוץ), i.e. perform a necessity of nature Dt 23^{14}. †**d.** *sit = be set* (as a jewel), יֹשְׁבוֹת עַל־מִלֵּאת Ct 5^{12} *set on a filling* (i.e. in a setting, De al.), in description of eyes; (> others *sitting by full streams*). **2. a.** *remain, stay, tarry* (for a limited or indef. time), c. אֵת pers. Gn 24^{55} (J), Ju 19^4 2 S 16^8; c. עִם pers. Gn 27^{44} (J), עִמָּדִי 29^{19} (E), Ju 17^{10}; c. בְּ loc. 1 S 7^2 (of ark), 13^{16} 14^2 24^4 (23^{25} rd. אֲשֶׁר for וַיֵּשֶׁב 𝔊 We Dr Klo Kit Bu), 2 S 10^5 19^{25} (where rd. שִׁבְתּוֹ for שִׁיבָתוֹ Dr Klo Bu, v. We), Nu 35^{25} (P), Jb 24^{13}; c. שָׁם 1 K 11^{16}, שָׁם עַד־עוֹלָם 1 S 1^{22}; c. על (*by*) 1 S 25^{13} 30^{24}; שְׁבוּ לָכֶם פֹּה עִם־ 2 K 7^4; הַחֲמוֹר Gn 22^5 (E); c. בֵּין Ju 5^{16}, מחוץ לְ Lv 14^8 (P), אֵצֶל 1 S 20^{19}; c. acc. בית 2 S 6^{11} 13^{20} Ru 2^7; abs. 1 S $1^{23.23}$; *abide, endure* Mi 5^3, וִיהוּדָה לְעוֹלָם תֵּשֵׁב Jo 4^{20}, so of Mt. Zion ψ 121^1. **b.** with special emphasis on qualifying phr., וַתֵּשֶׁב בְּאֵיתָן קַשְׁתּוֹ Gn 49^{24} *and his bow abode as a firm one* (poem in J); 1 K 22^{1} *and they continued* three years without war; of woman *remaining* בִּדְמֵי טָהֳרָה Lv 12^{4}, על־דמי וגו׳ v^{5}. **3.** *dwell, have one's abode* in (ב) a land, city, house, etc., Gn 4^{16} 13$^{7.12.12}$ 19^{29} 24$^{37.62}$ Dt 1^{4} 3^{2} Jos 20^{6} 2 S 7^{6} + oft. (on 2 S 21^{16} v. ישבו בְּנֹב, p. 444); in tents Je 35$^{7.10}$ 1 Ch 5^{10}; fig. of justice (צְדָקָה) Is 32^{16} (‖ וְשָׁכַן מִשְׁפָּט); in the midst of (בְּקֶרֶב) Gn 24^{3} Jos 13^{13} 16^{10} Ju 1$^{30.32.33}$ 3^{5}; so c. בְּתוֹךְ Gn 23^{10} (P); c. על + הארץ, of God 1 K 8^{27} = 2 Ch 6^{18}; of people Lv 25$^{18.19}$ 26^{35} (H); c. לְ Jb 15^{28}; c. בֵּין Gn 20^{1} (E); *dwell with* (אֵת) Gn 34$^{16.22}$ (P), Ex 2^{21} (E), Jos 15^{63} (JE), Ju 1$^{16.21}$ 17^{11}; יֵשְׁבוּ יְשָׁרִים אֶת־פָּנֶיךָ ψ 140^{14}; so c. עִם Jos 20^{4} Dt 23^{17} (+ בקרב), ψ 26^{4} (i.e. *assoc. with*); c. יַחְדָּו Gn 13$^{6.6}$ (J), 36^{7} (P), Dt 25^{5}; שֶׁבֶת גַּם־יָחַד ψ 133^{1}; *dwell* in their stead (תַּחְתָּם) Dt 2$^{12.21.22.23}$ 1 Ch 4^{41} 5^{22}; abs. לָשֶׁבֶת יְצָרָהּ Is 45^{18} *for dwelling he formed it* (the earth); (*thy*) *dwelling-place* is מְקוֹם שִׁבְתְּךָ 1 K 8^{30} = 2 Ch 6^{21}, also מְכוֹן ש׳ 1 K 8$^{39.43.49}$ = 2 Ch 6$^{30.33.39}$, so ψ 33^{14}; מָכוֹן לְשׁ׳ Ex 15^{17} 1 K 8^{13} = 2 Ch 6^{2}. *Pt.* יֹשֵׁב = subst., *dweller, inhabitant*, very oft. (c. 215 t.): e.g. יֹשֵׁב אהלים Gn 25^{27} (J); oft. coll. יֹשֵׁב אהל Gn 4^{20} (J), יֹשֵׁב הָאָרֶץ 34^{30} 50^{11} (both J), Ex 34$^{12.15}$ (JE); also poet. f., (as coll.; v. Dr on 1 S 17^{21}) יוֹשֶׁבֶת שָׁפִיר etc., Mi 1$^{11.11.12.13.15}$; יוֹשֶׁבֶת צִיּוֹן † Is 12^{6} Je 51^{35}; similarly † 10^{17} 21^{13} 22^{23} 48^{19} (cf. La 4^{21}) Zc 2^{11}; with בת in app. (Da § 28 R. 6), יוֹשֶׁבֶת בַּת־מִצְרַיִם † Je 46^{19}, so 48^{18}; more usu. pl. יֹשְׁבֵי הֶעָרִים Gn 19^{25} (J), cf. Dt 13^{14}; יֹשְׁבֵי הָאָרֶץ Ex 23^{21} (JE), cf. Ex 15$^{14.15}$ (poem in E); יוֹשְׁבֵי חָדֶל Is 18^{3}, יֹשְׁבֵי תֵבֵל 38^{11}, etc.; יֹשְׁבֶיהָ Lv 18^{25} 25^{10} (H), Nu 13^{32} (P); abs. יוֹשֵׁב (coll.) Am 1$^{5.8}$ Is 49^{19}; הַיּוֹשְׁבִים 1 Ch 9^{2}; also (strangely) יֹשְׁבוֹת הארץ 1 S 27^{8} = *the populations of the land* We Dr (elsewhere in this sense only fs. and poet., v. supr.); freq. in phr. *without inhabitant* (i.e. so that there shall be no inhab.), מֵאֵין יֹשֵׁב Is 5^{9} 6^{4} Je 4^{7} 26^{9} 33^{10} 34^{23} 44^{22} 46^{19} 51$^{29.37}$ Zp 2^{5} 3^{6}; מֵאֵין יוֹשֵׁב בָּהֵן Je 48^{9}; לְבִלְתִּי לֹא יִהְיֶה יוֹשֵׁב בָּהּ 50^{3}; מִבְּלִי יֹשֵׁב 2^{15} 9^{10}; הֱיוֹת־בּוֹ יוֹשֵׁב 51^{62}. **4.** of a land or city, *sit, abide seated in its place*, fig. for *be inhabited* Je 17$^{6.25}$ 50$^{13.39}$ Ez 26^{20} 29^{11} 36^{35} Is 13^{20} (‖ לֹא תִשְׁכֹּן), Zc 2^{8} 9^{5} 14^{11}; יָשְׁבָה תַחְתֶּיהָ 12^{6} 14^{10}; Ez 35^{9} Kt is תישבנה, Qr תָּשׁוֹבְנָה; Co תושבנה, i.e. Niph. תִּוָּשַׁבְנָה (cf. 36^{10}), or Hoph. תושבנה (cf. Is 44^{26}); of palace, וְאַרְמוֹן עַל־מִשְׁפָּטוֹ יֵשֵׁב Je 30^{18}.

†**Niph.** *Pf.* 3 fs. נוֹשָׁבָה Je 6^{8}; 3 pl. וְנֹשְׁבוּ consec. Ez 36^{10}, נוֹשָׁבוּ Ez 26^{19}, נוֹשָׁבָה Je 22^{6}; *Pt.* f. נוֹשֶׁבֶת Ez 26^{17} (< נִשְׁבַּתְּ 𝔊 Co, √שׁבת), נוֹשָׁבֶת Ex 16^{35}; pl. נוֹשָׁבוֹת Ez 12^{20} 38^{12};—*be inhabited*, of land Ex 16^{35} (perh. = *be habitable*), Je 6^{8}; of cities Je 22^{6} Ez 12^{20} 26^{19} 36^{10}; חֳרָבוֹת נוֹשָׁבוֹת Ez 38^{12};—Ez 26^{17} v. supr.; 35^{9} v. **Qal 4.**

†**Pi.** *Pf.* 3 mpl. וְיִשְּׁבוּ טִירוֹתֵיהֶם בָּךְ Ez 25^{4} *and they shall set their encampments in thee* (𝔊 𝔖 Co וְיָשְׁבוּ *inhabit*).

†**Hiph.** *Pf.* 3 ms. הֹשִׁיב Ezr 10^{14}, sf. הוֹשִׁיבַנִי La 3^{6} ψ 143^{3}; 1 s. הוֹשַׁבְתִּי Lv 23^{33}, וְה(וֹ)שַׁבְתִּים consec. Ho 11^{11} Je 32^{37}; וְהוֹשְׁבוֹתִים consec. Zc 10^{6} (Kö i. 413; but prob. txt. err., vid. Thes and Ges Lgb 464; rd. prob. וַהֲשִׁבוֹתִים as v^{10}, so Sta ZAW. 1881, 21 We), etc.; *Impf.* 3 ms. וַיּוֹשֶׁב Gn 47^{11}, וַיּוֹשֶׁב 2 Ch 8^{2} ψ 107^{36}; sf. וַיּוֹשִׁיבֵנִי 1 K 2^{24} (Kö i. 414, 224); וַיֹּשִׁיבֵם Jb 36^{7}; 1 pl. וַנֹּשֶׁב Ezr 10^{2}, etc.; *Imv.* ms. הוֹשֵׁב Gn 47^{6}; mpl. ה(וֹ)שִׁיבוּ 1 K 21$^{9.10}$; *Inf. cstr.* ה(וֹ)שִׁיב 1 S 2^{8} Ne 13^{27}; הוֹשִׁיבִי ψ 113^{8} (Ol § 123 d; rd. בוֹ-, v. Che); *Pt.* abs. מוֹשִׁיב ψ 68^{7}, cstr. מוֹשִׁיבִי ψ 113^{9} (Ol l.c. Ges l.c.);—**1.** *cause to sit* c. acc. pers. + עַל כסא 1 K 2^{24} 2 Ch 23^{20} so (without עַל כסא) + לָנֶצַח Jb 36^{7}; *set, place* c. acc. pers. + נֶגְדּוֹ 1 K 21^{10}, also v$^{9.12}$ (בְּרֹאשׁ הָעָם). **2.** *cause to abide* (acc. pers.) *at* (ב) 1 S 30^{21}. **3. a.** *cause to dwell*, c. acc. pers. + ב loc. 1 S 12^{8} 2 K 17^{6} Ho 12^{10}, Gn 47$^{6.11}$ (P), Lv 23^{43} (H), La 3^{6} ψ 143^{3}; בְּאֶרֶץ תַּחְתִּיּוֹת Ez 26^{20}; acc. pers. om. 2 K 17$^{24.26}$; acc. pers. + שָׁם 2 Ch 8^{2} ψ 107^{36}; acc. pers. + עַל־הַבָּתִּים Ho 11^{11} (but rd. וַהֲשִׁבֹתִים We); acc. pers. om., c. עִם pers. 1 S 2^{8} ψ 113^{8}; מוֹשִׁיב יְחִידִים בַּיְתָה ψ 68^{7} *causing solitary ones to dwell in a house* (or is מוֹשִׁיב for מֵשִׁיב Bae?); c. acc. pers. only מוֹשׁ׳ עֲקֶרֶת הַבַּיִת ψ 113^{9} *giving a dwelling to her that is barren of house;* abs. c. לָבֶטַח Je 32^{37} ψ 4^{9}; abs. c. כְּקַדְמוֹתֵיכֶם Ez 36^{11}. On Zc 10^{6}, v. supr. **b.** *cause* cities (עָרִים) *to be inhabited* Ez 36^{33} Is 54^{3}. **4.** *marry* (prop. *give a dwelling* to, cf. ψ 113^{9}), only Ezr Ne, and only c. acc. נָשִׁים נָכְרִיּוֹת *strange* or *foreign women* Ezr 10$^{2.10.14.17.18}$ Ne 13^{27}; so הֹשִׁיבוּ נָשִׁים אַשְׁדֳּוִדיּוֹת Ne 13^{23}.

†**Hoph.** *Pf.* וְהוּשַׁבְתֶּם לְבַדְּכֶם בְּקֶרֶב הָאָרֶץ Is 5^{8} *and ye be made to dwell alone in the midst of the land.* *Impf.* הָאֹמֵר לִירוּשָׁלַםִ תּוּשָׁב Is 44^{26} *he who saith of Jerusalem, she shall be inhabited.* Ez 35^{9} v. **Qal 4.**

†**1. שֶׁבֶת n.f. seat, dwelling, place** (pro- 7675
perly Inf. Qal from ישׁב)—מְקוֹם הַשָּׁבֶת 1 K 10^{19} = 2 Ch 9^{18} *the place of the seat;* שֶׁבֶת חָמָס Am 6^{3} *a seat* (*throne*, or *enthronement*) *of violence;* לְשֶׁבֶת עָר Nu 21^{15} *toward the dwelling* (i.e. *place*,

location) *of ʿÂr*; יִשָּׂרְפוּ בַּשָּׁבֶת 2 S 23[7] *they are burned in the* (same) *place*, i.e. *on the spot*, but del. ׳שׁ We Dr Bu; שִׁבְתּוֹ Ob[3] *his* (thy) *dwelling-*
7674 *place*.—II. שֶׁבֶת v. sub שׁבת. p. 992

7871 † I. [שִׁיבָה] **n.f.** sojourn (=*יְשִׁיבָה acc. to Thes)—only בְּשִׁיבָתוֹ 2 S 19[33] *during his sojourn*; but rd. בְּשִׁבְתּוֹ, v. יָשַׁב **Qal 2.**—II. שִׁיבָה v. sub שׁוב.

3428 †יֶשֶׁבְאָב **n.pr.m.** Levite of the 14th course 1 Ch 24[13]; but 𝔊 Γελβα, A 𝔊L Ισβααλ.

3429 †יֹשֵׁב בַּשֶּׁבֶת **n.pr.m.** one of David's heroes 2 S 23[8] 𝔊 Ιεβοσθε, 𝔊L Ιεσβααλ (‖ 1 Ch 11[11] has יָשָׁבְעָם, q. v. sub שׁוב); rd. אִישׁ־בֹּשֶׁת q. v.

3430 †ישבו בְּנֹב Kt, יִשְׁבִּי בְּנֹב Qr, **n.pr.m.** a gigantic Philistine 2 S 21[16]; but read וַיֵּשְׁבוּ בְנֹב *and they dwelt in Gob*, and tr. to v[15] We Dr Bu.

3436 †יָשְׁבְּקָשָׁה **n.pr.m.** a son of Heman 1 Ch 25[4.24]; 𝔊 Ιεβασακα(ταν), Βακατα, 𝔊L Ιεσβοκ.

3143 †יוֹשִׁבְיָה **n.pr.m.** (׳י *setteth, causeth to dwell*; cf. Ph. n.pr. ישבעל (?=ישבבעל))—a Simeonite 1 Ch 4[35] 𝔊 Ιωαβια, 𝔊L Ιωσαβια.

4186 †מוֹשָׁב **n.m.** [2 K 2, 19] **seat, assembly, dwelling-place, dwelling, dwellers**;—abs. ׳מ ψ 107[4] + 4 t.; cstr. מוֹשַׁב Ex 12[40] + 9 t.; sf. מוֹשָׁבִי Jb 29[7] etc.; pl. cstr. מוֹשְׁבֵי Ez 34[13]; sf. 2 mpl. מוֹשְׁבֹתֵיכֶם etc. Ex 12[20] + 11 t.; sf. 3 mpl. מוֹשְׁבֹתָם etc. 10[23] + 5 t.; מוֹשְׁבֹתֵיהֶם Ez 37[23], but read ׳מְשׁוּב *their apostasies* 𝔊 Comm., see VB; מוֹשְׁבוֹתֵיהֶם Ez 6[14];—**1. a.** *seat* 1 S 20[18.25.25] Jb 29[7]; fig. ׳מ אלהים יָשַׁבְתִּי Ez 28[2]. **b.** *sitting=those sitting, sitting company* or *assembly*, מוֹשַׁב עֲבָדָיו 1 K 10[5] (‖ מַעֲמַד מְשָׁרְתָיו)=2 Ch 9[4]; so ψ 1[1] 107[32] (‖ קהל). **2. a.** *dwelling-place* of people, tribe, etc., oft.=territory, district, or, later, city; Gn 10[30] 27[39] (both J), Ex 10[23] (E), Nu 24[21] (JE), Gn 36[43] (P), Ez 6[14] 48[15] 1 Ch 4[33] 6[39] 7[28]; ׳מ הָאָרֶץ Ex 34[13]=*habitable places of the land*; distinct from city עָרֵיהֶם בְּמוֹשְׁבֹתָם Nu 31[10], cf. Ez 6[6], but also עִיר מוֹשָׁב ψ 107[4.7.36]; of Zion as ׳מ׳ י 132[13]. **b.** alm.=abstr. *dwelling* בֵּית מוֹשָׁב עִיר Lv 25[29] (P); ׳אֶרֶץ מ Nu 15[2] *land of your dwelling-places* or *dwelling* (P). **c.** =house Ex 12[20] (‖ בית v[19]), 35[3] Lv 3[17] 7[26] 13[46] 23[3.14.21.31] Nu 35[29] (all P), Lv 23[17] (H). **3.** *situation* of city 2 K 2[19]; *location* of image Ez 8[3]. **4.** *time of dwelling* Ex 12[40] (P). **5.** coll.= *those dwelling*, ׳כֹּל מוֹשַׁב וגו 2 S 9[12] *all those dwelling in* the house of Ṣiba.—Ez 37[23] v. supr. and מְשׁוּבָה sub שׁוב.

†תּוֹשָׁב **n.m.** [Lv 25, 45] sojourner, only P (H) and late; abs. ׳ת Gn 23[4] + 6 t.; cstr. תּוֹשַׁב Lv 22[10]; sf. תּוֹשָׁבְךָ 25[6]; pl. תּוֹשָׁבִים v[6] + 2 t.; cstr. תֹּשָׁבֵי 1 K 17[1], but read תִּשְׁבֵּה (q. v.) 𝔊 Ew Th Hi;—*sojourner*, appar. of a more temporary and dependent (Lv 22[10] 25[6]) kind than the גֵּר (with which it is often joined): ‖ שָׂכִיר Ex 12[45] (P), Lv 22[10] (׳ת כֹּהֵן a priest's *sojourner*), 25[6.40] (all H); הַתּוֹשָׁבִים הַגָּרִים עִמָּכֶם v[45] (c. pt. גָּר also v[6]); c. עִם, also Lv 25[47.47] (H); c. בְּתוֹךְ Nu 35[15] (P). Fig. of one enjoying only a temporary tenure, c. עִם Gn 23[4], with ׳י Lv 25[23] ψ 39[13], c. לְפָנֶי 1 Ch 29[15].—1 K 17[1] v. supr. 8453

יִשְׁבָּח **n.pr.m.** v. שׁבח. p. 986 3431

יָשָׁבְעָם, יָשְׁבִי v. שׁוב. p. 1000 3432, 3434

יִשְׁבָּק v. שׁבק. p. 990 3435

ישׁה (√ of following; meaning uncertain; acc. to Fl De [Pr 2, 7]=Ar. أَسَا, III. آسَا, var. وَاسَا, *assist, support*: but this dubious; v. Lane [60] (cf. Wetzst [ZDMG 1868, 119]) acc. to whom this is a second sense from *to make equal* (viz. by giving to another of one's own property, etc.))

†תּוּשִׁיָּה **n.f.** **sound, efficient wisdom, abiding success** (on der., v. supr.; acc. to Fl De prop. *advancement*, or mental aptitude that *advances*: for the form, cf. תּוּגָה and תַּאֲנִיָּה; Sta [§ 262]), a technical term of the WisdLt;—**a.** *sound, efficient wisdom* Is 28[29] (of ׳י) הפליא עצה הגדיל תושיה; Pr 3[21] ׳נְצֹר ת׳ וּמְזִמָּה; 8[14] לִי עֵצָה ות׳; 18[1] בְּכָל ת׳ יִתְגַּלָּע; (Wisdom speaks) Jb 11[6] (of ׳י: v. Di), 12[6] עִמּוֹ עֹז ות׳; 26[3] ות׳ לָרֹב; יָעַצְתָּ לְלֹא חָכְמָה (‖ הוֹדָעְתָּ). **b.** of the *effect* of sound wisdom, *abiding success* (for the combination of meanings, cf. הִשְׂכִּיל *to shew wisdom*, and also *to achieve success*), Jb 5[12] ולא תעשינה ׳ידיהם ת do not achieve *abiding success*; 6[13] and *abiding success* (‖ עֶזְרָתִי) is driven from me; Pr 2[7] ׳יִצְפֹּן לַיְשָׁרִים ת; Mi 6[9] ותושיה יראה שמך, i.e. (si vera l.) he that seeth (heedeth) thy name is *well-advised* (Ges [§ 155, 2 b 3]; Dav [§ 29 e]).—תֻּשִׁיָּה Jb 30[22], v. sub שׁוא.

†יוֹשָׁה **n.pr.m.** a Simeonite 1 Ch 4[34]; 𝔊 Ιωσ(ε)ια, A Ιωσιας, 𝔊L Ιωας. 3144

†יוֹשַׁוְיָה **n.pr.m.** one of David's heroes 1 Ch 11[46]; 𝔊 Ιωσ(ε)ια, 𝔊L Σωσια. 3145

8454

3437-39 **יָשׁוּב** v. שׁוב; **יְשָׁוָה** v. שׁוה; **יְשׁוֹהָיָה** v. שׁוח. p. 1000-01, 1006

3440-42 **יִשְׁוִי** v. שׁוה; **יֵשׁוּעַ** v. יְהוֹשֻׁעַ supr. p. 221. p. 1001

ישׁח (√ of following, si vera l.)

3445 †[**יֶשַׁח**] **n.[m.]** ? **emptiness** (of hunger), meaning conjectured from context; Mi 6^{14} וְיֶשְׁחֲךָ בְּקִרְבֶּךָ (‖ תאכל ולא תִשְׂבָּע).

3447 †[**יָשַׁט**] **vb.** only **Hiph.** *Impf.* **extend, hold out** (late) (NH Hiph. *id.;* Aram. Aph. אוֹשִׁיט, ܐܘܫܛ *id.;* ? As. *aštu, extended, mighty* Lyon[Sargontexte 60] Dl[HWB 144]; Ar. وَسَطَ is *penetrate into the middle of*)—יוֹשִׁיט שַׁרְבִיט הַזָּהָב לְ׳ Est 4^{11} *hold out the golden sceptre to,* so (וַיּוֹשֶׁט) 5^{2} 8^{4}.

3448 **יִשַׁי** $_{41}$ **n.pr.m.** father of David (etym. dub.; Ol[§ 277 f.] conj. יֵשׁ יָהּ; We[1 S 14, 49] אבישי = אישי = ישי (but see this))—יִשַׁי 1 S 16^{3} + 29 t.; אִישַׁי v^{19} + 10 t.; 𝔊 Ιεσσαι; (ו)אִישַׁי 1 Ch 2^{13};—†בֵּית־יִשַׁי הַלַּחְמִי *Jesse the Bethlehemite* 1 S $16^{1.18}$ (בֶּן־יִשַׁי וגו׳, of David), 17^{58}†; ישי also 16^{3} + 14 t. 1 S 16, 17; †son of עוֹבֵד acc. to Ru $4^{17.22.22}$ = 1 Ch 2^{12}; דָּוִ(י)ד בֶּן־יִשַׁי 2 S 23^{1} 1 Ch 10^{14} 29^{26} ψ 72^{20}; אֱלִיאָב בֶּן־יִשַׁי 2 Ch 11^{18}; elsewhere בֶּן־יִשַׁי alone = David, 1 S $20^{27.30.31}$ $22^{7.8.9.13}$ 25^{10} 2 S 20^{1} 1 K 12^{16} = 2 Ch 10^{16}, 1 Ch 12^{18}; גֶּזַע יִשָׁי Is 11^{1}; שֹׁרֶשׁ יִשַׁי v^{10} of Jesse as ancestor of future (Messianic) king†.

3437 **יָשִׁיב** **n.pr.** v. יָשׁוּב sub שׁוב. p. 1000

3449 **יְשִׁיָּה(וּ)** v. נשׁה. p. 674

3456 †[**יָשַׁם**] **vb. be desolate** (cf. שָׁמֵם)—**Qal** *Impf.* 3 fs. תֵּשַׁם Ez 12^{19}; תֵּשָׁם Gn 47^{19}; וַתֵּשַׁם Ez 19^{7}; 3 fpl. תֵּישַׁמְנָה 6^{6} (Co תשמנה);—*be desolate,* subj. ארץ Ez 12^{19} 19^{7}; subj. אֲדָמָה Gn 47^{19} (J); subj. במות Ez 6^{6}.

3451 †[**יְשִׁימָה**] **n.f. desolation,** only intens. pl. יְשִׁימוֹת ψ 55^{16} Kt (Qr יַשִּׁיא מָוֶת), so Ges Hup al., cf. n.pr.loc. בית הישימות supr. p. 111 b; 𝔊 Ew Ol Pe De Bae al. follow Qr, *let death come deceitfully upon them,* v. נשׁא.

3452 †**יְשִׁימוֹן** **n.m. waste, wilderness;**—abs. יְשִׁימוֹן 1 S 23^{19} + 5 t.; יְשִׁימֹן Nu 21^{20} + 3 t.; יְשִׁמוֹן Is 43^{19}; יְשִׁמֹן Dt 32^{10}; cstr. יְשִׁימוֹן ψ 107^{4};—*waste, wilderness:* **a.** c. art., alm. n.pr. Nu 21^{20} (commanded by Pisgah), 23^{28} (by Peʿor; both JE), frequented by David as an outlaw 1 S $23^{19.24}$ $26^{1.3}$. Probably some part of the wilderness of Judah, bordering on Dead Sea (Conder[Tent Work, ch. 15]; Buhl[Geogr. § 61]); acc. to others, at least in Nu. (v. Di), part of the ʿArābah, NE. of the Dead Sea (in which was בֵּית הַיְשִׁימֹת Nu 33^{49} al.) **b.** without art., a *waste* or *wilderness* (only poet.), of scene of Israel's wanderings (after the Exodus), בְּתֹהוּ יְלֵל יְשׁ׳ Dt 32^{10} (‖ בְּאֶרֶץ מִדְבָּר), ψ 68^{8} 78^{40} 106^{14}; with ref. to returning exiles Is $43^{19.20}$; דֶּרֶךְ ׳י ψ 107^{4} *waste of a way* (= desert way).

†**יִשְׁמָא** **n.pr.m.** a name in Judah 1 Ch 4^{3}; 3457
𝔊 Ραγμα, A Ιεσμα, 𝔊L Σαμαα.

יִשְׁמַעְיָה(וּ), יִשְׁמָעֵאל v. שׁמע. p. 1035 3458

יִשְׁמְרַי v. שׁמר. p. 1038 3461

†[**יָשֵׁן**] **vb. sleep** (NH *id.;* Aram. n. ܫܢܬܐ 3462
sleep; Ar. وَسِنَ *be sleepy,* سِنَةٌ, وَسَنٌ *sleep;* As. *šittu, sleep,* Dl[HWB 246], *šunatu, šuttu, dream,* Id[ib], Flood[iv. 22] Asrb[Annals, v R. 2, 97])—**Qal** *Pf.* יָשַׁנְתִּי Jb 3^{13}; וְיָשֵׁנוּ consec. Je 51^{39} + 2 t.; *Impf.* יִישַׁן Is 5^{27} ψ 121^{4}; וַיִּישַׁן 1 K 19^{5}, etc.; *Inf. cstr.* לִישׁוֹן Ec 5^{11};—*sleep, go to sleep,* and *be asleep,* Gn 2^{21} (J), 41^{5} (E), Ez 34^{25} Jb 3^{13} ψ 3^{6} 4^{9} Pr 4^{16} Ec 5^{11}, also 2 S 4^{6} 𝔊 We Dr Kit Bu, vid. חָמֵשׁ; c. לֹא, of Ass. army Is 5^{27} (‖ נום); of Baal 1 K 19^{5}; of ׳י, עוּרָה לָמָּה תִישַׁן אֲדֹנָי ψ 44^{24}; לֹא יִישָׁן 121^{4} (‖ נום); c. acc. cogn. 8153
יִשְׁ׳ שְׁנַת עוֹלָם Je $51^{39.57}$ (v. שֵׁנָה), of death, cf. אִישַׁן הַמָּוֶת ψ 13^{4}. **Niph.** only in deriv. sense of *become inactive* or *stationary; Pf.* וְנוֹשַׁנְתֶּם consec. Dt 4^{25} *and ye be grown old* בָּאָרֶץ, i.e. (v. Di Dr) have lost freshness of first impressions; of inanimate things, *be old, stale,* only *Pt.* יָשָׁן נוֹשָׁן Lv 26^{10} (H), f. צרעת נוֹשֶׁנֶת Lv 13^{11} = *old leprosy* (P); these poss. denom. from יָשָׁן. **Pi.** causat. *Impf.* וַתְּיַשְּׁנֵהוּ Ju 16^{19} *and she made him sleep.*

† I. **יָשֵׁן** **adj. sleeping;**—ms. יָשֵׁן 1 S 26^{7} + 3 t., 3463
fs. יְשֵׁנָה 1 K 3^{20} Ct 5^{2}; pl. יְשֵׁנִים 1 S 26^{12} Ct 7^{10}; cstr. יְשֵׁנֵי Dn 12^{2};—*asleep, sleeping* 1 S $26^{7.12}$ 1 K 3^{20} Ct 5^{2} 7^{10}; so, fig., Ho 7^{6}, expl. as = יָעֵשָׁן *smoketh,* cf. Dt 29^{19}, by RS[J Phil. xvi. 1888, 72; Proph. iv, n. 19] Che with אַפֵּהֶם (Ges[§ 91. 1. R. 1a]) for אַפְּהֶם; but < We, *their anger sleepeth;* of Baal 1 K 18^{27}; in sim. of ׳י ψ 78^{65}; of dead, as sleeping in dust, Dn 12^{2}.

† II. **יָשֵׁן** **n.pr.m.** one of David's heroes, 2 S 3464
23^{32} = הָשֵׁם 1 Ch 11^{34} (in both del. בְּנֵי as dittogr., We Dr Bu); v. הָשֵׁם, and גּוּנִי.

†**יָשָׁן** **adj. old** (orig., as it seems, *withered,* 3465
flabby, like a lifeless plant with top hanging down, as if in sleep; cf. **Niph.** supr., and NH יִשֵּׁן Pi. *let a thing grow old*)—יָשָׁן Lv 25^{22} + 3 t.; f. יְשָׁנָה Is 22^{11} + 2 t.; pl. יְשָׁנִים Ct 7^{14};—*old:* הַבְּרֵכָה

הַיְשָׁנָה Is 22[11]; שַׁעַר הַיְשָׁנָה Ne 3[6]; so 12[39]; of choice fruits, Ct 7[14] (opp. חדש); subst. *old harvest, store*, Lv 25[22.22] 26[12.12] (H; opp. חדש).

3466 †יְשָׁנָה **n.pr.loc.** town on southern border of N. Israel, near Bethel, 2 Ch 13[19]; so rd. also 1 S 7[12] for MT הַשֵּׁן We Dr Klo Kit Bu; mod. *ʿAin Siniya*, 5 m. N. of Beitun, Cl. Ganneau[JAs. Avr.-Juin, 1870, 490-501] Socin[ZPV i, 1878, 41] Buhl[Geogr. § 95, p. 173].

8142, 8153 †שֵׁנָה, שֵׁנָא, שְׁנַת **n.f. sleep**;—שֵׁנָה ψ 90[5] + 3 t.; שֵׁנָא ψ 127[2], שְׁנַת ψ 132[4] (Ges[§ 80 g. h.]); cstr. שְׁנַת Je 51[39] + 3 t.; שְׁנָתִי Gn 31[40] Je 31[26], etc.; pl. abs. שֵׁנוֹת Pr 6[10] 24[33];—*sleep* Gn 28[16] (J), Ju 16[14.20] Pr 3[24] 6[9] 20[13] Ec 5[11] Je 31[26] Zc 4[1]; Pr 6[4] (‖ תְּנוּמָה); מְעַט שֵׁנוֹת מְעַט תְּנוּמוֹת Pr 6[10] = 24[33] (these two of sluggard אִישׁ עָצֵל; v. also 6[9] 20[13]); note also וַתִּדַּד שְׁנָתִי מֵעֵינָי Gn 31[40] (E) *and my sleep fled from mine eyes*; נָדְדָה שְׁנַת הַמֶּלֶךְ Est 6[1]; וְנִגְזְלָה שְׁנָתָם Pr 4[16]; וּשְׁנָתוֹ נִהְיְתָה עָלָיו Dn 2[1]; שֵׁנָה בְּעֵינָיו אֵינֶנּוּ רֹאֶה Ec 8[16]; אִם אֶתֵּן שְׁנַת לְעֵינָי ψ 132[4] (all of lack of sleep); יִתֵּן לִידִידוֹ שֵׁנָא ψ 127[2] = *he giveth to his beloved in sleep*, cf. Ges[§ 118, 3]; of sleep of death (so Ar. وَسَنٌ Dozy[ii, 806]) Jb 14[12] ψ 90[5] (cf. De Che); so, as acc. cogn., ψ 76[6] Je 51[39.57] (in these two שְׁנַת־עוֹלָם).

3467 †[יָשַׁע] **vb. Hiph.** deliver; **Niph.** intrans. and pass. (Ar. وَسِعَ *be capacious*, II. *make wide, spacious*, IV. *make sufficient*, V. VIII. *be* or *live in abundance* (v. Dr[1 S 14, 45]) Ph. n.pr. ישע; Sab. יתע (royal epith.), n.pr. עמיתע, יתעאל, אליתע, e.g. Mordt[ZMG 1876, 37; 1893, 409. 416. 417, etc.] (yet note strange equiv., ת = س); not in Aram.; MI[4] השעני *he delivered me*, l[3] (ב)משע *deliverance*, Sm and So, (but במת ClGann Dr); n.pr.m. משע l[1], also l[3 [4]] Sm and So, but ישע *deliverance*, ClGann Dr) — **Niph.** *Pf.* 3 m. נוֹשַׁע Dt 33[29] Is 45[17]; 2 pl. נוֹשַׁעְתֶּם Nu 10[9]; 1 pl. נוֹשָׁעְנוּ Je 8[20]; *Impf.* 3 ms. יִוָּשֵׁעַ Je 30[7] Pr 28[18] + 1 S 14[47] (for MT יַרְשִׁיעַ) 𝔊 We Klo Dr Kit Bu; 3 fs. תִּוָּשַׁע Je 23[6] 33[16]; אִוָּשֵׁעָה ψ 119[117] Je 17[14] + 8 t. Impf.; *Imv.* pl. הִוָּשְׁעוּ Is 45[22]; *Pt.* נוֹשָׁע ψ 33[16] Zc 9[9];—**1.** *be liberated, saved* (prop. *placed in freedom*; cf. for the fig. מֶרְחָב, הִרְחִיב), from external evils Pr 28[18], by God Is 30[15] 45[22] 64[4] Je 4[14] 8[20] 17[14] 23[6] 33[16] ψ 80[4.8.20] 119[117]; with מִן, Je 30[7]; מֵאֹיְבִים Nu 10[9] (P), 2 S 22[4] = ψ 18[4]. **2.** *be saved* in battle, *victorious* Zc 9[9] ψ 33[16] + 1 S 14[47] v. supr.; עַם נוֹשַׁע ביהוה Dt 33[29] *a people victorious in* י׳ (poem), cf. Is 45[17]. **Hiph.** *Pf.* 3 ms. הוֹשִׁיעַ 1 S 9[16] ψ 20[7]; הוֹשַׁע Zc 12[7]; sf. הוֹשִׁיעוֹ ψ 34[7]; 1 s. הוֹשַׁעְתִּי Is 43[12] + 4 t., + 14 t. Pf.; *Impf.* יְהוֹשִׁיעַ 1 S 17[47] (v. Dr) ψ 116[6]; יוֹשִׁיעַ Is 45[20] + 6 t.; וְיֹשַׁע (juss.) Pr 20[22]; וַיּוֹשַׁע Ex 14[30] + 7 t.; וַיֹּשַׁע 1 S 23[5] + 2 t.; sf. יוֹשִׁיעֶךָ Ho 13[10]; יוֹשִׁיעֻנוּ Is 46[7]; יֹשִׁעֵנוּ 1 S 10[27]; יֹשַׁעֲכֶם Is 35[4] (juss., Dr[§ 47. n. 4]), etc.; *Imv.* הוֹשַׁע Je 31[7] ψ 86[2]; הוֹשִׁיעָה 2 K 6[26] + 8 t.; הוֹשִׁעָה 2 S 14[4] + 19 t. Imv.; *Inf. abs.* הוֹשֵׁעַ 1 S 25[26] + 2 t.; cstr. הוֹשִׁיעַ 1 S 14[6] + 14 t. + 2 S 3[18] (where rd. אוֹשִׁיעַ Vrss. Ke We Klo Dr Bu al.), + 7 t. Inf.; *Pt.* מוֹשִׁיעַ Dt 22[27] + 21 t.; sf. מוֹשִׁיעָם ψ 106[21] + 8 t. sf.; pl. מוֹשִׁיעִים Ob[21] Ne 9[27];—**1.** *deliver, save* (prop. *give width and breadth to, liberate*), in peril, c. acc. pers. vel loc. Ex 2[17] (E) Ju 6[31] 1 S 23[2.5] 2 S 10[19] = 1 Ch 19[19], 2 K 6[27.27] ψ 36[7] 72[13] Jb 26[2]; with לְ pers. Jos 10[6] (E) Dt 22[27] Ju 10[14] 2 S 10[11] = 1 Ch 19[12] (with acc.), Je 11[12.12] ψ 72[4] 116[6]; abs. הוֹשִׁיעָה הַמֶּלֶךְ *Help, O king* 2 S 14[4] 2 K 6[26]. Specif. *save*, from evils and troubles: **a.** of heroic men, saving the nation in war Ju 3[31] 6[15] 10[1] 1 S 10[27] Ho 13[10] Je 14[9]; these are named מוֹשִׁיעַ *saviour* Ju 3[9.15] 2 K 13[5] Is 19[20] Ob[21] Ne 9[27]; phr. when they are lacking אֵין מוֹשִׁיעַ Ju 12[3] 1 S 11[3] 2 S 22[42] = ψ 18[42], Dt 28[29.31] Is 47[15]; they save מִיַּד *from the hand of* Ju 2[16] 8[22] 12[2] 13[5] 1 S 9[16] Ne 9[27]; מכף Ju 6[14] 1 S 4[3] 2 K 16[7]. **b.** of God, who saves his people from external evils Dt 20[4] Jos 22[22] Ju 3[9] 6[36.37] 7[7] 10[13] 1 S 14[23.39] 2 K 14[27] 19[34] = Is 37[35], Is 25[9] 33[22] 35[4] 43[12] 49[25] 63[9] Je 31[7] Ez 34[22] Ho 1[7.7] Hb 1[2] Zp 3[17.19] Zc 8[7.13] 9[16] 10[6] 12[7] ψ 28[9] 69[36] 106[8] 118[25] 2 Ch 20[9]; or the pious among them Is 38[20] Je 2[27] 17[14] ψ 3[8] 6[5] 7[2] 31[17] 54[3] 55[17] 57[4] 69[2] 71[2.3] 106[47] = 1 Ch 16[35], ψ 109[26] 119[94.146] 138[7] Pr 20[22]; and especially the king ψ 20[7.10]; David 2 S 8[6.14]; thy servant ψ 86[2.16]; חסיד 12[2]; דַּכְּאֵי־רוּחַ 34[19]; צדיקים 37[40]; חוסים 17[7]; יראי י׳ 145[19]; עם עני 18[28] = 2 S 22[28]; עַנְוֵי־אֶרֶץ ψ 76[10]; ישרי לב 7[11]; שַׁח עֵינַיִם Jb 22[29]; accordingly God is מוֹשִׁיעַ *saviour* Is 43[11] 45[15.21] 63[8] Ho 13[4]; מֹשִׁעִי 2 S 22[3]; מוֹשִׁיעָם ψ 106[21]; מוֹשִׁיעוֹ Je 14[8]; מוֹשִׁיעֵךְ Is 43[3] 49[26] 60[16] Je 30[10] = 46[27]; is with his people לְהוֹשִׁיעַ Je 15[20] 30[11] 42[11]; רַב לְהוֹשִׁיעַ Is 63[1]; בֵּית מְצוּדוֹת לְהוֹשִׁיעֵנִי ψ 31[3]; Isr. prays הוֹשִׁיעָה יְמִינְךָ *O save with thy right hand* ψ 60[7] = 108[7], cf. Is 59[1]; that fr. wh. one is saved constr. c. מִן: מִיַּד Ex 14[30] (J) Ju 2[18] 10[12] 1 S 7[8] 2 S 3[18] 2 K 19[19] = Is 37[20], ψ 106[10] 2 Ch 32[22]; מֵחָמָס 2 S 22[3]; מֵחֶרֶב Jb 5[15]: מִכָּל־צָרוֹת ψ 34[7]; מִכָּל־רָעוֹת 1 S 10[19]; מִפִּי אַרְיֵה 22[22]; מִצָּרֵינוּ ψ 44[8]; מִשֹּׁפְטֵי נַפְשׁוֹ 109[31]; מֵאַנְשֵׁי דָמִים 59[3]; מִמְּצוּקוֹת 107[13.19]. **c.** there is no other salvation, the sword saves not ψ 44[7], or a nation La 4[17], or astrologers Is 47[13], or Asshur Ho 14[4], or other gods Is 45[20] 46[7] Je 2[28]. **2.** *save from moral troubles*, only in Ez.

(מְשׁוּבוֹתֵיהֶם .rd., with Co Da al) מִכֹּל מוֹשְׁבֹתֵיהֶם 37^{23}; מִכֹּל טֻמְאוֹתֵיכֶם 36^{29}. **3.** *give victory to:* **a.** of *man*, c. לְ pers., *give victory to*, c. agent subj. יָד Ju 7^{2} 1 S 25$^{26.33}$, יָד om. v^{31}; יָמִין Jb 40^{14}; זְרוֹעַ ψ 44^{4}. **b.** of *God*, with לְ pers., subj. יָמִין ψ 98^{1}; זְרוֹעַ Is 59^{16} 63^{5}; Yahweh 1 Ch 18^{6}, with acc. v^{13}; abs. *gain victory* 1 S 14^{6} 17^{47}; וַיּוֹשַׁע תְּשׁוּעָה גְדוֹלָה 1 Ch 11^{14}.

3468 † יֵ֫שַׁע **n.m.** Is 51,5 **deliverance, rescue, salvation, also safety, welfare;**—יֵ֫שַׁע ψ 20^{7} + 4 t.; יֶ֫שַׁע Jb 5^{11} + 4 t.; sf. יִשְׁעִי 2 S 22^{3} + 11 t., + 14 t. sfs.;—**1.** *safety, welfare, prosperity* 2 S 23^{5} ψ 12^{6} Jb 5$^{4.11}$. **2.** *salvation*, i.e. primarily physical rescue, by God, oft. with added spiritual idea: Is 62^{11} ψ 69^{14} 85$^{8.10}$; יֵשַׁע אֱלֹהִים *salvation from God* ψ 50^{23}; used as infin. with acc. לְיֵשַׁע Hb 3$^{13.13}$ (see Ew § 239 a); accordingly Yahweh is אוֹרִי וְיִשְׁעִי *my light and my salvation* ψ 27^{1}; צוּר ישׁע 95^{1}; קֶרֶן ישׁע 18^{3} = 2 S 22^{3}; אֱלֹהֵי ישׁע Is 17^{10} Mi 7^{7} Hb 3^{18} ψ 18^{47} = אֱלֹהֵי צוּר ישׁע 2 S 22^{47}, ψ 24^{5} 25^{5} 27^{9} 65^{6} 79^{9} 85^{5} 1 Ch 16^{35}; מָגֵן יִשׁ׳ ψ 18^{36} = 2 S 22^{36}; על אלהים ישׁעי ψ 62^{8}; || צְדָקָה Is 45^{8} 51^{5} 61^{10}; שְׂשׂוֹן יִשְׁעֶךָ ψ 51^{14} *joy of thy salvation;* כֹּהֲנֶיהָ אַלְבִּישׁ יֶשַׁ׳ 132^{16} *her priests will I clothe with salvation.* **3.** *victory:* גְּבוּרוֹת יֵשַׁע יְמִינוֹ ψ 20^{7} *the mighty deeds of the victory of his right hand.*

3444 † יְשׁוּעָה **n.f. salvation;**—יְשׁ׳ ψ 119^{155} + 18 t.; יְשׁוּעָתָה 3^{3} Jon 2^{10}; יְשֻׁעָתָה ψ 80^{3}; cstr. יְשׁוּעַת Ex 14^{13} + 4 t.; sf. יְשֻׁעָתִי Jb 30^{15}; יְשׁוּעָתִי ψ 62^{2} + 12 t., + 25 t. sfs.; pl. יְשׁוּעוֹת 2 S 22^{51} + 6 t.; יְשׁוּעֹת 42^{12} + 3 t.; יְשֻׁעוֹת 53^{7};—**1.** *welfare, prosperity:* כעב עברה ישׁעתי Jb 30^{15} *as a cloud my prosperity passed away.* **2.** *deliverance:* והיתה לי לישׁועה *and thou wilt be to me for deliverance* 2 S 10^{11} = 1 Ch 19^{12}. **3.** *salvation* by God, primarily from external evils, but often with added spiritual idea: Gn 49^{18} (poem), Is 33^{2} 52$^{7.10}$ 59^{11} 60^{18} Jon 2^{10} ψ 3$^{3.9}$ 14^{7} = 53^{7}, 22^{2} 35^{3} 62^{2} 69^{30} 70^{5} (= תשׁועה 40^{17}), 78^{22} 80^{3} 91^{16} 96^{2} = 1 Ch 16^{23}, 106^{4} 140^{8} Jb 13^{16}; with verbs of rejoicing בישׁועה 1 S 2^{1} Is 25^{9} ψ 9^{15} 13^{6} 35^{9}; יְשׁוּעָה יָשִׁית חומות Is 26^{1} *salvation will he set as walls;* cf. phr. צוּר יְשׁ׳ Dt 32^{15} (song), ψ 89^{27}, cf. צוּרִי וִישׁוּעָתִי 62$^{3.7}$; אֵל יְשׁ׳ Is 12^{2}, אֱלֹהֵי יְשׁ׳ ψ 88^{2}, יוֹם יְשׁ׳ Is 49^{8}; מַעַיְנֵי הַיְשׁ׳ 12^{3} *wells of salvation;* pl. יְשׁוּעוֹת (intensive), of י׳: יְשׁוּעוֹת פָּנַי ψ 42^{6} *the salvation of my face* (person; פניו MT error, פני 𝔊 𝔖), v^{12} 43^{5}; כּוֹס ישׁועות 116^{13} *cup commemorating saving acts* (of drink-offering); further ψ 119$^{123.155.166.174}$; יְשׁוּעָתִי || צְדָקָה Is 51$^{6.8}$ 56^{1} 62^{1} ψ 98$^{2.3}$; יְשׁוּעָתִי עַד־קְצֵה הָאָרֶץ Is 49^{6} *my salvation unto the ends of the earth;* בְּכָל־גּוֹיִם יְשׁוּעָתֶךָ ψ 67^{3} *among all nations thy salvation.* **4.** *victory:* c. עָשָׂה *work victory* 1 S 14^{45} Is 26^{18}; elsewhere of victories wrought by Yahweh for his people Ex 15^{2} (song) Is 12^{2} Hb 3^{8} ψ 20^{6} 21$^{2.6}$ 44^{5} 68^{20} 118$^{14.15.21}$; phrases: פעל יְשׁוּעוֹת *do victories* 74^{12}; חֹסֶן יְשׁוּעֹת Is 33^{6} *store of victories;* מִגְדּוֹל יְשׁוּעוֹת 2 S 22^{51} Qr *tower of victories* (Kt מַגְדִּיל and so || ψ 18^{51}); מָעוֹז יְשׁוּעוֹת ψ 28^{8} *stronghold of victories;* רְאוּ אֶת־יְשׁוּעַת י׳ Ex 14^{13} (J) *see the victory of Yahweh,* 2 Ch 20^{17}; כּוֹבַע יְשׁוּעָה Is 59^{17} *helmet of victory;* יְפָאֵר עֲנָוִים בִּישׁוּעָה ψ 149^{4} *he will beautify the meek with victory.*—Cf. the syn. תְּשׁוּעָה, infr.

† I. שׁוֹעַ **adj. (free), independent, noble** 7771
(in station) (acc. to most from second. √ שׁוע = ישׁע, in sense of Ar. وَسِعَ (cf. תְּשׁוּעָה infr.); but actual existence of such a √ not proven; Thes allows שׁוֹעַ = (יָשׁוֹעַ)—*noble*, of rank (and, by implic., of character) Is 32^{5} (|| נָדִיב, opp. כִּילַי), Jb 34^{19} (Di al. *rich*, but || שָׂרִים, opp. דַּל).—II. שׁוֹעַ
Is 22^{5}, v. sub [שָׁוַע]. III. שׁוֹעַ **n.pr.gent.** 7772
Ez 23^{23}, v. ׳שׁ. p. 1003

† I. שׁוּעַ **n.pr.m.** father of Judah's wife, 7770
𝔊 Σαυα, Gn 38^{2} and (after cstr. בַּת) v^{12} 1 Ch 2^{3}; v. בַּת־שׁוּעַ p. 124 supr., and cf. on mng. (אֲבִי)שׁוּעַ p. 4, (אֱלִי)שׁוּעַ p. 46.

II. שׁוּעַ **n.[m.] opulence?** (cf. Ar. سَعَةٌ)— 7769
so AE al. Jb 30^{24} 36^{19}; but < v. sub [שָׁוַע]. p. 1002

† שׁוּעָא **n.pr.f.** a woman of Asher 1 Ch 7^{32}; 7774
𝔊 Σωλα, 𝔊L Σουα.

† יִשְׁעִי **n.pr.m.** (*salutary*)—**1.** one of the 3469
line of Jerahmeel 1 Ch 2$^{31.31}$, 𝔊 Ισεμιηλ, A Ιεσει, 𝔊L Ιεσσουει. **2.** a chief of Manasseh 1 Ch 5^{24}, 𝔊 Σεει, Ιεσ(σ)ει. **3.** a chief of Judah 1 Ch 4^{20}. **4.** a chief of Simeon 1 Ch 4^{42}.

יְשַׁעְיָ֫הוּ **n.pr.m.** (*salvation of Yah;* cf. 3470
אֱלִישָׁע p. 46 supr.; ישעאל on scarab ClGann JAs 1883, Fev.-Mars, 135, No. 8)—**1.** Isaiah, son of 'Amôs, the prophet: Is 1^{1} + 15 t. Is., 2 K 19^{2} + 12 t. K., 2 Ch 26^{22} 32$^{20.32}$, 𝔊 Ησαιας, 𝔙 *Isaias.* †**2.** one of the children of Jeduthun 1 Ch 25$^{3.15}$, 𝔊 Ισαια, etc. †**3.** a Levite ancestor of one of David's treasurers 1 Ch 26^{25}, 𝔊 Ωσαιας, 𝔊L Ιωσηε.

† יְשַׁעְיָה **n.pr.m.** (*salvation of Yah*)—**1.** 3470
grandson of Zerubbabel 1 Ch 3^{21}, 𝔊 Ιασαβα, Ιεσεια. **2.** chief of the sons of Elam, who went up with Ezra Ezr 8^{7}, 𝔊 Ιοσεια, Ησαια, etc. **3.** chief of sons of Merari in time of Ezra

Ezr 8^{19}, 𝔊 Ωσαια, etc. **4.** a Benjamite Ne 11^{7}, 𝔊 Ιεσια, etc.

1954 †**הוֹשֵׁעַ n.pr.m.** (*salvation;* on form, cf. הַמֹּשֵׁל, הַשְּׁמֵד; on pronunciation v. Hpt $^{ZA\ ii,261\ Anm.2}$ Jäger $^{BAS\ i,468}$)—**1.** orig. name of Joshua acc. to Nu $13^{8.16}$ (P), 𝔊 Αυση, cf. Dt 32^{44} (J; prob. err., v. Dr), 𝔊 Ιησους, v. יְהוֹשֻׁעַ p. 221 supr. **2.** last king of Israel 2 K 15^{30} $17^{1.3.4.6}$ $18^{1.9.10}$, 𝔊 Ωσηε. **3.** the prophet Hosea Ho $1^{1.2.2}$, 𝔊 Ωσηε. **4.** an Ephraimite chief under David 1 Ch 27^{20}, 𝔊 Ωση(ε). **5.** a chief under Nehemiah Ne 10^{24}, 𝔊 Ωσηθα, Ωσηε.

1955 †**הוֹשַׁעְיָה n.pr.m.** (*Yah has saved*)—**1.** a prince of Judah Ne 12^{32}, 𝔊 Ωσαια. **2.** father of Azariah or Jezaniah, a chief in time of Jeremiah Je 42^{1} 43^{2}, 𝔊 Μαασ(σ)αιος, etc.

3091,3442 **יֵשׁוּעַ, יְהוֹשֻׁעַ n.pr.**, see p. 221.

4190 †**[מוֹשָׁעָה] n.f.** only pl. מוֹשָׁעוֹת *saving acts* ψ 68^{21}.

4338 †**מֵישַׁע n.pr.m.** (*deliverance*)—Mesha, king of Moab 2 K 3^{4}=משע MI^{1}; 𝔊 Μωσα.—v. Sm and So^{MI,1886} Dr$^{Sm\ lxxxv\ ff.}$

4337 †**מֵישָׁע n.pr.m.** (*deliverance*)—son of Caleb 1 Ch 2^{42}, 𝔊 Μαρεισα, 𝔊L Μουσα.

8668 †**תְּשׁוּעָה** (+תְּשֻׁעָה 2 S 19^{3}) **n.f. deliverance, salvation** = יְשׁוּעָה (formed by false anal., as if from √ שׁוע, in sense of ישׁע; most assign it to שׁוע, but no sufficient evidence for existence of such a √; cf. Kö $^{ii.200}$)—abs. ת׳ 1 S 11^{9}+19 t.; cstr. Je 3^{23}+5 t.; sf. תְּשׁוּעָתִי Is 46^{13}+2 t.; תְּשׁוּעָתְךָ ψ 40^{11}+2 t.; תְּשׁוּעָתֵךְ v^{17} 71^{15};—**1.** *deliverance*, usually by God, through human agency, esp. from oppression 1 S 11^{9}, and in battle 1 Ch 19^{12} (הושׁיע in ‖ cl.), =*victory* Ju 15^{18} (נָתַתָּ ת׳ בְּיַד וגו׳), 2 K 5^{1}, י׳ עשׂה ת׳ י׳ 1 S 11^{13} *wrought a great victory*, so 19^{5} 2 S 19^{3} $23^{10.12}$ 1 Ch 11^{14} (as acc. cogn. after הושׁיע), Pr 21^{31} ψ 33^{17} (נושׁע in ‖ v^{16}); הַנּוֹתֵן ת׳ למלכים 144^{10}; so in phr. חֵץ־ת׳ ליהוה 2 K 13^{17}, חֵץ־ת׳ בַּאֲרָם v^{17}; of national *deliverance*, from exile, נוֹשַׁע יִשְׂרָאֵל ת׳ עולמים Is 45^{17} (Da$^{Synt.\ \S 67b}$), 46^{13} (‖ צְדָקָה), v^{13} (c. נתן; ‖ תִּפְאֶרֶת); in gen. of national *success* and *prosperity* Je 3^{23} Pr 11^{14}=24^{6}; of deliverance fr. personal trouble ψ 37^{39} La 3^{26} (תְּשׁוּעַת י׳), or of national deliverance under fig. of personal ψ 40^{11} (‖ אֱמוּנָתְךָ), v^{17} 71^{15} (‖ צְדָקָה), so תְּשׁוּעָתִי י׳ 38^{23}; contrasted with י׳'s deliverance is תְּשׁוּעַת אָדָם *deliverance of* (*through*) *man* ψ 60^{13}=108^{13}, cf. 146^{3}. **2.** more exclusively spiritual in sense, =*salvation*, appear to be אֱלֹהֵי תְּשׁוּעָתִי ψ 51^{16}, 119^{41} (‖ חַסְדֶּךָ), v^{81}, and כֹּהֲנֶיךָ יִלְבְּשׁוּ ת׳ 2 Ch 6^{41} (from כהניה אלביש יֶשַׁע ψ 132^{16}).

†**יָשְׁפֵה n.[m.] jasper** (loan-word fr. Pers. يَشْبْ; so Ar. يَشْبْ Lane^{2978}, also (and on forms يَشْمْ, يَشْفْ) Frey; perh. As. *ašpû* Dl$^{HA\ 36,\ HWB\ 147}$)—תַּרְשִׁישׁ וְשֹׁהַם וְיָשְׁפֵה Ex 28^{20} 39^{13} (both P) *beryl and onyx and jasper* (v. Di); וְיָשְׁפֵה (+*id.*) Ez 28^{13} (v. Sm). 3471

יִשְׁפָּה v. sub שׁפה; **יִשְׁפָּן** v. sub שׁפן. p. 1046, 1051 3472-76

†**יָשַׁר vb. be smooth, straight, right** (NH *id.*, and deriv.; Ar. يَسَرَ *be gentle, tractable, easy*, II. *make easy*; يَسَرٌ *manageable, easy*; but Sab. ותר, הותר, אהל יתרן Os$^{ZMG\ 1865,270}$ CIS^{iv,29,2}; As. *išâru*, *be* or *go straight, right*, *mêšêru*, *justice*, *mêšêriš*, *righteously*, Dl$^{HWB\ 310}$)—**Qal** *Pf.* יָשַׁר Je 18^{4}+2 t.; 3 f. יָשְׁרָה Ju 14^{3} Hb 2^{4}; 3 mpl. יָשְׁרוּ 1 K 9^{12}; *Impf.* יִישַׁר Nu 23^{27}+2 t.; יִשַׁר 1 S $18^{20.26}$; 3 fs. תִּישַׁר Ju 14^{7}; 3 fpl. יִשַּׁרְנָה 1 S 6^{12} (Ges $^{\S 47,\ n.3;\ 71}$)—**1.** *go straight*, בַּדֶּרֶךְ *in the way* 1 S 6^{12}. **2.** fig., *be pleasing, agreeable, right* (בְּעֵינֵי *in the eyes of*); said of a woman Ju $14^{3.7}$; a man Je 27^{5}; of matters and things (הַדָּבָר) 1 S $18^{20.26}$ 2 S 17^{4} 1 Ch 13^{4} 2 Ch 30^{4}; of cities 1 K 9^{12}; a place בְּעֵינֵי הָאֱלֹהִים Nu 23^{27} (E); with כַּאֲשֶׁר Je 18^{4}. **3.** in ethical sense, *straightforward, upright;* לֹא־יָשְׁרָה נַפְשׁוֹ בּוֹ Hb 2^{4} *his soul is not upright in him* (opp. עֻפְּלָה *swollen*). **Pi.** *Pf.* 1 יִשַּׁרְתִּי ψ 119^{128} (יִשְּׁרֵהוּ Jb 37^{3}, 3 m. sf. Thes; but < Ew Di Hi De Da, *Impf.* fr. שָׁרָה); *Impf.* יְיַשֵּׁר Pr 3^{6}; יְיַשֶּׁר־ 15^{21}; sf. וַיְיַשְּׁרֵם (Mas. abbrev. וַיְּשְׁרֵם) 2 Ch 32^{30}; 3 fs. תְּיַשֵּׁר Pr 11^{4}; 1 s. אֲיַשֵּׁר Is 45^{13}; אֲיַשֵּׁר v^{2} Qr (Kt Hiph. אושׁר Ges $^{\S 70,2}$ doubtless copyist's error); *Imv.* pl. יַשְּׁרוּ 40^{3}; *Pt.* pl. מְיַשְּׁרִים Pr 9^{15};—**1.** *make smooth, straight*, acc. מְסִלָּה Is 40^{3}; הֲדוּרִים 45^{2}; fig., with דֶּרֶךְ, *make smooth* or *straight*, i.e. free from obstacles, successful v^{13} Pr 11^{5}, אֹרַח 3^{6}; in ethical sense, הַמְיַשְּׁרִים אֹרְחוֹתָם 9^{15} *those making straight their paths*, going straightforward on their paths; יְיַשֶּׁר־לָכֶת 15^{21} *maketh straight his going, goeth straightforwards.* **2.** *lead straight along, direct*, waters of an aqueduct 2 Ch 32^{30}; (of the thunder Jb 37^{3} acc. to some; but v. rather שָׁרָה). **3.** *esteem right, approve* ψ 119^{128} (rd. כל פקודיך לי יִשַּׁרְתִּי). **Pu.** *Pt.* זָהָב מְיֻשָּׁר עַל־הַמְּחֻקֶּה 1 K 6^{35} *gold made level, laid smoothly out, upon the graven work.* **Hiph.** *Impf.* 3 pl. עַפְעַפֶּיךָ יַיְשִׁרוּ נֶגְדֶּךָ Pr 4^{25} *let thine eyelids look straight before thee; Imv.* הַיְשַׁר דַּרְכֶּךָ *make thy way even* ψ 5^{9} Qr (Kt הוֹשַׁר; v. Ges $^{70(2)}$). 3474

3477 **† יָשָׁר adj.** straight, right;—׳י 1 S 29^{6}+ 70t.; cstr. יְשַׁר Pr 29^{27}; f. יְשָׁרָה Ez 1^{7}+4t.; pl. יְשָׁרִים Nu 23^{10}+31 t.; cstr. יִשְׁרֵי ψ 7^{11}+8 t.; f. יְשָׁרוֹת Ez 1^{23} (del. Co);—**1.** *straight, level*, of a way Is 26^{7} Je 31^{9} ψ 107^{7} Ezr 8^{21}; foot Ez 1^{7}; wings v^{23} (? v. supr.) **2.** *right, pleasing*: **a.** *to God*, הַיָּשָׁר בעיני *that which is right, pleasing in the eyes of, agreeable to* (either cstr. before ׳י, or with sfs. referring to him), esp. in Deut. writers, Ex 15^{26} (R), Dt 12^{25} 13^{19} 21^{9} 1 K 11$^{33.38}$ 14^{8} 15$^{5.11}$ 22^{43} = 2 Ch 20^{32}, 2 K 10^{30}, 12^{3} 14^{3} 15$^{3.34}$ 16^{2} 18^{3} 22^{2} = 2 Ch 24^{2} 25^{2} 26^{4} 27^{2} 28^{1} 29^{2} 34^{2}, Je 34^{15}; הישר והטוב בעיני ׳י Dt 6^{18}; הטוב והישר בעיני ׳י 12^{28} 2 Ch 14^{1}; הטוב והישר והאמת לפני ׳י 31^{20}. **b.** *to man*, (ה)ישר בעיני Dt 12^{8} Ju 17^{6} 21^{25} 2 S 19^{7} Je 40^{5} Pr 12^{15} 21^{2}; (ה)טוב ו(ה)ישר בעיני Jos 9^{25} (D), Je 26^{14} 40^{4}; יֵשׁ דֶּרֶךְ יָשָׁר לִפְנֵי־אִישׁ Pr 14^{12} *there is a way which is pleasing before a man* = 16^{25}. **3.** *straightforward, just, upright*: **a.** *of God*, צַדִּיק וְיָשָׁר הוּא Dt 32^{4} (song); טוב וישר ׳י ψ 25^{8}; ישר ׳י 92^{16}; his ways Ho 14^{10}; his משפטים Ne 9^{13} ψ 119^{137}; פִּקּוּדִים 19^{9}; דָּבָר 33^{4}; the words of divine wisdom Pr 8^{9}. **b.** *of man*, God made him *upright* Ec 7^{29}; but יָשָׁר בָּאָדָם אָיִן Mi 7^{2} *an upright man among men there is none*, and yet Job is תָּם וְיָשָׁר Jb 1^{1} (v. Da), v^{8} 2^{3}, cf. ψ 37^{37}; זַךְ וישר Jb 8^{6}; so earlier of David as an upright man 1 S 29^{6}; of man's doings ‖ זַךְ Pr 20^{11}, cf. 21^{8}; of his way of life ‖ טובה 1 S 12^{23}; יְשַׁר־דַּרְכּוֹ Pr 29^{27}; יִשְׁרֵי־דָרֶךְ ψ 37^{14}; of his heart, mind, and will, יִשְׁרֵי לֵבָב *upright of heart* 2 Ch 29^{34}; יִשְׁרֵי־לֵב ψ 7^{11} 11^{2} 32^{11} 36^{11} 64^{11} 94^{15} 97^{11}; יְשָׁרִים בְּלִבּוֹתָם 125^{4}. **c.** as a noun, (1) with ref. to things, יָשָׁר הֶעֱוֵיתִי *the right I have perverted* Jb 33^{27}; הַיְשָׁרָה יְעַקֵּשׁוּ Mi 3^{9} *pervert the right* (lit. *twist* that which is *straight*); דֹּבֵר יְשָׁרִים *speaketh right things* Pr 16^{13}, cf. 2 K 10^{15}. (2) more commonly of men, in sg. (ה)יָּשָׁר Mi 2^{7} 7^{4} 2 K 10^{3} Pr 21^{29} Jb 23^{7}; collective, ψ 11^{7}; also in סֵפֶר הַיָּשָׁר *book of the upright* Jos 10^{13} 2 S 1^{18} (cf. 1 K 8^{53} 𝔊; Dr$^{Intr. 182}$), a collection of ancient national poetry; in pl. יְשָׁרִים *the upright*, of pious Israel Nu 23^{10} (song E); elsewhere of the upright among the people of God as distinguished from the wicked, in WisdLt, Jb 4^{7} 17^{8} Pr 2$^{7.21}$ 3^{32} 11$^{3.6.11}$ 12^{6} 14$^{9.11}$ 15$^{8.19}$ 16^{17} 21^{18} 28^{10} 29^{10}, in late ψψ 33^{1} 49^{15} 107^{42} 111^{1} 112$^{2.4}$ 140^{14} and Dn 11^{17}. **4.** abstr., *uprightness*, בֶּאֱמֶת וְיָשָׁר ψ 111^{8} (Thes), but read rather ישר with Hi Ri Bae, after 𝔊 𝔖 𝔗 Jer.

† יֹשֶׁר n.m. $^{ψ 25, 21}$ **straightness, uprightness;** 3476
—יֹשֶׁר Pr 2^{13}+11 t.; sf. יָשְׁרוֹ Jb 33^{23} Pr 14^{2};—**1.** *straightness, evenness*, of paths (with moral implication) Pr 2^{13} 4^{11}. **2.** *rightness, uprightness* Pr 17^{26}; תֹּם וָיֹשֶׁר ψ 25^{21}; of words, spoken Jb 6^{25}, written Ec 12^{10}; of the moral walk ב(ו)ישר 1 K 9^{4} Pr 14^{2}; יֹשֶׁר־לִבִּי Jb 33^{3}; ישר לבב Dt 9^{5} ψ 119^{7} 1 Ch 29^{17}:—on ψ 111^{8} v. יָשָׁר **4.** **3.** *what is due, right* Jb 33^{23} Pr 11^{24}.

† יֵשֶׁר n.pr.m. (*uprightness*) son of Caleb 3475
1 Ch 2^{18} (on pointing v. Baer), 𝔊 Ιωασαρ, 𝔊L Σαρ.

† [יִשְׁרָה] n.f. uprightness;—בְּיִשְׁרַת לֵבָב 3483
1 K 3^{6} (for form see Bö$^{§ 644 a}$ Kö$^{§ 90 (ii, 170)}$).

† יְשֻׁרוּן n.pr.m. (*upright one*) Dt 32^{15} 33$^{5.26}$ 3484
Is 44^{2}; poetic name of Israel, designating it under its *ideal* character, 𝔊 ὁ ἠγαπημένος, Aq Sym Theod εὐθύς, 𝔙 *rectissimus, dilectus*; Thes Ew$^{§ 167 a}$ Lag$^{BN 33}$ regard it as dimin. fr. יָשׁוּר = *good little people*; but no evidence that וּן- has a dimin. force, and most recent scholars De Di Dr MV Ges$^{§ 86 (2). 4}$ take as denom. = *Rechtvolk*; Bacher$^{ZAW v, 1885, 161 ff.}$ and Che rightly compare סֵפֶר הַיָּשָׁר (see יָשָׁר **3 e**).

† [מֵישָׁר] n.m. evenness, uprightness, 4339
equity;—only pl.: מֵשָׁרִים Pr 1^{3}; elsewhere מֵישָׁרִים Is 26^{7}+17 t.;—**1.** *evenness, level* Is 26^{7}, of path of righteous (in the future), fig. for free from difficulties; *smoothness*, of the flow of wine, בְּמ׳ Pr 23^{31}; למ׳ Ct 7^{10}. **2.** in ethical sense, *uprightness, equity*, as taught in the school of wisdom Pr 8^{6}, ‖ צֶדֶק 1^{3} 2^{9}; of government (ב)מ׳ ψ 9^{9} 58^{2} 75^{3} 96^{10} 98^{9} 99^{4}; of speech Is 33^{15} Pr 23^{16}; of Yahweh's promises Is 45^{19}; רצה מ׳ 1 Ch 29^{17} *have pleasure in equity*; עָשָׂה מ׳ Dn 11^{6} *make an equitable arrangement*. **3.** adv. *rightly*, with חזה ψ 17^{2}; אהב Ct 1^{4}.

† מִישׁוֹר n.m. $^{Je 48, 8}$ **level place, upright-** 4334
ness;—מ׳ ψ 27^{11}+9 t.; מִישֹׁר Zc 4^{7} (v. Baer)+12 t.;—**1.** *level country, table-land, plain*: antith. הר(ים) 1 K 20$^{23.25}$ Zc 4^{7}; עָקֹב Is 40^{4}; מַעֲקַשִּׁים 42^{16}; + שְׁפֵלָה 2 Ch 26^{10}; ‖ עֵמֶק Je 21^{13}; הַמִּישׁוֹר specifically of the elevated plateau or *table-land* between the Arnon and Heshbon Dt 3^{10} 4^{43} Jos 13$^{9.16.17.21}$ 20^{8} Je 48$^{8.21}$. **2.** *level place* (free from obstacles), fig. for place of safety, comfort, and prosperity ψ 26^{12}; ארח מ׳ 27^{11}; אֶרֶץ מ׳ 143^{10}. **3.** *uprightness* (cf. מֵישָׁר **2**), in government ψ 67^{5}; שֵׁבֶט מ׳ 45^{7}; ‖ צֶדֶק Is 11^{4}; שָׁלוֹם Mal 2^{6}.

8289 †שָׁרוֹן **n.pr.loc.** **Sharon** (plausibly connected with √ישׁר by Thes Ges[12] al., cf. GASm [Geogr. 52]; =*יְשָׁרוֹן; Ph. שרן)—strictly **n.m.**[Is 65, 10] **plain, level**;—**1.** הַשּׁ׳ (with art.), name of maritime plain on Mediterr., fr. Joppa northward, noted for fertility, Is 33[9] (‖ כַּרְמֶל, בָּשָׁן; 𝔊 ὁ Σαρων), cf. הֲדַר כַּרְמֶל וְהַשָּׁרוֹן 35[2]; 65[10] (‖ עֵמֶק עָכוֹר; 𝔊 τῷ δρυμῷ); חֲבַצֶּלֶת הַשּׁ׳ Ct 2[1] (𝔊 ἄνθος τοῦ πεδίου); הַבָּקָר הָרֹעִים בַּשּׁ׳ 1 Ch 27[29]; so also Jos 12[18], where rd. מֶלֶךְ אֲפֵק לַשּׁ׳, so Di We[Sam 55] Ges[12] after 𝔊, cf. RS[OTJC 2, 273, 435].—On this plain v. GASm [Geogr. 147 ff.] Buhl [Geogr. § 65]. **2.** מִגְרְשֵׁי שָׁרוֹן, region E. of Jordan 1 Ch 5[16] (‖ גִּלְעָד, בָּשָׁן; 𝔊 τὰ περίχωρα Γεριαμ, 𝔊A Σαρων); identified by many with הַמִּישׁוֹר (Dt 3[10] etc., v. supr.)

ישׁשׁ (√of foll.; cf. Ar. وَتْوَاتٌ *weak* or *impotent* man, وَتْوَتَةٌ *weakness, impotence*, Lane[2919]).

3486 †יָשֵׁשׁ **adj. aged, decrepit**, only זָקֵן וְיָשֵׁשׁ 2 Ch 36[17].

3453 †יָשִׁישׁ **adj. aged**, only Jb (NH once יְשִׁישִׁים *old, venerable* men, Levy Jastr);—abs. יָשִׁישׁ Jb 15[10]; pl. יְשִׁישִׁים 32[6] + 2 t.;—*aged*, as pred. adj. Jb 32[6] (opp. צָעִיר לְיָמִים); as subst. 15[10] (‖ שָׂב); 29[8] (opp. נְעָרִים); בִּישִׁישִׁים חָכְמָה 12[12] *among aged men is wisdom* (‖ אֹרֶךְ יָמִים תְּבוּנָה).

3454 †יְשִׁישַׁי **n.pr.m.** a Gileadite name 1 Ch 5[14].

יתד (√of foll.; mng. dub.; Ar. وَتَدَ *drive in peg, be firm* (of peg), is appar. denom.)

3489 †יָתֵד **n.f.**[Dt 23, 14] **peg, pin** (NH *id.*; Ar. وَتِدٌ)—יָתֵד Dt 23[14] + 9 t.; cstr. יְתַד Ju 4[21] 16[14] (where c. art. but v. Ges[§ 127, R. 4 a]); pl. יְתֵדֹת Ex 38[20]; cstr. יִתְדֹת 27[19] + 4 t.; sf. יְתֵדֹתָיו Is 54[2]; יְתֵדֹתַיִךְ Ex 27[19] Is 33[20]; וִיתֵדֹתֶיהָ Ex 39[40]; וִיתֵדֹתָם Nu 3[37] 4[32];—*pin, peg*, esp. **a.** *tent-pin* Ju 5[26] 4[21]; יְתַד הָאֹהֶל v[22]; rd. perh. also Jb 4[21] (fig.; cf. II. יֶתֶר); oft. of tabernacle Ex 27[19.19] 35[18.18] 38[20.31.31]; ‖ מֵיתָרָיו 39[40], cf. Nu 3[37] 4[32] (all P); of Zion under fig. of tent Is 33[20] 54[2]; fig. of ruler as support of state Zc 10[4]. **b.** a peg for hanging Ez 15[3]; so fig. of Eliakim Is 22[23.24]; of secure position Ezr 9[8] (cf. Ar., v. Thes Hi Hariri [361 Der.], ثَابِتُ الْأَوْتَادِ of a king). **c.** for digging Dt 23[14] (=spade). **d.** the *pin* or stick used in beating up the woof in the loom Ju 16[14a], vid. GFM [PAOS, Oct. 1889, clxxvi. ff.]; in היתד הארג v[b], del. היתד (Id[ib] and in Comm. ad loc.)

יְתוּר Jb 39[8], v. תור.

יִתְלָה v. תלה. p. 1068 3494

יתח (assumed by Thes as √of foll.; cf. Ar. وَتَخَ *beat with a club, chastise*; مِيتَخَةٌ *club*; Ba[NB 294] der. תותח as loan-word fr. As. *tartaḫu* = *club* (or *javelin*, cf. Dl[HWB 630])).

†תּוֹתָח **n.m.** name of a weapon, perh. **club, mace** (or *dart, javelin*; ‖ כִּידוֹן);—Jb 41[21]. 8455

יתם (√of foll.; cf. Ar. يَتِمَ, يَتَمَ *be alone, bereaved*, Aram. adj. and subst. ܝܬܡܐ, ܝܬܡ, 𝔗 יְתָם = יָתוֹם; vid. Lag[BN 30] Ba[NB 194]).

3490 †יָתוֹם **n.[m.]** orphan (NH *id.*; Aram. יַתְמָא, ܝܬܡܐ; Ph. יתם; Ar. يَتِيمٌ *pupil, orphan*)—יָתוֹם Ex 22[21] + 29 t.; pl. יְתוֹמִים v[23] + 8 t.; sf. יְתֹמֶיךָ Je 49[11]; יְתֹמָיו Is 9[16]; לִיתוֹמָיו ψ 109[12];—*orphan*, i.e. fatherless (‖ אַלְמָנָה) Ex 22[23] ψ 109[9] La 5[3] (‖ אֵין אָב); Jb 24[9] ψ 109[12]; prob. also Ex 22[21] Dt 10[18] 14[29] 16[11.14] 24[17.19.20.21] 26[12.13] 27[19] ψ 94[6] 146[9] Je 7[6] 22[3] Zc 7[10] Mal 3[5] (in all these, mentioned as helpless, exposed to injury, ‖ אַלְמָנָה and גֵּר); similarly, ‖ אַלְמָנָה Jb 22[9] 24[3] 29[12] 31[17] ψ 68[6] Is 1[17.23] 9[16] 10[2] Je 49[11] Ez 22[7]; without אלמנה Ho 14[4] Jb 6[27] 31[21] ψ 10[14.18] Pr 23[10] Je 5[28] (in no case clear that both parents are dead).

†יִתְמָה **n.pr.m.** one of David's valiant men, called הַמֹּאָבִי 1 Ch 11[46], 𝔊 (Ι)εθαμα; 𝔊L Ιεθαμ. 3495

יתן (√of foll.; cf. Ar. وَتَنَ *be perpetual, never-failing*, esp. of water, وَاتِنٌ *a permanent thing*: Ph. ירח אתנם CIS [I. i. 86 A]; W [PSBA 1886 (ix), 47]).

†I. אֵיתָן, אֵתָן **adj. perennial, ever-flowing**, fig. **permanent**, as subst. **steady flow,** 386
permanence;—abs. אֵיתָן Gn 49[24] + 8 t.; אֵתָן Jb 33[19]; sf. אֵיתָנוֹ Ex 14[27]; pl. אֵיתָנִים Jb 12[19]; אֵתָנִים 1 K 8[2] Mi 6[2]; (in form, an 'elative,' Ew[§ 162 b] = Arab. compar. and superl.);—**1.** *ever-flowing* (opp. אַכְזָב), נַחַל אֵיתָן Am 5[24] an *ever-flowing* wādy, Dt 21[4] (v. Dr); as subst. in נַהֲרוֹת אֵיתָן ψ 74[15] *rivers of steady flow*; as subst. also Ex
14[27] (J), the sea returned לְאֵיתָנוֹ to its *steady* 388
flow, יֶרַח הָאֵיתָנִים 1 K 8[2] month of *steady flowings* = 7th mo., Oct.–Nov. (post-Bibl. Tisri). **2.** fig. *permanent, enduring* גּוֹי אֵיתָן הוּא Je 5[15], i.e. a nation whose numbers never dwindle or fail, *imperishable*, וְרִיב עֲצָמָיו א׳ Jb 33[19] Kt the strife of his bones is *constant*, Gn 49[24] his bow abode א׳ as an *enduring, firm*, one, א׳ מוֹשָׁבֶךָ Nu 24[21] (‖ שִׂים בַּסֶּלַע), נְוֵה אֵיתָן Je 49[19] = 50[44] an

abode of *permanency* (of Edom, and Babylon, suddenly depopulated by foe, figured as lion); האיתנים מוסדי ארץ Mi 6[2] ye *ever-enduring* ones, the foundations of the earth (but rd. prob. with We הָאֲזִינוּ), Jb 12[19] אֵיתָנִים יְסַלֵּף he subverteth them that are *firmly seated* (i.e. men established in hereditary offices or dignities). Very uncertain is Pr 13[15] דֶּרֶךְ בֹּגְדִים אֵיתָן, perh. *firm, hard, rugged* (Ew De Hi Now: acc. to Str. the text is corrupt).

387 †II. אֵיתָן **n.pr.m.** a wise man 1 K 5[11] (where called הָאֶזְרָחִי) named with הֵימָן, כַּלְכֹּל, דַּרְדַּע; cf. 1 Ch 2[6] (where these 4 with זִמְרִי are בְּנֵי זֶרַח); also 2[8] 6[27]; called בֶּן־קִישִׁי 6[29] = בֶּן־קוּשָׁיָהוּ 15[17], where, and v[19], named as Levit. singer with הֵימָן and אָסָף (q.v.; יְדוּתוּן for אֵיתָן in this group 1 Ch 25[1.6] 2 Ch 5[12] 35[15], v. ידותון); לְאֵיתָן הָאֶזְרָחִי ψ 89[1] (title).

3496 יַתְנִיאֵל v. תנה. p. 1072

3497 †יִתְנָן **n.pr.loc.** (etym. dub.) city in the Negeb of Judah Jos 15[23] (foll. by זִיף v[24]), 𝔊A Ιθναζιφ, 𝔊L Ιθναν, Ζειφ; site unknown.

3498 [יָתַר]$_{107}$ **vb. remain over** (NH *id.*; Aram. יְתַר, ܝܬܰܪ *id.*; Zinj. יתר n. *rest, remainder*; Eth. ወተረ: As. [*atâru*], *remain over*, in der. conj., Dl [HWB]; in Sab. ותר CIS [iv, 15, 46, p. 77]; esp. n. ותר as epithet of king = *noble one*, and as n.pr. ותרם Mordt [ZMG, 1876, 37, 292] DHM [ZMG, 1883, 15] CIS [iv, 10]; Ar. وَتَرَ is *make single, make to be one*, or *an odd number*)—†**Qal** *Pt.* הַיּוֹתֵר 1 S 15[15] *the remainder*†. **Niph.** *be left over, remain over*; *Pf.* נוֹתַר Ex 10[15] + 8 t., etc.; *Impf.* יִוָּתֵר 2 K 20[17] + 2 t.; יִוָּתֶר בָּהּ Zc 13[8]; וַיִּוָּתֵר Gn 32[25] + 2 t.; וָאִוָּתֵר 1 K 19[10.14], etc.; *Pt.* נוֹתָר 1 S 2[36] + 17 t., נֹתָר Ex 12[10]; fs. נוֹתֶרֶת Lv 2[3] + 3 t.; mpl. נוֹתָרִים Ju 8[10] + 24 t., etc.;—*be left over, remain (over)*, abs. Ex 10[15] (J), Jos 11[11.22] (D), Ju 9[5] Is 1[8] 30[17] 1 K 18[22] 2 K 20[17] = Is 39[6], sq. לְבַדּוֹ *be left alone* Gn 32[25] (J), so 1 K 19[10.14]; sq. מִן *be left from* (= *of*) 2 S 13[30] Ex 29[34] Nu 26[65] (both P), ψ 106[11]; pt. sq. מִן Ju 8[10] + 10 t. P, 1 K 9[20] = 2 Ch 8[7], Zc 14[16] 1 Ch 6[46]; sq. לְ, *be left (surviving) to*, 1 S 25[34] 2 S 9[1], *of those belonging to* Gn 44[20] (J; לְבַדּוֹ לְאִמּוֹ); sq. בְּ *be left in* (= *of*) 2 S 17[12] Jos 18[2] (JE), also pt. Lv 8[32] 14[18] (P), Ez 48[15.15]; oft. sq. בְּ loc. Am 6[9] + 11 t.; sq. בֵּית *in the house of* Je 27[21]; sq. על־פני הארץ Ez 39[14] (pt.); sq. אַחֲרֵי = *be left behind* (of sons) 1 K 9[21] = 2 Ch 8[8]; sq. אֵצֶל + שָׁם Dn 10[13] *I was left over there beside the kings* (i.e. I had nothing more to do; cf. VB); elsewh. pt. abs., as adj. Gn 30[36] (J), Jos 17[2.6] (JE), Lv 10[12.16] 27[18] Jos 21[5.26.34] (all P), Je 34[7] 1 Ch 6[55.62] 22[20]; as subst. Ju 21[7.16] 1 S 30[9] Ex 28[10] 29[34] Lv 19[6] (all P), 1 K 20[30.30] 2 K 4[7] Ez 34[18] 48[21] 2 Ch 31[10].

†**Hiph.** *Pf.* הוֹתִיר Ex 10[15] Is 1[9], etc.; *Impf.* יוֹתִיר Dt 28[54]; juss. יוֹתֵר Ex 16[19]; וַיּוֹתֵר 2 S 8[4] 2 Ch 18[4]; 3 fs. וַתֹּתַר Ru 2[14]; 2 ms. juss. תּוֹתַר Gn 49[4]; 1 s. אוֹתִיר Ez 39[28]; 3 mpl. וַיּוֹתִרוּ Ex 16[20] 2 K 4[44]; 2 mpl. תּוֹתִירוּ Ex 12[10] + 2 t.; *Imv.* הוֹתֵר ψ 79[11]; *Inf. abs.* הוֹתֵר 2 K 4[43] + 2 t.; *cstr.* הוֹתִיר Je 44[7];—**1. a.** *leave over, leave* Ex 10[15] (J), Ru 2[14] (obj.om.), v[18] 2 K 4[43] (אָכוֹל וְהוֹתֵר, v. infr.), v[44] (obj.om. in both), 2 Ch 31[10]; יֶתֶר בָּנָיו אֲשֶׁר יוֹתִיר Dt 28[54]; sq. obj. שָׂרִיד + לְ pers. Is 1[9]; obj. שְׁאֵרִית + לְ pers. Je 44[7]; sq. מִן *from* (= *of*), 2 S 8[4] = 1 Ch 18[4], Nu 33[55] (P), Ez 12[16]; + עַד temp. Ex 12[10] 16[19.20] (all P), Lv 22[30] (H); + שָׁם loc. Ez 39[28]. **b.** abs. *leave a remnant* Ez 6[8] (denom. fr. יֶתֶר?). **c.** *save over*, i.e. *preserve alive* ψ 79[11]. **2.** *excel, shew pre-eminence* Gn 49[4] (poem in J). **3.** *shew excess* = *have more than enough* Ex 36[7] (P; vid. also 2 K 4[43] 2 Ch 31[10] supr.); *make abundant* Dt 28[11] 30[9] (sq. sf. pers. + בְּ rei).

יָתֵר Pr 12[26], v. תור. p. 1064 8446

I. יֶתֶר$_{94}$ **n.m.** [Ne 2, 16] **remainder, excellence, excess**;—abs. יֶתֶר Ne 2[16] + 2 t.; יָתֶר Pr 17[7]; cstr. יֶתֶר Gn 49[3] + 84 t.; יֶתֶר Is 56[12] (vid. Baer's note); sf. יִתְרוֹ Is 44[19]; יִתְרָם Ex 23[11] + 2 t. (not Jb 4[21], q.v. sub II. יֶתֶר);—**1.** †**a.** *remainder, remnant* (with implied inferiority in number or quality), of crops, etc. יִתְרָם Ex 23[11] (JE), *their remnant*, i.e. what they (the enemy) leave, so יֶתֶר הַגָּזָם Jo 1[4]; יֶתֶר הָאַרְבֶּה v[4]; יֶתֶר הַיֶּלֶק v[4]; יֶתֶר הַפְּלֵטָה הַנִּשְׁאֶרֶת Ex 10[5] (J); of vessels, יֶתֶר הַכֵּלִים הַנּוֹתָרִים Je 27[19]; of a tree Is 44[19] (= שְׁאֵרִית v[17]); elsewh. of pers. Dt 3[11] = Jos 12[4] 13[12] (both D), Dt 28[54] Jos 23[12] (D), 2 S 21[2] 2 K 25[11] = Je 52[15], Ez 34[18]; of a rescued remnant of Israel (Judah) Mi 5[2] Zp 2[9] (‖ שְׁאֵרִית), Zc 14[2]; יֶתֶר הַקָּדֵשׁ אֲשֶׁר נִשְׁאַר 1 K 22[47]; יֶתֶר הָעָם הַנִּשְׁאָרִים Je 36[9.9] 2 K 25[11] = Je 52[15]†. **b.** *remainder, rest, other part* of people, elders, etc., 2 S 10[10] = 1 Ch 19[11], 2 S 12[28] 1 K 12[23] Je 29[1] Hb 2[8] Ez 48[23]; sts. incl. a majority Ju 7[6] 1 S 13[2]; of common people (opp. rulers) Ne 2[16] 4[8.13], cf. 6[1]; of land Dt 3[13] Jos 13[27] (P); of other inanimate things Lv 14[17] (P), Nu 31[32] (*id.*), of years Is 38[10]; elsewhere in phr. 3499

יֶתֶר דִּבְרֵי *the rest of the affairs of*, in summaries of reigns of kings of Israel and Judah 1 K 11^{41} + 41 t. K Ch; יֶתֶר דְּבָרָיו 1 K 15^{23}; יֶתֶר כָּל־דִּבְרֵי 2 Ch 28^{26}. †**2. a.** *excess*, שְׂפַת יֶתֶר Pr 17^{7} *a lip of excess*=arrogant speech (see VB). **b.** in adv. phrases, עַל יֶתֶר ψ 31^{24} *on the basis of abundance=abundantly*, as adv. accus. גָּדוֹל יֶתֶר מְאֹד Is 56^{12} great, *in abundance*, exceedingly, Dn 8^{9} וַתִּגְדַּל־יֶתֶר and grew great *in excess, exceedingly* (cf. ܝܬܝܪ *much*, ܝܬܝܪ ܡܢ *more than*). **c.** specif. *what is over and above* immediate necessities, *abundance, affluence* Jb 22^{20} ψ 17^{14}. †**3.** *superiority, excellency* יֶתֶר שְׂאֵת וְיֶתֶר עָז Gn 49^{3}.—On Jb 4^{1} v. II. יֶתֶר.

3499 †II. יֶתֶר **n.m.**$^{\text{Ju 16, 7}}$ **cord** (prop. as *hanging over* or *down*; Aram. יַתְרָא part of the intestines, 𝔗 יַתְרַיָּא *ropes*, ܝܬܪܐ *cord, rope, chord* of arc; Ar. وَتَرٌ bow-*string*, lute-*string*; Eth. ወተር: *sinew, cord*; ወተረ: *stretch bowstring, strain* (eyes), *be intent, eager*, etc.)—יֶתֶר ψ 11^{2} + 3 t.; sf. יִתְרוֹ Kt Jb 30^{11} (יִתְרִי Qr); יִתְרָם Jb 4^{21};—*cord*, for binding a man Ju 16$^{7.8.9}$; *bowstring* ψ 11^{2} Jb 30^{11} (acc. to Qr, opp. 29^{20b}; Kt=*his cord*, with which he reins in my assailants; cf. Di Da). Jb 4^{21} *tent-cord* Ew De Di RV; yet rd. perh. יְתֵדָם *their tent-peg*, so Ol Hi Sgfr (>AV *their excellency*, fr. I. יֶתֶר).

3500 †III. יֶתֶר **n.pr.m.** (*abundance*; on form and mng. of this and the foll. n.pr. v. Lag$^{\text{BN 52, 198}}$)—**1.** father of Moses' wife Ex 4^{18a} (E; prob. txt. err., elsewhere יִתְרוֹ, q.v.) **2.** eldest son of Gideon Ju 8^{20}, 𝔊 Ιεθερ. **3.** father of Amasa 1 K 2$^{5.32}$ 1 Ch 2^{17}, 𝔊 Ιεθερ; =יִתְרָא 2 S 17^{25}, 𝔊 Ιοθερ, Ιοθορ; 𝔊L Ιεθερ. **4.** men of Judah, 𝔊 Ιεθερ: **a.** 1 Ch 2$^{32.32}$. **b.** 1 Ch 4^{17}. **5.** a man of Asher 1 Ch 7^{38} (=יִתְרָן v^{37}), 𝔊 Ιεθερ, A Ιεθηρ, 𝔊L [v^{39}] Εθραν.

3501 †יִתְרָא **n.pr.m.** father of Amasa 2 S 17^{25} (v. III. יֶתֶר **3**).

3502 †יִתְרָה **n.f. abundance, riches**;—יִתְרָה עָשָׂה Is 15^{7}=יִתְרַת עָשָׂה Je 48^{36} (on cstr. cf. Da$^{\text{Synt. § 25}}$) *the abundance* (which) *he hath gotten*.

3503 †יִתְרוֹ **n.pr.m.** father of Moses' wife Ex 3^{1} 4^{18b} 18$^{1.2.5.6.9.10.12}$ (all E), =יֶתֶר 4^{18}; in all 𝔊 Ιοθορ.

3505 †יִתְרִי **adj. gent.**, alw. c. art. הַיִּתְרִי 2 S 23^{38}, 𝔊 Αιθειραιος, etc.; v^{38}, 𝔊 Εθθεναιος, 𝔊L Ιεθεμ; rd. perh. הַיַּתִּירִי Th Klo Kit Bu; =1 Ch 11$^{40.40}$, 𝔊 Ηθηρει, Ιεθ(ε)ρι, etc.; coll. 1 Ch 2^{53}, 𝔊 Αιθαλειμ, 𝔊L Εθρι.

†יֹתֵר, יוֹתֵר **n.m. superiority, advantage,** 3148
excess (late) (prop. **Qal** pt. of יתר)—abs. יוֹתֵר Ec 7^{16} + 2 t.; יֹתֵר Ec 2^{15} + 4 t.;—*superiority, advantage* מַה־יּוֹתֵר לֶחָכָם מִן־הַכְּסִיל Ec 6^{8} *what advantage hath the wise over the fool?* prob. also יֹתֵר מֵהֵמָּה 12^{12} (as to) *what is more than these* (see VB); abs. מַה־יֹּתֵר לָאָדָם 6^{11}; יֹתֵר לְרֹאֵי הַשָּׁמֶשׁ Ec 7^{11}; elsewh. adv. *to excess, overmuch* Ec 2^{15} 7^{16}; sq. מִן (as oft. in NH), יוֹתֵר מִמֶּנִּי Est 6^{6} *more than me*; יֹתֵר שֶׁ׳=*besides that* Ec 12^{9}.

†יֹתֶרֶת **n.f. appendage** (term. techn. of 3508
P);—most prob. (fat) *appendage*, a (fatty) mass at opening of liver of sacrificial animal, extending to kidneys (v. Di Dr$^{\text{Polychr. Bible, Lv 3, 4}}$);—הַיֹּתֶרֶת עַל־הַכָּבֵד Ex 29^{13} Lv 3$^{4.10.15}$ 4^{9} 7^{4}; הַיּ׳ מִן־הַכָּבֵד Lv 9^{10}; cstr. יֹתֶרֶת הַכָּבֵד Ex 29^{22} Lv 8$^{16.25}$ 9^{19} (all P).

†יִתְרוֹן **n.[m.] advantage, profit, only Ec;** 3504
—abs. Ec 1^{3} + 4 t.; cstr. Ec 2^{13} + 4 t.;—*advantage* to (ל) any one, מַה־יִּתְרוֹן לָאָדָם Ec 1^{3}, i.e. *what advantage hath a man?* 5^{15} 10^{11}; sq. מִן compar.=*advantage beyond, more than* 2$^{13.13}$; cstr. יִתְרוֹן הָעוֹשֶׂה 3^{9} *advantage of* (for) *him that worketh*; יִתְרוֹן אֶרֶץ 5^{8}; יִתְרוֹן דַּעַת 7^{12} *advantage of knowledge*; וְיִתְרוֹן הַכְשֵׁיר חָכְמָה Ec 10^{10} *an advantage for giving success is wisdom*; abs. אֵין יִתְרוֹן תַּחַת הַשָּׁמֶשׁ Ec 2^{11}.

†יִתְרָן **n.pr.m. 1.** an Edomite Gn 36^{26}= 3506
1 Ch 1^{41}, 𝔊 Ι(ε)θραν, etc. **2.** a man of Asher 1 Ch 7^{37} (v. III. יֶתֶר **5**), 𝔊 Θερα, A Ιεθερ, 𝔊L [v^{38}] Ιεθραν.

†הוֹתִיר **n.pr.m.** (*abundance, superabund-* 1956
ance)—a son of Heman, acc. to 1 Ch 25$^{4.28}$ (but on the ostensible list of names v. Ew$^{\text{§ 274 b}}$ We$^{\text{Prol. 229; Hist. Isr. 219}}$ RS$^{\text{OTJC 224; 2nd ed. 143}}$).

†מוֹתָר **n.m.**$^{\text{Pr 14, 23}}$ **abundance, pre-emi-** 3195
nence;—**1.** *abundance, plenty* מוֹתָר Pr 14^{23} 21^{5} (in both opp. מַחְסוֹר). **2.** *pre-eminence, superiority*, מוֹתַר הָאָדָם מִן־הַבְּהֵמָה אָיִן Ec 3^{19} *the superiority of man over beast is nothing*.

†[מֵיתָר] **n.m. cord, string** (cf. II. יֶתֶר); 4340
of tent-*cords* מֵיתָרַי Je 10^{20}; מֵיתָרַיִךְ Is 54^{2}; specif. of *cords* of tabernacle, מֵיתָרָיו Ex 39^{40} Nu 3^{26}; מֵיתְרֵיהֶם Ex 35^{18} Nu 3^{37} 4$^{26.32}$ (all P); of bow-*strings* מֵיתָרֶיךָ ψ 21^{13}.

†יַתִּר, יַתִּיר **n.pr.loc.** town in Judah (√ 3492
dub.);—יַתִּיר Jos 15^{48}, 𝔊 Ι(ε)θερ; elsewh. יַתִּר,

Levitical city Jos 21^{14} (both P), 𝔊 Αιλωμ, A 𝔊L Ιεθερ, 1 Ch 6^{42}, 𝔊 [v^{43}] Ιεθθαρ, A Ιεθερ; prob. = יַתִּר 1 S 30^{27}, 𝔊 Γεθθορ, A Ιεεθερ;—acc. to Onom. = Ιεθειρα, village 20 miles from Eleutheropolis, Lag$^{Onom. 266, 133; ed. 2, p. 268}$; identified by Rob$^{BR\ i, 494}$ (who, however, questions ʿ (ע) = י) Bd$^{Pal. 3, 153}$ with ʿ*Attîr*, halfway between Hebron and Milḥ; so, 'perh.,' Buhl$^{Geogr. § 91, p. 164}$; this not certain, cf. Di.

†יִתְרְעָם **n.m.** 6th son of David 2 S 3^5 = 3507
1 Ch 3^3, 𝔊 Ιθ(α)ραμ, Ιεθρααμ, etc.

†יְתֵת **n.pr.m.** an Edomite chief Gn 36^{40}, 3509
𝔊 Ιεβερ = 1 Ch 1^{51}, 𝔊 Ιεθετ; 𝔊L in both Ιεθερ.

כ

כ, ךּ, eleventh letter; used as numeral 20 in postB Heb.; כא = 21, כב = 22, etc.

כְּ prop. **subst. the like of, like, as** (Aram. כְּ, Ph. כ, Ar. كَ, Sab. in כעד דא *as* till now DHM$^{ZMG\ xxix. 615}$, As. *ki, kima*, Dl$^{HWB\ 325\ f.}$)—before tone-syll. כָּ, as כָּזֶה, כָּאֵלֶּה, כָּהֵמָּה; c. sf. כָּכֶם Nu 15^{15} + 7 t. (Jb 16^4 כָּכֶם: Kö$^{ii. 1. 285}$), כָּהֶם † 2 K 17^{15}, כָּהֵן †Ez 18^{14} [also with nom. forms, כָּהֵמָּה, כָּהֶם, כָּהֵנָּה; v. הֵמָּה **8**; cf. Arab. كَأَنَا, كَأَنْتَ, etc.], before light sf., in the form כְּמוֹ (q.v.), viz. כָּמוֹנִי, כָּמֹנִי Gn 44^{15} + 16 t., כָּמוֹךָ Gn 41^{39} + 28 t., כָּמֹכָה †Ex $15^{11.11}$, כָּמֹהוּ 9^{18} + 23 t., כָּמוֹהָ 11^6 + 2 t., כָּמֹנוּ Gn 34^{15} + 3 t.; also כְּמוֹכֶם †Jb 12^3, כְּמוֹהֶם †Ju 8^{18} ψ 115^8 135^{18}. Prop. an undeveloped *subst.*, capable of standing in any case and followed (like كَ) always by a gen., as 1 S 20^3 כי כפשׂע for there is (nomin.) *the like of* a footstep (Ar. كَخَطْوَةٍ) between me and death, Gn 41^{38} הנמצא כזה shall we find (accus.) *the like of* this one? (v. esp. Fleischer$^{Kl. Schrr. i. 376 ff.}$ Mühlau, *ap.* Bö$^{ii. 64 f.}$, with many Arabic exx.; also W$^{AG\ i. § 356 R. c.; ii. § 63}$ Ges$^{§ 118. 6}$; compare, for both usage and constr., the Lat. *instar:* this view criticized by Kö$^{ii. 1. 279 ff.}$, who treats כְּ as demonstr. adv.); but Heb. having no case-endings, its proper sense was doubtless forgotten, and כְּ became practically equivalent to a prep. *like, as:*—**1. a.** *quantitatively* (like the Ar. قَدْرُ *measure, number, size, of . . .*: قَدْرُ مِائَةٍ *as many as* 100), to express exact or approx. equality, in the latter case *the like of* is = *about:* Dt 1^{11} Yahweh add to you ככם אלף פעמים *the like of you* (Saad. مِثْلَكُم) 1000 times (cf. 2 S 24^3), Ex 12^{37} כשׁשׁ מאות אלף רגלי *the like of* (i.e. *about*) 600,000 footmen, 32^{28} כשׁלשׁת אלפי אישׁ, Jos 4^{13} 7^3 1 S 9^{22} 25^{38} ויהי כעשׂרת הימים (nomin.) and there was *the like of* (= *about*) 10 days, and, etc. Ru 2^{17} כאיפה שׂערים, etc., cf. כַּמָּה *the like of* what? = *how many?* (v. מָה); as accus. of space or time, Nu 11^{31} כדרך יום *the like of* a day's journey, Jos 3^4; Jos 10^{13} כיום תמים *about* a whole day (Ar. نَحْوَ يَوْمٍ كَامِلٍ), Ru 1^4 כעשׂר שׁנים. So (as adv. accus.) with words denoting a *point* of time: often with עֵת, as כָּעֵת הַזֹּאת lit. at *the like of* this time = *about* this time, Jos 11^6 al., כָּעֵת מָחָר at *the like of* the time, (being) to-morrow = *about to-morrow*, Ex 9^{18} +, כָּעֵת חַיָּה (v. חי), Is 8^{23} כעת הראשׁון *at* the former time, כָּעֵת alone = *at the* (present) *time, now* Nu 23^{23} Ju 13^{23}, Is 23^5 (unusual) כְּשֵׁמַע צֹר; so כַּיּוֹם, כְּהַיּוֹם (v. יוֹם **7 h**), כְּרֶגַע, כִּמְעַט; and esp. with inf., v. **3 b. b.** *qualitatively* (like Ar. مَثَلُ *likeness of . . .*), to express resemblance in respect of some attribute, action, character, appearance, etc.: so very often; as subj. of a sentence, Nu 9^{15} כמראה אשׁ *the like of* (= *as it were*) an appearance of fire was, etc. (cf. Ez $1^{4.26 a. 27}$ Dn 8^{15} 10^{18}), 23^{22} כתועפות ראם לו, Ex 24^{10}, Dt 4^{32} הנהיה כדבר הגדול הזה hath there been *the like of* this great thing? 9^{10} Jos 10^{14}; Ho 9^1 Is 23^{15} ψ 58^5 Pr 16^{27} La 1^{20} בַּבַּיִת כַּמָּוֶת, Ec 8^{14}; Lv 14^{35} כְּנֶגַע נראה בביתי *the like of* (i.e. *a kind of*) mark; מִי כָמֹכָה who is *the like of* thee? Ex 15^{11} (Saad. مَنْ مِثْلُكَ) +; as gen. אֵין כָּמוֹךָ 1 S 10^{24} 2 S 7^{22} +; as pred., Ju 8^{21} כָּאִישׁ גְּבוּרָתוֹ, Hb 2^5 וְהוּא כַמָּוֶת, ψ 17^{14} 89^{30} וכסאו כימי שׁמים (of time: so v^{37}), 125^1, etc.; after a verb, היה כְּ to become *the like of* (*like*), Gn 3^5 + oft. (v. היה **II. 2 c**), cf. after שִׂים Gn 13^{16} +, נתן 42^{30} +, שִׁית ψ 83^{12} +, שִׁוָּה 18^{34}, נֶחְשַׁב 44^{23} +, נִמְשַׁל 49^{13}, הִרְבָּה Gn 22^{17} +; add כָּזֹאת, כָּאֵלֶּה *the like of* this (these), i.e. *tale, talia* (whether nom. or accus.) Ju 13^{23} 15^7 20^{30} Lv 10^{19} + (v. אֵלֶּה, זֹאת). Cases such as to give or reward a man כמעשׂהו, כרעתו, etc., *the like of* his doings, etc., 2 S 3^{39} 1 K 8^{32} ψ 18^{25} 28^{4}, to speak כדבר הזה or כדברים האלה Gn 18^{25} 24^{28} + oft., form the transition to **c.** as an accus. of mode or limitation, *in* or *with the like of* (=*like, as, according to,* κατά);—(1) expressing conformity to a standard or rule: Gn 1^{26} let us make man כדמותנו *according to* our likeness, 9^{3} Jos 19^{47} Ju 20^{10} 1 S 13^{14} hath looked out איש כלבבו a man *according to* his own heart (Je 3^{15}); to do a thing כמשפט הזה Jos 6^{15}, cf. Gn 40^{13} 2 K 11^{14}, etc., כדבר פ׳ Gn 44^{2} + oft., כְּצִדְקִי ψ 7^{9}, כְּחַסְדְּךָ 51^{3}, כַּכָּתוּב *according to* what is written Jos 8$^{31.34}$ +, בלא ככתוב (late) † 2 Ch 30^{18}, etc. (2) in comparisons: qualifying an adj., Ex 16^{14} דַּק כַּכְּפֹר, Ct 6^{10} יָפָה כַלְּבָנָה, cf. Gn 13^{10}; a verb ψ 7^{3} פֶּן־יִטְרֹף כְּאַרְיֵה, 19^{6} יָשִׂישׂ כְּגִבּוֹר, Is 42^{13}, etc.; with the *tertium compar.* attached in a relative clause, Dt 32^{11} כְּנֶשֶׁר יָעִיר קִנּוֹ *like* the great vulture, (that) stirreth up its nest, Jb 9^{26} 11^{16} Is 61^{10} *like* the bride, who putteth on, etc., 62^{1} כְּלַפִּיד יִבְעָר *like* a touch (that) burns (on the presence or absence of the art. in such cases, v. הַ **1 f**), ψ 42^{2} 83^{15} (infr. **2 d**) + oft. (cf. Dr$^{§ 34}$: כְּ is not in these cases to be construed as a conj. [=כַּאֲשֶׁר] with the verb: v. De$^{ψ 38, 14}$ Ges $^{§ 155, 2 b, 1 R.}$). **d.** sometimes כְּ is used in partic. to compare an object with the *class* to which it belongs, and express its correspondence with the idea which it ought to realize: Is 13^{6} (=Jo 1^{15}) of the יום י׳, כְּשֹׁד מִשַּׁדַּי יָבוֹא i.e. it comes as a *veritable*, or *ideal*, destruction from Shaddai, 29^{2} of Ariel (v^{1}) והיתה לי כאריאל i.e. shall be to me as a *true* Ariel (cf. Ges$^{§ 118 x}$): so also, acc. to Hi De, 10^{13} Ez 26^{10} Zc 14^{3} 2 S 9^{8} ψ 122^{3} Ct 8^{10} (v. De), Ec 10^{5} Ne 7^{2}. The older grammarians called this the *Kaph veritatis* (a translation of Ki's כ״ף לאמת הדבר, כ״ף הָאֲמִתּוּת, Michl $^{45 a (Lyck)}$, Comm $^{Jos 3, 4, 1 S 9, 13, Is 1, 7, Ho 5, 10}$, or כ״ף הָאֲמִתִּי, Lex s. v. יום): they extended it unduly (e.g. to Nu 11^{1} La 1^{20} Ho 11^{4}). **2.** repeated, כְּ . . . כְּ, to signify the completeness of the correspondency between two objects (peculiar to Heb.): **a.** in a principal clause, Gn 18^{25} וְהָיָה כַצַּדִּיק כָּרָשָׁע lit. that *the like of* the righteous be *the like of* the wicked, i.e. that the righteous be *as* the wicked, 44^{18} כמוך כפרעה *the like of* thee is *the like of* Pharaoh, i.e. *thou* art as Pharaoh, Lv 24^{22} כַּגֵּר כָּאֶזְרָח יִהְיֶה, 1 K 22^{4} כָּמוֹנִי כָמוֹךָ כְּעַמִּי כְעַמֶּךָ (Van Dyck مَثَلِي مَثَلُكَ), Hg 2^{3} הֲלוֹא כָמֹהוּ כְּאַיִן בְּעֵינֵיכֶם (شَعْبِي كَشَعْبِكَ), is not *the like of* it *the like of* nothing in your eyes? i.e. is it not like nothing in your eyes? ψ 139^{12} כַּחֲשֵׁיכָה כָּאוֹרָה i.e. the darkness (to thee) is *as* the light. Usu. the first term is the subj. and the second is the standard with which it is compared: but occas. the terms are inverted, as Lv 7^{7} Nu 15^{15} Ju 8^{18} כמוך כמוהם (Van Dyck مَثَلُهُم مَثَلُكَ), Ho 4^{9} Is 24^{2}, cf. 59^{18} (*Note*, infr.) **b.** in a subordinate clause (to be regarded as subordinated in the accus. to the principal verb); (*a*) attached to the *subj.* of the principal vb., Lv 24^{16} כגר כאזרח . . . יומת he shall be put to death, *the like of* the stranger (being) *the like of* the homeborn, Jos 8^{33}. (β) attached to its *object*, Dt 1^{17} כקטן כגדל תשמעון lit. ye shall hear (them), *the like of* the small (being) *the like of* the great. **c.** occas., for כְּ . . . כְּ, there occurs כְּ . . . וּכ: Jos 14^{11} כְּכֹחִי אָז וּכְכֹחִי עָתָּה *the like of* my strength then, and *the like of* my strength now, i.e. they are similar (cf. וְ **1 j**) 1 S 30^{24} Ez 18^{4} Dn 11^{29}. **d.** yet more distinct than כְּ . . . כְּ, is כְּ . . . כֵּן; in a nominal sentence (Ges$^{§ 140-1}$), 'כְּ with its genit. forming the predic., and כֵּן resuming it with emph. and connecting it with the subject;' 1 S 25^{25} כִּי כִשְׁמוֹ כֶּן־הוּא for *the like of* his name, *such* (or *so*) is he, Gn 44^{10} Jos 2^{21} Je 18^{6} ψ 48^{11} 127^{4} Pr 10^{26} +; in a verbal sentence, 'כְּ preceding, as an accusative of state, and giving the *secundum comparationis*, and כֵּן resuming it,' Jo 2^{4} כפרשים כן ירוצון '*instar* (accus.) equitum, *sic* currunt' (Fl$^{l. c.}$), Ho 4^{7} lit. *with* (or *in*) *the likeness of* their multiplying, *so* they sinned against me, Gn 6^{22} 1 S 8^{8} Is 38^{14} Ez 22^{22} ψ 42^{2} 83^{15} + oft. **3.** before an inf.: **a.** *like* (lit. *with* or *in the likeness of* . . .), Ju 14^{6} כְּשַׁסַּע הַגְּדִי *like* the rending of a kid, i.e. *as when* a kid is rent (by a lion), 2 S 3^{34} Is 5^{24} ψ 66^{10} 68^{3} Jb 2^{10}, etc.; =*as if*, Is 10^{15} or shall the saw magnify itself against him that wieldeth it כהניף שבט את־מרימיו *with the like of* a staff's shaking (=*as if* a staff were to shake) him that lifted it! **b.** of time, *about, at*, whether of the past or of the future: Gn 19^{17} כהוציאם אותם *at* their bringing them forth, i.e. *as* or *when* they brought them forth 24^{30} 29^{13} 39$^{10.13}$ + very often; of the future, 44$^{30.31}$ Dt 20$^{2.9}$ 2 S 13^{28} +; Is 28$^{20 b}$ (different from v$^{20 a}$) and the covering is (too) narrow *when one gathers oneself* in. Occasionally with the verbal noun, Ho 13^{6} כמרעיתם *at the time of* their feeding, Is 30^{19} כְּשָׁמְעָתוֹ; וּכְחֶזְקָתוֹ † 2 Ch 12^{1} 26^{16} Dn 11^{2} (Ew$^{§ 238 a, 239 a}$): cf. Is 23$^{5 b}$ כְּשֵׁמַע צֹר. With the ptcp. † Gn 38^{29} (si vera l.), perh. 40^{10}; cf. Dr$^{§ 135. 6, Obs. 2}$.

Note.—כְּ is rarely prefixed to preps., the only exx. which occur being the idiomatic כְּבָרִאשֹׁנָה, †Ju 20^{32} 1 K 13^{6} Is 1^{26} Jer 33$^{7.11}$; כְּבַתְּחִלָּה in the ‖ clause †Is$^{l.c.}$; כְּבְחֵצִי †1 S 14^{14} (apparently corrupt); כְּמִשְּׁלֹשׁ חֳדָשִׁים †Gn 38^{24} (and prob. כְּמֵחֹדֶשׁ 1 S 10^{27} 𝔊); כְּמִפְּנֵי †Lv 26^{37}; †כְּעַל (late): **a.** pleon. for כְּ (עַל = *according to*), Is 63^{7} כְּעַל כָּל־אֲשֶׁר עָשָׂה, 59^{18} כְּעַל גְּמֻלוֹת כְּעַל יְשַׁלֵּם *the like of* their deeds is *the like of* (that which) he will repay (ellipse of rel., as Jb 34^{32}, etc.); **b.** = *as over* ψ 119^{14}, = *as concerning* 2 Ch 32^{19}. Where logically a prep. would seem to be required after כ, it is in Heb. regularly omitted (Ges$^{\S 118.3R}$), the nature of כְּ, as explained above, not in fact admitting it; thus Is 1^{25} I will purge away thy dross כַּבֹּר [not, as in Engl., *like as with* lye, but] (with) *the like of* lye (כ being an accus. defining the mode in which אצרף takes place); 5^{17} כְּדָבְרָם in Engl. as *in* their pasture, Ju 20^{39}, כְּיוֹם as *in* the day of, Is 9^{3} ψ 95^{8}+, כִּימֵי, Jb 29^{3} who will set me as *in* the days of old! Is 51^{9}+, כְּנֹקֶף זַיִת as *at*, etc., 17^{6}: so with לְ ψ 83^{10} Jb 29^{23}, על 30^{5}. כְּ is used also pregnantly with substs., ψ 18^{34} who maketh my feet *like hinds* (for *like the feet of hinds*), Is 29^{4} 63^{2} בגדיך כדורך בגת, Je 50^{9} Jb 40^{9} al. Cf. Ges$^{\S\S 118.6; 141.2R.n}$.

834 **כַּאֲשֶׁר conj.** according as, as, when (cf. for the combin. Aram. כְּדִי, כַּד)—**1.** *according to that which, according as, as*: **a.** Gn 34^{12} I will give כאשר תאמרו אלי *according as* ye shall (*or* may) say unto me, 44^{1} Ex 8^{23} Nu 22^{8} 1 S 2^{16}; Gn 34^{22} if we are circumcised כאשר הם נמולים; 41^{21} כאשר בתחלה *as* at the beginning, so כ׳ Jos 8$^{5.6}$ 2 S 7^{10}; Ex 5^{13} כאשר בהיות התבן בראשונה: Gn 7^{9} they came in two by two כאשר צוה אלהים, *as* God commanded Noah; so, or similarly, very oft., esp. in P, v^{16} 8^{21} 12^{4} 17^{23} 21$^{1.1}$ Ex 16^{24} 39$^{1.5.7}$ Nu 3$^{16.42}$ etc.; כאשר דבר י׳ Dt 1^{21} 2^{1} 6$^{3.19}$ + oft. Dt. **b.** answered, for increased emph., by כֵּן (cf. כְּ **2 d**), Gn 50^{12} ויעשו כן כאשר צִוָּם, Ex 7$^{10.20}$; Gn 18^{5} (J) כן תעשה כאשר דברת, Ex 10^{10} (iron.), Am 5^{14} (do.); in opp. order, Ju 1^{7} כאשר עשיתי כן שלם לי, Ex 7^{6} כאשר צוה י׳ כן עשו, cf. 12$^{28.50}$ 39^{43} Nu 5^{4} 17^{26} 36^{10} (all P); with impf. (freq.) Nu 2^{17} (P) כאשר יחנו כן יסעו; of degree = *the more … the more*, Ex 1^{12} וכאשר יענו אתו כן ירבה וכן יפרץ, cf. 17^{11} (JE) והיה כאשר ירים . . . וגבר ישר׳ *according as* he held up, etc., Israel prevailed; in an oath or solemn promise, Nu 14^{28} אם לא כאשר דברתם כן אעשה, Dt 28^{63} (Je 31^{28}), 1 K 1^{30} Is 10^{11} 14^{24} 52$^{14f.}$ + (v. כֵּן **2 b**). **c.** answered by וְ (Dr$^{\S 127\gamma}$) †Ex 16^{34} Nu 1^{19}. **d.** oft. in *similes* (sq. impf. of habit) Ex 33^{11} כאשר ידבר איש אל רעהו, Nu 11^{12} Dt 1^{44} Is 9^{2} 66^{20}+, answered by כֵּן Is 31^{4} 55^{10} 66^{22} Am 3^{12}+; a second verb is, in such cases, in the pf. with וְ consec. (Dr$^{\S 115}$) Dt 22^{26} Is 29^{8} כאשר יחלם . . . והקיץ, 65^{8} Am 5^{19}. **e.** הָיָה כַּאֲשֶׁר (cf. הָיָה כְּ) to be *as if*, Jb 10^{19} כאשר לא הייתי אהיה, Zc 10^{6} והיו כאשר לא זנחתים. **2.** with a *causal* force, *in so far as, since* (Germ. *demgemäss dass*), Gn 26^{29} if thou doest us no harm כאשר לא נגענוך *according as, in so far as*, we have not touched thee; Nu 27^{14} כאשר מריתם פי *inasmuch as* ye have defied my mouth, Ju 6^{27} 1 S 28^{18} (answered by על כן), 2 K 17^{26} Mi 3^{4}. **3.** with a *temporal* force, *when*, Gn 18^{33} and Y. went away כאשר כלה *when* he had finished, etc., 32$^{3.32}$ 1 S 8^{6} 2 S 12^{21}+; answered by וְ (Dr$^{\S 127\beta}$), 1 S 6^{6} 12^{8}; ויהי כאשר . . . and it came to pass, when … Gn 12^{11} 20^{13} 24$^{22.52}$ 27^{30} Ex 32^{19} + oft.; Gn 43^{14} כאשר שכלתי שכלתי when I am bereaved, I am bereaved! an expression of resignation, so Est 4^{16} כאשר אבדתי אבדתי. Jos 2^{7} אחרי כאשר is a 'conflate' reading, omit either אחרי or כ. Of future time, Gn 27^{40} 40^{14} כאשר ייטב לך, Ho 7^{12} Ec 4^{17} 5^{3}, and without a verb Is 23^{5} כאשר שמע למצרים.—Mi 3^{3} כאשר is simply *as that which*, Jb 29^{25} *as one who*.

3644 **כְּמוֹ adv.** and **conj.** like, as, when (lit. *the like of what* (viz.) …, a pleon. form of כְּ (v. מוֹ), and, like it, prop. a **subst.**: cf. Aram. כְּמָא *like* ψ 78^{68} Levy, usually כְּמָא דְּ *like as*; ܐܝܟ ܡܐ (i.e. ܐܝܟ ܡܐ) *like what, like*, usu. sq. ܕ *like as*; Sam. ࠊࠌࠅ; Ar. كَمَا; Eth. ከመ፡ *kama, like as*, Di$^{Gr \S 63a}$ Sab. כמו $^{ZMG\ 1883,\ 394}$)—used **1.** (56 t.) as an indep. word (exc. Gn 19^{15} Ne 9^{11}, only in poetry); **2.** as an equivalent for כְּ before sfs., always before light ones, and occasionally before heavy ones (v. כְּ *ad init.*):—**1. a.** adv., as poet. syn. of כְּ, *like, as*, Ex 15^{5} they went down כמו־אבן *like* a stone (hence in prose Ne 9^{11}), v^{8} (ψ 78^{13}), Is 30^{22} 51^{6} (v. כֵּן), 26^{17} כְּמוֹ הָרָה תַּקְרִיב לָלֶדֶת (see כְּ **1 c** (2), on the constr.: so 41^{25} ψ 58$^{5.8a.9}$), v^{18} we have brought forth *the like of, as it were*, wind, Je 13^{21} 15^{18} 50^{26} Ez 16^{57} (כמו עת as *at* the time of: v. כְּ *Note*), Ho 7^{4} 8^{12} 13^{7} Hb 3^{14} (*as it were*), Zc 9^{15} 10$^{2.7}$ (as *with* wine: v. ib.) Elsewhere chiefly in ψψ (19 t.) and Jb (11 t.), as ψ 29^{6} 61^{7} 63^{6} 78^{69} 79^{5} 88^{6} 90^{9}, Jb 6^{15} 10$^{22.22}$ 12^{3} כמו אלה *the like of these things*, 14^{9} Ct 6^{10} 7^{2} La 4^{6} כמו רגע (in prose כרגע). Repeated, like כְּ . . . כְּ, † ψ 58[10]; and answered by כֵּן Is 26[17].—ψ 58[8b] כמו יתמוללו, *as it were* is against usage of כמו (with a vb.), and yields a lame sense: read perh. כמו [חָצִיר] יִת׳ (Lag Che); ψ 73[15] if I said, אֲסַפְּרָה כְמוֹ, the text is untranslateable, the rendering *thus* for כמו being indefensible: prob. הֵנָּה has dropped out before the following הִנֵּה: for כְּמוֹ הֵנָּה *the like of these things*, cf. Jb 23[14] כָּהֵנָּה, and 12[3] supr. **b. conj.** = כַּאֲשֶׁר: (*a*) of time, once, † Gn 19[15] כְּמוֹ עָלָה הַשַּׁחַר *when* the dawn arose; (β) of mode, *according as*, † Zc 10[8] וְרָבוּ כְּמוֹ רָבוּ Pr 23[7] (answered by כֵּן).—For **2** (before sfs.), see כְּ.

3510 **†כָּאַב** vb. **be in pain** (Aram. כְּאֵב, ܟܐܒ *id.*; Ar. كَئِبَ *be sorrowful, sad*; As. in deriv., *ikkibu, pain* Zim[BP 67], *kêbtu, ruin* Hpt in KAT[2 Gloss. I.])—**Qal** *Impf.* יִכְאַב־ Pr 14[13]; יִכְאָב Jb 14[22]; *Pt.* כּוֹאֵב ψ 69[30]; כֹּאֲבִים Gn 34[25];—**1.** *be in pain*, physical Gn 34[25] (J, as result of circumcision); Jb 14[22] (subj. בְּשָׂר; poet. of body in grave ‖ נַפְשׁוֹ תֶּאֱבָל). **2.** of *mental pain* Pr 14[13] (subj. לֵב); prob. also ψ 69[30] (‖ עָנִי). **Hiph.** *Pf.* 1 s. sf. הִכְאַבְתִּיו Ez 13[22]; 2 fpl. הִכְאַבְתֶּן v[22] 𝔊 𝔗 Co (MT הַכְאוֹת v. כָּאָה); *Impf.* יַכְאִיב Jb 5[18]; תַּכְאִבוּ 2 K 3[19]; *Pt.* מַכְאִב Ez 28[24];—*pain, mar;* **1.** of enemies of Isr. under fig. of thorn causing pain (no object expr.) קוֹץ מַכ׳ Ez 28[24] (‖ סִלּוֹן ‖ מַמְאִיר); of שַׁדַּי, no obj. expr., Jb 5[18] (opp. חָבַשׁ, ‖ מָחַץ). **2.** of *mental pain*, obj. לֵב, Ez 13[22] (subj. false prophetesses, v. supr.); cf. v[22] (subj. י׳). **3.** (si vera l.) of *marring* good land with stones 2 K 3[19], 𝔊 ἀχρειώσετε (Klo תְּאַבְּדוּ).

3511 **†כְּאֵב** n.m.[Jb 2, 13] **pain**;—כ׳ abs. Jb 2[13] Is 17[11]; cstr. 65[14]; sf. כְּאֵבִי Jb 16[6] + 2 t.;—*pain*, mental and physical Jb 2[13] 16[6] perh. also ψ 39[3]; כ׳ אָנוּשׁ (in disappointment and disaster) Is 17[11] (‖ נַחֲלָה from חָלָה); mental, כְּ׳־לֵב Is 65[14] (‖ שֵׁבֶר רוּחַ) so Je 15[18] (‖ מַכָּה fig.)

4341 **†מַכְאוֹב** n.m.[ψ 32, 10] **pain**;—מ׳ abs. Ec 1[18] + 2 t.; cstr. ψ 69[27]; sf. מַכְאֹבִי (מַכְאוֹבִי) ψ 38[18] + 3 t., etc.; pl. מַכְאוֹבִים ψ 32[10] Ec 2[23]; מַכְאֹבוֹת Is 53[3]; sf. מַכְאֹבָיו Ex 3[7]; מַכְאֹבֵינוּ Is 53[4];—**1.** *pain*, physical, Ex 3[7] (‖ עֳנִי; cf. מִפְּנֵי נֹגְשָׂיו in context); 2 Ch 6[29] (‖ נֶגַע); Jb 33[19]. **2.** of *mental pain*, ψ 32[10] (of troubles of wicked), of Babylon Je 51[8]; ψ 38[18] 69[27] (as result of sin; of י׳'s servant); in י׳'s word to Baruch Je 45[3] (‖ אֲנָחָה, יָגוֹן), cf. of Israel in distress Je 30[15] (‖ שֶׁבֶר), of Jerus. La 1[12.12.18], Ec 1[18] (יוֹסִיף דַּעַת יוֹסִיף מַכ׳); 2[23] (‖ כַּעַס עִנְיָנוֹ); partic. of suffering servant of י׳ Is 53[3.4] (both ‖ חֳלִי).

†[כָּאָה] vb. **Niph. be disheartened, cowed** (cf. Ar. كَأْكَأَ *draw back timidly*, كَأَى *abstain through timidity*)—**Niph.** *Pf.* וְנִכְאָה consec. Dn 11[30] *then shall he be cowed; Pt.* נִכְאֵה לֵבָב ψ 109[16] *downhearted* (‖ עָנִי וְאֶבְיוֹן). **Hiph.** *Inf. cstr.* הַכְאוֹת לֵב צַדִּיק Ez 13[22]; but 𝔊 𝔗 Co הכאבתן v. כָּאַב. 3512

†[כָּאֶה] adj. **cowed**, ψ 10[10] Qr חֵל כָּאִים; 2489
host of cowed ones, but rd. Kt חלכאים; v. p. 319. 2489

[כאר] v. II. כור. p. 468 3738

כָּאֹר Am 8[8], v. יְאֹר. p. 384 2975

כבב (√ of foll., cf. Sta[§ 116, 3]; meaning not wholly clear; Ar. كَبَّ is *roll threads into a ball*, كُبَّةٌ *ball* of thread, but also *troop* of horses, *band* of men, etc.; Eth. ከበበ: is *in orbem circumsistere*, ኩቡብ: ኩቡብ: *orbis, circulus*, etc.; hence perh. *star*, as *round*, or as collected in *bands, clusters, constellations;* As. *kabâbu* = *burn; kabâbê, shields*, is written *ḳabâbê* by Dl[HWB 578]).

†כּוֹכָב n.m.[Gn 15, 5] **star** (NH *id.*; Aram. כּוֹכְבָא, כּוֹכַבְתָּא, ܟܘܟܒܐ, ܟܘܟܒܬܐ, fem. form specifically of planet Venus, v. also We[Skizzen iii. 36, 38]; Ar. كَوْكَبٌ gen. of *single stars* and prob. Aram. loan-word, We[Skizzen iii. 173]; Eth. ኮከብ:; prob. for *כבכב v. Mahri *kubkob, kobkib*, etc., Maltzan[ZMG 1873, 227] and As. *kakkabu* Dl[HWB 336]; Pun. κακαβουμ (Dioscorides), name of a plant, prob. from shape of seed-cup, Blau[ZMG xxvii, 1873, 529]; on formation cf. Nö[M § 109] Ba[NB § 138. 1])—כ׳ abs. Nu 24[17]; cstr. כּוֹכַב Am 5[26]; pl. כּוֹכָבִים Gn 1[16] + 19 t.; cstr. כּוֹכְבֵי (כֹּכְבֵי) Gn 22[17] + 13 t.; כֹּכְבֵיהֶם Ez 32[7];—sg. only כ׳ אֱלֹהֵיכֶם Am 5[26] (where, however, כ׳ is prob. a gloss, so GFM Dec. 19, 1890, and now We; v. further כִּיּוּן), and כ׳ מִיַּעֲקֹב Nu 24[17] (JE; ‖ שֵׁבֶט בישראל, metaph. of future ruler); elsewhere pl. *stars*, ‖ sun and moon (cf. also infr.) Gn 1[16] (P) ψ 136[9] (to rule the night, cf. Gn 1[16]), Je 31[35] Gn 37[9] (E), Joseph's dream (כ׳ אַחַד עָשָׂר = 11 brethren); Dt 4[19] obj. of idol. worship (cf. infr.); observed in augury הַחֹזִים בַּכּ׳ Is 47[13] (of Babylon); Ec 12[2] (‖ (also) *light;* fig. of brightness of youth); ‖ sun Jb 9[7]; ‖ moon ψ 8[4]; sign of evening Ne 4[15] (מֵעֲלוֹת הַשַּׁחַר עַד צֵאת הַכּ׳) cf. כּוֹכְבֵי נִשְׁפּוֹ Jb 3[9] 3556 (appar. sign of dawn); numbered by God ψ 147^{4}; sim. of abundant posterity, Gn 15^{5} 22^{17} 26^{4} Ex 32^{13} (all JE); of Isr. Dt 1^{10} 10^{22} 28^{62} 1 Ch 27^{32} Ne 9^{23}; of number of merchants of Nineveh Na 3^{16}; as lofty, Jb 22^{12}; so in fig. of haughty nations Ob^{4} Is 14^{13}; cf. symbolic vision of Dn (צְבָא הַשָּׁמַיִם, צָבָא‖) Dn 8^{10}; sim. of brightness of righteous Dn 12^{3}; not pure (זַכּוּ) before God Jb 25^{5} (‖ moon); darkened in Yahweh's judgment Jo 2^{10} 4^{15} Ez 32^{7} (‖ sun and moon; so) Is 13^{10} (‖ also כְּסִילֵיהֶם); personified: as fighting Ju 5^{20}; shouting Jb 38^{7} (בְּרָן־יַחַד כּוֹכְבֵי בֹקֶר, ‖ בְּנֵי אֱלֹהִים); praising ψ 148^{3} (כּוֹכְבֵי אוֹר, ‖ sun and moon).—On stars in Arab. mythol. v. We Skizzen iii. 173 f.

3513 †**כָּבֵד vb. be heavy, weighty, burdensome, honoured** (NH Pi. *honour*, and deriv., כֹּבֶד *weight;* Ph. n.pr.f. כבדת = *honoured one*, and in cpd. n.pr.; Eth. **ከበደ:** *be heavy*, etc.; As. *kabâdu* or *kabâtu*, *grow* or *be heavy*, Dl ^{HWB}; cf. Ar. كَبَدٌ *difficulty, distress;* كَابَدَ III. *struggle with difficulties*, etc.; Zinj. כבדו *honour*, DHM$^{Sendsch. 58}$; Sab. כבודת *gifts of honour*, = Heb. נדבה *freewill offering* DHM$^{ZMG 1883, 341 f.}$)—**Qal** *Pf.* כ׳ Is 24^{20}; 3 fs. כָּֽבְדָה Gn 18^{20} + 4 t.; כָּבֵ֑דָה Ju 20^{34}; 3 mpl. כָּֽבְדוּ Gn 48^{10}; *Impf.* יִכְבַּד Ex 9^{7} Is 66^{5}; יִכְבָּ֑ד Jb 6^{3} 33^{7} + 10 t. Impf. (כָּבֵד Gn 12^{10} + is given as 3 m. Pf. by some; but it is prob. taken better as adj. SS make כָּבֵד ψ 38^{5} inf. abs.; < Thes adj.).—**1.** *be heavy*, in weight, of misfortune, heavier than sand Jb 6^{3}; of God's hand in punishment 1 S 5^{11}, with אֶל 1 S 5^{6}; עַל ψ 32^{4}; of man's hand in war Ju 1^{35}; יָדִי כָּֽבְדָה עַל־אַנְחָתִי *my hand is heavy upon my groaning* Jb 23^{2} is explained by 𝔗 Hrz Schlottm as *hand smiting me;* but read rather with 𝔊 𝔖 Ew De Reu Di יָדוֹ of God's hand; of pressure אַכְפִּי Jb 33^{7} (𝔊 כַּפִּי); = *vehement, sore*, of battle Ju 20^{34}; c. אֶל 1 S 31^{3} = עַל 1 Ch 10^{3}; *burdensome, grievous;* וְלֹא נִכְבַּד עָלֶ֑יךָ *lest we be burdensome unto thee* 2 S 13^{25}; of work laid upon one, bondage, with עַל Ex 5^{9} (JE) Ne 5^{18}; of sin conceived as a burden Gn 18^{20} (J), iniquities ψ 38^{5}; transgressions, with עַל Is 24^{20}. **2.** *heavy, insensible, dull*, of the eyes, so as to be unable to see Gn 48^{10} (JE); of the ears Is 59^{1}; of the לֵב, *hard, insensible* Ex 9^{7} (J; P and E's syn. is חָזַק, q. v.) **3.** *be honoured* (cf. βαρύς) of a man Jb 14^{21} (opp. יצערו: cf. Hiph. **3**), of Tyre Ez 27^{25}, of Yahweh Is 66^{5}.

Niph. *Pf.* נִכְבַּד 2 S 6^{20}, נִכְבָּד 2 S 23$^{19.23}$ 1 Ch 11^{21}; נִכְבַּדְתָּ Is 43^{4}; + 2 t. Pf.; *Impf.* אֶכָּבֵד Lv 10^{3} Is 49^{5}; אִכָּֽבְדָה Ex 14$^{4.17}$; אִכָּבֵ֑דָה 2 S 6^{22}; אִכָּֽבְדָה Hg 1^{8}; *Imv.* הִכָּבֵד 2 K 14^{10}; *Inf.* הִכָּֽבְדִי Ex 14^{18} Ez 39^{13}; *Pt.* נִכְבָּד Gn 34^{19} + 6 t.; pl. נִכְבָּדִים Nu 22^{15}; cstr. נִכְבַּדֵּי Is 23$^{8.9}$ Ps 8^{24}; נִכְבַּדֶּיהָ Na 3^{10}; נִכְבְּדֵיהֶם ψ 149^{8}; *Pl. f.* נִכְבָּדוֹת ψ 87^{3}—**1.** pass. **a.** *be made heavy* fr. abundance, מַעְיָנוֹת נִכְבַּדֵּי־מָ֑יִם *fountains abounding in water* Pr 8^{24}. **b.** *be honoured, enjoy honour*, of man 1 S 9^{6} 22^{14} 2 S 6$^{20.22}$ 23^{19} = 1 Ch 11^{21}, 2 S 23^{23} 2 K 14^{10} Is 43^{4} 49^{5} 1 Ch 4^{9} וַיְהִי נִכְבָּד, 11^{25} נִכְבָּד הוּא (altered from 2 S 23^{23}); but more frequent in *pt.* as subst. *honourable, honoured, distinguished man* Gn 34^{19} Nu 22^{15} (JE) Is 3^{5} 23$^{8.9}$ Na 3^{10} ψ 149^{8}; נִכְבָּדוֹת ψ 87^{3} *glorious things;* הַשֵּׁם הַנִּכְבָּד וְהַנּוֹרָא Dt 28^{58} *the glorious and awe-inspiring name* (of Yahweh). **2.** medial, *get oneself glory* (*or honour*), of God Is 26^{15} Ez 28^{22} 39^{13} Hg 1^{8}; with בְּ *in* or *by* any one Ex 14$^{4.17.18}$ (P); עַל־פְּנֵי Lv 10^{3} (P).

Piel *Pf.* 2 m. sf. כִּבַּדְתָּ֫נִי Is 43^{23}; 3 mpl. כִּבְּדוּ 1 S 6^{6}; + 3 t. Pf.; *Impf.* יְכַבֵּד Mal 1^{6} + 3 t.; sf. יְכַבְּדָ֫נְנִי ψ 50^{23}; 3 fs. sf. תְּכַבְּדֵנִי Is 43^{20}; אֲכַבְּדָה ψ 86^{12}; + 12 t. Impf.; *Imv.* כַּבֵּד Ex 20^{12} + 2 t.; + 3 t. Imv.; *Inf. abs.* כַּבֵּד Nu 22^{17}; + 2 t. Inf.; *Pt.* מְכַבֵּד 2 S 10^{3}; + 4 t. Pt.;—**1.** *make heavy, insensible* (cf. **Qal 2**) the לב(ב) 1 S 6$^{6.6}$. **2.** *make honourable, honour, glorify*, usu. c. human subj.: **a.** human obj., parents Ex 20^{12} = Dt 5^{16} (Dec.), Mal 1^{6}; Balaam Nu 22$^{17.17.37}$ 24$^{11.11}$ (JE); sons of Eli 1 S 2^{29}; Saul 1 S 15^{30}; Nahash 2 S 10^{3} = 1 Ch 19^{3}; Jerusalem La 1^{8}; more gen. ψ 15^{4}; subj. God 1 S 2^{30b} ψ 91^{15}, cf. Pr 4^{8}. **b.** obj. things, sacred place Is 60^{13} (God subj.); the Sabbath Is 58^{13}. **c.** God obj. 1 S 2^{30a} Is 24^{15} 25^{3} 43^{20} ψ 22^{24} 50$^{15.23}$ Pr 14^{31}; + acc. rei זבחיך Is 43^{23}; + בְּ instr. (lips) Is 29^{13}; + מִן (מֵהוֹנֶ֑ךָ) Pr 3^{9}; obj. the name of י׳, c. acc. ψ 86^{12}; c. לְ ψ 86^{9}; obj. the מַלְאַךְ י׳ Ju 13^{17}. **d.** subj. indef. (si vera l.), obj. God and man Ju 9^{9} (of olive; on text, esp. בּוֹ for בִּי, v. GFM). **e.** obj. a heathen god לֶֽאֱלֹהַּ Dn 11$^{38.38}$.

Pu. *be made honourable, honoured.* *Impf.* יְכֻבָּ֑ד Pr 13^{18} 27^{18}; *Pt.* מְכֻבָּד Is 58^{13}.

Hiph. *Pf.* הִכְבִּיד La 3^{7} + 5 t.; 2 f. הִכְבַּדְתְּ Is 47^{6}; + 4 t. Pf.; *Impf.* וַיַּכְבֵּד Ex 8^{28} 9^{34}; *Imv.* הַכְבֵּד Is 6^{10}; *Infin. abs.* הַכְבֵּד Ex 8^{11}; *cstr.* הַכְבִּיד 2 Ch 25^{19}; *Pt.* מַכְבִּיד Hb 2^{6}.—**1.** *make heavy*, a yoke 1 K 12$^{10.14}$ = 2 Ch 10$^{10.14}$, Is 47^{6}; ellipt. with עַל Ne 5^{15}; a chain La 3^{7}; pledges, with

עַל Hb 2^{6}. **2.** *make heavy, dull, unresponsive*, the ears Is 6^{10} Zc 7^{11}; the לֵב Ex 8$^{11.28}$ 9^{34} 10^{1}(J). **3.** *cause to be honoured*, of depopulated districts of NE. Israel, Is 8^{23}, of restored nation Je 30^{19} (‖לא יצערו); *shew* or *display honour*, 2 Ch 25^{19} לְהַכְבִּיד (in ‖2 K 14^{10} הִכָּבֵד).

Hithp. *Imv.* הִתְכַּבֵּד Na 3^{15}; *f.* הִתְכַּבְּדִי Na 3^{15}; *Pt.* מִתְכַּבֵּד Pr 12^{9};—**1.** *make oneself heavy, dense, numerous* (cf. כָּבֵד **1 b**) as locusts Na 3$^{15.15}$. **2.** *honour oneself* Pr 12^{9}.

3515 † כָּבֵד **adj.** heavy;—כ׳ Gn 41^{31} + 34 t.; cstr. כְּבַד Ex 4$^{10.10}$; כֶּבֶד Is 1^{4}; pl. כְּבֵדִים Ex 17^{12}; cstr. כִּבְדֵי Ez 3$^{5.6}$;—**1. a.** *heavy*, a burden ψ 38^{5}; hands (weary of holding up) Ex 17^{12} (E), hair of head 2 S 14^{26}, a corpulent old man 1 S 4^{18}; עַם כֶּבֶד עָוֺן Is 1^{4} *a people heavy with* (*the burden of*) iniquity; a cloud charged with rain Ex 19^{16} (E); a rock of large size Is 32^{2}; *oppressive, grievous, burdensome*, a yoke 1 K 12$^{4.11}$ = 2 Ch 10$^{4.11}$; a famine Gn 12^{10} 41^{31} 43^{1} 47$^{4.13}$ (J); the *vexation* (כַּעַס) of a fool Pr 27^{3}; *vehement, sore*, of a mourning Gn 50^{11} (J). **b.** *massive, abundant, numerous*, of a people עַם Nu 20^{20} (J) 1 K 3^{9}; army חיל 2 K 6^{14} 18^{17} = Is 36^{2}; insect swarm Ex 8^{20} (J). **c.** *heavy, dull* of speech and tongue Ex 4$^{10.10}$ (JE); of the לֵב, *hard* Ex 7^{14} (J). **d.** *hard, difficult*, of a thing to be done Ex 18^{18} (E) Nu 11^{14} (J); of a language to be understood Ez 3$^{5.6}$. **2.** in the usage of J כָּבֵד מְאֹד is frequent: **a.** *very oppressive, grievous*, of hail Ex 9$^{18.24}$; murrain Ex 9^{3}; lamentation Gn 50^{10}. **b.** *very numerous*, cattle Ex 12^{38}; army, מַחֲנֶה Gn 50^{9}; locusts Ex 10^{14}; so חַיִל 1 K 10^{2} = 2 Ch 9^{1}. **c.** *very rich*, במקנה *in cattle* Gn 13^{2}.

3516 † כָּבֵד **n.m.**$^{La\ 2,11}$ **liver** (explained by Thes (quoting Galen) as the *heavy* organ, *par excellence*, of the body; NH כָּבֵד; Aram. כַּבְדָּא, ܟܰܒ݂ܕܳܐ; Ar. كَبِدٌ, cf. أَكْبَدُ (anything) *large, thick* in the middle; Eth. ከብድ፡; As. *kabittu* Dl^{HWB} *temper, heart* (fig.), Aram. כְּבַד, ܐܬܟܒܕ *be angry*, because the liver was regarded as seat of emotions)—כ׳ Ex 29^{13} + 11 t.; כְּבֵדוֹ Pr 7^{23}; כְּבֵדִי La 2^{11};—*liver* of man, as pierced by arrow Pr 7^{23}; poured out in sorrow La 2^{11}; of animals as consulted by divination רָאָה בַכּ׳ Ez 21^{26}; elsewhere in P, in phrases (ה)יֹתֶרֶת (עַל־)הַכָּבֵד Ex 29$^{13.22}$ Lv 3$^{4.10.15}$ 4^{9} 7^{4} 8$^{16.25}$ 9^{19}; הַיֹּתֶרֶת מִן־הַכּ׳ Lv 9^{10}, of the animals suited for sacrifice.

† כֹּבֶד **n.[m.]** **1.** heaviness, *weight* of a 3514
stone Pr 27^{3}. **2.** *mass, abundance*, of corpses Na 3^{3}. **3.** *vehemence*, of war Is 21^{15}, of storm Is 30^{27}.

† I. [כָּבוּד] **adj.** glorious, only fs. כְּבוּדָּה, 3520
of a bed Ez 23^{41}; a queen in bridal array ψ 45^{14}. See also כְּבוּדָּה **n.f.** infr. p. 459

† II. כָּבוֹד **n.m.**$^{Is\ 60,1}$ and † **f.**$^{Gn\ 49,6}$ **abun-** 3519
dance, honour, glory;—כ׳ Jos 7^{19} + 70 t.; כָּבֹד Gn 31^{1} Na 2^{10}; cstr. כְּבוֹד Ex 16^{7} + 62 t.; כְּבֹד Pr 25$^{2.2}$; sf. כְּבוֹדִי Gn 45^{13} + 17 t.; כְּבֹדִי Gn 49^{6} + 3 t.; + 40 t. sfs.—**1.** *abundance, riches* Gn 31^{1} (J), Is 10^{3} 61^{6} 66$^{11.12}$ Na 2^{10} ψ 49$^{17.18}$. **2.** *honour, splendour, glory*, of external condition and circumstances: **a.** of men: of Joseph in Egypt Gn 45^{13} (E); of Job Jb 19^{9} 29^{20}; of Ephraim Ho 9^{11}, Samaria Ho 10^{5}; עֹשֶׁר וְכָבוֹד *wealth and splendour* 1 Ch 29$^{12.28}$ 2 Ch 17^{5} 18^{1} 32^{27} Pr 3^{16} 8^{18} 22^{4}; עֹשֶׁר (וּ)נְכָסִים וְכ׳ 2 Ch 1$^{11.12}$ = גם ע׳ גם כ׳ 1 K 3^{13}, Ec 6^{2}; ‖ עֹשֶׁר Pr 11^{16}; man was crowned with כ׳ וְהָדָר at his creation, ψ 8^{6}; the king is given כ׳ ‖ הוֹד וְהָדָר ψ 21^{6}. **b.** of things, כ׳ עָשְׁרוֹ Est 5^{11} *splendour of his wealth*, of a throne 1 S 2^{8} (poem), Is 22^{23} Je 14^{21} 17^{12}; a kingdom Est 1^{4}; chariots Is 22^{18}; priestly robes Ex 28$^{2.40}$ (P); Lebanon Is 35^{2} 60^{13}; forest Is 10^{18} (fig. of royal might); trees Ez 31^{18}; temple Hg 2$^{3.9}$; restored holy land ψ 84^{12} Is 4$^{2.5}$; Jerus. Is 62^{2}. **c.** of God, *glory*, (1) in historic theophanies: to Moses Ex 33$^{18.22}$ (J); ‖ אֹתֹת Nu 14^{22} (JE); ‖ גָּדְלוֹ Dt 5^{21}. P uses כ׳ יהוה for theophanies of the Exodus Ex 16$^{7.10}$ 24$^{16.17}$ 40$^{34.35}$ Lv 9$^{6.23}$ Nu 14^{10} 16^{19} 17^{7} 20^{6}, cf. 2 Ch 5^{14} = 1 K 8^{11}, 2 Ch 7$^{1.2.3}$; so Ezek., Ez 1^{28} 3$^{12.23}$ 10$^{4.4.18}$ 11^{23} 43$^{4.5}$ 44^{4}; with the variation כ׳ אֱלֹהֵי יִשְׂרָאֵל Ez 8^{4} 9^{3} 10^{19} 11^{22} 43^{2}, and הַכָּבוֹד Ez 3^{23}; the sacred tent was sanctified by the Glory Ex 29^{43} (P), and the temple was מְקוֹם מִשְׁכַּן כ׳ ψ 26^{8}; when the ark was captured, the Glory went into exile from Israel 1 S 4$^{21.22}$. (2) *in historic and ideal* manifestations to the pious mind Yahweh's name is a name of glory ψ 72^{19} Ne 9^{5}; his eyes eyes of glory Is 3^{8}; in the temple his glory is seen ψ 63^{3}; it is על השמים ψ 113^{4}; על כל הארץ ψ 57$^{6.12}$; in a thunderstorm he is אֵל הַכָּבוֹד ψ 29^{3}; his glory is לְעוֹלָם ψ 104^{31}; it is great ψ 138^{5}; above all the earth ψ 108^{6}; the whole earth is full of it Is 6^{3}; the heavens are declaring כְּבוֹד אֵל ψ 19^{2}; with reference to the divine reign כ׳ הֲדַר מַלְכוּתוֹ, ψ 145^{12}; הֲדַר כ׳ הוֹדֶךָ ψ 145^{5}. (3) he is מֶלֶךְ הַכָּבוֹד ψ 24$^{7.8.9.10.10}$;

he will appear in his glory ψ 102[17], his glory will be revealed in a march through the wilderness to the holy land Is 40[5], the land will see it Is 35[2], shine with it Ez 43[3], and it will dwell in the land ψ 85[10]; it will be to the rearward of Israel Is 58[8]; it will arise and be seen upon Jerusalem Is 60[1.2]; Yahweh will be the glory in the midst of her Zc 2[9]; the temple will be filled with it Hg 2[7]; the earth will be filled with a knowledge of it Hb 2[14], and with it Nu 14[21] (JE) ψ 72[19]; it will be declared among the nations and all will see it Is 66[18.19.19] ψ 97[6] and peoples and kings revere it ψ 102[16] Is 59[19]; י׳ will reign before his elders in glory Is 24[23]; the resting-place of the Messiah will be כָּבוֹד Is 11[10]. **3.** *honour, dignity* of position מנע מִכּ׳ *withhold from honour* Nu 24[11] (E); ירד מִכּ׳ *descend from* Je 48[18]; שלח אחר כ׳ *send after* Zc 2[12]; תמך כ׳ ψ 112[9]; רום בכ׳ Is 14[18]; שכב בכ׳ Pr 29[23]; יַרְבֶּה כ׳ Dn 11[39]; לקח כ׳ *take me to honour* ψ 73[24]; not becoming to fools Pr 26[1]; לפני כ׳ ענוה *before honour* (goeth) *humility* Pr 15[33] 18[12]; antithesis קלון Ho 4[7] Hb 2[16] Pr 3[35], קִיקָלוֹן Hb 2[16]; כָּבוֹד is used as collective, of honoured men, *dignitaries, nobility* כבוד ישראל Mi 1[15]; elsewhere as cstr. before various nations or with sfs. only Is 5[13] 8[7] 10[16] 16[14] 17[3.4] 21[16] 22[24]. **4.** *honour, reputation,* of character, of man וְלֹא־לְךָ לְכ׳ 2 Ch 26[18] *neither will it be for thine honour;* ‖ חכמה Ec 10[1]; צדקה Pr 21[21]; antith. כְּלִמָּה ψ 4[3]; וְחֵקֶר כְּבֹדָם כָּבוֹד Pr 25[27] *and searching out of their glory is* (not) *glory* כ׳ לאיש Pr 20[3]; כ׳ אֱלֹהִים הַסְתֵּר דָּבָר וכ׳ מְלָכִים חֲקֹר דָּבָר Pr 25[2] *the honour of God is to conceal a thing, but the honour of kings is to search out a thing.* **5.** *my honour,* poet. of the seat of honour in the inner man, the noblest part of man ‖ נפשׁי Gn 49[6] (poem) ψ 7[6]; לִבִּי ψ 16[9] 108[2]; it is called upon to זמר ψ 30[13] (rd. כְּבוֹדִי for כָּבוֹד); עוּרָה ψ 57[9]. **6.** *honour, reverence, glory,* as due to one or ascribed to one: **a.** of men, due to a father Mal 1[6]; honour done to David by Nathan's prophecy 1 Ch 17[18]; עשׂה כ׳ לְ 2 Ch 32[33] *do honour to;* נתן כ׳ לְ Pr 26[8]; ‖ ישׁע ψ 62[8]. **b.** of God, כְּבוֹדִי *the honour due to me* (Yahweh) Is 42[8] 43[7] 48[11] כ׳ שְׁמֶךָ ψ 79[9]; נתן כ׳ לְ 1 S 6[5] Je 13[16] Mal 2[2] ψ 115[1]; שׂים כ׳ לְ Jos 7[19] (J), Is 42[12]; שׂים כ׳ תהלתו ψ 66[2]; יהב כ׳ ועז לְ ψ 29[1] 96[7] = 1 Ch 16[28]; זמר כ׳ שְׁמוֹ ψ 29[2] 96[8] = 1 Ch 16[29]; יהב כ׳ שְׁמוֹ לְ ψ 66[2]; ספר כבודו בגוים ψ 96[3] = 1 Ch 16[24]; אמר כ׳ מלכותך ψ 145[11]; נתן כבודי בגוים Ez 39[21]; אֹמֵר כָּבוֹד ψ 29[9] *say Glory;* יַעְלְזוּ בְכ׳ *exult with* (ascriptions of) *glory* ψ 149[5]. **7.** *glory* as *the object* of honour, reverence and glorifying, כְּבוֹדִי ψ 3[4] *my glory* (the one whom I glorify); כְּבוֹדָם ψ 106[20] *their glory;* כְּבוֹדוֹ Je 2[11].

†כְּבֻדָּה **n.f.** *abundance, riches* Ju 18[21]. 3520
See also 1. [כָּבוֹד]. p. 458

כְּבֵדֻת **n.f. heaviness,** וַיְנַהֲגֵהוּ בִּכְ׳ Ex 14[25] (J) 3517
and they drave them with heaviness (*difficulty*).

†[כָּבָה] **vb. be quenched, extinguished,** 3518
go out, of fire or lamp (NH *id.;* Aram. כְּבָא *id.* of light of eyes (rare))—**Qal** *Pf.* 3 pl. כָּבוּ Is 43[17]; *Impf.* יִכְבֶּה 1 S 3[3] Pr 21[18]; 3 fs. תִּכְבֶּה Lv 6[5] + 10 t.; *Inf. cstr.* כְּבוֹתְךָ Ez 32[7] 𝔊 𝔖 𝔙 Co (MT כַּבּ׳ Pi.)—*be quenched, extinguished* (c. neg. exc. 1 S 3[3] Pr 26[20] Is 43[17]), of lamp (נֵר אֱלֹהִים) in sanctuary 1 S 3[3]; of altar-fire Lv 6[5.6]; of נֵרָהּ Pr 31[18]; of bodies of renegade Israelites Is 66[24] (cf. גֵּיא בֶן־הִנֹּם); subj. אֵשׁ fig. of contention Pr 26[20]; fig., subj. fire kindled by י׳ Ez 21[3.4]; subj. wrath (חֵמָה) of י׳ 2 K 22[17] = 2 Ch 34[25], Je 7[20]; wrath under fig. of fire (אֵשׁ) Je 17[27]; so of burning land of Edom Is 34[10]; of annihilation of Yahweh's enemies Is 43[17] (כַּפִּשְׁתָּה; ‖ דָּעַךְ), cf. Pharaoh Ez 32[7] (v. supr.) **Pi.** *Pf.* וְכִבּוּ consec. 2 S 14[7]; *Impf.* 3 ms. sf. יְכַבֶּנָּה Is 42[3]; 2 ms. תְּכַבֶּה 2 S 21[17]; וַיְכַבּוּ 2 Ch 29[7]; *Inf.* כַּבּוֹת Ct 8[7]; also MT כַּבּוֹתְךָ Ez 32[7] (but cf. supr.); *Pt.* מְכַבֶּה Is 1[31] + 3 t.;—*quench, extinguish,* fig. except 2 Ch 29[7] (of extinguishing lamps, נֵרוֹת, in temple); sq. נֵר יִשְׂרָאֵל (fig. for life of David) 2 S 21[17]; sq. גַּחַלְתִּי (*coal* = family-hope) 2 S 14[7] (of killing widow's only son); sq. פִּשְׁתָּה כֵהָה Is 42[3] *dimly-burning* wick (fig. of spiritually weak); implied obj. ref. to wrath of י׳ Am 5[6] Je 4[4] 21[12]; to people and idols Is 1[31]; sq. love אַהֲבָה Ct 8[7] (subj. מַיִם רַבִּים); Ez 32[7] cf. supr.

†כָּבוּל **n.pr.loc. 1.** city on border of Asher 3521
Jos 19[27], mod. *Kâbûl,* 4 h. (9 miles) SE. from Akko, Rob[BR iii. 88] Guérin[Gal. i. 422 f.] **2.** אֶרֶץ כָּבוּל district in Galilee 1 K 9[13] containing 20 cities given by Sol. to Hiram (popular etymol. poss. כּ *as* + בַּל = בַּל *not,* i.e. *as good as nothing,* cf. v[12], so Ew Th; Klo conject. ארץ גָּלִיל), Buhl[Geogr. § 116].

כבל (√ of foll. = *bind;* NH כָּבַל *bind,* כֶּבֶל *fetter;* Aram. כְּבַל *id.,* כַּבְלָא *id.,* ܟܒܠ, ܟܒܠܐ; Ar. كَبَلَ *bind,* كَبْلٌ *fetter*).

†כֶּבֶל **n.[m.]** fetter(s), late;—sg. coll. עִנּוּ 3525
בַכֶּ׳ רגליו ψ 105[18] *they humbled his feet with*

fetters (|| בַּרְזֶל); pl. cstr. אסר בְּכַבְלֵי בַרְזֶל 149[8] (|| זִקִּים).

כבן (√of foll., mng. dub.; NH כָּבַן, Aram. כבן, ܟܒܢ = *wrap round, wrap up*).

3522 †כַּבּוֹן **n.pr.loc.** in Judah Jos 15[40] poss.= foll., 𝔊 Χαβρα, 𝔊L Χαββω.

4343 †מַכְבֵּנָה (van d.H מַכְבֵּנָא) **n.pr.loc.** 1 Ch 2[49] (represented as having שְׁוָא for father; poss.= foregoing), 𝔊 Μαχαβηνα, 𝔊L Μαχβανα.

4344 †מַכְבַּנַּי **n.pr.m.** a hero of David 1 Ch 12[14].

3526 [כָּבַס] [51] **vb.** (tread), **wash** (NH *id.*; Ph. כבס as pt.; As. *kabâsu, tread (down), subjugate, kibšu, step, path,* Dl[HWB])—**Qal** *Pt.* only מְסִלַּת שְׂדֵה כוֹבֵס *highway of fuller's (=treader's, washer's) field* Is 7[3] 36[2]=2 K 18[17]. **Pi.** *Pf.* וְכִבֶּס consec. Lv 13[6]+11 t.; כִּבֵּס Gn 49[11] 2 S 19[25], etc.; *Impf.* יְכַבֵּס Lv 11[25]+16 t.; 2 ms.sf. תְּכַבְּסֵנִי ψ 51[9], etc.; *Imv.* sf. כַּבְּסֵנִי 51[4]; fs. כַּבְּסִי Je 4[14]; *Pt.* pl. מְכַבְּסִים Mal 3[2];—**1.** *wash* garments (i.e. by *treading*) Ex 19[10.14] (E), 2 S 19[25]; fig. of Judah Gn 49[11]; elsewhere chiefly P: Lv 6[20] 11[25.28] 13[6.34] 15[11] Nu 8[9]+; || רָחַץ (which=*wash person*) Lv 14[8.9] 15[5.6.7.8.10.11]+ (כ׳ in Lv 27 t., || ר׳ 15 t.; in Nu 8 t., || ר׳ 3 t.); Pt.=*fuller* (cf. Qal), only בֹּרִית מְכ׳ Mal 3[2]. †**2.** *wash* person, only poet. and fig. אִם תְּכַבְּסִי בַּנֶּתֶר Je 2[22]; כַּבְּסִי מֵרָעָה לִבֵּךְ 4[14]; c. sf. ψ 51[4] (|| טהר; + מֵעָוֹן); v[9] (|| חִטֵּא). †**Pu.** *Pf.* וְכֻבַּס consec. Lv 13[58] 15[17] *be washed,* of garment. †**Hothp.** (Ges[§ 54, 3]) *Inf.* אַחֲרֵי הֻכַּבֵּס אֶת־הַנֶּגַע Lv 13[55] *after the plague is washed out,* so v[56].

3527 †I. [כָּבַר] **vb. be much, many** (As. *kabâru, be great, mighty; kabru, great, huge;* Ar. كَبُرَ *be great,* in body, rank, or age, كَبِيرٌ *great, noble, aged;* Eth. ከብረ: *be honoured, magnified;* ክቡር: *honoured, glorious;* Sab. epith. כבר Hal[Ét. Sab. JAs. Dec. 1874, No. 90]; Syr. ܟܒܪ, ܟܒܪ, ܐܟܒܪ for Heb. רָבָה, הַרְבֵּה, ܟܒܝܪ (rare) *much;* Zinj. *be abundant, numerous*)—**Hiph.** (only Elihu) *make many,* Jb 35[16] בִּבְלִי דַעַת מִלִּין יַכְבִּר (cf. וַיֶּרֶב אֲמָרָיו 34[37])
4342 >*make great,* Bu[Beitr. 138], comparing 8[2]; מַכְבִּיר with the force of a subst. (Ew[§ 160c]) 36[31] יתן אכל לְמַכְבִּיר giveth food *in abundance* (=prose לָרֹב, e.g. 2 Ch 11[23]).

3524 †כַּבִּיר **adj.** great, mighty, much, only poet., and only Jb Is[1]:—Is 10[13] Qr (but rd. as Kt כְּאַבִּיר), 17[12] and 28[2] מים כבירים (usu. מַיִם רַבִּים), Jb 8[2] ורוח כביר אמרי פיך a *mighty* wind, 15[10] כביר מאביך ימים (Ges[§ 131, R 5a])=*aged:* of God, 34[17] כַּבִּיר צַדִּיק the just *mighty* one, 36[5a], v[b] כ׳ כֹּחַ לֵב *mighty* in strength of understanding; 34[24] כבירים *mighty men;* of quantity=*much,* Is 16[14] שְׁאָר מְעַט מִזְעָר לוא כַבִּיר, Jb 31[25] וכי כביר מצאה ידי had gotten *much.*

†[כִּבְרָה] **n.f.** appar. **distance,** only in the 3530
phr. כִּבְרַת (ה)ארץ a *distance of land* or *length of way,* Gn 35[16] וַיְהִי עוֹד כ׳ ה׳ לָבוֹא אֶפְרָתָה, 48[7] בְּעוֹד כ׳ א׳ לָבֹא אֶפְרָתָה, 2 K 5[19] וַיֵּלֶךְ מֵאִתּוֹ כ׳ אֶרֶץ. The distance meant is uncertain, but fr. 2 K 5[19] it would seem to have been a short one; v. further Di[Gn 35, 16] and Thes (As. *kibrâti* is a (widely extended) *territory, quarter of the world,* etc., Dl[HWB 315]; according to Hoffm.[GGAbh. xxxvi (1890), 23-25] perhaps the distance that one can see).

†I. כְּבָר **adv.** (late) **already** (freq. in Mish. 3528
and NH; 𝔗 כבר (rare); Syr. ܟܒܪ usu. *perhaps,* occas. *already* (Mt 11[21] Hb 10[2]); Mand. כבאר *already,* Nö[M. p. 202]. Der. uncertain, connexion with √כבר being dub.)—*already,* Ec 1[10] כְּבָר הָיָה it hath *already* been, 2[12.16] 3[15.15] 4[2] 6[10] 9[6.7].

†II. כְּבָר **n.pr.fl.** Kĕbār, a river (or perhaps 3529
a canal) of Babylonia, not at present identified, by wh. the exiles, among whom Ez. ministered, were settled; always in the phr. נְהַר כְּבָר Ez 1[1.3] 3[15.23] 10[15.20.22] 43[3] (cf. Sm[Ez 1, 1] Del[Par. 47 f., 184]).

II. **כבר** (√of foll.; ? *to intertwine, net;* NH כָּבַר *sift* is denom. fr. כְּבָרָה).

†[כָּבִיר] **n.[m.]** prob. something *netted,* i.e. 3523
either a **quilt** or (Ew[H. 3. 77] Ke) a **fly-net** (κωνωπεῖον) spread over the face while a person was
asleep; 1 S 19[13.16] כְּבִיר הָעִזִּים a *quilt* (or *fly-net*) 3523
of goats(' hair). Vid. further Dr[ad loc.]

†כְּבָרָה **n.f. a sieve** (a *net*-like implement), 3531
Am 9[9] כַּאֲשֶׁר יִנּוֹעַ בַּכְּבָרָה as it (corn) is shaken (i.e. sifted) in a *sieve.* Cf. Wetzst[ZPV xiv. 1 ff.]

†מַכְבֵּר **n.[m.]** a netted cloth or coverlet; 4345
2 K 8[15] of the cloth which Hazael dipped in water, and spread over Ben-hadad's face to smother him.

מִכְבָּר **n.m.** grating or lattice-work, cstr. 4346
מִכְבַּר;—Ex 27[4] and thou shalt make for it (the altar of burnt-offering in the tab.) מִכְבָּר מַעֲשֵׂה רֶשֶׁת נְחֹשֶׁת a *grating,* (even) a network of bronze, which surrounded the lower half of the altar (v[5b]): so 38[4]; מִכְבַּר הַנְּחֹשֶׁת 35[16] 38[5.30] 39[39].

3532 כֶּ֫בֶשׂ $_{107}$ **n.m.**$^{\text{Ex 29, 38}}$ lamb (√dub.: NH *id.*, *battering-ram;* As. *kabšu*, *lamb* acc. to COT^{Gloss}; Ar. كَبْش is *ram, leader;* Syr. ܟܒܫܐ *lamb*, with anom. ܫ, is very rare, and prob. loan-word; Nö in Frä^{109})—כ׳ abs. Ex 29^{39} + 43 t.; pl. כְּבָשִׂים v^{38} + 61 t.; sf. כְּבָשַׂי Jb 31^{20};—**1.** *lamb*, for sacrif.: Is 1^{11}; of daily offering Ex 29$^{38.39.39.40.41}$ Nu 28$^{3.4.4}$ + 12 t. Nu 28; sin-offering Lv 4^{32}; purification 12^{6} 14^{10} + 5 t. Lv 14; dedication of altar Nu 7^{15} + 25 t. Nu 7; offerings in 7th month 29^{2} + 22 t. Nu 29, etc. (87 t. Ex Lv Nu all P); in Ezekiel's temple Ez 46^{4} + 6 t. Ez 46; 1 Ch 29^{21} 2 Ch 29$^{21.22.32}$ 35^{7} Ezr 8^{35}, cf. sim. Je 11^{19}. **2.** *lambs*, as grazing; symb. of devastation Is 5^{17} (cf. Gie$^{\text{Beitr. 1890}}$), sim. of Isr. Ho 4^{16}; in predict. וְגָר זְאֵב עִם־כ׳ Is 11^{6}. **3.** *lambs*, as furnishing wool for clothing: Jb 31^{20} גֵּז כ׳, Pr 27^{26} כ׳ לִלְבוּשֶׁךָ.

3535 †כִּבְשָׂה, כַּבְשָׂה **n.f.** ewe-lamb; כּ׳ 2 S 12$^{3.6}$; כּ׳ Lv 14^{10} Nu 6^{14}; cstr. כִּבְשַׂת 2 S 12^{4}; pl. כְּבָשֹׂת Gn 21$^{29.30}$; cstr. כִּבְשֹׂת v^{28};—*ewe-lambs* (7) set in witness Gn 21$^{28.29.30}$ (E); used in sacrif. Lv 14^{10} (purif.), Nu 6^{14} (Nazirite; both P, and both ‖ כֶּבֶשׂ); for food, in Nathan's parable 2 S 12$^{3.4.6}$.

3775 †כֶּ֫שֶׂב **n.[m.]** lamb (transp. fr. preceding)—כ׳ abs. Lv 3^{7} + 5 t.; pl. כְּשָׂבִים Gn 30^{32} + 6 t.;—*lamb*, as property Gn 30$^{32.33.35.40}$ (J); for sacrif. Lv 1^{10} 3^{7} 4^{35} 22^{19} Nu 18^{17}, cf. Lv 22^{27}; for food Lv 7^{23}, cf. 17^{3} (all P); Dt 14^{4}.

3776 †כִּשְׂבָּה **n.f.** ewe-lamb Lv 5^{6} (P).

3533 †[כָּבַשׁ] **vb. subdue, bring into bondage** (NH *id.*, *press, oppress;* Aram. כְּבַשׁ, ܟܒܫ *tread down, beat* or *make a path, subdue;* Ar. كَبَسَ *press, squeeze, knead* (body or limb, as in the bath, *massage*), also *attack, assault*)—**Qal** *Pf.* 3 pl. וְכָבְשׁוּ consec. Zc 9^{15}; *Impf.* יִכְבּוֹשׁ Mi 7^{19}; וַיִּכְבְּשׁוּם Je 34^{11} Qr (Kt Hiph), etc.; *Imv.* pl. sf. כִּבְשֻׁהָ Gn 1^{28}; *Inf.* כְּבוֹשׁ 2 Ch 28^{10} Est 7^{8}; *Pt.* כֹּבְשִׁים Ne 5^{5};—**1.** *bring into bondage*, sq. acc. + לַעֲבָדִים Je 34$^{11.16}$ 2 Ch 28^{10} Ne 5^{5}. **2.** (late) *subdue, force*, a woman Est 7^{8} (= earlier עִנָּה). **3.** *subdue, dominate*, the earth Gn 1^{28} (P), Zc 9^{15} (of conquest); *tread down*, sq. אַבְנֵי־קֶלַע; fig. *subdue*, sq. עֲוֹנֹתֵינוּ Mi 7^{19}. **Niph.** *Pf.* 3 fs. נִכְבְּשָׁה Jos 18^{1} + 3 t.; *Pt.* fpl. נִכְבָּשׁוֹת Ne 5^{5};—pass. of **Qal 1**, subj. בְּנוֹתֵינוּ Ne 5^{5}; of **Qal 3**, subj. הָאָרֶץ (of conquest) Nu 32$^{22.29}$ Jos 18^{1} (all P), 1 Ch 22^{18}. **Pi.** *Pf.* כִּבֵּשׁ 2 S 8^{11}, obj. גּוֹיִם (of conquest). **Hiph.** *Impf. bring into bondage*, sq. acc. + לַעֲבָדִים Je 34^{11} Kt (Qr **Qal**).

†כֶּ֫בֶשׁ **n.[m.]** footstool (late) (NH *id.*, *step, stair;* Aram. כִּבְשָׁא, etc., a rude *seat* (rare))—כ׳ הַזָּהָב 2 Ch 9^{18} (of Solomon's throne). 3534

†כִּבְשָׁן **n.m.** kiln, for lime or pottery (so Ki, AW; Mishn$^{\text{Kel viii. 9}}$; √and original mng. dub.; acc. to Thes as *subduing, reducing* its contents, cf. *igne ferrum domatur* Plin$^{\text{Nat. Hist. 36. 27}}$)—alw. abs.; only in קִיטוֹר הַכּ׳ Gn 19^{28} (J; sim. of smoke of כִּכָּר, Sodom and Gom.); עֶשֶׁן הַכּ׳ Ex 19^{18} (E; sim. of smoke of Sinai); פִּיחַ כ׳ ashes of kiln Ex 9^{8}, cf. v^{10} (both P). 3536

כדד (√of foll.; Ar. كَدَّ is *toil severely; fatigue, weary, harass, tread;* كُدٌّ *mortar* in which things are *pounded, bruised;* كُدَادَةٌ *what remains in bottom of cooking-pot*).

†כַּד **n.f.** jar (NH *id.;* Aram. כַּדָּא)—כַּד abs. 1 K 17^{12} Ec 12^{6}; cstr. 1 K 17$^{14.16}$; כַּדָּהּ Gn 24$^{14.17.43}$ etc.; pl. כַּדִּים Ju 7$^{16.16}$ + 3 t.;—water-*jar*, carried on woman's shoulder Gn 24$^{14.15.16.17.18.20.43.45.46}$ (all J), 1 K 18^{34} Ec 12^{6}; empty (of water), containing lamps Ju 7$^{16.19.20}$; containing meal 1 K 17$^{12.14.16}$. (On extra-Palest. hist. of this word cf. Lag$^{\text{BN 104}}$.) 3537

†[כִּידוֹד] **n.m.** spark (fr. above √, = *strike out* a spark, acc. to Thes RobGes, cf. Sta$^{§ 216}$ (doubtfully), Lag$^{\text{BN 182}}$ Kö$^{\text{ii. 147, § 71. 1}}$, NH כִּדּוּר = *rod* (of iron, etc.); כִּדּוּרִיּוֹת שֶׁל אֵשׁ i.e. *red-hot rods;* but Ba$^{\text{NB § 142, 139}}$ der. this and כַּדְכֹּד fr. √כיד = Ar. كَادَ, كيد *emit fire* (said of a fire-stick, زَنْد, Lane$^{\text{2639 b, cf. 1257 b}}$), and so Buhl)—only pl. cstr. כִּידוֹדֵי אֵשׁ Jb 41^{11} of breath of crocodile (‖ לַפִּידִים). 3590

†כַּדְכֹּד **n.[m.]** a precious stone, perh. ruby (fr. *sparkle*?; Aram. ‖ is כַּדְכְּדָנָא); כ׳ Ez 27^{16} as article of commerce; כַּדְכֹּד Is 54^{12} fig. in promise to Zion. 3539

כַּדַּי v. דַּי. p. 191 1767

כדר (√of foll.; cf. Ar. كَدَرَ vii. *shoot* or *rush down* (of hawk, star, etc.; also of an attacking force) so Thes Fl in De$^{\text{Job 15, 24}}$ Buhl Di al.; v. also mod. Ar. كدّر *annoy, vex, reprimand*, Spiro$^{\text{Vocab.}}$; كدر oftener *be dark, gloomy, turbid*, whence > כידור = *seething* tumult, of battle, cf. Kö$^{\text{ii. 147, § 71. 1}}$).

†כִּידוֹר **n.[m.]** onset, מֶלֶךְ עָתִיד לַכּ׳ Jb 15^{24} *a king ready for the onset.* 3593

1754 †כַּדּוּר n.[m.] ball, acc. to Bö[NÄ ii, 134] De Or
al. Is 22[18], as in Talm.; **circle, cordon** (As.
1754 *kudûru*), acc. to Jastr[PAOS, Oct. 1888, xcvi]; v. also דּוּר
p. 189 b.

3540 †כְּדָרְלָעֹמֶר n.pr.m. king of Elam (=
Babylon. *Kudar-Laga*[*mar*] (*Lagamaru*=n.pr.
div.), v. Pinches[Vict. Inst. Jan. 20, 1896] Say[PSBA, June 1896, 176]
Scheil[Rev. Bibl. 1896, 600 f.], cf. Schr[COT])—Gn 14[1.4.5.9.17].

3541 **כֹּה** demonstr. adv. **thus, here** (BA כָּה;
𝔗 𝔖[Jerus.] Mand. כָּא *here:* in Syr. with prefixes ܠܟܐ *hither*, ܡܟܐ (𝔖[Jerus.] ܡܟܐ) *hence*, ܠܐܟܐ *where?* cf. אֵיכָה, p. 32, and Kö[ii. 1, 252])—
1. of manner, *thus* (so most freq., and usually pointing to what is to follow, while כֵּן points commonly to what has preceded), Gn 15[5] כה יהיה זרעך *thus* shall thy seed be, Nu 6[23] 1 K 2[30] כֹּה דִבֶּר יוֹאָב וְכֹה עָנָנִי, 5[25] Is 24[13] (answered by כֵּן, as Je 23[29]); with a subst. Is 20[6] הִנֵּה כֹה מַבָּטֵנוּ, Je 9[21] (si vera l.), 23[29] 1 S 27[11]. Mostly confined to particular phrases: thus **a.** with diff. forms of אמר, כה תאמר *thus* shalt thou say Ex 3[14.15] 19[3] 20[22] etc.; esp. כה אמר י״י thus saith (or said) י׳ Ex 4[22] 5[1] 7[17.26] 8[16] etc.; and continually in the prophets, as Is 7[7] 8[11] 18[4] etc.; Je 2[2.5] 4[27] 6[16] etc.; also in the idiom. formula אִם כֹּה יֹאמַר *if he say* (or *used to say*) (the words spoken following) †Gn 31[8] 1 S 14[9.10] 20[7] 2 S 15[26]. **b.** with עשׂה to do *thus*, Ex 5[15] Dt 7[5]; pointing back, Nu 22[30] Jos 6[14] 1 S 27[11] al.; esp. in the phrase כה יעשׂה אלהים וכה יוסיף (with variations), 1 S 3[17]+(v. יסף), in which כֹּה points to an imprecation understood but not expressed. With בְּ prefixed †1 K 22[20] ויאמר זה בְּכֹה וזה אמר בְּכֹה and one spake *in this wise*, and another spake *in that wise* (‖ 2 Ch 18[19] כָּכָה...כָּכָה; prob. rightly). †**2.** of place, *here* (rare, chiefly in E), Gn 31[37] שִׂים כֹּה place it *here* before my brethren, Nu 23[15.15] 2 S 18[30] Ru 2[8]. Repeated, Ex 2[12] וַיִּפֶן כֹּה וָכֹה and he turned *this way* and *that way;* כֹּה...כֹּה *on this side*...*on that side* Nu 11[31]. With עַד Gn 22[5] and we will go עַד־כֹּה *as far as here* (δεικτικῶς) i.e. *yonder.* †**3.** of time, עַד כֹּה *hitherto*, Ex 7[16] (cf. עַד־הֵנָּה), Jos 17[14]; עַד־כֹּה וְעַד־כֹּה till *now* and till *then*, i.e. meanwhile, 1 K 18[45].

3602 **כָּ֫כָה** [37] adv. **thus** (NH abbrev. to כָּךְ, with preps. בֵּין כָּךְ *meanwhile*, לְפִיכָךְ *therefore;* prob. either from כֹּה and כְּ, lit. *as thus*, Ol[§ 223 h]; or from כָּה כָּה Kö[ii. 1, 253]), somewhat more emph. than כֹּה, usu. prefixed to word which it qualifies:—Ex 12[11] וככה תאכלו אתו and *thus* shall ye eat it, 29[35] Nu 8[26] 11[15] ואם ככה את עשׂה לי, 15[11.12.13] Dt 25[9] 29[23] (cf. 1 K 9[8] Je 22[8]); so often with עשׂה: 1 S 19[17] למה ככה רמיתני why hast thou *thus* deceived me? 2 S 17[21] 1 K 1[6.48]; Je 13[9] 19[11] 28[11] 51[64]; once with an adj. 2 S 13[4] מדוע אתה כָּכָה דל why art thou *thus* lean? Ec 11[5] answering to כַּאֲשֶׁר; ψ 144[15] העם שֶׁכָּכָה לּוֹ the people to which it is *thus.* Once 2 Ch 18[19] repeated, *in this way*...*in that way* (‖ 1 K 22[20] בְּכֹה...בְּכֹה). Comp. the syn. כָּזֹאת. With a prep. once, in late Hebrew, Est 9[26] עַל־כָּ֫כָה concerning such a matter. With the interrog. אי, אֵיכָכָה *how?* (p. 32).

†I. [כָּהָה] vb. **be** or **grow dim, faint** 3543
(NH *id.;* Aram. כְּהָא; cf. Ar. كَهَى *be* اَكْهَى, i.e. *weak, cowardly*)—**Qal** *Pf.* 3 fs. כָּהֲתָה Dt 34[7]; *Impf.* יִכְהֶה Is 42[4]; 3 fs. תִּכְהֶה Zc 11[17]; וַתֵּכַהּ Jb 17[7]; וַתִּכְהֶיןָ Gn 27[1]; *Inf. abs.* כָּהֹה Zc 11[17];—*grow dim*, of eye Gn 27[1] (J), Dt 34[7] Jb 17[7]; of violent putting out of eye Zc 11[17.17]; *he shall not grow dim* Is 42[4], of servant of י׳ under fig. of lamp or fire (v. Kay Che De), or *grow faint* (cf. Di). **Pi.** *Pf.* 3 fs. וְכִהֲתָה consec. Ez 21[12] (subj. כָּל־רוּחַ; ‖ וְנָמֵס כָּל־לֵב) *grow faint* (Pi intrans., Ges[§ 52 k], Kö[i. 187]; but rd. perh. כָּהֲתָה).

†[כֵּהֶה] adj. **dim, dull, faint**; only f. כֵּהָה 3544
Lv 13[6]+6 t.; pl. כֵּהוֹת Lv 13[39] 1 S 3[2];—*dim*, of eyes 1 S 3[2]; of burning wick (פִּשְׁתָּה כ׳) Is 42[3]; *dull* (in colour, of plague-spots) Lv 13[6.21.26.39.56]; fig.=*faint* רוּחַ כ׳ Is 61[3] (opp. מַעֲטֵה תְהִלָּה).

†כֵּהָה n.f. **(dimming), lessening, allevia-** 3545
tion;—אֵין כ׳ לְשִׁבְרֵךְ of Nineveh Na 3[19] (read גֵּהָה, *healing*?).

†II. [כָּהָה] vb. **Pi. rebuke** (Syr. ܟܗܐ, 3543
Mand. כהא (Nö[M. 72]) *id.*), only 1 S 3[13] sq. בְּ, וְלֹא כִהָה בָּם.

כהן (√ of foll.; mng. dub., v. Dr[2 S 8, 18]; Ar. vb. كَهَنَ *is divine*, and كَاهِنٌ (Qor 52[29]) *is a seer*, the organ (mostly) of a jinn, rarely of a god: the كَاهِنٌ and the כֹּהֵן must have been orig. identical (both alike being guardians of an oracle, at a sanctuary); but their functions diverged: the كَاهِنٌ gradually lost his connexion with the sanctuary, and sank to be a mere diviner; the כהן acquired fuller sacrif. functions: v. RS[Enc. Brit. ed. 9, xix. 727]; We[Skizzen iii. 130 ff.],

^{107}; Now $^{\text{Arch. ii. 89 f.}}$; Ph. כחן is *priest*, כהנת *priestess*).

3548 כֹּהֵן$_{750}$ **n.m. priest** (NH כֹּהֵן; Aram. כָּהֵין, כַּהֲנָא, ܟܗܢ, ܟܗܢܐ; Eth. **ካህን:** all *id.;* on Ph. and Ar. v. supr.);—כ׳ Gn 14^{18} + 439 t.; pl. כֹּהֲנִים Ex 19^{6} + 272 t.; cstr. כֹּהֲנֵי 1 S 5^{5} + 13 t.; sf. כֹּהֲנַי La 1^{19} + 22 t. sfs.—†**1.** *priest-king:* e.g. Melchizedek Gn 14^{18} (E ?), cf. ψ 110^{4} (the Messianic priest-king like Melchizedek); Zc 6^{13} (Messianic priest and king); Israel מַמְלֶכֶת כֹּהֲנִים Ex 19^{6} (E) *a kingdom of priests* (priests and kings at once in their relation to the nations); cf. Is 61^{6} (of Israel ministering as a priest); or *a chieftain* (exercising priestly functions) כֹּהֵן מִדְיָן Ex 2^{16} 3^{1} 18^{1} (all JE); so also probably the sons of David 2 S 8^{18}, his grandson 1 K 4^{5}, and Ira the Jairite 2 S 20^{26}, who as princes performed priestly functions. With these we may class the כהנים Ex 19$^{22.24}$ (J). †**2.** *priests of other religions than* י׳*'s:* Potiphera כ׳ אֹן Gn 41$^{45.50}$ (E), 46^{20} (P); Egyptian כהנים Gn 47$^{22.22.26}$ (J); כ׳ דָגוֹן 1 S 5^{5}; Philistine כהנים וקסמים 1 S 6^{2}; כֹּהֲנָיו *his priests:* e.g. of Baal 2 K 10^{19} = of Ahab 2 K 10^{11}; of Chemosh Je 48^{7}; of Malcam Je 49^{3}; Mattan was כ׳ הבעל 2 K 11^{18} = 2 Ch 23^{17}; הכמרים עם הכהנים Zp 1^{4}; Josiah burned the bones of the priests of the Baalim and Asherim 2 Ch 34^{5}. †**3.** *priests of special orders in Israel:* **a.** Micah in the hill-country of Ephraim consecrated his own son וַיְהִי־לוֹ לְכֹהֵן Ju 17^{5}; but so soon as he could secure Jonathan ben Gershom, a descendant of Moses (see VB Ju 18^{30}), he consecrated him, הַכֹּהֵן היה ל׳ לכהן Ju 17$^{10.12.13}$ 18$^{4.19}$; v$^{6.17.18.20.24.27}$. He was captured by the Danites, and he and his line became priests at Dan until the Exile, v$^{19.19.30}$. **b.** Jeroboam עשׂה כהנים כ׳ (הַ)בָּמוֹת 1 K 12^{31} of those not מבני לוי, as *priests of (the) high places* 1 K 12^{32} 13$^{2.33.33}$ = כ׳ לבמות 2 Ch 11^{15}; Amaziah (of this class) was כ׳ בית־אל Am 7^{10}; v. also 2 Ch 13^{9}; called by Chr כ׳ לְלֹא אלהים v^{9}; yet Hosea rebukes them as priests of י׳ Ho 4$^{4.9}$ 5^{1} 6^{9}; at the Exile they were deported by the Assyrians 2 K 17$^{27.28}$. **c.** the people imported into Samaria made some of themselves כ׳ במות to worship י׳ the God of the land 2 K 17^{32}. †**4.** *priests in Israel* הכהנים who bore the ark and the trumpets Jos 3$^{13.14.15.17}$ 4$^{3.9.10.17.18.18}$ 6$^{4.4.6.6.8.9.12.13.16}$ (all JE), 1 K 8$^{3.6.10.11}$; Eli was הכהן 1 S 1^{9} 2^{11}; כ׳ יהוה 14^{3}; and his sons כ׳ ליהוה 1 S 1^{3}; a מִשְׁפַּט הַכֹּהֲנִים 1 S 2^{13} mentions the ministering priest הכהן and the נַעַר הַכּ׳ 1 S 2$^{13.14.15.15}$, Ahijah was הַכּ׳ in time of Saul 1 S 14$^{19.19.36}$; Abimelech הַכּ׳ at Nob, a priestly centre, 1 S 21$^{2.3.5.6.7.10}$ 22^{11}; where were many כֹּהֲנֵי י׳ 1 S 22$^{17.17.21}$, all slain by Saul except Abiathar son of Ahimelech 1 S 22$^{11.18.18.19}$, who became הַכּ׳ 1 S 23^{9} 30^{7} 1 K 1$^{7.19.25.42}$ 2$^{22.26}$; Zadok later was הַכּ׳ 2 S 15^{27} 1 K 1$^{8.26.32.34.38.39.44.45}$ 2^{35} 3^{2} 1 Ch 16^{39} 24^{6}: so that the two were (ה)כהנים 2 S 8^{17} = 1 Ch 18^{16} (rd. וְאֶבְיָתָר בֶּן־אח׳ 2 S 8^{17} 𝔖 We Dr, and correct 1 Ch 18^{16} accordingly) 2 S 15$^{35.35}$ 17^{15} 19^{12} 20^{25} 1 K 4^{4}; Sol. removed Abiathar 1 K 2^{27} and Zadok was anointed לְכֹהֵן acc. to 1 Ch 29^{22}; cf. prediction of rejection of house of Eli and selection of כ׳ נֶאֱמָן 1 S 2$^{28.35}$; Jehoiada הַכּ׳ led the revolution against Athaliah 2 K 11$^{9.9.10.15.15.18}$ 12$^{3.8.10}$ = 2 Ch 22^{11} 23$^{8.8.9.14.14}$ 24$^{2.20.25}$, perh. also Je 29^{26}; הכהנים sustaining him in his reforms 2 K 12$^{5.6.7.8.9.10.17}$; Uriah was הַכּ׳ in the reign of Ahaz 2 K 16$^{10.11.11.15.16}$ Is 8^{2}; Hilkiah of Josiah 2 K 22$^{10.12.14}$ 23^{24} 2 Ch 34$^{14.18}$. Other individual priests are named, e.g.: Pashhur of Jehoiachin Je 20^{1}; Zephaniah of Zedekiah Je 21^{1} 29$^{25.26.29}$ 37^{3}; הַכּ׳ is Ezekiel's title Ez 1^{3}. Priests are classed with officials of state: prophets and priests 2 K 23^{2} Is 28^{7} Je 5^{31} 6^{13} 8^{10} 14^{18} 23$^{11.33.34}$ 26$^{7.8.11.16}$ 29^{1} La 2^{20} 4^{13}; priests and elders La 1^{19} 4^{16}; king and priest La 2^{6}; kings, priests, and prophets Je 13^{13}; kings, princes, and priests Je 1^{18}; princes, eunuchs, and priests Je 34^{19}; priest, sage, and prophet Je 18^{18}; chiefs, priests, and prophets Mi 3^{11}; prophets, priests, and elders Ez 7^{26}; kings, princes, priests, and prophets Je 2^{26} 4^{9} 8^{1} 32^{32}; princes, judges, prophets, and priests Zp 3^{4}; seeming to exclude any other officials. Apparently in the same generic sense הכהנים Je 1^{1} 2^{8} 27^{16} 28$^{1.5}$ 29^{25} 31^{14}; כַּכֹּהֵן Is 24^{2}; כהנים Jb 12^{19}; כהניה La 1^{4} Ez 22^{26}; כהניו ψ 78^{64}. *Moses and Aaron among his priests* ψ 99^{6} includes Moses (against P). Zion's priests clothed with righteousness and salvation ψ 132$^{9.16}$ = 2 Ch 6^{41}, prob. here also. †**5.** *Levitical priests* הַכֹּהֲנִים הַלְוִיִּם Dt 17$^{9.18}$ 18^{1} 24^{8} 27^{9} Jos 3^{3} 8^{33} (all D), Je 33^{18} (inverted), v^{21} (neither in 𝔊), 2 Ch 5^{5} (= הַכּ׳ וְהַל׳ 1 K 8^{4}: Chronicler retains original Deuteronomic reading), Ez 43^{19} 44^{15} (cf. **6**); הַכּ׳ בְּנֵי לֵוִי Dt 21^{5} 31^{9}; לקח לכ׳ לל׳ Is 66^{21} *take for priests, for Levites* (of the nations in Messianic age). Doubtless of same class are: הַכֹּהֲנִים Dt 18^{3} 19^{17} Jos 3$^{6.8}$ 4^{11} (D); and הַכֹּהֵן, the priest officiating on a partic. occasion Dt 18^{3} 20^{2}; or holding a partic. dignity 17^{12} 26$^{3.4}$. The כהנים of the other cities of Judah, כ׳ הבמות, who were not allowed to minister in Jerusalem 2 K 23$^{8.8.9.20}$, may be an attempt to enforce an exclusion from the priesthood of all but Levitical priests. †**6.** *Zadokite priests:* Ezekiel distinguishes among הכהנים הלוים those of the seed of Zadok, בְּנֵי צָדוֹק; all but the latter excluded by him from priesthood 40^{46} 43^{19} 44^{15} 48^{11}; the priests of his code being all Zadokites 40$^{45.46}$ 42$^{13.14}$ 43$^{24.27}$ 44$^{21.22.30.30.31}$ 45$^{4.19}$ 46$^{2.19.20}$ 48$^{10.13}$. **7.** *Aaronic priests.* In H. it is taken for granted that a priest is of the seed of Aaron; the pl. is never used; כֹּהֵן is used for any priest Lv 21^{9} 22$^{10.11.12.13}$; הַכֹּהֵן for Aaron Lv 21^{21}, and for the official priest (acting for the priesthood, almost collective) Lv 17$^{5.6}$ 22^{14} 23$^{10.11.20.20}$ 27$^{8.8.8.11.12.12.14.14.18.21.23}$. The priests of P are בְּנֵי אַהֲרֹן Lv 1$^{5.8.11}$ 2^{2} 3^{2} 21^{1} Nu 3^{3} 10^{8} Jos 21^{19}; so in Chronicles 2 Ch 13$^{9.10}$ 26^{18} 29^{21} 31^{19} 35$^{14.14}$; הַכֹּהֵן is used of Aaron 22 t., Eleazar 29 t., Phinehas Jos 22^{30} and elsewhere; 180 t. of ministering priests, or generic of the priests; הכהנים Lv 6^{22} 7^{6} 13^{2} 16^{33} Jos 4^{16}; כהן Lv 6^{16}. Chronicles distinguishes הַכֹּהֲנִים וְהַלְוִיִּם 1 Ch 13^{2} 15$^{11.14}$ 23^{2} 24$^{6.31}$ 28$^{13.21}$ 2 Ch 8^{15} 11^{13} 13$^{9.10}$ 23^{4} 24^{5} 29^{4} 30$^{15.25}$ 31$^{2.2.4.9}$ 34^{30} 35$^{8.18}$ (the variants without וְ 2 Ch 23^{18} 30^{27} are due to copyists' errors), Ezr 1^{5} 2^{70} 3$^{8.12}$ 6^{20} 7^{7} 8$^{29.30}$ 9^{1} Ne 7^{72} 8^{13} 11^{3} 12$^{1.30.44.44}$ 13^{30}; הלוים והכהנים 2 Ch 19^{8} 30^{21}; priests, Levites, and others 1 Ch 9^{2} Ezr 10^{5} Ne 10$^{1.29.35}$ 11^{20}; בְּנֵי לֵוִי antith. to הַכֹּ׳ Ezr 8^{15}; הכהן בן אהרן עם הלוים Ne 10^{39}; (ה)כהנים in Chr 67 t. has the same reference, as also כֹּהֲנֵינוּ Ezr 9^{7} Ne 9$^{32.34}$; כֹּהֵן Ezr 2^{63}=Ne 7^{65}; כ׳ ליהוה 2 Ch 26^{17}; כהניו *His* (God's) *priests* 2 Ch 13^{12}; כ׳ מוֹרֶה *teaching priest* 2 Ch 15^{3}; הַכֹּהֵן is used of Jehoiada in time of David 1 Ch 27^{5}, and Azariah in the reign of Uzziah 2 Ch 26^{17}. In the literature of the restoration הַכֹּהֵן is used of Ezra, Ezr 7^{11} 10$^{10.16}$ Ne 8$^{2.9}$ 12^{26}; Uriah Ezr 8^{33}; Eliashib Ne 13^{4}; Shelemiah Ne 13^{13}; הכהנים Jo 1$^{9.13}$ 2^{17} Hg 2$^{11.12.13}$ Zc 7^{5} Mal 1^{6} 2^{1}; priests and prophets Zc 7^{3}; כהן Mal 2^{7}. **8.** *the high priest:* הַכֹּהֵן is frequently used (see **4**) to designate the priest who was at the head of priestly affairs. The adj. הַגָּדוֹל first appears of Jehoiada 2 K 12^{11}, then of Hilkiah 2 K 22$^{4.8}$ 23^{4} 2 Ch 34^{9}; after the exile, of Joshua Hg 1$^{1.12.14}$ 2$^{2.4}$ Zc 3$^{1.8}$ 6^{11}, and Eliashib Ne 3$^{1.20}$ 13^{28}. But P uses it of Aaron and his eldest descendants who are anointed with holy oil Lv 21^{10} (H; הכ׳ הַגָּדוֹל מֵאֶחָיו), Nu 35$^{25.28.28}$ Jos 20^{6}, and so הַכֹּ׳ הַמָּשִׁיחַ Lv 4$^{3.5.16}$ 6^{15}, cf. 16^{32}. כ׳ הָרֹאשׁ is used of Seraiah 2 K 25^{18}=Je 52^{24}; and, in Chronicler, of Amariah 2 Ch 19^{11}, Jehoiada 2 Ch 24^{11}, Azariah 2 Ch 26^{20} 31^{10}; of Aaron, Ezr 7^{5}. (We also supposes הרואה in 2 S 15^{27} to be a corruption of הראשׁ, which he regards as postexilic insertion. The text is corrupt [see Dr$^{Sm. l.c.}$]; but this correction is improbable. Lists of high priests occur 1 Ch 5$^{30-41}$ 6$^{35-38}$.) A priest of second rank (כֹּהֵן (ה)מִּשְׁנֶה) appears in 2 K 23^{4} (cstr. pl. incorrect), 25^{18}=Je 52^{24}; זִקְנֵי הַכֹּ׳ 2 K 19^{2}=Is 37^{2}, Je 19^{1}; שָׂרֵי הַכֹּ׳ 2 Ch 36^{14} Ezr 8$^{24.29}$ 10^{5}; רָאשֵׁי הַכֹּ׳ Ne 12^{7}.

† II. [כָּהַן] **vb.** only **Pi. denom.** **act as priest**; 3547
—*Pf.* כִּהֵן Ex 40^{13} 1 Ch 5^{36}; 3 mpl. כִּהֲנוּ Ex 28^{41} 40^{15}; *Impf.* 3 ms. יְכַהֵן Nu 3^{4}+2 t.; pl. יְכַהֲנוּ 1 Ch 24^{2}; *Inf. cstr.* כַּהֵן Ex 29^{1}+11 t.; sf. כַּהֲנוֹ Ex 28$^{1.3.4}$.—**1.** *minister as a priest,* abs. Ex 31^{10} 35^{19} 39^{41} Lv 16^{32} Nu 3$^{3.4}$ (all P); כ׳ לִי *minister to me* (י׳) Ex 28$^{1.3.4.41}$ 29$^{1.44}$ 30^{30} 40$^{13.15}$ (all P), Ez 44^{13} Ho 4^{6}; כ׳ ליהוה Lv 7^{35} (P), 1 Ch 5^{36} 24^{2} 2 Ch 11^{14} (alw. of Aaron and his sons, exc. Ez 44^{13} 2 Ch 11^{14}, where Levites are forbidden to minister; and Ho 4^{6} of Israel, whose national priesthood is taken away). **2.** *be* or *become priest* Dt 10^{6} (E ?). **3.** *play the priest:* כֶּחָתָן יְכַהֵן פְּאֵר Is 61^{10} *as a bridegroom (that) priests it with his turban,* decks himself with a splendid turban such as the priests wore.

†כְּהֻנָּה **n.f. priesthood**;—abs. כ׳ Ex 29^{9} 3550
+5 t.; cstr. כְּהֻנַּת Nu 25^{13}+2 t.; sf. כְּהֻנַּתְכֶם Nu 18$^{1.7.7}$; כְּהֻנָּתָם Nu 3^{10}; pl. כְּהֻנּוֹת 1 S 2^{36}.—כהנת יהוה *priesthood of* י׳, the portion of the Levites Jos 18^{7} (D); pl. *priest's offices* 1 S 2^{36}; elsewhere Ex 29^{9} 40^{15} Nu 3^{10} 16^{10} 18$^{1.7.7}$ 25^{13} (all P), Ezr 2^{62} =Ne 7^{64}, Ne 13$^{29.29}$.

† כּוּב **n.pr.gent.** Ez 30^{5}, rd. לוּב 𝔊 Sta$^{Pop. Jav. 6}$ 3552
Co, cf. Sm.

†כּוֹבַע **n.m. helmet** (√dub.; NH כּוֹבַע, Aram. 3553
כּוֹבְעָא *turban;* cf. קוֹבַע Ez 23^{24})—abs. כ׳ Ez 27^{10}; כּוֹבַע 38^{5}; cstr. כֹּובַע (Ew$^{§ 213, f.}$) 1 S 17^{5} Is 59^{17}; pl. כּוֹבָעִים Je 46^{4} 2 Ch 26^{14};—*helmet,* of bronze כ׳ נְחֹשֶׁת עַל־רֹאשׁוֹ 1 S 17^{5}; Je 46^{4} Ez 27^{10} 38^{5} 2 Ch 26^{14}; fig. of י׳, וַיִּלְבַּשׁ צְדָקָה כַּשִּׁרְיָן וְכ׳ יְשׁוּעָה בְּרֹאשׁוֹ Is 59^{17}.

†[כָּוָה] **vb. burn, scorch, brand** (NH *id.*; 3554
Aram. ܟܘܳܐ esp. Pa.; Ar. كَوَى *cauterize*)—**Niph.** *Impf.* 2 ms. תִּכָּוֶה Is 43^{2} thou shalt not *be scorched* (fig. of Isr., ‖ תִּבְעַר); 3 fpl. וְרַגְלָיו לֹא תִכָּוֶינָה Pr 6^{28} shall a man walk on the coals *and his feet not be burned?* (‖ שָׂרַף of garments v^{27}).

3587 †כִּי n.[m.] burning, branding (for form, cf. רִי from רָוָה, אִי, צִי, עִי: Kö II. 1. 04)—only כִּי
תַּחַת יֹ֫פִי Is 3[24] *branding instead of beauty*, in
3588 judgment on women of Jerusalem. p. 471

3555 †כְּוִיָּה n.f. id.; כ׳ תַּחַת כ׳ Ex 21[25].

4348 †מִכְוָה n.f. burnt-spot, scar of a burn; מִכְוַת־אֵשׁ Lv 13[24]; מִכְוָה v[24.25.28.28] (all P).

3556 כּוֹכָב v. sub ככב. p. 456

3557 †[כּוּל] vb. comprehend, contain (NH, Aram. *id., measure, measure out*, of dry or liquid measure; Syr. Aph. ܐܟܝܠ *id.*; Ar. كَالَ *measure grain*)—Qal *Pf.* only Is 40[12] מִי . . . כָּל בַּשָּׁלִשׁ עֲפַר הָאָרֶץ *who hath comprehended the dust of the earth in a shalish-measure?* Pilp. *Pf.* כִּלְכֵּל 2 S 19[33]; sf. כִּלְכְּלָם 1 K 18[4]; 2 ms. sf. כִּלְכַּלְתָּם Ne 9[21], etc.; *Impf.* יְכַלְכֵּל Zc 11[16]+, etc.; *Inf. cstr.* כַּלְכֵּל Je 20[9]+, etc.; *Pt.* מְכַלְכֵּל Mal 3[2];—*sustain, maintain, contain:* 1. *sustain, support, nourish*, sq. acc. pers. Gn 45[11] 50[21] (both E), 2 S 19[33.34] 20[3] 1 K 4[7a] (v[b] abs.), 5[7] 17[4.9] Ne 9[21] Ru 4[15] ψ 55[23] Zc 11[16] (of sheep); sq. acc. pers. + rei (food) Gn 47[12] (J), 1 K 18[4.13]. 2. *contain*, sq. acc. pers. 1 K 8[27] 2 Ch 2[5] 6[18] (heavens cannot contain י׳); *hold in, restrain* Yahweh's word within one, Je 20[9]. 3. *support, endure*, sickness רוּחַ אִישׁ יְכַלְ׳ מַחֲלֵהוּ Pr 18[14] Mal 3[2] (obj. אֶת־יוֹם בּוֹאוֹ); of *sustaining* a cause, in court, יְכַלְ׳ דְּבָרָיו בְּמִשְׁפָּט ψ 112[5]. Polp. *Pf.* 3 pl. כָּלְכְּלוּ *were supplied with food* 1 K 20[27] (Klo prop. בַּגִּלְבֹּעַ). Hiph. *Impf.* יָכִיל 1 K 7[26]+2 t. etc.; *Inf. cstr.* הָכִיל Je 6[11]+5 t.;—*contain, hold, hold in, endure;* 1. *contain*, sq. acc. (of liquid) 1 K 7[26.38] 2 Ch 4[5]; in fig. Je 2[13], abs. Ez 23[32]; (of burnt-offering) 1 K 8[64] 2 Ch 7[7]; *hold in* (wrath of י׳, obj. not expr., subj. Jeremiah) Je 6[11] (opp. שְׁפֹךְ). 2. *sustain, endure*, sq. acc. Am 7[10] Je 10[10] Jo 2[11].

3633 †כַּלְכֹּל n.pr.m. one of the wise men whom Solomon surpassed 1 K 5[11] 1 Ch 2[6] (on format. v. Ba NB 206).

כום (√ of foll.; Ar. كَامَ II. is *heap up, accumulate;* كُومَةٌ *heap;* كُومٌ *herd* of camels, hence perh. כִּימָה as a *group, herd*, or *flock* of stars, but uncertain (v. כִּימָה)).

3598 †כִּימָה n.f. perh. Pleiades (v. supr.; NH *id.*; 𝔗 כִּימָא, 𝔖 ܟܝܡܐ)—as made by י׳, Am 5[8] (|| כְּסִיל), Jb 9[9] (|| עָשׁ, כְּסִיל, חַדְרֵי תֵמָן); and under his control, מַעֲדַנּוֹת כ׳ Jb 38[31] (|| מֹשְׁכוֹת כְּסִיל).—(Stern Jüd. Zeitschr. f. Wissen. u. Leben. III. (1864-65) 258 ff. Nö in Schenkel BL Hoffm ZAW III. 107 ff. interpret עש as Pleiades, and כימה as Sirius).

†I. [כּוּן] 218 vb. prob. be firm, only in der. conj. (NH Aram. כּוּן, in der. conj., כַּיֵּן *arrange, direct;* ܟܘܢ *put right, correct;* As. *kânu, be firm, right* Dl HWB 321; Ar. كَانَ (med. و) *exist, occur, be;* so Eth. ኮነ: Sab. כון DHM ZMG 1875, 599, Ph. כון *be* (oft.));—Niph. *Pf.* (on 3 ms. v. *Pt.* infr.), 3 fs. נָכ֫וֹנָה 1 K 2[46]; 3 pl. נָכ֫וֹנוּ Pr 19[29]; נָכֹ֫נוּ Ez 16[7]; *Impf.* יִכּוֹן Pr 12[3]+; 3 fs. תִּכּוֹן Je 30[20]+; וַתִּכֹּן 1 K 2[12] 2 Ch 8[16], etc.; *Imv.* הִכּוֹן Am 4[12]; הִכֹּן Ez 38[7]; pl. הכונו 2 Ch 35[4] Kt (Qr הָכִינוּ Hiph.); *Pt.* נָכוֹן Gn 41[32]+ (in ψ 93[2] and perh. elsewh. the *Pf.* would be poss.); cstr. נְכוֹן Pr 4[18]; f. נְכוֹנָה ψ 5[10]+2 t.; pl. נְכֹנִים Ex 19[11]+2 t.; pass. or neut., and (less oft.) reflex.:—1. *be set up, established, fixed:* a. lit., of house upon (עַל) pillars Ju 16[26.29], so, in metaph., of temple-mt., sq. בְּרֹאשׁ Is 2[2]=Mi 4[1]; *be firm*, of breasts at puberty Ez 16[7]; *firmly established*, of תֵּבֵל ψ 93[1]=96[10]=1 Ch 16[30]; *firm*, i.e. a strong support, of י׳'s hand יָדִי תִּכּוֹן עִמּוֹ ψ 89[22] (|| זְרוֹעִי תְאַמְּצֶנּוּ). b. fig., of throne 2 S 7[16]=1 Ch 17[14], 1 K 2[45] ψ 89[38] 93[2] Pr 16[12] 25[5] 29[14]; of king, royal family, kingdom 1 S 20[31] 1 K 2[12.46] 2 S 7[26]=1 Ch 17[24]. c. of any persons, *be established, stable, secure, enduring* Jb 21[8] (c. לִפְנֵי), Pr 12[3], also v[19] (subj. שְׂפַת אֱמֶת), ψ 101[7] (c. לְנֶגֶד עֵינָי), 102[29] (c. לְפָנֶיךָ), 140[12] (c. בָּאָרֶץ); of plans Pr 16[3] 20[18]; 4[18] נְכוֹן הַיּוֹם *the established, stable,* (part) *of the day*, i.e. mid-day, when the sun seems motionless in mid-heaven.—2 S 6[6] v. נָכוֹן n.pr. infr. d. *fixed, securely determined* נ׳ הַדָּבָר מֵעִם הָאֱלֹהִים (|| אֱמֶת) Gn 41[32] (E); so כְּשַׁחַר נָכוֹן מֹצָאוֹ Ho 6[3] MT, but rd. כְּשַׁחֲרֵנוּ כֵּן נִמְצָאֵהוּ Gie Beiträge 208 We ad loc.; *substantiated, certain*, of an allegation Dt 13[15]=17[4]; עַל־נָכוֹן *acc. to* (what is) *certain*, =certainly, assuredly 1 S 23[23] 26[4] (v. Dr). 2. in moral sense, *be directed aright*, of ways Pr 4[26] ψ 119[5] (cf. Hiph. 3); *be fixed aright, stedfast* נָכוֹן לִבָּם לֹא נָכוֹן עִמּוֹ 78[37]; ψ 57[8.8] 108[2], so 112[7]; לִבִּי לֹא נָכוֹן לעשות כן; (|| לֵב טָהוֹר) 51[12] רוּחַ נָכוֹן Ex 8[22] (J) it is not *right, proper*, etc.; pt. f. נְכוֹנָה as subst.=*what is right, the right* Jb 42[7.8];=*uprightness* ψ 5[10]. 3. *prepare, be ready*, pers. Am 4[12] (c. לְ inf.); words Pr 22[18]; הִכֹּן וְהָכֵן לְךָ Ez 38[7]; 2 Ch 35[4] Kt (Qr Hiph.); pt. as adj.=*prepared*, 3559

ready, oft. c. הָיָה, of persons Ex 19$^{11.15}$ 34^{2} Jos 8^{4} (all JE); of things, sq. לְ pers. Jb 12^{5} Ne 8^{10}, לְ loc. Jb 18^{12}, לְ nom. act. ψ 38^{18}; בְּ loc. Jb 15^{23}; **4.** pass. *be prepared*, of judgments Pr 19^{29} (לְ pers.); of work *be arranged, settled* 2 Ch 8^{16}; fig. of prayer ψ 141^{2} *be arranged, set in order*, as incense before thee (> *present itself* as incense); *be arranged, ordered*, of temple service 2 Ch 29^{35} 35$^{10.16}$.

Hiph. *Pf.* הֵכִין Jos 4^{4}+; sf. הֱכִינַנִי 1 K 2^{24}; הֱכִינוֹ 2 S 5^{12} 1 Ch 14^{2}; הֱכִינָהּ Jb 28^{27}; 2 ms. הֲכִינוֹתָ Jb 11^{13}+; 3 pl. הֵכִינוּ 1 Ch 12^{39}+; וְהֵכִינוּ consec. Ex 16^{5}; 1 pl. הֲכִינוֹנוּ 1 Ch 29^{16}; הֵכַנּוּ (Ges$^{§ 72. R. 6}$) 2 Ch 29^{16}, etc.; *Impf.* יָכִין Ju 12^{6}+; וַיָּ֫כֶן 1 Ch 15^{1}+3 t., etc.; *Imv.* הָכֵן Gn 43^{16}+; pl. הָכִינוּ Jos 1^{11}+; *Inf. abs.* הָכֵן Jos 3^{17}, so הָכִין 4^{3} (rd. הָכֵין, v. Di), Je 10^{23} (v. Gie), Ez 7^{14} (v. Sm Co and infr.; see on all Kön$^{i. 468}$); *cstr.* הָכִין Is 9^{6}+; sf. הֲכִינוֹ Na 2^{4} Pr 8^{27}; הֲכִינָהּ Je 33^{2}; *Pt.* מֵכִין Je 10^{12}+4 t.;—(favourite word in Ch., in various applications) **1.** *establish, set up:* **a.** king (or, one as king) 2 S 5^{12} 1 K 2^{24} 1 Ch 14^{2}, royal seed ψ 89^{5}, kingdom 1 S 13^{13} 2 S 7^{12} = 1 Ch 17^{11}, 1 Ch 28^{7} 2 Ch 12^{1} 17^{5}, throne 1 Ch 22^{10}; the world תֵּבֵל Je 10^{12} = 51^{15}; mts. ψ 65^{7}; heavens Pr 8^{27}; an altar upon (עַל) its base Ezr 3^{3}. **b.** God's faithfulness ψ 89^{3}; heart of humble 10^{17}. **c.** = *accomplish, do* Je 33^{2} (‖ עשׂה), = *make* Is 40^{20} Jb 28^{27}. **d.** *make firm*, only inf. abs., as adv. = *firmly* הָכֵן Jos 3^{17}; הָכִין 4^{3} (v. supr.) **2. a.** *fix*, so as to be ready, *make ready, prepare*, a gift Gn 43^{25} (J), place Ex 23^{20} (JE), 2 Ch 3^{1}; c. לְ rei 1 Ch 15$^{1.3}$, also (obj. om.) v^{12} (vid. Be, and Da$^{Synt. § 144}$), 2 Ch 1^{4} (בַּהֵכִין, v. Ges$^{§ 138. 3. b}$); oft. *prepare* food, acc. + לְ pers. Jos 1^{11} (D), ψ 78^{20}; לְ om. Pr 6^{8} 30^{25}; obj. om. 1 Ch 12^{39} 2 Ch 35$^{14.14.15}$; both om. Gn 43^{16} (J), 1 Ch 9^{32}; *prepare* a road Dt 19^{3}, a sacrifice Zp 1^{7}, ambuscades Je 51^{12}, one's work Pr 24^{27}, materials for (לְ) temple 1 Ch 22$^{3.14}$, also v^{14b} (no לְ), 29$^{2.3}$; weapons (c. לְ pers.) 2 Ch 26^{14} and (hostile purpose) ψ 7^{14}, cf. 57^{7}, Is 14^{21} *prepare slaughter-place for* (לְ) *his children;* store-rooms 2 Ch 31^{11a}, also v^{11b} (obj. om.); gallows (c. לְ pers.) Est 6^{4} 7^{10}; corn (produce of land) ψ 65^{10}; land v^{10}, so (= *restore*) 68^{11}; c. acc. pers. 2 Ch 35^{6}; fig. of belly preparing deceit Jb 15^{35}; *make preparation* (for, לְ rei) 1 Ch 22^{5}, and v^{5} (לְ om.); sq. לִבְנוֹת 1 Ch 28^{2}, c. acc. material + לִבְנוֹת 1 K 5^{32} 1 Ch 29^{16}; without לְ, *make ready* 1 S 23^{22} Na 2^{4}; Ez 7^{14} (rd. הָכִינוּ הָכֵן Co, for ה׳ הַכֹּל לְ MT) = *make full preparation! make thee ready!* Je 46^{14} (לְ dat. eth.), Ez 28^{7} (*id.*), 2 Ch 35^{4}. **b.** *provide for, provide, furnish* Nu 23$^{1.29}$ 29^{7} Jos 4^{4} (all JE), Jb 27$^{16.17}$, food for (לְ) raven Jb 39^{41}, rain for (לְ) earth ψ 147^{8}; 1 Ch 29^{19} 2 Ch 2^{6} ψ 74^{16}. **3.** *direct* one's face towards (אֶל־) Ez 4$^{3.7}$; in moral and spiritual sense, *direct* one's step (צַעֲדוֹ) = *order aright*, Je 10^{23} (v. supr.), Pr 16^{9}, so (פְּעָמַי) ψ 119^{133}; הֵכִין דְּרָכָיו לִפְנֵי י׳ אֱלֹהָיו 2 Ch 27^{6}, also (sq. דרכיו only) Pr 21^{29} Kt (Qr יָבִין); עַל הַהֵכִין הָאֱלֹהִים לָעָם 2 Ch 29^{36} *that which God had ordered aright for the people* (on art. = pron. rel. v. Ges$^{§ 138. 3. b}$); sq. לֵב Jb 11^{13} ψ 78^{8}; + לְ, לֹא הֵכִין לִבּוֹ לִדְרוֹשׁ אֶת־י׳ 2 Ch 12^{14}, so 19^{3} 30^{19}; + לִדְרוֹשׁ אֶת־תּוֹרַת י׳ Ezr 7^{10}; הכין לבב אֶל־י׳ 1 S 7^{3} *direct the heart towards* י׳, 1 Ch 29^{18} (י׳ subj.), so (c. לֵאלֹהִים) 2 Ch 20^{33}; hence (no obj. expr.) = *give attention*, sq. inf. Ju 12^{6}. **4.** *arrange, order* 2 Ch 29^{19} (of sacred vessels; + הִקְדַּשְׁנוּ), 35^{20} (of temple).

Hoph. *Pf.* הוּכַן Is 30^{33}, וְהוּכַן consec. Is 16^{5} Zc 5^{11}; וְהֻכַּן Na 2^{6}; *Pt.* מוּכָן Pr 21^{31}, pl. מוּכָנִים Ez 40^{43};—**1.** *be established*, of throne Is 16^{5}; *be fastened*, of hooks Ez 40^{43}. **2.** *be prepared* for (לְ pers.) Is 30^{33} and (לְ temp.) Pr 21^{31}; abs. Na 2^{6}; *be ready* Zc 5^{11}.

Pôʿlēl. *Pf.* 3 ms. כּוֹנֵן ψ 9^{8}+3 t., וְכוֹנֵן consec. Hb 2^{12}; sf. כּוֹנְנָהּ Is 45^{18}; 2 ms. כּוֹנַנְתָּ ψ 99^{4} 119^{90}, כּוֹנַנְתָּה ψ 8^{4}, etc.; *Impf.* 3 ms. יְכוֹנֵן Is 62^{7}; sf. וַיְכֹנְנֶךָ Dt 32^{6}, יְכוֹנְנֶהָ ψ 24^{2}+, sf. 1 pl. וַיְכֻנֶנּוּ Jb 31^{15} (וַיְכוֹנְנֵנוּ van d. H); 2 ms. תְּכוֹנֵן ψ 7^{10} 21^{13}, etc.; *Imv.* כּוֹנֵן Jb 8^{8} (but on text v. infra), כּוֹנְנָה ψ 90^{17}, sf. כּוֹנְנֵהוּ ψ 90^{17};—orig. *make firm;*—**1.** *set up, establish:* **a.** of men, *found*, a city Hb 2^{12} (‖ בנה), ψ 107^{36}. **b.** of God, *establish*, king's throne 2 S 7^{13} = 1 Ch 17^{12}, his own throne ψ 9^{8} (לַמִּשְׁפָּט), sanctuary Ex 15^{7} (song), a nation Dt 32^{6} (poem; ‖ עשׂה, קנה), a city ψ 48^{9} 87^{5}, תֵּבֵל ψ 24^{2} (c. עַל ‖ יָסַד), אֶרֶץ 119^{90}, cf. Is 45^{18}, also ψ 68^{10} (obj. om., rd. perh. אֶרֶץ צִיָּה Bi Che), heavens Pr 3^{19} (‖ יָסַד־אָרֶץ), moon and stars ψ 8^{4}; fig., steps of men 40^{3}, work of men's hands 90$^{17.17}$, justice 99^{4}; *establish*, i.e. vindicate and make secure to righteous (צַדִּיק) 7^{10}. **2.** *constitute, make*, a man (in womb) Jb 31^{15} (‖ עשׂה), cf. ψ 119^{73} (‖ *id.*); c. acc. + לְ rei + לְ pers. reflex. 2 S 7^{24} *thou hast made* for thyself (לְךָ), thy people (אֶת־עַמְּךָ) Israel for thyself (לְךָ) into a people (לְעָם) for ever. **3.** *fix*, so as to be ready, arrow upon (עַל) string ψ 11², so (חִץ om.) ψ 21¹³ (c. עַל־פְּנֵיהֶם), and poss. (חִץ om.) Is 51¹³ (Di Che al.; but dub., cf. Du; verse corrupt acc. to Che [Intr. Is. 427]), a bow ψ 7¹³. **4.** *direct* (sc. לֵב), sq. לַחְקֹר Jb 8⁸, i.e. give attention to (but no ‖ in Po'l.; rd. perh. בּוֹנֵן, cf. Dt 32¹⁰, v. Ol Di). **Po'lal.** *Pf. be established:* מי׳ מִצְעֲדֵי־גֶבֶר כּוֹנָנוּ ψ 37²³ *from* י׳ *are a man's steps established;* =*be prepared* כּוֹנָנוּ Ez 28¹³ but del. Co Da after A B 𝔖 al. **Hithpo'l.** *Impf.; be established*, of house, 3 ms. יִתְכּוֹנָן Pr 24³ (‖ יִבָּנֶה), of nation, 2 fs. תִּכּוֹנָנִי (Ges [§ 54. 2. b]) Is 54¹⁴; 3 fs. תִּכּוֹנֵן=*be restored*, of city Nu 21²⁷ (JE; ‖ תִּבָּנֶה); *set oneself, take one's stand* 3 mpl. יִכּוֹנָנוּ ψ 59⁵.

3651 †**I. כֵּן** **adj. right, veritable, honest** (prop. *firm, upright;* Syr. ܟܐܢ *recte* PS [1662])—abs. כֵּן Ex 10²⁹ + (on poss. cstr. v. **2** ad fin.); pl. כֵּנִים Gn 42^{11.19.31.33.34};—**1.** *right*, usu. indecl., oft. as subst. *a right thing*, esp. c. vbb. *dicendi* Ex 10²⁹ (J) כֵּן דִּבַּרְתָּ, Nu 27⁷ כֵּן דֹּבְרֹת, 36⁵ (both P); כֵּן יַאֲרִיךְ Pr 28² (the) *right* (i.e. order and justice) *shall last long* (v. De Now VB); =adv. *aright*, of pronunciation Ju 12⁶; also c. vb. *agendi* Ec 8¹⁰ (on Is 33²³ v. III. כֵּן sub כנן); *right well* ψ 65¹⁰; (Che; al.=*so*); c. לֹא, as adj., *not right* דְּבָרִים אֲשֶׁר לֹא־כֵן 2 K 17⁹ *things which were not right* (vb. *agendi*); of heart of a fool Pr 15⁷; Je 23¹⁰; as subst.=*what is not right, upright* Je 8⁶; c. vb. *agendi* לֹא־כֵן 2 K 7⁹ *that which is not right we are doing*, Je 48^{30 b}. **2.** *veritable, true*, כֵּן־צְדָקָה Pr 11¹⁹ *the veritable of righteousness*=*true righteousness;* Is 16⁶=Je 48^{30 a} may be either *their boastings are not true* or (Thes Che Di Du Gr Gie al.) *the untruth of their boastings* (לֹא־כֵן as cpd. cstr.); abs., in assent to something already said, *Right! Correct! True!* Jos 2⁴. **3.** pl. concr. *honest* (men) Gn 42^{11.19.31.33.34}
651, 3653 (all E).—II. כֵּן *thus, so*, v. p. 485 infr.; III. כֵּן
3654 *place, base*, v. sub כנן; IV. [כֵּן], כַּנָּם, כִּנָּם, v. sub כנן. p. 487

3560 †**II. כּוּן** **n.pr.loc.** city of Hadarezer (מִטִּבְחַת וּמִכּוּן עָרֵי ה׳ 1 Ch 18⁸, 𝔊 ἐκ τῶν ἐκλεκτῶν πολέ(μ)ων (=בֵּרֹתַי 2 S 8⁸); =mod. *Kuna*, near *Bereitan* (betw. Laodicea and Heliopolis), acc. to Furrer
1268 [ZPV viii, 34], v. בֵּרוֹתָה p. 92 supr., and Thes.

3562 †**כּוֹנַנְיָהוּ** Kt, **כָּנַנְיָהוּ** Qr, **n.pr.m.** Levites. **1.** 2 Ch 31^{12.13} (v. Baer's note). **2.** 2 Ch 35⁹.—𝔊 Χωμενιας, Χωνενιας, A Χωχενιας.

†**יָכִין** **n.pr.m.** (*he will establish*);—**1.** a 3199
Simeonite Gn 46¹⁰=Ex 6¹⁵, Nu 26¹², 𝔊 Ιαχειμ(ν). **2.** name of right-hand pillar before temple 1 K 7²¹=2 Ch 3¹⁷, 𝔊 Ιαχουμ (opp. בֹּעַז, q.v. p. 126 f. supr.; v. also RS [Sem. i, 191 (208)]).

†**יָכִינִי** **adj. gent.** of יָכִין **1**, with art. as n. 3200
coll. הַיּ׳ Nu 26¹².

†**יְכוֹנְיָה** **n.pr.m.** (י׳ *is firm, enduring*);— 3204
Je 27²⁰=יְכָנְיָהוּ 24¹=יְכָנְיָה 28⁴ 29² 1 Ch 3^{16.17} 3204
Est 2⁶=כָּנְיָהוּ Je 22^{24.28} 37¹ (𝔊 Ιεχονιας throughout), all of last king but one of Judah, v. יְהוֹיָכִין p. 220 supr.

†**מָכוֹן** **n.m.** [Dn 8, 11] **fixed or established place,** 4349
foundation (chiefly poet.);—abs. מ׳ Ex 15¹⁷ + 2 t.; cstr. מְכוֹן 1 K 8³⁹ + 10 t.; sf. מְכוֹנִי Is 18⁴, מְכוֹנוֹ Ezr 2⁶⁸; pl. sf. מְכוֹנֶיהָ ψ 104⁵;—**1.** *fixed place* of י׳'s abode on earth Ex 15¹⁷ (song), 1 K 8¹³=2 Ch 6² (poet. fragm.: v. 𝔊 and Dr [Intr. 182]); =*place*, or *site* of God's house Ezr 2⁶⁸; כָּל־מְכוֹן הַר־צִיּוֹן Is 4⁵, appar.=*all the extent* of Mt. Zion; redund. (si vera l.) וְהֻשְׁלַךְ מְכוֹן מִקְדָּשׁוֹ Dn 8¹¹ *and the place of his sanctuary shall be thrown down* (on difficulties of v., see Bev); of heavens מְכוֹן שִׁבְתְּךָ 1 K 8^{39.43.49}=2 Ch 6^{30.33.39}, cf. ψ 33¹⁴; מְכוֹנִי alone Is 18⁴; fig. צֶדֶק וּמִשְׁפָּט מְכוֹן כִּסְאֶךָ ψ 89¹⁵, so 97². **2.** *foundation*, only pl., poet. יָסַד אֶרֶץ עַל־מְכוֹנֶיהָ ψ 104⁵.

מְכוֹנָה, מְכֹנָה, מְכֹנָה ₂₅ **n.f. fixed resting-place,** 4350
base;—abs. מ׳ 1 K 7²⁷ + 5 t.; מְכֹנָה 1 K 7^{34.34.35};
sf. מְכֻנָתָהּ Zc 5¹¹ (Ges [§ 27, 3. R. 1]); pl. מְכוֹנוֹת Je 27¹⁹, 4369
מְכֹנֹת 1 K 7²⁷ + 12 t.; sf. מְכוֹנֹתָיו Ezr 3³;—*base* or *stand* of laver כִּיּוֹר 1 K 7^{27.27} + 13 t. 1 K 7, 2 K 16¹⁷ 25^{13.16}=Je 52^{17.20}, Je 27¹⁹ 2 Ch 4^{14.14}; of altar Ezr 3³; of the symbol. ephah Zc 5¹¹.

†**נָכוֹן** **n.pr.m.** only in גֹּרֶן נ׳ 2 S 6⁶; 𝔊 Νωδαβ, 5225
A Ναχων, 𝔊L Ορνα τοῦ Ἰεβουσαίου;=כִּידֹן 1 Ch 13⁹.

†**תְּכוּנָה** **n.f. arrangement, preparation,** 8498-99
fixed place;—**1.** *arrangement, disposition* תְּכוּנָתוֹ Ez 43¹¹, i.e. the arrangement of the house (del. Co with 𝔊 codd.) **2.** *preparation*, וְאֵין קֵצֶה לַתְּכוּנָה Na 2¹⁰ *and no end to the preparation* (i.e. things prepared, supply, store). **3.** *fixed place*, i.e. dwelling-place, of God
(=מָכוֹן) תְּכוּנָתוֹ Jb 23³. 4349

†[**כַּוָּן**] **n.[m.] cake, sacrificial cake** (?√כון; 3561
cf. Hiph. **2. a.** *prepare* food, etc.)—only pl.

abs. עָשִׂינוּ לַעֲשׂוֹת כַּוָּנִים לִמְלֶכֶת הַשָּׁמַיִם Je 7[18]; לָהּ כ׳ לְהַעֲצִבָה 44[19].

3563 †I. **כּוֹס n.f.**[La 4, 21] **cup** (√unknown; perh. kindred with כִּיס, q.v.; NH *id.;* Ph. כסת; Aram. כָּס, ܟܣܐ; Ar. كَأْسٌ is Aram. loan-wd. acc. to Frä[171], but see DHM[VOJ i. 27])—כ׳ abs. Gn 40[11]+; כּוֹס Pr 23[31]; cstr. Gn 40[11]+; sf. כּוֹסִי ψ 16[5] 23[5] etc.; pl. abs. כֹּסוֹת Je 35[5];—*cup* 2 S 12[3]; for wine Gn 40[11.11.11.13.21] (all E), Pr 23[31] Je 35[5]; שְׂפַת־כּוֹס 1 K 7[26] 2 Ch 4[5]; כ׳ תַּנְחוּמִים Je 16[7] the *cup* offered to mourners; fig. (wine-) *cup* of judgment of י׳, from which the nations, or Isr., must drink Je 49[12] La 4[21] ψ 75[9]; כ׳ חֲמָתוֹ Is 51[17.22]; כ׳ הַיַּיִן הַחֵמָה Je 25[15], cf. v[17.28]; כ׳ הַתַּרְעֵלָה Is 51[17.22]; כ׳ שַׁמָּה וּשְׁמָמָה Ez 23[33], cf. v[31.32.33]; כ׳ יְמִין י׳ Hb 2[16]; by bold metaph. Babylon is such a cup כ׳ זָהָב בְּיַד י׳ Je 51[7]; so of wicked persons, fire, brimstone, and burning wind are מְנָת־כּוֹסָם ψ 11[6] *the portion of their cup;* כ׳ in good sense, *cup* of blessing ψ 23[5] (overflowing); י׳ מְנָת חֶלְקִי וְכוֹסִי ψ 16[5]; כ׳ יְשׁוּעוֹת ψ 116[13].

3563 †II. **כּוֹס n.[m.]** a kind of **owl** (acc. to Vrss.; v. Kn-Di Lv 11[17]; wd. perh. onomatop.)—unclean bird Lv 11[17] Dt 14[16], dwelling in ruins כ׳ חֳרָבוֹת ψ 102[7].

I. **כור** (√of foll.; perh. *be* or *make round,* hence *furnace, pot, basin,* fr. shape; Ar. كَارَ *wind about* (e.g. a turban), كَوَّرَ *turn* or *twist* (of turban), كُورٌ *blacksmith's fire-place, hornets'* or *bees' nest,* كَارَةٌ *bundle;* > Thes comp. Syr. ܐܬܟܘܪ *incaluit* (Lexx. *aestuavit, calefactus est*)).

3733 †I. **[כַּר] n.[m.] basket-saddle,** בְּכַר־הַגָּמָל Gn 31[34] *in the camel-basket,* i.e. the basket-saddle of the camel, a sort of palankeen bound upon the saddle proper (cf. Kn in Di and reff.).

3733 II. כַּר v. in alphabetical order. p. 499

3564 †כּוּר **n.[m.] smelting-pot or furnace** (Ar. كُور; NH *id.;* Aram. *id.*, ܟܘܪܐ; Eth. ኩውር:)—*pot* or *furnace* for smelting metals, but alw. in metaph. or sim. of human sufferings in punishment or discipline: iron (fig. of Egypt as place of bondage) מִתּוֹךְ כ׳ הַבַּ׳, מִכּ׳ הַבַּרְזֶל Dt 4[20] Je 11[4], 1 K 8[51]; gold כ׳ לַזָּהָב Pr 17[3]=27[21] (|| מַצְרֵף); various metals Ez 22[18.20.22]; once בְּכוּר עֹנִי Is 48[10] *in a smelting-pot of affliction.*

3565 כּוּר־עָשָׁן **n.pr.loc.** v. בּוֹר עָשָׁן supr. p. 92[b].

3600 †[כִּיר] **n.[m.] cooking-furnace** (Mishn. כִּירָה)—frangible, only du. כִּירַיִם Lv 11[35] (c. תַּנּוּר), perh. as supporting two pots (Ki); 𝔊 χυτρόποδες.

3595 †כִּיּוֹר, כִּיֹּר, כִּיּר **n.m.**[1 K 7, 38] **pot, basin** (NH כִּיּוֹר *wash-basin,* so Aram. כִּיּוֹרָא)—abs. כִּיּוֹר 1 K 7[30]+ 8 t.; כִּיּוֹר 1 S 2[14]+5 t.; cstr. כִּיּוֹר Ex 30[18]+2 t.; pl. abs. כִּיֹּרוֹת 1 K 7[40] (but v. infr.), 2 Ch 4[14]; כִּיּוֹרִים 1 K 7[43]; כִּיּוֹרִים 2 Ch 4[6]; cstr. כִּיֹּרוֹת 1 K 7[38];—**1.** *pot* for cooking 1 S 2[14] (|| קַלַּחַת, דּוּד, פָּרוּר). **2.** *fire-pot* כִּיּוֹר אֵשׁ Zc 12[6] (|| לַפִּיד אֵשׁ; fig. of chiefs of Judah). **3.** *basin* of bronze for washing, *laver;* set on a bronze support **a.** before tabernacle Ex 30[18.28] 31[9] 35[16] 38[8] 39[39] 40[7.11.30] Lv 8[11] (all P). **b.** 10 in number, 5 at each front corner of temple 1 K 7[30.38.38.38.43]= 2 Ch 4[14], 2 Ch 4[6] (1 K 7[40] rd. הַכִּיֹּרוֹת as v[45] and || 2 Ch 4[11.16], so Heb. Codd. 𝔊 𝔙 Th Ke Sta Klo al.) **4.** *platform* or *stage* of bronze (prob. round, bowl-like in shape) on which, acc. to Chr, Solomon stood and kneeled 2 Ch 6[13].

3738 †II. **[כּוּר] vb.** mng. dub., perh. *bore,* or *dig,* or *hew* (Dl[Prol. 121] comp. As. *kâru, fell* trees (Dl[HWB 324]))—only **Qal** *Pf.* 3 pl. כָּאֲרוּ = כארו for כָּרוּ ψ 22[17] (MT כָּאֲרִי, v. אֲרִי) *they have bored* (*digged, hewn*) my hands and my feet (si vera l.; cf. Vrss De Pe Che Bae al.; some, however, deriving from כרה in this sense); hence perhaps following.

4351 †[מְכוּרָה, מְכֹרָה] **n.f. origin** (i.e. *place of digging* out?)—sg. sf. אֶרֶץ מְכוּרָתָם Ez 29[14]; of a people, persons: pl. sf. בְּאֶרֶץ מְכֻרוֹתַיִךְ 21[35] (|| בִּמְקוֹם אֲשֶׁר נִבְרֵאת); of Jerus., מְכֹרֹתַיִךְ וּמֹלְדֹתַיִךְ מֵאֶרֶץ הַכְּנַעֲנִי 16[3].

4380 †[מְכֵרָה] **n.[f.]** prob. the name of a weapon, only pl. sf. כְּלֵי חָמָס מְכֵרֹתֵיהֶם Gn 49[5] *weapons of violence are their* מ׳ (other conjectures v. in Di).

3566 †כּוֹרֶשׁ and (Ezr 1[1.2]) כֹּרֶשׁ **n.pr.m. Cyrus** (Pers. *K'ur'u*(*š*), Spieg[APK 215]; Bab. *Kuraš* COT on Ezr 1[1], Dl in Baer[Dn. p. x])—king of (Anzan =Susiana, Tiele[Bab.-Assyr. Gesch. 469], and) Persia, conqueror of Babylon (Tiele[ib. 468 ff.]), restorer of Jews to Palestine Is 44[28] 45[1] Ezr 1[7]; called מֶלֶךְ פָּרַס 2 Ch 36[22.22.23] Ezr 1[1.1.2], also Ezr 1[8] 4[3.5] Dn 10[1]; simply הַמֶּלֶךְ Dn 1[21].

3568 †I. כּוּשׁ **n.pr.pers.m., gent. et terr.** (Egypt. *Kōš*, Steindorff[BAS i, 593], As. *Kûsu*, Id[ib.] Dl[Pa 251]; *Kaši* in Tel Amarna tablets, vid. Wkl

[Tel Am. 39*]);—**1.** 1st 'son' of חָם Gn 10$^{6.7}$(P)=1 Ch 1$^{8.9}$, 𝔊 Χους, 𝔙 *Chus*, from whom descended acc. to these vv. the southernmost peoples known to Hebrews. **2.** land and people of southern Nile-valley, or Upper Egypt, extending from Syene (Ez 29^{10}) indefinitely to the south, 𝔊 Αιθιοπια, Αιθιοπες: **a.** the land Is 11^{11} 18^{1} Zp 3^{10} Ez 29^{10} Jb 28^{19} Est 1^{1} 8^{9}. **b.** the people Is 20^{4} Je 46^{9} Ez 38^{5}; personif. ψ 68^{32}. **c.** indeterminate, either land or people, or including both: Is 20$^{3.5}$ 43^{3} 45^{14} 2 K 19^{9}=Is 37^{9} Na 3^{9} Ez 30$^{4.5.9}$ ψ 87^{4} (𝔊 λαὸς Αιθιοπων). **3.** in Gn 10^{8}(J)=1 Ch 1^{10} כּוּשׁ is err. for כַּשּׁ=Bab. *Kaššu*, acc. to Schr[COT] on Gn 10^{6}, Dl[Pa 51 ff. 72 f.] and most Assyriol.; so perh. also Gn 2^{13} (J), yet v. Hpt[Über Ld. u. Meer, 1894–5, No. 15].

3568 †II. כּוּשׁ **n.pr.m.** a Benjamite, ψ 7^{1} (title), 𝔊 Χουσει υἱοῦ Ιεμενει.

3569 †I. כּוּשִׁי **adj.gent.** of I. כּוּשׁ;—m. כּוּשִׁי Je
3571 13^{23}+13 t.; f. כֻּשִׁית Nu 12$^{1.1}$; pl. כּוּשִׁים Zp 2^{12} +6 t.; כֻּשִׁים Dn 11^{43}; כֻּשִׁיִּים Am 9^{7};—**a.** sg. agreeing with noun Nu 12$^{1.1}$ (E; only here fem.). **b.**=subst., *a Cushite* Je 13^{23}. **c.** id. c. art., *the Cushite*, of Joab's adjutant 2 S 18$^{21.21}$ (where rd. 'חֻכ, for MT 'כ, We Dr Kit Bu), v$^{22.23.31.31.32.32}$; in appos. with n.pr. Je 38$^{7.10.12}$ 39^{16} 2 Ch 14^{8}. **d.** pl. (הַ)כּוּשִׁים=subst. Zp 2^{12} 2 Ch 12^{3} 14$^{11.11.12}$ 16^{8} 21^{16}; so כֻּשִׁים Dn 11^{43}, כֻּשִׁיִּים (si vera l.) Am 9^{7}.

3570 †II. כּוּשִׁי **n.pr.m.** 𝔊 Χουσει—**1.** Je 36^{14} great-grandfather of יְהוּדִי, q.v. (perh. orig. appellat. *Cushite*). **2.** father of prophet Zephaniah Zp 1^{1}.

3572 †כּוּשָׁן **n. pr., gent.** vel **terr.**, only אָהֳלֵי כ׳ Hb 3^{7} (‖ מִדְיָן), 𝔊 Αιθιοπων.

3573 †כּוּשַׁן רִשְׁעָתַיִם **n.pr.m.** king of Aram Naharaim Ju 3$^{8.8.10.10}$; otherwise unknown, 𝔊 Χουσαρσαθαιμ, 𝔊L Χουσανρεσαμωθ.

3574 כּוּשָׁרוֹת v. [כּוֹשָׁרָה] sub כָּשֵׁר. p. 507

3575 †כּוּתָה, כּוּת **n.pr.loc.** whence king of Assyria (Sargon) transported colonists into N. Israel, מִכּוּתָה 2 K 17^{24}, אַנְשֵׁי־כוּת v^{30}; Bab. *Kûtû, Kûtê*, mod. Tel-Ibrahim, c. 20 m. NE. fr. Babylon, v. COT[2 K 17, 24] Dl[Par 217] M-A[JBL 1892, xi. 169].

3576 †[כָּזַב] **vb. lie, be a liar** (Ar. كَذَبَ; Aram. כַּדֵּב, ܟܰܕܶܒ *id.* chiefly Pa.; NH כִּזֵּב)—**Qal** *Pt.* כֹּזֵב כָּל־הָאָדָם ψ 116^{11} (cf. כָּזָב 62^{10}). **Niph.** *Pf.* 3 fs. תּוֹחַלְתּוֹ נִכְזָבָה Jb 41^{1} *his hope has been made deceptive*, i.e. been shewn to be so; 2 ms. consec. וְנִכְזָבְתָּ Pr 30^{6} lest he convict thee *and thou be proven a liar*. **Pi.** *Pf.* 3 ms. כִּזֵּב Mi 2^{11}; *Impf.* 3 ms. יְכַזֵּב Hb 2^{3} Pr 14^{5}; וִיכַזֵּב Nu 23^{19}, etc.; *Inf. cstr.* sf. (בְּ)כַזֶּבְכֶם Ez 13^{19};—**1.** *lie, tell a lie*, abs., Nu 23^{19} (JE), Mi 2^{11} Jb 6^{28} 34^{6} Pr 14^{5} Is 57^{11}; sq. לְ pers. *lie to* Ez 13^{19} ψ 78^{36} 89^{36}; sq. בְּ pers. *tell a lie with*, i.e. in intercourse, conversation with 2 K 4^{16}. **2.** *disappoint, fail*, of a divine revelation Hb 2^{3}; waters of a spring Is 58^{11}. **Hiph.** *Impf.* 3 ms. sf. יַכְזִיבֵנִי Jb 24^{25} who *will make me a liar?* i.e. prove me to be so (cf. **Niph.**)

†כָּזָב **n.m.**[Am 2,4] lie, falsehood, deceptive 3577
thing;—abs. 'כ Ho 12^{2}+19 t.; pl. abs. כְּזָבִים Ju 16^{10}+9 t.; sf. כִּזְבֵיהֶם Am 2^{4};—*lie, falsehood*, c. דִּבֶּר Ju 16$^{10.13}$ Ho 7^{13} Zp 3^{13} Dn 11^{27} ψ 5^{7} 58^{4}, so Ez 13^{8} Co (by transp. 'כ with שָׁוְא, cf. v$^{6.7.9}$); c. יָפִיחַ (in Pr) Pr 6^{19} 14$^{5.25}$ 19$^{5.9}$; of false prophecies (divinations) c. מִקְסַם כ׳, אָמַר Ez 13^{7}; c. קָסַם v^{9} 21^{34} 22^{28}+13^{6} 𝔊 Co (קְסוֹם כ׳, for MT קֶסֶם כ׳); c. שָׁמַע 13^{19}, בִּקֵּשׁ ψ 4^{3}; c. רָצָה *delight in* 62^{5}; so in the phr. דִּבְרֵי־כ׳ Pr 30^{8}, אִישׁ כ׳ 19^{22} =*liar*, עֵד כְּזָבִים 21^{28}=*false witness;* of idols as a *lie* (*res ementita*) Am 2^{4}, so prob. שָׂטֵי כ׳ *those turning aside to a lie* ψ 40^{5} (cf. אֱלִיל, אָוֶן, הֶבֶל, שֶׁקֶר); then of empty human pretensions כ׳ וָשֹׁד יַרְבֶּה Ho 12^{2}, Is 28^{15} (‖ שֶׁקֶר), v^{17} (מַחְסֵה כ׳), ψ 62^{10} (‖ הֶבֶל; cf. כֹּזֵב 116^{11}); לֶחֶם כְּזָבִים Pr 23^{3} =*deceptive* (disappointing) *bread*.

†כְּזִיב **n.pr.loc.** in plain of Judah Gn 38^{5}, 3580
𝔊 Χασβι, = אַכְזִיב **1.** v. infr.

†כֹּזֵבָא **n.pr.loc.** 1 Ch 4^{22} 𝔊 Σωχηθα, A𝔊L 3578
Χωζηβα, = אַכְזִיב **1.** v. infr.

†כָּזְבִּי **n.pr.f.** a woman of Midian Nu 25$^{15.18}$, 3579
𝔊 Χασβ(ε)ι.

†אַכְזָב **adj. deceptive, disappointing** (ela- 391
tive; opp. אֵיתָן q.v. sub יתן)—only abs. sg.:—Mi 1^{14} (with play on n.pr. אַכְזִיב); of a deceptive, disappointing stream (cf. Is 58^{11}) Je 15^{18} (‖ מַיִם לֹא נֶאֱמָנוּ; on meaning cf. Jb 6$^{15\,ff.}$)

†אַכְזִיב **n.pr.loc. 1.** in lowland of Judah 392
Jos 15^{44} (𝔊 Ακιεζει καὶ Κεζειβ, 𝔊L Αχζειβ), Mi 1^{14} (𝔊 οἴκους ματαίους; v. also כֹּזֵבָא, כְּזִיב). **2.** in Asher Ju 1^{31} (𝔊 Ασχαζει), and (אַכְזִיבָה) Jos

19^{29} (𝔊 Εχοζοβ, A. Αχζειφ, 𝔊L Αχαζειβ); it lay on the coast S. of Tyre, in As. *Akzibi*, COT $^{Jos\,19,29}$ Dl $^{Par.\,284}$; Gk. Εκδιππα; mod. *ez-Zîb*, Bd $^{Pal.\,272}$ Buhl $^{G.\,§\,120}$ and (on pronunciation) Kasteren $^{ZPV\,xiii.\,101}$.

כזר (√ of foll.; Aram. Ethpe. *be cruel* (𝔗 Jb 10^{1}), cf. Syr. ܟܙܝܪܐ, *miles, vir strenuus* PS^{1718}, who comp. Pers. گزیر *athleta, heros* (Vullers)).

393 †**אַכְזָר adj.** cruel, fierce, of poison (ראֹשׁ) Dt 32^{33}; elsewh. of men, *fierce* Jb 41^{2}; as subst. =*a cruel one* Jb 30^{21} (of God), La 4^{3}.

394 †**אַכְזָרִי adj.** cruel, always in this form;—Pr 12^{10} 17^{11} Je 6^{23} 50^{42}, also 30^{14} (rd. מוּסַר א׳, for MT מוּסַר, Gf Gie); as subst. Pr 5^{9} 11^{17}, perhaps also, in appos. with יוֹם י׳, Is 13^{9}.

395 †**אַכְזְרִיּוּת n.f.** cruelty, fierceness, only א׳ חֵמָה וְשֶׁטֶף אַף Pr 27^{4} *fierceness of rage and outpouring of anger*.

3581 †I. **כֹּחַ n.**[**m.**] a small reptile, prob. a kind of lizard, in list of unclean creeping things Lv 11^{30}; 𝔊𝔙 AV *chameleon;* on various opinions v. Di.

3581 II. **כֹּחַ** v. sub כחח. below

3582 †[**כָּחַד**] **vb.** not in **Qal**; **Pi. Hiph.** hide, **efface**; **Niph.** (usu.) pass. (Aram. אתכחדו *be effaced* †Jb 4^{7}; ܟܚܕ is *revere*, Pt. *venerable*, Pa. *put to shame*, Ethpa. *be ashamed;* Eth. ክሕደ: *deny, apostatize*)—**Niph.** *Pf.* 3 ms. נִכְחַד Ho 5^{3}+2 t.; 3 pl. נִכְחָ֑דוּ Jb 4^{7} ψ 69^{6}; *Impf.* 3 ms. יִכָּחֵד 2 S 18^{13}, etc.; *Pt.* נִכְחֶדֶת Zc 11^{9}; pl. נִכְחָדוֹת Zc 11^{16} Jb 15^{28};—**1.** *be hidden*, sq. מִן pers., 2 S 18^{13} Ho 5^{3} ψ 69^{6} 139^{15}. **2.** *be effaced, destroyed* Zc 11^{9} Jb 4^{7} 15^{28} (עָרִים נִכְחָדוֹת), 22^{20}, sq. מִן הָאָרֶץ Ex 9^{15} (J); *Pt.* intrans. of incomplete process = *going to ruin* Zc $11^{9.16}$. **Pi.** *Pf.* כִּחֵד 1 S 3^{18}; 1 s. כִּחַדְתִּי Jb 6^{10} ψ 40^{11}; 3 pl. כִּחֲדוּ Jb 15^{18}; כִּחֵ֑דוּ Is 3^{9}; *Impf.* 2 ms. תְּכַחֵד Jos 7^{19}+4 t.; 2 fs. תְּכַחֲדִי 2 S 14^{18}; 1 s. אֲכַחֵד Jb 27^{11}; 2 mpl. תְּכַחֵ֑דוּ Je 50^{2}; 1 pl. נְכַחֵד Gn 47^{18} ψ 78^{4};—*hide*, sq. מִן pers. Gn 47^{18} (J), Jos 7^{19} (JE), 1 S $3^{17.17.18}$ 2 S 14^{18} Je $38^{14.25}$ ψ 78^{4}; sq. לְ pers. ψ 40^{11} *conceal toward, with ref. to*, i.e. *from;* without prep. Is 3^{9} Je 50^{2} Jb 15^{18} 27^{11};=*disown* Jb 6^{10}. **Hiph.** *Pf.* 1 s. consec. sf. וְהִכְחַדְתִּיו Ex 23^{23}; *Impf.* 3 ms. וַיַּכְחֵד 2 Ch 32^{21}, sf. יַכְחִידֶ֫נָּה Jb 20^{12}; 1 s. וָאַכְחִד Zc 11^{8}; 1 pl. sf. וְנַכְחִידֵם ψ 83^{5}; *Inf. cstr.* לְהַכְחִיד 1 K 13^{34};—**1.** *hide*, in fig. יַכְחִידֶנָּה תַּחַת לְשׁוֹנוֹ Jb 20^{12} (obj. wickedness). **2.** *efface, annihilate* Ex 23^{23} (E), 1 K 13^{34} (‖ הַשְׁמִיד), Zc 11^{8} 2 Ch 32^{21}; sq. מִגּוֹי ψ 83^{5}, i.e. *from being* (so that they be not) *a nation*.

כחח (√ assumed by Thes Buhl al. for foll. Ba$^{NB\,79}$ prop. √כוח).

†II. **כֹּחַ** and (†Dn 11^{6}) **כּוֹחַ n.m.**$^{Dt\,4.37}$ **strength, power** (NH *id.*);—כ׳ abs. Dt 8^{18}+; cstr. Nu 14^{17}+; sf. כֹּחִי Gn 31^{6}+; כֹּחֲךָ Ju 16^{6}+, כֹּחֶ֑ךָ Pr 5^{10}, כֹּחֶ֑כָה Pr 24^{10}, etc.; alw. sg.;—**1.** *human strength:* **a.** physical, of Samson Ju $16^{5.6.9.15.17.19.30}$; strength in toil Is 44^{12} (וַיִּיעַף כֹּחוֹ), v^{12} Lv 26^{20} Ne 4^{4}; of manly vigour (in procreation) אַתָּה כֹּחִי וְרֵאשִׁית אוֹנִי Gn 49^{3} (poem in J; said to Reuben); vigour in gen. Jos $14^{11.11}$ (JE), Ju 6^{14} 1 S 28^{22} Jb $6^{11.12}$ ψ 31^{11} 38^{11} 71^{9} 102^{24} Pr 20^{29}; as sustained by food 1 K 19^{8}; lack of such vigour is לֹא־כֹחַ Jb 26^{2}, cf. מִכֹּחַ Je 48^{45} *without strength;* בְּלֹא־כ׳ La 1^{6}; יְגִיעֵי־כ׳ Jb 3^{17}; כֹּחַ לֹא־הָיָה בוֹ 1 S 28^{20}, cf. Dn $10^{8.17}$; in ψ 22^{16} rd. חִכִּי, so Ew Ol Che al.; specif. of *power* of voice Is 40^{9}. **b.** more inclusively, *ability, efficiency:* sq. inf., *ability* to weep 1 S 30^{4}; to get wealth Dt 8^{18}; to bring forth (a child; in fig.) 2 K 19^{3}=Is 37^{3}; sq. לַעֲמֹד Dn 1^{4} Ezr 10^{13}, cf. Dn 11^{15}; without inf. 1 Ch 29^{2} Ezr 2^{69}; of *efficiency* in battle 2 Ch 14^{10} 20^{12} 26^{13}; for porter's service in temple אִישׁ־חַיִל בַּכֹּחַ לַעֲבֹדָה 1 Ch 26^{8}; *ability* or *efficiency* in gen. Gn 31^{6} Pr $24^{5.10}$ Ec 4^{1} 9^{10}, so prob. כֹּחַ יְדֵיהֶם Jb 30^{2}; עָצַר כֹּחַ (late, cf. עצר) *retain ability* or *strength*, sq. inf.; נַעְצֹר כ׳ לְהִתְנַדֵּב 1 Ch 29^{14} that *we should retain* (have) *ability to make freewill-offerings;* to build 2 Ch 2^{5}; c. neg., without inf., Dn $10^{8.16}$ (cf. 11^{6}, **c**). **c.** *power* of a people, or king, Jos 17^{17} Na 2^{2} Hb 1^{11} Is 49^{4} (of servant of י׳), La 1^{14} Dn $8^{22.24\,a}$, also v$^{24\,b}$ (si vera l., v. Bev), 11^{25} (‖ לֵבָב); c. עָצַר 2 Ch 13^{20} 22^{9} Dn 11^{6} (לֹא תַעְצֹר כ׳ הַזְּרוֹעַ, cf. **b**); in Ho 7^{9} fig. of body seems combined with that of land yielding produce (v. **5** infr.) **d.** *power* opp. to that of God Am 2^{14} Is 10^{13} (כ׳ יָדִי), Dt 8^{17} 1 S 2^{9} Zc 4^{6} Jb 36^{19} ψ 33^{16}. **e.** *power* conferred by God Is 40^{29}, cf. v^{31} 41^{1}; of prophetic power Mi 3^{8}. **2.** *strength* of angels ψ 103^{20}. **3.** *power* of God: in creation Je 10^{12} 51^{15} (see also 32^{17} infr.), ψ 65^{7}; in governing the world 1 Ch 29^{12} 2 Ch 20^{6} ψ 29^{4}; in acts of deliverance and judgment Ex 9^{16} 15^{6} 32^{11} Nu $14^{13.17}$ (JE), Is 50^{2} 2 Ch 25^{8} Jb 9^{19} 24^{22} 26^{12} 30^{18} 36^{22}; in combin. כֹּחַ גָּדוֹל Dt 4^{37}; ‖ יָד חֲזָקָה Ex 32^{11} (JE), Ne 1^{10}; ‖ זְרוֹעַ נְטוּיָה Dt 9^{29} 2 K 17^{36} 3581

Je 27^{5} 32^{17}; he in רַב־כֹּחַ ψ 147^{5}, cf. רֹב כֹּחוֹ Is 63^{1} Jb 23^{6}; also גדול־כֹּחַ Na 1^{3}; אַמִּיץ כֹּחַ Is 40^{26} Jb 9^{4}, שַׂגִּיא־כֹחַ 37^{23}; כֹּחַ מַעֲשָׂיו ψ 111^{6} *the power of his works;* קוֹל י׳ בַּכֹּחַ ψ 29^{4} (of thunder); specif. of his wisdom (rather peculiarly, Elihu) כַּבִּיר כֹּחַ לֵב Jb 36^{5} *mighty in strength of mind.* **4.** of animals: wild ox Jb 39^{11}, horse v^{21}, hippopot. 40^{16}, bullock Pr 14^{4}; he-goat Dn 8^{6}, ram v^{7}. **5.** *strength,* of soil i.e. *produce,* Gn 4^{12} (J), Jb 31^{39}; (Ho 7^{9} v. **1. c** supr.);=*wealth* (cf. חַיִל) Pr 5^{10} Jb 6^{22}.

3583 †[כָּחַל] **vb.** paint (eyes) (NH *id.;* Aram. כְּחַל, ܟܚܰܠ; Eth. ኰሐለ: Ar. كَحَلَ)—only in רָחַצְתְּ כָּחַלְתְּ עֵינַיִךְ וגו׳ Ez 23^{40} (Co rds. 3 pl.);—v. also פּוּךְ.

3584 †כָּחַשׁ **vb. be disappointing, deceive, fail, grow lean** (NH כָּחַשׁ *grow lean;* Hiph. *convict of falsehood, refute;* Aram. כְּחַשׁ *grow lean;* כַּחֲשָׁא *leanness,* כְּחִישׁוּתָא *leanness, weakness;* Aph. as NH Hiph.)—**Qal** *Pf.* 3 ms. וּבְשָׂרִי כָּחַשׁ מִשָּׁמֶן ψ 109^{24} *my flesh hath grown lean (away) fr. fatness* (|| בִּרְכַּי כָּשְׁלוּ מִצּוֹם). **Niph.** *Impf.* וְיִכָּחֲשׁוּ אֹיְבֶיךָ לָךְ Dt 33^{29} *thine enemies shall cringe* (come cringing, i.e. orig. *act deceptively, feigning obedience*) *to thee* (cf. also **Pi. 3, Hithp.**) **Pi.** *Pf.* 3 ms. כִּחֵשׁ 1 K 13^{18} Hb 3^{17}; וְכִחֵשׁ consec. (bef. monosyll.) Lv 5^{22} Jb 8^{18}, etc.; *Impf.* (בָּהּ) יְכַחֶשׁ Ho 9^{2}; 3 fs. וַתְּכַחֵשׁ Gn 18^{15}, etc.; *Inf. abs.* כַּחֵשׁ Ho 4^{2} Is 59^{13}; *cstr.* Zc 13^{4};—**1.** *deceive,* abs. Gn 18^{15} (J), Jos 7^{11} (JE), Ho 4^{2} (אלה וכחשׁ together=*false swearing* acc. to We$^{Kl. Pr.}$; + וְרָצֹחַ וְגָנֹב וְנָאֹף), cf. לֹא תִגְנֹבוּ וְלֹא־תְכַחֲשׁוּ וְלֹא תְשַׁקְּרוּ אִישׁ בַּעֲמִיתוֹ Lv 19^{11} (H); לְמַעַן כ׳ Zc 13^{4} *in order to deceive;* sq. לְ pers. 1 K 13^{18} Jb 31^{28}; sq. בְּ pers. et rei Lv 5^{21}, בְּ rei v^{22}. **2.** *act deceptively* against (i.e. seem to acknowledge, but not really do so), sq. בְּ pers. Jos 24^{27} (E), Je 5^{12} Is 59^{13} Jb 8^{18}, appar. also וְתִירוֹשׁ יכ׳ בָּהּ Ho 9^{2} *and new wine shall deny her* (Isr.; i.e. refuse to acknowledge her as its mistress, not yield itself to her); abs. Pr 30^{9}. **3.** *cringe* =*come cringing* (make shew of obedience, v. Niph.), sq. לְ pers. ψ 18^{45} (Hithp. in || 2 S 22^{45}); sq. לְ pers. ψ 66^{3} 81^{16}. **4.** *disappoint, fail,* abs. כִּחֵשׁ מַעֲשֵׂה זַיִת Hb 3^{17} *the product of the olive hath failed* (in sense comp. Ho 9^{2} supr.)

Hithp. *Impf.* יִתְכַּחֲשׁוּ לִי 2 S 22^{45} *shall come cringing to me* (|| ψ 18^{45}, v. supr.)

†כַּחַשׁ **n.m.**$^{Jb 16, 8}$ **1. lying. 2. leanness;**—abs. כ׳ Ho 12^{1}+2 t.; כָּחַשׁ Ho 10^{13}; sf. כַּחְשִׁי 3585
Jb 16^{8}; pl. sf. כַּחֲשֵׁיהֶם Ho 7^{3};—**1.** *lying,* אֲכַלְתֶּם פְּרִי כ׳ Ho 10^{13} *ye have eaten the fruit of lying;* 7^{3} (|| רָעָה), 12^{1}; of Nineveh, כ׳ פֶּרֶק מְלֵאָה Na 3^{1} *of lying* (and) *robbery it is full;* ψ 59^{13} (|| אָלָה). **2.** of Job's affliction Jb 16^{8} *my leanness hath risen up against me* (cf. ψ 109^{24}; 𝔗 J Gn 41^{27}, Ec 12^{5}; Talm. כחשׁא; >*my lying,* i.e. my affliction regarded as a lying witness, Di Buhl al.)

†[כֶּחָשׁ] **adj. deceptive, false** (on format. v. 3586
Ba$^{NB 50}$ Ges$^{§ 84 b}$)—בָּנִים כֶּחָשִׁים Is 30^{9} (|| עַם מְרִי).

כִּי **conj. that, for, when** (Moab. *id.*: Ph. כ. 3588
Prob. from the same demonstr. basis found in ܟܳܐ *here,* and in certain pronouns, as Aram. דֵּךְ *this* (W$^{SG 110 f.}$); perh. also ultim. akin with كَىْ *that, in order that,* and ܟܰܝ *then,* enclit., like Lat. *nam* in *quisnam?*)—**1.** *that* (ὅτι, Germ. *dass*): **a.** prefixed to sentences depending on an active verb, and occupying to it the place of an accus.: so constantly, after vbs. of seeing, as Gn 1^{10} וַיַּרְא אֱלֹהִים כִּי טוֹב and God saw *that* it was good, 3^{6} 6$^{2.5}$ 12^{14}+oft., hearing 14^{14} 29^{33}, knowing 22^{12} 24^{14}, telling 3^{11} 12^{18}, repenting 6$^{6.7}$, swearing Gn 22^{16} Je 22^{5}, believing Ex 4^{5} La 4^{12}, remembering ψ 78^{35}, forgetting Jb 39^{15}; אָמַר=*command* (late; in early Heb. the words said are quoted) Jb 36$^{10.24}$ (זָכֹר in a command) 37$^{20 b}$ 1 Ch 21^{18} (contrast 2 S 24^{18}) etc.; טוֹב כִּי it is good *that* . . . 2 S 18^{3}+(v. p. 374^{b}: usu. the inf. c., as Gn 2^{18}; v. ibid.); Gn 37^{26} מַה־בֶּצַע כִּי נַהֲרֹג what profit *that* we should slay (impf.) . . .? Mal 3^{14} what profit כִּי שָׁמַרְנוּ *that* we have kept (pf.) . . .? Jb 22^{3} הַחֵפֶץ לְשַׁדַּי כִּי is it pleasure to Shaddai that . . .? after a pron., as ψ 41^{12} by *this* I know that thou hast pleasure in me, *that* my enemy cannot triumph over me, 42^{5} *these* things will I remember . . . *that* (or *how*) I used to go, etc., 56^{10} *this* I know *that* God is for me, Jb 13^{16} (הוּא). And with כִּי repeated pleon. after an intervening clause 2 S 19^{7} Je 26^{15}+; כִּי . . . וְכִי Gn 3^{6} 29^{12} Ex 4^{31} Jos 2^{9} 8^{21} 10^{1} 1 S 31^{7} 2 S 5^{12} 1 K 11^{21} Je 40$^{7.11}$; לֵאמֹר . . . וְכִי Gn 45^{26} Ju 10^{10}. **b.** כִּי often introduces the *direct* narration (like ܕ, إِنَّ, and the Gk. ὅτι *recitativum,* e.g. Luke 4^{21}), in which case it cannot be represented in English (except by inverted commas), Gn 21^{30} 29^{33} and she said, כִּי שָׁמַע י׳ Yahweh hath heard, etc.; Ex 3^{12}=Ju 6^{16} and he said, כִּי אֶהְיֶה עִמָּךְ I will

be with thee, Jos 2^{24} 1 S 2^{16} (v. Dr) 10^{19} and ye have said to him, כִּי מֶלֶךְ תָּשִׂים עָלֵינוּ Thou shalt set a king over us, 2 S 11^{23} 1 K 1^{13} 20^{5} Ru 1^{10}, cf. 2^{21} (but in reply to a qu. כִּי may= *because*, v. sub **3**; and so also in sentences giving the expl. of a proper name, Gn 26^{22} 29^{32} (but De *surely:* v. infr.), Ex 2^{10} (cf. Gn 4^{25} 41$^{51.52}$); in כִּי מָה, introducing an expostulation, 1 S 29^{8} 1 K 11^{22} 2 K 8^{13}, it gives the reason for a suppressed 'Why do you say this?'). **c.** esp. after an oath חַי י׳, חַי אָנִי, etc., introducing the fact sworn to, Gn 42^{16} by the life of Pharaoh, כִּי מְרַגְּלִים אַתֶּם (I say) *that* ye are spies; but though Heb. usage prob. gave it an asseverative force, Engl. idiom does not require it to be expressed: Nu 14^{22} 1 S 20^{3} as י׳ liveth, כִּי כְפֶשַׂע בֵּינִי וּבֵין הַמָּוֶת there is but a step between me and death! 26^{16} 29^{6} Is 49^{18}+; כֹּה־יַעֲשֶׂה אֱלֹהִים וְכֹה יוֹסִף כִּי מוֹת תָּמוּת 1 S 14^{44} thus may God do and more also: thou shalt surely die! 2 S 3^{35} 1 K 2^{23} Ru 1^{17} al.—Note that כִּי when thus used is oft. repeated after an intervening clause, in order that its force may be fully preserved: Gn 22$^{16 f.}$ 1 S 14^{39} חַי י׳ כִּי (אִם־יֶשְׁנוֹ בְּיוֹנָתָן בְּנִי) כִּי מוֹת יָמוּת 25^{34} 2 S 2^{27} כִּי (לוּלֵא דִּבַּרְתָּ) כִּי אָז וגו׳, 3^{9} 15^{21} Qr 1 K 1^{30} Je 22^{24}. **d.** כִּי is used sts. with advs. and interjs. to add force or distinctness to the affirmation which follows: (*a*) so esp. in אַף כִּי (v. אַף); הֲכִי† *is it that . . .?* (as a neutral interrog.) 2 S 9^{1}, (expecting a neg. answer) Gn 29^{15} *is it that* thou art my brother, and shalt (therefore) serve me for nothing? Jb 6^{22} *is it that* I have said, Give unto me? expressing surprise Gn 27^{36} *is it that* he is called Jacob, and has (hence) supplanted me twice? 2 S 23^{19} an affirm. answer is required (wh. would imply הֲלֹא כִי): rd. prob. with the ‖ 1 Ch 11^{25} הִנּוֹ *behold, he*, etc.; אִם־לֹא כִּי† Dt 32^{30} were it not *that . . .*; אָמְנָם כִּי† Jb 12^{2} of a truth (is it) *that* ye are the people, etc.; אַף כִּי† 1 S 8^{9}; אֶפֶס כִּי Nu 13^{28}+; גַּם כִּי† Ru 2^{21}; הֲלֹא כִי† 1 S 10^{1} (but v. 𝔊 Dr), 2 S 13^{28}; הִנֵּה כִי† ψ 128^{4}; cf. ψ 118$^{10-12}$ בְּשֵׁם י׳ כִּי אֲמִילַם in the name of י׳ (is it) *that*—or (I say) *that*—I will mow them down; Jb 39^{27} doth the vulture mount up at thy command, וְכִי יָרִים קִנּוֹ *and* (is it) *that* it (so) makes high its nest? Is 36^{19} have the gods of the nations delivered each his land etc.?... וְכִי הִצִּילוּ i. e. (Hi) *and* (is it) *that* they have delivered Samaria out of my hand? > (Ew §354c De Di) *and that* they have delivered Samaria out of my hand! = how much less (אַף כִּי) have they, etc.! (‖ 2 K 18^{34} כִּי alone, perhaps conformed by error to v^{35}; 2 Ch 32^{15} אַף כִּי, which however does not decide the sense of the orig. (וְכִי). 1 Ch 29^{14} וְכִי מִי rd. ומי or כי מי. (*b*) in introducing the apodosis, esp. in כִּי עַתָּה (chiefly after לוּלֵא) *indeed* then . . ., Gn 31^{42} 43^{10} for unless we had tarried כִּי עַתָּה שַׁבְנוּ *surely* then we had returned twice, Nu 22^{33} (rd. לוּלֵי for אוּלַי); so 1 S 14^{30} 𝔊 (after לוּא), and 13^{13} Hi We (לֹא for לוּא); after אִם Jb 8^{6} *surely* then he will awake over thee, etc. (But elsewhere כִּי עַתָּה is simply *for now*, Gn 29^{32} Jb 7^{21}+; or *for then* = *for in that case*, Ex 9^{15} Nu 22^{29} Jb 3^{13} 6^{3}+). It is dub. whether כִּי אָז has the same sense: for 2 S 2^{27} 19^{7} the כִּי in כִּי אָז may be merely resumptive of the כִּי *recitat.* preceding (vid. **a, c**). Rare otherwise: Ex 22^{22} if thou afflict him כִּי אִם־צָעֹק יִצְעַק 'tis *that* (= *indeed*), if he cries unto me, I will hear him, Is 7^{9} if ye believe not כִּי לֹא תֵאָמֵנוּ: *indeed* ye will not be established. **e.** there seem also to be other cases in which כִּי, standing alone, has an intensive force, introducing a statement with emph., *yea, surely, certainly* (Germ. *ja*—a lighter particle than these Engl. words): see in AV RV Ex 18^{11} Nu 23^{23} 1 S 17^{25} 20^{26} 2 K 23^{22} Is 32^{13} 60^{9} Je 22^{22} 31^{19} Ho 6^{9} 8^{6} 9^{12} 10^{3} Am 3^{7} ψ 76^{11} 77^{12} (Ew Che), Pr 30^{2} (but not if construed as RVm), Ec 4^{16} 7$^{7.20}$ Jb 28^{1}+; La 3^{22} (𝔖 𝔗 Ew Th Öt) the mercies of י׳, *surely* they are not consumed (rd. prob. תַּמּוּ or תָּמֵמּוּ for תמנו), Ru 3^{12} כִּי אָמְנָם *yea*, indeed. But it is doubtful whether כִּי has this force in all the passages for which scholars have had recourse to it, and whether in some it is not simply = *for*. De$^{Pr 30, 1}$ would restrict the usage to cases in which a suppressed clause may be understood. **f.** *that*, expressing consecution, esp. after a question implying surprise or deprecation: sq. perf., Gn 20^{9} what have I sinned against thee כִּי הֵבֵאתָ עָלַי *that* thou hast brought upon me? 1 S 22^{8} Is 22^{1} what aileth thee, *that* thou art gone up, etc.? v^{16} 36^{5} 52^{5} Mic 4^{9} Hb 2^{18}; sq. ptcp. Ju 14^{3} 1 S 20^{1} 1 K 18^{9} how have I sinned *that* thou art giving, etc.? 2 K 5^{7} Ez 24^{19}; usu. sq. impf. Ex 3^{11} who am I כִּי אֵלֵךְ *that* I should go, etc.? 16^{7} Ju 8^{6} 9^{28} 2 K 8^{13} Is 7^{13} 29^{16} (also pf.), ψ 8^{5} what is man כִּי תִזְכְּרֶנּוּ? Jb 3^{12} or why the breasts כִּי אִינָק: *that* I should suck? 6^{11} מַה־כֹּחִי כִּי אֲיַחֵל, 7$^{12.17}$ 10$^{5 f.}$ 13$^{25 f.}$ 15$^{12 f.14}$ 16^{3} 21^{15}+; after a neg., Gn 40^{15} here also I have done nothing

כִּי שָׂמוּנִי *that* they should have placed me in the dungeon, ψ 44$^{19f.}$ our heart has not turned backward, etc. כִּי דִכִּיתָנוּ *that* thou shouldst have crushed us, etc., Is 43^{22} not *me* hast thou called on, כִּי יָגַעְתָּ בִּי *that* thou shouldst have wearied thyself with me, Ho 1^{6} (v. RV), Jb 41^{2} Ru 1^{12} I am too old to have an husband כִּי אָמַרְתִּי *that* I should have said, etc. (cf. Ew $^{§ 337a}$; Dr $^{§ 39δ}$). **g.** added to preps. כִּי converts them, like אֲשֶׁר, into conjs...., as יַעַן כִּי because *that*...: v. sub יַעַן, עַד, עַל, עֵקֶב, תַּחַת.

2. a. Of time, *when*, of the past וַיְהִי כִּי Gn 6^{1} (cf. Bu $^{Urg. 6}$), 26^{8} 27^{1} 2 S 6^{13} 7^{1} 19^{26}+ (כַּאֲשֶׁר, and esp. כְּ c. inf., are more freq.); וְהָיָה כִּי (simple וְ!) 1 S 1^{12} 17^{48}; Jos 22^{7} Ju 2^{18}; 12^{5} והיה כי יאמרו and it would be, whenever (freq.) they said, Je 44^{19} (ptcp.), Ho 11^{1} ψ 32^{3} כי החרשתי *when* I was silent, Jb 31$^{21.26.29}$; of present (usu. with impf.) as Ex 18^{16} כִּי יִהְיֶה לָהֶם דָּבָר *when* they have a matter, 1 S 24^{20} Is 1^{12} 30^{21} Je 14^{12} Zc 7$^{5.6}$ Mal 1^{8} ψ 49^{19} and men praise thee כִּי תֵיטִיב לָךְ *when* thou doest well to thyself, 102^{1} 127^{5}+, with pf. Ez 3$^{19-21}$ 33^{9} Pr 11^{15} 23^{22}; esp. of future, as Gn 4^{12} כִּי תַעֲבֹד אֶת־הָאֲדָמָה *when* thou shalt till the ground it shall not, etc., 24^{41} 30^{33} 31^{49} 32^{18} Ex 7^{9} *when* Pharaoh shall speak unto you, Dt 4^{25} 6^{20}+; in phrase וְכִי תֹאמְרוּ (תֹאמַר וגו׳) Lv 25^{20} Dt 18^{21} Is 8^{19} 36^{7} Je 13^{22}; and esp. in ... וְהָיָה כִּי Gn 12^{12} 46^{33} Dt 6^{10} 15^{16} 1 S 10^{7} 25^{30} Is 8^{21} 10^{12}+oft.; with pf. Is 16^{12} 1 Ch 17^{11} (altered fr. impf. 2 S 7^{12}); with ptcp. (unusual) Nu 33^{51} 34^{2} Dt 11^{31} 18^{9}. **b.** elsewhere כִּי has a force approximating to *if*, though it usu. represents a case as more likely to occur than אִם:—(mostly with impf.) Gn 38^{16} Nu 5^{20} 10^{32} Dt 6^{25} 7^{17} 28$^{2.13}$ 1 S 20^{13} 2 S 19^{8} 2 K 4^{29} 18^{22} Je 38^{15} Pr 4^{8} Jb 7^{13} (כי אמרתי *when* I say), 19^{28}; oft. in laws, as Ex 21$^{14.33.35.37}$ 22$^{4.5}$ etc., Dt 13^{13} 14^{24} 15$^{7.12}$ 17^{2} 18$^{6.21}$ etc.; sometimes, in particular, to state a principle broadly, after which special cases are introduced by אִם, as Ex 21^{2} *when* (כִּי) thou buyest a Hebrew servant, he shall serve thee six years, after which v$^{3-5}$ follow four special cases with אִם *if*: so 21^{7} (כי), v$^{8-11}$ (אם); v^{18} (כי), v^{19} (אם); v^{20} (כי), v^{21} (אם); v$^{22f.28-32}$; Lv 1^{2} (כי), v$^{3.10}$ (אם) 4$^{2.3.13.27.32}$ 13$^{2ff.}$ Nu 30$^{3ff.}$+; though this distinction is not uniformly observed, contrast e.g. Ex 21^{5} with Dt 15^{16}; Nu 5^{19} and v^{20}.—N. B. with כִּי = *when* or *if*, the subject is oft. prefixed for distinctness and emph.: 1 K 8^{37} רָעָב כִּי־יִהְיֶה בָאָרֶץ דֶּבֶר כִּי יִהְיֶה וגו׳, Is 28^{18} Mi 5^{4} אַשּׁוּר כִּי־יָבֹא בְאַרְצֵנוּ, ψ 62^{11} Ez 3^{19} (וְאַתָּה), 14$^{9.13}$ 18$^{5.18.21}$ 33^{6} (cf. v^{2}); and esp. in laws of P, as אָדָם ... כִּי Lv 1^{2} 13^{2}, ... נֶפֶשׁ כִּי 2^{1} 4^{2} 5$^{1.4.15}$, similarly 15$^{2.16.19.25}$ 22$^{12.13.14}$ etc., rather differently Nu 5^{20}. **c.** *when* or *if*, with a concessive force, i.e. *though*:—(*a*) with impf. Je 4$^{30.30.30}$ 14^{12} 49^{16} כִּי־תַגְבִּיהַּ כַּנֶּשֶׁר קִנֶּךָ *though* thou make high like the vulture thy nest, I will bring thee down thence, 51^{53} Ho 13^{15} Zc 8^{6} ψ 37^{24} 49$^{19f.}$ *though* in his lifetime he bless himself... he shall come, etc., perh. also Je 46^{23} Ew (but Hi Gf Ke *for*), 50^{11} Ew Ke (Hi *yea*); and strengthened by גַּם, גַּם כִּי Is 1^{5} ψ 23^{4} (cf. Dr $^{§ 143}$); (*b*) with perf. (rare) Mi 7^{8} כִּי נָפַלְתִּי קָמְתִּי *though* I have fallen, I rise, Na 1^{10} (si vera l.), ψ 21^{12} (Hi Ew Now), 119^{83} (Ew De).

3. *Because, since* (ὅτι)—**a.** Gn 3^{14} *because* thou hast done this, cursed art thou, etc., v^{17} 18^{20} the cry of S. and G.—*because* it is great ... (subj. prefixed for emph.: cf. **2** N. B.) Is 28^{15}; in answer to a qu., Gn 27^{20} Ex 1^{19} 18^{15} 2 S 19^{43}+. Enunciating the conditions under which a fut. action is conceived as possible (Germ. *indem*) Lv 22^{9} Dt 4^{29} כי תדרשנו, 12^{20} (v. ^{Dr}), v$^{25.28}$ 13^{19} 14^{24} 16^{15} 19$^{6.9}$+, 1 K 8^{35} (cf. v^{33} אֲשֶׁר), v^{36} כִּי תוֹרֵם, Pr 4^{8b}. **b.** more commonly the causal sentence follows, as Gn 2^{3} and God blessed the seventh day כִּי בוֹ שָׁבַת וגו׳ *because* on it he rested, etc., 4^{25} etc., in which case it may oft. be rendered *for*, Gn 2$^{5.23}$ 3^{20} 5^{24} 6$^{7.12.13}$ ψ 6^{3} heal me כִּי נִבְהֲלוּ עֲצָמָי *for* my bones are vexed, 10^{14} 25^{16} 27^{10}+very oft. Spec. after vbs. expressive of mental emotions, as rejoicing Is 14^{29} ψ 58^{11}, being angry Gn 31^{35} 45^{5}, fearing 43^{18} ψ 49^{17} etc. Iron. 1 K 18^{27} *for* he is a god etc. (4 t.); Pr 30^{4} Jb 38^{5} כִּי תֵדָע *for* or *since* thou knowest. With subj. prefixed ψ 128^{2}. Repeated (with anacol.) Is 49^{19}. **c.** the causal relation expressed by כִּי is sometimes subtle, esp. in poetry, and not apparent without careful study of a passage. Thus sts. it justifies a statement or description by pointing to a pregnant fact which involves it, as Is 3^{8a} Jb 6^{21} (ground of the comparison v$^{15-20}$), 14^{16} (*For* ...: ground of the wishes expressed v$^{13-15}$), 16^{22} (ground of v$^{20f.}$) 30^{26} (*For* ...), or by pointing to a general truth which it exemplifies Jb 5^{6} (reason why complaining v$^{2-5}$ is foolish), 15^{34} 23^{14}; sts. it is *explicative*, justifying a statement by unfolding the particulars wh. establish or exemplify it 2 S 23^{5a} Is 1^{30} 5^{7} 7^{8} 9^{4} 10$^{8-11}$ 13^{10} (development of v^{9a}), 32$^{6f.}$ (developing the characters of the נָבָל and כִּילַי, and so explaining why they will no longer be esteemed v^{5}); Jb 11$^{16ff.}$ (explic. of v^{15b}), 18$^{8ff.}$ (justifying v^{7}), 22$^{26ff.}$ (justifying v^{25}); elsewhere the cause is expressed indirectly or figuratively Is 2^{6} (reason why invitation v^{5} is needed), 5^{10} (sterility of the soil the cause of the desolation v^{9}), 18^{5} 28^{8} (proof of the intoxication v^{7}), 31^{7} (reason for the exhortation v^{6}: the certainty that the folly of idolatry will soon be recognized), Jb 7^{21} (for soon it will be too late to pardon), 27$^{8-10}$ (Job wishes his enemy the lot of the wicked, *because* this is so hopeless); or כִּי relates not to the v. which immed. precedes or follows, but to several, as Is 7$^{16 f.}$ (v^{17} specially the ground of the people being reduced to simple fare v^{15}), 21$^{6 ff.}$ (ground of the statements v$^{1-5}$), Jb 4^{5} (ground of v^{2}), 14$^{7-12}$ (v$^{10-12}$ specially the ground for the appeal in v^{6}), 23$^{10-13}$ (ground why God cannot be found v$^{8 f.}$), ψ 73^{21} (ground not of v^{20}, but of the general train of thought v$^{2-14}$); similarly Gn 4^{24} Dt 18^{14} Je 30^{11} the reason lies not in the words immed. after כִּי, but in the second part of the sentence; or, on the other hand, it may state the reason for a partic. word, Is 28^{20} (justifying 'nought but terror' v^{19}), Jb 23^{17} (*God's* hostility v^{16} the cause of his misery, not the calamity as such). Sometimes also כִּי, in a poet. or rhet. style, gives the reason for a thought not expressed but implied, esp. the answer to a qu.; Is 28^{11} (the mockeries of v^{10} have a meaning) '*for* with men of strange lips, etc. he will speak unto this people,' who will retort the mockeries, charged with a new and terrible meaning, upon those who uttered them (v^{13}); = (no,) *for* Is 28^{28} (see RVm), Jb 22$^{2 b}$ *no*, he that is wise is profitable to himself, 31^{18} 39^{14} (see v$^{13 b}$), ψ 44^{24} (he cannot do this, v^{23}) *for* for thy sake are we killed, etc., 130^{4} *no*, with thee is forgiveness; = (yes,) *for* Is 49^{25} (see the qu. v^{24}), 66^{8}. **d.** כִּי . . . כִּי ἀσυνδέτως sts. introduce the proximate and ultimate cause respectively, Gn 3^{19} 26^{7} 43^{32} 47^{20} Ex 23^{33} *for* [else] thou wilt serve their gods, *for* it will be a snare to thee, Is 2$^{6.6}$ 3$^{8.8}$ 6$^{5 a, b}$ 10$^{22 f.}$ Jb 6$^{3 f.}$ 8$^{8.9.9}$ 24$^{17.17}$ 29$^{11 f.}$; sts. they introduce two co-ordinate causes (where we should insert *and*), Ex 23$^{21.22}$ Is 6$^{5 b, c}$ I am undone, *because* I am of unclean lips . . ., *because* mine eyes have seen ׳י of hosts, 15$^{5.5.6.6.8.9}$ Zp 3$^{8 f.}$ Jb 15$^{25.27}$ 20$^{19 f.}$ 31$^{11 f.}$. But כִּי . . . וְכִי also occurs, Gn 33^{11} Nu 5^{20} (if), Jo 7^{15} Ju 6^{30} 1 S 19^{4} 22^{17} 1 K 2^{26} Is 65^{16} +. **e.** after a neg. כִּי *for* becomes = *but* (Germ. *sondern*): Gn 17^{15} thou shalt not call her name Sarai, כִּי שָׂרָה שְׁמָהּ *for* (= *but*) Sarah shall be her name, 24$^{3 f.}$ 45^{8} Ex 1^{19} 16^{8} not against us are your murmurings, כי על־י׳ *for* (they are) agst. ׳י = *but* agst. ׳י, Dt 21^{17} 1 S 6^{3} (אַל), 27^{1} (v. Dr), 1 K 21^{17} Is 10^{7} 28^{27} 29^{23} 30^{5} ψ 44^{8} 118^{17} + oft.; so in לא כי *nay, for* = *nay, but*, as Gn 18^{15} לֹא כִּי צָחָקְתְּ *nay*, *but* thou didst laugh, 19^{2} 42^{12} Jos 5^{14} 1 S 2^{16} MSS 𝔊 (v. Dr), 12^{12} 2 S 16^{18} 24^{24} 1 K 2^{30} 3^{22} 11^{22} Is 30^{16} *nay, but* we will flee upon horses.

Note.—כִּי is sts. of difficult and uncertain interpretation, and in some of the passages quoted a different expl. is tenable. Authorities esp. read the Heb. differently, when the choice is between *for* and *yea*. E.g. Is 8^{23} Ges Ew$^{§ 330 b}$ *doch (no, but)*; Hi Di *for* (taking v^{22} as RVm); Ch *surely:* 15^{1} Ges Ew Hi Di *surely;* De *for:* 39^{8} Ges Hi De *surely;* Di *for* (expl. of טוֹב): Ez 11^{16} Hi Ke Co *surely;* Ew Sm *because.*—In Ex 20^{25} the tense of וַתְּחַלְלֶהָ makes it prob. that כִּי is *for* (Dr$^{§ 153}$). Jb 22^{29} is taken with least violence to usage (גֵּאָוָה) as Hi: *When* they humble thee, and thou sayest (= complainest) Pride! he will save, etc.

כִּי אִם־ (the אִם always foll. by makkeph, 3588+ 518
except Gn 15^{4} Nu 35^{33} Ne 2^{2}, where כִּי־אִם is read by the Mass.: Fr$^{MM 241}$)—**1.** each part. retaining its independent force, and relating to a *different* clause: **a.** *that if* Je 26^{15}; after an oath (כִּי not translated: v. כִּי **1 c**) *if* 1 S 14^{39} Je 22^{24}, *surely not* (אִם **1 b** 2) 2 S 3^{35} 1 S 25^{34} (כִּי being resumptive of the כִּי before לוּלֵי: v. כִּי **1 c**); Ex 22^{22} (in apod.) *indeed if* . . . (v. כִּי **1 d**). **b.** *for if* Ex 8^{17} 9^{2} 10^{4} Dt 11^{20} +, *for though* Is 10^{22} Je 37^{20} Am 5^{22}, *but if* Je 7^{5}.

2. (About 140 t.) the two particles being closely conjoined, and relating to the *same* clause—**a.** *limiting* the prec. clause, **except** (after a negative, or an oath, or question, the equivalent of a negative)—the most usual term for expressing this idea: sq. vb. Gn 32^{27} I will not let thee go; כִּי אִם־בֵּרַכְתָּנִי lit. *but* (כִּי **3 e**) *if* thou bless me (sc. I will let thee go), i.e., subordinating the second clause to the first, 'I will not let thee go, *except* thou bless me;' Lv 22^{6} he shall not eat of the holy things כִּי אִם־רָחַץ *except* he have washed his flesh, Is 65^{6} Am 3^{7} Ru 3^{18} La 5$^{21 f.}$ (Ew Näg Ke Che Öt), turn thou us unto thee, etc., *unless* thou have utterly rejected us, (and) art very wroth with us (= *Or* hast thou utterly rejected us? etc. Ew Öt); sq. a noun, *except, but*, Gn 28^{17} this is nothing כִּי אִם־בֵּית הָאֱ׳ *but* the house of God, 32^{9} he withholds from me nothing כִּי אִם־אוֹתְךָ *except* thee, Lv 21^{2} Nu 14^{30} (after אִם), 26^{65} (cf. 32^{12} בִּלְתִּי), Jos 14^{4} 1 S 30$^{17.22}$ 2 S 12^{3} אֵין כֹּל כִּי אִם־ (so 2 K 4^{2}), 19^{29} 1 K 17^{1} (after אִם), 22^{31} 2 K 5^{15} 9^{35} 13^{7} Je 22^{17} 44^{14} +; after אַל, 2 Ch 23^{6}; sq. an adv. clause, Gn 42^{15} Nu 35^{33} 2 S 3^{13} (but כִּי אִם and לִפְנֵי are mutually exclusive: rd. prob. with 𝔊 (כִּי אִם־הֲבִיאֹתָ); after an interrog. Is 42^{19} who is blind כִּי אִם־עַבְדִּי *but* my servant? (who is blind in comparison with him?), Dt 10^{12} Mi 6^{8} Ec 5^{10} 2 Ch 2^{5}. **b.** the *if* being neglected, and treated as pleonastic (cf. אִם **1 c**), so that the clause is no longer a limitation of the preceding clause but a contradiction of it: **but rather, but** (=a slightly strengthened כִּי), Gn 15^{4} this man shall not be thy heir; כִּי אִם־אֲשֶׁר וגו׳ *but* one that shall come forth from thy own bowels, he shall be thy heir (cf. 1 K 8^{19}), 32^{29} thy name shall no more be called Jacob כִּי אִם־יִשְׂרָאֵל *but* Israel (cf. כִּי alone 17^{15}), 47^{18} we will not hide it from my lord, *but* the money . . . is all made over to, etc., Ex 12^{9} not boiled in water, *but* roast with fire, Dt 7^{5} 12^{5} 16^{6} Jo 23^{8} 1 S 2^{15} he will not take of thee boiled flesh כִּי אִם־חָי׃ *but* raw, 8^{19} לֹא כִּי אִם־מֶלֶךְ יִהְיֶה עָלֵינוּ nay, *but* a king shall be over us (cf. כי alone, 10^{19} 12^{12}), 21^{5} 2 S 5^{6} 1 K 18^{18} 2 K 10^{23} (פֶּן), Is 33^{21} $55^{10.11}$ 59^{2} Je 3^{10} 7^{32} 9^{23} 16^{15} 20^{3} Ez 36^{22} 44^{10} Am 8^{11} ψ $1^{2.4}$ Pr 23^{17} (אַל)+; with the principal verb repeated (as Gn 15^{4} 1 K 8^{19}), Lv 21^{14} Ez 44^{22} Nu 10^{30} 2 K 23^{23} Je 39^{12} Kt (Qr om. אִם), cf. 7^{23}. Occas. in colloq. language, the neg., it seems, is left to be understood: 1 S 26^{10} as ׳י liveth, (by no means,) כִּי אִם *but* ׳י shall smite him, 2 S 13^{33} Kt (by no means,) *but* Amnon alone is dead (Qr om. אִם). Sq. imv. Is 65^{18} Ez 12^{23} Je 39^{12} 2 Ch 25^{8}. Sts. also, though rarely (and not certainly), כִּי אִם appears to have the force of *only* even without a previous neg.: Gn 40^{14} כִּי אִם־זְכַרְתַּנִי אִתְּךָ *only* have (?) me in remembrance with thyself (but rd. perh. אַךְ for כִּי; v Dr$^{§ 119 \delta n.}$, the use of a bare pf., without לוּ, or even waw consec., to express a wish or command is unexampled), Nu 24^{22} כִּי אִם־ יִהְיֶה לְבָעֵר קָיִן׃ *only, nevertheless,* the Kenite shall be for extermination (cf. Di), Jb 42^{8} (De Di) כִּי אִם־פָּנָיו אֶשָּׂא. **c.** after an oath כִּי אִם appears to=a strengthened כִּי (cf. בִּלְתִּי אִם, עַד אִם: אִם **1 c**), introducing the fact sworn to (v. כִּי **1 c**): 2 K 5^{20} as ׳י liveth, כִּי אִם־רַצְתִּי *surely* I will run (pf. of certitude) after him, etc., Je 51^{14} (Ges Hi Gf RV) *surely* I will fill thee with men (viz. assailants), etc. (but Ew Ke Ch treat the particles as separate (כִּי as כִּי **1 c**): though I have filled thee with men—i.e. increased thy population—, yet shall they—the assailants—lift up the shout against thee), 2 S 15^{21} Kt (Qr omits אִם); after an assever. part. Ru 3^{12} Kt וְעַתָּה כִּי אָמְנָם כִּי אִם גּוֹאֵל אָנֹכִי and now, yea indeed, *surely* I am thy kinsman (Qr omits אִם); the oath being understood, Ju 15^{7} if ye do thus, כִּי אִם־נִקַּמְתִּי *surely* (Ges *hercle*) I will avenge myself, 1 S 21^{6} כִּי אִם־אִשָּׁה עֲצֻרָה לָנוּ *of a truth* women have been kept from us, etc., 1 K 20^{6} *surely* tomorrow I will send, etc., Pr 23^{18} (v. De) *surely* there *is* a reward; perh. also Jb 42^{8}.

† כִּי עַל כֵּן *forasmuch as*, a peculiar phrase 3588+
found Gn 18^{5} 19^{8} 33^{10} 38^{26} Nu 10^{31} 14^{43} Ju 6^{22} 5921+
2 S 18^{20} Qr (rightly), Je 29^{28} 38^{4}—lit. *for there-* 3651
fore, emphasizing the ground pleonastically (Ew$^{§ 353 a}$). The orig. force of the phrase is traceable in some of the passages in which it occurs, as Gn 18^{5} let me fetch a morsel of bread, and comfort your heart; כִּי־עַל־כֵּן עֲבַרְתֶּם עַל עַבְדְּכֶם *for therefore* (sc. to partake of such hospitality) are ye come to your servant, Nu 14^{43} the Amalekite and the Canaanite are there, and ye will fall by the sword, כִּי־עַל־כֵּן שַׁבְתֶּם *for therefore* (to encounter such a fate) have ye turned back from ׳י, etc.: but in process of time the distinct sense of its component parts was no doubt gradually obscured, and it thus came to be used conventionally, as a *mere* particle of causation, even where there was no preceding statement to which עַל כֵּן *therefore* could be explicitly referred. אֲשֶׁר עַל כֵּן appears to be used similarly (cf. אֲשֶׁר **8 c**) +Jb 34^{27}.

I. כִּי, *branding*, v. sub כוה. p. 465 3587

†[כִּיד] **n.[m.]** only sf. כִּידוֹ Jb 21^{20}, meaning unknown; rd. prob. פִּידוֹ *his misfortune* 3589
(as 12^{5} etc.)

כיד (√ of foll.; cf. perh. Ar. كَادَ in sense *labour, take pains, strive,* or *struggle* with, كَيْدٌ *war*).

†I. כִּידוֹן **n.[m.]** dart, javelin (NH *id.*)— 3591
abs. כ׳ Jos 8^{18} + 6 t.; כִּידֹן Je 50^{42}; cstr. כִּידוֹן 1 S 17^{6};—*dart, javelin* (distinct fr. חֲנִית *spear, lance,* q.v.), נטה בַּכִּ׳ אשר בידך Jos $8^{18.18}$, cf. v^{26}; רַעַשׁ כ׳ Jb 41^{21} *the rushing sound of a dart;* בְּחֶרֶב וּבַחֲנִית וּבְכ׳ 1 S 17^{45} (weapons of Goliath), כ׳ נְחשֶׁת בֵּין כְּתֵפָיו v^{6} (חֲנִית in v^{7}); + חֲנִית Jb 39^{23} also; קֶשֶׁת וְכ׳ Je 6^{23} 50^{42}.

†II. כִּידֹן **n.pr.m.** 1 Ch 13^{9}, 𝔊L Χεδων, A 3592
Χειλω; = נָכוֹן 2 S 6^{6} (𝔊 Νωδαβ, A Ναχων, 𝔊L Ορνα).

כִּידוֹד v. sub כדד; כִּידוֹר v. sub כדר. p. 461 3590, 3593

†כִּיּוּן **n.pr.dei** Am 5^{26}, prob.=As. *kaivânu*, 3594
planet *Saturn* (Ar. and Pers. كَيْوَانُ, Syr. ܟܐܘܢ),

regarded as god; orig. pronunc. כֵּיוָן Schr$^{COT\ ad\ loc.}$, cf. Kö$^{ii.\ 151}$ (pointing כִּיּוּן intended to suggest √כון as something *established, firm*); *kaimânu*=*kaiânu*, acc. to Jen$^{Cosm.\ iii.\ 502}$ who der. fr. כון (cf. Thes; so Zim$^{BP\ 17}$); >Hpt$^{ZA\ ii.\ 266,\ 281\ f.}$ rds. כַּיָּוָן (for כְּאָמָן*), reading the Babyl. name *Ka'âmânu;* v. also M-A$^{JBL\ 1892,\ xi.\ 86\ n.\ 39}$.

3595 **כִּיּוֹר**, v. sub I. כור. p. 468

3596 **כִּילַי, כֵּלַי** Is $32^{5.7}$ v. נכל (Kö$^{ii.\ 118}$). p. 647

3597 †**כֵּילַפּוֹת** **n.[f.] axe** (loan-word (cf. Frä^{74}) fr. As. *kalappatu* v. Dl$^{HWB\ 333}$)—בְּכַשִּׁיל וְכ׳ יַהֲלֹמוּן ψ 74^{6} (‖ קַרְדֻּמּוֹת v^{5}).

3598 **כִּימָה** v. sub כום. p. 465

3599 †**כִּיס** **n.m.**$^{Pr\ 1,\ 14}$ **bag, purse** (perh. kindred with כּוֹס, q.v.; Ar. كِيسٌ (prob. fr. Pers. كِيسَهْ Lane^{2640}); Eth. ኪስ: NH כִּיס; Aram. כִּיסָא, ܟܝܣܐ; Palm. מן כיסה *from his purse*=at his own expense, Vog$^{p.\ 13\ al.}$)—*bag,* in which were carried: **a.** weights (v. אֶבֶן **5**) Dt 25^{13} Mi 6^{11} Pr 16^{11}; **b.** money, i.e. *a purse* Is 46^{6} Pr 1^{14}.

3595, 3600 **כִּיר, [כִּיר], כִּירַיִם** v. sub I. כור. p. 468

3601 **כִּישׁוֹר** v. sub כשר. p. 507

3602 **כָּכָה** v. sub כה p. 462 supr.

3603 **כִּכָּר** v. sub כרר; **כֹּל** v. sub I. כלל. p. 503

3607 †**[כָּלָא]** **vb. shut up, restrain, withhold** (NH *id.;* Aram. כְּלָא, ܟܠܐ; Eth. ከልአ: *restrain, hinder;* As. *kâlû, id.;* Ar. كَلَأَ *protect* Qor 21^{43} cf. Ba$^{ZMG\ 1887,\ 605\ Anm.\ 4}$)—**Qal** *Pf.* 3 ms. sf. כְּלָאוֹ Je 32^{3}; 3 fs. כָּלְאָה Hg 1^{10}; 2 fs. sf. כְּלִתְנִי 1 S 25^{33}; 1 s. כָּלָאתִי ψ 119^{101}; 3 pl. כָּלְאוּ Hg 1^{10}, כָּלוּ 1 S 6^{10}; *Impf.* 3 ms. יִכְלֶה Gn 23^{6}; 2 ms. תִּכְלָא ψ 40^{12}; 2 fs. תִּכְלָאִי Is 43^{6}; 1 s. אֶכְלָא ψ 40^{10}; *Imv.* sf. כְּלָאֵם Nu 11^{28}; *Inf. cstr.* לִכְלוֹא Ec 8^{8}; *Pt. pass.* כָּלוּא Je 32^{2}, כָּלֻא ψ 88^{9}; (on the metapl. forms, as if fr. כלה, v. Ges$^{§\ 75,\ 21\ c}$ Kö$^{i.\ 611}$);—**1.** *shut up,* c. acc. 1 S 6^{10} (+ בְּ loc.), Je 32^{3}; pt. pass. Je 32^{2} (בְּ loc.), fig. ψ 88^{9} (opp. יצא). **2.** *restrain,* c. acc. 1 S 25^{33} (+ מִבּוֹא בְדָמִים), ψ 119^{101} (+ מִכָּל־); כְּלָאֵם (sc. מִתְנַבְּאִים) Nu 11^{28}; כ׳ שְׂפָתַי ψ 40^{10}; כ׳ אֶת־הָרוּחַ Ec 8^{8}. On ψ 74^{11} v. כלה **Pi. 2.** **3.** *withhold,* כ׳ אֶת־קִבְרוֹ מִמְּךָ מִקְּבֹר מֵתֶךָ Gn 23^{6}(P), כ׳ רַחֲמֶיךָ מִמֶּנִּי ψ 40^{12}, Hg $1^{10\ b}$, prob. also v^{a} (rd. טַל for MT 𝔊 מִטַּל, We); abs. אַל־תִּכְלָאִי (sc. exiles) Is 43^{6} (‖ תְּנִי). **Niph.** *Impf.* וַיִּכָּלֵא הַגֶּשֶׁם מִן־הַשָּׁמַיִם Gn 8^{2} (J), *and the rain from heaven was restrained,* cf. וַיִּכָּלְאוּ מַיִם רַבִּים Ez 31^{15} (in fig.; ‖ מנע); וַיִּכָּלֵא הָעָם מֵהָבִיא Ex 36^{6} (P). **Pi.** [Pf. כִּלָּא and] *Inf. cstr.* לְכַלֵּא v. כלה **Pi.**

†**כֶּלֶא** **n.[m.] confinement, restraint, imprisonment;**—abs. כ׳ 1 K 22^{27} + 6 t.; sf. כִּלְאוֹ 3608
2 K 25^{29} Je 52^{33}; pl. כְּלָאִים Is 42^{22};—*confinement,* in combin. בֵּית (ה)כ׳ (cf. As. *bit kili, prison,* Dl$^{HWB\ 328}$) 1 K 22^{27} = 2 Ch 18^{26}, 2 K 17^{4} Je $37^{15.18}$
Is 42^{7}; בָּתֵּי כְלָאִים v^{22} (cf. בַּיִת **1** (ε) (2) p. 109 1004
supr.; v. also כלוא infr.); בִּגְדֵי כִלְאוֹ 2 K 25^{29} = Je 52^{33} *garments of imprisonment*=prison-garb.

†**כלוא** Kt, **כְּלִיא** Qr **n.[m.]** id.;—בֵּית הַכ׳ 1004, 3628
Je 37^{4} 52^{31} (v. כֶּלֶא supr.)

†I. **מִכְלָה** (incorrect for מכלא) **n. [m.] enclosure, fold;**—גָּזַר מִמִּ׳ צֹאן Hb 3^{17}; pl. cstr. 4356
מִמִּכְלְאֹת צֹאן ψ 78^{70} (obj. David); pl. sf. לקח
מִמִּכְלְאֹתֶיךָ 50^{9} (obj. he-goats).—II. מִכְלָה v. sub 4357
כלה. p. 479

†**כִּלְאַיִם** **n.[m.] du. two kinds** (Ar. كِلَانِ, 3610
كِلَا *both;* Eth. ክልኤ: *two;* perh. also כלאי MI^{23} *both, two,* Nö$^{LCB\ 1889,\ 61}$, cf. Dr$^{Sm\ xcii}$; Sm u. So$^{MI,\ 1886}$ suggest *reservoirs;* v. also כְּלִי)—בְּהֶמְתְּךָ לֹא־תַרְבִּיעַ כ׳ Lv 19^{19} *not cause thy cattle to breed* (in) *two kinds;* שָׂדְךָ לֹא תִזְרַע כ׳ v^{19}(H); לֹא תִזְרַע כַּרְמְךָ כ׳ Dt 22^{9} (both כִּלְאָיִם); בֶּגֶד כ׳ Lv 19^{19}(H);—only in law of H and D against mixtures.

†**כִּלְאָב** **n.pr.m.** second son of David, 2 S 3^{3} = 3609
דָּנִיֵּאל 1 Ch 3^{1}, v. דָּנִיֵּאל **1.** p. 193 supr.

כלב (√of foll.; meaning unknown; Thes regards כֶּלֶב as onomatop.)

†**כֶּלֶב** **n.m.**$^{1\ S\ 24,\ 15}$ **dog** (NH *id.;* Ph. כלב; 3611
Aram. כַּלְבָּא, ܟܠܒܐ; Ar. كَلْبٌ; Eth. ከልብ: As. *kalbu* Dl$^{HWB\ 328}$)—abs. כ׳ Ju 7^{5} + 16 t., כָּלֶב ψ $59^{7.15}$; pl. כְּלָבִים 1 K 14^{11} + 12 t.; cstr. כַּלְבֵי Jb 30^{1}; sf. כְּלָבֶיךָ ψ 68^{24};—*dog:* **a.** lit. 1 K 14^{11} 16^{4} $21^{19.19.23.24}$ 22^{38} 2 K $9^{10.36}$ (all of fierce, hungry dogs, devouring dead bodies and licking blood); cf. Je 15^{3} and (לְשׁוֹן כְּלָבֶיךָ) ψ 68^{24}; eating torn flesh, Ex 22^{30}(E), כַּלְבֵי צֹאנִי = *my sheep-dogs,* only Jb 30^{1} (in both these with implied inferiority); dog-sacrifice was a heathen rite Is 66^{3} (Di al.); v. esp. RS$^{Sem.\ i,\ 273\ (291),\ 325\ (343)}$; in various sim. Ju 7^{5} Pr $26^{11.17}$ ψ $59^{7.15}$; in proverbial sayings: לֹא יֶחֱרַץ־כ׳ לְשֹׁנוֹ Ex 11^{7} (v. I. חרץ); לְכ׳ מֵת טוֹב מִן־

הָאַרְיֵה הַמֵּת Ec 9^{4}. **b.** applied, fig., to men, in contempt 1 S 17^{43}, so of psalmist's enemies ψ $22^{17.21}$, or in excessive humility 2 K 8^{13}; still more emphatically כ׳ מֵת *a dead dog*, הַכּ׳ הַמֵּת 2 S 9^{8} 16^{9}; also רֹאשׁ כ׳ 3^{8}; כְּלָבִים אִלְּמִים Is 56^{10} (of misleading prophets), הַכּ׳ עַזֵּי נֶפֶשׁ v^{11} (*id.*); כ׳ was name given to male temple-prostitutes Dt 23^{19} (v. Dr; cf. קָדֵשׁ).

3612 †כָּלֵב **n.pr.m.** (Nab. n.pr. כלבא Eut (Nö)$^{p. 55}$. כלבו Vog$^{Nab. 6}$; cf. also We$^{Skizzen\ u. Vorarbeiten\ iii. 217}$; on כָּלֵב = *dog-clan*, v. RS$^{K\ 17, 190 f., 219, 254}$);—son of יְפֻנֶּה (𝔊 Χαλεβ; cf. Lag$^{BN\ 78}$), called הַקְּנִזִּי (v. קְנַז) in JE, Nu 32^{12} Jos $14^{6.14}$, cf. 15^{17} = Ju 1^{13}, Ju 3^{9} (where קְנַז is brother of כ׳), also 1 Ch 4^{15}; treated as full Judahite only in P Nu 13^{6} (v. GFM$^{Ju\ p. 30 f.}$) the one of the spies who (with Joshua) reported well of Canaan $14^{6.24.30.38}$; also 26^{65} 34^{19} Dt 1^{36} Jos 14^{13} $15^{13.14.16.18}$ 21^{12} (P = 1 Ch 6^{41}) Ju $1^{12.14.15.20}$ (‖ with Jos 15); = clan of Caleb 1 S 30^{14} (disting. from Judah). Caleb is called כָּלֵב בֶּן־חֶצְרוֹן 1 Ch 2^{18}, cf. $v^{19.42.46.48.49.50}$ = כְּלוּבָי v^{9}; אֶפְרָתָה 1 Ch 2^{24}, rd. perh. בָּא כ׳, so 𝔊 𝔙, cf. Kau^{AT} (v. אֶפְרָתָה p. 68 supr.)

3614 †כָּלִבִּי **adj.gent.** of כָּלֵב 1 S 25^{3} Qr (Kt כָּלִבּוֹ).

3620 †כְּלוּב **n.pr.m.** **1.** a name in Judah 1 Ch 4^{11}, 𝔊 Χαλεβ (acc. to We$^{Gentilb. 20, Hist. 218}$ = כָּלֵב בֶּן־חֶצְרוֹן; rd. also for כַּרְמִי v^{1}). **2.** father of one of David's officers, acc. to 1 Ch 27^{26} (𝔊 Χοβουδ, A Χελουβ, 𝔊L Χαλουβ).

3621 †כְּלוּבָי **n.pr.m.** a son of Hezron of Judah, acc. to 1 Ch 2^{9} (𝔊 Χαβελ, A Χαλεβ, 𝔊L Χαλωβι), = כָּלֵב v^{18} etc. (see כָּלֵב **2**).

3619 †כְּלוּב **n.m.**$^{Je\ 5, 27}$ **basket, cage** (√ dub.; NH *id.*, כְּלִיבָה; Aram. ܩܠܘܒܐ in Lexx.; Tel Am. *kilubi, bird-net*, cf. Zim$^{ZA\ vi. 145, 147}$)—abs. כִּכְלוּב מָלֵא עוֹף Je 5^{27} *like a cage full of birds*; cstr. כְּלוּב קַיִץ Am $8^{1.2}$ *a basket of summer fruit*.

3615 I. כָּלָה^{206} **vb. be complete, at an end, finished, accomplished, spent** (NH *id.*, Pi.; Ph. כלה; As. *kalû, put an end to*, and *cease, vanish* Dl$^{HWB\ 329}$; late Aram. כְּלָא *cease, perish* (not 𝔗); on root-meaning *enclose* cf. כלא and Ba$^{ZMG\ 1887, 605}$)—†**Qal** *Pf.* כ׳ 1 K 6^{38}+; 3 fs. כָּלְתָה 1 S 20^{7}+; 1 s. כָּלִיתִי ψ 39^{11}; 3 pl. כָּלוּ Jb 19^{27}+; 2 mpl. כְּלִיתֶם Mal 3^{6}; וְכִלִּיתֶם consec. Ez 13^{14}; 1 pl. כָּלִינוּ ψ 90^{7}, etc.; *Impf.* יִכְלֶה Pr 22^{8}; juss. יִכֶל Jb 33^{21} (v. Dr$^{§\ 171-173}$ Ges$^{§\ 109. 2\ b\ Anm.}$ Da$^{Synt. §\ 51\ R. 5;\ 64\ R. 6}$); 3 fs. תִּכְלֶה 1 K 17^{14}; וַתֵּכֶל Ex 39^{32} + 2 S 13^{39} (v. infr.); 3 mpl. יִכְלוּ Is 1^{28}+, יִכְלָיוּן Is 31^{3}, etc.; *Inf. cstr.* כְּלוֹת Ru 2^{23}+, etc.;—**1. a.** *be complete, at an end*, of a period of time Gn 41^{53} (E; opp. III. חלל Hiph. *begin* v^{54}), Je 8^{20} (‖ עבר); so of action or event, with emphasis on time Is 10^{25} 24^{13} Ru 2^{23} 2 Ch 29^{28} (opp. הֵחֵל v^{27}), v^{34} Dn 12^{7} (‖ קֵץ $v^{6.9}$);—vid. also **2 b** infr. **b.** *be completed, finished*, of a work: temple 1 K 6^{38} 1 Ch 28^{20} 2 Ch 8^{16} (‖ שָׁלֵם), tabernacle Ex 39^{32} (P). **c.** *be accomplished, fulfilled*, only of purposed wrath, or prediction of י׳, Ez 5^{13} (‖ כִּלּוֹתִי v^{b}, see **Pi.**), Dn 11^{36} 2 Ch 36^{22} = Ezr 1^{1}. **d.** be ideally complete, *be determined*, always in bad sense, *plotted*, subj. הָרָעָה: sq. מֵעִם of agent 1 S 20^{7}, also v^{9} (+ לָבוֹא עַל), + v^{33} (rd. כָּלְתָה, for MT כָּלָה הִיא, 𝔊 We Dr Kit Bu); כ׳ הָרָעָה אֶל־אֲדֹנֵינוּ וְעַל־כָּל־בֵּיתוֹ 25^{17}; sq. מֵאֵת of agent Est 7^{7} (+ אֵלָיו). **2. a.** *be spent, used up* (prop. *come to an end*), of water Gn 21^{15} (E), meal 1 K $17^{14.16}$. **b.** *waste away, be exhausted, fail*, lit. of fading grass Is 15^{6} (‖ יָבֵשׁ, לֹא היה), of vintage 32^{10} (opp. בּוֹא), of vanishing cloud Jb 7^{9} (in sim., ‖ הלך); fig. of fleeting days of life v^{6} (‖ קלל), cf. ψ 102^{4} and כָּלוּ בְיָגוֹן חַיַּי ψ 31^{11}, Je 20^{18}; v. also **1 a** supr.; of flesh Jb 33^{21}, cf. of vital strength ψ 71^{9}, כ׳ בְּשָׂרְךָ וּשְׁאֵרֶךָ Pr 5^{11}, כָּלָה שְׁאֵרִי וּלְבָבִי ψ 73^{26}, subj. רוּחִי 143^{7}; once of י׳'s compassion לֹא־כָלוּ רַחֲמָיו La 3^{22} (‖ תמם, on txt. see VB); esp. of eyes exhausted by weeping La 2^{11}, strained by looking (fig.) for relief or refreshment, *pine, languish* 4^{17} ψ 69^{4} Jb 11^{20} 17^{5} Je 14^{6} (of wild asses); sq. לְ La 4^{17} and, in spiritual sense, ψ $119^{82.123}$; similarly (sq. לְ) of נפשׁ exhausted by *longing* ψ 84^{3} (‖ נכסף), 119^{81}, כָּלוּ כִלְיֹתַי בְּחֵקִי Jb 19^{27}; so also 2 S 13^{29} where rd. וַתְּכַל רוּחַ הַמֶּלֶךְ (for MT וַתְּכַל דָּוִד הַמֶּ׳) *and the spirit of the king pined* to go forth unto Absalom, cf. 𝔊L We Klo Dr Kit Bu. **c.** *come to an end, vanish = perish, be destroyed*, by י׳'s judgment Is 1^{28} (‖ שֶׁבֶר), 16^{4} (‖ תָּמַם, אָפֵס), 29^{20} (‖ נִכְרַת, אָפֵס), 31^{3} (‖ נפל, כשׁל), וּבַחֶרֶב וּבָרָעָב יִכְלוּ Je 16^{4}, cf. 44^{27} (‖ תָּמַם), Ez 5^{12} (‖ נָפַל, מות), 13^{14} Mal 3^{6} ψ $37^{20.20}$ (‖ אבד), Jb 4^{9} (‖ *id.*), ψ 71^{13} (‖ בּוֹשׁ); hyperbol., of severe discipline 39^{11} 90^{7} (‖ נבהל); of prosperity of a people Is 21^{16}; שֵׁבֶט עֶבְרָתוֹ יִכְלֶה Pr 22^{8} *the rod of his wrath perishes*

(>Ew al. *is accomplished*, of God's wrath).—Dn 12^{7} rd. perh. וְכִכְלוֹת יַד נֹפֵץ עַם קֹדֶשׁ *and when the power of the shatterer of the holy people should come to an end*, so Bev after 𝔊 (for difficult MT וּכְכַלּוֹת נַפֵּץ יַד־עַם־קֹדֶשׁ)†.

3607 **Pi.** $_{140}$ *Pf.* כִּלָּה Gn 18^{33}+, כִּלָּא Pr 16^{30} Baer (van d. H כִּלָּה), sf. כִּלָּנוּ 2 S 21^{5}, כִּלָּם La 2^{22}; 3 fs. וְכִלְּתָה consec. Ho 11^{6}, sf. וְכִלַּתּוּ consec. Zc 5^{4}; 1 s. כִּלִּיתִי Nu 25^{11}, וְכִלֵּיתִי Is 49^{4}, וְכִלֵּיתִי Ez 6^{12}+ 2 t.; sf. כִּלִּיתִים Ez 22^{31}, וְכִלִּתִיךָ consec. Ex 33^{5}; 3 pl. כִּלּוּ Gn 24^{19}+, etc.; *Impf.* יְכַלֶּה Is 10^{18}; וַיְכַל Gn 2^{2}; 3 fs. וַתְּכַל Gn 24^{19}+2 S 13^{39} (but rd. וַתֵּכֶל We Dr al., and v. **Qal 2 b**); 1 s. אֲכַלֶּה Gn 24^{25}+4 t.; וָאֲכַל Ez 43^{8}; sf. אֲכֶלְךָ Ex 33^{3} (Kö $^{i. 545}$); 3 mpl. יְכַלּוּ Jb 36^{11}+21^{13} Qr (Kt יבלו; v. בלה p. 115 supr.), +, etc.; *Imv.* כַּלֵּה ψ $59^{14.14}$+74^{11} (but text dub., v. infr., **2**); mpl. כַּלּוּ Ex 5^{13}; *Inf. abs.* כַּלֵּה 1 S 3^{12}+5 t.; *cstr.*
3607 לְכַלֵּא Dn 9^{24} (metapl. form), כַּלּוֹת 1 S 2^{33}+, etc.; *Pt.* מְכַלֶּה Je 14^{12} Jb 9^{22}; fpl. מְכַלּוֹת Lv 26^{16};—**1.** †**a.** *complete, bring to an end, finish* a thing, task, work, etc., c. acc. rei Ex $5^{13.14}$ (+inf.; both J), 1 K $6^{9.14}$ 7^{1} Ez 42^{15}, Gn 2^{2} 16^{16} Ex 40^{33} (P), Ru 2^{21} 1 Ch 31^{1} 2 Ch 7^{11} Ezr 9^{1}, so לְכַלֵּא הַפֶּשַׁע Dn 9^{24} *to make an end of the transgression* (cf. VB Bev); Lv 23^{22} (modified from 19^{9} q.v. infr.); acc. om. 2 Ch 31^{7} (opp. הֵחֵל לְ), $24^{10.14}$ Ne 3^{34}. †**b.** *complete* a period of time יָמִים Ez $4^{6.8}$; *complete* one's days, enjoy the full measure of human life Jb 21^{13} 36^{11}, or *bring* one's years *to an end* ψ 90^{9}, with added idea of transitoriness. **c.** *finish* doing a thing, usu. sq. לְ inf. Gn 18^{33} $24^{15.19.19.22}$ (all J), 17^{22} Ex 31^{18} Nu 4^{15} (all P), Am 7^{2} 1 K 1^{41} 2 Ch 29^{29} Ru 3^{3}+31 t. incl. 2 S 11^{19}, where obj. of infin. precedes it, v. Dr, so Lv 19^{9} (cf. 23^{22} supr.); +1 Ch 27^{24} (לְ inf. om.; opp. הֵחֵל לְ), 2 Ch 29^{17}; +Dn 12^{7} (inf. without לְ; but see **Qal 2 c** ad fin.); sq. מִן inf., 1 S 10^{13} 2 S 6^{18}=1 Ch 16^{2}, Ex 34^{33} Lv 16^{20} Jos 19^{51} (all P), Ez 43^{23}. †**d.** *make an end, end,* sq. בְּ *make an end with,* finish dealing with 2 Ch 20^{23} Ezr 10^{17}; abs., opp. הֵחֵל, בַּגָּדוֹל הֵחֵל וּבַקָּטֹן כִּלָּה Gn 44^{12} (J) *he began with the eldest and with the youngest he ended;* so inf. abs. adverb. הָחֵל וְכַלֵּה 1 S 3^{12} *a beginning and an ending,* i.e. doing it thoroughly (v. Dr); also עַד־כַּלֵּה=*utterly* 2 K $13^{17.19}$, *to extremity* Ezr 9^{14} (of י׳'s anger), עַד־לְכַלֵּה (late) =*completely* 2 Ch 24^{10} (until all had given), 31^{1} (until all were destroyed). †**e.** *accomplish, fulfil, bring to pass,* a thing Ru 3^{18}; c. acc. of י׳'s wrath (חֲמָתוֹ) La 4^{11}; so (אַפִּי, חֲמָתִי) +בְּ pers. Ez 5^{13} 6^{12} 7^{8} 13^{15} $20^{8.21}$. †**f.** *accomplish* in thought, *determine* (cf. **Qal 1 d**) sq. רָעָה Pr 16^{30} (|| חשב). †**2. a.** *put an end to, cause to cease* Nu 17^{25} (מֵעָלַי+); וַיְכַל־בַּהֶבֶל יְמֵיהֶם ψ 78^{33} *and he consumed (caused to vanish) as vanity their days.* **b.** *cause to fail, exhaust, use up, spend,* חִצַּי אֲכַלֶּה־בָּם Dt 32^{23} *my arrows will I exhaust against them;* exhaust one's strength כֹּחַ Is 49^{4} (|| יָגַע); the eyes (by weeping; cf. **Qal 2 b**) 1 S 2^{33} Jb 31^{16}; of a disease, *consume* the eyes Lv 26^{16} (H). **c.** *destroy,* sts. *exterminate:* (1) men subj., c. acc. pers. 2 S 21^{5} 22^{39} (|| מחץ), Dt 7^{22} 2 Ch 8^{8} Je 10^{25} (|| אכל), La 2^{22} ψ 119^{87}; esp. in phr. עַד כַּלּוֹתָם 1 S 15^{18} (on txt. v. Dr), 2 S 22^{38} (|| השמיד)=ψ 18^{38}, 1 K 22^{11}=2 Ch 18^{10}; (2) God subj., c. acc. pers. Jos 24^{20} (E), Is 10^{18} (Assyrian host, under fig. of forest); Je 5^{3} Ex 32^{10} $33^{3.5}$ (JE), Nu 16^{21} 17^{10} 25^{11} (all P), Lv 26^{44} (H), Ez 20^{13} 22^{31} 43^{8} Jb 9^{22}; עַד כַּלֹּתוֹ אֹתְךָ Dt 28^{21}, עַד כַּלּוֹתִי אוֹתָם Je 9^{15} 49^{37}; abs. ψ $59^{14.14}$; so also (si vera l.) 74^{11} (see VB; Bi Che בְּקֶרֶב חֵיקְךָ תְּכַלֶּא and thy right hand (why) *keepest thou in thy bosom*); acc.+בְּ instr. Je 14^{12} (by sword, famine, and pestilence); sts. the instrument of י׳'s judgment becomes grammat. subj.; subj. הַחֶרֶב Ho 11^{6} (obj. בַּדָּיו, of city; || אכל), subj. עָגֵל Is 27^{10} (obj. סְעִפֶּיהָ; || רָעָה), subj. flying roll Zc 5^{4} (obj. house). †**Pu.** *Pf.* 3 pl. כֻּלּוּ ψ 72^{20} *be finished, ended; Impf.* 3 mpl. וַיְכֻלּוּ Gn 2^{1} *be completed* (P).

†כָּלָה **n.f.** **completion, complete destruction, consumption, annihilation;** alw. 3617
this form;—**1.** *completion,* but only as adv., and dubious: *completely, altogether* Gn 18^{21} (J; rd. כֻּלָּם Ol Kau Buhl), Ex 11^{1} (si vera l.) **2.** *complete destruction, consumption, annihilation:* **a.** almost alw. by God, esp. עָשָׂה כ׳ Is 10^{23} (וְנֶחֱרָצָה+), Na 1^{8} (2 acc., si vera l.; Buhl ^{ZAW} $^{1885, 181}$ prop. בְּקָמָיו for מְקוֹמָהּ v. Id $^{HWB\ 12}$ Kau $^{AT, Text Krit. Erläut. p. 65}$; v. also מָקוֹם sub קום), v^{9} Je 4^{27} Ne 9^{31} (2 acc.); +אֵת pers.=*with,* pregn. sense,=*in dealing with* (cf. II. אֵת **1 d**), Zp 1^{18} (כ׳ אַךְ נִבְהָלָה), Je 5^{18} 30^{11}=46^{28} (אִתְּךָ=אֹתְךָ), Ez 11^{13} 20^{17} (אִתָּם=אוֹתָם); +בְּכָל־גּוֹיִם Je 30^{11} 46^{28}; without עשׂה: כ׳ וְנֶחֱרָצָה שָׁמַעְתִּי Is 28^{22}, עַד־כ׳ וְנ׳ Dn 9^{27} (on both cf. Is 10^{23} Zp 1^{18}); לְכָלָה *for annihilation* Ez 13^{13} (si vera l., v. Co), וְכ׳ אַל־ 2 Ch 12^{12}. **b.** by men, וְלֹא לְהַשְׁחִית לְכ׳ תַּעֲשׂוּ Je 5^{10}; וְכ׳ בְיָדוֹ Dn 11^{16} *and* (i.e. *with*) *annihilation in his hand.*

3616 †[כָּלֶה] **adj.** failing with desire, longing, only fpl. וְעֵינֶיךָ רֹאוֹת וְכָלוֹת אֲלֵיהֶם Dt 28³² *while thine eyes look and fail longingly for them* (cf. vb. כלה **Qal 2 b**, and כִּלָּיוֹן infr.)

3622 †כלוהי Kt, כְּלוּהוּ Qr **n.pr.m.** (? √ I. כלה)—one of those who had strange wives Ezr 10³⁵, 𝔊 Χελκεια, A Χελια, 𝔊L Χελιασουβ.

3631 †כִּלָּיוֹן **n.m. 1.** failing, pining; **2.** annihilation (on format. cf. Lag^BN 200);—**1.** cstr. כִּלְיוֹן עֵינַיִם Dt 28⁶⁵ *failing of eyes* (in longing, cf. foregoing, and v. Dr). **2.** כִּלָּיוֹן חָרוּץ Is 10²² *annihilation, strictly decided.*

3630 †כִּלְיוֹן **n.pr.m.** one of Naomi's sons Ru 1^2.5 4⁹, 𝔊 Κελαιων, Χελαιων, Χελεων, 𝔊L Χελλαιων (on etym. cf. Jer.; vid. Lag^Onom. ed. 2, 62, 5).

4357 †II. [מִכְלָה] **n.[f.]** completeness, perfection;—only pl. cstr. intens. מִכְלוֹת זָהָב 2 Ch 4²¹
4356 *perfections of gold* = purest gold.—I. מִכְלָה v. sub כלא. p. 476

8502 †תִּכְלָה **n.f.** completeness, perfection;—לְכָל־ת׳ רָאִיתִי קֵץ ψ 119⁹⁶ *to all perfection have I seen an end.*

8503 †תַּכְלִית **n.f.** end, completeness;—ת׳ abs. Jb 11⁷ 28³; cstr. Ne 3²¹ + 2 t.;—**1.** *end,* וְעַד־ת׳ בֵּית וגו׳ Ne 3²¹ *even unto the end of the house of* Eliashib; עַד־ת׳ אוֹר עִם־חֹשֶׁךְ Jb 26¹⁰ *unto the end of* (=boundary betw.) *light and darkness;* וּלְכָל־ת׳ הוּא חוֹקֵר 28³ *and to every end* (=to the farthest limit) *he exploreth;* עַד־ת׳ שַׁדַּי תִּמְצָא Jb 11⁷ *unto the end of Shadday wilt thou reach* (so as to know him fully)? **2.** *completeness,* as acc. of manner (Da^Synt. § 70 b) ת׳ שִׂנְאָה שְׂנֵאתִים ψ 139²² *with completeness of hatred I hate them.*

3627 כְּלִי ₃₂₄ **n.m.**^Ho 8, 8 article, utensil, vessel (NH *id.*; acc. to Thes fr. כלה = *conficere,* like Ger. *Zeug* fr. *zeugen;* prop. therefore anything *finished, made, produced,* acc. to Ba^ZMG 1887, 605 fr. meaning *enclose, contain;* he finds pl. of כְּלִי in כלאי M-I²³ (cf. כלאים))—כ׳ abs. Je 18⁴ +; הַכֶּלִי 1 S 17⁴⁹ 21⁶; cstr. כְּלִי Ho 13¹⁵ +; sf. כֶּלְיְךָ Dt 23²⁵; pl. כֵּלִים Ex 22⁶ +; cstr. כְּלֵי Gn 24⁵³ +; sf. כֵּלַי Gn 31³⁷ + 2 t.; כֵּלֶיךָ Gn 27³ Ez 12⁴; כֵּלֵינוּ 1 S 9⁷; כְּלֵיכֶם Gn 43¹¹ +; כְּלֵיהֶם Jos 7¹¹ +;—**1.** in gen., *article, object,* made of any material, *thing,* esp. thing of value כ׳ זָהָב 1 S 6^8.15 (images of mice, etc.), personal or household property Gn 31^37.37 (E; v^b כֹּל כְּלֵי־בֵיתֶךָ), 45²⁰ (E), כְּלֵי בֵית־טוֹבִיָּהוּ Ne 13¹⁸, Jos 7¹¹ (JE), כֶּסֶף אוֹ כֵלִים Ex 22⁶ (E) *money or articles* (property), כְּלִי־פָז Jb 28¹⁷ (appar. coll.); *things carried,* pl. = *stuff, load, baggage* (*impedimenta*) 1 S 17^22.22, appar. = *baggage-train* 10²² 25¹³ 30²⁴ Is 10²⁸; (cf. Gn 31³⁷ supr.); כְּלֵי גוֹלָה *things of exile,* i.e. the most necessary articles, such as exiles may take, Je 46¹⁹ Ez 12^3.4 b.7 b, cf. v^4 a.7 a; = *ornaments* or *jewels* Gn 24⁵³ (J; כ׳ כֶּסֶף וכ׳ זָהָב, prob. = ornaments), כ׳ כסף וכ׳ זהב also Ex 3²² 11² 12³⁵ (all E); Is 61¹⁰, Ex 35²² Nu 31⁵⁰, כְּלִי מַעֲשֶׂה v⁵¹ (all P), כְּלִי יְקָר Pr 20¹⁵ (in fig.), כ׳ תִּפְאַרְתֵּךְ Ez 16^17.39 23²⁶ (all in fig.); כְּלִי נְחֹשֶׁת as merchandise Ez 27¹³; כסף וזהב וּכְלֵי נְחֹשֶׁת כֵּלִים as cargo of ship Jon 1⁵; וּבַרְזֶל Jos 6^19.24 (JE; spoil of war); of any household article (on which one sits) Lv 15^4.6.22.23.26 (all P); of skin Nu 31²⁰, or wood v²⁰ (P); כְּלִי חֶמְדָּה Na 2¹⁰ *precious thing,* so Ho 13¹⁵ (fig.), Je 25³⁴ (sim.), 2 Ch 32²⁷ Dn 11⁸, כלי חֲמֻדוֹת 2 Ch 20²⁵ (appar. = ornaments); also כְּלִי אֵין־חֵפֶץ בּוֹ Je 22²⁸ (fig. of Coniah, ‖ עֶצֶב נִבְזֶה נָפוּץ), Ho 8⁸ (sim.; cf. Je 48³⁸ infr.); † specif. of *garments* (one's 'things'): כְּלִי־גֶבֶר Dt 22⁵ (‖ שִׂמְלַת אִשָּׁה), so כְּלִי־עוֹר Lv 13⁴⁹ (cf. מְלֶאכֶת עוֹר v⁴⁸), v^52.53.57.58.59 (all P). **2.** *utensil, implement, apparatus:* † **a.** *implement* of hunting and (esp.) war, = *weapon* Gn 27³ (J), 1 S 20⁴⁰ 21⁹ (גַּם חַרְבִּי וְגַם כֵּלַי), 1 K 11⁸ = 2 Ch 23⁷, 1 K 11¹¹ Is 54^16.17 Je 22⁷; prob. also Nu 35³², כְּלִי בַרְזֶל v¹⁶, כְּלִי עֵץ־יָד v¹⁸ (all P); כְּלֵי חָמָס Gn 49⁵ (poem); כְּלִי מַשְׁחֵתוֹ Ez 9¹, כ׳ מַפָּצוֹ v²; fig. of God's weapons כְּלֵי־מָוֶת ψ 7¹⁴ (‖ חִצָּיו); כ׳ זַעְמוֹ Is 13⁵ Je 50²⁵; of entire equipment of warrior, *armour* or *armament* offensive and defensive 1 S 17⁵⁴ (cf. v^5 ff.), 21^6.6 (v. Dr^Sm 139.293), 31^9.10 = 1 Ch 10^9.10; hence (כֵּלָיו) נֹשֵׂא כֵלִים *armour-* or *weapon-bearer* Ju 9⁵⁴ 1 S 14^1.6.7.12.12.13.13.14.17 16²¹ 31^4.4.5.6 = 1 Ch 10^4.4.5, 2 S 18¹⁵ 23³⁷ = 1 Ch 11³⁹; fig. וְכֵלַי כֵּלָיו רָעִים Is 32⁷ *and a knave, his weapons* (i.e. devices, Che 'machinations') *are evil;* more precisely כְּלִי מִלְחָמָה Ju 18^11.16.17 1 S 8¹² 2 S 1²⁷ Dt 1⁴¹ Je 21⁴ 50²⁰ (fig.), Ez 32²⁷ 1 Ch 12³⁴ (van d. H v³³); כְּלֵי צְבָא מִלְחָמָה 1 Ch 12³⁸ (van d. H v³⁷); כְּלֵי קְרָב Ec 9¹⁸; בֵּית כֵּלָיו 2 K 20¹³ = Is 39² is perh. *armoury;* כ׳ Ez 40⁴² is sacrificial knife. † **b.** *instrument* of music כְּלֵי (הַ)שִּׁיר Am 6⁵ 1 Ch 15¹⁶ 16⁴² 2 Ch 5¹³ 7⁶ 23¹³ 34¹²; כְּלֵי דָוִיד 29^26.27, כ׳־שִׁיר דָּוִיד Ne 12³⁶; כְּלִי נֶבֶל ψ 71²², כ׳ נְבָלִים 1 Ch 16⁵; כֵּלִים alone 1 Ch 23⁵, cf. Nu 31[6] (P; כְּלֵי הַקֹּדֶשׁ);—for בִּכְלֵי עֹז (ליהוה) 2 Ch 30[21] rd. בְּכָל־עֹז (Kau[AT], cf. Be). †**c.** *implement* of labour, *tool* כ׳ בַּרְזֶל 1 K 6[7], or of one's calling, pursuit קַח־לְךָ כְּלִי רֹעֶה אֱוִלִי Zc 11[15] (otherwise 1 S 17[40], v. **3**). †**d.** *equipment* of oxen (yoke, etc.) 2 S 24[22] 1 K 19[21]. †**e.** כְּלֵי רִכְבּוֹ 1 S 8[12] *his chariot-equipments.* **f.** as gen. term for *utensils* and *furniture* of Sol.'s palace 1 K 10[21]=2 Ch 9[20]; esp. (very oft.) of tabern. Ex 25[9.39] 27[3]+ (in Hex alw. P), and temple 1 K 7[45.47.48] 2 K 12[14]+; of both palace and temple Je 27[18.19.21]; combinations are כְּלֵי הַמִּשְׁכָּן Ex 27[19], כ׳ בֵּית י׳ Is 52[11], כ׳ יהוה 38[3], כ׳ הַמִּזְבֵּחַ Je 27[16] 28[3.6] Ezr 1[7], כ׳ בֵּית י׳, כְּלֵי חֶמְדַּת בֵּית 2 Ch 36[10], כ׳ בֵּית אֱלֹהִים 2 Ch 28[24.24] 36[18] Ne 13[9] Dn 1[2], כ׳ הַמִּקְדָּשׁ Ne 10[40]; כ׳ הַשָּׁרֵת Nu 4[12] *utensil of ministry,* כ׳ עֲבוֹדַת בֵּית י׳ 1 Ch 9[28] 28[14.14], כ׳ עֲבֹדָתָם Nu 4[26] 1 Ch 28[13], כ׳ מִשְׁמֶרֶת מַשָּׂאָם Nu 4[32]; also כ׳ הַקֹּדֶשׁ 1 K 8[4] 1 Ch 9[29]; of *appliances* of idol-worship 2 K 23[4]. **3.** *vessel, receptacle,* of various materials and for various purposes Gn 43[11] (J); 1 S 9[7] Dt 23[25]; =*sack* Gn 42[25] (E; שַׂק in ‖ cl., cf. אַמְתַּחַת v[27]); כְּלִי הָרֹעִים *shepherd's bag* or *wallet* 1 S 17[40], cf. v[49]; כ׳ חֶרֶשׂ Je 32[14] is *earthenware receptacle* for deed of sale; for liquids 1 K 17[10] 2 K 4[3.3.4.6.6.6], כ׳ מַשְׁקֶה 1 K 10[21]=2 Ch 9[20], כְּלֵי שַׁמְנָהּ Nu 4[9], cf. v[10]; וְלֹא הוּרַק מִכְּלִי אֶל־כֶּלִי Je 48[11] (fig.), cf. v[12] (‖ נְבָלִים); for cooking Lv 6[21] (כ׳ חֶרֶשׂ), v[21] (כ׳ נְחֹשֶׁת); v. also (הַ)יּוֹצֵר 2 S 17[28] Je 19[11] (sim.), ψ 2[9] (sim.), כְּלִי לַצֹּרֵף Pr 25[4]; כ׳ פָּתוּחַ Nu 19[15] *an open (uncovered) vessel.* כ׳ טָהוֹר Is 66[20] *a clean vessel;* fig. of Eliakim's relatives כְּלֵי הַקָּטָן מִכְּלֵי הָאַגָּנוֹת וְעַד כָּל־כְּלֵי הַנְּבָלִים Is 22[24] *the vessels of smallness* (Da[Synt. § 32, R. 5]), *from the basin-vessels to all the pitcher-vessels.* †**4.** specif. כְּלֵי־גֹמֶא Is 18[2] *vessels* (boats) *of paper-reed.*

II. **כלה** (√ of foll.; meaning unknown).

3629 †[כִּלְיָה] **n.f.** only pl. **kidneys** (NH כִּלְיָה
(pl.); Aram. כּוּלְיָא or כּוֹלְיָא (only pl.), ܟܘܠܝܬܐ; Eth. ኵሊት: 𝔊 οἱ νεφροί);—abs. pl. כְּלָיוֹת Je 11[20] +5 t.; כְּלָית Ex 29[13] +13 t.; cstr. כִּלְיוֹת Dt 32[14] Is 34[6]; sf. כִּלְיוֹתַי Jb 16[13]+2 t.; כִּלְיֹתָי Jb 19[27]; כִּלְיוֹתָי ψ 16[7] Pr 23[16]; כִּלְיֹתָי ψ 139[13] La 3[13]; כִּלְיוֹתֵיהֶם Je 12[2];—*kidneys:* **1.** lit., as physical organ, **a.** of man, only poet., as created by י׳ ψ 139[13]; as the most sensitive and vital part, in metaph. of one wounded by י׳'s arrows Jb 16[13] La 3[13]. **b.** of sacrificial animals, offered as choice part to י׳ Lv 3[4.10.15] 4[9] 7[4] 9[10.19]; שְׁתֵּי הַכ׳ Ex 29[13.22] Lv 3[4.10.15] 4[9] 7[4] 8[16.25] (all P); in fig. of sacrif. Edomites חֵלֶב כִּלְיוֹת אֵילִים Is 34[6]; transferred to wheat, חֵלֶב כִּלְיוֹת חִטָּה Dt 32[14] *kidney-fat* (i.e. the choicest, richest) *of wheat.* **2.** fig., as seat of emotion and affection Jb 19[27] Pr 23[16] ψ 16[7] 73[21]; קָרוֹב אַתָּה בְּפִיהֶם וְרָחוֹק מִכּ׳ Je 12[2] *near art thou in their mouth, and far from their affections;* hence, as involving character, the obj. of God's examination, alw. ‖ לֵב: בֹּחֵן כ׳ וָלֵב Je 11[20] cf. ψ 7[10], בֹּחֵן צַדִּיק רֹאֶה כ׳ וָלֵב Je 17[10], חֹקֵר לֵב בֹּחֵן כ׳ 20[12], צָרְפָה כ׳ וְלִבִּי ψ 26[2].

כְּלוּלָה, כַּלָּה v. sub II. כלל. p. 483 3618, 3623

כלח (√ of I. כֶּלַח, mng. dub.; Ar. كَلَحَ is *contract the face, look hard, stern;* كُلَاحٌ, كَلَاحِ *a hard year* (through dearth, etc.)).

†I. **כֶּלַח** **n.m.** poss. **firm or rugged strength** 3624
(v. √ supr.), תָּבוֹא בְכֶ׳ אֱלֵי־קָבֶר Jb 5[26] *thou shalt come in firm strength* (with thy body vigorous, powers unimpaired) *unto the grave;* עָלֵימוֹ אָבַד כָּלַח 30[2] *upon whom vigour has perished.*

†II. [כֶּלַח], כָּלַח **n.pr.loc.** city in Assyria 3625
Gn 10[11.12]=As. *Kalḫu*, Schr[COT ad loc.] Dl[Par 261], mod. *Nimrûd*, at NE. angle of Upper Zab and Tigris (v. Billerbeck u. Jeremias BAS[iii. 1895, 130 ff.])

†כָּל־חֹזֶה† **n.pr.m.** **1.** father of one of the 3626
builders, Shallun Ne 3[15]. **2.** a name in Judah Ne 11[5] (relation to **1** unknown).

כְּלִי, כִּלָּיוֹן, etc., v. sub I. כלה. p. 479 3627, 3631

כְּלָיָה v. sub II. כלה. above 3629

כַּלְכֵּל **vb.**, **כַּלְכֹּל** **n.pr.m.** v. sub כול. p. 465 3557, 3633

†I. **כלל** **vb. complete, perfect** (NH *com-* 3634
prehend, include, Pi. *complete,* כְּלָל *a general rule,* בִּכְלָל *in general;* BAram. and Syr. Shaph. שַׁכלל, ܫܲܟܠܸܠ *complete, finish;* As. *kalâlu* III. 1. 2. *complete;* Ar. كَلَّ is *be wearied, fatigued;* Aram. כְּלִילָא, ܟܠܝܠܐ is *a crown,* hence den. אַכְלֵיל, ܟܲܠܸܠ *to crown;* Eth. I. 2 ከለለ: *to crown,* አክሊል: *a crown,* ተክሊል: *crowning* (of bride), *nuptials;* Ar. إِكْلِيلٌ *a crown,* loan-word (Frä[62])):—Ez 27[4] בֹּנַיִךְ כָּלְלוּ יָפְיֵךְ thy builders have *perfected* thy beauty (of Tyre, under fig. of ship), v[11].

3605 כֹּל כָּל once כּוֹל (Je 33^{9} Kt.), **n.m.** *the whole, all* (Moab., Ph., *id.*; Aram. כֹּל, ܟܠ; Ar. كُلٌّ; Sab. כל, cf. DHM$^{Epigr. Denk. 36-38}$; Eth. ኵሉ: As. *kullatu*)—abs. כֹּל, cstr. כֹּל Gn 2$^{5.16.20}$ + oft., once כֹּל־ ψ 138^{2} (v. Ba), but more usu. כָּל־ (with makk.: without it, † ψ 35^{10} Pr 19^{7}; Kö$^{i. 84, 95}$); sf. 2 ms. in p. כֻּלָּךְ †Mi 2^{12}; 2 fs. כֻּלֵּךְ †Is 14$^{29.31}$, כֻּלָּךְ †Is 22^{1} Ct 4^{7} (perh. for assonance with accompanying בָּךְ, לָךְ); 3 ms. כֻּלֹּה 2 S 2^{9} (v. Dr) + 17 t. (never in Pent.), כֻּלּוֹ Gn 25^{25} + 16 t.; 3 fs. כֻּלָּהּ Gn 13^{10} + 15 t., כֻּלָּא †Ez 36^{5}; כֻּלָּנוּ (16 t.); כֻּלְּכֶם (18 t.); כֻּלָּם (oft.), כּוּלָּם †Je 31^{34}, כֻּלָּהֵם †2 S 23^{6} (and prob. Je 15^{10} כֻּלְּהֶם); 3 fpl. כֻּלָּנָה †Gn 42^{36} Pr 31^{29}; כֻּלְּהֶנָה: † 1 K 7^{37}:—*the whole,* **1.** with foll. gen. (as usually) *the whole of*, to be rendered, however, often in our idiom, to avoid stiffness, *all* or *every*: **a.** Gn 2^{2} כָּל־צְבָאָם *the whole of* their host, v^{13} כָּל־אֶרֶץ כּוּשׁ *the whole of* the land of Kush; כָּל־הַלַּיְלָה *the whole of* the night; כָּל־יִשְׂרָאֵל *the whole of* Israel = *all* Israel; Dt 4^{29} בְּכָל־לְבָבְךָ with *the whole of* thy heart = with *all* thy heart; + very oft. With a *plural* noun, usu. determined by the art. or a genitive: Gn 5^{5} כל־ימי אדם *the whole of* (= *all*) the days of Adam, 37^{35} כל־בניו *the whole of* (= *all*) his sons, Is 2^{2} כל־הגוים *all* the nations; Gn 43^{9} + oft. כל הימים = *continually*. In poetry, however, the noun may remain undetermined, כָּל־יָדַיִם *the whole of* hands = *every* hand, Is 13^{7} Jer 48^{37} Ez 21^{12}; כל־פנים i.e. *every* face Is 25^{8} Joel 2^{6}; כל שלחנות Is 28^{8}; כל חוצות 51^{20} La 2^{19} al. Before an inf. †Gn 30^{41} Dt 4^{7} 1 K 8^{52} 1 Ch 23^{31}. Freq. with sfs., as כֻּלּוֹ (כֻּלֹּה) *the whole of him* Gn 25^{25} Jb 21^{23} Ct 5^{16}, *the whole of it* Lv 13^{13} Je 2^{21} Na 2^{1} Pr 24^{31}; כֻּלָּהּ *the whole of it* Gn 13^{10} Ex 19^{18} 25^{36} Am 8^{8}; כֻּלָּךְ *all of thee* Ct 4^{7} + (v. ad init.); כֻּלָּנוּ *the whole of us* Gn 42^{11} Dt 5^{3} Is 53$^{6.6}$; כֻּלְּכֶם Dt 1^{22} 4^{4} 1 S 22$^{7.7}$; כֻּלָּם Gn 11^{6} 43^{34} Jos 8^{24} ויפלו כֻלָּם, Ju 11^{6} בְּנֵי כֻלָּם, Is 7^{19} 31^{3} + oft.—Twice, strangely, with hyperb. intensive force, ψ 39^{6} כָּל־הֶבֶל *the whole of* vanity are all men (? om. כל, as v^{12}), 45^{14} כָּל־כְּבוּדָּה *the whole of* gloriousness is the king's daughter. **b.** followed often by a singular, to be understood *collectively*, whether with or without the art.: Gn 1^{21} את כל נפש החיה *the whole of* living souls = every living soul, 2^{9} כל עץ נחמד למראה *the whole of* trees (every kind of tree) pleasant to view, 6^{12} + כָּל־בָּשָׂר, 7^{14} כל צפור כל כנף *all* birds of *every kind of* wing (so Ez 17^{23}), v^{21} כל האדם the whole of mankind (so Nu 12^{3} 16^{29} Ju 16^{17} al.); poet. כל־אדם ψ 39^{6} 64^{10} +; 1 S 14^{52} כל איש גבור וכל־בן־חיל, 17$^{19.24}$ כל איש ישראל, 22^{2}; Is 9^{16} כל פה *the whole of* mouths = every mouth, 15^{2} 24^{10} כָּל־בַּיִת + oft. (in 2$^{12-16}$ the sg. and pl. interchange); ψ 7^{12} + בכל־יום, 10^{5} + בכל־עת = at *all* seasons. So כל־העץ Gn 1^{29}, כל־הבן Ex 1^{22} = *all* the sons, כל־המרכב 20^{24} Dt 11^{24} = *all* the places, כל־המקום Lv 15^{9}, v^{26} Dt 4^{3} כל־האיש אשר = all the *men* who . . ., 15^{19} כל־הבכור, Je 4^{29} כל־העיר עזובה *all* the cities (notice the foll. בָּהֵן); כל־היום = *all* the days (v. יום **7 f**), etc. In late Heb. extended to such phrases as בְּכָל־דּוֹר וָדוֹר † ψ 45^{18} 145^{13} Est 9^{28}; בכל־עיר ועיר † 2 Ch 11^{12} 28^{25} 31^{19} Est 8$^{11.17}$ 9^{28}; † 2 Ch 32^{28} Est 2^{11} 3^{14} 4^{3} 8$^{13.17}$ 9$^{21.27.28.28.28}$ (cf. וְ **1 i** *b*). **c.** the gen. after כל is oft. a rel. sentence, introduced by אשר: Gn 1^{31} את כל אשר עשה *the whole* of what he had made, 7^{22} 13^{1} + very oft. Sts., with a prep., כל אשר has the force of *wheresoever, whithersoever*, as Jos 1^{7} בְּכֹל אֲשֶׁר תֵּלֵךְ *wheresoever* thou goest, v^{16} אֶל־כָּל־אֲשֶׁר *whithersoever* (see אֲשֶׁר **4 b** γ). Very rarely in such cases is there ellipse of the rel., as Gn 39^{4} וְכָל־יֶשׁ־לוֹ נָתַן בְּיָדִי (contrast v$^{5.8}$), Ex 9^{4} מכל־לבני ישראל, Is 38^{16} ψ 71^{18} לְכָל־יָבוֹא, וּלְכָל־בָּהֶן חַיֵּי רוּחִי (74^{3}, v. **2 a**), 2 Ch 32^{31}; peculiarly also in Chr (Dr$^{Intr 505}$), 1 Ch 29^{3} מִכָּל־הֲכִינוֹתִי, 2 Ch 30$^{18 f.}$ Ezr 1^{6}; cf. with כֹּל (**2 a**) 1 Ch 29^{11a} 2 Ch 30^{17} Ezr 1^{5}. **d.** with a *suffix* two idiomatic uses of כל have to be noticed: (*a*) כל is often made more independent and emphatic by being placed with a suffix *after* the word which it qualifies, to which it then stands in apposition (cf. in Syr., Ar., Eth.), as 2 S 2^{9} יִשְׂרָאֵל כֻּלֹּה, Jer 13^{19} 48^{31} Is 9^{8} 14$^{29.31}$ פלשת כלך Philistia, *all of* thee! Mi 2^{12} Hb 2^{6} Jb 34^{13} ψ 67$^{4.6}$; esp. in Ezek., as 14^{5} 29^{2} מצרים כֻּלָּהּ 32$^{12.30}$; with change of person (cf. the idiom in Is 22^{16} 48^{1} 54^{1} etc.), 1 K 22^{28} = Mi 1^{2} שמעו עמים כלם Hear, nations, *all of* them! Mal 3^{9} הַגּוֹי כֻּלּוֹ. So even with כל preceding: Nu 16^{3} כָּל־הָעֵדָה כֻּלָּם, Is 14^{18} Jer 30^{16} Ez 11^{15} כל בית ישראל כֻּלֹּה *the whole of* the house of Israel, *the whole of* it (so 20^{40} 36^{10}), 35^{15} 36^{5} ψ 8^{8} (cf. Sab. DHM$^{l. c.}$); (*b*) with the sf. of 3 ms., understood as referring to the *mass* of things or persons meant, כֻּלֹּה or כֻּלּוֹ, lit. *the whole of it*, is equivalent to *all of them, every one*, †Ex 14^{7} and captains עַל־כֻּלּוֹ upon *the whole of it* (the רֶכֶב collectively)=*all of them*, Is 1^{23} *the whole of* it (the people) loveth bribes, 9^{16} 15^{3} Jer 6$^{13.13}$ 8$^{6.10.10}$ 20^{7} Hab 1$^{9.15}$ ψ 29^{9} and in his temple כֻּלּוֹ אֹמֵר כָּבוֹד *the whole of* it (=every one there) says, Glory! 53^{4} (‖ 14^{3} הַכֹּל); perh. Is 16^{7} Je 48^{38}; + Pr 19^{6} Ew Hi (וְכֻלֹּה רֵעַ): Je 15^{10} rd. כֻּלְּהֶם קִלְלוּנִי. **e.** Heb. idiom in certain cases affirms, or denies, of an *entire* class, where Engl. idiom affirms, or denies, of an *individual* of the class; thus in a compar. or hypoth. sentence כל is=*any*, and with a neg. =*none*: (*a*) Gn 3^{1} the serpent was more subtil מכל חית השׂדה than *all* beasts of the field (in our idiom: than *any* beast of the field), Dt 7^{7} 1 S 9^{2}; (*b*) Lv 4^{2} a soul when it sins through ignorance מכל מצות י״י in *all* the commandments of Jehovah (=in *any* of the commandments, etc.), 19^{23} when ye ... plant כל־עץ מאכל=*any* tree for food, Nu 35^{22} or if he have cast upon him כָּל־כְּלִי=*any* weapon, 1 K 8^{37b}; joined with a ptcp. in a hypoth. sense (Dr$^{§121 n.}$ Ges$^{§116.5 R.5}$), Gn 4^{14} כל מצאי *all my finders* (=if any one find me), he will slay me, v^{15a} Nu 21^{8} כָּל־הַנָּשׁוּךְ=*whosoever* (=if *any one*) is bitten, 1 S 2^{13}; (*c*) with a neg., Gn 2^{5} *all* plants of the field טֶרֶם יִהְיֶה were not as yet=no plant of the field as yet was, 4^{15b} לבלתי הכות־אתו כל־מצאו for the not-smiting him of all finding him= that none finding him should smite him, Ex 10^{15} ולא־נותר כל ירק=and no green things were left, 12^{16} כל־מלאכה לא יעשׂה *all* work shall not be done=no work shall be done, Dt 28^{14} Ju 13^{4} אַל־תֹּאכְלִי כָּל־טָמֵא eat not of *all that is* unclean, 19^{19} אֵין מַחְסוֹר כָּל־דָּבָר there is no lack of *all things* i.e. of *any thing*, ψ 143^{2} כי לא־יצדק לפניך כל־חי, + very oft. (so οὐ πᾶς, as a Hebraism, in the N. T., e.g. Mk 13^{20} οὐκ ἂν ἐσώθη πᾶσα σάρξ, Lk 1^{37} οὐκ ἀδυνατήσει . . . . πᾶν ῥῆμα, as Jer 32^{17} לֹא־יִפָּלֵא מִמְּךָ כָּל־דָּבָר, Gal 2^{16} οὐ δικαιωθήσεται...πᾶσα σάρξ, etc.) Usu., in such cases, כל (or its gen.) is without the art., being left purposely indef.: in ψ 49^{18} (**2 b** *a*) הַכֹּל is emph. (In Nu 23^{13} וְכֻלּוֹ לֹא תִרְאֶה the context shews that כֹּל is opp. to a part). **f.** very anomalously, severed from its gen., † 2 S 1^{9} כִּי־כָל־עוֹד נַפְשִׁי בִּי, Jb 27^{3} כִּי־כָל־עוֹד נִשְׁמָתִי בִי, Ho 14^{3} (si vera l.) כָּל־תִּשָּׂא עָוֺן. On Ec 5^{15} כָּל־עֻמַּת־שֶׁ׳ v. עֻמָּה.

Note.—When the gen. after כל is a noun fem. or pl., the pred. usu. agrees with this (as being the really important idea), e.g. Gn 5^{5} ויהיו כל ימי אדם, Nu 14^{1} וַתִּשָּׂא כָּל־הָעֵדָה, Nah 3^{1} ψ 150^{6} כֹּל הַנְּשָׁמָה תְּהַלֵּל; exceptions being very rare, Is 64^{10b} Pr 16^{2} (Ges$^{§141.1 R.2}$).

2. Absolutely: †**a.** without the art., *all things, all* (mostly neuter, but sts. m.), the sense in which 'all' is to be taken being gathered fr. the context, Gn 9^{3} נתתי לכם את כֹּל, 16^{12} וְיַד כֹּל בּוֹ, 20^{16} ואת כֹּל ונוכחת, 33^{11} וכי יש לי כל, Nu 8^{16} בכור כֹּל מבני ישראל, 11^{6} אֵין כֹּל *nought of all things!* = *there is nothing* (so †2 S 12^{3} Pr 13^{7}, cf. 2 K 4^{2}), 13^{2} כֹּל נשׂיא בהם (cf. 2 S 23^{28} 1 Ch 3^{9}: usu. so הַכֹּל), Dt 28^{47} מֵרֹב כֹּל, v$^{48.37}$ בְּחֹסֶר כֹּל (cf. Je 44^{18}), Is 30^{5} כֹּל הִבְאִישׁ *all* exhibit shame, 44^{24} י׳ עֹשֶׂה־כֹּל, Je 44^{12} וְתַמּוּ כֹל (unusual), Zp 1^{2} ψ 8^{7} 74^{3} (rd. כֹּל הֵרַע), 145^{15} עיני כל, Pr 16^{4} 26^{10} 28^{5} Jb 13^{1} הן כֹּל ראתה עיני, 42^{2} 1 Ch 29^{11b} 2 Ch 32^{22} (m.), Dn 11^{37} (v. also **1 c** *end*); מִכֹּל Gn 6$^{19.20b}$ שְׁנַיִם מִכֹּל, 14^{20} 27^{33} Je 17^{9} עקוב הלב מִכֹּל, Dn 11^{2} (m.) After a neg. = *anything*, Dt 4^{25} תְּמוּנַת כֹּל the likeness of *anything*, 8^{9} 28^{55} Pr 30^{30}. In the gen. also, very rarely, to express the idea of *all* as comprehensively as possible: Ez 44^{30} כָּל־בִּכּוּרֵי כֹל וְכָל־תְּרוּמַת כֹּל; ψ 119^{128} (si vera l.) כָּל־פִּקּוּדֵי כֹל all the statutes *about everything*. †**b.** with art. הַכֹּל: (*a*) where the sense is limited by the context to things (or persons) just mentioned, Ex 29^{24} ושׂמת הַכֹּל ביד אהרן, Lv 1^{9} והקטיר הכהן את הַכֹּל, v^{13} 8^{27} Dt 2^{36} את הַכֹּל נתן י׳ לפנינו, Jos 11^{19} (cf. 2 S 19^{31} 1 K 14^{26} = 2 Ch 12^{9}), 21^{43} הַכֹּל בָּא (cf. 23^{14}), 1 S 30^{19} הַכֹּל השׁיב דוד, 2 S 17^{3} (corrupt: v. 𝔊 Dr), 24^{23} (1 Ch 21^{23}), 1 K 6^{18} הַכֹּל ארז (cf. 7^{33} 2 K 25^{17}=Je 52^{22}), 2 K 24^{16} הַכֹּל גבורים, Is 65^{8} לבלתי השׁחית הַכֹּל, ψ 14^{3}; or implied, Gn 16^{12} יָדוֹ בַכֹּל, 24^{1} ברך את אברהם בַּכֹּל, 2 S 23^{5} (poet.) עֲרֻכָה בַכֹּל, Is 29^{11} (peculiarly) חָזוּת הַכֹּל the vision *of the whole*, Je 13$^{7.10}$ לא יצלח לַכֹּל, Ez 7^{14} וְהָכִין הַכֹּל (but Co וְהָכִינוּ הָכֵן), ψ 49^{18} לא במותו יקח הַכֹּל: more freq. later, viz. 1 Ch 7^{5} (as regards *all*), 28^{19} 29^{19} 2 Ch 28^{6} 29^{28} 31^{5} 35^{7} 36$^{17.18}$ Ezr 1^{11} 2^{42} 8$^{34.35}$ 10^{17} (וַיְכַלּוּ בַכֹּל: v. BeRy), Ec 5^{8} (בַּכֹּל, appar.=*in all respects*), 10^{19} 12^{13}. (*b*) in a wider sense, *all*, whether of all mankind or of all living things, the universe (τὸ πᾶν), or of all the circumstances of life (chiefly late), Je 10^{16}=51^{19} כי יוצר הַכֹּל הוא,

ψ 103^{19} (cf. 1 Ch 29^{12}), 119^{21} הַכֹּל עֲבָדֶיךָ, 145^{9} טוֹב י׳ לַכֹּל, 1 Ch 29$^{12.14.16}$ Dn 11^{2}, and esp. in Ec., as 1$^{2.14}$ 2$^{11.17}$ 3^{19} 12^{8} הַכֹּל הֶבֶל, 2^{16} הכל נשׁכח, 3^{1} לַכֹּל זְמָן, v$^{11.19.20}$ 6^{6} 7^{15} 9$^{1.2.2.3}$ 10$^{3.19}$ 11^{5}. כַּכֹּל, †Jb 24^{24} (si vera l.) כַּכֹּל יִקָּפְצוּן like *all* men (i.e. like men in general).

3632 †כָּלִיל **adj.** and **subst.** **entire, whole, holocaust,** cstr. כְּלִיל, fem. constr. כְּלִילַת:—**1. adj.** Ez 16^{14} (of Jerus.) the report כִּי כָּלִיל הוּא בְּיָפְיֵךְ, 28^{12} כְּלִיל יֹפִי׃ (of the king of Tyre) *entire, perfect* in beauty; 27^{3} אֲנִי כְּלִילַת יֹפִי׃ (of Tyre), La 2^{15} (of Jerus.) הֲזֹאת הָעִיר שֶׁיֹּאמְרוּ כְּלִילַת יֹפִי. **2. subst. a.** *entirety, whole,* Ex 28^{31} thou shalt make the robe of the ephod כְּלִיל תְּכֵלֶת a *whole* of purple (i.e. wholly purple); so 39^{22}; Nu 4^{6} בֶּגֶד כְּלִיל תְּכֵלֶת; Ju 20^{40} והנה עלה כְּלִיל־הָעִיר השׁמימה the *whole* of the city (perh. with allusion to mng. **b**); as adv. acc., Is 2^{18} וְהָאֱלִילִים כָּלִיל יַחֲלֹף will pass away *in entirety, wholly.* **b.** as a sacrif. term, *entire-* or *whole-*offering, *holocaust,* of a sacrifice consumed *wholly* on the altar (cf. Ph. כלל CIS$^{I. i, 165, 167}$; RS$^{Rel. Sem. 237}$), usu. a descriptive syn. of עוֹלָה: Dt 33^{10} יָשִׂימוּ קְטוֹרָה בְּאַפֶּךָ וְכָלִיל עַל מִזְבְּחֶךָ׃; ψ 51^{21} אז תחפץ זבחי צדק עולה וְכָלִיל, in app. 1 S 7^{9} ויעלה עולה כָּלִיל ליהוה; of the priests' מִנְחָה, Lv 6^{15} ליהוה כָּלִיל תָּקְטָר, v^{16} וְכָל־מִנְחַת כֹּהֵן כָּלִיל תִּהְיֶה לֹא תֵאָכֵל; fig. Dt 13^{17} (of idol. city) ושׂרפת באשׁ את־העיר ואת־כל שׁללה כָּלִיל לי׳ אלהיך and thou shalt burn the city and all its spoil as *a whole-offering* to י׳.

4358 †מִכְלוֹל **n.m. perfection,** i.e. (prob.) **gorgeous attire,** Ez 23^{12} 38^{4} (of warriors) לְבֻשֵׁי מִכְלוֹל.

4360 †[מַכְלֻל] **n.m. a thing made perfect,** i.e. (prob.) **gorgeous garment** (or **stuff**), Ez 27^{24} הֵמָּה רֹכְלַיִךְ בְּמַכְלֻלִים בִּגְלוֹמֵי תְּכֵלֶת וְרִקְמָה וג׳.

4359 †מִכְלָל **n.m. completeness, perfection,** ψ 50^{2} מִצִּיּוֹן מִכְלַל יֹפִי out of Zion, the *perfection* of beauty (cf. כָּלִיל **1**), hath God shined.

II. כלל (assumed as √ of foll., but dubious; cf. NH כַּלָּה; Aram. כַּלְּתָא, ܟܠܬܐ; Ar. كَنَّةٌ; As. *kallâtu,* expl. by Dl$^{Prol. 130 f.}$ (cf. Id$^{HWB 330}$) as prop. *closed bridal chamber* (ideogr. = *closed chamber*), fr. √ כלא or כלה, thence *bride* (cf. *harem*); acc. to RS$^{K 136 f. 292}$ כַּלָּה = *one closed in,* or *reserved* (sc. for her husband); Ges al. *one crowned* (cf. Aram. etc. כלילא *crown*), but form much against this; Nö$^{ZMG 1886, 737}$ 'ventures no explanation').

†כַּלָּה **n.f. daughter-in-law, bride**;—abs. 3618
כ׳ Je 2^{32} + 14 t.; sf. כַּלָּתוֹ Gn 11^{31} + 5 t.; כַּלָּתָהּ Ru 1^{22} + 2 t., etc.; pl. sf. כַּלֹּתֶיהָ Ru 1$^{6.8}$, כַּלּוֹתֶיהָ 1^{7}, כַּלּוֹתֵיהֶם Ho 4$^{13.14}$;—**1.** *daughter-in-law,* in ref. to husband's father Gn 38$^{11.16.24}$ (J), cf. 1 Ch 2^{4}, 1 S 4^{19} Ez 22^{11} Mi 7^{6} Gn 11^{31} (P), Lv 18^{15} 20^{12} (both H); husband's mother Ru 1$^{6.7.8.22}$ 2$^{20.22}$ 4^{15}. **2.** *bride,* usu. **a.** just before marriage Is 49^{18} 61^{10} 62^{5} Je 2^{32} (all in sim., etc.), ‖ חָתָן 7^{34} 16^{9} 25^{10} 33^{11} Jo 2^{16}; Ct 4$^{8.9.10.11.12}$ 5^{1}. **b.** also just after marriage = *young wife* Ho 4$^{13.14}$; rd. הַכַּלָּה likewise 2 S 17^{3} (for MT הַכֹּל), 𝔊 We Dr Klo Kit Bu.

†[כְּלוּלָה] **n. f. betrothal**; — only pl. 3623
כְּלוּלֹתָיִךְ (cf. '*espousals*') Je 2^{2} *thy betrothal-time* (‖ נְעוּרַיִךְ).

†כְּלָל **n.pr.m.** one of those who took strange 3636
wives Ezr 10^{30}, 𝔊 Χαηλ, A Χαληλ, 𝔊L Χαλαμαναι.

†[כָּלַם] **vb.** only **Niph. Hoph. be humi-** 3637
liated, Hiph. humiliate (NH Hiph., *id.*; Aram. כְּלַם Aph. Ithpe.; Ar. كَلَمَ is *wound;* كَلَّمَ also *speak to, converse with*);—**Niph.** *Pf.* 2 fs. וְנִכְלַמְתְּ consec. Je 22^{22} + 2 t.; 1 s. נִכְלַמְתִּי Je 31^{19} Ezr 9^{6}, נִכְלָמְתִּי Is 50^{7}; 3 pl. נִכְלְמוּ Is 45^{16} + 2 t.; *Impf.* 3 fs. תִּכָּלֵם Nu 12^{14}; 2 fs. תִּכָּלְמִי Is 54^{4}; 3 mpl. יִכָּלְמוּ Is 41^{11} + 5 t.; 2 mpl. תִּכָּלְמוּ Is 45^{17}; *Imv.* mpl. הִכָּלְמוּ Ez 36^{32}; *Inf. cstr.* הִכָּלֵם Je 3^{3} 8^{12}; *Pt.* נִכְלָם ψ 74^{21}; mpl. נִכְלָמִים 2 S 10^{5} + 2 t.; fpl. נִכְלָמוֹת Ez 16^{27};—*be humiliated, ashamed, put to shame, dishonoured, confounded:* **1.** *be humiliated, ashamed,* before men Nu 12^{14} (E), 2 S 10^{5} = 1 Ch 19^{5}, 2 S 19^{4}, cf. ψ 74^{21}; before enemies (by defeat, etc.) Is 45^{17} (‖ בושׁ), 50^{7} 54^{4} (‖ בושׁ, חפר); before God, sq. לְ inf., וְנִכְלַמְתִּי אֱלֹהַי לְהָרִים פָּנַי אֵלֶיךָ Ezr 9^{6} (‖ בושׁ); Je 3^{3} Ez 16$^{27.54}$ (‖ נָשָׂא כְלִמָּה), 43$^{10.11}$ (all + מִן caus.) 16^{61}, so prob. Levites, at Hezekiah's reforms 2 Ch 30^{15}. **2.** *be put to shame, dishonoured, confounded,* by judgments of י׳, all ‖ בושׁ: Je 22^{22} (מִן of cause), Ez 36^{32} (*id.*), Je 31^{19} (כִּי of cause), 8^{12} Is 41^{11} 45^{16} (+ הָלְכוּ בַכְּלִמָּה), ψ 35^{4} 69^{7}; + חפר ψ 40^{15} 70^{3}. **Hiph.** *Pf.* 3 ms. sf. הִכְלִמוֹ 1 S 20^{34}; 3 mpl. sf. הֶכְלַמְנוּם (Ges$^{§ 53, 3 R. 6}$) 1 S 25^{7}; *Impf.* יַכְלִים Pr 28^{7}; 2 ms. sf. וַתַּכְלִימֵנוּ ψ 44^{10}; 2 mpl.

sf. תַּכְלִימוּנִי Jb 19^{3}, -מוּהָ Ru 2^{15}; *Inf. cstr.* הַכְלִים Je 6^{15} Pr 25^{8}; *Pt.* מַכְלִים Ju 18^{7} (but v. infr.), מַכְלִם Jb 11^{3};—**1.** *put to shame = insult, humiliate*, c. acc. 1 S 20^{34} 25^{7} (cf. Hoph. v^{15}) Ru 2^{15} Jb 19^{3}; *humiliate* by rebuke Jb 11^{3}; *humiliate* by defeat Pr 25^{8} ψ 44^{10}; *cause shame to* Pr 28^{7};—Ju 18^{7} is crpt. (see Be VB GFM; Be prop. מַחְסוֹר כל־דבר there was no *lack of anything*, for MT מַכְלִים ד׳; GFM conjectures מַכְלָא מְדַבֵּר *there is no one to restrain* (us) *from anything* in the land). **2.** *exhibit shame* Je 6^{15} (‖ בוש). **Hoph.** *Pf.* **1.** 1 pl. לֹא הָכְלַמְנוּ 1 S 25^{15} *we were not insulted, humiliated* (cf. **Hiph. 1**). **2.** 3 pl. הָכְלְמוּ Je 14^{3} *they were put to shame, dishonoured, confounded* (‖ בוש).

3639 †כְּלִמָּה **n.f. insult, reproach, ignominy**;—abs. כ׳ Is 45^{16}+9t.; cstr. כְּלִמַּת Je 20^{11}+3t.; sf. כְּלִמָּתִי Jb 20^{3}+3t., etc.; pl. כְּלִמּוֹת Mi 2^{6} Is 50^{6};—**1.** specif., *insult, reproach,* לֹא יִסַּג כ׳ Mi 2^{6} *reproaches do not cease;* מוּסַר כְּלִמָּתִי Jb 20^{3}=*my beshaming* (*insulting*) *correction*, i.e. the correction which insults me. **2.** in gen., *reproach, ignominy*, opp. כָּבוֹד ψ 4^{3}; הלך בַּכ׳ Is 45^{16} *go into ignominy* (+ נִכְלַם, בּוֹשׁ); oft. ‖ בֹּשֶׁת Is 30^{3} 61^{7} ψ 44^{16}, subj. of כִּסָּה Je 3^{25} *our ignominy covereth us*, so under fig. of garment, after לָבַשׁ ψ 35^{26} (+ בוש, חפר in v^{a}), 109^{29}; ‖ חֶרְפָּה ψ 69^{8} (subj. of כִּסְּתָה פָּנָי), Je 51^{51} (*id.*; בוש in ‖ cl.), ψ 71^{13}(+ בוש in ‖ cl.); ‖ חֶרְפָּה + בֹּשֶׁת 69^{20}; ‖ אִוֶּלֶת Pr 18^{13}; ‖ רֹק Is 50^{6}; כ׳ עוֹלָם Je 20^{11} (בוש in ‖ cl.); כְּלִמָּתֵךְ Ez 16^{63} (*id.* ‖); oft. in Ezek. נשׂא כ׳ *bear ignominy*, Ez $16^{52.52}$ (‖ בוש), v^{54} (נִכְלַם in ‖ cl.); $32^{24.25.30}$ (all + אֶת־יוֹרְדֵי בוֹר *with those who go down to the pit;* ref. to ignominious death), 36^{7} 39^{26} (si vera l.=*bear the humiliating sense* of undeserved kindness from י׳; but txt. dub., Hi Co, q.v., [כ׳] נָשׁוּ; Sm Da defend); נשׂא כְּלִמַּת הַגּוֹיִם, i.e. caused by the nations, 34^{29} 36^{6}, also v^{15} (‖ חֶרְפַּת עַמִּים), prob. also ψ 89^{51} (rd. כְּלִמַּת, cf. VB Che Bae); וְכ׳ כְּלִמָּתָם וְתוֹעֲבוֹתָם אֲשֶׁר עָשׂוּ Ez 44^{13}.

3640 †כְּלִמּוּת **n.f. ignominy**;—only cstr. וּכְלִמּוּת עוֹלָם Je 23^{40} (‖ חֶרְפַּת עוֹלָם).

3638 †כִּלְמַד **n.pr.loc.** (si vera l.) Ez 27^{23}, named after אַשּׁוּר, 𝔊 Χαρμαν; =mod. *Kalwâdha* near Bagdad, acc. to G. Smith TSBA i, 61 Dl Pa 206, cf. Schr COT; but txt. dub. v. Co; 𝔗 ומדי, whence Mez Stadt Ḥarrân 34 כָּל־מָדַי *all Media;* JKi Hi Co כְּלִמּוּד (רְכֻלָּתֵךְ) Asshur was *as thine apprentice* (v. sub למד) *in trading;* but sense not very prob.

†כַּלְנֵה (van d. H, so Norzi; Baer כַּלְנֶה) 3641
n.pr.loc. in Babylonia, Gn 10^{10} (J), 𝔊 Χαλαννη; Dl Pa 225 prop. identif. with Bab. *Kul-unu=Zirlab* (conquered by Sargon in 710: COT Gn 10, 10; Am 6, 2), but dubious, and site of Zirlab unknown.

†כַּלְנֵה Am 6^{2}, prob.=כַּלְנוֹ Is 10^{9} **n.pr.loc.** 3641
city (conquered by Assyria under Sargon ?) poss.=כַּנֶּה (q. v.) Ez 27^{23}, 𝔊 om. in Am 6^{2}, Χαλαννη Is 10^{9}; perh.=Kullani (Wkl Gesch. Bab. 225) i.e. (Tomkins PSBA Jan. 1883, 61) Kullanhou, near Aleppo, conquered by Tiglath-Pileser III in 738 (COT ii, 195); or (Di) Kunulua (KG 217 KB i, 107), SE. of Antioch (cf. Dr Am 6, 2).

†כָּמַהּ **vb. faint** (Ar. كَمِهَ is *be pale* of face, 3642
gray (of daylight), *weak-eyed*, أَكْمَهُ *blind from birth;* Syr. ܟܡܗ *be blind*), only fig.—**Qal** *Pf.* 3 ms. כָּ׳ לְךָ בְשָׂרִי ψ 63^{2} *faint* (with longing) *for thee* (‖ צָמְאָה לְךָ נַפְשִׁי).

†כִּמְהָם **n.pr.m. 1.** attendant of David 3643
2 S $19^{38.39}$=כִּמְהָן v^{41}; 𝔊 in all Χιμααμ, 𝔊L Αχιμααμ. **2.** in **n.loc.** גֵּרוּת כִּמְהָם Je 41^{17} Qr (Kt כמוהם), cf. גֵּרוּת p. 158 supr.

כִּמְהָן 2 S 19^{41}, v. foregoing. 3643

כַּמָּה v. מָה. כְּמוֹ v. sub כְּ p. 455 supr. p. 553 3644, 4100

כמוהם Je 41^{17} Kt, v. כִּמְהָם. 3643

†כְּמוֹשׁ **n.pr.div. Chemosh** (כמש MI 3.5.9.12. 3645
13.14.18.19.32.33 also עשתר כמש l^{17} and n.pr.m. כמשמלך l^{1}; As. *Kammusunadbi*, a king of Moab Schr. COT i, 281; = KAT 2, 288; cf. further Bae Rel 13 f. 238, 256 Nö ZMG 1888, 471; 𝔊 Χαμώς);—god of the Moabites to whom Solomon erected a high place 1 K $11^{7.33}$ 2 K 23^{13} Je 48^{7} (Kt כמיש), v^{13}. Moab is עַם־כ׳ Nu 21^{29} (ode) *people of Chemosh*, and Moabites his sons and daughters, cf. Je 48^{46}. He is said to be also the God of the Ammonites Ju 11^{25} (probably an error Bae Rel 15 GFM).

כמז (√of foll.; mng. dub.; Ar. كُمْزَةٌ is *bunch, heap*).

†כּוּמָז **n.** [**m.**] name of a golden ornament; 3558
—אֶצְעָדָה וְצָמִיד טַבַּעַת עָגִיל וְכ׳ Ex 35^{22}; חָח וָנֶזֶם וְטַבַּעַת וְכ׳ Nu 31^{50} (both P).

כּמִישׁ Je 48^{7} Kt, v. כְּמוֹשׁ. above 3645

כמן (√of foll. (si vera l.); perh. *be hidden;* cf. Aram. כְּמַן, ܟܡܢ, *lie in ambush;* Ar. كَمَنَ *id.* is denom. fr. loan-word كمين acc. to Frä 243).

4362 †[מִכְמָן] **n.[m.]** only pl. **hidden stores,** מִכְמַנֵּי הַזָּהָב וְהַכֶּסֶף Dn 11^{43} (? rd. מַטְמֻנֵי).

3646 †כַּמֹּן **n.m. cummin,** plant grown as condiment (𝔊 *κύμινον, cuminum cyminum;* Plin. $^{NH\ xix.\ 8}$; Germ. '*römischer Kümmel;*' Löw$^{No.\ 152}$; √dub.; NH *id.;* Aram. כַּמּוֹנָא, ܟܡܘܢܐ; Ar. كَمُّون, Eth. ከሚን: on format. cf. Lag$^{BN\ 89}$; loan-word acc. to Di^{832});—Is 28$^{25.27.27}$.

3647 †[כָּמַס] **vb. store up** (si vera l.), in **Qal** *Pt. pass.* כָּמֻס Dt 32^{34} is not this *stored up* (*laid up in store*) with me (|| חָתוּם בְּאוֹצְרֹתָי); but rd. prob. כָּנֻס in same mng. (v. כנס, and Dr$^{Dt\ 32,\ 34}$).

4363 †מִכְמָס **n.pr.loc.** Ezr 2^{27} = Ne 7^{31}; = מִכְמָשׂ (v. Baer's notes) 1 S 13^{2} + 6 t. 1 S, + 2 t.;—city in Benjamin, N. fr. Geba and Jerusalem 1 S 13$^{2.5}$ (E. fr. Bethaven), v$^{11.16.23}$ 14$^{5.31}$ Is 10^{28} Ne 11^{31}; אַנְשֵׁי מ׳ Ezr 2^{27} = Ne 7^{31}. 𝔊 *Μαχ(ε)μας*, etc. (On *Mikmās* v. Rob$^{BR\ i.\ 440\ ff.}$ Buhl$^{Geogr.\ §\ 96}$.)

3648 †I. [כָּמַר] **vb. Niph. grow warm and tender, be or grow hot** (NH *id.* Pi. *heat* fruit in the ground, making it ripe, over-ripe, tender; Aram. כְּמַר *id.*, and more gen. *make warm* (one's flesh, or food); cf. *kemr, fermentation,* etc., in mod. Syria Wetzst$^{ZPV\ xiv\ (1891),\ 6}$)—**Niph.** *Pf.* 3 pl. נִכְמְרוּ Gn 43^{30} + 2 t., נִכְמָ֑רוּ La 5^{10};—**1.** *grow warm* and *tender*, fig., subj. רחמים; נ׳ רַחֲמָיו אֶל־אָחִיו Gn 43^{30} (J), so נ׳ רַחֲמֶיהָ עַל־בְּנָהּ 1 K 3^{26}; (רַחֲמַי We) יַחַד נ׳ נִחוּמָי Ho 11^{8} (|| נֶהְפַּךְ עָלַי לִבִּי). **2.** *be* or *grow hot,* עוֹרֵנוּ כְּתַנּוּר נ׳ מִפְּנֵי וגו׳ La 5^{10} *our skin has become hot like a furnace,* because of the famine.

II. כמר (? √ of foll.; cf. Syr. ܟܡܝܪ *black, dark,* usu. *gloomy, sad;* ܟܡܪ, ܐܬܟܡܪ *be sad*).

3650 †[כִּמְרִיר] **n.m. darkness, gloominess** (?), pl. intens. cstr. כִּמְרִירֵי יוֹם Jb 3^{5} *the deep gloom of day* (|| חֹשֶׁךְ, צלמות, עֲנָנָה);—rd. כַּמ׳, v. Di Sta$^{§\ 231}$.

III. כמר (√ of foll.; cf. As. *kamâru, overthrow, lay prostrate,* whence n. *kamâru, net, snare* Dl$^{HWB\ 336}$ and כֹּמֶר *priest* acc. to Dl$^{HA\ 42}$, i.e. one who prostrates himself; also Mand. כמר *turn round, bring back* Nö$^{M\ 443\ f.}$ and N. Syr. ܟܡܪ *pursue* Nö$^{ib.}$ PS^{1759}).

4364 †מִכְמָר **n.[m.] net, snare,** bringing an animal to its fall, כְּתוֹא מ׳ Is 51^{20} *like an antelope of (in) a net* or *snare* (cf. II. חֵרֶם p. 357, II. רֶשֶׁת p. 440).

†[מִכְמֹר] **n.[m.]** net, snare (v. foregoing)— 4364
pl. sf. יִפְּלוּ בְמַכְמֹרָיו רְשָׁעִים ψ 141^{10}; so Gr Che 140^{11} (במכמרות for MT בְּמַהֲמֹרוֹת, v. p. 243).

†[מִכְמֶרֶת] **n.f. net, fishing-net;** sg. sf. 4365
מִכְמַרְתּוֹ Hb 1^{15} (|| חֶרֶם, חַכָּה and), v^{16}, both in fig. of conquering Chaldeans.

†מִכְמֹרֶת **n.f.** id.; וּפֹרְשֵׂי מ׳ עַל־פְּנֵי־מַיִם Is 4365
19^{8} (|| מַשְׁלִיכֵי בַיְאוֹר חַכָּה).

†[כֹּמֶר] **n.m. (idol-)priest** (so NH כּוּמֶר; 3649
Aram. ܟܘܡܪܐ, כּוּמְרָא, is also priest of God; Nerab כמר Hal$^{Rev.\ Sém.\ 1896,\ 280,\ 282}$; Nab. כמר *priest* CIS$^{ii,\ No.\ 170}$, Teima כמרא *id.* CIS$^{ii,\ No.\ 113\ a,\ b,\ b\ bis}$; so כמר Neo-Pun. Eut$^{ZMG.\ 1875,\ 238,\ 239}$ Berger$^{JAs\ Apr.-June,\ 1887,\ 465}$; perh. Tel Am. *kamiru* Bez$^{BM.\ Tabl.\ xxvi;\ Or.\ Dipl.\ 92}$; Wkl$^{TA.\ 1,\ 15,\ 33}$ leaves untransl.);—pl. abs., in O.T. only of idol-priests; הַכְּמָרִים 2 K 23^{5}, כְּמָרָיו Ho 10^{5}, הַכּ׳ עִם־הַכֹּהֲנִים Zp 1^{4}. In Ho 4^{4} Beck (in Wü^{142}) We prop. וְעַמִּי כִּכְמָרָיו (for MT וְעַמְּךָ כִּמְרִיבֵי).

כמת (√ of foll., meaning unknown).

†מִכְמְתָת **n.pr.loc.** alw. הַמּ׳, Jos 16^{6} (𝔊 4366
Ικασμων, 𝔊L εις Αχθωθ, A Μαχθωθ), 17^{7} (מֵאָשֵׁר הַמּ׳; 𝔊 Δηλαναθ, A ἀπὸ Ασερ Μαχθωθ, and similarly 𝔊L), place in NE. Ephraim, near border of Manasseh, between Shechem and Taanath-Shilo; Buhl$^{Geogr.\ 109}$ conj. *Khirbet kefr beita.*

II. כֵּן **adv. so** (Ph. NH 𝔗 *id.;* Syr. ܟܢ is 3651
then, Ar. لَٰكِنْ, لَٰكِنَّ, *but:* prob. from the demonstr. √*ka,* found in כִּי etc., Kö$^{ii.\ 1,\ 254}$); כֵּן־הוּא (היא) Gn 44^{10} + 4 t.:—*so* (i.e. usu., as has been described or commanded, with ref. to what has preceded), mostly of manner, but sts. also of quantity, quality, or degree: **1. a.** Ju 5^{31} כן יאבדו *so* perish thy enemies, Jb 5^{27} כֶּן־הִיא, 8^{13} כן ארחות כל שכחי אל, Pr 6^{29} 8^{13} 2 S 16^{23} Is 36^{6} 47^{15} כן היו לך, Nu 13^{33} וכן היינו בעיניהם; Nu 9^{16} כן יהיה תמיד; Ex 10$^{14.14}$ לא היה כן ארבה לוֹ בא כמהו וג׳ (i.e. in such numbers), 1 K 10^{12} ולא מצאו כן עצי אלמגים, v^{20} 2 Ch 1$^{12.12}$, Ju 21^{14} להם כן and they did not suffice for them *so* (viz. in such numbers of them as there were); 1 K 6^{26} וכן הכרוב השני, Ez 41^{7}; וכן ל׳ Ex 27^{11} 1 K 10^{29} Ez 40^{16} 2 Ch 35^{12}, cf. 1 Ch 23^{30}; כן ל׳ Ex 25^{33} (cf. 26^{24}), Jos 21^{40}. **b.** the force of כֵּן has sts. to be elicited from the context: 1 K 2^{7} כי כן קרבו אלי (sc. with kindness such as that enjoined in v^{a}), 20^{40} כן משפטך, Je 14^{10} כן אהבו לנוע (i.e. not less than י׳ has withdrawn from

them v^{9}, Gf Ke; Gie prop. אָכֵן), ψ 61^{9} כֵּן אֲזַמְּרָה
כֵּן בַּקֹּדֶשׁ (Hi כְּצִדְקָךְ שִׁמְךָ, implied in v$^{6-8}$), 63^{3} כֵּן חֲזִיתִךָ (sc. with the longings of v^{2}), v^{5} כִּי כֵן תְּכִינֶהָ (sc. כְּרֹב חַסְדְּךָ v^{4}), 65^{10} אֲבָרֶכְךָ בְחַיָּי לִמְנוֹת יָמֵינוּ כֵּן הוֹדַע (i.e. so generously, v^{10}), 90^{12} (Hi כְּיִרְאַת י׳ v^{11}), 127^{2} כֵּן יִתֵּן לִידִידוֹ שֵׁנָא (sc. as abundantly; but Che אָכֵן), Pr 24^{14} (see v^{13}), Is 52^{14} כֵּן מִשְׁחַת מֵאִישׁ מַרְאֵהוּ (sufficiently to justify שממו עליך רבים). **c.** כן occurs freq. in partic. phrases, as (*a*) with הָיָה, esp. ויהי כן and it was *so* Gn 1$^{7.9.11}$+, 2 K 2^{10} if thou seest me taken from thee יהי־לך כן let it be to thee *so* (sc. as thou desirest), 7^{20}, with עשׂה (esp. וַיַּעַשׂ, וַיַּעֲשׂוּ) Gn 29^{28} 42^{20} 45^{21}+oft., Ju 7^{16} מִמֶּנִּי תִרְאוּ וְכֵן תַּעֲשׂוּ +, ויעשׂ להם כן Gn 42^{25} ל׳, Ex 22^{29} 23^{11} כן תעשׂה ל׳, Dt 22^{3} 2 S 12^{31} 1 K 11^{8} (cf. 6^{33} 7^{18}); Gn 29^{26} לֹא יֵעָשֶׂה כֵן במקומנו, 34^{7} 2 S 13^{12}; rarer usages, כֵּן אמרתם Ex 6^{9}, אמר כן 1 K 22^{8}, דִּבֶּר כֵּן Ez 11^{5} 33^{10}, אָמֵן כֵּן יֹאמַר י׳ 1 K 1^{36} (cf. Je 28^{6}), וגם שׁאול אבי יֹדֵעַ כֵּן 1 S 23^{17}; אָהֵב כֵּן (idiom.) to love (it) *so*, †Je 5^{31} Am 4^{5}; (*b*) Gn 50^{3} כי כן ימלאו ימי החנֻטים (cf. Ju 14^{10} 2 S 13^{18} Est 2^{12}); (*c*) alone, אִם כֵּן if it be *so* †Gn 25^{22} 43^{11}; וַיִּרְאוּ כִּי־כֵן 1 S 5^{7}, יָדַעְתִּי כִּי־כֵן Jb 9^{2}; (*d*) לא כן not *so* (viz. as has been described or implied), with a subst. Nu 12^{7} לֹא כֵן עבדי משׁה, 2 S 20^{21} 23^{5} ψ 1^{4} Jb 9$^{35\,b}$ כי־לא־כן אנכי עמדי not *so* am I with myself (i.e. I am not conscious of being one who would fear him, v^{a}), with a vb. Dt 18^{14} ואתה לא כן נתן לך י׳ (not *so*,—viz. as implied in v^{a}), 2 S 18^{14} Is 10^{7} לא כן יחשׁב, לֹא כֵן יְדַמֶּה, absol. Gn 48^{18} לֹא כֵן אבי, Ex 10^{11}.

2. Often, to emphasize the agreement, in answer to כְּ, and כַּאֲשֶׁר: viz. **a.** כְּ . . . כֵּן, (*a*) Gn 44^{10}=Jos 2^{21} כדבריכם כֶּן־הוּא acc. to your words, *so* be it, 1 S 25^{25} כִּי כשׁמו כֶּן־הוּא, ψ 48^{11} Pr 23^{7} כֶּן־הוּא (after conj. כְּמוֹ), Ez 42^{11} כְּאָרְכָּן כֵּן רָחְבָּן; (*b*) Lv 27^{12} כְּעֶרְכְּךָ כֵּן יִהְיֶה, 2 S 13^{35} Nu 8^{4} 9^{14} 15^{20} Dt 8^{20} Ju 11^{10}, so after כְּפִי Nu 6^{21}; (*c*) כְּכֹל . . . כֵּן . . . 1 S 8^{8} 2 S 7^{17} Je 42^{5}; (*d*) in similes, (*a*) 2 S 14^{17} כמלאך הא׳ כן אדני המלך, Je 18^{6} ψ 123^{2} 127^{4} Pr 10^{26} 26$^{8.19}$ 27$^{8.19}$ Ct 2$^{2.3}$; (*β*) Jo 2^{4} כְּפָרָשִׁים כֵּן יְרוּצוּן, Is 31^{5} 38^{14} ψ 103^{15} Pr 26$^{1.2}$; (*γ*) ψ 42^{2} כאיל תערג . . . כן נפשׁי וג׳ like the hind which etc., 83^{16} Is 61^{11} 63^{14} Jb 7^{3}, so after כמו Is 26^{17}; (*δ*) Je 2^{26} כְּבֹשֶׁת גַּנָּב . . . כֵּן הוֹבִישׁוּ, 6^{7} 34^{5} (rd. כְּמִשְׂרְפוֹת), Ez 22^{22} (cf. v^{20}), 23^{44} 34^{12}; cf. (of degree) 35^{15} (om. 𝔊 Co), Ho 4^{7} כְּרֻבָּם כֵּן חָטְאוּ לִי. Of *time* (uncommon) 1 S 9^{13} כְּבֹאֲכֶם הָעִיר כֵּן תִּמְצְאוּן אֹתוֹ. **b.** †Ezr 10^{12} כֵּן כדבריך עלינו לעשׂות. **c.** כַּאֲשֶׁר . . . , כֵּן . . . , (*a*) Ex 7^{6} כאשׁר צוה י׳ כן עשׂו, 12$^{28.50}$ 39^{43} (cf. 27^{8}), Nu 8^{22} (cf. 5^{4}), 17^{26} 36^{10} Jos 14^{5} (all P); Gn 41^{13} כאשׁר פתר כן היה, Jos 10$^{1.39}$ 11^{15} Ju 1^{7} 15$^{11\,b}$ ψ 48^{9}; (*b*) (freq.) Nu 2^{17} כאשׁר יַחֲנוּ כֵּן יִסָּעוּ, Ex 1^{12} (of degree=*the more . . . the more*) כַּאֲשֶׁר יְעַנּוּ אֹתוֹ כֵּן יִרְבֶּה וְכֵן יִפְרֹץ; (*c*) Gn 6^{22} ככל אשׁר צוה אתו אלהים כן עשׂה, Ex 39$^{32.42}$ 40^{16} Nu 1^{54} 2^{34} 8^{20} 9^{5} (all P), cf. Ex 25^{9} (וְכֵן), simil. 2 S 9^{11} 2 K 16^{11}, cf. Jos 1^{17} Je 42^{20}; (*d*) Ex 27^{8} כאשׁר הֶרְאָה אתך כן יעשׂו, 2 S 16^{19} 1 K 2^{38} Is 20^{4} 52$^{14\,f.}$; with the same vb. repeated Lv 24$^{19.20}$ Dt 28^{63} כאשׁר שׂשׂ . . . . כן יָשִׂישׂ, Jos 23^{15} 1 S 15^{33} 26^{24} 1 K 1^{37} Is 10^{11} Je 5^{19} 31^{28} 32^{42} 42^{18} Ez 12^{11} 20^{36} Zc 7^{13} Pr 24^{29}; Nu 14^{28} אם לא כאשׁר דברתם כן אעשׂה, Is 14^{24}, so after הלא 10^{11}, after asseverative כי 2 S 3^{9} 1 K 1^{30}; so כָּל־עֻמַּת שֶׁ׳ . . . . כֵּן †Ec 5^{15}; (*e*) Ju 7$^{17\,b}$ כאשׁר אעשׂה כן תעשׂון, Lv 27^{14} Nu 15^{14}, cf. Je 39^{12}; (*f*) in similes, Dt 12^{22} 22^{26} Am 3^{12} Is 65^{8} Je 13^{11}. †**d.** . . . כן כאשׁר, (*a*) Ex 7^{10} ויעשׂו כן כאשׁר צוה י׳, v^{20} Jos 4^{8} 2 S 5^{25} Ez 12^{7}, cf. Gn 50^{12} Nu 8^{3}; iron. Am 5^{14} יהי כן י׳ אתכם כאשׁר אמרתם, Ex 10^{10}; (*b*) Gn 18^{5} כן תעשׂה כאשׁר דברת, Ne 5^{12}.—Occasionally in poetry כאשׁר is not expressed: Is 54^{9} (De), 55^{9} Je 3^{20} Jb 7^{9} Ho 11^{2} קראו להם כן הלכו מפניהם (of degree: *so*=in the same proportion), ψ 48^{6} המה ראו כן תמהו (i.e. in the same measure that they saw); Je 33^{22} (acc. to many, but dub.; rd. prob. כאשׁר Gie) it is represented by אשׁר (so Is 54^{9} Hi Ew Di): Ju 5^{15} כ is not expressed.—Na 1^{12} is prob. corrupt; Zc 11^{11} for כן עניי rd. כְּנַעֲנִיֵּי.—כֹּה, כָּכָה, כָּזֹאת are syn., but differ considerably in usage.

3. With prepositions:—**a.** אַחֲרֵי־כֵן, אַחַר־כֵּן, מֵאַחֲרֵי־כֵן, lit. *after so*, i.e. *afterwards:* v. אַחַר. **b.** †בְּכֵן (late), lit. *in such circumstances*, i.e. *thereupon, then*, Ec 8^{10} Est 4^{16} (𝔗 בְּכֵין oft. for אָז; e.g. Ex 15^{1}; Syr$^{\text{Jerus.}}$ ܒܟܢ=τότε). **c.** †כְּמוֹ־כֵן Is 51^{6}, acc. to some, *like so*, i.e. (Vrss Rabb) *in like manner*, or (De) *like this* (accompanied by a contemptuous gesture)=like a mere nothing: but v. IV. כֵּן. **d.** לָכֵן$_{200}$ *according to such conditions, that being so, therefore* Nu 16^{11} 1 S 27^{6} ψ 16^{9} 73$^{6.10}$; esp. in proph., where it often introduces, after statement of the grounds, a divine declaration or command: Ju 10^{13} 2 K 1^{6} Am 4^{12} Is 5$^{13.14.24}$ 7^{14} 10^{16} 16^{7} 27^{9} Je 6^{15} 8^{10} etc.; לכן כה אמר י׳ 2 K 21^{12} Is 10^{24} 28^{16} 29^{22} 30^{12} 37^{33} Je 5^{14} 6^{21}+oft.; sq. נאם האדון Is 1^{24}; נאם י׳ 1 S 2^{30} Je 2^{9}; לכן הנה ימים באים נאם י׳ Je 7^{32} 16^{14} 19^{6}+; לכן חי אני נאם י׳ Ez 5^{11} 35$^{6.11}$ Zp 2^{9}; לכן הנני . . . . 1 K 14^{10} Ho 2$^{8.16}$ Is 29^{14} Je 16^{21} Ez 16^{37} 22$^{19\,b}$ 25$^{4.7.9}$+; לכן אֱמֹר †Ex 6^{6} Nu 25^{12} (both P),

Ez 11$^{16.17}$ 14^{6} 20^{30} 33^{25} 36^{22}; לָכֵן דַּבֵּר + Ez 14^{4}
20^{27}; לָכֵן הִנָּבֵא + Ez 11^{4} 36$^{3.6}$ 37^{12} 38^{11}; לָכֵן שִׁמְעוּ....
Is 28^{14} 51^{21} Je 6^{18} 44^{26} +. In answer to יען,
Nu 20^{12} (P), 1 K 14^{10} 2 K 1^{16} 21^{12} 22^{20} Is 29^{14}
30^{13} Je 19^{6} +, Ez 5^{8} 13^{23} +; so, once, וְלָכֵן Is 8^{7};
to כי Is 28^{16} Je 35^{17}; על Je 9^{14}; אם 23^{38} 42^{15}.
Special usages:—(*a*) idiom., in conversation, in reply to an objection, to state the ground upon which the answer is made; Gn 4^{15} *therefore*—this being so—whoso killeth Cain, etc., 30^{15} Ju 8^{7} 11^{8} 1 S 28^{2} 1 K 22^{19} Jb 20^{2} (𝔊 in Gn K Jb, not perceiving the idiom, renders *οὐχ οὕτως* (as though לא־כן): so also strangely, elsewhere, as 1 S 3^{14} 2 K 1$^{4.6}$ 21^{12}). (*b*) inferring the cause from the effect, or developing what is logically involved in a statement, Is 26^{14b} (cf. De) *therefore* thou hast visited and destroyed them (not a consequence of v^{a} 'the dead rise not,' but the development of what is implicit in it), 61^{7} Je 2^{33} 5^{2} (because viz. אין אמונה v^{1}), Jb 34^{25} 42^{3}.—Zc 11^{7} rd. לִכְנַעֲנֵי הַצֹּאן. **e.** † עַד־כֵּן *hitherto* (of time), *as yet* Ne 2^{16}. **f.** עַל־כֵּן$_{145}$ *upon ground of such conditions, therefore* (introducing, more generally than לָכֵן, the statement of a *fact*, rather than a *declaration*: never used in the phrases noted under לָכֵן), Gn 20^{6} 42^{21} Ex 5$^{8.17}$ 16^{29} 20^{11} 1 S 20^{29} 28^{18} 2 S 7$^{22.27}$ 1 K 20^{23} Is 5^{25} 9^{16} 13$^{7.13}$ 15$^{4.7}$ 16$^{9.11}$ 17^{10} 21^{3} Je 5$^{6.27}$ 10^{21} 12^{8} 20^{11} 31$^{3.20}$ Ez 7^{20} 22^{4} 31^{5} etc., ψ 1^{5} 42^{7} 45^{3c} (the poet's inference from v$^{a.b}$), v^{8} 110^{7} Jb 6^{3} 9^{22} 17^{4} 20^{21} etc., Ct 1^{3}; and regularly where the origin of a name, or custom, or proverb is assigned, Gn 2^{24} על־כן יעזב איש וג׳, 10^{9} על־כן יֵאָמַר, 11^{9} על־כן קרא שמה בבל, 16^{14} 19^{22} 21^{31} 25^{30} 26^{33} 29$^{34.35}$ 30^{6} 32^{33} 47^{22} Ex 13^{15} 15^{23} Nu 18^{24} 21$^{14.27}$ Dt 10^{9} (cf. 15$^{11.15}$ 19^{7} 24$^{18.22}$), Jos 7^{26} 14^{14} Ju 15^{19} 18^{12} 1 S 5^{5} 10^{12} 23^{28} (? rd. so 27^{6}) 2 S 5$^{8.20}$ etc.; הַעַל־כֵּן + Hb 1^{17}.—Est 9^{26} the 2nd על כן (unless dittogr.) points unusually onwards to על כל דברי האגרת *on this account, on account, viz.*, etc.

3651, 3653-54 I. כֵּן v. כון; III. כֵּן v. I. כנן; IV. כֵּן v. II. כנן. p. 467, below

3655 †[כָּנָה] **vb. Pi. betitle, title, give an epithet or cognomen** (NH *id.*; Aram. כְּנָא, ܟܢܳܐ; Ar. كَنَى)—**Pi.** *Impf.* 1 s. sf. וָאֲכַנְּךָ Is 45^{4} *I have called thee by thy name, giving thee a title* (of honour; cf. for construction Dr$^{§ 163}$); 3 ms. וּבְשֵׁם יִשְׂרָאֵל יְכַנֶּה 44^{5}, *and with the name Israel he titles* (himself), is hardly poss.; abs. *he betitles*, or *makes use of a title*, is unlikely; rd. prob. **Pu.**, v. infr., in bad sense =*give a flattering title*: וְאֶל־אָדָם לֹא אֲכַנֶּה Jb 32^{21} *and unto man I do not give flattering titles* (|| אַל־נָא אֶשָּׂא פְנֵי אִישׁ); abs. v^{22}. **Pu.** *Impf.* יְכֻנֶּה Is 44^{5} *he is betitled* (v. supr.; so 𝔗 Bi Che Du; || יקרא בשם יעקב, etc.)

כַּנָּה ψ 80^{16} v. sub כנן p. 488. 3657

†כַּנֵּה **n.pr.loc.** appar. in Mesopot., חָרָן וְכ׳ 3656
וָעֶדֶן Ez 27^{23}, 𝔊 Χαναα; identif. dub.; =כַּלְנֵה Thes and most; Co *rds.* כַּלְנֵה; Mez$^{\text{Stadt Ḫarrân 34}}$ prop. בְּנֵי עֶדֶן.

כְּנָוֹת v. כְּנָת p. 490. 3674

כָּנְיָהוּ v. יְהוֹיָכִין p. 220, and יְכָנְיָה sub כון. p. 467 3078, 3204

כִּנָּם, כִּנִּם v. IV. כֵּן sub II. כנן. below 3654

I. כנן (√ of foll.; parallel form of כון; *be firm, substantial*).

†III. כֵּן **n.m. base, pedestal, office** (NH 3653
כַּנָּה; Aram. כַּנְּתָא, ܟܰܢܳܐ)—abs. כ׳ Is 33^{23} 1 K 7^{31} (but v. infr.); sf. כַּנּוֹ Ex 30^{18} + 11 t.; כַּנֶּךָ Gn 40^{13}; כַּנִּי 41^{13};—**1.** lit. *base, pedestal*, 1 K 7^{31} (like) the work of *a pedestal* (Th VB), acc. to Sta$^{\text{ZAW iii, 1883, 161, 162}}$ מַעֲשֵׂה־כֵן is in wrong place, being orig. part of a gloss to v^{35};—כ׳ in v^{29}=*thus*, or is txt. err.;—כֵּן־תָּרְנָם Is 33^{23} *the base* (*support* or *socket*) *of their mast* (so Thes and most); esp. of base of laver of tabernacle Ex 30$^{18.28}$ 31^{9} 35^{16} 38^{8} 39^{39} 40^{11} Lv 8^{11} (all P). **2.** *office, place* Gn 40^{13} 41^{13} (both E); hence (late) עַל־כַּנּוֹ *in his place* Dn 11$^{20.21.38}$ (i.e. in his stead, as his successor, cf. Germ. *an seiner Stelle*); על om. v^{7}.

†כְּנַנְיָהוּ **n.pr.m.** (*י׳ is firm*);—**1.** a Levite 3663
1 Ch 15^{22} 𝔊 Κωνενια, A Χωνενια, 𝔊L Ιεχονιας; =כְּנַנְיָה v^{27}, 𝔊 Ιεχονιας, A Χενενιας, 𝔊L Χονενιας. **2.** an Izharite 1 Ch 26^{29}, 𝔊 Χωνεν(ε)ια(ς).

†כְּנָנִי **n.pr.m.** a Levite Ne 9^{4}, א$^{c.a}$ A Χανανι, 3662
𝔊L Χωνενιας (B om.)

כְּנַנְיָהוּ Qr **n.pr.m.** v. כּוֹנַנְיָהוּ sub כון. p. 467 3562

II. כנן (√ of foll.; meaning dubious; v. conj. in Kö$^{\text{ii. 1, 100 Anm.}}$)

†IV. כֵּן (?), כִּנִּם, כִּנָּם **n.**[**m.**], mng. dub.; 3654
either **gnat, gnats, gnat-swarm** (so 𝔊 𝔙 Philo$^{\text{Vita Mos. i, p. 97}}$, Origen$^{\text{Hom. 4, 6 in Ex.}}$, and most moderns), or [**louse,**] **lice** (so 𝔖 𝔗 Jos$^{\text{Ant. ii. 14. 13}}$ Boch$^{\text{Hieroz. II, ii, 572 f.}}$, as NH כִּנָּה, pl. כִּנִּים=*maggots*, and esp. *lice*)—abs. perh. כֵּן Is 51^{6} (v. infr.); pl. כִּנִּים Ex 8$^{13.14}$ ψ 105^{31}, כִּנָּם Ex 8^{12}; Ex 8$^{13.14}$ has, also, כִּנָּם prob. a mere Mas. device for כִּנִּם (cf. Di), on account of preceding וַתְּהִי (on which see Ges$^{§ 145. 4}$ Da$^{\text{Synt. § 116}}$); Sam. has כנים throughout:—of Egyptian plague Ex 8$^{12.13.13.14.14}$ (all P),

hence ψ 105[31]; כְּמוֹ־כֵן יְמוּתוּן Is 51[6] *like a gnat-swarm* (?) *shall they die* (cf. Di Du; Weir Che rd. כנים, cf. Buhl[p. 355]; >Brd De *like this*).

Note.—Nö[M 54] Ba[NB § 15, ES 53] Buhl[Ges HWB ed. 12] connect this word etymol. with Aram. כלמתא *vermin*, Ba and Buhl also with As. *kalmatu*, *id.* [Dl[HWB 333]], and even with Aram. קלמתא, ܩܠܡܬܐ, Ar. قَمْل, etc., Eth. ቍማል: *louse;* but these connexions, as well as that with NH כְּנִימָה, all involving radical מ, are most improb.

3657,3661 †כַּנָּה ψ 80[16] **n.f.** (si vera l.) **support** (of tree), i.e. *root, stock* (fem. of III. כֵּן; cf. Syr. ܟܢܐ m. *id.*, Che[Psalms 397], so Ges); al. take as vb., but 𝔊 καταρτισαι is ag. gramm. (should be כּוֹנְנָה), and √כנן=كَنَّ *protect* (HuRiDe; rd. then כַּנָּה) is improb. Txt. dubious.

3664 †[כָּנַס] **vb. gather, collect** (NH *id.;* Aram. כְּנַשׁ (v. also כנשׁ); Eth. ከነሰ: in der. conj. *assemble for worship*, etc.; Ar. كَنَسَ is *sweep, sweep away, destroy*)—**Qal** (late) *Pf.* 1 s. כָּנַסְתִּי Ec 2[8]; *Imv.* כְּנוֹס Est 4[16]; *Inf. cstr.* 1 Ch 22[2]+3 t.; *Pt.* כֹּנֵס ψ 33[7];—*gather* people 1 Ch 22[2] Est 4[16]; כֹּנֵס כַּנֵּד מֵי הַיָּם נֹתֵן בְּאוֹצָרוֹת תְּהוֹמוֹת ψ 33[7] (rd. perh., for כַּנֵּד, כַּנֹּאד *as in a wine skin*, v. נאד, נד); *gather, collect* portions of harvest for priests and Levites Ne 12[44]; stones Ec 3[5] (opp. השׁליך); silver and gold=*amass* wealth Ec 2[8]; abs. v[26] (‖ אסף). **Pi.** *Pf.* 1 s. וְכִנַּסְתִּי אֶתְכֶם Ez 22[21] *and I will gather you together* (for punishment; Co tr. to v[20] and rds. for וְהִנַּחְתִּי ‖ קבץ v[19.20]); of restoration וְכִנַּסְתִּים אֶל־אַדְמָתָם 39[28], and יְכַנֵּס ψ 147[2]. **Hithp.** *Inf. cstr.* וְהַמַּסֵּכָה צָרָה כְּהִתְכַּנֵּס Is 28[20] *and the covering is (too) narrow when one gathers oneself together* (‖ קָצַר הַמַּצָּע מֵהִשְׂתָּרֵעַ), i.e. the bed is too short to stretch oneself at full length, and when one (perforce) draws up the feet, the covering becomes too narrow.

4370 †[מִכְנָס] **n.m.**[Ez 44, 18] only du. (or pl.) **drawers** (connex. with above √כנס obscure; Di der. fr. כנס=גנז *cover up, hide* (cf. Du Is 28[20]), which Thes also comp.)—only cstr. מִכְנְסֵי;—a priestly garment of linen מִכְנְסֵי פִשְׁתִּים Ez 44[18]; מִכְנְסֵי (הַ)בָּד Ex 28[42] 39[28] Lv 6[3] 16[4] (all P).

3665 †[כָּנַע] **vb. be humble**, only in der. conj. (Aram. כְּנַע *id.;* Ar. كَنَعَ is *be contracted, wrinkled;* also *fold* wings (of eagle))—**Niph.** *Pf.* 3 ms. נִכְנַע 1 K 21[29]+3 t.; 3 pl. נִכְנְעוּ 2 Ch 12[7] 30[11]; נִכְנָֽעוּ 2 Ch 12[7]; *Impf.* יִכָּנַע Lv 26[41]+3 t.; 3 fs. וַתִּכָּנַע Ju 3[30]; 2 ms. וַתִּכָּנַע 2 K 22[19]+2 t.; 3 mpl. וְיִכָּנְעוּ 2 Ch 7[14]+5 t.; יִכָּנֵֽעוּ 1 Ch 20[4]; *Inf.* הִכָּנַע 2 Ch 33[23]; sf. הִכָּנְעוֹ 2 Ch 12[12] 33[19];—**1.** reflex. *humble oneself* Lv 26[41] (H; subj. לְבָבָם), 2 Ch 7[14] 12[6.7.7.12] 30[11] 32[26] 33[19.23]; *before* some one, לִפְנֵי 2 Ch 34[27]; מִלְּפָנַי 1 K 21[29] 2 Ch 33[12.23] 34[27] 36[12]; מִפָּנַי 1 K 21[29] 2 K 22[19]. **2.** pass. *be humbled, subdued* 1 S 7[13] 1 Ch 20[4] 2 Ch 13[18]; sq. לִפְנֵי pers. Ju 8[28]; מִפְּנֵי Ju 11[33]; *under* some one תַּחַת Ju 3[30] ψ 106[42]. **Hiph.** *Pf.* 3 ms. הִכְנִיעַ 2 Ch 28[19]; 1 s. הִכְנַעְתִּי 1 Ch 17[10]; *Impf.* 3 ms. וַיַּכְנַע Ju 4[23] ψ 107[12]; sf. יַכְנִיעֵם Dt 9[3]+2 t.; 2 ms. תַּכְנִיעַ Is 25[5]; וַתַּכְנַע Ne 9[24]; 1 s. אַכְנִיעַ ψ 81[15]; *Imv.* הַכְנִיעֵהוּ Jb 40[12];—**1.** *humble* 2 Ch 28[19] Jb 40[12] ψ 107[12] (obj. לֵב), Is 25[5] (obj. שְׁאוֹן זָרִים). **2.** *subdue* enemies 2 S 8[1]=1 Ch 18[1], 1 Ch 17[10] ψ 81[15]; sq. לִפְנֵי Dt 9[3] Ju 4[23] Ne 9[24].

†[כִּנְעָה] **n.f. bundle, pack** (cf. Ar. sense of √, supr.);—sf. אִסְפִּי מֵאֶרֶץ כִּנְעָתֵךְ Je 10[17] *pack thy bundle* (and take it) *out of the land.* 3666

I. כְּנַ֫עַן 90 **n.pr.m.** et **terr. Canaan** (𝔊 Χαναάν, Ph. כנען=*Phoenicia;* Χνα=כנע, Hecataeus, v. Müller[Fr. Hist. Gr. i, 17]al.; Egypt. *Ka-n-ʿ-na* WMM[Asien u. Europa, 205 ff.]; Tel Amarna *Kinaḫna, Kinaḫḫi*, etc., Bezold[BM Tablets, 150] Wkl[TA 39 :]; etym. dub. GFM[PAOS Oct. 1890, lxvii ff.]; v. also GASm[Geogr. 4 f.] Buhl[Geogr. § 42]);—†**1.** as **n.pr.m.,** son of Ham Gn 9[18.22.25.27] 10[15] (as ancestor of Canaanites and Phoenicians; all J); 10[6] (P); 1 Ch 1[8.13] (fr. Gn 10[6.15]). **2. a.** land, W. of Jordan, into wh. Hebrews came, and where they settled, subduing the inhabitants; מַלְכֵי כְנַעַן Ju 5[19], מֶלֶךְ כ׳ Ju 4[2.23.24.24]; hence מַמְלְכוֹת כ׳ ψ 135[11]; יֹשְׁבֵי כ׳ Ex 15[15] (song in E); cf. מִלְחֲמוֹת כ׳ Ju 3[1]; עֲצַבֵּי כ׳ ψ 106[38] *idols of Canaan*, i.e. of the former inhabitants; esp. אֶרֶץ(־) כ׳, אַרְצָה כ׳ Gn 44[8] 46[31] 47[1.4.13.14.15] 50[5.13] (all J), 35[6] 42[5.7.13.29.32] 45[17.25] Jos 24[3] (all E), Gn 11[31] 12[5.5] 13[12] (opp. עָרֵי הַכִּכָּר v[b]), 16[3] 17[8] (all P)+40 t. P, Ju 21[12] 1 Ch 16[18]=ψ 105[11]; also הָאָרֶץ כ׳ Nu 34[2] (P); בְּנוֹת כ׳ Gn 28[1] *daughters of Canaan* = women of the land, so v[6.8] 36[2] (all P); כנען is personif. Ho 12[8] = apostate Israel; שְׂפַת כ׳ Is 19[18]=the Hebrew lang. (without evil implication). **b.** the coast, esp. Phoenicia Is 23[11]; cf. כ׳ אֶרֶץ פְּלִשְׁתִּים Zp 2[5]. 3667

†II. כְּנַ֫עַן **n.[m.] merchant(s)** (because Canaanites, esp. Phoenicians, were traders);—כָּל־עַם כְּנַעַן Zp 1[11]; אֶרֶץ כ׳ Ez 16[29] (om. 𝔊 B al. Co), 17[4] *a land of merchants;* cf. כנעני *ad fin.* 3667

3669 †I. כְּנַעֲנִי **adj. et nom. gent.** of I. כְּנַעַן; —usu. ms. (הַ)כְּנַעֲנִי Gn 38^{2} Nu 21^{1} +; fs. הַכְּנַעֲנִית Gn 46^{10} = Ex 6^{15} 1 Ch 2^{3}; mpl. (הַ)כְּנַעֲנִים Ob^{20} Ne 9^{24}; —**1. adj.** אִישׁ כ׳ Gn 38^{2} (J). **2.** c. art. as **subst., a.** of individual, הַכּ׳ מֶלֶךְ־עֲרָד Nu 21^{1} (J) and hence 33^{40} (P or R); f. הַכְּנַעֲנִית Gn 46^{10} = Ex 6^{15} (P) בַּת־שׁוּעַ הַכְּנַעֲנִית 1 Ch 2^{3}. **b.** usu. coll. (c. art.) of pre-Isr. inhabitants of כְּנַעַן (q. v.) Gn 12^{6} 24$^{3.37}$ 50^{11} (all J), Nu 21^{3} (J), Jos 13^{3} (D), Ju 1$^{1.3.9.10.17}$, many of whom continued to live in the midst of Isr., v$^{27.28.29.29.30.32.33}$ Jos 16$^{10.10}$ 17$^{12.13.16.18}$ (all JE), 1 K 9^{16}; pl. only Ob^{20}, and יֹשְׁבֵי הָאָרֶץ הַכְּנַעֲנִים Ne 9^{24}; מִשְׁפְּחוֹת הַכּ׳ Gn 10^{18}, גְּבוּל הַכּ׳ v^{19} (both J), אֶרֶץ הַכּ׳ Ex 13^{11} (JE), Ez 16^{3}; oft. of *part* of the inhabit., הַכּ׳ וְכֹל יֹשְׁבֵי הָאָרֶץ Jos 7^{9} (JE), Dt 11^{30}; with other n.pr.gent., + הַפְּרִזִּי Gn 13^{7} 34^{30} (both J), Ju 1$^{4.5}$, + הָאֱמֹרִי Dt 1^{7} Jos 5^{1} 13^{4} (all D); + הַחִוִּי 2 S 24^{7}; + עֲמָלֵק(י) Nu 14$^{25.43.45}$; esp. in the list of peoples dispossessed by Isr., Gn 15^{21} Ex 3$^{8.17}$ 13^{5} 23$^{23.28}$ 33^{2} 34^{11} Nu 13^{29} (הַכּ׳ dwelling by the sea and along Jordan [cf. Dt 1^{7} 11^{30} Jos 5^{1} 11^{3} 13^{4}]; all these JE), Dt 7^{1} 20^{17} Jos 3^{10} 9^{1} 11^{3} 12^{8} 24^{11} (all JED), Ju 3$^{3.5}$; hence Ezr 9^{1} Ne 9^{8}. Cf. Dr$^{Dt. p. 11, 13 f., 97, 133}$.

3669 †II. כְּנַעֲנִי **n.m. trader, merchant** (cf. II. כְּנַעַן); only sg. (but v. infr.):—וְלֹא יִהְיֶה כ׳ עוֹד בְּבֵית י׳ Zc 14^{21} (prob.); וַחֲגוֹר נָתְנָה לַכּ׳ Pr 31^{24} (|| סָדִין עָשְׂתָה וַתִּמְכֹּר). In Zc 11$^{7.11}$ rd. perh. (לְ)כְנַעֲנִיֵּי for (לָ)כֵן עֲנִיֵּי, 𝔊 Χαναναῖοι, Χαναανῖτιν, Sta$^{ZAW, 1881, 26}$ (who comp. as to sense Ho 12^{8}), cf. Klo We Marti.

3668 †כְּנַעֲנָה **n.pr.m.** **1.** father of proph. Zedekiah 1 K 22$^{11.24}$ = 2 Ch 18$^{10.23}$ (𝔊 Χαναάν, Χαανα, Χανανα). **2.** a Benjamite 1 Ch 7^{10} (𝔊 Χαναάν, Χαναναν).

כנף √ of foll. (mng. dub.; Ar. كَنَفَ *fence in, enclose*, and Aram. כְּנַף *collect, assemble*, are denom.)

3671 כָּנָף$_{109}$ **n.f.** $^{1 K 6, 27}$ (**m.** Ez 7^{2} Kt, but cf. Qr and Co; also appar. 2 Ch 3$^{11.13}$, but v. Be), **wing, extremity** (NH *id.*; Aram. כַּנְפָּא, ܟܢܦܐ; Zinj. אחז בכנף מראה, fig. for *attached himself to the party of his lord*, Panammu$^{Inscr. l. 11}$, cf. Zc 8^{23} (**2 a** infr.); DHM$^{Sendsch. 58}$; Ar. كَنَفٌ, As. *kappu*, Eth. ክንፍ:);—abs. כ׳ Gn 1^{21} +; cstr. כְּנַף 1 K 6^{24} +; sf. כְּנָפִי Ez 16^{8}, כְּנָפֶךָ Ru 3^{9}, כְּנָפוֹ Hg 2^{12}; du. כְּנָפַיִם 1 K 8^{7} + (even of more than two, Is 6$^{2.2}$ Ez 1$^{6.21}$); cstr. כַּנְפֵי Ex 19^{4}; sf. כְּנָפֶיךָ Ez 5^{3}, כְּנָפַיִךְ Je 2^{34}, כְּנָפָיו Is 8^{8} +; כְּנָפֶיהָ Ho 4^{19} Mal 3^{20}; כַּנְפֵיהֶם 1 K 6^{27} +; כַּנְפֵיהֶן Ez 1$^{24.25}$; pl. cstr. כַּנְפוֹת Dt 22^{12} + 4 t.; —**1.** *wing*, †**a.** of birds Is 10^{14} (in fig.), Ex 19^{4} (E? R? fig.) Dt 32^{11} (in sim.), Zc 5^{9} Lv 1^{17} (P), Jb 39$^{13.26}$ ψ 68^{14}; in fig. of invading king Je 48^{40} 49^{22} Ez 17$^{3.7}$; so appar. Is 8^{8} of invader as overflowing river (but Du Che separate וְהָיָה מֻטּוֹת כְּנָפָיו from preceding); of riches, as flying away Pr 23^{5}; in phr. צִפּוֹר כָּנָף = *winged birds* Dt 4^{17} ψ 148^{10}, (עֵיט)צִפּוֹר כָּל־כ׳ Ez 39$^{4.17}$, כֹּל צִפּוֹר כָּל־כ׳ Gn 7^{14} (P), Ez 17^{23}, עוֹף כ׳ Gn 1^{21} (P), ψ 78^{27}; also בַּעַל כ׳ Pr 1^{17} = *winged thing*, cf. בַּעַל־הַכְּנָפַיִם Ec 10^{20}. †**b.** of insects (prob.), אֶרֶץ צִלְצַל כְּנָפָיִם Is 18^{1} *buzzing*, or *humming of wings*, i.e. Ethiopia, so called from its swarms of flies, with especial ref. poss. to the tsetse-fly (so Du, cf. Che; id., in gen., Hi De; > Kn Di of the tropical *shadow falling both ways;* Thes$^{1167 b}$ of *noise of the wings* of an army; ref. to sails as wings—cf. v^{2}—would be suitable, but צִלְצַל does not favour this). **c.** of cherubim 1 K 6$^{24.24.24.24}$ + 8 t. K, cf. 2 Ch 3$^{11.11.11.11}$ + 6 t. Ch, Ez 1^{6} + 17 t. Ez, Ex 25$^{20.20}$ 39$^{9.9}$ (all P). †**d.** of seraphim Is 6$^{2.2}$. †**e.** of women in Zec.'s vision Zc 5$^{9.9}$. †**f.** fig. of the wind, Ho 4^{19} ψ 18^{11} = 2 S 22^{11}, ψ 104^{3}. †**g.** fig. of the dawn (winged sun-disc?) ψ 139^{9}, cf. of sun of righteousness Mal 3^{20}. †**h.** fig. of י׳, as protector of his people ψ 17^{8} 36^{8} 57^{2} 61^{5} 63^{3} 91^{4} Ru 2^{12}. †**2.** *extremity:*—**a.** of garment = *skirt, corner*, or loose flowing end, 1 S 15^{27} 24$^{5.6.12.12}$ Dt 22^{12} 23^{1} 27^{20} Je 2^{34} (fig.), Ez 5^{3} 16^{8} (in fig.), Hg 2$^{12.12}$ Zc 8^{23} Nu 15$^{38.38}$ (P; cf. RS$^{Sem. i. 416, 2nd ed. 437}$). **b.** of the earth, מִכְּנַף הָאָרֶץ Is 24^{16} *from the end of the earth;* elsewhere pl. כַּנְפוֹת הָא׳ Jb 37^{3} 38^{13}, and, def. אַרְבַּע כ׳ הא׳ Is 11^{12} *the four corners of the earth;* so of the holy land Ez 7^{2}.—עַל־כְּנַף שִׁקּוּצִים מְשֹׁמֵם Dn 9^{27} is obscure; Meinh. reads, after Vrss., כָּנָף, *on the corner* (of the altar) *is a devastating abomination;* < Kue$^{Onderzoek 2, ii. 472}$ Bev, who rd. עַל־כַּנּוֹ *in its place, instead of it.*

†[כָּנַף] **vb. denom.** fr. כָּנָף **2.** only **Niph.** 3670
be cornered, thrust into a corner, or aside;— *Impf.* 3 ms. וְלֹא יִכָּנֵף עוֹד מוֹרֶיךָ Is 30^{20} *and no more shall thy teachers be thrust into a corner* (cf. Di); > others, who render *hide themselves*, (cf. Ar. كَنَفَ *enclose, guard*, but this rather for protection).

כנר (poss. √ of foll.; meaning unknown).

3658 †כִּנּוֹר **n.m.** [ψ 81, 3] **lyre** (on formation cf. Lag [BN 89, Anm.]; NH *id.;* Aram. כִּנָּרָא, ܟܢܳܪܐ; Mand. (א)כינאר Nö [M § 104] (who questions Shemitic origin); Ar. كِنَّارٌ, كَنَّارَةٌ; as loan-word in Hellen. Gk. κινύρα (𝔊 and Joseph.); in Egypt. *kn-an-aul* acc. to Bondi [79])—abs. כ׳ Gn 4^{21}+; sf. כִּנֹּרִי Jb 30^{31}; pl. כִּנֹּרוֹת 1 K 10^{12}+; sf. כִּנּוֹרַיִךְ Ez 26^{13}, כִּנֹּרוֹתֵינוּ ψ 137^{2};—*lyre,* stringed instrument used for popular as well as sacred music (cf. Benz [Arch. 273 ff.] Now [Arch. i. 273 ff.]);—כ׳ אִישׁ יֹדֵעַ מְנַגֵּן בַּכּ׳, Gn 4^{21}, 31^{27} בְּתֹף וּבְכ׳; וְעוּגָב 1 S 16^{16} *a man skilled in playing on the lyre,* cf. v^{23} (וְנִגֵּן בְּיָדוֹ); at banquets Is 5^{12} (+ נֶבֶל, תֹּף, חָלִיל), token of merriment 24^{8} (+ תֻּפִּים), Ez 26^{13}, cf. וַיְהִי לְאֵבֶל כִּנֹּרִי וְעֻגָבִי לְקוֹל בֹּכִים Jb 30^{31}, יִשְׂאוּ כְּתֹף וְכ׳ וְיִשְׂמְחוּ לְקוֹל עוּגָב Jb 21^{12}; carried by a loose woman Is 23^{16} (fig. of Tyre); in sim. Is 16^{11} (of murmuring sound of bowels=heart, in pity); used also in praising י׳, usu. as accompaniment of song (cf. 1 Ch 15^{16}) נֶבֶל וְתֹף וְחָלִיל וְכ׳ 1 S 10^{5}; Is 30^{32} (‖תֻּפִּים); esp. before the ark 2 S 6^{5} (+ תֻּפִּים, נְבָלִים, etc.) ‖ 1 Ch 13^{8}, and in sanctuary (usu. + נֶבֶל, etc.) 1 K 10^{12}, but esp. Chr ψψ:—1 Ch 13^{8} (pl., and so chiefly in Chr), $15^{16.21.28}$ 16^{5} $25^{1.3.6}$ 2 Ch 5^{12} 9^{11} 20^{28} 29^{25} Ne 12^{27}; ψ 33^{2} (sg., and so chiefly in ψψ), 43^{4} 49^{5} 57^{9} 71^{22} 81^{3} 92^{4} $98^{5.5}$ 108^{3} 147^{7} 149^{3} 150^{3}; cf. כִּנּוֹרוֹתֵינוּ ψ 137^{2}.—Vbs. used with כ׳ are:— תָּפַשׂ Gn 4^{21}, נִגֵּן בְּ 1 S 16^{16}, מְשַׂחֵק בְּ 2 S 6^{5}= 1 Ch 13^{8}, מְשַׁרֲרִים בּ 1 Ch 15^{16}, מַשְׁמִיעִים בְּ v^{28}, נִבָּא בְּ $25^{1.3}$, הוֹדָה בְּ ψ 33^{2} 43^{4}, זמּר בְּ ψ 71^{22} 98^{5} 147^{7} 149^{3}, הַלְלוּהוּ בְּ 150^{3}.—On ancient lyres v. reff. ap. Dr [Amos, p. 236 f.]

3672 †כִּנֶּרֶת, כִּנֲּרוֹת **n.pr.loc.** in Galilee (Naphtali), כִּנֶּרֶת Dt 3^{17} Jos 13^{27} Nu 34^{11}; כִּנֶּרֶת Jos 19^{35}; כִּנֲּרוֹת (so Baer; כִּנְּרוֹת Norzi) Jos 11^{2} 12^{3} 1 K 15^{20};—**1.** a city Jos 19^{35} (P; 𝔊B Κενερεθ, A Χενεροθ, 𝔊L Χενερεθ, as always exc. Jos 13^{27}), so prob. 11^{2} (D?; B Κενερωθ, A Χενερεθθι), Dt 3^{17} (B Μαχαναρεθ;—Μαχ-=מִכּ׳). **2.** יָם־כִּנֶּרֶת, lake near the city, Nu 34^{11} (P; 𝔊B Χεναρα, A Χενερεθ), Jos 13^{27} (P; 𝔊B Χενερεθ; A 𝔊L Χενερωθ), יָם כִּנֲּרוֹת Jos 12^{3} (D; 𝔊B Χενερεθ; A Χεννερεθ); כָּל־כִּנֲּרוֹת 1 K 15^{20} = all the territory about the city and lake, cf. πᾶσαν τὴν γῆν Χενερεθ 𝔊L,—𝔗 has גִּנֹּסַר, גְּנֵיסַר, גִּינֵסַר, cf. τὸ ὕδωρ τοῦ Γεννησαρ 1 Makk. 11^{67}; Γεννησαρετ Mk 6^{53} Mt 14^{34} Lu 5^{1}; etymol. connexion with כִּנֶּרֶת disputed by GASm [Geogr. 443 n.] Buhl [Geogr. 113 n.] —On the lake and surrounding region v. GASm [Geogr. ch. xxi.] Bd [Pal 254] Buhl [Geogr. 113 f. 225] Furrer [ZPV. 1879 (ii.), 52-74] Frei [ib. 1886 (ix.), 81-145] van Kasteren [ib. 1888 (xi.), 212-248].

†[כְּנָת] **n.** [of men, but **f.** in form, Ges [§122, 4. b]] 3674
associate, colleague (loan-wd. fr. BAram. כְּנָת; Syr. ܟܢܳܬܐ, cf. also Schwally [Idiot. 46]; on format. v. Lag [BN 82]);—only Aram. pl. שְׁאָר כְּנָוָתוֹ Ezr 4^{7} *the rest of his associates.*

כֵּס Ex 17^{16}, v. כִּסֵּא. below 3676

†כֶּסֶא Pr 7^{20}, כֶּסֶה ψ 81^{4} **n.** [**m.**] **full moon** 3677
(cf. Aram. ܟܶܣܳܐ; orig. dubious, cf. Lag [Symm. i. 93]; perh. As. loan-word; cf. As. *kusêu, headdress* or *cap,=agû, id.,* and also *full moon* (as tiara of moon-god?), Dl [HWB], sub *kusêu, kubšu, agû;* yet v. Brock)—לְיוֹם הַכּ׳ Pr 7^{20}; as a feast-day, בַּכּ׳ ψ 81^{4} (opp. בַּחֹדֶשׁ, *at the new moon*).

כִּסֵּא, כִּסֵּה [133] **n.m.** [2 S 7, 16] **seat** of honour, 3678
throne (NH *id.;* Ph. (pl.) כרסים; Aram. כּוּרְסְיָא, ܟܽܘܪܣܝܳܐ; BAram. כָּרְסֵא, Zinj. כרסא DHM [Sendsch. 58. 44]; Ar. كُرْسِيٌّ; but As. *kussu;* perh. Akkad. loan-word; ideogr. *is* GU. ZA, cf. Dl [HWB 343]);—abs. כִּסֵּא Gn 41^{40}+; כִּסֵּה 1 K $10^{19.19}$ Jb 26^{9}, הַכִּסֵּא Ez 1^{26}; cstr. כִּסֵּא 2 S 3^{10}+,
כֵּס Ex 17^{16} (si vera l.; v. infr.); sf. כִּסְאִי 1 K 3676
1^{13}+, כִּסְאֲךָ 2 S 7^{16}+, כִּסְאֶךָ 1 K 5^{19}+, כִּסְאוֹ Ex 11^{5}+; pl. כִּסְאוֹת ψ $122^{5.5}$; sf. כִּסְאוֹתָם Ez 26^{16} Is 14^{9};—*seat of honour,* usually **1. a.** of king=*throne* Gn 41^{40} (E), Ex 11^{5} 12^{29} (both J) 1 K 2^{19} Is 47^{1} Ez 26^{16}; of queen-mother 1 K 2^{19b}; כ׳ מַלְכוּתוֹ Est 5^{1} *his royal throne;* of future (Messianic) prince Zc 6^{13a} (in v^{b} read על־ימינו 𝔊 Sta [ZAW 1881, 10]); of dead kings in She'ôl Is 14^{9}; נָתַן כ׳, in, or against a place, said of king himself, (only Je) is a sign of conquest (Je 1^{15}); so שִׂים כ׳ 43^{10}, and (of י׳) 49^{38}; in Ju 3^{20}, though of king, not seat of office; 12 t. elsewhere, lit. †**b.** *throne* of י׳ (אלהים) as heavenly king, Is 6^{1} Ez $1^{26.26}$ 10^{1} 1 K 22^{19}=2 Ch 18^{18}; Jb 26^{9} ψ 11^{4} Is 66^{1} *heaven is my throne;* as seat of judgment ψ $9^{5.8}$; in
oath יָד עַל־כֵּס יָהּ Ex 17^{16} (cf. Di; >Cler JDMich 3676
Ges Buhl SS נֵס *banner;* 𝔊 κρυφαίᾳ √ כסה, favours כס); Jerusalem called throne of י׳ Je 3^{17}, so the sanctuary 17^{12} (כ׳ כָּבוֹד מָרוֹם), Ez 43^{7}. †**2.** of high priest 1 S 1^{9} $4^{13.18}$; of honoured guest 2 K 4^{10}; of governor Ne 3^{7}; of (unjust) judge כ׳ הַוּוֹת ψ 94^{20}; =conspicuous seat (lit.) Pr 9^{14}; =seat of distinction, explicitly כ׳ כָּבוֹד Is 22^{23}; כ׳ alone 2 K $25^{28.28}$=Je $52^{32.32}$ Est 3^{1}.

3. a. fig. = *royal dignity, authority, power,* הַמֶּלֶךְ וְכִסְאוֹ נָקִי 2 S 14^9; לְדָוִד וּלְזַרְעוֹ וּלְבֵיתוֹ וּלְכִ׳ 1 K 2^{33}; esp. *kingdom,* c. vbs. of *setting up, establishing,* ׳י subj., הָקִים כ׳ דָּוִד 2 S 3^{10}, וּבָנִיתִי כִסְאֲךָ ψ 89^5, so c. שִׂים v^{30}; king subj., סָעַד בַּחֶסֶד כִּסְאוֹ Pr 20^{28}; pass. כ׳ דָוִד יִהְיֶה נכון 1 K 2^{45} *the throne of David shall be established,* cf. 2 S 7^{16} = 1 Ch 17^{14}; וְהוּכַן בַּחֶסֶד כ׳ Is 16^5 (of Mess. reign); so (in gen.) בִּצְדָקָה יִכּוֹן כ׳ Pr 16^{12}, cf. 25^5 29^{14}; intrans. (c. הָיָה) ψ 89^{37}; more fully, כֹּנֵן כסאו) ׳י subj., וְכֹנַנְתִּי אֶת־כ׳ מַמְלַכְתּוֹ 2 S 7^{13} in ∥ 1 Ch 17^{12}), וַהֲקִמֹתִי אֶת־כ׳ מַמְלַכְתְּךָ עַל־יִשְׂרָאֵל 1 K 9^5, cf. ∥ 2 Ch 7^{18} and וַהֲכִינוֹתִי כ׳ מַלְכוּתוֹ עַל־יִשְׂרָאֵל 1 Ch 22^{10}; also מגר כ׳ ψ 89^{45} *cast down throne,* of Gentile nations וְהָפַכְתִּי כ׳ מַמְלָכוֹת Hg 2^{22}; יָשַׁב עַל־כ׳ *sit on the throne of* any one (esp. David) = be his successor 1 K 1$^{13.17.20.24.27.30.35.48}$ 2^{12} 3^6 2 K 13^{13}, esp. Je 13^{13} 17^{25} 22^2 + 5 t. Je; יֵשְׁבוּ לְכִ׳ לָךְ ψ 132^{12}; more fully 1 Ch 29^{23}; †caus. הוֹשִׁיב עַל־כ׳ 1 K 2^{24} 5^{19} 2 K 10^3; הֹשִׁיב לַכִּ׳ fig. Jb 36^7, of placing in honour; מִפְּרִי בִטְנְךָ אָשִׁית לְכִ׳ לָךְ ψ 132^{11}; †ישב עַל־כ׳ also = *take one's seat as king, become actual king, possess royalty* 1 K 16^{11}, oft. sit on the *throne of Isr.* 1 K 8$^{20.25}$ = 2 Ch 6$^{10.16}$, 1 K 10^9 2 K 10^{30} 15^{12}, Je 33^{17}; without ישב 1 K 2^4 9^5, cf. also Is 9^6 (Mess.); ישב על־כסא מַמְלַכְתּוֹ Dt 17^{18}, על־כסא הַמְּלוּכָה 1 K 1^{46}, and even לָשֶׁבֶת ישב עַל־כִּסֵּא מַלְכוּת ׳י עַל־יִשְׂרָאֵל 1 Ch 28^5; also עַל־כ׳ הַמְּלָכִים 2 K 11^{19}, ∥ כ׳ הַמַּמְלָכָה 2 Ch 23^{30}; of (royal) throne as judgment seat Pr 20^8, cf. also ψ 122^5; set one upon the throne of Isr. נתן פ׳ על־כ׳ יש׳ 1 K 10^9 cf. ∥ 2 Ch 9^8; in compar. sentence יְגַדֵּל אֶת־כִּסְאוֹ מִכ׳, i.e. make him a more powerful king than, 1 K 1^{37}, cf. v^{47}; of king of Babylon, מִמַּעַל לְכוֹכְבֵי־אֵל אָרִים כִּסְאִי Is 14^{13}. In ψ 45^7 כִּסְאֲךָ אלהים וגו׳ the text is prob. corrupt: AE Hi Ew Bae read *thy throne is (a throne) of God;* Bi Che insert נכונה יסודתו הקימו *thy throne* [*its foundation is firmly fixed*], God [has established it]; v. further Dr$^{§194, Obs.}$. †**b.** throne of ׳י (אלהים) = his royal dignity, sovereignty, La 5^{19} ψ 93^2 103^{19} (הֵכִין כ׳ ∥ מַלְכוּת); כ׳ כְּבוֹדֶךָ Je 14^{21}; יָשַׁב עַל־כ׳ קָדְשׁוֹ ψ 47^9; צֶדֶק וּמִשְׁפָּט מְכוֹן כִּסְאֶךָ ψ 89^{15} cf. 97^2.

3680 †I. [כָּסָה] **vb. cover** (NH כָּסָה Pi; Aram. כְּסָא chiefly Pa; ܟܣܐ Pa. *hide, cover;* ܟܣܘܝܐ *covering,* ܬܟܣܝܬܐ *garment;* Ar. كَسَا (كسو) *clothe,* كِسَاءٌ *garment;* As. *kusû,* cover; *kuṣîtu,* garment Dl$^{HWB 342}$)—**Qal,** only *Pt. act.* כֹּסֶה;—**1.** *conceal* shame Pr 12^{16}; knowledge Pr 12^{23}. **2.** *pass.* (cstr.) כְּסוּי חֲטָאָה ψ 32^1 *covered* in respect of sin (by God, which he thus puts out of sight) (∥ נְשׂוּי־פֶּשַׁע). **Niph.** *Pf.* 3 fs. נִכְסָתָה, *covered,* with waves Je 51^{42}; *Inf. cstr.* הִכָּסוֹת Ez 24^8, (blood) not to be covered. **Pi.** *Pf.* 3 ms. כִּסָּה Nu 9^{15} + 12 t.; sf. כִּסָּהוּ Lv 17^{13} Nu 17^7; כִּסָּמוֹ Ex 15^{10}; 3 fs. כִּסַּתָה Gn 38^{15} + 5 t.; 1 s. כִּסִּיתִי ψ 32^5 + 3 t.; כִּסֵּתִי Ez 31^{15} (del. Co); כִּסֵּיתִי Ez 32^7 + 13 t. Pf.; *Impf.* 3 ms. יְכַסֶּה Is 6^2 + 8 t.; וַיְכַס Ex 10^{15} + 4 t.; sf. יְכַסֶּךָּ Hab 2^{17}; יְכַסֶּנָּה Ez 30^{18}; 3 mpl. sf. יְכַסְיֻמוּ Ex 15^5 + 41 t. Impf.; *Imv.* sf. כַּסּוּנוּ Ho 10^8; *Inf. cstr.* כַּסּוֹת Mal 2^{13} + 11 t.; כַּסֹּת Nu 4^{15}; sf. כַּסֹּתוֹ Ex 26^{13}; *Pt.* מְכַסֶּה Pr 10^{18} + 12 t.; pl. מְכַסִּים Is 11^9; fpl. מְכַסּוֹת Ez 1$^{11.23.23}$;—**1.** *cover, clothe* Ju 4^{19} Ez 16^{10} (2 acc.), v^{18}; Jon 3^6 is appar. reflex., c. acc. of garment (strange; rd. perh. וַיְכַס); nakedness Gn 9^{23} (J), Ex 28^{42} (P), Ez 16^8 Ho 2^{11}; the naked Is 58^7 Ez 18$^{7.16}$ (+ acc. rei); the face and legs of seraphim Is 6$^{2.2}$; bodies of cherubim Ez 1$^{11.23.23}$; the face Gn 38^{15} (J), Ez 12$^{6.12}$, fig. Jb 23^{17}; earth with the great deep ψ 104^6; heavens with glory Hab 3^3; with בְּ of the clothing Gn 38^{14} (J), Dt 22^{12}, these two appar. reflex., cf. Jon 3^6 supr.; Ju 4^{18} 1 K 1^1; heaven with clouds ψ 147^8, with glory Ez 32^7. **2.** *cover, conceal* blood Gn 37^{26} (J), Jb 16^{18}; human ordure Dt 23^{14}; mts. conceal men from God Ho 10^8; *cover* transgressions Jb 31^{33} Pr 17^9 28^{13}; iniquity ψ 32^5; righteousness ψ 40^{11}; hatred Pr 10^{18}; a thing Pr 11^{13}; face of judge so that he cannot see justice Jb 9^{24}; rulers and seers Is 29^{10}; with בְּ of covering Lv 17^{13} (H), 1 S 19^{13}; face by fat Jb 15^{27}; sun by a cloud Ez 32^7; with מִן from whom Gn 18^{17} (J), Jb 33^{17}. **3.** *cover* (with covering of protection), a pit Ex 21^{33} (Covt. code); with cloud of incense, the Kapporeth Lv 16^{13} (P); coverings of the sacred tent, tabernacle, and their furniture Ex 26^{13} Nu 4$^{9.15}$ (P); with בְּ of the covering Nu 4$^{5.8.11.12}$ (P); Zion בְּצֵל יָדִי Is 51^{16}. **4.** *cover, spread over,* fat, the inwards Ex 29$^{13.22}$ Lv 3$^{3.9.14}$ 4^8 (with עַל), 7^3 (P); leprosy, the skin and flesh Lv 13$^{12.13}$ (P); the cloud of the theophany, the mount Ex 24$^{15.16}$ (P), the tent of meeting Ex 40^{34} Nu 17^7 (P), and the tabernacle Nu 9$^{15.16}$ (P); altar with tears Mal 2^{13} (2 acc.); Jerusalem with multitude of camels Is 60^6; of handiwork 1 K 7$^{18.41.42}$ = 2 Ch 4$^{12.13}$. **5.** *cover, overwhelm,* sq. accus., the sea the Egyptians Ex 14^{28} (P), 15$^{5.10}$ (song), Jos 24^7 (E), ψ 78^{53} 106^{11}; waters Jb 22^{11} 38^{34} ψ 104^9 Je 46^8 Ez 26^{19}; locusts the eye of the land Ex

$10^{5.15}$ (J), also Israel Nu $22^{5.11}$ (J); frogs the land Ex 8^{2} (P); quails the camp Ex 16^{13} (P); cloud the land Ez 30^{18} $38^{9.16}$; darkness the earth Is 60^{2}; dust a city Ez 26^{10}; the depths of the sea by God Jb 36^{30}; with a reference to a person's shame ψ 44^{16} 69^{8} Je 51^{51} Ob ^{10} Mi 7^{10}; horror ψ 55^{6} Ez 7^{18}; violence Pr $10^{6.11}$ Hb 2^{17}; confusion Je 3^{25}; mischief ψ 140^{10}; God *covers sin* ψ 85^{3} (|| נשׂא עון), cf. 32^{1} (Qal). **6.** sq. על of person or thing covered, *cover over:* cherubim over the ark 2 Ch 5^{8}; over the dead, the earth Nu 16^{33} (JE), ψ 106^{17} Is 26^{21}, worms Jb 21^{26}; dust over blood Ez 24^{7}; waters over the sea Hb 2^{14}, cf. לַיָּם Is 11^{9}; (v. Dr$^{§ 135.7 Obs.}$); love covereth over all sins Pr 10^{12}; God covereth over iniquity Ne 3^{37}; people not to cover over a guilty person Dt 13^{9}; + acc. of obj. covering (Da$^{Synt. § 75}$), fig. covering over the garment with violence Mal 2^{16}; God's hands with light Jb 36^{32}; + בְּ of covering ψ 44^{20}.

Note.—(אֵלֶיךָ) כִסִּתִי ψ 143^{9} is error for חָסִיתִי acc. to 𝔊 κατέφυγον SS, but חסה not cstr. wi. אֶל־; הֶאֱבַלְתִּי כִּסֵּתִי עָלָיו אֶת־תְּהוֹם Ez 31^{15} חִבֵּיתִי Bae; acc. to Co *I caused the deep to mourn for them* (del. כסתי). **Pual.** *Pf.* 3 mpl. כֻּסּוּ ψ 80^{11} Pr 24^{31}; *Impf.* יְכֻסֶּה Ec 6^{4}; *pl.* וַיְכֻסּוּ Gn $7^{19.20}$; *Pt.* pl. מְכֻסִּים 1 Ch 21^{16}; fpl. מְכֻסּוֹת Ez 41^{16}. **1.** sq. accus. *be covered*, hills with shadow ψ 80^{11}; mountains with water Gn $7^{19.20}$ (P); field with nettles Pr 24^{31}; abs., windows of temple Ez 41^{16}. **2.** sq. בְּ, *be clothed*, with sackcloth 1 Ch 21^{16}; name with darkness Ec 6^{4}.

Hithp. *Impf.* וַיִּתְכַּס Is 37^{1} = 2 K 19^{1}; 3 fs. תִּכַּסֶּה Pr 26^{26}; וַתִּתְכָּס Gn 24^{65}; pl. יִתְכַּסּוּ Is 59^{6} Jon 3^{8}; *Pt.* מִתְכַּסֶּה 1 K 11^{29}; pl. מִתְכַּסִּים Is 37^{2} = 2 K 19^{2};—*cover, clothe oneself*, abs. (of veil) Gn 24^{65} (J); with בְּ, of new garment 1 K 11^{29}; sackcloth 2 K $19^{1.2}$ = Is $37^{1.2}$; fig. of works Is 59^{6}, of hatred with guile Pr 26^{26}; with acc. Jon 3^{5} (שַׂקִּים).

3681 †[כָּסוּי] **n.[m.] covering**, only cstr. כְּסוּי עוֹר *covering of skins* Nu $4^{6.14}$ (P).

3682 †כְּסוּת **n.f. covering**—כ׳ Gn 20^{16} + 3 t.; sf. כְּסוּתְךָ Dt 22^{12} + 3 t. sfs.;—**1.** *covering, clothing* Ex 21^{10} 22^{26} (Covt. code), Dt 22^{12} Jb 24^{7} 31^{19}; of שַׂק as clothing of heavens Is 50^{3} in fig. **2.** *covering* for concealment, of Abaddon, the subterranean abode of the dead Jb 26^{6}; כ׳ עֵינַיִם, *covering of the eyes* Gn 20^{16} (so that they cannot see the wrong, fig. of a present offered in compensation for it; E).

†מִכְסֶה **n.[m.] covering**;—מ׳ Ex 26^{14} 36^{19}; 4372
cstr. מִכְסֵה Gn 8^{13} + 10 t.; sf. מִכְסֵהוּ Ex 35^{11} + 2 t.;—**1.** *covering* of the ark, deck-roof (𝔊 στέγη) Gn 8^{13} (J). **2.** of the skins of the tent of meeting Ex $26^{14.14}$ 35^{11} $36^{19.19}$ $39^{34.34}$ 40^{19} Nu 3^{25} $4^{8.10.11.12.25.25}$ (all P).

†מְכַסֶּה **n.m.**$^{Is 23.18}$ **covering**;—מ׳ Lv 9^{19} Is 4374
23^{18}; sf. מְכַסֵּךְ Ez 27^{7}; pl. sf. מְכַסֶּיךָ Is 14^{11}; of fat covering (the inwards) Lv 9^{19}; worms, covering the dead Is 14^{11}, deck of a ship Ez 27^{7} (Co *Kajütenwand*); garment Is 23^{18}.

II. כסה (√of foll.; prob. *bind;* cf. As. *kasû, take captive,* **Pi.** *fetter, kasîtu, kisittu, a fetter;* Zehnpfund$^{BAS i, 536}$ Dl$^{Baer's Ezech. xii, HWB 342}$).

†[כֶּסֶת] **n.f. band, fillet** (= charm or 3704
amulet acc. to Ephr. Syr., φυλακτήρια acc. to ὁ Ἑβραῖος of Hexapl., cf. RS$^{JPh xiii, 286}$; in NH כסת usu. = *cushion, bolster, pillow*), only pl. מְתַפְּרוֹת כְּסָתוֹת עַל־ Ez 13^{18} women *sewing bands upon* elbows; c. sf. 2 fpl. כִּסְּתוֹתֵיכֶנָה v^{20}.

כֶּסֶה v. כֶּסֶא. p. 490 3677

כֵּסֶה v. כֵּסֵא. p. 490 3678

כַּסּוּחָה Is 5^{25} v. סוּחָה. p. 691 5478

כְּסוּת, כָּסוּי v. sub I. כסה. above 3681-82

†[כָּסַח] **vb. cut off** or **away**, a plant 3683
(NH *id.;* Aram. כְּסַח, ܟܣܚ (for Heb. זָמַר); Ar. كَسَحَ *sweep off, away, destroy, do away with;* cf. Sab. כסח *overpower, conquer,* Hom$^{ZMG 1892, 532}$)—only **Qal** *Pt. pass.*, fs. כְּסוּחָה ψ 80^{17}, *cut away*, of Isr. under fig. of vine; mpl. קוֹצִים כְּסוּחִים Is 33^{12} *thorns cut away*, fig. of peoples destroyed by divine judgment.

†[כָּסַל] **vb. be** or **become stupid** (NH 3688
Aram. in deriv.; Ar. كَسِلَ *be sluggish*, so N Syr. in deriv.; orig. mng. possibly *thick, plump, fat;* hence in good sense: כֶּסֶל, כִּסְלָה, כְּסָלִים *loins, confidence;* in bad sense: כֶּסֶל, כִּסְלָה, כְּסִילוּת *stupidity, folly,* כְּסִיל *stupid fellow*)—**Qal** *Impf.* יִכְסָלוּ *they become stupid* Je 10^{8} (|| יִבְעֲרוּ *they become brutish*).

†כֶּסֶל **n.m. 1. loins, 2. stupidity, 3. con-** 3689
fidence (NH *id. loin;* Aram. כִּסְלָא *id.*);—**1.** *loins* כָּסֶל Jb 15^{27}; pl. כְּסָלִים Lv $3^{4.10.15}$ 4^{9} 7^{4}; sf. כְּסָלַי ψ 38^{8}. **2.** *stupidity, folly* כ׳ Ec 7^{25} (|| סִכְלוּת), כֶּסֶל ψ 49^{14}. **3.** *confidence*, sf. כִּסְלִי Jb 31^{24}; כִּסְלֶךָ Pr 3^{26}; כִּסְלוֹ Jb 8^{14}; כִּסְלָם ψ 78^{7}.

3690 †כִּסְלָה **n.f.** (Gie ZAW i, 1881, 304). **1. stupidity** ψ 85^{9} (but rd. לִבָּם לה 𝔊 Bae Che). **2. confidence,** sf. כִּסְלָתֶךָ Jb 4^{6}.

3684 I. כְּסִיל$_{70}$ **n.m. stupid fellow, dullard, fool;**—כ׳ ψ 49^{11} + 44 t.; pl. כְּסִילִים ψ 94^{8} + 25 t.; —|| בער ψ 49^{11} 92^{7} 94^{8}, elsewh. only in Wisd Lt.; he hates knowledge Pr 1^{22}; delights not in understanding 18^{2}; it is his sport to do mischief 10^{23}; his heart proclaimeth אִוֶּלֶת 12^{23}; his mouth poureth it forth 15^{2}, and feedeth on it 15^{14}.

3687 †כְּסִילוּת **n.f. stupidity;**—Pr 9^{13} אֵשֶׁת כ׳, *the woman Stupidity,* in antithesis with חָכְמוֹת the Supreme Wisdom personified as a woman.

3685 †II. כְּסִיל **n.m. Orion** (relation to above √ obscure);—Am 5^{8} Jb 9^{9}; also מֹשְׁכוֹת כ׳ תְּפַתֵּחַ 38^{31} *the cords of Orion wilt* (*canst*) *thou let out?* (appar. some mythological allusion, v. Di Che, to giant bound in skies; cf. Hom. Ὠρίωνα δοκεύει, and σθένος Ὠρίωνος); both times associated with the Pleiades; sf. כְּסִילֵיהֶם *their Orions* Is 13^{10}, Orion and other constellations of the same brilliancy.

3686 †III. כְּסִיל **n.pr.loc.** in S of tribe of Judah Jos 15^{30}, prob. corrupt for בְּתוּל Jos 19^{4}; see בְּתוּאֵל.

3693 †כְּסָלוֹן **n.pr.loc.** on border of tribe of Judah = הַר־יְעָרִים Jos 15^{10}; = *Kesla* 10 miles W. Jerus., Guérin Jud. ii. 11 ff. Mem iii. 25.26 Buhl G. § 92, p. 166.

3692 †כִּסְלוֹן **n.pr.m.** a prince of Benjamin Nu 34^{21}.

3694 †כְּסֻלּוֹת **n.pr.loc.** in the tribe of Issachar
3696 Jos 19^{18}, = כִּסְלֹת תָּבֹר (loins or flanks of Tabor),
8396 on the W. foot of Mt. Tabor, Jos 19^{12}; = תָּבוֹר Jos
19^{22} 1 Ch 6^{62}; = mod. *Iksâl* Rob BR iii. 182, Mem i. 365 Buhl G. § 113, p. 216.

3691 †כִּסְלֵו **n.pr.[m.] Kislew,** ninth month (postex.) = Nov.–Dec., Zc 7^{1}; בְּחֹדֶשׁ כ׳ Ne 1^{1} (𝔗 *id.*; loan-word from Bab. *kislimu, kislivu,* Muss-Arn JBL 1892, 167; conj. on etym. by Jen ZA ii, 210, Anm. 3 Hpt ib. 265, Anm. 2; Palm. כסלול Vog No. 24; Gk. χασελευ 1 Makk 1^{54}).

3695 †כַּסְלֻחִים **n.pr.gent.** Gn 10^{14} (𝔊D Χασμωνιειμ, 𝔊L Χασλωνιειμ, E Χαλοειμ) = 1 Ch 1^{12} (A Χασλωνιειμ, 𝔊L Χασλωειμ), among the sons of מִצְרַיִם; not identif.; conject. in Thes Di.

כִּסְלֹת תָּבוֹר v. כְּסֻלּוֹת supr. 3696

†[כָּסַם] **vb. shear, clip** (As. *kasâmu, cut in pieces,* acc. to Dl HWB 344);—only **Qal** *Impf.* and *Inf. abs.* כָּסוֹם יִכְסְמוּ אֶת־רָאשֵׁיהֶם Ez 44^{20} *they shall by all means clip their heads* (opp. יְגַלֵּחוּ *shave* and יְשַׁלֵּחוּ, i.e. *let grow freely*). 3697

†כֻּסֶּמֶת **n.f. spelt,** *triticum spelta* (NH pl. 3698
כּוּסְמִין, cf. 𝔗 𝔖 כּוּנְתָּא, ܟܘܢܬܐ; cf. Löw p. 104 ff. Di Ex 9, 23 Now Arch. i, 111);—abs. כ׳ Ex 9^{32} Is 28^{25} pl. כֻּסְּמִים Ez 4^{9} (in all disting. from wheat, barley, etc.)

†[כִּרְסֵם] **vb. quadril. = Pi., tear off** 3765
(cf. קִרְסֵם NH *cut* or *eat away,* Dt 28^{38} 𝔗 J for חָסַל; on form v. Ges § 56);—only *Impf.* 3 ms. sf.:—יְכַרְסְמֶנָּה חֲזִיר מִיָּעַר ψ 80^{14} *teareth it off* (sc. the vine, fig. of Israel).

†[כָּסַס] **vb. compute** (perh. orig. *divide* 3699
up, make small, fine; NH *chew;* Aram. ܟܣܣ *break small* (rare), usu. (Aph. etc.) *correct, convict;* Ar. كَسَّ *pulverize;* As. *kasâsu,* perh. *cut in two,* or *up,* whence *kissatu, fodder*)—only **Qal** *Impf.* 2 mpl. אִישׁ לְפִי אָכְלוֹ תָּכֹסּוּ עַל־הַשֶּׂה Ex 12^{4} (P) *each one according to his eating shall ye compute for the lamb.*

†מֶכֶס **n.m. computation, proportion to be** 4371
paid, tax (Palm. מכסא Reckendorf ZMG 1885, 379 ff.; NH מֶכֶס, Aram. מִכְסָא, ܡܟܣܐ *tax* (hence Ar. مَكْسٌ as loan-word Frä 283); As. *miksu,* Dl HWB 407 (√ מכס); NH מוֹכֵס *tax-collector;* so As. *makkasu,* cf. Ar. مَكَّاسٌ)—Nu 31^{28} וַהֲרֵמֹתָ מֶ׳ לַי׳ and thou shalt separate a *tax* (duty levied on the spoil) for י׳, v$^{37.38.39.40.41}$ (all P).

†מִכְסָה **n.f. computation** (f. of מֶכֶס); hence 4373
—**a.** *number,* Ex 12^{4} (P). **b.** *valuation, worth,* Lv 27^{23} (P).

†[כָּסַף] **vb. long** (for) (Ar. كَسَفَ *be* 3700
colourless, obscure, be eclipsed (of sun or moon); also *be depressed* in appearance Ba ES 61; mod. Ar. *disappoint;* refl. conjj. *be disappointed, ashamed,* v. Spiro Vocab.; NH כסף Hiph. *shew pallor, be pale, white;* Qal *be ashamed, long for,* cf. Aram. כְּסַף)—**Qal** *Impf.* 2 ms. לְמַעֲשֵׂה יָדֶיךָ תִכְסֹף Jb 14^{15} *for the work of thy hands thou wouldest long;* 3 ms. כְּאַרְיֵה יִכְסוֹף לִטְרֹף ψ 17^{12} *like a lion that longeth to rend.* **Niph.** *Pf.* 2 ms. + *Inf. abs.* נִכְסֹף נִכְסַפְתָּה לְבֵית אָבִיךָ Gn 31^{30} *thou didst long sorely for thy father's*

house; Pf. 3 fs. נִכְסְפָה... נַפְשִׁי לְחַצְרוֹת י׳ ψ 84^{4} *my soul longeth ... for the courts of* י׳; *Pf.* 3 ms. הַגּוֹי לֹא נִכְסָף Zp 2^{1} very dub.; but perhaps (Ges Ew Hi Ke al.), O nation *not turning pale,= not ashamed*, cf. etym. supr.; We thinks whole v. corrupt.

3701 **כֶּסֶף**$_{402}$ **n.m.** $^{\text{Gn 23, 9}}$ **silver, money** (NH *id.*; Ph. Zinj. כסף; Aram. כַּסְפָּא, ܟܣܦܐ; Palm. כספא Vog$^{\text{No. 23}}$; As. *kaspu;* prob. the *pale* metal Thes al., cf. RS$^{\text{JPh xiv, 125}}$)—כ׳ abs. Gn 20^{16} +, כָּסֶף Ex 21^{11} +; cstr. 43^{21} +; sf. כַּסְפִּי Gn 42^{28} + 3 t., כַּסְפְּךָ 1 K 20^{3} + 2 t., כַּסְפֶּךָ Gn 17^{13} Is 30^{22}, כַּסְפֵּךְ Is 1^{22}, כַּסְפֵּנוּ Gn 31^{15} + 2 t., כַּסְפָּם Ho 8^{4} + 6 t.; pl. sf. כַּסְפֵּיהֶם Gn 42$^{25.35}$;—*silver*, †**1.** = silver ore, raw silver (rare and mostly late) Jb 28^{1}, also (in fig.) Ez 22$^{20.22}$ Zc 13^{9} Pr 2^{4} 17^{3} 27^{21} Mal 3$^{3.3}$ ψ 12^{7} 66^{10} Is 48^{10}; הָגוֹ סִיגִים מִכֶּ׳ Pr 25^{4} *remove dross from silver*, cf. כ׳ סִיגִים 26^{23} and סִגִים כ׳ Ez 22^{18} (MT; 𝔊 כ׳ ס׳; Co del. in view of v^{20}); כ׳ נִמְאָס Je 6^{30} (cf. v^{29}), כַּסְפֵּךְ הָיָה לְסִיגִים Is 1^{22}. †**2.** silver as bright, shining, fig. of dove's wings כַּנְפֵי יוֹנָה נֶחְפָּה בַכֶּסֶף ψ 68^{14}. **3.** silver, as wealth, Gn 13^{2} (J) + oft. (c. 54 t. in all; frequently with gold, etc., v. זהב); מְלֹא בֵיתוֹ כ׳ וזהב Nu 22^{18} 24^{13}; fig. of a slave as valuable, כַּסְפּוֹ הוּא Ex 21^{21} (all JE); silver as less valuable than gold 1 K 10^{21} = 2 Ch 9^{20}; cf. also 1 K 10^{27} = 2 Ch 1^{15} 9^{27}; כ׳ נִבְחָר *choice silver*, Pr 18^{19} 10^{20}. **4.** silver as spoil of war (c. זהב, q.v.) Ju 5^{19} 2 S 8^{11} = 1 Ch 18^{11} + 11 t. †**5.** silver as merchandise Ez 27^{12} Pr 3^{14} (סְחַר־כ׳), Zp 1^{12}; cf. also 1 K 10^{22} = 2 Ch 9^{21}. **6.** silver as costly gift (c. זהב, q.v.) 1 K 15$^{18.19}$ = 2 Ch 16$^{2.3}$, 2 K 16^{8} 18^{15} 2 Ch 9^{14} 17^{11} 21^{3} Is 60^{9} Dn 11^{38} (other instances under **8**). **7.** silver as material (c. 117 t. in all; oft. c. זהב, q.v.), of cup Gn 44^{2} cf. v^{8} (J), trumpets Nu 10^{2} (P), כְּלֵי־כ׳ Gn 24^{53} (J)+; of idols Ex 20^{23} Is 2^{20} Dt 29^{16} Ez 16^{17} ψ 115^{4} 135^{15} + 4 t., cf. Dt 7^{25} Je 10^{4} Hb 2^{19}; esp. of fittings of tabern. Ex 26. 27. 36. 38 (19 t.), and those offered by chiefs of people Nu 7 (28 t.), etc. **8.** silver as measure of weight and value (c. 184 t.):—†**a.** shekels:—כ׳ שְׁלֹשִׁים שְׁקָלִים Ex 21^{32} (JE), cf. 2 S 24^{24} Lv 5^{15} Nu 18^{16} (both P), Ne 5^{15}; also (diff. order) חֲמִשָּׁה שקלים כ׳ Lv 27$^{6.6}$ (P), cf. Jos 7^{21} (JE), 2 K 15^{20}, and אַרְבַּע מֵאוֹת שֶׁקֶל כ׳ Gn 23$^{15.16}$, cf. Lv 27$^{3.16}$ (all P), 1 S 9^{8}; once שִׁבְעָה שְׁקָלִים וַעֲשָׂרָה הַכֶּ׳ Je 32^{9}. **b.** more oft. om. שקל Gn 20^{16} 45^{22} (E), 37^{28} (J), Ho 3^{2} Ct 8^{11} + 17 t. †**c.** talents:—כִּכַּר (הַ)כ׳ Ex 38^{27} (P), cf. 1 K 20^{39} 2 K 5^{22} 15^{19} 18^{14} 23^{33} = 2 Ch 36^{3}, 1 Ch 19^{6} 2 Ch 25^{6} 27^{5} Est 3^{9}; עֶשֶׂר כִּכְּרֵי־כ׳ 2 K 5^{5}; כִּכָּרַיִם כ׳ 1 K 16^{24} 2 K 5^{23}; כ׳ אלף אלפים ככרים 1 Ch 22^{14} cf. 29^{7} Ezr 8^{26}. †**d.** minas:—כ׳ מָנִים חֲמֵשֶׁת אֲלָפִים Ezr 2^{69} cf. Ne 7$^{70.71}$. **e.** more oft. = *money*, measure of value and exchange (c. 112 t.; not necess. *coined*) Gn 31^{15} 42$^{25.27}$ (E), 43$^{12.12.15.18}$ (J), Gn 23^{13} Lv 27^{18} Nu 3^{48} (P), Ju 16^{18} 1 K 21^{2} 2 K 12^{5} etc.; so ψ 68^{31} Che, but see De Grill Bae, and Che$^{\text{crit. n.}}$; מִקְנַת כ׳ *one bought for money* Gn 17$^{12.13.23.27}$ Ex 12^{44} (all P); כ׳ מִקְנָתוֹ Lv 25^{51} (H) *money for which he was bought;* כ׳ מָלֵא *full price* Gn 23^{9} (P) 1 Ch 21$^{22.24}$; כַּסְפֵּנוּ בְּמִשְׁקָלוֹ Gn 43^{21} i.e. our money in full; כ׳ מִמְכָּרוֹ Lv 25^{50} *the price of his sale;* כ׳ אָשָׁם 2 K 12^{7} *trespass-money*, כ׳ חַטָּאוֹת v^{7} *sin-money*, כ׳ הַכִּפֻּרִים Ex 30^{16} *atonement-money*, כ׳ הַפִּדְיוֹן Nu 3^{49} *redemption-money* (both P); כ׳ עֶרְכְּךָ Lv 27$^{15.19}$ i.e. estimated value, etc. **9.** among vbs. and phr. with כ׳ are:—צרף *try, refine*, Zc 13^{9} Is 48^{10} Mal 3^{3a} ψ 12^{7} 66^{10}; זִקֵּק Mal 3^{3b}, (cf. הִתּוּךְ Ez 22^{22}, √נתך, see v$^{20.21}$); יפה *beautify* בכ׳ Je 10^{4}; תָּפוּשׂ כ׳ Hb 2^{19} *encased with* gold and *silver;* שָׁקַל את־הַכּ׳ לְ *weigh out the silver to* or for a person Je 32^{9} Gn 23^{16} (P) Ezr 8^{25}, without לְ Je 32^{10}, cf. Ex 22^{16} (E), 1 K 20^{39}; שקל כ׳ ב׳ Is 55^{2} *= spend money for;* לֹא יִשָּׁקֵל כ׳ מְחִירָהּ Jb 28^{15}; וַיִּשְׁקְלוּ אֶת־שְׂכָרִי שלשים כ׳ Zc 11^{12}; כ׳ בַּקָּנֶה ישקלו Is 46^{6}, of weighing material for idol; מָכַר בכ׳ *sell for money* Am 2^{6} Gn 37^{28} (J), Dt 21^{14}; נָתַן בכ׳ Dt 2^{28b} 1 K 21$^{6.15}$ Gn 23^{9} (P), 1 Ch 21^{22}; also, of food, הִשְׁבִּיר ב׳ Dt 2^{28a}; נתן כ׳ השדה Gn 23^{13} (P) *pay the price of the field;* קָנָה בְכ׳ *buy* something *for money* Am 8^{6} Je 32$^{25.44}$ Is 43^{24} 1 Ch 21^{24}, cf. קָנָה נֶפֶשׁ קִנְיַן כ׳ Lv 22^{11} (H); שבר בכ׳ Dt 2^{6a} Is 55^{1}; כרה בכ׳ Dt 2^{6b}; peculiar is its use with פָּדָה, *redeem* (q.v.) in Nu 18^{16}; לקח כ׳ *receive money* 2 K 5^{26} 12$^{8.9}$; לָוָה כ׳ Ne 5^{4} *borrow money;* הִלְוָה Ex 22^{24} (JE) *lend* money *to* (c. 2 acc.); נתן כ׳ בְּנֶשֶׁךְ *give money on usury* Lv 25^{37} (H), ψ 15^{5}; cf. לֹא תַשִּׁיךְ לְאָחִיךָ נֶשֶׁךְ כ׳ Dt 23^{20}.

†**כַּסְפְּיָא** **n.pr.loc.** in Babylonia, site un- 3703
known:—בְּכ׳ הַמָּקוֹם Ezr 8$^{17.17}$ 𝔊 B ἐν ἀργυρίῳ, 𝔊L ἐν Μασφεν Esdr α, τῶν γαζοφυλακίων, γαζοφύλαξιν Esdr β.

כְּסֶת v. sub II. כסה. p. 492 3704

†**כָּעַס** **vb.** be vexed, angry (NH כָּעַס, 3707
Aram. כְּעַס (not Syr.));—**Qal** *Pf.* כ׳ ψ 112^{10} Ec 5^{16}; *Impf.* וַיִּכְעַס Ne 3^{33} 2 Ch 16^{10}; 1 s. אֶכְעַס Ez 16^{42};

Inf. לִכְעוֹס Ec 7^{9}.—**1.** *be vexed, indignant* ψ 112^{10} Ne 3^{33} Ec 5^{16}. **2.** *be angry* Ez 16^{42} Ec 7^{9}, c. אֶל pers. 2 Ch 16^{10}. **Piel.** *Pf.* 3 fs. sf. כִּעֲסַתָּה 1 S 1^{6}; 3 mpl. sf. כִּעֲסוּנִי Dt 32^{21} *provoke to anger.*

Hiph. *Pf.* הִכְעִיס Ho 12^{15} 1 K 15^{30}; sf. הִכְעִיסוֹ 2 K 23^{26} + 4 t. Pf.; הִכְעִסֻוּנִי Je 25^{7}; (scribal error for תַּכְעִיסוּנִי acc. to SS); *Impf.* וַיַּכְעֵס 1 K 22^{54} 2 Ch 28^{25}; 3 fs. sf. תַּכְעִסֶנָּה 1 S 1^{7} + 6 t. Impf.; *Inf. cstr.* הַכְעִיס 1 K 16^{13} + 5 t.; sf. הַכְעִ(י)סֵנִי Je 7^{18} + 11 t., + 6 t. sfs.; *Pt.* pl. מַכְעִיסִים Je 7^{19} + 4 t.—**1.** *vex*, c. acc. pers. 1 S 1^{7} Ez 32^{9}. **2.** *vex, provoke to anger*, esp. of provoking Yahweh by worship of other gods Ju 2^{12} 1 K 14$^{9.15}$ 16^{33} 22^{54} 2 K 17^{11} 23^{19} 2 Ch 28^{25} Ne 3^{37} Je 7$^{18.19}$ 11^{17} 32$^{29.32}$ 44^{3} Ez 8^{17} 16^{26} Is 65^{3} Ho 12^{15}; c. בְּ instr. בְּתוֹעֵבֹת Dt 32^{16}; בְּהַבְלֵיהֶם Dt 32^{21} 1 K 16$^{13.26}$; בחטאתם 1 K 16^{2}; במעשׂ(י) יד(יו) Dt 31^{29} 1 K 16^{7} Je 25$^{6.7}$ 32^{30} 44^{8}; בכל מעשׂ(ה) ידיהם 2 K 22^{17} = 2 Ch 34^{25}; בבמות ψ 78^{58}; בפסיליהם Je 8^{19}; במעלליהם ψ 106^{29}; cf. the phrases עשׂה הרע(ה) בעיני י׳ להכעיס(ו) *do the evil in the eyes of Yahweh to provoke* (him) *to anger* Dt 4^{25} 9^{18} 31^{29} 1 K 16^{7} 2 K 17^{17} 21^{6} = 2 Ch 33^{6}; so מכעסים 2 K 21^{15} Je 32^{30}; כעס(ים) אשׁר הכעיס 1 K 15^{30} 21^{22} 2 K 23^{26}.—The phrase is characteristic of D Je and the compiler of Kings; see Dr$^{\text{Intr 191; Dt 4, 25}}$ Holz$^{\text{Einl. Hex. 287}}$.

3708 † כַּ֫עַס **n.m.** vexation, anger;—כ׳ Dt 32^{27} + 13 t.; כָּ֑עַס Pr 21^{19} Ec 1^{18}; sf. כַּעְסִי 1 S 1^{16}, כַּעַסְךָ ψ 85^{5}, כַּעְסוֹ Pr 12^{16} 1 K 15^{30}; *pl.* כְּעָסִים 2 K 23^{26}.—*vexation:* **1.** of men, esp. caused by unmerited treatment, 1 S 1$^{6.16}$ Pr 12^{16} 17^{25} 21^{19} 27^{3} Ec 7^{9}. **2.** *vexation, anger of* Yahweh (caused esp. by worship of other gods) 1 K 15^{30} 21^{22} 2 K 23^{26}; כ׳ עִמָּנוּ ψ 85^{5} *anger (of Yahweh) with us;* כ׳ בָּנָיו Dt 32^{19} *anger against his sons,* כ׳ אוֹיֵב v^{27} *anger against the enemy* (both obj. gen. see Di; RV *provocation of*, cf. Dr); כ׳ קָרְבָּנָם Ez 20^{28} *provocation of their offering* (so RV but Co del., rightly). **3.** *vexation, grief* ψ 6^{8} 10^{14} 31^{10} Ec 1^{18} 2^{23} 7^{3} 11^{10}, also כעס 5^{16} acc. Ew al.

3708 † כַּ֫עַשׂ **n.m.** (dialectic variation of כַּעַס, only in Jb);—כ׳ Jb 17^{7}, כָּ֑עַשׂ Jb 5^{2}; sf. כַּעְשִׂי Jb 6^{2}; כַּעַשְׂךָ Jb 10^{17};—**1.** *vexation, grief* of men Jb 5^{2} (cf. Pr 12^{16} 27^{3}), 6^{2} 17^{7}. **2.** *vexation, anger,* of God; c. עִמָּדִי כַּעַשְׂךָ Jb 10^{17} *thine anger with me.*

3709 כַּף v. sub כפף. p. 496

3710 † [כֵּף] **n.[m.]** rock (As. *kâpu* Dl$^{\text{HWB 346}}$; Aram. כֵּיפָא, ܟܐܦܐ; perh. Aram. loan-word in Heb.; √ dub.);—only pl. כֵּפִים Je 4^{29} as place of refuge; Jb 30^{6} as dwelling-place.

† [כָּפָה] **vb.** prob. subdue (NH *overturn, hold under, compel;* Aram. כְּפָא, *id.;* ܟܦܐ *incline* (as face to ground), *overturn;* As. *kipû* perh. *id.*, Dl$^{\text{HWB 346}}$; cf. Ar. كَفَأَ *overturn, turn back*);—only **Qal** *Impf.* מַתָּן בַּסֵּתֶר יִכְפֶּה־אָף Pr 21^{14} *a gift in secret subdueth anger* (so Thes RobGes; Ew *beugt:* Fl De *averteth*, from the Ar., is more remote; 𝔊 ἀνατρέπει, cf. NH). 3711

כִּפָּה v. sub כפף. p. 497 3712

† כָּפַל **vb.** double, double over (late) (NH *id.;* Aram. כְּפַל; 𝔗 כּוּפְלָה, כִּיפְלָא, Nab. כפל Eut$^{\text{Nab. No. 20, 7}}$ *the double;* Christ. Pal. Aram. ܟܦܠ, Schwally$^{\text{Idiot. 46}}$; NSyr. *id.;* Ar. كِفْلٌ *the double,* كَفَلٌ *posteriors, buttocks;* Eth. ከፈለ: is *divide*, ክፍል: *a part*)—**Qal** *Pf.* 2 ms. וְכָפַלְתָּ Ex 26^{9} *and thou shalt double over* the sixth curtain, i.e. prob. use it double (Di); *Pt. pass.* כָּפוּל *folded double,* of the breast-piece (חֹשֶׁן) Ex 28^{16} 39$^{9.9}$. **Niph.** *Impf.* 3 fs. וְתִכָּפֵל Ez 21^{19} *and let* the sword *be doubled,* but very dub.; Co rds. plausibly תְּשַׁכֵּל *let* the sword *bereave* (cf. VB). 3717

† כֶּ֫פֶל **n.[m.]** the double:—כ׳ cstr.: בְּכ׳ רִסְנוֹ Jb 41^{5} *within the double of his jaw* (i.e. his double jaws) who can come? elsewhere du. כִּפְלַיִם (cf. Ar. كِفْلَانِ), לְתוּשִׁיָּה 11^{6} *double* in sound wisdom (beyond what Job imagines), of retribution Is 40^{2}. 3718

† מַכְפֵּלָה **n.pr.loc.** near Hebron, where the patriarchs and their wives were buried, only in P, alw. c. art.; שְׂדֵה אשׁר בַּמ׳ Gn 23^{17}, מְעָרַת הַמ׳ *the cave of Machpelah* v^{9}, 25^{9}, מְעָרַת שְׂדֵה הַמ׳ 49^{30}.—מְעָרָה אֲשֶׁר בִּשְׂדֵה הַמ׳ 23^{19} 50^{13}, cf. Buhl$^{\text{Geogr. 160, 161}}$.—(Evidently orig. appell., but meaning dub.; 𝔊 τὸ διπλοῦν; acc. to Thes = *part, lot, portion,* as Eth. መክፈልት:). 4375

† [כָּפַן] **vb.** be hungry, hunger, perh. also hungrily desire (Aram. loan-word; cf. Aram. כְּפֵין, כְּפַן, ܟܦܢ *be hungry;* Ar. كَفَنَ is *spin* wool, *wrap* a corpse *in the shroud*);—only **Qal** *Pf.* 3 fs. כָּֽפְנָה עַל Ez 17^{7} (si vera l.) this vine *stretched* its roots *hungrily* toward (‖ שִׁלְחָה לְ). 3719

† כָּפָן **n.[m.]** hunger, famine (Aramaism; on form cf. Lag$^{\text{BN 144}}$), Jb 5^{22} 30^{3}. 3720

כפס (perh. √ of foll.; cf. 𝔗 כְּפַס Est 1^{6} *bind, fasten* (so Levy, Jastrow)).

3714 †כָּפִיס **n.m.** appar. (si vera l.) term. techn. for some beam in a house, perhaps **rafter,** or **girder** (NH *id.,* Levy, Jastrow, but acc. to Hoffm $^{ZAW\ ii.\ 1881,\ 71}$ it is changed fr. oblong block of wood (O. T.) to a *building-stone,* or *brick* in Mish.);—only Hb 2^{11} *for a stone out of the wall crieth out,* וְכ׳ מֵעֵץ יַעֲנֶנָּה *and a rafter out of the timber-work answereth it.*

3721 †[כָּפַף] **vb. bend, bend down, be bent, bowed** (NH *bend, overturn,* As. *kapâpu, bend, bow,* Dl $^{HWB\ 347}$; Ar. كَفَّ *fell* a seam, also *turn back, avert,* كُفَّةٌ *selvage,* كِفَافٌ *circuit, rim;* Aram. כְּפַף, ܟܦ *bend, curve;* Palm. כפתא *niche,* from כפף *curve* acc. to Vog $^{No.\ 70,\ p.\ 50}$);—**Qal** *Pf.* כ׳ נַפְשִׁי ψ 57^{7} *my soul is bowed down; Inf. cstr.* (trans.) לָכֹף כְּאַגְמֹן ראשׁוֹ Is 58^{5} *to bend down, like a rush, his head. Pt. pass.* (הַ)כְּפוּפִים *those bowed down,* in distress, humiliation, etc., ψ 145^{14} 146^{8}. **Niph.** *Impf.* 1 s. אִכַּף לֵאלֹהֵי מָרוֹם Mi 6^{6} with what *shall I bow myself* (in worship) *toward the high God?*

3709 כַּף$_{192}$ **n.f.** $^{1\ K\ 8,\ 54}$ **hollow,** or **flat of the hand, palm, sole** of foot, **pan** (NH *id.;* Aram. *id.,* ܟܦܐ; As. *kappu, hand, pan, kippatu, hollow;* Ar. كَفّ *palm, hand*)—abs. כ׳ Jb 29^{9}+, so rd. prob. also Ez 29^{7b} for MT כָּתֵף (𝔊 𝔖 Sm Co, cf. v^{a}); כָּף 2 K 11^{12}+; more oft. cstr. כַּף Gn 40^{11}+; sf. כַּפִּי Ju 12^{3}, כַּפְּךָ Jb 13^{31}, etc.; in Ez 29^{7} rd. כַּף Qr for כפך Kt (so Ew Hi Sm Co Da); du. כַּפַּיִם Is 49^{16}+; cstr. כַּפֵּי Ex $29^{24.24}$+ 3 t.; sf. כַּפַּי Gn 20^{5}+, כַּפָּיו Nu 24^{10}+, כַּפֵּיהֶם Is 59^{6}+2 t., כַּפֵּימוֹ Jb 27^{23}, etc.; pl. כַּפּוֹת (esp. of *soles,* and in metaph. senses) abs. Nu 4^{7}+; cstr. 2 K 9^{35}+, sf. כַּפֹּתָיו Ex 25^{29} 37^{16};—**1. a.** of human beings, *hollow* or *flat of hand, palm,* (c. 116 t.) 2 K $4^{34.34}$; נָתַן אֶת הַכּוֹס עַל־כַּף פ׳ Gn $40^{11.21}$ (E), *set the cup upon the palm of Pharaoh* (cf. v^{11a} וְכוֹס פַּרְעֹה בְּיָדִי), similarly Lv $8^{27.27}$ (P)+; הַשֶּׁמֶן אֲשֶׁר עַל־כַּפּוֹ Lv $14^{16.17.18.27.28}$; as disting. from wrist and arm, Dt 25^{12}; rarely c. ידים (always כַּפּוֹת), שְׁתֵּי כַּפּוֹת ידיו 1 S 5^{4} (of Dagon), כַּף הַשְּׂמָאלִית, כ׳ הַיָּדַיִם 2 K 9^{35}, cf. Dn 10^{10}; Lv $14^{15.26}$; note esp. מְלֹא כ׳ קֶמַח 1 K 17^{12} *a handful of meal* (lit. *palmful*), cf. Ec 4^{6} (where disting. fr. מלא חָפְנַיִם *a double fistful;* in both these passages of a very small quantity); cf. מְלֹא קָמְצוֹ וַיְמַלֵּא כַפּוֹ מִן Lv 9^{17} (ref. to 2^{2} 5^{12} cf. 6^{8}). In Ex 4^{4} (JE), Pr 31^{19} Ez 21^{16} ψ 129^{7}, etc., the thought is that of grasping. **b.** anthropomorph. of י׳, covering Moses over with his palm, וְשַׂכֹּתִי כַפִּי עָלֶיךָ Ex 33^{22} (J), and so fig. (c. שׁית) ψ 139^{5}; withdrawing (הֵסִיר) his hand Ex 33^{23} (J); removing (הִרְחִיק) his afflicting hand Jb 13^{21}; עַל־כַּפַּיִם כִּסָּה אוֹר Jb 36^{32}, i.e. he (God) hath filled his palms with light. **c.** once of animals, הוֹלֵךְ עַל־כַּפָּיו Lv 11^{27} *going upon their palms,* i.e. paws (cats, dogs, etc.). **d.** phrases are:—†(1) הִכָּה כַּף = *clap the hands,* in applause 2 K 11^{12} so תָּקַע כ׳ ψ 47^{2}, מָחָא כ׳ Is 55^{12} (fig. of trees), ψ 98^{8} (fig. of rivers); but esp. in scorn, contempt, etc., סָפַק אֶת־כַּפָּיו Nu 24^{10} (J), יִשְׂפֹּק עָלֵימוֹ כַפֵּימוֹ Jb 27^{23}; so תָּקַע כַּף עַל־ Na 3^{19}, הִכָּה כַּפֵּי אֶל־ Ez 22^{13} (of י׳); abs., הַכֵּה בְכַפְּךָ Ez 6^{11} (as מחא יד 25^{6}), הַכֵּה כַּף אֶל־כַּף 21^{19}, אַכֶּה כַפִּי אֶל־כַּפִּי v^{22} (of י׳). †(2) תָּפַשׂ בַּכַּף *grasp, seize with the hand* Ez 29^{7} cf. v^{7} (on text v. supr.) †(3) of *hand-grasp* as pledge, תָּקַעְתָּ לַזָּר כַּפֶּיךָ Pr 6^{1} (*if*) *thou hast smitten thy palms* (given a double hand-grasp), *for another* (so De; ∥ עָרַבְתָּ לְרֵעֶךָ); so abs. תקע כף 17^{18} 22^{26} (cf. תקע ליד Jb 17^{3}). (4) oft. of hand *spread out* in prayer, as sign of longing to receive, c. פָּרַשׂ אֶל־ Ex $9^{29.33}$ (J), 1 K 8^{38} = 2 Ch 6^{29}, etc. (v. יד ψ 143^{6} La 1^{17} and יָד **1 d,** supr. p. 389; also שׁטח, נשׂא, פרשׂ). †(5) שִׂים כַּף לְפֶה, in respectful silence, Jb 29^{9}. †(6) fig. וָאָשִׂימָה נַפְשִׁי בְכַפִּי Ju 12^{3} = *I have taken my life in my hand* (i.e. hazarded it), so 1 S 19^{5} 28^{21} Jb 13^{14} and (without vb.) ψ 119^{109}. †(7) נִקְיֹן כ׳ Gn 20^{5} *cleanness of palms* is fig. for purity of act, cf. ψ 26^{6}, also Jb 9^{30} 22^{30} ψ 24^{4} 73^{13}; conversely, (לֹא)חָמָס בְּכַפָּי Jb 16^{17} 1 Ch 12^{18} Is 59^{6} Jon 3^{8}, cf. Is 59^{3} (so ידים 1^{15}), Jb 31^{7} ψ 7^{4}.—In many cases כַּף is not to be distinguished from יָד; so in phr. †יְגִיעַ כ׳ *toil of the hands* Gn 31^{42} Hg 1^{11} Jb 10^{3} ψ 128^{2}; פֹּעַל כ׳ ψ 9^{17}, חֵפֶץ כ׳ Pr 31^{13}; תְּבוּנוֹת כ׳ ψ 78^{72}, פְּרִי כ׳ Pr 31^{16}†; cf. Mi 7^{3}. †**2.** = *power* (i.e. grasp) of any one, נתן בכף Ju 6^{13} = *deliver into the power of,* so Je 12^{7}, cf. בּוֹא בכף Pr 6^{3}; usu. הִצִּיל, פָּדָה, הוֹשִׁיעַ etc., c. מִכַּף = *out of the power of* Ju 6^{14} 1 S 4^{3} 2 S 14^{16} $19^{10.10}$ $22^{1.1}$ = ψ 18^{1} (title), 2 K $16^{7.7}$ 20^{6} = Is 38^{6}, Mi 4^{10} Je 15^{21} 2 Ch 30^{6} 32^{11} Ezr 8^{31} ψ 71^{4} (cf. יָד **5 g,** p. 391 supr.) †**3.** כַּף רַגְלָהּ, etc., = *sole of foot,* Gn 8^{9} (J), Jos 3^{13} 4^{18} (both JE), 1 K 5^{17} 2 K 19^{24} = Is 37^{25}, Dt 11^{24} $28^{56.65}$ Jos 1^{3} (D), Ez 43^{7} Mal 3^{21}; מִכַּף רַגְלוֹ וְעַד קָדְקֳדוֹ 2 S 14^{25} Jb 2^{7}, cf. Is 1^{6} (fig.); מִדְרַךְ כ׳ ר׳ Dt 2^{5} *treading-place for the sole of a foot;* of the cherubim Ez 1^{7}, of a calf, (in sim.) v^{7}, (acc.

to MT; cf. however Co). **4.** of various *hollow, bending* or *bent* objects:—†**a.** *hollow* (i.e. socket), *of the thigh*-joint, כ׳ יָרֵךְ Gn 32$^{26.26.33.33}$ (J). **b.** *pan, vessel* (as hollow), used in ritual, Ex 25^{29} 37^{16} Nu 5^{7} 7^{14} + 15 t. Nu 7; 1 K 7^{50} = 2 Ch 4^{22}, 2 K 25^{14} = Je 52^{18}, Je 52^{19}, 2 Ch 24^{14}. †**c.** *hollow* of sling, 1 S 25^{29}. †**d.** כַּפּוֹת תְּמָרִים Lv 23^{40} = of huge *hand-shaped branches* (or *fronds*) *of palm-trees.* **e.** כַּפּוֹת הַמַּנְעוּל Ct 5^{5} *the* (bent) *handles of the bolt.*

3712 †כִּפָּה **n.f.** branch, frond (prob. of palm-tree, cf. כַּף **3 d**);—כ׳ Is 9^{13} 19^{15} fig. of nobles, rulers (both opp. אַגְמוֹן *rush,* i.e. high and low; ‖ רֹאשׁ וְזָנָב); c. sf. כִּפָּתוֹ Jb 15^{32} (of wicked under fig. of palm-tree).

I. **כפר** (of foll.; orig. mng. dub., but most prob. *cover,* cf. Ar. كَفَرَ *cover, hide;* > RS who thinks of Aram. כְּפַר, ܟܦܰܪ Pa. *wash away, rub off,* whence כֹּפֶר, כִּפֶּר of *washing away, obliteration* of sin: NH כִּפֶּר, Aram. כַּפֵּר and deriv.; Ar. كَفَّارَةٌ *an expiation* (see RS$^{\text{OTJC 438; 2. 381}}$ Kn on Lv 4^{20} Ri$^{\text{Begr. der Sühne}}$ We$^{\text{Comp. 335 f.}}$ Sm$^{\text{AT Rel. Gesch. 321}}$ Now$^{\text{Arch. ii, 192}}$ Dr$^{\text{Dt 425}}$ Schmoller$^{\text{St.Kr. 1891, 205 ff.}}$ Lag$^{\text{BN 230 ff.}}$)).

3724 † I. כֹּפֶר **n.m.** the price of a life, ransom (*ποινή, wergeld*);—כ׳ Ex 21^{30} + 10 t.; sf. כָּפְרְךָ Is 43^{3}; כָּפְרוֹ ψ 49^{8};—**1.** *a price for ransom of a life* Jb 33^{24} 36^{18}; כ׳ עַל Ex 21^{30} (Covt. code; ‖ פִּדְיֹן נַפְשׁוֹ); כ׳ נפשׁ Pr 13^{8}; כ׳ לְ *ransom for* Pr 6^{35} 21^{18} Nu 35$^{31.32}$ (P); כָּפְרוֹ *his ransom* ψ 49^{8} (‖ פדה); כָּפְרְךָ *thy ransom* Is 43^{3} (‖ תַּחְתֶּיךָ); כֹּפֶר alone 1 S 12^{3} Am 5^{12}. **2.** in the ritual of P כ׳ נַפְשׁוֹ Ex 30^{12} is a half shekel of the sanctuary paid by each male above twenty years at the census in order that there might be no plague upon them. It was offered to Yahweh, לְכַפֵּר על *to atone for them.*

3722 †כִּפֶּר **vb. Pi.** etc. **denom.** cover over (fig.), pacify, make propitiation;—**Pi.** *Pf.* כִּפֶּר Ex 30^{10} + 31 t.; 2 ms. sf. כִּפַּרְתָּהוּ Ez 43^{20}; 3 mpl. יְכַפְּרוּ Ez 43^{26}, 2 mpl. [illegible] Ez 45^{20}; *Impf.* יְכַפֵּר Ex 30^{10} + 10 t.; יְכַפֶּר־ Lv 7^{7} Nu 5^{8}; sf. יְכַפְּרֶנָּה Pr 16^{14}; 1 s. אֲכַפֵּר 2 S 21^{3}; אֲכַפְּרָה Gn 32^{21} Ex 32^{30}, etc.; *Imv.* כַּפֵּר Dt 21^{8} + 4 t.; *Inf.* כַּפֵּר Ex 30^{15} + 28 t.; sfs. כַּפְּרִי Ez 16^{63}; כַּפֶּרְךָ Ex 29^{36}; כַּפְּרָהּ Is 47^{11};—**1.** *cover over, pacify, propitiate;* אֲכַפְּרָה פָנָיו בַּמִּנְחָה Gn 32^{21} *let me cover over his face by the present* (so that he does not see the offence, i.e. *pacify* him; E; RS$^{\text{OTJC, 2d ed., 381}}$ 'wipe clean the face,' blackened by displeasure, as the Arabs say 'whiten the face'); וְתִפֹּל עָלַיִךְ הֹוָה לֹא תוּכְלִי כַּפְּרָהּ Is 47^{11} *and disaster will fall upon thee, thou wilt not be able to propitiate it* (by payment of a כֹּפֶר, see Is 43^{3}); pacify the wrath of a king Pr 16^{14} (e.g. by a gift). **2.** *cover over, atone for sin,* without sacrifice: **a.** man as subj., בַּמָּה אֲכַפֵּר 2 S 21^{3}, *with what shall I cover over* (viz. the bloodguiltiness of the house of Saul, says David. The answer is by a death penalty of seven sons of the guilty house); בְּעַד חטאתכם Ex 32^{30} *on behalf of your sins* (JE; Moses, by intercession); c. עַל of persons Nu 17$^{11.12}$ (P; by incense), 25^{13} (P when Phinehas slays the ringleaders). **b.** with God as subj., c. acc. pers., *cover,* i.e. treat as covered, view propitiously, Yahweh's land Dt 32^{43} (song); לְ pers. Dt 21^{8} (bloodguiltiness flows away in the stream), Ez 16^{63}; בְּעַד of person 2 Ch 30^{18}; c. acc. of *the sin* ψ 65^{4} 78^{38}, prob. also Dn 9^{24} (‖ חֹתם חטאת); עַל of sin, ψ 79^{9} Je 18^{23} (‖ מחה). It is conceived that God in his sovereignty may himself provide an atonement or covering for men and their sins which could not be provided by men. **3.** *cover over, atone for sin and persons by legal rites,* in the codes of H, P, and Ez: abs. וכ׳ הַכֹּהֵן *and the priest shall make atonement* Lv 16^{32}; **a.** c. acc. of sacred places (by the great sin-offering of the day of atonement), Lv 16$^{20.33.33}$; also Ez 43$^{20.26}$ 45^{20} (by the blood of the sin-offering ‖ חִטֵּא, טִהַר). **b.** usually c. עַל (1) of things, e.g. of the altar to which the blood of the sin-offering was applied Ex 29$^{36.37}$ 30^{10} Lv 8^{15} (‖ קִדֵּשׁ), 16^{18}; and specifically the horns of the altar Ex 30^{10}; the holy place of the tabernacle Lv 16^{16} (by the great sin-offering, because of (מִן) the uncleannesses of the children of Israel and because of their transgressions); for the leprous house by ceremony of purification Lv 14^{53} (‖ טִהַר); for the goat לעזאזל Lv 16^{10} (which was presented before Yahweh to consecrate him for the bearing away of the sins of the people). (2) of persons, עַל־נפשׁתיכם, *for your persons, yourselves,* e.g. by the payment of atonement-money כֶּסֶף הַכִּפֻּרִים at the census Ex 30$^{15.16}$; by the קרבן of the spoils Nu 31^{50}; by the blood upon the altar Lv 17^{11}; in the ritual עָלָיו, עֲלֵיהֶם by ministry of priest through the blood of the sin-offering Lv 4$^{20.31}$ 8^{34} 10^{17} 12$^{7.8}$ 14$^{19.31}$ 16$^{30.33}$ 23^{28} Nu 8$^{12.21}$ 15$^{25.28.28}$ 28$^{22.30}$ 29^{5} 2 Ch 29^{24} Ne 10^{34}; of the trespass-offering Lv 5$^{16.18.26}$ 7^{7} 14^{21} 19^{22} Nu 5^{8}; the whole burnt-offering Lv 1^{4} 14^{20} 16^{24}; by the oil used in purifying a leper Lv $14^{18.29}$; by the תרומה Ez 45^{15}; by the priestly ministry in general 1 Ch 6^{34}; by the substitution of the Levites for the firstborn Nu 8^{19}. Underlying all these offerings there is the conception that the persons offering are covered by that which is regarded as sufficient and satisfactory by Yahweh. (The purpose of the covering is stated Lv 16^{30} יְכַפֵּר עֲלֵיכֶם לְטַהֵר אֶתְכֶם מִכֹּל חַטֹּאתֵיכֶם לִפְנֵי י׳ תִּטְהָרוּ = *shall atonement be made for you to cleanse you, from all your sins shall ye be clean before Yahweh,* and Nu 8^{21} וַיְכַפֵּר עֲלֵיהֶם לְטַהֲרָם *and* (Aaron) *made atonement for them to cleanse them.*) **c.** the need of the atonement is expressed by מִן: מחטאתו *because of his sin* Lv 4^{26} $5^{6.10}$ 16^{34}; מטמאתו Lv 14^{19} 16^{16}; מזוב Lv $15^{15.30}$; מֵאֲשֶׁר חָטָא Nu 6^{11}; also עַל, עַל־חַטָּאתוֹ *on account of his sin* Lv 4^{35} 5^{13} 19^{22}; על־שׁגגתו Lv 5^{18}. **d.** c. בְּ instr. בְּאֵיל Lv 5^{16} 19^{22} Nu 5^{8}; *with* a trespass-offering Lv 7^{7}; כִּי־הַדָּם הוּא בַּנֶּפֶשׁ יְכַפֵּר Lv 17^{11} *for it is the blood with the living being that covers over* (H, see נפשׁ **3** (*a*); RV *by reason of the life* after De Di Kn Bähr Kau and most moderns; AV follows 𝔊 𝔙 𝔗, so Ges Ew § 282 a. Anm. 1: *'for the soul'*); c. בְּ loc. בַּקֹּדֶשׁ Lv 6^{23} $16^{17.27}$. **e.** c. בַּעַד pers., *on behalf of* Lv $9^{7.7}$ $16^{6.11.17.24}$ (by Aaron), Ez 45^{17} (by the prince). **Pu.** *Pf.* כֻּפַּר Ex 29^{33} Is 28^{18} (but rd. תֻּפַר,—√ I. פרר,—so 𝔗 Hu We Che SS al. v. Br MP 209); *Impf.* יְכֻפַּר Nu 35^{33} + 3 t.; 3 fs. תְּכֻפָּר Is 6^{7} *be covered over, atoned for.* **1.** apart from the ritual, חטאתך תכפר Is 6^{7} thy sin *shall be covered over* (‖ וְסָר עֲוֺנֶךָ; by the touch of the live coal from the altar); אִם־יְכֻפַּר הֶעָוֺן הַזֶּה לָכֶם Is 22^{14} *surely this iniquity shall not be covered over for you;* c. בְּ instr. בזאת יכפר עון Is 27^{9} by *this* shall the iniquity *of Jacob be covered over* (‖ הסר חטאתו; namely by the destruction of idolatrous objects); בחסד ואמת יכפר עון Pr 16^{6} *by mercy and fidelity iniquity is covered over.* **2.** c. לְ *for* whom, לארץ לא יכפר לדם Nu 35^{33} *for the land atonement cannot be made, in view of the blood* shed in it, except by the blood of the shedder of blood; in the ritual of P, c. בְּ instr. אֲשֶׁר כֻּפַּר בָּהֶם Ex 29^{33} *wherewith atonement was made* (ram of consecration).

Hithp. *Impf.* יִתְכַּפֵּר 1 S 3^{14}; c. בְּ instr. אִם־יִתְכַּפֵּר עֲוֺן בֵּית־עֵלִי בְּזֶבַח וּבְמִנְחָה *the iniquity of the house of Eli shall not be covered by peace-offering or minchah* (in other words there was no atonement for it; cf. **Pu.** Is. 22^{14}).

Niph. *Pf.* וְנִכַּפֵּר לָהֶם הַדָּם Dt 21^{8} *and the blood shall be covered for them.*

†כִּפֻּרִים **n.pl.abstr. atonement**, only in P: 3725
חַטַּאת הַכִּ׳ *sin-offering of the atonement* Ex 30^{10} Nu 29^{11}; יוֹם (ה)כ׳ *day of (the) atonement* Lv $23^{27.28}$ 25^{9}; אֵיל הַכִּ׳ Nu 5^{8}; עַל־הַכִּ׳ Ex 29^{36}; כֶּסֶף הכ׳ Ex 30^{16} *money of atonement.*

†כַּפֹּרֶת **n. propitiatory**, late techn. word 3727
from כפר *cover over sin:* the older explan. *cover, lid* has no justification in usage; 𝔊 ἱλαστήριον; only P: Ex $25^{17.18.19.20.20.21.22}$ 26^{34} 30^{6} 31^{7} 35^{12} $37^{6.7.8.9.9}$ 39^{35} 40^{20} Lv $16^{2.2.13.14.14.15.15}$ Nu 7^{89}, and 1 Ch 28^{11}; it was a slab of gold 2½ cubits × 1½ c. placed on top of the ark of the testimony. On it, and a part of it, were two golden cherubim facing each other, whose outstretched wings came together above and constituted the throne of Yahweh. When the high priest entered the Holy of Holies on the day of atonement it was necessary that this highest place of atonement should be enveloped in a cloud of incense. The blood of the sin-offering of the atonement was then sprinkled on the face of and seven times before it. The temple proper, as distinguished from porch etc., was called בֵּית הַכִּ׳ 1 Ch 28^{11}.

II. **כפר** (√ of following).

†II. כֹּפֶר **n.m. pitch** (Ar. كُفْرٌ (loan-wd., cf. 3724
Frä 150), Syr. ܟܘܦܪܐ, 𝔗 כּוּפְרָא; As. *kupru, kupur* Dl HWB 348; cf. גֹּפֶר?)—Gn 6^{14} (P).

†II. [כָּפַר] **vb. denom.** (from II. כֹּפֶר)—*Pf.* 3722
2 ms. וְכָפַרְתָּ בַּכֹּפֶר Gn 6^{14} *and thou shalt pitch it with pitch* (P).

III. **כפר** (√ of following).

†כְּפִיר **n.m. young lion**;—כ׳ Ju 14^{5} + 16 t.; 3715
pl. כְּפִרִים Je 2^{15} + 3 t.; כְּפִירִים Zc 11^{3} + 7 t.; sf. כְּפִירַיִךְ Na 2^{14}; כְּפִירֶיהָ Ez 38^{13} (Co rds. כנעניה);—lit. כ׳ אֲרָיוֹת Ju 14^{5} *young lion of lions;* Am 3^{4} ψ 17^{12}. It differs from whelp גּוּר Ez $19^{2.3}$ as old enough to hunt its prey, Je 25^{38} Is 11^{6} Zc 11^{3} ψ 104^{21}; in sim. of roar of hostile army Is 5^{29} (‖ לָבִיא) cf. Je 51^{38} (‖ גּוֹרֵי אריות); sim. of י׳'s invincible might Is 31^{4} (‖ אַרְיֵה); of Isr. among the nations, Mi 5^{7}; of Assyr. princes Na 2^{12}; of prince of Isr. Ez $19^{5.6}$; other cases are: ‖ לָבִיא Jb 38^{39}; ‖ שַׁחַל Ho 5^{14} ψ 91^{13} Jb 4^{10}; of bloodthirsty enemies ψ 34^{11} 35^{17} 58^{7} Je 2^{15}; כ׳ גוים Ez 32^{2}, of young warriors Na 2^{14} Ez 38^{13} (?; v. Co supr.); righteous compared with, Pr 28^{1}; king's wrath like roaring of, Pr 19^{12} 20^{2}; of one of faces of cherubim Ez 41^{19}.

3724 †III. כֹּפֶר **n.m.** name of a plant, *El Ḥenna* (√dub.; NH כּוֹפֶר; Aram. כּוּפְרָא, ܟܘܦܪܐ; Ar. *El Ḥenna*, see Löw[No. 159])—a shrub or low tree, with fragrant whitish flowers growing in clusters like grapes, אֶשְׁכֹּל הַכֹּפֶר *cluster of Ḥenna* Ct 1[14] (fragrant, fig. of a beloved one); pl. כְּפָרִים Ct 4[13].

3723 †[כָּפָר] **n.m. village** (√dub.; NH כָּפָר; Aram. כַּפְרָנָא; Syr. ܟܦܪܐ, ܟܘܦܪܢܐ; As. *kapru*
3726 Dl[HWB 348]);—sg. cstr. כְּפַר הָעַמּוֹנִי Jos 18[24] Kt *village of the Ammonites*, or כ׳ הָעַמֹּנָה Qri, a village of Benjamin, possibly *Kefr 'Âna'*, 3 miles N. of Bethel Surv[ii. 299]; *pl.* כְּפָרִים Ct 7[12] 1 Ch 27[25].

3724 †IV. כֹּפֶר **n.[m.] village**;—only sg. cstr. כֹּפֶר הַפְּרָזִי 1 S 6[18] *villages of the peasantry*.

3726 כְּפַר הָעַמּוֹנִי v. כָּפָר supr.

3716 †כְּפִירָה **n.pr.loc.** city of the Hivites subsequently assigned to Benjamin., Jos 9[17] 18[26] Ezr 2[25] = Ne 7[29]; 𝔊 Κεφειρα, etc.; = mod. *Kefîreh* Rob[BR iii. 146] Guérin[Jud. i. 283 ff.] Mem[iii. 36] Buhl[G. § 94, p. 169].

†כְּפִירִים Ne 6[2], prob. = foregoing (𝔊 al. n. appell. = *villages*).

IV. **כפר** (√of foll., = *dig*? cf. Sab. כפר, vb. *dig*, n. *cave*, DHM[Anzeiger d. Wiener Ak., phil.-hist. Cl., Dec. 17, 1884], quoted by Eut[Nab 27]; Nö[ib.] comp. also Eth. **ከፈር:** *basket, measure;* Nab. כפר *cave, sepulchre,* synon. of קברא Nö in Eut[Nab ib.])

3713 †I. כְּפוֹר **n.m. bowl** (NH *id.;* 𝔗 כְּפוֹרָא)—*bowl* of gold or silver, used in the temple (late), כ׳ 1 Ch 28[17.17.17.17]; pl. cstr. כְּפוֹרֵי 1 Ch 28[17.17] Ezr 1[10.10] 8[27].

3713 †II. כְּפוֹר **n.m. hoar frost** (NH *id.*)—כ׳ ψ 147[16]; כְּפֹר Ex 16[14] (P), Jb 38[29].

3728 †[כָּפַשׁ] **vb.** only **Hiph. make bent, press or bend together** (NH Hiph. *id.;* כָּפַשׁ *furnish* a vessel *with a bent rim,* כּוֹפֶשׁ *a broad-rimmed vessel;* Ar. كَفِسَ *have bent* or *crooked feet;* Tel Am. *kapâšu, sole* of foot Dl[HWB 348] (doubtfully), but inf. fr. כבש acc. to Wkl[Tel Am. Letters, Vocab.]);—**Hiph.** *Pf.* 3 ms. sf. הִכְפִּישַׁנִי בָּאֵפֶר La 3[16] *he made me cower in the ashes*.

3730 †I. כַּפְתּוֹר, כַּפְתֹּר **n.m. 1. capital, 2. knob, bulb** (**2.** perhaps earlier mng.; Hoffm[ZAW iii. (1883), 124], comp. Syr. ܟܦܬܪܐ *pear* (Löw[No. 153]), from shape);—**1.** כַּפְתֹּר Am 9[1] *capital* of pillar; so pl. sf. כַּפְתֹּרֶיהָ Zp 2[14]. **2.** כַּפְתֹּר, *knob* or bulb, ornament on the golden lampstand in tabernacle; 𝔊 σφαιρωτήρ, Jos[Arch. iii. 6, 7] ῥοΐσκος, *small pomegranate;* 𝔙 *sphaerula:*—Ex 25[33.33.35.35.35] = 37[19.19.21.21.21]; sf. כַּפְתֹּרֶיהָ 25[31.34] = 37[17.20], כַּפְתֹּרֵיהֶם 25[36] = 37[22] (all P).

†II. כַּפְתּוֹר, כַּפְתֹּר **n.pr.terr.** prob. **Crete,** 3731
so Ew Kiep Di[Gn 10. 14] Gie[Je 47. 4] al.; cf. A. J. Evans[Cretan Pictographs (1895), 100 ff.]; (> 𝔊 𝔖 𝔙 𝔗 *Cappadocia,* certainly wrong; Mich *Cyprus;* Eb[ÄgM 127 ff.] al. the coast of the *Nile-Delta;* WMM[As. Eu. 387 f.] Philistines, originally pirates from SW. coast of Asia Minor, and the Ægean islands);—כַּפְתּוֹר Am 9[7] (orig. home of Philistines), כַּפְתֹּר Dt 2[23] (home of Caphtorim, v. infr.); שְׁאֵרִית אִי כַּפְתֹּר Je 47[4] *the rest of the coast-land of Caphtor.*—Vid. also כְּרֵתִי infr.

†[כַּפְתֹּרִי] **adj.gent.**, only pl. as subst. 3732
כַּפְתֹּרִים **Cretans**; Gn 10[14] (J) = 1 Ch 1[12]; as expellers of the 'Awwim' from their homes about Gaza, Dt 2[23].

I. כַּר *basket-saddle,* v. sub כור. p. 468 3733

†II. כַּר **n.m.** [ψ 65, 14] **pasture** (√dub.; Thes 3733
der. fr. כַּר *lamb* (= lamb-pasturage); Schwally[ZAW x. (1890) 186] fr. כרה, and comp. As. *kirû* [which however = *nursery of trees, grove* Dl[HWB 353]], Ar. كُرّ *cistern;* Hom[NS 100] from כרר q. v., orig. = *round enclosure*);—sg. only כַּר נִרְחָב Is 30[23] *a roomy pasture;* pl. כָּרִים ψ 37[20], לָבְשׁוּ כ׳ הַצֹּאן 65[14] *the pastures are clothed with the sheep* (> Schwally[l. c.] who tr. *lambs* ψ 37[20] after Aq 𝔖 𝔗, and 65[14], and underst. Is 30[23] of a def. pl.).—III. כַּר *lamb* v. sub כרר.

†כֹּר **n.[m.]** kōr, a measure (usu. dry), = 3734
חֹמֶר (Ez 45[14] cf. v[11]) (NH כּוֹר, Aram. כּוֹרָא, ܟܘܪܐ; hence, as loan-words, Gk. κόρος, Ar. كُرّ Frä[207]; √ dub.; כרה, Lag[Or. ii. 30], cf. Id[BN 40. 156]; כרר, Nö[ZMG 1886, xl. 734]; Dl[Prol. 113] comp. As. *kâru,* and der. fr. כור (but see now *kâru* Dl[HWB 340]));—כ׳ סֹלֶת 1 K 5[2]; כ׳ קֶמַח v[2]; of חִטִּים v[25 a]; pl. כֹּרִים of ח׳ and שְׂעֹרִים 2 Ch 2[9.9] 27[5]; הַכֹּר as liquid measure (of oil) Ez 45[14]. See further Benz[Arch. 183 ff.] Now[Arch. i. 203], and, on capacity, v. III. חֹמֶר p. 330 f. supr.; in 1 K 5[25 b] rd. בַּת שֶׁמֶן for MT כֹּר שׁ׳ (cf. 𝔊 and 2 Ch 2[9]).

†[כרבל] **vb.** either **denom.** be-mantle 3736
(from BAram. כַּרְבְּלָא Dn 3[21], *if* this = *mantle,* and not (Marti[Gl.]) = Ass. *karballatu, cap* (but 'Kriegs[?]-mantel,' Zehnpfund[BAS ii, 535])), or

poss. **quadril.** bind round (from כבל, with ins. ר);—only **Pu.** *pt. pass.* מְכֻרְבָּל בִּמְעִיל בּוּץ 1 Ch 15^{27} *bemantled* with a robe of byssus.

3738 †I. כָּרָה **vb.** dig (NH *id.*; Aram. כְּרָא, Eth. ከረየ: Ar. كَرَا (c. و and esp. ى, Dozy[ii. 461]); Syr. ܟܪܳܐ is *be short, cut off* (i.e. *rounded off*?), Ar. كُرَةٌ *ball;* 𝔗 כְּרִי *heap* Dalm[Gr. 109]; Syr. ܟܪܺܝܳܐ, Mish. כרי *id.;* As. *karê*, large vessels for holding corn, etc., Dl[HWB 353], cf. *kirû* (dub.) Wkl[Tel Am. Vocab.]; Ba[ZMG 1887, 615] conjectures *be round* as orig. √ mng., and comp. Ar. كَرِيَتِ السَّاقُ *the leg is round*);—**Qal** *Pf.* 3 ms. כָּרָה 2 Ch 16^{14} ψ 7^{16}; 2 ms. כָּרִיתָ ψ 40^{7}; 1 s. כָּרִיתִי Gn 50^{5}; 3 pl. כָּרוּ Je 18^{20}+3 t.; sf. כָּרוּהָ Nu 21^{18}; *Impf.* 3 ms. יִכְרֶה Ex 21^{33}; 3 mpl. וַיִּכְרוּ Gn 26^{25}; *Pt.* כֹּרֶה Pr 16^{27} 26^{27};—*dig* a grave, קֶבֶר Gn 50^{5} (J), cf. 2 Ch 16^{14}; a well, בְּאֵר Gn 26^{25} (J), Nu 21^{18} (song in JE); a pit, בּוֹר Ex 21^{33}; fig. of plotting against others ψ 7^{16}; so sq. שׁוּחָה Je $18^{20.22}$, sq. שִׁיחָה 57^{7} 119^{85}; sq. שַׁחַת Pr 26^{27}; hence כֹּרֶה רָעָה Pr 16^{27} *one digging a calamity;* אָזְנַיִם כ׳ לִי ψ 40^{7} ears *hast thou dug* (with allusion to the cavity of the ear) *for me*, thou hast given me the means of hearing and obeying thy will.—On ψ 22^{17} v. II. כּוּר. **Niph.** *Impf.* 3 ms. עַד יִכָּרֶה שַׁחַת ψ 94^{13} *until the pit be digged* for the wicked, fig. of judgment.

3741 †[כֵּרָה] **n.f.** cistern (or well), only pl. cstr. in נְוֹת כְּרֹת רֹעִים Zp 2^{6} pastures of (=with) *wells of shepherds*, but text dub.; כ׳ a gloss acc. to Kö[ii. 176, (§ 94 a) Anm.]; 𝔊 κρήτη; We (והיתה כרת נות רעים, as 𝔊) *kereth*=Philistia; v. further כְּרֵתִי; Böhme[ZAW vii. 1887, 212] views כְּרֹת, plausibly, as erron. variant of preceding נְוֹת, so Schwally[ib. x. 1890, 185, 186]; Rothstein in Kau[AT].

4379 †[מִכְרֶה] **n.m.** pit (?), only cstr. מִכְרֵה־מֶלַח Zp 2^{9} *salt-pit* (but not certain).

3739 †II. [כָּרָה] **vb.** get by trade, trade (NH כִּירָה *act of buying, purchase* (so 'in den Küstenländern,' Levy[NWB ii. 323 f.]); Ar. كَرَى *let for hire*);—only **Qal** *Impf.* 1 s. sf. וָאֶכְּרֶהָ Ho 3^{2} (d. f. dirim., si vera punctat., Ges[§ 20. 2, b]; but cf. We); 3 mpl. יִכְרוּ Jb 40^{30}; 2 mpl. תִּכְרוּ Dt 2^{6} Jb 6^{27};—*get by trade, buy*, c. acc. Ho 3^{2} Dt 2^{6}; sq. עַל־ *trade in, make trade of* Jb 6^{27} 40^{30}.

3739 †III. [כָּרָה] **vb.** give a feast (lit. perhaps *bring* (guests), *invite;* cf. As. *karû, bring, kirêtu, feast, kireti iškun, he gave a feast*, Dl[HWB 352]);—only **Qal** *Impf.* c. acc. cogn., וַיִּכְרֶה לָהֶם כֵּרָה גְדוֹלָה 2 K 6^{23} *and he gave a great feast for them* (the context requires this sense, but text dubious, Nö[ZMG 1886, 724], cf. Klo).

†כֵּרָה **n.f.** a feast, 2 K 6^{23} (si vera l.; 3740
v. foregoing).

כְּרוּב 91 **n.m.** cherub;—כ׳ Ex 25^{19}+26 t.; 3742-43
pl. כְּרֻבִים ψ 99^{1}+33 t.; כְּרוּבִים Ex 25^{18}+29 t.; (NH *id.*; Aram. כְּרוּבָא, ܟܪܘܒܐ; √ dub.; As. *karâbu* = *be gracious to, bless* Dl[HWB 350], but adj. *karûbu* is *great, mighty*, Id[ib. 352]; on poss. connex. with כְּרוּב cf. Dl in Baer[Ezech. xiii.]; As. *kirubu*=*šêdu* (name of winged bull in Assyr.; v. Len[Origines i. 118, Eng. Tr. 126] Dl[Par 154]) has not been verified, cf. v.F.[ZA i. 68 f.] Budge[Expos. Apr. May, 1885] Teloni[ZA vi. 124 ff.]; the older view, connecting כ׳ with γρύψ, and deriving from Pers. *giriften, griffen*, lacks evidence and probability.—Possibly the *thunder-cloud* underlies the conception);—**1.** the living chariot of the theophanic God; possibly identified with the storm-wind ψ 18^{11}=2 S 22^{11} וַיִּרְכַּב עַל־כְּרוּב *and he rode upon a cherub* (‖ flew swiftly on the wings of the wind). **2.** as the guards of the garden of Eden Gn 3^{24} (J). **3.** as the throne of Yahweh Sabaoth, in phrase י׳ (צְבָאוֹת) יֹשֵׁב הַכְּרוּבִים *Yahweh Sabaoth throned on the cherubim* 1 S 4^{4} 2 S 6^{2}=1 Ch 13^{6}; the context shews that the cherubim of the ark of the covenant are referred to, and it is probable that the same reference is in 2 K 19^{15} = Is 37^{16}, ψ 80^{2} 99^{1}. **4.** P gives an account of: **a.** two cherubim of solid gold upon the slab of gold of the כַּפֹּרֶת facing each other with wings outstretched above, so as to constitute a basis or throne on which the glory of Yahweh appeared, and from whence He spake Ex 25^{18-22} 37^{7-9} Nu 7^{89}; **b.** numerous cherubim woven into the texture of the inner curtains of the tabernacle and the veils Ex $26^{1.31}$ $36^{8.35}$. **5.** K and Ch describe the cherubim of the temple: **a.** two gigantic images of olive wood plated with gold, ten cubits high, standing in the דְּבִיר facing the door, whose wings, five cubits each, extended, two of them meeting in the middle of the room to constitute the throne, two of them extending to the walls 1 K 6^{23-28} 8^{6-7} 2 Ch 3^{10-13} 5^{7-8}; Ch (doubtless influenced by Ez) represents them as the chariot of Yahweh 1 Ch 28^{18}; **b.** images of cherubim were carved on the gold plated cedar planks which constituted the inner walls of the temple, and upon the olive wood doors 1 K 6^{29-35} 2 Ch 3^{7}; and on the bases of the portable lavers, interchanging

with lions and oxen 1 K 7^{29-36}; Ch also represents that they were woven in the veil of the דְּבִיר 2 Ch 3^{14}. **6.** Ezekiel describes the cherubim: **a.** as four living creatures, each with four faces, lion, ox, eagle, and man, having the figure and hands of men, and the feet of calves. Each has four wings, two of which are stretched upward, meeting above and sustaining the throne of Yahweh; two of them stretched downwards so as to cover the creatures themselves. The cherubim never turn but go straight forward, as do the wheels of the cherubic chariot, and they are full of eyes and are like burning coals of fire, Ez 1^{5-28} 9^{3} 10^{1-20} 11^{22}; the king of Tyre is scornfully compared with one of these, and is assigned a residence in Eden and the mountain of God Ez $28^{14.16}$; **b.** Ez knows of no cherubic statues in the new temple, but represents the inner walls of the temple as carved with alternating palm trees and cherubim, each with two faces, the lion looking on one side, the man on the other. It is evident that the number and the form of the cherubim vary in the representations (cf. Ez 41^{18-25}). It is probable that the שְׂרָפִים of Is 6^{2-6} are another form of the cherubim. The Apoc. of the seals Rev 4–6 combines them in four *ζῷα*.

3746 †כָּרִי **adj. gent.** prob. = **Carian**, only c. art. as subst. coll. *Carians*, name given to foreign body-guard of king (cf. RS [OTJC 249, 2d ed. 262]) לַכָּרִי וְלָרָצִים 2 K 11^{4} cf. v^{19}; הכרי 2 S 20^{23} Kt (< Qr הַכְּרֵתִי, which We Dr Bu prefer).

3747-48 כְּרִית **n.pr.loc.** and כְּרִיתוּת v. sub כרת. p. 504

כרך (√ of following; cf. Aram. כְּרַךְ, ܟܪܰܟ *enwrap, surround*, כְּרָכָא, ܟܶܪܟܳܐ *bundle*, כְּרִיכָא, ܟܪܰܟܳܐ *city* (+many other deriv.); כְּרִיכָא, ܟܪܝܟܳܐ, NH כָּרֵךְ, *scroll*, etc.)

8509 †תַּכְרִיךְ **n.m.** robe וְתַכְרִיךְ בּוּץ וְאַרְגָּמָן Est 9^{15}.

כרכב **quadril.** (√ of following; cf. NH כִּרְכֵּב, *furnish with a rim, enclose, set*).

3749 †כַּרְכֹּב **n.[m.]** border, rim, of altar (NH *id.*);—cstr. כ׳ הַמִּזְבֵּחַ Ex 27^{5}; c. sf. כַּרְכֻּבּוֹ 38^{4} (both P).

3750 †כַּרְכֹּם **n.[m.]** saffron (*crocus sativus*) (NH *id.*; and *vb. denom.* כִּרְכֵּם; Hithp. *grow yellow, pale*; Aram. כּוּרְכְּמָא, ܟܘܪܟܡܐ; Ar. كُرْكُم = κρόκος, *crocus*; Lag [Ges. Abh. 58, No. 147]; so also JHMordt [Sab. Denkm. 83 f.]; otherwise DHM [ib.], who comp. Sab. כמכם, Ar. كَمْكَام = Gk. κάγκαμον);—Ct 4^{14}; on meaning v. esp. Löw [No. 162].

†כַּרְכְּמִישׁ, כַּרְכְּמִשׁ **n.pr.loc.**, city on Eu- 3751
phrates (As. *Kargamis, Gargamis*, cf. Dl [Par 265 ff.]; Egypt. *Ḳa-ri-ḳa-maï(?)-ša* WMM [Asien u. Europa 263]; etym. dub.; acc. to Hoffm [Auszüge Act. Pers. Märt. 163] RS [Proph. i, n. 5] = '*Castle of Mish*,' cf. Dl [l.c.]);—כַּרְכְּמִישׁ Is 10^{9} 2 Ch 35^{20} (𝔊L Χαρχαμεις), כַּרְכְּמִשׁ Je 46^{2} (𝔊 Χαρμεις, Καρχαμεις). Hittite capital, E. bank of Euphr., mod. *Jerabîs*, or *Jerbâs*; Schr [KGF 221 ff.; COT, on Is 10, 9] Dl [l.c.]; Jen [ZA vii. (1892), 365] thinks he reads *G(K)ar-g(k)a-mi-si(e)-ras* = 'king of Karkemish' on ('Hittite') inscr. from Karkemish.

†כַּרְכַּס **n.pr.m. Pers.**, a eunuch of Aha- 3752
suerus, Est 1^{10}.

כִּרְכָּרוֹת v. [כִּרְכָּרָה] sub כרר. p. 503 3753

כֶּרֶם 92 **n.m.** [Dt 28, 30] (**f.** [Is 27, 2]) vineyard (NH 3754
id.; Aram. כַּרְמָא, ܟܪܡܐ; Zinj. כרם DHM [Sendsch. 58]; Ar. كَرْمٌ, كَرْمَةٌ *vine*; Eth. ከርም: ከርም: *vine*; Jen [ZA vii. (1892), 217] comp. As. *karânu, vine*;—etym. dub.; Thes al. comp. Ar. كَرُمَ *noble, generous, fertile*, but precarious);—abs. כ׳ Ex 22^{4}+, כָּרֶם Gn 9^{20}+; cstr. כֶּרֶם 1 K 21^{7}+; sf. כַּרְמִי Is 5^{3}+, כַּרְמְךָ Ex 23^{11}+, etc.; pl. כְּרָמִים Jos 24^{13}+; cstr. כַּרְמֵי Am 5^{1}+2 t.; sf. כְּרָמֵינוּ Ne 5^{3}+3 t.; כַּרְמֵיכֶם Am 4^{9}+2 t., etc.;—*vineyard* Gn 9^{20} (J), 1 K 21^{1}+9 t. 1 K 21, Ct $2^{15.15}$+; so even Ju 15^{5} (where rd. כ׳ וזית; cf. GFM, who however doubts genuineness); + זַיִת Ex 23^{11} (E) and oft. (v. זית); + שָׂדֶה Ex $22^{4.5}$ (E), and oft.; fig. of Isr. under י׳'s care Is $5^{1 ff.}$, cf. 3^{14} Je 12^{10}; fig. of Shulamite's complexion Ct 1^{6}, of her heart 8^{12}.—Vbs. governing כ׳ are:—נָטַע Gn 9^{20} Am 5^{11}+16 t., cf. מַטָּעֵי כ׳ Mi 1^{6}; זָרַע Dt 22^{9} (c. 2 acc.); חִלֵּל = *begin to use fruit of*, Dt $20^{6.6}$ 28^{30} Je 31^{5}; זָמַר *prune*, Lv $25^{3.4}$; בָּצַר *gather, harvest* (lit. *cut off*, i.e. grapes, Lv $25^{5.11}$), Dt 24^{21} Ju 9^{27}, cf. לָקַשׁ Jb 24^{6}; עוֹלֵל *glean*, Lv 19^{10} Dt 24^{21}; אָכַל Jos 24^{13} (usu. 'eat *fruit* of' Is 65^{21}, etc.); locusts *devour* Am 4^{9} (si vera l.) On **n.pr.loc.** אָבֵל כְּרָמִים v. II. אָבֵל **4**; בֵּית הַכֶּרֶם v. p. 111 b.

†[כָּרַם] **vb. denom.** tend vineyards, dress 3755
vines, only **Qal** *Pt.* pl. *vinedressers* כֹּרְמִים 2 K 25^{12} = Je 52^{16} (‖ יֹגְבִים), Jo 1^{11} 2 Ch 26^{10} (both ‖ אִכָּרִים), כֹּרְמֵיכֶם Is 61^{5} (‖ *id.*)

†I. כַּרְמִי **n.pr.m.** **1.** a son of Reuben Gn 3756
46^{9} Ex 6^{14} Nu 26^{6} 1 Ch 5^{3}. **2.** a Judaite Jos $7^{1.18}$ 1 Ch 2^{7}; so 4^{1}, but rd. perh. כְּלוּבַי We (cf. 2^{9})—𝔊 throughout χαρμ(ε)ι.

3757 †II. כַּרְמִי **adj. gent.** of I. כַּרְמִי **1**; only c. art. הַכּ׳, as subst. Nu 26^{6}.

3759 †I. כַּרְמֶל **n.m.** [Is 29,17] **1. plantation, garden-land. 2. fruit, garden-growth** (כֶּרֶם + ל, cf. Ges [§ 85, 52] Sta [§ 299]);—abs. כ׳ Is 16^{10} + 12 t.; sf. כַּרְמִלּוֹ Is 10^{18} + 2 t.;—**1.** *garden-land*, Is 16^{10} (‖ כְּרָמִים), 10^{18} (‖ יַעַר), $29^{17.17}$ (opp. לְבָנוֹן, יַעַר), $32^{15.15}$ (opp. מִדְבָּר, יַעַר), v^{16} Je 4^{26} (opp. מִדְבָּר), 48^{33} 2 Ch 26^{10} (opp. הֶהָרִים); אֶרֶץ הַכּ׳ Je 2^{7} *the country of garden-land*, i.e. fertile; יַעַר כַּרְמִלּוֹ 2 K 19^{23} = Is 37^{24}, *the garden-like forest of it* (viz. of Lebanon). On Mi 7^{14} v. II. כַּרְמֶל. **2.** by meton. (*fresh*) *fruit, garden-growth*, 2 K 4^{42} (+ לֶחֶם שְׂעוֹרִים); Lv 2^{14} (+ אָבִיב קָלוּי בָּאֵשׁ, and גֶּרֶשׂ, q.v.); לֶחֶם וְקָלִי וכ׳ Lv 23^{14}.

3760 †II. כַּרְמֶל **n.pr.mont. et urb. Carmel**:—**1.** mt.-promontory on Mediterranean, with fertile slopes, Tel el-Amarna (*Ginti-*)*Kirmil*, Jastrow [JBL xi. 1892, 115]; Jos 19^{26}, הַר־הַכּ׳ 1 K $18^{19.20}$ 2 K 2^{25} 4^{25}; ראשׁ הַכּ׳ Am 1^{2} 9^{3} 1 K 18^{42}; c. art. also Jos 12^{22}; and, + בָּשָׁן, Je 50^{19}, as pasturage (in fig. of Isr. as flock of י׳), cf. (כ׳ without art.) Mi 7^{14} (less prob. rend. *garden-land*, I. כַּרְמֶל, so We GASm); הַכּ׳ Is 35^{2} (+ הַשָּׁרוֹן, הַלְּבָנוֹן); כ׳ Is 33^{9} (+ לְבָנוֹן, הַשָּׁרוֹן and בָּשָׁן, marking extent of land), Na 1^{4} (+ לְבָנוֹן, בָּשָׁן); כְּכַרְמֶל בַּיָּם Je 46^{18} (sim. of Nebuchad.); Ct 7^{6} רֹאשֵׁךְ עָלַיִךְ כַּכּ׳ (but v. כַּרְמִיל);—on Carmel v. GASm [G. 337 ff.] Buhl [G. 23]. **2.** city, 3 h. S. of Hebron, כַּרְמֶל Jos 15^{55}; בַּכּ׳ 1 S $25^{2.2.7}$; כַּרְמֶ֫לָה v^{5} (= *to Carmel*); הַכַּרְמֶ֫לָה 15^{12} 25^{40}.—Mod. *Kurmul*, Rob [BR i. 492–498, ii. 97] Buhl [G. 163].

3761 †כַּרְמְלִי **adj. gent.**, c. art., **the Carmelite**, of Nabal הַכּ׳ 1 S 30^{5} 2 S 2^{2} 3^{3}, so also 1 S 27^{3} (𝔊 We Klo Dr Bu Kit; MT הַכַּרְמְלִית, of Abi-
3762 gail); of חצרו 2 S 23^{35} = 1 Ch 11^{37}. **f.** הַכַּרְמְלִית *the Carmelitess*, 1 Ch 3^{1}, of Abigail.

3758 †כַּרְמִיל **n.[m.] crimson, carmine**, i.e. crimson stuff, cloth; late (prob. Pers. loan-word, and a deriv. fr. Pers. كِرْم *worm*, v. De [ZLuth. Th. 1878, 593]);—only 2 Ch $2^{6.13}$ 3^{14} (in all + אַרְגְּמָן(-וָן), תְּכֵלֶת, 2^{13} 3^{14} + בּוּץ also); rd. perh. also for כַּרְמֶל Ct 7^{6} (‖ אַרְגָּמָן: so Gi, of hair formed spirally, like shell-fish; Gr, of glossy hair).

3763 †כְּרָן **n.pr.m.**, an Edomite Gn 36^{26} = 1 Ch 1^{41}.

3765 כִּרְסֵם v. sub כסם. p. 493

†כָּרַע **bow down** (NH *id.*; Aram. כְּרַע; 3766
Ar. كَرَعَ *put one's mouth* into water, or water-vessel; i.e. kneel to drink? denom. fr. foll.?);—**Qal** *Pf.* 3 m. כ׳ Gn 49^{9} + 6 t.; 3 mpl. כָּֽרְעוּ Ju 7^{6} + 4 t.; *Impf.* יִכְרַע Ju 7^{5} + 3 t.; 1 s. וָאֶכְרְעָה Ezr 9^{5}; 3 mpl. יִכְרְעוּן Jb 31^{10}; 2 mpl. תִּכְרָ֑עוּ Is 65^{12}; 1 pl. וְנִכְרָ֫עָה ψ 95^{6} + 6 t. Impf.; *Inf. cstr.* כְּרֹעַ 1 K 8^{54}; *Pt.* כֹּרֵעַ Est 3^{5}; pl. כֹּרְעִים Est 3^{2}; f. כֹּרְעוֹת Jb 4^{4}.—**1.** *bow* על ברכים to drink Ju $7^{5.6}$, in supplication to Elijah 2 K 1^{13}; in the worship of God 1 K 8^{34} Ezr 9^{5}; c. ברכים subj. and לְ of God 1 K 19^{18} Is 45^{23}; without ברכים c. לִפְנֵי ψ 22^{30} 72^{9}; ‖ השׁתחוה 2 Ch 7^{3} 29^{29} ψ 95^{6}, worship of God, but Est $3^{2.2.5}$ in obeisance to Haman. **2.** *bow down*, of the couching lion Gn 49^{9} Nu 24^{9} (both poetry). **3.** preg. c. עַל, *bow down over* (in order to lie with) a woman Jb 31^{10}. **4.** *bow down*, of a woman in childbirth 1 S 4^{19}, so of animals Jb 39^{3}; idols, removed by enemies Is $46^{1.2}$; בִּרְכַּיִם כֹּרְעוֹת Jb 4^{4} *tottering* (feeble) knees; of enemies in death, כרע [ו]נפל *bow and fall down* Ju $5^{27.27.27}$ ψ 20^{9}, preg. without נפל 2 K 9^{24} Is 65^{12}, c. תַּחַת Is 10^{4}.—**Hiph.** *Pf.* 3 ms. הִכְרִיעַ ψ 78^{31}; 2 fs. sf. הִכְרַעְתִּנִי Ju 11^{35}; *Impf.* 2 ms. תַּכְרִיעַ 2 S 22^{40} = ψ 18^{40}; *Imv.* sf. הַכְרִיעֵהוּ ψ 17^{13}; *Inf. abs.* הַכְרֵעַ Ju 11^{35}.—**1.** cause to *bow in grief* Ju $11^{35.35}$. **2.** cause to *bow down in death* ψ 17^{13} 78^{31}, c. תַּחַת 2 S 22^{40} = ψ 18^{40}.

†[כֶּ֫רַע] **n.[f.] leg**, (NH כְּרַע, Aram. כַּרְעָא, 3767
ܟܪܥܐ);—only dual fem. כְּרָעַיִם Lv 11^{21} + 3 t.; כְּרָעָ֑יִם Lv 9^{14}; sf. כְּרָעָיו Ex 12^{9} + 3 t.;—*two* (bending) *legs*, of animals in ritual phrase of P, ראשׁוֹ עַל־כְּרָעָיו Ex 12^{9} *his head with his legs*, Lv 4^{11}; (ה)קרב(ו) ו(ה)כרע(יו) (*his*) *inwards* and (*his*) *legs* Ex 29^{17} Lv $1^{9.13}$ 8^{21} 9^{14}; Am 3^{12} (of legs of lamb in mouth of lion); of the long bending hinder legs of the Saltatorial Orthoptera (v. Tristr [Nat. Hist. Bib. 309]; Dr [Joel 84]) Lv 11^{21} אשׁר לוֹ כְרָעַיִם מִמַּעַל לְרַגְלָיו לְנַתֵּר בָּהֵן עַל הָאָרֶץ which have *bending legs* above their feet, etc.

†כַּרְפַּס **n.m. cotton (or fine linen)** (loan- 3768
word fr. Sk. *karpâsa, cotton*, Pers. كَرْپَاس *fine linen*; hence also κάρπασος, *carbasus*, Ar. كِرْبَاس, Talm. כַּרְפְּסָא; cf. Lag [Arm. Stud. § 1148]);—חוּר כ׳ וּתְכֵלֶת Est 1^{6} (𝔊 καρπασίνοις): cf. Cels. [Hierob. ii. 157 ff.]

†[כָּרַר] **vb.** √ of foll. (NH כִּרְכֵּר *use cir-* 3769
cumlocution; 𝔗 pl. כִּרְכְּרָן *dances*; Ar. كَرَّ *return, repeat, attack anew, advance and retreat*; كَرْكَرَ *id.*; II. *whirl about*; orig. perh. *move around*,

then *surround, enclose, recur,* etc.; Eth. ክርከረ: *turn* a mill, only pt.; ኮርኮረ: v. *rotate, revolve, roll,* and deriv. Di [838 f.]);—only **Pilpēl**, *Pt.* מְכַרְכֵּר *dancing* (lit. *whirling*) 2 S $6^{14.16}$ (|| מְפַזֵּז).

3733 †II. כַּר **n.[m.]** he-lamb, battering-ram (As. *kirru*, Zim in Schwally [ZAW x. (1890), 186]; perh. *lamb* fr. *dancing, skipping, gallopping* in field; (*battering-*)*ram* as in Eng., fr. butting; cf. Ar. كَبْش *ram* and *buttress,* Lane; also *battering-ram* cf. Dozy [ii. 440]);—sg. only Is 16^{1} *the lamb of the ruler* (as tribute); elsewh. pl. כָּרִים Am 6^{4} 1 S 15^{9} 2 K 3^{4} Je 51^{40} (in sim.), Ez 27^{21} 39^{18}; חֵלֶב כ׳ Dt 32^{14} *the fat of lambs;* דַּם כ׳ וְעַתּוּדִים Is 34^{6} *the blood of lambs and goats;* כָּרִים = *battering-rams* Ez 4^{2} $21^{27.27}$ (in vᵃ Co rds. שָׂרִים, cf. AV; MT RV as above).—Vid. also בֵּית כַּר p. 111 supr.

3753 †[כִּרְכָּרָה] **n.f.** dromedary (acc. to Ki Thes; perhaps from constantly *repeated undulating* movement);—only pl. abs. וּבַכִּרְכָּרוֹת Is 66^{20} (+ בַּסּוּסִים וּבָרֶכֶב וּבַצַּבִּים וּבַפְּרָדִים; the whole list is a gloss acc. to Du Che [Intr. Is.]).

3603 כִּכָּר **n.f.** [Gn 13, 10 Ex 29, 32]; a round: hence **1. a round district. 2. a round loaf. 3. a round weight, talent** (NH *id.; loaf, weight, talent;* Aram. כַּכְּרָא, ܟܰܟܪܳܐ, *talent;* Tel Am. *gaggaru* kaspu Wkl [No. 35, Rev. 14] Christ.-Pal.-Aram. ܟܟܪܐ, of honey-*comb* Schwally [Idiot. 46]; on format. v. Ba [NB 204]);—abs. כ׳ Gn 13^{12}+; cstr. כִּכַּר 1 S 2^{36}+; du. כִּכְּרַיִם כֶּסֶף 1 K 16^{24} 2 K 5^{23}, כִּכְּרָיִם v^{23}; pl. כִּכָּרִים 1 Ch $22^{14.14}$ + 7 t. Chr; cstr. כִּכְּרֵי 2 K 5^{5} + 2 t. Chr; כִּכְּרוֹת (*loaves*) Ju 8^{5} 1 S 10^{3};—†**1.** *the round* (or *oval*) esp. of the Jordan valley, כִּכַּר הַיַּרְדֵּן Gn $13^{10.11}$ 1 K 7^{46} = 2 Ch 4^{17}; abs. הַכִּכָּר Gn $19^{17.25}$ Dt 34^{3} 2 S 18^{23}; אֶרֶץ הַכּ׳ Gn 19^{28}; עָרֵי הַכּ׳ 13^{12} 19^{29}, v. GASm [G. 505] Buhl [G. 112]; district of Jerus., הַכּ׳ Ne 3^{22} 12^{28}. †**2.** *loaf* of bread (from round shape), כִּכַּר לֶחֶם 1 S 2^{36} Pr 6^{36}, cf. Ex 29^{23} Je 37^{21} 1 Ch 16^{3}; כִּכְּרוֹת לֶחֶם 1 S 10^{3} Ju 8^{5}. **3.** †**a.** *a weight* (also fr. shape), כִּכַּר עֹפֶרֶת Zc 5^{7} *a weight of lead,* serving as cover of an ephah. **b.** a particular unit of weight, *talent,* usu. of gold or silver:—כ׳ זָהָב 2 S 12^{30} 2 K 9^{14} + 18 t.; כ׳ כֶּסֶף 1 K 20^{39} 2 K 5^{5} + 21 t.; but also of iron, בַּרְזֶל 1 Ch 29^{7}, and bronze נְחֹשֶׁת Ex 38^{29} 1 Ch 29^{7}.—The weight of the talent was 58·944 kilogr. (= 129·97 lbs.) acc. to older (Bab.) standard, later 49·11 kg. (= 108·29 lbs.) and less; v. Benz [Arch. 187 ff. 194] Now [Arch. i. 208 f.].—See also שֶׁקֶל.

כרשׁ √ of foll. (Ar. كَرِشَ *be wrinkled*).

†[כָּרֵשׂ] **n.[m.]** belly (NH כָּרֵס *id.;* Aram. 3770
כַּרְסָא, ܟܰܪܣܳܐ *id.;* Mand. כארסא, כראס, *uterus,* Nö [M 151, 157]; Ar. كَرِش, Eth. ከርሥ: *wrinkled* or *folded stomach* of cud-chewing animals; cf. Lag [BN 20, 44]; As. *karšu, body, belly*);—only sf. כְּרֵשׂוֹ Je 51^{34} of Nebuchadrezzar under fig. of sea-monster.

כֹּרֶשׁ **n.pr.m.** v. כּוֹרֶשׁ. p. 468 3566

†כַּרְשְׁנָא **n.pr.m.** a Pers. prince Est 1^{14}. 3771

†כָּרַת 291 **vb. cut off, cut down** (NH *id.;* 3772-73
As. *karâtu,* II. *hew off* Dl [HWB 357]);—**Qal** *Pf.* כ׳ Gn 15^{18} + 19 t.; 2 ms. כָּרַתָּ Dt 20^{20}; 1 s. כָּרַתִּי Ex 34^{27} + 15 t.; + 8 t. Pf.; *Impf.* יִכְרֹת Jb 40^{28} + 21 t.; 2 ms. תִּכְרָת־ Is 57^{8}; 1 s. אֶכְרוֹת Is 61^{8} 1 S 11^{2}; אֶכְרְתָה Is 55^{3}; 3 mpl. יִכְרְתוּ Ho 12^{2} ψ 83^{6}; 1 pl. נִכְרְתָה Gn 26^{28} 31^{44}; sf. נִכְרְתֶנּוּ Je 11^{19}; + 31 t. Impf.; *Imv.* כְּרָת־ 1 S 11^{1}; כִּרְתָה 2 S 3^{12}; + 4 t. Imv.; *Inf. abs.* כָּרֹת Ho 10^{4}; כָּרוֹת Ne 9^{8}; *cstr.* כְּרֹת Je 34^{8} + 2 t.; כְּרָת־ Is 44^{14} + 2 t.; כְּרוֹת 2 Ch 2^{7} 29^{10}; sf. כָּרְתִי 1 S 24^{12}; *Pt. act.* כֹּרֵת Ex 34^{10} + 3 t.; + 3 t. Pt. act.; *pass.* כָּרוּת Lv 22^{24}; cstr. כְּרוּת Dt 23^{2}; pl. כְּרֻת[וֹ]ת 1 K 7^{12} + 3 t.;—**1.** *cut off:* **a.** *things:* c. acc. foreskin Ex 4^{25} (J); privy member Lv 22^{24} (H) Dt 23^{2}; cluster of grapes Nu $13^{23.24}$ (E); bough of tree Ju $9^{48.49}$; skirt 1 S $24^{5.6.12}$; head of man 1 S 17^{51} 31^{9} 2 S 20^{22}; garments 2 S 10^{4} = 1 Ch 19^{4}; palms of hands 1 S 5^{4}; sprigs Is 18^{5}. **b.** *persons,* c. acc. pers. מִן *loc.* Je 11^{19} 50^{16}. **2.** *cut down,* c. acc. trees Dt 19^{5} $20^{19.20}$ 2 K 19^{23} = Is 37^{24}, Is 44^{14} Je 6^{6} 10^{3} 22^{7} 46^{23} Ez 31^{12}; *asherim* Ex 34^{13} (J) Ju $6^{25.26.30}$ 1 K 15^{13} = 2 Ch 15^{16}; 2 K 18^{4} 23^{14}. **3.** *hew,* timber 1 K $5^{20.20}$ = 2 Ch $2^{7.15}$, Is 14^{8}; כֹּרְתֵי הָעֵצִים *hewers of timber* 2 Ch 2^{9}; כְּרֻת(וֹ)ת *hewn beams* 1 K 6^{36} $7^{2.12}$. **4.** כ׳ בְּרִית *cut, or make a covenant* (because of the cutting up and distribution of the flesh of the victim for eating in the sacrifice of the covenants, see בְּרִית); הָעֵגֶל אֲשֶׁר כ׳ *the calf which they cut* Je 34^{18} (referring to Gn 15^{10}); עֲלֵי־זֶבַח ψ 50^{5}; abs. Gn $21^{27.32}$ 31^{44} (E) 1 S 18^{3} 1 K 5^{26} Ho 10^{4}; c. אֵת *with* Gn 15^{18} Ex 34^{27} Dt 31^{16} (J) Dt 5^{3} $28^{69.69}$ 29^{13} 2 S $3^{12.13.21}$ 2 K $17^{15.35.38}$ Is 28^{15} Je 11^{10} $31^{31.32.33}$ $34^{8.13}$ Ez 17^{13} Zc 11^{10} ψ 105^{9} = 1 Ch 16^{16}; c. עִם Gn 26^{28} (J) Ex 24^{8} (E) Dt 4^{23} 5^{2} 9^{9} $29^{11.24}$ 1 K 8^{21} = 2 Ch 6^{11} 2 Ch 23^{3} Ne 9^{8} Ho 2^{20} 12^{2} Jb 40^{28}; בְּ׳ omitted 1 S 20^{16} 22^{8} 1 K 8^{9} = 2 Ch 5^{10}; c. לְ Ex 23^{32} $34^{12.15}$ Jos $9^{6.7.11.15.16}$ 24^{25} (JE) Dt 7^{2} Ju 2^{2} 1 S 11^{1} 2 S 5^{3} 1 K 20^{34}

2 K 11[4] 1 Ch 11[3] 2 Ch 21[7] 29[10] Ezr 10[3] Is 55[3] 61[8] Je 32[40] Ez 34[25] 37[26] Jb 31[1] ψ 89[4]; בְּ׳ omitted 1 S 11[2] 2 Ch 7[18]; נֶגֶד Ex 34[10] (J); לִפְנֵי 1 S 23[18] 2 K 23[3] = 2 Ch 34[31] Je 34[15.18]; בֵּין וּבֵין 2 K 11[17]; 2 Ch 23[16]; c. עַל *against*, ψ 83[6]; אֲמָנָה is used for ברית Ne 10[1]; and דָּבָר Hg 2[5].

Note.—וַתִּכְרָת־לְךָ מֵהֶם Is 57[8] is usually rendered as RV *made for thee a covenant with them*, with ellipsis of בְּ׳ as above. But מִן is not used in such a construction. The clause is commonly regarded as corrupt by recent critics. Gr emends עִמָּהֶם for מֵהֶם, this is easiest and gives the usual construction; Du, followed by Buhl, reads וַתִּכְרִי after Ho 3[2].

Niph. *Pf.* 3 ms. נִכְרַת Jo 1[5] + 5 t.; נִכְרָ֑ת Jo 1[16] + 2 t.; 3 fs. נִכְרְתָה Gn 17[14] + 16 t.; נִכְרָ֑תָה ψ 37[38]; 2 ms. נִכְרַתָּ Ob [10]; + 8 t. Pf.; *Impf.* יִכָּרֵת Gn 9[11] + 21 t.; יִכָּרֶת־ Ob [9]; 3 mpl. יִכָּרֵתוּ Zc 13[8]; יִכָּרֵתוּן Jos 3[13] ψ 37[9]; + 9 t. Impf.; *Inf.* הִכָּרֵת Nu 15[31] ψ 37[34].—**1.** *be cut off:* **a.** of *things*, froward tongue Pr 10[31]; burden from a nail Is 22[25]; chariots Zc 9[10]; dwelling Zp 3[7]. **b.** *of persons*, the people of the land by a famine (בְּ) Gn 41[36] (E); all flesh by waters of deluge (מִמֵּי) Gn 9[11] (P); the anointed Dn 9[26]; enemies Is 11[13] Mi 5[8]; the wicked Is 29[20] Ho 8[4] Na 2[1] ψ 37[9.22.28.34.38] Pr 2[22]; others Ob [9.10] Zp 1[11] Zc 13[8] 14[2]. **c.** in the technical phrases of H and P וְנִכְרְתָה הַנֶּפֶשׁ ההיא *that person shall be cut off* (by death penalty) מֵעַמֶּיהָ Gn 17[14] Lv 7[20.21.25.27] Nu 9[13] Lv 19[8]; מִיִּשְׂרָאֵל Ex 12[15] Nu 19[13]; מֵעֲדַת יִשְׂרָאֵל Ex 12[19]; מִקֶּרֶב עַמֶּיהָ Ex 31[14] Nu 15[30] (עַמָּהּ); מִלְּפָנַי Lv 22[3]; מִתּוֹךְ הַקָּהָל Nu 19[20]; similarly with variation of subject Ex 30[33.38] Lv 17[4.9] 18[29] 20[18] 23[29], and with omission of word with מִן Lv 17[14] 20[17] Nu 15[31.31]. **2.** *be cut down*, a tree Jb 14[7]. **3.** *be chewed* between the teeth Nu 11[33] (J). **4.** *be cut off*, in a more general sense, *fail:* of waters Jos 3[13.16] (JE) 4[7.7] (D); new wine Jo 1[5]; meat v[16]; hope Pr 23[18] 24[14]; a name Is 48[19] 56[5] Ru 4[10]; a sign Is 55[13]; faithfulness Je 7[28]; לֹא יִכָּרֵת לְךָ אִישׁ *there shall not fail thee a man* 1 K 2[4] 8[25] = 2 Ch 6[16], 1 K 9[5] = 2 Ch 7[18], Je 33[17.18] 35[19]; לא יכרת מן *there shall not fail of* Jos 9[23] (J) 2 S 3[29].

Pual *Pf.* כֹּרַת Ez 16[4]; 3 fs. כֹּרָ֑תָה Ju 6[28];—**1.** *be cut off*, navel string Ez 16[4]. **2.** *be cut down*, Asherah Ju 6[28].

Hiph. *Pf.* הִכְרִית 1 S 28[9] 1 K 11[16]; 3 fs. הִכְרִיתָה Lv 26[22]; 1 s. הִכְרַתִּי Jos 23[4] + 32 t.; + 4 t. Pf.; *Impf.* יַכְרִית Dt 12[29] + 2 t.; juss. יַכְרֵת ψ 12[4] + 4 t.; 1 s. וָאַכְרִ֫תָה 2 S 7[9]; 1 pl. sf. וְנַכְרִיתֶנָּה Je 48[2]; + 9 t. Impf.; *Inf.* הַכְרִית Je 44[8] + 15 t.; הַכְרִת 1 S 20[15]; + sf. 2 t.—**1.** *cut off*, flattering lips ψ 12[4]. **2.** *cut off, destroy* the life of: **a.** animals c. acc., cattle Lv 26[22] (H); c. acc. and מִן frogs Ex 8[5] (J); horses Mi 5[9] Zc 9[10]. **b.** of men abs. ψ 109[13], by men, c. acc. enemies Ju 4[24] 1 S 24[22] 1 K 11[16] 14[14] 18[4] 2 Ch 22[7] Is 10[7] Ez 17[17] Ob [14]; c. acc. and מִן enemies Jos 11[21] Je 48[2]; the wicked ψ 101[8]; a clan Nu 4[18] (P); young men by death Je 9[20]; people by the sword Na 3[15]; necromancers 1 S 28[9]; the name Jos 7[9]. **c.** of men, by God c. acc. (הַ)גּוֹיִם Dt 19[1] Jos 23[4] (D) Zp 3[6]; various persons and things Is 48[9] Je 44[11] 51[62] Ez 25[16] 30[15] Zc 9[6]; c. acc. and מִן Ez 25[7] Am 1[5.8] 2[3]; מֵאֶרֶץ Na 2[14] ψ 34[17] = 109[15]; מִיִּשְׂרָאֵל Is 9[13]; מִיַּד Mi 5[11]; מִפָּנֶיךָ Dt 12[29] 2 S 7[9] = 1 Ch 17[8]; מֵעַל פְּנֵי הָאֲדָמָה 1 S 20[15] 1 K 9[7] Zp 1[3]; מִקֶּרֶב עַמּוֹ Lv 17[10] 20[3.5.6] (H); מִתּוֹךְ עַמִּי Ez 14[8]; Ez says also הכ׳ מִן . . . אָדָם וּבְהֵמָה 14[13.17.19.21] 25[13] 29[8]; צדיק ורשע 21[8.9]; עבר ושב 35[7]; c. acc. and לְ, *cut off, to*, or *from* Is 14[22] Je 44[7.8] 47[4]; כ׳ לְ׳ מַשְׁתִּין בְּקִיר 1 K 14[10] 21[21] 2 K 9[8]; כ׳ ל׳ מעם מזבח 1 S 2[33]; יַכְרֵת י׳ לָאִישׁ מֵאָהֳלֵי יַעֲקֹב Mal 2[12] *may Yahweh cut off to the man—from the tents of Jacob*. **3.** *cut down, destroy*, cities Mi 5[10], sun-pillars Lv 26[30] (H); and other things used in idolatry Na 1[14] Zp 1[4]; מן הארץ Zc 13[2]; מִקִּרְבְּ Mi 5[12]. **4.** *take away*, חֶסֶד מֵעִם *kindness from* 1 S 20[15]. **5.** *permit to perish*, מֵהַבְּהֵמָה (some) *of the cattle* 1 K 18[5].

Hoph. *Pf.* הָכְרַת מִנְחָה וָנֶסֶךְ מִבֵּית י׳ Jo 1[9].

†כְּרִיתוּת **n.f.** divorcement;—כ׳ Is 50[1]; 3748
סֵפֶר כ׳ כְּרִיתֻת Dt 24[1.3]; pl. sf. כְּרִיתֻתֶיהָ Je 3[8]; *writing* (i.e. deed) *of divorcement*, Dt 24[1.3] Is 50[1] Je 3[8].

† כְּרִית **n.pr.** the brook where Elijah was 3747
hidden 1 K 17[3.5], identif. dub.; acc. Rob [BR ii. p. 288] Wady *el-Kelt*, near Jericho; acc. Buhl [Handw. 12] Wady ‘*Ajlun*, E. of Jordan, yet v. Buhl [G. 121].

כְּרֹת Zp 2[6] v. [כָּרָה] sub I. כרה. p. 500 3741

†כְּרֵתִי **adj. gent.**, always c. art., or pl., as 3774
subst., **Kerethites**, a name for Philistines or a part of them (perhaps = *Cretans*, cf. 𝔊 Zp 2[5] Ez 25[15]; on *Crete* as orig. home of Philistines, v. כַּפְתֹּר, פְּלִשְׁתִּי);—הַכְּרֵתִי = subst. coll.;—נֶגֶב הַכּ׳ 1 S 30[14] (cf. Dr; 𝔊B Χολθει, 𝔊L Χορρι, A Χερηθει); of soldiers of David's guard, הַכּ׳ וְהַפְּלֵתִי 2 S 8[18] (rd. עַל־הַכּ׳ Th We Dr al.) = 1 Ch 18[17], 2 S 15[18] 20[7] + v[23] Qr (> Kt הכרי), 1 K 1[38.44] (𝔊 Χελεθθει, Χερεθθει, etc.); pl. כְּרֵתִים Ez 25[16] (‖ פְּלִשְׁתִּים;

(𝔊 Κρῆτας); גּוֹי כְּרֵתִים Zp 2[5] (𝔊 Κρητῶν; || ארץ פלשׁתים): in v[6] We rds. כְּרֵת = Philistia (v. [כָּרָה], sub I. כרה).

3775-76 כִּשְׂבָּה, כֶּשֶׂב v. כֶּבֶשׂ, etc. p. 461

3777 †כֶּשֶׂד **n.pr.m.** son of Nahor acc. to Gn 22[22] (J; perh. orig. personif., or assumed ancestor, of following, v. Di Dl [Par 201]).

3679, 3778 † כַּשְׂדִּים **n.pr.gent. et terr. Kasdim = Chaldeans, Chaldea,** 𝔊 Χαλδαῖοι and (Je 50[10]) ἡ Χαλδαία (As. (mat) *Kaldu, Kaldû;* fr. earlier (Bab.) form [**Kašdu*]—*š* before dental becoming *l*, Dl [Par 128 f. 200 f.; As. Gr. § 51, 3]; Schr [KGF 94 ff.; COT on Gn 11, 28]);—**1.** *Chaldeans:* **a.** people dwelling on lower Euphrates and Tigris; in n.pr.loc. אוּר כ׳ Gn 11[28] (J), v[31] (P), 15[7] (J), Ne 9[7]. **b.** esp. the people ruled by Nebuchadrezzar;—כ׳ Je 37[10] 39[5] Ez 23[23] 2 K 24[2] 25[4.5.10.13] = Je 52[7.8.14.17] (2 K 24[5.10] = also Je 39[5.8]), 2 K 25[26] Is 13[19] 43[14] 48[14.20] Jb 1[17]; Kt. כַּשְׂדִּיִּים Ez 23[14] 2 Ch 36[17]; הַכּ׳ Je 21[4.9] 22[25] 32[4.5.24.25.28.29.43] 33[5] 35[11] 37[5.8.9.11.13.14] 38[2.18.19.23] 39[8] 40[9.10] 41[3.18] 43[3] 50[35] Hb 1[6] 2 K 25[24.25]; בַּת־כ׳ Is 47[1.5] = Babylon (in dirge); אֶרֶץ כ׳ ἡ γῆ Χαλδαίων (on locality v. Schr Dl [l.c.]) Je 24[5] 25[12] 50[1.8.25.45] 51[4.54] Ez 1[3] 12[3], also Is 23[13] (inauthentic, Di Che; rd. כְּנַעֲנִים Ew Schr, or כִּתִּים Du); סֵפֶר וּלְשׁוֹן כ׳ Dn 1[4]; מַלְכוּת כ׳ 9[1]. **c.** *Chaldeans* as learned class, skilled in interpretations Dn 2[2] (+ חַרְטֻמִּים, אַשָּׁפִים, מְכַשְּׁפִים), v[4]. **2.** *Chaldea,* וְהָיְתָה כַשְׂדִּים לְשָׁלָל Je 50[10] *and Chaldea shall be despoiled;* יוֹשְׁבֵי כ׳ 51[24.35]; כַּשְׂדִּים אֶרֶץ מוֹלַדְתָּם Ez 23[15]; c. ה loc.: כַּשְׂדִּימָה Ez 11[24] 16[29] 23[16].

3780 †[כָּשָׂה] **vb. be sated, gorged with food** (cf. Ar. كَشِيَ *be filled with food;* As. *kissatum, sustenance, provender, food,* Zehnpf [BAS i. 503]);—only **Qal** *Pf.* 2 ms. שָׁמַנְתָּ עָבִיתָ כָּשִׂיתָ Dt 32[15] *thou grewest fat, becamest thick, wast gorged!* fig. of Isr. as fat beast (cf. Dr).

3570 כּוּשִׁית, כֻּשִׁית v. כּוּשִׁי. p. 160

3782 †כָּשַׁל **vb. stumble, stagger, totter** (NH *id.;* Syr. [ܟܫܠ] *give offence* (occasion for stumbling), σκανδαλίζω, (chiefly Ethpe. Aph.), v. PS Brock Schwally; Ar. كَسِلَ is *be heavy, sluggish*);—**Qal** *Pf.* כ׳ Ne 4[4]+, (Ho 5[5b] rd. יִכָּשֵׁל, cf. We), כָּשְׁלָה Is 3[8] 59[14]; כָּשְׁלוּ Je 46[6]+, כָּשַׁלְנוּ Is 59[10], etc.; *Impf.* 3 mpl. יכשׁלו Pr 4[16] Kt (but rd. Hiph., q.v., so Qr); יכשׁלו Na 3[3] Kt (but rd. Pf. וְכָשְׁלוּ, so Qr); *Inf. abs.* כָּשׁוֹל Is 40[30] (c. Niph. Impf.); *Pt. act.* כּוֹשֵׁל Is 5[27] + 2 t., כֹּשֵׁל 2 Ch 28[15] ψ 105[37]; fpl. כֹּשְׁלוֹת Is 35[3];—**1.** *stumble* at, over, something, c. ב (lit. *by means of*), Na 3[3], גִּבּוֹר בְּגִבּוֹר כ׳ Je 46[12] (+ נָפַל), cf. Lv 26[37]; וּנְעָרִים בָּעֵץ כ׳ La 5[13] i.e. *stagger* (of toil in captivity); abs. Is 5[27] (|| עָיֵף), כָּשְׁלוּ וְנָפָלוּ Je 46[6], cf. הִרְבָּה כּוֹשֵׁל גַּם־נָפַל אִישׁ וגו׳ v[16] (strange; Gie, foll. in part 𝔊 𝔖, עֶרְבְּךָ כָּשַׁל וְנָפַל *thy mixed people*—cf. 25[20], etc.—*hath stumbled and hath fallen*); oft. fig. of overthrow, through divine judgment, c. בְּ *at,* (v. supr.) Je 6[21], so Is 8[15] (+ נָפַל etc.) acc. to Ges Hi Buhl Che Di; < בָּם = *among them,*—Isr. and Judah,—as ב in v[16], so Ew De Du EV; Ho 4[5.5] 5[5] 14[2] (בַּעֲוֺנֶךָ, בְּ prob. instr.); abs. of Babylon, under fig. of זָדוֹן, כ׳ ונפל Je 50[32]; כ׳ ונפל ψ 27[2] Is 3[8] 31[3] (both || נפל); of אֱמֶת Is 59[14]; in metaph. of anxiety, distress Is 59[10], ψ 107[12]. **2.** *totter,* of knees, lit. בִּרְכַּי כ׳ מִצּוֹם ψ 109[24] *my knees totter from fasting;* fig. Is 35[3] (|| יָדַיִם רָפוֹת); כּוֹשֵׁל *tottering one,* lit. Jb 4[4] 2 Ch 28[15] ψ 105[37]; hence fig., *fail,* of strength (כֹּחַ), Ne 4[4] ψ 31[11];—Inf. abs. כָּשׁוֹל, v. sub Niph. **Niph.** *Pf.* consec. וְנִכְשַׁל Dn 11[9], וְנִכְשְׁלוּ v[33], וְנִכְשְׁלוּ v[14]; *Impf.* יִכָּשֵׁל Ez 33[12] + Ho 5[5b] (𝔊 as v[a], so We; MT כָּשַׁל), 2 ms. תִּכָּשֵׁל Pr 4[12], יִכָּשְׁלוּ Ho 5[5a] + 9 t.; יִכָּשֵׁלוּ Is 40[30] + 3 t.; *Inf. cstr.* sf. בְּהִכָּשְׁלוֹ Pr 24[17] (yet v. Ges [§ 51, R. 1]), בְּהִכָּשְׁלָם Dn 11[34]; *Pt.* נִכְשָׁל Zc 12[8]; pl. נִכְשָׁלִים 1 S 2[4];—**1.** *stumble* (= **Qal**) Na 2[6] Is 63[13] Je 31[9]; usu. fig.: **a.** of misfortune Pr 24[17] (|| נפל), neg. 4[12]. **b.** of divine judgment (c. בְּ *at*) Pr 4[19] 24[16], neg. Ez 33[12]; see also Ho 14[10] (בְּ loc.), Je 20[11] Dn 11[14.35], יִכָּשְׁלוּ וְיֹאבְדוּ מִפָּנֶיךָ ψ 9[4]; esp. = *be overthrown,* of nations, armies, etc., Ho 5[5] (c. בַּעֲוֺנָם, cf. 14[2] **Qal**), Je 6[15] (|| נפל), cf. 8[12] (|| *id.*), Dn 11[19] (+ נפל), v[33] (בְּ instr.), v[34.41]. **2.** *be tottering, feeble,* כָּשׁוֹל יִכָּשֵׁלוּ Is 40[30] (opp. יַחֲלִיפוּ כֹחַ v[31]); so pt. 1 S 2[4] Zc 12[8]. **Pi.** only apparent, תְּשַׁכְּלִי, Ez 36[14], rd. תְּכַשְּׁלִי with Qr Vrss EV Sm Co Da (v. also **Hiph.** *ad fin.*). **Hiph.** *Pf.* הִכְשִׁיל La 1[14], הִכְשַׁלְתֶּם Mal 2[8]; *Impf.* 3 ms. sf. יַכְשִׁילְךָ 2 Ch 25[8]; 2 fs. תַּכְשִׁלִי Ez 36[15] (but del. 𝔊 Co; rd. תשׁכלי, as v[14] other Vrss Sm Da); 3 mpl. יַכְשִׁילוּ Pr 4[16] Qr (Kt v. sub **Qal**), וַיַּכְשִׁילֻהוּ ψ 64[9], וַיַּכְשִׁלוּם Je 18[15] (so 𝔗; Gie, after 𝔊 𝔖, וַיִּכָּשְׁלוּ, [< וַיִּכָּשְׁלוּ]); *Inf. cstr.* הַכְשִׁיל 2 Ch 25[8], sf. הַכְשִׁילוֹ 2 Ch 28[23];—**1.** *cause to stumble,* fig.: **a.** = *bring injury* or *ruin to,* abs. Pr 4[16]; of punishment ψ 64^{9} (indef. subj.; si vera l.; text prob. corrupt, v. Che Bae). **b.** = *overthrow*, of nation, army, etc., 2 Ch 25^{8} (sq. לִפְנֵי אוֹיֵב), cf. v^{8} (opp. עזר); *cause overthrow* 2 Ch 28^{23}.—On Ez 36^{15} v. supr. **c.** morally, Je 18^{15} (בְּ loc.), Mal 2^{8} (בְּ instr.) **2.** *make feeble, weak*, הִכְשִׁיל כֹּחִי La 1^{14} (of God's dealing with Jerus.) **Hoph.** only *Pt.* והיו מֻכְשָׁלִים לְפָנֶיךָ Je 18^{23} either *and let them be ones who have stumbled before thee*, i.e. regard them as such (Hi Gf VB), or *and let them be ones overthrown before thee* (Gie; so Qr acc. to Gf). So also in Ez 21^{20} acc. to Co, cf. Sm Da (MT מַכְשֹׁלִים, v. מִכְשׁוֹל).

3781 † כַּשִּׁיל **n.[m.]** axe (acc. to Vrss and context; NH *id.*; 𝔗 Je 46^{22}; prob. fr. *felling; Aram.* loan-word acc. to Frä^{74}; but word not common in Aram.)—בְּכ׳ וְכֵילַפּוֹת יַהֲלֹמוּן ψ 74^{6}.

3783 † כִּשָּׁלוֹן **n.[m.]** a stumbling; fig. = calamity Pr 16^{18}.

4383 † מִכְשׁוֹל **n.m.**$^{\text{Je 6, 21}}$ **a stumbling, means** or **occasion of stumbling, stumbling-block**;—מ׳ abs. Is 8^{14} + 3 t., מִכְשֹׁל Lv 19^{14}; cstr. מִכְשׁוֹל 1 S 25^{31} + 6 t. Ez; pl. מִכְשֹׁלִים Je 6^{21} + Ez 21^{20} MT (Co al. מֻכְשָׁלִים, v. *infr.*);—**1.** *stumbling*, צוּר מ׳ Is 8^{14} (fig.) *a rock of stumbling* (i.e. over which one stumbles); lit. הַרְבֵּה הַמִּכְשֹׁלִים Ez 21^{20} *an abundance of stumblings, falls* (si vera l.; 𝔊 οἱ ἀσθενοῦντες, appar. reading pt., cf. Sm; so Co Da (as a possibility), i.e. מֻכְשָׁלִים **Hoph.** *Pt.* of כשׁל = *those who have stumbled* or *been overthrown*). **2.** *means*, or *occasion of stumbling, stumbling-block;* **a.** lit. Lv 19^{14}. **b.** fig. of misfortune, calamity ψ 119^{165}; in divine judgment Je 6^{21} Ez 3^{20}, as a hindrance to restoration of people Is 57^{14}. **c.** in ethical sense מ׳ עֲוֹנָם Ez 7^{19} *a stumbling-block of* (i.e. occasioning) *their iniquity*, so $14^{3.4.7}$ 18^{30} 44^{12} (mostly with ref. to idols). **d.** מ׳ לֵב 1 S 25^{31} *a stumbling-block of heart* i.e. ground for remorse.

4384 † מַכְשֵׁלָה **n.f. 1. overthrown mass. 2. stumbling-block**;—**1.** fig. of kingdom Is 3^{6}. **2.** pl. הַמַּכְשֵׁלוֹת Zp 1^{3} *stumbling-blocks* = idols (cf. מִכְשׁוֹל **2 c**), but rather dub.; We thinks a gloss. Schwally$^{\text{ZAW x. (1890), 169}}$ rds. וְכִשַּׁלְתִּי *and I will cause* the wicked to *stumble*.

I. כשׁף (√ of foll.; cf. Ar. كَسَفَ *cut off, cut up*, Syr. ܐܬܟܫܦ *to pray* (lit. prob. *to cut oneself*, v. 1 K 18^{28}): so RS$^{\text{J Phil. xiv. 125, 126}}$ Nö$^{\text{ZMG 1886, 723}}$; acc. to RS כֶּשֶׁף is prop. herbs etc. *shredded* into a magic brew).

3785 † [כֶּשֶׁף] **n.m.**$^{\text{2 K 9, 22}}$ **sorcery**, only **pl.** (As. *kišpu, id.*);—כְּשָׁפִים Mi 5^{11} Na 3^{4}; sf. כְּשָׁפַיִךְ Is $47^{9.12}$; כְּשָׁפֶיהָ Na 3^{4} 2 K 9^{22};—*sorceries:* **1.** lit. וְהִכְרַתִּי כ׳ מִיָּדֶךָ Mi 5^{11}, said of Isr.; רֹב כ׳ Is $47^{9.12}$ (‖ חֲבָרַיִךְ), said of Babylon. **2.** fig. of seductive and corrupting influences: of Jezebel 2 K 9^{22} (‖ זְנוּנִים); of Nineveh personif. as harlot Na 3^{4} (‖ *id.*), called בַּעֲלַת כ׳ v^{4} (following מֵרֹב זְנוּנֵי זוֹנָה).

3784 † כִּשֵּׁף **vb. Pi. denom. practice sorcery** (As. *kašâpu, id.*);—*Pf.* 3 ms.: וְעוֹנֵן וְנִחֵשׁ וְכִשֵּׁף וְעָשָׂה אוֹב וְיִדְּעוֹנִי 2 Ch 33^{6} (of Manasseh); elsewh. only *Pt.* as subst. ms. *sorcerer*, in Israel, מְכַשֵּׁף Dt 18^{10} (following קֹסֵם קְסָמִים מְעוֹנֵן וּמְנַחֵשׁ); fs. מְכַשֵּׁפָה = *sorceress* Ex 22^{17} (E); mpl. מְכַשְּׁפִים Mal 3^{5} (named with adulterers and false-swearers); of diviners, or astrologers in Egypt (חַרְטֻמִּים q.v.) Ex 7^{11} (P; ‖ חֲכָמִים); in Babylon Dn 2^{2} (+ חַרְטֻמִּים, אַשָּׁפִים, כַּשְׂדִּים).

3786 † [כַּשָּׁף] **n.m.** sorcerer, only pl. sf. (As. *kaššapu, id.; kaššaptu, sorceress*);—אַל־תִּשְׁמְעוּ אֶל־נְבִיאֵיכֶם וְאֶל־קֹסְמֵיכֶם וְאֶל חֲלֹמֹתֵיכֶם וְאֶל־עֹנְנֵיכֶם וְאֶל־כַּשָּׁפֵיכֶם Je 27^{9}.

II. כשׁף (√ of following).

407 † אַכְשָׁף **n.pr.loc.** in (Northern) Canaan, with a king, Jos 11^{1} 12^{20}; situated on the border of Asher 19^{25}, Egypt. *'A-k-sap* WMM$^{\text{As. u. Eur. 181}}$; 𝔊B Αζειφ, A Ἀχσαφ, 𝔊L (Ἀ)χασαφ, etc.; site dub.; mod. *Iksâf* or *Kesâf*, Rob$^{\text{BR iii. 55}}$, c. 17 m. E. of Tyre, and nearly 3 m. SW. of the great bend of the Liṭâny, is phonetically suitable, but much too far NE. for Jos 19^{25}; poss. there were two *Akšaphs;* cf. Di$^{\text{Jos 11, 1}}$ Buhl$^{\text{Geogr. 237}}$. Vid. further Krall$^{\text{Tyrus u. Sidon 10}}$, Lag$^{\text{Onom. 218. 91, 3; 2d ed. 239}}$.

3787 † כָּשֵׁר **vb. be advantageous, proper, suitable, succeed**, late Aram. (NH *id.; Aram.* ܟܫܰܪ, כְּשַׁר);—**Qal** *Pf.* 3 ms. וְכָשֵׁר הַדָּבָר לִפְנֵי הַמֶּלֶךְ Est 8^{5} *and the thing be proper in the view of the king; Impf.* יִכְשָׁר Ec 11^{6} thou knowest not whether this *shall succeed*, or this. **Hiph.** *Inf. cstr.* וְיִתְרוֹן הַכְשֵׁיר חָכְמָה Ec 10^{10} *an advantage for giving success is wisdom.*

3788 †כִּשְׁרוֹן **n.[m.]** skill, success;—**1.** *skill*, בְּחָכְמָה וּבְדַעַת וּבְכִשְׁרוֹן Ec 2^{21}; cstr. כָּל־כִּשְׁרוֹן הַמַּעֲשֶׂה 4^{4} *all skill of work* = skilful work. **2.** *success, profit*, וּמַה־כִּשְׁרוֹן לִבְעָלֶיהָ Ec 5^{10} *and what profit have the owners of it?*

3574 †[כּוֹשָׁרָה] **n.f. prosperity** (cf. ܟܘܫܪܐ, *id.*). Only pl. intens. בַּכּוֹשָׁרוֹת ψ 68^{7} he bringeth out captives *into prosperity*.

3601 †כִּישׁוֹר **n.[m.] distaff** (etym. dub.; perh., if meaning correct, fr. כשׁר (cf. Sta ^{§216} Lag$^{BN 182}$) = *be straight*, because it stands erect, De Str; 𝔖 ܟܘܫܪܢܐ *industry;* whence 𝔗 כּוּשְׁרָא, and likewise 𝔗 כּוּנְשְׁרָא, also Pr 3^{8}, (for Heb. שֹׁר), where Levy *Wirbelsäule*, Str$^{ad\ loc.}$ Jastr *navel;* but Str doubts etymological connexion with כישור);—only in יָדֶיהָ שִׁלְּחָה בַכִּישׁוֹר Pr 31^{19} (|| פֶּלֶךְ: *whirl* of spindle).—As above De Now Str RV SS al.; > Ki AW Thes RobGes *whirl* of spindle (AV *spindle*); vid. פֶּלֶךְ.

3789 **כָּתַב** $_{223}$ **vb. write** (NH *id.;* Ph. כתב; Aram. כְּתַב, ܟܬܒ; Nab. כתב, v. esp. Nö in Eut$^{Nab.\ p.\ 43}$; thence Ar. كَتَبَ, Eth. ክታብ: *book*, Di$^{Lex.\ 852}$ (as loan-wds., Frä^{249} DHM$^{VOJ\ i\ (1887),\ 29}$); MV Buhl comp. Ar. كَتَبَ *draw* or *sew together, conjoin* (letters), etc., cf. Fl$^{ZMG\ 1873,\ 427}$)—**Qal** *Pf.* כ׳ Jos 8^{32}+, כָּתַבְתָּ Je 36^{6}+, sf. וּכְתַבְתָּם consec. Dt 6^{9} 11^{20}, etc. (Pf. 27 t.); *Impf.* יִכְתֹּב Is 44^{5}, וַיִּכְתֹּב Ex 24^{4}+, etc. (Impf. 39 t.); *Imv.* כְּתֹב Is 8^{1} + 5 t., כְּתָב־ Ex 34^{27} + 2 t.; sf. כָּתְבָהּ Is 30^{8}, כָּתְבֵם Pr 3^{3} 7^{3}; pl. כִּתְבוּ Dt 31^{9} + 3 t.; *Inf. abs.* כָּתוֹב Je 32^{44}; *cstr.* כְּתוֹב ψ 87^{8}, לִכְתֹּב Dt 31^{24} Jos 18^{8}; sf. כָּתְבוֹ Je 45^{1}; *Pt. act.* כֹּתֵב Je 36^{18}, pl. כֹּתְבִים Je 32^{12} Ne 10^{1}; *pass.* (113 t.), כָּתוּב Jos 1^{8}+, f. כְּתוּבָה 2 S 1^{18}+, pl. כְּתוּבִים 1 K 15^{7}+, כְּתֻבִים 1 K 11^{41}+; fpl. כְּתוּבוֹת 2 Ch 34^{24};—**1.** *write:* **a.** c. acc., words Ex 34^{27}, commandments 24^{12}, etc.; acc. cogn. מכתב Ex 39^{30}, cf. כמכתב Dt 10^{4}; with כְּ, giving purport of writing, also Est 8^{8}; but obj. also a book, סֵפֶר Ex 32^{32} Dt 24^{1}; מְגִלָּה Je 38^{6}, cf. pt. pass., וְהִיא כְתוּבָה פָּנִים וְאָחוֹר Ez 2^{10} (of מגלה; i.e. written on both sides); a letter, סֵפֶר 2 S 11^{14} 2 K 10^{1} + 4 t., אִגֶּרֶת 2 Ch 30^{1}; a divorce-certificate סֵפֶר כְּרִיתֻת Dt 24^{1}, etc.; even לֻחֹת כְּתֻבִים *tablets inscribed* by the finger of God Ex 31^{18} cf. Dt 9^{10}; לֻ׳ כ׳ מִשְּׁנֵי עֶבְרֵיהֶם Ex 32^{15} *tables inscribed on both sides* (cf. Ez 2^{10} supr.) Here belongs (prob.) וְזֶה יִכְתֹּב יָדוֹ לי׳ Is 44^{5} *and this one shall inscribe his hand, 'Yahweh's,'* so 𝔊 Hi Kn Che Br Du Di, > Ges Ew De, *shall sign* (with) *his hand unto* י׳. **b.** more often *write* something *on*, or *in* (עַל־ 85 t., בְּ 44 t., אֶל־ 3 t.) a tablet, roll, book, etc. (obj. various, as above):—(1) כ׳ עַל־ sq. סֵפֶר = *book* Dt 17^{18} + 55 t., esp. in phr. כתובים על־ספר דברי וגו׳ 1 K 11^{41} + oft. K Ch; כ׳ עַל־מְגִלָּה Je 36$^{2.28.32}$ 38^{29}; כ׳ עַל־לוּח(ות) Ex 34^{1} + 7 t., עַל־אֶבֶן Dt 27^{3} + 2 t., עַל־גִּלָּיוֹן Is 8^{1}; עַל־מְזֻזוֹת בֵּית Dt 6^{9} 11^{20}; עַל־מַטֶּה *on a rod* Nu 17$^{17.18}$; עַל־עֵץ Ez 37$^{16.16}$, עַל־צִיץ (high priest's plate) Ex 39^{30}; even (only Ch) עַל־ sq. name of book or its contents:—כ׳ עַל־דִּבְרֵי נָתָן 2 Ch 9^{29} cf. 33^{19}; עַל־מִדְרַשׁ וגו׳ 24^{27}; עַל־הַקִּינוֹת 35^{25}; fig., כ׳ עַל־לִבָּם Je 31^{33} *I will write them upon their heart;* cf. כ׳ עַל־לוּחַ לִבֶּךָ Pr 3^{3}. (2) כ׳ אֶל־ appears for כ׳ עַל־ only Je 36^{2} cf. Ez 2^{10}, Je 51^{60}. (3) כ׳ בְּ sq. ספר = *book* Jos 24^{26} (E) + 35 t.; = *letter, bill, deed*, 1 K 21^{9} + 5 t.; בִּמְגִלַּת סֵפֶר כָּתוּב עָלָי ψ 40^{8} *it is prescribed to me*, על as 2 K 22^{13} (N.B. כ׳ עַל־ not used with סֵפֶר = *letter*, and כ׳ בְּ not used with לוּחַ, אבן or עֵץ). **c.** other uses of prep. with כ׳ are:—בְּ instr., כ׳ בְּחֶרֶט אֱנוֹשׁ Is 8^{1}, כ׳ בְּעֵט בַּרְזֶל Je 17^{1}; כְּתֻבִים בְּאֶצְבַּע אֱלֹהִים Dt 9^{10} Ex 31^{18}; כ׳ אֶל־ *unto*, of person to whom letter, etc., is addressed 2 S 11^{14} 2 K 10^{6} Est 9^{13}; עַל־ subst. for אֶל־ (late) 2 Ch 30^{1} Ezr 4^{7} Est 8^{5}; the fuller construction is כ׳ ספר וישלח (אֶל־) 2 K 10^{1} Est 8^{10} 9^{20} +; כ׳ אֶל־ *write down for* the benefit or use of some one, Ju 8^{14}; לְ *to* or *for*, Dt 17^{18} 24^{1} +; note esp. אֶכְתָּוב־לוֹ רֻבּוֹ תּוֹרָתִי Ho 8^{12}, i.e. either, *I write* (*keep writing*) *for them ever so many* (We, רִב, cf. رُبَّ; Ew and most רִבּוֹ(א) a myriad) *of my directions*, or *'Though I write,' 'Were I to write,'* etc.; כ׳ sq. לְ c. inf. of purpose 2 Ch 32^{17} Est 8^{5}; c. מִן in phr. כ׳ מִפִּי פ׳ *write from the mouth of* any one, i.e. from dictation, †Je 36$^{2.32}$ 38$^{6.17.27}$ 45^{1}. **2.** = *write down, describe in writing*, ר׳ אֶת־הָאָרֶץ Ju 18$^{4.6.8.8.9}$. **3.** = *register, enroll* Is 10^{19} (= record the number), 1 Ch 24^{6}; esp. pass. הַכְּתוּבִים Nu 11^{26} *those enrolled* cf. Ne 12^{22}; הַכּ׳ בְּשֵׁמוֹת 1 Ch 4^{41} *those recorded by name;* in prediction, כ׳ אֶת־הָאִישׁ הַזֶּה עֲרִירִי Je 22^{30} *register this man as childless;* with eschatol. reference, כָּל־הַכָּתוּב לַחַיִּים Is 4^{3} *all those enrolled* (i.e. appointed) *unto life;* and, more explicitly, כָּל־הַנִּמְצָא כָּתוּב בַּסֵּפֶר Dn 12^{1}; י׳ יִסְפֹּר בִּכְתוֹב עַמִּים ψ 87^{6} *shall reckon, when he registers* (note absence of suffix) *the* peoples, etc. **4.** =*decree*, תִּכְתֹּב עָלַי מְרֹרוֹת Jb 13^{26} *thou* (′י) *decreest against me bitter things.* †**Niph.** (chiefly late, esp. Est.), *Impf.* יִכָּתֵב Est 1^{19}+, 3 fs. תִּכָּתֶב זֹאת ψ 102^{19}; 3 mpl. יִכָּתֵבוּ Je 17^{13}+3 t., יִכָּתֵבוּן Jb 19^{23}; *Pt.* נִכְתָּב Est 3^{12} +2 t.;—**1.** *be written*, subj. words, Jb 19^{23}, book Mal 3^{16}; *be written* בְּסֵפֶר Est 2^{23} 9^{23}, *in*, or *among* (ב) the laws Est 1^{19}; once, c. עַל־, עַל־סִפְרְךָ כֻּלָּם יִכָּתֵבוּ ψ 139^{16} *in thy* (′י's) *book all of them* (my members) *are written*, i.e. *written down, recorded* (v. infr.); abs. כְּתָב אֲשֶׁר נִכְתָּב בְּשֵׁם הַמֶּלֶךְ Est 8^8 *a writing which is written in the king's name*, cf. (impers.) 3^{12}; impers. also וַיִּכָּתֵב כְּכָל־אֲשֶׁר צִוָּה Est 3^{12} 8^9; יִכָּ׳ sq. לְ = *for* ψ 102^{19}; sq. לְ + inf. (really = a subject-cl.,—the contents of the letter) Est 3^9 8^5. **2.** *be written down, recorded*, Ezr 8^{34}; *enrolled*, בִּכְתָב בית ישראל לא יִכָּתֵבוּ Ez 13^9 *in the enrolment of the house of Israel they are not enrolled* (eschatolog.); וְעִם־צַדִּיקִים אַל־יִכָּתֵבוּ ψ 69^{29} (‖ יִמָּחוּ מִסֵּפֶר חַיִּים).—בָּאָרֶץ יִכָּתֵבוּ Je 17^{13} is difficult; Gie rds., plausibly, מֵאֶרֶץ יִכָּרֵתוּ (cf. ψ 34^{17} 101^8, etc.) †**Pi.** frequent., *Pf.* and *Pt.*, only וּמְכַתְּבִים עָמָל כִּתֵּבוּ Is 10^1 and *busy writers that make a business of writing* oppression (i.e. register unjust sentences, cf. **Qal 4**; ‖ הַחֹקְקִים חִקְקֵי־אָוֶן).

3791 †כְּתָב **n.m.** [Ezr 4,7] writing (late Aram.; BA. כְּתָב, Syr. ܟܬܒܐ);—כ׳ abs. 1 Ch 28^{19}+4 t.; cstr. Ez 13^9+4 t.; sf. כְּתָבָהּ Est 1^{22}+2 t.; כְּתָבָם Ezr 2^{62}+3 t.;—*writing:* **1.** *register, enrolment*, Ez 13^9 Ezr 2^{62}=Ne 7^{64}. **2.**=*mode of writing, character, letter*, וּכְ׳ הַנִּשְׁתְּוָן כָּתוּב אֲרָמִית Ezr 4^7 *and the writing of the letter was written in Aramaic* (characters; so prob., v. Be-Ry Ryle, cf. NH Hoffm [ZAW i. (1881), 334 ff.]); cf. Est 1^{22} 3^{12} $8^{9.9}$. **3.**=*letter*, 2 Ch 2^{10} Est 9^{27}. **4.** of a royal enactment, edict 2 Ch 35^4 (‖ מִכְתָּב), Est 3^{14} $8^{8.13}$; more fully כְּתָב־הַדָּת 4^8. **5.** of a writing with divine authority 1 Ch 28^{19}; כ׳ אֱמֶת Dn 10^{21}, i.e. a book of truth.

3793 †כְּתֹבֶת **n.f.** only cstr. וּכְתֹבֶת קַעֲקַע לֹא תִתְּנוּ בָּכֶם Lv 19^{28} i.e. *a writing* (mark or sign) *of imprintment*, scriptio stigmatis, perh. of tattooing, cf. Di (v. also Ba[NB 61]).

4385 †מִכְתָּב **n.m.** [2 Ch 21, 12] writing;—abs. מ׳ Dt 10^4+5 t.; cstr. מִכְתַּב Ex 32^{16}+2 t.;—**1.**=*handwriting* וְהַמִּכְתָּב מִכְתַּב אֱלֹהִים הוּא Ex 32^{16}. **2.** =thing written, Ex 39^{30} (acc. cogn. c. כְּתָב), Dt 10^4; specif. a royal enactment or edict (=כְּתָב 4), 2 Ch 35^4 (‖ כְּתָב), 36^{22}=Ezr 1^1; a prophetic writing 2 Ch 21^{12}. **3.** in a title, מ׳ לְחִזְקִיָּהוּ Is 38^9 *Writing of Hezekiah.*

†[כִּתִּי] **adj.gent.** alw. pl. כִּתִּיִּים, כִּתִּים; usu. 3794
as **n.gent.** = **Cypriotes** (cf. Ph. n.pr.loc. כת, כתי, *Citium;* on a connexion with *Kheta, Ḫ-tā, Ḫattê,* חִתִּי, v. WMM [Asien u. Europa, 345];—on *Citium* v. Cesnola [Cyprus 46 ff.]);—אֶרֶץ כִּתִּים Is 23^1, כִּתִּיִּים v^{12}; כִּתִּים (as son of Yawan) Gn 10^4=1 Ch 1^7; וְצִים מִיַּד כ׳ Nu 24^{24} *ships from the side* (direction) *of Kittim;* more generally, of coast-lands of Mediterranean, אִיֵּי כִתִּיִּים Je 2^{10}, אִיֵּי כִתִּים Ez 27^6; even of Macedonian Greece, צִיִּים כִּתִּים Dn 11^{30} (only here as adj., cf. Bev) i.e. Grecian ships.

כָּתִית v. sub כתת. p. 510 3795

כתל (√of foll.; cf. Ar. كَتَلَ *make into firm lumps* or *blocks, make compact;* Frey also *bind, imprison,* كَتِلَ *be joined together*).

†[כֹּתֶל] **n.[m.]** wall of house (NH כּוֹתֶל, 3796
Aram. כּוֹתְלָא);—only sf. כָּתְלֵנוּ Ct 2^9.

†כִּתְלִישׁ **n.pr.loc.** a city of Judah Jos 15^{40}, 3798
site unknown; 𝔊B Μααχως, A Χαθλως, 𝔊L Καθαλεις.

†I. [כָּתַם] **vb.** only **Niph.** be stained 3799
(NH Niph. *id.* (Jastr); כֶּתֶם *blood-stain;* 𝔗 כְּתִים (blood-)*stained* Is 1^{18}; כִּיתְמָא *blood-stain* Je 2^{22}; Syr. ܟܬܡ *stain, defile*, Pt., also Pa. Ethpa., and deriv.; Ar. كَتَمَ is *cover, conceal*, so As. *katâmu;* Zinj. כתם(?), DHM [Sendsch. p. 37]);—**Niph.** *Pt.*, fig., נִכְתָּם עֲוֹנֵךְ לְפָנַי Je 2^{22} *stained is thine iniquity before me* (cf. Eng. phr. *iniquity of deepest dye*).

II. **כתם** (√of foll.; meaning unknown).

†מִכְתָּם **n.[m.]** **Mikhtām**, a term. techn. 4387
in ψ-titles, meaning unknown (𝔊 στηλογραφία: cf. Bae [Ps. p. xiii f.]); alw. c. לְדָוִד:—מ׳ לְדָוִד ψ 16^1 60^1; לְדָוִד מ׳ 56^1 57^1 58^1 59^1.

†כֶּתֶם **n.m.** [La 4, 1] gold, poet. and late (perh. 3800
loan-word in Heb.; Ph. has n.pr.m. כתם; Sab. כתם Hal [Ét. Sab. 190]; *kaθâmā* as loan-wd. in Egypt., Bondi [80 f.]);—כ׳ abs. Jb 28^{19}+3 t., כָּתֶם Pr 25^{12}; cstr. כֶּתֶם Is 13^{12}+3 t.;—כ׳ אוֹפִיר Is 13^{12} *gold of Ophir* (‖ פָּז), so Jb 28^{16} ψ 45^{10}; כ׳ אוּפָז Dn 10^5 (rd. perh. אוֹפִיר for אוּפָז q.v.); כ׳ alone Jb 31^{24} (‖ זָהָב), חֲלִי־כ׳ Pr 25^{12} *ornament of gold* (‖ נֶזֶם זָהָב), כ׳ פָּז Ct 5^{11}, כ׳ טָהוֹר Jb 28^{19}; הַכּ׳ הַטּוֹב La 4^1 (‖ זָהָב).

כתן (√ of foll., = *clothe?* so Zehnpf.$^{BAS\ i.\ 532}$, who der. therefrom As. *kitinnê, linen, cloth,* = Ar. كَتَّانٌ; v. also Aram. כִּיתָּנָא, ܟܬܳܢܳܐ and infr.)

3801 †כְּתֹנֶת, כֻּתֹּנֶת **n.f. tunic** (NH *id.;* Aram. כִּתּוּנָא, etc., ܟܽܘܬܺܝܢܳܐ, etc.; Eth. ከተን: *tunic, linen;* cf. also √ supr.);—abs. כְּתֹנֶת Gn 37^{31} + 2 t.; כֻּתֹּנֶת Ex 28^{39}; cstr. כְּתֹנֶת Gn 37^{3} + 9 t.; sf. כֻּתָּנְתּוֹ Gn 37^{23} 2 S 15^{32}, כֻּתָּנְתֶּךָ Is 22^{21}, כֻּתָּנְתִּי Jb 30^{18} Ct 5^{3}; pl. abs. כֻּתֳּנֹת Ex 28^{40} + 3 t., הַכֻּתֳּנֹת 39^{27}; cstr. כָּתְנוֹת Gn 3^{21} + 2 t., כָּתְנֹת Ezr 2^{69}; sf. כֻּתָּנֹתָם Lv 10^{5};—*tunic,* principal ordinary garment (v. Benz$^{Arch.\ 98\ f.}$ Now$^{Arch.\ i.\ 121,193}$) of man and woman, worn next the person, כָּתְנוֹת עוֹר Gn 3^{21} *tunics of skin;* of man 2 S 15^{32}; כְּפִי כ׳ Jb 30^{18} *mouth of any tunic* (i.e. its collar); כ׳ פַּסִּים Gn 37$^{3.23.32}$ i.e. tunic with long skirts and sleeves (v. פַּס), cf. v$^{23.31.31.32.33}$; of woman Ct 5^{3} (put off at night); כ׳ פַּסִּים 2 S 13$^{18.19}$ (of king's daughter; rent, as sign of grief, cf. also 15^{32}, and v. קרע). Specif. of priest's tunic Ex 28$^{4.39}$ (embroidered, v. תַּשְׁבֵּץ, שׁבץ), v^{40} 29$^{5.8}$ 39^{27} (made of שֵׁשׁ, q.v.), 40^{14} Lv 8$^{7.13}$ 10^{5}; כּ׳־בַּד קֹדֶשׁ 16^{4} *a holy linen tunic,* of high priest; כ׳־כֹּהֲנִים Ezr 2^{69} Ne 7$^{69.71}$ (van d. H. v$^{70.72}$); of Shebna's official tunic Is 22^{21}.

כתף (√ of following; meaning unknown).

3802 †כָּתֵף **n.f.**$^{Ex\ 27,15}$ **shoulder, shoulder-blade, side** (NH *id.;* Aram. כַּתְפָּא, ܟܰܬܦܳܐ; Ar. كَتِفٌ);—abs. כ׳ Zc 7^{11}+; cstr. כֶּתֶף 1 K 6^{8}+, app. כָּתֵף Is 11^{14} (but regard as appos., or rd. כֶּתֶף); sf. כְּתֵפִי Jb 31^{22}; כְּתֵפָם 1 Ch 15^{15}; pl. abs. כְּתֵפֹת Ex 28^{7}+, כְּתֵפוֹת 1 K 7$^{30.34}$; cstr. כִּתְפֹת Ex 28^{12}+, כִּתְפוֹת Ez 41^{2}+; du. sf. כְּתֵפָיו Dt 33^{12} + 3 t., כְּתֵפֶיהָ 1 K 7^{34};—**1. a.** of man, *shoulder, shoulder-blade* (while שְׁכֶם, q.v. = *neck and shoulders*), כִּידוֹן נְחֹשֶׁת בֵּין כְּתֵפָיו 1 S 17^{6}; cf. fig. of י׳'s dwelling *between the shoulders* of Benj. Dt 33^{12} (v. Dr); כְּתֵפִי מִשִּׁכְמָה תִפּוֹל Jb 31^{22} *my shoulder-blade, from the shoulder let it fall;* as support for burdens Ju 16^{3} Ez 12$^{6.7.12}$ Is 46^{7} 49^{22} (in fig.), Ex 28^{12} Nu 7^{9} (both P), 1 Ch 15^{15} 2 Ch 35^{3}; cf. כָּל־כ׳ מְרוּטָה Ez 29^{18} *every shoulder was rubbed bare* (of Nebuch.'s soldiers chafed by armour and toil); as aim of bird of prey Is 11^{14} (fig.); cf. *shoulder of Moab* Ez 25^{9} (fig., i.e. the side of M. exposed to invasion): Ez 29$^{7\,b}$ rd. prob. כַּף (𝔊 𝔖 Sm Co, cf. v^{a}). **b.** of beasts, Is 30^{6} (carrying), Ez 34^{21} (thrusting, in fig.), כ׳ סֹרָרֶת Zc 7^{11} *a refractory shoulder* (refusing the yoke, fig.), so Ne 9^{29}; of choice meat Ez 24^{4} (‖ יָרֵךְ). **c.** = *shoulder-pieces* (alw. pl.) of ephod Ex 28$^{7.12.25.27}$ = 39$^{4.7.18.20}$ (P). **2. a.** *slope, side,* of mountain, כֶּתֶף יָם־כִּנֶּרֶת Nu 34^{11}, i.e. the mt.-slopes NE. of the lake, cf. Jos 15$^{8.10.11}$ 18$^{12.13.16.18.19}$ (all P). **b.** *opposite side(s),* sc. of door or entrance, of tabernacle-court Ex 27$^{14.15}$ = 38$^{14.15}$ (all P), of temple 1 K 6^{8} 7$^{39.39.39}$ = 2 Ch 4^{10}, 2 K 11$^{11.11}$ = 2 Ch 23$^{10.10}$; cf. Ez 40$^{18.40.40.41.44.44}$ 41$^{2.26}$ 46^{19} 47$^{1.2}$. **3.** *supports* of the bases for the lavers beside the temple 1 K 7$^{30.30.34.34}$.

3803 †[כָּתַר] **vb. surround** (in **Pi.**), (Aram. כַּתַּר Pa., *wait, hope* for; ܟܰܬܰܪ Pa. *wait, await, remain;* i.e. perh. *surround expectantly,* v. Jb 36^{2} infr.)—**Pi.** *Pf.* 3 pl. כִּתְּרוּ Ju 20^{43} of *surrounding* an enemy; sf. כִּתְּרוּנִי ψ 22^{13} (in fig.; ‖ סְבָבוּנִי); *Imv.* כַּתַּר־לִי Jb 36^{2} *wait, I pray* (as in Aram.) **Hiph.** *Impf.* 3 mpl. בִּי יַכְתִּרוּ צַדִּיקִים ψ 142^{8} dub., *throw out crowns* (Ges$^{§\ 53\ g}$), i.e. appear with crowns (denom. fr. כֶּתֶר; but this very late—only in Est.); fig. for *triumph,* because of me; but Gr Che יִתְפָּאֲרוּ (v. I. פאר); יַכְתִּרוּ דָעַת Pr 14^{18} dub., Thes De al. *throw out knowledge as a crown,* make knowledge their crown (denom. fr. כֶּתֶר; but v. supr.), Now, *encompass knowledge,* i.e. possess it (‖ נָחֲלוּ); sense good, but meaning of כ׳ without ‖. *Pt.* מַכְתִּיר *surrounding* (as **Pi.**) Hb 1^{4} (c. acc. of enemy).

3804 †כֶּתֶר **n.m. crown** ((perh. Pers. loan-word Lag$^{Ges.\ Abh.\ 207}$); NH *id.;* Aram. כִּתְרָא; Ar. كِتْرٌ *the higher hump* of a camel);—always cstr., in combin. כ׳ מַלְכוּת *royal crown* Est 1^{11} 2^{17} (both of queen), 6^{8} (of king).

3805 כֹּתֶרֶת, כּוֹתֶרֶת **n.f. capital** of pillar (as *surrounding, crowning* its top?);—abs. כֹּתֶרֶת 1 K 7$^{16.16}$ + 10 t.; הַכּוֹתֶרֶת Je 52$^{22\,c}$; pl. abs. כֹּתָרֹת 1 K 7^{16} + 7 t., כֹּתָרוֹת 2 Ch 4$^{12.12.13}$;—*capitals* of pillars יָכִין and בֹּעַז 1 K 7$^{16.16.16}$ + 12 t. 1 K 7 = 2 Ch 4$^{12.12.13}$; 2 K 25$^{17.17.17}$ = Je 52$^{22.22.22}$.

3806 †[כָּתַשׁ] **vb. pound, pound fine, bray** (NH *id.;* Aram. כְּתַשׁ; Syr. ܟܬܫ is *strive, contend;* Zinj. כתש *break in pieces, shatter,* DHM$^{Sendsch.\ 58}$);—**Qal** *Impf.* אִם־תִּכְתּוֹשׁ אֶת־הָאֱוִיל בַּמַּכְתֵּשׁ Pr 27^{22} *if thou shouldest bray the fool in the mortar.*

4388-89 †מַכְתֵּשׁ **n.m. mortar** (place of pounding, braying; cf. Palm. n.pr.m. מכתש = *contundens* Vog$^{No.\ 97}$)—abs. מ׳ Pr 27^{22} (v. foregoing); hollow resembling a mortar Ju 15^{19} (whence came forth a water-spring; cf. GFM), Zp 1^{11} = a part of Jerusalem, cf. Schwally$^{ZAW\ x.\ (1890),\ 173\ f.}$

3807 †[כָּתַת] **vb. beat, crush by beating** (NH *id.;* Aram. כְּתַת);—**Qal** *Pf.* 1 s. וְכַתּוֹתִי ψ 89^{24}; *Impf.* 1 s. וָאֶכֹּת Dt 9^{21}; *Imv.* mpl. כֹּתּוּ Jo 4^{10}; *Pt. pass.* כָּתוּת Is 30^{14} Lv 22^{24};—**1.** *beat* or *crush fine,* of a potter's vessel Is 30^{14}, the golden calf Dt 9^{21} (+ טָחוֹן הֵיטֵב); a sacrificial victim Lv 22^{24} (i.e. its testicles; + מָעוּךְ, נָתוּק, כָּרוּת); fig. of enemies ψ 89^{24}. **2.** *beat, hammer* (ploughshares into swords, cf. **Pi. 2**) Jo 4^{10}. **Pi.** *Pf.* 3 ms. כִּתַּת 2 K 18^{4} 2 Ch 34^{7}; 3 mpl. וְכִתְּתוּ consec. Is 2^{4} + 2 t.;—as **Qal 1.** *beat* or *crush fine* 2 K 18^{4} 2 Ch 34^{7} (of images); fig. of devastating the land Zc 11^{6}. **2.** *beat, hammer* (swords into ploughshares, cf. **Qal 2**) Is 2^{4} = Mi 4^{3}. **Pu.** *Pf.* 3 mpl. וְכֻתְּתוּ 2 Ch 15^{6} *and they were beaten in pieces,* one nation against another. **Hiph.** *Impf.* 3 mpl. וַיַּכְּתוּ Dt 1^{44} *beat in pieces* an enemy, sf. וַיַּכּוּם וַיַּכְּתוּם Nu 14^{45}. **Hoph.** *Impf.* 3 ms. וּשְׁאִיָּה יֻכַּת־שָׁעַר Is 24^{12} *and to ruins is the gate crushed;* 3 mpl. יֻכַּתּוּ Mi 1^{7} (of idol-images); fig. of warriors Je 46^{5}; of frail man Jb 4^{20}.

†כָּתִית **adj. beaten**;—only in combin. שֶׁמֶן כָּתִית *beaten oil,* i.e. oil made by beating or pounding the olives in a mortar; esp. fine and costly (cf. Levy [NHWB ii. 443] sub כָּתִית);—1 K 5^{25} Ex 29^{40} Nu 28^{5}; שֶׁמֶן זַיִת זָךְ כ׳ לַמָּאוֹר Ex 27^{20} *pure beaten olive oil for the lamp* = Lv 24^{2} (Hex only HP). 3795

†[מְכִתָּה] **n.f. the crushed or pulverized** = coll. **crushed fragments**;—sg. sf. מְכִתָּתוֹ Is 30^{14} (result of כָּתוּת, vᵃ). 4386

ל

ל, twelfth letter; used as numeral 30 in postB. Heb.

לְ prep. to, for, in regard to (Moab. Ph. ל, Aram. לְ, ܠ, Arab. لِ, Eth. ለ: As. *la* in *lapân* = לִפְנֵי, Dl [HWB 530]), before tone-syllables usu. לָ (Kö [ii. 276 f.]); with suff. לִי; לְךָ, לָכָה †Gn 27^{37} 2 S 18^{22} Is 3^{6}, לָךְ; f. לָךְ, לְכִי †2 K 4^{2} Ct 2^{13} Kt (prob. N. Pal. dialect: cf. Syr. ܠܟܝ); לוֹ (15 t., acc. to Mas., written incorrectly לֹא: v. לֹא *note*); לָהּ, לָהֿ †Nu 32^{42} Zc 5^{11} Ru 2^{14}; לָנוּ; לָכֶם; לָכֵ֫נָה †Ez 13^{18} (לָכֶן does not occur); לָהֶם, poet. לָמוֹ (55 t., incl. a few cases where, acc. to many, it stands for לוֹ: cf. Ges [§ 103. 2 a, n.], Di [Is 44, 15. 53, 8]), [also לָהֵ֫מָּה †Je 14^{16}]; לָהֶן [לָהֵן] (q.v.) †Ru 1$^{13.13}$, לָהֵ֫נָּה 5 t., v. הֵמָּה]. **Prep.** denoting **direction** (not properly *motion,* as אֶל) **towards,** or **reference to**; and hence used in many varied applications, in some of which the idea of *direction* predominates, in others that of *reference* (cf. Giesebrecht [Die Präp. Lamed, 1876]):—**1.** very often, with various classes of verbs, *to, towards, for:* viz. **a.** verbs of *looking, listening, attending, waiting,* etc., as האמין, הטה אזן, כלה (ψ 84^{3}+), נכסף, הוחיל, יחל, התחלל, שמע, הקשיב, קִוָּה, נתן (נטה, הכין, שׁת) לב (sts.), צמא to thirst *for* (Ex 17^{3} ψ 42^{3}), השתחוה (*to* Gn 37^{10}, *towards* ψ 99^{5}); sts. also with האזין, הביט, נִבַּט, ראה, נפשׁ, נשׂא (see these verbs; many are also construed with other preps.); Is 51^{6} ψ 44^{21}; pregn. Is 38^{14}; השתאה ל †Gn 24^{21}, החריש ל Nu 30$^{5.8}$: sts. without a vb., as Ju 5^{9} לִבִּי לְ, Je 5^{3} עיניך ל, ψ 33^{18} (|| אל), 39^{8} נפשי, 120^{7} המה למלחמה, 130^{6} תוחלתי לך היא לאדני (cf. Is 26^{8}), 143^{6} Dn 11^{27} 2 Ch 3^{13} 32^{2}. **b.** with verbs of *saying, calling, singing, vowing, sacrificing,* etc., as אמר, דבר (chiefly with God as subj. = *promise,* Gn 24^{7} 1 K 5^{26}+, esp. in D כאשר דבר לְ Dt 1^{11} (v. Dr), v^{21} etc.; with human subj. Gn 49^{28} Ju 14^{7} 1 K 2^{19} al. (Gie [42 f.]: דבר אל is more common), הגיד, הודה, זמר, זבח, נדר, נשׂא יד (in oath) Ez 20$^{5.6.23}$ ψ 106^{26}, קִטֵּר, שָׁר, נשׁבע, הריע etc. **c.** with vbs. of *giving, leaving, bringing, offering* etc., as הביא, הִפִּיל, *allot* (Jos 13^{6}), נתן, הסגיר, עזב ψ 16^{9} abandon *to* Sheol, Is 18^{6}, הקריב Lv 17^{4}, שׁוב = *to be returned* Dt 28^{31}, השׁיב = *bring back* 22^{1}, = *requite* 2 S 16^{12}, שִׁלַּח, etc. **d.** with vbs. of dealing, acting *towards* (whether with friendly or hostile intent), as עשׂה ל Gn 19^{8}+oft., גמל ל Is 3^{9}; so with הֵיטִיב, הֵרַע, הֵמַר, חָטָא to sin *against* (Gn 20^{9}+), אָשַׁם to be guilty *towards* (Lv 5^{19}), כִּחֵשׁ, שִׁקֵּר to lie *to,* כִּזֵּב; with vbs. of mocking or laughing, *against, at,* as לעג לְ ψ 2^{4}, שׂחק לְ 37^{13}, שׂמח לְ to rejoice *over* 35^{19} Ez 35^{15}, caus. שִׂמַּח לְ ψ 30^{2}, עלץ לְ †25^{2}: with other verbs denoting hostility (less common than ב or על), Gn 27^{42} מתנחם לך להרגך, 2 K 5^{7}, Ex 11^{7}

(so Jos 10[21]: cf. Jb 16[9]), Je 25[31] 50[9] ψ 7[14] 37[12] 56[3] 106[16] קנא לְ (usu. in good sense, **5 g** *c*) Jb 20[27] 34[37]. And with adjj., as ψ 73[1] טוב ל good *to*, Gn 13[13] רָעִים וְחַטָּאִים לי׳ *towards* י׳, 2 S 22[24] תָּמִים לוֹ (||ψ 18[24] עִמּוֹ), ψ 89[29] נֶאֱמֶנֶת לוֹ; with subst. (rare) Ex 32[12] La 3[60] (syn. v[61] עַל). **e.** with words denoting what is pleasurable or the reverse, as נעם לְ 2 S 1[26], ערב ל Ho 9[4], יֵמַר לְ Is 24[7], טוֹב לְ (adj.) 1 S 1[8], נָקֵל לְ 2 K 20[10], also הועיל ל, סכן ל, to be profitable *to;* and with neuter vbs., to denote the subj. of a sensation or emotion, as טוֹב לְ to be well *to* (with), Dt 5[30] 19[13] +, מַר לְ Ru 1[13], צַר לְ 1 S 13[6] + oft., כָּרֹב לְ Ho 10[1], רָוַח לְ 1 S 16[23], חַם לְ to be warm *to*, 1 K 1[1], רַע לְ ψ 106[32], חָרָה לְ it was hot (=anger arose) *to* Gn 4[6]+oft., חֲשֵׁכָה לְ Mi 3[6]. And with pass. vbs., נִסְלַח לוֹ it is forgiven *to him* = he is forgiven Lv 4[26] + oft.; otherwise rare, נִרְפָּא לָנוּ it is healed *to us* = we are healed Is 53[5], נִרְצָה לְ 1[4], הוּנַח לְ La 5[5], יְבֻלַּע לְ 2 S 17[16] (v. Dr). **f.** with verbs of *reaching to, touching, attaching* etc., as אסר ל to bind *to*, חבשׁ, דבק ψ 44[26], מצא to reach *to* Is 10[10.14] ψ 21[9], הגיע Ex 4[25], נצמד Nu 25[5], קרוב (adj.) Ru 2[20]; out of connexion with a vb. (almost = עַד), Jos 16[1] ψ 59[14] Jb 28[3] Ne 3[15] 2 Ch 33[14], and correl. to מִן (v. מִן **5**). **g.** with vbs. of *motion*, as שָׁב, בא, הלך etc. (not so common as אל, or the simple acc. with or without ה *loc.*)—(*a*) with *places*, rare in early prose, Jos 1[15] 8[14] Ju 1[34] 20[10] (but v. GFM), 1 S 9[12] 20[25] 2 K 3[27], exc. in partic. phrases, viz. למקומו Gn 18[33], לדרכו 32[2], לאהליו 1 S 4[10] (also with other sfs.: all these + oft., esp. with שׁוּב and הלך, or preceded by distrib. אִישׁ; לאהליו(ך), also, without vb., as exclam., 2 S 20[1] 1 K 12[16]), לארצו Gn 30[25] +, אִישׁ לִירֻשָּׁתוֹ Dt 3[20], אִישׁ לנחלתו Jo 24[28] +, אִישׁ לעירו 1 S 8[22] Ne 13[10]: oft. in late Heb., as Jb 4[5], 1 Ch 4[39.42] 5[26] 12[1.9] 22[18] 24[19] 2 Ch 1[3] 8[17] + oft. Chr, Ezr 2[68] +, Ne 10[35 ff.] Est 6[4] ψ 96[8] 132[7] 146[4]: לירושלם Je 3[17 b] (om. 𝔊), Zc 1[16], and oft. Ch Ezr Ne (as 2 Ch 11[14] 19[1] 30[3.11]), לשׁמרון 2 Ch 18[2] 28[8.9], לבבל Je 51[2] Ezr 2[1] 1 Ch 9[1] 2 Ch 36[7] (but earlier always שׁמרון, ירושלם, בבל or בבלה); and poet. Ju 5[11] Is 22[1] 23[17] 49[18] 51[14] (pregn.) ימות לשׁחת, 59[20] 60[4.5.7] 65[12] Je 31[17] 48[15] 50[27] Mi 1[12] Zc 9[12] ψ 7[8] 68[19] 74[3] Ct 4[16] 5[1] 6[2] 7[13] (pregn.) נשׁכימה לכרמים, Jb 10[19] 20[6]; הוציא לְ ψ 18[20] 66[12], לאור Mi 7[9] Jb 12[22]; יוּבַל ל Ho 10[6] +: without a vb., Is 23[5] Ho 7[12]. Also לָאָרֶץ, with many vbs., both in sense *down to* the earth, Is 14[12] 21[9] 28[2] Am 3[14] 5[7] Ez 26[11] ψ 7[6] +, c. חִלֵּל (pregn.) 74[7] 89[40], and idiom. c. ישׁב to sit *on* the earth, Is 3[26] 47[1] Jb 2[13] +, without vb. Is 26[9]: so לֶעָפָר Jb 7[21] ψ 7[6], הוריד לשׁחת Ez 28[8]. (*b*) with *persons*, not very common, Dt 32[35] Is 31[6] 57[9] Je 3[22] אָתָנוּ לָךְ, ψ 45[15] 119[79] Jb 18[14] 1 Ch 12[16] Ne 6[19], לְעַמִּי Nu 24[11] Ru 1[10]: בא לְ, esp. with pron. לָךְ, לָהּ etc. (friendly) 2 S 12[4] Zc 9[9] Am 6[1], (hostile) 2 S 5[23] Je 46[22] 49[9] 50[26] 51[48.53]; with a *thing* as subj. Dt 33[16] (לראשׁ), 2 S 24[13] Is 47[9] Jb 3[25] (cf. Is 66[4]), Je 4[12] 22[33] בְּבֹא לָךְ חֲבָלִים (so Ho 13[13] Is 66[7]). And with vbs. of placing (where עַל would be more usu.) ψ 21[4] תָּשִׁית לְרֹאשׁוֹ עֲטֶרֶת פָּז, 22[16] 66[12], with לְכִסֵּא ψ 9[5] 132[11.12] Jb 36[7]: cf. הִשְׁתַּחֲוָה, נָפַל לְאַפָּיו, Gn 48[12] + (also עַל א׳). **h.** expressing *direction towards* (without contact), לאחור back*wards* Je 7[24], לַחוּץ out*wards* ψ 41[7], למעלה up*wards*, למטה down*wards;* to scatter לכל רוח Je 49[32] cf. v[36] Ez 5[10] +, לארבע רוחות (שׁמים) Ez 42[20] Dn 8[8] 11[4] 1 Ch 9[24]: of the points of the compass (without vb.) לִפְאַת... *towards* the quarter of (the N., S., etc.) Ex 26[18] + oft. P (so Ez 47[15]), למזרח, לדרום etc. (late: earlier ממזרח, or מזרחה etc.) Ez 40[23] 41[11.14] 42[4] Ne 3[26] 1 Ch 5[9] 6[63] 7[28] 12[15] 26[16–18] 2 Ch 31[14], למדבר 2 Ch 20[24]; also (peculiarly) 1 S 14[40] 1 K 20[38] 2 K 11[11]. **i.** expressing *addition* (rare); Is 28[10.13] צַו לָצָו קַו לָקָו, 56[8] (resuming עַל), Ec 7[27] אחת לאחת (adding) one *to* another, Ezr 8[24] Ne 11[17] (עַל is more usual in this sense).

2. Expressing *locality, at, near,* idiom. in the phrases לִפְנֵי = *before* (sts. after vbs. of motion, as 1 K 1[23], but very oft. otherwise), לְעֵינֵי *in the sight of*, לְיַד, לִימִין, לִשְׂמֹאל (only Ec 10[2]), לפתח *at the entrance* (*of*), Gn 4[7] Nu 11[10] +; in other, rarer connexions, Nu 20[24] לְמֵי... (usu. עַל), Ju 5[16] (|| v[15] בְּ) לְחוֹף + Gn 49[13.13] Ju 5[17], לְפִי + ψ 141[7] Pr 8[3], Ho 5[1] לְמִצְפָּה, 2 Ch 35[15]. לִפְנִימָה = *within*, 1 K 6[30] Ez 40[16].

3. To denote the *object* of a vb.—**a.** with the Hif., mostly of intrans. vbs., properly (as it seems) a *dat. commodi*, as הֵנִיחַ לְ to *give rest to*, הִרְחִיב to *give width to*, הֵצַר לְ, הֵצִיק לְ, exceptionally also with other words, as הִרְגִּיז, הוֹכִיחַ, הִצְדִּיק to *give righteousness to*, Is 53[11], הֶחֱיָה Gn 45[7], הֵבִין *give understanding to* (late), הִצְלִיחַ (do.), הִרְבָּה Ho 10[1], הִשְׂגִּיא Jb 12[23], הִפְתָּה Gn 9[27] *give breadth to*. **b.** with other vbs., sporadically early (if the text be sound), but mostly late, in conseq. of Aram. influence (in Aram. the accus. being constantly denoted by ל), as אהב Lv 19$^{18.34}$ 2 Ch 19^{2}, הרג 2 S 3^{30} Jb 5^{2}, בוז (mostly), בזה 2 S 6^{16}, sts. also זכר *to remember*, עבד *to serve* (work or do service *for*), עזר (2 S 8^{5}, and esp. late), דרשׁ (esp. Chr), הִלֵּל (only Chr Ezr), רפא (prob. the dat. comm.), שִׁחֵת 1 S 23^{10} Nu 32^{15}, נִדָּה Am 6^{3}, גִּדֵּל ψ 34^{4}, פִּתַּח 116^{16}, כִּבֵּד 86^{9} Dn 11^{38}, חִזֵּק 1 Ch 26^{27} 29^{12}, בֵּרַךְ 29^{20} Ne 11^{2}, חֵרֵף 2 Ch 32^{17}; see also 1 S 22^{7} 2 K 8^{6} Je 16^{6} 40^{2} Jon 4^{6} ψ 69^{6} 73^{18} 135^{11} 136$^{19.20}$ Pr 17^{26} Jb 12^{23b} La 4^{5} 1 Ch 16^{37} 18^{6} (הושׁיע, altered fr. 2 S 8^{6}: so ψ 116^{6}), 25^{1} 29$^{22.22}$ 2 Ch 5^{11} 6^{42} 17^{7} 24^{5} 34^{13} (usu. על), Ezr 8^{16}; at the end of an enumeration, 1 Ch 28^{1b} 2 Ch 24^{12b} 26^{14b} 28^{23}; marking the defin. obj. in appos., 1 Ch 29^{18} 2 Ch 2^{12} 23^{1} ψ 135^{11} 136$^{19.20}$ (= earlier את, Gn 26^{34} Ju 3^{15} Is 7^{6} 8^{2}); after a sf. (in Syr. fashion), 1 Ch 5^{26} וַיַּגְלֵם לְ׳, 23^{6} 2 Ch 25$^{5.10}$ 28^{15}, cf. Ne 9^{32}; defining anom. the sf. of a *noun*, Nu 29$^{18.21.24\ etc.}$ 1 Ch 7^{5} הִתְיַחְשָׂם לַכֹּל, 2 Ch 31$^{16.18}$ Ezr 9^{1} 10^{14}. (But in sentences of the type אֵין דּוֹרֵשׁ לְנַפְשִׁי ψ 142^{5b} 72^{12} Is 51^{18} Je 14^{16} 49^{5} La 1$^{7.9.17.21}$, the ל belongs prob. to אין: cf. the ‖ types אֵין לִי מַכִּיר ψ 142^{5a} Dt 28^{31} Je 50^{32} La 1^{2}, דֹּרֵשׁ אֵין לָהּ Je 30^{17} La 4^{4}.) Cf. Ges^{§117n}.

4. *Into* (εἰς), of a transition into a new state or condition, or into a new character or office:— **a.** Gn 2^{22} וַיִּבֶן אֶת־הַצֵּלָע לְאִשָּׁה *into* a woman, 12^{2} וְאֶעֶשְׂךָ לְגוֹי גָּדוֹל *into* a great nation, and very oft. with this and similar verbs, as Ex 26^{7} Is 44$^{17.19}$, שָׂם Gn 46^{3} Is 5^{20} make bitter *into* sweet etc., 28^{17}, נָתַן 42^{6}, also in such phrases as שָׂם לְשַׁמָּה to make *into* a desolation Is 13^{9} Je 4^{7} etc. 19^{8}; הפך ל to change *into* Ex 7^{15} Dt 23^{6}+, to cut or divide *into* Gn 32^{8} Ju 19^{29} Is 11^{15}+, שָׂרַף לְ to burn *into* Am 2^{1}, Dt 9^{21} דַּק לְעָפָר, פעל ψ 7^{14} maketh *into* (or *to be*) flaming ones; היה ל *to become*, in many diff. connexions, as Gn 2^{7} ויהי האדם לנפשׁ חיה *became* a living soul (see היה **II. 2 e**, p. 226^{a}); משׁח למלך (לנגיד) to anoint *so as to be* king, *as* king (Germ. 'zum König': cf. Old Engl. *to*, as Ju 17^{13} and 'We have Abraham *to* our father'), 1 S 9^{16} 15^{1} etc., צִוָּה לְ to appoint *as* 13^{14} 25^{30}; שׁת לְ ψ 45^{17}; even more freely, as דִּבֶּר עָלַי לְמֶלֶךְ 1 K 14^{2}, cf. 2 S 3^{17} 1 Ch 29^{23}; חשׁב ל to count *for* (or *as*) Gn 38^{15}+oft.; Ex 21^{7} when a man sells his daughter לְאָמָה *for, as,* a female slave, Dt 6^{8} to bind לְאוֹת *for, as* a sign, הִתְיַצֵּב (יָצָא) לְשָׂטָן *so as to be* an adversary Nu 22$^{22.32}$, קום (הקים) לְאֹרֵב 1 S 22$^{8.13}$, עמד לְ Is 11^{10} Dn 11^{1}, יצא לַחָפְשִׁי to go forth *into the state of* one free Ex 21^{2} (cf. v$^{26.27}$ after שׁלח), 2 K 25^{12} Is 14^{2} Je 34^{11}, ψ 48^{4} נודע לְ hath made himself known *as*, 87^{4} הזכיר לְ to mention *as*, Ez 13^{20}; poet. Jb 39^{16} הִקְשִׁיחַ בָּנֶיהָ לְּלֹא־לָהּ treats her young ones hardly (turning them) *into* none of hers: without a vb. (poet., or late prose) Mi 1^{14} Na 1^{7} Hb 1^{11} זוּ כֹחוֹ לֵאלֹהוֹ, Zc 4^{7} La 4^{3} Jb 13^{12} Hg 1^{9} 1 Ch 21^{12} 26^{29} 28^{18b} 2 Ch 23^{4}. **b.** this usage is also combined idiomatically, with great freq., with a 2nd לְ, of reference (**5 a** *d*), giving rise to such phrases as Gn 1^{29} לָכֶם יִהְיֶה לְאָכְלָה to you it shall be *for food* (see היה **II. 2 f**, p. 226^{b}), 45^{8} וַיְשִׂימֵנִי לְאָב לְפַרְעֹה, 47^{26} Dt 28$^{9.25}$ Ju 1^{33} 1 S 2^{28} Is 21^{4} 28^{18b} יֹצְרִי מִבֶּטֶן לְעֶבֶד לוֹ, 49^{5} וִהְיִיתֶם לוֹ לְמִרְמָס, 63$^{8.10}$ וַיֵּהָפֵךְ לָהֶם לְאוֹיֵב (Jb 30^{21}), Je 15$^{4.20}$ 20^{4} 21^{9} Hb 2^{7} ψ 33^{12} 94^{22} 132^{13} 139^{22} Jb 13^{24} ותחשׁבני לאויב לך, 16^{12} etc.

5. *With reference to*, viz. **a.** defining those in reference to whom a predicate is affirmed, hence oft. = *belonging to, of:* (*a*) Dt 23^{3} דור עשׂירי לא יבא לו, v$^{4.9}$ La 1^{10}; הכרית לְ 1 S 2^{33} 1 K 14^{10}+; השׁבית לְ Je 48^{35}; לֹא יִכָּרֵת אִישׁ לְ 1 K 2^{4} 8^{25}+; אִם נוֹתַר לְ 1 S 25^{34}, המול לכם כל בשׂר Gn 17^{10}, 34$^{15.22}$ Ex 12^{48} 1 S 11^{2}; 1 K 14^{13}; ישׁב על כסא לְ 2 K 10^{30} 15^{12} Je 13^{13} 22^{4} ψ 132^{12} cf. v^{11}; ראה בנים לְ Gn 50^{23} ψ 128^{6}; אבד לְ to perish *belonging to* 1 S 9$^{3.20}$ Is 26^{14}; מצא לְ to find *belonging to* Dt 22^{14} 1 S 13^{22}; Gn 23^{16} money עֹבֵר לַסֹּחֵר current *to* (= with) the merchant, Nu 9^{10} Am 9^{1} Is 33^{14} Jb 12^{6}: note further the pron. in Ex 10^{5} הַצֹּמֵחַ לכם מן השׂדה, 12$^{2.5}$ 26^{33} Lv 11^{29} וְזֶה לָכֶם הַטָּמֵא (cf. v$^{4-8}$), 19^{23} 25^{30} 26$^{5.26}$ בְּשִׁבְרִי לָכֶם מַטֵּה לֶחֶם (Ez 14^{13}), Nu 28^{19} 32^{21} 34^{4} Dt 28^{66} Jos 2^{6} הָעֲרֻכוֹת לָהּ עַל הַגָּג, Ju 16^{9} 19^{14} (cf. זָרַח לְ Gn 32^{32}+), 1 S 5^{9} 2 S 15^{30} 2 K 4^{27b} נַפְשָׁהּ מָרָה־לָהּ (cf. Is 15^{4} Je 4^{19}), Is 23^{7} Je 2^{21} Mi 2^{4} איך ימישׁ לי, Ez 16^{14} 29^{7} ψ 110^{3}; also 40^{7} ears hast thou digged *to* (or *for*) me, 51^{12} (cf. 1 S 10^{9}), Is 50$^{4.5}$ יעיר לי אזן. (*b*) in such phrases as Nu 1^{4} אִישׁ אִישׁ לַמַּטֶּה a man *for* (or *of*) a tribe, 7^{11} 31^{4}, Dt 1^{23} Jos 3^{12} 18^{4} Ju 20^{10} ten men לַמֵּאָה *of* 100, 100 *of* 1000 etc.; רִאשׁוֹן לְ = first *of* Ex 12^{2} 2 S 19^{21}. (*c*) spec. of relationship, to define a man's family or tribe, esp. in genealogies, Nu 1^{6} לראובן אליצור, v$^{7.8}$ etc., v$^{22.24}$ etc., 3$^{21.27}$ 1 Ch 24$^{20.21}$ etc., 26$^{23.25}$ etc. + oft.; in the opp. order Ex 31^{2} Lv 24^{11} Nu 17^{23} אהרן לבית לוי 1 K 15^{27} etc., cf. 2 S 3$^{2.3.5}$, also 9^{3a} Gn 20^{18} 46$^{26.27}$; similarly הנשׁארים לְ 2 K 10$^{11.17}$, הַמֵּת לְ 1 K 14^{11}

16[4]+. (*d*) denoting *relation* (to be *to* or *towards* one in a particular regard or capacity) Ex 19[5] והייתם לי סְגֻלָּה ye shall be *to me* a special possession, 22[30] אנשי קדש תהיון לי, 1 S 18[18] 2 S 19[29] 1 K 5[15] 2 K 19[15] Je 12[9] 15[8] 22[6] גלעד אתה לי, 51[20] Is 54[9] Ez 24[19] ψ 12[5] מִי אָדוֹן לָנוּ, 35[14] כְּרֵעַ כְּאָח לִי, 99[8] Jb 24[17] 30[29] Ne 6[18]; with a ptcp. Nu 10[25] 25[18] 35[23] Dt 4[22] 19[4.6] Is 11[9] 14[2] (Dr § 135, 7 Obs.); מלך לְ Nu 22[4]; רַב לָכֶם it is (too) much *to* you, מְעַט לְ (too) little *to* . . .; in the phr. (מִי (מָה אֵלֶּה לָּךְ who (what) are these *to* thee?=*what meanest thou* by these things? Gn 33[5.8] 2 S 16[2] Ez 37[18], cf. Ex 12[26] Jos 4[6] Ez 12[22]; חלילה לי away be it *to* (or *for*) me! למה לי to what purpose *to* me is . . .? Gn 27[46] Is 1[11] Je 6[20] Jb 30[2]: oft. also in such phrases as מָגֵן לְ a shield *to* Gn 15[1] ψ 18[31], a strength *to* ψ 28[8], an abomination *to* Gn 43[32] Is 1[13]+, a grief *to* Pr 10[1] 17[21]; cf. Je 15[10] Mal 2[9] ψ 89[28] etc.: note also Jon 3[3] עיר גדולה לאלהים a city great *to* God (i.e. in his estimation: cf. Acts 7[20] ἀστεῖος τῷ θεῷ, and לפני Gn 10[9]), Est 10[3]. And with כְּ Ju 17[11] 2 S 12[3] וַתְּהִי לוֹ כְּבַת, Ex 22[24] (cf. **4 b**), Am 9[7] כבני כֻשִׁיִּים אַתֶּם לִי Ho 11[4] Is 29[2] Jb 33[6] הֵן־אֲנִי לָאֵל כְּפִיךָ lo, I am *to* God as thou art, etc. **b.** denoting possession, *belonging to*;—(*a*) as predicate, in הָיָה לְ (cf. Lat. *est mihi*), אֵין לְ, יֵשׁ לְ constantly (see these words); also alone, as Gn 31[16.43] לִי הוּא it is *mine*, 48[5] לי הם, Ex 19[5b] כי לי כל הארץ, 1 K 20[3.4] Is 43[1] לי אתה, 44[5] לי׳ אני, Ez 29[3] ψ 47[10] 50[10.12] Jb 12[13.16] Ct 2[16] 6[3]; 1 S 1[2] ולו שתי נשים and *he had* two wives, 25[7.36] Ju 3[16] 17[5] Jb 22[8] 2 S 17[18] Ho 6[10], +oft.; with לא, 1 K 22[17] Is 53[2] לא הדר לו, Je 5[10]+; with a neut. adj. (rare) Is 63[2] Je 30[10] אָנוּשׁ לְשִׁבְרֵךְ; note also such phrases as 2 K 10[19] זבח גדול לי לבעל, Is 2[12] כִּי יוֹם לי׳ על וג׳ for י׳ *hath* a day against, etc., 22[5] 28[2] הִנֵּה חָזָק וְאַמִּץ לי׳ י׳ *hath* a strong and mighty one (sc. at his disposal), 34[2] קֶצֶף לי׳ על וג׳, v[6b.8]; Ho 4[1] . . . כִּי רִיב לי׳ עם, 12[3] Mi 6[2]: מַה־לִּי וָלָךְ what is there *to* me and *to* thee? (i.e. what have we to do with each other?), v. מָה; שלום לך peace be *to thee!* Of that which *pertains to* one as a right, Lv 25[31.48] Dt 1[17] כי המשפט לאלהים הוא, 21[17] 1 S 17[47] Je 10[23] 32[7.8] Ez 21[32] ψ 3[9] לי׳ הישועה, Jon 2[10]; with an inf. 1 S 23[20] וְלָנוּ הַסְגִּירוֹ and it shall be *for us* (or *our place*) to deliver him, Mi 3[1] הלא לכם לדעת, Ezr 4[3] 2 Ch 13[5] 20[17] 26[18], cf. ψ 50[16] מַה־לְּךָ לְ. (*b*) here also belongs the so-called *Lamed auctoris*, Is 38[9] מִכְתָּב לְחִזְקִיָּהוּ a writing *belonging to, of*, or *by* H., Hb 3[1], ψ 3[1] and oft. מזמור לדוד a Psalm *of* or *by* D. (but possibly denoting orig., at least in some cases, a Psalm *belonging to* a collection known as David's: so certainly in לבני קרח ψ 42[1] al., and prob. also in לאסף ψ 50[1] al.); so לדוד מזמור 24[1]+, לדוד alone 10[1] 14[1]+. Comp. on Ph. coins לצדנם *of* the Sidonians, i.e. belonging to them, לצור (=Gk. Σιδονίων, Τύρου). Heb. idiom also uses the לְ of possession where we should write the simple name, as Ez 38[16] (written on a stick) ליהודה, v[17] ליוסף, in English 'Judah,' 'Joseph,' Is 8[1] למהר־שלל־חש־בז 'Maher-shalal-hash-baz.' **c.** as periph. for the *st. c.*:—(*a*) אשר לְ, as Ex 29[29] 39[1.39] Lv 7[20.21] 16[6.15] (see further exx. sub אשר **7**, p. 82 f.); so שֶׁלִּי †Ct 1[6] 8[12], שֶׁלָּנוּ †2 K 6[11]. (*b*) without אשר—(*a*) where it is desired to keep the first noun indeterm., 1 S 16[18] ראיתי בן לישי a son *to* or *of* Jesse, 22[20] Gn 41[12] Nu 1[4] 7[24] 1 K 2[39] שני עבדים לשמעי, 18[22] 2 K 3[11] Ru 2[1] etc.; (β) where the genit. is a *compound* term, to avoid a series of nouns in the *st. c.*, Nu 1[4] ראש לבית אבותיו, 7[24.30.36] etc., 1[21] פקדיהם למטה ראובן, v[23.25] etc., 2[9.16] etc., Jos 21[38]; 1 Ch 9[23] הַשְּׁעָרִים לְבֵית י׳, 27[3] הראשׁ לְ, 2 Ch 19[11] Ne 10[39] etc., occas. also besides, as 1 S 14[16] הצופים לשאול, Ex 31[7] (usu. ארון העדות); (γ) where the regens is a pr. name, or a compound term, which does not readily admit of being placed in the *st. c.*, as דברי הימים למלכי ישראל (יהודה) 1 K 14[19.29] +oft., 1 K 5[30] שרי הנצבים לְ, 2 K 11[4] שרי המאות לְ; ראשי האבות לְ Nu 36[1] Jos 19[51] 1 Ch 8[13]+oft. Ch Ne Ezr; in dates, as באחד לחדש Gn 8[5.14] Ex 12[3.6], Gn 7[11] בשנת . . . לחיי נח, 16[3] Ex 19[1] 1 K בשנת שתים לאסא, בחדש השלישי לצאת . . . 15[25.28] 16[8] (all+oft.); other cases, Ex 20[5.6] Lv 13[48] Nu 16[22] (=27[16]) 18[15] Ju 20[10] 2 K 5[9] Ez 45[19] Ru 2[3] 1 Ch 4[43] 9[19.21] 26[19] 2 Ch 22[10] 23[4]; (δ) with a neg., Gn 15[13] בארץ לא לכם, Je 5[19] Pr 26[17] Hb 1[6], poet. even alone, 2[6] who increaseth לֹא לוֹ (that which is) not *his*, Jb 18[15] בְּלִי לוֹ, 39[16] לְלֹא לָהּ as (**4**) those which are not *hers*; (ε) poet., Is 16[2] 26[7] ארח לצדיק Je 47[3] Ho 9[6] ψ 37[16] 49[14] 55[19] (Hi De Ch), 58[5] 73[6] 105[36] 116[15] המותה לחסידיו, 123[4] Jon 2[3] Ec 5[11]; cf. also מלך לְ Jos 12[18] (but v. 𝔊 Di), 2 K 19[13] (cf. Aram. Ezr 5[11]): v. further Ew § 292, Ges § 129, Giesebr § 19. **c.** attached to advbs., esp. those compounded with מִן, it forms preps., as מִקֶּדֶם לְ Gn 3[24] lit. off the front *with reference to* (or *of*)=*in front of*: so מִבֵּית לְ = *within*, מִחוּץ לְ = *without*,

סָבִיב לְ, מִצָּפוֹן לְ, מֵהָלְאָה לְ, מֵעֵבֶר לְ, מֵעַל לְ, מִמַּעַל לְ, מִבֵּינוֹת לְ, מִבַּעַד לְ, מֵאַחֲרֵי לְ (all oft.); more rarely, אֶל בֵּינוֹת לְ, מִזֶּה וּמִזֶּה לְ, הֵנָּה לְ Ex 38^{15}, Dn 12$^{5.5}$, תַּחַת לְ, מִסָּבִיב לְ, מִנֶּגֶד לְ, מִימִין לְ, מִזְרָח לְ, poet. נֶגְדָה־נָּא לְ †ψ 116$^{14.18}$. See בית, חוץ, etc.; and cf. Ju 7$^{1.8}$. **d.** construed with *passive* verbs, the ל of reference notifies the *agent*, as בָּרוּךְ לְ blessed *by*, Gn 14^{17} + oft.; otherwise not very common, Gn 31^{15} נֶחְשַׁב לְ to be reckoned *by* (so Is 40^{17}), Ex 12^{16} אַךְ אֲשֶׁר יֵאָכֵל לְכָל־נֶפֶשׁ הוּא לְבַדּוֹ, יֵעָשֶׂה לָכֶם, 1 S 2^{3} 25^{7} 2 S 19^{43} Je 8^{3} נִבְחַר לְ (Pr 21^{3}), 29^{22} ψ 73^{10} 111^{2} Pr 13^{13} יֵחָבֶל־לוֹ is pledged *by it*, 14^{20} Ne 6$^{1.7}$ נִשְׁמַע לְ, 13^{26} אָהוּב לְ, Est 4^{3} 5^{12} Ec 5^{12} שָׁמוּר לְ. So with נִרְאָה Ex 13^{7} (=Dt 16^{4}), נוֹדַע 1 S 6^{3} Ez 36^{32} Ne 4^{9} (but usu. with these words לְ is rather the dat. comm. *be known, appear, to*), נעתר Gn 25^{21} +, נדרש and נמצא Is 65^{1} + to let oneself be *entreated, sought, found, by*, נוֹסַר †Lv 26^{23}, נענה †Ez 14$^{4.7}$ (?). (Comp. in Syr. Nö $^{§ 247}$, esp. with pass. ptcp. $^{§ 279}$ (so Talm., Luz $^{§ 90}$), which in Mand. and New Syr. even unites with the ל to form a new tense, v. Nö $^{M § 263; NS § 104}$.) Analogously Gn 38^{15} וַתַּהַר לוֹ and was pregnant *by*, v^{18} הָרָה לְ (adj.) pregnant *by* (lit. *to*). **e.** *regarding, in respect of,* viz. (*a*) with verbs of *speaking, commanding, hearing,* etc.; *concerning, about* (syn. עַל, which is more usu.); so with אָמַר Gn 20^{13} Dt 33$^{12.13}$+ Ju 9^{54} Is 41^{7} ψ 3^{3} 41^{6}+, דִּבֵּר Ez 44^{5}, סִפֵּר ψ 22^{31}, דרשׁ Dt 12^{30} 2 S 11^{3}, חָלַם Gn 42^{9}, הִטִּיף Mi 2^{6}, צִוָּה Nu 8^{20} ψ 91^{11}+, שָׁמַע Gn 17^{20}, and oft. in the adjunct ...לאשׁר, ...לכל אשׁר Gn 27^{8} Jos 1^{18} 22^{2}+; שׁאל Gn 26^{7}+, esp. in phr. שׁאל לפ׳ לְשָׁלוֹם to ask *about* any one *with ref. to* (his) welfare; in the phr. לַדָּבָר הַזֶּה *in regard to* this thing (idiom.), Gn 19^{21} 1 S 30^{24}+, Ju 21$^{5.7}$ לנשׁים, 1 K 20^{7}; without a vb., Lv 7^{37} 14^{54} Dt 33^{7}, and in titles Je 23^{9} 46^{2} 48^{1} 49$^{1.7.23.28}$. (*b*) limiting the application of a term, esp. with כְּ to denote the *tertium comparationis*, as Gn 41^{19} לֹא רָאִיתִי כָהֵנָּה ... לָרֹעַ *as regards, in respect of* (in our idiom, simply *in* or *for*) badness, Ex 24^{10} כְּעֶצֶם הַשָּׁמַיִם לָטֹהַר *in brightness*, Dt 34$^{11.12}$ Ez 3^{3} (rd. לְמֹתֶק) Pr 25^{3} 1 Ch 24^{4}; with an inf., Gn 3^{22} היה כאחד ממנו לדעת *in respect of* knowing, etc., 34^{15} Is 21^{1} כַּסּוּפוֹת לַחֲלוֹף as whirlwinds *in respect of* sweeping through, Jos 10^{14} 2 S 14$^{17.25}$ Ez 38$^{9.16}$ Pr 26^{2} כצפור לָנוּד כדרור לָעוּף, 1 Ch 12^{9} כצבאים לְמַהֵר; with לָרֹב *in* multitude, Dt 1^{10} ככוכבי השׁמים לרב

Ju 7$^{12.12}$ + oft.; less freq. in comparisons with מִן, 1 K 10^{23} וַיִּגְדַּל ... מִכֹּל ... לְעֹשֶׁר וּלְחָכְמָה, Ct 1^{2} Jb 30^{1} צעירים ממני לימים (cf. the accus. 15^{10}), 32$^{4.6}$, cf. 11^{6} כִּפְלַיִם לְתוּשִׁיָּה; rarely after substs., 2 Ch 16^{8} 21^{3}, 3^{8} לְכִכָּרִים, v$^{9.11}$ Ezr 8^{26} (where the earlier language would use appos., or the accus. of specification, Dr $^{§ 194}$). (*c*) somewhat differently, Lv 5^{4b} and be guilty לְאַחַת מֵאֵלֶּה *as regards* one of these things, v^{5} 22^{5b} Nu 18^{7} (cf. 1 Ch 26^{32} 27^{1} 2 Ch 19$^{11.11}$) Je 2^{37} (peculiar) thou shalt not prosper להם *as regards* them, Ez 44^{14}, cf. Jb 9^{19}; after substs. Gn 47^{26} לַחֹמֶשׁ (but cf. 𝔊 Di) *with ref. to* the fifth, Lv 7^{26} 11^{46b} Nu 19^{11} 29^{39} 30^{13} Dt 19^{15} 23^{19} Ezr 8^{34} 1 Ch 27^{1} (לכל ח׳), 2 Ch 8^{15} Ne 11^{24}. (*d*) ... לְכֹל (לְכָל־), at the close of a description or enumeration, with a generalizing force, *as regards all ... =namely, in brief* (Ew $^{§ 310 a}$), chiefly in P and Chr (prob. a juristic usage): Gn 9^{10b} all that go out of the ark לְכֹל חַיַּת הָאָרֶץ *as regards* (*=namely, even*) all beasts of the earth, 23^{10b} Ex 14^{28} (cf. v^{9} !), 27$^{3.19}$ 28^{38} 30^{1b} Lv 5$^{3.4}$ (cf. 13^{51}) 11^{42} 16$^{16.21}$ 22^{18} Nu 3^{26b} (v$^{31.36}$!), 4$^{27.31.32}$ 5^{9} 18$^{4.8.9.11}$ (all P), 2 K 12^{6} Je 19^{13} Ez 44^{9} 1 Ch 13^{1} 2 Ch 5^{12} (לְכֻלָּם), 25^{5} 31^{16} 33^{8b} (‖ 2 K 21^{8} ולכל) Ezr 1^{5}. (*e*) introducing a new subj. (rare, and text sts. dub.; chiefly Chr), *as regards ...*, Is 32^{1} ולשׂרים (rd. prob. וְשָׂרִים; ל by error from foll. למשׁפט), Lv 11^{26} 1 Ch 3^{2} (rd. prob. אבשׁלום), 5^{2} (? v. Ke), 7^{1} (Ke ובני), v^{5a} (?), 24^{1} 26$^{1.23.25.26.31a.β}$ 2 Ch 5^{12} 7^{21} לְכָל־עֹבֵר עליו ישׁרק (‖ 1 K 9^{8} כָּל־עֹבֵר), cf. Dt 24^{5} (peculiar); Ec 9^{4} כִּי לְכֶלֶב חַי הוּא טוֹב וגו׳; cf. ψ 17^{4} (on 16^{3} v. Comm.). In Chr sts. used peculiarly as a periphr., 1 Ch 28$^{1b.21}$ לכל נדיב *as regards* every liberal man = every liberal man (cf. Ke), 29$^{5a.6b}$; cf. Ezr 6^{7} (Aram.), 7^{28}. **f.** in connexion with terms designating a cause or occasion, *with reference to* or *in view of* (Germ. *auf...hin*) becomes nearly equivalent to *on account of, through* (not common): so to cut oneself לָנֶפֶשׁ Lv 19^{28} *on account of* a (dead) person, Dt 14^{1} Je 16^{6b}, Lv 11^{24} לְאֵלֶּה תִּטַּמָּאוּ *on account of* these ye shall become unclean, 21$^{1.2.3}$+, Ez 20^{31} נִטְמָא לְ, Nu 5^{2} כָּל־טָמֵא לָנֶפֶשׁ Nu 9$^{6.7.10}$, cf. 2 Ch 23^{19}; לְשֵׁם י׳ *in view of* (i.e. determined by), *because of* י׳'s name, Jo 9^{9} Je 3^{17} Is 55^{5} (‖ לְמַעַן), Ez 36^{22} (do.); Gn 4^{23a} I have slain a man לְפִצְעִי *because of* my wound, v^{23b} Ex 4^{26} לַמּוּלֹת, Nu 35^{33} לַדָּם; לָכֵן = *therefore* (syn. עַל כֵּן), constantly (v. כֵּן); Job 30^{24} (si vera l.) לָהֶן: of the cause of an emotion, Is 15^{5} לִבִּי לְמוֹאָב

יִזְעָק *because of* Moab, 16$^{7.11}$ Je 31^{20} הָמוּ מֵעַי לוֹ (עַל Ct 5^{4}), Ho 10^{5}, לְזֹאת Jb 37^{1}. Cf. Nu 16^{34} נסו לקולם fled *at* the sound of them, Ez 27^{28} Hb 3^{16} ψ 42^{8}. **g.** marking the aim, object, or consequence of an action or thing, *in view of, for, unto*: (*a*) Gn 1^{16} לממשלת היום *for* the rule of the day, 22^{7} where is the sheep לְעֹלָה? 42^{25} provision לַדָּרֶךְ *for* the way; Ex 20^{7} לַשָּׁוְא i.e. *for* a vain or frivolous purpose, similarly לָרִיק and לַשֶּׁקֶר; Lv 1^{3} + לִרְצֹנוֹ *for* his acceptance; Nu 21^{23} and oft. יצא למלחמה *for* battle; יָשַׁב לְ to sit (wait) *for*, Ex 24^{14} Hos 3^{3} Je 3^{2}; 1 S 8^{16} to use לִמְלַאכְתּוֹ *for* his business; 2 S 15^{2} + בָּא לַמִּשְׁפָּט *for* judgment; ψ 69^{22} לִצְמָאִי *for* (i.e. to quench) my thirst, Ne 9^{15}; Ex 29^{36} + לַיּוֹם *for* each day; Is 4^{3} כָּל־הַכָּתוּב לַחַיִּים *for* life; Ho 9^{4} לַחְמָם לְנַפְשָׁם; לרעה and לטובה Je 21^{10} +; Is 58^{4} ψ 63^{10} לְשׁוֹאָה יבקשו נפשי: in the sense of *to secure, compass*, Gn 41^{55} cried to Ph. לַלָּחֶם *for* bread, 1 S 2^{36} Am 8^{11} Jb 15^{23} Is 10^{3}: so in לְמַעַן *for* the purpose of; and with an inf. oft. (v. **7 a**). (*b*) corresponding to the Lat. *dat. commodi*, (*a*) with vbs., Gn 2^{18} אעשה לו I will make *for* him, etc., v^{20} 3^{21}, etc., absol. עָשָׂה לְ 1 S 14^{6} Is 64^{3}, פָּעַל לְ ψ 68^{29}; מָצָא לְ Gn 8^{9}; בָּכָה לְ, נוּד, סָפַד לְ Je 16$^{5.6}$, לָקַח לְ 24$^{3.4}$ + oft.; 22^{10}, etc.; Ju 16^{25} וִישַׂחֶק־לָנוּ to sport *for* us (for our pleasure); Ho 2^{25} Mi 5^{1}, etc.; with a pron. of the same pers. as the vb., as 1 K 20^{34} תשים לך, 2 K 6^{7} 10^{24}, Zc 9^{13}, leading on to **h** *a*, below; oft. with prons. and imv., Nu 11^{16} אֶסְפָה־לִּי gather *me* 70 men, 22^{6} אָרָה־לִּי curse *me* this people, 23^{1} בְּנֵה לִי, 1 K 1^{28} קראו לי לבת־שבע call *me* B., 3^{24} 13^{13} 17^{10} Ct 2^{15} אֶחֱזוּ לָנוּ catch *us* the foxes, Is 49^{20} גְּשָׁה־לִּי retire *for* me, that I may dwell, 2 S 18^{5} לְאַט לִי לַנַּעַר (act) gently (**5 i** *b*) *for my sake* towards the young man, 2 K 4^{24} אַל־תַּעֲצָר־לִי לִרְכֹּב AV slacken *me* not the riding; (*β*) with substs., e.g. in such phrases as פסח הוא לי׳ Ex 12^{11} a passover is it *unto* י׳, 13^{6} חַג לי׳, 16^{25} שַׁבָּת לי׳, Is 23^{18} + קֹדֶשׁ לי׳, Lv 1^{9} and oft. אִשֵּׁה רֵיחַ נִיחוֹחַ לי׳, 1 S 1^{3} כהנים לי׳, etc.; (*γ*) also as a *dat. incommodi*, as to lie in wait, lay snares, dig a pit, etc., *for* any one, Ju 9^{25} 16^{2} ψ 35^{7} 57^{7} etc.; with vbs. of withholding or removing (rare), Ju 17^{2} לֻקַּח לָךְ 1 S 21^{6} (cf. [Syriac]) ψ 40^{11} 84^{12} Jb 12^{20}; note also the phr. לְכַד הַמַּיִם (הַמַּעְבָּרוֹת) לְ Ju 3^{28} (RV), 7^{24} 12^{5}: זכר ל, in both senses, to remember *for* (in one's favour) Je 2^{2} +, *against* ψ 137^{7} +, cf. גער לְ Mal 3^{11} and 2^{3}. (*c*) more distinctly *on behalf of*, as with קִנֵּא to be jealous *for*, Nu 11^{29} +, נִלְחַם Dt 3^{22} +, שָׁמַר 7^{12} +, רָב לְ to contend *for* Ju 6^{31}, יָרֵא Jos 9^{24}, הִתְפַּלֵּל 1 S 2^{25} +, דִּבֵּר to speak *for* one 2 K 4^{13}, Jb 13^{7} הַלָּאֵל תְּדַבְּרוּ עַוְלָה will ye speak wickedness *on God's behalf?* שָׁאַל to ask 1 S 22^{13} +, עָבַר to pass over *for* (=to pardon) Am 7^{8}; Dt 30^{12} מי יעלה לנו, v^{13} Ju 1^{1} 20^{18} Is 6^{8} מִי יֵלֶךְ־לָנוּ; see also Ex 2^{19} 4^{16a} Nu 35^{31} Dt 23^{6} Jos 18^{6} Ju 5^{13} 7$^{4.20}$ 2 S 15^{34b} Is 33^{21} Pr 16^{26} 31^{8}, etc.; ψ 94^{16} מִי יָקוּם לִי עִם מְרֵעִים; היה ל׳ to be *on one's side*, Hos 1^{9} ואנכי לא אהיה לכם, ψ 124$^{1.2}$, and without היה Gn 31^{42} Ex 32^{26}, מִי לי׳ אֵלָי who is on י׳'s side? (let him come) to me! Jos 5^{13b} 2 S 20^{11} 2 K 10^{6} אִם לִי אַתֶּם (syn. אִתִּי 9^{32}), ψ 56^{10} זה ידעתי כי י׳ לי, 118$^{6.7}$ י׳ לִי. **h.** used reflexively (the 'ethical' dative, or dative of feeling), throwing the action back upon the subj., and expressing with some pathos the interest, or satisfaction, or completeness, with which it is (or is to be) accomplished, esp. (but not exclusively) with imv. and 1 pers. impf. (oft. not expressible in Engl., sts. to be expressed by a paraphr.);—(*a*) with *trans.* verbs (a choice idiom, a development of **g** *b a*, common, esp. with imv., in best prose), עֲשֵׂה לְךָ Gn 6^{14} Nu 21^{8} + oft., וַיַּעֲשׂוּ לָהֶם, Dt 4$^{16.23}$ 9^{16} Am 5^{26}, עֲשִׂיתֶם לָכֶם Gn 3^{7} Ex 32^{31} Ho 13^{2}, Je 11^{17} the evil which עשו להם they have *loved to do* (cf. Hi), Gn 11^{4} Ju 3^{16} 2 S 15^{1}, etc.; קַח־לְךָ, קְחוּ לָכֶם Gn 6^{21} + oft., ויקח לו Gn 15^{10}, etc.; בָּזַז לוֹ Dt 2^{35} 20^{14} +; תְּנוּ לָכֶם Ex 7^{9} Jos 20^{2}; הָבוּ לָכֶם Dt 1^{13} (cf. Dr) +, שִׂימוּ לָכֶם Ju 19^{30}, cf. 2 K 10^{24} Ho 2^{2}; בָּחַר לוֹ, בַּחֲרוּ לָכֶם, etc. Gn 13^{11} 2 S 17^{1} 𝔊 (v. Dr) + oft.; קְנֵה לְךָ Je 32^{7} +, דַּע לְךָ Jb 5^{27}, cf. Ct 1^{8}; Dt 10$^{1.1}$ 16$^{9.13.18}$ 19$^{2.3.9}$, Jos 22^{23} לִבְנוֹת לָנוּ, 1 S 20^{20} לְשַׁלַּח לִי לְמַטָּרָה, 2 K 4^{3} שַׁאֲלִי לָךְ (cf. Is 7^{11}), 18^{23} Is 44^{7} יַגִּידוּ לָמוֹ, 59^{8} עִקְּשׁוּ לָהֶם, Je 2^{13} 22^{14} אֶבְנֶה־לִּי, 31^{21} 46^{14} Ho 10^{1} פְּרִי יְשַׁוֶּה־לּוֹ maketh fruit *freely*, v$^{11.12.12}$ Am 6$^{5.13}$ ψ 44^{11} שָׁסוּ לָמוֹ=plunder *at their will*, 64^{6} 83^{13} Pr 1^{22} Ec 8^{12} מַאֲרִיךְ לוֹ (denoting satisfaction), Jb 7^{3} הָנְחַלְתִּי לִי, 12^{11} יִטְעַם לוֹ, 13^{1} וַתָּבֶן־לָהּ, 24^{16}, etc.: rarely separated from the vb., Ho 12^{9} Pr 23^{20} Jb 3^{14}. (*b*) with verbs of *motion*, Gn 12^{1} 22^{2} לֶךְ־לְךָ *get thee* away, 27^{43} בְּרַח לְךָ Am 7^{12}, Nu 22^{34} אשובה לי lit. I will return *for myself*, Dt 1^{7} (cf. Dr) סְעוּ לָכֶם, v^{40} 2^{13} עברו לכם, 5^{27} שובו לכם, 1 S 22^{5} 26^{11} נְטֵה לְךָ, 2 S 2^{21} וַיֵּלְכוּ לָהֶם, v^{12} וְנֵלְכָה לָנוּ, v^{22} 1 K 17^{3} Is 31^{8} נָס לוֹ, 40^{9} עֲלִי לָךְ, Je 5^{5} אֵלְכָה לִי, Hos 8^{9} a wild ass בּוֹדֵד לוֹ going alone *at its* *pleasure*, Mi 1[11] ψ 58[8] כמים יתהלכו למו that *run apace*, Pr 20[14] אֹזֵל לוֹ=*goeth his way*, Jb 39[4] Ct 1[8b] 2[10.11.13] 4[6]. (*c*) with *neuter* verbs, esp. those signifying a state of mind or feeling (chiefly poet.), ψ 66[7] אל ירומו למו, 80[7] ילעגו למו mock *as they please*, 120[6] רַבַּת שָֽׁכְנָה לָּהּ נַפְשִׁי has *had her* dwelling with, etc., 122[3] שֶׁחֻבְּרָה לָּהּ is *well* compacted, 123[4] שָֽׂבְעָה לָּהּ is *but too* full, Is 2[22] חִדְלוּ לָכֶם, 2 Ch 25[16] 35[21] Je 7[4] אַל־תִּבְטְחוּ לָכֶם, v[8] 2 K 18[21], Ez 37[11] נִגְזַרְנוּ לָנוּ we are *quite* cut off, Jb 6[19] קִוּוּ לָמוֹ (implying that they *fed themselves* on hope), 15[28] יֵשְׁבוּ לָמוֹ which should not sit (be inhabited), 19[29] גּוּרוּ לָכֶם, Ct 2[17] 8[14] דְּמֵה לְךָ, and the freq. הִשָּׁמֶר־לְךָ take heed *to* thyself Gn 24[6]+; with an adj., Am 2[13] הַמְלֵאָה לָהּ עָמִיר. (Cf. Ew[§ 315 a]. Very common in Syriac, esp. *b*: Nö[§ 224].) **i.** of reference to a norm or standard, *according to, after, by*:—(*a*) Gn 1[11] + oft. P לְמִינוֹ *acc. to* its kinds, 8[19] + לְמִשְׁפְּחֹתֵיהֶם *acc. to* their families, 10[5] אִישׁ לִלְשֹׁנוֹ, v[31.32], Ex 30[12] + לִפְקֻדֵיהֶם *acc. to* them that are numbered of them, Nu 1[2] לְבֵית אֲבוֹתָם *by* their fathers' houses, v[2] לְגֻלְגְּלֹתָם, v[3] לְצִבְאֹתָם, v[20] + oft., esp. in enumerations and classifications; Gn 13[3] Abram went לְמַסָּעָיו *by* his journeyings (stages), so לְמַסְעֵיהֶם Ex 17[1]+; Gn 13[17] go through the land לְאָרְכָּהּ וּלְרָחְבָּהּ *acc. to* (i.e. to the full extent of) its length and breadth (cf. Hb 1[6]); 41[47] לִקְמָצִים *by* handfuls, Nu 24[2]+ לִשְׁבָטָיו *by* its tribes, 1 S 29[2] עברים למאות ולאלפים *by* hundreds and thousands, 2 S 18[4], לְעָרֶיהָ Nu 32[33] Jos 18[9]; Ju 19[19] לַעֲצָמֶיהָ *acc. to* her bones (i.e. limb by limb), Ez 24[6] לִנְתָחֶיהָ piece by piece; ψ 140[12] to hunt לְמַדְחֵפֹת thrust-*wise*, with thrust upon thrust, Is 27[12] לְאַחַד אֶחָד (Ges Ew) *by* one, one (i.e. one by one); hence, esp. with plurals, it acquires sts. a *distributive* force, as לַבְּקָרִים Is 33[2] *by* mornings = *every* morning (cf. **6**), so ψ 73[14] לַבְּקָרִים 101[8]+, לִרְגָעִים Is 27[3]+ *every* moment, לֶחֳדָשִׁים Is 47[13] *every* month, Ez 47[12] 1 K 10[22] אַחַת לְשָׁלוֹשׁ שָׁנִים once *every* three years, Am 4[4] לשלשת ימים *every* three days (but v. We), 1 Ch 9[25]; in Chr לעיר ועיר, לשער ושער, 2 Ch 8[14] 19[5], 26[11]. (*b*) denoting the *principle*, with regard to which an act is done, לְמִסְפַּר *acc. to* the number of ... Dt 32[8] Ju 21[23]+, Is 11[3] to judge לְמַרְאֵה עֵינָיו, לְמִשְׁמַע אָזְנָיו *acc. to* that which his eyes see, his ears hear (cf. Lv 13[12] Jb 42[5]), 28[26], 32[1] a king will reign לְצֶדֶק *acc. to* justice (‖ לְמשפט), 42[3] לֶאֱמֶת=*faithfully*, Je 9[2] לֶאֱמוּנָה=*honestly*, 15[15] 30[11] (=46[28]) וְיִסַּרְתִּיךָ לַמִּשְׁפָּט (synon. 10[24] בְּמשפט), Ho 2[12] (‖ לְפִי), Jo 2[23] לִצְדָקָה; Gn 38[24] pregnant לִזְנוּנִים=*unchastely*, Nu 15[24] לשגגה *by* error (elsewhere בשגגה), 2 Ch 30[3] 35[8], Ct 7[10] flowing down למישרים *straightly* (Pr 23[31] ב׳), לָרֹב Jb 26[3] 2 Ch 14[14], poet. לְמַכְבִּיר Jb 36[31] *in* abundance, לְאַט=*gently* 2 S 18[5]+; Ex 16[3] ψ 78[25] לָשֹׂבַע *acc. to* satiety; לְרֶגֶל *acc. to* the foot (pace) of Gn 33[14]+ (v. רֶגֶל); 1 S 23[20] לְכָל־אַוַּת נַפְשְׁךָ (Dt 12[15] al. בְּ׳), 2 S 15[11] לְתֻמָּם *acc. to* their simplicity, i.e. unsuspectingly (so 1 K 22[34]), 1 K 9[11] לְכָל־חֶפְצוֹ, Is 54[16] Ez 22[6] לִזְרֹעוֹ, Jb 12[5] ψ 119[91.154] לְאִמְרָתֶךָ (‖ כְּ׳ v[58.116.170]), Ec 1[10] long ago לְעולמים *acc. to* (measured by) the ages etc. (v. Hi): so also in the phr. לְפִי חֶרֶב *acc. to* a sword's mouth, i.e. as the sword would devour, without quarter, Jos 6[21]+oft.; לְפִי.... itself also, in various fig. applications, has the force of *acc. to*, Gn 47[12], etc. (v. פֶּה); and in יֵשׁ (אֵין) לְאֵל יָדְךָ it is (not) *acc. to* the power of thy hand (v. p. 43). Similarly Dt 11[11] לִמְטַר הַשָּׁמַיִם *after the manner of* the rain of heaven, i.e. as the rain permits (opp. to the artificial irrigation of v[10]), Ju 21[12]+ לְמִשְׁכַּב זָכָר, Ez 12[12] לַעַיִן i.e. *as* the eye sees it. **j.** designating a condition or state: לָבֶטַח *in a state of* confidence=confidently, Lv 25[18]+oft.; לְבָדָד, לְבַד, *in a state of* separation (=apart), so לְבַדּוֹ (v. pp. 94, 95); לְשָׁלוֹם Gn 44[17]+, לְפֶתַע suddenly †Is 29[5] 30[13]; לִבְלִי *in a condition of* no ...=without, Is 5[14]+ (v. בלי), so ... לְאֵין (late, v. p. 35), לְלֹא †2 Ch 15[3]; further Is 1[5] לָחֳלִי *in a state of* sickness, 50[11] לְמַעֲצֵבָה, ψ 45[15] לִרְקָמוֹת, Ezr 2[63]=Ne 7[65] a priest לאורים ולתמים *having relation to* (i.e. *with*) U. and Th., 2 Ch 20[21] לְהַדְרַת קֹדֶשׁ=*in* holy adornment (cf. בְּ׳ ψ 29[2] 96[9]). And of a concomitant circumstance (Germ. *bei*), *in presence of, at*, Jb 29[3] לְאוֹרוֹ, Hb 3[11], ... לקול Jb 21[12] Ezr 3[13].

6. Of time: **a.** *towards, against*, sts. with collat. idea of *in view of*, much rarer than בְּ, but expressing concurrence (*at*) rather than duration (*in*): Gn 3[8] לְרוּחַ הַיּוֹם *at* the breeze of the day, לְעֵת in various connexions, as לְעֵת עֶרֶב Gn 8[11]+ (v. עֵת); לְעִתִּים מְזֻמָּנִים+ Ezr 10[14] Ne 10[35]; לְעִתּוֹת בַּצָּרָה+ ψ 9[10] 10[1]; ... לְיוֹם *at, on* the day of, ψ 81[4] Pr 7[20]+, ... מה תעשׂו לְיוֹם Is 10[3] Ho 9[5] (cf. Je 5^{31}); ... לְיוֹם אֲשֶׁר ... ,לְיָמִים אֲשֶׁר + Ez 22^{14}; לתקופת † Mal 3^{17}; לתשובת השנה 2 S 11^{1} +; הימים † 1 S 1^{20}, לתקופת השנה + 2 Ch 24^{23} (Ex 34^{22} without לְ), לְקֵץ שָׁנִים (יָמִים) (late) 2 Ch 18^{2} Ne 13^{6} Dn $11^{6.13}$ (in early Heb. מִקֵּץ יָמִים); ... לשנת † 2 Ch 15^{10}; ψ לַבֹּקֶר 30^{6} 49^{15} + (Ex 34^{2} after הֱיֵה נָכוֹן = *against, for;* cf. 19^{11} Pr 21^{31}); (לַבְּקָרִים Is 33^{2}, v. **5 i**); לערב Gn 49^{27} (‖ בבקר) +; לְמָחָר † Ex 8^{6} (in answer to v^{5} לְמָתַי), v^{19} Est 5^{12} (Nu 11^{18} Jos 7^{13} after הִתְקַדְּשׁוּ = *against*), לְמָחֳרָת Jon 4^{7} (cf. 1 Ch 29^{21}); לְמוֹעֵד ... לָמוֹעֵד, לְאוֹר Jb 24^{14}; Gn 17^{21} Ex 23^{15} +; לְפָנִים and לִפְנֵי *before* (oft.); לְאָחוֹר *hereafter*, † Is 41^{23} 42^{23}; ψ 32^{6b}; with inf. (rare), in the phr. לִפְנוֹת (הַ)בֹּקֶר (עֶרֶב) Gn 24^{63} +, 2 S 18^{29} Is 7^{15} לְדַעְתּוֹ *when* he knoweth. **b.** to denote the *close* of a period (rare), Gn 7^{4} לימים עוד שבעה, v^{10} Ex 19^{15} 2 S 13^{23} Am 4^{4} לשלשת ימים (We); Ezr $10^{8.9}$ Ne 6^{15} Dn 12^{7} (cf. עד 7^{25}) 2 Ch 21^{19} (so Syr.: v. PS ⟍ 5). **c.** *towards, to,* Ex 34^{25} לא ילין לַבֹּקֶר (usu. עַד, as 23^{18}), Dt 16^{4} 1 S 13^{8} (after נוחל), Am 4^{7} בעוד שלשה חדשים לַקָּצִיר *to* the harvest; oft. in the expressions לְעוֹלָם, לְדֹר דֹּר, לְדוֹר וָדוֹר, לָנֶצַח; rather differently in ψ 96^{2} מִיּוֹם לְיוֹם (‖ 1 Ch 16^{23} אל), Est 3^{7} (i.e. passing from day to day), cf. 2 S 14^{26} (Gie $^{30f.}$). **d.** *for, during,* Is 63^{18} לַמִּצְעָר (si vera l.), 2 Ch 11^{17} לשנים שלוש, 29^{17}.

7. With an *inf.* (Ges ^{§114,2}), ל denotes **a.** most commonly the end or purpose of an action (= the Lat. gerund with *ad*, e.g. *ad faciendum*, to do): Gn 1^{17} and he placed them in the firmament לְהָאִיר וְלִמְשֹׁל ... וּלְהַבְדִּיל *to* give light ..., and *to* rule ..., and *to* divide, etc., 2^{15} set him in the garden לְעָבְדָהּ וּלְשָׁמְרָהּ *to* till it, and *to* keep it, v^{9} brought them to Adam לִרְאוֹת *to* see, etc., + very oft.; Gn 19^{20} קְרֹבָה לָנוּס שָׁמָּה near *for* fleeing thither, Ec 3^{2} עֵת לָלֶדֶת a time *for* bringing forth. The neg. is expressed by לְבִלְתִּי, q.v. **b.** *with reference to,* limiting or qualifying the idea expressed by the principal vb., and so resolvable sts. into *so as to, to,* sts. into *in respect of, in:*—(*a*) *so as to, to,* Dt 8^{6} and keep the commands of י׳ לָלֶכֶת בִּדְרָכָיו וּלְיִרְאָה אֹתוֹ *to* walk in his ways, and *to* fear him, 10^{15} 11^{22} 19^{9} 1 K $2^{3.4}$ 11^{2} 1 S $20^{20.36}$ Jo 2^{26} אֲשֶׁר עָשָׂה עִמָּכֶם לְהַפְלִיא *so as to* do wondrously, Ez 5^{6}; Ju 5^{18} עַם חֵרֵף נַפְשׁוֹ לָמוּת *so as to* die, *for* dying [not '*unto* death'], 16^{16} 2 K 20^{1} חָלָה לָמוּת; Gn 2^{3} לַעֲשׂוֹת *so as to* make (or *in* making) which, he created; and in the very freq. לֵאמֹר, introducing the words spoken, *so as to say = saying* (Germ. *indem* er sagte), Gn 1^{22}, etc. (*b*) *in respect of, in* (cf. **5 e** (*b*)) Gn 34^{7} 1 S 12^{17} your evil is great that ye have done לִשְׁאוֹל לכם מלך *in* asking for yourselves a king, v^{29} 14^{33} the people sin against **J.** לאכל על־הדם *in* eating with the blood, 19^{5} 2 S 19^{7} 2 K 4^{24} Je 44^{18} ψ 36^{3} 63^{3} 78^{18} 101^{8} 103^{20} Ne 13^{18}. And with the *tert. compar.*, above, **5 e** (*b*). Esp. with verbs expressing what with us would be denoted by an adv. adjunct, but in Heb. idiom forms the principal idea, as 1 S 1^{12} הִרְבְּתָה לְהִתְפַּלֵּל lit. did much *in respect of* praying (= prayed long *or* much), Is 55^{7} כִּי יַרְבֶּה לִסְלוֹחַ +; 2 K 2^{10} הִקְשִׁיתָ לִשְׁאוֹל thou hast done hardly *in respect of* asking (= asked a hard thing), 1 K 14^{9} הֵרַע לַעֲשׂוֹת; so with הקריב Gn 12^{11}, מִהַר 27^{20}, הרחיק Ex 8^{24} הֶעְפִּיל Nu 14^{44}, הֵהִין Dt 1^{41}, בֹּשֵׁשׁ Ju 5^{28}, הפליא 13^{19} 2 Ch 26^{15} (with *pass.* vb.), שוב 1 K 13^{17} Ezr 9^{14}, היטיב Je 1^{12} + (without לְ 1 S 16^{17}), העמיק Is 29^{15} +, קֵרֵב Ez 36^{9}, הגדיל Jo 2^{20} +, קִדַּמְתִּי לִבְרֹחַ Jon 4^{2}, הגביה ψ 113^{5}, השפיל v^{6}; Gn 31^{27} נַחְבֵּאתָ לִבְרֹחַ hast hidden thyself *in regard to* fleeing = hast fled secretly, 2 S 19^{4} וַיִּתְגַּנֵּב לָבוֹא = come in stealthily. (*c*) by an extension of (*b*), the inf. with לְ so forms the complement of a verb that, if the verb be trans., it becomes virtually its *object:* so very oft. with such verbs as הוסיף *to add* Gn $4^{2.12}$, הֵחֵל *to begin* 6^{1}, חדל 11^{8}, יכל 13^{6}, נתן 18^{7}, מִהַר *to permit* 20^{6}, אבה 24^{5}, בקש Ex 2^{15}, מֵאֵן 7^{14}, למד Dt 14^{23}, חפץ 25^{8}, ידע 1 K 5^{20} (these all occur also without לְ); הואיל *to undertake, consent,* Gn $18^{17.31}$, כִּלָּה *to finish,* תָּמַם Dt 2^{16} (to come to an end *in respect of*), קִוָּה Is 5^{2}; also צִוָּה Gn 50^{2}, אָמַר Ex 2^{14}, דִּמָּה Nu 33^{56}, חשב 1 S 18^{25}, יעץ ψ 62^{5}, לִמֵּד Je 12^{16}, אָהֵב Ho 12^{8}: Dt 10^{12} what doth י׳ ask of thee כי אם ליראה except *to* fear etc.? (cf. Mi 6^{8} after דרש without ל). (*d*) as the *subj.* of a sentence (rare): Is 10^{7} להשמיד בלבבו, 1 Ch 29^{12}; with טוב 1 S 15^{22} ψ $118^{8.9}$ Ec $7^{2.5}$ Pr 21^{9} (usu. without לְ, as v^{19} 25^{24} Ex 14^{12}); cf. Ex 8^{22} לא נכון לעשות כן; 2 S 18^{11} וְעָלַי לָתֵת, Ne 13^{13} Ezr 10^{12}; Mi 3^{1} הלא לכם לדעת, Ezr 4^{3} 2 Ch 13^{5} 20^{17} 26^{18}. (*e*) with אֵין, יֵשׁ (late), and (more rarely) לֹא, in sense of *it is* (*not*) *possible to ...*, or (sts.) *there is no need to ...:* see יֵשׁ **2 c** *c* (p. 442); אַיִן **5** (p. 34^{b}), adding Hag 1^{6} Est 8^{8} 2 Ch 22^{9}; לֹא **1 a** *b* (p. 518): and cf. Dr ^{§202} Ges $^{§114\,l}$ Dav $^{§94\,b,\,95\,b}$. (*f*) with הָיָה, to express the idea of *destination,* as Nu 24^{22} וקין יהיה

לְבָעֵר shall be *for consuming*, Dt 31^{17} Is 5^5 6^{13} 37^{26} Ez 30^{16} ψ 109^{13}+. Cf. מַה לַעֲשׂוֹת *what is (was) to be done?* Is 5^4 2 K 4^{13} 2 Ch 25^9+(Dr$^{§ 203}$). (*g*) expressing (acc. to the context) *tendency, intention,* or *obligation* (the 'periphrastic' future):—Ho 9^{13} וְאֶפְרַיִם לְהוֹצִיא אֶל הֹרֵג בָּנָיו *is for* bringing forth (=*must* bring forth), Is 10^{32} עוד היום בנב לעמד *is he for* tarrying (*must he* tarry), 38^{20} י׳ להושיעני *'י is* (*ready*) *to* save me, 44^{14} (si vera l.), Jer 51^{49} Hb 1^{17} ψ 32^9 49^{15} צוּרָם לְבַלּוֹת שְׁאוֹל = *must* Sheol waste away, 62^{10} בְּמֹאזְנַיִם לַעֲלוֹת, Pr 18^{24} 19^8 שומר תבונה למצא טוב *will be finding* prosperity, 20^{25} Jb 30^6 1 Ch 22^5 (לִבְנוֹת), Ec 3^{15}: of past time, Gn 15^{12} ויהי השמש לבוא *was about to* go down, Jos 2^5 1 S 14^{21b} (txt. dub.: Dr$^{§ 206 \, Obs.}$), 2 Ch 26^5 (strangely) ויהי לדרש אלהים RV *set himself to* seek; usu. without היה, 2 S 4^{10} אֲשֶׁר לְתִתִּי לוֹ to whom *it was for my* giving (*I ought to have* given), 2 K 13^{19} לְהַכּוֹת *percutiendum erat*, 1 Ch 9^{25}, and more freely 2 Ch 11^{22} כי להמליכו for (he was) *for making* him king, 12^{12} ולא להשחית and *was no longer for* destroying him, 36^{19}(?): in a question, Gn 30^{15} וְלָקַחַת and *art thou for* taking? Est 7^8 2 Ch 19^2 הֲלָרָשָׁע לַעְזֹר *wilt thou help* the wicked? Cf. Dr$^{§ 204}$, Ges$^{§ 114 \, h-k}$, Dav$^{§ 94}$. (*h*) with לְ, in contin. (mostly) of a finite vb. or ptcp., Ex 32^{29} מִלְאוּ יֶדְכֶם ... וְלָתֵת and *be for placing* etc. Lv $10^{10 f.}$ (?), 1 S 8^{12} יִקַּח ... וְלָשׂוּם, Je 19^{12} עשׂה ... וְלָתֵת, 44^{14} Ho 12^3 ψ 25^{14} 109^{16} Jb 34^8 Ec 7^{25} 9^1 (si vera l.), Dn 12^{11} Neh 8^{13} 1 Ch 10^{13} 2 Ch 2^8 7^{17} 8^{13} 30^9, Ez 13^{22}; Am 8^4 הַשֹּׁאֲפִים אֶבְיוֹן וְלַשְׁבִּית וגו׳ *and* (that are) *for making* the poor to cease, Is 44^{28} הָאֹמֵר ... וְלֵאמֹר, 56^6 ψ 104^{21} Je 17^{10} 44^{19} 1 Ch 6^{34} (cf. Dr$^{§ 206}$ Dav$^{§ 96 \, R. 4}$).—On לְמִן, v. מִן.

Note.—1 K 6^{19} לְתִתֵּן שָׁם, the supposition that לְ is a conj. (=למען) is too alien to Heb. usage to be justified by the Ar. لِ for لِكَى, and the view that תִּתֵּן here and 17^{14} is an anom. form for תֵּת (Ew$^{§ 238 c}$ Kö$^{i. 305}$) is against analogy: rd. with Ol$^{§ 224 d}$, Ges$^{§ 67 A. 3}$, Klo, לָתֵת (as 17^{14} Qr).

3926 †לְמוֹ poet. for לְ (v. מוֹ) Jb 27^{14} 29^{21} 38^{40} 40^4.

3808 **לֹא** or **לוֹא** **adv.** not (Ar. لَا, Aram. לָא, ܠܐ, Sab. לא, Ass. *lâ*; not in Eth.: cf. Kö$^{ii. 1. 236}$ Walker$^{AJSL \, 1896, 237 ff.}$)—לוֹא, acc. to Mass. (Fr$^{MM \, 248}$), 35 t., besides בְּלוֹא 6 t., and הֲלוֹא, the orthogr. of which varies much (*ib.*$^{p. 251}$), e.g. in S always הֲלוֹא, in Chr always הֲלֹא, on the whole הֲלוֹא 141 t., הֲלֹא 128 t.; twice, acc. to Mass., written לו (Qr לֹא), 1 S 2^{16} 20^2, once לה Dt 3^{11} Kt:—*not*—denying objectively, like οὐ (not μή = אַל):—**1.** in predication: **a.** with a *verb;* so most freq., and nearly always (*a*) with the finite tenses, whether pf. (Gn 2^{5b} 4^5 etc.) or impf. (3^4 $8^{21.22}$ etc.); in short circumst. clauses, as Gn 44^4 לא הרחיקו, Is 40^{20} לֹא יִמּוֹט, and with a final force 41^7 Ex 28^{32} (v. Ges$^{§ 156. 3 \, R. b, c}$ Dr$^{§ 162}$). Governing two closely connected verbs (Dr$^{§ 115, לא}$) Ex 28^{43} וְלֹא יִשְׂאוּ עָוֺן וָמֵתוּ, Lv $19^{12.29 b}$ Dt $7^{25.26}$ 19^{10} 22^1 al.; and two parallel clauses (Ges$^{§ 152. 3}$) Is 23^{4b} ψ 9^{19} 44^{19} Jb 3^{11} al. With the impf., esp. with 2 ps., לא often expresses (not, like אַל, a deprecation, *do not ..., let not ...*, but) a *prohibition*, as Gn 2^{17} לֹא תֹאכַל מִמֶּנּוּ thou *shalt not* eat of it, $3^{1.3}$ Ex 20^3 לֹא־יִהְיֶה לְךָ there *shall not* be to thee, etc., v^{13} לא תגנב, etc. With the coh. and juss. moods (which are negatived regularly by אַל), it occurs only exceptionally (Ges$^{§ 109. 1 b \, R. 1}$), Gn 24^8 1 S 14^{36} 2 S 17^{12} 18^{14} 1 K 2^6 Ez 48^{14}. (*b*) with the inf. (which is negatived by בִּלְתִּי, q.v.), only once, in בְּלֹא (**4 a**), and with לְ, in the sense of *cannot*, or *must not;* †Ju 1^{19} כי לא להוריש for it *was not* (possible) *to* dispossess, etc. Am 6^{10} לא להזכיר בשם י׳, 1 Ch 5^1 15^2 (Dr$^{§ 202. 2}$); cf. Aram. לָא Dan 6^9 Ezr 6^8. On its use with the ptcp., see **b** *c*. (*c*) לא always negatives properly the word immed. following: hence, in a verbal sentence, where this is not the verb, some special stress rests upon it, Gn 32^{29} לֹא יַעֲקֹב יֵאָמֵר עוֹד וגו׳ *not Jacob* shall thy name be called any more, but Israel, 45^8 לֹא אַתֶּם שְׁלַחְתֶּם אֹתִי *Not ye* (in our idiom: It is not ye who) have sent me hither, but God, Ex 16^8 1 S 8^7 כִּי לֹא אֹתְךָ מָאָסוּ כִּי אֹתִי וגו׳, ψ 115^{17}; without a foll. correcting clause, Gn 38^9 Nu 16^{29}: לֹא י׳ שְׁלָחָנִי *Not* י׳ (but another) hath sent me, Dt 32^{27} לא י׳ פָּעַל זֹאת, 1 Ch 17^4 Dt 8^9 Is 28^{28} ... לא לנצח *not for ever* (but only for a while) ... (so 57^{16} ψ 9^{19} 49^{18} 103^9; but Is 13^{20} לא תשב לנצח is, will *not be inhabited* for ever), Is 43^{22} Jb 13^{16} 32^9; hence rhetorically, insinuating something very different, not named, 2 K 6^{10} *not* once, and *not* twice (but repeatedly), Ezr 10^{13} Je 4^{11} a wind לֹא לִזְרוֹת וְלוֹא לְהָבַר: *not* to winnow, and *not* to cleanse (but to exterminate), Is 45^{13} 48^{1b} Jos 24^{12} Dn $11^{20.29}$ Jb 34^{20} לֹא בְיָד (but by a Divine agency: cf. Dn 2^{34}; also Jb 20^{26} אֵשׁ לֹא נֻפָּח fire *not* blown upon [but kindled from heaven],

Lam 4[6]; and אין Is 47[14]). (*d*) standing alone: (*a*) אִם־לֹא *if not*, Gn 18[21] וְאִם־לֹא אֵדָ֑עָה: , 29[49] 42[16] Jb 9[24] 24[25]; (*β*) הֲ . . . אִם־לֹא, *or not*, Gn 24[21] waiting to know הַהִצְלִיחַ י׳ דַּרְכּוֹ אִם־לֹא, 27[21] 37[32] Ex 16[4] Nu 11[23] Dt 8[2] Ju 2[22] (cf. אַיִן, אִם אַיִן **2 d** *β*, *δ*). In answer to a question or request, to deny, or decline, *Nay, No*: Ju 12[5] ויאמר לא, Hg 2[12]; לא אדני Gn 23[11] 42[10] 1 S 1[15]+; oft. sq. כי, *No: for* . . . = *No: but* . . ., Gn 18[15] ויאמר לֹא כִּי צָחָקְתְּ, 19[2] Jos 5[14] 24[21] 1 S 2[16] Qr (v. Dr), 10[19] (𝔊 MSS), 2 S 16[18] 24[24] 1 K 3[22.22]+; Jb 23[6] (strangely). (Cf., in deprecation, אַל.) (*e*) with an interrog. force, which however does not lie in לא as such, but (as in other cases) in the contrast with a preceding clause, or in the tone of voice (cf. וְ **1** *f*; Ew[§ 324 a] Ges[§ 150. 1] Dr[1 S 11, 12]): Jon 4[11] אַתָּה חַסְתָּ . . . וַאֲנִי לֹא אָחוּס וגו׳, Jb 2[10]; 22[11]; Ex 8[22]; 2 K 5[26] Je 49[9] (‖ Ob [5] הֲלוֹא), Mal 2[15] La 3[38]; and in passages, exeg. or text. doubtful (v. Comm.), 1 S 20[14] 2 S 23[5] (but v. Bu), Ho 10[9] (Ew We), 11[5] (Ew), Jb 14[16b] (but 𝔊 Ew Di תַעֲבֹר), La 1[12] (Ew Ke), 3[36] (Ke Bä). **b.** with *adjs.* and *substs.*: (*a*) Gn 2[18] לֹא טוֹב הֱיוֹת הָאָדָם לְבַדּוֹ *not good* is man's being alone, Ex 18[17]+oft. (*b*) Ex 4[16] לֹא אִישׁ דְּבָרִים אָנֹכִי, Am 7[14] לא נביא אנכי, Nu 23[9] לֹא אִישׁ אֵל וִיכַזֵּב, Dt 17[15] (v. אשר **2** *b*) 20[20] 32[47] 1 S 15[29] 2 S 18[20] לֹא אִישׁ בְּשֹׂרָה אַתָּה הַיּוֹם, 21[2] 1 K 22[33] 2 K 6[19] לא זה הדרך, Mi 2[10] Is 27[11] Ho 8[6]; והמה לא אלהים Je 2[11] 16[20] 2 K 19[18]; 1 K 19[11.11] לֹא בְרַעַשׁ י׳ ‖) לא כי היא, Dt 30[12.13] Jb 15[9] 28[14] אין עִמָּדִי), ψ 74[9] Je 5[10] לוא לי׳ המה, 10[16]; Dt 32[21] בָּנִים לֹא אֵמֻן בָּם, Je 10[14] Hb 1[14] Jb 16[17] 38[26] מִדְבָּר לֹא אָדָם בּוֹ; 1 K 22[17] לֹא אֲדֹנִים לָאֵלֶּה, Je 49[31] ψ 22[3] ולא עֹזֵר לוֹ, Jb 18[17.19] 29[12] וְלֹא דוּמִיָּה לִי, 30[13] 33[9]; Je 2[19] וְלֹא פַחְדָּתִי אֵלַיִךְ and (that) my terror reached not unto thee, Jb 21[9]; abs. Gn 29[7] לֹא־עֵת הֵאָסֵף הַמִּקְנֶה (Hg 1[2]), Nu 20[5] 2 K 4[23] לא חדש ולא שבת, Is 44[9] Je 5[12] ויאמרו לוא הוא, Jb 9[32] 22[16] 36[26] 41[2]; Pr 19[7] (si vera l.) מְרַדֵּף אֲמָרִים לֹא־הֵמָּה words which *are not*, which *are nought*. (*c*) with the ptcp. לא is rare, a finite vb. being usu. preferred (Ex 34[7] וְנַקֵּה לֹא יְנַקֶּה: Ew[§ 320 c] Dr[§ 162]): 2 S 3[34] יָדֶיךָ לֹא אֲסֻרוֹת, Ez 4[14] 22[24] Dt 28[61] ψ 38[15] כְּאִישׁ אֲשֶׁר לֹא שֹׁמֵעַ who is *not hearing*, Jb 12[3] 13[2] לֹא נֹפֵל אָנֹכִי מִכֶּם, Zp 3[5] (very anom.); 1 K 10[21] לא is prob. text. err. In וְהוּא לֹא שֹׂנֵא לוֹ or לא שנא הוא לו, Dt 4[42] 19[4.6] Jos 20[5] (cf. אֹיֵב Nu 35[23]), שֹׂנֵא is best construed as a subst., he being a *not-hater* to him aforetime.—In most of the cases under *b*, *c*, אין could have been employed; but the negation by לא is more pointed and forcible.

2. Not in predication: **a.** coupled to an adj. to negative it, like the Gk. ἀ-, but usu. by way of litotes: Ho 13[13] בן לא־חכם an *unwise* son, ψ 36[5] דֶּרֶךְ לֹא טוֹב a way *not good*, 43[1] גוי לא חסיד, Pr 16[29] 30[25.26] Ez 20[25] 2 Ch 30[17]: Is 16[14] לוֹא כַבִּיר, cf. 10[7] לֹא מְעַט. **b.** with a ptcp. Je 2[2] ארץ לא זרועה, 18[15] (the finite verb is more common: see Is 62[12] עִיר לֹא נֶעֱזָבָה (cf. 54[11]), Je 6[8] אֶרֶץ לוֹא נוֹשָׁבָה, 15[18] 22[6] 31[18] Zp 2[1]). **c.** †Gn 15[13] בארץ לא להם, Je 5[19] Hab 1[6] מִשְׁכָּנוֹת לֹא־לוֹ, Pr 26[17] רִיב לֹא־לוֹ. **d.** with a subst., in poetry, forming a kind of compound, expressing pointedly its antithesis or negation (Germ. *un-* is sts. used similarly): Dt 32[5(?).17.21a] they made me jealous בְּלֹא אֵל with a *not-God* (with what in no respect deserved the name of God), v[b] בְּלֹא עָם i.e. with an unorganized horde, Am 6[13] הַשְּׂמֵחִים לְלֹא דָבָר i.e. at a thing wh. *is not*, an unreality (of their boasted strength), Is 10[15] כְּהָרִים מַטֶּה לֹא עֵץ like a rod's lifting up *what is no wood* (but the agent wielding it), 31[8] חרב לא איש, חרב לא אדם, 55[2] בלוא לחם for *what is not bread*, בלוא לשׂבעה for *what is not* for satiety, Je 5[7] וַיִּשָּׁבְעוּ בְּלֹא אֱלֹהִים by *not-gods*, in late prose 2 Ch 13[9] כֹּהֵן לְלֹא אֱלֹהִים; ψ 44[13] תִּמְכֹּר עַמְּךָ בְלֹא־הוֹן for *no-value* (i.e. cheaply), Pr 13[23] Jb 10[12] צלמות וְלֹא סְדָרִים darkness and *disorder*; so לֹא־עַמִּי Ho 1[9] 2[25]: still more pregnantly Jb 26[2a] מֶה־עָזַרְתָּ לְלֹא־כֹחַ (poet. for לאשר אין לו כח) the *powerless*, v[2b.3a] (Ew[§ 286 g] Ges[§ 152. 1 n.]), 39[16] הִקְשִׁיחַ בָּנֶיהָ לְלֹא לָהּ useth hardly her young ones (making them) into *none of hers*; and even Hb 2[6] הַמַּרְבֶּה לֹא־לוֹ *what is not his own* (cf. Jb 18[15] מִבְּלִי לוֹ). Cf. with a verb, and ellipse of אשר, Is 65[1] לְלוֹא שָׁאָלוּ to those who have not asked, v[b] Je 2[8] אַחֲרֵי לֹא יוֹעִילוּ, v[11 b]; also לֹא רֻחָמָה Ho 1[6.8] 2[25], and prob. Jb 31[31] לֹא נִשְׂבָּע (pf. in p.) one *not satisfied*. **e.** in circ. clauses (Dr[§ 164]), poet. and rare: qualifying a subst., 2 S 23[4] בֹּקֶר לֹא עָבוֹת a morning *without clouds*, Job 12[24] בְּתֹהוּ לֹא דָרֶךְ in a *pathless* waste, 38[26a]; and a verb Jb 34[24] יָרֹעַ כַּבִּירִים לֹא חֵקֶר *without inquiry*, ψ 59[4] לא פשעי ולא חטאתי (cf. v[4] בלי עון), in late prose, twice, 1 Ch 2[30.32] וימת לא בנים (אַיִן and בְּלִי, q.v., are more usual in such cases).

3. Once (acc. to many MSS), as a subst., Jb 6^{21} כִּי־עַתָּה הֱיִיתֶם לֹא for now are ye become *nothing*, Hi De Kö (cf. Dn 4^{32} (Aram.) כְּלָה חֲשִׁיבִין, 𝔗 here הֲוֵיתוּן כְּלָא, and אַל Jb 24^{25}); but reading fluctuates (Orientals לֹא, Qr לוֹ, Westerns, Baer (v. pp. 37, 56) לוֹ [' now are ye become *that*,' viz. the נַחַל אַכְזָב of v^{15}]; but even לוֹ yields a forced sense; and text is prob. wrong: Mich Ew Ol Sgf Bu כֵּן...לִי (𝔊 𝔖 also rd. לִי); Bö Di כִּי...לְאַיִן. Cf. Kö $^{ii. 1. 236 f.}$

4. With prefixes:—**a.** †בְּלֹא$_{31}$ (chiefly poet. or late), acc. to the varying signif. of בְּ: (*a*) usu. *with not*=*without*, Je 22^{13} בונה ביתו בלא־צדק *without* justice (‖ בלא משפט; so Ez 22^{29} Pr 16^{8}), Is $55^{1.1}$ Pr 19^{2}, Jb 8^{11} הֲיִגְאֶה־גֹּמֶא בְּלֹא בִצָּה *without* mire (‖ בלי מים), 30^{28} בְּלֹא חַמָּה (= not *through* the sun), La 1^{6} וילכו בלא־כח, Nu 35^{22} בְּלֹא אֵיבָה...בְּלֹא צְדִיָּה, v^{23} (sq. inf.) בְּלֹא רְאוֹת, 2 Ch 21^{20} Ec 10^{11}; ψ 17^{1} תְּפִלָּתִי בְּלֹא שִׂפְתֵי מִרְמָה; used more freely in Chr, 1 Ch 12^{18} בְּלֹא חָמָס בְּכַפַּי; v^{34} בְּלֹא לֵב וָלֵב, 2 Ch 30^{18} בְּלֹא כַכָּתוּב. With ellipse of rel., La 4^{14} בְּלֹא יוּכְלוּ יִגְּעוּ *without* (that) men are able to touch, etc. (*b*) of time, *in not*, i.e. *outside of*, Lv 15^{25} בְּלֹא עֶת־נִדָּתָהּ, *before* Jb 15^{32} בלא־יומו, Ec 7^{17} בְּלֹא עִתֶּךָ: (*c*) where לֹא belongs to the foll. word, and is only accidentally preceded by ב (v. supr. **2 d**), Dt $32^{21.21}$ Je 5^{7} Pr 13^{23} בלא משפט through *injustice*; with בְּ *pretii*, ψ 44^{13} Is $55^{2.2}$ Je 2^{11} בְּלוֹא יוֹעִיל *for* (that which) *profiteth not*.

b. הֲלֹא *nonne?* Gn 4^{7}+oft. Inviting, as it does, an affirmative answer, it is often used, (*a*) esp. in conversation, for pointing to a fact in such a way as to arouse the interest of the person addressed, or to win his assent: Gn 13^{19} *Is not* the whole land before thee? 19^{20} 20^{5} 27^{36} 29^{25} Ex 4^{11} Who maketh dumb or deaf, etc.? *Do not* I? 33^{16} Ju $4^{6.14}$ 8^{2} $9^{28.38}$ 1 S $9^{20.21}$ 15^{17}etc.; with a vb. in 1 ps., Jos 1^{9} הלא צויתיך, Ju 6^{14} הלא שלחתיך, 1 S 20^{30} 2 S 19^{23} Ru 2^{9}: similarly in a poet. or rhet. style, Ju 5^{30} הלא ימצאו יחלקו שלל, Is 8^{19} $10^{8.9.11}$ 28^{25} 29^{17} $40^{21.28}$ 42^{24} 43^{19} etc., Jb $4^{6.21}$ 7^{1} $10^{10.20}$, etc. (*β*) it has a tendency to become little more than an affirm. particle, declaring with some rhetor. emph. what is, or might be, well known: Dt 3^{11} הֲלֹה הִיא בְּרַבַּת בְּנֵי עַמּוֹן, 11^{30} 1 S 21^{12} הלוא זה דוד וג׳ (cf. $29^{3.5}$ 2 S 11^{3}), 23^{19} 26^{1} 2 S 15^{35}; it is thus nearly=הִנֵּה (𝔊 sts. represents it by ἰδού, as Jos 1^{9} Ju 6^{14} Ru 2^{9} 2 S 15^{35}); so esp. in the phrase of the compiler of K, And the rest of the acts of ..., הֲלֹא הֵם (הֵמָּה) כְּתוּבִים *are* they *not* written in, etc.? 1 K 11^{41} 14^{29}+oft. (with which there interchanges הִנָּם כְּתוּבִים 1 K 14^{19} 2 K 15^{11} $15^{26.31}$, which is gen. used by the Chr, 2 Ch 16^{11} 20^{34}, etc.), Jos 10^{13} (cf. 2 S 1^{18} הִנֵּה), 1 K 8^{53} 𝔊, Est 10^{2}; ψ 56^{14}(strangely: contr. 116^{8}).—הֲלֹא הִנֵּה +Hb 2^{13} 2 Ch 25^{26} (הִנָּם).—On Ju 14^{15}, see הֲ **1** *end*.

c. †וְלֹא *and not*=*and if not*, 2 S 13^{26} 2 K 5^{17}. Comp. וְיֵשׁ. **d.** †כְּלוֹא Ob ^{16} והיו כלוא היו, poet. for כאשׁר, *as though* they had not been.

e. †לְלֹא *without*, lit. *in the condition of no* ... 2 Ch 15^{3} (comp. לְאַיִן, also in Chr). Elsewhere לֹא belongs to the foll. word, Am 6^{13} 2 Ch 13^{9} Is $65^{1.1}$ Jb $26^{2.3}$ 39^{16} (v. supr. **2 d**).

Note.—Fifteen times, acc. to Mas. (v. De $^{ψ 100, 3}$ Fr $^{MM 247}$ Str $^{Prol. Cr. 84}$), לֹא is written by error for לוֹ, viz. Ex 21^{8} Lv 11^{21} 25^{30} 1 S 2^{3} 2 S 16^{18} 2 K 8^{10} Is 9^{2} 63^{9} ψ 100^{3} 139^{16} Jb 13^{15} 41^{4} Pr 19^{7} 26^{2} Ezr 4^{2} (always with Qr לוֹ). The passages must be considered each upon its own merits: in some לוֹ yields a preferable sense; but this is not the case in all. There is the same קרי (rightly) on Is 49^{5} 1 Ch 11^{20}; but these were not considered to rest upon equal authority, and are hence not reckoned with the fifteen.—In Ju 21^{22} (v. GFM), 1 S 13^{13} $20^{14.14}$, and in Jb 9^{33} (לֹא יֵשׁ), rd. prob. לֻא for לֹא.

†לוֹ דְבָר, לֹא דְבָר **n.pr.loc.** in Gilead, 3810
near, perh. east of, Mahanaim (q.v.);—לֹא ד׳ 2 S 17^{27} (𝔊 Λωδαβαρ, Λαδαβαρ); Gr We rd. also לֹא דְבָר Am 6^{13}= same city (but v. Dr); =לוֹ ד׳ 2 S $9^{4.5}$ (𝔊 Λαδαβαρ); perh. also intended in לִדְבִר מִמַּחֲנַיִם עַד־גְּבוּל Jos 13^{26} (cf. Di Bla; 𝔊 Δαιβων, A Δαβειρ, 𝔊L Δεβηρ); v. II. דְּבִיר, p. 184 supr.

לֹא עַמִּי **n.pr.m.** (*not my people*: see לֹא 3818
2 d) symb. name of Hosea's son, Ho 1^{9}, cf. 2^{25} (v. also $2^{1.3}$).

לֹא רֻחָמָה **n.pr.f.** (*uncompassionated:* Ges 3819
$^{§ 152 a, N}$) symb. name of Hosea's daughter, Ho $1^{6.8}$, cf. 2^{25} (v. also 2^{3}).

לֻא 2 S 18^{12} Kt (Qr לוּ) **if**: v. לוּ. p. 530 3863

לאב (√of foll., cf. Ar. لَابَ (med. و) *be thirsty*, لَابَةٌ, لُوبَةٌ *a stony tract* of land (v. Wetzst $^{Reisebericht 99}$)).

†[תַּלְאֻבָה] **n.f. drought**;—only pl. intens., 8514
בַּמִּדְבָּר בְּאֶרֶץ תַּלְאֻבוֹת Ho 13^{5}.

3811 †[לָאָה] **vb.** be weary, impatient (cf. Ar. لَأَى *be slow, hesitating* (Frey); بَعْدَ لَأْيٍ *after difficulty*, لَأْيًا *with difficulty* (Lane^{3007}); Aram. (לְעֵי, לְעָא, לְאֵי);—**Qal** *Impf.* 2 ms. תִּלְאֶה Jb 4^{2}; וַתֵּלֶא Jb 4^{5}; 3 pl. וַיִּלְאוּ Gn 19^{11};—*be weary* (in vain endeavour) sq. Inf. Gn 19^{11}; *be weary, impatient* at attempted consolation abs. Jb 4^{2}; at calamity abs. Jb 4^{5} (|| תִּבָּהֵל). **Niph.** *Pf.* נִלְאָה Pr 26^{15} + 2 t.; 2 fs. נִלְאֵית Is 47^{13}; נִלְאֵיתִי Is 1^{14} + 3 t., etc.;—sq. inf. *be weary* of doing a thing, Ex 7^{18} (JE), *make oneself weary* in doing something Pr 26^{15} (of sluggard's laziness), *weary* (i.e. strenuously exert) *oneself* to Je 9^{4} 20^{9}; abs. of eager and hopeless prayer נִל׳ עַל־הַבָּמָה Moab, Is 16^{12} (|| וּבָא אֶל־מִקְדָּשׁוֹ לְהִתְפַּלֵּל ,נִרְאָה); of vain consultations, (sq. בְּ) Babylon Is 47^{13}; subj. י׳, sq. inf. Is 1^{14}; Je 6^{11} 15^{6}, always of exhausted patience; fig. of parched soil (abs.) ψ 68^{10}. **Hiph.** *Pf.* 3 ms. sf. הֶלְאָנִי Jb 16^{7}; 3 fs. הֶלְאָת Ez 24^{12} (del. 𝔊 Co), 1 s. sf. הֶלְאֵתִיךָ Mi 6^{3}; *Impf.* וַיַּלְאוּךָ Je 12^{5}; תַּלְאוּ Is 7^{13}; *Inf. cstr.* הַלְאוֹת Is 7^{13};—*weary, make weary, exhaust*, sq. acc. Jb 16^{7} (subj. God); *exhaust patience of*, obj. God Is 7^{13}; obj. men Is 7^{13} Je 12^{5} Mi 6^{3}.

8513 †תְּלָאָה **n.f.** weariness, hardship;—ת׳ Ex 18^{8} + 4 t.; of distress of Isr. in Egypt Nu 20^{14}; in wilderness Ex 18^{8} (both JE); from Assyr., Bab., etc. Ne 9^{32}; cf. La 3^{5} (|| רֹאשׁ, gall); Mal 1^{13}.

3812 לֵאָה$_{34}$ **n.pr.f.** Leah, elder daughter of Laban, and wife of Jacob (perh. = *wild-cow*, Ar. لَأًى, (لَآةٌ) [cf. רָחֵל *ewe*], Dl$^{Prol. 80}$ RS$^{K 219}$ and (doubtfully) Nö$^{ZMG\ xl.\ 1886,\ 167}$; also Gray$^{Heb.\ Names,\ 96}$; others, as Hpt$^{GGN\ 1883,\ 100}$ comp. As. *li'at*, in sense *mistress;* on poss. relation of לֵאָה to לֵוִי v. לֵוִי);—mother of Reuben, Simeon, Levi, Judah, Issachar, Zebulun and Dinah; Gn $29^{16.17.23.24.25.30.31.32}$ (cf. vv$^{33.34.35}$) 30^{9} + 15 t. Gn 31, 32, $33^{1.2.7}$ 34^{1} $35^{23.26}$ $46^{15.18}$ 49^{31} Ru 4^{11}; 𝔊 Λ(ε)ια.

3813 †לָאַט **vb.** cover, only **Qal** *Pf.* 3 ms. וְהַמֶּלֶךְ לָ׳ אֶת־פָּנָיו 2 S 19^{5}, rd. perh. לָאַט, fr. לוט We Dr Bu.

3814 לָאט Ju 4^{21}, etc., v. לוט. p. 532

328 לָאט, לַאַט *gently*, v. אַט sub אטט p. 31 supr.

לאך (√ of מַלְאָךְ, מְלָאכָה, cf. Ar. أَلَكَ, لَأَكَ *send*, مَلْأَكٌ *messenger*, Eth. ለአከ: *send a messenger*, v. ተለአከ: *be sent, wait on, minister;* መልአክ: = Heb. מַלְאָךְ; cf. Ph. מלאך *messenger;* NH מַלְאָךְ, Aram. מַלְאֲכָא, as in Heb.)

מַלְאָךְ$_{214}$ **n.m.** messenger;—מ׳ Ex 23^{20} + 4397
48 t.; cstr. מַלְאַךְ Gn 16^{7} + 69 t.; sfs. מַלְאָכִי Ex 23^{23} + 3 t.; מַלְאָכוֹ Gn $24^{7.40}$; pl. מַלְאָכִים Gn 32^{4} + 63 t. + מלאכים 2 S 11^{1} Kt (< Qr מלכים); cstr. מַלְאֲכֵי Gn 28^{12} + 11 t.; מַלְאָכֶיךָ Nu 24^{12}, 2 K 19^{23}; מַלְאָכֵכֵה Na 2^{14} error for מַלְאָכַיִכִי = מַלְאָכַיִךְ Ges$^{§ 91, (2) Anm. 2}$ or < for מַלְאָכֵךְ by dittogr. fr. foll. הוי Kö$^{ii. 1. 571}$). מַלְאָכָיו 2 Ch 36^{15} + 8 t.;—**1.** *messenger*, **a.** one sent with a message Gn 32^{4} + 8 t. JE; Dt 2^{26}, (not in P); Ju 6^{35} + 8 t.; 1 S 6^{21} + 51 t. S K, 1 Ch 14^{1} $19^{2.16}$ 2 Ch 18^{12} 35^{21} Ne 6^{3} Jb 1^{14} Pr 13^{17} 17^{11} Is 14^{32} 18^{2} 30^{4} $37^{9.14}$ Je 27^{3} Ez 17^{15} $23^{16.40}$ 30^{9} Na 2^{14}; מלאכי שלום, messengers of peace Is 33^{7}. **b.** a prophet Is 42^{19} 44^{26} 2 Ch $36^{15.16}$ Hg 1^{13}; the herald of the advent מלאכי Mal 3^{1}. **c.** priest Mal 2^{7}, prob. Ec 5^{5} (RV *angel*). **d.** || מֵלִיץ Jb 33^{23}, a messenger from God acting as an interpreter and declaring what is right (*angel* of RV too specific). **e.** fig. מ׳ רָעִים *messengers of evil* ψ 78^{49}; מ׳ מות *messengers of death* Pr 16^{14}; || רוחות *winds his messengers* ψ 104^{4}. **2.** *angel*, as messenger of God, מלאכים with God in theophanies Gn $19^{1.15}$ 28^{12} 32^{2} (JE), praising him; ψ 103^{20} 148^{2}; in his sight not without error Jb 4^{18} charged with the care of the pious ψ 91^{11}; elsewhere *sg.* sent to a prophet 1 K 13^{18} $19^{5.7}$ 2 K $1^{3.15}$ Zc 1^{9} + 18 t. in Zc 1–6; excellent, wise, powerful 1 S 29^{9} 2 S $14^{17.20}$ 19^{28} Zc 12^{8}; encamping about the faithful ψ 34^{8}; chasing his enemies ψ $35^{5.6}$; destroying by judgment of Yahweh 2 S $24^{16.17}$ = 1 Ch 21^{12-30}; 2 K 19^{35} = Is 37^{36} = 2 Ch 32^{21}. †**3.** *the theophanic angel* מ׳ (ה)אלהים in the story of E: Gn 21^{17} 31^{11} Ex 14^{19}, also in Ju 6^{20} $13^{6.9}$; מ׳ יהוה in the story of J: Gn $16^{7.9.10.11}$ $22^{11.15}$ Ex 3^{2} Nu $22^{22.23.24.25.26.27.31.32.34.35}$ and in Ju $2^{1.4}$ 5^{23} $6^{11.12.21.21.22.22}$ $13^{3.13.15.16.16.17.18.20.20.21}$, הַמַּלְאָךְ Gn 48^{16} (E); מַלְאָךְ Ex 23^{20} (E), 33^{2} Nu 20^{16} (JE), Ho 12^{5}; מַלְאָכִי Ex 23^{23} (E), 32^{34} (J); מַלְאָכוֹ Gn $24^{7.40}$ (J), מ׳ פניו Is 63^{9} (referring to the ancient מלאך); מ׳ הברית Mal 3^{1} (referring to the advent of י׳ for judgment, see Br$^{MP\ 473}$). The theophanic angel is not mentioned in D and P.

מְלָאכָה$_{167}$ **n.f.** occupation, work (for 4399
*מַלְאָכָה; cf. Ph. מלאכת *labour*)—מ׳ Ex 12^{16} + 102 t.; מְלֶאכֶת 2 Ch 13^{10}; cstr. מְלֶאכֶת Ex 35^{24} + 42 t.; sf. מְלַאכְתְּךָ Jon 1^{8}; מְלַאכְתֶּךָ Ex 20^{9} + 2 t.;

מְלַאכְתּוֹ Gn 2^2 + 13 t.; pl. cstr. מַלְאֲכוֹת 1 Ch 28^{19}; sf. מַלְאֲכוֹתֶיךָ ψ 73^{28};—**1.** *occupation, business*, מַה מְּלַאכְתְּךָ *what is thy occupation* Jon 1^8; business of a steward Gn 39^{11} (J); diligent in business Pr 22^{29}; slack in business 18^9. **2.** *property* in which one is occupied, מ׳ רעהו *his neighbour's property* Ex $22^{7.10}$ (E); possessions of herds and flocks Gn 33^{14} (J), 1 S 15^9 (cf. מִקְנֶה); מ׳ רבה *great property* 2 Ch 17^{13}. **3.** *work* as something done or made: **a.** of God in creation Gn $2^{2.2.3}$ (P), in judgment Je 50^{25}, in general ψ 73^{28}. **b.** of men, מ׳ עור *leather-work* Lv $13^{48.51}$ (P), מ׳ השדה *work in the field* 1 Ch 27^{26}; in building Pr 24^{27}+, the walls of Jerusalem Ne 4^5+, making the tabernacle and its furniture Ex 36^2+, the temple 1 K 5^{30}+; work of the potter Je 18^3, of the seaman ψ 107^{23}, of the Levites 1 Ch 26^{29}, of priests in the sacrifices 2 Ch 29^{34}; †מְלֶאכֶת (הָ)עֲבֹדָה phrase of P, Ex 35^{24} $36^{1.3}$ Lv $23^{7.8.21.25.35.36}$ Nu $28^{18.25.26}$ $29^{1.12.35}$ also 1 Ch $9^{13.19}$ $28^{13.20}$ 2 Ch 24^{12}; המ׳ לעבדה 1 Ch 23^{24}; עבדה למ׳ Ex 36^5 (P); cf. the phrase עֹשֵׂה המ׳ *workmen* Ezr 3^9 Ne 2^{16}; עֹשִׂים במ׳ 1 K 5^{30} 9^{23}+; כל מ׳ *any work* forbidden on the Sabbath Ex $20^{9.10}$ Lv 23^3 (P) Dt $5^{13.14}$ Je $17^{22.24}$; on holy convocations Ex 12^{16} Lv 16^{29} $23^{28.30.31}$ Nu 29^7 (P). †**4.** *workmanship*, כל מלאכה *in every kind of workmanship*, phrase of P: Ex $31^{3.5}$ $35^{29.31.33.35}$; and Chr: 1 Ch 22^{15} 28^{21} 29^5; 1 K 7^{14}. †**5.** *service, use* Lv 7^{24} 11^{32} Ju 16^{11} Ez 28^{13}. †**6.** *public business:* **a.** *political* 1 K 11^{28} 1 Ch 29^6 Dn 8^{27} Est 3^9 9^3. **b.** *religious*, putting away foreign wives Ezr 10^{13}; מ׳ יהוה 1 Ch 26^{30}; מ׳ הַקֹּדֶשׁ Ex 36^4 38^{24} (P), מ׳ קדש הקדשים 1 Ch 6^{34}; מ׳ אהל מועד Ex 35^{21} (P), מ׳ בית י׳ 1 Ch 23^4 Ezr 3^8 6^{22} Ne 10^{34} 11^{22}.

4400 †[מַלְאָכוּת] **n.f.** message, cstr. מַלְאֲכוּת Hg 1^{13}.

4401 †מַלְאָכִי appar. **n.pr.m. Malachi**, Mal 1^1, but in fact not historical name of author, nor pseudonym for Ezra; prob. a conjecture based on 3^1; so many moderns; see Dr[Intr.]

3815 †לָאֵל **n.pr.m.** (*belonging to God;* cf. Palm. לשמש: v. Nö[WZKM, 1892, 314] Gray[Heb. Names, 207]) a Gershonite-Levite; Nu 3^{24}, 𝔊 Δαηλ, Δαουηλ.

לאם (√ of foll.; cf. Ar. لَأَمَ *bind up*, or *together*, III. *reconcile, bring together* (Thes Ba[NB § 65 n. 2]); > Lag[BN 180] who comp. لَؤُمَ *be low, ignoble*, لِئَامٌ [pl.] *common ones*, hence לְאֹם prop. *common, vulgar people*).

†לְאֹם, לְאוֹם **n.m.** [Gn 25, 23] **people**, poet. and chiefly late;—ל׳ abs. Gn $25^{23.23}$ Pr 14^{28}, לְאוֹם Pr 11^{26}; sf. לְאֻמִּי Is 51^4; pl. לְאֻמִּים Gn 25^{23} + 28 t.; לְאוּמִּים Is 55^4;—*people*, both of Isr. and of Edom, Gn $25^{23.23.23}$ (J; Jacob and Esau; ‖ גּוֹי); elsewhere of Isr. only Is 51^4 (sg. ‖ עַם); usu. pl. of other peoples:—שְׁאוֹן ל׳ Is 17^{12} (‖ הֲמוֹן עמים), cf. v^{13}; ‖ גּוֹיִם Is 34^1 43^9 ψ 2^1 $44^{3.15}$ 105^{44} 149^7, cf. Is $55^{4.4}$ (גּוֹי in v^5); ‖ עַמִּים Gn 27^{29} (J), Hb 2^{13} Je 51^{58} ψ 47^4 57^{10} $67^{5.5}$ 108^4 Pr 24^{24}; further Is 41^1 49^1 (both ‖ אִיִּים), 43^4 (‖ אָדָם), 60^2 (‖ אֶרֶץ), ψ 9^9 (‖ תֵּבֵל), 148^{11} (‖ מַלְכֵי אֶרֶץ, etc.); עֲדַת לְאֻמִּים ψ 7^8, הֲמוֹן ל׳ 65^8; of any and all *peoples* Pr 14^{34}; sg. indef. = *people* in gen., as making public opinion, 11^{26} (coll., c. pl. vb.); = *population*, as subjects of prince 14^{28} (‖ עַם). 3816

†לְאֻמִּים **n.pr.gent.**, as 'son' of Dedan Gn 25^3. 𝔊𝔏 Λοωμ(ι)ειμ. (Sab. n.pr. trib. לאמם, לאימם SabDenkm [11]). 3817

לֵב v. sub לבב infr. p. 524 3820

לבא (√ of foll.; v. Ar. لَبُؤَةٌ, لَبْأَةٌ, لَبَاءَةٌ *lioness*, cf. לָבִיא; v. perh. also Ph. n.pr. לבא CIS [i. 147]; Jastrow [JBL xi. (1892) 120 f.] comp. Tel el-Am. n.pr. *Labâ'* (Bez [BM] *Labay[a]*); poss. is also *Lapaya*, which Wkl [TA, 1896] rds.; deriv. only poet.)

†[לָבִי] **n.[m., f.]** lion;—only pl. and fig. of foes נַפְשִׁי בְּתוֹךְ לְבָאִם ψ 57^5; of Assyrians Na 2^{13} (‖ גֹּרֹתָיו; sf. ref. to אַרְיֵה). 3833

†לְבִיָּא **n.f.** lioness (on format. v. Lag [BN 93]);—Ez 19^2 (‖ אֲרָיוֹת) fig. of mother of Isr. 3833

†לָבִיא **n.[m.]** lion, poss. also **[f.]** lioness (cf. Ar. usage, and Gn 49^9 Nu 24^9 Jb 4^{11}, etc.; but this by no means certain);—ל׳ abs. Gn 49^9 + 10 t.;—Is 30^6 (‖ לַיִשׁ), Jb 38^{39} (‖ כְּפִיר); Gn 49^9 in sim. of victor's repose (רָבַץ ‖ אַרְיֵה), cf. Nu 24^9 (c. שָׁכַב ‖ אֲרִי), Dt 33^{20} (שָׁכֵן וְטָרַף); v. also Nu 23^{24} (קוּם ‖ אֲרִי); fig. of Nineveh Na 2^{12} (‖ אַרְיֵה), cf. Is 5^{29} (שְׁאָגָה in sim.; ‖ כְּפִירִים); fig. of wicked Jb 4^{11} (+ לַיִשׁ, כְּפִיר, שַׁחַל, אַרְיֵה $v^{10.11}$); sim. of י׳, devouring (אָכַל) in judgment Ho 13^8; fig. of locusts מְתַלְּעוֹת ל׳ Jo 1^6 (‖ שִׁנֵּי אַרְיֵה). 3833

†לְבָאוֹת **n.pr.loc.** a city in S. Judah, Jos 15^{32}, 𝔊 Λαβως, 𝔊𝔏 Λαβωθ = בֵּית ל׳ (q.v. p. 111 supr.) Jos 19^6, 𝔊 Βαθαρωθ, 𝔊𝔏 Βηθλεβαωθ. Site unknown. 3822

†לבב (mng. dub.; Dl$^{Pr. 88 ff.}$ finds orig. mng. in As. *labâbu, in unruhiger Bewegung sein*;—√ of לֵב, לֵבָב; cf. NH *id.*, As. *libbu*, Aram. לִבָּא, ܠܶܒܳܐ, Eth. ልብ: Ar. لُبّ, Sab. לב, Sab. Denkm.$^{p. 13, No. 1, l. 7}$);—the literary usage of לֵב and לֵבָב is: **1.** earliest poetry, J and E chiefly, Eph doc. of Ju S K chiefly, Am Ho Zc 9–11 Is 15 use לֵב. **2.** לֵבָב first appears in Is and certain strata of E and Eph doc. of Ju S K, and is continued in Zp Na (prob.) D H Dt
3820 editors and some ψψ. **3.** Je Ez Jb prefer לֵב
3824 but use occasionally לֵבָב. **4.** Is$^{2.3}$ La and exilic ψψ use לֵב. **5.** Is 13–14^{23} Je 50–51 Hg Zc 1–8 Jo Jon ψ 25, 90, 104, use לבב. **6.** Mal Ob Zc 12–14 Memorials of Ezr and Ne Pr Ru Ct and many ψψ of Persian period use לֵב. **7.** Chr and Dn use לֵבָב. **8.** Ec Est and latest ψψ use לֵב. Exceptions will be noted and suspected passages indicated by ? under לבב and לב which are treated apart. See Br. 'Study of the use of לב and לבב in the O.T.' in *Semitic Studies in Memory of Dr. Kohut*, Berlin, 1897.

3824 †לֵבָב† 251 **n.m.** ψ$^{104, 15}$ inner man, mind, will, heart;—abs. ל׳ Dt 28^{28} + 31 t.; cstr. לְבַב Dt 20^{8} + 22 t.; sf. לְבָבִי Is 21^{4} + 24 t.; לְבָבְךָ Dt 4^{29} + 35 t.; לְבָבֶךָ Dt 4^{39} + 21 t.; לְבָבֵךְ 1 S 1^{8} + 3 t.; לְבָבוֹ Dt 2^{30} + 37 t.; לְבָבָהּ Zp 2^{15} + 3 t.; לְבָבֵנוּ Dt 1^{28} + 3 t.; לְבַבְכֶם Dt 10^{16} + 37 t.; לְבָבָם Lv 26^{41} + 22 t.; pl. לְבְבֵהֶן Na 2^{8} (Sta § 353 a rds. לִבְבֵהֶן, but see Kö ii. 78); pl. לְבָבוֹת 1 Ch 28^{9}.—*The inner, middle, or central part:* **I.** seldom of *things* בְּלֵבַב יַמִּים *in the midst of the seas*, Jon 2^{3} (poetry); עד לבב השמים *unto the midst of heaven* Dt 4^{11} (so Sam but MT לב). **II.** usu. *of men:* **1.** *the inner man* in contrast with the outer, כלה שארי ולבבי *my flesh and my heart (soul) doth fail* ψ 73^{26}; antithesis with garments Jo 2^{13}; hands ψ 73^{13} La 3^{41} (?); eyes Nu 15^{39} (H) 1 S 16^{7}; ears Ez 3^{10}; mouth Dt 30^{14}; speech ψ 28^{3} 78^{18}; מְתֹפְפֹת עַל־לִבְבֵהֶן *tabering upon their breasts* Na 2^{7} (inner for outer). **2.** the *inner man*, indef. the *soul*, comprehending mind, affections and will, or, in connexion with certain verbs, having more specific reference to some one of them. בכל־לבב ובכל־נפש *with all the heart and with all the soul* Dt 4^{29} 6^{5} 10^{12} 11^{13} 13^{4} 26^{16} 30$^{2.6.10}$ Jos 22^{5} 23^{14} 1 K 2^{4} 8^{48} (= 2 Ch 6^{38} לב ?) 2 K 23^{25} 2 Ch 15^{12} 34^{31} (= 2 K 23^{3} לב ?) Je 32^{41}; abbr. בכל־לבב 1 S 7^{3} 12$^{20.24}$ 1 K 14^{8} 2 K 10^{31} 2 Ch 15^{5} 22^{9} 31^{21} ψ 86^{12} 111^{1} Je 29^{13} Jo 2^{12}; אשר בלבב *what is in the heart* (mind) Dt 8^{2} 1 S 9^{19} 14^{7} 2 S 7^{3} (= 1 Ch 17^{2}) 2 K 10^{30}; 2 Ch 32^{31}; cf. Jb 10^{13}, ψ 84^{6} (?); שִׂיחַ עם לבב *with the heart* (mind), c. ידע Dt 8^{5}, ψ 77^{7}, usu. c. (היה), of a thought or purpose, Dt 15^{9} Jos 14^{7} 1 K 8$^{17.18.18}$ (= 2 Ch 6$^{7.8.8}$) 10^{2} (= 2 Ch 9^{1}) 1 Ch 22^{7} 28^{2} 2 Ch 1^{11} 29^{10} (cf. 24^{4} לב); כלבב *according to the heart* 1 S 13^{14} 14^{7} ψ 20^{7}. We may add Dt 5^{26} 11$^{16.18}$ 17^{17} 1 S 2^{35} 2 S 19^{15} 1 K 8$^{39.39}$ (= 2 Ch 6$^{30.30}$) 11$^{2.3}$ (לב an error) v$^{4.9}$ 1 Ch 12^{17} 22^{19} 28^{9} ψ 62^{9} 86^{11} 139^{23} Is 7^{2} Dn 11$^{27.28}$. **3.** specific ref. to *mind* (characteristic of לבב): **a.** אַנְשֵׁי לֵבָב *men of mind* Jb 34$^{10.34}$; גם לי לבב *I also have a mind* Jb 12^{3}; הוֹלֵלוֹת בְּל׳ *madness is in (their) mind* Ec 9^{3} (?); וַתִּגְנֹב לְבָבִי *and thou didst steal my mind* Gn 31^{26} (E, the לֵב of v^{20} should be corrected to לבב cf. 'steal me' v^{27}). **b.** *knowledge*, c. ידע Dt 8^{5} 23^{14} 1 K 2^{44}; הבין Is 6^{10} 32^{4}; חֲכַם לֵבָב *wise of mind* Jb 9^{4}; לְבַב חָכְמָה *mind of wisdom* ψ 90^{12}. **c.** *thinking, reflection*, c. חשב Is 10^{7} Zc 7^{10} 8^{17}; (שׂיח ψ 77^{7} supr.); יצר מחשבות ל׳ *conception of thoughts of mind* 1 Ch 29^{18}; מַשְׂכִּיּוֹת ל׳ *imaginations of (their) mind* ψ 73^{7}; מוֹרָשֵׁי ל׳ *possessions (thoughts) of (my) mind* Jb 17^{11}; שׂם לבב *set the mind, consider* Hg 2$^{15.18.18}$, c. לְ Dt 32^{46}, על Hg 1$^{5.7}$. **d.** of *memory* שׂם בלבב *lay up in the mind* 1 S 21^{13} Jb 22^{22}; השיב אל ל׳ *lay to heart, call to mind* Dt 4^{39} 30^{1} 2 Ch 6^{37} (= 1 K 8^{47} לב ?); עלה על ל׳ *come upon the mind* Je 51^{50} Ez 38^{10} (cf. לֵב **3 d**); סור מל׳ *depart from the mind* Dt 4^{9}; שמר בתוך ל׳ *keep in the midst of (thy) mind* Pr 4^{21}; על ל׳ *upon the mind* Dt 6^{6}. **4.** spec. ref. to *inclinations, resolutions, determinations of the will* (characteristic of ל׳): הכין ל׳ *set the mind*, c. אֶל 1 S 7^{3} 1 Ch 29^{18}, לְ 2 Ch 20^{33} לדרש 2 Ch 19^{3} 30^{19} Ezr 7^{10}; נתן ל׳ לדרש Jos 24^{23} (E) 1 K 8^{58}; הטה ל׳ אֶל 1 Ch 22^{19}, cf. 2 Ch 11^{16}; ל׳ פנה מעם *mind turn away from* Dt 29^{17} 30^{17}; יֵהָפֵךְ ל׳ פ׳ *Pharaoh's mind was changed* Ex 14^{5} (E). **5.** spec. ref. to *conscience* לא יחרף לבבי *my heart (conscience) shall not reproach me* Jb 27^{6}. **6.** spec. ref. to *moral character* (characteristic of ל׳): God tries the ל׳ 1 Ch 29^{17}: **a.** יֹשֶׁר ל׳ *uprightness of heart* Dt 9^{5} 1 Ch 29^{17}, ψ 119^{7} (?); יִשְׁרֵי ל׳ 2 Ch 29^{34}; יָשָׁר ל׳ 1 K 3^{6}; יִשְׁרַת ל׳ 2 K 10$^{15.15.15}$; תָּם־ל׳ *integrity of heart* Gn 20$^{5.6}$ (E) 1 K 9^{4} ψ 78^{72} 101^{2}; (עִם) ל׳ שָׁלֵם *heart perfect* (with) 1 K 8^{61} 11^{4} 15$^{3.14}$ (= 2 Ch 15^{17}) 2 K 20^{3} (= Is 38^{3} לֵב ?)

1 Ch 12^{39} 29^{19} 2 Ch 16^{9} 19^{9} 25^{2}; בַּר־ל׳ *pure in heart* ψ 24^{4}; בָּרֵי ל׳ ψ 73^{1}. We may add 2 K 22^{19} = 2 Ch 34^{27}, Ne 9^{8} Je 32^{40}. **b.** it is the seat of naughtiness 1 S 17^{28} (?), erring ψ 95^{10}; is froward ψ 101^{4}. **c.** seat of pride, ψ 101^{5} Is 9^{8} 10^{12}, 60^{5} (?) Ez 28$^{5.6(?)}$ Dn 8^{25}; רָם ל׳ *heart is lifted up* Dt 8^{14} 17^{20} Ez 31^{10} Dn 11^{12}. **d.** is circumcised Dt 10^{16} 30^{6} Je 4^{4}, or uncircumcised Lv 26^{41} (H); is hardened אמץ ל׳ Dt 2^{30} 15^{7} 2 Ch 36^{13}; כבד ל׳ 1 S 6^{6} (?); הקשה ל׳ ψ 95^{8}. **7.** = *the man himself* (meaning characteristic of נֶפֶשׁ) אמר בל׳ *say in the heart* (*to oneself*) Dt 7^{17} 8^{17} 9^{4} 18^{21} ψ 4^{5} Is 14^{3} 47^{8} 49^{21} Je 5^{24} 13^{22} Zp 1^{12} 2^{15}; ללבב Ho 7^{2} (?); דבר בל׳ ψ 15^{2}; ברכו בל׳ Jb 1^{5}; התברך בל׳ Dt 29^{18}; יְחִי לְבַבְכֶם *let your heart* (you yourselves) *live* ψ 22^{27} 69^{33} (cf. 119^{175}). **8.** spec. as the *seat of the appetites* (for which usually נֶפֶשׁ) סעד ל׳ *stay the heart* (with food) ψ 104^{15} Ju 19^{8} (?); יִיטַב לְבָבֶךָ *that thine heart may be merry* (with wine) Ju 19^{9} (?); יַיִן יְשַׂמַּח ל׳ *wine gladdens the heart* ψ 104^{15}. **9.** spec. of *seat of the emotions and passions* (for which usually נפש): **a.** of joy Is 30^{29} Je 15^{16} Ez 36^{5}, gladness Dt 28^{47}, desire Pr 6^{25} (?); דבר על ל׳ *speak into the heart* (comfortably) 2 Ch 32^{6} (elsewhere לֵב). **b.** of trouble 1 K 8^{38} ψ 25^{17} 73^{21}; weakness, faintness Lv 26^{36} (H) Dt 20$^{3.18}$ 2 Ch 13^{7} Is 1^{5} 7^{4} Je 51^{46}, grief Dt 15^{10} 1 S 1^{8}, sorrow ψ 13^{3}, fear Dt 28^{67}, dismay Is 21^{4}, astonishment Dt 28^{28}, anger 19^{6}, hate Lv 19^{16} (H); ימס ל׳ *the heart melteth* Dt 20^{8} Jos 2^{11} 5^{1} 7^{5} (all D) Is 13^{7} 19^{1}; המס ל׳ Dt 1^{28} (so rd. prob. also Jos 14^{8}, where לֵב error). **10.** *seat of courage* (for which usually רוּחַ), יָעֵר כֹּחוֹ וּלְבָבוֹ *stir up his power and his courage* Dn 11^{25}; יַאֲמֵץ לְבַבְכֶם *let your heart take courage* ψ 31^{25}.

3820 לֵב$_{599}$ **n.m.** $^{\text{Pr 23, 15}}$ (†**f.** Pr 12^{25}, fr. influence of נֶפֶשׁ v. De Now) **inner man, mind, will, heart**, abs. and cstr. לֵב Gn 8^{21} + 239 t.; לֶב־ Ex 15^{8} + 15 t.; sf. לִבִּי Gn 24^{45} + 102 t.; לִבְּךָ Ex 9^{14} + 28 t.; לִבֵּךְ Ju 19^{6} + 25 t.; לִבֵּךְ Is 47^{7} + 7 t.; לִבּוֹ Gn 6^{5} + 93 t.; לִבָּהּ Ju 19^{3} + 7 t.; לִבֵּנוּ Is 41^{22} + 5 t.; לִבְּכֶם Gn 8^{5} + 2 t.; לִבָּם Gn 42^{28} + 56 t.; לִבְּהֶן Ex 35^{26}; לִבְּהֶן Ez 13^{17}; pl. לִבּוֹת ψ 7^{10} Pr 15^{11} + 3 t. Pr.; sf. לִבֹּתָם Is 44^{18}; לִבּוֹתָם ψ 125^{4}.— *inner part, midst:* **I.** seldom of things, בְּלֶב־יָם *in the midst of the sea* Ex 15^{8} Pr 23^{34} 30^{19}; בְּלֵב יַמִּים ψ 46^{3} Ez 27$^{4.25.26.27}$ 28$^{2.8}$ בלב האלה 2 S 18^{14}; בְּלֵב אֹיְבֵי *in the midst of the enemies of* ψ 45^{2} (v. Br$^{\text{MP in loco}}$; AV RV al. *in the heart of*). **II.** elsewhere of men: †**1.** *the inner man* in contrast with outer לבי ובשׂרי ירננו *my heart and my flesh cry out* ψ 84^{3}; ‖ מעים ψ 22^{15} Je 4^{19}, the inner for outer מעים Je 49^{22}; as within the breast על לב Ex 28$^{3.29.30.30}$ (P); מלב 2 K 9^{24}; בלב ψ 37^{15} 2 S 18^{14}; סְגוֹר לִבָּם Ho 13^{8}; antithesis with בָּשָׂר Pr 14^{30} Ec 2^{3}; head Is 1^{5}, face Ez 14$^{3.4.7}$; arm Ct 8^{6}; hands Ez 22^{14}; bones ψ 102^{5}; eyes 1 K 9^{3} (= 2 Ch 7^{16}) Je 22^{17}; ear Pr 22^{17} 23^{12}; mouth ψ 55^{22}; lips Is 29^{13}; אֲנִי יְשֵׁנָה וְלִבִּי עֵר *I slept but my heart waked* Ct 5^{2}. **2.** *the inner man*, indef., *soul*, comprehending mind, affections and will, with occasional emphasis of one or the other by means of certain verbs: † בכל לב 1 K 8^{23} (= 2 Ch 6^{14}) ψ 9^{2} 119$^{2.10.34.58.69.145}$ 138^{1} Pr 3^{5} Je 3^{10} 24^{7}; † עם לב 2 Ch 24^{4} (see לבב **2**); † כלב 2 S 7^{21} (= 1 Ch 17^{19}) Je 3^{15}; תַּעֲלֻמוֹת לֵב *secrets of the heart* ψ 44^{22}; לֵב מְלָכִים אֵין חֵקֶר *the heart of kings is unsearchable* Pr 25^{3}; הַיֹּצֵר יַחַד לִבָּם ψ 33^{15} etc. **3.** specific reference to *mind:* **a.** † מִלִּבִּי of *one's own mind* Nu 16^{28} 24^{13} (JE) 1 K 12^{33} Ne 6^{8} Ez 13$^{2.17}$; † חֲסַר לֵב *destitute of mind* Pr 6^{32} 7^{7} 9$^{4.16}$ 10$^{13.21}$ 11^{12} 12^{11} 15^{21} 17^{18} 24^{30}; לִבּוֹ חָסֵר Ec 10^{3}; אֵין לֵב Je 5^{21} Ho 7^{11}; לב אין Pr 17^{16}; קנה לב *get a mind* Pr 15^{32} 19^{8}; כֹּחַ לב *power of mind* Jb 36^{5}; רֹחַב לב *breadth of mind* 1 K 5^{9}, גנב לב 2 S 15^{6} Gn 31^{20} (E? see לבב **3 a**). **b.** *knowledge*, c. † ידע Dt 29^{3} Pr 14^{10} 22^{17} Ec 1^{17} 7$^{22.25}$ 8$^{5.16}$ Je 24^{7}; ראה ψ 66^{18} Ec 1^{16}; חָכַם לב *mind is wise* Pr 23^{15}; † לֵב חָכָם *wise mind* 1 K 3^{12} Pr 16^{23} Ec 8^{5}; † חֲכַם לֵב Ex 31^{6} 35^{10} 36$^{1.2.8}$ (P) Pr 10^{8} 11^{29} 16^{21}; † חַכְמֵי לֵב Ex 28^{3} (P) Jb 37^{24}; † חכמת לב Ex 35$^{25.35}$ (P); לב חכמים Ec 7^{4} 10^{2}; לב כסילים Pr 12^{23} 15^{7} Ec 7^{4} 10^{2}; c. חכמה Ex 36^{2} (P) 1 K 10^{24} (= 2 Ch 9^{23}) Pr 2^{10} 17^{16} Ec 2^{3}; † לֵב נָבוֹן *intelligent mind* Pr 14^{33} 15^{14} 18^{15}; with הבין Pr 8^{5}; תְּבוּנָה Pr 2^{2}; שֵׂכֶל Jb 17^{4} etc. **c.** *thinking, reflection*, c. חשב ψ 140^{3} Pr 16^{9}; מחשבות Gn 6^{5} (J) ψ 33^{11} Pr 6^{18} 19^{21} cf. Gn 8^{21} (J); הגה *muse, study* Pr 15^{28} 24^{2} Is 33^{18} 59^{13}; הגיון ψ 19^{15}; הָגוּת ψ 49^{4}; † שׂם לב *set the mind, consider* Is 41^{22} Ez 44^{5}, c. לְ 1 S 9^{20} 2 S 13^{20} Ez 40^{4} 44^{5}; אֶל Ex 9^{21} (J) 1 S 24^{25} 2 S 18$^{3.3}$ Jb 2^{3} 34^{14}; עַל Jb 1^{8}; † שׁת לב ψ 62^{10} Pr 22^{17} 24^{32}, c. לְ Ex 7^{23} (JE) 1 S 4^{20} ψ 48^{14} Pr 27^{23} Je 31^{21}, אֶל Jb 7^{17}. **d.** *memory* † השיב אל לב *call to mind* Is 44^{19} La 3^{21}; על לב Is 46^{8}; † עלה על לב *come into mind* (occur to one) Is 65^{17} Je 3^{16} 7^{31}

19^5 32^{35} (cf. Acts 7^{23}), so בא על לב 2 Ch 7^{11}; †שׂם על לב *lay to heart* Is 42^{25} 47^7 57$^{1.11}$ Je 12^{11} Mal 2$^{2.2}$ Dn 1^8; אל לב 2 S 13^{33} 19^{20} כתב על לב Je 31^{33}; קשׁר על לב Pr 6^{21}; †לוּחַ לֵב *tablet of the memory* Pr 3^3 7^3 Je 17^1; נִשְׁכַּחְתִּי כְּמֵת מִלֵּב *I am forgotten as a dead man out of mind* ψ 31^{13}. **4.** spec. ref. to *inclinations, resolutions and determinations of the will;* †הכין לב *set the mind* 2 Ch 12^{14} ψ 10^{17} 78^8 Jb 11^{13}; †נכון לב ψ 57$^{8.8}$ (=108^2) 78^{37} 112^7; †נתן לב לְ Ec 1$^{13.17}$ 7^{21} 8$^{9.16}$; †נתן אל לב Ec 7^2 9^1; Ne 2^{12} 7^5, בלב Ex 35^{34} (P) Ezr 7^{27} Ec 3^{11}; †אֲשֶׁר־נְשָׂאוֹ לִבּוֹ *whose heart stirred him up* Ex 35^{21} 36^2 cf. 35^{26} (all P); †נְדִיב לֵב *willing of mind* Ex 35$^{5.22}$ (P) 2 Ch 29^{31} cf. Ex 25^2 35^{29} (P); †נטה לב אחרי *inclined to follow* Ju 9^3 ψ 119^{112}; †הטה לב 1 K 11^3 ψ 119^{36} 141^4 cf. 2 S 15^{13}:—גְּדֹלִים חִקְקֵי־לֵב *great resolves of heart* Ju 5^{15} etc. **5.** spec. ref. to *conscience,* וַיַּךְ לֵב דָּוִד אֹתוֹ *and David's heart* (*conscience*) *smote him* 1 S 24^6; מִכְשׁוֹל לֵב *offence of conscience* 1 S 25^{31}. **6.** spec. ref. to *moral character,* God tries the heart ψ 17^3 Je 12^3; sees the heart and reins Je 20^{12}, tries them ψ 7^{10} Je 11^{20}, refines them ψ 26^2; searches the heart and tries the reins Je 17^{10}. **a.** יִשְׁרֵי־לֵב Jb 33^3; †יִשְׁרֵי לֵב ψ 7^{11} 11^2 32^{11} 36^{11} 64^{11} (all c. דָּוִד in title), 94^{15} 97^{11}; †לֵב שָׁלֵם 1 Ch 28^9 29^9 Is 38^3 (all originally לבב, see לבב **6 a**); נִשְׁבְּרֵי־לֵב *broken of heart* ψ 34^{19} Is 61^1; לֵב־נִשְׁבָּר ψ 51^{19}; שְׁבוּרֵי לֵב ψ 147^3; לֵב נִדְכָּאִים Is 57^{15}; לֵב טָהוֹר *clean heart* ψ 51^{12}; †לֵב חָדָשׁ *new heart* Ez 18^{21} 36^{26} (prob. also 11^{19} for אֶחָד see Co) etc. **b.** לֵב רָע *evil heart* Pr 26^{23}; חַנְפֵי־לֵב *godless in heart* Jb 36^{13}; עקשׁ(י) לב *perverse in heart* Pr 11^{20} 17^{20}; †תַּרְמִת לִבָּם *deceit of their heart* Je 14^{14} 23^{26}; בלב ולב *with a double heart* ψ 12^3 etc. **c.** seat of pride Pr 21^4 Je 48^{29} 49^{16} Ho 13^6 Ob ^{3} גֹּבַהּ לב 2 Ch 32^{26}; גְּבַהּ־לֵב Pr 16^5; †גָּבַהּ לֵב 2 Ch 26^{16} 32^{25} ψ 131^1 Pr 18^{12} Ez 28$^{2.17}$. **d.** the heart is uncircumcised Je 9^{25} Ez 44$^{7.7.9}$ and hardened: †חזק לב Ex 4^{21} 10$^{20.27}$ (E), 9^{12} 11^{10} 14$^{4.8.17}$ (P), Jos 11^{20} (D^2 ?); †חִזְקֵי־לֵב Ez 2^4; †יְחַזֵּק לֵב Ex 7$^{13.22}$ 8^{15} 9^{35} (P); †הקשׁה לב Ex 7^3 (P) Pr 28^{14}; קְשֵׁי־לֵב Ez 3^7; הכביד לב Ex 8$^{11.28}$ 9^{34} 10^1 (J); כָּבֵד לב Ex 7^{14} 9^7 (J); כבד לב 1 S 6^6; הַשְׁמֵן לֵב־הָעָם הַזֶּה *make the heart of this people fat* Is 6^{10} (?); †שְׁרִ(י)רוּת לֵב Dt 29^{18} ψ 81^{13} after Je 3^{17} 7^{24} 9^{13} 11^8 13^{10} 16^{12} 18^{12} 23^{17}; †לב האבן *the heart of stone* Ez 11^{19} 36^{26} etc. **7.** for *the man himself,* †אמר בלב Gn 17^{17} (P), 27^{41} (JE), 1 K 12^{26} Est 6^6 ψ 10$^{6.11.13}$ 14^1 (=53^2) 35^{25} 74^8 Ec 2$^{1.15}$ 3$^{17.18}$ Is 47^{10} Ob ^{3} Zc 12^5; אֶל־לב Gn 8^{21} (J) 1 S 27^1; †דבּר בלב Ec 2^{15}; אֶל־לב Gn 24^{45} (J); על לב 1 S 1^{13} (?); עם לב Ec 1^{16}; נְאֻם־פֶּשַׁע לָרָשָׁע בְּקֶרֶב לִבִּי ψ 36^2. **8.** as *seat of appetites,* סָעַד לב *stay the heart* (with bread) Gn 18^5 (J) Ju 19^5. **9.** as *seat of the emotions and passions:* **a.** of joy and gladness, in various combinations of †טוב, Ju 16^{25} 18^{20} 19$^{6.22}$ Ru 3^7 1 S 25^{36} 2 S 13^{28} 1 K 8^{66} (=2 Ch 7^{10}) 21^7 Est 1^{10} 5^9 Pr 15^{15} Ec 7^3 9^7 11^9 Is 65^{14}; various combinations of †שׂמח, Ex 4^{14} (J) 1 Ch 16^{10} (=ψ 105^3) ψ 4^8 16^9 19^9 33^{21} Pr 15$^{13.30}$ 17^{22} 27$^{9.11}$ Ec 2$^{10.10}$ 5^{19} Ct 3^{11} Is 24^7 Zc 10^7; שׂושׂ ψ 119^{111} Is 66^{14} La 5^{15}; עלץ 1 S 2^1; עלז ψ 28^7 Zp 3^{14}; רנן Jb 29^{13}; גיל ψ 13^6 24^{17} Zc 10^7; of desire, ψ 21^3 37^4; †דבּר עַל לֵב *speak unto the heart* (kindly) Gn 34^3 50^{21} (JE) Ju 19^3 2 S 19^8 2 Ch 30^{22} Is 40^2 Ho 2^{16} Ru 2^{13}. **b.** of trouble 2 K 6^{11} Is 65^{14}, sorrow Ne 2^2 Pr 14^3, pain ψ 55^5, vexation Ec 11^{10}, trembling Dt 28^{65} (?) 1 S 28^5, faintness La 5^{17}; it is wounded ψ 109^{22}, dies within one out of fear 1 S 25^{37} etc.; †לב נמס *the heart melteth* (in fear) 2 S 17^{10} ψ 22^{15} Ez 21^{12} Na 2^{11}. †**10.** *seat of courage:* יַאֲמֵץ לִבֶּךָ *let thine heart take courage* ψ 27^{14}; אַמִּיץ לִבּוֹ Am 2^{16}; אַבִּירֵי לֵב *stout-hearted* ψ 76^6 Is 46^{12}; לִבּוֹ יָצוּק כְּמוֹ־אָבֶן *his heart as firm as a stone* Jb 41^{16}; לִבּוֹ כְּלֵב הָאַרְיֵה *his heart as the heart of the lion* 2 S 17^{10}.

†[לִבָּה] *sf.* לִבָּתֵךְ Ez 16^{30} should be corrected 3826
to לִבְרִיתֵךְ (see Co). >older view, as fem. of לֵב. 3820

לֵב קָמָי prob. late Atbash (cf. שֵׁשַׁךְ) for 6965, 8347
כשׂדים the original reading (𝔊) Je 51^1. p. 1058

†I. [לבב] **vb. denom.** **Niph.** *Impf.* יִלָּבֵב 3823
get a mind; וְאִישׁ נָבוּב יִלָּבֵב וְעַיִר פֶּרֶא אָדָם יִוָּלֵד *shall an empty man get a mind or a wild ass's colt be born a man?* Jb 11^{12}. **Pi.** encourage; *Pf.* לִבַּבְתִּנִי . . . . לִבַּבְתִּנִי בְּאַחַד מֵעֵינַיִךְ Ct 4$^{9.9}$ *thou hast encouraged me, thou hast encouraged me with one of thine eyes* Ew Gi Gr RVm (AV RV Ges Hi De Öt (cf. 5^6) *ravished my heart,*— Pi. *priv.* Ges$^{§ 52 h}$).

†[לְבִבָה] **n.pl.** cakes (prob. *pancakes,* 3834
from shape?) לְבִבוֹת 2 S 13$^{6.8.10}$.

†II. [לבב] **vb. denom.** **Pi.** make cakes. 3823
Impf. תְּלַבֵּב 2 S 13$^{6.8}$.

לְבַד *alone* v. בַּד sub בדד p. 94 supr.

[לַבָּה], לַבַּת Ex 3^{2} v. לֶהָבָה sub להב.

3832 [לָבַט] **vb. thrust down, out, or away**
(NH *id.;* Ar. لَبَطَ *strike the ground* with a person, i.e. throw one down; Syr. Pa. ܠܰܒܶܛ *incitavit, stimulavit*);—only **Niph.** *Impf. be thrust down, away,* i.e. ruined; עָם לֹא יָבִין יִלָּבֵט Ho 4^{14}; אֱוִיל שְׂפָתַיִם יִלָּבֵט Pr 10$^{8.10}$.

3833 לְבִיא, לָבִיא, לְבִי v. sub לבא. p. 522

3864 לְבִים v. לוּבִים. p. 530

3835 †[לָבֵן] **vb. be white** (on ـــَ v. Ba$^{NB\ 166}$; Lag$^{BN\ 33,\ cf.\ 53,\ 54}$ infers *לָבֵן from לְבֵנָה; NH *id.,* Pi. Hiph., and deriv.; Ph. לבן *white;* Ar. لَبَنٌ *milk;* لبن also *be white,* dial. of Yemen, Maltzan $^{ZMG\ xxvii,\ 1873,\ 247}$; appar. √ of foll. fourteen words, but this dub. esp. in case of II. III. לָבָן, לְבָנָא, II. לְבֹנָה, לְבוֹנָה, I. II. לִבְנִי);—**Hiph.** *Pf.* 3 pl. הִלְבִּינוּ Jo 1^{7}; *Impf.* 1 s. אַלְבִּין ψ 51^{9}; 3 pl. יַלְבִּינוּ Is 1^{18}; *Inf. cstr.* וְלַלְבֵּן (= וּלְהַלְבֵּן) Dn 11^{35};—**1.** *make white* = purify (ethical) Dn 11^{35} (no object expr., ‖ צָרַף, בָּרֵר). **2.** *shew whiteness, grow white,* of fig-tree, stripped by locusts, Jo 1^{7}; fig. of moral purity, כַּשֶּׁלֶג יַלְבִּ׳ Is 1^{18}; מִשֶּׁלֶג אַלְבִּ׳ ψ 51^{9}. **Hithp.** *Impf.* יִתְלַבְּנוּ Dn 12^{10} *be purified* (ethical, ‖ יִתְבָּרֲרוּ).—לָבֵן, *make brick,* v. infr.

3836 †I. לָבָן **adj. white;**—ל׳ abs. Gn 30^{35} + 13 t.; cstr. לְבֶן־ Gn 49^{12} (cf. Ges$^{§93,\ 2,\ R.\ 1}$ Kö$^{Lgb\ ii,\ 74}$ Ba$^{NB\ 166}$); f. לְבָנָה Lv 13^{4} + 6 t.; pl. לְבָנִים Zc 1^{8} + 3 t.; לְבָנוֹת Gn 30^{37} + 2 t.;—*white,* of wood under bark Gn 30$^{37.37}$ (cf. Jo 1^{7}); of spots on goats v^{35} (all J); of manna Ex 16^{31} (P); garments Ec 9^{8} (sign of cheerfulness and joy); of teeth וּלְבֶן־שִׁנַּיִם מֵחָלָב Gn 49^{12} (poem in J; ‖ חַכְלִילִי עֵינַיִם מִיָּיִן) of Judah (on interpr. v. Di and, differently, Marc. Jastr $^{JBL\ xi.\ (1892),\ 128}$); of horses Zc 1^{8} 6$^{3.6}$ (in vision); chfly. of diseased skin or flesh on body (בַּהֶרֶת Lv 13$^{4.19.24.25.26.38}$) Lv 13$^{4.10.13.16.17.19.24.38}$; and of hair on such spots 13$^{3.4.10.20.21.25.26}$; + אֲדַמְדֶּמֶת 13$^{19.24.43}$, cf. v^{42}; + כֵּהָה v^{39} (all P).

3842 †I. לְבָנָה **n.f.** moon, poet. (NH *id.*);—ל׳ Is 24^{23} + 2 t.; shall pale before י׳ Is 24^{23} (‖ חַמָּה); shall become like sun (חַמָּה) in day of י׳'s redemption 30^{26} (אוֹר הַל׳); sim. of woman's beauty, יָפָה כַל׳ Ct 6^{10} (‖ חַמָּה).

II. לָבָן$_{54}$ **n.pr.m.** son of Bethuel, brother of 3837
Rebekah, and father-in-law of Jacob (𝔊 Λαβαν), Gn 24$^{29.29.50}$ 27^{43} 28$^{2.5}$ + 17 t. J (Gn 29, 30, 31, 32); 29$^{15.16.19.21.22.26}$ + 18 t. E (Gn 31, 32, ל׳ הָאֲרַמִּי 31^{24}); 25^{20} (ל׳ הָאֲרַמִּי) 28^{5} (*id.*), also 28^{2} 29$^{24.29}$ 46$^{18.25}$ (all P).

† III. לָבָן **n.pr.loc.,** connected with desert- 3837
journey of Israelites Dt 1^{1}, 𝔊 Λοβον; poss. = לִבְנָה **2**, q. v.

†לְבָנָא Ne 7^{48} = II. לְבָנָה Ezr 2^{45};—head of 3838
a family of returning exiles, 𝔊 Λαβανα, Λαβανω, 𝔊L Λοβνα.

†לִבְנָה **n.pr.loc. 1.** city in SW. Judah, 3841
exact site unknown, captured by Joshua, acc. to D, Jos 10$^{29.29.31.32.39}$ 12^{15} (all D), 15^{42} (P); Levit. city 21^{13} (P) = 1 Ch 6^{42}; further 2 K 8^{22} = 2 Ch 21^{10}, 2 K 19^{8} = Is 37^{8}, 2 K 23^{31} 24^{18} = Je 52^{1}; 𝔊 Λεβνα. Vid. Lag$^{Onom.\ 274,\ 135,\ 26;\ 2nd\ ed.\ 273}$ Λεβνα; Buhl$^{Geogr.\ 193}$. **2.** station of Isr. in wilderness, between רִמֹּן פֶּרֶץ and רִסָּה Nu 33$^{20.21}$ (perh. = לָבָן Dt 1^{1}); 𝔊 Λεμωνα, A𝔊L Λεβωνα.

† I. לְבוֹנָה, לְבֹנָה **n.f. frankincense** (from 3828
white colour, cf. Lag$^{BN\ 33}$; NH *id.;* Aram. *id.,* לְבוֹנְתָא, ܠܒܘܢܬܐ; Ph. לבנת; Ar. لُبَانٌ (Lane^{3007}); Eth. ልብንት: is fr. λίβανος);—ל׳ Ex 30^{34} + 18 t.; לְבֹנָתָהּ Lv 2$^{2.16}$;—used in prep. of holy incense Ex 30^{34} (‖ סַמִּים); used as incense Je 6^{20}, on meal-offering Lv 2$^{1.2.15.16}$ 6^{8}, cf. 5^{11} Nu 5^{15}; also Je 17^{26} 41^{5} Is 43^{23} 66^{3}; with shew-bread Lv 24^{7}; Ne 13$^{5.9}$ 1 Ch 9^{29} (‖ בְּשָׂמִים); burned as perfume (art. of luxury) Ct 3^{6} (‖ מֹר); גִּבְעַת הַלְּבוֹנָה 4^{6} (‖ הַר הַמּוֹר); עֲצֵי לְבוֹנָה v^{14} (‖ נֵרְדְּ, כַּרְכֹּם, קָנֶה, קִנָּמוֹן, מֹר, אֲהָלוֹת); as tribute to Zion Is 60^{6} (‖ זהב).—In Hex only P.

† II. לְבוֹנָה **n.pr.loc.,** by which, among 3829
other places, loc. of Shiloh is fixed Ju 21^{19}, 𝔊 Λεβωνα; mod. *Lubban,* c. 3 m. WNW. fr. Shiloh (Seilûn), Rob$^{BR\ ii.\ 271\ f.}$ Guérin$^{Sam.\ ii,\ 164\ f.}$ Bd$^{Pal.\ 217}$ Buhl$^{Geogr.\ 175}$.

† I. לִבְנִי **n.pr.m.** a Levite, son of Gershom, 3845
Ex 6^{17} Nu 3^{18} 1 Ch 6$^{2.5.14}$ (𝔊 Λοβεν[ε]ι).

† II. לִבְנִי **adj. gent.** of foregoing, always 3846
c. art. הַלִּ׳ as subst. coll., Nu 3^{21} 26^{58}.

†לְבָנוֹן (Dt 3^{25} הַלְּבָנֹן van d. H.)$_{71}$ **n.pr.mont.** 3844
Lebanon (Ph. לבנן; As. *Labnanu,* etc., Schr^{COT} on 1 K 5^{13}, Dl$^{Par.\ 103\ ff.}$; Egypt. *Ra-m^{a} n-n* WMM

Asien u. Europa, 197 ff.; Ar. لُبْنَانٌ; cf. further Rob BR ii, 435 ff. 493 GASm[Geogr. 45 ff.] Buhl[Geogr. 110] and reff.; name prob. fr. *whiteness* of its cliffs Rob[BR ii, 493]);—wooded mountain-range on northern border of Isr. [usu. c. art. הַלּ׳ (51 t.); without art. לְבָנוֹן, poet. and late Ho 14[8] Na 1[4] 2 K 19[23]=Is 37[24], Ez 31[15.16] Is 14[8] 29[17] 33[9] 40[16] Je 18[14] Hb 2[17] Zc 10[10] 11[1] ψ 29[6] Ct 4[8.8.11.15]; c. ה loc. לְבָנוֹנָה 1 K 5[28a]]; perh. first mentioned in defining a locality, as הַר הַלְּבָנוֹן, Ju 3[3] (E acc. to GFM; this combination only here), but also in early proph., then in D, and later;—in defining a locality Jos 9[1]; בִּקְעַת הַלּ׳ Jos 11[17] 12[7] (side of Baal Gad); as a marked feature, in describing extent of land Dt 1[7] 3[25] 11[24] Jos 1[4] 13[5] (כָּל־הַלּ׳) v[6] (all D), 1 K 9[19]=2 Ch 8[6], Je 22[26] Zc 10[10]; רֹאשׁ הַלּ׳ Je 22[6] (fig. of royal house of Judah), as a height Ct 4[8.8]; מִגְדַּל הַלּ׳ Ct 7[5] i.e. a tower built on Lebanon; שֶׁלֶג ל׳ Je 18[14] *snow of L.;* L. as source of streams Ct 4[15]; יֵין ל׳ Ho 14[8]; most often, however, as bearing forests, esp. of cedars, אַרְזֵי הַלּ׳ Ju 9[15] (in allegory; perh. J, acc. to GFM), Is 2[13] 14[8] ψ 29[5] 104[16], cf. 1 K 5[13.20.23.28.28] 2 Ch 2[7.7.15], 2 K 14[9.9]=2 Ch 25[18.18] (in allegory), Je 22[23] Ez 17[3] 27[5] 31[3.15.16] Zc 11[1] Ezr 3[7] ψ 92[13] Ct 3[9] 5[15] (sim. of majestic figure); פֶּרַח ל׳ Na 1[4]; כְּבוֹד הַלּ׳ Is 35[2] 60[13]; וְשָׁב ל׳ לְכַרְמֶל 29[17] (יַעַר‖); יַרְכְּתֵי ל׳ with the same ref. Is 37[24]=2 K 19[23]; הַלּ׳=trees of Lebanon Ho 14[6] Is 10[34] 40[16] ψ 29[6] 72[16]; ל׳ Is 33[9] fig., as mourning; חֲמַס ל׳ Hb 2[17] i.e. *violence done to Lebanon*, prob. by cutting down its trees; בֵּית יַעַר הַלּ׳ a royal mansion of Sol., 1 K 7[2] and 10[17.21]=2 Ch 9[16.20]; ל׳ as home of wild beast 2 K 14[9]=2 Ch 25[18] (in allegory); רֵיחַ לְבָנוֹן, of the odour of cedar forests Ct 4[11], cf. Ho 14[7] (in sim.; We thinks ל׳ here to be a specific plant).

3839 †לִבְנֶה **n.[m.] poplar** (appar.=Ar. لُبْنَى; Eth. ልብን: *styrax officinalis;* but 𝔊 λεύκη, cf. 𝔖 and Löw[No. 107]);—Gn 30[37] מַקַּל ל׳ לַח וְלוּז וְעַרְמוֹן; as marking places of idolatrous incense-burning תַּחַת אַלּוֹן וְלִבְנֶה וְאֵלָה Ho 4[13].

3843 †לְבֵנָה **n.f. brick, tile** (NH *id.;* Aram. לְבֵינְתָּא, ܠܒܶܢܬܳܐ; Zinj. לבן (?) DHM[Sendsch. 37. 59]; As. *libittu;* Ar. لَبِنَةٌ, لِبْنَةٌ, لِبِنٌ, لَبِنٌ, لِبْنٌ (loan-words acc. to Frä[4 f.]); acc. to Thes and most from *whiteness* of clay, or light colour of sun-baked bricks; so Nö[ZMG xl, 1886, 735] Lag[BN 139]; >others regard as As. loan-word VOJ[i. 22 ff.]; in As. a deriv. fr. *labânu, throw down, prostrate,* is sought Dl[Pr. 93 f. (cf. HWB 369)]);—ל׳ Gn 11[3] Ez 4[1];
cstr. לִבְנַת Ex 24[10]; pl. לְבֵנִים Gn 11[3]+7 t.; sf. 3840
מִלִּבְנֵיכֶם Ex 5[19];—**1. brick,** as building-material, Gn 11[3] (sg. coll.; elsewh. pl.) v[3]; Ex 1[14]; straw used in making Ex 5[7], cf. v[8.16.18.19]; Is 9[9] (fig.; as inferior to גָּזִית *hewn stone*); incense burnt on Is 65[3] (=roof-tiles? cf. Che Di). **2.**=*tile,* on which plan of city could be engraved (חקק) Ez 4[1]. **3.**=*pavement,* Ex 24[10] (cf. Di).

†[לָבַן] **vb.denom. make brick** (as As. 3835
labânu fr. *libittu* Dl[HWB 370]);—**Qal** *Impf.* 1 pl. נִלְבְּנָה Gn 11[3] (c. acc. cogn.); *Inf. cstr.* לִלְבֹּן Ex 5[7] (c. acc. cogn.), v[14] (abs.)

†מַלְבֵּן **n.[m.] 1. brick-mould; 2. quad-** 4404
rangle (on meaning *brick-mould,* and fig. something *rectangular,* v. Hoffm[ZAW 1882, 53-72] Dr[2 S 12, 31], cf. NH מַלְבֵּן; Ar. مِلْبَنٌ; Syr. ܡܠܒܢܳܐ);—**1.** *brick-mould,* 2 S 12[31] Qr (Kt, by error, מלכן), Na 3[14]. **2.** *quadrangle,* Je 43[9] (at Tahpanhes).

לַבֵּן in עַל־מוּת ל׳ ψ 9[1] of dubious meaning, 4192
v. Thes Bae[Psalmen, p. xvii].

לִבְנַת, v. שִׁיחוֹר לִבְנָת. p. 1009 7884

†לָבֵשׁ, לָבַשׁ **vb. put on** (a garment), 3847
wear, clothe, be clothed (NH *id.;* Aram. לְבֵישׁ, ܠܒܶܫ; As. *labâšu;* Ar. لَبِسَ; Eth. ለበሰ:);—**Qal** *Pf.* 3 ms. לָבֵשׁ ψ 93[1.1], לָבַשׁ Jb 7[5]+2 t., וְלָבַשׁ (consec.) Lv 6[3]+3 t.; sf. וּלְבֵשָׁם (consec.) Lv 16[4]; 3 fs. לָבְשָׁה Ju 6[34]+2 t., etc. (Ez 42[14] rd. prob. וְלָבְשׁוּ Qr, for ילבשו Kt, but cl. perhaps interpol., v. Co); *Impf.* 3 ms. יִלְבַּשׁ Dt 22[5]+; sf. וַיִּלְבָּשֵׁנִי Jb 29[14], יִלְבָּשָׁם Ex 29[30]; 1 s. sf. אֲלְבָּשֶׁנָּה Ct 5[3]; 3 fpl. תִּלְבַּשְׁןָ 2 S 13[18], etc.; *Imv.* ms. לְבַשׁ 1 K 22[30], etc.; *Inf. abs.* לָבוֹשׁ Hg 1[6]; *cstr.* לִלְבֹּשׁ Gn 28[20] Lv 21[10]; *Pt. act.* pl. הַלֹּבְשִׁים Zp 1[8]; *pass.* abs. לָבוּשׁ 1 S 17[5] Dn 10[5]; לָבֻשׁ Ez 9[2]+3 t.; cstr. לְבוּשׁ Dn 12[6.7], לְבֻשׁ Ez 9[11]+3 t.; pl. cstr. לְבֻשֵׁי Ez 23[6]+2 t.;—**1. a.** lit. *put on* (one's own) garment (acc.) Gn 38[19] 1 S 28[8] 2 S 14[2] 1 K 22[30]=2 Ch 18[29], Ex 29[30] Lv 6[3.4] 16[4.4.23.24.32] 21[10] Dt 22[5] Ez 44[17.19], and so 42[14] Qr (v. supr.), Jon 3[5] Ct 5[3] Est 4[1] 5[1]; c. acc. garment+עַל־בְּשָׂרוֹ Lv 16[3]; of putting on armour Je 46[4];=*wear* (more or less habitually), c. acc. of garment,

Is 4^{1} Dt 22^{11} Zp 1^{8} Zc 13^{4}; of Jerus. under fig. of woman Je 4^{30}, of rulers under fig. of shepherds Ez 34^{3}, cf. כֵּן תִּלְבַּשְׁןָ 2 S 13^{18} (no acc.) **b.** very oft. fig., *put on, be clothed with*, c. acc. of garment;—לָבַשׁ בְּשָׂרִי רִמָּה Jb 7^{5} *my flesh is clothed* (i.e. covered) *with worms;* of Jerus., *be clothed with* inhabitants Is 49^{18}; of pasture, with flocks ψ 65^{14}; more oft. the garment is some abstract quality, e.g. righteousness, majesty, beauty, strength, etc.;—וַיִּלְבַּשׁ צְדָקָה כַּשִּׁרְיָן Is 59^{17} he (י׳) *hath put on righteousness as a breastplate*, cf. v^{17} (vengeance), ψ 93^{1} (majesty), v^{1} (strength), 104^{1} (honour and majesty), Is 51^{9} (strength); also Jb 40^{10}; said of men, 2 Ch 6^{41} (salvation), ψ 132^{9} (righteousness), Jb 29^{14} (*id.*); of Zion Is 52$^{1.1}$; also in bad sense, clothed with terror, trembling, shame, etc., Ez 7^{27} 26^{16} Jb 8^{22} ψ 35^{26} 109^{29}, cf. v^{18} (cursing). **c.** lit. *put on*, obj. om., נָתַן ... בֶּגֶד לִלְבֹּשׁ Gn 28^{20} Jb 27^{17}; *Inf. abs.* לָבוֹשׁ Hg 1^{6} (there is) *a clothing*, but he has nothing for warmth. **d.** once c. בְּ, לְבוּשׁ ... אֲשֶׁר לָבַשׁ בּוֹ Est 6^{8}. **e.** *Pt. pass., clothed with*, chiefly Ezek.;—c. acc. of garment, Ez 9$^{2.3}$ Zc 3^{3} Pr 31^{21} Dn 10^{5}; of wearing armour 1 S 17^{5}; cstr. before garment, לְבֻשׁ הַבַּדִּים Ez 9^{11} 10$^{2.6.7}$, cf. 23$^{6.12}$ 38^{4} Dn 12$^{6.7}$. **f.** fig.:—וְרוּחַ י׳ לָבְשָׁה אֶת־גִּדְעוֹן Ju 6^{34} *and the spirit of* י׳ *clothed itself with Gideon*, i.e. (GFM) took possession of him (cf. ܠܒܝܫ *possessed*); so 1 Ch 12^{18} 2 Ch 24^{20}; צֶדֶק לָבַשְׁתִּי וַיִּלְבָּשֵׁנִי Jb 29^{14} and it *clothed itself* in me, as it were, became incarnate in me. **Pu.** only *Pt.* pl. מְלֻבָּשִׁים *arrayed*, c. acc. of garment 1 K 22^{10} = 2 Ch 18^{9}, 2 Ch 5^{12}; abs. *in full apparel* Ezr 3^{10}. **Hiph.** *Pf.* 3 ms. sf. הִלְבִּישַׁנִי Is 61^{10}; 3 fs. הִלְבִּישָׁה Gn 27^{16}; 2 ms. וְהִלְבַּשְׁתָּ Ex 28^{41} + 3 t.; sf. וְהִלְבַּשְׁתָּם (consec.) Ex 29^{8} Nu 20^{26}; 1 s. sf. וְהִלְבַּשְׁתִּיו Is 22^{21}; 3 pl. הִלְבִּישׁוּ 2 Ch 28^{15}, וְהִלְבִּשׁוּ (consec.) Est 6^{9}; *Impf.* 3 ms. וַיַּלְבֵּשׁ Gn 41^{42} + 5 t.; sf. וַיַּלְבִּשֵׁם Gn 3^{21} Lv 8^{13}; 3 fs. תַּלְבִּישׁ Pr 23^{21}, etc.; *Inf. abs.* הַלְבֵּשׁ Zc 3^{4}; cstr. הַלְבִּישׁ Est 4^{4}; *Pt.* sf. הַמַּלְבִּשְׁכֶם 1 S 1^{24};—*clothe, array with.* **1.** usu. c. 2 acc., **a.** lit. וַיַּלְבֵּשׁ אֹתוֹ בִּגְדֵי־שֵׁשׁ Gn 41^{42} 2 S 1^{24} Is 22^{21} Ex 28^{41} 29$^{5.8}$ 40$^{13.14}$ Lv 8$^{7.13}$ Nu 20$^{26.28}$ Zc 3$^{4.5}$; of clothing Jerus. under fig. of infant Ez 16^{10}; of putting armour on some one 1 S 17$^{38.38}$. **b.** fig., Jb 10^{11} *thou hast clothed me with skin and flesh;* cf. 39^{19} (quivering of horse's neck); Is 50^{3} 61^{10} ψ 132$^{16.18}$. **2.** c. acc. garment only, Gn 27^{16} (+ עַל־יָדָיו); fig., Pr 23^{21}. **3.** c. acc. pers. only, Gn 3^{21} 27^{15} 2 Ch 28$^{15.15}$ Est 4^{4} 6$^{9.11}$.

† לְבוּשׁ, לְבֻשׁ **n.m.**$^{\text{Jb 30, 18}}$ **garment, clothing, raiment** (on format. cf. Ges$^{\text{§ 84a, 12}}$ Lag$^{\text{BN 64, 179}}$);—לְבוּשׁ abs. 2 K 10^{22} + 9 t.; cstr. לְבוּשׁ Est 3830
4^{2} + 2 t., לְבֻשׁ Is 14^{19}; sf. לְבוּשִׁי Jb 30^{18} + 3 t.; לְבוּשְׁךָ Is 63^{2} Pr 27^{26}; לְבוּשׁוֹ Is 63^{1} Jb 41^{5}, לְבֻשׁוֹ 2 S 20^{8} + 2 t.; לְבוּשָׁהּ ψ 45^{14} + 2 t.; לְבוּשְׁכֶן 2 S 1^{24}; לְבוּשָׁם Je 10^{9}; pl. sf. לְבֻשֵׁיהֶם La 4^{14};—*garment, clothing*, Gn 49^{11} (poem in J; ‖ סוּתֹה), Jb 24^{7} (‖ כְּסוּת), v^{10} 30^{18} 31^{19} Pr 27^{26} ψ 22^{19} La 4^{14}; of women's raiment 2 S 1^{24} Pr 31^{22}, also fig. עֹז וְהָדָר לְבוּשָׁהּ v^{25}; specif. of princess ψ 45^{14}; of warrior's tunic 2 S 20^{8}, cf. Is 63$^{1.2}$ (י׳ as warrior); raiment for worshippers 2 K 10^{22}; for mourners, לְבוּשִׁי שָׂק ψ 35^{13}, cf. 69^{12}; בִּלְבוּשׁ שָׂק Est 4^{2}; of royal apparel ל׳ מַלְכוּת Est 6^{8} 8^{15}, cf. (without מ׳) 6$^{9.10.11}$; scaly coat of crocod. פְּנֵי לְבוּשׁוֹ Jb 41^{5}; cover garment with violence Mal 2^{16}, fig. of putting away a wife, cf. RS$^{\text{K. 269}}$ We; in other fig. uses:—as changed ψ 102^{27} (sim. of heavens and earth), as covering 104^{6} (sim. of deep upon earth); of cloud as garment of sea Jb 38^{9}, sim. of terrestrial objects in the light v^{14}.

† מַלְבּוּשׁ, [מַלְבֻּשׁ] **n.m.**$^{\text{Zp 1, 8}}$ **raiment,** 4403
attire;—abs. 2 K 10^{22} + 2 t.; sf. מַלְבּוּשֵׁךְ Ez 16^{3}; pl. sf. מַלְבּוּשַׁי Is 63^{3}; מַלְבּוּשֵׁיהֶם 2 Ch 9$^{4.4}$, מַלְבֻּשֵׁיהֶם 1 K 10^{5};—*raiment*, 2 K 10^{22} (for worshippers, ‖ לְבוּשׁ), Jb 27^{16} (as wealth); of Jerus. under fig. of infant Ez 16^{13}; מַל׳ נָכְרִי Zp 1^{8} *foreign attire* (acc. with לָבַשׁ); pl. of *garments* of Sol.'s servants 1 K 10^{5} = 2 Ch 9^{4a}, + 2 Ch 9^{4b}; of י׳ under fig. of warrior Is 63^{3}.

† תִּלְבֹּשֶׁת **n.f.** raiment;—וַיִּלְבַּשׁ בִּגְדֵי נָקָם ת׳ 8516
Is 59^{17} *and he put on garments of vengeance as raiment* (of י׳ as champion of Israel).

† לֹג **n.m.**$^{\text{Lv 14, 10}}$ a liquid measure (NH *id.*; 3849
Aram. לוּגָּה; also ܠܓܢ, ܠܓܢܐ *a (dessert-)dish*, etc.; mng. of √ dub.; Thes comp. Ar. لَجَّ *be deep*, لُجّ *depth, abyss*);—ל׳ abs. Lv 14^{10}; cstr. v^{12} + 3 t. Lv 14; always of oil (שֶׁמֶן) Lv 14$^{10.12.15.21.24}$ (P; all in law of purif. of leper); acc. to Talm. = $\frac{1}{12}$ hin (v. הִין supr. p. 228; Zuckermann$^{\text{Jüd. Massystem, 49}}$) i.e. c. $\frac{1}{2}$ litre; Benz$^{\text{Arch. 182, 184}}$ Now$^{\text{Arch. i. 204 f.}}$

† לֹד **n.pr.loc.** = Λυδδα, 1 Makk 11^{34} Acts 3850
9$^{32.35.38}$, **Lydda**, mod. *Ludd*, c. 11 miles SE. fr. Jaffa, toward Jerusalem; Rob$^{\text{BR ii. 244–248}}$ GASm$^{\text{Geogr. 160 ff.}}$ Buhl$^{\text{Geogr. 197}}$ 1 Ch 8^{12} (ל׳ וּבְנֹתֶיהָ), Ezr 2^{33} (בְּנֵי לֹד) = Ne 7^{37}, cf. 11^{35}; 𝔊 Λωδ, Λοδ, Λυδδων, Λυδδα.

3810 †לְדְבִר **n.pr.loc.** only in גְּבוּל לְ׳ Jos 13[26]; E. of Jordan, in tribe of Gad; 𝔊B Δαιβων, A Δαβειρ, 𝔊L Δεβηρ; perh.=לֹא דְבָר q.v., and cf.
1688 II. דְּבִיר **2 b.** p. 184

3205 לֵדָה v. ילד, *Inf. cstr.* p. 408

3808 לֹה v. לֹא. p. 518

להב √ of foll. (cf. Ar. لَهِبَ *be thirsty* [prob. *burn with thirst* Lane 2674], II. *make* a fire *blaze fiercely*, cf. IV; v. *blaze fiercely* (of fire), cf. VIII; Aram. [להב, ܠܗܒ] *burn*, in Shaph. Ishtaph. and deriv.; also לַהֲבוּתָא, לַהֲבָא *flame;* Eth. ለሀበ:; As. *la'abu*, *flame*, Dl HWB 364).

3851 †לַהַב **n.m. flame, blade**;—לְ׳ abs. Ju 3[22.22] + 2 t.; cstr. Ju 13[20] + 5 t.; pl. לְהָבִים Is 13[8]; cstr. לַהֲבֵי Is 66[15];—**1.** *flame*, of altar, Ju 13[20.20] (לְ׳ הַמִּזְבֵּחַ); לְ׳ אֵשׁ אוֹכְלָה, of י׳'s judgment Is 29[6] 30[30] 66[15] (in all || forces of nature, whirlwind, thunder, earthquake, rain, hail, etc.); fig. פְּנֵי לְ׳ פְּנֵיהֶם Is 13[8] (i.e. hot with excitement, cf. Di); sim. Jo 2[5] כְּקוֹל לְ׳ אֵשׁ (of rush of locusts); fig. of breath of crocodile Jb 41[13]. **2.** of *flashing point* of spear Jb 39[23]; *blade* of sword Na 3[3]; in prose, Ju 3[22.22].

3852 †לֶהָבָה **n.f. id.**;—לְ׳ Nu 21[28] + 13 t., לֶהָבֶת
3827 abs. Jb 15[30]; cstr. Ez 21[3]; לַבַּת Ex 3[3] (=לַהֶבֶת; Sam. להבת, v. Di); pl. לֶהָבוֹת ψ 105[32]; cstr. לַהֲבוֹת ψ 29[7];—**1.** *flame*, poet. (|| or + אֵשׁ, exc. ψ 29[7] Dn 11[33]); of fire consuming (לָהַט) Dathan, etc. ψ 106[18] (cf. Nu 16[35]); wasting (לָהַט) mts. 83[15]; consuming (בָּעַר, אָכַל) chaff (in sim.) Is 5[24]; of lightning (with hail) אשׁ לְ׳ ψ 105[32] (cf. Ex 9[24]), ψ 29[7] לְ׳ אֵשׁ (on text of v. cf. Che); sim. of judgment, אֵשׁ לְ׳ La 2[3] (vb. אָכַל) Ho 7[6] (vb. בָּעַר) Is 47[14] (מִיַּד לְ׳); cf. 10[17] Ob[18]; לְ׳ שַׁלְהֶ׳ Ez 21[3]; fig. of drought Jo 1[19], of locusts' ravages 2[3] (vb. לִהַט in both); of war Nu 21[28] Je 48[4] (both vb. אָכַל); cf. Dn 11[33] (|| חֶרֶב); of calamity Is 43[2]; symb. נֹגַהּ אֵשׁ לְ׳ of י׳'s presence Is 4[5] (cf. Ex 13[21]); לַבַּת אֵשׁ Ex 3[2]. **2.** *point, head* of spear 1 S 17[7].

3852 לַבַּת אֵשׁ Ex 3[2] v. לֶהָבָה. above

7957 †שַׁלְהֶבֶת **n.f. flame** (Aram. שַׁלְהוֹבִיתָא, ܫܠܗܒܝܬܐ)—in שׁ׳ לֶהָבֶת Ez 21[3], of judgment; so שַׁלְהֶבֶת Jb 15[30]; רִשְׁפֵּי אֵשׁ שַׁלְהֶבֶתְיָה Ct 8[6] i.e. *Yahweh-flame* = powerful flame (> Jäger BAS i.471 Jastrow JBL xiii (1894), 111 expl. ־יָה here as encl. part.)

†לְהָבִים **n.pr.gent.** Gn 10[13] = 1 Ch 1[11], 3853
prob. = לוּבִים q.v.; 𝔊 Λαβιειμ.

להג √ of foll. (Ar. لَهِجَ *be devoted, attached* to a thing, *apply oneself assiduously* to it).

†לַהַג **n.m.** (late) **study, i.e. devotion to** 3854
books; לְ׳ הַרְבֵּה יְגִעַת בָּשָׂר Ec 12[12] (cf. Now).

†לַהַד **n.pr.m.** son of יַחַת of Judah 1 Ch 4[2], 3855
𝔊 Λααθ, 𝔊L Λααδ (etym. and mng. unknown).

†[לָהָה] **vb. languish, faint** (=לָאָה) 3856
(𝔗 לְהִי, *id.*);—**Qal** *Impf.* 3 fs. apoc. וַתֵּלַהּ אֶרֶץ Gn 47[13] (of famine).

[לְהַלְהַּ] **vb.quadril. amaze, startle** (cf. Syr. Palp. ܠܗܠܗ *confudit, obstupefecit;* Ethpalp. *stupore percussus est;* ܠܘܗܠܗܐ *consternatio*, all in Lexx., PS 1894)—**Hithpalp.** *Pt.* מִתְלַהְלֵהַּ as subst.=*madman*, sq. הַיֹּרֶה זִקִּים Pr 26[18] (v. Now).

†[לָהַט] **vb. blaze up, flame** (NH *id.;* Syr. 3857
ܠܗܛ; As. *la'âtu*, in der. forms);—**Qal** *Pt. act.* אֵשׁ לֹהֵט ψ 104[4] *a flaming fire* (so Bae; אֵשׁ וָלַהַט Bi Che, cf. Ol), made into י׳'s servants; pl. לֹהֲטִים 57[5] (fig. of enemies, cf. לְבָאִם v[a]). **Pi.** *Pf.* 3 ms. וְלִהַט Mal 3[19]; 3 fs. לִהֲטָה Jo 1[19]; *Impf.* 3 fs. תְּלַהֵט Jo 2[3] + 4 t.; וַתְּלַהֵט Dt 32[22]; sf. וַתְּלַהֲטֵהוּ Is 42[25];—*set ablaze*, usu. c. acc.;—foundation of mts., Dt 32[22] (subj. אֵשׁ, fig. of י׳'s judgment, || אָכַל, יָקַד, קָדַח), cf. תְּלַ׳ הָרִים ψ 83[15] (in sim., subj. לֶהָבָה || כְּאֵשׁ תִּבְעַר־יָעַר); of flame (לֶהָבָה) consuming trees Jo 1[19] (of effects of drought; || אֵשׁ אָכְלָה); persons Mal 3[19] (subj. הַיּוֹם הַבָּא || בָּעַר); cf. ψ 97[3] (subj. אֵשׁ), 106[18] (subj. לֶהָבָה || וַתִּבְעַר־אֵשׁ); hyperb. of י׳'s wrath (חֵמָה אַפּוֹ וֶעֱזוּז מִלְחָמָה) consuming Jacob Is 42[25]; of crocodile (hyperb.), נַפְשׁוֹ גֶּחָלִים תְּלַהֵט Jb 41[13] *his breath setteth coals ablaze;* abs. Jo 2[3], fig. of devastation by locusts (subj. לֶהָבָה || אָכְלָה אֵשׁ).

†לַהַט **n. [m.] flame**;—only cstr. לַהַט הַחֶרֶב 3858
הַמִּתְהַפֶּכֶת Gn 3[24] *the flame of the whirling sword.*

לְהָטִים v. לוט. p. 532 3874

†[לָהַם] **vb. swallow greedily** (=Ar. 3859
لَهِمَ; Di Lex. Eth. 25 comp. Eth. ለሀም: *ox, cow*);—only **Hithp.** *Pt.* מִתְלַהֲמִים Pr 18[8] i.e. *bits greedily*

swallowed, dainties, = 26^{22}, sim. of tale-bearer's words.

3860 †**לָהֵן** **conj. on this account, therefore,**
2004 Ru $1^{13.13}$ (either from לְ and הֵן (v. sub הֵ֫מָּה);
2005, 3861 or the Aram. לָהֵן Dn $2^{6.9}$ 4^{24}: see the Aram. Lex.) p. 242

3862 †[**לַהֲקָה**] **n.f.** dub.; acc.to 𝔊𝔖𝔗 Aq Symm **band, company** (perh. by transp. from קְהִלָּה, cf. Thes (קְהִלָּה) The Klo Bu; v. also HPS).—לַהֲקַת הַנְּבִיאִים 1 S 19^{20}.

3808 **לוֹ** (Kt 1 S 2^{16} 20^{2}), לוֹא, v. לֹא. p. 518

3863 †**לוּ**$_{17}$ and **לוּא** (†1 S 14^{30} Is 48^{18} 63^{19}), also לֻא (Qr לוּ), †2 S 18^{12} 19^{7} (Ar. لَوْ, Aram. ܠܘܺ, לְוַי, Mishn. לְוַי, As. *lû*, with opt. force, Dl[§§ 78 end, 93, 145]; cf. Kö[ii. 333]), **conj. if, O that**:—**1.** *if* (stating a case which has not been, or is not likely to be, realized): **a.** sq. pf. (so mostly), Dt 32^{29} לו חכמו ישכילו זאת *if* they had been wise (which they are not), they would understand this; Mi 2^{11} (apod. וְהָיָה); Ju 8^{19} 13^{23} לו חפץ י׳ להמיתנו לא לקח *if* J. had desired to slay us, he would not have taken, &c.; 1 S 14^{30} 2 S 19^{7}. **b.** sq. impf. Ez 14^{15} *if* I were to send, &c. (but rd. prob. אוֹ, cf. $v^{17.19}$). **c.** sq. ptcp., 2 S 18^{12} וְלֻא אָנֹכִי שֹׁקֵל and *though* I should be weighing 1000 pieces of silver upon my hand, I would not, &c.; ψ 81^{14-17} לו עמי שֹׁמֵעַ לִי *if* my people were hearkening to me, . . . quickly would I bow down, &c. **d.** sq. יֵשׁ Job 16^{4}.—With the apod. omitted, Gn 50^{15} לוּ יִשְׂטְמֵנוּ *if* Joseph were to hate us (how should we fare then?).

2. *If only . . . !* i.e. *O that! would that!* (cf. εἰ γάρ, εἴθε) usu. sq. perf., as Nu $14^{2.2}$ לוּ מַתְנוּ *if only* we had died in the land of Egypt! 20^{3} Jos 7^{7} וְלוּ הוֹאַלְנוּ וַנֵּשֶׁב Is 48^{18} 63^{19}; sq. יֵשׁ Nu 22^{29}; sq. impf. Gn 17^{18} לו יחיה *O that* Ishmael might live before thee! Jb 6^{2}; sq. juss. Gn 30^{34} לו יהי כדברך; sq. imv. 23^{13} אם אתה לוּ שמעני if thou—*O that* thou wouldst hear me! (+ prob. v^{5} לאמר לוּ : שׁ׳ for לאמר: לוּ שמעני, and similarly v^{15}).—Rd. also prob. לֻא for Mas. לא Ju 21^{22} (with כִּי עַתָּה for כָּעֵת), 1 S 13^{13} $20^{14.14}$ Jb 9^{33} (sq. יֵשׁ); and perh. 14^{4} (Ew Kö).

3884 †**לוּלֵא** Gn 43^{10} Ju 14^{18} 2 S 2^{27} ψ 27^{13}, elsewhere לוּלֵי$_{10}$ **if not, unless** (fr. לוּ *if*, and לֵא, by dissim. (Kö[ii. 236, 489]) for לֹא *not*; cf. Ar. لَوْلَا), the neg. of לוּ, and used similarly:—**a.** sq. pf., Ju 14^{18} לולא חרשתם . . . לא מצאתם *unless* ye had ploughed with my heifer, ye would not have found out my riddle, 1 S 25^{34} (second כי resumptive: כִּי **1 d**), ψ 106^{23}; with apod. introd. by כִּי עַתָּה Gn 31^{42} 43^{10}; by אָז 2 S 2^{27} (כי resumptive); by כִּמְעַט Is 1^{9}; with an aposiop. ψ 27^{13} *if I had not believed . . . !* **b.** sq. impf. Dt 32^{27} לולי . . . אמרתי אגור I should have said, &c. . . . *except* I dreaded, &c. **c.** sq. ptcp., 2 K 3^{14}. **d.** without a verb, ψ 94^{17} (apod. כמעט), 119^{92} (apod. אָז). In the later language, ψ $124^{1.2}$ לוּלֵי י׳ שֶׁ- (apod. אֲזַי) *except that . . .* (cf. Aram. ψ 106^{23}, אִילוּלֵי . . . דִּי ψ 27^{13} 𝔗).—Rd. also לוּלֵי for אוּלַי in Nu 22^{33} (apod. כִּי עַתָּה). See further on לוּ and לוּלֵא Dr[§§ 139–145] Kö[iii. 487 f. 565].

†**לְמוֹ** poet. for לְ, Job 27^{14} 29^{21} 38^{40} 40^{4}, like כְּמוֹ for כְּ, בְּמוֹ for בְּ: see מוֹ. 3926

†[**לוּב**], **לוּבִים**, **לֻבִים** **n.gent.pl. Lybians,** in N. Africa, W. of Egypt;—Na 3^{9} (+ פּוּט), 2 Ch 12^{3} (𝔊 Λίβυες; + מִצְרַיִם, סֻכִּיִּים, כּוּשִׁים), 16^{8} (𝔊 Λίβυες; (+ כּוּשִׁים); לֻבִים Dn 11^{43} (v. Baer; c. כֻּשִׁים, מִצְרַיִם), Theod. Λιβύων; prob. = לְהָבִים (q.v.) Gn 10^{13} = 1 Ch 1^{11} A𝔊L Λαβιειμ; read לוּבִים perh. also Je 46^{9} (for 𝔥 לוּדִים, cf. Sta[Javan 5 f.]), 𝔊 Λυδοί (פּוּט *ib.* = Λίβυες); 𝔊 Sm Co Sta[Javan 6] Berthol rd. לוּב Ez 30^{5} (for 𝔥 כּוּב, q.v.) See WMM[As. Eur. 115]. 3864

†**לוּד**, **לוּדִים** **n.pr.m.** et **gent. 1. Lud,** **Lydia,** As. *Luddu*:—אַרְפַּכְשַׁד וְלוּד וַאֲרָם Gn 10^{22} = 1 Ch 1^{17} 𝔊 Λούδ. **2.** appar. a people in NE. Africa תַּרְשִׁישׁ פּוּל וְלוּד Is 66^{19}, 𝔊 Λούδ; פָּרַס וְל׳ Ez 27^{10}; כּוּשׁ וּפוּט וְלוּד 30^{5} (+ לוּב q.v.), in both 𝔊 Λ(ο)υδοί; also pl. לוּדִים a 'son' of Miṣraim, Gn 10^{13} 𝔊 Λουδιειμ (‖ לְהָבִים) = 1 Ch 1^{11} (לוּדִיִּים); Je 46^{9} (‖ כּוּשׁ, פּוּט) v. לוּב supr.—On this African לוּד v. Di[Gn 10, 13], opp. Sta[Javan 5 ff.] cf. WMM[As. Eur. 115]. 3865-66

לֹא דְבָר **n.pr.loc.** v. לֹא דְבָר. p. 520 3810

†I. [**לָוָה**] **join** (intr.), **be joined** (NH Pi. לִוָּה (ליוה) trans., Hithp. intr.; Aram. לְוֵי *accompany;* so ܠܘܳܐ; Ba[ES 12] comp. Ar. وَلِيَ *be near*);—**Qal** (late) *Impf.* 3 ms. sf. יִלְוֶנּוּ Ec 8^{15}, *be joined to, attend* (of mirth). **Niph.** נִלְוָה ψ 83^{9} Is 14^{1}; 3 mpl. consec. וְנִלְווּ Nu 18^{4} + 2 t., + Je 50^{5} (Ges[Lbg.] Bö Kö[i. 588] Gf Gie; > *Imv.* Ki Ew[§ 226 c] Ol[§ 264]); *Impf.* יִלָּוֶה Gn 29^{34}; יִלָּווּ Nu 18^{2}; *Pt.* נִלְוֶה Is 56^{3} (pointed as Pf., rd. prob. נִלְוֶה); pl. נִלְוִים Est 9^{27} Is 56^{6};—*join oneself* or *be joined* unto, sq. עַל Nu $18^{2.4}$ (מַטֵּה לֵוִי) to Aaron, by 3867

word-play), Is 14[1] (strangers to Isr.), Dn 11[34] (flatterers to the people), cf. Est 9[27]; Is 56[6] (to 'י); sq. ־אֶל Is 56[3] (to 'י), Zc 2[15] (to 'י), Je 50[5] (to 'י), Gn 29[34] (J; husband to wife); sq. עִם ψ 83[9] (Asshur with enemies of Isr.)

3867 †II. [לָוָה] **vb.** **borrow** (NH *id.*; cf. Ar. لَوَى *delay payment of debt* (cf. Ba[ES 12]));—**Qal** *Pf.* 1 pl. לָוִ֫ינוּ Ne 5[4]; *Impf.* 2 ms. תִּלְוֶה Dt 28[12]; *Pt.* לֹוֶה Pr 22[7]+2 t.;—*borrow*, עֶבֶד לֹוֶה לְאִישׁ מַלְוֶה Pr 22[7] *a borrower is slave to a man who lends*; abs. Dt 28[12] Is 24[2] ψ 37[21]; sq. כֶּסֶף Ne 5[4]. **Hiph.** *Pf.* 2 ms. consec. וְהִלְוִיתָ Dt 28[12]; *Impf.* 3 ms. sf. יַלְוְךָ Dt 28[44]; 2 ms. תַּלְוֶה Ex 22[24]; sf. תַּלְוֶנּוּ Dt 28[44]; *Pt.* מַלְוֶה ψ 37[26]+3 t., cstr. מַלְוֵה Pr 19[17];—*cause to borrow*, i.e. *lend to*, c. acc. pers.+rei Ex 22[24] (E); c. acc. pers. Dt 28[12.44.44]; abs. ψ 37[26] 112[5]; אִישׁ מַלְוֶה Pr 22[7] (v. **Qal** supr.); as subst. Is 24[2]; מַלְוֵה י׳ Pr 19[17] *a lender to* 'י is one shewing favour to the poor.

III. **לוה** (√ of foll.; cf. Ar. لَوَى *turn, twist, wind*; As. *lamû, surround, encircle*; Dl[HWB 368] Jen[ZMG xliii (1889), 201]).

3880 †[לִוְיָה] **n.f. wreath**;—cstr. לִוְיַת חֵן only fig. Pr 1[9] (‖ עֲנָקִים) of instruction of parents, 4[9] (‖ עֲטֶרֶת תִּפְאֶרֶת) of work of Wisdom.

3914 †[לֹיָה] **n.f. wreath**? (mng. dubious, cf. Sta[ZAW iii. 1883, 161]; poss.=לִוְיָה);—pl. לֹיוֹת 1 K 7[29.30.36] of carved work on bases of lavers in Solomon's temple.

3882 †לִוְיָתָן **n.m.**[Jb 40, 25] **serpent, dragon, leviathan**, poet. and rare (on format. fr. לוה c. fem. ת+ ָן—v. Thes and cf. Ges[§ 85, 54] Kö[ii. p. 99] Ba[NB § 207 c]; Lag[BN 205] thinks foreign loan-word);—*sea-monster*=crocodile Jb 40[25]; whale ψ 104[26] (v. Che); *dragon* producing eclipses (mythol.) Jb 3[8]; fig. of Egypt as all-engulfing ψ 74[14] (‖ תַּנִּינִים v[13]); cf. Is 27[1.1] (‖ נָחָשׁ בָּרִחַ, נָחָשׁ עֲקַלָּתוֹן), v. Che Di and esp. (on ל׳ in gen.) Barton[Tiamat, JAOS xv (1891), 22 ff.] Gunkel[Schöpf. u. Chaos 46].

3868 †[לוּז] **vb.** (poet., mostly WsdLt) **turn aside, depart** (NH Niph., Hiph.; Ar. لَاذَ *have recourse* to, *take refuge* in);—**Qal** *Impf.* אַל־יָלֻזוּ מֵעֵינֶיךָ Pr 3[21] *let them not* (i.e. sound wisdom, etc., si vera l., cf. VB) *depart from thine eyes* (v. Hiph.). **Niph.** *Pt.* נָלוֹז Pr 3[32] Is 30[12]; cstr. נְלוֹז Pr 14[2]; pl. נְלוֹזִים 2[15];—fig., *devious, crooked*, נ׳ בְּמַעְגְּלוֹתָם Pr 2[15] (‖ עִקְּשִׁים); נ׳ דְּרָכָיו 14[2]; as subst. of pers. 3[32]; of course of action Is 30[12] (‖ עֹשֶׁק), i.e. *crookedness=craftiness, cunning*, cf. De Che Di. **Hiph.** *Impf.* אַל־יַלִּיזוּ מֵעֵינֶיךָ Pr 4[21] (subj. דְּבָרַי) *let them* [my words] *not depart* (on form v. Ges[§ 72 R. 9]) *from thine eyes* (strictly, *let them not practise, exhibit, deviation*, direct causat., Kö[i. 205]).

†[לָזוּת] **n.f. deviation, crookedness** (fig.); 3891
—only cstr. לְזוּת שְׂפָתַיִם Pr 4[24] (on form cf. Ol[§ 219 a] Kö[ii. 166, 474]).

†I. לוּז **n.**[m.] **almond-tree, almond-wood** 3869
(NH *id.*; Aram. לוּזָא, ܠܘܙܐ *almond* (Löw[No. 319]), whence Ar. لَوْز as loan-wd. (Frä[145] Lag[BN 157 f.]), Eth. ሎዝ:);—Gn 30[37] (J; + לִבְנֶה, עַרְמוֹן לַח) of rods stripped by Jacob.

†II. לוּז **n.pr.loc. 1.** former name of Bethel 3870
Gn 28[19] (J), 35[6] (E), 48[3] (P), Jos 18[13.13] (P), Ju 1[23]; appar. distinct fr. B. מִבֵּית־אֵל לוּזָה Jos 16[2] (JE; but ל׳ here perh. explan. gloss, v. Di); 𝔊 Λουζα, Gn 28[19] [Ουλαμ]μαυς. **2.** city in hands of Hittites Ju 1[26] (on conject. as to site v. GFM); 𝔊 Λουζα.

לוח (√ of foll., mng. unknown; cf. perh. Ar. لَاحَ *shine, gleam, flash* (of star, lightning, etc.), or Syr. ܠܚܐ *wipe out, efface*, with ref. to smooth surface; but this=לחה).

†לוּחַ **n.m. tablet, board** or **plank, plate** 3871
(NH *id.*, Aram. לוּחָא, ܠܘܚܐ; Ar. لَوْح (mod. pron. *lûḥ, lôḥ*, cf. e.g. Spiro[Arab.-Eng. Vocab.] Buhl), Eth. ሉሕ:, but As. *li'û* (as if from לחה) in Dl[HWB 366]; see, however, *lêjum* (*lêyum*) Jäger[BAS i, 486]);—ל׳ abs. Is 30[8]; cstr. Pr 3[3]+4 t.; du. לֻחֹתַיִם Ez 27[5]; pl. לֻחֹת (לוּחוֹת) abs. Ex 32[16]+17 t.; cstr. Dt 4[13]+16 t.;—**1.** chiefly of stone tablets on which ten words were written Ex 24[12] 31[18b] 32[16.16.19] (all E), 34[1.1.1.4.4.28] (all J), Dt 4[13] 5[19] 9[9.10.11.17] 10[1.2.2.3.3.4.5] 1 K 8[9] 2 Ch 5[10]; ל׳ הָעֵדֻת Ex 31[18a] 32[15] cf. v[15], 34[29] (all P); ל׳ הַבְּרִית Dt 9[9.11.15]; tablet for writing prophecy Is 30[8] (‖ סֵפֶר), Hb 2[2], and fig., לוּחַ לִבֶּךָ Pr 3[3] 7[3] (for writing wise counsel), cf. Je 17[1] (inscribing sin of Judah); (vb. mostly כָּתַב Ex 31[18b] 32[15] Dt 9[10]; כ׳ עַל Ex 34[1.28] Dt 4[13] 5[19] 10[2.4] Pr 3[3] 7[3] Is 30[8]; חָרַשׁ עַל Je 17[1]; חָרַת sq. acc. Dt 9[9] cf. 1 K 8[9]=2 Ch 5[10]; חָרַת עַל Ex 32[16]; בֵּאֵר עַל Hb 2[2]). **2.** wooden *boards*, composing altar of tabern. Ex 27[8] 38[7]; *planks* composing ship (fig. of Tyre) Ez 27[5]; cf. נָצוּר עָלֶיהָ לוּחַ אָרֶז Ct 8[9], of door. **3.** (metal)

plates on bases of lavers in Solomon's temple 1 K 7^{36}.

3872 † לוּחִית **n.pr.loc.** in Moab; c. art. מַעֲלֵה הַלּוּחִית Is 15^{5} Je 48^{5} Qr (הַלֻּחִית; Kt. הלחות); it lay S. of the Arnon; cf. Buhl$^{Geogr. 24, 272}$ and reff.; 𝔊 Λουειθ.

3874 [לוּט] **vb. wrap closely, tightly, enwrap, envelope** (Ar. لَاطَ *cleave, stick* to a thing; also trans. *make to stick*, or *adhere*);—**Qal** *Pf.* 3 ms. לָאט 2 S 19^{5} (so rd., for MT לָאַט, We Klo Dr Bu); *Pt. act.* לוֹט Is 25^{7} (cf. Kö$^{i. 445}$); *Pt. pass.* f. לוּטָה 1 S 21^{10};—לוּטָה בַשִּׂמְלָה 1 S 21^{10} it is *wrapped up in a garment* (of sword of Goliath); fig. of covering as sign of mourning, פְּנֵי־הַלּוֹט הַלּוֹט עַל־כָּל־הָעַמִּים Is 25^{7} *the surface of covering which covereth over all the peoples* (|| הַמַּסֵּכָה הַנְּסוּכָה). **Hiph.** *Impf. envelope, wrap* וַיָּלֶט פָּנָיו בְּאַדַּרְתּוֹ 1 K 19^{13}.

3814,3909 † לָט, לָאט **n.[m.] secrecy, mystery**;— abs. לָט 1 S 18^{22} + 2 t., לָאט Ju 4^{21}; pl. sf. לָטֵיהֶם
3858 Ex 7^{22} + 2 t.; לַהֲטֵיהֶם Ex 7^{11};—alw. c. בְּ: **1.** בַּלָּט = *secretly* 1 S 18^{22} 24^{5} Ru 3^{7}; so בַּלָּאט Ju 4^{21}. **2.** בְּלָטֵיהֶם *with their mysteries* = enchantments (i.e. of חַרְטֻמֵּי מִצְרַיִם) Ex 7^{22} 8$^{3.14}$ = בְּלַהֲטֵיהֶם 7^{11} (all P).

3875 † I. לוֹט **n.m.** envelope, covering;—Is 25^{7} v. sub vb. supr.

3876 II. לוֹט$_{33}$ **n.pr.m.** Lot son of Haran, and nephew of Abram; 𝔊 Λωτ;—Gn 11$^{27.31}$ 12$^{4.5}$ 13$^{1.5.7.8.10.11.11.12.14}$ 14$^{12.16}$ + 15 t. Gn 19; † בְּנֵי לוֹט = Moabites Dt 2^{9}; = Ammonites Dt 2^{19}; = both, ψ 83^{9}.

3877 † לוֹטָן **n.pr.m.** 𝔊 Λωταν; a son of שֵׂעִיר Gn 36$^{20.22}$ = 1 Ch 1$^{38.39}$, and father of חֹרִי etc. Gn 36^{22} = 1 Ch 1^{39}; called a chief (אַלּוּף) of הַחֹרִי Gn 36^{29}.

3878 † I. לֵוִי **n.pr.m. Levi** (√ and mng. dubious; Gn 29^{34} (J) interpr. as *joined*, i.e. husband to wife; Nu 18$^{2.4}$ (P; appar. in word-play) of Levites as *joined to, attendant upon*, Aaron; orig. as *attached to, accompanying* Isr. fr. Egypt, Lag$^{Or. ii. 20 f.}$; as *attached to, attending upon* the ark, Bau$^{Priest. 74}$; in this case I. לֵוִי would be derived fr. II. לֵוִי in priestly sense; Hom$^{A. u. A. 1890, 30 f.}$ prop. Minaean לוא, *lau'ân, priest*, cf. Id$^{Süd-Arab. Chrest. 127}$; ag. all such views v. Kau$^{SK 1890, 771 f.}$; We$^{Prol. ed. 5, 141; Hist. Isr. 145}$ Sta$^{ZAW i (1881), 112 ff.}$ Gray$^{Prop. Names, p. 96}$, cf. Nö$^{ZMG xl (1886), 167}$, make לֵוִי n. gent. fr. לֵאָה (q.v.); cf. a further sugg. We$^{Skizzen iii. 114}$)—𝔊 Λευ(ε)ι(ν);—**1. a.** *Levi*, son of Jacob and Leah, as individual, Gn 29^{34} 34$^{25.30}$ 35^{23} 49^{5} (all J); 35^{23} 46^{11} Ex 1^{2} 6$^{16.16}$ Nu 3^{17} 16^{1} (all P); 1 Ch 2^{1} 5^{22} 6$^{1.4.23.28.32}$ 23^{6} Ezr 8^{18}; so [אֶת־] בַּת־ל׳ Ex 2^{1} (E), Nu 26^{59} (P). **b.** as head of a family of descendants, in phr. בֵּית לֵוִי Ex 2^{1} (E), and (with ref. to tribe; late) Nu 17^{23}, מִשְׁפַּחַת בֵּית ל׳ Zc 12^{13}. **c.** oft. בְּנֵי(־)ל׳ Ex 32$^{26.28}$ (E), Jos 21^{10} (P), בְּנֵי(־)ל׳ with tribal ref. Nu 3^{15} 4^{2} 18^{21} (charged with service of tabern., and hence to receive tithes; all P); as priests הַכֹּהֲנִים בְּנֵי לֵוִי Dt 21^{5} 31^{9}, cf. Mal 3^{3}, and לֹא הָיוּ מִבְּנֵי ל׳ 1 K 12^{31}; from the בְּנֵי ל׳ the Zadokites are selected as priests Ez 40^{46}; acc. to 1 Ch 9^{18} 23$^{24.27}$ בְּנֵי ל׳ are subordinate officials in temple (cf. v$^{28 f.}$), cf. 24^{20}; sharply disting. from priests Ezr 8^{15}, Ne 12^{23} (cf. v^{22}); so also in later stratum of story of Korah's revolt Nu 16$^{7.8.10}$ (P^{2}). **2.** as name of tribe, שֵׁבֶט ל׳ Dt 18^{1} (priestly tribe), מַטֵּה ל׳ Nu 1^{49} (in charge of tabern.), 3^{6} 18^{2} (ministers unto Aaron); לֵוִי alone = (tribe of) Levi Dt 27^{12} 33^{8} (earlier poem), Nu 26^{58} (P), Ez 48^{31} Mal 2^{4} (priestly tribe, cf. v^{1}), 1 Ch 21^{6} 27^{17}; מַטֵּה ל׳ = *rod* of (the tribe of) *Levi* Nu 17^{18} (P); also (no inheritance, because charged with service of tabernacle) Dt 10^{9}.

II. לֵוִי$_{291}$ **adj.gent. Levite**;—לֵוִי, 40 t.; pl. 3881
לְוִיִּם 250 t.; sf. 1 pl. לְוִיֵּנוּ Ne 10^{1};—† **1.** sg. of individual, אִישׁ ל׳ Ju 19^{1} *a certain Levite*; pred. וְהוּא ל׳ Ju 17^{1} *and he was a Levite*, so v^{9}; c. art. הַל׳ as subst. *the Levite* Ex 4^{14} (J), Ju 17$^{10.11.12.13}$ (as priest), Dt 18^{6} 2 Ch 20^{14} 31$^{12.14}$, Ezr 10^{15}; הָאִישׁ הַל׳ Ju 19$^{3.15}$; הַנַּעַר הַל׳ 20^{4}. Sg. usu. † **2.** c. art. הַלֵּוִי as subst. coll. *the Levites*: Ex 6^{19} Nu 3$^{20.32}$ 26^{57} (all P); 18^{23} (P; charged with service of tabern.); esp. D, Dt 12$^{12.18.19}$ 14$^{27.29}$ 16$^{1.14}$ 26$^{10.12.13}$; also 1 Ch 24^{6}; Mal 2^{8} (as priestly tribe); שֵׁבֶט הַל׳ Dt 10^{8} *tribe of the Levites* (set apart for service), cf. Jos 13$^{14.33}$ 1 Ch 23^{14}; בְּנֵי־הַלֵּוִי 1 Ch 12^{27} (van d. H v^{26}) *sons of the Levites* (i.e. of the tribe); so Ne 10^{40} (as tithe-collectors); בֵּית הַלֵּוִי ψ 135^{20} *house* (family, tribe) *of the Levites*. **3.** pl. הַלְוִיִּם chiefly Chr and P;—alw. c. art. except sf. לְוִיֵּנוּ Ne 10^{1}; the art. is om. by 𝔊𝔅 and most in Is 66^{21}; always = subst. *Levites*;— **1.** † **a.** earlier usage:—as bearing the ark 1 S 6^{15} 2 S 15^{24} Dt 31^{25}, so (with priests) 1 K 8^{4} = 2 Ch 5^{5} (𝔊 הכהנים הַל׳; rd. prob. וְהַל׳ as in K, 𝔊𝔖𝔅 cf. Öt VB); also 1 Ch 15$^{2.26.27}$ 23^{26} 2 Ch 5^{4} (for הכהנים || 1 K 8^{3}). † **b.** not disting. from priests by D: הַכֹּהֲנִים הַל׳ Dt 17$^{9.18}$ 18^{1} 24^{8} 27^{9},

Je 3^{3} 8^{33} (both D; as bearing ark), also Je 33$^{18.21}$ (הַלְ׳ הַכֹּ׳), Ez 43^{19} 44^{15}; cf. Dt 18^{7} 27^{14} Je 33^{22}; הַכֹּ׳ הַלְ׳ likewise 2 Ch 23^{18} 30^{27} (but rd. prob. וְהַלְ׳ after 𝔊𝔖𝔙, cf. Öt and infr.) †**c.** as tribal designation, Ex 6^{25} Nu 3^{39} 4$^{18.46}$ Jos 21^{1} (all P), 1 Ch 9$^{33.34}$ 15^{12} 2 Ch 35^{5} Ne 11$^{15.16}$ 12^{24}; with ref. to share in land Lv 25$^{32.32.33.33}$ (H), Nu 1^{47} 2^{33} Jos 14$^{3.4}$ 21$^{3.4.8.20.27.34.38.39}$ (all P), 18^{7} (D), 1 Ch 6^{49}; cf. also 2 Ch 11^{14}†. **d.** set apart for service in tabern., Ex 38^{21} Nu 1$^{50.51.51.53.53}$ 2^{17} 7$^{5.6}$ 8^{6} + 18 t. Nu 8 (all P), cf. 1 Ch 6^{33} 16^{4}; ministers to Aaron and his sons Nu 3^{9} 8^{19} 18^{6} (P); set apart for י׳ (as redemption for first-born) Nu 3$^{12.12}$ + 7 t. Nu 3 (P); with certain perquisites Nu 18$^{24.26.30}$ + 9 t. Nu (P). **2.** in Chr. the tribal idea is in the background, and thought of Levites as official class is prominent: **a.** disting. from priests הַכֹּ׳ וְהַלְ׳ 1 Ch 9^{14} (cf. v^{10}), 13^{2} 15$^{4.11.14}$ 23^{2} 24$^{6.31}$ + 67 t. Chr.; also Is 66^{21} (acc. to Vrss., but dub.), Ez 44^{10} 45^{5} (cf. v^{4}), 48$^{11.12.13.22}$. **b.** as porters, 1 Ch 9^{26} 26^{17}, cf. 34^{9}; as in charge of music, 1 Ch 15$^{16.17.22}$ 2 Ch 5^{12} 29$^{25.30}$ 34^{12} Ne 12^{27}; yet disting. fr. porters and singers, Ne 7^{1} 13$^{5.10}$; disting. also fr. נְתִינִים 1 Ch 9^{2} Ezr 8^{20} Ne 10^{29}; further (with various official functions) 1 Ch 9^{31} + 29 t. Chr.; of groups of individuals, 2 Ch 17$^{8.8}$ 29^{12} 34^{12} Ezr 2^{40} = Ne 7^{43}, Ezr 8^{33} Ne 3^{17} 9^{5} 10^{10} 12^{8}, also 8^{7} (om. וְ; 𝔙 BeRy Ryle). **c.** בְּנֵי־הַלְוִיִּם 1 Ch 15^{15} (bearing ark), 24^{30} (tribal designation).—See, on Levites, esp. Gf Gesch. d. Stammes Levi in Me Archiv i. 68 ff. 208 ff. We Prol. Cap. iv RS OTJC. 435 f., 2nd ed., 360 f. Bau Priesterthum 50 f., 68 f., and oft.

3883 †[לוּל] **n.[m.] shaft or enclosed space** (poss. in wall), **with steps or ladder**, only pl. לוּלִים 1 K 6^{8} (וּבְלוּלִים יַעֲלוּ), on mng. v. Sta ZAW iii, 1883, 136 ff. > 𝔊𝔙 *winding-stair*, cf. Buhl, v. Sta l.c. (NH לוּל *winding passage* or *stair*, or enclosed space in which is *a winding stair*, acc. to Levy NHWB ii. 486, but v. Sta l.c.; √ dubious; hardly לולו infr.)

3884 לוּלֵא, לוּלֵי v. sub לוּ. p. 530

לולו (appar. secondary √ from III. לוה *turn, twist, wind*, whence following).

3924 †[לוּלָי] **n.f. loop** (probably from לולו; cf. [דּוּדַי] p. 188 supra; Zehnpf BAS i. 635, comp. As. *lu-lu*, '*Schleife*');—only pl. abs. לֻלָאֹת Ex 26$^{5.5.5}$ + 8 t., cstr. לֻלְאֹת Ex 26^{4} 36^{11};—*loops* on edges of curtains of tabernacle, matching the hooks (קְרָסִים), for joining the curtains: Ex 26$^{4.5.5.5.10.10.11}$ 36$^{11.12.12.12.17.17}$ (all P).

לוּלֵי v. לוּלֵא sub לוּ. p. 530 3884

I. לִין, לוּן **vb. lodge, pass the night**, fig. 3885
abide (NH לִינָה n. *lodging, spending the night*; cf. Nö ZMG xxxvii (1883), 535 ff.; acc. to Thes kindred with לַיְלָה (q.v. infra), with change of ל and ן)—**Qal** *Pf.* לָן Gn 32^{22} 2 S 12^{16}; 3 fs. וְלָנָה consec. (before monosyl.) Zc 5^{4}; 1 pl. וְלַנּוּ consec. Ju 19^{13} (v. Ges §73. R. 1 Kö i. 508); *Impf.* יָלִין Ex 23^{18} + 13 t. + 2 S 17^{8}, but cf. **Hiph.**; וַיָּלֶן Gn 28^{11} + 4 t.; 3 fs. תָּלִין Lv 19^{13} + 4 t.; תָּלַן Jb 17^{2} (v. Kö i. 509); 2 ms. juss. אַל־תָּלֶן 2 S 17^{16}; תָּלַן Ju 19^{20} (v. Kö l.c.), etc.; *Imv.* לִין Ju 9$^{6.19}$, etc.; *Inf. cstr.* לָלוּן Gn 24^{25} + 5 t.; לָלִין 24^{23}; *Pt.* pl. לֵנִים Ne 13^{21};—**1.** *lodge, pass the night*: **a.** lit., human subj., oft. c. prep. or adv. of place, Gn 19^{2} 28^{11} Ju 19$^{13.15}$ 2 S 17^{16} Jb 24^{7} + oft. (on 2 S 17^{8} v. **Hiph.**); c. ה loc., וְלָן וְשָׁכַב אָרְצָה 2 S 12^{16}; c. ב loc. + ב temp. בַּלַּיְלָה הַהוּא Gn 32$^{14.22}$ Jos 8^{9}; c. הַלָּיְלָה (accus. temp.), Nu 22^{8} Jos 4^{3} 2 S 17^{16} 19^{8} Ru 3^{13}; of the wicked ψ 59^{16}, acc. to Hup DePe al.; < fr. II. לון 𝔊𝔙 Aq Che Bae al., cf. AV; sim. of temporary sojourn Je 14^{8} (of י׳ in Isr.) **b.** of animals: wild ox (רְאֵם) Jb 39^{9} (sq. עַל־אֲבוּסֶךָ), porcupine (קִפֹּד) Zp 2^{14}. **c.** inanim. subj. = *remain all night*: of fat of sacrifice Ex 23^{18} (E; sq. עַד־בֹּקֶר), passover meal 34^{25} (P; sq. לַבֹּקֶר), Dt 16^{4} (sq. לַבֹּקֶר; all these without local designation), wages of hireling Lv 19^{13} (H; אֵת = *with* + עַד־בֹּקֶר); of dead body Dt 21^{23} (עַל loc.); dew Jb 29^{19} (ב loc.); bunch of myrrh Ct 1^{13} (בֵּין loc.) **d.** fig. בָּעֶרֶב יָלִין בֶּכִי ψ 30^{6} *at evening weeping may come to lodge* (opp. וְלַבֹּקֶר רִנָּה). †**2.** fig. *abide, remain*, subj. עַיִן (= *look upon*), c. ב Jb 17^{2}; of error, 19^{4} (c. prep. אֶת pers.), strength 41^{14} (of crocod.; c. ב); of righteousness, Is 1^{21} (c. ב); נַפְשׁוֹ בְּטוֹב תָּלִין ψ 25^{13}; of hearkening ear Pr 15^{31}, c. בְּקֶרֶב; of thoughts Je 4^{14}, c. id.; abs., of man, *continue, endure*, ψ 49^{13}, שָׂבֵעַ יָלִין Pr 19^{23} *he shall continue satisfied*. **Hiph.** *Impf.* יָלִין *cause to rest, lodge*, sq. acc., 2 S 17^{8} v. Kö i. 509. **Hithpalp.** *Impf.* יִתְלֹנָן Jb 39^{28} *dwell, abide*, of eagle; fig. בְּצֵל שַׁדַּי יִתְלוֹנָן ψ 91^{1} of one trusting in י׳.

†מָלוֹן **n.m. lodging-place, inn, khan**;— 4411
abs. מ׳ Gn 42^{27} + 5 t.; cstr. מְלוֹן 2 K 19^{23} Je 9^{1};—*lodging-place, inn, khan* (?) Gn 42^{27} 43^{21} Ex 4^{24}; מְ׳ אֹרְחִים Je 9^{1}; = camp (of Isr.) for a night, Jos 4^{3} (+ לִין), v^{8}; of Assyrians Is 10^{29}; fig. מְלוֹן קִצֹּה 2 K 19^{23}, i.e. its (Lebanon's) remotest camping-ground, hyperb. of Assyrian conquest; so rd.

prob. in ‖ Is 37[24] for MT מְרוֹם קִ׳, cf. Di Du Kit Che[Hpt.]

4412 †מְלוּנָה **n.f.** **lodge, hut**;—מ׳ בְּמִקְשָׁה Is 1[8] (i.e. a watchman's hut); sim. of frail, insecure structure וְהִתְנוֹדְדָה כַּמְּלוּנָה Is 24[20] *and it* [the earth] *shall shake* (or *totter*) *like a hut.*

3885 †II. [לוּן] **vb. murmur**, only Ex 15, 16, 17, Nu 14, 16, 17, and Jos 9[18] (Sam. always defect., hence Nö[ZMG xxxvii. 1883, 535 n.] thinks poss. לנן [cf. רנן?]; from limited occurrence, he supposes it disappeared early; but found chiefly in P);—**Niph.** *Impf.* 3 mpl. וַיִּלֹּנוּ Ex 15[24] + 3 t. + Ex 16[2] Qr (Kt וילינו) + Nu 14[36] Kt (Qr וַיַּלִּינוּ, **Hiph.**); 2 mpl. תִּלֹּונוּ Ex 16[7] Nu 16[11], both Kt (Qr תַּלִּינוּ); on forms v. Ges[§ 72 Anm. 8] Kö[i. 509];—*murmur* against, sq. עַל Ex 15[24] (JE), 16[2.7] Nu 14[2] 16[11] 17[6] Jos 9[18] (all P; all of people Isr.); abs. ψ 59[16] (v. I. לון **1 a**). **Hiph.** *Pf.* 2 mpl. הֲלִינֹתֶם Nu 14[29]; *Impf.* וַיָּלֶן Ex 17[3]; וַיַּלִּינוּ Ex 16[2] Kt, Nu 14[36] Qr; 2 mpl. תַּלִּינוּ Ex 16[7] Qr, Nu 16[11] Qr (on all vid. supr.); *Pt.* pl. מַלִּינִים Ex 16[8] + 3 t.;—*murmur* = Niph., sq. עַל Ex 17[3] (E), elsewhere P: 16[8] Nu 14[27.27.29] 17[20]; *cause to murmur*, sq. acc. + עַל Nu 14[36] Qr; (cf. also supra **Niph.**)

8519 †[תְּלֻנָּה] **n.f. murmuring**;—pl. cstr. תְּלֻנּוֹת (תְּלוּנֹּת) Ex 16[12] + 2 t.; sf. תְּלֻנֹּתֵיכֶם 16[7] + 3 t.; תְּלוּנֹּתָם Nu 17[25];—*murmurings* of Isr. against י׳ (only P); Ex 16[9.12] Nu 17[25]; sq. עַל Ex 16[7.8], cf. v[8], Nu 14[27] 17[20] (+ מַלִּינִם עַל).

3886 †I. [לוּעַ, or לָעַע] **vb. swallow, swallow down** (Syr. ܠܥܐ, ܠܥ *lap* or *lick up* Ju 7[5-7]);—**Qal** *Pf.* 3 pl. וְלָעוּ consec. Ob[16] (Ges[§ 67 R. 12]);—abs., fig. of nations drinking (cup of judgment).—Hi De *talk wildly*, vid. II. לוע; We Now נָעוּ *reel, totter* (cf. Is 24[20] 29[9]).

3930 †[לֹעַ] **n.[m.]** prob. **throat** (external) (cf. NH לוֹעַ *jaw, cheek*, Aram. לוֹעָא, ܠܘܥܐ *id.*);—וְשַׂמְתָּ שַׂכִּין בְּלֹעֶךָ Pr 23[2] *and thou shalt put a knife to thy throat* (fig. for restraining oneself from indulgence in food).

3886 †II. [לוּעַ, or לָעַע] **vb. talk wildly** (MT יָלַע, לָעוּ; perh. better wd. be יִלְעֶה, לָעוּ (√לעה), cf. Thes and Ar. لَغَا, لَغِيَ *make mistakes in talking*, Ba[ZMG xli. 1887, 605, 614]);—**Qal** *Pf.* 3 mpl. לָעוּ Jb 6[3], subj. דברים (v. Di); *Impf.* מוֹקֵשׁ אָדָם יָלַע קֹדֶשׁ
3216

Pr 20[25] it is *a snare to a man* that *he should rashly cry, Holy!* (construction unusual, and perh. text. err., cf. Frankenberg; on form v. Ol[§ 243 a Anm.]; Bö[i. 296] Kö[i. 375 f.] der. fr. לעע; Str., Hiph. fr. לעע).

לוץ v. ליץ. p. 539 3887

†לוּשׁ **vb. knead** (NH *id.*; Aram. לוּשׁ, ܠܫ, Eth. ለውሰ: or ለሰ:);—**Qal** *Impf.* 3 fs. וַתָּלָשׁ 1 S 28[24] 2 S 13[8] Qr (Kt ־ושׁ); *Imv.* fs. לוּשִׁי Gn 18[6]; *Inf. cstr.* מִלּוּשׁ Ho 7[4]; *Pt.* fpl. לָשׁוֹת Je 7[18];—*knead* (obj. not expr. = קֶמַח סֹלֶת) Gn 18[6] (J), cf. 1 S 28[24]; obj. בָּצֵק *dough* Ho 7[4] Je 7[18] cf. 2 S 13[8]. 3888

לושׁ (Kt) **n.pr.m.**, לַיִשׁ v. ליש. p. 539 3889, 3919

לָז, לָזֶה, לֵזוּ v. הַלָּז etc., p. 229 supra. 1975-77

לְזוּת v. לוז supra. p. 531 3891

לַח v. sub לחח. p. 535 3892

לחה (√ of foll., poss. fr. *smoothness*, cf. Ar. لَحَى *peel off*; Syr. ܠܚܐ *strip off, erase*).

†I. לְחִי **n.m.** [Ct 1, 10] **jaw, cheek** (NH *id.*; Aram. לוֹחָא; Ar. لَحْيٌ; on As. *laḫû* cf. Dl[HWB 375], but ح = *ḥ*?);—ל׳ abs. Ju 15[17] Mi 4[14]; cstr. Ju 15[15] + 2 t.; לְחִי 1 K 22[24] + 3 t. + Ju 15[19.19]; *sf.* לְחָיוֹ Jb 40[26]; לֶחְיָהּ La 1[2]; du. לְחָיַיִם Dt 18[3]; cstr. לְחָיֵי Is 30[28]; sf. לְחָיַי Is 50[6], cf. Jb 16[10], etc.; לְחֵיהֶם Ho 11[4];—**1.** *jaw, jawbone*, of animal, Ju 15[15.16.16.17] (under jaw of ass), cf. n.pr.loc. רָמַת לֶחִי v[17]; in sim. כִּמְרִימֵי עֹל עַל־לְחֵיהֶם Ho 11[4] *like those lifting up a yoke from upon* (rd. מֵעַל?) *their jaws* (Isr. under fig. of oxen); of sacrificial ox or sheep Dt 18[3]; of crocodile Jb 40[26]; of Pharaoh under fig. of תַּנִּים Ez 29[4] (cf. v[3]); cf. 38[4] Is 30[28]. **2.** *cheek*, of man 1 K 22[24] = 2 Ch 18[23], Jb 16[10] ψ 3[8] Ct 5[13] Is 50[6] La 3[30] Mi 4[14]; of woman Ct 1[10] La 1[2] (fig. of Jerusalem). 3895

†II. לְחִי **n.pr.loc.** scene of an exploit of Samson;—ל׳ Ju 15[19.19] (𝔊 Σιαγων), לֶחִי v[14]; c. art. בַּלֶּחִי v[9] (𝔊 Λευει, 𝔊L Λεχει), cf. רָמַת לֶחִי v[17] = *height of Leḥi* (expl. as fr. לְחִי *jawbone*, cf. GFM, 𝔊 Ἀναίρεσις σιαγόνος); also 2 S 23[11], where read לֶחְיָה *to Leḥi*, for לַחַיָּה, vid. II. חַיָּה, p. 312 supr.; (𝔊 θηρία; 𝔊L σιαγόνα). It must have lain in the Shephelah, near the border of the hill-country of Judah (Buhl[Geogr. 91]); site unknown; conjectures are cited and criticized by GFM[Ju 15, 19] q.v. 3896

לחח (√of foll.; cf. Eth. ለሐሐ: II. I. *moisten, cool;* ሰሐለሐ: *be moistened* Di[Lex. 30]; NH לִחְלַח Pilp. *moisten thoroughly*, Aram. לַחְלַח *id.*, NH לַח *moist, fresh;* לֵיחָה *moisture, freshness*, etc.)

3892 †לַח **adj. moist, fresh, new**;—לַ׳ Gn 30[37] Ez 21[3]; לָח 17[24]; pl. לַחִים Nu 6[3]+2 t.;—**1.** *moist, fresh*, of trees, fruit, etc.; לִבְנֶה לַח Gn 30[37] (J); עֵץ לַ׳ Ez 17[24] 21[3]; grapes עֲנָבִים לַ׳ Nu 6[3]. **2.** *new*, of cords, יְתָרִים לַ׳ Ju 16[7.8], prob. made of *fresh* sinews of animal (cf. Syr. ܠܚܐ PS[1652]; GFM[ad loc.])

3893 †[לֵחַ] **n.m. moisture, freshness** (i. e. *force, vigour*);—sf. וְלֹא נָס לֵחֹה Dt 34[7] *and his freshness had not fled;* rd. prob. also בְּלֵחוֹ for MT בְּלַחְמוֹ Je 11[19] (v. לֶחֶם ad fin.; on Zp 1[17] v. לְחוּם).

3895-96 לְחִי, לֶחִי v. sub לחה. p. 534

3897 †[לָחַךְ] **vb. lick** (NH *id.;* so Aram. לְחַךְ, ܠܚܟ; Ar. (لَحِكَ);—**Qal** *Inf. cstr.* כִּלְחֹךְ Nu 22[4] (E), sq. acc.; of ox licking up grass. **Pi.** *Pf.* 3 fs. לִחֵכָה 1 K 18[38]; *Impf.* 3 mpl. יְלַחֲכוּ Nu 22[4] Mi 7[17]; יְלַחֵכוּ ψ 72[9] Is 49[23]; *lick up* (sq. acc.), fire fr. heaven the water in trench 1 K 18[38]; of Isr. consuming produce of land Nu 22[3] (E); esp. לִ׳ עָפָר *lick the dust*, sign of humiliation Mi 7[17] ψ 72[9] Is 49[23].

3898 I. [לָחַם] [171] **vb. fight, do battle** (NH Hithp.; ואלתחם MI[11.15.19]; perh. = *order the battle*, cf. Nö[ZMG xl. 1886, 721]; Ar. لَحَمَ *fit close together*, so NH לחם Pi., Syr. ܠܚܡ Pa. *unite*, ܠܚܡ *fit; also threaten;* Gerber[Verb. Denom. 59] thinks vb. in Heb. denom. fr. מִלְחָמָה *battle-line*, but dub.);—†**Qal** (poet.) only *Imv.* ms. and *Pt. act.*—*fight, do battle* with, rare, only ψψ, appar. later usage:—לְחַם אֶת־לֹחֲמָי ψ 35[1] *do battle with those battling with me* (dub. whether את is acc. sign or prep. *with*, cf. Ol; ‖ רִיבָה אֶת־יְרִיבַי); לֹחֲמִים לִי 56[3] *doing battle against me;* לֹחֵם v[2] as subst. *fighter*.† **Niph.** [167] *Pf.* נִלְחַם Ju 9[17]+, וְנִלְחַמְתָּ 11[8] 1 S 15[18], וְנִלְחַמְנוּ Dt 1[41] consec., etc.; *Impf.* יִלָּחֵם Ex 14[14] Dt 1[30]; יִלָּחֶם לָנוּ Ne 4[14], וַיִּלָּחֶם Ex 17[8]+19 t.; 3 fs. תִּלָּחֵם Zc 14[14]; 3 mpl. וַיִּלָּחֲמוּ Ju 1[5]+13 t.; sf. וַיִּלָּחֲמוּנִי ψ 109[3]; 2 mpl. תִּלָּחֲמוּ 1 K 22[31]+4 t.; תִּלָּחֲמוּן 1 K 12[24], etc.; *Imv.* הִלָּחֶם Ex 17[9] 1 S 18[17]; הִלָּחֶם בּוֹ Ju 9[38]; pl. הִלָּחֲמוּ 2 K 10[3] Ne 4[8]; *Inf. abs.* נִלְחֹם Ju 11[25]; *cstr.* הִלָּחֵם 1[9]+35 t.; הִלָּחֶם בּוֹ etc., Nu 22[11]+6 t.; sf. הִלָּחֲמוֹ 2 K 8[29]+3 t.; *Pt.* נִלְחָם Ex 14[25]+10 t.; pl. נִלְחָמִים Jos 10[25]+10 t. (but 1 S 31[1] rd. rather נִלְחֲמוּ, so ‖ 1 Ch 10[1] We Klo Bu, cf. Dr);—*engage in battle* (recipr.), sometimes *wage war* (Jos 10[5] Ju 11[5] 1 K 14[19] 22[46] 2 K 6[8] 14[28] etc.), oft. c. בְּ of enemy (60 t.) Ex 1[10] 17[9.10] Nu 21[23.26] 22[11] (all E), Ju 11[8.25] 1 S 15[18] 2 S 8[10]+(49 t.); less oft. c. בְּ of city attacked or besieged †Ju 9[45] 1 S 23[1] 2 S 12[26.27.29] Is 20[1] Jos 10[31] (D), 1 K 20[1] Ne 4[2]; of tower Ju 1[52]; sq. בְּאַרְצִי 11[12]+; also c. עִם of enemy (26 t.): Ju 5[20] 11[4.5.20] Jos 11[5] (JE), 1 S 13[5] 17[19], also 1 S 17[32.33] (of single combat), Dt 20[4] Jos 9[2] (both D), 2 K 13[12] 14[15] 2 Ch 11[1] 17[10] 27[5] Dn 10[20] 11[11]+; c. עִם of city †Jos 10[29] (D), 19[47] (JE)†; c. אֶת־ = *with*, of enemy, †Jos 24[8] (E), 1 S 17[9] (single combat), Je 21[5] 1 K 20[23] 2 K 19[9] = Is 37[9], Je 37[10]; also Ju 12[4] 2 S 11[17] 21[15] 1 K 22[31] 2 K 8[2] 9[15] Je 21[4] 32[5] 33[5] 2 Ch 18[30] 22[6], and c. אוֹתָם (= אִתָּם) Jos 10[25] (D), 1 K 20[25] (Kö[Lgb. ii. 296])†; c. עַל, *against*, of enemy only Je 21[2]; elsewhere (16 t.) of city: †Jos 10[5] (JE), Is 7[1] 2 K 12[18] 19[8] = Is 37[8]; esp. D and Je: Dt 20[10.19] Jos 10[34.36.38] (all D), Je 32[24.29] 34[1.7.8.22]†; c. אֶל־ of enemy †Je 1[19] 15[20]†; c. sf. וַיִּלָּחֲמוּנִי †ψ 109[3] *and they have fought against me*†; c. יַחַד i.e. fight *together* = with (against) one another †1 S 17[10]; abs. c. acc. cogn. מִלְחָמוֹת *fight battles* †1 S 8[20] 18[17] 25[28] 2 Ch 32[8]†; abs. elsewhere Ju 5[19.19.20] Dt 1[41] Zc 10[5] +26 t.+ וַיָּסֹרוּ עָלָיו לְהִלָּחֵם 1 K 22[32]; †c. עַל *for, in behalf of*, Ju 9[17] 2 K 10[3] Ne 4[8]; c. לְ = *id.*, Ex 14[14] (J), v[25] (J; + בְּ of enemy), Dt 1[30] 3[22] 20[4] (+ עִם of enemy, vid. supra), Jos 10[14.42] 23[3.10] (all D), Ne 4[14]+; יָכֹל לְהִלָּ׳ *be able to fight*, c. את of enemy 1 S 17[9], c. בְּ of enemy Nu 22[11], = *be successful in fighting*, prevail against; so c. עַל of city Is 7[1], and abs. 2 K 16[5] (after וַיָּצֻרוּ עַל *besiege*).

†לָחֶם **n.[m.]** only in אָז לָחֶם שְׁעָרִים Ju 5[8] 3901 (so Mass.; Codd. לְחֵם, לָחֵם), usu. tr. *then* was there *war* of (= at) the *gates*, but improb.; text and meaning dub.; A𝔊L rd. ὡς ἄρτον κρίθινον, whence Bu[RS 103] אָז לֶחֶם שְׂעֹרִים *then* they used to eat *barley bread;* but Bu[Comm.] אָזַל לֶ׳ שְׂ׳ *the barley bread was exhausted;* Mayer Lambert[RÉJ xxx, 115] אז לחמש ערים *then for (in) 5 cities* no shield was seen, etc.; other conj. in Kau[AT]; cf. GFM[ad loc.]

†[לְחוּם] **n.[m.]** perh. **intestines, bowels** 3894 (mng. and √ not wholly certain, cf. Nö[ZMG xl. 1886, 721]; from לחם = *press together*, acc. to Dl[Prol. 193]);—

only sf.: וּלְחֻמָם כַּגְּלָלִים Zp 1[17] their blood shall be poured out like water, *and their bowels like dung*, Hi-St (cf. 2 S 20[10]), Dl[l.c.] We ('ihr Mark'), Rothstein[KauAT] Di[Jb 20. 23]; Gr חֵילָם cf. v[12] (to wh. Now incl.); Now suggests also וְלֵחָם *and their moisture* (*freshness, vigour*, cf. Dt 34[7]); >al. who render *flesh*, 𝔊 τὰς σάρκας (cf. Ar. لَحْمٌ *flesh, meat*, v. sub לֶחֶם); וְיַמְטֵר עָלֵימוֹ בִּלְחוּמוֹ Jb 20[23] to fill his belly, God sendeth into him his burning anger, *and raineth* it *upon him, into his* (very) *bowels* Hi Dl[l.c.] Bae[KauAT] (cf. Di, and *into his flesh* De, v. supr.); >disting. from Zp 1[17] Di (in transl.) Da Hoffm Bu *his food* (as obj. of ימטר; rd. then לַחְמוֹ); 𝔊 ὀδύνας, whence Me Sgfr חֲבָלִים, Schwally[ZAW x. 1890. 179] בַּלָּהָה; Nö[l.c.] *wrath*, cf. Syr. ܠܚܡ *threaten*.

4421 **מִלְחָמָה**[319] **n.f. battle, war**;—abs. מ׳ Gn 14[2.8] Ex 1[10]+; cstr. מִלְחֶמֶת 1 S 13[22] (מ׳ מִכְמָשׁ 𝔊 Th We Bu HPS Ew[§ 188 c] Kö[ii. 182] > abs. Thes al.); sf. מִלְחַמְתִּי 2 Ch 35[21]; מִלְחַמְתְּךָ 2 S 11[25]; מִלְחַמְתֶּךָ Is 41[12], etc.; pl. מִלְחָמוֹת Is 42[13] + 7 t. Ch ψψ; cstr. מִלְחֲמוֹת Ju 3[1]+, etc.;—*battle*, Gn 14[8] 1 S 17[1.2.8] 31[3] 1 K 20[14.18.29.39]+oft.; *war*, Gn 14[2] Ex 1[10] Dt 20[12] Jos 11[23] 14[15] 2 S 3[1] (וַתְּהִי הַמִּלְחָמָה)+; סֵפֶר מִלְחֲמֹת י׳ Nu 21[14] (JE); acc. cogn. c. נלחם †1 S 8[20] 2 Ch 32[8] and (מִלְחֲמוֹת י׳) 1 S 18[17] 25[28]†; =*art of war*, למד מ׳ Is 2[4] *learn war*=Mi 4[3]; למד מ׳ Ju 3[2] *teach war, fighting*; מְלַמֵּד יָדַי לַמִּ׳ 2 S 22[35]=ψ 18[35], cf. ψ 144[1]; לִמּוּדֵי מ׳ 1 Ch 5[18], מְלֻמְּדֵי מ׳ Ct 3[8] *instructed in war*; once=*battlefield* וַיָּבֹאוּ עַד הַמִּ׳ 1 S 14[20] (so Kit[KauAT]). The most freq. phrases are: †אִישׁ מ׳ Is 3[2] 1 S 16[18] 17[33] 2 S 17[8] Ez 39[20] Jos 17[1] (P), also (coll.) Ju 20[17], of י׳ Ex 15[3] (poem); אַנְשֵׁי הַמִּ׳ Jos 6[3] 10[24] (both JE), Dt 2[14.16] Jos 5[4.6] (all D), Je 38[4] 39[4] 41[3.16] 49[26] 51[32] 52[7.25], also 1 K 9[22] 2 K 25[4] Nu 31[28.49] (P), Jo 4[9]; late אַנְשֵׁי מ׳ Jo 2[7] 1 Ch 12[39] (v[38] van d. H) 2 Ch 8[9] 17[13]; אַנְשֵׁי מִלְחַמְתֵּהּ Is 42[13] 1 Ch 28[3]; אִישׁ מִלְחָמוֹת Je 50[30] *her men of war*, cf. Is 41[12] Ez 27[10.27]; אִישׁ מִלְחֲמוֹת תֹּעִי 2 S 8[10] *a man of battles of Toi*, i.e. his frequent opponent (v. Dr), =1 Ch 18[10]; seldom גִּבּוֹר מ׳ ψ 24[8] (of י׳), גִּבּוֹרֵי מ׳ 2 Ch 13[3]; שָׂרֵי מִלְחָמוֹת 2 Ch 32[6]; עַם הַמִּ׳ Jos 8[1.3] 10[7] 11[7], cf. 8[11] (all JE), cf. also 1 S 13[16] add. 𝔊 We Dr, cf. Klo; אַנְשֵׁי חַיִל לַמִּ׳ Je 48[14]; צְבָא מ׳ *battle-host* Is 13[4], so צ׳ הַמִּ׳ Nu 31[14] (P); also גְּדוּדֵי צְבָא מ׳ 1 Ch 7[4], יֹצְאֵי צ׳ לַמִּ׳ v[11], אַנְשֵׁי צָבָא לַמִּ׳ 1 Ch 12[9] (v[8] van d. H)†; *weapons of war*, כְּלֵי (ה)מ׳ Ju 18[11.17] Je 21[4] 51[20] 1 Ch 12[34] (v[33] van d. H), also fig. 2 S 1[27] (|| גִּבּוֹרִים); כְּלֵי צְבָא מ׳ 1 Ch 12[38] (v[37] van d. H); קֶשֶׁת מ׳ Zc 9[10] 10[4]; כְּלֵי מִלְחַמְתּוֹ *his weapons of war* 1 S 8[12] Dt 1[41], cf. Ju 18[16] Ez 32[27]; דִּבְרֵי הַמִּ׳ =*the news of the battle* 2 S 11[18.19]+v[22] add. 𝔊 The We Klo Dr Bu. Freq. combin. with vbs. are: עָרַךְ מ׳ *draw up battle*-line Ju 20[22]+, sq. אֵת *with*=*against* Gn 14[8] Ju 20[20], sq. עִם 2 Ch 13[3]; אסר המ׳ i.e. begin the battle 1 K 20[14], cf. 2 Ch 13[3]; וַתִּקְרַב הַמִּ׳ 1 K 20[29] *and the battle was joined*; עָשָׂה מ׳ *make war* Pr 20[8] 24[6] 1 Ch 22[8], sq. אֵת *with* Gn 14[2] Jos 11[18] (D), sq. עִם Dt 20[12.20] 1 Ch 5[10.19]; †יָצָא לַמִּ׳ עִם Ju 20[14.20.28], c. עַל 1 K 8[44] 2 Ch 6[34]; הָלַךְ לַמִּ׳ עִם 2 K 8[28]; נגשׁ לַמִּ׳ עִם Ju 20[23], c. בְּ 1 S 7[10] 2 S 10[3], abs. Je 46[3]†; וַתְּהִי הַמִּ׳ עִם 2 S 21[18.19], c. בֵּין 2 S 3[1], cf. v[6]+; †קִדֵּשׁ מ׳ *consecrate war*, i.e. open a campaign (with sacred rites, Che) Mi 3[5] Je 6[4] (both c. עַל), Jo 4[9]; cf. †וְהַמִּ׳ הִדְבִּיקַתְהוּ Ju 20[42] *and the battle clung to them*; וַתַּעַל הַמִּ׳ 22[35] *and the battle rose* (high)=2 Ch 18[34]; וַתִּטֹּשׁ הַמִּ׳ 1 S 4[2], rd. וַתֵּט הַמִּ׳ (𝔊 We Klo Bu, cf. Dr) *and the battle inclined* (in favour of one side); נָפוֹצֶת הַמִּ׳ 2 S 18[8] Qr *the battle was spread* (extended), so read 1 S 14[24] add. 𝔊 The We Klo Dr; תָּקוּם עָלַי מ׳ ψ 27[3] if *war rise against me*†; הַמִּ׳ כָּבְדָה Ju 20[34] *the battle was severe*, cf. וַתִּכְבַּד הַמִּ׳ אֶל־שָׁאוּל 1 S 31[3]=1 Ch 10[3] (אל for עַל); so וַתְּהִי הַמִּ׳ חֲזָקָה 1 S 14[52], חָזַק מִמֶּנּוּ הַמִּ׳ 2 K 3[26]; וַתְּהִי הַמִּ׳ קָשָׁה 2 S 2[17]: cf. כֹּבֶד מ׳ Is 21[15], עֱזוּז מ׳ 42[25].

†II. [**לָחַם**] **vb. use as food, eat**, poet. 3898
(so Thes Buhl, cf. Frä[30] Guidi[Della Sede 33]; this would explain diff. between לֶחֶם and لَحْمٌ; yet verb rare and chiefly late);—**Qal** *Pf.* 3 pl. לָחֲמוּ Pr 4[17]; *Impf.* 2 ms. תִּלְחַם Pr 23[6], 1 s. אֶלְחָם ψ 141[4]; *Imv.* mpl. לַחֲמוּ Pr 9[5]; *Inf. cstr.* לְחוֹם Pr 23[1]; *Pt. pass.* pl. cstr. לְחֻמֵי Dt 32[24]; *eat* (mostly Pr), abs. Pr 23[1]; sq. acc. cogn. לֶחֶם 4[17] 23[6]; sq. בְּלַחְמִי 9[5]; sq. בְּמַנְעַמֵּיהֶם ψ 141[4] eat *of their dainties*; לְחֻמֵי רֶשֶׁף Dt 32[24] (poem) *eaten up with the Fire-bolt*, fig. of pestilence (Dr).

לֶחֶם[296] **n.m.**[1 S 9, 7] and (rarely) **f.**[Gn 49, 20] (vid. 3899
infr., and Dr[1 S 10, 4]) **bread, food** (Ph. לחם *bread*; NH לֶחֶם; Aram. לַחְמָא, ܠܰܚܡܳܐ, as Heb.; Ar. لَحْمٌ *flesh, meat* (cf. Frä[30]));—abs. ל׳ Gn 3[19]+; לָחֶם Gn 31[54]+; לָחֶם ψ 14[4]+2 t.; cstr. לֶחֶם Ho 9[4]+; sf. לַחְמִי Jb 3[24]+, לַחְמְךָ Ob[7]+, לַחְמָם Ho 9[4b], +v[4a] (for MT לָהֶם), We GASm Now, +etc.;—**1. a.**

bread, the ordinary food of early Hebrews (Benz [Arch. 84 ff.] Now[Arch. i. 109 ff.]) Ex 21[14] (E), Nu 21[5] Jos 9[5.12] (JE), Dt 8[3] 23[5] Ex 16[3] (P) +; כִּכַּר־ל׳ *loaf of bread* 1 S 2[36] + (vid. כִּכָּר sub כרר), and without ככר (always c. num.) †1 S 10[4] 16[20] (v. Dr), 17[17] 21[4] 25[18] 2 S 16[1] 1 K 14[3] 2 K 4[42]†; חַלַּת ל׳ *cake of bread* 2 S 6[19] Ex 29[23] + (v. חַלָּה sub I. חלל); made from barley (שְׂעֹרִים) Ju 7[13] 2 K 4[42] (v. also לֶחֶם supr.); from wheat-flour (סֹלֶת חִטִּים) Ex 29[2] (P); cf. the mixture Ez 4[9]; made by baking (אפה) Is 44[15.19] Lv 26[26] (H; cf. Je 37[21]); פַּת־ל׳† *a bit of bread* 1 S 2[36] 1 K 17[11] Pr 28[21], cf. Ez 13[19], as modest term for a hospitable meal Gn 18[5] (J), Ju 19[5] 1 S 28[22]†; disting. from meat (flesh), Gn 27[17] (J), 1 S 25[11] 1 K 17[6.6] Ex 16[8.12] (also v[3] supr.), 29[32.34] Lv 8[31] (all P), 23[18] (H), 1 Ch 12[40] ψ 78[20] Dn 10[3]; = a meal 1 S 20[27], אָכַל ל׳ = *take a meal* Gn 31[54.54] 37[25] 43[25.32] +; אכל לַחְמִי ψ 41[10] *eat my bread*, establishing an obligation, cf. Ob[7] (rd. אֹכְלֵי ל׳ acc. to Marti [KauAT]; del. ל׳ 𝔊 Hi We, cf. VB) עשׂה ל׳ = *make a feast* Ec 10[19]; מַטֵּה ל׳ *staff of bread* (as *support* of life), only late †Ez 4[16] 5[16] 14[13] Lv 26[26] (H), ψ 105[16]; cf. מִשְׁעַן ל׳ Is 3[1] (gloss)†; *leavened bread* is ל׳ חָמֵץ Lv 7[13]; *unleavened bread* is ל׳ מַצּוֹת Ex 29[2] (both P); ל׳ (הַ)פָּנִים† *bread of the face* (of י׳; i. e. in his presence, Di[Lv 24, 9] Dr[1 S 21, 7]): in the sanctuary 1 S 21[7] 1 K 7[48] = 2 Ch 4[19], Ex 25[30] 35[13] 39[36], without פ׳ 40[23] (all P); = ל׳ הַתָּמִיד Nu 4[7] (P), ל׳ קֹדֶשׁ 1 S 21[5]; in Chr ל׳ הַמַּעֲרֶכֶת 1 Ch 9[32] cf. 23[29] Ne 10[34], מ׳ ל׳ 2 Ch 13[11]; opp. ל׳ חֹל 1 S 21[5]†; ל׳ תְּנוּפָה Lv 23[17] *wave-loaf*; ל׳ (הַ)בִּכּוּרִים v[20] 2 K 4[42] *bread of first-fruits*. †**b.** = *bread-corn*, the material from which bread is made, i.e. wheat, barley, etc.: Gn 41[54.55] (E), 47[13.15.17.17.19] (J), 49[20] (poem in J), Is 28[28] 30[23] 55[10] Je 5[17] Ez 48[18] Jb 28[5] Pr 28[3] ψ 104[14]; ל׳ הָאָרֶץ Nu 15[19] (P), ארץ ל׳ 2 K 18[32] = Is 36[17]†. **2.** *food* in general: **a.** of man, Ju 13[16] (kid, v[15]), 1 S 14[24.24.28] (honey), 28[20] 30[12] Pr 22[9] 27[27.27] (goat's milk) +; נֹתֵן ל׳ לְכָל־בָּשָׂר ψ 136[25]. †**b.** of animals, Pr 6[8] 30[25] 65[25] Jb 24[5] ψ 147[9]†. **c.** of God (in sacrifices): ל׳ אֱלֹהֵיהֶם† (cf. RS[Sem. i. 207, 2nd ed., 224]) Lv 21[6] cf. v[8.17.21.22], 22[25] (all H), cf. Nu 28[2] (P), Ez 16[19] 44[7], and ל׳ מְגֹאָל Mal 1[7]; also (ל׳) ל׳ אִשֶּׁה Lv 3[11.16] Nu 28[24] (all P)†. **3.** other phrases and fig. uses are: **a.** ל׳ רֶשַׁע Pr 4[17] (acc. cogn. c. לָחַם), prob. = *food gained by wickedness* (‖ יֵין חֲמָסִים), cf. ל׳ שֶׁקֶר 20[17], ל׳ כְּזָבִים 23[3]; ל׳ עַצְלוּת 31[27] = *bread of idleness*, i. e. unearned; ל׳ חֻקִּי Pr 30[8] (opp. to riches and poverty, v. חֹק); ל׳ לַחַץ 1 K 22[27] = 2 Ch 18[26], vid. לַחַץ infr.; ל׳ הָעֲצָבִים ψ 127[2], vid. II. עֶצֶב; ל׳ אוֹנִים Ho 9[4], vid. אָוֶן, p. 20a; ל׳ אֲנָשִׁים Ez 24[17.22] of food offered to mourners, cf. Je 16[7] (where ins. ל׳ 𝔊 Gf Gie); שַׁלַּח לחמך על־פני המים Ec 11[1] usually interpr. of benevolent giving (cf. Now); De al. of sea-commerce in bread-stuffs, cf. Pr 31[14]. **b.** fig. לַחְמֵנוּ הֵם Nu 14[9] (JE) *our food are they*, i. e. we will devour, destroy, them (cf. Dt 7[16]); דִּמְעָתִי ל׳ ψ 42[4] cf. 80[6] (vid. אכל, p. 37[b] supr.); ל׳ of evil deeds of wicked Jb 20[14]; עֵץ בְּלַחְמוֹ Je 11[19] appar. fig. of destroying the *prophet and his house*, but read prob. בְּלֵחוֹ *in its freshness* (i. e. untimely), so Hi Gf Che Gie (vid. לַח sub לחח supra).

†לַחְמִי **n.pr.m.** brother of Goliath of Gath (q.v.) slain by Elhanan, acc. to 1 Ch 20[5] (את לחמי; 𝔊 Ελεμεε, Λεεμει, Λοομι); orig. reading prob. (as in ‖ 2 S 21[19]) בֵּית הַלַּחְמִי q.v. p. 112[a] supra. 3902

†לַחְמָס **n.pr.loc.** in Judah (32 Codd. לחמם);—Jos 15[40], 𝔊 Μαχες, A𝔊L Λαμ(μ)ας; perh. = *El-laḥm*, c. 13 miles WNW. from Hebron, Kn[ad loc.] PEF[Mem. iii. 261] Buhl[Geogr. 192]. 3903

†לָחַץ **vb. squeeze, press, fig. oppress** (Ar. لَحَصَ; Chr.-Pal. ܠܚܨ Schwally [Idioticon 48] (with which Nö[M 74] comp. Mand. הלאצא, *torture*, NS. ܠܚܨ *press together, urge, exert oneself*); see also rare deriv. in Syr. PS[1932]);—**Qal** *Pf.* ל׳ Ju 4[3] + 2 t. etc.; *Impf.* sf. יִלְחָצֵנִי ψ 56[2]; 3 fs. וַתִּלְחַץ Nu 22[25], etc.; *Pt.* pl. לֹחֲצִים Ex 3[9] + 2 t., etc.—**1.** *squeeze, press:* sq. acc. + אֶל Ju 1[34] Nu 22[25 b] (J); sq. acc. + בְּ instr. 2 K 6[32] shut the door *and press him* (back, out) *with the door.* **2.** *oppress:* sq. acc. pers. Ex 22[20] (‖ הוֹנָה), 23[29] (both E), ψ 56[2]; of people Ex 3[9] (E; + acc. cogn.), Ju 2[18] 4[3] 6[9] 10[12] 1 S 10[18] Am 6[14] 2 K 13[4.22] Je 30[20] ψ 106[42]; abs. Is 19[20]. **Niph.** *Impf.* 3 fs. וַתִּלָּחֵץ Nu 22[25 a] (J) *squeeze oneself*, of Balaam's ass, sq. אֶל־הַקִּיר. 3905

†לַחַץ **n.m. oppression, distress**;—ל׳ abs. 1 K 22[27.27] + 5 t.; cstr. 2 K 13[4] + 2 t.; sf. לַחֲצֵנוּ Dt 26[4] ψ 44[25];—*oppression* of Isr. Ex 3[9] (E; + vb. cogn.), 2 K 13[4] cf. Dt 26[7] (‖ עָמָל, עֳנִי) ψ 44[25] (‖ עֳנִי); *oppr. of* (i.e. by) an enemy, ψ 42[10] 43[2]; in gen. Jb 36[15] (‖ עֳנִי); לֶחֶם ל׳ וּמַיִם ל׳ 1 K 22[27] 3906

$=$ 2 Ch 18^{26} *bread of oppression and water of oppression*, i.e. prison-fare ($>$ Klo *scanty* fare); cf. לֶחֶם צַר וּמַיִם ל׳ Is 30^{20}, appar. of privations of a siege (cf. Che Di Du; on the apposition in these passages v. Ges$^{\S 131. 2 (b)}$ Kö$^{iii, \S 333 p. q.}$ Da$^{Synt. \S 29. e}$).

3907 †[לָחַשׁ] **vb. whisper, charm** (NH *id.*; Aram. לְחַשׁ, ܠܚܫ; Eth. ለሐሰ: *whisper*, v. RS $^{JPh\ xiv. 1885, 122}$, possibly originally serpent-charming);—**Pi.** *Pt.* pl. קוֹל מְלַחֲשִׁים ψ 58^{6} *voice of whisperers* (i.e. *serpent-charmers*; ‖ חוֹבֵר חֲבָרִים). **Hithp.** *whisper together*, *Impf.* יִתְלַחֲשׁוּ c. עַל ψ 41^{8}; *Pt.* pl. מִתְלַחֲשִׁים 2 S 12^{19}.

3908 †לַ֫חַשׁ **n.[m.] a whispering, charming**;—ל׳ Is 26^{16}; לָ֑חַשׁ Ec 10^{11} Is 3^{3} Je 8^{17}; pl. לְחָשִׁים Is 3^{20}.—**1.** *serpent-charming* Ec 10^{11}; נְבוֹן לָחַשׁ Is 3^{3} (prob. more general). **2.** *charms, amulets*, worn by women, Is 3^{20}. **3.** *whisper of prayer*, צָקוּן לַחַשׁ Is 26^{16} *they pour forth a whisper of prayer* (but Koppe Bö Gr Di Du rd. צָקוֹן לָחַשׁ '*Zauberzwang*,' *compulsion of (by) magic*).

3873 †לוֹחֵשׁ **n.pr.m.** ($=$ *whisperer*) only c. art. הַל׳, a chief of the people Ne 3^{12} 10^{25}.

3909 לָט v. sub לוט. p. 532

3910 †לֹט **n.[m.]** myrrh, or '*ladanum*' (Gk.), an aromatic gum exuded by leaves of *cistus-rose, cistus villosus*, Tristr$^{FFP, 235, and\ esp.\ Nat.\ Hist.\ Bib., 458\ ff.}$; Ri$^{HWB\ 897}$, cf. Löw$^{No. 79}$ Di$^{Gn\ 37, 25}$ Now$^{Arch.\ i.\ 64}$ (Sab. לדן, Sab. Denkm.^{84}; As. *ladunu* (fr. Damascus) cf. Schr$^{COT\ Gn\ 37,\ 25,\ MBAk.\ 1881,\ pp.\ 413\ ff.}$; Ar. لَاذَنٌ, whence Gk. λήδανον, λάδανον Hdt$^{iii.\ 112}$);—נְכֹאת וּצְרִי וָלֹט Gn 37^{25}, merchandise of Ishmaelite caravan, cf. 43^{11}, present to Joseph (both J; 𝔊 στακτή).

לטא (√of following; meaning unknown).

3911 †לְטָאָה **n.f.** a kind of **lizard** (NH *id.*);—named as unclean Lv 11^{30} (with כֹּחַ, אֲנָקָה, צָב, חֹמֶט, תִּנְשֶׁמֶת), 𝔊 χαλαβώτης, 𝔙 *stellio*.—Vid. Di$^{ad\ loc.}$ Tristr$^{Nat.\ Hist.\ Bib.\ 266\ ff.}$

3913 †[לָטַשׁ] **vb. hammer, sharpen, whet** (NH *id.*, *hammer, tap*; Aram. לְטַשׁ, ܠܛܫ *sharpen*; Ar. لَطَسَ *strike, tap*);—**Qal** *Impf.* יִלְטוֹשׁ Jb 16^{9} ψ 7^{13}; *Inf. cstr.* לִלְטוֹשׁ 1 S 13^{20}; *Pt.* לֹטֵשׁ;—**1.** *hammer*, only *Pt.* $=$ *hammerer*, sq. כָּל־חֹרֵשׁ Gn 4^{22} (J). **2.** *sharpen* sword, חֶרֶב (acc.) ψ 7^{13}; cf. 1 S 13^{20}, obj. קַרְדֹּם, אֵת, מַחֲרֵשָׁת, מַחֲרֵשָׁה; fig. ל׳ עֵינַיִם לִי Jb 16^{9} my foe *whets his eyes for me*. **Pu.** *Pt.* תַּעַר מְלֻטָּשׁ ψ 52^{4} *a sharpened razor* (in sim. of evil tongue).

†לְטוּשִׁם **n.pr.gent.** Gn 25^{3}, descendants of Abraham and Keturah; 𝔊 Λατουσιειμ. 3912

[לִיָה], לִיוֹת v. sub III. לוה. p. 531 3914

לַיְלָה, לַ֫יִל$_{242}$ **n.m.**$^{Gn\ 40,\ 5}$ **night** (NH *id.*; MI^{15} (ב)ללה; Aram. לֵילְיָא, ܠܠܝܐ, ܠܠܝܐ; Ar. لَيْلَةٌ, لَيْلٌ; Eth. ሌሊት: all $=$ *night*; As. *lîlâtu*, *evening* Dl^{HWB}; meaning of √dubious; form probably לילי, and ending ־ָה radical, and not ה loc., Nö$^{M\ 127}$ Dl$^{Prol.\ 128}$ Ges$^{\S 90,\ 2.\ c.\ R.}$ Kö$^{ii.\ p.\ 57,\ R.\ 1}$);—abs. לַ֫יְלָה Gn 19^{33} + 214 t. + 2 t. Qr (v. infr.); לָ֑יְלָה Gn 1^{5} + 3 t.; לַ֫יִל Is 16^{3} + Pr 31^{18} La 2^{19} Kt (Qr לַ֫יְלָה); לֵיל Is $15^{1.1}$ 21^{1}; cstr. לֵיל Ex 12^{42} Is 30^{29}; pl. abs. לֵילוֹת 1 S 30^{12} + 4 t.; cstr. *id.*, Is 21^{8} + 5 t.;—**1.** lit. *night*, opp. day, Gn 8^{22} (J), Dt 1^{33} + very oft. (v. יוֹם); alternation of day and night divinely ordained Gn 1^{5} (P), Je $33^{20.20.25}$ +; מִיּוֹם עַד־ל׳ Is $38^{12.13}$ i.e. within one whole day; as close of day, עַד־ל׳ 2 Ch 35^{14}; as time of sacred (לֵיל) חַג Is 30^{29}; of suffering and weeping לֵילוֹת עָמָל Jb 7^{3}, cf. ψ 6^{7} 77^{3} etc.; of pious desires, prayer, praise, meditation, etc. (sts. ‖ *by day*) Is 26^{9} Jb 35^{10} ψ 1^{2} 22^{3} 42^{9} 77^{7} 88^{2} 92^{3} 119^{55}, cf. 16^{7} 17^{3}; of night-service in Temple 134^{1}; of sudden assault, or destruction, Is 15^{1} Je 6^{5} Ob ^{5} Jb 27^{20} $34^{20.25}$ 36^{20}; divided into watches ψ 90^{4}; לֵיל שִׁמֻּרִים Ex 12^{42} v. sub שׁמר; c. num., denoting duration of time, †*forty days and forty nights* Gn $7^{4.12}$ Ex 24^{18} 34^{28} Dt $9^{9.11.18.25}$ 10^{10} 1 K 19^{8}; *three days and three nights* (שְׁלֹשָׁה לֵילוֹת) 1 S 30^{12} Jon 2^{1}; *seven days and seven nights* (שִׁבְעַת לֵילוֹת) Jb 2^{13} †; מַרְאֹת הַל׳ †Gn 20^{3} 31^{24} (both E), 1 K 3^{5}; חֲלוֹם הַל׳ Gn 46^{2} (E); חֶזְיוֹן ל׳ Jb 20^{8} 33^{15}, חֶזְיֹנוֹת ל׳ 4^{13}, חֲלוֹם חֲזוֹן ל׳ Is 29^{7} (cf. Mi 3^{6} infr.)†; בִּן־ל׳ Jon $4^{10.10}$ v. בֵּן **8.** p. 121 b. Chiefly in adverb. phr.:—בַּחֲצִי הַל׳ *at midnight* Ex 12^{29} + (v. חֲצִי, חֲצוֹת p. 345 b), cf. בְּתוֹךְ הַל׳ † 1 K 3^{20}, בְּאִישׁוֹן ל׳ Pr 7^{9} †; בַּל׳ הַזֶּה Ex $12^{8.12}$ *on this night* (P; the night of which one is speaking); בַּל׳ הַהוּא *on that night* Gn 19^{35} (J) + oft., (P only Nu 14^{1}); בַּל׳ הוּא Gn 19^{33} 30^{16}; so הַל׳ alone † 1 S 14^{34}, but del. 𝔊 We Kit, cf. Dr; Klo Bu rd. לַיהוה; הַל׳ *to-night* †Gn $19^{5.34}$ 30^{15} (all J), Nu $22^{8.19}$ (E), Jos 2^{2} 4^{3} 3915 (both JE), 2 S 17[1.16] 19[8] Ru 1[12] 3[2.13], opp. מָחָר *to-morrow* 1 S 19[11]; הַלּ׳ = *this night* just past, *last night* 1 S 15[16] (cf. Dr); כָּל־הַל׳ *all night* Ho 7[6] (opp. בֹּקֶר), Ex 14[20.21] (J), Nu 11[32] Jos 10[9] (both JE), Ju 16[2.2] 19[25] 1 S 15[11] 31[12] 2 S 2[29.32] 4[7]; opp. כל־היום ההוא (of continuous action) 1 S 19[24] 28[20] Is 62[6], opp. יומם ψ 78[14]; בְּכָל־ל׳ ψ 6[7] *every night* (prob.); cf. כָּל־הַלֵּילוֹת Is 21[8] *all the nights* (opp. יוֹמָם)†; esp. לַיְלָה *by night* Nu 22[20] (E) Jos 8[3] (JE), Dt 16[1] Nu 9[16] (P) + 51 t.; of these Gn 14[15] and Ex 13[21.22] (J) + 25 t. opp. יוֹמָם, covering all the time; otherwise Ju 6[27] (opp. יוֹמָם); לַיְלָה וָיוֹם *night and day* 1 K 8[29] Is 27[3] Est 4[16]; less oft. לֵילוֹת ψ 16[7]; הַל׳ *by night* †2 K 25[4] (ל׳ in ‖ Je 52[7]), Zc 1[8] Ne 4[16] (opp. הַיּוֹם)†; בַּל׳ *id.*, Je 6[5] + 18 t. (chfly late; oft. opp. יוֹמָם, בַּיּוֹם, etc.); בַּלַּיְלָה †ψ 92[3] (opp. בַּבֹּקֶר), 134[1] Ct 3[1.8]; בַּלֵּילוֹת Ne 9[19] (opp. בְּיוֹמָם); בְּלֵיל Is 15[1.1]; כַּל׳ *as at night* Jb 5[14] (opp. צָהֳרַיִם)†. **2.** fig. שִׁיתִי כַלַּיִל צִלֵּךְ Is 16[3] sim. of shadow of Zion as protection; more oft. in gloomy sense, of avenging calamity without divine guidance or comfort לַיְלָה מֵחָזוֹן Mi 3[6]; personal distress Jb 35[10]; judgment perh. also Jb 36[20] (Ew De Di Da; night of death Bu; 'unintelligible' Siegf); מַה־מִּלַּיְלָה מַה־מִּלֵּיל Is 21[11] i.e. what hour of the night of calamity is it? cf. v[12] (opp. בֹּקֶר).

3917 †**לִילִית**† **n.f. Lilith** (Milton Che *night-hag*), name of a female night-demon haunting desolate Edom; prob. borrowed fr. Bab., Is 34[14] (NH *id.;* As. *lilîtu*, Dl[HWB 377]; Syr. ܠܶܠܺܝܬܳܐ PS[1951]; on the development of legends of Lilith in later Judaism, v. Bux[Lex. Talmud., s.v.] Che[ad loc.] Grünbaum[ZMG xxxi. 1877, 250 f.]—Connexion with לילה perhaps only apparent, a popular etymology).

3885 **לִין** v. לוּן. p. 533-34

3887, 3045 †[**לִיץ**] **vb. scorn** (NH *id.;* vb. not in cognates; cf. Ph. מליץ *interpreter* CIS[22.44.88]; Ar. لَاصَ is *turn aside* (intrans.); hence perh. prop. *speak indirectly* or *obliquely*, Fl[De Pr. 1, 6]);—**Qal** *Pf.* 3 m. לָצְתָּ Pr 9[12]; *Impf.* יָלִיץ 3[34] + 2 t.; *Pt.* לֵץ 9[7] + 11 t.; pl. לֵצִים ψ 1[1] + 3 t.;—*scorn*, וְלַצְתָּ לְבַדְּךָ תִשָּׂא Pr 9[12] *if thou scornest thou alone shalt bear it* (opp. חָכַמְתָּ), c. acc. 14[9] 19[28]; c. לְ, לַלֵּצִים הוּא־יָלִיץ *scorners he (God) scorneth* 3[34]; הַלֵּץ the scorner is proud and haughty 21[24], delights in scorning 1[22], is incapable of discipline 9[7], reproof 9[8] 15[12], or rebuke 13[1], cannot find wisdom 14[6]; is an abomination 24[9], should be avoided ψ 1[1]; smitten and punished for the benefit of the simple Pr 19[25] 21[11] and banished for the removal of contention 22[10]; judgment is prepared for him 19[29]; ‖ עָרִיץ Is 29[20]; wine is a scorner Pr 20[1].—**Hiph.** *Pf.* 3 mpl. sf. הֱלִיצֻנִי ψ 119[51]; *Pt.* מֵלִיץ Gn 42[23] Jb 33[23]; pl. cstr. מְלִיצֵי 2 Ch 32[31]; sf. מְלִיצַי Jb 16[20]; מְלִיצֶיךָ Is 43[27];—**1.** *deride* Jb 16[20] ψ 119[51]. **2.** Pt. *interpreter* Gn 42[23] (E); fig. of intermediaries between God and man, Jb 33[23] Is 43[27]; *ambassador* 2 Ch 32[31]. **Po'lel** *Pt.* pl. לֹצְצִים 3945
(מְ dropped Kö[ii. 479]) *scorners* Ho 7[5]. **Hithp.**
Impf. תִּתְלוֹצָצוּ *act as a scorner, shew oneself a* 3945
mocker, Is 28[22].

†**לָצוֹן** **n.[m.] scorning**, Pr 1[22]; אַנְשֵׁי לָצוֹן 3944
men of scorning, scorners = לֵצִים 29[8] Is 28[14].

†**מְלִיצָה** **n.[f.] satire, mocking-poem** Hb 4426
2[6], also Pr 1[6] (al. here *figure, enigma*).

ליש (√of foll., Thes לוּשׁ; perhaps = *be strong* (Thes) cf. Ar. لَيْثٌ, لَوْثٌ, **strength**; لَاثَ (med. י) III. v. *be strong*, etc., appar. denom. = *be lion-like*).

†I. **לַיִשׁ** **n.m.**[Jb 4, 11] **lion** (Ar. لَيْثٌ, 𝔗 לֵיתָא; 3918
As. *nešu, lion* is comp. by Hal (cf. Hpt[KAT 2, 510]) Ba[ZA iii. 1888, 60]);—*lion* Jb 4[11] Is 30[6] (‖ לָבִיא), ל׳ גִּבּוֹר בַּבְּהֵמָה Pr 30[30].

†II. **לַיִשׁ** **n.pr.loc.** (on meaning *lion*, cf. 3919
RS[Sem. i. 156 (om. 2nd ed.)]);—former name of Dan, in extreme north of Canaan, Ju 18[7.14.27.29] (v. דָּן p. 192 b); 𝔊 Λαισα; = לֶשֶׁם q.v.; cf. Buhl[Geogr. § 124].

†III. **לַיִשׁ** **n.pr.m.** father of Michal's second 3919
husband, 1 S 25[44] + 2 S 3[15] Qr (Kt לוּשׁ), 𝔊 Αμεις, 3889
Σελλης, A Λα(ε)ις, 𝔊L Ιωας, Σελλειμ.

†**לַיְשָׁה** **n.pr.loc.** N. of Jerus. Is 10[30] (perh. 3919
akin to III. לַיִשׁ, v. Di); site unknown; v. Kasteren[ZPV xiii. 101] conj. *'Isawiye*, village two miles NE. fr. Jerus. (PEF[Map; Mem. iii. 27] Rob[BR i. 437] cf. Buhl[Geogr. 175]), 𝔊 ἐν Σα, Λαισα.

לֵךְ = לְכָה *Imv.* of הָלַךְ q.v. p. 229 1980

לָכַד [121] **vb. capture, seize, take (by lot)** 3920
(Ph. לכד *take out, choose* (?); 𝔗 לְכַד as BH; Ar. لَكَدَ is *strike, push*, with the hand, etc., مِلْكَدٌ *pestle*, cf. mod. لَكَدَ *attack* Wetzst[ZMG xxii. 1868, 140];

לָכַד stick or cleave to);—**Qal** *Pf.* ל׳ Jos 8^{1}+, לְכַדְתִּי 2 S 12^{27} etc.; *Impf.* 3 ms. יִלְכּוֹד Am 3^{5}; וַיִּלְכֹּד Ju 8^{12}+, etc.; *Imv.* ms. sf. לָכְדָהּ 2 S 12^{28}, mpl. לִכְדוּ; *Inf. abs.* לָכוֹד Am 3^{5}; *cstr.* sf. לְלָכְדֵנִי Je 18^{22}, לְלָכְדָהּ 32^{24}; *Pt.* לֹכֵד Jb 5^{13} Pr 16^{32};—**1.** *capture, seize* (not in P) c. acc., usu. a city or town, in war Ju $1^{8.12}$ Jos 8^{21} 10^{1} (JE), Dt 2^{35} + 48 t. (but Ju 1^{18} del. as gloss Bu Kit GFM al.); land Jos 10^{42} (D), Dn 11^{18}; water-courses (fords), Ju 3^{28} $7^{24.24}$ 12^{8}; obj. men (usu. princes, kings) in battle Ju 7^{25} $8^{12.14}$ Jos $11^{12.17}$ (D), 2 Ch 22^{9} 33^{11}; captives and spoils 2 S 8^{4} = 1 Ch 18^{4}; of Saul's seizing the kingdom (הַמְּלוּכָה), i.e. acquiring it actually by force of arms 1 S 14^{47}; also of Samson's *catching* the foxes Ju 15^{4}; of a lion *catching* his prey Am 3^{4}; of a trap, snare, לָכוֹד יִלְכּוֹד 3^{5}. †**2.** fig. of entrapping men Je 5^{26} ψ 35^{8}, cf. Pr 5^{22} Jb 5^{13} and (of a pit) Je 18^{22}. †**3.** of *taking* by lot Jos $7^{14.14.14.17}$ (JE; v. **Niph. 3**).

†**Niph.** *Pf.* נִלְכַּד La 4^{20}; 3 fs. נִלְכְּדָה 1 K 16^{18}+, etc.; *Impf.* יִלָּכֶד בָּהּ Is 24^{18} Je 48^{44}; וַיִּלָּכֵד Ec 7^{26}; וַיִּלָּכֵד Jos 7^{16}+, etc.; *Pt.* נִלְכָּד Jos 7^{15};—**1.** *be captured* in war, of city 1 K 16^{18} 2 K 18^{10} Je $38^{28.28}$ $48^{1.41}$ $50^{2.9.24}$ $51^{31.41}$ Zc 14^{2}; of men Je 51^{56} La 4^{20} (cf. **Qal 1**). **2.** of men, *be caught*, viz. in a snare or trap, only fig., usu. by divine judgment Is 8^{15} 24^{18} 28^{13} ψ 9^{16} 59^{13} Pr 6^{2} 11^{6} Je 6^{11} 8^{9}; so of Moab Je $48^{7.44}$; of being *ensnared* by a woman Ec 7^{26}; of being *caught* by cords of distress, בְּחַבְלֵי עֹנִי, Jb 36^{8}. **3.** *be taken* by lot Jos $7^{15.16.17.18}$ (all JE), 1 S $10^{20.21.21}$ $14^{41.42}$ (cf. **Qal 3**).

†**Hithp.** *Impf.* 3 mpl.; יִתְלַכְּדוּ וְלֹא יִתְפָּרָדוּ Jb 41^{9} *they grasp each other, and cannot be separated*, of crocodile's scales (‖ אִישׁ בְּאָחִיהוּ יְדֻבָּקוּ); פְּנֵי תְהוֹם יִתְלַכָּדוּ Jb 38^{30} *the face of the deep compacts* (of freezing; ‖ כָּאֶבֶן מַיִם יִתְחַבָּאוּ; vbs. transp., plausibly, by Me Bi Siegf Bu).

3921 †[לֶכֶד] **n.[m.]** a taking, capture (cf. ψ 9^{16}) וְשָׁמַר רַגְלְךָ מִלָּכֶד Pr 3^{26} (subj. י׳).

4434 †[מַלְכֹּדֶת] **n.f.** a catching instrument, i.e. a snare, trap, only fig.; sf. מַלְכֻּדְתּוֹ עֲלֵי נָתִיב Jb 18^{10} of the wicked (‖ טָמוּן בָּאָרֶץ חַבְלוֹ).

1980 לְכָה, לְכָה *Imv.* fr. הָלַךְ q.v.; לְכָה also for לָךְ *to thee* †Gn 27^{37}. p. 229

3922 †לֵכָה **n.pr.loc.** in Judah 1 Ch 4^{21}; unknown. 𝔊 Ληχα, Λαιχα.

3923 †לָכִישׁ **n.pr.loc.**—so Jos 10^{3}+; c. ה loc. לָכִישָׁה Jos 10^{31} + 5 t.;—Canaanitish (Amorit.) city, with king, Jos $10^{3.5.23}$ (all JE), v ^{31} 12^{11} (both D); (= Tel el-Amarna *Lakiša, Lakisi* Wkl[TA Tablets, Nos. 217, 218, 180, 181]); captured by Jos $10^{32.33.34.35}$ (all D); reckoned to Judah Mi 1^{13} Je 34^{7} Jos 15^{39} (P), cf. 2 K $14^{19.19}$ = 2 Ch $25^{27.27}$, 2 Ch 11^{9} Ne 11^{30}; base of Assyrian operations 2 K 18^{14}, cf. 2 Ch 32^{9}, also 2 K 18^{17} 19^{8} = Is 36^{2} 37^{8} (= As. *Lakisi* Schr[COT 2 K 18, 13]); prob. = mod. *Tell el-Hesy*, c. 33 miles SW. from Jerusalem FJB[Mound of Many Cities, 1893] Buhl[Geogr. § 103] GASm[Geogr. 234]; > *Umm el-Lâkis* vdVelde[Mem. 320] Guérin[Judeé ii. 299 ff.]; *Um Lâkis* opp. by Rob[BR ii. 47].—𝔊 Λαχεις.

לָכֵן v. כֵּן. לְלָאוֹת v. [לוּלִי] sub לולו. 3651, 3924
p. 485, 533

†לָמַד **vb.** exercise in, learn (NH *id.*, *be* 3925
accustomed to, learn; Aram. לְמַד (rare) *learn*; Syr. ܠܡܕ Pa. *accustom, combine*; Ettaph. *be taught*, etc.; As. *lamâdu*, *learn*, Dl[Prol. 29]);—

Qal *Pf.* 3 ms. ל׳ Is 26^{10}; 1 s. לָמַדְתִּי Pr 30^{3} + 3 t. Pf.; *Impf.* 3 ms. יִלְמַד Dt 17^{19}; 1 s. אֶלְמְדָה ψ 119^{73}; 3 pl. יִלְמְדוּן Dt 4^{10} + 12 t. Impf.; *Imv.* לִמְדוּ Is 1^{17}; *Inf. abs.* לָמֹד Je 12^{16}; *cstr.* sf. לָמְדִי ψ 119^{7}; *Pt. pass.* cstr. לְמוּדֵי 1 Ch 5^{8};—*learn* something, c. acc. Dt 5^{1} ψ $119^{7.71.73}$ 106^{35} Pr 30^{3} Is 2^{4} $26^{9.10}$ 29^{24} Je $12^{16.16}$ Mi 4^{3}; c. אֶל Je 10^{2}; c. *inf.* Dt 18^{9} Is 1^{17} Ez $19^{3.6}$; לְיִרְאָה Dt 4^{10} 14^{23} 17^{19} 31^{13}; וְיָרְאוּ Dt 31^{12}; לְמוּדֵי מִלְחָמָה *trained* to war 1 Ch 5^{18}. **Piel** *Pf.* 3 ms. לִמַּד Ec 12^{9}; 2 m. sf. לִמַּדְתָּנִי ψ 71^{17} + 7 t. Pf.; Impf. יְלַמֵּד ψ 25^{9}; יְלַמֶּד־ Jb 21^{22}; 2 ms. sf. תְּלַמְּדֶנּוּ ψ 94^{12}; 1 s. אֲלַמְּדָה ψ 51^{15}; 3 mpl. יְלַמְּדוּן Dt 4^{10} + 12 t. Impf.; *Imv.* sf. לַמְּדֵנִי ψ 25^{4} + 12 t. Imv.; *Inf.* לַמֵּד Je 32^{33} + 9 t.; *Pt.* מְלַמֵּד Dt 4^{1} + 7 t. Pt.;—*teach*, abs. 2 Ch $17^{7.9.9}$ ψ 60^{1}; *teach* some one something, c. double acc. Dt $4^{5.14}$ 5^{28} 11^{19} $31^{19.22}$ Ju 3^{2} 2 S 1^{18}(?), ψ $25^{4.9}$ 34^{12} 51^{15} 94^{10} $119^{12.26.64.66.68.108.124.135.171}$ 132^{12} Ec 12^{9} Is 40^{14} Je 2^{33} $9^{13.19}$ 13^{21} Dn 1^{4}; c. acc. pers. Dt 4^{10} ψ 25^{5} 71^{17} Ct 8^{2} Is 48^{17} Je 31^{34} $32^{33.33}$ Ezr 7^{10}; acc. rei Jb 21^{22}; acc. pers. לְ rei 2 S 22^{35} = ψ 18^{35}, ψ 144^{1}; acc. rei לְ pers. Jb 21^{22}; acc. pers. מִן rei ψ 94^{12}; acc. pers. בְּ rei Is 40^{14}; acc. pers. inf. rei Dt 4^{1} 6^{1} 20^{18} ψ 143^{10} Je 9^{4} 12^{16}; מְלַמְּדַי *my teachers* ψ 119^{99} Pr 5^{13}. **Pual** *Pf.* 3 ms. לֻמַּד Je 31^{18}; *Pt.* pl. cstr. מְלֻמְּדֵי 1 Ch 25^{7} Ct 3^{8}; f. מְלֻמָּדָה Is 29^{13} Ho 10^{11};—*trained*, as soldiers Ct 3^{8}; singers 1 Ch 25^{7}; a bullock to the yoke Ho 10^{11}; *taught*, of a human command Is 29^{13}.

3928 **לָמֻד adj.** taught;—לִ׳ Je 2^{24}; pl. לִמּוּדִים Is $50^{4.4}$; cstr. לִמּוּדֵי Is 54^{13}; לִמֻּדֵי Je 13^{23}; sf. לִמֻּדָי Is 8^{16};—**1.** *taught,* as disciples Is 8^{16} $50^{4.4}$ 54^{13}. **2.** *accustomed to* something, לִמֻּד מִדְבָּר Je 2^{24} (wild ass) *accustomed to the wilderness;* לִמֻּדֵי הָרֵעַ 13^{23} *accustomed to do evil.*

4451 †[מַלְמֵד] **n.[m.] ox-goad**;—cstr. מַלְמַד Ju 3^{31}.

8527 †תַּלְמִיד† **n.[m.] scholar** (late; NH) 1 Ch 25^{8}.

4100 לָמָּה, לָמָה, לָמָּה, לָמָה v. מָה **4 d.** p. 554

3926 לְמוֹ poet. for לְ, v. p. 518 a.

3927 †לְמוּאֵל, לְמוֹאֵל† **n.pr.m.** king of Massa (prob., v. מַשָּׂא); לְמוֹ׳ Pr 31^{1}, לְמוֹ׳ v^{4}.

4136, 8040 לְמוֹאל Ne 12^{38} rd. לִשְׂמֹאל, v. שׂמאל. p. 969

3929 †לֶמֶךְ **n.pr.m.** (on orig. form cf. Lag[BN 77]; conj. as to meaning Bu[Urgesch. 102, 129]);—לֶ׳ Gn 4^{19} + 7 t.; לָמֶךְ 4^{18} + 2 t.;—**1.** son of מְתוּשָׁאֵל (Cainite) Gn $4^{18.19.23.23.24}$ (all J). **2.** son of מְתוּשֶׁלַח (Sethite) Gn $5^{25.26.28.30.31}$ (all P), 1 Ch 1^{3}.—𝔊 Λαμεχ.

4480 לְמִן, לְמִנִּי v. מִן **9 b.** p. 583

4616 לְמַעַן v. מען sub ענה. p. 775

3930 לֹעַ v. sub I. לוע. p. 534

3931 †[לָעַב] **vb. jest** (NH Hiph. *id.;* 𝔗 לְעַב Ethpa. *id.;* Syr. ܠܥܒ Ethpa. *mock, delight oneself, be greedy;* Ar. لَعِبَ *play, sport, jest*);—only **Hiph.** *Pt.* וַיִּהְיוּ מַלְעִבִים בְּ׳ 2 Ch 36^{16} *and they were* (continually) *making jest at* the messengers of God.

3932 †[לָעַג] **vb. mock, deride**; also (Niph.) **stammer,** poet. (NH Hiph. *id.;* 𝔗 לְעַג Aph. *id.;* ܠܥܓ *stutter* (cf. NH לִגְלֵג *mock,* 𝔗 לַגְלֵג *id.;* Syr. ܠܓܠܓ *stutter,* Ar. لَجْلَجَ *id.*));—**Qal** *Pf.* 3 fs. לָעֲגָה 2 K 19^{21} Is 37^{22}; *Impf.* יִלְעַג־ Jb 22^{19} ψ 2^{4}, יִלְעָג Jb 9^{23}; 3 fs. תִּלְעַג Pr 30^{17}; 2 ms. תִּלְעָג ψ 59^{9}, וַתִּל׳ Jb 11^{3}; 1 s. אֶלְעַג Pr 1^{26}; 3 mpl. יִלְעֲגוּ־ ψ 80^{7}; *Pt.* לֹעֵג Pr 17^{5} Je 20^{7};—*mock, deride, have in derision,* of Jerus. triumphing over enemy (c. לְ pers. vel rei) 2 K 19^{21} = Is 37^{22} (‖ בוז); of the innocent Jb 22^{19} (‖ שׂמח); of God (c. לְ) 9^{23} ψ 2^{4} 59^{9}; abs. of wisdom Pr 1^{26} (‖ שׂחק); of wicked (c. לְ) Pr 17^{5} (‖ שׂמח), 30^{17} (‖ בוז), Je 20^{7} (‖ שׂחק); so also perh. ψ 80^{7} (read לָנוּ for לָמוֹ with 𝔊 𝔖 𝔙), cf. (abs.) Jb 11^{3}. **Niph.** *Pt.* עַם . . . נִלְעַג לָשׁוֹן Is 33^{19} *a people stammering of tongue* (i.e. barbarians, cf. v^{a}; but rd. נעלג [עלג √] Gr[Monatsschr. 1884, 45]; ‖ עִמְקֵי שָׂפָה). **Hiph.** (late; cf. NH) *Impf.* 3 ms. וַיַּלְעֵג Ne 3^{33}; 2 ms. תַּלְעִיג Jb 21^{3}; 3 mpl. יַלְעִגוּ ψ 22^{8}, וַיַּלְעִגוּ Ne 2^{19}; *Pt.* מַלְעִגִים 2 Ch 30^{10};—*mock, deride,* always in bad sense: c. לְ pers. Ne 2^{19} (‖ בזה), ψ 22^{8}; c. עַל־ pers. Ne 3^{33}; c. בְּ pers. 2 Ch 30^{10} (‖ השׂחיק); abs. Jb 21^{3}.—So also יַלְעִיג (or יִלְעַג) Pr 18^{1} for MT יִתְגַּלָּע Gr[l.c.] (v. גלע, p. 166 supra).

†לַעַג **n.[m.] mocking, derision,** (barbarous) **stammering**;—abs. לַ׳ Jb 34^{7} + 2 t. + ψ 123^{4} (הַלַּ׳ MT cstr. c. art.—so Kö[Synt. § 303 e]—but prob. insert לְ foll. Hup Now Bae, cf. also Ges[§ 127 g]), + Ez 23^{32} (but del. 𝔊B Hi Co Berthol), + 36^{4} (where Co reads בלע, but less prob., cf. Berthol); sf. לַעְגָּם Ho 7^{16} (v. infr.); pl. cstr. לַעֲגֵי Is 28^{12} (v. infr.);—**1. a.** *mocking, derision,* ψ 123^{4} (‖ בוז); so appar. c. sf. as gen. obj. Ho 7^{16} (but very dub., probably corrupt, cf. We Now); nearly = *blasphemy* Jb 34^{7}. **b.** = obj. of derision ψ 44^{14} = 79^{4} (‖ קֶלֶס, חֶרְפָּה); so also Ez 23^{32} (‖ צחק; si vera l., v. supr.), 36^{4}. **2.** *stammerings* (of barbarous language), לַ׳ שָׂפָה Is 28^{11} (‖ לָשׁוֹן אַחֶרֶת; so Ew Brd Di Hup-Now[ψ 35, 16], De al. sub לָעֵג); but Gr[Monatsschr. 1884, 45] reads עלגי, עלג √. 3933

†[לָעֵג] **adj. mocking,** only pl. cstr. as noun (si vera l.), לַעֲגֵי מָעוֹג ψ 35^{16} *mockers of* מָעוֹג (q.v.), but text dub.; Che reads לַעֲגֵי, Schwally ZAW xi. 1890, 258 לָעֲגוּ.—To [לָעֵג] is also referred לַעֲגֵי Is 28^{11} by Ges De Che Du, < sub לַעַג q. v. 3934

†לַעְדָּה† **n.pr.m.** a man of Judah 1 Ch 4^{21}, 𝔊 Μαδαθ, A Λαδα, 𝔊L Λαδηι. 3935

†לַעְדָּן† **n.pr.m. 1.** an Ephraimite 1 Ch 7^{26} 𝔊 Λαδ(δ)αν. **2.** a Gershonite 1 Ch $23^{7.8.9}$ $26^{21.21.21}$ 𝔊 Εδαν, A Λ(ε)αδαν, Χαδαν, 𝔊L Λααδαν. 3936

לַעֲנָה v. לוע. p. 534 3886

†[לָעַז] **vb. talk indistinctly, unintelligibly** (NH *id.*, in deriv. (לַעַז *foreign language,* לָעוֹז *foreigner*), also *murmur, remonstrate;* Syr. ܠܥܙ *talk indistinctly;* Ar. لَغَزَ *distort;* IV. *talk obscurely, ambiguously*);—only **Qal** *Pt.* עַם לֹעֵז ψ 114^{1} *a people talking unintelligibly* (‖ מִצְרַיִם). 3937

3938 †[לָעַט] **vb. swallow (greedily)** (NH *id.*, Hiph. *stuff* cattle with food; Syr. ܠܘܥܐ *jaw;* cf. Ar. لَغَطَ *speak confusedly, utter indistinct sounds*);—only **Hiph.** *Imv.* ms. sf. causat. הַלְעִיטֵנִי Gn 25[30] (J) *let me swallow*, sq. מִן rei.

3939 †לַעֲנָה **n.f. wormwood** (NH *id.*; Ar. لَعْنٌ is *curse* (vb. لَعَنَ *id.*), so Nab. לענת (vb. לען) cf. Cook[Gloss.]);—only fig. of bitter things:—of perverted justice, Am 5[7] 6[12] (‖ ראשׁ); of result of idolatry, Dt 29[17] (‖ *id.*); of י׳'s chastisement Je 9[14] (‖ מֵי־רֹאשׁ), 23[15] (‖ *id.*), La 3[15] (‖ מְרוֹרִים), v[19] (‖ ראשׁ); sim. of bitter (מָרָה) result of intercourse with strange woman Pr 5[4].—On *wormwood* (*Artemisia absinthium*, etc., Gk. ἀψίνθιον) cf. Löw[80 f. 401, 421] Tristr[Nat. Hist. Bib. 493].

3886 לָעַע v. לוע. p. 534

לפד (√ of following; meaning unknown).

3940 †לַפִּיד **n.m.**[Ju 15, 4] **torch** (NH *id.*);—ל׳ abs. Ju 15[4] Is 62[1]; cstr. Gn 15[17] Zc 12[6]; pl. לַפִּידִים Ju 15[5] + 2 t., לַפִּדִם Ex 20[18], לַפִּדִים Ju 7[16] + 3 t.; cstr. לַפִּידֵי Dn 10[6]:—*torch*, Ju 7[16.20] 15[4.4.5] (kindled, הִבְעִיר אֵשׁ בְּ׳); לַפִּיד אֵשׁ Gn 15[17] (+ תַּנּוּר עָשָׁן; JE), Zc 12[6] (sim. of conquering power of [chiefs of] Judah; ‖ כִּיּוֹר אֵשׁ), לַפִּידֵי אֵשׁ Dn 10[6] (sim. of eyes of angel in vision; ‖ וּפָנָיו כְּמַרְאֵה בָרָק); sim. of flashes (reflected from) darting chariots Na 2[15] (‖ בְּרָקִים); ל׳ of lightning-flashes Ex 20[18] (E; + קוֹלֹת *thunder-peals*); of flashing water-drops expelled by snortings of crocodile Jb 41[11] (‖ כִּידוֹדֵי אֵשׁ); of flame between cherubim Ez 1[13] (‖ גַּחֲלֵי אֵשׁ, אֵשׁ); sim. of Zion's glorious deliverance Is 62[1] (‖ נֹגַהּ).—לַפִּיד Jb 12[5] v. sub פִּיד.

3941 †לַפִּידוֹת **n.pr.m.** husband of Deborah Ju 4[4]; 𝔊 Λαφ(ε)ιδωθ.—On fem. form cf. GFM.

3942, 6440 לִפְנַי 1 K 6[17] v. sub [פָּנֶה], פָּנִים. p. 815f

6441 לִפְנִים 1 K 6[29] v. sub פְּנִימָה. p. 819

3943 †[לָפַת] **vb. twist, turn, grasp with a twisting motion** (Ar. لَفَتَ *twist, wring;* As. *lapâtu, overthrow*, Dl[HWB 382]);—**Qal** *Impf.* וַיִּלְפֹּת Ju 16[29] sq. acc., Samson *grasped* the two middle columns. **Niph.** *Impf.* 3 ms. וַיִּלָּפֵת Ru 3[8] the man started up *and twisted himself;* 3 mpl. יִלָּפְתוּ Jb 6[18] the paths of their way [i.e. of the streams] *turn aside* (*twist, wind*, with lessening force), so AV Hi De Da Bu > Ew Ol Di Siegf Du, who read Qal יִלְפְּתוּ or Pi. יְלַפְּתוּ, making ארחות, = *caravans*, subj.

לָצוֹן, לֵץ v. sub ליץ. p. 539 3887

†לַקּוּם **n.pr.loc.** northern border-town of Naphtali, Jos 19[33] (P), 𝔊 Δωδαμ, 𝔊L Λακουμ. so also Lag[Onom. 275, 24]; site unknown. 3946

לָקַח [965] **vb. take** (NH *id.*, esp. *buy*, and (Niph.) *be taken in marriage;* MI[17.20] Impf. ואקח; Ph. לקח; As. *liḳû, laḳû* Dl[HWB 384]; Ar. لَقِحَ *conceive* (of female), IV. *impregnate;* Eth. ለቀሐ: *receive;* Zinj. לקח DHM[Sendsch. 59]; Aram. also Inscr. of Carpentr.[3] (Imv. קחי); cf. Cook[Gloss. Aram. Inscr.]);—**Qal** *Pf.* ל׳ Gn 2[22] +, לָקָחְ 27[36] + (קָח Ez 17[5] is textual error; om. 𝔊 𝔖 Co, cf. Ges[§ 19, 3. a]); sf. לְקָחַנִי Gn 24[7], לְקָחָם Je 27[20] (for קָחָם Ho 11[3] rd. prob. אֶקָּחֵם 𝔊 𝔗 Ew St Sta[§ 384, 4] Now Che Or We); 2 ms. לָקַחְתָּ Gn 20[3] +, etc.; *Impf.* יִקַּח Ex 21[10] +, וַיִּקַּח Gn 2[15] + (Nu 16[1] read וַיָּקָם Bö We Di Dr[2 S 18, 18]; 1 S 30[20] read וַיִּקְחוּ We Dr Kit Bu); sf. יִקָּחֵנִי 2 S 22[17] +; יִקָּחֲךָ Jb 15[12]; 3 fs. תִּקַּח Gn 38[23] +; 1 s. אֶקַּח 14[23] +, וָאֶקְחָה Zc 11[13]; 1 pl. נִקַּח Gn 34[6] +, נִקְחָה 1 S 4[3] +; וַנִּקַּח Dt 3[8] 29[7]; *Imv.* קַח Ex 29[1] Pr 20[16] + Ez 37[16] (Co וְלָקַחְתָּ, after 𝔊); fs. קְחִי 1 K 17[11]; usually קַח Gn 6[21] +, קְחָה 15[9], sf. 3 ms. קָחֶנּוּ 1 S 16[11] + 2 t.; sf. 3 fs. קָחֶנָּה Je 36[14]; sf. 3 mpl. קָחֶם־נָא Gn 48[9] (cf. Kö[i. 330] Ges[§ 61, 2]); fs. קְחִי Is 23[16] + 3 t.; mpl. קְחוּ Gn 42[33] +, sf. 3 ms. קָחֻהוּ 1 K 20[33]; *Inf. abs.* לָקוֹחַ Je 32[14] + 2 t., לָקֹחַ Dt 31[26]; *cstr.* קַחַת Je 5[3] +; קַחַת־ 2 K 12[9] (Kö[i. 318]); usually c. prep. לָקַחַת Gn 4[11] +, מִקַּחַת 1 K 22[3] +, etc.; sf. קַחְתִּי Ez 24[25], קַחְתְּךָ Gn 30[15] +, etc.; *Pt. act.* לֹקֵחַ 27[46] +, etc.; *pass.* pl. לְקֻחִים Pr 24[11];—**1.** *take, take in the hand*, sq. acc. rei, Ex 7[15] (J), 17[5] (E), Nu 25[7] (P), 2 K 4[29] (all c. בְּיַד) 2 S 18[14] (c. בְּכַף), cf. Gn 8[9] (J), Ex 4[17] 12[22] (JE), Dt 15[17] + oft.; Gn 40[11] (E; of plucking grapes. 2 S 4[6] read סֹקְלָה for לֹקְחֵי, v. חִטָּה, p. 334 supra, and סקל). This easily passes into **2.** *take and carry along* with oneself, כֶּסֶף קְחוּ בְיֶדְכֶם Gn 43[12] (J), Jos 9[11] (JE), 1 K 14[3] 2 K 5[5] 8[8.9] 9[1] Pr 7[20] (all c. בְּיַד); cf. Gn 43[15] Jos 9[4] (both JE), +. **3. a.** *take* from, or out of, sq. acc. rei vel pers., + מִן loc.: Gn 2[22] (rib from man), 3[22] (man from ground; both J); Dt 19[12] 1 S 17[49] 1 K 17[19] +; וַיִּקַּח אֶת־הַחֶרֶב מֵעַל יֶרֶךְ יְמִינוֹ Ju 3[21] (i.e. *drew* it); c. בְּ instr. בְּמֶלְקָחַיִם ל׳ מֵעַל הַמִּזְבֵּחַ Is 6[6]; sq. מִן partit. 2 S 12[4]. **b.** *take, carry away:* Ez 3[14] *spirit lifted me up and carried me away;* fig. of passion carrying one away Jb 15[12]. **c.** *take away* from, so as to 3947 deprive of, sq. acc. Gn 42[36] (E); sq. acc. + מִן, Gn 44[29] (מֵעִם; J), 1 K 11[34] ψ 51[13]; י׳ לֹקֵחַ אֶת־ אֲדֹנֶיךָ מֵעַל רֹאשֶׁךָ 2 K 2[3] *is about to take away thy lord from over thy head*, so v[5]; cf. abs. אֵינֶנּוּ כִּי־ל׳ אֹתוֹ אלהים Gn 5[24] (P); more oft. without מִן, Gn 27[36.36] 30[15.15] 31[1] (all J), Ju 11[13.15] 15[6] 18[24] 1 S 12[3.3] 2 S 12[4] 1 K 11[34] Jb 12[20]; abs. Jb 1[21]; אֶתֶּן־לְךָ מֶלֶךְ בְּאַפִּי וְאֶקַּח בְּעֶבְרָתִי Ho 13[11]; of the sword, taking away its victims Ez 33[4.6]; fig. of taking away understanding Ho 4[11]. **d.** esp. *take away* life 1 K 19[10.14] ψ 31[14] Pr 1[19] Jon 4[3]. **4.** *take* to or for a person: **a.** for oneself, sq. acc. + לְ, =*appropriate* to oneself Dt 7[25] Nu 8[16] (P), Dt 22[7] 2 K 12[6]; c. לְ as dat. comm., Zc 11[7]; ל׳ אֶת־שְׁנֵי יְלָדַי לוֹ לַעֲבָדִים 2 K 4[1] *to take my two sons for himself for slaves;* so (without לְ reflex.), תִּקָּחֶנּוּ לְעֶבֶד עוֹלָם Jb 40[28] *wilt thou take him as slave for ever?* **b.** =*procure, get*, sq. acc. + לְ, קְחוּ לָכֶם תֶּבֶן Ex 5[11] (J) *get you straw;* לֹקֵחַ לוֹ קָלוֹן Pr 9[7] *getteth to himself shame;* so oft., esp. קַח לְךָ, etc., Gn 6[21] 12[19] 16[21] 45[19]+; without לְ, Ne 5[2] *let us procure corn*, and eat and live; of acquiring a field Pr 31[16]. **c.** *take possession of*, sq. acc., of land Dt 29[7] Jos 11[16.23] (all D), 2 Ch 16[5]; cf. פְּקֻדָּתוֹ יִקַּח אַחֵר ψ 109[8] *his office let another take;* fig. הַלַּיְלָה הַהוּא יִקָּחֵהוּ אֹפֶל Jb 3[6] *that night—let darkness take possession of it!* **d.** =*select, choose*, וְאֶתְכֶם ל׳ י׳ Dt 4[20], cf. v[34] (+לוֹ), 1 K 11[37]; of men Dt 1[15] Jos 3[12] (JE; +לָכֶם); + מִן Dt 1[23] Jos 4[2] (JE). **e.** esp. *take* in marriage: (1) for another, esp. a son, c. לְ, וְלָקַחְתָּ אִשָּׁה לִבְנִי Gn 24[4] *and thou shalt take a wife for my son*, so v[7.38.40.48] (all J), 21[21] (E), Je 29[6b]; (2) more oft. for oneself, usu. c. לְ reflex. (sts. + לְאִשָּׁה), Gn 4[19] 6[2] 11[29] 12[19] (all J), + oft.; without לְ Gn 20[2.3] (E), etc. **f.** =*receive, accept*, esp. a bribe, gift, ransom, etc., 1 S 8[3] 12[3c.4] (both sq. מִן), Am 5[12] 2 K 5[15.16.20.23.26.26] ψ 15[5]; interest-money Ez 18[13.17] 22[12]; inheritance Jos 13[8] 18[7] (both D), Nu 34[14.14.15] (P); of earth, receiving Abel's blood Gn 4[11] (J); chastisement Is 40[2]; of *perceiving* a sound, Jb 4[11] *mine ear received a whisper of it;* *receive* mentally: וְלָקַח בְּעָלָיו Ex 22[10] (E) i.e. shall accept the oath as satisfactory; בָּרֵךְ לָקָחְתִּי Nu 23[20] (JE), i.e. *I have received* (commandment by revelation) *to bless;* *receive* instruction Pr 24[32] Je 2[30]+; entanglements of temptation Pr 22[25]. **g.** *take*, as preliminary to further action: Gn 31[34] (E), *she took them* and put them; Ju 3[25] *take* key and open; Jos 2[4] *she took* the two men and hid them; 1 K 18[4] Obadiah *took* 100 prophets and hid them; 19[21] Elisha *took* the yoke of oxen and slew them, cf. 2 S 17[19] 18[18]; sts. wholly redundant, קְחוּ וַעֲשׂוּ עֲגָלָה חֲדָשָׁה 1 S 6[7] *take and prepare a new cart*, etc.; somewhat different is הַלֹּקְחִים לְשׁוֹנָם וַיִּנְאֲמוּ נְאֻם Je 23[31], i.e. *they take* (=make use of) their own tongues, and talk oracles. **5.** *take* up, upon=*put* upon, sq. עַל: וַתִּקַּח תָּמָר אֵפֶר עַל־רֹאשָׁהּ 2 S 13[19] *and Tamar put ashes upon her head;* וַיִּקָּחֶהָ עַל־הַחֲמוֹר Ju 19[28]; cf. יִפְרֹשׂ כְּנָפָיו יִקָּחֵהוּ Dt 32[11] *he spreadeth his wings, he taketh him up.* **6.** =*fetch:* קְחִי־נָא לִי מְעַט־מַיִם 1 K 17[10] *fetch me, pray, a little water*, cf. v[11.11], 2 K 2[20] 4[41]; וְקַח־לִי מִשָּׁם שְׁנֵי גְּדָיֵי עִזִּים Gn 27[9] *and fetch me thence two kids*, cf. v[13] (J); + בְּיָדִי 1 S 21[9]; an offering Lv 12[8] (P; ‖ הֵבִיא v[6]); c. human obj. oft. nearly=*summon*, לָקֹב אֹיְבַי לְקַחְתִּיךָ Nu 33[11] (JE) *to curse mine enemies did I summon thee*, Ju 11[5] 1 S 16[11]; שְׁלַח וְקַח אֹתוֹ אֵלַי 1 S 20[31] *send and bring him unto me;* 2 K 3[15] 6[13]+; of י׳, summoning his people from exile, מִשָּׁם יִקָּחֶךָ Dt 30[4]. **7.** *take=lead, conduct* (with or without contact): וַיִּקַּח אֶת־שְׁנֵי בָנָיו עִמּוֹ Gn 48[1]; גַּם בְּקַרְכֶם קְחוּ Ex 12[32] (both E); וְאֶת־עַמּוֹ לָקַח עִמּוֹ Ex 14[6] (J) *and his people he took with him;* cf. v[7] (J), Jos 8[1] (JE), Ju 4[6]; אֶקָּחֲךָ אֶל־מָקוֹם אַחֵר Nu 23[27] *I will take thee unto another place*, cf. v[14.28] (all JE); י׳ subj., וָאֶקַּח אֶת־אֲבִיכֶם Jos 24[3] (E) *and I took your father* Abraham from beyond the river; הַצֵּל לְקֻחִים לַמָּוֶת Pr 24[11] *rescue those led to death.* **8.** *take=capture, seize:* לָקַחְתִּי בְחָזְקָה 1 S 2[16] *I will take by force*, sc. flesh; of spoils, בֶּצַע כֶּסֶף לֹא ל׳ Ju 5[19] *gain of silver they took not;* of capture of ark 1 S 5[1]; bronze 2 S 8[8], etc.; territory Gn 48[22] (E), Dt 3[14]; cities Nu 21[25] (JE), Dt 3[14] Jos 11[19] (D), 1 S 7[14] 2 S 8[1]; of capture of hippopotamus Jb 40[24]; of seductions of woman, וְאַל־תִּקָּחֲךָ בְּעַפְעַפֶּיהָ Pr 6[25] *and let her not capture thee with her eyelids.* **9.** *take=carry off:* **a.** as booty Gn 14[11] 1 S 27[9] 30[16.18.19.20] 1 K 14[26.26]. **b.** as prisoners Gn 14[12] 2 K 18[32]=Is 36[17], 2 K 23[34]=2 Ch 36[4]. **10.** in phr. *take* vengeance: וְנִקְחָה נִקְמָתֵנוּ מִמֶּנּוּ Je 20[10] *and we will take our vengeance upon him;* abs. נָקָם אֶקָּח Is 47[3] *vengeance will I take.*

†**Niph.** *Pf.* נִלְקַח 1 S 4[22]; נִלְקָח 4[11] Ez 33[6]; 3 fs. נִלְקְחָה 1 S 4[17]; *Impf.* 3 fs. וַתִּלָּקַח Est 2[8.16]; 1 s. אֶלָּקַח

2 K 2^{9}; *Inf. cstr.* הִלָּקַח 1 S 4$^{19.21}$, sf. הִלָּקְחוֹ 1 S 21^{7};—**1.** *be captured,* of ark 1 S 4$^{11.17.19.21.22}$. **2.** *be taken away, removed,* of shewbread 1 S 21^{7}; of removal by death Ez 33^{6}; of translation of Elijah 2 K 2^{9} (c. מֵעִם pers.) **3.** *be taken, brought* unto (אֶל־), only Est 2$^{8.16}$.

†**Pu.** *Pf.* לֻקַּח Gn 3^{23}+, 3 fs. לֻקְחָה־ 2^{23}, 2 ms. לֻקָּחְתָּ 3^{19}, etc.;—**1.** *be taken* from, out of (מִן of source) Gn 2^{23} 3$^{19.23}$ (all J); cf. וְלֻקַּח מֵהֶם קְלָלָה Je 29^{22} *and there shall be taken from them* (derived from their case) *a curse-formula.* **2.** =*be stolen* from, Ju 17^{2} (לְ pers.) **3.** *be taken captive,* Je 48^{46}, cf. Is 52^{5}. **4.** *be taken away, removed* (=**Niph. 2**), of Elijah's translation 2 K 2^{10} (c. מֵאֵת pers.), of death Is 53^{8} (c. מִן, prob. instr.)

†**Hoph.** *Impf.* יֻקַּח Gn 18^{4}+, etc.;—**1.** *be taken, brought* unto Gn 12^{15} (J; sq. בֵּית *to the house of*), 18^{4} (abs.) **2.** *be taken* out of Jb 28^{2} (מִן of source), from, of Ez 15^{3} (מִן partit.) **3.** *be taken away* from Is 49^{24} (מִן pers.); abs. v^{25}.

†**Hithp.** *Pt.* fs. אֵשׁ מִתְלַקַּחַת lit. fire *taking hold of itself,* of lightning Ex 9^{24} (JE), Ez 1^{4}, exact signif. dub.; *in close succession, incessant* Di Sm, *infolding itself,* i.e. a mass of fire, Thes RobGes AV VB SS, >of *quivering* flashes Buhl, of *forked* or *zigzag* lightning Da.

3948 †לֶקַח **n.m.**$^{Pr. 4, 2}$ **learning, teaching** (concrete; prob. *what is received*);—לֶ׳ abs. Is 29^{24}+ 5 t.; sf. לִקְחִי Dt 32^{2} Jb 11^{4}; לִקְחָהּ Pr 7^{21};—**1.** *instruction,* subjective, as personal acquirement; יִלְמְדוּ לֶקַח Is 29^{24}, they *shall learn instruction* (|| בִּינָה); וְיוֹסֶף לֶקַח Pr 1^{5} a wise man will hear *and will increase* (his) *learning,* so 9^{9}. **2.** *teaching,* obj., as thing taught, יַעֲרֹף כַּמָּטָר לִקְחִי Dt 32^{2} (|| אִמְרָתִי), Jb 11^{4}; לֶ׳ טוֹב נָתַתִּי לָכֶם Pr 4^{2}; also=*teaching-power, persuasiveness,* מֶתֶק שְׂפָתַיִם יֹסִיף לֶ׳ Pr 16^{21} *sweetness of lips increaseth persuasiveness* (v. מתק), וְעַל שְׂפָתָיו יֹסִיף לֶקַח v^{23}; in bad sense, of seductive words of adulteress, בְּרֹב לִ׳ Pr 7^{21} (|| בְּחֵלֶק שְׂפָתֶיהָ).

3949 †לִקְחִי **n.pr.m.** a Manassite, 1 Ch 7^{19}, 𝔊 Λακεειμ, A Λακεια, 𝔊L Λοκεειμ.

4455 †I. מַלְקוֹחַ **n.m.**$^{Is 49, 25}$ **booty, prey** (cf. לקח 9);—מַ׳ הֲיֻקַּח מִגִּבּוֹר Is 49^{24} (|| שְׁבִי), cf. v^{25} (|| *id.*); Nu 31^{26} (|| *id.*), 31^{11} (|| שָׁלָל), v^{12} (|| *id.* + שְׁבִי, i.e. here, only, disting. fr. captives), v^{32} (|| יֶתֶר הַבָּז), v^{27}.

†II. [מַלְקוֹחַ] **n.[m.] jaw** (as *taking, seizing* food);—du. sf. וּלְשׁוֹנִי מֻדְבָּק מַלְקוֹחָי ψ 22^{16} *and my tongue is made to cleave to my jaws,* i.e. my gums. 4455

†מֶלְקָחַיִם, [מַלְקָחַיִם] **n.[m.]du. tongs, snuffers**;—**1.** tongs used at altar of temple, for lifting coal, in Is.'s vision, Is 6^{6}. **2.** lamp-*snuffers,* in temple 1 K 7^{49}=2 Ch 4^{21}; in tabern. sf. (ref. to lamp-stand, מְנוֹרָה) מַלְקָחֶיהָ Ex 25^{38} 37^{23} Nu 4^{9} (all P). 4457

†[מִקָּח] **n.[m.] a taking, receiving**;—cstr. מִקַּח־שֹׁחַד 2 Ch 19^{7} *a taking of a bribe.* 4727

†[מַקָּחָה] **n.f. ware** (prop. thing *received,* sc. in trade; cf. לָקַח in NH); only pl. הַמַּקָּחוֹת Ne 10^{32} (*their*) *wares.* 4728

†[לָקַט] **vb. pick or gather up,** specif. **glean** (NH *id.* and נָקַט; Ar. لَقَطَ *pick up* (as a bird, grains, etc.); Aram. לְקַט, and נְקַט; ܠܩܛ; Mand. לנט (Nö$^{M 54}$, also on Talm. נקט); cf. As. *lakâtu* Dl$^{HWB 385}$ (but ט=*t*?));—**Qal** *Pf.* 3 pl. לָקְטוּ Ex 16^{22} Nu 11^{8}, וְלָ׳ consec. Ex 16^{4}, לָקְטוּ Ex 16^{18}; *Impf.* 3 mpl. יִלְקְטוּ Ex 16^{5}, וַיִּלְקְטוּ Ex 16$^{17.21}$; 2 mpl.sf. תִּלְקְטֻהוּ ψ 104^{28}, יִלְקֹטוּן Ex 16^{26}; *Imv.* mpl. לִקְטוּ Gn 31^{46} Ex 16^{16}; *Inf. cstr.* לִלְקֹט Ex 16^{27}+2 t.;—**1.** *pick up, gather,* c. acc., stones Gn 31^{46} (J), lilies Ct 6^{2}; usu. the manna: Ex 16$^{4.5.26}$ (J), v$^{21.22}$ (P); sq. מִן partit. v^{16} (P); so abs. v^{27} Nu 11^{8} (both JE), Ex 16$^{17.18}$ (P); of animals gathering food תִּתֵּן לָהֶם יִלְקֹטוּן ψ 104^{28}. **2.** specif. *glean,* abs., Ru 2^{8} (c. בְּ loc.; usu. Pi. in this sense). **Pi.** *Pf.* 3 fs. וְלִקְּטָה consec. Ru 2^{16}, לִקֵּטָה Ru 2$^{17.18}$; 2 fs. לִקַּטְתְּ Ru 2^{19}; *Impf.* וַיְלַקֵּט Gn 47^{14}+2 t.; 3 fs. תְּלַקֵּט Ru 2^{15}, וַתְּ׳ Ru 2$^{3.17}$; 2 ms. תְּלַקֵּט Lev 19^{9}+2 t.; 1 s. אֲלַקֲּטָה Ru 2$^{2.7}$ (cf. Ba$^{NB 152, 489}$); *Inf. cstr.* לְלַקֵּט Ru 2^{15}+2 t.; *Pt.* מְלַקֵּט Is 17^{5}, pl. מְלַקְּטִים Ju 1^{7} Je 7^{18};—**1.** *gather, gather up,* fallen grapes, Lv 19^{10} (H), arrows 1 S 20^{38}, (fire-)wood Je 7^{18}; abs. (food from ground) Ju 1^{7} (cf. GFM);=*pick, pick off,* 2 K 4$^{39.39}$ (+מִן of source). **2.** fig. *collect* (money) Gn 47^{14} (J). **3.** specif. *glean,* after the reapers, usu. abs. Ru 2$^{3.7}$ (|| אָסַף), v^{17} (all c. בְּ loc.), v^{15} (בֵּין loc.), v^{19} (adv. loc.), also v^{2} (where בְּ may be loc. or partit., cf. Be), also v$^{15.16.23}$; c. acc. Is 17^{5} (שִׁבֳּלִים, sim. of devastation of land; || אָסַף קָצִיר), Ru 2$^{17.18}$; c. acc. cogn. לֶקֶט Lv 19^{9}=23^{22} (H). **Pu.** *Impf.* 2 mpl. תְּלֻקְּטוּ 3950

Is 27[12] *ye shall be picked up* (of Isr. under fig. of grains or berries, after the threshing process of י׳'s judgment). **Hithp.** *Impf.* וַיִּתְלַקְּטוּ Ju 11[3] and *there collected themselves* worthless men unto (אֶל) Jephthah (*were raked together* GFM).

3951 †לֶ֫קֶט **n.[m.] gleaning,** i.e. what is or may be gleaned, only cstr. לֶ׳ קְצִירְךָ, as acc. cogn. with לקט Pi., (q.v.) Lv 19[9] = 23[22] (H).

3219 †יַלְקוּט **n.[m.] receptacle, wallet**(?) (prop. *collector*) (on form cf. Lag[BN p. 127] Ba[NB § 156 b] Kö[ii. 1, § 76, 4])—only in 1 S 17[40] and he put them [the stones] בִּכְלִי הָרֹעִים אֲשֶׁר־לוֹ וּבַיַּלְקוּט *in the shepherd's receptacle which he had, even* (?) *in the wallet* (? such as every shepherd carried, hence art.); but prob. del. ו before בַּיַּל׳ (𝔊 The We Klo Bu HPS), and regard בִּכְלִי . . . לוֹ as gloss (We Bu HPS).

3952 †[לָקַק] **vb. lap, lick** (NH *id.*, Pi.; Ar. لَقَّ *lick, lap* of dog (Wahrm));—**Qal** *Pf.* 3 ms. לָקְקוּ 1 K 21[19]; *Impf.* 3 ms. יָלֹק Ju 7[5.5]; 3 mpl. יָלֹקּוּ 1 K 21[19], וַיָּלֹקּוּ 1 K 22[38];—*lap*, יָלֹק בִּלְשׁוֹנוֹ מִן־הַמַּיִם Ju 7[5], like a dog v[5] (abs.); of dogs *lapping up* blood (acc.), 1 K 21[19.19] 22[38]. **Pi.** *Pt.* pl. c. art. הַמְלַקְקִים Ju 7[6] (בְּיָדָם אֶל־פִּיהֶם is erron. gloss, v. GFM), v[7]; in both = *lap, lap up* (= **Qal** v[5]).

לקשׁ (√ of foll.; NH לקשׁ *be late* (Hiph. and deriv.); Aram. ܠܰܩܶܫ *make* or *do late*, לְקִישָׁא, ܠܰܩܽܫܳܐ *late*; vulg. Ar. لَقَسَ *be late* (Hauran), Wetzst in De[Job 24, 6], so II. Wahrm; لَقِّيسَ *late*, Dozy[Suppl. ii. 543]).

3954 †לֶ֫קֶשׁ **n.[m.]** prob. **after-growth, aftermath, i.e. spring-crop** (cf. GASm[12 Proph. i. 109]);—only (2 t.) Am 7[1], בִּתְחִלַּת עֲלוֹת הַלָּ֫קֶשׁ וְהִנֵּה לֶ֫קֶשׁ אַחַר גִּזֵּי הַמֶּלֶךְ׃.—> Other interpr. are: *late-rain growth* (fr. מַלְקוֹשׁ q.v.), Hoffm[ZAW iii. (1883) 116]; *leaf-and-herb-gathering* in spring, We after Klein[ZPV iv. 1881, 83]; Anderlind[viii. 1886, 62].

4456 †מַלְקוֹשׁ **n.m.**[Je 3, 3] **latter-rain, spring-rain** (i.e. showers of March–April; important, as strengthening and maturing crops); מ׳ Ho 6[3] + 7 t.;—related to גֶּשֶׁם as particular to general, opp. יוֹרֶה (*former rain*, q.v.): Ho 6[3] Je 5[24]; so opp. מוֹרֶה Jo 2[23]; particular under מָטָר Dt 11[14] (opp. יוֹרֶה), Zc 10[1] (+ מְטַר־גֶּשֶׁם), Jb 29[23]; || רְבִבִים Je 3[3]; עָב מ׳ Pr 16[15] *spring-rain-cloud* (sim. of king's favour).

†[לִקֵּשׁ] **vb.** only **Pi.** 3 mpl., prob. denom. 3953
tr. לֶ֫קֶשׁ = **take the aftermath,** i.e. *take every thing* (Wetzst in De[Hiob 20, 6]) (> Buhl II. לקשׁ, cf. Ar. لَقَشَ *schnell zusammenraffen* [cf. Lane[2668]]);—*despoil*; וְכֶרֶם רָשָׁע יְלַקֵּשׁוּ׃ Jb 24[6] *and the vineyard of the wicked* (but rd. prob. עָשִׁיר *the rich* Bu Du) *they despoil* (|| קָצַר).

לשׁד (√ of foll., cf. Ar. لَسَدَ *suck, lick* (Eth. ሰስዴ: *butter*); so Thes and on ψ 32[4] De Bae, also Di[Nu 11, 8]).

[לָשָׁד] **n.m. juice, juicy** or **dainty bit,** 3955
dainty;—cstr. כְּטַעַם לְשַׁד הַשָּׁמֶן Nu 11[8] (J) sim. of taste of manna (𝔊 ἐγκρίς, 𝔙 *panis oleatus*), i.e. a dainty prepared with oil (cf. Di); נֶהְפַּךְ לְשַׁדִּי בְּחַרְבֹנֵי קַיִץ ψ 32[4] *my juice* (sap, life-moisture) is transformed, etc.

לשׁך (√ of foll.; meaning unknown).

†לִשְׁכָּה **n.f. room, chamber, hall, cell,** 3957
lishka (NH *id.* 𝔗 לִשְׁכְּתָא; cf. also נִשְׁכָּה; on the *lishka* v. Now[Arch. ii. 37, 52, 79]; Bo[Geogr. I, xvii. 438 (ed. Leusd.)] comp. Gk. λέσχη, cf. RS[Sem. i. 236 (2nd ed. 254)] al.);—ל׳ Ez 40[38] +; cstr. לִשְׁכַּת 2 K 23[11] +; c. ה loc. לִשְׁכָּ֫תָה 1 S 9[22]; pl. לְשָׁכוֹת Ez 40[17] +; cstr. לִשְׁכוֹת Ne 10[38] +;—**1. a.** of room connected with a sanctuary (בָּמָה), where sacrif. meal was eaten 1 S 9[22], insert also prob. 1[18] (𝔊 We Dr Klo Bu). **b.** connected with Sol.'s temple, where wine offered to Rechabites Je 35[2.4], cf. v[4.4]; one where prophecy read 36[10] (both these appar. open, cf. Gie[Je 35, 2]); cf. לִשְׁכַּת נְתַן־מֶלֶךְ הַסָּרִיס . . בַּפַּרְוָרִים 2 K 23[11]; used of Levites' cells 1 Ch 9[33]; = store-rooms v[26] (|| אֹצָרוֹת), 23[28] 28[12] 2 Ch 31[11]. **c.** in Ezek.'s temple, cells for priests, singers, etc. Ez 40[17.17.38.44.45.46] + 41[10] (del. Co Bthl), 42[1.4.7.7.8.11] + v[12] (del. Co Bthl); in three tiers, cf. הַלְּ׳ הָעֶלְיוֹנֹת 42[5] (vid. v[3]), (45[5] rd. עָרִים לָשֶׁבֶת 𝔊 Sm Co Sgfr[KauAT] Bthl); ל׳ הַקֹּדֶשׁ for sacred uses 42[13.13.13] 44[19] 46[19]. **d.** in second temple, as store-rooms Ezr 8[29] Ne 10[38.39] (|| בֵּית הָאוֹצָר), v[40]; used by individuals Ezr 10[6] Ne 13[5] (ל׳ גְּדוֹלָה), v[8], in gen. v[4.9]. **2.** of scribe's room in royal palace Je 36[12.20.21].

†I. לֶ֫שֶׁם **n.[m.]** a precious stone in h. p.'s 3958
breast-plate Ex 28[19] 39[12] (√ and mng. dub.; 𝔊 λιγύριον, Joseph[Ant. iii. 7, 5] λίγυρος, 𝔙 *ligurius*, and this (= λυγκούριον, *lyncurion* ?) compared with *carbuncle* Plin[NH viii. 57 (38)]; identif. with *amber*

Demostratus in Plin[NH xxxvii. 11 (2)], or with *jacinth* (Rev 21[20]) Braun[De Vest. Sacerd. ii. 14] Winer[RWB i. 332]; cf. further, Di[Ex 28, 19]).

3959 † II. לֶ֫שֶׁם **n.pr.loc.** variant of לַ֫יִשׁ (whence We[De gent 37] Di rd. לֶ֫שֶׁם; Lag[BN 20 Anm.] thinks ם remnant of *Mimmation*, לֶ֫שֶׁם fr. לַ֫יִשׁ = *Laišum*), old name of city דָּן (v. לַ֫יִשׁ), Jos 19[47.47] (cf. Di), 𝔊B Λαχεις, לֶ֫שֶׁם דָּן = Λασεννδακ, A𝔊L Λεσεν(μ).

לשׁן (√ of foll.; Thes conj. orig. mng. *lick* (cf. لسّ, لسب, لسم), so Hup-Now[ψ 32, 4]).

3956 † לָשׁוֹן **n.m.**[Jos 7, 29] and (more oft.) **f.**[Is 28, 11] **tongue** (NH *id.*; also As. *lišânu*; Ar. لِسانٌ; Eth. ልሳን:; Aram. לִשָּׁן, לִישָּׁן, ܠܶܫܳܢܳܐ (all *li*-); Zinj. לשן DHM[Sendsch. 59]);—abs. ל׳ Ex 4[10]+; הַלָּשׁוֹן Jos 15[2]; cstr. לְשׁוֹן Jos 7[21]+; sf. לְשׁוֹנִי 2 S 23[2]; לְשׁוֹנוֹ Ex 11[7]+2 t.; לְשׁוֹנוֹ Ju 7[5] Est 1[22]; לְשׁוֹנְךָ ψ 34[14]; לְשׁוֹנְכֶם Is 59[3], etc.; pl. לְשֹׁנוֹת abs. ψ 31[21] Is 66[18]; cstr. Zc 8[23]; sf. לְשֹׁנֹתָם Gn 10[20.31];—**1.** *tongue* of men, **a.** used in lapping Ju 7[5]; cleaving to the palate (חֵךְ), in thirst La 4[4], so as to produce dumbness Jb 29[10] (|| קוֹל נֶחְבָּא), ψ 137[6] Ez 3[26] (|| נֶאֱלַם); cleaving to jaws (מַלְקוֹחַ) ψ 22[16]; ל׳ בַּצָּמָא נָשָׁתָּה Is 41[17] *their tongue for thirst is parched;* ל׳ תִּמַּק בְּפִיהֶם Zc 14[12] (of י׳'s judgment); a choice morsel is held תַּחַת ל׳ Jb 20[12] (fig. of mischief), cf. ψ 10[7] (ready to be uttered), 66[17] (|| פֶּה), Ct 4[11]. **b.** usu. as organ of speech, both good and bad (esp. ψ Pr, oft. || פֶּה, שָׂפָה);—כְּבַד ל׳ Ex 4[10] (J) *heavy of tongue;* מַעֲנֵה ל׳ Pr 16[1], מִלָּתוֹ עַל־לְשׁוֹנִי 2 S 23[2], cf. Pr 31[26], ψ 139[4]; (בְּל׳) הֲיֵשׁ בִּלְשׁוֹנִי עַוְלָה Jb 6[30]; מָוֶת וְחַיִּים בְּיַד ל׳ Pr 18[21], cf. 21[23] 25[15]; of (false) proph., הַלֹּקְחִים ל׳ Je 23[31]; subj. of vb. of speaking, דִּבֵּר:—דִּבְּרָה לְשׁוֹנִי בְחִכִּי Jb 33[2] ψ 12[4] 37[30]; cf. (Je 9[7] infr. and) ל׳ . . תְּמַהֵר לְדַבֵּר Is 32[4], לְשׁוֹנִי עֵט סוֹפֵר מָהִיר ψ 45[2], i.e. as swift as a rapid scribe's stylus; subj. of הָגָה Is 59[3] Jb 27[4] ψ 35[28] 71[24]; subj. of נִשְׁבַּע Is 45[23]; ל׳ תִּהֲלַךְ בָּאָרֶץ ψ 73[9]; of hostile speech, insolence, etc., Jos 10[21] (JE; obj. of I. חָרַץ q.v., cf. **3** infr.), Je 18[18] Is 3[8]; זַעַם ל׳ Ho 7[16] (but text dub., cf. We Now), ל׳ חֶרֶב חַדָּה ψ 57[6], cf. 64[4]; שָׁנְנוּ ל׳ כְּמוֹ נָחָשׁ 140[4]; כָּל־ל׳ תָּקוּם אִתָּךְ Is 54[17]; הֶאֱרִיךְ ל׳ 57[4]; further, Je 9[2.4]; as instr. of seductive flattery (הֶחֱלִיק), without בְּ, ψ 5[10] Pr 28[23], cf. חֶלְקַת ל׳ נָכְרִיָּה Pr 6[24]; of falsehood ψ 78[36] (cf. infr.); of slander (cf. לוֹשְׁנִי) רָגַל עַל־ל׳ ψ 15[3], אִישׁ לָשׁוֹן 140[12], cf. ל׳ סָתֶר Pr 25[23]; חָטָא בִל׳ ψ 39[2]; cf. 64[9] (text dub., v. Hup Che Bae); moral qualities ascribed to:—as arrogant ψ 12[5] (cf. v[4] supr.); as devising injuries, הַוּוֹת תַּחְשֹׁב ל׳ ψ 52[4], cf. ל׳ הַוֹּת Pr 17[4]; ל׳ תַּצְמִיד מִרְמָה ψ 50[19] *nectere fraudem;* נְצֹר ל׳ מֵרָע ψ 34[14] (|| וּשְׂפָתֶיךָ מִדַּבֵּר מִרְמָה); oft. of lying tongue: לְשׁוֹן שָׁקֶר Pr 6[17] 12[19] 21[6] 26[28] ψ 109[2]; ל׳ תַּרְמִית Zp 3[13]; ל׳ רְמִיָּה Mi 6[12] ψ 120[2.3]; ל׳ מִרְמָה 52[6]; ל׳ תַּהְפֻּכוֹת Pr 10[31], and נֶהְפָּךְ בִּל׳ Pr 17[20]; ל׳ עֲרוּמִים Jb 15[5]; also ל׳ מִרְמָה דִּבֵּר Je 9[7]; on the other hand ל׳ צַדִּיק Pr 10[20]; ל׳ חֲכָמִים 12[18] 15[2]; מַרְפֵּא ל׳ v[4]; ל׳ לִמּוּדִים Is 50[4].—Note phrases שׁוֹט ל׳ Jb 5[21] *scourge of* (the) *tongue,* רִיב לְשֹׁנוֹת ψ 31[21]; פַּלַּג לְשׁוֹנָם ψ 55[10]: also בַּעַל הַל׳ Ec 10[11] (of serpent-charmer), and וַתַּעֲלוּ עַל־שְׂפַת ל׳ Ez 36[3].—On tongue of י׳ (once), v. **4** infr. †**c.** organ of singing, subj. of רִנֵּן ψ 51[16] 126[2] Is 35[6], עָנָה ψ 119[172]. **2.** = *language* Dt 28[49] Je 5[15] and later, viz.: Ez 3[5.6] (כִּבְדֵי ל׳ || עִמְקֵי שָׂפָה, but del. 𝔊 Codd. Co Sgfr[KauAT]), Is 28[11] (|| ל׳ אַחֶרֶת, לַעֲגֵי שָׂפָה, fig. of י׳'s unintelligible dealings); עַם . . . נִלְעַג ל׳ 33[19] (|| עִמְקֵי שָׂפָה); 66[18] (|| גּוֹיִם), Zc 8[23] Gn 10[5.20.31] (all P), Ne 13[24] Est 1[22.22] 3[12] 8[9.9] Dn 1[4]. **3.** *tongue* of animals: dog Ex 11[7] (J; obj. of I. חָרַץ q.v.; cf. **1 b**), ψ 68[24]; adder Jb 20[16] (subj. of תַּהַרְגֵ); crocodile 40[25]. **4.** *tongue* of fire, devouring, כֶּאֱכֹל קַשׁ לְשׁוֹן אֵשׁ Is 5[24]; cf. of י׳, (שְׂפָתָיו מָלְאוּ זַעַם ||) וּלְשׁוֹנוֹ כְּאֵשׁ אֹכָלֶת 30[27]. **5.** = (*tongue*-shaped) *wedge* of gold Jos 7[21.24] (JE). **6.** = (*tongue*-shaped) *bay* of sea Is 11[15] Jos 15[2.5] 18[19] (all P).

3960 † [לָשַׁן] **vb. denom.** use the tongue, only specif., **slander**;—**Po'el** *Pt.* מְלָושְׁנִי בַסֵּתֶר רֵעֵהוּ ψ 101[5] (on form, cf. Ges[§ 90, 3] Kö[Lgb. i. § 26]). **Hiph.** *Impf.* 2 ms. juss. אַל־תַּלְשֵׁן עֶבֶד וגו׳ Pr 30[10].

3962 † [לֶ֫שַׁע] **n.pr.loc.** near Sodom and Gomorrah, only לָ֫שַׁע Gn 10[19]; 𝔊D Λασα; E𝔊L Λασα; site unknown; = *Kallirrhoë*, with hot-springs, Jerome[Quaest in Gen. (10, 19)], cf. Buhl[Geogr 123 and reff.]

8289 לַשָּׁרוֹן Jos 12[8] v. שָׁרוֹן. p. 450

לתח (√ of foll.; meaning unknown; Thes conj. *spread out*, cf. Sam. נתח *spread out garment*, v. also Di[Lex. Eth. 45 f.], but this word very dubious).

4458 †מֶלְתָּחָה **n.f.** appar. **wardrobe, wearing apparel** (Eth. አልታት፡ *tunic*);—only in וַיֹּאמֶר לַאֲשֶׁר עַל־הַמֶּ׳ הוֹצֵא לְבוּשׁ 2 K 10^{22}; 𝔊 ἐπὶ τοῦ [οἴκου] μεσθααλ (μισθ'); 𝔙 *super vestes.*

לתך (√ of foll., mng. unkn., cf. Lag$^{Or. ii, 32 f.}$).

†לֶתֶךְ **n.[m.]** **a barley-measure** (NH *id.*, a corn-measure); only in חֹמֶר־שְׂעֹרִים וְלֶ׳ שְׂעֹרִים 3963
Ho 3^{2}; acc. to 𝔙 = ½ כֹּר = ½ חֹמֶר (q.v.), cf. Mish. (Levy$^{NHWB ii. 531}$), but this tradition is uncertain (cf. Now$^{Arch. i. 203}$); 𝔊 νέβελ οἴνου, for לֶ׳ שׂ׳.

מ

מ, ם, *Mēm*, thirteenth letter; used as numeral 40 in postB. Heb.

4100, 4480 מַ־ v. מָה. מִ־ v. מִן. p. 552, 577

3965, 4124 מַאֲבוּס v. אבס. [מַאֲבוּס] v. מוֹאָב. מֹאָב p. 7, 555

מאד (√ of following As. *ma'âdu, be many, increase; ma'adu, many; ma'adiš, in abundance*, Dl$^{HWB, 388 f.}$; cf. Sab. מאד *to add*, DHM $^{ZMG 1883, 342 f.}$ Hom$^{Süd-Ar. Chr. 127}$; Ar. مَأَدَ *begin to grow*, of plant).

3966 מְאֹד **n.m. muchness, force, abundance, exceedingly** (cf. As. *mu'du, abundance*, Hom $^{ZMG 1878, 711}$ ('treasures *ana mu'di, in abundance*') Dl$^{HWB 399}$):—**1.** *force, might*, †Dt 6^{5} וּבְכָל־מְאֹדֶךָ and with all thy *might;* hence 2 K 23^{25}. **2.** in diff. idioms (298 t.) to express the idea of *exceedingly, greatly, very* (whether of magnitude or degree): **a.** (so mostly) as adv. acc., qualifying both adjj. and obs., Gn 1^{31} טוֹב מְאֹד good *exceedingly*, 4^{5} וַיִּחַר לְקַיִן מְאֹד and Cain was wroth *exceedingly*, 7^{18} וַיִּגְבְּרוּ הַמַּיִם וַיִּרְבּוּ מְאֹד, 12^{14} 13^{2} וְאַבְרָם כָּבֵד מְאֹד בַּמִּקְנֶה, v^{13} חַטָּאִים לי׳ מאד, 18^{20} $19^{3.9}$ 21^{11} $24^{16.35}$, + oft., ψ 46^{2} עֶזְרָה בְצָרוֹת נִמְצָא מְאֹד as a help in troubles, to be found (= present) *exceedingly;* with an inf. Is 47^{9} בְּעָצְמַת חֲבָרַיִךְ מְאֹד despite of thy spells being *very* numerous, Jos 9^{13} מֵרֹב הַדֶּרֶךְ מְאֹד, 1 K 7^{47}; הַרְבֵּה מְאֹד Gn 15^{1} 41^{49} Dt 3^{5} +, for which in the later language is found לָרֹב מְאֹד †Zc 14^{14} 2 Ch 4^{18} 9^{9} (in 1 K 10^{10} הַרְבֵּה מְאֹד), 24^{24} 30^{13}, and even לְהַרְבֵּה מְאֹד †2 Ch 11^{12} 16^{8}. מְאֹד is not usually separated from the word it qualifies by more than one or two words (as Gn 20^{8} וייראו האנשים מאד, Nu 11^{10} (ויחר אף י׳ מאד); see, however, Dt 30^{14} Ju 12^{2} 2 S 12^{5} 1 K 11^{19} ψ 31^{12}. It precedes its verb, †ψ 47^{10} מְאֹד נַעֲלָה (hence 97^{9}), 92^{6}. **b.** עַד־מְאֹד *up to abundance, to a great degree, exceedingly*, †Gn 27^{33} חֲרָדָה גְּדֹלָה עַד־מ׳, v^{34} 1 S 11^{15} וישמח . . . עד מ׳, 25^{36} וְהוּא שִׁכֹּר עַד־מ׳, 2 S 2^{17} 1 K 1^{4} Is 64^{8} (cf. La 5^{22}), v^{11} ψ $38^{7.9}$ $119^{8.43.51.107}$ Dn 8^{8} 11^{25}. **c.** עַד־לִמְאֹד (v. עַד לְ) †2 Ch 16^{14}. **d.** duplicated (Ges$^{§ 133 k}$), †Gn 7^{19} וְהַמַּיִם גָּבְרוּ מ׳ מ׳, 30^{43} Nu 14^{7} 1 K 7^{47} 2 K 10^{4} Ez 37^{10}. **e.** בִּמְאֹד מְאֹד lit. *with muchness, muchness*, †Gn $17^{2.6.20}$ Ex 1^{7} (all P), Ez 9^{9} 16^{13}.

I. מֵאָה $_{583}$ **n.f. hundred** (NH *id.;* MI^{20} 3967
מאתן (du.); SI^{5} מאת, מאתים (du.); Ph. מאת, מאתם (du.); As. *mê* (prob., Dl$^{§ 75}$), TelAm. *mê-at* Wkl$^{TelAm 20*}$; Ar. مِائَةٌ; Sab. מאת, מאתם Os $^{ZMG x. 1856, 49; CIS iv. i. 6, 4; 46, 6}$; מאה Eut$^{Sin 457}$; Eth. ምእት፡; Aram. מְאָה, ܡܐܐ; Palm. תלת מאה 300 Vog$^{Palm 6, 4}$; Nab. מאה Eut$^{Nab 8, 9}$);—מ׳ Gn 6^{3} + 144 t.; cstr. מְאַת 5^{3} + 30 t. (on מְאַת Ec 8^{12} v. **2 d** infr.); pl. abs. מֵאוֹת Gn 5^{9} + 324 t. (מֵאֹת only $5^{4.30}$); המאיות Kt 2 K 11^{4} + 3 t. 2 K 11; du. מָאתַיִם (-תַיִם) Gn 11^{19} + 76 t. (but 1 S 18^{27} rd. מֵאָה (מְאַת) 𝔊 We Dr Kit Bu HPS);—*hundred:*—**1.** as simple number: **a.** abs. sg., (1) foll. by sg. of noun enumerated: מֵאָה קְשִׂיטָה Gn 33^{19} Jos 24^{32} (both E); מ׳ אִישׁ Ju 7^{19} 1 K 18^{13} 2 K 4^{43}; מֵאָה אַמָּה 1 K 7^{2} Ez 40^{19} +; מ׳ כִּכָּר 2 K 23^{33} 2 Ch 25^{6} 27^{5} 36^{3} Ezr 8^{26}; מ׳ אֶלֶף = 100,000 1 K 20^{29} + 6 t. K Ch; cf. also Gn 17^{17} (P), 2 S 8^{4} Is $65^{20.20}$, and sq. n. coll. רֶכֶב 2 S 8^{4} = 1 Ch 18^{4}, צֹאן 1 K 5^{3}; (2) less oft. sq. pl. מֵאָה שְׁעָרִים Gn 26^{12} (J), מ׳ פְּעָמִים 2 S 24^{3} = 1 Ch 21^{3}, מ׳ נְבִיאִים 1 K 18^{4}, etc.; (3) seldom, and late, preceded by n.pl.: אַמּוֹת הַמֵּאָה Ez 42^{2}, הָרִמֹּנִים מֵאָה Je 52^{23}, cf. Ezr 2^{69} 2 Ch 3^{16} 4^{8} 29^{32}; (4) exceptional is כְּלֵי כֶסֶף מֵאָה לְכִכָּרִים Ezr 8^{26}; also, with ellipsis, מֵאָה כֶסֶף Dt 22^{19} (i.e. shekels); מֵאָה קַיִץ 2 S 16^{1} (i.e. cakes);

(5) מֵאָה without noun enumerated, esp. = *a hundred* (men, persons) Ju $20^{10.10}$ Am $5^{3.3}$ Lv $26^{8.8}$ (H), 1 Ch 12^{14}; מ׳ Pr 17^{10} = 100 (blows), Ec 6^{3} = 100 (children), 8^{12} = 100 (times).—On Ne 3^{1} 12^{39} v. infr. **b.** abs. du., (1) foll. by sg., מָאתַיִם אִישׁ 1 S 18^{27} 30^{10} 2 S 15^{11}, מ׳ לֶחֶם 1 S 25^{18} 2 S 16^{1}, מ׳ צְנָה 1 K 10^{16} = 2 Ch 9^{15}, מ׳ אֶלֶף 1 S 15^{4}+, מ׳ שָׁנָה Gn 11^{23} (P); (2) less oft. sq. pl. מ׳ שְׁקָלִים Jos 7^{21} (JE), 2 S 14^{26}, מ׳ דְּבֵלִים 1 S 25^{18}, מ׳ אֲנָשִׁים 1 S 30^{21}, cf. Ezr 8^{4}; (3) also preceded by n.pl.: הָרִמּוֹנִים מ׳, רְחֵלִים מ׳ עִזִּים מ׳ Gn 32^{15}, v^{15} (E), 1 K 7^{20}, cf. 1 Ch 15^{8} 2 Ch 29^{32} Ezr 2^{65}; (4) c. ellipsis מ׳ כֶּסֶף Ju 17^{4}; (5) as pred., רָאשֵׁיהֶם מ׳ 1 Ch 12^{32} (v^{33} van d. H). **c.** abs. pl. מֵא(וֹ)ת:—(1) alone, = *hundreds,* לְמֵאוֹת 1 S 29^{2} *by hundreds,* so 2 S 18^{4} (both + thousands); esp. שָׂרֵי (הַ)מ׳ *captains of* (*the*) *hundreds* Ex $18^{21.25}$ (E), 2 K $11^{4.9.10.15}$+; (2) multiplied, sq. noun enumerated, in sg.: שְׁלֹשׁ מ׳ אִישׁ Ju 7^{6} 300 *men,* cf. $v^{7.8.16}$ 8^{4} Ex 12^{27} (E), etc.; אַרְבַּע מ׳ שָׁנָה Gn 15^{13} (JE) 400 *years;* חֲמֵשׁ מ׳ אֶלֶף 2 S 24^{9} 500,000, cf. 2 Ch 13^{17}; שֵׁשׁ מ׳ רֶכֶב Ex 14^{7} (J) 600 *chariots;* שְׁבַע מ׳ אִישׁ Ju $20^{15.16}$ 700 *men;* שְׁמֹנֶה מ׳ חָלָל 2 S 23^{8} 800 *slain;* תְּשַׁע מ׳ רֶכֶב Ju $4^{3.13}$ 900 *chariots;* (3) less oft. sq. n.pl.: שְׁלֹשׁ מ׳ שׁוּעָלִים Ju 15^{4} 300 *foxes;* חֲמֵשׁ מ׳ אֲתוֹנוֹת Jb 1^{3} 500 *she-asses,* etc.; (4) rare, and chiefly late, after n.pl. פִּלַגְשִׁים שְׁלֹשׁ מ׳ 1 K 11^{3} 300 *concubines,* cf. 7^{42} = 2 Ch 4^{13}, 1 Ch 4^{42} 2 Ch 14^{8} etc.; after n.coll. בָּקָר חֲמֵשׁ מ׳ 2 Ch 35^{9}; (5) rare is חֲמֵשׁ מ׳ בַּשֶּׁקֶל Ex 30^{24} (P); (6) ellipsis of n., שְׁלֹשׁ מ׳ כֶּסֶף Gn 45^{22} (E), etc. **d.** cstr. sg., only sq. sg., and late: מְאַת־שָׁנָה Gn 11^{10} 21^{5} 25^{7} (all P) + 25 t. P, 1 Ch 25^{9} Est 1^{4} (Dr^Intr. 124) (also c. other numerals, v. **2** infr.); מְאַת Ec 8^{12} = 100 *times* (מֵאָה פְּעָמִים), sc. פַּעַם, or perhaps only appar. cstr. (Kö^ii. 228 cf. Ew^§ 269 b. 279 e).—Ne 5^{11} v. **3** infr. **2.** as part of larger number: **a.** usually preceding tens and units, (1) with noun expressed once, or not at all, earlier usage, usu. c. וְ before ten if no unit follows, otherwise without וְ before ten (see Kö^ii. 218 ff.): שֵׁשׁ מֵאוֹת מֵאָה וְעֶשֶׂר שָׁנִים Ju 2^{8}; שִׁשִּׁים וָשֵׁשׁ כִּכַּר 1 K 10^{14} 666 *talents,* etc. (exceptions are Ne 7^{24} and v^{31}); (2) chiefly late, with noun and וְ repeated: מֵאָה שָׁנָה וְעֶשְׂרִים שָׁנָה וְשֶׁבַע שָׁנִים Gn 23^{1} (P) (cf. ואלף אמה ומאת אמה SI^5.6 Da^Expos. Times, May, 1898). **b.** less oft., foll. tens and units, chiefly late, c. וְ repeated:—שֶׁבַע וּשְׁלֹשִׁים וּמְאַת שָׁנָה Nu 7^{86} (P); עֶשְׂרִים וּמֵאָה Ex 6^{16} (P), etc.; **c.** noun after ten and after hundred, חָמֵשׁ וְשִׁשִּׁים שָׁנָה וּשְׁלֹשׁ מֵאוֹת שָׁנָה Gn 5^{23} (P), etc.—On these usages v., further, Kö^ii. 217 ff. Da^Synt. §§ 36 R. 3, 37 (d) Ges^§§ 97, 134 and esp. Herner^Synt. d. Zahlwörter im AT (1893). †**3.** מְאַת הַכֶּסֶף Ne 5^{11} = *a hundredth* part *of the money;* but read quite poss. מַשַּׁאת *the debt* (Gei^Jüd. Zeitschr. viii. 1870. 227 Gr.)

†II. **מֵאָה n.f.** used as n.pr. of tower on northern wall of Jerus., מִגְדַּל הַמֵּאָה Ne 3^{1} 12^{39}. 3968

[מַאֲוַי], מַאֲוַיֵּי v. sub I. אוה, p. 16 supr. 3970

מאם (√ of following, mng. unkn.; Ol^§ 205 prop. √ אום = חום *black,* cf. already Ew^§ 160 d).

†**מְאוּם n.m.** ^Jb 31, 7 **blemish, defect** (for 3971
מְאוּם, which, although found only late, is (si vera l.) appar. original form, Kö^ii. 146);—מ׳ abs.: **1.** of physical defect Dn 1^{4}. **2.** fig. בְּכַפַּי דָּבַק מ׳ Jb 31^{7} of moral stain; usually

†**מוּם n.m.** ^Lv 21, 17 (= foregoing; quiesc. א 3971
om.) (NH *id.;* Aram. מוּמָא, ܡܘܡܐ);—abs. מ׳ Lv 21^{17} + 16 t.; sf. מוּמוֹ Pr 9^{7}; מוּמָם Dt 32^{5};—*blemish, defect* (chiefly H): **1.** physical, **a.** in man, as excluding from priestly service, Lv $21^{17.18.21.21.23}$; disfiguring man 2 S 14^{25}, woman Ct 4^{7}; (in all היה מ׳ בְּ); as caused by man upon man Lv $24^{19.20}$. **b.** in beast (ref. to sacrifice) Lv $22^{20.21.25}$ Nu 19^{2} Dt $15^{21.21}$ 17^{1} (in all היה מ׳ בְּ). **2.** fig. of moral blemish Dt 32^{5} (but text very dubious, cf. Dr); תִּשָּׂא פָנֶיךָ מִמּוּם Jb 11^{15}; of shame of repulse Pr 9^{7} (‖ קָלוֹן).

מְאוּמָה ^32 **pron. indef. anything** (acc. to 3972
Thes from מָה וּמָה, like *quidquid,* against which is the *Milʿel* tone; acc. to Ol^254, 255, 386 Kö^ii. 146 an old accus. from מאום in sense of *speck, particle,* cf. Fr. *point:* in As. *manman* (prop. *who? who?*), assim. *mamman,* or *manma* (*man, who?* + generalizing *ma*), *mamma,* is *any one, minma* (*min, what?* + *ma*), *mimma,* is *anything,* Dl^§ 60, HWB 418 f. Wsg^125 f.);—*anything,* usually in negative sentences, as Gn 22^{12} ואל־תעשׂ לו מאומה (euphem. for *something bad*), 30^{31} לֹא־תִתֶּן־לִי מאומה, $39^{6.9}$ 40^{15} (euphem.), 1 S $12^{4.5}$ $20^{26.39}$ $25^{7.15.21}$ 29^{3} etc., Ju 14^{6} ומאומה אין בידו, Ec 5^{14} ומ׳ לא ישׂא בעמלו, 1 K 18^{43} אין מ׳ lit. nought of *anything!* Je 39^{12} ואל תעשׂ לו מאומה רָע; strengthened by כֹּל + Gn 39^{23} 2 S 3^{35}; after אִם = *surely not,* 2 S 3^{35}; in interrog. sentence Nu 22^{38}; in affirm. sentence Dt 24^{10} כִּי־תַשֶּׁה בְרֵעֲךָ מַשַּׁאת מ׳ a pledge of (= consisting in)

anything, 2 S 13^{3} (euphem.), 2 K 5^{20}. Used adverbially, 1 S 21^{3} איש אל ידע מ׳ את הדבר let no one know of the matter *in anything at all*.

3974 מָאוֹר, [מְאוּרָה] v. אור. p. 22

3976 [מאזן], מֹאזְנַיִם v. II. אזן. p. 24

3967 מְאָיוֹת Kt v. מֵאָה. p. 547

3978-80 מַאֲכָל, מַאֲכֶלֶת, מַאֲכֹלֶת v. אכל. p. 38

3981 [מַאֲמָץ, מַאֲמַצִּים] v. אמץ. p. 55

3982 [מַאֲמָר] v. אָמַר. p. 57

3985 †[מָאֵן] **vb. Pi.** refuse (**Qal** perhaps *be distasteful*, cf. Syr. ܡܐܢ *taeduit, piguit*, Aph. *be slothful;* NH Pi., as term. techn. of girl, *refuse* to acknowledge marriage contract; poss. akin to Eth. መአነ: *reject;* Ar. مَأَنَ is *sustain, maintain*);—**Pi.** *Pf.* מֵאֵן Ex 7^{14}+4 t.; fs. מֵאֲנָה Je 15^{18}+3 t.; מֵאַנְתָּ Ex 10^{3}, etc.; *Impf.* יְמָאֵן Ex 22^{16}; וַיְמָאֵן Gn 37^{35}+8 t. etc.; *Inf. abs.* מָאֵן Ex 22^{16};—*refuse*, (sq. Inf. except 6 t. v. infr.) human subj. Gn 37^{35} (J), Je 31^{15} Ex 22$^{17.17}$ Nu 20^{21} 22^{14} (all E), Dt 25^{7} 1 S 8^{19} 2 S 2^{23} 13^{9} 1 K 20^{35} 21^{15} Est 1^{12} Je 50^{33} cf. Jb 6^{7} ψ 77^{3} Pr 21^{25} Je 15^{18}; without Inf. וַיְמָאֵן וַיֹּאמֶר Gn 39^{8} 48^{19} (both J), 1 S 28^{23}; also 2 K 5^{16}; esp. of refusing to obey י׳'s commands Ex 4^{23} 7^{14} 10^{3} 16^{28} (all J), Ne 9^{17}; also ψ 78^{10} Pr 21^{7} Ho 11^{5}, v. esp. Je 3^{3} 5$^{3.3}$ 8^{5} 9^{5} 11^{10} cf. 25^{28}, Zc 7^{11}; without Inf. = *be recusant* Pr 1^{24} Is 1^{20}; once subj. י׳ Nu 22^{13} (E).

3986 †מָאֵן **adj. verb.** refusing, sq. Inf., and alw. of disobeying י׳; Ex 7^{27} 9^{2} 10^{4} (all J), Je 38^{21}.

3987 †[מֵאֵן] **adj.** id. pl. מֵאֲנִים sq. Inf., of disobeying י׳ Je 13^{10}.

3988 †I. [מָאַס] **vb.** reject (NH *id.;* Aram. מְאַס *reject, despise;* BA$^{ES 15}$ comp. (dub.) Ar. مَعَسَ *lightly esteem* (Kam.); As. *ma'âsu* is perhaps *destroy* Meissn$^{Suppl. 55}$);—**Qal** *Pf.* 3 ms. מָאַס Is 8^{6}+4 t.; sf. מְאָסָם ψ 53^{6}; 2 ms. מָאַסְתָּ Je 14^{19}+3 t.; מְאַסְתָּה Ju 9^{38} 1 S 15^{26}+22 t. Pf.; *Impf.* יִמְאַס Jb 8^{20}+3 t.; יִמְאָס ψ 36^{5} Jb 36^{5}; sf. וַיִּמְאָסְךָ 1 S 15$^{23.26}$; for וְאֶמְאָסְאךָ Ho 4^{6} (so Baer, cf. De Complut.Var. 18 f.; not וָא׳ van d. H) rd. וְאֶמְאָסְךָ; 3 mpl. יִמְאָסוּ Je 6^{19}+2 t.; יִמְאָסוּן Is 31^{7}; +12 t. Impf.; *Inf. abs.* מָאוֹס Is 7$^{15.16}$ מָאֹס Je 14^{19} La 5^{22}; *cstr.* מָאָסְכֶם Is 30^{12}; מָאֳסָם Am 2^{4}; *Pt.* מוֹאֵס Pr 15^{32}; מֹאֵס Is 33^{15}, f. מֹאֶסֶת Ez 21^{15} (text dub., Co מוֹאֶסֶת; Berthol וּמְאַסֵּף), v^{18} (also dub., Co מְטֻמְאָתָם; Berthol מְאַסֵּף);—**1.** *reject, refuse,* **a.** c. acc.: God rejects men Ho 4^{6} 9^{17} 1 S 15$^{23.26}$ 16$^{1.7}$ 2 K 23^{27} Je 7^{29} 14$^{19.19}$ 33$^{24.26}$ Lv 26^{44} (H), ψ 53^{6} Jb 8^{20} 10^{3} La 5$^{22.22}$; זָנַחְתָּ וַתִּמְאָס ψ 89^{39}; men reject God Nu 11^{20} (J), 1 S 8^{7} 10^{19}; men 1 S 8^{7} Jb 30^{1}; idols Is 31^{7}, evil ψ 36^{5}, knowledge Ho 4^{6}, divine תורה Am 2^{4} Is 5^{24}; דבר 1 S 15$^{23.26}$, חקות Ex 20^{24}, חקים 2 K 17^{15}; מוסר Jb 5^{17} Pr 3^{11}; var. things Is 8^{6} Ez 21^{15} ψ 118^{22} Jb 31^{13}. **b.** c. בְּ God rejects men 2 K 17^{20} Je 6^{30} 31^{37} ψ 78$^{59.67}$, that in which man confides Je 2^{37}; men reject evil Is 7$^{15.16}$, divine תורה Je 6^{19}, דבר Is 30^{12} Je 8^{9}, חקות Lv 26^{15} (H); משפטים v^{43} (H), Ez 5^{6} 20$^{13.16}$; var. things, Nu 14^{31} (J) Is 33^{15} Je 4^{30} ψ 106^{24}. **2.** *despise*, c. acc., God subj. שָׂנֵאתִי מאסתי חגיכם Am 5^{21} *I hate, I despise your feasts;* elsewhere men subj. גם עוילים מ׳ בי Jb 19^{18} *even young children despise me;* אמ׳ חיי 9^{21} *I despise my life*, cf. מואס נפשׁוֹ Pr 15^{32}; הלא זה העם אשר מ׳ בו Ju 9^{38} *is not this the people that thou despisedst?* מ׳ עָרִים Is 33^{8}; obj. om. Jb 7^{16} (< join to preceding Me Siegf Du); 34^{33} 36^{5} 42^{6} (𝔖 Siegf אֶשְׁתֹּק; 𝔊 𝔙 Symm Bö אֶמָּאֵס) Ez 21^{18} (but v. supr.).—**Niph.** *be rejected:* *Impf.* תִּמָּאֵס Is 54^{6} (wife); *Pt.* נִמְאָס Je 6^{30} (silver), ψ 15^{4} (= *reprobate;* opp. יִרְאֵי י׳); + f. נִמְאֶסֶת, נִמְאָסָה 1 S 15^{9} *rejected*, i.e. *worthless* (for 𝔊 נָמֵס) acc. to We Klo Dr Kit Bu HPS
(‖ נמבזה, rd. נִבְזָה; cf. בזה, מסס **Niph.**) 4549

†מָאוֹס **n.[m.]** refuse סְחִי וּמָאוֹס תְּשִׂימֵנוּ 3973
La 3^{45} *offscouring and refuse thou makest us.*

†II. [מָאַס] **vb. Niph.** flow, run (Aram. 3988
id., but rare and dub.;—secondary form of מסס q.v.);—*Impf.* 3 ms. וַיִּמָּאֵס Jb 7^{5} my skin hath hardened *and run* (i.e. again, afresh; > GHoffm Du rd. וַיִּמַּס, Bu וַיִּמָּאֵס, √מסס); 3 mpl. יִמָּאֲסוּ כְּמוֹ מַיִם ψ 58^{8} (fig. of annihilation of wicked).

[מַאֲפֶה] v. אפה. p. 66 3989

מַאֲפֵלְיָה, מַאֲפֵל v. אפל. p. 66 3990

מאץ (cf. Ar. مَأْصٌ a kind of *white* camel, whence Lag$^{BN 29}$ prop. מָאֵץ for the difficult אָמֹץ (אֲמֻצִּים) Zc 6$^{3.7}$).

†[מָאַר] **vb.** (cf. Ar. مَأَرَ *excite hostility,* 3992
irritate, مَئِرَ *break open*, of a wound);—**Hiph.** prick, pain *Pt.* מַמְאִיר Ez 28^{24}; f. מַמְאֶרֶת Lv 13^{51}+2 t.;—of thorn סִלּוֹן מ׳ Ez 28^{24} (fig. of oppressors of Isr., ‖ קוֹץ מַכְאִב); elsewh. of leprosy (צָרַעַת) = *malignant?* Lv 13$^{51.52}$ 14^{44} (all P; but Sam. in all these has מרראת, √מרא = מרה *be obstinate*, cf. Thes$^{816 b}$ Di).

3993-94 מַאֲרָב v. ארב. מְאֵרָה v. ארר. p. 70, 76

3995 [מִבְדָּלָה], מִבְדָּלוֹת v. בדל. p. 95

3996, 3998 מָבוֹא v. בוא. מְבוּכָה v. בוך. p. 99-100

3999 †מַבּוּל n.m.[Gn 7, 6] flood in time of Noah (NH *id.;* Jew.-Aram. מַבּוּלָא; Syr. ܡܰܒܘܼܠܳܐ; der. dub.; Thes al. √יבל, but improb., v. Dl [Prol. 122 f.]; poss. old As. (Bab.) loan-word (yet form unkn. in As.), or fr. √נבל = As. *nabâlu, destroy* Dl [HWB 443 f.]; cf. Dl[Par. 156; Prol. 122] Che[ψ 29, 10 crit. n., Hbr. iii. 3, 175 f.], O. Whitehouse[COT ii. 293]);—מ׳ only Gn and ψ 29[10]; alw. abs. and alw. c. art. exc. Gn 9[11.15]; —וַיְהִי הַמּ׳ Gn 7[17]; לֹא יִהְיֶה עוֹד מ׳ 9[11]; foll. by מַיִם as appos. Gn 6[17] 7[6]; מֵי הַמּ׳ Gn 7[7.10] 9[11]; לֹא־יִהְיֶה עוֹד הַמַּיִם לְמ׳ Gn 9[15]; as epoch, in phr. אַחַר הַמּ׳ Gn 9[28] 10[1.32] 11[10] (del. as gloss Bu Di); י׳ לַמּ׳ יָשָׁב ψ 29[10] *at the flood sat enthroned* (so most; Che[v. crit. n.] *'at the storm'* (*destruction = destructive storm* Id[Hbr. l.c.]), but הַמּ׳ seems in all the other passages to be almost = n. pr. of the flood; cf. also מֵי נֹחַ Is 54[9.9]).

4000-01 מבונים Kt v. בין. מְבוּסָה v. בוס. p. 101, 108

4002 מַבּוּעַ v. נבע. מְבוּקָה v. בוק. p. 101, 616

4016 [מְבוּשִׁים, מבושׁ] v. בושׁ. p. 102

4004 מִבְחוֹר, I, II. מִבְחָר v. בחר. p. 104

4007-08 מַבָּט v. נבט. מִבְטָא v. בטא. p. 105, 613

4009-10 מִבְטָח v. בטח. [מַבְלִיגִית] v. בלג. p. 105, 114

1110, 4011 מְבֻלָּקָה v. בלק. [מִבְנֶה] v. בנה. p. 118, 125

4012-13 מְבֻנַּי v. סִבְּכַי. I. מִבְצָר v. בצר. p. 125, 131, 687

4014 II. מִבְצָר n.pr.m. Edomite chief Gn 36[42] = 1 Ch 1[53]; A𝔊L Μαζαρ, A (in Ch) Μαβσαρ;—on n.pr.loc. *Mabsar* (Onom.[277, 63; 137, 11]) cf. Buhl [Edom. 38]).

4015, 4017 [מִבְרָח] v. ברח. מְבֻשָּׁם v. בשׂם. p. 138, 142

4016, 4018 [מְבֻשִׁים] v. בושׁ. מְבַשְּׁלוֹת v. בשׁל. p. 102, 143

7248 †מָג n.m. soothsayer, magian (loan-word fr. As. *maḫḫu, soothsayer,* Dl[HWB 397]; perh. orig.

7248 Sumerian, Dl[HA 14]);—רַב־מָג Je 39[3.13] *chief-soothsayer,* in train of Nebuchadrezzar.

4019-20 מַגְבִּישׁ v. גבשׁ. מִגְבָּלֹת v. גבל. p. 148, 150

4021 מִגְבָּעוֹת v. גבע. p. 149

מגד (√of foll.; cf. Ar. مَجَدَ, مَجُدَ, *be glorious, excel in glory*).

†מֶגֶד n.m. excellence (NH *id., choice fruit;* Syr. ܡܓܕܐ *fruit;* Ar. مَجْدٌ *glory, honour, nobility*);—מ׳ cstr. Dt 33[13] + 4 t. Dt 33; pl. מְגָדִים Ct 4[13] 7[14]; sf. מְגָדָיו Ct 4[16]—*excellence:* excellent or choice things; always of gifts of nature: מ׳ שָׁמַיִם Dt 33[13] i.e. (natural) gifts of heaven; מ׳ תְּבוּאֹת שָׁמֶשׁ v[14]; מ׳ גֶּרֶשׁ יְרָחִים v[14]; מ׳ גִּבְעוֹת עוֹלָם v[15] (רֹאשׁ הַרְרֵי קֶדֶם ‖); מ׳ אֶרֶץ וּמְלֹאָהּ; pl. abstr. פְּרִי מ׳ (= excellent fruit) Ct 4[13.16]; מ׳ alone = foreg., 7[14]. 4022

†[מִגְדָּנָה] n.f. choice or excellent thing;—pl. abs. מִגְדָּנוֹת, as gifts, Gn 24[53] 2 Ch 21[3] 32[23] (‖ מִנְחָה), Ezr 1[6]. 4030

†מַגְדִּיאֵל n.pr.m. a chief of Edom, Gn 36[43] = 1 Ch 1[54]; 𝔊[B] Μεδιηλ (Ch), 𝔊[A] Μετοδιηλ (Gn), Μαγεδιηλ (Ch, cf. 𝔊L)—(cf. Sab. מגדעל Derenb [Études i. 65], Palm. מגדת (? מנרת) Cook [Aram. Gloss. 70]). 4025

מִגְדּוֹ, מְגִדּוֹן v. גדד. p. 151 4023

מִגְדָּל, מִגְדּוֹל, מִגְדָּל v. גדל. p. 153 4026

מָגוֹג n.pr. v. גוג. p. 156 4031

I, II. מָגוֹר, מְגוּרָה, מְגוּרָה v. I, III. גור. p. 158-59 4032, 4034-35

[מַגְזֵרָה] v. גזר. מַגָּל v. נגל. p. 160, 618 4037-38

מְגִלָּה v. גלל. [מְגַמָּה] v. גמם. p. 166, 169 4039, 403-

מָגֵן, מְגִנָּה, מָגֵן v. גנן. p. 171 4043-44

מִגְעֶרֶת v. גער. מַגֵּפָה v. נגף. p. 172, 620 4045-46

†מַגְפִּיעָשׁ n.pr.m. a chief of the people, Ne 10[21], 𝔊 Βαγαφης, A Μαιαφης, 𝔊L Μεγαιας. 4047

†[מָגַר] vb. cast, throw, toss (Aram. ܡܓܪ *lapsus est et cecidit* Lexx.; 𝔗 Pa מַגַּר *hurl down* 2 K 9[33], *overthrow*);—**Qal** *Pt.* pass. pl. cstr. מְגוּרֵי אֶל־חֶרֶב הָיוּ Ez 21[17] *they are thrown to the sword* (on cstr. before prep. v. Ges[§ 130. 1] Da[Synt. § 28 R 1]). **Pi.** *Pf.* 2 ms. וְכִסְאוֹ לָאָרֶץ מִגַּרְתָּה ψ 89[45] and his throne to earth *thou hast hurled.* 4048

†מִגְרוֹן n.pr.loc. **1.** 1 S 14[2] district (?) near Gibeah (home of Saul), cf. Buhl[Geogr. 176]; 𝔊 Μαγων, 𝔊L Μαγεδδω (We thinks n.pr. not required, and prop. מִגְרָן (= 𝔖 גֹּרֶן *threshing-floor;* so Bu, but word not in Hebrew; Klo, improb., מִגְרָשׁ). **2.** Is 10[28], place north of Michmash (and Gibeah), 𝔊 Μαγεδω, perhaps modern ruin *Makrun* Di[ad loc.] Bd[Pal 3. 121] Buhl[l.c.] 4051

4050 **מְגֵרָה** v. גרר. p. 176

4052 **[מְגְרָעָה]**, **מִגְרָעוֹת** v. גרע. p. 175

4053-54 **[מֶגְרָפָה]** v. גרף. **מִגְרָשׁ** v. גרשׁ. p. 175, 177

4055, 4057 **מַד** v. מדד. I, II. **מִדְבָּר** v. דבר. below, p. 184

4058-59 **מָדַד** vb. **measure** (NH *id.*; Ph. מדד; Ar. مَدَّ *extend, stretch*, مُدّ *a corn-measure*, etc.; As. *madâdu, measure*; Jew.-Aram. n. מִידָּה *measure, proportion, rule*);—**Qal** *Pf.* מ׳ (מָדַד) Is 40^{12} + 9 t. Ez; sf. מְדָדוֹ Ez $42^{15.20}$; 1 s. וּמַדֹּתִי Is 65^{7}; וּמָדְדוּ consec. Dt 21^{2} Ez 43^{10}; וּמַדֹּתֶם consec. Nu 35^{5}; *Impf.* וַיָּמָד Ru 3^{15} + 22 t. Ez; 2 ms. תָּמוֹד Ez 45^{3}; וַיָּמֹדּוּ Ex 16^{18}; תָּמֹדּוּ Ez 47^{18}; *Inf.* לָמֹד Zc 2^{6};—*measure*, chiefly lit. (usu. sq. acc. *rei*; obj. om. Ex 16^{18} Dt 21^{2} Ez 40^{35}, cf. 47^{18} (but v. Co); sq. acc. of measure Ru 3^{15} Ez 42^{19} $47^{3.4.4.5}$);—**1.** measure of length, distance Nu 35^{5} (P), Dt 21^{2} (D), Ez $40^{5.6.8.20}$ + 32 t. Ez 40–47 Zc 2^{6}. **2.** of dry measure Ex 16^{18} (P), Ru 3^{15}. **3.** fig. of measuring waters Is 40^{12} (of ׳י); of requital Is 65^{7}. †**Niph.** *Impf.* יִמַּד Ho 2^{1} Je 33^{22}; יִמַּדּוּ Je 31^{37};—*be measured*, of sand of sea Ho 2^{1} Je 33^{22}; of heavens Je 31^{37}. †**Pi.** *Pf.* וּמִדַּד־ consec. Jb 7^{4} (cf. Ges$^{§ 52. 2. R. 1}$); *Impf.* וַיְמַדֵּד 2 S 8^{2}; וַיְמַדְּדֵם v^{2}; אֲמַדֵּד ψ 60^{8} 108^{8};—**1.** *extend, continue* (=make extent *or* continuation), subj. עֶרֶב Jb 7^{4}. **2.** *measure, measure off*, בַּחֶבֶל, of apportioning Moabites to death and life, sq. sf. 2 S 8^{2}; also obj. חֲבָלִים v^{2}; metaph. of conquest, sq. acc., ψ 60^{8} = 108^{8} (‖ חִלֵּק). **Po.**
4128 *Impf.* וַיְמֹדֶד Hb 3^{6} (subj. God, obj. אֶרֶץ), *measured* (viz. with eye) 𝔙 Hi AV RV, but dub.; 𝔊 ἐσαλεύθη, 𝔗 אֲזִיעַ, hence *shook* Ew Ke Or al. (fr. √ [מוּד =] מוט, but rd. then rather וַיְמֹטֵט, although מוט not elsewhere in this conj.; We, plausibly, וַיְמֹגֵג √ מוג, cf. Na 1^{5}). †**Hithpo.** וַיִּתְמֹדֵד sq. עַל־הַיֶּלֶד 1 K 17^{21} *measured* (=extended, stretched) *himself* upon the boy.

4055 **[מַד]** **n.m.**$^{1 S 4, 12}$ measure, also **cloth garment** (as *extended, wide*);—sf. מַדּוֹ ψ 109^{18}; מִדּוֹ Lv 6^{3} 2 S 20^{8} (מִדָּה Jb 11^{9}, v. sub מִדָּה); pl. מִדִּין Ju 5^{10} (v. infr.), 2 S 21^{20} Kt (Qr מָדוֹן; rd. perh. מִדָּה, v. 1 Ch 20^{6}, cf. Dr); sf. מִדֶּיךָ Je 13^{25}; מַדָּיו 1 S 4^{12} + 4 t.;—**1.** *measure* (only pl.) =apportionment Je 13^{25}, מְנָת־מִדַּיִךְ (of lot of Judah, ‖ גּוֹרָל); cf. lit. 2 S 21^{20} Kt (but v. מִדָּה). **2.** perh. *cloth, carpet* (for sitting on), Ju 5^{10} (so most, conj. fr. context; on pl. in ין, v. Ges$^{§ 87. 1. a}$). **3.** *garment*, outer garment Ju 3^{16} 1 S 4^{12}, cf. (sim.) ψ 109^{18}; of fighting-attire 1 S 17^{38} (c. vb. הִלְבִּישׁ), v^{39} 18^{4} 2 S 20^{8} (‖ לְבוּשׁ); of priest's garment וְלָבַשׁ הַכֹּהֵן מִדּוֹ בַד Lv 6^{3}; cf. [מַדְוֶה, מָדוּ] sub מדה.

†I. **מִדָּה** **n.f.** **measure, measurement,** 4060
stature, size, garment (mostly late)—מ׳ Ex 26^{2} + 35 t.; cstr. מִדַּת Ez 40^{21} + 2 t.; pl. מִדּוֹת Ez 41^{17} + 12 t.; מִדּוֹתָיו ψ 133^{2}; מִדּוֹתֶיהָ Ez 48^{16};—**1.** *measure, act of measurement*, i.e. long measure Ez 41^{17} (del. Co), 42^{15} $48^{30.33}$; cf. Jos 3^{4} (P), 1 Ch 23^{29}, v. also Lv 19^{35} (H); once of liquid measure, fig., Jb 28^{25}; קָוֵה הַמּ׳ Je 31^{39} *measuring-line*; חֶבֶל מ׳ Zc 2^{5} (*id.*); קְנֵה הַמּ׳ *measuring-reed* Ez $40^{3.5}$ 42^{16} (del. Co), $v^{16.17.18.19}$. **2.** *measurement, size* of curtains in tabern. Ex $26^{2.8}$ $36^{9.15}$ (all P); cf. 1 K 6^{25} 7^{37} (both ‖ קֶצֶב), $v^{9.11}$ 2 Ch 3^{3} Ez $40^{10.10.21.22.24.28.29.32.33.35}$ 43^{13} 46^{22} 48^{16}; once of time, מִדַּת יָמַי ψ 39^{5}; prob. also Jb 11^{9} (fig. of God's wisdom) where מִדָּהּ = מִדָּתָהּ, cf. Sta$^{§ 347, c. 2}$; בֵּית מִדּוֹת = *house of size* Je 22^{14}; אִישׁ מִדָּה = *man of size, stature*, 1 Ch 11^{23} 20^{6};
so also prob. ‖ 2 S 21^{20} (for 𝔊 מדין, Qr מָדוֹן, 4067
v. [מַד]), We Dr Kit Bu; pl. Nu 13^{32} Is 45^{14}. **3.** *measured portion, extent*, stretch (of wall) Ne $3^{11.19.20.21.24.27.30}$, cf. Ez 45^{3}. **4.** *garment* (pl. poet.) ψ 133^{2}.

†**[מֵמַד]** **n.[m.]** measurement;—מִי שָׂם 4461
מְמַדֶּיהָ Jb 38^{5}, i.e. of the earth (‖ מִי־נָטָה עָלֶיהָ קָו).

†**מִדִּין** **n.pr.loc.** city of Judah Jos 15^{61}, site 4081
unknown, A Μαθων; 𝔊L Μαδδειν.

†II. **[מִדָּה]** **n.f.** tribute (loan-word fr. As. 4060
mandattu, id., √ *nadânu* = נָתַן Dl$^{HWB 451}$, cf. Schr$^{COT Ezr 4, 13}$; also in BAram. מִנְדָּה, מִדָּה *id.*);—מִדַּת הַמֶּלֶךְ Ne 5^{4}.

מדה (secondary form of מדד; √ of foll.)

†**[מָדוּ]**, II. **[מַדְוֶה]** **n.m.** garment;—pl. sf. 4063
מַדְוֵיהֶם 2 S 10^{4} = 1 Ch 19^{4}.

†**מַדְהֵבָה** Is 14^{4}, rd. מַרְהֵבָה v. רהב. p. 923 4062

† I. **[מַדְוֶה]** v. דוה. **מַדּוּחִים** v. נדח. p. 188, 623 4064-65

I, II. **מָדוֹן** v. דין. p. 193 4066

† III. **מָדוֹן** **n.[m.]** 2 S 21^{20} Qr, v. I. מִדָּה. above 4067

מַדּוּעַ v. ידע, p. 396. 4069

מְדוּרָה v. דור. **מִדְחֶה** v. דחה. p. 190-91 4071-72

[מַדְחֵפָה], **מַדְחֵפֹת** v. דחף. p. 191 4073

4074 †מָדַי **n.pr.gent.** et **terr.** **Medes, Media** (OPers. *Mâda* Sp^{APK}, As. *Madai* COT$^{Gloss, and on Gn 10. 2}$ Dl$^{Par. 247}$);—**1.** people, as 'son' of Japhet Gn 10^{2} (P) = 1 Ch 1^{5}; as hostile power Is 13^{17} 21^{2}; זֶרַע מָדָי Dn 9^{1}; land and people, מַלְכֵי מָדַי Je 25^{25} (+מַלְכֵי עֵילָם), 51$^{11.28}$; מַלְכֵי מ׳ וּפָרַס Dn 8^{20}; cf. פָּרַס וּמָדַי Est 1$^{3.14.18.19}$ 10^{2}; 𝔊 Μαδαι. **2.** of land alone = *Media* 2 K 17^{6} 18^{11} (both עָרֵי מָדָי).

4075 †מָדִי **adj.gent.** **Mede, Median,** דָּרְיָוֶשׁ הַמָּדִי Dn 11^{1}.

1767, 4078, 4100 מַדַּי (i.e. מַה־דַּי) 2 Ch 30^{3}, v. מה **1 e.** p. 553

1767 מִדֵּי v. דַּי. p. 191

4079-80, 4082 מְדָיָן, מְדִינָה v. דין. p. 193

4066,4085 מִדְיָנִים v. I. מדון. מְדֻכָה v. דוך. p. 189, 193

4086-89 מַדְמֵן, I, II. מַדְמֵנָה, מַדְמַנָּה v. דמן. p. 199

4066, 4084, 4090-91 מְדָן v. דין. מְדָנִים v. מדון, מִדְיָנִי. p. 193

4093 4129-30 מַדַּע, מֹדַע, מוֹדַעַת v. ידע. p. 396

4094 [מַדְקָרָה], pl. cstr. מַדְקְרוֹת v. דקר. p. 201

4071, 4095 מַדְרֵגָה v. דרג. מְדֻרָה v. דור. p. 190, 201

4096-97 [מִדְרָךְ] v. דרך. [מִדְרָשׁ] v. דרשׁ. p. 204-05

4098 [מְדֻשָׁה] v. דושׁ. p. 190

4100 מָה, rarely מָה־ (e.g. Gn 31^{43} Jos 22^{16} Ju 8^{1}), מַ·, מֶה, מַה·, מַה־ (+Ex 4^{2} Is 3^{15} Mal 1^{13} 1 Ch 15^{13} 2 Ch 30^{3}), מָ (only in מָהֶם +Ez 8^{6} Kt., Qr. מָה הֵם)—on the distinction in the use of these forms, see Ges$^{§ 37}$—**pron. interrog.** and **indef.** **what? how? aught;** used of things, as מִי of persons (Aram. ܡܳܢܳܐ, מָא, Ar. مَا; prob. apoc. from a longer form with *n* or *nt*, As. *minû* (Dl$^{HWB 417 f.}$), Eth. ምንት: *ment;* cf. W$^{CG 123 ff.}$ Kö$^{ii. 368}$):—**1.** interrog. *what?* **a.** in a direct question, before either verbs or nouns Gn 4^{10} מֶה עָשִׂיתָ *what* hast thou done? 15^{2} מה־תתן־לי *what* wilt thou give me? Ex 3^{13} מַה־שְּׁמוֹ, 12^{26} 13^{14} and so very often: מַה־הִיא Zc 5^{6}; מה אלה Zc 1^{9}; מָה אַתָּה רֹאֶה Je 1^{11} Am 7^{8}+; Jl 4^{14} מה אתם לי; Ju 18^{8} מה אתם vid. Comm., v^{24} מה לי עוד *what* have I still? Is 21^{11} מה־מלילה *what* (= how much) of the night (is past)? = *as what? (qualem?)* Hg 2^{3} (cf. מִי Am 7^{2}); to express surprise, Jb 9^{12} who shall say to him, מה תעשׂה *what* doest thou? 22^{13} Ec 8^{4} Is 45$^{9.10}$; sq. כִּי, Gn 20^{10} מה ראית כי עשׂית *what* hadst thou in view, that thou hast done, etc.? 31^{36} Ex 16^{7} וְנַחְנוּ מָה כִּי and *what* are we, that . . .? 32^{21} Nu 22^{28} Hb 2^{18}, etc. Note in partic.—(*a*) מָה is followed sometimes by a subst. in appos. (against Arabic usage, which does not permit this: W$^{AG. ii. § 170}$), so that it becomes virtually an adj.: מַה־בֶּצַע *what* profit . . .? Gn 37^{26} ψ 30^{10} Mal 3^{14}; Is 40^{8} מַה־דְּמוּת, Mal 1^{13} ψ 89^{48} זְכָר־אֲנִי מֶה חָלֶד (inverted for מַה חֶלֶד אָנִי) remember (of) *what* (short) duration I am, Ec 1^{3} 5$^{10.15}$ 6$^{8.11}$ (Da$^{§ 8, R. 2}$ Kö$^{iii. 23 f.}$); as exclam., ψ 89$^{48 b}$ Jb 26^{14}. And with the subst. idiom. at the end (in Arabic preceded then by مِنْ: W$^{AG. ii. § 49. 7}$), 1 S 26^{18} ומה־בידי רעה and what is there in my hand, evil? 20^{10} (vid. **3**), 2 S 19^{29} 24^{13} 1 K 12^{16} Je 2^{5} מה־מצאו אבותיכם בי עָוֶל, Ec 11^{2} Est 6^{3}. (*b*) מַה־זֶּה *what, now?* 1 S 10^{11}, contr. מַזֶּה +Ex 4^{2} (זֶה **4 c**); Gn 3^{13} מַה־זֹּאת עָשִׂית; 12^{18} 29^{25} מַה־זֹּאת עָשִׂיתָ לִּי; similarly 26^{10} 42^{28}+, either *what, now,* hast thou done? or *what is this* that thou hast done? (vid. זֶה **4 d**). (*c*) מַה־לְּךָ *what* to thee? i.e. *what aileth* thee? or *what dost thou want?* Gn 21^{17} מַה־לָּךְ הָגָר; Jos 15^{18} 2 S 14^{5} 1 K 1^{16} 2 K 6^{28} Ez 18^{2} (accents); sq. כִּי, Ju 18^{23} מה־לך כי נזעקת, Gn 20^{9} (cf. 1 S 11^{5} מה לעם כי יבכו), Is 22^{1} מַה־לָּךְ כִּי עָלִית (cf. τί παθὼν τοῦτο ποιεῖς;), ψ 114^{5}; without כִּי Is 3^{15} (cf. Qor 57$^{8.10}$); with a ptcp., Jon 1^{6} *what is it to thee* as a sleeper? (accus.: Da$^{§ 70a}$ cites Qor 74^{50}), Ez 18^{2} (if אתם be treated as strengthening לכם). (*d*) מַה־לְּךָ (לִּי) פֹּה = *what* hast thou (have I) here? Ju 18^{3} 1 K 19^{9} Is 22^{16} 52^{5}. (*e*) in the genit., Jer 8^{9} וְחָכְמַת־מֶה לָהֶם, and wisdom of *what* (= what kind of wisdom) is theirs? Nu 23^{3} (v. infr. **3**). **b.** often in an *indirect* question, as after ראה, Gn 2^{19} to see מה־יקרא־לו *what* he would call it, 37^{20} וְנִרְאֶה מה־יהיו חלמֹתיו *to what* his dreams will come, Nu 13$^{19 f.}$ Hb 2^{1}; הִכִּיר Gn 31^{32}; ידע 39^{8} Ex 2^{4} לדעת מה־יֵּעָשֶׂה לו, 16^{15} 32^{1} Jb 34^{4}; שׁמע Nu 9^{8} וְאשׁמעה מה־יצוה י׳ (cf. ψ 85^{9}), 2 S 17^{5}; פֵּרַשׁ Nu 15^{34}; שׁאל 1 K 3^{5} 2 K 2^{9}; הֵבִין Jb 6^{24} 23^{5}: Nu 13^{18} וראיתם את הארץ מה היא, ψ 39^{5} Is 41^{22} הראשׁנות מָה הֵנָּה הַגִּידוּ.—In some such cases it approximates in meaning to the simple rel., as Jer 7^{17} 33^{24} Mi 6$^{5.8}$ Jb 34^{33}. **c.** = *of what kind?* (Germ. *was für ein . . .?*), with an insinuation of blame, or reproach, or contempt: Gn 37^{10} מה החלום הזה *what* is this

dream which thou hast dreamt? 44^{15} Jos 22^{16} Ju 8^{1} 15^{11} 20^{12} 1 S 29^{3} מָה הָעִבְרִים האלה, 1 K 9^{13} מה הערים האלה אשר נתתה לי, 2 K 9^{22} 18^{19}. **d.** מה is often used in questions to which the answer *little*, or *nothing*, is expected, and it thus becomes equivalent to a *rhetorical negative* (cf. הֲ **b**, מִי **f** *c*): (*a*) Gn 23^{15} land worth 400 shekels..., מה היא *what is it?* (i.e. it is something quite insignificant), 27^{37} Ju 8^{3} ומה־יכלתי עשׂות ככם, 14^{18} Ho 9^{5} 10^{3} ψ 30^{10} 56^{5} Jb 15^{9} 16^{6} 21^{21} $22^{13.17}$ La 2^{13} Ct 5^{9} מַה־דּוֹדֵךְ מִדּוֹד *what* is thy beloved (more) than a(nother) beloved? ‖ לא, 1 K 12^{16} מַה־לָּנוּ חֵלֶק בְּדָוִד וְלֹא־נַחֲלָה בְּבֶן יִשַׁי (2 S 20^{1} אֵין־לָנוּ חֵלֶק וגו׳), Jb 16^{6}. (*b*) sq. כִּי (כִּי **1 f**), Gn 20^{9} 37^{26} מַה־בֶּצַע כִּי נַהֲרֹג *what* profit (is it) that we should slay him? Ex 16^{7} Nu 16^{11} Hb 2^{18} 2 K 8^{13} *what* is thy servant, the dog, *that he should do*, etc.? and often in poetry, as ψ 8^{5} מָה אנושׁ כי תזכרנו *what* is man *that* thou rememberest him? Jb 6^{11} מַה־כֹּחִי כִּי אֲיַחֵל, v^{11b} 7^{17} $15^{12f.14}$ 16^{3} 21^{15}+ (cf. מִי **f** *b*). Hence, (*c*) in the formula of repudiation, or emphatic denial, מַה־לִּי וָלָךְ (וְלָכֶם) *what* is there (common) to me and to thee? i.e. what have I to do with thee? †Ju 11^{12} 2 S 16^{10} מה לי ולכם, 19^{23} 1 K 17^{18} 2 K 3^{13} 2 Ch 35^{21}; cf. Jos 22^{24} 2 K $9^{18.19}$; rather differently, without וְ, †Je 2^{18} מה לך לדרך מ׳ *what* is there to thee *with reference to* the way to Egypt? Ho 14^{9} מַה־לּוֹ לָעֲצַבִּים, cf. ψ 50^{16} (לְסַפֵּר); with את, †Je 23^{28} מַה־לַתֶּבֶן אֶת־הַבָּר *beside* (or *in comparison with*) the wheat? cf. τί ἐμοὶ (ἡμῖν) καὶ σοί; Mt 8^{29} Mk 5^{7} Jn 2^{4}; and Ar. مَا لِى وَلَكَ. **e.** =*whatsoever* (cf. מִי **g**): (*a*) Ju 9^{48} מה אתם ראיתם עשׂיתי מהרו עשׂו כמוני, lit. *what* do you see (that) I have done? hasten, and do like me (=*whatever* ye see, etc.), 2 S 21^{4} מה אתם אמרים אעשׂה לכם, Jb 6^{24}; with the apod. introd. by וְ, 1 S 20^{4} מה תאמר נפשׁך ואעשׂה לך; Est 5^{3} מַה־בַּקָּשָׁתֵךְ ... וְיִנָּתֵן לָךְ, v^{6} 7^{2} 9^{12}; hence in the late and strange idiom of Ch., it sinks twice almost to the rel. *what*, 1 Ch 15^{13} כי לְמַבָּרִאשׁוֹנָה לא אתם because ye were not (employed) for *what* was at first (on the former occasion), J. etc., 2 Ch
4078 30^{3} לְמַדַּי acc. to *what* was sufficient (=in sufficient numbers), cf. Est 9^{26}. (*b*) מַה־שֶּׁ־ (late: frequently in Mishn., etc.), *whatever, what* (cf. מִי, מִי אֲשֶׁר **g** *end*): †Ec 1^{9} מַה־שֶּׁהָיָה הוּא שֶׁיִּהְיֶה, lit. *what* is that which hath been? it is that which shall be (=*whatever* hath been, it is that which shall be), v^{9} $3^{15.22}$ 6^{10} 7^{24} 8^{7} 10^{14}.

2. Used adverbially: **a.** as an *interrogative*: (*a*) *how?* especially in expressing what is regarded as an impossibility, Gn 44^{16} מַה־נִּצְטַדָּק *how* shall we justify ourselves? Nu $23^{8.8}$ 1 S 10^{27} מַה־יֹּשִׁעֵנוּ זֶה, 2 K 4^{43} Jb 9^{2} $25^{4.4}$ 31^{1} I made a covenant with my eyes, וּמָה אֶתְבּוֹנֵן עַל ב׳ and *how* should I look upon a maid? (𝔊 οὐ, 𝔙 *non*), Pr 20^{24} וְאָדָם מַה־יָּבִין דַּרְכּוֹ; in an indirect question, Ex 10^{26} ψ 39^{5} אֵדְעָה מֶה־חָדֵל אָנִי; מַה־זֶּה *how, now?* (in surprise), Gn 27^{20} מַה־זֶּה מִהַרְתָּ לִמְצֹא בְּנִי, Ju 18^{24} 1 K 21^{5} 2 K 1^{5}. (*b*) *why?* Ex 14^{15} מַה תִּצְעַק אֵלָי, $17^{2.2}$ 2 K 6^{33} 7^{3} ψ 42^{6} מַה־תִּשְׁתּוֹחֲחִי עלי, Jb 15^{12}+; Ct 8^{4} I adjure you מַה־תָּעִירוּ וּמַה־תְּעוֹרְרוּ, *why* will ye stir up, etc.? (i.e. *do not*: ‖ אִם 2^{7} 3^{5}).—The transition from the interrog. to the neg., to which in Heb. there is an approx. (v. supr.: esp. 1 K 12^{16} Jb 31^{1} Ct 8^{4}), is in Ar. complete, مَا being there used constantly in the sense of *not* (cf. Walker$^{Hbr. xii. 244 ff.}$; Kö$^{iii. 478}$). **b.** as an *exclam.*, *how ...!* with adjectives and verbs, Gn 28^{17} מַה־נּוֹרָא הַמָּקוֹם הַזֶּה *how* dreadful is this place! 38^{29} Nu 24^{5} מַה־טֹּבוּ אֹהָלֶיךָ, Is 52^{7} ψ 3^{2} מה רבו, 8^{2} מה אדיר, 21^{2} 36^{8}, etc., Ct $4^{10.10}$ 7^{2}; ironically, 2 S 6^{20} Je $2^{33.36}$ Jb $26^{2.3}$.

3. Indef. pron. *anything, aught*, Nu 23^{3} וּדְבַר־מַה־יַּרְאֵנִי וְהִגַּדְתִּי לָךְ and he will shew me the matter of *aught*, and I will tell thee (=if he shew me ... I will, etc., Dr$^{§ 149}$), 1 S 19^{3} וְרָאִיתִי מָה וְהִגַּדְתִּי לָךְ=and if I see aught, I will, etc., 20^{10} אוֹ מַה־יַּעַנְךָ אָבִיךָ קָשָׁה if perchance thy father shall answer thee *aught* that is harsh (order, **1 a** *a*), 2 S 18^{22} וִיהִי־מָה אָרוּצָה־נָּא but let there happen *what may* (lit. *aught*), I will run, v^{23} (cf. Jb 13^{13} (וְיַעֲבֹר עָלַי מָה), v^{29} וְלֹא יָדַעְתִּי מָה (cf. Pr 9^{13}), Pr 25^{8}. Cf. Kö$^{iii. § 65}$.

4. With preps.: **a.** בַּמֶּה$_{9}$, בַּמָּה$_{19}$ *wherein?* Ex 22^{26} Ju 16^{5} 1 S 14^{38} (indirect question; We בְּמִי); and so acc. to the various senses of בְּ: *whereby?* Gn 15^{8} Ex 33^{16} Mal $1^{2.6.7}$ 2^{17} 3^{7-8}; *wherewith?* 1 S 6^{2} 2 S 21^{3} Mi 6^{6}; *by what means?* Ju 16^{5} וּבַמֶּה נוכל לו; *at what* (worth)? Is 2^{22}; *for what?* 2 Ch 7^{21} (‖ 1 K 9^{8} על־מה). **b.** יַעַן מֶה †Hg 1^{9} *because of what?* †**c.** כַּמֶּה, כַּמָּה, prop. *the like of what?* (Ar. كَمْ, Syr. ܟܡܐ); hence (*a*) *how much? how many?* כַּמָּה יְמֵי וגו׳ Gn 47^{8} 2 S 19^{35} ψ 119^{84} Jb 13^{23}; עַד כַּמֶּה פְעָמִים 1 K 22^{16} (=2 Ch 18^{15}); כַּמָּה *how often?* Jb 21^{17} (i.e. how seldom!); in an indirect question, *how much?* Zc $2^{6.6}$. As an exclamation, Zc 7^{3} as

I have done זֶה כַּמֶּה שָׁנִים now (זֶה **4 i**), *how many* years! ψ 78^{40} כַּמָּה *how often!* (*b*) *for how long?* ψ 35^{17} כמה תראה, Jb 7^{19}. **d.** לָ֫מָּה, לָמָ֫ה (לָ֫מָּה) mostly before the gutturals א, ה, ע, and ׳י [i.e. אֲדֹנָי], but twice besides, ψ 42^{10} 43^{2}; לָ֫מָּה also occurs before gutt., in five places noted by Mas. on ψ 43^{2}, viz. 1 S 28^{15} 2 S 2^{22} 14^{31} ψ 49^{6} Je 15^{18}, and before ח †Gn 4^{6} 2 S 14^{13} 24^{3} Ec 2^{15}), לָ֫מָּה †Jb 7^{20}, לָ֫מֶּה †1 S 1$^{8.8.8}$, *for what reason? why?* Gn 4^{6} למה חרה לך *why* art thou angry? 24^{31}, etc.; often strengthened by זֶה (זֶה **4 e**), Gn 18^{13} 32^{30} (=Ju 13^{18}) למה זה תשאל לשמי, 33^{15} Ex 2^{20} 5^{22} 17^{3}, etc., Je 6^{20} 20^{18}+; Gn 25^{22} אם כן למה־זה אנכי if so, *why, then,* am I? (why do I continue to live?); =*to what purpose* (sq. לְ pers.), Gn 27^{46} למה לי חיים, Is 1^{11} Je 6^{20} Am 5^{18} למה זה לכם יום ׳י, Jb 30^{2}; in an indirect question, 1 S 6^{3} Dn 10^{20}. Note especially (*a*) in expostulations, Gn 12^{18} למה לא הגדת לי *why* didst thou not tell me, etc.? v^{19} 29^{25} 31^{27} 42^{1} 43^{6} 1 S 21^{15} 22^{13} 24^{10} ψ 22^{2} 44$^{24.25}$ 74$^{1.11}$+oft.; (*b*) with an impf., oft. deprecating, or introducing rhetorically, the reason why something should, or should not, be done, *why should . . .?* 1 S 19$^{5.17}$ 20^{8} but to thy father (emph.) למה זה תביאני, *why shouldst* thou bring me? 20^{32} למה יומת מה עשׂה *why should* he be put to death? 2 S 13^{26} 16^{9} 20^{19} 2 K 14^{10}, etc.: in such cases, it approximates in meaning to *lest* (cf. Ph. CIS$^{i.\ 2,\ 21}$ לָם יסגרינם אלנם *ne* tradant eos dii), and is in 𝔊 often rendered by μήποτε, as Gn 27^{45} למה אשכל *why should* I be bereaved, etc.? Ex 32^{12} למה יאמרו מצרים Ne 6^{3} ψ 79^{10} 115^{2} Ec 7^{16}, μή, Jer 40^{15}, ἵνα μή, Gn 47^{19} 2 S 2^{22} 2 Ch 25^{16} Ec 5^{5} 7^{17}, or ὅπως μή, Jo 2^{17} (in 1 S 19^{17} 2 S 13^{26}, paraph. by εἰ μή); and, connected with the foreg. sentence by אשׁר, or שֶׁ, in late, or dial., Heb. it actually has that mng., Dn 1^{10} אֲשֶׁר לָמָּה יִרְאֶה *lest* he see, Ct 1^{7} שַׁלָּמָה אֶהְיֶה *lest* I become (so in Aram. דִּי לְמָה Ezr 7^{23}, דִּילְמָא 𝔗, Syr. ܕܠܡܐ, both regularly=*lest*). **e.** עַד־מֶה (ψ 4^{3} עַד־מָה) *until when? how long?* †Nu 24^{22} (aposiop.), ψ 4^{3} 79^{5} 89^{47}; in indirect qu., ψ 74^{9} (cf. עד מתי, עד אנה). **f.** עַל־מָה, and עַל־מֶה, *upon what?* Jb 38^{6} 2 Ch 32^{10}; *upon what ground? wherefore?* Nu 22^{32} עַל־מָה הִכִּיתָ אֶת־אֲתֹנְךָ, Dt 29^{23} (cf. 1 K 9^{8} Je 22^{8}), Is 1^{5} Je 8^{14} 9^{11} 16^{10} Ez 21^{12} ψ 10^{13} Jb 13^{14} (probably dittogr. from v^{13}); על־מה־זה Ne 2^{4}. In an indirect question, Jb 10^{2} הוֹדִיעֵנִי עַל מַה־תְּרִיבֵנִי, Est 4^{5} לָדַעַת מַה־זֶּה וְעַל־מַה־זֶּה.

†[מָהַהּ] **vb.** only **Hithpalp.** linger, 4102
tarry (cf. Ar. مَهَّ *slow walk, delay* (Ḳam.));—**Hithpalp.** *Pf.* 1 s. הִתְמַהְמָהְתִּי ψ 119^{60}; 3 pl. הִתְמַהְמְהוּ Ju 19^{8}; 1 pl. הִתְמַהְמָהְנוּ Gn 43^{10}; *Impf.* יִתְמַהְמַהּ Hb 2^{3}; וַיִּתְמ׳ Gn 19^{16}; *Imv.* mpl. הִתְמַהְמְהוּ Is 29^{9}; *Inf.* לְהִתְמַהְמֵהַּ Ex 12^{39}; *Pt.* מִתְמַהְמֵהַּ 2 S 15^{28};—*linger, tarry, wait,* of pers., Gn 19^{16} 43^{10} (J), Ex 12^{39} (E), Ju 3^{26} 19^{8} 2 S 15^{28} Is 29^{9} ψ 119^{60} (c. לֹא, opp. חָשַׁתִּי); subj. חָזוֹן *vision* Hb 2^{3}

מְהוּמָה v. הום. מְהוּמָן v. אמן. p. 54, 223 4106-04

מְהֵיטַבְאֵל v. יטב. p. 406 4105

†[מָהַל] **vb.** circumcise, weaken (si 4107
vera l.; cf. NH מָהַל *circumcise,* Aram. מְהַל *id.*);—only fig. **Qal** *Pt. pass.* סָבְאֵךְ מָהוּל בַּמָּיִם Is 1^{22} *thy choice wine weakened with water,* so Thes De Che^{Comm} Di Du; cf. *vinum castrare,* Plin$^{xix.\ 53}$: Ba$^{Erkl.\ d.\ Jes.}$ Che^{Hpt} (cf. Nö$^{ZMG\ xl.\ 1886,\ 741}$) comp. NH מוֹהַל, *juice* (of fruit, esp. olives); Ar. مُهْلٌ *oil, liquid pitch, suppurating matter;* v. against this Di.

[מַהֲלָךְ] v. הלך. p. 237 4109

[מַהֲלָל], מַהֲלַלְאֵל v. II. הלל. p. 239 4110-11

מַהֲלֻמוֹת v. הלם. p. 240 4112

[מַהֲמֹרָה], מַהֲמֹרוֹת v. המר. p. 243 4113

[מַהְפֵּכָה], מַהְפֶּכֶת v. הפך. p. 246 4114-15

†I. [מָהַר] **vb.** hasten (NH Pi., and 4116
deriv.; Ar. مَهَرَ *be practised, skilled* (with As. *mâru, send, order, govern,* cf. II. מהר); Eth. ምሀረ: *train, teach;* Syr. ܡܗܪ Pa. *id.;* cf. also Egypt. *māhar, trained warrior* Bondi^{57});—**Niph.** *Pf.* 3 fs. נִמְהָרָה Jb 5^{13}; *Pt.* נִמְהָר Hb 1^{6}; pl. נִמְהָרִים Is 32^{4}; cstr. נִמְהֲרֵי Is 35^{4};—*be hurried*=anxious, disturbed נִמְהֲרֵי־לֵב Is 35^{4}; *hasty, precipitate,* subj. עֵצָה Jb 5^{13}; so pt. as subst. Is 32^{4}; *impetuous,* of Chaldeans, Hb 1^{6} (‖ מַר). **Pi.** *Pf.* מִהַר 1 S 4^{14} Is 51^{14}; 3 fs. מִהֲרָה Je 48^{16} etc.; *Impf.* יְמַהֵר Is 5^{19}+2 t.; וַיְמַהֵר Gn 18^{6}+8 t. (1 S 28^{30} v. infr.); 3 fpl. תְּמַהֵרְנָה Je 9^{17} etc.; *Imv.* ms. מַהֵר Gn 19^{22}+; מַהֲרָה 1 S 23^{27} 1 K 22^{9}, etc.; *Inf. cstr.* מַהֵר Pr 7^{23}+; *Pt.* מְמַהֵר Gn 41^{32} Mal 3^{5} (on מַהֵר Zp 1^{14} [1 S 23^{22}] cf. Kö$^{i.\ 268}$, Schwally$^{ZAW\ x.\ 1890,\ 176}$ vid. 1. מַהֵר p. 555), fpl. מְמַהֲרוֹת Pr 6^{18};—**1.** *hasten, make haste,* =go or come quickly Gn 18^{6} 1 S 9^{12} (but del. 𝔊 We

Dr Kit Bu HPS), Na 2[6] Is 49[17] 1 Ch 12[9]; =go eagerly, (sq. Inf. of purpose) Pr 1[16] Is 59[7]; *Pt.* =swift, prompt Mal 3[5]; of bird Pr 7[23]; fig. of calamity Is 5[19] (‖ חוּשׁ), Je 48[16], cf. מַהֵר שָׁלָל חָשׁ בַּז Is 8[1.3], infr. **2.** *hasten* + vb., (מ׳ having really adverbial force): sq. Inf. Gn 18[7] (מִהַר לַעֲשׂוֹת); cf. 27[20] 41[32] (subj. God), Ex 2[18] 10[16] 12[33] 2 S 15[14] Is 32[4] 51[14] Pr 6[18] Ec 5[1]; more often sq. vb. c. ו Gn 24[18.20.46] 44[11] (all J), 45[9.13] (E), prob. 43[30] (J), also Ex 34[8] (J), Jos 4[10] 8[14.19] (all JE), Ju 13[10] 1 S 4[14] 17[48] 23[27] 25[18.23.34.34] 28[24] 2 S 15[14] 19[17] 1 K 20[33.41] 2 K 9[13] Je 9[17]; so even when act. is not wholly voluntary 1 S 28[20] (but rd. prob. וַיִּבָּהֵל 𝔊 We Dr Kit Bu); also, ו om., ψ 106[13]; esp. c. Imv. Gn 19[22] (J), Ju 9[48] Est 6[10]; so also מַהֵר עֲנֵנִי ψ 69[18] 102[3] 143[7]; cf. 79[8] (v. Ol[ad loc.]). **3.** trans. *hasten,* = prepare quickly Gn 18[6]; =bring quickly 1 K 22[9] = 2 Ch 18[8], Est 5[5]; = do quickly 2 Ch 24[5.5].

4116 † I. מַהֵר **adj. hastening, speedy, swift** (strictly **Pi.** *Pt.* for מְמַהֵר v. sub מהר);—of יוֹם י׳, קָרוֹב וּמ׳ מְאֹד Zp 1[14]; rd. also f. (רַגְלוֹ) הַמְּהֵרָה 1 S 23[22] *his swift foot* (for MT (ר׳ מִי רָאָהוּ) Th We Dr Bu; deeper corruption assumed by HPS.

4118 † II. מַהֵר **adv. quickly, speedily** (strictly **Pi.** inf. abs.) always immediately after vb.; Ex 32[8] (J), Dt 4[26] 7[4.22] 9[3.12.12.16] 28[20] Jos 2[5] (J), Ju 2[17.23] Pr 25[8] (on ψ 69[18] 79[8] 102[3] 143[7], where מ׳ precedes, v. supr. sub מָהַר).

4106 †מָהִיר **adj. quick, prompt, ready, skilled;**—סוֹפֵר מ׳ ψ 45[2] Ezr 7[6]; אִישׁ מ׳ בִּמְלַאכְתּוֹ Pr 22[29]; cstr. מְהִר צֶדֶק Is 16[5] *prompt in justice.*

4120 †מְהֵרָה **n.f. haste, speed;**—usually as adverb. acc. *hastily, quickly:* Jos 8[19] 10[6] 23[16] (all JE), Nu 17[11] (P), Dt 11[17] Ju 9[54] 2 S 17[16.18.21] Je 27[16] Ec 8[11] (in all these cases after vb.); before vb. (poet.) Is 5[26] (‖ קַל), ψ 31[3] 37[2] Is 58[8] Jo 4[4] (‖ קַל); so also 1 S 20[38] מ׳ הוּשָׁה (cf. Dr); 2 K 1[11] מ׳ רְדָה;—but perhaps rd. מַהֲרָה, i.e. *Pi. Imv.* of מהר (cf. 1 S 23[27]); c. prep. (late): בִּמ׳ *in haste* = quickly Ec 4[12]; עַד־מ׳, *id.* ψ 147[15].

4121 †מַהֲרַי **n.pr.m.** one of David's heroes; 2 S 23[28] 1 Ch 11[30] 27[13]; 𝔊 Νοερε, Μαεραει, Μααρναν, Μααρι, etc.

4122 †מַהֵר שָׁלָל חָשׁ בַּז as **n.pr.m.** Is 8[1.3] (lit. *Swift* is booty, *speedy* is *prey*).

II. מהר (√ of foll.; cf. prob. As. *mâru, send,* whence *tamirtu, tamartu,* (*missive,*) *gift,* Dl[HWB 389 f.]; v. Nö[ZMG xl. 1886, 154]).

†מֹהַר **n.m. purchase-price** of wife (NH *id.*; Ar. مَهْر RS[K 78 f. Proph. iv. n. 13] Nö[l.c.] Sta[Gesch. i. 381] Dr[Dt 22, 23] and reff.; Aram. מוֹהֲרָא, ܡܗܪܐ);—abs. מ׳ Gn 34[12] (J; ‖ מַתָּן) 1 S 18[25]; cstr. מֹהַר הַבְּתוּלֹת Ex 22[16] (E). 4119

†III. [מָהַר] **vb. denom. acquire by paying purchase-price** (Ar. مَهَرَ *give a dowry,* marry for a مَهْرٌ; cf. Gerber[Verb. denom. 12] Buhl SS);—**Qal** *Pf.* 3 pl. מָהָרוּ ψ 16[4] usu. *obtain* another *in exchange* (or, by paying a price, cf. Che), but txt. dub.; *Impf.* 3 ms. sf. + *Inf. abs.* מָהֹר יִמְהָרֶנָּה לּוֹ לְאִשָּׁה Ex 22[15] (E). 4117

מַהֲתַלּוֹת v. תלל. p. 251, 1122 4123

I. מוֹ a paragogic syllable, attached to בְּ, כְּ, לְ (q.v.), so as to form with them independent words, בְּמוֹ, כְּמוֹ, לְמוֹ (q.v.) These forms, except sometimes כְּמוֹ, are exclusively poetical. In origin מוֹ is identical with מָה *what,* Ar. مَا, which is used similarly, pleonastically, with certain prefixes, e.g. بِمَا, كَمَا, عَمَّا. See Qor 3[153] 71[25]; Fl[Kl. Schr. i. 473 f., 479, 558]; W[AG ii. § 70, Rem. f; SG 126 f.]; Kö[ii. 250 f.]; and cf. Eth. ሐመ:, Syr. ܐܝܟܡܐ, Sab. בנמו = مِمَّا, DHM[ZDMG 1883, 396 f.], Hom[Chrest. § 18].

II. [מוֹ] = מַי *water.* p. 565 4325

מוֹאָב, מֹאָב[180] **n.pr. gent. et terr. Moab** (MI[1.2.5.6.12.20] מאב; As. *Ma'aba, Ma'bu, Mu'âba,* etc., Schr[COT Gloss., and on Gn 19, 37] Dl[Par. 294 f., 296];—on etym. cf. Lag[BN 90 Anm.], Ne[SK 1892, 573], Gray[Prop. N. 25]);—מוֹ׳ Gn 19[37] + 178 t.; מֹאָב 2 S 8[12]; 𝔊 Μωαβ;—**1.** *Moab* as son of Lot by his elder daughter acc. to Gn 19[37]. **2.** *Moab:* **a.** = nation of which Lot's son is represented as ancestor Gn 19[37] Nu 21[29] 22[3.3] Am 2[1.2] Je 48[1.2] + 30 t. Je 48 + oft.; having a king, Nu 21[26] 22[4.10] Ju 3[12] 1 S 12[9] +. **b.** = territory of Moab Nu 21[11.13.13.15] +; שְׂדֵה מ׳ †Gn 36[25] Nu 15[20] Ru 1[1.2.6.6.22] 2[6] 4[3] 1 Ch 1[46] 8[8]; אֶרֶץ מ׳ †Dt 1[5] 28[69] 32[49] 34[5.6] Ju 11[15.18.18] Je 48[24.33]; מִדְבַּר מ׳ †Dt 2[8]; עַרְבוֹת מ׳ †Nu 26[3.63] 31[12] 33[48.49.50] 35[1] 36[13] Dt 34[1.8] Jos 13[32]. 4124

†מוֹאָבִי, מוֹאֲבִיָּה **adj. gent. Moabitish;** 4125
—מ׳ Dt 23[4] + 2 t., מֹאָבִי Ezr 9[1]; pl. מֹאָבִים Dt 2[11]; מוֹאָב׳ Dt 2[29]; fs. מוֹאֲבִיָּה Ru 1[22] + 4 t.; מֹאֲב׳ Ru 4[10]; מוֹאָבִית 2 Ch 24[26]; fpl. מוֹאֲבִיּוֹת 1 K 11[1] Ne

13^{23}; מֹאֲבִ׳ Ru 1^4:—m. =*a Moabite* Dt 23^4 Ne 13^1; הַמּ׳ =*the Moabite* 1 Ch 11^{46}; coll. =*the Moabites* Ezr 9^1, so pl. Dt $2^{11.29}$; fpl. as adj. נָשִׁים מ׳ Ru 1^4; as subst., 1 K 11^1 Ne 13^{23}; fs. as adj. 2 Ch 24^{26}; esp. רוּת הַמּ׳ Ru 1^{22} $2^{2.21}$ $4^{5.10}$; מ׳ as n.fs. Ru 2^6.

4136 **מוֹאל** v. מול. p. 541

4126 [**מוֹבָא**] v. מָבוֹא sub בוא. p. 99

4127 †**מוּג** vb. **melt** (𝔗 מוג Ithp., ψ 46^7 107^{26}; cf. Ar. مَاجَ *surge* (of the sea), Qor 18^{99}; مَوْجٌ *a wave*);—**Qal** *Impf.* 3 fs. תָּמוּג ψ 46^7; וַתָּמוֹג Am 9^5; 2 ms. sf. וַתְּמוּגֵנוּ Is 64^6 (but rd. prob. וַתְּמַגְּנֵנוּ, v. [מָגַן] p. 171 supr., and cf. Di > Du תְּמוֹגְגֵנוּ); *Inf.* לָמוֹג Ez 21^{20};—**1.** *melt*, subj. אֶרֶץ, at touch of י׳ Am 9^5; at voice of י׳ ψ 46^7; =*faint* (of heart), Ez 21^{20}. **2.** trans. *cause to melt* Is 64^6 (but v. supr.) **Niph.** *Pf.* נָמוֹג Na 2^7 + 2 t.; 3 pl. נָמֹגוּ Ex 15^{15} + 3 t.; *Pt.* pl. נְמֹגִים ψ 75^4;—*melt away*, fig. for be helpless, disorganized (through terror, etc.) Ex 15^{15} (cf. context), Jos $2^{9.24}$ 1 S 14^{16} (cf. We Dr), Je 49^{23}, cf. Na 2^7 Is 14^{31} ψ 75^4. **Po'l.** *soften, dissolve*, act.: only Impf. 2 ms. sf. (subj. God): בִּרְבִיבִים תְּמֹגְגֶנָּה ψ 65^{11} *thou softenest it* [the earth] *with showers;* fig., =*dissipate* וּתְמֹגְגֵנִי Jb 30^{22}—We rds. וַיְמֹגֵג Hb 3^6 for וַיְמֹדֶד, v. מדד **Po'.** **Hithpo'l.** *Pf.* 3 pl. הִתְמֹגָגוּ Na 1^5; *Impf.* 3 fs. תִּתְמוֹגָג ψ 107^{26}; 3 fpl. תִּתְמוֹגַגְנָה Am 9^{13};—*melt*, subj. hills (before י׳) Na 1^5; subj. נֶפֶשׁ ψ 107^{26} (in terror); hyperb. for *flow* Am 9^{13} (of fertile hills, || הִטִּיפוּ הֶהָרִים).

I. **מוד** (√ of foll.; appar. secondary form of מדד, cf. Ba$^{NB\ §190c}$, and Ar. مَدَّ *stretch, extend,* also *prolong, make to continue*).

8548 †**תָּמִיד** n.m.$^{Dn\ 12,11}$ **continuity** (perh. orig. *extent;* NH as BH, Ecclus תמיד 45^{14});—ת׳ alw. abs.;—**1.** earliest and oftenest as adv., *continually:* **a.** of going on without interruption =*continuously*, Ho 12^7 Je 6^7 Na 3^{19} Is 21^8 49^{16} 51^{13} (+ כָּל־הַיּוֹם), 52^5 (+ *id.*), 60^{11} (|| יוֹמָם וָלַיְלָה), 62^6 (+ כָּל־הַיּוֹם וְכָל־הַלַּיְלָה), 65^3 Ob ^{16} Hb 1^{17} Dt 11^{12} 1 K 10^8=2 Ch 9^7, 1 Ch $16^{11.37}$; esp. (sometimes hyperbol.) in ψψ: ψ 16^8 25^{15} 34^2 (|| בְּכָל־עֵת), 35^{27} cf. 40^{17} 70^5, 38^{18} 40^{12} 50^8 51^5 69^{24} $71^{6.14}$ 72^{15} 73^{23} 74^{23} 105^4 $109^{15.19}$ 119^{44} (+ לְעוֹלָם וָעֶד), v$^{109.117}$ (so also ψ 16^5, for MT תומיך, Bi Che; תוסיף Ol Bae); Pr 5^{19} (|| בְּכָל־עֵת), 6^{21} 15^{15} 28^{14}; also Ez 38^8 (del. 𝔖 Co Toy$^{Hpt.}$ Berthol), Lv 6^6 (P; of fire, || לֹא תִכְבֶּה), and 46^{14} (but חֻקַּת ת׳ 𝔊 Co Berthol); also in ritual, Lv 24^8 (H), cf. Ex 25^{30} (P; shew-bread), Lv $24^{2.3.4}$ (H), cf. Ex 27^{20} (P; of lamp), Ex $28^{29.30.38}$. **b.** of regular repetition: meals 2 S $9^{7.10.13}$ 2 K 25^{29}=Je 52^{33}; journeys 2 K 4^{19}; cf. Nu 9^{16} ψ 71^3; of ritual: sacrifice, לַיּוֹם תָּמִיד Ex 29^{38}; cf. 1 Ch 16^{40} 23^{31} 2 Ch 24^{14}. **2.** as subst.: **a.** of uninterrupted continuity, אַנְשֵׁי ת׳ Ez 39^{14} *men of continuity,* i.e. men continually employed for the purpose; לֶחֶם הַתּ׳ Nu 4^7 *the bread of continuity,* i.e. the bread that is always there, so מַעֲרֶכֶת ת׳ 2 Ch 2^3, and perh. חֲצֹצְרוֹת ת׳ 1 Ch 16^6. **b.** of regular repetition אֲרֻחַת מ׳ 2 K 25^{30}, i.e. a regular allowance, =Je 52^{34}; esp. of ritual: קְטֹרֶת ת׳ Ex 30^8 (P); most often עֹלַת ת׳ Ez 46^{15} (every morning), Ex 29^{42} (morning and evening, so) Nu 28^6 Ezr 3^5, so rd. also Nu 28^3 (Di) for MT עֹלָה ת׳ (לַיּוֹם); עֹלַת הַתּ׳ Nu $28^{10.15.23.24.31}$ $29^{6.11.16.19.22.25.28.31.34.38}$ Ne 10^{35}; rarely מִנְחַת ת׳ Nu 4^{16}(P), Ne 10^{34}; as appos., מִנְחָה ת׳ Lv 6^{13} *meal-offering as a regular observance* (cf. Ges$^{§131,2(b)}$ Da$^{Synt.\ §29(b)}$; on text v. Di, Now$^{Arch.\ ii.\ 124\ f.}$), (and Nu 28^3 MT, but v. supr.) **c.** (late) הַתּ׳ alone= *daily* (morning and evening) *burnt-offering* (Now$^{Arch.\ ii.\ 222\ f.}$) Dn $8^{11.12.13}$ 11^{31} 12^{11} (so Talm., even in pl. תְּמִידִין).

†II. **מוד** vb. assumed by Ke Or al. (=מוט) 4128
as √ of וַיְמֹדֶד Hb 3^6, but v. מדד **Po.** p. 551

מוֹדַע v. ידע. p. 396 4129

†[**מוֹט**] vb. **totter, shake, slip** (usu. poet.) 4131
(NH *id.*, der. species; Aram. ܡܳܛ, מוט; Ar. مَاطَ (med. י) *remove, retire; deviate from right course; repel, push, thrust;* Eth. ሞጥ: *turn;* As. *maṭû* is *dwindle, diminish, grow weak* Dl$^{HWB\ 405}$; > denom. fr. מוט *pole, bar* Dl$^{Prol.\ 184}$ Gerber$^{Verb.\ denom.\ 195\ f.}$, cf. Buhl);—**Qal** *Pf.* 3 fs. מָטָה ψ 60^4 + 2 t.; 3 pl. מָטוּ ψ 46^7; *Impf.* 3 fs. תָּמוּט Dt 32^{35} Is 54^{10}; 3 fpl. תְּמוּטֶינָה Is 54^{10}; *Inf. cstr.* מוֹט ψ 38^{17} 46^3; *abs.* id. Is 24^{19}; *Pt.* מָט Pr 25^{26}; pl. מָטִים Pr 24^{11};—*totter, slip,* subj. רֶגֶל (fig. of insecurity) Dt 32^{35} ψ 38^{17} 94^{18}: cf. (without רֶגֶל) Pr 24^{11} מ׳ לַהֶרֶג; מ׳ לִפְנֵי־רָשָׁע 25^{26}; *shake,* intr., subj. יָד Lv 25^{35} (H; of feebleness); subj. גְּבָעוֹת Is 54^{10} (|| מוּשׁ); מ׳ הָרִים בְּלֵב יַמִּים ψ 46^3 (|| הָמִיר, cf. מור) (both symb. of extreme insecurity); cf. subj. בְּרִית Is 54^{10}; subj. מַמְלָכוֹת ψ 46^7; subj. אֶרֶץ (=land) ψ 60^4; cf. Is 24^{19} (v. sub Hithp.) **Niph.** *Pf.* 3 pl. נָמוֹטוּ ψ 17^5;

Impf. יִמּוֹט ψ 15[5]+8 t., etc.;—all poet., mostly c. neg. (בַּל 13 t.; לֹא 6 t.), *be shaken, moved, overthrown,* of idols Is 40[20] 41[7]; of scales of crocodile Jb 41[15]; of תֵּבֵל 1 Ch 16[30]=ψ 93[1] 96[10]; of אֶרֶץ ψ 104[5]; of הַר־צִיּוֹן ψ 125[1], cf. 46[6]; fig. of general disorder (no neg.), subj. מוֹסְדֵי אֶרֶץ ψ 82[5]; oft. of righteous, as secure, ψ 10[6] 15[5] 16[8] 21[8] 30[7] 62[3.7] 112[6] Pr 10[30] 12[3] (subj. שֹׁרֶשׁ צַדִּיקִים); cf. (without neg.) ψ 13[5] 140[11] Qr (so appar. 𝔊 AV RV; but mng. of Niph. not suitable; Kt Hiph. q.v.); fig. of steadfast obedience (subj. פְּעָמַי) ψ 17[5]. **Hiph.** *Impf.* 3 mpl. יָמִיטוּ ψ 55[4] 140[11] Kt (Qr **Niph.**);—*dislodge, let fall, drop* יָמִיטוּ עָלַי אָוֶן ψ 55[4]; cf. וימיטו עֲלֵיהֶם גֶּחָלִים 140[11] Kt, *and may they drop coals upon them,* De al.; <rd. יַמְטֵר (Hup Gr Bae Dr), wh. Bi Che *insert.* **Hithpo'l.** *Pf.* 3 fs. מוֹט הִתְמוֹטְטָה Is 24[19] *be greatly shaken* (subj. אֶרֶץ, in judgment of י׳; ‖ רעע, פרר, Hithp.)

4132 †מוֹט **n.[m.]** shaking, pole, bar of yoke;—abs. מ׳ Nu 4[10]+5 t.; sf. מֹטֵהוּ Na 1[13];—**1.** *a shaking, tottering* (c. neg., of security) לֹא־יִתֵּן מ׳ לַצַּדִּיק ψ 55[23]; לֹא נָתַן לַמּ׳ רַגְלֵנוּ ψ 66[9], cf. 121[3]. **2.** *pole,* or *bar* for carrying (named from springing motion) Nu 4[10.12] cf. esp. 13[23]. **3.** *bar* of yoke Na 1[13] (אֶשְׁבֹּר מֹטֵהוּ מֵעָלָיִךְ), fig. of oppression. Cf. following.

4133 †מוֹטָה **n.f.** pole, bar of yoke, mostly late (cf. מוֹט);—מ׳ Je 28[10]+4 t.; pl. מֹטוֹת etc., abs. Je 27[2] 1 Ch 15[15]; cstr. Ez 30[18]+4t.;—**1.** *pole,* pl., staves, for bearing ark 1 Ch 15[15]. **2.** *bar* of yoke, symb., of oppression Je 27[2] (‖ מוֹסֵרוֹת, cf. עֹל v[8.11.12]), 28[10.12] (cf. עֹל v[11]); מ׳ עֵץ 28[13]; מ׳ בַּרְזֶל v[13] (cf. עֹל v[14]); fig. of oppression, Is 58[6.9] Ez 30[18]; cf. (thongs of yoke) אֲגֻדּוֹת מ׳ Is 58[6]; מֹטֹת עֻלְּכֶם Lv 26[18] cf. Ez 34[27].—On form of yoke v. Schumacher[ZPV xii. 1889, 160], Benz[Arch. 207].

4134 †[מוּךְ] **vb.** be low, depressed, grow poor (NH *id.*, Niph.; Aram. מוּךְ, *sink* or *bend down;* cf. מָכַךְ, Syr. ܡܳܟ, ܡܰܟܶܟ, *be brought low, humble*);—**Qal** *Pf.* consec. וּמָךְ Lv 27[8] (P); *Impf.* יָמוּךְ Lv 25[25.35.39] (all H); *Pt.* מָךְ Lv 25[47] (P): all of impoverished Israelites.

4136 †I. מוּל, מֹל (†Dt 1[1]), מוּאל (†Ne 12[38]) **subst.** and **prep.** front, in front of (deriv. dub.; acc. to Ol[§ 223 c] Sta[§ 378 a], for מְאוֹל from אול *to be in front:* v. further Kö[ii. 300 f.] Hpt[BAS i. 172]);—**1. subst.** only 1 K 7[5] (si vera l.: v. Sta[ZAW 1883, 151]) וּמוּל מֶחֱזָה אֶל־מֶחֱזָה and the *front* of (one) window was towards (the other) window, and Ne 12[38] לְמוֹאל = *in the opposite direction* (but rd. prob. לִשְׂמֹאול, cf. לְיָמִין v[31]). **2.** as **prep.**, Dt 1[1] 2[19] מול בני עמון *in front of* the Ammonites, 3[29] (=4[46] 34[6]) מול בית פעור, 11[30] Jos 18[18] 19[46] מוּל יָפוֹ, 1 S 14[5.5]; fig. Ex 18[19] הֱיֵה אַתָּה לעם מול האלהים *in front of* God, i.e. representing God to them. With prefixes:—**a.** אל־מול *towards the front of,* 1 S 17[30] וַיִּסֹּב מֵאֶצְלוֹ אֶל־מוּל אַחֵר *to the front of* another; *on the front of,* Ex 34[3] (pregn.) וְאַל־יִרְעוּ אל־מול ההר, Jo 8[33.33] 9[1] 22[11] (v. WAW[JPh. xiii. 117 ff.]); spec. אֶל־מוּל פְּנֵי *towards* or *on the forefront of,* Ex 26[9] 28[25] (‖ 39[18]), v[37] Lv 8[9] Nu 8[2.3] 2 S 11[15] set ye Uriah אל־מול פני המלחמה. **b.** מִמּוּל:—(*a*) *from the front of,* Mi 2[8] (text dub.: rd. prob. מֵעַל). (*b*) of position, *off* (v. מן **1 c**) *the front of,* Lv 5[8] מִמּוּל עָרְפּוֹ *off the front of* its neck, i.e. close in front of it, Nu 22[5] והוא יושב מִמֻּלִי *close in front of* me, 2 S 5[23] (1 Ch 14[14]) ובאת להם ממול בכאים come to them *off the front of* the mulberry-trees, 1 K 7[39] (2 Ch 4[10]) מִמּוּל נֶגֶב; מִמּוּל פָּנָיו *on the forefront of,* Ex 28[27] (‖ 39[20]).

†II. [מוּל] **vb. circumcise** (NH *id.*; 4135
𝔗 מוּל *cut off* (grass, etc.: only for III. מָלַל, q.v.); cf. NH מָהַל, Aram. מְהַל, acc. to Thes Nö[ZMG xl. 1886, 741] Ba[ib. xli. 1887, 626] v. also מהל supr.);—**Qal** *Pf.* 3 ms. מָל Jos 5[4]+2 t.; 2 ms. מַלְתָּה Ex 12[44]; 3 mpl. מָ֫לוּ Jos 5[5.7]; 2 mpl. מַלְתֶּם Dt 10[16]; *Impf.* וַיָּמָל Gn 17[23]+2 t.; *Imv.* מֹל Jos 5[2]; *Pt. pass.* מוּל Je 9[24]; pl. מֻלִים Jos 5[5];—*circumcise,* c. acc. בשׂר ערלה (flesh of foreskin) Gn 17[23] (P), acc. pers. Gn 21[4] Ex 12[44] (P), Jos 5[2.3] (J), v[4.5.7.7] (D); fig. ערלת לבב (foreskin of the heart) Dt 10[16]; לבב Dt 30[6]; pass. מול בערלה Je 9[24]; מֻלִים Jos 5[5] (D). **Niph.** *Pf.* 3 ms. נִמּוֹל (Ges[§ 72, R. 9]) Gn 17[26]; 3 mpl. נִמֹּ֫לוּ Gn 17[27]; 2 mpl. וּנְמַלְתֶּם (consec.) Gn 17[11] (for וּנְמַלְתֶּם מלל √ Ew[§ 234. e.] Ges[§ 67, R. 11]; but Bö[1146 B] for וּנְמוֹלְתֶּם); *Impf.* יִמּוֹל Gn 17[12]+3 t.; 3 mpl. וַיִּמֹּלוּ Gn 34[24]; *Imv.* הִמֹּ֫לוּ Je 4[4]; *Inf.* הִמּוֹל Gn 17[10]+5 t.; הִמֹּל Gn 34[15]; sf. הִמֹּלוֹ Gn 17[24.25]; *Pt.* pl. נִמֹּלִים Gn 34[22];—*be circumcised,* of בשׂר ערלה Gn 17[14.24.25] Lv 12[3]; elsewhere of pers. Gn 17[10.10.12.13.13.26.27] 34[15.17.22.24] Ex 12[48] (P), Jos 5[8] (J): reflex. הִמֹּלוּ לי׳ Je 4[4] *circumcise yourselves to Yahweh* (and take away the foreskin of

your heart). **Hiph.** *Impf.* 1 s. בשם י׳ כי אֲמִילַם ψ 118$^{10.11.12}$ *in the name of* ׳י, *yea I will make them to be circumcised* (enemies, by force of arms; but De *cut to pieces* (from מָלַל=מול), Che *mow*, Bae *annihilate* (?), 𝔊 Aq ἠμυνάμην, Symm διέθρυψα, Jer *ultus sum eas*). **Hithp.** *Impf.* 3 mpl. יִתְמֹלָלוּ ψ 58^8 *be cut off*, of arrows, i.e. made blunt.

4139 †[מוּלָה] **n.f.**, only pl. **circumcision**: חתן דמים למולֹת Ex 4^{26} (J) *a bridegroom of blood because of* (or *in regard of*) *the circumcision*; cf. We$^{Prol. ed. 4 (1895) 345 f.; Hist. 340}$.

4137-38, 4140 מוֹלָדָה, מוֹלֶדֶת, מוֹלִיד v. ילד. p. 409f

3971, 4462 מוּם v. מְאוּם. מוּמכן Kt, v. מְמוּכָן. p. 548, 577

4141, 4327 מוּן v. מין. מוּסַב v. סבב. p. 568, 687

4143-45 מוּסָד, מוּסָדָה, [מוּסָד] v. יסד. p. 414

4329, 4561 מוּסָר v. יסר. [מוּסָךְ] v. סכך. p. 416, 697

4147 [מוֹסֵר], מוֹסֵרָה v. אסר. p. 64

4148 מוּסָר v. יסר. p. 416

4150-52 מוֹעֵד, [מוֹעָד], מוֹעָדָה v. יעד. p. 417f

4153, 4573 מוֹעַדְיָה v. מַעַדְיָה. p. 588

4155-56 מוּעָף v. II. עוף. [מוֹעֵצָה] v. יעץ. p. 420, 734

4157, 6338 מוּעָקָה v. עוק. מוּפָז v. פזז. p. 734, 808

4158 מופעת Kt, v. מיפעת sub יפע. p. 422

4159 מוֹפֵת v. אפת. p. 68

מוץ (√of following, meaning unknown).

4671 †[מוֹץ], מֹץ **n.m.**$^{Is 29,5}$ **chaff** (Talm. 𝔗 מוֹצָא, Ar. مَوْصٌ *straw*);—מ׳ abs. Ho 13^3 + 6 t.; cstr. Is 17^{13};—*chaff*, always as driven by wind, and alw. c. כְּ, in sim.; of wicked Jb 21^{18} (|| תֶּבֶן לִפְנֵי רוּחַ), cf. ψ 1^4 35^5 Ho 13^3; of hostile nations Is 17^{13} (מ׳ הָרִים), 29^5 (|| אָבָק דַּק); hyperb. of Judah's power, תָּדוּשׁ הָרִים וְתָדֹק || Is 41^{15} (גְּבָעוֹת כַּמֹּץ תָּשִׂים); of passing time, יוֹם Zp 2^2.

4161-63 I, II. מוֹצָא, [מוֹצָאָה] v. יצא. p. 425f

4165-66 I. מוּצָק, [מוּצֶקֶת] v. יצק. p. 427

4164 II. מוּצָק v. צוק. p. 848

4167 †[מִיק, מוּק] **vb. mock, deride** (Aram. Pa. מַיֵּק, ܡܰܝܶܩ, and Aph. אָמֵיק);—*Impf.* 3 mpl. (prob. Hiph.) יָמִיקוּ ψ 73^8 (|| וִידַבְּרוּ בְרָע).

4168-69 מוֹקֵד, מוֹקְדָה v. יקד. p. 428f

4170 מוֹקֵשׁ v. יקשׁ. p. 430

4171 †[מוּר] **vb. change** (NH *id.*, Hiph.; Ar. مَارَ (med. و) is *move to and fro* (intransitive); مَارَ (med. ي) *procure* food, Aram. ܡܳܪ *buy* or *import* food, Nö$^{ZMG xl. 1886, 154}$);—**Niph.** *Pf.* נָמָר (as if fr. מרר) *be changed*, Je 48^{11} subj. רֵיחוֹ (of wine, fig. of Moab); **Hiph.** *Pf.* הֵמִיר Je 2^{11}; on הֲהֵימִיר *ib.*, v. Kö$^{i. 457}$; *Impf.* יָמִיר ψ 15^4 + 3 t.; juss. יָמֵר Ez 48^{14}; sf. יְמִירֶנּוּ Lv 27$^{33.33}$; אָמִיר Ho 4^7; וַיָּמִירוּ ψ 106^{20}; *Inf. cstr.* הָמִיר ψ 46^3; abs. הָמֵר Lv 27$^{10.33}$;—**1.** *change, alter*, Mi 2^4 (obj. חֵלֶק עַמִּי; but 𝔊 יִמַּד בַּחֶבֶל, so Sta$^{ZAW 1886, 122 f.}$); ψ 15^4 (no obj. expr.); Hiph. declar. 46^3 (ארץ subj., Hup Che Bae al., Ges$^{§ 115, 2, R. 2}$) *when the earth shews change;* Krochm Gr prop. הִמּוֹג (cf. מוג v^{7b} || מוט), but needless. **2.** *exchange* (sq. acc. of obj. relinquished, + בְּ before obj. acquired) Lv 27$^{10.10.10.10}$ (2 t. as Inf. abs.); Ho 4^7 ψ 106^{20}; cf. c. one obj. Lv 27$^{33.33.33}$ (once as Inf. abs.); Je 2$^{11.11}$ (cf. supr.); without obj. Ez 48^{14} (but Ew Co יוּמַר, Hoph.). **Hoph.** *Impf.* יוּמַר Ez 48^{14} Ew Co, cf. Berthol.

8545 †תְּמוּרָה **n.f. exchange, recompense**;—ת׳ Ru 4^7; sf. תְּמוּרָתוֹ Lv 27^{10} + 3 t.; תְּמוּרָתָהּ Jb 28^{17};—*exchange*=thing acquired by exchange Lv 27$^{10.33}$ Jb 28^{17}; חֵיל תְּמוּרָתוֹ Jb 20^{18} *wealth acquired by exchange* (fig.; rd. poss. חֵילוֹ as *his wealth* (so) *his exchange*, Bu); *recompense* (for worldliness) Jb 15^{31}; abstr. *exchanging* Ru 4^7 (|| גְּאוּלָּה).

4753 מוֹר, מֹר v. מרר. p. 600

4172 מוֹרָא, I. מוֹרָה v. יָרֵא. p. 432

4173 †מוֹרָג **n.m.**$^{Is 41, 15}$ **threshing-sledge** (NH *id.*; 𝔗 *id.*, S.Ar. نَيْرَجٌ, نَوْرَجٌ, Frä^{133}, cf. Ba$^{ZA ii. 117}$ (loan-word in Ar. = *ploughshare*); mod. مَوْرَجٌ Dozy$^{ii. 623}$, and نَوْرَجٌ Wetzst$^{Z. für Ethnol. 1873, 270 ff.}$, Anderlind$^{ZPV ix. 41 f.}$ (*ploughshare and harrow*));—abs. מ׳ Is 41^{15}; pl. מֹרִגִּים 2 S 24^{22} (+ כְּלֵי הַבָּקָר); מוֹרִגִּים 1 Ch 21^{23};—*threshing-sledges* of Araunah, given by him to David for wood of sacrifice 2 S 24^{22} = 1 Ch 21^{23}; fig. of Israel as instr. of ׳י's judgment Is 41^{15}. On form of threshing-sledge (mod.; slightly turned up in front, and set with sharp stones or pieces of iron), and threshing-rollers, v. Benz$^{Arch. 209 f.}$ Now$^{Arch. i. 232 f.}$ Dr$^{Amos, 227 f.}$

4172, 4174 מוֹרָד v. ירד. I. מוֹרָא v. יָרֵא. p. 432, 434

4177 †II. מוֹרָה **n.m.** razor (√dub.; We$^{Sm\ p.146}$ thinks = מַעֲרָה);—*razor*, always in phr. מ׳ לֹא יַעֲלֶה (עָלָה) עַל־רֹאשׁ Ju 13^{5} 16^{17} 1 S 1^{11}.

I, II. מוֹרֶה v. ירה. מֹרִיָּה v. מוֹרִיָּה.

4180-83 [מוֹרָשׁ], מוֹרָשָׁה, מוֹרֶשֶׁת, מוֹרַשְׁתִּי v. ירשׁ. p. 440

4185 †I. [מוּשׁ, מִישׁ Bö$^{ii.512f.}$; but Thes Kö$^{i.511}$ think purely ע״ו] **vb. depart, remove** (Ar. مَاسَ (ى) is *walk with elegant, proud, self-conceited gait*);—**Qal** *Pf.* וּמָשׁ consec. Zc 14^{4}; וּמַשְׁתִּי Zc 3^{9}; מָשׁוּ Nu 14^{44}; *Impf.* יָמוּשׁ Jos 1^{8} Is 54^{10}, etc.;—*depart*, mostly of inanimate things (= *be removed*) sq. מִן Jos 1^{8} Is 59^{21} Je 31^{36}; without prep. Pr 17^{13} Qr, Is 22^{25} $54^{10.10}$ (‖ מוט); sq. ה loc. Zc 14^{4}; sq. מִן pers. Ju 6^{18}; of both Nu 14^{44}; trans. *remove*, sq. acc. Zc 3^{9}. **Hiph.** *Impf.* יָמִישׁ Ex 13^{22} + 6 t., etc.; *remove, take away*, sq. מִן Mi 2^{3}; sq. לְ v^{4} (but 𝔊 Sta$^{ZAW\ vi.1886,122f.}$ אֵין מֵשִׁיב for אֵיךְ יָמִישׁ); *depart*, sq. מִן pers. Ex 33^{11}; fig. *recede* Jb 23^{12}; of idol, *leave its place*, Is 46^{7}; of other inanimate things, sq. מִן Ex 13^{22}; fig. ψ 55^{12} Pr 17^{13} Kt (Qr יָמוּשׁ); without prep., abs., Na 3^{1}, subj. טֶרֶף; of righteous under fig. of tree, לֹא יָמִישׁ מֵעֲשׂוֹת פֶּרִי Je 17^{8}, i.e. shall not cease.

4184 †II. [מוּשׁ] **vb. feel** (NH *id.*; Aram. מוּשׁ, ܡܫ *id.*; secondary form of משׁשׁ q.v.);—**Qal** *Impf.* 1 s. sf. וַאֲמֻשְׁךָ Gn 27^{21} draw near *that I may feel thee.* **Hiph.** *Impf.* 3 mpl. יְדֵיהֶם וְלֹא יְמִישׁוּן ψ 115^{7} *as for their hands, they do not feel* (of idols; ‖ רַגְלֵיהֶם וְלֹא יְהַלֵּכוּ); *Imv.* sf. וַהֲמִישֵׁנִי Ju 16^{26} Qr (Kt והימשׁני, v. ימשׁ), but rd. וַהֲמִשֵּׁנִי, v. משׁשׁ.

4186 מוֹשָׁב v. ישׁב. p. 444

4187 †I. מוּשִׁי, מֻשִׁי **n.pr.m.** a Levite, son of Merari, מוּשִׁי Ex 6^{19} Nu 3^{20} 1 Ch 6^{32} $23^{21.23}$ $24^{26.30}$; מֻשִׁי 1 Ch 6^{4}; 𝔊 Ομουσ(ε)ι, rarely Μουσ(ε)ι, Μοουσι.

4188 †II. מוּשִׁי **adj. gent.** c. art. as n. coll. מִשְׁפַּחַת הַמּ׳ Nu 3^{33} 26^{58}.

4190 [מוֹשָׁעָה], מוֹשָׁעוֹת v. ישׁע. p. 448

4191 מוּת **vb. die** (NH *id.* (rare); As. *mâtu* Dl$^{HWB\ 395}$, Ar. مَاتَ, Eth. ሞተ:, Aram. מוּת, מִית, ܡܝܬ; Nab. מות Eut$^{Nab\ 14,6}$; Zinj. מת DHM $^{Sendsch.\ Gloss.}$);—**Qal** *Pf.* 3 ms. מֵת Gn 42^{38} +; 3 fs. מֵתָה Gn 35^{18}+; 2 ms. מַתָּה Ez 28^{8}; 1 s. וָמַתִּי Gn 19^{19}; 3 mpl. מֵתוּ Gn 7^{22}+; 1 pl. מַתְנוּ Nu 14^{2} 2 K 7^{4}; מָתְנוּ Nu 14^{9}+; *Impf.* יָמוּת Gn 38^{11}+; יָמֹת Dt 33^{6}+; וַיָּמָת Gn 11^{28}+; 1 s. אָמוּת Gn 26^{9}+; אָמֻת 2 S 19^{38}; אָמוּתָה Gn 46^{30}; 3 mpl. יָמוּתוּ 1 S 2^{23}+; יְמֻתוּן Nu 16^{29}; 3 fpl. תְּמוּתֶנָה Ez 13^{19} (Ges ^{§72,5}) +; *Imv.* מֻת Dt 32^{50} Jb 2^{9}; *Inf. abs.* מוֹת Gn 2^{17}+; *cstr.* מוּת Gn 25^{32}+; sf. מוֹתִי 2 S 19^{1}; מֻתָן 2 S 20^{3}, etc.; *Pt.* מֵת Gn 20^{3}+; sf. מֵתִי Gn 23^{4}+; fs. מֵתָה Gn 30^{1} Zc 11^{9}; pl. מֵתִים Ex 12^{33}+; cstr. מֵתֵי Is 22^{2}+; sf. מֵתֶיךָ Is 26^{19};—**1.** *die*, of natural or other causes: **a.** (1) of man, †וַיִּגְוַע וַיָּמָת *and he expired and died* Gn 25^{8} (+ בְּשֵׂיבָה טוֹבָה, v. infr.), v^{17} 35^{29} (P); †וַיָּמָת וַיִּקָּבֵר Ju $10^{2.5}$ 8^{32} $12^{7.10.12.15}$ 2 S 17^{23}; †וימת וימלך תַּחְתָּיו *and he died and — reigned in his stead* Gn $36^{33.34.35.36.37.38.39}$ (P), 2 S 10^{1} = 1 Ch 19^{1}, 2 K 1^{17} 8^{15} 13^{24} 1 Ch $1^{44.45.46.47.48.49.50}$; וימת בְּשֵׂיבָה טוֹבָה *and he died in a good old age* 1 Ch 29^{28} (+ Gn 25^{8}, v. supr.); as the result of smiting הכה Ex $21^{18.20.22}$ (E); +במלחמה Dt $20^{5.6.7}$ 2 S 19^{11}; בַּחֶרֶב Je 11^{22}; ברעב v^{22}; מפני הרעב 38^{9}; באבן 21^{6}; בַּדֶּבֶר Nu $35^{17.23}$ (P); †בַּמַּגֵּפָה Nu 14^{37} 17^{14} 25^{9} (P). (2) fig. of wisdom, עִמָּכֶם תָּמוּת חָכְמָה Jb 12^{2}; of courage, וַיָּמָת לִבּוֹ בְּקִרְבּוֹ *and his heart died within him* 1 S 25^{37}.—2 S 2^{31} del. מֵתוּ We Dr Kit Bu, cf. 𝔊. **b.** of animals Lv 11^{39}; cattle Gn 33^{13} (J), fish Ex 7^{18} (E), frogs Ex 8^{9} (J), lion Ec 9^{4}, worm Is 66^{24}; כֶּלֶב מֵת, *dead dog* (in proverb) 1 S 24^{15} 2 S 9^{8} 16^{9}. **c.** a tree Jb 14^{8}. **d.** וְזִבְחֵי מֵתִים ψ 106^{28} *sacrifices to the dead* (idols). **2.** *die* as a penalty = *be put to death*: **a.** by human authority Gn 42^{20} Ex 10^{28} 21^{14} (E), Gn 44^{9} Jos 2^{14} (J), Lv 20^{20} (H), Nu $35^{12.30.30}$ (P), esp. D, Dt $17^{2.6}$ 18^{20} 19^{12} $22^{22.25}$ 24^{7} Ju 6^{30} 1 S $14^{43.45.45}$ 19^{24} Je 38^{24}; מוֹת יָמוּת, *die = be put to a violent death* (> AV RV *surely die*), 1 S $14^{39.44}$ 22^{16} 1 K $2^{37.42}$ (all Judaic), Je 26^{8}, all of capital punishment; 2 K 8^{10} (Ephr.) cf assassination; מוֹת יוּמַת *be put to a violent death*, in the codes of Ex $21^{12.15.16.17}$ 22^{18} (E), Lv $20^{2.9.10.11.12.13.15.16.27}$ $24^{16.17}$ (H), Ex $31^{14.15}$ Nu 15^{35} $35^{16.17.18.21.31}$ Lv 27^{29} (P; never in D; D uses verb, either Qal or Hiph., without inf. abs.); it is used in narratives Gn 26^{11} (J), Ex 19^{12} (E), Ju 21^{5}. מ׳ is preceded by רגם Nu 15^{36} (P), Dt 21^{21} 1 K 12^{18} = 2 Ch 10^{18}, 1 K 21^{13}; סקל Dt 13^{11} 17^{5} $22^{21.24}$ 1 K $21^{10.13.14.15}$; פגע 1 K $2^{25.46}$; רמס 2 K $7^{17.20}$; בְּיַד גֹּאֵל Jos 20^{9} (P). **b.** inflicted by God, Gn $20^{3.19}$ Jos 10^{11} (E), Gn 3^{3} 38^{11} Ex

11^{5} 12^{36} (J), 28^{35} 30$^{20.20}$ Lv 8^{35} 10$^{2.6.7.9}$ 16$^{1.2.13}$ Nu 3^{4} 4$^{19.20}$ 14^{35} 17$^{14.28.35}$ 18$^{3.32}$ 26$^{11.61}$ (P), Dt 5$^{22.22}$ 18^{16} Ju 6^{23} 1 S 5^{12} 12^{19} 25$^{17.38.39}$ 2 S 6^{7} 12^{13} 1 K 19^{4} 2 K 14^{6} = 2 Ch 25^{4}, 1 Ch 24^{2} 2 Ch 13^{20} 2 K 19^{35} = Is 37^{36}, Ez 3^{20} 18$^{4.20.21.28}$ 33^{15}; מוֹת יָמוּת Gn 2^{17} 3^{4} (J), 20^{7} (E), Ju 13$^{21.22}$ 2 S 12^{14} 14^{14} 2 K 1$^{4.6.16}$ (all Judaic), Nu 26^{65} (P), Ez 3^{18} 33$^{8.14}$; מות יומת 18^{13}, ביד יהוה Ex 16^{3} (P); בחטא Lv 22^{9} (H), Nu 27^{3} (P), 2 K 14^{6} = 2 Ch 25^{4}; לשׂאת חטא למות Nu 18^{22} (P); בחטאת Ez 3^{20} 18^{24}; בטמאה Lv 15^{21} (P); בעון Je 31^{30} Ez 3$^{18.19}$ 18$^{17.18}$ 33$^{8.9}$; לא ישׂאו עון ומתו Ex 28^{43} Nu 4^{15} (P); בעול Ez 18^{26} 33$^{13.18}$; על עול 18^{26}; במעל 1 Ch 10^{13}. **c.** *die, perish,* of a nation by divine judgment, Moab Am 2^{2}, Ephraim Ho 13^{1}; בית ישׂראל Ez 18^{31} 33^{11}. **d.** *die prematurely,* by neglect of wise moral conduct Pr 5^{23} 10^{21} 15^{10} 19^{16} 23^{13} Ec 7^{17}.—*Note.* On (לַבֵּן) עַל־מוּת ψ 9^{1} 48^{15} v. עַלְמָה sub II. עלם.

Po'lel. *Pf.* 3 ms. sf. מוֹתְתָנִי Je 20^{17}; 1 s. מֹתַתִּי 2 S 1^{16}; *Impf.* 3 ms. sf. יְמֹתְתֵהוּ 1 S 17^{51}; 3 fs. תְּמוֹתֵת ψ 34^{22}; 1 s. sf. אֲמֹתְתֵהוּ 2 S 1^{10}; *Imv.* sf. מוֹתְתֵנִי Ju 9^{54}; מֹתְתֵנִי 2 S 1^{9}; inf. מוֹתֵת ψ 109^{16}; *Pt.* מְמוֹתֵת 1 S 14^{13};—*kill, put to death, despatch* (intens.), abs. 1 S 14^{13}, elsewhere c. acc. Ju 9^{54} 1 S 17^{51} 2 S 1$^{9.10.16}$ Je 20^{17} ψ 34^{22} 109^{16}.

Hiph. *Pf.* 3 ms. הֵמִית Ju 16^{30}+; sf. וֶהֱמִתָנִי 2 S 14^{32}; הֱמִיתָם Je 41^{8}; 3 fs. sf. הֱמִיתָתְהוּ 2 Ch 22^{11}; 2 ms. הֵמַתָּה Nu 14^{15}; 1 s. sf. הֲמִיתִּיו (rd. הֲמִתִּיו) 1 S 17^{35}; 3 mpl. הֵמִיתוּ 1 S 30^{2}+, etc.; *Impf.* יָמִית Nu 35^{19}+; וַיָּמֶת Gn 38^{10}+; sf. יְמִיתֵהוּ 1 K 13^{24}+; יְמִתֶנּוּ Nu 35^{19}+; *Imv.* sf. הֲמִיתֵנִי 1 S 20^{8}; pl. הָמִיתוּ 1 S 22^{17}; *Inf. abs.* הָמֵת 2 K 11^{15}+; *cstr.* הָמִית Lv 20^{4}+; *Pt.* מֵמִית 1 S 2^{6}; pl. מְמִיתִים 2 K 17^{26} Jb 33^{22}; מְמִתִים Je 26^{15};—*kill, put to death:* **1.** abs. Jb 9^{23}, elsewhere c. acc., subj. man, **a.** of killing men in personal combat, or in war, often preceded by הכה smite Jos 10^{26} 11^{17} 17^{50}+; of destroying a city 2 S 20^{19} (||השׁחית v^{20}). **b.** by authority, espec. in capital punishment Ex 1^{16} (E), Lv 20^{4} (H), Nu 35$^{19.19.21}$ (P), Dt 9^{10} 17^{7} Ju 20^{13} 1 S 11^{12} 28^{9} 2 S 14$^{7.32}$ 21^{4} 1 K 2$^{26.34}$ 11^{40} 19$^{17.17}$ 2 K 14^{6} = 2 Ch 25^{4}; Is 11^{4} Je 26$^{15.21.24}$ 38$^{15.16.25}$ Est 4^{11}; בֶּחָרֶב 1 K 1^{51} 2^{8} 2 K 11^{20} = 2 Ch 23^{21}; הָמֵת יָמִית Ju 15^{13} 1 K 3$^{26.27}$ Je 26^{19} 38^{15}. **2.** subj. God, by inflicting penalty, abs. Dt 32^{39} 1 S 2^{6} 2 K 5^{7}, elsewh. c. acc. Gn 18^{25} 38$^{7.10}$ Ex 4^{24} Nu 14^{15} (J), Dt 9^{28} Ju 13^{23} 1 S 2^{25} 5$^{10.11}$ 1 Ch 2^{3} 10^{14} Is 65^{15} Ho 9^{16}; ברעב Is 14^{30}; בצמא Ho 2^{5}; of killing fish ψ 105^{29}; מְמִיתִים Jb 33^{22} *executioners,* angels of death. **3.** of animals killing men, e. g. ox Ex 21^{29} (E), lion 1 K 13$^{24.26}$ 2 K 17^{26}. **4.** bring to a premature death Pr 19^{18} 21^{25}.

Hoph. *Pf.* הוּמַת 2 K 11^{2}+; 3 mpl. הֻמְתוּ 2 S 21^{9}; *Impf.* יוּמַת Lv 20^{10}+; יוּמָת Gn 26^{11}+; *Pt.* מוּמָת 1 S 19^{11}, pl. מוּמָתִים 2 K 11^{2} (Qr), 2 Ch 22^{11};—*be killed, put to death:* **1.** by conspiracy 2 K 11$^{2.2}$ = 2 Ch 22^{11}, 2 K 11$^{8.15.16}$ 2 Ch 23$^{7.14}$. **2.** by capital punishment Ex 21^{29} (E), 35^{2} Nu 1^{51} 3$^{10.38}$ 18^{7} (P), Lv 19^{20} 24$^{16.21}$ (H), Dt 13^{6} 17$^{6.6}$ 21^{22} 24$^{16.16.16}$ = 2 K 14$^{6.6}$, Jos 1^{18} (all D) Ju 6^{31} 1 S 11^{13} 19$^{6.11}$ 20^{32} 2 S 19$^{22.23}$ 21^{9} 1 K 2^{24} 2 Ch 15^{13} Je 38^{4}, and the phrase מות יומת (see **Qal 2 a**). **3.** by divine infliction, in the phrase מות יומת (see **Qal 2 b**). **4.** *die prematurely* Pr 19^{16}.

מָ֫וֶת$_{161}$ **n.m.**$^{Ex\ 10,\ 17}$ death;—abs. מ׳ Dt 19^{6}+; מָ֫וְתָה ψ 116^{15}; cstr. מוֹת Gn 25^{11}+; sf. מוֹתִי Gn 27^{2}+; pl. cstr. מוֹתֵי Ez 28^{10}; sf. בְּמֹתָיו Is 53^{9};—**1.** *death,* opp. life, Dt 30$^{15.19}$ 2 S 15^{21}; †מ׳ כל האדם *the death of all men* (that all go to) Nu 16^{29} (J), as distinguished from violent death; יוֹם מ׳ *day of death* Gn 27^{2} (J) Ju 13^{7} 1 S 15^{35}+; שְׁנַת מ׳ Is 6^{1} 14^{28}; עד מ׳ Nu 35$^{25.28.32}$ Jos 20^{6} (P), 1 K 11^{40}; לפני מ׳ Gn 27$^{7.10}$ 50^{16} (JE); אחרי מ׳ Gn 26^{18} (J), 25^{11} Lv 16^{1} Nu 35^{28} (P), Dt 31$^{27.29}$ (D)+; בכור מ׳ Jb 18^{13} *firstborn of death* (deadly disease); of flies Ec 10^{1}, unclean animals Lv 11$^{31.32}$ (P). **2.** *death by violence* as a penalty: †מִשְׁפַּט מ׳ + לְ or בְּ pers.: *a case of death to,* or *in* a man, guilty of capital crime Dt 19^{6} 21^{22} Je 26$^{11.16}$; †חֵטְא מ׳ Dt 22^{26}; †מ׳ בנ(י) 1 S 20^{31} 26^{16} 2 S 12^{5}; איש מ׳ 2 S 19^{29}; אנשי מ׳ 1 K 2^{26}; מַלְאֲכֵי מ׳ Pr 16^{14} *messengers of death;* במותיו Is 53^{9} *in his* (*martyr-*)*death* (v. Br$^{MP\ 359}$). †**3.** *state of death* or *place of death* (||שׁאול) Is 28$^{15.18}$ 38^{18} Ho 13^{14} Hb 2^{5} ψ 6^{6} 49^{15} Ct 8^{6} Pr 5^{5} 7^{27}; (||אבדון) Jb 28^{22}; שַׁעֲרֵי מ׳ *gates of death* ψ 9^{14} 107^{18} Jb 38^{17}. 4194

†[מָמוֹת] **n.[m.]** only pl. **death** (cf. Ar. مَمَات);—cstr. מְמוֹתֵי תַחֲלֻאִים Je 16^{4} of painful *death by diseases;* מ׳ חָלָל Ez 28^{8}.—For הַמְּמוֹתִים (Kt) 2 K 11^{2}, *the slain,* Qr. הַמּוּמָתִים is certainly correct (v. מות **Hoph.** supr.) 4463

†תְּמוּתָה **n.f.** death;—בְּנֵי ת׳ *children of death,* those worthy of death and appointed to death, ψ 79^{11} 102^{21} (see מָוֶת **2**). 8546

מוֹתָר v. יתר. מִזְבֵּחַ v. זבח. p. 258, 452 4195-96

מַזָּבֵל v. I. זְבֻל sub זבל. p. 259 2083

מזג (√of foll.=*mix*, cf. Syr. ܡܙܓ, and deriv.; 𝔗 מְזַג *mix, prepare by mixing*.—Ar. مَزَجَ *id.* is denom. fr. مِزَاجٌ v. foll., Frä[172]).

4197 **[מֶ֫זֶג] n.m. mixture,** i.e. **mixed wine** (NH *id.*, Aram., and thence מִזְגָּא, מְזִיגָא, ܡܘܙܓܐ; Ar. مِزَاجٌ *water mixed with wine, mixture* (Frä l.c.), cf. مِزْجٌ, مُزْجٌ);—אַל־יֶחְסַר הַמָּ֑זֶג Ct 7[3] (Tosafoth here *spiced wine*: cf. Levy[NHWB iii. 61]).

מזה (√of foll.; prob. cf. Ar. مَزَّ *suck out*, cf. Dr[Dt 32, 24]).

4198 †**[מָזֶה] adj.** (si vera l.) **sucked out, empty,** מְזֵי רָעָב Dt 32[24] *sucked out, empty, from hunger* (|| לְחֻמֵי רֶשֶׁף) so Is 5[13] Ew De Che Di Du (for MT מְתֵי; 𝔊𝔙 מֵתֵי).

4199 †**מִזָּה n.pr.m.** grandson of Esau Gn 36[13.17] (𝔊 Μοζε); 1 Ch 1[37] (𝔊 Ομοζε, 𝔊L Μαζε).

4200-01 **[מָזוּ]**, **מְזָוֵינוּ** v. זוה. **מְזוּזָה** v. זוז. p. 265

4202, 4205 **מָזוֹן** v. זון. I. **מָזוֹר** v. III. זור. p. 266-67

4204 II. **מָזוֹר** v. II. מזר infra. below

4206 †**מֵ֫זַח n.m. girdle** (acc. to Bondi[11] WMM[As. u. Eur. 104] loan-word fr. Egypt *mdḥ*, cf. Lag[GGN 1889, 310]);—abs. מ׳:—in sim. of curse enfolding the wicked ψ 109[19] (|| בֶּגֶד); fig.=restraint Is 23[10] (but text dubious).

4206 †**[מְזִיחַ] n.m.** *id.* (of like orig.):—only cstr. מ׳ אֲפִיקִים רִפָּה Jb 12[21] *loosen the girdle of mighty;* i.e. weaken them, make them defenceless, by ungirding.

2142 **מַזְכִּיר** v. זכר. hiphil p. 270

4208 †**מַזָּלוֹת n.[f.]pl. constellations,** perhaps **signs of the zodiac** (prob. loan-word fr. As. *manzaltu, mazaltu, station, abode* (of gods) Dl[HWB 457; Prol. 142] Jen[Kosmologie 348]; cf. NH מַזָּלוֹת, *id.;* מַזָּל Aram. מַזָּלָא, *star of fortune* or *fate*, Ph. [מ]זל נעם CIS[95, 8] (Vogüé; bilingual inscr.; Gk. ἀγαθῇ τύχῃ); Syr. ܡܘܙܠܬܐ *zodiac* PS[109] ܡܘܙܠܐ *mansiones lunae*, Lexx, PS[2332]; Ar. مَنَازِلُ (loan-word acc. to Hoffm[ZAW iii. 1883, 110]. Suidas *μαζουρωθ=ζωδία*);—only לַמַּזָּלוֹת 2 K 23[5] as obj. of worship (+ בַּעַל, שֶׁמֶשׁ, יָרֵחַ, and כָּל־צְבָא הַשָּׁמָיִם) 𝔊 *τοῖς μαζουρωθ;* prob.=מַזָּרוֹת Jb 38[32].

4207, 4209 **מַזְלֵג**, **[מִזְלָגָה]** v. זלג. **מְזִמָּה** v. זמם. p. 272-73

4210 **מִזְמוֹר** v. I. זמר. p. 274

מְזַמֶּרֶת, **מְזַמְּרָה** v. II. זמר. p. 275 4211-12

מִזְעָר v. זער. p. 277 4213

I. **מזר** (? √of foll. so Thes[781] cf. Ba[NB §164 c]; otherwise Gei[Urschrift 52]: NH מָזַר and Aram. ܡܙܪ *be bad* (of eggs), Ar. مَذِرَ *be foul, corrupt*).

†**מַמְזֵר n.m. bastard,** specif. **child of incest** (NH *id.* (v. Levy), מַמְזֵרוּת *incest;* Aram. (loan-word) מַמְזֵרָא *bastard*):—**1.** lit. *bastard*, Dt 23[3] (v. Dr). **2.** perh. fig. coll., of mixed population Zc 9[6] 𝔊 ἀλλογενεῖς (cf. also Gei[Urschrift, 52 f.]) 4464

II. **מזר** (√of foll., si vera l.; poss.=*spread out;* Aram. ܐܬܡܙܪ *stretch oneself*, cf. Ar. مَزَرَ *aequaliter distendit* utrem).

†II. **מָזוֹר n.m.** Ob[7] יָשִׂימוּ מ׳ תַּחְתֶּיךָ, very dub., perh. **net** (as something *extended*): 𝔊 (ἔνεδρα), 𝔖𝔙 *ambush* (? מָצוֹד or מְצוּדָה *net*, Vollers[ZAW 1884, 16]; מָצוֹר *siege* Prince[JBL xvi. 1897, 177]), Aq Theod *fetter, bond*, 𝔗 (תקלא) *stumbling-block;* Gr מַכְמֹר, מִכְמָר; We Now leave untranslated; Dl[Prol. 67, HWB 396] comp. As. *mazûru*, appar. *a pole with an iron hook*, but improb.—I. מָזוֹר v. sub II. זור, p. 267. 4204

מִזְרֶה v. זרה. p. 280 4214

†**מַזָּרוֹת n.[f.]pl.** prob.=מַזָּלוֹת q.v. supr. (on ר=ל v. W[SG 67], yet also Nö[ZMG xl. 1886, 185]) only הֲתֹצִיא מ׳ בְּעִתּוֹ Jb 38[32], where treated as ms., and perh. understood of some particular star or constellation. 𝔊 *μαζουρωθ.* 4216

מִזְרָח v. זרח. **מְזָרִים** v. זרה **Pi. 1.** p. 280 2219, 4217

[מִזְרַע] v. I. זרע. **מִזְרָק** v. זרק. p. 283-84 4218-19

[מֹחַ], **מֵחַ** v. מחח. p. 562 4220-21

†**[מְחָא] vb. strike,** only=**clap** (the hand) (Aram. form of II. מָחָה q.v.);—**Qal** *Impf.* 3 mpl. only fig., of joy of inanimate things before י׳: נְהָרוֹת יִמְחֲאוּ־כָף ψ 98[8]; וְכָל־עֲצֵי הַשָּׂדֶה יִמְחֲאוּ־כָף׃ Is 55[12].—**Pi.** *Inf. cstr.* sf. *id.*, of exultation over foe יַעַן מַחְאֲךָ יָד Ez 25[6] (|| וְרַקְעֲךָ בְּרֶגֶל). 4222

מַחֲבָא, **[מַחֲבֹא]** v. חבא. p. 285 4224

מַחְבֶּרֶת, **[מְחַבְּרָה]** v. חבר. p. 289 4225

מַחֲבַת v. חבת. **מַחֲגֹרֶת** v. חגר. p. 290, 292 4227-28

4229 †I. **מָחָה** **vb.** **wipe, wipe out** (NH *id.*; Ar. مَحَا, *efface, erase, cancel, obliterate;* Aram. מְחָא (I), cf. Ph. למחת *acc. to stroke = exactly* Hoffm [Ph. Inschr., Abh. GGW. xxxvi. May 1889, 9]).—**Qal** *Pf.* 3 ms. מָחָה Nu 5[23] + 3 t.; 3 fs. מָֽחֲתָה Pr 30[20] + 4 t. *Pf.; Impf.* יִמְחֶה 2 K 21[13]; וַיִּמַח (Baer; var. וַיִּמַּח) Gn 7[23]; 1 s. sf. אֶמְחֶנּוּ Ex 32[33]; + 4 t. Impf.; *Imv.* מְחֵה ψ 51[3.11]; sf. מְחֵנִי Ex 32[32]; *Inf. abs.* מָחֹה Ex 17[14]; *cstr.* לִמְחוֹת 2 K 14[27]; *Pt.* מֹחֶה Is 43[25]; fpl. (לְ)מֹחוֹת Pr 31[3] (Ges Fl Nö De Str for MT לַמְחוֹת);—**1.** *wipe,* the mouth Pr 30[20]; tears from (מעל) the face Is 25[8]; written curse, into the water (אל־מים) for drinking Nu 5[23] (P); Moses' name from the book (מספר) of God Ex 32[32.33] (J); וּמָחִיתִי אֶת־יְרוּשָׁלַםִ כַּאֲשֶׁר יִמְחֶה אֶת־הַצַּלַּחַת מָחָה וְהָפַךְ עַל־פָּנֶיהָ 2 K 21[13] *and I will wipe Jerusalem as one wipeth a dish,—he doth wipe and turn it* (but rd. prob. מָחֹה וְהָפֹךְ) *upside down.* **2.** *blot out = obliterate* from the memory, מִתַּחַת הַשָּׁמַיִם *from under heaven* e.g. the name Dt 9[14] 29[19] 2 K 14[27]; the remembrance Ex 17[14.14] (J), Dt 25[19]; the name for ever ψ 9[6]; transgressions (פשע; no more remembered by God against sinner) ψ 51[3] Is 43[25] 44[22]; עָוֺן ψ 51[11]. **3.** *blot out = exterminate,* כל־היקום all existing things Gn 7[23] (J) and mankind, מֵעַל פְּנֵי הָאֲדָמָה Gn 6[7] 7[4] (J); מֹחוֹת מְלָכִין Pr 31[3] (with the text-change, v. supr.) = *destroyers of kings* (i.e. impure women), but expression strange and dubious.

Niph. *Pf.* 3 mpl. נִמְחוּ Ez 6[6]; *Impf.* יִמָּחֶה Dt 25[6] Ju 21[17]; יִמַּח ψ 109[13]; 3 fs. תִּמָּח ψ 109[14]; + 4 t. Impf.;—**1.** *be wiped out* מִסֵּפֶר חַיִּים ψ 69[29]. **2.** *be blotted out,* מִיִּשְׂרָאֵל of a name Dt 25[6], a tribe Ju 21[17]; name (‖ posterity) ψ 109[13]; from memory, of sins Ne 3[37] ψ 109[14]; reproach, Pr 6[33]. **3.** *be exterminated,* מִן־הָאָרֶץ Gn 7[23] (J); of idolatrous works of Israel Ez 6[6].

Hiph. *Impf.* 2 ms. תֶּמַח Ne 13[14]; תֶּמְחִי Je 18[23] (but tone suggests תֶּ֫מַח cf. Ges [§ 75. R. 17]; Gie reads Qal and doubts Hiph. altogether); *Inf.* לִמְחוֹת Pr 31[3] (= לְהַמְחוֹת but see **Qal 3**);—*blot out,* from the memory; pious acts Ne 13[14]; sins Je 18[23].

4229 †II. **מָחָה** **vb.** **strike** (Aram. מְחָא (II), ܡܚܳܐ; acc. to L Gei [Urspr. d. Spr. 416] Lag [Sem. i. 26, BN 142] Nö [ZMG xxxii, 1878, 409] weakened fr. ܡܚܰܨ = مخض, Heb. מָחַץ q.v., cf. Dr [§ 178 n.]; As. *maḫû = crush, oppress,* acc. to Dl [HWB 396]);—*Pf.* 3 ms. consec., וּמָחָה עַל־כֶּתֶף וגו׳ Nu 34[11] (P) *and the border shall strike upon (reach unto) the shoulder of the sea of Chinnereth* (> Di al. der. fr. I. מָחָה *rub along by, brush past, skirt*).

†**מְחִי** **n.[m.]** only in מְחִי קָבָלּוֹ Ez 26[9] *the stroke of his battering ram* (cf. (מ)מחיו Ecclus 42[5] *smiting* a deceitful servant, marg. מוסר). 4239

III. **מָחָה** v. מֹחַ sub מחח. **מְחוּגָה** v. חוג. 4229-30
below, p. 295

†**[מָחוֹז]** **n.[m.]** **city** (As. loan-word; fr. *maḫâzu, city,* Asrb [Annals iii. 115] and oft.; v. Dl [HWB 271]; cf. 𝔗 מְחוֹזָא *market-place, province,* ܡܚܘܙܐ *small town*)—only cstr. וַיַּנְחֵם אֶל־מְחוֹז חֶפְצָם ψ 107[30] *and he guided them unto the city of their desire.* 4231

†**מְחוּיָאֵל** **n.pr.m.** great-grandson of Cain Gn 4[18a] = מְחִיָּיאֵל v [18b] (J; A 𝔊L in both Μαιηλ, E Μαουιηλ; cf. further Lag [Or. ii, 35 BN 96] (Μαιουιαηλ) Bu [Urgesch. 125]).—(Etym. dub.; Thes [Add. 97] perhaps *smitten of Ēl* √ מחה; Bu [Urgesch. 128] Kerber [Eigennam. d. AT. 91] מְחִיָּאֵל, or מְחַיָּאֵל *Ēl maketh alive;* DHM [MV 10] thinks of n. pr. div. יאל,—cf. Ph. n. pr. יאלפעל, and CIS [I. 132, 4; esp. p. 163 b], = *god* יאל *giveth life* (against this Gray [Prop. N. 164])). 4232

מַחֲוִים v. sub II. חוה. I. **מָחוֹל** v. I. חול. 4233-34
p. 296, 298

†II. **מָחוֹל** **n.pr.m.** father of Heman, etc., 1 K 5[11], 𝔊 Μαλ, A Μαουλ, 𝔊L Μααλα. 4235

מְחוֹלָה v. II. אָבֵל p. 6 supr.; v. also מְחֹלָה. 65, 4246
p. 298

מַחֲזֶה, מֶחֱזָה, מַחֲזִיאוֹת v. חזה. 4236-38

מחח (√ of foll.; cf. Ar. مخّ IV. *be fat,* also *contain marrow*).

†**[מֵחַ]** **n.[m.]** **fatling** (Ph. מח *fat* (adj.); NH מֵיחָא fig. of *choice flour*);—only pl. abs.: עֹלוֹת מֵיחִים ψ 66[15] *burnt offerings of fatlings;* so מֵחִים Is 5[17] (‖ כְּבָשִׂים) acc. to Hi Du Che [Hpt] (rd. חֲרָבוֹת and del. גָּרִים); most, *fat ones,* fig. for *rich men.* 4220

†**מֹחַ** **n.m.** **marrow** (NH מוֹחַ, Ar. مُخّ, Aram. מוֹחָא, ܡܘܚܳܐ all *marrow, brain*);—only cstr. מֹחַ עַצְמוֹתָיו יְשֻׁקֶּה Jb 21[24] fig. of prosperity. 4221

†III. **מָחָה** **vb.** **denom.** only **Pu.** *Pt.* מְמֻחָיִם (Ges [§ 75. R. 13]) in phr. שְׁמָנִים מ׳ Is 25[6] fat pieces *full of marrow.* 4229

מְחִי v. II. מחה. p. 562 4239

4240 †מְחִידָא **n.pr.m.** head of a family of returning exiles Ezr 2^{52} (𝔊 Μαουδα, 𝔊L Μεειδα) = Ne 7^{54} (𝔊 Μεειδα).

4232, 4241 מִחְיָה v. חיה. מְחִיָּיאֵל v. מְחוּיָאֵל. p. 313, 562

4244 †מַחְלָה **n.pr.f. 1.** a daughter of Zelophehad Nu 26^{33} 27^{1} 36^{11} Jos 17^{3}, 𝔊 Μα(α)λ(α)α. **2.** a Gileadite name (poss. **m.**) 1 Ch 7^{18} 𝔊 Μαελα, 𝔊L Μααλαθ.

4245 [מַחֲלֶה], מַחֲלָה v. I. חלה. p. 318

65, 4246-47 מְחֹלָה v. I. חול. [מְחִלָּה] v. I. חלל. p. 298, 320

4248 †מַחְלוֹן **n.pr.m.** son of Elimelech and Naomi, first husband of Ruth, Ru $1^{2.5}$ $4^{9.10}$, 𝔊 Μααλων.

4249 †I. מַחְלִי **n.pr.m. 1.** Levite, son of Merari Ex 6^{19} Nu 3^{20} 1 Ch $6^{4.14}$ $23^{21.21}$ $24^{26.28}$ Ezr 8^{18} (prob.), 𝔊 Μοολλει. **2.** son of Mushi, and grandson of Merari 1 Ch 6^{32} 23^{23} 24^{30}, 𝔊 Μοολει, Μοολ(λ)ι.

4250 †II. מַחְלִי **adj.gent.** of above; only c. art. as coll. הַמּ׳ Nu 3^{33} 26^{58}.

4251 מַחֲלֻיִים v. [מַחֲלוּי] sub I. חלה. p. 318

4252-53 [מַחֲלָף], [מַחֲלָפָה] v. חלף. p. 322

4254 מַחֲלָצוֹת v. [מַחֲלָצָה] sub I. חלץ. p. 323

4256, 5555 II. מַחְלְקוֹת v. II. חלק. מַחֲלֹקֶת v. I. חלק. p. 324-25

4257 I. מַחֲלַת v. sub II. חלה. p. 318

4258 †II. מַחֲלַת **n.pr.f. 1.** daughter of Ishmael Gn 28^{9}, 𝔊 Μαελεθ. **2.** granddaughter of David 2 Ch 11^{18}, 𝔊 Μολλαθ; 𝔊L Μαελλεθ.

4246 מְחֹלַת v. מְחוֹלָה sub I. חול. p. 298

4259 †מְחֹלָתִי **adj.gent.** only c. art. הַמּ׳ *the Mĕḥolathite*, of ʽAdriel 1 S 18^{19}, A τῷ Μοουλαθειτῃ; 𝔊L τοῦ Μαολλαιου; of Barzillai 2 S 21^{8}; 𝔊 τῷ Μωουλαθει, 𝔊L τοῦ Μααθει.

4260 †מַחֲמָאֹת **n.f.pl.** only (appar. cstr.) חָלְקוּ מ׳ פִּיו ψ 55^{22}, acc. to Ew De Hup = *curd-like* (i.e. smooth, hypocritical) *words, smooth are the butter-words of his mouth;* but read prob. חלק(ו) מֵחֶמְאָת (or מֵחֶמְאָה) פִּיו (פניו) *his face is smoother than curds* (Vrss Ki Thes Ol Che Bae We).

4261-62 מַחְמָד [מַחְמֹד, מַחֲמַדִּים] v. חמד. p. 326-27

4263 [מַחְמָל] v. חמל. מַחְמֶצֶת v. I. חמץ. p. 328, 330

4264-66 מַחֲנֶה, מַחֲנֵה־דָן, מַחֲנַיִם v. חנה. p. 334

4267-68 מַחֲנָק v. חנק. מַחֲסֶה, מַחְסֶה v. חסה. p. 338, 340

4269-70 מַחְסוֹם v. חסם. מַחְסוֹר v. חסר. p. 340-41

4271 מַחְסֵיָה v. חסה. p. 340

4272 †מָחַץ **vb. smite through, wound severely, shatter** (poet.) (As. *maḫâṣu, smite, wound,* Dl$^{HWB\ 398}$; Ar. مَخَضَ *churn; beat* or *agitate* the milk, etc.; Sab. מחץ DHM$^{ZMG\ xxx.}$ 1876, 684; xxxvii. 1883, 338; Burgen u. Schlösser (SB. xcvii. 1881), 965 (of stone-cutter's work), Hom$^{Chrestom.\ 127}$; Eth. መሐጸ:);—**Qal** *Pf.* 3 ms. מ׳ Jb 26^{12} + 3 t.; וּמָחֲצָה Ju 5^{26} etc.; *Impf.* יִמְחַץ Jb 5^{18} ψ 68^{22}; 1 s. sf. אֶמְחָצֵם ψ 18^{39}; וָא׳ 2 S 22^{39};—*smite through,* sq. רֹאשׁוֹ, of Jael, Ju 5^{26} (|| הָלְמָה, מָחֲקָה, חָלְפָה); of Isr., *shattering* enemies, מ׳ חִצָּיו Nu 24^{8} (obj. om.; || עַצְמֹתֵיהֶם יְגָרֵם) cf. v^{17} (obj. פַּאֲתֵי מוֹאָב); cf. ψ 18^{39} = 2 S 22^{39}; of י׳, *smiting through* or *shattering* his foes, ψ 110^{5}, their heads v^{6} 68^{22} Hb 3^{13}, loins Dt 33^{11}; cf. Jb 26^{12} obj. רַהַב, q.v.; abs., Dt 32^{39} (opp. רָפָא; || cl. אָמִית וַאֲחַיֶּה) cf. Jb 5^{18} (opp. רָפָא, || cl. יַכְאִיב וְיֶחְבָּשׁ). For תִּמְחַץ (רגלך בְּדָם) ψ 68^{24}, rd. תִּרְחַץ (58^{11}), Ol Br Che Bae We.

4273 †מַחַץ **n.[m.] severe wound;**—only cstr. מַחַץ מַכָּתוֹ יִרְפָּא Is 30^{26} of י׳'s restoration of his people (|| חָבַשׁ שֶׁבֶר עַמּוֹ).

4274-76 מַחְצֵב v. חצב. מֶחֱצָה, מַחֲצִית v. חצה. p. 345

4277 †[מָחַק] **vb. utterly destroy, annihilate** (cf. GFM) (NH *id., wipe* or *rub off, erase;* Aram. מְחַק *id.;* Ar. مَحَقَ *utterly destroy, annihilate*);—only 3 fs.: מָחֲקָה רֹאשׁוֹ Ju 5^{26} (|| הָלְמָה, מָחֲצָה, חָלְפָה).

4278 [מֶחְקָר] v. חקר. p. 350

מחר (√of foll.; *be in front of, meet,* cf. As. *maḫâru,* Dl$^{HWB\ 400}$ *come to meet, receive* [cf. קִבֵּל], and Id$^{Prol.\ 93}$; Sab. מחר *receive,* etc., n. *id., token of favour,* || *gift,* נחלת; DHM$^{ZMG\ xxxvii.\ 1883,\ 408}$).

4279 מָחָר$_{52}$ **n.m.,** used oft. as **adv., to-morrow, in time to come** (Aram. מְחַר, ܡܚܪ; prob. properly *time in front,* Kö$^{ii.\ 263}$, cf. √, and As. *maḫru, front,* oft. of time, though alw. of *former time, of old,* Dl$^{HWB\ 402}$):—**1.** *to-morrow* (the day following the *present* day), **a.** as *subst.* Ex 16^{23}

שַׁבָּתוֹן שַׁבַּת קֹדֶשׁ לַי׳ מָחָר *to-morrow* is a sabbath, etc., 1 S 20^{5} חֹדֶשׁ מָחָר *to-morrow* is the new moon, v^{18}; in יוֹם מָחָר †Gn 30^{33} Pr 27^{1} Is 56^{12}; in the idiom. phr. כָּעֵת מָחָר at the like of the time, (being) *to-morrow,* = *about to-morrow* (v. כְּ **1 a)** †Ex 9^{18} 1 S 9^{16} 20^{12} 1 K 19^{2} 20^{6} 2 K 7$^{1.18}$ 10^{6}; and in לְמָחָר †Ex 8^{19} לְמָחָר יִהְיֶה הָאֹת הַזֶּה, = *for, against, to-morrow,* Ex 8^{6} Nu 11^{18} Jos 7^{13} Est 5^{12}. **b.** as *adv. acc.* Ex 8^{25} 9^{5} מָחָר יַעֲשֶׂה, הִנְנִי מֵבִיא מָחָר אַרְבֶּה 10^{4} ,י׳ הַדָּבָר הַזֶּה 17^{9} 32^{5} Nu 14^{25} 1 S 11^{9} etc., Jos 11^{6} מָחָר כָּעֵת הַזֹּאת; opp. to הַיּוֹם Ex 19^{10} הַיּוֹם וּמָחָר, Jos 22^{18} 2 S 11^{12a}; rhetorically, Is 22^{13} כִּי מָחָר נָמוּת. **2.** = *in future time,* Ex 13^{14} כִּי יִשְׁאָלְךָ בִנְךָ מָחָר לֵאמֹר = Dt 6^{20}, Jos 4$^{6.21}$ 22$^{24.27.28}$; so בְּיוֹם מָחָר Gn 30^{33}.

4283 †מָחֳרָת **n.f. the morrow** (the day following a *past* day)—abs. מ׳ Gn 19^{34}+, cstr. מָחֳרַת Lv 23^{11}+;—*the morrow,* Nu 11^{32} וְכֹל יוֹם הַמָּחֳרָת; מִמָּחֳרָת = *on the morrow,* so וַיְהִי מִמָּחֳרָת, Gn 19^{34} Ex 18^{13} 32^{30} Nu 17^{23} Ju 9^{42} 21^{4} 1 S 11^{11} 18^{10} 31^{8} (= 1 Ch 10^{8}) 2 K 8^{15} Je 20^{3}; וַיַּשְׁכִּמוּ (וַיַּשְׁכִּמוּ) ויעש י׳ את מִמָּחֳרָת, Ex 32^{6} Ju 6^{38} 1 S 5$^{3.4}$; Ex 9^{6} מִמָּחֳרָת, הדבר הזה ממ׳ Nu 17^{6} Jos 5^{12}; 2 S 11^{12b}: הַשַּׁבָּת *on the morrow of* (= *after*) the sabbath, Lv 23$^{11.15.16}$, מִמָּחֳרַת הַפֶּסַח ממ׳ Nu 33^{3} Jos 5^{11}, הַחֹדֶשׁ [𝔊 בַּיּוֹם] הַשֵּׁנִי (MT falsely מִמָּחֳרַת) 1 S 20^{27}; of the morrow after a day specified in a law, Lv 19^{6} בְּיוֹם זִבְחֲכֶם יֵאָכֵל וּמִמָּחֳרָת, 7^{16}. Twice (late) with לְ, Jon 4^{7} לַמָּחֳרָת *on the morrow,* 1 Ch 29^{21} לְמָחֳרַת הַיּוֹם הַהוּא.—1 S 30^{17} strangely וַיַּכֵּם דָּוִד מֵהַנֶּשֶׁף וְעַד־הָעֶרֶב לְמָחֳרָתָם from the dawn to the evening *of their following day* (We Bu לְהַחֲרִימָם).

4242 †I. מְחִיר **n.m. price, hire** (as that which is *placed in front* of one, *presented, offered;* As. *maḫîru, price; maḫirânu, buyer,* Dl$^{HWB\ 404,\ Prol.\ 94}$);—מ׳ abs. Mi 3^{11} + 9 t.; cstr. Dt 23^{19} + 2 t.; sf. מְחִירָהּ Jb 28^{15}; pl. sf. מְחִירֵיהֶם ψ 44^{13};—**1.** *price,* oft. בִּמְחִיר *for a price;* in trade 2 S 24^{24} 1 K 10^{28} 2 Ch 1^{16}; cf. La 5^{4} (‖ כֶּסֶף), also (no בְּ) 1 K 21^{2} and מ׳ שָׂדֶה עַתּוּדִים Pr 27^{26}; of wisdom Jb 28^{15} (‖ סְגוֹר כֶּסֶף) cf. Pr 17^{16} (no בְּ); fig. בְּלוֹא־כֶסֶף וּבְלוֹא מ׳ Is 55^{1} in purchase of blessings fr. י׳; of price of people, fig. ψ 44^{13}, cf. Je 15^{13}. **2. hire,** מ׳ כֶּלֶב (i.e. of male prostitute) Dt 23^{19} (‖ אֶתְנַן זוֹנָה) v. Di Dr; of venal priests Mi 3^{11} (‖ שֹׁחַד); = *reward, gain,* denied of Cyrus Is 45^{13} (‖ *id.*); affirmed of Ant. Epiph. Dn 11^{39}.

4243 †II. מְחִיר **n.pr.m.** 1 Ch 4^{11}, 𝔊 Μα(χ)ειρ.

[מַחֲרָאָה], מחראות v. חרא. p. 351 4280

[מַחֲרֶשֶׁת, מַחֲרֵשָׁה] v. I. חרש. p. 361 4281-83

מַחְשֹׂף v. חשׂף. p. 362 4286

מַחֲשָׁבָה, מַחֲשֶׁבֶת v. חשב. p. 364 4284

מַחְשָׁךְ v. חשך. מְחִתָּה, מְחִתָּה v. חתה. p. 365, 367 4285, 4287, 4289

מַחְתָּה v. חתת. מַחְתֶּרֶת v. חתר. p. 367 4288, 4290

מַט v. מֹטָּה sub נטה. p. 641 4295

מְטַאֲטֵא v. טאטא. מַטְבֵּחַ v. טבח. p. 370-71 4292-93

מַטֶּה, מִטָּה, מֻטָּה, מֻטֶּה v. נטה. p. 641-42 4294-96, 4298

מְטַוֶּה v. טוה. p. 376 4299

מטל (√ of foll.; cf. Ar. مَطَلَ *strike, beat, extend by beating, shape iron into a helmet,* Frey, مَمْطُول iron, or a sword, *beaten into a long shape,* Lane^{3021}).

†מְטִיל **n.m. wrought-metal rod** (Aram. (𝔗) מְטַל);—cstr. מְטִיל בַּרְזֶל Jb 40^{18} fig. of bones (‖ עֲצָמָיו אֲפִיקֵי נְחוּשָׁה) of hippopot. (גְּרָמָיו). 4300

מַטְמוֹן v. טמן. מַטָּע v. נטע. p. 380, 642 4301-02

[מַטְעָם], מַטְעַמִּים v. טעם. p. 381 4303

מִטְפַּחַת v. טפח. p. 381 4304

†מָטָר **n.m.**$^{Ex\ 9,33}$ **rain** (As. *meṭru,* Dl^{HWB} 406; Ar. مَطَرٌ; Sab. (Min.) מטר Hom$^{Chrestom.\ 127}$; Aram. מִטְרָא, ܡܶܛܪܳܐ);—מ׳ Ex 9^{33} + 30 t.; cstr. מְטַר Dt 11^{11} + 5 t.; pl. cstr. מִטְרוֹת Jb 37^{6};—*rain,* as watering earth, esp. Canaan, Dt 11^{11} מ׳ הַשָּׁמַיִם; as blessing sent (vb. usu. נָתַן) and withheld by י׳, Dt 11^{14} (‖ מַלְקוֹשׁ, יוֹרֶה); v^{17} (here מ׳ אַרְצְכֶם); 28^{12} 1 K 8$^{35.36}$ 17^{1} (‖ טַל), 18^{1} 2 Ch 6$^{26.27}$ 7^{13} Jb 5^{10} (‖ מַיִם), cf. 28^{26} 36^{27} ψ 147^{8} (vb. הֵכִין); so מ׳ זַרְעֲךָ Is 30^{23} Zc 10^{1} (‖ מַלְקוֹשׁ), v^{1} גֶּשֶׁם מָטָר; מְטַר־גֶּשֶׁם Jb 37^{6}, גֶּשֶׁם מִטְרוֹת עֻזּוֹ v^{6} (‖ שֶׁלֶג); 38^{28} (‖ אֶגְלֵי־טָל) הֲמוֹן מַיִם ‖); לַמּ׳ בְּרָקִים ψ 135^{7} Je 10^{13} = 51^{16} also in נָתַן אֶת מְ׳ אַרְצְךָ אָבָק וְעָפָר Dt 28^{24}; cf. Is 5^{6} (where acc. cogn. with הִמְטִיר); wish of David 2 S 1^{21} (‖ טַל); מ׳ בַּקָּצִיר sim. of the unseasonable, Pr 26^{1} (‖ שֶׁלֶג בַּקַּיִץ); sent by extraord. supernat. power as sign Ex 9$^{33.34}$ (J; both ‖ קֹלוֹת, בָּרָד) cf. 1 S 12$^{17.18}$ (‖ קֹלוֹת); sim. of refreshment Dt 32^{2} (‖ טַל), Jb 29^{23} (‖ מַלְקוֹשׁ), ψ 72^{6} (‖ רְבִיבִים), cf. 2 S 23^{4}; as destructive Ps 28^{3} (מָטָר סֹחֵף); also fig., Is 4^{6} (‖ זֶרֶם). 4306

4305 †[מָטַר] **vb. denom.** (cf. Gerber$^{\text{Verb. denom. 106}}$) [**rain**] (Ar. مَطَرَ; Syr. ܡܛܪ; 𝔗 Aph. אַמְטַר);—**Niph.** *Impf.* *be rained upon* חֶלְקָה אַחַת תִּמָּטֵר Am 4^{7}. **Hiph.** *Pf.* הִמְטִיר Gn 2^{5} 19^{24}; וְהִמְטַרְתִּי Am 4^{7}; *Impf.* יַמְטֵר ψ 11^{6} Jb 20^{23}; וַיַּמְטֵר Ex 9^{3} + 2 t.; 3 fs. תַּמְטִיר Am 4^{7} (but rd. אַמְטִיר 𝔊 𝔙); 1 s. אַמְטִיר Am 4^{7} + v^{7} (for תַּמְטִיר), Ez 38^{22}; *Inf. cstr.* הַמְטִיר Is 5^{6} Jb 38^{26}; *Pt.* מַמְטִיר Gn 7^{4} + 2 t.;—*send rain, rain* (sq. עַל exc. Ex 9^{18} 16^{4}); subj. ׳י (no dir. obj.) Gn 2^{5} 7^{4} (both J), Am $4^{7.7.7}$, cf. Jb 38^{26}; subj. clouds עָבִים by divine command Is 5^{6} (acc. cogn. מָטָר); הִמְ׳ מָן ψ 78^{24}; שְׁאֵר v^{27}; לֶחֶם Ex 16^{4} (J; מִן־הַשָּׁמַיִם; no עַל); as act of judgment הִמ׳ בָּרָד *rain hail, send hail,* subj. ׳י Ex 9^{23} (J); cf. v^{18} (J; no עַל); obj. גָּפְרִית וָאֵשׁ Gn 19^{24} (J), cf. Ez 38^{22} וְגֶשֶׁם שׁוֹטֵף וְאַבְנֵי אֶלְגָּבִישׁ אֵשׁ וְגָפְרִית אַמ׳; fig. ψ 11^{6} (obj. פַּחִים; but rd. פַּחֲמֵי אֵשׁ v. Ew Che Bae al.); Jb 20^{23} (‖ cl. יְשַׁלַּח בּוֹ חֲרוֹן אַפּוֹ).

4309 †מַטְרִי **adj. gent.** only c. art. as subst. coll. הַמ׳ 1 S 10^{21a} + v^{21b} 𝔊 The We Klo Dr Kit Bu HPS. 𝔊 Ματταρι.

4307, 4807 מַטָּרָא, מַטָּרָה v. נטר. מְטֹרָד v. טרד.

p. 382, 643

4325 [מַי] ^{580} **n.m.** $^{2 S 14, 14}$ only pl. מַיִם **waters, water** (NH *id.*; MI^{23} [מ[ין]; SI^{5} המים; Aram. מַיִן, מַיָּא, ܡܝܐ; As. *mû*, pl. *mê*, also *mâmu* Dl$^{\text{HWB 394}}$; Ar. مَاءٌ; Eth. ማይ:, pl. ማያት:; Sab. [מו], מום, pl. מון, Min. [מה], pl. מהן DHM$^{\text{6th Or. Congr. (Leiden) ii. 1, 451 f.}}$ (v. on these forms Ba$^{\text{ZMG xlii. 1888, 341 ff.}}$));—מַיִם (מָיִם) Gn 1^{2}+; הַמַּ֫יְמָה Ex 7^{15} 8^{16}; cstr. מֵי Gn 7^{7} + 71 t.; מֵימֵי Ex 4^{9} + 10 t. + Qr 2 K 18^{27} = Is 36^{12}; sf. מֵימַי Ho 2^{7} + 1 S 25^{11} (but rd. here יֵינִי 𝔊 Ew Th We Klo Dr Kit Bu); מֵימֶיךָ Ex 23^{25} + 3 t.; מֵימָיו Nu 20^{8} + 6 t.; מֵימֶיהָ Je 6^{7} 50^{38}; מֵימֵינוּ La 5^{4}; מֵימֵיהֶם Ex 7^{19} + 4 t.;—*waters, water* (c. adj. pl. Gn 26^{19} Ex 15^{10} Lv $14^{5.6.50}$ + oft., so alw. c. adj.; also c. pt. pl. Nu $5^{18.19.24}$ 2 K 3^{20}+; c. pron. pl. Nu 20^{13} 27^{14} 2 K 2^{21}+; cf. sf. Jos 4^{18}; before pl. vb. Gn $1^{9.20.21}$ 7^{17} + oft.; after pl. vb. Jos 3^{13} Is 28^{17} Pr 9^{17} Ez 31^{4}+; rarely c. sg. vb.; before, Gn 9^{15} Lv 11^{34} Nu 20^{2} 24^{7} 33^{14} 2 K 3^{9}; after, Nu $19^{13.20}$);—**1. a.** *water,* of a spring or well (בְּאֵר, עַיִן) Gn 16^{7} $24^{11.13.13.43}$ Ex $15^{27.27}$ (J), Gn $21^{19.25}$ Nu 20^{17} 21^{16} (E), etc.; for drinking, also Am 4^{8} 8^{11} Jon 3^{7} + oft.; out of rock Ex 17^{6} (E), Nu $20^{8.8.10.11}$ (P), Dt 8^{15} etc.; מֵי מְרִיבָה (RS$^{\text{Sem. i. 165; 2nd ed. 181}}$) Nu $20^{13.24}$ 27^{14} (P), Dt 33^{8} ψ 81^{8} 106^{32}; cf. Dt 32^{51} Ez 47^{19} 48^{28}; for washing (hands, feet, person) Gn 18^{4} 24^{32} 43^{24} (J), 2 K 3^{11}, Ex 29^{4} 30^{20} Lv $15^{5.6}$ + (P); (victims) Lv $1^{9.13}$ 8^{21} (P); (vessels) Lv 6^{21} $12^{32.34}$ (P); (garments) Lv 15^{17} Nu 19^{8} (P); for cooking Ex 12^{9} (P), cf. Is 64^{1} Ez 24^{3} (symbol.); for purification Nu 8^{7} (מֵי חַטָּאת), 19^{9} (מֵי נִדָּה), cf. $v^{13.18.20.21.31}$ $31^{23.23}$ (all P), Ez 36^{25} (fig.). **b.** of a river, Nile Ex 2^{10} $4^{9.9}$ (J), Je 2^{18} etc.; Jordan Jos 3^{8} (D), $v^{15.16}$ (JE), etc.; Euphrates Is 8^{7} (fig.), Je 2^{18}; Ezek.'s river Ez $47^{1.1.2}$+, etc.; of streams, canals, etc., esp. as condition of fertility Dt 8^{7} 10^{7} Is 1^{30} Pr 30^{16} 2 K 3^{17}+, etc. **c.** of sea Am 5^{8} 9^{6}; Red Sea Ex $15^{8.10.19}$ (song), $14^{21.22.26}$ + (P), Jos 2^{10} (D), etc. **d.** of flood Gn $7^{7.10}$ $8^{3.7.8.9.11}$ (J), 6^{17} $7^{6.17.18.18.19}$ 8^{5} $9^{11.15}$ (P); so מֵי־נֹחַ Is $54^{9.9}$ *waters of Noah.* **e.** subterranean Ex 20^{4} (E), Dt 4^{18} 5^{8}, cf. Jb 26^{5} ψ 136^{6}. **f.** in clouds Je 10^{13} Jb 26^{8} ψ $29^{3.3}$ 104^{3} 148^{4}, etc. **g.** of rain Ju 5^{4} 2 S 21^{10} Dt 11^{11} ψ 65^{10} Jb 5^{10} (‖ מָטָר), etc. **h.** of dew Ju 6^{38}. **i.** primæval deep Gn $1^{2.6}$ (P). **2.** c. nomm. pr. loc. (q. v.), to denote springs, streams, or seas belonging to, near, such places: מֵימֵי מִצְרַיִם Ex 7^{19} 8^{2}; מֵי מְרִיבָה (v. supr. **1 a**); מֵי מֵרוֹם Jos $11^{5.7}$; מֵי עֵין־שֶׁמֶשׁ Jos 15^{7}; מֵי נֶפְתּוֹחַ 15^{9} 18^{15}; מֵי יְרִיחוֹ 16^{1}; מֵי מְגִדּוֹ Ju 5^{19}; מֵי נִמְרִ(י)ם Is 15^{6} Je 48^{34}; מֵי דִימוֹן Is 15^{9}; cf. מֵי הַשִּׁלֹחַ Is 8^{6}; מֵימֵי גִּיחוֹן הָעֶלְיוֹן 2 Ch 32^{30}; cf. also n. pr. loc. מִשְׂרְפוֹת מַיִם Jos 11^{8} 13^{6}. **3.** special uses are: מֵי רַגְלַיִם *water of the feet* = urine 2 K 18^{27} = Is 36^{12}; cf. בְּמֵי מַדְמֵנָה Is 25^{10} Kt *in water of a dunghill* (> Qr כְּמוֹ); מַיִם לַחַץ *water* (which is) *distress,* because drunk in imprisonment 1 K 22^{27} (‖ לֶחֶם לַחַץ) = 2 Ch 18^{26}; בְּמֵי־שָׁלֶג *in snow-water* Jb 9^{30} Qr (Kt במו; Me Hoffm Siegfr כְּמוֹ), מֵימֵי שֶׁלֶג 24^{19}; מַיִם קְדֹשִׁים †Nu 5^{17} *holy water* (cf. RS$^{\text{Sem. 165, 2nd ed. 181}}$, but text dubious, v. Di); מֵי הַמָּרִים *bitter water* †Nu $5^{18.19.23.24}$; cf. Ex 15^{23} (כִּי מָרִים הֵם), opp. וַיִּמְתְּקוּ הַמָּיִם v^{25} *and the waters were sweetened;* מֵי נִדָּה, מֵי חַטָּאת v. supr. **1 a**; מַיִם חַיִּים *living* (i.e. running) *water* Lv $14^{5.6.50.51.52}$ Nu 19^{17}, also (fig.) Zc 14^{8} (cf. Ez 47), and (fig.) Je 2^{13} 17^{13}. See also infr. (cf. Nu $21^{17.18}$; v. RS$^{\text{Sem. i. 127, 157; 2nd ed. 135, 176}}$). **4.** among fig. uses are: **a.** of distress Is 43^{2} ψ 66^{12} (‖ אֵשׁ), 69^{2} La 3^{54}; usu. *many waters* 2 S 22^{17} = ψ 18^{17}, cf. Jb 22^{11} ψ 32^{6} 144^{7}, or *deep waters* ψ $69^{3.15}$, cf. v^{16}; also מֵי־רֹאשׁ *water of gall* Je 8^{14} 9^{14} 23^{15}. **b.** פֶּרֶץ מַיִם 2 S 5^{20} = 1 Ch 14^{11} of outbursting force. **c.** שְׁאוֹן מַיִם Is $17^{12.13}$ of rushing nations. **d.** of what is impetuous, violent, overwhelming Is $28^{2.17}$ Ho 10^{7} Jb 27^{20} ψ $124^{4.5}$ 88^{18}; sim. of impetuousness פַּחַז כַּמַּיִם Gn 49^{4}. **e.** (as running away) of heart in timidity Jos 7^{5}, cf. ψ 22^{15}, of knees Ez 7^{17} 21^{12}. **f.** of transitoriness Jb 11^{16} 24^{18} ψ 58^{8}. **g.** of refreshment Is 32^{2} 49^{10}; spiritual 12^{3}. **h.** מֵי מְנֻחוֹת ψ 23^{2} in fig. of rest and peace, cf. Je 31^{9}. **i.** of reckless bloodshed (poured out like water) ψ 79^{3}; cf. pouring away (and not eating) blood Dt 12$^{16.24}$ 15^{23}. **j.** בְּאֵר מַיִם חַיִּים Ct 4^{15} fig. of bride; מַיִם מִבּוֹרֶךָ Pr 5^{15} of enjoyment of one's own wife; of harlotry מַיִם גְּנוּבִים Pr 9^{17} *stolen waters.* **k.** of outpoured wrath of ׳י Ho 5^{10}. **l.** of abundant justice Am 5^{24}. **m.** of outpoured feelings Jb 3^{24}; שִׁפְכִי כַמַּיִם לִבֵּךְ La 2^{19}.—Is 48^{1} rd. prob. מִמְּעֵי for MT מִמֵּי, so Secker Du Che ^{Hpt} Skinner, cf. Di.

4314 †מֵי זָהָב **n.pr.m.** an Edomite Gn 36^{39} (𝔊 Μεζοοβ, 𝔊L Μαιζοοβ) = 1 Ch 1^{50} (𝔊L Μαιζααβ).

4313 †מֵי הַיַּרְקוֹן **n.pr.loc.** in Dan, near Joppa Jos 19^{46} (reading dubious; 𝔊 ἀπὸ θαλάσσης [i. e. מִיָּם = מים] Ιερακων).

4310 מִי$_{423}$ **pron. interrog.** who? of persons, as מָה (q.v.) of things (Eth. **መኑ**: but only = *What?* and *How?* As. *mî, me* (rare) Jäger$^{BAS. ii. 277}$, the usu. Sem. form for *Who?* has *n*, viz. As. *mannu, manu* (Dl$^{HWB 419}$), Eth. **መኑ**: *manū*, Aram. ܡܰܢ, Arab. مَنْ, vulg.-Arab. *min, mīn*, from a form resembling which, by rejection of *n*, prob. Heb. מִי: W$^{SG 123 f.}$):—*who?* (*τίς; quis?*) Gn 3^{11} מִי הִגִּיד לְךָ *who* told thee? 24^{65} מִי הָאִישׁ הַלָּזֶה *who* is this man? 27^{18} מי אתה בני *who* art thou, my son? Nu 22^{9} Ju 1^{1} 6^{29} 15^{6} 18^{3} 20^{18} 2 S 1^{8}+oft.; Ru 3^{9} מִי אָתְּ *who* art thou (fem.)? Is 51^{12}; of more than one, מִי אֵלֶּה *who* are these? Gn 33^{5} 48^{8} Is 60^{8}; מי אתם 2 K 10^{13}; once, more explicitly, מִי וָמִי הַהֹלְכִים Ex 10^{8}; =*as who?* (i.e. in what condition, or capacity), Am 7^{2} מי יקום יעקב, v^{5} Is 51^{19} מִי אֲנַחֲמֵךְ (but Vrss Che Lag Brd Du ׳מִי יְ, as ‖ מִי יָנוּד), Ru 3^{16} (Be Ke Kö$^{iii. 388}$). Note in partic.: **a.** מִי is rarely used of *things*, and usually where persons are understood or implied: Gn 33^{8} מי לך כל־המחנה הזה *who* (or *what*) to thee is all this camp? Dt 4^{7} Ju 9^{28} מִי שְׁכֶם *who* is Shechem (i.e. the Shechemites)? Mi 1^{5} מִי־פֶשַׁע יַעֲקֹב הֲלֹא שֹׁמְרוֹן, v^{b} Ct 3^{6} Ju 13^{17} מִי שְׁמֶךָ (but מה Gn 32^{28} Ex 3^{13}: with מִי cf. מַן in Aram. Ezr 5^{4} Gn Ex. *ll. cc.* 𝔗; and see Nö$^{M. p. 341}$). On 1 S 18^{18}, v. II. חַי. **b.** in the gen., בַּת־מִי אַתְּ *whose* daughter art thou? Gn 24$^{23.47}$ 1 S 12$^{3.3.3}$ 17^{55} Je 44^{28} Jb 26^{4} 33^{28}; after various preps., as מִי אַחֲרֵי 1 S 24$^{15.15}$; אֶל־מִי 1 S 6^{20} 2 K 9^{5}+; בְּמִי by *whom?* †1 K 20^{14}, לְמִי$_{20}$ *to whom? whose?* Gn 32^{18} לְמִי אַתָּה, 38^{25} Pr 20^{29} (6 t.)+; מִמִּי †Ez 32^{19} ψ 27$^{1.1}$; עַל־מִי 2 K 18^{20} 19^{22} Is 57^{4}+; אֶת־מִי (so alw. in acc.), 1 S 12$^{3.3}$ 28^{11} Is 6^{8}; =*with whom?* Jb 12^{3}. **c.** in an indirect qu., as Gn 21^{26} 43^{22} לֹא ידענו מי שם we do not know *who put*, etc., Dt 21^{1} ψ 39^{7} Jos 24^{15} בַּחֲרוּ . . . אֶת־מִי תַעֲבֹדוּן choose *whom* ye will serve, after ראה 1 S 14^{17}, שׁאל 17^{56}, הגיד 1 K 1^{20}, הודיע v^{27}. **d.** ׳מי ב *who among . . . ?* 1 S 22^{14} Is 36^{20}; 43^{9} 48^{14} (בהם); 42^{23} 50^{10} Hg 2^{3} (all בכם); מי מן *who of . . . ?* Ju 21^{8} 2 K 6^{11} Is 50^{1}. **e.** strengthened and emph. forms of interrog.: (*a*) מי זה (v. זה **4 b**), מי הוא (v. הוא **4 b** β), מִי הוא זה †ψ 24^{10} Je 30^{21} Est 7^{5} (v. *ibid.*); (*b*) מִי אֶחָד *what single one . . . ?* Ju 21^{8}, cf. 2 S 7^{23} (=1 Ch 17^{21}). **f.** various *rhetorical* uses (oft. *repeated* in ‖ cl., as ψ 15^{1} 18^{32} Is 28^{9} 29^{15}):—(*a*) sq. impf. it expresses a *wish* (the question implying a desire that the person asked for were present), 2 S 15^{4} מִי יְשִׂמֵנִי שֹׁפֵט *who* will set me judge? i.e. *would that* some one would make me judge! 23^{15} מִי יַשְׁקֵנִי מַיִם = *O that* one would give me to drink, etc.! cf. Nu 11$^{4.18}$ Mal 1^{10} ψ 4^{7} 60^{11} 94^{16} Is 42^{23}, and very oft. in the phr. מִי יִתֵּן *who will give?* i.e. *would that there were . . .!* as Nu 11^{29} ומי יתן כל עם ׳י נביאים = and *would that* all ׳י's people were prophets! Dt 28^{67} מי יתן ערב = *would it were* even! Ju 9^{29}+ (v. נָתַן). (*b*) it expresses *contempt* (*who?* implying the answer *no one at all*), Ex 5^{2} ׳מי י אשר אשמע בקולו *who* is ׳י that I should listen to his voice? Ju 9^{28} מִי אֲבִימֶלֶךְ וּמִי שְׁכֶם כִּי נַעַבְדֶנּוּ, v^{38} 1 S 17^{26} *who* is this Phil. that he should have reproached, etc.? 25^{10} מי דוד ומי בן ישי, Is 28^{9} Jb 26^{4} Pr 30^{9} ׳מי י; or *modesty* (real or assumed), Ex 3^{11} מִי אָנֹכִי כִּי אֵלֵךְ אֶל־פַּרְעֹה, 1 S 18^{18} מי אנכי ומי חיי who am I, and who is my clan (חַיַּי), that I should be the king's son-in-law? 2 S 7^{18} 1 Ch 29^{14} 2 Ch 2^{5}; or *surprise*, Is 44^{10} 49^{21}. (*c*) in impassioned prose, and esp. in poetry, implying the answer *few* or *none*, it is equiv. to a rhetorical negative, Dt 9^{2} מִי יִתְיַצֵּב לִפְנֵי בְּנֵי עֲנָק *who* can stand, etc.? 30^{12} מִי יַעֲלֶה־לָּנוּ הַשָּׁמַיְמָה, v^{13} 1 S 4^{8} מִי יַצִּילֵנוּ וגו׳, 6^{20} 22^{14} 26$^{9.15}$ 2 S 16^{10}; מי יאמר *who* shall (or can) say? Jb 9^{12} Pr 20^{9} Ec 8^{4}; with the perfect (of experience), *who has ever . . . ?* Nu 23^{10} Dt 5^{23} Is 36^{20} 66$^{8.8}$ Je 18^{13} מִי שָׁמַע כָּאֵלֶּה, 23^{18} (MT), 30^{21} Jb 4^{7} 9^{4} מִי הִקְשָׁה אֵלָיו וַיִּשְׁלָם, 41^{3} Pr 30^{4} La 3^{37}; poet., very oft., as Gn 49^{9} וּכְלָבִיא מִי יְקִימֶנּוּ *who* can rouse him up? (i.e. no one), Ex 15$^{11.11}$ מִי כָמֹכָה (so ψ 35^{10} al.), Nu 24$^{9.23}$ 1 S 2^{25} מי יתפלל לו *who* shall intercede for him? (i.e. no one), Is 1^{12} 10^{3} 40$^{13.14.18}$ 41^{26} 42^{19} 43^{9} 48^{14} 50^{1} 53^{1} מִי הֶאֱמִין לִשְׁמֻעָתֵנוּ (i.e. few or none), etc.; ψ 18^{32} ׳מִי אֱלוֹהַּ מִבַּלְעֲדֵי י, 76^{8} 89^{7} 130^{3} Jb 21^{31}

34^{29} Jo 17^{9} Jo 2^{11} Mal 3^{2}; ... מִי לֹא Am 3^{8} Je 10^{7} Jb 12^{9} (cf. 25^{3} Na 3^{19}); (יְשִׁיבֶנָּה) מִי יְשִׁיבֶנּוּ *who* shall (can) turn it back? †Jb 9^{12} 11^{10} 23^{13} Is 14^{27} 43^{13} Je 2^{24}; implying the answer, *no one but God*, Is 40^{12} 41^{2} Jb $38^{5.6.25}$, etc.; defiantly, Is 50^{9} מִי הוּא יַרְשִׁיעֵנִי, Je 21^{13} 49^{4} מִי יָבוֹא אֵלַי, v^{19} וְאִם לְמִשְׁפָּט Ob^{3} ψ 12^{5} מִי אָדוֹן לָנוּ, 59^{8} 64^{6} Jb 9^{19} מִי הוּא יָרִיב עִמָּדִי, 13^{19} מִי יוֹעִידֵנִי *who* is he that will contend with me? 17^{3} 41^{2}. Notice in examples of this kind the freq. *order* of words: Pr 20^{6} ואיש אמונים מי ימצא, 24^{22} ופיד שניהם מי יודע, 31^{10} Na 1^{6} לפני זעמו מי יעמד, ψ 147^{17} לפני קָרָתוֹ מי יעמד, Jb 4^{2} וַעְצֹר בְּמִלִּין מִי יוּכָל, 26^{14} 38^{37} 39^{5} $41^{5.6}$ ψ 6^{6} בִּשְׁאוֹל מִי יוֹדֶה־לָּךְ, 19^{13}; and with the *nom. pendens*, Je 2^{24} תַּאֲנָתָהּ מִי יְשִׁיבֶנָּה, Pr 18^{14} Jb 17^{15} וְתִקְוָתִי מִי יְשׁוּרֶנָּה, 38^{29} וּכְפֹר שָׁמַיִם מִי יְלָדוֹ. (*d*) מִי יוֹדֵעַ *who knoweth?* (ψ 90^{11} Pr 24^{22}), sq. a verbal clause, becomes (cf. *nescio an*) = *it may be, perchance*, †2 S 12^{22} מִי יוֹדֵעַ יְחָנַּנִי י׳ (Qr וְחַנַּנִי), Jo 2^{14} (= Jon 3^{9}) מי יודע ישוב ונחם, Est 4^{14} מי יודע אם. (*e*) especially in poetry, a question with מִי, to which the answer follows, is an effective mode of affirming a fact, or introducing a description: ψ $15^{1.1}$ (see v$^{2-5}$), $24^{3.8.10}$ Is 23^{8} מי יעץ זאת וג׳ (v^{9} the answ., י׳ צ׳ יְעָצָהּ), 33^{14} (see v$^{15\,f.}$), 37^{23} $41^{2.4}$ 60^{8} 63^{1} Je 46^{7} Ct 3^{6}, cf. 6^{10} 8^{3}; answered by הֲלֹא Ex 4^{11} Is 42^{24} 45^{21} Mi $1^{5.5}$. **g.** מִי may sometimes be rendered *whosoever*, though, as the examples will shew, it does not really mean it: Ex 24^{14} מי בעל דברים יִגַּשׁ אליהם, lit. *Who* hath a cause? let him draw nigh unto them, i.e. *whoso* hath a cause, let him, etc., Is 50^{8b} מִי בַעַל מִשְׁפָּטִי יִגַּשׁ אֵלָי, 54^{15} Ju 7^{3} מִי יָרֵא וְחָרֵד יָשֹׁב וג׳ *who* is fearful and trembling? let him return, Pr $9^{4.16}$ מִי־פֶתִי יָסֻר הֵנָּה, Ezr 1^{3} (cf. with וְ in apod. Je 9^{11} Ho 14^{10} ψ 107^{43}; Zc 4^{10} is dubious, on account of anom. tense and construct.); so with מי האיש אשר ... Dt $20^{5.6.7}$ Ju 10^{18}, cf. ψ 25^{12}. With 1 ps. in apod., Ex 32^{33} מִי אֲשֶׁר חָטָא לִי אֶמְחֶנּוּ מִסִּפְרִי, Je 49^{19} (= 50^{44}) וּמִי בָחוּר אֵלֶיהָ אֶפְקֹד and *who* is chosen? I will appoint him over her! Is 50^{8a}; with an imv. in the apod. Ex 32^{24} (against accents; v. Ra) למי זהב התפרקו *who* hath gold? break it off you! Gn 19^{12} 1 S 11^{12}, cf. ψ $34^{13\,f.}$; without a verb, Ex 32^{26} מי לי׳ אלי *who* is on J.'s side? (let him come) to me! so 2 S 20^{11} (מי אשר); Ec 5^{9} 9^{4} (מי אשר). **h.** once, following a verb (cf. מָה **3**), *any one*, 2 S 18^{12} שִׁמְרוּ־מִי בַּנַּעַר באבשלום Have a care, *whosoever ye be*, of, etc. (but 𝔊 𝔖 𝔙 Bu לִי; cf. v^{5}).

†מִיכָאֵל **n.pr.m.** Michael, 𝔊 Μειχαηλ, 4317
Μιχαηλ (*Who is like God?* cf. מִיכָיָהוּ, and As. proper names, as *Mannu-kî-Rammân*, 'Who is like Rammân?' *Mannu-kî-ilu-rabu*, 'Who is like the great God?' Dl$^{\text{Prol. 210; HWB 419}}$; Schr$^{\text{COT 478}}$; cf. Cook$^{\text{Aram. Gloss. 74}}$):—**1.** Nu 13^{13} (P). **2.** 1 Ch 5^{13}. **3.** 5^{14}. **4.** 6^{25}. **5.** 7^{3}. **6.** 8^{16}. **7.** 12^{21}. **8.** 27^{18}. **9.** 2 Ch 21^{2}. **10.** Ezr 8^{8}. **11.** the 'prince,' or patron-angel, of Israel, Dn $10^{13.21}$ 12^{1} (cf. Jude^{9} Rev 12^{7}; Levy$^{\text{NHWB iii. 100}}$).

†מִיכָיָהוּ **n.pr.** (*Who is like Yah?* cf. 4322
מִיכָאֵל):—**1. m.** a prince under Jehosh. 2 Ch 17^{7}. **2. f.** 2 Ch 13^{2} f. l. for מַעֲכָה **2 b**, q. v. Of this name, the following are abbreviated, or softened, forms—

†מִיכָיְהוּ **n.pr.m.** (so on an Isr. scarab, 4321
Ganneau$^{\text{JAS 1883, 156, No. 42}}$)—**1.** an Ephraimite, Ju $17^{1.4}$ (in $17^{5\,ff.}$ $18^{2\,ff.}$ called מִיכָה). **2.** a prophet, the son of Imlah (𝔊 Μειχαίας), 1 K 22^{8-26} (9 t.),
‖ 2 Ch 18^{7-25} (7 t.) + v^{8} Qr (Kt מיכהו). **3.** a con- 4319
temp. of Jer., Je 36^{11} (מִכָיְהוּ), v^{13}.

†מִיכָיָה **n.pr.m.** **1.** the canon. prophet, 4320
Micah, Je 26^{18} Kt (Qr מִיכָה, as Mi 1^{1}). **2.** Ne 12^{35} (called מִיכָא, $11^{17.22}$). **3.** Ne 12^{41}. **4.** 2 K 22^{12} (‖ 2 Ch 34^{20} מִיכָה).

†מִיכָה **n.pr.m.** **1.** Micha, the Ephraimite 4318
(𝔊 Μειχαίας), Ju $17^{5.8.9.10.12.12.13}$ $18^{2\,ff.}$ (12 t.), called מִיכָיְהוּ $17^{1.4}$. **2.** the prophet Micah (𝔊 Μειχαίας), Mi 1^{1} (Je 26^{18} Kt מִיכָיָה). **3.** 1 Ch 5^{5}. **4.** son of Meribbaal (Mephibosheth) $8^{34\,f.}$ (𝔊 Μιχια), $9^{40\,f.}$ (𝔊 Μειχα), called מִיכָא 2 S 9^{12}. **5.** 23^{20} (𝔊 Μειχας), $24^{24.25}$ (𝔊 Μειχα). **6.** 2 Ch 18^{14} (= מִיכָיְהוּ **2**). **7.** 34^{20} (‖ 2 K 22^{12} מִיכָיָה).

†מִיכָא **n.pr.m.** (so in Palm., Vog$^{\text{No. 36a}}$). 4316
1. son of Mephibosheth (𝔊 Μειχα), 2 S 9^{12} (= מִיכָה **4**). **2.** Ne 10^{12}. **3.** Ne 11^{17} (= 1 Ch 9^{15}), v^{22} (called מִיכָיָה 12^{35}).

†מִישָׁאֵל **n.pr.m.** (*Who is what God is?* 4332
Ass. form., cf. מְתוּשָׁאֵל: note also in Thothmes' list of towns *Ba-ti-ša-'-ra*, i.e. prob. בֵּיתְשָׁאֵל, Heb. בֵּיתְאֵל WMM$^{\text{As. Eur. 193}}$):—**1.** a cousin of Moses Ex 6^{22} Lv 10^{4} (P). **2.** one of Daniel's companions Dn $1^{6.7.11.19}$ + 2^{17} (Aram.), elsewhere in c. 2–3 called מֵישַׁךְ (1^{7}). **3.** Ne 8^{4}.

†מֵידְבָא **n.pr.loc.** city in Moab (MI^{8} 4311
מהדבה)—Nu 21^{30} Is 15^{2}; Jos $13^{9.16}$ assigned to

Reuben (𝔊 Δαιδαβαν, Μαιδαβα, 𝔊L Μεδαβα); 1 Ch 19[7] meeting-place of Ammonites (𝔊 Μαιθαβα, A 𝔊L Μηδαβα).

4312 **מֵידָד** v. II. ידד. p. 392

4129 **מירע** Kt Ru 2[1] v. מודע sub ידע. p. 396

4220 **מֵיחִים** v. מֵחַ sub מחח. p. 562

4315 **[מֵיטָב]** v. יטב. p. 406

4316, 4318, 4320-21 **מִיכָא, מִיכָה, מִיכָיָה, מִיכָיְהוּ** v. מִי. p. 567

4317 **מִיכָאֵל** v. מִי. p. 567

4323 †**[מִיכָל]** **n.[m.] brook, stream**(?) (dubious word, cf. Dr[ad loc.] HPS), cstr. מִיכַל הַמָּיִם 2 S 17[20].

4324 †**מִיכַל** **n.pr.f.** (acc. to Ol[§ 277 f.], contr. from מִיכָאֵל):—younger daughter of Saul, wife of David (𝔊 Μελχολ), 1 S 14[49] 18[20.27.28] 19[11.12.13.17.17] 25[44] 2 S 3[13.14] 6[16] = 1 Ch 15[29], 2 S 6[20.21.23]; also 21[8] (𝔊 Μιχολ), but err. for מֵרַב (𝔊L Μεροβ).

4325 **מַיִם** v. מַי. p. 565

4326, 4509 †**מִיָּמִן, מִיָּמִין, מִנְיָמִן, מִנְיָמִין** **n.pr.m.** **1.** priestly name: **a.** מִיָּמִן assigned to David's time, 1 Ch 24[9]. **b.** Neh.'s time Ne 10[8]=מִנְיָמִין 12[17.41]. **c.** מִנְיָמִן assigned to Hezekiah's time 2 Ch 31[15]. **d.** מִיָּמִין went up with Zerub. Ne 12[5]. **2.** one of those who took strange wives Ezr 10[25].—𝔊 Βενιαμειν and (esp. A𝔊L) Μιαμειν.

מון, מין (√ of foll.; dubious; Fl in Levy NHWB[iii. 310], comp. Ar. مَانَ (med. *i*) *split* the earth (in ploughing), cf. Dr[Dt 14, 13]).

4327 †**[מִין]** **n.[m.] kind, species** (NH *id.* (Ecclus 43[25] *id.*), also *schismatic, heretic;* Jewish-Aram. מִינָא, *species,* so Syr. (Edessa) ܡܙܢܐ; Palest. Syr. = *nation* PS[2094] Schwally[Idioticon 50]; yet not Aram. loan-wd. in Heb.; v. Lag[BN 183 f.]);—alw. sf. + prep. לְמִינֵהוּ Gn 1[12.12] + 2 t.; לְמִינוֹ Gn 1[11] (om. 𝔊) + 3 t.; לְמִינָהּ Gn 1[24.24] + 9 t.; לְמִינֵהֶם Ez 47[10] (**del.** Co); לְמִינֵהֶם Gn 1[21];—*kind, species,* of plant Gn 1[11.12.12]; usu. of animal (beast, bird, fish, insect) Gn 1[21.22.24.24.25.25.25] 6[20.20.20] 7[14.14.14.14]; Lv 11[14.15.16.19.22.22.22.22.29] (all P); also Dt 14[13.14.15.18] (cf. Lv) Ez 47[10] (on text, cf. Co).

8544 †**תְּמוּנָה** **n.f. likeness, form**;—ת׳ Ex 20[4] + 4 t.; cstr. תְּמוּנַת (תְּמֻנַת) Dt 4[16] + 3 t.; sf. תְּמוּנָתֶךָ ψ 17[15];—*likeness, representation* (‖ פֶּסֶל) Ex 20[4] = Dt 5[8], cf. 4[16.23.25]; *form, semblance* of י׳ Nu 12[8] ψ 17[15], cf. Dt 4[12] (vid. Dr), v[15]; of nocturnal apparition Jb 4[16].

מֵינֶקֶת v. ינק **Hiph.** p. 413 3243

מיסך v. [מוּסָךְ] sub סכך. p. 697 4329

מֵיפַעַת, מֵפַעַת, מופעת v. יפע. p. 422 4158

†**[מִיץ]** (√ of foll. = *press, squeeze,* cf. NH *id., press, suck;* Ar. مَاصَ (med. ו) is *wash gently, rub* with the hand).

†**מֵץ** **n.m. squeezer,** i. e. **extortioner, oppressor,** only הַמֵּץ Is 16[4]. 4160

†**מִיץ** **n.m. squeezing, pressing, wringing** (3 t.) מִיץ חָלָב יוֹצִיא חֶמְאָה וּמ׳־אַף יוֹצִיא דָם וּמ׳ אַפַּיִם יוֹצִיא רִיב׃ Pr 30[33] *the squeezing of milk produceth curd* (v. Thomson[Land and Book, Centr. Pal. 456] Rob[BR i. 485; ii. 418]), *and the squeezing of the nose produceth blood,* and (so) *the squeezing of anger* (i. e. pressure, insistence) *produceth strife.* 4330

מִישׁ v. מוּשׁ. p. 559 4185

†**מֵישָׁא** **n.pr.m.** of Benjamite in Moab 1 Ch 8[9]. 𝔊 Μισα; A Μωσα. 4331

מִישָׁאֵל v. מִי. p. 567 4332

מִישׁוֹר, [מֵישָׁר], מֵישָׁרִים v. ישר.

†**מֵישַׁךְ** **n.pr.m.** (acc. to Dl[Baer, Dan. xi] for *Mî-sha-aku* 'who is what Aku (the moon-god) is?' cf. מִישָׁאֵל, p. 567);—the new (Bab.) name given to Mishael, Dn 1[7] (+ Aram. 2[49] and c. 3). 4335

מֵישַׁע, מֵישָׁע v. ישע. **[מֵיתָר]** v. יתר. p. 448, 452 4337-38, 4340

מַכְאוֹב v. כאב. **מַכְבִּיר** v. I. כבר **Hiph.** p. 456, 460 4341-42

מַכְבֵּנָה, מַכְבַּנַּי v. כבן. p. 460 4343

מִכְבָּר, מַכְבֵּר v. II. כבר. p. 460 4345-46

מַכָּה v. נכה. **מִכְוָה** v. כוה. p. 646 4347-48

מָכוֹן, מְכוֹנָה v. כון. p. 467 4349-50

[מְכֹרָה, מְכוּרָה] v. II. כור. p. 468 4351

†**מָכִי** **n.pr.m.** a Gadite Nu 13[15]. 𝔊 Μα(κ)χι. 4352

†**[מָכַךְ]** **vb. be low, humiliated** (Aram. מְכַךְ, ܡܟ; Ar. مَكَّ is *suck entirely out, diminish, consume*)—**Qal** *Impf.* וַיָּמֹכּוּ ψ 106[43] of perverse Isr. **Niph.** *Impf.* יִמַּךְ Ec 10[18] *sink* (in decay) of house-timbers. **Hoph.** *Pf.* וְהֻמְּכוּ Jb 24[24] *be brought low,* of wicked. 4355

4356-57 I. מִכְלָה v. כלא. II. [מִכְלָה] v. כלח. p. 476, 479

4358-60 מִכְלוֹל, מִכְלָל, [מַכְלֻל] v. כלל. p. 483

4361-62 מַכֹּלֶת v. אכל. [מִכְמָן], מִכְמַנֵּי v. כמן. p. 38, 485

4363 מִכְמָשׂ, מִכְמָס v. כמס. p. 485

4364-65 מִכְמָר, [מַכְמֹר], [מִכְמֶרֶת], מִכְמֹרֶת v. III. כמר. p. 485

4366 מִכְמְתָת v. כמת. p. 485

4367 †מַכְנַדְבַי **n.pr.m.** one of those who had taken strange wives Ezr 10^{40} (Gray Expos. Times, Feb. 1899, p. 233 prop. מכרנבו = *possession of Nebo*); 𝔊 Μαχαδναβου, A Μαχναδααβου; 𝔊L Ναδαβου.

4368 †מְכֹנָה **n.pr.loc.** in Judah Ne 11^{28}. 𝔊L Μαμη.—
4350 מְכֹנָה = מְכוֹנָה v. כון. p. 467

4370 [מִכְנָס], מִכְנְסֵי v. כנס. p. 488

4371, 4373 מֶכֶס, [מִכְסָה] v. כסס. p. 493

4372, 4374 מִכְסֶה, מְכַסֶּה v. I. כסה. p. 492

4375 מַכְפֵּלָה v. כפל. p. 495

4376 †מָכַר **vb. sell** (NH *id.*; Ph. מכר; Zinj. מכרו *price*, DHM Sendsch. 60; Aram. מְכַר, ܡܟܰܪ *marry* (i.e. *buy* as a wife); cf. As. *makkûru, namkur(r)u, nakkuru, possession, property*, Dl HWB 408);—**Qal** *Pf.* מ׳ Lv 27^{20} + 2 t.; sf. מְכָרוֹ Ex 21^{37} + 2 t.; 1 s. מָכַרְתִּי Is 50^{1} + 2 t., etc.; *Impf.* יִמְכֹּר Ex 21^{7} +, etc.; *Imv.* מִכְרָה Gn 25^{31}; fs. מִכְרִי 2 K 4^{7}; *Inf. abs.* מָכֹר Dt 14^{21} 21^{14}; *cstr.* מְכֹר Ne 10^{32}; sf. מָכְרָהּ Ex 21^{8}; מִכְרָם Am 2^{6} Ne 13^{15} (cf. Ba NB 104); *Pt.* מֹכֵר (מוֹכֵר) Lv 25^{16} + 3 t.; f. מֹכֶרֶת Na 3^{4}, etc.;—*sell* (c. בְּ *pret.* Am 2^{6} Jo 4^{3} ψ 44^{13}) sq. acc. e.g. land Gn $47^{20.22}$ (J), Lv 25^{14} (acc. cogn.), v^{25} (H; sq. מֵאֲחֻזָּתוֹ) cf. Ez 48^{14} (sq. מִן partit.), Lv 25^{15} (no obj. expr.), so v^{27}; 27^{20} (H), Ru 4^{3}; house Lv 25^{29} (H); beast Ex $21^{35.37}$ (E); flesh Dt 14^{21} (no obj.); crop Lv 25^{16} (H); food Ne 10^{32} $13^{15.16}$, cf. v^{20} (sq. מִמְכָּר); oil 2 K 4^{7}; linen Pr 31^{24}; birthright Gn $25^{31.33}$ (J); most oft. human beings, e.g. as slaves Gn $37^{27.28.36}$ $45^{4.5}$ (all JE), Ex 21^{16} (E), Dt $21^{14.14}$ 24^{7}, cf. Am 2^{6} Ne 5^{8} Zc 11^{5} Jo $4^{3.6.7.8.8}$; esp. daughters Ex $21^{7.8}$ (E); in marriage Gn 31^{15} (E); *Pt.* = *seller* Is 24^{2} Ez $7^{12.13}$; fig., obj. truth Pr 23^{23}; of Nineveh, selling nations גּוֹיִם Na 3^{4}; esp. י׳ selling his people (to enemies), i.e. giving it entirely into their power: Dt 32^{30} ψ 44^{13} Is 50^{1}, also (מ׳ בְּיַד) Ju 2^{14} 3^{8} 4^{2} 10^{7} 1 S 12^{9}; cf. Ju 4^{9} (Sisera to woman); also Ez 30^{12} (del. Co after B al.) **Niph.** *Pf.* נִמְכַּר Lv 25^{48} | 5 t., etc.; *Impf* יִמָּכֵר Lv 25^{34} + 3 t., etc.; *Inf.* הִמָּכְרוֹ Lv 25^{50}; *Pt.* pl. נִמְכָּרִים Ne 5^{8};—*be sold*, of land Lv $25^{23.34}$; beast Lv 27^{27}; cf. v^{28} (all P); of human beings as slaves Ex 22^{2} for (בְּ) theft (E), Lv 25^{42} (P), ψ 105^{17} Est 7^{4}; *sell oneself* Lv $25^{39.47.48.50}$ (PH), Dt 15^{12} Je 34^{14} Ne $5^{8.8}$; fig. of Isr., *sold* by י׳, Is 50^{1} for (בְּ) their sins, 52^{3}; cf. Est 7^{4} = *given over* to death. **Hithp.** *Pf.* הִתְמַכֵּר 1 K 21^{25}; וְהִתְמַכַּרְתֶּם consec. Dt 28^{68}; וַיִּתְמַכְּרוּ 2 K 17^{17}; *Inf.* הִתְמַכֶּרְךָ 1 K 21^{20}; *sell oneself* as slave Dt 28^{68}; fig. 1 K $21^{20.25}$ 2 K 17^{17}, all sq. לַעֲשׂוֹת הָרַע.

†מֶכֶר **n.m.** Pr 31, 10 **merchandise, value**;— 4377
מ׳ abs. Ne 13^{16}; מִכְרָהּ Pr 31^{10}; מִכְרָם Nu 20^{19}; prob. also מִמְכָּרָיו (rd. מִמְּכָרָיו) Dt 18^{8}, v. Di Dr;— **1.** *merchandise* Ne 13^{16}; *value, price*, of water Nu 20^{19} (JE), cf. Dt 18^{8} (v. supr.); of capable woman Pr 31^{10}.

†מָכִיר **n.pr.m.** 𝔊 Μαχειρ (Sab. מכר Hal[4]). 4353
1. eldest son of Manasseh;— Gn 50^{23} Nu $26^{29.29}$ 27^{1} $32^{39.40}$ 36^{1} Dt 3^{15} Jos $13^{31.31}$ $17^{1.3}$, cf. 1 Ch $1^{21.23}$ $7^{14.15.16.17}$; v. also Ju 5^{14} (poet.) where = Manasseh. **2.** son of ʿAmmiel 2 S $9^{4.5}$ 17^{27}.

†מָכִירִי **adj.gent.** only c. art. הַמּ׳ as subst. 4354
coll. *the Machirites* Nu 26^{29}.

†מִכְרִי **n.pr.m.** a Benjamite 1 Ch 9^{8}. 𝔊 4381
Μαχειρ; A Μοχορε; 𝔊L Μαχειρι.

†מִמְכָּר **n.m.** Lv 25, 28 **sale, ware**;—abs. מ׳ Lv 4465
25^{14} + 2 t.; cstr. מִמְכַּר Lv $25^{25.33}$; מִמְכָּרוֹ Lv 25^{27} + 3 t.; pl. sf. מִמְכָּרָיו Dt 18^{8} (but v. sub מֶכֶר);—*sale* Lv $25^{27.29.50}$; *thing sold* Lv 25^{14} (acc. cogn.), $v^{25.28}$ Ez 7^{13} Ne 13^{20}; מִמְכַּר בַּיִת Lv 25^{33} (Hex. only PH). On Dt 18^{8} v. מֶכֶר.

†מִמְכֶּרֶת **n.f. sale**;—cstr. יִמָּכְרוּ מִמְכֶּרֶת 4466
עָבֶד Lv 25^{42} (H).

[מַכָּר] v. נכר. [מְכֵרָה] v. I. כרה. p. 500, 648 4378-79

[מְכֻרָה], [מְכֹרָה] v. II. כור. p. 468 4351, 4380

†מְכֵרָתִי **adj.gent.** 1 Ch 11^{36}. 𝔊 Μοχορ, 4382
𝔊L ὁ Μεχωραθι.

מִכְשׁוֹל, מִכְשֹׁל, מַכְשֵׁלָה v. כשל. p. 506 4383-84

מִכְתָּב v. כתב [מִכְתָּה] v. כתת. p. 508, 510 4385-86

מִכְתָּם v. II. כתם. מַכְתֵּשׁ v. כתשׁ. p. 508-09 4387-89

מָלֵא 249 **vb. be full, fill** (NH *id.* (Pi. trans.); 4390
Zinj. מלא (Pi. trans.) DHM Sendsch. 60; As. *malû*

(trans. and intrans.) Dl $^{HWB\ 409}$; Ar. مَلَأَ (trans.) مَلُؤَ, مَلِئَ (intrans.); Eth. መልአ: (trans. and intrans.); Aram. ܡܠܐ (trans.), מְלָא (intrans. and trans.), Palm. n.pr. מלא = *plenitude*, Vog $^{Palm\ 7,2\ al.}$; Sab. מלא Os ^{14} Levy-Os $^{ZMG\ xix.\ 1865,\ 211\ f.}$ DHM $^{ZMG\ xxix.\ 1875,\ 595}$);—**Qal** $_{99}$ *Pf.* מ׳ Ex 40^{34}+; sf. מְלָאוֹ Est 7^{5}; מָלֵאתָ Jb 36^{17}; מָלֵאתִי Mi 3^{8} Je 6^{11}; מָלֵתִי Jb 32^{18}; מָלְאוּ Gn 29^{21}+; מָלוּ Ez 28^{16} (מָלְאָתָ 𝔊 𝔖 Co); מָלְאוּ Is 1^{15}, etc.; *Impf.* 3 fs. sf. תִּמְלָאֵמוֹ Ex 15^{9}; יִמְלְאוּ Gn 50^{3}+2 t.; וַיִּמְלְאוּ Gn 25^{24} 50^{3}; *Imv.* מִלְאוּ Gn 1^{22}+5 t.; *Inf. cstr.* מְלֹאת (מְלֹאות) Lv 8^{33}+12 t.; *Pt.* מָלֵא Je 23^{24}; מְלֵאִים Is 6^{1}; (cf. also sub מָלֵא *adj.*);—**1.** *be full*, usu. c. acc. material: **a.** lit., subj. houses Ex 8^{17} 10^{6} (both J) Ju 16^{27} Is 13^{21} 2 Ch 5^{13}, cf. Ez 10^{4} (del. Co); winepress Jo 4^{13}; threshing-floor Jo 2^{24}; vessel 2 K 4^{6} Jb 21^{24}, etc.; Jb 20^{22} מְלֹאות (cf. מְלֹא), i.e. *fulness, abundance.* **b.** fig., earth full of violence Gn 6^{13}, cf. Lv 19^{29} (both P), Mi 6^{12} Is 1^{15} Je 23^{10} 51^{5} ψ 26^{10} Ez 7$^{23.23}$ Ec 9^{3}, etc.; earth full of glory, mercy, goodness, knowledge, of י׳ ψ 33^{5} 119^{64} Is 11^{9} Hb 3^{3}; cf. also ψ 48^{11} 104^{24}, etc.; subj. נֶפֶשׁ = desire be satisfied (full) c. sf. Ex 15^{9}; וְדִין רָשָׁע מ׳ Jb 36^{17} *and of judgment on the wicked art thou full* (hast thou thy fill), cf. Di Du; מָלֵא לֵב לַעֲשׂוֹת רָע Ec 8^{11}; esp. of days, years, *be full, accomplished, ended*, Gn 25^{24} 29^{21} 50$^{3.3}$ (JE); Lv 8^{33} 12$^{4.6}$ 25^{30} Nu 6$^{5.13}$ (P); 1 S 18^{26} 2 S 7^{12}; Je 25^{12} 29^{10} La 4^{18} Ez 5^{2} 1 Ch 17^{11} Est 1^{5} 2^{12} Dn 10^{3}; cf. also with other subj. (lit.) Je 25^{34} Is 40^{2}. **2.** trans. *fill*, of populating sea and earth Gn 1$^{22.28}$ 9^{1} (all P); *consecrate* מִלְאוּ יֶדְכֶם ליהוה; (lit. fill the hand) Ex 32^{29} (cf. infr.); esp. of glory of י׳ filling tabern. and temple; Ex 40$^{34.35}$ (P) 1 K 8$^{10.11}$, cf. Is 6^{1}; v. also Je 23^{24}, esp. lit. Ez 10^{3} 43^{5} 44^{4} 2 Ch 5^{14} 7$^{1.2}$; sq. 2 acc. *fill* jars (with) water 1 K 18^{34}; abs. *overflow* מ׳ עַל־כָּל־גְּדוֹתָיו Jos 3^{15} (cf. 1 Ch 12^{16} **Pi.**); fig. *fill* land with sin Je 16^{18}, cf. 19^{4} Ez 8^{17} 28^{16}, cf. 30^{11}; מְלָאוֹ לִבּוֹ לַעֲשׂוֹת־כֵּן Est 7^{5} (cf. Ec 8^{11} supr.); מִלְאוּ הַשְּׁלָטִים Je 51^{11} meaning obscure, v. [שֶׁלֶט]; Gie prop. מִרְטוּ הַשׁ׳ *polish.*

†**Niph.** *Pf.* נִמְלָא־ Ct 5^{2}; *Impf.* יִמָּלֵא 2 S 23^{7}+9 t.; וַיִּמָּלֵא Ex 7^{25}+5 t.; יִמָּלְאוּ Pr 3^{10}+2 t.; יִמָּלְאוּ Pr 24^{4}; יִמָּלְאוּן Ez 32^{6};—**1.** *be filled*, usu. c. acc. mat. (c. מִן of source Ec 1^{8}, cf. Ez 32^{6}; c. לְ Hb 2^{14}); land, with people Ex 1^{7}; cf. 2 K 3$^{17.20}$ Is 2$^{7.7.8}$; house with smoke Is 6^{4}, cf. Ez 10^{4}; v. also Pr 3^{10} 24^{4} Je 13$^{12.12}$ Zc 8^{5} Ct 5^{2} Ec 11^{3} 2 K 10^{21} Ez 32^{6}; =*be armed* 2 S 23^{7} (lit. *be filled* or *fill himself*, i.e. his hand, with weapon, cf. **Pi. 2**); *be satisfied*, subj. נֶפֶשׁ = appetite Ec 6^{7}; subj. אֹזֶן Ec 1^{8}; fig. earth filled with violence (cf. **Qal**) Gn 6^{11}, cf. Ez 9^{9} 23^{33}; with glory and knowledge of י׳ Nu 14^{21} Hb 2^{14} ψ 72^{19}; v. also 1 K 7^{14} ψ 71^{8} 126^{2} Est 3^{5} 5^{9} Pr 20^{17}; abs. Ez 26^{2} (but Co sub מָלֵא *adj.*, so 𝔊 𝔗) 27^{25}. **2.** *be accomplished, ended*, subj. days Ex 7^{25}; of an exchange, requital, Jb 15^{32}.

Pi. $_{112}$ *Pf.* מִלֵּא Ex 35^{35}+; מִלָּא Je 51^{34}; מִלֵּאתָ Dt 6^{11}+; מִלְאוּ Nu 32^{11}+, etc.; *Impf.* יְמַלֵּא Lv 8^{33}+; יְמַלֵּה* Jb 8^{21}; וַיְמַלְאוּ Gn 42^{25} Ex 39^{10}; יְמַלֵּאוּ Ez 7^{19}, etc.; *Imv.* מַלֵּא Gn 29^{27}+5 t.; מַלְאוּ Je 4^{5} Ez 9^{7}; *Inf. cstr.* מַלֵּא Ex 29^{29}+5 t.; מַלֹּאות (-את) Ex 31^{5}+5 t.; sf. מַלְּאָם Je 33^{5}; *Pt.* מְמַלֵּא Je 13^{13} 1 Ch 12^{15}; pl. מְמַלְאִים Is 65^{11} +2 t.;—**1.** *fill* (oft. c. 2 acc.; lit., c. בְּ 2 K 9^{24} Ezr 9^{11} Jb 40^{31}; c. מִן Je 51^{34} ψ 127^{5}): Gn 21^{19} 24^{16} 26^{15} 42^{25} 44^{1} Ex 2^{16} Dt 6^{11} Jos 9^{13} 1 K 18^{35} 20^{27} 2 K 3^{25} 23^{14} Is 23^{2} Jb 3^{15} 22^{18} Je 41^{9} Ez 3^{3} 7^{19} 9^{7} 10^{2} 24^{4} Na 2^{13} Hg 2^{7} ψ 129^{7} 2 Ch 16^{14}, etc. (indef. subj.); *fill* (cup) *with drink* for libation Is 65^{11}; fig. *fill with spirit* Ex 28^{3} 31^{3} 35^{31} cf. v.^{35}, ψ 107^{9} Is 33^{5} Je 15^{17}; fill (with blood) 2 K 21^{16}; with abominations Ezr 9^{11} (c. בְּ). **2.** special uses are: *satisfy* appetite Jb 38^{39} ψ 17^{14} Pr 6^{30} Jb 20^{23} Je 51^{14} (fig.); *take a handful of* מ׳ כַּפּוֹ מִן Lv 9^{17}; *grasp* מ׳ יָדוֹ בְּ 2 K 9^{24}, cf. (of laying arrow on bow) fig. מ׳ הַקֶּשֶׁת בְּאֶפְרַיִם Zc 9^{13}; *overflow* מְמַלֵּא עַל־כָּל־גְּדִיֹתָיו 1 Ch 12^{16} (cf. Jos 3^{15} **Qal**); *give in full* וַיְמַלְאוּם לַמֶּלֶךְ 1 S 18^{27} (rd. וַיְמַלְּאֵם A𝔊L 𝔙 We Dr Kit Bu); מִלֵּא יַד פ׳ fig. for *institute to a priestly office, consecrate* Ex 28^{41} 29$^{9.29.33.35}$ Lv 8^{33} 16^{32} 21^{10} Nu 3^{3} Ju 17$^{5.12}$ 1 K 13^{33} Ez 43^{26} (altar), 1 Ch 29^{5} 2 Ch 13^{9} 29^{31} (cf. As. *umallu ḳatu, confer upon*, Dl $^{HWB\ 409}$); מ׳ אַחֲרֵי *wholly follow* י׳ Nu 14^{24} 32$^{11.12}$ Dt 1^{36} Jos 14$^{8.9.14}$ 1 K 11^{6}; *fill in*, i.e. *set* precious stones Ex 28^{17} (מ׳ בּוֹ מִלֵּאת אֶבֶן) cf. 31^{5} 35^{33} 39^{10} (all P); etc. **3.** *fulfil, accomplish, complete*, obj. week, year, day, Gn 29$^{27.28}$ Ex 23^{26} Is 65^{20} Jb 39^{2} 2 Ch 36^{21} Dn 9^{2}; obj. word, promise, etc.; subj. י׳ 1 K 8$^{15.24}$ 2 Ch 6$^{4.15}$ ψ 20$^{5.6}$; subj. men 1 K 2^{27} Je 44^{25} 2 Ch 36^{21}. **4.** *confirm* words 1 K 1^{14}.

†**Pu.** *Pt. filled*, i.e. *set* with jewels מְמֻלָּאִים בַּתַּרְשִׁישׁ Ct 5^{14}.

†**Hithp.** *Impf.* עָלַי יִתְמַלָּאוּן Jb 16^{10}, *mass themselves* against me; perh. denom. fr. מְלֹא **2.**

†מָלֵא **adj.** full;—מ׳ Gn 23^{9}+15 t.; cstr. 4392
מְלֵא Je 6^{11}; f. מְלֵאָה Nu 7^{14}+20 t.; cstr. מְלֵאַתִי Is 1^{21} cf. Ges $^{§ 90. 3 a.}$; pl. מְלֵאִים Nu 7^{13}+18 t.;

f. מְלֵאוֹת (-את) Gn 41^{7} + 4 t.;—*full*, abs. of ears of corn Gn 41$^{7.22}$; of value, price, Gn 23^{9} 1 Ch 21$^{22.24}$; of wind (=strong) Je 4^{12} sq. acc. mat., bowls of fine flour (סֹלֶת) Nu 7$^{13.19.25.31.37.43.49.55.61.67.73.79}$; spoons of incense Nu 7$^{14.20.26.32.38.44.50.56.62.68.74.80.86}$; bowls of wine Je 35^{5}, cf. fig. ψ 75^{9}; houses, of contents Dt 6^{11} Ne 9^{25} cf. Pr 17^{1}; cage, of birds Je 5^{27} (in sim., v. infr.); cart, of sheaves Am 2^{13} (in sim.) 1 Ch 11^{13} 2 K 7^{15}; Ez 1^{18} 10^{12} 17^{3} 36^{38} 37^{1}; as pred., of storehouses ψ 144^{13}; cf. fig. of Naomi Ru 1^{21}; of sea Ec 1^{7}; with art., of *full vessel* 2 K 4^{4}; מְלֵאָה pregnant woman Ec 11^{5}; fig. *full* of blessing Dt 33^{23}; wisdom 34^{9}; justice Is 1^{21}; commotion 22^{2}; fury 51^{20}; lies, etc. Na 3^{1}; wisdom Ez 28^{12} (del. A B Co); only twice in cstr. before that with which a thing is filled Is 1^{21} מ׳ מִשְׁפָּט; Je 6^{11} מְלֵא יָמִים (as subst.); as subst. in genit. (Ges §128 n) ψ 73^{10} מֵי מָלֵא; as adv.=*fully* Na 1^{10} Je 12^{6} (loudly, cf. 4^{5}).

4393 †מְלֹא, [מְלוֹא] **n.m.**$^{Is\ 31,4}$ **fulness, that which fills** (Ar. مِلْءٌ Lane^{2729});—מ׳ cstr. Gn 48^{19} + 19 t.; מְלוֹ Ez 41^{8}; sf. מְלוֹאוֹ Is 42^{10} + 3 t.; מְלֹאָהּ Dt 33^{16} + 12 t.;—**1.** *fulness* of hand (=handful) Ec 4$^{6.6}$ sq. acc. mat. מ׳ חָפְנֵיכֶם פִּיחַ Ex 9^{8} cf. Lv 16^{12} 1 K 17^{12}; so homer-full of manna; Ex 16^{33} cf. Lv 16^{12} Nu 22^{18} 24^{13} Ju 6^{38}; simil. מְלֹא בִגְדוֹ 2 K 4^{39}; rarely sq. מִן Lv 2^{2} 5^{12}, cf. Ex 16^{32} (but rd. perh. מְלָאוֹ so 𝔊 Sam. v. Di). **2.** *mass* of shepherds Is 31^{4} (in sim.); *multitude* of nations Gn 48^{19} (cf. Ar. مَلَأٌ Qor 2^{247} al.) **3.** *fulness* =*that which fills, entire contents*, of אֶרֶץ Dt 33^{16} ψ 24^{1} Is 6^{3} 8^{8} 34^{1} Mi 1^{2} Je 8^{16} 47^{2} Ez 12^{19} 19^{7} 30^{12} 32^{15}; תֵּבֵל ψ 50^{12} 89^{12}; יָם Is 42^{10} 1 Ch 16^{32} ψ 96^{11} 98^{7}; עִיר Am 6^{8}. **4.** phrases:—מ׳ קוֹמָתוֹ =*at full length* 1 S 28^{20}; *full line*, or portion מ׳ הַחֶבֶל 2 S 8^{2}; מ׳ הַקָּנֶה Ez 41^{8} *full rod* (reed).

4395 †מְלֵאָה **n.f. fulness, full produce**;—מ׳ Nu 18^{27} Dt 22^{9}; מְלֵאָתְךָ Ex 22^{28}; =*full produce* of field Ex 22^{28}, מ׳ הַזֶּרַע *the full produce of the seed* Dt 22^{9}; of winepress Nu 18^{27}.

4396 †[מִלֻּאָה] **n.f. setting** of jewel (cf. **vb. Pi. 2, Pu.**);—cstr. מִלֻּאַת Ex 28^{17} מ׳ אֶבֶן (as acc. cogn. with מִלֵּא); cf. sf. מִלּוּאֹתָם (מִלֻּא׳) Ex 28^{20} 39^{13}.

4394 †[מִלֻּא, מִלּוּא] **n.m. setting, installation**; (cf. **vb. Pi. Pu.**);—pl. מִלֻּאִים (מִלּוּ׳) Ex 25^{7} + 13 t.; מִלֻּאֵיכֶם Lv 8^{33};—**1.** *setting*, אַבְנֵי מ׳ *stones for setting* Ex 25^{7} 35$^{9.27}$ cf. 1 Ch 29^{2} (אַבְנֵי שֹׁהַם וּמ׳). **2.** installation (of priests): Lv 7^{37} 8^{33}; =installation-offering 8^{28} (|| אִשֶּׁה) cf. סַל־הַמּ׳ v^{31}; אֵיל הַמּ׳ Ex 29$^{22.26.27.31}$ Lv 8$^{22.29}$; בְּשַׂר הַמּ׳ Ex 29^{34}.

†מִלּוֹא **n. pr. loc.** (Thes '*fill*' of earth, 4407
earthwork, but v. GFM$^{Ju\ 9,6}$);—**1.** בֵּית מִלּוֹא Ju 9^{6} 1037
(|| בַּעֲלֵי שְׁכֶם) so v$^{20.20}$; near Shechem, site unknown; 𝔊 οἶκος Βηθμααλων. **2.** citadel in Jerus. הַמִּלּוֹא 2 S 5^{9} 1 K 9$^{15.24}$ 11^{27} 1 Ch 11^{8} 2 Ch 32^{5}. 𝔊 usu. ἡ ἄκρα (A 1 K 9$^{15.24}$ also Μελω).
3. בֵּית מִלֹּא 2 K 12^{21} (+ הַיֹּרֵד סִלָּא) dub.; = **2**? 1037
𝔊 οἴκῳ Μααλω.

†מִלֵּאת **n.f.** dub.: only יֹשְׁבוֹת עַל־מ׳ Ct 5^{12} 4402
of lover's eyes; AE De Bae^{Kau} **setting**, perh. better **border, rim**, Öt Wild *fulness, abundance*, of surrounding of eye.

†יִמְלָה, יִמְלָא **n.pr.m.** father of prophet 3229
Micaiah of Isr.:—יִמְלָה 1 K 22$^{8.9}$ 𝔊 Ιεμια, 𝔊L Ναμαλι; = יִמְלָא 2 Ch 18$^{7.8}$. 𝔊 Ιεμαα, A Ιεμλα, 𝔊L Ναμαλι.

מַלְאָךְ, מְלָאכָה, [מַלְאֲכוּת], מַלְאָכִי v. לאך. p. 521-22 4397, 4399-401

מַלְבֵּד v. II. בַּד. מַלְבּוּשׁ v. לבשׁ. p. 94, 528 905, 4403

מַלְבֵּן v. לבן. מִלָּה v. I. מלל. p. 527, 576 4404-05

מִלּוֹ v. מְלֹא. מְלוּנָה, מָלוֹן v. לון. above, p. 533-34 4393, 4411-12

מַלּוֹתִי **n. pr.** v. I. מלל. p. 576 4413

†I. [מָלַח] **vb. tear away,** fig. **dissipate** 4414
(cf. Ar. مَلَخَ *pull out* eye, tooth, &c.; esp. Dozy *tear off branch* to plant it, &c. so Eth. መለኀ: *evellere*);—**Niph.** fig. *be dispersed in fragments, dissipated, Pf.* שָׁמַיִם כֶּעָשָׁן נִמְלָחוּ Is 51^{6}.

†I. [מֶלַח or מָלַח] **n.[m.] rag**; only pl. 4418
מְלָחִים Je 38$^{11.12}$ (|| סְחָבוֹת).

II. מלח (√ of foll.; meaning dubious).

†II. מֶלַח **n.m. salt** (NH *id.*; Ar. مِلْحٌ; 4417
Aram. מִלְחָא, ܡܠܚܐ);—מ׳ abs. Gn 19^{26} +; cstr. Lv 2^{13};—*salt* for seasoning food Jb 6^{6}; offering Lv 2$^{13.13.13}$ cf. Ez 43^{24}; בְּרִית מֶלַח Nu 18^{19} 2 Ch 13^{5} (cf. Lv 2^{13} v. Di); used in purifying waters 2 K 2$^{20.21}$; strewn on site of devoted city Ju 9^{45} cf. Zp 2^{9} (מִכְרֵה־מ׳) Dt 29^{22} (|| גָּפְרִית); produced in marshes reserved for purpose Ez 47^{11}; pillar of salt נְצִיב מ׳ Gn 19^{26}; usu. in combin. יָם(־) הַמֶּלַח Gn 14^{3} (עֵמֶק הַשִּׂדִּים), Nu 34$^{3.12}$ Dt 3^{17}

(‖ יָם הָעֲרָבָה), Jos 3^{16} 12^{3} 15$^{2.5}$ 18^{19}; also גֵּיא־מ׳ 2 S 8^{13} 2 K 14^{7} Qr, ψ 60^{2} (title), גֵּיא הַמּ׳ 1 Ch 18^{12} 2 Ch 25^{11} 2 K 14^{7} Kt.

4414 †III. [מָלַח] **vb. denom.** salt, season; **Qal** *Impf.* 2 ms. תִּמְלָח sq. acc. Lv 2^{13} (obj. offering). **Pu.** *Pt.* מְמֻלָּח Ex 30^{35} *salted*, i.e. the incense (v. Di.) **Hoph.** *Pf.* 2 fs. + *Inf. abs.* הָמְלֵחַ לֹא הֻמְלַחַתְּ Ez 16^{4}, i.e. *rubbed* or *washed with salt* (of infant, in personification).

4420 †מְלֵחָה **n.f.** saltness, barrenness;—Jb 39^{6} (‖ עֲרָבָה) as dwelling-place of wild ass, *salt-plain;* אֶרֶץ מְלֵחָה Je 17^{6} (‖ לֹא תֵשֵׁב); ψ 107^{34} (opp. אֶרֶץ פְּרִי).

4408 †מַלּוּחַ **n.[m.]** mallow; plant growing in salt-marsh; Jb 30^{4} (cf. Now$^{Arch. i. 67, 112}$).

4419 †[מַלָּח] **n.m.** mariner (loan-word from As. *malaḫu* Dl$^{HWB 412}$ cf. Id$^{Prol. 178}$; Hal$^{ZA iv. 1889, 53}$; so also Aram. ܡܠܚܐ (v. Brock.), whence Ar. مَلَّاحٌ Frä^{221});—pl. מַלָּחִים Jon 1^{5} Ez 27^{29}; מַלָּחַיִךְ Ez 27^{27}; מַלָּחֵיהֶם v^{9} (Ba$^{NB 49 Anm. 3}$);—*mariners, sailors* of ship going to Tarshish Jon 1^{5} (cf. רַב הַחֹבֵל v^{6}); to Tyre Ez 27^{9}, cf. v$^{27.29}$ (‖ חֹבְלִים).

4421 מִלְחָמָה v. I. לחם. p. 536

4422 †[מָלַט] **vb.** slip away (not in **Qal**) (NH מִילּוּט *rescue;* 𝔗 מְלַט (rare) = BH; Ar. مَلِطَ is *have scanty hair;* IV. *cast the foetus without hair;* [*slip away, escape* fr. hand is مَلِصَ]);—**Niph.** *Pf.* 3 ms. נִמְלַט Ju 3^{26} + 6 t.; 3 fs. נִמְלְטָה ψ 124^{7}, with וְ cons. וְנִמְלָ֑טָה Je 48^{19}; 3 mpl. נִמְלָ֑טוּ 2 S 4^{6} + 8 t. Pf.; *Impf.* יִמָּלֵט Am 9^{1} + 13 t.; וַיִּמּ׳ Ju 3^{26} + 7 t.; 1 s. אִמָּלְטָה Gn 19^{20} +; 3 mpl. וַיִּמָּלֵ֑טוּ Mal 3^{15} + 12 t. Impf.; *Imv.* הִמָּלֵט Gn 19$^{17.17.22}$; f. הִמָּלְטִי Zc 2^{11}; *Inf. abs.* הִמָּלֵט 1 S 27^{1} (but rd. אִם אִמָּלֵט 𝔊 We Dr Löhr HPS; > Th Kit Bu ins. אִם bef. הִמּ׳); cstr. *id.*, Gn 19^{19} Est 4^{3}; *Pt.* נִמְלָט 1 K 19$^{17.17}$;—**1.** *slip away* אִמָּלְטָה נָּא וְאֶרְאֶה אֶת־אֶחָי 1 S 20^{29} *let me slip away to see my brethren; slip through,* or *past* (into the house) 2 S 4^{6} (cf. Dr HPS and **Pi. 1, Hiph. 2**; > Klo *נִלְאָטוּ, √לאט, after 𝔊 ἔλαβον). **2.** *escape,* Ju 3^{29} 1 S 19^{10} (‖ נוּס), v$^{12.18}$ (both ‖ בָּרַח), v^{17} 22^{20} (‖ בָּרַח), 30^{17} 1 K 18^{40} 20^{20} (‖ נוּס), 2 K 10^{24} Is 20^{6} (‖ נוּס, נִצַּל), 49$^{24.25}$ Je 46^{6} 48$^{8.19}$ (‖ נוּס), Ez 17$^{15.15.18}$ Am 9^{1} Jo 3^{5} Zc 2^{11} Mal 3^{15} ψ 124^{7} Pr 19^{5} Jb 1$^{15.16.17.19}$; c. מִן of place whence 1 S 23^{13} 2 S 1^{3} ψ 124^{7}; c. אֶל־ = whither 1 S 22^{1} 27$^{1.1}$; c. עַד Ju 3^{26}; c. ־ָה loc., Gn 19$^{17.19.20.22}$ (J), Ju 3^{26}; c. acc. 2 K 19^{37} = Is 37^{38}, Est 4^{13}; c. מִן of person fr. whom Ec 7^{26}; c. מִיַּד 1 S 27^{1} 2 Ch 16^{7} Je 32^{4} 34^{3} 38$^{18.23}$ Dn 11^{41}; מִפְּנֵי Je 41^{15}; מֵחֶרֶב 1 K 19$^{17.17}$; c. עַל־נֶפֶשׁ *for one's life* Gn 19^{17}. **3.** pass. *be delivered* ψ 22^{6} Pr 11^{21} 28^{26} Jb 22^{30} Dn 12^{1} (later usage). **Pi.** *Pf.* 3 ms. מִלֵּט Ez 33^{5}; וּמִלַּט־ Ec 9^{15}; sf. מִלְּטָ֑נוּ 2 S 19^{10}; *Impf.* יְמַלֵּט Am 2^{14} + 8 t., sf. יְמַלְּטֵ֑הוּ ψ 41^{2}; + 5 t. Impf.; *Imv.* מַלְּטָה ψ 116^{4}; f. מַלְּטִי 1 K 1^{12}; + 4 t. Imv.; *Inf. abs.* מַלֵּט Is 46^{2} Je 39^{18}; *Pt.* מְמַלֵּט 1 S 19^{11}; pl. מְמַלְּטִים 2 S 19^{6};—**1.** *lay* (eggs; i.e. let them slip out; of arrow-snake) Is 34^{15}. **2.** *let escape:* וימלטו עצמתיו 2 K 23^{18} *and so they let his bones* (the prophet's) *escape* (from the burning). **3.** *deliver*, abs. Is 46^{4}; c. acc. Is 46^{2} Je 39$^{18.18}$ ψ 41^{2} Jb 22^{30} 29^{12} Ec 8^{8} 9^{15}; c. מִיַּד Jb 6^{23}; מִכַּף 2 S 19^{10}; מִשְּׁחִיתוֹתָם ψ 107^{20}; elsewh. מִלֵּט נֶפֶשׁ *deliver, save, life* 1 S 19^{11} 2 S 19^{6} 1 K 1^{12} Je 48^{6} 51$^{6.45}$ Ez 33^{5} Am 2$^{14.15}$ ψ 89^{49} 116^{4}; נפש om. Am 2^{15} ψ 33^{17} Jb 20^{20}.—(This form not in Hex., Ju., Ch., Is.^{1}) **Hiph.** *Pf.* 3 ms. הִמְלִיט Is 31^{5}; 3 fs. הִמְלִיטָה Is 66^{7}. **1.** *give birth to* a male child Is 66^{7} (‖ יָלְדָה, cf. **Pi. 1**). **2.** *deliver:* abs. Is 31^{5} (‖ הִצִּיל, גָּנַן, פָּסַח). **Hithp.** *Impf.* 1 s. וָאֶתְמַלְּטָה Jb 19^{20}; 3 mpl. יִתְמַלָּ֑טוּ Jb 41^{11}. **1.** *slip forth, escape* (sparks of fire from jaws of crocodile; RV *leap forth*) Jb 41^{11}. **2.** *escape* (with the skin of the teeth, the gums; only these left unattacked by leprosy) Jb 19^{20}.

†מֶלֶט **n.[m.]** mortar, cement (etym. dub.; 4423
Aram. ܡܠܛܐ *id.*, whence Ar. مِلَاطٌ Frä^{10});—Je 43^{9}.

†מְלַטְיָה **n.pr.m.** (*Yahweh delivered*, cf. 4424
Gray$^{Prop. N. 267, 293}$) a Gibeonite, a builder at the wall Ne 3^{7}; 𝔊L Μαλτιας.

מְלִיצָה v. ליץ. p. 539 4426

I. מלך (√of foll.; mng. dub.; Thes comp. Ar. مَلَكَ *possess, own exclusively*, cf. Eth. መለከ: so Bae$^{Rel. 144}$ (cf. בַּעַל), and Nö$^{ZMG xl. 1886, 727}$; Lyon$^{Bib. Sacr., Apr. 1884}$ Dl$^{Prol. 30}$ al. comp. As. *malâku*, *counsel, advise* Dl$^{HWB 412}$, BH and NH מְלַךְ, Aram. מְלַךְ, ܡܠܟ, whence king as orig. *counsellor*, he whose opinion is decisive).

I. מֶלֶךְ 2513 **n.m.** king (NH *id.;* MI$^{1.5.10.18.23}$ 4428
מלך; 1^{4} המלכן; Ph. מלך; Zinj. מלך DHM$^{Sendsch. 60}$;

As. *maliku, malku, prince* (As. *šarru—king*); Ar. مَلِك *king* (orig. Heb. *מַלִךְ inferred, Lag$^{BN 73}$ Ba$^{NB § 112}$ WMM$^{As. u. Europ. 76}$); Sab. מלכן Sab Denkm$^{No. 1}$; cstr. מלך, pl. אמלך CIS$^{iv. 37}$; cf. Eth. አምላክ: *God* (and Nö$^{l. c.}$); Aram. ܡܠܟܐ, מְלֵךְ; Palm. מלך מלכא Vog$^{No. 28}$; Nab. מלכא Eut$^{Nab. 1}$);—מ׳ abs. Gn 14^{7}+ (ins. also 2 S 13^{17} 𝔊 Th We Dr Kit Bu, and v^{34} 𝔊 We Dr Kit Bu); in p. alw. מֶלֶךְ
4429 Gn 49^{20}+238 t. (so also n. pr. in מֶלֶךְ-); cstr. Gn 14^{1}+; sf. מַלְכִּי 2 S 19^{44}+6 t., etc.; pl. מְלָכִים Gn 14^{9}+; מְלָכִין Pr 31^{3}; cstr. מַלְכֵי Gn 17^{16}+; sf. מְלָכֶיהָ Is 7^{16}+3 t.; מַלְכֵיהֶם Dt 7^{24}+16 t., etc.;—**1.** *king:* of Egypt Gn 39$^{20 f.}$ Ex 1$^{8 f.}$ Dt 11^{3} 1 K 3^{1}; of Mesopotamia, Shinar, Assyr., Babyl., Pers., etc. Ju 3$^{8.10}$ Gn 14$^{1 f.}$ 2 K 15$^{19.20.29}$ 17$^{3 f.}$ 18$^{13 f.}$ 24$^{1.11 f.}$ Ezr 1$^{1 f.}$ 4$^{3 f.}$ Est 1^{2}+, 1 K 11$^{18.40}$ 14^{25} 2 K 17$^{4 f.}$ 23^{29}+; of Canaan, Philist., Edom, Moab, etc. (often of single city): Gn 14$^{2 f.}$ v^{18} 20^{2} 26$^{1.8}$ 36^{31} Nu 20^{14} 21$^{1 f.}$ 22$^{4.10}$ Dt 1^{4} 3$^{1 f.}$ Jos 2^{2} (oft. in Jos), Ju 1^{7} 5^{19} 8$^{5.12}$ 11$^{12 f.}$ 2 K 3$^{4 f.}$+; of Aram, Hamath, etc. 2 S 8$^{3 f.}$ v^{9} 1 K 15^{18} 20$^{1 f.}$ 22^{3} 2 K 5$^{1 f.}$ 8$^{7 f.}$ v^{29} 9$^{14.15}$ 15^{37} 16$^{5 f.}$+; of Tyre, etc. 2 S 5^{11} 1 K 5^{15} 9^{11} 16+, etc.; esp. of Israel (undivided, and of both divisions) Gn 36^{31} Nu 23^{21} 24^{7} Dt 17$^{14 f.}$ Ju 17^{6} 18^{1} 19^{1} 21^{25} 1 S 2^{10} 8$^{5 f.}$ 2 S 2$^{4 f.}$ 1 K 1$^{33.34 f.}$ +very often; cf. also Ju 9^{5}.—2 S 18$^{29 b}$ del. הַמּ׳ We Klo Dr Kit Bu. Note that in early books המלך דוד is nearly always said; in late books usually דוד (שלמה וגו׳) המלך; cf. Aram. כּוֹרֶשׁ מַלְכָּא, etc. **2.** of Davidic king, as under divine protection, 1 S 2^{10} (|| מְשִׁיחוֹ), ψ 2^{6} 18^{51} 89^{19} 61^{7}, cf. 99^{4}; so in (Messianic) prediction Ho 3^{5} Is 32^{1} Je 23^{5} Ez 37$^{22.24}$ Zc 9^{9}. **3.** used of י׳ as king of Israel 1 S 12^{12}; poet. Dt 33^{5} cf. ψ 5^{3} 10^{16} 29^{10} 44^{5} 48^{3} 68^{25} 74^{12} 84^{4} 145^{1} 149^{2} Is 41^{21} 43^{15} 44^{6} Zp 3^{15}; מֶלֶךְ הַכָּבוֹד ψ 24$^{7.8.9.10.10}$; universal king ψ 47$^{3.8}$ 95^{3} 98^{6} Je 10$^{7.10}$, cf. 46^{18} 48^{15} 51^{57} Zc 14$^{9.16.17}$ Mal 1^{14}; of false god Am 5^{26}. **4.** in fable, king of trees Ju 9$^{8.15}$; fig. of crocodile Jb 41^{26}; מ׳ אֵין לָאַרְבֶּה Pr 30^{27}; of death, מֶלֶךְ בַּלָּהוֹת Jb 18^{14}. **5.** combinations are:—**a.** הַמּ׳ הַגָּדוֹל 2 K 18$^{19.28}$ = Is 36$^{4.13}$ (of Assyrian king: cf. As. *šarru rabu*); מ׳ גָּדוֹל Ec 9^{14} (indef.); of י׳ Mal 1^{14}, מ׳ ג׳ עַל־כל־אלהים ψ 95^{3}; מ׳ עוֹלָם Je 10^{10} (of י׳); מ׳ מְלָכִים Ez 26^{7} (king of Babyl.) **b.** יְחִי הַמֶּלֶךְ 1 S 10^{24} 2 S 16$^{16.16}$ 1 K 1$^{34.39}$ 2 K 11^{12} 2 Ch 23^{11}; מֶלֶךְ בירושלם Ec 1^{1}, cf. 15^{26} 2 S 5^{2} 1 K 14^{2} 1 Ch 29^{25} 2 S 2^{11} (היה מ׳ בחברון על־) 1 K 11^{37} 2 Ch 28^{4} Ec 1^{12}. **c.** following a verb (one or two acc.) שִׂים מ׳ עַל Dt 17$^{14.15.15}$ 1 S 10^{19}; שִׂים לָנוּ מ׳ 1 S 8^{5}; שִׂים לְמ׳ 1 K 10^{9}; נָתַן מ׳ לְ 1 S 8^{6} Ho 13$^{10.11}$; נָתַן עַל 1 S 12^{13} 2 Ch 2^{10} Ne 9^{37} 13^{26}; הִמְלִיךְ לְמֶלֶךְ Ju 9^{6} 1 S 15^{11}; הִמְלִיךְ מ׳ עַל 1 S 12^{1}; הִמְלִיךְ מ׳ לְ 1 S 8^{22}; מָשַׁח מ׳ עַל Ju 9^{8}; מָשַׁח לְמ׳ 1 K 1^{45}; מָשַׁח לְמ׳ עַל Ju 9^{15} 1 S 15$^{1.17}$ 2 S 2^{4} 5$^{3.12}$ 12^{7} 1 K 1^{34} 1 Ch 11^{3} 14^{8}; מ׳ יִהְיֶה עַל 1 S 8^{19}; בִּקֵּשׁ לְמ׳ עַל 2 S 3^{17}; הֵכִין לְמ׳ עַל 2 S 5^{12} 1 Ch 14^{2}; הֵקִים מ׳ עַל 1 K 14^{14} Dt 28^{36}; יָשַׁב עַל־כִּסֵּא י׳ לְמ׳ תַּחַת וגו׳ 1 Ch 29^{23}, cf. Pr 20^{8}; נָתַן עַל־כִּסֵּא לְמ׳ לי׳ אלהיך 2 Ch 9^{8}. **d.** מַעֲדַנֵּי־מֶלֶךְ Gn 49^{20} *royal dainties*, fig.; מִשְׁתֵּה הַמּ׳ 1 S 25^{36} *royal feast* (in sim.); אֶבֶן הַמּ׳ 2 S 14^{26} *king's weight*; יַד־הַמּ׳ 1 K 10^{13} *royal bounty* (in sim.); גִּזֵּי הַמּ׳ Am 7^{1} *king's mowings*; מִקְדַּשׁ מ׳ Am 7^{13} *royal sanctuary*; עֲטֶרֶת מַלְכָּם 2 S 12^{30} *crown of their king* = 1 Ch 20^{2} (but rd. מִלְכֹּם 𝔊 We Klo Dr Kit Kau—not Bu Kit$^{Chr. Hpt}$); cf. also בַּיִת, שָׁוֵה, בֵּן, עֵמֶק, etc.—N.pr. אחימלך, אבימלך, אלימלך, נתן מלך, עבד מלך, v. sub אח, אב, etc.

מַלְכָּה$_{35}$ **n.f.** queen:—abs. מ׳ Est 1^{9}+24 t. Est.; cstr. מַלְכַּת 1 K 10^{1}+7 t.; pl. מְלָכוֹת Ct 6$^{8.9}$;—*queen* of Sheba 1 K 10$^{1.4.10.13}$ = 2 Ch 9$^{1.3.9.12}$; of Persia, Vashti Est 1^{9}+7 t. Est 1; Esther Est 2^{22}+16 t. Est 4–9 (in Esther mostly appos. of n.pr.; it precedes n.pr. Est 1$^{12.15}$; follows n.pr. Est 1^{9}+17 t.); of Isr. queens only pl. and only Ct 6$^{8.9}$ (both || פִּילַגְשִׁים). Cf. גְּבִירָה. 4436

† מְלֶ֫כֶת n.f. queen (form difficult; cf. Ol § 147 d Kö$^{ii, 169 n.}$ Gie$^{Je 7, 18}$ Ba$^{NB 165, Anm. 2; ZMG xli. 1887, 606}$);—only cstr. מ׳ הַשָּׁמַיִם Je 7^{18}+4 t. Je = *queen of the heavens*, a goddess; identif. dub.; perhaps = Ištar, Venus, cf. Schr$^{infr.}$ al.; (> = מְלֶאכֶת (Codd.), cstr. of מְלָאכָה (v. לאך), *worship of the heavens* (Cast$^{Lex. Syr.}$), or creative *work of the heavens*, coll. = צְבָא הַשּׁ׳ *host of heaven*, Sta$^{infr.}$ (cf. 𝔊); v. Schr$^{COT Je 7, 18; SBAk 1886, 477 ff.; ZA iii. 1888, 353 ff., iv. 1889, 74 ff.}$ Sta$^{ZAW 1886, 123 ff. 289 ff.}$ Kue$^{Ges. Abh. 186 ff.}$ We$^{Skizzen iii. 38}$ Nö$^{ZMG xli. 1889, 710 f.}$ RS$^{Sem. i. 57, 172 (ed. 2, 57, 189)}$ Grünb$^{ZMG xlii. 1888, 45}$);—only as worshipped by people of Jerusalem לַעֲשׂוֹת כַּוָּנִים לְמ׳ הַשּׁ׳ Je 7^{18} (|| הַסֵּךְ נְסָכִים לֵאלֹהִים אֲחֵרִים); לְקַטֵּר לְמ׳ הַשּׁ׳ Je 44$^{17.18.19.25}$ (all || הַסֵּךְ לָהּ נְסָכִים). 4446

II. **מָלַךְ**$_{346}$ **vb. denom.** be, or become king, or queen, reign;—**Qal**$_{296}$ *Pf.* מ׳ Jos 13^{10}+, etc.; *Impf.* יִמְלֹךְ (-לוֹךְ) Ex 15^{18}+; וַיִּמְלֹךְ Gn 36^{32}+; 2 ms. תִּמְלֹךְ Gn 37^{8}+, (הֲתִמְלֹךְ Je 22^{15} Baer); *Imv.* מְלָךְ־ Ju 9^{14}; מָלְכָה Ju 9^{8}; מָלְכִי Ju 9$^{10.12}$; *Inf. abs.* מָלֹךְ Gn 37^{8} 1 S 24^{21}; *cstr.* 4427

מְלֹךְ 1 K 2^{15}+; sf. מָלְכוֹ 1 S 13^{1}+; *Pt.* מֹלֵךְ Je 22^{11}+2 t.; מֹלֶכֶת 2 K 11^{3}=2 Ch 22^{12};—*be* (become) *king, reign,* mostly of Hebrew kings, 2 S 2^{10} 1 K 16^{22} 2 K 3^{1} 9^{13}, but also gen. Pr 8^{15} 30^{22}; of Can., Edom., Aram., Assyr., Pers. kings, etc.: Ju 4^{2} Gn 36^{31} 1 K 11^{25} 2 K 8^{15} 19^{37} Est 1^{1}+; sq. בְּ loc. (usu. city) Jos $13^{10.12}$ Ju 4^{2} 2 S 5^{5} 1 K 11^{24} 14^{21}+oft.; but also Gn $36^{31.32}$ 1 Ch 1^{43} בְּארץ, and even בְּכֹל אֲשֶׁר־תְּאַוֶּה נַפְשֶׁךָ 2 S 3^{21}; sq. עַל c. people or land 1 S $8^{9.11}$ 12^{14} 13^{1} 1 K $15^{1.9}$ 16^{23}+oft.; sq. בְּ loc.+עַל territ. (or pop.) 2 S 5^{5} 1 K 11^{42}; sq. תַּחַת (תַּחְתָּיו) 2 S 16^{8} Gn $36^{33 f.}$=1 Ch $1^{44 f.}$, 1 K $14^{20.31}$ 2 K 8^{15} 13^{24} Je 22^{11}+oft.; †subj. God, sq. עַל ψ 47^{9} Mi 4^{7} Ez 20^{33} 1 S 8^{7}; sq. בְּ Is 24^{23}; abs. Ex 15^{18} Is 52^{7} ψ 93^{1} 96^{10}=1 Ch 16^{31}, 97^{1} 99^{1} 146^{10}†; subj. future (Mess.) king Is 32^{1} Je 23^{5}; †subj. a woman (=*be queen*) 2 K 11^{3}=2 Ch 22^{12} (both sq. עַל), Est 2^{4} sq. תַּחַת†; Imv. only in fable, king of trees, Ju $9^{8.10.12.14}$ all sq. עַל; בְּמָלְכוֹ esp.= *when he began to reign, became king* 1 S 13^{1} 2 S 2^{10} 1 K 14^{21}+oft.; Inf. also=*reign:* בִּשְׁנַת שְׁמֹנֶה לְמָלְכוֹ 2 K 24^{12} 25^{1}, cf. v^{27}; 1 K 6^{1} 2 Ch 16^{13} 17^{7} 29^{3} $34^{3.8}$, cf. עַד מְלֹךְ דָּוִד 1 Ch 4^{31}; עַד מְלֹךְ מַלְכוּת פָּרָס 2 Ch 36^{20}; *began to reign and reigned* מָלַךְ וַיִּמְלֹךְ 1 K 15^{25} 16^{29} 2 K 3^{1}+; oft. מָלַךְ alone with *same meaning* 1 K 16^{23} 2 K $13^{1.10}$ 14^{23}+. †**Hiph.** *Pf.* הִמְלִיךְ 1 S 15^{35}+2 t.; הִמְלַכְתָּ 1 K 3^{7}, etc.; Impf. וַיַּמְלֵךְ 2 K 33^{34}+4 t.; וַיַּמְלִיכוּ Ju 9^{6}+etc.; *Inf. cstr.* הַמְלִיךְ 1 K 12^{1}+etc.; *Pt.* מַמְלִיךְ Ez 17^{16};—*make king,* or *queen, cause to reign,* sq. acc. pers. Ju 9^{16} 1 S 11^{15} 1 K 1^{43} 12^{1} 16^{21} 2 K 10^{5} 11^{12} (anointing and coronation)=2 Ch 23^{11}, 2 K 17^{21} 1 Ch 11^{10} $12^{32.39}$ 2 Ch 10^{1} 11^{22} Ez 17^{16}; sq. לְשלמה (לְ of dir. obj., as Aram.) 1 Ch 29^{22}; sq. acc. cogn. 1 S 8^{22} (+לָהֶם), 12^{1} (+עַל), Is 7^{6} (+בְּתוֹךְ); sq. לְמֶלֶךְ Ju 9^{6} 1 S 15^{11}; sq. acc. pers.+בְּ loc. Je 37^{1}; +עַל Ju 9^{18} 1 S 15^{35} 1 K 12^{20} 16^{16} 2 K 8^{20} 1 Ch 12^{38} 28^{4} (acc. om.), 23^{1} 2 Ch $1^{9.11}$ 21^{8} $36^{4.10}$, cf. 2 S 2^{9} (3 t. עַל־, 3 t. אֶל־); +תַּחַת 1 K 3^{7} 2 K 14^{21} 21^{24} 23^{30} (anointing), v^{34} 24^{17} 2 Ch 1^{8} 22^{1} 26^{1} 33^{25} 36^{1}; Est 2^{17} (=*make queen* at coronation); abs. Ho 8^{4}. †**Hoph.** *Pf.* הָמְלַךְ עַל מַלְכוּת כַּשְׂדִּים Dn 9^{1}.

4429 †II. מֶ֫לֶךְ **n.pr.m.** son of Micah, a Benjamite (on מ׳ as individ. name v. Gray[Prop. N. 116, 122 n. 4]; cf. Ph. n. pr. מלך (v. Bloch); Sab. n. pr. מלכם CIS[iv. 1]; Palm. n. pr. מלכו Vog[Palm. 92 al.] Nab. *id.*, Eut[Nab 21, 4 al.] Vog[Nab 1, 2]);—1 Ch 8^{35} (𝔊 Μελχηλ), 9^{41} (𝔊 Μαλαχ; 𝔊L Μελχιηλ in both).

†מֹ֫לֶךְ **n.pr.div. Molech** (𝔊 Μολοχ, 𝔙 *Moloch*) 4432
(=מֶלֶךְ i.e. (*divine*) *King*, with vowels of בֹּשֶׁת 1322,
to denote abhorrence, Hoffm[ZAW iii. 1883, 124] RS[Sem. 4428
i. 353; 2nd ed. 372]; cf. Hoffm[GG Abh. xxxvi. 1890 (May, 1889), 25]; Ph. n. pr. div. מלך *Milk*, in n. pr. cf. Bloch, Dr[Dt 222 f.]);—c. art. הַמֹּ׳:—the god to whom Isr. sacrif. children with fire (in valley of Hinnom); העביר לַמֹּ׳ 2 K 23^{10}; העביר בָּאֵשׁ לַמֹּ׳ Je 32^{35} (‖ הַבַּעַל), Lv 18^{21} (H); נתן לַמֹּ׳ Lv $20^{2.3.4}$ (H); more gen. לִזְנוֹת אַחֲרֵי הַמֹּ׳ v^{5} (H). In 1 K 11^{7} rd. prob. מִלְכֹּם, q.v.

†מֹ֫לֶכֶת **n.pr.f.** c. art. הַמֹּלֶכֶת 1 Ch 7^{18} (of 4447
Manasseh). 𝔊 ἡ Μαλέχεθ, 𝔊L Μελχαθ.

†מִלְכָּה **n.pr.f.** 𝔊 Μελχα (=מַלְכָּה? Nö 4435
ZMG xlii. 1888, 484 comp. Ph. n. pr. deæ מלכת; cf. Gray[Prop. N. 116]);—**1.** wife of Nahor Gn $11^{29.29}$ $22^{20.23}$ $24^{15.24.47}$ (all J). **2.** daughter of Zelophehad (of Manasseh), Nu 26^{33} 27^{1} 36^{11} Jos 17^{3} (all P).—Perhaps orig. town-name, Gray[l. c.]

†מְלוּכָה **n.f. kingship, royalty**;—מ׳ 4410
abs. 1 S 10^{16}+23 t.;—*kingship, kingly office, royalty:* 1 S $10^{16.25}$ 11^{14} 18^{8} 1 K $2^{15.15.22}$ 11^{35} 1 Ch 10^{14} Is 34^{12}; belonging to י׳ Ob ^{21} ψ 22^{29} (‖ וּמֹשֵׁל בַּגּוֹיִם); לְכַד מ׳ עַל 1 S 14^{47} *assume sovereignty over;* נָתַן מ׳ בְּיַד 2 S 16^{18} *give kingship to* (subj. י׳); הֵשִׁיב מ׳ לְ׳ 1 K 12^{21} *restore kingship to;* עָשָׂה מ׳ עַל 1 K 21^{7} *exercise kingship over;* metaph. of Jerus. וַתִּצְלְחִי לִמְלוּכָה Ez 16^{13} (del. 𝔊 Co); עִיר הַמּ׳ 2 S 12^{26}=*royal city;* cf. כִּסֵּא הַמּ׳ 1 K 1^{46}; זֶרַע הַמּ׳ 2 K 25^{25} so Je 41^{1} Ez 17^{13} Dn 1^{3}; צְנוֹף מ׳ Is 62^{3} (‖ עֲטֶרֶת תִּפְאֶרֶת).

†מַלְכוּת **n.f. royalty, royal power, reign,** 4438
kingdom (chiefly late);—מ׳ abs. Est 1^{9}+; cstr. 1 Ch 12^{23}+; sf. מַלְכוּתִי 1 Ch 17^{14}, etc.; pl. מַלְכֻיוֹת Dn 8^{22};—**1.** *royal power, dominion* Nu 24^{7} (c. תִּנַּשֵּׂא), 1 S 20^{31} (c. תִּכּוֹן), 1 K 2^{12} (c. *id.*); cf. Je 10^{7} Ec 4^{14}; 1 Ch 11^{10} 12^{23} 29^{30} (‖ גְּבוּרָה), 2 Ch 33^{13} Est 1^{19}, *royal* (queenly) *dignity* 4^{14}; 1 Ch 14^{2} (c. נִשֵּׂאת); c. לְכַד Dn 11^{21}; c. הֵכִין (subj. י׳) 1 Ch 17^{11} 28^{7}; 2 Ch 12^{1} (subj. Rehob.); Isr. royalty as belonging to י׳ 1 Ch 17^{14}; dominion of י׳ ψ 103^{19} (c. מָשְׁלָה), ψ $145^{13.13}$; כְּבוֹד מ׳ v^{11}; כְּבוֹד הֲדַר מ׳ v^{12}; שֵׁבֶט מ׳ ψ 45^{7}; כִּסֵּא מ׳ 1 Ch 22^{10} 28^{5} 2 Ch 7^{18}; of Pers. Est 1^{2} 5^{1}; בֵּית לְמ׳ 2 Ch 1^{18} 2^{11}; בֵּית מ׳ Est 1^{9} 2^{16} 5^{1} (cf. As. *bit šarruti* Dl[HWB 171]); יֵין מ׳ *royal wine* Est 1^{7}; דְּבַר מ׳ *royal command* Est 1^{19}; הוֹד מ׳ *royal honour, majesty* 1 Ch 29^{25} Dn 11^{21}; so perh. also

הֲדַר מ׳ Dn 11^{20} v. Bev; עֹשֶׁר כְּבוֹד מ׳ Est 1^{4}; כֶּתֶר מ׳ *royal crown* Est 1^{11} 2^{17} 6^{8}; לְבוּשׁ מ׳ *royal apparel* Est 6^{8} 8^{15}; מ׳ (לְבוּשׁ om.) Est 5^{1} (*queenly attire*). **2.** *reign:* 40th year of reign of David 1 Ch 26^{31} cf. 2 Ch 3^{2} 15$^{10.19}$ 16$^{1.12}$ 35^{19} Je 49^{34} Dn 1^{1}; also 2 Ch 29^{19}; of Babyl. and Pers. kings Je 52^{31} (בִּשְׁנַת מ׳ ‖ 2 K 25^{27} מָלְכוֹ) Dn 2^{1} 8^{1} Ezr 4$^{5.6.6}$ 7^{1} 8^{1} Ne 12^{22} Est 2^{16}; cf. עַד־מְלֹךְ מַלְכוּת פָּרָס 2 Ch 36^{20}. **3.** *kingdom, realm* 2 Ch 1^{1} 11^{17} 20^{30} Ne 9^{35}; esp. realm of Babyl. and Pers. 2 Ch 36^{22} = Ezr 1^{1}, Est 1$^{14.20}$ 2^{3} 3$^{6.8}$ 5$^{3.6}$ 7^{2} 9^{30} Dn 8^{22} 9^{1} 10^{13}; cf. 11$^{2.4.4.9.17}$; v^{20} הֲדַר מ׳ = Jerus. acc. to Hi., but v. **1** supr.

4467 †מַמְלָכָה **n.f. kingdom, sovereignty, dominion, reign**;—abs. מ׳ Jos 10^{2}+; cstr. מַמְלֶכֶת Ex 19^{6} + 11 t. (incl. Mi 4^{8} before לְ); sf. מַמְלַכְתִּי Gn 20^{9}+, etc.; pl. מַמְלָכוֹת Dt 3^{21}+; cstr. מַמְלְכוֹת Dt 28^{25}+;—**1.** *kingdom, realm*, chiefly non-Isr.: Gn 10^{10} (J), 20^{9} (E), Nu 32$^{33.33}$ (P), Dt 3$^{4.10.13.21}$ 28^{25} Jos 11^{10} (D), 1 S 10^{18} 1 K 5^{1} 10^{20} 18$^{10.10}$ (both ‖ גּוֹי), Is 10^{10} 1 Ch 16^{20} = ψ 105^{13} (‖ עַם and גּוֹי), ψ 135^{11} Is 14^{16} 19$^{2.2}$ 23^{11} 2 Ch 9^{19} 14^{4} 29^{21} 32^{15} (‖ גּוֹי), Ne 9^{22} (‖ עַם), ψ 46^{7} (‖ גּוֹי), 79^{6} (‖ *id.*), 102^{23} (‖ עַם), Is 60^{12} (‖ גּוֹי), so Je 1^{10} 18$^{7.9}$ 27^{8} 28^{8}; Je 49^{28} 51$^{20.27}$ Am 6^{2} Na 3^{5} Zp 3^{8} Hg 2^{22} Ez 17^{14} 29$^{14.15}$ 37^{22}; מַמְלְכוֹת הַגּוֹיִם 2 Ch 20^{6}, cf. Is 13^{4}; מַמְלְכוֹת הָאָרֶץ 2 K 19$^{15.19}$ = Is 37$^{16.20}$, 2 Ch 36^{23} = Ezr 1^{2}, ψ 68^{33} Is 23^{17} Je 15^{4} 24^{9} 25^{26} 29^{18} 34$^{1.17}$; מַמְלְכוֹת הָאֲרָצוֹת 1 Ch 29^{30} 2 Ch 12^{8} 17^{10} 20^{29}; of Isr. Am 9^{8} Dt 17^{20} 2 S 3^{28} La 2^{2} 2 Ch 21^{4}; cf. מַמְלֶכֶת כֹּהֲנִים Ex 19^{6} (‖ גּוֹי קָדוֹשׁ); of Mess. king Is 9^{6}; צְבִי מַמְלָכוֹת (of Babylon) Is 13^{19}, מִשְׁפְּחוֹת מַמְלְכוֹת צָפוֹנָה Je 1^{15}. גְּבֶרֶת מ׳ (*id.*) 47^{5}; **2.** *sovereignty, dominion* 1 S 13^{14} (Isr.; c. תָּקוּם), cf. 24^{21}; 2 Ch 13^{8} מ׳ י׳ בְּיַד בְּנֵי דָוִיד; לְךָ י׳ הַמַּמ׳; 1 Ch 29^{11}; ח׳ עַל 2 K 14^{5}; חָזְקָה בְּיָדוֹ 2 Ch 25^{3} הֶחֱזִיק בְּיַד 2 K 15^{19} cf. 2 Ch 22^{9}; הֵכִין מ׳ אֶל (subj. י׳) 1 S 13^{13} (Isr.), cf. 2 S 7$^{12.16}$ (‖ בַּיִת); 2 Ch 17^{5} (בְּיָד) cf. 1 K 2^{46} (נְכוֹנָה בְּיַד); נִשֵּׂא מ׳ (subj. י׳) 2 S 5^{12}; נָתַן מ׳ לְדָוִד עַל (subj. י׳) 2 Ch 13^{5}, cf. 21^{3}; קָרַע הַמ׳ מִן (subj. י׳) 1 S 28^{17} (Isr.), 1 K 11^{11} (sq. מֵעַל), v^{31} 14^{8}; מִן om. 11^{13}; לָקַח מִיָּדוֹ 11^{34} (or = *kingdom?*), הֶעֱבִיר מ׳ מִן (subj. י׳), 2 S 3^{10} (Isr.); נִשְׁבַּת מ׳ מִן Is 17^{3}; cf. תָּשׁוּב הַמ׳ לְ 1 K 12^{26}; עדיך כִּסֵּא...מ׳ Mi 4^{8}; הֵשִׁיב מ׳ לְ 2 Ch 11^{1}; תאתה ובאה כִּסֵּא מ׳ Dt 17^{18} (Isr.; יָשַׁב עַל), 2 S 7^{13} (כּוֹנֵן י׳), 1 K 9^{5} (הֵקִים י׳) 2 Ch 23^{20}, כִּסֵּא מַמְלָכוֹת Hg 2^{22}; בֵּית מ׳ *royal house* Am 7^{13}; עָרֵי הַמ׳ *royal cities* Jos 10^{2} cf. 1 S 27^{5}; זֶרַע הַמ׳ *royal seed, children*, 2 K 11^{1} = 2 Ch 22^{10}. **3.** *reign*, בְּרֵאשִׁית מ׳ Je 27^{1} 28^{1} *in the beginning of the reign of* (cf. מַלְכוּת **2**, מַמְלָכוּת **3**).

†[מַמְלָכוּת] **n. f. kingdom, dominion, reign** (on form cf. We$^{1 S 15, 28}$ Dr$^{ad loc. id.}$);—cstr. מַמְלְכוּת Jos 13^{12} + 8 t.; **1.** *kingdom* of Og Jos 13$^{12.30.31}$; of Sihon v$^{21.27}$. **2.** *dominion, royal power* c. קָרַע מֵעַל (subj. י׳) 1 S 15^{28}; c. הֵשִׁיב לְ (hum. subj.) 2 S 16^{3}; c. הִשְׁבִּית Ho 1^{4}. **3.** *reign* בְּרֵאשִׁית מַמ׳ Je 26^{1} (cf. מַמְלָכָה **3**, מַלְכוּת **2**). 4468

†מַלְכִּיאֵל **n.pr.m.** son of Beriah (of Asher) (*my king is Ēl;* cf. Tel Am. *Milkili* Wkl$^{Tel Am. 39*}$, v. Jastr$^{JBL 1892, 120; 1893, 61 f.}$; cf. further, Gray$^{Prop. N. 118 f., 206}$, v. also Ph. n.pr. מלכבעל, Palm. n.pr. מלכבל Vog$^{Palm. 3, 4; 140}$ and BH אֱלִימֶלֶךְ);—Gn 46^{17} Nu 26^{45} 1 Ch 7^{31}. 𝔊 Μελχιηλ. 4439

†מַלְכִּיאֵלִי **adj.gent.** c. art. as subst. coll. מִשְׁפַּחַת הַמ׳ Nu 26^{45}. 4440

†מַלְכִּיָּהוּ (only Je 38^{6}), מַלְכִּיָּה **n.pr.m.** (*my king is Yah;* cf. Gray$^{Prop. N. 119 f., 146 al.}$);—𝔊 Μελχ(ε)ια(ς).—**1.** father of Pashhur Je 21^{1} 38^{1}, cf. 1 Ch 9^{12} (priest), Ne 11^{12}. **2.** a prince Je 38^{6}. **3.** priests: **a.** 1 Ch 24^{9}. **b.** Ne 12^{42}. **4.** one of the sealed Ne 10^{4}; perh. also 8^{4}. **5.** a Levite 1 Ch 6^{25}. **6.** various men: **a.** Ezr 10$^{25 a}$. **b.** Ezr 10$^{25 b}$. **c.** Ezr 10^{31} = Ne 3^{11}. **d.** Ne 3^{14}. **e.** Ne 3^{31}. 4441

†מַלְכִּי־צֶדֶק **n.pr.m.** king of שָׁלֵם (q. v.), 4442
(*my king is Ṣedek*)—Gn 14^{18} ψ 110^{4}. 𝔊 Μελχι- 6664
σεδεκ. 4428

†מַלְכִּירָם **n.pr.m.** son of Jeconiah (= 4443
Jehoiakin) (*my king* (= Yahweh) *is high*, cf. 4428, 7311
Gray$^{Prop. N. 146 f.}$; Ph. n. pr. מלכרם);—1 Ch 3^{18}. 𝔊 Μελχ(ε)ιραμ.

†מַלְכִּישׁוּעַ **n.pr.m.** son of Saul (*my king* 4428, 4444
(= י׳) *is opulence*, cf. Gray$^{Prop. N. 147}$);—1 S 14^{49} 7769
31^{2} 1 Ch 8^{33} 9^{39} 10^{2} (in Ch. מַלְכִּי־שׁוּעַ). 𝔊 Μελχεισα, Μελχεσουε, etc.

†מַלְכָּם **n.pr.m.** a Benjamite 1 Ch 8^{9}. 𝔊B Μελχας, A Μελχαμ, 𝔊L Μελχομ. On Je 49$^{1.3}$ Zp 1^{5} v. מִלְכֹּם. 4445

†מִלְכֹּם **n.pr.div. Milcom**, god of Ammonites (cf. RS$^{Sem. i. 67}$)—מ׳ שִׁקֻּץ עַמֹּנִים 1 K 11^{5} (‖ עַשְׁתֹּרֶת); cf. מ׳ אֱלֹהֵי בְנֵי עַמּוֹן v^{33} (‖ כְּמוֹשׁ + ע׳), so rd. also (for MT מֹלֶךְ) v^{7} (‖ כְּמוֹשׁ); מ׳ תּוֹעֲבַת בְּנֵי־עַמּוֹן 2 K 23^{13} (‖ as 1 K 11^{33}); rd. מִלְכֹּם also 4445

for מַלְכָּם Je $49^{1.3}$ (𝔊 Μελχολ, Μελχομ), cf. Gie, and Zp 1^{5} (𝔖 𝔙, cf. Now), prob. 2 S 12^{30} = 1 Ch 20^{2} (v. מֶלֶךְ **5 d**), and perh. Am 1^{15} (whence Je 49^{3}; cf. Dr Now;—not We GASm).

3230 †יַמְלֵךְ **n.pr.m.** a Simeonite (cf. Palm. n.pr. ימלכו Vog Palm. 36 a);—1 Ch 4^{34}. 𝔊 Ιεμολοχ.

4409 †מַלּוּךְ **n.pr.m.** 𝔊 Μαλωχ, Μαλουχ, etc. **1.** Levites: **a.** 1 Ch 6^{29}. **b.** Ne 12^{2} (priest ?). **2.** various men: **a.** Ezr 10^{29}. **b.** Ezr 10^{32}. **c.** Ne 10^{5}. **d.** Ne 10^{28}.

4409 †מלוכי Kt, מְלִיכוּ Qr **n.pr.m.** a priest Ne 12^{14}. 𝔊 Μαλουχ, 𝔊L Μαλουκ.

4427 †II. [מָלַךְ] **vb. counsel, advise** (loan-wd. from Aram. ܡܠܟ, מְלַךְ; cf. As. *malâku*, Dl HWB 412);—only **Niph.** (so NH) *Impf.* וַיִּמָּלֵךְ לִבִּי עָלַי i. e. I considered carefully, Ne 5^{7}.

4434 [מַלְכֹּדֶת] v. לכד. p. 540

4404 מַלְכֵּן v. מַלְבֵּן sub לבן. p. 527

4448 †I. [מָלַל] **vb. Pi. speak, utter, say** (NH Pi. *id.*; Aram. ܡܲܠܸܠ (and many deriv.), מַלֵּל; perh. cf. Ar. مَلَّ IV. *dictate* (a letter, etc.), (ملو) مَلَا IV. *id.* Nö ZMG xl. 1886, 725);—**Pi.** *Pf.* מִלֵּל Gn 21^{7}; cf. 1 s. מִלּוֹתִי (Ew § 274 b. N) as **n.pr.** infr.; מִלֵּלוּ Jb 33^{3}; *Impf.* יְמַלֵּל ψ 106^{2}; תְּמַלֶּל־ Jb 8^{2};—**say**, sq. dir. quot. + לְ of ind. obj. Gn 21^{7}; **utter**, obj. דַּעַת Jb 33^{3}; cf. 8^{2}; obj. גְּבוּרוֹת י׳ ψ 106^{2}.

4405 †מִלָּה **n.f. word, speech, utterance** (poet., esp. Jb; common in Aram.);—מ׳ ψ 139^{4} Jb 30^{9}; sf. מִלָּתִי Jb 13^{17} + 3 t.; מִלָּתוֹ 2 S 23^{2}; pl. מִלִּים Jb 6^{26} + 9 t. (all Jb); מִלִּין Jb 4^{2} + 12 t. (all Jb); pl. sf. מִלָּי Jb 19^{23} + 4 t.; מִלֶּיךָ Jb 4^{4} Pr 23^{9}; מִלֵּיהֶם ψ 19^{5};—*word* בִּלְשׁוֹנִי *in* (*on*) *my tongue* ψ 139^{4}; *word* (of י׳), עַל־לְשׁוֹנִי *on my tongue* 2 S 23^{2}; שֵׂכֶל מ׳ Pr 23^{9}; fig. ψ 19^{5} (|| קַוָּם; but rd. קוֹלָם v. Che crit. n.); elsewhere only Jb (34 t.); sg. *speech, utterance* Jb 13^{17} 21^{2} 24^{25} 29^{22}; also *word = by-word,* וָאֱהִי לָהֶם לְמִלָּה Jb 30^{9}; pl. *words,* Jb 4^{4} 6^{26} 8^{10} 12^{11} 15^{3} (|| דָּבָר), 16^{4} $19^{2.23}$ $32^{11.14}$ $33^{1.8}$ (קוֹל מ׳), $34^{2.3.16}$ (קוֹל מ׳), $36^{2.4}$; words of God Jb 23^{5}; *words = speech, speaking,* וַעְצֹר בְּמִלִּין מִי יוּכָל Jb 4^{2}, cf. 29^{9}; *utter words,* וְהֹצֵאתָ מִפִּיךָ מִלִּין 15^{13}; הִגַּדְתָּ מ׳ 26^{4}; *lay snares for words* הְשִׂימוּן קִנְצֵי לְמִלִּין Jb 18^{2}, cf. Jb 32^{15} הֶעְתִּיקוּ מֵהֶם מִלִּים; מָלֵתִי מִלִּים Jb 32^{18} *I am full* *of words,* cf. אִם־יֵשׁ־מִלִּין הֲשִׁיבֵנִי 33^{32}; אֲשִׁיבְךָ מִלִּין Jb 35^{4}; בִּבְלִי־דַעַת מִלִּין יַכְבִּר 35^{16}, cf. 38^{2}.

†מַלּוֹתִי as **n.pr.m.** a son of Heman (*I have* 4413
uttered = מִלֵּלְתִּי Ew § 274 b. N. v. מלל);—1 Ch 25^{4} (on this appar. list of names v. Ew l.c. RS OTJC 422; 2nd ed. 143) v^{26}.

†מִלֲלַי **n.pr.m.** a priest's son, Ne 12^{36}. 4450

†II. [מָלַל] **vb. rub, scrape** (NH *id., rub* 4448
ears of wheat, *scrape*);—only **Qal** *Pt.* מֹלֵל in קֹרֵץ בְּעֵינָו מֹלֵל בְּרַגְלָו מֹרֶה בְּאֶצְבְּעֹתָיו Pr 6^{13} *he that winketh with his eyes, that scrapeth with his feet* (making signs), etc., so De Now Str < Ew Wild fr. I. מלל *that speaketh with his feet.*

†[מְלִילָה] **n.f. ear** of wheat, etc. (perh. as 4425
rubbed or *scraped*, cf. NH הַמּוֹלֵל מְלִילוֹת);—only pl. abs. מְלִילֹת Dt 23^{26} (cf. Di).

†III. [מָלַל] **vb. languish, wither, fade** 5243
(apparently secondary √ of אמל q.v.);—**Qal** *Impf.* 3 ms. יִמַּל Jb 18^{16}; וַיִּמָּל Jb 14^{2}; 3 mpl. יִמָּלוּ Jb 24^{24} ψ 37^{2} (so Hup De and most; > Niph. fr. IV. מלל Thes);—*hang down, wither,* fig. of man Jb 14^{2} (כְּצִיץ); of wicked מִתַּחַת שָׁרָשָׁיו יִבָשׁוּ וּמִמַּעַל יִמַּל קְצִירוֹ 18^{16}; כְּרֹאשׁ שִׁבֹּלֶת יִמָּלוּ 24^{24} (|| הֻמְּכוּ, יִקָּפְצוּן); כֶּחָצִיר מְהֵרָה יִמָּלוּ ψ 37^{2} (|| יִבּוֹלוּן). **Po'l.** *Impf.* יְמוֹלֵל ψ 90^{6} *it withereth* (of grass; + וְיָבֵשׁ).

†IV. [מָלַל] **vb. circumcise** (= מוּל);— 5243
to this are sts. assigned: **Qal** *Imv.* מֹל Jos 5^{2}. **Niph.** *Pf.* נְמַלְתֶּם Gn 17^{11}. **Hithpo.** *be cut off*: *Impf.* יִתְמֹלָלוּ ψ 58^{8}. Vid. מוּל.

[מַלְמֵד, מַלְמָד] v. למד. p. 541 4451

†[מָלַץ] **vb.** prob. **be smooth, slippery** 4452
(Ar. مَلِصَ *slip*);—**Niph.** *Pf.* מַה־נִּמְלְצוּ לְחִכִּי אִמְרָתֶךָ ψ 119^{103} *how smooth* (agreeable, pleasant) *are thy words to my palate* (|| מִדְּבַשׁ לְפִי).

†מֶלְצַר **n.m.** a Bab. title; dubious; perhaps 4453
guardian? (Schr COT Dn 1, 11 Dl Baer Dn xi conj. loan-word fr. As. *maṣ(ṣ)aru, keeper, guardian*, cf. Dl HWB 423; hardly connected with (mod.) Pers. *mulsaru* 'kellermeister' (cf. Meinh.), v. against this Bevan);—only c. art. הַמּ׳ Dn $1^{11.16}$.

4454 †מָלַק **vb. nip, nip off** (head of bird; without *necessarily* severing it fr. body, cf. Lv 5^{8}) (NH *id.*, Aram. מְלַק, ܡܠܰܩ);—**Qal** *Pf.* consec. וּמָלַק אֶת־רֹאשׁוֹ Lv 1^{15}, i. e. head of dove; cf. וּמָלַק אֶת־רֹאשׁוֹ מִמּוּל עָרְפּוֹ וְלֹא יַבְדִּיל Lv 5^{8}. Cf. Di-Ry. 𝔊 ἀποκνίζω.

4455, 4457 I, II. מַלְקוֹחַ, מֶלְקָחַיִם, מַלְקָחַיִם v. לקח. p. 544

4456, 4458 מַלְקוֹשׁ v. לקשׁ. מֶלְתָּחָה v. לתח. p. 545, 547

4459, 4973 [מַלְתָּעוֹת] v. מְתַלְּעוֹת sub תלע. p. 1069

4460-61 מַמְּגֻרוֹת v. I. גור. [מֵמַד] v. מדד. p. 158, 551

4462 †מְמוּכָן **n.pr.m.** a prince of Persia and Media—Est 1$^{14.21}$ also v^{16} Qr; Kt מומכן. 𝔊 Μουχαιος, Μαμουχαιος.

4463 [מָמוֹת], מְמוֹתִים v. מות. p. 560

4464 מַמְזֵר v. I. מזר. p. 561

4465-66 מִמְכָּר, מִמְכֶּרֶת v. מכר. p. 569

4467 מַמְלָכָה, [מַמְלָכוּת] v. מלך. p. 575

4469, 4480 מִמֶּנִּי, etc. v. מִן. מִמְסָךְ v. מסך. below, p. 587

4470, 4472 מֶמֶר, [מַמְרוֹר], מַמְּרוֹרִים v. מרר. p. 601

4471 †מַמְרֵא **n.pr.m. et loc.** Mamre, only in Gn: **1.** in J only אֵלֹנֵי מַמְרֵא *terebinths of M.* (n.pr.m.?), Gn 13^{18} (defined by אֲשֶׁר בְּחֶבְרוֹן), 18^{1} (in both the dwelling-place of Abraham). **2. n.pr.m.** in Gn 14^{13} (אֵלֹנֵי מ׳ הָאֱמֹרִי), cf. v^{24} (where ally of Abr.) **3. n.pr.loc.** in P: near Abr.'s place of burial Gn 23^{17} 25^{9} 49^{30} 50^{13}; appar. identified with Hebron 23^{19} 35^{27}, cf. Di.—𝔊 Μαμβρη.

4473 מִמְשָׁח v. משׁח. p. 603

4474-75 מִמְשָׁל, מֶמְשָׁלָה, מֶמְשֶׁלֶת v. משׁל. p. 606

4476-77 [מִמְשָׁק] v. משׁק. מַמְתַּקִּים v. מתק. p. 606, 609

4478 †I. מָן **n.m.**$^{Nu\ 11,\ 9}$ **manna** (=Ar. مَنّ, known to Beduin in Sin. Penin.; a juice exuding in heavy drops from twigs (some say also the leaves) of *Ṭarfa* (Ṭŭrfa) tree (*tamarix gallica mannifera*) in W. Sin. Penin., end of May and in June, sweet, sticky, honey-like; cf. Di$^{Ex\ 16,\ 36}$ Rob$^{BR\ i.\ 75,\ 115,\ 590}$ Eb$^{GS\ 233\ ff.,\ 574\ ff.}$ Soc$^{ZMG\ xxxv.\ 1881,\ 254}$);—מ׳ abs. Ex 16^{15} + 12 t., sf. מַנְךָ Ne 9^{20}:—*manna*: וַיֹּאמְרוּ מָן הוּא כִּי לֹא יָדְעוּ מַה־הוּא Ex 16^{15}; v$^{31.33.35.35}$ Nu 11$^{6.7.9}$ (described Ex 16$^{14.31}$ Nu 11^{7}; accomp. dew Ex 16^{14} Nu 11^{9}); ceased after Israel reached Canaan Jos 5$^{12.12}$; as 2nd acc. הֶאֱכִלְךָ אֶת־הַמָּן Dt 8^{3}, cf. v^{16}; וַיַּמְטֵר עֲלֵיהֶם מָן לֶאֱכֹל ψ 78^{24}; וּמַנְךָ לֹא־מָנַעְתָּ מִפִּיהֶם Ne 9^{20}.

†II. מָן in Ex 16^{15} (with reference to the manna) וַיֹּאמְרוּ אִישׁ אֶל־אָחִיו מָן הוּא כִּי לֹא יָדְעוּ מַה־הוּא, most prob. '**What is it?**' the question being intended as a popular etym. of מָן 'manna,' based upon the *late* Aram. ܡܰܢ *What?* (*man* is 'Who?' in Arab., Aram. (מַן, ܡܰܢ), Mand. (מאן), Eth. (*manu*), 'What?' in these dialects being مَا, מָה, ܡܳܐ, מָא (Eth. *ment*); מָן in the sense of 'What?' must correspond to the later Syr. ܡܰܢ, contr. from ܡܳܐ ܗܽܘ, 𝔗 מָדֵין: Nö$^{§\ 68}$ W$^{SG\ 125}$). 4478

†I. [מֵן] **n.[m.] string** (of harp) (prob. loan-word fr. Aram. ܡܶܢܬܳܐ, *hair, string* PS^{2163}); pl. מִנִּים ψ 150^{4}, so also prob. 45^{9} (rd. מִנִּים for MT מִנִּי, cf. Che Bae We > Ges$^{§\ 87,\ 1.b}$ Hup al., who think מִנִּי an apoc. pl.) 4482

II. [מֵן], מִנְּהוֹ v. מנן. p. 577 4482

מִן־, and מִ·, before ׳ (exc. Dn 12^{2} 2 Ch 4480
20^{11}) contr. to מִי (as מִידֵי from מִיְּדֵי), before gutt. and ר, mostly מֵ, occasionally מִ (Ges$^{§\ 102,\ 1\ R.}$; more fully Kö$^{ii.\ 291\ ff.}$), מִן before art. in all books much commoner than מֵ־; מִן before other words most freq. in Ch [51 t.: elsewhere 47 t. (Kö^{292})]; poet. also מִנִּי, with the old ׳ of the gen. (Ges$^{§\ 90.\ 3\ a}$) Ju 5$^{14.14}$ Is 46$^{3.3}$ ψ 44$^{11.19}$ 68^{32} 74^{22} 78$^{2.42}$ 88^{10} + 19 t. Jb, and in לְמִנִּי †Mi 7$^{12.12}$, and מִנֵּי (on anal. of עֲלֵי, עֲדֵי) †Is 30$^{11.11}$, **prep.** expressing the idea of *separation*, hence **out of, from, on account of, off, on the side of, since, above, than, so that not** (Ph. מ; Aram. ܡܶܢ; Ar. مِنْ; Eth. እምነ:; Sab. בן (DHM$^{ZMG\ xxix.\ 606\ ff.;\ xxxvii.\ 375}$)); with suff. מִמֶּנִּי (the מִן reduplicated, Ol$^{§\ 223\ c}$, al., Kö$^{ii.\ 289\ f.}$), poet. מִנִּי †Is 22^{4} 30^{1} 38^{12} Jb 16^{6}, מֶנִּי †ψ 18^{23} 65^{4} 139^{19} Jb 21^{16} 22^{18} 30^{10}; מִמְּךָ, מִמֶּךָּ, מִמֵּךְ; מִמֶּנּוּ (מֶנְהוּ †Jb 4^{12}), מִמֶּנָּה; 1 pl. מִמֶּנּוּ (acc. to Orientals מִמֶּנּוּ: v. Baer Job, p. 57 Kö^{290}); מֵהֶם, מִכֶּם (מִנְּהֶם †Jb 11^{20}), מֵהֵמָּה †Je 10^{2} Ec 12^{12}; מֵהֵנָּה 7 t. (v. הֵמָּה **8 c**), מֵהֶן (edd. מֵהֵן) †Ez 16$^{47.52}$ (v. Zerweck$^{Heb.\ Präp.\ Min,\ 1894}$): —**1.** with verbs expressing (or implying) *separation* or *removal*, whether from a person or place, or in any direction, also from guilt, calamity, etc.:—thus **a.** to descend *from* a mountain Ex 19^{14}, to fall *from* a roof Dt 22^{8}, *from* heaven Is 14^{12}, to go up *from* a valley

Jos 10[7], to raise up *from* the dunghill 1 S 2[8], or the ground 2 S 12[17]. So constantly with vbs. of *going*, as בא, הלך, שב, ברח (sq. a person, usu. מפני), of *calling*, as Is 24[14] צָהֲלוּ מִיָּם, 42[10.11] ψ 148[1], of *asking* or *exacting*, as שאל, בקשׁ, דרשׁ, הִנָּקֵם, נָקַם, of *delivering*, as הושׁיע, הציל, etc., of *hiding*, as נעלם, העלים, etc., of *taking* or *withholding*, as לקח, חשׂך, מנע, of *keeping* (*from*), as שׁמר, נצר, of *being far*, or *desisting*, as רחק Ex 23[7], חֲדַל מִמֶּנּוּ desist *from* us, 14[12], so הֶרֶף Dt 9[14], הֵנִיחַ 12[10], השׁקיט ψ 94[13], שׁבת Gn 2[2], cf. 5[29]; note esp. the pregn. constructions, שׁפט to judge (and save) *from* ψ 43[1], sq. מִיַּד 1 S 24[16]+, ענה to answer (and save) *from* ψ 22[22], חרשׁ and חשׁה to be silent (turning) *from* ψ 28[1.1], החרישׁו ממני Jb 13[13] Je 38[27], ψ 18[22] ולא רשׁעתי מאלהי nor did wickedly (turning) *from* my God, 30[4] Kt., 73[27] כל־זוֹנֶה ממך, Je 3[20] בָּגַד מִן (𝔊 εἰς=ב), 31[13] c. שִׂמַּח (2 Ch 20[27]), Ez 27[34] Pr 25[17] הֹקַר רַגְלְךָ מִבֵּית רֵעֶךָ, Is 29[4] 63[17] Jo 1[12]; Je 51[5] אַלְמָן מֵאֱלֹהָיו widowed (and severed) *from* etc., Ez 44[22]; also Ju 7[17] מִמֶּנִּי תִרְאוּ וְכֵן תַּעֲשׂוּ ye shall *see from* me, i. e. learn what to do by observing me. Some of the verbs mentioned above are construed more precisely with מֵאֵת, מֵעִם, מֵעַל, q.v.: and others, esp. לקח, דרשׁ, הושׁיע, הציל, פדה, פִּלֵּט, idiom. with מִיַּד. With inff., v. infr. **7 b**. Often also with adverbs, as מִשָּׁם *thence*, מֵאַיִן *whence?* מִזֶּה, מִפֹּה *hence*. Cf. also חָפְשִׁי מִן free (safe) *from* Jb 3[19], עֵזֶר מִצָּרָיו a help *from* his foes Dt 33[7], Na 3[11] מָעוֹז מֵאוֹיֵב, ψ 32[7] סֵתֶר מִצַּר, 60[13] עֶזְרָת מִצָּר, Is 4[6] צֵל מֵחֹרֶב a shadow *from* the heat, 25[4]. Here also belong Is 40[15] מַר מִדְּלִי a drop *from* (hanging from) a bucket; Ct 4[1] goats שֶׁגָּלְשׁוּ מהר גלעד that sit up (seeming to hang) *from* the hills of Gilead (cf. Od. 21. 420 ἐκ δίφροιο καθήμενος: also the Arabic idiom قَرُبَ مِنْ, lit. to be near *from* a thing): prob. also the difficult passage Dn 8[9], and from one of them there came forth קֶרֶן אַחַת מִצְּעִירָה a horn *from* (being) a little one, i. e. gradually increasing from small beginnings (but ? rd. אַחֶרֶת צְעִירָה Bev cf. 7[8]). **b.** מן also, without a verb of similar significance, sometimes expresses the idea of separation, *away from, far from* (cf. Il. 2. 162 φίλης ἀπὸ πατρίδος αἴης): Pr 20[3] שֶׁבֶת מֵרִיב to sit *away from* strife (cf. قَعَدَ عَنْ *ap.* De), Nu 15[24] if the thing be done מֵעֵינֵי הָעֵדָה *away from* the eyes of etc., Ju 5[11] De RV (but Be RVm *because of*), Is 14[19] cast out מִקִּבְרְךָ *away from* thy sepulchre, Jb 28[4] דַּלּוּ מֵאֱנוֹשׁ, Gn 4[11] cursed art thou מן־האדמה, De Di *away from* the (tilled) soil, cf. v[14] (but Kn Ke *from*, cf. v[12a]), 27[39] (prob.) מִשְׁמַנֵּי הָאָרֶץ *away from* the fatness of the earth shall be thy dwelling; almost=*without*, Jb 11[15] then shalt thou lift up thy face מִמּוּם *away from, without* spot, 19[26] (prob.) מִבְּשָׂרִי *without* my flesh shall I see God, 21[9] בָּתֵּיהֶם שָׁלוֹם מִפָּחַד are at peace *without* fear, Pr 1[33] Je 48[45] fleeing עָמְדוּ מִכֹּחַ they stand *without* strength, Is 22[3] מִקֶּשֶׁת אֻסָּרוּ (Hi De Di Che) they were bound *without* the bow (being used) (but Ges as **2 e**: *by* the bowmen), Zp 3[18]. (On 2 S 13[16] v. We or Dr). See also **7 b**. **c.** of position, *off, on the side of, on*, esp. with ref. to quarters of the heavens (cf. πρὸς Νότου, ἐκ δεξιῶν, *a* fronte, *a* tergo, etc.): Gn 2[8] י׳ planted a garden in Eden מִקֶּדֶם *off, on* the east, 12[8] בֵּיתְאֵל מִיָּם וְהָעַי מִקֶּדֶם Bethel *off* (*on*) the West and ʿAi *off* (*on*) the East; so מִנֶּגֶב, מִצָּפוֹן, מִמִּזְרָח Jos 11[3] 15[8] 18[5] 1 S 14[5], etc.: similarly מִיָּמִין *on* the right, מִשְּׂמֹאול *on* the left, מִמּוּל and (more rarely) מִפָּנִים *on* the front, מֵאָחוֹר = behind (2 S 10[9]), מִסָּבִיב Dt 12[10]+ *round about*, מִלְמַעְלָה, מִמַּעַל, and מֵעָל (rare)=*above*, מִתַּחַת Ex 20[4]+*beneath*, מִבַּיִת *on* the inside, מִחוּץ *on* the outside Gn 6[14]+, מִנֶּגֶד *in front, at* a distance, Gn 21[16]+, מֵרָחוֹק Ex 2[4]+ *afar off*, מִפְּנִימָה *within*, מִזֶּה ... מִזֶּה and מִפֹּה ... מִפֹּה *on* this side ... *on* that side. And so even with verbs of motion, as Gn 11[2] ויהי בנסעם מִקֶּדֶם as they journeyed—not *from*, but—*on the side of* the east, virtually=*eastwards*, 13[11] and Lot journeyed מקדם *east*, Is 17[13] 22[3] מֵרָחוֹק ברחו they fled—not *from* afar but—*afar*, 23[7] whose feet used to carry her מֵרָחוֹק *afar off* to sojourn, 57[9] thou didst send thy messengers עד־מרחוק *even to afar*. With a foll. לְ (or sf.), most of these words are freq. in the sense of *on the east* (*west*, etc.) *of* . . . , as Jos 8[13] מִיָּם לָעִיר *on* the west of the city, מִקֶּדֶם לְ Gn 3[24], מִצָּפוֹן לְ (cstr. Ges [§ 130 a. n.]) Jos 8[11.13] 24[30], מִימִינֶךָ ψ 91[7], מִתַּחַת לְ Gn 1[7], מִמַּעַל לְ 22[9], מִבֵּית לְ Lv 16[2]: מֵאַחֲרֵי *behind* Ex 14[19], מִצַּד בֵּיתְאֵל *beside* Bethel Jos 12[9], מִצִּדּוֹ *beside* it 1 S 6[8], מֵעֵבֶר לַיַּרְדֵּן *on* the other side of Jordan Nu 21[1]+; מֵהָלְאָה לְ *beyond* Am 5[27]; tablets written מִשְּׁנֵי עֶבְרֵיהֶם *on* both their sides, מִכָּל־עֲבָרָיו Je 49[32]+ (v. further the words cited). So מֵהַבַּיִת *on the side of the* house Ez 40[7.8.9], מֵאֵצֶל *beside* Ez 40[7]; 1 S 20[21] the arrows are טוֹבְךָ וָהֵנָּה *from thee* and hither—on this side of thee, v^{22} מִמְּךָ וָהָלְאָה, cf. Nu $32^{19.19}$.

2. Out of, Gk. ἐκ, Lat. *ex:* thus **a.** מִמִּצְרַיִם *out of* Egypt: so (*a*) with verbs of *proceeding, removing, expelling*, etc., as יָצָא, הוֹצִיא (v. יָצָא), שִׁלַּח Gn 3^{23}, לָקַח 34^{26}, גָּנַב 40^{15}, הִכְרִית Ex 8^{5} ψ 101^{8}, גֵּרֵשׁ Ju 11^{7}, etc.; to draw *out of* water, a pit, etc. Ex 2^{10} ψ 40^{3}; to cast *out of* the hand Ju 15^{17}; to rescue *out of* the mouth Am 3^{12}; to drink מִכּוֹס 2 S 12^{3}; Dt 30^{3} וְקִבֶּצְךָ מִן־הָעַמִּים, Ez 11^{17} 36^{24}+: pregn. with חָרֵד Ho $10^{10.11}$, רגז Mi 7^{17} to tremble (and come) *out of*, חרג ψ 18^{46} (‖ 2 S 22^{46} חגר), 74^{11} Is 38^{17} חָשַׂךְ (ni חָשַׂךְ leg.), Ez 28^{16} חִלֵּל, Ezr 2^{62}; cf. נִשְׁכַּח מִפֶּה Dt 31^{21}, מִלֵּב ψ 31^{13}. In this applic., often made more definite by the use of מִקֶּרֶב . . . , מִתּוֹךְ . . . *out of* the midst of. (*b*) of the place *out of* which one looks, speaks, exerts power, etc., Gn 4^{10} Nu 24^{19} (ψ 110^{1}), Dt 4^{36} מן־השמים השמיעך את־קלו, Am 1^{2} י׳ מציון ישאג, ψ 14^{2} 20^{3} send thee help מִקֹּדֶשׁ, v^{7} יַעֲנֵהוּ מִשְּׁמֵי קָדְשׁוֹ, 42^{7} 68^{36} 85^{12} 109^{10} ודרשו מחרבותיהם seek (their bread) *out of* their desolate homes (but Ew De as **1 b** *far from;* 𝔊 Gr Che יְגֹרְשׁוּ let them *be driven from*), 128^{5} 130^{1} Jb 27^{23} Is 29^{18} to see *out of* darkness, Ct 2^{9} to look out מִן־הַחַלֹּנוֹת *from* the windows (usu. בעד), 5^{4} he put forth his hand מִן־הַחוֹר *from* (i.e. *in through*) the hole (in the door or wall). (*c*) with בָּחַר to choose *out of*, Ex 18^{25}+oft., cf. with הִבְדִּיל Dt 29^{20} 1 K 8^{53}, with יָדַע Am 3^{2}, Ex 19^{5} ye shall be to me סְגֻלָּה מכל־העמים a treasure (chosen) *out of* all peoples (cf. with בָּחַר Dt 7^{6} 14^{2}). **b.** of the material *out of* which anything is formed, or from which it is derived: (*a*) Gn 2^{19} to form מן־האדמה *out of the* soil, v^{23} עֶצֶם מֵעֲצָמַי וּבָשָׂר מִבְּשָׂרִי, Ex 39^{1} Nu 6^{4} Ho 13^{2} to make images מִכַּסְפָּם, ψ 16^{4} נִסְכֵּיהֶם מִדָּם, 45^{14} Ct 3^{9}; Is 40^{17} מאפס ותהו נחשבו־לו as *made of* nought and unreality are they reckoned by him (‖ כְּאַיִן נֶגְדּוֹ), 41^{24} הֵן אַתֶּם מֵאַיִן ‖ מֵאֶפַע, rd. מֵאֶפֶס), ψ 62^{10} מֵהֶבֶל (*al.* **6 c**), Pr 13^{11}; Ex $25^{19.31}$ its cups, its knops, etc., ממנה יהיו shall be *from it* (i.e. of one piece with it), so $v^{35.36}$ 27^{2} 30^{2} *al.*; (*b*) with verbs of eating, filling, etc., as שתה Gn 9^{21}, Jb 21^{20} מֵחֲמַת שַׁדַּי יִשְׁתֶּה, Ct 8^{2} הַשְׁקָה, ψ 36^{9}+, רָוָה Is 34^{7}, שׂבע Pr 18^{20}+, השׂביע ψ 81^{17}+, מִלֵּא רִוָּה (rare) 127^{5}: cf. Dt 32^{42} אַשְׁכִּיר חִצַּי מִדָּם, Is 51^{21}; ψ 28^{7} (peculiar) וּמִשִּׁירִי אֲהוֹדֶנּוּ *out of* my song I will thank him (69^{31} ב׳), also (unusual) Is 2^{3} וְיֹרֵנוּ מִדְּרָכָיו i.e. *out of* (the treasure of) his ways

(*al.* part.=*some of*), ψ 94^{12b} מִתּוֹרָתְךָ תְלַמְּדֶנּוּ; Ec 7^{10} to speak מֵחָכְמָה (cf. Rabb. מִתּוֹךְ). **c.** of the *source* or *origin:* viz. (*a*) of parents, Gn 16^{2} אִבָּנֶה ממנה I shall be built up *out of* her (so 30^{3}), 17^{16} מלכי עמים ממנה יהיו, 35^{11a}: often of coming forth מִבֶּטֶן Jb 1^{21}, מֵחֲלָצֶיךָ Gn 35^{11b}, ממעיך 15^{4}, 1 S 2^{20} י׳ give thee seed *from* this woman; cf. Jb 14^{4} מִי יִתֵּן טָהוֹר מִטָּמֵא. (*b*) of the tribe or people, *from* which a person comes (cf. **1 a**), Nu 3^{12} כל בכור . . . מבני ישׂר׳, Jos 12^{4} 2 S 4^{2} 21^{2} Je 1^{1}+; and so of a person's native place, as Ju 12^{8} אבצן מבית לחם Ibzan *from* B., 13^{2} אִישׁ מִצָּרְעָה, $17^{1.7}$ 1 S 1^{1} 9^{1} 2 S $23^{20.30}$ Am 1^{1}+, cf. Je 46^{25} אָמוֹן מִנֹּא; Is 48^{1} וּמִמֵּי יְהוּדָה יָצָאוּ, v^{2} מֵעִיר הַקֹּדֶשׁ נִקְרָאוּ, 58^{12} וּבָנוּ מִמְּךָ (those) *from* thee shall build, ψ 68^{27} מִמְּקוֹר ישׂראל ye (sprung) *from* the fountain of Israel, Mi 5^{1} Na 1^{11} (v^{14} fig. מִשִּׁמְךָ), Zp 3^{18}; Je 30^{21} Zc 10^{4}. (*c*) of beasts and things, Gn 2^{7} עָפָר מִן־הָאֲדָמָה, Je 5^{6} אַרְיֵה מִיַּעַר a lion *from* the forest, ψ 80^{14} חֲזִיר מִיָּעַר; cf. 10^{18} אֱנוֹשׁ מִן־הָאָרֶץ man *from* the earth (*terrenus*), 72^{16} יָצִיצוּ מֵעִיר; Jb 28^{12} וְהַחָכְמָה מֵאַיִן תִּמָּצֵא. (*d*) מִלֵּב Is 59^{13} Jb 8^{10}, esp. with reference to what is self-devised, Nu 16^{28} כִּי לֹא מִלִּבִּי, 24^{13} 1 K 12^{33} Ne 6^{8}; נְבִיאֵי מִלִּבָּם Ez 13^{2}. **d.** of the *source* or *author* of an action, counsel, or event: 1 S 24^{14} מֵרְשָׁעִים יֵצֵא רֶשַׁע, 2 S 3^{37} לא היתה מהמלך it was not *from* the king to, etc.; spec. of י׳, Gn 24^{50} כי מי׳ יצא הדבר, Ju 14^{4} knew כי מי׳ הוא that it was *from* J., 1 K 2^{15} כי מי׳ היתה לו, Pr 16^{1} 20^{24} מי׳ מִצְעֲדֵי גָבֶר, ψ 37^{39} 62^{2} וְלֹא מִמֶּנּוּ יְשׁוּעָתִי, Ho 8^{4} they have made kings, מִמֶּנִּי not *from me*, i.e. not at my prompting, Is 30^{1} 50^{11} (מִיָּדִי), Ez $3^{17\,end}$=33^{7} and warn them *from me*, 1 Ch 5^{22} 13^{2} 2 Ch 22^{7} 25^{20} (syn. מֵאֵת, מֵעִם, which are more frequent in this sense); poet. Ho 7^{5} חֲמַת מִיָּיִן heat *from wine*, ψ 9^{14} עָנְיִי מִשֹּׂנְאַי *at the hands of* my haters, 74^{22} Jb 4^{13} שְׂעִפִּים מֵחֶזְיֹנוֹת לָיְלָה thoughts (arising) *out of*, etc., 6^{25} הוֹכֵחַ מִכֶּם reproof *proceeding from* you, $20^{29.29}$, ψ 78^{2} חִידוֹת מִקֶּדֶם indirect lessons (springing) *out of* antiquity; Dn 11^{31} וּזְרֹעִים מִמֶּנּוּ (Kö$^{iii.\,241}$). As marking the author of a judgment or estimate (rare), Nu 32^{22} נְקִיִּם מי׳ וּמִיִּשְׂרָאֵל guiltless *at the hands of* (=in the judgment of) J. and Israel (cf. מֵעִם 2 S 3^{28} Jb 34^{33}), Jb 4^{17} shall man be just מֵאֱלוֹהַּ *at God's hands?* (‖ מֵעֹשֵׂהוּ), Je 51^{5b} (Ges Gf); so in חָלִילָה לִּי מי׳. **e.** of the immediate, or *efficient*, cause (chiefly poet.), *in consequence of, at, by* (cf. Gk. ἀπό, as Hd. 2^{54}

ζήτησιν ἀπὸ σφέων γενέσθαι): (*a*) the cause, a *person* Gn 19^{36}+ הָרָה מִן to be pregnant *by*, 49^{25} 1 S 31^{3} וַיָּחֶל מֵהַמּוֹרִים was in anguish *from* the archers, Ho 7^{4} בֹּעֵרָה מֵאֹפֶה (ni בֹּעֵר הֵם leg.: v. We), ψ 18^{9} Na 1^{5} הרים רעשו ממנו, Dn 11^{31} (accents); with pass. vb., Na 1^{6} הצורים נִתְּצוּ ממנו, ψ 37^{23} (cf. Pr 20^{24} **d**), Jb 24^{1} Ec 12^{11} Dn 8^{11}. (*b*) the cause, a *thing*, Gn 49^{24} his arms were agile מידי אביר יעקב *from* the hands, etc., Is 6^{4} the thresholds shook מִקּוֹל הַקּוֹרֵא (so מקול elsewhere, as 30^{31} 33^{3} Je 8^{16}), 28^{7} תָּעוּ מִן־הַשֵּׁכָר (ב ‖), 31$^{4.9}$ Je 10^{10} Ez 19^{10} became fruitful מִמַּיִם רַבִּים, 31^{5} Jb 4^{9} מִנִּשְׁמַת אֱלוֹהַּ יֹאבֵדוּ *at* the breath of God, 14^{9} מֵרֵיחַ מַיִם יַפְרִחַ, 31^{23} 39^{26} הֲמִבִּינָתְךָ יַאֲבֶר־נֵץ, ψ 39^{11} 73^{19} סָפוּ תַמּוּ מִן־בַּלָּהוֹת, 78^{65} מִתְרוֹנֵן מִיָּיִן, 104^{15} להצהיל פנים משמן *from* oil, 107^{39}, cf. Jb 7^{14} (ב ‖); so with מִגַּעֲרַת י׳ *at* J.'s rebuke, 18^{16} 76^{7}+; with a pass. vb., Gn 9^{11} to be cut off מִמֵּי הַמַּבּוּל, 2 S 7^{29} וּמִבִּרְכָתְךָ יְבֹרַךְ, Is 28^{7} נבלעו מן־היין are undone *through* wine (22^{3} is dub.: see **1 b**), Ob^{9} Jb 28^{4} הַנִּשְׁכָּחִים מִנִּי רָגֶל; cf. Is 34^{3} Ho 6^{8}. (*c*) with verbs of *fearing*, to express the source of the emotion, as ירא ψ 3^{7}+ oft. (also c. מִפְּנֵי), פָּחַד 27^{1}, נִבְהַל Ez 26^{18}, גּוּר Dt 18^{22} Jb 41^{17}, Est 5^{9} ולא־קם ולא זָע ממנו; with בּוֹשׁ *to be disconcerted* or *disappointed*, to express the source of the disappointment, Is 1^{29} +oft.; with שָׂמַח †Pr 5^{18} Ec 2^{10}. **f.** of the remoter cause, the ultimate ground *on account of* which something happens or is done. (N.B. The line between **e** and **f** is not always clearly defined): Ex 2^{23} they sighed מן־העבדה *on account of* the bondage, 6^{9} 15^{23} Dt 7^{7} not מֵרֻבְּכֶם *through, by reason of*, your numbers did J. set his love upon you, Jos 22^{24} to do a thing מִדְּאָגָה *out of* carefulness, 2 S 23^{4} מִנֹּגַהּ, 1 K 14^{4} Is 53^{5} wounded מִפְּשָׁעֵנוּ *on account of* our transgressions, bruised מֵעֲוֺנֹתֵינוּ, v^{8} Jb 4^{19} Ob^{10} Hb 2^{17} ψ 6^{8} עששה עיני מִכַּעַס *from* vexation (cf. Jb 17^{7}: ψ 31^{10} ב׳), 31^{12} 38^{19} I am concerned *on account of* my sin, Pr 20^{4} מֵחֹרֶף עצל לא יחרש *by reason of* the winter, Jb 22^{4} הֲמִיִּרְאָתְךָ יֹכִיחֶךָ *on account of* thy fear of him? Ct 3^{8} Ru 1^{13} כִּי־מַר־לִי מְאֹד מִכֶּם *because of you:* see also Dt 28$^{34.67}$ 32^{19} Ju 2^{18} Is 65^{14} Je 12^{4} 24^{2} מֵרֹעַ, 50^{13} 51$^{5\,b}$ (Ew Ke), Ez 7^{27} (but read prob. with 𝔊 𝔖 𝔙 Co כְּדַרְכָּם), 16^{61} 35^{11} (AV *out of*), 45^{20} Mi 2^{12} 7^{13} ψ 5^{11} 12^{6} 107^{17} 119^{53}; Gn 49^{12} red of eyes מִיָּיִן, and white of teeth מֵחָלָב. Often also in מֵרֹב *from* the abundance of, abs. *for* abundance, with many different verbs, as Gn 16^{10} לֹא יִסָּפֵר מֵרֹב Jos 9^{13} 1 S 1^{16}, etc. Similarly in מִבְּלִי, מִבִּלְתִּי, מֵאֵין (pp. 35, 115, 117); and before an inf. (**7 a**), and in מֵאֲשֶׁר (p. 84). **g.** the cause being conceived as regulative, מן occasionally approaches in sense to *according to* (cf. Lat. *ex* more, *ex* lege), Jon 3^{7} proclaimed in Nineveh מטעם המלך וגדליו *at, by, in accordance* with, the decree of the king (cf. Aram. Ezr 6^{14} Dn 2^{8}): so Jb 39^{26} (**2 e** (*b*)) acc. to Ges Hi.

3. *Partitively* (a sense connecting with **2 a** (*c*), above):—**a.** Gn 6^{19} שְׁנַיִם מִכֹּל two *out of, from*, all, 7^{8}; 39^{11} . . . איש מן a man (or one) *of* . . . (so Nu 25^{6} 1 S 24^{28}+, . . . אנשים מן Nu 16^{2} Jos 2^{2}+, 2 K 2^{7}, etc.); Gn 42^{16} send מִכֶּם אֶחָד Lv 1^{2a} 17^{12} כָּל־נֶפֶשׁ מִכֶּם, 19^{34} 26^{8}, Ju 8^{14} נַעַר מֵאַנְשֵׁי סֻכּוֹת, 1 S 22^{8}, etc.; Ju 14^{19} 2 K 2^{24} Is 66^{19}; . . . אֶחָד מִן 1 S 16^{18}+, . . . אחד מן (Ges$^{§\,130,\,1}$) Dt 25^{5}+; אַחַת מֵהֵנָּה ψ 34^{21} Is 34^{16}; . . . מִי מִן Jb 5^{1} Is 50^{1}, . . . אֵין מִן 1 S 14^{39} Is 51^{18}; Is 21^{11} מַה־מלילה how much *of* the night? 2 Ch 31^{3} וּמְנָת הַמֶּלֶךְ מִן־רְכוּשׁוֹ. **b.** the number being omitted, מִן is used indefinitely:—(*a*) = *some of*,—as subj. Ex 16^{27} יצאו מן־העם there went out (some) *of* the people, Lv 25^{49} 2 S 11$^{17.24}$, esp. in late Hebrew Ezr 2$^{68.70}$ 7^{7} Ne 11$^{4.25}$ 1 Ch 4^{42} 9$^{30.32}$ 2 Ch 17^{11} 32^{21} Dn 11^{35}; more freq. as obj., esp. with לקח, Gn 4^{3} וַיָּבֵא מִפְּרִי האדמה brought *of* the fruit of the ground, 30^{14} give me מִדּוּדָאֵי בְּנֵךְ (some) *of* thy son's love-apples, 33^{15} Ex 12^{7} 17^{5} Lv 18^{30} 20^{2} Nu 11^{17} 13^{23} 1 K 12^{4} Is 39^{7} 47^{13} Am 2^{11} Dn 8^{10}+, Ct 1^{2} ישקני מִנְּשִׁיקוֹת פִּיהוּ let him kiss me (with) *some of* the kisses etc., ψ 72^{15} 137^{3} מִשִּׁיר צִיּוֹן (some) of the songs of Zion, Jb 11^{6} (Ges RVm) +oft.; in late Hebr. note also . . . יֵשׁ מִן there are *some of* . . . Ne 5^{5}; . . . מֵהֶם . . . מֵהֶם *some* . . . *others* . . . 1 Ch 9$^{28\,f.}$ (as in Aram. Dn 2^{33}, and PS^{2155}); . . . מִקְצָת *some of* . . . (as in NH) †Dn 1^{2} Ne 7^{69}. (*b*) to designate an individual (rare), Gn 28^{11} and he took מֵאַבְנֵי הַמָּקוֹם (one) of the stones of the place (see v^{18}), Ex 6^{25} מבנות פוטיאל (one) *of* the daughters of P., Ez 17$^{5.13}$ Ne 13^{28} ψ 132^{11}; as subj. Lv 25^{33} Dn 11^{5} the king of the south וּמִן־שָׂרָיו and (one) of his captains, v^{7}, cf. Je 41^{1} Est 4^{5} 2 Ch 26^{11}; Ru 2^{20} מִגֹּאֲלֵנוּ הוא he is (one) of our kinsmen, Ex 2^{6}. (*c*) in a neg. or hypoth. sentence (whether subject or object) = *any, aught*, Dt 16^{4} ולא ילין מן־הבשׂר and there shall *not* remain *any* of the flesh, 1 K 18^{5} ולא נכרית

מן־הבהמה and we shall not destroy *any* of the beasts, 2 K 10^{10} (cf. Jos 21^{43} 23^{14} 1 S 3^{19} 1 K 8^{56} Est 6^{10}), v^{23} פֶּן־יֶשׁ־פֹּה מֵעַבְדֵי י׳, Jb 27^{6} לֹא יֶחֱרַף לְבָבִי מִיָּמָי my heart reproacheth not *one* of my days: with אֹם, etc. Ex 29^{34} Lv 4^{2a} (cf. v$^{22.27}$), 11^{32} (מהם), v$^{33.35.37-39}$ 18^{29} 25^{25} Nu 5^{6}; מִכֹּל *anything whatever*, Lv 5^{24} 11^{34}; cf. 1 S 23^{23} (?). (*d*) peculiarly, with a noun of unity, esp. אֶחָד, to express forcibly the idea of a *single one:* Dt 15^{7} if there be a poor man in thy midst, מֵאַחַד אַחֶיךָ *any one* of thy brethren, Lv 4^{2b} if he doeth מֵאַחַת מֵהֵנָּה *any one* of these things, 5^{13} Ez 18^{10} וְעָשָׂה אָח מֵאַחַד מֵאֵלֶּה (where אח is a *vox nihili*) and doeth *aught* of these things; 1 S 14^{45} if there shall fall מִשַּׂעֲרַת ראשׁו אַרְצָה *a single* hair of his head to the ground! (for שַׂעֲרָה as a nom. unit. v. Ges^{§122t} Dr), cf. 2 S 14^{11} 1 K 1^{52}. (Probably a rhetorical application of the partitive sense, though the explanation '*starting from* one' = '*even* one' would also be possible. مِنْ is used similarly after neg. and interrog. particles, not merely with collective nouns, as مَا لَهُمْ مِنْ عِلْمٍ nought have they of knowledge (Qor 18^{4}), but also with nouns of unity, as Qor 3^{55} Ye have not مِنْ إِلَهٍ *aught of* (= *any*) god, except Him; 19^{19} dost thou perceive مِنْهُمْ مِنْ أَحَدٍ *even one* of them? 6^{59} there falleth not مِنْ وَرَقَةٍ *even a single* leaf (nom. unit.) without His knowing it. See further Thes, and W$^{AG. ii. §48 f. b}$). (*e*) (rare) specifying the objects, or elements, of which a genus consists (the Ar. مِنْ لِلْبَيَانِ, *min* of *explication*, W$^{AG. ii. §48 g}$): Gn 6^{2} מכל אשׁר בחרו *consisting of* all whom they chose, 7^{22} 9^{10} Lv 11^{32} (מכל), 1 Ch 5^{18} Je 40^{7} (מאשׁר); 44^{28} דְּבַר־מִי יָקוּם מִמֶּנִּי וּמֵהֶם and they shall know whose word shall stand, *consisting of me and of them* (defining the genus embraced by מי: cf. كُلٌّ مِنْ هَابِيلَ وَقَابِيلَ both (of them), Abel as well as Cain, and Qor 3^{193}: W$^{l.c.}$).—On מֵאַיִן Je 10$^{6.7}$, v. אַיִן *ad fin.*, p. 35.

4. Of *time*—viz. **a.** as marking the *terminus a quo*, the anterior limit of a continuous period, *from, since* Dt 9^{24} מִיּוֹם דַּעְתִּי אֶתְכֶם *from* the day of my (first) knowing you (so 1 S 7^{2} 8^{8}+); 1 S 18^{9} מהיום ההוא וָהָלְאָה *from* that day and onwards, simil. †Lv 22^{27} Nu 15^{23} Ez 39^{22}; Is 18$^{2.7}$ (where מִן־הוּא = מֵאֲשֶׁר הוּא; cf. Na 2^{9} מִימֵי אֲשֶׁר הִיא = מִימֵי הִיא); מהיום ההוא וָמָעְלָה †1 S 16^{13} 30^{25} (Hg 2$^{15.18}$ appar. of time *back-wards*); מֵאָז *from* the time of .... (v. p. 23); מִבֶּטֶן אִמִּי מִן־הַבֶּטֶן *from* the womb Ju 13$^{5.7}$, 16^{17}+; .... מִימֵי Ho 10^{9} Is 23^{7} Je 36^{2}+; מִיָּמֶיךָ idiom. = *since* thou wast born †1 S 25^{28} 1 K 1^{6} (מִיָּמָיו), Jb 38^{12}; מִקֶּדֶם *from* antiquity Hb 1^{12} ψ 74^{12}, Is 42^{14} הֶחֱשֵׁיתִי מֵעוֹלָם I have been silent *since* old time; מֵעַתָּה *from* now, hence-*forth* Je 3^{4}+, מִיּוֹם *from* to-day †Is 43^{13} Ez 48^{35}, מן־היום הזה Hg 2^{19}. See also **5 c, 7 c.** Cf. Ex 33^{6} מֵהַר חוֹרֵב *from* Horeb, Ho 13^{4} I am י׳ thy God מֵאֶרֶץ מִצְרָיִם. **b.** as marking the period immediately succeeding the limit, *after:* Gn 38^{24} כְּמִשְׁלֹשׁ חֳדָשִׁים *after* about three months it was told Judah, מִיָּמִים רַבִּים †Jos 23^{1} Ez 38^{8}, מִיָּמִים *after* (some) days, †Ju 11^{4} 14^{8} 15^{1}, מִיֹּמַיִם *after* two days †Ho 6^{2}; מֵרֹב יָמִים Is 24^{22}: more freq. with קֵץ or קָצֶה, Gn 4^{3} מִקֵּץ יָמִים, 8^{3} Jos 3^{2}+oft.; Dt 14^{28} מִקְצֵה שָׁלֹשׁ שָׁנִים, 15^{1} מִקְצֵה שֶׁבַע שָׁנִים (by which is meant not the actual *end* of the three or seven years, but the period when the third or seventh year has arrived); מִמָּחֳרָת *after* the morrow (had arrived) = *on* the morrow, Gn 19^{34}+oft.; מֵהַבֹּקֶר 2 S 2^{27}.—2 S 23^{4} מִמָּטָר; Is 53^{11} מֵעֲמַל נַפְשׁוֹ; perhaps 29^{18} (Kö^{581}). Cf. 2 S 20^{5} and he delayed מן־המועד *beyond* the appointed time. **c.** in such phrases, however, מִן sometimes (cf. **1 c**) loses its signif.: thus מֵאָז 2 S 15^{34} Is 16^{13} not *from* former time, but *in* former time, formerly, Gn 6^{4} הַגִּבֹּרִים אֲשֶׁר מֵעוֹלָם which were *of old*, Jos 24^{2} dwelt *of old*, ψ 77^{6} days מִקֶּדֶם *aforetime*, מֵאַחֲרֵי Dt 29^{21} (p. 30).—†מִקָּרוֹב lit. *from near*, i.e. recently Dt 32^{17}, of short duration Jb 20^{5}, shortly Ez 7^{8}; at hand (in a *local* sense, **1 c**) Je 23^{23}.

5. מִן ... עַד (וְעַד) *from ... even to:* very oft.:—**a.** in geogr. or local sense, Gn 10^{19} 15^{18} מנהר מצרים עד הנהר הגדול, 25^{18} Ex 23^{31} Dt 2^{36} 1 S 3^{20} 2 S 5^{25} Je 31^{38} ψ 72^{8}+oft.; so with מִלְּבוֹא †1 K 8^{65} (2 Ch 7^{8}), 2 K 14^{25} Am 6^{14}; Dt 13^{8} מִקְצֵה הָאָרֶץ וְעַד קְצֵה הָאָרֶץ, 28^{64} Je 12^{12}; Gn 47^{21} מִקְצֵה גְבוּל־מִצְרַיִם וְעַד־קָצֵהוּ, 1 K 6^{24} 7^{23} מִשְּׂפָתוֹ וְעַד שְׂפָתוֹ; Lv 13^{12} מראשׁו ועד רגליו, Dt 28^{35} מכף רגלך ועד קדקדך (similarly 2 S 14^{25} Jb 2^{7} Is 1^{6}). Cf. 1 S 9^{2} מִשִּׁכְמוֹ וָמַעְלָה, 2 S 5^{9} Jos 15^{46}. **b.** metaph. not of actual space, but of *classes of objects*, to express idiomatically the idea of *comprehension*, so that the two preps. may be often represented by *both ... and:* Gn 19^{4} מִנַּעַר וְעַד־זָקֵן *from* young *to* old (i.e. both included) = *both* young *and* old, v^{11} 1 S 5^{9}+ מִקָּטֹן וְעַד־גָּדוֹל = *both* great *and* small, Je 6^{13} מִקְּטַנָּם וְעַד־גְּדוֹלָם *from* the least of them *even to* the greatest of them, ib. מִנָּבִיא וְעַד־כֹּהֵן *from* the proph. *even to* the priest every one dealeth falsely, Ex 9^{25}+ מאדם ועד בהמה *both* man *and* beast, 11^{5} מבכור פרעה . . . עד מחטב עציך, 13^{15} Nu 6^{4} Dt 29^{10} בכור השפחה וגו׳, עד שׁאב מימיך, Jos 8^{25}+ מאיש ועד אשה, 1 S 15^{3} (4 pairs), 22^{19} 1 K 5^{13} 2 K 17^{9} = 18^{8}, Is 10^{18} מנפש ועד בשׂר = *both* soul *and* body, Je 9^{9}; after a word implying a negative = *either* . . . *or* Gn 14^{23} $31^{24.29}$ מטוב עד רע *either* good *or* evil. The עַד may be repeated, if required: Gn 6^{7} מאדם עד־בהמה עד רמשׂ ועד־עוף השמים (so 7^{23}), Ex 22^{3} Jos 6^{21} Ju 15^{5} מִגָּדִישׁ וְעַד־קָמָה וְעַד־כֶּרֶם זָיִת, 20^{48} 1 S 30^{19}: without מִן, Lv 11^{42} Nu 8^{4}. Similar is the use of מן in the idiom (וָמַ֫טָּה) מִבֶּן...שָׁנָה וָמַ֫עְלָה (also וְעַד־בֶּן . . . שָׁנָה): v. p. 122^{a}; and cf. 2 K 3^{21}. **c.** of *time*, Gn 46^{34} מִנְּעוּרֵינוּ וְעַד עַתָּה *from* our youth even until now, 1 S 12^{2} Je 3^{25}; Nu 14^{19}; Ex 10^{6}; 18^{13} מן־הבקר עד־הערב, 1 S 30^{17} 1 K 18^{26}; Is 9^{6} ψ 90^{2}; + oft.; with two inff. Hos 7^{4}: and implying *intervals* (not duration) Ez $4^{10.11}$ (cf. with לְ Est $3^{7.7}$). **d.** there occur further (1) מִן . . . אֶל־, Jos 15^{21}, Ex 26^{28} = 36^{33} מִן־הַקָּצֶה אֶל־הַקָּצֶה *from* end *to* end, Ez $40^{23.27}$ Ezr 9^{11} מִפֶּה־אֶל־פֶּה; ψ 144^{13} מִזַּן אֶל זַן *from* kind *to* kind = kinds of every sort; with a verb of motion, Je 48^{11} ψ 105^{13} 1 Ch 17^{5}, and expressing a climax, ψ 84^{8} יֵלְכוּ מֵחַיִל אֶל־חָיִל, Je 9^{2} (cf. Rom 1^{17}): of time, מיום־אל־יום + Nu 30^{15}, cf. 1 Ch 16^{23} (‖ ψ 96^{2} לְ); implying *intervals*, מֵעֵת אֶל־עֵת + 1 Ch 9^{25}. (2) מִן . . . לְ Ex 32^{27} Ez 40^{13} Zc 14^{10}: of time ψ 96^{2}; Jb 4^{20}: with *intervals*, 2 S 14^{26}. (3) מִן...ה ֿ Nu 34^{10} Ez 6^{14} מִמִּדְבַּר רִבְלָ֫תָה (so Ges Ew Hi etc.) *from* the wilderness *to* Riblah, 21^{3} 25^{13} מִתֵּימָן וּדְדָ֫נֶה (Co Kö Berthol); without ה ֿ, 1 K 5^{1}. And of time in the phrase (implying *intervals*) מִיָּמִים יָמִ֫ימָה Ex 13^{10} + 4 t.

6. In *comparisons*, *beyond*, *above*, hence in Engl. *than:* so constantly; viz. **a.** when an object is compared with another distinct from itself, Ju 14^{18} מַה־מָּתוֹק מִדְּבַשׁ what is sweet *away from, beyond, in excess of*, honey? i.e. in our idiom, what is *sweeter than* honey? Lv 21^{10} הַכֹּהֵן הַגָּדוֹל מֵאֶחָיו the priest that is great *above* his brethren, Nu 14^{12} Ez 28^{3} חָכָם מִדָּנִאֵל wiser *than* Daniel, ψ 119^{72} + very oft.; Ho 2^{9} כִּי טוֹב לִי אָז מֵעָתָּה; with an inf. (sts. c. לְ) as subj., Gn 29^{19} טוב תִּתִּי אֹתָהּ לָךְ מִתִּתִּי אֹתָהּ וגו׳ better is my giving her to thee *than* my giving her to another, Ex 14^{12} 1 S 15^{22} Pr $21^{9.19}$ 25^{7} ψ $118^{8.9}$ +; with verbs, Gn 19^{9} עתה נָרַע לְךָ מֵהֶם now we will harm thee *beyond* them, *more than* them, 25^{23} לְאֹם מִלְאֹם יֶאֱמָץ, 26^{16} 29^{30} ויאהב גם־את־רחל מִלֵּאָה, 38^{26} צָדְקָה מִמֶּנִּי, 48^{19} יִגְדַּל מִמֶּנּוּ, Ju 2^{19} השחיתו מאבותם they have done corruptly *more than* their fathers, 1 S 2^{29} 2 S 20^{6} 1 K 1^{37} 14^{9} Je 5^{3} Ez 5^{6} + oft.; = *in preference to, above*, ψ 45^{8} $52^{5.5}$ Ho 6^{6} Hb 2^{16}, after בחר Je 8^{3} Jb 7^{15} 36^{21} ψ 84^{11} (מִדּוּר) +: note also נֹפֵל מִן Jb 12^{3} 13^{2} = inferior *to* (Ew Ges: al. Hi; al. De); שֹׁנָה מִן different *from* Est 1^{7} 3^{8}. **b.** when an obj. is compared with a group or multitude of which it forms one, esp. with מִכֹּל, Gn 3^{1} עָרוּם מִכֹּל חַיַּת הַשָּׂדֶה subtil *out of* all beasts of the field, or *beyond*, *above* all (other) beasts, v^{14} cursed *above* all cattle (but without implying any judgment whether other cattle are cursed likewise), 37^{3} Israel loved Joseph מִכָּל־בָּנָיו *out of* all his sons, or *above* all his (other) sons, Dt 7^{7} 33^{24} בָּרוּךְ מִבָּנִים אָשֵׁר blessed above sons be Asher, Ju 5^{24} תְּבֹרַךְ מִנָּשִׁים blessed *above* women be Jael, 1 S 9^{2b} 15^{33} כֵּן תִּשְׁכַּל מִנָּשִׁים אִמֶּךָ, 18^{30} Je 17^{9} עָקֹב מִכֹּל deceitful *above* all things, ψ 45^{3} Ct 5^{10} דָּגוּל מֵרְבָבָה (cf. בָּחַר מִן supr. **2 a** *c: ex* in eximius, egregius; Il. 18^{431} ὅσσ', ἐμοὶ ἐκ πάσεων Κρονίδης Ζεὺς ἄλγε' ἔδωκεν, 3^{227} ἔξοχος Ἀργείων . . . κεφαλήν). **c.** sometimes in poetry the idea on which מן is logically dependent, is unexpressed, and must be understood by the reader, Is 10^{10} ופסיליהם מירושלם and their idols are (more) *than* (those of) Jerusalem, Mi 7^{4} יָשָׁר מִמְּסוּכָה the uprightest is (sharper) *than* a thorn-hedge (but We *from*), Jb 11^{7} 28^{18}; ψ 4^{8} מֵעֵת *beyond* (that of) the time when etc. Ec 4^{17} 9^{17}; cf. Ez 15^{2}. **d.** מִן not unfrequently expresses the idea of a thing being *too much for* a person, or surpassing his powers: Gn 18^{14} הֲיִפָּלֵא מי׳ דָּבָר can a thing be *too hard for* J.? (so Dt 17^{8}+; cf. ψ 131^{1} 139^{6}+), 32^{11} קָטֹנְתִּי מִן, Dt 14^{24} כִּי יִרְבֶּה מִמְּךָ הַדֶּרֶךְ = is *too great for* thee (1 K 19^{7}), 32^{47} רֵק מִכֶּם: so c. עָצֵם Gn 26^{16}, כָּבֵד be *too heavy for* Ex 18^{18} ψ 38^{5}, מָךְ Lv 27^{8} (too poor to pay), קָשָׁה Dt 1^{17}, צַר be *too narrow for*, 2 K 6^{1} Is 49^{19}, קצר Is 50^{2}, אָמֵץ ψ 18^{18}, ירום ממני is *too high for* me 61^{3}, גָּבַר 65^{4}; הַמְעַט מִמְּךָ + Jb 15^{11} *too little for* thee? הַמְעַט מִכֶּם + Nu 16^{9} Is 7^{13} Ez 34^{18} (v. מְעַט; also on 16^{20}); oft. with an inf., as Gn 4^{13} גָּדוֹל עֲוֺנִי מִנְּשֹׂא is *greater than* I can bear, 30^{7} their substance was רַב מִשֶּׁבֶת יַחְדָּו lit. *great beyond* dwelling together = *too great for* (their) dwelling together, Ex 12^{4} Ju 7^{2} רַב מִתִּתִּי = *too great for* me to give, 1 S 25^{17b} 1 K 8^{64} רַב מֵהָכִיל, Is 28^{20} 33^{19} 59^{1} Hb 1^{13} ψ 40^{6} Ru

1[12]: note esp רַב מִן it is *more than that* . . . (=there is enough of), Ex 9[28] 1 K 12[28], sq. subst. Ez 44[6] (v. רַב); and Is 49[6] נָקֵל מִהְיוֹתְךָ לִי עֶבֶד לְהָקִים וגו׳ *too light for thy being* my servant was it to raise up, etc., Ez 8[17] הֲנָקֵל לְבֵית יִשְׂר׳ מֵעֲשׂוֹת וגו׳ was it *too trifling* to the house of Isr. *for* the doing etc. (less than the doing etc. deserved)? (but ?rd. עֲשׂוֹת on anal. of 1 K 16[31]).

7. מִן is prefixed to an *infin.*: **a.** with a *causal* force (rare), *from, on account of, through* (cf. **2 f**): Dt 7[7.8] מֵאַהֲבַת י׳ אֶתְכֶם *through* J.'s loving you = *because* J. *loved* you, 9[28] (cf. 1[27] בְּ) 2 S 3[11] מִיִּרְאָתוֹ אֹתוֹ = *because* he feared him, Is 48[4] . . . מִדַּעְתִּי = *because* I knew . . . So in מִבִּלְתִּי, מִבְּלִי . . . . **b.** after verbs implying *restraint, prevention, cessation*, etc., as עֲצָרַנִי מִלֶּדֶת Gn 16[2] hath restrained me *from* bearing, וַתַּעֲמֹד מִלֶּדֶת 29[35] 30[9]: so with חשׂך 20[6]+, חדל Ex 23[5]+, כָּלָה 34[33]+, נִכְלָא 36[6], מָנַע 1 S 25[26]+, שִׁמְרוּ מִן־הַחֵרֶם †Jos 6[18], יָרֵא מֵהַבִּיט Ex 3[6]+, שׁבת Je 31[36]+, הֵשִׁיב מִלֶּכֶת 2 Ch 25[13]. Esp. (*a*) after similar verbs, expressing concisely a *negative consequence*, lit. *away from* . . ., i.e. *so as not to, so that not*: Gn 23[6b] 27[1] Jacob's eyes were dim, מֵרְאֹת *away from* seeing = *so that* he could not see, 31[29] נִשְׁמַר מִן (‖ v[24] פֶּן), Ex 14[5] Lv 26[13] Nu 32[7] Dt 28[55] (his eye shall be envious etc.) מִתֵּת *from* giving = *so that he will not* give, Ju 6[27] 1 S 2[31] 7[8] do not be silent from us מִזְּעֹק *so as not to* call (cf. 1 K 22[3]), 8[7] me have they rejected מִמְּלֹךְ עליהם, 16[1] (Ho 4[6]), 2 S 14[11] (rd. מֵהַרְבּוֹת), Is 5[6] 8[11] 21[3] 23[1] is destroyed מִבּוֹא *so that none* can enter in, 24[10] 33[15] 44[18] 49[15] 54[9] 56[6] 58[13] Je 10[14] נִבְעַר . . . מִדַּעַת is stupefied *so that he has no knowledge*, 13[14] 33[21.24.26] Ez 20[17] Mi 3[6] Zc 7[11.12] ψ 30[4] Qr, 39[2] 69[24] 102[5] (after שָׁכַח, peculiarly), 106[23] La 3[44] 4[18] Jb 34[30a] 2 Ch 36[13]. So in חָלִילָה־לִּי מֵעֲשׂוֹת *that I should not* do Gn 44[17]+. (*b*) still more concisely, esp. in poetry, with a noun alone: 1 S 15[23] has rejected thee מִמֶּלֶךְ *from* (being) king (v[26] מִהְיוֹת מֶלֶךְ), Lv 26[43] מֵהֶם, Is 7[8] יֵחַת מֵעָם shall be shattered *from* (being) a people, *that it be no more* a people, 17[1] מוּסָר מֵעִיר, 25[2b] 52[14] כֵּן מִשְׁחַת מֵאִישׁ מַרְאֵהוּ marred *away from* (being) a man('s), Je 2[25] מִיָּחֵף, 17[16] מֵרֹעֶה, 48[2] וְנַכְרִיתֶנָּה מִגּוֹי, v[42] מֵעָם, ψ 8[6] hast made him lack but little מאלהים *ut non esset* Deus, 83[5] מִגּוֹי, Pr 30[2] בַּעַר אָנֹכִי מֵאִישׁ *too* boorish *to be* a man; cf. Dn 4[13]; 1 K 15[13] וַיְסִרֶהָ מִגְּבִירָה removed her *from* (being) queen-mother, Ez 16[41] וְהִשְׁבַּתִּיךְ מִזּוֹנָה; and even to express absol. the non-existence of a thing not named in the principal clause, as Is 23[1] כִּי שֻׁדַּד מִבַּיִת *so that there is no* house, Ez 12[19] (32[15]), 25[9] מֵהֶעָרִים, Ho 9[11.11.11.12] Mi 3[6] Hg 1[10] מִטָּל, Zc 7[14] 9[8] ψ 39[3] 49[15] מִזְּבֻל־לוֹ *so that it has no* dwelling, 52[7] יִסָּחֲךָ מֵאֹהֶל pluck thee up *tentless*, 109[24] is lean מִשָּׁמֶן *so that there is no* fatness, Jb 28[11] 33[21] 34[30b]. Oft. strengthened by pleon. אַיִן or בְּלִי, as מֵאֵין יוֹשֵׁב Is 5[9], מִבְּלִי יוֹשֵׁב v. pp. 35[a], 115[b]. Cf. Kö[iii. 592 ff.] **c.** with a *temporal* force, *since, after* (cf. **4**), chiefly late: Nu 24[23] מִשֻּׂמוֹ אֵל *after* God's establishing him, Is 44[7] מִשּׂוּמִי עַם־עוֹלָם *since* I appointed the ancient people, Ho 7[4] Hg 2[16](?) Ru 2[18] Ne 5[14] 1 Ch 8[8] מִן־שִׁלְחוֹ אוֹתָם (cf. 6[16]) 2 Ch 31[10] Dn 11[23] 12[1] (cf. 9[25]), ψ 73[20] כַּחֲלוֹם מֵהָקִיץ *after* (one's) awaking, Jb 20[4].

8. Once Dt 33[11] as a **conj.** before a finite verb. Smite . . . his haters מִן־יְקוּמוּן *that* they rise not again, poet. for מִקּוּם (**7 b**): cf. Dr[§ 41].—On מֵאֲשֶׁר **adv.** and **conj.**, v. p. 84.

9. In compounds:—**a.** מֵאַחֲרֵי, מֵאֵת, מִבֵּין, מִבַּלְעֲדֵי, מִבַּעַד, מִל (common in NH, esp. before inf.; in O.T. only in מִלְּבַד, מִלְּבוֹא (supr. **5 a**), מִלְמַעְלָה, מִלְמַטָּה, מִלְּעֻמַּת, מִלְּפָנִים, מִלִּפְנֵי, and, si vera l., מִלְמַעֲלֵה הֶחָרֶס Jd 8[13], v. מַעֲלֶה), מִנֶּגֶד, מֵעַל, מֵעִם, מִתַּחַת; see אַחֲרֵי, אֵת, etc. **b.** לְמִן (לְמִנִּי †Mi 7[12.12]), with לְ pleon., *from* = מִן, but used almost exclusively of the *terminus a quo*, whether of space or time (cf. מִן **5**);—(1) of *space*, Dt 4[32] Ju 20[1] לְמִדָּן וְעַד־בְּאֵר שֶׁבַע, Mi 7[12.12] (both לְמִנִּי), Zc 14[10] 1 Ch 5[9]; לְמֵרָחוֹק *from* afar Jb 36[3] 39[29] (on Ezr 3[13] 2 Ch 26[15], v. sub עַד לְ); לְמִתַּחַת לְ = *underneath* 1 K 7[32]. Idiom., esp. sq. וְעַד, to denote comprehensively an entire class, לְמֵאִישׁ וְעַד בְּהֵמָה †Ex 11[7] Je 51[62] (לְמֵאָדָם), לְמִקָּטֹן וְעַד גָּדוֹל, לְמֵאִישׁ וְעַד אִשָּׁה †2 S 6[19] 2 Ch 15[13], †2 K 23[2] Je 42[8], simil. 2 Ch 15[13] Je 31[34] Est 1[5.20], לְמִבֶּן עֶשְׂרִים שָׁנָה, לְמֵרַע וְעַד־טוֹב †2 S 13[22], וּלְמַטָּה †1 Ch 27[23], cf. 2 Ch 25[5].—On לְמִבֵּית Nu 18[7], see p. 110[b]. (2) of *time* (oft. foll. by עַד), לְמִן הַיּוֹם אֲשֶׁר . . . *from* the day when . . ., †Dt 4[32] 9[7] 2 S 7[11] (‖ 1 Ch 17[10] וּלְמִיָּמִים אֲשֶׁר) Je 7[25] 32[31] Hg 2[18]; לְמִקְצָת הַיָּמִים אֲשֶׁר . . . †Dn 1[18]; לְמִן הַיּוֹם sq. inf. (in appos.) †Ex 9[18] 2 S 19[25]; לְמִיּוֹם sq. inf. (genit.) †Ju 19[30] 2 S 7[6] Is 7[17]; לְמִימֵי . . . †2 K 19[25] (‖ Is 37[26] מימי) Mal 3[7]; למן־עולם ועד עולם †Je 7[7] 25[5]; לְמֵרָחוֹק *from* afar = long before, 2 S 7[19] = 1 Ch 17[17], 2 K 19[25] = Is 37[26].

4521 **מְנָאוֹת** v. מְנָת sub מנה. below

4485 **[מְנַגִּינָה]** v. נגן. p. 618

4487 † **מָנָה** **vb.** count, number, reckon, assign (NH *id.;* As. *manû* Dl[HWB 416]; Ar. مَنَى *assign, apportion;* Aram. ܡܢܳܐ, מְנָא);—**Qal** *Pf.* מָנָה Nu 23[10]; וּמָנִ֫יתִי Is 65[12]; *Impf.* 2 ms. תִּמְנֶה־ 1 K 20[25]; וַיִּמְנוּ 2 K 12[11]; *Imv.* מְנֵה 2 S 24[1]; *Inf. cstr.* לִמְנוֹת Gn 13[16] + 4 t.; *Pt.* מוֹנֶה Je 33[13] ψ 147[4];—**1.** *count, number* (cf. סָפַר) dust (grains) Gn 13[16] (J), cf. עֲפַר יַעֲקֹב Nu 23[10] (JE); money 2 K 12[11]; stars (מ׳ מִסְפָּר לַכּוֹכָבִים) ψ 147[4]; flock Je 33[13] (symb. of peace); days ψ 90[12]; people, army 2 S 24[1] 1 Ch 21[1.17], cf. 27[24] (object om.); 1 K 20[25]. **2.** *reckon, assign, appoint* לֶחָרֶב Is 65[12] (with play on מְנִי v[11]). **Niph.** *Pf.* נִמְנָה Is 53[12]; *Impf.* יִמָּנֶה Gn 13[16] 1 K 3[8]; יִמָּנוּ 1 K 8[5] = 2 Ch 5[6]; *Inf. cstr.* הִמָּנוֹת Ec 1[15];—**1.** *be counted, numbered,* of descendants Gn 13[16] (J), of people 1 K 3[8] (‖ יִסָּפֵר); of sacrificial animals 1 K 8[5] = 2 Ch 5[6] (both ‖ *id.*); indef. Ec 1[15]. **2.** *be reckoned, assigned* (a place), of servant of י׳ Is 53[12] (c. אֶת פֹּשְׁעִים). **Pi.** (late and poet.) (B Aram. and 𝔗 מַנִּי);—*Pf.* מִנָּה Dn 1[10.11]; מִנּוּ Jb 7[3]; *Impf.* וַיְמַן Jon 2[1] + 4 t.; *Imv.* מַן ψ 61[8]; *appoint, ordain,* food Dn 1[10], v[5] (sq. לְ), officer v[11] (sq. עַל); nights of weariness (לֵילוֹת עָמָל) Jb 7[3] (subj. indef.; sq. לְ); in story of Jonah, obj. fish Jon 2[1], ricinus 4[6], worm v[7], wind v[8] (all subj. י׳); obj. חֶסֶד וֶאֱמֶת ψ 61[8] (subj. י׳). **Pu.** *Pt.* pl. מְמֻנִּים 1 Ch 9[29] *appointed,* of porters (sq. עַל).

4490 † **מָנָה** **n.f.** part, portion;—מ׳ Ex 29[26] + 4 t.; (on מְנָת־ Je 13[25], cf. ψ 16[5], v. מְנָת); pl. מָנוֹת 1 S 1[4] + 5 t.; sf. מָנוֹתֶ֫הָ Est 2[9];—*part, portion,* esp. choice portion, Ex 29[26] Lv 7[33] 8[29] (all of sacrificial animal; all P); cf. 2 Ch 31[19]; also 1 S 1[4.5]; of distrib. of choice bits Ne 8[10.12] Est 9[19.22]; cf. also Est 2[9] (v. Dn 1[5.10]).

4488 † **מָנֶה** **n.m.** maneh, mina, a weight (perh. orig. *a* specific *part;* NH *id.;* As. *manû* Dl [HWB 417]; Aram. ܡܢܝܳܐ, מָנְיָא);—מ׳ Ez 45[12]; מָנִים 1 K 10[17] + 3 t.; = 50 shekels Ez 45[12] (on חֲמִשִּׁים for חֲמִשָּׁה v. Hi Co); of gold 1 K 10[17]; of silver Ezr 2[69] Ne 7[71.72].—The weight of the mina was $\frac{1}{60}$ of talent; i.e. acc. to older (Bab.) standard, 982·2 grammes (= 60 shekels at c. 16·37 g.) = c. 2 lbs.; in Ezekiel's time the mina = 50 shekels = 818·6 g. = c. $1\frac{2}{3}$ lb. (cf. שֶׁקֶל, כִּכָּר). Vid. Benz[Arch. 187 ff. 194] Now[Arch. i. 208 f.]

† **[מֹנֶה]** **n.[m.]** counted number, time;— 4489
only הֶחֱלִף . . . עֲשֶׂרֶת מֹנִים Gn 31[7.41] *changed ten times.*

† **מְנִי** **n.pr.div.** Menî, god of fate (*award,* 4507
apportionment; cf. Ar. n. pr. div. *Maniyyât,* and perh. *Manât,* We[Skizzen iii. 22 f. 189], مَنَوَاتٌ Nö [ZMG xl. 1886, 709]; in Nab. מנותו Eut[Nab. No. 2, l. 5], etc.);— מְמַלְּאִים לַמְנִי מִמְסָךְ Is 65[11] (‖ לַגַּד)—v. Che Di Bae [Sem. Rel. 79].

† **[מְנָת]** **n.f.** portion (= מָנָה, chiefly late; 4521
on form cf. Ges[§ 95 n.] Lag[BN 81, 150]);—cstr. מְנָת 2 Ch 31[3] + 5 t.; *Pl.* cstr. מְנָאוֹת Ne 12[44]; מְנָיוֹת Ne 12[47] 13[10];—*portion* of king, for sacrifice, 2 Ch 31[3]; of priest v[4]; also Ne 12[44] מְנָאוֹת הַתּוֹרָה לַכֹּ׳; of Levites 13[10]; of singers 12[47]; fig. מְנָת כּוֹסָם ψ 11[6] (of judgment of wicked), cf. מ׳ שֻׁעָלִים ψ 63[11]; so מְנָת־מִדַּיִךְ Je 13[25] *portion of thy measure* = thine allotted portion; rd. also מְנָתוֹ(-ה) for מִנֵּהוּ ψ 68[24] (so Ol Dy Bi Che We); in good sense, י׳ מְנָת חֶלְקִי וְכוֹסִי ψ 16[5] י׳ *is the portion of my lot and my cup.*

† **תִּמְנָ֫תָה, תִּמְנָה** **n.pr.loc.** (prob. = *por-* 8553
tion, territory);—(תִּמְנָה) Jos 15[10.57] 2 Ch 28[18]; תִּמְנָ֫תָה [as nomin. v. GFM[Ju 14, 1]] Jos 19[43] Ju 14[1.2.5]; c. ה loc. תִּמְנָ֫תָה Gn 38[12.13.14] Ju 14[1.5]; 𝔊 Θαμνα, Θαμναθα):—**1.** place in hill-country of Judah Gn 38[12.13.14] prob. = Jos 15[57]. Site unknown (cf. Di[Gn 38, 12] Rob[BR ii. 17 n.]). **2.** place on border of Judah Jos 15[10] 19[43] (assigned to Dan), Ju 14[1.1.2.5.5] 2 Ch 28[18]. Mod. *Tibneh,* c. 15 m. S. of W. fr. Jerusalem cf. Rob [BR ii. 17] Buhl[Geogr. 196].

† **תִּמְנִי** **adj.gent.** הַתִּ׳ Ju 15[6] *the Timnite.* 8554

† **תִּמְנַת חֶ֫רֶס** **n.pr.loc.** (prob. = (sacred) 8556
territory of the Sun; WMM[As. u. Eur. 165] thinks perh. Eg. *Ḥï-ra-tà*); in hill-country of Ephr., westward, Ju 2[9] = foll. (cf. GFM) = Θαμναθα 1 Makk 9[50] = mod. *Tibneh,* c. 17 m. W. of N. fr. Jerusalem, v. also Buhl[Geogr. 170].

† **תִּמְנַת סֶ֫רַח** **n.pr.loc.** by metath. from 8556
foregoing, to avoid idolatr. suggestion (GFM [Ju 2, 9]), Jos 19[50] 24[30].

מִנְהָג v. נהג. **[מִנְהָרָה]** v. II. נהר. 4491-92
p. 624, 626

מָנוֹד v. נוד. p. 627 4493

I, II. **מָנוֹחַ, מְנוּחָה** v. נוח. 4494-96

† **מָנוֹן** **n.m.** dub.; only in וְאַחֲרִיתוֹ יִהְיֶה מ׳ 4497
Pr 29[21] Ew Now *thankless one* (Eth. መኒን: Di[189]);

De "*Brutstätte*" i.e. father of numerous progeny (√נון); < Be Str (who cites A. Müller), cf. Wild., rd. מָדוֹן *strife.*

מְנוּסָה, מָנוֹס v. נוס. **מָנוֹר** v. ניר.

מְנוֹרָה v. נור. **[מִנְּזָרִים]** v. נזר.

מנח (√of foll.; cf. Ar. مَنَحَ *lend, give a gift,* مِنْحَةٌ *loan, gift* esp. of she camel, sheep, or goat for milking, Ph. מנחת, *gift, offering*).

4503 **מִנְחָה**$_{153}$ **n.f. gift, tribute, offering** (NH *id.;* Ph. מנחת; 𝔗 מִנְחָתָא; on Ar. v. supr.);—abs. מ׳ Gn 4^{3} + 81 t.; cstr. מִנְחַת Lv 2^{7} + 22 t.; sf. מִנְחָתִי Gn 33^{10} + 3 t.; + 41 t. sfs. sg.; pl. sf. מִנְחֹתֶיךָ ψ 20^{4}; מִנְחֹתֵיכֶם Nu 29^{39} Am 5^{22};—†**1.** *gift, present* Gn 32$^{14.19.21.22}$ (E), 33^{10} 43$^{11.15.25.26}$ (J), Ju 6^{18} 1 S 10^{27} 1 K 10^{25} = 2 Ch 9^{24} 2 K 8$^{8.9}$ 20^{12} = Is 39^{1}, ψ 45^{13} 2 Ch 32^{23}. †**2.** *tribute* Ju 3$^{15.17.18.18}$ 2 S 8$^{2.6}$ = 1 Ch 18$^{2.6}$, 1 K 5^{1} 2 K 17$^{3.4}$ 2 Ch 17$^{5.11}$ 26^{8} Ho 10^{6} ψ 72^{10}. †**3.** *offering* made to God, of any kind, whether grain or animals Gn 4$^{3.4.5}$ Nu 16^{15} (J), 1 S 2$^{17.29}$ 26^{19} Is 1^{13} ψ 96^{8} Zp 3^{10}; + (prob.) (לַ)עֲלוֹת הַמִּנְחָה 1 K 18$^{29.36}$ 2 K 3^{20} (Ephr.; usually regarded as = מִנְחַת עֶרֶב, but that much later usage). This gen. meaning poss. also in foll.: זבח ומנחה 1 S 2^{29} (see v^{29b}), 3^{14} Is 19^{21}; עלה ומנחה Je 14^{12}; עולה ‖ ψ 20^{4}; שֶׁלֶם ‖ Am 5^{22} (עֹלוֹת gloss, to explain אָרִיחַ); or these may shew early stage of discrimination. †**4.** *grain offering* (whether raw, roasted, ground to flour, or prepared as bread or cakes, see below. AV *meat offering,* misleading < RV *meal-offering.* GFM $^{Judges\ 322}$ renders *cereal oblation*);—יָבִיאוּ אֶת־הַמִּנְחָה בִּכְלִי טָהוֹר Is 66^{20} *they bring the grain offering in clean vessels* (restored Jews are brought as such an offering), cf. מנחה טהורה Mal 1^{11}; brought in hands Je 41^{5} (late addit. Co); received from hands Mal 1^{10}; חִטִּים למנחה 1 Ch 21^{23} *wheat for grain offering;* סֹלֶת 1 Ch 23^{29}, mixed with oil Ez 46^{14}, baked v^{20}; disting. from other offerings 1 K 8$^{64.64}$ = 2 Ch 7^{7}, 2 K 16$^{13.15.15.15}$ Is 43^{23} 57^{6} 66^{3} Je 17^{26} 33^{18} 41^{5} (late editors Co), Ez 42^{13} 44^{29} 45$^{15.17.17.25}$ Dn 9^{27} ψ 40^{7}; used alone Ne 13$^{5.9}$ Ez 45^{24} 46$^{5.5.7.11.14.14.15}$ Mal 1^{13} 2$^{12.13}$ 3$^{3.4}$ Ju 13$^{19.23}$ (R, GFM $^{Judges\ 322}$); מִנְחַת (הָ)עֶרֶב *evening grain offering* 2 K 16^{15} Ezr 9$^{4.5}$ Dn 9^{21} ψ 141^{2}; מִנְחַת הַתָּמִיד *continual grain off.* Ne 10^{34}, cf. Lv 6^{13} Nu 4^{16} (all cases under **4** exilic or post-exilic). **5.** *grain-offering,* always with this meaning in P, in classifications Ex 30^{9} 40^{29} Lv 7^{37} 23^{37} Nu 18^{9} 29^{39} Jos 22$^{23.29}$:—**a.** אָבִיב grain in the ear parched with fire, with oil and frankincense Lv 2$^{14.15}$. **b.** סֹלֶת fine flour with oil and frankincense Lv 2^{1} 6^{7}; elsewhere בְּלוּלָה בַשֶּׁמֶן mingled with oil Lv 14$^{10.21}$ 23^{13} Nu 7$^{13+10\ t.}$ 8^{8} 15$^{4.6.9}$ Nu 28$^{5+6\ t.}$ 29$^{3.9.14}$, except sin offering of very poor where offered without oil and frankincense Lv 5$^{11-13}$. **c.** סֹלֶת baked in an oven as חַלּוֹת perforated cakes, or רְקִיקִים flat cakes Lv 2^{4} 7^{9} Nu 6^{15}, על הַמַּחֲבַת *on a flat pan* Lv 2^{5} 6^{14} 7^{9}, or מַרְחֶשֶׁת *frying pan* Lv 2^{7} 7^{9}. All these always unleavened (מַצּוֹת) and mixed with oil and salt Lv 2$^{11-13}$. **d.** at Pentecost to consecrate new bread, מִנְחָה חֲדָשָׁה *new grain offering* of two loaves of leavened bread Lv 23$^{16.17}$ Nu 28^{26}. **e.** barley meal without oil or incense; מִנְחַת קְנָאֹת *grain offering of jealousy,* מ׳ זִכָּרוֹן Nu 5$^{15.18.25}$. Cf. phrases מִנְחַת הַבֹּקֶר *morning oblation* Ex 29^{41} Nu 28^{8}; מ׳ בִּכּוּרִים Lv 2^{14}; קָרְבַּן מ׳ Lv 2$^{1.4.13}$; מ׳ כֹּהֵן Lv 6^{14}. **6.** vbs. of *offering* are הֵבִיא Gn 4^{3} (J), Lv 2$^{2.8}$ (P), Is 1^{13} 66$^{20.20}$ Je 17^{26} Mal 1^{13}; הִקְרִיב Lv 2$^{1.8.11}$ 6^{7} Nu 5^{25}; עשׂה Nu 6^{17} 28^{31} 1 K 8^{64} = 2 Ch 7^{7}, Ez 45^{24} 46$^{7.14.15}$; הקטיר 2 K 16$^{13.15}$ Je 33^{18}; העלה Is 57^{6} 66^{3} Je 14^{12}; הגישׁ Am 5^{25} Mal 2^{12} 3^{3}; הוביל Zp 3^{10}; נשׂא ψ 96^{8}, also (מ׳ = *tribute*) 2 S 8$^{2.6}$ and ‖.

מְנֻחָה v. מְנוּחָה sub נוח. **מְנַחֵם** v. נחם.

מָנַחְתִּי, מְנֻחוֹת, מָנַּחַת v. נוח.

מִנִּי v. מנה.

†I. **מִנִּי** **n.pr.terr.** region of Armenia;—Je 51^{27} (אַשְׁכְּנַז ‖ ,אֲרָרָט); = As. *Mannai* Schr. COT ad loc.; KGF 174.212.520. 4508

II. **מִנִּי, מִנֵּי** v. מִן. **מִנִּי** ψ 45^{9} v. I. [מֵן]. p. 577 4480, 4482

מִנְיוֹת v. מְנָת sub מנה. p. 584 4521

מִנְיָמִן, מִנְיָמִין v. מִיָּמִן. p. 568 4509

מִנְלָם v. [מִנְלָה] sub נלה. p. 649 4512

מנן (of foll.; Ar. مَنَّ is *praecidit* funem, *diminuit* numerum, *debilitavit;* also *be bounteous,* Qor 3^{158} al., مَنٌّ *a gift;* whence Zerweck $^{Präp.\ Min\ 4}$ *assumes* a primary mng. *to separate*—either *from* or *for* ("zutheilen"), as the case might be).

†II. **[מֵן]** **n.[m.]** **portion** (Sim Hup al.);—מִנֵּהוּ ψ 68^{24}, but rd. מְנָתוֹ (ـָה) Ol Dy Bi Che We (v. מְנָת supr.).—ψ 45^{9} 154^{4} v. I. מֵן supr. 4482

† **מִנִּית** **n.pr.loc.** in Ammonite territory, site unknown (4 Rom. m. fr. Heshbon Euseb. 4511

Onom. 253, 33; cf. Buhl$^{Geogr. 266}$);—Ju 11^{33} (𝔊 ἄχρις Ἀρνών, A εἰς Σεμωειθ, 𝔊L Σεμενειθ); חִטֵּי מ׳ Ez 27^{17} *wheat of Minnîth* (cf. wheat fr. Ammon 2 Ch 27^{5}) so Berthol, but dub.; Co conj. חִטִּים וּנְכֹאת *wheat and storax.*

4499 [מְנֻסָּה] v. מְנוּסָה sub נוס. p. 631

4513 †**מָנַע vb. withhold, hold back** (NH *id.*; Zinj. מנע DHM$^{Sendsch. 60}$; Ar. مَنَعَ; Sab. מנע Levy-Os$^{ZMG\ xix.\ 1865,\ 268}$; Aram. מְנַע);—**Qal** *Pf.* מ׳ Gn 30^{2}; sf. מְנָעַנִי 1 S 25^{34}; מָנַעְתָּ ψ 21^{3} Ne 9^{20}, etc.; *Impf.* יִמְנַע־ ψ 84^{12}; sf. יִמְנָעֵנִי 2 S 13^{13} etc.; *Imv.* מְנַע Pr 1^{15}; מִנְעִי Je 2^{25} 31^{16}; *Pt.* מֹנֵעַ Pr 11^{26} Je 48^{10};—*withhold*, sq. מִן Gn 30^{2} (obj. פְּרִי־בֶטֶן), Am 4^{7} (rain), Ne 9^{20} (manna; all subj. י׳); Jb 22^{7} (bread), 1 K 20^{7} (obj. om.; both hum. subj.), so Je 48^{10} (sword), Ec 2^{10} (heart), Je 5^{25} (good), Pr 3^{27} (*id.*), 1^{15} (foot); Je 2^{25} (*id.*) 31^{16} (voice); further, 2 S 13^{13} (woman), Je 42^{4} (knowledge), Jb 31^{16} (poor), Pr 23^{13} (correction), obj. om. י׳ subj. Pr 30^{7}; מִן om. Pr 11^{26} (obj. corn); cf. ψ 21^{3} subj. י׳ (obj. אֲרֶשֶׁת שְׂפָתָיו ‖ נָתַן תַּאֲוַת לֵב), Jb 20^{13} fig. (wickedness), Ez 31^{15} י׳ subj. (obj. rivers); obj. pers. י׳ subj. sq. מן Nu 24^{11}; sq. מִן + inf. 1 S 25$^{26.34}$; sq. לְ, subj. י׳ ψ 84^{12} (good). **Niph.** *Pf.* נִמְנַע Jo 1^{13}; *Impf.* יִמָּנַע Jb 38^{15}, etc.; *be withholden* sq. מִן, subj. מִנְחָה etc. Jo 1^{13}; light from wicked Jb 38^{15}; Nu 22^{16} (sq. מִן + inf.); subj. showers (רְבִבִים) Je 3^{3}.

3234 †**יִמְנָע n.pr.m.** son of Helem (of Asher) 1 Ch 7^{35}. 𝔊 Ιμανα, 𝔊L Ιαμνα.

8555 †**תִּמְנָע n.pr.m.** and **f.** Edomite name. 𝔊 Θαμνα:—**1.** תִּמְנָע **n.pr.m. a.** a chief of Edom Gn 36^{40} = 1 Ch 1^{51}. **b.** son of Eliphaz 1 Ch 1^{36} (for Korah Gn 36$^{15.16}$). **2.** תִּמְנָ֑ע **f.** Gn 36^{22} = 1 Ch 1^{39} sister of Lotan (of Seir); Gn 3^{12} concubine of Eliphaz son of Esau.

4514-15 מַנְעוּל, [מִנְעָל] v. נעל. p. 653

4516-17 [מַנְעַמִּים] v. נעם. מְנַעַנְעִים v. נוע. p. 631, 654

4518 [מְנַקִּית], מְנַקִּיָּה v. נקה. p. 667

3243 מֵנֶקֶת v. ינק **Hiph.** p. 413

4501 מְנֹרָה v. מְנוֹרָה sub נור. p. 633

4519 **מְנַשֶּׁה** $_{136}$ **n.pr.m. et trib. Manasseh** (interpr. Gn 41^{51} as Pi. causat. √II. נשה q. v.);— מ׳ Gn 46^{20}+; מְנַשֶּׁ֑ה 41^{51}+ (on Ju 18^{30} v. מֹשֶׁה); c. art. (strangely), הַמְּ׳ Jos 1^{12} + 10 t. (v. infr.); 𝔊 Μαν(ν)ασση;—**1.** †**a.** *Manasseh*, eldest son of Joseph Gn 41^{51} 48$^{1.13.14.14.17.20.20}$, also 50^{23} (father of Machir; all E), 46^{20} 48^{5} (both P). **b.** of tribe, oft. + Ephraim (v. אֶפְרַיִם): (1) the part W. of Jordan: †*a.* בְּנֵי מ׳ Jos 16^{9} 17^{2a} (בני־מ׳) הַנּוֹתָרִים), v$^{2b.6.12}$ (all JE), 1 Ch 7^{29} 9^{3} (בְּנֵי אֶפְרַיִם וּמ׳; Jos 13^{29} v. infr.); *β.* מ׳ alone, Jos 17$^{5.8.8.9b.11.17}$ Dt 34^{2} (אֶרֶץ אֶפְרַיִם וּמ׳; all JE), 2 Ch 30^{10} (*id.*), Jos 16^{4} 17$^{7.9a.10}$ (all P), also appar. Dt 33^{17} (poem), Ju 1^{27} 6$^{15.35}$ 7^{23} Is 9$^{20.20}$ ψ 80^{3} + 10 t. Chr; †*γ.* מַטֵּה מ׳ 1 Ch 6^{55}; חֲצִי מַטֵּה מ׳ Jos 21$^{6.25}$ 1 Ch 12^{32} (van d. H v^{31}); מַחֲצִית מַטֵּה חֲצִי מ׳ 6^{46} (but on text v. Kit); שְׁנֵי מַטּוֹת מ׳ וְאֶפְרַיִם Jos 14^{4} (P); †*δ.* חֲצִי שֵׁבֶט מ׳ 1 Ch 27^{20}; c. art. הַשֵּׁבֶט הַמְּ׳ Jos 13^{7} (D). †(2) of Manasseh E. of Jordan; *a.* בְּנֵי מ׳ Jos 22$^{30.31}$ (P); *β.* מ׳ alone, Ju 11^{29} (distinctly of territory), 12^{4} (but on text v. GFM), ψ 60^{9} = 108^{9}; חֲצִי הַמְּ׳ 1 Ch 27^{21}; *γ.* מַטֵּה מ׳ Jos 17^{1a} 20^{8} (both P), 1 Ch 6^{47}; חֲצִי מַטֵּה מ׳ Jos 22^{1} (D), Nu 34^{14} Jos 21$^{5.27}$ (all P), 1 Ch 6^{56}; חֲצִי מַטֵּה בְּנֵי מ׳ Jos 13^{29} (P); *δ.* חֲצִי שֵׁבֶט מ׳ Dt 3^{13} (D), Jos 13^{29} 22$^{13.15}$ (all P), 1 Ch 15$^{18.23.26}$ 12^{38} (van d. H v^{37}); חֲצִי שֵׁבֶט מ׳ בֶּן־יוֹסֵף Nu 32^{33} (P); c. art. חֲצִי שֵׁבֶט הַמְּ׳ Jos 1^{12} 4^{12} 12^{6} 18^{7} 22$^{1.7}$ (all D), 22$^{9.10.11.21}$ (all P). Here belong also (chiefly) reff. to מ׳ as father of Machir (cf. Gn 50^{23} supr.): † Nu 27^{1} 32$^{39.40}$ 36^{1} Jos 13^{31} 17$^{1.3}$ (all P), 1 Ch 7$^{14.17}$; and of Jair Dt 3^{14} (D), Nu 32^{41} (P), 1 K 4^{13} (cf. יָאִיר, מָכִיר). †(3) of undivided tribe (never שֵׁבֶט מ׳): *a.* בְּנֵי מ׳ Nu 1^{34} 2^{20} 7^{54} 26^{29} 36^{12} (all P); *β.* מ׳ alone, Nu 1^{10} 26$^{28.34}$ 27^{1b} (all P), Ez 48$^{4.5}$; *γ.* מַטֵּה מ׳ Nu 1^{35} 2^{20} 13^{11}, מַטֵּה בְנֵי מ׳ Nu 10^{23} 34^{13} (all P). **2.** son of Hezekiah, and king of Judah (As. *Menasê*, *Minsê* Schr COT 2 K 21, 1);—2 K 20^{21} 21^{1} + 9 t. Kings, 12 t. Chr, Je 15^{4}. †**3.** two who had taken strange wives: **a.** Ezr 10^{30}. **b.** 10^{33}.

†**מְנַשִּׁי adj. gent.** of מ׳ **1**; only c. art. הַמְּ׳, 4520
as n. coll., of tribe E. of Jordan: Dt 4^{43} 2 K 10^{33}; שֵׁבֶט הַמְּ׳ Dt 29^{7} 1 Ch 26^{32}.

מְנָת v. מנה. p. 584 4521

†I. **מַס n.m.** $^{1\ K\ 5,\ 27}$ usu. **coll. body of forced** 4522
labourers, task-workers, labour-band or **gang,** also (late) **forced service, task-work, serfdom** (𝔗 מִסָּא, esp. in phr. מַסְּקֵי מִסִּין (implying late and [for BH] false sense 'tribute,' so NH מַעֲלֵי מִסִּים; √ unknown, prob. loan-wd.; follows anal. of ע״ע);—abs. מ׳ 1 K 5^{27}+; לָמַס Jos 17^{13}+, הַמַּ֑ס 2 S 20^{24}+; pl. מִסִּים Ex 1^{11};—**1.** *labour-band, labour-gang,* body of task-workers for public service, formed

by levy upon the people by Sol. וַיַּ֫עַל הַמֶּלֶךְ שְׁלֹמֹה מַס מִכָּל־יִשְׂרָאֵל 1 K 5^{27}, amounting to 30,000 men v^{27}; וַיַּעֲלֵם שׁ׳ 9^{15}; הַמ׳ אֲשֶׁר הֶעֱלָה לְמַס עֹבֵד v^{21} *and Sol. levied them for a toiling labour-band* (cf. Gn 49^{15} Jos 16^{10}) = וַיַּעֲלֵם שׁ׳ לְמַס 2 Ch 8^{8}; appar. instituted, earlier, by David, cf. וַאֲדֹרָם עַל־הַמַּס 2 S 20^{24}, i.e. had charge of the body of labourers, so 1 K 4^{6} 5^{28} 12^{18} = 2 Ch 10^{18}. **2. a.** of *labour-bands, slave-gangs* of Isr. in Egypt, only שָׂרֵי מִסִּים Ex 1^{11} (J) *gang-overseers.* **b.** of conquered populations, subject to forced labour: יִהְיוּ לְךָ לָמַס וַעֲבָדוּךָ Dt 20^{11} cf. Ju 1$^{30.33.35}$ (v. GFM), Is 31^{8} La 1^{1}; so ויהי לְמַס וַיִּתְּנוּ אֶת־הַכְּנַעֲנִי עֹבֵד Jos 16^{10} (cf. Gn 49^{15} 1 K 9^{21}); וַיָּשִׂ֫ימוּ (וגו׳) לָמַס Jos 17^{13}, cf. (וַיָּ֫שֶׂם וגו׳) Ju 1^{28}. **3.** in gen.: וַיְהִי לְמַס־עֹבֵד Gn 49^{15} *and he* (Issachar) became *a slaving labour-band* (poem in **J**; cf. Jos 16^{10} 1 K 9^{21}); cf. רְמִיָּה תִּהְיֶה לָמַס Pr 12^{24} (here appar. of individ.) **4. forced service,** *serfdom* (or poss. (in late passage) *tribute = enforced payment*, cf. NH, 𝔗, v. supr.), only of Ahasuerus: וַיָּשֶׂם הַמֶּלֶךְ מַס עַל־הָאָרֶץ וגו׳ Est 10^{1}.

4523-24 II. מַס v. מסס. מֵסֵב, מֵסַב v. סבב. p. 588, 687

4525-26 מִסְגֶּ֫רֶת, מַסְגֵּר v. סגר. p. 689

4527-28 מַסַּד v. יסד. [מִסְדְּרוֹן] v. סדר. p. 414, 690

4529 †[מָסָה] **vb.** melt, dissolve, be liquefied (Eth. መሰወ: *liquefy;* Aram. מְסָא *melt away,* ܡܣܳܐ *dissolve, decay, coagulate;* As. *masû* is *wash;* v. also מסס);—only **Hiph.** *Pf.* 3 pl. הִמְסִיו Jos 14^{8} (on form v. Ges$^{§ 75 R. 17}$). *Impf.* sf. יַמְסֵם ψ 147^{18}; 2 ms. וַתֶּ֫מֶס ψ 39^{12}; אַמְסֶה ψ 6^{7};—*cause to dissolve, melt,* ice ψ 147^{18}; hyperb. בְּדִמְעָתִי עַרְשִׂי אַמְסֶה ψ 6^{7} *with my tears I cause my bed to dissolve;* וַתֶּמֶס כָּעָשׁ חֲמוּדוֹ ψ 39^{12} = *consume, cause to vanish;* fig. sq. לֵב = *intimidate* Jos. 14^{8}.

4531-32 I. [מַסָּה] v. מסס. II, III. מַסָּה v. נסה. p. 588, 650

4530, 4533 [מִסָּה] v. מִסַּת. מַסְוֶה v. סוה. p. 588, 691

4534 מְסוּכָה = מְשׂוּכָה v. II. סוך (שׂוך). p. 692

4535 †מַסָּח dub. word., only in וּשְׁמַרְתֶּם אֶת־מִשְׁמֶרֶת הַבַּיִת מַסָּח 2 K 11^{6}; Thes al. sub √נסח = *for plucking away,* i. e. repulse, defence, but very uncertain; prob. text. err.; om. 𝔊^{B} We Sta$^{p. 354}$; 𝔊L Μεσσαε.

4536 [מִסְחָר] v. סחר. p. 695

†מָסַךְ **vb.** mix, produce by mixing (cf. perh. מזג, מֶזֶג Ba$^{ES 33, 51}$);—**Qal** *Pf.* 3 ms. מ׳ Is 19^{14}; מָסְכָה Pr 9^{2}; מָסַ֫כְתִּי Pr 9^{5} ψ 102^{10}; *Inf. cstr.* מְסֹךְ Is 5^{22};—**1.** *pour,* only fig., מ׳ בְּקִרְבָּהּ רוּחַ עִוְעִים Is 19^{14} (subj. י׳); *mix,* c. acc. שֵׁכָר Is 5^{22}; i. e. make a choice drink by mixing with spices, etc. (mixing with water came later, cf. 2 Macc 15^{39}) Löw$^{p. 419}$ Frä$^{162 f. 171 f.}$ Now$^{Arch. 1, 120}$ Benz$^{Arch. 95}$; obj. יַיִן fig., subj. wisdom Pr 9$^{2.5}$; שִׁקֻּוַי בִּבְכִי מָסָ֫כְתִּי ψ 102^{10} *my drink with weeping have I mixed* (v. As. [*akâl*] *ul âkul, bikîtum kurmati, mê ul aštî, dîmtu maštîtî* Zim$^{BP 34}$). 4537

†מֶ֫סֶךְ **n. [m.]** mixture, i. e. wine mixed with spices; כּוֹס בְּיַד י׳ וְיַיִן חָמַר מָלֵא מ׳ ψ 75^{9} (fig. of י׳'s judgment). 4538

†מִמְסָךְ **n.m.** mixed drink (v. מָסָךְ);—מִמְסָךְ Pr 23^{30} *mixed* (wine), as beverage; Is 65^{11} as libation to M^{e}nî. 4469

מָסָךְ, [מְסֻכָּה] v. סכך. p. 697 4539-40

I. מַסֵּכָה v. I. נסך. p. 651 4541

II. מַסֵּכָה, [מַסֶּ֫כֶת] v. II. נסך. p. 651 4541, 4545

†מִסְכֵּן **adj.** poor, only Ec. (NH *id.;* Aram. *id.,* ܡܣܟܢܐ PS^{2632}; Ar. مِسْكِين; Eth. ምስኪን: Di^{382}; √dub.; usu. der. fr. III. סכן q.v.; perh. loan-wd.; acc. to Jen$^{ZA iv (1889), 271 f}$ Zim$^{ib. vii (1892), 353}$ = As. *muškênu, beggar, needy one*);—alw. abs. יֶלֶד מ׳ וְחָכָם—:מ׳ Ec 4^{13} (opp. מֶלֶךְ זָקֵן וּכְסִיל); אִישׁ מ׳ חָכָם 9^{15}, הָאִישׁ הַמ׳ v^{15}; as subst. הַמ׳ v^{16} *the poor man.* 4542

†מִסְכֵּנֻת **n.f.** poverty, scarcity, Dt 8^{9}. 4544

מִסְכְּנוֹת v. I. סכן. p. 698 4543

מְסִלָּה, מַסְלוּל v. סלל. p. 700 4546-47

[מַסְמֵר], מַסְמְרִים etc. v. סמר (שׂמר). p. 702 4548

†[מָסַס] **vb.** dissolve, melt, intr. (𝔗 מְסַם; cf. מסה, and II. מאס);—**Qal** *Inf. cstr.* מְסֹס נֹסֵס Is 10^{18}; *like the melting* (wasting away) of a נֹסֵס (q.v.) **Niph.** *Pf.* וְנָמֵס consec. Ez 21^{12}; וְנָמָ֑ס Ex 16^{21} ψ 112^{10}; נָמַ֫סּוּ ψ 97^{5} + 2 t.; *Impf.* יִמַּס Dt 20^{8} +; וַיִּמַּסּוּ Ju 15^{14}; *Inf. abs.* הִמֵּס 2 S 17^{10}; *cstr. id.* ψ 68^{3}; *Pt.* נָמֵס ψ 22^{15} + 2 t.;—**1.** *melt* (intr.) of manna Ex 16^{21}; wax ψ 68^{3} (sim. of wicked); manacles Ju 15^{14} (= *vanished, dropped off*); wicked ψ 112^{10} (*melt away*); esp. of hills and mts. Mi 1^{4} ψ 97^{5} Is 34^{3}. **2.** most oft. fig. of heart = *faint, grow fearful,* Na 2^{11} 2 S 17$^{10.10}$ (cf. Dr), Dt 20^{8} Jos 2^{11} 5^{1} 7^{5} Is 13^{7} 4549

19^1 Ez 21^{12} ψ 22^{15}. **3.** *Pt.* = *wasted, consumptive* (?), 1 S 15^9 (‖ נְמִבְזָה, rd. נִבְזָה v. בזה **Niph.**)
3988 < rd. נִמְאֶסֶת *worthless*, lit. *rejected* (v. מאס **Niph.**) **Hiph.** *Pf.* 3 pl. הֵמַסּוּ אֶת־לְבָבֵנוּ Dt 1^{28} *cause to melt* (= intimidate).

4523 † II. [מַס] **adj. despairing** (lit. *melting*, i.e. *failing, collapsing*);—לַמָּס Jb 6^{14} *to him who despaireth* belongeth kindness, etc.

4531 † I. [מַסָּה] **n.f. despair** (lit. *melting, failing*);—only לְמַסַּת נְקִיִּם יִלְעָג Jb 9^{23} *at the despair of innocent ones he mocketh;* so 𝔗 Ew Di Bu Du > Ges Hi al. *trial* (by calamity), √ נסה.

8557 † תֶּמֶס **n.m. melting** (away);—כְּמוֹ שַׁבְּלוּל תֶּ׳ יַהֲלֹךְ ψ 58^9 like a snail that goeth *into melting* (leaving slimy track).

4550-51 מַסַּע, I. מַסָּע v. I. נסע. II. מַסָּע v. II. נסע. p. 652

4552-53 מִסְעָד v. סעד. מִסְפֵּד v. ספד. p. 703-04

4554 מִסְפּוֹא v. ספא. p. 704

4555-56 מִסְפָּחוֹת, מִסְפַּחַת v. ספח. p. 705

4557-59 I, II. מִסְפָּר, מִסְפֶּרֶת v. ספר. p. 708-09

4560 † [מָסַר] **vb.** si vera l. **deliver up, offer** (NH מָסַר; Aram. ܡܣܰܪ *deliver up, denounce, betray*, מְסַר; Hom $^{ZMG\ xlvi.\ 1892,\ 530}$ comp. Sab. מסר *take away*);—**Qal** *Inf. cstr.* לִמְסָר־מַעַל בי׳ Nu 31^{16} *offer* (commit) *a trespass against* י׳, but rd. לִמְעֹל, cf. Thes Di (v. Nu 5^6 2 Ch 36^{14}). **Niph.** *Impf.* וַיִּמָּסְרוּ Nu 31^5 *delivered over to, assigned to* (of warriors), rd. perh. וַיִּסָּפְרוּ (𝔊 ἐξηρίθμησαν) cf. Thes.

4149, 4562 מֹסֵרוֹת, מָסֹרֶת v. אסר. p. 64

4561 [מֹסָר] v. מוּסָר sub יסר. p. 416

4530 † מִסַּת **n. sufficiency** (der. obscure: Aram. מִיסַּת, ܡܣܰܬ, common in 𝔗 𝔖, both absol. and cstr., in sense of *sufficiency, enough;* e.g. for Heb. רַב 2 S 24^{16} 𝔗, דַּי Ex 36^7 𝔗 𝔖, Ob^5 𝔗 𝔖, for לְפִי Ex 12^4 𝔖; ܡܣܰܬ ܡܰܘܙܦܳܐ the *amount* of the debt, PS^{2183});—Dt 16^{10} and thou shalt keep the pilgrimage of weeks מִסַּת נִדְבַת יָדְךָ *acc. to* (adv. acc.) *the sufficiency of* the free-will offering of thy hand, which thou shalt give, i.e. with the full amount that thou canst afford (cf. דֵּי שֶׂה Lv 5^7 12^8; 𝔗 כְּמִיסַּת אִימְּרָא).

4563-65 מִסְתּוֹר, מַסְתֵּר, מִסְתָּר v. סתר. p. 712

4566, 4568 [מַעְבָּד] v. עבד. [מַעֲבֶה] v. עבה. p. 716

4569 [מַעֲבָר], מַעְבָּרָה v. עבר. p. 721

4570 מַעְגָּל, מַעְגָּלָה v. עגל. p. 722

† [מָעַד] **vb. slip, slide, totter, shake** 4571
(only Heb.);—**Qal** *Pf.* 3 pl. מָעֲדוּ 2 S 22^{37} = ψ 18^{37}; *Impf.* 3 fs. תִּמְעַד ψ 37^{31}; אֶמְעָד ψ 26^1; *Pt.* pl. cstr. מוֹעֲדֵי Jb 12^5;—*slip*, subj. feet, (fig.) 2 S 22^{37} = ψ 18^{37}, Jb 12^5; subj. אֲשֻׁרָיו ψ 37^{31};
cf. ψ 26^1. **Pu.** *Pt.* מוּעָדֶת (= מְמוֹ׳ Ges $^{§\,53\,s}$; 4154
or old **Qal** *Pt. pass.*,—cf. Ba $^{NB\ 273}$;—but pass. not needed here, read perh. מוֹ׳ **Qal** *Pt. act.* v. Schwally $^{ZAW\ x,\ 1890,\ 176}$);—רֶגֶל מ׳ Pr 25^{19} (sim. of untrustworthiness). **Hiph.** *Pf.* וְהַמְעַדְתָּ
(so rd. for 𝔥 והעמדת, cf. Sm Co Da Berthol) Ez 5976
29^7; *cause to shake* obj. כָּל־מָתְנַיִם, i.e. *make them totter;* cf. *Imv.* הַמְעַד (obj. *id.*) ψ 69^{24}.

† מַעַדְיָה (van d. H מַעֲדַי) **n.pr.m.** one of 4572
those who had taken strange wives Ezr 10^{34}. 𝔊 Μοδεδ(ε)ια, A 𝔊 L Μοο(υ)δεια (perh. = foll., q.v.)

† מַעַדְיָה **n.pr.m.** a priest of Zerubbabel's 4573
time acc. to Ne 12^5; 𝔊 א Μααδιας, 𝔊 L Μαασιας;
appar. = מוֹעַדְיָה v^{17}, 𝔊 L Μασαι (etym. dub.; 4153
Thes puts sub עדה = *ornamentum Jovae*, but prop. מַע׳ = מוֹע׳, √ יעד = *conventus Jovae*).

מֹעֵד v. מוֹעֵד sub יעד. p. 417 4150

[מַעֲדָן], מַעֲדַנִּים v. עדן. p. 726 4574

† מַעֲדַנּוֹת **n.[f.]pl.** Jb 38^{31} v. sub ענד; p. 772 4575
מַעֲדַנֹּת 1 S 15^{32} is dub.; = above, as adv. acc. *in bonds, fetters*, Ki Gr Klo; 𝔗 Sym We Dr assign to √ עדן = *delicately, voluptuously;* but 𝔊 τρέμων, whence Lag $^{Proph.\ Chald.\ li}$ prop. מֹעֲדֹנֹת (cf. אֲחֹרַנִּית) √ מעד = *totteringly*, so HPS.

מַעְדֵּר v. עדר. p. 727 4576

מעה (√ of foll.; meaning dubious).

† [מֵעָה] **n.m.** $^{Is\ 16,\ 11}$ only **pl. internal or-** 4578
gans, inward parts (intestines, bowels), belly (NH *id.;* Aram. מְעָא, מַעֲיָא, ܡܥܳܐ, ܡܥܰܝܳܐ; Ar. مِعًى; Eth. **አምዐት:**;—on form cf. Lag $^{BN\ 156}$ Ba $^{ZMG\ xlii.\ 1888,\ 345}$);—pl. [מֵעִים] cstr. מְעֵי ψ 71^6 + 3 t.; sf. מֵעַי 2 S 16^{11} + 9 t., מֵעָי ψ 22^{15} 40^9; מֵעֶיךָ Gn 15^4 + 6 t.; מֵעַיִךְ Gn 25^{23} Nu 5^{22}; מֵעָיו 2 S 20^{10} + 5 t.; מֵעֵיהֶם Ez 7^{19};—**1.** lit.: **a.** וַיִּשְׁפֹּךְ מֵעָיו אַרְצָה 2 S 20^{10} *and he poured out his inward parts on the ground* (through a wound); cf. מַחֲלֵה מ׳ 2 Ch $21^{15.18}$, יֵצְאוּ מ׳ $v^{15.19}$. **b.** as digestive organs, but without precision, nearly = *stomach,*

belly, Jb 20^{14}; Ez 3^{3} (|| בֶּטֶן), 7^{19} (|| נֶפֶשׁ; both c. מִלֵּא), Nu 5^{22}; so of fish that swallowed Jonah Jon $2^{1.2}$. **2.** source of procreation: אשר יצא מִמּ׳ (said of offspring) Gn 15^{4} (JE), 2 S 7^{12} (|| זַרְעֲךָ), 16^{11}; צֶאֱצָאֵי מ׳ Is 48^{19} (|| *id.*); מִיּצִיאֵי מ׳ 2 Ch 32^{21}. **3.** = *womb*, שְׁנֵי לְאֻמִּים מִמֵּעַיִךְ יִפָּרֵדוּ Gn 25^{23} (J; || בֶּטֶן), cf. Is 49^{1} (|| *id.*), ψ 71^{6} (|| *id.*), Ru 1^{11}. **4.** in gen. = *inwards, inward part*, לִבִּי . . . נָמֵס בְּתוֹךְ מ׳ ψ 22^{15}, cf. תּוֹרָתְךָ בְּתוֹךְ מ׳ 40^{9}. **5.** fig. = seat of emotions: pity, Is 16^{11} (|| קֶרֶב); of God's compassion, Je 31^{20} (|| רחם; in both subj. of vb. הָמוּ); הֲמוֹן מֵעֶיךָ Is 63^{15} (|| רַחֲמֶיךָ); distress, Je $4^{19.19}$ (|| לֵב), מֵעַי חֳמַרְמָרוּ La 1^{20} (|| לֵב), 2^{11} (|| כָּבֵד *liver*); מֵעַי רֻתְּחוּ Jb 30^{27} (dub., v. Bu); love, מֵעַי הָמוּ עָלָיו Ct 5^{4}. **6.** the external belly, מֵעָיו עֶשֶׁת שֵׁן Ct 5^{14}.

4579 †[מְעָה] **n.f. grain** (of sand), si vera l. (NH מָעָה, *seed* (of melon, etc.), *coin*, Aram. ܡܽܥܳܐ, מָעָא *coin*);—only fpl. sf.: וַיְהִי כַחוֹל זַרְעֶךָ וְצֶאֱצָאֵי מֵעֶיךָ כִּמְעֹתָיו Is 48^{19} *and thy seed had been like the sand, and the offspring of thy bowels like the grains thereof*, cf. 𝔙 𝔗 De Di Du al. > pl. of [מֵעֶה] *the entrails of it* (i.e. the sea) AE Ges Hi Che[Comm.].—𝔊 ὡς ὁ χοῦς τῆς γῆς, whence Gr כְּעפרותיו.

4580-81 מָעוֹג v. עוג. מָעֹז, מָעוֹז v. עוז (cf. עזז). p. 728, 732

4583-85, 4587 מָעוֹן I, II., מְע(וֹ)נָה, מְעוֹנֹתַי v. עון. p. 732-33

4586 †מְעוּנִים **n.pr.gent.** Me'unim, Me'unites (usu. connected with מָעוֹן (v. עון), but dub., cf. Buhl[Edom. 41 f.]);—a people S. (SE?) of Canaan (cf. Buhl[l.c.]);—הַמְּ׳ 2 Ch 26^{7} and 1 Ch 4^{41} Qr (Kt המעינים, 𝔊[B] τοὺς Μιναίους, 𝔊[L] τ. Κιναίους); rd. also מֵהַמְּעוּנִים 2 Ch 20^{1} (for MT מֵהָעַמּוֹנִים), so 𝔊[BA] (𝔊[L] Αμμανιειμ), Ew Be Ke Öt Kau Kit; בְּנֵי־מְעוּנִים (among Nethinim who went back with Zerub.) Ezr 2^{50} = Neh 7^{52} are perhaps descendants of those named above (2 Ch 26^{7}). 𝔊 οἱ Μιναῖοι, but against מ׳ = Minæans (Glaser[Skizze ii. 450 f.] al.) v. Sprenger[ZMG xliv (1890), 505].

4588-89 [מָעוּף] v. I. עיף. מָעוֹר v. II. עור. p. 734-35

מעז (√of following).

4590 †מַעַזְיָה, מַעַזְיָהוּ† **n.pr.m.** of priests. **1.** 1 Ch 24^{18} ascribed to David's time, A Μοοζαλ, 𝔊[L] Μοοζια. **2.** Neh 10^{9}, Nehemiah's time, A Μααζεια, 𝔊[L] Μααζίας.

4591 †[מָעַט] **vb. be or become small, diminished, few** (NH, Talm., *id.*; Ar. مَعِطَ is *to be without hair on the body*)—**Qal** *Impf.* יִמְעַט Ex 12^{4}, 2 mpl. תִּמְעָטוּ Je 29^{6}, 3 mpl. יִמְעָטוּ Is 21^{17}+, וַיִּמְעֲטוּ ψ 107^{39}; *Inf.* מְעֹט Lv 25^{16};—Ex 12^{4} אִם־יִמְעַט הַבַּיִת מִהְיוֹת מִשֶּׂה if the house be *too small* for a lamb; Ne 9^{32} אַל־יִמְעַט לְפָנֶיךָ אֵת כָּל־הַתְּלָאָה (cf. Ges[§117 l]); of a people, Je 29^{6} וּרְבוּ שָׁם וְאַל־תִּמְעָטוּ and *become* not *few*, 30^{19} וְהִרְבִּתִים וְלֹא יִמְעָטוּ, Is 21^{17} ψ 107^{39}; Pr 13^{11} הוֹן מֵהֶבֶל יִמְעָט *diminishes* (opp. יַרְבֶּה); Lv 25^{16} וּלְפִי מְעֹט הַשָּׁנִים acc. to the *fewness* of the years. **Pi.** *become few* (Ges[§52k]), *Pf.* 3 pl. Ec 12^{3} וּבָטְלוּ הַטֹּחֲנוֹת כִּי מִעֵטוּ. **Hiph.** *Pf.* 3 fs. consec. וְהִמְעִיטָה (Ges[§49k]), Lv 26^{22}, 1 s. with sf. וְהִמְעַטְתִּים Ez 29^{15}; *Impf.* 2 ms. תַּמְעִיט Lv 25^{16}, תַּמְעִטֵנִי Je 10^{34}, 2 fs. תַּמְעִיטִי 2 K 4^{3}, etc.;—*make small* or *few, diminish*: **a.** Lv 26^{22} (of the sword) וְהִמְעִיטָה אֶתְכֶם, Ez 29^{15} וְהִמְעַטְתִּים, Je 10^{24} אַל־בְּאַפְּךָ פֶּן־תַּמְעִטֵנִי lest thou *make me* (the people) *small*, ψ 107^{38} וּבְהֶמְתָּם לֹא יַמְעִיט; Lv 25^{16} וּלְפִי מְעֹט הַשָּׁנִים תַּמְעִיט מִקְנָתוֹ acc. to the smallness (fewness) of the years, thou shalt *make small* its price, Nu 26^{54} לָרַב תַּרְבֶּה נַחֲלָתוֹ וְלַמְעַט תַּמְעִיט נַחֲלָתוֹ and to the small (few) thou shalt *make small* his inheritance (so 33^{54}). **b.** qualifying an *action* (sts. to be understood from the context), Ex 16^{17} וַיִּלְקְטוּ הַמַּרְבֶּה וְהַמַּמְעִיט and they gathered, he that made much, and he that *made little* (sc. לִלְקֹט), v[18] Nu 11^{32} הממעיט אסף עשרה חמרים, 2 K 4^{3} כֵּלִים רֵקִים אַל־תַּמְעִיטִי empty vessels *make not few* (sc. in borrowing); Ex 30^{15} הֶעָשִׁיר לֹא יַרְבֶּה וְהַדַּל לֹא יַמְעִיט מִמַּחֲצִית הַשָּׁקֶל לָתֵת וגו׳ *shall not diminish* from the half shekel to give, i.e. shall not give less, Nu 35^{8} מֵאֵת הָרַב תַּרְבּוּ וּמֵאֵת הַמְעַט תַּמְעִיטוּ and from the few ye shall *make few* (sc. לָתֵת), i.e. ye shall give few (cities).

מְעַט[101] **subst. a little, fewness, a few**;— 4592
מ׳ abs. and cstr., מְעָט Is 10^{7}+, pl. מְעַטִּים †ψ 109^{8} Ec 5^{1};—**1. a.** Gn 30^{30} מעט אשר היה לך לְפָנַי *the little* that thou hadst, 47^{9} מעט ורעים היו ימי שני חיי *few* and evil, Lv 25^{52} Nu 26^{54} (cf. 33^{54}) וְלַמְעַט תמעיט נחלתו and *to the small* (few) thou shalt make small his inheritance, v[56] 35^{8} וּמֵאֵת הַמְעַט תמעיטו, Dt 7^{7} כי אתם הַמְעַט מכל־העמים ye are *the fewest* out of all peoples, 1 S 14^{6} לְהוֹשִׁיעַ בְּרַב אוֹ בִמְעָט, Je 42^{2} כִּי נִשְׁאַרְנוּ מְעַט מֵהַרְבֵּה we are left *as few* out of many, Ez 5^{3} וְלָקַחְתָּ מִשָּׁם מְעַט בְּמִסְפָּר, Hg 1^{6} זְרַעְתֶּם הַרְבֵּה וְהָבֵא מְעָט (cf. v[9]), ψ 8^{6} ותחסרהו מעט מאלהים, 37^{16} טוֹב מְעַט לַצַּדִּיק

(cf. Pr 15^{16} 16^{8}), 2 Ch 29^{34} רַק הַכֹּהֲנִים הָיוּ לִמְעָט; as pred. Nu 13^{18} הַמְעַט הוּא אִם־רָב, Jos 7^{3} כִּי מְעַט הֵמָּה, Jb 10^{20} Ru 2^{7} Ne 7^{4}; Is 16^{14} וּשְׁאָר מְעַט מִזְעָר.—Ho 8^{10} וַיָּחֵלּוּ מְעַט and they begin *as littleness* (= *to be minished*) because of, &c.; but rd. prob. (𝔊) וְיֶחְדְּלוּ מְעַט מִמְּשֹׁחַ and they shall cease *for a little* (**d**) from anointing, etc. **b.** as subst. with foll. gen., Gn 18^{4} מְעַט מַיִם *a little of* water, 24$^{17.43}$, מְעַט אֹכֶל 43^{2} 44^{25} 1 S 14^{43} 17^{28} מְעַט הַצֹּאן הָהֵנָּה lit. *the fewness of* those sheep, Pr 6^{10}+; as gen. to a previous subst., מְתֵי מְעָט men *of fewness* †Dt 26^{5} 28^{62}; in appos., †Is 10^{7} לְהַכְרִית גּוֹיִם לֹא מְעָט, Ezr 9^{8} מִחְיָה מְעַט, Ne 2^{12} וַאֲנָשִׁים מְעַט עִמִּי, Ec 9^{4}; either gen. or appos., 10^{1} Dn 11^{34} יֵעָזְרוּ עֵזֶר מְעָט with a help *of smallness*. **c.** twice declined as an adj., ψ 109^{8} יִהְיוּ יָמָיו מְעַטִּים, Ec 5^{1} על־כן יהיו דבריך מְעַטִּים. **d.** as adverb. acc., of place, 2 S 16^{1} וְדָוִד עָבַר מְעַט; of time, Jb 10$^{20\,b}$; of degree, 2 K 10^{18} אַחְאָב עָבַד אֶת־הַבַּעַל מְעָט, Ez 11^{16} and have been to them for a sanctuary *but little*, Zc 1^{15}; repeated מְעַט מְעַט *by little, by little*= gradually, Ex 23^{30} Dt 7^{22}. **e.** phrases:—*a.* with the interr. הֲ, †Gn 30^{15} הַמְעַט קַחְתֵּךְ אֶת־אִישִׁי וְלָקַחַת was thy taking my husband (too) little? and (wilt thou be) for taking also my son's love-apples? Nu 16$^{9-10}$ הַמְעַט מִכֶּם כִּי הִבְדִּיל ... וּבִקַּשְׁתֶּם גַּם כְּהֻנָּה is it *too little for you* that J. hath separated, etc., ... and do ye seek, etc.? v^{13} הַמְעַט כִּי הֶעֱלִיתָנוּ ... כִּי תִשְׂתָּרֵר גַּם הִשְׂתָּרֵר, Jos 22$^{17\,f.}$ הַמְעַט לָנוּ ... וְאַתֶּם תָּשֻׁבוּ וגו׳, Is 7^{13} הַמְעַט מִכֶּם הַלְאוֹת אֲנָשִׁים כִּי תַלְאוּ וגו׳ is wearying men *too little* for you, that you will weary also my God? Ez 34^{18} (as Ew Co AV RV), Jb 15^{11} הַמְעַט מִמְּךָ תַּנְחֻמוֹת אֵל. But Ez 16^{20} (si vera l.) was it (too) little *because of* thy whoredom? (was that insufficient for thee? Kö$^{iii. 406\,m}$). *b.* עוֹד מְעַט וְ׳, †Ex 17^{4} עוֹד מְעַט וּסְקָלֻנִי *yet a little, and* they will stone me, Je 51^{33} Ho 1^{4} ψ 37^{10}; עוֹד מְעַט מִזְעָר וְ׳ †Is 10^{25} 29^{17}; cf. Hg 2^{6} Jb 24^{24}.

2. †כִּמְעַט *like a little:* hence **a.** *within a little, almost* (cf. ὀλίγου), Gn 26^{10} כִּמְעַט שָׁכַב ... *almost* had lain ..., ψ 73^{2} Qr, 94^{17} 119^{87} Pr 5^{14} (all sq. pf.); Ez 16^{47} כִּמְעַט קָט וַתַּשְׁחִתִי מֵהֶן *like a little*, and thou hadst done more corruptly than they; Ct 3^{4} כִּמְעַט שֶׁעָבַרְתִּי מֵהֶם = *hardly* had I passed. **b.** with impf., *just*, 2 S 19^{37} כמעט יעבר עבדך *just* would thy servant pass over; *lightly, easily, quickly* (cf. δι' ὀλίγου), ψ 2^{12} כִּי יִבְעַר כִּמְעַט אַפּוֹ, 81^{15} Jb 32^{22}. **c.** =*shortly*, 2 Ch 12^{7}. **d.** =*little worth*, Pr 10^{20} ולב רשעים כמעט. **e.** pleon. for מְעַט, Is 1^{9} (accents) שָׂרִיד כִּמְעָט a *little* remnant, ψ 105^{12} (=1 Ch 16^{19}) כִּמְעַט וְגָרִים בָּהּ; כִּמְעַט רֶגַע *like the littleness of* a moment=*for a little* moment, Is 26^{20} Ezr 9^{8}.

מְעֻטָּה Ez 21^{20} textual error, v. sub מרט. 4803
p. 598

מַעֲטֶה v. עטה. [מַעֲטָפָה] v. I. עטף. 4594-95
p. 742

†מְעִי only in והיתה מ׳ מַפָּלָה Is 17^{1}; acc. to 4596
AV RV Thes al. **n.[m.]** = עִי *ruin-heap*, but form very strange; 𝔊 om. (ἔσται εἰς πτῶσιν); Gr prop. כְּעִי, Di לְעִי; < dittogr. from מעיר Lag$^{Sem. i. 29}$ Che Nö$^{ZMG\ xxxii. 1878, 401}$ Brd SS Buhl Gu$^{in\ Kau}$ Du.

†מָעַי **n.pr.m.** a musician Ne 12^{36}; 𝔊א$^{c.a}$ 4597
Μααι, 𝔊L Μαια.

מֵעִים v. מעה. מַעְיָן v. sub עין. p. 588, 745 4578, 4599

מעינים 1 Ch 4^{41} Kt v. מְעוּנִים. p. 589 4586

†[מָעַךְ] **vb.** press, squeeze (NH *id.*; 4600
𝔗 מְעַךְ; Ar. مَعَكَ *rub*);—**Qal** *Pt. pass.* וּמָעוּךְ וְכָתוּת וְנָתוּק וְכָרוּת Lv 22^{24} (H), not to be offered to י׳, reference to emasculation (cf. Di); וַחֲנִיתוֹ מְעוּכָה־בָאָרֶץ 1 S 26^{7} *and his spear pressed* (thrust) *into the ground*. **Pu.** *Pf.* 3 mpl. שָׁמָּה מֹעֲכוּ שְׁדֵיהֶן Ez 23^{3} *there were their breasts squeezed* (‖ עִשּׂוּ; unchastely; fig. of intercourse of Samaria and Jerus. with Egypt, involving idolatry).

†מָעוֹךְ **n.pr.m.** father of Achish of Gath 4582
(on form cf. Lag$^{BN\ 32}$);—1 S 27^{2} (𝔊 Αμμαχ, A Μωαβ, 𝔊L Αχιμααν) = מַעֲכָה 1 K 2^{39} (𝔊 Αμησα, A 𝔊L Μααχα).

†מַעֲכָה **n.pr.m., f. et gent. 1. n.pr.m.** 4601
𝔊 Μ(ο)ωχα, Μα(α)χα: **a.** son of Nahor by his concubine רְאוּמָה Gn 22^{22} (J), ancestor of people v. **3.** **b.** father of חָנָן, a hero of David 1 Ch 11^{43}. **c.** Simeonite name 1 Ch 27^{16}. **d.** father of Achish 1 K 2^{39} (v. מָעוֹךְ supra). **2. n.pr.f.** 𝔊 Μ(ο)ωχα, Μααχα, etc.: **a.** Geshurite princess, wife of David, mother of Absalom, 2 S 3^{3}=1 Ch 3^{2}. **b.** daughter of Absalom, wife of Rehoboam, mother of Abijam, 1 K 15^{2} 2 Ch 11$^{20.21.22}$; rd. also מ׳ 2 Ch 13^{2} (so 𝔊 𝔖) for MT מִיכָיָה, where called daughter of Uriel of Gibeah (on this difficulty v. Be Öt, and cf. **c**). **c.** mother of Asa, and called also daughter of Absalom (as **b**) 1 K 15^{10}, cf. v^{13} = 2 Ch 15^{16}, (on this difficulty v. Th Kmp$^{in\ Kau}$). **d.** concubine of Caleb acc. to 1 Ch 2^{48}. **e.** wife of

Machir 1 Ch 7[16], cf. v[15] (corrupt, v. Be). **f.** wife of (יעיאל), father of Gibeon, 1 Ch 8[29] 9[35]. **3. n.pr.gent.**, 𝔊 Μοοχα, Μωχα, Μα(α)χα; dwelling W. of Bashan, near *Soba*, and *Geshur* (cf. esp. adj. gent. infr.), 2 S 10[6.8] = 1 Ch 19[7],
758 אֲרַם מ׳ v[6] (cf. Gn 22[24] supr.); = מַעֲכַת Jos 13[13]
1038 (+ גְּשׁוּר), 𝔊 ὁ Μαχατει, Μαχαθι.—אָבֵל בֵּית מַעֲכָה
59 v. sub בַּיִת, p. 112 supr., and אָבֵל, p. 5.

4601 מַעֲכָת v. supr. מַעֲכָה **3.**

4602 †מַעֲכָתִי **adj.gent.** הַמּ׳ 1 Ch 4[19]; so בֶּן־הַמַּעֲכָתִי 2 S 23[34] of one of David's heroes, We del. בן; rd. prob. בֵּית הַמּ׳ Klo HPS; v. also Dr; of associate of Ishmael the Judaean 2 K 25[23] = Je 40[8]; coll. = *the Maachathites* Dt 3[14] Jos 12[5] 13[11.13] (all + הַגְּשׁוּרִי; cf. מַעֲכָה **3**).—𝔊 Μαχ(ε)ι, Μαχατ(ε)ι, Μααχαθι, etc.

4603 †מָעַל **vb. act unfaithfully, treacherously**, a priestly word (P Ez. Ch.), chiefly late (NH *id.*, *act unfaithfully; Ar.* مَغَلَ *whisper, backbite*, مَغَالَةٌ *perfidy, fraud*);—**Qal** *Pf.* 3 ms. מָעַל Jos 22[20] + 4 t.; 3 fs. מָעֲלָה Lv 5[21] Nu 5[12] + 13 t. Pf.; *Impf.* יִמְעַל Pr 16[10] 2 Ch 26[16]; 3 fs. תִּמְעֹל Lv 5[15] Nu 5[27]; 3 mpl. יִמְעֲלוּ, וַיִּמְעֲלוּ Jos 7[1], 1 Ch 5[25]; 2 mpl. תִּמְעָלוּ Ne 1[8]; *Inf. cstr.* לִמְעֹל, so rd. for 𝔐 למסר Nu 31[16] Thes Di;—*act unfaithfully, treacherously*, usu. **1.** מָעַל מַעַל: **a.** abs. בַּחֵרֶם *in the matter of the devoted thing* (the sin of Achan) Jos 7[1] (JE), 22[20] (P), cf. Lv 5[15] (P), 2 Ch 36[14] Ez 14[13] 15[8] 18[24]. **b.** wife against (בְּ) husband Nu 5[12.27] (P; marital infidelity). **c.** elsewhere ag. (בְּ) God, Lv 26[40] (H), 5[21] Nu 5[6] 31[16] (?) Jos 22[16.31] (all P), 1 Ch 10[13] 28[19] Ez 17[20] 20[27] 39[26] Dn 9[7]. **2.** usage without מַעַל (only late): **a.** במשפט לא ימעל פיו Pr 16[10] *let not his* (the king's) *mouth act treacherously against justice* (RV *in judgment*). **b.** elsewhere against God, c. בְּ, Dt 32[51] (P), 1 Ch 5[25] 12[2] 26[22] 30[7] Ezr 10[2] Ne 13[27] Ez 39[23]; without בְּ, 2 Ch 26[18] 29[6] Ezr 10[10] Ne 1[8]; בַּחֵרֶם 1 Ch 2[7].

4604 †I. מַ֫עַל **n.m.**[Ezr 9, 2] **unfaithful, treacherous act** (NH מְעִילָה);—מ׳ Lv 5[15] + 16 t.; מָעַל Nu 5[12] + 2 t.; sf. מַעֲלוֹ Ez 17[20] + 4 t.; מַעֲלָם Ez 39[26] + 3 t.;—**1.** ag. man: נשאר מעל Jb 21[34] *faithlessness remains* (cf. Nu 5[12.27] Pr 16[10] under מָעַל). **2.** elsewhere ag. God, c. בְּ, Jos 22[22] (P); without בְּ, 1 Ch 9[1] 2 Ch 29[19] 33[19] Ezr 9[2.4] 10[6].—מַעַל elsewhere only c. מָעַל q.v. (**1**; all cited).

†מְעִיל **n.m.**[152, 10] robe (Thes conj. orig. meaning *cover* for √מעל, cf. בגד; Ba[NB 15] comp. Ar. مِعْلَاةٌ *an outer garment*, but against this Sta[ThLz, Apr. 28, 1894, 235]);—מ׳ Ex 28[31] + 18 t.; sf. מְעִילוֹ 1 S 15[27]; מְעִלוֹ Jb 1[20] 2[12] + 4 t. sg.; pl. מְעִילִים 2 S 13[18], (but del. We Klo Kit Bu SS; orig. gloss מֵעוֹלָם We Kit Bu); מְעִילֵיהֶם Ez 26[16];—exterior garment, *robe*, worn over the inner tunic כְּתֹנֶת: **1.** worn by men of rank: Saul and Jonathan 1 S 18[4] 24[5.12.12]; princes of the sea Ez 26[16]; Job Jb 1[20] 2[12]; Samuel 1 S 15[27] 28[14]; Ezra Ezr 9[3.5]; David clothed with מ׳ בוץ 1 Ch 15[27] (in the procession of the ark); the child Samuel had מ׳ קָטֹן 1 S 2[19];—(it had a skirt כנף 1 S 15[27] 24[5.12.12]). **2.** worn by the daughters of David 2 S 13[18] (but prob. del., v. supr.) **3.** robe of high priest (only P): מְעִיל הָאֵפוֹד, made of purple stuff, Ex 28[31] 29[5] 39[22]; אפוד ומעיל 28[4]; הַמְּעִיל Lv 8[7], having שׁוּלֵי הַמְּעִיל skirts Ex 28[34] 39[24.25.26], around which were alternate coloured pomegranates and golden bells, and פִּי הַמְּעִיל, an opening or hole by which it might be drawn over the head 39[23]. **4.** fig. of attributes (of י׳, and of men), קנאה Is 59[17]; צדקה 61[10]; משפט Jb 29[14]; בשת ψ 109[29]. 4598

II. מַ֫עַל v. sub עלה. מֵעַל v. עַל. p. 751, 758f 4605, 5921

[מֹעַל], מַעֲלָה, מַעֲלֶה v. sub עלה. p. 751-52 4607-09

[מַעֲלָל, מַעֲלִיל] v. עלל. p. 760 4611

[מַעֲמָד], מָעֳמָד v. עמד. מַעֲמָסָה v. עמס. p. 765, 770 4612-14

מַעֲמַקִּים v. עמק. מַ֫עַן v. מַעֲנֶה sub I. עָנָה. p. 771, 775 4615-16

מַעֲנֶה, מַעֲנָה, מַעֲנִית v. I. ענה. p. 775-76 4617-18

מְעֹנָה v. עון. p. 733 4585

מעץ (√of foll.; perhaps = *be wrathful*, cf. Ar. مَعِضَ *be enraged*; cf. also **n.pr.m.** אֲחִימַעַץ, supr. p. 27). 290

†מַ֫עַץ **n.pr.m.** in Judah 1 Ch 2[27]; 𝔊 Μαας. 4619

מַעֲצֵבָה v. עצב. מַעֲצָד v. עצד. p. 781 4620-21

[מֹעֵצָה] v. [מוֹעֵצָה] sub יעץ. p. 420 4156

מַעְצוֹר, מַעְצָר v. עצר. מַעֲקֶה v. עקה. p. 784-85 4622-24

מַעֲקַשִּׁים v. עקש. מַ֫עַר, מַעֲרָה v. ערה. p. 786, 789 4625-26, 4629

I. מַעֲרָב v. I. ערב. p. 786 4627

II. מַעֲרָב, מַעֲרָבָה v. III. ערב. p. 788 4628

4631 מְעָרָה v. I. ערר. p. 792

4630 מערות 1 S 17^{23} Kt v. מערכה sub ערך. p. 790

6206 [מַעֲרִיץ] v. ערץ. p. 792

4633-35 מַעֲרָךְ, מַעֲרָכָה, מַעֲרֶכֶת v. ערך. p. 790

4636-37 [מַעֲרֻמִּים] v. II. עור. מַעֲרָצָה v. ערץ. p. 736, 792

4638 מַעֲרָת v. ערה. p. 789

4639-41 מַעֲשֶׂה, מַעְשַׂי, מַעֲשֵׂיָה, מַעֲשֵׂיָהוּ v. עשׂה. p. 795-96

4642-43 מַעֲשֵׂר v. עשׂר. מַעֲשַׁקּוֹת v. עשׁק. p. 798-99

4644 † מֹף **n.pr.loc. Memphis** (Eg. *Mr-nfr*, i.e. *Mĕnnūfĕr*, **Mĕnnū́fĕ*, Steindorff$^{BAS\ i.\ 594\ f.}$; As. *Mêmpi*, *Mimpi*, Schr$^{COT\ Is\ 19,\ 13}$ Dl$^{Par.\ 314}$; cf. Erman$^{Ægypten\ 48,\ 243}$ Eb$^{Cicerone\ i.\ 114\ f.}$; 𝔊 (and Gk) Μεμφις, on coins Μενφι(ς) Steind.$^{l.c.}$);—מ׳ Ho 9^{6}

5297 = נֹף Is 19^{13} Je 2^{16} 44^{1} 46$^{14.19}$ Ez 30^{13}, and וְנֹף צָרֵי יוֹמָם v^{16} (without clear meaning, prob. txt. err. Siegfr$^{in\ Kau}$; 𝔊 (appar.) וְנָפֹצוּ מֵימֵיהֶם *and their waters shall be dispersed* (cf. Na 3^{8}); Co ונפרצו חומותיה *and its walls shall be torn down*); נֹף also v^{15} (for MT נא) 𝔊 Co.

4645-47 מִפְגָּע v. פגע. מַפָּח, מַפֻּחַ v. נפח. p. 656, 803

4648 מְפִי(י)בֹשֶׁת v. מְרִיב׳ sub ריב. p. 937

4649 † מֻפִּים **n.pr.m.** family name in Benjamin, Gn 46^{21}, 𝔊 Μαμφειν; but 1 Ch 7^{12} שֻׁפִּם q.v.

4650 מֵפִיץ v. פוץ p. 807

4651, 4654, 4658 מַפָּל, מַפָּלָה, מַפֶּלֶת v. נפל. p. 658

4652-53 [מִפְלָאָה] v. פלא. [מִפְלַגָּה] v. פלג. p. 811

4655-56 מִפְלָט v. פלט. מִפְלֶצֶת v. פלץ. p. 812, 814

4657 [מִפְלָשׂ] v. פלשׂ = פלס. p. 814

4659 [מִפְעָל, מִפְעָלָה] v. פעל. p. 821

4158 מֵיפַעַת v. מֵיפַעַת sub יפע. p. 422

4660-63 [מַפָּץ], מַפֵּץ v. נפץ. מִפְקָד v. פקד. p. 658-59, 824

4664-65 [מִפְרָץ] v. פרץ. [מַפְרֶקֶת] v. פרק. p. 830

4666-67 [מִפְרָשׂ] v. פרשׂ. מִפְשָׂעָה v. פשׂע. p. 831-32

4668-69 מַפְתֵּחַ, [מִפְתָּח] v. פתח. p. 836

4160, 4670 מִפְתָּן v. פתן. מֵץ Is 16^{4} v. מיץ. p. 568, 837

4671 מֹץ v. מוץ. p. 558

4672 מָצָא^{452} **vb. attain to, find** (NH *id.*; As. *maṣû*, Dl$^{HWB\ 421}$, Eth. **መጽአ:** *come, arrive;* Aram. [ܡܛܳܐ *find*], Pt. pass. ܡܛܝܳܐ *able, powerful*, and deriv.; cf. Nö$^{ZMG\ xl.\ 1886,\ 736}$ Dr$^{1\ S\ 23,\ 17}$);—**Qal** *Pf.* מ׳ Gn 2^{20}+, sf. מְצָאוֹ Jb 31^{29}, 3 fs. מָצְאָה Gn 8^{9}+, sf. מְצָאַתְנוּ Ju 6^{13} Ne 9^{32}, מְצָאָתַם Ex 18^{8}; 2 ms. מָצָאתָ Gn 31^{37}+; 1 s. מָצָאתִי Gn 18^{3}+, מָצָתִי Nu 11^{11}, sf. מְצָאתִיו Ct 3$^{1.2}$, מְצָאתִיהוּ Ct 5^{6}; 3 pl. מָצְאוּ Ju 21^{14}+; sf. מְצָאֻהוּ Jb 37^{23}, etc.; *Impf.* יִמְצָא 1 S 24^{20}+, 3 fs. תִּמְצָא 1 S 1^{18}+; 3 mpl. יִמְצְאוּ Ju 5^{30}+, sf. יִמְצָאֻהוּ Jb 20^{8}, יִמְצָאֻנְנִי Pr 1^{28} 8^{17}, יִמְצָאוּנְהָ Je 2^{24}; 3 fpl. תִּמְצֶאןָ Dt 31^{21} etc.; *Imv.* מְצָא 1 S 20$^{21.36}$, וּמְצָא־ Pr 3^{4}; mpl. מִצְאוּ Je 6^{16}; fpl. וּמְצֶאןָ Ru 1^{9}; *Inf.* מְצֹא, מְצוֹא ψ 32^{6} Gn 19^{11}+, sf. בְּמֹצַאֲכֶם Gn 32^{20} [= מָצְאֲכֶם Ges $^{§\ 74,\ 3,\ R.\ 2}$]; *Pt.* מוֹצֵא ψ 119^{162}, מוֹצֶה Ec 7^{26}, sf. מֹצְאִי Gn 4^{14} Pr 8^{35}; fs. abs. מֹצֵאת 2 S 18^{22}, מוֹצֵאת Ct 8^{10}; mpl. מֹצְאִים Nu 15^{33}, cstr. מֹצְאֵי Pr 8^{9}; fpl. abs. מֹצְאוֹת Jos 2^{23}, etc.;—**1.** *find*: **a.** thing sought, c. acc. rei, straw Ex 5^{11} (J), water Gn 26^{32} (J), cf. v^{19}, Ex 15^{22} (J), grass 1 K 18^{5}, help, consort, Gn 2^{20} (J), cf. Pr 18^{22}+; with idea of attaining to, arriving at, a resting-place Gn 8^{9} (J) Is 34^{14} cf. צִפּוֹר מָצְאָה בַיִת ψ 84^{4}, Je 45^{3} La 1^{3}; of marriage Ru 1^{9}; of finding place for temple ψ 132^{5}; fig. וּמִצְאוּ מַרְגּוֹעַ לְנַפְשְׁכֶם Je 6^{16} *and find quiet for yourselves;* find grave Jb 3^{22}; reach cities 2 S 20^{6} (where rd. יִמְצָא Vrss Th Dr Kit Bu), cf. ψ 107^{4}; *find* = secure prey, booty, plunder Gn 27^{20} (J), Ju 5^{30} 21^{12} 1 S 14^{30} cf. 2 Ch 20^{25} Pr 1^{13} ψ 119^{162}; of securing gain Ho 12^{9} (+ לִי; ‖ עשׁר), Jb 31^{25}; so perhaps also abs. אֵין בְּשׂוֹרָה מֹצֵאת 2 S 18^{22} *there is no news securing* gain i.e. such as to bring you a reward (cf. Th Dr; but text dub.); secure as crop Gn 26^{12} (J), cf. Ec 11^{1}; = *acquire, get* wounds and dishonour Pr 6^{33}; מ׳ חֵן בְּעֵינֵי פ׳ *find* (= gain, secure) *favour in the eyes of* any one: of י׳, †Gn 6^{8} Ex 33$^{12.13.13.16.17}$ 34^{9} (all J), Nu 11$^{11.15}$ (JE), Ju 6^{17} 2 S 15^{25}+; oftener of men Gn 18^{3} 19^{19} 30^{27} 32^{6} + 8 t. Gn (all J), Nu 32^{5} (JE), Dt 24^{1} 1 S 1^{18} + 7 t. S, 1 K 11^{19} Ru 2$^{2.10.13}$ Est 5^{8} 7^{3}; מ׳ חֵן לִפְנֵי פ׳ †Est 8^{5}; אָז הָיִיתִי בְעֵינָיו כְּמוֹצְאֵת שָׁלוֹם †Ct 8^{10}; abs. מָצָא חֵן †Je 31^{2} Pr 3^{4} 28^{23}†: = *seek and find* 1 S 20^{21} (arrows), so v^{36}; fig. of grounds of accusation Jb 33^{10} *he succeeds in finding;* so also Is 58$^{3.13}$; *find* knowledge of God Pr 2^{5} cf. 8^{9}, word of י׳ Am 8^{12}, words of wisdom Pr 4^{22}, wisdom Jb 32^{13} Pr 24^{14} (v. also infr.); ransom Jb 33^{24}; life Pr 8^{35} (Qr מָצָא; >Kt מצאי, i.e. מֹצְאִי De Str Wild), 21^{21}; c. acc. pers. Gn

18$^{26.28.30}$ (J), 41^{38} (E), 1 S 9$^{13.13}$ 1 K 1^{3} 13^{14} cf. v^{28},+; of pursuit Jos 2^{22} (J), *find* 'י Ho 5^{6} Dt 4^{29} Je 29^{13} Jb 23^{3} ψ 32^{6}+Ho 6^{3} (rd. כְּשַׁחֲרֵנוּ כֵּן נִמְצָאֵהוּ, for MT כְּשַׁחַר נָכוֹן מֹצָאוֹ Gie$^{Beitr. z. Jes. Krit. 208}$ We Now); so poss. also (obj. om.) Je 10^{18} (so Gf.; 𝔊 Or rd. Niph.; Gie יֶאְשָׁמוּ), (Jb 37^{23} 11$^{7.7}$ v. infr.); *find* wisdom (personif.) Pr 1^{28} 8$^{17.35}$ cf. 3^{13}. **b.** what is lost, missed, c. acc. rei, Gn 31$^{32.33.34.35.37}$ (E), 1 S 9$^{4.4}$ Dt 22^{3} Lv 5$^{22.23}$ (P), Gn 36^{24} (P)+; וַיִּלְאוּ לִמְצֹא הַפָּתַח Gn 19^{11} *and they grew weary in finding the door; find* a word (to say) Ne 5^{8} Ec 12^{10}, answer Jb 32^{3}, vision from 'י La 2^{9}; c. acc. pers. Gn 38$^{20.22.23}$(J), 2 S 17^{20} 1 K 18$^{10.12}$ 21$^{20.20}$ 2 K 2^{17} Ez 22^{30} Pr 7^{15} Ct 3$^{1.2.4}$ 5^{6}+. **c.** *meet, encounter,* c. acc. pers. (one expected), Gn 32^{20} (E), 2 K 9^{21} Je 41^{12} 2 Ch 20^{16}; cf. also Nu 35^{27} (P). **d.** *find* a condition, *find* one in a situation; וְלֹא מ׳ לָהּ בְּתוּלִים Dt 22^{14} cf. v^{17} 24^{1}; וַיִּמ׳ אֶת־מֶלֶךְ . . . נִלְחָם 2 K 19^{8} *and he found the king* of Assyria *warring* against Lachish = Is 37^{8}; וּמ׳ אֶת־לְבָבוֹ נֶאֱמָן Ne 9^{8}; מ׳ כָּתוּב בספר Ne 7^{5} 8^{14}; esp. late, 1 Ch 20^{2} 2 Ch 25^{5} Dn 1^{20} Ec 7^{26}. **e.** = *learn, devise* Ec 7$^{27.27.29}$. **f.** = *experience* sorrow ψ 116^{3}, cf. Ec 7^{14}. **2.** *find out:* **a.** find out thoroughly, explore: obj. God Jb 11$^{7.7}$ 37^{23}; God's works Ec 3^{11} 8$^{17.17.17}$, cf. 7^{24}. †**b.** = *detect* sin, crime, usu. *in* (ב) one, 2 K 17^{4} 1 S 29$^{3.6.8}$ Ho 12^{9}; לֹא מ׳ בְּיָדִי מְאוּמָה 1 S 12^{5}; detect evil in God Je 2^{5}; subj. God Je 2^{34} 23^{11}; מ׳ עֲוֹן עֲבָדֶיךָ Gn 44^{16}(J), cf. ψ 36^{3}; abs. ψ 10^{15} 17^{3}†. **c.** = *guess,* solve riddle Ju 14$^{12.18}$ cf. Pr 8^{12}. **3.** = *come upon, light upon:* **a.** often unexpectedly = *happen upon,* c. acc. rei, money Gn 44^{8} (J), book 2 K 22^{8} 23^{24} = 2 Ch 34$^{14.15}$, cf. Ne 7^{5}; honey Pr 25^{16}, ship Jon 1^{3}; a plain Gn 11^{2} (J), jawbone Ju 15^{15}; ark of 'י ψ 132^{6} (acc. to some, but dub.; Bae prop. הוֹצֵאנוּהָ); indef. Ez 3^{1} (del. 𝔊 Co); c. acc. pers. = *meet, fall in with* Gn 4$^{14.15}$ cf. Je 50^{7} Gn 37$^{15.17}$ (all J), 1 S 9^{11} 30^{11} Dt 22$^{23.25.27.28}$ 1 K 13^{24} 20^{36} 2 K 4^{29} 10$^{13.15}$ Ct 3^{3} 5$^{7.8}$ 8^{1}; come upon = *discover,* Nu 15$^{22.33}$; of 'י meeting (finding) Isr. in desert Ho 9^{10} cf. 12^{5} Dt 32^{10}; angel finding Hagar Gn 16^{7} (J); 'י finding David ψ 89^{21}. **b.** *hit,* c. acc. pers., subj. bowmen 1 S 31^{3} = 1 Ch 10^{3}; subj. axe Dt 19^{5}. **c.** subj. hand Is 10^{14} (fig., in metaph., of reaching nests), cf. v^{10}, 1 S 23^{17} (of Saul's taking David), ψ 21^{9} (sq. לְ), v^{9} (c. acc.); כֹּל אֲשֶׁר תִּמְצָא יָדְךָ לַעֲשׂוֹת Ec 9^{10}; sin (i.e. its punishment) *will light upon* you Nu 32^{23}. **d.** †subj. fire, כִּי תֵצֵא אֵשׁ וּמָצְאָה קֹצִים Ex 22^{5} (E). †**e.** *befal,* c. acc. pers. Jos 2^{23} (JE); of evil Gn 44^{34} (J), Dt 4^{30} 31$^{17.17.21}$ Ju 6^{13} 2 K 7^{9} Jb 31^{29} ψ 116^{3} 119^{143} Est 8^{6}; subj. תְּלָאָה Ex 18^{8} (E), Nu 20^{14} (JE), Ne 9^{32}†. **4.** noteworthy phrases are: כַּאֲשֶׁר תִּמ׳ יָדֶךָ Ju 9^{33} *acc. to what thy hand findeth,* i.e. as the occasion may demand, so 1 S 10^{7} (c. acc.; cf. Ec 9^{10} **3 c**); but 25^{8} = *what thou chancest to have,* cf. אֲשֶׁר מ׳ כְּלִי זָהָב Nu 31^{50} (P); וְלֹא יִמְצָאֻהוּ Jb 20^{8} = *and he shall not be,* shall no longer exist, cf. Is 41^{12}; Ec 9^{15} *they found in it* = there happened to be in it; מ׳ אֶת־לִבּוֹ לְהִתְפַּלֵּל 2 S 7^{27} *he found the heart* (took courage) *to pray* = 1 Ch 17^{25} (om. את־לבו, perh. ancient text. err.); לֹא מָצְאוּ יְדֵיהֶם ψ 76^{6} *they did not find their hands,* were not able to use them, were paralyzed; חַיַּת יָדֵךְ מָצָאת Is 57^{10} = (perh.) *experience renewal of thy strength* (cf. I. חַיָּה p. 312 supr. Che$^{Comm.}$; for other interpr. of ח׳, ידך, v. Ew Di Du Che^{Hpt}); וּמָצָא כְּדֵי גְאֻלָּתוֹ Lv 25^{26} = *and he find* (that he has) *enough for its redemption* (cf. דַּי), so מָצְאָה יָדוֹ v^{28}, תִּמ׳ יָדָהּ דֵּי שֶׂה 12^{8} (cf. תַּגִּיעַ 5^{7}); without דַּי, וְלֹא מָצְאוּ לָהֶם כֵּן Ju 21^{14} = (prob.) *and they* (the Israelites) *did not find* enough *for them,* even *so* (cf. GFM); also וּמָצָא לָהֶם Nu 11$^{22.22}$ (JE) *and so one find* (= there be found) enough *for them* (cf. Niph. Jos 17^{16} Zc 10^{10}).

†**Niph.** *Pf.* נִמְצָא 1 S 13^{22}+; 3 fs. נמצאה Je 48^{27} Kt Gf; < נִמְצָא Qr Gie; 2 fs. נִמְצֵאת Je 50^{24}; 1 s. נִמְצֵאתִי Is 65^{1}, וְנִמְצֵאתִי consec. Je 29^{14}; 3 pl. נִמְצְאוּ Dt 22^{20}+, הַנִּמְצְאוּ 1 Ch 29^{17} (הַ· = rel., cf. Da$^{Synt. § 22 R. 4}$ Kö$^{Synt. § 52}$); *Impf.* יִמָּצֵא Gn 44^{9}+; 3 fs. תִּמָּצֵא Ex 22^{3}+; 2 fs. תִּמָּצְאִי Ez 26^{21}; 3 mpl. יִמָּצְאוּן Gn 18$^{29.30.31.32}$, וַיִּמָּצְאוּ 1 Ch 24^{4} 2 Ch 4^{16}; 3 fpl. תִּמָּצֶאינָה Je 50^{20}; *Inf.* הִמָּצֵא Ex 22^{3} (= Inf. abs. cf. Ba$^{NB 74}$), sf. הִמָּצְאוֹ Is 55^{6}; *Pt.* נִמְצָא Ju 20^{48}+, fs. נִמְצָאָה 2 K 19^{4} = Is 37^{4}; pl. נִמְצְאִים 1 S 13^{15}+11 t.; נִמְצָאִים only Ezr 8^{25}; sf. 2 fs. נִמְצָאַיִךְ Is 22^{3}; נִמְצָאוֹת Gn 19^{15} Ju 20^{48};—pass. of Qal, *be found:* **1. a.** of a thing lost (asses) 1 S 9^{20} 10$^{2.16}$; stolen Gn 44$^{9.10.12.16.17}$ (J), Ex 21^{16} (all c. בְּיַד); sought, wisdom Jb 28$^{12.13}$ Pr 10^{13}. **b.** of thing found unexpectedly, book 2 K 22^{13} 23^{2} = 2 Ch 34$^{21.30}$; of corpse Dt 21^{1}. **c.** = *be lighted upon, encountered;* of breaches in temple 2 K 12^{6}; of cities Ju 20$^{48 b}$; of persons in captured city 2 K 25$^{19.19}$ = Je 52$^{25.25}$, Dt 20^{11}, cf. Ex 9^{19} (J), Ju 20$^{48 a}$ Is 13^{15} 22^{3} Je 41^{8}; *be discovered,* of a condition, situation Dt 22^{20} (בתולים); נִמְצָא־בוֹ דָּבָר טוֹב 1 K 14^{13}, cf. 2 Ch 19^{3}. **d.** *be found* written (כתוב), Ne 13^{1} Est 6^{2}; of persons Dn 12^{1}.

e.=*appeared, were recognised*, of words of י׳ Je 15^{16}. **f.** of persons sought Gn 18$^{29.30.31.32}$ (J), Jos 10^{17} (JE), 1 S 10^{21} 2 S 7^{12} 1 Ch 26^{31}; in geneal. register Ezr 2^{62}=Ne 7^{64}; of י׳, specif., *let himself be found of (by)* any one: sq. לְ pers. Is 65^{1} Je 29^{14} 1 Ch 28^{9} 2 Ch 15$^{2.4.15}$, abs. Is 55^{6}. **g.**=*be discovered, detected:* (1) of iniquity, crime: Ex 22$^{3.3}$ (E), 1 S 25^{28} 1 K 1^{52} Je 2^{34} Ez 28^{15} Jb 19^{28} Mal 2^{6}, cf. Mi 1^{13}, 2 Ch 36^{8} Est 2^{23}. (2) of wrong-doers Ex 22$^{1.6.7}$ (E), Dt 22$^{22.28}$ 24^{7} Je 2^{26} 48^{27} 50^{24} (‖ נִתְפַּשְׂתְּ, נִלְכַּדְתְּ), Pr 6^{31} Ezr 10^{18}. **h.**=*be gained, secured*, as a crop, of fruit, fig. מִמֶּנִּי פֶּרְיְךָ נִמְצָא Ho 14^{9} (cf. Qal Gn 26^{12} Ec 11^{1}). **i.**=*be discoverable, to be found* Jb 42^{15} Dn 1^{19} (cf. Is 55^{6} supr. **1 f**). **2.** *be found*=*be:* **a.** c. בְּיַד *be found in* one's *hand*=one happens to have 1 S 9^{8} 13$^{22.22}$, cf. (without ביד) 23^{4}. **b.** c. לְ pers.,=be in the possession of: Dt 21^{17}, c. אֶת־ (prep.) pers. Ex 35$^{23.24}$ 1 Ch 29^{8}. **c.** *be found in* (בְּ) a place, esp. of wealth, treasure, Gn 47^{14} (J), 2 K 12$^{11.19}$ 14^{14} 16^{8} 18^{15} 20^{13}=Is 39^{2}, 2 K 22^{9} 2 Ch 21^{17} 25^{24} 34^{17}; cf. Ex 12^{19} Je 41^{3} 1 Ch 4^{41};=*happen to be, be*, Dt 17^{2} 18^{10} Je 5^{26} Is 35^{9} 51^{3} 65^{8}; c. neg.=*be no more* Zp 3^{13} Ez 26^{21} ψ 37^{36} (‖ אֵינֶנּוּ), Dn 11^{19}. **d.**=*be left* after war, violence, etc., 1 S 13^{19} 2 S 17^{13} Is 30^{14} 2 K 19^{4}=Is 37^{4}. **e.**=*be present* Gn 19^{15} (J), 1 S 13$^{15.16}$ 21^{4}; esp. late, 1 Ch 29^{17} 2 Ch 5^{11} 29^{29} 30^{21} 31^{1} 34$^{32.33}$ 35$^{7.17.18}$ Ezr 8^{25} Est 1^{5} 4^{16}. **f.**=*prove to be*, after numbering, 1 Ch 24^{4} 2 Ch 2^{16}; of י׳, עֶזְרָה בְצָרוֹת נִמְצָא ψ 46^{2}. **3.** *be (found) sufficient:* לֹא יִמָּצֵא לָנוּ הָהָר Jos 17^{16} (JE), cf. Zc 10^{10} (also Qal Nu 11^{22} Ju 21^{14}).

†**Hiph.** *Pf.* 1 s. sf. הִמְצִיתִךָ 2 S 3^{8}; 3 mpl. הִמְצִיאוּ Lv 9^{13}; *Impf.* 3 ms. sf. 3 ms. יַמְצִאֶנּוּ Jb 34^{11}, יַמְצִאֵהוּ Jb 37^{13}; 3 mpl. וַיַּמְצִאוּ Lv 9$^{12.18}$; *Pt.* מַמְצִיא Zc 11^{6};—**1.** *cause to find, attain*, c. acc. pers. Jb 34^{11} (subj. God). **2.** *cause to light upon, come upon, come* c. acc. of cloud Jb 37^{13} (dub.) **3.** *cause to encounter*, deliver up to, c. acc. pers., + בְּיַד 2 S 3^{8} (subj. man), Zc 11^{6} (subj. God). **4.** *present* unto (אֶל־), of Aaron's sons ministering unto him, c. acc. of offering, and of blood, Lv 9$^{12.13.18}$.

4161-62 **מוֹצָא** v. מוֹצָא sub יצא. p. 425f

4673-76, 4678 **מַצָּב, מֻצָּב, מַצָּבָה, מַצֵּבָה, מַצֶּבֶת** v. נצב. p. 662-63

4677 †**מְצֹבָיָה** c. art. הַמְּ׳ 1 Ch 11^{47}, dub.; the preceding n.pr. seems to call for adj. gent., but form not suitable, and poss. deriv. unknown; Be conj. מִצֹּבָה, *from Ṣôba;* 𝔊 ὁ Μειναβεια, Μεσωβια, Μασαβια; 𝔙 *de Masobia.*

מָצַד, [מְצָדָה], מְצוּדָה v. צוד. p. 844-45 4679, 4685-86

†[**מָצָה**] **vb. drain, drain out** (NH *id.*, *press or drain out;* Aram. מְצָא, مصا *id.;* Ar. مصو 4680
II. *drain to the last drop* (Dozy); cf. מָצַץ);—**Qal** *Pf.* 2 fs. מָצִית Is 51^{17}, וּמָצִית consec. Ez 23^{34}; *Impf.* 3 ms. apoc. וַיִּמֶץ Ju 6^{38}, 3 mpl. יִמְצוּ ψ 75^{9};—*drain, drain out*, וַיִּמֶץ טַל מִן־הַגִּזָּה Ju 6^{38} *and drained dew out of the fleece;* so fig., obj. קֻבַּעַת *bowl, goblet*, of bewilderment fr. י׳, Is 51^{17} (+שׁתה; of personif. Jerusalem), cf., obj. כּוֹס, Ez 23^{24} (+שׁתה); obj. שְׁמָרֶיהָ *the dregs of it* (viz. כּוֹס) ψ 75^{9} (subj. the wicked). **Niph.** *Pf.* וְנִמְצָה consec. Lv 1^{15} *and* the blood (of the bird) *shall be drained out;* so *Impf.* יִמָּצֵה 5^{9} (both P); וּמֵי מָלֵא יִמָּצוּ לָמוֹ ψ 73^{10} *water of abundance is drained* (i. e. drunk) *by them* (Gr Che Buhl rd. יָמֹצּוּ or יִמְצוּ (מצץ) *they drain*).

I. **מַצָּה** v. מצץ. II. **מַצָּה** v. נצה. p. 595, 663 4682-83

†**מֹצָה** **n.pr.loc.** in Benj., Jos 18^{26}; 𝔊 Αμωκη, A Αμωσα, 𝔊L Μασσα. Site unknown. 4681

[**מִצְהָלָה**] v. צהל. p. 843

[**מָצוֹד**], **מְצוֹדָה, מְצוּדָה** v. צוד. p. 844-45 4685-86

מִצְוָה v. צוה. p. 846 4687

[**מְצוֹלָה**], **מְצוּלָה, מְצֻלָה** v. צול. p. 846 4688

מָצוֹק, מְצוּקָה v. I. צוק. p. 848 4689, 4691

מָצוּק v. II. צוק. p. 848 4690

I. **מָצוֹר, מְצוּרָה** v. I. צור. p. 848 4692

II. **מָצוֹר** *Egypt*, v. מצר, מִצְרַיִם. p. 596 4693

[**מַצּוּת**] v. נצה. p. 663 4695

מצח (√ of foll.)

†**מֵצַח** **n.m.**$^{Ez\,3,8}$ **brow, forehead**;—מ׳ abs. Ez 3^{7}, cstr. Ex 28^{28} Je 3^{3}; sf. מִצְחֲךָ Ez 3^{8} Is 48^{4}, מִצְחֶךָ Ez 3^{9}; מִצְחוֹ Ex 28^{38}+4 t.; מִצְחָם Ez 3^{8}; pl. cstr. מִצְחוֹת Ez 9^{4};—*brow, forehead*, struck by stone fr. David's sling 1 S 17$^{49.49}$; Aaron's forehead Ex 28$^{38.38}$; place where leprosy appears 2 Ch 26$^{19.20}$; place for a distinguishing mark or cross Ez 9^{4}; חִזְקֵי־מ׳ 3^{7} the house of Isr. are *stout of forehead* (i. e. obstinate; ‖ קְשֵׁי־לֵב), cf. v^{8}; so מִצְחֵךְ נְחוּשָׁה Is 48^{4} *thy brow* (is) *brass* 4696

(גִּיד בַּרְזֶל עָרְפֶּךָ ||); also of boldness, firmness of prophet v[8], and v[9] (but del. 𝔊 Co); מ׳ אִשָּׁה זוֹנָה הָיָה לָךְ Je 3^3, i. e. thou wast shameless (|| מֵאַנְתְּ הִכָּלֵם).

4697 †[מִצְחָה] **n.f. greave(s)**;—only sg. cstr. וּמִצְחַת נְחֹשֶׁת עַל־רַגְלָיו 1 S 17^6 *and greaves of bronze upon his legs*; < מִצְחֹת Vrss Th We Klo Dr Bu.

4698, 4700 [מְצִלָּה], מְצִלְתַּיִם v. I. צלל. p. 853

4688, 4701 מְצֻלָּה v. צול. מִצְנֶפֶת v. צנף. p. 846f, 857

4702-03 [מַצָּע] v. יצע. [מִצְעָד] v. צעד. p. 427, 857

4705-06 מִצְעָר v. צער. p. 859

4708-09 I, II. מִצְפָּה, מִצְפֶּה v. צפה. p. 859

4710 [מַצְפּוּנִים] v. צפן. p. 861

4711 †[מָצַץ] **vb.** drain out (cf. מָצָה; NH *id.*; Ar. مَصَّ *suck, suck up*; Aram. מְצַץ, مْصَ *suck* or *press out*);—only **Qal** *Impf.* 2 mpl. תָּמֹצּוּ וְהִתְעַנַּגְתֶּם מִזִּיז כְּבוֹדָהּ Is 66^{11} that *ye may drain out and delight yourselves*, etc. (|| תִּינְקוּ וּשְׂבַעְתֶּם).

4682 †I. מַצָּה **n.f. unleavened bread, or cake(s)**;—abs. מ׳ Lv 2^5 8^{26} (חַלַּת מ׳ אַחַת), Nu 6^{19} (*id.*), v[19]; usu. pl. מַצּוֹת Ex 12^{15} + 44 t.; מַצֹּת Ex 12^{18} + 3 t.;—*unleavened bread*, prepared in form of לֶחֶם Ex 29^2; חַלָּה Ex 29^2 + 4 t. P; רקיקים Ex 29^2 1 Ch 23^{29} + 4 t. P; ענה Ex 12^{39}; used at ordinary meals (prepared hastily): אפה מ׳ Gn 19^3 (J), Ex 12^{39} (J), 1 S 28^{24}; prob. also Ju $6^{19.20.21.21}$; elsewhere at sacrificial meals, e. g. ritual peace-offerings Lv $2^{4.4.5}$ 6^9 $7^{12.12}$ 10^{12}; consecration of priesthood Ex $29^{2.2.2.23}$ Lv $8^{2.26.26}$; at peace-offering of Nazirite Nu $6^{15.15.17.19.19}$; at Passover Ex 12^8 Nu 9^{11} (all P); esp. at feast of *unleavened bread* [*cakes*] for 7 days after Passover שמר חג המ׳ Ex 23^{15} (E), 34^{18} (J); שמר מ׳ Ex 12^{17} (P), עשׂה (ה)מ׳ חג 2 Ch $30^{13.21}$ 35^{17} Ezr 6^{22}, בחג המ׳ Dt 16^{16} 2 Ch 8^{13}; חג המ׳ לי׳ Lv 23^6. During these seven days all Israel ate מצות Ex $12^{15.18.20}$ (P), 23^{15} (E), $13^{6.7}$ 34^{18} (J), Lv 23^6 Nu 28^{17} (P), Dt $16^{3.8}$ Jos 5^{11} Ez 45^{21}.—2 K 23^9 rd. prob. מַצּוֹת or מָנָיוֹת for MT מ׳ (אכל); so Gei Kue Kmp Bu.

4690 [מָצֹק] v. מָצוֹק sub II. צוק. p. 848

4691 [מְצָקָה] v. מצוקה sub I. צוק. p. 848

4166, 4712 [מֻצֶּקֶת] v. מוּצ׳ sub יצק. מֵצַר v. I. צרר. p. 427, 865

מצר (√ of foll.)

מִצְרַ֫יִם[681] **n.pr.terr. et gent. f.**[Ex 10, 7], 4714
m.[Ex 12, 33], **mpl.**[Gn 41, 55] etc. (v. infr. **2**), **Egypt, Egyptians** (Ph. מצרם; As. *Mŭṣŭr(u)*, *Muṣru*, *Miṣir*, Dl[Par 308] Schr[COT Gloss. KGF 246 ff.], TelAm *Miṣrî*, Wkl[TA 39*] Bez[BM 152], and *Mašrî* Wkl[l.c.]; Ar. مِصْر Cairo, Egypt (Spiro); Min. *Miṣru* Hom[A. and A. (1892), 125]; v. also Eb[ÄgM 71 ff.]; 𝔊 Αἴγυπτος;—deriv. and form dub.; ־ַיִם usu. regarded as dual term. (Upper and Lower Egypt? cf. Di[Gn 10, 6]), but as loc. ending EMey[Gesch. i, § 42] Ba[NB p. 319 R. 5]; Jen[ZA iv (1889), 268 ff.] thinks מִצְרַיִם abs. formed by anal. of מַיִם, שָׁמַיִם from *Miṣrî* (cf. TelAm); v. further Wkl[infra, ad fin.]);—מ׳ Gn 13^1+; מִצְרָ֑יִם 37^{36}+; מִצְרַ֫יְמָה 12^{10} + 12 t., מִצְרָ֑יְמָה 12^{11} + 14 t.;—**1. a.** of land, *Egypt*, Gn 13^1 + 500 t., +, in all periods, incl. אֶרֶץ מ׳ 13^{10} + c. 220 t. (of course f., $47^{6.13}$); אַדְמַת מ׳ *the soil of Egypt* †$47^{20.26}$; מֵימֵי מ׳ †Ex 7^{19} 8^2; יְאֹרֵי מ׳ †Am 8^8 9^5; יְאֹר מ׳ נְהַר מ׳ †Gn 15^{18}; †Is 7^{18} (cf. מָצוֹר); שִׁיחוֹר מ׳ †1 Ch 13^5; לְשׁוֹן יָם־מ׳ †Is 11^{15}; נַחַל מ׳ Jos 15^4 + 6 t. (v. these various wds.); land as productive Gn 45^{20} 49^{23}, cf. שֵׁשׁ בְּרִקְמָה מִמּ׳ Ez 27^7, אֵטוּן מ׳ Pr 7^{16}; oft. || כּוּשׁ, esp. in proph. and poet. Is $20^{3.4.5}$ 45^{14} Ez $30^{4.9}$+; || אַשּׁוּר Ho 11^{11} 12^1 Is 7^{18} Je 2^{18}+; incl. Upper Egypt (פַּתְרוֹס), as well as Lower, Je 44^1, cf. Ez 29^{10} 30^6; appar. disting. fr. Upper Egypt Is 11^{11}, and poss. also Je 44^{15} (cf. Gf Gie Buhl SS Che[Hpt Isaiah]); but פתרוס etc. in these vv. somewhat dub. (cf. Du Gie). **b.** combinations are: (1) מ׳ as limit of motion: יָרַד מצרימ(ה) Gn 43^{15} Jos 24^4 + c. 12 t.; בּוֹא מ׳ 1 S 12^8 + c. 26 t., בּוֹא בְמ׳ †Is 19^{23}, בּוֹא לְמ׳ †Je 44^{28}; שׁוּב מ׳ Ho 8^3 + 9 t., שׁוּב אֶל־מ׳ †Ho 11^5, שׁוּב שָׁלַח מ׳ †Je 37^7; בָּרַח מ׳ †1 K 11^{40}; לְאַרְצוֹ מ׳ †Je 26^{22}, so (+ אֶל־) v[22]. In Je 42^{16b} rd. בְּמ׳ with Gie. (2) מ׳ as point of departure (הֶעֱלָה) (הוֹצִיא) יָצָא מִן־(ארץ) מ׳ עָלָה מִן־(ארץ) מ׳ Gn 13^1 + c. 43 t.; מִן־(ארץ) מ׳ Ex 12^{39} + c. 96 t.; פָּדָה מִמּ׳ †2 S 7^{23} (but del. Gei[Urschr. 288] We Dr Kit Bu) = 1 Ch 17^{21}; בּוֹא מִמּ׳ †2 Ch 12^3 20^{10}; שׁוּב מִמּ׳ †Je 44^{28} 2 Ch 10^2; קָרָא מִמּ׳ †ψ 68^{32}; אָתָה מִמּ׳ †Ho 11^1. **2.** of people: **a.** in table of nations, personif. as second son of Ham †Gn 10^6 = 1 Ch 1^8, cf. Gn 10^{13} = 1 Ch 1^{11}. **b.** = *Egypt* (as a people), *Egyptians* Gn 41^{56} + c. 134 t., incl. use = Egyptian kingdom, empire, i. e. land and people as political power; so c. vb. fs. אָבְדָה מ׳ Ex 10^7, cf. Ho 9^6 Jo 4^{19} and (pron. fs.) Ez 30^{18}; c. vb. ms. Ex 12^{33} 14^{25} Is $19^{16.23.25}$ Je 46^8; oft. c. vb. mpl. Gn 41^{55} Is $19^{21.23}$ + 22 t.; בְּנֵי מ׳ Ez 16^{26};

מ׳ בְּתוּלַת בַּת +Je 46[11], cf. v[19.24].—In 1 K 10[28]= 2 Ch 1[16.17], 2 K 7[6] Wkl[Alttest. Unters. 171 f.] thinks of As. *Muṣri* in N. Syria. (On מִצְרַיִם as oft.= *Muṣri* in N. Arabia v. Wkl[Altor. Unters. i. 24 ff., ii. 195, iii. 289, iv. 337 f.; MVG 1898, 1. 4]).

4693 †מָצוֹר **n.pr.terr.** = מִצְרַיִם; only poet.: מ׳ יְאֹרֵי Is 19[6] 2 K 19[24]=Is 37[25]; וְעָדֶיךָ יָבוֹא לְמִנִּי אַשּׁוּר וְעָרֵי מ׳ וּלְמִנִּי מ׳ וְעַד נָהָר Mi 7[12] (𝔊 misunderstands everywhere).

4713 †מִצְרִי **adj.gent.** Egyptian;—ms.מ׳ Gn 39[1] +16 t.; fs. מִצְרִית 16[1]+3 t.; mpl. מִצְרִים 12[12]+ 5 t.; fpl. מִצְרִיֹּת Ex 1[19];—**1.** adj. אִישׁ מ׳ = *an Egyptian* Gn 39[1] Ex 2[11.19] Lv 24[10] 1 S 30[11] 2 S 23[30]; עֶבֶד מ׳ 1 Ch 11[23]; נַעַר מ׳ 1 S 30[13], הָאִישׁ הַמּ׳ 1 Ch 2[34]; שִׁפְחָה מִצְרִית Gn 16[1], הַמִּצְרִיֹּת בַּנָּשִׁים Ex 1[19]. **2.** c. art.=subst. *the Egyptian* Gn 39[2.5] Ex 2[12.14] 2 S 23[30.30] 1 Ch 11[23.23]; so once without art. מִצְרִי Dt 23[8]; הַמִּצְרִי once (late) coll.=*the Egyptians* Ezr 9[1] (where with Canaanitish peoples); pl.=*the Egyptians,* הַמִּצְרִים Gn 12[12.14] 43[32] Dt 26[6] Jos 24[7]; fs. הָגָר הַמִּצְרִית *Hagar the Egyptian woman* Gn 16[3] 21[9] 25[12].

4694 [מְצָרָה] v. מְצוּרָה sub I. צור. p. 849

4695, 4715 מַצְרֵף v. צרף. [מַצָּה] v. מַצּוֹת sub נצה. p. 663, 864

4716, 4718 מַק, מָק v. מקק. I, II. מַקֶּבֶת v. נקב. p. 597, 666

4719 †מַקֵּדָה **n.pr.loc.** in Judah Jos 15[41], near Beth Horon Jos 10[10], and Libnah v[29], where was a cave v[16.17], cf. v[21], captured by Joshua v[28], with a king v[28] 12[16]. 𝔊 Μακηδα. Site dubious, Warren[Survey Mem. ii. 411 ff., 427] comp. *El-mughâr*, c. $2\frac{3}{4}$ miles SW. from Ekron.

4720 מִקְדָּשׁ v. קדשׁ. p. 874

4721-22 מַקְהֵלִים, I, II. מַקְהֵלֹת v. קהל. p. 875

4723-24 מִקְוֵא, I, II. מִקְוֶה, מִקְוָה v. קוה. p. 876

4725-26 מָקוֹם v. קום. מָקוֹר v. קור. p. 879, 881

4757-58 [מִקָּחָה, מִקָּח] v. לקח. p. 544

4729-30 [מִקְטָר], מִקְטֶרֶת v. קטר. p. 883

4731 †מַקֵּל **n.m.**[Zc 11,7] (appar. **f.** Gn 30[37], where בָּהֶן, but Sam. בָּהֶם) rod, **staff** (√ dub.; Thes assumes √ מקל *sprout;* Schwally[ZAW xi. 1891, 170 f.] from קלל=*shake,* with ref. to oracle of the lot (cf. קִלְקַל בַּחִצִּים Ez 21[26]); Ba[ZMG xli. 1887, 616] gives √ קל, and comp. قُلَةٌ *stick driven* by another, in sport; Frä[ZA iii. 52], comp. Eth. **በቀልት:** *growth, stem, palm-tree* (interchange of ב and מ));—מ׳ abs. Nu 22[27]; cstr. Je 1[11]+2 t., מַקַּל Gn 30[37]; sf. מַקְלִי 32[11]+2 t.; מַקְלוֹ 1 S 17[40] Ho 4[12]; מַקֶּלְכֶם Ex 12[11]; pl. abs. מַקְלוֹת Gn 30[37]+6 t.;—**1.** branch of tree as *rod, stick,* used by Jacob in breeding his flocks, Gn 30[37] (מ׳ לִבְנֶה לַח), v[37.38.39.41.41]; of symbolic rod (מ׳ שָׁקֵד *almond-rod*) in Jerem.'s vision Je 1[11]; symbolic rods or staves, with names, used by proph. Zc 11[7.10.14]; fig. of Moab מ׳ תִּפְאָרָה Je 48[17] (|| מַטֵּה־עֹז). **2.** *staff,* used in journeying Gn 32[11] Ex 12[11], 1 S 17[40] cf. v[43]; carried even when riding Nu 22[27]; so also מַקֵּל יָד Ez 39[9] (=*riding-stick*) acc. to Hi Da Berthol; < a weapon (+מָגֵן, צִנָּה, קֶשֶׁת, חִצִּים, רֹמַח). **3.** *wand* of diviner Ho 4[12].

4732 †מִקְלוֹת **n.pr.m.** **1.** a Benjamite 1 Ch 8[32] (read perh. also v[31 ad fin.], so 𝔊, cf. 9[37]), 9[37.38].—𝔊 Μακαλωθ, Μακελλωθ, etc. **2.** an officer of David acc. to 1 Ch 27[4] (om. 𝔊B; 𝔊L Μακελλωθ).

4733 מִקְלָט v. II. קלט. p. 886

4725, 4734 מִקְלַעַת v. קלע. מָקֹם v. מָקוֹם sub קום. p. 879, 887

4735-37 מִקְנֵיָהוּ, מִקְנָה, מִקְנֶה v. קנה. p. 889

4738, 5362 [מִקְסָם] v. קסם. מַקְּפִים v. נקף. hiphil p. 668, 890

4739 †מָקַץ **n.pr.loc.** in Israel, site unknown, 1 K 4[9]; 𝔊 Μαχεμας, A Μαχμας (i. e. מִכְמָס), 𝔊L Μαγχας.

4740-42 מִקְצֹעַ, מִקְצָע, [מִקְצוֹעָה, מִקְצֹעַת] v. קצע. p. 893

7117 מִקְצָת v. קְצָת. p. 892

4743 †[מָקַק] **vb. decay, rot, fester,** fig. **pine away** (NH *id.;* Aram. (𝔗) מְקַק);—**Niph.** *Pf.* 3 pl. נָמַקּוּ ψ 38[6], וְנ׳ consec. Is 34[4] Ez 4[17]; 2 mpl. וּנְמַקֹּתֶם consec. Ez 24[23]; *Impf.* 3 fs. תִּמַּק Zc 14[12]; 3 mpl. יִמַּקּוּ Lv 26[39], יִמָּקּוּ v[39]; 3 fpl. תִּמַּקְנָה Zc 14[12]; *Pt.* pl. נְמַקִּים Ez 33[10];—**1.** *fester,* of wounds ψ 38[6] (+הבאישׁ, v. באשׁ). **2.** *rot, rot away,* עֵינָיו תִּמַּקְנָה בְחֹרֵיהֶן וּלְשׁוֹנוֹ תִּמַּק בְּפִיהֶם: Zc 14[12] (plague upon foes of Jerusalem). **3.** *moulder away,* of צְבָא הַשָּׁמַיִם Is 34[4] (|| וְנָגֹלּוּ כַסֵּפֶר הַשָּׁמָיִם). **4.** of *pining away* by reason of (בְּ), as punishment for, iniquity Ez 4[17] 24[23] 33[10] Lv 26[39.39]. **Hiph.** *Inf. abs.* הָמֵק, trans. ה׳ בְּשָׂרוֹ Zc 14[12] *a causing his flesh to rot.*

4716 †מַק (c. art. מָק) **n.m.** **decay, rottenness**;—תַּחַת בֹּשֶׂם מַק יִהְיֶה Is 3[24] *instead of perfume rottenness shall there be;* fig. שָׁרְשָׁם כַּמָּק יִהְיֶה 5[24] (|| וּפִרְחָם כָּאָבָק יַעֲלֶה).

4744-46 מִקְרָא v. I. קרא. מִקְרֶה, מִקְרֶה v. קרה. p. 896-97, 900

4747-49 מְקָרָה v. קרר. I. מִקְשֶׁה, מִקְשָׁה v. קשה. p. 903-04

4750 II. מִקְשָׁה v. [קִשֻּׁאָה]. p. 903

4751, 4753, 4755 I. מַר, מֹר, מָרָא Ru 1[20], v. I. מרר. p. 600

4752 II. מַר v. II. מרר. p. 601

4754 †I. [מָרָא] **vb.** only **Hiph.** *Impf.* 3 fs.: mng. dub., perh. *beat* the air, or *flap* the wings, cf. Di De (and Wetzst in De), Bu Du (cf. Ar. مَرَى *whip, urge on* a horse?);—תַּמְרִיא תִּשְׂחַק לַסּוּס וּלְרֹכְבוֹ׃ Jb 39[18] *she* (the ostrich) *flaps away,* she laughs at the horse and his rider.

II. מרא (√ of foll., *be fat;* cf. As. *marû* III. causat., adj. *marû, well-fed, fat;* Ar. مَرِئَ *be digestible, agree with* (of food)).

4806 †מְרִיא **n.[m.]** **fatling, fatlings**;—abs. מ׳ 2 S 6[13] + 3 t.; pl. abs. מְרִיאִים Is 1[11], cstr. מְרִיאֵי Ez 39[18]; sf. מְרִיאֵיכֶם Am 5[22];—*fatling:* עֵגֶל וּכְפִיר וּמְרִיא Is 11[6]; elsewh. only of sacrificial animals, חֵלֶב מְרִיאִים Is 1[11] (|| עֹלוֹת אֵילִים, דַּם פָּרִים, etc.); שֶׁלֶם מְרִיאֵיכֶם Am 5[22] (|| עֹלוֹת, מִנְחֹתֵיכֶם); מְרִיאֵי בָשָׁן Ez 39[18] (+ אֵילִים, פָּרִים, etc.); also sg. coll., וַיִּזְבַּח שׁוֹר וּמְרִיא 2 S 6[13], so (+ צֹאן וּבָקָר) 1 K 1[9], and (+ שׁוֹר, צֹאן) v[19.25].

4760 †[מֻרְאָה] **n.f.** **crop or alimentary canal,** of bird, cf. Di-Ry (on form cf. Lag[BN 81]);—וְהֵסִיר אֶת־מֻרְאָתוֹ בְּנֹצָתָהּ Lv 1[16].

4172 מֹרָא v. מוֹרָא sub ירא. p. 432

4757 מְרֹאדַךְ v. מְרֹדַךְ. below

4758-59 מַרְאָה, מַרְאֶה v. ראה. p. 909

84, 8112 מֹרְאָה v. מרה pt. f. מְראוֹן v. שִׁמְרוֹן... p. 598, 1038

4762-63 מָרֵאשָׁה v. מָרֵשָׁה. [מְרַאֲשׁוֹת] v. ראשׁ. p. 601, 912

4764 †מֵרַב **n.pr.f.** elder daughter of Saul 1 S 14[49], promised to David 18[17], but given to Adriel v[19] (rd. also 2 S 21[8] for מִיכַל 𝔊L 𝔖 Th Dr Klo Kit Bu Löhr HPS). 𝔊 Μεροβ.

4765 מַרְבַדִּים v. II. רבד. p. 915

מַרְבֶּה, מַרְבִּית, מִרְבָּה v. רבה. p. 916 4766-68

מַרְבֵּץ v. רבץ. מַרְבֵּק v. רבק. p. 918 4769-70

מַרְגּוֹעַ v. II. רגע. [מַרְגְּלוֹת] v. רגל. p. 920-21 4771-72

מַרְגֵּמָה v. רגם. מַרְגֵּעָה v. II. רגע. p. 920-21 4773-7

†[מָרַד] **vb.** rebel (NH *id.;* Ar. مَرَدَ *be* 4775
bold and audacious in acts of rebellion or disobedience; Eth. ወረደ: *run strenuously, attack;* መረድ: *rebellion,* Prä[Beiträge iii. 44]; Sab. מרד *rebellion* Hal[535, 16] Sab.Denkm.[38] Hom[Chrestom. 127]; Aram. ܡܪܕ, מְרַד; *rebel*);—**Qal** *Pf.* 3 ms. מָרַד 2 Ch 36[13], 2 ms. מָרַדְתָּ 2 K 18[20] = Is 36[5], etc.; *Impf.* וַיִּמְרֹד 2 K 18[7] + 3 t., וַיִּמְרָד־ 2 K 24[1] Ez 17[15], etc.; *Inf. cstr.* לִמְרֹד Jos 22[29], לִמְרוֹד Ne 6[6]; *Pt.* pl. מֹרְדִים Ne 2[19] Ez 20[38], מוֹ׳ Ez 2[3]; cstr. מֹרְדֵי Jb 24[13];—*rebel, revolt:* **1.** against human king, c. בְּ pers. 2 K 18[7.20] = Is 36[5], 2 K 24[1.20] = Je 52[3], cf. Ez 17[15] 2 Ch 36[13], Ne 9[26]; less oft. (late) c. עַל pers. 2 Ch 13[6] Ne 2[19]; abs. Gn 14[4] Ne 6[6]. **2.** against God, c. בְּ Nu 14[9] (JE), Jos 22[16.18.19.29] (all P), Ez 2[3] (Co מָרוּ), Dn 9[9]; abs. Ez 2[3] (pt., Co מורים), 20[38] Dn 9[5]. **3.** poet., against light, only מֹרְדֵי אוֹר Jb 24[13].

†I. מֶרֶד **n.[m.]** rebellion, revolt, against י׳, 4777
אִם בְּמֶ׳ וְאִם־בְּמַעַל ביהוה Jos 22[22] (P; cf. מָרַד **2**).

†II. מֶרֶד **n.pr.m.** name in Judah acc. to 4778
1 Ch 4[17], מֶרֶד v[18]. 𝔊 Πωραδ, Νωρωηλ, A Μωραδ, Μωρηδ, 𝔊L Βαραδ, Μαρω.

†מַרְדּוּת **n.f.** **rebellion, rebelliousness,** 4780
only in בֶּן־נַעֲוַת הַמּ׳ 1 S 20[30], where read prob. בֶּן־נַעֲרַת הַמַּרְדּוּת *son of a girl of rebelliousness = rebellious girl,* cf. 𝔊 𝔙 Th We Dr HPS; > Lag[M i. 236 f.] Bu (cf. also Dr Kit) der. מ׳ fr. רדה, and, retaining MT, rd. *a woman gone astray* (v. II. עָוָה) *from discipline* (Aram. sense: √ רְדָא).

†מְרֹדָךְ **n.pr.div.** chief god of Babylon in 4781
Nebuchadrezzar's time (As. *Mar(u)duk(u)* Schr[COT Gloss] Tiele[Bab.-Ass. Gesch. 530 ff.] Say[Rel. Bab. 96 ff.]; cf. Muss-Arnolt[JBL xi. 1892, 164 f.]);—נִלְכְּדָה בָּבֶל הֹבִישׁ בֵּל חַת מְרֹדָךְ Je 50[2] (𝔊 Μαιωδακ).

†מְרֹדַךְ בַּלְאֲדָן **n.pr.m.** king of Babylon 4757
(As. *Marduk-abal-idinna, Marduk has given a son* Schr[COT 2 K 20, 12]);—Is 39[1] (> van d. H מְרֹאדַךְ ב׳, v. Baer's n.) = 2 K 20[12] (where read מרדך for בראדך); 𝔊 (in both) Μαρωδακ(χ) Βαλ(α)δαν; 1255
cf. also בַּלְאֲדָן. p. 114 1081

4782 †מָרְדֳּכַי (van d. H מָרְדְּכַי) **n.pr.m. Mordecai** (perh. fr. n. div. *Marduk* (מְרֹדָךְ), Zim[ZAW xi. 161 ff.]; cf. further Wild (citing Jensen)[Comm. Est. 173 f.]);—מ׳ Ezr 2² Est 2⁵+; מָרְדֳּכָי Est 2²²+;—**1.** companion of Zerub., acc. to Ezr 2² = Ne 7⁷. 𝔊 Μαραθχαιος, Μαρδοχαιος, etc. **2.** cousin and adoptive father of Esther Est 2^{5.7.10} + 55 t. Est. 𝔊 Μαρδοχαιος.

4783 מֻרְדָּף v. רדה, רדף. p. 923

4784 †מָרָה **vb. be contentious, refractory, rebellious** (NH *id.*, Hiph.; Ar. مَرَى III. *dispute with;* Syr. ܡܪܐ Pa. *contend with*);—**Qal** *Pf.* 3 ms. מָרָה 1 K 13²⁶; f. מָרְתָה Ho 14¹; מָרָתָה Je 4¹⁷; 2 ms. מָרִיתָ 1 K 13²¹ + 11 t. pf.; *Inf. abs.* מָרוֹ La 1²⁰; *Pt.* מֹרֶה 2 K 14²⁶ (but rd. מַר, √מרר, Kmp[Kau] כִּי מַר הוּא); מוֹרֶה Dt 21¹⁸ + 3 t.; f.
4754 מֹרְאָה Zp 3¹ (rd. מֹרָה; metapl. form acc. to Ges[§ 75 R. 22]); pl. מֹרִים Nu 20¹⁰;—*be disobedient, rebellious:* **1.** בֵּן סוֹרֵר וּמוֹרֶה Dt 21^{18.20} *stubborn and rebellious son* (towards father). **2.** elsewhere towards God: דּוֹר סוֹרֵר וּמֹרֶה ψ 78⁸; לֵב סורר ומ׳
4754 Je 5²³; מוֹרְאָה ונגאלה הָעִיר Zp 3¹; הַמֹּרִים Nu 20¹⁰ *ye rebels* (P); abs. Is 50⁵ 63¹⁰ La 1^{20.20}; ‖ מאן Is 1²⁰; פשׁע La 3⁴²; c. בְּ pers. Ho 14¹ ψ 5¹¹, elsewh. acc. pers. Je 4¹⁷; ׳י׳s words ψ 105²⁸; מרה (את) פי Nu 20²⁴ 27¹⁴ (P), 1 S 12¹⁵ 1 K 13^{21.26} (D²) La 1¹⁸. —In Ho 4⁴ rd. perh. מָרוּ בִי *have rebelled against me* (for MT כִּמְרִיבֵי), so RS[Proph. iv. n. 8] Che (for other views v. ריב). **Hiph.** *Pf.* 3 mpl. הִמְרוּ ψ 106³³ 107¹¹; *Impf.* יַמְרֶה Jos 1¹⁸; f. וַתֶּמֶר Ez 5⁶; 2 ms. תַּמֵּר (as if √מרר) Ex 23²¹, rd. תַּמֶר Di al.; 3 mpl. יַמְרוּ ψ 106⁴³ + 6 t.; sf. יַמְרוּהוּ ψ 78⁴⁰; 2 mpl. תַּמְרוּ 1 S 12¹⁴ + 3 t.; *Inf. cstr.* לַמְרוֹת Is 3⁸ ψ 78¹⁷; sf. הַמְּרוֹתָם (Ges[§ 20. 2 b]) Jb 17²; *Pt.* pl. מַמְרִים Dt 9⁷ + 2 t.;—*shew disobedience, rebelliousness,* always toward God: abs. Ne 9²⁶ (‖ מרד), ψ 106^{7.43} Jb 17²; c. בְּ pers. Ex 23²¹ Ez 20^{8.13.21}; עִם Dt 9^{7.24} 31²⁷; elsewhere acc. of God or his commands: Is 3⁸ Ez 5⁶ ψ 78^{17.40.56} 107¹¹; המרה את פי Dt 1^{26.43} 9²³ Jos 1¹⁸ 1 S 12¹⁴ (D²), את־רוחו ψ 106³³ (cf. Eph 4³⁰); perh. 139²⁰ (v. אָמַר **1**).

4805 †מְרִי **n.m.**[Pr 17, 11] **rebellion;**—מְרִי Is 30⁹ + 10 t.; מֶרִי Nu 17²⁵ + 9 t.; sf. מֶרְיְךָ Dt 31²⁷; מְרָיָם Ne 9¹⁷;—*rebellion* Dt 31²⁷ 1 S 15²³ Ne 9¹⁷ Jb 23²; עם מרי *rebellious people* Is 30⁹; בית (ה)מרי *rebellious house* (referring to Israel) Ez 2^{5.6.8} 3^{9.26.27} 12^{2.2.3.9.25} 17¹² 24³, בית omitted (restored by Co) 2⁷ 44⁶; בְּנֵי מרי *rebellious sons* Nu 17²⁵ (P); with omission of בֵּן (or abstr. for concrete), אל תהי מֶרִי *be not a rebellious person* Ez 2⁸; אך מרי יבקשׁ רע *a rebellious man seeketh only evil* Pr 17¹¹.

†יִמְרָה **n.pr.m.** 1 Ch 7³⁶ a chief of Asher. 3236
𝔊 Ιμαρη, A Ιεμρα, 𝔊L Ιεμβρα.

מָרָה, מָרָּה, מֹרָה v. I. מרר. p. 598, 600-01 4784-87

מֹרֶה v. ירה **Hiph.** Pt., and II. מוֹרָה p. 435. 4175-76

[מָרוּד] v. רוד. מֵרוֹז v. ארז. p. 72, 924 4788-89

†[מָרוֹחַ] **n.[m.]** dub., only cstr. מְרוֹחַ אָשֶׁךְ 4790
Lv 21²⁰; √ either מָרַח *rub = a rubbing away of the testicle;* or רָוַח *be roomy, enlarged = enlargement* (read then מְרֻוַּח); v. further Di.

מָרוֹם v. רום. p. 928 4791

†מֵרוֹם **n.pr.loc.** only in מֵי מֵרוֹם Jos 11^{5.7} 4792
waters of Merom, in N. Canaan; = Lake *Ḥule,* acc. to Rel and many, but dub., cf. Di Bäd[Pal. 3. 259] GASm[Geogr. 481] Buhl[Geogr. 113].

מֵרוֹן v. שִׁמְרוֹן. מֵרוֹץ, I. [מְרוּצָה] v. רוץ. 4793-94, p. 930, 1038 8112
II. מְרוּצָה v. רצץ. [מְרוּקִים] v. I. מרק. 4795, 4835 p. 599, 954

†מָרוֹת **n.pr.loc.** in (Shephelah of) Judah 4796
Mi 1¹²; form attested by 𝔊 ὀδύνας (√ מרר).

מַרְזֵחַ v. רזח. p. 931 4798

†[מָרַח] **vb. rub** (NH *id.;* Aram. (Talm.) 4799
מְרַח; cf. Ar. مَرَخَ *anoint, smear*);—**Qal** *Impf.* יִשְׂאוּ דְּבֶלֶת תְּאֵנִים וְיִמְרְחוּ עַל־הַשְּׁחִין Is 38²¹ let them take a cake of figs *and rub* it upon the eruption (שִׂים in ‖ 2 K 20⁷).—On מרוח v. supr.

מֶרְחָב, מֶרְחַבְיָה v. רחב. p. 932 4800

מֶרְחָק v. רחק. מַרְחֶשֶׁת v. רחשׁ p. 935 4801-02

†[מָרַט] **vb. make smooth, bare, bald;** 4803
scour, polish (NH *id.; pull out, off* (feathers, hair); Aram. ܡܪܛ, מְרַט *id.;* Ar. مَرِطَ *have little hair,* مَرَطَ *pluck out hair*);—**Qal** *Impf.* 1 s. וָאֶמְרְטָה Ezr 9³, sf. 3 mpl. וָאֶמְרְטֵם Ne 13²⁵; *Inf. cstr.* מָרְטָה Ez 21¹⁶; *Pt.* pl. מֹרְטִים Is 50⁶; *pass.* f. מְרוּטָה Ez 21¹⁴ + 2 t.;—**1.** *make bare* כָּל־כָּתֵף מְרוּטָה Ez 29¹⁸ *every shoulder is laid bare* (fr. chafing of burden; ‖ כָּל־רֹאשׁ מֻקְרָח); the cheek (by plucking out beard) גֵּוִי נָתַתִּי לְמַכִּים וּלְחָיַי לְמֹרְטִים Is 50⁶; c. acc. pers. וָאֶמְרְטֵם Ne 13²⁵ (both acts of violence); of hair and beard וָאֶמְרְטָה מִשְּׂעַר רֹאשִׁי וּזְקָנִי Ezr 9³ (sign of grief). **2.** *scour, polish,* a sword, only Ez 21:

v[14] (+ הוּחַדָּה; Co rds. 'מ as Pu), v[16] (del. Co),
4603 v[22], + v[20] מֹרָטָה for MT מְעֻטָּה (Ew Sm Co Berthol). **Niph.** *Impf.* יִמָּרֵט רֹאשׁוֹ Lv 13[40.41] *his
head is made bald* (by leprosy). **Pu.** *Pf.* 3 fs.
4178 מֹרָטָה Ez 21[15.16]; *Pt.* מְמֹרָט 1 K 7[45], מוֹרָט Is 18[2.7]
(Ges[§ 52 R. 6]):—*scoured, polished,* of bronze utensils of temple 1 K 7[45]; of human skin Is 18[2.7]; of
sword Ez 21[15.16] (both + הוּחַדָּה, v. **Qal** supr.)

4805 מְרִי v. מרה. p. 598

4807, 4810 מְרִיב־בַּ֫עַל, מְרִי־בַ֫עַל v. ריב. p. 937

4808-09 I, II. מְרִיבָה v. ריב. p. 937

4811 †מְרָיָה **n.pr.m.** a priest in days of h.p. Joiakim Ne 12[12]; 𝔊 Μαρεα, Μαρ(α)ια, 𝔊L Αμαριας.

4179 †מֹרִיָּה, מוֹרִיָּה **n.pr.loc.** אֶרֶץ הַמּ׳ Gn 22[2] (E), place for sacrificing Isaac, 𝔊 τ. γῆν τ. ὑψηλήν (text dub., v. Di); הַר הַמּוֹ׳ 2 Ch 3[1] site of temple, 𝔊 Αμορ(ε)ια (cf. Jos[Ant. i. 13, 1 f.])

4812 †מְרָיוֹת **n.pr.m.** (on form cf. Lag[BN 51]);— **1.** descendant of Aaron: **a.** grandfather of Ahitub and great-grandfather of Zadok 1 Ch 5[32.33] 6[37] Ezr 7[3]; 𝔊 Μαρειηλ, Μαρερωθ, Μαραιωθ, etc. **b.** as son of Ahitub and father of Zadok 1 Ch 9[11] Ne 11[11]; 𝔊 Μαρμωθ Μαρ(α)ιωθ. **2.** name of a priestly house Ne 12[15] (prob. err. for מְרֵמוֹת, q. v., 12[3]), 𝔊L Μαριμωθ.

4813 †מִרְיָם **n.pr.f.** et **m.** **1. f.** sister of Aaron Ex 15[20] (E), and of Moses and Aaron Nu 26[59] (P), 1 Ch 5[29]; named also Ex 15[21] (E), Nu 12[1.4.5.10.10.15.15] 20[1] (all JE), Dt 24[9] Mi 6[4]. 𝔊 Μαριαμ. **2. m.** (prob.) a Judahite 1 Ch 4[17]. 𝔊 τὸν Μαιων, 𝔊L Μωεωρ.

4814-15 מְרִירִי, מְרִירוּת v. מרר. p. 601

4816-18 מֹ֫רֶךְ v. רכך. מֶרְכָּב, מֶרְכָּבָה v. רכב. p. 939-40

4820 [מַרְכֹּ֫לֶת] v. רכל. I. מִרְמָה v. רמה. p. 941

4821 †II. מִרְמָה **n.pr.m.** a Benjamite 1 Ch 8[10]; 𝔊 Ιμαμα, A 𝔊L Μαρμ(ι)α.

4822 †מְרֵמוֹת **n.pr.m. 1.** priest, time of Zerub. Ne 12[3] (= מְרָיוֹת, q.v., v[15]) 𝔊L Μαρειμωθ. **2.** priest, time of Ezra and Neh., Ezr 8[33] Ne 3[4.21] 10[6] (prob. same). 𝔊 Μερειμωθ, Μεραμωθ, etc. **3.** one of those who had taken strange wives Ezr 10[36]. 𝔊 Ιεραμωθ, A Μαρεμωθ.

4823 מִרְמָס v. רמס. p. 942

†מֵרֹנֹתִי **adj. gent.** (deriv. unknown) c.art. 4824
as subst. = *the Merothonite* **1.** 1 Ch 27[30]; 𝔊 ὁ ἐκ Μεραθων. **2.** Ne 3[7]; 𝔊L ὁ Μηρωναθαιος.

†מֶ֫רֶס **n.pr.m.** a Persian noble Est 1[14]. 4825

†מַרְסְנָא **n.pr.m.** a Persian noble Est 1[14]. 4826

[מֵרֵעַ] v. רעה. p. 946 4828

מִרְעֶה, [מַרְעִית] v. רעה. p. 945 4829

†מַרְעֲלָה **n.pr.loc.** on border of Zebulun 4831
Jos 19[11]. 𝔊 Μαραγελδα, A Μαριλα, 𝔊L Μαραλα.

מַרְפֵּה, מַרְפֵּא v. רפא. p. 951 4832

[מִרְפָּשׂ] v. רפשׂ. p. 952 4833

†[מָרַץ] **vb. be sick**, only in der. species 4834
(As. II. *marâṣu* Dl[HWB 426]; Ar. مَرِضَ; Sab. מרץ̇ *sick person, sickness,* Mordt[ZMG 1876, 32]; Aram. vb. ܡܪܰܥ, מְרַע);—**Niph.** *Pf.* 3 pl. נִמְרְצוּ Jb 6[25] (but v. infr.); *Pt.* נִמְרָץ Mi 2[10]; f. נִמְרֶ֫צֶת 1 K 2[8];— חֶבֶל נִמְרָץ Mi 2[10] *a sore, grievous* destruction (lit. *made sick,* cf. מַכָּה נַחְלָה Je 14[17]); קְלָלָה נִמְרֶ֫צֶת 1 K 2[8] *a grievous curse.*—In Jb 6[25] this mng. unsuit., Bu *are strong, effective* [cf. As. I. *marâṣu, be difficult, inaccessible* Dl[HWB 425 f.]; always of something repelling]. More prob. נמרצו = נמלצו *be sweet* (cf. ψ 119[103]) or rd. נמלצו (q.v.), Che[JQ July, 1897] Du. **Hiph.** *Impf.* sf. מַה־יַּמְרִיצְךָ Jb 16[3] *what sickens thee* (what disturbs, vexes thee) that thou answerest?

[מְרֻצָּה] v. מְרוּצָה sub רוץ. p. 930, 954 4794, 4835

מַרְצֵעַ v. רצע. מַרְצֶ֫פֶת v. רצף. p. 954 4836-37

†I. [מָרַק] **vb. scour, polish** (NH *id.;* 4838
Aram. מְרַק, ܡܪܰܩ; cf. Ar. مَرَقَ *scrape off wool from a skin*);—**Qal** *Imv.* מִרְקוּ הָרְמָחִים Je 46[4] *polish the lances!* *Pt. pass.* מָרוּק 2 Ch 4[16] *polished,* of bronze utensils of temple (= מְמֹרָט 1 K 7[45]). **Hiph.** *Impf.* 3 fs. תַּמְרִיק only Pr 20[30] Kt, fig., in cl. חַבֻּרוֹת פֶּצַע ת׳ בְּרָע *blows that cut in, cleanse away evil* (cf. De Now Wild VB); Qr תַּמְרוּק i.e. (are) *a cleansing.* (𝔊 συναντᾷ κακοῖς, whence Gr תַּקְדִּים, Frankenb. תִּקְרֶינָה, but improb.). **Pu.** *Pf.* וּמֹרַק consec. Lv 6[21] *be well scoured,* of bronze vessel (‖ וְשֻׁטַּף בַּמָּיִם).

†[מָרוּק] (Kö[ii. 138]) **n.[m.] a scraping,** 4795
rubbing;—only pl. sf. יְמֵי מְרוּקֵיהֶן Est 2[12] lit. *the days of their* (bodily) *rubbings,* i.e. the year's preparation of girls for the harem.

8562 †תַּמְרוּק **n.[m.]** id.;—abs. sg. only Pr 20^{30} Qr, v. מרק **Hiph.**; elsewhere pl. cstr. תַּמְרוּקֵי הַנָּשִׁים Est 2^{12}; sf. תַּמְרוּקֶיהָ v^{9}, תַּמְרוּקֵיהֶן v^{3}.

II. **מרק** (✓ of foll.; cf. Ar. مَرَقَ *fill a pot with rich broth* (Frey Wahrm)).

4839 †מָרָק (van d. H מְרַק) **n.m. juice stewed out of meat, or broth** (on form cf. Lag$^{BN\ 50}$);—וְאֶת־הַמָּרָק שָׂם בַּפָּרוּר Ju 6^{19} (v. GFM); וְהַמָּרָק שְׁפוֹךְ v^{20}; cstr. מְרַק Is 65^{4} Qr, so Vrss (Kt פרק) *broth* of unclean things.

4840-42 [מֶרְקָח], מֶרְקָחָה, מִרְקַחַת v. רקח. p. 955

4843 † I. **מָרַר** **vb. be bitter** (NH *id.*; As. *marâru* and deriv. Dl$^{HWB\ 427}$; Ar. مَرَّ *become roused* (of bile), II. *make bitter*, IV. *become bitter*; مُرٌّ *bitter*; Eth. መረረ: ; Aram. ܡܰܪ, (מְרַר);—**Qal** *Pf.* 3 ms. מַר Is 38^{17} + 2 t.; 3 fs. מָרָה 1 S 30^{6} 2 K 4^{27}; *Impf.* 3 ms. יֵמַר Is 24^{9};—*be bitter*: **1.** lit. יֵמַר שֵׁכָר לְשֹׁתָיו Is 24^{9}. **2.** fig. מָרָה נֶפֶשׁ 1 S 30^{6} *the soul* of all the people *was bitter* against (עַל־); נַפְשָׁהּ מָרָה־לָהּ 2 K 4^{27} *her soul, it is bitter to her* (i.e. she is in bitter distress); impers. מַר־לִי מְאֹד מִכֶּם Ru 1^{13} *it is very bitter to me on your account* (I am much distressed), cf. La 1^{4}.—לְשָׁלוֹם מַר־לִי מָר Is 38^{17} is dub.; Che$^{Comm.}$ *for (my) welfare was it (so) bitter to me, (so) bitter*, cf. Brd; so De Kau (treating מר appar. as adj.); < Drechsl. Di *for my welfare did the bitter become bitter to me* (מָר adj.); Lo Gr, cf. Buhl (sub מַר adj.), rd. מָר for מַר (✓מוּר), the bitter *is changed* for me into welfare; Che^{Hpt} del. מָר; Du (after 𝔊) del. cl. as gloss.

Pi. *Impf.* 1 s. אֲמָרֵר Is 22^{4}; 3 mpl. וַיְמָרְרוּ Ex 1^{14}, sf. וַיְמָרֲרֻהוּ Gn 49^{23};—*make bitter, shew bitterness*:—**1.** וַיְמ׳ Gn 49^{23} (poem) and the archers *shewed bitterness* (i.e. bitter hostility) *toward him* (sf. of indir. obj.); אֲמָרֵר בַּבֶּכִי Is 22^{4} *I will shew bitterness in weeping* (=weep bitterly). **2.** וַיְמ׳ אֶת־חַיֵּיהֶם Ex 1^{14} (P) *and they made their lives bitter* by slavery.

Hiph. *Pf.* 3 ms. הֵמַר Ru 1^{20} Jb 27^{2}; *Impf.* 2 ms. תַּמֵּר Ex 23^{21} (but rd. תַּמֶר ✓מרה **Hiph.** q.v.); *Inf. abs.* הָמֵר Zc 12$^{10.10}$;—*make bitter, shew bitterness*: **1.** שַׁדַּי הֵמַר נַפְשִׁי Jb 27^{2} *Shadday, who hath embittered my soul*; הֵמַר שַׁדַּי לִי מְאֹד Ru 1^{20}. **2.** וְהָמֵר עָלָיו כְּהָמֵר עַל־הַבְּכוֹר Zc 12^{10} *and a bitter outcry* (=lit. shewing bitterness; ‖ סָפַד, מִסְפֵּד) over him, like a *bitter outcry* over the first-born.

Hithpalp. *Impf.* וְיִתְמַרְמַר Dn 11^{11} *and the* king of the south *shall embitter himself* (be enraged); וַיִּתְמ׳ אֶל־ 8^{7} *and he was enraged against.*

†I. **מַר** **adj.** and **subst. bitter, bitterness**;—abs. מ׳ Pr 27^{7} +, הַמַּר Hb 1^{6}, מָר ψ 64^{4} +; 4751
cstr. מַר 1 S 22^{2} +; f. מָרָה Gn 27^{34} +, מָרָא Ru 1^{20}; 4755
cstr. מָרַת 1 S 1^{10}; mpl. מָרִים Ex 15^{23} +; cstr. מָרֵי Ju 18^{25} Pr 31^{6};—*bitter*: **1.** lit., of water Ex 15^{23} (J); food Pr 27^{7} (opp. מָתוֹק); wormwood (לַעֲנָה) Pr 5^{4} (in sim. of end of harlot, cf. Ec 7^{26} infr.); as subst. pl., of physical pain, result of curse לְמָרִים Nu 5$^{24.27}$, whence מֵי הַמָּרִים v^{18} (cf. Di) v$^{19.23.24}$; of harmful result of ruthless fighting 2 S 2^{26}; of wickedness Je 2^{19} 4^{18}; = *injurious, hurtful* Is 5$^{20.20}$ (opp. מָתוֹק). **2.** fig., **a.** of cry (זְעָקָה, צְעָקָה) Gn 27^{34} (J), Est 4^{1}; מִסְפֵּד מָר Ez 27^{31} (del. Co); דָּבָר מָר ψ 64^{4}; as adv. (cry, weep) *bitterly* Ez 27^{30} (מָרָה), Zp 1^{14} Is 33^{7} (both מַר). **b.** of feeling, temper, esp. c. נֶפֶשׁ: אֲנָשִׁים מָרֵי נֶפֶשׁ Ju 18^{25} *men fierce* (GFM *acrid*) *of temper*, so 2 S 17^{8} (like a bear robbed of whelps); הַגּוֹי הַמַּר Hb 1^{6} *the fierce nation*; מַר־נֶפֶשׁ = *discontented* 1 S 22^{2}; מָרֵי נֶפֶשׁ = *the bitterly wretched* Jb 3^{20} Pr 31^{6}, so מָרַת נ׳ 1 S 1^{10}; cf. יוֹם מָר Am 8^{10}; as subst. abstr. מַר־נֶפֶשׁ *bitterness of soul* Is 38^{15} Ez 27^{31} (del. Co), Jb 7^{11} 10^{1} = נפשׁ מָרָה 21^{25}; cf. מָרָא Ru 1^{20} (name given to Naomi by herself); מַר־הַמָּוֶת 1 S 15^{32} *the bitterness of death*; מַר־מִמָּוֶת Ec 7^{26} (metaph. of harlot); in Ez 3^{14} *I went bitterly*, del. מַר Co.—Is 38^{17} v. מרר.

†**מֹר, מוֹר** **n.m.**$^{Ct\ 5,5}$ **myrrh** (fr. *bitter* taste; 4753
As. *murru* Meissn$^{Suppl.\ 60}$; Ar. مُرٌّ; cf. Lag$^{BN\ 40}$);—abs. מֹר ψ 45^{9} + 5 t., מוֹר Ct 4^{6} + 3 t. Ct; cstr. מָר־ Ex 30^{23}; sf. מוֹרִי Ct 5^{1};—*myrrh* (late), an Arabian gum, exuding from the bark of a tree, *Balsamodendron Myrrha* (v. Sigismund$^{Aromata\ 12\ f.}$ Ri$^{HWB\ s.v.}$):—as flowing, i.e. fine, choice (carefully prepared by pressing and mixing, cf. Di$^{Ex\ 30,\ 23}$ Ri^{HWB}): מָר־דְּרוֹר Ex 30^{23} (v. I. דְּרוֹר), ingredient of sacred oil; מוֹר עֹבֵר Ct 5$^{5.13}$ (as perfume); cf. (as perfume) Ct 1^{13} 4^{14} 5$^{1.5}$; הַר־הַמּוֹר 4^{6}, i.e. where it is gathered; as perfume also ψ 45^{9} Pr 7^{17}, as incense מְקֻטֶּרֶת מֹר וּלְבוֹנָה Ct 3^{6}; שֶׁמֶן הַמּוֹר as unguent Est 2^{12}.

מָרָא Ru 1^{20}, v. I. מַר supr. 4755

†**מָרָה** **n.pr.f.** of bitter spring in Sinaitic 4785
penins. Ex 15$^{23.23}$ (J), Nu 33$^{8.9}$ (P), + ־ָה loc. מָרָתָה Ex 15^{23} (J); prob. mod. *ʽAin Hawwâra*^{tun}. (Cf. Rob$^{BR\ I.\ 67}$ Palmer$^{Desert\ I.\ 40}$ Eb$^{GS\ 125\ f.}$)

4787 †[מָרָּה] **n.f. bitterness** (on form v. Ges §22,5 R);—cstr. לֵב יוֹדֵעַ מָרַּת נַפְשׁוֹ Pr 14[10] the heart knoweth *the bitterness of its soul* (its own misery).

4786 †[מֹרָה] **n.f.** id., cstr. מֹרַת רוּחַ Gn 26[35] (P) *bitterness of spirit* (= grief of mind).

4844 †[מָרֹר] **n.m. bitter thing, bitter herb** (cf. NH *id., bitter herb;* on form v. Ba[NB 194]);—only pl. מְרֹרִים Ex 12[8] Nu 9[11], מְרוֹרִים La 3[15];—*bitter herbs,* in Passover meal Ex 12[8] Nu 9[11] (both P); cf. הִשְׂבִּיעַנִי בַמְּ׳ La 3[15], fig. of distress inflicted (‖ לַעֲנָה).

4846 †[מְרֹרָה] **n.f. bitter thing, gall, poison;** cstr. מְרוֹרַת Jb 20[14]; sf. מְרֹרָתוֹ v[25]; pl. מְרֹרֹת Dt 32[32], מְרוֹרוֹת Jb 13[26];—**1.** *gall,* i.e. seat of gall, gall-bladder Jb 20[25] (‖ גֵּוָה *back;* cf. מְרֵרָה 16[13]). **2.** =*poison,* מְ׳ פְּתָנִים Jb 20[14]. **3.** מְרֹרוֹת *bitter things* Jb 13[26] (of God's edict of judgment). **4.** pl. abstr.=*bitterness;* אַשְׁכְּלֹת מְ׳ Dt 32[32] *clusters of bitterness* (‖ עִנְּבֵי רוֹשׁ).

4845 †[מְרֵרָה] **n.f. gall;** only sf. יִשְׁפֹּךְ לָאָרֶץ מְרֵרָתִי Jb 16[13] *he poureth on the ground my gall* (‖ יְפַלַּח כִּלְיוֹתַי), fig. of God's cruel treatment (cf. מְרֹרָה 20[25]).

4815 †מְרִירִי **adj.** bitter;—קֶטֶב מְ׳ Dt 32[24] *bitter destruction.* (On Jb 3[5] v. כִּמְרִיר sub II. כמר.)

4814 †מְרִירוּת **n.f.** bitterness;—וּבִמְ׳ תֵּאָנַח Ez 21[11] *and in bitterness* (bitterly) *shalt thou groan.*

4470 †מֶמֶר **n.[m.]** bitterness;—מְ׳ לְיוֹלַדְתּוֹ Pr 17[25] of a fool-son (‖ כַּעַס לְאָבִיו).

4472 †[מַמְרוֹר] **[n.m.]** bitter thing;—only pl. יַשְׂבִּעַנִי מַמְּרֹרִים Jb 9[18] (on dagh. f. dirim. cf. Ges §20.2.b), he sateth me with *bitter things* (bitter experiences; cf. מָרֹר La 3[15]).

8563 †I. [תַּמְרוּר] **n.m.** bitterness;—only pl. intens. תַּמְרוּרִים Ho 12[15] + 2 t.;—מִסְפַּד תּ׳ Je 6[26] *mourning of bitterness* (bitter mourning), so בְּכִי תּ׳ 31[15] (cf. the vb. Is 22[4] Zc 12[10]); as adv. *bitterly* Ho 12[15] (si vera l.).—II. [תַּמְרוּר] v. sub ת.

4847 †I. מְרָרִי **n.pr.m.** a son of Levi, and head of a chief Levit. family: 𝔊 Μεραρ(ε)ι, Μαραρει;—Gn 46[11] Ex 6[16.19] Nu 3[17.20.33.33.35.36] 4[29.33.42.45] 7[8] 10[17] 26[57] Jos 21[7.34.38] (all P), 1 Ch 5[27] 6[1.4.14.29.32.48.62] 9[14] 15[6.17] 23[6.21] 24[26.27] 26[10.19] 2 Ch 29[12] 34[12] Ezr 8[19].

4848 †II. מְרָרִי **adj. gent.** of above, only c. art. as subst. coll. הַמְּ׳ Nu 26[57].

II. מרר (√ of foll.; perhaps (so Thes) cf Ar. مَرَّ *pass by, go,* sts. *flow,* مَرْمَرَ *cause to flow,* مَمَرّ *water-course*).

†II. מַר **n.[m.]** drop, only גּוֹיִם כְּמַר מִדְּלִי Is 40[15] *nations are like a drop* hanging *from a bucket.* 4752

†מָרֵשָׁה and (Jos 15[44]) מָרֵאשָׁה **n.pr.loc.** (etym. dub.) in (the Shephelah of) Judah, Mi 1[15] (where named with אַכְזִיב etc.), Jos 15[44] (*id.*), cf. 2 Ch 11[8] 14[8.9] 20[37]; so appar. (as n.pr.m. in geneal. scheme) 1 Ch 2[42] 4[21].—Cf. 2 Macc. 12[35] (Μαρισα), 1 Macc 5[66] (rd. Μαρισα for Σαμαρια, cf. Var. Apocr.).—Joseph[Ant. xii. 8, 6] (Μαρισσα). 𝔊A Jos 15[44] Μαρησα; 𝔊L βαρσηα; 𝔊 1 Ch 2[42] Μαρ(ε)ισα 𝔊L Μαρησα, etc. Prob.=mod. *Merāsh* 1 m. S. of Beit Jibrin (Eleutheropolis), cf. Rob BR ii. 31 Be[1 Ch 2, 42] GASm[Geogr. 233] (who identif. with (גַּת) מוֹרֶשֶׁת Mi 1[14] q.v. sub ירשׁ p. 440 supr., but v. Lag[Onom. 139, 141, 279, 282]) Buhl[Geogr. 192]. 4762

מִרְשַׁעַת v. רשׁע. מֹרָשְׁתִּי v. ירשׁ. p. 440, 958 4183, 4849

†מְרָתַיִם used as **n.pr.f.**=Babylon, עַל־הָאָרֶץ מְ׳ עֲלֵה עָלֶיהָ Je 50[21]; perh.=*Double rebellion* (du.) √ מרה q.v.; De[Par 182] thinks=Bab. *Marrâtim,* i.e., land by the *nar Marrâtu, the bitter river* (Pers. Gulf)=Southern Babylonia. 4850

†I. מַשָּׂא **n.pr.gent. et terr. 1.** 'son' of Ishmael Gn 25[14] = 1 Ch 1[30]. 𝔊 Μασση, Μασσα, etc. **2.** realm of king Lemuel Pr 31[1] De Now Str Wild.—Perh.=N. Arab. *Mas'u* Schr[COT Gn 25, 14; KGF 102, 262 ff., 364] Dl[Par 302 f.] II, III, p. 672 4854

II, III. מַשָּׂא, מַשָּׂא, מַשָּׂאָה, מַשְׂאֵת v. נשׂא. p. 672-73 4853, 4855-56, 4858, 4864

מַשֻּׂאוֹת v. מַשּׁוּאוֹת sub נשׁא. p. 674 4876

מִשְׂגָּב v. שׂגב. [מְשׂוּכָה] v. III. שׂכך. p. 960, 962, 968 4869, 4881

מַשּׂוֹר v. נשׂר. p. 673 4883

†מְשׂוּרָה **n.f.** measure, of water, Ez 4[11.16] (‖ מִשְׁקָל); capacity in gen., Lv 19[35] (+ מִדָּה, מִשְׁקָל), 1 Ch 23[29] (deriv. dub.) 4884

מָשׂוֹשׂ v. שׂושׂ. מִשְׂחָק v. שׂחק. p. 965-66 4885, 4890

מַשְׂטֵמָה v. שׂטם. [מְשֻׂכָּה] v. שׂוך. p. 962, 966, 968 4881, 4895

מַשְׂכִּיל v. שׂכל. מַשְׂכִּית v. שׂכה. p. 967-68 4905-06

[מַשְׂכֹּרֶת] v. שׂכר. [מַשְׂמֵר] v. שׂמר. p. 969, 971 4548, 4909

מִשְׂפָּח v. שׂפח. מִשְׂרָה v. שׂרה. p. 705, 976 4839, 4951

4955-56 [מִשְׂרְפוֹת], מִשְׂרְפוֹת מַיִם v. שׂרף. p. 977

4957 מַשְׁרֵקָה v. שׁרק. p. 977

4958 †מַשְׂרֵת **n.m.** appar. = **pan, dish,** Pal.-Aram. מסרית, only וַתִּקַּח הַמּ׳ 2 S 13[9] *and she took the pan;* perh. = *מִשְׁאֶרֶת, orig. *dough*-pan (שׁאר), kneading-trough, Gei[Urschr. 382 f.] We (not Dr); > Klo Bu Ry in Di[Ex 12, 34 (3te Aufl.)] וַתִּקְרָא (אֶת־) הַמְּשָׁרֵת *and she called the servant* (HPS del. v.)

4851 †מַשׁ **n.pr.loc.** vel **gent.** מָ֑שׁ Gn 10[23], as son of Aram, Sam. משא; 𝔊 Μοσοχ; so rd. in ‖ 1 Ch 1[17] for MT מֶ֑שֶׁךְ A 𝔊L Μοσοχ; v. Kau Kit. Loc. dub. Bo Mich *Mons Mas-ius*, N. of Nisibis (between Armen. and Mesop.), but name not certainly old Aram. (unknown in As.) cf. Di[ad loc.]. As. *Maš* (Syro-Ar. desert Dl[Par 242 f.]) is hardly poss., cf. מֵשָׁא.

4855, 4859 מַשָּׂא, מַשָּׂאָה v. I. נשׂא. p. 673

4852 †מֵשָׁא **n.pr.loc.** limiting territory of Joktanites, Gn 10[30]; Dl[Par 243] identif. with As. *Maš* (Syro-Ar. desert); > district *Mesene,* on Pers. Gulf, Thes[823] (cf. Di); 𝔊 Μασση(ε), whence Di I. מַשָּׂא q. v. (after Hal[Mél. 91 f.])

4857, 4875 [מַשְׁאָב] v. שׁאב. מַשָּׁאָה v. מַשּׁוּאָה. p. 980, 996

4860, 4876 מַשְּׁאוֹן, מַשָּׁאוֹת v. II. נשׁא. p. 674

4861 †מִשְׁאָל **n.pr.loc.** in Asher (Eg. *Mi-ša'a-ra* WMM[As. u. Eur. 181]);—Jos 19[26] (𝔊 Μαασα, A Μασαψ, 𝔊L Μασαλ) 21[30] (𝔊 Βασελλαν, A Μασααλ,

4913 𝔊L Μισαλα); = (1.) מָשָׁל 1 Ch 6[59] (𝔊 Μαασα, A Μασαλ, 𝔊L Μασιλ).

4862 [מִשְׁאָלָה] v. שׁאל. p. 982

4863 †[מִשְׁאֶרֶת] **n.f.** a household vessel, AV (Ex), RV *kneading-trough;* vessel in which was dough before it was leavened (Ex 12[34]) (hence usu. der. fr. שְׂאֹר *leaven* (with שׁ—by error?—for שׂ), but this not certain; cf. מַשְׂרֵת supr.);—only sf. מִשְׁאַרְתֶּךָ Dt 28[5.17] (both + טַנְאֲךָ); pl. sf. מִשְׁאֲרוֹתֶיךָ Ex 7[28] (J; + תַּנּוּרֶיךָ), מִשְׁאֲרֹתָם 12[34] (E).

4865, 4878 מַשְׁבָּה v. מְשׁוּבָה. מִשְׁבְּצוֹת v. שׁבץ. p. 990, 1000

4866-67 מַשְׁבֵּר, [מִשְׁבָּר] v. שׁבר. p. 991

4868, 4870' [מִשְׁבָּת] v. שׁבת. מִשְׁגֶּה v. שׁגה. p. 992-93

4871 †[מָשָׁה] **vb.** draw (Ar. مَسَى *cleanse uterus* of camel, Aram. ܡܫܐ *clean, stroke, the face,* etc.; מְשָׁא (Talm.) *wash* the hands; Zinj. מש[י] perhaps *wash* oneself, DHM[Sendsch. 60]);—**Qal** *Pf.* sf. מִן־הַמַּיִם מְשִׁיתִהוּ Ex 2[10] *out of the water I drew him* (used to explain מֹשֶׁה, but v. this infr.) **Hiph.** *Impf.* sf. = **Qal**, fig. יַמְשֵׁנִי מִמַּיִם רַבִּים 2 S 22[17] = ψ 18[17] (subj. י׳).

מֹשֶׁה[767] **n.pr.m. Moses,** the great Hebrew leader, prophet and lawgiver (prob. = Eg. *mes, mesu, child, son,* Eb[GS 539], cf. Di[Ex 2, 10], where see also older (abandoned) etymol.);—מ׳ Ex 2[10] + מֹשֶׁה v[15] +; name occurs 706 t. in Hex. (Ex. 290 t., Lv. 86 t., Nu. 233 t., Dt. 38 t., Jos. 59 t.), Ju. 4 t. + 18[30] where read מֹשֶׁה for מְנַשֶּׁה (cf. GFM); 1 S 12[6.8], Kings 10 t., Mi 6[4] Je 15[1] Is 63[11.12] Mal 3[22] ψ 77[21] + 7 t.; Chr. 3 t., Dn 9[11.13];—*Moses* was son of Amram and Jochebed Ex 6[20] Nu 26[59] (both P), 1 Ch 5[29] 23[13]; of tribe of Levi Ex 2[1] (E; cf. also foregoing); (younger) brother of Aaron 4[14] (J), 7[1.2.7] (P), etc., and brother of Miriam Nu 26[59] (P), 1 Ch 5[29] (cf. Ex 15[20] E); called prophet Dt 18[15.18] 34[10]; agent by whom י׳ gave law Ex 20[19.20.21.22] (E) +; esp. P (כַּאֲשֶׁר צִוָּה י׳ אֶת־מ׳, etc.), Ex 39[1.5.7.21.26.29.31] 40[19.21.25.27.29.32] Lv 7[38] 8[9.13.17.27.29] + oft.; lawgiver Dt 33[4] Jos 1[7.13] (D) +; priest, מ׳ וְאַהֲרֹן בְּכֹהֲנָיו ψ 99[6]. Phrases are—(עַבְדִּי, עַבְדּוֹ, etc.) מ׳ עֶבֶד י׳ Ex 14[31] (J), Nu 12[7] (E), Dt 34[5] (JE), Jos 1[1] (D) + 15 t. Jos. (D); 1 K 8[53.56] 2 K 18[12] 21[8] Mal 3[22] 2 Ch 1[3] 24[6] Ne 1[8] 9[14] ψ 105[26]; מ׳ עֶבֶד אלהים 1 Ch 6[34] 24[9] Ne 10[30] Dn 9[11]; מ׳ אִישׁ הָאֱלֹהִים Ezr 3[2] ψ 90[1]; תּוֹרַת מ׳ Jos 8[32] (D), 1 K 2[3] 2 K 23[25] Mal 3[22] 2 Ch 23[18] 30[16] Ezr 3[2] 7[6] Dn 9[11.13]; סֵפֶר מ׳ 2 Ch 25[4] 35[12] Ne 13[1]; סֵפֶר תּוֹרַת מ׳ Jos 8[31] (D), 23[6] (D), 2 K 14[6] Ne 8[1].

[מַשֶּׁה] v. נשׁה. p. 674 4874

מַשּׁוּאָה, מְשׁוֹאָה v. II. שׁוא. p. 996 4875

מַשּׁוּאוֹת v. II. נשׁא. מְשׁוֹבָב v. שׁוב. p. 674 4876

מְשׁוּבָה v. שׁוב. [מְשׁוּגָה] v. שׁוג. p. 1000 4878-79

מָשׁוֹט, [מִשּׁוֹט] v. שׁוט. p. 1002 4880

מְשׁוֹסָה Kt. = מְשִׁסָּה v. שׁסס. p. 1042 4882

†מָשַׁח **vb. smear, anoint** (NH *id.;* orig. prob. as Ar. مَسَحَ *wipe* or *stroke with the hand* (cf. RS[Sem. i. 215; 2nd ed., 233]), *anoint,* Aram. ܡܫܚ, מְשַׁח *anoint;* on משח, *id.* (?) in Aram. inscr. v. CIS[ii. 1, No. 145, C, 1]; Palm. משחא *oil* Vog[No. 16]; Eth. መስሐ: *anoint, feast, dine* Di[Lex 176]; (As. *mašâḫu* is *measure;* Aram. מְשַׁח *id.;* Ar. مساحة *measure-* 4886

ment, cf. Dl$^{Prol. 178}$ Frä^{282}));—**Qal** *Pf.* 3 ms. מ׳ Nu 3^{25} + 2 t.; sf. מְשָׁחֲךָ ψ 45^{8} 1 S 10^{1}; מְשָׁחוֹ 2 Ch 22^{7}; 2 ms. מָשַׁחְתָּ Gn 31^{13} + 12 t., + 9 t. Pf.; *Impf.* 3 ms. יִמְשַׁח Lv 16^{32} + 6 t.; 3 mpl. יִמְשָׁחוּ Am 6^{6}, + 13 t. Impf.; *Imv.* sf. מְשָׁחֵהוּ 1 S 16^{12}; pl. מִשְׁחוּ Is 21^{5}; *Inf. abs.* מָשׁוֹחַ Je 22^{14}; *cstr.* מְשֹׁחַ Ju 9^{8} Dn 9^{24} + Ho 8^{3} 𝔊 We GASm Now; מָשְׁחוֹ מָשְׁחָה Ex 29^{29}; sf. מָשְׁחֲךָ 1 S 15^{1} (Baer); מָשְׁחוֹ Lv 7^{36}; מָשְׁחָתָם Ex 40^{15}; *Pt.* pl. משחים Ju 9^{15}; *pass.* מָשׁוּחַ 2 S 3^{39} (We suggests deriv. from שׁח, defect. משח (מְשַׁח), wrongly read as מָשַׁח; or by transposition משוח may have been mistaken for an unexampled מוּשָׁח Hoph. Pt. of שׁוח); מָשִׁיחַ 2 S 1^{21} (but rd. מָשֻׁחַ (or נמשח) Codd. We Dr Kit Bu HPS); pl. מְשֻׁחִים Ex 29^{2} + 4 t.;—**1.** *smear*, house with colour (paint) Je 22^{14}; shield with oil (anoint) Is 21^{5} 2 S 1^{21} (cf. Dr; Gr כְּלִי מָשׁוּחַ *weapon anointed;* Peters$^{JBL\ 1893, 56}$ כְּלֵי מָשׁוּחַ *weapons of one* (the king) *anointed*); the person, with ointments Am 6^{6}; unleavened cakes, with oil Ex 29^{2} Lv 2^{4} 7^{12} Nu 6^{15} (P). **2.** *anoint*, as consecration, solemn setting apart to an office, always by the use of oil poured on the head: לנביא as a prophet 1 K 19^{16} (Elisha by Elijah) Is 61^{1}; elsewh. of king, c. acc., מֶלֶךְ Ju 9^{8} (E), so Ho 8^{3} reading מִמְּשֹׁחַ מֶלֶךְ (for MT מִמַּשָּׂא מ׳) We GASm Now; also Ho 7^{3} reading יִמְשְׁחוּ (for MT יְשַׂמְּחוּ) We Now; elsewhere acc. pers. 1 S 16$^{3.12.13}$ 1 K 1^{39} 2 K 11^{12} 23^{30} 2 Ch 22^{7} 23^{11}; בְּשֶׁמֶן קָדְשִׁי ψ 89^{21} *with my holy oil;* שמן שָׂשׂוֹן ψ 45^{8} (fig.); c. עַל, 2 S 19^{11} whom *we have anointed over* us; לְמֶלֶךְ 1 K 1^{45} 5^{15}; c. לְמֶלֶךְ עַל, Ju 9^{15} 2 S 2$^{4.7}$ 1 K 19^{15}; על ישׂראל *over Israel* 1 S 15$^{1.17}$ 2 S 5^{3} = 1 Ch 11^{3}, 2 S 5^{17} 12^{7} 1 K 1^{34} 19^{16}; אֶל־ישׂראל 2 K 9$^{3.6.12}$ (Ephr.); לנגיד 1 Ch 29^{22}; על 1 S 9^{16} 10^{1}; מָשׁוּחַ מֶלֶךְ 2 S 3^{39} (? v. supr.) **3.** *anoint, consecrate* to religious service: **a.** Aaronic priests, only P, c. acc. pers. Ex 28^{41} 29^{7} 30^{30} 40$^{13.15.15.15}$ Lv 7^{36} 8^{12} 16^{32}; abs. Ex 29^{29}; הכהנים הַמְּשֻׁחִים Nu 3^{3}. **b.** sacred things: מַצֵּבָה Gn 31^{13} (E); tabernacle and its sacred vessels Ex 29^{36} 30^{26} 40$^{9.10.11}$ Lv 8$^{10.11}$ (all P); קדשׁ קדשׁים Dn 9^{24}. **Niph.** *Pf.* 3 ms. נִמְשַׁח 1 Ch 14^{8}; *Inf.* הִמָּשַׁח Lv 6^{13} + 3 t.;—*be anointed*, למלך על כל ישׂראל 1 Ch 14^{8}; Aaron and his sons Lv 6^{13} (P); altar Nu 7$^{10.84.88}$.

4888 †מִשְׁחָה **n.f.** **1.** ointment; **2.** consecrated portion;—abs. מ׳ Ex 25^{6} +; cstr. מִשְׁחַת Ex 30^{25} +;—**1.** *ointment*, the holy oil used in the consecration of the Aaronic priests, only in P; שֶׁמֶן הַמִּשְׁחָה Ex 25^{6} 29$^{7.21}$ 31^{11} 35$^{8.15.28}$ 37^{29} 39^{38} 40^{9} Lv 8$^{2.10.12.30}$ 21^{10} Nu 4^{16}; שׁ׳ מִשְׁחַת קֹדֶשׁ Ex 30$^{25.25.31}$; שׁ׳ מ׳ יהוה Lv 10^{7}; שׁ׳ מ׳ אֱלֹהָיו 21^{12}. **2.** *consecrated portion*, of Aaron and his sons Lv 7$^{35.35}$ (P).

†מָשְׁחָה **n.f.** consecrated portion (Ew$^{§ 238 a}$ poss. error of pointing);—Nu 18^{8} (P). 4888

†מָשִׁיחַ **n.m.** anointed;—abs. מ׳ Lv 4^{3} + 4899
5 t.; cstr. מְשִׁיחַ La 4^{20} + 11 t.; sf. מְשִׁיחִי ψ 132^{17} 1 S 2^{35}; מְשִׁיחֶךָ Hb 3^{13} + 5 t.; מְשִׁיחוֹ ψ 2^{2} + 9 t.; pl. sf. מְשִׁיחָי 105^{15} 1 Ch 16^{22};—**1.** king of Israel *anointed* by divine command, מ׳ יהוה 1 S 24$^{7.7.11}$ 26$^{9.11.16.23}$ 2 S 1$^{14.16}$ 19^{22} La 4^{20}; מ׳ אלהי יעקב 2 S 23^{1}; so c. sfs. ref. to י׳, 1 S 12$^{3.5}$ 16^{6} ψ 20^{7} 28^{8} Hb 3^{13}; Davidic dynasty with Messianic ideals attached ψ 2^{2} 18^{51}, = 2 S 22^{51}, ψ 89$^{39.52}$ 132^{10} = 2 Ch 6^{42}, ψ 132^{17} 1 S 2$^{10.35}$. **2.** high priest of Israel, הַכֹּהֵן הַמָּשִׁיחַ, Lv 4$^{3.5.16}$ 6^{15} (P); מְשִׁיחֶךָ ψ 84^{10}. **3.** Cyrus as commissioned by י׳, מְשִׁיחוֹ Is 45^{1}. **4.** *Messianic prince*, עַד־מָשִׁיחַ נָגִיד Dn 9^{25} = מָשִׁיחַ v^{26} (see Br$^{MP\ 422\ f.}$; others disting. מ׳ v^{25} fr. v^{26} and refer v^{25} to Cyrus [as **3**; so Ew v. Leng Schü Co Behrm], or h. p. Joshua [as **2**; so Gr Bev], v^{26} to Seleucus IV [Ew v. Leng], or h. p. Onias III. [Hi Gr Co Bev Behrm]). **5.** patriarchs, regarded as anointed kings ψ 105^{15} = 1 Ch 16^{22}.

†מִמְשַׁח **n.[m.]** dub.; only in כְּרוּב מִמְשַׁח 4473
הַסּוֹכֵךְ Ez 28^{14} *cherub of expansion* (then cf. As. *mašâhu, measure*, Aram. מְשַׁח *id.*, etc.) *that covereth*, after 𝔙 *cherub extentus* (far-reaching wings), "*far-covering cherub*," Ew (Or "*umspannender*"); *the anointed cherub that covereth*, AV RV, so Hä. Co thinks gloss, and reads אֶת־כְּרוּב נְתַתִּיךָ; text dub. acc. to Siegf^{Kau} SS Buhl Berthol.

מַשְׁחִית, [מַשְׁחֵת], מִשְׁחַת, [מָשְׁחָת] 4889, 4892-93
v. שׁחת. p. 1008

מִשְׁחָר v. שׁחר. p. 1007 4891

מִשְׁטוֹחַ, [מִשְׁטָח] v. שׁטח. p. 1009 4894

[מִשְׁטָר] v. שׁטר. p. 1009 4896

†מֶשִׁי **n.[m.]** a costly material for garments, 4897
acc. to Rabb. **silk**, (so Now$^{Arch. i. 124}$); whether this is based on actual tradition is dub. (etym. unknown);—abs. מ׳ Ez 16^{13} (‖ שֵׁשׁ), מֶשִׁי v^{10} (‖ *id.*) Vid., further Thes Sm Da Berthol. 𝔊 τρίχαπτα.

מֹשִׁי v. מוּשִׁי. p. 559 4187

4898 †מְשֵׁיזַבְאֵל **n.pr.m.** Jewish name in Persian period (*God delivers;* from Aram. שֵׁיזִיב, ܫܘܙܒ *deliver*, As. *šûzubu*, Shaph. from *ezêbu*, *deliver*, Dl[HWB 35]; cf. the Bab. names *Mušizib-Marduk*, 'Marduk delivers,' *Mušizib-ilu*, KB [ii. 281, iv. 129]):—grandfather of one of the wall-builders Ne 3^{4}; one of those sealed 10^{22}; father of royal officer (a Judaean) 11^{24}; the relation of these to each other is unknown; 𝔊 Μασεζεβηα, Μεσωζεβηλ, 𝔊L Μασσιζαβελ, etc.

4900 †מָשַׁךְ **vb. draw, drag** (NH *id.;* Aram. מְשַׁךְ (rare) *be extended*, also *conduct, take*, Syr. ܡܫܟ is *be dry, shrivelled* (of fruit, etc.); Eth. መሰከ: *bend* (the bow); Ar. مَسَكَ *grasp and hold* i. Frey; iv. Frey Lane; cf. also As. *mašku*, *skin* (perh. also *march* Dl[HWB 431]), Ar. مَسْك *id.*, Aram. ܡܫܟܐ, מַשְׁכָּא *id.*);—**Qal** *Pf.* 3 ms. מ׳ 1 K 22^{34} + 2 t., וּמָשַׁךְ consec. Jb 24^{22}; 3 fs. מָֽשְׁכָה Dt 21^{3}, etc.; *Impf.* יִמְשׁוֹךְ Jb 21^{33}; וַיִּמְשֹׁךְ Ju 20^{37}; 2 ms. sf. תִּמְשְׁכֵנִי ψ 28^{3}; 1 s. sf. אֶמְשְׁכֵם Ho 11^{4}, etc.; *Imv.* מְשֹׁךְ ψ 36^{11}, sf. מָשְׁכֵנִי Ct 1^{4}; mpl. מִשְׁכוּ Ex 12^{21}, מָשְׁכוּ Ez 32^{20}; *Inf. cstr.* מְשֹׁךְ Ex 19^{13} Jos 6^{5}, לִמְשׁוֹךְ Ec 2^{3}; *Pt.* מֹשֵׁךְ Am 9^{13} ψ 109^{12}; pl. מֹשְׁכִים Ju 5^{14}; cstr. מֹשְׁכֵי Is 5^{18} 66^{19};—**1.** *draw* and lift out of (מִן), c. acc. pers., וַיִּמְשְׁכוּ וַיַּעֲלוּ אֶת־יוֹסֵף מִן הַבּוֹר Gn 37^{28} (E), so Jeremiah (+ בַּחֲבָלִים, ב instr.) Je 38^{13}; cf. תִּמְשֹׁךְ לִוְיָתָן בְּחַכָּה Jb 40^{25}; *draw, drag along* מֹשְׁכֵי עָוֹן בְּחַבְלֵי הַשָּׁוְא Is 5^{18} (fig.); בְּמָשְׁכוֹ בְּרִשְׁתּוֹ ψ 10^{9} (fig. of wicked catching and *dragging* the poor); *draw, lead along* (with hostile purpose) c. acc. pers. Ju 4^{7} (subj. י׳; + אֶל־ pers. et rei); *lead* or *drag off* (to doom, subj. י׳) ψ 28^{3} (cf. 26^{9}); similarly, or = *draw down* to death, מָשְׁכוּ אוֹתָהּ וגו׳ Ez 32^{20} (si vera l.; ref. to fall of Egypt), but rd. perh. a form of שכב for משכו, 𝔊 Co Berthol, cf. Sm.; abs., subj. heifer, מָֽשְׁכָה בְּעֹל Dt 21^{3} (ב instr.); *draw, lead* (in love), (fig., subj. י׳) בְּחַבְלֵי אָדָם אֶמְשְׁכֵם Ho 11^{4}, cf. Je 31^{3} (al. as **5** infr.) **2.** *draw* the bow, מ׳ בַּקֶּשֶׁת 1 K 22^{34} = 2 Ch 18^{33}, but מֹשְׁכֵי ק׳ Is 66^{19} (where text dub., 𝔊 Μοσοχ καὶ εἰς (Θοβελ), so Lo Sta[Javan 8] Du Che[Hpt],—not Gr Che[Comm] Di). **3.** *proceed, march* (cf. Germ. *ziehen*) וּמָשַׁכְתָּ בְּהַר תָּבוֹר Ju 4^{6} cf. 20^{37} (abs.), Jb 21^{33} (אַחֲרָיו); so also (perh.) Ex 12^{21} *proceed* (i.e. forthwith), and take you a sheep; and prob. מֹשְׁכִים בְּשֵׁבֶט Ju 5^{14} *those marching with the staff*, etc. (most under **2.** *drawing with*, i.e. wielding). **4.** *draw out* a sound, *give a sound*, בִּמְשֹׁךְ הַיֹּבֵל Ex 19^{13} (E) *when the ram('s horn) sounds*, בִּמְ׳ בְּקֶרֶן הַיֹּבֵל Jos 6^{5} (JE). **5.** *draw out, prolong, continue*, מְשֹׁךְ חַסְדְּךָ לְיֹדְעֶיךָ ψ 36^{10} *prolong, continue thy kindness to them that know thee;* אַל־יְהִי לוֹ מֹשֵׁךְ חָסֶד 109^{12}; (so poss. מְשַׁכְתִּיךְ חָסֶד Je 31^{3} *I have prolonged kindness to thee*, cf. Ryle Ne 9^{30}; al. as **1** supr.); cf. וַתִּמְ׳ עֲלֵיהֶם שָׁנִים רַבּוֹת Ne 9^{30} (חֶסֶד omitted); תִּמְ׳ אַפְּךָ לְדֹר וָדֹר 85^{6} (|| הַלְעוֹלָם תֶּאֱנַף בָּנוּ); וּמ׳ אַבִּירִים בְּכֹחוֹ Jb 24^{22} i.e. *he* (God) *prolongeth* the life of *the mighty* (Du *draggeth* them *off*, as ψ 28^{3} **1** supr.,—reading also אֹבְדִים for אַבּ׳, with 𝔊 Bi); cf. **Niph.** **6.** *trail* seed (draw along in sowing) Am 9^{13} (opp. דֹּרֵךְ עֲנָבִים; cf. מֶשֶׁךְ infr.) **7.** (late) *cheer* (draw, attract, gratify) מ׳ בַּיַּיִן אֶת־בְּשָׂרִי Ec 2^{3},—so De (who cites NH, Chag[14 a]) Now Wild.—מָשַׁךְ יָדוֹ אֶת־לֹצְצִים Ho 7^{5} is difficult, 𝔊 AV RV *he stretcheth out his hand with*, maketh common cause with, is hardly poss., text prob. corrupt We Now. **Niph.** *Impf.* 3 mpl. לֹא יִמָּשֵׁכוּ Is 13^{22} *they shall not be prolonged* (days of Babylon); 3 fs. לֹא תִמָּשֵׁךְ Ez $12^{25.28}$ *it shall not be postponed.* **Pu.** *Pt. long drawn out:* מְמֻשָּׁךְ Is $18^{2.7}$ of persons, = *tall;* תּוֹחֶלֶת מְמֻשָּׁכָה Pr 13^{12} *hope postponed, deferred.*

†I. [מֶשֶׁךְ] **n.[m.] a drawing, drawing** 4901
up, a trail;—**1.** cstr. מֶשֶׁךְ חָכְמָה מִפְּנִינִים Jb 28^{18} *the drawing up* (fishing up, i.e. securing after effort) of wisdom is beyond corals. **2.** cstr. *a trail* (of seed), מֶ׳ הַזָּרַע ψ 126^{6} bearing the *trail* of seed; cf. מָשַׁךְ **6.**

†II. מֶשֶׁךְ **n.pr.gent. the Moschi** (Gk. 4902
Μοσχοι, v. infr.; As. *Mušku, Muški*, Dl[Par 250] Schr[COT Gn 10, 2; KGF 155 ff.]; cf. Sab. משך Hal[243]);—'son' of Japheth Gn 10^{2} (P), between תֻּבַל and תִּירָס, = 1 Ch 1^{5}; also, מֶשֶׁךְ, prob. err., v[17] (v. מַשׁ); מֶשֶׁךְ ψ 120^{5} (|| קֵדָר; here without תֻּבַל); תּוּבַל וּמ׳ Ez 27^{13} cf. 32^{26} 38^{2} (both + תֻּבַל); so also 𝔊 Is 66^{19} (Lo Sta[Javan 8] Du Che[Hpt]; v. supr. מָשַׁךְ **2**); גּוֹג נְשִׂיא רֹאשׁ מ׳ וְתֻבָל Ez 38^{3} 39^{1}. 𝔊 Μοσοχ (Μεσοχ), Sam. מוש(י)ך.—On identif. cf. Boch.; in Assyr. times they dwelt in W. (or NW.) Armenia (cf. Schr[l. c.]); in Pers. times appar. farther NE. (SE. of Euxine Sea), cf. Μοσχοι καὶ Τιβαρηνοι Herod[iii. 94; vii. 78]; also Di Gn 10, 2 and Che[Encycl. Bib. Art. Geogr. (Biblical)].

†[מֹשֶׁכֶת] **n.f. cord**;—only pl. cstr. מֹשְׁכוֹת 4189
כְּסִיל Jb 38^{31} *the cords of Orion*, i.e. prob. those by which (acc. to some legend) he is dragged along in the sky (cf. Di).

4904,4908 מִשְׁכָּב v. שכב. מִשְׁכָּן v. שכן. p. 1012, 1015

4913 I. מָשָׁל **n.pr.loc.** v. מִשְׁאָל.

4911 †I. [מָשַׁל] **vb. represent, be like** (Ar. مَثَلَ *stand erect* (cf. Fl$^{De\ Pr\ 1,1}$), II. *effigiavit, repraesentavit* (rem alicui), V. *imitate, use a verse as a proverb;* مَثَلٌ *description by way of comparison;* As. *mašâlu*, Dl$^{HWB\ 431\ f.}$; Eth. መሰለ: *become like;* Aram. מְתַל *be like,* ܡܬܠ *compare*). **Niph.** *Pf.* 3 ms. נִמְשַׁל ψ 49$^{13.21}$; 2 ms. נִמְשַׁלְתָּ Is 14^{10}; 1 s. נִמְשַׁלְתִּי ψ 28^{1} 143^{7}:—*be like, similar,* c. אֶל Is 14^{10}; עִם ψ 28^{1} = 143^{7}; כְּ ψ 49$^{13.21}$. **Hiph.** *Impf.* 2 mpl. sf. וְתַמְשִׁלוּנִי *compare* Is 46^{5}. **Hithp.** *Impf.* 1 s. וָאֶתְמַשֵּׁל Jb 30^{19} (c. כְּ) *and I have become like dust.*

4912 †II. מָשָׁל **n.m.**$^{Is\ 14,4}$ **proverb, parable** (of sentences constructed in *parallelism,* usu. of Hebrew Wisdom, but occas. of other types);—abs. מ׳ Ez 17^{2} + 20 t.; cstr. מְשַׁל 1 S 24^{14}; sf. מְשָׁלוֹ Nu 23^{7} + 8 t.; pl. מְשָׁלִים Ec 12^{9} + 2 t.; cstr. מִשְׁלֵי Pr 1^{1} + 3 t.;—**1.** *proverbial saying,* brief terse sentence of popular sagacity 1 S 10^{12} Ez 12$^{22.23}$ 18$^{2.3}$; מ׳ הַקַּדְמֹנִי 1 S 24^{14} *proverb of the ancients.* **2.** *by-word* ψ 44^{15} 69^{12}; לְמָשָׁל וְלִשְׁנִינָה Dt 28^{37} 1 K 9^{7} 2 Ch 7^{20} Je 24^{9}; לְאוֹת וּלְמָשָׁל Ez 14^{8}. **3.** prophetic figurative discourse: נָשָׂא מָשָׁל *lift up, utter a* מ׳ Nu 23$^{7.18}$ 24$^{3.15.20.21.23}$ (all of Balaam); Is 14^{4} Mi 2^{4} (|| נהי) Hb 2^{6} (|| חידה), (cf. Jb 27^{1} 29^{1} for same phrase under **6**). **4.** *similitude, parable,* Ez 17^{2} 21^{5} 24^{3}. **5.** *poem,* of various kinds: the ode (Nu 21$^{27-30}$), the 3,000 pieces traditionally ascribed to Solomon 1 K 5^{12}, didactic psalms ψ 49^{5} 78^{2}. **6.** *sentences of ethical wisdom* דִּבְרֵי חֲכָמִים collected in the מִשְׁלֵי שְׁלֹמֹה Pr 10^{1} 25^{1} (10^{1}–22^{16} consisting of 376 couplets chiefly antithetical; 25–29 chiefly couplets of an emblematic type, but also occasional tristichs, tetrastichs, pentastichs, and decastichs. To these are appended דְּבָרִים of a more mixed character as to size and content in 22^{7}–24^{22}; 24$^{23-34}$; 30$^{1-14}$; v$^{15-33}$; 31$^{1-9}$; v$^{10-31}$; the Praise of Wisdom 1$^{8-9}$ is prefixed, and an introduction to the whole 1$^{1-7}$, in which the whole contents are represented as) משלים Pr 1^{1}, cf. v^{6}. The references in Jb 13^{12} 27^{1} 29^{1} Pr 26$^{7.9}$ Ec 12^{9} are to the same type of wisdom.

4911 †II. מָשַׁל **vb. denom. use a proverb, speak in parables or sentences of poetry,** esp. Ezek.;—**Qal** *Impf.* יִמְשֹׁל Ez 16^{44}; 3 mpl. יִמְשְׁלוּ 12^{23}; *Imv.* מְשֹׁל 17^{2} 24^{3}; *Inf. cstr.* מְשֹׁל 18^{3}; *Pt.* מֹשֵׁל 16^{44}, pl. מֹשְׁלִים 18^{2} Nu 21^{27};—*use a proverb:* מ׳ מָשָׁל אֶל־ Ez 12^{23} 18^{3}; a parable c. אֶל־ 17^{2} (|| חוּד חִידָה), 24^{3}; c. עַל־ 18^{2}, and (מָשָׁל appar. om.) הִנֵּה כָּל־ הַמֹּשֵׁל עָלַיִךְ יִמְשֹׁל 16^{44} (but this is awkward; point הִנֵּה כֹּל הַמָּשָׁל); מֹשְׁלִים Nu 21^{27} (JE). **Pi.** *Pt.* הֲלֹא מְמַשֵּׁל מְשָׁלִים הוּא Ez 21^{5} *is he not a maker of parables?*

†I. [מֹשֶׁל] **n.[m.] likeness, one like**; only 4915
sf. מָשְׁלוֹ Jb 41^{25} *his likeness,* i.e. *one like him.* II p. 605

†מְשֹׁל **n.[m.]** by-word, only cstr. (strictly 4914
Inf.) לִמְשֹׁל עַמִּים Jb 17^{6} (they) *have made me a by-word of the peoples.*

†III. מָשַׁל **vb. rule, have dominion, reign** 4910
(NH *Pt. id.;* Ph. משל);—**Qal** *Pf.* 3 ms. וּמָשַׁל consec. Zc 6^{13} + 2 t., מָשָׁל Dn 11^{4}, וּמָשַׁל consec. v^{5}; 3 fs. מָשָׁלָה ψ 103^{19}; 2 ms. מָשַׁלְתָּ Is 63^{19}, וּמָשַׁלְתָּ Dt 15^{6}; 3 pl. מָשְׁלוּ Is 3^{5} La 5^{8}; *Impf.* 3 ms. יִמְשֹׁל Ex 21^{8} + 3 t., יִמְשׁוֹל Pr 22^{7}; יִמְשָׁל־ Gn 3^{16}, etc.; *Imv.* מְשָׁל־ Ju 8^{22}; *Inf. abs.* מָשׁוֹל Gn 37^{8}; *cstr.* מְשֹׁל Ju 9^{2} +, לִמְשָׁל־ Jo 2^{17}, etc.; *Pt.* מֹשֵׁל Gn 45^{26} +, etc.;—**1.** human subj., *rule, have dominion* over (בְּ) Gn 3^{16} 4^{7} 24^{2} (all J), 45$^{8.26}$ (E), מָשׁוֹל תִּמְשֹׁל בּ׳ 37^{8} (E); Dt 15$^{6.6}$ Jos 12^{5} (D); Ju 8$^{22.23.23}$ 9$^{2.2}$ 14^{4} 15^{11} 2 S 23^{3} (Pt. abs. = *when one ruleth,* cf. Dr), 1 K 5^{1} 2 Ch 7^{18} 9^{26} 23^{20} Is 3$^{4.12}$ 19^{4} Mi 5^{2} Hb 1^{14} Je 22^{30} La 5^{8} Jo 2^{17} Pr 16^{32} (מֹשֵׁל בְּרוּחוֹ), 17^{2} 19^{10} 22^{7} ψ 19^{14} 105^{21} 106^{41} Dn 11^{43} Ec 9^{17}; rarely other preps.: ל (c. inf.) Ex 21^{8} (E); עַל־ Pr 28^{15} Ne 9^{37}, אֶל־ Je 33^{26}; c. sf. Is 52^{5} Je 30^{21}; c. acc. cogn. מ׳ מִמְשָׁל רָב Dn 11$^{3.4}$; מָשַׁל מִן . . . וְעַד Jos 12^{2} (D); abs. 2 S 23^{3} (cf. Dr), Ez 19^{14} Zc 6^{13} (עַל loc.), Pr 12^{24} 29^{2} Dn 11^{5}; esp. Pt. as subst. = *ruler,* מֹשֵׁל־אֶרֶץ Is 16^{1}, מֹשֵׁל עַמִּים ψ 105^{20}; abs. Is 14^{5} 49^{7} Je 51$^{46.46}$ Ez 19^{11} Pr 6^{7} 23^{1} 29$^{12.26}$ Ec 10^{4}; מֹשְׁלֵי הָעָם הַזֶּה Is 28^{14}. **2.** of heavenly bodies, c. בְּ Gn 1^{18}. **3.** of God, c. בְּ Ju 8^{23} Is 63^{19} ψ 22^{29} 59^{14} 89^{10} 103^{19} 1 Ch 29^{12} 2 Ch 20^{6}; abs. ψ 66^{7}; וּזְרֹעוֹ מ׳ לוֹ Is 40^{10} *his arm ruling for him.* **Hiph.** *Pf.* 3 ms. sf. consec. וְהִמְשִׁילָם Dn 11^{39}; *Impf.* 2 ms. sf. תַּמְשִׁילֵהוּ ψ 8^{7}; *Inf. abs.* הַמְשֵׁל Jb 25^{2};—*cause to rule,* sq. acc. pers. + בְּ ψ 8^{7} (subj. י׳), Dn 11^{39}; *exercise dominion,* only inf. abs. as n. abstr. *the exercise of dominion* Jb 25^{2} (attrib. of God).

4915 †II. [מֹשֶׁל] **n.[m.]** dominion;—sf. מָשְׁלוֹ מִיָּם כְּמָשְׁלוֹ אֲשֶׁר מָשָׁל עַד־יָם Zc 9[10] (of Mess. king); Dn 11[4] (of Alexander).

4474 †מִמְשָׁל **n.[m.]** dominion, ruler (late);—abs. מ׳ Dn 11[3.5]; pl. הַמִּמְשָׁלִים 1 Ch 26[6];—**1.** מ׳ רב *great dominion* Dn 11[3] (acc. cogn. c. מָשַׁל), v[5] (pred. of מֶמְשַׁלְתּוֹ). **2.** abstr. for concr. (pl.) = *rulers* 1 Ch 26[6] (? rd. הַמֹּשְׁלִים).

4475 †מֶמְשָׁלָה **n.f.** rule, dominion, realm (cf. Dr JPhil. xi. 1882, 215);—abs. מ׳ Mi 4[8]; cstr. מֶמְשֶׁלֶת ψ 136[8] (before בְּ Ges §130.1 Kö ii. 182), Je 34[1] + 2 t.; sf. מֶמְשַׁלְתְּךָ Is 22[21] ψ 145[13]; מֶמְשַׁלְתּוֹ 1 K 9[19] + 6 t.; pl. cstr. מֶמְשְׁלוֹת ψ 136[9]; sf. מַמְשְׁלוֹתָיו ψ 114[2];—**1.** *rule, dominion* (human) Is 22[21] Mi 4[8]; וְכָל־מֶמְשַׁלְתּוֹ עִמּוֹ 2 Ch 32[9] *and all his imperial might with him* (i.e. display of might—soldiers, court, luxury, etc.; of Sennach.); כֹּל אֶרֶץ מֶמְשַׁלְתּוֹ 1 K 9[19] = 2 Ch 8[6], Je 51[28], מַמְלְכוֹת אֶרֶץ מֶמְשֶׁלֶת יָדוֹ Je 34[1]; hence מ׳ alone = *realm, domain* 2 K 20[13] = Is 39[2], Dn 11[5]. **2.** *rule* of heavenly bodies לְמֶמְ׳ הַיּוֹם Gn 1[16] the sun *for the rule of the day*, cf. v[16]; also sq. בְּ ψ 136[8.9]. **3.** God's *rule, dominion:* ψ 145[13] (|| מַלְכוּת), בְּכָל־מְקֹמוֹת מֶמְשַׁלְתּוֹ 103[22]; pl. = *realm* הָיְתָה יְהוּדָה לְקָדְשׁוֹ יִשְׂרָאֵל מַמְשְׁלוֹתָיו׃ 114[2].

4916-17 [מִשְׁלָח], מִשְׁלַח, מִשְׁלַחַת v. שׁלח. p. 1020

4918-20 מְשֻׁלָּם, מְשִׁלֵּ(י)מוֹת, מְשֶׁלֶמְיָה(וּ) v. שׁלם. p. 1024

4921-22 מְשִׁלֵּמִית, מְשֻׁלֶּמֶת v. שׁלם. p. 1024

834, 4480, 7969 מִשֶּׁלָּנוּ v. -שֶׁ. מְשֻׁלָּשׁ Gn 38[24] v. שׁלשׁ. p. 980, 1025

4923 מְשַׁמָּה v. שׁמם. p. 1031

4924-25 מִשְׁמָן, מִשְׁמַנָּה, מַשׁ׳, מַשְׁמַנִּים v. שׁמן. p. 1032

4926-28 I, II. מִשְׁמָע, [מִשְׁמַעַת] v. שׁמע. p. 1036

4929, 4931 מִשְׁמָר, [מִשְׁמֶרֶת] v. שׁמר. p. 1038

4932-33 מִשְׁנֶה v. שׁנה. מְשִׁסָּה v. שׁסס. p. 1041-42

משׁע (cf. As. *misû, cleanse, wash*, cf. Dl HWB; whence *might* come foll.—though שׁ = s is surprising—cf. Dl Baer, Ezech. xiv).

4935 †מִשְׁעִי **n.f.** (? = מִשְׁעִית cf. Thes Sm) cleansing, only לְמִ׳ לֹא רֻחַצְתְּ Ez 16[4] *thou wast not washed for cleansing* (cf. 𝔗 Thes and Add[98] Sm RV al.; 𝔙 *ad salutem*, as if from ישׁע; 𝔊 om., and so Co Be SS, cf. Buhl; form strange, and word at best dub.)

4934 מִשְׁעוֹל v. I. שׁעל. p. 1043

4936 †מִשְׁעָם **n.pr.m.** name in Benjamin 1 Ch 8[12]. 𝔊 Μεσσααμ, 𝔊L Μεσοαμ.

4937-38 מַשְׁעֵן, מַשְׁעֵן, מַשְׁעֵנָה, מִשְׁעֶנֶת v. שׁען. p. 1044

4940-41 מִשְׁפָּחָה v. שׁפח. מִשְׁפָּט v. שׁפט. p. 1046, 1048

4942 מִשְׁפְּתַיִם v. שׁפת. p. 1046

משׁק (assumed as √ of two following, but wholly dubious).

4943 †מֶשֶׁק **n.[m.]** acquisition, possession (?; meaning conject. fr. context, fr. analogy of מִמְשָׁק q.v., and of משׁך), only וּבֶן־מֶשֶׁק בֵּיתִי הוּא דַּמֶּשֶׂק אֱלִיעֶזֶר Gn 15[2] (cf. בן **8** (λ), supr. p. 121[b]; Ges §128.2, R.2.c) *and the son of acquisition* (= *he who is to acquire, the heir of*) *my house is*, etc.; מ׳ poss. changed from משׁך (cf. Jb 28[18]) for word-play with דמשׂק, Kau and So Gn. Anm. 62, or by copyist's error, but very dubious. 𝔊 Μασεκ (n.pr., cf. Lag BN 78).

4476 †[מִמְשָׁק] **n.[m.]** possession (? so RV), perh. better *place of possession, place possessed by*; only cstr. מִמְשַׁק חָרוּל Zp 2[9] *a place possessed by* chickpeas (> AV *breeding* of nettles), 𝔊 Δαμασκος. Word very dubious (We GASm); text prob. corrupt; Schwally ZAW x. 1890, 188 conj. meaning *place of growth*; Gr (so Now) prop. קִמּוֹשׂ, or קִמְּשֹׂנִים.

4944-45 מַשָּׁק v. שׁקק. מַשְׁקֶה v. שׁקה. p. 1052, 1055

4946, 4948, 4949 מִשְׁקוֹל, מִשְׁקָל, מִשְׁקֶלֶת, מִשְׁקֹלֶת v. שׁקל. p. 1054

4947, 4950 מַשְׁקוֹף v. שׁקף. [מִשְׁקָע] v. שׁקע. p. 1054

4952 מִשְׁרָה v. שׁרה. p. 1056

4339 מֵישָׁרִים v. מֵישָׁרִים sub ישׁר. p. 449

4954 †מִשְׁרָעִי **adj.gent.** (deriv. unknown), only c. art. as n.coll. הַמִּ׳ 1 Ch 2[53] *the Mishra'ites*, a family of Kirjath Jearim, 𝔊 Ἡμασαρειμ, 𝔊L Μασερεθι.

4959 †[מָשַׁשׁ] **vb.** feel, grope (NH *id.* Pi.; Ar. مَسَّ *feel*; Eth. መርሰሰ: Di[166]; Aram. ܡܫ, מְשַׁשׁ Pa., Palp.—v. also ימשׁ, II. מושׁ);—**Qal** *Impf.* 3 ms. sf. יְמֻשֵּׁנִי Gn 27[12] perhaps my father *will feel me*; וַיְמֻשֵּׁהוּ v[22] *and he felt of him* (both J). **Pi.** *Pf.* 2 ms. מִשַּׁשְׁתָּ; *Impf.* 3 ms. יְמַשֵּׁשׁ Dt 28[29], וַיְמַשֵּׁשׁ Gn 31[34]; 3 mpl. יְמַשְׁשׁוּ Jb 5[4] 12[25]; *Pt.* מְמַשֵּׁשׁ Dt 28[29];—*feel over* or *through, grope*:—

1. וַיְמ׳ לָבָן אֶת־כָּל־הָאֹהֶל Gn 31[34] *and Laban felt through the whole tent* (i.e. searched it); so (obj. כֵּלַי) v[37] *thou hast felt through* all my possessions (or baggage; both E). **2.** *grope*, of blind Dt 28[29 b] (in sim.), periphr. conj., וְהָיִיתָ מְמַשֵּׁשׁ v[29a] *and thou shalt become one that gropes* at noonday (fig. of judicial blindness); cf. Jb 5[14] 12[25]. **Hiph.** *Impf.* וְיָמֵשׁ חֹשֶׁךְ Ex 10[21] *that one may feel* (the) *darkness;* rd. also *Imv.* sf. הֲמִשֵּׁנִי (for והימשׁני, v. ימשׁ, p. 413 supr.) Ju 16[26] *and let me touch* the pillars (2 acc.)

4191, 4960 **מִשְׁתֶּה** v. שׁתה. **מֵת** v. מות. p. 559, 1059

4962 †[**מַת**] **n.m.** male, man (מְתוּ־ in n.pr.; Zinj. מת coll. *males, male offspring;* As. *mutu, husband;* Eth. **ምት፡** *id.;* cf. Eg. *m-t, phallus, male*, Steindorff in Ba[NB § 2b, δ]);—only pl. מְתִים Jb 11[3] + 3 t., מְתִם Dt 2[34] 3[6] + Ju 20[48] (probably),
4974 for MT מְתֹם, so GFM; cstr. מְתֵי Gn 34[30] + 13 t.; sf. 2 fs. מְתַיִךְ Is 3[25]; 3 ms. מְתָיו Dt 33[6];— **1.** *males, men*, Is 3[25] (‖ גְּבוּרָתֵךְ); more distinctly, עִיר מְתִם (וְ)הַנָּשִׁים וְהַטָּף Dt 2[34] 3[6] every *city of males* (male population, cf. Dr), *and the women*, etc.; Ju 20[48] (v. supr.; opp. בְּהֵמָה). **2.** usu. less emphasis on sex, in prose only phr.: **a.** מְתֵי מִסְפָּר *men of number* (numerable, i.e. few) Gn 34[30] (J; appos. of אֲנִי = Jacob, representing his family), Dt 4[27] Je 44[28], also ψ 105[12] = 1 Ch 16[19]; cf. וִיהִי מְתָיו מִסְפָּר Dt 33[6] *and (but) let his men be few.* **b.** בִּמְתֵי מְעָט = *consisting of a few men* Dt 26[5] 28[62]. **3.** elsewhere only poet., sex usually not emph.: **a.** Jb 11[3] 24[12] ψ 17[14.14] (but text prob. corrupt, cf. Bae We; at least om. ממתים ידך Ol Bi Che, cf. Hup-Now); מְתֵי יִשְׂרָאֵל Is 41[14]. **b.** poet. phr.: מְתֵי שָׁוְא *men of falsehood* Jb 11[11] ψ 26[4]; מ׳ אָוֶן 22[15] *men of wickedness;* מ׳ סוֹדִי 19[19] *men of my circle;* מ׳ אָהֳלִי Jb 31[31] *men of my tent* (household); מ׳ רָעָב Is 5[13] *men of hunger*, but read probably מְזֵי ר׳ *sucked out, empty* from hunger (as Dt 32[24]) Ew De Che Di Du (cf. מָזֶה).

4967 †**מְתוּשָׁאֵל** **n.pr.m.** descendant of Cain (Bab. form., *mutu-ša-ili* 'man of God,' Len Orig. ed. 2, i. 262 f. Eng. Tr. 268);—Gn 4[18.18] (J), 𝔊 Μαθουσαλα (i.e. מְתוּשֶׁלַח? so Di; otherwise Bu[Urgesch. 125 f.])

4968 †**מְתוּשֶׁלַח** **n.pr.m.** descendant of Seth (? *man of the dart:* more prob. Bab.; see conj. in Hom[PSBA 1893, 243 ff.]);—מ׳ Gn 5[22.25.26.27] (P), 1 Ch 1[3], מְתוּשָׁלַח Gn 5[21] (P). 𝔊 Μαθουσαλα.

4963 **מַתְבֵּן** v. תבן. p. 1062

מתג (√ of foll.; meaning unknown).

†**מֶ֫תֶג** **n.m.** bridle (Aram. (𝔗) מִתְגָּא; NH 4964
מֶתֶג of secondary accent ֽ; מִתֵּג Pi. denom. *put on a bridle*);—**1.** lit. *bridle*, for animals; מֶתֶג לַחֲמוֹר Pr 26[3] a whip for the horse, *a bridle for the ass*, etc.; בְּמ׳ וָרֶסֶן ψ 32[9] *with bridle and halter* (on text of verse cf. Che); of י׳'s *bridle* for Sennach. (under fig. of beast), וּמִתְגִּי בִּשְׂפָתֶיךָ 2 K 19[28] and I will put (וְשַׂמְתִּי) my hook in thy nose *and my bridle in thy lips* = Is 37[29] (v. Dr Is. ed. 2, 220). **2.** fig. = *control, authority*, only
in מ׳ הָאַמָּה 2 S 8[1] *authority of the mother city,* 4965
acc. to MV Buhl, cf. esp. We Dr; Bu om. as corrupt (v. 1. אַמָּה, p. 52 supr.); vid., further, HPS.

מְתוּשָׁאֵל, מְתוּשֶׁלַח v. sub מַת supr. 4967-68

†[**מָתַח**] **vb.** spread out (NH *id.;* Aram. 4969
מְתַח, ܡܬܚ; Ar. مَتَحَ *be long*, مَتَّاح *long* (prob. loan-word); cf. perhaps As. *matâḫu, direct* the eyes toward);—only **Qal** *Impf.* 3 ms. sf. וַיִּמְתָּחֵם Is 40[22] *and he* (י׳) *hath spread them* (the heavens) *out* as a tent to dwell in.

†**אַמְתַּ֫חַת** **n.f.** sack, only Gn 42–44;—א׳ 572
constr. Gn 44[2.12]; sf. אַמְתַּחְתִּי 42[28], אַמְתַּחְתּוֹ 42[27] + 2 t.; pl. cstr. אַמְתְּחֹת 44[1]; sf. אַמְתְּחֹתֵינוּ 43[18] + 3 t.; אַמְתְּחֹתֵיכֶם 43[12.23];—*sack*(s) in wh. brethren of Joseph carried corn from Egypt; in phr. בְּפִי אַמ׳ Gn 42[27] *in the mouth of the sack*, so 43[12.21] 44[1.2.8]; elsewhere 42[28] 43[18.21.22.23] 44[1.11.11.12] (all J).

מָתַי [43] **interrog. adv.** when? (Ar. مَتَى; 4970
As. *mati:* in NH and Aram. with the interrog. אֵימָתַי, אֵימַת, ܐܡܬܝ), in OT only of future time: **a.** alone, †Gn 30[30] מָתַי אעשׂה גם אנכי לביתי *when* shall I also do, etc.? Am 8[5] ψ 41[6] 42[3] 94[8] 101[2] 119[82.84] Pr 6[9b] 23[35] Jb 7[4] מָתַי אָקוּם, Ne 2[6]. **b.** לְמָתַי *against when?* †Ex 8[5] לְמָתַי אַעְתִּיר לְךָ. **c.** עַד־מָתַי *until when? how long?* sq. impf. Ex 10[7] עד מתי יהיה זה לנו למוקשׁ, 1 S 1[14] Je 4[14.21] ψ 74[10] 82[2] 94[3] Pr 1[22] +, sq. ptcp. 1 S 16[1] 1 K 18[21] עַד־מָתַי אַתֶּם פֹּסְחִים עַל־שְׁתֵּי הַסְּעִפִּים, sq. pf. †Ex 10[3] ψ 80[5]; עַד מָתַי לֹא †2 S 2[26] Ho 8[5] Zc 1[12]; alone, Is 6[11] וָאֹמַר עַד־מָתַי אֲדֹנָי, Hb 2[6] הוֹי הַמַּרְבֶּה לֹּא־לוֹ עַד־מָתַי; with an aposiop., ψ 6[4] וְאַתָּה י׳ עַד־מָתָי, 90[13]. **d.** אַחֲרֵי מָתַי עוֹד *after how long yet?* †Je 13[27].

מְתִים v. מַת. **מַתְכֹּנֶת** v. תכן. 4962, 4971
above, p. 1069

4972-73 מַתְּלָאָה v. תְּלָאָה. מְתַלְּעוֹת v. תלע. p. 521, 1069

4962, 4974 מְתֹם v. תמם; Ju 20^{48} v. מַת. p. 607, 1071

מתן (√of foll.; Ar. مَتُنَ *be stout, firm, enduring* (Frey Wahrm), II. *make stout, firm* (Lane)).

4975 †מָתְנַיִם **n.m.du.** loins (Ar. مَتْنٌ *back*, مَتْنَتَانِ *the two sides of the back*, etc.; Syr. ܡܰܬܢܳܐ);—abs. מ׳ Dt 33^{11} + 7 t., מָתְנָ֑יִם Ez 29^{7} 47^{4}; cstr. מָתְנֵי Je 13^{11} + 3 t.; sf. מָתְנַי Is 21^{3}, מָתְנֶ֑יךָ Je 13^{2}; מָתְנֵיהֶם 1 K 20^{32} + 4 t., etc.;—*loins:* **1. a.** place of wearing girdle 1 K 2^{5} 2 K 1^{8} Je 13$^{1.2.4.11}$ Ez 23^{15}; fig. Is 11^{5} *righteousness shall be the girdle of his loins.* **b.** hence place of things attached to girdle:—sword girded on (אסר, חגר על) 2 S 20^{8} Ne 4^{12}; opp., וּמָתְנֵי מְלָכִים אֲפַתֵּחַ Is 45^{1} *and the loins of kings I will loosen,* i.e. will disarm them (י׳ before Cyrus; cf. Che); ink-horn Ez 9$^{2.3.11}$. **c.** girding up *loins* = make ready for action, וַיְשַׁנֵּס מָתְנָיו 1 K 18^{46}; more oft. חָגַר מ׳ 2 K 4^{29} 9^{1} Ex 12^{11} (P), Dn 10^{5}; אָזַר מ׳ Je 1^{17}. **d.** זַרְזִיר מ׳ Pr 30^{31} that which is *girt in the loins,* i.e. prob. either a *greyhound* Ew Bö De (contracted, as if by a belt), or a war-horse, charger, Bo Ges Hi Str Wild (with a saddle); cf. also זרזיר, p. 267 supr.; text perh. corrupt (Wild). **e.** girded with sackcloth (in mourning) Gn 37^{34} (J), Am 8^{10} Is 20^{2} 1 K 20$^{31.32}$ Je 48^{37}. **f.** linen breeches of priests were to extend מִמָּתְנַיִם וְעַד יְרֵכַיִם Ex 28^{42} (P); to be עַל־מָת׳ Ez 44^{18}; loins of slaves are girt with waistcloth, cf. Jb 12^{18} (v. also אֵזוֹר). **g.** in gen. of the middle of the body, מֵי מָת׳ Ez 47^{4} (i.e. water reaching to the loins); so of the appearance of י׳ in Ezek.'s visions Ez 1$^{27.27}$ 8$^{2.2}$. **2. a.** *loins* as seat of strength, Dt 33^{11} 1 K 12^{10} = 2 Ch 10^{10}; חַזֵּק מָתְנַיִם Na 2^{2} (‖ אַמֵּץ כֹּחַ); כֹּחוֹ בְמָתְנָיו Jb 40^{16} (of hippopotamus); in combin. with **1 a** (fig.) חָגְרָה בְעוֹז מ׳ Pr 31^{17} *she girdeth her loins with strength,* she puts on energy with her girdle; cf. also בְּשִׁבְּרוֹן מ׳ Ez 21^{11} sigh *with breaking of loins,* i.e. in entire collapse of strength; so וּמ׳ תָּמִיד הַמְעַד ψ 69^{24} *and make their loins continually to shake,* make them totter; cf. Ez 29^{7} (where rd. וְהִמְעַדְתָּ for וְהַעֲמַדְתָּ, v. מָעַד). **b.** as seat of keenest pain, due to grief or dread Na 2^{11} Is 21^{3} (as in travail); so prob. also ψ 66^{11} (cf. Bae; and v. מוּעָקָה sub עוק).

4981 †מִתְנִי **adj.gent.** (deriv. unknown);—only יוֹשָׁפָט הַמִּ׳ 1 Ch 11^{43}. 𝔊 ὁ Βαιθανει, A Μαθθανει, 𝔊L Ματθανι.

4976-77, 4979-80, 4982-83 מַתַּנְיָה(וּ), מַתְּנַי, מַתָּנָה I, II. מַתָּן I, II. v. נתן. p. 682

4985, 4988 †[מָתֹק] **vb.** become or be sweet, pleasant (NH מתק, esp. Pi.; As. [*matâḳu*] *be sweet,* in deriv.; Eth. ምጥቅ: *sweet;* Aram. ܡܨ *suck* (with pleasure), מְתַק *id., be sweet;* Ar. مطق (ط before ق) v. *smack* the lips (with pleasure), مُطْقَةٌ *sweetness*);—**Qal** *Pf.* 3 ms. sf. מְתָקוֹ Jb 24^{20}; 3 pl. מָתְקוּ 21^{33}; *Impf.* 3 mpl. יִמְתָּ֑קוּ Pr 9^{17}, וַיִּמְתְּקוּ Ex 15^{25};—**1.** lit. *become sweet,* of water (opp. מָרִים) 15^{25} (J); *are* (i.e. taste) *sweet,* מַיִם גְּנוּבִים יִמ׳ Pr 9^{17} (fig. of delights of illicit pleasure). **2.** = *be pleasant,* מָתְקוּ לוֹ Jb 21^{33} *sweet* (pleasant) *to him* are the clods of the valley (said of one resting in the grave). **3.** *suck* (Aram. sense, cf. Syr. supr.) מְתָקוֹ רִמָּה Jb 24^{20} the worm *doth suck him,* feast on him (on vb. masc. cf. Ges$^{§ 145.7}$ Kö$^{Synt. § 345a}$ Da$^{Synt. § 113(b)}$), Di De Buhl (cf. Kau Da; also SS who render 'angenehm finden'), but this sense in Heb. dub.; txt. perh. crpt. (cf. conject. by Bu Du). **Hiph.** *Impf.* 3 fs. אִם תַּמְתִּיק בְּפִיו רָעָה Jb 20^{12} *if evil gives a sweet taste in his mouth* (declarative Hiph.); 1 pl. אֲשֶׁר יַחְדָּו נַמְתִּיק סוֹד ψ 55^{15} *we who used to make sweet* (our) *intimacy.*

4986 †מֶ֫תֶק **n.m.**$^{Pr 16.21}$ **sweetness**; cstr. מ׳ שְׂפָתַיִם Pr 16^{21} i.e. agreeable, attractive speech, so prob. מ׳ רֵעֵהוּ 27^{9} *the sweetness of one's friend,* i.e. of his speech.

4987 †[מֹ֫תֶק] **n.[m.] sweetness**;—only sf. מָתְקִי Ju 9^{11} *my sweetness* (fig-tree loquitur), i.e. sweetness of the fruit.

4966 †מָתוֹק **adj.** sweet, and **n.[m.] sweetness** (on form v. Lag$^{BN 30, 60}$, cf. Ba$^{NB 13, 36}$);—abs. מ׳ Ju 14^{14} + 9 t.; f. מְתוּקָה Ec 5^{11}; pl. מְתוּקִים ψ 19^{11};—**1.** *sweet,* of honey Ju 14^{14} (where מ׳ = subst. *a sweet thing*), v^{18} (both Samson's riddle), Pr 24^{13}; so = *sweetness,* Ez 3^{3}; more gen., כָּל־מַר מ׳ Pr 27^{7} *every bitter thing is sweet* to one hungry; fig. ψ 19^{11} (God's commandments, sweeter than honey), cf. Pr 16^{24} (sim. of pleasant words) וּפִרְיוֹ מ׳ לְחִכִּי Ct 2^{3} (i.e his caresses); שָׂמִים מַר לְמ׳ וּמ׳ לְמָר Is 5^{20} *making bitter into sweet and sweet into bitter* (obscuring moral distinctions; ‖ הָאֹמְרִים לָרַע טוֹב וְלַטּוֹב רָע).

2. =*pleasant*, sleep of the toiler Ec 5^{11}; light 11^{7} (|| טוֹב לַעֵינַיִם לִרְאוֹת אֶת־הַשָּׁמֶשׁ).

4989 **†מִתְקָה n.pr.loc.** a station of Isr. in desert Nu $33^{28.29}$. 𝔊 Ματεκκα, A Μαθεκκα, 𝔊L Ματτεκα.

4477 **†מַמְתַּקִּים n.[m.]pl. sweetness = sweet things**; — of drinks וּשְׁתוּ מ׳ Ne 8^{10} (|| אִכְלוּ מַשְׁמַנִּים); of lover's kisses חִכּוֹ מ׳ Ct 5^{16} (|| כֻּלּוֹ מַחֲמַדִּים).

†מִתְרְדָת n.pr.m. name of two Persians; 4990
1. Cyrus' time Ezr 1^{8}. **2.** Artaxerxes' time Ezr 4^{7}.—𝔊 Μιθρα[ι]δατης in both.

מַתַּת, מַתַּתָּה, מַתִּתְיָה(וּ) v. **נתן.** p. 682-83 4991-93

נ

נ, ן, *Nûn*, fourteenth letter; used as numeral 50 in postB.Heb.

4994 I. **נָא part. of entreaty** or **exhortation, I (we) pray, now** (enclitic) (Syr. ܢܳܐ, ܢܳܐ; cf. Eth. ነዐ: *veni, age!* Di$^{§160.1}$ Lex^{675} Kö$^{ii.244}$);—attached: **1.** to the imv., esp. in colloquial style, when it expresses an entreaty or admonition, as Gn 12^{13} אִמְרִי־נָא say, *I pray*, 13^{9} הִפָּרֶד־נָא מֵעָלַי, v^{14} שָׂא־נָא עֵינֶיךָ, 15^{5} הַבֶּט־נָא השמימה, 24^{2} + oft., Nu 20^{10} שמעו־נא המורים, Ju 13^{4} $16^{6.10.28}$ 18^{5}, etc., Is 1^{18} 5^{3} Am $7^{2.5}$; rarely in a command, Gn 22^{2} Is 7^{3}. Ironically, in a challenge, Is 47^{12} Jb 40^{10}. Once anomalously attached to a subst., or (accents) prefixed to a verb, Nu 12^{13} אֵל נָא רְפָא נָא (Ew^{§246a} Di אַל־נָא; v. **3 b**). **2.** to the pf. with *waw* consec., in a precative sense (Dr^{§119δ}) Gn 40^{14}. **3.** to the impf., when leave is asked, or a prayer or desire expressed; **a.** in 1 pers., esp. with ה cohort., Gn 19^{8} אוציאה־נא let me, *I pray*, bring out, v^{20} אִמָּלְטָה־נָּא שָׁמָּה, 24^{12} הַקְרֵה־נָא לְפָנַי, v^{14} הַטִּי־נָא, v$^{17.23.43.45}$ 25^{30} $32^{12.30}$ + oft., Ex 3^{18} נלכה־נא let us go, *I pray*, Nu 20^{17} Is 5^{5}; and in self-deliberation, Gn 18^{21} ארדה־נא I will go down, *now!* Ex 3^{3} אסורה־נא ואראה I will turn aside, *now*, and see, 2 S 14^{15} Ct 3^{2} Is 5^{1}; with אַל Jb 32^{21}. **b.** in 2 pers., with אַל, in deprecation, Gn 18^{3} אל־נא תעבר מעל עבדך, 19^{7} 47^{29} Nu 10^{31}, etc.; hence ellipt. אל־נא do not, *I pray*, (do this,) Gn 19^{18} 33^{10} Nu 12^{13} Ew Di. **c.** in 3 pers., Gn 18^{4} יֻקַּח־נָא let there be brought, *I pray*, 26^{28} 33^{14} $44^{18.33}$, etc., 2 S $14^{11.12.17}$ 1 K 17^{21} 2 K 2^{9} ψ 7^{10} $118^{2.3}$; ironically Is 19^{12} 47^{13}, or defiantly Jer 17^{15} where is the word of J.? יָבוֹא נָא; with אַל־נָא Gn 13^{8} אַל־נָא תְהִי מְרִיבָה, 18^{30} אַל־נָא יִחַר לַאדֹנָי, 37^{27} Nu 12^{12}. **4.** joined to conjunctions and interjections: **a.** [אָהּ־נָא, contr.] אָנָּא; v. p. 58. **b.** אַל־נָא, see above **3 b, c.** **c.** אִם־נָא, esp. in the phrase אם נא מצאתי חן בעיניך, used by one craving a favourable hearing †Gn 30^{27} 33^{10} Ju 6^{17} 1 S 27^{5}, and with נא repeated in the request itself †Gn 18^{3} 47^{29} 50^{4} Ex 33^{13} 34^{9}; otherwise Gn 24^{42}. **d.** הִנֵּה־נָא behold, *I pray*, craving a favourable consideration of the fact pointed to by הִנֵּה, and of the request founded upon it (with which נא is often repeated), Gn 12^{11} 16^{2} $18^{27.31}$ $19^{2.8.19.20}$ 27^{2} Ju 13^{3} 19^{9} 1 S 9^{6} 16^{15} 2 S 13^{24} 2 K $2^{16.19}$ 4^{9} +, Jb 13^{18} 33^{2} $40^{15.16}$. **e.** אוי־נא לי (לנו) Woe, *now*, to me (us)! †Je 4^{31} 45^{7} La 5^{16}. **f.** אַיֵּה־נָא where, *pray?* †ψ 115^{2}. **g.** נֶגְדָה־נָּא, peculiarly, †ψ $116^{14.18}$ my vows to J. I will perform, נגדה־נא לכל־עמו *O that* (it may be) before all his people!

II. **נָא adj.** v. **ניא.** p. 644 4995

†נֹא n.pr.loc. No = Thebes (Eg. *nt, city,* i.e. prob. *nē(t)*, v. Steind$^{BAS\ i.\ 596\ f.}$; As. *Ni-'u, Ni-i'* Dl$^{Par\ 318}$ Steind$^{l.c.}$ Schr$^{COT\ gloss.}$; Tel Am. Nî (Ni-i) Wkl$^{Tel\ Am.\ 39*}$ Bez$^{Tel\ Am.\ in\ BM\ 153}$);—הִנְנִי פוֹקֵד אֶל־אָמוֹן מִנֹּא Je 46^{25} *Amon from (of,* 𝔊 ἐν = בְּ) *No;* נֹא אָמוֹן Na 3^{8} *No of Amon* (= *city of god Ammon,* = 𝔊 Διόσπολις Ez $30^{14.16}$ Steind$^{l.c.}$; v. also Jerem. and Billerbeck$^{BAS\ iii.\ 104\ f.}$); Ez 30^{14} (|| צֹעַן, פַּתְרוֹס) v^{15} וְהִכְרַתִּי אֶת־הֲמוֹן נֹא (|| סִין; but 𝔊 Co Berthol נֹף q.v. for נֹא) v^{16} (|| סִין, Co סון). It lay on the right bank of the Nile, c. 400 miles (by the river) S. of Memphis. 4996

4997 **†נֹאד** (Ju 4^{19} Kt נאוד, i.e. prob. נְאוֹד), **n.m.**$^{Jos\ 9,\ 4}$ **skin-bottle, skin** (√unknown; NH נוֹד; As. *nâdu*, Dl$^{HWB\ 438}$; Aram. נוֹדָא);—נ׳ abs. ψ 119^{83}; cstr. Ju 4^{19} 1 S 16^{20}; sf. נֹאדְךָ ψ 56^{9}; pl. נֹאדוֹת Jos $9^{4.13}$;—*skin*, נ׳ יַיִן Jos $9^{4.13}$ 1 S 16^{20}; נ׳ הֶחָלָב Ju 4^{19}; for tears ψ 56^{9} (fig.; v. Che); נ׳ בְּקִיטוֹר i.e. shrivelled and useless ψ 119^{83} (in sim.; cf. [De] Che Schu DeWitt We > as thrust aside, out of the way Now (in Hup), cf. De, or as black and wrinkled outwardly, while retaining the choice wine within Bae, after Rosenm. Hup).—Vid. Winer[RWB. Art. *Schlauch*] Kmp[Bl HWB *id.*]

4998 †[נָאָה] **vb.** only **Piʿlel** be comely, befitting (Thes Ol[§ 251 a, 187 a] Sta[§ 416 b] Ges[§ 73.2.R.4] SS Bae[ψ 33,1] > AE Ki Hartm[Plurllt.-bildungen (1875) 13 ff.] Nö[ZMG xxx. 1876, 185] Now Hup[ψ 31,1. 93,5] Buhl **Niph.** √ I. אוה *desire*, i.e. *desirable, beautiful;* NH נאה Pi. Hithp.; 𝔗 נוֹאִי *beauty*);—**Piʿlel** *Pf.* נַאֲוָה ψ 93^{5} (so van d. H Ginsb; Mass Baer De[ad loc.] נָאֲוָה = נָאוָה v. נָאוֶה **adj.**, but v. Sta [§ 155 b.n]); נָאווּ Is 52^{7} Ct 1^{10} (on form cf. Ges[l. c.]);—**1.** *be comely;* of feet of messenger, (fig.) Is 52^{7}; of cheeks Ct 1^{10}. **2.** *be befitting:* לְבֵיתְךָ נ׳־קֹדֶשׁ ψ 93^{5}.

5000 †נָאוֶה **adj. comely, seemly;**—נ׳ m. Ct 2^{14} + 3 t.; f. נָאוָה ψ 33^{1} + 4 t., נָוָה Je 6^{2};—**1.** *comely, beautiful,* of woman Ct 1^{5} 6^{4} (‖ יָפָה); of face 2^{14} (מַרְאֶה); so נָוָה Je 6^{2} (fig. of Jerus.; ‖ מְעֻנָּגָה); of mouth Ct 4^{3} (‖ שִׂפְתוֹת). **2.** *seemly,* of praise תְּהִלָּה ψ 33^{1} 147^{1}; subj. שְׂפַת־יֶתֶר Pr 17^{7} (cf. Ct 4^{3}); תַּעֲנוּג 19^{10}; כָּבוֹד 26^{1}. So also ψ 93^{5} Mass. (anom. fem.) v. [נאה] supr.

5116 נְאוֹת v. II. [נָוָה] sub II. נוה. p. 627

נאם (√ of foll.; cf. نَأَمَ *groan, sigh;* perhaps also NH נוּם *speak*).

5002 נְאֻם 376 **n.m.** utterance (Ba[NB 82e] Kö[Lgb ii. 501] > older expl. as *Pt. pass.*);—נ׳ always thus, as cstr.:—**1.** *utterance, declaration, revelation,* of prophet in ecstatic state נ׳ בלעם Nu $24^{3.15}$; נ׳ הַגֶּבֶר v$^{3.15}$ 2 S 23^{1} Pr 30^{1}; נ׳ שֹׁמֵעַ אִמְרֵי אֵל v$^{4.6}$; נ׳ דוד 2 S 23^{1}; נ׳ פֶּשַׁע ψ 36^{2} (transgression personified, speaking with proph. voice בְּקֶרֶב לִבּוֹ); elsewh. alw. **2.** before divine names (exc. Je 23^{31} see **vb.**): נ׳ יהוה *utterance, declaration* of י׳ (prophet citing divine word given through him), Gn 22^{16} (J), Nu 14^{28} (P), 2 K $9^{26.26}$ 19^{33} = Is 37^{34}, 2 K 22^{19} = 2 Ch 34^{27}, Is 14^{22} 30^{1} 31^{9} Ez $13^{6.7}$ 16^{58} 37^{14} Ho $2^{15.18.23}$ 11^{11} Jo 2^{12} Ob$^{4.8}$ Mi 4^{6} 5^{9} Zp $1^{2.3.10}$ 3^{8} Zc 8^{17} 10^{12} 11^{6} $12^{1.4}$ 13^{8} Mal 1^{2} + Is^{2} 12 t., Je 162 t., Am 14 t., Hg 5 t., Zc^{1} (1–8) 6 t.; sq. אלהי ישראל 1 S 2^{30} Is 17^{6}; י׳ אֱלֹהֵי (הַ)צְבָאוֹת Am $6^{8.14}$; נ׳ י׳ צְבָאוֹת Is $14^{22.23}$ 17^{3} 22^{25} Je 8^{3} 25^{29} 30^{8} 49^{26} Na 2^{14} 3^{5} Zc $13^{2.7}$ + Hg 5 t., Zc^{1} (1–8) 7 t.; sq. אלהי ישראל Zp 2^{9}; האדון י׳ צ׳ Is 1^{24} 19^{4}; אדני י׳ צ׳ אֲדֹנָי י׳ אֱלֹהֵי הַצ׳ Am 3^{13}; Is 3^{15} Je 49^{5}; הַמֶּלֶךְ י׳ צ׳ 46^{18} 48^{15} 57^{57}; נ׳ אדני יהוה Is 56^{8} Je 2^{22} Am 4^{5} $8^{3.9.11}$ + Ez 82 t. נְאֻם begins sentence only Is 56^{8} ψ 110^{1}; often in middle Is 49^{18} Am 3^{10} +; most frequently at end Is 54^{17} Am 2^{11} 4^{3} +; found in all proph. except Hab., Jon.; not in HD of Hex., Chr. (except ‖ Kings), Dan., Job or the five Megilloth.

†[נָאַם] **vb. denom. utter a prophecy,** 5001
speak as prophet;—**Qal** *Impf.* 3 mpl. וַיִּנְאֲמוּ נְאֻם Je 23^{31} *and they uttered* (in the prophetic manner), it *as an utterance* (of י׳); they used the prophetic formula (cf. אֹמְרִים נְאֻם י׳ Ez $13^{6.7}$).

†[נָאַף] **vb. commit adultery** (NH *id.;* 5003
Aram. נְאַף (rare));—**Qal** *Impf.* 3 ms. יִנְאַף Lv $20^{10.10}$; 3 mpl. וַיִּנְאָפוּ Je 5^{7} + 3 t. Impf.; *Inf. abs.* נָאוֹף 23^{14}; נָאֹף Ho 4^{2} Je 7^{9}; *Pt.* נֹאֵף Pr 6^{32} Jb 24^{15}; fs. נֹאָפֶת Lv 20^{10}; fpl. נֹאֲפוֹת Ez 16^{38} + 2 t.;—**1.** lit. *commit adultery:* **a.** usu. of *man,* always with wife of another; c. acc. woman, Lv $20^{10.10}$ (H), Pr 6^{32}; elsewh. abs. Ex 20^{14} = Dt 5^{17} (Ten Words), Je 5^{7} 7^{9} 23^{14} Ho 4^{2}; pt. m. Lv 20^{10} (H), Jb 24^{15}. **b.** of *women,* only pt. Lv 20^{10} (H), Ez 16^{38} $23^{45.45}$. **2.** fig. of *idolatrous worship,* את האבן ואת העץ Je 3^{9}.

Piel *Pf.* 3 fs. נִאֲפָה Je 3^{8}; 3 mpl. נִאֵפוּ Ez $23^{37.37}$; *Impf.* 3 mpl. יְנָאֲפוּ Je 29^{23}; 3 fpl. תְּנָאַפְנָה Ho $4^{13.14}$; *Pt.* מְנָאֵף Is 57^{3}; pl. מְנָאֲפִים Je 9^{1} + 4 t.; f. מְנָאֶפֶת Pr 30^{20} + 2 t.;—**1.** lit. *commit adultery:* **a.** of *man,* c. acc. woman, Je 29^{23}; abs. Ez 23^{37}; pt. pl. Je 9^{2} 23^{10} Ho 7^{4} Mal 3^{5} ψ 50^{18}. **b.** of *woman,* abs. Ho $4^{13.14}$; pt. 3^{1} Pr 30^{20}; pl. Ez 16^{32}. **2.** fig. of *idolatrous worship,* אֶת־גִּלּוּלֵיהֶם Ez 23^{37}; abs. Je 3^{8}, זֶרַע מְנָאֵף Is 57^{3}.

†[נִאֻף] **n.[m.] adultery;**—only pl. נִאֻפִים 5004
Ez 23^{43} (but 𝔊 𝔖 Co נִאֻפוּ, cf. Berthol); sf. נִאֻפַיִךְ Je 13^{27} (Kö[i. 151]); fig. of idolatrous worship.

†[נַאֲפוּף] **n.[m.] adultery;**—only pl. sf. 5005
נַאֲפוּפֶיהָ Ho 2^{4} (Ba[NB 216]), of idolatrous worship of Baal.

†נָאַץ **vb. contemn, spurn** (NH *id.*, Pi.; 5006
𝔗 נִיאוּצָא *reviling*);—**Qal** *Pf.* נ׳ Pr 5^{12}; 3 pl. נָאֲצוּ Pr 1^{30}; נָאֲצוּ ψ 107^{11}; *Impf.* יִנְאַץ Pr 15^{5}; יִנְאָצוּן Je 33^{24}, etc.;—*contemn,* subj. wicked and foolish, obj. תּוֹכַחַת Pr 1^{30} 5^{12}; obj. מוּסָר Pr 15^{5}; עֵצָה ψ 107^{11}; Je 33^{24} (obj. עַם י׳; cf. Gie); subj. י׳ Dt 32^{19} Je 14^{21} La 2^{6}. **Pi.** *Pf.* נִאֵץ ψ $10^{3.13}$; נִאַצְתָּ 2 S 12^{14}, etc.; *Impf.* יְנָאֵץ ψ 74^{10}; sf. יְנַאֲצֻנִי Nu 14^{11}; *Inf. abs.* נִאֵץ (Sta[§ 221]) 2 S 12^{14}; *Pt.* sf. מְנַאֲצַי Nu 14^{23}; מְנַאֲצַי Je 23^{17}; מְנַאֲצַיִךְ Is 60^{14};—

contemn, spurn, subj. men, obj. 'י, etc.: Nu 14[11.23] 16[30] (all J), Dt 31[20] Is 1[4] ψ 10[3.13] Je 23[17]; obj. שֵׁם י' ψ 74[10.18]; אִמְרַת י' Is 5[24]; מִנְחַת י' 1 S 2[17]; once obj. Jerus. Is 60[14]; *cause to contemn* (blaspheme AV RV) 2 S 12[14.14] (but אֹיְבֵי prob. interp.; v. Comm).

Hiph. *Impf.* יָנֵאץ v. נצץ.

Hithpo'el *Pt.* כל־היום שְׁמִי מִנֹּאָץ Is 52[5] *every day is my name contemned.*

5007 †נְאָצָה **n.f. contempt, contumely**;—יום צָרָה וְתוֹכֵחָה וּנ' 2 K 19[3]=Is 37[3].

5007 †[נֶאָצָה] **n.f. contempt** (toward 'י), **blasphemy**;—pl. נֶאָצוֹת Ne 9[18.26] c. עָשָׂה, of Isr.; נָאָצוֹתֶיךָ Ez 35[12] of Mt. Seir, spoken against הרי ישׂראל.

5008 †נָאַק **vb. groan** (Aram. נְאַק (rare));—**Qal** *Pf.* וְנָאַק consec. Ez 30[24] c. acc. cogn. fig. of Pharaoh before king of Babylon (emend. Co v. נְאָקָה) *Impf.* Jb 24[12] יִנְאָקוּ.

5009 †[נְאָקָה] **n.f. groan, groaning**;—cstr. נַאֲקַת Ex 6[5]; sf. נַאֲקָתָם Ex 2[24] Ju 2[18]; pl. cstr. נַאֲקוֹת Ez 30[24];—*groaning* of oppressed people Ex 2[24] 6[5] Ju 2[18]; of a wounded man Ez 30[24]; (𝔊 Co וּבֹז בִּזָּה for MT וְנָאַק נַאֲקוֹת, but cf. Berthol).

5010 [נָאַר] **vb.** only **Pi.** exact mng. uncertain; prob. (from context) **abhor, spurn** (De comp. Ar. نار *abhor*, but this is med. و);—**Pi.** *Pf.* subj. 'י, נֵאֵר י' La 2[7] (obj. מִקְדָּשׁוֹ ‖ זָנַח); 2 ms. נֵאַרְתָּה ψ 89[40] (obj. בְּרִית עַבְדֶּךָ ‖ חִלֵּל, and זָנַח, מָאַס v[39]; doubts cast on text by Hup (reading נאץ), Now, Bu[La 2, 7]).

5011 †נֹב **n.pr.loc. 1.** ancient priestly city 1 S 22[19] cf. v[11] c. ה loc. נֹבֶה (Ges[§ 90, 2 ad fin.]), 21[2] 22[9]; 𝔊 Νομβα, Νομμα, Νοβα, etc.; perh.=נְבוֹ (q.v.) Ezr 2[29]=Ne 7[33], Ezr 10[43], 𝔊 Ναβου, Ναβια, etc. Site dub.; on Jerome's identif. with *Nobe* near Lydda cf. Buhl[Geogr. 189]; a Bēt Nūbā lies c. 13 m. WNW. fr. Jerus., c. 10 SE. fr. Lydda. **2.** Is 10[32] just N. of Jerus., station in (ideal) Assyr. march; cf. Ne 11[32] (inhab. by Benjamites); perhaps=**1.**—2 S 21[6] read גֹּב (q. v. p. 146 supr.)

נבא (√of foll.; Ew Fl De Kö[Lgb ii. 1, 133] al. comp. Ar. نَبَأَ [نَبَأَ *utter a low voice*, or *sound*, (esp. of dog); *announce;* but also *be exalted, elevated* (نُبَاوَة *eminence*); III, IV. *acquaint, inform,* نَبَأ *information, announcement, intelligence*]; As. *nabû, call, proclaim, name,* Dl[HWB 441]; Eth. ነበበ: *speak;* Sab. תנבא ? cf. Levy-Os[ZMG xix. 1865, 208] CIS[iv. 1, No. 31]; Ges Kue al. think weakened form of נבע *bubble up, pour forth* (of flow of words under excitement of inspiration); Hup Ri Sch cf. נאם; v. careful discussions by RS[Proph. ii, n. 18] Kö[OB i. 71 ff.])

נָבִיא[306] **n.m. spokesman, speaker, prophet** 5030
—נ' Gn 20[7]+155 t.; sf. נְבִיאֶךָ Ex 7[1]; pl. נְבִיאִים Nu 11[29]+82 t.; נְבִאִים Je 27[18]+16 t.; sf. נְבִיאַי ψ 105[15]; נְבִיאָיו 1 K 22[22]; נְבִיאָו 2 K 17[13], etc.;—**1.** genuine *prophet* of 'י, נביא, anciently called רֹאֶה, 1 S 9[9] (antiquarian note); change prob. occurred in times of Elijah and is first reflected in Ephr. lit. as applied to Abraham Gn 20[7]; Moses Dt 34[10], M. and other early proph. Ho 6[5] 12[11.11.14.14] Am 2[11.12]; of proph. in ecstatic state Nu 12[6] (E), 11[24] (JE). So in Judaic lit., of prophet like Moses Dt 18[15.18] (D), of Aaron (as mouthpiece of M.) Ex 7[1] (P), of Sam. 1 S 3[20], an unknown Ju 6[8]; in time of Sam. proph. were organized in bands: †חֶבֶל נביאים 1 S 10[5.10]; †להקת הנ' 1 S 19[20]; and in time of Elijah were †בְּנֵי הַנְּבִיאִים = members of prophets' guilds 1 K 20[35] 2 K 2[3.5.7.15] 4[1.38.38]; נָבִיא of genuine proph. (besides phrases), in Judaic prophets, only of Jer., Je 1[5]; Ezekiel, Ez 2[5]=33[33]; of ancient prophets Je 28[8.9.9.9] Zc 1[6] 8[9]; esp. †הנביאים הראשׁנים Zc 1[4] 7[7.12], cf. †עבדי(ו) הנביאים *my* (*his*) *servants the prophets* 2 K 9[7] 17[13.23] 21[10] 24[2] (all R[D]) Ezr 9[11] Dn 9[10] Je 7[25] 25[4] 26[5] 29[19] 35[15] 44[4] Am 3[7] Zc 1[6], cf. Ez 38[17] Dn 9[6]; †עבדו הַנּ' *his servant the prophet* 1 K 14[18] 2 K 14[25]; הַנָּבִיא with n. pr.: Jer., 2 Ch 36[12] Dn 9[2]+31 t. Je (but 𝔊 only 4 t., the rest prob. redactional, see Gie[Jer. xxvii]); Elijah 1 K 18[36] (om 𝔊), 2 Ch 21[12] Mal 3[23]; Nathan 2 S 7[2]+10 t. S. and K.; 4 t. Chr. ψ 51[2] (title); Isaiah, 2 K 19[2] 20[1.14]=Is 37[2] 38[1] 39[1]; 2 K 20[11] 2 Ch 26[22] 32[20.32]; Habakkuk Hb 1[1] 3[1] (titles); Haggai, Hg 1[1.3.12] 2[1.10]; Zech., Zc 1[1.7] (titles); elsewh. several others in S., K. and Chr. 15 t.; נביא is used elsewh. of genuine proph. only 1 S 9[9]+34 t. S. and K.; 1 Ch 16[22]=ψ 105[15], +13 t. Chr.; ψ 74[9] complains of absence of נ'; לַחְתֹּם חָזוֹן וְנָבִיא Dn 9[24] v. חתם. **2.** *false prophets:* †prophets as official class, beside priests, charact. as false prophets: Is 28[7] Je 2[26] 4[9] 6[13] 8[1.10] 13[13] 14[18] 18[18] 23[11.33.34] 26[7.8.11.16] 32[32] Zc 7[3], app. also 2 K 23[2] Ne 9[32] La 2[20] Je 29[1] Ez 7[26] (in these not characterized); alw. false (exc. of ancient and special prophets given above) in Am 7[14] Ho 4[5] 9[7.8] Mi 3[5.6.11] Is 3[2] 9[14] 29[10] Je 2[8.30]

5[13.31] 14[13.14.15.15] 23[9+16 t.] 27[9.14.15.16.18] 29[8.15] 37[19] Ez 13[2.2.3.4.9.16] 14[4.7.9.9.10] 22[25.28] Zp 3[4] La 2[9.14] 4[13]; especially discredited Dt 13[2.4.6] 18[20.20.22.22] Zc 13[2.4.5]; such a prophet Hananiah called הַנָּבִיא Je 28[1.5.10.12.15.17] (𝔊 omits in all but v[1], where ψευδοπροφήτης). Usage of prophets themselves gives such a bad flavour to נביא, that we are not surprised that it is absent from exilic Isaiah, the Wisd. Lit., and ψψ (except for special reasons in 3 ψψ given under **1**). †**3.** *heathen prophets* 1 K 18[20] 19[1] 2 K 3[13.13]; נביאי האשרה 1 K 18[19]; נביאי הבעל 1 K 18[19.22.25.40] 2 K 10[19]; 1 K 22[6.10.12.13.22.23] = 2 Ch 18[5.9.11.12.21.22].

5012 †[נָבָא] **vb. denom.** prophesy (in oldest forms, of religious ecstasy with or without song and music; later, essentially religious instruction, with occasional predictions);—**Niph.** *Pf.* 3 ms. נִבָּא Je 20[1] + 7 t.; 2 ms. נִבֵּאתָ Je 20[6] + 2 t.; נִבֵּיתָ Je 26[9]; 1 s. נִבֵּאתִי Ez 37[7]; 3 pl. נִבְּאוּ Je 2[8] + 3 t.; נִבָּאוּ Je 23[21]; *Impf.* 3 ms. יִנָּבֵא Am 3[8] + 9 t. Impf.; *Imv.* הִנָּבֵא Am 7[15] + 27 t.; *Inf.* הִנָּבֵא Am 7[13]; sf. הִנָּבְאוֹ Zc 13[3]; הִנָּבְאֹתוֹ Zc 13[4], + 4 t. Inf.; *Pt.* נִבָּא Je 26[18] + 20 t. Pt.;—**1.** *prophesy* under influence of divine spirit: **a.** in the ecstatic state, with song 1 S 10[11] 19[20] and music 1 Ch 25[1.2.3]. **b.** the word of ׳י: abs. Am 2[12] 3[8] (emend. יחרד We Now needless), 7[12.13] Jo 3[1] Je 19[14] 26[18] 28[9] 32[3] Ez 11[13] 12[27] 21[19] 37[7] 38[17] but esp. in phr. הִנָּבֵא וְאָמַרְתָּ Ez 12[27] 21[14.33] 30[2] 34[2] 36[3] 37[7.12] 38[14.17]; c. acc. Je 20[1] 25[30] 28[6]; sq. עַל *against* Am 7[16] Je 25[13] 26[20] Ez 4[7] 11[4] 13[17] 25[2] 28[21] 29[2] 34[2] 35[2] 36[6] 38[2] 39[1]; *unto* Ez 37[4]; אֶל *unto* Am 7[15] Je 26[11.12] 28[8] Ez 36[1] 37[9]; *against* 6[2] 13[2] 21[2.7]; בְּשֵׁם ׳י Je 11[21] 14[15] 23[25] 26[9]. **2.** of false prophets: abs. Je 23[21] Ez 13[2] Zc 13[3.3.4]; c. acc. 1 K 22[12] = 2 Ch 18[11]; לַשֶּׁקֶר Je 14[14] 23[25] 27[10.14.16] 29[21]; לְ 27[15]; בַּשֶּׁקֶר 5[31] 20[6] 29[9]; נִבְאֵי הַשׁ׳ 23[26], cf. v[32]; c. לְ 14[16] 23[16] 27[15.16] 29[31] 37[19]; sq. אֶל *concerning* Ez 13[16]. **3.** cf. *heathen prophets*, בַּבַּעַל Je 2[8]. **Hithp.** *Pf.* 2 ms. הִתְנַבִּיתָ 1 S 10[6]; 1 s. הִנַּבֵּאתִי Ez 37[10]; *Impf.* יִתְנַבֵּא 1 S 10[10] + 7 t.; 3 mpl. יִתְנַבְּאוּ Nu 11[25] + 5 t.; *Imv.* הִנַּבְּאוּ Je 23[13]; *Inf.* הִתְנַבּוֹת 1 S 10[13]; *Pt.* מִתְנַבֵּא Je 26[20] + 9 t. Pt.;—**1.** *prophesy* under influence of divine spirit: **a.** in the ecstatic state Nu 11[25.26.27] (J), with music 1 S 10[5.6.10.13], in frenzy 1 S 19[20.21.21.23.24]; excited to violence 1 S 18[10] (= מְשֻׁגָּע *mad* 2 K 9[11]); Je 29[26]. **b.** apart from ecstatic state, abs. Ez 37[10], c. לְ 1 K 22[8] Je 29[27]; עַל 1 K 22[18] = 2 Ch 18[17], 2 Ch 18[7] 20[37]; בְּשֵׁם ׳י Je 26[20]. **2.** of heathen prophets of Baal in ecstatic state 1 K 18[29]; בַּבַּעַל Je 23[13]. **3.** of false prophets 1 K 22[10] = 2 Ch 18[9], Je 14[14] Ez 13[17].

†נְבוּאָה **n.f. prophecy** (late: earlier syn. 5016
חָזוֹן);—**1. a.** specific and genuine 2 Ch 15[8]. **b.** false Ne 6[12]. **2.** prophetic writing עַל־נְבוּאַת אֲחִיָּה 2 Ch 9[29].

†נְבִיאָה **n.f. prophetess**;—**1. a.** of the 5031
ancient type endowed with gift of song, Miriam Ex 15[20]; Deborah Ju 4[4]. **b.** of the later type consulted for a word of ׳י, Huldah 2 K 22[14] = 2 Ch 34[22]. **2.** false prophetess, Noadiah Ne 6[14]. **3.** wife of Isaiah Is 8[3].

†[נָבַב] **vb. hollow out** (cf. As. *imbubu,* 5014
flute, Dl[HWB 443], NH אַבּוּב *id.*, Aram. ܐܒܘܒܐ, אַבּוּבָא *id.;* hence also Ar. أُنْبُوبٌ *knots* in reed, *part of* reed *between knots, reed;* vid. Hoffm [LCB 1882, 321] Frä[23] Fl in Levy[TW i. 417]);—**Qal** *Pt. pass.* נָבוּב Jb 11[12] Je 52[21]; נְבוּב Ex 27[8] 38[7];—*hollowed, hollow:* of altar of tabern. נְבוּב לֻחוֹת Ex 27[8] 38[7] (P); of pillar in temple Je 52[21]; fig. אִישׁ נָבוּב Jb 11[12], i.e. *empty, hollow-minded* man.

נֹבַה v. נֹב. p. 611 5011

†I. נְבוֹ **n.pr.loc.** (prob. connex., at least 5015
for **2**, with (Bab.) god *Nebo, Nabû,* cf. II. נְבוֹ and Bae[Rel. 15, 89, 259]; yet not certain, Nö[ZMG xlii. 1888, 470] comp. Ar. النَّبَاوَةُ *the height,* etc.): 𝔊 Ναβαυ;—**1. a.** city in Moab Nu 32[3.38] (where assigned to Reuben; both JE = נבה MI[14]) Is 15[2] Je 48[1.22] 1 Ch 5[8]; prob. on or near Mt. Nebo (v. infr.), cf. Buhl[Geogr. 266 f.] Tristr[Moab 338]. **b.** city in Judah, בְּנֵי נ׳ Ezr 2[29] = אַנְשֵׁי נ׳ אַחֵר Ne 7[34] (*the men of the other N.,* so disting.—si אחר vera l., cf. Ryle—fr. **a**? or fr. another נֹב?), Ezr 10[43];—this נבו in Judah perhaps = נֹב **1** q. v. **2.** mt. in Moab, where Moses died Nu 33[47] Dt 32[49] (הַר־נְבוֹ), 34[1] (*id.;* all P), six miles W. of Heshbon acc. to Onom. (ed. Lag[283]). Prob. = mod. *Nebâ* at NE. corner of Dead Sea, Survey [E. Pal. i. 198 ff.] GASm[Geogr. 562 ff.] Buhl[Geogr. 266 f.] Tristr [Moab 318, 338] Merrill[E. of Jordan, 242 ff.].—Cf. פִּסְגָּה.

†II. נְבוֹ **n.pr.div.** Nebo (loan-wd. in Heb., 5015
cf. Ph. n.pr.m. נבו; = As. *Nabû,* Schr[COT Gloss. and Is 46, 1] Jastrow[Rel. Bab. 124 ff.] Jen[Kosmol. pass.] Tiele[Ass. u. Bab. Gesch. 532 f.] Say[Rel. Bab. 112 ff.] (cf. Palm. n.pr. נבוזבד, ברנבו Vog[Palm. No. 73]), and this perh. √ *nabû, call, name,* v. נבא);—Babylonian god כָּרַע בֵּל קֹרֵס נְבוֹ Is 46[1].

5018 †נְבוּזַרְאֲדָן **n.pr.m.** (= *Nabû-zêr-iddin, Nebo hath given seed,* Schr[COT 2 K 25, 8]);—general of Nebuchadrezzar, always entitled רַב־טַבָּחִים 2 K 25[8.11.20] = Je 52[12.15.26]; Je 39[9.10.11.13] 40[1] 41[10] 43[6] 52[16.30].

5019 †נְבוּכַדְרֶאצַּר† and (incorrectly) נְבוּכַדְנֶאצַּר (v. also infr.) **n.pr.m. Nebuchadrezzar, Nebuchadnezzar** (Bab. *Nabû-kudurri-uṣur* = (prob.) *Nebo, protect the boundary!* Dl[Calwer BL] Budge[Nebuchadn.] (on *kudurru, boundary,* v. Dl[HWB 319]); poss. is also *crown,* and so Schr[COT 2 K 24, 1]; Jäger[BAS i. 471] prop. (*thy*) *servant*);—𝔊 Ναβουχοδονοσ(σ)ορ; Can. Ptol. Ναβοκολασσαρου Schr[COT 490], Abydenos etc. Ναβουκοδρόσορος, v. Schr[ib. 2 K 24, 1];—the great king of Babylon (reigned B.C. 605–562), who captured Jerus. and carried Judah captive: most oft. נְבוּכַדְרֶאצַּר מֶלֶךְ בָּבֶל (נ׳ oft. om. in 𝔊) Je 21[2.7] (but om. 𝔊 Gie), 22[25] 25[1.9] 29[21] 32[28] 34[1] (v. Baer's note; van d. H נבוכדנ׳), 35[11] 37[1] 39[1.5] (v. on 34[1]), v[11] 43[10] 44[30] 46[2.13.26] 49[30] 50[17] 51[34] 52[4.12] Ez 26[7] 29[18.19.30]; so Qr Je 49[28] (Kt נבוכדראצור מ׳ ב׳); נְבוּכַדְרֶאצַּר (מֶלֶךְ בָּבֶל om.) Je 32[1] 52[28.29.30]. Spelt corruptly with *n,* נְבוּכַדְנֶאצַּר מ׳ ב׳ (cf. Schr[COT 2 K 24, 1 n.]) 2 Ch 36[6] Dn 1[1] Je 27[6.8.20] 28[3] 29[3] Ezr 2[1] Qr (Kt נבוכדנצור מ׳ ב׳, cf. Je 49[8] supr.); נְבוּכַדְנֶאצַּר alone 2 Ch 36[7.10.13] (הַמֶּלֶךְ נ׳), Je 29[1]; נְבֻכַדְנֶאצַּר 2 K 24[1.10.11] 25[1.8.22] Je 28[11.14]; נְבֻכַדְנֶאצַּר מ׳ ב׳ 1 Ch 5[41]; נְבוּכַדְנֶצַּר מ׳ ב׳ Ne 7[6] Est 2[6]; נְבוּכַדְנֶצַּר Ezr 1[7] (מ׳ ב׳ om.), נְבֻכַדְנֶצַּר Dn 2[1.1], נְבֻכַדְנֶצַּר 1[18] (v. also Tobit 14[5], Jud 1[1] + oft., as 𝔊 supr.)—On N. v. further Tiele[Bab.-Ass. Gesch. 421 ff., 454 ff.]

5021 †נְבוּשַׁזְבָּן **n.pr.m.** (= *Nabû-šêzib-anni, Nebo delivers me,* Schr[COT Je 39, 13]);—officer of Nebuchadrezzar, called רַב־סָרִים (q.v.) Je 39[13].

5022 נָבוֹת[22] **n.pr.m.** a Jezreelite;—1 K 21[1.2.3] + 16 t. 1 K 21; 2 K 9[21.25.26]. 𝔊 Ναβουθαι.

5024 †[נָבַח] **vb. bark** (of dogs) (NH *id.;* Ar. نَبَحَ; Eth. ነበሐ:; Aram. ܢܒܚ, נְבַח);—**Qal** *Inf. cstr.* only כֻּלָּם כְּלָבִים אִלְּמִים לֹא יוּכְלוּ לִנְבֹּחַ Is 56[10] fig. of helpless prophets.

5025 †נֹבַח **n.pr.m. et loc.** **1. m.** a Manassite Nu 32[42] (JE), 𝔊 Ναβαυ. **2. loc.** in Gilead Ju 8[11], 𝔊 Ναβαι, Ναβε(θ); Nu 32[42] (formerly קְנָת, q.v.), 𝔊 Ναβωθ.

5026 †נִבְחַז **n.pr.div.** god of men of Avva, 2 K 17[31]; name otherwise unknown, cf. Sch[COT ad loc.]; 𝔊B τὴν Ἐβλαζέρ, 𝔊L Ἐβλαιεζέρ, A Ἀβααζέρ καὶ τὴν Ναιβας; Thes comp. Mand. denom. נבאז = ܢܒܙ (Cod. Nasar. Norberg.) Codd. give variant נבחן cf. Baer[ad loc.] Frensdorff[Mas. Magna i. 306].

†[נָבַט] **vb. Pi., Hiph.** look (NH Pi. *id.;* 5027
Ar. نَبَطَ is *well* or *issue forth* (of water). As. *nabâṭu* is *shine* Dl[HWB 443]; Sab. epith. נבט *protector* (? lit. looking with consideration upon Mordt[ZMG xxx. 1876, 37]); n.pr. נבטאל *God has seen,* i.e. *considered* Levy-Os[ZMG xix. 1865, 231]);—**Pi.** *Pf.* consec. וְנִבַּט Is 5[30] *look* (lit.), sq. לְ. **Hiph.** *Pf.* הִבִּיט Nu 21[9] + 3 t.; וְהִבַּטְתָּ 1 S 2[32], etc.; *Impf.* יַבִּיט Nu 12[8] + 4 t.; וַיַּבֵּט 1 S 17[42] + 4 t., etc.; *Imv.* הַבֵּט 1 K 18[43] +; הַבִּיט ψ 142[5] (or *Inf. abs.*), cf. La 5[1] Kt; הַבִּיטָה ψ 13[4] +, etc.; *Inf. cstr.* הַבִּיט Ex 3[6] +, etc.; *Pt.* מַבִּיט ψ 104[32];—*look:* **1.** lit., **a.** human subj., sq. אֶל־ Ex 3[6] (E), Nu 21[9] (JE), Is 8[22] (|| פָּנָה לְמָעְלָה v[21]), cf. 51[6], Jon 2[5]; sq. עַל־ Hb 2[15]; sq. אַחֲרֵי Gn 19[17.26] (J), Ex 33[8] (E), 1 S 24[9]; sq. ה ָ loc., Gn 15[5] (שָׁמַיְמָה), cf. Jb 35[5] (שָׁמַיִם); sq. דֶּרֶךְ־יָם 1 K 18[43]; sq. acc. = *look upon, behold* Nu 12[8] (E), Is 38[11]; abs. Jb 6[19] 1 S 17[42] (|| רָאָה), 1 K 18[43] 19[6] (sq. הִנֵּה), 1 Ch 21[21] (|| רָאָה), so ψ 22[18]. **b.** subj. eagle, abs. Jb 39[29] (sq. adv. לְמֵרָחוֹק). **2.** fig.: sq. אֶל *regard, shew regard to* 1 S 16[7] (אֶל־מַרְאֵהוּ), cf. 2 K 3[14] (|| רָאָה); *pay attention to,* sq. אֶל־ Is 22[8]; = *consider* Is 51[1.2]; *look unto* י׳, sq. אֶל־ ψ 34[6] (read Imv. pl. 𝔊 𝔖 Che), Is 22[11] Zc 12[10]; cf. ψ 119[6] sq. אֶל־כָּל־מִצְוֹת; cf. also Jb 36[25] (abs., sq. מֵרָחוֹק); sq. acc. אֹרְחֹתֶיךָ ψ 119[15], cf. v[18], Is 5[12]; sq. acc. וַתַּבֵּט בְּשׁוּרַי בְּ׳, עֵינִי אָוֶן Nu 23[21] (|| רָאָה); subj. ψ 92[12] *see its desire upon, gloat over* (cf. רָאָה בְּ), diff. 1 S 2[32]; sq. acc. adv. ψ 142[5] (יָמִין) *to the right;* || רָאָה); abs. Is 42[18] (sq. לִרְאוֹת of purpose); 63[5] Hb 1[5] (|| רָאָה), so ψ 91[8] (בְּעֵינֶיךָ), cf. Pr 4[25], sq. לְנֹכַח (subj. עֵינֶיךָ || יַיְשִׁרוּ נֶגְדֶּךָ). **3.** subj. י׳: sq. מִשָּׁמַיִם + אֶל ψ 102[20]; sq. אֶל־ = *look upon,* i.e. endure to see Hb 1[13] (|| רָאָה); so sq. acc. v[13], cf. 1[3] (or *causat.* Ew; || תַּרְאֵנִי); sq. לְ, ψ 104[32] Jb 28[24]; ψ 74[20] (לַבְּרִית); sq. acc. Is 64[8] (|| הֵן), La 3[63] ψ 10[14] (|| רָאָה); = *regard, shew regard to,* Am 5[22] ψ 84[10] La 4[16], cf. ψ 13[4]; sq. אֶל־ *id.* Is 66[2]; abs. ψ 94[9] i.e. *have power of sight,* Is 18[4]; sq. מִשָּׁמַיִם ψ 33[13] 80[15] Is 63[15] (|| רָאָה), La 1[11] (|| רָאָה), so v[12] 2[20] 5[1].

†[מַבָּט] **n.m.**[Zc 9, 5] **expectation** = object of 4007
hope or confidence (lit. *thing looked to*);—sf. מַבָּטֵנוּ Is 20[6], מַבָּטָם v[5], מֶבָּטָהּ Zc 9[5];—of Cush

as ally of Judah Is $20^{5.6}$; of Tyre as ally of Philistia Zc 9^{5}.

5028 †נְבָט **n.pr.m.** father of Jerob. I (cf. Sab. נבטאל, נבט, v. נָבַט supr.);—only in phrase יָרָבְעָם בֶּן־נְבָט 1 K 11^{26} $12^{2.15}$ 15^{1} $16^{3.26.31}$ 21^{22} 22^{53} 2 K 3^{3} 9^{9} 10^{29} $13^{2.11}$ 14^{24} $15^{9.18.24.28}$ 17^{21} 23^{15} 2 Ch 9^{29} $10^{2.15}$ 13^{6}. 𝔊 Ναβαθ, Ναβατ.

5032 †נְבָיוֹת **n.pr.gent.** (Nab. נבטו = *Nabataean* and *Nabataeans*, Eut[Nab 1, 4] and oft., cf. נבט of Jewish trad. Nö[ZMG xxv. 1871, 124], נבט 𝔗[Is 60, 7] (on form of name, and on ט = ת cf. Lag[BN 51 f.]); in As. *Nabaitai*, etc., Schr[COT Gn 25, 13; KGF 99 ff.] Dl[Par 296 f.]);—as (eldest) son of Ishmael (brother of Kedar) Gn 25^{13} 28^{9} 36^{3} (all P), 1 Ch 1^{29}; people (‖ Kedar) Is 60^{7}, cf. *Nabataei* + *Cedrei* Plin[NH v. 11, 65]; 𝔊 Ναβαιωθ; Gk. Ναβαταῖοι.—See further Nö[ZMG xxv. 1871, 122 f.] Eut[Nab p. 78] GASm[Geogr. 547–629 pass.]

5033 †[נֵבֶךְ] **n.[m.] spring** (si vera l.) (√unknown);—only pl. cstr. נִבְכֵי־יָם Jb 38^{16} *the springs, sources of the ocean* (‖ חֵקֶר תְּהוֹם);—Ol Siegf נִבְלֵי; Bu suggests מַבֻּעֵי = נבעי as poss.; but Gr Perles rd. נִבְכֵי Jb 28^{11}, also, for Mass. מִבְּכִי, cf. נָהָר **2**.

†I. נבל (√of foll.; meaning dubious).

5035 I. נֵבֶל **n.m.**[Je 13, 12] **1. skin-bottle, skin**; **2. jar, pitcher**;—נֵבֶל abs. 1 S 10^{5}+; cstr. v³+(on נֶבֶל v. Baer[1 S 1, 24]);—**1.** *skin of wine,* נֵבֶל יַיִן 1 S 1^{24} 10^{3} 2 S 16^{1}, cf. also Je $13^{12.12}$; pl. נִבְלֵי יַיִן 1 S 25^{18}: fig. נִבְלֵי שָׁמַיִם Jb 38^{37} i.e. *clouds* (‖ שְׁחָקִים). **2.** earthen *jar, pitcher*: fig. of connexions of Eliakim כְּלֵי נְבָלִים Is 22^{24}; נִבְלֵיהֶם יְנַפֵּצוּ Je 48^{12} (‖ כֵּלִים יָרִיקוּ) in fig. of Moab (cf. ψ 2^{9}); נִבְלֵי־חֶרֶשׂ La 4^{2} sim. of men of Judah (‖ מַעֲשֵׂה יְדֵי יוֹצֵר); sim. of destruction of Judah, שֵׁבֶר נֵבֶל יוֹצְרִים Is 30^{14}.

5035 †II. נֵבֶל, נֶבֶל **n.m.**[ψ 57, 9] a musical instrument, either a portable **harp**, or a **lute, guitar** (with bulging resonance-body at lower end); (perh. = I. נֵבֶל, and then shape seems to favour *lute*; perh. independent word, e.g. Egyptian loan-word, cf. *nfr, lute,* We[Hpt 222]);—abs. נֵבֶל 1 S 10^{5} + 3 t., נֶבֶל ψ 71^{22} + 3 t.; נָבֶל Am 6^{5} + 2 t.; pl. נְבָלִים 2 S 6^{5} + 4 t.; sf. נְבָלֶיךָ Am 5^{23} Is 14^{11};—*harp* (or *lute*), played at feasts and religious ceremonies, probably less simple, cheap and common than כִּנּוֹר (q.v.; oft. named with נ׳):—as mark of luxury, revelry Am 5^{23} 6^{5} Is 14^{11}, so 5^{12} (כִּנּוֹר נ׳ תֹּף חָלִיל), also (not in bad sense) 1 K 10^{12}; played by wandering band of prophets 1 S 10^{5} (list as Is 5^{12}); in worship 2 S 6^{5}; elsewh. only ψψ Chr. always in worship: ψ 57^{9} 81^{3} 92^{4} 108^{3} 150^{3}; כְּלִי נֶבֶל 71^{22}; נ׳ עָשׂוֹר *a harp with ten strings* 33^{2} 144^{9}; 1 Ch 13^{8} $15^{16.20.28}$ 16^{5} (כְּלֵי נְבָלִים), $25^{1.6}$ 2 Ch 5^{12} 9^{11} 20^{28} 29^{25} Ne 12^{27}.—Cf. further Benz[Arch. 273 ff.] Now[Arch. i. 273 ff.] Dr[Amos 234 ff.] We[Hpt 222 ff.]

†II. נָבֵל **vb. be senseless, foolish** (NH 5034
נְבָלָה, נַבְלוּת of immodesty; Ar. نَبُلَ = (per contra) *be noble, distinguished,* نَبَلَ also *be gracious* (Frey); Aram. נְבַל Pa. *reject, despise,* v. 𝔗 Ne 3^{6} Je 14^{21}; in deriv. as NH);—**Qal** *Pf.* 2 ms. נָבַלְתָּ Pr 30^{32} *if thou hast been foolish* in lifting up thyself (opp. זַמּוֹתָ). **Pi.** *Pf.* 1 s. sf. consec. וְנִבַּלְתִּיךְ Na 3^{6}; *Impf.* 3 ms. וַיְנַבֵּל Dt 32^{15}; 2 ms. תְּנַבֵּל Je 14^{21}; *Pt.* מְנַבֵּל Mi 7^{6};—*regard* or *treat as a* נָבָל (q.v.), i.e. *with contumely,* c. acc.: בֵּן מְנַבֵּל אָב Mi 7^{6} *son treateth father as a fool* (with contumely); וַיְנַ׳ צוּר Dt 32^{15} *and he treated with contumely the Rock* of his salvation (i.e. י׳; ‖ נטשׁ); י׳ subj., Na 3^{6} *I will treat thee* (Nineveh) *with contumely* (‖ וְהִשְׁלַכְתִּי עָלַיִךְ שִׁקֻּצִים); Je 14^{21} do not *treat with contumely* the throne of thy glory (‖ נאץ).

†I. נָבָל **adj. foolish, senseless,** esp. of the 5036
man who has no perception of ethical and religious claims, and with collat. idea of *ignoble, disgraceful*;—abs. נ׳ 2 S 3^{33} + 14 t.; mpl. נְבָלִים 13^{13} Ez 13^{3} (𝔊 Co מִלִּבָּם); fpl. נְבָלוֹת Jb 2^{10};—*senseless,* esp. of religious and moral insensibility: עַם נ׳ Dt 32^{6} (of Isr., unappreciative of J.'s benefits; opp. חָכָם), so of heathen nation ψ 74^{18} (blaspheming name of י׳), גּוֹי נ׳ Dt 32^{21} (‖ לֹא עָם) הַנְּבִאִים הַנְּ׳ Ez 13^{3} (si vera l., v. supr.); elsewh. as **subst.** (impious and presumptuous) fool, Is 32^{5} (opp. נָדִיב *noble-minded*), characterized as at once irreligious and churlish, v⁶; denying God ψ 14^{1} = 53^{2}; insulting God 74^{22}, and God's servant 39^{9}; Pr 17^{7} arrogant speech becometh not *the* (impious and presumptuous) *fool* (whose faults it only makes the more conspicuous), much less do lying lips him that is noble (נדיב), v²¹ (‖ כְּסִיל), 30^{22} ונבל כי ישׂבע לחם (one of the things under which the earth trembles), בְּנֵי נָבָל Jb 30^{8} i.e. ignoble men (‖ בְּנֵי בְלִי־שֵׁם); as one who might be expected

to have a contumelious end, הַכְּמוֹת נ׳ ימות אבנר ? 2 S 3^{33} was Abnor (destined) to die, as a נ׳ dieth ? of the man who amasses riches unjustly ובאחריתו יהיה נבל Je 17^{11} i.e. will prove himself to be a נ׳; as acting immorally (with collat. idea of disgracefully) 2 S 13^{13} ואתה תהיה כְּאַחַד הַנְּבָלִים בישׂראל (cf. נְבָלָה); f. only in כְּדַבֵּר אחת הַנְּבָלוֹת Jb 2^{10} (of Job's wife). Cf. Dr $^{Dt 22, 21. 32, 6. 15. 21; Psalt. 457}$.

5037 II. נָבָל **n.pr.m.** (on popular etymol. see 1 S 25^{25} infr.);—a churlish man of Carmel, whose widow David married 1 S $25^{3.4.5.9.10.14.19.25.25}$ (כִּשְׁמוֹ כֶּן־הוּא נָבָל שְׁמוֹ וּנְבָלָה עִמּוֹ), v^{26} + 10 t. 1 S + 2 S 2^2 3^3. 𝔊 Ναβαλ.

5039 †נְבָלָה **n.f. senselessness** (as shewn in disregard of moral and religious claims), esp. of disgraceful sins; also **disgrace**;—alw. abs. נ׳;—**1.** *disgraceful folly*, esp. of sins of unchastity Ju 19^{23} (*wanton deed* GFM), so דְּבַר הַנּ׳ הַזֹּאת v^{24}, 2 S 13^{12}; oft. עָשָׂה נ׳ בְּיִשְׂרָאֵל i.e. do a thing disgraceful acc. to Isr.'s standard: Gn 34^7 (J), Dt 22^{21} (cf. Dr on mng. of wd.; only here of woman), Ju 20^6 (+ זִמָּה), v^{10} Je 29^{23} (cf. לֹא יֵעָשֶׂה כֵן בְּיִשְׂרָאֵל 2 S 13^{12}); also of inhospitable churlishness 1 S 25^{25} (v. I, II. נָבָל, and esp. Is 32^6); of profane action Jos 7^{15} (Achan; עָשָׂה נ׳ בְּיִשְׂרָאֵל); of senseless and irreligious language Is 9^{16} דֹּבֵר, 32^6 (יְדַבֵּר). **2.** *contumely, disgrace* עֲשׂוֹת עִמָּכֶם נ׳ Jb 42^8 (of י׳), i.e. *deal out to you disgrace*, expose you and punish you as נְבָלִים (cf. 2 S 3^{33}, sub נָבָל), because of your utterances about me.

5040 †נַבְלוּת **n.f. immodesty, shamelessness,** *lewdness* of Isr. under fig. of adulteress Ho 2^{12}.

5034 †נָבֵל **vb. sink or drop down, languish, wither and fall, fade** (NH *id.*; As. *nabâlu*, *destroy*, Dl $^{HWB\ 443\ f.}$ Ar. نَبَلَ v, VIII. *die*; Aram. נְבֵילָא *corpse*);—**Qal** *Pf.* 3 ms. נ׳ Is $40^{7.8}$ Je 8^{13}; 3 fs. נָבְלָה Is $24^{4.4}$; *Impf.* 3 ms. יִבּוֹל ψ 1^3 + 4 t. (on form cf. Ges $^{§ 43, 3, R. 1, h}$ Ol $^{§ 246 e}$), 2 ms. תִּבֹּל Ex 18^{18}; 3 mpl. יִבְּלוּ 2 S 22^{46} = ψ 18^{46}, יִבּוֹלוּן ψ 37^2; 1 pl. וַנָּבֶל Is 64^5 (on form cf. Di and Ol $^{§ 236 e}$); *Inf. abs.* נָבֹל Ex 18^{18}; cstr. נְבֹל Is 34^4; *Pt.* נֹבֵל Is $28^{1.4}$; f. נֹבֶלֶת abs. Is 34^4; cstr. Is 1^{30};—**1.** *sink* or *drop down*, fr. exhaustion נָבֹל תִּבֹּל Ex 18^{18} (Moses and Isr.); fr. discouragement 2 S 22^{46} = ψ 18^{46} (of foreigners, foes of Isr.); of mt. הַר־נֹפֵל יִבּוֹל Jb 14^{18} (but נָפוֹל יִפּוֹל Lag $^{Proph. Chald.}$ Siegf Baer, after 𝔊, so Bu [or יִבְלֶה]; Du נָבוֹל יִבּוֹל). **2.** usu. *fall* like a leaf, or flower *wither and fall, fade*: כְּאֵלָה נֹבֶלֶת עָלֶהָ Is 1^{30} *like an oak falling as to its leaves* (sim. of people of Jerus.); the host of heaven יִבּוֹל כִּנְבֹל עָלֶה מִגֶּפֶן וּכְנֹבֶלֶת מִתְּאֵנָה Is 34^4; לֹא יִבּ׳ עָלֵהוּ Ez 47^{12} (trees in Ezek.'s vision), so fig. of good man ψ 1^3; of Isr. Je 8^{13}, וַנָּבֶל כֶּעָלֶה Is 64^5; also צִיץ נֹבֵל $40^{7.8}$ (both ‖ יָבֵשׁ חָצִיר), נֹבֵל צִיץ 28^1, cf. v^4; of wicked ψ 37^2 כְּיֶרֶק דֶּשֶׁא יִבּ׳ (‖ כֶּחָצִיר יִמָּלוּ); of devastated earth אָבְלָה נָבְלָה הָאָרֶץ אֻמְלְלָה נָבְלָה תֵּבֵל Is 24^4.

†נְבֵלָה **n.f. carcass, corpse** (as *inert, flabby*);—נ׳ abs. 1 K 13^{24}+; cstr. נִבְלַת v^{29}+; sf. נְבֵלָתִי Is 26^{19}; נִבְלָתְךָ Dt 28^{26} 1 K 13^{22}; נִבְלָתוֹ Jos 8^{29} + 6 t.; נִבְלָתָהּ Lv $11^{39.40.40}$; נִבְלָתָם Is 5^{25} + 14 t.;—*carcass, corpse*: **1. a.** human (not in Ez P, (H), which use פֶּגֶר); Jos 8^{29} (JE), 1 K $13^{22.24.24.25.25.28.28.28.29.30}$ 2 K 9^{37} Je 26^{23} 36^{30} Dt 21^{23} 28^{26}; coll. *corpses* Is 5^{25} 26^{19} (wish for restoration to life), Je 7^{33} 9^{21} 16^4 19^7 34^{20} ψ 79^2. **b.** of lifeless idols, coll. נִבְלַת שִׁקּוּצֵיהֶם וגו׳ Je 16^{18}. **2.** of animals (clean and unclean, wild animals, cattle, birds and reptiles, chiefly Lv Ez), Dt 14^8; Lv $5^{2.2.2}$ $11^{8.11.24.25.27.28.35.36.37.38}$ 17^{15} (all P); נ׳ specif. = body of animal dying of itself Dt 14^{21}; Lv 7^{24} $11^{39.40.40}$ (P), 22^8 (H), Ez 4^{14} 44^{31}. 5038

†נְבַלָּט **n.pr.loc.** place where Benjamites dwelt Ne 11^{34}. 𝔊L Ναβαλατ. Mod. Beit Nebâlâ, 6 m. NE. from Lydda, acc. to Guérin $^{Sam. ii. 67 f.}$; Mishn. בית נבלטא Buhl $^{Ges\ 12;\ Geogr.\ 197}$. 5041

†[נָבַע] **vb. flow, spring, bubble up,** poet. and late (NH *id.* (rare); As. *nabû*, *id.*, Dl $^{HWB\ 442}$; Ar. نَبَعَ *well* or *issue forth* (of water); Aram. ܢܒܰܥ, נְבַע; Eth. ነብዐ: II. *weep*, አንብዐ: *tear(s)*);—**Qal** *Pt.* נַחַל נֹבֵעַ Pr 18^4 *a flowing wady*, metaph. of מְקוֹר חָכְמָה. **Hiph.** *Impf.* יַבִּיעַ ψ 19^3 + 3 t.; אַבִּיעָה ψ 78^2 Pr 1^{23}; יַבִּיעוּ ψ 94^4 145^7; יַבִּיעוּן ψ 59^8; 3 fpl. תַּבַּעְנָה ψ 119^{171};—*pour out, emit, cause to bubble, belch forth*: **1.** *pour out*, fig. אַבִּיעָה לָכֶם רוּחִי Pr 1^{23} (‖ אוֹדִיעָה דְבָרַי אֶתְכֶם). **2.** *cause to bubble, ferment* זְבוּבֵי מָוֶת יַבְאִישׁ יַבִּיעַ שֶׁמֶן רוֹקֵחַ Ec 10^1. **3.** fig., usually of speech, *pour forth, emit, belch forth*, emphat. expression: פִּי רְשָׁעִים יַבִּיעַ רָעוֹת Pr 15^{28} (opp. לֵב צַדִּיק יֶהְגֶּה לַעֲנוֹת) i.e. the righteous 5042

considers before he speaks, the wicked bursts out with reckless utterance; כִּי כְסִילִים יַבִּיעַ אִוֶּלֶת Pr 15^{2} (opp. לְשׁוֹן חֲכָמִים תֵּיטִיב דָּעַת); יַבִּיעוּ יְדַבְּרוּ עָתָק ψ 94^{4} (|| יִתְאַמְּרוּ כָּל־פֹּעֲלֵי אָוֶן); יַבִּ׳ בְּפִיהֶם 59^{8} (|| חֲרָבוֹת בְּשִׂפְתוֹתֵיהֶם); in good sense, אַבִּיעָה חִידוֹת 78^{2} (|| אֶפְתְּחָה בְמָשָׁל פִּי); תַּבַּעְנָה שְׂפָתַי תְּהִלָּה 119^{171}; זֵכֶר רַב־טוּבְךָ יַבִּיעוּ 145^{7} (|| וְצִדְקָתְךָ יְרַנֵּנוּ), cf. also v^{6}); metaph. יוֹם לְיוֹם יַבִּ׳ אֹמֶר 19^{3}, i. e. though silent, it really *pours forth* speech.

4002 †מַבּוּעַ **n.[m.]** spring of water (As. *nambaʾu* Dl$^{HWB\,442}$, Ar. مَنْبَعٌ, Syr. ܡܒܘܥܐ);—abs. מ׳ Ec 12^{6}; pl. cstr. מַבּוּעֵי מַיִם Is 35^{7} 49^{10} (for returning exiles).

5044 נִבְשָׁן v. בשׁן. p. 143

נגב (√ of foll. = *be dry, parched*, NH נָגַב, Aram. נְגִיב, נְגוּב, ܢܓܒ).

5045 †נֶ֫גֶב **n.[m.]** south-country, Negeb, south (cf. Lag$^{BN\,78}$);—נ׳ abs. Gn 20^{1}+; cstr. Jos 11^{2}+; נֶ֫גְבָּה Gn 13^{14}+;—**1.** *south-country*, i.e. **a.** specif. the region S. of Judah, boundaries not exactly defined (see cities in it Jos 15$^{21-32}$), but c. fr. hills S. of Hebron to Ḳadesh, אֶרֶץ הַנֶּ׳ Gn 20^{1} (E), 24^{62} (J), Nu 13^{29} (JE), Ju 1^{15} Jos 15^{19}; alm. = n.pr. הַנֶּ׳, הַנֶּ֫גְבָּה, Gn 12^{9} 13^{1} Nu 13$^{17.22}$ 21^{1} (all J), Dt 34^{3} (JE), Dt 1^{7} Jos 10^{40} 11^{16} 12^{8} (all D), Nu 33^{40} Jos 15^{21} (both P), Ju 1^{9} 1 S 20^{41} (but rd. הָאַרְגָּב, i.e. *the mound* 𝔊 (ἀργαβ) Th We Klo Dr Kit Bu HPS), Je 13^{19} 17^{26} 32^{44} 33^{13} Zc 7^{7} Ob^{20} ψ 126^{4} (sim.), Ez 21^{3a} (= Judah); נ׳ (no art.) Gn 13^{3} (J), 1 S 30^{1}, Is 30^{6} (cf. Di); of particular districts in the Negeb: נ׳ עֲרָד Ju 1^{16} (cf. GFM), נ׳ יהוּדָה etc. 1 S 27$^{10.10.10}$ (cf. Dr), 30$^{14.14}$ 2 S 24^{7} 2 Ch 28^{18}; v. also Zc 14^{10}; רָמַת נ׳ Jos 19^{8}, רָמוֹת נ׳ 1 S 30^{27}; coll. c. pl. vb. = *people of south-land* Ob^{19}. **b.** land S. of Babylon Is 21^{1} (cf. Di). **c.** = Egypt Dn 11$^{5.6.9.11.14.15.25.25.29.40}$ (v. Meinh Bev Behrm, cf. v^{43}). **2.** hence *south* (opp. N., E., W.) Gn 13^{14} 28^{14} (both J), Jos 17^{10} (P), 1 K 7^{25} = 2 Ch 4^{4}, 1 Ch 9^{24} 26$^{15.17}$ (cf. v$^{14.16.18}$), Ez 21$^{3b.9}$ Dn 8$^{4.9}$, further 1 K 7^{39} Zc 14^{4}; פְּאַת נֶ֫גְבָּה תֵּימָ֫נָה Ex 26^{18}, cf. 27^{9} 36^{23} 38^{9} 40^{24} (of S. side of tabernacle); שַׁעַר נ׳ Ez 46$^{9.9}$; פְּאַת נ׳ *south side* or *border* Nu 34^{3} 35^{5} Jos 18^{15} (all P), Ez 47^{19}, cf. v^{19} 48$^{16.28.33}$; גְּבוּל נ׳ *south boundary* Nu 34^{3} Jos 15$^{2.4}$ 18^{19} (all P), cf. (הַגְּבוּל) מִנֶּ֫גֶב לְ *on the south of* Nu 34$^{4.4}$ Jos 15^{3} (אֶל־מִנֶּ׳ לְ), v$^{3.7}$ 18^{3} (all P), Ju 21^{19}; מִנֶּ׳ abs. *on the south* Jos 18^{5} (JE), 19^{34} (P), 1 S 14^{5} Ez 40^{2}; כֶּ֫תֶף הַיְבוּסִי מִנֶּ׳ Jos 15^{8}, cf. 18$^{13.16}$ (all P); נֶ֫גְבָּה 15$^{1.2}$ 18$^{14.14.19}$ (all P), 2 Ch 4^{10} Ez 21^{2} (Co; 𝔖 נגב), 48$^{10.17}$; נֶ֫גְבָּה לְ Jos 17^{9} (P).—For כִּנֲרוֹת נ׳ 11^{2} rd. נֶגֶד (𝔊 Di).

[נָגַד]$_{363}$ **vb. be conspicuous** (NH in deriv.; Ph. n.pr.m. נגד; Ar. نَجَدَ *conquer, overcome*, also *be apparent, conspicuous*; نَجْدٌ *high land* or *country*; نَجُدَ *be courageous, vigorous, effective*, نَجِدٌ *courageous, efficient*; Aram. ܢܓܕ, נְגַד *drag, draw, lead*; נָגוֹדָא, ܢܳܓܽܘܕܳܐ *leader*; Eth. ነገደ: is *travel*);—**Hiph.**$_{328}$ *Pf.* הִגַּ֫דְתָּ, הִגִּיד Gn 3^{11}+, 3 fs. הִגִּ֫ידָה 1 S 25^{19}+, Gn 12^{8}+, etc.; *Impf.* יַגִּיד 1 S 9^{6}+; וַיַּגֵּד Gn 9^{22}+; sf. יַגִּידֶ֫הָ Is 44^{7}; יַגִּדֵהּ Je 9^{11}; יַגֶּדְךָ Dt 32^{7} (juss.), etc.; *Imv.* הַגֵּד 2 S 18^{21}+; הַגִּ֫ידָה Gn 29^{15}+, etc.; *Inf. abs.* הַגֵּד Ju 14^{12} + 2 t.; הַגִּיד Je 36^{16}; *cstr.* לְהַגִּיד Gn 32^{6}+; לגיד 2 K 9^{15} Kt. (Qr לְהַגִּ׳); *Pt.* מַגִּיד Gn 41^{24}+; f. מַגֶּ֫דֶת Est 2^{20}; pl. cstr. מַגִּידֵי Ju 14^{19};—*declare, tell* [usu. sq. לְ of indir. obj. Gn 3^{11} + oft.; ins. also 1 S 12^{7} 2 S 13^{34} 𝔊 Th We Klo Dr Kit Bu, so HPS 2 S 13^{34} (1 S 12^{7} he foll. 𝔖 as more diff.); sq. אֶל Ex 19^{9} 1 S 3^{15}; sq. לִפְנֵי 1 S 17^{31} ψ 142^{3}; עַל־פָּנָיו Jb 21^{31}; בְּאָזְנֵי Je 36^{20}; sq. בְּ loc. (instead of indir. obj.) chiefly proph. Je 4^{5} 5^{20} 31^{10}+; also 1 S 4^{13} 2 S 1^{20} 2 K 9^{15} Mi 1^{10}; rarely sq. acc. pers. 2 S 15^{31} (but rd. וּלְדָוִד הִגִּיד HPS (indef. subj.), or ולד׳ הֻגַּד We Dr Kit, 𝔊𝔙 Th Klo Bu favour הֻגַּד), 2 K 7$^{9.11}$ Ez 43^{10} Jb 17^{5} 26^{4} 31^{37}; sq. dir. obj. in acc. Gn 45^{13} + oft.; sq. cl. wi. כִּי Gn 3^{11} + oft.; sq. cl. wi. כִּי = אֲשֶׁר (late) Est 3^{4} 6^{2}; sq. cl. wi. מַה Gn 29^{15} Ju 16^{15} Est 8^{1}+; sq. cl. wi. מִי 2 K 6^{11}; sq. cl. wi. אֵיכָה Ct 1^{7}, once sq. cl. wi. הֲ Gn 43^{6}, etc.; oft. no dir. obj., sq. לֵאמֹר Ex 13^{8} 1 S 25^{14}+; sq. וַיֹּאמֶר Gn 47^{1}+; אמר then foll. by *orat. rect.*; הִגִּ׳ alone sq. *orat. rect.* Zc 9^{12}; sq. עַל *concerning*, 1 S 27^{11} Est 6^{2}; oft. indir. obj. om. 1 S 24^{19}+; dir. obj. om. Ju 13^{10}+; both om. Lv 5^{1}+]. In Hex. rarely P, †Lv 5^{1} 14^{35} Ex 16^{22}†; J, Gn 3^{11} 12^{18} Ex 13^{8} + 18 t.; E, Gn 21^{6} 31^{20} 41^{25} + 15 t.; D, Dt 17^{9} 26^{3} 30^{18} + 5 t.;—**1.** *tell, announce, report*, usu. human subj. Gn 9^{22} 24^{23} 32^{6} Lv 14^{35} Ju 13^{6} 1 S 3^{18} 1 K 1^{23} Ne 2^{12} Est 2$^{10.10}$ Jb 12^{7} ψ 142^{3} Is 19^{12} Je 5^{20} Ez 24^{19}+. **2.** *declare, make known, expound*, esp. of something before not understood, concealed or mysterious, Gn 3^{11} 12^{18}, etc.; 1 K 10^{3} = 2 Ch 9^{2}; a riddle Ju 14$^{12.15.16.16.16.19}$; dream Dn 2^{2}; secret Jb 11^{6}, etc.; of י׳ as revealing, Gn 41^{25} 2 S 7^{11} 2 K 4^{27} Mi 6^{8} Je 42^{3} ψ 147^{19}; of declaring by י׳'s agents Dt 5^{5} Mi 3^{8} 1 S 15^{16} 2 S 24^{13} Je 50^{28} Is 58^{1}; by divin. Ho 4^{12}. 5046

3. *inform of* (play the informer concerning) Jos $2^{14.20}$ Je 20^{10} Jb 17^{5} Lv 5^{1} Pr 29^{24}. **4.** *publish, declare, proclaim,* esp. of proclaiming wisdom, power, loving-kindness, etc., of ׳י (esp. ψψ): ψ 9^{12} 22^{32} 51^{17} $92^{3.16}$ 145^{4}+, subj. heavens ψ 19^{2} 50^{6} 97^{6}; Is 42^{12} 57^{12}. **5.** *avow, acknowledge, confess:* Is 3^{9} ψ 38^{19}, cf. Is 48^{6}. —Pt.=*messenger* 2 S 15^{13} Je $51^{31.31}$ cf. הַנַּעַר הַמַּגִּיד 2 S $1^{5.6.13}$; הָאִישׁ הַמַּ׳ 2 S 18^{11}. †**Hoph.** *Pf.* הֻגַּד Jos 9^{24}+; *Impf.* וַיֻּגַּד Gn 22^{20}+; *Inf. abs.* הֻגֵּד Jos 9^{24} Ru 2^{11};—*be told, announced, reported,* alw. sq. לְ (sts. impers., logical subj. in acc., cf. Gn 27^{42} 2 S 21^{11}, c. fem. Is 21^{2}; not in P): Gn 27^{42} (J), 31^{22} (E), Dt 17^{4} Jos $9^{24.24}$ (D), Ru $2^{11.11}$ Ju 9^{25} 2 S 10^{17} 19^{2} 21^{11} 1 K 10^{7} 18^{13} 1 Ch 19^{17} 2 Ch 9^{6} Is 21^{2} 40^{21}; sq. לֵאמֹר Gn 22^{20} $38^{13.24}$ (all J), Jos 10^{17} (JE), 1 S 15^{12} 19^{19} 2 S 6^{12} 1 K 1^{51} 2 K 6^{13} 8^{7} Is 7^{2}; sq. cl. with כִּי Ex 14^{5} (J), Ju 9^{47} 1 S $23^{7.13}$ 27^{4} 1 K $2^{29.41}$.

5048 נֶ֫גֶד $_{151}$ **subst.** what is conspicuous or in front, always as **adv.** or **prep.** in front of, in sight of, opposite to, נֶגֶד, cstr. נֶגֶד, sf. נֶגְדִּי ψ 38^{11}+, נֶגְדְּךָ 38^{10}+, etc.; with ה *loc.* נֶגְדָּה †ψ $116^{14.18}$;—**1.** as adv. accus. *in front of,* **a.** locally (rather stronger and distincter than לִפְנֵי), (*a*) Gn 31^{32} נֶגֶד אַחֵינוּ הַכֶּר־נָא *in front of* our brethren own it, now, v^{37} 47^{15} ולמה נמות נגדך why should we die *in thy sight?* Ex 19^{2} Isr. encamped נגד ההר *in front of* the mountain, 34^{10} נגד כל־עמך אעשׂה נִפְלָאֹת *before, in sight of, all thy people* (cf. ψ 78^{12}), Jos 3^{16} the people passed over נגד ירחו *in front of* J., 1 K 20^{27}, etc.; Ne 3^{23} *in front of* their house, v^{29}; (כל) נגד ישׂראל Dt 31^{11} Jos 8^{35} 1 S 15^{30} 2 S 12^{12}+; 1 K 21^{13} set Naboth נֶגֶד הָעָם; נגד י׳ 1 S 12^{3} 16^{6} אַךְ נֶגֶד י׳ מְשִׁיחוֹ, so נֶגְדִּי ψ 89^{37}, נֶגְדּוֹ 18^{13}; נגד השׁמשׁ Nu 25^{4} 2 S 12^{12}; ψ 22^{26} נ׳ יראיו, 52^{11} (so poet. נֶגְדָה לְּ ψ $116^{14.18}$); hostilely, Jb 10^{17}; with collat. idea of *to the mortification of,* ψ 23^{5} 31^{20}, cf. Jo 1^{16}; with collat. idea of being *open* or *known to,* Pr 15^{11} שׁאול ואבדון נגד י׳, Jb 26^{6}, ψ 38^{10} נגדך כל־תאותי (||ממך לא נסתרה), 69^{20} (||יָדַעְתָּ), 119^{168} Is 59^{12}; so נֶגֶד פָּנַי הָיוּ Ho 7^{2}. (*b*) with reflex. sf., and vb. of motion, to go *in front of oneself,* i.e. *straightforward,* Jos 6^{5} ועלו העם איש נגדו each *straightforward,* v^{20} Am 4^{3} Je 31^{39} Ne 12^{37}, cf. Pr 4^{25}. **b.** mentally,=vividly present to, ψ 38^{18} ומכאובי נגדי תמיד, 44^{16} 51^{5} וחטאתי נגדי תמיד, 109^{15} נ׳ י׳ (remembered by): nearly=בְּעֵינָיו, כְּאַיִן נֶגְדּוֹ Is 40^{17} ψ 39^{6}; so וְנ׳ פְּנֵיהֶם נְבוֹנִים Is 5^{21}. But Ex 10^{10} כי רעה נגד פניכם before your face is=in your view, or purpose (cf. לא אשׁית לְנֶגֶד עֵינַי דבר־בליעל ψ 101^{3}).

2. With preps.: **a.** †כְּנֶגֶד *acc. to what is in front of=corresponding to,* Gn 2^{18} I will make him עֵזֶר כְּנֶגְדּוֹ a help *corresponding to* him i.e. equal and adequate to himself, v^{20} among the animals there was no עֵזֶר כְּנֶגְדּוֹ. **b.** לְנֶגֶד *in front of, before,* Gn 33^{12} וְאֵלְכָה לְנֶגְדֶּךָ, Nu 22^{32} 2 K 1^{13} fell on his knees לנגד אליהו, Is 1^{7} your ground לנגדכם זרים אכלים אותהּ; with עָמַד Jos 5^{13} Dn 8^{15} 10^{16}, in a hostile sense v^{13}, cf. Pr 21^{30}; *in the sight* or *presence of,* Hb 1^{3} וְשֹׁד וְחָמָס לְנֶגְדִּי, ψ 39^{2} בעוד רשׁע לנגדי, 50^{8} ועולתיך לנגדי תמיד, Ne 3^{37}; *opposite to* (prob. of opposite choirs), Ne $12^{9.24}$;=*parallel to,* 1 Ch 5^{11};=*over, for,* a business (peculiar) Ne 11^{22}; fig. of what is visible morally, ψ 18^{23} כי כל משׁפטיו לנגדי (||לֹא אָסִיר מֶנִּי), with *to set* or *place* ψ 16^{8} 54^{5} לא שָׂמוּ אלהים לנגדם (cf. 86^{14}), 90^{8}; oft. in the phrase לְנֶגֶד עֵינֵי..., both lit., as Jb 4^{16} תְּמוּנָה לְנ׳ עֵינָי, ψ 5^{6} לא יתיצבו הוללים לנ׳ עיניך (cf. 101^{7}); and in a moral sense, ψ 18^{25} כְּבֹר ידי לנ׳ עיניו, 26^{3} כי חסדך לנ׳ עיני i.e. is ever present to my mind, 36^{2} אין פחד אלהים לנ׳ עיניו i.e. he has no eye to discern God's awe-inspiring judgments (cf. 10^{5}); with לא אשׁית i.e. have in view, purpose (||שׂנאתי) 101^{3}. **c.** †מִנֶּגֶד (*a*) **adv.** *off* (מִן **1 c**) *the front, in front, opposite, ex adverso,* Gn 21^{16} ותשׁב לה מנגד sat her down *opposite,* v^{16}, 2 K 2^{7}; Dt 28^{66} והיו חייך תלואים לך מנגד shall be hung up for thee *in front* (i.e. suspended, as by a thread, in front of thee); Ju 9^{17} וישׁלך נפשׁו מנגד and flung away his life *in front* or *straight away* (i.e. hazarded it);=*some way off, from* or *at a distance,* Nu 2^{2} Dt 32^{52} כי מִנֶּגֶד, תראה את הארץ, 2 K 2^{15} וַיִּרְאֻהוּ מנ׳ *at a distance,* 3^{22} 4^{25}; *aloof,* 2 S 18^{13} ואתה תתיצב מנגד, Ob 1^{11}. (*b*) as a **prep.** (*α*) *from the front of, away from,* Ct 6^{5} הָסֵבִּי עֵינַיִךְ מִנֶּגְדִּי, 1 S 26^{20} אל־יפל דמי ארצה מנ׳ פני י׳; מנגד עיני, *from before the eyes of,* with verbs of removing Is 1^{16}, cutting off ψ 31^{23} Jon 2^{5}, hiding Am 9^{3} Je 16^{17}. (*β*) *opposite to,* Ne $3^{19.25.27}$; *at a distance from,* ψ 10^{5} מרום משׁפטיך מנגדו, 38^{12} מנגד נגעי יעמדו. (*γ*) מִנֶּגֶד לְ *from before,* Pr 14^{7}, *in front of* Ju 20^{34}. **d.** †עַד נֶגֶד *as far as the front of,* Ne $3^{16.26}$.

†נָגִיד **n.m.** leader (lit. prob. *one in front*), 5057
ruler, prince;—abs. נ׳ 1 S 9^{16} + 31 t.; cstr. נְגִיד (נְגַד) 2 K 20^{5} + 6 t.; pl. נְגִידִים Jb 29^{10} + 3 t.; נְגִידֵי 2 Ch 35^{8};—*ruler, prince* ψ 76^{13} Pr 28^{16} Jb

29^{10} 31^{37} (in sim.). Esp. **1.** of king of Isr.: of Saul מָשַׁח לְנ׳ עַל (+acc. pers.), 1 S 9^{16} (subj. proph.), cf. of Sol., subj. people, 1 Ch 29^{22}; 10^{1} (subj. ׳י); of David צִוָּהוּ לְנ׳ עַל 1 S 13^{14} 25^{30}, נ׳ עַל 2 S 6^{21} (in these ׳י subj.), היה לנ׳ על 5^{2}, היה נ׳ על 7^{8} 1 Ch 11^{2} 17^{7}; cf. also 5^{2} 2 Ch 6^{5}; of David also נָתַן נ׳ לְ׳ Is 55^{4}; of Sol. צִוָּה אֹתוֹ לִהְיוֹת נ׳ על 1 K 1^{35} (׳י subj.); of Jerob. נתן נ׳ על (+acc. pers.) 1 K 14^{7} (׳י subj.); so 16^{2} of Baasha; of Hezekiah נְ׳ עַמִּי 2 K 20^{5}; הֶעֱמִיד לְנ׳ בְּאֶחָיו (+acc. pers.) 2 Ch 11^{22} (of Abijah, subj. Rehob.); of Judah 1 Ch 28^{4}. **2.** of a foreign *ruler* or *prince* Ez 28^{2} Dn 9$^{25.26}$. **3.** the title of some high official connected with the temple Je 20^{1} (of Pashḥur) וְהוּא פָקִיד נָגִיד בבית ׳י and he was *prince-overseer* in, etc. (for פ׳ see 29^{26}); hence נ׳ בית האלהים 1 Ch 9^{11} 2 Ch 31^{13} 35^{8} (three נגידי ב׳ ה׳, including the high-priest), Ne 11^{11}; of high-priest Dn 11^{22} נ׳ בְּרִית. **4.** *ruler* in other capacities (late): of tribe 1 Ch 27^{16} 2 Ch 19^{11}; of Ḳoraḥites 9^{20}; of Aaronite warriors 12^{27}; of division of army 1 Ch 13^{1} 27^{4} 2 Ch 11^{11} (commandant of fortress), 32^{21} (in Ass. army: ‖ שַׂר); of temple-treasuries 1 Ch 26^{24}, cf. 2 Ch 31^{12}; נ׳ הבית 2 Ch 28^{7} (i.e. of palace?). **5.** *princely things*, pl. abstr. Pr 8^{6}.

5050 †[נָגַהּ] **vb. shine** (As. *nagû, shine, beam, be joyful*, Dl$^{HWB\ 446}$; Eth. ነገሀ: ; Aram. ܢܓܗ; NH 𝔗 נוֹגְהָא planet *Venus*)—**Qal** *Pf.* ועל-דרכיך נ׳ אור Jb 22^{28}; אור נ׳ עליהם Is 9^{1}; *Impf.* ולא-יִגַּהּ שְׁבִיב אִשּׁוֹ Jb 18^{5}. **Hiph.** *Impf.* **1.** *enlighten* יהוה אלהי יַגִּיהַּ חשכי 2 S 22^{29} = ויהוה יַגִּיהַּ חָשְׁכִּי ψ 18^{29}. **2.** *cause to shine* (of moon) וְיָרֵחַ לֹא־יַגִּיהַּ אוֹרוֹ Is 13^{10} (‖ חָשַׁךְ).

5051 †I. נֹגַהּ **n.f.**$^{Hb\ 3,4}$ **brightness**;—נ׳ abs. Am 5^{20}+; cstr. Is 4^{5}+; sf. נָגְהָם Jo 2^{10} 4^{15};—*brightness* of a (clear, sunshiny) day Am 5^{20} (‖ אוֹר; opp. חשֶׁךְ, אָפֵל), 2 S 23^{4} (מִמָּטָר *after rain*); so fig. of Zion's dawning, נ׳ זַרְחֵךְ Is 60^{3} (‖ אוֹר); of her righteousness כַּנֹּגַהּ 62^{1} (c. art. only here and Ez 1^{28}), ‖ כְּלַפִּיד יִבְעָר; of moon Is 60^{19}, of stars Jo 2^{10} 4^{15}; of theophany 2 S 22^{13} = ψ 18^{13} (in storm); cf. Ez 1$^{4.27.28}$, נ׳ כְּבוֹד ׳י 10^{4}; נ׳ כאור Hb 3^{4}; נ׳ לָאֵשׁ Ez 1^{13}, נ׳ אֵשׁ לֶהָבָה Is 4^{5}; נ׳ בְּרַק חֲנִיתֶךָ Hb 3^{11} (of glitter of ׳י's spear; ‖ אוֹר חִצֶּיךָ); of individ., וְאֵין נ׳ לוֹ Is 50^{10} (fig. of distress ‖ חֲשֵׁכִים); so וְאֹרַח צַדִּיקִים כְּאוֹר נ׳ Pr 4^{18} *the path of righteous men is like a light of brightness.*

5052 †II. נֹגַהּ **n.pr.m.** a son of David acc. to 1 Ch 3^{7} 14^{6}. 𝔊 Ναγαι, Ναγεθ, etc.

†[נְגֹהָה] **n.f. brightness**; fig. of prosperity;—pl. לַנְּגֹהוֹת Is 59^{9} (opp. אֲפֵלוֹת; ‖ אוֹר). 5054

†נָגַח **vb. push, thrust, gore** (NH *id.;* Ar. نَجَحَ *succeed, attain, make progress;* 𝔗 as BH);—**Qal** *Impf.* יִגַּח Ex 21$^{28.31.32}$ (E), יִגָּח v^{31};—*gore*, subj. שׁוֹר, sq. acc. pers. **Pi.** *Impf.* יְנַגַּח Dt 33^{17}; 2 ms. תְּנַגַּח 1 K 22^{11} 2 Ch 18^{10}; תְּנַגְּחוּ Ez 34^{21}; נְנַגֵּחַ ψ 44^{6}; *Pt.* מְנַגֵּחַ Dn 8^{4};—*push* or *thrust at*, sq. acc.: of Joseph under fig. of wild ox Dt 33^{17}, cf. 1 K 22^{11} = 2 Ch 18^{10} ψ 44^{6} (‖ בוס); v. also Ez 34^{21} (of Isr. under fig. of sheep), cf. Dn 8^{4} (of ram in vision; obj. not expr.). **Hithp.** *Impf.* יִתְנַגַּח עִמּוֹ מֶלֶךְ הַנֶּגֶב Dn 11^{40} *engage in thrusting with,* wage war with. 5055

†נַגָּח **adj. addicted to goring,** pred. of שׁוֹר Ex 21$^{29.36}$ (E), cf. Ba$^{NB\ 49}$. 5056

נגל (√ of foll., mng. unknown; Ar. نَجَلَ is *strike, split, pierce,* but v. infr.).

†מַגָּל **n.[m.] sickle** (Ar. مِنْجَل (yet poss. Aram. loan-word Frä^{133}), Aram. ܡܓܠܐ);—c. תָּפַשׂ *handle, wield* Je 50^{16} (‖ זֹרֵעַ); c. שָׁלַח Jo 4^{13} fig. of judgment. 4038

†[נָגַן] **vb. touch** (strings), **play** a stringed instrument (NH Pi.; Aram. נַגֵּן Pa.);—**Qal** *Pt.* נֹגְנִים ψ 68^{26} *players* (‖ שָׁרִים, עֲלָמוֹת תּוֹפֵפוֹת). **Pi.** *Pf.* וְנִגֵּן 1 S 16^{16} (consec.), v^{23}; *Impf.* 1 pl. נְנַגֵּן Is 38^{20}; *Inf. cstr.* נַגֵּן 1 S 16^{17}+5 t.; *Pt.* מְנַגֵּן 1 S 16^{16}+4 t.;—*play* בַּכִּנּוֹר 1 S 16^{16}; בְּיָדוֹ v$^{16.23}$ (כִּנּוֹר in context), 18^{10} 19^{9}; c. acc. cogn. Is 38^{20}; in sim. מֵטִב נַגֵּן Ez 33^{32} (‖ שִׁיר עֲגָבִים יְפֵה־קוֹל); אִישׁ מֵיטִיב לְנ׳ 1 S 16^{17}, cf. ψ 33^{3} Is 23^{16} (both ‖ שִׁיר), יָדַע נ׳ 1 S 16^{18}; also 2 K 3^{15}; Pt. = *player, minstrel* (cf. Qal) 2 K 3$^{15.15}$; cf. also אִישׁ יֹדֵעַ מְנַגֵּן בַּכִּנּוֹר 1 S 16^{16} (Ges$^{§\,120b}$). 5059

†[נְגִינָה] **n.f. music**;—abs. נְגִינַת ψ 61^{1} (v. infr.); sf. נְגִינָתִי ψ 77^{7}; נְגִינָתָם Jb 30^{9} + 2 t.; pl. נְגִינוֹת ψ 4^{1}+6 t.; נְגִינוֹתַי Is 38^{20}; ־תָי Hb 3^{19};—**1.** *music* (of stringed instr.) acc. cogn. Is 38^{20}; as occupation La 5^{14}; esp. בִּנְגִינוֹת in ψ-titles; ψ 4^{1} 6^{1} 54^{1} 55^{1} 67^{1} 76^{1}; so Hb 3^{19}; cf. עַל־נְגִינַת ψ 61^{1} (rd. perh. pl. Ges$^{§\,80f.}$). **2.** *song* (with string accomp.?) ψ 77^{7}; *subject of* mocking *song* Jb 30^{9} (‖ מִלָּה), ψ 69^{13} (נ׳ שׁוֹתֵי שֵׁכָר), La 3^{14} (‖ שְׂחֹק). 5058

†[מַנְגִּינָה] **n.f.** (**mocking, derisive**) **song** (cf. foreg.);—מַנְגִּינָתָם La 3^{63}, i.e. *subject of their mocking song.* 4485

5060 **נָגַע** [150] **vb. touch, reach, strike** (NH *id.*; Ar. نَجَعَ is *agree* with one (of food), *produce effect*; Aram. נְגַע Ithpa. *be struck* (sc. w. leprosy), cf. Pi. infr.);—**Qal** *Pf.* נ׳ Gn 32[33]+; נָגְעָה Ju 20[41]+; 1 pl. sf. נְגַעֲנוּךָ Gn 26[29]; *Impf.* יִגַּע Lv 5[3]+; וַיִּגַּע Gn 32[26]+, etc.; *Imv.* גַּע ψ 144[5]+2 t.; *Inf. cstr.* נְגֹעַ, לִנְגּוֹעַ Gn 20[6]+3 t.; גַּעַת 2 S 14[10] Ez 17[10]; sf. נָגְעֵךְ Ru 2[9], etc.; *Pt. act.* נֹגֵעַ 1 K 19[5]+; נֹגְעִים Je 12[14]; f. נֹגַעַת Nu 19[22]+2 t.; pl. נֹגְעֹת 1 K 6[27]; *pass.* נָגוּעַ ψ 73[14] Is 53[4];—**1. a.** *touch*, usu. sq. בְּ Gn 3[3] (J), 32[26.33] Ex 19[12.12.13] (all E), 29[37] 30[29] (P), Lv 5[2.3]+25 t. Lv; Nu 16[26]+7 t. Nu (P)+19[22] (no בְּ or obj.), Dt 14[8] Ju 6[21] 2 S 23[7] 1 K 6[27.27] 19[5.7] 2 K 13[21] Est 5[2] Dn 8[5.18] 10[10.18] La 4[14]; sq. אֶל־ Hg 2[12] Nu 4[15] 1 K 6[27] Dn 9[21], cf. Ho 4[2]; sq. עַל־פֶּה Is 6[7]; עַל־שָׂפָה Dn 10[16]; sq. acc. Is 52[11]; abs. (no obj. expr.) Jb 6[7] La 4[15]. **b.** of י׳ *touching* earth, mountains, etc., sq. בְּ Am 9[5] ψ 104[32] 144[5]; fig. of י׳ *touching* the heart, sq. בְּ 1 S 10[26]. **2.** nearly=*strike*, pass. *stricken*, ψ 73[14] Is 53[4] (‖ מֻכֵּה), of wind Jb 1[19] Ez 17[10]; of divine chastisement 1 S 6[9] Jb 1[11] 19[21]; sq. אֶל 2[5]. **3.** *touch*=harm, sq. בְּ, Gn 26[11] (J), Jos 9[19] 2 S 14[10] 1 Ch 16[22] (‖ הָרֵעַ)=ψ 105[15], Je 12[14] Zc 2[12.12]; sq. אֶל־ Gn 20[6] (*touch* a woman), so Pr 6[29] (sq. בְּ); sq. acc. Gn 26[29] (J, sf.), so Ru 2[9]; v. also Jb 5[19] (subj. רַע, sq. בְּ), Ju 20[34.41] (both subj. רָעָה, sq. עַל־). **4.** *reach, extend to*, 2 S 5[8], sq. בְּ (but crpt. v. Dr HPS); in metaph., sq. עַד, of vine Is 16[8] Je 48[32]; of sword Je 4[10], cf. v[18]; of chastisement Mi 1[9], cf. Jb 4[5] (‖ בּוֹא אֶל־); also (sq. אֶל) Je 51[9]; =*come*, sq. אֶל־ Jon 3[6]; *arrive* (of time), abs. Ezr 3[1] Ne 7[73].

†**Niph.** *Impf.* וַיִּנָּגְעוּ Jos 8[15] *be stricken, defeated* (in battle), i.e. feign to be so, but rd. prob. וַיִּנָּגְפוּ, v. נגף **Niph.**

†**Pi.** *Pf.* sf. נִגְּעוֹ 2 Ch 26[20] *strike* (with leprosy, 2 acc.), subj. י׳; so *Impf.* וַיְנַגַּע 2 K 15[5]; Gn 12[17] (subj. י׳; acc. pers. + acc. cogn.).

†**Pu.** *Impf.* יְנֻגָּעוּ *be stricken* by diseases (?; cf. **Pi.** and נֶגַע **2. 3.** esp. 2 S 7[14]) ψ 73[5].

†**Hiph.** *Pf.* הִגִּיעַ Is 25[12]+6 t.; 2 fs. הִגַּעַתְּ Est 4[14]; 1 s. sf. וְהִגַּעְתִּיהוּ Ez 13[14], etc.; *Impf.* יַגִּיעַ Is 8[8]+3 t.; וַיַּגַּע Is 6[7] Je 1[9], etc.; *Inf. cstr.* הַגִּיעַ Est 2[12.15]; *Pt.* מַגִּיעַ Gn 28[12]+; f. מַגַּעַת 2 Ch 3[11];—*cause to touch; reach, approach, arrive*: **1.** *cause to touch, apply*, Ex 12[22] (JE; אֶל־, מִדָּם); *cause to touch* (sq. לָאָרֶץ, עַד עָפָר), i.e. bring to ground, Is 25[5.12], cf. La 2[2], Ez 13[14] (sq. אֶל־), Ex 4[25] (J; sq. לְרַגְלָיו); sq. עַל־פֶּה Is 6[7] Je 1[9]; sq. בְּ Is 5[8]. **2.** intr. *reach, extend*, Gn 28[12] (sq. ה__ loc.); sq. אֶל־ Zc 14[5], sq. עַד Is 8[8]; cf. תַּגִּ׳ יָדוֹ דֵּי שֶׂה Lv 5[7] *if his hand do not reach enough for a lamb* (i.e. he be not able to furnish a lamb); sq. לְ Jb 20[6] (hyperb.) 2 Ch 3[11.11.12]; sq. עַד לְ 28[9]; *attain*, sq. לְ Est 4[14], *arrive, come*, sq. acc. loc. Is 30[4] Est 4[3] 8[17], sq. לְ (of time) Dn 12[12], sq. אֶל־ 1 S 14[9], sq. עַד־ ψ 107[18], abs. Est 6[14]; sq. אֵצֶל Dn 8[7]. **3.** *approach*, of time, abs. Ec 12[1] Ct 2[12] Ez 7[12] (‖ בּוֹא); v. also Est 9[1] (sq. Inf.), cf. 2[12.15] ψ 88[4] (sq. לְ). **4.** of fate or lot, =*befal*, sq. אֶל־ Est 9[26] Ec 8[14.14] ψ 32[6].

נֶ֫גַע [78] **n.m.** [Gn 12, 17] **stroke, plague, mark, plague-spot**;—נ׳ abs. Ex 11[1]+, נָ֫גַע Lv 13[13]+; cstr. Dt 24[8]+; sf. נִגְעִי ψ 38[12]; נִגְעֶ֫ךָ 39[11]; נִגְעוֹ Lv 13[44] 2 Ch 6[29]; pl. נְגָעִים Gn 12[17] ψ 89[33]; cstr. נִגְעֵי 2 S 7[14];—**1.** *stroke, wound*, inflicted by man on man Dt 17[8] 21[5] (‖ רִיב), Pr 6[33]. **2.** *stroke*, metaph., esp. of a disease, regarded as sent by a divine chastisement, Gn 12[17] (J), Ex 11[1] (E), 2 S 7[14] (שֵׁבֶט אֲנָשִׁים ‖ נ׳ בְּנֵי אָדָם, i.e. customary, ordinary), 1 K 8[37] = 2 Ch 6[28] (both ‖ מַחֲלָה); 1 K 8[38] (נ׳ לְבָבוֹ)=2 Ch 6[29] (נִגְעוֹ); ψ 91[10] (‖ רָעָה); of Israel 38[12] 39[11] (‖ תִּגְרַת יָדְךָ), 89[33] (‖ שֵׁבֶט); v. also Is 53[8] (of suffering servant of י׳, נֶ֫גַע לָ֫מוֹ). **3.** *mark* (60 t. Lv 13, 14), indeterm. Lv 13[5.6] (מִסְפַּחַת), v[17.29.30.32.43.44]; of leprosy, regarded as the *heavy touch* or *stroke* of a disease, נ׳ צָרַ֫עַת Lv 13[2]+; v[51] (צָרַעַת מַמְאֶרֶת הַנֶּ׳), v[59] 14[3.32.54], Dt 24[8]; also נ׳ לָבָן אֲדַמְדָּם Lv 13[31]; נ׳ הַנֶּתֶק v[42]; identif. with person having it 13[4.12.13.17.31]; in garment, etc. v[47]+15 t. Lv 13; in house 14[34.35.36.43.44.48.48]; i.e. house-wall v[37.37.39]; in stones of wall v[40]; = garment, etc., with plague-spot 13[50]. 5061

†**נָגַף** **vb. strike, smite** (Aram. נְגַף);— 5062
Qal *Pf.* נ׳ 2 Ch 13[15] Is 19[22] (וְ consec.); sf. נְגָפוֹ 2 Ch 21[18], etc.; *Impf.* יִגֹּף Ex 21[35]+2 t.; וַיִּגֹּף Ex 32[35]+4 t.; אֶגּוֹף ψ 89[24]+, etc.; *Inf. abs.* נָגֹף Is 19[22]; *cstr.* לִנְגֹּף Ex 12[23.23]; נָגְפּוֹ v[27];—*strike, smite*, of serious (even fatal) injury, sq. acc. pers. Ex 21[22.35] (E); one's foot against (בְּ) stone ψ 91[12]; abs. (stumble) Pr 3[23]; esp. of judgment, subj. י׳, obj. individ. (fatal stroke) 1 S 25[38] 26[10] 2 S 12[15] 2 Ch 13[20] 21[18] (לָחֳלִי); obj. people (abs.) Ex 12[23.23.27] (JE), 32[35] Jos 24[5] (E), Is 19[22], cf. v[22]; v. also ψ 89[24]; cf. c. acc. cogn. מַגֵּפָה Zc 14[12.18] 2 Ch 21[14] (sq. also בְּעַמְּךָ); c. בְּ instr. Ex 7[27]; of causing defeat in battle, sq. acc. + לִפְנֵי Ju 20[35] 1 S 4[3] 2 Ch 13[15] 14[11].

Niph. *Pf.* נִגַּף 2 S 10^{15}; נִגְּפוּ v^{19} + 2 t., etc.; *Impf.* יִנָּגֵף 2 Ch 6^{24}; וַיִּנָּגֵף 1 S 4^{2} + 4 t.; *Inf. abs.* נִגּוֹף Ju 20^{39}; cstr. הִנָּגֵף 1 K 8^{33}; *Pt.* נִגָּף Dt 28^{25} Ju 20^{39}, etc.;—*be smitten*, bef. enemy, in battle, sq. לִפְנֵי Ju $20^{32.39.39}$ 1 S 4^{2} 7^{10} 2 S $10^{15.19}$ 18^{7} 1 K 8^{33} 2 K 14^{12} 1 Ch $19^{16.19}$ 2 Ch 6^{24} 25^{22} Lv 26^{17} Nu 14^{42} Dt 1^{42}; abs. Ju 20^{36} 1 S 4^{10} 2 S 2^{17} 2 Ch 20^{22}; Pt. after נָתַן, sq. לִפְנֵי Dt $28^{7.25}$. Vid. נָגַע **Niph.**

Hithp. *Impf.* יִתְנַגְּפוּ Je 13^{16} = *stumble*, subj. רַגְלֵיכֶם, sq. עַל (loc.); cf. **Qal** (ψ 91^{12}) and נֶגֶף **2.**

5063 **†נֶגֶף n.m.**$^{Ex\ 12,13}$ **blow, striking** (as judgment, only P);—נ׳ abs. Ex 12^{13} + 6 t.;—**1.** fatal *blow, plague*, Ex 12^{13} (death of first-born); 30^{12} Nu 8^{19} (indef.); = pestilence Nu $17^{11.12}$ Jos 22^{17}. **2.** *striking*, אֶבֶן נ׳ Is 8^{14} i.e. against which the foot strikes and so stumbles (‖ צוּר מִכְשׁוֹל).

4046 **†מַגֵּפָה n.f. blow, slaughter, plague, pestilence**;—מ׳ abs. Nu 14^{37} + 23 t.; cstr. מַגֵּפַת Zc 14^{15}; pl. sf. מַגֵּפֹתַי Ex 9^{14};—**1.** *blow*, = fatal stroke Ez 24^{16}; in divine judgment (plague) Ex 9^{14} (J). **2.** *slaughter* in battle, 1 S 4^{17} 2 S 17^{9} 18^{7}. **3.** *plague, pestilence* (divine judgment), of tumours on Philistines 1 S 6^{4}; against Isr Nu 14^{37} $17^{13.14.15}$ $25^{8.9.18.19}$ 31^{16} 2 S $24^{21.25}$ (ins. also v^{15} 𝔊 Th We Klo Dr Kit Bu), 1 Ch 21^{22} ψ $106^{29.30}$; specif. disease of bowels 2 Ch 21^{14}; מ׳ = infected people 1 Ch 21^{17}; wasting of flesh, eyes and tongue, of hostile peoples Zc $14^{12.18}$; attacking beasts $v^{15.15}$.

5064 **†[נָגַר] vb. pour, flow, run** (Aram. ܢܓܪ *be long* (of time), Aph. *prolong, protract;* נְגַר *endure, flow, stream*);—**Niph.** *Pf.* 3 fs. נִגְּרָה ψ 77^{3} La 3^{49}; *Pt.* pl. נִגָּרִים 2 S 14^{14}; נִגָּרוֹת Jb 20^{28};—**1.** *be poured, spilt*, 2 S 14^{14} (כַּמַּיִם הַנִּגָּרִים אַרְצָה in sim. of mortality). **2.** *pour oneself, flow, trickle*, of eye (in tears) La 3^{49}. **3.** fig. *vanish*, Jb 20^{28} (‖ גָּלָה). **4.** *be stretched out* (?) יָדִי לַיְלָה נִגְּרָה ψ 77^{3} (or rd. עֵינִי ?). **Hiph.** *Pf.* וְהִגַּרְתִּי Mi 1^{6}; *Impf.* וַיַּגֵּר ψ 75^{9}; וַתַּגֵּר Ez 35^{5}; יַגִּירֻהוּ ψ 63^{11}; *Imv.* sf. הַגִּרֵם Je 18^{21};—*pour down, hurl down* the stones of Samaria, subj. י׳ Mi 1^{6}; *pour out*, fig. of י׳'s wine-cup, ψ 75^{9}; sq. עַל־יְדֵי חֶרֶב = *deliver over to* Je 18^{21} ψ 63^{11} Ez 35^{5}. **Hoph.** *Pt.* כְּמַיִם מֻגָּרִים בְּמוֹרָד Mi 1^{4} in sim., of mountains melting at theophany.

5065 **†[נָגַשׂ] vb. press, drive, oppress, exact** (As. *nagâšu, throw down, overthrow*, Dl$^{HWB\ 448}$; Ar. نَجَشَ *rouse* and *drive* game, *drive vehemently;* Eth. ነገሠ: *reign, wield power*, ንጉሥ: *king*);—**Qal** *Pf.* נ׳ 2 K 23^{35}; *Impf.* יִגֹּשׂ Dt 15^{2}; 2 ms. תִּגֹּשׂ Dt 15^{3}; 2 mpl. תִּנְגֹּשׂוּ Is 58^{3};—*Pt.* נֹגֵשׂ Is 9^{3} +, etc.;—**1.** *press, drive* to work (obj. עַצְּבֵיכֶם your workmen), Is 58^{3} (Ges$^{Comm.}$, De Di Du; *exact* [changing ע׳, q.v.] Che, etc.); v. **3.** **2.** *exact* c. acc. כֶּסֶף, 2 K 23^{35}; sq. acc. pers. only Dt $15^{2.13}$. **3.** Pt. (= subst.) *driver, taskmaster* Ex 3^{7} $5^{6.10.13.14}$ Jb 3^{18}; (ass-)driver Jb 39^{7}; of (arbitrary) *ruler* Is 3^{12}, *ruler* (good sense) Zc 10^{4}; = foreign *oppressor, tyrant* Is 9^{3} (c. בְּ) $14^{2.4}$ Zc 9^{8}; *exactor* of tribute, Dn 11^{20}; pl. abstr. *lordship = lord, ruler*, fig. of צְדָקָה (personif.) Is 60^{17} (‖ פְּקֻדָּתֵךְ שָׁלוֹם). **Niph.** *Pf.* נִגַּשׂ 1 S 13^{6} + 2 t. + Is 3^{5} (וְ consec.);—*hard pressed* by enemy 1 S 13^{6}, and so 14^{24} (but om. by emend., after 𝔊, Th We Dr Kit Bu HPS); *treated harshly*, of suffering servant of י׳ Is 53^{7}; recipr. *tyrannize over* (ב׳) *each other* Is 3^{5}.

[נָגַשׁ]$_{125}$ **vb. draw near, approach**, less 5066
freq. syn. of קרב q.v. (NH *id.* Hiph. (rare) and deriv.);—**Qal**$_{68}$ *Impf.* יִגַּשׁ Ex 24^{14} +, יִגָּשׁ ψ 91^{7}, וַיִּגַּשׁ Gn 18^{23} +; 3 fs. וַתִּגַּשׁ Gn 33^{7}; 2 ms. תִּגַּשׁ־ Is 65^{5}; 3 mpl. יִגְּשׁוּ Is 41^{1} +, יִגָּ֑שׁוּ Ex 24^{2}, יִגָּשׁוּ Jb 41^{8} (Baer; van d. H. יִגַּ֑שׁוּ); 3 fpl. וַתִּגַּשְׁןָ Gn 33^{6}, etc.; *Imv.* גַּשׁ 2 S 1^{15}, גֶּשׁ־ Gn 19^{9}, גְּשָׁה Gn 27^{21} + 2 t.; fs. גְּשִׁי Ru 2^{14}, etc.; *Inf. cstr.* לָגֶשֶׁת Ju 20^{23} +; sf. גִּשְׁתּוֹ Gn 33^{3}; גִּשְׁתָּם Ex 28^{43} + 2 t.;—*draw* or *come near*, **1.** human subj.: sq. אֶל־ pers. Gn 27^{22} 43^{19} 44^{18} 45^{4} (all J), Ex 19^{15} (of sexual intercourse), 24^{2} Nu 32^{16} Jos 14^{6} (all E), Ex 34^{30} Jos 21^{1} (P), + 10 t. elsewh. (not D), + ψ 91^{7} (subj. pestilence personif.); of priestly approach to י׳ Ez 44^{13}, cf. Je 30^{21b}, also sq. אֶל־ of altar Ex 28^{43} 30^{20} Lv 21^{23} and abs., v^{21} (all P or H); sq. אֶל־ rei also Nu 8^{16}; sq. עַד־ pers. Gn 33^{3} (J), rei Ju 9^{52}; sq. עַל־ pers. Ez 9^{6}, rei 44^{13}; sq. בְּ pers. Is 65^{5} (‖ קְרַב אֶל־); in Am 9^{10} rd. תִּגַּשׁ בַּעֲדֵנוּ (for MT תַּגִּישׁ **Hiph.** cf. We GASm Dr Now; ‖ קִדֵּם); sq. לַמִּלְחָמָה *draw near for battle* Ju 20^{23} Je 46^{3} 2 S 10^{13} = 1 Ch 19^{14} (+ לִפְנֵי pers.); sq. acc. pers. 1 S 9^{18} 30^{21}, rei Nu 4^{19} (P), but acc. difficult; Dr rds. אֶל־ for אֶת־ 1 S 9^{18} Nu 4^{19}, cf. Klo HPS; in 1 S 30^{21} Dr takes אֶת־ = *with;* sq. הֲלֹם *hither*, 1 S 14^{38} Ru 2^{14}; abs. Gn 18^{23} 27^{21} 29^{10} $33^{6.7}$ 45^{4} (all J), Ex 24^{2} (E), Jos 8^{11} (E; + ויבאו), + 9 t. (not P, D), + Gn $27^{26.27}$ (E), Jos 3^{9} (J), 2 S 1^{15} 2 Ch 29^{31} (all Imv. sq. 2nd Imv.), + Gn 19^{9} (J), Lv $21^{21.21}$ (H), 2 K 4^{27} (all sq. Inf. purpose). Note esp. גֶּשׁ־הָלְאָה Gn 19^{9} lit. *approach thither!*

i.e. move away! cf. גְּשָׁה־לִּי וְאֵשֵׁבָה Is 49[20] *move away for me* (make room for me) *that I may dwell* (‖צַר־לִי הַמָּקוֹם). **2.** inanim. subj. אֶחָד בְּאֶחָד יִגַּשׁוּ Jb 41[8] *one to another they approach* (fit closely together; of scales of crocodile).—**Qal** not in D.

Niph. *Pf.* נִגַּשׁ Gn 33[7]+; 3 fs. וְנִגְּשָׁה Dt 25[9]; 3 mpl. נִגְּשׁוּ Ex 34[32]+; נִגַּשְׁתֶּם 2 S 11[20.21]; *Pt.* pl. נִגָּשִׁים Ex 19[22];—*draw near* = **Qal** (and substit. for it in D):—sq. אֶל־ pers. Dt 25[9] 1 K 20[13] Ezr 9[1], of priestly approach to Yahweh Ex 19[22] (J), Je 30[21]; sq. אֶל־ rei Ex 20[21] 24[2] (both E), 2 S 11[20.21], אֶל־הַמִּשְׁפָּט Dt 25[1]; sq. בְּ pers. Am 9[13]; sq. לַמִּלְחָמָה 1 S 7[10]; abs. Gn 33[7] (J), Dt 20[2] (‖קרב), 21[5] Ex 34[32] (P), so fig. of worship Is 29[13].

†**Hiph.** *Pf.* 3 ms. sf. consec. וְהִגִּישׁוֹ Ex 21[6.6], וְהִגִּישָׁהּ Lv 2[8]; 3 pl. הִגִּישׁוּ 2 S 17[29]; 2 mpl. הִגַּשְׁתֶּם Am 5[25]; *Impf.* juss. יַגֵּשׁ Jb 40[19]; וַיַּגֶּשׁ־ Gn 27[25]; וַיַּגֵּשׁ Ju 6[19]; 3 fs. תַּגִּישׁ Am 9[10], וַתַּגֵּשׁ 1 S 28[25] 2 S 13[11]; 3 mpl. יַגִּישׁוּ Is 41[22]; 2 mpl. תַּגִּישׁוּ Mal 1[8], תַּגִּישׁוּן v[8], וַתַּגִּישׁוּן Am 6[3], etc.; *Imv.* ms. הַגִּישָׁה Gn 27[25]+; mpl. הַגִּישׁוּ 1 S 13[9]+; *Pt.* מַגִּישׁ Mal 2[12]; pl. cstr. מַגִּישֵׁי Mal 3[3], etc.;—*cause to approach, bring near, bring*, sq. אֶל־ pers. (usu. obj. acc. rei, rarely pers. Ex 21[6.6] 1 S 15[32] Gn 48[10] cf. v[13]):—Gn 48[10.13] (E), Ex 21[6.6] (E), 1 S 13[9] 14[34] 15[32] 2 S 13[11] (+Inf. purpose), 2 K 4[5.6]; sq. אֶל־הַמִּזְבֵּחַ Lv 2[8] (P; of sacrifice); עַל־מִזְבְּחִי Mal 1[7] (sacrif.); לְ pers. Gn 27[25.25] (E), 1 S 30[7] 2 S 17[29] (rd. וַיַּגִּישׁוּ 𝔊 Th We Klo Kit, cf. Dr), of sacrifice Am 5[25] Mal 2[12] 3[3]; לִפְנֵי pers. 1 S 28[25] 2 Ch 29[23]; no prep. Ex 32[6] (J), 1 S 14[18.34] 23[9] 30[7] Ju 6[19] (foll. הוציא אֶל־), Am 6[3] 1 K 5[1] Lv 8[14] (P), of sacrif. also Mal 1[8] (לִזְבֹּחַ), v[8] (‖הקריב); fig. (obj. *proofs, evidences*) Is 41[21] (‖קרב), v[22] (+וְיַגִּידוּ), cf. 45[21] (‖הַגִּידוּ); הָעֹשׂוֹ יַגֵּשׁ חַרְבּוֹ Jb 40[19] let him that made him (the hippot.) *draw near* his sword, is dub.; Du הֶעָשׂוּ[י] נֹגֵשׂ חֲבֵרָיו *wh. is made ruler of its fellows* (other conject. v. Di Bu); Am 9[10] rd. תִּגַּשׁ **Qal** q.v.). †**Hoph.** *Pf.* 3 mpl. לֹא־לִנְחֻשְׁתַּיִם הֻגָּשׁוּ 2 S 3[34] (Ginsb הֻגָּשׁוּ) thy feet *have not been brought near* (put into) *fetters; Pt.* מֻגָּשׁ לשמי Mal 1[11] *it* (impers.) *is offered to my name.* †**Hithp.** *Imv.* mpl. הִתְנַגְּשׁוּ Is 45[20] *draw near!* (‖הִקָּבְצוּ וָבֹאוּ).

067, 5112 נֵד v. II. נדד. נֹד v. נוד. p. 622, 627

5077 †[נָדָא] **vb. drive away, thrust aside** (‖form of נדה, q.v., or text. err.; Eth. ነደአ: *drive* cattle, etc.);—only **Hiph.** *Impf.* 3 ms. וידא . . . אֶת־יִשְׂרָאֵל מֵאַחֲרֵי י׳ 2 K 17[21] Kt (Qr וַיַּדַּח ✓נדח **Hiph.**). p. 622

†נָדַב **vb. incite, impel** (NH *id.;* Ar. نَدَبَ *call, impel, incite* (نَدُبَ *be noble, willing, generous*, is denom. fr. [نَدْبٌ cf.] נָדִיב acc. to Ba[NB § 125 e]); VIII. نتدب *ready, willing;* As. *nidbu, freewill-offering* Dl[HWB 448]; Aram. נְדַב *be willing* Pa. Ithpa.; Zinj. נדב *inciting, instigation* DHM[Sendsch. 60]);—**Qal** *Pf.* 3 ms. נָדַב Ex 35[29]; 3 fs. נָדְבָה v[21]; *Impf.* 3 ms. sf. יִדְּבֶנּוּ 25[2];—אֲשֶׁר נָדַב לִבּוֹ 25[2] *whose heart incited*, cf. 35[29]; subj. רוּחַ 35[21] (all P). **Hithp.** *Pf.* 1 s. הִתְנַדַּבְתִּי 1 Ch 29[17]; 3 mpl. הִתְנַדְּבוּ Ezr 2[68] 1 Ch 29[9]; *Impf.* 3 mpl. יִתְנַדְּבוּ v[6]; *Inf.* הִתְנַדֵּב Ju 5[2] +2 t.; הִתְנַדֶּב־ 1 Ch 29[17]; sf. הִתְנַדֶּבְכֶם v[9]; *Pt.* מִתְנַדֵּב Ezr 3[5]+2 t.; pl. מִתְנַדְּבִים Ju 5[9] Ne 11[2];—**1.** *volunteer* for war Ju 5[2.9]; for service of other kinds 2 Ch 17[16] Ne 11[2]. **2.** *offer freewill-offerings* for the first temple 1 Ch 29[5.6.9.9.14.17.17]; for the second Ezr 1[4] 2[68] 3[5] (cf. BAram.). 5068

†נָדָב **n.pr.m.** (*generous, noble*)—**1.** eldest son of Aaron Ex 6[23] 24[1.9] 28[1] Lv 10[1] Nu 3[2.4] 26[60.61] 1 Ch 5[29] 24[1]. 𝔊 Ναδαβ (so **3, 4**). **2.** son of Jeroboam I 1 K 14[20] 15[25.27.31]. 𝔊 Ναβατ, Ναβαθ, 𝔊L Ναδαβ. **3.** a Jerahmeelite 1 Ch 2[28.30]. **4.** a Gibeonite 1 Ch 8[30] 9[36]. 5070

†נְדָבָה **n.f. voluntariness, freewill-offering**;—abs. נ׳ Ex 35[29]+14 t.; cstr. נִדְבַת Dt 16[10]; pl. נְדָבוֹת Am 4[5] ψ 68[10]; נְדָבֹת 110[3]; cstr. נִדְבוֹת 119[108] 2 Ch 31[14]; sf. נִדְבֹתֶיךָ Dt 12[7] +4 t. sfs.;—**1.** *voluntariness* אֹהֲבֵם נְדָבָה Ho 14[5] *I* (י׳) *will love them freely;* עַמְּךָ נְדָבֹת בְּיוֹם חֵילֶךָ ψ 110[3] *thy people will be* (all) *voluntariness in the day of thy host* (be ready to volunteer, v. Br[MP 133]); גֶּשֶׁם נדבות 68[10] *generous* (copious) *rain;* בנדבה 54[8] *voluntarily*, and adverb. acc. נדבה Dt 23[24] (v. Dr). **2.** *freewill, voluntary, offering:* **a.** incl. gifts used in erection and furnishing of tabernacle Ex 35[29] 36[3] (P); for first temple 2 Ch 31[14], second Ezr 1[6] 8[28]. **b.** incl. עולה and שלמים Ez 46[12]; prob. also Am 4[5], נדבות פי ψ 119[108]. **c.** usu. a זֶבַח for festival meals, at Passover 2 Ch 35[8], Pentecost Dt 16[10], Tabernacles Ezr 3[5] (besides the ritual offerings); disting. from נֶדֶר votive offering Lv 7[16] Nu 15[3] 29[39] (P), Lv 22[18.21.23] 23[38] (H), Dt 12[6.17].—(Verbs used are הביא נ׳ Ex 35[29] 36[3]; הקריב נ׳ Lv 22[18]; עשׂה נ׳ Nu 15[3] Ez 46[12]; נתן נ׳ Lv 23[38] Dt 16[10].) 5071

5081 †**נָדִיב adj.** and **n.m.**$^{Is\ 32,8}$ **inclined, generous, noble**;—abs. נ׳ Is 32^{5} + 6 t.; cstr. נְדִיב Ex 35^{5} + 2 t.; f. נְדִיבָה ψ 51^{4}; pl. נְדִיבִים Is 13^{2} + 9 t.; cstr. נְדִיבֵי Nu 21^{18} + 2 t.; sf. נְדִיבֵמוֹ ψ 83^{12};—**1.** *incited, inclined, willing*, נְדִיב לֵב Ex 35$^{5.22}$ (P), 1 Ch 29^{31} (v. נָדַב **Qal**), נְדִיב בְּחָכְמָה 28^{21}; רוּחַ נְדִיבָה ψ 51^{14} *a willing spirit*. **2.** *noble, princely*, in rank 1 S 2^{8} (poem), Jb 12^{21} = ψ 107^{40}, Jb 34^{18} Pr 8^{16} ψ 47^{10} 83^{12} 113$^{8.8}$ 118^{9} 146^{3}; פְּנֵי נדיב Pr 19^{6} 25^{7}; בית נ׳ Jb 21^{28}; פתחי נ׳ Is 13^{2}; בת נ׳ Ct 7^{2}; נְדִיבֵי הָעָם Nu 21^{18} (poem). **3.** *noble* in mind and character ‖ צדיק Pr 17^{26}; opp. נָבָל Is 32$^{5.8}$.

5082 †[**נְדִיבָה**] **n.f. nobility, nobleness**;—sf. נְדִבָתִי Jb 30^{15}; pl. נְדִיבוֹת Is 32$^{8.8}$;—**1.** *nobility* of rank, *honour* Jb 30^{15}. **2.** pl. = *noble things* as counselled by the נדיב in character Is 32$^{8.8}$.

5114 †**נוֹדָב n.pr.gent.** Arab tribe acc. to 1 Ch 5^{19} (+ יְטוּר, נָפִישׁ q.v. Gn 25^{15} 1 Ch 1^{31}); 𝔊 Ναδαβαιων. (Connex. with above ✓ quite uncertain.)

5072 †**נְדַבְיָה n.pr.m.** (*whom Yah impels;* in As. *Na-ad-bi-ia-a-u* Jäger$^{BAS\ i.\ 468}$);—son of Jeconiah 1 Ch 3^{18}. 𝔊 Δενεθει, 𝔊L Ναδαβια.

5074 †I. [**נָדַד**] **vb. retreat, flee, depart, stray, wander, flutter** (NH *id.;* Ar. نَدَّ *flee, run away;* Aram. ܢܕ *hate, abominate, shrink from*, Aph. *put to flight*, etc.; נְדַד *flee*);—**Qal** *Pf.* 3 fs. נָדְדָה Is 10^{31} Est 6^{1}; 3 pl. נָדְדוּ Ho 7^{13} + 4 t., נָדָדוּ Is 21^{15} Je 4^{25}; *Impf.* יִדּוֹד Na 3^{7}; 3 fs. וַתִּדַּד Gn 31^{40}; 3 mpl. יִדֹּדוּן ψ 68$^{13.13}$; *Inf. cstr.* נְדֹד ψ 55^{8}; *Pt.* נֹדֵד Je 49^{5} +; f. נוֹדֶדֶת Pr 27^{8}; pl. נֹדְדִים Ho 9^{17};—**1.** *retreat, flee* Is 21^{15} *fr. before* (מִפְּנֵי) *swords;* 33^{3} *at the sound* (מִקּוֹל) *of tumult;* abs. 10^{31} 22^{3} ψ 68$^{13.13}$, of birds and beasts Je 4^{25} 9^{9} (+ הָלָכוּ); pt. = *fugitive* Is 16^{3} 21^{14}; of fleeing in horror, disgust, c. מִן pers. Na 3^{7} ψ 31^{12}. **2.** *flee, depart*, Isr. fr. (מִן) י׳ Ho 7^{13}; of sleep (מֵעֵינַי) Gn 31^{40} (E), abs. Est 6^{1}. **3.** *wander, stray* (homeless, cf. נוד), עוֹף נוֹדֵד Is 16^{2} (in sim.), so Pr 27^{8} (מִן loc., in sim.), cf. v^{8} (מִן loc.); of scattered Isr. Ho 9^{17} Je 49^{5}; (searching) for food Jb 15^{23} (wicked man); אַרְחִיק נְדֹד ψ 55^{8} *I will wander afar.* **4.** trans. *flutter* wings (of bird, in fig.) Is 10^{14}. **Po'ēl** *Pf.* consec. שֶׁמֶשׁ זָרְחָה וְנוֹדַד Na 3^{17} the sun hath arisen and it (the locust swarm) *fleeth away.* **Hiph.** *chase away*, *Impf.* 3 mpl. sf. וּמִתֵּבֵל יְנִדֻּהוּ Jb 18^{18} (of wicked, ‖ יֶהְדְּפֻהוּ מֵאוֹר). **Hoph.** *be chased away*, *Impf.* 3 ms. וְיֻדַּד כְּחֶזְיוֹן Jb 20^{8} (of wicked); קוֹץ מֻנָד 2 S 23^{6} *thorns thrust away* (si vera l., cf. Dr.; Klo Bu HPS (ק׳ מִדְבָּר). **Hithpo'l.** *Impf.* יִתְנוֹדְדוּ ψ 64^{9} *flee away* (in horror, disgust, cf. **Qal** Na 3^{7} ψ 31^{12}).

†[**נְדוּד**] **n.**[**m.**] **tossing** of sleeplessness, 5076
only pl. נְדֻדִים Jb 7^{4} I am sated with *tossings*.

†**נִדָּה n.f. impurity** (as *abhorrent*, 5079
shunned);—abs. נ׳ Ez 18^{6} +; cstr. נִדַּת Lv 12^{2} +; sf. נִדָּתָהּ v^{5} +;—*impurity* (esp. P and Ezek.): **1.** of ceremonial impurity, as union with brother's wife, Lv 20^{21}; esp. of menstruation Ez 18^{6} (rd. אִשָּׁה בְּנִדָּתָהּ for MT א׳ נִדָּה 𝔊 Co), טֻמְאַת הַנּ׳ 22^{10}, cf. 36^{17}, נִדַּת דְּוֹתָהּ Lv 12^{2}, cf. v^{5} 15$^{19.20.24.25}$ (עֵת־נִדּ׳), v$^{25.25}$, v^{26} (מִשְׁכַּב נִדּ׳), v^{26} (טֻמְאַת נִדּ׳), v^{33} 18^{19}; of defilement contracted by contact with a corpse, מֵי (הַ)נִּדָּה *water of impurity* (i.e. to remove it, cf. Di) Nu 19$^{9.13.20.21.21}$ 31^{23}. **2.** fig. (with allusion to cerem. usage), *impure thing*, Ez 7$^{19.20}$ (of gold), La 1^{17} (of Jerus.); of idolatry, immorality, etc., 2 Ch 29^{5} Ezr 9^{11} (אֶרֶץ נִדָּה), v^{11}, Zc 13^{1} (לְחַטַּאת וּלְנִדָּה).

†**נִידָה n.f. id.** (on form cf. Ges$^{§20,3,R.1}$ Kö 5206
$^{ii.\ 1,\ 497}$);—of Jerusalem La 1^{8} (= נִדָּה v^{17}). 5079

II. **נדד** (✓ of foll., v. Kö$^{ii.\ 1,\ 42}$; cf. Ar. نَدٌّ *high hill, hill rising high into the sky*, Lane^{2778}; also *earth-heap, sand-heap*).

†**נֵד n.m.**$^{Jos\ 3,\ 13}$ **heap** of waters; of Red Sea 5067
Ex 15^{8} (song), ψ 78^{13}; of Jordan Jos 3$^{13.16}$ ψ 33^{7} (sim.). נֵד קָצִיר Is 17^{11} *harvest-heap* is perhaps corrupt: Ges Ew Di Du der. from נוד, reading (probably) נָד (Di) *fled is the harvest;* Che^{Hpt} proposes לָכֵן *therefore;* Buhl$^{Lex\ 13}$ עַד, after 𝔊 𝔗.

†I. [**נָדָה**] **vb. Pi. put away, exclude** (NH 5077
Pi. (*excommunicate*) Hithp. Niph.; As. *nadû*, *throw, overthrow, destroy*, etc., Dl$^{HWB\ 448\ f.}$);—**Pi.** *Pt.* הַמְנַדִּים לְיוֹם רָע Am 6^{3} *they that thrust off the evil day* (i.e. refuse to think of it); lit. מְנַדֵּיכֶם Is 66^{5} *thrust away, exclude* from association in worship (on usage v. Che).

II. **נדה** (✓ of foll.; cf. Ar. نَدِىَ *be moist, moistened*, and also *betide, befal;* نَدًى *rain, dew*, and also *bounty, liberality, a gift*, Lane^{3030}).

†**נֵדֶה** (so Baer Ginsb; van d. H. נֵדֶה), **n.m.** 5078
gift (on format. cf. Ges^{§84ac} Ol^{§144a} Kö$^{ii.\ 1,\ 65}$ Ba$^{NB\ §12a}$);—לְכָל־זֹנוֹת יִתְּנוּ־נֵדֶה Ez 16^{33} (‖ נְדָבִים).

5080 †[נָדַח] **vb.** impel, thrust, banish (esp. Dt. Je. and later) (NH *id., beguile,* Hiph. Niph.; Aram. נְדַח (rare)=BH; Eth. ነድሐ: *thrust;* Ar. نَدَخَ is *drive* a ship to *shore*);—**Qal** *Impf.* יִדַּח 2 S 14[14]; *Inf.* לִנְדֹּחַ Dt 20[19];—trans. **1.** *impel* (i.e. *wield*) an axe, sq. עַל־ Dt 20[19]; **2.** *thrust away, banish,* sq. מִן־ 2 S 14[14]. **Niph.** *Pf.* 3 fs. נִדְּחָה Jb 6[13], etc.; (*Impf.* יִדַּחוּ Je 23[12] v. דחח); *Pt.* נִדָּח 2 S 14[14]; נִדָּחָה Mi 4[6] + 2 t.; נִדַּחַת Ez 34[4.16], etc. On נִדְחֵי Is 11[12] 56[8] ψ 147[2] v. Ki Kö[i. 317];—**1.** *be impelled:* וְנִדְּחָה יָדוֹ בַגַּרְזֶן *be impelled* with the axe Dt 19[5]. **2.** *be thrust out, banished:* of dispersion in exile, sq. שָׁם Je 40[12] 43[5] (|| שׁוּב); sq. לִפְנֵי 49[5] (|| קִבֵּץ); cf. also fig. תֻּשִׁיָּה נִדְּחָה מִמֶּנִּי Jb 6[13] *is banished from me,* i.e. is non-existent; esp. Pt. *banished one(s), outcast(s),* as acc. cogn. c. נָדַח 2 S 14[14]; c. קִבֵּץ Mi 4[6] Dt 30[4] Zp 3[19] Ne 1[9]; נ׳ יִשְׂרָאֵל, c. אָסַף Is 11[12] (|| נְפֻצוֹת יְקַבֵּץ); c. קִבֵּץ 56[8]; c. כִּנֵּס ψ 147[2]; c. הֵשִׁיב 2 S 14[13] Ez 34[4.16] (both || אֹבֵד); c. בּוֹא Is 27[13] (|| *id.*); v. also Is 16[3.4] Je 49[36]; *outcast = neglected one,* fig. of Zion 30[17] (|| דֹּרֵשׁ אֵין לָהּ). **3.** *driven away* (fr. herd, i.e.) *straying* Dt 22[1]. **4.** *thrust away, aside,* from י׳ to idolatry Dt 4[19] 30[17] (sq. וְהִשְׁתַּחֲוָה).

Pu. *Pt.* אֲפֵלָה מְנֻדָּח Is 8[22] *thrust into darkness.*

Hiph. *Pf.* וְהִדִּיחַ consec. 2 S 15[14]; הִדַּחְתִּי Je 23[3] 29[14], etc.; *Impf.* sf. וַיַּדַּח 2 Ch 21[11] + 2 K 17[21] Qr; וַיַּדִּיחוּ Dt 13[14], etc.; *Imv.* sf. הַדִּיחֵמוֹ ψ 5[11]; *Inf.* הַדִּיחַ 62[5], etc.;—**1.** *thrust, move, impel,* fig., obj. רָעָה 2 S 15[14] (sq. עַל־). **2.** *thrust out, banish,* esp. of exile, subj. י׳, c. acc. sq. שָׁמָּה Dt 30[1] Je 46[28]; 16[15] (|| הֶעֱלָה); sq. שָׁם Je 8[3] 24[9] 29[18] Dn 9[7] + Ez 4[13] (om. 𝔊 Co); Je 23[3] (|| קִבֵּץ), v[8] (|| הֵבִיא, הֶעֱלָה), 29[14] (|| הֵשִׁיב, קִבֵּץ), so 32[37]; also 27[10] (|| הִרְחִיק), v[15] (|| אָבַד), cf. 23[2] (Judah under fig. of flock, subj. evil shepherd, || הֵפִיץ), 50[17] (Isr. as sheep, subj. enemies as lions); of driving out priests 2 Ch 13[9]; invader Jo 2[20] (sq. אֶל־); wicked ψ 5[11] (|| הַאֲשִׁימֵם); good man from his eminence ψ 62[5] (sq. מִן). **3.** *thrust away, aside,* from י׳ to idolatry, c. acc., Dt 13[14]; sq. מִן־הַדֶּרֶךְ v[6]; מֵעַל י׳ v[11]; מֵאַחֲרֵי י׳ 2 K 17[21] Qr (Kt v. נדא); cf. 2 Ch 21[11] (|| הִזְנָה). **4.** *compel, force,* subj. adulteress (by flattery), sq. acc. Pr 7[21] (|| הִטָּה).

Hoph. *Pt.* מֻדָּח *chased, hunted,* צְבִי מ׳ Is 13[14], sim. of fugitive Babylonians.

4065 †[מַדּוּחַ] **n.[m.]** a thing to draw aside, enticement (cf. √ **Hiph. 3, 4**);—pl. מַדּוּחִים La 2[14], וַיֶּחֱזוּ לָךְ מַשְׂאוֹת שָׁוְא וּמ׳ (cf. || שָׁוְא וְתָפֵל v[a]).

† I. [נָ֫דֶן, נֵ֫דֶן, נָדָן] **n.[m.]** **gift** (prob. As. 5083
loan-word, cf. As. *nudnu, dowry* Dl[HWB 451], √*naddânu* = נתן, Dl[Baer Ezech. xiv]);—נְדָנַיִךְ Ez 16[33], of bribe from harlot (|| נֵדֶה), metaph. of Jerusalem.

† II. [נָדָן] **n.[m.]** **sheath** (NH *id.;* Aram. 5084
נִדְנָא (𝔗 Talm.); Pers. loan-word Nö[GGA, 1884, 1022]);—וַיָּשֶׁב חַרְבּוֹ אֶל־נְדָנָהּ׃ 1 Ch 21[27].

†[נָדַף] **vb.** **drive, drive asunder** (NH 5086
id., spread, be diffused, disseminated (of odour); Ar. نَدَفَ *strike, beat,* esp. bow-string with mallet, to clean cotton; also *play* the lyre; Aram. נְדַף = NH; Eth. ነደፈ: *throw, hurl*);—**Qal** *Impf.* sf. יִדְּפֶנּוּ Jb 32[13] (juss.); 3 fs. sf. תִּדְּפֶנּוּ ψ 1[4]; 2 ms. תִּנְדֹּף ψ 68[3];—*drive about,* chaff, subj. wind ψ 1[4]; wicked, subj. God 68[3] (כְּהִנְדֹּף עָשָׁן, v. infr.); cf. Jb 32[13] (= defeat, anguish).

Niph. *Pf.* נִדַּף Is 19[7]; *Inf.* כְּהִנְדֹּף ψ 68[3] (v. Kö[i. 306 f.]); *Pt.* נִדָּף Lv 26[36] + 3 t.;—*be driven, driven about* (esp. by wind) ψ 68[3], v. supr. (like a driving [Che *drift*] of smoke); of breath (הֶבֶל) fig. of deceitful gain Pr 21[6] (𝔊 Hi Ew רֹדֵף; v. De Now); of withered plant Is 19[7] (where subj. מִזְרַע, עָרוֹת i.e. place; whence Che trans. נ׳ *vanish;* but ref. prob. to plant-life in these places, v. Di); of leaf Lv 26[36] (as making slight sound), Jb 13[25] (fig. of sufferer, || קַשׁ יָבֵשׁ), of chaff (קַשׁ) Is 41[2] (sim. of bow of hostile kings || עָפָר).

†נָדַר **vb.** **vow** (NH *id.;* Ph. נדר; || form 5087
of נָזַר, q.v.);—**Qal** *Pf.* 3 ms. נ׳ ψ 132[2] 2 S 15[8]; נָדַר Ju 11[39]; 3 fs. נָדְרָה Nu 30[11]; 2 ms. נָדַרְתָּ Gn 31[13] + 5 t. Pf.; *Impf.* 3 ms. יִדֹּר Nu 6[21] + 5 t.; 2 ms. תִּדֹּר Dt 12[17] + 4 t., תִּדּוֹר Ec 5[4] + 4 t. Impf.; *Imv.* pl. נִדְרוּ ψ 76[12]; *Inf.* לִנְדֹּר Nu 6[2] Dt 23[23]; Pt. נֹדֵר Lv 27[8] Mal 1[14];—*vow a vow* נָדַר נֶדֶר Gn 28[20] 31[13] (both E), Nu 21[2] (J), Nu 6[2] 30[3.4] (P), Ju 11[30] 1 S 1[11] 2 S 15[8.7] Is 19[21]; נֶדֶר om. Lv 27[8] Nu 30[11] (P); Dt 23[23] ψ 76[12] Ec 5[4.4]; c. לְ *to whom* Nu 6[21] Dt 23[24] Mal 1[14] ψ 132[2] Ec 5[3]; נֶדֶר אֲשֶׁר נָדַר *vow which he vowed* Dt 12[11.17] 23[22.22] Ju 11[39] Je 44[25] Jon 1[16]; cf. אֲשֶׁר נ׳ אֲשַׁלֵּמָה Jon 2[10], אֵת אֲשֶׁר תִּדֹּר שַׁלֵּם Ec 5[3].

†נֶ֫דֶר, נֵ֫דֶר **n.m.**[Nu 30, 5] **vow;**—נֶ֫דֶר Gn 28[20] 5088
+ 17 t.; נֵ֫דֶר Nu 30[10] + 4 t.; sf. נִדְרִי 2 S 15[7] + 5 t. sfs.; pl. נְדָרִים Jon 1[16] Pr 20[25]; sf. נְדָרַי ψ 22[26]

+3 t.; נִדְרֵיהֶם Lv 22^{18} + 24 t. sfs.;—*vow:* **1.** of personal service to י׳ Gn 28^{20} 31^{13} (of Jacob at Bethel), 2 S $15^{7.8}$ (at Hebron); Lv 27^{2} (P, any one), of Nazirite Nu $6^{2.5.21}$; Hannah's consecration of her son 1 S 1^{11}, cf. בר נדרי Pr 31^{2}. **2.** in gen. of any kind of votive offerings or promised gifts to י׳ Nu $30^{3.4.5.5.6.7.8.9.10.12.13.14.15}$ (P) Dt $12^{11.17.26}$ $23^{19.22}$ Is 19^{21} Na 2^{1} ψ 22^{26} $61^{6.9}$ 65^{2} $116^{14.18}$ Pr 20^{25} Jb 22^{27} Ec 5^{3}. **3.** Jephthah's daughter as עולה Ju $11^{30.39}$. **4.** the ban Nu 21^{2} (E). **5.** ‖ עֹלָה ψ 66^{13}; תּוֹדָה ψ 50^{14} 56^{13}; שְׁלָמִים Nu 15^{8}; opp. נדבה Lv 7^{16} Nu 15^{3} 29^{39} (P), Lv $22^{18.21.23}$ 23^{38} (H), Dt $12^{6.17}$ 1 S 1^{21} Jon 1^{16}. **6.** once of idolatry Je 44^{25} (נ׳ לְקַטֵּר לִמְלֶכֶת הַשָּׁמַיִם).—Vbs. used are: נָדַר q.v.; שִׁלֵּם *pay* 2 S 15^{7} + 12 t.; עשׂה Ju 11^{39} Je 44^{25}; נשׂא Dt 12^{26}; קום Nu $30^{5.8.12.15}$; הֵקִים Je 44^{25}; אפר Nu 30^{14}; פִּלֵּא Lv 22^{21} 27^{2} Nu $15^{3.8}$ פלא לנ׳ נ׳ Nu 6^{2}; הֵפֵר Nu 30^{9}. (See these vbs.)

5089 נָהּ v. נוה. p. 627

5090 †I. **נָהַג vb. drive, conduct** (NH *conduct oneself, behave, be accustomed;* Ar. نَهَجَ *go along the road, keep to the road;* Aram. נְהַג *lead*);—**Qal** *Pf.* נ׳ La 3^{2}; נָהֲגוּ 1 S 30^{20}; *Impf.* יִנְהַג Is 20^{4}, etc.; *Imv.* נְהַג 2 K 4^{24}; *Pt. act.* נֹהֵג Is 11^{6} + 2 t., etc.; *pass.* נְהוּגִים Is 60^{11};—**1.** *drive,* flocks Ex 3^{1}; cf. (in predict.) Is 11^{6} (sq. בְּ); fig., obj. Joseph, ψ 80^{2} (sim. of flock); hence, obj. human being, *lead on,* Ct 8^{2} (‖ הֵבִיא אֶל־); also fig., subj. י׳, La 3^{2} (‖ הוֹלִיךְ); pass. pt. of kings *led* in procession Is 60^{11} cf. Di (rather than as captives, Che, as earlier usage; ‖ הֵבִיא); *drive away, off,* (obj. מִקְנֶה) Gn 31^{18} (of Jacob, going by stealth); usually as booty (obj. flocks and herds) 1 S 23^{5}, חמור יתומים ינהגו Jb 24^{3} (unjustly); cf. 1 S $30^{2.20}$ (rd. וַיִּנְהֲגוּ We Dr Kit Bu, cf. Th, not HPS q.v.), v^{22} (no obj. expr. but really captives ‖ הָלַךְ), Is 20^{4}; *drive* an ass for riding 2 K 4^{24} (‖ הָלַךְ); a cart (עֲגָלָה) 2 S 6^{3} = 1 Ch 13^{7} (where בְּע׳); abs. of driving chariot 2 K 9^{20}; *lead out* an army to battle (late) 1 Ch 20^{1} 2 Ch 25^{11}. **2.** fig. וְלִבִּי נֹהֵג בַּחָכְמָה Ec 2^{3} my heart *behaving itself* in wisdom (cf. NH supr.). **Pi.** *Pf.* נִהַג Ex 10^{3}; נִהַגְתָּ Is 63^{14}; *Impf.* יְנַהֵג Dt 4^{27}, etc.;—**1.** *drive away, lead off,* sq. acc., daughters of Laban Gn 31^{26} (‖ גָּנַב); of י׳, *leading off* people into exile, sq. שָׁמָּה Dt 4^{27} (‖ הֵפִיץ), 28^{37} (‖ הוֹלִיךְ). **2.** *lead on, guide,* sq. acc., subj. י׳, ψ 78^{52} (כַּעֵדֶר ‖ הִסִּיעַ כַּצֹּאן); Is 49^{10} (‖ נִהֵל, cf. ψ 23^{2}); 63^{14}; ψ 48^{15}; *guide on,* a wind, Ex 10^{13} (sq. בָּאָרֶץ), ψ 78^{26} (‖ הִסִּיעַ). **3.** *cause to drive* (cf. **Qal**, 2 K 9^{20}) Ex 14^{25} (JE; subj. י׳, v. Di).

†מִנְהָג **n.m.** **driving, charioteering**;—abs. מ׳ 2 K 9^{20}; cstr. מִנְהַג v^{20}. 4491

†II. [נָהַג] **vb. Pi. moan, lament** (Ar. نَهَجَ *be out of breath, pant, breathe heavily;* Aram. ܢܗܩ *sigh, groan*);—**Pi.** *Pt.* fpl. מְנַהֲגוֹת Na 2^{8} (כְּקוֹל יוֹנִים). 5090

†נָהָה **vb. wail, lament** (prob. onomatop., cf. Sta$^{Gesch. i. 388}$; Aram. ܢܗܐ, (in Lexx); Eth. ነሀየ: is *recreari, respirare,* etc. Di^{632});—**Qal** *Pf.* וְנָהָה Mi 2^{4} *lament* sq. acc. cogn.; *Imv.* נְהֵה Ez 32^{18}, sq. עַל, *concerning, for.* **Niph.** *Impf.* וַיִּנָּהוּ 1 S 7^{2} sq. אַחֲרֵי *went mourning after* (so most, cf. Th Dr, who argue against Thes *were gathered*), < rd. וַיִּפְנוּ, ויפנ(ה) *turned after* = *submitted* to (as Ez 29^{16}) 𝔊 (perh.), We Kit Bu HPS. 5091

†נְהִי **n.[m.] wailing, lamentation, mourning song**;—נ׳ abs. Am 5^{16} + 5 t.; וְנֶהִי Je 9^{9};—*wailing,* at י׳'s judgment Mi 2^{4} as acc. cogn.; Je 9^{9} (c. נָשָׂא עַל־ + ‖ בְּכִי, קִינָה), v^{17} (c. *id.,* ‖ דִּמְעָה), v^{18} (קוֹל נ׳), 31^{15} (‖ בְּכִי, תַּמְרוּרִים); *mourning song* יוֹדְעֵי נ׳ Am 5^{16} of professional mourners, skilled in mourning song; cf. Je 9^{19}, where taught (‖ קִינָה), also הִי Ez 2^{10} (‖ אֵבֶל, מִסְפֵּד) q.v. (Ol Co rd. נהי, cf. Berthol). 5092

†נִהְיָה **n.f.** *id.* (si vera l.);—only Mi 2^{4} נָהָה נְהִי נִהְיָה, where, however, Thes al. der. נהיה fr. היה (Niph., v. p. 228 a supr.); but prob. corrupt, del. 𝔊 Sta$^{ZAW\ 1886,\ 122\ f.}$ We Now as dittogr. 5093

†[נִי] **n.[m.]** si vera l., **wailing** (AV RV) (= נְהִי);—וְנָשְׂאוּ אֵלַיִךְ בְּנִיהֶם קִינָה Ez 27^{32}, but improb.; 𝔊 𝔖 בְּנֵיהֶם, v. MV; so Co, who, however, del. as gloss, cf. Buhl Berthol. 5204

†הִי **n.[m.]** si vera l., **wailing** (= (נְ)הִי q.v.) Ez 2^{10} וָהִי, where probably read וּנְהִי Ol Co, cf. Berthol (‖ קִינִים והגה).

†[נָהַל] **vb. Pi. lead, guide to a watering-place** or station, **and cause to rest there; bring to a station** or **place of rest; lead, guide; refresh** (cf. Ar. مَنْهَلٌ *watering-place,* نَهَلَ *take a first drink;* likewise (Dozy) مَنْهَلَةٌ *station, stage* of the road; perh. also As. *nâlu, lie down* Dl$^{HWB\ 438}$; Dl$^{HA\ 5\ f.;\ Prol.\ 17\ ff.}$ tries to ex- 5095

plain all the passages from this As. *nâlu*; against him v. Frä[ZDPh i. 105] Che[Acad., April 10, 1881] DHM[ZKF i. 357 f.] Nö[ZMG xl. 1886, 728]; *two* √√ prop. by RDWilson[Presb. Rev. (N.Y.), April, 1885] (careful art.), cf. Che[ψ 23. 2, crit. n.]);—**Pi.** *Pf.* 2 ms. נֵהַלְתָּ Ex 15[13]; *Impf.* 3 ms. יְנַהֵל Is 40[11]; sf. יְנַהֲלֵנִי ψ 23[2], יְנַהֲלֵם Is 49[10]; וַיְנַהֲלֵם Gn 47[17] 2 Ch 32[22]; 2 ms. sf. תְּנַהֲלֵנִי ψ 31[4]; 3 mpl. sf. וַיְנַהֲלוּם 2 Ch 28[15]; *Pt.* מְנַהֵל Is 51[18];—**1.** *lead to a watering-place* (*or station*), *and cause to rest there*, subj. י׳ as shepherd, Is 49[10] (עַל־ loc.; ‖ נהג), ψ 23[2] (c. עַל־ loc.; ‖ הִרְבִּיץ), Is 40[11] (‖ קִבֵּץ, רעה). **2.** *lead* or *bring to a station, a goal*, י׳ subj. Ex 15[13] (song; no obj. expressed, אֶל־ loc.; ‖ נחה); human subj. 2 Ch 28[15] *and they conducted* all the feeble of them *by means of* (ב) *asses* (‖ הֵבִיא). **3.** *lead, guide:* fig., אֵין מְנַהֵל לָהּ Is 51[18] *there is no one to be a guide for her*, i.e. for Jerus., drunk with cup of י׳'s fury (‖ מַחֲזִיק בְּיָדָהּ); י׳ subj. ψ 31[4] *lead me* (‖ תַּנְחֵנִי). **4.** *give rest to* (?) וַיְנ׳ מִסָּבִיב 2 Ch 32[22] *and he gave them rest on every hand*, cf. 𝔊 𝔙 (=וַיָּנַח לָהֶם מִסּ׳ 1 Ch 22[18]+, prob. so read here, v. Be DHM Öt). **5.** *refresh* with food, וַיְנ׳ בַּלֶּחֶם Gn 47[17] (J).

Hithp. *Impf.* prob. *journey by stations, stages*, only 1 s. אֶתְנַהֲלָה Gn 33[14] (J), *I will proceed, journey on, by stages* (i.e. deliberately, with family and cattle).

5096 נַהֲלָל v. II. נַהֲלֹל. below

5097 †I. נַהֲלֹל **n.m. pasture,** or perh. (EncBi[614]) *watering-place* (see √), only pl. נַהֲלֹלִים Is 7[19].

5096 II. נַהֲלֹל **n.pr.loc.** Ju 1[30] in Zebulun, 𝔊 Δωμανα, A Εναμμαν, 𝔊L Αμμαν; = נַהֲלָל Jos 19[15] 21[35], 𝔊 Ναβααλ, Νααλωλ, 𝔊L Αναλωθ, Αλωμ;—site unknown, cf. GFM[Ju 1. 30].

5098 †[נָהַם] **vb. growl, groan** (NH *id.*; Ar. نَهَمَ; Aram. ܢܗܡ, נְהַם);—**Qal** *Pf.* וְנָהַמְתָּ Pr 5[11]; וּנְהַמְתֶּם Ez 24[23]; *Impf.* יִנְהֹם Is 5[29.30]; *Pt.* נֹהֵם Pr 28[15];—**1.** *growl*, of a lion (viz. while it is devouring its prey: opp. שׁאג, of *roar* with which it springs upon it RS[Proph. 243]) Pr 28[15], of Assyr. (under fig. of lion) Is 5[29]; sq. עַל (*over*), v[30]. **2.** *groan*, of sufferer Pr 5[11] Ez 24[23].

5099 †נַ֫הַם† **n.[m.]** growling of lion;—fig. of king's wrath Pr 19[12], cf. 20[2].

5100 †[נְהָמָה] **n.f. growling, groaning;**—only cstr. נַהֲמַת: **1.** Is 5[30] of sea, in sim. of growling of Assyr. lion. **2.** fig. *groaning* ψ 38[9] of heart (שַׁאֲגְתִּי מִנ׳).

†[נָהַק] **vb. bray, cry** (NH *id.*; Ar. نَهَقَ 5101
bray (of ass); Aram. נְהַק *cry out* (of men), נְהִיקָא *braying*);—**Qal** *Impf.* יִנְהַק Jb 6[5] of wild ass; יִנְהָקוּ 30[7] of cries of destitute outcasts.

†I. [נָהַר] **vb. flow, stream** (Ar. نَهَرَ *run*, 5102
flow; perh. denom. fr. نَهْرٌ *river*, and this loan-wd. (cf. Frä[285]); As. *nâru, stream, river*, Dl[HWB 440]; Aram. ܢܗܪܐ, נַהֲרָא *river*);—**Qal** *Pf.* 3 pl. consec. וְנָהֲרוּ Is 2[2] + 2 t.; *Impf.* 3 mpl. יִנְהֲרוּ Je 51[44];—*flow, stream*, only fig.: of restored Isr. streaming אֶל־טוּב י׳ עַל־דָּגָן וגו׳ Je 31[12]; nations to (אֶל־) Bel 51[44]; to temple-hill at Jerus. Is 2[2] (אֵלָיו) = Mi 4[1] (עָלָיו).

נָהָר 120 **n.m.**[Gn 2, 10] **stream, river;**—abs. נ׳ 5104
Gn 2[10]+; cstr. נְהַר Dt 1[7]+; pl. נְהָרִים Is 18[27] + 4 t., cstr. נַהֲרֵי Is 18[1] + 2 t.; but oftener נְהָר(וֹ)ת Is 19[6] + 23 t.; cstr. נַהֲרוֹת 2 K 5[12] + 2 t.; sf. נַהֲרוֹתֶיךָ Ez 32[2], נַהֲרֹתַיִךְ Is 44[27], נַהֲרֹתֶיהָ Ez 31[4.15], נַהֲרֹתָם Ex 7[19], נַהֲרוֹתָם Ez 32[2.14]; appar. du. נַהֲרַיִם Gn 24[10] + 2 t., נַהֲרָיִם Ju 3[8] (v. infr.) (all in אֲרַם נ׳);—**1.** *stream, river*, Nu 24[6] (JE), Jb 14[11] 40[23] ψ 105[41] (in sim.), Is 48[18] (*id.*), 59[19] (*id.*) + oft.; freq. of partic. rivers; r. of Eden Gn 2[10] and its branches v[13.14] (all J); נְהַר מִצְרַיִם 15[18] (J; i.e., si vera l., the Nile) but rd. prob. נַחַל מ׳, whence נהר through infl. of foll. נהר—cf. 2 K 24[7]—Nö[ZMG xl. 1886, 699] (alternat.), Lag[BN 140] Ball[Hpt]; נָהָר of Nile Is 19[5]; esp. of Euphrates נְהַר פְּרָת Gn 15[18] Dt 1[7] (both + הַנּ׳ הַגָּדוֹל) Jos 1[4] + 8 t. + 2 S 8[3] (Qr 𝔊 and ‖ 1 Ch 18[3]; Kt om. פְּרָת;—cf. also Gn 2[14 b] supr.); oftener (of Euphr.) without פ׳: הַנָּהָר κατ' ἐξοχήν, Gn 31[21] Ex 23[31] Nu 22[5] Jos 24[2.3.14.15] (all E), poss. also Gn 36[37] (P; cf. Di) = 1 Ch 1[48], + 13 t. + 2 S 8[3] Kt (v. supr.); and even without art. (poet.) † Is 7[20] Je 2[18] Mi 7[12] Zc 9[10] ψ 72[8]; הַנּ׳ הַגּ׳ once of Tigris † Dn 10[4]; † נְהַר גּוֹזָן (חבור) 2 K 17[6] 18[11] cf. 2 Ch 5[26]; pl. נַהֲרֵי כוּשׁ Zp 3[10]; perh. of a *canal:* נְהַר־כְּבָר Ez 1[1.3] + 6 t. Ez; הַנָּהָר אַהֲוָא Ezr 8[21], נְהַר א׳ v[31]; cf. נַהֲרוֹת בָּבֶל ψ 137[1]; *canals* poss. also in שַׁעֲרֵי הַנּ׳ Na 2[7] (of Nineveh); of *canals* of Egypt Ex 7[19] (‖ יְאֹרִים etc.), 8[1] (‖ *id.*). **2.** נְהָרוֹת (מִבְּכִי) Jb 28[11] usu. understood of (*underground*) *streams;* Szold[Comm. Jb] Gr[Monatsschr. 1887, 410] and Perles[Analekten 69] prop. נִבְכֵי נ׳ *sources of rivers* (cf. 36[16]); Wetzst Hoffm Bu מַבְּכֵי נ׳

(not elsewh.) with similar meaning. **3.** fig. of י׳'s favour ψ 46[5].—On נַהֲרַיִם ending appar. du., v. אֲרָם; Tel Am. *Na-ri-ma, Nahrima* (Wkl [Tel Am. 40*]), and Eg. *Nhrina* (WMM [As. u. Eur. 249 ff.]) point however to orig. ending ַ־יִם; this inconsistent with view of EMey [Gesch. § 180] that ָ־יִם here a *locative* ending (cf. Ba [§ 194 c. Anm. 1] Buhl [Ges 12]), v. also Di [Gn 24, 10].

5102 †II. נָהַר **vb. shine, beam** (Aram.) (NH *id.*, esp. in deriv.; As. *nûru, light*, Dl [HWB 440]; Ar. نَهَرٌ *daytime*, نَهَارٌ *day, daytime;* Aram. ܢܗܰܪ *shine*, נְהַר *id.;* Palm. נהירא *illustrious*, e.g. Vog [Palm. No. 22]);—**Qal** *Pf.* 2 fs. consec. וְנָהַרְתְּ Is 60[5]; 3 pl. נָהָרוּ ψ 34[6];—*beam, be radiant*, fig. of joy: תִּרְאִי וְנ׳ Is 60[5], הִבִּיטוּ אֵלָיו וְנ׳ ψ 34[6] (rd. הַבִּ׳, וּנְהָרוּ, v. 𝔊 𝔖 𝔙 Che Bae Du).

5105 †נְהָרָה **n.f. light, daylight** (as Aram. נְהוֹרָא, ܢܘܗܪܐ m.);—וְאַל־תּוֹפַע עָלָיו נ׳ Jb 3[4] (opp. חֹשֶׁךְ).

4492 †[מִנְהָרָה] **n.f.** dub., only pl. הַמִּנְהָרוֹת אֲשֶׁר בֶּהָרִים Ju 6[2] (+ הַמְּעָרוֹת *caves*, הַמְּצָדוֹת *strongholds*)—(clearly, si vera l., fr. a √נהר, but with what meaning? Schultens [Jb 49] comp. Ar. مِنْهَرٌ, مِنْهَرَةٌ [which means *a place hollowed out by water*], and rend. *crevices, ravines*, so Thes al.; Rashi Ki Wetzst [Hauran, 46] think of caves with a *light*-opening; R. Levi ben Gerson *beacons*, i.e. towers for fire-signals, GFM; but II. נהר late in Heb.; 𝔊 *τρυμαλίας*, 𝔙 *antra;* Bu thinks הַמְּעָרוֹת a gloss explaining הַמִּנ׳).

5106 †[נוא] **vb. hinder, restrain, frustrate** (Ar. نَاءَ (نوأ) (or نَأَى) *rise with difficulty, rise against one* (Frey), III. *contend with*, Lane [2861]);—**Qal** *Impf.* 2 mpl. תנואון Nu 32[7] Kt, but read Hiph. (so Qr), cf. Di. **Hiph.** *Pf.* הֵנִיא Nu 30[6], etc.; *Impf.* יָנִיא v[9], יָנִי ψ 141[5], תְּנִיאוּן Nu 32[7] Qr;—**1.** *restrain, forbid* (performance of vow), sq. acc. pers. Nu 30[6.6.9.12]; *frustrate* (device of people), subj. י׳, sq. acc. rei, ψ 33[10] (‖ הֵפִיר); *refuse* 141[5] (text dub. v. Che). **2.** *restrain, make averse* the heart (acc.) Nu 32[7] (sq. מֵעֲבֹר), v[9] (sq. לְבִלְתִּי־בֹא).

8569 †[תְּנוּאָה] **n.f. opposition;**—sf. תְּנוּאָתִי Nu 14[34] *my opposition*, of י׳; pl. תְּנוּאוֹת עָלַי יִמְצָא Jb 33[10] = occasions for hostility (‖ count as enemy).

5107 †[נוּב] **vb. bear fruit** (poet.) (Aram. נוֹבָא *fruit* (rare));—**Qal** *Impf.* יָנוּב ψ 62[11] Pr 10[31]; יְנוּבוּן ψ 92[15];—only fig., abs. of righteous under fig. of tree ψ 92[15]; חַיִל כִּי יָנוּב 62[11] if wealth *beareth fruit;* Pr 10[31] פִּי צַדִּיק יָנוּב חָכְמָה *beareth the fruit of* wisdom. **Po'l.** *Impf.* יְנוֹבֵב Zc 9[17], דָּגָן בַּחוּרִים וְתִירוֹשׁ יְנ׳ בְּתֻלוֹת fig. for *makes to flourish.*

†נוֹב Kt (Qr נִיב, q.v.) **n.[m.] fruit;**—cstr. Is 57[19] *fruit of lips* (fig. for thanksgiving). 5108

†[נִיב] **n.[m.] fruit;**—ניב cstr. Is 57[19] Qr, v. supr.; נִיבוֹ Mal 1[12] of offerings to י׳ as fruit of his table (‖ אכלו). 5108

†נוֹבָי **n.pr.m.** a chief of people Ne 10[20] Qr נֵיבָי (Baer; נֵיבַי van d. H., Ginsb; 𝔊 Νωβαι (cf. Palm. נבי n.pr.f. Cook [124] Lzb [321]). 5109

תְּנוּבָה **n.f. fruit, produce;**—abs. Is 27[6]; cstr. תְּנוּבַת Ez 36[30]; תְּנוּבָתִי Ju 9[11]; pl. תְּנוּבֹת Dt 32[13], ־וֹת La 4[9]; esp. ת׳ שָׂדָי *fruit, produce, of field* Dt 32[13] La 4[9]; cf. ת׳ הַשָּׂדֶה Ez 36[30] (‖ פרי העץ); of fig-tree Ju 9[11]; metaph. of Isr. וּמָלְאוּ פְנֵי־תֵבֵל ת׳ Is 27[6] (‖ יַשְׁרֵשׁ יעקב יציץ ופרח יש׳). 8570

†נוּד **vb. move to and fro, wander, flutter, shew grief** (NH *id.* (rare); Aram. נוּד, ܢܳܕ, *shake, move to and fro, be disturbed, agitated;* BAram. *flee* (v. infr.); Ar. نَادَ (نود) *waver, totter*);—**Qal** *Pf.* 3 ms. נָד, so rd. for MT נֵד Is 17[11] Ges Hi Ew Di Kit Che [Hpt] RV; 3 pl. נָדוּ Je 50[3]; *Impf.* 3 ms. יָנוּד 1 K 14[15] + 3 t.; 2 ms. תָּנוּד Je 4[1], juss. תָּנֹד 16[5]; 3 mpl. וַיָּנֻדוּ Jb 42[11]; 2 mpl. תָּנֻדוּ Je 22[10]; *Imv.* fs. נוּדִי ψ 11[1] Qr (Kt נודו); mpl. נֻדוּ Je 48[17] + 2 t. Je; *Inf.* לָנוּד Jb 2[11] + 2 t.; *Pt.* נָד Gn 4[12.14];—**1. a.** *move to and fro, wander* aimlessly, as fugitive, נָע וָנָד Gn 4[12.14] (J), Je 4[1] (Gie, as apod., so RV; but Ew Hi Gf Che Ke, as prot., *if thou wanderest not* [morally], and swearest, etc.,—Ew Hi reading with 𝔊 שקוציך מִפִּיךָ וּמִפָּנַי לא תנוד; Co del. v[1.2]); *take flight* (perh. metaplast. form of נדד q.v.), נָסוּ נָּדוּ מְאֹד Je 49[30] (on dagh. v. Ges [§ 20 g]), of harvest Is 17[11] i.e. be destroyed, in fig. (v. supr.); Je 50[3] (‖ הלך), v[8] (sq. מִתּוֹךְ; ‖ יצא). **b.** *flutter*, of bird Pr 26[2] (‖ עוּף); fig. of soul ψ 11[1]. **c.** *waver, wave, shake*, of reed 1 K 14[15] (sim. of smitten Isr.). **2.** *shew grief* (i.e. by shaking or nodding head), usu. sq. לְ pers.: **a.** *lament* for the dead (Josiah) Je 22[10] (‖ בכה), for Jerus. Je 15[5] (‖ חמל), 16[5] (‖ ספד), Is 51[19]; for Nineveh Na 3[7]; Moab Je 48[17]. **b.** *condole, shew sympathy* with Jb 2[11] 42[11]; abs. ψ 69[21]. **Hiph.** *Impf.* 3 ms. יָנִיד Je 18[16]; 3 fs. sf. תְּנִדֵנִי ψ 36[12]; *Imv.* ms. sf. הֲנִידֵמוֹ ψ 59[12] (so rd. for MT הורידמו 𝔖 Lag [Proph. Chald. xlviii.] Dr [2 S 15, 20] cf. Che [crit. n.] Hup-Now Bae Du); *Inf.* לְהָנִיד 2 K 21[8];— 5110

1. *cause to wander* aimlessly, as fugitives, c. acc. pers. ψ 36^{12} 59^{12} (v. supr.), sq. רֶגֶל 2 K 21^{8}. **2.** *make a wagging, wag* with the head, בְּרֹאשׁ Je 18^{16}. **Hoph.** *Pt.* כְּקוֹץ מֻנָּד 2 S 23^{6} and the worthless, *like briers made to flutter* (tossed away) are they (text dub.; Klo Bu HPS rd. מדבר). **Hithpo'lel** *Pf.* 3 fs. וְהִתְנוֹדְדָה consec. Is 24^{20}; *Impf.* 2 ms. תִּתְנוֹדָד Je 48^{27}; *Pt.* מִתְנוֹדֵד Je 31^{18};—**1.** *move oneself to and fro, sway, totter,* Is 24^{20} (of earth). **2.** *shake oneself,* in excitement Je 48^{27} (perh. of scorn = *wag* the head, as Hiph. Je 18^{16} cf. Gf RV). **3.** *bemoan oneself* (cf. **Qal 2**), Je 31^{18} (the lament follows in orat. recta).

5112 †I. [נֹד, נוֹד] **n.[m.] wandering** of aimless fugitive;—only sf. נֹדִי ψ 59^{9} *my wandering* (word-play with נֹאדֶךָ v^{b}).

5113 †II. נוֹד appar. **n.pr.terr.** ארץ־נ׳ Gn 4^{16} of region into which Cain wandered (cf. v$^{12.14}$); 𝔊 (strangely) Ναιδ; 𝔙 appellat., *profugus* in terra, cf. Symm Theod, v. Ne$^{Marg. 9}$.

5205 †נִיד **n.m.**$^{(v. infr.)}$ **quivering motion** of lips;—only cstr. נ׳ שְׂפָתַי Jb 16^{5} *the motion of my lips* (in expressing sympathy).—MT makes subj. of יחשׂך, but rd. prob. אחשׂך, v. חשׂך.

5206 נִידָה v. נִדָּה sub נדד. p. 622

4493 †[מָנוֹד] **n.[m.] a shaking, wagging**;—only cstr. מְנוֹד רֹאשׁ ψ 44^{15} *object of head-shaking,* in derision (of Isr.; ‖ מָשָׁל; v^{14} קֶלֶס, לַעַג, חֶרְפָּה).

נוה (prob. √of foll., si vera l., cf. Ar. نَاهَ (نوه) *be high, eminent*).

5089 †נֹהַּ **n.[m.] eminency, distinction**;—לֹא נֹהַּ בָּהֶם Ez 7^{11} *no eminency is left in them* (so A 𝔊 Theod Symm Ges Ke), < del. 𝔊B Co Berthol Toy, cf. also Da.

5115 †I. [נָוָה] **vb.** only **Hiph.** (si vera l.) lit. **beautify** (then connected with נאה *be comely,* so Buhl SS; cf. NH נוה Niph. *shew oneself beautiful,* Nithp. *adorn oneself,* נָוֶה adj. *beautiful,* Levy^{NHWB});—*Impf.* 1 s. sf. אַנְוֵהוּ Ex 15^{2} *I will beautify, adorn him* (with praises; obj. י׳; ‖ רוממ; 𝔊 δοξάσω, 𝔙 *glorificabo*).—Adj. נָוֶה Je 6^{2}, v. נָאוֶה sub [נָאָה].

II. **נוה** (√of foll., mng. dub.; Ar. نَوَى is *aim at, propose to oneself as aim* (e.g. of journey), VIII. *betake oneself to a place of alighting,* or *abode;* نِيَّةٌ, نَوًى *place to which one purposes journeying* Lane^{3040}; hence poss. I. נָוֶה as goal of shepherd; cf. Sab. נוי *meadow, pasture,* DHM $^{Südar. Alt. 32}$; see however Dr$^{1 S 19, 18}$ HPS$^{ib.}$; NH נָוֶה *dwelling, habitation*).

†I. נָוֶה **n.m.**$^{Is. 27, 10}$ **abode of shepherd, or** 5116
flocks, poet. **habitation**;—abs. Is 27^{10}+; cstr. נְוֵה Ex 15^{13}+; נְוַת Jb 8^{6} (as if fr. נָוָה; or rd. נְוֵה ?); sf. נָוְךָ Jb 5^{24}, נָוֵהוּ 2 S 15^{25}+, נְוֵהֶם Je 49^{20} Ez 34^{14} (cf. Sta$^{§ 351 c.}$), נְוֵהֶן Je 23^{3} (so Baer Ginsb; נְוֵיהֶן van d. H., pl. acc. to Kö$^{ii. 1, p. 77}$);—**1. a.** *abode,* of sheep 2 S 7^{8} (‖ מֵאַחַר הַצֹּאן) = 1 Ch 17^{1}; Is 65^{10} (‖ רֵבֶץ); of people under fig. of sheep Je 23^{3} 49^{20} = 50^{45}, 50^{19} Ez 34$^{14.14}$ (‖ רֵבֶץ, מִרְעֶה); of camels Ez 25^{5} (‖ מִרְבַּץ צֹאן). **b.** *abode of shepherds* Je 33^{12} (+ מַרְבִּיצִים צֹאן). **c.** = *meadow,* in fig. of Ephr. planted (שָׁתוּל) as tree Ho 9^{13}. **2.** *habitation,* usu. of country, or of domains in the country (chiefly poet.), Jb 5^{3} 8^{6} (נְוַת צִדְקֶךָ, v. supr.), Pr 21^{20}; ‖ אֹהֶל Jb 5^{24} 18^{15}; ‖ בַּיִת Pr 3^{33}; ‖ רֵבֶץ 24^{15}; of י׳ in Canaan 2 S 15^{25}; of Can. as place of י׳'s sanctuary, נ׳ קָדְשֶׁךָ Ex 15^{13}; fig. of י׳ himself, נ׳ צֶדֶק Je 50^{7}; habit. of nation Je 10^{25} 25^{30} Is 32^{18} (נ׳ שָׁלוֹם), ψ 79^{7}; = city Is 27^{10}, esp. Jerus. Is 33^{20} (אֹהֶל ‖ נ׳ שַׁאֲנָן); נ׳ אֵיתָן Je 49^{19} (fig. of Edom) = 50^{44} (of Bab.); of land of Isr., נ׳ צֶדֶק Je 31^{23} (‖ הַר הַקֹּדֶשׁ). Twice of habitation of jackals Is 34^{13} 35^{7} (both ‖ חָצִיר).

†II. [נָוָה] **vb. denom. dwell, abide** (si vera 5115
l.);—only **Qal** *Impf.* 3 ms. לֹא יִנְוֶה Hb 2^{5} *he shall not abide,* so Ke; Hi *rest* (cf. Da); We prop. יִרְוֶה *be satiated,* cf. 𝔖; Krochm יָנוּחַ.

†II. [נָוֶה] **adj. dwelling, abiding**;—only 5116
(si vera l.) נְוַת בַּיִת ψ 68^{13} *she that is abiding at home.*—נָוָה Je 6^{2} v. נָאוָה sub [נָאָה].

†II. [נָוָה] **n.f. pasture, meadow**;—pl. 4999, 5116
cstr. נְוֹת Zp 2^{6}, usu. נְאוֹת ψ 23^{2}+11 t.;—**1.** *pasture, meadow:* נ׳ הָרֹעִים Am 1^{2}, cf. Zp 2^{6} (‖ גִּדְרוֹת צֹאן; v. also [כָּרָה] p. 500 supr.); esp.
נ׳ דֶּשֶׁא ψ 23^{2} *grassy pastures;* נְאוֹת (הַ)מִּדְבָּר Je 9^{9} 23^{10} ψ 65^{13} Jo 1$^{19.20}$ 2^{22}; 4999
נ׳ אֱלֹהִים ψ 83^{13} *pastures of God,* i.e. the land of Canaan, נ׳ יַעֲקֹב La 2^{2}; נ׳ הַשָּׁלוֹם Je 25^{37} *meadows of peace;* נ׳ חָמָס ψ 74^{20} appar. *habitations* (?) *of violence,* but rd. prob. נַאֲוָה וְח׳, so Bi Che (v. 73^{6}).—Je 6^{2} v. foll.; Jb 8^{6} v. I. נָוֶה.

†נוית Kt (i.e. נְוָיִת, or נְוָיַת, Ginsb), נָיוֹת 5121
Qr; prob. **n.pr.loc.** in Ramah (poss. = *habitations,* but dub., v. Dr$^{1 S 19, 18}$ HPS);—abode of prophets 1 S 19$^{18.19.22.23.23}$ and 20^{1} (where Baer

נוות Kt); sq. בָּרָמָה (exc. 19^{18}); 𝔊 Ἀναθ (ν dropped out after ἐν), so 𝔊L; A Ναυιωθ.

5117 † **נוּחַ** **vb. rest** (NH *id.*; Aram. נוּחַ, ܢܳܚ;
Ph. נחת n. *rest*; poss. also vb. ינח (Iph. Pf.), cf. Levy cited CIS$^{i.\ 118}$ Lzb^{322}; As. *nâḫu*, *rest* (*inûḫ*), and deriv.; Eth. ኖኀ: *be extended, long*, rarely *rest*; Ar. ناخ iv. is *make camel lie down* on his breast; مُنَاخٌ *resting-place of camel*, cf. Doughty$^{Arab.\ Des.\ i,\ 397,\ ii,\ 63,\ 486,\ 642}$);—**Qal** *Pf.* 3 fs. נָ֫חָה Is 7^{2} + 2 t., consec. וְנָחָה Is 11^{2}; 1 s. נַחְתִּי Jb 3^{26}; 3 pl. נָ֫חוּ Est 9^{22}, consec. וְנָחוּ Is 7^{19}; *Impf.* 3 ms. יָנוּחַ Ex 23^{12} + 6 t., וַיָּ֫נַח Ex 10^{14} 20^{11}; 3 fs. תָּנוּחַ Is 25^{10} Pr 14^{33}, וַתָּ֫נַח Gn 8^{4} Nu 11^{26}; 2 ms.
5118 תָּנוּחַ Dn 12^{13} etc.; *Inf. abs.* נוֹחַ Est 9$^{16.17.18}$; *cstr.* לָנוּחַ 2 S 21^{10}; כְּנוֹחַ Nu 11^{25} Jos 3^{13} Ne 9^{28}; sf. 3 ms. בְּנֻחֹה Nu 10^{36};—לְנוּחֶ֫ךָ 2 Ch 6^{41} v. מְנוּחָה;—**1.** *rest, settle down and remain*, sq. עַל; of birds 2 S 21^{10}; ark Gn 8^{4} (P); נָ֫חָה אֲרָם עַל־אֶפְרָ֫יִם Is 7^{2} *Aram hath settled down upon Ephraim*; of spirit of י׳ Nu 11$^{25.26}$ (E), Is 11^{2}; spirit of Elijah 2 K 2^{15}; sceptre of wicked ψ 125^{3} (in fig.); sq. בְּ loc.: of insects Ex 10^{14} (J), Is 7^{19} (fig. of invaders); of soles of feet *resting* in water Jos 3^{13} (JE); hand of י׳ Is 25^{10}; wisdom Pr 14^{33}; anger Ec 7^{9}; בִּקְהַל רְפָאִים יָנוּחַ Pr 21^{16} *in the assembly of Shades shall he settle down*; abs., = *stop*, of ark at stages of journey Nu 10^{36} (JE); *cease* speaking 1 S 25^{9}. **2.** *repose, be quiet, have rest:* after labour Ex 20^{11} (E; of God), 23^{12} (E; of cattle), Dt 5^{14} (of slave); *have rest from* (מִן) enemies Est 9^{16} (inf. abs. נוֹחַ, + הָרוֹג, עָמוֹד), v^{22}, cf. (abs.) v$^{17.18}$ (in both + עָשֹׂה), Ne 9^{28}; *be at rest* (from trouble), abs., Jb 3^{26} (+ שָׁקַטְתִּי, שָׁלַוְתִּי); of the earth Is 14^{7}; in couch of the grave 57^{2}; in Sheʾôl Jb 3^{17}, so prob. Dn 12^{13}; also לֹא תָנוּחַ לָךְ Is 23^{12} = *thou shalt not be at rest*, cf. impers. יָנוּחַ לִי Jb 3^{13} = *I should be at rest* (in Sheʾôl).—אָנוּחַ לְיוֹם צָרָה Hb 3^{16} is dub.: *I wait quietly for the day of distress* De Ke Hi-St SS, so Now, doubtfully; We conj. אֶנָּחֵם as Is 1^{24} *I will appease me*, GASm leaves untransl. **Hiph. A.** *Pf.* 3 ms. הֵנִיחַ Jos 22^{4} +; 1 s. וַהֲנִיחֹתִי 2 S 7^{11} +; הֵנִ֫יחוּ Zc 6^{8}; *Impf.* 3 ms. יָנִיחַ Ex 17^{11} +; וַיָּ֫נַח Jos 21^{42} +; sf. וַיְנִיחֵנִי Ez 37^{1} 40^{2}; 3 fs. sf. תְּנִיחֶ֫נּוּ Is 63^{14} (but v. infr.), etc.; *Imv.* mpl. הָנִ֫יחוּ Is 28^{12}; *Inf. cstr.* הָנִיחַ Is 14^{3} +, sf. הֲנִיחִי Ez 24^{13}; *Pt.* מֵנִיחַ Jos 1^{13};—**1.** *cause to rest* = *give rest* to: **a.** sq. acc. יָדוֹ Ex 17^{11} (E), רוּחִי Zc 6^{8}; so appar. sq. חֲמָתִי + בְּ pers., *quiet* (i.e. sate) *my fury by* (wreak it upon) Ez 5^{13} (del. Co), 16^{42} 24^{13}, also 21^{22} (Co adds בְּ pers.). **b.** usu. sq. לְ pers.: (1) *give rest to* i.e. bring to resting-place Ex 33^{14} (J), Dt 3^{20} Jos 1$^{13.15}$ 22^{4} (all D), 1 Ch 23^{25}; so, c. sf., Is 63^{14} (si vera l.; Vrss Lo Ew Brd Che^{Hpt} rd. תַּנְחֶנּוּ, *leadeth him*, √נחה); (2) of freedom from enemies, Is 28^{12} 2 Ch 14^{5}; + מִכָּל־אֹיְבִים [מִסָּבִיב] Dt 12^{10} 25^{19} Jos 23^{1} (D), 2 S 7$^{1.11}$ 1 Ch 22^{9}; so + מִסָּבִיב alone 1 K 5^{18} Jos 21^{42} (P), 1 Ch 22^{18} 2 Ch 14^{6} 15^{15} 20^{30}, so also prob. 32^{22} (for MT וַיְנַהֲלֵם מִסָּבִיב); (3) of freedom from suffering, + מֵעָצְבְּךָ וגו׳ Is 14^{3}. **c.** *make quiet* in mind, *set at rest* וִינִיחֶ֫ךָ Pr 29^{17} discipline thy son, *that he may give thee quiet* (of mind; ‖ יִתֵּן מַעֲדַנִּים לְנַפְשֶׁ֫ךָ). **2.** *cause to rest* (i.e. *light*) upon, c. acc. *staff* + עַל pers. Is 30^{32}; c. acc. *blessing* + אֶל־ Ez 44^{30}; *cause to alight, set down*, c. sf. pers. + בְּתוֹךְ loc. Ez 37^{1}; + אֶל־ loc. 40^{2}.—For this mng. v. esp. **B.** infr. **B.** *Pf.* 3 ms. הִנִּיחַ Ju 3^{1} +, הִנַּח 1 K 8^{9}, sf. וְהִנִּיחוֹ Dt 26^{4}, וְהִנִּיחָם Lv 16^{23} both consec.; 2 ms. וְהִנַּחְתָּ֫ Dt 14^{28}, sf. וְהִנַּחְתּוֹ 26^{10} consec., etc.; *Impf.* 3 ms. יַנִּיחַ Lv 7^{15}, וַיַּנַּח Ju 2^{23} +, sf. וַיַּנִּיחֵהוּ Ex 16^{34}; 3 fs. וַתַּנַּח Gn 39^{16}; 2 ms. juss. אַל־תַּנַּח Ec 7^{18} + 2 t., etc.; *Imv.* ms. הַנַּח Ho 4^{7} + 2 t., הַנִּ֫יחָה Ex 32^{10} Ju 16^{26}, etc.; *Inf. cstr.* sf. לְהַנִּיחוֹ Nu 32^{15}, לְהַנִּיחָם Est 3^{8}; *Pt.* מַנִּיחַ Ec 5^{11};—**1.** *lay* or *set down, deposit, let lie*, c. acc. rei, usu. + word of place: stones at ford of Jordan Jos 4$^{3.8}$ (JE), ark 1 S 6^{18}, garments Gn 39^{16} (J), Lv 16^{23} (P), Ez 42^{14} 44^{19}; cf. Ex 16$^{23.24.33.34}$ Nu 17$^{19.22}$ (all P), Dt 26$^{4.10}$ 1 K 8^{9} 13^{31} Ez 40^{42} 42^{13}; so, acc. om., Ju 6$^{18.20}$ Dt 14^{28} Nu 19^{9} (P), 1 S 10^{25}; *place, put*, sq. acc. pers. + local modif., Gn 2^{15} (J), 19^{16} (J), Jos 6^{23} (JE), Lv 24^{12} Nu 15^{34} (both P), Is 14^{1} 46^{7} Ez 37^{14}; prob. also Zc 5^{11} (rd. וְהִנִּיחָהָ, v. Ges$^{§\ 72\ ee}$); rd. וַיַּנִּיחֵם also 2 K 18^{11} (𝔊 ἔθετο; for MT וַיַּנְחֵם; cf. ‖ וַיֹּשֶׁב אוֹתָם 2 K 17^{6}); *place* corpse on (אֶל־) ass 1 K 13^{29}, in grave v^{30}; horsemen and chariots in cities 2 Ch 1^{14} 9^{25}, so rd. also ‖ 1 K 10^{26} (𝔊 3240
ἔθετο; for MT וַיַּנְחֵם); tables in temple 2 Ch 4^{8}; idols in shrines 2 K 17^{29} (acc. om.). Here belongs perh. also וְגַם מִזֶּה אַל־תַּנַּח אֶת־יָדֶ֫ךָ Ec 7^{18} *and also from this do not let thy hand lie* (idle), i.e. engage in it, cf. 11^{6}; *lay down forcibly, thrust down* הִנִּיחַ לָאָרֶץ בְּיָד Is 28^{2}, cf. Am 5^{7}; perh. also Ez 22^{20} (abs.; but del. Co Berthol, after 𝔊). **2.** *let remain, leave* (in present condition), obj. nations Ju 2^{23} 3^{1} Je 27^{11}, people in wilderness Nu 32^{15} (JE); וְהִנִּיחוּךָ עֵירֹם וְעֶרְיָה

Ez 16^{39}; sq. acc. rei Lv 7^{15} 1 K 7^{47} (*leave unweighed*); *leave behind* sq. acc. pers. Gn 42^{33} (E), 2 S 16^{21} 20^{3} 1 K 19^{3} Je 43^{6}; + אֶת־פְּנֵי 1 S 22^{4} (rd. וַיַּנִּחֵם, for MT וַיַּנְחֵם, *and he left them with* 𝔖𝔗𝔙 We Dr Klo Bu Löhr HPS; *leave* name, for a curse Is 65^{15}; *leave* or *bequeath* to (ל), c. acc. rei, ψ 17^{14} Ec 2^{18}. **3.** *leave* = depart from, מְקוֹמְךָ אַל־תַּנַּח Ec 10^{4} *do not leave thy place.* **4.** *abandon*, sq. acc. pers. Je 14^{9}; בַּל־תַּנִּיחֵנִי לְעֹשְׁקָי ψ 119^{121} *abandon me not to my oppressors.* **5.** *let alone* (refrain from interfering with), sq. ל pers. Ex 32^{10} (JE; obj. י׳), Ho 4^{17} 2 S 16^{11} 2 K 23^{18}; sq. acc. pers. Est 3^{8}; = *avoid* יַנִּיחַ חֲטָאִים גְּדוֹלִים Ec 10^{4} (but rd. perh. יָנִיחַ, *causeth to rest* = *allayeth* cf. Wild). **6.** *permit*, c. acc. pers. Ju 16^{26}; + inf. לֹא הִנִּיחַ אָדָם לְעָשְׁקָם ψ 105^{14} = 1 Ch 16^{21}, but here הִנִּיחַ לְאִישׁ, cf. מַנִּיחַ לוֹ לִישׁוֹן Ec 5^{11}. **Hoph. A.** *Pf.* 3 ms. הוּנַח־לָנוּ La 5^{5} i.e. *no rest is granted to us;* for 3 fs. וְהֻנִּיחָה Zc 5^{11} [so Baer Ginsb; van d. H. וְהֻנִּ׳] rd. prob. וְהִנִּיחֻהָ v. supr. **Hiph. B 1.** **B.** *Pt.* מֻנָּח as subst. = *space left, open space* Ez 41$^{9.11.11}$.

5118 נֹחַ v. נוח *Inf. abs.* נוּחַ 2 Ch 6^{41} v. מְנוּחָה. below, p. 628

5119 †נוֹחָה† **n.pr.m.** 4th son of Benjamin acc. to 1 Ch 8^{2}. 𝔊 Ιωα, A Νωα, 𝔊L Νοναα.

5183 †I. נַחַת **n.[f.]** (appar. **m.** Jb 36^{16}, but v. infr.) **quietness, rest** (under this √ Thes Ol §164 c Sta §201 d Kö ii. 172 f.; > sub נחת Dl Prol. 118 ff.);—נ׳ Is 30^{15} + 2 t., נָחַת Jb 17^{16} + 2 t.; cstr. נַחַת Jb 36^{16};—**1.** *quietness, quiet attitude* Is 30^{15} (|| הַשְׁקֵט); דִּבְרֵי חֲכָמִים בְּנ׳ נִשְׁמָעִים Ec 9^{17}; opp. עָמָל וּרְעוּת רוּחַ 4^{6}; opp. שָׂחַק, רָגַז Pr 29^{9}; of comfort of one's table, i.e. its satisfying plenty, וְנ׳ שֻׁלְחָנְךָ מָלֵא דָשֶׁן Jb 36^{16} *the comfort of thy table, which* (i.e. the table) *was full of fat* (Di, cf. Bu; > *that which is set on thy table shall be,* etc. De al., making נ׳ subj. of מָלֵא, and so masc.). **2.** *rest* of death Jb 17^{16}; of a still-
5183-84 born child Ec 6^{5}.—II, III. נַחַת v. נחת.

5146 נֹחַ$_{46}$ **n.pr.m. Noah** (Nab. n.pr. נוח Lzb 322, Syr. n.pr. ܢܘܚ Meissn VOJ viii, (1894), 303 ad fin. (No. 116));—Gn 5^{29} (where trad. etym.), + 40 t. Gn 5–10 (not in ED); 1 Ch 1^{4}; נֹחַ דָּנִאֵל וְאִיּוֹב Ez 14$^{14.20}$; מֵי נֹחַ = flood Is 54$^{9.9}$; 𝔊 Νωε.—On hist. of interpret. of name v. Goldziher ZMG xxiv. (1870), 207 ff.

5207 נִיחֹחַ and (Lv 1^{9}) נִיחוֹחַ$_{43}$ **n.[m.] a quieting, soothing, tranquillizing** (cf. I. נַחַת Jb 36^{16}) (ריח ניחח also Ecclus 45^{16c}; on format. v. Ol §187 b Sta §233 Ba NB §142 Kö ii. 1, 151. 489, where, after Philippi DAS ii. 362, ־ֹ expl. as dissim. from וֹ);—abs. נ׳ Gn 8^{21} +; sf. נִיחֹחִי Nu 28^{2}, נִיחֹחֲכֶם Lv 26^{31}, נִיחֹחֵיהֶם Ez 20^{28};—*a soothing, tranquillizing,* only in phr. רֵיחַ נ׳ = *soothing, tranquillizing odour* of sacrifices acceptable to י׳ Gn 8^{21} (J), Ex 29$^{18.25.41}$ Lv 1$^{9.13.17}$ + 32 t. P. Ez 20^{41}; of sacrif. to idols †Ez 6^{13} 16^{19} 20^{28}.

†הֲנָחָה† **n.f. a giving of rest,** i.e. perh. **holiday-making** (cf. נוח **Hiph. A**; prop. Inf., Sta §621 c Ba NB 90, cf. Kö ii. 1, 402);—וַהֲ׳ לַמְּדִינוֹת עָשָׂה Est 2^{18} *and a holiday-making for the provinces be enacted,* 𝔙 *requies;* but 𝔊 ἄφεσις, whence al. *release* from taxes, or *amnesty.* 2010

†יָנוֹחַ† **n.pr.loc.** in extreme N. of Isr. 2 K 15^{29}; site dub., *Yânûḥ* (Conder Lists 38) near Tyre is prob. too far W.; Guérin Gal. ii. 371 f. prop. *Hunîn*, W. of upper Jordan, cf. Buhl Geogr. 237; 𝔊 Ανιωχ, A 𝔊L Ιανωχ. 3239

†יָנ֫וֹחָה† **n.pr.loc.** on border of Ephraim Jos 16$^{6.7}$, identif. with *Yânun* SE. fr. Shechem Rob BR iii. 297 cf. Buhl Geogr. 178; 𝔊 Ιανωχα, Ιανωκα. 3239

†I. מָנוֹחַ **n.m. resting-place, state,** or **condition of rest;**—abs. מ׳ Gn 8^{9} + 4 t.; cstr. מְנוֹחַ 1 Ch 6^{16}; pl. sf. 2 fs. מְנוּחָ֑יְכִי ψ 116^{7} (Ges §91 l);—**1.** *resting-place* לְכַף רַגְלָהּ Gn 8^{9} (J), cf. Dt 28^{65} La 1^{3}; Is 34^{14} (cf. also מְנֻחָה Gn 49^{15}). **2.** *rest, repose* of soul ψ 116^{7} (pl. abstr. vel intens.); *condition of rest* and security attained by marriage Ru 3^{1}. **3.** with force of inf. (cf. Aram. inf. c. מ pref.) מִמְּנוֹחַ הָאָרוֹן 1 Ch 6^{16} *from the coming to rest of the ark.* 4494

II. מָנוֹחַ$_{18}$ **n.pr.m.** father of Samson Ju 13$^{2.8}$ + 15 t. Ju 13, 16^{31}, 𝔊 Μανωε. 4495

†מְנֻחָה, מְנוּחָה† **n.f. resting-place, rest;**—abs. מ׳ Mi 2^{10} +, מְנֻחָה Gn 49^{15} (but v. infr.), 2 S 14^{17}; sf. מְנוּחָתִי ψ 95^{11} + 2 t., מְנוּחָתֶךָ ψ 132^{8} 4496
= 2 Ch 6^{41} (where rd. as in ψ, for anom. לְנוּחֶךָ 5118
MT), מְנֻחָתוֹ Is 11^{10} Zc 9^{1}; pl. מְנוּחֹת Is 32^{18}, מְנֻחוֹת ψ 23^{2};—**1.** *resting-place* Mi 2^{10} Nu 10^{33} (JE), Dt 12^{9} (+ הַנַּחֲלָה) so ψ 95^{11} (י׳'s resting-pl.), cf. 132^{8} = 2 Ch 6^{41} (v. supr.), ψ 132^{14} Is 66^{1} (|| בֵּית מ׳ לַאֲרוֹן וגו׳, cf. בַּיִת אֲשֶׁר תִּבְנוּ לִי) 1 Ch 28^{2}; also Is 11^{10}; prob. also Gn 49^{15} (|| הָאָרֶץ) טוֹב here is appar. subst., Sam. rds. adj. טוֹבָה; but rd. perh. מְנֻחֹה, *his resting-place,* fr. מָנוֹחַ, Ball Hpt Holz after 𝔊); מְנוּחֹת שַׁאֲנַנּוֹת Is 32^{18} (+ נְוֵה שָׁלוֹם, מִשְׁכְּנוֹת מִבְטַחִים); of י׳'s word Zc 9^{1}; resting-

place on journey, in שַׂר מ׳ Je 51^{59} (Ew Gf Gie al.); fig. for security, assurance 2 S 14^{17} (taken from *resting*, equilibrium, of scale acc. to Klo). **2.** *rest, quietness*, pl. מֵי מְנֻחוֹת ψ 23^{2}; = refreshment Is 28^{12} (‖ מַרְגֵּעָה); *rest* (fr. enemies) = peace 1 K 8^{56} (cf. 5^{18}), אִישׁ מ׳ 1 Ch 22^{9} *a man of peace* (cf. הֵנִיחַ vb); = relief fr. sorrow Je 45^{3}; *condition of rest* and security attained by marriage Ru 1^{9} (= מָנוֹחַ 3^{1}).—מ׳ Ju 20^{43} is perh. n. pr., cf. GFM.

2679 **מְנֻחוֹת** **n.pr.** v. מָנַחְתִּי infr.

4506 †I. **[מָנַ֫חַת]** **n. pr. loc.** (= *resting-place, settlement*), מָנָ֑חַת 1 Ch 8^{6}, site unknown, 𝔊 Μαχαναθει, 𝔊L Μανουαθ.

†**מָנַחְתִּי** **adj.gent.** perh. fr. foregoing, only
2680 c. art. as n. coll. חֲצִי הַמ׳ 1 Ch 2^{54} of a Judaean
tribe (𝔊 Μαλαθει, A 𝔊L Μαναθ(ι)); so rd. also
2679 prob. for חֲצִי הַמְּנֻחוֹת v^{52} (𝔊 Μωναιω, A Αμμανιθ).

4506 †II. **מָנַ֫חַת** **n.pr.m.** in Edom Gn 36^{23} = 1 Ch 1^{40}; 𝔊 Μαν(ν)αχαθ, Μαναaθ.

5120 †**[נוּט]** **vb.** **dangle, shake** (𝔗 [נוט] Aph. *scare*, sld., Levy $^{ChWB\ ii.\ 97}$ Jastr$^{Dict.\ 886}$; Ar. نَوْطٌ *a bag hanging down*, نَاطَ *suspend, hang*);—**Qal** *Impf.* 3 fs. תָּנוּט ψ 99^{1} *let* (the earth) *shake* (‖ רָגַז).—Ol We prop. תָּמוּג.

5121 **נֵוִית** v. sub I. נוה. p. 627

5123 †**נוּם** **vb.** **be drowsy, slumber** (NH נוּם, נִמְנֵם *id.*; Aram. נוּם, نُم; Ar. (نوم) نَامَ *id.*; Eth. ኖመ:);—**Qal** *Pf.* 3 pl. נָמוּ Na 3^{18} ψ 76^{6} (Ges$^{§72\,l}$); *Impf.* יָנוּם ψ 121^{3} + 2 t.; 3 fs. וַתָּנָם 2 S 4^{6} (so rd. for 𝔐 וַיַּכֻּהוּ, with other radical changes, 𝔊 Th We Dr Kit Bu HPS); *Inf. cstr.* לָנוּם Is 56^{10}.—*be drowsy, slumber*, lit. וַתָּנָם וַתִּישָׁן 2 S 4^{6} (emend., v. supr.) *and she grew drowsy and slept*; fig. of inactivity, indolence, Is 5^{27} (‖ יִשַׁן), ψ 121$^{3.4}$ (of י׳; ‖ *id.*); Na 3^{18} (‖ שָׁכְנוּ); אֹהֲבֵי לָנ׳ Is 56^{10} (‖ שֹׁכְבִים); sq. acc. cogn. שֵׁנָה ψ 76^{6} (of death, ‖ נִרְדָּם).

5124 †**נוּמָה** **n.f.** **somnolence**, fig. for **indolence**, Pr 23^{21}.

8572 †**תְּנוּמָה** **n.f.** **slumber**;—abs. ψ 132^{4} Pr 6^{4}; pl. תְּנוּמוֹת Pr 6^{10} + 2 t.;—*slumber* as time of visions Jb 33^{15} (‖ תַּרְדֵּמָה); of indolent slumber ψ 132^{4} (‖ שְׁנָת) Pr 6^{4} (‖ שנה) in both c. נָתַן, sq. acc. + לְ; 6^{10} 24^{33} (both ‖ שנות, שכב).

3241 †**יָנוּם** **n.pr.loc.** city in Judah, Jos 15^{53} Qr;
3241 Kt ינים (so van d. H. Ginsb; Baer only יָנוּם); 𝔊 Ιεμαειν, A 𝔊L Ιανουμ.

†**[נִין, נוּן]** **vb.** **propagate, increase** (si 5125
vera l.) (> denom. fr. נִין Hup-Now SS;—NH נוּן = *fish*, so Aram. נוּנָא, نُونٌ, As. *nunu*);—**Qal** (or **Hiph.**?) *Impf.* ינין Kt; > **Niph.** יִנּוֹן Qr ψ 72^{17} let his name *have increase* (or, if Niph., *be propagated, spread*); but dub., Vrss perh. יִכּוֹן *be established, endure*.

†**נוּן** and (1 Ch 7^{27}) **נוֹן** **n.pr.m.** father of 5126
Joshua 1 Ch 7^{27}; elsewh. alw. (יְהוֹשֻׁעַ) בִּן־נוּן Ex 33^{11} Nu 11^{28} 13$^{8.16}$ + 22 t. Nu Dt Jos (JEDP); also Ju 2^{8} 1 K 16^{34} Ne 8^{17}; 𝔊 Ναυη (for Ναυν by err., cf. Thes).

†**נִין** **n.[m.]** **offspring, posterity**;—abs. 5209
Jb 18^{19} Is 14^{22}; sf. נִינִי Gn 21^{23} (all ‖ נֶכֶד).

מָנוֹן v. p. 584 supr.

נוּס $_{160}$ **vb.** **flee, escape** (Syr. ܢܳܣ *tremble* 5127
(rare), cf. Brock; Ar. نَاسَ, نوس *move to and fro, be in commotion, dangle*, Lane^{2866});—**Qal** *Pf.* נָס Nu 35^{25} +; נַסְתָּה 2 K 9^{3}; נַסְתִּי 1 S 4^{16}, etc.; *Impf.* יָנוּס Ex 21^{13} +; וַיָּנָס Gn 39^{12} +; יְנוּסוּן ψ 104^{7}, etc.; *Imv. mpl.* נֻסוּ Je 48^{6} + 4 t. Je Zc; *Inf. abs.* נוֹס 2 S 18^{3}; *cstr.* (לָנֻס) לָנוּס Gn 19^{20} +; *Pt.* נָס Am 9^{1} +; נָסִים Ex 14^{27} +;—**1.** *flee*, abs. Gn 39$^{12.15}$ Nu 16^{34} (all J); Jos 10^{16} (JE); Lv 26$^{17.36}$ (H); fig. of sea ψ 114$^{3.5}$ cf. 104^{7}; sq. acc. cogn. מָנוֹס Je 46^{5}, sq. דֶּרֶךְ Jos 8^{15} (J), 2 K 9^{27}; sq. בְּדֶרֶךְ Dt 28$^{7.25}$; נ׳ אֶל־נַפְשָׁם 2 K 7^{7} *flee for their life*, נ׳ בְּרַגְלָיו Ju 4^{15} *flee on foot*; + 44 t. abs. (not elsewh. Hex); sq. אֶל־ loc. Dt 4^{42} 19$^{5.11}$ (D), Nu 35^{32} Jos 20^{4} (both P), Ju 4^{17} 1 K 2$^{28.29}$ Is 13^{14}; sq. לְ 1 S 4^{10} + 6 t. + לִקְרָאתוֹ Ex 14^{27} (E; not elsewh. Hex); sq. עַד Ju 7^{22} + Pr 28^{17} (עַד־בּוֹר, v. בּוֹר); sq. עַל־ Is 10^{3}; sq. ־ָה loc. Gn 14^{10} + 4 t. JE, Nu 35^{6} + 6 t. P, Dt 4^{42} 19$^{3.4}$ (D), + 6 t.; sq. שָׁם Is 20^{6}; sq. acc. loc. Jos 8^{20} (J), + 4 t.; sq. מִמֶּרְחָק Is 17^{13} = *far away*; sq. מִן *from*, Jos 20^{6} (P), 1 S 4^{16} + 3 t.; מִתּוֹךְ Je 51^{6}; esp. מִפְּנֵי *from before* Ex 4^{3} 14^{25} Nu 10^{35} Jos 10^{11} (all JE),
1 S 17^{24} Je 48^{44} (Qr הַנָּס, > Kt הנים), + 19 t.; sq. 5211
מִלִּפְנֵי לִפְנֵי Jos 7^{4} 8$^{5.6.6}$ (all J), 1 S 4^{17} 2 S 24^{13}, 1 Ch 19^{18}. **2.** *escape* Am 9^{1} (‖ נמלט) so Je 46^{6}; hence **3.** *take flight, depart, disappear*, only fig.; Dt 34^{7} (JE) *his freshness* (לֵחֹה *vigour*) *was not gone* (‖ לֹא כָהֲתָה עינו); of shadows (at evening), Ct 2^{17} 4^{6}; of sorrow etc. Is 35^{10} 51^{11}. **4.** נ׳ עַל־סוּס Is 30^{16} *fly* (to the attack) *on horseback*. †**Po'lel** *Pf.* Is 59^{19} רוּחַ י׳ נֹסְסָה בוֹ *the breath of* י׳ *driveth at it, driveth it on* (cf.

Hiph. 2). †**Hithpo'l.** *Inf. cstr.* לְהִתְנוֹסֵס ψ 60[6] *in order to take flight before* the bow (so Vrss Hup-Now Che Bae al.). †**Hiph.** *Pf.* הֵנִיס Ex 9[20]; *Impf.* יָנִיסוּ Dt 32[30] + Ju 7[21] Kt (Qr וַיָּנוּסוּ **Qal**); *Inf. cstr.* לְהָנִיס Ju 6[11];—**1.** *put to flight*, sq. acc. Dt 32[30] (‖רדף). **2.** *drive hastily* to a safe place Ex 9[20], sq. acc. + אֶל־. **3.** *cause to disappear, hide* Ju 6[11] (no obj. expr.) sq. מִפְּנֵי.

4498 †מָנוֹס **n.m.**[Am 2, 14] **1. flight. 2.** place of **escape, refuge**;—abs. מ׳ Am 2[14] + 5 t.; sf. מְנוּסִי 2 S 22[3] Je 16[19];—**1.** *flight*, acc. cogn. c. נוס Je 46[5]. **2.** (*place of*) *escape;* אָבַד מ׳ מִן *escape perished from*, = *there was no escape for*, Am 2[14] Je 25[35] Jb 11[20] ψ 142[5]; of י׳ as a *refuge* 2 S 22[3] (‖ משׂגב; מנוס וגו׳ not ‖ ψ 18[3]; txt. disputed, Kit Bu retain in Sm, Klo Bae Löhr Du ins. in ψ; < del. in Sm De Hup-Now HPS cf. Che), ψ 59[17] (‖*id.*); Je 16[19] (‖ מעוז, עז).

4499 †מְנוּסָה **n.f. flight**;—מ׳ Is 52[12] (‖ חִפָּזוֹן); מְנֻסַת־חֶרֶב Lv 26[36] = *flight from sword*, acc. cogn. c. נוס.

5128 †נוּעַ **vb. quiver, wave, waver, tremble, totter** (NH Pilp. נִעְנַע *shake*, Aram. נוּעַ *waver, stagger* (rare); Ar. نَاعَ, نوع *bend* (of boughs), v. commotus fuit (of *id.*), so Kam Frey; also *change*, نَوْعٌ *kind, species, variety;* Di cp. Eth. ነወ: *hunt*);—**Qal** *Pf.* נָעוּ Jb 28[4] +; וְנָעוּ Am 4[8] + 2 t.; *Impf.* וַיָּנַע Is 7[2]; 3 fs. תָּנוּעַ Is 24[20]; יָנֻועוּ אֲנוּעֲךָ 2 S 15[20] Kt (but rd Qr Hiph q.v.); ψ 109[10]; יְנִיעוּן ψ 59[16] Kt (so rd.; not Qr Hiph.), etc.; *Inf. abs.* נוֹעַ Is 24[20] ψ 109[10]; *cstr.* נוּעַ Ju 9[9] + 3 t.; נוֹעַ Is 7[2]; *Pt.* נָע Gn 4[12.14]; נָעִים Pr 22[19]; נָעוֹת 1 S 1[13]:—**1.** *wave*, of trees, sq. עַל Ju 9[9.11.13]; sq. מִפְּנֵי of cause Is 7[2]; *quiver, vibrate*, of lips 1 S 1[13]; *swing* (to and fro) of miners Jb 28[4] (‖דלל); *stagger* like drunkard, of mariners in storm ψ 107[27] (‖ חגג), cf. Is 29[9] (‖ שכר); hence *be unstable*, fig. of ways of harlot Pr 5[6]; *tremble*, of doorposts, Is 6[4] (sq. מִן caus.), idols 19[1] (sq. מִפְּנֵי), earth Is 24[20] (‖ התנודד), people Ex 20[18] (E); fig. of heart Is 7[2]. **2.** *totter, go tottering* (faint and uncertain) La 4[14] v[15] (‖ נוּד), Am 8[12] (‖ שׁוטט); as beggars ψ 109[10] (‖ שָׁאַל), cf. 59[16]; Am 4[8] sq. אֶל־; *pt. vagabond* Gn 4[12.14] (both ‖ נָד); fig. = *err, sin*, Je 14[10]. **Niph.** *Impf.* יִנּוֹעַ Am 9[9] *be tossed about* (of corn) in a sieve; יִנּוֹעוּ *id.*, of bulwarks as fig-trees Na 3[12] (‖ נפל). **Hiph.** *Pf.* 3 fs. הֵנִיעָה 2 K 19[21] = Is 37[22]; וַהֲנִעוֹתִי Am 9[9]; *Impf.* יָנִיעַ Zp 2[15]; juss. יָנַע 2 K 23[18]; אֲנִיעֲךָ 2 S 15[20] Qr (cf. **Qal**); יְנִיעוּן ψ 109[25] + 59[16] Qr (rd. Kt **Qal** q.v.), etc.; *Imv.* sf. הֲנִיעֵמוֹ ψ 59[12];—**1.** *toss about* Am 9[9] subj. י׳, obj. Isr. sq. בַּגּוֹיִם (cf. **Niph.**). **2.** *shake, cause to totter:* = *set me tottering* Dn 10[10] *on my knees and hands;* esp. *shake* or *wag* the head, in mockery 2 K 19[21] = Is 37[22] (‖ לעג, בוז) cf. ψ 22[8] 109[25]; sq. עַל־ Jb 16[4] (בְּמוֹ ר׳ [Ges[§ 119 q]]), also La 2[15] (‖ שרק), Zp 2[15] יָדוֹ (‖ *id.*), [v. also Ecclus 12[18] 13[7] (ר׳ [בְּ])]. **3.** (*shake*), *disturb*, bones of dead 2 K 23[18]. **4.** *cause to wander* Nu 32[13] (J); 2 S 15[20] (sq. ללכת); ψ 59[12] (‖ הוריד, for which Lag[Proph. Chald. xlviii.] prop. הניד).

†נֵעָה **n.pr.loc.** in Zebulun; הַנֵּעָה Jos 19[13]. 5269
𝔊 Αοζα, Α Αννουα, 𝔊L Νουα; site unknown.

†נֹעָה **n.pr.f.** a daughter of Zelophahad 5270
(of Manasseh), Nu 26[33] 27[1] 36[11] Jos 17[3], 𝔊 Νουα.

†[מְנַעֲנֵעַ] **n.[m.]** appar. a kind of **rattle**, 4517
only וּבִמְנַעַנְעִים 2 S 6[5], in list of musical instruments; 𝔊 κύμβαλα, but this usu. (12 t.) = מְצִלְתַּיִם; 𝔙 *sistra;* the sistrum (Gr. σεῖστρον, fr. σείω) was much used in Egypt; it was a small metal frame with loose metal bars carrying loose rings, borne and *swung* or *shaken* in the hand, v. Wilkinson [Anc. Egyptians (1878), i. 497 ff.] Now [Arch. i. 273] Benz [Arch. 278] We [ψψ Eng. Trans. p. 233].

נוֹעַדְיָה v. יעד. p. 418 5129

I. [נוּף] **vb. move to and fro, wave,** 5130
besprinkle (NH Hiph., Pilp. *wave, blow, fan*, cf. נָפָה *sift*, נָפָה n. *sieve* (as BH); 𝔗 Aph. as BH; Syr. ܢܦ *bend, wave, shake;* Di cp. Eth. quadril. ነፍነፈ: *distil, drop like dew;* ነፈየ: *sift*);—**Qal** *Pf.* 1 s. נַפְתִּי מִשְׁכָּבִי מֹר וגו׳ Pr 7[17] *I have besprinkled my couch with myrrh*, etc. **Po'lel** *Impf.* 3 ms. יְנֹפֵף יָדוֹ הַר וגו׳ Is 10[32] *he brandisheth his hand toward the mt.* (on acc. הַר cf. Ges [§ 118 f.] Da[Synt. § 69, R 2]). **Hiph.** *Pf.* 3 ms. הֵנִיף Jos 8[31] +, 2 ms. הֲנַפְתָּ Ex 20[25] (Ges[§ 72 k]), וְהֵנַפְתָּ Ex 29[24] + 3 t.; 1 s. הֲנִיפֹתִי Jb 31[21]; *Impf.* וַיָּנֶף Lv 8[27] Nu 8[21], sf. וַיְנִיפֵהוּ Lv 8[29]; 2 ms. תָּנִיף Dt 23[26] + 2 t., etc.; *Imv.* mpl. הָנִיפוּ Is 13[2]; *Inf. cstr.* הָנִיף Is 10[15] + 2 t.; לַהֲנָפָה Is 30[28] (Ges[§ 72 z] BA[NB 90], v. also הֲנָחָה), etc.; *Pt.* מֵנִיף Is 19[16] Zc 2[13], etc.;—*swing, wield, wave:*—**1.** *wield*, move tool to and fro in using it, c. עַל־ of material: כִּי חַרְבְּךָ הֵנַפְתָּ עָלֶיהָ Ex 20[25] (E), i.e. over stone, so Dt 27[5] Jos 8[31] (D), and Dt 23[26]

a sickle *thou shalt not wield over* the standing grain of thy neighbour; abs. מְנִיפוֹ Is 10[15] against *him that wieldeth it* (i.e. a saw), and כְּהָנִיף שֵׁבֶט וְאֶת־מְרִימוֹ v[15] (rd. אֶת־) *like a rod's wielding him that lifteth it.*

2. *Shake* or *wave* the hand; **a.** *wave* hand אֶל־הַמָּקוֹם 2 K 5[11], in healing ceremony (i.e. prob. toward sanctuary Kmp[Kau]; > *toward the spot* [where leprosy appears], so most). **b.** c. עַל־, *shake* or *brandish against*, Is 11[15] 19[16] Zc 2[13] (all of י׳), Jb 31[21] [cf. Ecclus 12[18] (without עַל) in mockery]. **c.** *wave* hand, as a signal, Is 13[2]. **3.** *swing* to and fro בְּנָפַת, *in a sieve*, Is 30[28] (fig., of nations).

4. Oft. term. techn. in P (H), of rite in which originally the priest lifted his share of offering and *waved* it, i.e. moved it toward altar and back, in token of its presentation to God and its return by him to priest: in H, וְהֵנִיף אֶת־הָעֹמֶר לִפְנֵי י׳ Lv 23[11 a] cf. v[11 b. 12], also v[20] (on text v. Di Dr-Wh[Hpt]); in P, וְהֵנַפְתָּ אֹתוֹ תְּנוּפָה לִפְנֵי י׳ Ex 29[26], so Lv 7[30] 8[29] 9[21] 10[15] (obj. om.), Nu 6[20]; thus also Levites are set apart for service of the priests Nu 8[11] (Di del. v.), v[13.21], cf. v[14] (לִפְנֵי י׳ om.); but same phr. of entire lamb, with oil, Lv 14[12.24], and of offerings wh. were burnt, entirely Ex 29[24] (cf. v[25]), Lv 8[27] (cf. v[28]), or in part Nu 5[25] (הֵנִיף הַמִּנְחָה לִפְנֵי י׳), —in these the orig. signif. seems lost; so, clearly, of contributions for tabernacle, = *offer*, הֵנִיף תְּנוּפַת זָהָב לַי׳ Ex 35[22].—Cf. תְּנוּפָה infr.

5. *Shed abroad* (si vera l.) גֶּשֶׁם נְדָבוֹת תָּנִיף ψ 68[10] *bounteous rain thou didst shed abroad* [cf. Ecclus 43[17 c]], but vb. not wholly suitable; Lag Gr prop. תַּטִּיף, yet this also questionable. **Hoph.** *Pf.* 3 ms. הוּנַף, *be waved*, Ex 29[27] (P), pass. of **Hiph. 4.**

5299 †I. [נָפָה] **n.f.** **sieve** or other winnowing implement, Di Du *Schwinge*, Che[Hpt] *fan* (as *swung*);—only cstr. לַהֲנָפָה גוֹיִם בְּנָפַת שָׁוְא Is 30[28] *to swing* nations in a sieve of worthlessness.

8573 תְּנוּפָה[30] **n.f.** **a swinging, waving, wave-offering, offering**;—abs. ת׳ Is 30[32]+; cstr. תְּנוּפַת Is 19[16] Ex 35[22]; pl. cstr. תְּנוּפֹת Nu 18[11];—**1.** *a swinging, brandishing,* ת׳ יַד י׳ Is 19[16] *the brandishing of* י׳*'s hand* (in hostility); מִלְחֲמוֹת ת׳ 30[32] *battles of brandishing* (brandished weapons). **2. a.** *waving, wave-offering,* term. techn. in P (H), orig. of priest's share of sacrifice (cf. נוף **Hiph. 4**), לְכָל־תְּנוּפֹת בְּנֵי יִשׂ׳ לְךָ נְתַתִּים Nu 18[11]; oft. as 2nd acc. after הֵנִיף Ex 29[26]+5 t.; even of Levites Nu 8[11.13.15.20] (on all v. נוף **Hiph. 4**); חֲזֵה הַתּ׳ Ex 29[27] *the wave-breast*, so Lv 7[34] 10[14.15] Nu 6[20] (all + שׁוֹק הַתְּרוּמָה); 18[18] (+ שׁוֹק הַיָּמִין); עֹמֶר הַתּ׳ Lv 23[15]; לֶחֶם הַתּ׳ v[17]; ת׳ alone v[20] (all H); less accurately Ex 29[24] Lv 8[27] 14[12.21.24] (v. נוף[l.c.]). **b.** *offering*, of gold and brass for tabern., Ex 35[22] 38[24.29].—On ת׳ v. Di[Lv 7, 30] Benz[Arch. 459 f.] and esp. Now[Arch. ii. 239 f.]; also תְּרוּמָה.

II. נוף (√of foll.; cf. Ar. نوف, نَافَ I, IV. *overtop* (Frey), نَوْفٌ *camel-hump* (ib.); مُنِيفٌ *high, lofty* (of mt. and building, Lane[3039])).

†נוֹף **n.[m.]** **elevation, height** (NH נוֹף is *tree-top, bough*, so 𝔗 נוֹפָא);—יְפֵה נ׳ ψ 48[3] 5131
beautiful in elevation (of Mount Zion).

II. [נָפָה] **n.f.** **height**;—only cstr. in combin. 5299
נָפַת דּוֹר Jos 12[23] = נ׳ דֹּאר 1 K 4[11], pl. cstr. נָפוֹת ד׳ Jos 11[2]; cf. II. דּוֹר, and Di[Jos 11, 2]; v. also [נֶפֶת].

†[נֶפֶת] **n.f.** id.;—only הַנָּ֫פֶת Jos 17[11] (but 5316
rd. perh. הַנָּפֹת, fr. foregoing, v. Di; 𝔊 Μαφετα, A Ναφεθα, 𝔊L Νοφεθ, cf. 12[23] [supr. sub II. נָפָה], 𝔊L Ναφαθδωρ).—נֹפֶת *honey*, v. נפת.

נוֹצָה v. I. נצה. p. 663 5133

[נוק] **vb.** whence (si vera l.) might come, 5134
Hiph. suckle, nurse;—*Impf.* 3 fs. sf. וַתְּנִיקֵ֫הוּ Ex 2[9], but v. ינק and Ges[§ 70 e]; rd. prob. וַתֵּינ׳ (Sam. ותיניקהו).

נור (√of foll.; cf. NH נוּר, *flame, fire*, 𝔗 *id.*; Ar. نَارَ, نور *give light, shine*, I. (Kam Frey), IV. Lane[2864], نَارٌ *fire*, نُورٌ *light*; Syr. ܢܘܪܐ *fire*; also in n.pr. Palm. Pun. v. Lzb[322] Cook[81]; Min. מנורת *torches* (?) Hom[Südar. Chrest. 128]; As. *tinûru, furnace, oven* (Dl[HWB 711]) belongs here acc. to Jäger[BAS ii. 294]).

I. נֵר[43] **n.m.**[Ex 25, 37] **lamp**;—נ׳ abs. Ex 27[20]+, 5216
cstr. 1 S 3[3]+; sf. נֵרִי ψ 18[29], †נִירִי† || 2 S 22[29], etc.; pl. נֵרוֹת abs. Lv 24[4]+; cstr. Ex 39[37]; sf. נֵרֹתֶיהָ Ex 25[37.37]+, נֵרֹתֵיהֶם 1 Ch 28[15] 2 Ch 4[20];—*lamp* in shrine at Shiloh 1 S 3[3]; esp. of *lamps* in temple 1 K 7[49]+7 t. Ch, and in tabern. Ex 25[37.37]+15 t. P; cf. in Zech.'s vision Zc 4[2.2]; as token of merrymaking Je 25[10]; used in search Zp 1[12], cf. (fig.) נֵר י׳ נִשְׁמַת אָדָם Pr 20[27]; used in household work Pr 31[18]; fig. of prosperity נ׳ יִשְׂרָאֵל 2 S 21[17] (embodied in David); also Jb 18[6] 21[17] 29[3] ψ 18[29] = 2 S 22[29], ψ 132[17] Pr 13[9] 20[20] 24[20]; of God's word as a guide ψ 119[105], cf. Pr 6[23].

5369 †II. נֵר **n.pr.m.** 𝔊 Νηρ: **1.** father of Abner 1 S $14^{50.51}$ $26^{5.14}$ 2 S $2^{8.12}$ $3^{23.25.28.37}$ 1 K $2^{5.32}$ 1 Ch 26^{28}. **2.** father of Kish 1 Ch 8^{33} $9^{36.39}$.

5216 †I. נִיר **n.**[**m.**] **lamp**;—alw. fig. לְמַעַן הֱיוֹת־נ׳ לְדָוִיד 1 K 11^{36}, i.e. that his family may remain on the throne; cf. 15^4 2 K 8^{19} = 2 Ch 21^7; = happiness, delight (cstr.) נִר רְשָׁעִים Pr 21^4 (so Vrss Thes Buhl Now Wild, > Ew Del SS Frankenb = II. נִיר sub II. ניר infr.).

5374 †נֵרִיָּהוּ†, נֵרִיָּה **n.pr.m.** father of Baruch: נֵרִיָּהוּ Je $36^{14.32}$ 43^6 45^1, = father of Seraiah 51^{59}; נֵרִיָּה $32^{12.16}$ $36^{4.8}$ 43^3; 𝔊 Νηριου; cf. Gray[Prop N. 294.]

4501 מְנוֹרָה, מְנֹרָה$_{42}$ **n.f. lampstand** (Ecclus מנורה *fire*, 43^{4d});—abs. מְנֹ׳ 2 K 4^{10} + 9 t., מְנֹרָה Ex $25^{32.32}$ + 19 t.; cstr. מְנוֹרַת Zc 4^2 2 Ch 13^{11}, מְנֹרַת Ex 25^{31} + 2 t.; pl. מְנֹרוֹת abs. 1 K 7^{49} + 2 t.; cstr. 1 Ch $28^{15.15}$ 2 Ch 4^7;—*lampstand:* **1.** in private house 2 K 4^{10}. **2.** ten *lampstands* in temple, pl. 1 K 7^{49} = 2 Ch 4^7, Je 52^{19} (so also 𝔊; om. ‖ 2 K $25^{14.15}$, del. here Now[Arch. ii. 40] < retain Gf Gie), cf. 2 Ch 4^{20}, also 1 Ch $28^{15.15.15.15.15.15.15}$, but 2 Ch 13^{11} has מ׳ in sg. (as **3**); cf. sg. in Zech.'s vision Zc 4^2. **3.** seven-branched *lampstand* in tabern. Ex $25^{31.31.32.32}$ + 15 t. Ex, Lv 24^4 (with lamps upon it), Nu 3^{31} 4^9 $8^{2.3.4.4}$ (all P).—מָנוֹר v. II. ניר.

5136 †[נוּשׁ] **vb. be sick,** si vera l. (= I. אנשׁ acc. to Thes who comp. Syr. ܢܫ);—**Qal** *Impf.* 1 s. וָאָנוּשָׁה ψ 69^{21}, but rd. perh. וַאֲנוּשָׁה [מַכַּת נַפְשִׁי] (‖ חֶרְפָּה שָׁבְרָה לִבִּי), Bi Che[crit. n.], cf. 𝔊, v. I. אנשׁ; or (< קִוָּה) וְאָנוּשׁ הוּא קַוֵּה (with different word-division), Weir[Acad. 1870, 257] (who cp. Je 17^9 8^{15}).

5137 †I. [נָזָה] **vb. spurt, spatter; Hiph. sprinkle** (NH **Hiph.** *sprinkle;* Aram. נְדָא, אַדֵּי Lv 4^6 and oft., for הִזָּה; Syr. ܢܕܐ is *erupit, stillavit* Is 63^3, also *prominuit,* etc. PS[2291]);—**Qal** *Impf.* 3 ms. יִזֶּה Lv $6^{20.20}$, וְיֵז Is 63^3 (but rd. וַיֵּז Che Di Du Ges[§ 53, p. N., 107 b N.] al.), וַיִּז 2 K 9^{33};—*spurt, spatter,* alw. of blood:—וַיִּז מִדָּמָהּ אֶל־ 2 K 9^{33} *and some of her blood spurted against* the wall; so ויז נִצְחָם Is 63^3 (c. עַל־ rei, in metaph.); יִזֶּה מִדָּמָהּ Lv 6^{20}, cf. v^{20} (both c. עַל־ rei). **Hiph.** *Pf.* 3 ms. וְהִזָּה consec. Lv 4^6 + 12 t.; 2 ms. וְהִזֵּיתָ Ex 29^{21}; *Impf.* יַזֶּה Lv 16^{14} (Is 52^{15}, v. infr.); וַיַּז Lv $8^{11.30}$; *Imv.* הַזֵּה Nu 8^7; *Pt.* cstr. מַזֵּה Nu 19^{21};—*cause to spurt, sprinkle* upon, in ceremonials of P: c. acc. + עַל־ pers. Nu 8^7 (water), + עַל־ rei, לִפְנֵי rei Lv 16^{15}; obj. oft. מִן partit., or implied in context; sq. עַל־ Lv 5^9 14^7 $16^{14.19}$ (all of blood); 8^{11} (oil); Nu $19^{18.19}$ (water), Ex 29^{21} Lv 8^{30} (both blood and oil); sq. אֶל־ Lv 14^{51} (blood and water), אֶל־נֹכַח פְּנֵי Nu 19^4 (blood); sq. לִפְנֵי Lv $4^{6.17}$ 16^{14} (blood), $14^{16.27}$ (oil); once without prep. מַזֵּה Nu 19^{21} *the sprinkler of* the water.—Is 52^{15} v. II. נזה.

†יְזִיָּה **n.pr.m.** (*may* י׳ *sprinkle,* rd. prob. 3150
יִזִּ׳, 𝔊 Αζεια, א Αδεια, 𝔊L Ιαζιας);—one of those who took strange wives Ezr 10^{25}.

II. [נָזָה] **vb.** (dub.) **spring, leap** (cf. Ar. 5137
نَزَا *leap, leap up, upon,* Thes Frey[Prov. Ar. 1, 171. 297; 22, 138; 25, 11]);—hence, acc. to many, **Hiph.** *Impf.* 3 ms. כֵּן יַזֶּה גּוֹיִם רַבִּים Is 52^{15} *so shall he cause to leap* (i.e. in joyful surprise, or = *startle*) *many nations;* but perh. crpt.; Che[Comm.] יַתִּר in like sense; < יִרְגְּזוּ (for יזהגוים) *many shall tremble* (v. רגז), GFM[JBL 1890, 216 ff.] cf. Che[Hpt].

נָזִיד v. זיד. p. 268 5138

†[נָזַל] **vb. flow, trickle, drop, distil** 5140
(poet.) (𝔗 נְזַל of *flowing* water; Syr. ܢܙܠ *descendit, defluet* PS[2331]; Ar. نَزَلَ *descend* (milk into udder, but also in gen.));—**Qal** *Pf.* נָזְלוּ Ju 5^5; *Impf.* יִזַּל Nu 24^7, etc.; *Pt.* נֹזְלִים Ex 15^8 +, etc.;—**1.** *flow,* subj. water, Nu 24^7 (JE); ψ 147^{18}; cf. Je 18^{14}; subj. clouds, Jb 36^{28} sq. rain as acc. mat. Ges[§ 117 z] (‖ רעף and, v^{27}, זקק), cf. Je 9^{17} (of eyelids); so fig. Is 45^8 sq. צֶדֶק (‖ רעף); of mts. (i.e. their torrents) Ju 5^5 acc. to 𝔙 Ew GFM al., but v. I. זלל; esp. pt. as subst., = *streams, floods,* Ex 15^8 (‖ מים, תהום of Red Sea); ψ 78^{44} (‖ יְאֹר); for drinking ψ 78^{16} (‖ מים כַּנהרות, תהום v^{15}), Pr 5^{15} out of well (‖ מים); for irrigation Is 44^3 (‖ מים); fig. of Shulamite נ׳ מִן־לְבָנוֹן Ct 4^{15} (‖ באר מים, מעין גנים). **2.** *distil,* of spices בְּשָׂמִים Ct 4^{16}; fig. of words, like dew Dt 32^2 (‖ ערף). **Hiph.** *Pf.* הִזִּיל Is 48^{21} *cause to flow,* water from rock (‖ זוב).—Vid. also I. זלל.

נזם (√ of foll.; meaning unknown).

†נֶ֫זֶם **n.m.**[Jb 42, 11] **ring,** always of gold when 5141
material mentioned;—נ׳ abs. Gn 24^{30} +; cstr. v^{22} +; sf. נִזְמָהּ Ho 2^{15}; pl. נְזָמִים Gn 35^4; cstr. נִזְמֵי Ex 32^2 +;—**1.** *nose-ring* (Syr. ܩܕܫܐ) woman's ornament, נ׳ עַל־אַפָּהּ Gn 24^{47} cf. $v^{22.30}$ (J); נִזְמֵי הָאָף Is 3^{21} (‖ טַבַּ֫עַת seal-ring); perh. also Ho 2^{15}; Ez 16^{12} fig. of י׳'s adorning Jerus. (‖ עֲגִילִים עַל־אָזְנָיִךְ); cf. נ׳ בְּאַף חֲזִיר Pr 11^{22}.

2. *earring*, ornament of men and women, Gn 35[4], נ׳ אֲשֶׁר בְּאָזְנֵיהֶם so Ex 32[2.3] (all E); cf. Pr 25[12] (in sim. of wise reprover), and perh. Ex 35[22] (P; ‖ טַבַּעַת); prob. also Ju 8[24.24.25.26] (of men, cf. GFM), Jb 42[11].—Cf. further Gei [Jüd. Zeitschr. x (1872), 45 ff.] RS [Sem. i. 434, 2d ed. 453]; also ref. sub נזר.

5143 †[נֵ֫זֶק] **n.[m.] injury, damage** (Aram. loan-word v. BAram.);—only cstr. בְּנֵזֶק הַמֶּלֶךְ Est 7[4] *at the price of injury to the king.*

5144 [נָזַר] **vb. dedicate, consecrate,** (cf. We [Skizzen iii. 118]), **separate,** in relig. and ceremonial sense (NH only as denom., cf. ɪɪ. נזר; Ar. نَذَرَ *make a vow*, cf. We [Skizzen iii. 117 f.], RS [i. 463 f., 2d ed. 482 f.]; Sab. נדר *vow* Levy [ZMG xxii (1868), 196] Min. *id.*, Hom [Südar. Chrest. 128]; Aram. נְדַר, ܢܕܪ, *vow*; As. *nazâru*, *curse* Dl [HWB 457]);—**Niph.** *Impf.* יִנָּזֵר Ez 14[7], וְיִנָּזְרוּ Lv 22[2]; וַיִּנָּזְרוּ Ho 9[10]; *Inf. abs.* הִנָּזֵר Zc 7[3];—*devote, dedicate oneself* unto (לְ), הַבֹּשֶׁת, i.e. Baʿal Ho 9[10]; from (מִן) י׳ Ez 14[7] (of apostasy); *hold sacredly aloof* from, (מִן) Lv 22[2] (H); abs. Zc 7[3] *consecrating my(self)*, i.e. by fasting. **Hiph.** *Pf.* וְהִזַּרְתֶּם אֶת־בְּנֵי־יִשׂ׳ מִטֻּמְאָתָם Lv 15[31] (P) *and ye shall keep the sons of Isr. sacredly separate from their uncleanness* (but rd. perh. וְהִזְהַרְתֶּם *warn* away from—as Ez 3[18] 33[8.9],—so Sam 𝔊—as to sense—Di Kau).—Vid. also ɪɪ. [נָזַר].

5145 †נֵ֫זֶר **n.m.** [ψ 132, 18] **consecration, crown, Naziriteship**;—נ׳ abs. 2 S 1[10]+; cstr. Ex 29[6]+; sf. נִזְרוֹ ψ 89[40]+, נִזְרֵךְ Je 7[29];—**1.** *crown* (sign of consecration; We [Skizzen iii. 118] cp. Syr. קדשא [ܩܕܫܐ], *earring*; v. also Gei [Jüd. Zeitschr. x. 45 ff.] on נֶזֶם): **a.** of kg. 2 S 1[10] 2 K 11[12] = 2 Ch 23[11]; symbol of royal power ψ 89[40] 132[18]; cf. Pr 27[24]; אַבְנֵי נ׳ Zc 9[16] *stones of a crown, diadem* (prob.; > We Now—who del., cf. GASm—*stones of charming*, fr. use of precious stones as charms. **b.** of high priest, נ׳ הַקֹּדֶשׁ Ex 29[6], made of gold 39[30] Lv 8[9] (all P). **2.** woman's *hair* (orig. prob. of long hair as sign of consecration, as in Nazirite vow, cf. Nu 6[19] infr., and נָזִיר, also We [Skizzen iii. 117, 167; Arab. Heidenthum 2, p. 143] RS [Sem. i. 464, 2d ed. 483]), Je 7[29] (of personif. Jerus.). **3.** *consecration* **a.** of h. p. נ׳ שֶׁמֶן מִשְׁחַת א׳ עליו Lv 21[12] (P) *the consecration of the oil of anointing of his God is upon him.* **b.** in Nu 6 (P), specif. of Nazirite consecration (cf. נָזִיר): נ׳ אֱלֹהָיו עָלָיו Nu 6[7], נֶדֶר נִזְרוֹ v[5], טִמֵּא נ׳ v[12], ראשׁ נ׳ (because of unshorn hair) v[9.18.18], (כָּל־) יְמֵי נ׳ v[4.8.12.13], תּוֹרַת נ׳ v[21 b] cf. עַל־נ׳ v[21 a]; in v[19] נ׳ = *the hair of his consecration* (cf. Je 7[29] supr.).

†נָזִיר **n.m.** [Gn 49, 26] **one consecrated, devoted** 5139
(נזיר י׳ Ecclus 46[13 c] (of Samuel); cf. Syr. ܢܙܝܪܐ RS [Sem. i. 463, 2d ed. 483]);—נ׳ abs. Nu 6[2]+5 t.; cstr. נְזִיר Gn 49[26]+4 t.; sf. נְזִירֶךָ Lv 25[5]; pl. נְזִרִים Am 2[11.12]; sf. נְזִרֶיהָ Lv 25[11], נְזִירֶיהָ La 4[7];—**1.** of prince, ruler, as *consecrated*: נְזִיר אֶחָיו Gn 49[26] (poem in J), *one consecrated among his brethren*, = Dt 33[16]; cf. נְזִירֶיהָ La 4[7] *her princes.* **2.** specif. of one dedicated to י׳ by vow involving abstinence fr. intoxicants, fr. touching corpse, and fr. cutting hair (cf. נֵזֶר **2**), *devotee* (GFM), *Nazirite*: נ׳ אֱלֹהִים *God's devotee*, of Samson Ju 13[5.7] 16[17] (exceptionally, from birth); usu. voluntary Am 2[11.12], and for limited time, cf. נ׳ נֶדֶר Nu 6[2] (of man or woman; cf. Peritz [JBL xvii (1898), 128]), תּוֹרַת נ׳ v[13.21], also v[18.19.20] (all P; cf. also נֵזֶר).—On Naz. v. GFM [Ju 13, 5] Dr [Am 2, 11], esp. Grill [JPTh. 1880, 645–680] Now [Arch. ii, § 97] Benz [Arch. 429 f.] Gray [JThS. Jan. 1900, 201 ff.] **3.** = *untrimmed vine* (like Nazirite with unshorn hair) Lv 25[5.11] (HP).

†[נָזַר] **vb. denom. Hiph.** *be a Nazirite, live as Nazirite*, sq. מִן (abstaining) *from* (so 5144
NH);—only Nu 6 in law of Naz.: *Pf.* וְהִזִּיר לי׳ consec. v[12]; *Impf.* יַזִּיר לי׳ v[5]; also מִיַּיִן . . . יַזִּיר v[3] *from wine . . . he shall abstain as a Nazirite*; *Inf.* לְהַזִּיר לי׳ v[2], כָּל־יְמֵי הַזִּירוֹ לי׳ v[6].

†[מִנְּזָר] **n.[m.]pl.** perh. **consecrated** (i.e. 4502
anointed) **ones, princes**;—only sf. מִנְּזָרַיִךְ Na 3[17] with d. f. dirim. Ges [§ 20 h] (of Nineveh);—form dub.; Kö [ii. 1, 90] prop. מְנֻזָּרַיִךְ = *thy crowned ones*; Gr רוֹזְנַיִךְ; Now GASm leave untranslated.

נַחַ **n.pr.** v. נוח   נַחְבִּי **n.pr.** v. חבה. 5146-47
p. 286, 629

†[נָחָה] **vb. lead, guide** (Ar. نَحَا *go in* 5148
direction of, turn (eyes) *toward*);—**Qal** *Pf.* sf. נָחַ֫נִי Gn 24[27]+2 t.; וְנָחֲךָ Is 58[11]; נָחָם Ex 13[17]; 2 ms. נָחִיתָ Ex 15[13] ψ 77[21]; *Imv.* נְחֵה Ex 32[34]; sf. נְחֵנִי ψ 5[9]+2 t.;—*lead, bring*, sq. acc. pers., subj. man Ex 32[34] (sq. אֶל־), cf. ψ 60[11] 108[11] (both sq. עַד־; ‖ הוביל); usu. subj. י׳ Gn 24[27] (J; also sq. בַּדֶּרֶךְ + acc. loc.), Ex 13[17] (E; sq. דֶּרֶךְ), 15[13] (song; ‖ נהל), ψ 77[21]; fig. of guidance in prosperity and righteousness ψ 5[9] (‖ הושׁר דרך), 27[11] (sq. בְּאֹרַח ‖ הורה דרך), 139[24] (sq. בדרך עולם); cf. Is 58[11]. **Hiph.** *Pf.* sf. הִנְחַ֫נִי Gn 24[48]; 2 ms. sf. הִנְחִתָם Ne 9[12]; *Impf.* sf. יַנְחֵ֫נִי Nu 23[7] ψ 23[3]; יַנְחֶ֫נּוּ Dt 32[12] Pr 18[16]; 3 fs. תַּנְחֶה Pr 6[22], etc.; *Inf. cstr.* sf. לְהַנְחֹתָם Ne 9[19]; לַנְחֹתָם Ex

13^{21};—*lead, guide* (= Qal) sq. acc. pers. Nu 23^7 (JE; + מִן).—1 S 22^4 (+ אֶת־פְּנֵי), 1 K 10^{26} 2 K 18^{11} v. sub נוח **Hiph.** B.—; of guiding = treating kindly (the helpless) Jb 31^{18}, of guiding constellations 38^{32} (‖ הוציא); usu. subj. י׳ Gn 24^{48} (J; sq. בַּדֶּרֶךְ) Dt 32^{12} ψ $78^{14.53.72}$ (Isr. as flock; ‖ רעה); Is 57^{18} ψ 107^{30} (sq. אֶל־); cf. of pillar of cloud Ex 13^{21} (J), Ne $9^{12.19}$; also Jb 12^{23} (‖ שׁטח), ψ 67^5; esp. in path of blessing ψ 23^3 31^4 (‖ נהל), 61^3 (sq. בְּ), 73^{24}; cf. 43^3 139^{10} (‖ אחז), 143^{10} (sq. בְּ); also of instruction, etc., Pr 6^{22} 11^3 18^{16} (sq. לִפְנֵי).

I. נחל (√ of foll.; cf. Ar. نَحَلَ *give for one's own, bestow,* so Sab. נחל Sab. Denkm. No. 9, l. 10; No. 15, l. 4; cf. pp. 41, 65; hence נַחֲלָה orig. *gift,* as Sab. נחלת Levy-Os ZMG xix (1865), 284 Sab. Denkm. l.c.; Min. *id.*, Hom Südar. Chrest. 128).

5159 נַחֲלָה 224 **n.f. possession, property, inheritance** (orig. *gift;* NH = BH);—נ׳ Nu 18^{23}+; נַחֲלַת ψ 16^6 (Ges §90g), rd. נַחֲלָתִי EwSSWeKö ii. 1, 425; cstr. נַחֲלַת Jos 13^{23}; sf. נַחֲלָתִי Ru 4^6; נַחֲלַתְכֶם ψ 105^{11}; pl. נְחָלוֹת Is 49^8, נְחָלֹת Jos 19^{51};—**1.** *property:* **a.** in Canaan given by י׳ to Israel, †נחלת ישׂראל Ju 20^6; †נ׳ יעקב Is 58^{14}, esp. †אֲשֶׁר נֹתֵן לְךָ נַחֲלָה Dt 4^{21} 15^4 19^{10} 20^{16} 21^{23} 24^4 25^{19} 26^1 (all D); הנחלה אשׁר הנחלתי את עמי Je 12^{14}. **b.** distrib. among tribes: נתן נ׳ לְ Nu 16^{14} 36^2 Jos 14^3 (restore לְ), $17^{4.14}$ 19^{49} (all P); נתן לנ׳ לְ Dt 29^7 Jos 11^{23} 14^{13} (all D²); נִחֲלוּ נחלה Jos 17^6 (J); תְּחַלֵּק בנ׳ Nu $26^{53.56}$ (P); נפל בנחלה Nu 34^2 (P), Ju 18^1 Ez 47^{22}; הפיל בנ׳ Jos 13^6 23^4 (D²), Ez 45^1 47^{22}, also v^{29} (Co rds. ב for מ). **c.** nations as possession of the people, ψ 111^6; of the king 2^8. **d.** Levites have no property in the land Nu $18^{23.24}$ Dt 10^9 12^{12}; their possession is י׳ Nu 18^{20} (P); י׳ הוא נחלתו Dt 10^9 18^2 Jos $13^{14.33}$ (all D); the tithes Nu $18^{21.24.26}$ (P). **e.** †י׳ takes Isr. as his property, 1 S 10^1 1 K 8^{53} 2 K 21^{14} Is 19^{25} Mi 7^{18} ψ 33^{12} 68^{10} 106^5; עם נחלה Dt 4^{20} (D²); עַמְּךָ וְנַחֲלָתְךָ Dt $9^{26.29}$ (D), 1 K 8^{51}; ‖ עם Is 47^6 Jo 2^{17} 4^2 Mi 7^{14} ψ 28^9 $78^{62.71}$ $94^{5.14}$ 106^{40}; נחלת י׳ 1 S 26^{19} 2 S 20^{19} 21^3; נ׳ אלהים 2 S 14^{16}; יעקב חבל נ׳ Dt 32^9; שֵׁבֶט נ׳ Je 10^{16} = 51^{19}, ψ 74^2; שבטי נ׳ Is 63^{17}; also, the holy mt. Ex 15^{17} (song), temple Je 12^7 ψ 79^1, land Je 2^7 $12^{8.9}$ 16^{18} 50^{11}. †**2.** *portion, share:* **a.** assigned by God, Is 54^{17} ψ 37^{18} 127^3; elsewh. ‖ חֵלֶק Jb 20^{29} 27^{13} 31^2. **b.** by choice, ‖ חֵלֶק, לא נ׳ לנו בבן ישׁי 2 S 20^1 *we have no share in the son of Jesse* = 1 K 12^{16} = 2 Ch 10^{16}. **3.** *inheritance* (45 t.) חֵלֶק וְנַחֲלָה בְּבֵית אָבִינוּ Gn 31^{14} (E) *portion or inheritance in the house of our father;* העביר נ׳ לְ Nu $27^{7.8}$ (P) *cause the inheritance to pass unto;* נתן נ׳ לְ Nu $27^{9.10.11}$ (P), Jb 42^{15}; †נחלת אבות Nu $36^{3.8}$ 1 K $21^{3.4}$ Pr 19^{14}; נ׳ לבניו תהיה Ez 46^{16}.

† נָחַל **vb. denom.** get or take as a possession (cf. Gerber 236 ff.; Ecclus נחל 45^{22b}+; NH *id.* (rare));—**Qal** *Pf.* נ׳ Zc 2^{16}; 2 ms. נָחַלְתָּ Ex 23^{20} + 8 t. Pf.; *Impf.* 3 ms. יִנְחַל Is 57^{13}; 3 mpl. יִנְחָלוּ Nu 18^{23} + 5 t.; יִנְחָלוּ 26^{55} + 2 t.; + 8 t. Impf.; *Inf.* נְחֹל Nu 34^{18} Jos 19^{49};—**1.** *take possession, inherit:* **a.** land of Canaan, Ex 23^{30} (E), 32^{13} (J), Is 57^{13} Ez 47^{14}; Zion and Judah ψ 69^{37}. **b.** special sections in the land, of tribes and individuals, נחל נחלה Jos 17^6 (J); נחלה אשׁר נ׳ Dt 19^{14} (D), Nu 35^8 (P), cf. Jos 14^1 (P); without acc., *have or get a* (landed) *property,* Nu $18^{20.23.24}$ 26^{55} 32^{19} Jos 16^4 19^9 (all P), Ju 11^3. **c.** land of Moab and Ammon by conquest Zp 2^9; landed property בכל הגוים ψ 82^8. **d.** God takes possession of Israel as his private property Ex 34^9 (J); Judah Zc 2^{16}. **2.** fig. *have or get as a possession, property:* testimonies ψ 119^{111}, glory Pr 3^{35}, good things 28^{10}, lies Je 16^{19}, wind Pr 11^{29}, simplicity 14^{18}. **3.** *divide the land for a possession,* Nu $34^{17.18}$ Jos 19^{49} (all P; incorrect pointing for Piel, so SS). 5157

Pi. *divide for a possession: Pf.* 3 ms. נִחַל Jos 13^{32}; 3 pl. נִחֲלוּ Jos 14^1 19^{51}; *Inf.* נַחֵל Nu 34^{29} (all P); also Nu $34^{17.18}$ Jos 19^{49} (v. **Qal 3**).

Hithp. *Pf.* 3 pl. sf. הִתְנַחֲלוּם Is 14^2; 2 mpl. הִתְנַחַלְתֶּם Lv 25^{46} Nu 33^{54}; *Impf.* תִּתְנַחֲלוּ Nu 34^{13} Ez 47^{13}; תִּתְנֶחָלוּ Nu 33^{54}; *Inf.* הִתְנַחֵל Nu 32^{18}; *possess oneself of* land (acc.), Nu 33^{54} 34^{13} (P) Ez 47^{13}; נחלה Nu 32^{18} (P); slaves Lv 25^{46} (P) Is 14^2; abs., ref. to land Nu 33^{54} (P); all c. לְ pers. (for whose benefit), exc. Nu 32^{18} 34^{13} Is 14^2.

Hiph. *Pf.* 1 s. הִנְחַלְתִּי Je 3^{18} + 3 t. Pf.; *Impf.* 3 ms. יַנְחִיל Dt 3^{28}; יַנְחֵל Ez 46^{18}; 2 ms. sf. תַּנְחִילֶנָּה Dt 31^7 + 5 t. Impf.; *Inf. cstr.* הַנְחִיל Is 49^8 Pr 8^{21}; בְּהַנְחֵל Dt 32^8 (on form cf. Ew §238d Kö i. 315 Ges §53k; rd. בְּהַנְחִל?); sf. הַנְחִילוֹ Dt 21^{16}; *Pt.* מַנְחִיל Dt 12^{10};—**1.** *give as a possession:* **a.** land of Canaan (given by י׳ or his servants), acc. pers. et rei, Dt 1^{38} 3^{28} 12^{10} 19^3 31^7 Jos 1^6 (all D), Je 3^{18} 12^{14}. **b.** various things, acc. pers. et rei, espec. blessings, Zc 8^{12} 1 S 2^8 Pr 8^{21}; acc. rei Is 49^8; acc. pers. Dt 32^8. **2.** *cause to inherit, give as an inheritance,* c. acc. pers. et rei, Dt 21^{16}; acc. pers. + מן rei, Ez 46^{18}; acc. pers. Pr 13^{22}; לְ

pers. 1 Ch 28^{8}. **Hoph.** *Pf.* 1 s. הָנְחַלְתִּי Jb 7^{3} *made to possess*, c. acc. rei, e.g. *months of vanity*.

5155 [נְחִילָה] **n.f.** meaning unknown; only pl. in phr. אֶל־הַנְּחִילוֹת ψ 5^{1} (title); most conj. = נְחִלּוֹת √חָלִיל=חלל *flute*; v. against this Bae$^{Einl. xi}$, who thinks (cf. 𝔊 ὑπὲρ τῆς κληρονομούσης = אֶל־הַנַּחֲלָת [cf. 𝔙], Jerome [Aq. Symm] *pro hereditatibus* = אֶל־הַנְּחָלֹת) possibly designation of a melody.

II. נָחַל (√of foll.; meaning unknown).

5158 †I. נַ֫חַל **n.m.**$^{2 K 3, 16}$ **torrent, torrent-valley, wady** (Ecclus 40$^{13.16}$; NH *id.*, *stream* (rare); 𝔗 נַחְלָא, Syr. ܢܚܠܐ, = BH; As. *naḫlu* = BH; Lag$^{BN 140 Anm.}$ thinks Νεῖλος may be from Νεέλ = נַחַל pronounced *נְחֵל; on נ׳ in Sab. n.pr.loc., v. Hal$^{Rev. Sémit. iv (1896), 80, l. 14}$);—abs. נ׳ Gn 32^{24}+, נַ֫חְלָה ψ 124^{4}; cstr. נַחַל Gn 26^{17}+; c. ה loc. Nu 34^{5}; so read also Ez 47^{19} 48^{28} (where MT נַחֲלָה; v. Thes); du. נַחֲלַיִם Ez 47^{9}, but rd. הַנַּחַל 𝔊 𝔗 𝔖 𝔙 Co Berthol; pl. נְחָלִים Nu 21^{4}+; נַחֲלֵי Dt 8^{7}+; sf. נְחָלֶיהָ Is 34^{9};—**1.** *torrent*, of rushing water in narrow channel Ju 5$^{21.21.21}$ 4$^{7.13}$ ψ 83^{10} (all of קִישׁוֹן, q.v.); mountain torrent Dt 9^{21} (cf. Ex 32^{20}); so Am 5^{24} (sim. of righteousness); הַנּ׳ הַשּׁוֹטֵף 2 Ch 32^{4} (‖ מַעְיָנוֹת); נֶהֶפְכוּ נ׳ לְזֶפֶת Is 34^{9}; sim. of tears La 2^{18}; hyperb. נ׳־שָׁ֑מֶן Mi 6^{7} *torrents of oil*, cf. of honey and curd Jb 20^{17} (‖ נְהָרִים, פְּלַגּוֹת); fig. נ׳ בְלִיַּעַל 2 S 22^{5} *torrents of worthlessness* (‖ מִשְׁבְּרֵי מָ֫וֶת), = ψ 18^{5}; נ׳ שׁוֹטֵף sim. of glory of nations Is 66^{12}, fig. of invaders Je 47^{2} (‖ מַיִם), or foes ψ 124^{4} (נַ֫חְלָה, v. supr.); 1 K 17$^{4.6}$ (for drinking), drying up in summer v^{7} (יָבֵשׁ; all of Elijah's stream כְּרִית, q.v.); for drinking also ψ 110^{7}, and (fig.) נ׳ עֲדָנֶיךָ 36^{9}; Jb 6$^{15.15}$ (אֲפִיק נְחָלִים; in sim.); of water bursting from rock ψ 78^{20} (‖ מַיִם, שָׁטַף), cf. 74^{15} (+ מַעְיָן); fig. of מְקוֹר חָכְמָה Pr 18^{4} (נ׳ נֹבֵעַ ‖ מַיִם עֲמֻקִּים); more gen. = stream, brook, river (chiefly late) Is 11^{15} (divisions of river, נָהָר), in desert 35^{6} (‖ מַיִם), Je 31^{9} (נַחֲלֵי מַיִם), Ez 47$^{5.5.9b}$ (all del. Co), v$^{6.7.9a}$ (rd. הַנַּחַל, v. supr.), v^{12}; containing fish, etc. Lv 11$^{9.10}$ (‖ יַמִּים, מַיִם), Ec 1$^{7.7}$; fig. of רוּחַ י׳ Is 30^{28} (נ׳ שׁוֹטֵף), 30^{33} (נ׳ גָּפְרִית).

2. *Torrent-valley, wady*, as stream-bed 1 S 17^{40} Ne 2^{15} Is 57^{6}; with torrent flowing through it, נ׳ אֵיתָן Dt 21$^{4.4.6}$, אֶרֶץ נַחֲלֵי מַיִם Dt 8^{7} (‖ עֲיָנֹת וּתְהֹמֹת יֹצְאִים בַּבִּקְעָה), cf. 10^{7}, 1 K 18^{5} (‖ מַעְיְנֵי הַמַּיִם), ψ 104^{10}; abode of Elijah 1 K 17$^{3.5}$ (cf. v$^{4.6.7}$ supr.); עֹרְבֵי נ׳ Pr 30^{17} (cf. 1 K 17$^{4.6}$); נ׳ הַכַּתּוֹת Is 7^{19} as home of bees; fertile, נ׳ אֶשְׁכֹּל Nu 13$^{23.24}$ (E); אִבֵּי הַנּ׳ Ct 6^{11}; עַרְבֵי־נ׳ *poplars of the wady* Lv 23^{40} (H), Jb 40^{22}; נ׳ עֲרָבִים Is 15^{7}; needing water Gn 26^{17} (נ׳ גְּרָר), v^{19} (J), cf. 2 K 3$^{16.17}$; place for refuse, ruins, etc. 2 S 17^{13}; poet. also as wild, remote *ravine* Jb 30^{6}, cf. בְּצוּר הַנְּחָלִים 22^{24}; place of child-sacrifice Is 57^{5}; burial-place Jb 21^{33} (רִגְבֵי נ׳).—Nu 24^{6} v. II. נַחַל.

Particular wadys designate localities: אַרְנוֹן Nu 21^{14} (E), Dt 2$^{24.36.36}$ 3$^{8.12.16.16}$ 4^{48} Jos 12$^{1.2.2}$ 13$^{9.9}$ (all D), v$^{16.16}$ (P), 2 K 10^{33}; אֶשְׁכֹּל Nu 32^{9} (J), Dt 1^{24}; בְּשׂוֹר 1 S 30$^{9.10.21}$; גָּד 2 S 24^{5}; זֶרֶד Nu 21^{12} (E), Dt 2$^{13.13.14}$; יַבֹּק Gn 32^{24} (J), Dt 2^{37} 3^{16} Jos 12^{2} (all D); קִדְרוֹן 2 S 15^{23} 1 K 2^{37} 15^{13} 18^{40} 23$^{6.6.12}$ 2 Ch 15^{16} 29^{16} 30^{14} Je 31^{40}; קָנָה Jos 16^{8} 17$^{9.9.9}$ (all P); שׂוֹרֵק Ju 16^{4}; נ׳ הַשִּׁטִּים Jo 4^{18}; נ׳ מִצְרַיִם is SW. limit of Pal. (As. *naḫal* [*mat*] *Muṣri*, Dl$^{Par. 310}$ Schr$^{COT Nu 34, 5}$) Nu 34^{5} (P), Jos 15^{4} (D), v^{47} (P), 1 K 8^{65} 2 K 24^{7} 2 Ch 7^{8} Is 27^{12}, + (om. מצרים) Ez 47^{19} 48^{28} (v. supr.); so rd. also poss. Am 6^{14} (v. עֲרָבָה: usually identified with *Wâdy el-Arîsh;* on Wkl's different view, v. reff. sub מִצְרַיִם *ad fin.*); on identif. of נ׳ Jos 15^{7} 19^{11} (both P), 2 S 23^{30} = 1 Ch 11^{32}, 2 Ch 20^{16} 33^{14}, v. Comm.; אֶשֶׁד הַנְּחָלִים Nu 21^{15}, v. אֶשֶׁד.

3. *Miner's shaft*, פָּרַץ נ׳ Jb 28^{4}.

5158 †II. [נַ֫חַל] **n.[m.]** perh. **palm-tree** (Ar. نَخْلٌ, n. unit. نَخْلَةٌ; v. Perles$^{JQ. July, 1899, 688}$);—only pl. abs., כִּנְחָלִים נִטָּיוּ Nu 24^{6} *like palm-trees, which are stretched out, spread out* (as to foliage). So Perles$^{l.c.}$, who compares כערבי נחל Ecclus 50^{12e}, 𝔊 ὡς στελέχη φοινίκων.

5160 נַחֲלִיאֵל† **n.pr.loc.** (= *valley*—or *palm*—*of Ēl*);—station of Isr. E. of Dead Sea Nu 21$^{19.19}$ (JE), poss. (if = *valley*) one of main tributaries of Arnon, e.g. *W. Wâle* (v. Bliss$^{PEF 1895, 204, 215}$).

5161 נֶחֱלָמִי† **adj.gent.** (noun not found);—Je 29^{24}; also v$^{31.32}$ (where van d. H. נֶחְלָמִי).

5158 נחלת v. נַחֲלָה. p. 635

5162 †[נחם] **vb. Niph. be sorry, console oneself**, etc. (only in der. species) (NH Pi. *comfort;* Ph. in n.pr. Lzb^{322}; 𝔗 Pa. = NH, and deriv.; Chr Pal Aram. Pa. *id.*, Schwally$^{Idiot. 54}$; Ar. نَحَمَ *breathe pantingly* (of horse));—**Niph.** *Pf.* נִחַם Am 7^{3}+4 t.; נִחָ֑ם Je 20^{16}+2 t.; 1 s. נִחַמְתִּי Gn 6^{7}+8 t.; נִחָ֫מְתִּי Zc 8^{14}; 2 mpl. נִחַמְתֶּם Ez 14^{22}; *Impf.* יִנָּחֵם Ex 13^{17}+6 t.; וַיִּנָּ֫חֶם Gn 6^{6}+6 t.; +5 t. Impf.; *Imv.* הִנָּחֵם Ex 32^{12} ψ 90^{13}; *Inf.* הִנָּחֵם Je 31^{15} 1 S 15^{29}; *Pt.* נִחָם Ju 21^{15}+3 t.;

—**1.** *be sorry, moved to pity, have compassion,* for others, abs. Je 15[6]; c. על ψ 90[13]; אֶל Ju 21[6]; לְ v[15]; מִן 2[18]. **2.** *be sorry, rue, suffer grief, repent,* of one's own doings, abs. Ex 13[17] (E), ψ 106[45] Je 20[16] Jo 2[14] Zc 8[14]; ‖ שׁקר 1 S 15[29.29]; מאס Jb 42[6]; שׁוב Je 4[28] 31[19] Jon 3[9]; חוס Ez 24[14]; לא נ׳, ‖ נשׁבע ψ 110[4]; c. על Am 7[3.6] Je 8[6] 18[10]; על־הרעה for ill done to others Ex 32[12.14] (J), Je 18[8] Jo 2[13] Jon 3[10] 4[2]; אל־הרעה 2 S 24[16] = 1 Ch 21[15] (על), Je 26[3.13.19] 42[10]; כִּי Gn 6[6.7] (J), 1 S 15[11.35]. **3.** *comfort oneself, be comforted:* abs. Gn 38[12] (J) ψ 77[3] Ez 31[16]; c. על 2 S 13[39] Je 31[15]; על הרעה, *concerning the evil* Ez 14[22] 32[31]; אחרי Gn 24[67] (J). **4.** *comfort oneself, ease oneself,* by taking vengeance c. מן Is 1[24]; על 57[6].

Piel *Pf.* נִחַם Is 49[13]; + 8 t. Pf.; *Impf.* יְנַחֵם Jb 29[25]; 3 mpl. יְנַחֲמוּ Jb 42[11]; יְנַחֲמוּן Zc 10[2] + 13 t. Impf.; *Imv.* נַחֲמוּ Is 40[1.1]; *Inf.* נַחֵם Is 61[2]; sf. נַחֲמוֹ Gn 37[35] + 9 t. Inf.; *Pt.* מְנַחֵם La 1[2], pl. מְנַחֲמִים ψ 69[21], + 11 t. Pt.—*comfort, console,* abs. Gn 37[35] (J), 1 Ch 19[3] = 2 S 10[3]; ψ 69[21] Ec 4[1.1] Zc 10[2] Na 3[7] La 1[16]; c. acc. pers. Gn 50[21] (E) 2 S 12[24] 1 Ch 7[21] 19[2] Jb 2[11] 7[13] 21[34] 29[25] Ru 2[13] ψ 23[4] 71[21] 119[76.82] Is 12[1] 22[4] 40[1.1] 51[3.3.12.19] 61[2] 66[13.13] Ez 14[23] 16[54] Zc 1[17] La 2[13]; ‖ עזר ψ 86[17]; רִחַם Is 49[13]; גאל Is 52[9]; שׂמח Je 31[13]; מן rei Gn 5[29] (J); על Je 16[7] 42[11]; אל 2 S 10[2] = על 1 Ch 19[2]; מְנַחֲמֵי עמל Jb 16[2]; אֵין מְנַחֵם לְ La 1[2.9.17.21].

Pual *Pf.* נֻחָ֫מָה Is 54[11]; *Impf.* תְּנֻחָ֫מוּ Is 66[13]; *be comforted, consoled.*

Hithpa. Pf. 1 s. וְהִנֶּחָמְתִּי (for הִתְנ׳; but del. Co) Ez 5[13]; *Impf.* יִתְנֶחָ֫ם Dt 32[36] + 2 t.; 1 s. אֶתְנֶחָם ψ 119[52]; *Inf.* הִתְנַחֵם Gn 37[35]; *Pt.* מִתְנַחֵם Gn 27[42]—**1.** *be sorry, have compassion* עַל־עֲבָדָיו *upon his servants* Dt 32[36] = ψ 135[14]. **2.** *rue, repent of,* ‖ כִּזֵּב, Nu 23[19] (poem). **3.** *comfort oneself, be comforted,* abs. Gn 37[35] (J), ψ 119[52]. **4.** *ease oneself,* by taking vengeance Ez 5[13] (?); c. לְ pers. Gn 27[42] (JE): cf. **Qal 4.**

5163 †נַ֫חַם **n.pr.m.** (*comfort*), a chieftain of Judah 1 Ch 4[19]; 𝔊 Ναχεθ, A Ναχεμ, 𝔊L Ναουμ.

5164 †נֹ֫חַם **n.m.** *sorrow, repentance,* Ho 13[14].

5151 †נַחוּם **n. pr. m.** (*comfort*) the prophet Nahum, Na 1[1], 𝔊 Ναουμ.

5149 †נְחוּם **n.pr.m.** (*comfort*) a returned exile Ne 7[7] 𝔊 Ναουμ = רְחוּם Ezr 2[2].

5150 †[נִחוּם] **n.m. 1.** *comfort,* pl. נִחֻמִים Is 57[18] Zc 1[13]. **2.** *compassion,* sf. נִחוּמָ֑י Ho 11[8] (We rds. רַחֲמַי).

†נְחֶמְיָה **n.pr.m.** (*Yah comforts,* 𝔊 Νεε- 5166
μιας (-ου), etc.;—n.pr. נחמיה(ו) on Isr. scarab in BM, Cl-Gann[JAs 1883, Fév.-Mars. 156 No. 42]);—**1.** the son of Hachaliah, governor of Judah under Artaxerxes Longimanus Ne 1[1] 8[9] 10[2] 12[26.47]. **2.** ruler of half the district of Bethzur Ne 3[16]. **3.** one of twelve heads of people who returned with Zerubbabel Ezr 2[2] = Ne 7[7].

†נַחֲמָנִי **n.pr.m.** (*compassionate*) a returned 5167
exile Ne 7[7]; 𝔊 Νεεμιου (gen.).

†[נֶחָמָה] **n.f.** comfort, sf. נֶחָמָתִי ψ 119[50] 5165
Jb 6[10].

†מְנַחֵם **n. pr. m.** (*comforter*), king of 4505
Northern Israel, 2 K 15[14.16.17.19.20.21.22.23]; 𝔊 Μαναημ.

†[תַּנְחוּם] **n.m.** [ψ 94, 19] *consolation,* only in 8575
pl. (usually abstr. and intensive) תַּנְחוּמִים Je 16[7]; sf. תַּנְחוּמֶיךָ ψ 94[19]; תַּנְחֻמֶיהָ Is 66[11]; תַּנְחוּמוֹת Jb 15[11]; תַּנְחוּמֹתֵיכֶם 21[2].

†תַּנְחֻ֫מֶת **n.pr.m.** (? Lag[BN 126 f.] thinks **f.**) 8576
parent of Seraiah, a Hebr. captain, after fall of Jerus. Je 40[8] = 2 K 25[23] (Lag[l. c.] conj. תכחמת, Egyptian name).

נַחְנוּ v. אֲנַחְנוּ p. 59 b supr. 5168

†[נָחַץ] **vb.** urge (?), whence (si vera l.);— 5169
Qal *Pt. pass.* (*active* Pt. in *u,* acc. to Ba[NB 175]), דְּבַר הַמֶּלֶךְ נָחוּץ 1 S 21[9] *the king's business was urgent* (𝔊 κατὰ σπουδήν, A κατασπεῦδον). (Thes cp. Ar. نَحَضَ *ursit institique rogando* [Kam Frey]); text dub.; HPS נָאוּץ (from אוץ), > נחושׁ.

נחר (prob. onomatop. √ of foll.; cf. As. *naḫîru, nostril;* Ar. نَخَرَ *snort,* نُخَرٌ *nostril;* Eth. ነኀረ: *snort;* Syr. ܢܚܪ *id.,* ܢܚܝܪܐ *nostril;* 𝔗 נְחִירָא *id.;* also NH Pi. *snort*).—נָחַר Je 6[29] etc., v. I. חרר.

†[נַ֫חַר] **n.[m.]** a snorting; sf. נַחְרוֹ Jb 39[20] 5170
(of horse).

†[נַחֲרָה] **n.f.** id.;—cstr. נַחֲרַת סוּסָיו Je 8[16]. 5170

†נָחוֹר **n.pr.m.** (connexion with √ ob- 5152
scure);—**1.** father of Teraḥ Gn 11[22.23.24.25] (all P), 1 Ch 1[26]. **2.** son of Teraḥ and brother of Abr. Gn 11[26.27] (P), v[29.29] 22[20.23] 24[15.24.47] cf. 29[5] (all J), Jos 24[2] (E); עִיר נ׳ Gn 24[10] (J); אֱלֹהֵי נ׳ 31[53] (E).—𝔊 always Ναχωρ.

5156 †[נָחִיר] **n.[m.]** nostril (appar. fr. above √, and not connected with Ar. نَحَرَ *stab* camel in wind-pipe, etc., Aram. נְחַר *kill by stabbing* in nose or throat, cf. NH נָחַר *perforate, kill by stabbing*, so that נָחִיר would=*perforation*, and נחר *snort* wd. be denom.);—only du. sf. מִנְּחִירָיו יֵצֵא עָשָׁן Jb 41^{12} (of crocodile).

5171 †נַחֲרַי **n.pr.m.** one of David's heroes, 2 S 23^{37}; 𝔊 Γελωρε, 𝔊L Αραια; =†נַחְרַי 1 Ch 11^{39}; 𝔊 Ναχωρ, A Νααραι, 𝔊L Νοαραι.

I. **נחשׁ** (appar. onomatop. √of foll.=*hiss*, so Thes Bau$^{\text{Sem. Rel. i. 287}}$ al.).

5175 †I. **נָחָשׁ** **n.m.** $^{\text{Gn 3, 1}}$ **serpent** (NH *id.*; Ar. حَنَشٌ *serpent, viper* (Lane^{406} anything *hunted*) is cp. by Lag$^{\text{M. i. 230; BN 50, 188}}$ Ba$^{\text{ES 48}}$, but improb.; Ar. نَحِسَ v. sub [נָחַשׁ] infr.; on formation cf. Lag$^{\text{BN 50}}$);—abs. נ׳ Am 5^{19}+; cstr. נְחַשׁ Nu 21^{9}+ 2 t.; pl. נְחָשִׁים Nu 21^{6} Je 8^{17};—**1.** *serpent*: **a.** as biting, Am 5^{19} Ec 10^{8}, in spite of charm (לָחַשׁ) v^{11} [cf. Ecclus 12^{13}], Je 8^{17} (+צִפְעֹנִים; fig. of enemies); so הַנְּחָשִׁים הַשְּׂרָפִים Nu 21^{6} (deadly; JE; cf. Jacob$^{\text{Arab. Dicht. iv. 10 ff.}}$), and sg. v^{9}, also (coll.) v^{7}, cf. נ׳ שָׂרָף Dt 8^{15} (+עַקְרָב); נ׳ fig. of oppressor, מִשֹּׁרֶשׁ נָחָשׁ יֵצֵא צֶפַע וּפִרְיוֹ שָׂרָף מְעוֹפֵף Is 14^{29}; fig. of Dan Gn 49^{17} (poem in J; ‖ שְׁפִיפֹן); חֲמַת נ׳ ψ 58^{5} (sim. of perniciousness of ungodly), cf. נ׳ 140^{4}; sim. of effect of wine Pr 23^{32} (‖צִפְעֹנִי). **b.** rod becomes נ׳ Ex 4^{3} (J), cf. 7^{15} (E); דֶּרֶךְ נ׳ עֲלֵי צוּר Pr 30^{19}. **c.** נ׳ (appar.) as hissing Je 46^{22} (in sim., cf. Gie); as eating dust Is 65^{25} cf. Mi 7^{17} (in sim.; v. also Gn 3^{14}). **d.** as crafty tempter Gn 3$^{1.2.4.13.14}$. **2.** (הַ)נְּחֹשֶׁת (הַ)נ׳, bronze image of serpent Nu 21$^{9.9}$ 2 K 18^{4} (cf. נְחֻשְׁתָּן). **3.** mythol. נ׳ בָּרִחַ Jb 26^{13} *fleeing serpent*, of eclipse-dragon (cf. לִוְיָתָן 3^{6}); also לִוְיָתָן נ׳ בָּרִחַ ... לִוְיָתָן נ׳ עֲקַלָּתוֹן Is 27^{1} (symbol. of world-powers); נ׳ of sea-monster Am 9^{3}.—נ׳ c. vb. נָשַׁךְ *bite* Nu 21^{6}+8 t. On supernat. character of serpents in Arab. belief v. Nö$^{\text{Zeitschr. für Völkerpsychol. i (1860), 412–416}}$ RS$^{\text{Kinship 197; Sem. i. 421 f., 2d ed. 442}}$ We$^{\text{Skizzen iii. 147; Arab. Heid. 2, 152 f.}}$ Jacob$^{\text{Arab. Dicht. iv. 5}}$

5176 †II. **נָחָשׁ** **n.pr.m.** **1.** king of Ammon 1 S 11$^{1.1.2}$ 12^{12} 2 S 10^{2} 1 Ch 19$^{1.2}$; perh. also 2 S 17^{27}; 𝔊 Ναας. **2.** father of Abigail and Zeruiah 2 S 17^{25}, si vera l.: 𝔊 Ναας, but 𝔊L Ιεσσαι (cf. 1 Ch 2^{16}); We$^{\text{Gesch. 2. 57 Anm. 1}}$ Löhr defend נחשׁ; dub. We^{Sm} HPS. **3.** giving name to a city,
5904 עִיר נ׳ 1 Ch 4^{12}, 𝔊 *πόλεως Ναας*; 𝔊L Ηρναας.
5177 †נַחְשׁוֹן **n.pr.m.** son of Aminadab, of Judah, brother-in-law of Aaron Ex 6^{23} Nu 1^{7} 2^{3} 7$^{12.17}$ 10^{14} (all P), Ru 4$^{20.20}$ 1 Ch 2$^{10.11}$. 𝔊 Ναασσων (DHM$^{\text{ZMG xxxvii (1883), 15}}$ cp. Sab. tribal name נחסן).

†II. **[נָחַשׁ]** **vb.** only **Pi.** *practise divination, divine, observe signs* (denom. from נָחָשׁ acc. to Nö$^{\text{Zeitschr. f. Völkerpsychol. i (1860), 413}}$ Bau$^{\text{Sem. Rel. i. 287}}$ Lag$^{\text{BN 188}}$ Gerber$^{\text{Verb. Denom. 29}}$; otherwise We$^{\text{Skizzen iii. 147}}$ Me$^{\text{Chrest. Targ. s.v.}}$ Ba$^{\text{ES 48}}$ (agst. him v. Sta$^{\text{Th Lz. April 28, 1894, 235}}$); chief difficulty is that Aram., which has נַחֵשׁ, has no נְחָשׁ, cf. RS$^{\text{JPh. xiv. 115}}$;—NH Qal Pt. נוֹחֵשׁ, and Pi.; Aram. Pa. נַחֵשׁ, ܢܰܚܶܫ, all=*divine, learn by omens*; perh. cp. also Ar. نَحِسَ *be unlucky* Lane^{2775} cf. Me$^{\text{l.c.}}$);—*Pf.* 3 ms. וְנִחֵשׁ 2 K 21^{6} 2 Ch 33^{6}; 1 s. נִחַשְׁתִּי Gn 30^{27}; *Impf.* יְנַחֵשׁ Gn 44$^{5.15}$; 3 mpl. וַיְנַחֲשׁוּ, יְנַחֲשׁוּ 1 K 20^{33}, 2 K 17^{17}; 2 mpl. תְּנַחֲשׁוּ Lv 19^{26}; *Inf. abs.* נַחֵשׁ 1 K 20^{33}; *Pt.* מְנַחֵשׁ Dt 18^{10} (cf. esp. RS$^{\text{JPh. xiv. 113 ff.}}$);—**1.** *practise divination* Gn 44^{5} (J; by means of cup, i.e. by hydromancy), with implied power to learn secret things v^{15}; condemned by proph. writer 2 K 21^{6}=2 Ch 33^{6} (+וְעָשָׂה אוֹב עוֹנֵן), 2 K 17^{17} (וַיִּקְסְמוּ קְסָמִים ‖ וַיְנַחֵשׁוּ); forbidden in D and H: Dt 18^{10} (+קֹסֵם קְסָמִים מְעוֹנֵן וּמְכַשֵּׁף), Lv 19^{26} (H; ‖ תְעוֹנֵנוּ). **2.** *observe the signs or omens* Gn 30^{27} (J); so prob. יְנַחֲשׁוּ 1 K 20^{33} now the men *were observing the signs*. 5172

†נַחַשׁ **n.[m.]** **divination, enchantment,** only abs. נ׳ Nu 23^{23} (JE; ‖ קֶסֶם), and pl. abs. נְחָשִׁים Nu 24^{1} (JE), both in story of Balaam. 5173

III. **נחשׁ** (√of foll., meaning unknown).

I. **נְחֹשֶׁת** $_{137}$ **n.m.** $^{\text{1 K 7, 45}}$ (cf. Albrecht$^{\text{ZAW xvi (1896), 108}}$; **f.** 1 Ch 18^{8}) **copper, bronze** (NH=BH; Ph. נחשת; Palm. נחשא Lzb^{322}; Syr. ܢܚܳܫܳܐ, 𝔗 נְחָשָׁא, Ar. نُحَاسٌ, Eth. ናሐስ: (so also OEth. DHM$^{\text{Epigr. Denkm. aus Abess. (1894), 52}}$); WMM$^{\text{As. u. Eur. 127}}$ cites Egypt. *teḥ(ḥ)ost, copper* (=**tenḥost*), as loan-wd. fr. נְחֹשֶׁת+fem. art.);—נ׳ abs. Gn 4^{22}+; cstr. Ex 38^{29}; sf. נְחֻשְׁתִּי La 3^{7}, נְחֻשְׁתֵּךְ Ez 16^{36}, נְחֻשְׁתָּהּ 24^{11}, נְחֻשְׁתָּם 2 K 25^{13}+2 t.; du. נְחֻשְׁתַּיִם Ju 16^{21}+6 t.;—**1.** *copper*, as ore Dt 8^{9}, cf. Zc 6^{8}; worked by artificer Gn 4^{22} (J) 1 K 7$^{14.14}$ 2 Ch 24^{12}; material—doubtless hardened with alloy, prob. tin, making *bronze*, cf. Now$^{\text{Arch. i. 243}}$ Benz$^{\text{Arch. 214}}$—of armour 1 S 17$^{5.6}$ 1 K 14^{27}, utensils 2 K 25^{14}=Je 52^{18}, Lv 6^{21} Nu 17^{4}+very oft., altar 2 K 16$^{14.15}$ Ex 38^{30} 39^{39}, etc., and other objects Nu 21$^{9.9}$ (JE), 2 K 18^{4} 1 K 4^{13} 7$^{15\text{ ff.}}$+, esp. in description of tabernacle and temple; cast 1 K 7^{14}; polished מְמֹרָט v^{45}, מָרוּק 2 Ch 4^{16} (cf. Lv 6^{21}); and shining מֻצְהָב Ezr 8^{27}. On 5178

נ׳ קָלָל Ez 1⁷ Dn 10⁶ v. קלל; נ׳ as spoil of war 2 S 8⁸ 2 K 25¹³=Je 52¹⁷·²⁰ etc. †**2.** *fetters of copper* or *bronze*, usu. du. Ju 16²¹ 2 S 3³⁴ 2 K 25⁷=Je 39⁷ 52¹¹ 2 Ch 36⁶, also 33¹¹; sg. only La 3⁷ (fig. of oppression). **3.** as less in value than gold but more than wood Is 60¹⁷·¹⁷; fig. of worthless people Je 6²⁸ (+בַּרְזֶל), *id.* (as dross of silver) Ez 22¹⁸ (+עוֹפֶרֶת, בַּרְזֶל, בְּדִיל).—On Ez 16³⁶ v. IV. נחשׁ. **4.** fig. of pitiless sky Dt 28²³.

5153 † נָחוּשׁ **adj. of bronze**;—אִם־בְּשָׂרִי נ׳ Jb 6¹² *or is my flesh of bronze?* fig. for strong, enduring (|| אֲבָנִים; cf. 40¹⁸).

5154 † נְחוּשָׁה and (Lv 26¹⁹ Jb 40¹⁸) נְחֻשָׁה **n.f. copper, bronze** (only poet.; cf. I. נְחֹשֶׁת);—נ׳ alw. abs.;—**1.** *copper* produced from ore by melting Jb 28². **2.** *copper*, doubtless hardened with alloy, =*bronze*, as material of bow 2 S 22³⁵=ψ 18³⁵, Jb 20²⁴; gates Is 45²; fig. of strength Jb 40¹⁸ (bones of hippopotamus), cf. 41¹⁹, Mi 4¹³ (hoofs of Zion); of obstinate brow Is 48⁴ (|| גִּיד בַּרְזֶל עָרְפֶּךָ); unproductive earth Lv 26¹⁹.

5179 † נְחֻשְׁתָּא **n.pr.f.** mother of king Jehoiakin 2 K 24⁸; 𝔊 Νεσθα, A Ναισθα, 𝔊L Νεεσθαν.

5180 † נְחֻשְׁתָּן **n.pr.** given to bronze serpent 2 K 18⁴ prob. =*bronze*-god (so Thes, v. also Bau^Sem. Rel. i. 288^; cf. נְחַשׁ נְחֹשֶׁת v⁴ Nu 21⁹·⁹);—chief arg. ag. this are vocalization of 𝔊 Νεσθαλει, A𝔊L Νε(ε)σθαν, and comparat. unimportance of material of wh. image was made; others think of נָחָשׁ *serpent* (Nö^ZMG xlii (1888), 482^ נחש+תן, Klo^ad loc.^ נחש+יתן); Lag^BN 188, 205^ thinks loan-wd.

IV. נחשׁ (poss. √of foll., si vera l.; but precise meaning uncertain; Gei^Urschrift 392^ cp. Ar. نَخَسَ [=*goad, prick;* نِخَاسٌ a certain piece of *perforated wood* (Frey)], NH נְחֹשֶׁת [*bottom* of vessel, Levy^NHWB iii. 374^]).

5178 †II. [נְחֹשֶׁת] **n.[f.]** sf. נְחֻשְׁתֵּךְ Ez 16³⁶ where context (|| עֶרְוָה) favours mng. *lust, harlotry*, or specif. sens. obscoen. (Co [citing Ki Ra] Berthol, v. also Da); text perh. crpt. (cf. Nö^ZMG xl (1886), 730^); Sm prop. תַּזְנוּתַיִךְ, so appar. Toy^Hpt^; Or בָּשְׁתֵּךְ.

5181 †[נָחַת] **vb.** (Aram. and poet.) **go down, descend** (Aram. נְחֵת, ܢܚܬ; Palm. נחת Lzb³²³);—**Qal** *Impf.* 3 ms. יֵחַת Je 21¹³; 3 fs. תֵּחַת Pr 17¹⁰, וַתִּנְחַת ψ 38³; 3 mpl. יֵחָתּוּ Jb 21¹³ (forms יֵחַת, יֵחָתּוּ v. also חתת);—**1.** *go down, descend,* to attack Je 21¹³; into She'ôl Jb 21¹³. **2.** fig. *descend* in chastisement ψ 38³ (hand of י׳; || **Niph.** v. infr.); sq. בְּ *descend into* i.e. make impression on, Pr 17¹⁰ (of reproof). **Niph.** *Pf.* 3 mpl. נִחֲתוּ sq. בְּ=*penetrate* ψ 38³, (of arrows of י׳). **Pi.** *Pf.* 3 ms. consec. וְנִחַת 2 S 22³⁵ (v. Ges^§ 145. 7^); =3 fs. וְנִחֲתָה ψ 18³⁵; *Inf. abs.* נַחֵת ψ 65¹¹;—*cause to descend*=*press down*, acc. to most, in וְנ׳ קֶשֶׁת נְחוּשָׁה זְרֹעֹתָי 2 S 22³⁵=ψ 18³⁵ *so that my arms press down, stretch,* a bow of bronze, but dub.; Bu conj. Hiph. וְהִנְחִת; HPS וַיָּשֶׁת *and makes my arms a bow of bronze;* of *pressing down*, smoothing out, furrows of land ψ 65¹¹. **Hiph.** *Imv.* הַנְחַת Jo 4¹¹ thither *bring down* thy heroes, י׳! (on form cf. Ges^§ 64 R. 3^ Kö^i. 314 f.^).

†II. נַחַת **n.[m.]** descent;—only cstr., of י׳'s arm in judgment Is 30³⁰.—I. נַחַת v. sub נוח p. 629 5183

†[נָחֵת] **adj.** descending;—mpl. נְחִתִּים (on form cf. Kö^ii. 81^), 2 K 6⁹ (to battle); but rd. prob. with Th Klo Benz after 𝔊 נֶחְבִּים *hidden.* 5185

†III. נַחַת **n.pr.m. 1.** son of Reuel, grandson of Esau Gn 36¹³·¹⁷ (P; 𝔊 Ναχομ, Ναχοθ, 𝔊L Ναχεθ), 1 Ch 1³⁷ (𝔊 Ναχες, A 𝔊L Ναχεθ). **2.** grandson of Elkanah 1 Ch 6¹¹, 𝔊 Καιναθ, 𝔊L Νααθ;—prob. crpt. for תּוֹחַ v¹⁹, or תֹּחוּ 1 S 1¹ (v. these words and We^de gent. 37 f.^ [who prop. תַּחַת for נַחַת], Dr^1 S 1. 1^). **3.** an overseer, Hezekiah's time 2 Ch 31¹³, 𝔊 Μαεθ, A Ναεθ, 𝔊L Νααθ. 5184

נָטָה₂₁₅ **vb. stretch out, spread out, extend, incline, bend** (NH *id., incline, spread tent*, etc.; Ar. نطو, نَطَا *stretch out*);—**Qal**₁₃₇ *Pf.* 3 ms. נ׳ Gn 33¹⁹+; 3 fs. נָטְתָה Nu 22³³; 2 ms. נָטִיתָ Ex 15¹²; 3 pl. נָטוּ ψ 21¹² Is 45¹², נָטָיוּ ψ 73² Qr, etc.; *Impf.* יִטֶּה Jb 15²⁹, juss. יֵט Zp 2¹³; וַיֵּט Gn 12⁸+, וַיֶּט־ Gn 26²⁵ 1 Ch 15¹; 3 fs. תִּטֶּה Jb 31⁷, וַתֵּט Nu 22²³+2 t.; 2 ms. juss. תֵּט Pr 4⁵·²⁷; 3 mpl. וַיִּטּוּ 1 S 8³; 1 pl. נִטֶּה Nu 20¹⁷ 21²²; *Imv.* נְטֵה Ex 8¹+; *Inf. cstr.* נְטוֹת Ju 19⁸+4 t., נְטֹת Ex 23²; sf. נְטֹתִי Ex 7⁵, נְטוֹתוֹ ψ 109²³; *Pt. act.* נֹטֶה Je 10²⁰+6 t., נוֹטֶה Ez 25¹⁶+3 t.; sf. נוֹטֵיהֶם Is 42⁵; *pass.* נָטוּי ψ 62⁴+2 t.,+ψ 73² (v. infr.); fs. נְטוּיָה Is 5²⁵+24 t.; pl. נְטֻיוֹת Is 3¹⁶ Qr (Kt נטוות):—**1. a.** *stretch out, extend*, hand, rod, usu. c. acc.+עַל of direction Ex 9²²·²³ 10¹²·¹³·²¹·²² (all E), 7¹⁹ 14¹⁶·²¹·²⁶·²⁷ (all P), abs. Jos 8¹⁹ (JE), Ex 8¹² (P); c. בּ of dart or rod נ׳ יָדְךָ בְּמַטְּךָ עַל־ Jos 8¹⁸·¹⁸ (JE), נ׳ בַּכִּידוֹן אֶל־ Ex 8¹ (P), cf. v² and (עַל om.) v¹³ (all P), Jos 8²⁶ (JE); fig. of hostility to God נ׳ יָדוֹ אֶל־ Jb 15²⁵; 5186 esp. of God *stretching out* his hand *over* (עַל), oft. with idea of *against*, i.e. in judgment, Is 5^{25} 23^{11} Zp 1^{4} 2^{13} Ez 6^{14} + 7 t. Ez, Ex 7^{5} (P); c. אֶל־ *against* Je 51^{25}, cf. sword Ez 30^{25}; abs. Ex 15^{12} (song); pt. pass. נ׳ גָּרוֹן Is 3^{16} *outstretched of neck;* oft. זְרוֹעַ נְטוּיָה *arm stretched out* (of י׳) to deliver, Dt 4^{34} + 14 t. (v. זְרוֹעַ); אֶזְרוֹעַ נ׳ Je 32^{21}; יָד נ׳, to oppose, Je 21^{5}; עוֹד יָדוֹ נְטוּיָה in judgment, Is 5^{25} (‖ לֹא שָׁב אַפּוֹ), so $9^{11.16.20}$ 10^{4} (all ‖ *id.*), cf. 14^{27}; הַיָּד הַנְּטוּיָה עַל־ v^{26}; נָטִיתִי יָדִי Pr 1^{24} (of wisdom's appeal; ‖ קָרָאתִי). **b.** *stretch* line and plummet, c. עַל, 2 K 21^{13} (subj. י׳; fig. of destruction), cf. Is 34^{11} La 2^{8}; line, of artisan's measurements (abs.) Is 44^{13}, and (c. עַל) Jb 38^{5}. **c.** = *offer*, only שָׁלוֹשׁ אֲנִי נֹטֶה עָלֶיךָ 1 Ch 21^{10} *three* things *do I offer unto thee* (so rd. prob. also ‖ 2 S 24^{12}, v. נטל).

2. *Spread out*, i.e. *pitch*, tent Gn 12^{8} 26^{25} 35^{21} (all J), 33^{19} (E), Ju 4^{11}, cf. Je 43^{10}; fig. of establishing people Je 10^{20}; of sacred tent Ex 33^{7} (JE), 2 S 6^{17} = 1 Ch 16^{1}, 1 Ch 15^{1} 2 Ch 1^{4}; obj. heavens (spread out by י׳ as tent) Je 10^{12} + 9 t., cf. Jb 26^{7}; obj. likeness of firmament in Ezek.'s vision Ez 1^{22}.

3. *Bend, turn, incline:* **a.** intrans., of wady Nu 21^{15} (JE; c. לְ); *turn aside*, of Balaam's ass 22^{23} (מִן־הַדֶּרֶךְ), v^{33} (מִפָּנַי), cf. v^{33} (לְפָנַי); c. adv. acc. 22^{26}, so of Isr. 20^{17}, and (c. מֵעָלָיו) v^{21}; c. בְּ *into*, 21^{22}; of individ. 2 S 2^{19} (לָלֶכֶת עַל), v^{21} (עַל), Je 14^{8} (c. inf.); cf. Gn 38^{1} (עַד), v^{16} (אֶל־); fig. of deviating from path of loyalty 1 K 2^{28} (c. אַחֲרֵי), cf. Ju 9^{3} (of heart), or of righteousness Ex 23^{2} [yet on text cf. Bu ZAW xi (1891), 113 Ry ad loc.], 1 S 8^{3} (all c. אַחֲרֵי); c. מִן Jb 31^{7} ψ 44^{19}, cf. Pr 4^{5} and (c. adv. acc.) v^{27}; מֵעִם י׳ 1 K 11^{9} (of heart), cf. ψ $119^{51.157}$; *incline*, of heart, c. לְ 1 S 14^{7} (rd. לִבְבְךָ נָטָה or לְ׳ נֹטֶה Th We Dr Klo Bu HPS Löhr); *decline*, of shadow on dial 2 K 20^{10} (‖ הָלַךְ, opp. שׁוּב אֲחֹרַנִּית), fig. of failing life ψ 102^{12} 109^{23}; of day Ju 19^{8} + v^{9} (txt. emend., v. GFM); *bend down*, יִטֶּה לָאָרֶץ Jb 15^{29}, לִנְטוֹת בָּאָרֶץ ψ 17^{11} (both dub., v. Comm.); appar. וַיֵּט בְּכֹחַ Ju 16^{30} *and he bowed with* all his *might* (after וַיִּסְמֹךְ, וַיִּלְפֹּת; al. *stretched himself*, i.e. *gave a thrust*, Be GFM, but vb. less oft. intrans. in this sense); of י׳, וַיֵּט אֵלַי ψ 40^{2} *and he inclined unto me*,—וַתֵּט הַמִּלְחָמָה is rd. 1 S 4^{2} by 𝔊 Dr Klo Bu, cf. נָטַשׁ. **b.** less oft. trans., *bend, bow*, וַיֵּט שִׁכְמוֹ לִסְבֹּל Gn 49^{15} (Issachar under fig. of ass); קִיר נָטוּי ψ 62^{4} (sim. of fate of wicked; ‖ גָּדֵר הַדְּחוּיָה); here belongs also prob. וַאֲנִי כִּמְעַט נָטוּי רַגְלָי ψ 73^{2} (Kt) *and I was almost prostrated as to my feet* (i.e. by stumbling; Qr נָטָיוּ Pf. 3 mpl. but needless, cf. Ol Bae; נ׳ לִבִּי ψ 119^{112} *I have inclined my heart* (c. inf.); of י׳, וַיֵּט שָׁמַיִם וַיֵּרַד ‖ :כְּאַיִן שִׁפְכָה אֲשֻׁרָי); 2 S 22^{10} = ψ 18^{10}; also fig., *hold out, extend* unto, of י׳, obj. חֶסֶד Gn 39^{21} (J), שָׁלוֹם, etc., Is 66^{12} (both c. אֶל־); of men רָעָה ψ 21^{12} (עַל).

†**Niph.** *be stretched out;—Pf.* 3 mpl. נִטָּיוּ Nu 24^{6} (JE; cf. II. נַחַל); *Impf.* 3 ms. יִנָּטֶה עַל־ Zc 1^{16} (of measuring line, for building); *stretch themselves out*, i.e. grow long, 3 mpl. יִנָּטוּ Je 6^{4} (of shadows, ‖ פָּנָה הַיּוֹם).

Hiph. 75 *Pf.* הִטָּה Ezr 7^{28} ψ 116^{2}, sf. הִטָּהוּ; 3 fs. sf. הִטַּתּוּ Pr 7^{21}; 1 s. הִטִּיתִי Pr 5^{13}; 3 pl. הִטּוּ Am 5^{12} + 8 t.; 2 mpl. הִטִּיתֶם Je 25^{4} 35^{15}; *Impf.* יַטֶּה Is 31^{3}, וַיַּט 2 S 9^{15} Ezr 9^{9}; 2 ms. תַּטֶּה Ex 23^{6} + 3 t., juss. תַּט ψ 27^{9} 141^{4}; 1 s. אַטֶּה Je 6^{12} ψ 49^{5}, אַט Jb 23^{11}, וָאַט Ho 11^{4}, but rd. perh. וָאַט (cf. Now) as Je 15^{6}; etc.; *Imv.* הַטֵּה 2 K 19^{16} + 7 t., הַט ψ 17^{6} + 5 t. ψψ Pr; fs. הַטִּי Gn 24^{14} ψ 45^{11}; mpl. הַטּוּ Jos 24^{23} + 3 t.; *Inf. cstr.* לְהַטּוֹת Is 10^{2} + 4 t., לְהַטֹּת Ex 23^{2}; sf. לְהַטּוֹתָהּ Nu 22^{23}; *Pt.* מַטֶּה Dt 27^{19}; mpl. מַטִּים ψ 125^{5}, cstr. מַטֵּי Mal 3^{5};—**1.** rarely *stretch out* (as **Qal 1**), hand Is 31^{3} (of י׳ in hostility), c. עַל Je 6^{12} 15^{6}. **2.** rarely *spread out* cloth on (אֶל) rock 2 S 21^{10}; as **Qal 2**: tent 16^{22} (+ לְ pers.), tent-curtains (fig. of growth) Is 54^{2}. **3.** usu. *turn, incline*, c. acc., in many senses: **a.** lit. *turn* ass into (acc.) road Nu 22^{23} (JE); *take aside* 2 S 3^{27} (acc. pers. + אֶל־), 6^{10} (acc. rei + acc. = *to*) = 1 Ch 13^{13} (אֶל־); *incline, turn* jar of water Gn 24^{14} (J; to give drink); intrans. only יַטּוּ עַל־ Am 2^{8} *on* garments taken in pledge *they recline*, and הַטּוּ מִנֵּי־אֹרַח Is 30^{11} *turn aside, out of the path* (i.e. do not interfere with us; ‖ סוּרוּ מִנֵּי־דֶרֶךְ). **b.** fig., הַמַּטִּים עֲקַלְקַלּוֹתָם ψ 125^{5} *those turning aside their crooked* (ways), i.e. making their ways crooked; cf. (neg.) Jb 23^{11}. **c.** *turn*, = influence, heart 2 S 19^{15}; *turn* (away) heart (cause to apostatize) 1 K $11^{2.4}$ (c. אַחֲרֵי), v^{3} (abs.); לֵב subj., c. acc. pers. Is 44^{20} cf. Jb 36^{18} (acc. pers.); of persuasion, c. acc. pers. Pr 7^{21} (‖ תַּדִּיחֶנּוּ). **d.** *incline* one's own heart unto (אֶל) God and his commands, Jos 24^{23} (E), cf. Pr 2^{2} (לְ); subj. י׳, 1 K 8^{58} ψ 119^{36}, c. עַל־ Pr 21^{1}; neg. (c. לְ) ψ 141^{4}. **e.** esp. *incline* the ear, of men (in obedience to God), usu. ‖ שָׁמַע: abs.

Je 7^{24}+6 t. Je (all neg.), so 25^{4} 44^{5} (+inf.), Is 55^{3}; to inspired teacher Pr 4^{20} (‖ הִקְשִׁיב), 5^{1} (‖ *id.*) v^{13} (all c. לְ), 22^{17} ψ 45^{11} 78^{1} (‖ הַאֲזִינָה); to receive revelation ψ 49^{5}; of God, listening to men, sts. ‖ שָׁמַע: 2 K 19^{16}=Is 37^{17}, Dn 9^{18}, c. לְ ψ 17^{6}; also (c. אֶל־) 31^{3} 71^{2} 102^{3}, c. לְ 88^{3} 116^{2}, abs. 86^{1}; once וְאַט אֵלָיו Ho 11^{4} *and I used to incline* etc. (either rare intrans., or obj. om., e.g. אָזְנִי; rd. perh. וְאֵט (וָאַט?) *and I inclined*, after וָאֶהְיֶה). **f.** *bend down* heavens, of י׳ (cf. **Qal 3 b**), ψ 144^{5};=*hold out, extend* unto (from above, עַל) Ezr 7^{28} 9^{9} (obj. חֶסֶד). **g.** *thrust aside*, esp. c. acc. מִשְׁפָּט, of *perverting* or *wresting* justice: Ex 23^{6} (E), 1 S 8^{3} Dt 16^{19} 24^{17} 27^{19} La 3^{35}, cf. Am 2^{7}; לְהַטּוֹת אָרְחוֹת מִשְׁפָּט Pr 17^{23}; also c. acc. pers. לְהַטּוֹת מִדִּין דַּלִּים Is 10^{2} Am 5^{12} Is 29^{21} Mal 3^{5}, יַטּוּ אֶבְיֹנִים מִדָּרֶךְ Jb 24^{4}, לְהַטּוֹת צַדִּיק בַּמִּשְׁפָּט Pr 18^{5}; here belongs prob. לְהַטּוֹת Ex 23^{2} (E; abs.), perh. ins. מִשְׁפָּט (cf. Bu$^{ZAW\ xi.\ (1891),\ 113}$ Ry$^{ad\ loc.}$). **h.** *thrust away*, of י׳, אַל־תַּט בְּאַף עַבְדֶּךָ ψ 27^{9}; cf. עֲוֹנוֹתֵיכֶם הִטּוּ־אֵלֶּה Je 5^{25} *your iniquities have thrust away* (deprived you of) these (harvests).

3194 †יֻטָּה Jos 21^{16}, יוּטָּה (so Baer) 15^{55} **n.pr. loc.** town in Judah (15^{55} 𝔊 Ιταν, A 𝔊L Ιεττα, 21^{16} 𝔊 Τανυ, 𝔊L Ιεττα).

4295 †מַ֫טָּה, מַ֫טָּה **adv.** downwards (from [מַט] for [מַטֶּה] *a place of declension* (cf. נָטָה, **3 a**), with ה ָ *loc.*, Ol$^{222\,b}$ Kö$^{ii.\,260}$: cf. the opp. מַ֫עְלָה, sub עָלָה):—**1.** alone, Dt 28^{43} and thou shalt descend מַ֫טָּה מָּ֫טָּה *downwards, downwards*, i.e. lower and lower, Pr 15^{24} לְמַעַן סוּר מִשְּׁאוֹל מ׳. **2.** לְמַ֫טָּה: **a.** *downwards* Dt 28^{13} וְלֹא תִהְיֶה לְמ׳, Is 37^{31}=2 K 19^{30} שֹׁרֶשׁ לְמ׳ (cf. Ph CIS$^{I.\,i.\,2,\,11\,f.}$ אל יכן לם שרש למט ופר למעל let them not have root *downwards*, or fruit upwards), Je 31^{37} Ec 3^{21} 2 Ch 32^{30}; Ezr 9^{13} כי אתה חָשַׂכְתָּ לְמַטָּה מֵעֲוֹנֵנוּ either (Be) hast kept back, *downward*, part of our iniquity (prevented it from appearing, and being counted against us), or, held us (Ges), or thy anger (Ke), back, *below* (cf. לְמַ֫עְלָה מֵעַל *above*, 2 Ch 34^{4}) our iniq. (punished us less than our iniq. deserved). **b.** וּלְמַ֫טָּה, (*a*) of space, *and downwards*, Ez 1^{27} וּמִמַּרְאֵה מָתְנָיו ול׳, 8^{2}; (*b*) of age, *and under*, 1 Ch 27^{23} לְמִבֶּן עֶשְׂרִים שָׁנָה ול׳. **3.** מִלְּמַ֫טָּה *beneath* (v. מִן **9 a**: opp. מִלְמַ֫עְלָה *above*), Ex 26^{24} = 36^{29}, 27^{5} = 38^{4}, 28^{27}=39^{20}.

מַטֶּה$_{251}$ **n.m.**$^{Ex\,4,\,17}$ (**f.** Mi 6^{9} acc. to MT, but 4294
dub., v. infr.) **1. staff, rod, shaft. 2. branch. 3. tribe** (Ecclus 48^{2} *staff*, 45$^{6.25}$ *tribe*);—abs. מ׳ Gn 38^{25}+; cstr. מַטֵּה Ex 4^{20}+; sf. מַטְּךָ Gn 38^{18} +5 t., מַטֶּ֫ךָ Ex 8^{1}, מַטֵּ֫הוּ Is 10^{24}+10 t.; pl. מַטּוֹת 1 K 8^{1}+, etc.; sf. מַטּוֹתָם Ex 7^{12} Nu 17^{21}; also מַטָּיו Hb 3^{14} (but rd. מַטֶּיךָ, or—Gr—מַטּוֹתֶיךָ);—**1.** (cf. שֵׁבֶט, מַקֵּל) *staff* of traveller Gn 38$^{18.25}$ (J); in gen. Is 10^{15} (sim.; ‖ שֵׁבֶט); from staff as support comes fig. מַטֵּה־לֶחֶם *staff of bread* (food supply) Ez 4^{16} 5^{16} 14^{13} Lv 26^{26} ψ 105^{16}; of staff or rod, Moses as shepherd Ex 4$^{2.4}$ 7^{15} (J), 4^{17} 7$^{17.20}$ 9^{23} 10^{13} 17^{5} (all E); cf. also Is 10^{26}; Ex 14^{16} Nu 20$^{8.9.11}$ (all P); called מ׳ הָאֱלֹהִים Ex 4^{20} 17^{9} (both E), because of miraculous power connected with it; cf. mirac. rod of Aaron 7$^{9.10.12.19}$ 8$^{1.12.13}$ (all P), and of Egyptian magicians 7$^{12.12}$ (P); cf. Aaron's rod that budded Nu 17$^{18.21.23.25}$ (cf. RS$^{Sem.\ i.\ 180;\ 2d\ ed.\ 197}$); carried even by warrior 1 S 14$^{27.43}$; מַטֵּה שִׁכְמוֹ Is 9^{3} i.e. rod that strikes his shoulder, task-master's rod (‖ שֵׁבֶט הַנֹּגֵשׂ בּוֹ), cf. 10^{5} and v^{24} 14^{5} (‖ שֵׁבֶט), all fig. of oppression; מַטֵּה מוּסָדָה 30^{32} *appointed rod* (of punishment); cf. מ׳ Ez 7$^{10.11}$ (but text obscure, Co—q.v.—*sceptre*), also Mi 6^{9} acc. to MT, but v. sub **3**; used in beating out (חבט) fennel Is 28^{27}; *staff* as badge of leader or ruler מַטֵּה־עֹז Je 48^{17} (‖ מַקֵּל), cf. ψ 110^{2}; so Nu 17$^{17.17.17.17}$+10 t. Nu 17; appar. *shafts*, i.e. arrows or spears, Hb 3$^{9.14}$ (cf. Now Da GASm). †**2.** *branch* of vine Ez 19$^{11.12.14.14}$. **3.** *tribe* (183 t.), orig. company led by chief with *staff*: specif. of tribes of Isr. in both sg. and pl., 1 K 7^{14} 8^{1}=2 Ch 5^{2}, Ex 31^{2} +5 t. Ex; Lv 24^{11}; Nu 1^{4}+89 t. Nu; Jos 7^{1} +56 t. Jos (all P); 1 Ch 6^{45}+21 t. 1 Ch 6, 12^{31}; prob. also Mi 6^{9} (vocative; so 𝔊 We Now GASm).—Cf. שֵׁבֶט, and on relation of these two words for *tribe* in Hebr. usage Dr$^{JPh.\ xi.\ (1882),\ 213\ f.}$

†מִטָּה **n.f.** couch, bed (*place of reclining*; 4296
מטותם Ecclus 18^{6}); abs. מִטָּה Am 3^{12}+14 t.; cstr. מִטַּת 2 K 4^{21}; sf. מִטָּתִי ψ 6^{7}, מִטָּתֶ֑ךָ Ex 7^{28}, מִטָּתוֹ 2 S 4^{7}+6 t.; pl. מִטּוֹת abs. 2 K 11^{2} 2 Ch 22^{11}, cstr. Am 6^{4} Est 1^{6};—*couch, bed*, common article of furniture 2 K 4^{10}, cf. v$^{21.32}$ 1 K 17^{19}, for repose, esp. at night, or in illness Gn 47^{31} (J; רֹאשׁ הַמּ׳), cf. 48^{2} (J), 49^{33} (P), ψ 6^{7} Pr 26^{14} 2 Ch 24^{25} (prob.), and for sitting, or reclining by day 1 S 28^{23} 1 K 21^{4}; פְּאַת מ׳ Am 3^{12}; seat of King Solomon Ct 3^{7}; in bed-chamber (חֲדַר מִשְׁכָּב) Ex 7^{28} (J), 2 S 4^{7}; sts. portable 1 S 19^{15} cf. v$^{13.16}$, hence=*bier*

2 S 3^{31}; sts. high 2 K 1$^{4.6.16}$ (עָלָה שָׁם, opp. יָרַד מִן); sts. costly, (with frames) of ivory Am 6^{4}; for reclining at feasts, made of gold and silver Est 1^{6}; cf. מ׳ כְּבוּדָּה Ez 23^{41} *glorious couch;* חֲדַר הַמִּטּוֹת 2 K 11^{2} = 2 Ch 22^{11} (v. חֶדֶר).—Cf. also עֶרֶשׂ, מִשְׁכָּב (שׁכב).

4298 †[מֻטָּה] **n.f. spreading, outspreading;**—only pl. cstr. מֻטּוֹת כְּנָפָיו Is 8^{8} *the outspreading of his wings* (cf. Ges$^{§ 147, 7 a}$ Kö$^{ii. 1, 192, 399}$), fig. of invading Assyrian army.

4297 †מֻטֶּה **n.[m.] that which is perverted, perverted justice** (see √**Hiph. 3 g**);—only וְהָעִיר מָלְאָה מ׳ Ez 9^{9} (as above Ke Sm Da Berthol Toy RV > *perverseness* AV) > Co חָמָס (as 7^{23}).

5190 †נָטַל **vb. lift, bear** (rare synon. of נָשָׂא; BAram. 𝔗 נְטַל *lift;* hence specif., Syr. ܢܛܰܠ *sustulit* (aquam), further, *be heavy;* also borrowed and denom. forms in Ar. and NH, cf. Frä$^{65 f.}$);—**Qal** *Pf.* 3 ms. נ׳ La 3^{28}; *Impf.* 3 ms. יִטּוֹל Is 40^{15}; *Pt. act.* נוֹטֵל 2 S 24^{12};—*lift,* c. acc. Is 40^{15} (fig. subj. י׳); *lift over thee* (על) i.e. offer 2 S 24^{12}, but rd. נוֹטֶה (as ‖ 1 Ch 21^{10}) We Bu HPS; *lift (and lay) upon* (עַל) La 3^{28}. **Pi.** *Impf.* sf. וַיְנַטְּלֵם Is 63^{9} *and he bare them,* fig. of י׳ bearing his people (‖ וַיְנַשְּׂאֵם).

5192 †נֵטֶל **n.[m.] burden, weight;**—נ׳ cstr., of sand, Pr 27^{3} (‖ כֹּבֶד).

5187 †[נָטִיל] **adj. laden,** only pl. cstr. נְטִילֵי כֶסֶף Zp 1^{11} *those laden with silver.*

5193 †נָטַע **vb. plant** (NH *id.*, and deriv.; cf. Sab. נטעת *pavilion* [? as planted, established] DHM$^{ZMG\ xxxvii.\ (1883),\ 337,\ 349}$);—**Qal** *Pf.* 3 ms. Nu 24^{6} +, 2 ms. נָטַעְתָּ Dt 6^{11}, sf. 3 mpl. נְטַעְתָּם Je 12^{2}; 1 s. נָטַעְתִּי Je 45^{4} + 2 t., וְנָטַעְתִּי Je 42^{10} Ec 2^{5}, sf. נְטַעְתִּיךְ Je 2^{21}, וּנְטַעְתִּיו consec. 2 S 7^{10} = וּנְטַעְתִּיהוּ 1 Ch 17^{9}, וּנְטַעְתִּים consec. Am 9^{15} + 2 t., etc.; *Impf.* 3 ms. יִטַּע Dn 11^{45}, וַיִּטַּע Gn 2^{8} + 2 t., sf. וַיִּטָּעֵהוּ Is 5^{2}; 2 ms. תִּטַּע Dt 16^{21} + 2 t., sf. 3 fs. וַתִּטָּעֶהָ ψ 80^{9}; sf. 3 mpl. וְתִטָּעֵמוֹ Ex 15^{17}, וַתִּטָּעֵם ψ 44^{3}, etc.; *Imv.* נִטְעוּ Je 29^{5} + 3 t.; *Inf.* לִנְטֹעַ Is 51^{16} Je 18^{9}, לִנְטוֹעַ Je 1^{10} 31^{28}, לָטַעַת Ec 3^{2}; *Pt. act.* נוֹטֵעַ Je 11^{17}, נֹטַע ψ 94^{9} (shewing orig. *a* acc. to Lag$^{BN\ 84}$); pl. נֹטְעִים Je 31^{5}; *pass.* נָטוּעַ Ec 3^{2}, pl. נְטוּעִים Ec 12^{11};—**1.** *plant,* c. acc. of tree or vine Nu 24^{6} (JE; subj. י׳), Gn 21^{33} (J), Lv 19^{23} (H), Is 44^{14} ψ 106^{16} (subj. י׳), Ec 2^{5} also (fig. of people) Je 2^{21} 11^{17} ψ 80$^{9.16}$; c. acc. of vineyard Gn 9^{20} (J), Am 5^{11} 9^{14} 2 K 19^{29} = Is 37^{30} Zp 1^{13} Dt 20^{6} 28$^{30.39}$ Je 31$^{5.5.5}$ 35^{7} Ez 28^{26} Is 65^{21} Pr 31^{16} ψ 107^{37} Ec 2^{4}; olive trees and vineyards Dt 6^{11} Jos 24^{13} (D); garden Gn 2^{8} (י׳), Je 29$^{5.28}$; so c. acc. אֲשֵׁרָה כָּל־עֵץ Dt 16^{21}; נ׳ נִטְעֵי נַעֲמָנִים Is 17^{10} (fig. of idolatry); abs. (lit.) Is 65^{22} Ec 3$^{2.2}$ (opp. עָקַר); c. 2 acc. Is 5^{2} (*plant vineyard* with *vine*). **2.** *plant,* fig. = establish, usu. of establishing people, c. acc. 2 S 17^{10} = 1 Ch 17^{9} Am 9^{15} (opp. נָתַשׁ), Ez 36^{36} Ex 15^{17} (song), esp. Je 24^{6} 32^{41} (ב loc.), 42^{10} (opp. נָתַשׁ), 45^{10} (opp. *id.*), ψ 44^{3} (all of establishing Isr.); of establishing wicked Je 12^{2}; abs. of establishing people Je 1^{10} 18^{9} 31^{28}; more lit., *establish* heavens Is 51^{16} (‖ לִיסֹד אָרֶץ); *plant* i.e. fix (late use) tents Dn 11^{45}; מַשְׂמְרוֹת נְטוּעִים Ec 12^{11} *nails planted,* i.e. fixed in; even נ׳ אֹזֶן ψ 94^{9} *he that planted* the *ear.* **Niph.** *Pf.* 3 pl. נִטָּעוּ Is 40^{24} *be planted,* fig., = be established.

†[נֶטַע] **n.[m.] plantation, planting, plant;**—abs. נָטַע Jb 14^{9}; cstr. נְטַע Is 5^{7}; sf. נִטְעֵךְ Is 17^{11}; pl. cstr. נִטְעֵי Is 17^{10};—**1.** *plantation* Is 5^{7} (fig. of Judah, planted by י׳); 17^{10} (fig. of idolatry), so **2.** act of *planting* Is 17^{11}. **3.** *plant* Jb 14^{9} (in sim.). 5194

†נְטָעִים **n. pr. loc.** 1 Ch 4^{23}, 𝔊 Αζαειμ, A Αταειμ, 𝔊L Εταειμ. 5196

†[נָטִיעַ] **n.[m.] plant;**—only pl. נְטִעִים ψ 144^{12} (fig. of vigorous sons). 5195

†מַטָּע **n.m. place, or act of planting; plantation;**—abs. מ׳ Ez 34^{29}; cstr. מַטַּע Is 61^{3}; sf. מַטָּעוֹ Is 60^{21} (Kt; Qr מַטָּעַי); מַטָּעָהּ Ez 17^{7}, also 31^{4}, but rd. מַטָּעָהּ 𝔊 Hi Co Berthol Toy; pl. cstr. מַטָּעֵי Mi 1^{6};—**1.** *planting-place,* מַטָּעֵי כָרֶם Mi 1^{6} *planting-place for a vineyard,* so Ez 31^{4} (rd. מַטָּעָהּ, v. supr.); prob. also מ׳ לְשֵׁם < rd. מ׳ שָׁלֹם 𝔊 Co Berthol Toy i.e. *peaceful* (fruitful) *planting-place;* cf. עֲרֻגוֹת מ׳ 17^{7} = *beds where it was planted.* **2.** act of *planting* נֵצֶר מ׳ Is 60^{21} *shoot of his (my) planting* (fig. of people). **3.** מ׳ י׳ Is 61^{3} *plantation of* י׳ (*id.*). 4302

†[נָטַף] **vb. drop, drip,** fig. (esp. of prophet) **discourse** (NH *id.;* 𝔗 נְטַף *drop, drip;* Syr. ܢܛܰܦ *drip,* ܢܶܛܳܦܬܳܐ *drop* (Nö$^{Syr.\ Gr.\ §\ 105}$) etc.; Ar. نَطَفَ *id.;* Eth. ነጠበ: *id.,* ነጠፈ: *colare* (stillando), *expercolare*);—**Qal** *Pf.* 3 mpl. נָטְפוּ Ju 5^{4} + 2 t.; נָטָפוּ Ju 5^{4}; *Impf.* 3 fs. תִּטֹּף Jb 29^{22}; 3 mpl. יִטְּפוּ Jo 4^{18}; 3 fpl. תִּטֹּפְנָה Pr 5^{3} Ct 4^{11}; 5197

Pt. נֹטְפוֹת Ct 5^{13};—*drop, drip*, usu. trans., c. acc., of clouds *dropping* water (מַיִם), in storm Ju 5^{4}, ‖heavens v^{4} (obj. om.), ψ 68^{9} (*id.*; all theoph.); of hands *dripping* myrrh (מוֹר) Ct 5^{5}; in predict. יִטְּפוּ עָסִיס Jo 4^{18} the mts. *shall drip must*; fig. of (seductive) speech נֹפֶת תִּטֹּ׳ Pr 5^{3} the lips of the strange woman *drop honey*, so perh. Ct 4^{11} (Bu of kisses); שִׂפְתוֹתָיו נ׳ מוֹר 5^{13} *his lips drip myrrh* (perh. of sweet breath). Intrans. only עָלֵימוֹ תִּטֹּף מִלָּתִי Jb 29^{22} *upon them my speech used to drop*. **Hiph.** *Pf.* 3 mpl. וְהִטִּיפוּ consec. Am 9^{13}; *Impf.* 2 ms. תַּטִּיף Am 7^{16}; 1 s. אַטִּף Mi 2^{11}; 3 mpl. יַטִּיפוּן v^{6}; 2 mpl. תַּטִּיפוּ v^{6}, תַּטִּפוּ v^{6}; *Pt.* מַטִּיף Mi 2^{11};—**1.** *drip*, וְהִטּ׳ עָסִיס Am 9^{13} and the mts. *shall drip must* (=**Qal** Jo 4^{18}). **2.** of speech, esp. prophecy (without acc.): c. עַל *against*, Am 7^{16} (‖הִנָּבֵא), c. אֶל־ *toward*, Ez 21^{2} (‖*id.*), v^{7} (‖*id.*); c. לְ *concerning* Mi 2^{11} cf. v^{11};—אַל־תַּטִּפוּ יַטִּיפוּן לֹא־יַטִּפוּ לָאֵלֶּה Mi 2^{6} '*talk not'—so they talk—'they* (rd. *ye*?) *shall not talk of these things'* (where תַּטּ׳, יַטִּפוּ ref. to prophets).

5198 †I. [נָטָף] **n.m. drop**;—נִטְפֵי־מָיִם Jb 36^{27} (‖מָטָר, *rain*).

5198 †II. נָטָף **n.[m.]** an odorif. gum (gathered in *drops*), used in sacred incense Ex 30^{34} (P). Identif. dub.; 𝔊 στακτή, 𝔙 *stacte*, i.e. (Hesych.) a kind of myrrh, so Kn, cf. Ri^{HWB}; Rosenm Thes Ke al. *storax*; Rabb. *opobalsamum* (cf. Di$^{ad\ loc.}$ Now$^{Arch.\ ii.\ 64,\ 248}$).

5188 †[נְטִיפָה?] **n.[f.] drop, i.e. pendant**, an ornament (or *pearl* = Ar. نُطْفَةٌ, fr. likeness to drop of water; cf. GFM);—only pl. abs. נְטִיפוֹת Ju 8^{26}, נְטִפוֹת Is 3^{16}.

5199 †נְטֹפָה **n.pr.loc.** in Judah (*dropping, dripping*, cf. Lewy$^{Sem.\ Fremdwörter\ 40}$);—Ezr 2^{22} = Ne 7^{26}; 𝔊 Νετωφα, 𝔊L Νετωφατι (as adj. gent. Ne 12^{28}).

5200 †נְטוֹפָתִי, נְטֹפָתִי† **adj. gent.**;—נְטֹפ׳ 2 S 23^{28} + 5 t., נְטוֹפ׳ 1 Ch 2^{54} + 4 t. Ch;—הַנּ׳ *the Netophathite* 2 S 23$^{28.29}$ 2 K 25^{23} = Je 40^{8} 1 Ch 11$^{30.30}$; sg. coll. (the) *Netophathites* (no art.) 1 Ch 2^{54} 9^{16} Ne 12^{28}.

5201 †[נָטַר] **vb. keep** (less common ‖ of נָצַר) (NH *id.*; 𝔗 נְטַר, Syr. ܢܛܰܪ *id.*; Nab. in n.pr. Lzb^{323} (cf. also infr.), Ar. نَطَرَ *id.* (obj. garden, etc.));—**Qal** *Pf.* 1 s. נָטַרְתִּי Ct 1^{6}; *Impf.* 3 ms. יִטּוֹר ψ 103^{9}, יִנְטוֹר Je 3^{5}; rd. וַיִּטֹּר also Am 1^{11} (for MT וַיִּטְרֹף) Ol$^{ψ\ 103.9}$ We Now GASm Dr; 2 ms. תִּטֹּר Lv 19^{18}; 1 s. אֶטּוֹר Je 3^{12}; *Pt. act.* נֹטֵר Na 1^{2}; f. נֹטֵרָה Ct 1^{6}; mpl. נֹטְרִים Ct 8$^{11.12}$;—**1.** *keep, maintain* (sc. wrath), of י׳, Je 3$^{5.12}$ Na 1^{2} (c. לְ *for*), ψ 103^{9}; of Edom Am 1^{11} (rdg. וַיִּטֹּר לָעַד אַפּוֹ *and he kept his anger perpetually*, v. supr.). **2.** *keep, guard* a vineyard Ct 1$^{6.6}$ (in fig.), abs. 8^{11}, obj. פִּרְיוֹ v^{12}.

†מַטָּרָה and (La 3^{12}) מַטָּרָא **n.f. 1. guard,** 4307
ward, prison. 2. target, mark (as *kept* in the eye, *watched*, cf. נָצַר Pr 23^{26}, and σκόπος (*watcher, mark*) from σκέπτομαι; perh. Nab. מט[רתא] Lzb^{323});—always abs.:—**1.** *guard, ward, prison*, usu. חֲצַר הַמּ׳ *court of guard* (v. I. חָצֵר) Je 32$^{2.8.12}$ 33^{1} 37$^{21.21}$ 38$^{6.13.28}$ 39$^{14.15}$; שַׁעַר הַמּ׳ Ne 12^{39}. **2.** *target, mark* Jb 16^{12} (fig. of י׳'s chastisement), כַּמַּטָּרָא לַחֵץ La 3^{12} (sim. *id.*); lit. only 1 S 20^{20}.

†נָטַשׁ **vb. leave, forsake, permit** (𝔗 *for-* 5203
sake; draw off skin of dead animal; Ar. نَطِسَ = *abstinens ab impuro* acc. to Kam (Frey));—**Qal** *Pf.* 3 ms. נ׳ 1 S 10^{2}, sf. 1 pl. נְטָשָׁנוּ Ju 6^{13}; 2 ms. נָטַשְׁתָּ 1 S 17^{28}, נָטַשְׁתָּה Is 2^{6}, sf. נְטַשְׁתַּנִי Gn 31^{28}, וּנְטַשְׁתָּהּ consec. Ex 23^{11}, etc.; *Impf.* יִטֹּשׁ 1 S 12^{22} ψ 94^{14}, יִטּוֹשׁ Ho 12^{15}, sf. 1 pl. יִטְּשֵׁנוּ 1 K 8^{57}; 1 pl. נִטֹּשׁ Ne 10^{32}, etc.; *Imv.* נְטוֹשׁ Pr 17^{14}; *Pt. pass.* f. נְטוּשָׁה Is 21^{15}; mpl. נְטֻשִׁים 1 S 30^{16};—**1.** *leave, let alone* Ex 23^{11} (E; = let field lie fallow, ‖שָׁמַט), cf. וְנִטֹּשׁ אֶת־הַשָּׁנָה הַשְּׁבִיעִית וּמַשָּׁא כָל־יָד Ne 10^{32} (i.e. leave field fallow and debts unclaimed); obj. quails, *let them lie*, (עַל loc.) Nu 11^{31} (JE), of Amalekites נְטֻשִׁים עַל־פְּנֵי כָל־הָאָרֶץ 1 S 30^{16} *left to themselves over all the land*; וְדָמָיו עָלָיו יִטּוֹשׁ Ho 12^{15} and his mortal guilt *shall he leave upon him*; *leave in charge of, entrust to* (עַל pers.): sheep 1 S 17$^{20.28}$; baggage v^{22}. **2.** usu. *forsake, abandon*, נ׳ דִּבְרֵי הָאֲתֹנוֹת 1 S 10^{2} thy father *hath abandoned the matter of the asses* (ceased to be concerned about them); הָרִיב נְטוֹשׁ Pr 17^{14} *abandon contention*; oft. subj. י׳, c. acc. pers. Ju 6^{13} Is 2^{6} 1 S 12^{22} 1 K 8^{57} (‖ עָזַב) 2 K 21^{14} Je 7^{29} 12^{7} (‖עָזַב), 23$^{33.39}$ ψ 27^{9} (‖עָזַב), 94^{14} (‖*id.*); of י׳ leaving Phar. forsaken (on ground, cf. **Niph. 1**) Ez 29^{5} (+ ה loc.), 32^{4} (+ בְּ loc.); abandoning the sanctuary at Shiloh ψ 78^{60}; of men *forsaking* God Dt 32^{15} (poem), Je 15^{6}; cf. אַל־תִּטֹּשׁ תּוֹרַת אִמֶּךָ Pr 1^{8} 6^{20}; of men *abandoning* kg. (under fig. of cedar)

Ez $31^{12.12}$. **3.** *permit*, only וְלֹא נְטַשְׁתַּנִי לְנַשֵּׁק לְבָנַי וגו׳ Gn 31^{28} (E) *and hast not permitted me to kiss my sons*, etc.—For וַתִּטֹּשׁ הַמִּלְחָמָה 1 S 4^{2} rd. prob. וַתֵּט (𝔊 ἔκλινεν) Dr Klo Bu, or < וַתִּקֶשׁ (קשׁה) *grew fierce* HPS (Löhr prop. תִּנָּטֵשׁ cf. Ju 15^{9} etc.). For חֶרֶב נְטוּשָׁה Is 21^{15} (‖ קֶשֶׁת דְּרוּכָה) rd. perh. ח׳ לְטוּשָׁה. **Niph.** *Pf.* 3 fs. נִטְּשָׁה Am 5^{2}; 3 pl. נִטְּשׁוּ Is 16^{8} 33^{23}; *Impf.* 3 mpl. וַיִּנָּטְשׁוּ Ju 15^{9} + 2 t.;—**1.** *be forsaken*, Am 5^{2} *she* (Isr.) *lieth forsaken* (עַל loc.). **2.** *be loosened* or *loose* (prop. *be let alone*, left to hang down) of ship's tackle Is 33^{23}. **3.** *be let go, spread abroad*, of warriors, Ju 15^{19} 2 S $5^{18.22}$ (all c. ב loc., for purpose of plunder); of tendrils of vine Is 16^{8} (fig. of Moab). **Pu.** *Pf.* only אַרְמוֹן נֻטָּשׁ Is 32^{14} *palaces are abandoned, deserted* (‖ הֲמוֹן עִיר עֻזָּב).

5189 †[נְטִישָׁה] **n.f. twig, tendril** of vine (as *spreading*, cf. √**Niph. 3**);—only pl. הַנְּטִישׁוֹת הֵסִיר הֵתַז Is 18^{5} *the tendrils he hath removed*, cf. הָסִירוּ נְטִישׁוֹתֶיהָ Je 5^{10} (appar. cited from Is.; expl. by Finn[Journ. Trans. Vict. Inst. xxii. 306 f.] from use by shepherds of *poterium spinosum*, called *nettsh*, as defence of sheepfolds),—in both of destroying city (under fig. of vineyard); נְטִישֹׁתַיִךְ עָבְרוּ יָם Je 48^{32} *thy tendrils went over the sea* (fig. of prosperity of Moab).

5204 [נִי] v. נהה. p. 624

4995 **ניא** (√of foll., cf. Ar. نَاءَ (med. י), *be raw*).

4994 †II. **נָא** **adj. raw**, of flesh Ex 12^{9} (P; opp. בָּשֵׁל). I. נָא p. 609

5108-09 [נִיב], נִיבַי, נֵיבָי v. נוב. p. 626

5205-06 נִיד v. נוד. נִידָה v. II. נדד. p. 622, 627

5121 נָיוֹת v. נוית sub I. נוה. p. 627

5207, 5209 נִיחֹחַ, נִיחוֹחַ v. נוח. נִין v. נון. p. 629-30

5210 †נִינְוֵה **n.pr.loc. Nineveh**, capital of Assyria (As. *Ninâ, Ninua, Ninû*, cf. Schr[COT Gloss.] Dl[Par 260]);—Gn $10^{11.12}$ (J), 2 K 19^{36} = Is 37^{37}, Na 1^{1} 2^{9} 3^{7} Zp 2^{13} Jon 1^{2} $3^{3a.4.5.6.7}$, called הָעִיר הַגְּדוֹלָה v^{3b} 4^{11} (cf. $3^{4f.}$); 𝔊 Νινευη, 𝔊L Νινευι. Site on E. bank of Tigris marked by mounds *Neby Yunus* and *Kuyundjik*, opposite Mosul. Cf. Layard[Nineveh and its Remains, 1848; Monuments of N. 1849 f.] Billerbeck u. Jeremias[BAS iii. 1 (1895), 107 ff.]

נִיס v. נוס **Qal 1.** ad fin.

5212 †נִיסָן **n.pr.** of 1st month (loan-wd. fr. Bab. *Nisannu*, cf. Schr[COT Ne 1, 1] Muss-Arnolt[JBL xi. 1 (1892), 76]; NH = BH; so Nab. Palm. v. Lzb[323]);—only post-exil.: חֹדֶשׁ נ׳ Ne 2^{1} Est 3^{7} (+ הַחֹדֶשׁ הָרִאשׁוֹן), = pre-exil. חֹדֶשׁ הָאָבִיב (חֹדֶשׁ).—On sacredness of Nisan cf. also RS[Sem. i. 387; 2d ed. 406 f.]

נִיצוֹץ v. נצץ. נִיר v. נֵר.

†I. [נִיר] **vb. break up, freshly till**;— 5214
Qal *Imv.* mpl. נִירוּ, c. acc. cogn. נִיר Ho 10^{12} Je 4^{3}.

†II. נִיר **n.[m.] the tillable, untilled** or 5215
fallow ground;—נ׳ abs. as acc. cogn. נִירוּ לָכֶם נִיר Ho 10^{12} Je 4^{3} *till you the untilled ground* (fig. of unaccustomed moral action); cstr. only רָב־אֹכֶל נִיר רָאשִׁים Pr 13^{23} *abundant food* (yields) *the fallow ground of poor men* (i.e. with י׳'s
blessing).—I. נִיר v. נור. p. 632f 5216

II. **ניר** (√of foll.; cf. NH נִיר, Ar. نِيرٌ, Syr. ܢܝܪܐ (in Lexx), all = the system of *heddles* or 'apparatus [of small cords with loops, or eyes] by wh. the threads of the warp are raised and lowered to make an opening for the passing of the woof' GFM[PAOS Oct. 1889, clxxix. f.]; cf. As. *nîru*, Syr. ܢܝܪܐ, *yoke*).

†[מָנוֹר] **n.m. beam** (prob. round) carrying 4500
the heddles (in loom), = Lat. *jugum*, so GFM[l. c.];—only cstr. in phr. כִּמְנוֹר אֹרְגִים *beam of weavers* 1 S 17^{7} 2 S 21^{19} = 1 Ch 20^{5}, 1 Ch 11^{23}, all sim. of thick and heavy shaft of spear.

†[נָכָא] **vb. smite, scourge** (rare Arama- 5217
izing form of נָכָה);—only **Niph.** *Pf.* 3 pl. נִכְּאוּ מִן־הָאָרֶץ Jb 30^{8} *they are scourged out of the land.*

†[נָכָא] **adj. stricken**;—mpl. נְכָאִים Is 16^{7} 5218
(Kö[ii. 1, 73]), of Moab prostrated by conquest.

†[נָכֵא] **adj. id.**, alw. f. רוּחַ נְכֵאָה *a stricken* 5218
spirit, Pr 15^{13} 17^{22} (both opp. לֵב שָׂמֵחַ), 18^{14}.

†נְכֹאת **n.f.** a spice, (usu. understood of 5219
tragacanth gum, exuding fr. *astralagus* bush, Di[Gn 27, 25] and reff.; Now[Arch. i. 64 (and 249)]; cf. also Löw[§ 24]; but = Ar. نَكَعَةٌ = نُكَاعَةٌ *summitas rubicunda* sive *flores plantae* (i.e. a certain plant, Frey), acc. to Hom[Aufsätze 4]);—abs. נ׳ Gn 37^{25} (+ צְרִי, לֹט, as merchandise), 43^{11} (+ *id.*, also דְּבַשׁ, בָּטְנִים, שְׁקֵדִים, as gift).

נכד (√of foll., mng. uncertain; Eth. ንገድ: = *gens, stirps*, [cf. Sam. נגד Gn 21^{23}]).

5220 †[נֶ֫כֶד]† **n.[m.]** **progeny, posterity,** alw. c. נִין in standing phr. (Ecclus 41⁵ 47²²ᶜ, both c. (נין);—abs. לֹא נִין לוֹ וְלֹא נֶ׳ בְּעַמּוֹ Jb 18¹⁹, cf. שֵׁם וּשְׁאָר וְנִין וָנֶ׳ Is 14²²; sf. לִי וּלְנִינִי וּלְנֶכְדִּי Gn 21²³ *to me and to my offspring and to my posterity.*

5221 **[נָכָה]**₅₀₁ **vb. smite** (not in **Qal**) (NH Hiph. *id.*; Pf. 3 pl. הכו SI⁴, Inf. להכ[ת] ib.⁹; Syr. ܢܟܐ, *laesit, nocuit, repugnavit;* Aph. *laesit, vulneravit;* Eth. ነከየ: *laesit, nocuit;* cf. Ar. نَكِىَ *be defeated,* نِكَايَةٌ *the inflicting of injury* on an enemy Lane³⁰³⁸);—†**Niph.** *Pf.* וְנִכָּה וָמֵת consec. 2 S 11¹⁵ *and he shall be smitten* [struck by weapon in battle] *and die.*

†**Pu.** *Pf.* 3 fs. נֻכָּ֫תָה Ex 9³¹; 3 pl. נֻכּוּ v³² (J), both *be smitten down* by the hail.

Hiph.₄₈₂ *Pf.* 3 ms. הִכָּה Ex 9²⁵+; sf. וְהִכַּ֫נִי consec. Gn 32¹², הִכָּם Je 5⁶; 2 ms. הִכִּ֫יתָ Ex 17⁵+; 1 s. הִכֵּיתִי Ju 15¹⁶+, וְהִכֵּיתִ֫י Ex 3²⁰+; 3 pl. הִכּוּ Gn 19¹¹+; 2 mpl. הִכִּיתֶם Je 37¹⁰+3 t. consec.; etc.; *Impf.* 3 ms. יַכֶּה Ex 21²⁰+, יַךְ Ho 6¹ (but rd. וַיַּךְ We Now GASm); וְיַךְ Ho 14⁶ (v. infr.); יַכֶּ֫הָ וַיַּכֶּה Jos 10⁴⁰+, usu. וַיַּךְ Ex 2¹²+; sf. 2 ms. יַכְּכָה Je 40¹⁵+2 t., 3 ms. וַיַּכּוֹ 2 S 14⁶ (but rd. וַיַּךְ 𝔊𝔖𝔙 Th We Dr Klo Kit Bu HPS), יַכֵּ֫נּוּ 1 S 17²⁵ +2 t.; usu. וַיַּכֵּ֫הוּ Nu 21²⁴+; 3 fs. וַתַּךְ Jon 4⁷·⁸; 2 ms. תַּכֶּה Ex 2¹³+; sf. 3 ms. תַּכֶּ֫נּוּ Pr 23¹³·¹⁴; 1 s. אַכֶּה 1 S 18¹¹+; וָאַכֶּה Ne 13²⁵, וָאַךְ Ex 9¹⁵; 3 mpl. יַכּוּ Mi 4¹⁴; usu. וַיַּכּוּ Gn 14⁵+ (1 S 4² rd. prob. **Hoph.** q.v.); 1 pl. נַכֶּה־ Nu 22⁶; וַנַּךְ Dt 2³³, etc.; *Imv.* הַכֵּה Ez 6¹¹, הַךְ Am 9¹+; mpl. הַכּוּ 2 S 13²⁸, etc.; *Inf. abs.* הַכֵּה Dt 3¹⁶+, הַכּוֹת 2 K 3²⁴ (Ges§⁷⁵ᶠᶠ); *cstr.* הַכּוֹת Gn 4¹⁵+, etc.; *Pt.* מַכֶּה Ex 2¹¹+; cstr. מַכֵּה Ex 21¹²+; pl. מַכִּים 1 S 4⁸+, etc.;—**1. a.** lit., *smite* (with a single, non-fatal, blow), *strike,* sq. acc., ass Nu 22²³·²⁵·²⁷ (בַּמַּקֵּל), v²⁸·³² (all J); man Ex 21¹⁵·¹⁹ (E); cheeks Jb 16¹⁰; man (on) cheek (2 acc.) La 3³⁰ ψ 3⁸; man עַל־לְחִי Mi 4¹⁴ (ב instr.), 1 K 22²⁴=2 Ch 18²³; eye Ex 21²⁶ (E); שֵׁבֶט מַכֵּךְ Is 14²⁹ (fig. of conqueror); with (ב) stone or fist Ex 21¹⁸ (E), cf. (fig.) Is 58⁴ (abs.); *smite* lion or bear 1 S 17³⁵; *strike* river (with rod מַטֶּה) 7¹⁷ (c. עַל obj., +ב instr.), v²⁰ Ex 17⁵ (E; ב instr.), also (with mantle) 2 K 2⁸·¹⁴·¹⁴, cf. ׳י *smiting* Euphrates into (ל) seven streams Is 11¹⁵; dust Ex 8¹²·¹³ (P); rock 17⁶ (E), Nu 20¹¹ (P; ב instr.), ψ 78²⁰; fig. *smite* earth בְּשֵׁבֶט פִּיו Is 11⁴ (of future Davidic kg.); *strike* on ground (אַ֫רְצָה; with arrows) 2 K 13¹⁸, also (abs.) v¹⁸·¹⁹; *strike* weapons out of (מִן) hands, Ez 39³ (׳י; fig. of making powerless); lintol of door Am 9¹, barley-loaf *strikes* tent Ju 7¹³ (in dream); in fig. of regret, remorse וַיַּךְ לֵב דָּוִד אֹתוֹ 2 S 24¹⁰ *and David's heart smote him,* so 1 S 24⁶ (+עַל־אֲשֶׁר *because*); of goat smiting (butting with horn) the ram, so as to break its horns Dn 8⁷ (in vision); *smite*=*hit* with missile, sling-stone 1 S 17⁴⁹ (c. acc. pers. +אֶל־מִצְחוֹ), cf. 2 K 3²⁵ (but text perh. corrupt, v. Benz); arrow, 1 K 22³⁴=2 Ch 18³³ (c. acc. pers.+בֵּין), 2 K 9²⁴ (c. *id.*); of piercing, הַכּוֹת בַּחֲנִית בְּדָוִד וּבַקִּיר 1 S 19¹⁰ *smite with the dart into D. and into the wall,* pin D. to the wall, וַיַּךְ אֶת־הַח׳ בַּקִּיר v¹⁰, cf. 18¹¹, אַכֶּנּוּ בַחֲנִית וּבָאָרֶץ 26⁸. **b.** *smite* repeatedly, *beat,* a man Ex 2¹¹·¹³ (E), 5¹⁶ (J), Ne 13²⁵ (מִן partit.), cf. Dt 25¹¹; here prob. also 1 K 20³⁵·³⁵·³⁷·³⁷ (הַכֵּה וּפָצֹעַ *beating and bruising him*); of Assyr. under fig. of taskmaster Is 10²⁴; *beat* a woman so as to bruise her (פָּצַע) Ct 5⁷; *beat* by authority, *scourge* Je 20² 37¹⁵ Dt 25²·³ (c. acc. pers.+acc. cogn. מַכָּה רַבָּה), v³ cf. בִּן הַכּוֹת v² i.e. *worthy of scourging,* bastinado, (cf. Dr); 2 Ch 25¹⁶; Pr 17¹⁰ 19²⁵ 23¹³·¹⁴ (ב instr.); cf. גֵּוִי נָתַתִּי לְמַכִּים Is 50⁶; of hail, *beat down* herbage etc. Ex 9²⁵·²⁵ (cf. **Pu.**). **c.** וַיַּכּוּ כָף 2 K 11¹² *and they clapped hands* (in applause); elsewhere only Ezek., in mockery; כַּף אֶל־כַּף Ez 21¹⁹·²² ; בְּכַפְּךָ 6¹¹ (|| רְקַע בְּרַגְלְךָ); acc. כַּפִּי 22¹³. **d.** *give a thrust* (with fork) into (ב) pot 1 S 2¹⁴; *strike* roots Ho 14⁶ (in fig., but וְיֵלְכוּ We Now). **e.** rarely *smite* (in battle) so as (merely) to wound 1 K 8²⁸, so (+acc. cogn. מַכָּה) v²⁹ 9¹⁸=2 Ch 22⁶; fig. of ׳י's wounding Isr. Ho 6¹ (opp. חָבַשׁ, *bind up*), Je 30¹⁴ (c. acc. cogn.). Cf. *smite with* (ב) *the tongue* Je 18¹⁸. **f.** *smite,* of sun, etc., c. acc. pers. Is 49¹⁰ ψ 121⁶; c. עַל Jon 4⁸.

2. *Smite* fatally: **a.** (subj. man) *smite,* c. acc., +word of killing (dying):—obj. lion and bear 1 S 17³⁵; man Ex 21¹²·²⁰ (E), Jos 10²⁶ (JE), 11¹⁷ (D), 1 S 17⁵⁰ 2 S 1¹⁵ 2³¹ (מִן partit. +ב *among*), 4⁷ 14⁶ 18¹⁵ 21¹⁷ 1 K 16¹⁰ 2 K 12²² 15³⁰ 25²¹=Je 52²⁷, 2 K 25²⁵ Je 41² Nu 35¹⁶·¹⁷·¹⁸·²¹ (P; all c. ב instr.); c. acc.+אֶל־הַחֹמֶשׁ+ב instr. 2 S 2²³ *smote him* (fatally) *in the belly with* (on text v. HPS), 20¹⁰, cf. 3²⁷ 4⁶ (but del. 𝔊 Ew Th We Dr Bu HPS); וְהִכָּהוּ נֶפֶשׁ Dt 19¹¹ *and he smite him in his life* (mortally), and he die, cf. (without word of dying) v⁶ Gn 37²¹ (J), Je 40¹⁴·¹⁵ [otherwise Lv 24¹⁷·¹⁸ Nu 35¹¹·¹⁵·³⁰ Dt 27³⁵ Jos 20³·⁹]; with prolepsis לְהַכּוֹת חֲלָלִים *smite the slain*

Ju $20^{31.39}$; + אַ֫רְצָה *smite to the ground* i.e. kill 2 S 2^{22} 18^{11}. **b.** *smite*, of worm gnawing or boring so as to kill plant Jon 4^{7}. **c.** very oft. = *kill, slay, man or beast* (c. 150 t.): Gn 4^{15} 8^{21} (exterminate; both J), Ex 2^{12} Nu 21^{35} (E), Jos 7^{5} (מִן partit.), v^{5} (JE), Dt 19^{6} 21^{1} $27^{24.25}$ Jos 11^{10} (ב instr.; all D), Lv $24^{17.18.21.21}$ (H), Nu $35^{11.15.21.24.30}$ Jos 9^{18} $20^{3.9}$ (all P), Ju 15^{16} 1 S $17^{9.9.36}$ 2 S 12^{9} (ב instr.), 2 K 9^{7} (exterminate), etc.; c. ב *among* 1 S 23^{5}, מִן partit. Ju 14^{19} 20^{45}; c. ב partit. *slay at, work slaughter among* 2 S 23^{10} (ins. also in ‖ 1 Ch 11^{13} v. $Be^{ad\ loc.}$ $Dr^{2\ S\ 23,\ 10}$), but also ב of dir. obj. 1 S 18^{7} 21^{12} 29^{5}; subj. lion 1 K $20^{36.36}$ cf. Je 5^{6} (fig. of judgment); ׳י subj. 1 S $6^{19\,b}$ (ב *among*, + acc. cogn.; 1 S $6^{19\,a}$ וַיַּךְ crpt. v. 𝔊 Th We Dr Kl Kit Bu HPS); *slay* firstborn Ex 12^{2} (J), v^{29} Nu 3^{13} 8^{17} 33^{4} (all P), ψ 78^{51} 105^{36} 135^{8}; God *slays* for (עַל) sin 2 S 6^{7} = 1 Ch 13^{10} (עַל־אֲשֶׁר); *slay* לְפִי־חֶרֶב Dt 13^{16} 20^{13} Jos $11^{11.12.14}$ (all D), Ju 18^{27} 21^{10} 1 S 22^{9} 2 K 10^{25} Je 21^{7} Jb $1^{15.17}$; *kill, slay*, c. acc. cogn. (מַכָּה) 1 S 14^{14} 1 K 20^{21} (ב *among*), 2 Ch 13^{17} (בָּהֶם), 25^{13} (מֵהֶם); c. acc. pers. + acc. cogn. Jos 10^{20} (JE), Est 9^{5}, etc.; *kill unwittingly, unintentionally* הִכָּה בִבְלִי דַ֫עַת Dt 19^{4} Jos 20^{5} (both D).

3. *Smite* = *attack, attack and destroy* a company Gn $32^{9.12}$ 34^{30} Jos 8^{21} Ju 8^{11} 9^{43} 2 K 8^{21} 2 Ch 21^{9}; *attack and capture* a city Ju 1^{8} v^{12} = Jos 15^{16} (JE), Jos 7^{3} 10^{4} (JE), 1 S 30^{1} 1 K 15^{20} = 2 Ch 16^{4}, 2 K $15^{16.16}$ 1 Ch 20^{1} 2 Ch 14^{13} Je 47^{1}; tents 1 Ch 4^{41} 2 Ch 14^{14}; = *sack* a city לְפִי־חֶרֶב (slaying inhab.), Jos 8^{24} 19^{47} (both JE), $10^{28.30.32.35.37}$ cf. v^{39} (all D), Ju 1^{25} 20^{37} 2 S 15^{14}; esp. *defeat* kg. or army (involving oft. overthrow, pursuit and slaughter),—c. 95 t.,—Gn $14^{5.15.17}$ Nu 14^{45} 21^{24} (JE), Jos 8^{12} 10^{10} (+acc. cogn.), v^{10} (עַד loc.), $11^{8.8}$ (all JE), Dt 1^{4} 2^{33} 3^{3} 4^{46} 7^{2} 29^{6} Jos $10^{33.40}$ (מִן—ועד loc.), $12^{1.6.12}$ 13^{12} (all D); Ju $1^{5.17}$ 1 S 11^{11} (עד temp.), 1 K 13^{17} (עַד־כַּלֵּה), 2 K $3^{24\,a}$ + $v^{24\,b}$ (where rd. וַיָּבֹאוּ בוֹא וְהַכּוֹת *and they went on defeating*), Is 10^{20} Je 37^{10}, etc.; ins. וַיַּךְ or הִכָּה in 2 S 8^{13} Th Ke Kit Bu cf. Dr, after 𝔊; c. ב obj. 1 S 14^{31} $23^{2.2}$ (ה loc.—מִן); + לְפִי חֶרֶב Ju 20^{48}, etc.; of gods *causing defeat* 2 Ch 28^{23}; *smite* land = conquer, subjugate, sts. ravage, Gn 14^{7} Jos 10^{40} (D), 1 S 27^{9} Je 43^{11} 46^{13}, cf. Is 14^{6} (acc. cogn.); subj. ׳י Nu 32^{4} (P); of ׳י *smiting* sea וְהִכָּה בַיָּם גַּלִּים Zc 10^{11} ($Bev^{JPh.\ xviii.\ 35\ (1889),\ 88}$ prop. נבלים).

4. Of God, **a.** *smite* with (ב) a plague, disease, etc.:—blindness Gn 19^{11} (J), 2 K $6^{18.18}$ cf. Zc $12^{4.4}$ (symbol.); of Egyptian plagues Ex 3^{20} 9^{15} (both J), 1 S 4^{8}, without ב Ex 7^{25} (J), 12^{13} (P), ψ 136^{10} (acc. + בִּבְכוֹרֵיהֶם); other plagues Nu 14^{12} (JE), Dt $28^{22.27.28.35}$ 1 S 5^{6} 2 S 24^{17} Jb 2^{7} Am 4^{9} Hg 2^{17} Mal 3^{24}; without ב, 1 S 5^{9} 2 K 19^{35} = Is 37^{26}; Nu 11^{33} (JE; בָּעָם + acc. cogn.); *smite* vines with (ב) blight ψ 105^{33}. **b.** *smite* = *chastise*, or *send judgment upon*, usu. c. acc., 1 K 14^{15} 1 Ch 21^{7} Is 5^{25} 9^{12} 27^{7} (הַכְּמַכַּת מַכֵּהוּ הִכָּהוּ), 30^{31} (ב instr.) 57^{17} 60^{10} (opp. רִחַם) Je 2^{30} 5^{3} 14^{9} Ez 32^{15} (𝔊 Co זֵרָה scatter); c. עַל *punish for*, (sin) Lv 26^{24} (H). **c.** of God's *destroying* palaces Am 3^{15} 6^{11} (2 acc.), cf. Zc 9^{4}.

†**Hoph.** *Pf.* הֻכָּה Ho 9^{16} Nu 25^{14}, הוּכָּה ψ 102^{5}; וְהֻכָּה consec. Ex 22^{1}; 3 fs. הֻכְּתָה Ez 33^{21} 40^{1}; 1 s. הֻכֵּ֫יתִי Zc 13^{6}; 3 pl. הֻכּוּ 1 S 5^{12}; *Impf.* 3 mpl. וַיֻּכּוּ Ex 5^{14}; 2 mpl. תֻכּוּ Is 1^{5}; *Pt.* מֻכֶּה Nu 25^{14}, cstr. מֻכֵּה Is 53^{4}; f. מֻכָּה Nu $25^{15.18}$; pl. מֻכִּים Ex 5^{16}, cstr. מֻכֵּי־ Je 18^{21};—*be smitten:* **1.** = *receive a blow* Is 1^{5} (Judah under fig. of man). **2.** *be wounded* Zc 13^{6}. **3.** *be beaten* Ex $5^{14.16}$ (J). **4.** *be* (fatally) *smitten* + vb. of dying Ex 22^{1} (E); *be killed, slain* Nu $25^{14.14.15.18}$ (c. עַל, *for*), מֻכֵּי־חֶרֶב Je 18^{21} (‖ הֲרֻגֵי מָ֫וֶת); so also (abs.) prob. 1 S 4^{2} (rd. וַיֻּכּוּ 𝔊𝔖𝔙 Th Dr Klo Kit, for MT וַיַּכּוּ). **5.** *be attacked and captured*, of city Ez 33^{21} 40^{1}. **6.** *be smitten* with disease (by God) 1 S 5^{12}; abs., of ׳י's servant Is 53^{4}. **7.** *be blighted*, of plant (in fig.) Ho 9^{16} (Ephr.), ψ 102^{5} (heart, כָּעֵשֶׂב; both + יָבֵשׁ).

†[נָכֶה] **adj. smitten, stricken** (cf. [נָכָא]);— 5223
only cstr.: נְכֵה רַגְלַיִם 2 S 4^{4} 9^{3} *crippled of feet;* נְכֵה־רוּחַ Is 66^{2} *contrite of spirit* (+ עָנִי).

†[נֵכֶה] **adj.** id.;—pl. נֵכִים ψ 35^{15} *smitten* 5222
ones, but rd. prob. נָכְרִים *aliens* Ol Che Bae al.

†I. נָכוֹן **n.[m.]** = **blow** Jb 12^{5} acc. to Schult Di Bu, but precarious; < Niph. fr. כון q.v.

†מַכָּה **n.f. blow, wound, slaughter;**— 4347
abs. מ׳ 1 S 4^{8}+; cstr. מַכַּת Is 10^{26}+; sf. מַכָּתִי Je 10^{19} 15^{18}, etc.; pl. מַכּוֹת abs. 2 K 8^{29}+; cstr. Dt 29^{21}+; sf. מַכֹּתְךָ Dt 28^{59}, מַכּוֹתַיִךְ Je 30^{17}, etc.;—**1. a.** *blow, stripe*, lit. of scourging, chastising Dt 25^{3} Pr 20^{30} (‖ חַבֻּרוֹת פֶּצַע); מַכַּת חֶרֶב Est 9^{5} (as acc. cogn.). **b.** *beating, scourging*, fig. of defeat of Midian Is 10^{26} (‖ עוֹרֵר שׁוֹט). **c.** oft. *wound* 1 K 22^{35} 2 K 8^{29} 9^{15} = 2 Ch 22^{6} (rd. מִן־הַמ׳), Zc 13^{6} (בֵּין יָדֶיךָ); symbol. of violence Je 6^{7} (+ חֳלִי); פֶּצַע וְחַבּוּרָה וּמַכָּה טְרִיָּה Is 1^{6} (of Judah, under fig. of maltreated man), cf. Mi 1^{9} (מ׳ אֲנוּשָׁה),

Na 3^{19}(שֶׁבֶר||; of Nineveh), esp. in Je (of Judah): Je 10^{19} 14^{17} 30^{12} (all + נַחְלָה *severe*; || שֶׁבֶר), 15^{18} (מ׳ אֲנוּשָׁה), 19^{8} 47^{17} 50^{13}, as acc. cogn. 30^{14}, c. vb. רָפָא *heal* v^{17}; also מַחַץ מ׳ Is 30^{26} (שֶׁבֶר||); of wounds made by י׳'s arrows ψ 64^{8}. **2.** = *slaughter* 1 S 4^{10} 14^{30}, usu. as acc. cogn. c. הִכָּה Jos 10^{20} 1 S 6^{19} 14^{14} 19^{8} 23^{5} 1 K 20^{21} 2 Ch 13^{17}. **3.** = *defeat*, as acc. cogn. c. הִכָּה Jos 10^{10} 11^{33} 15^{8} 2 Ch 28^{5}; = *conquest* (of י׳) Is 14^{6}. **4.** *plague*, esp. disease, as punishment (of י׳), 1 S 4^{8} Dt $28^{59.59.59}$ (חֳלִי||), v^{61} (||*id.*), 29^{21}(תַּחֲלֻאִים||), Lv 26^{21} (H), as acc. cogn. Nu 11^{33}.—מַכּוֹת 2 Ch 2^{9} rd. מַכֹּלֶת (v. אכל) as || 1 K 5^{25}, so 𝔊𝔙 Be Öt and Th[1 K 5, 25].

5224 †נְכֹה, נְכוֹ **n.pr.m. Necho** (II), king of Egypt (Egypt. *Nkw*, i.e. (Steindorff[BAS i. 346 f.]) *Nekawō*; As. *Nikû* Id.[ib.] Schr[COT 2 K 23, 29] is grandfather of Bibl. Necho);—contemp. of Josiah and Nebuchad. [B.C. 611–605]: נְכוֹ 2 Ch 35^{20} (𝔊 Φαραω Νεχαω), נְכֹה 2 Ch 35^{22} 36^{4} (𝔊 Φαραω
6549 Νεχαω); פַּרְעֹה נְכוֹ Je 46^{2}, פַּרְעֹה נְכֹה 2 K $23^{29.33.34.35}$ (all 𝔊 *id.*).

3592, 5225 נָכוֹן **n.pr.m.** v. sub כון, and v. כִּידֹן.

נכח (√ of foll.: prob. *be in front of*; Lag[BN 30] cp. Ar. نَكَحَ *marry* (perh. orig. in phys. sense); Syr. ܢܟܺܝܚ is *gentle*, ܢܰܟܺܝܚܽܘܬܳܐ *gentleness*).

5226-27 †נֹכַח **subst.** front, always in **prep.** or **adv.** phrases, with sf. נִכְחוֹ Ex 14^{2} Ez 46^{9}:—**1.** as adv. acc. *in front of, opposite to*, Ex 14^{2} נִכְחוֹ תַּחֲנוּ, 26^{35} the candlestick נֹכַח הַשֻּׁלְחָן, 40^{24}, Jos 18^{17} (in the || 15^{7}, לְנֹכַח: v. לְ **5 c**), 1 K 20^{29} וַיַּחֲנוּ אֵלֶּה נֹכַח אֵלֶּה, 22^{35} (= 2 Ch 18^{34}), Est $5^{1.1}$; Ez 46^{9} Qr כִּי נִכְחוֹ יֵצֵא shall go out *in front of himself*, i.e. straightforward; cf. נֶגֶד, נֶגְדּוֹ **1 a** (*b*). Fig. Pr 5^{21} כִּי נֹכַח עֵינֵי י׳ דַּרְכֵי אִישׁ *in the sight* of י׳'s eyes are, etc., Ju 18^{6} נֹכַח י׳ דַּרְכְּכֶם *before* י׳ is your way, i.e. under his eye and favourable regard. In the phr. נֹכַח פְּנֵי, Je 17^{16} מוֹצָא שְׂפָתַי נֹכַח פָּנֶיךָ הָיָה was *before* thy face, La 2^{19}, Ez 14^{3} מִכְשׁוֹל עֲוֹנָם נָתְנוּ נֹכַח פְּנֵיהֶם (i.e. they contemplate it with pleasure), $v^{4.7}$. **2.** combined with preps.:—**a.** אֶל־נֹכַח, Nu 19^{4} וְהִזָּה אל־נ׳ פני אהל מועד and sprinkle it *towards the front* of, etc. **b.** לְנֹכַח: (*a*) as **adv.** Pr 4^{25} עיניך לנ׳ יביטו let thine eyes look *to the front* or *right on* (ועפעפיך|| יַיְשִׁרוּ נֶגְדֶּךָ); (*b*) as **prep.** Gn 30^{38} לְנֹכַח הַצֹּאן *in front of* the flocks, 25^{21} וַיֶּעְתַּר . . . לְנֹכַח אִשְׁתּוֹ *in front of*, i.e. *on behalf of* (cf. *pro*), his wife; (*c*) עַד־נֹכַח, Ju 19^{10} וַיָּבֹא עַד־נ׳ יְבוּס *as far as in front of* Jebus, 20^{43} Ez 47^{20} (עַד־נֹכַח לְ). Syn. נֶגֶד, q.v.

†[נָכֹחַ] **adj.** and **subst. straight, right,** 5228
straightness, f. נְכֹחָה, pl. נְכֹחִים, ־וֹת:—Is 57^{2} 5229
הֹלֵךְ נְכֹחוֹ he that walks *in* (cf. 33^{15} 50^{10}) *his straightness* (Ges 'der seinen *geraden* Weg geht'), fig. for straightforwardly (cf. Pr 4^{25}); נְכֹחָה *what is straight in front*, fig. *straightforwardness, honesty*, Am 3^{10} לֹא יָדְעוּ עֲשׂוֹת נ׳, Is 59^{14} (אֱמֶת||) ונ׳ לא תוּכַל לָבוֹא; 2 S 15^{3} דבריך טובים וּנְכֹחִים thy pleadings are good and *right* (i.e. *true*), Pr 8^{9} (of words of Wisdom) כֻּלָּם נְכֹחִים לַמֵּבִין i.e. they lead *straight* to the right goal (אֵין בָּהֶם נִפְתָּל וְעִקֵּשׁ || יְשָׁרִים; comp. $v^{8\,b}$), 24^{26} מֵשִׁיב דְּבָרִים נְכֹחִים i.e. either *correct* (leading to the right point), or *honest* answers; Is 30^{10} לֹא־תֶחֱזוּ לָנוּ נְכֹחוֹת *true* things (opp. חֲלָקוֹת, מַהֲתַלּוֹת *illusions*), 26^{10} בְּאֶרֶץ נְכֹחוֹת יְעַוֵּל in a land of *rectitude* (Che) he will do wickedly.

†[נָכַל] **vb. be crafty, deceitful, knavish** 5230
(As. *nakâlu*, *be crafty, cunning*; 𝔗 נְכֵל *be crafty*, Pa. *deceive*; Syr. ܢܟܰܠ *deceive, plot*; cf. perh. ወሰከለ *act faithlessly*, ወሰካል *faithless*, Prä Amhar. Spr. 90);—**Qal** *Pt.* נוֹכֵל Mal 1^{14} *knave*. **Pi.** *Pf.* 3 mpl. c. acc. cogn. נִכְלֵיהֶם אֲשֶׁר נִכְּלוּ לָכֶם Nu 25^{18} *their wiles with which they beguiled you*. **Hithp.** *Impf.* וַיִּתְנַכְּלוּ אֹתוֹ לַהֲמִיתוֹ Gn 37^{18} *they knavishly planned* against him (Kö[iii. 9]), etc.; *Inf. cstr.* לְהִתְנַכֵּל בְּ ψ 105^{25} *to deal knavishly with*.

†[נֵכֶל] **n.** [**m.**] **wiliness, craft, knavery;**— 5231
only pl. sf. נִכְלֵיהֶם Nu 25^{18} *their craft, their wile* (as acc. cogn. c. נִכֵּל).

†כֵּלַי, כִּילַי **n.m. knave** (for נְכִילַי v. Kö 3596
ii. 1, 118);—abs. כִּילַי Is 32^{5} (opp. שׁוֹעַ || נָבָל); כֵּלַי v^{7} (assonance with כֵּלָיו, fr. כְּלִי q.v.).

†[נֶכֶס] **n.m.**[Jos 22, 8] only pl. נְכָסִים **riches,** 5233
treasures (prob. As. or Aram. loan-word, cf. As. *nikâsu*, *property, wealth, gain*, Dl[HWB 463], Syr. ܢܶܟܣܶܐ *wealth*; on deriv. fr. As. *nikâsu*, *cut off, hew down, behead*, etc., Syr. ܢܟܰܣ *slay*, 𝔗 נְכַס, NH נֶכֶס *id.*, through meaning *cattle for slaughter*, cf. Frä 98 Hpt[Hbr. iii (Jan. 1887), 107 ff.] Schwally Idiot. 120 f. Brock[ad voc.]);—Jos 22^{8} (P), 2 Ch $1^{11.12}$ Ec 6^{2} (all || כָּבוֹד, עֹשֶׁר), 5^{18} (עֹשֶׁר||).

†I. [נָכַר] **vb.** (not **Qal**) **regard, recognize** 5234
(NH Hiph. *know, be acquainted with*; 𝔗 Aph.

id.; Syr. Aph. ܐܰܟܰܪ *id.;* cf. also Ar. نَكِرَ in sense *be shrewd, cunning*);—**Niph.** *Pf.* 3 mpl. לֹא נִכְּרוּ La 4[8] *they are not recognized.* **Pi.** *Pf.* לֹא נִכַּר שׁוֹעַ לִפְנֵי־דָל Jb 34[19] *he regardeth not the opulent above the poor* (‖לֹא־נָשָׂא פְּנֵי שָׂרִים); *Impf.* לֹא תְנַכֵּרוּ Jb 21[29] *do ye not recognize their tokens.* **Hiph.** *Pf.* הִכִּיר Dt 33[9] Dn 11[39] Kt; sf. הִכִּירוֹ Gn 27[23]; 3 pl. הִכִּירוּ Ju 18[3] + 2 t., sf. הִכִּירֻהוּ Jb 2[12], הִכִּרֻהוּ Gn 42[8]; *Impf.* יַכִּיר Dt 21[17] + 3 t. + Dn 11[39] Qr; וַיַּכֵּר Gn 38[26]+; sf. וַיַּכִּרֵהוּ 1 K 18[7], יַכִּירֶנּוּ Jb 7[10], וַיַּכִּירָהּ Gn 37[33], etc.; *Imv.* הַכֶּר־ Gn 31[32] + 2 t.; *Inf. abs.* הַכֵּר־ (Ginsb van d. H. הַכֶּר־) Pr 24[23] 28[21]; *cstr.* sf. הַכִּירֵנִי Ru 2[10]; *Pt.* מַכִּיר ψ 142[5], sf. מַכִּירֵךְ Ru 2[19], etc.;—**1.** *regard, observe,* esp. with a view to recognition, c. obj. cl., Gn 31[32] 37[32] 38[25]; *pay attention to,* c. acc. pers. Ru 2[10.19]; acc. rei (of God) Jb 34[25]; acc. rei om. 2 S 3[36]; י׳ subj. כֵּן אַכִּיר ... לְטוֹבָה Je 24[5] *so will I regard* the exiles ... *for good;* Antiochus subj. Dn 11[39]; הִכִּיר פָּנִים *pay regard to* (shew partiality, = נָשָׂא פְּנֵי פ׳) Dt 1[17] 16[19] (‖הִטָּה מִשְׁפָּט), Pr 24[23] 28[21].

2. *Recognize* (as formerly known) c. acc. pers. vel rei, Gn 27[23] 37[33] 38[26] (all J), 42[7.8.8] (E), 1 K 18[7] 20[41] Jb 2[12]; proverb. בְּטֶרֶם יַכִּיר אִישׁ אֶת־רֵעֵהוּ Ru 3[14] *before a man could recognize his fellow* (i.e. before dawn); *recognize* voice (קוֹל), Ju 18[3] 1 S 26[17]; = *perceive* the true situation, וָאַכִּירָה וְהִנֵּה Ne 6[12] *and I perceived, and lo!* God had not sent him.

3. *Be willing to recognize, acknowledge* Dt 21[17] 33[9] Is 63[16] (‖יָדַע), ψ 142[5]; *acknowledge with honour* Is 61[9].

4. *Be acquainted with,* לֹא יַכִּירֶנּוּ עוֹד מְקוֹמוֹ Jb 7[10] *his place shall be acquainted with him no more* (he shall be gone and forgotten), cf. ψ 103[16]; c. acc. rei Jb 24[17].

5. *Distinguish, understand,* הִכִּיר קוֹל ... לְקוֹל Ezr 3[13] could not *distinguish,* etc.; cf. Jb 4[16] *could not distinguish its appearance;* הִכִּיר לְדַבֵּר Ne 13[24] *understand* how *to speak,* etc.

Hithp. *Impf.* יִתְנַכֶּר־נָעַר Pr 20[11] by his deeds *a youth maketh himself known,* whether his doing be pure, etc.

1971 †[הַכָּרָה] **n.f. look (or expression?);**—cstr. הַכָּרַת פְּנֵיהֶם Is 3[9] *a look at their face* witnesses against them (𝔙 Che[Comm.] al.), or *the expression of their face* (Ges[Comm.] De Gu SS, cf. Kit-Di), > *their regarding of persons* 𝔖 𝔗 Thes Hi Du Che[Hpt] (v. against this Kit-Di); Ew Di *the impudence of their face* (√הכר), but this very dub.

†[מַכָּר] **n.m. acquaintance, friend** (dub., cf. Benz[ad loc.]);—sf. מַכָּרוֹ 2 K 12[6]; pl. sf. מַכָּרֵיכֶם v[8]. 4378

II. נכר (√of foll., poss. = I. נכר, whence the *foreign, strange,* as that which is intently regarded, so Thes, but precarious; cf. As. *nakâru, rebel,* Pa. *change, nakiru,* and *nakaru, enemy, nukurtu, enmity,* etc.; Ar. نَكِرَ in sense *be bad, evil;* II. *change, alter* a thing; Sab. נכר II. *reject, injure,* etc., נכרם *injury* Sab Denkm [76] CIS[iv. 81. 9; 29. 5]; Min. נכר *alter* Hom[Südarab. Chrest. 128]; Syr. ܢܟܰܪ *reject,* ܢܘܟܪܳܝܳܐ *alienus,* etc.; 𝔗 נוּכְרַי *strange, foreign*).

†נֵכֶר, [נֹכֶר] **n.[m.] misfortune, calamity;**—abs. נֵכֶר Jb 31[3] *calamity* (‖אֵיד); sf. נָכְרוֹ Ob[12] *his calamity.* 5235

†נֵכָר **n.[m.] that which is foreign, foreignness** (on format. cf. Lag[BN 51, 154]);—abs. נ׳ Ju 10[16]+, cstr. נֵכַר־ Dt 31[16];—*foreignness* (of another family, tribe, or nation), esp. **1.** אֱלֹהֵי (הַ)נֵּכָר = *foreign gods* Gn 35[2.4] Jos 24[20.23] (all E, = א׳ אֲחֵרִים of D, cf. אַחֵר), Ju 10[16] 1 S 7[3] Je 5[19] 2 Ch 33[5]; א׳ נֵכַר־הָאָרֶץ Dt 31[16] = *foreign gods of the land;* sg. אֵל נֵכָר Dt 32[12] Mal 2[11] ψ 81[10]; אֱלוֹהַּ נ׳ Dn 11[39]. **2.** בֶּן־(הַ)נֵּכָר = *foreigner* Gn 17[12] (‖לֹא מִזַּרְעֲךָ), v[27] Ex 12[43] (all P), Lv 22[25] (H), Ez 44[9.9] Ne 9[2] Is 56[3]; בְּנֵי (ה)נ׳ 2 S 22[45.46] = ψ 18[45.46], Ez 44[7] Is 56[6] 60[10] 61[5] 62[8] ψ 144[7.11]. **3.** other combin.: הַבְלֵי נ׳ Je 8[19] *foreign vanities* (idolatries); מִזְבְּחוֹת הַנּ׳ 2 Ch 14[2] *foreign altars;* אַדְמַת נ׳ ψ 137[4] *foreign soil;* מִכָּל־נ׳ Ne 13[30] *from everything foreign.* 5236

†נָכְרִי **adj. foreign, alien** (NH נָכְרִי = *Gentile*);—נ׳ abs. m. Zp 1[8]+; f. נָכְרִיָּה Ex 2[22]+; mpl. נָכְרִים Is 2[6] + 2 t. + Pr 20[16] Kt (> Qr נָכְרִיָּה), + 27[13] (so read for MT נָכְרִיָּה); fpl. נָכְרִיּוֹת Gn 31[15]+;—**1. a.** *foreign:* עַם נָכְרִי Ex 21[8] (E) *a foreign* (non-Isr.) people, אִישׁ נ׳ Dt 17[15] (‖לֹא אָחִיךָ); מַלְבּוּשׁ נ׳ Zp 1[8]; אֶרֶץ נָכְרִיָּה Ex 2[22] (J) *foreign land,* so 18[3] (E); esp. נָשִׁים נָכְרִיּוֹת *foreign* (non-Isr.) *women* 1 K 11[1.8] Ezr 10[2.10.11.14.17.18.44] Ne 13[26.27]. **b.** as subst. נָכְרִי *foreigner* (non-Isr.) Ju 19[12] (+אֲשֶׁר לֹא מִבְּנֵי יִשְׂרָאֵל), 1 K 8[41] (+אֲשֶׁר לֹא מֵעַמְּךָ), = 2 Ch 6[32] (+*id.*), 1 K 8[43] = 2 Ch 6[33], Dt 14[21] (‖גֵּר), 15[3] 23[21] (opp. אָחִיךָ), 29[21] (+אֲשֶׁר יָבֹא מֵאֶרֶץ רְחוֹקָה); as predicate, 2 S 15[19] (‖גֹּלֶה), נָכְרִיָּה Ru 2[10]; pl. נָכְרִים *foreigners* La 5[2] (‖זָרִים), Ob[11] (‖*id.*); cf. יַלְדֵי נָכְרִים Is 2[6]; fpl. *alien women* Gn 31[15] (E; i.e. not of one's 5237

father's family). **2.** נָכְרִיָּה *foreign woman*, as term. techn., in Pr, for *harlot* (perh. because harlots were orig. chiefly foreigners): Pr 2[16] (|| אִשָּׁה זָרָה), 7[5] (|| *id.*), 5[20] (|| זָרָה), 6[24] (|| אֵשֶׁת רָע), 23[27] (|| זוֹנָה).—On 20[16] 27[13] v. infr. **3.** fig. *unknown, unfamiliar*: נָכְרִי הָיִיתִי בְעֵינֵיהֶם Jb 19[15] *an alien am I become in their eyes*; נ׳ לִבְנֵי אִמִּי ψ 69[9] (|| מוּזָר הָיִיתִי לְאֶחָי); אִישׁ נ׳ Ec 6[2]; of ׳י's judgment, נָכְרִיָּה עֲבֹדָתוֹ Is 28[21] *strange is his task!* (|| זָר מַעֲשֵׂהוּ); גֶּפֶן נָכְרִיָּה Je 2[21] *an alien vine* (opp. זֶרַע אֱמֶת), fig. of degenerate Israel; as subst., נָכְרִים Pr 20[16] Kt (> Qr נָכְרִיָּה), *aliens*, persons unknown to him (|| זָר), so read also (for MT נָכְרִיָּה) || 27[13].

5234 †[נכר] **vb.denom.** act or treat as foreign, or strange; disguise, misconstrue;—**Niph.** *Impf.* יִנָּכֵר Pr 26[24] with his lips a hater *disguiseth himself* (dissembles, speaks what is *foreign* to his thought). **Pi.** *Pf.* נִכַּר 1 S 23[7], but v. infr.; *Impf.* וַיְנַכְּרוּ Je 19[4] *and they have treated* this place *as foreign* (profane); יְנַכְּרוּ צָרֵימוֹ Dt 32[27] lest *their adversaries should misconstrue* (it).—נִכַּר אֹתוֹ א׳ בְּיָדִי 1 S 23[7] *God hath alienated him into my hand*, but improbable; 𝔊 מָכַר (cf. Ju 4[9]) *hath sold him*, so Th Klo HPS (cf. We); < סִכַּר (as Is 19[4]) Krochm Dr; Kit either of these; > סִגַּר Bu; Löhr either סִגַּר or סִכַּר. **Hithp.** *Impf.* וַיִּתְנַכֵּר אֲלֵיהֶם Gn 42[7] *he acted as a stranger toward them*; *Pt.* f. מִתְנַכֵּרָה 1 K 14[5.6] *feign to be a stranger-woman.*

5238 †[נְכֹת] **n.[f.]** treasure (so context demands) (𝔊L 2 K 20[13] τῆς ὑπάρξεως, cf. 𝔖 𝔗; der. uncertain; Dl[Prol. 141] cp. As. *bit nakamti* (*nakanti*), *house of treasure*, √ *nakâmu*, *heap up* [Dl[HWB 462]], whence ב׳ נ׳ perh. borrowed; this favoured by Nö [ZMG xl (1886), 731] Hpt[ZA ii. 266] (reading *nakavâti* = *nakamâti*, and Heb. ב׳ נְכוֹתָיו or (ב׳ נְכוֹתוֹ).—Only sf. בֵּית נְכֹתֹה = *his treasure-house* 2 K 20[13] = Is 39[2].

5239 **נלה** doubtful √ (Ar. نَالَ, نَيْل is *obtain, attain*, نَيْل *what one obtains* by another's bounty, Lane[3040]);—for supposed **Hiph.** *Inf.* sf. כַּנְּלֹתְךָ Is 33[1] = כְּהַנְלֹתְךָ (Ki Ges[Lgb. 87] Kö[i. 574]), read כְּכַלֹּתְךָ (**Pi.** Inf. of כלה; so Ra Capp Ges[Thes] Ew Kn Che Brd Di Du), cf. || כַּהֲתִמְּךָ.

4512 †[מִנְלֶה] **n.[m.]?** gain, acquisition?—Only sf. לֹא יִטֶּה לָאָרֶץ מִנְלָם Jb 15[29] (si vera l.) *their acquisition*, but very dub.; Di (formerly) שִׁבֳּלִים, Hi מְלִלִים *ears*, cf. Bu; other conj. v. in Di; Du thinks hopelessly corrupt.—𝔊 σκιάν [i.e. צִלָּם], 𝔖 *their word* [מִלָּתָם].

נִמְבְזָה 1 S 15[9] v. בזה **Niph.** p. 102 5240

†נְמוּאֵל **n.pr.m.** (cf. Gray[Prop. N. 307]);—**1.** son of Simeon Nu 26[12] 1 Ch 4[24] (= יְמוּאֵל, q.v., Gn 46[10] Ex 6[15]), 𝔊 Ναμουηλ. **2.** a Reubenite (brother of Dathan and Abiram) Nu 26[9], 𝔊 *id.* 5241

†נְמוּאֵלִי **adj.gent.** of **1** supr., only c. art. הַנּ׳ as n.coll. Nu 26[12], 𝔊 Ναμουηλει. 5242

נמל (√ of following, meaning unknown).

†נְמָלָה **n.f.unit.** (Lag[BN 81]) **ant** (NH *id.*; Ar. نَمْلَة (nom. unit. of نَمْل); Syr. ܢܡܠܐ);—abs. נ׳ Pr 6[6]; pl. הַנְּמָלִים 30[25]. 5244

נמר (√ of foll., meaning dub.; poss. cp. As. *namâru, shine, gleam* (fr. glossy coat of panther and leopard), [v. Ar. نَمِرَ *pardus*, and *limpidus, purus* (of water; cf. infr. נמרים)] so Hom [NS 294 f.]; ag. this Nö [ZMG xl (1886), 736] Schwally[Idiot. 121]; נָמֵר is comm. Sem.: As. *nimru* Dl [HWB 468]; Ar. نَمِرٌ, نِمْرٌ Lane[2853]; Eth. ነምር: Syr. ܢܡܪܐ, 𝔗 נִמְרָא; NH נָמֵר).

†נָמֵר **n.m.**[Is 11, 6] **leopard**;—abs. נ׳ Ho 13[7] + 3 t.; pl. נְמֵרִים Hb 1[8] Ct 4[8];—*leopard*, as spotted Je 13[23], swift Hb 1[8], keen-eyed Je 5[6] (symb. of calamities of Isr.), so Ho 13[7] (sim. of ׳י); נ׳ עִם־גְּדִי יִרְבָּץ Is 11[6] (predict.); הַרְרֵי נְמֵרִים Ct 4[8] (|| מְעֹנוֹת אֲרָיוֹת). 5246

†נִמְרָה **n.pr.loc.** place E. of Jordan Nu 32[3] (+ חֶשְׁבּוֹן, דִּיבֹן, עֲטָרוֹת, etc.), 𝔊 Ναμβρα, A Αμβραμ, 𝔊L Μαμβραν. Perh. = *Tel Nimrîn*, c. 6 m. E. of Jordan, nearly opp. Jericho, cf. Buhl[Geogr. 264].—Cf. בֵּית נ׳ (q.v.), also in NH (cf. נמרה n.pr.m. Sinait. Inscr. SACook[81] Lzb[323]; meaning dub.; Nö [ZMG xxix (1875), 437] thinks from *spotted* or *striped* appearance of ground; *place of leopard* also Gray[Prop. Names 92] (on tribal names from leopard v. RS[K 201] also Sab n.pr. אנמרם Levy-Os[l.c.], etc.); We[Heid. 2, 82] thinks of *clear water* [cf. foll.]). 5247

†נִמְרִים **n.pr.loc.** in Moab (cf. Sab. נמרן attrib. of Bark[m], DHM [ZMG xxix (1875), 592], v. also CIS[iv. No. 103, p. 169]; مَآءٌ نَمِيرٌ *wholesome water* Lane[2853], also We[l.c.]);—only מֵי נִמְרִים Is 15[6] Je 48[34]; prob. = Βηνναμαρειμ Lag [Onom. 284, 33], in *Wady Numêre* at SE. end of Dead Sea, Buhl[Geogr. 272]. 5249

5248 †נִמְרֹד, נִמְרוֹד **n.pr.m.** Nimrod (etym. and meaning wholly unknown; Thes (dub.) sub מָרַד *rebel* (of which Hebr. may have thought [cf. Lag[BN 105]]); in fact prob. Bab. name; **1.**=a god e.g. Marduk, We[Comp. Hex. (2), 308 f.; Nimrod, Encycl. Brit. (9), xvii. 511], RS[Sem. i. 91 n.; 2d ed. 92]; Hom[PSBA xv (1893), 291-300] prop. *Narûdu*=**Namra-uddu*, a star-god. **2.** < name of Bab. king or prince: *Nu-marad*= 'Man of Marad' cf. Dl[Pa 220] De[Gn 10, 8 [1887]]; more plausibly=*Nazi-maraddash* (*marattash, murudas*), Hpt[Andover Rev. July, 1884, 93 f.] Dl[K (1884)] Say[Athen. Feb. 16, 1895, Acad. Mar. 2, 1895] (cf. Che[ib. Mar. 9]),—i.e. a Kashite kg., B.C. 1378, but dub., cf. Hpt[BAS i (1889), 183], Jeremias[Izdubar-Nimrod, 1891, 1 ff.]);—son of כּוּשׁ (q.v.), hero and hunter Gn $10^{8.9}$ (J; kg. in Babylonia, builder of Nineveh, etc. $v^{10 f.}$), נִמְרוֹד 1 Ch 1^{10}; אֶרֶץ נִמְרֹד Mi 5^{5} (‖ אֶרֶץ אַשּׁוּר); 𝔊 Νεβρωδ.

5250 †נִמְשִׁי **n.pr.m.** grandfather of Jehu 2 K $9^{2.14}$; יֵהוּא בֶּן־נ׳ 1 K 19^{16} 2 K 9^{20} 2 Ch 22^{7}; 𝔊 Ναμεσθει, Ναμεσ(σ)ει.

5251-52 נֵס v. נסס. נְסִבָּה v. סבב. p. 651, 687

5375 נְסָה v. נשׂא. qal impv p. 670

5254 †[נָסָה] **vb. Pi.** test, try (NH *id.*, Pi.; 𝔗 Pa. נַסִּי; Syr. Pa. ܢܰܣܺܝ; cf. Eth. መንሱት: *temptation*);—**Pi.** *Pf.* 3 ms. נִסָּה Dt 4^{34}+3 t.; sf. נִסָּהוּ Ex 15^{25}; 3 fs. נִסְּתָה Dt 28^{56}; 1 s. נִסִּיתִי Ec 7^{23}, +4 t. Pf.; *Impf.* 3 ms. sf. יְנַסֵּם Dn 1^{14}; 1 s. אֲנַסֶּה Ju 6^{39}; sf. אֲנַסְּכָה Ec 2^{2}; 3 mpl. יְנַסּוּ Nu 14^{22}; 2 mpl. תְּנַסּוּן Ex 17^{2}, +7 t. Impf.; *Imv.* נַס Dn 1^{12}; sf. נַסֵּנִי ψ 26^{2}; *Inf. cstr.* נַסּוֹת Ex 20^{20}, +8 t. Inf.; *Pt.* מְנַסֶּה Dt 13^{4};—**1.** *test, try* (syn. בחן), abs. 1 S 17^{39} (a sword); c. בְּ Ju 7^{39} Ec 2^{1}; c. acc. Dn $1^{12.14}$; acc.+ בְּ 1 K 10^{1} =2 Ch 9^{1}, Ec 7^{23}. **2.** *attempt, assay, try* to do a thing, c. Inf. Dt 4^{34} 28^{56}; c. acc. Jb 4^{2} (*venture* a word). **3.** *test, try, prove, tempt* [but not in modern sense of the word: v. Dr[Dt 6, 16; ψψ 453, 483]] **a.** God *tests* or *proves* Abr. Gn 22^{1} (E), Isr. Ex 15^{25} 20^{20} (E), 16^{4} (J), Dt $8^{2.16}$ 13^{4}; c. בְּ Ju 2^{22} $3^{1.4}$; tribe of Levi Dt 33^{8} (poem); Hezekiah 2 Ch 32^{31}; psalmist ψ 26^{2}. **b.** Isr. *tests*, or *tries* God: Ex $17^{2.7}$ Nu 14^{22} (J), Dt 6^{16} ψ $78^{18.41.56}$ 95^{9} 106^{14}; so Ahaz, Is 7^{12}.

4531 †II. מַסָּה **n.f.** test, trial, proving;—מ׳ ψ 95^{8}; cstr. מַסַּת Jb 9^{23}; pl. מַסֹּת Dt 4^{34} 7^{19}, מַסּוֹת Dt 29^{2};—*testings* or *provings* of Pharaoh and Egyptians at Exodus, Dt 4^{34} (v. Dr), 7^{19} 29^{2} (‖ אֹתֹת);—*test, trial*, of innocent person Jb 9^{23} acc. to Hi al., but v. I. מַסָּה sub מסס.

†III. מַסָּה **n.pr.loc.** where Israel tried י׳ in the wilderness, Ex 17^{7} (JE), Dt 6^{16} 9^{22} ψ 95^{8} (all 𝔊 (ὁ) πειρασμός), where Levi was tested Dt 33^{8} (𝔊 πείρᾳ). 4532

†[נָסַח] **vb.** pull or tear away (NH נָסַח, 𝔗 נְסַח both *remove*; As. *nasâḫu* = BH, so OAram. נסח Cook[82] Lzb[323]; Ar. نَسَخَ *annul, supersede, change by substitution, copy*; cf. As. *nisḫu, nusḫu, extract, excerpt* Dl[HWB 472] Meissn[ZA iv (1889), 267]; NH נֻסְחָה, Nab. נסחת *id.*, also Aram. נוסחא (whence Ar. نُسْخَة) Hoffm[ZMG xxxii. 760] cf. Frä[251]; Syr. ܢܣܰܚ *copy*);—**Qal** *Impf.* 3 ms. בֵּית גֵּאִים יִסַּח י׳ Pr 15^{25} *the house of proud men will* י׳ *tear down*; וְיִסָּחֲךָ מֵאֹהֶל ψ 52^{7} *yea, he* [י׳] *shall tear thee away, without a tent*; 3 mpl. יִסְּחוּ מִן Pr 2^{22} transgressors *shall* (men) *tear away from* the land (rd. perh. יִנָּסְחוּ *shall be torn away*; ‖ יִכָּרֵתוּ; cf. Ges[§ 144, 3 b. R] Da[Synt. § 108. b]). **Niph.** *Pf.* 2 mpl. consec. וְנִסַּחְתֶּם מֵעַל הָאֲדָמָה Dt 28^{63} *and ye shall be torn away from off the land.* 5255

מַסָּח 2 K 11^{6}, v. p. 587 a supr. 4535

†I. נָסַךְ **vb.** pour out (NH *id.*, *pour, cast* (metals, Pi. *make libation*; Ph. נסך *cast* gold or iron Lzb[323 f.]; 𝔗 נְסַךְ *make libation*; Syr. ܢܣܰܟ *pour out*; Ar. نَسَكَ, orig. *be-pour, water* Nö[ZMG xli (1887), 719] (rare), usu. *worship* Lane[3032] (cf. RS[Sem. i. 213; 2d ed. 229]), i.e. *pour out* blood of victim, *pour out* wine We[Heid. 2, 114, 118, 142];—**Qal** *Pf.* 3 ms. נָסַךְ Is 29^{10} 40^{19}; נָסָךְ 44^{10}; *Impf.* 3 mpl. יִסְּכוּ Ho 9^{4}; 2 ms. תִּסְּכוּ Ex 30^{9}; *Inf.* לִנְסֹךְ Is 30^{1}; *Pt. pass.* f. נְסוּכָה 25^{7};—**1.** *pour out*, c. עַל (the spirit of deep sleep) Is 29^{10}. **2.** *pour out libations*, c. acc. נֶסֶךְ Ex 30^{9} (P); מַסֵּכָה Is 30^{1}; יַיִן Ho 9^{4}. **3.** *cast metal images*, c. acc. פֶּסֶל Is 40^{19} 44^{10}. 5258

Piel *Impf.* וַיְנַסֵּךְ 1 Ch 11^{18} *pour out as libation*, c. acc. מַיִם + ליהוה (=2 S 23^{16} Hiph.).

Hiph. *Pf.* 3 mpl. הִסִּכוּ Je 32^{29}; *Impf.* 3 ms. וַיַּסֵּךְ Gn 35^{14}+2 t.; 1 s. אַסִּיךְ ψ 16^{4}; 3 mpl. וַיַּסִּיכוּ Ez 20^{28}; *Imv.* הַסֵּךְ Nu 28^{7}; *Inf. abs.* הַסֵּךְ Je 44^{17}; הַסֵּךְ Je 7^{18}+3 t.; *cstr.* לְהַסֵּךְ Je $44^{19.25}$ (Kö[i. 309]);—*pour out libations*, c. acc. נֶסֶךְ Gn 35^{14} (E), 2 K 16^{13} Nu 28^{7} (P), מַיִם 2 S 23^{16} ליהוה; elsewhere, נְסָכִים to other gods Je 7^{18} 19^{13} 32^{29} $44^{17.18.19.19.25}$ Ez 20^{28} ψ 16^{4}.

Hoph. *Impf.* 3 ms. יֻסַּךְ *be poured out*, Ex 25^{29} 37^{16}, of holy wine, c. בְּ of vessels.

5262 †נֶ֫סֶךְ **n.m.** drink-offering;—abs.'נ Gn 35^{14} + 6 t.; נֶ֫סֶךְ Ex 29^{40} 30^{9} Ez 45^{17}; נָ֑סֶךְ Nu 4^{7} Jo 1^{13}; cstr. נֶסֶךְ Nu 28^{7}; sf. נִסְכִּי Is 48^{5}, etc.; pl. נְסָכִים Je 7^{18} + 9 t.; sf. נִסְכָּהּ Nu 29^{31}, נִסְכֵּיהֶם v^{39}, etc.;—**1.** *drink-offering*, c. עַל (on Jacob's מַצֵּבָה at Bethel) Gn 35^{14} (E); elsewhere in worship of 'י only P and related doc.; once of vessels of holy table קְשׂוֹת הַנָּ֑סֶךְ Nu 4^{7}; elsewh. in classifications Lv 23^{37} Nu 29^{39}, usu. offered with the עלה Ex 29^{40} Lv $23^{13.18}$ Nu $15^{5.7.10.24}$ $28^{7.14.31}$ $29^{18.21.24.27.30.33.37}$, esp. עֹלַת הַתָּמִיד $28^{9.10.15.24}$ $29^{6.11.16.19.22.25.28.31.34.38}$; מִנְחַת הַבֹּקֶר Ex 29^{41} Nu 28^{8}; but sts. also with (שׁלמים) זבח $6^{15.17}$ $15^{15.10}$; usu. + מִנְחָה; elsewhere only 1 Ch 29^{21} 2 Ch 29^{35} Ez 45^{17}; מִנְחָה 'וְנ Jo $1^{9.13}$ 2^{14}. Offered to other gods 2 K $16^{13.15}$ Is 57^{6} Je 7^{18} 19^{13} 32^{29} $44^{17.18.19.19.25}$ Ez 20^{28} ψ 16^{4}. **2.** *molten images*, Is 41^{29} 48^{5} Je 10^{14} 51^{17}.—Combinations are: 'הִסִּיךְ נ', נָסַךְ נ (see vb.); 'שָׁפַךְ נ Is 57^{6}.

5257 †I. [נָסִיךְ] **n.m. 1. libation; 2. molten image**;—**1.** sf. יֵין נְסִיכָם *wine of their drink-offering* Dt 32^{38}. **2.** *molten image*, sf. נִסְכֵּיהֶם Dn 11^{8}.

4541 †I. מַסֵּכָה **n.f. 1. molten metal, or image; 2. libation**;—'מ Ex 32^{4}+; cstr. מַסֵּכַת Is 30^{22}; pl. מַסֵּכוֹת 1 K 14^{9}+; sf. מַסֵּכֹתָם Nu 33^{52};—**1.** *libation*, with covenant sacrif. in making covenant Is 30^{1} (= **1.** נֶסֶךְ; see, however, sub II. [נָסַךְ]). **2.** *molten metal*, or *image*: עֵגֶל מַסֵּכָה *molten calf* Ex $32^{4.8}$ Dt 9^{16} Ne 9^{18}, cf. ψ 106^{19}; אֱלֹהֵי מַסֵּכָה *molten gods* Ex 34^{17} Lv 19^{4}; 'צַלְמֵי מ Nu 33^{52}; פֶּסֶל וּמַסֵּכָה Dt 27^{15} Ju $17^{3.4}$ 18^{14} Na 1^{14} 2 Ch $34^{3.4}$, elsewh. (variously) Dt 9^{12} Ju $18^{17.18}$ 1 K 14^{9} 2 K 17^{16} 2 Ch 28^{2} Is 30^{22} 42^{17} Ho 13^{2} Hb 2^{18}.

5259 †II. [נָסַךְ] **vb. weave** (Ar. نَسَجَ has same meaning);—**Qal** *Pt. pass.* f. נְסוּכָה Is 25^{7}; perh. also *Inf. cstr.* לִנְסֹךְ 30^{1}; on both v. foll.

4541 †II. מַסֵּכָה **n.f. woven stuff, web, esp. as covering**;—abs. הַמּ' הַנְּסוּכָה עַל־ Is 25^{7} *the web that is woven over* all the nations (i.e. *mourning-veil*, symb. of distress; || הַלּוֹט הַלּוֹט); = *bed-covering* 28^{20} (in fig.). Perhaps also 'לִנְסֹךְ מ 30^{1} *weave a web* (|| לַעֲשׂוֹת עֵצָה), ref. to negotiations with Egypt (so 𝔙 Aq Ew De Che Di; > 𝔊 Ges Hi Kn Brd Du *pour a libation*; 'מ not elsewhere = נֶסֶךְ).

†[מַסֶּ֫כֶת] **n.f.** web of unfinished stuff, on loom (v. GFM $^{JAOS, Oct. 1889, clxxvii}$);—only abs. מַסָּ֫כֶת Ju $16^{13.14}$.—מָסָךְ, מְסֻכָּה v. סכך. 4545

†III. [נָסַךְ] **vb. set, install** (As. *nasâku*, *id.*, whence *nasîku*, *prince*, Dl $^{HWB\,472}$; v. also Muss-Arnolt $^{Hbr.\,vi.\,89.\,R.\,17}$ and reff.);—**Qal** *Pf.* 1 s. נָסַכְתִּי מַלְכִּי עַל־צִיּוֹן ψ 2^{6} *I have installed my king upon Zion*. **Niph.** *Pf.* 1 s. נִסַּכְתִּי Pr 8^{23} *I was installed* (of Wisdom). 5258

†II. [נָסִיךְ] **n.m. prince**;—pl. cstr. נְסִיכֵי Jos 13^{21} Ez 32^{30} Mi 5^{4}; sf. נְסִיכֵמוֹ ψ 83^{12}. 5257

נִסְמָן v. סמן. p. 702 5567

†I. [נָסַס] **vb. be sick** (?; cf. Syr. ܢܰܣ *id.*, and esp. ܢܰܣܺܝܣܳܐ *debilis, infirmus, aegrotans*, etc., PS ^{2387}; 𝔗 נְסַס *be sad*; As. *nasâsu*, *wail*, *lament* Dl $^{HWB\,472}$; Ar. نَسَّ is *go at a gentle pace*);—only **Qal** *Pt. act.* (si vera l.) כִּמְסֹס נֹסֵס Is 10^{18} like the wasting away *of a sick man* (so Thes Ew De Che Di Du). 5263

II. נסס (√ of foll. = *be high* or *conspicuous?* **Hithpo'l.** *Inf.* לְהִתְנוֹסֵס ψ 60^{6}, acc. to some denom. from נֵס *that it may be displayed*, AV, cf. De; < v. נוס; *Pt.* מִתְנוֹסְסוֹת Zc 9^{16} *raised? prominent?* (עַל־אַדְמָתוֹ; of precious stones, in fig.) very dub.; We Now del.; Gr מִתְנוֹצְצוֹת). 5264

†נֵס **n.[m.] standard, ensign, signal, sign** (NH *id.*, *flag*, usu. *sign*, i.e. *miracle*; 𝔗 נֵס, נִסָּא *sign, miracle*);—'נ abs. Nu 21^{8}+; cstr. Is 11^{10}; sf. נִסִּי Ex 17^{15} Is 49^{22};—**1. a.** *standard*, as 5251
rallying-point, 'י' נִסִּי Ex 17^{15} (E), 'י *my standard* 3071
(name of altar); conspicuously set on hill Is 30^{17} (sim. of solitariness; || הַתֹּרֶן עַל־רֹאשׁ הָהָר); signal of war [v. Schumacher $^{ZPV\,ix.\,232,\ Across\ the\ Jordan,\ 104\,f.}$] (esp. to the nations, for destruction or deliverance of Judah, Is Je), נָשָׂא נ' לַגּוֹיִם Is 5^{26} 11^{12} cf. 18^{3} (on mts., || תְּקֹעַ שׁוֹפָר); אֶל־עַמִּים אָרִים נ' 49^{22} (|| אֶשָּׂא אֶל־גּוֹיִם יָדִי),—in all these subj. 'י; cf. עֹמֵד לְנֵס עַמִּים Is 10^{11} (of Mess. kg.); 'שְׂאוּ נ 13^{2} (on mt.), Je 50^{2} 51^{12} (c. אֶל־ *against*), v^{27} (|| תִּקְעוּ שׁוֹפָר בַּגּוֹיִם), הָרִימוּ נ' עַל־עַמִּים Is 62^{10}, cf. Je 4^{21} (|| קוֹל שׁוֹפָר); נָתַתָּה . . . נ' לְהִתְנוֹסֵס ψ 60^{6} *thou hast set a standard* (only) *for fleeing*. **b.** *signal*, שְׂאוּ נ' צִיּוֹנָה Je 4^{6} (i.e. to direct refugees to Zion). **2.** *standard*, as pole, supporting serpent of bronze Nu $21^{8.9}$ (JE). **3. a.** *ensign*, *signal*, שֵׁשׁ . . . מִמִּצְרַיִם הָיָה מִפְרָשֵׂךְ לִהְיוֹת לָךְ לְנֵס Ez 27^{7} *byssus from Egypt was thy sail, to serve*

thee for an ensign (so DaToy; on lack of pennon on ancient ships v. Co; > del. Co Berthol); so **b.** (since sails were the only ensign) = *sail* Is 33^{23} (Che Di al.; > *pennon* Ges Hi Ew De Du). **4.** *sign* (cf. NH) = *warning* Nu 26^{10} (P).

5265 I. **נָסַע** $_{147}$ **vb. pull out or up, set out, journey** (NH *id., move, march;* As. *nisû, set out, withdraw,* etc. Dl$^{HWB\,470}$; Nö$^{ZMG\,xl\,(1886),\,723}$ cp. also Ar. نَزَعَ, Eth. ንሕዐ: [rare] *pull up, away,* so Ba$^{ES\,51}$); — **Qal**$_{137}$ *Pf.* 3 ms. נ׳ Gn 33^{17}+, 3 mpl. נָסְעוּ Dt 10^{6}, נָסָ֑עוּ Nu 2^{34}+, etc.; *Impf.* יִסַּע Is 33^{20}, וַיִּסַּע Gn 12^{9}+, sf. וַיִּסָּעֵם Ju 16^{3}; 3 mpl. יִסְעוּ Ex 40^{36}+, יִסָּ֑עוּ Nu 2^{9}+; 2 mpl. תִּסְעוּ Jos 3^{3}; 1 pl. נִסְעָה cohort. Gn 33^{12}, וַנִּסַּע Dt 1^{19} 2^{1}, וַנִּסְעָה Ezr 8^{31}, etc.; *Imv.* סְעוּ Dt 2^{24}+; *Inf. abs.* נָסוֹעַ Gn 12^{9}; *cstr.* נְסֹעַ Jos 3^{14}+; sf. נָסְעָם Gn 11^{2} Nu 10^{34}; *Pt.* נֹסֵעַ Ex 14^{10} Nu 10^{33}; pl. נֹסְעִים Nu 10^{29};—**1.** *pull out* or *up,* city-gate and gate-posts Ju 16^{3}; loom v^{14} (on text cf. GFM), tent-pegs Is 33^{20} (fig. of Jerusalem; cf. also **Niph.**). **2.** hence (from pulling up tent-pegs), **a.** *set out* Gn 35^{5} Nu 12^{15} (both E), Je 4^{7} (‖ יָצָא מִמְּקוֹמוֹ); even of lifeless things, e.g. the ark, הָאָרוֹן Nu 10^{35} (JE); oft. in P: Ex 14^{15} 40^{37} Nu 1^{51} $4^{5.15}$ 9^{17} + 8 t. Nu 9, $10^{5.6.17.18.21.22.25}$, so prob. also 2^{8} + 6 t. Nu 2 (v. infr.; even of lifeless things, אֹהֶל מוֹעֵד 1^{51}, מִשְׁכָּן $10^{18.22}$, דֶּגֶל 2^{17}), 33^{3}; וַיִּסַּע . . . וַיָּבֹא Gn 46^{1} (E) *and* Isr. *set out, and came,* etc., Ex 16^{1} 19^{2} Nu 20^{22} Jos 9^{17} (all P), Dt 1^{7}, נִסְעָה וְנֵלֵכָה 33^{12} (J); (וַיַּעֲלוּ . . . וַיִּסְעוּ) Ju 18^{11}, סְעוּ וְעִבְרוּ Dt 2^{24}; נ׳ oft. c. מִן Gn 35^{16} (E), Nu 10^{34} (JE), נ׳ מֵאָהֳלֵיהֶם לַעֲבֹר Jos 3^{14} (JE), *set out from their tents, to cross,* etc., cf. נ׳ מִן . . . לָלֶכֶת Ezr 8^{31}; c. ויבא + מִן, Jos 3^{1} (JE), Nu 33^{9} (P), + וַיֵּלֶךְ v^{3} (D), Dt 1^{19}, + וַיַּעַבְרוּ Nu 33^{8} (P); + וַיַּחֲנוּ + וַיֵּשְׁבוּ Nu 33^{7} (P). **b.** *depart,* c. מִן Gn 37^{17} (J), 2 K 3^{27} $19^{8.36}$ = Is $37^{8.37}$; even of עַמּוּד הֶעָנָן Ex 14^{19} (J); of angel v^{19} (E; + וַיֵּלֶךְ). **3.** *journey, march* (by stages) Gn 12^{9} 35^{21} (both J), Nu $10^{13.14.28}$ (P), (poss. also Nu 2^{9} etc., cf. **2** supr.); + לְמַסְעֵיהֶם *acc. to their stations,* i.e. by stages Ex 17^{1} Nu 10^{12} (+ מִן), cf. Ex 40^{36} (all P); sq. ה loc. Gn 12^{9} 33^{17} (both J), Dt 1^{40} 2^{1}; סְעוּ לָכֶם הַמִּדְבָּר Nu 14^{25} (JE); sq. מִקֶּדֶם *eastward* (v. מִן **1. c**) Gn 11^{2} 13^{11} (both J), אֶל־אַחֲרֵי Ex 14^{10} (J), Nu 10^{29}, לִפְנֵי v^{33} (of ark; all J); sq. ה + מִן loc. Gn 20^{1} (E), Dt $10^{6.7}$ Ex 12^{37} (P), + acc. loc. Nu 11^{35} (JE); sq. מִן + acc. of distance, דֶּרֶךְ 10^{33} (JE), 21^{4} (P); esp. וַיִּסְעוּ מִן . . . וַיַּחֲנוּ Nu $21^{12.13}$ (JE), Ex 13^{20} Nu 21^{11} 33^{5} + 37 t. Nu 33 (all P); of shepherds Je 31^{24}.—נָסְעוּ כְמוֹ צֹאן Zc 10^{2} is dub.; We נָעוּ or יָנֻעוּ, so Now. **4.** of wind, נ׳ רוּחַ מֵאֵת י׳ Nu 11^{31} *there set forth* (sprang up) a wind from י׳.

†**Niph.** *Pf. be pulled up, removed:* 3 ms. דּוֹרִי נִסַּע וְנִגְלָה מִנִּי כְּאֹהֶל רֹעִי Is 38^{12}; of tent-peg הֲלֹא נִסַּע יִתְדָם Jb 4^{21} (reading יִתְדָם for יִתְרָם, v. II. יֶתֶר).

†**Hiph.** *Impf.* 3 ms. יַסַּע ψ 78^{26}, וַיַּסַּע Ex 15^{22} + 2 t.; 2 ms. תַּסִּיעַ ψ 80^{9}, 3 fs. תַּסִּיעִי 2 K 4^{4}; 3 mpl. וַיַּסִּעוּ 1 K 5^{31}; *Pt.* מַסִּיעַ Ec 10^{9}; — **1.** *cause to set out, lead out,* c. acc. pers. Ex 15^{22} (J; + מִן, וַיֵּצְאוּ), ψ 78^{52} (וַיְנַהֲגֵם ‖ כַּצֹּאן), 80^{9} (מִן; fig. of vine); fig. of a wind, *cause to spring up,* יַסַּע קָדִים ψ 78^{26} (‖ וַיְנַהֵג; cf. **Qal 4**). **2.** *remove,* c. acc. rei 2 K 4^{4}; וַיַּסַּע כָּעֵץ תִּקְוָתִי Jb 19^{10}; specif., *remove* from quarry, *quarry:* 1 K 5^{31} *and they quarried* great stones, cf. Ec 10^{9}.

†**מַסַּע n.[m.] pulling up, breaking camp, setting out, journey**;—abs. מ׳ Nu 10^{2} Dt 10^{11}; 4550
pl. cstr. מַסְעֵי Nu 10^{28} 33^{1}; sf. מַסָּעָיו Gn 13^{3}, מַסְעֵיהֶם Ex 17^{1} + 6 t.;—**1. a.** *pulling up, breaking* camp (c. acc. מַחֲנֶה; Ges$^{§\,45e,\,115d}$) Nu 10^{2}. **b.** *setting out* Nu 10^{6}, cf. v^{28}. **2.** *station, stage, journey* (by stages), וַיֵּלֶךְ לְמ׳ Gn 13^{3} *and he went by* (acc. to) *his journeyings* (cf. הלך, p. 231 a supr.); לְמַסְעֵיהֶם Ex 17^{1} cf. $40^{36.38}$ Nu 10^{12} (all P; all c. נָסַע), $33^{1.2}$ (‖ מוֹצָאֵיהֶם), v^{2} (‖ *id.*); קוּם לֵךְ לְמַסַּע Dt 10^{11} *for journeying* (v. Dr).

†I. **מַסָּע n.[m.] quarry or quarrying**;— 4551
only abs. as adv. acc., אֶבֶן שְׁלֵמָה מַסָּע 1 K 6^{7} *stone perfect* (at the) *quarry* (or *at quarrying,* i.e. when it was quarried; cf. Benz; text dub.).

II. **נסע** (√ of foll.; poss. Ar. نَسَغَ *throw* (*puncture, wound,* etc.), Kam Frey, so Buhl^{13}).

†II. **מַסָּע missile, dart**;—only abs. Jb 41^{18} (+ חֲנִית, שִׁרְיָה). 4551

נסך whence אֶסַּק ψ 139^{8} acc. to Thes al.; but v. סלק. p. 701 5266

†**נִסְרֹךְ n.pr.div.** Assyr. god, worshipped by Sennach., 2 K 19^{37} = Is 37^{38}; 𝔊 Εσδραχ, A Εσθραχ, 𝔊L Ασραχ (K); 𝔊 Νασαραχ, א Ασαρακ, A Ασαραχ (Is); Jos$^{Ant.\,x.\,1,\,5}$ Αρασκη; no such god in cuneif. inscr.; see views in Meinh$^{Jesaiaerzählungen\,(1898)\,ad\,loc.}$; crpt. form of *Nusku* (= נסוך) acc. to Hal$^{JAs.\,xiii\,(1879),\,387\,=\,Mél.\,de\,Crit.\,177}$ Muss-Arnolt$^{JBL\,xi.\,1\,(1892),\,86;\,Hbr.\,vii.\,89\,R.\,17}$; *Nusku* is a solar deity, cf. Jastr$^{Rel.\,Bab.\,220\,f.}$ 5268

נֵעָה, נֹעָה v. נוע. p. 631 5269-70

5272 †נְעִיאֵל **n.pr.loc.** on border of Asher Jos 19[27]; 𝔊 Ιναηλ, A Ανιηλ, 𝔊L Νασιηλ.

5274 †נָעַל **vb.** bar, bolt, lock (NH *id.*);—**Qal** *Pf.* 3 ms. נָעַל 2 S 13[18], נָעָ֑ל Ju 3[23]; *Imv.* נְעֹל 2 S 13[17]; *Pt. pass.* נָעוּל Ct 4[12.12]; fpl. נְעֻלוֹת Ju 3[24];—*bar, bolt, lock,* usu. c. acc. דֶּלֶת, דַּלְתוֹת: Ju 3[23], + אַחֲרֵי *after, behind,* v[24] 2 S 13[17.18]; elsewh. only גַּן נָעוּל Ct 4[12] *a garden barred* (fig. of Shulamite), so also v[12 b] (reading גַּן for גַּל, Vrss Gr Bu).

5275 †נַ֫עַל **n.f.**[Jos 9, 5] **sandal, shoe** (NH *id.*; Ar. نَعْلٌ *id.* (also *horse-shoe,* etc.); Syr. ܢܥܠܐ appar. only *horse-shoe* (rare; also NS) PS[2405]; cf. poss. Eth. ነዐልት: (obsol.) *wife of Levirate marriage* Di[676]);—abs. נ׳ Gn 14[23], נָ֑עַל Dt 25[10]; sf. נַעֲלִי ψ 60[10] 108[10], נַעַלְךָ Jos 5[15], etc.; du. נַעֲלַ֫יִם Am 2[6] 8[6]; pl. נְעָלִים Is 11[15] Ct 7[2], נְעָלוֹת Jos 9[5]; sf. נְעָלֶיךָ Ex 3[5] Ez 24[17], נְעָלָיו Is 5[27], נְעָלֵינוּ Jos 9[13], נַעֲלֵיכֶם Ex 12[11] Ez 24[23];—*sandal* Ju 9[13], Am 2[6] 8[6] (du. = pair of sandals; mentioned as of little worth); Dt 29[4]; on (ב) feet Jos 9[5] (JE), 1 K 2[5] Ez 24[23] Ex 12[11] (P); cf. וְהִדְרִיךְ בַּנ׳ פְּעָמַיִךְ בַּנְּעָלִים Ct 7[2], Is 11[15]; *put on sandal* is שִׂים נ׳ בְּרֶגֶל Ez 24[17]; *loose the sandal* is חָלַץ Is 20[2] Dt 25[9] cf. v[10]; שַׁל (Imv.) Ex 3[5] (E), Jos 5[15] (JE); שָׁלַף Ru 4[7.8] (cf. Burton[Midian ii. 197]); *sandal-thong* is שְׂרוֹךְ Gn 14[23] Is 5[27]; עַל־אֱדוֹם אַשְׁלִיךְ נַעֲלִי ψ 60[10] *upon Edom do I cast my sandal* = 108[10], denotes either contempt (Hup; עַל = *unto,* fig. of slave), or taking possession of (Fl in De, Che Bae), ‖ מוֹאָב סִיר רַחְצִי favours former.—On symbolic use of sandal v. further Goldziher[Abh. z. Arab. Philol. i. 47 f.] Jacob[Arab. Dicht. iv. 23].

5274 †[נָעַל] **vb. denom.** furnish with sandals, shoe (𝔗 נְעַל (rare), *bind on sandal;* Ar. نَعَّلَ *furnish with sandals, shoe* horse or camel; Syr. ܢܰܥܶܠ *shoe* horse);—**Qal** *Impf.* 1 s. sf. וָאֶנְעָלֵךְ תַּ֑חַשׁ Ez 16[10] *and I shod thee with* תחשׁ (q.v.). **Hiph.** *Impf.* 3 mpl. sf. וַיַּנְעִלוּם 2 Ch 28[15] *and gave them sandals.*

4514 †מַנְעוּל **n.[m.]** bolt;—abs. כַּפּוֹת הַמּ׳ Ct 5[5] (of house-door); pl. sf. מַנְעוּלָיו Ne 3[3], מַנְעֻלָיו v[6.13.14.15], all of city-gates, in phr. דַּלְתֹתָיו (וּ)מַנ׳ וּבְרִיחָיו.

4515 †[מִנְעָל] **n.m.** id., only sf. בַּרְזֶל וּנְחֹשֶׁת מִנְעָלֶ֑ךָ Dt 33[25] (song).

†I. [נָעֵם] **vb. be pleasant, delightful,** 5276
lovely (Ph. נעם *good* Lzb[324] (and many n.pr.); Ar. نَعِمَ be *plentiful, easy, pleasant;* أَنْعَمَ على *shew gracious favour toward,* oft. in Qor; Sab. נעם *be lovely, agreeable, well* Levy-Os[ZMG xix (1865), 178] CIS[iv. 19, 11], so Min. Hom[Südar. Chrest. 128]; OAram. in n.pr. Lzb[222, 324] Cook[82] (נעמתי *my darling* [or *my songs,* cf. II. נ׳]); 𝔗 נְעִים *pleasant, lovely,* נְעִימְתָּא *loveliness;* Prä[BAS i. 46 f.] cp. Eth. አዳመ: *be pleasant,* = *አነዐመ:);—**Qal** *Pf.* 3 fs. נָעֵ֫מָה Gn 49[15] (poem in J; of land); 2 ms. (of delightful friend) נָעַמְתָּ לִּי מְאֹד 2 S 1[26], also (of physical beauty) מִמִּי נָעָ֑מְתָּ Ez 32[19]; 2 fs. (*id.*) מַה־נָּעַמְתְּ Ct 7[7] *how lovely art thou!* (‖ מַה־יָּפִית); 3 pl., of pleasant words, נָעֵ֫מוּ ψ 141[6]; *Impf.* 3 ms. יִנְעָם: לֶחֶם סְתָרִים יִנ׳ Pr 9[17] (‖ יִמְתָּקוּ); יִנ׳ לְנַפְשְׁךָ Pr 2[10] (of knowledge); 24[25] is impers. c. לְ, *to them . . . shall be delight.*

†נֹ֫עַם **n.m.**[ψ 90, 17] **delightfulness, pleasantness** (Ecclus נועם תירוש 32[6]);—נ׳ abs. Zc 11[7] 5278
+ 4 t.; cstr. ψ 27[4] 90[17];—**1.** *delightfulness* of י׳: contemplated in temple ψ 27[4], shewn in his favour, וִיהִי נ׳ אדני . . . עָלֵינוּ 90[17]. **2.** name of one of two symbol. staves Zc 11[7.10]. **3.** *pleasantness,* as defining genit.: דַּרְכֵי־נ׳ Pr 3[17]; אִמְרֵי־נ׳ 15[26] 16[21].

†נַ֫עַם **n.pr.m.** son of Caleb, 1 Ch 4[15]; 𝔊 5277
Νοομ, A Νααμ.

†I. נָעִים **adj. pleasant, delightful** (poet.);— 5273
abs. נ׳ Pr 22[18] +; cstr. נְעִים 2 S 23[1]; pl. נְעִמִים ψ 16[6], נְעִימִים 2 S 1[23], נְעִימִם Pr 23[8]; f. נְעִמוֹת ψ 16[11];—**1.** *delightful* הַנֶּאֱהָבִים וְהַנּ׳ בְּחַיֵּיהֶם 2 S 1[23] (of Saul and Jonath.); of wealth, הוֹן יָקָר וְנ׳ Pr 24[4]; words Pr 23[8]; of acts, etc.: מַה־טּוֹב וּמַה־נּ׳ שֶׁבֶת אַחִים גַּם־יָחַד ψ 133[1]; singing praises to י׳, 135[3] 147[1]; keeping wise teachings Pr 22[18]; as subst. = *delight* יְכַלּוּ יְמֵיהֶם בַּטּוֹב וּשְׁנֵיהֶם בַּנְּעִימִים Jb 36[11] (of earthly prosperity); of spiritual delights ψ 16[6.11]. **2.** *lovely, beautiful* (physically), Ct 1[16] (‖ יָפֶה).—ψ 81[3] 2 S 23[1] v. II. נָעִים sub II. נעם.

†I. נַעֲמָה **n.pr.f. 1.** sister of Tubal Cain 5279
Gn 4[22] 𝔊 Νοεμα, 𝔊L Νοεμμα. **2.** Ammonitess, mother of Rehoboam 1 K 14[21] 𝔊 Μααχαμ, A Νααμα, 𝔊L Νaava = 2 Ch 12[13], 𝔊 Νοομμα, 𝔊L Νaαμα; also 1 K 14[31] but prob. gloss (om. 𝔊B, 𝔊L, etc.).

5279 †II. נַעֲמָה **n.pr.loc.** city assigned to Judah in Philist. plain Jos 15^{41}; 𝔊 Νωμαν, A Νωμα, 𝔊L Νομα.

5280 נַעֲמִי v. infr.

5281 נָעֳמִי **n.pr.f.** mother-in-law of Ruth, Ru 1$^{2.3.8}$ + 18 t. Ru; 𝔊B Νωεμειν; A Νωεμμειν 1^{2}, Νοεμμειν v^{3}, usu. Νοομει(ν); 𝔊L Νοομι.

5282 †I. [נַעֲמָן] **n.[m.]** usu. **pleasantness** (so Thes *amoenitas*), but perh. epithet of **Adonis** (so Mo$^{\text{Phoen. i. 227}}$ Lag$^{\text{Symm. i. 468; Semit. i. 32}}$ who cp. red flower called شقايق النعمان [v. Lane^{1578}], i.e. *wound of Adonis*, whence ἀνεμώνη; cf. Ew$^{\text{Proph. i. 364}}$ RS$^{\text{Proph. vi. n. 10}}$ and v. Lewy$^{\text{Fremdwörter, 49}}$); —only pl. נִטְעֵי נַעֲמָנִים Is 17^{10} (𝔊 φύτευμα ἄπιστον) perh. = *Adonis-plantations*, or gardens (on double pl. v. Ges$^{\S\text{ 124 q}}$; and on Ἀδώνιδος κῆποι v. Rochette$^{\text{Rev. Archéol. viii. 1851, 105–123}}$ Daremberg et Saglio$^{\text{Dict. des Antiquités (1877), i. 73, and reff.}}$ WSmith$^{\text{Dict. Antiq. (3) i. 25}}$ Fl in Levy$^{\text{NHWB iv. 229}}$).

5283 II. נַעֲמָן$_{16}$ **n.pr.m. 1.** son of Benj. Gn 46^{21}, 𝔊 Νοεμ(μ)αν; = grandson of Benj. Nu 26$^{40.40}$, 𝔊 Νοεμα(νει), 1 Ch 8$^{4.7}$ (so 𝔊 Gn 46^{21}), 𝔊 in Ch Νοομα, 𝔊L Ναμει, Νααμαν. **2.** Aramaean general 2 K 5$^{1.2.6}$ + 8 t. 2 K 5; 𝔊 Ναιμαν, 𝔊L Νεεμαν.

5280 †נַעֲמִי **adj.gent.** from II. נַעֲמָן **1,** Nu 26^{40}, rd. doubtless נעמני (so Sam.).

5284 †נַעֲמָתִי **adj.gent.** (from unused n.pr.);— צוֹפַר הַנּ׳ Jb 2^{11} (𝔊 ὁ Μειναίων βασιλεύς), 11^{1} 20^{1} 42^{9} (all 𝔊 ὁ Μειναῖος); Hom$^{\text{Aufsätze 48}}$ prop. מְעוּנִי.

4516 †[מַנְעַמִּים] **n.[m.]pl. delicacies, dainties**;—only sf. וּבַל־אֶלְחַם בְּמַנְעַמֵּיהֶם ψ 141^{4}.

II. נעם (perh. to be assumed as √ of foll., Ne$^{\text{Marg. 10}}$; Ar. نَغَمَ *speak in a low, gentle voice*, نَغْمَةٌ *note, melody*; Syr. ܢܚܡ *rugivit*, ܢܶܥܡܬܳܐ *gentle sound, note*; NH נְעִימָה *melody*; Ecclus 45^{9} לתת נעימה *to make music*; cf. Hiph. 47$^{\text{9 b marg.}}$).

5273 †II. נָעִים **adj.** perh. **singing, sweetly sounding, musical**;—abs. כִּנּוֹר נ׳ ψ 81^{3} *sweetly-sounding lyre*; cstr., as subst., נְעִים זְמִרוֹת יִשׂ׳ 2 S 23^{1} *Israel's sweet singer of songs* (cf. Dr$^{\text{2 S 8, 10}}$ Löhr; 𝔙 *egregius psaltes Israel*, and so Ges Ew al., from I. נעם; *joy of the songs of Isr.* HPS, cf. Klo Kit).

נעץ (√ of foll.; NH נָעַץ *prick, stick* or *thrust in, wedge in*; 𝔗 נְעַץ *id.*; NH נַעֲצוּץ fig. of *wicked person*; 𝔗 נַעֲצוּצָא = BH).

†נַעֲצוּץ **n.[m.] thorn-bush** (on form cf. Ba$^{\text{NB 213}}$);—abs. נ׳ Is. 55^{13}; pl. נַעֲצוּצִים 7^{19}. 5285

†I. [נָעַר] **vb. growl** (NH *id. cry, bray*; cf. Syr. ܢܥܰܪ; Ar. نَعَرَ *make a noise* Lane^{2815}; poss. As. *na'ru, cry, roar* (?) Dl$^{\text{HWB 439}}$);—only **Qal** *Pf.* 3 pl. נָעֲרוּ כְּגוֹרֵי אֲרָיוֹת Je 51^{38} (‖ כַּכְּפִרִים יִשְׁאָגוּ). 5286

†II. [נָעַר] **vb. shake, shake out** or **off** (NH נָעַר *shake, stir up*, esp. Pi. Niph.; 𝔗 נְעֹרֶת *tow* (v. infr.); Ar. نَغَرَ, نَغِرَ *boil, be in violent commotion, be very angry*);—**Qal** *Pf.* 1 s. נָעַרְתִּי Ne 5^{13}; *Pt. act.* נֹעֵר Is 33$^{9.15}$; *pass.* Ne 5^{13};—*shake out*, to shew emptiness, חָצְנִי נ׳ Ne 5^{13} (symbol.), נ׳ כַּפָּיו מִתְּמֹךְ בַּשֹּׁחַד Is 33^{15}; pt. *shaken out, emptied* נ׳ וָרֵק Ne 5^{13} (i.e. stripped of possessions); *shake off* (leaves) Is 33^{9} (cf. ‖ cl.). **Niph.** *Pf.* 1 s. נִנְעַרְתִּי כָּאַרְבֶּה ψ 109^{23} *I am shaken out like a locust* (fr. fold of a garment; sim. of perishing helplessly); cf. *Impf.* 3 mpl. וְיִנָּעֲרוּ רְשָׁעִים מִמֶּנָּה Jb 38^{13} to seize the corners of the earth *that wicked men may be shaken out of it*; 1 s. אִנָּעֵר Ju 16^{20} *I will shake myself* (free? cf. Hithp. and GFM). **Pi.** *Impf.* 3 ms. juss. יְנַעֵר Ne 5^{13} *so may* God *shake utterly out* every man from (מִן) his house, etc.; וַיְנַעֵר Ex 14^{27} *and* י׳ *shook off* the Egypt. into (בְּ) the sea, = *Pf.* נִעֵר ψ 136^{15} (also c. acc. + בְּ). **Hithp.** *Imv.* fs. הִתְנַעֲרִי מֵעָפָר Is 52^{2} *shake thyself* (*free*), etc. (of personif. Zion). 5287

†I. נֹ֫עַר **n.[m.]** usu. interpr. as **a shaking, scattering**, abst. for concr. = *scattered ones*, only Zc 11^{16}, but text corrupt, v. We Now. 5288

†נְעֹ֫רֶת **n.f. tow** (as *shaken off* from the flax when beaten; on form cf. Ba$^{\text{NB 64}}$);—in sim. פְּתִיל־הַנּ׳ Ju 16^{9} *a thread of tow* (snapping from heat); נ׳ Is 1^{31} (fig.; as inflammable). 5296

III. נער (√ of foll.; meaning unknown).

II. נַ֫עַר$_{239}$ **n.m. 1. boy, lad, youth. 2. retainer** (not in P) (NH as BH; Ph. נער Lzb^{324}); —נ׳ abs. Gn 37^{2}+; cstr. 1 S 2^{13}+; sf. נַעֲרוֹ Ju 19^{3}+, נַעֲרָהּ 2 K 4^{24}; pl. נְעָרִים 1 S 25^{5}+, cstr. נַעֲרֵי Ex 24^{5}+; sf. נְעָרַי Ne 4^{10} 5^{10}, etc.;— **1.** *boy, lad, youth* (c. 133 t.) **a.** of infant Ex 2^{6} (E; 3 months old), to be born Ju 13$^{5.7.8.12}$, just born 1 S 4^{21}, not weaned 1 S 1^{22}; also Is 8^{4}, cf. 7^{16}+. **b.** of lad just weaned 1 S 1^{24} (del. 2nd נער, cf. further Dr Bu HPS), v$^{25.27}$, etc. **c.** = 5289 youth: of young Ishmael Gn 21$^{12f.}$ (E), Isaac 22$^{5.12}$(E), Joseph Gn 37^{2}(E; 17 years old), Benj 43^{8} 44$^{22f.}$ (J), sons of Samuel 1 S 2^{17}, of Jesse 1 S 16^{11}; נ׳ קָטֹן *little lad* 1 S 20^{35} 1 K 3^{7} 2 K 5^{14} Is 11^{6}, נ׳ קָטָן 1 K 11^{17}, pl. 2 K 2^{23}. **d.** נ׳ with special stress on youthfulness Ju 8^{20} 1 S 17$^{33.42}$ Ho 11^{1} Is 3^{4} cf. Ec 10^{16} Is 3^{5} 10^{19} Je 1$^{6.7}$ 1 Ch 22^{5} 29^{1} 2 Ch 13^{7} 34^{3}; so in phr. מִנּ׳ וְעַד זָקֵן Gn 19^{4} (J), Jos 6^{21} (J), Est 3^{13} cf. Ex 10^{9} (E), Dt 28^{50} Is 20^{4} 65^{20} Je 51^{22} La 2^{21} ψ 37^{25} 148^{12} Pr 22^{6}. **e.** of marriageable age Gn 34^{19} (J), warrior Absalom 2 S 18$^{5.12}$+, Zadok 1 Ch 12^{28}, etc. **2.** *servant, retainer* (c. 105 t.): **a.** = personal attendant, household servant, Nu 22^{22} (J), Ju 7$^{10.11}$ 19^{3} 1 S 9$^{3f.}$ 2 K 4$^{12.25}$+oft. **b.** = retainer, follower Gn 14^{24} 1 S 25$^{5f.}$ 2 S 2$^{14f.}$ 1 K 20$^{14f.}$ 2 K 19^{6} = Is 37^{6}, Jb 1$^{15.16.17}$ Ne 4$^{10.17}$+oft.—Zc 11^{16} is corrupt, cf. We Now.—*Note.* נער occurs in Pent. as Kt with Qr perpet. נַעֲרָה q.v.

5290 † נֹ֫עַר **n.m.** youth, early life (rare poet. synon. for נְעוּרִים);—abs. נ׳ Jb 33^{25} (=youthful vigour), 36^{14}, מִנּ׳ Pr 29^{21} ψ 88^{16} *from youth up.*

5291 † II. נַעֲרָה **n.f.** girl, damsel;—abs. נ׳ Ju 19^{3} + 22 t., also Qr Gn 24^{14} + 20 t. Gn Dt (נַעֲרָה Kt in Pent. only Dt 22^{19}, v. infr.); pl. abs. נְעָרוֹת 1 S 9^{11}+, cstr. נַעֲרוֹת Est 4^{4}; sf. נַעֲרֹתָיו Ru 2^{22} 3^{2}, נַעֲרֹתֶיהָ Gn 24^{61} Ex 2^{5}, etc.;—**1.** *girl, damsel;* נ׳ קְטַנָּה *little girl* only 2 K 5^{2}, cf. v^{4}, perh. = young daughters Jb 40^{29}; elsewh. = young woman 1 S 9^{11}; esp. as marriageable, Gn 24$^{14.16.28.55.57}$ 34$^{3.12}$ (all J), Dt 22$^{15.15.16.19.20.21.24.26.26.29}$ 1 K 1$^{3.4}$ Est 2$^{4.7.8.9.12.12.13}$; specif. virgin נ׳ בְתוּלָה Ju 21^{12} Dt 22$^{23.28}$ 1 K 1^{2} Est 2$^{2.3}$ (cf. Dt 22$^{15b.20}$); נ׳ מְאֹרָשָׂה *betrothed girl* Dt 22$^{25.27}$; young widow Ru 2^{6} 4^{12}; of a concubine Ju 19$^{3.4.5.6.8.9}$, a prostitute Am 2^{7}. **2.** of female attendants, *maids* (alw. pl.), Gn 24^{61} (J), Ex 2^{5} (E), 1 S 25^{42} Pr 9^{3} 27^{27} 31^{15} Est 2$^{9.9}$ 4$^{4.16}$; gleaners Ru 2$^{5.8.22.23}$ 3^{2}.—*Note.* נער Kt in Pent. as fem. (Qr נַעֲרָ֫) is prob. not original; it is not found in Sam. Pent., and fpl. נַעֲרֹתֶיהָ occurs Gn Ex; cf. Ges$^{§§2n, 17c}$.

5271 † נְעוּרִים **n.[m.] pl.** youth, early life;—abs. נ׳ Is 54^{6} ψ 127^{4}; elsewhere sf. נְעֻרַי 1 S 12^{2}, נְעוּרַי Jb 31^{18}+, נְעֻרֶיךָ 2 S 19^{8}, נְעוּרֶךָ Pr 5^{18}+, נְעוּרַיִךְ Je 2^{2}+, נְעוּרָיְכִי ψ 103^{5}, נְעוּרֵיהֶן Ez 23^{3}, etc.;—*youth, early life*, esp. in phr. מִנּ׳ *from one's youth up* Gn 8^{21} (J), 1 S 17^{33} 1 K 18^{12} Je 3^{24} Zc 13^{5} Jb 31^{18} (extreme youth; ‖ מִבֶּטֶן אִמִּי); fig. of Babylon Is 47$^{12.15}$, Moab Je 48^{11}, Judah 22^{21}, cf. ψ 71$^{5.17}$ 129$^{1.2}$; מִנּ׳ וְעַד־עַתָּה Gn 46^{34} (J), 2 S 19^{8} Ez 4^{14}; מִנּ׳ וְעַד־הַיּוֹם הַזֶּה 1 S 12^{2} Je 3^{25}; as time in or during which Lv 22^{13} (H), Nu 30$^{4.17}$ (P), La 3^{27} ψ 144^{12}, fig. of Judah and Sam., personif., Ez 23$^{2.8}$; cf. יְמֵי נ׳ (in fig. of Isr.) Ho 2^{17} (‖ יוֹם עֲלוֹתָהּ מֵאֶרֶץ מִצְרָיִם), Ez 16$^{22.43.60}$ 23^{19}; other phr. are: אַלּוּף נ׳ Je 3^{4} *friend of my youth,* cf. Pr 2^{17}, עֲוֹנוֹת נ׳ Jb 13^{26}, חַטֹּאות נ׳ ψ 25^{7}, חֶסֶד נ׳ Je 2^{2}, חֶרְפַּת נ׳ 31^{19}, זִמַּת נ׳ Ez 23^{21}, שְׁדֵי נ׳ v^{21}, בַּעַל נ׳ Jo 1^{8}, and esp. אֵשֶׁת נ׳ Pr 5^{18} Mal 2$^{14.15}$ Is 54^{6} (fig.); בְּנֵי נ׳ ψ 127^{4} sons of (a man's) *youth;* = *youthful vigour* ψ 103^{5}.

† [נְעֻרוֹת] **n.[f.] pl.** id.;—only מִנְּעֻרֹתֵיהֶם 5271
Je 32^{30} (fig. of nation).

† II. [נַעֲרָה] **n.pr.loc.** on border of Ephr.:— 5292
only c. ה loc., נַעֲרָ֫תָה Jos 16^{7} (𝔊 αἱ κῶμαι αὐτῶν; 𝔊L id. + Αναραθα); appar. = נַעֲרָן, q.v. infr.; Νοοραθ lay 5 Rom. miles fr. Jericho Lag$^{Onom. 283, 11}$ cf. Buhl$^{Geogr. 181}$.

† III. נַעֲרָה **n.pr.f.** in Judah 1 Ch 4$^{5.6.6}$; 5292
𝔊 Θοαδα, A Νοορα, 𝔊L Νοερα.

† נַעֲרַי **n.pr.m.** one of David's heroes, נ׳ 5293
בֶּן־אֶזְבָּי 1 Ch 11^{37}; 𝔊 Ναaραι, A Νοορα, 𝔊L Ναραι (= פַּעֲרַי הָאַרְבִּי 2 S 23^{35}).

† נְעַרְיָה **n.pr.m.** **1.** a descendant of David 5294
1 Ch 3$^{22.23}$, 𝔊 Νωαδεια, 𝔊L Νεαριου. **2.** a Simeonite 1 Ch 4^{42}; 𝔊 *id.*, 𝔊L Νααριας (cf. Sinait. n.pr. נערת Cook^{82}).

† נַעֲרָן **n.pr.loc.** in E of Ephr., 1 Ch 7^{28} 5295
(𝔊 Νααρναν, A Νααραν, 𝔊L Νοαραν), appar. = [נַעֲרָה] q.v.

נֹף v. מֹף. p. 592 5297

† נֶ֫פֶג **n.pr.m.** **1.** a Levite Ex 6^{21} (P), 𝔊 5298
Ναφεκ, F Ναφεγ. **2.** a son of David 2 S 5^{15} (𝔊 *id.*, 𝔊L Ναφεθ), 1 Ch 3^{7} (𝔊 Ναφαθ, A Ναφεγ, 𝔊L Νεεγ), 14^{6} (𝔊 *id.*, א Ναφατ, A Ναφαγ, 𝔊L Ναφεκ).

I, II. נָפָה v. I, II. נוף. p. 632 5299

נְפוּסִים, נפושסים v. נפיסים infr. 5300

† [נָפַח] **vb.** breathe, blow (כור נפוח Ecclus 5301
43^{4} *a furnace blown upon* (heated hot); NH נָפַח, *id.*, 𝔗 נְפַח, Syr. ܢܦܰܚ; As. *napâḫu, inflame, nappaḫu, smith* Dl$^{HWB 474}$; Ar. (نَفَحَ and) نَفَخَ *blow;* Eth. ነፍኀ: or ነፍሐ: Di^{712});—**Qal** *Pf.* 3 fs. נָפְחָה Je 15^{9}; וְנָפַ֫חְתִּי Hg 1^{9}; וְנָפַחְתִּי Ez 22^{21};

Impf. וַיִּפַּח Gn 2^{7}; *Imv.* fs. פְּחִי Ez 37^{9}; *Inf.* (לָ)פַחַת Ez 22^{20}; *Pt. act.* נֹפֵחַ Is 54^{16}; *pass.* נָפוּחַ Je 1^{13} Jb 41^{12};—*breathe, blow,* וַיִּפַּח בְּאַפָּיו נִשְׁמַת חַיִּים Gn 2^{7} (J); sq. ב also Ez 37^{9} Is 54^{16} and Hg 1^{9} *blow* into it (to scatter it); sq. עַל־: לָפַחַת עָלָיו אֵשׁ Ez 22^{20} *to blow fire upon it* (ore, for melting), so fig. Ez 22^{21} *and I will blow upon you with* (ב) *the fire of my wrath;* נ׳ נַפְשָׁהּ Je 15^{9} *she hath breathed out her life* (of a mother, cf. **Hiph.**); abs. סִיר נָפוּחַ Je 1^{13} *a blown* (i. e. well-heated, boiling) *pot,* cf. דּוּד נ׳ Jb 41^{12} (sim.). **Pu.** *Pf.* אֵשׁ לֹא נֻפָּח Jb 20^{26} *a fire not blown* (by any human breath). So perh. also Nu 21^{30} (reading עַד־נֻפַּח אֵשׁ וגו׳ *until fire was blown* [hot] as far as Medeba), cf. Di. **Hiph.** *Pf.* 1 s. נֶפֶשׁ בְּעָלֶיהָ הִפָּחְתִּי Jb 31^{39} (or if) *the life of its* (the land's) *owners I have caused them to breathe out;* וְהִפַּחְתֶּם אוֹתוֹ Mal 1^{13} *and ye have sniffed at it* (in contempt).

5302 נֹפַח appar. **n.pr.loc.** Nu 21^{30} (= נֹבַח ?) perhaps נֻפַּח (𝔊 προσεξέκαυσαν), v. נפח **Pu.**

4646 †[מַפָּח] **n.[m.]** breathing out;—only cstr. מַפַּח נֶפֶשׁ Jb 11^{20} *a breathing out of life* = expiring (cf. נפח Jb 31^{39} Je 15^{9}).

4647 †מַפֻּחַ **n.m.** bellows;—נָחַר מ׳ Je 6^{29} (fig. of vain prophetic labour).

8598 †I. תַּפּוּחַ **n.[m.] apple-tree, apple** (from aromatic *scent* (breath), Thes Lag$^{BN\ 111,\ 129}$ Post (v. infr.); Ar. تُفّاح is loan-wd. Frä^{140}; on meaning *apple* v. Löw$^{No.\ 109}$ RS$^{JPh\ xiii.\ 65\ f.}$ Post$^{Hast.\ Dict.\ Bib.\ 'Apple'}$)—**1.** sg. תַּפּוּחַ *apple-tree* Jo 1^{12} Ct 2^{3} 8^{5}. **2.** pl. תַּפּוּחִים *apples* Ct 2^{5}, רֵיחַ אַפֵּךְ כַּתּ׳ 7^{9}; תַּפּוּחֵי זָהָב Pr 25^{4} (in sim.).

8599 †II. תַּפֻּחַ **n.pr.m.** son of Hebron, acc. to 1 Ch 2^{43}; 𝔊 Θαπους, A Θαφφου, 𝔊L Φεθρουθ.

8599 †III. תַּפּוּחַ **n.pr.loc.** **1.** in lowland of Judah Jos 12^{17} (𝔊 Ταφουτ, A Θαφφου, 𝔊L Θαπφου), 15^{34} (𝔊 Ιλουλωθ, 𝔊L Θαφφουα). **2.** on border between Ephraim and Manasseh Jos 16^{8} (𝔊 Ταφου, 𝔊L Θαπφουε), $17^{8.8}$ (𝔊 Θαφεθ, A Θαφθωθ, 𝔊L Θαφωθ), = עֵין ת׳ v^{7} (𝔊 Θαφθωθ, 𝔊L Ναφθωθ); so read also perh. 2 K 15^{16} (for MT תִּפְסַח; 𝔊L Th Kmp^{Kau} Benz; 𝔊 Θερσα, A Θαιρα, but 𝔊L τὴν Ταφωε). On locality v. Buhl$^{Geogr.\ 178}$.—Vid. also בֵּית תַּפּוּחַ.

5300,5304 †נפיסים **n.pr.** Kt, in phr. בְּנֵי נ׳ Ezr 2^{50}, Qr נְפוּסִים, of family of returned exiles; 𝔊 Ναφεισων, A Νεφουσειμ, 𝔊L Νεφωσειμ; = נפושסים Ne 7^{52} Kt, Qr נְפִישְׁסִים, 𝔊 Νεφωσασει, etc., 𝔊L Νεφουσειμ;—Kt Ezr and Qr Ne, respectively, are prob. to be preferred (cf. נָפִישׁ sub נפשׁ), but Ne has mixture of two variants, נפישים, נפיסים.

נְפִישְׁסִים v. foregoing. 5300

†נֹפֶךְ **n.[m.]** a precious stone which Tyre gained by trade Ez 27^{16} (where נ׳ doubted by Berthol, queried by Toy^{Hpt}), cf. 28^{13} (symbol. of wealth and honour of king of Tyre); in high priest's breastplate Ex 28^{18} 39^{11}. Perh. = *ruby* or *carbuncle* 𝔊 Joseph. ἄνθραξ, 𝔙 *carbunculus*, cf. Di^{Ex} Kau^{Ex} Sgfr^{Ezek} Co Berthol; 𝔗 AV *emerald.* 5306

נָפַל$_{433}$ **vb. fall, lie** (NH = BH, 𝔗 נְפַל, Syr. ܢܦܰܠ; cf. also Ar. نَفَلَ *dedit praedam* (Nö$^{ZMG\ xl\ (1886),\ 725}$ Frä$^{153\ f.}$), Min. נפל *remove* Hom$^{Sudar.\ Chrest.\ 128}$);—**Qal** $_{366}$ *Pf.* נ׳ Ju 5^{27}+, 3 fs. נָפְלָה Gn 15^{12}+, etc.; *Impf.* יִפֹּל 1 S 14^{45}+, וַיִּפֹּל Ju 4^{16}+; 1 s. אֶפֹּל 1 Ch 21^{13} (needless change fr. 1 pl. נִפְּלָה ‖ 2 S 24^{14} We Dr); 3 mpl. יִפְּלוּ Ho 7^{16}+, יִפֹּלוּ Is 3^{25}+, 3 fpl. תִּפֹּלְנָה Ez 13^{11} 30^{25}, etc.; *Imv.* mpl. נִפְלוּ Ho 10^{8} Je 25^{27}; *Inf. abs.* נָפוֹל Est 6^{13}; *cstr.* נְפֹל Is 30^{25}+; לִנְפֹּל Je 51^{49}+; sf. נָפְלוֹ 1 S 29^{3}, נִפְלוֹ 2 S 1^{10}, נִפְלָם Je 49^{21} (on these forms cf. Ba$^{NB\ 104}$); *Pt.* נֹפֵל Ju 4^{22}+; f. נֹפֶלֶת Gn 15^{12}+; pl. נֹפְלִים Jos 8^{25}+ (ins. also 1 S 28^{19b} 𝔊 Th We Dr Kit Bu HPS; Klo כֹּרְעִים), etc.;—**1.** *fall,* by accident, וְנ׳־שָׁמָּה Ex 21^{33} (E) *and there fall into it* (a pit) an ox or an ass, cf. Dt 22^{4} (בַּדֶּרֶךְ, *on the way*), bird עַל־פַּח Am 3^{5}; subj. pers., 1 S 4^{18} (fr. seat, מֵעַל), Dt $22^{8.8}$ (fr. roof, מִן); oft. into (ב) pit (usu. fig.) Pr 26^{27} 28^{10}, also (abs.), 22^{14}, Ec 10^{8} ψ 7^{16} 57^{7} (בְּתוֹךְ), cf. 35^{8} 141^{10} (net), also, c. אֶל, Is 24^{18} = Je 48^{44}; fall בְּלֵב יַמִּים Ez 27^{27} (of Tyrian people); abs. 2 S 4^{4} Gn 14^{10} Je 25^{27}; opp. קוּם Je 8^{4} cf. Ec $4^{10.10}$; c. אָחוֹר *fall backward* Gn 49^{17} (poem); c. בְּעַד *through* 2 K 1^{2} cf. (of locusts) Jo 2^{8}; †נ׳ עַל־חֶרֶב causing death 1 S $31^{4.5}$ = 1 Ch $10^{4.5}$; †נ׳ עַל־פָּנָיו אַרְצָה 1 S 17^{49} (Goliath); subj. rei, 2 K $2^{13.14}$ (מֵעַל), 6^{5} (אֶל־ *into* water), v^{6} (abs.); c. עַל Lv $11^{32.35.37.38}$, אֶל־ v^{33}; abs. of tent Ju 7^{13} + v^{13} (gloss, GFM, Bu); of wall Jos 6^{5} (JE), Je 51^{44}, fig. Ez 13^{11} (del. 𝔊 𝔖 Sm Co Berthol), v$^{12.14}$, לָאָרֶץ Ez 38^{20}; +תַּחְתֶּיהָ i.e. *flat* Jos 6^{20}; נ׳ of bricks Is 9^{9} (in fig.), פֶּרֶץ 30^{13}, towers v^{25}, foundations Je 50^{15}; *wall fell upon* 5307

(על) 1 K 20^{30}, so of house Ju 16^{30} Jb 1^{19}, mts. Ho 10^{8}; mt. also abs. Jb 14^{18} (cf. נָבֵל), height Ez 38^{20}; tree Ec 11$^{3.3}$ (ב loc.), cf. Is 10^{34} (בְּ instr., in fig.), Zc 11^{2} (abs.); branches Ez 31^{12} (fig.); a grain Am 9^{9} (אֶרֶץ = *to earth*); of dew 2 S 17^{12} (c. עַל), hailstones Ez 13^{11}; blood (אַרְצָה) 1 S 26^{20}; †hair of head (ארצה) 1 S 14^{45} 2 S 14^{11} 1 K 1^{52}; horns of altar Am 3^{14} (לָאָרֶץ); peg Is 22^{25}; fruit עַל־פֶּה Na 3^{12}; crown La 5^{16}; arm from (מִן) shoulder Jb 31^{22}; of sword (appar.) 2 S 20^{8} (but on text v. Comm.); †fire from heaven, abs. 1 K 18^{38} c. מִן Jb 1^{16}†; †hand of י׳ Ez 8^{1} (c. עַל־; but rd. וַתְּהִי 𝔊 Co Berthol); spirit of י׳ Ez 11^{5} (עַל־); of lot (גּוֹרָל) Ez 24^{6} Jon 1^{7} (both c. עַל), 1 Ch 26^{14} (c. לְ; ‖ יָצָא), + Est 3^{7} 𝔊 Ry Wild (עַל); cf. **Hiph. 3**; hence (of share, inheritance) *fall*, be allotted, to (לְ) Ju 18^{1} (ב = *as*: בְּ **I 7 c**; so Nu 34^{2} Ez 47^{14}), ψ 16^{6}, abs. Jos 17^{5}.—On Ez 47$^{22\,b}$ v. **Hiph. 3**.

2. a. Esp. of violent death (c. 96 t.), Ju 5$^{27.27.27}$ (+ שָׁדוּד), 1 S 4^{10} 14^{13} 2 S 11^{17} 21^{9}, 1 K 22^{20} = 2 Ch 18^{9}, etc.; + וַיָּמֹת, etc., 2 S 1^{4} 2$^{23.23}$; נ׳ חָלָל *fall pierced* (fatally) Ju 9^{40} 1 S 17^{52} 31^{1} = 1 Ch 10^{1}+; חַלְלֵי חֶרֶב Ez 35^{8}; cf. בְּתוֹךְ חֲלָלִים 32^{20}; נ׳ תַּחַת הֲרוּגִים Is 10^{4}; נ׳ פְּגָרִים *corpses fall* Je 9^{21} Nu 14^{29} (P), v^{32} (JE); by the sword, בַּחֶרֶב Am 7^{17} Ho 7^{16} 14^{1} Is 3^{25} 2 S 1^{12} Ez 5^{12} 6^{11} Nu 14$^{3.43}$ (JE), (+ בַּדֶּבֶר, בָּרָעָב), etc.; נ׳ לְפִי חֶרֶב †Jos 8^{24} (JE), Ju 4^{16}†; בְּיַד *by the hand of* †2 S 21^{22} 24$^{14.14}$ = 1 Ch 21$^{13.13}$, 1 Ch 5^{10} 20^{8}†; נ׳ תַּחַת רגלי *fall under my feet* 2 S 22^{39} = ψ 18^{39}. **b.** fig. = go to ruin, perish, etc. (c. 30 t.); Am 5^{2} 8^{14}+; oft. ‖ כָּשַׁל Is 3^{8} 8^{15} (+ other words), 31^{3} Je 8^{12} 46^{12} 50^{32} ψ 27^{2} Pr 24^{17}; ‖ כָּרַע ψ 20^{9}; fig. of earth Is 24^{20} (opp. קום); Haman *falls* before (לִפְנֵי) Mordecai Est 6$^{13.13}$; cf. Is 14^{12} (abs.); peculiar to Pr are נ׳ בְּרִשְׁעָה Pr 11^{5}, בְּרַע 13^{17}, בְּרָעָה 17^{20} 28^{14}. **c.** fig. = experience calamity Mi 7^{8} (opp. קום), ψ 37^{34} 145^{14} Pr 24^{16}. **d.** *fall*, of a city Je 51^{8} (‖ וַתִּשָּׁבֵר).

3. a. *Fall prostrate*, Ju 19$^{26.27}$, + אַרְצָה Jb 1^{20}; *fall at full length* (in a faint) וַיִּפֹּל מְלֹא־קוֹמָתוֹ 1 S 28^{20}; *sink down* Nu 24$^{4.16}$ (JE; supernat. influence); of arms of Pharaoh Ez 30^{25} (opp. חָזַק). **b.** *fall* = *prostrate oneself before* (לִפְנֵי) man Gn 50^{18} (E), 2 S 19^{19} Gn 44^{14} (J; + אַרְצָה); before י׳ 2 Ch 20^{18}; נ׳ אֶל־פָּנָיו אַרְצָה before י׳ or his representative Jos 5^{14} 7^{6} (both JE); also (ארצה om.) Ez 43^{3} 44^{4}; before man 2 S 14^{22}; more oft. נ׳ עַל־פָּנָיו, before man 2 S 9^{6} 1 K 18$^{7.39}$ Ru 2^{10}, before י׳ Gn 17$^{3.17}$ + 6 t. P, Ez 3^{23} 9^{8} 11^{13} 1 Ch 21^{16} Dn 8^{17}; + אַפַּיִם, before man 2 S 14^{4}, before י׳ Ju 13^{20}; לְאַפָּיו אַרְצָה 1 S 20^{41}, לְאַפֵּי דָוִד עַל־פָּנֶיהָ 1 S 25^{23}, נ׳ ארצה 2 S 1^{2} (all before man); נ׳ עַל־רַגְלָיו *fall at* one's *feet* 1 S 25^{24} 2 K 4^{37}, לִפְנֵי ר׳ Est 8^{3}. Vid. syn. sub קדד. **c.** *fall upon* (עַל) one's neck, in embrace Gn 33^{4} 46^{29} (both J), 45^{14} (E), עַל־פְּנֵי אָבִיו 50^{1} (J).

4. a. *Fall upon* (עַל) = attack Je 48^{32} (fig.), cf. Is 16^{9}; c. בְּ Jos 11^{7} (D), abs. Jb 1^{15}; נ׳ אִישׁ אֶל־רֵעֵהוּ Je 46^{16}. **b.** †*desert* or *fall away to, go over to*, c. עַל־ 2 K 25$^{11.11}$ = Je 52$^{15.15}$, Je 21^{9} 37^{14} 39^{9} 1 Ch 12$^{20.21.21}$ (van d. H. v$^{19.20.20}$), 2 Ch 15^{9}, c. אֶל־ 2 K 7^{4} Je 37^{13} 38^{19}, abs. 1 S 29^{3} Je 39^{9}. **c.** נ׳ בְּיַד *fall into the hand* (power) *of* Ju 15^{18} La 1^{7}:—cf. also **2. a.** supr.

5. †Fig., of deep sleep, c. עַל Gn 15^{12} (J), 1 S 26^{12} Jb 4^{13} 33^{15}; face, countenance (in displeasure) Gn 4$^{5.6}$ (J); נ׳ לֵב אָדָם עָלָיו 1 S 17^{32} (of *sinking* heart); וַיִּפְּלוּ בְעֵינֵיהֶם Ne 6^{16} *and they were cast down in their* (*own*) *eyes* (cf. Be-Ry, Ryle); †of calamity sq. עַל־ Is 47^{11} Ec 9^{12}; terror, etc., sq. עַל־ Gn 15^{12} (J), Jos 2^{9} (JE), Ex 15^{16} (song), 1 S 11^{7} Jb 13^{11} ψ 55^{5} 105^{38} Est 8^{17} 9$^{2.3}$ Dn 10^{7}; reproach, sq. עַל־ ψ 69^{10}; † = *fail* to be accomplished Jos 21^{43} 23$^{14.14}$ (all D), 1 K 8^{56} 2 K 10^{10} (+ אַרְצָה); = not to be reckoned Nu 6^{12} (P); †of word (דָּבָר) *falling* into (ב) Isr. Is 9^{7}; † = *fall out, turn out, result* Ru 3^{18} (subj. דָּבָר).

6. Other idiomatic uses are: נ׳ לְמִשְׁכָּב *take to one's bed* Ex 21^{18} (E); *settle* Gn 25^{18} (J); = *alight quickly*, מֵעַל הַגָּמָל Gn 24^{64} (J), מֵעַל הַמֶּרְכָּבָה 2 K 5^{21}; *waste away* Nu 5$^{21.22.27}$; = *be born* Is 26^{18} (cf. **Hiph.** v^{19}); = *be offered*, of supplication (לִפְנֵי י׳) Je 36^{7} 37^{20} 42^{2} (cf. **Hiph. 6**); c. מִן = *be inferior to* Jb 12^{3} 13^{2}.

†**7.** = *lie*, of Midianites, etc. (like locusts; ב loc.) Ju 7^{12}; = *lie prostrate*, 1 S 19^{24}; usu. pt. Jos 7^{10} (JE; עַל־פָּנֶיךָ), 1 S 5$^{3.4}$ (לְפָנָיו), Am 9^{11}, עַל־הַמִּטָּה Est 7^{8}; of the dead 1 S 31^{8} = 1 Ch 10^{8} Dt 21^{1} Ez 32^{27} (Co conj. נְפִילִים [cf. Gn 6^{4}], v. also Berthol Toy^{Hpt}); נֹפֵל אַרְצָה מֵת Ju 3^{25} cf. 4^{22} (om. ארצה); פְּגָרִים נ׳ אַרְצָה 2 Ch 20^{24}; cf. also Ez 32$^{22.23.24}$ (del. in v^{22} Hi Co Berthol, in v^{23} Toy^{Hpt}).

Hiph. *Pf.* הִפִּיל 1 S 3^{19}+; 2 ms. sf. הִפַּלְתָּם ψ 73^{18}; 3 pl. הִפִּילוּ Ju 2^{19}+; 1 pl. הִפַּלְנוּ Ne 10^{35}, etc.; *Impf.* יַפִּיל Ex 21^{27}, וַיַּפֵּל Gn 2^{21}+, sf. יַפִּלֵם

ψ 140[11]; 3 mpl. יַפִּילוּ 2 K 3[25] ψ 22[19], יַפִּלֻן Jb 29[24], etc.; *Imv.* ms. sf. הַפִּלֶהָ Jos 13[6]; mpl. הַפִּילוּ 1 S 14[42]; *Inf. cstr.* לְהַפִּיל 1 S 18[25]+; לַנְפֵּל Nu 5[22] rd. לִנְפֹּל (Di Ol[§ 78 c] Sta[§ 114 a, 2] Kö[i. 309] Ges[§ 66, 2 R 1]); *Pt.* מַפִּיל 2 K 6[5]+2 t., pl. מַפִּילִים Dn 9[18]; —**1.** *cause to fall*, c. acc., lit.: **a.** *fell* tree 2 K 3[19.25] cf. 6[5]. **b.** *throw down* wall 2 S 20[15]. **c.** *knock out* tooth Ex 21[27] (E). **d.** *lay prostrate* Dn 25[2] (for bastinado). **e.** *cast* (cedar pillars) into (עַל־) fire Je 22[7]; so (c. בּ), wicked men ψ 140[11]. **f.** *make* sword *drop* from (מִן) hand Ez 30[22] (fig.), cf. 39[3]. **g.** *cause* stone *to fall* עַל Nu 35[23], flesh ψ 78[28] (בְּקֶרֶב), stars Dn 8[10] (in vision).

2. Of causing death בַּחֶרֶב 2 K 19[7]=Is 37[7], Je 19[7] Ez 32[12] (all י׳ subj.), 2 Ch 32[21] (human subj.); בְּיַד 1 S 18[25]; + חֲלָלִים Ez 6[4] Pr 7[26]; also ψ 106[26] Dn 11[12]=*overthrow*, bring to destruction, ψ 37[14] 73[18] (c. לְ), 106[27].

3. Esp. of *casting* lot (גּוֹרָל), Is 34[17] (c. לְ *for*), Ne 10[35] (c. עַל+inf.), 11[1] (c. inf.), 1 Ch 26[14] (c. לְ; so rd. Kit[Hpt] cf. 𝔊𝔙 Be Öt), ψ 22[19] (c. עַל), Est 9[24] (c. inf.); abs. Jon 1[7.7] 1 Ch 24[31] 25[8] 26[13] Est 3[7]; + בְּתוֹכֵנוּ Pr 1[14] (i.e. share with us); om. גּוֹרָל 1 S 14[42] (c. בֵּין), Jb 6[27] (c. עַל); hence הִפּ׳ = *assign, apportion, by lot*, usu. c. לְ pers., Jos 13[6] 23[4] (both D), Ez 45[1] 47[22 a]+v[22 b] (rd. יַפִּילוּ 𝔙 𝔗 Hi-Sm Co Berthol), 48[29] (read בְּנַחֲלָה for מִנּ׳, 𝔊 𝔙 Hi-Sm, etc.), ψ 78[55] (cf. **Qal 1** end; and בְּ **I 7 c**).

4. Fig., *let drop, cause to fail* (cf **Qal 5**), Ju 2[19] Est 6[10], + אַ֫רְצָה 1 S 3[19].

5. *Cause* deep sleep *to fall* (עַל־) Gn 2[21] (J), Pr 19[15] (abs.), *make* countenance *fall*, look displeased at (בּ), Je 3[12], cf. Jb 29[24] (obj. אוֹר פָּנַי); *cause* terror, etc., *to fall* (עַל־) Je 15[8].

6. Other idioms are: *bring to life* (prop. *drop* young) Is 26[19] (fig.); *present* supplication Je 38[26] 42[9] Dn 9[18.20] (all c. לִפְנֵי);—on both cf. **Qal 6.**

Hithp. *throw*, or *prostrate oneself*, **1.** *Inf. cstr.* הִתְנַפֵּל *throw himself upon* (עַל) Gn 43[18] (J; i.e. attack). **2.** *Pf.* 1 s. הִתְנַפָּ֫לְתִּי Dt 9[25]; *Impf.* 1 s. וָאֶתְנַפַּל Dt 9[18.25]; *Pt.* מִתְנַפֵּל Ezr 10[1]; —*prostrate oneself* and *lie prostrate*, לִפְנֵי י׳.— **Pil'el.** וְנִפְלַל Ez 28[23], rd. וְנָפַל Hi-Sm Co Berthol.

5309 †נֵ֫פֶל **n.m.**[Jb 3, 16] **untimely birth, abortion**;— נֵ֫פֶל abs. Jb 3[16] (Baer, Ginsb., > van d. H. נֶפֶל), נָ֑פֶל Ec 6[3]; cstr. נֵפֶל אֵשֶׁת ψ 58[9].

†[מַפָּל] **n.m.**[Jb 41, 15] **refuse, hanging parts**; 4651
—**1.** *fallings, refuse*, cstr. מַפַּל בַּר Am 8[6] *the refuse* of wheat. **2.** pl. cstr. מַפְּלֵי בְשָׂרוֹ Jb 41[15] *the hanging* (falling, drooping) *parts of his flesh* (of crocodile).

†מַפָּלָה **n.f. a ruin**;—abs. מ׳ of city Is 17[1]. 4654

†מַפֵּלָה **n.f. id.**;—abs. מ׳ of city Is 23[13] 25[2]. 4654

†מַפֶּ֫לֶת **n.f. carcass, ruin, overthrow**;— 4658
1. *carcass*, of lion, מ׳ cstr. Ju 14[8]. **2.** elsewh. sf. **a.** *a ruin*, מַפַּלְתּוֹ Ez 31[13] (kg. under fig. of tree). **b.** *overthrow, id.* v[16] (same fig.); מַפַּלְתֶּ֑ךָ (kg.) 32[10]; מַפַּלְתֵּךְ (of Tyre) 26[15.18] 27[27]; מַפַּלְתָּם (of wicked) Pr 29[16].

†נְפִלִים **n.m.pl. giants**, acc. to 𝔊 γίγαντες, 5303
so 𝔖𝔙; הַנְּפִלִים Gn 6[4] (J), הַנְּפִילִים בְּנֵי עֲנָק מִן־הַנְּפִלִים Nu 13[33] (JE); 𝔊 om. בְּנֵי וגו׳, and so Di; these words perhaps doublet, but already in Sam., also 𝔙 (etym. dub.; cf. Aram. נִיפְלָא, נִפְלָא *Orion;* conject. v. in Thes Di[ad loc.]; Tuch Kn Len[Or. i. 344, Eng. Tr. 345 f.]; Che[Hbr. iii (1887), 175, 176]; all very precarious).

†I. [נָפַץ] **vb. shatter** (NH *id., dash,* 5310
beat; As. *napâṣu, shatter, destroy* Dl[HWB 475]; 𝔗 נְפַע Pa. *shatter*, but also נְפַץ Pa., *id.*, Syr. ܢܦܨ *shake, break*, so Mand., Nö[M. 240, and ZMG xxxii (1878), 406]); —**Qal** *Inf. abs.* וְנָפוֹץ c. acc. Ju 7[19] *and a shattering* (=*and shattered*) the jars; *Pt. pass.* עֶצֶב נִבְזֶה נָפוּץ Je 22[28] (fig.) *a vessel to be despised* (*and*) *shattered* (cf. Ew Gie Rothstein[Kau]); also *Pt. act.* נֹפֵץ *shatterer* of the holy people Dn 12[7] (Bev Marti[Kau], rdg. כְּכַלּוֹת יַד נֹפֵץ). **Pi.** *dash to pieces: Pf.* 3 ms. וְנִפֵּץ consec. ψ 137[9] c. acc. infants ag. (אֶל) rock; 1 s. וְנִפַּצְתִּי of י׳ dashing all in pieces with (בּ) Babyl. as war-club Je 51[20.21.21.22.22.22.23.23.23]; sf. וְנִפַּצְתִּים אִישׁ אֶל־אָחִיו 13[14]; *Impf.* 2 ms. sf. כִּכְלִי יוֹצֵר תְּנַפְּצֵם ψ 2[9] (i.e. nations); 3 mpl. נִבְלֵיהֶם יְנַפֵּ֑צוּ Je 48[12] (symbol. of destroying Moab); *Inf.* נַפֵּץ יַד־עַם־קֹדֶשׁ Dn 12[7] *when* (*they*) *finish shattering the hand* (fig. for *power*) *of the holy people*, but rd. poss. נֹפֵץ, v. **Qal.** **Pu.** *Pt.* fpl. מְנֻפָּצוֹת Is 27[9] like chalk-stones *pulverized.*

†נֶ֫פֶץ **n.[m.] driving storm** (lit. *bursting* 5311
of clouds, Che[Comm.]), נ׳ וָזֶרֶם וְאֶבֶן בָּרָד Is 30[30] (theoph.).

†[מַפָּץ] **n.[m.] shattering**;—כְּלִי מַפָּצוֹ Ez 4660
9[2] with *his shattering-weapon* in his hand.

4661 †מַפֵּץ **n.m. war-club** (lit. *a shatterer*);—מַפֵּץ־אַתָּה לִי Je 51^{20} *a war-club art thou to me* (′י addressing Babylon, cf. Gf Gie).

5310 †II. **נָפַץ vb. disperse, be scattered** (oft. taken as secondary √fr. Niph. of פוץ, yet cf. NH נפץ, Qal (Pt.), Pi., *scatter;* Syr. ܢܦܨ *pour out, throw down,* 𝔗 נְפַץ; Ar. نَفَضَ *shake* (irreg. correspondence of sibilants cf. Nö$^{l.c.}$), Eth. ነፍጸ: *dissipari, aufugere* Di^{713});—**Qal** *Pf.* 3 ms. נ׳ הָעָם מֵעָלָי 1 S 13^{11} *the people were scattered from me;* 3 fs. נָפְצָה כָל־הָאָרֶץ Gn 9^{19} (J) thence *dispersed all* (the population of) *the earth;* 3 pl. נָפְצוּ גּוֹיִם Is 33^{3} *nations were scattered; Pt. pass.* fpl. cstr. נְפֻצוֹת יְהוּדָה Is 11^{12} *the dispersed of Judah* he shall collect (‖ נִדְחֵי יִשְׂרָאֵל).

נפשׁ (√of foll.; cf. Ar. نَفْسٌ *soul, life, person, living being, blood, desire,* نَفَسٌ *breath, sweet odour,* نَفُسَ *be high in estimation, become avaricious;* III. *desire a thing, aspire to it,* V. *breathe, sigh.* As. *napâšu, get breath, be broad, extended; napištu, life,* less frequently *soul, living being, person.* Vbs. appar. denom.; nouns in all Semitic languages: Ph. נפשׁ, CIS $^{1.86\ B\ 5}$, Eth. ነፍስ:; in the foll. = both *soul, person,* and *tombstone, monument* (as representing person, v. esp. Duval $^{Rev.\ Sémit.\ ii\ (1894),\ 259\ ff.}$): NH נפשׁ v. Levy $^{ZMG\ xii\ (1858),\ 215}$; O Aram. נפשׁ, Nab. Palm. נפשׁ, v. Lzb^{325} Cook^{82}; Syr. ܢܦܫܐ, v. 1 Macc 13$^{27.28}$; Sab. נפס Levy-Os $^{ZMG\ xix\ (1865),\ 255.290}$ Mordtm $^{ib.\ xxxii\ (1878),\ 202}$ cf. Lihyan., DHM $^{Epigr.\ Denkm.\ 67}$, Min. Hom $^{Südarab.\ Chrest.\ 128}$).

5315 נֶ֫פֶשׁ$_{756}$ **n.f.**$^{Gn\ 49,6}$ (so even Gn 2^{19} Nu 31^{28} 1 K 19^{2} v. Albrecht$^{ZAW\ xvi\ (1896),42}$ SS) **soul, living being, life, self, person, desire, appetite, emotion,** and **passion** (Ecclus 3^{18} 4$^{1.1.2.2}$ 13^{12} 14^{11});—נ׳ Gn 1^{20}+; נָ֑פֶשׁ Gn 37^{21}+; sf. נַפְשִׁי Gn 12^{13}+; pl. נְפָשׁוֹת Ez 13^{18}+13 t.; נְפָשֹׁת Ex 12^{4} Lv 27^{2}; *cstr.* נַפְשׁוֹת Gn 36^{6}+4 t.; נַפְשֹׁת Lv 21^{11}; נְפָשִׁים Ez 13^{20} (but rd. חָפְשִׁים, v. Co Berthol Toy); sf. נַפְשֹׁתָם Nu 17^{3}+; נַפְשׁוֹתָם 2 S 23^{17}+:—

1. = *that which breathes, the breathing substance or being* = ψυχή, anima, *the soul, the inner being of man:* **a.** disting. fr. בָּשָׂר: מִנֶּ֫פֶשׁ וְעַד בָּשָׂר Is 10^{18}; הַנֶּפֶשׁ עִם הַבָּשָׂר Dt 12^{23}; fr. שְׁאֵר Pr 11^{17}; fr. בֶּ֫טֶן *body* ψ 31^{10}. **b.** both the inner נפשׁ and the outer בשׂר are conceived as resting on a common substratum: אַךְ בְּשָׂרוֹ עָלָיו יִכְאָב וְנַפְשׁוֹ עָלָיו תֶּאֱבָל׃ Jb 14^{22} *only his flesh upon him is in pain, and his soul upon him mourneth;* cf. ψ 42$^{5.7}$ 131^{2} Jb 30^{16} La 3^{20} [v. עַל **1 d**], all poetical (cf. **6 c**). **c.** נ׳ departs at death and returns with life: וַיְהִי בְּצֵאת נַפְשָׁהּ כִּי מֵתָה Gn 35^{18} (E) *and it came to pass when her soul was going forth* (*for she died*); נָפְחָה נַפְשָׁהּ Je 15^{9} *she breathed out her soul,* cf. 1 K 17$^{21.22}$ Jb 11^{20} 31^{39}. **d.** oft. desired that the נפשׁ may be delivered: fr. She'ôl ψ 16^{10} 30^{4} 49^{16} 86^{13} 89^{49} Pr 23^{14}; fr. שַׁחַת, the pit of She'ôl, Is 38^{17} Jb 33$^{18.22.28.30}$.

2. The נפשׁ becomes a living being: by God's breathing נשׁמת חיים into the nostrils of its בשׂר; of man Gn 2^{7} (J); by implication of animals also Gn 2^{19} (J); so ψ 104$^{29.30}$ cf. 66^{9}; man is נֶ֫פֶשׁ חַיָּה, a living, breathing being Gn 2^{7} (J); elsewh. נפשׁ חיה alw. of animals Gn 1$^{20.24.30}$ 9$^{12.15.16}$ (all P), Ez 47^{9}; so נפשׁ החיה Gn 1^{21} 9^{10} (both P), Lv 11$^{10.46}$ (H); נפשׁ השׁרצת Lv 11^{46} (H); נפשׁ כל חי Jb 12^{10}. נפשׁ is frequently used with the verb חיה: †וחיתה נפשׁי Gn 12^{13} 19^{20} (both J), 1 K 20^{32} (E), ψ 119^{175} Je 38$^{17.20}$; †חֵי נַפְשְׁךָ 1 S 1^{26} 17^{55} 20^{3} 25^{26} 2 S 11^{11} 14^{19} 2 K 2$^{2.4.6}$ 4^{30} (all JE); cf. †יְחִיֶה נ׳ 1 K 20^{31} (E), Ez 18^{27} ψ 22^{30}; also Gn 19^{19} Is 55^{3} Pr 3^{22}.

3. The נפשׁ (without חיה noun or verb) is specif.: **a.** a living being whose life resides in the blood [so in Arab. We$^{Skizzen\ iii.\ 217}$ G. Jacob $^{Arab.\ Dicht.\ iv.\ 9\ f.}$] (hence sacrificial use of blood, and its prohib. in other uses; first in D), Dt 12$^{23.24}$ *only be sure that thou eat not the blood, for the blood is the living being* (הַדָּם הוּא הַנָּ֑פֶשׁ); *and thou shalt not eat the living being with the flesh* (הַנֶּ֫פֶשׁ עִם הַבָּשָׂר); *thou shalt pour it upon the earth as water;* this is enlarged in H, Lv 17$^{10.11.12.14}$ and in P Gn 9$^{4.5}$, cf. Je 2^{34}. **b.** a serious attack upon the life is an attack upon this inner living being 2 S 1^{9} Je 4^{10} Jon 2^{6} ψ 69^{2} 124$^{4.5}$ Jb 27^{3}. **c.** נפשׁ is used for life itself 171 t., of animals Pr 12^{10}, and of man Gn 44^{30} (J); נפשׁ תחת נפשׁ *life for life* Ex 21^{23} (E), Lv 24^{18} (H), 1 K 20$^{39.42}$ 2 K 10^{24}; נפשׁנו תחתיכם Jos 2^{14} (J); נפשׁ בנפשׁ Dt 19^{21}; בנפשׁ *for the life of* 2 S 14^{7} Jon 1^{14}; שׂם נפשׁ בכף *put life in one's own hand* Ju 12^{3} 1 S 19^{5} 28^{21} Jb 13^{14}; חרף נפשׁו למות Ju 5^{18} *risked his life to die;* †בנפשׁ *at the risk of life* Nu 17^{3} (P), 2 S 23^{17} = 1 Ch 11$^{19.19}$, 1 K 2^{23} Pr 7^{23} La 5^{9}; †בקשׁ נפשׁ Ex 4^{19} (J), 1 S 20^{1} 22$^{23.23}$ 23^{15} 25^{29} 2 S 4^{8} 16^{11} 1 K 19$^{10.14}$ Je 4^{30} 11^{21} 19$^{7.9}$ 21^{7} 22^{25} 34$^{20.21}$ 38^{16} 44$^{30.30}$ 46^{26} 49^{37} ψ 35^{4} 38^{13} 40^{15} 54^{5} 63^{10} 70^{3} 86^{14} Pr 29^{10}; †שׁאל נ׳ 1 K 3^{11} = 2 Ch 1^{11}, 1 K 19^{4} = Jon 4^{8}; †הִכָּה נפשׁ *smite mortally* Gn 37^{21} (J), Dt 19$^{6.11}$ Je 40$^{14.15}$; †לקח נ׳ 1 K 19^{4} Jon 4^{3} ψ 31^{14} Pr 1^{19}; †הִצִּיל

נֶפֶשׁ מִמָּוֶת *deliver life from death* Jos 2[13] ψ 33[19] 56[14]; †מלט נפשׁ 1 S 19[11] 2 S 19[6.6.6.6] 1 K 1[12.12] Je 48[6] 51[6.45] Ez 33[5] Am 2[14.15] ψ 89[49] 116[4]; †פדה נ׳ 2 S 4[9] 1 K 1[29] ψ 34[23] 49[16] 55[19] 71[23]; †שׁמר נ׳ ψ 25[20] 97[10] Jb 2[6] Pr 13[3] 16[17] 19[16] 22[5].

4. The נפשׁ as the essential of man stands for *the man himself:* **a.** paraphrase for pers. pron. esp. in poetry and ornate discourse, 70 t.; (1) נַפְשִׁי = *me:* אל תבא נפשׁי Gn 49[6] *let me not enter* (poem in J); תָּמֹת נ׳ מות ישׁרים Nu 23[10] *let me die,* etc. (poem); תָּמוֹת נַפְשִׁי Ju 16[30] (J); אמרה נפשׁי La 3[24] *I say.* (2) נַפְשְׁךָ = *thee:* לְאֻמִּים תַּחַת נַפְשֶׁךָ Is 43[4] *peoples instead of thee;* אִמְרוּ לְנַפְשֵׁךְ 51[23]. (3) נַפְשׁוֹ = *he:* נפשׁו בטוב תלין ψ 25[13] *he will not dwell in good circumstances.* (4) נַפְשֵׁנוּ = *we:* נַפְשֵׁנוּ כְּצִפּוֹר נִמְלְטָה מִפַּח יוֹקְשִׁים ψ 124[7]. (5) נַפְשָׁם = *they, them:* נַפְשָׁם בַּשְּׁבִי הָלָכָה Is 46[2] *they are gone into captivity;* אוי לנפשׁם Is 3[9]. **b.** = reflexive, *self,* 53 t.: אסר על נפשׁ *bind oneself* Nu 30[3.5.5.6.7.8.9.10.11.12]; לְעַנֹּת נ׳ Nu 30[14] *to afflict oneself.* (1) נַפְשִׁי = *myself:* לא אדע נפשׁי Jb 9[21] *I know not myself.* (2) נַפְשְׁךָ = *thyself:* שׁמר נ׳ Dt 4[9] *keep thyself.* (3) נַפְשׁוֹ = *himself:* אהב כנ׳ 1 S 18[1.3] 20[17] *loved as himself.* (4) נַפְשָׁהּ = *herself:* צדקה נ׳ Je 3[11] *justified herself.* (5) נַפְשָׁם = *themselves:* הציל נ׳ *deliver themselves* Is 47[14] Ez 14[14.20]. (6) נַפְשֹׁתֵיכֶם, נַפְשְׁכֶם = *yourselves:* אַל־תַּשִּׁאוּ נ׳ Je 37[9] *deceive not yourselves,* also 42[20] 44[7]; ענה נ׳ Lv 16[29.31] 23[27.32] Nu 29[7] (P); נשׁמרתם לנ׳ Dt 4[15] Jos 23[11] (D). (7) נַפְשׁוֹתֵינוּ = *ourselves:* על נ׳ Je 26[19] *against ourselves.* **c.** = *person* of man, individual, 144 t., first in D[2]; esp. in H, P, and kindred writers: (1) c. אָדָם: נ׳ אדם Lv 24[17] opp. נ׳ בהמה 24[18] (both H), and so נ׳ אדם *human persons* Nu 31[35.40.46] (P) 1 Ch 5[21] Ez 27[13]. Elsewhere without אדם: נ׳ ברכה Pr 11[25] *one who blesses;* נ׳ רְמִיָּה Pr 19[15] *idle person;* נ׳ תחת נ׳ *person in place of person,* Jb 16[4]; כפר על נ׳ Ex 30[15.16] Nu 15[28] 31[50] (all P) Lv 17[11] (H). †(2) נפשׁ = *person, any one:* Dt 24[7] 27[25] Pr 28[17] Ez 18[4.4.4] 33[6]; elsewhere only H P: Lv 2[1] 4[2.27] 5[1.2.4.15.17.21] 7[18.20.21.25.27] 23[29.30.30] Nu 5[6] 15[27.30] 19[22] 31[19.28] 35[11.15.30.30] Jos 20[3.9] (all P), Lv 17[10.12.15] 20[6.6] 22[6.11] (all H); נכרתה הנ׳ הַהִוא מן *that person shall be cut off from:* only in Gn 17[14] Ex 12[15.19] 31[14] Lv 7[20.21.27] Nu 9[13] 15[30.31] 19[13.20] (all P), Lv 19[8] 22[3] (both H). †(3) נפשׁ coll. for *persons,* in enumerations: Dt 10[22] Jos 10[28.30.32.35.37.37.39] 11[11] (all D[2]) Je 43[6] 52[29.30.30] Ez 22[25]; elsewhere only Gn 12[5] 46[15.18.22.25.26.26.27.27] Ex 1[5.5] 12[16] Nu 31[35.40] (all P). †(4) נְפָשׁוֹת *persons* Gn 36[6] Ex 12[4] 16[16] Nu 19[18] (all P), Lv 18[29] 20[25] 27[2] (all H), 2 K 12[5] Pr 11[30] 14[25] Ez 13[18.18.18.19.19.20.20] 17[17] 18[4] 22[27] (נפשׁים 13[20] v. supr.). †(5) נפשׁ = *deceased person,* sts. c. מֵת, נֶפֶשׁ מֵת Nu 6[6] (P), נַפְשֹׁת מֵת (נֶפֶשׁ 𝔖 𝔊) Lv 21[11] (H); usu. without מֵת, נפשׁ (ה)אדם Nu 9[6.7] 19[11.13] (P); or simply נפשׁ, Lv 19[28] 21[1] 22[4] (all H) Nu 5[2] 6[11] 9[10] (all P); elsewhere only Hag 2[13].

5. נפשׁ = *seat of the appetites,* in all periods (46 t.)—**a.** hunger: נ׳ רְעֵבָה *hungry soul* ψ 107[9] Pr 27[7]; with noun or verb of שׂבע *satisfy* Is 56[11] 58[10] Je 50[19] Ez 7[19] ψ 63[6] 107[9] Pr 13[25] 27[7]; מתוק לנ׳ Pr 16[24] *sweet to the taste.* **b.** thirst: נ׳ עֲיֵפָה *weary soul* Pr 25[25] Je 31[25]; כארץ עיפה נ׳ ψ 143[6]; צמאה נ׳ ψ 42[3] 63[2]. **c.** appetite in general: אֹיְבַי בנ׳ יַקִּיפוּ עָלָיו ψ 17[9] *my enemies compass me about with greed;* הִרְחִיבָה שְׁאוֹל נַפְשָׁהּ וּפָעֲרָה פִיהָ Is 5[14] *She'ôl enlarged her appetite,* etc., cf. Hb 2[5]; בַּעַל נֶפֶשׁ Pr 23[2]; Ec uses נפשׁ only in the sense of **a, b, c**; the נפשׁ craves, lacks, and is filled with good things: Ec 2[24] 4[8] 6[2.3.7.9] 7[28].

6. נ׳ = *seat of emotions and passions* (151 t.)—**a.** desire: †אִוְּתָה נ׳ *soul desires* Dt 12[20] 14[26] 1 S 2[16] 2 S 3[21] 1 K 11[37] Jb 23[13] Pr 13[4] 21[10] Mi 7[1]; תַּאֲוַת נ׳ ψ 10[3] Is 26[8]; †אַוַּת נ׳ Dt 12[15.20.21] 18[6] 1 S 23[20] Je 2[24]; so also לנפשׁ *according to one's desire* Dt 21[14] ψ 78[18] Je 34[16]; כנפשׁ Dt 23[25]; האח נפשׁנו *ah, our desire* ψ 35[25]; בנפשׁ *at one's desire* ψ 105[22] Ez 16[27]; נ׳ יָצְאָה בְדַבְּרוֹ Ct 5[6]; †נשׂא נ׳ *lift up the soul, desire* Dt 24[15] 2 S 14[14] (rd. אליהם, not אלהים), ψ 24[4] 25[1] 86[4] 143[8] Pr 19[8] Je 22[27] 44[14] Ho 4[8]. †**b.** abhorrence, loathing: נעלה נ׳ *soul abhorreth* Lv 26[11.15.30.43] (H) Je 14[19]; וגם נ׳ בחלה בי Zc 11[8] *and their soul also fell a loathing against me.* **c.** sorrow and distress: †מרי נ׳ *bitter, gloomy, discontented of soul* Ju 18[25] (E) 2 S 17[8] Jb 3[20] Pr 31[6]; †מר נ׳ 1 S 22[2] cf. Jb 7[11] 10[1] Is 38[15] Ez 27[31]; עָגְמָה נ׳ Jb 30[25] *grieved;* אנמי נ׳ *sad of soul* Is 19[10]; תבכה נ׳ *my soul shall weep* Je 13[17]; נ׳ ירעה *his soul trembleth* Is 15[4]; צרת נ׳ *distress of soul* Gn 42[21] (E). †**d.** joy: נ׳ תגיל *my soul rejoiceth* ψ 35[9] Is 61[10]; שׂמח נ׳ *rejoice the soul* ψ 86[4]; also ψ 94[19] 138[3] Pr 29[17]. †**e.** love: אהבה נ׳ *my soul loveth* Ct 1[7] 3[1.2.3.4]; יְדִדוּת נ׳ *darling of my soul* Je 12[7]; דבקה נ׳ ב׳ *his soul clave unto* Gn 34[3] (J), c. אחרי ψ 63[9]; חשׁקה נ׳ ב׳ *soul is attached to* Gn 34[8] (P). **f.** alienation, hatred, revenge: †תֵּקַע נ׳ מן *the soul is* *alienated from* Je 6[8] Ez 23[17.18]; נקעה נ׳ מן Ez 23[18.22.28]; שׂנאה נ׳ שְׂנֻאֵי נ׳ *hated of soul* 2 S 5[8] (Qr); ψ 11[5] Is 1[14]. **g.** other emotions and feelings: השׁיב נ׳ *bring back soul* La 1[11.19] (*i.e.* revive, cf. c. שׁוּב 1 K 17[21 f.]), hence fig. *refresh, cheer,* v[16] ψ 19[8] Pr 25[13] Ru 4[15]; שׁובב נ׳ ψ 23[3]; מַחְמַל נ׳ *your souls' compassion* Ez 24[21]; קצרה נ׳ *soul was impatient* Nu 21[4] (E), Ju 10[16] 16[16] Zc 11[8]; כי אאריך נ׳ *that I should prolong my patience* Jb 6[11]; ידעתם את־נ׳ הגר *ye know the feeling of the stranger* Ex 23[9] (R[D]).

7. נפשׁ is used occasionally for mental acts + לבב (see **10**); poss. also alone, owing to unconscious assimilation by late writers; but most, if not all, exx. may be otherwise explained: נפשׁי ידעת מאד ψ 139[14] *my soul knoweth well* (or *I know well;* cf. **4 a**); בלא דעת נ׳ לא טוב Pr 19[2] *that the soul be without knowledge is not good* (but RV[m] *desire without knowledge,* cf. **6 a**); דעה חכמה לנ׳ Pr 24[14] *know wisdom for thy soul* (or *according to thy desire,* cf. **6 a**); אל תדמי בנ׳ Est 4[13] *think not in thy soul* (or *in thyself,* cf. **4 b**); כמו שׁער בנ׳ Pr 23[7] *as he reckoneth in his soul* (but RV *in himself,* cf. **4 b**); מה תאמר נ׳ 1 S 20[4] (but AV RV foll. 𝔊 ἐπιθυμεῖ = תְּאַוֶּה; v. **6 a**).

8. נפשׁ for acts of the will is dub.: אם ישׁ (את) נפשׁכם *if it is your purpose* Gn 23[8] (P) 2 K 9[15] (or *if it is your desire,* **6 a**); בחרה נ׳ *my soul chooseth* Jb 7[15]; מאנה נ׳ *my soul refuseth* Jb 6[7] ψ 77[3]; נ׳ חפצה *their soul delighteth in* Is 66[3]; נ׳ רצתה *my soul delighteth in* Is 42[1]; (all perhaps emotional, **6 b, d, g**).

9. נפשׁ = character is still more dub.: לֹא־יָשְׁרָה נ׳ בּוֹ Hb 2[4] *his soul is not right in him* (but 𝔊 οὐκ εὐδοκεῖ ἡ ψυχή μου ἐν αὐτῷ [εὐδοκεῖ = רצתה], v. **6**); נַפְשִׁי לֹא מְטֻמָּאָה Ez 4[14] *my soul hath not* (or *I have not,* **4 a**) *been polluted.*

†**10.** נ׳ in D, when used with לבב, is assim. to it, and shares with it the mngs. of **7, 8, 9**; and so in later writers influenced by D (unless we may think that ל׳ is used of intellect, while נ׳ is used of the feelings): thus, בכל לבב ובכל נפשׁ (see לבב): c. דרשׁ Dt 4[29] 2 Ch 15[12]; עשׂה Dt 26[16]; אהב Dt 6[5] 13[4] 30[6]; ידע Jos 23[14]; עבד Dt 10[12] 11[13] Jos 22[5]; שׁמע בקלו Dt 30[2]; שׁוב אל Dt 30[10] 1 K 8[48] = 2 Ch 6[38], 2 K 23[25]; שׁמר מצות 2 K 23[3] = 2 Ch 34[31]; הלך לפני 1 K 2[4]; and Dt 11[18] 1 S 2[35] 1 Ch 22[19] 28[9] Je 32[41] ψ 13[8] Pr 2[10] 24[12]. *Note.*—In three cases is generally found closer approach to supposed radical meaning *breath:*—**a.** שׁמן וקטרת ישׂמח לב ומתק רעהו מעצת נפשׁ Pr 27[9]. Ges (after Döderlein) renders מעצת נ׳ *more than odorous trees,* so later edds., even Buhl; but 𝔅 De SS transp. וּמֶתֶק נ׳ מֵעֲצַת רֵעֵהוּ. 𝔊 Hi Bi ומתקרעה = *the soul is rent asunder by cares.* In any case נפשׁ is ‖ לב, cf. **10**. **b.** נַפְשׁוֹ גֶּחָלִים תְּלַהֵט Jb 41[13] *his breath kindleth coals* (of the crocodile). The piece is one of the latest in the book; primitive meaning hardly in such a passage; context favours ref. to *passion* or *fury;* perhaps sub **6 f**, *his passion* or *fury* kindleth coals. **c.** בָּתֵּי הַנֶּפֶשׁ Is 3[20] *perfume boxes;* mng. evident fr. context; but not necessarily *scent* (*breath*)-*boxes;* may be **6 a**, *boxes of desire,* or **5**, *boxes exciting the sense of smell;* = *smelling* boxes or bottles. No sufficient evid. in BH, therefore, for meaning *breath, odour.*—See, for complete study of נֶפֶשׁ (all passages), Br [JBL 1897, 17 ff.]

†[נָפַשׁ] **vb.denom.** (cf. Syr. ܢܦܫ *refresh;* ܐܬܢܦܫ, ܐܬܢܦܫ *be refreshed;* Eth. ነፍሰ:);— 5314
Niph. *Impf.* 3 ms. יִנָּפֵשׁ Ex 23[12] (E) 2 S 16[14]; וַיִּנָּפַשׁ Ex 31[17] (P);—*take breath, refresh oneself.*

†נָפִישׁ **n.pr.m.** son of Ishmael, acc. to Gn 5305
25[15] (P), = 1 Ch 1[31] (𝔊 Ναφες, 𝔊L Ναφεις); = (Arab) tribe 5[19] (𝔊 Ναφεισαδαιων, A 𝔊L Ναφισαιων).

נֹפֶת v. II. נוף. p. 632 5316

†נֹפֶת **n.m.** [Pr 24,13] **flowing honey, honey** 5317
from the comb (Ph. נפת CIS[i. 166, 8 b]);—נ׳ abs. Pr 5[3] + 3 t., cstr. ψ 19[11];—sweet Pr 24[13] (‖ דְּבַשׁ), cf. 27[7]; fig. of sweet words Pr 5[3], and perh. Ct 4[11] (Bu of kisses; ‖ דְּבַשׁ, חָלָב); in full נ׳ צוּפִים ψ 19[11] *honey of* (*the*) *combs* (comp. with דְּבַשׁ ‖ מִשְׁפְּטֵי י׳).

נֶפְתּוֹחַ v. פתח. p. 836 5318

נַפְתּוּלִים ,נַפְתָּלִי v. פתל. p. 836 5319, 5321

†נַפְתֻּחִים **n.pr.loc.** Gn 10[13] = 1 Ch 1[11] (𝔊 5320
Νεφθαλ(ι)ειμ, but 𝔊L in Ch Νεφθωσειμ); = *p3 t3mḥi, the northern land,* i.e. Lower Egypt, acc. to Brugsch [Hierogl. WB. Suppl. 633], and esp. Erman [ZAW x (1890), 118, 119] rdg. פתמחים. Other conj. v. Di[Gn].

I. [נֵץ] v. II. נצץ. II. נֵץ v. II. נצץ. p. 665 5322

†[נָצָא] **vb.** = נָצָה = **fly**, acc. Thes Gf al.;— 5323
only **Qal** *Inf. abs.* (si vera l.) נָצֹא תֵּצֵא Je 48[9], but improb.; 𝔗 Symm יָצֹא cf. Ol[§ 245 h] Gie; > Schwally[ZAW viii (1888), 197] נָצֹה תִּצֶּה, √III. נצה.

5324 † [נָצַב] **vb. Niph.** take one's stand, stand (NH נִצָּב *id.* (rare), הַצָּבָה n. *taking a stand;* Ph. (Pun.) מצבת, מנצבת, נצב *monument* Lzb^{325}; Nab. Palm. נצב *set up;* Zinj. *id., statue,* all Lzb^{325} Cook^{82}; Palm. מצבא *image,* Nab. נצב *id.,* DHM$^{\text{VOJ viii (1894), 12}}$, cf. Lzb$^{\text{l.c.}}$; perhaps As. *naṣâbu* Tel Am, Wkl$^{\text{TA 24*b}}$; Aram. נְצַב, ܢܨܒ; Ar. نَصَبَ *set up, erect,* نُصْبٌ *sign, mark, way-mark;* Sab. נצב *cippus* CIS$^{\text{iv. 23}}$ Sab Denkm^{95} DHM$^{\text{ZMG xxx (1876), 115 f.}}$ Derenb$^{\text{JAs. 1883, Aug.-Sept. 244}}$; Min. מצב *statue* (=מנצב) Hom$^{\text{Südar. Chrest. 128}}$);—**Niph.** *Pf.* 3 fs. נִצְּבָה ψ 45^{10}, נִצָּבָה Gn 37^{7} Pr 8^{2}; 2 ms. וְנִצַּבְתָּ Ex 7^{15} + 2 t.; 3 pl. נִצְּבוּ 15^{8}, וְנִצְּבוּ consec. 33^{8}; *Pt.* נִצָּב Gn 24^{13} +, f. נִצָּבָה Zc 11^{16}, נִצֶּבֶת 1 S 1^{26}; mpl. נִצָּבִים Ex 5^{20} +; fpl. נִצָּבוֹת 1 S 1^{26};—**1. a.** *station oneself, take one's stand,* for definite purpose, c. עַל loc. (*by, on*) Gn 24$^{13.43}$ 28^{13} Ex 7^{15} 33^{21} 34^{2} (all J), Ex 17^{9} 18^{14} (E), Nu 23$^{6.17}$ (JE); Am 7^{7} 9^{1} Pr 8^{2}; of י׳ Is 3^{13} *taketh his stand to plead;* c. בּ loc. Ex 5^{20} ψ 82^{1} (of God), cf. Nu 22$^{23.31.34}$; נ׳ עִמְּכָה 1 S 1^{26}; לִפְנֵי י׳ Dt 29^{9}; c. פֶּתַח Nu 16^{27} (JE), Ju 18$^{16.17}$; abs. La 2^{4} (on text v. Löhr). **b.** *stand = be stationed* (by appointment, or in fulfilment of duty), c. עַל pers. (sitting or lying) Gn 45^{1} 1 S 4^{20} 22$^{6.7.17}$; נ׳ עַל־מִשְׁמַרְתִּי Is 21^{8} *stand at my watchman's post* (|| עֹמֵד); לִימִינְךָ ψ 45^{10}; abs. 2 S 13^{31}. **c.** *take an upright position, stand,* יָקוּמוּ וְנ׳ Ex 33^{8} (E; + פֶּתַח loc.), cf. Gn 37^{7} (E; of sheaf); of waters, נ׳ כְּמוֹ־נֵד Ex 15^{8} (song). **2.** *be stationed = appointed* over (עַל), 1 S 22^{9} Ru 2$^{5.6}$; with Samuel *presiding over* (עַל) *them* 1 S 19^{20}. Hence **3.** Pt. as subst. *deputy, prefect* (as *appointed, deputed*), only 1 K 4$^{5.7}$ 5$^{7.30}$ 9^{23} 2 Ch 8^{10} (all of Sol.'s officers; so also 2 Ch 8^{10} Qr, < Kt נציב), 1 K 22^{48} (of Edom). **4.** *stand firm,* fig. כָּל־אָדָם נִצָּב ψ 39^{6} *every man,* (even) *the firm-standing,* is wholly vanity (but expression strange, and text dub.); נ׳ בַּשָּׁמָיִם 119^{89} (of י׳'s word); *that which stands firm* Zc 11^{16} (Isr. under fig. of sheep), but dub.; We GASm leave untranslated; Now prop. הַנַּחְלָה *the diseased.*

Hiph. *Pf.* הִצִּיב 1 K 16^{34}; 2 ms. הִצַּבְתָּ Gn 21^{29} ψ 74^{17}; 3 mpl. הִצִּ֫יבוּ Je 5^{26}; *Impf.* יַצִּיב Jos 6^{26}, יַצֵּב Dt 32^{8} (dub.; poet. for וַיּ׳ Ew$^{\text{§ 233a}}$ Di; rhythmical shortening Ges$^{\text{§ 109k}}$; read יַצֵּב Dr Da$^{\text{Synt. p. 94}}$), וַיַּצֶּב־ 2 S 18^{18}; sf. וַיַּצִּיבֵ֫נִי La 3^{12}; *Imv.* fs. הַצִּ֫יבִי Je 31^{21}; *Inf. cstr.* הַצִּיב 1 S 13^{21} 1 Ch 18^{3}; *Pt.* מַצִּיב 1 S 15^{12} (but rd. הִצִּיב 𝔊 We Dr Bu Kit HPS);—**1.** *station, set:* c. acc., ewes Gn 21$^{28.29}$ (E; לְבַד *apart*), trap Je 5^{26}; fig. *set me before thee* (לְפָנֶיךָ) ψ 41^{13}; *set me* as a target La 3^{12}. **2.** *set up, erect* pillar (מַצֵּבָה) Gn 35$^{14.20}$ (E), 2 S 18^{18}, + אֲשֵׁרִים 2 K 17^{10}; altar Gn 33^{20} (E), stone-heap 2 S 18^{17}; monument (יָד) 1 S 15^{12}; city-gates (c. בּ), Jos 6^{26} (JE) = 1 K 16^{34}. **3.** *cause to stand erect,* waters, כְּמוֹ־נֵד ψ 78^{13} (cf. **Qal** Ex 15^{8}). **4.** *fix, establish* boundary (subj. י׳) Dt 32^{8} ψ 74^{17} Pr 15^{25}; dominion (יָד) 1 Ch 18^{3} (of king).—1 S 13^{21} is dub.; AV *sharpen,* RV *set;* Kit *'gerade machen';* Klo נִצָּב subst., v. infr.; cf. HPS.

Hoph. *Pf.* 3 ms. הֻצַּב Na 2^{8} *it is fixed, determined* (Kl Or), but very dub.; perh. n.pr., or epith., of queen, cf. We Now GASm, q.v.; *Pt.* סֻלָּם מֻצָּב אַרְצָה Gn 28^{12} (E) *a ladder set up on the earth;* אֵלוֹן מֻ׳ Ju 9^{6}, read אֵלוֹן הַמַּצֵּבָה GFM, v. infr.—Cf. also יצב **Hithp.**

5325 † נִצָּב **n.m. 1.** haft, hilt of sword Ju 3^{22} (Ar. نِصَابٌ *handle of knife,* 'in wh. the سِيلَان [i.e. the *shank*] is set' Lane^{2800}). **2.** prefect, deputy, v. נצב **Niph. 3.**

5333 †I. נְצִיב **n.m.** pillar, prefect, also appar. garrison, post (Ecclus 46^{18} ויכנע נציבי צר *and he subdued garrisons, posts, of the foe*);—נ׳ abs. 1 K 4^{19}; cstr. 1 S 13^{3} + 3 t.; pl. נְצִיבִים 2 S 8^{6} + 2 t. + 2 Ch 8^{10} Kt, נְצִבִים 2 S 8$^{14.14}$; cstr. נְצִבֵי 1 S 10^{5} MT, but rd. נְצִיב 𝔊𝔖𝔙 Th We Dr Klo Kit Bu HPS;—**1.** *pillar,* נ׳ מֶלַח Gn 19^{26} (J). **2.** *prefect, deputy* 1 K 4^{19} (on text cf. Klo Benz), so perh. also 1 S 10^{5} (HPS; *pillar* 𝔊 Th Dr Klo Kit), and appar. 13$^{3.4}$ (> al. *pillar*); this mng. serves also for 2 S 8$^{6.14.14}$ (so Ki; Th HPS *garrison*) 1 Ch 11^{16} 18^{13} 2 Ch 8^{10} (where rd. Kt), 17^{2} (Kau *garrison* in 11^{16} 17^{2}; Ecclus 46^{18}—v. supr.—would favour this meaning in other passages).

5334 †II. נְצִיב **n.pr.loc.** in Judah on border of Philist. Jos 15^{43}; 𝔊 Νασειβ, A𝔊L Νεσ(ε)ιβ; v. also Lag BN$^{\text{95 Anm. *}}$; mod. *Beit Naṣîb,* c. 8 m. NW. of Hebron Buhl$^{\text{Geogr. 193}}$.

4673 † מַצָּב **n.m.**$^{\text{1 S 13, 23}}$ **standing-place, station, garrison;**—מ׳ abs. 1 S 14^{15}, cstr. מַצַּב Jos 4$^{3.9}$ + (Baer in Sm מַצָּב, cf. on 1 S 13^{23}, but v. Ginsb); sf. מַצָּבְךָ Is 22^{19};—**1.** *standing-place* of feet Jos 4$^{3.9}$ (JE). **2.** *station, office* Is 22^{19} (|| מַעֲמָד). **3.** *garrison, post,* or *outpost* (of Philistines) 1 S 13^{23} 14$^{1.4.6.11.15}$ 2 S 23^{14}; so rd. also 1 S 14^{12} (for MT מַצָּבָה) 𝔊 Th We Bu HPS.

4674 מִצָּב n.[m.] palisade or intrenchment;—only Is 29^{3} (of siege-works; ‖ מְצֻרֹת).

4675 מַצָּבָה n.f. אַנְשֵׁי מ׳ 1 S 14^{12} v. מַצָּב.

4675 †מִצָּבָה n.f. guard, watch?—only וְחָנִיתִי לְבֵיתִי מ׳ Zc 9^{8} *and I encamp as watch for my house* (so We Now GASm, but dub.; Kue Sta Marti^{Kau} GASm rd. מַצָּבָה, but this prob. non-existent, v. supr.; MT appar. intends *because of a host* = מִצָּבָא).

4676, 4678 †מַצֵּבָה, מַצֶּבֶת n.f. pillar, maṣṣēbā, stump;—abs. מַצֵּבָה Ho 3^{4} +, מַצֶּבֶת 2 S 18$^{18\,a}$ (rd. הַמּ׳ 𝔊 Dr Bu Kit), v$^{18\,b}$ Is 6^{13}, cstr. מַצֵּבַת 2 K 3^{2} 10^{27}, מַצֶּבֶת Gn 35$^{14.20}$; sf. מַצַּבְתָּהּ Is 6^{13}; pl. abs. מַצֵּבוֹת 1 K 14^{23}, cstr. מַצְּבוֹת 2 K 10^{26}, etc.;—**1. a.** pillar, as monument, personal memorial 2 S 18$^{18.18}$. **b.** a stone, set up (הציב, שׂים), and anointed as memorial of divine appearance Gn 28$^{18.22}$ 31^{13} (all E), 35^{14} (J); so also 33^{20} (E), where ins. מ׳, or rd. מ׳ for MT מִזְבֵּחַ (We Di Now$^{Arch.\ ii.\ 18}$), set up (הציב, הרים, שׂים), in token of an agreement 31$^{45.51.52.52}$ (all E); over grave 35$^{20.20}$ (E). **c.** esp. of sacred stones or pillars in connexion with altar, erected (בנה) by Moses Ex 24^{4} (E; 12 pillars), Ho 3^{4} 10$^{1.2}$ Is 19^{19}; conj. also 2 K 12^{10} for MT מִזְבֵּחַ Sta$^{ZAW\ v\ (1885),\ 296}$ Now$^{Arch.\ l.c.}$, but dub., v. Benz$^{ad\ loc.}$; (usu. + אֲשֵׁרִים etc.): of Canaanites Ex 23^{24} (E), 34^{13} (J), Dt 7^{5} 12^{3}, cf. מ׳ הַבַּעַל 2 K 3^{2} 10$^{26.27}$; Tyre, מ׳ עֻזֵּךְ, Ez 26^{11}, of obelisks of Heliopolis in Egypt; condemned for Isr. by Deut. code, and Deut. redaction of K: Dt 16^{22} 1 K 14^{23} 17^{10} 18^{4} 23^{14}, 2 Ch 14^{2} 31^{1}; cf. Mi 5^{12} Lv 26^{1} (H).—On *maṣṣēbā* v. further Now$^{Arch.\ ii.\ 18\ f.}$ Benz$^{Arch.\ 380\ f.}$ Dr$^{Dt.\ 16,\ 21\ f.}$ We Skizzen iii. 99, 165 RS$^{Sem.\ i.\ 184\ ff.\ 437\ f.;\ 2d\ ed.\ 204\ ff.\ 456\ f.;\ K.\ 50}$.—Ju
5324 9^{6} v. [נָצַב] **Hoph.** **2.** *stock, stump* of tree Is 6$^{13\,a}$ (in sim.), so v$^{13\,b}$ (fig.; but prob. del. as gloss).

5132 †I. [נָצָה] vb. fly (?);—only **Qal** Pf. 3 pl. (si vera l.) נָצוּ גַּם־נָעוּ La 4^{15} (of homeless exiles); text very dub.; rd. perh. נָדוּ (cf. Gn 4$^{12.14}$), so Bu; Löhr (more venturesomely) כִּי לֹא יִמְצְאוּ מָנוֹחַ; Buhl^{13} perhaps כִּי גַּם נָגְעוּ.

5133 †נוֹצָה n.f. plumage (cf. poss. Ar. نَاصِيَةٌ *hair over forehead, fore-lock* of horse, Lane^{3033}; v. also As. *na-aṣ kappe*);—of eagle מְלֹא הַנּ׳ Ez 17^{3} (fig. of Nebuch.; + אֵבֶר, כָּנָף); also רַב נ׳ v^{7} (fig. of kg. of Egypt; + כָּנָף); of ostrich נֹצָה Jb 39^{13} (‖ אֶבְרָה, + כנף; cf. Di Bu). Here belongs prob. also בְּנֹצָתָהּ Lv 1^{16}, rd. בְּנֹצָתהֹ (Dr-Wh^{Hpt}), בנצתו (Sam), or וְ(אֶת־) נֹצָתוֹ (cf. Di), *its feathers*, of bird for burnt-offering; 𝔊 σὺν τοῖς πτεροῖς, 𝔙 *et plumas;* so AV RVm; > with *its filth* (i.e. of the crop) 𝔗^{Onk} 𝔖 Ges Kn Ke Kal Ew RV, meaning without evidence elsewhere.

†II. [נָצָה] vb. **Niph.** **Hiph.** struggle 5327
(NH *id.*, Hithp. (Jastrow^{928}); Aram. נְצָא, ܢܨܳܐ *quarrel;* Ar. نَصَا *apprehendit, arripuit aliquem antiis suis*, Eth. ነጸየ: *vellere, evellere*, are perh. denom. from نَاصِيَةٌ (v. נוֹצָה), so Thes);—**Niph.** recipr. *struggle with each other: Impf.* 3 mpl. יִנָּצוּ Ex 21^{22} (E), Lv 24^{10} (H), 2 S 14^{6}; יַחְדָּו יִנּ׳ Dt 25^{11}; *Pt.* נִצִּים Ex 2^{13} (E); all of physical struggle, wrestling, and the like. **Hiph.** *engage in a struggle* against: *Pf.* 3 pl. הִצּוּ Nu 26^{9} (עַל); *Inf. cstr.* sf. הַצֹּתָם v^{9} (עַל); הַצּוֹתוֹ אֶת ψ 60^{2} (title); only here of *war*, hence Klo's suggestion (cf. Buhl^{13}) הַכּוֹתוֹ is plausible (cf. 2 S 8$^{3.5.9}$).

†II. מַצָּה n.f. strife, contention;—abs. מ׳ 4683
Is 58^{4} Pr 13^{10} 17^{19}.—I. מַצָּה v. מצץ.

†[מַצּוּת] n.f. id.;—only sf. אַנְשֵׁי מַצֻּתֶךָ Is 4695
41^{12} i.e. *the men who strove with thee* (‖ אַנְשֵׁי מִלְחַמְתֶּךָ).

†III. [נָצָה] vb. fall in ruins;—**Qal** 5327
Impf. 3 fpl. עָרַיִךְ תִּצֶּינָה מֵאֵין יוֹשֵׁב Je 4^{7} *thy cities shall fall in ruins* (read prob. תִּנָּצֶינָה **Niph.**). **Niph.** *Pt.* pl. גַּלִּים נִצִּים *ruined heaps*, i.e. ruin-heaps, 2 K 19^{25} = Is 37^{26}.—On Je 2^{15} 9$^{9.11}$ 46^{19} v. יצת.

נִצָּה v. נצץ. נֹצָתָהּ Lv 1^{16} v. נוֹצָה supr. 5133, 5328
p. 665

†I. [נָצַח] vb. be pre-eminent, enduring 5329
(Ecclus [Pi.] *make brilliant* 43$^{5.13}$ [?] (cf. Oxford ed.^{xxxiii}); NH נָצַח *conquer*, etc.; Ph. נצח, Aram. נְצַח, ܢܨܰܚ *shine, be illustrious, pre-eminent, victorious;* Ar. نَصَحَ *be pure, reliable;* Eth. ነጽሐ: *be pure, innocent;* both classes of meaning prob. derived from *shine, be bright, brilliant*, v. also Dr$^{1\ S\ 15,\ 29}$);—**Niph.** *Pt. act.* f. נִצַּחַת Je 8^{5} *enduring* (מְשֻׁבָה *apostasy*).

Piel = *act as overseer, superintendent, director*, only Chr. and ψ-titles;—*Inf.* לְנַצֵּחַ 1 Ch 15^{21} + 4 t.; pt. לַמְנַצֵּחַ Hb 3^{19} ψ 4^{1} + 54 t. ψψ; *pl.* מְנַצְּחִים 2 Ch 2$^{1.17}$ 34^{13};—**1.** in building temple 2 Ch 2$^{1.17}$ Ezr 3$^{8.9}$, cf. 2 Ch 34$^{12.13}$. **2.** in ministry of house of י׳ 1 Ch 23^{4}. **3.** in liturgical service of song, על־השמינית, over the bass voices, leading them with לְנַצֵּחַ בְּכִנֹּרוֹת 1 Ch 15^{21}; לַמְנַצֵּחַ in titles of ψψ has prob. sim. meaning, = *musical director* or *choirmaster;* Gk. Vrss. of 2nd cent. A.D., Aq Theod Sym, and so Jer, think of Aram. *victorious*, but no clear explan.; 𝔊 εἰς τὸ τέλος (prob. לַמְּנֶצַח) follows ordinary meaning of noun נֶצַח, which may be expl. in eschatological sense as referring to end of age of world after Euseb Theod; or for *full rendering* after De; neither satisfactory. Chr., near in date, gives the clue which is intrinsically prob.: לְ indicates, not assignment (nothing special in these ψψ to suggest it, and assignment of ψψ for such use a matter of course), but that these ψψ were taken by final editor from an older major Psalter known as the Director's Collection, cf. the still earlier collections known as (ל)דוד, (ל)בני קרח, (ל)אסף. The 55 ψψ with למנצח were taken 39 from Davidic, 9 from Korahite, and 5 from Asaphic Psalters; only 2 anonymous. Hb 3 originally belonged to Director's Psalter. This and other Director's ψψ have musical directions in titles. The Director's Psalter was prob. the prayer-book of synagogue of Gk. period, presupposed by our Hab., the collection of the twelve Minor Prophets, the prophetic canon, and Daniel (v. Br$^{Gen. Intr. 123}$).

5331 † I. נֵ֫צַח **n.m.**$^{La 3, 18}$ **eminence, enduring, everlastingness, perpetuity** (לנצח Ecclus 40^{14} as **4** infr.);—נֵ֫צַח 1 S 15^{29} + 3 t.; נֶ֫צַח Am 1^{11} + 36 t.; sf. נִצְחִי La 3^{18}; pl. נְצָחִים 34^{10};—**1.** *eminence:* נצח ישראל *the Eminence of Israel* (י׳) 1 S 15^{29} (Dr$^{Sam. 98}$ *glory of Israel*); attribute of God 1 Ch 29^{11} (‖ הוד, תפארת et al.). **2.** *enduring of life*, and so *life* itself as enduring: אָבַד נִצְחִי La 3^{18} *my endurance doth vanish* (De *sap* of life, v. II. נ׳). **3.** *endurance in time:* משאות נ׳ ψ 74^{3} *perpetual desolations;* לנ׳ יְדַבֵּר Pr 21^{28} *speaketh continually* (?; v. Toy); עד־נ׳ ψ 49^{20} *unto the end* (a long duration), so Jb 34^{36}. **4.** *everlastingness, ever*, usu. לָנֶצַח *for ever*, 2 S 2^{26} Is 13^{20} 25^{8} 28^{28} 33^{20} 57^{16} Je 3^{5} 50^{39} Am 8^{7} Hb 1^{4} ψ 9$^{7.19}$ 10^{11} 44^{24} 49^{10} 52^{7} 68^{17} 74$^{1.10.19}$ 77^{9} 79^{5} 89^{47} 103^{9} Jb 4^{20} 14^{20} 20^{7} 23^{7} 36^{7} La 5^{20}; לנצח נצחים (cf. עולם עולמים) Is 34^{10}; seldom abbr. נֶצַח Am 1^{11} (לָנ׳ 𝔊 We Now GASm), Je 15^{18} ψ 13^{2} 16^{11}.

II. נצח (√ of foll.; cf. Ar. نَضَحَ, نَضَخَ Lane$^{2806, 2807}$ *sprinkle;* Ba$^{ES 52}$ cp. Eth. ነዝኀ: *spargere, aspergere* Di^{677} (rare)).

† II. [נֵ֫צַח] **n.m. juice of grapes, fig. of blood, gore;**—only sf. נִצְחָם Is 63$^{3.6}$. 5332

† נְצִיחַ **n.pr.m.** head of a family of Nethinim 5335
Ezr 2^{54} (𝔊 Νασους, A Νεθιε) = Ne 7^{56} 𝔊 Ασεια, A Νεισεια; 𝔊L Νεσια in both.

[נָצַל]$_{212}$ **vb.** not in **Qal**; **Pi. strip, plun-** 5337
der; Niph. deliver oneself, be delivered; Hiph. snatch away, deliver (Ecclus Hiph. Pt. מצלת *delivering* 40$^{24 b}$ (Levi conj. יציל 40$^{24 a}$); NH Hiph. = BH; BAram. Haph. *id.;* Syr. ܢܨܠ *pour out;* Ar. نَصَلَ intrans. *tincturam exuit emisitque* barba, ex cuspide *excidit* sagitta, etc., Kam Frey; Eth. III. ተነጽለ: *evulsum vel abruptum excidere e suo loco*, Di^{698});—† **Niph.** *Pf.* 1 pl. נִצַּלְנוּ Je 7^{10}; *Impf.* יִנָּצֵל Dt 23^{16}, + 1 s. אִנָּצְלָה ψ 69^{15}, + 8 t. Impf.; *Inf.* הִנָּצֵל Is 20^{6} + 3 t. —**1.** reflex. *tear oneself away, deliver oneself:* abs. Pr 6^{3} Ez 14$^{16.18}$ 2 K 19^{11} = Is 37^{11}; c. מִיַּד Pr 6^{5}; מֵעִם . . . אֶל *escape from—unto* Dt 23^{16}. **2.** passive, *be torn out or away* מִפִּי הָאֲרִי Am 3^{12}; *be delivered*, abs. Gn 32^{31} Je 7^{10} ψ 33^{16} Mi 4^{10}; מִפְּנֵי Is 20^{6}; מִכַּף Hb 2^{9}; מִן ψ 69^{15}.

† **Pi.** *Pf.* 2 mpl. נִצַּלְתֶּם Ex 3^{22}; *Impf.* יְנַצֵּל Ez 14^{14} + 2 t.;—**1.** *strip off, spoil*, abs. 2 Ch 20^{25}; c. acc. pers. Ex 3^{22} 12^{36} (J). **2.** *deliver*, c. acc. נַפְשָׁם Ez 14^{14}.

Hiph.$_{190}$ *Pf.* הִצִּיל Ex 12^{27}; 2 ms. הִצַּ֫לְתָּ Ex 5^{23} + 50 t. Pf.; *Impf.* יַצִּיל 2 K 17^{39}; יַצֵּל Gn 31^{9}; + 63 t. Impf.; *Imv.* הַצֵּל Pr 24^{11}; הַצִּ֫ילָה ψ 22^{21}; sf. הַצִּילֵנִי Gn 32^{12} + 24 t. Imv.; *Inf. abs.* הַצֵּל 2 K 18^{30} + 4 t.; *cstr.* הַצִּיל Gn 37^{22} + 23 t. Inf.; *Pt.* מַצִּיל Dt 32^{39} + 16 t. Pt.—†**1.** *take away, snatch away*, e.g. property Gn 31$^{9.10}$ (E) Ho 2^{11}, prey from the mouth of animals 1 S 17^{35} Am 3^{12} Ez 34^{10}, words of י׳ from the mouth ψ 119^{43}; וְאֵין מַצִּיל בֵּינֵיהֶם 2 S 14^{6} *and there was none to tear them apart* (two fighting); וְהִצִּיל עֵינֵנוּ 2 S 20^{6} *and take away our eye* (elude our sight, Ges; Ew We after 𝔊 *cast shadow* over our eye, denom. from צֵל; Bö Th after 𝔖 *tear away* our eye, harm us irretrievably, v. Dr$^{1 S 26, 2}$; HPS *escape from us* [מִמֶּנּוּ, as 𝔊L], cf. Bu [וְנִצַּל]). †**2.** *rescue, recover*, e.g. cities Ju 11^{26}; wives and property 1 S 30$^{8.18.22}$. **3.** *deliver from:* **a.** *enemies and troubles*, abs. 1 S 12^{21} Pr 19^{19} Is 50^{2} Je 39^{17}; + אֵין מַצִּיל Ju 18^{28} Jb 5^{4} 10^{7} ψ 7^{3} 50^{22} 71^{11} Is 5^{29} 42^{22} 43^{13} Dn 8$^{4.7}$ Ho 5^{14} Mi 5^{7}; c. acc. Gn 18^{8} (E), Ex 5^{23} 12^{27} (J), Dt 23^{15} + 39 t.;

†הַצִּיל נַפְשׁוֹ Is 44^{20} 47^{14} Ez 3$^{19.21}$ 14^{20} 33^{19}; c. מִן *from* Mi 5^{6} + 25 t.; מִיַּד *from the hand* or *power of* Gn 32^{12} Ex 2^{19} (J) + 57 t.; מִתַּחַת יַד Ex 18^{10} (E); † מִכַּף 2 S 14^{16} 19^{10} 22^{1} = ψ 18^{1}, 2 K 20^{6} = Is 38^{6}, 2 Ch 32^{11} Ezr 8^{31}. †**b.** *from death* Pr 11^{6} 12^{6}; מִמּוֹת Jos 2^{13} (J), ψ 33^{19} 56^{14} Pr 10^{12} = 11^{4}; מִשְּׁאוֹל ψ 86^{13} Pr 23^{14}. †**4.** *deliver from sin and guilt* (in late writings), מִכָּל־פְּשָׁעַי ψ 39^{9} *from all my transgressions;* מִדָּמִים ψ 51^{16} *from bloodguiltiness;* הַצִּילֵנוּ וְכַפֵּר עַל־חַטֹּאתֵינוּ ψ 79^{9} *deliver us and cover over all our sins;* prob. also כְּאִמְרָתְךָ הַצִּילֵנִי ψ 119^{170}.

†**Hoph.** *Pt.* מֻצָּל;—כְּאוּד מֻצָּל מִשְּׂרֵפָה Am 4^{11} *as a brand plucked out of the burning;* מֵאֵשׁ Zc 3^{2} *from the fire.*

†**Hithp.** וַיִּתְנַצְּלוּ אֶת־עֶדְיָם Ex 33^{6} (E) *and they stripped themselves* of their ornaments.

2020 †הַצָּלָה **n.f. deliverance** Est 4^{14} (old Sem. Inf. in *â* acc. to Ba$^{NB\ 90}$; Inf. also Sta$^{§\ 621\ c}$ cf. Ges$^{§\ 85\ c}$ Kö$^{ii.\ 1,\ 402}$; prob. here by Aram. infl.).

5339 [נָצַן] v. II. נצץ. below

5340 †I. [נָצַץ] **vb. shine, sparkle** (NH נִצְנֵץ; akin to Ar. نَاصَ *sparkle, flash,* 𝔗 נְצָא);—**Qal** *Pt.* וְנֹצְצִים כְּעֵין נְחֹשֶׁת Ez 1^{7} (of cherubim);—Perles$^{Anal.\ 45}$ prop. נוֹצָתָם *their plumage* (נ׳ ‖ form of נוֹצָה), cf. Ew.

5213 †נִיצוֹץ **n.[m.] spark**;—Is 1^{31} (fig.).

5322 †I. [נֵץ] **n.m.** only sf. נִצָּהּ Gn 40^{10}, v. foll.

5328 †נִצָּה **n.f. blossom** (perhaps fr. above √, blossom, flower, as *shining* amid leaves);—abs. נ׳ of vine Is 18^{5} (‖ פֶּרַח; = *berry-cluster* acc. to Di Kit Che^{Hpt} cf. J. Derenb$^{ZAW\ v\ (1885),\ 301\ f.;\ vi\ (1886),\ 98\ f.}$); sf. נִצָּתוֹ Jb 15^{33} (of olive); read also נִצָּתָהּ Gn 40^{10} (of vine) for MT נִצָּהּ, cf. Di Holz.

5339 †[נִצָּן] **n.[m.]** id., only pl. נִצָּנִים Ct 2^{12}.

006,5132 †[נָצַץ] **vb. denom.** bloom, blossom (NH *id.*; Jewish-Aram. נְצַץ *id.*);—**Hiph.** *Pf.* 3 pl. הֵנֵצוּ Ct 6^{11} (no dagh., v. Kö$^{i.\ 381}$ Ges$^{§\ 67,\ 8,\ R.\ 11}$) the pomegranates *have put forth blossoms,* so 7^{13}; *Impf.* 3 ms. יָנֵאץ Ec 12^{5} the almond-tree *wears blossoms.*

II. נצץ (√ of foll.; cf. Ph. n.pr.loc. אי־נצם *isle (coast) of hawks,* Lzb$^{213,\ 325}$; Syr. ܢܨܐ *hawk;* 𝔗 נַצָּא (cf. Me$^{Chrest.\ 241}$)).

†II. נֵץ **n.m.** a bird of prey, generic name, incl. **hawk** and **falcon** (Tristr^{NHB}; *accipiter* Bo$^{Hieroz.\ ii.\ 266\ ff.;\ ed.\ Rosenm.\ iii.\ 5\ ff.}$ cf. Now$^{Arch.\ i.\ 116}$);—unclean bird, Lv 11^{16} (P), Dt 14^{15} (varieties, לְמִינֵהוּ); bird of passage Jb 39^{26}. 5322

†I. [נָצַר] **vb. watch, guard, keep** (NH 5341
id., observe; As. *naṣâru, watch over, protect;* OAram. נצר *protect* Lzb^{325} Cook^{83}; Palm. in n.pr. Vog$^{150,\ 4}$ Cook^{124}; Aram. נְטַר, ܢܛܪ (cf. Wetzst in De$^{Job\ (2)}$ on 27^{18}); Ar. نَظَرَ *look at, consider, examine* (نَاطُورٌ, *overseer* is Aram. loan-word Frä^{138}); Sab. להנצרהמו *to aid them* Hal$^{Rev.\ Sém.\ iv\ (1896),\ 71}$; Eth. ነጸረ: *spectare, intueri,* etc., Di^{701};—cf. also נטר);—**Qal** *Pf.* 3 ms. sf. נְצָרָתַם ψ 119^{129}; 1 s. נָצַרְתִּי ψ 119$^{22.56.100}$; 3 mpl. נָצְרוּ Pr 22^{12}; *Impf.* יִצֹּר Pr 3^{1}; sf. יִצְּרֶנְהוּ (Ges$^{§\ 58,\ 4\ R.}$) Dt 32^{10}; f. sf. תִּנְצְרֶכָּה Pr 2^{11} (Ges$^{§\ 58,\ 4\ R.}$); 1 s. אֶצֹּר ψ 119^{69}; אֶצְּרָה ψ 119$^{34.115}$; אֶצְּרָה ψ 119^{145}; sf. אֶצָּרְךָ Is 42^{6} 49^{8} (Ges Bö Ew al. from יצר); אֶצְּרֶנָּה Is 27^{3}; 3 mpl. יִצְּרוּ Pr 20^{28}; יִנְצֹרוּ Dt 33^{9} (on forms v. Ges$^{§\ 66,\ 2,\ R.\ 1}$) + 15 t. Impf.; *Imv.* נְצֹר ψ 34^{14} + 3 t.; נִצְּרָה ψ 141^{3} (d. f. dirim. Ges$^{§\ 20,\ 2\ b}$); sf. נִצְּרֶהָ Pr 4^{13}; *Inf. abs.* נָצוֹר Na 2^{2}; *cstr.* נְצֹר Pr 2^{8}; *Pt.* נוֹצֵר Pr 27^{18}; נֹצֵר Ex 34^{7} + 7 t.; sf. נֹצְרָהּ Is 27^{3}; pl. נֹצְרִים 2 K 17^{9} 18^{8}, etc.; *pass.* נָצוּר Ez 6^{12}; pl. נְצוּרִים Is 65^{4} (𝔊 ἐν τοῖς σπηλαίοις, בַּמְּעָרוֹת); cstr. נְצוּרֵי (Kt נְצִירֵי only here) Is 49^{6}; f. נְצוּרָה Is 1^{8} (Di rds. נְצוֹרָה Niph. Pt. √צור); cstr. נְצֻרַת Pr 7^{10}; pl. נְצֻרוֹת Is 48^{6} (Che rds. בְּצֻרוֹת).

1. *Watch, guard, keep,* a vineyard Jb 27^{18} (cf. Wetzst in De$^{Job\ (2)\ ad\ loc.}$), Is 27$^{3.3}$, fig-tree Pr 27^{18}, fortification Na 2^{2}; נֹצְרִים *watchmen* Je 31^{6}; מִגְדַּל נ׳ *tower of watchmen* 2 K 17^{9} 18^{8}; in ethical sense of men, guarding the mouth Pr 13^{3}, the way Pr 16^{17}, לֵב Pr 4^{23}; the tongue מֵרָע ψ 34^{14}; c. עַל, over the door of the lips ψ 141^{3}; of God נֹצֵר הָאָדָם Jb 7^{20} (thou) *watcher of men* (iron.).

2. *Guard from dangers, preserve,* c. acc., subj. God or his attributes Dt 32^{10} ψ 25^{21} 31^{24} 40^{12} 61^{8} Is 26^{3} 42^{6} 49^{8} Pr 2^{8} 20^{28} 22^{12}; נֹצֵר נֶפֶשׁ Pr 24^{12}; c. acc. and מִן *from* which ψ 12^{8} 32^{7} 64^{2} 140$^{2.5}$. In WisdLit. subj. is abstr.: חכמה Pr 4^{6}; תבונה Pr 2^{11}; צדקה Pr 13^{6}; נְצוּרֵי ישׂראל Is 49^{6} *preserved of Israel.*

3. *Guard with fidelity, keep, observe:* of י׳, נֹצֵר חֶסֶד לאלפים Ex 34^{7} (J); elsewhere of man observing the covenant Dt 33^{9} (poem) ψ 25^{10}, the divine law ψ 78^{7} 105^{45} 119$^{2.22.33.34.56.69.100.115.129.145}$;

commands of parents Pr 6^{20} 28^{7}; and discipline of Wisdom Pr $3^{1.21}$ 4^{13} 5^{2}.

4. *Guard, keep secret*, dub.: נְצֻרוֹת *secret things* Is 48^{6}; נְצוּרִים *secret places* Is 65^{4} (see forms above); נְצֻרַת לֵב *secret, wily minded* Pr 7^{10} (of harlot, so RVm *close*, i.e. *secretive*).

5. *Kept close, blockaded*, dub.: הַנָּצוּר *the blockaded* (so Ew Hi Co Toy; but Ke Bth Kau *preserved;* Hi Co Bth Toy del. (והנשאר) Ez 6^{12}; עִיר נְצוּרָה *blockaded city* Is 1^{8} (see form above); נֹצְרִים *blockaders* Je 4^{16} (but 𝔊 συστροφαί = צררים i.e. *foes*).

5341 נְצוּרִים v. I. נצר **Qal** *Pt. pass.* p. 665

5336 †[נָצִיר] **adj.** preserved;—only pl. cstr. נצירי Is 49^{6} Kt, Qr נְצוּרֵי q.v. נצר *Pt.*

נִצְּרָה ψ 141^{3} v. I. נצר Qal Imv.

II. **נצר** (√of foll.; cf. perh. Ar. نَضُرَ *be fresh, bright, grow green;* Ecclus 40^{15} נוצר, marg. נצר, *branch;* NH נֵצֶר = BH).

5342 †**נֵ֫צֶר** **n.m.** sprout, shoot, in fig. uses:—'נ abs. Is 11^{1} 14^{19} (sim.); cstr. 60^{21} (נ׳ מַטָּעַי), Dn 11^{7} (מִנּ׳ שָׁרָשֶׁיהָ; but 𝔊 Bev 'poss.' נ׳ מִשָּׁרָשֶׁיהָ).

5344 †I. [**נָקַב**] **vb.** pierce (NH *id.;* SI$^{1.1.4}$ הנקבה *the piercing, boring through;* Aram. נְקַב, ܢܩܒ *id.;* נִקְבָּא *hole*, etc.; Sinait. n.pr.m. נקבו Eut^{441,2}, נקיבו Eut$^{99,2;\ 153,2}$ (Lzb$^{325.326}$ Cook^{83}); As. *nakbu, depth, spring* of water; Ar. نَقَبَ *perforate, pierce, scrutinize*, etc., نَقِيبَةٌ *sagacity*, etc.; نَقِيبٌ *leader, chief* (one who *scrutinizes*));—**Qal** *Pf.* 3 fs. sf. נְקָבָהּ 2 K 18^{21} Is 36^{6}; 2 ms. נָקַבְתָּ Hb 3^{14}; *Impf.* יִנְקָב־ Jb 40^{24}, וַיִּקֹּב 2 K 12^{10}; sf. יִקֳּבֶ֫נּוּ Is 62^{2}; 2 ms. תִּקֹּב Jb 40^{26}; *Imv.* ms. נָקְבָה Gn 30^{28}; *Pt. pass.* נָקוּב Hg 1^{6}; pl. cstr. נְקֻבֵי Am 6^{1};—**1.** *pierce, bore*, c. acc. 2 K 18^{21} = Is 36^{6}, Hb 3^{14} (all in fig.), Jb $40^{24.26}$; c. acc. cogn. + ב, וַיִּקֹּב חֹר בְּדַלְתּוֹ 2 K 12^{10} *and he bored a hole in its lid;* צְרוֹר נָקוּב Hg 1^{8} *a bag pierced*, i.e. with a hole in it. **2.** *prick off*, designate, wages Gn 30^{28} (J), name Is 62^{2} (׳י subj.; cf. **Niph.**); pt. pass. *noted, distinguished* Am 6^{1}. **Niph.** *Pf.* 3 pl. in phr. (אֲשֶׁר) נִקְּבוּ בְּשֵׁמוֹת *who were pricked off, designated, by name* Nu 1^{17} 1 Ch 12^{32} (v^{31} van d. H), 16^{41} 2 Ch 28^{15} 31^{19}, cf. Ezr 8^{20}.

5345 †I. [**נֶ֫קֶב**] **n.[m.]** term. techn. of jeweller's work, prob. some hole or cavity (Hi-Sm Co Berthol; Toy^{Hpt} leaves untransl.),—only pl. sf. תֻּפֶּיךָ וּנְקָבֶיךָ Ez 28^{13} *thy sockets and thy grooves* (Da), or *thy settings and thy sockets.*

†II. **נֶ֫קֶב** **n.pr.loc.** only in אֲדָמִי הַנּ׳ Jos 5346
19^{33} (𝔊 Αρμε καὶ Ναβωκ; A Αρμαι καὶ Νακεβ; 𝔊L Αδεμμη αννεκβ); on border of Naphtali; appar. a *pass* (Ar. نَقْبٌ, *road between mountains*).

†**נְקֵבָה** **n.f.** female (*perforata* (Ba$^{NB\ 166}$); 5347
so Thes and most; > another view in Schwally ZAW xi (1891), 181 f.; Idiot. 57; NH = BH; Aram. נוּקְבָא, ܢܩܒܬܐ, ܢܘܩܒܐ, נוּקְבְּתָא);—alw. abs. 'נ Je 31^{22} + 21 t. (all Pent., and all P exc. Dt 4^{16}): **1.** *woman* (or female child) Je 31^{22} (opp. גֶּבֶר), Gn 1^{27} 5^{2} Lv $12^{5.7}$ 15^{33} $27^{4.5.6.7}$ Nu 5^{3} (all opp. זָכָר), Nu 31^{15}. **2.** *female animal* Gn 6^{19} $7^{3.9.16}$ Lv $3^{1.6}$ (all opp. זָכָר), $4^{28.32}$ 5^{6}.—Dt 4^{16} (opp. זָכָר) may include both women and animals.

†I. **מַקֶּ֫בֶת** **n.f.** hammer (by means of which 4717-18
one *drives in* nails and pegs);—abs. 'מ Ju 4^{21} (+ יָתֵד); elsewhere pl. מַקָּבוֹת 1 K 6^{7} (+ גַּרְזֶן); Is 44^{12} Je 10^{4} (+ מַסְמְרוֹת).—On name *Maccabee* v. Schürer$^{Gesch.\ i.\ 158}$.

†II. **מַקֶּ֫בֶת** **n.f.** hole, excavation;—only 4718
cstr. מ׳ בּוֹר Is 51^{1} (fig.), *excavation of a pit*, = quarry (‖ צוּר).

†II. [**נָקַב**] **vb.** curse (perh. akin to I. 5344
נקב; perh. secondary format. fr. קָבַב, q.v. for forms קֹב, יִקֹּב, etc.);—**Qal** *Inf.* sf. נָקְבוֹ שֵׁם Lv 24^{16}; *Pt.* נֹקֵב שֵׁם י׳ v^{16} (on text v. Di, Gei Urschrift 274 Dalman$^{Adonai\ 44\ f.}$).

I. **נקד** (√of foll.; NH נָקַד *point, furnish with points;* cf. Syr. ܢܩܕ (very rare) PS^{2453}; n. ܢܘܩܕܐ, but also ܢܘܩܙܐ *point, mark;* vbs. perh. denom.; Ar. نَقَطَ *point* or *dot* (letter, word, etc.), II. *make specks, spots*, on garment, etc., prob. loan-word Frä^{195}; Di$^{Lex.\ 648}$ cp. Eth. ነቀዘ: *be decayed, worm-eaten* (of wood, bread, etc.)).

†**נָקֹד** **adj.** speckled;—only of sheep and 5348
goats; 'נ Gn $30^{32.32}$, fpl. נְקֻדּוֹת v^{35} (all ‖ טָלוּא), mpl. נְקֻדִּים v^{39} (‖ *id.* + עֲקֻדִּים;—all these J); mpl. also $31^{8.8}$ and (+ עֲקֻדִּים, בְּרֻדִּים) $v^{10.12}$ (all E).

†[**נִקּוּד**] **n.[m.]** perh. what is crumbled 5350
or easily crumbles, crumb (cf. נְקֻדָּה);—only pl. **1.** *crumbs:* כֹּל לֶחֶם צֵידָם יָבֵשׁ הָיָה נִקֻּדִים Jos 9^{5} *all the bread of their provision was dry* (and) *become crumbs* (𝔊 βεβρωμένος[οι]; 𝔙 *in frusta comminuti*), cf. יָבֵשׁ וְהָיָה נ׳ v^{12} (v. Di Benn). **2.** appar. a kind of (hard) biscuit or cake 1 K 14^{3} (brought as present; + לֶחֶם, etc.).

5351 †[נְקֻדָּה] **n.f.** point, or drop;—only pl. cstr. תּוֹרֵי זָהָב נַעֲשֶׂה־לָּךְ עִם נְקֻדּוֹת הַכָּסֶף Ct 1^{11} rows (strings or chains) of gold will we make for thee, with *points of silver*.

II. נקד (√of foll.; cf. Ar. نَقَدٌ *a kind of small sheep* with very abundant wool (Jacob Altarab. Bed. Leben, 1897, 83), whence نَقَّادٌ *shepherd* of this kind of sheep; נקד perh. MI^{30}; As. *nâḳidu* Dl$^{HWB\ 479}$; cf. NH נוֹקֵד (rare)).

5349 †נֹקֵד **n.m.** sheep-raiser, -dealer, or -tender (Lag$^{NB\ 108}$);—abs. נ׳ only 2 K 3^{4} (of Mesha, king of Moab); pl. אֲשֶׁר בַּנֹּקְדִים מִתְּקוֹעַ Am 1^{1} (of Amos, v. Dr; cf. 7^{14}, where read נוקד for בוקר acc. to We Now Dr, not GASm, v. Bu infr.); perh. gloss, cf. Bu$^{Kohut\ Memorial,\ 106\ f.}$ Now$^{ad\ loc.}$

5353 †נְקוֹדָא **n.pr.m.** head of a family of Nethinim Ezr 2$^{48.60}$ = Ne 7$^{50.62}$, 𝔊 Νεκωθα, Νεχωδα.

5352 †[נָקָה] **vb.** be empty(?), clean (Ecclus 16^{11b} Niph. *Impf.* ינקה *be unpunished*, so 40^{15} 31^{5} = Pr 28^{20}; NH Pi. = BH; Aram. נְקָא Pa. = BH, adj. נְקֵא *clean;* Ph. נקי adj. *pure;* Palm. נקא *be clean* (perh.) in n.pr. Sachau$^{ZMG\ xxxv\ (1881),\ 735}$ Lzb^{325}; As. *nâḳû, pour out, pour libation, make offering, niḳû, libation, offering;* OAram. נקיה perhaps = נוֹקָיָה *libation* (Lzb^{326}), cf. Syr. ܢܩܘܡܐ Cook^{83}; Syr. ܢܩܐ Pa. *pour out, make a libation;* on the other hand, Ar. نَقِيَ *purus, mundus fuit* Kam Frey; II. *cleanse*, etc., Lane^{3037}.—Orig. meaning prob. *empty out*, hence *pour* and *be empty, clean*);—**Qal** *Inf. abs.* נָקֹה Je 49^{12} (נָקֹה תִּנָּקֶה, prob. err. for הנקה ת׳, cf. Je 25^{29}).

Niph. *Pf.* 3 ms. נִקָּה Zc 5^{3} + 5 t.; f. נִקְּתָה Nu 5^{28}; נִקָּתָה Is 3^{26}; 2 ms. נִקִּיתָ Gn 24^{8}; 1 s. נִקֵּיתִי Ju 15^{3} + 2 t.; *Impf.* יִנָּקֶה Pr 6^{29} + 6 t.; 2 ms. תִּנָּקֶה Gn 24^{41} + 2 t.; pl. תִּנָּקוּ Je 25$^{29.29}$; *Imv.* הִנָּקִי Nu 5^{19}; *Inf.* הִנָּקֵה Je 25^{29};—**1.** *be cleaned out*, of a plundered city Is 3^{26}; *purged out*, of liars and perjurers Zc 5$^{3.3}$. **2.** *be clean, free from guilt, innocent*, Je 2^{35} c. מִן, מִפֶּשַׁע ψ 19^{14}; מֵעָוֹן Nu 5^{31} (P); מִפְּלִשְׁתִּים *from* (at the hands of) *the Philistines* Ju 15^{3}. **3.** *be free, exempt from punishment*, abs. Ex 21^{19} (E) Nu 5^{28} (P) 1 S 26^{9}; לֹא יִנָּקֶה Pr 6^{29} 11^{21} 16^{5} 17^{5} 19$^{5.9}$ 28^{20} Je 25$^{29.29.29}$ 49^{12b}, נָקֹה תִּנָּקֶה v^{12a}. **4.** *free, exempt from obligation*, c. מִן, from oaths Gn 24$^{8.41}$ (J); מִמֵּי הַמָּרִים from effects of drinking the bitter water Nu 5^{19} (P).

Piel *Pf.* 1 s. נִקֵּיתִי Jo 4^{21} (𝔊 𝔖 נִקַּמְתִּי; so Now SS Buhl); *Impf.* 3 ms. יְנַקֶּה Ex 20^{7} + 2 t.; יְנַקֶּה Nu 14^{18} Na 1^{3}; 2 ms. sf. תְּנַקֵּנִי Jb 9^{28} 10^{14}; תְּנַקֵּהוּ 1 K 2^{9}; 1 s. sf. אֲנַקֶּךָּ Je 30^{11} 46^{28}; *Imv.* sf. נַקֵּנִי ψ 19^{13}; *Inf. abs.* נַקֵּה Ex 34^{7} + 4 t.;—**1.** *hold innocent, acquit*, Jb 9^{28}; מֵעֲוֹנִי Jb 10^{14}; מִנִּסְתָּרוֹת ψ 19^{13}. **2.** *leave unpunished:* of man, c. acc. 1 K 2^{9}; elsewhere of God: abs. נַקֵּה לֹא יְנַקֶּה Ex 34$^{7.7}$ = Nu 14$^{18.18}$ (all J) = Na 1$^{3.3}$; c. acc. לֹא יְנַקֶּה Ex 20^{7} = Dt 5^{11}; נַקֵּה לֹא אֲנַקֶּךָּ Je 30$^{11.11}$ = 46$^{28.28}$, cf. Jo 4$^{21.21}$ (but v. supr.).

†נָקִי **adj.** clean, free from, exempt;—נ׳ Gn 24^{41} + 31 t.; cstr. נְקִי ψ 24^{4}; pl. נְקִיִּם Je 2^{34}; נְקִיִּם Gn 44^{10} + 6 t.;—**1.** *free from guilt, clean, innocent*, ‖ צַדִּיק: נָקִי וְצַדִּיק Ex 23^{7} (E), נָקִי *innocent person* Jb 4^{7} 17^{8} 22$^{19.30}$ 27^{17} ψ 10^{8} 15^{5} Pr 1^{11}; נקיים Jb 9^{23}; דם נקי *innocent blood*, first used in D, Dt 19^{10} 27^{25} 1 S 19^{5} 2 K 21^{16} 24^{4} ψ 94^{2} 106^{38} Pr 6^{17} Is 59^{7} Je 7^{6} 22^{3} 26^{15}; דם הנקי Dt 19^{13} 1 K 24^{4} Je 22^{17}; הדם הנקי Dt 21^{9}; דם נקיים Je 19^{4}; נְקִי מִדְּמֵי 2 S 3^{28} (+ מֵעִם י׳); נְקִי כַפַּיִם ψ 24^{4}; אביונים נקיים Je 2^{34}. **2.** *free from punishment* Ex 21^{28} (E) 2 S 14^{9}. **3.** *free, exempt from obligations* Gn 44^{10} (J); from service in war Nu 32^{22} (P; + מִן pers., v. מִן **2 d**), Dt 24^{5} 1 K 15^{22} (cf. Ar. نَقِيَ and Wetzst ZMG xxii (1868), 129); c. מִן, from oaths Gn 24^{41} (J) Jos 2$^{17.19.20}$ (JE). 5355

†נָקִיא **adj.** innocent;—דָּם נָקִיא *innocent blood* Jo 4^{19} Jon 1^{14} (both Kt; Qr נָקִי). 5355

†נִקָּיוֹן **n.[m.]** innocency;—נ׳ ψ 26^{6} 73^{13}; 5356 נִקָּיֹן Ho 8^{5}; cstr. נִקְיוֹן Am 4^{6}; נִקְיֹן Gn 20^{5};—**1.** *freedom from guilt, innocency:* נ׳ כַּפַּי Gn 20^{5} (R^{JE}); אֶרְחַץ בנ׳ כַּפָּי ψ 26^{6} *I will wash my hands in innocency* = 73^{13}. **2.** *freedom from punishment* Ho 8^{5}. **3.** in physical sense, נִקְיוֹן שִׁנַּיִם *cleanness of teeth* (without food) Am 4^{6} (but read perh. after 𝔊 𝔖 𝔗 קֵהָיוֹן *bluntness*, so Lag$^{BN\ 201}$).

†[מְנַקִּיָּה] **n.f.** sacrificial bowl;—pl. 4518 מְנַקִּיֹּת Je 52^{19}; מְנַקִּיֹּת Nu 4^{7}; sf. מְנַקִּיֹּתָיו Ex 25^{29} 37^{16}.

נקט v. קוט. p. 876 5354

†[נָקַם] **vb.** avenge, take vengeance 5358 (Ecclus 46^{1e} להנקם נקמי אויב (Niph. + acc. cogn.); נקם n. also 12^{6} (cf. Dt 32^{41}), 39^{30} 48^{7}; NH נָקַם esp. in deriv.; Aram. נְקַם (rare), ܢܩܡ in der. species; Ar. نَقَمَ *take vengeance* (عَلَى *upon*), Lane^{3037}; cf. Eth. ቂም: Di^{458} *vindictae studium, ultionis cupido;* As. *iḳḳimu, ven-*

geance, requital, is poss. fr. √אקם Jäger $^{BAS\,ii.\,279}$);—**Qal** *Pf.* 3 ms. sf. נְקָמַנִי 1 S 24^{13}; *Impf.* יִקּוֹם Dt 32^{43}; יִקֹּם Jos 10^{13}; 2 ms. תִּקֹּם Lv 19^{18}; *Inf. abs.* נָקֹם Ex 21^{20}; cstr. נְקֹם Ez 24^{8} 25^{12}; *Imv.* נְקֹם Nu 31^{2}; *Pt.* נֹקֵם Na 1^{2} + 3 t.; f. נֹקֶמֶת Lv 26^{25};—**1.** *avenge, take vengeance:* **a.** God subj. דַּם עֲבָדָיו יִקּוֹם Dt 32^{43} *the blood of his servants he avengeth* (against those who slew them) (+ 1 K 2^{5} 𝔊L Klo); נ׳ abs. Na 1$^{2.2}$ c. לְ (agst. Nineveh) Na 1^{2}; נ׳ נָקָם (agst. Jerus.) Ez 24^{8}; עַל־עֲלִילוֹתָם *on their doings* (his people's) ψ 99^{8}; נ׳ נְקַם בְּרִית Lv 26^{25} (H) *the vengeance of the covenant* (against those who break it); נְקָמַנִי, 1 S 24^{13}, c. מִן of pers. *from* whom vengeance is taken (cp. Je 20^{10}). **b.** *Israel and its leaders against their enemies,* נ׳ נקמה c. מִן against whom Nu 31^{2} (P); c. acc. יִקֹּם אֹיְבָיו Jos 10^{13} (poem). **c.** Edom against Judah נ׳ נקם לְ Ez 25^{12}. **d.** in administration of justice agst. murder Ex 21^{20} (E). **2.** *entertain revengeful feelings* (opp. אהב) against neighbour forbidden Lv 19^{18} (H).

Niph. *Pf.* 1 s. נִקַּמְתִּי Ju 15^{7} 1 S 14^{24}; 3 mpl. נִקְּמוּ Ez 25^{12}; *Impf.* יִנָּקֵם Ex 21^{20}; 1 s. אִנָּקְמָה Ju 16^{28} Is 1^{24}; 3 mpl. יִנָּקְמוּ Ez 25^{15}; *Inf.* הִנָּקֵם Je 46^{10} + 2 t.; *Imv.* הִנָּקֵם Je 15^{15}; pl. הִנָּקְמוּ Je 50^{15}:—**1.** *avenge oneself,* **a.** י׳ subj. c. מִן of adversary Is 1^{24} Je 46^{10}; c. מִן advers., לְ for whom Je 15^{15}; c. בְּ adversary Je 50^{15}. **b.** of Israel and champions c. מִן Ju 16^{28} 1 S 14^{24} Est 8^{13}; c. בְּ Ju 15^{7} 1 S 18^{25}. **c.** of enemies against Israel נ׳ נקם Ez 25^{15}; c. בְּ Ez 25^{12}. **2.** *suffer vengeance* (of law against murder) Ex 21^{20} (E).

Piel *Pf.* 1 s. נִקַּמְתִּי 2 K 9^{7} Je 51^{36};—*avenge,* י׳ subj. דְּמֵי מיד 2 K 9^{7} *blood at hands of;* נ׳ נִקְמָתֵךְ Je 51^{36} *take vengeance for thee.*

Hoph. *Impf.* יֻקַּם Gn 4^{24} Ex 21^{21}, יֻקָּם Gn 4^{15} *be avenged, vengeance be taken* (for blood).

Hithp. *Impf.* תִּתְנַקֵּם Je 5$^{9.29}$ 9^{8}; *Pt.* מִתְנַקֵּם ψ 8^{3} 44^{17}; *avenge oneself,* י׳ subj. לֹא תִתְנַקֵּם נַפְשִׁי בְּ׳ Je 5$^{9.29}$ 9^{8}; of Israel's enemies אוֹיֵב וּמִתְנַקֵּם ψ 8^{3} 44^{17}.

5359 †נָקָם **n.m.** vengeance;—נ׳ Dt 32^{35} + 14 t.; cstr. נְקַם Lv 26^{25} Ju 16^{28};—**1.** taken by God, abs. Ez 24^{8} ψ 58^{11}; נ׳ בְּרִית *vengeance of the covenant* Lv 26^{25} (H); יום נקם Is 34^{8} 61^{2} 63^{4}; בִּגְדֵי נ׳ Is 59^{17}; לִי נָקָם וְשִׁלֵּם Dt 32^{35}; לקח נ׳ Is 47^{3}; נ׳ יבוא Is 35^{4}; c. acc. adversary עשׂה נ׳ Mi 5^{14}; c. לְ advers. השׁיב נ׳ Dt 32$^{41.43}$. **2.** Samson against Philistines, נקם נ׳ Ju 16^{28}. **3.** enemies against Judah, abs. Ez 25$^{12.15}$; individual enemy יום נ׳ Pr 6^{34}.

†נְקָמָה **n.f.** vengeance (on format. cf. Lag $^{BN\,143}$);—נ׳ Je 46^{10} + 3 t.; cstr. נִקְמַת Nu 31^{2} + 7 t.; *sf.* נִקְמָתִי Ez 25^{14} + 7 t. sfs.; pl. נְקָמוֹת Ju 11^{36} + 5 t.; נְקָמֹת 2 S 22^{48};—**1.** *vengeance* of God, abs. Ez 25^{14}; נקם נ׳ Je 51^{36}; נִקְמַת יום נ׳ Je 51^{6}; עֵת נ׳ ψ 79^{10}; אֵל נְקָמוֹת 94$^{1.1}$; דַּם Je 46^{10}; נ׳ יהוה 50$^{15.28}$ 51^{11}; נ׳ הֵיכָלוֹ 50^{28} 51^{11}; c. בְּ of adversary, נתן נ׳ Ez 25$^{14.17}$; עשׂה נ׳ Ez 25^{17}; c. מִן of adversary נתן נ׳ 2 S 4^{8} עשׂה נ׳ Ju 11^{36}; נִקְמָתְךָ מֵהֶם Je 11^{20} 20^{12}; c. לְ for whom נתן נ׳ 2 S 22^{48} = ψ 18^{48}. **2.** of Israel and its chiefs נקם נ׳ מן Nu 31^{2} (P); c. בְּ׳, נתן נ׳ Nu 31^{3} (P); עשׂה נ׳ ψ 149^{7}. **3.** enemies of Israel abs. La 3^{60}; עשׂה בנקמה Ez 25^{15}; of Jeremiah לקח נ׳ מן Je 20^{10}. 5360

†[נָקַע] **vb.** be [severed, fig.] alienated, estranged (cf. Ar. نَقَعَ *split, rend, sacrifice* RS $^{Sem.\,i.\,471\,f.;\,2d\,ed.\,491}$; Eth. ነቀዐ: *split up, open* (intrans.) Di ^{647}; NH נָקַע *cleft,* Syr. ܢܩܥ *id.*);—**Qal** *Pf.* 3 fs. נָקְעָה נַפְשִׁי מֵעַל Ez 23^{18} *my soul was estranged from* her sister (‖ יָקַע), cf. v$^{22.28}$ (both c. מִן). 5361

†I. [נָקַף] **vb. strike off** (NH *strike, wound,* Aram. נְקַף *id.;* Ar. نَقَفَ *fregit* caput, ut cerebrum appareret; Vulg. Ar. *snap* with the finger (Dozy $^{ii.\,716}$); As. *nakpu* prob. = *mutilated;* Eth. ነቀፈ: *peel, flay* Di ^{649});—**Niph.** *Pf.* 3 ms. וְנִקַּף סִבְכֵי הַיַּעַר consec. Is 10^{34} and the thickets of the forest shall be *struck away* (on sg. vb. cf. Ges $^{§\,145\,o}$ Da $^{Synt.\,§\,113\,b}$; or rd. נִקְּפוּ;—form poss. Pi., but cf. Di Du Che ^{Hpt}). **Pi.** *Pf.* 3 pl. וְאַחַר עוֹרִי נִקְּפוּ־זֹאת Jb 19^{26} *after my skin, which they* (Ges $^{§\,144\,g}$) *have struck off* (alluding to ravages of his disease)—*this!* but text dub.; Bu נִקַּף כָּזֹאת (**Niph.**) *which has been thus struck off.* 5362

†נֹקֶף **n.[m.]** striking off;—only cstr. כְּנֹקֶף זַיִת *as (at) the striking of olive-trees* Is 17^{6} 24^{13} (sim. of fewness of people after י׳'s judgment). 5363

II. [נָקַף] **vb.** go around (intrans.), (Ecclus 45^{9} Hiph. ויקיפהו *surround something with* (2 acc.); Pf. 3 fs. הקיפה 43^{12} (acc. + ב instr.); NH Hiph. הִקִּיף = BH; also = *cling to, be attached, joined to,* and so Aram. אַקֵּיף (Aph.), ܢܩܦ);—**Qal** *Impf.* חַגִּים יִנְקֹפוּ Is 29^{1} (fig.) *let feasts go around,* i.e. run the round (of the year). **Hiph.** *Pf.* הִקִּיף Jb 19^{6}; 3 fs. הִקִּיפָה Is 15^{8}; 3 pl. הִקִּיפוּ Jb 1^{5} ψ 88^{18}, וְהִקִּיפוּ consec. 2 Ch 23^{7}, sf. הִקִּיפוּנִי ψ 22^{17}; 2 mpl. וְהִקַּפְתֶּם 5362

consec. 2 K 11^{8}; *Impf.* וַיַּקֵּף La 3^{5}; 3 mpl. יַקִּ֫יפוּ ψ 17^{9}, וַיַּקִּ֫פוּ 2 K 6^{14}; 2 mpl. תַּקִּ֫פוּ Lv 19^{27}; *Imv.* mpl. sf. הַקִּיפ֫וּהָ ψ 48^{13}; *Inf. abs.* הַקֵּיף Jos 6^{3}, הַקֵּף v^{11}; *Pt.* pl. מַקִּ(י)פִים 1 K 7^{24} 2 Ch 4^{3};—**1.** *go around, surround, encompass:* **a.** *go around,* c. acc. of city, Jos 6^{3} cf. v^{11} (acc. om.), ψ 48^{13} (all ‖ סָבַב); also (fig.) הִקִּיפָה הַזְּעָקָה אֶת־ Is 15^{8} *the cry hath gone about* the border of Moab. **b.** *surround, encompass, enclose,* usu. c. עַל־: וַיַּקִּ֫פוּ עַל־הָעִיר 2 K 6^{14} *and they closed in upon the city* (beleaguered it); c. עַל pers. 2 K 11^{8} (+ סָבִיב), ψ 17^{9} 88^{18} (‖ סָבַב), + acc. rei Jb 19^{6} *he hath closed his net in upon me,* cf. La 3^{5}; less oft. c. acc. pers. ψ 22^{17} (‖ סָבַב), 2 Ch 23^{7} (‖ 2 K 11^{8}; + סָבִיב), also of inanim. things 1 K 7^{24} = 2 Ch 4^{3} (both + סָבִיב, ‖ סָבַב). **2.** *make the round,* i.e. *complete the circuit* הִקּ׳ יְמֵי הַמִּשְׁתֶּה Jb 1^{5} when *the days of feasting had completed their circuit.* **3.** *make round, round off* (lit.): לֹא תַקִּ׳ פְּאַת רֹאשְׁכֶם Lv 19^{27} (‖ לֹא תַשְׁחִית אֵת פְּאַת זְקָנֶךָ), of heathen rite.

5364 †נְקָפָה **n.f. encircling rope** (of captive), תַּחַת חֲגוֹרָה נִקְפָּה Is 3^{24}.

נקק (√ of foll. cf. Eth. ንቅቅ: *rima, fissura,* Di^{645}; NH נָקִיק (rare) *cleft of rock*).

5357 †[נָקִיק] **n.m. cleft** of **rock**;—only cstr.: sg. נְקִיק הַסֶּלַע Je 13^{4}; pl. נְקִיקֵי הַסְּלָעִים Is 7^{19} (‖ נַחֲלֵי הַבַּתּוֹת), Je 16^{16}.

5365 †[נָקַר] **vb. bore, pick, dig** (NH *id.,* Aram. נְקַר, ܢܩܪ *id.;* Ar. نَقَرَ *perforate, bore out, hollow out* Lane^{2838}; Eth. ነቈረ: *be one-eyed* Di^{645});—**Qal** *Impf.* 3 mpl. sf. יִקְּרוּהָ Pr 30^{17}; *Inf.* נְקוֹר 1 S 11^{3}, both of *boring,* or *picking out* eye (acc.). **Pi.** *Impf.* 2 ms. תְּנַקֵּר Nu 16^{14} (JE), 3 mpl. וַיְנַקְּרוּ Ju 16^{21} both of *boring out* eyes (acc.); *Pf.* 3 ms. נִקַּר Jb 30^{17} *he* (or *it,* i.e. the night) *boreth* my bones מֵעָלָי (of effects of elephantiasis; Bu rds. נִקַּר). **Pu.** *Pf.* 2 mpl. נֻקַּרְתֶּם Is 51^{1} the quarry (fr. wh.) *ye were digged.*

5366 †[נְקָרָה] **n.f. hole, crevice**;—cstr. נִקְרַת הַצּוּר Ex 33^{22}; pl. cstr. נִקְרוֹת הַצֻּרִים Is 2^{21} (‖ סְעִפֵי הַסְּלָעִים).

5367 †[נָקַשׁ] **vb. knock, strike,** only in specif. sense of **hit, strike** or **bring down** (a bird), and only fig. (Ecclus ינקש 41^{2c} *striketh* against (ב; marg. ונוקש), so נוקש ב 13^{2c}; NH *knock, strike* e.g. the knees, or a door (so Hiph.); Aram. (incl. BAram.) נְקַשׁ *id.,* ܢܩܫ *fixit, impegit, percussit,* etc. (Ar. نَقَشَ *strike in, carve,* etc., is loan-wd. Frä^{194});—the Heb. vb. appar. means *bring down with a* [certain kind of] *stick,* perh. like a boomerang, v. descript. and illustr. in Wilkinson$^{\text{Manners and Customs of Egypt, (new ed. 1878), ii. 103 f. 109 f.}}$ Erman$^{\text{Ægypten 323}}$ WMM$^{\text{Asien u. Europa 123 f.}}$);—**Qal** *Pt.* נוֹקֵשׁ ψ 9^{17} he (י׳) *striketh down* the wicked (so Hup-Now De Che); Vrss Ol Ew Bae Kau We Buhl^{Lex} rd. נוֹקַשׁ, **Niph.** fr. יקשׁ. **Niph.** *Impf.* 2 ms. תִּנָּקֵשׁ אַחֲרֵיהֶם Dt 12^{30} lest *thou be thrust* (impelled) *after them.* **Pi.** *Impf.* יְנַקֵּשׁ ψ 109^{11} let the creditor *strike* at, *take aim* at (לְ); 3 mpl. וַיְנַקְשׁוּ 38^{13} (abs.). **Hithp.** *Pt.* מִתְנַקֵּשׁ בְּנַפְשִׁי 1 S 28^{9} why *art* thou *striking at my life?*

I, II. נֵר, נִר, (נִיר) v. נור. p. 632f 5215-16

†נֵרְגַל **n.pr.div.** (Ph. נרגל CIS$^{\text{i. 119. 2}}$)—wor- 5370
shipped by men of Cuth, 2 K 17^{30} (v. Schr$^{\text{COT 2 K 17. 30}}$ Jen$^{\text{Kosmol. 476–490}}$ Muss-Arnolt$^{\text{JBL xi (1892), 168}}$).

†נֵרְגַל שַׂרְאֶ֫צֶר **n.pr.m.** (so Baer Ginsb; 5371
van d. H. ׳שַׁר), chief soothsayer (רַב־מָג) in train of Nebuchad. Je 39^{3a} (del. Gie, plausibly) v$^{3b, 13}$ (cf. Schr$^{\text{COT ad loc.}}$).

נִרְגָּן v. רגן. p. 920 5372

†נֵרְדְּ **n.m. nard,** an odorif. plant fr. India 5373
(*via* Persia) (Skr. *naladâ;* Pers. *nârdîn;* Sab. Ar. transp. رَنْد acc. to DHM$^{\text{Burgen u. Schlösser 975 (SB xcvii)}}$ v. also Sab. Denkm^{82}; Gk. νάρδος [so 𝔊] (through Semites) Lewy$^{\text{Fremdwörter 40}}$; cf. Löw$^{\text{No. 316}}$ Lag$^{\text{M. ii. 25}}$);—abs. ׳נ Ct 4^{14}; sf. נִרְדִּי נָתַן רֵיחוֹ 1^{12}; pl. נְרָדִים 4^{13}.

נְרִיָּה v. נֵר sub נור. p. 633 5374

נָשָׂא$_{655}$ **vb. lift, carry, take** (NH = BH; 4984, 5375
Ph. נשא *id.* Lzb^{326}; As. *našû, id.* Dl$^{\text{HWB 484}}$; BAram. נְשָׂא (rare); Syr. in ܡܣܐܬܐ *scales;* Palm. נסא, נשא n.pr. Lzb^{326} Cook$^{81, 83}$ (cp. נשא *forget*); Ar. نَشَأَ intrans. *rise, be high,* etc.; Sab. in n.pr., e.g. CIS$^{\text{iv. 5. 1}}$; also נשא vb. Hal$^{\text{Rev. Sém. iv (1896), 69}}$ Min. נשא *take,* Hom$^{\text{Südar. Chrest. 128}}$; Eth. ነሥአ: *suscipere, tollere* Di^{635}, so OEth., DHM$^{\text{Epigr. Denkm. aus Abess. (1894), 52}}$);—**Qal**$_{599}$ *Pf.* ׳נ Gn 13^{6}+; 2 ms. נָשָׂאתָ 1 K 2^{26}+, נָשָׂאתָה Nu 14^{19}, sf. נְשָׂאתַ֫נִי ψ 102^{11}; 2 fs. sf. נְשָׂאתִים Ez 16^{58}; 3 pl. נָשְׂאוּ 2 S 18^{28}+, נָשׂוּא ψ 139^{20}, וְנָשׂוּ consec. Ez 39^{26}, sf. נְשָׂאוּם 2 Ch 12^{11}, etc.; *Impf.* 3 ms. יִשָּׂא Gn 32^{21}+, וַיִּשָּׂא 13^{10}+, sf. יִשָּׂאֵהוּ Dt 32^{11}+;

3 mpl. יִשְׂאוּ Ho 4^{8}+, יִשָּׂאוּ Hb 2^{6}+, וַיִּשְׂאוּ Ju 2^{4}+; sf. יִשָּׂאֻנוּ Is 64^{5}; 3 fpl. תִּשֶּׂנָה Je 9^{17}, וַתִּשֶּׂאנָה Ru 1^{9}, וַתִּשֶּׂנָה Zc 5^{9} Ru 1^{14}; 2 fpl. תִּשֶּׂאינָה Ez 23^{49}, etc.; *Imv.* ms. שָׂא Gn 13^{14}+, נְשָׂא ψ 10^{12}, נְסָה 4^{7}; sf. שָׂאֵהוּ Nu 11^{12} 2 K 4^{19}; fs. שְׂאִי Gn 21^{18}+, etc.; *Inf. abs.* נָשׂוֹא Je 10^{5}, נָשֹׂא Ho 1^{6}+ 2 t.; cstr. נְשֹׂא Is 1^{14}+ 2 t., שׂוֹא ψ 89^{10} (rd. perh. שְׁאוֹן *roar* Ri Bi Che, cf. Hi שׁוֹא), usu. שְׂאֵת Gn 4^{7}+; sf. נָשְׂאִי ψ 28^{2}, שְׂאֵתִי Je 15^{15} ψ 89^{51}, etc.; Aramaizing Inf. לְמַשְׂאוֹת Ez 17^{9} (si vera l.; Co Berthol לְיוֹם שְׂאֵת); *Pt. act.* נֹשֵׂא Ex 34^{7}+, f. נֹשֵׂאת 1 K 10^{22}, נשֵׂאת Est 2^{15}, etc.; *pass.* cstr. נְשׂוּא Is 3^{3}+, נְשׂוּי ψ 32^{1}, etc.;—**1.** *lift, lift up:* **a.** lit., c. acc. pers. vel rei; the flood lifts ark Gn 7^{17} (J), י׳ lifts standard (נֵס) Is 5^{26} 11^{12}+ (oft. sq. לְ pers.), rod Is 10^{26}, c. עַל *against* v^{24}, נ׳ חֶרֶב אֶל־ Mi 4^{3}=Is 2^{4}, etc.;—esp. *lift* in order to hold, carry away, etc. Gn 21^{18} (E), Ju 9^{48} Am 6^{10} 2 S 2^{32} 4^{4} 1 K 13^{29} 2 K $9^{25.26}$ Ez $3^{12.14}$ 8^{3} 11^{24}+; *lift up* wings to fly Ez $10^{16.19}$ 11^{22}; †נ׳ רַגְלָיו וַיֵּלֶךְ Gn 29^{1} *he lifted up his feet and went; lift up, upon* (עַל) Gn 31^{17} 42^{26} (both E), fig. Jb 31^{36}; נ׳ בְּמֹאזְנַיִם Jb 6^{2} *put* a thing into scale; נ׳ בוֹ אָלָה *put on him* (require of him) *an oath* 1 K 8^{31}=2 Ch 6^{22}, so van d. H., 𝔊; correct MT נָשָׁא (Baer Ginsb), but sense hardly possible; אֶשָּׂא בְשָׂרִי בְשִׁנָּי Jb 13^{14} *I will take up my flesh in my teeth* (fig. for hazarding life). **b.** in many phr., lit. and fig., e.g.: (1) *lift up hand;* against (בְּ) 2 S 18^{28} 20^{21}, c. לְ ψ 106^{26}; אֶל־ (as signal) Is 49^{22}; abs., in display of power ψ 10^{12}; freq. in oath (esp. Ez P; of י׳; usu. sq. inf., oft. + לְ pers.) Ex 6^{8} Nu 14^{30} (both P), Ez $20^{5.5.6.15.23.28.42}$ 36^{7} 44^{12} 47^{14} Ne 9^{15}, + אֶל־שָׁמַיִם Dt 32^{40} *lift hand to heaven;* in prayer (c. אֶל־) ψ 28^{2} La 2^{19}, so (בְּשִׁמְךָ) ψ 63^{5}, abs. 134^{2}, and, remarkably, אֶל־מִצְוֺתֶיךָ 119^{48}; also fig. of the deep (תְּהוֹם) Hb 3^{10}; in blessing Lv 9^{22} (P; c. אֶל). (2) *lift up one's head*=shew boldness, independence Ju 8^{28} Zc 2^{4} Jb 10^{15} ψ 83^{3}; of another=restore to honour Gn $40^{13.20}$ (E), but *lift thy head* from off thee (מֵעָלֶיךָ), v^{19}, by word-play;—+ מִבֵּית כֶּלֶא 2 K 25^{27}=Je 52^{31}; fig. of gates, *lift up your heads* ψ $24^{7.9}$. (3) *lift up one's face, countenance* (פָּנִים), lit., 2 K 9^{32} (אֶל־); sign of good conscience 2 S 2^{22} (אֶל־), abs. Jb 11^{15}; of י׳, sign of favour, נ׳ פָּנֶיךָ אֶל־ Nu 6^{26} (P; form of benediction); cf. נ׳ אוֹר פָּנֶיךָ עַל־ ψ 4^{7}; esp. *lift up face* of another (orig. prob. of one prostrate in humility; opp. הֵשִׁיב פָּנִים *repel*), in various shades of mng.: =grant a request Gn 19^{21} (J; + לַדָּבָר הַזֶּה), 1 S 25^{35} Jb $42^{8.9}$; =be gracious to, Gn 32^{21} (E), Mal $1^{8.9}$; hence phr. נְשׂוּא פָנִים *graciously received, held in honour* †2 K 5^{1} (of Naaman), and, as subst., *honourable, eminent one* Is 3^{3} 9^{14} (but del. as gloss), Jb 22^{8}†; =shew consideration for Dt 28^{50} La 4^{16}; also in bad sense=be unduly influenced by Jb 32^{21}, and, specif.,=shew partiality (towards) Dt 10^{17} (denied of י׳), Lv 19^{15} (H), Mal 2^{9} (בַּתּוֹרָה), Jb $13^{8.10}$ 34^{19} Pr 18^{5} ψ 82^{2} (syn. הִכִּיר פ׳); even נ׳ פְּנֵי כָל־כֹּפֶר Pr 6^{35} i.e. regard any bribe. (4) *lift up eyes,* on high 2 K 19^{22}=Is 37^{23}, cf. ψ 121^{1} (אֶל־); לַשָּׁמַיִם Is 51^{6} (‖ הַבִּיטוּ אֶל־); sq. ה loc. Dt 3^{27} 4^{19} cf. Ez $8^{5.5}$; toward (אֶל־) idols Ez $18^{6.12.15}$ 33^{25}, cf. 23^{27}; toward (אֶל־) י׳ ψ 123^{1} (these with implied worship); נ׳ עֵינֶיהָ אֶל־ Gn 39^{7} i.e. she gazed at him with desire; usu.+vb. of seeing (35 t.) Gn $13^{10.14}$ 18^{2}+ (Hex only JE), Is 40^{26} (+מָרוֹם), 49^{18} 60^{4} (both+סָבִיב), Je 3^{2} (+עַל־). (5) *lift up voice* (קוֹל), give (loud) utterance Is 52^{8}, of floods ψ 93^{3}, +*and weep* Gn 21^{16} (E) 27^{38} 29^{11} (both J), Ju 2^{4}, + וַתִּשָּׂא וַיִּתְּנוּ אֶת־קוֹלָם וַיִּבְכּוּ Nu 14^{1} (P), + 9 t.; + יָרֹנּוּ Is 24^{14}; + קָרָא Ju 9^{7}; קוֹל om. Is 3^{7} 42^{2}, v^{11} (‖ יָרֹנּוּ); also (6) *lift up* (+vb. of saying, usu. אָמַר), oft. of formal and solemn utterance, נ׳ מָשָׁל Nu $23^{7.18}$ $24^{3.15.20.21.23}$ Jb 27^{1} 29^{1} +עַל Mi 2^{4} Hb 2^{6} Is 14^{4}; ונשׂא־בוֹ אָלָה 1 K 8^{31} *and he shall lift up against him an oath*= 2 Ch 6^{22} (MT וְנָשָׁא v. Baer Ginsb, but sense difficult; read rather וְנָשָׂא); י׳ נ׳ עָלָיו הַמַּשָּׂא הַזֶּה 2 K 9^{25}; נ׳ קִינָה+עַל־ Je 7^{29} Ez 26^{17} 27^{2} 28^{12} 32^{2}, +אֶל־ 19^{1} 27^{32}; *lift up* word Am 5^{1} (עַל, +קִינָה); weeping Je 9^{9} (עַל־); lamentation (נְהִי) v^{17} (עַל־), reproach ψ 15^{3} (עַל־). (7) *lift up, take up*= utter: name of י׳, לַשָּׁוְא Ex $20^{7.7}$ = Dt $5^{11.11}$ (Decalogue); cf. ψ 139^{20} (read prob. שְׁמֶךָ Bö Ol Che Kau); בַּל־אֶשָּׂא שְׁמוֹתָם עַל־שְׂפָתָי ψ 16^{4}; נ׳ בְּרִיתִי עֲלֵי־פִיךָ ψ 50^{16}; prob. also נ׳ שֵׁמַע שָׁוְא Ex 23^{1} (E). (8) *lift up* prayer in behalf of (בְּעַד) †2 K 19^{4}=Is 37^{4}, Je 7^{16} 11^{14}. (9) *lift up* soul (נֶפֶשׁ), i.e. direct the desire (נֶפֶשׁ **1 d**) towards (אֶל) a thing, Dt 24^{15} Pr 19^{18}, אֶל־עָוֺן Ho 4^{8}, לַשָּׁוְא ψ 24^{4} (cf. **Pi.** and II. מַשָּׂא **2**); אֶל־י׳ ψ 25^{1} 86^{4} 143^{8}, so the heart La 3^{41}. (10) *take up* (incur) sin, iniquity, (only HP) †Ex 28^{43} Nu 18^{22}, c. עַל *for* Lv 19^{17} 22^{9} Nu 18^{32} (cf. also **2 b**). (11) of heart *lifting* one *up,* (inciting), Ex $35^{21.26}$ 36^{2} (all P); of presumption 2 K 14^{10} =2 Ch 25^{19}.—MT appar. requires intrans. or reflex. meaning, *lift oneself up,* in foll., text dub.

in all: Ho 13[1] rd. perh. נָשִׂיא Oort We cf. Now; Na 1[5] Now (after Bi) וַתִּשָּׂא (rd. ?וַתִּשָּׁא √שאה); ψ 89[10] rd. שְׁאוֹן Bi Ri Che; Hb 1[3] יִשָּׂא queried by We Gr Buhl al., cf. Gunkel[Schöpfung 33].

2. *Bear, carry:* **a.** lit., a load or burden (usu. acc.) Gn 37[25] 44[1] (both J), 45[23.23] (E), 1 S 10[3.3.3] Je 10[5] 17[21.27] + very oft.; נֹשֵׂא כֵלִים *armour-bearer* Ju 9[54] 1 S 14[1] + oft. S; bearing weapons 1 Ch 5[18] 12[24] 2 Ch 14[7.7]; La 3[27] (נ׳ עֹל fig.), Is 1[14] (fig., cf. **d** infr.); a load of care, responsibility Dt 1[9.12]; *share a burden with* נ׳ אֶת־ Ex 18[22] (E; no acc.); with ב׳, יִשָּׂא בְשִׂיחִי מִשְׁכָּבִי Jb 7[13] *my bed shall carry at* (help carry) my grief, Nu 11[17]; *take up and carry* (idolatrous images) Am 5[26] Is 46[7]; *bear* ephod, 1 S 2[28] 14[3]+v[18] (𝔊), 22[18] (v. Dr in Hastings Dict. 726); in triumph Is 8[4]. **b.** esp. *bear* guilt, or punishment Gn 4[13] (J, עֲוֺנִי), oft. Ez HP: † נ׳ עָוֺן Lv 5[1.17] 7[18] Nu 5[31] 14[34], cf. 15[31] (all P), Lv 17[16] 19[8] 20[17.19] (H) Ez 14[10] 44[12] (cf. **Hiph.** Lv 22[16]); נ׳ חֵטְא Lv 20[20] 24[15] (H) Nu 9[13] (P), cf. Ez 23[49]; cf. נ׳ כְּלִמָּה 16[52.52], נ׳ עֹנֶשׁ Pr 19[19], נ׳ abs. 9[12]; נ׳ עֲוֺן ... = *be responsible for* Ex 28[38] Nu 18[1.1] cf. v[23]; = *bear guilt* for others Lv 10[17] 16[22] (of goat; + אֶל־ארץ, cstr. praegn.), Nu 30[16] (all P), Ez 4[4.5.6], cf. נ׳ זְנוּתֵיכֶם Nu 14[33]; נ׳ חֵטְא Is 53[12], cf. נ׳ חֳלָיֵנוּ v[4]; also נ׳ בַּעֲוֺן ... *bear at* (share in), Ez 18[19.20.20]. **c.** *support, sustain,* on (עַל) wings Ex 19[4] Dt 32[11] ψ 91[12] (all fig.); land could not *support* them Gn 13[6] (J), 36[7] (P). **d.** *endure* Je 15[15] 31[19] Ez 36[6] Jb 34[31] ψ 55[13] 69[8] 88[16] Pr 18[14] 30[21]; *suffer, bear with, permit* Jb 21[3]. **e.** *bear, carry,* וַיִּשָּׂא מַאֵת פָּנָיו אֲלֵהֶם Gn 43[34] (J) *and they* (indef.) *carried* portions *from his presence unto them; carry* gifts as tribute 2 S 8[2.6]; later, *bring* an offering ψ 96[8] = 1 Ch 16[29], Ez 20[31] (𝔊 Co בראשית; Toy foll. MT). **f.** *carry* = contain, hold: bath to hold 1/10 homer Ez 45[11]. **g.** *bear* fruit, of tree Hg 2[19] Jo 2[22], fig. Ez 36[8]; boughs 17[23] (in fig.); *produce, yield,* of mountains Jb 40[20] ψ 72[3] (both c. לְ *for*).

3. *Take, take away:* **a.** lit. c. מִן 1 S 17[34] Nu 16[15] (unjustly). **b.** *take away, carry off,* Ju 21[23] 1 K 15[22] = 2 Ch 16[6], 1 K 18[12] La 5[13] Mi 2[2] Je 49[29] (לְ pers.), Is 40[24] 41[16]+; *take away* head (מֵעַל pers.) Gn 40[19] (v. supr.); *sweep away* = destroy Jb 32[22] (cf. **Niph. 4**); life 2 S 14[14]. **c.** *take away,* guilt, iniquity, transgression, etc., i.e. *forgive,* c. acc. Gn 50[17] (E), Ex 32[32] (E), 10[17] 34[7] (J), Nu 14[18] (JE), 1 S 15[25] Ho 14[3] Jb 7[21] (‖ הֶעֱבִיר עָוֺן), ψ 32[5]; + לְ pers. Mi 7[18]; לְ pers., acc. om., Gn 18[26] (J), Nu 14[19] (JE; ‖ סלח עָוֺן), Ho 1[6] Is 2[9] (prob. gloss.), ψ 99[8]; c. לְ of sin Gn 50[17] Ex 23[21] (both E), 1 S 25[28] ψ 25[18]; נְשֻׂא עָוֺן Is 33[24]; נְשׂוּי־פֶּשַׁע ψ 32[1]. [In this sense נ׳ used in E; סלח in D P; both in J; נ׳ also in early proph., S. and Jb, and in earlier and latest ψψ; not in Je K Is[2] La Chr Dn, which use סלח; v. Br[Hex. 155].] **d.** *take* as wife (usu. c. לְ *for*), late: Ezr 9[2.12] 10[44] Ne 13[25] 2 Ch 11[21] 13[21] 24[3] Ru 1[4]. **e.** *take* an enumeration, usu. c. ראשׁ *sum* Ex 30[12] Nu 1[2.49] 4[2.22] 26[2] 32[26.49] (all P); c. מִסְפָּר Nu 3[40] 1 Ch 27[23]. **f.** *take and carry away, receive,* Dt 33[3] 1 K 5[23] ψ 24[5]; hence, *obtain* favour (חֵן, חֶסֶד) Est 2[9.17] (both + לִפְנֵי), 5[2] (+ בְּעֵינָיו).— לְמַשְׂאוֹת אוֹתָהּ מִשָּׁרָשֶׁיהָ Ez 17[9] (Co Berthol לְיוֹם שְׂאֵת וגו׳) is usu. rendered *plucking it up* (tearing it away) *by the roots,* but dub.; נ׳ not elsewhere in this sense.

†**Niph.** *Pf.* נִשָּׂא Je 51[9], וְנ׳ consec. Ex 25[28]+; *Impf.* יִנָּשֵׂא Is 40[4]; 3 mpl. יִנָּשְׂאוּ Ez 1[19.20.21], יִנָּשׂוּא Je 10[5], יִנָּשֵׂאוּ Pr 30[13]; 3 fpl. תִּנָּשֶׂאנָה Is 49[22], etc.; *Imv.* הִנָּשֵׂא ψ 7[7] 94[2], mpl. הִנָּשְׂאוּ ψ 24[7]; *Inf.* הִנָּשֵׂא Ez 1[19], sf. הִנָּשְׂאָם Ez
1[21]; *Pt.* נִשָּׂא Is 2[2]+, f. נִשָּׂאָה Is 30[25], נִשֵּׂאת Zc 5379
5[7] 1 Ch 14[2], etc.;—2 S 19[43] is dub., and pt. (Ol[§ 192 c] Kö[i. 632 f.]) inexplicable; rd. נִשֹּׂא (Inf. abs. **Niph.**) Dr (cf. Th), or מַשְׂאֵת *portion* Gr HPS; >Ba[NB 90] thinks נִשֵּׂאת Inf. Niph. with compensative ending;—**1.** *be lifted up,* **a.** lit. Zc 5[7] Ez 1[19.21] (both מֵעַל הָאָרֶץ), v[19.20.21] (all in vision), of valleys Is 40[4]; of gates ψ 24[7] + v[9 b] (rd. **Niph.**); of eyelids Pr 30[13] (*superciliousness*); metaph. of judgment on Babylon *reaching up* to the sky (עַד); pt. = *elevated, exalted* Is 6[1] (of י׳'s throne, in vision); of lofty hills Is 2[14] 30[25] 57[7], cf. Mi 4[1] = Is 2[2] (מִן, *lifted from out* the hills), once of trees 2[13] (text dub.); gen., Is 2[12]. **b.** fig., *be exalted,* of kg., 2 Ch 32[23], kingdom 1 Ch 14[2], servant of י׳ Is 52[13], י׳ himself 57[15]. **2.** refl. *lift oneself up* = *rise up,* of י׳, to display power in judgment: Is 33[10] ψ 94[2]. **3.** *be borne, carried* Je 10[5] Ex 25[28] (P), Is 49[22] 66[12]. **4.** *be taken away, carried off,* 2 K 20[17] (ה loc.) = Is 39[6]; *be swept away* (of multitude) Dn 11[12] (cf. Bev Behrm, Prince, v. also **Qal 3**; Ew Hi as **2**, v. Dr).

†**Pi.** *Pf.* נִשֵּׂא 2 S 5[12], נִשָּׂא (anal. of ל׳ ה) 2 S 19[43] 1 K 9[11], וְנִשֵּׂא consec. Am 4[2], etc.; *Impf.* 3 ms. sf. וַיְנַשְּׂאֵהוּ Est 3[1], וַיְנַשְּׂאֵם Is 63[9]; 3 mpl. sf. יְנַשְּׂאוּהוּ Ezr 1[4]; *Imv.* ms. sf. נַשְּׂאֵם ψ 28[9]; *Pt.* pl. מְנַשְּׂאִים Je 22[27] + 2 t.;—**1.** *lift up* = exalt,

kingdom 2 S 5^{12} (‖ **Niph.** 1 Ch 14^{2}), pers. Est 5^{11} (עַל), cf. 3^{1}; =*support, aid, assist* Ezr 8^{36} Est 9^{3}; c. ב *aid with trees* (supply with) 1 K 9^{11}, so Ezr 1^{4}. **2.** fig. נ׳ נֶפֶשׁ = desire, long, Je 22^{14} 44^{14}. **3.** *carry, bear continuously* Is 63^{9}, ψ 28^{9}. **4.** *take, take away* 2 S 19^{43} (ל *for;* but v. **Niph.** supr.); Am 4^{2} (ב instr.; We Now וְנִשְּׂאוּ).—†**Hithp.** *Impf.* יִתְנַשָּׂא Nu 23^{24}; 3 fs. תִּנַּשֵּׂא 24^{7}; 2 ms. תִּתְנַשֵּׂא Ez 29^{15}; 3 mpl. יִנַּשְּׂאוּ Dn 11^{14}; 2 mpl. תִּתְנַשְּׂאוּ Nu 16^{3}; *Inf.* הִתְנַשֵּׂא Ez 17^{14} Pr 30^{32}; *Pt.* מִתְנַשֵּׂא 1 K 1^{5} 1 Ch 29^{11};—*lift oneself up*, like a lion Nu 23^{24} (JE); pt. *he who exalts himself* 1 Ch 29^{11} (+ לְכֹל לְראֹשׁ) as human ruler (Kau), > (sc. אַתָּה) of י׳ as ruler; Ew§ 160 e Ke Be as subst. [inf. of Aram. form], *the exaltation;* of a kingdom Nu 24^{7} (JE), cf. Ez 17^{14}; in arrogance 1 K 1^{5} Nu 16^{3} (P; c. עַל־), Ez 29^{15} (c. עַל), Pr 30^{32} Dn 11^{14}. †**Hiph.** *Pf.* 3 ms. consec. **1.** *cause one to bear* iniquity (2 acc.) וְהִשִּׂיאוּ Lv 22^{16}. **2.** appar. *cause to bring, have brought,* וְהִשִּׂיאוּ 2 S 17^{13} (c. acc. rei + אֶל loc.), but very dub.; Ki Kit Bu וְיָשִׂימוּ; HPS וְהֵבִיאוּ; > We הֵשִׂימוּ.

5379 **נְשֵׂאת** 2 S 19^{43} v. נשׂא **Niph.** p. 671

5385 †[נְשׂוּאָה] **n.f.** what is borne about;—pl. sf. נְשֻׂאֹתֵיכֶם עֲמוּסוֹת Is 46^{1}, *your things* (formerly) *borne about* in procession (i. e. idols) are now loaded on beasts for exile.

5387 I. **נָשִׂיא** 128 **n.m.** one lifted up, i.e. a chief prince;—abs. נ׳ Ex 22^{27}+; cstr. נְשִׂיא Gn 23^{6}+; pl. נְשִׂיאִם Jos 22^{32}+, נְשִׂאִים Ex 34^{31}+7 t., נְשִׂיאִם Gn 17^{20}+3 t., נְשִׂאִם Ex 35^{27}; cstr. נְשִׂיאֵי Ex 16^{22}+; sf. נְשִׂיאַי Ez 45^{8}, נְשִׂאֶיהָ Ez 32^{29}, נְשִׂיאֵיהֶם Nu 17^{21}, נְשִׂאֵהֶם v^{17}, etc.;—mostly in Isr.: **1.** נ׳ בְּעַמְּךָ of any chief man, Ex 22^{27} (E; human ruler, over ag. אֱלֹהִים). **2.** of Solom. 1 K 11^{34}. Elsewhere only Ez P Chr:—**3.** of Abr. Gn 23^{6}, and heads of Ishmaelite tribes 17^{20} 25^{16}. **4.** rulers of the congregation, נְשִׂיאֵי הָעֵדָה Ex 16^{22} Jos $9^{15.18}$ 22^{30}, הַנּ׳ בָּעֵדָה 34^{31}, cf. 35^{27} Lv 4^{22} Jos $9^{18\,b.\,19.21.21}$ 17^{4} $22^{14.14.14.32}$ (all P); esp. **5.** tribal chiefs and representatives, acc. to the religious organization of P, Nu $1^{16.44}$ 2^{3}+57 t. Nu (esp. chaps. 2, 7, 34; note נְשִׂיא נְשִׂיאֵי הַלֵּוִי 3^{32}); cf. 1 Ch 2^{10} 4^{38} 5^{6} 7^{40} 2 Ch 1^{2}, also 1 K 8^{1} (prob. gloss, om. 𝔊 Benz), 2 Ch 5^{2}. **6.** in Ezek.: **a.** of Zedekiah (for מֶלֶךְ; v. Böhmer SK 1900, 112 ff.), 7^{27} $12^{10.12}$ 21^{30}, + 19^{1} (rd. sg. 𝔊 Ew Hi Co Berthol Toy). **b.** chief men of Judah 21^{17} 22^{6} $45^{8.9}$. **c.** future Davidic kg. 34^{24} 37^{25}, cf. $44^{3.3}$ + 16 t. Ez 45, 46, 48. **d.** foreign princes 26^{16} 27^{21} 30^{13} 32^{29} $38^{2.3}$ $39^{1.18}$. **7.** leader of exiles returning under Cyrus, acc. to Ezr 1^{8}. **8.** non-Isr. chiefs in P: Gn 34^{2} Nu 25^{18} Jos 13^{21}.

†II. [נָשִׂיא] **n.[m.]** rising mist, vapour 5387
(Ar. نَشْءٌ, (نَشِيٌّ);—only pl. נְשִׂאִים *vapours*, forming clouds, and portending rain, Je 10^{13} = 51^{16}, ψ 135^{7}, נְשִׂיאִים Pr 25^{14}.

†II. **מַשָּׂא** **n.m.** ψ 38, 5 load, burden, lifting, 4853
bearing, tribute;—מ׳ abs. Ne 13^{19}+; cstr. 2 K 5^{17}+; sf. מַשָּׂאוֹ Ex 23^{5}+2 t.; מַשַּׂאֲכֶם Dt 1^{12}; מַשָּׂאָם Nu 4^{27}+2 t.;—**1.** *load, burden* of ass Ex 23^{5} (E), mules 2 K 5^{17}, camels 8^{9}, cf. Is $46^{1.2}$; hanging on a peg Is 22^{25} (fig.); forbidden on Sabbath Je $17^{21.22.24.27}$ Ne $13^{15.19}$; fig. of people as burden Nu $11^{11.17}$ (JE), Dt 1^{12}, cf. הָיָה לְמ׳ עַל־ 2 S 15^{33} 19^{36} (אֶל־), also וָאֶהְיֶה עָלַי לְמַשָּׂא Jb 7^{20}; of iniquities ψ 38^{5}.—Ho 8^{10} rd. מְשֹׁחַ, so 𝔊 We Now GASm. **2.** n. verb., *lifting, uplifting*, only מ׳ נַפְשָׁם Ez 24^{25} *the uplifting of their soul*, i. e. that to which they lift up their soul, their heart's desire. **3.** n. verb., *bearing, carrying*, Nu 4^{24} (+ לַעֲבֹד), 2 Ch 20^{25} 35^{3} (בַּכָּתֵף), so prob. 1 Ch $15^{22.22.27}$ (cf. Be Kau; > *singing, uplifting of voice*, e.g. Öt); esp. of *responsibility and duty of bearing* sacred vessels (oft. ‖ עֲבֹדָה, מִשְׁמֶרֶת מ׳, פְּקֻדָּה) Nu $4^{15.19.27.27.49}$, עֲבֹדַת מ׳ v^{47}, $v^{31.32}$. **4.** perhaps *what is carried, brought*, i.e. *tribute* כֶּסֶף מ׳ 2 Ch 17^{11} *silver* as *tribute* (+ מִנְחָה; cf. נשׂא **Qal**; others, *silver by the load*, i.e. in great quantity).—I. מַשָּׂא v. supr. p. 601 b. 4854

†III. **מַשָּׂא** **n.m.** Is 14, 28 utterance, oracle 4853
(cf. נשׂא **1 b** (6); Gf Je 23, 33);—מ׳ abs. Is 14^{28}+; usu. cstr. 13^{1}+;—of prophetic *utterance:* 2 K 9^{25} Is 14^{28} Ez 12^{10} 2 Ch 24^{27} (c. עַל); מ׳ בָּבֶל Is 13^{1}, מ׳ מוֹאָב 15^{1}, cf. 17^{1} 19^{1} $21^{1.11}$ 22^{1} 23^{1} 30^{6} Na 1^{1}; מ׳ בערב Is 21^{13} is later ins. (Di); מ׳ = *revelation*, הַמּ׳ אֲשֶׁר חָזָה חֲבַקּוּק הַנָּבִיא Hb 1^{1}; מ׳ י׳ *utterance of* י׳ Je $23^{33.34.36.38.38.38}$ (cf. 2 K 9^{25}), vid. also $v^{33\,b}$ (rd. אַתֶּם הַמַּשָּׂא), with word-play, —sq. וְנָטַשְׁתִּי, $v^{36\,b}$; מ׳ דְּבַר י׳ Zc 9^{1} (+ בארץ), 12^{1} (+ עַל־יִשְׂרָאֵל), Mal 1^{1} (+ אֶל־יִשׂ׳).—Pr 31^{1} v. I. מַשָּׂא, p. 601 supr.; in 30^{1} rd. מִמַּשָּׂא *from Massa* (Mühlau, De), or הַמַּשָּׂאִי (Wild), which however is perhaps not original, but borrowed from 31^{1} (cf. Wild ad loc. Frankenberg Spr. p. 5; corrupt name of Agur's home or tribe, Kau).

4856 †מַשֹּׂא **n.m.** lifting up;—only cstr. מ׳ פָּנִים 2 Ch 19^{7} = *regarding of persons* (partiality, see √**1 a** (3); || מִקַּח־שֹׁחַד).

4858 †מַשָּׂאָה **n.f.** the uplifted (cloud);—כֹּבֶד מ׳ Is 30^{27} *weight of uplifted clouds.*

4864 †מַשְׂאֵת **n.f.** uprising, utterance, burden, portion (on format. cf. Ol^{§109a} Sta^{§272b} Kö$^{ii.1,183}$; Ph. (Pun) has משאת = *payment, tax* v. Lzb^{326});—abs. מ׳ Ju 20^{40}+; cstr. מַשְׂאַת Gn 43^{34}+; pl. abs. מַשְׂאֹת Gn 43^{34}, + (prob.) מַשְׂאוֹת La 2^{14} (v. infr.); cstr. מַשְׂאֹת Gn 43^{34};—**1.** *that which rises, uprising, uplifting:* **a.** מ׳ הֶעָשָׁן Ju 20^{38} *uprising of smoke*, cf. (הֶע׳ om.) v^{40}. **b.** in gen. = *signal* Je 6^{1} (= נֵס Gf.). **c.** *uplifting* of hands (כַּפַּי) in prayer ψ 141^{2} (|| תְּפִלָּה). **2.** *utterance, oracle* (= III. מַשָּׂא), La 2^{14} (Bu Löhr). **3.** *burden* Zp 3^{18} (of reproach, fig.). **4. a.** *portion* (carried to some one), esp. from table of king or superior, Gn 43$^{34.34.34}$ (J; on custom v. Di and reff.), 2 S 11^{8}; so rd. perh. also 2 S 19^{43} (for MT נִשֵּׂאת) Gr HPS. **b.** perh. also more gen., *present, largess* from a superior Je 40^{5} (+ אֲרֻחָה *food-allowance*), Est 2^{18} (כְּיַד הַמֶּלֶךְ). **c.** exacted or enforced *gift*, from inferior, מ׳ בַּר Am 5^{11} (cf. Ph. supr.; v. also מנחה). **d.** sacred *contribution, tax* מ׳ מֹשֶׁה עֶבֶד (י׳) 2 Ch 24$^{6.9}$. **e.** *offering* to י׳ Ez 20^{40}.

7863 †[שִׂיא] **n.m.** *loftiness*, fig. of pride:—אִם־יַעֲלֶה לַשָּׁמַיִם שִׂיאוֹ Jb 20^{6} (of wicked).

7865 †שִׂיאֹן **n.pr.mont.**, i.e. Hermon, הַר שׂ׳ הוּא חֶרְמוֹן Dt 4^{48} (cf. Di Dr).

7613 †שְׂאֵת **n.f. 1.** exaltation, dignity. **2.** swelling. **3.** uprising;—שׂ׳ abs. Gn 4^{7}+, cstr. Lv 13^{28}+; sf. שְׂאֵתוֹ Jb 13^{11}+; (מִ)שְּׂתוֹ 41^{17};—**1.** *dignity* Gn 49^{3} (dignity of first-born), ψ 62^{5}, of Chaldeans Hb 1^{7}; of God, *his exaltation, loftiness* Jb 13^{11} 31^{23}. **2.** *swelling*, eruption, בְּעוֹר בְּשָׂרוֹ Lv 13^{2} (+ סַפַּחַת, בַּהֶרֶת), cf. 14^{56} (+*id.*); also 13$^{10.10.19.28}$, שׂ׳ הַנֶּגַע v^{43} (all P). **3.** *uprising*, Jb 41^{17} *at his uprising the mighty are in dread.* **4.** Gn 4^{7} is dub.;—is there not *acceptance?* 𝔖 𝔙 al.; *forgiveness* 𝔗 Holz al.; *uplifting* of countenance, cheerfulness, Ew De Ke Di Kau.

5381 †[נָשַׂג] **vb.** only **Hiph.** reach, overtake (Ecclus 14^{13} והשגת ידך, 35^{10} ובהשגת יד (cf. Schechter on 14^{13}), cf. **3** infr.; ישיג מענה 32^{14} *shall obtain an answer;*—**Hiph.** *Pf.* 3 ms. וְהִשִּׂיג consec. Lv 25^{6}, sf. וְהִשִּׂיגוֹ consec. Dt 19^{6}; 2 ms. sf. וְהִשַּׂגְתָּם consec. Gn 44^{4}, etc.; *Impf.* יַשִּׂיג Lv 26^{5}, וַיַּשֵּׂג Gn 31^{25}, sf. וַיַּשִּׂגֵם Gn 44^{26}, etc.; *Inf. abs.* הַשֵּׂג 1 S 30^{8}; *Pt.* מַשִּׂיג 1 S 14^{26}, sf. מַשִּׂיגֵהוּ Jb 41^{18}; f. מַשֶּׂגֶת Lv 14^{21} 1 Ch 21^{12} (but rd. וְאִם הֱיוֹת as || 2 S 24^{13} We^{Sm} Kit);—**1.** *overtake*, c. acc., oft. after רָדַף: **a.** lit. Gn 31^{25} (E), 44$^{4.6}$ (J), Ex 14^{9} (P), 15^{9} (song), Dt 19^{6} Jos 2^{5} (JE), 1 S 30$^{8.8.8}$ 2 S 15^{14} 2 K 25^{5} = Je 39^{5} = 52^{8}, Ho 2^{9}, cf. ψ 7^{6} 18^{38} (וָאַשְׁמִידֵם in || 2 S 22^{38}), La 1^{3} (metaph.). **b.** fig. of battle Ho 10^{9}, sword Je 42^{16}; on 1 Ch 21^{12} v. supr.; of blessings Dt 28^{2}, curses v$^{15.45}$, predictions Zc 1^{6}, justice Is 59^{9}, wrath of י׳ ψ 69^{25}, iniquities 40^{13}, calamities Jb 27^{20}. **2. a.** *reach, attain to*, Jb 41^{18} (if one) *reach it* (crocodile) with the sword (2 acc.); fig. paths of life Pr 2^{19}, joy, etc., Is 35^{10} also 51^{11} (Che^{Hpt} יַשִּׂיגוּם, for MT יַשִּׂיגוּן; Perles$^{Analekten\ 64}$ יְשֻׂגּוּן, fr. שׂגה); of time Gn 47^{9} my days *have not reached* the days . . . of my fathers, cf. Lv 26$^{5.5}$. **b.** *cause to reach, bring, put,* מַשִּׂיג יָדוֹ אֶל־פִּיו 1 S 14^{26} no one *put his hand to his mouth,* but rd. מֵשִׁיב 𝔊 𝔗 Klo Dr Bu Kit HPS Löhr. **3.** fig. הִשִּׂיגָה יָדוֹ *one's hand has reached,* i.e. one is able, or has enough, Lv 5^{11} (c. לְ), 14^{21} 25$^{26.49}$; c. acc. = *able to secure, get* 14$^{22.30.31.32}$ 27^{8} Nu 6^{21} (all P), Ez 46^{7}; abs. = gain (riches) Lv 25^{47} (H).—Jb 24^{2} v. סוג.

נשק v. שׂלק. p. 969 5400

נשר (√ of foll.; NH נָסַר *saw* (Qal Pi.); Aram. נְסַר, ܢܣܰܪ *saw;* cf. Eth. ወሰረ: *id.;* Ar. مِنْشَار n. *a saw*).

†מַשּׂוֹר **n.m.** saw;—abs. Is 10^{15}. 4883

†I. [נָשָׂא] **vb.** lend on interest, or usury, 5378
be a creditor (cf. Ar. نَسَأَ *postpone, delay; sell on credit;* || form of I. נָשָׁה, v. Ges^{§75oo});—**Qal** *Pt. act.* נֹשֶׁא (anal. ל׳ ה) 1 S 22^{2} every man that had *a creditor;* אֲשֶׁר נֹשֶׁא בוֹ Is 24^{2} *against whom is a creditor,* and pl. נֹשְׁאִים Ne 5^{7} Kt (נֹשִׁים Qr, from נָשָׁה), + acc. cogn. מַשָּׁא. **Hiph.** *Impf.* 5383
3 ms. לֹא־יַשִּׁא אוֹיֵב בּוֹ ψ 89^{23} *an enemy shall not act the creditor against him, make exactions of him* (|| יְעַנֶּנּוּ).—1 K 8^{31} 2 Ch 6^{22} v. נשׂא **Qal 1 b** (5).

†מַשָּׁא **n.m.**$^{Ne\ 5,10}$ lending on interest, or 4855
usury;—Ne 5^{7} (as acc. cogn.), v^{10}.

†[מַשָּׁאָה] **n.f.** loan (on pledge);—cstr. 4859
כִּי תַשֶּׁה בְרֵעֲךָ מַשַּׁאת מְאוּמָה Dt 24^{10}; pl. עֹרְבִים מַשָּׁאוֹת Pr 22^{26} *those pledging* (giving security for) *debts.*

5377 †II. נָשָׁא **vb.** only **Niph. Hiph. beguile,
deceive**;—(kindred with I. שׁוא, from which,
however, the forms can hardly be derived (conj.
We $^{Comp. 2. 351}$));—**Niph.** *Pf.* 3 pl. נִשְּׁאוּ Is 19^{13}
the princes *have been beguiled* (|| נוֹאֲלוּ, הִתְעוּ).
Hiph. *Pf.* הִשִּׁיא Je 49^{16}, sf. הִשִּׁאַנִי Gn 3^{13},
הִשִּׁיאֶךָ Ob^{3}; 2 ms. הִשֵּׁאתָ Je 4^{10}; 3 pl. sf. הִשִּׁיאוּךָ
Ob^{7}; *Impf.* only juss. יַשִּׁיא 2 Ch 32^{15}, so ψ 55^{16}
Qr (v. infr.); יַשִּׁא 2 K 18^{29} Is 36^{14}, sf. יַשִּׁאֲךָ
2 K 19^{10} Is 37^{10}; 2 mpl. תַּשִּׁאוּ Je 37^{9}; *Inf. abs.*
הַשֵּׁא Je 4^{10};—*beguile*, usu. c. acc. pers. Gn 3^{13}
(J; not elsewh. Hex); Je 49^{16} Ob$^{3.7}$; אַל־יַשִּׁאֲךָ
2 K 19^{10} *let not thy God beguile thee* = Is 37^{10},
of Hezekiah 2 Ch 32^{15} (cf. infr.), אַל־תַּשִּׁאוּ
נַפְשֹׁתֵיכֶם Je 37^{9} *do not deceive yourselves;* also
sq. לְ pers. אַל־יַשִּׁא לָכֶם 2 K 18^{29} = Is 36^{14}
(= 2 Ch 32^{15}, v. supr.), Je 29^{8}; הַשֵּׁא הִשֵּׁאתָ לָעָם
הַזֶּה 4^{10} *thou hast utterly beguiled this people;*
ישימות עָלֵימוֹ ψ 55^{16} Kt appar. = *desolations* (*be*)
upon them! (but elsewh. only in n.pr.loc., cf.
p. 445 supr.), < Qr יַשִּׁיא מָוֶת עלימו Ew Ol Pe
De Now ^{Hup}, cf. 𝔊, *let death* (*beguile them*, i.e.)
come deceitfully upon them! Brüll Che, cf. Bae,
conj. plausibly יַשִּׁיא מָוֶת יִבְלָעֵמוֹ.

4860 †מַשָּׁאוֹן **n.[m.] guile, dissimulation** (>
acc. to Lag $^{BN 196}$ der. fr. מַשָּׁא, *lending on usury*);
תִּכַּסֶּה שִׂנְאָה בְּמַשָּׁאוֹן Pr 26^{26} *hatred may hide
itself with dissimulation.*

4876 †מַשּׁוּאוֹת **n.f.pl.** *deceptions* ψ 73^{18} 74^{3},
but meaning not suitable; read prob. מְשֹׁאוֹת,
4875 v. מְשׁוֹאָה sub שׁוא (so Klo Now ^{Hup} Bae). p. 996

5382 III. [נָשָׁא] *forget*, v. II. נָשָׁה. below

5380 †[נָשַׁב] **vb. blow** (NH = BH; 𝔗 נְשַׁב
(but also נְתַב), Syr. ܢܫܒ, all *blow;* || form of
נָשַׁף);—**Qal** *Pf.* 3 fs. רוּחַ י׳ נָשְׁבָה בּוֹ Is 40^{7} *the
breath of* י׳ *has blown upon it.* **Hiph.** *Impf.*
3 ms. יַשֵּׁב רוּחוֹ ψ 147^{18} *he causes* his wind *to
blow;* וַיַּשֵּׁב אֹתָם Gn 15^{11} *and he drove them
away* (perh. orig. *blow away*, drive away by
blowing, or by a sound like blowing).

†I. נָשָׁה **vb. lend, become a creditor**
(cf. I. נשא);—**Qal** *Pf.* 1 s. נָשִׁיתִי Je 15^{10}; 3 pl.
נָשׁוּ v^{10}; *Pt.* נֹשֶׁה Ex 22^{24} + 4 t.; pl. נֹשִׁים Ne
5378 5$^{10.11}$ + v^{7} Qr (Kt נשׁאים, v. I. נשא), sf. נוֹשַׁי Is
50^{1};—*lend*, usu. c. בְּ pers.: לֹא־נָשִׁיתִי וְלֹא־נָשׁוּ־בִי
Je 15^{10} *I have not lent, and they have not lent
to me*, Dt 24^{11} Ne 5^{7} (Qr; + acc. cogn.), v$^{10.11}$
(both + acc. rei); pt. as subst. *creditor, usurer*
Ex 22^{24} (E), 2 K 4^{1} Is 24^{2} 50^{1} ψ 109^{11}. **Hiph.**
Impf. 3 ms. יַשֶּׁה בְּ Dt 15^{2} *who lendeth to* his
neighbour; 2 ms. תַּשֶּׁה בְ 24^{10} when *thou lendest
to* thy neighbour (+ acc. cogn.).

†[נְשִׁי] **n.[m.]** debt;—only sf. 2 fs. נשיכי 5386
Kt, נִשְׁיֵךְ Qr 2 K 4^{7} (so Baer; van d. H. Ginsb
נִשְׁיֵךְ) *pay* (שַׁלְּמִי) *thy debt.*

†[מַשֶּׁה] **n.m.** loan;—only cstr. שָׁמוֹט כָּל־ 4874
בַּעַל מַשֵּׁה יָדוֹ אֲשֶׁר יַשֶּׁה בְּרֵעֵהוּ Dt 15^{2} *every possessor of a loan of his hand shall renounce
what he lends to his neighbour* (cf. Dr).

†II. [נָשָׁה] **vb.** forget (NH *id.;* As. 5382
nišîtu perh. *forgottenness* Dl $^{HWB 486}$; Aram.
נְשָׁא (esp. Ithpe., Aph.), ܢܫܐ *forget;* Ar. نَسِيَ
forget, neglect; cf. Eth. ናሕሰየ፡ *ignoscere, con-
donare, indulgere* Di ^{633});—**Qal** *Pf.* 1 s. וְנָשִׁיתִי
אֶתְכֶם נָשֹׁא Je 23^{39} *I will forget you finally*
(but 𝔊 𝔙 𝔖 Che Gie וְנָשָׂאתִי, sq. וְנָטַשְׁתִּי as v$^{33 b}$,
v. III. מַשָּׂא); נָשִׁיתִי טוֹבָה La 3^{17} *I have forgotten
prosperity; Impf.* 1 s. הַאֶשֶּׁה *shall I forget?* i.e.
overlook, rd. by We Mi 6^{10} plausibly for MT הַאִשׁ;
Inf. abs. נָשֹׁא (ל״א) Je 23^{39} (v. supr.). **Niph.**
Impf. 2 ms. sf. תִּנָּשֵׁנִי Is 44^{21} *thou shalt not be
forgotten of me*, but dub.; Ges $^{§ 117*}$ תִּנְשֵׁנִי (Qal);
Che ^{Hpt} תִּטְשֵׁנִי (cf. Dt 32^{15}). **Pi.** *Pf.* 3 ms.
sf. נַשַּׁנִי Gn 41^{51} (E) *God hath made me forget*
+ acc. rei (ַ in 1st syllable only here, infl. of
מְנַשֶּׁה Ges $^{§ 52 m}$). **Hiph.** *Pf.* 3 ms. sf. הִשָּׁהּ
חָכְמָה Jb 39^{17} *God caused her* (the ostrich) *to
forget* wisdom, i.e. did not endow her with it.
Impf. יַשֶּׁה לְךָ מִן־ Jb 11^{6} Eloah *allows a part
of* thy guilt *to be forgotten thee*, i.e. does not
reckon it to thee in full (𝔊 = יִשְׁוֶה לְךָ מֵאֱלוֹהַּ
כַּעֲוֺנֶךָ [Du] *there is equivalent to thee from
Eloah, acc. to thine iniquity*, cf. Bi Che $^{Job and Sol.}$;
Bu reads נָשָׁה for יַשֶּׁה; Du rejects ver. as gloss).

†נְשִׁיָּה **n.f. forgetfulness, oblivion,** אֶרֶץ נ׳ 5388
ψ 88^{13} (|| חֹשֶׁךְ), designation of שְׁאוֹל (cf. v$^{11.12}$).

†יִשִּׁיָּה, יִשִּׁיָּהוּ **n.pr.m.** **1.** †יִשִּׁיָּהוּ 1 Ch 3449
12^{7} (van d.H. v^{6}) one of David's heroes, 𝔊 Ιησου-
νει, A Ιεσια, 𝔊L Ιεσσουε. **2.** יִשִּׁיָּה, a man
of Issachar 1 Ch 7^{3}, 𝔊 Εισια, Ιεσια, 𝔊L Ιωσια
(and so in foll.). **3.** Levites: **a.** 1 Ch 23^{20}
24$^{25.25}$. **b.** 1 Ch 24^{21}, 𝔊 Ιεσεια, etc. **4.** one
of those strange wives Ezr 10^{31}, 𝔊 Ιεσσ(ε)ια.

†נָשֶׁה **n.[m.] a vein (or nerve) in the** 5384
thigh (etym. dub.; on format. cf. Lag $^{BN 50}$;
Ar. نَسًا appar. *the portion of the principal*

vein of the leg which is in the thigh, vulg. *sciatic vein*, or (mod.) *sciatic nerve* and even *sciatica*, Lane ^{3033});—only גִּיד הַנָּשֶׁה Gn 32^{33a} *the sinew of the thigh-vein* (or *thigh-nerve*, אֲשֶׁר עַל־כַּף הַיָּרֵךְ), cf. v^{33b}.—On sacredness of thigh, cf. RS $^{Sem\ i.\ 360;\ 2nd\ ed.\ 380}$ We $^{Held\ (2),\ 168}$.

נָשִׁים v. אִשָּׁה p. 61 supr.

5391 † **נָשַׁךְ vb. bite** (NH = BH, but also transp. נָכַשׁ Hiph.); As. *našâku* Dl$^{HWB\ 486}$; ℭ נְכֵית (esp. of snakes); Syr. ܢܟܬ, ܢܟܬ; Eth. ነከሰ: Di^{642}; Ba$^{ZMG\ xliii\ (1889),\ 188}$ cp. Ar. نَكَثَ, *undo* threads, *untwist* rope, *disintegrate, dissolve*);—**Qal** *Pf.* 3 ms. נָשַׁךְ Nu 21^9, sf. וּנְשָׁכוֹ consec. Am 5^{19}, וּנְשָׁכָם consec. 9^3; *Impf.* 3 ms. יִשֹּׁךְ Ec 10^{11}, יִשָּׁךְ Pr 23^{32}, sf. יִשְּׁכֶנּוּ Ec 10^8; *Pt. act.* נֹשֵׁךְ Gn 49^{17}; pl. נֹשְׁכִים Mi 3^5, sf. נֹשְׁכֶיךָ Hb 2^7; *pass.* נָשׁוּךְ Nu 21^8;—*bite*, chiefly of serpent, c. acc., Am 5^{19} 9^3 Gn 49^{17} (poem in J), Nu 21^8 (pt. pass., abs.), v^9, Ec 10^8 also v^{11} (abs.), Pr 23^{32} (sim. of wine); fig. of prophets הַנּ׳ בְּשִׁנֵּיהֶם Mi 3^5 *who are biting with their teeth*, and crying, Peace! fig. of oppression, etc., נֹשְׁכֶיךָ Hb 2^7 (with play on sense *thy debtors, those that give thee interest*). **Pi.** *Pf.* 3 pl. וְנִשְּׁכוּ אֶתְכֶם Je 8^{17} *and they shall bite you fatally* (fig.); *Impf.* 3 mpl. וַיְנַשְּׁכוּ אֶת־הָעָם Nu 21^6 *and they bit the people fatally* (both of serpents).

5392 † **נֶשֶׁךְ n.[m.] interest, usury** (lit. *something bitten off*);—נ׳ abs. Ex 22^{24} +; cstr. Dt 23^{20};—c. שִׂים עַל־ Ex 22^{24} (E); c. לָקַח מִן Lv 25^{36}, הֵשִׁיב מִן Ez 18^{17}, לָקַח 22^{12} (no prep.), בְּנֶשֶׁךְ Lv 25^{37} *at interest*, so ψ 15^5 Ez $18^{8.13}$; בְּנ׳ Pr 28^8 *by usury*; as acc. cogn. Dt $23^{20.20.20}$.

5391 † [**נָשַׁךְ**] **vb. denom.** pay, give interest (cf. Gerber$^{Verba\ denom.\ 89}$);—**Qal** *Impf.* 3 ms. יִשָּׁךְ Dt 23^{20} interest of anything off which *one giveth interest* (cf. Dr). **Hiph.** *make* one *give interest*; *Impf.* 2 ms. תַשִּׁיךְ Dt 23^{20} (+ acc. cogn.) $v^{21.21}$, all c. לְ pers.

5393 † **נִשְׁכָּה n.f. chamber** (rare ∥ of לִשְׁכָּה, q.v.; cf. W$^{SG\ 67}$);—abs. נ׳ Ne 13^7, sf. נִשְׁכָּתוֹ Ne 3^{30}, both rooms of individuals; pl. abs. נְשָׁכוֹת 12^{44} (Chr) = treasuries, storehouses.

5394 † **נָשַׁל vb. 1.** intrans. **slip** or **drop off**; also trans.: **2. draw off. 3. clear away** (NH נָשַׁל prob. intrans., Qal not used, but n. נְשִׁילָה *a falling off*, etc.; Pi. Hiph. *cast off, let fall off*, Niph. *be cast off, fall off*; ℭ Aph. אַשִּׁיל *cast out* (fr. house); Ar. نَسَلَ *excidit* pluma, etc.; but also trans., avis *mutavit rejecitque* plumas (Frey);—نَشَلَ *celeriter extraxit*, etc., is denom. fr. loan-word acc. to Frä^{88});—**Qal** *Pf.* וְנָשַׁל consec. Dt 7^1 + 2 t.; *Impf.* 3 ms. יִשַּׁל Dt 28^{40}; *Imv.* ms. שַׁל Ex 3^5 Jos 5^{15};—**1.** *slip or drop off*, וְנָשַׁל הַבַּרְזֶל מִן־הָעֵץ Dt 19^5 *and the iron slippeth off from the wood* (i.e. axe-head from helve); יִשַּׁל זֵיתֶךָ Dt 28^{40} *thine olives shall drop off* (abs.). **2.** *draw off* sandal fr. (מֵעַל) foot Ex 3^5 (E), Jos 5^{15} (JE). **3.** *clear away* nations מִפָּנֶיךָ Dt $7^{1.22}$. **Pi.** *Impf.* 3 ms. וַיְנַשֵּׁל 2 K 16^6 *he cleared* the Jews *entirely* out of (מִן) Elath.

† [**נָשַׁם**] **vb. pant** (NH in nn. נְשָׁמָה, נְשִׁימָה, ℭ נִשְׁמְתָא, נִשְׁמָא; late Aram. Ithpe.; Syr. ܢܫܡ *breathe, blow*; Ar. نَسَمَ *gently breathe* (of wind), etc.; v. *seek a thing with labour and perseverance* (Lane^{3032}); نَسَمَةٌ *a soul*, Lane$^{ib.}$);—*pant*, of the deep and strong breathing of a woman in travail; **Qal** *Impf.* 1 s. אֶשֹּׁם Is 42^{14}. 5395

† **נְשָׁמָה n.f. breath**;—נ׳ Dt 20^{16} + 9 t.; cstr. נִשְׁמַת (cf. Lag$^{BN\ 82}$) Gn 2^7 + 10 t.; sf. נִשְׁמָתִי Jb 27^3; נִשְׁמָתוֹ Jb 34^{14}; pl. נְשָׁמוֹת Is 57^{16};—**1.** *breath* of God as hot wind kindling a flame Is 30^{33}; as destroying wind 2 S 22^{16} = ψ 18^{16}, Jb 4^9; as cold wind producing ice Jb 37^{10}; as creative, giving breath to man Jb 32^8 33^4. **2.** *breath of* man 1 K 17^{17} Is 42^5 Jb 27^3 Dn 10^7; breath of life נשמת חיים Gn 2^7 (J); cf. נִשְׁמַת רוּחַ חַיִּים Gn 7^{22} (J); as breathed in by God it is God's breath in man Jb 34^{14} 36^4; and is characteristic of man אדם אשר נשמה באפו Is 2^{22} *man in whose nostrils is* but *a breath* (late gloss). **3.** syn. נפש כָּל נְשָׁמָה *every breathing thing* Dt 20^{16} Jos $11^{11.14}$ 1 K 15^{29}; כָּל־הַנְּשָׁמָה Jos 10^{40} ψ 150^6; נְשָׁמוֹת Is 57^{16}. **4.** *spirit* of man, ∥ רוּחַ, נֵר י׳ נ׳ אָדָם Pr 20^{27} *the spirit of man is a lamp of* י׳. 5397

† **תִּנְשֶׁמֶת n.f.** an animal;—ת׳ Lv 11^{18}, תִּנְשָׁמֶת Lv 11^{30} Dt 14^{16}:—**1.** unclean bird, the *ibis, water-hen*, 𝔊 πορφυρίων, (acc. Tristr $^{NHB\ 249}$); or species of *owl* (Di Bu SS); *pelican* (Ges): Lv 11^{18} = Dt 14^{16}. **2.** unclean שֶׁרֶץ Lv 11^{30}, *lizard* (Saad Tristr$^{NHB\ 120}$), or *chameleon* (Bo$^{Hieroz.\ i.\ 1078\ ff.;\ ed.\ Rosenm.\ ii.\ 503\ ff.}$), so most; (deriving name from alleged living on air, Plin$^{NH\ viii.\ 51}$; but this not applicable to **1**; cf. Lag$^{BN\ 130\ f.}$). 8580

5398 †נָשַׁף vb. blow (NH = BH; Chr.-Pal.-Aram. ܢܫܦ Schwally[Idiot. 58]; Ar. نَسَفَ (vulg.) *id.* (Dozy[ii. 667]; on usu. mng. cf. Wetzst[ZPV xiv. 7]); ‖ form of נשב, cf. Jen[ZA iv (1889), 268]);—**Qal** *Pf.* 3 ms. נ׳ בָּהֶם Is 40^{24} *he hath blown upon them* (of י׳ under fig. of wind); 2 ms. נָשַׁפְתָּ בְרוּחֲךָ Ex 15^{10} (song).

5399 †נֶ֫שֶׁף n.m. twilight (prop. *twilight-breeze*, cf. לְרוּחַ הַיּוֹם Gn 3^{8}; NH *id.;* 𝔗 נִשְׁפָּא, נְשַׁף);—נ׳ abs. 1 S 30^{17}+, נָ֑שֶׁף Je 13^{16}; cstr. Is 21^{4}; sf. נִשְׁפּוֹ Jb 3^{9};—**1.** *evening twilight* 2 K 7$^{5.7}$ (cf. לַיְלָה v^{12}); opp. בֹּקֶר Is 5^{11}; time of concealment Jb 24^{15} Pr 7^{9} (+אִישׁוֹן לַיְלָה וַאֲפֵלָה, עֶרֶב יוֹם+, to emphasize sin that shuns the day); of refreshing Is 21^{4} (נ׳ חִשְׁקִי); of stumbling, in dim light Is 59^{10} (opp. צָהֳרַיִם), so הָרֵי נָ֑שֶׁף Je 13^{16} (both fig.); כּוֹכְבֵי נִשְׁפּוֹ Jb 3^{9} *the stars of its twilight* (i.e. of night of Job's birth).—so מֵהַנּ׳ וְעַד־הָעֶרֶב לְמָחֳרָתָם 1 S 30^{17} Klo Kit HPS (rd. לְהַחֲרִמָם for לְמָח׳, We Kit Bu); Th, after Luth, sub **2**, so Buhl[Lex] SS; Löhr allows either. **2.** *morning twilight* Jb 7^{4} (opp. עֶרֶב), appar. also ψ 119^{147}.

3244 †יַנְשׁוּף and (Is 34^{11}) יַנְשׁוֹף n.[m.] a bird (with harsh, *strident* note? Bo[Hieroz. ii. 284; ed. Rosenm. iii. 29], Tristr[NHB 192] think of נֶשֶׁף—i.e. a *twilight* bird; on format. cf. Lag[BN 127] Ba[NB 231]);—unclean Lv 11^{17} Dt 14^{16}; inhabiting deserts Is 34^{11}. Prob. a kind of *owl* Bo[l.c.], '*Great Owl*,' Egyptian *Eagle-owl* (*bubo ascalaphus*) Tristr[l.c.] cf. 𝔖𝔗 Di Dr-White[Hpt] (Lv), > 𝔊 𝔙 Lv Is *ibis*.

5401 †I. נָשַׁק vb. kiss (NH *id.*, As. *našâku*, 𝔗 נְשַׁק, נְשֵׁיק, Syr. ܢܫܩ, *kiss* (orig. *smell* [نَشِقَ] acc. to Lag[Nov. Psalt. Spec. 24 f.]): Ar. نَسَقَ is *fasten together, arrange in order*, Eth. ንሱቅ: pt. *ordine dispositus, apte sertus* Di[641], poss. akin to II. נשק);—**Qal** *Pf.* 3 ms. נ׳ 1 K 19^{18} 2 S 15^{5}; 3 fs. נָֽשְׁקָה Pr 7^{13}; 3 pl. נָשָׁ֑קוּ ψ 85^{11}; *Impf.* יִשַּׁק Gn 41^{40}, וַיִּשַּׁק 27^{27}+; sf. יִשָּׁקֵנִי Ct 1^{2}; 1 s. cohort. אֶשְּׁקָה־ 1 K 19^{20}; 3 mpl. יִשָּׁקוּן Ho 13^{2}, etc.; *Imv.* וּשְׁקָה Gn 27^{26}; *Inf. cstr.* נְשֹׁק־ 2 S 20^{9};—*kiss*, usu. c. לְ pers.: Gn 27$^{26.27}$ 29^{11} 50^{1} Ex 4^{27} (all J), Gn 48^{10} Ex 18^{7} (both E), 2 S 15^{5} 14^{33} 19^{40} 20^{9} 1 K 19^{20} Pr 7^{13} Ru 1$^{9.14}$; so of idol-worship 1 K 19^{18} (cf. We[Skizzen iii. 105; Heid. 109]), cf. וַתִּשַּׁק יָדִי לְפִי Jb 31^{27} *and my hand hath kissed my mouth;* rarely c. acc. pers. 1 S 20^{41} (אִישׁ אֶת־רֵעֵהוּ), sf. pers. 1 S 10^{1} Ct 1^{2} (+מִנְּשִׁיקוֹת), 8^{1}, also Gn 33^{4} וַיִּשָּׁקֵהוּ (J; Holz E; wd. suspicious, Di rejects); עֲגָלִים יִשּׁ׳ Ho 13^{2} *calves do they kiss;* שְׂפָתַיִם יִשָּׁק Pr 24^{26} *lips he kisses;* abs. ψ 85^{11} (fig., recipr.).—עַל־פִּיךָ יִשַּׁק Gn 41^{40} is dub., Di 'to thy mouth all my people shall yield' (fit, adapt themselves, cf. Ar. √), so Kau Buhl[Lex], but this meaning uncertain, and text perh. corrupt, v. Di Holz). **Pi.** *Impf.* 3 ms. וַיְנַשֵּׁק Gn 32^{1} 45^{15}, וַיְנַשֶּׁק־ 29^{13}; *Imv.* mpl. נַשְּׁקוּ־ ψ 2^{12}; *Inf. cstr.* נַשֵּׁק Gn 31^{28};—*kiss* = **Qal**: c. לְ pers. Gn 29^{13} (J), 31^{28} 32^{1} 45^{15} (all E); נַשְּׁקוּ־בַר ψ 2^{12} is dub., cf. 1. בַּר p. 135 a supr. **Hiph.** *Pt.* מַשִּׁיקוֹת Ez 3^{13} of wings of cherubim, *gently touching* each other (c. אֶל־).

5390 †[נְשִׁיקָה] n.f. kiss;—only pl. cstr.: יִשָּׁקֵנִי מִנְּשִׁיקוֹת פִּיהוּ Ct 1^{2}; נְשִׁיקוֹת שׂוֹנֵא Pr 27^{6} *kisses of an enemy*.

5401 †II. [נָשַׁק] vb. exact meaning uncertain; prob. either handle, or be equipped with (cf. perh. Ar. نَسَقَ, etc., sub I. נשק);—only **Qal** *Pt.* pl. cstr. נֹשְׁקֵי: נ׳ קֶשֶׁת 1 Ch 12^{2} *equipped with the bow*, so 2 Ch 17^{17} (+מָגֵן); נ׳ רוֹמֵי קֶשֶׁת ψ 78^{9} is difficult, ר׳ appos. of נ׳ acc. to Hup-Now Bae al. (Ges[§ 130 e]); del. רוֹמֵי as explan. gloss Hup Hi Che Kau; del. ver. as gloss Hup Kau Bae.

5402 †נֶשֶׁק, נֵ֫שֶׁק n.[m.] equipment, weapons (coll.), armoury;—abs. נֶ֫שֶׁק Ez 39^{9}+2 t., נֵשֶׁק 1 K 10^{25} 2 Ch 9^{24}, נָ֑שֶׁק 2 K 10^{2}+2 t., cstr. נֶ׳ Is 22^{8}, נֵ׳ Jb 20^{24};—**1.** *equipment, weapons* 1 K 10^{25} 2 K 10^{2} Is 22^{8} 2 Ch 9^{24} Ez 39^{9} (gen. term, foll. by specif.), v^{10}; נ׳ בַּרְזֶל Jb 20^{24} (‖קֶשֶׁת נְחוּשָׁה); יוֹם נָ֑שֶׁק ψ 140^{8} i.e. day of battle; so נ׳ alone Jb 39^{21}. **2.** appar. *armoury* Ne 3^{19}.

5404 †נֶשֶׁר n.m. [Dt 32, 11] griffon-vulture, eagle (NH *id.;* As. *našru;* 𝔗 נִשְׁרָא; Syr. ܢܫܪܐ; Ar. نَسْرٌ *vulture* (Lane[2780]), vulg. نِسْر; Eth. ንስር: Di[641]; Sab. נסר n.pr. dei, and ביתן נסר DHM[ZMG xxix (1875), 600; xxxvii (1883), 356]);—abs. נ׳ Ho 8^{1}+; נָ֑שֶׁר Dt 28^{49}+; pl. נְשָׁרִים 2 S 1^{23}+, cstr. נִשְׁרֵי La 4^{19};—sts. (perhaps not always) the *griffon-vulture* (Tristr[NHB 172 ff.] Dr[Dt 14, 12] Now[Arch i. 84] Lane[2780]), Mi 1^{16} (bald, in sim.), flying swiftly to prey Hb 1^{8} Jb 9^{26}, cf. Pr 30^{17} (בְּנֵי־נ׳), unclean Lv 11^{13} Dt 14^{12}; soaring Jb 39^{27}, also in sim. Pr 23^{5} Is 40^{31} Ob^{4}, building nest high Je 49^{16} (cf. also Jb 39^{27}); as swift also 2 S 1^{23}, esp. of Bab. and Assyr. invader Je 4^{13} La 4^{19}, cf. Ho 8^{1} Dt 28^{49} Je 48^{40} 49^{22} (all in comparisons), הַנֶּשֶׁר הַגָּדוֹל Ez 17^{3} (fig. of Nebuch.), v^{7} (fig. of king of Egypt); leaving no trace of flight Pr 30^{19}; as renewing youth (by moulting) ψ 103^{5}; as training and supporting its young Ex 19^{4} (E), Dt 32^{11} (song); פְּנֵי נ׳ of cherubim in vision Ez 1^{10} 10^{4}.—Only Mi 1^{16} seems to compel ref. to vulture (on eating fresh carrion by eagles v. reff. in Di$^{Lv 11, 13}$), and נ׳ may be a more comprehensive word, incl. both vulture and eagle.

5405 †**נָשַׁת** **vb. be dry, parched**;—**Qal** *Pf.* 3 fs. לְשׁוֹנָם בַּצָּמָא נָשָׁתָּה Is 41^{17} (on D. f. affect. v. Ges$^{§20 l}$); also fig. נָשְׁתָה גְבוּרָתָם Je 51^{30}, *their might is dry*, i.e. fails. **Niph.** *Pf.* 3 pl. consec. וְנִשְּׁתוּ־מַיִם מֵהַיָּם Is 19^{5} *and water shall be dried up from the sea;* cf. *Impf.* יִנָּתְשׁוּ מַיִם Je 18^{14}, where read prob. יִנָּשְׁתוּ (Gf Gie al.).

5406 †**נִשְׁתְּוָן** **n.[m.] letter** (usu. der. fr. Pers. نِبِشْتَن, نُوِشْتَن i.e. *writing*, Hoffm$^{ZA ii (1887), 52}$ yet cf. Meyer$^{Judenthum 22}$);—abs. נ׳ Ezr 4^{7} 7^{11}.

נתב (√ of foll.; Ar. نَتَبَ *swell forth, become prominent, protuberant*, Lane^{2760}).

5410 †**נָתִיב** **n.m.** $^{Jb 28, 7}$ **path, pathway** (as *raised*);—abs. נ׳ Jb 18^{10}+3 t.; cstr. נְתִיב ψ 119^{35}; sf. 3 fs. נְתִיבָהֿ Pr 12^{28} (si vera l., v. infr.; on om. of Mappik v. Ges$^{§91 e}$, v. infr.);—*path* Jb 18^{10} (fig.), 28^{7} 41^{24} (track); ψ 78^{50} (fig.); נְתִיב מִצְוֹתֶיךָ ψ 119^{35} *the path of thy commands;* דֶּרֶךְ נְתִיבָה אַל־מָוֶת Pr 12^{28} *the journey of her pathway* is *no-death!* (|| בְּאֹרַח צְדָקָה חַיִּים) Ew Be De, v. אַל p. 39 a supr.; others rd. אֶל־, and either transl. נ׳ *by-paths* (Hi Str), or substitute a syn. of 'wickedness' (cf. Now Frankenb; Perles$^{Analekten 87 f.}$ נִתְעָבִים after Levy$^{ChWB i. 28 b}$).

5410 †**נְתִיבָה** **n.f. id.**;—abs. נ׳ Is 43^{16}, sf. נְתִיבָתִי Jb 30^{13} + 2 t., נְתִיבָתָם Pr 1^{15}; pl. abs. נְתִיבוֹת Pr 8^{2}+; cstr. *id.* Jb 38^{20}+; sf. נְתִיבֹתַי Jb 19^{8} La 3^{9}, נְתִיבֹתָיו Jb 24^{13}, etc.;—*path:* **1.** lit. הֹלְכֵי נְתִיבוֹת Ju 5^{6} *goers on paths*, i.e. travellers, Pr 8^{2} Is 58^{12} (Oort Lag Klo נְתִיצוֹת but against this Du); *path* through sea Is 43^{16} (in fig.); of path to house of (personif.) light and darkness Jb 38^{20}. **2.** oft. || דֶּרֶךְ: **a.** = course of life Jb 19^{8} 30^{13} La 3^{9} ψ 119^{105} 142^{4}, of Isr. Ho 2^{8}; of path of God's appointment Is 42^{16}. **b.** of moral action, and character: paths of wisdom Pr 3^{17}, justice 8^{20} (|| אֹרַח צְדָקָה); light Jb 24^{13}; נ׳ עוֹלָם Je 6^{16} (|| דֶּרֶךְ הַטּוֹב); path of wicked Pr 1^{15}, Is 59^{8} (crooked), path of adulteress Pr 7^{25}; נְתִיבוֹת Je 18^{15} is rendered 'by-paths,' by Gf Rothst al.; < Gie makes cstr. bef. foll. דֶּרֶךְ לֹא סְלוּלָה.—נְתִיבָה Pr 12^{28} v. נָתִיב.

†**[נָתַח]** **vb.** only **Pi. cut up, cut in** 5408
pieces, divide by joints (Dr$^{1 S 11, 7}$; NH *id.*, Pi.; rare);—**Pi.** *Pf.* נִתַּח Lv 8^{20}, וְנִתַּח consec. Lv $1^{6.12}$; *Impf.* 3 ms. וַיְנַתַּח 1 K 18^{33}, sf. וַיְנַתְּחֵהוּ 1 S 11^{7}, וַיְנַתְּחֶהָ Ju 19^{29}, etc.;—*cut up, cut in pieces*, c. acc. of animals 1 S 11^{7}, of woman Ju 20^{6} (all these to be sent about as token for assembling warriors; on signif. of the practice cf. RS$^{Sem i. 383; 2nd ed. 402}$); elsewh. usu. + לִנְתָחִים, *cut up into pieces*, of woman Ju 19^{29}; of sacrificial animals 1 K $18^{23.33}$ (acc. only), Ex 29^{17} Lv $1^{6.12}$ 8^{20} (all P).

†**נֵתַח** **n.m.** $^{Ez 24, 4}$ **piece of a divided car-** 5409
cass (Ecclus נתחים 50^{12a});—abs. נ׳ Ez 24^{4}; pl. נְתָחִים Ju 19^{29} + 2 t.; sf. נְתָחָיו Ex $29^{17.17}$ + 2 t., נְתָחֶיהָ Lv 1^{6} + 3 t.;—usu. pl. *pieces:* of meat in a caldron (symbol. of Jerusalem) Ez $24^{4.4}$ (sg. only v^{4b}), v$^{6.6}$; of sacrif. animals Ex 29^{17b} Lv 1^{8} 8^{20b} 9^{13}; elsewh. לִנ׳ after vb. נִתַּח (q.v.): of woman Ju 19^{29}; Ex 29^{17a} Lv $1^{6.12}$ 8^{20a}.

†**[נָתַךְ]** **vb. pour forth** (intrans.), **be** 5413
poured out (NH *id.*, Niph. *flow*, Hiph. *melt* (trans.); As. *natâku, flow* Dl$^{HWB 487}$ Jäger$^{BAS ii. 292}$; 𝔗 Aph. *pour out*, esp. *melt;* Zinj. ליתכה (Haph.) Nö$^{ZMG xlvii (1893), 98}$ Cook^{83}; Syr. ܢܬܟ (rare) PS^{2480});—**Qal** *Impf.* 3 fs. תִּתַּךְ Je 42^{18} + 3 t., וַתִּתַּךְ Je 44^{6} Dn 9^{11}; 3 mpl. וַיִּתְּכוּ Jb 3^{24};—*pour forth*, alw. fig., וַיִּתּ׳ כַּמַּיִם שַׁאֲגֹתָי Jb 3^{24} *and my groans have poured forth like water;* usu. of divine wrath (חֵמָה) Je 42^{18} (c. עַל־ pers.), 44^{6} (abs.), 2 Ch 12^{7} 34^{25} (both c. בְּ loc. *against*); cf. also Dn 9^{11} v^{27} (both c. עַל־ pers.). **Niph.** *Pf.* 3 ms. נִתַּךְ Ex 9^{33} + 2 t.; 3 fs. נִתְּכָה Na 1^{6} 2 Ch 34^{21}, וְנִתְּכָה consec. Ez 24^{11}; 2 mpl. וְנִתַּכְתֶּם Ez 22^{21}; *Pt.* f. נִתֶּכֶת Je 7^{20};—*be poured*, of rain, אָרְצָה Ex 9^{33} (J), cf. נ׳ מַיִם עֲלֵיהֶם 2 S 21^{10}; *be poured out*, of wrath of י׳ Na 1^{6} (abs.), Je 7^{20} (c. אֶל־ loc.), 42^{18} (c. עַל־ pers.), 2 Ch 34^{21} (c. בְּ pers.); *be poured forth* i.e. melted, annihilated in the midst of (בְּתוֹךְ) the fire of י׳'s fury Ez 22^{21} (subj. persons), so 24^{11} (subj. impurity, fig. of caldron). **Hiph.** *Pf.* 3 mpl. הִתִּיכוּ עֲבָדֶיךָ אֶת־הַכֶּסֶף 2 K 22^{9} *thy servants have poured out the money* (||2 Ch 34^{12} infr.); 1 s. וְהִתַּכְתִּי אֶתְכֶם consec. Ez 22^{20} *and I will melt you* (fig. of judgment); *Inf. cstr.* לְהַנְתִּיךְ Ez 22^{20} *in order to melt* it (i.e. metal in furnace; Co after 𝔊 𝔖 reads

לְהִנָּתֵךְ **Niph.** *Inf.*, so Berthol, cf. Toy); *Impf.* 3 mpl. וַיִּתִּיכוּ 2 Ch 34^{17} (‖ 2 K 22^{9} supr.); הֲלֹא כֶּחָלָב תַּתִּיכֵנִי Jb 10^{10} *dost* (= didst) *thou not pour me out like milk?* (of beginnings of life). **Hoph.** *Impf.* 2 mpl. כֵּן תֻּתְּכוּ Ez 22^{22} *so shall ye be melted* (fig. of judgment).

2046 †הִתּוּךְ† **n.[m.]** *a melting* (Hophal-format., dissim. from הֻתּוּךְ, acc. to Ba[NB § 102 d]);—cstr. כְּהִתּוּךְ כֶּסֶף בְּתוֹךְ כּוּר Ez 22^{22} *like a melting of silver in a smelting-pot.*

5414 **נָתַן** [2007] **vb. give, put, set** (Ecclus נתן 44^{19} + oft.; OHeb. נתן־יהו n.pr.m. Lzb[327]; NH = BH; Ph. יתן, נתן in n.pr. מתנת, etc., Lzb[292, 327]; As. *nadânu* Dl[HWB 450] (rarely *ittan* Id[ib. 488]); Zinj. נתן, also in n.pr., Lzb[327] Cook[84]; Nab. Impf. ינתן, and n.pr.; Palm., also n.pr. Lzb[l. c.] Cook[l. c.]; 𝔗 Impf. יִתֵּן, Inf. מִתַּן; Sab. נתן Hal[154], Liḥ n.pr. נתנבעל [North-Sem. form] DHM[Epigr. Denkm. 80, No. 35]; Chr Pal Aram. ܢܬܠ (rare) Schwally[Idiot. 58]; Syr. Impf. ܢܬܠ, Inf. ܡܬܠ Lindberg[Vergl. Sem. Gram. 93 f.], but Mand. נתן Nö[M 52]);—**Qal** [1917] *Pf.* נ׳ Gn 24^{53} +; 2 ms. נָתַתָּה, נָתַתָּ Ju 15^{18} +, Gn 3^{12} +, תַּתָּה 2 S 22^{41} (defended as vulg. form with aphaer. of נ׳ by Th Ges[Lgb. 139] Ew[§ 195 b] Kö[i. 300] De[ψ 18, 41] al.; < txt. err. for נָתַתָּה (so ‖ ψ 18^{41}) Ol[§ 89] Sta[§ 127 b] Ges[§ 19 i] (hesitantly), Klo Bu Löhr HPS, cf. Hup-Now[ψ 18, 41]); 2 fs. נָתַתְּ Ez $16^{33.36}$, נָתַתִּי v[18], sf. נְתַתִּיהוּ v[19]; 1 s. נָתַתִּי Ju 1^{2} +, etc.; *Impf.* יִתֵּן Gn 43^{14} +, וַיִּתֵּן 15^{10} +; sf. 3 ms. יִתְּנֶנּוּ Lv 5^{24} Ec 2^{21}; 1 s. אֶתֵּן Gn 12^{7} +; 1 pl. נִתֵּן 34^{21} +, נִתֶּן־ Ju 16^{5}, etc.; *Imv.* ms. תֵּן 2 K 4^{42} +, תֶּן־ Gn 14^{21}, תְּנָה 1 S 2^{15} +, sf. תְּנֵהוּ Ne 1^{11} 1 Ch 21^{22}, תְּנֶנָּה 1 S 21^{10}; fs. תְּנִי Gn 30^{14} +, תֵּנִי Is 43^{6}; mpl. תְּנוּ Gn 34^{8} +; *Inf. abs.* נָתוֹן Dt 15^{10} +, נָתֹן Nu 21^{2} +; cstr. נְתֹן 20^{21}, נְתָן־ Gn 38^{9}, לְתִתֵּן 1 K 6^{19} (but read לָתֵת so Ol[§ 224 d] Ges[§ 67 i] Benz), תתן also 17^{14} Kt (Qr תֵּת)—> these forms retained by Ew[§ 238 c] Kö[i. 305];—תֵּת Gn 4^{12} +, esp. לָתֵת 15^{7} +, לָתֶת־ Ju 21^{18}, לָתֶת־ Ex 5^{21} (so Ginsb, van d. H. לָתֶת־, cf. also Ki in Kö[i. 304 f.]) +; sf. תִּתִּי Gn 29^{19} +, תִּתְּךָ Dt 15^{10} +, etc.; *Pt.* נֹתֵן Ju 21^{18} +, etc.;—**1.** *give:* **a.** = give personally, deliver or hand to, c. acc. rei + ל pers. 1 S 10^{4} 22^{10} 2 K 22^{10} Lv 5^{16} (P) 22^{14} (H) Ru 4^{7} + oft.; in trade Pr 31^{24}; אֶל־ pers. Gn 21^{14} (E), Je 3^{8} Lv 15^{14} + oft.; explicitly נ׳ בְּיַד Dt $24^{1.3}$ (bill of divorce); c. acc. rei alone Ju 5^{25}. **b.** = *bestow* upon, c. acc. rei + ל pers. Gn 24^{53} (J) 20^{16} (E) 1^{29} (P) + oft.; an understanding heart 1 K $3^{9.12}$, blessing Dt 12^{15}, mercy 13^{18}, cf. Je 16^{13} 42^{12}; strength Dt 8^{18} ψ 68^{36}; the sabbath Ex 16^{29} (J) Ez 20^{12}; = procure for (לְ) one 1 S 17^{10} 1 K 21^{7}; יִתֵּן לָכֶם רַחֲמִים לִפְנֵי Gn 43^{14} (J) *he will give you compassion in the eyes of* the man (cf. also **2 b, 3 b**); give persons $46^{18.25}$ (P); of Levites given to (לְ) Aaron and his sons Nu 3^{9} cf. 8^{19}, to י׳ 8^{16} cf. 18^{6} (all P); esp. of י׳'s giving land to Abr. and his descendants Gn 15^{18} 26^{4} (J) 17^{8} (P) Ex 6^{8} (P; + מוֹרָשָׁה) + oft. (pt. in this sense 37 t. Dt.), + לְרִשְׁתָּהּ Dt 3^{18} +; אַל־תִּתֵּן לַנָּשִׁים חֵילֶךָ Pr 31^{3}; + מִן of source נָתַתִּי מִמֶּנָּה לְךָ בֵּן Gn 17^{16} (P); c. acc. alone ψ 61^{6} Ec 12^{7} (רוּחַ); give something to (ל) one for (ל) sthg., in some capacity, אֶת־כָּל־אֶחָיו נ׳ לוֹ לַעֲבָדִים Gn 27^{37} +; prob. also נ׳ בְּבָרוּתִי רֹאשׁ ψ 69^{22} *they gave, as my food, gall* (בְּ essentiae), cf. supr. בְּ **7 c**, Hup-Now[ad loc.]; acc. + inf. נ׳־לִי לֶחֶם לֶאֱכֹל וּבֶגֶד לִלְבֹּשׁ Gn 28^{20} (J), cf. Ex 16^{15} (P), Ne $9^{15.20}$; לֹא נ׳ לָכֶם לֵב לָדַעַת וְעֵינַיִם לִרְאוֹת וְאָזְנַיִם לִשְׁמֹעַ Dt 29^{3}. Esp. **c.** *give* woman to (ל) man as (ל) wife, Gn 29^{28} (E), $34^{8.12}$ (J), Jos $15^{16.17}$ (JE), = Ju $1^{12.13}$ +; without 2nd ל Gn $29^{19.19}$ (E), Gn 38^{21} Ex 2^{21} (J), Gn $34^{9.14.16}$ (P), Ju $15^{2.6}$ +; c. acc. alone, Gn 29^{26} (E), 1 S 25^{44}. **d.** of (gracious) bestowals of various kinds: *give* = grant, send rain, מְטַר־אַרְצְכֶם, Dt 11^{14}, גִּשְׁמֵיכֶם Lv 26^{4} (H), מָטָר עַל־אַרְצְךָ 1 K 8^{36}, etc.; also of sending plague of hail Ex 9^{23} (E); send herbage (עֵשֶׂב) in (בְּ) your field for (לְ) your cattle Dt 11^{15}; grant a remnant to (לְ) Judah Je 40^{11}; וְנָתַתִּי לְךָ אֶת־נַפְשְׁךָ לְשָׁלָל 45^{5} *and I will grant thee thy life as spoil;* grant revenge (acc.) to (לְ) the king on (מִן) Saul, etc. 2 S 4^{8}, cf. הָאֵל הַנֹּתֵן נְקָמוֹת לִי 2 S 22^{48} = ψ 18^{48}; other gifts Ju 15^{18} (בְּיַד), 1 S 1^{11} (לְ), Ru 4^{13}. **e.** *grant* a request, שְׁאֵלָה 1 S $1^{17.27}$ Est 5^{3} ψ 106^{15} (+ ל pers.), בַּקָּשָׁה Ezr 7^{6}, תַּאֲוָה Pr 10^{24}, (רָשָׁע) מַאֲוַיֵּי ψ 140^{9}, תִּקְוָה Jb 6^{8}, יִתֵּן י׳ לָכֶם וּמְצֶאןָ מְנוּחָה ψ 37^{4}, cf. מִשְׁאֲלֹת לִבֶּךָ Ru 1^{9}. Esp. †**f.** מִי יִתֵּן *who will give* or *grant,* in expressions of wish = O that (I had! etc.; = As. *mannu inamdin* Jäger[BAS ii. 279]), esp. (9 t.) Jb.: c. acc. מִי־יִתֵּן עֶרֶב Dt 28^{67} cf. v[67], Jb 14^{4} ψ 14^{7} = 53^{7}, 55^{7} Je 9^{1}; c. 2 acc. כָּל־עַם י׳ נְבִיאִים Nu 11^{29} (JE), lit. *who will make all* י׳'s *people prophets?* cf. Je 8^{23}; c. acc. + כְּ, מִי יִתֶּנְךָ כְּאָח לִי Ct 8^{1}, cf. Jb 29^{2}; c. acc. + בְּ, אֶת־הָעָם הַזֶּה בְּיָדִי Ju 9^{29} *O that this people were in my charge!* c. acc. + לְ Jb 31^{35}, lit. *who will give to me* (לִי) one hearing me? also מִי יִתְּנֵנִי Is 27^{4} where sf. appar. = לִי; c. inf. מִי יִתֵּן מוּתֵנוּ Ex 16^{3} (P), so

2 S 19[1], מִי יִתֵּן אֱלוֹהַּ דַּבֵּר Jb 11[5]; c. impf. תָּבוֹא שֶׁאֱלָתִי Jb 6[8] *O that my request might come to pass!* 14[13] 31[31]; impf. + וְ 19[23.23]; c. pf. יָדַעְתִּי 23[3] *O that I knew!* (+ וְאֶמְצָאֵהוּ); c. pf. consec. Dt 5[26]†. **g.** *permit,* c. acc. + inf., לֹא־נְתַתִּיךָ לִנְגֹּעַ אֵלֶיהָ Gn 20[6] (E), cf. 31[7] (E) Ex 3[19] (J) Nu 20[21] 21[23] (JE) + oft.; c. לְ pers. + inf. 2 Ch 20[10]; other constructions are: לֹא כֵן נ׳ לְךָ י׳ Dt 18[14] *not thus hath* י׳ *permitted to thee;* אִם־אֶתֵּן שְׁנָת לְעֵינָי וגו׳ ψ 132[4] Pr 6[4]; *give thyself* (לְ) *no rest* La 2[18], *give him* (לְ) *no rest* Is 62[6]. **h.** = ascribe glory, etc. (acc.) to (לְ) God 1 S 6[5] Jb 36[3], esp. imv. Je 13[16] Ezr 10[11] ψ 68[35] cf. 115[1] (so הָבוּ, v. יהב **4**); to man 1 S 18[8.8]; unseemliness (תִּפְלָה) to God Jb 1[22]. **i.** = apply, devote heart to seek out, acc. + inf. Ec 1[13.17] 8[9.16] Dn 10[12], נ׳ לֵב לְ Ec 7[21] = attend to; conversely אֶת־כָּל־זֶה נָתַתִּי אֶל־לִבִּי Ec 9[1] = *all this I set before my mind,* 7[2]; also (with subj. diff. fr. ind. obj.) מָה אֱלֹהַי נֹתֵן אֶל־לִבִּי לַעֲשׂוֹת Ne 2[12] cf. 7[5]. **j.** = employ, devote money (acc.) עַל־עֲבֹדַת אֹהֶל מוֹעֵד Ex 30[16] (P). **k.** *give* offerings, לי׳ Nu 18[12] (P), תְּרוּמַת י׳ Ex 30[15] (P), cf. give spoil to (לְ) י׳ Dt 20[14] (י׳ subj.); מִיָּדְךָ נָתַנּוּ לָךְ 1 Ch 29[14]; offering to (לְ) idols Ez 6[13]; esp. to Moloch Lv 20[2.4], to pass through fire to (לְ) M. 18[2], etc. **l.** = consecrate, dedicate to (לְ) י׳ 1 S 1[11] Ex 22[29] (E). **m.** *give* a sign or wonder, acc. 1 K 13[3.5], + לְ pers. Jos 2[12] (JE), with reflex. לְ Ex 7[9] (P), alm. = display, exhibit; cf. נָתְנוּ הֲדָרֵךְ Ez 27[10] *they set forth, exhibit* thy splendour; כִּי יִתֵּן בַּכּוֹס עֵינוֹ Pr 23[31] *when it sheweth its sparkle in the cup.* **n.** = pay, wages (acc., + sf.), נ׳ שְׂכָרִי Gn 30[18] (E) *he hath paid my hire,* Ex 2[9] (E) Dt 24[15], cf. Is 61[8]; + לְ pers. Je 22[13]; a price, נ׳ מִכְרָם Nu 20[19] (JE), וַיִּתֵּן שְׂכָרָהּ Jon 1[3], i.e. paid his fare, passage-money; money (as) price (מחיר) 1 K 21[2], cf. נ׳ כֶּסֶף הַשָּׂדֶה Gn 23[13] (P); pay money for (ב) something Dt 14[26]; wealth for (ב) love Ct 8[7]; tax or rent, c. acc. rei + לְ pers. Gn 47[24] (J); fine (c. *id.*) Ex 21[32] (E) Dt 22[29], acc. om. v[19], cf. וְנָתַן בִּפְלִלִים Ex 21[22] (v. פָּלִיל), נ׳ שִׁבְתּוֹ v[19] (i.e. pay for his lost time), נ׳ פִּדְיֹן נַפְשׁוֹ v[30] (pay redemption-money; all E), cf. וְנ׳ אִישׁ כֹּפֶר נַפְשׁוֹ לי׳ 30[12] (P); pay votive offering (c. acc. + לְ) Lv 27[23] (P); a wager (c. acc. + לְ) Ju 14[12.13]. **o.** c. בְּ, *give* for (ב) money = sell, תְּנָה־לִּי אֶת־כַּרְמְךָ בְּכֶסֶף 1 K 21[6], cf. Dt 2[28] 14[25] 1 Ch 21[22]; — נ׳ Ez 27 is trading term, but sts. connexion obscure and text dub.: *give* wares for (בְּ) 27[12] (but rd. prob. ך for ב 𝔊 𝔖 Co Berthol), v[13.16] (del. 2nd ב), v[17.19.22] (cf., further, Co Berthol and esp. Sm); נ׳ הֵילְלוּ בַּגּוֹיִם Jo 4[3] (|| מָכַר); ב instr., give בַּגּוֹרָל *by lot* Jos 21[8]. **p.** *give* instead of, exchange for, c. תַּחַת Ex 21[23] (E) 1 K 21[2.6] Is 43[4] 61[3], בְּעַד Jb 2[4]. **q.** give, i.e. lend, at interest, כַּסְפּוֹ לֹא נ׳ בְּנֶשֶׁךְ Lv 25[37] ψ 15[5], so (acc. om.) Ez 18[8.13]. **r.** = commit, entrust to, c. acc. + אֶל־ pers. Ex 22[6.9] (E), c. לְ pers. Ct 8[11], c. בְּיַד Gn 30[35] 39[4.8.22] (all J), 2 S 10[10]. **s.** *give over,* deliver up, c. acc. Nu 21[3] (JE) Ju 20[13] 1 S 11[12] 2 S 14[7] 20[21] 1 K 14[16] Ho 11[8] (|| מִגֵּן), Mi 5[2]; נ׳ בָּנָיו פְּלֵיטִים וּבְנֹתָיו בַּשְּׁבִית לְמֶלֶךְ אֱמֹרִי Nu 21[29] (JE); + לְ, נ׳ פ׳ לַמָּוֶת ψ 118[18]; + לִפְנֵי Dt 7[2.23] 31[5] + (see Dr[Dt. lxxxiii, No. 52], and v. further **2 b** *ad fin.*); esp. נ׳ בְּיַד, c. acc., Nu 21[34] (JE) Jos 2[24] (JE) Dt 2[24] + oft. **t.** *yield* produce, fruit, etc., esp. of land, ground, Gn 4[12] (J), Lv 25[19] 26[4.20] (all H), Dt 11[17] Is 55[10] (+ לְ pers.) Zc 8[12] ψ 67[7] 85[13] cf. Ez 36[8]; of tree Ez 34[27] Lv 26[4.20] (H) ψ 1[3], + vine Jo 2[22], vine Zc 8[12]; abs. root of righteous *yields,* יִתֵּן Pr 12[12] acc. to De Str (dub.; prop. to insert פְּרִי); Dy Kau Wild prop. אֵיתָן (as ψ 74[15], etc.), cf. as to sense Ew; other conj. v. Now; cf. Nu 20[8] (P) Zc 8[12] Ct 1[12] 2[13] 7[14]. **u.** = occasion, produce, שֵׂכֶל טוֹב יִתֶּן־חֵן Pr 13[16] cf. 29[15], חֶרְדַּת אָדָם יִתֵּן מוֹקֵשׁ v[25] *trembling before man occasioneth a snare.* **v.** *requite* to (לְ) a man, acc. to (כְּ) character 1 K 8[39] = 2 Ch 6[33] Je 17[10] 32[19] ψ 28[4.4]; c. עַל־ + כְּ Ez 7[9]; c. עַל־ pers. + acc. of sin 7[3.4.8] 23[49] (cf. **2 b**). **w.** = report, mention, וַיִּתֵּן אֶת־מִסְפַּר... אֶל־הַמֶּלֶךְ 2 S 24[9] *he reported the number unto the king;* וָאֶתְּנָה לוֹ זְמָן Ne 2[6] *and I mentioned to him a time.* **x.** = utter, usu. c. acc. קוֹל, utter a sound, lift up the voice: Je 4[16] (+ עַל *against*), 22[20] 48[34] La 2[7]; in weeping, וַיִּתֵּן אֶת־קֹלוֹ בִּבְכִי Gn 45[2] (E), וַיִּבְכּוּ Nu 14[1] (P); + לְ pers. Pr 2[3] (|| לַבִּינָה תִּקְרָא); of wisdom Pr 1[20] 8[1] (|| קרא); of י׳, esp. in thunder of theoph. Am 1[2] 2 S 22[14] (|| יַרְעֵם), = ψ 18[14], Je 25[30] Jo 2[11]; of clouds ψ 77[18], the deep Hb 3[10]; of young lion's roaring Am 3[4] Je 2[15]; of birds ψ 104[12]; קוֹל om., נ׳ דָּוִד... לְהֹדוֹת לי׳ 1 Ch 16[7]; so of י׳'s voice in thunder, לְקוֹל תִּתּוֹ Je 10[13] (sc. קוֹלוֹ) *at the sound of his uttering* (his voice) = 51[16]; נ׳ בְּקוֹל Je 12[8] (+ עַל־ *against*), of י׳ ψ 46[7], הֵן־יִתֵּן בְּקוֹלוֹ קוֹל עֹז 68[34]; נ׳ with other words, אֹמֶר v[12] (of י׳); of confession, (acc. + לְ pers.) Jos 7[19] (JE) Ezr 10[11]. **y.** *give* = stretch out, extend, וַיִּתֶּן־יָד Gn 38[28] (J) *it put out a hand;* וַיִּתֵּן צִפָּרְתּוֹ אֶל־בֵּין עֲבֹתִים

(read עָבוֹת) Ez $31^{10.14}$ *and it stretched its top amid the clouds.* **z.** combinations are: יִתֵּן וַיִּתְּנוּ לְמַכֵּהוּ לֶחִי La 3^{30} (humiliation), cf. Is 50^{6}; וַיִּתְּנוּ כָתֵף סֹרֶרֶת Zc 7^{11} (of stubbornness), so Ne 9^{29} (וְעָרְפָּם הִקְשׁוּ ‖); also וַיִּתְּנוּ עֹרֶף 2 Ch 29^{6} *gave*, i.e. *turned* (their) *back* (on '‏י; ‖ וַיַּסֵּבּוּ פְנֵיהֶם מִמִּשְׁכַּן י'); of compact, תְּנָה אֶת־יָדֶךָ 2 K 10^{15} cf. v^{15}, so מִצְרַיִם נָתַנּוּ יָד La 5^{6}; of submission, נָתְנָה יָדָהּ Je 50^{15} = *she* (Babyl.) *hath surrendered;* תְּנוּ יָד לַי' 2 Ch 30^{8} = *submit to* '‏י; more explicitly, נ' יָד תַּחַת שְׁלֹמֹה 1 Ch 29^{24}; נ' מָקוֹם לְ Ju 20^{36} *give place to* (retire before); of sexual relation, אֶל־אֵשֶׁת . . . לֹא־תִתֵּן שְׁכָבְתְּךָ לְזָרַע Lv 18^{20} (H), וַיִּתֵּן אִישׁ בָּךְ אֶת־שְׁכָבְתּוֹ Nu 5^{20} (P), so (בְּכָל־בְּהֵמָה) Lv 18^{23} (H), cf. 20^{15} (H).—יִתֵּן is taken impers. = 'es giebt,' *there is, there are,* in Jb 37^{10} Pr 10^{24} 13^{10} by De, citing Ew$^{\S 295\,d}$, Now$^{Pr\,13,10}$ Str Frankenb (in transl., dub. in note), Bae$^{Jb\ in\ Kau}$ Ges$^{\S 144\,b}$; but improb., Kau^{Pr} Di^{Jb}, so Hi Bu Du (on Jb 37^{10}), reading יֻתַּן; cf. Kö$^{Synt.\ \S 324\,d\,\beta}$.

2. *Put, set,* nearly = שִׂים, and sts. ‖ with it: **a.** lit., (esp. oft. in Ez P): c. acc. + עַל־ *on,* ring on hand Gn 41^{42} (E), cf. Ez 16^{11}, helmet on head 1 S 17^{38}, also Je 27^{2} 28^{14} (in fig.), 1 K $12^{4.9}$ (in fig.), 18^{23} (‖ שִׂים), Ex 12^{7} (acc. om.), cf. $25^{12.26.30}$ + oft. P; c. עַל־ = *above* Ex 25^{21} 26^{34} (P), = *for,* נ' גֹּרָלוֹת עַל־ Lv 16^{8} (P), *cast lots for;* = *against* Ez 26^{8}; c. אֶל־ *into:* ark into cart 1 S 6^{8}, *put* one in the stocks Je 29^{26} (also c. עַל־ 20^{2}), in prison 37^{18} 38^{11}, cf. Ex 25^{16} 28^{30} (P); *put* water upon (עַל־) sthg. *into* (אֶל־) vessel Nu 19^{17}; = *toward* וַיִּתֵּן פְּנֵי הַצֹּאן אֶל־עָקֹד Gn 30^{40} (J; del. Ol Di al.); c. בְּ, cup into hand Gn 40^{13} (E), cf. Ju 7^{16}, also Gn 41^{48} (E), cf. 1 K 7^{51}, Gn 1^{17} (P), 9^{13} (P), 2 K 19^{18}, Je 27^{8}, נָתַתִּי שִׂפְתָתִי בְּחִיקֶךָ Gn 16^{5} (J), נ' בֶּעָפָר פִּיהוּ La 3^{29} (in fig.), וְנָתַתָּה בְאָזְנוֹ וּבַדֶּלֶת Dt 15^{17} *and thou shalt put* (the awl) *into his ear and into the door* (pin his ear to the door); put disease into one Dt 7^{15} (‖ שִׂים); inflict blemish (מוּם) on (בְּ), Lv $24^{19.20}$; וּכְתֹבֶת קַעֲקַע לֹא תִתְּנוּ בָּכֶם 19^{28}; c. לְ + בְּ, שֶׂרֶט לָנֶפֶשׁ לֹא תִתְּנוּ בִּבְשַׂרְכֶם v^{28} (all H); c. לִפְנֵי *before, in front of, set food before* one, 2 K $4^{43.44}$; cf. Zc 3^{9} Ez 3^{20} Ex 30^{6} $40^{5.6}$ (all P); c. בֵּין *between,* Ex 30^{18} 40^{17} (P); c. לְ, מִגְרָעוֹת נ' לַבַּיִת סָבִיב 1 K 6^{6} *he put ledges to the house;* c. other preps. הָאִשָּׁה אֲשֶׁר נָתַתָּ עִמָּדִי Gn 3^{16} (J), *the woman whom thou hast set at my side,* cf. Ex 31^{6} (נ' אִתּוֹ; fig. of association, assistance); c. לִקְרַאת Gn 15^{10} (J), *lay* each piece *to meet* its fellow; he set the sea מִכֶּתֶף הַבַּיִת 1 K 7^{39}; c. ה loc. put money שָׁמָּה *into it* 2 K 12^{10}, so of water Ex 30^{18} (P), cf. 40^{7} (שָׁם); c. 2 acc. נ' אוֹתוֹ בֵּית הַכְּלוּא Je 37^{4} cf. v^{15}; *put, place,* abs. Ex 40^{8} (P; ‖ שִׂים, cf. 26^{32}); *set up,* אֶבֶן מַשְׂכִּית בְּ Lv 26^{1} (H; ‖ הֵקִים); + לְ pers., *lay snare for me* ψ 119^{110} (in fig.). **b.** fig., in many phr.: c. עַל, *put my spirit upon him* Is 42^{1}, reproach *upon* one Je 23^{40}, blessing on Mt. Gerizim, etc., Dt 11^{29}, curses on enemies 30^{7}; impose tax upon Ne 10^{33} cf. 2 K 23^{33}; נָתַן הוֹד עַל *put majesty upon* one 1 Ch 29^{25} Dn 11^{21} Nu 27^{20} (P; מֵהוֹד; cf. ψ 21^{6}); so also perh. ψ 8^{2} *hast set thy majesty upon* (over) *the heavens,* cf. 𝔖 𝔙 𝔗 (rd. נָתַתָּה for תְּנָה, Hup De Pe Bae al.; other views v. in Thes Ew Ol Now Che We Du); = *above,* וּנְתָנְךָ עֶלְיוֹן עַל־כָּל־גּוֹיֵי הָאָרֶץ Dt 28^{1} cf. 26^{19}; put (sthg.) *over* mouth Mi 3^{5} (i.e. stop one's mouth, by a gift); = *against* נ' מָצוֹר עַל־ Ez 4^{2} (siege), cf. v^{2b}; c. אֶל־, וָאֶתְּנָה אֶת־פָּנַי אֶל־אֲדֹנָי . . . לְבַקֵּשׁ Dn 9^{3}; c. בְּ, words into mouth Dt 18^{18} Je 1^{9}, cf. 1 K 22^{23}; wisdom into heart, or person, 1 K 10^{24} Ex 31^{6} $36^{1.2}$ (all P), cf. ψ 4^{8}; set peace in earth Lv 26^{6} (H); (the idea of) perpetuity (עוֹלָם) in heart Ec 3^{11}; a purpose, וּלְהוֹרֹת נ' בְּלִבּוֹ Ex 35^{34} (P); וְנָתַתִּי אֶת־יָדִי בְּמִצְרָיִם Ex 7^{4} (P); אַל־תִּתֵּן דָּם נָקִי בְּקֶרֶב עַמְּךָ Dt 21^{8}; וַיִּתֵּן חִנּוֹ בְּעֵינֵי Gn 39^{21} (J), *and he put his favour in the eyes of the prison-keeper* (made the keeper favourable to him), cf. Ex 3^{21} 11^{3} 12^{36} (all E; cf. also **1 b, 3 b**); c. בְּ pers. = *against,* in phr. *set my face against,* oppose Ez 14^{8} 15^{7} Lv 17^{10} 20^{6} (both H); c. בֵּין, = *put,* i.e. *make* a covenant *between* Gn 17^{2} (P), cf. Lv 26^{46} (H); נ' אֶרֶץ לִפְנֵיכֶם i.e. place at your disposal Dt $1^{8.21}$ cf. 2^{36}; *set* ordinances, etc., before, לִפְנֵי (for observance), 1 K 9^{6} Je 26^{4} 44^{10} Dn 9^{10}; blessings and cursings (for choice) Dt $30^{1.15.19}$; נ' דֶּרֶךְ בְּרֹאשׁ פ' *set* or *place* one's *way upon his head,* i.e. requite him, Ez 9^{10} 11^{21} 16^{43} 22^{31} cf. 17^{19}, also 1 K 8^{32} = 2 Ch 6^{23} + (cf. **1 v**); לָתֵת נִקְמַת י' בְּמִדְיָן Nu 31^{3} *to set the vengeance of* '‏י *upon Midian;* נ' ב' ψ 50^{20} = *set in,* i.e. *impute to* (usu. שִׂים ב'). **c.** *set, appoint,* c. acc. + עַל־ *over,* '‏י *hath set a king over you* 1 S 12^{13} cf. Gn 41^{41} (E); c. עַל־ *on,* נ' יֹשֵׁב עַל־כִּסְאִי 1 K 1^{48}; c. בְּ *in* = over, 1 Ch 12^{9} Ne 13^{4}; c. לְ, Nethînîm לַעֲבֹדָה Ezr 8^{20}; c. acc. alone, idol-priests 2 K 23^{5}, prophet Je 1^{5} (2 acc.), leader Nu 14^{4}; one instead of (תַּחַת) another 1 K 2^{35}. **d.** = assign, designate, c. לְ: God *hath* *assigned* victim-flesh to (לְ) you, in order to bear sins of people Lv 10^{17}, cf. Nu 18^{8} (both P); cities for (לְ) flight of man-slayer Nu 35^{6} (P); נָתַתִּי לָכֶם עַל־הַמִּזְבֵּחַ לְכַפֵּר Lv 17^{11} (H).

3. *Make, constitute,* **a.** c. 2 acc., וְנָתַתִּי נְעָרִים שָׂרֵיהֶם Is 3^{4} *and I will make boys their princes,* cf. Gn 17^{5} Ex 7^{1} (both P), ψ 18^{33} (> וַיַּתֵּר in ‖ 2 S 22^{33}), 39^{6} 69^{12} 135^{12}, etc.; + בֵּין Jos 22^{25} (P); + אֶל־ pers. וְנָתַתִּי אֶת־כָּל־אֹיְבֶיךָ אֵלֶיךָ עֹרֶף Ex 23^{27} (E), *and I will make all thine enemies unto thee a back,* i.e. make them shew thee their back, flee from thee, so c. לְ ψ 18^{41} = 2 S 22^{41}. **b.** c. acc. + לְ, וְנָתַתִּי אֶת־יְרוּשָׁלִַם לְגַלִּים Je 9^{10} *and I will make Jerusalem into ruin-heaps,* cf. Dt 28^{13} Is 42^{24} Gn $17^{6.20}$ 48^{4} Nu 5^{21} Jos 17^{3} (all P) +; נ׳ פ׳ לְרַחֲמִים לִפְנֵי 1 K 8^{50} *make* persons an object of *compassion before* (in the eyes of), so Ne 1^{11} ψ 106^{46} Dn 1^{9} (cf. also **1 b, 2 b**); + לְ pers. *for* (esp. Je.), וּנְתַתִּים לְזַוָעָה לְכֹל מַמְלְכוֹת הָאָרֶץ Je 15^{4} *and I will make them a terror for all kingdoms of the earth,* cf. 24^{9} 29^{18} 34^{17}. **c.** c. acc. + כְּ, וְאֵת הָאֲרָזִים נ׳ כַּשִּׁקְמִים 1 K 10^{27} *and the cedars he made like the sycomores,* i.e. as common, = 2 Ch 1^{15}, cf. 1 K 16^{3} Ez 28^{6} Lv 26^{19} (H), Ru 4^{11}; וַיִּתֵּן אֹתָנוּ כִּמְרַגְּלִים Gn 42^{30} (E), i.e. regarded, treated us as spies, but ins. בְּמִשְׁמָר 𝔊 Ol Di Ball Holz,—אַל־תִּתֵּן אֶת־אֲמָתְךָ לִפְנֵי בַּת בְּלִיַּעַל 1 S 1^{16} difficult, (notwithstanding Jb 3^{24} 4^{19}), rd. prob. כְּ (HPS), or לְ, for לִפְנֵי. **d.** rarely c. acc. alone: וּמִבְּנֵי יִשׂ׳ לֹא נ׳ שְׁלֹמֹה עֶבֶד 1 K 9^{22} *and of the sons of Israel Sol. made no slave,* but rd. prob. לְמַס עֹבֵד (as v^{21}; 𝔊A εἰς πράγμα, om. B 𝔊L; cf. Klo Benz), וָאֶתֵּן עֲלֵיהֶם קְהִלָּה Ne 5^{7} *and I made* (held) *over their case a* great *assembly; make a decree,* חֹק, ψ 148^{6}; perh. also וַתִּתֵּן אֹתֹת בְּפַרְעֹה Ne 9^{10} *and thou didst perform signs* and wonders *against Pharaoh,* etc. (cf. שִׂים אוֹתֹת בְּ Ex 10^{2} ψ 78^{43}).

Niph.$_{82}$ *Pf.* נִתַּן Is 9^{5}+; 3 fs. נִתְּנָה Gn 38^{14}+; 2 mpl. וְנִתַּתֶּם consec. Lv 26^{25}; 1 pl. נִתַּנּוּ Ezr 9^{7}, etc.; *Impf.* יִנָּתֵן Ex 5^{18}+, יִנָּתֶן לוֹ 2 Ch 2^{13} (Ginsb van d. H. יִנָּתֶן־לוֹ), etc.; *Inf. abs.* הִנָּתֹן Je 32^{4} 38^{3}; *cstr.* לְהִנָּתֵן Est 3^{14} 8^{13};—**1.** *be given* to (usu. c. לְ pers.): **a.** = bestowed upon Jos 24^{33} (E), Ez 11^{15} (+ לְמוֹרָשָׁה), 33^{24} (+ *id.*), Jb 15^{19}; Ez 16^{34} Nu 26^{62} (P), Is 9^{5}, portion from sacrifice Lv 10^{14} (P), glory Is 35^{2}, birthright 1 Ch 5^{1}, freedom Lv 19^{20} (H). **b.** *given* to one (לְ) for wife (לְ) Gn 38^{14} (J), 1 S 18^{19}. **c.** *provided,* usu. c. לְ Ex $5^{16.18}$ (J); 1 S 25^{27} 2 K 25^{30} = Je 52^{34}, Is 33^{16} Ne 13^{10}; נ׳ מֵרֹעֶה אֶחָד Ec 12^{11} *they are given from one shepherd* (i.e. words of wise) acc. to Ew De Hi-Now Rüetschi^{Kau}; Wild underst. subj. of *compilers.* **d.** = entrusted to Je 13^{20} cf. 2 Ch 2^{13}; c. עַל־יָדָם 2 K 22^{7}, בְּיַד 2 Ch 34^{16}. **e.** = give into the power of (usu. c. בְּיַד), esp. of city (kg., people) given into the hand of foe 2 K 18^{30} (+ אֶת־ acc.), 19^{10} = Is 36^{15} 37^{10}, Je 21^{10} + 18 t. Je Lv Chr Dn; earth into hand of wicked Jb 9^{24}; in good sense Gn 9^{2} (P); delivered to death (לְ), unto lower world (אֶל־), Ez 31^{14}; *given to us* (לְ) *for devouring* (לְ) 35^{12}; חֶרֶב נ׳ Ez 32^{20} *delivered to the sword* (del. 𝔊 𝔖 Co Sgfr^{Kau} Toy); abs., of צָבָא, Dn 8^{12} (al. *was appointed,* v. esp. Dr), 11^{6}. **f.** of request, *be granted* to (לְ), Est 2^{13} 5^{3} (בַּקָּשָׁה), v^{6} 7^{2} 9^{12} (all שְׁאֵלָה), cf. 7^{3} (בְּבַקָּשָׁה, בִּשְׁאֵלָה). **g.** = be permitted Est 9^{13} (+ inf.). **h.** = be issued, published (of royal decree), abs. Est $3^{5.14}$ 4^{8} $8^{13.14}$ 9^{14}; of law given בְּיַד מֹשֶׁה Ne 10^{30}. **i.** = be uttered, נ׳ שְׁאוֹן קוֹלָם Je 51^{55} (of stormers of Babylon). **j.** *be assigned* for (לְ), Ez 47^{11}.

2. *Be put, set:* **a.** lit., crown בְּרֹאשׁ Est 6^{8}; of personif. folly נ׳ הַסֶּכֶל בַּמְּרוֹמִים Ec 10^{6}. **b.** in imagery of Ezek. נ׳ . . . בְּיַרְכְּתֵי־בוֹר Ez 32^{23}, c. אֶת (with) v^{29}, c. בְּתוֹךְ v^{25}, vine put (cast) לָאֵשׁ לְאָכְלָה Ez 15^{4} *into the fire for consuming;* fig. of terror נ׳ בארץ 32^{25}. **c.** = be made, בֶּן־אָדָם חָצִיר יִנָּתֵן Is 51^{12}. **d.** = be inflicted, of blemish (מוּם) Lv 24^{20} (c. בְּ pers.).

†**Hoph.** (or **Qal** *pass.* Ges^{§53a}) *Impf.* יֻתַּן 1 K 2^{21} + 5 t. + 2 S 21^{6} Qr (Kt ינתן); וַיֻּתַּן 2 S 18^{9};—**1. a.** *be given, bestowed,* abs. Nu 26^{54}; c. לְ pers. 2 K 5^{17}, Nu 32^{5} (אֶת־ c. acc.; both P); in exchange for (תַּחַת) Jb 28^{15}. **b.** = *be given* to one (לְ) for wife (לְ) 1 K 2^{21} (Abishag, אֶת־ c. acc.). **c.** = *be given, delivered, up* to (לְ) 2 S 21^{6}. **2.** *be put* upon (עַל־) Lv 11^{38} (P); of Absalom וַיֻּתַּן בֵּין הַשָּׁמַיִם וגו׳ 2 S 18^{9}, < וַיִּתָּל (√תלה) 𝔊 𝔖 We Dr (?), Klo Kit Bu HPS.

נָתָן$_{42}$ **n.pr.m.** 𝔊 Ναθαν;—†**1.** a son of David 5416
2 S 5^{14} = 1 Ch 3^{15}, 1 Ch 14^{4}. **2.** the prophet of David's time 2 S $7^{2.3.4.17}$ = 1 Ch $17^{1.2.3.15}$, 2 S 12^{1} + 6 t. 2 S 12, 1 K 1^{8} + 10 t. 1 K 1, 2 Ch 29^{25} ψ 51^{2} (title); דִּבְרֵי נָתָן הַנָּבִיא as name of a book 1 Ch 29^{29} 2 Ch 9^{29}. †**3.** father of one of David's heroes 2 S 23^{36}. †**4.** father of officers of Solomon, 1 K $4^{5.5}$ (= **2** ?). †**5.** name in Judah: **a.** 1 Ch $2^{36.36}$. **b.** 11^{38}. †**6.** companion

of Ezra from Babylon Ezr 8^{16}. †**7.** one of those who took strange wives 10^{39}. †**8.** head of a family Zc 12^{12}.

5419 †נְתַן־מֶ֫לֶךְ **n.pr.m.** an official of Judah, Josiah's time 2 K 23^{11}; 𝔊 Ναθαν βασιλέως (τοῦ εὐνούχου), 𝔊L Ναθαν εὐνούχου τοῦ βασιλέως.

5411 †נְתִינִים **n.m.pl. Nethinim** (prop. *those given* to the service of the sanctuary, as Levites are called נְתוּנִים Nu 3^9, $8^{16.19}$);—only 1 Ch 9^2 (where disting. from priests and Levites) + 16 t. Ezr Ne (oft. disting. from priests, Levites and porters; Ezr 8^{17} Kt has הנתונים, Qr הַנְּתִינִים), viz.: Ezr $2^{43.58.70}$ = Ne $7^{46.60.72}$ (so Baer, Ginsb; van d. H. v^{73}), Ezr 7^7 $8^{17.20}$ (appointment ascribed to David, cf. 1 Ch 9^2), v^{20} Ne 10^{29} 11^3; living on the Ophel 3^{26} 11^{21}, with their own overseers v^{21}, having a house known (in part) by their name 3^{31}.—On נ׳ v. further Bau Priesterthum 100, 142 f.

5417 †נְתַנְאֵל **n.pr.m.** (v. Gray Prop. N. 181, 192, 205; on n.pr. of this kind cf. RS Sem i. 100 n., 2nd ed. 108, Gray Prop. N. 264);—𝔊 Ναθαναηλ;—**1.** a chief of Issachar Nu 1^8 2^5 $7^{18.23}$ 10^{15}. **2.** 4th son of Jesse 1 Ch 2^{14}. **3.** name of priests: **a.** 1 Ch 15^{24}. **b.** Ne 12^{21}. **4.** priest's son (who had strange wife) Ezr 10^{22}, perh. = Ne 12^{36}. **5.** Levite name: **a.** 1 Ch 24^6. **b.** 26^4. **c.** 2 Ch 35^9. **6.** a prince of Jehoshaphat 2 Ch 17^7.

5418 †נְתַנְיָה, נְתַנְיָ֫הוּ **n.pr.m.** (cf. Gray Prop. N. 294), 𝔊 Ναθανιας;—**1.** נְתַנְיָ֫הוּ father of Jehudi Je 36^{14}. **2.** נ׳ father of Ishmael Gedaliah's murderer Je 40^8 41^9 = נְתַנְיָה 2 K $25^{23.25}$ Je $40^{14.15}$ 41^1 + 9 t. Je 41. **3.** נְתַנְיָ֫הוּ Levite name: **a.** 2 Ch 17^8. **b.** 1 Ch 25^{12} = נְתַנְיָה v^2.

4976 †I. מַתָּן **n.m.** Pr 18, 16 **coll. gift(s)**;—abs. מ׳ Gn 34^{12} + 2 t.; cstr. *id.* Pr 18^{16} (v. Baer ad loc. Ges § 92 g Kö ii. 1, 98); sf. מַתָּנָם Nu 18^{11};—*marriage-gifts* Gn 34^{12} (J; + מֹהַר); *offerings* Nu 18^{11} (P; תְּרוּמַת מ׳); elsewh. gen., *gifts, presents,* Pr 18^{16} 21^{14} (‖שֹׁחַד); אִישׁ מַתָּן 19^6 = *a giver of gifts.*

4977 †II. מַתָּן **n.pr.m. 1.** priest of Baal at Jerusalem 2 K 11^{18} = 2 Ch 23^{17}; 𝔊 Μαγθαν, Ματθαν, 𝔊L Ματθαν. **2.** father of Shephatiah, in Judah Je 38^1; 𝔊 Ναθαν, Μαθθᾶ.

4979 †I. מַתָּנָה **n.f.** gift;—abs. מ׳ Nu 18^6 + 4 t.; cstr. מַתְּנַת Dt 16^{17}; pl. מַתָּנֹת Gn 25^6 +, cstr. מַתְּנֹת Ex 28^{38}, sf. מַתְּנֹתֵיכֶם Ez 20^{31} +, etc.;—*gift,* Gn 25^6 (J) Ez $46^{16.17}$ 2 Ch 21^3; offerings to י׳ Ex 28^{38} (מַתְּנֹת קָדְשֵׁיכֶם), Lv 23^{38} (disting. from נֶדֶר and נְדָבָה), 18^{29} (cf. מַתָּנָם v^{11};—all P); rejected (idolatrous) offerings Ez $20^{26.31.39}$; אִישׁ כְּמַתְּנַת יָדוֹ Dt 16^{17} *each man acc. to the gift of his hand,* i.e. acc. to his ability; cf. לָקַחְתָּ מ׳ בָּאָדָם ψ 68^{19} *thou* (י׳) *hast received gifts among men* (i.e. either tribute gained by battle, cf. Che, or the offerings of those who turn to י׳ Hup-Now; >*gifts consisting of men* JDMich Hgst Bö Ew DeWette); מ׳ used of Levites, as God's *gift* to Aaron and his sons, Nu 18^6, whose priesthood is עֲבֹדַת מ׳ v^7, i.e. a service which is a gift from God; מַתָּנוֹת לָאֶבְיֹנִים Est 9^{22} *gifts to the poor;* = bribe Pr 15^{27} Ec 7^7.

†II. מַתָּנָה **n.pr.loc.** a station of Isr. E. of Jordan Nu $21^{18.19}$ (JE), 𝔊 Μανθαναειν. 4980

מַתְּנַי v. מַתַּנְיָה infr. 4982

†[מַתָּת] **n.f.** id.;—abs. מַתָּת 1 K 13^7; cstr. 4991
מַתַּת Pr 25^{14} + 4 t.;—*gift* = reward 1 K 13^7; מַתַּת יָדוֹ *the gift of his hand,* i.e. of his power, what he is able to give Ez $46^{5.11}$ (cf. מַתָּנָה and יָד **2**); מ׳ אֱלֹהִים Ec 3^{13} *the gift of God* (of the enjoyment of man), so 5^{18}; מ׳ שָׁקֶר Pr 25^{14} *a gift of falsity,* i.e. one promised and not given.

†מַתַּנְיָה, מַתַּנְיָ֫הוּ **n.pr.m.** (cf. Gray Prop. N. 4983
294, No. 82);—𝔊 Μαθθας, Μανθανιας, Ματθανιας, etc.;—**1.** מַתַּנְיָה, last king of Judah, name changed to Zedekiah 2 K 24^{17}. **2.** מַתַּנְיָ֫הוּ, Levite name: **a.** son of Heman 1 Ch 25^4. **b.** Asaphite 1 Ch 25^{16}. **c.** *id.*, 2 Ch 29^{13} (Hezekiah's time). **3.** מַתַּנְיָה, Levite name: **a.** Asaphite 1 Ch 9^{15} Ne $11^{17.22}$ $12^{8.35}$, perh. = **2 b, c** (but much confusion and uncertainty; e.g. מ׳ is of Hezekiah's time 2 Ch 29^{13}, and 4th generation before Neh., Ne 11^{22} 12^{35}; while contemp. of Zerub. 12^8 and of Neh. 11^{17}). **b.** other Levites: (1) 2 Ch 20^{14}, (2) Ne 12^{25}, (3) 13^{13}. **4.** מַתַּנְיָה, name of several who took strange wives: **a.** Ezr 10^{26}. **b.** v^{27}. **c.** v^{30}. **d.** v^{37}.

†מַתְּנַי **n.pr.m.** (abbrev. fr. foregoing);— 4982
𝔊 Μαθ(θ)ανια, Μαθθαναι;—**1.** a priest Ne 12^{19}. **2.** name of two who took strange wives: **a.** Ezr 10^{33}. **b.** v^{37}.

†מַתִּתְיָה, מַתִּתְיָ֫הוּ **n.pr.m.** (cf. Gray Prop. 4993
N. 294, No. 81);—𝔊 Ματταθιας, etc.;—**1.** a Levitical musician, מַתִּתְיָ֫הוּ 1 Ch $15^{18.21}$ $25^{3.21}$ = מַתִּתְיָה 16^5. **2.** מַתִּתְיָה, Levitical name 1 Ch 9^{31}. **3.** מ׳, attendant of Ezra (also Levite?) Ne 8^4. **4.** one of those who took strange wives Ezr 10^{43}.

4992 †מַתַּתָּה **n.pr.m.** one of those who took foreign wives Ezr 10^{33}, 𝔊 Αθα, A 𝔊L Μαθθαθ(α).

5420 †[נָתַס] **vb. tear or break down** (=נָתַץ);—**Qal** *Pf.* 3 pl. נָתְסוּ נְתִיבָתִי Jb 30^{13} *they have broken down my path*, made it impassable (fig.).

5421 †[נָתַע] **vb. break, break down, or out;**—**Niph.** *Pf.* 3 pl. שִׁנֵּי כְפִירִים נִתָּעוּ Jb 4^{10},—Aramaic (?) form, or < textual error for נִתָּצוּ.

5422 †נָתַץ **vb. pull down, break down** (NH Hoph., and deriv.; cf. perh. Eth. ነሠተ: (with transp. and weakening of sibilant), *destruere, demoliri, excidere* Di ^{634});—**Qal** *Pf.* 3 ms. נ׳ Ju 6^{30}+, 3 pl. נָתְצוּ 2 K 25^{10} Je 52^{14}, etc.; *Impf.* 3 ms. יִתֹּץ Ez 26^{9}+v^{12} (Co, for MT יִתְּצוּ); וַיִּתֹּץ Ju 9^{45} 2 K 23^{7}; sf. יִתְּצֵנִי Jb 19^{10}, יִתָּצְךָ ψ 52^{7}; 1 s. אֶתֹּץ Ju 8^{9}; 3 mpl. וַיִּתְּצוּ 2 K $10^{27.27}$; 2 mpl. תִּתֹּצוּ Dt 7^{5}, תִּתֹּצוּן Ex 34^{13} Ju 2^{2}; וַתִּתְּצוּ Is 22^{2}, etc.; *Imv.* נְתָץ ψ 58^{7}; *Inf. cstr.* לִנְתוֹץ Je 1^{10} 18^{7}, לִנְתֹּץ 31^{28} (on תֹ v. Ges ^{§45g}); *Pt. pass.* pl. הַנְּתֻצִים Je 33^{4};—**1.** lit. *pull down* a structure (acc.): altar Ju 2^{2} $6^{30.31.32}$ Ex 34^{13} (J), Dt 7^{5} 2 K 23^{12}; high place (במה) v^{8}, מִזְבֵּחַ+בָּמָה v^{15}; מַצֵּבָה 10^{27}; בֵּית הַבַּעַל v^{27} 11^{18}=2 Ch 23^{17}, cf. 2 K 23^{7}; a tower Ju $8^{9.17}$, cf. Ez 26^{9} (בְּחַרְבוֹתָיו); (any) house Is 22^{10} Ez 26^{12} Lv 14^{45}, so הַנְּתֻצִים Je 33^{4} (strangely + אֶל, cf. Gf Gie); city-wall Je 39^{8} 2 K 25^{10}=Je 52^{14}; city Ju 9^{45}. **2.** fig.: **a.** *pull down* a nation, break its power, וְלִנְתוֹשׁ וְלִנ׳ וּלְהַאֲבִיד (וְלַהֲרוֹס) (obj. not expressed) Je 1^{10} (so Ecclus 49^{7b}), =18^{7}, cf. 31^{28}. **b.** an individual, subj. God, יִתְּצֵנִי סָבִיב Jb 19^{10}, יִתָּצְךָ ψ 52^{7}. **c.** jaw-teeth of lions (metaph.) ψ 58^{7} (*break down, break off*, so only here, but v. נָתַע). **Niph.** *be pulled, broken, down: Pf.* 3 pl. נִתְּצוּ מִפְּנֵי י׳ Je 4^{26} (of cities), so נ׳ מִמֶּנּוּ Na 1^{6} (of rocks). **Pi.** *Pf.* 3 ms. נִתַּץ 2 Ch 33^{3}; 3 pl. וְנִתְּצוּ Ez 16^{39} (consec.); 2 mpl. וְנִתַּצְתֶּם Dt 12^{3}; *Impf.* 3 ms. וַיְנַתֵּץ 2 Ch 34^{7}; 3 mpl. וַיְנַתְּצוּ 31^{1}+2 t.;—*tear down* (chiefly late): c. acc. altars Dt 12^{3}, + בָּמוֹת 2 Ch 31^{1}, + הַחַמָּנִים, etc., 34^{4}, + אֲשֵׁרִים v^{7}; בָּמוֹת alone 33^{3}, רָמֹתַיִךְ Ez 16^{39}; city wall 2 Ch 36^{19}. **Pu.** *be torn down: Pf.* 3 ms. נֻתַּץ Ju 6^{28} (of altar + אֲשֵׁרָה). **Hoph.** (or **Qal** *pass.* Ges ^{§53u}) *be broken down, broken*, only *Impf.* 3 ms. יֻתָּץ Lv 11^{35} (of תַּנּוּר, v. Dr-White ^{Hpt}, and כִּירַיִם, v. supr., p. 468 b).

5423 †[נָתַק] **vb. pull, draw, tear away, apart, off** (NH *id.*, 𝔗 נְתַק in der. species (rare), *pull off, tear off;* Chr Pal Aram. ܢܬܩ *shake off*, Schwally $^{Idiot. 58}$; Ar. نَتَقَ *pull off, draw out, shake;* Di ^{660} cp. Eth. ነተገ: ነተቀ: *detrahere*, etc.);—**Qal** *Pf.* 1 pl. sf. וּנְתַקְּנוּהוּ consec. Ju 20^{32} (on d. f. dirim. v. Ges ^{§20h}); *Impf.* 1 s. sf. אֶתְּקֶנְךָּ Je 22^{24} (cf. Ges ^{§58,1}); *Pt. pass.* נָתוּק Lv 22^{24};—**1.** *draw away* warriors from (מִן) city, unto (אֶל־) high road Ju 20^{32}. **2.** *draw* or *pull off* ring from (מִן) finger Je 22^{24} (fig. of rejection of king of Judah by י׳). **3.** *pull, tear away* Lv 22^{24} (pass., of testicles, + כָּרוּת, כָּתוּת, מָעוּךְ). **Niph.** *Pf.* 3 ms. נִתַּק Is 5^{27}; 3 pl. נִתְּקוּ Jos 4^{18} Jb 17^{11}, נִתָּקוּ Je 6^{29} 10^{20}; *Impf.* 3 ms. יִנָּתֵק Ju 16^{9} + 2 t.; 3 mpl. וַיִּנָּתְקוּ Jos 8^{16}, יִנָּתֵקוּ Is 33^{20};—**1.** *be drawn away* from (מִן) city Jos 8^{16} (cf. **Qal 1**); of soles of feet, *be drawn out* (from water) unto (אֶל־) dry ground 4^{18}. **2.** *be torn apart*, or *in two, snapped:* of sandal-thong Is 5^{27}, strand of tow Ju 16^{9} (sim.), cord Ec 4^{12}; esp. tent-cord (in fig.) Is 33^{20} Je 10^{20}, so יִנָּתֵק מֵאָהֳלוֹ מִבְטַחוֹ Jb 18^{14}; metaph. of plans (זִמּוֹת) 17^{11}. **3.** *be separated*, in smelting, fig., רָעִים לֹא נִתָּקוּ Je 6^{29}. **Pi.** *Pf.* 1 s. נִתַּקְתִּי Je 2^{20}; 3 pl. נִתְּקוּ 5^{5}; *Impf.* 3 ms. יְנַתֵּק Ez 17^{9} ψ 107^{14}, וַיְנַתֵּק Ju 16^{9}, sf. וַיְנַתְּקֵם v^{12}; 2 fs. תְּנַתֵּקִי Ez 23^{34}; 1 s. אֲנַתֵּק Na 1^{13}; 1 pl. נְנַתְּקָה cohort. ψ 2^{3}; 2 mpl. תְּנַתֵּקוּ Is 58^{6};—**1.** *tear apart, snap*, c. acc. הַיְתָרִים Ju 16^{9} *the cords*, v^{12} (+ מֵעַל זְרֹעֹתָיו); esp. c. acc. מוֹסֵרוֹת, *bonds* (fig.) Na 1^{13} Je 2^{20} 5^{5} 30^{8} ψ 2^{3} 107^{14}; obj. מוֹטָה Is 58^{6} (|| פַּתֵּחַ, and הַתֵּר אֲגֻדּוֹת מוֹטָה). **2.** *tear out, up*, obj. roots Ez 17^{9} (in fig.); *tear out, away*, obj. breasts 23^{34} (in violent fig. of Jerus. as drunken woman). **Hiph.** **1.** *Inf. cstr.* sf. הַתִּיקֵנוּ: *draw away* warriors from (מִן) city Jos 8^{6} (=**Qal 1**). **2.** *Imv.* ms. sf. הַתִּקֵם *drag them away* like sheep to slaughter Je 12^{3} (of י׳'s dealing with wicked). **Hoph.** *Pf.* (si vera l.) הָנְתְּקוּ מִן־הָעִיר Ju 20^{31} *they were drawn away from the city* (cf. **Niph. 1**), but prob. gloss, v. GFM.

5424 †נֶ֫תֶק **n.m.** $^{Lv 13, 32}$ **scab, an eruption of skin, on head or in beard, causing suspicion of leprosy** (lit. *a tearing off*, i.e. what one is inclined to scratch or tear away, cf. *scabies* fr. *scabere, Krätze* fr. *kratzen*, etc., v. Di $^{Lv 13, 30}$);—נ׳ abs. Lv $13^{30.32.32.33.34.34.35.36.37.37}$; נֶגַע נֶתֶק 14^{54}; הַנֶּתֶק $13^{31.31}$ (all P).

5425 †I. [נָתַר] **vb.** spring or start up;—**Qal** *Impf.* וְיִתַּר מִמְּקוֹמוֹ Jb 37^{1} *yea, it* (the heart) *starts up from its place* (‖ יֶחֱרַד). **Pi.** *Inf.* לְנַתֵּר בָּהֵן עַל־הָאָרֶץ Lv 11^{21} (P), *to leap with them* (i.e. its legs) *upon the earth* (of locust). **Hiph.** *Impf.* וַיַּתֵּר גּוֹיִם Hb 3^{6} he (י׳) looked, *and made nations start up.*

5425 †II. [נָתַר] **vb.** be free, loose (? usu. placed sub I., but connexion not obvious; cf. also NH Niph. *free oneself*, Hiph. = BH; perh. cp. Ar. نَتَرَ *rend* a garment, *break* string (of bow), etc.);—**Hiph.** *Impf.* 3 ms. juss. יַתֵּר Jb 6^{9}, sf. וַיַּתִּירֵהוּ ψ 105^{20}; *Inf. abs.* הַתֵּר Is 58^{6}; *Pt.* מַתִּיר ψ 146^{7};—**1.** *unfasten, loosen,* c. acc. rei; thongs of yoke Is 58^{6} (‖ פַּתֵּחַ, תְּנַתֵּקוּ). **2.** *set free, unbind* c. acc. pers., prisoners ψ 105^{20} (‖ וַיְפַתְּחֵהוּ), 146^{7}; fig. יַתֵּר יָדוֹ Jb 6^{9} *that he would let loose his hand* and cut me off,—וַיַּתֵּר 2 S 22^{33} was poss. connected by Mass. with תור (v. Comm.), but rd. וַיִּתֵּן (as ‖ ψ 18^{33}).

5427 †נֶתֶר **n.[m.]** natron, or carbonate of soda, a mineral alkali (NH = BH; Aram. נִתְרָא, ܢܬܪܐ; cf. Gk. νίτρον, λίτρον, Lat. *nitrum* (v. Lexx.));—אִם־תְּכַבְּסִי בַּנֶּתֶר Je 2^{22} though thou wash thyself with *natron* (fig.; ‖ בֹּרִית; on use of 'nitrum' for handwashing among Greeks v. Meineke Fragm. Comicorum ii. 638); חֹמֶץ עַל־נָתֶר Pr 25^{20} (fig. of the incompatible).

†נָתַשׁ **vb.** pull or pluck up, root out, 5428
esp. in Je and later (Ecclus *Impf.* 3 fs. תנתש נטע 3^{9}; NH=BH; 𝔗 נְתַשׁ *id.*; Syr. ܢܬܫ *tear off, away;* Ar. نَتَشَ is loan-wd. Frä 137);—**Qal** *Pf.* 3 ms. וְנָתַשׁ consec. 1 K 14^{15}; 2 fs. נָתַשְׁתְּ ψ 9^{7}, etc.; *Impf.* 3 ms. sf. וַיִּתְּשֵׁם Dt 29^{27}; 1 s. אֶתּשׁ Je 12^{14}, אֶתּוֹשׁ 24^{6} 42^{10}; *Inf. abs.* נָתוֹשׁ Je 12^{17}; *cstr.* לִנְתוֹשׁ Je 1^{10} 18^{7}, לִנְתֹּשׁ 31^{28} (on ת v. Ges §45 g); sf. נָתְשִׁי 12^{15}; *Pt. act.* נֹתֵשׁ 45^{4}, sf. נֹתְשָׁם 12^{14};—*pull* or *pluck up*, c. acc. Asherim Mi 5^{13} (מִקִּרְבֶּךָ); esp. of nation, וְנ׳ אֶת־יִשׂ׳ מֵעַל הָאֲדָמָה 1 K 14^{15}, so Dt 29^{27} Je 12^{14} 2 Ch 7^{20}; אֶתּשׁ מִתּוֹכָם Je 12^{14}; without מֵעַל וגו׳ Je 12$^{15.17}$; opp. נָטַע 45^{4}; obj. om. 24^{6} 42^{10} (both opp. נָטַע); so inf. abs. נָתוֹשׁ וְאַבֵּד 12^{17}; inf. cstr. לִנְתוֹשׁ Je 1^{10} = 18^{7} cf. 31^{28} (v. נתץ **Qal 2 a**); once of cities עָרִים נ׳ ψ 9^{7} *thou hast uprooted cities.* **Niph.** *Impf.* 3 ms. יִנָּתֵשׁ Je 31^{40} *it shall not be rooted up* (‖ יֵהָרֵס, ref. to the city Jerus.); 3 fs. תִּנָּתֵשׁ Dn 11^{4} of kingdom; 3 mpl. יִנָּתְשׁוּ מֵעַל אַדְמָתָם Am 9^{15} (of Isr.; opp. נָטַע).—For יִנָּתְשׁוּ Je 18^{14} rd. יִנָּשְׁתוּ √ נשת q.v. **Hoph.** *Impf.* 3 fs. וַתֻּתַּשׁ Ez 19^{12} *and she was rooted up* (of Isr., under fig. of vine).

ס

ס, *Samekh,* fifteenth letter; used as numeral 60 in postB. Heb.

5429 †סְאָה **n.f.** (v. *infr.*) seʾāh, a measure of flour, grain, etc. (√ unknown; perh. foreign word; NH *id.;* Aram. סְאָה, סָאתָא, ܣܐܬܐ, ܣܐܬܐ, ܣܐܬܐ (Gk. σάτον, Lewy Fremdwörter 116 f.));—abs. סְאָה־ 2 K 7$^{1.16}$, וּסְאָה־ v^{18} (Baer Ginsb cf. Ges §10 h); du. סָאתַיִם 1 K 18^{32} + 3 t.; pl. סְאִים Gn 18^{6} 1 S 25^{18};—alw. c. appos. of thing measured, Gn 18^{6} (J), 1 S 25^{18} 1 K 18^{32} 2 K 7$^{1.1.16.16.18.18}$ (where appar. masc., perh. after anal. of other measures of capacity, כֹּר, חֹמֶר, הִין, etc., Al-
5432 brecht ZAW xvi (1896), 95);—סַאסְּאָה Is 27^{8} v. סאסא.
—On size of *seʾāh* = ⅓ ephah, = 12·148 *litres* (= 10·696 qts.), v. Now Arch. i. 203 Benz Arch. 183.

5430 †[סְאוֹן ?] **n.[m.]** sandal, boot of soldier (prob. loan-word from As. *šênu, shoe, sandal* (of leather), Dl HWB 634 Wkl Tel Amarna, Gloss., whence (denom.) *šênu, put on sandals* Dl l. c.; cf. Aram. סֵינָא, ܣܐܢܐ, ܣܐܘܢܐ, ܣܐܢܐ, *sandal* (vb. denom. ܣܐܢ); Eth. ሣእን: *sandal*);—prob. cstr. כָּל־סְאוֹן סֹאֵן Is 9^{4} *every boot of one tramping* (abs. Du al.).

†[סָאַן] **vb.** prob. **denom.** tread, tramp;— 5431
only **Qal** *Pt.* סֹאֵן בְּרַעַשׁ Is 9^{4} (v. foregoing).

†[סַאסֵא] **vb.** **Pilpēl,** whence *Inf.* 5432
בְּסַאסְאָהּ (MT בְּסַאסְּאָה) Is 27^{8} = *by driving her* (it) *away* (conj. fr. ‖ בְּשַׁלְּחָהּ), acc. to Hi Ew Di Du Che Hpt Am RVm; > = בְּסְאָה סְאָה *by the seʾāh, the seʾāh,* i.e. (Ges §123 c, 133 k) *by exact measure* Vrss (not 𝔊), Ges De cf. AV RV, which is prob. Rabbin. conceit. (On format. cf. טאטא, and v. Ges §55 f. Sta §§112 a Anm. 2; 238.)

†[סָבָא] **vb.** imbibe, drink largely (NH 5433
id.; Aram. סְבָא *id.* (rare); cf. As. *sabû, sesame-wine* Dl HWB;—Ar. سَبَأٌ *wine,* is prob. loan-wd. and سَبَأَ *import foreign wine* denom.,

Frä[157 f]);—**Qal** *Impf.* 1 pl. cohort. נִסְבְּאָה Is 56[12]; *Pt. act.* סֹבֵא Dt 21[20] Pr 23[21]; pl. סובאים Ez 23[42] Kt (Qr סָבָאִים, v. infr.); cstr. סֹבְאֵי Pr 23[20]; *pass.* סְבוּאִים Na 1[10];—*imbibe*, c. acc. שֵׁכָר Is 56[12]; pt. act.=subst. wine-*bibber, drunkard* Dt 21[20] Pr 23[21] (both + זוֹלֵל); fully, סֹבְאֵי יַיִן 23[20] (+ זֹלְלֵי בָשָׂר); so also Ez 23[42] Kt (Qr perh. n.gent., so 𝔊 AV, v. infr.), which rd. Sm RV Sgfr[Kau] Da; Co thinks dittogr. of מוּבָאִים, but perh. the reverse (Toy[Hpt] om. מוּבָאִים); > Berthol (q.v.) מְסֻבְּאָ; other conj. v. in Sm; וּכְסָבְאָם סְבוּאִים Na 1[10] is prob. corrupt, pt. pass. of person dub., and sense obscure; del. both as dittogr. Gunkel[ZAW xiii (1893), 235] Now; om. in transl. We Kau. On Ho 4[18] v. סֹבֶא.

5433 †[סָבָא] only pl. סָבָאִים Ez 23[42] Qr=*drunkards, wine-bibbers*(?) so Thes al., but v. סְבָאִים.

5435 †[סֹבֶא] **n.m.** [Is 1, 22] **drink, liquor**;—only sf. סָבְאֵךְ Is 1[22]; סָבְאָם Ho 4[18] (but v. infr.), Na 1[10] (but v. סָבָא);—*liquor* (appar. strong, choice) Is 1[22]; סָר ס׳ Ho 4[18] *their liquor* (i.e. their drunkenness) *is gone* Thes Hi Che RV[m], but very dub., 𝔊 quite diff. (ἡρέτισεν Χαναναίους), We Gu[Kau] Now om. in transl.; conj. of Houtsma[TTijdschr ix (1875), 60] סֹד סֹבְאִים, *a company of wine-bibbers*, makes good sense.

5434 †סְבָא **n.pr.m.** 1st son of Cush, poet. and late;—Gn 10[7] (P) (𝔊 Σαβα, as שְׁבָא)=1 Ch 1[9] (𝔊 *id.*, but B Σαβατ); =nation (or territory) ψ 72[10] (𝔊 Σαβα; + שְׁבָא, 𝔊 Αραβων), so (+ כּוּשׁ, ‖ מִצְרַיִם) Is 43[3] (𝔊 Σοηνη); clearly situated in south; most prob.=λιμὴν Σαβά, and Σαβαὶ πόλις εὐμεγέθης, in Adulic gulf on W. coast of Red Sea; v. Strabo[xvi. 4.8.10] Ptol[iv. 7, 7 f.] Di[Gn] Bae[ψ] Du[Is]; > *Meroë* Jos[Ant. ii. 10, 2] al.

5436 †סְבָאִים **n.pl.gent.** S[e]bā'im, 𝔊 οἱ Σαβαειμ, A Σεβωειμ;—וס׳ אַנְשֵׁי מִדָּה Is 45[14] (+ כּוּשׁ, ‖ מִצְרַיִם, cf. 43[3] supr.); this perh. intended also by Ez 23[42] Qr (v. סָבָא), perh. confounding it with שְׁבָא, cf. 𝔊.

5437 †סָבַב **vb. turn about, go around, surround** (NH *id.*, Pi. Hiph., and deriv.; Aram. סוּבְּבָא *rim, border;* Ar. سَبَبٌ *rope,* سَبِيبٌ *lock of hair;* poss. also سَبَّ II. *prepare a means of attaining* sthg. Lane[1284]);—**Qal** *Pf.* 3 ms. ס׳ Ez 42[19]+; 1 s. סַבֹּתִי 1 S 22[22] (but v. infr.), סַבּוֹתִי Ec 2[20] 7[25]; 3 pl. סָבְבוּ Jos 6[15] + 1 S 14[21] 2 S 24[6] (v. infr.), sf. סְבָבוּנִי ψ 18[6]+, סַבּוּנִי 88[18] + 2 t., סַבֻּנִי 2 S 22[6]; 2 mpl. וְסַבֹּתֶם consec. Jos 6[3], etc.; *Impf.* יָסֹב 1 K 7[15]+, sf. יְסֻבֵּנִי ψ 49[6]; oftener יִסֹּב 1 S 5[8]+, וַיִּסֹּב Gn 42[24]+; 3 mpl. יָסֹבּוּ Jb 16[13], וַיָּסֹבּוּ Jos 6[14]+, 3 fpl. תְּסֻבֶּינָה Gn 37[7], etc.; *Imv.* ms. סֹב 1 S 22[18], fs. סֹבִּי Is 23[16], etc.; *Inf. cstr.* לִסְבֹב Nu 21[4], סֹב Dt 2[3]; *Pt.* סוֹבֵב 2 K 6[15]+, הַסֹּבֵב 8[21] (Ginsb הַסְּבִיב Kt, הַסֹּבֵב Qr), etc.;—**1.** *turn*, intrans. (Impf. of form יִסֹּב in this sense only): **a.** *turn about*, oft. as preliminary to something else 1 S 15[12.27] (sq. inf.), 1 Ch 16[43] (*id.;* וַיָּשָׁב in ‖ 2 S 6[20]) + 1 S 14[21] (rd. סָבְבוּ גַם for MT סָבִיב וְגַם, 𝔊 𝔖 𝔙 Th We, etc.), Je 41[14a] (+ שׁוּב v[b], but 𝔊 om. v[a] cf. Gie), Ec 1[6.6]; of door, Pr 26[14] *turn on* (עַל) *its hinge* (cf. Niph. Ez 26[2]); *turn* (toward one) 1 S 22[17.18.18] 2 S 18[30.30] Ct 2[17] (v. Bu); also c. אֶל־ 2 S 14[24.24] + 24[6] (rd. סָבְבוּ for סָבִיב We Dr Bu Kit HPS; Klo יָסֹבּוּ, cf. Löhr), Ez 42[19] Ec 1[6], אֶל־אַחֲרַי 2 K 9[18.19]; of cup of י׳, *it shall come round unto* (עַל־, with hostile implic.; עָבַר עַל La 4[22]) Hb 2[16]; of Jordan, turn לְאָחוֹר ψ 114[3.5]; *turn about* from (מֵעַל) Gn 42[24], (מִן) 1 S 18[11], + אֶל־ 17[30]; so of inheritance Nu 36[7] it *shall not go about from* (מִן) *tribe to* (אֶל־) *tribe*, also v[9] (לְ for אֶל־); cf. (abs.) וַתִּסֹּב הַמְּלוּכָה וַתְּהִי לְאָחִי 1 K 2[15] (cf. **Hiph. 1 b**); = *be brought round*, c. acc. loc. 1 S 5[8] (of ark). **b.** *turn = change*, only Zc 14[10] (of land, changed like [כְּ, i.e. *into*] a plain), cf. **Hiph. 1 c.** **c.** fig. *turn* (in a new direction) to do something (inf.) Ec 2[20] 7[25].—ψ 71[21] is dub.; Bae reads וְתָשֹׁב for וְתִסֹּב after 𝔊 𝔖 𝔙; Hup-Now Che al. sub **a.** supr.: *turn, comfort me.*—Jb 10[8] rd. אַחַר תְּסֹב for MT יחד סביב De al. **2. a.** *march*, or *walk, around*, c. acc. (city) Jos 6[3.4.7.14.15.15] (all JE), ψ 48[13]; poss. also נָסֹב 1 S 16[11] (of marching about altar? so HPS; *turn* to do something else Th), but cf. תסוב Ecclus 32[1] *sit about* a table (v. Schechter [BS p. 56], and cf. מֵסַב), or rd. נֵשֵׁב Weir in Dr Kit Bu Löhr (perh.). **b.** *go partly round, circle about, skirt*, c. acc. (land) Nu 21[4] (JE) Ju 11[18], also Dt 2[1.3]; of rivers Gn 2[11.13]. **c.** *make a round*, or *circuit, go about to*, c. acc. loc. 1 S 7[16]; *go about in* (בְּ) 2 Ch 17[9], cf. also (c. בְּ) 23[2] Ct 3[5] 5[7] Ec 12[5], so c. acc. Is 23[16]; =*make a circuitous march* 2 K 3[9] (c. acc. דֶּרֶךְ).—Vid. also 2 S 5[23] 1 Ch 14[14] **Hiph. 2 a.** **d.** *surround, encompass*, abs. Gn 37[7] (E); c. acc. Jb 40[22]; with hostile purpose, 2 K 6[15] Ec 9[14] (both of siege), cf. 2 K 3[25]; acc. om. Ju 16[2], cf. 2 S 18[15]; c. acc. rei + עַל־ pers. Ju 20[5]; c. עַל־ pers. alone Jb 16[13] 2 Ch

18^{31}; c. אֶל־ pers. 2 K 8^{21}=2 Ch 21^{9}; oft. fig. in poetry, c. acc. Ho 7^{2} 2 S 22^{6}=ψ 18^{6}, ψ 22$^{13.17}$ 49^{6} 88^{18} 118$^{10.11.11.12}$; so also ψ 17^{11} (Kt סְבָבוּנִי, Qr סְבָבוּנוּ; on text v. esp. Hup-Now); lit. of cord *surrounding* (measuring circumf. of), c. acc. 1 K 7^{15} = Je 52^{21}, 1 K 7^{23} = 2 Ch 4^{2}; of ornaments, etc., *surrounding* something (acc.) 1 K 7^{24} 2 Ch 4^{3}; *surround* one *with* something (2 acc.) 1 K 5^{17} ψ 109^{3}; acc. + בְּ instr. Ho 12^{1}; ס׳ לָעֹפֶל 2 Ch 33^{14} (i.e. build a wall around it). —1 S 22^{22} rd. חַבְתִּי (√חוב), 𝔊 𝔖 Th We Dr Kit Bu Löhr HPS.

Niph. *Pf.* 3 ms. נָסַב Jos 15^{3}+; 3 fs. נָסַבָּה Ez 26^{2} (Ges^{§67t} St^{§410b} Kö$^{i. 342}$); וְנִסְבָה 41^{7} (but rd. וְנוֹסְפָה Ew Sm Co Toy^{Hpt}, cf. Berthol); 3 pl. נָסַבּוּ Gn 19^{4}+; *Impf.* 3 mpl. יִסַּבּוּ Ez 1^{9}+5 t.;—**1. a.** *turn oneself* against (עַל־), *close round* upon (עַל) Gn 19^{4} (J) Jos 7^{9} (JE); c. acc. Ju 19^{22}. **b.** *turn round* (from a direct course), of wheels Ez 1$^{9.12.17}$ 10$^{11.11}$, also v^{16} (but dub., Co ישׁבו, Toy^{Hpt} *leave*, Symm ἀπελείποντο); נָסַבָּה אֵלָי Ez 26^{2} of Jerus. under fig. of door (Sm Co Berthol Toy^{Hpt}). **c.** esp. of boundary (Hex only P): *turn round* from (מִן), toward (לְ) Nu 34^{4}, +ה loc. Jos 18^{14}; c. מִן + ה loc. + אֶל־ 15^{10}; c. מִן alone Nu 34^{5}; c. ה loc. alone Je 31^{39} Jos 15^{3} 16^{6}; *circle about, skirt,* c. acc. Jos 19^{14}. **2.** pass. *be turned over* to (לְ), into the power of, Je 6^{12}.

Pi. *Inf. cstr.* סַבֵּב אֶת־פְּנֵי הַדָּבָר 2 S 14^{20} *to change, transform, the aspect of the matter.*

Poʿ. *Impf.* 3 ms. sf. יְסֹבְבֶנְהוּ, יְסֹבְבֵנִי Jon 2$^{4.6}$, Dt 32^{10}, יְסוֹבְבֻנוּ ψ 32^{10}; 3 fs. תְּסוֹבֵב Je 31^{22}, etc.;—*encompass, surround* (poet. and chiefly late):—**1.** *encompass* (with protection), c. acc. Dt 32^{10} (י׳ subj.), c. 2 acc. חֶסֶד יְסוֹבְבֶנּוּ ψ 32^{10}, cf. v^{7} (but 2nd obj. here dub.); similarly נְקֵבָה תְּסוֹבֵב גָּבֶר Je 31^{22} i.e. *either shall protect* (so most) or (Che, cf. Gf) the woman (fig. of Isr.), instead of holding aloof (הַבַּת הַשּׁוֹבֵבָה v^{22}), will, in the new future which י׳ creates, with affection *press round* her divine husband. **2.** *come about, assemble round* (acc. pers. י׳) ψ 7^{8}. **3.** *march* or *go about,* city (acc.) ψ 55^{11} 59$^{7.15}$; altar (in solemn procession) 26^{6}; *go about* in (בְּ) city Ct 3^{2}. **4.** *enclose, envelop,* c. acc. pers. Jon 2$^{4.6}$ (of waters).

Hiph. *Pf.* 3 ms. הֵסֵב 2 K 16^{18}+; 2 ms. הֲסִבֹּתָ 1 K 18^{37}; 3 pl. הֵסַבּוּ 1 S 5$^{9.10}$, etc.; *Impf.* 3 ms. וַיַּסֵּב Ex 13^{18}+, sf. וַיְסִבֵּנִי Ez 47^{2}; 3 mpl. וַיַּסֵּבּוּ Ju 18^{23}+2 t.; 1 pl. נָסֵב 2 Ch 14^{6}, cohort. נָסֵבָּה 1 Ch 13^{3}; *Imv.* ms. הָסֵב 2 S 5^{23} 1 Ch 14^{14} (but v. infr.); fs. הָסֵבִּי Ct 6^{5}; *Inf. cstr.* הָסֵב 2 S 3^{12} 1 Ch 12^{23}; *Pt.* מֵסֵב Je 21^{4}; perh. also pl. sf. מְסִבָּי ψ 140^{10} (Ginsb);—**1. a.** *turn* (trans.), *cause to turn: turn* face (acc.) Ju 18^{23} 1 K 8^{14}=2 Ch 6^{3} (all=*turn toward*); = *turn round* face 1 K 21^{4}, +אֶל־הַקִּיר 2 K 20^{2}=Is 38^{2}; +מִן Ez 7^{22} (subj. י׳), 2 Ch 29^{6} (of neglect), 35^{22} (of avoiding battle); *turn away* eyes from (מִן), Ct 6^{5}; *turn* (back), *change* heart 1 K 18^{37} (recall from apostasy; +אֲחֹרַנִּית), Ezr 6^{22} (+עַל־); *turn back, reverse* (weapons) Je 21^{4}. **b.** *bring over* (i.e. to allegiance), c. acc.+אֶל־ pers., 2 S 3^{12} 1 Ch 12^{24} (van d. H. v^{23}); of י׳, *turn over* kingdom to (לְ) 1 Ch 10^{14} (cf. **Qal 1 a**, 1 K 2^{15}). **c.** *turn into,* of changing name, 2 acc. 2 K 23^{24}=2 Ch 36^{4}, 2 K 24^{14}. **d.** =*bring round,* c. acc. 1 S 5$^{8.9}$; +מִן 2 S 20^{12}; +אֶל־ 1 S 5^{10} 1 Ch 13^{3}; +acc. loc. 2 K 16^{18} (sense obscure). **2. a.** *cause to go around:* of carrying ark around city (2 acc.) Jos 6^{11} (JE; but **Qal** 𝔊 𝔖 𝔙); *lead round,* i.e. by a round-about way, acc. pers.+acc. דֶּרֶךְ Ex 13^{18} (E) Ez 47^{2}; c. acc.+inf. of purpose 2 Ch 13^{13}; acc. om., *lead round* toward (אֶל־) 2 S 5^{23}, away from (מֵעַל־) ‖ 1 Ch 14^{14} (where, however, perh. read as S, so Be Öt, and, in both, סֹב for הָסֵב Dr Kit$^{Kau\ Hpt}$ Bu HPS Löhr). **b.** *surround* with (acc.) wall, 2 Ch 14^{6} (acc. of city om.). **c.** perh. also *encompass* (as foe), מְסִבָּי ψ 140^{10} *those*
encompassing me (others sub מֵסַב infr.). 4524

Hoph. *Impf.* 3 ms. יוּסַב Is 28^{27}; *Pt.* fpl. 4142
cstr. מֻסַבֹּת Ex 28^{11} 39^{6}; מוּסַבֹּת v^{13} Nu 32^{38} (v. infr.); מוּסַבּוֹת Ez 41^{24};—**1.** *be turned,* of cart wheel, c. עַל־ *upon, over;* מוּסַבּוֹת דְּלָתוֹת Ez 41^{24} pt. appar. as gerundive, *that can be turned, movable* (Ges^{§116e}; Co rds. צלעות מ׳, cf. Toy^{Hpt}); מוּס׳ שֵׁם Nu 32^{38} *turned* (i.e. changed) *as to name,* but gloss, v. Di. **2.** *surrounded,* i.e. *set,* of jewels (pt. cstr.) Ex 28^{11} 39$^{6.13}$ (all P).

†סִבָּה **n.f.** turn of affairs;—only abs. 5438
הָיְתָה סִבָּה מֵעִם י׳ 1 K 12^{15} *it was a turn* (an ordering) from י׳ (=נְסִבָּה q.v., in ‖ 2 Ch 10^{15}).

סָבִיב$_{336}$ **subst.,** used mostly as **adv.** and 5439
prep., circuit, round about:—cstr. סְבִיב †Am 3^{11}; pl. cstr. סְבִיבֵי †Je 32^{44} 33^{13}, sf. סְבִיבֶיךָ etc. (10 t.), much oftener סְבִיבוֹת Ex 7^{24}+22 t., סְבִיבוֹתַי, ־תֶיךָ, etc., Dt 17^{14}, etc. (48 t.):—**1.** in *sg.:*—**a.** as **subst.** 1 Ch 11^{8} מִן־המלוא וְעַד־הַסָּבִיב and to *the parts round about.* **b.** as **adv. acc.** סָבִיב (in) *a circuit,* i.e. *round about,* Gn 23^{17}

בְּכָל־גְּבֻלוֹ סָבִיב Ex 19^{12} 25$^{11.24.25}$, Lv 1$^{5.11}$ עַל הַמִּזְבֵּחַ
סָבִיב, Ju 20^{29} 1 K 3^{1} 5^{11} ψ 3^{7} אֲשֶׁר ס׳ שָׁתוּ עָלָי, 12^{9}
34^{8} + oft.; sometimes doubled, for the sake of
emphasis, 2 Ch 4^{3}, Ez 8^{10} עַל הַקִּיר ס׳ ס׳, 37^{2} 40^{5}
and oft. in Ez 40–43. **c.** as **prep.:** (*a*) †Am
3^{11} צַר וּסְבִיב הָאָרֶץ *distress*, and that *in the circuit*
of (=*round about*) the land (but rd. prob. with
𝔖 יְסֹבֵב *will encircle*). (*b*) סָבִיב לְ׳ Ex 16^{13} 40^{33}
Nu 1$^{50.53}$ 2^{2} Ju 7^{21} 1 K 6^{5} 18$^{32.35}$ Ez 41$^{10.16}$ Jb 19^{12}
ψ 34^{8} 78^{28} 125$^{2.2}$ י׳ סָבִיב לְעַמּוֹ, 128^{3} Ct 3^{7} Na 3^{8}.
(*c*) strangely, סָבִיב אֶת † 1 K 6^{5} (om. 𝔊), Ez 43^{17}.
d. מִסָּבִיב$_{42}$, *from round about, from every side,*
Ez 16$^{33.37}$ 23^{22} 37^{21}, but usu. (מִן **1 c**) = *on every*
side, Je 4^{17} הָיוּ עָלֶיהָ מִסָּבִיב, Is 42^{25} וַתְּלַהֲטֵהוּ מ׳,
4036 Jo 4$^{11.12}$; †מָגוֹר מִסָּבִיב terror *on every side!* Je
6^{25} 20$^{3.10}$ 46^{5} 49^{29} ψ 31^{14}, cf. La 2^{22}; esp. in the
Deut. phrases אוֹיְבִים מ׳, or הֵנִיחַ מ׳ (sts. in
combin.), as Dt 12^{10} והניח לכם מכל־אויביכם מ׳,
25^{19} Jos 21^{42} וַיָּנַח י׳ לָהֶם מ׳, 23^{1} Ju 2^{14} 8^{34} 1 S
12^{11}+; מִסָּבִיב לְ׳ *from round about*, †Nu 16$^{24.27}$.
5437 —On 1 S 14^{21} 2 S 24^{6} Jb 10^{8} v. סָבַב.

2. In *plur.*:—**a.** †סְבִיבִים: (*a*) in masc.
sense, *those round about*, ψ 76^{12} כָּל־סְבִיבָיו יֹבִילוּ שַׁי,
89^{8} Je 48$^{17.39}$. (*b*) in neuter sense, *the parts*
round about, Je 49^{5} מִכָּל־סְבִיבָיִךְ, בִּסְבִיבֵי ירושלם
32^{44} 33^{13}; 21^{14} וְאָכְלָה כָּל־סְבִיבֶיהָ, 46^{14}; with the
force of a **prep.**, ψ 50^{3} וסביביו נשׂערה מאד, 97^{2}
La 1^{17}. **b.** סְבִיבוֹת: (*a*) as **subst.** (*α*) *cir-*
cuits, Ec 1^{6} ועל סביבותיו שָׁב הָרוּחַ; (*β*) *the parts*
round about, Nu 22^{4} ילחכו הקהל את־כל־סְבִיבֹתֵינוּ,
Je 17^{26} 50^{32} (cf. 21^{14} supr.); with ref. to their
inhabitants, ψ 44^{19} = 79^{4} לעג וקלס לסב׳, Ez
16^{57} 28^{24} Dn 9^{16}. (*b*) with the force of a **prep.**
Ex 7^{24} סְבִיבֹת הַיְאֹר lit. (in) *the circuits of* the
Nile = *round about* the Nile, Nu 11$^{24.31.32}$ 35^{2}
סְבִיבֹתֵיהֶם, Ju 7^{18} 1 S 26$^{5.7}$ 2 K 6^{17} סביבֹת אלישע,
ψ 18^{12} 27^{6} עַל אֹיְבַי סביבותי, etc.; oft. idiom. preceded by אשׁר, as Gn 33^{5} הערים אשׁר סביבותיהם
41^{48} Lv 25^{44} Nu 16^{34} Dt 6^{14} 13^{8} 17^{14} 21^{2}+. In
the same sense מִסְּבִיבוֹתָם †Ez 28^{26}.

4524 †מֵסַב **n.[m.]** that which surrounds, or
is round;—**1. a.** pl. *surrounding places*, מְסִבֵּי
ירוּשׁ׳ 2 K 23^{5} *places round about Jerus.* **b.** as
adv. מֵסַב *round about* 1 K 6^{29}; fpl. מְסִבּוֹת *on*
all sides, in all directions, Jb 37^{12} (of cloud Di
< of lightning Bu Du). **2.** sf. מְסִבּוֹ Ct 1^{12}
dub.: *round table* Ew De; *cushion, divan* Bae
5437 Kau; cf. on all these Bu.—מְסִבָּי ψ 140^{10} v. סבב
Hiph. p. 686

†[מוּסַב] **n.m.** encompassing, surround- 4141
ing (?);—only cstr. מוּסַב הַבַּיִת Ez 41^{7} *the encom-*
passing of the house, but mng. wholly obscure;
*מוּסָף *enlargement* Ew Berthol Toy^{Hpt} after 𝔊;
Co del. clause as dittogr. Niph. p. 686 5437

†נְסִבָּה **n.f.** turn of affairs;—abs. 2 Ch 10^{15} 5252
(= סִבָּה q.v., ∥ 1 K 12^{15}).

†[סָבַךְ] **vb.** interweave (∥ form to שׂבך 5440
q. v.);—**Qal** *Pt. pass.* pl. סִירִים סְבֻכִים Na 1^{10}
interwoven (entangled) *thorns* (cf. Da); Gunkel
ZAW xiii (1893). 235 prop. (after 𝔊𝔗 Vollers) כְּסוּחִים
i. e. *cut off, away* (Is 33^{12}) cf. Now; text very
dub. **Pu.** *Impf.* 3 mpl. עַל־גַּל שָׁרָשָׁיו יְסֻבָּכוּ
Jb 8^{17} *are interwoven* (in a tangled mass).

†סְבַךְ **n.[m.]** thicket;—abs. (נֶאֱחַז) בַּסְּבַךְ 5442
Gn 22^{13} (so Ginsb; Baer בַּסְּבָךְ, van d. H. בַּסְּבָךְ) 5442
a ram *caught in the thicket* by its horns; pl.
cstr. סִבְכֵי הַיַּעַר Is 9^{17} *thickets of the forest*, 10^{34}.

†[סְבֹךְ] **n.[m.]** id.;—cstr. ψ 74^{5} בִּסְבָךְ־עֵץ 5441
in the thicket of trees; sf. מִסֻּבְּכוֹ Je 4^{7} (abode
of lion; on בְּ v. Ges$^{§ 20 h}$; on — Kö$^{ii. 1, 512}$).

†סִבְּכַי **n.pr.m.** a captain of David; 𝔊 5444
Σοβοχαι, etc.; 2 S 21^{18} = 1 Ch 20^{4}, 1 Ch 11^{29} +
∥ 2 S 23^{27} where rd. ס׳ for MT מְבֻנַּי Th We Dr 7145
Klo Bu Kit Löhr cf. HPS (B ἐκ τῶν υἱῶν, but
𝔊L Σαβενι); also 1 Ch 27^{11}.

†[סָבַל] **vb.** bear a heavy load (NH *id.*; 5445
Ar. סָבַל, ܣܒܰܠ *id.*; cf. also sub זבל p. 259 b
supr.);—**Qal** *Pf.* 3 ms. sf. סְבָלָם Is 53^{4}; 1 pl.
סְבָלְנוּ La 5^{7};—*Impf.* 3 ms. יִסְבֹּל Is 53^{11}; 1 s.
אֶסְבֹּל 46^{4}; 3 mpl. sf. יִסְבְּלֻהוּ 46^{7}; *Inf. cstr.*
לִסְבֹּל Gn 49^{15};—*bear* a load, וַיֵּט שִׁכְמוֹ לִסְבֹּל
Gn 49^{15} (poem in J; of Issachar under fig. of
ass); of carrying an idol Is 46^{7}; of י׳ carrying
Isr. v$^{4.4}$; servant of י׳ carrying load of pain 53^{4}
and guilt v^{11}; Isr. bearing iniquities of fathers
La 5^{7}. **Pu.** *Pt.* pl. מְסֻבָּלִים *laden*, ψ 144^{14} (i.e.
pregnant Ges Hi Ew Hup-Now Che al.; perh.
better, token of abundant harvest, so many,
v. esp. Bae). **Hithp.** *Impf.* וְיִסְתַּבֵּל הֶחָגָב Ec
12^{5} *drag oneself along*, as a burden (v. חָגָב).

†סֵבֶל **n.[m.]** load, burden;—abs. Ne 4^{11} 5447
ψ 81^{7} (enforced burden); cstr. *id.*, = *burdensome*
labour (of *corvée*) 1 K 11^{28}.—Vid. also סַבָּל. p. 688 5449

†[סֹבֶל] **n.m.**$^{Is\ 10,\ 27}$ burden (always fig. 5448
of burden of tyranny);—only sf. סֻבֳּלוֹ, Is 10^{27}

(v. reff. on סִבְּכוֹ, [סֻבְּךָ]), על ס׳ 9^{3} 14^{25} (in all conceived as burden resting on shoulders).

5449 †**סַבָּל** **n.[m.] burden-bearer,** (late);—only abs. ס׳ coll. Ne 4^{4} 2 Ch 2$^{1.17}$; mpl. abs. סַבָּלִים 2 Ch 34^{13};—נשֵׂא סַבָּל 1 K 5^{29} is certainly wrong; 𝔊 αἴροντες ἄρσιν, 𝔙 *qui onera portabant*, hence prob. נשֵׂא סֵבֶל; > אִישׁ סַבָּל, as ‖ 2 Ch 2^{1}.

5450 †**[סִבְלָה]** **n.f. burden;**—pl. cstr. סִבְלֹת מִצְרַיִם Ex 6^{6} (P), of the heavy labours imposed on Isr. by Egypt., v^{7}; sf. סִבְלֹתֵיכֶם 5^{4} (J), סִבְלֹתָם 1^{11} 5^{5} (both J), 2^{11} (E); (cf. ψ 81^{7}, סֵבֶל).

5451 †**סִבֹּלֶת** **n.f.** prob. **ear** of wheat, etc., only Ju 12^{6} dial. form of II. שִׁבֹּלֶת q.v. (> = late wd. שִׁבֹּלֶת *tide, flood*); cf. Marquardt[ZAW viii (1888), 151 ff.] but also GFM Bu.

5453 †**סִבְרַיִם** **n.pr.loc.** city between the border of Damascus and that of Hamath Ez 47^{16}; identif. by v. Kasteren[Revue Bibl. Internat. 1895, 23 ff.] with *Khirbet Sanbariye* on the river Ḥâṣbâni, SW. of Hermon, cf. Buhl[Geogr. 67, 238], but this appar. too far SW.; 𝔊 Σεβραμ, A Σεφραμ. A city *Šabara'in* is named in Bab. Chron.[i. 28] (Schr[KB ii. 276]); but location not given.

5454 †**סַבְתָּה, סַבְתָּא** **n.pr.gent.** 3rd 'son' of Cush acc. to Gn 10^{7} (ה ָ), = 1 Ch 1^{9} (א ָ); identif. with Σαββαθα [Periplus maris Erythr.[27]], Σαυβαθα Ptol[vi. 7. 38], or Σαβατα [Strabo[xvi. 42]], Sabota [Plin[NH vi. § 155, xii. 63]], old commercial city of S. Arabia, by Tuch Ku, but this = Sab. שבות (not ס׳) Levy-Os[ZMG xix (1865), 253; xx (1866), 273], cf. Hal[JAs 7, iv. 525]; Glaser[Skizze ii. 252 f.] prop. Σαφθα (Ptol[vi. 7, 30]), near W. shore of Pers. Gulf; 𝔊 Σαβαθα, Σαβατα, Σεβαθα. All uncertain conjectures.

5455 †**סַבְתְּכָא** **n.pr.gent.** 5th 'son' of Cush acc. to Gn 10^{7} = 1 Ch 1^{9} (ה ָ acc. to Baer; א ָ, as Gn, van d. H. Ginsb); location quite unknown; 𝔊 Σαβακαθα, Σεβεκαθα.

5456 †**[סָגַד]** **vb. prostrate oneself** in worship (only Is 44, 46) (perh. Aram. loan-word in Heb., cf. Nö[ZMG xli (1887), 719]; Aram. סְגִד, ܣܓܶܕ, so OAram. סגד, ܣܓܕ (Sachau) Lzb[328]; Eth. ሰገደ: all *id.*; Ar. سَجَدَ *be lowly, submissive, prostrate oneself in prayer*, etc., مَسْجِدٌ *mosque*, Nab. מסגדא *shrine* (?) Lzb[152.328], Syr. ܡܣܓܕܐ = Ar.; cf. We[Skizzen iii. 165; Heid. 141]);—**Qal** *Impf.* 3 ms. יִסְגּוֹד לוֹ Is 44^{17} Kt *he prostrateth himself to it* (an idol; Qr יִסְגָּד־לוֹ; + יִתְפַּלֵּל, יִשְׁתַּחוּ; (וַיִּסְגְּדוּ־לָמוֹ v^{15} ‖ וַיִּשְׁתַּחוּ); 1 s. אֶסְגּוֹד לְבוּל עֵץ v^{19}; 3 mpl. יִסְגְּדוּ אַף־יִשְׁתַּחֲווּ 46^{6} (abs.).—Cf. BAram. סְגִד.

סִגִים, סִגִּים v. סִיג sub I. סוג. p. 691 5509

סגל (√of foll.; cf. NH סְגוּלָּה as BH; סִגֵּל *acquire property;* Aram. סְגוּלָא, ܣܓܘܠܐ, *bunch of grapes*, As. *sugullâtê, herds;* also Ar. سَجْلٌ [*a full bucket, bucketful*], *share, portion*).

†**סְגֻלָּה** **n.f. possession, property** (on format. v. Ba[NB § 95 b] Kö[ii. 1, 168]);—abs. ס׳ Ex 19^{5} 5459
+ 5 t.; cstr. סְגֻלַּת Ec 2^{8}; sf. סְגֻלָּתוֹ ψ 135^{4};—**1.** *valued property, peculiar treasure,* which י׳ has chosen (בחר) and taken to himself; always of people of Israel, first Ex 19^{5} (E; 𝔊 λαὸς περιούσιος = Tit 2^{14}; 1 Pet 2^{9} λαὸς εἰς περιποίησιν = περιποίησις Eph 1^{14} cf. Br[MP 102; MA 52, 235]); then עַם ס׳ Dt 7^{6} 14^{2} 26^{18}; later ס׳ alone, Mal 3^{17} ψ 135^{4}. **2.** *treasure* (very late), of kings 1 Ch 29^{3} (gold and silver), Ec 2^{8}.

†**[סֶגֶן, סָגָן]** **n.m. prefect, ruler** (loan-word 5461
fr. As. *šaknu, prefect* of conquered city or province (√*šakânu, set, appoint*) Dl[HWB 659], cf. Schr[COT Is 41, 25]; appar. = NH סֶגֶן, סְגָן, Aram. סִגְנָא *a superior* (not *high*) *priest;* Mand. אשגאנדא WBrandt[Mand. Schriften 169] *a candidate for priesthood;* cf. Jen in Brandt[ib.]; hence perh. Gk. ζωγάνης, cf. Lewy[Fremdw. 129]);—only pl. סְגָנִים Ez 23^{6} + 14 t.; sf. סְגָנֶיהָ Je 51^{57} + v^{58} (where rd. prob. סְגָנָיו 𝔊 Gie);—**1.** *prefects* of Assyr. and Bab. Ez 23$^{6.12.23}$ Je 51$^{23.57}$ (all + פַּחוֹת), Is 41^{25}, of king of Medes Je 51^{28} (+ פַּחוֹת). **2.** *petty rulers, officials* of Judah (only Ne Ezr in sources): disting. from חֹרִים *nobles* Ne 2^{16} 4$^{8.13}$ 5^{7} 7^{5}; alone, 2^{16} 12^{40} 13^{11}; + יְהוּדִים 5^{17} (v. also 2^{16}); + שָׂרִים Ezr 9^{2}. Cf. BAram. סְגַן.

I. **סָגַר** **vb. shut, close** (NH *id.*, Aram. סְגַר, 5462
ܣܓܰܪ *id.;* Zinj. מסגרת *prison* Lzb[328]; Ph. סגר Pi. or Hiph. *deliver over;* poss. Eth. ሠግራት: (prison) *guard* Prä[BAS i. 371]);—**Qal** *Pf.* 3 ms. ס׳ Gn 19^{6} +, 3 pl. סָגְרוּ 2 Ch 29^{7}, סָגְרוּ ψ 17^{10} (cf. Baer's n., Ges[§ 29 o] Kö[ii. 1, 535 Anm.]), סָגָרוּ Gn 19^{10} Jos 2^{7}; *Impf.* יִסְגֹּר Jb 12^{14} Mal 1^{10}, 1 pl. cohort. נִסְגְּרָה Ne 6^{10}, etc.; *Imv.* ms. סְגֹר ψ 35^{3} Is 26^{20} (וּסְגֹר Baer Ginsb), mpl. סִגְרוּ 2 K 6^{32}; *Inf. cstr.* לִסְגּוֹר Jos 2^{5}; *Pt. act.* סֹגֵר Is 22^{22}; f. סֹגֶרֶת Jos 6^{1} (but v. infr.); *pass.* סָגוּר 1 K 6^{20} + 12 t.; —**1.** *shut* door (דֶּלֶת) Gn 19^{10} (J) 2 K 6^{32} Mal 1^{10} Ne 6^{10} 2 Ch 28^{24} 29^{7}; gate (שַׁעַר) Jos 2^{7} (JE) Ez 46^{12},

cf. 44$^{1.2.2}$ 46^{1}, וַיְהִי הַשּׁ׳ לִסְגּוֹר Jos 2^{5} (JE), also (שַׁעַר om.) Jos 6^{1} (si vera l.; סֹגֶרֶת dittogr. acc. to Buhl$^{Lex 13}$); door after one (אַחֲרֵי), on leaving room Gn 19^{6} (J); upon, behind, oneself, from within (בְּעַד q.v.) 2 K 4$^{4.5.33}$ Is 26^{20} (fig.), also (דֶּלֶת om.) Ju 9^{51} 2 K 4^{21}; c. בְּעַד + דֶּלֶת upon one left inside Ju 3^{23}, and (דֶּלֶת om.) Gn 7^{16} (J); fig. ס׳ בְּעַד 1 S 1^{5}, cf. ס׳ רַחְמָהּ Jb 3^{10}, ס׳ דַּלְתֵי בִטְנִי רַחְמָהּ v^{6}; abs. *shut* (opp. פָּתַח) Is 22$^{22.22}$; metaph. חֶלְבָּמוֹ ס׳ ψ 17^{10} *their fat* (i.e. gross, unreceptive heart) *they have closed.* **2. a.** *close* in upon (בְּעַד) Ju 3^{22} (fat upon blade of sword), so poss. also וַיִּסְגֹּר בָּשָׂר תַּחְתֶּנָּה Gn 2^{21} (J) *and flesh closed in*, in place of it (usu. and he closed flesh, i.e. closed the gap with flesh); ס׳ עֲלֵיהֶם הַמִּדְבָּר Ex 14^{3} *the wilderness hath closed in upon them;* obj. om., יִסְגֹּר עַל־אִישׁ Jb 12^{14} *he closeth in upon a man*, fig. of imprisonment. **b.** *close up* breach (פֶּרֶץ) [in wall] of city 1 K 11^{27}; poss. *close* up [path] (si vera l.) ψ 35^{3} Vrss Ol De Bae; JDMich DeW Ew Hup-Now Che take סְגֹר here as weapon, usu. *battle-axe* [Gk. σάγαρις] of Massagetae Herod$^{i. 215}$ cf. Lag$^{Ges. Abh. 203}$, also Egypt. *sagartá* (loan-word) Bondi^{55}; both improb., text prob. corrupt; Schwally$^{ZAW\ xi\ (1891),\ 258}$ reads חֲגֹר > Hal$^{Rev. Sém. iii (1894), 47}$ עֶזְרָה (cf. ψ 59^{5}). **3.** *Pt. pass., closed up = closely joined* with tight seal, Jb 41^{7} (of scales of crocodile). **4.** elsewhere only *Pt. pass.* in זָהָב סָגוּר (gold *shut up*, and so *prized, rare, fine*?), only of temple adornment and utensils 1 K 6$^{20.21}$ 7$^{49.50}$ 10^{21} = 1 Ch 9^{20}, 1 Ch 4$^{20.22}$; perh. read סָגוּר (abbrev. for ז׳ ס׳) Jb 28^{15} (for MT סְגוֹר, so Hoffm Bu Du): cf. As. *ḫurâṣu sakru*, Dl$^{HWB\ 499}$.

Niph. *Pf.* 3 ms. נִסְגַּר 1 S 23^{7}; *Impf.* 3 ms. יִסָּגֵר Ez 46^{2}; 3 fs. juss. תִּסָּגֵר Nu 12^{14}, וַתִּסָּגֵר v^{15}; 3 mpl. יִסָּגֵרוּ Is 45^{1} 60^{11}, וַיִּסָּגְרוּ Ne 13^{19}; *Imv.* ms. הִסָּגֵר Ez 3^{24};—**1.** subj. pers. *be shut up* [in city] 1 S 23^{7}, מִחוּץ לַמַּחֲנֶה Nu 12$^{14.15}$ (E); בְּתוֹךְ בֵּיתֶךָ Ez 3^{24}. **2.** *be shut, closed*, of city gates Ez 46^{2} Is 45^{1} 60^{11} and (דלתות) Ne 13^{19}.

Pi. *Pf.* 3 ms. סִגַּר 1 S 26^{8} 2 S 18^{28}; sf. סִגְּרַנִי 1 S 24^{19}; *Impf.* 3 ms. sf. יְסַגֶּרְךָ 1 S 17^{46};—*deliver up* to (leave no other opening for one, shut one
4042 up to), cf. [מָגַן], מִגֵּן, p. 171 b supr.), only S: c. acc. pers. + בְּיַד 1 S 17^{46} 24^{19} 26^{8}; בְּיַד om. 2 S 18^{28}
5462 (v. also **Hiph.**). p. 698

Pu. *Pf.* 3 ms. סֻגַּר Is 24^{10}; 3 pl. סֻגְּרוּ Je 13^{19}, וְסֻגְּרוּ consec. Is 24^{22}; *Pt.* f. מְסֻגֶּרֶת Jos 6^{1};—*be shut up:* **1.** of cities Je 13^{19} (opp. פָּתַח), of beleaguered city Jos 6^{1} (JE), of houses Is 24^{10} (+ מִבּוֹא). **2.** of prisoners עַל־מַסְגֵּר Is 24^{22}—*down into* a dungeon. **3.** of doors Ec 12^{4}.

Hiph. *Pf.* 3 ms. הִסְגִּיר Lv 14^{46} +; 2 ms. sf. הִסְגַּרְתַּנִי ψ 31^{9}; 1 s. וְהִסְגַּרְתִּי Am 6^{8}, etc.; *Impf.* 3 ms. יַסְגִּיר Jb 11^{10}, וַיַּסְגֵּר ψ 78$^{48.62}$; 2 ms. תַּסְגִּיר Dt 23^{16}, juss. תַּסְגֵּר Ob^{14}, etc.; *Inf. cstr.* הַסְגִּיר Am 1^{6}, sf. הַסְגִּירוֹ 1 S 23^{20}, הַסְגִּירָם Am 1^{9};—**1.** *deliver up* to (cf. **Pi.**), c. acc. pers. + בְּיַד 1 S 23$^{11.12.20}$ 30^{15} Jos 20^{5} (D) ψ 31^{9}; + לְ Am 1^{9} ψ 78$^{50.62}$, and (acc. pers. om.) Am 1^{6}; + אֶל־ Dt 23^{16} Jb 16^{11}; c. acc. of animal + לְ ψ 78^{48}; c. acc. pers. alone Dt 32^{30} Ob^{14}, acc. om. 1 S 23^{12}; c. acc. urb. alone Am 6^{8}. **2.** *shut up* (late; chiefly Lv 13, 14, P): **a.** c. acc. pers. Lv 13$^{5.11.21.26}$ cf. v$^{4.31.33}$, so (abs.) = *imprison* Jb 11^{10}; c. acc. rei Lv 13^{54} cf. v^{50}. **b.** c. acc. הַבַּיִת Lv 14^{38} and (indef. subj.) v^{46}.

† סְגוֹר **n.[m.]** enclosure, encasement;— 5458
cstr. סְגוֹר לִבָּם Ho 13^{8} *the encasement of their heart* (*pericardium;* i.e. their vitals).—סְגוֹר Jb 28^{15} must = *fine gold*, si vera l., but v. סגר, **Qal** ad fin.; סְגֹר ψ 35^{3} v. *id.*, **Qal 2 b.**

† סוּגַר **n.[m.]** cage, prison (poss. loan-word 5474
from As. *šigaru, cage* (Ba$^{NB 22}$); NH סוּגַר *dog-collar* or *chain* = Syr. ܣܘܓܪܐ (*clog of*) *dog-collar;* whence Ar. سَاجُور *dog-collar* (as loan-word), Frä^{114} Prä$^{BAS\ i. 372}$);—וַיִּתְּנֻהוּ בַסּוּגַר Ez 19^{9} *and they put him into a cage.*

† מַסְגֵּר **n.[m.]** **1.** locksmith, smith. **2.** 4525
dungeon:—alw. abs.: **1.** coll. *smiths*, וְכָל־הֶחָרָשׁ וְהַמַּ׳ 2 K 24^{14} cf. v^{16}, Je 24^{1} 29^{2}. **2.** *dungeon* Is 24^{22} (cf. סגר **Pu.**); fig. of exile 42^{7} (הוֹצִיא מִמּ׳); הוֹצִיאָה מִמּ׳ נַפְשִׁי ψ 142^{8}.

† מִסְגֶּרֶת **n.f.** **1.** border, rim. **2.** fast- 4526
ness;—abs. מ׳ Ex 25^{27} 37^{14}; cstr. מ׳ 25^{25} 37^{12}; sf. מִסְגַּרְתּוֹ 25^{25} 37^{12}; pl. abs. מִסְגְּרוֹת 1 K 7^{28} +; sf. מִסְגְּרֹתֶיהָ v$^{35.36}$, etc.;—**1.** *border, rim* (enclosure), of sacred table in tabern. Ex 25$^{25.25.27}$ = 37$^{12.12.14}$; of bases of the sea, in temple 1 K 7$^{28.28.29.31.32.35.36}$ (cf. Benz), also 2 K 16^{17}. **2.** *fastness*, וְיַחְרְגוּ מִמּ׳ ψ 18^{46} = 2 S 22^{46} (v. חרג) *and they shall come quaking out of their fastnesses*, so Mi 7^{17} (יִרְגְּזוּ, like reptiles), all of nations, in awe of ׳י.

II. סגר (√ of foll.; cf. appar. Ar. سَجَرَ *fill with water* Lane^{1308}, سَاجِرٌ torrent *that fills everything* Id$^{ib.}$; Syr. ܣܓܪܐ *imber vehemens*, and Sam. אַסְגַּר, cf. Gei$^{Nachgel.\ Schr.\ iv.\ 186}$).

5464 †סַגְרִיר n.[m.] steady, persistent rain (on format. cf. Ba[NB 215]);—abs. יוֹם ס׳ Pr 27[15] *a day of steady rain, rainy day.*

5465 †סַד n.[m.] stocks, for confining feet of culprits (prob. loan-word fr. Aram. סַדָּא, סַדָּנָא, ܣܕܐ; NH סַד, pl. סַדִּין); = Lat. *nervus*, Gk. ποδοκάκη;—abs. שִׂים בַּסַּד רַגְלָיִם Jb 13[27] (𝔊 κώλυμα), 33[11] (𝔖 ξύλον); (cf. syn. מַהְפֶּכֶת, and Gk. equiv. there cited).

5467 סְדֹם[39] n.pr.loc. Sodom, important Canaanitish city named (usu.) with Gomorrha (עֲמֹרָה, q.v.);—𝔊 Σόδομα (inflected Σοδόμων, Σοδόμοις):—ס׳ (on format. cf. Lag[BN 54]), Gn 13[10.12.13] + 7 t. Gn 18, 19, + סְדֹמָה (ה loc.) Gn 10[19] 18[22] 19[1] (all J), + 8 t. Gn 14; fr. 8th cent. onwards, used as illustrating י׳'s judgments, Am 4[11] Is 1[9] 13[19] Dt 29[22] Je 49[18] 50[40] Zp 2[9] La 4[6]; as proverbial for open sin Is 3[9] Je 23[14], so metaph. קְצִינֵי ס׳ Is 1[10] (i.e. rulers as corrupt as in Sodom), גֶּפֶן ס׳ Dt 32[32] (i.e. wickedness like Sodom's); Judah cp. with ס׳ to her disadvantage Ez 16[46.48.49.53.55.56]. Site prob. at S. end of Dead Sea, where are now *Jebel Usdum* (SW.), and *Zoar* (SE.) cf. Di[Gn 19, 20 ff.] Rob[BR ii. 187 ff.] GASm[Geogr. 505 ff.] Blankenhorn[ZPV xix (1896), 53 ff.] Bd[Pal. 3, 146] Buhl[Geogr. 117, 271, 274]. Vid. also שִׂדִּים.

5466 †סָדִין n.[m.] linen wrapper (perh. foreign word; cf. As. *sudinnu* Dl[HWB 490], a garment; NH סָדִין, 𝔗 סְדִינָא, Syr. ܣܕܝܢܐ, ܣܕܢܐ (rare) Mk 15[46]; > cf. Ar. سَدِينٌ, سِدْنٌ *veil, saddle-cover* (v. Lane[1335]), or ܣܘܕܪܐ, Gk. [and 𝔊] σινδών, cf. Frä[48] Lewy[Fremdw. 85]);—abs. ס׳ Pr 31[24]; pl. סְדִינִים Ju 14[12.13] Is 3[23];—*wrapper* or rectangular piece of fine *linen*, worn as outer, or (at night) as sole garment (cf. GFM[Ju 14, 12]), + חֲלִפֹת בְּגָדִים Ju 14[12.13], in list of women's finery Is 3[23], made and sold by the capable woman Pr 31[24].

סדר (√of foll.; cf. As. *sadâru, arrange in order, sidru, sidirtu, row, battle-line;* NH סָדַר *arrange, order,* Aram. סְדַר, ܣܕܪ, all c. deriv.).

5468 †[סֵדֶר] n.[m.] arrangement, order (on vocaliz. cf. As. *sidru, sidirtu,* and Ba[NB § 77 c]);—only pl. לֹא סְדָרִים Jb 10[22] = *disorder, confusion,* of the dark underworld.

7713 †[שְׂדֵרָה] n.f. 1. row, rank of soldiers in line. 2. architectural term. (prob. for סְדֵרָה, v. supr. and cf. Ba[§ 92 a]);—only pl. abs. שְׂדֵרוֹת 2 K 11[8] 2 Ch 23[14]; -רֹת 1 K 6[9] 2 K 11[15];—**1.** *rows, ranks,* 2 K 11[8], and v[15] = 2 Ch 23[14] (where thought to be gloss by Benz, on account of מִבֵּית, *within*). **2.** term. techn. of building, גֵּבִים וּשְׂדֵרֹת בָּאֲרָזִים 1 K 6[9], meaning unknown.

†[מִסְדְּרוֹן] n.[m.] porch, colonnade? (*place* 4528
of a row (of pillars)?);—only c. ה loc.: וַיֵּצֵא אֵהוּד הַמִּסְדְּרוֹנָה Ju 3[23] precise meaning dub., cf. GFM.

סהר (√of foll. = *be round*?; cf. NH סַהַר *a round place;* As. *sîru, enclosing wall;* also Ph. סהרו n.pr.loc.).

†סַהַר n.[m.] roundness;—אַגַּן הַסּ׳ Ct 7[3] 5469
a bowl of roundness = a round bowl (in sim.).

†סֹהַר n.[m.] roundness (?);—only in 5470
בֵּית הַסּ׳ Gn 39[20.20.21.22.23] (all J), 40[3.5] (R[J]), *the round house* (name of a prison: but ס׳ perh. an Egypt. word Hebraized, cf. Dr in Hastings DB ii. 768 n. and Eb[Äg. M. 318 f.]).

†סוֹא n.pr.m. (𝔊 Σηγωρ, A Σωα, 𝔊L Αδρα- 5471
μελεχ τὸν Αἰθίοπα τὸν κατοικοῦντα ἐν Αἰγύπτῳ (!); Jos[Ant. ix. 14, 1] Σωαν; 𝔙 *Sua;* all acc.), called מֶלֶךְ מִצְרַיִם 2 K 17[4], with whom Hoshea had intrigue; poss. = *Šab-'-ê,* or *Sib-'-ê* mentioned by Sargon (KB[ii. 54, l. 25, 26] COT[ad loc.]) as a ruler (appar.) under *Pir'u* king of *Muṣuri;* hence Schr[COT l. c.] prop. to rd. סֶוֶא, and, further, identif. *Šab-'-ê* = סֶוֶא with *Šabaku,* founder of 25th (Ethiop.) dynasty, cf. Wied[Äg. Gesch. 583 f.]; very uncertain is Wkl's conj. of סוא = *Sib-'-ê* as general of kg. *Pir'u* of *Muṣri* in NArab. (Wkl[MVG 1898, 3 ff.]).

I. [סוּג, seldom שׂוּג] vb. move away, 5253, 5472, 7734
backslide (שׂ׳ erron.; Ar. (سوج), سَاجَ *go and come* Lane[1459], سَوْجَانٌ *abitus et adventus* Frey (Kam));—**Qal** *Pf.* 3 ms. סָג ψ 53[4]; *Impf.* 1 pl. נָסוֹג ψ 80[19]; *Pt. act.* cstr. סוּג Pr 14[14] (Ba[NB § 124 c] Ges[§§ 50 f, 72 p]);—*backslide, prove recreant to* י׳, c. מִן ψ 80[19]; so abs. 53[4]; סוּג לֵב Pr 14[14] *a backslider in heart.* **Niph.** *Pf.* 3 ms. נָסוֹג ψ 44[19], נָשׂוֹג 2 S 1[20] (שׂ for ס); 1 s. נְסוּגֹתִי Is 50[5]; 3 pl. נָסֹגוּ Is 42[17] Je 38[22]; *Impf.* 3 ms. יִסַּג Mi 2[6] (Ges[§ 72 dd], but v. infr.); 3 mpl. יִסֹּגוּ ψ 35[4] + 3 t., וַיִּסֹּגוּ ψ 78[57]; *Inf. abs.* נָסוֹג Is 59[13]; *Pt.* pl. נְסוֹגִים Zp 1[6] Je 46[5];—**1.** refl. *turn oneself away, turn back:* **a.** lit. of Jonathan's bow 2 S 1[22], c. מִן (v. HPS). **b.** fig. = prove faithless (as **Qal**): (1) of human friends, נס׳ אָחוֹר Je 38[22] (abs.); usu. (2) נס׳ מֵאַחֲרֵי י׳ Zp 1[6] cf. Is 59[13]; so abs. ψ 78[57] (+ בָּגַד), c. אָחוֹר Is 50[5] (|| מָרִיתִי), ψ 44[19]

(נָטָה מִן ||).—לֹא יִסַּג כְּלִמּוֹת Mi 2^{6} could mean *reproaches do not depart*, i.e. cease (Hi-St Che GASm Now RV); Now prop. also (emending foll. v.) *shall not disgrace depart from Jacob's house?* Buhl$^{Lex 13}$ conj., plausibly, יַשִּׂיג (√נשׂג) *disgrace shall not overtake* us. **2.** *be turned* or *driven back, be repulsed*, of י׳'s foes: אָחוֹר+ Je 46^{5} Is 42^{17} ψ 35^{4} 40^{15} = 70^{3}, 129^{5}. **Hiph.** **1.** usu. of *displacing, moving back* a boundary mark (גְּבוּל), *Impf.* 2 ms. תַּסִּיג Dt 19^{14}, juss. תַּסֵּג Pr 22^{28} 23^{10}; 3 mpl. יַשִּׂיגוּ Jb 24^{2} (שׂ for ס); *Pt.* מַסִּיג ג׳ Dt 27^{17}, מַסִּיגֵי ג׳ Ho 5^{10}. **2.** *remove, carry away*, valuables, to rescue them, juss., 2 ms. תַּסֵּג Mi 6^{14} si vera l. (on synt. v. Dr$^{§§ 152, 1. 2; 155 Obs.}$). **Hoph.** *Pf.* 3 ms. וְהֻסַּג אָחוֹר מִשְׁפָּט Is 59^{14} *and justice is driven back* (|| צְדָקָה מֵרָחוֹק תַּעֲמֹד).

5509 **סוג** Ez 22^{18} v. following.

5509, 7873 **†סִיג, שִׂיג** **n.[m.] 1. a moving back or away; 2. dross** (*what is removed from metal*);—abs. סִיג Ez 22^{18} Qr (סוג Kt), שִׂיג 1 K 18^{27} (שׂ for ס, but v. infr.); pl. סִיגִים (van d. H. סִגִּים) Is 1^{22} + 3 t.; סִגִים Ez 22^{18} + 2 t.; sf. סִיגָיִךְ Is 1^{25};—**1.** *a moving back, away:* שִׂיג לוֹ 1 K 18^{27} *there is a moving back to him = he has moved back, away* (prob. of temporary withdrawal, diff. from דֶּרֶךְ *journey*). **2.** *dross*, usu. of silver Pr 25^{4} (מִכָּסֶף), 26^{23} (כֶּסֶף ס׳), so (fig. of Isr.) Is 1^{22} cf. v^{25}, Ez 22^{18b} (בְּתוֹךְ סִיגִים כֶּסֶף MT, כ׳ ס׳ 𝔊 Co Berthol;—Co del. ס׳, not so Berthol Toy), cf. v$^{18a. 19}$; indef. ψ 119^{119}.

5473, 7735 † II. **[שׂוּג, סוּג] vb. fence about** (Aram. word; ܣܳܓ, ܣܺܝܓ *sepsit, circumsepsit, clausit*, סְיָיגָא ܣܝܳܓܳܐ *sepes*, cf. 𝔗 סיג Pa. *fence about, fence;* NH סוג *fence about;* Ar. سِيَاجٌ *enclosure made with thorns*, etc., *around grape-vines*, etc. Lane^{1460}, سَوَّجَ II. *make a* (سِيَاجٌ);—only **Qal** *Pt. pass.* f. בִּטְנֵךְ עֲרֵמַת חִטִּים סוּגָה בַּשּׁוֹשַׁנִּים Ct 7^{3} *thy body a heap of wheat fenced about with lilies* (cf. esp. De Bu). **Pilp.** intens. *Impf.* 2 fs. תְּשַׂגְשֵׂגִי Is 17^{11} *thou dost fence it carefully about* (>*make it grow*, as if שׂוג=שׂגה, AE Ki Brd Du).

סוד (√ of foll.; perh. kindred with יסד (cf. יסד **Niph.**), v. Kö$^{ii. 1, 49}$; Ecclus 42^{12} Hithp. הִסְתַּיֵּד (marg. הסתיד) *converse*, is perh. denom.; Syr. ܣܘܳܕܳܐ, ܣܰܘܕܳܐ *friendly, confidential speech*, ὁμιλία, ܐܶܣܬܰܘܕܺܝ = ὁμιλεῖν; Sab. מסוד *place of speaker, oracle*, Hom$^{ZMG xlvi (1892), 529}$, who finds connexion with سَيِّدٌ *lord, chief* (and سَادَ *be lord*), properly *speaker;* NH=BH).

†סוֹד **n.[m.] council, counsel**;—ס׳ abs. 5475
Pr 11^{13} +; cstr. Je 6^{11} +; sf. סוֹדִי Je 23^{22} Jb 19^{19}; סוֹדוֹ Am 3^{7} Pr 3^{32}; סֹדָם Gn 49^{6};—**1.** *council*, in familiar conversation;—**a.** *divan* or *circle* of familiar friends, ס׳ בַּחוּרִים Je 6^{11}, ס׳ משׂחקים 15^{17}; מְתֵי סוֹדִי Jb 19^{19} *men of my intimate circle;* עמד בסוד (י׳) Je 23$^{18.22}$ *in the intimate circle of* י׳; בסוד אלוה Jb 15^{8}; in bad sense, ס׳ מְרֵעִים ψ 64^{3}. **b.** *assembly, company*, ס׳ יְשָׁרִים ψ 111^{1} (|| עֵדָה); סוד עמי Ez 13^{9}; ס׳ קדשׁים ψ 89^{8} (of angels); in bad sense, בסוד בא Gn 49^{6} (|| קהל). **2.** *counsel*, taken by those in familiar conversation: **a.** *counsel* itself, מחשׁבות באין סוד Pr 15^{22} *thoughts without counsel;* of intimate friendship, ψ 55^{15} נַמְתִּיק סוד; in bad sense, of crafty plotting 83^{4} יַעֲרִימוּ סוד. **b.** *secret counsel*, which may be revealed (גלה), Am 3^{7} Pr 11^{13} 20^{19} 25^{9}. **c.** *familiar converse* with God, *intimacy*, ס׳ י׳ ליראיו ψ 25^{14} *intimacy with* י׳ *have those who fear him* (|| ברית), את־ישׁרים סודו Pr 3^{32} *with the upright is his intimacy;* here also Jb 29^{4} (si vera l.) Di De al.; Siegf Du cf. Buhl^{Lex} בְּסֹךְ *when Eloah sheltered* my tent.

†סוֹדִי **n. pr. m.** a Zebulunite Nu 13^{10} 5476
(=*סוֹדִיָּה *intimacy of Yah*);—𝔊 Σουδ(ε)ι.—
Vid. also בְּסוֹדְיָה p. 126 supr. 1152

סוה (√ of foll.; cf. Ph. סוית *curtain, veil?* Bloch^{46} Lzb^{328}).

†[סוּת] **n.[m.] vesture** (NH, but dub.; 5497
v. Levy$^{s.v.}$);—sf. 3 ms. סוּתֹה Gn 49^{11} (poem in J; || לְבֻשׁוֹ).

†מַסְוֶה **n.[m.] veil**;—abs. מ׳ עַל־פָּנָיו Ex 4533
34^{33} cf. v$^{34.35}$ (P).

סוח (√ of following; =סחה q.v.). p. 695 5500

†סוּחָה **n.f.** offal;—abs. in sim. נִבְלָתָם 5478
כַּסּוּחָה בְּקֶרֶב חוּצוֹת Is 5^{25}.

†סוּחַ **n.pr.m.** an Asherite 1 Ch 7^{36}; 5477
𝔊 Χουχι, A 𝔊L Σουε.

†סֹטַי, סוֹטַי **n.pr.m.**; בְּנֵי־סֹטַי among re- 5479
turned captives Ezr 2^{55} = בְּנֵי סוֹטַי Ne 7^{57}; 𝔊 Σατει, Σουτει, 𝔊L Σωται.

†I. **[סוּךְ, סִיךְ] vb. pour in anointing,** 5480
anoint (NH Aram. סוּךְ *anoint*);—**Qal** *Pf.* 2 fs. וָסַכְתְּ consec. Ru 3^{3}; 1 s. סַכְתִּי Dn 10^{3};

Impf. 2 ms. תָּסוּךְ Dt 28^{40} Mi 6^{15}; 2 fs. תָּסוּכִי 2 S 14^{2}; 1 s. sf. וָאֲסֻכֵךְ Ez 16^{9}; 3 mpl. sf. וַיְסֻכוּם 2 Ch 28^{15}; also (prob.) 3 ms. וַיָּסֶךְ 2 S 12^{20} (Ges[§ 73 f.]); *Inf. abs.* סוֹךְ Dn 10^{3}; appar. *Impf. pass.* is יִיסָךְ rd. יוסך Sam., cf. Kö[i. 436] (and not **Hoph.**, cf. Ges[l. c.]);—*anoint*, in the toilet, oft. after washing; usu. **1.** refl. *anoint oneself*, 2 S 12^{20}, Ru 3^{3}, סוֹךְ לֹא־סָכְתִּי Dn 10^{3}; + שֶׁמֶן as acc. mat. 2 S 14^{2} Mi 6^{15} Dt 28^{40}. **2.** act., *anoint* another Ez 16^{9} (בַּשֶּׁמֶן), 2 Ch 28^{15}. **3.** pass., *be poured*, Ex 30^{32} (P; subj. the sacred oil).

610 †אָסוּךְ **n.[m.] flask** (*for pouring, anointing*);—appar. cstr. אָ׳ שֶׁמֶן 2 K 4^{2}, cf. Kö[ii. 1, 139, 401, 494]; yet form unusual and text dub.; Gr מֶסֶךְ, or מִסְכָּה; Klo כַּךְ.

5526 †II. [סִיךְ, סוּךְ] **vb. hedge, or fence about, shut in** (‖ form of שׂוּךְ; prob. not connected with Ar. شَوْكٌ, Eth. ሦክ: *thorns;* poss. cf. Syr. ܣܘܟ *finish*, Pa. ܣܰܘܶܟ *finish, conclude, comprehend*, and Ar. سَكَّ *close, close up, stop, stop up, lock up*, Lane[1386]);—**Qal** (al. **Hiph.**, but cf. שׂוּךְ) *Impf.* 3 ms. וַיָּסֶךְ אֱלוֹהַּ בַּעֲדוֹ Jb 3^{23}, c. acc. + בְּ instr. וַיָּסֶךְ בִּדְלָתַיִם יָם 38^{8} *and (who) shut in the sea with doors?* (Bi Bu וּמִי סָךְ, Me מִי סָךְ).

4534 †מְסוּכָה **n.f. hedge** (‖ form of מְשֻׂכָּה q.v. sub שׂוּךְ);—only in fig. יָשָׁר מִמְּסוּכָה Mi 7^{4}, rd. (טוֹבָם כְּחֵדֶק ‖) יְשָׁרָם מְס׳, *their most upright one is a hedge* (an obstruction).

5482 †[סְוֵן, < סְוָן], סְוֵנֵה **n. pr. loc. Syene**, city on S. border of Egypt, toward Ethiopia, only in phr. (מִמִּגְדֹּל ס׳ (וְעַד־גְּבוּל כּוּשׁ Ez 29^{10} cf. 30^{6}, rd. prob. סְוֵנָה or < סְוָנָה (Copt. *Suan*), c. ה loc. (JDMich Sm Co Berthol) = Egypt. *Sun*, Copt. *Suan*, mod. أَسْوَان, *Aswân;* 𝔊 ἕως Συηνης; rd. prob. סְוֵן also 30^{16} (for MT סִין q.v.) 𝔊 Συηνη.—See further Jos[BJ iv. 10, 5] Strabo[xxxii. 817–820], Brugsch[Geogr. Inscr. i. 155; Reiseber. aus Aegypt. 247] Bd[Egypt. 4, 324 f.] Budge[Nile 284].

5515 †סְוֵנִים **adj. gent. pl. Syenites**, so (or
5515 סְוָנִים) rd. prob. for סִינִים (q.v.) Is 49^{12}. p. 696

5483 †I. סוּס **n.[m.] swallow or swift** (*cypselus*, Tristr[FFP 82 ff.]) (𝔗 סוּסְיָא Is 38^{14});—as twittering Is 38^{14} (in sim.); 𝔊 χελιδών, 𝔙 *pullus hirundinis;* so Je 8^{7} Kt (Qr סִיס wrongly; perhaps to distinguish from foll., so Gie), 𝔊 *id.*, 𝔙 *hirundo*.

5483 II. סוּס$_{138}$ **n.m.**[Ex 15, 1] **horse** (NH סוּס, סוּסָה, Aram. סוּסְיָא, ܣܘܣܝܐ, Mand. סוסיא, Sin. *id.*, Lzb[328]; As. *sisû* (*sîsû?*) Dl[HWB 506]; Tel Am. *su-u*[*su*] Wkl[TA. 191, 24]; prob. foreign word cf. Nö[M 147] Erman[Ägypten 649; Eng. tr. 490]);—ס׳ abs. 1 K 20^{20} +; cstr. Ex 15^{19} +; pl. סוּסִים Gn 47^{17} +, סֻסִים 2 S 15^{1}; cstr. סוּסֵי 2 K 2^{11}; sf. סוּסַי 1 K 22^{4} 2 K 3^{7}, סוּסֶיךָ Mi 5^{9} + 4 t., סוּסָיו Is 5^{28} +, סוּסֵיכֶם Am 4^{10}, סוּסֵיהֶם Jos 11^{6} +;—*horse:* **1.** non-Isr.; *chariot-horses* of Canaanites Ju 5^{22} (cf. v^{28} 4$^{3.13}$; עִקְּבֵי ס׳; ס׳ coll., as oft.), Jos 11$^{4.6.9}$ (JE); *horses* as property of Egyptians Gn 47^{17} Ex 9^{3} (both J), cf. Zc 14^{15}; merchandise of Tyre Ez 27^{14}; *chariot-horses* of Egypt [cf. Hom[Il. ix. 384]], Ex 14$^{9.23}$ (P), 15$^{1.21}$ (poem), v^{19} (P; on all v. Di), Dt 11^{4} Is 31$^{1.3}$ Je 46$^{4.9}$ Ez 17^{15}; of Aram 1 K 20^{1} + 11 t. K (1 K 20^{20} *ridden*, for flight), Assyr. Is 5^{28} + 3 t., Chaldeans Je 4^{13} + 6 t.; other nations Na 3^{2} Je 50^{42} + 5 t.; as ridden 1 K 20^{20} (v. supr.), Je 8^{23} Ez 38$^{4.15}$ + 13 t. (late). **2.** in Isr.; chariot-horses of Absalom 2 S 15^{1}, esp. of Sol., and later, 1 K 5$^{6.8}$ 10$^{25.28.29}$, and ‖Chr; 18^{5} and (as war-equipment) 22^{4} 2 K 3^{7} 9^{33} 10^{2} Pr 21^{31}; סוּסֵי אֵשׁ 2 K 2^{11} (Elijah), cf. 6^{17}; consecr. to sun 2 K 23^{11} (cf. RS[Sem. 275; 2nd ed. 293]); sign of luxury and apostasy Am 4^{10} Ho 1^{7} 14^{4} Is 2^{7} Mi 5^{9} Zc 9^{10}, cf. Dt 17$^{6.16}$, but v. Zc 14^{20}; in vision Zc 6$^{2.2.3.3.6}$; ridden 2 K 9$^{18.19}$ 18^{23} = Is 36^{8}, Am 2^{15} + 4 t. Is Je; in vision Zc 1$^{8.8}$; שַׁעַר הַסּ׳ Je 31^{40} Ne 3^{28}, cf. 2 K 11^{16} = 2 Ch 23^{15}; property of returned exiles Ezr 2^{66} = Ne 7^{68} van d. H. (om. Mass. Baer Ginsb q.v.); description of horse Jb 39^{19}; in various sim. and fig. Am 6^{12} Je 5^{8} 8^{6} 12^{5} Ez 23^{20} Is 63^{13} Jo 2^{4} Pr 27^{3} ψ 32^{9} 147^{10}. **3.** *chariot-horses* of י׳ Hb 3^{15} (fig. of clouds), cf. Zc 10^{3}.—Cf. also חֲצַר סוּסִים, and רֶכֶשׁ, פָּרָשׁ.

†[סוּסָה] **n.f. mare**;—c. sf. סֻסָתִי Ct 1^{9}.— 5484
Cf. also חֲצַר סוּסָה.

†סוּסִי **n.pr.m.** (Gray[Prop. N. 92]);—a Manassite 5485
Nu 13^{11}; 𝔊 Σουσ(ε)ι;—but text dub. Nes[Eg. 209] Di[ad loc.] (cf. Gray[l. c.]).

†[סוּף] **vb. come to an end, cease** (𝔗 5486
סוּף, Syr. (ܣܘܦ) ܣܳܦ, *cease, stop* (oft.), 𝔗 סוֹפָא, Syr. ܣܰܘܦܳܐ, NH סוֹף *end*);—**Qal** *Pf.* 3 pl. סָפוּ ψ 73^{19}, וְסָפוּ consec. Am 3^{15}; *Impf.* 3 ms. יָסוּף Est 9^{28}; 3 mpl. יָסֻפוּ Is 66^{17};—*come to an end* Am 3^{15} Is 66^{17} ψ 73^{19} (+ תַּמּוּ), וְזִכְרָם לֹא־יָסוּף מִזַּרְעָם Est 9^{28}. **Hiph.** *make an end of*, only (if text correct) *Impf.* 1 s. (+ Inf. abs. אָסֹף, chosen for assonance, v. אסף), cohort. = juss. in form, אָסֹף אָסֵף Zp 1^{2}, אָסֵף v$^{3.3}$, אָסֹף אֲסִיפֵם Je 8^{13} (on these forms v. Gf Bö[§ 988, 1] Kö[i. 445, 466]); but rd. perhaps, for אָסֵף, אֶאֱסֹף, We Buhl[Lex 13], or אֹסֵף,

Ges[§§ 72 aa, 113 w n. 3] Now[Zp 1,2], and in Je אָסֹף אֹסִפֵם Ges[l. c.] (against Gie v. Hi).

5490 † סוֹף **n.m.**[Ec 7,2] **end**, late synon. of קֵץ;—ס׳ abs. Ec 3[11], cstr. 2 Ch 20[16] + 2 t.; sf. סֹפוֹ Jo 2[20];—*end* of wady 2 Ch 20[16], of invading swarm Jo 2[20]; of God's work מֵרֹאשׁ וְעַד־סוֹף Ec 3[11]; death as *end* of all men 7[2]; = *conclusion, sum* of instruction 12[13]. Cf. BAram.

5492 † I. סוּפָה **n.f. storm-wind** (that *makes an end*?);—abs. ס׳ Is 5[28] +; סוּפָתָה Ho 8[7] (Ges[§ 90 f.]); sf. סוּפָתְךָ ψ 83[16]; pl. סוּפוֹת Is 21[1];—*storm-wind*, כְּסַעַר בְּיוֹם ס׳ Am 1[14], Na 1[3] (|| שְׂעָרָה), Is 17[13] (|| רוּחַ), Jb 37[9] Is 21[1], as driving chaff Jb 21[18] (vb. גָּנַב; in sim.), sim. of rushing chariots Is 5[28] 66[15] Je 4[13], of ruin Pr 1[27] cf. 10[25]; symbol. of י׳'s judgments, רוּחַ יִזְרָעוּ וְס׳ יִקְצֹרוּ Ho 8[7], ψ 83[16] (|| סַעַר), Jb 27[20] (vb. גָּנַב), Is 29[6] (+ סְעָרָה).

5488 † I. סוּף **n.m.**[Jon 2,6] **reeds, rushes** (coll.) (prob. loan-word from Egypt. *ṯwfi*, *reeds*, Steindorff [BAS i. 603] Erman[ZMG xlvi (1892), 122]; Semitic acc. to WMM[As. u. Eur. 101]);—**1.** *rushes*, in Nile Ex 2[3.5] (E); קָנֶה וָסוּף Is 19[6] (of Egypt). **2.** usu. in combin. יַם־סוּף prob. = *sea of rushes* or *reeds* (> *sea of* (city) *Suph*), which Gk. incl. in wider name θάλασσα ἐρυθρά, **Red Sea** (cf. Di[Ex 13, 18] and esp. WMM[As. u. Eur. 42 f.], who expl. as name orig. given to upper end of Gulf of Suez, extending into Bitter Lakes, shallow and marshy, whence *reeds* (prob. also reddish colour));—name applied only to arms of Red Sea; most oft. **a.** to *Gulf of Suez* Ex 10[19] Jos 2[10] (both J), Ex 13[18] 15[4.22] 23[31] (all E), Dt 11[4] Jos 4[23] (D), Nu 33[10.11] (P), elsewh. late Ne 9[9] ψ 106[7.9.22] 136[13.15]. **b.** sts. to *Gulf of Akaba* 1 K 9[26], and דֶּרֶךְ יַם־סוּף Nu 21[4] (E), prob. also 14[25] (E), Dt 1[40] 2[1]; perh. Ju 11[16] Je 49[21]; poss. rd. מְיַם־סוּף for מוֹל ס׳ Dt 1[1] (v. infr.).

5489 † II. סוּף **n.pr.loc.** (si vera l.) named in defining loc. of Deut. law-giving Dt 1[1] (מוֹל סוּף, where מוֹל by dissimil. for מוּל); but read perh. מְיַם סוּף (𝔊 πλησίον τῆς ἐρυθρᾶς, 𝔊L + θαλάσσης, 𝔙 *contra mare rubrum*), v. I. סוּף.

5492 † II. סוּפָה **n.pr.loc.** E. of Jordan;—only in phr. וָהֵב בְּס׳ in ancient poet. fragment Nu 21[14]; Tristr[Moab 50] cp. *Ṣâfieh* (صافيه), SE. oasis of Dead Sea, but ס = ص is most improb.

5493-94 **סוּר** and (Ho 9[12]) [**שׂוּר**][300] **vb. turn aside** (NH Hiph. *cause to turn aside*, or *apostatize;* Tel Am. *sûru*, n. *rebel* Wkl[Gloss]);—**Qal**[161] *Pf.* 3 ms. סָר Ex 3[4] +; 3 fs. סָרָה 1 S 16[14] +; 1 s. סַרְתִּי ψ 119[102]; 3 pl. סָרוּ Dt 9[12] +; 2 mpl. סַרְתֶּם

v[16] +, etc.; *Impf.* 3 ms. יָסוּר Gn 49[10] +, וַיָּסַר Ju 3249
4[18] +; 3 fs. תָּסוּר 1 S 6[3] +; 1 s. cohort. אָסֻרָה Ex 3[3]; 3 mpl. יָסֻרוּ Ex 25[15] +, etc.; *Imv.* ms. סוּר 2 S 2[22] +, etc.; *Inf. abs.* סוֹר Dn 9[5], סֹר v[11]; *cstr.* סוּר Is 7[17] +; sf. שׂוּרִי Ho 9[12] (Ges[§ 6 k] Now); *Pt.* סָר Jb 1[1] +; f. cstr. סָרַת Pr 11[22]; mpl. cstr.
סָרֵי Je 6[28] (or from סרר, or שָׂר); *pass.* f. סוּרָה 5637
Is 49[21], c. intrans. meaning (Ges[§ 50 f] Kö[ii. 1, 137]), pl. sf. סוּרַי Je 17[13] Qr; and cstr. סוּרֵי 2[21];—**1.** *turn aside*, out of one's course 1 S 6[12] Dt 2[27], *from following*, מֵאַחֲרֵי pers. 2 S 2[21.22], abs. v[23], *from attacking*, מֵעַל 2 Ch 20[10]; *turn in unto* (for shelter, refuge, etc.), c. אֶל־, Gn 19[2.3] (J) Ju 4[18.18.18] 19[11.12] 2 K 4[11], c. לְ Ju 20[8], c. שָׁם 18[3] 19[15], שָׁמָּה 18[15] 2 K 4[8] (+ inf.), v[10]; c. הֵנָּה Pr 9[4.16] (in fig.); for purpose implied Ex 3[3] (J) Ru 4[1.1], or expr. by inf. Ex 3[4] (J) Ju 14[8] Je 15[5] (in fig.); esp. fig. *turn aside* from right path, from י׳, his commands, etc., usu. c. מִן Ex 32[8] (J) Ju 2[17] Dt 9[12] + 7 t. D, Pr 13[14] + 5 t. Pr, + 10 t. elsewhere, + 2 Ch 8[15] (ins. מִן); c. מֵאַחֲרֵי 1 S 12[20] + 4 t.; c. מֵעַל Je 32[40] Ez 6[9]; יָמִין + מִן etc. Dt 5[29] 17[11] 2 K 22[2] = 2 Ch 34[2]; abs. (sts. = *revolt*) ψ 14[3] Je 5[23] Dt 11[16] 17[17] (subj. לֵבָב), וְסוּרַי Je 17[13] Qr (> יסורי Kt) read prob. וְסוּרֶיךָ *those revolting from thee* (Ew Gie); סוּרֵי הַגֶּפֶן נָכְרִיָּה Je 2[21] *degenerate* (shoots) *of the foreign vine* (fig.); סָרַת טָעַם Pr 11[22] a woman *turning aside as to discretion*, shewing lack of it; also from wrong path, sins (of Jerob.), etc., c. מִן 2 K 3[3] 14[24] + 7 t. 2 K; c. מֵעַל 2 K 10[31] 15[18]; c. מֵאַחֲרֵי 2 K 10[29]; סָר מֵרָע+ (pt.) Jb 1[1.8] 2[3] also Is 59[15]; סוּר מֵרָע (inf. and imv.) Jb 28[28] Pr 3[7] 13[19] 16[6.17] ψ 34[15] 37[27]. **2.** *depart*, usu. c. מִן, of frogs Ex 8[7], flies v[25] (both J), sword 2 S 12[10]; sceptre from Judah Gn 49[10] (poem in J): י׳'s hand 1 S 6[3], his kindness 2 S 7[15] (MT, but rd. אָסִיר 𝔊𝔖𝔙 || 1 Ch 17[13] Th We Dr Klo Bu Kit HPS), his wrath Ez 16[42] (but del. Co Siegf Toy), *depart from way* = get out of the way, cease to obstruct Is 30[11], etc.; c. מִתּוֹךְ 1 S 15[6.6]; c. מֵעַל Is 7[17] Ju 16[19] Nu 12[10], etc.; of י׳ *departing*, מִן pers., Ho 9[12], מֵעַל Ju 16[20] 1 S 28[16], מֵעִם 1 S 18[12]; God, c. מִן Jb 21[14] 22[17], c. מֵעַל 1 S 28[15]; רוּחַ י׳, c. מֵעִם 1 S 16[14]; evil spirit, c. מֵעַל v[23]; abs. *depart* [from Babyl.] Is 52[11.11]; = *avoid* contact La 4[15.15.15]; of wicked Jb 15[30] *he shall not depart out of* (מִנִּי) *darkness*, i.e. shall not avoid it, escape it; pt. pass. *made to depart, thrust away*, of Isr. under fig. of wife Is 49[21] (> act., acc. to Ba[NB § 124 c]). **3.** of life-

less things = *be removed*, oppressor's yoke, c.
מֵעַל Is 14^{25} cf. v^{25} 10^{27}; staves from (מִן) ark
Ex 25^{15}; abs. iniquity Is 6^{7}; esp. of בָּמוֹת 1 K
15^{14} 22^{44} 2 K 12^{4} 14^{4} $15^{4.35}$ 2 Ch 15^{17} 20^{33}. **4.**
= *come to an end*, Am 6^{7} Is 11^{13}.—For סָר אֶל־
1 S 22^{14} read שַׂר עַל־ 𝔊 Th Dr Klo Bu Kit Löhr
HPS; in 15^{32} Th HPS del. סָר (after 𝔊 𝔙 𝔖)
as dittogr.; סָר סָבְאָם Ho 4^{18} v. סֹבֶא; Ho 7^{14} rd.
יָסוֹרוּ for יָסוֹרוּ (√ סרר q.v.); Je 6^{28}, it is uncertain whether (סוֹרְרִים) סָרֵי belongs here, *revolters*
8269 *among the rebellious*, or sub סרר, or even = שָׂרֵי
princes, chiefs (cf. 1 S 22^{14}).

†**Pôlēl** *Pf.* 3 ms. סוֹרֵר דְּרָכַי La 3^{11} *he
turned aside my ways* (my steps).

Hiph.$_{133}$ *Pf.* 3 ms. הֵסִיר 2 K 18^{4}+; 2 ms.
וַהֲסִרֹתָ consec. (Dr §110(5) Obs.) 1 K 3^{31}; 1 s. הֲסִירֹתִי
2 K 23^{27}+, וַהֲסִרֹתִי 1 S 17^{46}+; 3 pl. הֵסִירוּ 2 Ch
30^{14}, etc.; *Impf.* 3 ms. יָסִיר Is 3^{18}+, juss. יָסֵר
Ex 8^{4}+, וַיָּסַר Gn 8^{13}+; sf. וַיְסִרֵהוּ 1 S 18^{13},
וַיְסִרֶהָ 1 K 15^{13}, יְסִירֶנָּה Lv 3^{4}+; 3 mpl. יָסִירוּ Is
5^{23}+, etc.; *Imv.* ms. הָסֵר 1 K 20^{24}+, הָסִיר Ez
21^{31} (rd. הָסֵר, הָסִיר); fs. הָסִירִי 1 S 1^{14}, etc.; *Inf.
abs.* הָסֵר Gn 30^{32}+; *cstr.* הָסִיר 2 K 6^{32}+, etc.;
Pt. מֵסִיר Is 3^{1} + 3 t.;—**1.** *cause to* (turn aside,)
depart, common word for *remove, take away*:
c. מִן, Ex $8^{4.27}$ 33^{23} (all J), 23^{25} (E) Dt 7^{15} 1 S 28^{3}
Jos 7^{13} (J) Ju 10^{16} Is 3^{1} ψ 18^{23} (+ ‖ 2 S 22^{23}, rd.
אָסִיר מִמֶּנִּי De Hup-Now HPS); shoulder from
burden ψ 81^{7}; מֵסִיר אָזְנוֹ מִשְּׁמֹעַ Pr 28^{9}; + oft.,
+ Jb 33^{17} (ins. מִן 𝔊 Ew Di De Hi Bu al.); c. מֵעַל,
take off ring Gn 41^{42} (E) Est 3^{10}, also 8^{2} (abs.);
garments Gn $38^{14.19}$ (J) Dt 21^{13} Zc 3^{4} 1 S 17^{39}
(armour), also Ex 34^{34} (P; abs.) and Ez 26^{16} (Co
ins. מֵעַל); *take off* head, מֵעַל 1 S 17^{46}, abs. 2 S 4^{7}
16^{9} 2 K 16^{32}; c. מֵעַל also oft. fig. (*from upon* =
from resting on, or burdening), plagues Ex 8^{4}
10^{17} (J), cf. Nu 21^{7} (E), also 1 S 1^{14} Am 5^{23} 1 K
2^{31}; reproach 1 S 17^{26} Is 25^{8}; c. מֵעִם = from one's
presence 1 S 18^{13}, also of ׳י removing his kindness 1 Ch 16^{13} + ‖ 2 S 7^{15} (v. **Qal 2**); c. מֵעַל פָּנָיו,
of ׳י removing Isr. 2 K $17^{18.23}$ 23^{27} 24^{3} Je 32^{31};
abs. 2 K 23^{27}; oft. abs., Gn 8^{13} *Noah removed
the covering*; remove = *depose* c. מִן 1 K 15^{13} =
2 Ch 15^{16} (v. מִן **7 b** (*b*)), abs. 2 Ch 36^{3}, cf. Ju 9^{29}
Jb 34^{20}; remove בָּמוֹת, etc., 2 K 18^{4}, v^{22} = Is 36^{7} =
2 Ch 32^{12}, 2 K 23^{19} 2 Ch 30^{14} 14^{2}, cf. 14^{4} 17^{5} (both
c. מִן); = *put away* strange gods, etc., Gn 35^{2}
Jos $24^{14.23}$ (all E), 1 S 7^{4}, c. מִתּוֹךְ v^{3} Is 58^{9}; once
c. לְ, מֵסִיר שָׂפָה לְנֶאֱמָנִים Jb 12^{20}. **2.** rarer
uses are: *put aside* = leave undone Jos 11^{15} (D);
retract words Is 31^{2} (of ׳י); *reject* prayer ψ 66^{20};
abolish sacrifice Dn 11^{31}; *turn* one *away* מֵאַחֲרֵי,
i.e. from following Dt 7^{4}; c. אֶל־ pers., *remove the
ark unto* 2 S 6^{10} = 1 Ch 13^{13}.

†**Hoph.** *Pf.* 3 ms. הוּסַר Lv 4^{31} Dn 12^{11};
Impf. 3 ms. יוּסַר Lv 4^{35}; *Pt.* מוּסָר Is 17^{1}; pl.
מוּסָרִים 1 S 21^{7} (but final ם prob. dittogr. before מ
We Dr Klo Kit HPS);—*be taken away, removed*:
c. מִן Lv 4^{35}, מֵעַל v^{31}, מִלִּפְנֵי ׳י 1 S 21^{7}; מוּסָר מֵעִיר
Is 17^{1} *Damascus is removed from* being *a city*;
abs. *be abolished* Dn 12^{11} (cf. 11^{31} Hiph.).

I. סוּר **adj.verb.** properly *Pt.* of סור q.v. 5493-94

†II. סוּר **n.pr.** of a temple-gate;—שַׁעַר ס׳ 5495
2 K 11^{6} (> ‖ 2 Ch 23^{5} שַׁעַר הַיְסוֹד, v. יְסוֹד), but
del. ver. as gloss We Bleek, Einl. 4, 258 Kmp Kau Benz.

†סָרָה **n.f.** **a turning aside, defection,** 5627
apostasy, withdrawal;—alw. abs. ס׳;—**1.** *defection*, used appar. of any moral or legal offence
Dt 19^{16}, so prob. Is 59^{13} (+ דִּבְרֵי שֶׁקֶר, עֹשֶׁק). **2.**
apostasy, Dt 13^{6} Is 1^{5} 31^{6} Je 28^{16} 29^{32}. **3.** בִּלְתִּי
סָרָה *non-withdrawal* Is 14^{6} (cf. vb., v^{25} Am 6^{7}).

סרה v. בּוֹר הַס׳ p. 92 supr. יסור, only in 953, 5626
יסורי Je 17^{13} Kt, but v. Qr סור **Qal** *Pt.* 5493-94

†[סוּת] **vb.** **Hiph.** **incite, allure, instigate** 5496
(NH Hiph., *id.*);—**Hiph.** *Pf.* 3 ms. sf. הֱסִיתְךָ
1 S 26^{19}, הֱסִיתְךָ Jb 36^{16}; 3 fs. הֵסַתָּה 1 K 21^{25}
(Ges §72 w Kö i. 460); 3 pl. sf. הִסִּיתוּךָ Je 38^{22} (Ges
§72 ee); *Impf.* 3 ms. יַסִּית 2 K 18^{32} + 2 t., but also
וַיָּסֶת 2 S 24^{1} 1 Ch 21^{1}, sf. יְסִיתְךָ Dt 13^{7} Jb 36^{18},
etc.; *Pt.* מַסִּית Je 43^{3} 2 Ch 32^{11};—**1. a.** *incite*
to make a request (c. acc. pers. + inf.) Ju 1^{14}
(on text v. GFM) = Jos 15^{18}. **b.** *allure* וַיְסִיתֵם
מִמֶּנּוּ 2 Ch 18^{31} *and* God *allured them away fr.
him* (si vera l.; del. cl. as gloss Be Kit); so
also Jb 36^{16} acc. to De Hi Bu al.; *he allureth
thee* out *of the mouth of distress*, but Di Du
freedom hath seduced thee; for meaning *seduce,
entice*, cf. also v^{18}. **2.** *instigate*, in bad sense,
c. acc. pers., + בְּ *against*, 1 S 26^{19} 2 S 24^{1} Je 43^{3}
Jb 2^{3}; c. acc. pers. alone 1 K 21^{25} 2 K 18^{32} =
Is 36^{18}, cf. 2 Ch 32^{15}, Dt 13^{7} Je 38^{22}; + inf. 1 Ch
21^{1} 2 Ch 18^{2} 32^{11}.

סוּת **n.** v. סוה. p. 691 5497

†[סָחַב] **vb.** **drag** (*Impf.* consec. 1 s. 5498
ואסחב MI ^{18}, sf. ואסחבה Ib $^{12.13}$; Ph. סחב Lzb ^{328};
Ar. سَحَبَ, Eth. ሰሐበ:);—**Qal** *Pf.* 1 pl. וְסָחַבְנוּ
consec. 2 S 17^{13}; *Impf.* 3 ms. sf. יִסְחָבוּם Je 49^{20}
50^{45}; *Inf. abs.* סָחוֹב Je 22^{19}; *cstr.* לִסְחֹב Je 15^{3};
—*drag*, a city עַד־הַנַּחַל 2 S 17^{13}, corpses Je 15^{3}

22^{19}, captives, under fig. of sheep dragged off by wild beast $49^{20}=50^{46}$ (𝔊 pass., whence Schwally Gie suppose a **Niph.** יִסָּחֲבוּ).

5499 †סְחָבָה **n.f. rag, clout** (stuff *pulled* or *dragged about;* > Lag$^{BN\ 143}$ √ شَحُبَ, شَحَبَ *become altered for the worse*);—only pl. סְחָבוֹת Je $38^{11.12}$ (both + מְלָחִים).

5500 †[סָחָה] **vb. scrape** (Ar. سَحَا (سحو), and سحى Lane^{1322}) *scrape off, clear away;* cf. Talm. סְחוּתָא, סְחִיתָא *refuse,* 𝔗 סְחִיתָא *dirt, dung*);—only **Pi. scrape clean, scour,** *Pf.* 1 s. consec. וְסִחֵיתִי עֲפָרָהּ מִמֶּנָּה Ez 26^4 *and I will scrape clean her dust from her.*

5501 †סְחִי **n.[m.] offscouring;**—ס׳ וּמָאוֹס תְּשִׂימֵנוּ La 3^{45}.

7823 †סָחִישׁ **n.[m.]** grain that shoots up of itself in 2nd year (√unknown);—‖ סָפִיחַ, 2 K 19^{29} (= שָׁחִיס ‖ Is 37^{30}); on use of this for food, cf. Strabo$^{xi.\ 4,\ 3}$ (of Albanians).

5502 †[סָחַף] **vb. prostrate** (NH סחף, Aram. סְחַף, ܣܚܦ (for ἐδαφίζω, Lk 19^{42}); As. *saḫâpu, throw down, overwhelm*);—**Qal** *Pf.* מָטָר סֹחֵף Pr 28^3 *a prostrating rain* (beating down grain), וְאֵין לָחֶם *and* (so) *there is no bread.* **Niph.** *Pf.* 3 ms. נִסְחַף אַבִּירֶיךָ Je 46^{15} *why are thy mighty ones* (or, *why is thy bull,* i.e. Apis, Hi Ew Gf) *prostrated?* but rd. perh. נָס חָף אַבִּירְךָ לֹא עָמַד (𝔊 Mich Gie Co) *why hath Apis fled, thy bull doth not stand?*

5503 †[סָחַר] **vb. go around, about, travel about in** (NH *id., go about as merchant, pedlar,* perh. denom. from סוֹחֵר (Jastr); Syr. ܣܚܰܪ *go about as beggar, be beggar* PS^{2593} (rare), esp. ChrPalAram. v. Schwally$^{Idiot.\ 61\ f.}$; As. *saḫâru, turn, surround,* Tel Am. *return* Wkl$^{TA\ Gloss.}$; 𝔗 *surround* (oft.), and deriv.; Ar. سَخِرَ is *mock at, deride*);—**Qal** *Pf.* 3 pl. סָחֲרוּ Je 14^{18}; *Impf.* 3 mpl. יִסְחֲרוּ Gn 34^{21}; 2 mpl. תִּסְחָרוּ Gn 42^{34}; *Imv.* mpl. sf. סְחָרוּהָ Gn 34^{10}; *Pt.* סֹחֵר Gn 23^{16}, סוֹחֵר Pr 31^{14}; cstr. סֹחֵר Is 23^2; fs. sf. סֹחַרְתֵּךְ Ez $27^{12.16.18}$ + סֹחֲרֹתַיִךְ v^{15} (v. infr.); mpl. סֹחֲרִים Gn 37^{28} + 2 t.; cstr. סֹחֲרֵי 1 K 10^{28} + 3 t.; sf. סֹחֲרַיִךְ Is 47^{15}, ־רַיִךְ Ez 27^{21}, ־רֶיהָ Is 23^8;—**1.** *go about, to and fro* (i.e. go about one's affairs, carry on one's business) *in,* c. acc. אֶרֶץ Gn 42^{34} (E), $34^{10.21}$ (P); c. אֶל־אֶרֶץ Je 14^{18}, but dub., 𝔊 Gf Hi Or Co^{Hpt} Rothst^{Kau} *journey unto a land which* they have not known. **2.** *Pt.* = subst. *a trafficker, trader* (who *goes about* with wares, etc.) Gn 23^{16} (P), 37^{28} (E), Is $23^{2.8}$ 47^{15} 1 K 10^{28} = 2 Ch 1^{16}, Ez $27^{21.21.36}$ 38^{13}; + תָּרִים 2 Ch 9^{14}; f., of a city or country, Ez $27^{12.16.18}$; also in v^{15} rd. סֹחֲרֹתַיִךְ for MT (ידך) סְחֹרַת Sm Co Berthol Toy. **Pilp.** *Pf.* 3 ms. לִבִּי סְחַרְחַר ψ 38^{11} (Ges$^{§\ 55\ e}$) *my heart palpitates* (+ עֲזָבַנִי כֹחִי).

†[סַחַר] **n.m.**$^{Pr\ 3,\ 14}$ **traffic, gain;**—cstr. סְחַר Is 23^3 + 2 t.; sf. סַחְרָהּ Pr 3^{14} + 3 t.;—*traffic,* i.e. *gain* from traffic, Is $23^{3.18}$ (+ אֶתְנַנָּהּ), v^{18} 45^{14} Pr 3^{14} 31^{18}. 5504-05

†[סְחֹרָה] **n.f. merchandise;**—cstr. סְחֹרַת Ez 27^{15}, but v. סחר *Pt.* 5506

†סֹחֵרָה **n.f. buckler;**—ψ 91^4 (+ צִנָּה; fig. of י׳'s faithfulness). 5507

†[מִסְחָר] **n.m.** appar. **merchandise;**—cstr. מִסְחַר הָרֹכְלִים 1 K 10^{15}, but text prob. crpt.; Klo prop. מִסַּחַר, so Buhl$^{Lex\ 13}$; ‖ 2 Ch 9^{14} has הַסֹּחֲרִים, and so Benz here (for both wds. of MT). 4536

†[סֹחֶרֶת] **n.f.** a stone used (with marble) in paving (cf. As. *siḫru,* a precious stone, Dl $^{HWB\ 495}$);—סֹחָרֶת Est 1^6. 5508

[סֵט], סֵטִים v. שֵׂט sub שׂוט. סִיג v. סוג.

†סִיוָן **n.pr.** of 3rd month, **Sîwān** = May–June (loan-word from As.-Bab. *Simânu,* cf. Schr$^{COT\ Ne\ 1,1}$ Muss-Arnolt$^{JBL\ xi\ (1892),\ 82\ ff.}$; Palm. סיון Lzb^{328} Cook^{84});—בַּחֹדֶשׁ הַשְּׁלִישִׁי הוּא־חֹדֶשׁ ס׳ Est 8^9. 5510

סִיחוֹן, סִיחֹן $_{35}$ **n.pr.m. Sihon** (on format. cf. Lag$^{BN\ 198}$);—סִיחוֹן Nu 21^{27} + 18 t., סִיחֹן v^{21} + 17 t.;—king of Amorites, Nu 21^{21} + 7 t. Nu 21 (JE), 32^{33} (R) Dt 1^4 + 10 t. Dt, Ju 2^{10} + 4 t. Ju (D) + $13^{21.21.27}$ (P), $11^{19.20.20.21}$ Je 48^{45} 1 K 4^{19} Ne 9^{22} ψ 135^{11} 136^{19}. 𝔊 Σηων, 𝔊L Σιων. 5511

†I. סִין **n.pr.loc. Sin,** i.e. *Pelusium,* E. frontier city of Egypt (Egypt. *'Imt = clay,* of which סין is transl. (cf. Aram. סְיָן *clay*), acc. to Steindorff$^{BAS\ i.\ 599}$, who cp. Πηλούσιον (πηλός = *dirt, mud*), cf. Brugsch$^{Dict.\ Géogr.\ 1081\ ff.}$);—Ez 30^{15} (𝔊 Σαιν acc.), + v^{16}, but here Co Toy rd. plausibly סון, i.e. סְוֵן = Syene (v. [סְוֵן], סְוֵנֵה), 𝔊 Συηνη.—On Pelusium v. Bd$^{Egypt.\ 4\ (1898),\ 169}$. 5512

†II. סִין **n.pr.loc.** wilderness between Elim and Sinai, מִדְבַּר־סִין, acc. to P, Ex 16^1 17^1 Nu $33^{11.12}$; 𝔊 Σειν, A 𝔊L Σιν; cf. Eb$^{GS\ 2.\ 155\ ff.}$ and esp. Di$^{Ex\ 16,1}$. 5512

5514 †סִינַי **n.pr.mont.** Sinai;—name of mt. of law-giving in J and esp. P (חֹרֵב in E and esp. D): Ju 5[5] ψ 68[9] Dt 33[2] (poem), also Ex 16[1] (P); usu. הַר־סִינַי (סִינָ֑י Lv 7[38]+), rarely J, Ex 19[20.23] and perh. 34[2.4], elsewh. mostly P, 24[16] 31[18] 34[29.32] Lv 7[38] 25[1] 27[34] and 26[46] (H), Nu 3[1] 28[6], also Ne 9[13]; מִדְבַּר סִינַי (סִינָ֑י Nu 1[19]+), Ex 19[1.2] Lv 7[38] Nu 1[1.19] 3[4.14] 9[1.5] 10[12] 26[64] 33[15.16] (all P);—in view of these facts, and of E's use of חֹרֵב (q.v.), it is prob. that Ex 19[11.18] (in E passages) are from R.—𝔊 Σ(ε)ινα. Identif. dub.; local tradition names *Jebel Musa*, mt. at S. end of peninsular between the two arms of Red Sea, so Rob[BR i. 90 ff., esp. 119–122] cf. Stanley[Sinai and Pal. 42 f.] al., specif. its N. spur, *Ras Ṣafṣâfeh;* but Lepsius[Briefe 345 ff., 416 ff.] Eb[GS esp. 392 ff.] al. advocate *Serbal*, NW. from *Jebel Musa* (on trad., cf. Eb[ib. 413 ff.]); v. discussion Di[Ex 19, 1]. Against both is the working of Egypt. mines in the penins. as late as the 19th dyn. (v. Eb[GS 135, 148 ff., 159, etc.]), involving presence of soldiers there. This, and connex. with Midian (cf. also Ju 5[5]), have led to search for Sinai further NE, near head of Gulf of Aḳaba, or even in Seir, so Say[Monuments 263 ff.], cf. GFM[Ju 5, 5; 6, 1] and *Yakut*, cited by Id[179 n. §], also v. Gall[Altisr. Kultst. 12]; on sanctity of mt. v. further RS[Sem i. 110 f., 2nd ed. 117 f.] Sm[Rel. Gesch. 30].

5513 †סִינִי **adj.gent.** only c. art. = subst. Gn 10[17] = 1 Ch 1[15] a Canaanite people, in north, 𝔊 τὸν Ἀσενναῖον; cf. city *Siânu*, 'on shore of sea,' in As. inscr. Dl[Pa 282], Σιννᾶν (acc.) in possession of those holding Lebanon Strabo[xvi. 2. 8] (v. Di[Gn]).

5515 †סִינִים **adj.gent.pl.** = subst.; אֶרֶץ ס׳ Is 49[12], identif. with *Chinese* by Thes[948–950] De Che[Comm.] al.; but see v. Richthofen[China i. 436 f., 504], rev. by Yule[Acad. xiii. 339]; Di Du; T. de Lacouperie[BOR i. 45 ff., 183 ff.], who thinks of *Šina*, at foot of Hindu Kush, but unlikely; rd. prob. סְוֵנִים (or סְוָנִים), so Che[Intr. Is. 275, and Hpt.], cf. already JDMich.

סִים Je 8[7] Qr v. I. סוּס. p. 692

5516 סִיסְרָא[21] **n.pr.m.** (GFM[Ju 4, 2; PAOS xix (1898), 160] cp. Hittite names in *-sira*);—**1.** general of Jabin, king of Hazor Ju 4[2] + 12 t. Ju 4; appar. himself king 5[20.26.28.30]; cf. 1 S 12[9] ψ 83[10];—on ס׳ v. GFM[Ju, 107 ff.; PAOS l. c.]; 𝔊 Σ(ε)ισαρα. †**2.** בְּנֵי־סִיסְרָא, returned exiles, Ezr 2[53] = Ne 7[55]; 𝔊 Σεισαραθ, Σισαρα, etc.

5517 †סִיעָא, סִיעֲהָא **n.pr.m.** בְּנֵי־סִיעָא returned exiles Ne 7[47] = בְּנֵי־סִיעֲהָא Ezr 2[44]; 𝔊 Ne Ασουια, א Ιασουια, A Σιαια, 𝔊L Ιωσιου; 𝔊 Ezr Σωηλ, A Ασαα, 𝔊L Ιωσια.

†I. סִיר **n.m.**[Je 1, 13] et **f.**[2 K 4, 38] **pot** (probably 5518
foreign wd. (Egypt.?), Ar. زِيرٌ a large water-jar Lane[1276] is perh. loan-wd.; on Gk. deriv. σιρός, σίρινος, v. Lewy[Fremdw. 107]);—ס׳ abs. 2 K 4[38]+, cstr. Ex 16[3]+; pl. סִירֹת 38[3], סִירוֹת 1 K 7[45]+; sf. סִירֹתָיו Ex 27[3], סִירֹתֵיכֶם ψ 58[10];—*pot:* **1. a.** household utensil for boiling 2 K 4[38.39.40.41.41], ס׳ הַבָּשָׂר Ex 16[3] (P), Zc 14[21]; ס׳ נָפוּחַ Je 1[13] (cf. נפח; in vision), symbol. of Jerus. Ez 11[3.7.11] 24[3.6]; fig. also ψ 58[10] (cf. Che); in sim. Mi 3[3] Jb 41[23] Ec 7[6]. **b.** ס׳ רַחְצִי ψ 60[10] *my washing-pot*, 108[10]. **2.** *pots* used in sanctuary, Ex 27[3] 38[3] (both P), 1 K 7[40] (rd. סִירוֹת for MT כִּיֹּרוֹת, so Codd. of 𝔊 𝔊 𝔙 Th Ke Klo Kmp Benz), v[45] = 2 Ch 4[11.16], 2 K 25[14] = Je 52[18], also Je 52[19] 2 Ch 35[13] Zc 14[20].—Here belongs prob. סִרָה in בּוֹר הַסִּרָה, v. p. 92 b.

†II. [סִיר] **n.[m.]** thorn, hook (𝔗 *id.;* cf. סירם 5518
in Sab. n.pr. Hom[ZMG xlvi (1892), 532]);—**1.** pl. סִירִים, *thorns*, sign of desolation Is 34[13], a barrier Ho 2[8], on Na 1[10] v. [סָבַךְ]; כְּקוֹל הַסּ׳ תַּחַת הַסִּיר Ec 7[6] *as the sound of thorns* (crackling as they burn) *under the pot.* **2.** pl. סִירוֹת *hooks* Am 4[2] (cf. דּוּגָה sub דגה; ‖ צִנּוֹת; on relation of meanings v. חוֹחַ, צֵן).

סָךְ, [סֹךְ], סֻכָּה, סֻכּוֹת v. II. סכך. p. 697

†סִכּוּת **n.pr.div.** Am 5[26] read prob. *סַכּוּת, 5522
= As. *Sakkut* (epithet of Adar-Ninip = Saturn), Schr[SK 1874, 332; COT Am 5, 26], cf. Tiele[Gesch. 528] Bae[Rel 239] Rogers[Ency. Bib. 749] (Vrss Thes al. = סֻכָּה, סֻכּוֹת).

†סֻכּוֹת בְּנוֹת **n.pr.div.** 2 K 17[30], As.-Bab. 5524
deity, worshipped by Babylonians in Samaria; text of name corrupt; Schr[COT ad loc.] (after H. Rawlinson) prop. *Zîr-bânit*, or *Zarpanituv*, wife of *Marduk* (cf. Hpt[Andover Rev., May 1886] Muss-Arnolt[JBL xi (1892), 167]), rejecting *Sakkut-binûtu* = Marduk Dl[Par 215]; Jen[ZA iv. 352] makes בְּנוֹת = *banîtu*, epithet of Ištar; all doubtful.

†סֻכִּיִּים **n.pr.m.pl.** a people in army of 5525
Shishak acc. to 2 Ch 12[3] (between לוּבִים and כּוּשִׁים); 𝔊 Τρωγλοδυται, so 𝔙; 𝔊L Σουχιειμ.

†I. [סָכַךְ] **vb. overshadow, screen,** 5526
cover (‖ √ to I. שׂכך (which is prob. orig., cf. Ar. شَكَّ, and Frä[90]); NH הֵסִיךְ *cover*, and perh. סָכַךְ *roof over*);—**Qal** *Pf.* only 2 ms. סַכֹּתָה Ex 40[3], סַכֹּתָה La 3[43.44], סַכֹּתָה ψ 140[8]; *Impf.* 3 mpl. וַיָּסֹכּוּ 1 K 8[7], sf. יְסֻכֻּהוּ Jb 40[22]; *Pt. act.* סוֹכֵךְ

Ez 28$^{14.16}$, pl. סֹכְכִים Ex 25^{20} + 2 t.;—**1.** *screen, cover*, usu. c. עַל־ of thing covered, 1 K 8^{7} 1 Ch 28^{18}; + acc. of covering Ex 40^{3} (P); + בְּ of covering 25^{20} 37^{9} (both P); c. לְ of thing covered ψ 140^{8}; so (+ בְּ instr.) ס׳ בֶּעָנָן לָךְ La 3^{44} *thou hast screened thyself with the clouds;* c. acc. Jb 40^{22} *lotus-trees, as its shade, screen it;* abs. Ez 28$^{14.16}$ (difficult, text prob. corrupt, Co Toy del. as gloss). **2.** reflex. *cover oneself* ס׳ בָאַף La 3^{43} *thou hast covered* (clothed, panoplied) *thyself with anger* (si vera l.; cf. v^{44} *supr.*). **Hiph.** *Impf.* 3 ms. יָסֶךְ לָךְ ψ 91^{4}, וַיָּסֶךְ Ex 40^{1} + 2 t.; 2 ms. תָּסֵךְ ψ 5^{12}; *Inf. cstr.* הָסֵךְ 1 S 24^{4}; *Pt.* מֵסִיךְ Ju 3^{24} (Ges[§ 67 v]);—*screen, cover*, **1.** specif. c. אֶת־רַגְלָיו, i.e. with long garments, euphemism for evacuating the bowels, from posture assumed, so inf. Ju 3^{24}, pt. 1 S 24^{4} (cf. NH הֵסִיךְ, and v. GFM, HPS). **2.** elsewhere Impf., as **Qal** (expl. as Qal Ba[ZMG xliii (1889), 178]), c. עַל־ Ex 40^{21}, of protection ψ 5^{12}; c. לְ pers. + בְּ instr. 91^{4} (of protection). **Pilp.** סִכְסֵךְ, denom., v. sub **IV.** שׂכך. p. 967-68

4539 †מָסָךְ **n.[m.] covering, screen**;—abs. מ׳ 2 S 17^{19} + 11 t.; cstr. מָסַךְ Is 22^{8} + 12 t.;—**1.** *covering*, large cloth spread (פרשׂ) over well to hide persons within 2 S 17^{19}; fig. of protection, or of eye-screen, וַיְגַל אֵת־מ׳ יְהוּדָה Is 22^{8}; *screen*, of cloud ψ 105^{39} (פרשׂ). **2.** name given (in P) to each of three *screens*, of tabern.: **a.** at gate (שַׁעַר) of court Ex 27^{16} 35^{17} 38^{18} 39^{40} 40$^{8.33}$ Nu 3^{26} (פֶּתַח), 4^{26}. **b.** at entrance (פֶּתַח) of tent Ex 26$^{36.37}$ 35^{15} 36^{37} 39^{38} 40$^{5.28}$ Nu 3$^{25.31}$ 4^{25}. **c.** פָּרֹכֶת הַמּ׳ (v. פ׳), dividing off the Most Holy Place within the tent, Ex 35^{12} 39^{34} 40^{21} Nu 4^{5}.

4540 †[מְסֻכָה] **n.f. that with which one is covered, covering**;—sf. מְסֻכָתֶךָ Ez 28^{13} (so Baer Ginsb; van d. H. מְסֻכ׳) *all precious stones were thy covering* (= *thou wast covered* with them);—the tradition is strong in favour of *Raphē*, but sense favours deriv. from סכך.

4329 †[מוּסָךְ] **n.m.** architect. term (si vera l.) of some *covered* structure, otherwise unknown;—only cstr. מוּסַךְ־הַשַּׁבָּת 2 K 16^{18} Qr (Kt מיסך i.e. מֵיסַךְ);—𝔊 τὸν θεμέλιον τῆς καθέδρας, i.e. מוּסַד הַשֶּׁבֶת?

5526 †II. [סָכַךְ] **vb. weave together** (‖ form of II. שָׂכַךְ; NH Hiph. הֵסִיךְ *weave*, סוּכָּה, *booth*);—**Qal** *Pf.* 2 ms. sf. תְּסֻכֵּנִי ψ 139^{13} *thou didst weave me together* in my mother's womb. p. 968

5519 †[סַךְ] **n.[m.] throng** (prop. *an interwoven mass*);—אֶעֱבֹר בַּסָּךְ ψ 42^{5} *I used to pass along in the throng*, so most; but word dub.

5520 †[סֹךְ] **n.[m.] thicket, covert, lair**;—only sf. סֻכּוֹ Je 25^{38} *lair* of י׳, under fig. of lion (but Gie סֻכְּכוֹ cf. 4^{7}), סֻכֹּה ψ 10^{9} of lion (sim. of wicked; Bae סֻכָּה; Lag Che We סֻכְּכוֹ); סוּכּוֹ 76^{3} *his covert* (of י׳ under fig. of lion; ‖ מְעוֹנָתוֹ); for סֻכֹּה *in his covert* ψ 27^{5} Qr rd. perh., with Kt סֻכָּה *a booth* (Ol Hup-Now Bae cf. 31^{21}).

5521 †סֻכָּה **n.f. thicket, booth** (prop. of *interwoven* boughs cf. Ne 8^{15});—abs. ס׳ Is 1^{8}+; cstr. סֻכַּת Am 9^{11}; sf. סֻכָּתוֹ Jb 36^{29} ψ 18^{12}, and so rd. ‖ 2 S 22^{12} (for MT סֻכּוֹת; De Hup-Now HPS); usu. pl. סֻכֹּת Gn 33^{17}+; סֻכּוֹת 2 S 11^{11}+;—**1.** *thicket*, lurking-place of lions Jb 38^{40} (cf. [סֹךְ] **1**). **2.** *booth*, rude or temporary shelter, for cattle Gn 33^{17} (J; distinct fr. בַּיִת), but also for warriors in the field 2 S 11^{11} 1 K 20$^{12.16}$; for watchers in vineyards Is 1^{8} (sim.) Jb 27^{18} (sim. of frailty), for man's shelter from sun Jon 4^{5}, cf. (fig.) Is 4^{6} ψ 31^{21}, prob. also 27^{5} (v. [סֹךְ]); poet. of fallen house (dynasty) of David Am 9^{11}; of clouds as (temporary) enclosure (AV 'pavilion') of י׳ in storm ψ 18^{12} = 2 S 22^{12} Jb 36^{29}. **3.** specif. of *booths*, made of boughs, in which people lived at harvest-feast Lv 23$^{42.42.43}$ (H), Ne 8$^{14.15.16.17.17}$, hence called חַג הַסֻּכּוֹת Dt 16$^{13.16}$ 31^{10} Lv 23^{34} (P), Zc 14$^{16.18.19}$ 2 Ch 8^{13} Ezr 3^{4}.

5523 סֻכּוֹת 18 **n.pr.loc.**;—**1.** סֻכֹּתָה (ה loc.) Gn 33$^{17.17}$ (J; expl. from Jacob's making *booths*), elsewhere סֻכּוֹת;—city E. of Jordan Ju 8^{5} + 6 t. Ju 8, Jos 13^{27} (P); prob. also 1 K 7^{46} = 2 Ch 4^{17} (reading מַעְבֶּרֶת אֲדָמָה *ford of Adamah* GFM[Ju 7, 22] cf. Buhl[Geogr. 206] Benz[1 K 7, 46]); עֵמֶק ס׳ ψ 60^{8} = 108^{8} is Jordan-valley near *Succôth;* on identif. cf. GFM[Ju 8, 5] Buhl[Geogr. 260] GASm[Geogr. 585], and reff.; acc. to Talm. *Dêr ʿalla*, 1 m. N. of Jabbok Nbr[Géogr. du Talm. 248], so S. Merrill[East of Jordan 385 ff.]; 𝔊 Σοκχωθ (Σκηναί Gn 33 cf. ψψ). †**2.** סֻכֹּתָה (ה loc.) Ex 12^{37}, elsewh. סֻכֹּת;—first station of Isr. at Exodus, Ex 12^{37} 13^{20} Nu 33$^{5.6}$ (all P); = Egypt. *Thku(t)* WMM[As. u. Eur. 70], *Thkw* Steindorff[BAS i. 603]; on site v. Naville[Pithom (1885), esp. pp. 6. 23 f.] Guthe[ZPV viii (1885), 219 f.]; 𝔊 Σοκχωθ.

5526 †סֹכֵךְ **n.[m.] protector**;—term. techn. of structure shielding stormers of city (Lat. *testudo*) הַסּ׳ Na 2^{6}; 𝔊 τὰς προφυλακὰς αὐτῶν.

5527 †סְכָכָה **n.pr.loc.** in wilderness of Judah Jos 15[61]; A Σοχοχα, 𝔊L Σχαχα. Site unknown.

5528 †[סָכַל] **vb. be foolish, or a fool,** usu. in moral or spiritual sense (Syr. ܣܟܠ, Aph. *act foolishly;* ܣܟܠܐ *foolish,* etc., 𝔗 סְכַל der. species, *act foolishly;* סִכְלָא *fool;* ChrPalAram. ܣܟܠ, Aph. = ἁμαρτάνω, also deriv. Schwally[Idiot. 62]; As. *saklu,* perh. *foolish,* Dl[HWB 498]; Aram. ܣܟܠ, סְכַל *know, be intelligent, cause to understand,* etc. (der. species), cf. שׂכל; Me[Chrest. Targ.] derives both these opp. mngs. fr. Ar. شَكْلٌ *form, likeness.* Gerber[178] thinks Heb. vb. denom.);—**Piel** *Impf.* יְסַכֵּל Is 44[25], *Imv.* סַכֶּל־נָא 2 S 15[31], *make foolish, turn into foolishness.* **Niph.** *Pf.* 2 ms. נִסְכַּלְתָּ 2 Ch 16[9]; נִסְכָּ֑לְתָּ 1 S 13[13]; 1 s. נִסְכַּלְתִּי 2 S 24[10] = 1 Ch 21[8], *act or do foolishly.* **Hiph.** *Pf.* 2 ms. הִסְכַּלְתָּ Gn 31[28] (E), 1 s. הִסְכַּלְתִּי 1 S 26[21], *do foolishly, play the fool.*

5530 †סָכָל **n.m. fool** (on format. cf. Lag[BN 48]);—Je 5[21] Ec 2[19] 7[17] 10[3.3.14]; pl. adj. סְכָלִים Je 4[22].

5529 †סֶ֫כֶל **n.m. folly**;—Ec 10[6].

5531 †סִכְלוּת, שִׂכְלוּת **n.f. folly**;—ס׳ Ec 2[3.12.13] 7[25] 10[1.13]; שׂ׳ Ec 1[17] (שׂ erroneously for ס).

5532 †I. [סָכַן] **vb. be of use or service, benefit** (Tel Am. *sakânu, care for* (c. prep. *ana*) Zim[ZA vi. 248] Wkl[TA Gloss.]; Ph. סכן *prefect* Lzb[329]; cf. perh. Tel Am. *zukini* as loan-word Wkl[l.c.]);—**Qal** *Impf.* 3 ms. only Jb.: יִסְכָּן 22[2], ־ן 15[3], יִסְכָּן־ 22[2] + 2 t.; *Pt.* סֹכֵן Is 22[15]; f. סֹכֶנֶת 1 K 1[2.4];—**1.** *be of use* or *service,* only pt. וּתְהִי לוֹ ס׳ 1 K 1[2] *and let her become servitress to him,* so v[4] (+ וַתְּשָׁרְתֵהוּ); סֹכֵן Is 22[15] = *servitor, steward.* **2.** *benefit, profit,* abs. Jb 15[3]; c. לְ pers. 22[2] 35[3], עַל־ pers. 22[2]; c. acc. 34[9] (or abs. *gain benefit,* גבר subj.). **Hiph.** *Pf.* 1 s. הִסְכַּ֫נְתִּי Nu 22[20]; 2 ms. הִסְכַּ֫נְתָּה ψ 139[3]; *Imv.* הַסְכֶּן־נָא Jb 22[21]; *Inf. abs.* הַסְכֵּן Nu 22[30];—*be used, wont,* strictly *exhibit use,* or *habit,* הַהַסְכֵּן הִסְכַּנְתִּי לַעֲשׂוֹת לְךָ כֹּה Nu 22[30] (J) *have I ever shewn the habit of doing thus to thee?* hence *shew harmony with* (עִם) one Jb 22[21], *be familiar with, know intimately* (subj. י׳) ψ 139[3] (c. acc. דְּרָכַי).

4543 †מִסְכְּנוֹת **n.f.pl. supply, storage** (Dl[Pr 186]);—(הַ)מ׳ עָרֵי Ex 1[11] (J), 1 K 9[19] = 2 Ch 8[6], 2 Ch 8[4] 17[12]; מ׳ ע׳ 16[4] prob. corrupt (Be al.; v. עִיר); מ׳ alone 32[28] *storage-places, magazines.*

5533 II. [סָכַן] **vb. incur danger** (late) (NH *id.* Pi. *endanger,* Hiph. *be endangered,* סַכָּנָה *danger,* etc.; Aram. סְכַן *id.,* cf. Levy[NHWB iii. 526 f.] De[HL und Koheleth 203; Eng. Trans. 194]);—**Niph.** *Impf.* 3 ms. יִסָּכֶן־בָּם Ec 10[9] he that cleaveth (logs of) wood *endangers himself by them.*

†III. [סָכַן] **vb.** (so most) **be poor,** but v. infr.;—**Pu.** *Pt.* הַמְסֻכָּן תְּרוּמָה Is 40[20] usu., *he who is impoverished in respect to offering,* but very dub.; v. conject. in Du (against him Di-Kit) Skinner Zim[ZA ix. 111] Che[Heb. Hpt.].—מִסְכֵּן *poor,* מִסְכֵּנֻת *poverty,* v. p. 587. 5533 4544

[סִכְסֵךְ] v. sub IV. שׂכך. p. 697, 968 5526

†I. [סָכַר] **vb. shut up, stop up** (Aram. סְכַר, ܣܟܪ *shut up, stop up, dam up;* Ar. سَكَرَ *fill, stop up, dam* (river), etc., also *close, stop up* door, Lane[1390]; As. *sikêru, dam up,* II. 2. *stop ears;* cf. *sikkuru, bolt* Dl[HWB 499]; appar. kindr. with סגר;—hence Egypt. *t'akar, barrier,* Bondi[88]);—**Niph.** *Impf.* 3 ms. יִסָּכֵר פִּי וגו׳ ψ 63[12] *the mouth* of liars *shall be stopped;* 3 mpl. וַיִּסָּֽכְרוּ Gn 8[2] (P) *and* the springs of the deep etc., *were shut up.* **Pi.** *Pf.* וְסִכַּרְתִּי אֶת־מִצְרַיִם בְּיַד Is 19[4] *and I will shut up* (*deliver*) *Egypt into the hand of,* etc. (cf. סגר, מגן). p. 171, 689 5534 4042, 5462

†II. [סָכַר] **vb. hire** (= שָׂכַר; ס erroneously for שׂ);—only **Qal** *Pt.* pl. וְסֹכְרִים Ezr 4[5] *and hiring* against (עַל) them agents. p. 968 7936

†[סָכַת] **vb. be silent** (Ar. سَكَتَ *id.,* Lane[1389]; Sam. ࠎࠊࠕ *pay attention,* cf. Thes; Ar. = also *be quiet* (in gen.), = Syr. ܫܟܬ, a differentiated √?);—**Hiph.** declar. *shew silence: Imv.* ms. הַסְכֵּת Dt 27[9] *keep silence* and listen (cf. נִסְכַּת Ecclus 13[23]). 5535

סַל v. סלל. p. 700 5536

†סִלָּא word in (unintelligible) design. loc., בֵּית מִלֹּא הַיֹּרֵד ס׳ 2 K 12[21]; Th conj. מְסִלָּה *highway,* Klo בְּמוֹרַד מִלֹּא other conj. in Benz. 5538

†[סָלָא] **vb. weigh** (Ar. سَلَأَ *pay promptly* Lane[1398]; cf. Sab. סלא *consecrate, devote* Hom ZMG xlvi (1892), 531; Süd-Arab. Chrest. 124);—only **Pu.** *Pt.* הַמְסֻלָּאִים בַּפָּז La 4[2] *they who were weighed against gold,* reckoned of such value.—Cf. also II. סלה. 5537

†[סָלַד] **vb.** very dubious, perh. **spring** (NH *start* or *spring back,* as hand from fire; v. Levy);—**Pi.** *Impf.* 1 s. וַאֲסַלְּדָה Jb 6[10] *and I would spring* (for joy) in (my) anguish. 5539

5540 †סֶ֫לֶד **n.pr.m.** in Judah 1 Ch 2[30.30], 𝔊 Σαλαδ, 𝔊L Σαλεδ.

5541 †I. [סָלָה] **vb. make light of, toss aside** (cf. As. *salû, throw off, shake off* (yoke) Dl[500]; Ar. سلو, سَلَا is *be forgetful, neglectful* Lane[1417]; Aram. סְלָא *despise*, ܣܠܐ *reject*);—**Qal** *Pf.* 2 ms. סָלִיתָ ψ 119[118] *thou dost make light of* all those that err from thy statutes.—Cf. also סִלּוֹן infr. **Pi.** intens. *Pf.* 3 ms. סִלָּה La 1[15] Adonay *hath flouted at* my mighty ones.

5541 †II. [סָלָה] **vb. weigh, balance** (‖ form of סָלָא q.v.);—**Pu.** *Impf.* 3 fs. לֹא־תְסֻלֶּה בְּכֶתֶם Jb 28[16] *it cannot be weighed against* (estimated in) *gold* of Ophir, cf. v[19].

5542 סֶ֫לָה v. סלל. below

5543 †סַלּוּ **n.pr.m.** a priest, Zerub.'s time, acc. to Ne 12[7] (𝔊L Σαλουια), = סַלַּי v[20] (𝔊L Σαλουαι; om. BA in both).

5543 †סָלוּא **n.pr.m.** a Simeonite Nu 25[14], 𝔊 Σαλμων, A Σαλω, 𝔊L Σαλωμ.

5543 †סַלּוּא **n.pr.m.** a post-exil. Benjamite 1 Ch 9[7] (𝔊 Σαλωμ, A Σαλω) = סַלֻּא Ne 11[7] (𝔊 Σηλω, 𝔊L Σαμαα).

5544 †[סַלּוֹן], סִלּוֹן **n.m. brier** (√unknown);—סִלּוֹן מַמְאִיר Ez 28[24] *a pricking brier* (fig. of national distress; ‖ קוֹץ מַכְאִב); pl. סַלּוֹנִים 2[6] (+ סָרָבִים; Co [after Vrss] Berthol [not Toy] rd. סֹרְבִים וְסֹלִים (אותך) *resisting and despising thee;* סל׳ is then *Pt.* from I. סלה).

5543 †סַלַּי **n.pr.m. 1.** Ne 12[20] = סַלּוּ q.v. **2.** סַלַּי a Benjamite Ne 11[8], 𝔊 Σηλε(ε)ι.

5545 †[סָלַח] **vb. forgive, pardon** (𝔗 סְלַח *id.*, NH סְלִיחָה *forgiveness*);—**Qal** *Pf.* 2 ms. סָלַחְתָּ Ex 34[9] + 9 t., סָלָ֑חְתָּ La 3[42] + 2 t.; 1 s. סָלַחְתִּי Nu 14[20] + 2 t.; *Impf.* 3 ms. יִסְלַח 30[6] + 4 t.; 1 s. אֶסְלַח Je 31[34] + 3 t. + 5[7] Qr (Kt אֶסְלוֹחַ); *Imv.* סְלַח Nu 14[19] Am 7[2]; סְלָ֫חָה Dn 9[19]; *Inf.* סְלֹחַ Dt 29[19] 2 K 24[4]; סְלוֹחַ Is 55[7]; *Pt. act.* סֹלֵחַ ψ 103[3];—*forgive, pardon*, always of God: abs. Nu 14[20] (J), 1 K 8[30.39] = 2 Ch 6[21.30], 2 K 24[4] Is 55[7] Am 7[2] La 3[42] Dn 9[19]; c. לְ, of the sin Ex 34[9] Nu 14[19] (both J), Je 31[34] 33[8] 36[3] ψ 25[11] 103[3] 1 K 8[34.36] = 2 Ch 6[25.27], 2 Ch 7[14]; + לְ, of sinner Dt 29[19] 1 K 8[50] = 2 Ch 6[39], 2 K 5[18.18] Je 5[1.7] 50[20], and in law, Nu 30[6.9.13] (P). **Niph.** *Pf.* 3 ms. נִסְלַח, c. לְ, term. techn. in code of P, *it shall be forgiven him* לוֹ Lv 4[26.31.35] 5[10.13.16.18.26] 19[22] Nu 15[28]; *them* לָהֶם Lv 4[20] Nu 15[25]; לְכָל־עֲדַת וגו׳ v[26].

†סַלָּח **adj. ready to forgive, forgiving;**— 5546
ψ 86[5] אַתָּה אֲדֹנָי טוֹב וְס׳ thou Lord art *kind and forgiving*.

†סְלִיחָה **n.f. forgiveness** (late; on format. 5547
v. Kö[ii. 1, 197]);—ס׳ ψ 130[4]; pl. abstr. intens. *abundant forgiveness*, סְלִיחוֹת Ne 9[17], סְלִחוֹת Dn 9[9].

†סַלְכָה **n.pr.loc.** city on E. border of 5548
Bashan, Dt 3[10] Jos 12[5] 13[11] (all D), 1 Ch 5[11]; = Nab. צלחד (Lzb[358] Cook[101]), mod. *Ṣalḫad, Ṣarḫad*, on S. spur of *Jebel Hauran*, c. 63 m. due E. of Jordan; cf. Buhl[Geogr. 252] Dr[Dt 3, 10]; 𝔊 Σελχα, Ελχα, etc. (Σ lost often after ἕως).

†I. [סָלַל] **vb. lift up, cast up** (NH סִלְסֵל 5549
esteem highly, סִלְסוּל *loftiness, distinction;* סוּלָּם *ladder;* 𝔗 סוּלְּמָא *id.;* MI[26] מסלת *highway;* Ph. סלמת *stair* (?) Lzb[329]; As. *sellu, sillu*, perh. *breast-works* Dl[HWB 501]; Ar. سَلَّ is *draw out, forth* Lane[1395] = שָׁלַל, but سُلَّمٌ *ladder* (a loan-wd. acc. to Schwally[ZMG liii (1899), 197]), cf. סֻלָּם; v. also *ṭrry, siege-wall*, Egypt. loan-word from סֹלְלָה acc. to WMM[As. u. Eur. 101]);—**Qal** *Impf.* וַיָּסֹ֫לּוּ Jb 19[12] 30[12]; *Imv.* mpl. סֹ֫לּוּ Is 57[14] + 4 t.; sf. סַלּוּהָ Je 50[26] (cf. סֶ֫לָה); *Pt. pass.* סְלוּלָה Je 18[15]; סְלֻלָה Pr 15[19];—**1.** *cast up a highway:* ס׳ מְסִלָּה Is 62[10.10], without obj. Is 57[14.14], דֶּרֶךְ לֹא סְלוּלָה Je 18[15]; fig. of path of upright Pr 15[19]. **2.** *cast up a way:* דֶּרֶךְ, c. על *against*, Jb 19[12] (of besieger, in fig.), ארח Jb 30[12] (of besetting foe); Bab. as a heap of garbage Je 50[26]. **3.** *lift up* (a song) ψ 68[5], c. לְ pers. (‖ זמר, שיר; most as **1**). **Pilp.** *Imv.* sf. סַלְסְלֶהָ Pr 4[8] *exalt her* (i.e. Wisdom), i.e. (cf. Toy) *esteem highly, prize.* **Hithp.** *Pt.* מִסְתּוֹלֵל Ex 9[17] (J) *exalt oneself*, c. בְּ *against* (denom. from סֹלְלָה acc. to Gerber[52]); cf. Ecclus 39[24] 40[28].

†סֶ֫לָה **vb. lift up** (voices in ברוך לעולם), or 5542
exalt (לעולם י׳) (*Imv.* of סָלַל (cf. Pr 4[8] ψ 68[5]; הִגּ׳ 9[17], v. הִגָּיוֹן סלה), properly סֹ֫לָּה, סֶ֫לָה poss. Qr = נֶצַח, Hexapla σελ; but cf. הֶ֫רָה Ew[554] Kö[ii. 1, 539]; 𝔊 Sym Theod διάψαλμα, expl. Suidas μέλους ἐναλλαγή; Theodoret Hippolytus μέλους μεταβολή (cf. Hexapla Hb 3[3] μεταβολὴ διαψάλ-

ματος; Syr. Hexapla Aq. עוניתא in 5 ψψ, Field in ψ 38^{12}); 𝔊 adds *διάψαλμα*, e.g. 2^{2} 34^{11} 94^{15}, after final editing of Heb. Psalter; so Psalms of Sol. 17^{31} 18^{10} on same principles as in MT; used therefore with full knowledge that it indicated some kind of interruption or change in the regular rendering. סלה is used in שמונה עשרה after Benedictions 3, 18, and after other early Jewish prayers, shewing knowledge, c. 100 A.D.; Aq. gives *ἀεί* (Theod. also ψ 9^{17}); Sexta *διαπαντός* (except 20^{4} *εἰς τέλος*); Quinta *εἰς τοὺς αἰῶνας*; Jer. *semper*, 𝔗 usu. לעלמין, לעלמא; but 39^{6} לחיי עלמא, 44^{9} לעלמי עלמין, 48^{9} עד עלמי עלמין, 49^{14} לעלמא דאתי; uniform tradition best expl. by closing contents of the Benedictions, מהעולם ועד העולם. So Jer. classes *sela* with *amen* and *salom*; and Jacob of Edessa in Bar Hebr. 10^{1} cp. Christian *Amen* of the people after *Gloria*);—this interpr. agrees with usage: 71 t. in 39 ψψ, 3 t. Hb 3 (taken from Minor Psalter למנצח, v. נצח); it occurs at end of 3^{9} 24^{10} 46^{12} (om. 𝔊), 9^{21} (𝔊 combines 9 and 10); elsewh. at close of strophe, $3^{3.5}$ $4^{3.5}$ 7^{6} 9^{17} 24^{6} $32^{4.5.7}$ $39^{6.12}$ $46^{4.8}$ 47^{5} 48^{9} 49^{13} (so rd. MT v^{14} by error) v^{16} 50^{6} $52^{5.7}$ 54^{5} $59^{6.14}$ 61^{5} $62^{5.9}$ $66^{4.7.15}$ 67^{5} 68^{20} $76^{4.10}$ $77^{4.10.16}$ 81^{8} 82^{2} 83^{9} $84^{5.9}$ $88^{8.11}$ $89^{38.46}$ $140^{4.6.9}$ 143^{6}; or where citations have been made, 44^{9} 55^{8} 57^{7} 60^{6} 67^{2} $68^{8.33}$ 89^{5} Hb $3^{3.9}$; or where extracts might be made for liturgical purposes, 20^{4} 21^{3} 55^{20} 75^{4} 85^{3} $87^{3.6}$ 89^{49}; so 57^{3} (𝔊 for MT v^{4}) Hb 3^{13}.—Of ψψ c. סֶלָה, 23 used in Elohistic Psalter, 28 in Director's Psalter, 39 in final editing of Psalter. These editors found it in earlier Psalters. Davidic Psalter uses 20 of them, so few in proportion that it is not characteristic of this Psalter; but Korahite 9 (out of 12), and Asaph 7 + 80^{8} [𝔊] (prob. 8 out of 12); appar. it came into use in time of these editors. In Director's Psalter musical terms are added to 19 of the 28 it uses (and only to ten others, of which some could hardly use סלה); ψψ with סלה all (except 61, 81) name the kind of ψ in title: 3 מִכְתָּם, 7 מַשְׂכִּיל, 10 שִׁיר, 26 (27) others מִזְמוֹר, Hb 3 תְּפִלָּה; ס׳ is esp. frequent with שִׁיר and מַשְׂכִּיל, terms associated with musical rendering. It prob. came into use in late Persian period in connexion with ψψ used with musical accompaniment in public worship, to indicate place of benedictions. It was not added by later editors to other psalms; but was revived in first century B.C., and continued in use for some time (v. Jacob [ZAW xvi (1896), 129 f.] Br [JBL 1899] EGBriggs [Am. J. Sem. Lang. Oct. 1899, 1 ff.]).

†**סֹלְלָה** **n.f. mound**;—ס׳ 2 S 20^{15} + 7 t.; סוֹלְלָה Dn 11^{15}; pl. סֹלְלוֹת Je 32^{24} 33^{4}.—שָׁפַךְ ס׳ עַל־הָעִיר *cast up mound against the city*, besieging it, 2 K 19^{32} = Is 37^{33}, Je 6^{6} Ez 4^{2} 26^{8}; c. אֶל 2 S 20^{15} (error for עַל); without על העיר Ez 17^{17} 21^{27} Dn 11^{15}; without vb. Je 32^{24} 33^{4}. 5550

†**סֻלָּם** **n.m. ladder**;—Gn 28^{12} (E). 5551

†**מְסִלָּה** **n.f. highway**;—מ׳ Is 11^{16} + 12 t.; cstr. מְסִלַּת Is 7^{3} + 3 t.; sf. מְסִלָּתוֹ Jo 2^{8}; pl. מְסִלּוֹת Is 33^{8} + 5 t.; sf. מְסִלֹּתַי Is 49^{11}; מְסִלּוֹתָם Ju 5^{20} Is 59^{7};—*raised way, highway, public road* (never of street in city) Nu 20^{19} Ju $20^{31.32.45}$ 21^{19} 1 S 6^{12} 2 S $20^{12.12.13}$ 2 K 18^{17} = Is 36^{2}, 1 Ch $26^{16.18}$ Is 7^{3} 11^{16} 19^{23} 33^{8} 49^{11} 59^{7} Je 31^{21}; ישׁר מ׳ Is 40^{3}; סלל מ׳ Is 62^{10}; in a fig. sense, of the courses of the stars Ju 5^{20}; the march of locusts Jo 2^{8}; the conduct of the upright Pr 16^{17}; of the ascents to Zion in the mind of the pious ψ 84^{6} (𝔊: Bae rds. מַעֲלוֹת).—In 2 Ch 9^{11} מסלות is error for מִסְעָד(ות) of ‖ 1 K 10^{12}. 4546

†**מַסְלוּל** **n.m. highway**;—Is 35^{8} (foll. ודרך corrupt; 𝔊 *ὁδὸς καθαρά*). 4547

II. **סלל** (√ of foll.; cf. NH סִלְסֵל *plait, curl* hair; NH סַל, 𝔗 סַלָּא, Talm. סִילְתָּא, Syr. ܣܠܐ, Chr Pal Aram. ܣܠܐ, all = *basket*; Ar. سَلّ, سَلَّة prob. loan-wd. Frä [75 f.]; cf. Schwally [Idiot. 63]).

†**סַל** **n.m.** [Gn 40, 16] **basket**;—ס׳ abs. Gn 40^{17} +; cstr. Ex 29^{23} +; pl. סַלִּים Gn 40^{18}; cstr. סַלֵּי v^{16};—*basket* Gn $40^{16.17.17.18}$ (E), Ju 6^{19}; Ex $29^{3.3.23.32}$ Lv $8^{2.26.31}$ Nu $6^{15.17.19}$. 5536

†[**סַלְסִלָּה**] **n.**[**f.**] **basket** acc. to 𝔊𝔙 AV RV; but prob. **shoot, branch** Ew Hi Gf Gie al.; only pl. abs. הָשֵׁב יָדְךָ (rd. prob. יָד) כְּבוֹצֵר עַל־סַלְסִלּוֹת Je 6^{9}. 5552

סלע (√ of foll.; cf. Ar. سَلَعَ *cleave, split*, سِلْعٌ *cleft, fissure*, Lane [1406], hence סֶלַע *split, jagged cliff, crag*, oft. *isolated* (split off) *rock* (cf. Wetzst [De Is 3, 696–707; and esp. ZAW iii (1883), 273]); then of smaller fragments, NH סֶלַע *rock, stone*, also *scale* (of serpent), *weight* (in trade); Aram. סִלְעָא specif. *weight* for coin; Nab. סלע, a coin Lzb [329] Cook [85]).

I. **סֶלַע** [61] **n.m.** [Ju 6, 20] **crag, cliff**, synon. צוּר;—abs. ס׳ Ju 6^{20} +, סָלַע Nu 20^{10} +; cstr. סֶלַע 1 S 5553

23[23]; sf. סַלְעִי 2 S 22[2]+, סַלְעוֹ Is 31[9]; pl. סְלָעִים Is 2[21]+;—**1.** lit. *cliff, crag* Ju 6[20] Is 2[21] 7[19] Am 6[12] Nu 20[8.8.10.10.11] (cf. Ne 9[15] ψ 78[16], and contr. the צוּר of Ex 17[6]), Nu 24[21] Dt 32[13] (not elsewh. Hex), + 10 t.; שֵׁן הַסּ׳ 1 S 14[4.4] *tooth of the crag,* i.e. sharp crag, so Jb 39[28]; excav. in cliff as place of burial Is 22[16]; abode of wild animals, יַעֲלֵי־ס׳ v[1], cf. ψ 104[18] Pr 30[26], of birds Jb 39[28] Ct 2[14] (in fig.), cf. Je 48[28], so of Edom Ob[3] = Je 49[16]; cf. (Nu 24[21] *supr.* and) Is 42[11]; particular cliffs are: ס׳ עֵיטָם Ju 15[8.11] cf. v[13], ס׳ (הָ)רִמּוֹן 20[45.47.47] 21[13] ס׳ הַמַּחְלְקוֹת 1 S 23[28] cf. v[25]; v. also II. סֶלַע. †**2.** fig., esp. סַלְעִי of י׳ (only ψψ), ψ 18[3] = 2 S 22[2], ψ 31[4] 42[10] 71[3]; of As. god Is 31[9] (prob.; cf. צוּר Dt 32[31.37]); צֵל ס׳ כָּבֵד Is 32[2] (sim. of protecting care); fig. of security ψ 40[3] (feet on cliff), מְצָדוֹת סְלָעִים מִשְׂגַּבּוֹ Is 33[16]; symb. of obstinacy חִזְּקוּ פְנֵיהֶם מִס׳ Je 5[3]; צְחִיחַ ס׳ (*bare cliff,* lit. *glare of* [*the*] *cliff*), in fig. of openness, flagrancy Ez 24[7.8], of razed city 26[4.14] (only here Ez); in fig. of fall of Bab. Je 51[25].

5554 †II. סֶלַע **n.pr.loc.** in Edom, מֵהַסּ׳ Ju 1[36] (del. מֵ, cf. GFM); הַסּ׳ captured in war 2 K 14[7] (and called יָקְתְאֵל); מִס׳ Is 16[1]; site dub.; old identif. with *Petra* denied, plausibly, by Buhl [Edom] GFM[Ju 1, 36] (who thinks of an actual *cliff*), but held Benz[2 K 14, 7] Bd[Pal (1898), 206]; 𝔊 (ἡ) πέτρα.

5556 †סָלְעָם **n.m.** an edible, winged, **locust** (NH *id.; swallower, consumer,* cf. 𝔗 סַלְעֵם *swallow up, destroy;* Ar. سَلْغَفَ vb. *swallow,* Kö[ii. 1, 404]);—Lv 11[22] (+ אַרְבֶּה, חַרְגֹּל, חָגָב).

5557 סָלַף **vb. twist, pervert, overturn** (𝔗 סְלַף *twist* (rare); Ar. سَلَفَ is *pass, pass away, come to naught* Lane[1407 f.]);—**Pi.** *Impf.* 3 ms. יְסַלֵּף Jb 12[19] + 2 t., וַיְסַלֵּף Pr 22[12]; 3 fs. תְּסַלֵּף Pr 13[6] 19[3]; *Pt.* מְסַלֵּף Pr 21[12];—**1.** *pervert,* Ex 23[8] (E) a bribe *perverteth* the case (cause, דִּבְרֵי) of righteous, = Dt 16[19]. **2.** *subvert, turn upside down, ruin* (only WisdLt): c. acc. pers. Jb 12[19] Pr 13[6] (opp. תִּצֹּר), 21[12]; אִוֶּלֶת אָדָם תּ׳ דַּרְכּוֹ 19[3] *a man's folly subverteth his way;* וַיְסַלֵּף דִּבְרֵי בֹגֵד 22[12] *and he* (י׳) *subverteth the affairs of a treacherous* man.

5558 †סֶלֶף **n.m.**[Pr 11, 3 Qr] **crookedness, crooked dealing**:—ס׳ abs. Pr 15[4] (of tongue); cstr. ס׳ בֹּגְדִים 11[3].

†[סָלַק] **vb. ascend** (loan-word from Aram. סְלֵיק, ܣܠܶܩ; Palm. סלק *id.,* Lzb[329] Cook[85]; NH סלק Pi. *remove;* Ar. سَلِقَ *ascend,* Lane[1410] (also loan-word?));—only **Qal** *Impf.* 1 s. אֶסַּק ψ 139[8] 5266
if I ascend to heaven (שָׁמַיִם), thou art there (on form, = *אֶסְלַק, v. Ges[§ 66 e] Kö[i. 301] Kau[§ 44]).

סֹלֶת [53] **n.f.**[Lv 2, 5] (cf. on gender Albrecht 5560
ZAW xvi (1896), 106) **fine flour** (𝔊 σεμίδαλις, 𝔙 *simila*) (NH *id.;* Aram. סוּלְתָּא; Ar. سُلْتٌ *a kind of barley without husks* Lane[1401]; As. *sillatu,* or *šillatu,* a kind of grain (?) Meissner-Rost[BAS iii. 361]; also *tultà, turuti, flour,* as loan-word in Egypt., Bondi[84] WMM[As. u. Eur. 101]);—abs. ס׳ Gn 18[6]+, cstr. ס׳ Ex 29[9]+; sf. סָלְתָּהּ Lv 2[2];—*fine flour,* used in king's household 1 K 5[2] (|| קֶמַח), for honoured guests קֶמַח ס׳ Gn 18[6] (J), a *s^e'āh* of it sold for a shekel in time of scarcity 2 K 7[1.16.18] (v. Benz); luxurious food Ez 16[13.19] (of Jerus. under fig. of woman); elsewh. only in offerings Ez 46[14] 1 Ch 9[29] 23[29], and P; ס׳ חִטִּים Ex 29[2], ס׳ v[40], Lv 2[1] + 13 t. Lv., Nu 6[15] + 26 t. Nu.

סַם v. סמם. p. 702 5561

†סַמְגַּר נְבוֹ **n.pr.m.** an officer of Nebuchad. 5562
acc. to MT Je 39[3] = (assumed) *Šumgir Nabu* (Schr[COT]), but prob. text. err.; Gie (plausibly) takes סמגר as crpt. dittogr. of רב מג, and joins נבו to foll., נבושרסכים = נְבוּשַׁזְבָּן, cf. v[13] and 𝔊 Σαμαγωθ (Σαμαγάδ, Σαμαγαρ, etc.) καὶ Ναβουσαχαρ.

†[סְמָדַר ?], also סְמָדַר, סְמָדָר **n.m.**[Ct 7, 13] 5563
blossom of grape (just at flowering Duval[REJ xiv (1887), 227 ff.] NH *id.;* Aram. סמדר, ܣܡܕܪܐ, Mand. סימאדרא Nö[M. 128]);—alw. abs. ס׳, only Ct: הַגְּפָנִים סְמָדַר 2[13] *the vines are* (all) *blossom;* כְּרָמִים סְמָדַר v[15] (on bold predicate cf. Ges[§ 141 d]); פִּתַּח הַסְּמָדַר 7[13] *the blossom has opened* (its buds).

סָמַךְ [48] **vb. lean, lay, rest, support** (NH 5564
id.; Ph. in n.pr. Lzb[317, 329]; Aram. סְמַךְ, ܣܡܰܟ; also Eth. (ሰመከ:) አስመከ: *cause to lean upon,* etc. Di[335]; Ar. سَمَكَ is *be high, ascend, raise, uplift,* سَمْكٌ *roof*);—**Qal** [41] *Pf.* 3 ms. ס׳ Dt 34[9] Ez 24[2], וְסָמַךְ consec. Am 5[19]+; 3 fs. סָמָכָה ψ 88[8], sf. סְמָכָתְהוּ Is 59[16], סְמָכָתְנִי 63[5], etc.; *Impf.* 3 ms. וַיִּסְמֹךְ Lv 8[14] Nu 27[23], sf. יִסְמְכֵנִי ψ 3[6], etc.; *Imv.* ms. sf. סָמְכֵנִי ψ 119[116]; *Pt. act.* סוֹמֵךְ Is 63[5] + 3 t.; pl. cstr. סֹמְכֵי Ez 30[6] ψ 54[6]; *pass.* סָמוּךְ Is 26[3] ψ 112[8]; pl. סְמוּכִים 111[8];—**1. a.** *lean* or *lay* hand upon (עַל־): Am 5[19]; elsewh. in sacred rite: on head of sacrif. victim, as those who share in sacrif., Ex 29[10.15.19] Lv 1[4] + 12 t. Lv, Nu 8[12] (all P), 2 Ch 29[23]; so of Levites,

presented to י׳ Nu 8[10] (P); on head of blasphemer Lv 24[14] (P; as witnesses of his guilt); on head of Joshua in consecration (Moses subj.) Nu 27[18.23] Dt 34[9] (all P). **b.** intrans. ψ 88[8] thy wrath *hath rested* upon me (עָלַי); also סָמַךְ מֶלֶךְ־בָּבֶל אֶל־ Ez 24[2] *hath leaned against, rested his weight upon*, Jerusalem, i.e. invested (Toy), begun the siege of it. †**2.** *support, uphold, sustain*, only fig.: c. 2 acc. Gn 27[37] (J) with corn and must *have I sustained him*, provided sustenance for him, cf. (of י׳) ψ 51[14]; *uphold* Egypt Ez 30[6]; abs. Is 63[5]; esp. of י׳ *upholding, sustaining* Is 59[16] 63[5] ψ 3[6] 37[17.24] 54[6] (on בְּ *essentiae* v. Ges[§ 119i], בְּ supr. **7 a**), 119[116] 145[14]; so pt. pass. ψ 111[8] *they are sustained*, i.e. maintained (י׳'s commands), סָמוּךְ לִבּוֹ 112[8] *his heart is sustained*, firm, and so יֵצֶר ס׳ Is 26[3].

†**Niph.** *Pf.* 1 s. נִסְמַכְתִּי ψ 71[6]; 3 pl. נִסְמָכוּ Is 48[2]; *Impf.* יִסָּמֵךְ 2 K 18[21] Is 36[6], וַיִּסָּמֵךְ Ju 16[29]; 3 mpl. וַיִּסָּמְכוּ 2 Ch 32[8]; — reflex. *support*, or *brace oneself*, also c. עַל־: Ju 16[29] *and he braced himself* against (upon) them (the pillars); 2 K 18[21] (if) a man *support himself* on it (Egypt as a cracked reed) = Is 36[6]; on cheering words 2 Ch 32[8]; on God Is 48[2] ψ 71[6].

†**Pi.** *Imv.* mpl. sf. + בְּ instr.: סַמְּכוּנִי Ct 2[5] *sustain* (refresh, revive) *me with raisin-cakes.*

5565 †סְמַכְיָהוּ **n.pr.m.** (cf. Gray[Prop. N. 294, No. 89]; = י׳ *hath sustained*);—Korahite name 1 Ch 26[7]; 𝔊 Σαβχεια, A 𝔊L Σαμαχια(ς).

3253 †יִסְמַכְיָהוּ **n.pr.m.** (י׳ *sustaineth*, but perh. rd. סמ׳ as foreg. Gray[Prop. N. 291, No. 60]); — Levite name 2 Ch 31[13]; 𝔊 Σαμαχ(ε)ια.

5566 †סֶמֶל **n.m.**[Ez 8, 5] perh. orig. n.pr.div., then gen. **image, statue** (Ph. סמל *id.*, f. סמלת, Lzb[151, 329], also פנסמלת Id[329]; Bau[Rel. i. 88] understands ס׳ to be design. of foreign god);—abs. הַסּ׳ 2 Ch 33[7.15], סָמֶל Dt 4[16]; cstr. סֵמֶל Ez 8[3.5];—*image, figure* of anything, פֶּסֶל תְּמוּנַת כָּל־ס׳ Dt 4[16]; *idol-image* פֶּסֶל הַסּ׳ 2 Ch 33[7] and (פֶּסֶל om.) v[15]; סֵמֶל הַקִּנְאָה Ez 8[3] *the statue of jealousy*, i.e. that rouses י׳'s jealousy, = v[5].

סמם (√of foll.; meaning dub.; if akin to Ar. شَمّ *smell* Lane[1593], مَشْمُومٌ any *fragrant plant* Id[1594], then ס must be for שׁ; in that case ס׳ perh. loan-word in Heb.; NH *id., spice, drug* (Ecclus ש׳ 38[4 m.]); Aram. סַמָּא *id.; ܣܡܐ drug, pigment;* Ar. سَمّ *poison* is appar. loan-word Frä[262]).

5561 [סַם]₁₆ **n.m.** spice, used in incense;—only pl. abs. סַמִּים, and only P Ch; Ex 30[34.34], elsewh. קְטֹרֶת (הַ)סַּמִּים *incense of spices* 25[6] + 8 t. Ex, Lv 4[7] 16[12] Nu 4[16] 2 Ch 2[3] 13[11].

5567 †סמן **vb.** whence **Niph.** *Pt.* נִסְמָן Is 28[25] (si vera l.) barley *in an appointed place*, or *a determined portion* (cf. Ges Hi De al.), but נ׳ lacking in 𝔊 and plausibly taken as dittogr. for כֻּסֶּמֶת by We[Prol. 417; Gesch. Isr. i. 409] Che[Comm. and Hpt.] Du; cf. Brd Gu[Kau].

5568 †סָמַר **vb. bristle up** (Lag[BN 106] cp. Ar. شَمَّرَ *contract;* in that case ס׳ for ש׳);—**Qal** *Pf.* 3 ms. ס׳ מִפַּחְדְּךָ בְשָׂרִי ψ 119[20] *from fear of thee did my flesh bristle up*, 'creep.' **Pi.** *Impf.* תְּסַמֵּר שַׂעֲרַת בְּשָׂרִי Jb 4[15].

5569 †סָמָר **adj. bristling, rough**;—יֶלֶק ס׳ Je 51[27] *bristling locust*, perh. with allusion to horn-like sheaths enclosing wings of the pupa, v. Dr[Joel and Amos, 58] (on format. cf. Lag[BN 50]).

4548 †[מַסְמֵר] **n.m.**[Ec 12, 11] **nail** (connexion with above √dub.; 𝔗 מַסְמְרָא, ChrPalAram. ܡܣܡܪܐ Schwally[63.122]; NH vb. סמר *nail on* or *up;* Ar. مِسْمَار is perh. loan-word Frä[89]);—pl. abs. מַסְמְרִים Is 41[7], מִסְמְרִים 1 Ch 22[3] (of iron; on ־ v. Ges[§ 85 f.]); also מַסְמְרוֹת Je 10[4] (+ מַקָּבוֹת), מַשְׂמְרוֹת נְטוּעִים, Ec 12[11] (sim.; + דָּרְבֹנוֹת), and 4930

מַסְמְרוֹת 2 Ch 3[9] (of gold).

5570 †סְנָאָה appar. **n.pr.m.** בְּנֵי ס׳ Ezr 2[35] = Ne 7[38], בְּנֵי הַסּ׳ Ne 3[3]; 𝔊 Σαανα, Σαναυα(τ), etc., 𝔊L Σενναα; Mey[Judenth. 150, 154] rds. סְנֻאָה (ס׳ for ש׳, cf. שְׂנוּאָה) = *sons of the hated* (rejected) *woman*, i.e. the poorer classes of Jerusalem.

5571 †סַנְבַלַּט (so Baer; van d. H. Ginsb סַנְבַלַּט) **n.pr.m.** leader of Samaritan opponents of Nehemiah: Ne 2[10.19] 3[33] 4[1] 6[1.2.5.12.14] 13[28]; (Bab., = *Sin-uballiṭ, Sin gave life* Schr[COT Ne 2, 10]).

5572 †סְנֶה **n.m.**[Ex 3, 2] a thorny bush, perh. **blackberry bush** (cf. Löw[No. 219]; *rubus fruticosus* Linn.; Aram. סַנְיָא, ܣܢܝܐ *thorn-bush*, As. *sinû*, Meissner[ZA vi. 293] *blackberry bush* (M. thinks Aram. ס׳ loan-word from this); Ar. سَنًا *senna*, Lane[1449]);—abs. ס׳ Ex 3[2.2.4], סְנֶה v[2.3] (all E) Dt 33[16] (akin to E).

5573 †סֶנֶּה **n.pr.rup.** (= *thorny*, cf. GASm[Geogr. 250 n.] HPS[ad loc.]);—a cliff opp. the cliff called בּוֹצֵץ, 1 S 14[4] (Ginsb as here; Baer סֶנֶּה, van d. H. סֶנָּה); 𝔊 Σενναάρ.

5570, 5574 †סְנוּאָה n.pr.m. (but v. סְנָאָה);—בֶּן־הַסּ׳ Ne 11^{9} (𝔊 Ασανα, 𝔊L Ασεννα), בֶּן־הַסְּנֻאָה 1 Ch 9^{7} (𝔊 Αανα, A Ασανουα, 𝔊L Σααυα). p. 702

5575 †סַנְוֵרִים **n.[m.] pl. intens.** vel **abstr.** (Sta[§ 324 b]) **sudden blindness** (etym. dub.; der. fr. נור highly improb., whether *antiphr.* Wetzst[De ψψ 4, 886] Kö[ii. 1, 404], or fr. *dazzling*, cf. 'flimmern' Hoffm[ZAW ii (1882), 68]; but also view of Hal[RÉJ xi. 66] deriv. fr. √סנר *cover with a skin*, i.e. *produce film over*, lacks demonstration; at present we must be content with assuming quadrilit. √, Thes Sta[§ 243]);—הִכּוּ בַּסּ׳ Gn 19^{11} (J) *they smote* the men *with sudden blindness*, cf. 2 K 6$^{18.18}$ (all cases miraculous, and in K temporary).

5576 †סַנְחֵרִיב **n.pr.m. Sennacherib** (=*Sin-aḫê-irba, Sin multiplied brothers*, Schr[COT 2 K 18, 13]);—son of Sargon and father of Esarhaddon, king of Assyria (B.C. 705–681; cf. Tiele[Gesch. 285 ff.]); 2 K 18^{13} 19$^{16.20.36}$ = Is 36^{1} 37$^{17.21.37}$ 2 Ch 32$^{1.2.9.10.22}$ (all as above, exc. סַנְחֵרֽב 2 K 19^{20}); 𝔊 Σενναχηρειμ, 𝔊L Σενναχειρειμ; Σεναχήριβος Jos[Ant. x. 1 ff.]; Σαναχάρβου (acc.) Herodot.[ii. 141].

7158 סַנָּה v. קִרְיַת־סַנָּה. p. 900

5578 סַנְסַנָּה **n.pr.loc.** in S. Judah;—Jos 15^{31}, 𝔊 Σεθεννακ, A Σανσαννα, 𝔊L Σεεvακ; prob. = חֲצַר סוּסָה 19^{5}, חֲצַר־סוּסִים 1 Ch 4^{31}; conj. on loc. (near Gaza), v. in Di[ad loc.] Buhl[Geogr. 163] and reff. (*Simsum*, NE. of Gaza, cp. by J. Schwarz[Das heilig. Land (1852), 72] van d. Velde[Mem, 346], is too far north).

5577 †[סַנְסִנִּים] **n.[m.]pl. fruit-stalk** of date (Löw[p. 119]) (Aram. loan-word fr. ܣܢܣܢܐ PS[2617] *racemus dactylorum*, cf. As. *sissinnu*, part of the date-palm Dl[507]);—sf. אֹחֲזָה בְּסַנְסִנָּיו Ct 7^{9}.

5579 †סְנַפִּיר **n.[m.] fin** (NH *id.*; quadrilit. acc. to Sta[§ 243]; Fl in Levy[NHWB iii. 725 a] cp. Aram. סְמְפּוּרִין *points, nails*, and der. this fr. סַמֵּר vb. *nail*, with infixed פ (Levy[ChWB ii. 570 b]));—Lv 11$^{9.10.12}$ = Dt 14$^{9.10}$.

5580 †סָס **n.m. moth** (𝔗 סָסָא, Syr. ܣܣܐ; As. *sâsu*, Dl[HWB 506]; Ar. سُوسٌ, سُوسَةٌ; Eth. ፀፀ: Thes Lag[Armen. Stud. § 2262] cp. Armen. *zez* = Gk. σής, wh. is der. fr. סָס by Bo[Hieroz. iii. 514] Lewy[Fremdw. 16 f.]);—וְכַצֶּמֶר יֹאכְלֵם סָס Is 51^{8}.

5581 †סַסְמַי **n.pr.m.** name in Judah (on Ph. n. pr. div. (ססמ(י v. Lzb[330] Ren in CIS[i. No. 95, 3, al.] Bae[Rel. 64 f.] Kit[1 Ch 2, 40]);—ס׳ 1 Ch 2$^{40\,b}$, סִסְמָי v$^{40\,a}$; 𝔊 Σοσομαι, 𝔊L Σασαμει.

†סָעַד **vb. support, sustain, stay** (NH *id.*, esp. *take a meal*; Aram. סְעַד *support, stay*; Zinj. סעד *strengthen* Lzb[330], *support*, perh. *feed* Cook[85]; ChrPalAram. n. ܣܥܕܘܢ *aid*, Schwally[Idiot. 64]; Ar. سَعِدَ, سُعِدَ III, IV. *aid, assist*, Lane[1360], سَاعِدٌ *forearm* Id[1362]; Sab. סעד DHM[Südar. Alt. p. 16]);—**Qal** *Pf.* 3 ms. וְסָעַד consec. Pr 20^{28}; 5582
Impf. 3 ms. יִסְעָד; 3 fs. sf. תִּסְעָדֵנִי ψ 18^{36}, rd. also in ‖ 2 S 22^{36}, etc.; *Imv.* ms. סְעָד Ju 19^{5} (on ָ prob. ŏ, by err., v. Kö[i. 261 f.] GFM[ad loc.]), סְעָד־נָא v^{8} (cf. *id.*), וּסְעָדָה 1 K 13^{7}; sf. סְעָדֵנִי ψ 119^{117}; *Inf. cstr.* sf. וּלְסַעֲדָהּ Is 9^{6};—*support, sustain*, alw. fig.: **1.** *sustain, stay*, the heart (cf. לֵב **8**, לֵבָב **8**), with food Gn 18^{5} (J), Ju 19^{5} (c. 2 acc.), v^{8}, ψ 104^{15}; obj. om. 1 K 13^{7}. **2. a.** *support* throne (subj. kg.) Pr 20^{28}, coming ruler Is 9^{6}. **b.** *support, uphold* c. acc. pers. (subj. י׳, his hand etc.) ψ 18^{36} + ‖ 2 S 22^{36} (v *supr.*), ψ 20^{3} 41^{4} 94^{18} 119^{117}.

†מִסְעָד **n.[m.] support**;—abs. מ׳ 1 K 10^{12}; 4552
precise meaning unintelligible.

†[סָעָה] **vb.** (dub.) **rush**, of storm-wind 5584
(cf. Ar. سَعَى (and سعو), *go quickly, run, be energetic*; Syr. ܣܥܐ *make an attack upon*);—**Qal** *Pt.* fs. מֵרוּחַ סֹעָה ψ 55^{9} *from rushing wind* (and) from tempest (סָעַר); Hup (not Now) Gr Dy סוּפָה or סְעָרָה.

סעף (√of foll.; appar. = *cleave, divide*; cf. perh. Ar. سَعِفَ, of hand, *become cracked around nails* etc., Lane[1364], سَعَفٌ *palm-branches with leaves on them*, Id[1365]; Ba[ES 56] GFM[Ju 15, 8] cp. شُعْبَةٌ *cleft, (forked) branch*, cf. Buhl[Lex 13]).

†[סָעִיף] **n.[m.] 1. cleft. 2. branch**;— 5585
1. *cleft* of a crag, cstr. סְעִיף סֶלַע Ju 15$^{8.11}$; pl. cstr. וּבִסְעִפֵי הַסְּלָעִים Is 2^{21}; סְעִיפֵי הַסּ׳ 57^{5}. **2.** *branches, boughs*, pl. cstr. סְעִפֵי הַפֹּרִיָּה Is 17^{6} (so divide, Hi Kn Di Dr[Sm xxx] Du al.) *the boughs of the fruit-tree*; sf. סְעִיפֶיהָ 27^{10} (of ruined city; cf. קְצִירָהּ v^{11}).

†[סְעַפָּה] **n.f. bough, branch**;—pl. sf. 5589
סְעַפֹּתָיו Ez 31$^{6.8}$ (of king under fig. of cedar).

†I. [סָעַף] **vb. Pi. denom. lop off boughs**;— 5586
Pt. מְסָעֵף פֻּארָה Is 10^{33} י׳ . . . *shall lop off* (the) crown of branches.

†סַרְעַפָּה **n.f. bough** (with infixed ר; cf. 5634
Ges[§ 85 w], as transition-cons. Kö[ii. 1, 472]; cf. BAram., Kau[§ 62] F. Selle[De Aramaismis Lib. Ezech. 17]);—pl. sf.

סַרְעַפֹּתָיו Ez 31^{5} (of Pharaoh under fig. of tree, cf. Co Berthol Toy).

5588 † II. [סֵעֵף] (Kö $^{ii.\ 106}$) **adj. divided, half-hearted**;—pl. abs. as subst., in religious sense, סֵעֲפִים שָׂנֵאתִי ψ 119^{113} *half-hearted ones do I hate.*

5587 † [סְעִפָּה] **n.f. division, divided opinion**;—pl. abs. עַל־שְׁתֵּי הַסְּעִפִּים 1 K 18^{21} how long are ye limping *on the two divided opinions* (as on unequal legs; 𝔊 ταῖς ἰγνύαις seems an attempt to interpret the fig.; acc. to Albrecht $^{ZAW\ xvi\ (1896)\ 75}$ ס׳ really = *legs*).

5590 † [סָעַר] **vb. storm, rage** (Ecclus. סער Hiph. 47^{17} *move tempestuously;* סְעָרָה *storm-wind* 43^{17} 48^{9}; NH Pi. *stir up, blow,* סְעָרָה *storm-wind;* =II. שָׂעַר, but relation obscure; As. *šâru, wind,* favours originality of ש׳, but this only late in Heb., and for ס׳ Frä^{189} cp. Ar. سَعَرَ *kindle fire, excite, inflame, be vehemently hungry and thirsty, be mad, insane,* etc. Lane ^{1363});—**Qal** *Impf.* 3 mpl. fig., יִסְעֲרוּ Hb 3^{14} *they* [my foes] *storm along* to scatter me; *Pt. act.* סֹעֵר Jon 1^{11} the sea *was growing* more and more *stormy,* so v^{13} (+ עֲלֵיהֶם); f. סֹעֲרָה Is 54^{11} *storm-tossed* (fig. of Jerusalem). **Niph.** *Impf.* 3 ms. וַיִּסָּעֵר 2 K 6^{11} and the heart of the king ... *was enraged* because of (עַל־) this thing. **Pi.** *Impf.* 1 s. sf. וְאֲסָעֲרֵם עַל־ Zc 7^{14} (on form v. Ges$^{§§\ 23\ h,\ 52\ n}$) *and storm them away* (hurl them by a storm-wind) *upon* the nations. **Po.** *Impf.* 3 ms. כְּמֹץ יְסֹעֵר Ho 13^{3} shall be *like chaff* (which) *is storm-driven* from a threshing-floor.

5591 † סַ֫עַר **n.m.** $^{Je\ 23,19}$ **tempest**;—abs. ס׳ Am 1^{14} + 5 t.; סָעַר ψ 55^{9}; pl. sf. סַעֲרֶךָ 83^{16};—*tempest,* esp. fig.: of passionate acts of men, מֵרוּחַ סֹעָה מִסָּעַר ψ 55^{9} (מִס׳ here awkward, without ו); of י׳'s wrath Je 23^{19} (ס׳ מִתְחוֹלֵל), cf. 25^{32} 30^{23}; *tempest* as instr. of י׳'s wrath, ψ 83^{16} (‖ סוּפָה); v. also בְּסַעַר בְּיוֹם סוּפָה Am 1^{14} and Jo $1^{4.12}$.

5591 † סְעָרָה **n.f. tempest, storm-wind**;—abs. סְעָרָה Is 29^{6}+ (so also 2 K $2^{1.11}$ Ginsb; Baer בַּסְּעָרָה); cstr. סַעֲרַת Je 23^{19} 30^{23}; pl. סְעָרוֹת Ez $13^{11.13}$; cstr. סַעֲרוֹת Zc 9^{14};—*tempest, storm-wind,* as instr. of י׳'s wrath, Is 29^{6} (+ סוּפָה), cf. 40^{24} 41^{16}, also רוּחַ סְעָרוֹת Ez $13^{11.13}$ (against nation under fig. of wall); storm-wind of Elijah's translation 2 K $2^{1.11}$; of theophany Ez 1^{4} (רוּחַ סְעָרָה), Jb 38^{1} 40^{6}, and סַעֲרוֹת תֵּימָן Zc 9^{14}; סַעֲרַת י׳ as fig. of י׳'s wrath Je 23^{19} 30^{23}; of ordinary tempests only in late ψψ: רוּחַ סְעָרָה 107^{25} 148^{8}, ס׳ opp. דְּמָמָה 107^{29}.

I, II, III. סַף v. ספף. p. 706 5592-93

ספא (√ of foll.; cf. NH ספי, סָפָא *give to eat,* 𝔗 סְפִי *id.;* perh. Palm. ספא *feed, nourish,* Lzb^{330} Cook^{85}).

† מִסְפּוֹא **n.m.** $^{Gn\ 24,\ 25}$ **fodder**;—alw. abs. מ׳, 4554
Gn 24^{25}, elsewhere obj. of נָתַן v^{32} 43^{24} (all J) 42^{27} (E) Ju 19^{19}.

† [סָפַד] **vb. wail, lament** (NH *id.;* 𝔗 5594
סְפַד, ChrPalAram. ܣܦܕ *id.,* Schwally$^{Idiot.\ 64}$; As. [*sapâdu*], *sipdu, sipittu, mourning* Dl$^{HWB\ 507}$; cf. Amhar. ሰደፈ: *dirge* Prä$^{ZMG\ xxxv\ (1881),\ 762}$);—**Qal** *Pf.* 3 fs. וְסָפְדָה consec. Zc 12^{12}, 3 pl. וְסָפְדוּ consec. 1 K 14^{13} Zc 12^{10}; *Impf.* 3 fs. וַתִּסְפֹּד 2 S 11^{26}, 2 ms. תִּסְפֹּד Ez 24^{16}, 1 s. cohort. אֶסְפְּדָה Mi 1^{8}, 3 mpl. יִסְפְּדוּ Je 6^{16}+, etc.; *Imv.* mpl. סִפְדוּ 2 S 3^{31} + 2 t.; fpl. סְפֹ֫דְנָה Je 49^{3}; *Inf. abs.* סָפוֹד Zc 7^{5}; cstr. סְפוֹד Ec 3^{4}, לִסְפֹּד Gn 23^{2} 1 K 13^{29}, לִסְפּוֹד Je 16^{5}; *Pt. act.* pl. סֹפְדִים Is 32^{12}, סוֹ׳ Ec 12^{5};—*wail, lament* (with loud cries, etc., v. Mi 1^{8}, and cf. Dr$^{Am\ 5,\ 16}$), esp. for dead, c. לְ, 1 S 25^{1} 28^{3} 1 K $14^{13.18}$ Gn 23^{2} (P) Je 16^{6} $22^{18.18}$ 34^{5}, cf. וְאַל־תֵּלֵךְ לִסְפּוֹד וְאַל־תָּנֹד לָהֶם 16^{5}; c. עַל־ *over* 2 S 1^{12} 11^{26} 1 K 13^{30}, cf. Zc 12^{10} (see v^{12} infr.); c. לִפְנֵי i.e. marching *before* (bier) 2 S 3^{31} (v. Dr); c. acc. cogn. Gn 50^{10} (J); abs. 1 K 13^{29} Ez 24^{16} cf. v^{23} Ec 3^{4} (opp. רקד; cf. ψ 30^{12}), and pt. as subst. Ec 12^{5} *wailers;* also, with idea of guilt on part of those wailing, Zc 12^{12} (cf. v^{10} supr.); over calamity, judgment, c. עַל־ Mi 1^{8}, abs. Je 4^{8} (both + הֵילִיל), 49^{3} and (with fasting) Zc 7^{5} Jo 1^{13}.—עַל־שָׁדַיִם סֹפְדִים עַל־שְׂדֵי־חֶמֶד וגו׳ Is 32^{12} is dub.; Thes Ew De Che al. *upon the breasts smiting* (?) *for the fields,* etc., but rd. prob. שָׂדִים (־ִים, ־וֹת) Ges$^{Comm.}$ (q.v.) Buhl$^{Lex\ 13}$ Skinner al.: *over the fields wailing, over the delightful fields,* etc. **Niph.** *Impf.* 3 mpl. לֹא יִסָּפְדוּ Je 16^{4} *they shall not be bewailed,* so 25^{33}.

מִסְפֵּד **n.m.** $^{Gn\ 50,10}$ **wailing**;—abs. מ׳ Am 5^{16} 4553
+ 11 t.; cstr. מִסְפַּד Mi 1^{11} + 2 t.; sf. מִסְפְּדִי ψ 30^{12};—*wailing:* **1.** for dead, Gn 50^{10} (J; as acc. cogn.), Zc 12^{10} (c. עַל־; cf. v$^{11.11}$ infr.). **2.** for calamity experienced Am $5^{16.16}$ (‖ אֵבֶל), v^{17} Mi 1^{8} (מ׳ כַּתַּנִּים ‖ אֵבֶל), v^{11} Je 48^{38} Ez 27^{31}, anticipated Je 6^{26} Est 4^{3}. **3.** in contrition Is 22^{12} (+ בְּכִי), Jo 2^{12} (+ בְּכִי, צוֹם), cf. Zc $12^{11.11}$. **4.** in gen., ψ 30^{12} (opp. מָחוֹל, cf. Ec 3^{4}).

5605 †[סָפָה] **vb. swoop** or **snatch away, catch up** (NH סָפָא ,ספי *collect* (rare), 𝔗 סְפֵי (rare), Syr. ܣܦܐ *collect, pick up;* Ar. سَفَا of wind, *raise dust and carry it away* Lane 1377);—**Qal 1.** intrans.: *Pf.* 3 fs. סָפְתָה Je 12[4] *be snatched away* (rd. poss. סָפָה [סוּף]). **2.** trans.: *Impf.* 3 fs. תִּסְפֶּה Is 7[20] *sweep away* beard; 2 ms. תִּסְפֶּה Gn 18[23.24] *sweep away* indiscriminately (good and bad); *Inf. cstr.* סְפוֹת Dt 29[18] *to snatch away* the moist with the dry (proverb. expression, cf. Dr), sf. לִסְפּוֹתָהּ ψ 40[15] *to snatch it away* (i.e. my life).—וְסָפוּ Am 3[15] v. סוּף. **Niph.** *Pf.* 3 ms. וְנִסְפָּה consec. 1 S 26[10]; *Impf.* 2 ms. תִּסָּפֶה Gn 19[15.17]; 1 s. אֶסָּפֶה 1 S 27[1]; 2 mpl. תִּסָּפוּ Nu 16[26], תִּסָּפוּ 1 S 12[25]; *Pt.* נִסְפֶּה Is 13[15] Pr 13[23] (1 Ch 21[12] v. infr.);—**1.** *be swept away, destroyed,* Gn 19[15] (בַּעֲוֺן הָעִיר *by reason of the iniquity of the city*), v[17] (both J), Nu 16[26] (JE) 1 S 12[25] 26[10] (in battle), + בְּיַד of agent 1 S 27[1]; cf. וְיֵשׁ נִסְפֶּה בְּלֹא מִשְׁפָּט Pr 13[23] *and there is that is swept away for lack of justice.*—1 Ch 21[12] rd. נֹסְךָ (as ‖ 2 S 24[13], v. נוּס). **2.** *be caught up, captured,* Is 13[15] (‖ נִמְצָא). **Hiph.** *Impf.* 1 s. אַסְפֶּה עָלֵימוֹ רָעוֹת Dt 32[23] *I will catch up against them calamities,* but read אֹסְפָה *I will gather* (√ אסף), or < אֹסִפָה (Di Dr Buhl[Lex 13]) *I will add,* i.e. *multiply* (√ יסף; v. Ges[§ 69 h, note]).

5596 †I. [סָפַח] **vb. join, attach to**;—**Qal** *Imv.* ms. sf. סְפָחֵנִי נָא אֶל־וגו׳ 1 S 2[36] *attach me, pray, to* one of the priest's offices. **Niph.** *Pf.* 3 pl. וְנִסְפְּחוּ עַל־ consec. Is 14[1] *and they shall attach themselves to* the house of Jacob (‖ נִלְוָה). **Pi.** *Pt.* מְסַפֵּחַ חֲמָתְךָ Hb 2[15] *joining* (to it?) *thy fury,* but read prob. מִסַּף (ח dittogr.) *from the goblet of thy fury* (so We Gr Now GASm Da). **Pu.** *Impf.* 3 mpl. יְסֻפָּחוּ Jb 30[7] *are joined together, hold themselves together* (yet rd. perh. Niph. יִסָּפְחוּ Bu). **Hithp.** *Inf. cstr.* מֵהִסְתַּפֵּחַ 1 S 26[19] they have driven me out *from joining myself* with (בְּ) the inheritance of י׳.

II. **ספח** (√ of foll.; appar. *pour out;* cf. Ar. سَفَحَ *pour out, shed* (blood; Qor 6[146]); NH סִפֵּחַ of river, *cast out* alluvial soil, make new land).

5599 †I. [סָפִיחַ] **n.[m.] outpouring** (?);—pl. sf. תִּשְׁטֹף־סְפִיחֶיהָ עֲפַר הָאָרֶץ Jb 14[19] (si vera l.) *its outpourings sweep away the dust of the earth,* so most, but dub.; Bu prop. *סְחִיפָה, cf. מָטָר סֹחֵף Pr 28[3].

†II. סָפִיחַ **n.[m.] growth from spilled kernels** ((kernels) *poured out,* accidentally, in harvesting, acc. to most; Buhl[Lex 13] al. think of *additional* growth, √ I. ספח);—it is what springs up of itself in second year, and serves as food when no grain could be sown: abs. ס׳ 2 K 19[29] = Is 37[30]; cstr. סְפִיחַ קְצִירְךָ Lv 25[5]; sf. תִּקְצְרוּ אֶת־סְפִיחֶיהָ v[11]. 5600

†מִשְׂפָּח **n.[m.]** prob. **outpouring** (of blood), **bloodshed** (שׂ subst. for ס; word chosen for assonance with מִשְׁפָּט);—abs., וַיְקַו לְמִשְׁפָּט וְהִנֵּה מ׳ Is 5[7] *and he waited for justice and lo! bloodshed,* so Ges Hi Ew Di Gu Du Che[Comm.] Che[Hpt.] (dub.). 4939

III. **ספח** (√ of foll.; meaning dubious).

†סַפַּחַת **n.f. eruption, scab,** either malignant or harmless;—abs. שְׂאֵת אוֹ ס׳ אוֹ בַהֶרֶת Lv 13[2] cf. 14[56]. 5597

†מִסְפַּחַת **n.f.** id.;—abs. Lv 13[6.7.8]. 4556

†שִׂפַּח **vb. Pi. denom. cause a scab upon, smite with scab** (שׂ subst. for ס);—וְשִׂפַּח אֲדֹנָי קָדְקֹד וגו׳ (consec.) Is 3[17] *and Adonay shall smite with scab the crown of* the daughters of Zion. 5596

†[מִסְפָּחָה] **n.f. long veil** (prop. *sheathing?*) covering whole person; pl. abs. וְעֹשׂוֹת הַמִּסְפָּחוֹת עַל־רֹאשׁ Ez 13[18]; sf. מִסְפְּחֹתֵיכֶם v[21]. 4555

סַפִּי v. ספף. p. 706 5598

†סַפִּיר **n.[m.] sapphire,** perh. also **lapis lazuli** (cf. Di[Ex 24, 10] Now[Arch. i. 131]) (NH *id.,* and סַמְפִּירִינוֹן; 𝔗 סַפִּירִינוֹן; 𝔖 ܣܦܝܠܐ; loan-word from Skr. *çanipriya* acc. to Lag[Ges. Abh. 72] Lewy[Fremdw. 56] cf. Gk. σάπφειρος);—abs. ס׳ Ex 24[10] + 8 t.; pl. סַפִּירִים Is 54[11] Ct 5[14];—with other jewels as ornaments of prince Ez 28[13]; in high priest's breastplate Ex 28[18] 39[11]; found in mines Jb 28[6], costly Jb 28[16] cf. Is 54[11]; taking high polish La 4[7] (in fig.); שֵׁן מְעֻלֶּפֶת סַפִּירִים Ct 5[14] *ivory covered with sapphires* (in fig.); *lapis lazuli,* acc. to Hi Bu Du al. in Jb 28[6] (עַפְרֹת זָהָב לוֹ being understood of sparkling crystals of iron pyrites in this), but v. Di; *lapis lazuli* may be intended in לִבְנַת הַסּ׳ Ex 24[10] (J) *pavement of sapphire* (in theoph.), cf. אֶבֶן־ס׳ Ez 1[26] 10[1]. 5601

†סֵפֶל **n.[m.] bowl** (√ unknown; perhaps foreign word; As. *saplu, bowl, basin* (Dl[HWB 508] Schr[COT 2 K 9, 2]) [occurs as object of tribute or 5602

plunder]; NH = BH; 𝔗 סִיפְלָא *bowl, basin,* ChrPalAram. ܣܦܠܐ (wash-)*basin* Schwally Idiot. 64; Ar. سِفْل *bowl, jar* Fl[Levy NHWB iii. 320; Kl. Schr. ii. 556 f.] is perh. loan-word Frä[67 f.]);—abs. מְלֹא הַסּ׳ Ju 6[38]; for drinking, cstr. סֵפֶל אַדִּירִים 5[25] *a bowl of* (fit for) *nobles, huge bowl* (GFM).

5603,8226 †[סָפַן, once, erron., 'שׂ] **vb. cover, cover in, panel** (NH סָפַן is *respect, care for;* Ph. מספנת *roof,* Lzb[330]; Aram. סְפַן Ithpe. *be covered, overlaid;* As. *sapânu* (sts. *šapânu!*), *cover, overwhelm* Dl[508]; *sapannu, concealment, obscurity, depth* (of sea); Eth. ሰፈነ: *invalescere, percrebescere, praevalere,* Di[406]);—**Qal** *Impf.* 3 ms. וַיִּסְפֹּן אֶת־הַבַּיִת גֵּבִים 1 K 6[9] *and he covered in the house with beams* (?); *Inf. abs.* סָפוּן בָּאָרֶז Je 22[14] (rdg. with JDMich Hi Gf Or Gie Co, חַלּוֹנָיו סָפוּן, for MT חַלּוֹנָי וְסָפוּן, cf. Dr[Sm xxx]) *covering* (it) *in, panelling* (it) with cedar; *Pt. pass.* סָפוּן בָּאָרֶז 1 K 7[7], סָפֻן בָּאָרֶז v[3]; pl. בְּבָתֵּיכֶם סְפוּנִים Hg 1[14] *in your panelled houses.*—סָפוּן strangely = *reserved, laid up,* Dt 33[21], and = *hidden* v[19] שְׂפֻנֵי טְמוּנֵי חוֹל (only here with שׂ; both in sense of צָפוּן [rd. this ?], cf. Dr).

5604 †סִפֻּן **n.[m.] ceiling**;—abs. הַסּ׳ 1 K 6[15].

5600 †סְפִינָה **n.f. vessel, ship** (*covered in, overlaid,* with sheathing, deck, etc.; Aram. ܣܦܝܢܬܐ; on Ar. سَفِينَةٌ as loan-word v. Frä[216]);—only יַרְכְּתֵי הַסּ׳ Jon 1[5].

ספף (√of foll., meaning unknown).

5592 †I. סַף **n.m. basin, goblet** (NH סַף; Ph. ספ (Inscr. of Tyre (1), 5, 6) Schröd[ZMG xxxix (1885), 317 f.] Cl-Gann[Annales du Musée Guimet x. 511 = Recueil d'arch. orient. (1886), 89] Hal[RÉJ xii. 107] Bloch; but Lzb[330] *door-sill*);—ס׳ abs. *basin* Ex 12[22.22] (J; containing blood of passover lamb); cstr. סַף־רַעַל Zc 12[2] *goblet of reeling* (intoxicating, fig.), prob. also Hb 2[15], where rd. מִסַּף חֲמָתְךָ *from the goblet of thy fury* (for MT מְסַפֵּחַ ח׳, v. I. ספח); pl. abs. סִפּוֹת 2 S 17[28] *basins* for ordinary use; הַסִּפִּים Je 52[19], הַסִּפּוֹת 1 K 7[50] and cstr. סִפּוֹת כֶּסֶף 2 K 12[14], of temple utensils.

5592 II. סַף[24] **n.m.**[Am 9, 1] **threshold, sill** (NH *id.;* Ph. v. Lzb I. סף; Aram. סִפָּא, ܣܦܐ, Ar. *sippu* Dl[509], all *id.*);—abs. ס׳ 2 K 12[10]+, also הַסָּף Ju 19[27]+3 t. (Baer Ginsb), הַסָּף 2 K 25[8]; sf. סִפִּי Ez 43[8], סִפָּם v[8]; pl. סִפִּים Am 9[1] Is 6[4]+6 t. Ez Ch;—*threshold, sill* Ju 19[27] Am 9[1] Is 6[4] Ez 41[16.16] 43[8.8] 2 Ch 3[7], ס׳ הַבַּיִת 1 K 14[17], ס׳ הַשַּׁעַר Ez 40[6.7], cf. v[6 b]; שֹׁמֵר הַסַּף = *door-keeper,* an important temple official, Je 35[4], so שֹׁמְרֵי הַסּ׳ 2 K 12[10] (priests), 22[4] = 2 Ch 34[9] (Levites!), 2 K 23[4] 25[18] = Je 52[24]; in Persia, of palace Est 2[21] 6[2]; of tabern. שֹׁ׳ הַסִּפִּים 1 Ch 9[19]; שַׁעֲרֵי הַסּ׳ 2 Ch 23[4] (Levites), שֹׁעֲרִים בַּסּ׳ 1 Ch 9[22]; coll. חֹרֶב בַּסַּף Zp 2[14] *desolation in the thresholds.*

†[ספף] **vb. denom. Hithpô'. stand at,** or **guard, the threshold**;—*Inf. cstr.* בָּחַרְתִּי הִסְתּוֹפֵף בְּבֵית אֱלֹהַי ψ 84[11] *I choose standing at the threshold in the house of my God.* 5605

†III. סַף, סִפַּי **n.pr.m.** a Philistine, 2 S 21[18] (𝔊 τὸν Σεφ(ε); 𝔊L τοὺς ἐπισυνηγμένους), = סִפַּי 1 Ch 20[4] (𝔊 τὸν Σαφουτ, A Σεφφι, 𝔊L Σαπφι). 5593, 5598

†סָפַק, [שָׂפַק], **vb. slap, clap** (NH Pi. *id.;* Ar. سَفَقَ *slap* (face), *strike* (hands) Lane[1373]);—**Qal** *Pf.* 3 ms. וְסָפַק consec. Je 48[26], sf. סְפָקָם Jb 34[26]; 1 s. סָפַקְתִּי Je 31[19]; 3 pl. סָפְקוּ La 2[15]; *Impf.* 3 ms. יִשְׂפֹּק (שׂ subst. for ס) Jb 27[23], יִסְפּוֹק 34[37], וַיִּסְפֹּק Nu 24[10]; *Imv.* ms. סְפֹק Ez 21[17];—**1.** *slap,* sq. עַל־יָרֵךְ *on* the *thigh,* in remorse and sorrow Je 31[19] Ez 21[17]; c. כַּפַּיִם *clap* one's *hands* Nu 24[10] (in anger), c. עַל *at,* La 2[15] Jb 27[23] (in mockery); כ׳ om. Jb 34[37] (in presumptuousness, against God). **2.** *slap, chastise,* c. acc. pers. Jb 34[26] (subj. God). **3.** *splash* וְס׳ מוֹאָב בְּקִיאוֹ Je 48[26] *and Moab shall splash* (fall with a splash) *into his vomit,* > Thes Buhl[Lex 13] *empty himself* (?), *throw up* (cf. Syr. ܣܦܩ Pa.). **Hiph.** *Impf.* 3 mpl. וּבְיַלְדֵי נָכְרִים יַשְׂפִּיקוּ Is 2[6] (rd. perh. וּבִידֵי Hi Du Che, *and into the hands of foreigners they clap,* lit. *cause to clap,* sc. their hands; > 𝔊 𝔖 from I. שׂפק q.v., *they abound in, have a sufficiency of*). p. 974 5606, 8210

†[שֶׂפֶק] **n.[m.]** doubtful word; **hand-clapping, i.e. mockery** (?) (cf. vb. Jb 27[23]);—שָׂפֶק Jb 36[18] in difficult cl. כִּי־חֵמָה פֶּן־יְסִיתְךָ בְשׂ׳ *because* there is *passion,* (beware) *lest it incite thee to mockery,* Bae[Kau] Da (but הסית בְּ = *incite against,* hence Bu reads לְשָׂפֶק); De is not clear; others (as Di): *lest it* (passion) *excite thee at the chastisement* (v. √**2**; cf. Thes); Du reads מִשְׂפָּק לְחֵמָה lest *chastisement* incite thee *to wrath.*—On Jb 20[22] (edd.) v. שֶׂפֶק. p. 974 5607

סֵפֶר[185] **n.m.**[Is 29, 11] **missive, document, writing, book** (prob. ancient loan-word from As. *šipru, missive, message* Dl[HWB 683], TelAm. *šipru, šipirtu, id.* Wkl[TA Gloss]; √*šâpâru, send, send message* or *letter* Dl[HWB 683], Wkl[l. c.], whence also 5612

šâpiru, writer, and (perh.) *ruler, šapirûtu, rule;* v. Hom Aufsätze (1892), 34 Buhl Lex 13; perh. cf. Ar. سَفَرَ *go forth to journey*, II. *send on a journey* Lane 1370; NH סֵפֶר = BH; so Aram. סִיפְרָא, ܣܶܦܪܳܐ; ChrPalAram. ܣܦܪܐ Schwally Idiot. 64; Ar. سِفْرٌ);—ס׳ abs. 2 S 11^{14}+; cstr. Ex 24^{7}+; sf. סִפְרִי Ex 32^{33}, סִפְרְךָ v^{33} ψ 139^{16}; pl. סְפָרִים 1 K 21^{8}+;—†**1.** *missive:* **a.** *letter* of instruction, *written order, commission*, or *request*, usu. fr. king, 2 S 11$^{14.15}$ 1 K 21$^{8.8.9.11}$ 2 K 5$^{5.6.6.7}$ 10$^{1.2.6.7}$, 19^{14} = Is 37^{14} cf. 2 Ch 32^{17}, 2 K 20^{12} = Is 39^{1}; = *written decree* for publication Est 1^{22} 3^{13} 8^{5} 9$^{20.25.30}$ (= אִגֶּרֶת v$^{26.29}$, vid. p. 8 b supra), cf. וַיִּשְׁלַח סְפָרִים בְּיַד הָרָצִים בַּסּוּסִים רֹכְבֵי הָרֶכֶשׁ 8^{10}.—[כָּתַב ס׳ 2 S 11^{15} 1 K 21^{8} 2 K 10$^{1.6}$ 2 Ch 32^{17}; כָּתַב בַּסּ׳ (of specif. contents) 2 S 11^{15} 1 K 21$^{9.11}$; קָרָא אֶת־הַסּ׳ 2 K 5^{7} *read the letter*].—**b.** fr. prophet Je 29^{1}, other influential persons v$^{25.29}$†. †**2.** *legal document*, ס׳ כְּרִיתֻת *certificate of divorce* Dt 24$^{1.3}$ and (fig.) Je 3^{8} Is 50^{1}; ס׳ הַמִּקְנָה *deed of purchase* Je 32$^{11.12}$ (del. art.), v$^{12.14.16}$, cf. בַּסּ׳ v^{10}, הַסְּפָרִים v^{14} (si vera l.; del. 𝔊 Gie cf. Gf), סֵפֶר v$^{16 b. 44}$; ס׳ = *indictment* Jb 31^{35} (obj. of כָּתַב; כָּתַב בְּ׳ = *sign* Je 32$^{10.12.44}$). **3.** *book*, or *scroll*, in which something is written to preserve it for future use Ex 17^{14} (E), Jos 18^{9} (JE), 1 S 10^{25} Is 30^{8} Jb 19^{23}+; in form of roll, cf. וְנָגֹלּוּ כַסֵּפֶר הַשָּׁמָיִם Is 34^{4}, הַסּ׳ הֶחָתוּם 29$^{11.12}$ (v. Je 36, etc., infr.); partic.: **a.** *book of prophecies* Je 25^{13} 30^{2}+6 t. Je 36, Dn 12^{4}; ס׳ חֲזוֹן נַחוּם Na 1^{1}; סֵפֶר י׳ Is 34^{4}; so מְגִלַּת סֵפֶר Je 36$^{2.4}$ (= מְגִלָּה v^{6}+6 t.; with many columns, דְּלָתוֹת v^{23}), Ez 2^{9}, cf. ψ 40^{8}. **b.** *geneal. register*, ס׳ תּוֹלְדוֹת Gn 5^{1} (P), ס׳ הַיַּחַשׂ Ne 7^{5}. **c.** *law-book*, †ס׳ הַבְּרִית Ex 24^{7} (E), 2 K 23^{2} = 2 Ch 34^{30}, 2 K 23^{21}; †ס׳ הַתּוֹרָה Dt 28^{61} 29^{20} 30^{10} 31^{26} Jos 1^{8} 8^{34} (all D), 2 K 22^{8} = 2 Ch 34^{15}, 2 K 22^{11} Ne 8^{3}; †ס׳ תּוֹרַת אֱלֹהִים Jos 24^{26} (E), Ne 8^{8} (rdg. ס׳ תּוֹרַת, so 𝔊, cf. Talm. Nedarim 37 b), v^{18} 9^{3}; †ס׳ תּוֹרַת י׳ 2 Ch 17^{9} 34^{14}; †ס׳ תּוֹרַת מֹשֶׁה Jos 8^{31} 23^{6} (both D), 2 K 14^{6} Ne 8^{1}; †ס׳ מֹשֶׁה 2 Ch 25^{4} 35^{12} Ne 13^{1}. **d.** *book* of poems, ס׳ מִלְחֲמֹת י׳ Nu 21^{14} (JE), ס׳ הַיָּשָׁר Jos 10^{13} (JE), 2 S 1^{18}. **e.** *book* concerned with kings, ס׳ דִּבְרֵי שְׁלֹמֹה 1 K 11^{41}, and esp. ס׳ דִּבְרֵי הַיָּמִים לְמַלְכֵי וגו׳ 1 K 14$^{19.29}$+31 t. K (18 t. of Isr., 15 t. of Judah), cf. Est 10^{2} (of Media and Pers.); also ס׳ דִּבְרֵי הַיָּמִים לַמֶּלֶךְ דָּוִיד 1 Ch 27^{24} (rdg. ס׳ for מִסְפַּר, 𝔊 Kit Hpt); ס׳ הַמְּלָכִים לִיהוּדָה וְיִשְׂרָאֵל 2 Ch 16^{11}; ס׳ מַלְכֵי יְהוּדָה וְיִשׂ׳ 25^{26} 28^{26} 32^{32}; ס׳ מ׳ יִשׂ׳ וִיהוּדָה 27^{7} 35^{27} 36^{8}; ס׳ מ׳ יִשׂ׳ 1 Ch 9^{1} 2 Ch 20^{34}; מִדְרַשׁ ס׳ 24^{27}; also ס׳ דִּבְרֵי הַיָּמִים הַמְּלָכִים Ne 12^{23} Est 2^{23}; ס׳ הַזִּכְרֹנוֹת דִּבְרֵי הַיָּמִים Est 6^{1}. **f.** once בַּסְּפָרִים Dn 9^{2} *by means of the Scriptures* (canonical books) cf. Ew Meinh Bev Marti Kau. **g.** God's *record-book*, ψ 139^{16}, ס׳ זִכָּרוֹן Mal 3^{16}; God's register of living, Ex 32$^{32.33}$ (E), ס׳ חַיִּים ψ 69^{29}; הַסּ׳ Dn 12^{1} (citizens of Mess. kingdom). **4.** ס׳ = *book-learning*, esp. *writing:* יָדַע (הַ)סֵּפֶר Is 29$^{11.12.12}$ (of ability to read); so לְלַמְּדָם סֵפֶר וּלְשׁוֹן כַּשְׂדִּים Dn 1^{4} *to teach them the writing and speech of the Chaldeans* (on constr. v. Ges § 128 a); more gen. הַשְׂכֵּיל בְּכָל־ס׳ וְחָכְמָה v^{17}.—[סֵפֶר *book* is joined with vbs. thus: it is written (יִכָּתֵב) Mal 3^{16}; a thing is written בַּסּ׳ Ex 17^{14}+20 t., עַל־ס׳ 2 S 1^{18}+50 t. (+Je 36^{32}; בַּדְּיוֹ *with ink* v^{18}), אֶל־ס׳ +Je 30^{2} 51^{60}; conversely דָּרַשׁ מֵעַל ס׳ Is 34^{16}, שָׁמַע מֵעַל ס׳ Je 36^{11}; v. also †וְיֻחָקוּ בַּסּ׳ Jb 19^{23} *inscribe in a book*, †עַל־ס׳ חֻקָּהּ Is 30^{8} (|| כָּתְבָהּ עַל־לוּחַ); †מָחָה מִס׳ *blot out of a book* Ex 32$^{32.33}$ ψ 69^{29}; †קָרָא אֶת־הַס׳ Je 51^{63} *read the book*, scroll, but usu. †קָרָא בַס׳ 36$^{8.10.13}$ Ne 8$^{8.18}$
9^{3} 13^{1}].—ס׳ in קִרְיַת ס׳, v. ק׳. p. 900 7158

†[סִפְרָה] **n.f.** book;—sf. הֲלֹא בְּסִפְרָתֶךָ 5612
ψ 56^{9} (cf. סֵפֶר **3 g**); del. as gloss Bi Che
Hup-Now Du.—Cf. also [סְפֹרָה] infr. p. 708 5615

סָפַר$_{107}$ **vb. count, Pi. recount, relate** (prob. 5608
ancient denom. from סֵפֶר; NH = BH; Eth. ሰፈረ: *measure* Di 404);—**Qal**$_{27}$ *Pf.* 3 ms. ס׳ 2 S 24^{10}, 2 ms. סָפַרְתָּה ψ 56^{9}, וְסָפַרְתָּ Lv 25^{8}, etc.; *Impf.* יִסְפֹּר ψ 87^{6}+Jb 38^{37} where read prob. יִסְפֹּר (Bu) for MT יְסַפֵּר; וַיִּסְפֹּר Jb 31^{4}, 2 Ch 2$^{1.16}$, sf. וַיִּסְפְּרֵם Ezr 1^{8}; 2 ms. תִּסְפֹּר Jb 39^{2}, תִּסְפּוֹר 14^{16}, תִּסְפָּר־ Dt 16^{9}, etc.; *Imv.* ms. סְפֹר Gn 15^{5}; mpl. סִפְרוּ 1 Ch 21^{2} ψ 48^{13}; *Inf. cstr.* לִסְפֹּר Gn 15^{5}+2 t.; *Pt.* סֹפֵר Is 33$^{18.18}$ (v. also סֹפֵר **n.** infr.);—**1.** *count* things, to learn their number, c. acc., Gn 15$^{5.5}$ (J) 2 S 24^{10}+10 t. (+acc. cogn. 2 Ch 2^{16}); acc. om. Gn 41^{49} (E); +ל (dat. comm. vel eth.), Lv 15$^{13.28}$ 23^{15} 25^{8} (all PH), Dt 16^{9} Ez 44^{26} Ezr 1^{8} ψ 87^{6} Is 33^{18} (abs.), v^{18} (but text suspicious, conjj. in Du Che Hpt). **2.** *number* = *take account of*, carefully observe and consider, *reckon:* צְעָדַי תִּסְפּוֹר Jb 14^{16} *of my steps thou takest account*, so 31^{4}; v. also 38^{37} (cf. supr.); נֹדִי סָפַרְתָּה ψ 56^{9} *my wandering hast thou reckoned*, taken into account (Che reads סְפַרְתִּי after 𝔊).

†**Niph.** *Impf.* 3 ms. יִסָּפֵר Ho 2^{1}+4 t.; 3 mpl. יִסָּפְרוּ 1 K 8^{5} 2 Ch 5^{6}, וַיִּסָּפְרוּ 1 Ch 23^{3};—

be counted, numbered, usu. c. neg., to indicate multitude, לֹא יִסּ׳ מֵרֹב Gn 16^{10} (J) *it is not to be counted, for multitude,* so 32^{13} (J), 1 K 3^{8} (‖ לֹא־יִמָּנֶה), 8^{5} (+*id.*), 2 Ch 5^{6} (+*id.*); cf. Ho 2^{1} (+לֹא־יִמַּד), Je 33^{22} (‖ לֹא יִמַּד); positively, only וַיִּסָּפְרוּ הַלְוִיִּם 1 Ch 23^{3}.

Pi. $_{67}$ *Pf.* 1 s. סִפַּרְתִּי ψ 119^{26}, סִפַּרְתִּי v ^{13}; 3 pl. סִפְּרוּ Ju 6^{13} + 3 t.; *Impf.* 3 ms. יְסַפֵּר Jb 38^{37} +, 1 s. אֲסַפֵּר ψ 22^{18} +; cohort. אֲסַפְּרָה Jb 15^{7}; 1 pl. וּנְסַפֵּר־ Ex 10^{2}, etc.; *Imv.* סַפֵּר Is 43^{26}, etc.; *Inf. cstr.* (לְ)סַפֵּר ψ 50^{16} + 5 t.; *Pt.* מְסַפֵּר Ju 7^{13} 2 K 8^{5}; pl. מְסַפְּרִים ψ 19^{2} 78^{4};—*recount, rehearse, declare*: **1.** *recount* something (acc.), to (לְ pers.) Ju 6^{13} 7^{13} Gn 24^{66} (J), 1 S 11^{5} + 18 t. (of *rehearsing* glorious deeds of י׳ ψ 44^{2} 73^{28} $78^{3.4}$ 79^{13}); c. acc. + בְּ loc. Ez 12^{16}, elsewhere of rehearsing name or praise of י׳ Ex 9^{16} (J) ψ 9^{15} 96^{3} = 1 Ch 16^{24}, ψ 102^{22} Je 51^{10}; c. acc. alone ψ 9^{2} 19^{2} 119^{13} (+ בְּ instr.), 145^{6} + 8 t. ψψ + Is 43^{21}, all of rehearsing praise of י׳; cf. עָצְמוּ מִסַּפֵּר ψ 40^{6} *they are too great to rehearse,* c. acc. also Je $23^{28.32}$ Jb 15^{17} 28^{27} ψ 119^{26}; acc. om. Is 43^{26}, c. לְ pers. Gn 40^{8} (E) + 6 t., c. אֶל־ pers. Gn 37^{10} (E), c. בְּאָזְנֵי Ex 10^{2}; c. כְּמוֹ (q. v.) ψ 73^{15}; c. אֶל־ *concerning* ψ 2^{7}, cf. 69^{27} (𝔊 𝔖 Ew Ol Gr Bi Che Bae *add;* in that case read יֹסִפוּ); c. עַל־ *concerning,* + לְ pers. Jo 1^{3}. **2.** appar., in weakened sense, *talk* ψ 59^{13}, 64^{6} (c. לְ *concerning*), 73^{15} (c. כְּמוֹ). **3.** *count exactly, accurately,* אֲסַפֵּר כָּל־עַצְמוֹתָי ψ 22^{18} *I can count exactly all my bones* (in wasted body).—ψ 40^{6} v. sub **1**, Jb 38^{37} read יִסְפֹּר.

†**Pu.** *be recounted, related, rehearsed: Pf.* 3 ms. סֻפַּר לְ Is 52^{15}; *Impf.* 3 ms. יְסֻפַּר לְ Jb 37^{20} (cl. as subj.), + לְ *concerning* ψ 22^{31}; c. בְּ loc. 88^{12}; abs. יְסֻפָּר Hb 1^{5}.

5608 †סוֹפֵר, סֹפֵר **n.m.** $^{\psi 45,2}$ **enumerator, muster-**
5608 **officer, secretary, scribe** (prop. pt. of סָפַר; Aram. סָפְרָא, ܣܳܦܪܳܐ *id.*, cf. ܣܦܰܪ *doctus, literatus;* OAram. ספרא *id.*, Lzb ^{330} Cook ^{85}; Ph. ספר Lzb ^{330});—abs. סֹפֵר Ju 5^{14} +, סוֹפֵר 2 S 8^{17} +; cstr. סֹפֵר 2 K 12^{11} + 2 t., + Je 52^{25} (Gie GFM rd. הַסּ׳ as ‖ 2 K 25^{19}); pl. סֹפְרִים 1 K 4^{3} Je 8^{8}, סוֹ׳ 1 Ch 2^{55} 34^{13}; cstr. סֹפְרֵי Est 3^{12} 8^{9};—**1. a.** *enumerator, muster-officer,* in description of leaders of Isr. מֹשְׁכִים בְּשֵׁבֶט ס׳ Ju 5^{14}. **b.** king's official = *secretary* 2 S 8^{17} = 20^{25} = 1 Ch 18^{16}, 2 K $18^{18.37}$ = Is $36^{3.22}$; Sol. had two 1 K 4^{3} (in all these disting. from מַזְכִּיר); also 2 K 19^{2} = Is 37^{2}, Je $36^{10.12}$, cf. לִשְׁכַּת הַסּ׳ v $^{12.20.21}$, בֵּית הַסּ׳ $37^{15.20}$; acting as treasurer and paymaster 2 K 12^{11} = 2 Ch 24^{11},—cf. Zadok Ne 13^{13};—2 K $22^{3.8.9.10.12}$ = 2 Ch $34^{15.18.20}$; 1 Ch 24^{6} (Levite); הַסּ׳ שַׂר הַצָּבָא 2 K 25^{19} = Je 52^{25} (si vera l. in K) implies military authority (but שַׂר הַצ׳ perh. gloss GFM $^{Ju\ 5,14}$); Ew Sta al. read (as Je) *scribe of general.* **c.** in Persia, *secretaries* who wrote out (king's) decrees, acc. to Est 3^{12} 8^{9}. **d.** 2 Ch 26^{11} uses ס׳ for muster-officer; 1 Ch 2^{55} mentions families of סוֹפְרִים; 2 Ch 34^{13} knows ס׳ as Levites; ס׳ 1 Ch 27^{32} = *man of learning.* **2.** professional class of *learned men, 'scribes,'* able to read and write Je $36^{26.32}$; with writing implements, עֵט ס׳ ψ 45^{2}, מָהִיר קֶסֶת הַסּ׳ Ez $9^{2.3}$, תַּעַר הַסּ׳ Je 36^{23}; esp. *learned* in the law, and assuming to issue its precepts, עֵט שֶׁקֶר סֹפְרִים 8^{8}. **3.** specif. of Ezra, at once priest (כֹּהֵן) and learned in the law (סֹפֵר), Ezr 7^{11}, ס׳ דִּבְרֵי מִצְוֹת י׳ v ^{11} [cf. Aram. v $^{12.21}$], ס׳ מָהִיר בְּתוֹרַת משֶׁה v ^{6}; Ne $8^{1.4.9.13}$ $12^{26.36}$.

†I. סְפָר **n.[m.]** **enumeration, census** 5610
(late; on format. cf. Lag $^{BN\ 175}$);—abs. ס׳, sq. אֲשֶׁר as acc. cogn. with סָפַר 2 Ch 2^{16}.

†II. [סְפָר] **n.pr.loc.** in S. Arabia;—only 5611
c. ה loc. סְפָרָה Gn 10^{30}, 𝔊 Σωφηρα; usu. indentif. with *Ṭafâr* (ظَفَار, pronounced إِسْفَار, إِصْفَار acc. to Thes), ancient city of Ḥimyarite kings (Ptol. Σαπφαρ μητρόπολις v. Sprenger $^{Alte\ Geogr.\ Arab.\ §\ 301\ et\ pass.}$), so Thes Tuch $^{Comm.\ Gen.\ 2,\ 212}$, but dub. Glaser $^{Skizze\ ii.\ 437}$, ס = צ improb. Di $^{ad\ loc.}$ Lag $^{BN\ 61}$.

†[סְפֹרָה] **n.f.** number;—pl. abs. לֹא יָדַעְתִּי 5615
סְפֹרוֹת ψ 71^{15} *I know not (the) numbers* (of י׳'s acts of righteousness and deliverance, i.e. they are *innumerable;* cf. 𝔗 Symm.); > Du (after 𝔊
Bab א 𝔖 𝔙) reads סְפָרוֹת (cf. סִפְרָה supr.). p. 707 5612

I. מִסְפָּר $_{133}$ **n.m.** $^{1\ Ch\ 27,24}$ **number, tale;**—abs. 4557
מ׳ Gn 34^{30} +; cstr. מִסְפַּר Ex 16^{16} +; sf. מִסְפַּרְכֶם Nu 14^{29}, מִסְפָּרָם Ju 21^{23} +; pl. cstr. מִסְפְּרֵי 1 Ch 12^{23};—**1. a.** *number,* Ju 7^{6} *the number of those lapping,* מֹנֶה מִס׳ לַכּוֹכָבִים ψ 147^{4}, + oft. (37 t. PH); לֹא עָלָה הַמִּסְפָּר בְּמִסְפַּר דִּבְרֵי וגו׳ 1 Ch 27^{24} (read בְּסֵפֶר) *the number did not come up into* (was not recorded in) *the book of the daily doings,* etc.; redund. after num., †2 S 21^{20} *twenty-four (in) number;* אֵין מ׳ *it was (they were) innumerable* Gn 41^{49} (E), c. לְ Ju 6^{5} 7^{12} 1 Ch 22^{16} 2 Ch 12^{3}, לִתְבוּנָתוֹ אֵין מ׳ ψ 147^{5} (of י׳); abs. Je 2^{32} Jb 21^{33} Ct 6^{8}; †עַד־אֵין מ׳ = *id.*, Jb 5^{9} 9^{10} ψ 40^{13}, וְאֵין מ׳ Je 46^{23}; לְאֵין מ׳ †1 Ch 22^{4}; וְאֵין לָהֶם מ׳ †ψ 104^{25} 105^{34} Jo 1^{6}; הֲיֵשׁ מ׳ לִגְדוּדָיו Jb 25^{3} *can his bands be numbered?* without אֵין = *numerable,*

i.e. *few*, וִיהִי מְתָיו מ׳ Dt 33[6] but *let his men be few*, יָמִים מ׳ Nu 9[20], מ׳ alone Is 10[19], usu. in combin., מְתֵי מ׳ = *a few men* Gn 34[30] (J), Dt 4[27] Je 44[28] 1 Ch 16[19] ψ 105[12], אַנְשֵׁי מ׳ Ez 12[16]; so שְׁנוֹת מ׳ Jb 16[22]; adv. phr. מִסְפַּר יְמֵי חַיֵּיהֶם Ec 2[3] = *during all their lives*, cf. 5[17] 6[18]; = *appointed* (normal) *number*, מ׳ יָמֶיךָ אֲמַלֵּא Ex 23[26] (E). **b.** c. prep. בְּ: בְּמ׳ מְעַט Ez 5[3] *few in number*; בְּמ׳ *by* (exact) *count, tale* 2 S 2[15] Dt 25[2] 1 Ch 9[28.28], so prob. Ez 20[37] rd. בְּמִסְפָּר 𝔊 Toy for MT מָסֹרֶת; *in* (prescribed) *number* Nu 29[18] + 6 t. Nu 29 (P), Ezr 3[4]; = *acc. to* (proportioned to) *the number of* Lv 25[15.15] + oft.; לְמִס׳ *acc. to number* Ju 21[23] Jos 4[5.8] (JE) Nu 14[29] (P) Ez 4[5] 1 Ch 27[1]; כְּמִס׳ = *id.*, 1 K 18[31] Nu 15[12.12] (P); so מ׳ alone (adv. acc.) Ex 16[16] (P) Jb 1[5] Je 2[28] 11[13].—Nu 23[10 b] rd. מִי סָפַר, cf. v[a], so 𝔊 Di So[Kau]. †**2.** *recounting, relation*, מִסְפַּר הַחֲלוֹם Ju 7[15] *the recounting of the dream*.

4558 †II. מִסְפָּר **n.pr.m.** a returned exile Ezr 2[2]
4559 (𝔊 Μαλσαρ, A 𝔊L Μασφαρ), = מִסְפֶּ֫רֶת Ne 7[7] (𝔊 Μασφεραν, א Μασφαραδ, A Μαασφαραθ, 𝔊L Μασφαρ).

4559 מִסְפֶּ֫רֶת v. foregoing.

5618 †סֹפֶ֫רֶת **n.pr.m.** in בְּנֵי־הַס׳ Ezr 2[55] a family of returned exiles (𝔊 Ασεφηραθ, A Ασεφοραθ, 𝔊L Ασωφερεθ) = בְּנֵי־ס׳ Ne 7[57] (𝔊 Σαφαραθ(ι), 𝔊L Ασοφερεθ).

5614 †[סְפָרֵד?], סְפָרַד **n.pr.loc.** Ob[20] 𝔊 Εφραθα, Q[a] Σαφαραδ; loc. dub.; Spieg[APK 242] Nö[ZMG xxxiii (1879), 323] Che[Founders 312] Say[Monuments 483] al. cp. *Sparda* in Asia Minor (= *Sardis?* Behistun[i, 15] Persep. I[12] NR[a 28]); Schr[COT ad loc. (cf. KGF 116 ff.)] Dl[Par 249], cf. GASm[12 Proph. ii. 176], cp. *Šaparda* in SW. Media (time of Sargon); a *Saparda* also NE. from Nineveh (Esarhaddon's time), cf. Knudtzon[Ass. Gebete, Nos. 8, 11, 30].

5617 †סְפַרְוַ֫יִם **n.pr.loc.** city conquered by king of Assyr.;—ס׳ 2 K 17[14] 18[34] = סְפַרְוָ֑יִם Is 36[19], עִיר סְפַרְוָיִם 2 K 19[13] = Is 37[13]; סְפַרְוָ֑יִם also 2 K 17[31 b] Qr (Kt. ספרים); 𝔊 Σεπφαρουαιν, Επφαρουαιμ, etc., 𝔊L Σεπφαρειμ;—usu. identif. with *Sippara* (on a canal), between Bagdad and Babyl., a city in two parts, *Sipp. of Šamaš* (mod. *Abbu Habba*), and *Sipp. of Anunitu(m)*, on opp. side of canal, hence du. ס׳ = *the two Sipparas*, Schr[COT 2 K 17, 24], cf. Dl[Par 209–212] Tiele[Gesch. 88]; this recently disputed, in view of mention with Hamath and other northern cities (2 K 17[24] and esp. 18[34]), v. Hal[ZA ii 401 ff] Di[Is 36, 19] Wkl[Alttest. Unters. 101] Benz[2 K 17, 24] al., who cp. *Šabara'in*, city conquered by Ṡalmanašarid IV (Wkl in Schr[KB ii. 276]); but this by no means certain.

†[סְפַרְוִי] **adj.gent.** of Sepharvaim, only 5616
pl. c. art. = subst., הַסְפַרְוִים 2 K 17[31 a].

†[סָקַל] **vb.** stone, put to death by 5619
stoning, also (**Pi.**) free from stones (appears like denom., but noun unknown; NH סְקִילָא *execution by stoning*);—**Qal** *Pf.* 2 ms. sf. וּסְקַלְתּוֹ consec. Dt 13[11]; 3 mpl. sf. וּסְקָלֻנִי consec. Ex 17[4]; 2 mpl. וּסְקַלְתֶּם consec. Dt 22[24], etc.; *Impf.* 3 mpl. יִסְקְלוּ Jos 7[25], sf. יִסְקְלֻהוּ 1 K 21[13], etc.; *Imv.* mpl. sf. סִקְלֻהוּ 1 K 21[10]; *Inf. abs.* סָקוֹל Ex 19[13] 21[28]; *cstr.* sf. סָקְלוֹ 1 S 30[6];—*pelt with stones, stone to death*, (as penalty) c. acc. pers. vel animal., Ex 8[22] 17[4] (both JE) 1 S 30[6] 1 K 21[10], abs. Ex 19[3] 21[28] (JE); c. acc. pers. + בְּ instr. בָּאֲבָנִים Dt 13[11] 17[5] 22[21.24] Jos 7[25] 1 K 21[13]. **Niph.** *Impf.* 3 ms. יִסָּקֵל *be stoned to death* Ez 19[13] 21[28.29.32] (JE). **Pi.** *Impf.* 3 ms. יְסַקֵּל 2 S 16[6.13], sf. יְסַקְּלֵהוּ Is 5[2]; *Imv.* mpl. סַקְּלוּ Is 62[10];—**1.** *stone, pelt with stones*, c. acc. pers. + בָּאֲבָנִים 2 S 16[6], acc. om. v[13] (|| עִפַּר בֶּעָפָר). **2.** *free* vineyard (acc.) *from stones* (Ges[§ 52 h]) Is 5[2]; so also 2 S 4[6], reading pt. f. מְסַקְּלָה חִטִּים ·lo, the portress *was cleansing wheat from stones* (for MT לֹקְחֵי ח׳), so We Dr Bu Kit Löhr HPS, after 𝔊; (>rdg. however mostly סֹלְקָה, **Qal** *Pt.*); סַקְּלוּ מֵאֶבֶן Is 62[10] *free* (highway) *fr. stones*. **Pu.** *Pf.* סֻקַּל *be stoned to death* 1 K 21[14.15].—Not in HP; these and other writings (exc. above) use syn. רגם, cf. Br[Hex 73].

סַר v. סרר. p. 711 5620

†[סָרָב] **n.m.** rebel? acc. to Thes al. (prob. 5621
Aram. loan-word, cf. Aram. ܣܪܒ *contradict, chatter, prattle, tell lies*; Pa. סָרֵב and NH Pi. סֵרֵב = BH; cf. סרב Ecclus 41[2d] *loving contradiction*);—pl. abs. (i.e. אִתָּךְ) סָרָבִים וְסַלּוֹנִים אוֹתָךְ Ez 2[6] *rebelles et* quasi *spinae sunt erga te* Thes; Vrss rd. ptcp., Co Berthol סֹרְבִים וְסֹלִים *resisting and despising* thee (cf. סַלּוֹן); AV RV *briers and thorns*, cf. Ew Hi-Sm Siegf[Kau] Da Toy.

†סַרְגוֹן **n.pr.m.** Sargon (As. *Šargânu*, and 5623
(prob. by pop. etymol.) *Šarrukênu* = *firm, faithful, king*, v. reff. infr.);—king of Assyria B.C. 722–705, conqueror of Samaria, father of

Sennacherib, only Is 20^{1} (𝔊 Αρνα, Aq Theod Σαραγῶ, Symm Σαργων [Q^{mg}]); Ptol^{Canon} Ἀρκεάνου (genit.); cf. Schr$^{COT\ ad\ loc.}$ Tiele$^{Gesch.\ 238\ ff.}$.

סרד (√of foll.; Thes. cp. Syr. ܣܪܕ *be frightened*).

5624 †**סֶ֫רֶד** **n.pr.m.** son of Zebulun;—Gn 46^{14} (𝔊 Σερεδ, 𝔊L Σεδεκ), Nu 26^{26} (𝔊 Σαρεδ).

5625 †**סַרְדִּי** **adj.gent.** of foregoing, only c. art. הַסּ׳ as n. coll., Nu 26^{26}.

5627 **סָרָה** v. סוּר. p. 694

953, 5626 **סִרָה** v. בּוֹר הַסִּרָה supr. p. 92 b.

5628 †[**סָרַח**] **vb. go free, be unrestrained, overrun, exceed** (NH סָרוּחַ *overhanging, flapping;* Ar. سَرَحَ of camels, etc., *pasture where they please;* also *send forth* to pasture; II. *let* a wife *go free; let down* the hair; سُرُحٌ *easy.*—NH סָרַח, Aram. ܣܪܚ usu. = *corrupt, sin*);—**Qal** *Impf.* 3 fs. תִּסְרַח Ex 26^{12}; *Pt. act.* f. סֹרַ֫חַת Ez 17^{6}; *pass.* סָרוּחַ (cf. Kö$^{ii.\ 1,\ 137}$ Ges$^{§\ 50\ f.}$ Ba$^{NB\ 180}$) Ex 26^{13}; pl. סְרוּחִים Am 6^{7}, סְרֻחִים v^{4}; cstr. סְרוּחֵי Ez 23^{15};—**1.** *go free, be unrestrained:* וּסְרֻחִים עַל־עַרְשׂוֹתָם Am 6^{4} i.e. prob. = *and are sprawling* upon their couches (in contempt. hyperbole), מִרְזַח ס׳ v^{7} *the revelry of sprawlers;* pt. act. of *overrunning, spreading* vine Ez 17^{6}. **2.** of *overhanging* stuffs (prop. *overrunning, exceeding, extended beyond limits*) תִּסְרַח עַל אֲחֹרֵי הַמִּשְׁכָּן Ex 26^{12} (P) *it shall overrun (overhang),* over the back of the tabern., so יִהְיֶה סָרוּחַ עַל־צִדֵּי הַמּ׳ v^{13}; סְרוּחֵי טְבוּלִים Ez 23^{15} *overhung of turbans,* extended with respect to turbans, = with pendant turbans (cf. [טְבוּל]). **Niph.** *Pf.* 3 fs. נִסְרְחָה חָכְמָתָם Je 49^{7} usu. *is their wisdom let loose* (i.e. *dismissed, gone*)? (‖ הַאֵין עוֹד חָכְמָה בְּתֵימָן אָבְדָה עֵצָה מִבָּנִים); but Nö$^{Expos.\ May,\ 1897,\ 363}$ *is corrupt* (cf. NH, and esp. Aram.).

5629 †**סֶ֫רַח** **n.m. excess**;—ס׳ הָעֹדֵף Ex 26^{12} (P) *the excess* (sc. of tent-covering), *which remains over.*

5630 †[**סִרְיֹן**] **n.[m.] armour** (‖form of שִׁרְיוֹן q.v.);—sf. יִתְעַל בְּסִרְיֹנוֹ Je 51^{3} *let him raise himself in his armour;* pl. לִבְשׁוּ הַסִּרְיֹנוֹת 46^{4}.

5631 **סָרִיס**$_{45}$ **n.m. eunuch** (NH *id.*, 𝔗 סָרִיסָא, Syr. ܡܣܪܣܐ (all c. vb. denom. = *emasculate*), OAram. סרסא Lzb^{331} Cook^{86}; Ar. سَرِيسٌ, سَرِسٌ (vb. سَرِسَ *be impotent*), Kam Frey (not Lane); prob. foreign word; acc. to Jen$^{ZA\ vii.\ 174}$ = As. *ša rêši (rîši), he who is the head, chief,* cf. Brock$^{Lex\ 239\ b}$ Dl$^{HWB\ 694}$ (*ša-riš*?), Zim$^{ZMG\ liii.\ 1899,\ 116}$; *eunuch* being specialized meaning; in any case Ar. is Aram. loan-word);—abs. ס׳ 1 K 22^{9} + 7 t.; cstr. סְרִיס Gn 37^{36} + 3 t.; pl. סָרִיסִים 2 K 9^{32} + 17 t.; cstr. סְרִיסֵי Gn 40^{7} + 4 t.; sf. סָרִיסָיו Gn 40^{2} + 4 t., סָרִיסֶ֫יהָ Est 4^{4};—*eunuch,* of Pharaoh Gn 37^{36} 40$^{2.7}$ (all E), married 39^{1} (R^{JE}); of Isr. kings 1 S 8^{15} (predict.), 1 K 22^{9} = 2 Ch 18^{8}, 2 K 8^{6} 9^{32} (all of N. Isr.); 1 Ch 28^{1} (in David's time), 2 K 23^{11} 24$^{12.15}$ cf. Je 29^{2}, also 34^{19} 38^{7} 41^{16} (all in Judah; so likewise) 2 K 25^{19} (military officer) = Je 52^{25}; of Bab. kings 2 K 20^{18} = Is 39^{7} (predict.); ascribed to Nebuch. in Dn, רַב סָרִיסָיו Dn 1^{3}, שַׂר הַסָּרִיסִים v$^{7.8.9.10.11.18}$; to king of Persia in Est, 1$^{10.12.15}$ + 9 t. Est; promises made to eunuchs Is 56$^{3.4}$. (Term never used in law codes; on contrary cf. exclusion of פְּצוּעַ דַּכָּא, and כְּרוּת שָׁפְכָה Dt 23^{2} [v. Dr$^{ad\ loc.}$], also מְרוֹחַ אָשֶׁךְ Lv 21^{20}.)—רַב־סָרִיס is title of high military officer 2 K 18^{17} (As.), Je 39$^{3.13}$ (Bab.).—Vid. further, Thes Smith^{DB} Art. '*Eunuch,*' Di$^{Gn\ 39,\ 1}$ Dr Dt$^{23,\ 1}$.

I. [**סֶ֫רֶן**]$_{21}$ **n.m. tyrant, lord** (Philist. loan- 5633
word);—pl. abs. הַסְּרָנִים Ju 16^{30} + 2 t.; cstr. סַרְנֵי Ju 3^{3} + 16 t.; sf. סַרְנֵיכֶם 1 S 6^{4};—only of *tyrants, lords* of the Philistines, five in no. Ju 3^{3} Jos 13^{3} (D), 1 S 6$^{16.18}$ cf. v^{4}, i.e. appar., one ruling each of the five cities (named 1 S 6^{17}); without the numeral Ju 16^{5} + 6 t. Ju 16, 1 S 5^{8} + 7 t. 1 S, + 1 Ch 12^{20} (Baer Ginsb; v^{19} van d. H.).

†II. [**סֶ֫רֶן**] **n.[m.] axle** (Aram. ܣܪܢܐ; √un- 5633
known);—סַרְנֵי נְחֹשֶׁת 1 K 7^{30} *axles of brass* (𝔊 τὰ προσέχοντα, 𝔙 *axes*).

[**סַרְעַפָּה**] v. סעף. **סרף** v. שׂרף. p. 703, 977 5634-35

†**סִרְפַּד** **n.[m.]** a desert-plant, contrasted 5636
with הֲדַס, *myrtle:* תַּחַת הַסּ׳ יַעֲלֶה הֲדַס Is 55^{13}; not clearly identif.; 𝔊 κόνυζα, 𝔖 ܙܘܢܐ, 𝔙 *urtica.*

†**סָרַר** **vb. be stubborn, rebellious** (usu. 5637
towards י׳) (NH *id.*, (rare); As. *sarâru*);—**Qal** *Pf.* 3 ms. ס׳ יִשְׂרָאֵל Ho 4^{16} *Isr. is stubborn; Pt. act.* בֵּן סוֹרֵר וּמוֹרֶה Dt 21^{18}, cf. v^{20}; בָּנִים סוֹרְרִים Is 30^{1}, עַם סוֹרֵר 65^{2}, דּוֹר ס׳ וּמֹרֶה ψ 78^{8} (all of Isr.); לֵב ס׳ וּמוֹרֶה Je 5^{23}; פָּרָה סֹרֵרָה Ho 4^{16} (sim. of Isr., v. supr.); as pred. שָׂרֵיהֶם סוֹרְרִים Ho 9^{15} cf. Is 1^{23}; סָרֵי סוֹרְרִים Je 6^{28} *revolters among the rebellious* (? cf. סור **Qal** ad

fin., and סַר infr.); of loose woman הֹמִיָּה הִיא וְסֹרָ֑רֶת Pr 7[11]; as subst. = *the stubborn*, ψ 66[7] 68[7.19]; fs. וַיִּתְּנוּ כָתֵף סֹרֶרֶת Ne 9[29] *and they presented a stubborn shoulder* (of Isr.) = Zc 7[11] (סֹרָ֑רֶת).

5620 †**סַר adj. stubborn, resentful, sullen, implacable**;—סַר וְזָעֵף 1 K 20[43] 21[4]; f. מַה־זֶּה רוּחֲךָ סָרָה v[5] why then *is thy spirit sullen?* poss. also pl. cstr. סָרֵי סוֹרְרִים Je 6[28] *revolters* (*stubborn ones*) among, etc. (v. supr. and סור **Qal** ad fin.).

5638 †**סתו** Kt, **סְתָיו** Qr **n.m. winter** (loan-wd. fr. Aram.; cf. Syr. ܣܬܘܐ, 𝔗 סִיתְוָא; Ar. شِتَاءٌ Lane[1504]; prob. orig. שׁ׳, cf. Schwally[Idiot. 64]; on ו as old nominat. ending (ס׳ for *šutayu*) cf. Lag[BN 190 Anm.]);—הַסְּתָו עָבָ֑ר Ct 2[11].

5640 †**סָתַם vb. stop up, shut up, keep close** (NH *id.*; 𝔗 סְתַם *id.*; Syr. ܣܬܡ (very rare); Ar. سَدَمَ *close* door Lane[1334], and سَطَمَ Kam Frey, are perh. loan-words);—**Qal** *Pf.* 3 ms. ס׳ 2 Ch 32[30]; *Impf.* 2 mpl. תִּסְתֹּ֫מוּ 2 K 3[19]; 3 mpl. יִסְתְּמוּ v[25], וַיִּסְתְּמוּ 2 Ch 32[4]; *Imv.* ms. סְתֹם Dn 8[26] 12[4]; *Inf. cstr.* לִסְתּוֹם 2 Ch 32[3]; *Pt. pass.* סָתוּם Ez 28[3], סָתֻם ψ 51[8], pl. סְתֻמִים Dn 12[9];—**1.** *stop up* springs of water 2 K 3[19.25] 2 Ch 32[3.4], cf. v[30]. **2.** *shut up, keep close,* prophetic words Dn 8[26] 12[4.9]; בְּסָתֻם ψ 51[8] *in* (the) *closed* (chamber of the breast; ‖ טֻחוֹת).—כָּל־סָתוּם Ez 28[3] usu. no *secret* is too dark for thee, but doubtful (v. II. עמם); 𝔊 σοφοί, Co חַרְטֻמִּים < Toy חֲכָמִים, or Berthol. קֹסְמִים. **Niph.** *Inf. cstr.* לְהִסָּתֵם Ne 4[1] the breaches [in the walls] had begun *to be stopped up.* **Pi.** *Pf.* 3 pl. sf. סִתְּמוּם Gn 26[16]; *Impf.* 3 mpl. sf. וַיְסַתְּמוּם v[18], both of *stopping* wells *quite up* (R[JE]).

5641 †**סָתַר vb. hide, conceal** (NH *id.*, der. species; 𝔗 סְתַר Pa. Ithpa., Syr. ܣܬܪ Pe. Pt. pass., chiefly Pa. Ithpa., *id.*; Ar. سَتَرَ *veil, conceal, hide,* Lane[1304]; Eth. ሰተረ: (rare) Di[364]);—**Niph.** *Pf.* 3 ms. נִסְתָּ֑ר Pr 27[12] + 22[3] Qr (Kt וְנִסְתָּר); 2 ms. נִסְתַּ֫רְתָּ 1 S 20[19]; 1 pl. נִסְתָּ֑רְנוּ Is 28[15], etc.; *Impf.* 3 ms. יִסָּתֵר Ho 13[14] +; 1 s. אֶסָּתֵר Gn 4[14] +; 3 mpl. יִסָּתְרוּ Am 9[3]; 1 pl. נִסָּתֵר Gn 31[49], etc.; *Imv.* ms. הִסָּתֵר Je 36[19]; *Inf. cstr.* לְהִסָּ֫תֶר שָׁם Jb 34[22]; *Pt.* נִסְתָּר ψ 19[7]; pl. נִסְתָּרִים Dt 7[20]; fpl. נִסְתָּרֹת Dt 29[28], ־וֹת ψ 19[13];—**1.** *hide oneself,* c. בְּ loc., 1 S 20[5.24] 1 K 17[3] Je 23[24], so (fig.) Is 28[15]; c. שָׁם 1 S 20[19] Jb 34[22]; abs. Je 36[19] Pr 22[3] 27[12] 28[28] ψ 89[47]; c. מִפְּנֵי pers. Dt 7[20] Jb 13[20], c. מִן pers. ψ 55[13]. **2.** *be hid, concealed,* esp. fig. of escaping God's notice, c. מִפְּנֵי pers. Gn 4[14] (J), מִלְּפָנַי Je 16[17], מִנֶּגֶד עֵינַי Am 9[3], מֵעֵינָ֑י Is 65[16] Ho 13[14] (subj. נֹחַם, i.e. I will not repent, change my purpose of judgment), מִן ψ 38[10] Is 40[27]; fr. heat of sun ψ 19[7] (i.e. it penetrates everywhere); fr. birds Jb 28[21] (of place of wisdom); recipr. נִס׳ אִישׁ מֵרֵעֵהוּ Gn 31[49] (J) when *we are hidden each from the other* (i.e. separated); abs. Nu 5[13] Jb 3[23] (*whose way is hid* sc. from himself), Zp 2[3] (i.e. escape י׳'s judgment); pt. *hidden, secret things,* in gen. Dt 29[28]; of sins ψ 19[13].

Pi. *Imv.* fs. סַתְּרִי Is 16[3] *carefully hide* (i.e. *shelter*) the outcasts (Moab speaks to Zion).

Pu. *Pt.* fs. אַהֲבָה מְסֻתָּ֑רֶת Pr 27[5] *love carefully concealed.*

Hithp. *Impf.* 3 fs. תִּסְתַּתָּ֑ר Is 29[14]; *Pt.* מִסְתַּתֵּר 1 S 23[19] + 3 t.;—*hide oneself carefully,* of David's taking refuge with (עִם) Ziphites 1 S 23[19] = ψ 54[2] (title), in (בְּ) a hill 1 S 26[1]; אֵל מִ׳ Is 45[15] *a God that completely hides himself.*

Hiph. *Pf.* 3 ms. הִסְתִּיר ψ 10[11] 22[25]; 2 ms. הִסְתַּ֫רְתָּ ψ 30[8] Is 64[6], etc.; *Impf.* 3 ms. יַסְתִּיר 1 S 20[2], וַיַּסְתֵּר Ex 3[6] Jb 3[10], sf. יַסְתִּרֵ֫נִי ψ 27[5], וַיַּסְתִּרֵם Je 36[26]; 3 fs. sf. וַתַּסְתִּירֵ֫הוּ 2 Ch 22[11]; 1 s. וָאַסְתִּר Ez 39[23.24], etc.; *Imv.* ms. הַסְתֵּר ψ 51[11]; *Inf. abs.* הַסְתֵּר Dt 31[18] Is 57[17]; *cstr.* הַסְתֵּר Pr 25[2] (v. Kö[i. 213] and reff.; yet cf. inf. abs. אָכֹל v[27]), לַסְתִּר Is 29[15] (Ges[§ 53 q]); *Pt.* מַסְתִּיר Is 8[17];—*conceal, hide*: **1.** a person from (מִפְּנֵי) enemy 2 K 11[2] = 2 Ch 22[11]; subj. י׳, c. מִן ψ 64[3], abs. Je 36[26]; *hide* anything from (מִן) one 1 S 20[2], a thing, in gen., Pr 25[2]; anything (fr. י׳; מִן in ‖ cl.) Is 29[15]; in gen. = *shelter* a person Jb 14[13], c. בְּ loc. (subj. י׳) ψ 17[8] 27[5] 31[21] (all metaph.); toil (עָמָל), מֵעֵינָ֑י Jb 3[10]; commands fr., מִן pers. (subj. י׳) ψ 119[19]; *hide* one as arrow in quiver Is 49[2]. **2.** esp. *hide* the face: **a.** lit., of Moses Ex 3[6] (E), usu. fig.: **b.** subj. י׳, c. מִן, i.e. be not observant of sin ψ 51[11], abs. ψ 10[11]; more oft. **c.** י׳ *hides* his face from (מִן pers.), i.e. withdraws his favour, Mi 3[4] Is 8[17] 54[8] 64[6] Dt 31[17] 32[20] Je 33[5] Ez 39[23.24.29] ψ 13[2] 22[25] 27[9] 69[18] 88[15] 102[3] 143[7]; abs. Dt 31[18] Jb 13[24] 34[29] ψ 30[8] cf. 104[29], 44[25]; פָּנִים om. Is 57[17]; cf. Is 59[2] your sins *have hidden* (his) *face* from (מִן) you; of hiding one's face from (מִן) shame, i.e. avoiding it Is 50[6] (of servant of י׳).

5643 **†סֵ֫תֶר†** **n.[m.] covering, hiding-place, secrecy**;—abs. ס׳ Ju 3^{19}+, סָ֑תֶר 2 S 12^{12} Pr 25^{23}, סָ֫תֶר ψ 139^{15}; cstr. סֵ֫תֶר 1 S 25^{20}+; sf. סִתְרוֹ ψ 18^{12} (ins. also ‖ 2 S 22^{12} 𝔊 𝔖 Th Bu HPS), סִתְרִי ψ 119^{114}; pl. סְתָרִים Pr 9^{17};—**1.** *covering, cover*, בְּס׳ הָהָר 1 S 25^{20} *under cover of the mt.*, concealed by it; of clouds as covering for י׳ (shutting out his view) Jb 22^{14}, of darkness (i.e. dark clouds) as י׳'s *hiding-place* (in theoph.) ψ 18^{12} (= 2 S 22^{12} v. supr.), so ס׳ רַ֫עַם 81^{8} *hiding-place of thunder;* of adulterer ס׳ פָּנִים יָשִׂים Jb 24^{15} i.e. disguiseth himself. **2. a.** *hiding-place*, 1 S 19^{2} Is 28^{17} ס׳ הַמַּדְרֵגָה Ct 2^{14} (in fig.; ‖ חַגְוֵי הַסֶּ֫לַע), of hippopot. Jb 40^{21}; fig. of Isr. as shelter to Moab c. מִפְּנֵי Is 16^{6}, of ideal Israelite, as ס׳ זָ֫רֶם 32^{2}, esp. of י׳ as *shelter:* ס׳ אָהֳלוֹ ψ 27^{5}, ס׳ פָּנֶיךָ 31^{21}, ס׳ כְּנָפֶיךָ 61^{5}, ס׳ עֶלְיוֹן 91^{1}, אַתָּה ס׳ לִי 32^{7} cf. 119^{114}. **b.** *secret place*, of womb ψ 139^{15} (‖ תַּחְתִּיּוֹת אָ֑רֶץ). **3.** *secrecy:* דְּבַר־ס׳ Ju 3^{19} *a matter of secrecy*, secret matter; pl. abstr. intens. לֶחֶם סְתָרִים Pr 9^{17} *bread of utter secrecy* (i.e. gained stealthily, ‖ מַיִם גְּנוּבִים); לְשׁוֹן סָ֑תֶר 25^{23} *tongue of secrecy*, i.e. slanderous; elsewhere בַּס׳ *in secrecy, secretly* Dt 13^{7} $27^{15.24}$ 28^{57} 2 S 12^{12} Je 37^{17} 38^{16} 40^{15} Is 45^{19} 48^{16} Jb 13^{10} 31^{27} Pr 21^{14} ψ 101^{5}.

†סִתְרָה† **n.f. shelter, protection,** יְהִי עֲלֵיכֶם ס׳ 5643
Dt 32^{38} (rd. perh. יהיו, cf. Dr) *let them* (the strange gods) *be over you as a shelter.*

†סְתוּר† **n.pr.m.** a spy, from Asher;— 5639
Nu 13^{13}, 𝔊 Σαθουρ, 𝔊L Θασουρ.

†סִתְרִי† **n.pr.m.** a Levite;—Ex 6^{22}, 𝔊 5644
Σεγρει, A Σεθρει, 𝔊L Σετρι.

†מִסְתּוֹר† **n.[m.] place of shelter**; abs. 4563
מִסְתּוֹר מִזֶּרֶם Is 4^{6} (fig. of י׳'s protection; cf. סֵתֶר Is 32^{2}).

†מִסְתָּר† **n.[m.] secret place, hiding-** 4565
place;—abs. מ׳ ψ 10^{9} Hb 3^{14}; usu. pl. מִסְתָּרִים Je 13^{17} + 6 t.; sf. מִסְתָּרָיו Je 49^{10};—**1.** *secret place(s)*, concealed from view, Je 13^{17}; where treasures are stored Is 45^{3}. **2.** *hiding-place(s)*: **a.** for protection Je 23^{24} 49^{10}. **b.** for perpetration of crime, esp. murder: ψ 10^{8} (‖ מַאֲרָב), sim. of lion v^9 17^{12}, cf. Hb 3^{14}; ψ 64^{5}; of י׳ lying in wait La 3^{10} (as a lion).

†מַסְתֵּר† **n.[m.] hiding, act of hiding**;— 4564
cstr. וּכְמַסְתֵּר פָּנִים מִמֶּנּוּ Is 53^{3} *and like a hiding of face from him* i.e. like one before whom the face is hidden (e.g. a leper, cf. Che[Hpt]).

ע

ע, *'Ayin*, sixteenth letter; used as numeral 70 in postB. Heb.

עבב (√ of foll., cf. Kö[ii. 1, 40]; meaning unknown).

5646 **†I. עָב, [עֹב]** **n.m.** archit. term, meaning unknown; **projecting roof** is conjectured (Sm Co Berthol); others **landing** (Da); AV RV *thick beam* or *plank*, RVm *threshold;* Benz Kit Toy leave untranslated; in any case a structure of wood;—abs. וְעַמֻּדִים וְעָב 1 K 7^{6}; appar. cstr. וְעָב עֵץ אֶל־פְּנֵי הָאוּלָם מֵהַחוּץ Ez 41^{25}; pl. (si vera l.) הָעֻבִּים v^26.

5645 II. עָב v. עוּב. p. 728

5647 **עָבַד**₂₉₀ **vb. work, serve** (OAram. עבד *do, make*, esp. Nab.Palm. (oft.), Lzb[331 f.] Cook[86], so 𝔗 עֲבַד, Syr. ܥܒܰܕ (very oft.); but also OAram. Ph. עבד *slave, vassal* (and in many n.pr.), 𝔗 עַבְדָּא, Syr. ܥܰܒܕܳܐ *id.;* As. *abdu, id.* (rare); NH עָבַד *serve, perform acts of worship* (c. acc. cogn.), and deriv.; Ar. عَبَدَ *worship, obey* (God); cf. We[Skizzen iii. 165; Heid. 141], II. *enslave;* عَبْدٌ *slave, worshipper;* Sab. עבד *id.* DHM[Südar. Alt. p. 18]; Gerber[Verb. Denom. 14 ff.] thinks *be slave, serve* (Qal) and *enslave* (Hiph.) are denom., cf. also Nö[ZMG xl (1886), 741]);—**Qal**₂₇₂ *Pf.* 3 ms. ע׳ Ez 29^{18}+; sf. עֲבָדוֹ Mal 3^{18}+; 3 mpl. עָבְדוּ Dt 7^{4}; עָבָ֑דוּ Nu 4^{26}, +64 t. Pf.; *Impf.* 3 ms. יַעֲבֹד Gn 25^{23}+; sf. יַעַבְדֵ֫נִי Ex 4^{23}; יַעַבְדֶ֫נּוּ ψ 22^{31} 2 K 10^{18}; 3 mpl. יַעַבְדוּ Dt 12^{30}+; יַעֲבֹ֑דוּ Gn 15^{14} (Dr[§ 103]) Jb 36^{11}; 2 mpl. תַּעַבְדוּן Ex 3^{12}, תַּעֲבֹ֑דוּן Jos 24^{15}, +99 t. Impf.; (נָעָבְדֵם, תָּעָבְדֵם v. **Hoph.**); *Imv.* עֲבֹד 1 S 26^{19}; sf. עָבְדֵהוּ 1 Ch 28^{9}; עִבְדוּ Ex 5^{18} + 15 t.; עֲבֹ֑דוּ Ez 20^{39}; sf. עִבְדֻהוּ 1 S 7^{3}; *Inf. cstr.* עֲבֹד Mal 3^{14}+; עֲבָד־ Je $34^{9.10}$; sf. עָבְדוֹ Je 27^{6}+, etc.; *Pt.* עֹבֵד Gn 4^{2}+; pl. עֹבְדִים Nu 18^{21}+; cstr. עֹבְדֵי ψ 97^{7}+; sf. עֹבְדָיו 2 K 10^{19}; עֹבְדֵיהֶם Zc 2^{13};

—†**1.** *labour, work, do work:* abs. Ex 20^{9}=34^{21}=Dt 5^{13} (4th word); Ex 5^{18} (E) Ec 5^{11}; c. acc. rei, *till* the ground Gn 2^{5} 3^{23} 4$^{2.12}$ (J), 2 S 9^{10} Is 30^{24} Je 27^{11} Zc 13^{5} Pr 12^{11} 28^{19}; obj. om. Dt 15^{19} Ez 48^{19}; vineyard Dt 28^{39}; garden Gn 2^{15} (J); עֹבְדֵי פִשְׁתִּים Is 19^{9} *workers in flax;* עֹבֵד(י) הָעִיר Ez 48$^{18.19}$ *labourers of the city;* ע׳ עֲבֹדָתוֹ Is 28^{21} *work his work* (only here of God, ‖ עשׂה מַעֲשֵׂהוּ); ע׳ עבדה על Ez 29^{18} *serve a military service against.* †**2.** *work for another, serve him by labour:* abs. Ex 21^{2} (E); c. acc. pers. Gn 29^{15} 31^{6} Ex 21^{6} (E) Dt 15$^{12.18}$ Mal 3^{17} Je 34^{14}, king his people 1 K 12^{7}; subj. animals Je 27^{6} Jb 39^{9}; c. acc. pers. et rei Gn 30$^{26.26.29}$ (J); c. לְ pers. 2 S 16^{19}; עִם Gn 29$^{25.30}$ (E) Lv 25^{40} (P); עִמָּדִי Gn 29^{27} (E); לִפְנֵי 2 S 16$^{19.19}$; c. בְּ of price Gn 29$^{18.20.25}$ 31^{41} (E) Ho 12^{13} Ez 29^{20}; c. בְּ pers. *work by means of another, use him as slave,* Ex 1^{14} Lv 25$^{39.46}$ (P) Je 22^{13} 34$^{9.10}$. **3.** *serve as subjects:* usu. c. acc., their own chiefs or kings Ju 9$^{28.28.38}$ 1 S 11^{1} 1 K 5^{1}+; other kings, by tribute ψ 18^{44}=2 S 22^{44}, Je 27^{7} 28^{14} 2 K 25^{24}+, other nations 2 S 10^{19} Je 40^{9} Zc 2^{13}+, kings other kings 2 K 18^{7}+, c. לְ, 1 S 4$^{9.9}$; †מַס עֹבֵד Gn 49^{15} (J) Jos 16^{10} 1 K 9^{21} (see מַס); †c. בְּ pers., *work with,* i.e. use as subjects, impose tribute upon, Je 25^{14} 27^{7} 30^{8} Ez 34^{27}. **4.** *serve* God: **a.** c. acc. י׳, Ex 3^{12} 4^{23} 7$^{16.26}$ (JE), ψ 22^{31} Jb 21^{15} Mal 3^{14}+; c. acc. pers. et rei Ex 10^{26} (E); acc. pers. om., Je 2^{20} (rd. אֶעֱבוֹד Kt), עבד זבח ומנחה Is 19^{21} *serve with peace-offering and grain-offering;* עבד עֲבֹדָה Ex 13^{5} (of מַצֹּת). **b.** other gods, c. acc. א׳ †Dt 7^{16} 12$^{2.30}$+; אלהים אחרים 7^{4} 8^{19} 11^{16} 13$^{7.14}$ 17^{3} 28$^{14.36.64}$ 29^{25} 30^{17} 31^{20} Jos 23^{16} 24$^{2.16}$ Ju 2^{19} 10^{13} 1 S 8^{8} 26^{19} 1 K 9$^{6.9}$ 2 K 17^{35} 2 Ch 7$^{19.22}$ Je 11^{10} 13^{10} 16$^{11.13}$ 22^{9} 25^{6} 35^{15} (all D and Je); אֱלֹהֵי הַגּוֹיִם Dt 29^{17}; זָרִים Je 5^{19}; †כל צבא השׁמים Dt 4^{19} 2 K 21^{3} 2 Ch 33^{3} Je 8^{2}; †הבעל(ים) Ju 2^{11} 3^{7} 10$^{6.10}$ 1 S 12^{10} 1 K 16^{31} 22^{54} 2 K 10$^{18.18.19.19.[illegible]}$ 17^{16}; †אלהי נֵכָר Jos 24^{20} Je 5^{19}; †(הַ)גִּלּוּלִים 2 K 17^{12} 21$^{21.21}$ Ez 20^{39}; †האשׁרים 2 Ch 24^{18}; עצבים ψ 106^{36}; †פסיל(ים) 2 Ch 33^{22} 2 K 17^{41}; פסל ψ 97^{7}; c. לְ, †לבעל Ju 2^{13}; †לאלהים אחרים Je 44^{3}. **5.** *serve* י׳ *with Levitical service* (all P; cf. RS$^{Sem\ i.\ 69}$): c. acc. עבד עֲבֹדָה (v. עֲבֹדָה) Nu 3$^{7.8}$ 4$^{23.30.47}$ 7^{5} 8$^{11.19.22.26}$ 16^{9} 18$^{6.21.23}$ Jos 22^{27}; acc. om. Nu 4$^{24.26.37.41}$ 8^{15} (but Sam 𝔊 עבדה), v^{25} 18^{7}.

†**Niph.** *Pf.* 3 ms. נֶעֱבַד Ec 5^{8}; 2 mpl. נֶעֱבַדְתֶּם Ez 36^{9}; *Impf.* 3 ms. יֵעָבֵד Dt 21^{4}; 3 fs. תֵּעָבֵד Ez 36^{34};—**1.** *be tilled,* of land Dt 21^{4} Ez 36$^{9.34}$. **2.** Ec 5^{8} מֶלֶךְ לְשָׂדֶה נֶעְבָּד dub.: a king for (devoted to) the *cultivated* field (Hi); a king *that maketh himself servant* to the field (devoted to agriculture), De: v. Comm., esp. De.

†**Pual** *Pf.* 3 ms. עֻבַּד Dt 21^{3} Is 14^{3}; pass. of **Qal**, c. בְּ: impers. Dt 21^{3} of a calf with which *it has not been worked;* hard *service* with which it *was worked with captives* Is 14^{3}.

†**Hiph.** *Pf.* 3 ms. הֶעֱבִיד Ez 29^{18}; 2 ms. sf. הֶעֱבַדְתַּנִי Is 43^{24}, הֶעֱבַדְתִּיךָ v^{23}, וְהַעֲבַדְתִּיךָ Je 17^{4}; *Impf.* 3 ms. וַיַּעֲבֵד 2 Ch 34^{33}; 3 mpl. יַעֲבִדוּ Ex 1^{13}; *Inf. cstr.* הַעֲבִיד 2 Ch 2^{17}; *Pt.* pl. מַעֲבִדִים Ex 6^{5};—**1.** *compel to labour* as slaves Ex 1^{13} 6^{5} (P) 2 Ch 2^{17}, +Gn 47^{21} (reading הֶעֱבִיד לַעֲבָדִים), 2 S 12^{31} (reading וְהֶעֱבִיד, + בְּ *at;* on both these v. עבר **Hiph.** ad fin.); *cause to serve,* of army's service against, c. acc. + אל (על) Ez 29^{18}; *cause to labour, weary,* c. בְּ of means Is 43$^{23.24}$ (perh. play on meanings **2, 3**). **2.** *make to serve as subjects,* c. 2 acc. Je 17^{4}, +Je 15^{14} (rd. וְהַעֲבַרְתִּיךָ, v. עבר **Hiph.** ad fin.). **3.** *cause to serve* God 2 Ch 34^{33}.

Hoph. *Impf.* 2 ms. sf. תָּעָבְדֵם Ex 20^{5}=Dt 5^{9}, Ex 23^{24}; 1 pl. sf. נָעָבְדֵם Dt 13^{3} (Kö$^{i.259}$ Sta^{§549g} Thes; < Nes$^{Marg.\ 12f.}$ Qal anom. pointed (cf. W$^{AG.\ ed.\ 2,\ i.\ 62\ n.}$ Fl$^{Kl.\ Schr.\ i.\ 98}$); Ges$^{§60,\ R.1}$ Dr Qal falsely pointed as Hoph.);—*be led* or *enticed to serve* other gods Ex 20^{5}=Dt 5^{9} Ex 23^{24} Dt 13^{3}.

I. עֶ֫בֶד $_{799}$ **n.m.** slave, servant (on format. 5650
Lag$^{BN\ 77}$);—ע׳ Gn 9^{25}+, עָ֑בֶד 44^{10}+; sf. עַבְדִּי 26^{24}+; עַבְדְּךָ 19^{19}+; עַבְדֶּ֫ךָ 18^{3}+; pl. עֲבָדִים 9^{25}+, עֲבָדֵי 21^{25}+; sf. עֲבָדַי Lv 25^{42}+, עַבְדֵיכֶם Jos 9^{11}+, etc.;—**1.** *slave, servant* of household Gn 39$^{17.19}$ 41^{12} 50^{2} Ex 21^{2}+; *man-servant,* ‖ אמה Ex 20^{10} Lv 25^{6} Dt 5^{14} Jb 31^{13}+; ‖ שׁפחה Gn 12^{16} 32^{6} Je 34^{11} Is 14^{2}+; + אדון Dt 23^{16} Is 24^{2} Mal 1^{6}+; מִקְנַת כֶּסֶף Ex 12^{44} or יְלִיד בַּיִת Je 2^{14}; עֶבֶד עֲבָדִים *servant of servants, humblest servant,* Gn 9^{25}; †בֵּית עֲבָדִים *house of slaves,* esp. Israel in Egypt Ex 13$^{3.14}$ (D?) Dt 5^{6} 6^{12} 7^{8} 8^{14} 13$^{6.11}$ Jos 24^{17} Ju 6^{8} Je 34^{13} Mi 6^{4}, ‖ וזכרת כי עבד היית ב(ארץ) מצרים *and thou shalt remember that thou wast a slave in* (the land of) *Egypt* Dt 5^{15} 15^{15} 16^{12} 24$^{18.22}$; king of Babylon is slave to י׳ Je 25^{9} 27^{6} 43^{10}; the borrower to the lender Pr 22^{7}; fig. of beast Jb 40^{28}; of things Gn 47^{19}.

2. *Subjects,* of chief Gn 26$^{15.19.25.32}$ 27^{37} 32$^{17.17}$+; of king 21^{25} Ex 7$^{28.29}$ 1 K 9^{27} Dt 29^{1}+; vassal kings 2 S 10^{19}; tributary nations 8$^{2.6.14}$=1 Ch 18$^{2.6.13}$; specif. officers of king 1 S 19^{1} 21^{8} 2 S 11^{13} Pr 14^{35}+; עַבְדֵי פַרְעֹה Gn 40^{20} 41^{10}; ע׳ שָׁאוּל 1 S 16^{17} 18^{22} 28^{7}; ע׳ הַמֶּלֶךְ 1 K 1^{47} Est

3[3] +; עֶבֶד הַמֶּלֶךְ 2 K 22[12] = 2 Ch 34[20] (a court official); opp. שַׂר Pr 19[10] Ec 10[7]; מֶלֶךְ Pr 30[22]; ambassadors Nu 22[18] 2 S 10[2]; soldiers of army 1 S 17[8] 25[10] 2 S 2[12], + officers of army 1 S 29[3] 1 K 11[26] 2 K 25[8] Is 36[9].

3. *Servants, worshippers,* of God: †עַבְדֵי יהוה 2 K 9[7] 10[23] Is 54[17], cf. Gn 50[17] Is 56[6]; עֲבָדָיו Dt 32[36] = ψ 135[14], Is 65[15] 66[14] ψ 34[23] 69[37] Ne 2[20]; ‖ עַמּוֹ ψ 105[25] cf. Dt 32[43]; עֲבָדַי Is 65[8.9.13.13.13.14]; עֲבָדֶיךָ 1 K 8[23] Is 63[17] (‖ שִׁבְטֵי נחלתך), ψ 89[51] 90[13.16] 102[15.29] 119[91], 79[2.10] (‖ חֲסִידֶיךָ); delivered from Egypt Lv 25[42.55.55] 26[13] (P); עַבְדְּךָ ψ 119[125] 143[2], ‖ בֶּן־אֲמָתֶךָ 86[16] 116[16.16]; specif. angels Jb 4[18]; and ancient worthies, patriarchs Ex 32[13] (J) Dt 9[27]; Abraham Gn 26[24] (J) ψ 105[6.42]; Isaac Gn 24[14] (J); Jacob, Israel Ez 28[25] 37[25] 1 Ch 16[13]; Moses †Ex 14[31] Jos 18[7] (J) Nu 12[7.8] (E) Dt 34[5] (?) Jos 1[1.2.7.13.15] 8[31.33] 9[24] 11[12.15] 12[6.6] 13[8] 14[7] 22[2.4.5] (all D), 1 K 8[53.56] 2 K 18[12] 21[8] 1 Ch 6[34] 2 Ch 1[3] 24[6.9] Ne 1[8] 9[14] 10[30] ψ 105[26] Mal 3[22] Dn 9[11]; Joshua † Jos 24[29] (E) Ju 2[8]; Caleb † Nu 14[24] (J); Job † Jb 1[8] 2[3] 42[7.8.8.8]; David 2 S 3[18] 7[5.8.26] + 27 t.; Hezekiah † 2 Ch 32[16]; Zerubbabel † Hag 2[23]; Eliakim † Is 22[20].—The צֶמַח Zc 3[8] cf. 6[12] is also servant of י׳ as Messianic builder of temple (see Br[MP 442 ff.]).

†**4.** *Servant* of י׳, in a special sense: of Levitical singers using benedictions in temple ψ 113[1] 134[1] 135[1]; usu. of prophets, עֲבָדַי הַנְּבִיאִים *my servants the prophets* 2 K 9[7] 17[13] Je 7[25] 26[5] 29[19] 35[15] 44[4] Ez 38[17] Zc 1[6]; עֲבָדָיו הַנְּבִיאִים 2 K 17[23] 21[10] 24[2] Je 25[4] Am 3[7] Dn 9[10]; עֲבָדֶיךָ הנביאים Ezr 9[11] Dn 9[6]; specif. Ahia 1 K 14[18] 15[29]; Elijah 2 K 9[36] 10[10]; Jonah 2 K 14[25]; Isaiah Is 20[3]; עַבְדּוֹ, ‖ מלאכיו 44[26]; as one calling to fear י׳ 50[10].

†**5.** Israel as a people is *servant* of י׳: יִשְׂרָאֵל Is 41[8.9] 44[21.21] 49[3] ψ 136[22]; יעקב Is 44[1.2] 45[4] 48[20] Je 30[10] 46[27.28]; עֶבֶד יהוה = עַבְדִּי ‖ מַלְאָכִי, as having a mission to the nations Is 42[19.19]; and chosen as witness of י׳ 43[10]. But there is also an ideal servant chosen and endowed with the divine Spirit to be a covenant of Israel and a light of the nations Is 42[1] (cf. v[2–6]); formed to bring back Jacob, raise up the tribes, and become salvation to the end of the earth 49[5.6.7]; bearing the sins of all as a lamb and a trespass-offering, and yet prospering and justifying many as interposing martyr 52[13] 53[11]: many understand of ideal Israel, contr. with the actual; al. of personif. ‖ with Zion the wife and mother, disting. from unworthy Israel as Zion from her apostate children; al. of ideal prophetic writer; al. of ideal prophetic person; al. (esp. in Is 53) of an actual proph. known to writer and his readers; [in any case it is Messianic, v. Mt 8[16.17] 12[16–21] Lk 4[17–22] Phil 2[5–11]]; see De[Is ii. 174] Da[Expos. 1884, 358 ff.] Di Du Che al. on Is 42, 53, Dr[Is 168 ff.] Br[MP 345 ff.], also Gie[Beitr. 146 ff.] Berthol[Is 53].

6. In polite address of equals or superiors the Hebrews used עַבְדְּךָ *thy servant* = 1 pers. sing., *I*, Gn 18[3] 1 S 20[7.8.8] 2 K 8[13] +; עֲבָדֶיךָ *thy servants* = *we* Gn 42[11] Is 36[11]; also עַבְדּוֹ *his servant* = *I*, 1 S 26[18.19] 2 S 14[22] 24[21] +; also in addressing God, esp. in prayer Ex 4[10] Nu 11[11] Ju 15[18] 1 S 3[9.10] 25[39] 2 S 24[10] ψ 19[12.14] 27[9] 31[17] 35[27] 69[18] 109[28] 143[2] +.

7. Phrases are: †עבד (היה), c. לְ pers., *become servant to* Gn 9[26.27] 44[10.16.17.33] 47[19.25] (J) Dt 6[21] 15[17] 2 S 8[14] 2 K 17[3] 24[1] 1 Ch 18[2.6.13] 2 Ch 10[7] Pr 11[29] 12[9] 22[7]; †היה לעבד, c. לְ pers., Gn 44[9] (J) 50[18] (E) 1 S 8[17] 17[9.9] 27[12] 2 S 8[2.6] Je 34[16]; †כבשׁ לעבדים 2 Ch 28[10] Ne 5[5] Je 34[11]; לקח לעי׳ Gn 43[18] (J) 2 K 4[1] Jb 40[28].

†II. עֶ֫בֶד **n.pr.m.** (*servant* of God = עַבְדְּאֵל); 5651
—**1.** father of Gaal Ju 9[26.28.30.31.35] (GFM, after Hollenb[ThLz 1891, 371] [cf. Bu[Ib. 1892, 63]] עֶבֶד, as 𝔊L; v. also Gray[Prop. N. 184, 272]); 𝔊 Ιωβηλ, A 𝔊L Αβεδ. **2.** a companion of Ezra Ezr 8[6]; 𝔊 Ωβηθ, 𝔊L Αμιναδαβ. — For list of Ar. names beginning with عبد v. Nö[ZMG xli (1887), 724 ff.], cf. also Id[ib. xlii (1888), 486] We[Heid. 2, 2 ff.]

†[עֲבַד] **n.m.** **work** (late; Aram. form); 5652
pl. sf. עֲבָדֵיהֶם Ec 9[1] (cf. Syr. ܥܒܕ).

†עוֹבֵד, עֹבֵד **n.pr.m.** (*worshipper*; cf. Sab. 5744
עבד Os[22] and DHM[ZMG xxxvii (1883), 14];—**1.** son of Boaz and Ruth Ru 4[17], v[21] = 1 Ch 2[12], Ru 4[22] (only here עֹבֵד) = 1 Ch 2[12], 𝔊 Ωβηδ. **2.** names in Judah, 𝔊 Ωβηδ: **a.** 1 Ch 2[37.38]. **b.** 2 Ch 23[1]. **3.** a mighty man of David 1 Ch 11[47], 𝔊 Ιωβηθ, A Ιωβηδ. **4.** a doorkeeper 1 Ch 26[7], 𝔊 Ωβηδ.

†עֹבֵד אֱדֹם, and (2 Ch 25[24]) ע׳ אֱדוֹם **n.pr.m.** 5654
(*servant of* (god) *Edom*, cf. עבד אדם CIS[No. 295]; Dr[Sm 206, 293] and reff., RS[Sem i. 43; 2nd ed. 42] and reff., HPS[286, 10]; but Bae[Rel 10] *servant of man*, אֱדֹם = אָדָם, which is thought possible by Nö[ZMG xlii (1888), 470] Buhl[Edomiter 49]);—**1.** the Gittite who harboured the ark 2 S 6[10.11.11.12.12] = 1 Ch 13[13.14.14], 1 Ch 15[25]; 𝔊 Αβεδδαρα, 𝔊L Αβεδδαδαν. **2.** (= **1**?) one of the chief Levitical singers and doorkeepers 1 Ch 15[18.21.24] 16[5.38.38] 26[4.8.8.15]; 𝔊 Αβαεδωμ, Αβδεδωμ, etc., 𝔊L Αβεδδομ. **3.** the family of the same 2 Ch 25[24] (not in ‖ 2 K 14[14]).

5663 †עֶ֫בֶד מֶ֫לֶךְ **n.pr.m.** (=*servant of the king*, or < *of* (god) *Melek*, cf. Gray$^{Prop. N. 117, 147 ff.}$);—Eth. official of Zedekiah Je 38$^{7.8.10.11.12}$ 39^{16}; 𝔊 Αβδεμελεχ.

5664 †עֲבֵד נְגוֹ **n.pr.m.** (*servant of* (God) *Nebo*, נְגוֹ being corrupt (intent. or unintent.) for נבו (q.v.), COT$^{Dn 1,7}$ Bev$^{Dn 1,7}$);—Babylonian name of Azariah, one of the three companions of Daniel Dn 1^{7} (v. also BAram); 𝔊 Theod Αβδεναγω.

5653 †עַבְדָּא **n.pr.m.** (*servant of* י׳ (= עֹבַדְיָה 1 Ch 9^{16} = Ne 11^{17}), but form dub., v. 𝔊);—**1.** father of Adoniram 1 K 4^{6}; 𝔊 Εφρα, A Αβαω, 𝔊L Εδραμ. **2.** a Levite Ne 11^{17}; 𝔊 Ωβηβ, A Ιωβηβ, 𝔊L Αβδιας.

5655 †עַבְדְּאֵל **n.pr.m.** (*servant of Ēl*, cf. עַבְדִּיאֵל) name in Judah Je 36^{26}; 𝔊 Εσ(δ)ριηλ.

5656 †עֲבֹדָה, and (Chr) עֲבוֹדָה n.f. **labour, service** (on format. v. Lag$^{BN 179}$ Ba$^{NB 61}$);—ע׳ Ex 1^{14} + 41 t.; cstr. עֲבֹדַת 30^{16} + 43 t.; sf. עֲבֹדָתִי Gn 30^{26} + 33 t. sfs.; in Chr עֲבוֹדָה 1 Ch 28^{14} + 7 t.; cstr. עֲבוֹדַת 6^{33} + 13 t.; sf. עֲבוֹדָתִי 2 Ch 12^{8}; עֲבוֹדָתָם 1 Ch 6^{17} 2 Ch 31^{16};—**1.** †*labour, work*, ψ 104^{23}; in the field Ex 1^{14} 1 Ch 27^{26}, prob. Ne 10^{38} (ע׳ עָרֵי), ψ 104^{14} (עֵשֶׂב לע׳); in fine linen 1 Ch 4^{21}; in erection of tabernacle Ex 35^{24} 36$^{1.3.5}$ 39^{42} (P); in repairing temple 2 Ch 34$^{13.13}$; כל מלאכת עבדה לא תעשׂוּ *ye shall do no laborious work* Lv 23$^{7.8.21.25.35.36}$ Nu 28$^{18.25.26}$ 29$^{1.12.35}$ (P); fig. of man, ע׳ הַצְּדָקָה Is 32^{17} (|| מַעֲשֵׂה הַצּ׳); of God's work of judgment Is 28$^{21.21}$. †**2.** *labour of servant or slave:* of Jacob for Laban Gn 29^{27} 30^{26} (JE); ע׳ עֶבֶד of bondservant Lv 25^{39} (P); of the Nethinim Ezr 8^{20}; *service* of things, vessels of tabernacle and temple Nu 4$^{26.32}$ (P) 1 Ch 9^{28} 28$^{14.14.15}$. †**3.** *labour, service of captives or subjects:* of Israel in Egypt Ex 1^{14} 2$^{23.23}$ (P), 5^{11} (E), 6^{6} (P); כבד(ה) הע׳ 5^{9} (E) Ne 5^{18}; ע׳ קשׁה Ex 1^{14} 6^{9} (P) Dt 26^{6} 1 K 12^{4} = 2 Ch 10^{4}, Is 14^{3}; מֵרֹב ע׳ La 1^{3}; ע׳ ממלכות 2 Ch 12^{8}; ע׳ המלך 1 Ch 26^{30}; ע׳ אדניהם Ne 3^{5}; military service Ez 29$^{18.18}$. **4.** *service* of God, in P Chr Ez: by people Jos 22^{27} (P) 2 Ch 12^{8}, feast of passover Ex 12$^{25.26}$ 2 Ch 35$^{10.16}$, unleavened bread Ex 13^{5}; Levites and priests Nu 4$^{19.49}$ 8^{11} 1 Ch 24$^{3.19}$ 2 Ch 8^{14} 31^{16}; ע׳ מתנה Nu 18^{7}; Levites Ex 38^{21} Nu 4$^{24.27.27.28.33.47.47}$ 7$^{7.8}$ 8^{26} 18^{21} 1 Ch 6^{17} 2 Ch 31^{2}; c. בְּאֹהֶל מוֹעֵד v$^{4.23.31.33.35.39.43}$ 8$^{19.22}$ 18^{31}; אֹהֶל מוֹעֵד Ex 30^{16} Nu 4^{30} 7^{5} 8^{24} 18$^{4.6.21.23}$, cf. Ex 35^{21} Nu 7^{5}; (ה)מִּשְׁכָּן Ex 39$^{32.40}$ Nu 3$^{7.8}$ 16^{9} 1 Ch 6^{33}, cf. Ex 27^{19} Nu 3^{36} 1 Ch 23^{26}; ע׳ חַקֹּדֶשׁ Nu 7^{9}, cf. 3^{31}, of its court v^{26}; more specif. ע׳ משׂא 4^{47}; צבא הע׳ 8^{25}; ע׳ בית י׳ (ה)אלהים 1 Ch 23$^{24.28.32}$ 25^{6} 28$^{13.13.21.21}$ 29^{7} 2 Ch 29^{35} 31^{21} 35^{2} Ne 10^{33}; מלאכת ע׳ בית האלהים 1 Ch 9^{13} 28^{20} 2 Ch 24^{12}; מעשׂה ע׳ 1 Ch 23^{28}; its service Ez 44^{14} 1 Ch 9^{19}; specif. service of Levit. singers 25$^{1.1}$, and doorkeepers 26^{8} 2 Ch 35^{15}.

†עֲבֻדָּה **n.f. service** (on format. v. Lag 5657
$^{BN 151}$);—of household servants as a body, || cattle, etc., Gn 26^{14} (J) Jb 1^{3}.

†עַבְדּוֹן **n.pr.** I. **n.pr.m.** **1.** a judge Ju 5658
12$^{13.15}$, 𝔊 Αβδων, A 𝔊L Λαβδω(μ); (Ew cp. בְּדָן 1 S 12^{11}, but read בָּרָק, v. בְּדָן supr.). **2.** a Benjamite 1 Ch 8^{23}, 𝔊 Αβαδων, A 𝔊L Αβδων. **3.** son of Jehiel a Gibeonite 1 Ch 8^{30} 9^{36}; 𝔊 Αβαλων, Σαβαδων, A Αβδων, Σαβδων, 𝔊L Αβδων. **4.** son of Micah 2 Ch 34^{20}, 𝔊 Αβδοδομ, A 𝔊L Αβδων (= עַכְבּוֹר 2 K 22^{12}). II. **n.pr.loc.** Levitical city in Asher Jos 21^{30} 1 Ch 6^{59}, 𝔊 Δαββων, Αβαραν, A 𝔊L Αβδων (20 Codd. rd. עַבְדֹּן Jos 19^{28} for עֶבְרֹן), *ʿAbde*, Guérin$^{Gal 2, 37}$ cf. Buhl$^{Geogr. 230}$. 5683

†[עַבְדוּת] **n.f. servitude, bondage**;—sf. 5659
עַבְדֻתֵנוּ Ez 9$^{8.9}$; עַבְדֻתָם Ne 9^{17} (cf. Syr. ܥܒܕܘܬܐ).

†עַבְדִּי **n.pr.m.** (= עֹבַדְיָה *servant of Yah;* 5660
v. however, Gray$^{Prop. N. 149 ff.}$ and cf. OAram. עבדו, Nab. Palm. עבדי Lzb$^{333, 334}$ Cook^{87});—**1.** a Levite 1 Ch 6^{29} 2 Ch 29^{12}; 𝔊 Αβδ(ε)ι, 𝔊L 1 Ch Αβδια. **2.** one with a foreign wife Ezr 10^{26}; 𝔊 Αβδε(ι)α.

†עַבְדִּיאֵל **n.pr.m.** (*servant of Ēl;* on this 5661
and foll. cf. Ph. עבדאלם, Nab. עבדאלהא, Sin. עבדאלהי, etc., Lzb^{332} Cook^{87}; Sab. עבדלת = [עבדאלת] Hal^{168} DHM$^{ZMG xxxvii (1883), 16}$; v. also Gray$^{Prop. N. 309, No. 53}$);—a Gadite 1 Ch 5^{15}; 𝔊 Αβδεηλ, A 𝔊L Αβδιηλ.

†עֹבַדְיָה, עֹבַדְיָ֫הוּ **n.pr.m.** (*servant of* 5662
Yah, cf. Gray$^{Prop. N. 295, No. 90}$; also Ph. עבדבעל, Palm. עבדבל, OAram. עבדההד Lzb^{333}, OHeb. עבדיהו Id.^{334});—I. עֹבַדְיָ֫הוּ: **1.** chief of Ahab's household 1 K 18$^{3.3.4.5.6.7.16}$, 𝔊 Αβδ(ε)ιου. **2.** father of one of the chiefs of Zebulun 1 Ch 27^{19}, 𝔊 Αβδ(ε)ιου (genit.). **3.** a Levite overseer in time of Josiah 2 Ch 34^{12}, 𝔊 Αβδ(ε)ια, A 𝔊L Αβδιας. II. עֹבַדְיָה: **1.** the prophet Ob^{1}, 𝔊 Οβδ(ε)ιου (genit.), Αβδ(ε)ιου. **2.** a descendant of David 1 Ch 3^{21}, 𝔊 Αβδεια, 𝔊L Οβδιας. **3.** chief of tribe of Issachar 1 Ch 7^{3}, 𝔊 Μειβδεια, A Οβδια, 𝔊L Αβδια. **4.** a Benjamite 1 Ch

8[38] 9[44], 𝔊 Αβδ(ε)ια. **5.** a Levite 1 Ch 9[16] (‖ עַבְדָּא Ne 11[17]), 𝔊 Αβδεια, A Οβδια, 𝔊L Αβια. **6.** a Gadite chief 1 Ch 12[9], 𝔊 Αβδ(ε)ια. **7.** a prince in time of Jehoshaphat 2 Ch 17[7], 𝔊 Αβ(δ)ιαν. **8.** priestly companion of Ezra Ezr 8[9] Ne 10[6], 𝔊 Αδεια, Αβ(α)δ(ε)ια, 𝔊L Αβδιου, Αβιας. **9.** a doorkeeper Ne 12[25], א Οβδιας, 𝔊L Αβδιας.

4566 †[מַעְבָּד] **n.[m.]** work (late form; BAram. מַעֲבַד);—pl. sf. מַעְבָּדֵיהֶם Jb 34[25].

5666 †עָבָה **vb.** be thick, fat, gross (NH Pi. עִבָּה *make thick*, and deriv.; Syr. ܥܒܐ *swell up*, pt. pass. *swollen, thick, dense, stupid*, and many deriv.; Ar. غَبِيَ *be dense, stupid*, أَغْبَى *dense foliage;* Eth. ዐቢየ: *be great* Di[985]);—**Qal** *Pf.* 3 ms. קָטָנִּי ע׳ מִמָּתְנֵי אָבִי 1 K 12[10] *my little finger is thicker* (stouter) than, etc., = 2 Ch 10[10]; *be thick, gross*, of rebell. Isr. under fig. of highly fed beast, 2 ms. שָׁמַנְתָּ עָבִיתָ כָּשִׂיתָ Dt 32[15].

5672 †עֲבִי **n.[m.]** thickness;—cstr. ע׳ גַּבֵּי מָגִנָּיו Jb 15[26] *the thickness* (stoutness) *of the bosses* of his shields (in fig.); sf. עָבְיוֹ *its thickness*, of the molten sea 1 K 7[26] = 2 Ch 4[5]; of pillar Je 52[21].—2 Ch 4[17] v. foll.—Under עבה belongs perh.
5645 also בְּעַב הֶעָנָן Ex 19[9] (rd. בַּעֲבִי ?) in *the thickness* of the clouds, cf. Bu[Th Lz 1892 (3), 63] Kö[ii. 1, 86].

4568 †מַעֲבֶה **n.[m.]** si vera l., thickness, compactness;— בְּמַעֲבֵה הָאֲדָמָה 1 K 7[46] *in the compactness of the soil*, i.e. *clayey ground* or *clay mould* = 2 Ch 4[17] (where MT בַּעֲבִי הָ׳); but read doubtless in both בְּמַעְבֶּרֶת אֲדָמָה *at the ford of Adamah*, v. GFM[Ju 7, 22] Benz[K].

5688 עֲבֹות v. עבת. p. 721

עבט (perh. √ of foll.; cf. As. *ubbuṭu'* (II. of אבט [= עבט?]) *be pledged* Dl[HWB 6]; Aram. (Talm.) עֲבִיטָה *pledge*, עֲבַט Ithpe. *be taken in pledge;* but We[Jo 2, 7] thinks עֲבוֹט Aram. loanword, and cp. Ar. ضَبَطَ *hold, keep, guard*).

5667 †עֲבוֹט **n.[m.]** pledge, article pledged as security for debt;—abs. ע׳ Dt 24[11.13]; sf. עֲבֹטוֹ v[10] (as acc. cogn.), v[12].

5671 †עַבְטִיט **n.[m.]** **intens.** weight of pledges, heavy debts;—abs. מַכְבִּיד עָלָיו ע׳ Hb 2[6].

5670 †[עָבַט] **vb. denom.** take or give a pledge;—**Qal** *Inf. cstr.* לַעֲבֹט Dt 24[10] *to take possession of a thing pledged* (c. acc. cogn.); *Impf.* 2 ms. *give a pledge* תַּעֲבֹט Dt 15[6] (i.e. *borrow*). **Hiph.** *Pf.* 2 ms. וְהַעֲבַטְתָּ גּוֹיִם רַבִּים v[6] *and thou shalt cause many nations to give pledges* (i.e. lend to them); *Impf.* 3 ms. sf. + *Inf. abs.* הַעֲבֵט תַּעֲבִיטֶנּוּ v[8] *thou shalt surely lend to him* (lit. as above). **Pi.** *Impf.* יְעַבְּטוּן Jo 2[7] hardly makes sense (*lend on pledge = interchange?*); most rd. יְעַבְּתוּן; יְעַוְּתוּן We, cf. Now Dr GASm; Gr. יַטּוּן.

עבל (√ of foll.; cf. poss. Ar. عَبُلَ *be bulky, stout;* Pun. n. pr. עבל Lzb[335]).

†עוֹבָל, I. עֵיבָל **n. pr. gent.** Arabian people, descended from Joktan acc. to Gn 10[28] (𝔊L Γαιβαλ); = עֵיבָל 1 Ch 1[22] (𝔊L Ηβηλ). On loc. cf. Glaser[Skizze ii. 426]. 5658, 5745

I. עֵיבָל v. עוֹבָל supr. 5658

†II. עֵיבָל **n.pr.m.** vel **gent.** name in Edom, 5658
Gn 36[23] (𝔊 Γαιβηλ), = 1 Ch 1[40] (𝔊 Γαιβηλ, A Γαοβηλ, 𝔊L Ουβαλ); acc. to Glaser[Skizze ii. 426] poss. = foregoing (cp. with name of (god) *Bēl*, Wkl[Gesch. Isr. 120; Alttest. Unters. 117 f.]).

†III. עֵיבָל **n.pr.mont.** Ebal, the mt. of 5658
cursing, N. of Shechem (Nabulus), and opp. Mt. Gerizim (mt. of blessing, S. of Shechem), Dt 11[29], also Jos 8[30.33] (D); 𝔊 Γαιβαλ (connex. with above √dub.; on בל = *Bēl*, cf. Gray[Prop. N. 124 n., and reff.]);—on Ebal v. Rob[BR ii. 275 ff.] GASm[Geogr. Ch. vi.] Di[Dt 11, 29] Dr[ib.] Bd[Pal. (1898), 257].

עבץ (√ of foll.; meaning unknown).

†יַעְבֵּץ **n.pr. 1. m.** Jabez, a man of the 3258
Calebites, 1 Ch 4[9.9.10] (where interpr. as akin to עצב; on position of this family cf. Mey[Judenthum 118]); 𝔊 Ιγαβης, A Ιαγβης, Γαβης, GL Ιαβιης, Ιαβηλ, Ιαβεις. **2. loc.** in Judah, appar. near Bethlehem 1 Ch 2[55] (cf. v[54]); 𝔊 Γαμες, A Γαβης, 𝔊L Ιαβις.

עָבַר [548] **vb.** pass over, through, by, pass 5674
on (NH = BH; Zinj. עבר Haph. Lzb[336] Cook[88], perh. also Nab. עבר Id[ib.]; 𝔗 עֲבַר, Syr. ܥܒܪ *id.;* As. *ebêru, id.* Dl[HWB 10], and deriv.; Ar. عَبَرَ *id.*, and deriv.; Sab. עבר = Heb. עִבֵּר **1.** Mordt[Sab Denkm 49]; עברת *passage, march through* DHM[ZMG xxix (1875), 614] also *bank* or *neighbourhood of a stream* Sab Denkm[49]);—**Qal**[465] *Pf.* 3 ms. ע׳ Gn 15[17] +, sf. עֲבָרוֹ Je 23[9]; 1 s. עָבַ֫רְתִּי 1 S 15[24] +; 2 mpl. עֲבַרְתֶּם Gn 18[5] +; 1 pl. עָבַ֫רְנוּ Jos 24[17] +, etc.; *Impf.* 3 ms. יַעֲבֹר Am 8[5] +, יַעֲבָר־ Gn 33[14] +, sf. 3 ms. יַעַבְרֶנּוּ Is 33[21] 35[8], יַעַבְרֻ֫נְהוּ Je 5[22], וַיַּעֲבֹר Gn 12[6] +; 1 s. אֶעֱבֹר Am 5[17] +, cohort. אֶעְבְּרָה

Nu 21^{22}+, אֶֽעֱבְּרָה Nu 20^{19} Ju 12^{5}, etc.; *Imv.* ms. עֲבֹר Ex 17^{5}+; fs. עִבְרִי Mi 1^{11}+2 t.; עֲבֹ֫רִי Is 23^{12}; mpl. עִבְרוּ Am 6^{2}+; *Inf. abs.* עָבוֹר 2 S 17^{16}; *cstr.* עֲבֹר Am 7^{8}+, לַעֲבָר־ 1 K 18^{6}+Na 2^{1} Qr (Kt לעבור); sf. עָבְרִי Ex 33^{22} Dt 4^{21}, etc.; *Pt.* עֹבֵר Ju 8^{4}+, etc.;—**1.** *pass over:* **a.**=*cross* (stream, wady, sea, etc.), (1) c. acc. Gn 31^{21} (E), 32^{11} (J), Jos 3$^{14.17}$ 4^{1} (all JE), Dt 2^{14} (D), Nu 32^{29} (P), 2 S 17$^{20.22.24}$ Is 16^{8}, + 37 t., + Gn 32^{23} (E; acc. מַעֲבַר), וְעָבְרָה הָעֲבָרָה לַעֲבִיר 2 S 19^{19} (rd. וַיַּעַבְרוּ We Dr Kit Löhr, *and they crossed the ford*, or וְעָבְרוּ frequent., HPS; >𝔊 Klo Bu וַיַּעַבְדוּ הָעֲבֹדָה *and they performed the service*); also c. acc.+acc. loc. 1 S 13^{7},+ה loc. Dt 4^{26} 31^{13} 32^{47}. (2) acc. om. Ju 3^{28} 2 S 17$^{16.16}$+32 t., +עֹבֵר Ju 8^{4} (rd. וַיַּעֲבֹר Vrss, or del. as gloss GFM Bu), 2 S 15$^{23\,a}$ (where rd. עֹמֵד for MT עֹבֵר We Dr Bu Kit Löhr HPS, but del. עֹבְרִים, plausibly, Klo HPS); c. אֶל־ †Nu 32^{7} (JE), Dt 27^{2} (D), Jos 4^{13} 22^{19} (both P), c. אֶל־עֵבֶר Dt 30^{13}, c. הָעֵבֶר 1 S 26^{13}; c. ה loc. †Dt 3^{21} 4^{14} 6^{1} 11$^{8.11}$ 34^{4} Is 23^{6}; c. acc. loc. †Is 23^{12} Je 2^{10} Nu 32^{32} (P). †**b.** *cross* border, boundary, c. acc. Nu 20$^{17\,b}$ 21$^{22\,b}$ (both JE), + אֶל־ 1 S 27^{2}; of invasion, acc. om., c. אֶל־ Ju 11^{32} 12^{3} 1 S 14$^{1.6.8}$, c. ה loc. 2 K 8^{21}, abs. 2 Ch 21^{9}. **c.** *cross over* (sc. intervening space) against (עַל־) 1 S 14^{4}, unto 2 S 24^{20} (rd. אֶל־ for עַל־ Bu HPS, cf. 𝔊L), so perh. also Is 45^{14} (עַל; rd. אֶל?); c. acc. of goal Am 5^{5} 6^{2}. †**d.** *pass, march over* (sc. bodies of captives), Is 51$^{23.23}$. †**e.**=*overflow*, fig., Is 23^{10}, abs. of invasion (like a flood) Is 8^{8}, hence Dn 11$^{10.40}$, Na 1^{8} (cf. **4 c**); of evil thoughts ψ 73^{7}; cf. עָֽבְרוּ דִבְרֵי־רָע Je 5^{28} *they overflow with evil matters.* †**f.** *pass, go, over,* of waves, over one's head, usu. c. עַל־ Is 54^{9} ψ 42^{8} 88^{17} 124$^{4.5}$ (all fig.), Jon 2^{4}; c. acc. ψ 38^{5}, cf. Je 23^{9} *over whom wine hath gone* (=overcome with wine). †**g.** of razor *passing over* head, c. עַל Nu 6^{50}; fig. of time *passing over* one, c. עַל־ 1 Ch 29^{30} (cf. BAram. חלף על Dn 4^{13}+). †**h.** *pass over upon* (עַל־), in weakened sense, nearly =come or light upon; of spirit Nu 5$^{14.14.30}$; abs. + מֵאֵת 1 K 22^{24} = 2 Ch 18^{23}; c. עַל־ also *light upon* in chastisement or judgment, Ho 10^{11} Jb 13^{13}, cf. Na 3^{19}; Dt 24^{5} *no affair shall pass over upon* (עַל־) *him*, i.e. no duty be laid upon him. †**i.** *overstep, transgress,* c. acc. of covenant, command, etc. (usu. divine); Nu 14^{41} Jos 7$^{11.15}$ (all JE), Dt 17^{2} 26^{13} Jos 23^{16} (all D), Ju 2^{20} 1 S 15^{24} Ho 6^{7} 8^{1} 2 K 18^{12} Je 34^{18} Is 24^{5} ψ 148^{6} 2 Ch 24^{20} Dn 9^{11}, command of earthly king Est 3^{3}; abs. ψ 17^{3}. †**j.** *pass over*=*overlook, forgive* עַל־פֶּשַׁע Mi 7^{18} (+ לְ pers.), Pr 19^{11}; c. לְ pers. only, Am 7^{8} 8^{2}.

†**2.** *Pass beyond,* c. acc. 1 S 14^{23} (of battle), Je 5$^{22.22}$ (of sea); + אֶל Gn 31$^{52.52}$ (E); *pass a little beyond* כִּמְעַט ע׳ מְעַט מֵהָרֹאשׁ 2 S 16^{1}, שֶׁעָבַרְתִּי מֵהֶם Ct 3^{4}; c. acc. of God's command (פֶּה), Pr 8^{29} (of sea), Nu 22^{18} = 24^{13} (JE); acc. om. Jb 14^{5} ψ 104^{9}.

3. *Pass through, traverse,* usu. **a.** c. בְּ of land, city, etc.: Nu 22^{21} (E), 20^{21} Jos 18^{9} (JE), Ex 12^{2} (P), 1 S 9$^{4.4.4.4}$ 2 S 20^{14} (+ה loc.), + 31 t.; c. בְּתוֹךְ †Ez 9^{4} Jb 15^{19}; c. בְּקֶרֶב of camp, nation(s) †Jos 1^{11} 3^{2} (D), 24^{17} (E), Am 5^{17} Dt 29^{15}; c. acc. †Dt 2^{18} 29^{15} Ju 11$^{29.29}$ Is 10^{29} Jb 14^{5}; abs. Ex 12^{23} (J), Nu 20$^{19.20}$ (JE), Dt 2^{28} Mi 5^{7} La 3^{44} Ez 14^{15} 33^{28}; †opp. שׁוּב, *pass through* and return, go to and fro, Ex 32^{27} (E; מִשַּׁעַר לָשַׁעַר בְּ׳), pt. abs. *those going to and fro* Ez 35^{7} Zc 7^{14} 9^{8}. †**b.** c. בְּ of river 2 S 19^{19}+15^{23} (but rd. עֹמֵד We Dr Bu al.), of sea Zc 10^{11}, cf. Is 43^{2} ψ 66^{6}, c. בְּתוֹךְ Nu 33^{8} (P), Ne 9^{11}; c. בְּ of gates Is 62$^{10.10}$; cf. עֹבְרֵי הָעֹבְרִים בְּעֵמֶק ψ 84^{7} (Ges$^{§130\,a}$). **c.** pt. abs. הָעֹבְרִים *the passers-through* Ez 39$^{11\,a}$, rd. prob. הָעֲבָרִים (JDMich Hi Co Berthol), v$^{11\,b}$ (Co rds. אֶת־הַגַּיְא; Toy del. as gloss), v^{14} (del. 𝔊𝔖 Co Toy Berthol). †**d.** *pass through* between (בֵּין) parts of victim, in covenant Gn 15^{7} (J), Je 34$^{18.19}$. **e.** *traverse* c. acc. of expanse of water Is 33^{21} (of ship).

4. a. *pass along* by (עַל־), Gn 18^{5} (J; not אֶל־ סְרָהֶם Ball after 𝔊), 1 K 9^{8} Je 18^{16}+14 t.; c. עַל־פָּנָיו †Ex 34^{6} (J); c. acc. †Gn 32^{32} Ju 3^{26} (on other possibilities v. GFM), 2 K 6^{9}; abs. *pass by* Ex 33$^{22.22}$ (J), 2 K 4^{8}+15 t., + (of wind) Jb 37^{21} Pr 10^{25} and (of waters,=*flow past*) Hb 3^{10} (cf. Jb 6^{15}), Jb 11^{16}, hence מוֹר עֹבֵר Ct 5$^{5.13}$ *flowing myrrh* (liquid, opp. hard = מ׳ דְּרוֹר Ex 30^{23}); pt.=*passer-by* Mi 2^{8} Ez 5^{14} 36^{34} 39^{15}+6 t. (Pr 26^{10} v. Toy), + עֹבֵר אֹרַח Is 33^{8}, עֹבְרֵי דֶרֶךְ †La 1^{12} 2^{15} Jb 21^{29} Pr 9^{15} ψ 80^{13} 89^{42}; *pass by*=*overtake and pass* c. acc. †2 S 18^{23}. **b.** *pass by,* בְּ rei, ψ 103^{16} (of wind). **c.** *sweep by,* of scourge (fig.) Is 28$^{15.18.19}$ (cf. מַעֲבָר **3**). **d.** *be past, over,* of time, etc., Am 8^{5} 1 K 18^{29} Gn 50^{4} Ct 2^{11}+7 t. **e.** *pass along* (from hand to hand), only pt. שֶׁקֶל כֶּסֶף עֹבֵר לַסֹּחֵר Gn 23^{16} i.e. *current* money *of the merchant* (or, money *passing over to* merchant? Bu$^{Th\,Lz\,1892\,(3),\,63}$); כֶּסֶף עוֹבֵר 2 K 12^{5}.

5. *Pass on, go on:* **a.** abs. Gn 18^{5} (J), Nu 22^{26} (E), Ju 12^{1} + 20 t., + Ju 11^{29} 18^{13} Jos 10^{29} (D; all c. acc. of goal + מִן), Gn 18^{3} (J; c. מֵעַל pers.); also c. אֶל־ pers. vel rei, *proceed unto* 1 K 19^{19} 2 K 4^{8} Ne 2^{14}, c. עַל־ pers. (rd. אֶל־?) La 4^{21}; c. מִן Ru 2^{8}, *out of the city* 2 S 15^{24}; c. ה loc. Ju 12^{1} 2 S 19^{41}, c. ה loc. + מִן Jos $10^{31.34}$ (D); ע׳ מֵעִיר לָעִיר בארץ 2 Ch 30^{10}; abs. 2 S 19^{41} *all the people of Judah proceeding with the king* (rd. עֹבְרִים for ויעברו, v. **Hiph.** ad fin.). †**b.** specif. of boundary-line, *pass on*, c. ה loc. Nu $34^{4.4}$ Jos $15^{3.4}$ 16^{6} (om. אוֹתוֹ 𝔊𝔙 cf. Benn^{Hpt} Steuern); + מִן 19^{13} + מִן + אֶל־ 18^{13}; c. מִן + לְ 15^{6}; c. אֶל־ $15^{7.10}$ 16^{2} $18^{18.19}$; c. acc. loc. $15^{3.10.11}$ (all P, exc. Jos 16^{2} JE). **c.** c. לִפְנֵי *pass on before, go in advance of* Gn 32^{17} Ex 17^{5} (both E), Gn 32^{22} $33^{3.14}$ (all J), Dt 9^{3} + 7 t., + Dt $3^{18.28}$ $31^{3.3}$ Jos 1^{14} (all D) where ref. may be to *crossing* in advance of; c. עַל־פְּנֵי 2 S 15^{18} so v$^{23\,b}$ (reading עַל־פָּנָיו 𝔊L We Dr Klo Bu Kit HPS). †**d.** *pass on* as far as (עַד), Ju 19^{12}, + מִן v^{18}; c. אַחֲרֵי *after* 2 S 20^{13}; תַּעֲבָר־כּוֹס עַל La 4^{21} *pass on unto* (cf. תִּסּוֹב Hb 2^{16}). †**e.** *pass on* into (בְּ), Jos 3^{11} (+ לִפְנֵי), 4^{7} (both JE), cf. Ju 9^{26} Jb 33^{28}, so also ע׳ בִּבְרִית י׳ Dt 29^{11} *enter into a covenant with* י׳; (Klo rds. וַיַּעֲבֹר בַּבּ׳ also 2 K 23^{3} for MT ויעמד). †**f.** *pass on* away from (מֵאֵת) Dt 2^{8} (+ ה loc.). †**g.** *pass on* in order, for counting 2 S 2^{15}, עַל־יְדֵי מוֹנֶה Je 33^{13}, עֹבֵר עַל־הַפְּקֻדִים Ex $30^{13.14}$ 38^{26}, also *pass on* under (תַּחַת) rod Lv 27^{32} (for counting; all P; cf. **Hiph. 3 d**). †**h.** *pass along, travel* c. acc. of way Is 35^{8} cf. 51^{10}; עֹבֵר אָרְחוֹת יַמִּים ψ 8^{9}; c. בְּ of way Jos 3^{4} Pr 4^{15} 7^{8}. **i.** *pass on, advance*, abs., ψ 48^{5} (Ol We *pass away, perish*), Mi 2^{13a} (acc. loc.).

†**6.** *Pass away:* **a.** *emigrate*, leave one's territory or city Mi 1^{11}. **b.** vanish, of chaff, Is 29^{5} cf. Je 13^{24}, shadow ψ 144^{4}, brooks Jb 6^{15} (all in sim.), Ct 5^{6}. **c.** = cease to exist, perish Na 1^{12} Jb 30^{15} 33^{18} (בְּ instr.), 36^{12} (*id.*), 34^{20} ψ 37^{36} (but rd. ואעבר *and I passed by*, cf. **4 a**), cf. Is 31^{9} (סלעו subj.), מֵאֱלֹהֵי מִשְׁפָּטִי יַעֲבוֹר 40^{27} *pass away from.* **d.** = become invalid, obsolete, of law, decree, Est 1^{19} 9^{27}, also v^{28} (+ מִתּוֹךְ הַיְּהוּדִים). **e.** c. מִן of hands ψ 81^{7} (i.e. they were freed from). **f.** = *be alienated, pass into other hands* Ez 48^{14} (rdg. Kt; > Qr **Hiph.**).—Je 2^{20} rd. אֶעֱבוֹד Kt (not אֶעֱבוֹר Qr); וָאֶתֵּן לָהֶם יַעַבְרוּם 8^{13} *and I gave to them that which they transgress* 𝔖𝔙𝔗 Aq Symm Ew, *those that shall pass over them* Hi Gf Ke RVm, *those that shall consume, devour them* Rothst^{Kau} (rdg. יְבַעֲרוּם) but all very dub.; 𝔊 Co del.; 11^{15} rd. Hiph. q. v.; מִנֹּגַהּ נֶגְדּוֹ עָבָיו עָבְרוּ ψ 18^{13} is difficult; perhaps best, as Che Kit^{Kau} Löhr, *out of the brightness before him issued forth* hailstones, etc. (del. עָבָיו); > ‖ 2 S 22^{13} בָּעֲרוּ and so here Bu HPS cf. Woods$^{Hbr\,1887,\,262}$, *his clouds burned* with hailstones, etc.; rd. rather עברו in 2 S.

†**Niph.** *Impf.* 3 ms. נַחַל אֲשֶׁר לֹא יֵעָבֵר Ez 47^{5} *a stream which cannot be forded.*

Pi. 1. *Pf.* 3 ms. שׁוֹרוֹ עִבַּר Jb 21^{10} *his bull impregnateth* (cf. NH) abs. (prop. *causeth to pass over*, sc. *semen*). **2.** *Impf.* 3 ms. וַיְעַבֵּר בְּ׳ 1 K 6^{21} *he made to pass across* with chains of gold.—**Hithp.** v. [עָבַר] infr.

†**Hiph.** *Pf.* 3 ms. הֶעֱבִיר 2 S 12^{13} +; 2 ms. הֶעֱבַרְתָּ Jos 7^{7} (Ges$^{§\,63\,p}$), וְהַעֲבַרְתָּ Ez 5^{1} +; 1 s. הֶעֱבַרְתִּי Zc 3^{4}, וְהַעֲבַרְתִּי Ez 20^{37} + Je 15^{14} (but rd. והעבדתי 𝔊𝔖𝔗 Codd Ew Hi Gf Gie), etc.; *Impf.* 3 ms. וַיַּעֲבֵר Gn 8^{1} +, וַיַּעֲבֶר־ 2 Ch 36^{22} = Ezr 1^{1}, sf. וַיַּעֲבִרֵנִי Ez 46^{21} +, etc.; *Imv.* ms. הַעֲבֵר ψ 119^{37} + 2 t., הַעֲבֶר־ 2 S 24^{10} = 1 Ch 21^{8}; mpl. sf. הַעֲבִירוּנִי 2 Ch 35^{23}; *Inf. abs.* הַעֲבִיר Jos 7^{7} (rd. prob. הַעֲבֵיר); *cstr.* הַעֲבִיר 2 S 3^{10} +, לַעֲבִיר 2 S 19^{19} (Ges$^{§\,53\,q}$), etc.; *Pt.* מַעֲבִיר Dt 18^{10} Dn 11^{20}, pl. מַעֲבִרִים 1 S 2^{24} (v. infr.);—**1.** *cause to pass over, bring over:* **a.** *cause* one *to cross* river, c. 2 acc., Gn 32^{24} (J), Nu 32^{5} Jos 7^{7} (both JE), 2 S $19^{16.42}$; acc. of river om. Gn 32^{24} (J), Jos 4^{3} 7^{7} (+ Inf. abs.; both JE), 4^{8} (JE; + אֶל־), 2 S 2^{8} (+ acc. loc.). **b.** *cause* something *to pass over* (עַל־): razor (acc.) Nu 8^{7} (P), cf. Ez 5^{1} (where Co rds. sf. of razor), wind Gn 8^{1} (P). **c.** *make over* to (לְ), acc. of inheritance Nu $27^{7.8}$ (P); of *making over, dedicating*, something to (לְ) deity Ex 13^{12} (JE; = קִדֵּשׁ). Esp. **d.** *devote* children to (לְ) heathen god Je 32^{35} Ez 23^{37} (+ לְאָכְלָה), Lv 18^{21} (H), cf. Ez 16^{21}; + בָּאֵשׁ *by fire* 2 K 23^{10}; c. acc. alone *devote* Ez 20^{26}; c. acc. + בָּאֵשׁ alone, *devote by fire* Dt 18^{10} 2 K 16^{3} 17^{7} 21^{6} = 2 Ch 33^{6}, Ez 20^{31} (on the practice cf. Now$^{Arch.\,ii.\,205\,f.}$ Benz$^{Arch.\,433\,f.}$ Toy$^{Ez\,16,\,20;\,20,\,26}$ GFM$^{JBL\,xvi\,(1897),\,161\,ff.}$).

2. a. *cause to pass through*, c. acc. + בְּ Ez 14^{15} $47^{3.4}$ + v^{4} (where ins. בְּ, cf. Co Berthol Toy), Nu $31^{23.23}$ (P); c. acc. + בְּתוֹךְ ψ 136^{14}; c. acc. pers. alone 78^{13}, + אֶל־ Ez 46^{21}, + עַד־אֲשֶׁר Ne 2^{7}; c. acc. of (sound of) שׁוֹפָר Lv 25^{9} (H), + בְּ v^{9} (P); c. acc. קוֹל = *proclamation*, + בְּ Ex 36^{6} (P), 2 Ch 30^{5} 36^{22} = Ezr 1^{1}, Ezr 10^{7} (+ לְ pers.), Ne 8^{15}. **b.** *let pass through*, c. acc. + בְּ pers. Dt 2^{30}.

3. a. *cause to pass by*, c. acc. + עַל־, Ez 37^{2}

(+סָבִיב סָבִיב), + עַל־פְּנֵי Ex 33^{19} (J), + לִפְנֵי 1 S 16$^{8.10}$ and (לִפְנֵי om.) v^{9}. **b.** *let pass by*, c. acc. מוֹעֵד Je 46^{17} *he hath let the set time pass by* (in mocking appell. of Pharaoh). **c.** *cause* arrow *to pass beyond* one 1 S 20^{36}. **d.** *cause to pass* under rod, for counting, Ez 20^{37} (cf. **Qal 5 g**).

4. *Cause to pass away, take away*, kingdom (acc.) + מִן pers. 2 S 3^{10}, cf. Est 8^{2}, + מֵעַל Jon 3^{6} (of putting off garment); c. acc. of sin 2 S 12^{13} 24^{20} = 1 Ch 21^{8}, Jb 7^{21}, + מֵעַל pers. Zc 3^{4} Je 11^{15} (rdg. יַעֲבִרוּ מֵעַל Ew Gf Gie); *put away* evil things (acc.) from (מִן), 1 K 15^{12} cf. ‖ 2 Ch 15^{8}, Zc 13^{2} Ec 11^{10}; c. acc. alone ψ 119^{39} Est 8^{3}; also *take me away* (sf.) 2 Ch 35^{23} (c. מִן) v^{24}; *turn away* eyes (acc.) + מִן ψ 119^{37}.—Gn 47^{21} rd. הֶעֱבִיד לַעֲבָדִים Sam 𝔊 𝔙 Ol Kn Di Kau Holz; Je 15^{14} rd. וְהַעֲבַדְתִּיךָ 𝔊 𝔗 Codd Gie; 2 S 12^{31} rd. וְהֶעֱבִיד Hoffm ZAW ii (1882), 53 f. Gr Klo Bu Kit HPS, cf. Dr Löhr; 2 S 19^{41} (for ויעברו Kt, הֶעֱבִרוּ Qr) rd. עֹבְרִים 𝔊 We Bu Löhr HPS, וַיַּעַבְרוּ Kit (v. **Qal 5 a**); Ez 48^{14} rd. **Qal** (so Kt; v. **Qal 6 e**); מַעֲבִרִים עַם־י׳ 1 S 2^{24} not good is the report which I hear *the people of* י׳ *spreading* (cf. **2**), so Ew Th We Dr Kit Löhr RVm, but order of words difficult; > (ye) *make the people of* י׳ *transgress* 𝔙 AV RV; text dub.; מַעֲבִיר נוֹגֵשׂ Dn 11^{20} *one causing an exactor to pass through* Ew al. RV, Bev prop. נוֹגֵשׂ מ׳ *an exactor causing to pass away* the glory, etc.

5676 **I. עֵ֫בֶר** $_{91}$ **n.m.** $^{1 S 14, 40}$ **region across** or **beyond, side** (on format. cf. Ba$^{NB\ 144}$; cf. esp. As. *êbru, êbirtu, id.*, *êbirtan*, adv. *beyond*);—ע׳ abs. 1 S 14^{4}+; cstr. Jos 24^{4}+; sf. עֶבְרוֹ Is 47^{15}; pl. cstr. עֶבְרֵי Is 7^{20} Je 48^{28} (si vera l., v. infr.); sf. עֲבָרָיו 1 K 5^{4} Je 49^{32} (read probably עֶבְרֵיהֶם, so Vrss), עֶבְרֵיהֶם Ex 32^{15};—**1.** *region across* or *beyond* anything (usu. wady, river, or sea), mostly c. prep.: בְּעֵבֶר אַרְנוֹן Nu 21^{13} (JE) Ju 11^{18}, cf. Je 25^{22}; אֶל־ע׳ הַיָּם Dt 30$^{13\,b}$, מֵעֵבֶר לַיָּם v$^{13\,a}$ *beyond the sea;* מֵע׳ לְנַהֲרֵי־כוּשׁ Is 18^{1}, cf. עַד־מֵע׳ 1 K 4^{12} (מִן *on the side of, on*, v. מִן **1 c**; so usu. c. ע׳); but also (rarely) מֵע׳ *from the other side of* Zp 3^{10} Jb 1^{19} 2 Ch 20^{2}; abs. הָע׳ 1 S 26^{13} *to the other side* (sc. of a ravine; after וַיַּעֲבֹר); בְּעֵבֶר הָעֵמֶק 1 S 31^{7}, read perh. בְּעָרֵי הָע׳, so Klo Bu HPS; בְּעֶבְרֵי פִי־פָחַת Je 48^{28} *beyond the mouth of a chasm* is dub.; Gie prop. בְּחֹרֵי כֵּפֵי בַּחֹת *in the rock-holes of the precipices;* esp. (chiefly Hex, 37 t.) ע׳ הַיַּרְדֵּן (30 t.), or (less oft., Jos 13^{32} + 13 t.), לַיַּרְדֵּן יְרֵחוֹ, לַיַּרְדֵּן (only c. מֵע׳), of either E. Jordan (36 t.) or W. Jordan land (9 t.) acc. to standpoint of speaker or writer: **A.** E. Jordan (fr. standpoint of writer) Gn 50$^{10.11}$ (J) Jos 17^{5} (JE) Dt 1$^{1.5}$ 4$^{41.46.47.49}$ Jos 1^{14} 12^{1} 13^{8} (D), Nu 22^{1} 32^{19} 34^{15} Jos 13$^{27.32}$ 14^{3} 20^{8} (P), Ju 7^{25} 10^{8} 1 S 31^{7} Is 8^{23} 1 Ch 6^{63} 12^{37}; fr. standpoint of speaker, Jos 7^{7} (JE), 24^{8} (E), 1^{15} 2^{10} 9^{10} 18^{7} 22^{4} (D), Ju 5^{17}; in Nu 35^{14} (Moses speaks) it is *land opp.* to Can., cf. Nu 32^{32}; in Dt 3^{8} (Moses speaks) writer (D) ascribes his own standpoint to Moses; (oft. further topogr. note is added, e.g. מִזְרָ֫חָה Dt 4^{49}+, מִזְרַח הַשֶּׁמֶשׁ Jos 1^{15}+, etc.); אֶל־עֵבֶר בְּנֵי יִשְׂר׳ Jos 22^{11} *toward the region opposite the sons of Israel* appar. also refers to E. side (v. Steuernagel on text). **B.** W. Jordan (9 t.), from standpoint of speaker Dt 3$^{20.25}$ (Moses), also 11^{30} (but here + מְבוֹא הַשֶּׁמֶשׁ, and in all foll. some special designation of *West*), + יָ֫מָּה Jos 5^{1} (D; from standpoint of those just crossed), 12^{7} (*opposite* East v$^{1-6}$), 22^{7} (*id.;* Kt מעבר, Qr בְּעֵבֶר), cf. 9^{1} (as 5^{1}); + וָהָ֫לְאָה Nu 32$^{19\,a}$ (*opposite* East v^{b}); in 1 Ch 26^{30} מֵע׳ לַיַּר׳ מַעְרָבָה ע׳ seems = *side* (v. infr.). Also בְּע׳ הַנָּהָר *beyond the river* (Euphrates) Jos 24$^{2.14.15}$ (E; Kt Qr מֵע׳), מֵע׳ 2 S 10^{16} = 1 Ch 19^{16} *beyond*, and 1 K 14^{5} *to the other side of* (v. מִן **1 c**); מֵע׳ *from beyond* the river only Jos 24^{3} (E), in all these = beyond the Euphr. *eastward*, from standpoint of those west of Euphr.; so pl. בְּעֶבְרֵי הַנּ׳ Is 7^{20}; poss. also ע׳ alone (si vera l.) in the difficult passage Nu 24^{24}; ע׳ הַנָּהָר = *region beyond the river* (Euphr.) westward (from standpoint of those in Babylonia or Persia) Ne 2$^{7.9}$ 3^{7} Ezr 8^{36}; also 1 K 5$^{4.4}$ (written in Bab.; cf. BAram. עֲבַר, and Dr $^{Intr\ (6)\ 504}$).

2. (Opposite) *side, side:* מֵע׳ הַלָּז 1 S 14^{1} *on yonder side* seems transition to this meaning; מֵהָע׳ מִזֶּה twice, v^{4} = *on one side, on the other side*, so לְע׳ אֶחָד twice v^{40}; even מִשְּׁנֵי עֶבְרֵיהֶם Ex 32^{15} (E) *on their two sides* (i.e. of tablets); אֶל־ע׳ הָאֵפוֹד בָּ֫יְתָה Ex 28^{26} (P) *toward the inner side of the ephod;* in 1 K 7$^{20.30}$ ע׳ appar. = *at the side of* or *opposite*, but the archit. details are obscure; מִכָּל־עֲבָרָיו מִסָּבִיב 1 K 5^{4} *on all sides of him*, round about, מִכָּל־עֲבָרָיו Je 49^{32} (rd. עֶבְרֵיהֶם Vrss Gie) *from all sides of them* (all directions, מִכָּל־סְבִיבֶיךָ = v^{5}); אֶל־עֵבֶר פָּנָיו יֵלֵכוּ *to the side of their faces* (i.e. in front, straight forward) *they* (always) *went* Ez 1$^{9.12}$ 10^{22}, cf. עַל־ע׳ פָּנֶיהָ Ex 25^{37} to give light *upon the space in front of it;* אִישׁ לְעֶבְרוֹ תָּעוּ Is 47^{15} *they wander away each in his own direction* (regardless of thee).—On 1 Ch 26^{30} v. supr.

5677 †II. עֵ֫בֶר **n.pr.m. Eber** (perh. eponym of *Hebrews,* form inferred from עִבְרִי, cf. reff. there);—**1.** 'son' of Shelaḥ, and 'grandson' of Arpachshad Gn 10^{24} (J) = 1 Ch 1^{18}, Gn 11$^{14.15}$ (P); 'father' of Peleg and Joktan 10^{25} (J; with esp. ref. to Joktan v$^{26 ff.}$, i.e. to Arabians) = 1 Ch 1^{19} (cf. v$^{20 ff.}$), of Peleg specif. Gn 11$^{16.17}$ (P; with esp. ref. to Abr. v$^{26 f.}$) cf. 1 Ch 1^{25} (see v$^{27 f.}$); in Gn 10^{21} (J) Shem is called אֲבִי כָּל־בְּנֵי־עֵבֶר; 𝔊 Εβερ.—ע׳ Nu 24^{24} perh. (si vera l.) belongs not here (= עִבְרִים *Hebrews,* 𝔊 Ἐβραίους, so Thes), but sub I. עֵבֶר = the (land) beyond (the river), ‖ אַשּׁוּר, so Di Kau. **2.** a Gadite chief 1 Ch 5^{13}, 𝔊 Ωβηδ, 𝔊^{L} Εβερ. **3.** Benjamite names: **a.** 1 Ch 8^{12}, 𝔊 Ωβηδ, 𝔊^{L} Αβερ. **b.** 1 Ch 8^{22} (עֵבֶר van d. H. Ginsb; עֶבֶד Baer), 𝔊 Ωβδη, A Ωβηδ, 𝔊^{L} Αβερ. **4.** a priest Ne 12^{20} 𝔊^{L} Αβεδ.

5680 †I. עִבְרִי **adj.** et **n. gent. Hebrew,** either **a.** put into the mouth of foreigners (Egypt. and Philist.), or **b.** used to distinguish Isr. from foreigners (= *one from beyond, from the other side,* i.e. prob. (in Heb. trad.) *from beyond the Euphrates* (cf. Jos 24$^{2.3}$ E), but poss. in fact (if name given in Canaan) *from beyond the Jordan;* cf. Ges^{§2b} Sta^{§1b} Kö$^{i. 18 ff.}$ We$^{Isr. u. Jüd. Gesch. 7}$ Kau$^{'Eber' and 'Hebräer'}$ in Ri$^{HWB 332, 600}$.—On connexion of ע׳ (in wide sense) with *Ḥabiri* (Tel Am.) v. Wkl$^{Gesch. Isr. 17 ff.; Sem. Studies in Mem. of Kohut, 605 ff.}$ EMey$^{Aegyptica [Ebers], 75}$ cf. Glaser$^{MVG 1897, 255 ff.}$ Kö$^{Exp. Times xi. 238}$; opp. Jastr$^{JBL xi (1892), 118 ff.}$ Say$^{Monuments 188, 333}$ WMM$^{As. u. Eur. 396}$);—ms. ע׳ Gn 39^{14}+; fs. עִבְרִיָּה Dt 15^{12} Je 34^{9}; mpl. עִבְרִים Gn 43^{32}+, עִבְרִיִּים Ex 3^{18}; fpl. עִבְרִיֹּת Ex 1^{15}+2 t., ־וֹת 1^{16}; word not in P;—**1. adj. a.** אִישׁ עִבְרִי Gn 39^{14} cf. v^{17} (both J), 41^{12} (E). **b.** אִישׁ עִבְרִי Ex 2^{11} cf. v^{13} 21^{2} (all E), Dt 15^{12} Je 34$^{9.14}$; f. Dt 15^{12} Je 34^{9}. **2. n. a.** Ex 1$^{16.19}$ 2^{7} (all f.) 2^{6} (all E), 1 S 4$^{6.9}$ 13^{19} 14^{11} 29^{3}. **b.** Gn 40^{15} Ex 1^{15} (f.; both E), 1 S 13^{3} 14^{21}, Gn 43^{32} (J); esp. in אֱלֹהֵי הָעִבְרִים Ex 3^{18} 5^{3} 7^{16} 9$^{1.13}$ 10^{3} (all J); sg. only אַבְרָם הָע׳ Gn 14^{13}, ע׳ אָנֹכִי Jon 1^{9}.—𝔊 Ἑβραῖος, Ἑβραία, Gn 14^{13} τῷ περάτῃ.—1 S 13^{7} read prob. for וְעִבְרִים וגו׳, וַיַּעַבְרוּ מַעְבְּרוֹת הַיַּרְדֵּן (We), or, better, וַיַּעַבְרוּ Dr Kit Löhr; > וְעָם רַב Klo Bu HPS.

5681 †II. עִבְרִי **n.pr.m.** Levite name, 1 Ch 24^{27}; 𝔊 Αβαι, A Ωβδι, 𝔊^{L} Αβαρια.

5679 †עֲבָרָה **n.f. ford,** rare synon. of מַעֲבָר, מַעְבָּרָה;—abs. הָע׳ 2 S 19^{19} *and they crossed the ford* (v. עבר **Qal 1 a**); pl. cstr. עַבְרוֹת הַמִּדְבָּר 2 S 15^{28} Kt (Qr עַרְבוֹת), so 17^{16} van d. H. (but Baer Ginsb עַרְבוֹת Kt also), עב׳ preferable (so Th We Dr Bu Kit Löhr HPS), *the fords of the desert* (HPS 17^{16} n.pr.).

†עֶבְרָה **n.f. overflow, arrogance, fury;**— 5678
abs. ע׳ Is 13^{9}+; cstr. עֶבְרַת Zp 1^{18}+; sf. עֶבְרָתִי Is 10^{6}+, etc.; pl. עֲבָרוֹת Jb 21^{30}; cstr. עַבְרוֹת ψ 7^{7} Jb 40^{11};—**1.** *overflow, excess, outburst,* ע׳ זָדוֹן Pr 21^{24} *excess of insolence;* עַבְרוֹת אַפֶּךָ Jb 40^{11} *outbursts of thine anger.* **2.** *arrogance,* of Moab Is 16^{6} (+ גַּאֲוָה, גָּאוֹן), hence Je 48^{30} (+ *id.* v^{29}). **3.** *overflowing rage, fury:* **a.** of men, Gn 49^{7} (poem in J), Am 1^{11} (both ‖ אַף), Is 14^{6} Pr 14^{35}, שֵׁבֶט עֶבְרָתוֹ 22^{8} (i.e. rod wielded by him in fury, v. also La 3^{1} infr.), עַבְרוֹת צוֹרְרָי ψ 7^{7} *the outbursts of fury of my foes.* **b.** of י׳ Ho 5^{10} 13^{11} (‖ אַף), Hb 3^{8} (‖ *id.*), Is 9^{18} La 2^{2} ψ 90$^{9.11}$; + חֲרוֹן אַף Is 13^{9}, ‖ *id.* v^{13} ψ 78^{49} (+ זַעַם), 85^{4}; אֵשׁ עֶבְרָתִי Ez 21^{36} (‖ זַעַם), 22^{31} (‖ *id.*), v^{21} 38^{19}; שֵׁבֶט עֶבְרָתוֹ La 3^{1} (cf. Pr 22^{8} supr.); עַם עֶבְרָתִי Is 10^{6} (i.e. obj. of my rage), cf. דּוֹר עֶבְרָתוֹ Je 7^{29}; יוֹם עֶבְרַת י׳ Zp 1^{18} *day of* י׳*'s fury* (coming judgment), so Ez 7^{19} (del. Co Berthol, after 𝔊, as gloss from Zp); so יוֹם עֶבְרָה Zp 1^{15} Pr 11^{4}; יוֹם עֲבָרוֹת Jb 21^{30}; cf. עֶבְרָה Pr 11^{23}.

†[עָבַר] **vb. denom. Hithp. be arrogant,** 5674
infuriate oneself;—*Pf.* 3 ms. הִתְעַבָּר ψ 78^{62}; 2 ms. הִתְעַבַּ֫רְתָּ 89^{39}; *Impf.* 3 ms. וַיִּתְעַבֵּר Dt 3^{26}, וַיִּתְעַבָּר ψ 78$^{21.59}$; *Pt.* מִתְעַבֵּר Pr 14^{16} 26^{17}; sf. מִתְעַבְּרוֹ 20^{2};—**1.** *be arrogant,* Pr 14^{16} (opp. יָרֵא). **2. a.** *put oneself in a fury, become furious,* c. בְּ pers. Dt 3^{26} ψ 78^{62}; c. עִם pers. 88^{39}; abs. 78$^{21.59}$ (all of God); of man, c. עַל rei Pr 26^{17}. **b.** *incite* one *to fury for oneself* Pr 20^{2} (si vera l.; cf. De Ges$^{§54 f.}$).

†עֲבָרִים **n.pr.loc. 'Abarîm** (prop. *regions* 5682
beyond river or sea);—usu. הַר הָע׳ Nu 27^{12} Dt 32^{49} (= הַר־נְבוֹ; both P), and הָרֵי הָע׳ 33^{47} (לִפְנֵי נְבוֹ), v^{48} (P); alone only צַעֲקִי מֵעֲבָרִים Je 22^{20}; the mountainous district in NW. Moab, just NE. of Dead Sea, GASm$^{Geogr. 548 and EBi}$ Buhl$^{Geogr. 122}$; 𝔊 Αβαρειμ (-ειν), but τὸ ἐν τῷ πέραν Nu 33^{47}, εἰς τὸ πέραν τῆς θαλάσσης Je 22^{20}.—Vid. also sub עִיִּים.

עֶבְרֹן **n.pr.loc.** Jos 19^{38} (𝔊 Ελβων, A 𝔊^{L} 5683
Αχραν); read probably עַבְדֹּן q.v. p. 715 5658

†עַבְרֹנָה **n.pr.loc.** a station of Israelites in 5684
wilderness, one march from Ezion-geber, on Gulf of Aḳaba Nu 33$^{34.35}$ (P); 𝔊 (Σ)εβρωνα.

5669 †I. [עָבוּר] **n.[m.]** produce, yield (cf. As. *ebûru, id.*, Dl $^{HWB\ 11}$; Syr. ܥܒܘܪܐ *corn*);—cstr. עֲבוּר הָאָרֶץ Jos $5^{11.12}$ (P).

5668 II. [עָבוּר] **n.** only in בַּעֲבוּר ,בַּעֲבֻר$_{47}$ (Gn $27^{10.31}$), **prep.** and **conj.** *for the sake of, on account of, in order that* (perh. orig. *for the produce* or *gain of*), sf. בַּעֲבוּרִי, 1 S 23^{10}, etc.;—**1.** as **prep.**: **a.** Gn 3^{17} ארורה האדמה בעבורך *for* thy *sake*, 8^{21} בעבור האדם *for* man's *sake*, 12^{13} לְמַעַן יִיטַב־לִי בַעֲבוּרֵךְ, v ^{16} $18^{26.29}$ 26^{24}, Ex 9^{16} ב׳ זאת ,ב׳ זה, 13^{8}, 1 S 12^{22} 2 S 5^{12} 6^{12} 7^{21} $9^{1.7}$ Am 2^{6} 8^{6} ואביון ב׳ נַעֲלָיִם, Mi 2^{10} ב׳ טָמְאָה *on account of* uncleanness, ψ 106^{32} 132^{10}, etc.; 2 S 12^{21} ב׳ הַיֶּלֶד חַי *because of* the child, (being) alive (=while he was alive), Je 14^{4} ב׳ הָאֲדָמָה חַתָּה *on account of* the ground, (which) is dismayed, Jb 20^{2} וב׳ זאת ובַעֲבוּר חוּשִׁי בִּי rd. ,וב׳ זאת, or וּבַעֲבוּרָהּ. †**b.** sq. inf. (cf. לְמַעַן), *in order to*, Ex 9^{16} ב׳ הַרְאֹתְךָ אֶת־כֹּחִי, 1 S 1^{6} 2 S 10^{3} ב׳ חֲקֹר את־העיר, 18^{18}: so לְבַעֲבוּר Ex 20^{20} 2 S 14^{20} 17^{14}; לְ בעבור 1 Ch 19^{3} (‖ 2 S 10^{3}, no לְ). †**2.** as **conj.** Gn 27^{10} ב׳ אֲשֶׁר יְבָרֶכְךָ; without אשר, Gn 21^{30} ב׳ תִּהְיֶה לִּי לְעֵדָה *in order that* it may be a witness for me, 27^{4} ב׳ תְּבָרֶכְךָ נפשי, v $^{19.31}$ 46^{34} Ex 9^{14} 19^{9} 20^{20} ψ 105^{45}.

4569 †[מַעֲבָר] **n.[m.]** ford, pass, passing;—only cstr.: **1.** מַעֲבַר יַבֹּק Gn 32^{23} (J) *the ford of* (the) *Jabbok*. **2.** *pass*, מַעֲבַר מִכְמָשׂ 1 S 13^{23} *the pass of M.* **3.** *passing, sweep*, כֹּל־מַעֲבַר מַטֵּה Is 30^{32} *every sweep of the rod* (עָבַר **4 c**).

†מַעְבָּרָה **n.f.** ford, pass, passage;—abs. מ׳ Is 10^{29}; pl. מַעְבְּרוֹת Is 16^{2} Je 51^{32}, מַעְבָּרוֹת abs. Jos 2^{7} 1 S 14^{4}; cstr. Ju 3^{28}+2 t.;—**1.** *ford*, only pl. Jos 2^{7} (JE), Ju 3^{28} $12^{5.6}$ Is 16^{2}; so also 1 S 13^{7} (for MT עִבְרִים) We Dr Kit Löhr; + מַעְבֶּרֶת 1 K 7^{46}=2 Ch 4^{17}, v. סֻכּוֹת. **2.** *pass* (wady, ravine), 1 S 14^{4} Is 10^{29}. **3.** *passage* in defensive works of Bab. Je 51^{32}.

5685 †[עָבַשׁ] **vb. shrivel** (cf. Ar. عَبَسَ *contract* (esp. face), *frown*);—**Qal** *Pf.* 3 mpl. עָבְשׁוּ פְרֻדוֹת Jo 1^{17} *the grains have shrivelled* (cf. Dr Now).

5686 †[עָבַת] **vb. Pi.** wind, weave (cf. derivatives);—*Impf.* 3 mpl. sf. וַיְעַבְּתוּהָ Mi 7^{3} *and (so) they wind it* (or *weave it;* i.e. mischief); so Hi Che GASm, but dub.; Ew rds. עבט= *twist, pervert* (cp. Jo 2^{7}, but v. עבט), We וַיְעַוְּתוּהָ =*id.*, cf. Now (?), Dr.

†עָבוֹת **adj.** having interwoven foliage, 5687
leafy;—עֵץ עָבוֹת *leafy trees* Ez 20^{28} Ne 8^{15}; עֵץ עָבֹת Lv 23^{40} (H); f. אֵלָה עֲבֻתָּה Ez 6^{13} *a leafy terebinth.*—עָבוֹת 2 S 23^{4} ψ 77^{18} v. II. עָב sub עוב.

†עֲבֹת **n.m.** $^{Ju\ 15,13+}$ et **f.** $^{Ju\ 15,14+}$ (twisted) 5688
cord, rope; cordage; interwoven foliage (?);—abs. ע׳ Ex 28^{14}+2 t.; cstr. עֲבוֹת Is 5^{18} ψ 129^{4}; sf. 3 ms. עֲבֹתוֹ Jb 39^{10}, 3 mpl. עֲבֹתֵימוֹ ψ 2^{3}; pl. עֲבֹתִים Ju 15^{13}+, עֲבֹתֹת Ex 28^{14}+, etc.;—**1.** *cord, rope:* **a.** as fetter, Ju $15^{13.14}$ $16^{11.12}$ Ez 3^{25} 4^{8} Jb 39^{10} (of wild ox), so also prob. ψ 118^{27} *bind the festal victim* (חַג) *with cords* Ew Ol De Hup-Now Dr al.; >*with branches* Che, cf. Bae Du; fig. of authority ψ 2^{3} (‖ מוֹסְרוֹתֵימוֹ), 129^{4}. **b.** עֲבוֹת הָעֲגָלָה Is 5^{18} i.e. with which a cart is drawn (in sim.; ‖ חַבְלֵי הַשָּׁוְא); fig. עֲבֹתוֹת אַהֲבָה Ho 11^{4} *with the cords of love*, of י׳'s drawing Isr. (‖ חַבְלֵי אָדָם). **c.** *cordage, cord*, of (twisted) golden chains on high priest's breast-piece (all P): מַעֲשֵׂה עֲבֹת, *cordage-work* Ex $28^{14.22}$ 39^{15}; שַׁרְשְׁרֹת הָעֲבֹתֹת 28^{14} *the chains of cords* (cordlike chains); שְׁתֵּי (הָ)עֲבֹתֹת *the two cords* v $^{24.25}$ $39^{17.18}$. **2.** *interwoven foliage* (?) in phr. (עַל־)בֵּין עֲבֹתִים of top of a vine Ez 19^{11} (*clouds* Ew Hi-Sm Toy, rd. then עָבוֹת); of cedar, $31^{3.10.14}$, but in these certainly *clouds*, so 𝔊 Ew Hi-Sm Co al.

עֹג v. עוּג. p. 728 5747

†[עָגַב] **vb.** have inordinate affection, 5689
lust (cf. Ar. عَجِبَ *wonder, admire*, عَجِيبٌ *beloved;* and (on sens. obsc. in NH) Levy $^{NHWB\ iii.\ 616}$);—**Qal** *Pf.* 3 fs. עָגְבָה Ez $23^{7.9.12}$; *Impf.* 3 fs. וַתַּעְגַּב v ^{5}, + v ^{16} Kt (Qr וַתַּעְגְּבָה), וַתַּעְגְּבָה v ^{20} (Ew $^{§ 191\ c}$ Ol $^{§ 228\ b}$); *Pt.* pl. עֹגְבִים Je 4^{30};—*lust* after (עַל־), only in fig. of relations of Samaria and Jerus. (personif.) with foreigners Ez $23^{5.9.12.16.20}$, so c. acc. v ^{7}; pt. as subst. *paramours* Je 4^{30}.

†[עֲגָב] **n.[m.]** (sensuous) love (on form 5690
cf. Lag $^{BN\ 143}$);—only pl. intens. שִׁיר עֲגָבִים Ez 33^{32} thou art to them as a *love-song.*—For עֲגָבִים v ^{31} rd. כְּזָבִים 𝔊 𝔖 Co Berthol Toy.

†[עֲגָבָה] **n.f.** lustfulness;—sf. עַגְבָתָהּ Ez 5691
23^{11} (of personif. Jerus.; ‖ תַּזְנוּתֶיהָ).

†עוּגָב **n.m.** a musical instr. (poss. from 5748
above √, because of *sensuous* or *appealing* tones);—Gn 4^{21} (J; + כִּנּוֹר), Jb 21^{12} (‖ כִּנּוֹר ,תֹּף), ψ 150^{4} (+ מִנִּים), sf. עֻגָבִי Jb 30^{31} (‖ כִּנֹּרִי);—acc. to 𝔗 a reed-pipe or flute (אַבּוּבָא), 𝔙 a *Pan's*

pipe (*organon*, made up of several reeds together); Now[Arch. i. 277] Benz[Arch. 276] think of *bag-pipe* (=סוּמְפֹּנְיָה Dn 3$^{5.10.15}$), cf. also in We ψψ [Eng. Tr. 219]; >a stringed instr. 𝔊𝔖 (Gn 4^{21}).

5692 **עָגָה** v. עוג. p. 728

עגל (√of foll.; cf. NH עָגַל Niph. *be rounded;* Pi. *roll* a thing, etc.; Aram. Pa. ܥܰܓܶܠ *roll* a thing, and deriv.; 𝔗 עֲגוּלָא *rolled* cake, עֲגִילָא *shield*, בַּעֲגָלָא, Syr. ܒܥܓܠܐ, *in swiftness, swiftly;* Ar. عَجِلَ *hasten, be swift*, cf. Lag[BN 31, 143]).

5695 †**עֵ֫גֶל n.m.**[Ex 32, 24] **calf** (as *rolling* or *circling* about? cf. כַּר fr. כָּרַר; NH *id.;* Ph. (Pu.) עגל *id.* Lzb^{336}; עגילו Palm. n.pr. *id.* Cook^{89}; Aram. עִגְלָא, עֲגַלְתָּא, ܥܶܓܠܳܐ, ܥܶܓܠܬܳܐ, *id.;* As. [*agalu*], pl. *agalê* prob. *calves* Dl[HWB 16] (cf. against this Jen [Kosmol. 110], but v. also Jäger[BAS ii. 2, 286]); Ar. عِجْلٌ, *id.;* Eth. **ዕጐል: ዕጐልት:**, cf. also Hom[NS 226]);—ע׳ abs. Ex 32^{19}+; cstr. 1 S 28^{24}+; sf. עֶגְלֵךְ Ho 8^{5}; pl. עֲגָלִים Ho 13^{2}+; cstr. עֶגְלֵי 1 K 12^{28}+;—*calf*, Is 11^{6} 27^{10} in sim. of leaping mts. ψ 29^{6}; in sim. of foot-sole of cherubim Ez 1^{7}; ע׳ מַרְבֵּק i.e. a *stall*-fed (fatted) *calf*, 1 S 28^{24}, in sim. Je 46^{21} Mal 3^{20}, cf. ע׳ מִתּוֹךְ מַרְבֵּק Am 6^{4}; ע׳ לֹא לֻמָּד Je 31^{18} *an untrained calf;* עֶגְלֵי עַמִּים ψ 68^{31} *calves of peoples*, i.e. peoples like calves, so most; perh. rd. בַּעֲלֵי עמ׳ Matthes Che Gunkel[Schöpf. 66 f.] cf. Bae; *calf* as sacrif. victim Mi 6^{6} Lv 9$^{2.3.8}$(P); cut in two, in ratifying covenant Je 34$^{18.19}$ (cf. עֶגְלָה Gn 15^{9}); elsewh. *image* of calf: made at Horeb, ע׳ מַסֵּכָה Ex 32$^{4.8}$ Dt 9^{16} Ne 9^{18}; ע׳ alone Ex 32$^{19.20.24.35}$ Dt 9^{21} ψ 106^{19}; two set up by Jerob. I in N. Isr., 1 K 12$^{28.32}$ 2 K 10^{29} 17^{16} 2 Ch 11^{15} 13^{8}, cf. Ho 8$^{5.6}$ (ע׳ שֹׁמְרוֹן, עֶגְלֵךְ), 13^{2}; also 10^{5} (v. I. עֶגְלָה ad fin.).

5697 †I. **עֶגְלָה n.f. heifer**;—abs. ע׳ Gn 15^{9}+; cstr. עֶגְלַת Is 7^{21}+; sf. עֶגְלָתִי Ju 14^{18}; pl. cstr. עֶגְלוֹת Ho 10^{5} (but v. infr.);—*heifer*, Is 7^{21}, used in ploughing Ju 14^{18} (fig.), threshing Je 50^{11} (ע׳ דָּשָׁא, in sim., v. דוש, read perh. דָּשָׁה), fig. of stateliness etc. Je 46^{20}; ע׳ מְלֻמָּדָה Ho 10^{11} *a trained heifer* (sim. of Ephr.); used for sacrif. 1 S 16^{2} (עֶגְלַת בָּקָר); cut in two for ratifying covenant Gn 15^{9} (J; ע׳ מְשֻׁלֶּשֶׁת; cf. עֵגֶל Je 34$^{18.19}$); in cleansing city from blood-guiltiness Dt 21^{3} (ע׳ בָּקָר), v$^{4.4.6}$; once of *calves* worshipped in N. Isr. Ho 10^{5} (where read prob. עֵגֶל, so 𝔊 We Now GASm, cf. Che, v. also the foll. sfs. ms.).

†II. **עֶגְלָה n.pr.f.** wife of David (on sense *heifer* cf. רָחֵל, לֵאָה; v. also Gray[Prop. N. 92, No. 27]);—2 S 3^{5} (𝔊 Αιγαλ, A Αιγας, 𝔊L Αγλα) = 1 Ch 3^{3} (𝔊 Αλα, A Αγλα, 𝔊L Εγλα). 5698

†**עֶגְלַת n.pr.loc.**;—ע׳ שְׁלִשִׁיָּה (the) *third Eglath* Is 15^{5} (𝔊 δάμαλις τριετής) Je 48^{34} (𝔊 ἀγγελίαν Σαλασεια), near Zoar and S. border of Moab. 5697, 7992

†**עָגֹל, עָגוֹל adj. round**;—abs. עָגֹל 1 K 7^{23} + 2 t., עָגוֹל 10^{19} 2 Ch 4^{2}; fpl. עֲגֻלּוֹת 1 K 7^{31};—*round* 1 K 7$^{31.31}$ (opp. מְרֻבָּעוֹת), 10^{19}; ע׳ סָבִיב *round in circuit* (perimeter) 7^{23} = 2 Ch 4^{2}, 1 K 7^{35}. 5696

†**עֲגָלָה n.f. cart** (from *rolling* of wheels; NH *id.;* Ph. (Pu.) עגלת (?) Lzb^{336}; Aram. עֲגַלְתָּא, ܥܓܠܬܐ; Sem. loan-word in Egypt. *āgarϑâ* Bondi^{38}, *ʿagolt* Erman[Egypt, 491]; cf. also Wilkinson [Anc. Egypt. (1878), i. 223–241, esp. 235, also 249] (illustr. vehicles drawn by cattle, cf. 1 S 6^{7} Nu 7^{3}));—abs. ע׳ 1 S 6^{7}+, sf. עֶגְלָתוֹ Is 28^{28}; pl. עֲגָלוֹת Gn 45^{19}+; cstr. עֶגְלֹת Nu 7^{3};—*cart*, used for transporting persons and things Gn 45$^{19.21.27}$ 46^{5} (E), 1 S 6$^{7.7.8.10.11.14.14}$, 2 S 6$^{3.3}$ = 1 Ch 13$^{7.7}$; Nu 7^{3} (ע׳ צָב *covered carts*), v$^{3.6.7.8}$ (P); in sim. Am 2^{13}, עֲבוֹת הָעֲ׳ Is 5^{18} *cart-rope*, אוֹפַן ע׳ 28^{27} of (*threshing-*) *wagon* (cf. Dr[Am. p. 228]), גַּלְגַּל ע׳ v^{28} *id.;*—ע׳ = *war-chariots* only ψ 46^{10} (Du *transport-wagons*). 5699

†**עָגִיל n.** [**m.**] **hoop, ring**;—abs. ע׳ Nu 31^{50} prob. *ear-ring* (+ טַבַּעַת, etc.); pl. עֲגִילִים עַל־אָזְנָיִךְ Ez 16^{12} (+ נֶזֶם עַל־אַפֵּךְ *nose-ring*). 5694

עֶגְלוֹן$_{13}$ **n.pr.** (cf. Gray[Prop. N. 92, No. 27]);—†**1. m.** a king of Moab, Ju 3$^{12.14.15.17.17}$, 𝔊 Εγλωμ. **2. loc.** Jos 10$^{3.5.23.37}$ 12^{12} 15^{34}, c. ה loc. 10^{34}, מֵעֶגְלוֹנָה v^{36}; 𝔊 Οδολλαμ Jos 10; Αιλαμ 12^{12}, A Εγλωμ, 𝔊L Εγλων, and so 15^{39}; site *ʿAǵlân*, N. of *Tel-el-Ḥesy*, Buhl[Geogr. 192]. 5700

עֶגְלַיִם Ez 47^{10} in עֵין ע׳ q.v. p. 745 5882

†**מַעְגָּל n.m.** [ψ 65, 12] **1. entrenchment; 2. track**;—abs. מ׳ 1 S 26^{5}+, c. ה loc. הַמַּעְגָּלָה 17^{20}; cstr. מַעְגַּל Pr 5^{26}+; pl. cstr. מַעְגְּלֵי ψ 23^{3} Pr 4^{11}; sf. מַעְגָּלֶיךָ ψ 65^{12}, elsewh. מַעְגְּלוֹתֶיהָ 17^{5}, מַעְגְּלֹתָיו Pr 5^{21}, ־תֶיהָ 2^{12} 5^{6}, ־תָם 2^{15} Is 59^{8};—**1.** *circumvallation, entrenchment* 1 S 17^{20} 26$^{5.7}$. **2.** *track* (prop. *wagon*-track), only fig.: **a.** in fig. of snares of wicked ψ 140^{6}. **b.** = course of action, or life, מ׳ רַגְלֶךָ Pr 4^{26}, מ׳ 5^{21} (|| דַּרְכֵי־אִישׁ); specif. good, right, מ׳ צֶדֶק ψ 23^{3}, מ׳ יֹשֶׁר Pr 4^{11}, מ׳ צַדִּיק Is 26^{7}; מ׳ טוֹב 2^{9}, bad sense Pr 2$^{15.18}$ 5^{6} 4570

Is 59[8]; *tracks* of 'י are those approved by him ψ 17[5]; or those traversed by him, מַעְגָּלֶיךָ יִרְעֲפוּן דָּשֶׁן 65[12] fig. of richly-laden cart dropping its contents in its track.

5701 †[עָגַם] **vb.** be grieved (NH *id.*; Aram. עֲגַם, and ܥܓܡ (in Lexx.) *id.*; cf. perh. also As. *agâmu, be vexed* Dl[HWB 16] (rare; cited under אגם)); —**Qal** *Pf.* 3 fs. אִם־לֹא . . . עָגְמָה נַפְשִׁי לָאֶבְיוֹן Jb 30[25] *was not my soul grieved for the poor?* (‖ בָּכִיתִי).

5702 †[עָגַן] **vb. Niph.** shut oneself in or off (NH *id.*, Pt. pass. *restrained* (esp. from marriage), also עוֹגִין *anchor*; 𝔗 עֲגַן *be imprisoned*); —*Impf.* 2 fpl. תֵּעָגֵנָה לְבִלְתִּי הֱיוֹת לְאִישׁ Ru 1[13] *would ye shut yourselves off, so as not to belong to a man?*

עגר (√of foll., meaning dubious; conject. in Meier[WurzelWB 38] Lag[BN 59]; on Gk. ἀγορ cf. Lewy[Fremdw. 8]).

5693 †עָגוּר **n.[m.]** appar. understood by Mass. as name of a bird; very uncertain; **crane** acc. to Saad. (Is), but note of crane not suitable (Tristr[NHB 239 f.]); —וְתוֹר וְסוּס וְעָגוּר Je 8[7]; כְּסוּס עָגוּר Is 38[14] (but here gloss Klo Brd Di Dn Che[Hpt]); Thes and (in Je) Hi Gf Gie del. ו and take ע׳ as adj. of סוס = *twittering* or the like; Thes assumes transpos. fr. גער, Eth. ገዐረ: *cry*.

5703-04, I, II, III. עַד v. I. עדה. עֵד v. עוד.
5706-07 p. 729
5714, 5750 עֹד v. עוד. עִדֹּא v. עדד. below, p. 728

עדד (√of foll.; cf. Ar. عَدَّ *count, reckon*, عِدَّةٌ *number, period*; Aram. עִדָּנָא *time*).

5708 †[עִדָּה] **n.f.** menstruation, so Vrss (prop. *time, period*); —pl. abs. בֶּגֶד עִדִּים Is 64[5] i.e. stained garment (fig. of best deeds of guilty people; ‖ טָמֵא).

5714 †עִדּוֹ, עִדֹּא, עִדּוֹא **n.pr.m.** Iddo; —**1.** father of an officer of Sol. עִדֹּא 1 K 4[14]; 𝔊 Αχελ, A Σαδωκ, 𝔊L Αχιαβ. **2.** grandfather of prophet Zechariah עִדּוֹ Zc 1[1], עִדּוֹא v[7]; 𝔊 Αδδω. **3.** a Levite עִדּוֹ 1 Ch 6[6]; 𝔊 Αδει, 𝔊L Αδδω. **4.** a priestly name עִדּוֹא van d. H. Ginsb (Baer עִדּוֹ) Ne 12[4]; 𝔊א etc. Αδαιας; also עִדִּיא v[16] Kt (עִדְּיָא?), Qr עִדּוֹא; 𝔊א τῷ Αδδαι, 𝔊L τῷ Αδαια. **5.** a seer עִדּוֹ הַחֹזֶה 2 Ch 12[15] = עִדּוֹ הַנָּבִיא 2 Ch
3260 13[22]; 𝔊 Αδ(δ)ω; = יֶעְדּוֹ 2 Ch 9[29], Ιωηλ(δ).

5752 עֹדֵד v. עוד. p. 729

†I. עָדָה **vb.** pass on, advance (Ar. عدو) عَدَا *pass by,* also *run* = Eth. ዐደወ: *pass by;* Aram. עדי *go along, go by* (oft. for Heb. 5710
עָבַר), Aph. *remove;* Syr. ܥܕܐ *pass by, come,* c. ܥܠ *fall upon*); —**Qal** *Pf.* 3 ms. עָדָה Jb 28[8] the fierce lion *hath not advanced* upon it (sc. the way). **Hiph.** *Pt.* מַעֲדֶה בֶּגֶד Pr 25[20] *removing a garment* (cf. Gn 38[19] 𝔗, Jon 3[6] Heb. and 𝔗).

†I. עַד and וָעֶד (so alw.) **n.m. perpetuity** 5703
(=*advancing* time, cf. As. *adû, time, at the present time*); —**1.** of *past time:* מִנִּי עַד Jb 20[4]; הררי עד Hb 3[6] *ancient mountains* (cf. עולם **1**). **2.** of *future time,* לָעַד (usu. לָעַד) *for ever:* **a.** during lifetime, of king ψ 21[7] Pr 29[14]; of others ψ 9[19] 22[27] 61[9] Pr 12[19]. **b.** of things, לָעַד בַּצּוּר יֵחָצְבוּן Jb 19[24]. **c.** *of continuous existence,* of nations, גְּבֶרֶת עַד (of Babylon, cf. עולם **2 c**) Is 47[7] (yet v. III. עַד **II 3**); anger, לעד Am 1[11]; elsewh. עֲדֵי עַד ψ 83[18] 92[8] Is 26[4] 65[18]. **d.** of divine existence, שֹׁכֵן עַד Is 57[15]; attributes, לָעַד ψ 111[3.10] 112[3.9]; residence in Zion, עֲדֵי עַד 132[14]; law of God, לָעַד 19[10]; promise as to dynasty of David, לָעַד 89[30]; עֲדֵי עַד 132[12]; inheritance of land, לָעַד 37[29]; continuous relations between God and his people 1 Ch 28[9] Is 64[8] Mi 7[18] לעד. **e.** phrases (see עולם **2 m**): (לְ)עוֹלָם וָעֶד ψ 9[6] 10[16] 21[5] 45[7.18] 48[15] 52[10] 104[5] 119[44] 145[1.2.21] Ex 15[18] Mi 4[5] Dn 12[3]; לָעַד לְעוֹלָם ψ 111[8] 148[6]; עַד־עוֹלְמֵי עַד Is 45[17].—Is 30[8] rd. (עַד־עוֹלָם) לְעֵד *for a witness* (𝔖 𝔙 𝔗 Ges Ew Di Che Du) for MT לָעַד.

†II. עַד **n.[m.]** booty, prey (upon which one 5706
advances, falls); —יֹאכַל עַד Gn 49[27] *devour prey* (‖ שָׁלָל); עַד שְׁלַל מַרְבֶּה Is 33[23] *prey of great spoil;* קוּמִי לְעַד Zp 3[8] (of God) my *rising up to the prey* (Br[MP]); אֲבִי עַד Is 9[5] *father* (i.e. *distributor*) *of booty* (Hi Kn Kue Br[MP] Du Che[Hpt]; > Ges Ew Di al. *everlasting father*).

III. עַד, in poetry עֲדֵי (†Nu 24[20.24] ψ 104[23] 5704
147[6] Jb 7[4] 20[5], and in עֲדֵי עַד Is 26[4] 65[18] ψ 83[18] 92[8] 132[12.14]: cf. עֲלֵי, אֱלֵי), **prep. as far as, even to, up to, until, while** (Aram. עַד, ܥܕ; Sab. עד, עדי, Mordtm[ZMG xxx (1876), 27]; DHM[xxxvii (1883), 414], As. *adi* Dl[§ 81 a] (Ar. عَدَا is *except*); perh. akin to عَدَا *pass on, advance to,* Kö[ii. 304, 309]: עֲדֵי prob. from ground-form *'ădăy,* Ol[428, 431] Kö[ii. 309 ff.]; but Lag[Sym. ii. 101–3, Mitth. i. 231 f.], as plur. like אַחֲרֵי); —with sf. עָדַי Nu 23[18]+, עָדֶיךָ Mi 4[8]+, etc., עֲדֵיכֶם †Jb 32[12]; 2 K 9[18] עַד־הֵם occurs;

—*as far as, even to* (differing from אֶל, in that the limit is *in*cluded, as in Ar. حَتَّى Fl[Kl. Schr. i. 402 f.]): **I. prep. 1.** of *space*:—**a.** Gn 11[31] ויבאו עד חרן *as far as* Haran, 12[6] 13[3.12] + oft., Is 8[8] עד צואר יגיע, 15[4] עד יהץ נשמע קולם, 25[12] 26[5] ψ 36[6] אמונתך עד שחקים, 69[2] באו מים עד נפש (cf. Jon 2[6] Mi 1[9] Je 4[10.18]), 90[3] תָּשֵׁב אֱנוֹשׁ עַד דַּכָּא, Jb 11[7], etc.; pregn. ψ 118[27] אִסְרוּ חַג עַד וגו׳ *bind* ... (and lead) *up to* ...; Is 57[9] עַד מֵרָחוֹק *even to* afar (מִן **1 c**); with the goal a *person*, Ex 22[8] עד האלהים יָבֹא דְּבַר שְׁנֵיהֶם, 1 S 9[9] ψ 65[3] עָדֶיךָ כָּל־בָּשָׂר יָבֹאוּ, Is 45[24] Jb 4[5], שׁוּב עַד י׳ Ho 14[2] *al.* (v. שׁוּב, stronger than שׁוּב אֶל־י׳); poet. Nu 24[20] וְאַחֲרִיתוֹ עֲדֵי אֹבֵד shall be *even unto* destruction, shall issue in destruction, v[24]; rarely with verbs of *attending*, הֶאֱזִין עַד † Nu 23[18], הִתְבּוֹנֵן עַד † Jb 32[12] 38[18] (usu. אֶל). Before another prep., 1 S 7[11] עַד מִתַּחַת ל׳, 1 K 4[12] עַד מֵעֵבֶר ל׳, עַד מֵעַל Ez 41[20], עַד לִפְנֵי Est 4[2], and even (si vera l.) עַד אֲלֵיהֶם 2 K 9[20]: cf. עַד נֶגֶד Ne 3[16.26], עד נכח Ju 19[10] +.

b. In the combin. מִן . . . (וְ)עַד, as Gn 10[19] מצידון . . . עַד עַזָּה *from* Sidon ... *as far as* Gaza + oft. (v. מן **5 a**); and idiom., not of actual space, but of *classes of objects*, to express the idea of *both ... and*, as Gn 19[4] מִנַּעַר וְעַד זָקֵן *from* young *to* old (inclusively) = *both* young *and* old (v. מִן **5 b**); without מִן, *even to* = *including*, Lv 11[42] Nu 8[4] *even to* (i.e. including) its base and its flowers, cf. 1 S 18[4].

2. Of *time*: **a.** (*a*) *even to, until* Gn 8[5] *even to* the 10th month, Ex 12[6] *unto* the 14th day, etc., v[15.18], etc.; עד היום *unto this day*, Gn 19[37.38], עד היום הזה 26[33] 32[33], both + oft.; עד יום sq. inf. Ex 40[37] Jos 6[10] Ju 18[30]; עד בקר *till* morning, Ex 12[10] + (15 t.), עד הבקר 16[23] + (11 t.); so עד (ה)ערב Ex 18[13.14] +, poet. עֲדֵי ערב ψ 104[23]; עַד עוֹלָם Gn 13[15] + oft.; עַד שֶׁבַע פְּעָמִים 2 K 4[35]; עַד דּוֹר וָדוֹר Is 13[20]; v. also בְּלִי, and בִּלְתִּי, *ad fin.* And sq. another prep., Lv 23[16] עַד מִמָּחֳרַת הַשַּׁבָּת, Ne 13[9] עַד אַחַר הַשַּׁבָּת. With the force of *against*, Ju 6[31] יוּמַת עַד הַבֹּקֶר; cf. (*b*) *end*. (*b*) sq. inf., both of past time, as Gn 8[7] 32[25] עַד עֲלוֹת הַשַּׁחַר, 33[3] 34[5], and esp. of future time, as 3[19] עַד שׁוּבְךָ *until* thy returning, 19[22] 27[45] Dt 7[20.23] 20[20] 22[2] 28[20.22],—both + oft.; cf. עַד תֻּמָּם Lv 25[29] + 10 t.; עַד תֹּם . . . Ju 3[25] +; עַד בּוֹשׁ Dt 2[15] +; עַד כַּלֵּה † 2 K 13[17.19] Ezr 9[14]; עַד כַּלּוֹתָ(ם) 1 S 15[18] Je 9[15] +; עַד אוֹר הַבֹּקֶר Ju 16[2] +; also in עַד הִשְׁמִדְךָ אֹתָם Dt 7[24] (cf. 28[48] Jos 11[14] 1 K 15[29] 2 K 3[25] 10[17] 24[20] [|| Je 52[3] הִשְׁלִיכוֹ]; on the anom. הִ׳, v. Dr, rd. prob. הַ׳); and most prob. (cf. Kö[iii. 583]) in עַד בִּלְתִּי הִשְׁאִיר לוֹ (לָהֶם) שָׂרִיד Dt 3[3] (v. Dr), + 5 t. (v. supr. p. 117), rd. prob. הַשְׁאִיר. With the force of *towards the end of, against*, esp. in עַד בֹּאֲ(ם), Gn 43[25] Ex 22[25] Nu 10[21] והקימו את המשכן עד בֹּאָם used to set up the tab. *against* their coming, 2 K 16[11], Ez 33[22]; cf. 2 S 17[22]. Ellipt. Ju 16[2] עַד אוֹר הַבֹּקֶר וַהֲרַגְנֻהוּ (wait) *till* the morning dawn, and we slay him! (GFM; Dr[§115]). (*c*) with various adverbs of time (q.v.), as עַד הֵנָּה, עַד מָתַי, עַד־מָה, עַד אָנָה, עַד עַתָּה, עַד כֵּן, עַד כֹּה, cf. עַד כַּמֶּה פְּעָמִים (v. מָה **4 b**). (*d*) to suggest also *degree* (cf. **3**), עַד אֵין מָקוֹם *until* there is no place Is 5[8], עַד אֵין מִסְפָּר † ψ 40[13] Jb 5[9] 9[10]; cf. Lv 26[18] וְאִם־עַד־אֵלֶּה and if *even up to these things*, even the end of all these punishments, you do not hearken to me.

b. *During* (rare; prop. *as far as* the limit indicated, including the time previous, cf. ἕως: so oft. Aram. עַד, ܥܕ, *while*), 2 K 9[22] what is peace עַד זְנוּנֵי אִיזֶבֶל *during*, etc.? Jb 20[5] עֲדֵי רָגַע *during* a moment; sq. inf. Ju 3[26] עַד הִתְמַהְמְהָם *during* their delaying, Ex 33[22] Jb 7[19] עַד בִּלְעִי רֻקִּי Jon 4[2].

3. Of *degree*, to suggest a higher or the highest; as עַד מְאֹד *even to* muchness, i.e. exceedingly (v. מְאֹד), עַד מְהֵרָה *even to* haste † ψ 147[15]; Est 5[6] וּמַה־בַּקָּשָׁתֵךְ עַד־חֲצִי הַמַּלְכוּת וְתֵעָשׂ, v[3] 7[2]. See also עַד לְ, below. With a neg., to express *not even as much as*, Dt 2[5] לא אתן לכם מארצם עד מִדְרַךְ כַּף רָגֶל, and with אֶחָד, † Ex 9[7] לֹא מֵת . . . עַד־אֶחָד, simil. 14[28] Ju 4[16] 2 S 17[22] (rd. אֶחָד for אַחַד: v. Dr). Sts. almost = Lat. *adeo*, 1 S 2[5] (si vera l.) עַד עֲקָרָה ילדה שבעה *even to* the barren, she hath borne seven, i.e. *even* the barren hath, etc., Jb 25[5] הֵן עַד־יָרֵחַ ולא יאהיל, Hg 2[19]. In comparisons, *to the degree of, even like* (rare), Na 1[10] עַד סִירִים סְבֻכִים (text dub.) entangled *even like* thorns, 1 Ch 4[27] לֹא הִרְבּוּ עַד בני יהודה did not multiply *to the degree of* (i.e. *like*), etc. Cf. 2 S 23[19] עַד הַשְּׁלֹשָׁה לֹא בָא did not *attain* (in prowess) *unto* the three.

II. Conj. 1. *until*:—**a.** עַד אֲשֶׁר *until that*: (*a*) with pf., of *past time*, Ex 32[20] ויטחן עד אשר דָּק (Dt 9[21]), Dt 2[14] עַד אֲשֶׁר עָבַרְנוּ, Jos 3[17] 8[26] Ju 4[24] 1 K 10[7] (2 Ch 9[6]), 2 K 17[20.23] 21[16]; with suggestion of *degree*, 1 S 30[4] (sq. אֵין), 1 K 17[17]; rarely of *future* time (the 'future perfect,' Dr[§17]), 2 S 17[13] (of degree), Ez 34[21]. So עַד שֶׁ־ (oft. in NH; v. שֶׁ), † Ju 5[7] Ct 3[4.4]; עַד כִּי † Gn 26[13] עַד כִּי־גָדַל מְאֹד, 41[49] 2 S 23[10]

2 Ch 26^{15}; and (of future time) עַד אֲשֶׁר אִם †Gn 28^{15} Nu 32^{17} Is 6^{11}. (*b*) with impf., usu. of *future* time, Gn 27^{44} עַד אֲשֶׁר תָּשׁוּב חֲמַת אָחִיךָ, 29^{8} Ex 23^{30} 24^{14} Lv 22^{4} Nu 11^{20} 20^{17} 1 S 22^{3} Ho 5^{15}+; rarely of *past* time, Jon 4^{5} עד אשר יראה *till he should* see, Ec 2^{3}. So (of the future) עַד שֶׁ- †Ct 2$^{7.17}$ 3^{5} 4^{6} 8^{4} ψ 123^{2}; and עַד כִּי †Gn 49^{10} עַד כִּי־יָבֹא שִׁילֹה.

b. עַד alone, *until:* (*a*) with pf., of *past* time, Jos 2^{22} 4^{23} עַד־עָבְרֵנוּ, 1 S 20^{41} עַד דָּוִד הִגְדִּיל, 2 S 21^{10} 1 K 11^{16} Ez 28^{15}; of the *future* (rare), 2 K 7^{3} עַד מָתְנוּ, Ez 39^{15} Dn 11^{36} עַד כָּלָה זָעַם. So עַד אִם (of the fut.), †Gn 24$^{19.33}$ Is 30^{17} Ru 2^{21}. (*b*) with impf., of *future* time, 1 S 1^{22} (ellipt.: cf. Ju 16^{2}, **I 2 a** (*b*) *end*), Is 22^{14} 26^{20} 32^{15} 62$^{1.7}$ ψ 57^{2} 71^{18} Jb 27^{5}+; of the *past* (rare), Ex 15^{16} עד יעבור עמך, v^{16} Jos 10^{13} (poet.) עַד יִקֹּם גּוֹי אֹיְבָיו, ψ 73^{17}.—N.B. In poetry, עַד is sts. used to mark not an absolute close, but an epoch, or turning-point, in the fut., as ψ 110^{1} (v. De) עַד אָשִׁית אֹיְבֶיךָ הֲדֹם לְרַגְלֶיךָ, Ho 10^{12} Jb 14^{6} (but v. **3**); after a neg. cl., Gn 49^{10} Nu 23^{24} Is 42^{4} ψ 71^{18} 112^{8} Jb 8^{21} (but rd. prob. with Ew Hi Di Du *al.* עֹד he will *yet*, etc., understanding v^{20} as present, not future).

2. *While* (rare: cf. **I 2 b**):—**a.** with pf., 1 S 14^{19} עד דִּבֶּר שאול *while* Saul spake. **b.** with impf., ψ 141^{10} יַחַד אָנֹכִי עַד אֶעֱבוֹר *while I* at the same time pass by. **c.** with ptcp., Jb 1^{18} עַד זֶה מְדַבֵּר (but rd. prob. עֹד, as v$^{16.17}$), Ne 7^{3}. **d.** עַד שֶׁ- (without vb.) †Ct 1^{12}. So עַד לֹא *while not = ere yet* (of past time) †Pr 8^{26} עד לא עשה ארץ (so עַד לָא, حَتَّى لا, oft., e.g. Gn 24^{15} 𝔗, Mt 1^{18}); and עד אשר לא (of the fut.) †Ec 12$^{1.2.6}$ (cf. Talm. עַד דְּלָא, Mishn. עַד שֶׁלֹּא).

3. Of degree, *to the point that, so that even* (rare), Is 47^{7} Thou saidst, I shall be for ever a lady, עַד לֹא שַׂמְתְּ אֵלֶּה עַל לִבֵּךְ *to the point that* (going so far in thy pride that) thou didst not, etc. (but Hi Che Du *al.* join גְּבֶרֶת עַד I shall be for ever, a lady *perpetually;* v. I. עַד); Jb 14^{6} (Di De Bu Du) *to the point that* he may enjoy, etc., Is 22^{14} (Du). In Jos 17^{14} עַד אֲשֶׁר עַד כֹּה בֵּרְכַנִי י׳, rd. עַל אֲשֶׁר *because* that (Ges Buhl; cf. Di).

†**III.** עַד לְ, a strengthened form for עַד, found chiefly in Ch Ezr, and occurring in most of the above senses. Thus **1.** of *space:* עַד לְבוֹא חֲמָת Jos 13^{5} Ju 3^{3} 1 Ch 13^{5}, עד ל׳ מִדְבָּרָה 5^{9}, עַד לְמִזְרַח הַגָּיְא 1 Ch 4^{39}, עד ל׳ מצרים 2 Ch 26^{8}; עַד לַשָּׁמַיִם 2 Ch 14^{12}; עַד לִגְרָר 12^{17}; עַד לְמַעְלָה 2 Ch 28^{9} Ezr 9^{6}.

2. Of *time:* עד לעולם 1 Ch 23^{25} 28^{7}; עַד לְמֵרָחוֹק 2 Ch 26^{15} Ezr 3^{13}; Ezr 9^{4} עד למנחת הערב; עד לַדָּבָר הַזֶּה Ezr 10^{14} prob. *during* (Keil: Ges Be *with regard to*, strengthened for לְ); sq. inf. עַד לַעֲלוֹת הַמִּנְחָה 1 K 18^{29}; עַד לִכְלוֹת 1 Ch 28^{20} 2 Ch 29^{28}; עַד לְכַלֵּה 2 Ch 24^{10} 31^{1}; עד להשחית 26^{16}; עַד לָמוּת 32^{24} (‖ 2 K 20^{1} לָמוּת alone); Ezr 10^{14} עד להשיב.

3. Of *degree:* עד לְמַחֲנֶה גָדוֹל *even unto* (till there was) a great camp, 1 Ch 12^{23}; עַד לְמַעְלָה = *exceedingly* 2 Ch 16^{12} 17^{12} 26^{8}; עַד לִמְאֹד 2 Ch 16^{14}; עַד לָרֹב 29^{30}; עַד לְשִׂמְחָה 31^{30}; עַד לְאֵין מַרְפֵּא 36^{16}.

†עֲדֶנָּה Ec 4^{2} Baer Ginsb (al. עֲדֶנָּה), abbrev. 5728
עֲדֶן Ec 4^{3} (from עַד־הֵן, עַד־הֵנָּה; cf. NH עֲדַיִן, e.g. Ned. 9^{10}), **adv. hitherto, still.**

†II. **עָדָה** **vb. ornament, deck oneself** 5710
(Aram. in deriv. עִידוּת, *ornament;* cf. perh. עֲדִיתָא, *scurf, scab;* Ar. عَدْوَى *mange, scab*, etc. [as sheathing, or excrescence ?], also عِدَّى, *broad stone* for covering grave, etc., Lane 1979);—**Qal** *Pf.* 2 fs. וְעָדִית Ez 23^{40}; *Impf.* 3 fs. תַּעְדֶּה Is 61^{10}, וַתַּעַד Ho 2^{15}; 2 fs. תַּעְדִּי Je 4^{30} 31^{4}, וַתַּעְדִּי Ez 16^{13}; 1 s. sf. וָאֶעְדֵּךְ v^{11}; *Imv.* ms. עֲדֵה־נָא Jb 40^{10};—*ornament;* usu. **1. a.** reflex., *deck oneself* with, c. acc. of (woman's) ornaments, of bride Is 61^{10} (sim.; cf. הִלְבִּישׁ v^{a}); fig. of Isr. Ho 2^{15} Je 31^{4}; Jerus. Je 4^{30} (c. acc. cogn.; ‖ לָבַשׁ), Ez 16^{13} (מַלְבּוּשֵׁךְ in ‖ clause), 23^{40} (c. acc. cogn.). **b.** metaph., עֲדֵה־נָא גָאוֹן וגו׳ Jb 40^{10} *deck now thyself* [Job] *with majesty.* **2.** c. 2 acc., וָאֶעְדֵּךְ עֶדִי Ez 16^{11} *and I decked thee* [Jerus.] *with finery* (? rd. **Hiph.** וָאַ׳).

†עָדָה **n.pr.f.** (*ornament;* or (Ar. غُدْوَةٌ, 5711
غَدْوَةٌ) *morning*) 𝔊 Ἀδ(δ)α;—wife, **1.** of Lamech Gn 4$^{19.20.23}$ (J). **2.** of Esau 36$^{2.4.10.12.16}$ (P^{R}).

†עֲדִי **n.[m.] coll. ornaments** (with which 5716
one is *decked*);—ע׳ abs. Is 49^{18}, עֲדִי Ez 16^{11} 23^{40}; cstr. 2 S 1^{24}+; sf. עֶדְיוֹ Ex 33^{4}+, עֶדְיְךָ Ex 33^{5}, etc.;—*ornaments:* **1.** of women 2 S 1^{24} (ע׳ זָהָב), Je 2^{32}; of Jerus. under fig. of woman 4^{30} (ע׳ זָהָב), Ez 16^{11} 23^{40} (all acc. cogn. c. עָדָה), Is 49^{18} (sim.).—עֲדִי עֲדָיִים Ez 16^{7}, rd. prob. עַד עִדִּים *unto menstruation* (maturity), JDMich Co Berthol (rdg. בְּעֵת עִדּ׳), Toy. עֶדְיֵךְ ψ 103^{5} [sf. ref. to נַפְשִׁי] is dub., 𝔊 τ. ἐπιθυμίαν σου [rdg. אַוָּתֵךְ ? this usu. c.

[נַפְשֶׁ]; *thine age, prime* (cf. I. עד) JDMich Thes; conject. in Hup-Now Che Du. **2.** of men Ex 33[4.5.6] (JE). **3.** in gen., as feeding pride Ez 7[20] (צְבִי עֶדְיוֹ, sf. ref. to silver and gold, v[19]). **4.** *trappings* of horse ψ 32[9] (De Hup, cf. Du), si vera l., but prob. corrupt; Che (after v. Ortenb.) לְבְלֹם עַד יוּבַל אֵלֶיךָ must be curbed *till he can be brought*, etc.

5717 †עֲדִיאֵל **n.pr.m.** (*an ornament is Ēl;* cf. Sab. n. pr. עדאל Hal[51, 2]);—**1.** a Simeonite 1 Ch 4[36], 𝔊A Εδιηλ, 𝔊L Αδαηλ. **2.** a priest 9[12], 𝔊 Αδιηλ. **3.** father of officer, David's time 27[25], 𝔊 Ωδιηλ.—Cf. Gray[Prop. N. 225, 231].

5718 †עֲדָיָה(וּ) **n.pr.m.** (י׳ *has decked himself*);— **1.** עֲדָיָהוּ father of a Judaean captain 2 Ch 23[1], 𝔊 Αζεια, A Αδαια, 𝔊L Αδαιου (genit.). Elsewhere עֲדָיָה: **2.** grandfather of Josiah 2 K 22[1], 𝔊 Εδειva, A Ιεδιδα, 𝔊L Οζιου (genit.). **3.** a Levite 1 Ch 6[26], 𝔊 Αζεια, A 𝔊L Αδ(α)ια. **4.** a Benjamite 8[21], 𝔊 Αβια, A Αλαια, 𝔊L Αδαια. **5.** a priest 9[12] Ne 11[12], 𝔊 Αδαια(ς). **6.** two with foreign wives: **a.** Ezr 10[29], 𝔊 Αδα, 𝔊L Αδαιας. **b.** v[39], 𝔊 Αδαια, 𝔊L Αδδαιας. **7.** a Judahite Ne 11[5], 𝔊 Οζ(ε)ια, 𝔊L Αδαια.

5723 †עֲדִיתַיִם **n.pr.loc.** town of Judah in the שְׁפֵלָה Jos 15[36], 𝔊A Αδιαθαειμ, 𝔊L Αγεθθαιμ.

5712-13 I. עֵדָה v. יעד. II. III. עֵדָה v. עוד. p. 417, 729f

5708, 5714-15 [עִדָּה], עִדּוֹ(א), עֵדֻת עֵדוּת v. עדד. עֵדוֹת v. עוד. p. 723, 730

5716-18 עֲדִי, עֲדִיאֵל, עֲדָיָה(וּ) v. II. עדה. p. 725, above

5708, 5714 עדיא v. עִדּוֹא. עִדִּים v. עִדָּה. p. 723

5723 עֲדִיתַיִם v. עדה. p. 726

I. עדל (√ of foll.; poss. = Ar. عَدَلَ *act equitably* (so Thes), or As. *edlu, hero*).

5724 †עַדְלַי **n.pr.m.** 1 Ch 27[29], 𝔊 Αδαι, 𝔊L Αδλι.

II. עדל (√ of foll.; cf. Ar. عَدَلَ *turn aside*, whence עֲדֻלָּם = *retreat, refuge*, so Lag[BN 54], cf. Dr[Sm, p. 293] Buhl[Geogr. 97]).

5725 †עֲדֻלָּם **n.pr.loc.** old Canaanite city, 𝔊 Οδολλαμ, with king Jos 12[15] (D), in the שְׁפֵלָה 15[35] (P; 𝔊L Αδαλαμ), cf. Mi 1[15] Ne 11[30]; (re-)built by Rehob. acc. to 2 Ch 11[7] (Οδολαμ); מְעָרַת ע׳ (rd. מְצָדַת, מְצֻדַת, v. מְעָרָה sub I. ערר) 1 S 22[1] 2 S 23[13] 1 Ch 11[15]; site prob. *'Îd-el-Mîye* (*'Aid el-Ma*), c. 13 miles WSW. from Bethlehem, v. GASm[Geogr. 229] Buhl[Geogr. 193] and reff.

†עֲדֻלָּמִי **adj.gent.** Adullamite;—אִישׁ ע׳ Gn 38[1], הָע׳ as subst. v[12.20]. 5726

I. עדן (√ of foll.; cf. Ar. غَدَنٌ *mollities, languor*, etc., Frey (Ḳam.); Palm. עדנא (good) *fortune* Cook[89]; NH עִידּוּן *luxuriousness*).

†I. [עֵדֶן] **n.[m.]** luxury, dainty, delight;—pl. abs. עֲדָנִים *luxuries* 2 S 1[24] si vera l. (rd. perh. סְדִינִים [v. סָדִין] Klo Gr HPS); pl. sf. Je 51[34] he hath filled his belly מֵעֲדָנָי *from my dainties* (fig. of Nebuchad.'s plunder; Gie reads מַעֲדַנַּי); 𝔗 Gf Rothst join with foll.: *from my dainties hath he thrust me forth;* fig. of *delights* of worshipping י׳, נַחַל עֲדָנֶיךָ ψ 36[9] (|| דֶּשֶׁן בֵּיתֶךָ). 5730

†[עָדַן] **vb.denom.Hithp.** luxuriate (NH Pi. *delight* (act.), so Syr. ܥܕܢ);—*Impf.* 3 mpl. וַיִּתְעַדְּנוּ בְּטוּבְךָ Ne 9[25] *and they luxuriated in thy great goodness* (+ וַיֹּאכְלוּ וַיִּשְׂבְּעוּ וַיַּשְׁמִינוּ). 5727

†II. עֵדֶן **n.pr.m.** Levite name 2 Ch 29[12] (𝔊 Ιω(α)δαν), 31[15] (𝔊 Οδομ, 𝔊L Ιαδαν). 5729

†עַדְנָא **n.pr.m.** **1.** man with foreign wife 5733
Ezr 10[30] (Ginsb; עַדְנָה van d. H. Baer), 𝔊 Αιδαινε, 5734
𝔊L Εδνα. **2.** Ne 12[5], 𝔊א Αδανας, 𝔊L Εδνας.

†עֶדְנָה **n.f.** delight;—Gn 18[12] (sexual). 5730

†עַדְנָה **n.pr.m.** **1.** a prince of Judah 2 Ch 5734
17[14], 𝔊 Εδνα(α)ς. **2.** a Manassite 1 Ch 12[21], prob. (rdg. ע׳, with Codd., for עַדְנַח; van d. H.
עַדְנַח, 𝔊 Εδνα).—Vid. also עַדְנָא. above 5733

†I. [עָדִין] **adj.** voluptuous;—fs. עֲדִינָה as 5719
subst. Is 47[8], of Bab. personified, (thou) *voluptuous one.*—עֲדִינוֹ העצנו 2 S 23[8], read עוֹרֵר אֶת־ 5722
חֲנִיתוֹ, || 1 Ch 11[11] Th We Dr, cf. Ginsb[note].

†II. עָדִין **n.pr.m.** **1.** in בְּנֵי ע׳, returned 5720
exiles Ezr 2[15] = Ne 7[20], Ezr 8[6], 𝔊 Αδ(δ)ιν, Ηδ(ε)ιν, etc. **2.** a chief Ne 10[17], 𝔊 Ηδ(ε)ιν, Αδειν.

†עֲדִינָא **n.pr.m.** Reubenite captain, David's 5721
time, acc. to 1 Ch 11[42], 𝔊 Αδ(ε)ινα.

†[מַעֲדָן] **n.[m.]** dainty (food), delight;— 4574
only pl.;—מַעֲדַנֵּי מֶלֶךְ Gn 49[20] (poem) *royal dainties;* הָאֹכְלִים לְמַעֲדַנִּים La 4[5] those who ate (*acc. to dainties*) *daintily;* more gen. וְיִתֵּן מַעֲדַנִּים לְנַפְשֶׁךָ Pr 29[17] he shall give *delight* to thy soul (|| וִינִיחֶךָ).—מַעֲדַנּוֹת, v. p. 588, also sub ענד. p. 772 4575

II. עדן (√ of foll.; cf. perh. As. *edinu, plain* (in word-lists), Schr[COT Gn 2, 8], Dl[Pa 79 f.]; other views v. Di[Gn 2, 8]).

5731 † III. עֵ֫דֶן **n.pr.terr.** (prob. associated by Heb. with I. עֵדֶן); —district in which lay garden of ׳י, home of Adam and Eve: וַיִּטַּע גַּן־בְּעֵדֶן Gn 2⁸, river יֹצֵא מֵע׳ v¹⁰, קִדְמַת־ע׳ 4¹⁶; גַּן־ע׳ 2¹⁵ 3²³·²⁴ (all 𝔊 Εδεμ); cf. כְּגַן־ע׳ Ez 36³⁵ Jo 2³ and כְּע׳ Is 51³ (‖ גַּן־י׳), all sim. of fertility; ע׳ גַּן־אֱלֹהִים Ez 28¹³, עֲצֵי ע׳ 31⁹, עֲצֵי ע׳ אֲשֶׁר בְּגַן הָאֱלֹהִים v¹⁶·¹⁸·¹⁸ (𝔊 Ez Jo ἡ τρυφή; Is παράδεισος).

5729 † עֶ֫דֶן **n.pr. (? urb. et) terr.** conquered by Assyria (prob. = IV. עֵדֶן; pointed עֶדֶן, to differentiate from III. ע׳, cf. WMM As. u. Eur. 291); —בְּנֵי־ע׳ 2 K 19¹² (𝔊 υἱοὺς Ἔδεμ) = Is 37¹² (in Telassar), ע׳ alone Ez 27²³ (+ חָרָן וְכַנֵּה); prob. = (*Bit-*)*Adini* on Middle Euphrates Schr COT 2 K 19, 12 Dl Pa 263 f.—

1040 בֵּית ע׳, v. p. 112.

5728 עֲדֶ֫נָה, עֲדֶן v. עַד **prep.** sub I. עדה. p. 725

5734 עַדְנַח v. עַדְנָה sub I. עדן. p. 726

5735 עַדְעָדָה v. II. עֲרוֹעֵר sub II. ערר. p. 793

5736 † [עָדַף] **vb. remain over, be in excess,** syn. of סרח q.v., only PH (NH *id.*, Aram. עֲדִיף *superior* (to); Ar. غَدَفَ *be profuse*, IV. *let down* veil, or curtain, etc.; غَدَفٌ *plentifulness*);—**Qal** *Pt.* סֶרַח הָעֹדֵף Ex 26¹² *the surplus* (of curtains) *that remains over*, so f. הָעֹדֶ֫פֶת v¹², and הָעֹדֵף as subst. v¹³ *the excess* in (ב) length; הָעֹדֵף = *the surplus* of food Ex 16²³, of price of field Lv 25²⁷; הָעֹדְפִים עַל־ *those over and above*, Nu 3⁴⁶·⁴⁹, cf. v⁴⁸ (no עַל־). **Hiph.** *Pf.* 3 ms. הֶעְדִּיף Ex 16¹⁸ *have a surplus* (of manna; opp. הֶחְסִיר).

5737 † I. [עָדַר] **vb.** prob. (si vera l.) **help** (Aram. loan-word, Syr. ܥܕܰܪ, 𝔗 עֲדַר (rare) = Heb. עזר q.v.; > Thes, assuming mng. *arrange, order*);—**Qal** *Inf. cstr.* לַעֲדֹר 1 Ch 12³⁴ (Baer Ginsb; van d. H. v³³; this mng. also 𝔊 𝔙); but < Codd. לַעֲזֹר (cf. v¹⁸·²²·²³, van d. H. v¹⁷·²¹·²²), so Kau Buhl; *Pt.* pl. cstr. עֹדְרֵי מַעֲרָכָה v³⁹ (van d. H. v³⁸), rd. עֹרְכֵי (q.v. v³⁴) 𝔊 Kau; see ערך.

5741 † עַדְרִיאֵל **n.pr.m.** son-in-law of Saul (appar. Aram. name, *my help is God* = Heb. עַזְרִיאֵל q.v.; so Ne Am. Jour. Sem. Lang, xiii (1897), 173 HPS cf. Gray Prop. N. 309; cf. OAram. יעדראל ClGann JAs, 1883, Fev.-Mar., 139, No. 13);—1 S 18¹⁹ (𝔊A Ιηλ, 𝔊L Εδριηλ), 2 S 21⁸ (𝔊 Σερει, A Εσδρι, 𝔊L Εζρι).

5737 † II. [עָדַר] **vb. hoe** (NH *id.*; so Ar. (in Syria) عَدَرَ, مَعْدُور *pick, hoe,* Cuche (معدور also Dozy ii. 101b); cf. Fl Kl. Schr. ii. 628); —**Niph.** *Impf.* 3 ms. לֹא יֵעָדֵר Is 5⁶ *it* (the vineyard) *shall not be hoed* (‖ יִזָּמֵר); 3 mpl. בַּמַּעְדֵּר יֵעָדֵרוּן 7²⁵ which *used to be hoed with the hoe* (subj. הֶהָרִים).

† מַעְדֵּר **n.[m.]** hoe Is 7²⁵, v. foregoing. 4576

† III. [עָדַר] **vb. Niph.** be lacking, fail 5737
(Ar. غَدَرَ *remain* or *lag behind*);—**Niph.** *Pf.*, all c. לֹא, 3 ms. נֶעְדַּר לָהֶם 1 S 30¹⁹ not anything *was lacking to them;* נֶעְדָּר none *was lacking* 2 S 17²² Is 40²⁶; of ׳י, Zp 3⁵ *he doth not fail;* 3 fs. נֶעְדָּ֫רָה Is 34¹⁶ no wild beast *is lacking. Pt.* f. נֶעְדֶּ֫רֶת Is 59¹⁵ truth has become *lacking.* **Pi.** *Impf.* 3 mpl. לֹא יְעַדְּרוּ דָּבָר 1 K 5⁷ *they left nothing lacking.*

† I. עֵ֫דֶר **n.m.** Gn 29, 2 **flock, herd** (NH *id.*; 5739
Aram. עֶדְרָא; on 𝔊 Γαδερ Gn 35¹⁶ (= 𝔖 v²¹) v. Lag BN 76 f., who assigns ע׳ therefore, plausibly, to III. עדר (غدر), as *lagging, loitering*);—ע׳ abs. Gn 32¹⁷·¹⁷ +, cstr. Ct 4¹ +; sf. עֶדְרוֹ Is 40¹¹ +; pl. עֲדָרִים Gn 29² +, cstr. עֶדְרֵי Mi 5⁷ +, etc.;—**1.** *flock:* **a.** of sheep, ע׳ צֹאן Gn 29² (J), Mi 5⁷, ע׳ הַצֹּ׳ Jo 1¹⁸; cf. Gn 29²·³·⁸ 30⁴ (all J), 1 S 17³⁴ Je 51²³ Mal 1¹⁴; ‖ צֹאן Ez 34¹² (sim.), Pr 27²³; + בְּהֵמָה 2 Ch 32²⁸; ע׳ הָרְחֵלִים Ct 6⁶ = 4² (ins. prob. הָר׳); sign of desolation Is 17² 32¹⁴ (מִרְעֵה ע׳), Zp 2¹⁴ Je 6³, of peace 31²⁴; in sim. also Mi 2¹² Je 31¹⁰ ψ 78⁵²; fig. of Isr. Is 40¹¹ Je 13²⁰ (‖ צֹאן), ע׳ יהוה v¹⁷, so עֶדְרוֹ Zc 10³. **b.** of goats, ע׳ הָעִזִּים Ct 4¹ 6⁵. **c.** undefined Ju 5¹⁶ Jb 24² Ct 1⁷. **2.** *herds, flocks and herds:* **a.** incl. sheep, cattle, etc., Gn 32¹⁷·¹⁷·¹⁷·¹⁷·²⁰ (cf. v¹⁴; all E). **b.** specif. ע׳ בָּקָר Jo 1¹⁸.—מִגְדַּל־עֵדֶר v. p. 154 supr.

† II. עֵ֫דֶר **n.pr.m.** (cf. Nab. n.pr. עדרו = Ar. 5740
غَدَرٌ Lzb 337);—a Levite 1 Ch 23²³ 24³⁰, 𝔊 Αιδαθ, Ηλα, A 𝔊L Εδερ.

† III. עֵ֫דֶר **n.pr.loc.** in extreme S. of Judah 5740
Jos 15²¹, site unknown; 𝔊 Αρα, A Εδραι, 𝔊L Εβερ.

† [עֵ֫דֶר] **n.pr.m.** a Benjamite, עָ֫דֶר 1 Ch 8¹⁵; 5738
𝔊 Ωδηδ, A Ωδερ, 𝔊L Αδαρ.

† [עֲדָשָׁה] **n.f. lentile** (NH עֲדָשָׁה *id.*; Löw 5742
No. 140; Ar. عَدَسٌ; on formation v. Lag BN 50);—pl. עֲדָשִׁים growing 2 S 23¹¹; art. of food, 2 S 17²⁸ Ez 4⁹; נְזִיד ע׳ Gn 25³⁴ (J) *pottage of lentiles.*

עָוָא v. עַוָּה. p. 731 5755

עוב (√ of foll.; cf. Ar. غَابَ, غيب *be absent, hidden*, of sun, *set;* غَابَةٌ *hidden place, thicket, wood,* so Syr. ܥܒܐ; hence *obscuring clouds,* cf. NH עָב, Aram. עֵיבָא *cloud(s)*).

5645 II. עָב [33] **n.m.**[Is 19,1] and (1 K 18[44] Kö[Synt. 163]) **f. dark cloud, cloud-mass, thicket**;—ע׳ abs. 1 K 18[44]+, cstr. Is 18[4] Pr 16[15]; pl. עָבִים Ju 5[4]+, עָבוֹת 2 S 23[4] ψ 77[18]; cstr. עָבֵי 2 S 22[12] ψ 18[12]; sf. עָבָיו ψ 18[13] (but prob. del., v. עבר **Qal** ad fin.);—**1.** *dark cloud*: **a.** rain-cloud Ju 5[4] Is 5[6] 1 K 18[44.45]+9 t. **b.** as high Is 14[14] Jb 20[6], +Ez 19[11] 31[3.10.14] (rdg. עָבוֹת, v. עֲבֹת). **c.** chariot of י׳ Is 19[1] ψ 104[3]; covering his eyes Jb 22[14]. **d.** casting shadow Is 25[5], cf. 2 S 23[4]. **e.** as swift Is 60[8], and transient 44[22] Jb 30[15] (all sim.). **f.** disposed by God Jb 36[29] 37[16]. **g.** ע׳ טל Is 18[4] *cloud of dew, dew-mist* (sim.). **2.** (cloud-) *mass*, ע׳ שְׁחָקִים 2 S 22[12] *masses of clouds* (enwrapping י׳)=ψ 18[12] (v[13] v. supr.). **3.** *thicket* as refuge Je 4[29] (perh. under Aram. influence).—

5646, 5672 עב Ex 19[9] v. עֲבִי sub עבה. I. עָב v. p. 713 supr.

5743 †[עוּב] **vb. denom. Hiph.** becloud, *Impf.* 3 ms. יָעִיב בְּאַפּוֹ אֲדֹנָי אֶת־בַּת־צִיּוֹן La 2[1] (Bu הֵעִיב).

עוג (√of foll., cf. NH *id. draw a circle*, עוּגָה (circular) *ditch*; Aram. עוּגִית *id.*; Ar. عَوِجَ *be crooked, curved, bent*, عَاجٌ *elephant's tusk, tortoise-shell*).

5692 †**עֻגָה** **n.f. disc or cake of bread**;—abs. ע׳ Ho 7[8] 1 K 17[13], cstr. עֻגַת 19[6] Ez 4[12]; pl. עֻגוֹת Gn 18[6] Nu 11[8]; cstr. עֻגֹת Ex 12[39];—*bread-cake*, made of קֶמַח סֹלֶת Gn 18[6] (J), of קֶמַח 1 K 17[13], of manna Nu 11[8] (JE; vb. בִּשֵּׁל), of barley Ez 4[12] (sim.); unleavened, עֻגֹת מַצּוֹת Ex 12[39] (E; vb. אָפָה); ע׳ רְצָפִים 1 K 19[6] *cake of hot-stones*, i.e. baked on them; metaph. ע׳ בְּלִי הֲפוּכָה Ho 7[8] Ephr. is *a cake not turned* (i.e. burnt, ruined).—On ע׳ v. Benz[Arch. 85 f.] Now[Arch. i. 111] Kennedy[Ency. Bib. BREAD] and synonyms, Ib.[CAKE].

5746 †[עוּג] **vb. denom.** bake (a cake; lit. *make a cake of*);—**Qal** *Impf.* 2 ms. sf. 3 fs. תְּעֻגֶנָּה (so Baer Ginsb, > van d. H. תְּעֻגֶנָּה) *thou shalt bake it* (on form v. Kö[i. 496 f.] Ges[§ 59 k]) Ez 4[12].

4580 †**מָעוֹג** **n.[m.] cake**;—abs. 1 K 17[12]; לַעֲגֵי מ׳ ψ 35[16] *mockers of* (for) *a cake*, i.e. buffoons, but 𝔊 Che al. rd. לָעֲגוּ (לַעֲגֵי) לַעַג.

5747 †**עוֹג** and (1 K 4[19]) עֹג **n.pr.m.** (orig. n.pr. div. acc. to RS[Sem i. 91, 2nd ed. 93]);—**Og**, giant king of Bashan (i.e., peculiarly, of a country, v. RS[l.c.]), usu. + סִיחוֹן (q.v.); Nu 21[33] (JE), 32[33] (P), Dt 1[4] 3[1.3.4.10.11.13] 4[47] 29[6] 31[4] Jos 2[10] 9[10] 12[4] 13[12.30.31] (prob. all D), 1 K 4[19] Ne 9[22] ψ 135[11] 136[20]; 𝔊 Ωγ (Γωγ B Dt 3[1] 4[47]).

5748 **עוּגָב, עֻגָב** v. עגב. p. 721

5749 †[עוּד] **vb.** prob. **return, go about, repeat, do again** (Ar. عود, عَادَ *return, do again*, IV. *restore*, also *say again, iterate*, عَادَةٌ *habit*; Eth. ዐደ: *turn about, surround*, ዐውድ: *circuit, circle*; Syr. Pa. ܥܰܝܶܕ *accustom*, Ethpe. Aph. *be accustomed*, ܥܝܳܕܳܐ *usage, ceremony*, ܥܐܕܳܐ *festival* (Brock), whence Ar. عِيد *id.*, as loan-word, Frä[276]; Palm. עידא *usage* Lzb[337] Cook[90]; NH עֵד, and esp. עֵדוּת=BH, also עִיד *festival*, 𝔗 עִידָא; cf. prob. As. Shaph. *uš-id*, *he solemnly affirmed* Dl[HWB 32]);—only intens.: **Pi.** *surround* (cf. Eth.), *Pf.* 3 ms. sf. עִוְּדֻנִי ψ 119[61] (cf. סְבָבוּנִי 18[6]). **Pōlēl**, *restore, relieve* (cf. Ar. IV.), *Impf.* 3 ms. יְעוֹדֵד, c. acc. pers. ψ 146[9] (|| שָׁמַר, opp. עִוֵּת), 147[6] (opp. הִשְׁפִּיל). **Hithpōl.** *be restored*, *Impf.* 1 pl. וַנִּתְעוֹדָד ψ 20[9] (+קוּם, opp. נָפַל; 𝔊 ἀνωρθώθημεν).

5750 **עוֹד** and (14 t.: Fr[MM 256]) עֹד, **subst. a going round, continuance, but used mostly as adv. acc. still, yet, again, besides**: with sf. עוֹדֶנִּי (with appar. verbal form, like אֵינֶנִּי: Ol[§ 222 g] Sta[§ 352 b] Kö[ii. 444, iii. 360] Ges[§ 100. 5]), †Dt 31[27] Jos 14[11] 1 S 20[14], עוֹדִי †Gn 48[15] ψ 104[33] 139[18] 146[2]; עוֹדְךָ Gn 46[30]+4 t., f. עוֹדָךְ †1 K 1[14]; עוֹדֶנּוּ Gn 18[22]+20 t. (never עוֹדוֹ), עוֹדֶנָּה †1 K 1[22], עוֹדָהּ †Is 28[4]; עוֹדָם †Ex 4[18] Est 6[14], 3 fpl. עוֹדֵינָה †La 4[17] Kt (Qr 1 pl. עוֹדֵינוּ); there occur also עוֹד אֲנִי †2 S 14[32] Dn 9[20.21], and עוֹד הֵם †Is 65[24]:—**1.** as *adv.*: **a.** (*a*) expressing *continuance, persistence*, usu. of the past or present, *still, yet*, Gn 18[22] ואברהם עודנו עֹמֵד and A., he was *still* standing before י׳ (note oft. so עוֹדֶנּוּ after cas. pend., 44[14] 1 S 13[7] 1 K 12[2] Je 33[1] 2 Ch 34[3]), 29[7] הן עוד היום גדול the day is *still* high, 31[14] 43[7] הַעוֹד אֲבִיכֶם חַי, v[27] 45[3] Ex 4[18] 9[2] Nu 19[13] Ju 6[24] 8[20] 1 K 20[32] הַעוֹדֶנּוּ חַי; 2 S 14[32] (but Kö[iii. 558] עַד), 18[14]; Is 5[25] ועוד יָדוֹ נְטוּיָה; 10[32] עוֹד הַיּוֹם בְּנֹב לַעֲמֹד *still* to-day (such is his haste) will he tarry in Nob; 1 K 22[44] עוד העם מְזַבְּחִים the people were *still* sacrificing, etc. (so 2 K 12[4]+); 2 S 1[9] כי־כל־עוד נפשי בי, Jb 27[3] (v. כֹּל **1 f**); Mi 6[10] (v. הֲ **1 b** *end*, and Ke; but also We Now); La 4[17] the sf. is anticipatory, either of *eyes* (Kt) or *our* (Qr 𝔊), poet. for עוֹד עֵינֵינוּ כָּלוֹת; but Dys Löhr *al.* rd. עַד מָה for ע׳, Bi[1] Wild simply עוֹד. 2 Ch 14[6] rd. either עוֹדֶנּוּ (sf. 1 pl. antic. of לְפָנֵינוּ), or עוֹד. Twice, peculiarly, עוד לא *still not* (Germ. *noch nicht*) i.e. *not yet* (in class. Heb. טֶרֶם), Je 40[5] עוֹדֶנּוּ לא ישוב, 2 Ch 20[33] ועוד העם לא הֵכִינוּ לבבם (the vb. fin. on acc. of לֹא). Sq. וְ, Nu 11[33] הבשׂר עודנו בין שניהם . . . ואף י׳ חרה בעם the flesh was *still* between their teeth . . ., *and* (=*when*) etc., (cf. ψ 78$^{30 f.}$ Jb 8^{12}); and oft. in the phr. עוֹדֶנּוּ (עוֹדָם וגו׳) מְדַבֵּר (מְדַבְּרִים) he (they, etc.) was (were) *still* speaking, *and* (=*when*) etc., Gn 29^{9} עודנו מְדַבֵּר עמם ורחל באה, 1 K 1$^{22.42}$ 2 K 6^{33} Est 6^{14} Dn 9$^{20.21}$, so עוֹד זֶה . . . Jb 1$^{16.17}$ (+v^{18} for עַד): and of the future, 1 K 1^{14} Is 65^{24} (עוֹד הֵם מְדַבְּרִים ואני אשׁמע); cf. Ex 9^{17}.

(*b*) Expressing *addition* or *repetition, still, yet, more,* Gn 7^{4} כי לימים עוד שׁבעה after *yet* seven days, 8$^{10.12}$ 29$^{27.30}$ עוד שׁבע שׁנים אחרות, 45^{6} 2 K 6^{33} Is 1^{5} Hb 2^{3} כִּי עוֹד חָזוֹן לַמּוֹעֵד (cf. Dn 10^{14} 11$^{2.27.35}$), Je 13^{27} אַחֲרֵי מָתַי עוֹד after how long *still?* with stress on the idea of *continuance*, Gn 46^{29} וַיֵּבְךְּ עַל צַוָּארָיו עוֹד *still going on* (AV. *a good while*), Ru 1^{14}, ψ 84^{5} עוד יהללוך they will be *still praising* thee, Jb 34^{23}; with עוד prefixed for emph., Ex 11^{1} עוד נגע אחד אביא על פ׳, Is 49^{20} 56^{8} עוֹד אֲקַבֵּץ וגו׳, Ez 8$^{13.15}$ ψ 42^{6} 92^{15}+; in the phr. עוֹד מְעַט ו sq. pf. consec., †Ex 17^{4} עוד מעט וּסְקָלֻנִי *yet* a little, *and* they will stone me, Ho 1^{4} Je 51^{33}, cf. ψ 37^{10}, Is 10^{25} 29^{17}; simil. Jon 3^{4} (cf. בְּעוֹד Is 21^{16}), 2 Ch 10^{5} (but see 𝔊 and ‖ 1 K 12^{5}); עוד . . . לא *no more*, both of the past, as Ex 2^{3} Jos 5$^{1.12}$ 1 K 10^{5}, and of the fut., as Gn 17^{5} לֹא יִקָּרֵא עוד שׁמך א׳, 32^{29} Dt 31^{2} Is 2^{4} 30^{20} 62^{4} Je 3^{16}+oft., עוד . . . לא Gn 8^{22}; so with אַיִן Is 23^{10} Je 10^{20} 48^{2} ψ 74^{9} *al.*

b. When the continuance is limited by its nature to a single occurrence, עוד becomes= *again*, Gn 4^{25} 9^{11} לֹא יִכָּרֵת כל בשׂר עוד, 18^{29} וַיֹּסֶף עוֹד לְדַבֵּר and he added *still* to speak, i.e. he spake yet *again* (so oft. with יָסַף; v. √), 24^{20} וַתָּרָץ עוֹד and she ran *again*, 29^{33} וַתַּהַר עוֹד, 35^{9} 37^{9} Ex 3^{15} 4^{6} Dt 3^{26} 1 S 10^{22}+oft.; with עוד prefixed, Ho 12^{10} Je 31$^{4.5.23}$ 32^{15} 33$^{12.13}$; עוד . . . לא *not again, no more,* Dt 13^{17} 34^{10}.

c. *Still, moreover, besides* (not in temporal sense); Gn 19^{12} עוֹד מי לך פה whom hast thou here *besides?* 43^{6} הַעוֹד לָכֶם אָח Am 6^{10}; 1 S 10^{22} הֲבָא עוֹד הֲלֹם אִישׁ is there *still* a man come hither? (sc. besides ourselves: but 𝔊 We al. הֲבָא הֲלֹם הָאִישׁ), 16^{11} עוֹד שָׁאַר הַקָּטָן, 18^{8} ועוד לו אך המלוכה, 1 K 22$^{7.8}$ 2 K 4^{6} אֵין עוֹד כֶּלִי, Is 5^{4} Je 36^{32} Ez 20^{27} 23^{38} 36^{37} Pr 9^{9} Ec 12^{9} 1 Ch 29^{3} 2 Ch 17^{6}+; וְאֵין עוֹד and there is none *besides*, †Dt 4^{39} (cf. v^{35}), 1 K 8^{60} Is 45$^{5.6.14.18.22}$ (cf. v^{21}), 46^{9} Jo 2^{27}; אֲנִי וְאַפְסִי עוֹד †Is 47$^{8.10}$ Zp 2^{15}.

2. With prefixes:—†**a.** בְּעוֹד, lit. *in the continuance of . . .*, i.e. (*a*) *while yet:* Gn 25^{6} בְּעוֹדֶנּוּ חַי *while* he was *yet alive,* Dt 31^{27} 2 S 12^{22} בְּעוֹד הַיֶּלֶד חַי, Is 28^{4} ψ 39^{2} Jb 29^{5}; בְּעוֹדִי alone, =*so long as I live,* ψ 104^{33} 146^{2} (‖ בְּחַיַּי); 2 S 3^{35} בעוד היום, Je 15^{9} בעוד יומם, Pr 31^{15}. (*b*) *within yet,* usu. of time, Gn 40^{13} בְּעוֹד שְׁלֹשֶׁת יָמִים יִשָּׂא וגו׳ *within yet* three days, etc., v^{19} Jos 1^{11} Is 7^{8} 21^{16} בְּעוֹד שָׁנָה (sq. pf. cons.), Je 28$^{3.11}$ Am 4^{7}; but also of distance, Gn 48^{7} בְּעוֹד כִּבְרַת ארץ לבוא אפרתה (cf. 35^{16} ויהי עוד וגו׳); cf. SI^{2} ובעוד שׁלשׁ אמה לה[נָּקֶב]. **b.** †מֵעוֹד, lit. *from the continuance of . . .*, only in the phr. מֵעוֹדִי (מֵעוֹדְךָ) עד היום הזה *ever since I was* (*thou wast*) unto this day, Gn 48^{15} Nu 22^{30}.

†עוֹדֵד, עֹדֵד† n.pr.m. (*restorer*);—𝔊 Ωδηδ, Αδαδ: **1.** עֲזַרְיָהוּ בֶּן־עו׳ 2 Ch 15^{1}, so read also v^{8} (MT עֹדֵד alone). **2.** עֹדֵד a prophet 2 Ch 28^{9}. 5752

עֵד $_{69}$ **n.m.**$^{Dt 17,6}$ **witness** (prob.fr.*reiterating*, hence *emphatically affirming*);—ע׳ abs. Gn 31^{48}+, cstr. Ex 20^{16}+; sf. עֵדִי Jb 16^{19}; pl. עֵדִים Nu 35^{30}+, cstr. עֵדֵי ψ 27^{12} 35^{11}; sf. עֵדַי Is 43$^{10.12}$, etc.;—†**1.** *witness, testimony, evidence,* of things: heap of stones Gn 31$^{44.48.52}$ (JE), torn animal Ex 22^{12} (E), song of Moses Dt 31$^{19.21}$ (J), law-book v^{26} (D), witness of י׳ against Israel; altar E. of Jordan, c. בֵּין, Jos 22$^{27.28.34}$ (P), cf. Is 19^{20}; Job's evil condition Jb 16^{8}; the moon ψ 89^{38}. **2.** *witness,* a person: †**a.** God, in heaven for Job Jb 16^{19}; on earth, for Samuel 1 S 12$^{5.5}$+v^{6} 𝔊 Th and most, Jeremiah Je 42^{5}; see also 1 S 20^{12} (ins. עֵד bef. י׳ 𝔖 Dr Bu Kit Löhr HPS); against persons Je 29^{23} Mal 3^{5}, nations Mi 1^{2}; between (בֵּין) persons Gn 31^{50} (E). **b.** Davidic dyn., to nations Is 55^{4}. **c.** *witnesses,* of transfer of property Je 32$^{10.12.25.44}$, betrothal Ru 4$^{9.10.11}$; usu. of testimony in court, and in civil and social relations, c. בְּ against, Nu 5^{13} Jos 24^{22} 1 S 12^{5}+, c. קוּם *rise up against* ψ 27^{12} 35^{11}; †עָנָה עֵד שֶׁקֶר בְּ *answer* (in court) *as a false witness against* Ex 20^{16}=עֵד שָׁוְא Dt 5^{17}, Pr 25^{18}; †לְפִי עֵדִים Nu 35^{30} (P); †עַל־פִּי עֵד(ים) Dt 17$^{6.6}$ *at the mouth of witnesses,* so 19$^{15.15}$.—*False witness* is ע׳ שֶׁקֶר Ex 20^{16} Dt 19$^{18.18}$ ψ 27^{12} Pr 6^{19} 14^{5}; ע׳ שְׁקָרִים [illegible] 12^{17} 19$^{5.9}$; ע׳ כְּזָבִים 21^{28}; ע׳ חִנָּם 24^{28}; ע׳ בְּלִיַּעַל 19^{28}; ע׳ חָמָס *witness of* (i.e. supporting) *violence* Ex 23^{1} (E) Dt 19^{16} ψ 35^{11}. *Faithful witness* is ע׳ אֱמוּנִים Pr 14^{5}; ע׳ אֱמֶת Je 42^{5} Pr 14^{25}. 5707

†II. עֵדָה n.f. testimony, witness, of things (only E);—Gn 21^{30} 31^{52} Jos 24$^{27.27}$ (J uses עֵד for feminine things).—I. עֵדָה v. יעד. p. 417 5713 5712

†[עוּד] vb. denom. (Gerber$^{42 f.}$) **bear witness**;—**Qal** *Impf.* 1 s. sf. אֲעִידֵךְ La 2^{13} Kt; 5749

<**Hiph.** Qr Bu. **Hiph.** *Pf.* 3 ms. הֵעִיד 2 K 17^{15} Mal 2^{14}; הֵעַד Gn 43^{3}; 2 ms. הַעִידֹתָ Ne 9^{34}; הַעֲדֹתָה Ex 19^{23}; 1 s. הַעִידֹתִי Dt 4^{26} Je 42^{19}; 3 mpl. הֵעִידוּ Ne 9^{26}, etc.; *Impf.* וַיָּעַד 2 K 17^{13} Zc 3^{6}; 3 fs. sf. וַתְּעִידֵנִי Jb 29^{11} + 15 t. Impf.; *Inf. abs.* הָעֵד Gn 43^{3} + 4 t.; *Imv.* הָעֵד Ex 19^{21} + 2 t. Imv. *Pt.* מֵעִיד Dt 32^{46}.—**1.** *testify, bear witness,* c. sf. against one 1 K 21$^{10.13}$; in favour of Jb 29^{11} La 2^{13} (Qr); c. בֵּין Mal 2^{14}. **2.** *cause to testify, take as witness,* c. acc. pers. Is 8^{2} Je 32$^{10.25.44}$; *call as witness, invoke,* c. acc. את השמים ואת הארץ + בְּ *against* Dt 4^{26} 30^{19} 31^{28}. **3.** *protest, affirm solemnly, warn:* subj. men, abs. Je 6^{10} Ne 13^{15}; c. בְּ pers. Gn 43$^{3.3}$ (J) Ex 19^{21} (E) 1 S 8$^{9.9}$ 1 K 2^{42} 2 Ch 24^{19} Ne 9^{26} 13^{21} Je 42^{19} Am 3^{13}; *exhort solemnly, admonish, charge,* ׳י subj., c. בְּ pers., Ex 19^{23} (J) Dt 8^{19} 2 K 17^{13} Ne 9$^{29.30}$ Je 11$^{7.7.7}$ Zc 3^{6} ψ 50^{7} 81^{9}; *enjoin solemnly,* c. בְּ pers. + acc. rei עֵדוֹת 2 K 17^{15} Ne 9^{34}, דברים Dt 32^{46}. **Hoph.** *Pf.* 3 ms. וְהוּעַד consec. Ex 21^{29} (E) impers. *and protest be entered,* c. בְּ pers.

5713 †III. [עֵדָה] **n.f.** only *pl.* MT **testimonies** (always of laws as divine testimonies or solemn charges);—pl. abs. עֵדֹת Dt 4^{45} 6^{20}; sf. (of ׳י), עֵדֹתַי ψ 132^{12} (Ges §91 n.), עֵדֹתָיו Dt 6^{17} ψ 25^{10} 99^{7} 119^{2}, עֵדוֹתָיו 78^{56}; עֵדֹתֶיךָ 93^{5} 119$^{22.24.46.59.79.95.119.125.138.146.152.167.168}$ (MT pointing artificial, der. prob. fr. עֵדוּת, reading עֵדֹת for עֵדֹת, or regarding עֵדֹת as contr. from עֵדְוֹת, pl. of עֵדוּת [Sta §320 b SS Buhl]; v. also Dr$^{Dt 4, 45}$; Dt 4^{45} 6$^{17.20}$ are redactional).

5715 † עֵדוּת$_{19}$ and עֵדֻת$_{27}$ **n.f. testimony**;—׳ע abs. Ex 16^{34} +, cstr. ψ 19^{8} +; pl. sf. עֵדְוֹתֶיךָ 119^{14} +, עֵדְוֹתָיו Je 44^{23} + 4 t.;—**1.** *testimony* of the Ten Words on the tables as a solemn divine charge, לֻחֹת הע׳ Ex 31^{18} 32^{15} 34^{29} (P), הע׳ 25$^{16.21}$ 40^{20} (P); ark as containing tables, אֲרוֹן הע׳ 25^{22} 26$^{33.34}$ 30$^{6.26}$ 39^{35} 40$^{3.5.21}$ Nu 4^{5} 7^{89} (all P), Jos 4^{16} (JE; Kue הברית [ag. him Di], so Benn Steuernag), הארן לע׳ Ex 31^{7} (P); abbrev. לִפְנֵי הע׳ 16^{34} 30^{36} Nu 17$^{19.25}$ (P); עַל הע׳ Ex 27^{21} (= הע׳ Lv 24^{3}), 30^{6} Lv 16^{13} (P); tabernacle as containing ark of testimony, מִשְׁכַּן הע׳ *tabernacle of the testimony* Ex 38^{21} Nu 1$^{50.53.53}$ 10^{11} (P); so אֹהֶל הע׳ 9^{15} 17$^{22.23}$ 18^{2} (P) 2 Ch 24^{6}. **2.** the code of law in gen. (late), as a *testimony* of God: ψ 19^{8} 119^{88} 122^{4}; || תּוֹרָה 78^{5}; || חֹק 81^{6}. In titles, עַל־שׁוּשַׁן ע׳ ψ 60^{1}, אֶל־שֹׁשַׁנִּים ע׳ 80^{1} = melody whose first line cp. law as testimony to a choice flower. Special laws of the code are denoted by pl.; + חֻקּוֹת etc. 1 K 2^{3} 2 K 23^{3} = 2 Ch 34^{31} (+ חקים etc.), Je 44^{23}; חֻקִּים etc. 1 Ch 29^{19}; מִצְוֹת Ne 9^{34}; pl. of contents of covenant 2 K 17^{15}; pl. elsewh. ψ 119$^{14.31.36.99.111.129.144.157}$. Vid. also III. [עֵדָה].—For הָעֵדוּת 2 K 11^{12} = 2 Ch 23^{11} rd. prob. הַצְּעָדוֹת (cf. 2 S 1^{10} We al.).

8584 † תְּעוּדָה **n.f. testimony, attestation**;— **1.** *testimony,* prophet. *injunction,* || תּוֹרָה Is 8$^{16.20}$. **2.** *attestation,* Ru 4^{7} (> *fixed usage* Buhl^{Lex}).

5753 †I. [עָוָה] **vb. bend, twist** (so Ar. عَوَى);— **Niph.** *Pf.* 1 s. נַעֲוֵיתִי Is 21^{3} ψ 38^{7}; *Pt.* cstr. נַעֲוֵה Pr 12^{8}; f. cstr. נַעֲוַת 1 S 20^{30} (but rd. נַעֲרַת 𝔊 We Dr SS Bu HPS);—*be bent, bowed down, twisted,* || שחח ψ 38^{7}; || נבהל Is 21^{3}; נַעֲוֵה לֵב Pr 12^{8} *one perverted of mind.* **Pi.** *Pf.* 3 ms. עִוָּה, subj. ׳י:— La 3^{9} my paths *hath he twisted;* וְע׳ Is 24^{1} *its surface will he distort* (|| בּוֹקֵק הָאָרֶץ). **Hiph.** *Pf.* 1 s. יָשָׁר הֶעֱוֵיתִי Jb 33^{27} *the right have I perverted* (|| חָטָא); so 3 pl. הֶעֱווּ אֶת־דַּרְכָּם Je 3^{21}.

5754 †I. עַוָּה **n.f. distortion, ruin**;—עַוָּה עַוָּה עַוָּה אֲשִׂימֶנָּה Ez 21^{32} (cf. √**Pi.** Is 24^{1}).

5773 † עִוְעִים **n.pl. abstr. distorting, warping** (for *עֲוָעִים);— רוּחַ עִוְעִים Is 19^{14} *temper of distorting,* i.e. *warped* judgment.

5856 † עִי **n.[m.] ruin, heap of ruins**;—׳ע abs.
1164 Jb 30^{24}, cstr. Mi 1^{6}; pl. עִיִּין (Aram. form) 3^{12}, but עִיִּים in the quotation Je 26^{18}, and ψ 79^{1}.

4596 † מְעִי **n.[m.] ruin** (si vera l.);—וְהָיְתָה מְעִי מַפָּלָה consec. Is 17^{1} *Damascus shall become a ruinous heap* (but del. ׳מ 𝔊 Lag Che SS Buhl).

cf p. 590

II. עוה (√ of foll., cf. Ar. غَوَى *err from the way,* Eth. **ዐየ:** *err;* distinct from I. עוה, cf. Lag$^{M. i. 236 f.}$ Dr$^{1 S 20, 30}$ Gerber^{90}).

5771 † עָוֹן **n.m.**$^{Is 22, 14}$ **iniquity, guilt,** or **punishment of iniquity**;—׳ע abs. Ex 21^{43} +; עָווֹן 2 K 7^{9} ψ 51^{7}; cstr. עֲוֹן Gn 15^{16} +; עֲווֹן 1 Ch 21^{8}; sf. עֲוֹנִי Gn 4^{13} + (2 S 16^{12} read בְּעָנְיִי), עֲוֹנְךָ Ho 9^{7} +; עֲוֹנֵכִי ψ 103^{3}; עֲוֹנָהּ Nu 15^{31} (Ges §91 e), etc.; pl. עֲוֹנוֹת abs. ψ 130^{3} +, cstr. Jb 13^{26} +; עֲוֹנֹת abs. ψ 65^{4}, cstr. Lv 16^{21} +; sf. עֲוֹנֹתֶיךָ Is 43^{24}, עֲוֹנֹתֵיכֶם Nu 14^{34} +, etc.; also עֲוֹנַיִךְ Ez 28^{18}; עֲוֹנֵינוּ Is 64^{6} +, etc. (SS doubt all these);—**1.** *iniquity,* Jb 15^{5} 20^{27} Je 11^{10} 14^{7} 16^{17} La 2^{14} Ez 7^{13}; || חטאת 1 S 20^{1} Jb 13^{23} Is 5^{18} 43^{24} 59^{2} Je 5^{25} 16^{10} La 4$^{6.13}$ Dn 9^{16} Ho 4^{8} 13^{12}; || פשע Jb 14^{17} 31^{33} ψ 107^{17} Is 50^{1} 53^{5}; || אשמה Ezr 9$^{6.7.13}$; רעה Jb 22^{5} Ho 7^{1}. **a.** ע׳ נְעוּרַי Jb 13^{26} *iniquities of my youth;* ע׳ חֶרֶב 19^{29} *iniquities* calling *for the sword;* ע׳ פְּלִילִ(ים) 31$^{11.28}$ *iniquity for* (to be punished by) *judges;* שְׁתֵּי עֲוֹנֹתָם Ho 10^{10} (so rd. Vrss Hi al.); כשל בע׳

stumble by iniquity Ho 5^{5} 14^{2}; cf. מִכְשׁוֹל ע׳ Ez 7^{19} $14^{3.4.7}$ 18^{30} 44^{12}; לרל־ינון מע׳ אוֹשתמרה Dt 19^{15}; 2 S 22^{24} = ψ 18^{24}; עָוֹן אֲשֶׁר־חֵטְא Ho 12^{9}. **b.** *iniquity* as recognized, ידע ע׳ 1 S 3^{13} Is 59^{12} Je 3^{13} 14^{20}; confessed, התודה ע׳ Lv 16^{21} $26^{40.40}$ (P), Ne 9^{2}; הגיד ע׳ ψ 38^{19}; לא כסה ע׳ 32^{5}; brought to remembrance, הזכיר ע׳ Nu 5^{15} (P) 1 K 17^{18} Ez $21^{28.29}$ 29^{16}; causing shame, יִכָּלְמוּ מע׳ Ez 43^{10}; turned from, שׁוּב מע׳ Dn 9^{13}, cf. השיב מע׳ Mal 2^{6}. **c.** (1) phrases of punishment: פקד ע׳ על Ex 20^{5} = Dt 5^{9}, Ex 34^{7} Nu 14^{18} (J), Lv 18^{25} (H) 2 S 3^{8} Is 13^{11} 26^{21} Je 25^{12} 36^{31} Am 3^{2}; without על, La 4^{22}, פקד ע׳ ב ψ 89^{33}; Jb 11^{6} v. II. [נשׁא]; יסר על ע׳ ψ 39^{12} *chastise for iniquity;* שַׁתָּ ע׳ לנגדך 90^{8} *set our iniquities before thee;* גמל כע׳ 103^{10}; שמר ע׳ 130^{3}; שִׁלַּם ע׳ Is $65^{7.7}$ Je 16^{18} 32^{18}; מַטְבֵּחַ בע׳ Is 14^{21}; (2) of forgiveness or removal: העביר ע׳ 2 S 24^{10} = 1 Ch 21^{8}, Jb 7^{21} Zc 3^{4}; משתי ע׳ 3^{9}; סלח לע׳ Ex 34^{9} Nu 14^{19} (J), ψ 25^{11} 103^{3} Je 31^{34} 33^{8} 36^{3}; נשׂא ע׳ Ex 34^{7} Nu 14^{18} (J), ψ 32^{5} 85^{3} Is 33^{24} Ho 14^{3} Mi 7^{18}; סר ע׳ Is 6^{7}; יכבושׁ ע׳ Mi 7^{19}; (3) of covering over, כסה על ע׳ Ne 3^{37}; כִּפֶּר ע׳ ψ 78^{38} Pr 16^{6} Is 22^{14} 27^{9} Dn 9^{24}; יתכפר ע׳ כפר על ע׳ Je 18^{23}; 1 S 3^{14}; (4) of cleansing from: כבס מע׳ ψ 51^{4}; מחה ע׳ v^{11}; טהר מע׳ Je 33^{8} Ez 36^{33}; (5) of imputing, reckoning to one: חשׁב ע׳ ל 2 S 19^{20} ψ 32^{2}; (ל) זכר ע׳ 79^{8} Is 64^{8} Je 14^{10} Ho 8^{13} 9^{9}; יִזָּכֵר ע׳ ψ 109^{14}; בקשׁ (ל)ע׳ Jb 10^{6} Je 50^{20}; (6) פדה מע׳ ψ 130^{8} *ransom from iniquity.*

2. *Guilt of iniquity* (not always easy to disting. from **1**; SS give more, Buhl fewer, sub **2**);—|| תועבות Ez 36^{31}; || דם Is 59^{3}; || חמס Ez 9^{9}; ע׳ בצעו ע׳ פעור Jos 22^{17} (P); ע׳ סדם Ez 16^{49}; Is 57^{17}; שְׁנֵי עונם Ez 4^{4}; נִכְתָּם עֲוֹנֵךְ לְפָנַי Je 2^{22} *the guilt of thine iniquity is marked before me;* מצא ע׳ Gn 44^{16} (E) ψ 36^{3}. **a.** ע׳ בְּ: *guilt of iniquity upon one* Nu 15^{31} (P) 1 S 20^{8} 2 S 14^{32}; לא ע׳ לִי Jb 33^{9} (|| זַךְ); בלי־עון ψ 59^{5} *without my guilt.* **b.** *guilt,* as great, increased: רֹב עָוֹן Je 13^{22} $30^{14.15}$ Ez 28^{18} Ho 9^{7}; לֹא־שָׁלֵם ע׳ Gn 15^{16} (J); ע׳ הִשִּׂיגוּנִי ψ 38^{5}; ע׳ עֲקֵבַי יְסוּבֵּנִי 49^{6}; ע׳ עָבְרוּ ראשׁי 40^{13}; ע׳ גברו מני 65^{4}; עַם כֶּבֶד ע׳ Is 1^{4}; בע׳ נלקח Ez 33^{6}. **c.** as a condition, בע׳: c. חוללתי *was I brought forth* ψ 51^{7}; **c.** גָּוַע *expire* Jos 22^{20} (P); c. מות *die* Je 31^{30} Ez $3^{18.19}$ $18^{17.18}$ $33^{8.9}$.

3. *Consequence of, or punishment for, iniquity* (SS include most of these under **2**, and do not recognize **3**; Buhl thinks this meaning rare, giving only Gn 4^{13} Is 5^{18});—אם יִקְרְךָ ע׳ בדבר הזה 1 S 28^{10} *no punishment shall happen unto thee for,* etc.; נשׂא ע׳ *bear the punishment for iniquity* of others Ex 28^{38} Lv 10^{17} (*take away* ע׳ Di Now $^{ii. 233 n.}$) 16^{22} Nu 30^{16} (P), Ez $4^{4.5.6}$; בע׳ $18^{19.20.20}$; one's own, Ex 28^{43} Lv $5^{1.17}$ 7^{18} 17^{16} 19^{8} $20^{17.19}$ 22^{16} Nu 5^{31} 14^{34} $18^{1.1.23}$ (P), Ez 14^{10} $44^{10.12}$; גדול ע׳ מנשׂוא Gn 4^{13} (J) *my punishment is greater than I can bear;* נִרְצָה עֲוֹנָהּ Is 40^{2} *her punishment is accepted,* cf. רצה ע׳ Lv $26^{41.43}$ (H); ומצאנו ע׳ 2 K 7^{9} *punishment will overtake us;* תנה ע׳ על ע׳ ψ 69^{28} *add punishment to their punishment;* ע׳ הוא יסבל Is 53^{11} *the consequences of their iniquities he shall bear,* cf. ע׳ סָבָלְנוּ La 5^{7}; הפגיע בו ע׳ Is 53^{6}; נִקָּה מע׳ *freed from punishment* Nu 5^{31} (P) Jb 10^{14}; בי אני העון 1 S 25^{24} *on me the punishment;* עלי הע׳ 2 S 14^{9}; בע׳ c. various vbs.: Gn 19^{15} (J) Lv $26^{39.39}$ (H) ψ 31^{11} 106^{43} Je 51^{6} Ez 4^{17} 7^{16} 24^{23} 39^{23}; עת ע׳ קֵץ $21^{30.34}$ 35^{5}; see also: Pr 5^{22} (|| חַבְלֵי חטאת), Is 30^{13} $64^{5.6}$ La 4^{22} Ez 4^{4} $14^{10.10}$ 32^{27}.

† [עָוָה] **vb. denom.** (Gerber^{90}) **commit iniquity, do wrong** (Aram. עוי *commit sin,* עֲוָיָא *sin,* cf. Levy$^{NHWB\ iii.\ 626}$);—**Qal** (late) *Pf.* 3 fs. עָוְתָה Est 1^{16} *she hath done wrong* (c. עַל); 1 pl. עָוִינוּ Dn 9^{5} *we have committed iniquity* (|| חָטָא). **Hiph.** *commit iniquity;*—*Pf.* 3 ms. הֶעֱוָה 2 S 19^{20}, 1 s. הֶעֱוֵיתִי 24^{17} (|| חָטָא); 1 pl. הֶעֱוִינוּ 1 K 8^{47} = 2 Ch 6^{37}, ψ 106^{6} (all || חָטָא); *Inf. abs.* הַעֲוֵה Je 9^{4}, *cstr.* sf. הַעֲוֹתוֹ 2 S 7^{14}.—Jb 33^{27} v. I. עָוָה. p. 730 5753

† II. עִוָּה, עַוָּה **n.pr.loc.** city conquered by Assyrians;—עַוָּה 2 K 17^{24} (van d. H. עַוָּא=עִוָּה) 18^{34} 19^{13} = Is 37^{13}; 𝔊 Αια(ν), Αυα, and (2 K 19^{13}) Ουδου, A Αυτα, 𝔊L Αιναγ, etc.; site in N. Syria Wkl$^{Alttest.\ Unters.\ 102\ f.}$ Benz; Sachau$^{ZA\ xii\ (1897),\ 48}$ prop. *Emma* (Tab. Pent.) = Ἴμμα Ptol$^{v.\ 15,\ 15}$, mod. *'Imm* betw. Antioch and Aleppo.—I. עַוָּה v. sub I. עוה. p. 730 5755 5754

† [עַוִּי] **adj.gent.** only pl. הָעַוִּים as subst., inhab. of II. עַוָּה 2 K 17^{31} (another עַוִּים infr.). p. 732 5757 5761

עֹז n. v. עֹז sub עזז. p. 738 5797

† [עוּז], עוֹז **vb. take or seek refuge** (Ar. عوذ, عَاذَ *take refuge, seek protection,* مَعَاذٌ *a refuge*);—**Qal** *Inf. cstr.* לָעוֹז בְּמָעוֹז Is 30^{2} (|| לַחְסוֹת בְּ). **Hiph.** *bring into safety,* Pf. 3 mpl. הֵעִיזוּ Is 10^{31}, obj. om., and so *Imv.* mpl. הָעִיזוּ Je 4^{6}, הָעִזוּ מִקֶּרֶב 6^{1}; c. acc., ms. הָעֵז Ex 9^{19}. 5756

† מָעוֹז **n.m.**$^{Ju\ 6,\ 26}$ **place or means of safety, protection** (MT sfs. as if from עזז, but prob. erron., cf. Buhl$^{Lex\ 13}$ Ges$^{§\ 85\ k}$);—מ׳ abs. Ju 6^{26} +, cstr. Is 30^{2} +; sf. מָעוּזִּי 2 S 22^{33} (but rd. הַמְאַזְּרֵנִי as || ψ 18^{33}), מָעוּזִּי ψ 31^{3} +, מָעֻזִּי Is 27^{5} +, מָעוּזּוֹ ψ 52^{9} +, מָעֻזָּה Dn 11^{10}, etc. (rd. prob. מָעוֹזִי, etc.); pl. מָעֻזִּים $v^{38.39}$, sf. מָעֻזְּנֶיהָ Is 23^{11}, read מָעֻזֶּיהָ (Ges $§\ 20\ o$ Che$^{Heb.\ Hpt.}$ al.; del. d. f. in all, v. supr.);— 4581

1. lit. *place of safety* Ju 6^{26}, hence (c. collat. idea of *strength*, as if fr. עזז) = *fastness* Is 23$^{11.14}$ (in v^{14} Che$^{Heb. Hpt.}$ prop. מְחוֹזְכֶם *your city*), Ez 24^{25} 30^{15} Dn 11$^{7.10.19}$, הַמִּקְדָּשׁ הַמּ׳ v^{31}, מִבְצְרֵי מָעֻזִּים v^{39}; מ׳ הַיָּם i.e. *harbour* Is 23^{4}, but del. Ol Du Che$^{Hpt.}$; מ׳ מֵאוֹיֵב Na 3^{11}; cf. עָרֵי מ׳ Is 17^{9}. **2. a.** fig., of God (י׳) as *refuge* Na 1^{7} ψ 27^{1} 31^{5} 37^{39} 52^{9} Is 25$^{4.4}$ Jo 4^{16}, י׳ עֻזִּי וּמָעֻזִּי וּמְנוּסִי Je 16^{19}, מ׳ יְשׁוּעוֹת מְשִׁיחוֹ ψ 28^{8} (|| עֹז); so צוּר מ׳ Is 17^{10} ψ 31^{3}, אֱלֹהֵי מ׳ 43^{2}; also יַחֲזֵק בְּמָעֻזִּי Is 27^{5} *let him lay hold of my refuge* (me as refuge); cf. חֶדְוַת י׳ הִיא מָעֻזְּכֶם Ne 8^{10}, מ׳ לַתֹּם דֶּרֶךְ י׳ Pr 10^{29}. **b.** of a heathen god, אֱלוֹהַּ מָעֻזִּים Dn 11^{38} (rd. מְחוֹזִים *cities* Che$^{Is 23, 1, Heb. Hpt.}$). **3.** fig. of human *protection*, מ׳ פַּרְעֹה Is 30$^{2.3}$ (both || צֵל מִצְרַיִם); אֶפְרַיִם מ׳ רֹאשִׁי ψ 60^{9} = 108^{9}, i.e. my helmet; also (of angel) Dn 11^{1} (|| מַחֲזִיק).

5759 עֲוִיל v. II. עול. below

5757, 5761 † עַוִּים **n.pr. 1. gent.** הָע׳ people on SW. coast of Mediterr. before the כַּפְתֹּרִים (q.v.) came Dt 2^{23}, and remaining thereafter Jos 13^{3} (D^{2}),
5761 𝔊 Ευαιοι. **2. loc.** הָע׳ city in Benj. Jos 18^{23} (= הָעַי ?), 𝔊 Αιειν, Αυειμ.—Vid. also [עַוִּי] supr.

5762 † עֲוִית **n.pr.loc.** in Edom Gn 36^{35} = Qr 1 Ch 1^{46} (Kt עיות); 𝔊 Γεθθαιμ, but 𝔊L 1 Ch 1^{46} Ευιθ.

5763 † I. [עוּל] **vb. give suck** (Ar. غَالَ, غيل *give suck* (while pregnant); cf. Aram. ܥܘܠܐ *foetus, sucking child*; ܥܝܠܐ *foal*, so Eth. ዐዋል: Talm. עִילָה);—**Qal** *Pt.* fpl. עָלוֹת *giving suck*, of cows 1 S 6$^{7.10}$; ewes ψ 78^{71} and (fig. of returning exiles) Is 40^{11}; of both Gn 33^{13} (J).

5764 † עוּל **n.m. sucking child, suckling**;—cstr. ע׳ יָמִים Is 65^{20} *a suckling of days*, i.e. a few days old; sf. עוּלָהּ 49^{15} (|| בֶּן־בִּטְנָהּ).

II. עול (√of foll.; cf. Ar. عول, عَالَ *feed, nourish*; v. Wetzst in De$^{Jb 16, 11}$).

5759 † I. [עֲוִיל] **n.m. young boy**;—pl. עֲוִילִים Jb
5760 19^{18}; sf. עֲוִילֵיהֶם 21^{11}.—II. עֲוִיל sub III. עול. below

III. עול (√of foll., cf. Ar. عول, عَالَ *deviate from* (right course); Aram. ܥܘܠ Aph. *act unjustly*, and many deriv., עַוְלָא *unrighteousness*; Eth. ዐለወ: *pervert, corrupt*).

5766 † עָוֶל **n.m. injustice, unrighteousness** (opp. צְדָקָה);—ע׳ Lv 19^{15}+; cstr. עֲוֶל Ez 28^{18} (van d. H. עָוֶל, but v. Baer Ginsb); sf. עַוְלוֹ 18^{26} 33^{13};—עשׂה עול Lv 19$^{15.35}$ (H) Dt 25^{16} Ez 3^{20} 18$^{24.26.26}$ 33$^{13.13.15.18}$; פעל ע׳ Jb 34^{32}; הִתְעִיבוּ ע׳ ψ 53^{2} (|| עֲלִילָה 14^{2}); שׁפט ע׳ 82^{2}; אישׁ ע׳ Pr 29^{27}; ע׳ בְּכַפַּי ψ 7^{4}; מצא ע׳ בְּ Je 2^{5}, read prob. also Ez 28^{15} (for MT עולתה); מע׳ ישׁיב ידו 18^{8}; בְּעֶוֶל רְכֻלָּתְךָ 28^{18}; of God, אין עול (|| אֱמוּנָה) Dt 32^{4}; חָלִלָה מע׳ Jb 34^{10}.

† עָוַל **vb. denom.** (Gerber^{31}) **act wrong-** 5765
fully;—**Pi.** *Impf.* 3 ms. יְעַוֵּל Is 26^{10} (opp. נְכֹחוֹת); *Pt.* מְעַוֵּל ψ 71^{4} (+ חוֹמֵץ, || רָשָׁע).

† עַוְלָה **n.f.**$^{Jb 11, 14}$ (? **m.** Mal 2^{6} Kö$^{ii. 2, 453, § 345 d}$ 5766
Ez 28^{15} [עולתה; but ע׳ only here Ez, error for עול] questioned by SS, v. Albrecht$^{ZAW xvi (1896), 117}$) **injustice, unrighteousness, wrong**;—ע׳ ψ 37^{1}
+ 24 t., + 1. עוֹלָה Is 61^{8} (rd. prob. עַוְלָה); עַוְלָתָה 5766
ψ 125^{3} 92^{16} (Qr) + 2 t.; עֹלָתָה v^{16} (Kt) Jb 5^{16}; pl. עוֹלוֹת ψ 58^{3} 64^{7};—**1.** *violent deeds of injustice*, בְּנֵי עַוְלָה 2 S 3^{34} 7^{10} = 1 Ch 17^{9}; בֶּן־ע׳ ψ 89^{23}, cf. בְּנֵי עַלְוָה Ho 10^{9} (rd. עַוְלָה Now); אישׁ מרמה וע׳ ψ 43^{1}; בע׳ Is 61^{8}; || דָּם Mi 3^{10} Hb 2^{11}; עשׂה ע׳ ψ 37^{1} Zp 3$^{5.13}$; פעל ע׳ ψ 58^{3} 119^{3} Jb 36^{23}; שׁלח בע׳ ידים ψ 125^{3}. **2.** *injustice* of speech: דבר ע׳ Jb 13^{7} 27^{4}; לשׁונכם ע׳ תהגה Is 59^{3}; בלשׁוני ע׳ Jb 6^{30}; ע׳ לא נמצא בשׂפה Mal 2^{6}; ע׳ קפצה פיה ψ 107^{42} Jb 5^{16}. **3.** *injustice*, in general, ψ 64^{7} Jb 6^{29} 11^{14} 15^{16} 22^{23} 24^{20}, + 36^{33} (for MT עוֹלֶה) acc. to 𝔊 Di Bu Du al., Pr 22^{8} Ho 10^{13}; of God, אֵין עִם י׳ ע׳ 2 Ch 19^{7}; לא ע׳ בּוֹ ψ 92^{16}.

† II. עֲוִיל **n.m.** unjust one, Jb 16^{11} (v. foll.). 5760

† עַוָּל **n.m. unjust, unrighteous one**;— 5767
esp. of oppressive ruler Zp 3^{5} Jb 18^{18} 27^{7} (|| רָשָׁע), 29^{17} 31^{3} (|| פֹּעֲלֵי אָוֶן); prob. also 16^{11} (for MT עֲוִיל, so Di; || רְשָׁעִים).

I. [עוֹלָה] v. II. עול. II. עוֹלָה v. עלה. p. 750f 5766, 5930
עוֹלֵל, עוֹלָל v. II. עלל. עוֹלָם v. עלם. p. 760-61 5768-69

† [עוּן] **vb. dwell** (prob.; √of foll.; Ar. 6030
عون, عَانَ is *support, help*, v. esp. Fl$^{Kl. Schr. i. 87 ff.}$);—**Qal** *Pf.* 3 fs. consec. וְעָנָה (rd. וְעָנָה ?) Is 13^{22} *and* jackals *shall dwell*, etc. (on agreement v. Ges$^{§ 145 k}$; || שׁכן v^{21}), so 𝔊 Buhl; Che$^{Heb. Hpt.}$
^{124} וְשָׁכְנוּ; > 𝔖𝔗𝔙 al. √ IV. ענה.—ψ 87^{7} v. מַעְיָן. 6030

† I. מָעוֹן **n.[m.] dwelling, habitation**;— p. 777 4583
abs. מ׳ ψ 71^{3}+, cstr. מְעוֹן Je 25^{30}+, sf. מְעוֹנְךָ ψ 91^{9}, etc.;—**1.** *lair* of jackals Je 9^{10} 10^{22} 49^{33} 51^{37} (all of desolated cities); מ׳ אֲרָיוֹת Na 2^{12} (|| מִרְעֶה; fig. of Nineveh). **2.** *dwelling* of י׳:

a. in heaven מ׳ קָדְשְׁךָ Dt 26[15] cf. Je 25[30] (‖ מָרוֹם), Zc 2[17] ψ 68[6] 2 Ch 30[27]. **b.** in temple מ׳ בֵּיתֶךָ ψ 26[8], מְעוֹנוֹ 2 Ch 36[15] (only here alone). **3.** fig. of י׳ as abode of his people, צוּר מ׳ ψ 71[3], מ׳ alone 90[1] 91[9].—מ׳ 1 S 2[29.32] is unintellig. (v. Comm.), poss. rd. מְעוֹיֵן (*eyeing* [enviously], v. עין denom.) Klo HPS, cf. 𝔊 Bu. מְעוֹנָהּ Zp 3[7] is difficult in context, 𝔊 We Now rd. מֵעֵינֶיהָ (cf. Jos 9[23] 2 S 3[29]).

4584 †II. מָעוֹן **n.pr. 1. loc.** in Judah Jos 15[55] (P), 1 S 25[2] (𝔊 Μααν, Μαων), now *Ma'în* (Buhl Geogr. 163 and reff.), 8 miles S. of Hebron; hence מִדְבַּר מ׳ 23[24.25.25], so rd. also 25[1] (for MT פארן) 𝔊 Th We Dr Bu Klo Kit Löhr; cf. **2. m.** in Judah 1 Ch 2[45.45], 𝔊 Μεων, Μαων. **3. gent.** Ju 10[12] named with Sidonians and Amalek as ancient foes of Isr.; poss. intended by writer as = מְעוּנִים q. v. p. 589 supr.; many read מִדְיָן (𝔊 BA 𝔊L Μαδιαμ); v. GFM.—בֵּית בַּעַל מְעוֹן v. מְעוֹן p. 111 supr.; 1 Ch 4[41] v. מְעוּנִים p. 589.

4585 †מְעֹנָה **n.f.** id.;—**1.** *den, lair* of wild beasts: of כְּפִיר, מְעֹנָתוֹ Am 3[4], so pl. abs. מְעוֹנוֹת Jb 38[40] (‖ סֻכָּה), sf. מְעוֹנֹתָם ψ 104[22]; cstr. מְעֹנוֹת אֲרָיוֹת Ct 4[8]; מְעֹנָתָיו Na 2[13] (‖ חֹרָיו; of אַרְיֵה, fig. of Nineveh); of חַיָּה in gen., בִּמְעוֹנֹתֶיהָ תִשְׁכֹּן Jb 37[8] (‖ אָרֶב); so appar. fig. of men, hunted by י׳, מְעוֹנוֹתֵינוּ Je 21[13], fig. also of י׳ dwelling in temple, sg. sf., מְעוֹנָתוֹ בְּצִיּוֹן ψ 76[3] (‖ סֻכּוֹ). **2.** fig. מְעֹנָה אֱלֹהֵי קֶדֶם Dt 33[27] *the ancient God is a dwelling-place* (for his people; cf. I. מָעוֹן **3**).

4587 †מְעוֹנֹתַי **n.pr.m.** name in Judah 1 Ch 4[14], 𝔊 Μα(ω)ναθει.

5772 †[עוֹנָה] Qr, [עֵינָה] Kt **n.f.** only sf. Ho
10[10]: Qr pl. עוֹנֹתָם Baer, sg. עוֹנָתָם Ginsb;
5771, 5869 > עֵינֹתָם Kt; but rd. עֲוֹנֹתָם, v. עָוֹן **1 a.** p. 730.

5869 עֹיֵן Kt 1 S 18[9] v. עין. p. 744

5773 עִוְעִים v. sub I. עוה. p. 730

5774 †I. עוּף **vb.** fly (NH *id.*, (rare) *flicker, flutter*, עוֹף *fowl;* Aram. עוֹפָא, ܥܘܦܐ *id.;* Eth. ዖፍ: *id.;* Ar. عَوْفٌ *augury*, from birds (cf. We Heid. 2, 202), *fortune*, عاف، عيف *practice augury*, عائف *augur;* also عاف، عوف *fly about*, of birds);—**Qal** *Pf.* 3 mpl. וְעָפוּ consec. Is 11[14]; *Impf.* 3 ms. יָעוּף Jb 20[8] ψ 91[5] + Pr 23[5 b] Qr (> Kt ועוף [van d. H.], or ועיף [Ginsb]); וַיָּעֹף 2 S 22[11] = ψ 18[11], Na 3[16], וַיָּעָף Is 6[6]; 3 fs. (הֲ)תָעוּף Pr 23[5a] Kt (v. infr.); 3 fpl. תְּעוּפֶינָה Is 60[8], etc.; *Inf. cstr.* עוּף Jb 5[7] Pr 26[2]; *Pt.* fs. עָפָה Zc 5[1.2]; pl. עָפוֹת Is 31[5];—**1. a.** *fly*, of birds Dt 4[17], specif. of swallow (in sim.) Pr 26[2] (‖ נוּד); of seraph Is 6[6] (cf. **Pōʿl.**); י׳ riding (רכב) on cherub 2 S 22[11] = ψ 18[11]; roll (in vision) Zc 5[1.2]; arrow ψ 91[5]; of swift army Is 11[14] (under fig. of bird, sq. בְּכָתֵף) Hb 1[8] (sim. of vulture); fig. of ships (like cloud, or doves) Is 60[8]; בְּנֵי־רֶשֶׁף יַגְבִּיהוּ עוּף Jb 5[7] *make high to fly*, i.e. make their flight high, soar aloft (sim. of irresistible tendency). **b.** *hover* (protectingly) Is 31[5] (birds, sim. of י׳; on sense cf. Dt 32[11]). **2.** *fly away*, to a distance, ψ 55[7] (fig.; ‖ אַרְחִיק נְדֹד v[8]); = vanish, of locusts Na 1[16] (fig.); כְּנֶשֶׁר יָעוּף הַשָּׁמָיִם Pr 23[5 b] (Qr) sim. of riches (v. Toy); of wicked Jb 20[8] (כַּחֲלוֹם); end of life, in gen., וַנָּעֻפָה ψ 90[10].—הֲתָעוּף Pr 23[5a] Kt, *do thine eyes fly* (*light*) upon it? (הֲתָעִיף **Hiph.** Qr *dost thou cause thine eyes to fly*, etc.?) is difficult, and line perhaps not original (v. Toy). **Pōʿl. 1.** *fly about, to and fro; Impf.* 3 ms. יְעוֹפֵף of birds Gn 1[20] (P); seraphim Is 6[2]; *Pt.* שָׂרָף מְעוֹפֵף *flying* fiery serpent Is 14[29] 30[6]. **2.** *cause to fly to and fro, brandish, Inf. cstr.* sf. בְּעוֹפְפִי חַרְבִּי Ez 32[10] *when I brandish my sword* before them. **Hithpōʿl.** *Impf.* 3 ms. כָּעוֹף יִתְעוֹפֵף כְּבוֹדָם Ho 9[11] *like a bird their glory shall fly away.* **Hiph.** *Impf.* 2 ms. Qr, v. **Qal** ad fin.

עוֹף 70 **n.m.** Gn 40, 17 **coll. flying creatures,** 5775
fowl, insects;—ע׳ abs. Gn 1[20]+, cstr. v[21]+; —**1.** *fowl, birds*, Gn 40[17.19] (E), 7[8] (J), 1[20.22] (P), 1 K 5[13]+; esp. (38 t.) ע׳ הַשָּׁמַיִם *fowl of the sky*, Gn 2[19.20] (J), 1[26.28.30] (P), Ho 2[20] Ec 10[20]+, carrion birds 1 S 17[44.46] 2 S 21[10] 1 K 14[11]+11 t.; ע׳ הָרִים ψ 50[11], ע׳ נוֹדֵד Is 16[2], כִּכְלוּב מָלֵא ע׳ Je 5[27]; redundantly ע׳ כָּנָף *fowl of wing* Gn 1[21] (P), ψ 78[27] (for food); for food also Lv 7[26] (P), 17[13] 20[25] (both H), cf. Lv 11[13.46] (H, clean and unclean); for offering Gn 8[20] (J; הָע׳ הַטָּהוֹר), Lv 1[14] (P). **2.** *winged insects* (clean and unclean) שֶׁרֶץ הָע׳ הַהֹלֵךְ עַל־אַרְבַּע Lv 11[20.21] (H), שׁ׳ הָע׳ Dt 14[19], so prob. הָע׳ alone v[20]; שׁ׳ הָע׳ אֲשֶׁר־לוֹ אַרְבַּע רַגְלַיִם Lv 11[23] (H).

†[עַפְעַף] **n.m.** Je 9, 17 **eyelid** (NH *id.;* from 6079
fluttering?);—only du. cstr. (v. infr.) and sf. עַפְעַפֵּי Jb 16[16] ψ 132[4], עַפְעַפֶּיךָ Pr 4[25] 6[4], etc.;—*eyelids*, usu. nearly = *eyes* (6 t. ‖ עֵינַיִם), as weeping, עַפְעַפֵּינוּ Je 9[17]; closed in sleep ψ 132[4] Pr 6[4], cf. of צַלְמָוֶת Jb 16[16]; looking Pr 4[25] cf. ψ 11[4] (of י׳, testing men); used seductively by wanton women Pr 6[25]; raised, in arrogance

('*superciliousness*') 30[13]; fig. עַפְעַפֵּי־שָׁחַר Jb 3[9] *eyelids of dawn*, break of dawn, 41[10] (sim.).

5774 †II. [עוּף], I. [עִיף] **vb. be dark**;—only **Qal** *Impf.* 2 ms. תָּעֻפָה Jb 11[17] (though) *it be dark*, but rd. prob. תְּעֻפָה, subst., v. infr.

5890 †I. עֵיפָה **n.f. darkness**;—עֹשֵׂה שַׁחַר עֵיפָה Am 4[13]; אֶרֶץ עֵפָתָה Jb 10[22] (Ges [§ 90 g]; || צַלְמָוֶת).

5891 †II. עֵיפָה **n.pr. 1. gent.** 'son' of Midian Gn 25[4] (J) = 1 Ch 1[33], cf. Is 60[6], 𝔊 Γαφερ, Γεφαρ, Γαιφα(ρ). **2. m.** name in Judah 1 Ch 2[47], 𝔊 Γαιφα. **3. f.** concubine of Caleb 1 Ch 2[46], 𝔊 Γαιφαηλ, A Γαιφα ἡ, 𝔊L Γαιφα.

4155 †מוּעָף **n.[m.] gloom**;—Is 8[23].

4588 †[מָעוּף] **n.[m.] id.**;—cstr. מְעוּף צוּקָה Is 8[22] (|| הֲשֵׁכָה); Che [Hpt.] rds. מוּעָף.

†תְּעֻפָה **n.f. id.**;—so rd. prob. for תָּעֻפָה Jb 11[17] (opp. בֹּקֶר).

5778 †עוֹפַי Kt, עֵיפַי Qr **n.pr.m.** a Neṭophathite, Je 40[8], 𝔊 Ιωφε, Ωφε, Ωφετ.

5779 †[עוּץ] **vb. counsel, plan** (Aram. *id.*; || form of יעץ);—only **Qal** *Imv.* mpl. עֻצוּ Ju 19[30] (GFM rds. עֵצָה, but v. Bu), Is 8[10] c. acc. cogn. עֵצָה. (Sta [ThLz 1894, Apr. 28, 235] der. עֻצוּ fr. יעץ).

5780 †עוּץ **n.pr. 1. m. a.** (eldest) 'son' of Aram Gn 10[23] (P), = 'son' of Shem 1 Ch 1[17], 𝔊 Ως, 𝔊L Ch Ουζ. **b.** eldest 'son' of Naḥor Gn 22[21] (J), A Ωξ, 𝔊L Ωζ. **c.** Edomite name Gn 36[28] = 1 Ch 1[42], 𝔊 Ως, 𝔊L Ους. **2. loc.** (= **1. a**, **b**, poss. also **c**), מַלְכֵי אֶרֶץ הָעוּץ Je 25[20] (𝔊 om.); בְּאֶרֶץ־עוּץ Jb 1[1] (home of Job), 𝔊 Αυσιτις; La 4[21] (del. עוּץ 𝔊 cf. Bu and reff.); on Uz as vague name for E. country v. esp. Bu [ix. f.]; Dl [Pa 259, ZKF ii. 87 ff.] puts in Ḥauran, or N. (NE.) therefrom, = As. *Uṣṣu*, but dub. With name עוּץ RS [K 261] cp. Ar. n.pr. div. عَوْض, so We [Heid. 2, 146]; against this Nö [ZMG xl (1886), 183 f.], but v. reply RS [Sem i. 43].

3263 †יְעוּץ **n.pr.m.** Benjamite name 1 Ch 8[10], 𝔊 Ιδως, A Ιεους, 𝔊L Ιωας.

5781 †[עוּק] **vb.** dub. (if correct, Aram. form (cf. עוּק, ܥܳܩ) for צוּק *press*, so Thes al.);—only **Hiph.** *Impf.* 3 fs. תָּעִיק Am 2[13], *Pt.* מֵעִיק v[13]; but read prob. תָּפוּק, מֵפִיק *totter, cause tottering* Hi We Now Dr.

6125 †[עָקָה] **n.f. pressure** (si vera l., Aram. word, 𝔗 עָקְתָא, Syr. ܥܳܩܬܳܐ);—only cstr. מִפְּנֵי עָקַת רָשָׁע ψ 55[4] *because of the pressure of the wicked*; > rd. צַעֲקַת (|| קוֹל; Ol al.), which means *cry for help*.

†מוּעָקָה **n.f. compression, distress** (si 4157
vera l., Aram. word, = מְצוּקָה);—שַׂמְתָּ מ׳ בְּמָתְנֵינוּ ψ 66[11], 𝔊 θλίψεις, 𝔙 *tribulationes*; but word dub.

†[עָוַר] **vb. Pi. make blind, blind** (orig. 5786
meaning of √ dub.; Thes עור = *dig* (Ar. غَارٌ etc. *cave*); Hal [RÉJ xi, 67] cp. עוֹר *skin*, whence *blindness* as cataract;—Aram. adj. עֲוִיר, ܥܰܘܝܪܳܐ *blind*, Pa. עַוַּר, ܥܰܘܰܪ = Heb. Pi.; Ar. عَوِرَ *be one-eyed*, Eth. ዐወረ: *be blind* Di [995]);—**Pi.** *Pf.* 3 ms. עִוֵּר 2 K 25[7], c. עֵינֵי *put out the eyes of* = Je 39[7] = 52[11]; *Impf.* 3 ms. יְעַוֵּר fig., Ex 23[8] (E) a bribe *blindeth*, c. acc. pers. (Sam 𝔊 ins. עֵינֵי); Dt 16[19], c. עֵינֵי.

†עִוֵּר **adj. blind**;—only abs. ע׳ Ex 4[11] +, 5787
pl. עִוְרִים 2 S 5[6] +, f. עִוְרוֹת Is 42[7]; (c. art. הָעִוֵּר Dt 28[29], elsewh. הָע׳ Baer Ginsb; van d. H. לָעִוֵּר Jb 29[15], הָעִוְרִים 2 S 5[6.8] Is 42[18]);—*blind*, usu. as subst. = *the blind*: **1.** lit., physically *blind*: **a.** of men Ex 4[11] (J; opp. פִּקֵּחַ), 2 S 5[6.8.8] Lv 19[14] (H), Dt 27[18] Je 31[8] Jb 29[15]; in sim. Dt 28[29] Zp 1[17] Is 59[10], cf. La 4[14] (appos.); as adj. attribute אִישׁ ע׳ Lv 21[18] (H). **b.** of sacrif. animal Dt 15[21] Mal 1[8]. **2.** fig., **a.** of the helpless, groping Is 29[18] 35[5] 42[16] ψ 146[8]; as adj. attribute, עֵינַיִם עִוְרוֹת Is 42[7]. **b.** of the dull, unreceptive, Is 42[18.19.19.19] (but v[19c] rd. חֵרֵשׁ q.v.); as adj. attrib. עַם עִוֵּר 43[8]; as predicate 56[10].

†עִוָּרוֹן **n.[m.] blindness**;—only in phr. 5788
(subj. י׳), *smite* (הִכָּה) *with blindness*: fig. of 'blind incapacity' (Dr) בְּע׳ Dt 28[28]; of smiting horses בע׳ Zc 12[4], i.e. with *blind staggers*, making them helplessly wild.

†עַוֶּרֶת **n.f. id.**;—of sacrif. animals, abstr. 5788
for concr., Lv 22[22] (H).

†I. [עוּר] **vb. rouse oneself, awake** (NH 5782
id.; Aram. עוּר, ܥܳܪ; Ar. عير, غَارَ, v. עִיר, עַיִר; غير, غَارَ is *be jealous*, cf. Syr. ܥܽܘܪܳܐ *hate, revenge*);—**Qal** *Impf.* 3 ms. sf. יְעוּרֶנּוּ Jb 41[2] Baer Ginsb, and Qr van d. H., but Kt יעירנו (Hiph.), Bab. Mass. (v. Baer [p. 58]), so Ginsb [marg.] van d. H.; rd. thus, or יְעוֹרְרֶנּוּ (Pōʿl.) Bu; > contr. form of Pōʿl. Ges [§ 72 cc] Di; cf. Sta [§ 484 e]; *Imv.* ms. עוּרָה ψ 7[7] +, fs. עוּרִי Ju 5[12.12] + 3 t., עוּרִי Ju 5[12.12] + 5 t. (for rhythm); *Pt.* עֵר Ct 5[2] + Mal 2[12] (read prob. עַד We Now GASm, cf. 𝔊 ἕως = עַד);—*rouse oneself* to activity, of Deborah Ju 5[12.12.12.12]; of י׳ ψ 7[7] (|| קוּמָה, הִנָּשֵׂא), 59[5] (sq. inf.), 44[24] (opp. יָשֵׁן), of י׳'s arm Is 51[9.9.9], of oneself ψ 57[9], of Zion Is 52[1.1], of stone (idol),

Hb 2^{19}, sword Zc 13^{7} (+ עַל *against*), wind Ct 4^{16}, harp and lyre ψ 57^{9} = 108^{3}; לִבִּי עֵר Ct 5^{2} *my heart waketh* (opp. יְשֵׁנָה).—Jb 41^{2} Mal 2^{12} v. supr. **Niph.** *Pf.* 3 ms. נֵעוֹר Zc 2^{17}; *Impf.* 3 ms. יֵעוֹר Je 6^{22} Zc 4^{1}; 3 mpl. יֵעֹרוּ Je 50^{41} Jb 14^{12}, יֵעוֹרוּ Jo 4^{12};—*be roused* Zc 4^{1} (fr. [מִן] sleep, in sim.), so Jb 14^{12} (sleep of death, ‖ יָקוּם, יָקִיצוּ); *be incited* to activity, c. מִן loc.: of ׳י Zc 2^{17}, of nation Je 6^{22}, kings 50^{41}, whirlwind 25^{32}; abs. of nations Jo 4^{12}. **Pōʿl.** *Pf.* 3 ms. עוֹרֵר 2 S 23^{18}+, ׳וְע consec. Is 10^{26}, 1 s. וְעוֹרַרְתִּי Zc 9^{13}, sf. עוֹרַרְתִּיךָ Ct 8^{5}; *Impf.* 3 fs. תְּעֹרֵר Pr 10^{12}, 2 mpl. תְּעוֹרְרוּ Ct 2^{7} 3^{5}, תְּעֹרְרוּ 8^{4} (fem. subj. Ges ^{§144a}); *Imv.* ms. עוֹרְרָה ψ 80^{3}; *Inf.* עֹרֵר Jb 3^{8};—*rouse, incite* to activity, c. acc. pers. Zc 9^{13} (+ עַל *against*), acc. רְפָאִים Is 14^{9} (subj. שְׁאוֹל v. Ges ^{§145t}); ׳ע אֶת־גְּבוּרָתֶךָ ψ 80^{3} (of ׳י); הָעֲתִידִים עֹרֵר לִוְיָתָן Jb 3^{8}; esp. *rouse, excite* love Ct 2^{7} 3^{5} 8^{4} (all ‖ תָּעִירוּ; fem. subj. v. Ges ^{§144a}); עוֹרַרְתִּיךָ 8^{5} is dubious, of exciting love De, arousing from slumber Bu, so, reading עוֹרַרְתִּיךְ, Siegf; שִׂנְאָה תְּע׳ מְדָנִים Pr 10^{12} *hatred stirreth up strifes;* c. acc. of weapon 2 S 23^{18} *rouse, awaken,* i.e. *wield, brandish* (+ עַל *against*), so read also v^{8} (v. חֲנִית **1**) = 1 Ch $11^{11.20}$, so Is 10^{26}.—Is 23^{13} v. ערר. **Pilp.** *Impf.* 3 mpl. זַעֲקַת־שֶׁבֶר יְעֹעֵרוּ Is 15^{5}, usu. expl. as = יְעַרְעֵרוּ (wh. some rd.), *rouse* (i.e. *raise?*) *a cry of destruction,* Ges $^{Comm. Thes.}$ De Di Du Ges ^{§72cc} Kö $^{i. 500; ii. 497}$; Pilp. not elsewhere, very dub.; rd. perh. יְעוֹרֵרוּ; Lag $^{Proph. Chald. II}$ Che Gu ^{Kau} SS rd. יְרֹעָעוּ *shout,* but improb. with זַעֲקַת. **Hithpōʿl.** *Pf.* וְהִתְעֹרַרְתִּי כִּי consec. Jb 31^{29} *and I was* (joyfully) *excited, triumphant,* that (‖ אֶשְׂמַח), so perh. *Impf.* 3 ms. Jb 17^{8}, rdg. וְחָנֵף עַל־נָקִי יִתְעֹרָר Me Di Beer (MT וְנָקִי עַל־חָנֵף יִתְע׳, i.e. *be excited with displeasure*); *rouse oneself* to activity, *Pt.* מִתְעוֹרֵר לְהַחֲזִיק בָּךְ Is 64^{6}. **Hiph.** *Pf.* 3 ms. הֵעִיר Is 41^{2}+; 1 s. הַעִירֹוֹתִי Is 41^{25} (v. Kö $^{i. 500}$ Ges ^{§72x}), sf. הַעִירֹתִהוּ 45^{13}; *Impf.* 3 ms. יָעִיר Dt 32^{11}+, וְיָעֵר Dn 11^{25}, וַיָּעַר Hg 1^{14}+, sf. וַיְעִירֵנִי Zc 4^{1}, etc.; *Imv.* ms. הָעִירָה ψ 35^{23}; mpl. הָעִירוּ Jo 4^{9}; *Inf.* בָּעִיר (= בְּהָעִיר) ψ 73^{20} (Ges ^{§53q}); *Pt.* מֵעִיר Is 13^{17}+, sf. מְעִירָם Jo 4^{7};—**1.** *rouse,* c. sf. Zc 4^{1} (as if from sleep, v. **Qal**); *rouse, stir up,* to activity, כְּנֶשֶׁר יָעִיר קִנּוֹ Dt 32^{11}; c. acc. pers., or equiv., expressed or implied, esp. subj. ׳י: Is 45^{13}; c. מִן loc. $41^{2.25}$ Jo 4^{7}; + עַל *against* Is 13^{17}, cf. Je 50^{9} 51^{1} Ez 23^{22}; הֵעִיר אֶת־רוּחַ פ׳ Je 51^{11} Hg 1^{14} 1 Ch 5^{26} 2 Ch 21^{16} (+ עַל *against*), 36^{22} = Ezr 1^{1}, cf. v^{5}; ׳י subj. also in foll.: יָעִיר קִנְאָה Is 42^{13}, יָעִיר $50^{4.4}$ (+ לִי אֹזֶן); human subj., c. acc. pers. Jo 4^{9}, Dn 11^{2} (+ אֵת in conflict *with,* 𝔙 deW Meinh Behrm, cf. Bev. who thinks יערך לקראת poss.); perh. also, obj. crocodile Jb 41^{2} (rdg. יְעִירֶנּוּ v. **Qal**); וְיָעֵר כֹּחוֹ וּלְבָבוֹ Dn 11^{25} (+ עַל *against*); esp. of *rousing* love Ct 2^{7} 3^{5} 8^{4} (all ‖ **Pōʿl.** q. v.); fig. אָעִירָה שָּׁחַר ψ 57^{9} *I will arouse the dawn* (‖ Imv. **Qal** q.v.); pt. abs. = *stirring up* (a fire) Ho 7^{4} (si vera l.; cf. Ges ^{§120b}; but text dubious cf. We Now GASm). **2.** declarative or exhibitive sense, *act in an aroused manner, awake,* הָעִירָה וְהָקִיצָה לְמִשְׁפָּטִי ψ 35^{23}, cf. Jb 8^{6} (+ עַל *over = for;* both subj. ׳י); abs. ψ 73^{20}.

†I. **עִיר n.[m.] excitement;**—of terror, 5892
ע׳ וּבֶהָלוֹת Je 15^{9}; of rage (si vera l.), לֹא אָבוֹא בְּעִיר Ho 11^{9}, but St prop. לְבָעֵר cf. We Oort Now GASm.—בָּעִיר ψ 73^{20} v. עור **Hiph.**—II, III. עִיר v. p. 746 infr.

†**עֵר n.pr.m.** Hρ (cf. עוּר Qal Pt.);—**1.** eldest 6147
son of Judah Gn $38^{3.6}$ = 1 Ch $2^{3.3}$, Gn 38^{7} $46^{12.12}$ Nu $26^{19.19}$. **2.** son of Judah's son Shelah 1 Ch 4^{21}.—Vid. also **Qal** *Pt.* עֵר supr.

†I. **עֵרִי n.pr.m.** a son of Gad Gn 46^{16} 6179
Nu 26^{16}, Ἠδις, Αδδει.

II. **עֵרִי adj.gent.** of I. עֵרִי, c. art. as subst. 6180
coll. הָעֵרִי Nu 26^{16}, Αδδει.

†**עֵרָן n.pr.m.** (si vera l.) an Ephraimite 6197
Nu 26^{36}, but עדן Sam Ginsb $^{marg.}$, 𝔊 Εδεν.

†**עֵרָנִי adj.gent.** of עֵרָן, c. art. as subst. coll. 6198
Nu 26^{36}, עדני Sam Ginsb $^{marg.}$, 𝔊 Εδενει.

†**יָעוּר** Kt, **יָעִיר** Qr, **n.pr.m.** father of 3265
Elhanan the giant-slayer 1 Ch 20^{5} (Ιαειρ) + ‖ 2 S 21^{19} (where read יעיר for יַעְרֵי, and del. אֹרְגִים, v. Th We Dr Bu Kit HPS).

†II. **[עוּר] vb. be exposed, bare** (akin 5783
to עָרָה, ערר; Ar. عَوْرَةٌ = *pudenda*);—**Niph.** *Impf.* 3 fs. עֶרְיָה תֵעוֹר קַשְׁתֶּךָ Hb 3^{9} *into nakedness* (i.e. utterly) *is thy bow laid bare,* made ready; We prop. עוֹרֵר תְּעוֹרֵר (cf. 2 S 23^{18}, I. עור **Pōʿl.**), and so Now [from √ערר, *lay bare*] *thou layest,* etc.

† **[מָעוֹר] n[.m.] nakedness, pudendum;**— 4589
only pl. sf. מְעוֹרֵיהֶם Hb 2^{15}.

†**עֵירֹם, עֵרֹם adj.** and **n.[m.] 1. naked;** 5903
2. nakedness (√עור Ew ^{423,426} Ges ^{§85t} Sta $^{§§295, 327a}$; > √ערם (not Heb. in this sense) Ba $^{NB §27g}$ Kö $^{ii. 84, 120}$);—abs. עֵירֹם Gn $3^{10.11}$ + 4 t., עֵרֹם Ez 16^{7} + 2 t. Ez; pl. עֵירֻמִּים Gn 3^{7};—**1. adj.** *naked*

Gn 3[7.10.11] (all pred.); as subst. concr. Ez 18[7.16]. **2. n.abstr.** *nakedness* Dt 28[48]; ע׳ וְעֶרְיָה *nakedness and bareness* (=naked and bare, of personified Jerusalem), Ez 16[7.22.39] 22[29].

6174 †עָרוֹם, עָרֹם **adj. naked** (perh. secondary form from עֵירֹם Ew[§ 163 c] Sta[§ 327 a]; or from √עָרָה, q.v.);—abs. עָרוֹם Am 2[16] + 8 t., עָרֹם 1 S 19[24] + 3 t.; f. עֲרֻמָּה Ho 2[5]; pl. עֲרוּמִּים Gn 2[25] Jb 22[6];—*naked* Gn 2[25] (J) 1 S 19[14] Ho 2[5]; adverb. (Ges[§ 118 n]) c. הָלַךְ Is 20[2.3.4] Mi 1[8], cf. Am 2[16] Jb 24[7.10]; =subst. concr. Is 58[7] Jb 22[6]; = without possessions Jb 1[21.21] = Ec 5[14]; of She'ôl, open before י׳ Jb 26[6].

4636 †[מַעֲרֹם, Kö[ii. 1, 121]] **n.m. naked thing**;—pl. abstr. sf. מַעֲרֻמֵּיהֶם 2 Ch 28[15] *their nakedness* (denom. fr. foreg. Sta[§ 273 a]; > √ערם Ba[NB § 166 b]).

III. עור (√of foll.; meaning unknown).

5785 עוֹר [99] **n.m.** [Jb 7, 5] **skin** (NH *id.*; Ph. ערת Lzb[346]);—ע׳ abs. Gn 3[21] +, cstr. Ex 34[29] +; sf. עֹרוֹ 29[14] +, עוֹרוֹ Je 13[23], עֹרָהּ Nu 19[5], etc.; pl. cstr. עֹרֹת Gn 27[16] +, עוֹרֹת Ex 39[34], sf. עֹרֹתָם Lv 16[27];—*skin*: **1.** of men (55 t.), שִׂמְלָתוֹ לְעֹרוֹ Ex 22[26] (E), ע׳ פָּנָיו 34[29.30] cf. v[35] (all P); (dark) skin of Cushite Je 13[23]; v. also Ez 37[6.8] La 3[8] Jb 7[5] 10[11] +; in hyperb. Mi 3[2.3]; עוֹר שִׁנָּי Jb 19[20 b] *the skin of my teeth*, i.e. gums (si vera l.); also Lv 13[2] + 33 t. Lv 13 (P), in tests for leprosy (v. esp. ע׳־בְּשָׂרוֹ v[2.2.3.4.11], cf. v[3.38.39.43]); עוֹר בְּעַד עוֹר Jb 2[4] *skin in behalf of, for, skin*, appar. proverb. phrase of barter, = everything has its price (on varieties of interpr. v. Comm.). **2.** *hide* of animals (44 t.), alw.—exc. Jb 40[31]—after skinning: Gn 27[16] (J); of sacrif. victims Ex 29[14] Lv 4[11] + 5 t. (all P); prepared for use (by some process of tanning, cf. Now[Arch. i. 242]), sts. = *leather*: material of garments Gn 3[21] (J), girdle 2 K 1[8], any article Lv 11[32] 13[48 ff] Nu 31[20] (P); covering of tabern. Ex 25[5.5] + 10 t. Ex 26, 35, 36, 39, of ark, sacred utensils, etc., Nu 4[6] + 5 t. Nu 4.

5895 עוֹרִים Is 30[6] v. עַיִר. p. 747

5789 †[עוּשׁ] **vb.** si vera l., **lend aid, come to help** (Ar. غَاثَ IV. *aid, succour*; Sab. עות n. *help*, Sab Denkm[91]; Nab. Sin. עות in n.pr. Lzb[337] Cook[90]);—**Qal** *Imv.* mpl. עוּשׁוּ וָבֹאוּ Jo 4[11] but dub.; Gr Dr, plausibly, חוּשׁוּ; Che[Expos., Nov. 1897, 365] גֹּשׁוּ (√נגשׁ); עוּרוּ We Now.

3266,3274 †יְעוּשׁ (also Kt יעישׁ) **n.pr.m.** (prob. *he comes to help*, Nö[ZMG xl (1886), 168]; = Ar. n.pr.div. يَغُوث, We[Skizzen iii, 171; Heid. 2, 146] RS[K 218 (cf. Sem i. 43)] Nö[l.c.], yet against this 𝔊 Ιεους (i.e. ع; not Ιαγους, غ), and ־ֻ (not ־ִ), Lag[M ii. 77; BN 133] Buhl[Edom. 48 f.]);—**1.** son of Esau Gn 36[5.14] (both Kt יעישׁ), v[18] 1 Ch 1[35]. **2.** Benjamites: **a.** 1 Ch 7[10] (Kt יעישׁ). **b.** 1 Ch 8[39]. **3.** a Levite 1 Ch 23[10.11]. **4.** son of Rehoboam 2 Ch 11[19].—יוֹעָשׁ v. supr., p. 222 b.

†[עָוַת] **vb. be bent, crooked** (NH *id.*, Pi. Nithp.; Aram. עַוֵּית Pa.; cf. ܥܘܬ, ܥܘܬ *deceive* PS[3008]);—**Pi.** *Pf.* 3 ms. sf. עִוְּתַנִי Jb 19[6], עִוְּתוֹ Ec 7[13]; 3 pl. sf. עִוְּתוּנִי ψ 119[78]; *Impf.* 3 ms. יְעַוֵּת ψ 146[9] Jb 8[3], יְעַוֵּת־ v[3]; *Inf.* לְעַוֵּת Am 8[5] La 3[22];—**1. a.** *make crooked* = falsify, scales Am 8[5]; *pervert* justice (מִשְׁפָּט, צֶדֶק) Jb 8[3.3] 34[12] (all God subj.); c. acc. pers. *subvert* (i.e. deprive of justice), לְעַ׳ אָדָם בְּרִיבוֹ La 3[36], cf. ψ 119[78]; so עִוְּתַנִי Jb 19[6] (י׳ subj.). **2.** *bend, make crooked*, דֶּרֶךְ רְשָׁעִים ψ 146[9] (י׳ subj.); in gen. Ec 7[13] (God subj.; opp. תִּקֵּן). **Pu.** *Pt.* מְעֻוָּת Ec 1[15] *what is bent* (opp. תִּקֵּן). **Hithp.** *Pf.* 3 pl. consec. וְהִתְעַוְּתוּ Ec 12[3] *and* the strong men *bend themselves*. 5791

†[עַוָּתָה] **n.f. subversion,** i.e. deprivation of justice;—sf. עַוָּתָתִי La 3[59] (opp. מִשְׁפָּטִי). 5792

†עוּת **vb.** very dub.; only in לָדַעַת לָעוּת אֶת־יָעֵף דָּבָר Is 50[4] usu. *to help*, so Ges Del Di Ry[Kau] al., but in that case an Aramaism (Aram. *עוּת = Ar. غَاثَ, q.v. sub עוּשׁ); text prob. corrupt, 𝔊 Oort[Th T 1891, 469] לְעַתּוֹ, and del. אֶת־יָעֵף; Klo Che[Comm.] לִרְעוֹת '*teach, edify*,' Gr לַעֲנוֹת, Che[Hpt.] לְהַחֲיוֹת. 5790

†עוּתַי **n.pr.m. 1.** name in Judah 1 Ch 9[4], Γωθει (= עֲתָיָה Ne 11[4]). **2.** Ezr 8[14], Ουθι. 5793

עַז, עֹז, עַזָּא v. עזז. עֵז v. ענז. p. 738-39, 777 5794-95, 5797-98

†עֲזָאזֵל **n.[m.]** entire removal (redupl. intens. (Ges[§ 30 n.] Sta[§ 124 a]), abstr., √[עזל] = Ar. عزل *remove*, v. Bähr[Symb. ii. 668] Win[ii. 659 ff.] Me in Schenkel[BL. i. 256]; > most, n.pr. of spirit haunting desert, Thes Di Dr[Hastings, DB] [a fallen angel, Lv 16[8 ff.] being late, acc. to Che[ZAW xv (1895), 153 ff., Ency. Bib.], who der. fr. עזז־אל; cf. Benz[Ency. Bib.]], as in Jewish angelology, where prob. based on interpret. of Lv 16[8 ff.]; name not elsewhere);—ע׳ Lv 16[8.10.10.26] in ritual of Day of Atonement, = *entire removal* of sin and guilt from sacred places into desert on back of goat, symb. of entire forgiveness. 5799

I. עָזַב [213] **vb. leave, forsake, loose** (NH *id.* (rare); Ar. عَزَبَ *be remote, absent, depart*, As. *ezêbu, leave*, Shaph. *ušezib, rescue*, cf. BAram. שֵׁיזִב;—Eth. መዐበ: *widowed* Di[973]);—**Qal** *Pf.* 3 ms. ע׳ Gn 24[27] +, sf. עֲזָבַנִי Is 49[14] ψ 38[11]; 5800

3 fs. עָזְבָה Ez 23^{8}; 1 s. sf. עֲזַבְתִּיךְ Is 54^{7}; 2 fpl. עֲזַבְתֶּן Ex 2^{20}, etc., *Impf.* 3 ms. יַעֲזֹב Is 55^{7}+, יַעֲזָב־ Gn 2^{24}, sf. 1 s. וַיַּעַזְבֵנִי 1 S 30^{13}, etc.; *Imv.* עֲזֹב ψ 37^{8}, עָזְבָה Je 49^{11}, עִזְבוּ Je 48^{28} Pr 9^{6}, etc.; *Inf. abs.* עָזוֹב Je 14^{5}, עָזֹב Ex 23^{5}; *cstr.* עֲזֹב Gn 44^{22}+, sf. עָזְבֵךְ Je 2^{17}+, etc.; *Pt. act.* עֹזֵב Pr 10^{17}+, cstr. עֹזְבֵי (Ges $^{§90 l}$); f. cstr. עֹזֶבֶת Pr 2^{17} etc.; *pass.* עָזוּב Dt 32^{36}+, etc.;—†**1.** *leave,* c. acc. (on order of meanings cf. Nö $^{ZMG. xl (1886), 726}$): **a.** = *depart from,* acc. pers. Gn 44$^{22.22}$ (J), 2 K 2$^{2.4.6}$ 4^{30} Nu 10^{31} (P), Ru 1^{16} Je 9^{1} (|| הָלַךְ מֵאֵת); acc. loc. 1 K 8^{6} Je 25^{38} ('י as lion leaving lair); c. מִן loc. intrans. (strangely) Je 18^{14} (of snow). **b.** *leave behind,* acc. pers. Ex 2^{20} (J), 2 S 15^{16} (+ inf.), Ez 24^{21}; acc. rei + בְּיַד Gn 39$^{12.13}$, + אֶצְלִי v$^{15.18}$ (all J); + בְּ loc. 50^{8} (J); acc. pers. et rei Ex 9^{21} (J). **c.** *leave* in the presence of (לִפְנֵי) 1 Ch 16^{37} (לְ of accus., cf. לְ **3 b** supr.), 2 Ch 28^{14}. **d.** *leave in safety,* וְאָנָה תַעַזְבוּ כְבוֹדְכֶם Is 10^{3}. **e.** *leave* in a given condition, situation, ע׳ אֹתוֹ בְּמַחֲלֻיִים 2 Ch 24^{25} *they left him in* great *suffering;* c. adv. acc. Ez 23^{29}; a city פְּתוּחָה Jos 8^{17}. **f.** *leave undisturbed, let alone* Ru 2^{16}. **g.** *leave* unexercised, Gn 24^{27} pregn. *he hath not left his kindness and his faithfulness from* (being) *with* (מֵעִם) *my master;* so ע׳ חַסְדּוֹ אֶת־ Ru 2^{20} (both of 'י); הֶרֶף מֵאַף || ע׳ חֵמָה ψ 37^{8}. **h.** *leave* in the hand of, entrust to, acc. rei + בְּיַד Gn 39^{6} (J), + אֶל־ Jb 39^{11} (|| בָּטַח בְּ), + עַל־ ψ 10^{14} (acc. om., *his cause*).—So also poss. (c. לְ) Ne 3^{34} (reading לֵאלֹהִים for MT לָהֶם), but text prob. otherwise corrupt. **i.** *leave* to (לְ) one (unaided), וְחָדַלְתָּ מֵעֲזֹב לוֹ Ex 23^{5a} (E) *thou shalt refrain from leaving* it (sc. the affair) *to him;* cf. תַּעֲזֹב לָאָרֶץ בֵּיצֶיהָ Jb 39^{14} (of ostrich). **j.** *leave over, remaining,* acc. pers. Jos 2^{21} (JE); acc. rei + לְ pers. Lv 19^{10} 23^{22} (H), Mal 3^{19}. **k.** *leave* = have nothing to do with Pr 9^{6}. **2.** *leave, abandon, forsake:* †**a.** *abandon,* acc. rei: (1) land, house, city, tent, etc., 1 S 31^{7} = 1 Ch 10^{7}, 2 K 7^{7} Je 9^{18} 48^{28} 51^{9} 2 Ch 11^{14}, Is 17^{9} (+ מִפְּנֵי of enemy); pt. pass. of cities v^{2} Je 4^{29} Zp 2^{4}, cf. עֲזוּבָה Is 17^{9} pt. = subst. = *deserted region.* (2) oxen 1 K 19^{20}, idol-images (+ שָׁם) 2 S 5^{21} = 1 Ch 14^{12}, flock Zc 11^{17}; pt. pass. of eggs Is 10^{14}. †**b.** *forsake,* (1) human subj. and obj.: Gn 2^{24} (J; a man his parents), 1 S 30^{13} Jos 22^{3} (D), Je 49^{11} ψ 27^{10} (parent a child), Pr 2^{17} (wife her husband, אַלּוּף), cf. אִשָּׁה עֲזוּבָה Is 54^{6}, and ע׳ of personif. Zion Is 60^{15} 62^{4}. (2) an animal its young Je 14^{5} (obj. om.). †**c.** = neglect, Levite Dt 12^{19} 14^{27}, poor Jb 20^{19}. **d.** esp. (1) fig. of *forsaking* God ('י), apostatizing, Ju 10^{10} Dt 28^{20} 31^{16} Je 1^{16} + 38 t. (oft. Je and later); + Jon 2^{9} (obj. חֲסָדִים, i.e. God, v. חֶסֶד **II**); c. לְ + inf. only אֶת־י׳ עָזְבוּ לִשְׁמֹר Ho 4^{10} (Oort We Now doubt לִשְׁמֹר). (2) obj. 'י's law, commands, covenant, etc., Dt 29^{24} 1 K 19$^{10.14}$ + 14 t.; house of 'י 2 Ch 24^{18} Ne 10^{40}. †(3) *forsake,* fail to follow, obey advice, instruction, wisdom, reproof: 1 K 12$^{8.13}$ = 2 Ch 10$^{8.13}$ Pr 2^{13} 4$^{2.6}$ 10^{17} 15^{10} 27^{10}. †(4) but also of *forsaking* idols Ez 20^{8}, sins of various kinds 23^{8} Is 55^{7} Pr 28^{13} (obj. om.; + מוֹדֶה *confess*); הַמַּשָּׁא *usury* Ne 5^{10}. **e.** of God's *forsaking, abandoning* men: Dt 31^{17} Is 42^{16} 49^{14} 54^{7} 2 Ch 12^{5} Ezr 9^{9} ψ 9^{11} 22^{2} + 8 t. ψψ; + בְּיַד Ne 9^{28} ψ 37^{33}; ψ 16^{10} *thou wilt not abandon my soul* לִשְׁאוֹל; of temporary abandonment 2 Ch 32^{31} (+ inf. of purpose); etc. (34 t. in all); + Je 12^{7} ('י abandoning his house). †**f.** of God's *leaving,* i.e. ceasing to regard, the earth, thus giving impunity to crime, Ez 8^{12} 9^{9}. †**g.** of strength (כֹּחַ) *forsaking* one ψ 38^{11}, courage (לֵב) 40^{13}, kindness and faithfulness (חֶסֶד וֶאֱמֶת) Pr 3^{3}. †**3.** *let loose, set free, let go* עָזֹב תַּעֲזֹב עִמּוֹ Ex 23^{5b} (E) *thou shalt by all means free* it (sc. the beast) *with him,* (aid him to set it free; on sense, cf. Dt 22^{4}; DHM sub II. עזב); עָצוּר וְעָזוּב *shut up and freed,* proverb. phr., = all classes of people Dt 32^{36} 1 K 14^{10} 21^{21} 2 K 9^{8} 14^{26} (exact meaning dub.; prob. either = bond and free, or [v. RS $^{Sem\ i.\ 437,\ 2nd\ ed.\ 456}$] under taboo and free from it); *let go* Jb 20^{13} (c. acc. of wickedness as morsel in mouth); *let loose* my complaint Jb 10^{1} (עָלַי *apud me,* cf. עַל **II 1 d**); אֶעֶזְבָה פָנַי Jb 9^{27} *I will loosen, relax, my face,* (cf. Thes De Me Stu Di Buhl ^{Lex} Bu; > *abandon my* [gloomy] *countenance* AV RV SS Bae ^{Kau} Du). †**Niph.** *Pf.* 3 ms. נֶעֱזַב Ne 13^{11}; 3 fs. נֶעֱזָבָה Is 62^{12}; *Impf.* 3 fs. תֵּעָזֵב Is 7^{16} Lv 26^{43}, תֵּעָזַב Jb 18^{4}; 3 mpl. יֵעָזְבוּ Is 18^{6}; *Pt.* נֶעֱזָב Is 27^{10} ψ 37^{25}; fpl. נֶעֱזָבוֹת Ez 36^{4};—**1.** *be left to* (לְ), i.e. to the possession of, Is 18^{6}. **2.** *be forsaken,* of house of God Ne 13^{11}, a city Ez 36^{4} Is 27^{10} (|| מְשֻׁלָּח), 62^{12}; the earth Jb 18^{4}, land Is 7^{16}, Lv 26^{43} (+ מִן of exiles); of man ψ 37^{25}. †**Pu.** (or **Qal pass.**, v. Ges $^{§52 e}$) *be deserted,* of city: *Pf.* 3 ms. הֲמוֹן עִיר עֻזָּב Is 32^{14} (|| נֻטָּשׁ); 3 fs. עֻזָּבָה Je 49^{25}.

†I. עֲזוּבָה **n.f.** forsakenness, desolation;— 5805
וְרַבָּה הָע׳ בְּקֶרֶב הָאָרֶץ Is 6^{12}.—17^{9} v. √**2 a.**

5806 † II. עֲזוּבָה **n.pr.f. 1.** Ἀζαεβα, Ἀζουβα, mother of Jehoshaphat 1 K 22^{42} = 2 Ch 20^{31}. **2.** (Γ)αζουβα, wife of Caleb 1 Ch $2^{18.19}$.

5801 † [עִזָּבוֹן] **n.[m.]** only pl. **wares** (as *left* in the purchaser's hand; cf. As. *uzub(b)u*, a specif. *payment*);—sf. 2 fs. עִזְבוֹנַיִךְ Ez $27^{27.33}$, -נָיִךְ v^{12} + 4 t.;—*wares*, only Ez 27 (oft. ‖ מַעֲרָב q. v. sub ערב); בַּרְזֶל בְּדִיל וְעוֹפֶרֶת נָתְנוּ ע׳ Ez 27^{12} *iron, tin and lead they furnished as thy wares;* similarly v$^{14.22}$; also v^{16} (MT בְּע׳, but prob. del בְּ); בְּע׳ נָתְנוּ v^{19} *at the price of (in exchange for) thy wares they furnished,* etc.; הוֹנֵךְ וְע׳ (as subj. of sentence) v^{27}; בְּצֵאת ע׳ מִיַּמִּים v^{33} *when thy wares came forth,* etc.

5800 † II. [עָזַב] **vb. restore, repair** (?) (cf. perhaps Sab. עדב *restore,* Sab Denkm^{90} DHM Öster. Monatsschr. f. d. Orient 1885, 226; also NH מַעֲזִיבָה *restoration, erection* Levy NHWB iii. 186, Ar. معزب *building-stone* Kremer Beitr. ii. 18);—**Qal** *Impf.* 3 mpl. וַיַּעַזְבוּ Ne 3^{8} *and they repaired* (?) Jerus. as far as the broad wall; > *paved* Gu ZPV viii (1885). 282 f., or fr. √ I. עזב (see views in Be Ryle).

5798, 5802-03 עַזְבּוּק, עַזְגָּד, עִזָּה v. עזז. p. 739

5804 † עַזָּה **n.pr.loc. Gaza**, Γαζα (As. *Ḫazzutu*, etc., COT i. 97 Dl Pa 290, TelAm *Ḫazati, Azzati* Wkl^{38*}; Egypt. *Gaḏatu* WMM As. u. Eur. 87, 96, 159, 392; 𝔊 Γαζα, so Jos Ant. xiii. 5, 5, etc.; Herod. ii. 159; iii. 5 Κάδυτις);—Philistine city (mod. غَزَّة, Ghazze, Razze), c. Lat. 31° 3′ N, Long. 34° 28′ E, c. 50 miles WSW. from Jerus., near the sea (Rob BR ii. 36 ff. GASm Geogr. 181 ff. Buhl Geogr. 190 f.), Ju $16^{1.21}$ (both עַזָּתָה), southernmost of the famous five cities, Gn 10^{19} (J), Ju 6^{4} 1 K 5^{4} 2 K 18^{8}, cf. Dt 2^{23} Jos 10^{41} (D); also 11^{22} (D), 15^{47} (P), Ju 1^{18} 1 S 6^{17} Am $1^{6.7}$ Zp 2^{4} Je 25^{20} $47^{1.5}$ Zc $9^{5.5}$;—On commercial importance v. DHM B und S 989 Gatt ZPV vii (1884), 1 ff., 293 ff.; viii (1885), 69 ff., 179 ff..—For עַזָּה 1 Ch 7^{28} van d. H., read עַיָּה Baer Ginsb (q. v.), Be Oettli Kau Kit Hpt.; v. עַי.

5841 † עַזָּתִי **adj.gent.** of foreg., c. art. as subst. coll. Jos 13^{3} (D); pl. לָעַזָּתִים Ju 16^{2}.

5810 † [עָזַז] **vb. be strong** (NH *id.*, Hiph., esp. in bad sense, and esp. deriv. עַז; Ph. עז *strength*, also in n.pr. Lzb^{338}; Aram. עַז *be mighty, strong*, cf. OAram. Nab. Palm. n.pr. עזיזו Lzb ^{338} Cook^{90}; Ar. عَزَّ *be mighty, strong*, Eth. **ዐዘዘ:** *id.;* As. *ezêzu, be furious, ezzu, fierce*);—**Qal** *Impf.* 3 ms. יָעֹז ψ 9^{20} 52^{9}, יָעוֹז Dn 11^{12}; 3 fs. תָּעֹז ψ 89^{14} Ec 7^{19}, וַתָּעָז Ju 3^{10} 6^{2}; *Imv.* ms. עוּזָּה ψ 68^{29} (but v. infr.); *Inf. cstr.* עֲזוֹז Pr 8^{28};—*be strong, prevail,* וַתָּעָז יָדוֹ עַל־ Ju 3^{10} *and his hand prevailed against,* so 6^{2}; אַל־תָּעֹז אֱנוֹשׁ ψ 9^{20}, Dn 11^{12}; abs. תָּעֹז יָדְךָ ψ 89^{14} (of י׳); of appar. strength of wicked 52^{9}; בַּעֲזוֹז עִינוֹת תְּהוֹם Pr 8^{28} *when the fountains of the deep grew strong,* i. e. firm, fixed; but Oort Bi Toy rd. בְּעַזְּזוֹ *when he made firm, fixed fast* (‖ בְּאַמְּצוֹ); עוּזָּה אֱלֹהִים ψ 68^{29} Che Bae al. *shew thyself strong, O God,* who, etc., cf. Kö i. 363; < עוֹז הָא׳ *the might, O God,* wh., etc., Hup Du; הַחָכְמָה תָּעֹז לֶחָכָם Ec 7^{19} *wisdom is strong for the wise.*—לָעוֹז Is 30^{2} v. עוז. **Hiph.** *Pf.* 3 ms. הֵעֵז אִישׁ רָשָׁע בְּפָנָיו Pr 21^{29} *a wicked man maketh firm (sheweth boldness) with his face;* so 3 fs. הֵעֵזָה פָנֶיהָ 7^{13} (Ges § 67 dd Kö i. 372) *she maketh bold her face.*

† עַז **adj. strong, mighty, fierce**;—ע׳ abs. 5794
Nu 13^{28} + 2 t., עָז Ju 14^{18}, עָז Am 5^{9} + 4 t.; עַז cstr. Dt 28^{50} Dn 8^{23}; f. עַזָּה Ex 14^{21} + 2 t.; pl. עַזִּים Ez 7^{24} + 3 t.; f. עַזּוֹת Pr 18^{23}; cstr. עַזֵּי Is 56^{11};—*strong, mighty,* wind Ex 14^{21} (J); border Nu 21^{24} (JE), but rd. prob. יַעְזֵר (𝔊 Di al.) *Ya'zer was t. border;* of people Pr 30^{25} (fig. of ants), מַיִם עַזִּים Is 43^{16} (‖ הַיָּם), Ne 9^{11}; of love Ct 8^{6}; = subst. *the mighty* Am 5^{9} Ez 7^{24} + Pr 24^{5} (of physical force; rdg. טוֹב מֵעַז or the like 𝔊 𝔖 𝔗 Kmp Kau Wild Toy); *formidable, fierce,* of lion Ju 14^{18}, so (= subst.) v^{14}, of king Is 19^{4} (‖ אֲדֹנִים קָשֶׁה), of people Nu 13^{28} (JE), Is 25^{3} (‖ עָרִיצִים); of enemy 2 S 22^{18} = ψ 18^{18}, so as subst. ψ 59^{4}; עַז פָּנִים Dt 28^{50} *fierce of countenance,* Dn 8^{23}, so perh. = *impudent* Ec 8^{1} (rdg. עַז for עֹז q.v.); of anger (אַף) Gn 49^{7} (poem in J), wrath (חֵמָה) Pr 21^{14}; הַכְּלָבִים עַזֵּי־נֶפֶשׁ Is 56^{11} *dogs fierce of appetite* (‖ לֹא יָדְעוּ שָׂבְעָה); fpl. as adv. accus. יַעֲנֶה עַזּוֹת Pr 18^{23} the rich *answereth fiercely.*

† עֹז, and (rarely) עוֹז **n.m. strength,** 5797
might;—abs. ע׳ Ju 9^{51} +, עוֹז ψ 84^{6} +, עָז־ Is 26^{1}, once עָז Gn 49^{3}; cstr. עֹז Mi 5^{3} +, עָז־ ψ 28^{8}; sf. עָזִּי Ex 15^{2} + 2 t., עֻזִּי ψ 28^{7} +; עָזְּךָ 21^{2} + 2 t., עֻזְּךָ 66^{3} +; sf. 1 pl. עוּזֵּנוּ 81^{2}; 3 mpl. עֻזָּמוֹ 89^{18}, etc.;—*strength, might* (usu. poet., 44 t. ψψ): **1.** material and physical, מִגְדַּל־עֹז Ju 9^{51}, and fig. (of י׳), ψ 61^{4} Pr 18^{10}, מַחֲסִי־עֹז ψ 71^{7}, cf. עִיר עָז־לָנוּ Is 26^{1}, עֹז מִבְטָחָה קִרְיַת־עֹז Pr 18^{19} (sim.), 10^{15} = 18^{11} (fig.); Pr 21^{22} (of a city, read poss. מעוז Toy); צוּר עֻזִּי ψ 62^{8} (fig.); מְרוֹם עֻזָּהּ Je 51^{53} (of Bab.), מַצְּבוֹת עֻזֵּךְ Ez 26^{11} (of Tyre), cf. ψ 30^{8} (rdg. לְהַרְרֵי־עֹז 𝔗 Hup Che Kau We; but no obj. for vb.; Gie in Bae prop. הֶעֱמַדְתִּי for הֶעֱמַדְתָּה); רְקִיעַ עֻזּוֹ ψ 150^{1} *his*

mighty firmament (De Hup Kau al.; Ki AV RV Che *the f. of his power*, where his power dwells); בְּכָל־עֹז *with all* one's *might* 2 S 6^{14} = 1 Ch 13^{8}, + 2 Ch 30^{21} (where so read, for MT כְּלֵי עֹז, Kau Kit cf. Be Oettli); בְּעוֹז Pr 31$^{17.25}$; abstr. for concr. Ju 5^{21} si vera l., but prob. crpt., cf. GFM Bu; of crocodile Jb 41^{14}; קוֹל עֹז ψ 68^{34} *a mighty voice;* זְרוֹעַ עֻזּוֹ = *his mighty arm* (fig. of י׳) Is 62^{8}, cf. 51^{9} ψ 89^{11} Jb 26^{2}, גֶּשֶׁם מִטְרוֹת עֻזּוֹ Jb 37^{6}; מַטֵּה־עֹז, fig. of political power Je 48^{17} (|| מַקֵּל תִּפְאָרָה), Ez 19$^{11.12.14}$ (vine-branches, in fig.), ψ 110^{2}. **2.** personal, social, and political: **a.** Am 3^{11}, גְּאוֹן ע׳ Lv 26^{19} (H), Ez 24^{21} 30$^{6.18}$ 33^{28}. **b.** bestowed by י׳, 1 S 2^{10} (song), ψ 29^{11} 68^{36} 86^{16} 138^{3}, עוֹז־לוֹ בָךְ 84^{6} 138^{3}; so (implic.) of Zion Is 52^{1}. **c.** of י׳ as strength of his servants Mi 5^{3} Is 49^{5} ψ 81^{2} 84^{6}, also Ex 15^{2} (|| יְשׁוּעָה) = Is 12^{2} = ψ 118^{14}, cf. Is 45^{24}, עֹז יְשׁוּעָתִי ψ 140^{8}, תִּפְאֶרֶת עֻזָּמוֹ 89^{18}; sts. as their stronghold, for defence Je 16^{19} (+ מָעֻזִּי), ψ 28^{7} (+ מָגִנִּי), v^{8} (|| מָעוֹז), 46^{2} (+ מַחֲסֶה), 59^{10} (rdg. עֻזִּי, v. Comm. and Ginsb$^{marg.}$; || מִשְׂגַּבִּי), v^{18} (|| *id.*), cf. Pr 14^{26} (|| מַחְסֶה); v. also sub **1**.—Pr 24^{5} v. עַז. **3.** *might* of י׳ (esp. ψψ): **a.** as essential attribute Hb 3^{4} Jb 12^{16} ψ 62^{12} 63^{3} 68^{35} 93^{1} 96^{6} = 1 Ch 16^{27}; עֹז מֶלֶךְ ψ 99^{4} (title of י׳). **b.** theme of ascription in praise ψ 29^{1} (c. יָהַב) = 96^{7} = 1 Ch 16^{28}, ψ 59^{17} (c. שִׁיר), 68^{35} (c. נָתַן). **c.** exerted for his people and against his foes Ex 15^{13} (song), ψ 21^{2} (|| יְשׁוּעָה), v^{14} 66^{3} 68^{29} + v^{29} (rdg. עוֹז for עוּזָּה, v. עזז), 74^{13} 77^{15} 78^{26} 105^{4} = 1 Ch 16^{11}, Ezr 8^{22} (+ אַפּוֹ), cf. עֹז אַפֶּךָ ψ 90^{11}. **d.** manifested in connex. with the ark, אֲרוֹן עֻזֶּךָ 2 Ch 6^{41} = ψ 132^{8}, עֹז = ark 78^{61}. **4.** עֹז פָּנָיו = *boldness, impudence* Ec 8^{1}, changed by wisdom, De Wild al.; < rd. עַז פ׳ *he who is impudent* 𝔊 Siegf (cf. עזז **Hiph.**). **5.** = *stronghold* (cf. **2 c**): ψ 8^{3} *out of the mouth of babes . . . thou hast founded strength, or a stronghold* (for thy defence, cf. v^{b}), so Ew De Hup Kau Sch Che Dr, cf. Du; > *praise* Vrss Bae.—מָעוֹז v. עוז.

5807 † עֱזוּז **n.[m.] strength, might, fierceness** = עֹז;—cstr. ע׳ מִלְחָמָה Is 42^{25} *fierceness of battle* (fr. י׳; + חֲמַת אַפּוֹ), ע׳ נוֹרְאֹתֶיךָ ψ 145^{6}; sf. עֱזוּזוֹ וְנִפְלְאֹתָיו 78^{4}.

5808 † עִזּוּז **adj. mighty, powerful;**—of an army Is 43^{17}; of י׳ ψ 24^{8}.

5811 † עָזָז **n.pr.m.** Reubenite name 1 Ch 5^{8}, Οζους, 𝔊L Ιωαζαζ. (Ginsb$^{marg.}$ עָזֵז, עָזָן, עָזֻן, cf. Baer^{100}.)

5798 † עֻזָּא **n.pr.m.** Οζα, Αζα: **1.** driver of the ark 2 S 6^{3} = עֻזָּה v$^{6.7.8}$ = עֻזָּא 1 Ch 13$^{7.9.10.11}$. **2.** in גַּן־עֻזָּא burial-place of Manasseh and Amon 2 K 21$^{18.26}$ (ע׳ perh. = עֻזִּיָּה, cf. Sta$^{G\ i.\ 569,\ ii.\ 679}$ Kit). **3.** Benjamite name 1 Ch 8^{7}. **4.** head of family of returned exiles Ezr 2^{49} = Ne 7^{51}.

† עֻזָּה **n.pr.m.** **1.** Levite name 1 Ch 6^{14}, 5798
Οζ(ι)α, Αζα. **2.** v. עֻזָּא.

† עֲזִיזָא **n.pr.m.** one with foreign wife 5819
Ezr 10^{27}, Οζει(α), Αζιζα.

† עֲזַזְיָהוּ **n.pr.m.** (י׳ *is mighty*);—Οζ(ε)ιας 5812
(= עֻזִּיָּהוּ): **1.** Levite names: **a.** 1 Ch 15^{21} (del. Kit). **b.** 2 Ch 31^{13} (? Kit). **2.** a Benjamite 1 Ch 27^{20} (Kit עֻזִּיָּהוּ; v. also Gray$^{Prop. N. 295}$).

† עֻזִּיאֵל **n.pr.m.** (*my strength is Ēl*);— 5816
Οζ(ε)ιηλ: **1.** Levites: **a.** Ex 6$^{18.22}$ Lv 10^{4} Nu 3$^{19.30}$ 1 Ch 5^{28} 6^{3} 15^{10} 23$^{12.20}$ 24^{24}. **b.** 1 Ch 25^{4} (= עֲזַרְאֵל v^{18}), 𝔊^{B} Αζαραηλ. **c.** 2 Ch 29^{14}. **2.** Simeonite 1 Ch 4^{42}. **3.** Benjamite 1 Ch 7^{7}.
4. repairer of wall Ne 3^{8}.—Vid. יַעֲזִיאֵל. below 3268

† עָזִּיאֵלִי **adj. gent.** of foregoing, c. art. as 5817
subst. coll. Nu 3^{27} (Ginsb$^{marg.}$ הָעֻזִּ׳); לָעָזִּ׳ 1 Ch 26^{23}.

† עֻזִּיָּה, עֻזִּיָּהוּ **n.pr.m.** (*my strength is* י׳; 5818
cf. OHeb. עזיו Lzb^{338});—**1.** Οζειας, but also Αζαριας: king of Judah = עֲזַרְיָהוּ: **a.** עֻזִּיָּהוּ 2 K 15$^{32.34}$ 2 Ch 26$^{1.3.8.9.11.14.18.18.19.21.22.23}$ 27^{2} Is 1^{1} 6^{1} 7^{1}. **b.** עֻזִּיָּה 2 K 15$^{13.30}$ Ho 1^{1} Am 1^{1} Zc 14^{5}. **2.** עֻזִּיָּהוּ father of an officer of David 1 Ch 27^{25}. **3.** עֻזִּיָּה Levite name 1 Ch 6^{9}. **4.** *id.*: priest with foreign wife Ezr 10^{21}. **5.** *id.*: name in Judah Ne 11^{4} (also v^{5} 𝔊 for חזיה).—Vid. also יַעֲזִיָּהוּ.

† עֻזִּיָּא **n.pr.m.** (= foregoing; cf. Gray 5814
$^{Prop. N. 295}$);—hero of David 1 Ch 11^{44}, Οζεια(ς).

† עֻזִּי **n.pr.m.** Οζει: **1.** Levites: **a.** 1 Ch 5$^{31.32}$ 5813
6^{36} Ezr 7^{4}. **b.** Ne 11^{22}. **c.** priestly name Ne 12$^{19.42}$. **2.** name in Issachar 1 Ch 7$^{2.3}$. **3.** Benjamite name 1 Ch 7^{7} 9^{8}.

† (ו)יַעֲזִיאֵל **n.pr.m.** Οζειηλ, Levite name 3268
1 Ch 15^{18} = (ו)עֲזִיאֵל v^{20}, both prob. err. for עֻזִּיאֵל 5815
Gray$^{Prop. N. 210, 224, 307, 309}$.

† יַעֲזִיָּהוּ **n.pr.m.** Οζεια(ς), Levite name 1 Ch 3269
24$^{26.27}$, perhaps for עֻזִּיָּהוּ Gray$^{Prop. N. 291}$.

† עַזְבּוּק **n.pr.m.** father of one Nehemiah, 5802
a wall-builder Ne 3^{16}, Αζαβουχ, 𝔊L Εζδουκ.

† עַזְגָּד **n.pr.m.** Ασγαδ, Αζγαδ (*Gad is mighty;* 5803
Gray$^{Prop. N. 145}$);—**1. a.** head of family returning with Zerub. Ezr 2^{12} = Ne 7^{17}. **b.** returning with Ezra Ezr 8^{12}. **2.** one of those sealed Ne 10^{16}.

5820 †I. עַזְמָ֫וֶת **n.pr.m.** A𝔊L usu. Αζμωθ, Ασμωθ: **1. a.** one of David's heroes 2 S 23^{31} 1 Ch 11^{33}, B Ασβωθ. **b.** father of two of David's men 1 Ch 12^{3}. **c.** officer of David 1 Ch 27^{25}. **2.** Benjamite name 1 Ch 8^{36} 9^{42}, B Σαλμω, Γαβαωθ.

1011, 5820 †II. עַזְמָ֫וֶת **n.pr.loc.** v. בֵּית־ע׳ p. 112 supr.

5821 †עַזָּן **n.pr.m.** Οζα, Οζα, in Issachar Nu 34^{26}.

5822 †עָזְנִיָּה **n.f.** (unclean) bird of prey, appar. akin to vulture (Now$^{Arch. i. 84, 116}$), named + נֶשֶׁר, פֶּרֶס Dt 14^{12} Lv 11^{13} (H); = *osprey* Tristr$^{NHB 184}$ Dr$^{Dt 14, 12}$ (others *vulture* Di$^{Lv 11, 13}$) (√ unknown; conject. v. in Di; perhaps foreign word).

5823 †[עָזַק] **vb. dig about** (NH *id.*, also *surround, enclose;* Aram. עִזְקְתָא, ܥܙܩܬܐ, ܥܙܩܬܐ *ring;* Ar. عَزَقَ *cleave* or *furrow the earth* with implement مِعْزَقَة; Eth. **ዐዘቅት:** *well, cistern*);—**Pi.** *Impf.* 3 ms. sf. וַיְעַזְּקֵהוּ Is 5^2 (intens.) *and he dug it carefully about.*

5825 †עֲזֵקָה **n.pr.loc.** Αζηκα, in the Shephelah of Judah, near שׂוֹכֹה, Jos $10^{10.11}$ (JE), 15^{35} (P), 1 S 17^1 Je 34^7 2 Ch 11^9 Ne 11^{30}; not identified.

5826 I. [עָזַר] $_{82}$ **vb. help, succour** (NH n. עֶזְרָה *help;* Ph. in deriv. and cpds. Lzb$^{338 f.}$; Ar. عَذَرَ *excuse, exculpate,* also *aid;* Aram. ܥܕܪ *help,* Palm. עדר, rarely עזר Lzb^{338} Cook$^{89.90}$);—**Qal** *Pf.* 3 ms. sf. עֲזָרָ֫נִי ψ 118^{13}, עֲזָרְךָ 1 Ch 12^{19}; 3 pl. sf. עֲזָרֻם 1 Ch 12^{20}, etc.; *Impf.* 3 ms. יַעֲזָר־ Is $50^{7.9}$, sf. יַעְזְרֶךָּ Is 44^2; 3 mpl. יַעְזֹ֫רוּ Is 30^7 41^6, וַיַּעְזְרוּ 1 K 1^7, sf. יַעְזְרֻנִי ψ 119^{175}, etc.; *Imv.* ms. sf. עָזְרֵ֫נִי ψ 109^{26} 119^{86} + Jos 10^4 Kt, mpl. sf. עִזְרֻנִי Qr, etc.; *Inf. cstr.* לַעְזֹר 1 Ch 22^{17}, לַעְזוֹר 18^5, לַעְזוֹר Jos 10^{33} + 5 t., לַעְזוֹר 2 Ch 25^8 + 2 S 18^3 Qr (> Kt לַעְזִיר **Hiph.**); sf. לְעָזְרֵנִי 1 Ch 12^{17} + 2 t., etc.; *Pt. act.* עֹזֵר 1 K 20^{16}+, etc.; *pass.* עָזוּר Is 31^3;—*help,* c. acc. pers. 1 K 20^{16} Jos 1^{14} (D), Is 41^6 + 2 Ch 28^{23} (rdg. עֹזְרִים Ges$^{§ 53 o}$, for MT מַעְזְרִים, appar. **Hiph.**; subj. false gods); c. acc. loc. (city) Jos 10^{33} (D); esp. c. sf. pers. Jos $10^{4.6}$ (+ הוֹשִׁיעַ; both JE), 1 Ch $12^{18.20.23}$ (van d. H. v$^{17.19.22}$), 2 Ch 32^3 Ezr 8^{22} (+ מִן of enemy), 10^{15} Dn 10^{13} (subj. Michael); subj. oft. God (י׳), c. acc. pers. ψ 10^{14} 1 Ch 15^{26}, usu. sf. Gn 49^{25} (poem in J), 1 S 7^{12} Is $41^{10.13.14}$ + 12 t. + 2 Ch 26^7 (c. עַל *against*), ψ 37^{40} (+ פִּלֵּט), 46^6 (sf. of city), 109^{26} (|| הוֹשִׁיעַ); subj. false gods Dt 32^8 2 Ch 28^{23}; c. לְ pers. 2 S 8^5 + 1 Ch 18^5 + 4 t. + 2 S 18^3 (rd. Qr לַעְזוֹר, or לְעָזֵר? cf. HPS); subj. י׳ Is $50^{7.9}$; c. עִם pers. 1 Ch 12^{22} (van d. H. v^{21}; + עַל *against*); c. אַחֲרֵי pers. (constr. praegn.) 1 K 1^7; c. בְּ pers. against whom 2 Ch 20^{23} (+ inf.); c. לְ . . . בֵּין, of י׳, 2 Ch 14^{10}; abs. Is 30^7 2 Ch 26^{13} (+ עַל *against*), 28^{16}; ע׳ לְרָעָה Zc 1^{15} *they helped, with evil result;* י׳ subj., 2 Ch 25^8 (opp. הִכְשִׁיל); also pt. c. sf. Ez 30^8 + 3 t.; c. לְ pers. 2 K 14^{26} + 5 t., of י׳ ψ 30^{11} 54^6; abs. Is 31^3 63^5 Je 47^4 ψ 22^{12} 107^{12}; cstr. עֹזְרֵי הַמִּלְחָמָה 1 Ch 12^1, עֹזְרֵי רָ֑הַב Jb 9^{13} (v. רהב); Pt. pass. abs. as subst. *he who is helped* Is 31^3. †**Niph.** *Pf.* וְנֶעֱזָ֑רְתִּי ψ 28^7 *I am helped* (sc. by י׳); *Impf.* 3 mpl. וַיֵּעָֽזְרוּ 1 Ch 5^{20} (sc. *id.;* + עַל *against*), c. n. cogn. יֵעָֽזְרוּ עֵזֶר מְעָט Dn 11^{34}; *Inf. cstr.* הִפְלִיא לְהֵעָזֵר 2 Ch 26^{15} *he was wonderfully helped* (lit. *made wonderful to be helped*). †**Hiph.** dub.: *Inf. cstr.* 2 S 18^3 Kt, *Pt.* pl. מַעְזְרִים 2 Ch 28^{23}, v. **Qal.**

†I. עֵ֫זֶר **n.m.** $^{ψ 121, 1}$ **help, succour**;—ע׳ abs. 5828
Gn 2^{18}+, sf. עֶזְרִי Ex 18^4, עֶזְרֹה Ez 12^{14}, etc.;—**1.** *help, succour* Is 30^5 (|| הוֹעִיל, opp. בֹּשֶׁת, חֶרְפָּה), Dn 11^{34}; fr. י׳ ψ 20^3 $121^{1.2}$ 124^8; in 89^{20} rd. נֵזֶר for ע׳ Dy Gr Kau (עֹז Bi Che), cf. Hup; מָגֵן עֶזְרֶךָ Dt 33^{29} (=י׳). **2.** concr. = *one who helps* (cf. I. עֶזְרָה **2**) בְּעֶ׳ (בְּ essent., v. **ב I 7 b**, Ges$^{§ 119 h, i}$) Gn $2^{18.20}$ (J) + Ho 13^9 (rd. מִי בְּעֶ׳ Che We Gu^{Kau} Now); coll. (without בְּ) Ez 12^{14} (si vera l.; Co עֹזְרָיו); esp. of י׳ ע׳ מִצָּרָיו Dt 33^7 (poem), ע׳ + מָגֵן ψ 33^{20} $115^{9.10.11}$, + מְפַלֵּט 70^6; בְּעֶ׳ (v. supr.) Ex 18^4 (E), Dt 33^{26} (poem), ψ 146^4.

†II. עֵ֫זֶר **n.pr.m.** (Ph. and OHeb. עזר Lzb 5829
^{338});—**1.** a wall-builder Ne 3^{19}, Αζουρ. **2.** name in Judah 1 Ch 4^4, Αζηρ, Εζερ. **3.** hero of David 1 Ch 12^{10} (van d. H. v^9), Αζερ, etc.

†עֶ֫זֶר **n.pr.m. 1.** Ephraimite 1 Ch 7^{21}, Εζερ. 5827
2. עֶ֑זֶר, a priest, Ne 12^{42}, Ιεζουρ.

†עֶזְרָא **n.pr.m.** Εσρας, Εσδρας, Εζδρας; 5830
1. Ezra Ezr $7^{1.10}$ $10^{1.2.5.6}$ Ne 8^6; called (ה)סֹּפֵר Ezr 7^6 Ne $8^{1.4.5.13}$ 12^{36}, הַכֹּהֵן Ezr $10^{10.16}$ Ne $8^{2.9}$, both Ezr 7^{11} Ne 12^{26}. **2.** priest with Zerub. Ne $12^{1.13}$. **3.** Ne 12^{33}.

†I. עֶזְרָה, עֶזְרַת, עֶזְרָ֫תָה **n.f. help, suc-** 5833
cour, assistance;—abs. ע׳ Is 10^3+, עֶזְרָת ψ 60^{13} 108^{13} (Ges$^{§ 80 g}$), עֶזְרָ֫תָה ψ 63^8 + 2 t.; cstr. עֶזְרַת Is 31^2+; sf. עֶזְרָתִי ψ 22^{20}+, etc.;—**1.** *help, succour* Is 10^3 20^6 (+ לְהִנָּצֵל), 31^1 Je 37^7 La 4^{17} Jb 6^{13} 2 Ch 28^{21}; ע׳ פֹּעֲלֵי אָ֑וֶן Is 31^2 *help from,* etc.; ע׳ י׳ Ju $5^{23.23}$ *help of* (for) י׳; from

י׳ ψ 22^{20} 38^{23} 40^{14} (|| לְהַצִּילֵנִי), 70^{2} (|| *id.*), 71^{12}, + מִצָּר 60^{13} (|| תְּשׁוּעָה) = 108^{13}. **2.** concr., embodied *help, one who helps* (cf. I. עֵזֶר **2**): **a.** coll. Jb 31^{21} *when I saw my help* (assistance, support) in the gate; בְּע׳ (v. I. עֵזֶר **2**) Na 3^{9}. **b.** of י׳ ψ 27^{9} 40^{18} (+ מְפַלֵּט), 46^{2} (|| מַחֲסֶה, עֹז), 44^{27} 63^{8} 94^{17}; בְּע׳ 35^{2}.

5834 †II. עֶזְרָה **n.pr.m.** Εσρει, Ιεζραα, in Judah 1 Ch 4^{17}.

5809 †עַזּוּר and (once) עַזֻּר **n.pr.m.** Αζωρ, Εζερ, Ιαζερ: **1.** father of Hananiah Je 28^{1}. **2.** עַזֻּר Ez 11^{1}. **3.** a chief of people Ne 10^{18}.

5832 †עֲזַרְאֵל **n.pr.m.** (*Ēl hath helped*);—Οζρειηλ, Εζριηλ, etc.: **1.** warrior of David 1 Ch 12^{7} (van d. H. v^{6}). **2.** Levite musician 1 Ch 25^{18} (= עֻזִּיאֵל v^{4}), B Αζαρια, A Εζριηλ. **3.** a Danite 1 Ch 27^{22}, Αζαραηλ, Εζριηλ. **4.** one with foreign wife Ezr 10^{41}. **5.** priestly name: **a.** Ne 11^{13}. **b.** 12^{36}.

5837 †עַזְרִיאֵל **n.pr.m.** (*my help is Ēl*);—Εσ(δ)ριηλ, etc.: **1.** Je 36^{26}. **2.** a Manassite 1 Ch 5^{24}. **3.** name in Naphtali 27^{19}.

5838 †עֲזַרְיָהוּ, עֲזַרְיָה **n.pr.m.** (*'י hath helped*); **Azariah** (OHeb. עזריהו, Ph. עזרבעל, OAram. הדעדר, הדדעזר, Lzb $^{338.\ 258}$ Cook ^{42});—Αζαριας: **1.** king of Judah (As. *Azriyâ'û* COT $^{2\,K\,15,1}$ Jäger $^{BAS\,i.\,468}$) עֲזַרְיָהוּ 2 K 15$^{6.8}$; עֲזַרְיָה 14^{21} 15$^{1.7.17.23.27}$ 1 Ch 3^{12} (v. עֻזִּיָּה). **2.** יָהוּ- officer of Sol. 1 K 4^{5}. **3.** *id.* prophet 2 Ch 15^{1}. **4.** sons of Jehosh.: **a.** *id.*, 2 Ch 21^{2}. **b.** יָה- v^{2}. **5.** priests: **a.** יָהוּ- 1 K 4^{2} = יָה- 1 Ch 5$^{36.37}$ Ezr 7^{3}. **b.** יָה- 1 Ch 5$^{35.35}$. **c.** *id.*, 1 Ch 5$^{39.40}$ 9^{11} Ezr 7^{1}. **d.** *id.*, Ne 10^{3}. **e.** יָהוּ- 2 Ch 31$^{10.13}$, = יָה- 26$^{17.20}$. **6.** Levites, יָהוּ-: **a.** 2 Ch 29^{12}. **b.** v^{12}. יָה-: **c.** 1 Ch 6^{21}. **d.** Ne 8^{7}. **7.** יָהוּ- a temple captain 2 Ch 23$^{1\,a}$ (van d. H. יָה- cf. Ginsb $^{marg.}$), v$^{1\,b}$. **8.** יָה- wall-builder Ne 3$^{23.24}$. **9.** יָה- one with Zerub. 7^{7} (שְׂרָיָה || Ezr 2^{2}). **10.** יָה- 12^{33}. **11.** יָהוּ- Ephraimite 2 Ch 28^{12}. **12.** יָה- name in Judah: **a.** son of Ethan (!) 1 Ch 2^{8}. **b.** v$^{38.39}$.—For עֲזַרְיָהוּ 2 Ch 22^{6} rd. אֲחַזְיָה, cf. v^{7}.

5836 †עֶזְרִי **n.pr.m.** 1 Ch 27^{26}, Εσδρει, Εζραι.

5840 †עַזְרִיקָם **n.pr.m.** Εζρεικαν, Εζρικαμ, etc.: **1.** descendant of David 1 Ch 3^{23}. **2.** prince in Judah 2 Ch 28^{7}. **3.** Benjamite 1 Ch 8^{38} 9^{44}. **4.** Levite 9^{14} Ne 11^{15}.

3270 †יַעְזֵר and (1 Ch 6^{66} 26^{31}) יַעְזֵיר **n.pr.loc.** Ιαζηρ, E. of Jordan (**Qal** *Impf.* in ـَ acc. to Ba $^{NB\,104}$);—oft. + Heshbon and other important towns, Nu 21^{31} + v^{24} (v. עַז) 32^{1} (אֶרֶץ יַע׳), v$^{3.35}$ (all JE), 2 S 24^{5}, Jos 13^{25} (P), 21^{39} (Ginsb, v^{37} van d. H. Baer; P); with vineyards Is 16$^{8.9}$ = Je 48$^{32.32}$ (where del. יָם before יַע׳ 𝔊 Hi Gf Gie Rothst). Site dub., cf. Buhl $^{Geogr.\ 264}$.

II. עזר (√ of foll.; connexion with I. ע׳ dub.; cf. Sab. מעדר, 'Einfassung' Sab Denkm ^{97}; NH עֲזָרָה *temple-court*, 𝔗 עֲזַרְתָּא).

†עֲזָרָה **n.f.** appar. enclosure;—abs. ע׳: 5835
1. *ledge surrounding* Ezekiel's altar; הָע׳ הַגְּדוֹלָה הָע׳ הַקְּטַנָּה = הַתַּחְתּוֹנָה Ez 43^{14}, below v^{14}; הָע׳ alone v$^{17.20}$ 45^{19} (v. Comm.). **2.** outer *court* of temple, הָע׳ הַגְּדֹלָה 2 Ch 4^{9}; with doors v^{9}; 6^{13} (v. I. חָצֵר **3 b**, and on ע׳ in Herod's temple Now $^{Arch.\ ii.\ 78\ ff.}$).

עַזָּתִי v. sub עַזָּה. p. 738 5841

†עֵט **n.m.** $^{Je\,8,8}$ **stylus** (√dub.; Kö $^{ii.\,1,83}$ (after 5842
older authorities) cp. Ar. غوط, غَاطَ *sink, penetrate*);—ע׳ only cstr.: **1.** of iron, for use on stone or metal Je 17^{1} (בְּצִפֹּרֶן שָׁמִיר *with diamond-point*), Jb 19^{24} (v. also חֶרֶט). **2.** prob. = reed-pen (used on roll, cf. Je 36$^{2.23}$ etc.), ע׳ שֶׁקֶר סֹפְרִים Je 8^{8}, fig., לְשׁוֹנִי ע׳ סוֹפֵר מָהִיר ψ 45^{1} (cf. Now $^{Arch.\ i.\ 290}$ Benz $^{Arch.\ 290}$).

† I. עָטָה **vb.** wrap oneself, enwrap, en- 5844
velop oneself (Ar. غَطَا *cover, conceal*; Aram. ܥܛܐ *extinguish, destroy*; As. *eṭû, be dark, eṭûtu, darkness*);—**Qal** *Pf.* 3 ms. וְע׳ (consec.) Je 43^{12}; 3 pl. וְעָטוּ (consec.) Mi 3^{7}; *Impf.* 3 ms. יַעְטֶה Lv 13^{45} + 2 t., וַיַּעַט Is 59^{17}; 2 ms. תַּעְטֶה Ez 24^{17}; 3 mpl. יַעֲטוּ (Baer יַע׳) ψ 71^{13} 109^{29}; 2 mpl. תַעְטוּ Ez 24^{22}; *Pt. act.* עֹטֶה 1 S 28^{14} ψ 104^{2}; fs. עֹטְיָה Ct 1^{7};—**1.** *wrap, envelop* oneself *with* sthg. (acc., like לבשׁ): וְהוּא עֹטֶה מְעִיל 1 S 28^{14} an old man ascending, *and he is enwrapped in a robe;* so יַע׳ הָרֹעֶה בִּגְדוֹ Je 43^{12} (sim.), and וְע׳ אֶת־אֶרֶץ מִצְרַיִם v^{12} *he will wrap himself in the land of Egypt* (use it as a robe, fig., of Nebuchadnezzar; so completely will it be in his power, Gf); so fig. of י׳, וַיַּעַט כַּמְעִיל קִנְאָה Is 59^{17} (|| לָבַשׁ), ע׳־אוֹר כַּשַּׂלְמָה ψ 104^{2}; of men, כְּבֶגֶד יַע׳ 109^{19} (sim. || לָבַשׁ v^{18}), וְיַע׳ כַּמְעִיל בָּשְׁתָּם v^{29} (|| *id.*), יַע׳ חֶרְפָּה וגו׳ 71^{13}; **c.** עַל of part covered, in phrase וְעָטוּ עַל־שָׂפָם Mi 3^{7} *they shall envelop themselves upon their beard* (cover the beard, sign of mourning or shame Che Now Benz $^{Arch.\ 165}$ Now $^{Arch.\ i.\ 195}$), so Ez 24$^{17.22}$ and (of leper) Lv 13^{45} (P);

pt. f. עֹטְיָה Ct 1^{7} as subst., *one wrapping* (a veil about her), i.e. a mourner; > a harlot (cf. Gn 38^{14}); but rd. perh. טֹעִיָּה *wandering woman*, v. טעה.—וַיַּעַט etc., v. also עיט; מַעֲטֶה, v. מרט. **Hiph.** *Pf.* 2 ms. הֶעֱטִיתָ עָלָיו בּוּשָׁה ψ 89^{46} (of ׳י) *thou hast wrapped shame upon him* (enwrapped him in shame); *Impf.* 3 ms. בְּרָכוֹת יַעְטֶה מוֹרֶה ψ 84^{7} *early rain enwrappeth* (it, עֵמֶק הַבָּכָא v^{a}) *with blessings* (𝔊 δώσει, as if from Ar. عطو, عَطَا, III, IV. *give*, cf. $Ne^{Marg. 41}$); read prob. also יַעְטֵנִי Is 61^{10} (for MT יְעָטָנִי, v. יעט) *with a robe of rightness he envelopeth me*, so Brd Di Ry^{Kau} Du; >**Qal** *Pf.* עָטָנִי Klo $Che^{Hpt.}$

4594 †[מַעֲטֶה] **n.[m.] wrap, mantle**;—only cstr. fig. מַעֲטֵה תְהִלָּה Is 61^{3} *a mantle of praise.*

5844 †II. [עָטָה] **vb. grasp** (Ar. عَطَا, عطو I, VII. *take with hands*);—**Qal** *Inf. abs.* + *Pt. act.* sf. וְעֹטְךָ עָטֹה Is 22^{17} *he shall grasp thee forcibly*, cf. $Ges^{Comm.}$ Hi Ew De $Che^{Comm.}$ Di Gu ^{Kau}; > Thes RobGes $Buhl^{Lex (13)}$ fr. I. עטה (*he shall wrap, roll thee tight together*) for this vb. not trans.

5847 †עֲטַלֵּף **n.[m.] bat** (quadrilit., $Ges^{§85w}$ $Sta^{§243,8}$; NH *id.;* Ph. οθολαβαδ $Ges^{Mon. Ph. 391}$; $Lewy^{Fremdw. 17}$ cp. ἀττέλεβος, name of a locust in N. Africa $Herod^{iv. 172}$);—׳ע abs. Lv 11^{19} (H), = Dt 14^{18} (unclean creature); pl. עֲטַלֵּפִים Is 2^{20}.

עטן (√of foll.; NH עָטַן *put* olives into vat or press, or in vessel; Ar. عَطَنَ *put skin into tan*).

5845 †[עֲטִין] **n.[m.]** prob. **pail, bucket** (NH מַעֲטָן *vessel for olives*);—עֲטִינָיו מָלְאוּ חָלָב Jb 21^{24} *his pails are full of milk.*

5848 †I. [עָטַף] **vb. turn aside** (Syr. ܥܛܦ *turn, return;* Ar. عَطَفَ *incline, bend*);—**Qal** *Impf.* 3 ms. יַעְטֹף *turn aside* (so Ew Di De Bae ^{Kau} al.), Jb 23^{9} *he turneth aside* to the right (שְׂמֹאול בַּעֲשֹׂתוֹ ‖ יָמִין), rd. prob. 1 s. אֶעֱטֹף Me Bu Du, *I turn* . . . and do not see him (and ‖ שׁ׳ בְּבַקְּשָׁתוֹ).

5848 †II. [עָטַף] **vb. envelop oneself** (Aramaism) (NH *id.;* Aram. עֲטַף, ܥܛܦ; Eth. ዐጥፈ: *covered*, also n. *web, texture*);—**Qal** *Impf.* 3 ms. יַעֲטָף־ ψ 73^{6}; 3 mpl. יַעַטְפוּ 65^{14};—*envelop oneself:* ψ 65^{14} *the valleys cover themselves with corn* (‖ לָבְשׁוּ); יַעֲ־שִׁית חָמָס לָמוֹ 73^{6} *they put on for themselves* (each) *a garb of violence.*

†[מַעֲטָפָה] **n.f. overtunic** (so Ar. مِعْطَفٌ, Aram. ܡܥܛܦܐ, ܥܛܦܐ);—pl. abs. מַעֲטָפוֹת Is 3^{22}. 4595

†III. [עָטַף] **vb. be feeble, faint** ($Ba^{ES 27}$ 5848
cp. Ar. عَطِبَ *perish, flag*);—**Qal** *Impf.* 3 ms. יַעֲטֹף ψ 102^{1}, יַעֲטוֹף Is 57^{16}; *Inf. cstr.* עֲטֹף ψ 61^{3}; *Pt. pass.* ($Ges^{§50f}$) pl. עֲטֻפִים Gn 30^{42}, עֲטוּפִים La 2^{19};—lit. *be feeble* Gn 30^{42} (J; opp. קְשֻׁרִים); הָעֲטוּפִים בְּרָעָב La 2^{19}; fig. רוּחַ מִלְּפָנַי יַעֲ׳ Is 57^{16} *the spirit would faint before me* (׳י); בַּעֲטֹף לִבִּי ψ 61^{3}, 102^{2} (title). **Niph.** *Inf. cstr.* בֵּעָטֵף עוֹלֵל La 2^{11} *when infants faint* (for בְּהֵעָ׳; but read perh. בַּעֲטֹף **Qal**, so Buhl). **Hiph.** *Inf. cstr.* בְּהַעֲטִיף הַצֹּאן Gn 30^{42} when the flock *shewed feebleness.* **Hithp.** *Impf.* 3 fs. תִּתְעַטֵּף ψ 77^{4}, 143^{4}, תִּתְעַטָּף 107^{5}; וַתִּתְ׳ *Inf. cstr.* הִתְעַטֵּף 142^{4} Jon 2^{8}, sf. הִתְעַטְּפָם La 2^{12};—*faint, faint away*, La 2^{12} (כֶּחָלָל *like the wounded*); subj. רוּחַ ψ 77^{4} 142^{4} (+ עָלַי, v. עַל **II 1 d**), 143^{4} (+ *id.*); subj. נֶפֶשׁ Jon 2^{8} (+ *id.*), ψ 107^{5} (+ בָּהֶם).

†[עָטַר] **vb. surround** (NH *id.*, and 5849
deriv.; Ph. עטרת *wreath*, עטר Pi. denom. *crown* Lzb^{339}; Aram. עֲטַר; As. *etêru, spare, rescue*);—**Qal** *Impf.* 2 ms. sf. כַּצִּנָּה רָצוֹן תַּעְטְרֶנּוּ ψ 5^{13} *as with a shield, with favour wilt thou surround him; Pt.* pl. עֹטְרִים אֶל־דָּוִד 1 S 23^{26} Saul and his men *were surrounding* (closing in) *upon David.*

†I. עֲטָרָה **n.f. crown, wreath**;—abs. ׳ע Ez 5850
21^{31} Ct 3^{11}; cstr. עֲטֶרֶת 2 S 12^{30} + 17t.; pl. עֲטָרוֹת Zc 6^{11} Jb 31^{36}, עֲטָרֹת Zc 6^{14};—*crown:* **1.** of idol-image (*Milcom*, 𝔊 We Klo Dr Kit Löhr HPS) 2 S 12^{30} = 1 Ch 20^{2}; golden, ׳ע פָּז ψ 21^{4}; ׳ע תִּפְאַרְתְּכֶם of king and queen, Je 13^{18} *the crown of your splendour;* cf. Ez 21^{31}; wedding-crown Ct 3^{11}. **2.** ׳ע זָהָב Est 8^{15} (of Mordecai); of silver and gold Zc $6^{11.14}$; ׳ע תִּפְאֶרֶת *crown of splendour*, on personif. Jerus. Ez 16^{12} (in allegory), Jerus. and Samaria 23^{42}; ׳ע as appos. (= sim.) Jb 31^{36}. **3.** fig. of honour, etc., Jb 19^{9} (‖ כְּבוֹדִי) La 5^{16}; אֵשֶׁת חַיִל ע׳ בַּעְלָהּ Pr 12^{4}, cf. 14^{24} 17^{6}; ׳ע תִּפְאֶרֶת 16^{31} (of שֵׂיבָה); gift of wisdom 4^{9}; fig. of Jerus. Is 62^{3} (‖ צְנִיף מְלוּכָה), cf. ׳ע גֵּאוּת $28^{1.3}$ fig. of Samaria; fig. of ׳י, ׳ע צְבִי v^{5} (‖ צְפִירַת תִּפְאָרָה).

†II. עֲטָרָה **n.pr.f.** 1 Ch 2^{26}, Ατάρα. 5851

†[עִטֵּר] **vb.denom. crown**;—**Pi.** *Pf.* 3 fs. 5849
שֶׁעִטְּרָה לוֹ Ct 3^{11} *with which* his mother *crowned him* (v. I. עֲטָרָה **1**); elsewh. fig.: 2 ms. עִטַּרְתָּ שְׁנַת טוֹבָתֶךָ ψ 65^{12} *thou* (׳י) *hast crowned the year of*

thy goodness; Impf. 2 ms. sf. וְכָבוֹד וְהָדָר תְּעַטְּרֵהוּ 8^{6}; *Pt.* sf. הַמְעַטְּרֵכִי חֶסֶד וְרַחֲמִים 103^{4} (of ′י). **Hiph.** *Pt.* f. צֹר הַמַּעֲטִירָה Is 23^{8} usu. *Tyre the crown-bestower* (Ges Ew De Che$^{Comm.}$ Di Du Gu^{Kau} Skinner), but dub.; < *the crown-wearer* Hi Gr (after 𝔖), so Ren Che$^{Hpt.}$ (rdg. הַמְּעֻטָּרָה).

5852 †עֲטָרוֹת and (Nu 32^{34}) עֲטָרֹת **n.pr.loc.** Αταρωθ, etc.: **1.** E. of Jordan (MI$^{10.11}$);—**a.** Nu 32^{3} (+ דִּיבֹן, etc.)—mod. *Aṭṭarûs*, c. 8 miles NNW. from Dibon—built by Gad Nu 32^{34} (+ ′ד,
5855 עֲרֹעֵר, and also) **b.** עַטְרֹת שׁוֹפָן v^{35} (Sam. ע′ שפים, v. Di; site unknown). **2.** W. of Jordan, conject. as to sites v. in Di Buhl$^{Geogr. 172}$: **a.** on border between Ephr. and Benj. Jos 16^{2}, = עַטְרוֹת
5853 אַדָּר v^{5} 18^{13}. **b.** on E. border of Ephr. Jos 16^{7}.
5854 **c.** עַטְרוֹת בֵּית יוֹאָב 1 Ch 2^{54} in Judah; a 'son' of Salma (+ Bethlehem, al.).

עטשׁ (√ of foll.; NH עָטַשׁ *sneeze;* Aram. ܥܛܫ in deriv. n.; Ar. عَطَسَ *id.*, Eth. [ዐጠሰ:], ዐጥሰ:, ዕጥስ: *sneezing*).

5846 †[עֲטִישָׁה] **n.f.** sneezing;—pl. sf. עֲטִישֹׁתָיו Jb 41^{10}, v. I. הלל (Bi Siegf Bu Du rd. sg.).

5857 עַי, עַיָּת, עַיָּה $_{40}$ **n.pr.loc.** Αγγαι (Gn), Γαι: **1.** old Canaanit. city, ע′ alw. c. art. הָעַי (הָעָי) Gn 13^{3}+), near Bethel to the SE. (exact site unknown, cf. Di$^{Jos. 7, 2}$ Buhl$^{Geogr. 177}$), Gn 12^{8} (J), 13^{3} (J), Jos $7^{2.2.3.4.5}$ $8^{1.1.2.3}$ + 18 t. Jos 8 (+ Qr $v^{12.16}$, but improb., Kt עיר, cf. Di), 9^{3} $10^{1.1.2}$ (all JE), 12^{9} (D), Ezr 2^{28} = Ne 7^{32}; = עַיָּת Is 10^{28}; עַיָּה (so Baer Ginsb, > עַיָּא van d. H.) Ne 11^{31}, so rd. also (for עַזָּה q.v. ad fin.) 1 Ch 7^{28}. **2.** E. Jordan city Je 49^{3} (+ חֶשְׁבּוֹן), but rd. עָר *city* (?) Gf Rothst^{Kau} Co (הָעִיר ?).

5743, 5856-57 עַי v. I. עוה. עַיָּא v. עַי. עיב v. עוב. p. 728, 730, above
5857-58 עֵיבָל v. עוֹבָל sub עבל. עַיָּה v. עַי. p. 716, above

5859 †עִיּוֹן **n.pr.loc.** Αιν, in Naphtali;—1 K 15^{20} = 2 Ch 16^{4}, 2 K 15^{29} (on 2 S 24^{6} v. דָּן p. 193 a supr.). Perh. = *Tell Dibbin*, on the plateau *Merj ʿayyûn* (Buhl$^{Geogr. 11, 110}$), between the Lîṭânî and the Ḥâsbânî (Id$^{ib. 237 f.}$).

5762 עיות Kt v. עֲוִית. p. 732

5860 †[עִיט] **vb. scream, shriek** (Ar. عيط, عَاطَ II. *scream, scold,* عِيَاطٌ *screaming, scolding,* Frey Dozy$^{ii. 195}$; Syr. ܚܡܬܐ *anger, reviling*);—only **Qal** *Impf.* 3 ms. וַיַּעַט בָּהֶם 1 S 25^{14} *and he screamed at them* (of Nabal).

†עַיִט **n.m.** $^{Je 12, 19}$ bird(s) of prey (from *scream*);—abs. ע′ Gn 15^{11}+, עָיִט Jb 28^{7}, c. art. (perh.) הַע′ Je 12^{9b} (cf. Gie; הַע′ interrog. v^{a}); cstr. עֵיט Is 18^{6} Ez 39^{4};—usu. coll. Gn 15^{11} (JE), Is 18^{6} Jb 28^{7}, עֵיט הָרִים Is 18^{6}, צִפּוֹר כָּל־כָּנָף Ez 39^{4}; fig. of foes of Judah Je 12^{9b}; of single bird v^{9a} (fig. of Judah), Is 46^{11} (fig. of invader, ‖ אִישׁ עֲצָתִי). 5861

†[עִיט] **vb.denom.** dart greedily (like a bird of prey);—**Qal** *Impf.* 3 ms. וַיַּ֫עַט Qr (Kt erron. ויעשׂ) 1 S 14^{32} *and* the people *darted greedily* upon the spoil (אֶל־הַשָּׁלָל), so 2 ms. וַתַּ֫עַט 15^{19} (on forms v. Ges$^{§ 72 ff.}$). 5860

†עֵיטָם **n.pr.loc.** (perh. animal-name, fr. עַיִט, cf. Gray$^{Prop. Names 93}$);—**1.** Ηταμ, 𝔊L Ιταμ, a cliff, סְעִיף סֶלַע ע′ Ju $15^{8.11}$ perh. near town עֵיטָם, v. foll., but at *ʿArāḳ Ismaʿîn* near edge of Shephelah, WSW. fr. Jerus. acc. to Schick $^{ZPV x (1887), 143 ff.}$ **2.** Αιταν[μ], etc., city fortified by Rehob. 2 Ch 11^{6}, between Bethlehem and Tekoa, = *ʿAin ʿAṭān* c. 2 miles SSW. from B., Buhl$^{Geogr. 92}$ GFM$^{Ju 15, 8}$, near Ŭrṭâs Rob$^{BR i. 477}$; clan in Judah 1 Ch 4^{3}. **3.** Αιταν[μ], in Simeon 1 Ch 4^{32} (Be [not Oettli Kau Kit] rds. עֶתֶר fr. Jos 15^{42}). 5862

†עִיִּים **n.pr.loc.** Γαι, etc. (as if עַי′): **1.** station of Isr. on E. border of Moab, before דִּיבֹן גָּד Nu 5864
33^{45}, = עִיֵּי הָעֲבָרִים v^{44} 21^{11} (all P; 𝔊 ignores 5863
הָעֲבָרִים). **2.** city in Judah Jos 15^{29} (P).

עִילוֹם v. עוֹלָם sub עלם. p. 761 5865

†עִילַי **n.pr.m.** one of David's heroes 1 Ch 11^{29}, Ηλει, Ηλα (= צַלְמוֹן 2 S 23^{28}). 5866

†I. עֵילָם **n.pr.gent. et terr. Elam,** Αιλαμ, Ἐλαμεῖται, well-known country and people NE. of Lower Tigris (As. *Elamtu* Dl$^{Pa 320 ff.}$ COT$^{Gn 10, 22}$);—as early invaders of Palestine Gn $14^{1.9}$, allies of Assyr. Is 22^{6}; foe of Babylon 21^{2}; abode of dispersed Israelites 11^{11}; prophesied against Je $49^{34.35.36.36}$ (Qr, Kt עולם), $v^{37.38.39}$ Ez 32^{24}, cf. כָּל־מַלְכֵי ע′ Je 25^{25}; called 'son' of Shem Gn 10^{22} (P) = 1 Ch 1^{17}; purely local designation ע′ הַמְּדִינָה Dn 8^{2}. 5867

†II. עֵילָם **n.pr.m.** Ηλαμ, Αιλαμ: **1.** heads of families of returned exiles: **a.** Ezr 2^{7} = Ne 7^{12}. **b.** Ezr 2^{31} = Ne 7^{34}. **c.** Ezr 8^{7} 10^{2} (Qr; Kt עולם), v^{26}. **2.** a chief of people Ne 10^{15}. **3.** name in Benjamin 1 Ch 8^{24}. **4.** Levite name 1 Ch 26^{3}. **5.** a priest Ne 12^{42}. 5867

5868 †[עָיִם] **n.[m.]** dub., poss. glow (Ar. غيم, غَامَ to *thirst*, غَيْمَةٌ *thirst, internal heat*), si vera l. (so Du; on form cf. Nö$^{\text{ZMG xxxvii (1883), 526}}$);—cstr. בַּעְיָם רוחוֹ Is 11^{15}, rd. perh. בְּעֹצֶם (so appar. Vrss) Thes Luzz Krochm Che Gu^{Kau} Gr Perles$^{\text{Anal. 52}}$.

5869 I. עַ֫יִן$_{859}$ **n.f.**$^{\text{Gn 3, 7}}$ and (Zc 3^{9} 4^{10} Albr$^{\text{ZAW xvi (1896), 75}}$) **m. eye** (ancient Sem. word; √ and relation to II. ע׳ unknown; NH *id.*; Ph. ען; 𝔗 עֵינָא, עַיְנָא; Palm. עינא, Zinj. sf. עיני, עינך; Syr. ܥܰܝܢܳܐ; As. *ênu, enu*, TelAm. sf. *inaya* and (appar. Can. gloss) *ḫinaya*; Ar. عَيْنٌ; Eth. ዐይን:);—abs. ע׳ Ex 21^{4}+, cstr. עֵין v^{26}+; sf. עֵינִי Gn 44^{21}+ (2 S 16^{12} rd. עָנְיִי Vrss Comm.), עֵינְךָ Dt 7^{16}+, עֵינֵנוּ ψ 35^{21} (2 S 20^{6} v. נצל Hiph.); sf. 3 mpl. עֵינָם Is 13^{18} (Zc 5^{6} rd. עֲוֹנָם 𝔊 We Gr Now), עֵינֵמוֹ ψ 73^{7} (but rd. עֲוֹנָמוֹ v. Comm.); usu. du. עֵינַיִם Gn 20^{16}+, עֵינָיִם Is 3^{16}+, esp. cstr. עֵינֵי Gn 3^{7}+, עֵנֵי Is 3^{8}; sf. עֵינַי Gn 31^{10}+, עֵינֶיךָ Ju 6^{17}+, etc. (Ho 10^{10} rd. עֲוֹנֹתָם cf. 𝔊 𝔙 Che We Gr Now);—*eye*: **1.** lit. as physical organ, **a.** of man Ex 21$^{6.6.6}$(E), Gn 3^{6}(J)+, Lv 21^{20} 24$^{20.20}$ 26^{16}(H; very rarely P, e.g. Dt 34$^{4.7}$), 2 K 4$^{34.34}$+; once שְׁתֵּי עֵינַי Ju 16^{28}. **b.** anthropomorph. of י׳ ψ 33^{18} 34^{16}+. **c.** of idols ψ 115^{5} 135^{16}. **d.** of beasts Gn 30^{41}(J), Jb 40^{24} (hippop., si vera l., but prob. crpt. Di Siegf Bu Du where see conj.), 41^{10} (crocod.); bird Jb 28^{7} 39^{29} Pr 1^{17}. †**e.** in wheels Ez 1^{18} cf. 10^{12}; on stone Zc 3^{9} (all in visions). **f.** subj. of ראה *see* Gn 45$^{12.12}$ (E), +(oft. Dt), c. חזה ψ 11^{4}; men *see* בְּע׳ Dt 3^{27} 2 K 7^{12}+; esp. ע׳ נָשָׂא + ראה Gn 13$^{10.14}$ (J)+; cf. לְכָל־מַרְאֵה עֵינֵי הַכֹּהֵן Lv 13^{12} = *as far as the priest can see*, מַרְאֵה ע׳ Dt 28^{34} *what is seen by the eyes* = v^{67} Ec 6^{9}. **g.** as affected by sleep, v. שֵׁנָה sub [יָשֵׁן]. **h.** as weeping, ע׳ מְקוֹר דִּמְעָה Je 8^{23}, ע׳ נִגְּרָה La 3^{49}, דָּלְפָה ע׳ Jb 16^{20}; v. also Je 31^{16} ψ 116^{8}, and ירד **Qal 3 c.** **i.** as growing dim, v. I. כָּהָה, חָשַׁךְ **3**; c. כָּבֵד Gn 48^{10} (E), קוּם 1 S 4^{15} 1 K 14^{4}, שָׁעַע Is 32^{3} 6^{10} (Hiph.); c. כָּלָה *pine, languish*, v. כ׳ **Qal 2 b, Pi. 2 b**, c. דָּאַב ψ 88^{10}, עָשֵׁשׁ 6^{8} 31^{10}, דָּלַל Is 38^{14}. †**j.** c. פָּקַח *open*, after sleep Jb 27^{19}, sleep of death 2 K 4^{35}; = *keep awake* Pr 20^{13} (opp. שֵׁנָה); of new power of vision Gn 3$^{5.7}$ (J), given by God 21^{19} (E), 2 K 6$^{17.17}$; so (c. וַיְגַל) Nu 22^{31} (JE); = *give sight to* blind 2 K 6$^{20.20}$ Is 35^{5} 42^{7} ψ 146^{8}; of God (י׳) opening his eyes, פָּקַח ע׳ 2 K 19^{16} = Is 37^{17}, Dn 9^{18}, + עַל־ Je 32^{19} Zc 12^{4} Jb 14^{3}; c. פָּתַח, + אֶל־ 1 K 8^{29} = 2 Ch 6^{20}, 1 K 8^{52} Ne 1^{6}, + לְ v^{40} 7^{15}; + inf. Ne 1^{6}.—Nu 24$^{3.15}$ v. שׁתם. **k.** ע׳ אוֹר etc., = *revive*, v. אור **vb. Qal, Hiph.**; **noun, 10.** †**l.** קָרַץ ע׳ = *wink* ψ 35^{19} Pr 10^{10}, ק׳ בְּע׳ 6^{13}. †**m.** יִרְזְמוּן ע׳ Jb 15^{12} i.e. *roll* (in anger). †**n.** לָטַשׁ ע׳ לְ׳ Jb 16^{9} *whet eyes against* = 'look daggers at.' **o.** *put out* eye, v. נקר, עִוֵּר. **p.** as feature of beauty, יְפֵה ע׳ Dt 16^{12}; cf. Ct 4^{9} 7^{5}, ע׳ יוֹנִים 1^{15} 4^{1} and 5^{12} (כְּיוֹנִים); on other hand, ע׳ לֵאָה רַכּוֹת Gn 29^{17}(E); וַתָּשֶׂם בַּפּוּךְ ע׳ †2 K 9^{30} (v. פּוּךְ), cf. Je 4^{30}, כָּחַל ע׳ Ez 23^{40} *paint the eyes*†. **q.** *apple of the eye*, v. אִישׁוֹן, [בָּבָה], בַּת **6.** **r.** גַּבֹּת ע׳ Lv 14^{9} *eyebrows*. **s.** חַכְלִילִי ע׳ מִיַּיִן Gn 49^{12}, חַכְלִלוּת ע׳ Pr 23^{29} (v. ח׳); מְאוֹר ע׳ Pr 15^{30}, v. Toy.

2. a. eyes as shewing mental qualities: arrogance גַּבְהוּת ע׳ Is 2^{11}, ע׳ גְּבֹהִים 5^{15}, גְּבַהּ־ע׳ ψ 101^{5}, תִּפְאֶרֶת רוּם ע׳ Is 10^{12}; c. רוּם also ψ 18^{28} (so read also ‖ 2 S 22^{28} Hup HPS), 131^{1} Pr 6^{17} 21^{4}; humility, שַׁח ע׳ Jb 22^{29}; mockery, ע׳ תִּלְעַג לְ Pr 30^{17}; cf. רָעָה ע׳ בְּ Dt 15^{9} (grudging), 28$^{54.56}$ (*id.*); esp. ע׳ אַל־תָּחֹס (עַל) *not have pity on* Dt 7^{16} + 4 t. Dt, Ez 5^{11} + 8 t. Ez, Is 13^{18}, also Gn 45^{20} (E; = not regret); cf. נֹחַם יִסָּתֵר מֵע׳ Ho 13^{14}. **b.** מַחְמַד ע׳ Ez 24^{16} *desire of the eyes*, so v$^{21.25}$; שִׁקּוּצֵי ע׳ 20^{7} *abominations of the eyes*, so v^{8}.—ψ 73^{7} v. חֵלֶב.

3. Fig. of mental and spiritual faculties, acts and states: **a.** תִּפָּקַחְנָה ע׳ Gn 3$^{5.7}$ (J) Is 42^{7}, גְּלוּי ע׳ Nu 24$^{4.16}$ (JE); also טַח מֵרְאוֹת ע׳ Is 44^{18}; ע׳ אֶל־י׳ ψ 123^{2} (see v$^{2.2}$ for origin of fig.), +; of י׳, 33^{18} (i.e. his favour) 34^{16} (*id.*)+. **b.** ע׳ הַזֹּנוֹת Ez 6^{9}; ע׳ לְנֹכַח יַבִּיטוּ Pr 4^{25}; ע׳ לֹא תִשְׂבַּע Ec 1^{8} 4^{8}; שָׁאֲלוּ ע׳ 2^{10}; טוֹב־ע׳ 22^{9} = *bountiful*, רַע עָ֫יִן 23^{6} = *niggardly one*, so 28^{22}; eye as avenue of temptation Jb 31$^{1.7}$; שִׁית ע׳ ψ 17^{11} = design. **c.** esp. בְּעֵינֵי, c. adj. and intrans. verbs, *in the view, opinion, of* Gn 16$^{4.5}$ (J), 21$^{11.12}$ (E), 34^{18} (P), + oft.; c. act. vb. 2 S 10^{3} = 1 Ch 19^{3}, Est 1^{17} 3^{6}; הַטּוֹב בְּע׳ Gn 16^{6} 19^{14} (J), +, i.e. what one pleases, Nu 36^{6} (P) whom they please; הַיָּשָׁר בְּע׳ Dt 12$^{8.25}$+, הַטּוֹב וְהַיָּשָׁר בְּע׳ v^{28} Jos 9^{25} (D), הָרַע בְּע׳ Ju 2^{11} 3^{7} Dt 4^{25} + esp. D and K (R^{D}); so לְנֶגֶד עיניו 2 S 22^{25} = ψ 18^{25}; אַחֲרֵי עֵינֵיכֶם Nu 15^{39} = acc. to your wish, fancy (+ לְבַבְכֶם). **d.** נֶעְלַם מֵע׳ Lv 4^{13} i.e. hid from knowledge of, so Nu 5^{13} (both P), Jb 28^{21}; מֵע׳ Nu 15^{24} (P) *without the knowledge of*; אַעְלִים ע׳ מִן Is 1^{15} = disregard, pay no attention; cf. Lv 20^{4} (H) Ez 22^{26}; without מִן, abs., Pr 28^{27}; אַעְלִים ע׳ בּוֹ Is 65^{16}, וַיַּסְתֵּר עָמָל מֵע׳ Jb 3^{10}; נִסְתְּרוּ מֵע׳ (i.e. בַּכֹּפֶר) 1 S 12^{3} (נעלים *sandals* + ענו בי 𝔊 Th We Kit, cf. Ecclus$^{\text{xlvi. 19}}$; Bu HPS ins. ענו בי); הַשֹּׁחַד יְעַוֵּר ע׳ Dt 16^{19}, cf. כְּסוּת ע׳ Gn 20^{16} (E).

4. Transferred mngs.: **a.** visible *surface* of earth Ex 10$^{5.15}$ (J) Nu 22$^{5.11}$ (JE). **b.** *appearance* Lv 13^{5} (P; rdg. בְּעֵינוֹ Di Kau Dr-Wh), v^{37}

(P; rdg. *id.*), v^{66} (P) Nu $11^{7.7}$ (JE); so appar. dual 1 S 16^{7}. **c.** *gleam, sparkle* (of metal, jewels, etc.) Ez $1^{4.7.16.22.27}$ 8^{2} 10^{9} Dn 10^{6}; of wine Pr 23^{31}.

5. Other phrases are: ע׳ תַּחַת ע׳ Ex 21^{24} (E)=Lv 24^{20} (H), =ע׳ בְּע׳ Dt 19^{21}, all=*an eye for an eye*; ע׳ בְּע׳=*eye to eye*, Nu 14^{14} (P) Is 52^{8} (fig.), cf. וְע׳ אֶת־ע׳ תִּרְאֶינָה Je 32^{4} 34^{3}; esp. לְעֵינֵי *in the presence of, in full view of* Gn 42^{24} (E) 47^{19} (J) Ex 4^{30} (J) Nu 19^{5} (P), + oft.; of business transaction Je $32^{12.12}$ Gn $23^{11.18}$ (P); so נֶגֶד ע׳ Jo 1^{16}, לְנֶגֶד ע׳ Jb 4^{16}, and even בְּע׳ 1 S 21^{14} Ezr 3^{12}; נִגְרַזְתִּי מִנֶּגֶד ע׳ ψ 31^{23}; בֵּין ע׳=*on the forehead* Ex $13^{9.16}$ (JE) Dt 6^{8} 11^{18} 14^{1} Dn $8^{5.21}$.

5770 †[עִין] **vb. denom.** eye (enviously), look (askance) at;—**Qal** *Pt.* (or **Pôʿēl**, מ om., v. Dr), c. acc. עוֹיֵן 1 S 18^{9} Qr (Kt עון).

5869, 5871 †II. עַ֫יִן **n.f.** spring (of water) (connexion with I. ע׳ dub.; NH *id.*, Ph. ען; As. *ênu, înu*; Ar. عَيْنٌ; Eth. ዐይን:; Palm. עינא, 𝔗 עֵינָא, עַיְינָא; Syr. ܥܶܝܢܳܐ;—abs. ע׳ 1 S 29^{1}+, עָ֑יִן Gn 49^{22}+, הָעַ֫יְנָה $24^{16.45}$; cstr. עֵין v^{13}+; pl. עֲיָנֹת Dt 8^{7}, -וֹת 2 Ch 32^{3}; cstr. עֵינוֹת Ex 15^{27}=Nu 33^{9}, עִינוֹת Pr 8^{28} (Ges$^{§ 93 v}$);—*spring* Gn 16^{7} $24^{16.29.30.42.45}$ (all J) 49^{22} (poem in J), 1 S 29^{1}; עֵין הַמַּיִם Gn 16^{7} $24^{13.43}$ (J), cf. Ex 15^{27} (J) Nu 33^{9} (P); נַחֲלֵי מַיִם ע׳ וּתְהֹמֹת Dt 8^{7}; מֵימֵי הָעֲיָנוֹת 2 Ch 32^{3}; ע׳ תְּהוֹם Pr 8^{28} (i.e. of the sea); fig. עֵין יַעֲקֹב Dt 33^{28} (poem), i.e. Jacob's descendants. Particular springs
5878 are: **a.** ע׳ חֲרֹד Ju 7^{1} (on loc. cf. GFM). **b.**
5875 ע׳ הַקּוֹרֵא (*partridge-spring*) Ju 15^{19} (cf. *id.*).
5883 **c.** ע׳ רֹגֵל near Jerus. (early sanctuary RS$^{Sem\ i. 157,}$
2nd ed. 172) 2 S 17^{17} cf. 1 K 1^{9}, on border of Judah
5886 Jos 15^{7}, and Benj. 18^{16}. **d.** ע׳ הַתַּנִּין (*dragon-*
spring) Ne 2^{13} (=**c**? so RS$^{l.c.}$).—On שַׁעַר הָעַיִן
8179 Ne 2^{14} 3^{15} 12^{37} v. שַׁעַר. p. 1044

5871 †III. עַ֫יִן **n.pr.loc.** **1.** לָעָ֑יִן, on NE. border of Can. Nu 34^{11}, 𝔊 ἐπὶ πηγάς. **2. a.** in Negeb of Judah Jos 15^{32} (+וְרִמּוֹן), Levit. city 21^{16} (but 𝔊^{B} Ασα rd. עָשָׁן, as 1 Ch 6^{44}), appar.= **b.** 19^{7} (+ר׳; assigned to Simeon), וְעַ׳ ר׳ 1 Ch 4^{32} (rd. prob. וְעֵין ר׳); prob. mod. *Umm er-Ramāmīn*, c. 18 miles SW. from Hebron, Buhl$^{Geogr. 183}$.—
5884 Vid. עֵין רִמּוֹן. below

5872 †עֵין גֶּ֫דִי **n.pr.loc.** Εγγαδδει, etc.;—מְצָדֹת עֵין גֶּדִי 1 S 23^{29}, מִדְבַּר ע׳ 24^{1}, כַּרְמֵי ע׳ Ct 1^{14}; עֵין גֶּ֫דִי ע׳=חַצְצוֹן תָּמָר (q.v.) acc. to 2 Ch 20^{2}; Ez 47^{10}; mod. *ʿAin ğidî*, on W. shore of Dead Sea, GASm$^{Geogr. 269 f., 512}$ Buhl$^{Geogr. 41, 164 f.}$

†עֵין גַּנִּים **n.pr.loc.** **1.** in the Shephelah 5873
of Judah Jos 15^{34}, perh. *Umm-ğîna*, c. 1 mile S. of W. from Bethshemesh Cl-Gann Buhl$^{Geogr. 194 f.}$. **2.** in Issachar 19^{21} (A Ηνγαννιμ), Levit. city
21^{29} (πηγὴν γραμμάτων); hence by txt. err. עָנֵם 6046
1 Ch 6^{58}; *Gennin*, near SE. end of plain of Jezreel, c. 15 m. NNE. fr. Samaria, Buhl$^{Geogr. 202}$

†עֵין־דֹּאר **n.pr.loc.** in Manasseh Jos 17^{11} 5874
(JE; om. 𝔊), =ע׳ דּוֹר 1 S 28^{7} (Αελδωρ, 𝔊L Αενδωρ),
ע׳־דֹאר ψ 83^{11} (Gr ע׳ חֲרוֹד), Αενδωρ; *Endûr*, c. 5878
14 miles NNE. from foregoing.

†עֵין חַדָּה **n.pr.loc.** in Issachar Jos 19^{21}, 5876
Αιμαρεκ, A Ηναδδα, 𝔊L Αναδδα.

†עֵין חָצוֹר **n.pr.loc.** in Naphtali Jos 19^{37}, 5877
πηγὴ Ασορ.

†עֵין מִשְׁפָּט **n.pr.loc.** Gn 14^{7} = (בַּרְנֵעַ) קָדֵשׁ 5880, 6947
q.v. (𝔊 τὴν πηγὴν τὴν κρίσεως; on signif. of name cf. RS$^{Sem\ i. 165, 2nd\ ed. 181}$).

†עֵין עֶגְלַיִם **n.pr.loc.** on Dead Sea Ez 5882
47^{10}, Εναγαλειμ.

עֵין רִמּוֹן **n.pr.loc.** in post-exil. Judah Ne 5884
11^{29} (A (εν)Ρεμμιον), prob.= III. עַיִן **2** q.v. and 5871
רִמּוֹן Zc 14^{10}. p. 942 7416

†עֵין שֶׁ֫מֶשׁ **n.pr.loc.** on border betw. Judah 5885
Jos 15^{7} (πηγῆς ἡλίου) and Benj. 18^{17} (πηγὴν Βαιθσαμυς, 𝔊L [πη]γὴν Σαμες); conj. in Buhl$^{Geogr. 98}$.

עֵין תַּפּוּחַ **n.pr.loc.** v. III. תַּפּוּחַ sub נפח. p. 656 5887, 8598

†עֵינַ֫יִם **n.pr.loc.** (on form v. Ges$^{§ 88 c}$);—Gn 5879
$38^{14.21}$ (J), Αιναν = following.

†עֵינָם **n.pr.loc.** in the Shephelah of Judah, 5879
הָעֵ׳ Jos 15^{34} (Μαιανει, A 𝔊L Ηναειμ) = עֵינַיִם. above

†עֵינָן **n.pr.m.** Αιναν, name in Naphtali Nu 2704, 5881
1^{15} 2^{29} $7^{78.83}$ 10^{27}.—Vid. also חֲצַר עֵינוֹן. p. 347 2703

עֵינוֹן v. חֲצַר עֵינוֹן. p. 347 2703

†עָנִים **n.pr.loc.** in hill-country of Judah 6044
Jos 15^{50}, Αισαμ, Ανειμ[β], perh. *Ghuwain*, c. 17 miles W. of S. from Hebron, Buhl$^{Geogr. 163 f.}$

†מַעְיָן **n.m.**$^{Pr\ 8, 24}$ spring;—abs. מ׳ ψ 74^{15}+; 4599
cstr. מַעְיַן 2 K 3^{25}+, מַעְיְנוֹ ψ 114^{8} (Ges$^{§ 90 n}$); sf. מַעְיָנוֹ Ho 13^{15}; pl. מַעְיָנוֹת Is 41^{18}+, מַעְיָנִים ψ 104^{10}; cstr. מַעְיְנוֹת Gn 7^{11}+, מַעְיְנֵי 1 K 18^{5} 2 K 3^{19}, מַעַיְנֵי Is 12^{3}; sf. מַעְיָנַי ψ 87^{7} (but v. infr.), מַעְיְנֹתֶיךָ Pr 5^{16};—*spring*, cstr. before מַיִם 1 K 18^{5} 2 K $3^{19.25}$, Jos 15^{9} 18^{15} (both P), ψ 114^{8},

cf. Pr 8^{24}; מַעְ׳ alone Is 41^{18} Lv 11^{36} (P), ψ 74^{15} 104^{10} 2 Ch 32^{4}, cf. Jo 4^{18} (in eschatol. picture); in sim. Pr 25^{26}; מ׳ תְּהוֹם Gn 7^{11} 8^{2} (cf. Pr 8^{28}); fig. of source of happiness, enjoyment Ho 13^{15} (‖ מְקוֹרוֹ) ψ 84^{7} Pr 5^{16} (of wife, v. Toy), cf. מ׳ חָתוּם Ct 4^{12}, מ׳ גַּנִּים v^{15}; also ψ 87^{7} (si vera l.; so De Che Du; Hup Bae We rd. form of מָעוֹן *dwelling*); מ׳ הַיְשׁוּעָה Is 12^{3}.

5774, 5778, 5890-91 I. [עִיף] = II. עוּף q.v. for עֵיפָה, עֵיפַי etc. p. 734

5774, 5888 †II. [עִיף] **vb.** be faint (cf. Syr. ܥܐܦ **3**, PS^{2835}; ‖ form of יעף q.v.; occurrences dub.);—**Qal** *Pf.* 3 fs. עָיְפָה נַפְשִׁי לְ Je 4^{31} (? rd. עָֽיְפָה); *Impf.* 3 ms. וַיָּעַף Ju 4^{21} (< וַיָּעַף GFM Bu), 1 S 14^{28} (del. We Bu Kit Löhr, emend. HPS), v^{31} (rd. וַיִּעַף [√יעף] Buhl HPS), 2 S 21^{15} (corrupt, HPS; for Philist. name We Dr Bu Kit).

5889 †עָיֵף **adj.** faint, weary;—ע׳ abs. Gn 25^{29}+; f. עֲיֵפָה Je 31^{25}+; pl. עֲיֵפִים Ju 8^{4}+;—fr. exertion and hunger Gn 25$^{29.30}$ (J), Ju 8$^{4.5}$ Dt 25^{18} (+יָגֵעַ), cf. Is 5^{27}, הָנִיחוּ לֶעָ׳ 28^{12} (fig.), 2 S 16^{14} (si vera l., n.pr.loc. needed, cf. We Dr HPS); + רָעֵב, צָמֵא 17^{29}; specif. from thirst Is 29^{8} (sim.), Jb 22^{7}, נֶפֶשׁ ע׳ Pr 25^{25} and (fig.) Je 31^{25} (‖ דָּֽאֲבָה); hence אֶרֶץ צִיָּה וְעָיֵף ψ 63^{2} (fig., on masc. v. Kö Synt. § 334 f.), cf. 143^{6} (sim.), Is 32^{2} (opp. צֵל, in sim.); ע׳ sc. beast 46^{1}.—Vid. also foregoing.

5892 I. עִיר v. sub I. עור. p. 735

5892 II. עִיר 1092 **n.f.** Gn 10,12 (Albrecht ZAW xvi. 49 f.) city, town (√unkn.; NH *id.*; ? Ph. ער Lzb^{345}; Sab. ער *fortified height* (cf. **3**) Prä ZMG xxvi (1872), 437, ערן, ערהן *city* CIS iv. pp. 94, 95, 173);—ע׳ abs. Gn 4^{17}+, cstr. 24^{10}+; הָעִ֫ירָה 1 K 14^{12}+7 t.; sf. עִירִי 2 S 19^{38}+2 t., etc.; pl. עָרִים Is 6^{11}+, עֲיָרִים Ju 10^{4} (txt. err., or word-play, cf. GFM); cstr. עָרֵי Gn 19^{29}+; sf. עָרַי Zc 1^{17}, עָרֵיכֶם Is 1^{7}+, etc.;—**1.** *city, town,* abode of men Gn 4^{17} (J) and oft.; גְּדֹלָה 10^{12} (J), +, or קְטַנָּה Ec 9^{14} (cf. Gn 19^{20}); esp. **a.** fortified: עָרִים בְּצֻרוֹת 2 S 20^{6}+, etc., v. בָּצַר, מִבְצָר; עִיר מִבְצַר־צֹר Jos 19^{29} (P) *fortified city (of) Tyre,* ע׳ מָצוֹר ψ 31^{22}+, etc., v. מָצוֹר, מְצוּרָה sub צוּר (Mi 7^{12} v. מָצוֹר p. 596 a); ע׳ עֻזֵּ֫נוּ Is 26^{1}, עָרֵי מָעֻזּוֹ 17^{9}; ע׳ דְּלָתַיִם וּבְרִיחַ 1 S 23^{7}; ע׳ חוֹמָה Lv 25^{29}, cf. v^{30} (P), 1 K 4^{13}; on Ho 10^{14} v. I. עַם **2 b** (1 S 9^{14} rd. הַשַּׁעַר 𝔊 We Dr al.). **b.** opp. ע׳ הַפְּרָזוֹת, עָרֵי הַפּ׳ Dt 3^{5}, כֹּפֶר הַפְּרָזִי 1 S 6^{18}, Est 9^{19}; disting. fr. dependencies חֲצֵרִים Jos 13^{23} + oft. P. **c.** עָרֶיהָ are dependent towns Jos 13^{17} (P), Je 19^{15}. †**d.** עָרֵי הַמַּמְלָכָה Jos 10^{2} (JE) *royal cities* (i.e. with a king, cf. Tel Am. *al šarri*), so sg. 1 S 27^{5}, opp. עָרֵי הַשָּׂדֶה v^{5} *rural towns;* ע׳ הַמְּלוּכָה 2 S 12^{26} (but rd. ע׳ הַמַּיִם We Bu Kit Löhr HPS, v. **2** infr.). †**e.** עָרֵי מִסְכְּנוֹת Ex 1^{11} *storage-cities,* so 1 K 9^{19} = 2 Ch 8^{6}, 2 Ch 8^{4} 17^{12}; for מ׳ ע׳ נַפְתָּלִי 16^{4} rd. prob. כִּנְּרוֹת עַל־וגו׳ (as 1 K 15^{20}; Be Kit Buhl); cf. ע׳ הָרֶכֶב 1 K 9^{19} 10^{26} = 2 Ch 8^{6} 9^{25}, 2 Ch 1^{14}; ע׳ הַפָּרָשִׁים 1 K 9^{19} = 2 Ch 8^{6}. †**f.** ע׳ (הַ)מִּקְלָט (P) *asylum-cities* Nu 35$^{11.13.14}$ Jos 20^{2}, cf. Nu 35$^{25.26.27.28.32}$, ע׳ לְמִקְלָט v^{12}; ע׳ מִקְלַט הָרֹצֵחַ Jos 21^{13}+4 t. 21. **g.** ע׳ (הָ)אֱלֹהִים = Jerus.: ψ 46^{5} 87^{3}, cf. 48$^{2.9}$; ע׳ י׳ Is 60^{14} ψ 101^{8}; ע׳ י׳ צְבָאוֹת 48^{9}. **h.** *city* = inhabitants 1 S 4^{13} 5^{12} Is 22^{2} Ru 1^{19}, so 2 S 20^{22} (rdg. הָעִיר for MT הָעָם) 𝔊 We Dr al. (cf. also foll.). **i.** combinations are: ע׳ רֹכְלִים Ez 17^{4} *city of merchants;* ע׳ מוֹשָׁב ψ 107$^{4.7.36}$ *city for dwelling;* esp. of character or condition: †ע׳ הַצֶּדֶק Is 1^{26}, †ע׳ הָאֱמֶת Zc 8^{3}; †ע׳ הַקֹּדֶשׁ Is 48^{2} 52^{1} Ne 11$^{1.18}$, cf. Dn 9^{24}, all of Jerus.; עָרֵי קָדְשֶׁךָ Je 5^{17} of Judaean cities; of foreign cities, ע׳ תְּהִלָּה Je 49^{25}, הָע׳ הַהֻלָּלָה Ez 26^{17}, הָע׳ הָעַלִּיזָה Zp 2^{15}; of Jerus. also הָע׳ הַיּוֹנָה Zp 3^{1} *oppressive city,* ע׳ (הַ)דָּמִים *bloody city* Ez 22^{2} 24$^{6.9}$ and (of Nineveh) Na 3^{1}. **2.** of fortress in a city esp. עִיר דָּוִד 2 S 5$^{7.9}$ 6^{10} + oft. (v. דָּוִד); ע׳ בֵּית הַבַּעַל 2 K 10^{25} (crpt.; Klo prop. דְּבִיר for ע׳, cf. Kmp Benz Kit); ע׳ הַמַּיִם 2 S 12^{27} (so rd. also v^{26}, see **1 d**). **3.** appar. fortified place, of any size, בְּכָל־עָרֵיהֶם מִמִּגְדַּל נוֹצְרִים עַד־עִיר מִבְצָר 2 K 17^{9} = 18^{8}; cf. Nu 13^{9} (P; but on comp. of ver. see Di); perh. also ע׳ עֲמָלֵק 1 S 15^{5} (HPS).—Ho 7^{4} v. I. עור **Hiph.** p. 249

עִיר הַהֶרֶס v. הֶרֶס. 2041, 5892

†עִיר־הַמֶּ֫לַח **n.pr.loc.** (*city of salt*) in 5898
desert of Judah, Jos 15^{62} (P; + Ên-gedi), πόλεις Σαδων (A 𝔊L [τῶν] ἁλῶν); site unknown.

עִיר נָחָשׁ as **n.pr.m.** v. II. נָחָשׁ. 3, p. 638 5904

†עִיר שֶׁ֫מֶשׁ **n.pr.loc.** (*city of the sun(-god)*), 5905
assigned to Dan Jos 19^{41} (P), = בֵּית שׁ׳ q.v.; 1053
πόλεις Σαμμαυς, A 𝔊L πόλις Σαμες.

עִיר הַתְּמָרִים (*city of palms*) = יְרִיחוֹ q.v. 3405, 5899

†III. עִיר **n.pr.m.** in בְּנֵי ע׳ 1 Ch 7^{12}, txt. 5893
dub., v. Be Kau.

עיר (√of foll.; cf. Ar. عَارَ, عَيْر *go away, go hither and thither, escape through sprightliness,* whence عَيْرٌ *ass,* esp. *wild ass* De Jb (2), 149 Hom NS 121–123).

5895 †עַיִר **n.m.**$^{\text{Gn 32, 16}}$ **male ass** (young and vigorous);—pl. וַעְיָרִם Gn 32^{16} (E); cf. עִירֹה 49^{11} (poem; ‖ בְּנִי אֲתֹנוֹ); cstr. עַיִר פֶּרֶא (Ges$^{§ 131 c \text{ N. } 2}$; or appos. Kö$^{\text{Synt. § 333 s}}$ Di al.) Jb 11^{12} *wild ass's colt;* pl. עֲיָרִים, for riding Ju 10^{4a} (v^{4b} see II. עִיר), עֲיָרִם 12^{14}, sg. abs. עַיִר Zc 9^{9}; עֲיָרִים for carrying Is 30^{6} Qr (Kt עורים), עֲיָרִם for tillage v^{24}.

5896 †עִירָא **n.pr.m.** (v. Sab. n.pr.m. עיר Hal 159);—**1.** כֹּהֵן (q.v. **1**) of David 2 S 20^{26}; on poss. ident. with **2 b** v. Th Klo HPS, opp. We Dr; Ειρας, ⅏L Ιωδαε. **2.** heroes of David (Ειρας, etc., ⅏L Ιδαε, Οιαδ, etc.): **a.** 2 S 23^{26} = 1 Ch 11^{28}, 1 Ch 27^{9}. **b.** 2 S 23^{38} = 1 Ch 11^{40}.

5897 †עִירָד **n.pr.m.** a Cainite Gn 4$^{18.18}$ Γαιδαδ.

5900 †עִירוּ **n.pr.m.** in Judah 1 Ch 4^{15}, Ηρ(α).

5901 †עִירִי **n.pr.m.** Benjamite 1 Ch 7^{7}, Ουρ(ε)ι.

5902 †עִירָם **n.pr.m.** in Edom Gn 36^{43} = 1 Ch 1^{54}, Ζαφω(ε)ιν (A Gn Ηραμ).

5903 עֵירֹם v. II. עור. p. 735

5906 †עַיִשׁ **n.f.** a constellation, perh. **Great Bear** (cf. esp. Di) (point perh. עִיֻּשׁ (v. Bu and reff.), cf. Syr. ܥܝܘܬܐ PS^{2866}, ܥܝܘܬܐ Brock., name of a star);—וְע׳ עַל־בָּנֶיהָ Jb 38^{32} = עָשׁ 9^{9} (both +
6211 כְּסִיל, כִּימָה etc.). p. 799

5857 עַיָּת **n.pr.loc.** v. עַי. p. 743

5907 †עַכְבּוֹר, עַכְבֹּר **n.pr.m.** (*mouse*, cf. עַכְבָּר, v. Gray$^{\text{Prop. N. 93}}$; עכבר OH and Ph. as n.pr. Lzb 340 (cf. also on simil. Lat. n.pr. Cl-Gann$^{\text{JAs 1883, Fev.-Mar. 128}}$));—⅏ Αχοβωρ: **1.** Edomite Gn 36$^{38.39}$ (P) = עַכְבֹּר 1 Ch 1^{49} (Baer Ginsb). **2.** courtier of Josiah 2 K 22$^{12.14}$, perh. also Je 26^{22} 36^{12} (cf. Gie and Ency. Bib.).

5909 †עַכְבָּר **n.m.**$^{\text{1 S 6, 4}}$ **mouse** (NH *id.;* Aram. עַכְבְּרָא; Syr. (in Lexx) ܥܘܟܒܪܐ, ܥܟܒܪܐ (PS^{22}); Ar. عَكَابِرُ pl. *mares murum* Frey (Kam), cf. also Hom$^{\text{AS 338}}$; Ar. of *jerboa* RS$^{\text{K 302}}$; v. Tristr$^{\text{NHB 122}}$ FFP$^{\text{10 ff.}}$);—abs. הָע׳ unclean Lv 11^{29} (H), Is 66^{17} (cf. RS$^{\text{Sem i. 275, 2nd ed. 293}}$); pl. cstr. עַכְבְּרֵי (ה)זָּהָב 1 S 6$^{4.11.18}$; sf. צַלְמֵי עַכְבְּרֵיכֶם v^{5}.

5908 †עַכָּבִישׁ **n.m. spider** (𝔗 עַכָּבִיתָא, עַכּוּבִיתָא; whence Ar. عَنْكَبُوتٌ as loan-wd.; NH עַכְשׁוּב prob. *tarantula*, acc. to Levy$^{\text{NHWB iii. 648}}$);—בֵּית ע׳ Jb 8^{14} i. e. web, so prob. 27^{18} (rdg. ע׳ for MT עָשׁ); cf. קוּרֵי ע׳ Is 59^{5} *filaments of a spider.*

5910 †עַכּוֹ **n.pr.loc.** Ακχω, **Acco**, in Asher, Ju 1^{31}, + Jos 19^{30} (P), rdg. ע׳ for MT עֻמָּה, Di Kau Benn Ency. Bib., after ⅏ Codd.; a seaport N. of Carmel (= Acre, Ptolemais), mod. *'Akka*, cf. Buhl$^{\text{Geogr. 228}}$ (Egypt. *'A-ka*, 'Ακη WMM$^{\text{As. u. Eur. 181}}$; As. *Akkû*, COT^{Gloss}, TelAm. *Ak-ka*).

עכן (√ of foll.; meaning unknown).

†עָכָן **n.pr.m.** man of Judah;—Jos 7^{1} (P), 5912
v$^{18.19.20.24}$ (JE), 22^{20} (P); = עָכָר 1 Ch 2^{7} (fr. עָכוֹר 5917
Jos 7^{26}, v. also עָכָר); Αχαρ, Αχαν.

†יַעְכָּן **n.pr.m.** Gadite 1 Ch 5^{13}, Χιμα, Ιαχᾱ. 3275

עכס (√ of foll.; Ar. عَكَسَ is *reverse, tie backward*, whence عِكَاسٌ *hopple*, of camel).

†[עֶכֶס] **n.[m.] anklet, bangle**;—pl. abs. 5914
הָעֲכָסִים Is 3^{18} *bangles, anklets* (as ornaments); for sg. abs. ע׳ Pr 7^{22} read עֵגֶל Toy.

†[עָכַס] **vb. denom. Pi. shake bangles,** 5913
rattle, tinkle;—*Impf.* 3 fpl. וּבְרַגְלֵיהֶם תְּעַכַּסְנָה Is 3^{16} *and with their feet they rattle their bangles.*

†עַכְסָה **n.pr.f.** daughter of Caleb Jos 15$^{16.17}$ 5915
(JE) = Ju 1$^{12.13}$, 1 Ch 2^{49}, Ασχα, Αχσα, Αζα, Οξα.

†עָכַר **vb. stir up, disturb, trouble** (NH 5916
id., make turbid; Ar. عَكِرَ *be turbid*);—**Qal** *Pf.* 3 ms. ע׳ 1 S 14^{29}; 2 ms. sf. עֲכַרְתָּנִי Jos 7^{25}, etc.; *Impf.* 3 ms. sf. יַעְכָּרְךָ v^{25}; *Pt.* עֹכֵר 1 K 18^{17} + 3 t., עוֹכֵר 1 Ch 2^{7}; pl. sf. עֹכְרָי Ju 11^{35};—*disturb, trouble*, c. acc. pers. Gn 34^{30} (J), Jos 6^{18} 7$^{25.25}$ (all JE; v^{25b} subj. י׳), Ju 11^{35}; cf. Pr 11^{17} (opp. גֹּמֵל), v^{29} 15^{27} (opp. חָיָה); ע׳ יִשְׂרָאֵל 1 K 18$^{17.18}$ 1 Ch 2^{7} (cf. Jos 7^{18} etc., supr.); ע׳ אֶת־הָאָרֶץ 1 S 14^{29}. **Niph.** *Pf.* 3 ms. וּכְאֵבִי נֶעְכָּר ψ 39^{3} *my pain was stirred up; Pt.* f. נֶעְכֶּרֶת Pr 15^{6} usu. as n. abstr. *disturbance, calamity*, but < read וּתְבוּאַת רָשָׁע נִכְרָת[ה] *the income of the wicked is cut off* (Toy).

†עָכוֹר **n.[m.] disturbance, trouble,** only 5911
in עֵמֶק ע׳ *valley of trouble*, W. or SW. from Jericho Jos 7$^{24.26}$ (JE; name explained), on border of Judah 15^{7} (P), cf. Ho 2^{17} Is 65^{10}; on identif. cf. esp. Di$^{\text{Jos 7, 24}}$ Buhl$^{\text{Geogr. 98}}$; Εμεκαχωρ, φάραγξ (or κοίλας) Αχωρ.

עָכָר **n.pr.m.** v. עָכָן. above 5917

†עָכְרָן **n.pr.m.** name in Asher Nu 1^{13} 2^{27} 5918
7$^{72.77}$ 10^{26}; Εχραν.

†עַכְשׁוּב **n.m.** usu. **asp, viper** (so ⅏ 𝔙; 5919
perh. conject. fr. sense and ‖ נָחָשׁ), but perh. =

(? crpt. for) **עַכָּבִישׁ spider** (q.v.; cf. 𝔗$^{ad\ loc.}$);—חֲמַת ע׳ ψ 140^{4} *a viper's* (? *spider's*) *venom* is under their lips (v. esp. Che and reff.).

5920-21,
5923 **עַל** v. עלה. **עֹל** v. III. עלל. p. 752, 760

5925 † **עֻלָּא n.pr.m.** in Asher 1 Ch 7^{39}, Ωλα.

45 **עַלְבוֹן** only in אֲבִי־עַלְבוֹן q.v. p. 3 b supr.

עלג (√ of foll., cf. לעג, and v. esp. Lag$^{M\ iii.\ 29\ ff.}$ Nö$^{ZMG\ xli\ (1887),\ 718\ f.}$, who cites Mand. **אלגא**).

5926 †**[עִלֵּג] adj. speaking inarticulately**;—pl. לְשׁוֹן עִלְּגִים Is 32^{4} (𝔊 ψελλίζουσαι; Lag$^{l.c.}$).

5927 **עָלָה** 890 **vb. go up, ascend, climb** (NH *id.*; MI$^{33(?)}$; Ph. עלה; As. *elû*; Ar. عَلَا; 𝔗 and Syr. in der. species; cf. perh. Eth. **ዐለለ:** (for **ዐለወ: ዐልዐለ:** Di^{54}); Sab. עלי = عَلِيَ DHM$^{ZMG\ xxxvii.\ 415}$, cf. עלוהו = عُلُوٌّ Sab Denkm^{91});—**Qal** *Pf.* 3 ms. ע׳ Gn 19^{15}+; 3 fs. עָלְתָה 40^{10}+; עָלָ֫תָה Je 14^{2} 1 S 1^{22}; 2 ms. עָלִיתָ Gn 49^{4}+, etc.; *Impf.* 3 ms. יַעֲלֶה 2^{6}+, יַ֫עַל 44^{33}+, וַיַּעַל 13^{1}+; sf. יַעֲלֶנָּה Is 35^{9}, etc.; *Inf. abs.* עָלֹה Gn 46^{4}+2 t.; cstr. עֲלוֹת 32^{25}+, etc.; *Imv.* עֲלֵה 35^{1}+; fs. עֲלִי Nu 21^{17}+, pl. עֲלוּ Gn 44^{17}+; *Pt.* עֹלֶה 38^{13}+; עוֹלֶה Is 24^{18}+, pl. עֹלִים Gn 28^{12}+, etc.;—**1.** of persons, *go up, ascend*, in local relations: **a.** from low place to high, c. מִן, מִמִּצְרַיִם Gn 45^{25} (E)+ 6 t.; מארץ מצרים Ex 13^{18} (E)+3 t.; †מִבָּבֶל Ezr 7^{6} 8^{1}; מִן הירדן Jos 4$^{16.17.19}$ (P); מ(ן־ה)מדבר Ct 3^{6} 8^{5} etc. **b.** out of a place, c. מִן הארץ, 1 S 28^{13}; מ(תוֹךְ) הַפַּחַת Is 24^{18} Je 48^{44}; מֵהַבְּאֵר 2 S 17^{21}. **c.** c. acc. of place whither: a city ביתאל Gn 35$^{1.3}$ (E); באר שבע 26^{23} (J); a mountain ההר Nu 13^{17} (JE) Dt 1^{24}+, etc.; a bed Gn 49$^{4.4}$ (J) 2 K 1$^{4.16}$, gate Ru 4^{1}; (הַ)שָּׁמַיִם Dt 30^{12} 2 K 2^{11} Am 9^{2}+4 t.; c. אֶל־, אל (ה)הר Ex 19^{23} 34$^{2.4}$ (J) 24$^{15.18}$ (P)+5 t. P; אֶל־הַמָּקוֹם Dt 17^{8}, אל ירושלם Ezr 7^{7}, Is 2^{3} =Mi 4^{2} (אל הר), c. acc. loc.+ אֶל־י׳ (v. **2 b**) Je 31^{6}, of going up to Jerusalem (from a distance), etc.; c. לְ *to*, לירושלם Ezr 1^{3} (from Babylon); לבית 1 S 25^{35}, etc.; c. עד *unto*, עד־נחל Nu 32^{9} (J); †c. בְּ, בְּאַחַת עָרֵי 2 S 2^{1} (constr. praegn.); בְּבַעַל פרצים 1 Ch 14^{11} (del. בְּ); בְּגוֹרָלִי Ju 1^{3}. **d.** to sacred places, Ex 34^{24}, c. acc. †בית יהוה, from palace 2 K 19^{14} 20$^{5.8}$ 23^{2} 2 Ch 29^{20} 34^{30} Is 37^{14} 38^{22} Je 26^{10}; במה 1 S 9$^{13.14.19}$; c. אֶל, אל הר האלהים Ex 24^{13} (E); בבית י׳ 1 S 1^{7} (בּ dittogr.); בהר יהוה ψ 24^{3}. **e.** c. acc. דֶּרֶךְ *by the way to* †Nu 21^{33} (E) Dt 3^{1} Ju 8^{11} 1 S 6^{9} 2 K 3^{8}; מעלה Je 48^{5}; חוֹמָה Jo 2^{7}. **f.** *ascend, climb*, c. בְּ *by*, a ladder Gn 28^{12} (E), Ez 40$^{6.22.49}$, etc.; c. עַל *upon*, altar by (ב) steps, of priest, Ex 20^{23} (Gi; van d. H. v^{26}; E) the roof Jos 2^{8} Ju 9^{51}, bed ψ 132^{3}; עַל־יָדָיו *on his hands* 1 S 14^{13}; על במתי עב Is 14^{14} (|| ממעל לכוכבי אֵל), etc. **2.** *go up*, in personal relations: **a.** *to meet* or *visit*, c. אֶל pers., Gn 44$^{17.24.34}$ 45^{9} (J) Jos 10$^{4.6}$ (all with implication of *ascent*), Dt 25^{7} (to gate of city), +; c. †על pers., Gn 38^{12} (+ה loc., up *to Timnah*); לקראת 46^{29} (J) Ju 6^{35} 2 K 1$^{3.6.7}$. †**b.** *go up* unto (אֶל) God, on a height, אל האלהים Ex 19^{3} (E) 1 S 10^{3}; אל יהוה Ex 24^{1} (E) 19^{24} 32^{30} (J) Ju 21$^{5.5.8}$ (to war); אֵלַי Ex 24^{12} (E) Dt 10^{1}; unto Deborah Ju 4^{5}. **c.** *go up*, in war, c. אֶל *against* Nu 13^{31} (E) Ju 1^{1} 12^{3} 1 S 7^{7} Is 36^{10} (= על 2 K 18^{25})+; oftener c. על, 1 S 14^{10} Ju 6^{3} 15^{10} 18^{9} 1 K 14^{25}+; c. על+לַצָּבָא Jos 22$^{12.33}$ (P); c. בְּ, Is 7^{6} Je 48^{18}; c. לְ, Hb 3^{16}; +למלחמה Ju 20^{18} +3 t.; +במלחמה 1 S 29^{9}; וַתַּעַל(ה) המלחמה 1 K 22^{35}=2 Ch 18^{34}. **d.** *go up* after, c. אחרי = *follow* 1 S 25^{13} 1 K 1$^{35.40}$. **e.** *go up, depart*, c. מֵעַל (q.v.) 1 S 6^{20} Gn 17^{22} 35^{13} (P)+, subj. כבוד י׳ Ez 11$^{23.24}$; =*withdraw, retreat*, 1 K 15^{19} 2 K 12^{19} Je 21^{2}, abs. 2 S 23^{9}, and so read || 1 Ch 11^{13} (v. Dr^{Sm}). †**3.** of animals, *go* or *come up*: abs. frogs Ex 7^{28} (J) 8^{2} (P), quails Ex 16^{13} (P); lion Is 35^{9}; fox Ne 3^{35}; *rise up, fly up*, eagle Is 40^{31} Je 49^{22}; c. מִן, cattle out of water Gn 41$^{2.3.18.19}$ Ct 4^{2} 6^{6}, lion מִגְּאוֹן הַיַּרְדֵּן Je 49^{19}=50^{44}, מִסֻּבְּכוֹ Je 4^{7}, from prey Gn 49^{9} (J); *climb up* into (ב) houses, locusts Jo 2^{9}; frogs, on (ב) persons Ex 7^{29} (J); c. על, of cattle, sexually Gn 31$^{10.12}$ (E); locusts upon the land Ex 10$^{12.14}$ (E) Jo 1^{6}. †**4.** of vegetation, *spring up, grow, shoot forth*: trees Is 55$^{13.13}$ Ez 47^{12}; קיקיון Jon 4^{6}; grass Dt 29^{22} Am 7^{1}; ears of grain Gn 41$^{5.22}$ (E), also Gn 40^{10} (E) Is 5^{6} 32^{13} cf. sim. 53^{2}, Ho 10^{8} Pr 26^{9}; ע׳ כֻלּוֹ קמשׂנים Pr 24^{31} *all of it grown up with thorns*, Is 34^{13}; fig. קֶרֶן Dn 8$^{3.8}$. **5.** of natural phenom., *go up, rise*: dew, Ex 16^{14}, i.e. disappear (P); אֵד ע׳ מִן־הָאָרֶץ Gn 2^{6} (J), cloud 1 K 18^{44} Je 4^{13}; ע׳ הַשַּׁחַר dawn, etc. Gn 19^{15} (JE) Ju 19^{25} 1 S 9^{26}+; smoke Gn 19^{28} Ex 19^{18} (J) Ju 20^{40}+; fire 6^{21}; flame 13^{20}; stench Is 34^{3} Jo 2^{20}; incense Ez 8^{11}; well Nu 21^{17} (E); waters Je 47^{2}; Nile Je 46$^{7.8}$ Am 8^{8} 9^{5}; c. על, of overflow Is 8^{7}+. †**6.** of inanimate things (instead of passive construction), abs., shock of grain (to גֹּרֶן) Jb 5^{26}; of בָּשָׂר (covering bones in Ezek.'s vision) Ez 37^{8}; c. על, of garments upon the body Lv 19^{19} (P) Ez 44^{17}; razor on head Ju 13^{5} 16^{17} 1 S 1^{11}; yoke upon oxen

Nu 19^{2} (P) 1 S 6^{7}; lot upon an animal Lv 16$^{9.10}$ (P); c. בְּ, weight in balance ψ 62^{10}; entry in (ב) a book 1 Ch 27^{24}; =*be offered* (of sacrif.) 1 K 18^{29} 2 K 3^{20} Is 60^{7}; אֲרוּכָה (q.v.) in healing, Je 8^{22}, fig. 2 Ch 24^{13} Ne 4^{1}. **7.** of thoughts, ע׳ על לב 2 K 12^{5} Is 65^{17} + 5 t.; ע׳ על לבב Je 51^{50} Ez 38^{10}; ע׳ אל לב 14^{7}; ע׳ על רוּחַ 20^{32}; of anger 2 S 11^{20} 2 Ch 36^{16} (ב pers.) + 3 t.; temper Ec 10^{4} (עָלֶיךָ). **8.** *come up* before God, arrogance, בְּאָזְנָיו 2 K 19^{28}=Is 37^{29}; cry, אֶל־א׳ Ex 2^{23} (P), c. acc. 1 S 5^{12}, abs. Je 14^{2}; tumult ψ 74^{23}; of evil Jon 1^{2} (לְפָנָי). †**9.** *go up, extend,* of boundary, c. מִן *whence*, + acc., לְ, אֶל and even בְּ *whither* Jos 15$^{3.6.8}$ 18$^{12.12}$ + (all P). †**10.** *excel: thou excellest* (עַל) *them* Pr 31^{29}; *be superior to* יעלה עליך מעלה מעלה Dt 28^{43}.—עוֹלֶה Jb 36^{33} is difficult, cf. Comm., and v. עוֹלָה.

†**Niph.** *Pf.* 3 ms. נַעֲלָה Nu 10^{11}+; 2 ms. נַעֲלֵיתָ ψ 97^{9}; *Impf.* יֵעָלֶה Ex 40^{37}, etc.; *Inf. cstr.* הֵעָלוֹת Nu 9^{17}+, etc.; *Imv.* mpl. הֵעָלוּ 16^{24};—**1. a.** *be brought up:* מבבל לירושלם Ezr 1^{11}. **b.** *be taken up,* וַתֵּעָלוּ על שפת לשון Ez 36^{3} (Kö$^{i. 553}$; talked about). **c.** (1) pass., *be taken up, away,* of (pillar of) cloud, sq. מֵעַל of tabern. Ex 40^{36} Nu 9^{17} 10^{11} (P); abs. Ex 40$^{37.37}$ Nu 9$^{21.21.22}$ (P); of the glory from upon the cherubim Ez 9^{3}; (2) reflex., *take oneself away from, get up from:* מִסָּבִיב Nu 16^{24}; מֵעַל v^{27}; of a besieging army Je 37$^{5.11}$. **2.** reflex.: *take oneself away* מאחרי pers., from following after, 2 S 2^{27}. **3.** *be exalted,* of God ψ 47^{10}; c. עַל, *over* all gods 97^{9}.

Hiph. *Pf.* הֶעֱלָה Nu 8^{3}+, הֶעֱלָה Hb 1^{15} (Ges$^{§ 63p}$); sf. הֶעֶלְךָ Ne 9^{18}, הֶעֱלָנוּ Ex 32^{1} + 2 t.; 3 fs. וְהַעֲלְתָה 1 S 2^{19} consec.; sf. הֶעֱלָתַם Jos 2^{6}; 2 ms. הֶעֱלִיתָ Ex 33^{1}+; וְהַעֲלִיתָ consec. Dt 27^{6}+; הֶעֱלִיתָ Ex 32^{7}; וְהַעֲלִיתָ consec. 40^{4}; 2 mpl. sf. הֶעֱלִיתֻנוּ Nu 20^{5} 21^{5}, etc.; *Impf.* יַעֲלֶה Lv 17^{8}+; וַיַּעַל 2 S 24^{22}; וַיַּעֲלֶה Je 10^{13}; וַיַּעַל Gn 8^{20}+, sf. יַעֲלֵם Dt 28^{61}, etc.; *Inf. abs.* הַעֲלֵה Ez 23^{46}; cstr. הַעֲלוֹת 1 Ch 23^{31}+, etc.; *Imv.* הַעַל Ex 33^{12} + 2 t.; fs. הַעֲלִי 1 S 28$^{8.11}$+, etc.; *Pt.* מַעֲלֶה 7^{10}+; cstr. מַעֲלֵה Lv 11^{4}+; sf. מַעַלְךָ Dt 20^{1} ψ 81^{11}; f. מַעֲלָה Lv 11^{26}; cstr. מַעֲלַת Lv 11$^{3.6}$ Dt 14^{6}, etc.;—**1.** *bring up* persons: **a.** from a place, c. מִן: מִן הַסֶּלַע Ju 15^{13}; מִמִּצְרַיִם Ex 17^{3} (E) + 3 t. E, + 8 t.; מארץ מצרים Ex 32^{1} (J) + 5 t. J, + Lv 11^{45} (P), Dt 20^{1} Jos 24^{17} (E), + 13 t.; מארץ צפון Je 16^{15}=23^{8}. **b.** (1) out of a place, c. מִן: †מִ(ן) הַ(בּ)וֹר Gn 37^{28} (E) ψ 40^{3} Je 38$^{10.13}$; משחת Jon 2^{7}; מקברות Ez 37$^{12.13}$; מִן־שְׁאוֹל ψ 30^{4}, etc.; (2) c. בְּ *by means of,* בְּחֶרְמִי Ez 32^{3} (Hb 1^{15} v. **3** infr.). **c.** c. acc. of place whither, Nu 20^{25} (P) 22^{41} (E) Jos 2^{6} 7^{24} (J) Ezr 4^{2}; השמים 2 K 2^{1}; c. אֶל: אֶל־הָעֲלִיָּה 1 K 17^{19}; c. לְ: לבית 2 Ch 8^{11}. **d.** *cause to ascend, climb:* על המרכבה 1 K 20^{33} (אֶל 2 K 10^{15} prob. error), על־המגדלות 2 Ch 32^{5} (𝔊 *built towers thereon,* i.e. ע׳ עָלָיו); מֵעַל לחומה Ne 12^{31} vid. עַל **IV 2 c.** †**2.** in personal relations: **a.** *bring up,* c. אל, 1 S 19^{15} 2 K 10^{15} 25^{6} Je 39^{5} 52^{9}; c. לְ, 1 S 28$^{8.11.11}$. **b.** in war, c. עַל *against* 2 Ch 36^{17} Je 50^{9} Ez 16^{40} 23^{46} 26^{3}. **c.** *take away* (from life) ψ 102^{25} Jb 36^{20}. †**3.** *bring up* animals, c. על, frogs על הארץ Ex 8$^{1.3}$ (P); *bring up* horses to a charge Je 51^{27}, cf. Na 3^{3}; *draw up* men, under fig. of fish (בְּחַכָּה) Hb 1^{15}; *train,* young lion Ez 19^{3}; of cattle, מעלה גֵרָה, i.e. *chewing the cud* Lv 11$^{3.4.4.5.6.26}$ Dt 14$^{6.7.7}$. **4.** *cause to ascend:* c. acc. rei, smoke מן העיר Ju 20^{38}; stench באף Am 4^{10}, etc.; *bring waters* upon, על Is 8^{7}; *bring up* from (מן loc.) 2 S 6$^{2.12}$ 1 K 8^{1} Gn 50^{25} (JE), +; c. אֶל loc., Ju 16^{3} 1 Ch 15$^{3.12}$, c. acc. loc. 2 Ch 2^{15}; c. אל pers. 1 S 6^{21}; c. לְ pers. Ju 16^{8} 1 S 2^{19}; c. על, *bring* sickness *upon* Dt 28^{61}; †הע׳ עפר על ראש *throw dust on the head* Jos 7^{6} La 2^{10} Ez 27^{30}; *clothe* sackcloth *upon* Am 8^{10}; flesh upon Ez 37^{6}; *put* ornaments *on* 2 S 1^{24}; cf. also 1 K 10$^{16.17}$= 2 Ch 9$^{15.16}$, 2 Ch 3$^{5.14}$; הע׳ נֵר *light lamp* (make flame go up; Thes al. of *raising* lamp upon the lamp-stand) Ex 25^{37} 27^{20} + 6 t. P; *bring up* new flesh (heal; v. אֲרוּכָה) Je 30^{17} 33^{6}. †**5.** mentally: הע׳ גִּלּוּלִים על לב Ez 14^{3}, אל לב v^{7}, i.e. make object of thought; *rouse, stir up,* c. acc. אַף, *anger* Pr 15^{1}, cf. Ez 24^{8}. †**6.** הע׳ מנחה ל׳ 2 K 17^{4} *offer* a present; *bring up* tithe to (ל) Ne 10^{39}; הע׳ מַס *raise a levy* 1 K 5^{27} 9^{15}, למס v^{21} 2 Ch 8^{8}. †**7.** *exalt:* ψ 137^{6} *if I exalt not Jerus. above* (עַל) *my chief joy;* אנכי אַעַלְךָ גם־(מ)עלה Gn 46^{4} (E) *I will exalt thee exceedingly* (cf. **Qal 10**; מ lost in MT, after ם; Di and most *bring up*). **8.** *cause to ascend* (in flame; Thes al. to go up on altar), *offer* sacrifice, usu. עֹלָה, either alone or foll. by other sacrif.: העלה עלות Ex 24^{5} (E) 32^{6} (J) Lv 17^{8} (H) Dt 12$^{13.14}$ + (see עֹלָה); seldom: †קטרת Ex 30^{9} (P), cf. ψ 66^{15}; †מנחה Is 57^{6} 66^{3}, also prob. 1 K 18$^{29.36}$ 2 K 3^{20} (>**Qal**); פר(ים) Nu 23$^{2.4.14.30}$ (E) ψ 51^{21}; הטוב בעיניו 2 S 24^{22}; הע׳ ליהוה Ju 13^{16}; abs. 2 Ch 8^{13} 29^{29}; †הע׳ לעולה Gn 22$^{2.13}$ (E); c. acc. loc. מַעֲלֶה בָמָה Je 48^{35}; מזבח(ה) Lv 14^{20} (P) Is 60^{7} (>**Qal**); c. לְ loc. 2 Ch 29^{27}; c. בְּ loc. Gn 8^{20} (J) Nu 23$^{2.4.14.30}$ (E); עַל־הַחֹמָה 2 K 3^{27}; usu. על loc., על הַצּוּר Ju 13^{19}, הע׳ על מזבח 1 K

$12^{32.33.33}$ 2 K 16^{12} 2 Ch 1^6 29^{21} 1 S 2^{28}, פרים על מזבח ψ 51^{21}; elsewh. הע׳ עלות על מזבח Ex 40^{29} (P) Jos 22^{23} 1 K 3^4 9^{25} 2 Ch 1^6 35^{16} Ezr 3^2 Ez 43^{18}, הע׳ עלות ליהוה על מז׳ Dt 27^6 Jos 8^{31} 1 Ch 16^{40} 2 Ch 8^{12} Ezr 3^3.

†**Hoph.** *Pf.*;—**1.** *be carried away*, 3 fs. הֹֽעֲלָ֫תָה Na 2^8. **2.** *be taken up* into, *inserted* in, 3 ms. הֹֽעֲלָה 2 Ch 20^{34} (על ספר) (pass. of **Qal 6**). **3.** 3 ms. *be offered*, of פר Ju 6^{28} (על המזבח).

†**Hithp.** *lift oneself*: *Impf.* 3 ms. אֶל־יִתְעַל Je 51^3 *against* (him that) *lifts himself*, but corrupt; either rd. אַל־, *let him not*, etc. (𝔊𝔗𝔙 Hi Gf Gie Rothst), or del. אל (𝔊 $Co^{Hpt.}$).

5929 †עָלֶה **n.m.** leaf, leafage (v. עלה **Qal 4**);—ע׳ Lv 26^{36}+; cstr. עֲלֵה Gn 3^7 8^{11}; sf. עָלֵהוּ Je 17^8+; pl. cstr. עֲלֵי Ne 8^{15}+; sf. עָלֶהָ Is 1^{30};—*leaf, leafage*, of various trees Gn 3^7 8^{11} Ne $8^{15.15.15.15.15}$; green Je 17^8, flourishing Pr 11^{28}; but usu. fading Is 1^{30} 34^4 64^5 Je 8^{13} Ez 47^{12} ψ 1^3; *driven leaf* Lv 26^{36} Jb 13^{25}; עלה לִתְרוּפָה *leaf for healing* Ez 47^{12}.

5940 †עֱלִי **n.[m.]** pestle (as *rising* before the blow);—Pr 27^{22}.

5941 עֵלִי **n.pr.m.** Eli, priest at Shiloh 1 S 1^3 (+ v^3 𝔊 Th Klo HPS), $v^{9.12}$ + 28 t. 1–4 + 14^3 1 K 2^{27}; Ηλει.

5930 II. $עֹלָה_{286}$ **n.f.** whole burnt-offering (*that which goes up* (√**6**) to heaven (al. on altar));—ע׳ Gn 22^3 + 141 t.; עוֹלָה Nu 28^{37} + 33 t.; cstr. עֹלַת Ex 29^{42} + 27 t., עוֹלַת Nu 28^{24} + 2 t.; sf. עוֹלָתְךָ ψ 20^4, etc.; pl. עלות Jos 8^{31} + 42 t., עֹלֹת Gn 8^{20} + 3 t.; עולת Dt 27^6, עולות Am 5^{22}+; sf. עֹלוֹתֵיכֶם Je 6^{20}+, etc.;—the *whole burnt-offering* (beast or fowl) is entirely consumed and goes up in the flame of the altar to God expressing the ascent of the soul in worship. All of the victim is laid on the altar except the hide and such parts as could not be washed clean. If beast the ע׳ must be a male without blemish Lv $1^{3.10}$ $22^{18.19}$, of herd or flock; if of flock, either sheep or goat; if fowl, either turtle-dove or young pigeon Lv 1^{14}, the latter usu. offered by the poor + 5^7 12^8 14^{22} $15^{14.15.29.30}$ Nu $6^{10.11}$. A lamb was offered by individuals Lv 12^6 Nu 6^{14}, and by the nation at the עֹמֶר offering Lv 23^{12}, and daily at the עֹלַת הַבֹּקֶר 9^{17} Nu 28^{23} 2 K 16^{15} Ez 46^{13}, and at morning and evening עלה תמיד Nu 28^3, †עֹלַת (הַ)תָּמִיד Ex 29^{42} Nu $28^{6.10.15.23.24.31}$ $29^{6.11.16.19.22.25.28.31.34.38}$ Ezr 3^5 Ne 10^{34} Ez 46^{15}. These were doubled at the עֹלַת שַׁבָּת Nu 28^{10}. A ram was offered by Aaron and his sons †Ex 29^{18} Lv 8^{18} 9^2 $16^{3.5}$; but a young bullock was of greater value Nu $15^{8.24}$ 2 S 24^{22} = 1 Ch 21^{23}, at consecration of Levites Nu 8^{12}, so calves Mi 6^6; on great occasions bullocks + rams Nu $23^{1-6.14.15}$, bullocks + rams + lambs Is 1^{11}; one of each kind offered by tribal chiefs Nu $7^{15.21.27.33.39.45.51.57.63.69.75.81.87}$. In ritual of עֹלַת (ה)חֹדֶשׁ Nu 28^{14} 29^6 and at מצות and Pentecost 2 bullocks, 1 ram, and 7 lambs were added to daily offering Nu $28^{11.19.27}$; at offering of new bread at Pentecost 1 bullock, 2 rams, and 7 lambs Lv 23^{18}; on the 1st and 10th of the 7th month and at עצרת 1 bullock, 1 ram, and 7 lambs, in addition to the offerings of new moon Nu $29^{2.8.36}$; the system culminated in 70 bullocks, 14 rams, 98 lambs for the 7 days of Tabernacles $29^{13ff.}$ Acc. to Ezek. the prince was to offer on each of 7 days of מצות 7 bullocks and 7 rams Ez 45^{23}, and on Sabbath 6 lambs and 1 ram 46^4. At the reconsecration of temple 70 bullocks, 100 rams, and 200 lambs were offered 2 Ch 29^{32}, and at the return of exiles 12 bullocks, 96 rams, and 77 lambs Ezr 8^{35}. In early times whole burnt-offerings of children were sometimes made, e.g. Jephthah's daughter Ju 11^{31}; Isaac proposed as, Gn 22^2 but ram substituted v^{13}; made to other gods 2 K 3^{27} Je 19^5+. The ע׳ was anciently made on any altar used for worship, but in P confined to †מִזְבַּח הָעֹלָה Ex 30^{28} 31^9 35^{16} 38^1 $40^{6.10.29}$ Lv $4^{7.10.18.25.25.30.34}$ 1 Ch 6^{34} 16^{40} $21^{26.29}$ 2 Ch 29^{18} (not in other lit.); מזבח לעלה Jos 22^{29} 1 Ch 22^1. The offerer imposed his hands on head of animal, then slaughtered it Lv $1^{4.5}$; †שחט ע׳ $4^{24.33}$ 6^8 7^2 9^{12} $14^{13.19.31}$ Ez $40^{39.42}$ 44^{11}, and flayed it †הִפְשִׁיט ע׳ Lv 1^6 2 Ch 29^{34}. The priest washed the pieces Ez 40^{38}; arranged them on the altar above the wood Lv 6^5; the fire devoured them v^{2-6} 9^{24} 1 K 18^{38} 2 Ch 7^1, they went up in the flame ריח ניחח ליהוה (ל) Lv $1^{9.13.17}$ 8^{21} Nu 28^{13}; לְרָצוֹן, according to character of offerer Is 56^7 Je 6^{20}; see also ψ 20^4 40^7 51^{18} 1 S 15^{22}.

Phrases: †העלה ע׳ Gn 8^{20} Ex 32^6 (J) 24^5 (E) 30^9 40^{29} Lv 14^{20} 17^8 (P) Dt $12^{13.14}$ 27^6 Jos 8^{31} 22^{23} Ju 6^{26} 20^{26} 21^4 1 S $6^{14.15}$ $7^{9.10}$ 10^8 $13^{9.10.12}$ 2 S $6^{17.18}$ $24^{24.25}$ 1 K $3^{4.15}$ 9^{25} 10^5 2 K 3^{27} 1 Ch $16^{2.40}$ $21^{24.26}$ 23^{31} 29^{21} 2 Ch 1^6 8^{12} 9^4 23^{18} 24^{14} $29^{7.27}$ $35^{14.16}$ Ezr $3^{2.3.6}$ Jb 1^5 42^8 ψ 66^{15} Je 14^{12} 33^{18} Ez $43^{18.24}$ Am 5^{22} (cf. העלה **9**); †זבח ע׳ Ex 20^{24} (E); עשה לע׳ Lv 23^{12} Nu 6^{11} 15^{24} 29^{39}; †עָשָׂה ע׳ Lv 5^{10} $9^{7.22}$ $15^{15.30}$ $16^{24.24}$ Nu 6^{16} 8^{12} $15^{3.8}$ 29^2 Dt 12^{27} Ju 13^{16} 1 K 8^{64} 2 K 5^{17} $10^{24.25}$ 2 Ch 7^7 Ez 43^{27} $45^{17.23}$ $46^{2.12.12.13}$; †הִקְרִיב ע׳ Lv 7^8 9^{16} 10^{19} 23^{37} Nu $28^{3.11.19.27}$ $29^{8.13.36}$ 1 Ch 16^1 Ezr 8^{35} Ez 46^4; הקריב לע׳

Lv 22^{18} Nu 6^{14}; †ע׳ הביא Dt 12$^{6.11}$ 2 Ch 29$^{31.32}$ 30^{15} Is 43^{23} Je 17^{26}; †ע׳ הקטיר 2 K 16$^{13.15}$ 2 Ch 13^{11}.—עֹלָתָה, עולות v. also עַוְלָה sub I. עול.

5930 †II. [עֹלָה] **n.f. ascent, stairway,** עלותו Ez 40^{26} Kt, עֹלוֹתָיו Qr; rd. prob. מַעֲלָתוֹ (𝔊 Co SS לוֹ, Toy עֹלָתוֹ).

5942 †[עִלִּי] **adj. upper**;—fs. עִלִּית Ju 1^{15}; pl. עִלִּיּוֹת Jos 15^{19} (opp. תַּחְתִּית, תַּחְתִּיּוֹת).

5944 †עֲלִיָּה† **n.f.** (c. adj. masc. Je 22^{14}, cf. Albrecht ZAW xvi (1896), 83 Kö$^{Synt. § 251 k}$) **roof-chamber** (NH *id.*, 𝔗 עִלִּיתָא, Syr. ܥܶܠܺܝܬܳܐ (whence Ar. عُلِّيَّة *dining-room* as loan-wd. Frä$^{20 f.}$); Sab. עלית DHM$^{Epigr. Denkm. 27}$);—chamber on roof, cool and secluded: abs. ע׳ Ju 3$^{23.24.25}$ (cf. Nes$^{Marg. 13}$), 1 K 17$^{19.23}$ 2 K 4^{11}; cstr. עֲלִיַּת הַמְּקֵרָה Ju 3^{20}, ע׳־קִיר 2 K 4^{10} *roof-chamber with walls* (permanent); ע׳ הַשַּׁעַר 2 S 19^{1}, i.e. over the gateway; ע׳ הַפִּנָּה Ne 3$^{31.32}$ i.e. at a corner of the wall; ע׳ אָחָז 2 K 23^{12} (prob. built by A.); sf. עֲלִיָּתוֹ 1^{2} (belonging to Ahaziah);—2 Ch 9^{4} rd. עֹלָתָיו (cf. ‖ 1 K 10^{5}); pl. abs. עֲלִיּוֹת מְרֻוָּחִים Je 22^{14} *spacious roof-chambers;* in Sol.'s temple acc. to 2 Ch 3^{9}, so sf. עֲלִיֹּתָיו 1 Ch 28^{11}; more gen. עֲלִיּוֹתָיו Je 22^{13}; י׳'s chambers in sky ψ 104^{3}, containing rain, v^{13}.

5945 I. עֶלְיוֹן$_{22}$ **adj. 1. high**;—ms. ע׳ Dt 26^{19} 28^{1} 1 K 9^{8} (? rdg. הַבַּיִת הַזֶּה הָע׳ as 𝔊L Benz) = 2 Ch 7^{21}, of י׳ ψ 97^{9}. **2.** *upper* Bethhoron, ע׳ Jos 16^{5}, העליון 1 Ch 7^{24} 2 Ch 8^{5}, *the upper* (opp. lower), of house Ne 3^{25}; cf. 2 K 15^{35} 2 Ch 23^{20} + 5 t., + Gn 40^{17} (*uppermost* basket); fs. הָעֶלְיוֹנָה *the upper* pool 2 K 18^{17} = Is 36^{2}, Is 7^{3}; *the highest* side-chamber (צֵלָע) Ez 41^{7}; fpl. הָעֶלְיוֹנֹת 42^{5} *the upper* chambers (לְשָׁכוֹת). **3.** of Davidic king exalted above monarchs ψ 89^{28} (cf. Dt 28^{1}, supr.).

5945 †II. עֶלְיוֹן **n.m. Highest, Most High** (prob. = foreg.);—**1.** name of God Nu 24^{16} Dt 32^{8} ψ 18^{14} = 2 S 22^{14} ψ 9^{3} 21^{8} 46^{5} 50^{14} 73^{11} 77^{11} 78^{17} 83^{19} 87^{5} 91$^{1.9}$ 92^{2} 107^{11} Is 14^{14} La 3$^{35.38}$; with other divine names: אל עליון Gn 14$^{18.19.20.22}$ (v. Di) ψ 78^{35}; יהוה עליון ψ 7^{18} 47^{3}; אלהים עליון ψ 57^{3} 78^{56}. **2.** of rulers, either monarchs or angel-princes, בְּנֵי עֶלְיוֹן = אלהים ψ 82^{6}.

4607 †מֹעַל† **n.[m.] lifting**;—בְּמֹעַל יְדֵיהֶם Ne 8^{6}.

4608 מַעֲלֶה$_{19}$ **n.m.**$^{Is 15, 5}$ **ascent**;—מ׳ Ne 12^{37}; cstr. מַעֲלֵה Jos 10^{10} + 14 t.; מַעֲלָו Ez 40$^{31.34.37}$; **1.** *ascent* of hill or mt.: to a city 1 S 9^{11}, to the

royal sepulchres (in Jerus.) 2 Ch 32^{33}; מ׳ הַזֵּיתִים
2 S 15^{30} (v. זַיִת **3**); מ׳ עַקְרַבִּים = *Scorpion-pass*, on 4610
S. border of Pal., Ju 1^{36} Nu 34^{4} Jos 15^{3} (both P),
i.e. prob. the *Naḳb eṣ-ṣafâ* SW. from Dead Sea
Buhl$^{Geogr. 16.66}$ Di and GFM ad loc., and reff.; oft.
def. by n.pr.loc.: מ׳ אֲדֻמִּים 15^{7} 18^{17}, S. of valley 131
of Achor, between Jerusalem and Jericho, cf.
mod. *Tel'at ed-dâm* Buhl$^{Geogr. 98}$; v. also בֵּית חוֹרֹן, 1032
I. גּוּר, II. חֶרֶס, לוּחִית, II. צִיץ. **2.** of stairs Ez 1483, 2776,
40$^{31.34.37}$; to a wall Ne 12^{37}; מַעֲלֵה הַלְוִיִּם Ne 9^{4}. 3872, 6731

p. 111, 158, 357, 532, 851

מַעַל$_{140}$ **subst., higher part,** only in **adv.** 4605
and **prep.** phrases, **above, upwards** (Ph. מעל, v. sub מַטָּה p. 641: abbrev. from מַעְלָה; cf. מַעַן in לְמַעַן from עָנָה: Kö$^{ii. 116}$):—†**1.** מִמַּעַל = *above* (v. מִן **1 c**): **a.** as *adv.* Am 2^{9} וָאַשְׁמִיד פִּרְיוֹ מִמַּעַל his fruit *above* (opp. שָׁרָשָׁיו מִתַּחַת), Jb 18^{16}; 1 K 7$^{3.20.29}$; oft. in the phr. הַשָּׁמַיִם מִמַּעַל Dt 4^{39} 5^{8} (= Ex 20^{4}), Jos 2^{11} 1 K 8^{23} Is 45^{8} Je 4^{28}; cf. שְׁחָקִים מ׳ ψ 78^{23} Pr 8^{28}, אֱלוֹהַּ מ׳ Jb 3^{4} 31^{2}, אֵל מ׳ 31^{28}. **b.** מִמַּעַל לְ, as *prep.* (מִן **1 c**), *on the top of, above,* Gn 22^{9} ממעל לָעֵצִים *above* the wood, Ex 28^{27} = 39^{20}, Lv 11^{21} כְּרָעַיִם מִמַּעַל לְרַגְלָיו, Is 6^{2} שְׂרָפִים עֹמדים מִמַּעַל לוֹ, 14^{13} Je 43^{10} Ez 1^{26} Dn 12$^{6.7}$; = *on higher ground than,* Je 35^{4}; fig. Je 52^{32} (‖ 2 K 25^{28} מֵעַל).

2. With ה— *loc.* מַעְלָה, מַ֫עְלָה, *upwards* (opp. מַטָּה p. 641): †**a.** fig. Dt 28^{43} יַעֲלֶה עָלֶיךָ מַעְלָה מָּ֫עְלָה *upwards, upwards,* i.e. *higher and higher* (opp. מַטָּה מָּטָּה). †**b.** וָמַ֫עְלָה (*a*) of direction in *space,* Ju 1^{36} מֵהַסֶּלַע וָמָ֫עְלָה from the rock *and upwards* (cf. Bu), 1 K 7^{31} (corrupt: v. Sta VB Benz), 1 S 9^{2} = 10^{23} מִשִּׁכְמוֹ וָמַ֫עְלָה from his shoulder *and upwards:* so וּלְמ׳, †Ez 1^{27} מִמַּרְאֵה מָתְנָיו וּלְמָ֫עְלָה, 8^{2} 43^{15}. (*b*) of direction in *time,* or age:—(*a*) מִבֶּן עֶשְׂרִים שָׁנָה וָמָ֫עְלָה Ex 30^{14} Nu 1^{3} + 19 t. P, מִבֶּן חֹדֶשׁ וָמ׳ Nu 3$^{15.22}$ + 6 t. P, simil. 4^{3} 8^{24} + 7 t. P; elsewhere only 1 Ch 23$^{3.24}$ Ezr 3^{8}, and with וּלְמַעְלָה † 1 Ch 23^{17} 2 Ch 31$^{16.17}$; מִכֹּל חֹגֵר חֲגֹרָה † 2 Ch 25^{5}; and 2 K 3^{21} לְמִבֶּן...וָמ׳ וָמ׳. †(β) מהיום ההוא וָמ׳ from that day *and onwards,* 1 S 16^{13} 30^{25}. †(γ) מִן היום הזה וָמ׳ from this day *and upwards* (i.e. *and back*), Hg 2$^{15.18}$. †**c.** לְמַ֫עְלָה *upwards,* more common than מ׳ alone (**a**): (*a*) Ex 25^{20} (= 37^{9}) פֹּרְשֵׂי כְנָפַיִם לְמ׳, Ju 7^{13} ויהפכהו לְמ׳ overthrew it *upwards,* i.e. turned it downside up, Is 7^{11} אוֹ הַגְבֵּהַּ לְמ׳ or make it (the request) high *upwards,* 8^{21} וּפָנָה לְמ׳, 37^{31} (2 K 19^{30}) ועשׂה פרי לְמ׳ (cf. Am 2^{9}, **1 a**), Ez 41$^{7 a β}$ (v$^{a a}$ *bis* לְמ׳ לְמ׳

=*higher and higher*), ψ 74^{5}; fig. וְהָיִיתָ רַק לְמ׳ Dt 28^{13} (cf. **a**), Pr 15^{24} אֹרַח חַיִּים לְמ׳ (opp. שְׁאוֹל לְמ׳ : מָ֑טָּה), cf. Ec 3^{21}; sq. a noun, Ezr 9^{6} לְמ׳ ראשׁ *over* the head, sq. מֵעַל (cf. *Aboth* 2^{1} לְמַעְלָה מִן)= *above*, 2 Ch 34^{4}: v. also **b** *a*, *b a*. (*b*) metaph. =*exceedingly*, only in Chr, 1 Ch 14^{2} 22^{5} the house must be built to J. לְהַגְדִּיל לְמ׳ so as to shew greatness *exceedingly*, 23^{17} וּבְנֵי ר׳ רָבוּ לְמ׳, 29^{3} (sq. מִן; =*over and above* . . .), v^{25} 2 Ch 1^{1} וַיְגַדְּלֵהוּ לְמ׳, 20^{19}; עַד לְמַ֫עְלָה, 16^{12} 17^{12} 26^{8}. †**d.** מִלְמַ֫עְלָה (v. מִן **9 a**), adv., *above* (the more usual *prose* syn. of מִמַּעַל): Gn 6^{16} אֶל־אַמָּה תְּכַלֶּנָּה מ׳, 7^{20} 15 cubits מ׳ (i.e. above the mountain-tops), Ex 25^{21} (40^{20}) וְנָתַתָּ֫ה אֶת־הַכַּפֹּרֶת על הארון מ׳ upon the ark *above*, 26^{14} (36^{19} 40^{19} Nu 4^{25}) a covering of skins on the tent מ׳ *above*, 39^{31} Nu 4^{6}, 1 K 7^{11} 7^{25} 8^{7} (2 Ch 4^{4} 5^{8}), Je 31^{37} אִם יִמַּדּוּ שָׁמַיִם מ׳ (cf. **1 a**), Ez 1^{11} פְּרֻדוֹת מ׳ separate *above*, v$^{22.26}$ 10^{19} 11^{22} 37^{8}; *from above*, Jos 3$^{13.16}$ הַמַּיִם הַיֹּרְדִים מ׳.

4609 †I. [מַעֲלָה] **n.f. what comes up**;—pl. cstr. מַעֲלוֹת רוּחֲכֶם Ez 11^{5}, i.e. your thoughts.

4609 II. מַעֲלָה$_{46}$ **n.f.** step, stair;—מ׳ Ezr 7^{9} 1 Ch 17^{17}; pl. מַעֲלוֹת Is 38^{8}+, sf. מַעֲלֹתָו Am 9^{6}, etc.;—**1.** *step, stair* of temple Ez 40^{6}+5 t. 40, and temple porch 40^{49}; of altar Ex 20^{26} (E) (forbidden, cf. RS$^{OTJC\ xii,\ n.\ 1;\ 2nd\ ed.\ 358}$) Ez 43^{17} (prescribed); of house 2 K 9^{13}, of throne 1 K 10$^{19.20}$ 2 Ch 9$^{18.19}$; to the city of David Ne 3^{15} 12^{37}. **2.** *steps* (forming sun-dial, cf. Di^{Is}) 2 K 20$^{9.9.10.10}$ $^{11.11.11}$= Is 38$^{8.8.8.8.8}$. **3.** *stories* of heaven Am 9^{6}. **4.** *ascent* מִבָּבֶל Ezr 7^{9}. **5.** שִׁיר (ל)הַמַּעֲלוֹת *song of ascents*, to the three great pilgrim feasts, i.e. to be sung on way up to Jerusalem, titles of ψψ 120–134+84^{6} We al.—כְּתוֹר האדם המעלה 1 Ch 17^{17} is crpt., v. Comm.$^{ad\ loc.}$ (and on ‖ 2 S 7^{19}).

8585 †I. תְּעָלָה **n.f. water-course**;—ת׳ Je 30^{13}+; cstr. תְּעָלַת Is 7^{3}+2 t.; pl. sf. תְּעָלֹתֶיהָ Ez 31^{4};—**1. a.** *water-course*, conducted for irrigation Ez 31^{4}; hence poet., channel for rain Jb 38^{25}. **b.** *conduit*, 2 K 18^{17}=Is 36^{2}, Is 7^{3}, cf. 2 K 20^{20}. **c.** *trench*, 1 K 18$^{32.35.38}$.

8585 †II. תְּעָלָה **n.f. healing** (of new flesh and skin forming over wound);—(fig.) Je 30^{13} 46^{11}.

5920-21 עַל, עַ֫ל (cf. Kö$^{ii.\ 261\ f.}$) **I. subst. height** (poet.) †Ho 7^{16} יָשׁוּבוּ לֹא עָל they return (but) not *up*wards (i.e. not God-wards), 11^{7} וְאֶל־עַל יִקְרָאֻהוּ they (the prophets) call it (the people) *up*wards, (but) none striveth to rise; as adv. accus., 2 S 23^{1} the man הֻקַם עָל (that) is raised up *on high*. With מִן, מֵעַל+ (ה)שמים מֵעָ֑ל (the) heavens *above* Gn 27^{39} 49^{25} ψ 50^{4} (opp. מִתַּחַת Ex 20^{4}. In prose מִמַּעַל).

II. As **prep. upon, and hence on the** 5921
ground of, according to, on account of, on behalf of, concerning, beside, in addition to, together with, beyond, above, over, by, on to, towards, to, against (SI$^{4.6}$; Moab. Aram. *id.*; Ph. על, and עלת; Palm. Nab. על; Sab. עלי, Ar. عَلَى;—abbrev. from עֲלֵי (cf. אֱלֵי, עֲדֵי), which is preserved in poetry, Gn 49$^{17.17.22.22}$ Nu 24$^{6.6}$ Dt 32$^{2.2}$ Is 18^{4} Je 8^{18} Mi 5^{6} La 4^{5} 1 K 20^{41} Qr, Jb 7^{1} Qr+10 t. ψ, 3 t. Pr, 15 t. Jb; with sf. עָלַי; עָלֶיךָ, עָלַ֫יִךְ (+ψ 116^{7} the Aramaizing form עָלָ֫יְכִי); עָלָיו, עָלוֹ +1 S 2^{10}, עָלֶיהָ; 1 pl. עָלֵינוּ; 2 mpl. עֲלֵיכֶם, +Ex 12^{13} עֲלֵכֶם, 2 fpl. עֲלֵיכֶן +Ez 23^{49}; 3 mpl. עֲלֵיהֶם, 13 t. in Pent. עֲלֵהֶם Gn 45^{15}, etc. (Kö$^{ii.\ 305}$), poet. עָלֵ֫ימוֹ Dt 22^{23}+11 t. ψ, Jb (perh. sts. sg., Ges$^{§\ 103\ f,\ N.}$); 3 fpl. עֲלֵיהֶן, +Lv 3$^{4.10.15}$ עֲלֵהֶן (on the appar. *plur.* form of עֲלֵי, עָלַי, etc., v. Kö$^{ii.\ 309\ ff.}$, and cf. sub עַד).

1. Upon, of the substratum *upon* which an object in any way rests, or *on* which an action is performed; as על־הארץ *upon* the earth Gn 1$^{11.26}$ 7^{6}, etc., ψ 110^{6} על ארץ רבה *over* a wide country; על האדמה *upon* the ground Ex 20^{12} +oft., Am 7^{12} עַל אֲדָמָה טְמֵאָה, Is 14^{2} על אדמת י׳, ψ 137^{4} עַל אַדְמַת נֵכָר (אֲדָמָה being properly *ground, soil*, is construed regularly with עַל, על פני באדמה being very rare), more definitely על פני האדמה Gn 6^{1} Nu 12^{3}+oft.; על מקום Lv 14^{28} Je 45^{5} (uncommon: usu. בְּ); Dt 17^{20} Is 9^{6} עַל מַמְלַכְתּוֹ *upon* his realm, 2 Ch 1^{1}; עַל בָּתִּים very strangely Ho 11^{11} (rd. וַהֲשִׁבֹתִים with 𝔊: v. **7 c** *a β*); constantly after such vbs. as נוח, ישׁב, רכב, etc., Gn 8^{4} Ex 11^{5}; כתב על to write (idiom.) *on* a book or other surface, Jos 10^{13}, etc.; יצא על go forth *over* Gn 41^{45} Zc 5^{3} ψ 81^{6}; with נִשְׁעַן, נִסְמַךְ, בָּטַח (fig.), to lean or trust *upon*: Gn 3^{14} to go עַל גְּחֹנְךָ *upon* thy belly, 32^{32} to limp עַל יְרֵכוֹ *upon* his thigh, 1 S 14^{13} Ez 37^{10}; Ju 15^{8} to smite שׁוֹק עַל יָרֵךְ leg *upon* thigh, i.e. so that the scattered limbs fall one upon another, Am 3^{15}. And with ref. not to a horizontal surface but to a *side*, Lv 1^{5}+זָרַק עַל to pour *against* the altar, 1 K 6$^{5.18}$ to build *against* the temple, Jos 10^{27}, etc. Fig. Ex 23^{13} let it not be heard עַל פִּיךָ *upon* thy mouth (in our idiom, *upon thy lips*, as Pr 22^{18}), ψ 15^{3} לֹא רָגַל עַל לְשֹׁנוֹ he slandereth not (i.e. prepares not slander) *upon* his tongue, 2 S 23[2] וּמִלָּתוֹ עַל לְשׁוֹנִי, Pr 16[23.27] 31[26] Ec 5[1]; cf. נָשָׂא עַל שְׂפָתַיִם or עַל פֶּה ψ 16[4] 50[16]; Ez 36[3 b].

Specially **a.**—(*a*) of *clothing*, etc., which any one wears, Gn 37[23] the tunic אשר עליו which was *upon* him, Jos 9[5] 1 K 11[30] Ru 3[15]+; Gn 24[30] 38[30] 2 S 13[18], of a sword 20[8] Ct 3[8]; so הָיָה עַל Lv 16[4] Dt 22[5] Ez 44[18] 1 Ch 15[27] 18[7] (‖ 2 S 8[7] אֶל: see p. 41 a); cf. לֹא יַעֲלֶה עָלֶיךָ Lv 19[19] Ez 44[17], and with הֶעֱלָה, below, **7 b**.

(*b*) With verbs of *covering* or *protecting*, even though the cover or veil be not *over* or *above* the thing covered, but *around* or *before* it ('upon' referred to a *side*): v. סָכַךְ, כָּסָה, גָּנַן, עָטָה; Ne 2[8] יד אלהי הטובה עלי, cf. v[18] Ezr 7[6.9] 8[18.22.31]; Ex 27[21] the veil that is *over* (i.e. *before*) the testimony, 1 S 25[16] חוֹמָה הָיוּ עָלֵינוּ they were a wall *about* us; סָגַר עַל to shut *in* (or *down*) *upon* Ex 14[3] Jb 12[14]; Ez 13[5] Jb 13[27] 26[9] 36[30] he spreadeth his light עָלָיו *about* him.

b. Of what rests heavily *upon* a person, or is a burden to him, Is 1[14] הָיוּ עָלַי לָטֹרַח they are a cumbrance *upon* me, Jb 7[20] I am a burden עָלַי *upon* myself, 2 S 15[33] (cf. with אֶל 19[36]); כָּבֵד עַל to be heavy *upon* Ex 5[9] al. (v. כָּבֵד); of sin, calamity, etc. Is 53[5] Ez 33[10] ψ 88[8] Jb 21[9] 2 Ch 15[5] 28[13] Ec 6[1] 8[6] (cf. **5 a** β); Lv 7[20] וְטֻמְאָתוֹ עָלָיו 22[3]: idiomatically, Gn 48[7] מֵתָה עָלַי רָחֵל Rachel died *upon* me (i.e. to my sorrow), 33[13] וְהַבָּקָר עָלוֹת עָלָי are giving suck *upon* me (i.e. as a care to me), Nu 11[13] יִבְכּוּ עָלַי they weep *upon* me (vexing me), Ju 14[16.17] 19[2] (v. Be), 1 S 21[16] to play the mad man *upon* me, Je 12[11].

c. Of a duty, payment, care, etc., imposed *upon* a person, or devolving *on* him, as שִׂים עַל to lay *upon* Ex 5[8] 21[22.30] (שִׁית), 22[24], cf. Gn 47[26] 2 Ch 35[25]; with other verbs, Jb 38[10] Dt 24[5] 26[6] 2 K 15[20] 18[14] 23[33] Ne 10[33.33] Est 1[8] 9[21.27.31]; with צִוָּה enjoin *upon* Gn 2[16]+oft., כתב prescribe *to* 2 K 22[13] ψ 40[8], נטשׁ cast *upon* 1 S 17[20] (v[22] על יד), נתן על יד (fig.) Gn 42[37] 2 K 12[12] 22[5], cf. 1 K 14[27], עזב ψ 10[14], גלל 37[5], השליך 55[23], פקד Jb 34[13] al.; Gn 30[28] נָקְבָה שְׂכָרְךָ עָלַי fix thy wages *upon* me (*name* thy wages *to* me), 34[12] הַרְבּוּ עָלַי מְאֹד מֹהַר וּמַתָּן multiply *upon* me, etc., 2 S 19[39] (pregn.) whatsoever thou choosest (and layest) *upon* me; without a verb, Ju 19[20] רַק כָּל־מַחְסֹרְךָ עָלַי only let all thy wants be *upon* me, Ezr 10[4] ψ 56[13] עָלַי נְדָרֶיךָ thy vows are *upon* me (i.e. I owe them: cf. Nu 30[7.9.15]), Pr 7[14] זִבְחֵי שְׁלָמִים עָלָי peace-offerings were *upon* me (=were due from me); perh. ψ 62[1] 77[1] (to the charge of); with an inf. 2 S 18[11] וְעָלַי לָתֵת and it would have been *incumbent on* me to give, etc., 1 K 4[7] Ezr 10[12] (accents [Baer], RV[m]), Ne 13[13], cf. Zc 12[2] (Ew RV[m]); Nu 7[9] (P) the service of . . . was *upon* them, Ez 45[17], so especially late 1 Ch 9[27.33] 23[31] 2 Ch 2[3] לעולם זאת על ישראל, 8[15] 24[9] Ezr 7[11] Ne 11[23]; Is 9[5] and the government is *upon* his shoulder (cf. 22[22]), 2 Ch 25[3]; ψ 7[11] מָגִנִּי עַל־א׳ my shield rests *upon* God (he has undertaken my defence), 62[8] עַל־אלהים יִשְׁעִי וּכְבוֹדִי.

d. עַל is used idiom. to give pathos to the expression of an emotion, by emphasizing the person who is its subject, and who, as it were, feels it acting *upon* him: ψ 42[6] why art thou cast down, O my soul, וַתֶּהֱמִי עָלָי and disquieted *upon me?* v[7] my soul *upon me* is cast down, v[12] 43[5] La 3[20]; ψ 131[2] כְּגָמֻל עָלַי אִמּוֹ כַּגָּמוּל עָלַי נַפְשִׁי is my soul *upon me;* 142[4] בְּהִתְעַטֵּף עָלַי רוּחִי when my spirit faints *upon me,* 143[4] Jon 2[8]; Je 8[18] עָלַי לִבִּי דַוָּי׃ my heart *upon me* is sick, Jb 14[22.22] (cf. Di), Hos 11[8] נהפך עלי לבי my heart is turned (altered) *upon me,* 1 S 17[32] 25[36] Ne 5[7] וַיִּמָּלֵךְ לִבִּי עָלַי and my heart took counsel *upon me:* cf. ψ 42[5] I will pour out my soul *upon me,* Jb 30[16]; 10[1] אעזבה עלי שׂיחי I will let loose my complaint *upon me.* (Thes *apud me, mecum.* The rend. '*within* me' alters entirely the point of view of the Heb. expression, and is incorrect.) Denoting with some emph. the subj. of an experience, Jb 30[2] עלימו אבד כָּלַח, Dn 2[1] his sleep נִהְיְתָה עָלָיו was done with *upon* him (cf. Aram. 6[19] נַדַּת עֲלוֹהִי), 10[8] וְהוֹדִי נֶהְפַּךְ עָלַי (cf. 5[9] 7[28]): also, rather differently, Lv 18[18 b] Je 49[20] אִם לֹא יַשִּׁים עֲלֵיהֶם נְוֵהֶם, Mi 7[13] ψ 90[17 b]; ψ 7[9] acc. to my perfectness *upon* me, Ez 18[20]; 22[3] 2 Ch 36[8].

e. חָיָה עַל to live *upon* (as upon a foundation or support; cf. Is 3[1], and ζῆν ἐπί τινος), Dt 8[3] עַל־הַלֶּחֶם, Is 38[16] (cf. Hi), Gn 27[40] על חרבך תחיה *upon* (=*by*) thy sword thou shalt live (cf. Kazwini[ii. 17] *ap.* Tuch), Ez 33[19], cf. v[26].

f. Of the *ground*, or *basis*, *on* which a thing is done, as Gn 24[9] על הדבר הזה, Lv 7[12] if he offers it עַל תּוֹדָה *on the ground of* a thanksgiving, Nu 6[21] עַל נִזְרוֹ, v[b] Ez 16[15] 28[17] Dn 8[25] עַל שִׂכְלוֹ, 9[18] על צדקותינו (with عَلَى this use is extended so as to denote explicitly *on condition of*). Hence (*a*) the basis being conceived as *regulative*, על comes to denote the *norm* or *standard* (cf. Germ. '*auf* die Art'; W AG ii. § 59 *i*): the transition may be seen in a passage like Ex 24^{8} the covenant which ׳י made with you *on the basis of* (על), or *in agreement with*, all these words (cf. על פי 34^{27}), Nu 35^{24} על המשפטים האלה, Dt 17^{11} Je 30^{18} the palace shall sit (i.e. be inhabited: v. ישב) עַל מִשְׁפָּטוֹ *in accordance with* its manner, ψ 94^{20} who frames mischief עֲלֵי־חֹק *in accordance with* a law, . . . על פי *acc. to* the mouth (i.e. command, Gn 45^{21} + oft., evidence Dt 17^{6} 19^{15}, sentence 21^{5}) of . . .; . . . עַל שֵׁם *acc. to* the name of . . . (mostly with *call, be called*) Gn 48^{6} Ex 28^{21} 2 S 18^{18} +, cf. 1 Ch 23^{14}; Ex 6^{26} 12^{51} עַל צִבְאֹתָם *acc. to* their hosts (usu. לְ), Nu 1^{18} על משפחתם (usu. לְ), v^{52} 2$^{2.34}$ 7^{3} (‖ לְ), Dt 18^{8} (prob.); עַל יְדֵי *acc. to* the hands (direction) of Je 5^{31} 33^{13} *al.* (v.p. 391 b); ψ 110^{4} עַל דִּבְרָתִי מ׳ *after* the manner of M.; Pr 25^{11} (prob.) a word spoken עַל אָפְנָיו *in accordance with* its circumstances = appositely; of the tune *acc. to* which a song is to be sung (RV. *set* to) ψ 6^{1} (1 Ch 15^{21}), 8^{1} 9^{1} 12^{1} 45^{1} 46^{1} (1 Ch 15^{20}) עַל־עֲלָמוֹת (perh., however, *in the manner of* maidens = for 'sopranos'), 53^{1} 56^{1} 60^{1} 69^{1} 81^{1} 84^{1} 88^{1} (cf. in Syr. ܥܠ ܩܠܐ ܕ).

(*b*) The basis being conceived as involving the *ground*, על denotes the cause or reason, *on account of, because of*, Gn 20^{3} lo thou shalt die עַל הָאִשָּׁה *on account* of the woman, 21^{12} 26$^{7.9}$ 27^{41} 42^{21} Lv 4$^{3.28}$ 5^{18} 19^{17} 26$^{18.24.28}$ Dt 9^{18} 24^{16} fathers shall not be put to death על־בנים *on account of* children, 31^{18} Jos 9^{20} Je 1^{16} 5^{9} Ez 18^{26} עליהם (‖ 33^{18} בָּהֶם), Pr 28^{21} ψ 39^{12} 50^{8} + oft.; ψ 44^{23} עָלֶיךָ הֹרַגְנוּ *on thy account* are we slain all the day, 69^{8} Je 15^{15}; in the phrases על דְּבַר, על אודות, על זאת and עַל זֶה . . . *on* this *account*, עַל מָה *on* what *account?* עַל־כֵּן = *therefore* (v. דָּבָר, אוֹדָה, etc.); before an inf., as Ex 17^{7} וְעַל נַסֹּתָם אֶת־י׳ and *on account* of their trying ׳י, Am 1^{3} עַל דּוּשָׁם *on account of* their threshing = because they threshed, v$^{6.9.11.13}$, etc., Je 2^{35} עַל אָמְרֵךְ *because of* thy saying, 9^{12} 16^{18} +; and as a conj. both with and without אֲשֶׁר or כִּי (v. infr. **III**). And so often of the ground or cause of fear, grief, delight, or other emotions, e.g. Ex 18^{9} 32^{14} (נִחַם *repent:* so oft.), 1 S 4^{13} 30^{6} 2 S 1^{26} 3^{8} 1 K 21^{4} 2 K 6^{11} Je 10^{19} Am 6^{6}.

(*c*) Somewhat more strongly, *on behalf of, for the sake of*, Gn 19^{17} escape על נפשך *for* thy life; Ju 9^{17} 2 K 10^{3} נִלְחַם עַל (usu. לְ); 1 K 2^{18} I will speak *on thy behalf* to the king, v^{19} (2 K 4^{13} לְ); Est 4^{16}; 4^{8} 7^{7}; 8^{11} 9^{16} Dn 12^{1} עמד על stand up (in late Heb.) *on behalf of;* התפלל על intercede *for* (usu. בעד) Jb 42^{8} Ne 1^{6} 2 Ch 30^{18}; 29^{21} Ezr 8^{35}; and very often with כִּפֶּר (q.v.) make atonement *for*. (Not very common with other verbs.)

(*d*) Sometimes it acquires almost a final force, *for;* Ex 12^{4} 29^{36} 30^{16} Dt 27^{13} there shall stand עַל־הַקְּלָלָה (‖ v^{12} לְבָרֵךְ), ψ 89^{48} עַל־מַה־שָּׁוְא בָּרָאתָ כָל־בְּנֵי־אָדָם *unto* what vanity hast thou created, etc.! Pr 29$^{5\,b}$ 2 Ch 23^{18} Ec 3^{17}.

(*e*) Of a *condition*, or *attendant circumstances* (rare; so عَلَى, W AG ii. § 59 *e*): ψ 50^{5} עֲלֵי זָבַח׃ *upon, with* sacrifice, 92^{4} עֲלֵי עָשׂוֹר וגו׳ *with* a ten-stringed instr., *with* a harp, *with* sounding music on a lyre; עַל רִיב *upon occasion of* a law-suit Ex 23^{2} Ez 44^{24}, על יום טוב 1 S 25^{8} (cf. عَلَى حِينٍ *at a time of* . . . Qor 28^{14}), Ne 12^{22} (? rd. עַד BeRy), Is 18^{4} כְּחֹם צַח עֲלֵי אוֹר *at time* of sunshine, 64^{11} עַל אֵלֶּה, Je 8^{18} עֲלֵי יָגוֹן *at time of* sorrow, 16^{7} (but Gie עַל אֵבֶל *to*): with abstr. substs. to form a periphr. for adverbs, Lv 5^{22} and swear עַל שָׁקֶר *upon* falseness = falsely, Je 6^{14} = 8^{11} to heal a wound עַל נְקַלָּה *lightly, easily*, ψ 31^{24} עַל יֶתֶר = *abundantly*, Is 60^{7} עַל רָצוֹן = *acceptably* (cf. عَلَى لَذَّةٍ = *with* delight).

(*f*) It hence acquires the force of *in spite of, notwithstanding* (so عَلَى, W AG ii. § 59 *h*), Jb 10^{7} עַל דַּעְתְּךָ *in spite of* thy knowing, 34^{6} על משפטי *notwithstanding* my right I am to be a liar (Di De Da RV: otherwise Hi RV^{m}). Cf. below, **III c** *b*.

(*g*) *Upon, concerning*, with vbs. of speaking, as דִּבֶּר Ju 9^{3} 1 K 5^{13}, אָמַר Je 16^{3} 27^{19} (‖ אל) 33^{4}, hearing Gn 41^{15} שָׁמַעְתִּי עָלֶיךָ I have heard *concerning* thee, saying, etc., 1 K 10^{6} Is 37^{9} (‖ 2 K 19^{9} אל), disputing Gn 26^{21}, telling 1 S 27^{11} Jo 1^{3}, commanding 2 S 14^{8} 1 K 11^{10}, being vexed 21^{4} 2 K 6^{11}, crying 8^{5}, confessing ψ 32^{5} Ne 1^{6}; of the object of a prophecy or vision 1 K 22^{8} Is 1^{1} 2^{1}; and often with similar verbs.

(*h*) In a somewhat weaker sense, *in the matter of, as regards*, Gn 41^{32} וְעַל הִשָּׁנוֹת הַחֲלוֹם, Ex 22^{8} Ru 4^{7} Lv 5$^{22.26}$ Dn 9$^{14\,b}$ Ne 9^{33}; חָטָא עַל Lv 4^{14} (‖ בָּהּ v^{23}, cogn. acc. v^{28}), 5^{5} Nu 6^{11} Ne 13^{26}; עַל־דְּבַר . . . *in the matter of*, Nu 25^{18} 31^{16}.

2. It expresses *excess* (synon. מִן q.v.); Gn 48^{22} I give thee שְׁכֶם אַחַד עַל אַחֶיךָ one shoulder (ridge) *above* thy brethren, Ex 16^{5} מִשְׁנֶה עַל double *above* or *beyond*, Nu 3^{46} Dt 25^{3} stripes עַל־אֵלֶּה *beyond* these, Jos 3^{15} Jordan מָלֵא עַל was full *over* all its banks (cf. 4^{18} Is $8^{7\,b}$ עלה ,הלך על), ψ 138^{2} Ec 1^{16} Dn 1^{20} עֶשֶׂר יָדוֹת עַל ten times *above* (cf. in Aram. 3^{19}, and عَلَى Qor 37^{153}), Ezr 1^{6} +עַל לְבַד = *beside* (v. בַּד); ψ 16^{2} (si vera l.) טוֹבָתִי בַּל עָלֶיךָ my welfare is not *beyond* thee, i.e. does not lie outside thee.—Of *time*, Lv 15^{25} if she has an issue עַל נִדָּתָהּ *beyond* her time of impurity (cf. Is 32^{10}, **4 b**).

3. It denotes *elevation* or *pre-eminence*, as עליון על high (fig.) *above*, Dt 26^{19} *al.*, 28^{43} יעלה עליך will go up *above* thee, cf. Pr 31^{29}; ψ $57^{6.12}$ be thou exalted *above* the heavens, 89^{8} 95^{3} 96^{4}, etc., Ne 9^{5}; with words (q.v.) such as גבר ,גדל ,חזק ,נשׂא (Ni. Pi. Hithp.), עזז, and esp. those denoting rule or superintendence, as מלך ,הפקיד; so with שִׁית ,היה ,נתן, Gn $41^{33.40.43}$, שׂם 1 S 18^{5}; with פָּקִיד ,שַׂר ,מֶלֶךְ, etc., Gn 41^{34} Ex 1^{11} 18^{21}, etc.; abs. 2 S 8^{16} Joab was על־הצבא *over* the host, $20^{23\,b.24}$ 1 K 4^{4-6} 5^{30}; Nu $10^{14\,ff.}$ 1 Ch $9^{23.26\,ff.}$ $27^{25\,ff.}$ 2 Ch 30^{17} 31^{12}; אֲשֶׁר עַל בֵּיתוֹ of Joseph's steward Gn $43^{16.19}$ $44^{1.4}$; and in the official titles אֲשֶׁר עַל־הַבַּיִת = the Governor of the Palace Is 22^{15} al. (v. בַּיִת **6**); אֲשֶׁר עַל־הַמַּס the overseer of the forced labour 1 K 12^{18}; אשׁר על־העיר the governor of the city 2 K 10^{5}, אשׁר על המלתחה v^{22}.

4. It expresses *addition* (cf. ἐπί in Gk., e.g. ἐπὶ τούτοις); viz. **a.** introducing the complement of a verb, as with יָסַף to add *upon* or *to*, ψ 61^{7} + oft. (v. יָסַף), שִׁית to put *to* Gn 30^{40}, נִלְוָה to be joined *to* Nu $18^{2.4}$ Is 14^{1} (also c. אֶל), נָפַל to fall *to*, i.e. desert to, Je 21^{9} +, עבר to pass *over to* Ex $30^{13.14}$ Is 45^{14} (cf. 60^{5}); also Hb 2^{16} תִּסֹּב כּוֹס עַל La 4^{21}, Est 4^{7}; נֶחְשַׁב to be reckoned *to* Lv 25^{31} 2 S 4^{2}, היה על Nu 36^{12}; ψ 69^{28} תְּנָה עָוֹן עַל עֲוֹנָם, Is 56^{8} עוֹד אֲקַבֵּץ עָלָיו I will yet gather (others) *unto* him.

b. Used absol., as Gn 28^{9} he took Maḥalath עַל נָשָׁיו *in addition to* his (other) wives, 31^{50} (cf. אל Lv 18^{18}), Nu 31^{8} עַל חַלְלֵיהֶם *in addition to* their slain (‖ Jos 13^{22} אֶל), Dt 23^{14} Ez $16^{37.43}$ 25^{10}; Is 32^{10} יָמִים עַל שָׁנָה days *upon, in addition to*, a year, 2 Ch 31^{16} יָמִים עַל יָמִים, Ez 7^{26} הֹוָה עַל הֹוָה תָּבוֹא (‖ אל), Je 4^{20} (if נִקְרָא = *be proclaimed*), Jb 16^{14} יִפְרְצֵנִי פֶרֶץ עַל־פְּנֵי־פָרֶץ (cf. Lag [M iii. 112]; also Il. 14^{130} ἕλκος ἐφ' ἕλκει, Odyss. $7^{120\,f.}$, Qor 31^{13}). So often in laws of P (cf. **c**), Lv 7^{12} he shall offer עַל־זֶבַח הַתּוֹדָה *in addition to* the sacrifice of thanksgiving, etc., $v^{13\,b}$ Nu 6^{20} 15^{9} $28^{10.15.24}$ (cf. מִלְּבַד v^{31} 29^{6}), 35^{6}; Ez 16^{43} (Hi Sm RV: cf. 44^{7} אל).

c. Hence by an easy transition it denotes *together with, with*, Ex 35^{22} men *together with* (על) women, Jb 38^{32} וְעַיִשׁ עַל־בָּנֶיהָ תַנְחֵם and the Bear *with* her children, wilt thou lead them? 1 K 15^{20} Je 3^{18} the house of Isr. *with* the house of Judah, Mi 5^{2} (Ca Ke Kue; but al. as **7 c** *a*), Gn 32^{12} lest he come and smite me, אֵם עַל בָּנִים the mother *with* the children (cf. Ho 10^{14} Dt 22^{6}); and as a techn. term in the regulations for sacrifice, esp. with אכל, Ex 12^{8} עַל־מְרֹרִים יֹאכְלֻהוּ *together with* bitter herbs they shall eat it, v^{9} his head *with* (על) his legs, etc., Nu 9^{11} Dt 16^{3} לֹא־תֹאכַל עָלָיו חָמֵץ (cf. Ex 23^{18} 34^{25}), v^{3}; in the phrase אכל על הדם to eat *with* the blood 1 S $14^{32.33}$ (v^{34} אל), Lv 19^{26} Ez 33^{25} (cf. in Gk. e.g. ἐπὶ τῷ σίτῳ πίνειν ὕδωρ); see also Lv $2^{2.16}$ 3^{4} (so $v^{10.15}$ 4^{9} 7^{4}), 4^{11} $7^{13\,a.30}$ 10^{15} 14^{31} $23^{18.20}$ Nu 6^{17} 19^{5}; 1 Ch 7^{4}.

5. It expresses the idea of being suspended, or extended, *over* anything, without however being in contact with it, **above, over**: Gn 1^{20} let fowl fly *over* the earth, 19^{23} השׁמשׁ יצא על had come forth *upon* the earth (cf. זרח על Ex 22^{2} +; בא על go down [set] *upon* Dt 24^{15} Mi 3^{6}; Jb 25^{3}), Nu 10^{34} 14^{14} and thy cloud stood עליהם *over* them, Dt 28^{23} the heavens על־ראשׁך *above* thy head, Is 4^{5} $60^{1.2}$ Zp 2^{11} Zc 9^{14} ψ 7^{8} *over* it return thou on high, Jb 29^{3} בְּהִלּוֹ נֵרוֹ עֲלֵי רֹאשִׁי (cf. דעך על be extinguished *over*, 18^{6}), Ct 2^{4} his banner *over* me: fig. of protection Dt 32^{38} ψ 68^{35}: with vbs. of motion (expressed or implied), נשׁקף על to incline *over* 1 S 13^{18} +, נטה ידו על Ex 14^{16} Is 23^{11} + (cf. ψ 21^{12}), הניף על to swing *over* Is 11^{15} 19^{16}; השׁמיע על to proclaim *over* Je 4^{16} Am 3^{9}, cf. Nu 10^{10} 2 Ch 13^{12}, נקרא שׁם על a name to be called *over* 2 S 12^{28} + (v. קרא).

6. From the sense of *inclining* or *impending over*, על comes to denote *contiguity* or *proximity*, Engl. *by* (or sts. *on*):—**a.** in designating localities, esp. those beside water, Gn 14^{6} עַל־הַמִּדְבָּר *by* the wilderness, 16^{7} עַל עֵין הַמַּיִם *by* the spring of water, $24^{13.30}$ 29^{2} three flocks lying עָלֶיהָ *by* it (the well), 41^{1} Nu 3^{26} 13^{29} עַל־הַיָּם *by* the sea, 22^{5} 24^{6} gardens עֲלֵי נָהָר

Dt 3^{12} 33^{8} Ju 5^{19} 7^{1} 1 S 1^{9} על מזוזת היכל י׳ (Ez 46^{2}), 4^{1} 2 K 2^{7} and they stood על־הירדן *by* the Jordan, 25^{4} Is 19^{7} 38^{20} ψ 1^{3} planted *by* water-courses, Je $17^{2.8}$ Jb 30^{4} 31^{9} על פתח *by* the entrance, Pr 14^{19}, + oft.; על הדרך *by* the way Gn 38^{21} 1 S 24^{4}; Ez $48^{24\,ff.}$ על גבולו *adjoining* his border; עבר על to pass *by* a place 1 K 9^{18} Je 18^{16} +, fig. עבר על פשע to pass *by* transgression, i.e. to overlook it, Mi 7^{18} al.: על יְמִין . . . *on* the right of . . . ψ 110^{5} +, עַל יֶרֶךְ . . . , עַל יַד . . . , עַל כֶּתֶף . . . *on* the side of . . . (see these words): less freq. (exc. as **c**) with ref. to persons, Nu 2^{5} וְהַחֹנִים עָלָיו and those encamping *next* him, v$^{12.20.27}$ 6^{9} וכי ימות מת עליו, 2 K 11^{11} *by* the king round about (cf. Nu 3^{26} supr.), עבר על פ׳ Gn 18^{5} 2 K 4^{9} +.

b. 2 S $9^{7.10}$ to eat bread עַל שֻׁלְחַן פ׳ *at* any one's table, Ex 16^{3} when we sat עַל־סִיר הַבָּשָׂר, 1 S 20^{24} Kt to sit עַל־הַלֶּחֶם *at* meat; 25^{13} 30^{24} to remain עַל־הַכֵּלִים; Pr 23^{30} to tarry long על־היין *at* (or *over*) the wine, Jb 39^{9} עַל־אֲבוּסֶךָ׃ *at* thy crib: cf. הַיּוֹשֵׁב עַל הַמִּשְׁפָּט Is 28^{6}.

c. Idiomatically, with עָמַד and נִצַּב to stand *by* (lit. *over*,—orig. no doubt with ref. to one supposed to be seated), Gn 18^{2} three men נִצָּבִים עָלָיו standing *by* him, v^{8} and he עֹמֵד עליו standing *by* him under the tree, 24^{30} *by* the camels, 28^{13} 1 S 4^{20} 2 S 1^{9} 12^{17} $20^{11.12}$ Am 7^{7}; esp. of persons standing *about* a superior, as servants or courtiers, Gn 45^{1} Ju 3^{19} 1 S $22^{6.7.17}$, of persons surrounding a judge Ex $18^{13.14}$, of י׳'s heavenly ministers, 1 K 22^{19} (cf. Is 6^{2} ממעל לו), Zc 4^{16}, and with התיצב 6^{5} Jb 1^{6} 2^{1}; also of one standing *by* (prop. leaning *over*) an altar or sacrifice Nu $23^{3.6}$ 1 K 13^{1} (cf. **7 b**) Am 9^{1}; of an Ashêrah *by* an altar Ju $6^{25.28}$ (cf. אֵצֶל Dt 16^{21}).

7. In connexion with verbs of *motion* (actual or fig.):—**a.** of motion from a higher place downwards, *down upon:* thus (*a*) המטיר על to rain *upon* Gn 2^{5} 19^{24}, ירד על 15^{11}, יצק על to pour *upon* Gn 28^{18}, נפל על צוארי פ׳ Gn 33^{4}, נפל על פניו to fall *on* his (own) face $17^{3.17}$, שׂם על to put *upon*, 21^{14} $22^{6.9}$ 24^{47} (v^{22} Sam Di), נתן על כף to place *on* the hand of . . . $40^{11.21}$, השליך על 2 S 20^{12}, etc.; cf. Jb 29^{22} וְעָלֵימוֹ תִּטֹּף מִלָּתִי, Mi 3^{5} Na 3^{12}.

(*b*) In diff. fig. connexions, as of sleep falling *upon* one, Gn 2^{21} 15^{12}; of fear 9^{2} 1 S 11^{7} (v. אֵימָה, חֲרָדָה, פַּחַד); of good or bad fortune, esp. the latter, coming *upon* one, as with בוא and הביא, Gn 27^{12} Dt 28^{2} (in good sense), v^{15}, Je 5^{12} 19^{3} (רעה, as oft.); of retribution, reproach, the Divine wrath, etc., with diff. verbs (הביא, נתן, ירד, חול, היה, etc.), as Gn 20^{9} Nu 12^{11} חטאה; Gn 42^{36} עָלַי הָיוּ כֻלָּנָה *upon me* are they all; Nu 18^{5} + (היה קֶצֶף על); Dt 19^{10} דם (cf. אל 2 S 21^{2} 𝔊 We Dr), Ju 9^{24} 1 K 2^{32} 2 S 16^{8} Ho 12^{15}; 2 S 3^{29}; 15^{14}; 1 S 11^{2} חרפה; Je 14^{16}; 26^{15} דם נקי (אל‖), Jon 1^{14}; Ez $7^{3.4.8}$ 23^{49} 36^{29}; ψ 7^{17} $94^{2.23}$ 109^{5} וישׂימו עלי רעה תחת טובה (*lay* upon me: but Hu וישיבו, Pr 17^{13}), 140^{11}; שָׁפַךְ חֵמָה על Ez 7^{8} + oft.; without a verb, Gn 16^{5} חֲמָסִי עָלֶיךָ my wrong be *upon* thee, Je 51^{35} (אל‖); Gn 27^{13} עלי קללתך; 38^{29} (accents, RV^{m}); 2 S 1^{16} דמיך על ראשך; 14^{9} עָלַי הֶעָוֹן; Is 24^{17} Je 48^{43}; 50^{27}; Ez 13^{3} הוֹי עַל . . .; ψ 55^{16} Kt.; of a blessing, Ex 32^{29} ψ 3^{9}, a curse Dt 30^{7}, mercies (prob. conceived spec. as descending *from heaven*) ψ 33^{22} 86^{13} 90^{17} 103^{17} (with גבר be mighty *over* or *upon*, v^{11} 117^{2}), 116^{12} 145^{9} Ezr 3^{11}, שלום ψ 125^{5} 128^{6} 1 Ch 22^{9}.

(*c*) Introducing the object *upon* which an action, or emotion, esp. if accompanied by a gesture, is conceived as being directed (but with some of these words, esp. when they refer to an *event*, rather than a person, as Ex 18^{9}, על is to be explained from **1 f** *b*). Thus with verbs denoting the manifestation of joy or grief, as שׂוש to rejoice *over*, התפאר, התענג, שׂמח, גיל, שׂחק, אבל, ספד, שׁמם, בכה Ju 11^{37} +, נשׂא קינה (משׁל) to take up a lament, or proverb, *over* (see these words); prob. also in הִנָּבֵא על prophecy *over* Ez 11^{4} 13^{17}+; with חום, חָמַל, רִחַם to shew compassion *on* (cf. 1 K 3^{26} [Gn 43^{30} אל], Ct 5^{4} [Je 31^{20} ל]); with שׁמר, שׁקד, הֵעִיר (Jb 8^{6}) to guard or watch *over;* with יעץ to counsel *upon* Is 14^{26} +, חשׁב to devise (usu. in bad sense, Je 29^{11} in good), דִּבֶּר (רעה Je 11^{17} +, טובה 18^{20} 32^{42}), הֵקִים דָּבָר Je 29^{10}. Of more distinctly phys. acts, with בכה to weep *on* Gn $45^{14.15}$ +, שׁרק *to hiss*, ספק or תקע כף *to clap the hand*, הִכָּה כף Ez 22^{13} (אל‖); Is 5^{30} to growl *over*, 31^{4} Ez 36^{2} Jb 30^{5}; הִתְוַדָּה to confess *over* (the goat), Lv 16^{21}; Ex $30^{10\,a}$ (prob.); Dt 21^{6}; Jb 6^{27} 40^{30}.

b. From a lower place upwards, *up upon*, *up to*, as עלה על to go up *upon:* Ex 20^{26} 1 S 2^{28} 1 K $12^{33\,b}$ 2 K $16^{12\,b}$ 2 Ch 1^{6} (an *altar*, i.e. to a ledge beside it; cf. 2 K 23^{9}, and ירד Lv 9^{22} 1 K 1^{53}); Ju 9^{51} Is 14^{14} 40^{9}, etc.; to come up *upon* (in diff. connexions) Ex 10^{12} Lv 16^{9} (fig.), 19^{19} 1 S 1^{11} 6^{7} 1 K $10^{16.17}$; fig. עלה על לב Is 65^{17} +

(v. לב, לבב, **3 d**); in Hiph. 1 K 20^{33} ויעלהו על הַמֶּרְכָּבָה, Am 8^{10} (cf. **1 a** *a*), 2 S 1^{24} Ez 37^{6} ψ 137^{6} (fig.), 2 Ch 3$^{5.14}$ (=*ornamented with*); Dt 28^{61} (cf. Ex 15$^{26\,b}$); 2 Ch 20^{34} the history of Jehu which הָעֳלָה על *was brought up upon* (i.e. inserted in) the book of, etc. (cf. 32^{32}; and כתב על supr. **1**); cf. נטה יד על־השמים *up to* heaven Ex 9^{22} 10^{21}; 17^{16}.

c. Expressing direction *towards* (not common, exc. in sense *against*: v. infr.)—(*a*) with verbs of motion, properly of a person (or thing) moving to another so as either to stand *above*, or rest *upon*, it (cf. Pusey$^{\text{Min. Pr. 333}}$), Ex 34^{12} הארץ אשר אתה בא עליה (simil., of a land, or place, 18^{23} Nu 11^{12} 1 K 2^{26} עֲנָתֹת לֵךְ עַל־שָׂדֶיךָ, Ez 32^{9} Je 3$^{18\,b}$ 16^{13} 22^{26}, and after שׁוּב or הֵשִׁיב 16^{15} 22^{27} 23^{3} 24^{6} [but אֶל 27^{22} 30^{3} *al.*], Ez 29^{14}; Gn 40^{13} וֶהֱשִׁיבְךָ עַל־כַּנֶּךָ, 41^{13}; 30^{33} כִּי תָבוֹא עַל שְׂכָרִי *to view* my hire; בא על נפש מֵת to enter in *upon* or *beside* a corpse; בא על אשה Gn 19^{31} Dt 25^{5} (usu. אל); Jos 3^{16} מַיִם יֹרְדִים עַל יָם, Ez 47^{8} 1 K 18^{12} יִשָּׂאֲךָ עַל־אֲשֶׁר לֹא־אֵדָע, ψ 19^{7}; 2 K 16^{12}; 2 Ch 20^{24}; Is 53^{1} *upon* whom (coming from above) was י׳'s arm revealed? 62^{10} הרימו נֵס על העמים *over towards* (but 49^{22} אל): but often it is dub. if this force is perceptible; and in gen. על in such cases seems to be used merely as a syn.—perh. as a slightly more graphic syn.—of אֶל (cf. p. 41); in the later language, also, it may be due partly to the infl. of Aram., which does not use אֶל; thus (*a*) with a *personal* obj., with *assemble* or *be assembled*, Ex 32^{1} 2 S 17^{11} 1 K 8^{5} 11^{24} 2 K 22^{20} (2 Ch 34^{28} and usu. אל), 2 Ch 13^{7}, עלה Gn 38^{12} Jos 2^{8} 1 S 14^{10} (v$^{9.12}$ אל), עבר 1 S 14^{4} (v^{1} אל), בא 2 S 15^{4} (v. Dr) 1 Ch 12$^{23\,f.}$, יצא 2 K 24^{12}, הוליך 25^{20}, נגע Ju 20$^{34.41}$ (cf. Is 6^{7} Je 1^{9}), נם Is 10^{3}, הלך 22^{15} (אל . . . על), נשׂא 30^{6}, שׁלח 2 K 18^{27} (על . . . אל . . . על: ‖ Is 36^{12} אל . . . אל . . . על), Je 26^{15} 29^{31} 1 Ch 13^{2} 2 Ch 28^{16} 30^{1} 32$^{9.31}$ 36^{15} Ne 6^{3}, נגשׁ Ez 9^{6}, שׁב, השׁיב Ne 4^{6} Ml 3^{24} (v. *c*), sq. על י׳ 2 Ch 15^{4} 30^{9}, התיצב 2 Ch 11^{13}; letters going על פ׳ Ne 2^{7} 6$^{17\,a}$ (v^{b} אל). (*β*) of *places*, Gn 24^{49} 2 S 2^{19}+ על ימין *to* the right; with הלך 1 S 2^{11} 1 K 20^{43} על־ביתו (21^{4} אל), 2 S 15^{20} ואני הולך על אשר אני הולך, Je 1^{7} Ez 1^{20} (v^{12} אל), הוליך 1 K 1^{38} (v^{33} אל), נהר Mi 4^{1} (‖ Is 2^{2} אל), עלה Je 31^{12} (אל . . . על), נגשׁ Ez 44^{13} (‖ אל), 1 S 24^{23} 2 S 19^{1} 1 K 6^{8} (‖ אל), Ez 41^{7}, בא Je 14^{3} 51^{51}, הביא (על הר) Is 66^{20} (56^{7} אל), ירד Je 36^{12}, הִטָּה Pr 21^{1}, הסיר 2 S 6^{10} (‖ 1 Ch 13^{13} אל), נתן Is 29^{12} (v^{11} אל) Mi 1^{14} 3^{5} Gn 42^{37}, שׁב, השׁיב Nu 33^{7} Je 11^{10} (fig., על עֲוֹנוֹת), ψ 35^{13} Jb 31^{15} (Gn 3^{19} אל), Pr 26^{11} Ec 1^{6}, 1 K 17$^{21.22}$ (cf. 1 S 30^{12} אל), השׁתחוה Lv 26^{1} (prob.), Is 60^{14}; pregn. Is 24^{22} אֻסְּפוּ על בּוֹר be collected (and delivered) *into* a dungeon: cf. חוּשׁ על Jb 31^{5} (fig.), also to requite עַל־חֵיק Is 65$^{6.7\,\text{Kt.}}$ (Je 32^{18} ψ 79^{12} אל). After נראה *appear*, ψ 90^{16} (אל . . . על). And *as far as, unto* (nearly = עַד) Gn 49^{13} וְיַרְכָתוֹ עַל צִידֹן, Jos 2^{7} 18^{13} 19^{12} Je 31^{39} Ez 47^{18} 48$^{21.28}$ ψ 48^{11} 1 Ch 5^{16}.

(*b*) With אמר say *to*, 2 K 22^{8} Je 18^{11} (אל . . . על), 22^{6} 23$^{2.35}$ (על . . . אל), 36^{29} 44^{20} (אל . . . על), דבר 1 S 1^{13} (Gn 24^{45} אל), 1 K 9^{5} Ho 12^{11} Je 6^{10} 10^{1} 11^{2} (אל . . . על), speak *to* 25^{2} (על . . . אל), 26^{2}, cf. Est 1^{17}, היה דבר י׳ Je 25^{1} 1 Ch 22^{8} cf. 11^{10}, ענה 2 S 19^{43}, קרא Is 34^{14} 2 Ch 32^{18}, שִׁוַּע ψ 18^{42}, הֵרַע 1 K 17^{20}, שׁוֹרֵר, שָׁר *sing* Pr 25^{20} Jb 33^{27}, החליק Pr 29^{5} (ψ 36^{3} אל), התפלל 1 S 1^{10}, כתב 2 Ch 30^{1} Ezr 4^{7} Est 8^{8}, שׁמע 2 K 20^{13} (=Is 39^{2}), 22^{13} Je 23^{16} 26^{5} 35^{18} Hg 1^{12}; v. also הקשׁיב, האזין, הבין, התבונן, השׂכיל.

(*c*) Expressing (or implying) the direction of the mind, 2 S 14^{1} לב המלך על אבשלם; Mal 3^{24} Ezr 6^{22}; Ct 7^{11} וְעָלַי תְּשׁוּקָתוֹ (Gn 3^{16} 4^{7} אל); שָׂם לִבּוֹ על Jb 1^{8} (2^{3} אל), 1 S 25^{25} (אל . . . על); Je 22^{17} thy eyes and thy heart are only (set) *upon* (על) . . ., 1 Ch 12^{17} 1 K 1^{20} 2 Ch 20^{12} כִּי עָלֶיךָ עֵינֵינוּ (elsewhere אל), 1 K 2^{15} עָלַי שָׂמוּ פניהם, ψ 146^{5} שִׂבְרוֹ על י׳; Is 10^{25} וְאַפִּי עַל־תַּבְלִיתָם be (directed) *towards* their destruction, Je 32^{31} (Gf Ew: cf. RV); cf. שׁעה על look *to* (trustfully) Is 17^{7} 31^{1}. (The uses *a*, *b*, *c* are all exceptional: אל would be regularly employed.)

(*d*) With the force of *over* and *towards* (cf. **5** and **7 a** *b*, *end*): ψ 65^{5} נוֹרָא עֲלִילָה על; to shine, etc. *on*, ψ 31^{17} הָאִירָה פָנֶיךָ על (Nu 6^{25} אל); רָאָה עַל Ex 5^{21}; הוֹפִיעַ על Jb 10^{3}; וְשַׂמְתִּי עֵינִי עַל Am 9^{4}+ (cf. Jb 14^{3} 24^{3} 34^{21}); הִשְׁקִיף עַל look out *over* ψ 14^{3}+.

d. In a hostile sense, *upon, against:* so very often, after every kind of verb expressing or implying attack, as בא Gn 34$^{25.27}$, נֶאֱסַף v^{30}, קצף to be angry 40^{2}, לון to murmur Ex 15^{24}, עמד stand up Lv 19^{16}+, קָם rise up Dt 19^{11} Am 7^{9}, נלחם Dt 20^{10}, חנה 1 S 11^{1} ψ 27^{3}, עלה 2 K 17^{3}, חרה אף Zc 10^{3} (usu. בְּ), שׁפך סללה Is 37^{33}, צור besiege Dt 20^{12}, חשׁב to devise Gn 50^{20} Je 11^{19}, דִּבֶּר Dt 13^{6}+, etc.: add Jb 16$^{4.4.9.10.13}$ 19^{12} 21^{27} 30^{12}, etc.; היה על 2 S 11^{23} Nu 31^{3}: הִנְנִי עָלַיִךְ (v. אֶל **4**); note also Ju 9^{31} 20^{5}: without a verb

Is 9^{20}; Ju 16^{12} פלשׁתים עליך the Philistines are *upon* thee, 20^{9} עָלֶיהָ בְּגוֹרָל Against it by lot!

8. By writers of the silver age, על is sts. used with the force of a *dative*, 1 Ch 13^{2} אִם עֲלֵיכֶם טוֹב (in classical Heb. בְּעֵינֵיכֶם) if it seems good *to* you, אִם עַל הַמֶּלֶךְ טוֹב †Ne $2^{5.7}$ Est 1^{19} 3^{9} $5^{4.8}$ 7^{3} 8^{5} 9^{13} (cf. in Aram. Ezr 5^{17} 7^{18}); שָׁפַר עַל ψ 16^{6} (cf. in Aram. Dn 4^{24}); עָרַב עַל ψ 104^{34} (elsewhere לְ); רַע עַל Ec 2^{17} (v. De; cf. בְּאֵשׁ עַל Dn 6^{15}): comp. Jb 22^{2} סָכַן עַל be profitable *to*, 33^{23}; also גָּמַל עַל (in both good and bad sense: v. גמל), Ne 5^{19} עשׂה על, 9^{30} משׁך על prolong (mercy) *to;* הִטָּה חֶסֶד עַל Ezr 7^{28} 9^{9} (Gn 39^{21} אל): 1 S 20^{8} rd. prob. עם for על. Cf. Mish. חביב על, dear *to;* סני על hateful *to;* Syr. ܫܦܝܪ ܥܠ, ܡܩܒܠ ܥܠ, pleasant, acceptable *to.*—Comp. in gen. the uses of عَلَى, W^{AG ii. § 59}.

9. With other particles:—עַל אַחֲרֵי Ez 41^{15}; עַל בֵּין Ez 19^{11} (cf. אל $31^{10.14}$); עַל לִפְנֵי Ez 40^{15}; עַל מֵעַל Ez 41^{17} (txt. dub.), v^{20}; עַל עֵבֶר Ex 25^{37} (cf. אל Ez $1^{9.12}$); עַל־כָּכָה Est 9^{26} (v. p. 462).—On עַל־יַד, עַל־יְדֵי, עַל פִּי, עַל־פְּנֵי, v. יָד, פֶּה, פָּנִים.

834 **III.** As **conj.**: **a.** עַל אֲשֶׁר *because that*... (cf. above, **II 1 f** *b*), Ex 32^{35} and י׳ plagued the people על אשׁר עשׂו *because* they had made, etc., Nu 20^{24} Dt 29^{24} (in answer to על מה: so 1 K 9^{9} Je 16^{11} 22^{9}), $32^{51.51}$ 1 S 24^{6} 2 S 3^{30} 6^{8} 8^{10} 12^{6} ψ 119^{49}+.

3588 **b.** עַל כִּי similar in meaning, but less frequent: †Dt 31^{17} Ju 3^{12} Je 4^{28} Mal 2^{14} ψ 139^{14}.

c. על alone: (*a*) *because*, †Gn 31^{20} (E) עַל בְּלִי הִגִּיד, ψ 119^{136} עַל לֹא. (*b*) *notwithstanding that* (above, **1 f** *f*), *although*, †Is 53^{9} עַל לֹא חָמָס עָשָׂה *although* he did no violence, Jb 16^{17} עַל לֹא חָמָס בְּכַפַּי.

IV. Compounds:—**1.** with כְּ (rare and late), **a.** *as concerning, as upon* †ψ 119^{14} כְּעַל כָּל־הוֹן, 2 Ch 32^{19}. **b.** (pleon. for כְּ), †Is 59^{18} כְּעַל גְּמֻלוֹת כְּעַל יְשַׁלֵּם *the like of* their deeds is *the like of* (that which) he will repay (כְּעַל repeated on the anal. of כְּ Nu 15^{15} Ho 4^{9}: v. כְּ) =*according to* their deeds is (that which) he will repay, Is 63^{7} *according to.*

2. מֵעַל$_{304}$ **from upon, from over, from by**—used with much delicacy of application in many different connexions, corresponding mostly with the different senses of על. Thus **a.** *from upon* idiomatically, when removal, motion, etc., from a *surface* is involved, as מעל פני האדמה ,מעל האדמה *from upon* (the face of) the ground, usu. with expel, destroy, perish, etc. Gn 4^{14} 6^{7} 7^{4} Ex 32^{12} Dt 6^{15} $28^{21.63}$ + oft. esp. Je and compiler of K; to be lifted up מעל הארץ Gn 7^{17} Ez $1^{19.21}$+, to return or be dried (of water) מעל הארץ Gn $8^{3.7.11.13}$; to roll a stone מֵעַל פִּי הַבְּאֵר 29^{3}; of the cloud departing מעל האהל Nu 9^{17} 12^{10}, cf. Ne 9^{19}; to rise up מֵעַל הַכִּסֵּא Ju 3^{20} 1 K 2^{4}, מֵעַל מִשְׁכָּבוֹ 2 S 11^{2}; to alight מֵעַל הַגָּמָל (נָפַל) Gn 24^{64} (cf. Jos 15^{18} צנח, 1 S 25^{23} (נפל), ירד מֵעַל הַמֶּרְכָּבָה Ju 4^{15} 2 K 5^{21} (נפל); to take מֵעַל ראשׁ Gn 40^{19} 2 S 12^{30}, מֵעַל הַמִּזְבֵּחַ Lv 16^{12} Nu 17^{11} Is 6^{6}; to see מֵעַל הַגָּג 2 S 11^{2}; to shoot מֵעַל הַחוֹמָה $v^{20.24}$; to speak מֵעַל הַכַּפֹּרֶת Ex 25^{22} Nu 7^{89}; to cast down מֵעַל יָדַיִם Dt 9^{17} Lv 8^{28} (כַּפַּיִם); to break, remove, etc., a yoke מעל שׁכמך (צווארך) Gn 27^{40} Is 10^{27} Je $28^{10.11}$; to wipe tears מֵעַל כָּל־פָּנִים Is 25^{8}; to take a bandage מעל עיניו 1 K 20^{41} (cf. על v^{38}); often of putting off a garment or ornament, as Gn $38^{14.19}$ וַתָּסַר צְעִיפָהּ מֵעָלֶיהָ, הוֹרֵד עֶדְיְךָ מֵעָלֶיךָ Ex 33^{5}, a sandal Ex 3^{5} Jos 5^{15}, a ring מֵעַל יָדוֹ Gn 41^{42}; to seek (דרשׁ), or hear, words מֵעַל הַסֵּפֶר Is 34^{16} Je 36^{11} (cf. כתב על ספר above); pregn. with בָּלָה to wear away (and fall) *from off*, Dt 8^{4} 29^{4}, cf. of the bones or skin in disease Jb 30^{17} עֲצָמַי נִקַּר מֵעָלָי are pierced (and drop) *from off* me, v^{30} עוֹרִי שָׁחַר מעלי is black (and falls) *from off* me; fig. 1 S 1^{11} הָסִירִי יֵינֵךְ מֵעָלָיִךְ remove thy wine *from off* thee; Nu 14^{9} סָר צִלָּם מֵעֲלֵיהֶם; Ju $16^{19.20}$ י׳ סר מעליו (with allusion to the hair, as the seat of Samson's strength), 1 S 16^{23} (cf. על in v^{16}).

b. Of relief from a burden or trouble: as of a plague, stroke, rod, etc., removed *from* (resting) cn one, Ex 10^{17} וְיָסֵר מֵעָלַי אֶת־הַמָּוֶת הַזֶּה, Nu 21^{7} 25^{8} וַתֵּעָצַר הַמַּגֵּפָה מֵעַל ישׂר׳ (2 S $24^{21.25}$), ψ 39^{11} הָסֵר מֵעָלַי נִגְעֶךָ, Jb 9^{34} 13^{21} Jo 2^{20}; of reproach Jos 5^{9} Is 25^{8} ψ 119^{22}, iniquity Ez 18^{31} Zc 3^{4}, bloodguiltiness, 1 K 2^{31}, wrath Ju 8^{3} Nu 25^{11} Pr 24^{18}, murmurings Nu $17^{21.25}$; הֵקַל מֵעַל to lighten *from upon* one Ex 18^{22}+; Am 5^{23} הָסֵר מֵעָלַי הֲמוֹן שִׁירֶיךָ; pregn. Jon $1^{11.12}$ that the sea יִשְׁתֹּק מֵעָלֵינוּ may be calm *from off* us; to remove, etc., מֵעַל פְּנֵי (v. פָּנִים); 1 S 6^{20} to whom shall he go up מֵעָלֵינוּ—not merely 'from us,' but—*from upon us* (relieving us of his presence), so often of an army retiring from a country or raising a siege, 2 S 10^{14} וַיָּשָׁב יוֹאָב מֵעַל בְּנֵי עַמּוֹן,

20^{21} וְאֵלְכָה מֵעַל הָעִיר, v^{22} 2 K 3^{27} 18^{14}, esp. with נַעֲלָה, עָלָה, 1 K 15^{19} Je 21^{2} 37$^{5.11}$ +; 2 S 19^{10} David fled מעל אבשׁלום *from* Absalom (whom his presence had encumbered), Ne 13^{28} וָאַבְרִיחֵהוּ מֵעָלָי, cf. Gn 13^{11} 25^{6} Nu 20^{21} וַיֵּט ישׂר׳ מֵעָלָיו, 2 Ch 20^{10}; Ex 10^{28} לֵךְ מֵעָלָי (contemptuously; be no more obnoxious to me), similarly 2 S 13^{17} שִׁלְחוּ־נא את־זאת מעלי (Amnon of Tamar).

c. *From beside* (cf. על **6 c**), in different *nuances:* Gn 17^{22} God went up מעל אברהם *from beside* A., 35^{13}; 18^{3} אל נא תעבר מעל עבדך (cf. על v^{5}), 42^{24} Nu 16$^{26.27}$; 1 K 1^{53} to come down מֵעַל הַמִּזְבֵּחַ (cf. על 13^{1}; **6 c** and **7 b**); *from attendance on* Gn 45^{1} (cf. על *ib.*), Ju 3^{19} וַיֵּצְאוּ מֵעָלָיו כָּל־הָעֹמְדִים עָלָיו 1 S 17^{15} (v. Dr), 2 S 13^{9}, cf. 1 S 13$^{8.11}$ 2 K 25^{5} (Je 36^{21} rd. עַל, מ being dittogr.), cf. 2 Ch 35^{15}; *from attachment to,* סָר מֵעַל י׳ Je 2^{5} Ez 11^{15} 44^{10}, cf. 8^{6}, רָחַק מֵעַל י׳ Je 32^{40} Ez 6^{9}, תָּעָה מֵעַל י׳ Ez 44$^{10.15}$, cf. 14^{5} Dt 13^{11}; also סָר מֵעַל חַטֹּאות 2 K 10^{31} 15^{18} (usu. מֵחטאות), cf. Ez 14^{6} 23^{18}; *from companionship with,* Jb 19^{13} אַחַי מֵעָלַי הִרְחִיק; *from accompanying protectingly* 1 S 28^{15} וֵאלֹהִים סָר מֵעָלַי, v^{16} (cf. על ψ 110^{5}; and v. Dr); *from adhesion to* 2 K 17^{21} קָרַע ישׂראל מֵעַל בֵּית דָּוִד, Is 7^{17} 56^{3} יַבְדִּילַנִי; זָנִיתָ מֵעַל אֱלֹהֶיךָ Hos 9^{1}, י׳ מֵעַל עַמּוֹ.

d. In late Heb., = עַל *above:* 2 K 25^{28} נָתַן כִּסְאוֹ מֵעַל כִּסֵּא וגו׳ (|| Je 52^{32} more class. מִמַּעַל לְ), Est 3^{1} ψ 108^{5} גדול מעל שׁמים (|| 57^{11} עד), 148^{4} Ec 5^{7} גָּבֹהַּ מֵעַל גָּבֹהַּ שֹׁמֵר, Ne 3^{28} 8^{5} 2 Ch 34^{4} לְמַעְלָה מֵעֲלֵיהֶם on high *above* them; Ez 41$^{17.20}$.—Pr 14^{14} rd. with De Now Str וּמִמַּעֲלָלָיו.

e. מֵעַל לְ (chiefly late, and pleon. for עַל, or else = the more class. syn. מִמַּעַל לְ): (*a*) Gn 1^{7} מֵעַל לָרָקִיעַ (Ez 1^{26} מִמַּעַל לְ׳), Ez 1^{25} (txt. dub.; v. Comm.), 1 S 17^{39} Jon 4^{6} Mal 1^{5} *upon, over* the border (territory) of Israel (so Köhl Ke: but Hi Ew We *beyond*), 2 Ch 13^{4} *upon* mount Zemaraim, 31^{20}. (*b*) *beside* 2 Ch 26^{19} מֵעַל לְמִזְבַּח הַקְּטֹרֶת; Ne 12$^{31.31.37.38.38.39}$ dub.: BeRy (in all) *off the side of* (מִן **6**) = *at a little distance from;* Ke in v$^{31.38 a}$ *upon,* in v$^{37.38 b.39}$ *by the side of* (*an … vorüber*).

5766, 5932 †I. עֲלָוָה transp. fr. עַוְלָה (q.v.) Ho 10^{9}. p. 732

5933 †II. עַלְוָה **n.pr.m.** in Edom Gn 36^{40} (P) = 1 Ch 1^{51} Qr (Kt עליה), 𝔊 Γωλα; 𝔊L^{Chr} Αλουα.

5935 †עַלְוָן **n.pr.m.** in Edom Gn 36^{23} (P), 𝔊 Γωλων, Γωλαμ = 1 Ch 1^{40} Qr (Kt עלין), 𝔊 Σωλαμ, A Ιωλαμ, 𝔊L Αλουαν.

†[עָלַז] **vb.** exult (|| form of עלץ q.v.; cf. 5937
Ph. n.pr.m. נבעלז);—**Qal** *Impf.* 3 ms. יַעֲלֹז ψ 96^{12}; 1 s. וְאֶעְלֹז Je 15^{17}; אֶעֱלֹזָה ψ 60^{8} 108^{8}; 3 mpl. יַעְלְזוּ 149^{5}, יַעֲלֹזוּ Je 51^{39} ψ 94^{3}, etc.; *Imv.* fs. עִלְזִי Zp 3^{14}; mpl. עִלְזוּ ψ 68^{5}; *Inf. cstr.* לַעֲלוֹז Is 23^{12};—*exult, triumph* Is 23^{12} Je 15^{17}; of Isr.'s foes 2 S 1^{20} Je 50^{11} (|| שׂמח), of wicked ψ 94^{3} Je 11^{15}; of Isr. Zp 3^{14} (+ שִׂמְחִי), בְּי׳ אֶע׳ Hb 3^{18} *in* י׳ *will I exult* (|| אָגִילָה), ψ 149^{5}; ע׳ לְפָנָיו 68^{5}; subj. לִבִּי 28^{7}, כִּלְיוֹתָי Pr 23^{16}; fig. of field ψ 96^{12} (|| רַנֵּן); of י׳ ψ 60^{8} = 108^{8}.

†עָלֵז **adj.** exultant, jubilant; as **n.** Is 5^{14}. 5938

†[עַלִּיז] **adj.** exultant, jubilant (on form 5947
cf. Lag$^{BN 110}$);—fs. עַלִּיזָה *jubilant city* Is 22^{2} (|| עִיר הוֹמִיָּה), 32^{13}, cf. Zp 2^{15} and (*city* om.) Is 23^{7}; of pers., pl. שְׁאוֹן עַלִּיזִים 24^{8}; cstr. עַלִּיזֵי גַּאֲוָתִי 13^{3}, cf. Zp 3^{11}, v. גַּאֲוָה.

†עֲלָטָה **n.f.** thick darkness (NH עֲלָטָה 5939
(rare); acc. to Ba$^{ES 5}$ transp. fr. Ar. غَطَلَ [*be cloudy*]; غَيْطَلَةٌ *darkness*);—abs. ע׳, attending sunset Gn 15^{17} (c. vb. masc.; Albr$^{ZAW xv (1895), 325}$ Kö$^{Synt. § 350 e}$ rd. הָיְתָה); בָּע׳ Ez 12^{7} (|| בָּעֶרֶב), v$^{6.12}$.

עֶלְיוֹן, עֲלִיָּה, עֲלִי, עֱלִי, עֵלִי v. עלה. p. 750f 5940-42, 5944-45
עֲלֵי v. עַל. עַלְיָן, עַלְיָה v. עלוה, עלון. p. 752 5921, 5933, 5935

†I. [עָלַל] **vb.** **Pô'ēl,** act severely 5953
(toward) (NH *id.*, *deal with* (rare), and deriv.; Ar. عَلَّ *do a thing* (drink, beat, give) *a second time,* II. *divert, occupy,* V. *divert, occupy oneself with* (food, a woman, etc.); Syr. ܥܠܬܐ *cause, occasion, affair*);—*act severely,* alw. c. ל pers.: *Pf.* 2 ms. עוֹלַלְתָּ לִי La 1^{22} *as thou hast acted severely to me* (in punishment, subj. י׳); לְמִי ע׳ 2^{20} *to whom hast thou acted thus severely?* 3 fs. עֵינִי עוֹלְלָה לְנַפְשִׁי 3^{51} *my eye deals severely with me,* i.e. gives me pain (?; text dub.; cf. Perles$^{Anal. 18}$ Bu). *Imv.* ms. עוֹלֵל לָמוֹ La 1^{22} *deal severely with them.*—Vid. also ע׳ **denom.** infr. **Pō'al** *Pf.* 3 ms. מַכְאֹבִי אֲשֶׁר עוֹלַל לִי La 1^{12} *my pain which is severely dealt out to me.* **Hithpa.** *Pf.* **1.** *busy, divert oneself* with (cf. Ar. v.), alw. c. ב pers.: 1 s. אֵת־אֲשֶׁר הִתְעַלַּלְתִּי בְּ׳ Ex 10^{2} (J) *how I* [י׳] *have made a toy of* Egypt; esp. *deal wantonly, ruthlessly* with (ב pers.): 3 ms. הִתְעַלֵּל 1 S 6^{6}; 2 fs. הִתְעַלַּלְתְּ Nu 22^{29} (JE; Balaam's ass); 3 pl. וְהִתְעַלְּלוּ consec. 1 S 31^{4} = 1 Ch 10^{4}, Je 38^{19}; *Impf.* 3 mpl. וַיִּתְעַלְּלוּ־בָהּ Ju 19^{25} (of abusing a woman;

(|| וַיֵּדְעוּ אֹתָהּ). **Hithpō῾.** *Inf. cstr.* לְהִתְעוֹלֵל עֲלִלוֹת ψ 141^{4} *to practise practices* in wickedness (perhaps denom.).

5955 † עוֹלֵלוֹת **n.f. pl. intens.** gleaning (*going over a second time*);—*gleaning* (of grapes and olives; לֶקֶט of grain), always fig. of remnant: abs. ע׳ Is 17^{6} (|| כְּנֹקֶף זַיִת), 24^{13} (sim.; || *id.*, + בָּצִיר), Je 49^{9} (cf. בֹּצְרִים v^{a}) = Ob^{5} (*id.*); cstr. עֹלְלוֹת בָּצִיר Mi 7^{1}; fig. of warlike achievement עֹלְלוֹת אֶפְרַיִם Ju 8^{2} (opp. בָּצִיר).

5953 † [עָלַל] **vb. denom. Pō῾.** glean (grapes or olives; לִקֵּט of grain);—*Impf.* 2 ms. תְּעוֹלֵל Lv 19^{10} (obj. כֶּרֶם; || תְּלַקֵּט), Dt 24^{21} (abs., + אַחֲרֶיךָ); 3 mpl. fig. (+ *Inf. abs.*) עוֹלֵל יְעוֹלְלוּ כַגֶּפֶן שְׁאֵרִית יִשְׂרָאֵל Je 6^{9}; וַיְעֹלְלֻהוּ Ju 20^{45} *they made a gleaning of them* (i.e. smote the fugitives).

5949 † עֲלִילָה **n.f.** wantonness, deed;—abs. ע׳ ψ 14^{1} 66^{5}; elsewh. pl. עֲלִלוֹת 1 S 2^{3} ψ 141^{4}; cstr. עֲלִילֹת Dt 22$^{14.17}$; sf. עֲלִילוֹתָם ψ 77^{13}, עֲלִילוֹתֶיךָ Zp 3^{7}+, etc.;—**1.** *wantonness*, ע׳ דְּבָרִים Dt 22$^{14.17}$ *wantonness of words*, i.e. baseless charges (cf. Di, esp. Dr). **2.** *deed*: **a.** in gen., of men 1 S 2^{3}. **b.** of י׳ (only ψψ) ψ 9^{12} = 105^{1} = Is 12^{4} = 1 Ch 16^{8}, ψ 77^{13} (|| פָּעֳלֶךָ), 78^{11} (|| נִפְלְאוֹתָיו), 103^{7}; נוֹרָא ע׳ עַל 66^{5} *he is terrible in deed toward*, etc. **c.** usu. *practices = evil deeds* (esp. Ez 8 t.): Ez 14$^{22.23}$ 20^{43} 24^{14} 36$^{17.19}$ (all || דֶּרֶךְ), fully ע׳ הַנִּשְׁחָתוֹת 20^{44} (|| ד׳ הָרָעִים); 21^{29} Zp 3^{11}; הִשְׁחִיתוּ כֹּל ע׳ v^{7}.

5950 † עֲלִילִיָּה **n.f.** (Kö$^{ii.1,204}$) deed;—of י׳, רַב הָע׳ Je 32^{19} (|| גְּדֹל הָעֵצָה); but rd. prob. הָעֲלִילָה.

4611 [מַעֲלָל] $_{41}$ **n.m.** $^{Ne\ 9,35}$ **deed, practice;**—only pl. מַעֲלָלִים 1 S 25^{3}; cstr. מַעַלְלֵי ψ 77^{12} 78^{1}; sf. מַעֲלָלֶיךָ Dt 28^{20}, מַעֲלָלָיו Ho 4^{9}+, מַעַלְלֵיכֶם Is 1^{16}+, מַעַלְלֵיהֶם 3^{10}+, etc.;—**1.** usu. (esp. Je 17 t.) bad *practices* of men, רַע מַעֲלָלִים 1 S 25^{3} he was *evil in his practices;* Ju 2^{19} (|| דַּרְכָּם), Ho 5^{5} 7^{2} Is 3^{8} Je 11^{18} ψ 106$^{29.39}$ (|| מַעֲשֵׂיהֶם); מ׳ הָרָעִים Ne 9^{35}; רֹעַ מ׳ *the evil of your* (their, etc.) *practices* Ho 9^{15} Is 1^{16} Je 4^{4} 21^{12} (sf. 3 mpl. Kt, 2 mpl. Qr), +; מ׳ הָרָעִים Zc 1^{4} Qr (+ ד׳ הָרָעִים; Kt מעליליהם), מ׳ אֲשֶׁר לֹא טוֹבִים Ez 36^{31} (+ *id.*); הֵרֵעוּ מ׳ Mi 3^{4}; פְּרִי מ׳, i.e. their consequences, Is 3^{10} Je 17^{10} 21^{14} 32^{19} (+ דֶּרֶךְ). **2.** *deeds* of י׳ ψ 77^{12}, of אֵל 78^{7}; cf. Mi 2^{7}. **3.** *acts*, in gen., of youth Pr 20^{11} (|| פָּעֳלוֹ).

4611 [מַעֲלִיל], מעליליהם Zc 1^{4} Kt, v. foreg. **1.**

8586 † תַּעֲלוּלִים **n.m.pl. abstr.** wantonness, caprice;—ת׳ יִמְשְׁלוּ בָם Is 3^{4} *caprice shall rule over them;* sf. תַּעֲלֻלֵיהֶם 66^{4} *their wanton dealing*, i.e. that inflicted on them.

II. עלל (√ of foll.; poss. = I. עלל (Kö$^{ii.1,106}$) whence child as *capricious, mischievous*, but dub.; > foll. fr. עול; in either case orig. meaning quite forgotten; prob. distinct √, meaning unknown).

5768 † עוֹלֵל, עוֹלָל **n.m.** $^{La\ 2,19}$ child;—abs. עוֹלֵל 1 S 15^{3}+, עוֹלָל Je 6^{11} 9^{20}; usu. pl. עוֹלְלִים ψ 8^{3}, עֹלְלִים Jb 3^{16}, עוֹלָלִים La 4^{4} Jo 2^{16}; cstr. עֹלְלֵי La 2^{20}; sf. עֹלָלַיִךְ ψ 137^{9}, עֹלָלֶיהָ Mi 2^{9}+, עֹלְלֵיהֶם 2 K 8^{2}+, etc.;—*child* Mi 2^{9} La 2$^{19.20}$ 4^{4}; + יוֹנֵק (sts. disting. from men and women), 1 S 15^{3} 22^{19} ψ 8^{3} Je 44^{7} La 2^{11} Jo 2^{16}, || בַּחוּרִים Je 6^{11} 9^{20}; || בָּנִים ψ 17^{14} (heirs of father); dashed in pieces (רטשׁ) by foe 2 K 8^{12} Ho 14^{1} Na 3^{10} Is 13^{16}, cf. ψ 137^{9} (נִפֵּץ); taken captive La 1^{5}; stillborn Jb 3^{16}.

† [עָלַל] **vb. denom.** act or play the child;—only **Pō῾.** *Pt.* עַמִּי נֹגְשָׂיו מְעוֹלֵל Is 3^{12} *my people—its ruler is acting the child.* 5953

† III. [עָלַל] **vb. insert, thrust in** (Ar. غَلَّ, whence غُلٌّ *yoke;* cf. OAram. עלל, 𝔗 עֲלַל, Syr. ܥܠ, all *enter*);—only **Pō῾.** *Pf.* 1 s. וְעֹלַלְתִּי בֶעָפָר קַרְנִי Jb 16^{15} fig. of humiliation. 5953

† עֹל $_{39}$ **n.m.** $^{1\ K\ 12,4}$ yoke;—ע׳ abs. Ho 11^{4}+; cstr. Is 9^{3}+; sf. עֻלְּךָ Je 2^{20} Is 47^{6}, עֻלּוֹ Gn 27^{40}+, עֻלְּכֶם 1 K 12^{11}, etc.;—*yoke*, for cattle, עָלָה עֲלֵיהֶם ע׳ 1 S 6^{7}, cf. Nu 19^{2} (P), מָשְׁכָה בְּע׳ Dt 21^{3}; usu. fig. of servitude 1 K 12$^{4.10.11.11.14.14}$ = 2 Ch 10$^{4.10.11.11.14}$; נָתַן ע׳ עַל 1 K 12$^{4.9}$ = 2 Ch 10$^{4.9}$; וְנָתַן ע׳ בַּרְזֶל עַל־צַוָּארֶךָ Dt 28^{48}, so Je 28^{14}; עַל־זָקֵן הִכְבַּדְתְּ ע׳ Is 47^{6}; also נָתַן (הֵבִיא) אֶת־צַוָּארוֹ בְּעֹל Je 27$^{8.11.12}$; שָׁבַר ע׳ *break the yoke* Je 2^{20} 5^{5} 28$^{2.4.11}$ 30^{8} (+ מֵעַל צ׳), so מֹטוֹת ע׳ Lv 26^{13} (H), Ez 34^{27} (v. מוֹטָה); פָּרַק ע׳ Gn 27^{40} (J; + מֵעַל צ׳); הֵחַת ע׳ Is 9^{3}; cf. הֵרִים ע׳ Ho 11^{4}; also יָסוּר ע׳ מֵעַל צ׳ Is 10^{27}, and 14^{25}; fig. of transgressions La 1^{14}, del. ע׳ 𝔊 𝔙 Löhr Bu, but read עַל v^{b} (v. *id.*); of hardship, נָשָׂא ע׳ 3^{27}. 5923

† עֲלִיל appar. **n.[m.]**, only כֶּסֶף צָרוּף בַּע׳ לָאָרֶץ ψ 12^{7}, usu. (after 𝔗 כּוּרָא) *furnace, crucible* (Hup fr. III. עלל; De al. *workshop*, fr. I. עלל), but wholly dub.; NH *openly* Levy$^{NHWB\ iii.\ 654}$; Che Du del. as gloss; cf. discussion Che Expos. T. viii. 236, 336 Ne$^{ib.\ 287,379}$. 5948

5956 †I. [עָלַם] **vb.** conceal (NH *id.*, der. spec.);—**Qal** *Pt. pass.* עֲלֻמֵנוּ ψ 90^{8} as subst. *our secret*, i.e. hidden sin (‖ עֲוֹנֹת). **Niph.** *Pf. be concealed*, of wisdom, 3 fs. נֶעֶלְמָה מֵעֵינֵי Jb 28^{21}; of a fact or condition, נֶעְלַם 2 Ch 9^{2}, וְנ׳ consec. Lv 5$^{2.3.4}$ (all c. מִן pers.), וְנ׳ מֵעֵינֵי Lv 4^{13} Nu 5^{13} (all P); *Pt.* **1.** נֶעְלָם *concealed*, c. הָיָה in periphrastic conjug. 1 K 10^{3} (מִן pers.); abs. כָּל־נֶעְלָם Ec 12^{14}. **2.** fs. תְּהִי נַעֲלָמָה Na 3^{11} *mayest thou become obscured* (as to the senses; fig. for *swoon*), but very doubtful, read perhaps נעלפה? [Dr]. **3.** pl. נַעֲלָמִים ψ 26^{4} *those who conceal themselves*, i.e. their thoughts, *dissemblers* (‖ מְתֵי שָׁוְא). **Hiph.** *Pf.* 3 ms. הֶעְלִים 2 K 4^{27}; 3 pl. הֶעְלִימוּ Ez 22^{26}; *Impf.* 2 ms. תַּעְלִים ψ 10^{1}, תַּעְלֵם La 3^{56}; 3 mpl. יַעְלִימוּ Lv 20^{4}, etc.; *Inf. abs.* הַעְלֵם v^{4}; *Pt.* מַעְלִים Jb 42^{3} Pr 28^{27};—*conceal, hide*, c. מִן pers. 2 K 4^{27} (‖ לֹא הִגִּיד לִי); usu. *hide* the eyes from (מִן), i.e. *disregard* Is 1^{15} Ez 22^{26}, הַעְלֵם יַע׳ וגו׳ Lv 20^{4}, מִן om. Pr 28^{27}; *hide* the eyes by (בְּ) a bribe 1 S 12^{3} (i.e. pervert justice, but v. I. עַיִן **3 d**); *hide* (cover) the ear La 3^{56} (turn a deaf ear); *hide* (obscure) counsel (עֵצָה) Jb 42^{3}; לָמָּה תַּע׳ ψ 10^{1} *why dost thou* [י׳] *hide*, sc. thine eyes (so most), or *practise concealment* (=hide thyself)? **Hithp.** *Pf.* 2 ms. consec. וְהִתְעַלַּמְתָּ מֵהֶם Dt 22$^{1.4}$ *and thou hide thyself completely from them* (utterly neglect to aid), so *Inf. cstr.* (מֵהֶם om.) לְהִתְעַלֵּם v^{3}; so also *Impf.* c. מִן, תִּתְעַלַּם ψ 55^{2}, תִּתְעַלָּם Is 58^{7}; once lit. יִתְעַלֶּם־שָׁלֶג Jb 6^{16} wherein *snow hides itself*.

8587 †תַּעֲלֻמָה **n.f. hidden thing, secret** (so, c. ה, van d. H. Bu, הּ- Baer Ginsb);—תּ׳ *what is hidden* Jb 28^{11}; pl. cstr. תַּעֲלֻמוֹת חָכְמָה Jb 11^{6} *secrets of wisdom*, תּ׳ לֵב ψ 44^{22}.

5960 †עַלְמוֹן **n.pr.loc.** (cf. Sab. n.pr. עלמן Hal^{192});—priestly city in Benj. Jos 21^{18} (P), 𝔊 Γαμαλα, A Αλμων, 𝔊L Ελμων; = עָלֶמֶת in ‖ 1 Ch 6^{45} (𝔊 Γαλεμεθ, 𝔊L Αλαμωθ); mod. ʿ*Almît*, c. 1 hour NE. of Jerusalem, v. Buhl$^{\text{Geogr. 175}}$.

5963 †עַלְמֹן דִּבְלָתָיְמָה **n.pr.loc.** in Moab, Nu 33$^{46.47}$ (P), 𝔊 Γελμων Δεβλαθαιμ; = בֵּית ד׳ q.v.

4192, 5921, 5961 עַל־מוּת, עֲלָמוֹת etc., v. עַלְמָה sub II. עלם. below

5964 †עָלֶמֶת **1. n.pr.m.** a Benjamite 1 Ch 8^{36} 9^{42}, עָלֶמֶת 7^{8}; 𝔊 Σαλαμαιθ, Γαλεμαθ, Αλαμωθ, etc. **2. n.pr.loc.** (= עַלְמוֹן q.v.) 1 Ch 6^{45} Baer Ginsb (van d. H. עַלֶּמֶת).

†יַעְלָם **n.pr.m.** Edomite Gn 36$^{5.14.18}$ = 1 Ch 3281
1^{35}, Ιεγλομ.

II. עלם (√ of foll.; perh. orig. *be mature* (sexually); Aram. עֲלֵם *be strong*, ܥܠܡ *rejuvenate* (certainly denom.), Ar. غَلِمَ *be lustful* (*id.*); cf. Sab. עלם, עלמן *young man* CIS$^{\text{iv. pp. 30, 42}}$, Ar. غُلَامٌ *id.*; Ph. עלמת *girl*; Nab. Palm. עלם, עלים *slave*, Palm. fpl. *harlots*; 𝔗 עוּלֵימָא, עוּלֵימְתָּא, Syr. ܥܠܝܡܐ, ܥܠܝܡܬܐ *young man, young woman*).

†עֶלֶם **n.m. young man**;—ע׳ abs. 1 S 20^{22}, 5958
הָעָלֶם 17^{56}; ע׳ prob. also v^{42} 16^{12} (for MT עִם) Gr Krenkel$^{\text{ZAW ii (1882), 309}}$ Bu HPS.

†עַלְמָה **n.f. young woman** (ripe sexually; 5959
maid or newly married);—ע׳ Gn 24^{43} (J), Ex
2^{8} (E), Pr 30^{19} Is 7^{14}; pl. עֲלָמוֹת ψ 68^{26} Ct 1^{3} 6^{8}; 5961
עַל־עֲלָמוֹת *to* (the voice of) *young women*, either
lit., or of soprano or falsetto of boys: 1 Ch 15^{20}
ψ 9^{1} (rd. עַל־עֲלָמוֹת לַבֵּן [for עַל־מוּת לַבֵּן], '*voce* 4192
virginea a pueris decantandum,' Thes), 46^{1} 48^{15}
(rd. עַל־עֲלָמוֹת [for עַל־מוּת]; tr. prob. to 49^{1}). 4192

†[עֲלוּמִים] **n.pl.abstr. youth, youthful** 5934
vigour;—only sf. עֲלוּמָיו Jb 20^{11} Qr (Kt עֲלוּמוֹ); עֲלוּמָיו ψ 89^{46} Jb 33^{25}; עֲלוּמַיִךְ Is 54^{4}.

III. עלם (√ of foll., meaning dub.; cf. NH עוֹלָם (chiefly *world, age*); MI$^{7.10}$ עלם, Ph. *id.*, Aram. עָלְמָא, ܥܠܡܐ, Nab. עלם, Palm. עלמא; Ar. عَالَمٌ *creation, world*, etc.; Eth. ዓለም: *aevum, saeculum*, etc.; acc. to Thes al. from I. עלם *the hidden*, cf. Kö$^{\text{ii. 1, 87}}$; Lag$^{\text{BN 115}}$ cp. quadril. عألم *primitive waters*; Ew$^{\S 77\text{a}}$ cp. Eth. ዐለተ: *time* [√ ועל Di^{923}]; Ba$^{\text{ZMG xliv (1890), 685}}$ cp. As. *ullûti, ullâ* [*ullânu, remote time*], cf. Dl$^{\text{HWB 65}}$ Jen$^{\text{ZA vii}}$).

עוֹלָם$_{439}$ **n.m. long duration, antiquity,** 5769
futurity;—ע׳ Gn 9^{12} + 405 t.; עֹלָם 3^{22} + 19 t.;
עֵילוֹם 2 Ch 33^{7}, rd. prob. עוֹלָם (for other explan. 5865
v. note in Kit^{Hpt}); sf. עֹלָמוֹ Ec 12^{5}; pl. עוֹלָמִים Is 26^{4} + 7 t., עֹלָמִים ψ 145^{13} + 2 t.; cstr. עוֹלְמֵי Is 45^{17};—†**1.** of past time: **a.** *ancient time*: יְמֵי ע׳ *days of old* Is 63$^{9.11}$ Am 9^{11} Mi 5^{1} 7^{14} Mal 3^{4}; יְמוֹת ע׳ Dt 32^{7}; עַם ע׳ Is 44^{7} *ancient people*; גּוֹי מֵע׳ Je 5^{15}; חָרְבוֹת ע׳ *old waste places* Is 58^{12} 61^{4}, cf. Ez 26$^{20\text{ b}}$; פִּתְחֵי ע׳ *ancient gates* ψ 24$^{7.9}$; שְׁבִילֵי ע׳ Jb 22^{15}; נתבות ע׳ Je 6^{16}; ארח ע׳ 18^{15}; גבול ע׳ Pr 22^{28} 23^{10}; במות ע׳ Ez 36^{2}; מִן (מֵ)ע׳ *from of old* Is 64^{3} Je 2^{20} Jo 2^{2}, of the fathers Jos 24^{2}, the prophets Je 28^{8}, the ancient נפלים

Gn 6^{4}; (Ez 32^{27} 𝔊 Co for מערלים; but 1 S 27^{8} read מִטֶּלֶם for מעולם We Dr HPS); בהם ע׳ *long in them* Is 64^{4} (text dub.). **b.** מֵתֵי ע׳ *the long dead* ψ 143^{3} La 3^{6}; so עַם ע׳ Ez 26^{20}. **c.** of God, מֵע׳: former acts Is 46^{9}; as redeemer Is 63^{16}; of love ψ 25^{6}, judgment 119^{52}, dominion Is 63^{19}; long silence 42^{14} 57^{11}; his wisdom personif. Pr 8^{23}; his existence ψ 93^{2}. **d.** of things: גבעות ע׳ *ancient hills* Gn 49^{26} (J), Hb 3^{6} (‖ הררי־עד), Dt 33^{15} (‖ הררי קדם). **e.** pl. שְׁנוֹת עולמים ψ 77^{6} *years of ancient times;* דורות עולמים Is 51^{9}; לעלמים Ec 1^{10} *in olden times.* **2. a.** indef. *futurity*, c. prep. *for ever, always* (sts. = *during the lifetime*); עֶבֶד עולם *slave for ever* Dt 15^{17} 1 S 27^{12} Jb 40^{28}; עֶבֶד לע׳ *serve for ever* Ex 21^{6} (E), Lv 25^{46}; עד ע׳ 1 S 1^{22}; גְּאֻלַּת ע׳ Lv 25^{32} *redemption at any time;* הֲרַת ע׳ Je 20^{17} *ever pregnant* (womb); כְּלִמַּת ע׳ v^{11} of persecutors of Jeremiah; חרפת ע׳ 23^{40}; שַׁלְוֵי ע׳ ψ 73^{12} *alway at ease;* יְחִי לע׳ (יחיה) *may the king live alway* 1 K 1^{31} Ne 2^{3}; cf. אֹרֶךְ יָמִים עולם ועד ψ 21^{5}; ישב עולם לפני אלהים 61^{8}; so of the pious, לע׳ לא ימוט 15^{5}; בל ימוט Pr 10^{30}, cf. ψ 30^{7}; other phr.: ψ $37^{27.28}$ 41^{13} 55^{23} 61^{8} 73^{26} 121^{8} Pr 10^{25}; אשירה ע׳ ψ 89^{2} *I will sing for ever* (as long as I live), cf. 52^{10} 115^{18} $145^{1.2}$; הודה לע׳ 30^{13} 44^{9} 52^{11} 79^{13}; other emotions and activities continuous through life 5^{12} 31^{2} = 71^{1}, 75^{10} 86^{12} $119^{44.93.98.111.112}$ Mi 4^{5}, cf. לע׳ 2^{9}. **b.** = *continuous existence,* (1) of things: the earth, הָאָרֶץ לְעוֹלָם עֹמָדֶת Ec 1^{4}; other phr.: ψ 78^{69} 104^{5}, heavens and contents 148^{6}, ruined cities Is 25^{2} 32^{14} Ez 26^{21} 27^{36} 28^{19}, ruined lands Je 18^{16} $25^{9.12}$ $49^{13.33}$ $51^{26.62}$ Ez 35^{9} Zp 2^{9}; לעד עד ע׳ Is 30^{8} *for a witness for ever,* in a book; (2) of nations: לעולם אהיה 47^{7} (Babylon loqu.), cf. ψ 81^{16} Ob ^{10}; ישב לע׳ of Judah Jo 4^{20}; (3) families ψ 49^{12} Is 14^{20}; the dynasty of Saul 1 S 13^{13}; house of Eli 2^{30}; (4) national relations: איבת ע׳ *continual enmity* Ez 25^{15} 35^{5}; of exclusion from קהל י׳, עד ע׳ Dt 23^{4} = Ne 13^{1}; various relations Is 32^{17} 34^{10}; חרפת ע׳ *perpetual reproach* ψ 78^{66}, of dynasty of David 2 S 3^{28} 12^{10} 1 K 2^{33}, families v^{33} 2 K 5^{27} ψ 106^{31} Je 35^{6}. **c.** of divine existence: אל עולם Gn 21^{33} (J); אלהי ע׳ Is 40^{28}; חי אנכי לע׳ Dt 32^{40}; חֵי הע׳ Dn 12^{7}; of divine name, זה שמי לְע׳ Ex 3^{15} (E), cf. 2 Ch 33^{7} (v. supr.); blessing and praise of it 2 S 7^{26} = 1 Ch 17^{24}, ψ 72^{19} 135^{13}; of י׳ himself 89^{53}; attributes, אהבה Je 31^{3} 1 K 10^{9}; חסד Is 54^{8} ψ 89^{2} 138^{8}; לע׳ חַסְדּוֹ 1 Ch $26^{34.41}$ 2 Ch 5^{13} $7^{3.6}$ 20^{21} Ezr 3^{11} ψ 100^{5} 106^{1} 107^{1} $118^{1.2.3.4.29}$ 136^{1} + 25 t., Je 33^{11}; כבוד ψ 104^{31}; אמת 117^{2} 146^{6}; צדק 119^{142}; עצה 33^{11}; reign Ex 15^{18} (E), ψ 10^{16} 66^{7} 92^{9} 146^{10} Je 10^{10} Mi 4^{7}; ישב יהוה לע׳ ψ 9^{8} 29^{10} 102^{13} La 5^{19}; presence in Zion 1 Ch 23^{25} Is 33^{14} $60^{19.20}$ Ez 37^{28} $43^{7.9}$; his salvation Is $51^{6.8}$; זרעת ע׳ Dt 33^{27} *everlasting arms;* כל אשר יעשה האלהים יהיה לע׳ Ec 3^{14}. **d.** of God's covenant: בְּרִית ע׳ *everlasting covenant* Gn 9^{16} $17^{7.13.19}$ Ex 31^{16} Lv 24^{8} Nu 18^{19} (all P), 2 S 23^{5} 1 Ch 16^{17} = ψ 105^{10}, Is 24^{5} 55^{3} 61^{8} Je 32^{40} 50^{5} Ez 16^{60} 37^{26}; covenant with Noah, לְדֹרֹת ע׳ Gn 9^{12} (P); God remembers it 1 Ch 16^{15} = ψ 105^{8}, ψ 111^{5}; will not break it, לע׳ Ju 2^{1}; אות ע׳ Ex 31^{17} (P); אות עד ע׳ Dt 28^{46}. **e.** of God's laws: דבר(ים) Is 59^{21} ψ 119^{89}; משפט 119^{160}; עדות $v^{144.152}$; חק ע׳ Ex 29^{28} 30^{21} (E), Lv $6^{11.15}$ 7^{34} 10^{15} 24^{9} Nu $18^{8.11.19}$ (P), also Je 5^{22} (of bounds of sea); חק עד ע׳ Ex 12^{24} (J), חֻקַּת ע׳ $v^{14.17}$ 27^{21} 28^{43} 29^{9} Lv 3^{17} 7^{36} 10^{9} $16^{29.31.34}$ 17^{7} $23^{14.21.31.41}$ $24^{3.8}$ Nu 10^{8} 15^{15} 18^{23} $19^{10.21}$ (P) (most of these in fact specif. Jewish and temporary); temple to bear God's name, עד ע׳ 1 K 9^{3} = 2 Ch 7^{16}; לע׳ 2 K 21^{7} 2 Ch 33^{4}; consecrated לע׳ 30^{8}; its ceremonies לע׳ 2^{3}; Levit. priesthood, לשרתו עד ע׳ 1 Ch 15^{2}; Aaronic priesthood, לברך בשמי עד ע׳ $23^{13.13}$. **f.** of God's promises: his word, יקום לע׳ Is 40^{8}; promised dynasty of David, עד (ה)ע׳ 2 S $7^{13.16.16.25}$ = 1 Ch $17^{12.14.14.23}$, ψ 18^{51} = 2 S 22^{51}, 1 K $2^{33.45}$ 1 Ch 22^{10} ψ 89^{5}; לע׳ 1 K 9^{5} 1 Ch $28^{4.7}$ 2 Ch 13^{5} ψ $89^{29.37}$ 2 S $7^{29.29}$ = 1 Ch $17^{27.27}$; of holy land 1 Ch 28^{8}, אֲחֻזַּת ע׳ Gn 17^{8} 48^{4} Lv 25^{34} (P); given לע׳ Ex 32^{13} (J) 2 Ch 20^{7}; עד ע׳ Gn 13^{15}, inherited לע׳ Is 60^{21} ψ 37^{18}; עד ע׳ Is 34^{17}; dwelt in עד ע׳ Ez 37^{25}; other blessings, לע׳ Dt 5^{26} Ho 2^{21}; עד ע׳ Dt 12^{28} 2 S 7^{24} = 1 Ch 17^{22}, ψ 133^{3}; שִׂמְחַת ע׳ Is 35^{10} 51^{11} 61^{7}; דֶּרֶךְ ע׳ ψ 139^{24}; שם ע׳ Is 56^{5} 63^{12}; אות ע׳ 55^{13}; גאון ע׳ 60^{15}; Jerus. to abide לע׳ Je 17^{25} ψ 125^{1}, cf. Je 31^{40}; עד ע׳ ψ 48^{9}. **g.** of relations between God and his people, לע׳ 1 Ch 29^{18} ψ 45^{18} 85^{6} 103^{9} 145^{21} Is 57^{16} Je $3^{5.12}$ La 3^{31} Jo $2^{26.27}$; עד (ה)ע׳ ψ 28^{9} Mal 1^{4}. **h.** of Messianic dynasty and king: (ל)ע׳ ψ 110^{4}; having divine throne 45^{7}; name endures 72^{17}; established 89^{38}; God blesses him 45^{3}; of his reign, מעתה ועד ע׳ Is 9^{6}. **i.** = *indefinite, unending future:* live לע׳ Gn 3^{22} Jb 7^{16}; הנביאים הלע׳ יִחְיוּ Zc 1^{5} *the prophets, can they live for ever?* cf. חדל לע׳ ψ 49^{9}; c. neg. *never* Ezr 9^{12} Pr 27^{24}. **j.** after death: שנת ע׳ Je $51^{39.57}$; בית ע׳ Ec 12^{5}; חַיֵּי ע׳ Dn 12^{2}; דראון ע׳ v^{2}; also v^{3} Jon 2^{7} Ec 2^{16} 9^{6}. **k.** = *age* (*duration*) *of the world:* את העלם נתן בְּלִבָּם Ec 3^{11} *the age of the world he hath set,* etc. (cf. esp. NH; others **i**). **l.** pl. intens. *everlastingness, eternity:* תשועת עולמים Is 45^{17}; צדק עלמים Dn 9^{24}; צור עולמים

Is 26[4] (RVm *rock of ages*); מלכות כל עלמים ψ 145[13], also 61[5] 77[8] 1 K 8[13] = 2 Ch 6[2]. **m.** special phr.: (מן) מ(ה)עולם (ו)עד (ה)עולם *from everlasting to everlasting*, of חסד י׳ ψ 90[2], 103[17]; benedictions 1 Ch 16[36] = ψ 106[48], Ne 9[5] 1 Ch 29[10] ψ 41[14]; the land given למן עולם ועד עולם Je 7[7] 25[5]; מעתה ועד עולם *from now and for ever* ψ 115[18] 121[8] (i.e. as long as one lives); of people's hope in God 131[3]; dynasty of David Is 9[6]; of God's acts, words, etc. Mi 4[7] Is 59[21] ψ 125[2], cf. 113[2];—v. further I. עַד p. 723.

5865, 5961 עילום v. עוֹלָם. עֲלָמוֹת v. עַלְמָה, II. עלם. p. 761

4192, 5921 עַל־מוּת לַבֵּן, עַל־מוּת v. עַלְמָה, II. עלם. p. 761

5965 †[עָלַס] **vb. rejoice** (|| with עָלַז, עָלַץ, q.v.; NH עֲלִיסָה *rejoicing* (once Levy[NHWB iii. 657]));—**Qal** *Impf.* 3 ms. יַעֲלֹס Jb 20[18] *he shall* not *rejoice*. **Niph.** *Pf.* 3 fs. נֶעֱלָסָה Jb 39[13] (of ostrich's wing) = *flap joyously*. **Hithp.** *Impf.* 1 pl. cohort. נִתְעַלְּסָה Pr 7[18] *let us delight ourselves* in (ב) love.

5966 †[עָלַע] **vb.** assumed as √ of **Pi.** *Impf.* 3 mpl. יְעַלְעוּ־דָם Jb 39[30] *they drink* (?) *blood*, but rd. prob. יְלַעְלְעוּ (√ I. לוע) Thes Ol De Me Di al.

5968 †[עָלַף] **vb. cover** (NH *id., cover, faint;* Ar. غَلَفَ *smear*, II. *cover*, غِلَافٌ *sheath;* As. *elpitu, pining, exhaustion*);—**Pu.** *Pt.* f. *covered, encrusted*, cstr. מְעֻלֶּפֶת Ct 5[14] his belly of ivory *encrusted with* sapphires. *Pf.* 3 pl. בָּנַיִךְ עֻלְּפוּ Is 51[20] *thy sons are enshrouded, enwrapped*, i.e. their senses obscured = *have swooned away;*
5969 so also Ez 31[15], rdg. 3 fs. עֻלָּפָה for subst. עֻלְפֶּה (Kö[ii. 1, 118]), all the trees *have fainted* for (עַל) him (so 𝔊 𝔖 𝔙 Hi Co al.). **Hithp.** *enwrap oneself, Impf.* 3 fs. וַתִּתְעַלָּף Gn 38[14] (J); = *swoon away,* 3 ms. וַיִּתְעַלָּף Jon 4[8]; 3 fpl. תִּתְעַלַּפְנָה Am 8[13].

5969 עֻלְפֶּה Ez 31[15] v. foregoing.

5970 †עָלַץ **vb. rejoice, exult** (NH *id.* (rare); Hiph. Impf. יעליצו Ecclus 40[20]; As. *elêṣu, exult;* Sab. מעלץ *joys* CIS[iv, No. 197, l. 5. 7]; v. also עלז, עלס);—**Qal** *Pf.* 3 ms. ע׳ לִבִּי בי׳ 1 S 2[1] *my heart exulteth in* י׳; *Impf.* 3 ms. יַעֲלֹץ הַשָּׂדֶה 1 Ch 16[32] *the field exulteth;* cf. 3 fs. תַּעֲלֹץ קִרְיָה Pr 11[10] (|| רנן); 1 s. אֶעֶלְצָה בָּךְ ψ 9[3] (i.e. in י׳; + שׂמח, || זמר); 3 mpl. יַעַלְצוּ בְךָ ψ 5[12] (in י׳ || רנן, שׂמח); יַעַלְצוּ לִפְנֵי אֱלֹהִים 68[4] (+ שׂמח, || שׂישׂ); + לִי 25[2] *exult at me; Inf. cstr.* בַּעֲלֹץ Pr 28[12] *when* the righteous *exult*.

†[עֲלִיצוּת] **n.f. exultation**;—sf. עֲלִיצֻתָם כְּמוֹ לֶאֱכֹל עָנִי Hb 3[14] *their exultation was as it were to devour the poor.* 5951

עלק (√ of foll.; cf. Ar. عَلِقَ *hang, be suspended, cleave, adhere;* عَلَقٌ *leech;* n. unit. عَلَقَةٌ; As. *ilḳitu*, of some inferior animal (word list); Syr. ܥܠܘܩܐ, etc., 𝔗 עֲלוּקָא all *leech*).

†עֲלוּקָה **n.f. leech** (perh. Aram. loan-wd.; > vampyre-like demon, Ew al. = Ar. ʿ*Aulaḳ* We[Heid. 2, 149], or name of sage, as some Rabb.; v. discussion De Toy);—לַע׳ שְׁתֵּי בָנוֹת Pr 30[15]. 5936

עֹלָתָה Jb 5[16] etc., v. עַוְלָה sub עָוַל. p. 732 5766

I, II. עַם, עִם v. sub I. עמם. p. 766-67, 769 5971, 5973

עָמַד[520] **take one's stand, stand** (NH *id.;* Ph. עמד; As. *emêdu, stand, set up;* Ar. عَمَدَ *prop up, support,* and deriv.; Eth. ዐምድ: *pillar;* 𝔗 עַמּוּדָא *pillar*, Syr. ܥܡܘܕܐ, Palm. עמודא, cf. also n.pr. תימעמד; Sab. עמד *pillar*, acc. to CIS[iv. 91] (or other deriv. fr. √ עמד DHM[ZMG xxxvii (1883), 5]), pl. אעמדן *pillars* DHM[Epigr. Denkm. aus Abess. 80]);—**Qal**[435] *Pf.* ע׳ Gn 19[27] +, 3 fs. עָֽמְדָה 2 K 13[6] +, etc.; *Impf.* יַעֲמֹד Ex 21[21], יַעֲמוֹד Na 1[6] +, יַעֲמָד־ 1 S 16[22] +; 1 s. אֶעֱמֹדָה Hb 2[1], וָאֶעֱמֹד 2 S 1[10]; 3 mpl. יַעַמְדוּ Je 32[14] +, יַעֲמֹדוּ Ez 1[21] +, 2 mpl. וַתַּעַמְדוּן Dt 4[11], etc.; *Imv.* עֲמֹד 1 S 9[27] +, עֲמָד־ 2 S 1[9]; fs. עִמְדִי Is 47[12] Je 48[19], etc.; *Inf. abs.* עָמֹד Est 9[16]; *cstr.* עֲמֹד Ex 18[23] +, sf. עָמְדִי Je 18[20], עֲמָדְךָ Ob[11], etc.; *Pt.* עֹמֵד Is 3[13] +, f. עֹמֶדֶת Hg 2[5] +, etc.;—**1. a.** *take one's stand,* and (esp. pt.) *stand, be in a standing attitude:* c. עַל *by*, 1 S 26[13] 2 S 2[25] 2 K 2[7] +, so pt. Gn 18[8] (J), 41[1.17] (E) +, עַל *on*, Ex 3[5] (E), Dt 27[12] +; c. ב loc. Ex 32[26] Nu 22[24.26] (all JE), +; c. אֶל loc. 1 K 20[38] (+ לְ pers.), Je 48[19] Ez 21[26] 27[29]; c. אֶל pers. 1 S 17[51] 2 K 5[25]; c. אֵצֶל Gn 41[3] (E), Ez 9[2] 10[6] Ne 8[4]; c. לִפְנֵי Gn 18[22] 1 K 3[16] 8[22] +; before י׳, for intercession Gn 19[27] (J), Dt 4[10] Je 15[1] 18[20], etc.; *take one's stand* and do a thing 1 S 17[8] 1 K 8[55] 2 K 18[28] = Is 36[13] +; sq. inf. 1 K 8[11] = 2 Ch 5[14] +. **b.** *stand forth* (to speak, etc.) 2 K 10[9] +. **c.** *take a stand* against (עַל), in opposition to, Ju 6[31] Ezr 10[15] (but *stand* over, = have charge of, acc. to Kue[Ges. Abh. 247 f.]) 2 Ch 26[18]; cf. עַל־דַּם Lv 19[16] (H) *against the blood of*, i.e. seek one's blood, life; c. יַחַד Is 50[8] *together*, i.e. against each other. **d.** *present* oneself before (לִפְנֵי) Gn 43[15] (J), Ex 9[10] (E), Nu 27[2.21] (P), 1 S 16[21] +; before י׳ (in sanctuary) Dt 19[17] Je 7[10] cf. 18^{20} Lv 9^{5} (P); so in heaven 1 K 22^{21} = 2 Ch 18^{20}; c. ב loc. of child at birth Ho 13^{13}, in palace (as retainer, courtier) Dn 1^{4}. **e.** c. לִפְנֵי *attend upon, be(come) servant of* 1 S 16^{22} (v. Dr), 1 K 1^{2}+; servant of י׳ 1 K 17^{1} 18^{15} 2 K 3^{14} 5^{16} Je 15^{19}; priests (לְשָׁרְתוֹ) לִפְנֵי י׳ Dt 10^{8} Ju 20^{28} Ez 44^{15} 2 Ch 29^{11}; of Levites, *stand* before congreg. for menial duties Ez 44^{11} Nu 16^{9} (P). **f.** *stand* afar מֵרָחוֹק Ex 20$^{18.21}$ (E), Is 59^{14} ψ 38^{12}, בְּר׳ ψ 10^{1}; מִנֶּגֶד מֵר׳ 2 K 2^{7}; *stand* aloof, מִנֶּגֶד Ob^{11} ψ 38^{12}. **g.** *stand* (silent) Jb 32^{16}. **h.** *stand* (appealingly) Jb 30^{20} (but rd. עָמַדְתָּ, of God, Me Hi Du). **i.** *stand*, subj. רֶגֶל Zc 14^{4} (עַל loc.), ψ 122^{2} (ב loc.) so 26^{12} (fig.). **j.** *stand*, of water, עַל־הָרִים ψ 104^{6}. Vid. also preps. עִם, מִמַּעַל, עַל, אֵצֶל, אֶל, etc. **2. a.** *stand still, stop*, cease moving, of moon Jos 10^{13} (JE; ‖ וַיִּדֹּם), sun v^{13}, both, Hb 3^{11}; of pers. 1 S 9^{27} (opp. עָבַר), 2 S 2^{28} (opp. רָדַף), עִמְדוּ עֲמֹדוּ Na 2^{9}+; *stop* flowing (of oil) 2 K 4^{6}; *remain standing*, c. תַּחְתֵּינוּ Ju 7^{21} 1 S 14^{9} etc.; of eruption in skin = remain unchanged Lv 13$^{23.28}$; so (without ת׳) 13$^{5.37}$ (all P). **b.** = be inactive 2 Ch 20^{17} (opp. הִתְיַצְּבוּ + ,לְהִלָּחֵם). **c.** = be attentive Jb 37^{14}. **d.** *stop, cease* doing a thing 2 K 13^{18}; c. מִן Gn 29^{35} 30^{9} (both J), Jo 1^{15}. **3. a.** *tarry, delay* Gn 45^{9} (E), Jos 10^{19} (JE; opp. רָדַף), 1 S 20^{38} (opp. חוּשָׁה, מְהֵרָה), +. **b.** *remain*, c. ב loc. 2 K 15^{20} Dt 10^{10}; c. עִמָּדִי Dt 5^{28} (opp. שׁוּב); +inf. purpose Est 7^{7}. **c.** *continue, abide* Je 32^{14} Is 66^{22} ψ 102^{27} (opp. אָבַד); = dwell Ex 8^{18} (J; עַל loc.); לָעַד ψ 19^{10} 111$^{3.10}$ 112$^{3.9}$; לְעוֹלָם ψ 33^{11} Ec 1^{4}; בְּתוֹךְ Hg 2^{5}; of plan = be established ψ 33^{11} (earlier קוּם, as Is 14^{24}), so Est 3^{4} Dn 11^{17b}; = maintain itself (earlier קוּם Jos 2^{11}) Ec 2^{9}; לֹא יַעֲמָד־בִּי כֹחַ Dn 10^{17}. **d.** *endure* Ex 18^{23} (E), Ez 22^{14} (‖ חָזַק). **e.** *be steadfast* Dt 25^{8} Ru 2^{7}. **f.** *persist* Ec 8^{3}. **4.** *make a stand, hold one's ground*, Am 2^{15} 2 K 10^{4} Mal 3^{2}+; c. לִפְנֵי Ju 2^{14} 2 K 10^{4}+, בִּפְנֵי Jos 10^{8} 21^{44} (Ginsb; van d. H. Baer v^{42}), 23^{9} (all D); c. עַל, for one's life Est 8^{11} 9^{16}. **5.** *stand upright*: **a.** *remain standing* 2 K 13^{6}; of head 6^{31} *remain upright* upon him (עָלָיו); of house (fig. of endurance) Jb 8^{15}, Pr 12^{7}. **b.** *stand up*, opp. sit, Ne 8^{5} Jb 29^{8} (+קוּם); opp. lie prostrate Ez 2^{1} (עַל־רַגְלֶיךָ), so 37^{10} (*id.*), Dn 10^{11}, v^{11} (עַל־עָמְדֶךָ), Est 8^{4}; of revival after death Dn 12^{13} (late for קוּם). **c.** *stand up, rise*, of water Jos 3^{13} (+appos. נֵד אֶחָד), v^{16} (+קָמוּ + *id.*; both JE). **d.** *be erect, upright*, of boards Ex 26^{15} 36^{20} (P). †**6. a.** *arise, appear, come on the scene* (= קוּם; late) Ezr 2^{63} = Ne 7^{65}, ψ 106^{30} (cf. Ecclus 47$^{1.12}$), esp. Dn 8$^{22.22.23}$ 11$^{2.3.4}$ 12^{1}, cf. 11^{7} (כַּנּוֹ), v$^{20.21}$ (עַל־כַּנּוֹ); c. תַּחַת *instead of* Ec 4^{15}; of war 1 Ch 20^{4}, deliverance Est 4^{14}. **b.** *stand forth, appear* = come into being Is 48^{13} ψ 33^{9} 119^{90}. **c.** *rise up* as foe (earlier קוּם Am 7^{9} Gn 4^{8}), c. עַל *against* 1 Ch 21^{1} 2 Ch 20^{23} Dn 8^{25} 11^{14}, c. לְנֶגְדִּי *against* 10^{13}. **7.** rare usages are: **a.** ע׳ אֶת־ *stand with*, as attendant, servitor Gn 45^{1} (E), Nu 1^{5} (P). **b.** *take one's stand* in covenant, בַּבְּרִית 2 K 23^{3}. **c.** *stand* עַל־חֶרֶב Ez 33^{26} (resort to the sword). **d.** *stand* בְּסוֹד י׳ Je 23$^{18.22}$ (v. סוֹד). **e.** *be appointed* Ezr 10^{14}. **f.** *stand* before (לִפְנֵי) beast Lv 18^{23} (carnal intercourse) **g.** *grow flat, insipid* (Gie), taste of wine Je 48^{11} (fig. of Moab), or *remain unchanged* (so most, in that case cf. **3 b**).—עָמְדִי Dn 11^{1b} is crpt., rd. prob. עֲמַדְתִּי, or עָמַד (מִיכָאֵל subj.), join then to 10^{21} and del. 11^{1a}; so Bev Behrm Marti^{Kau}.

Hiph.$_{83}$ (cf. Dr$^{Intr.(6)\,535}$) *Pf.* 3 ms. הֶעֱמִיד 1 K 12^{32}+, 2 ms. הֶעֱמַדְתָּה ψ 30^{8}, וְהַעֲמַדְתָּ Nu 3^{6}+, etc.; *Impf.* יַעֲמִיד Pr 29^{4}+, וַיַּעֲמֵד 2 K 8^{1}+; 3 fs. sf. וַתַּעֲמִדֵנִי Ez 2^{2} 3^{24}, 1 pl. וַנַּעֲמִיד Ne 4^{3}, etc.; *Imv.* הַעֲמֵד Is 21^{6}; sf. הַעֲמִידָהּ Ez 24^{11}; *Inf. abs.* הַעֲמֵיד Ne 7^{3}; *cstr.* הַעֲמִיד 1 K 15^{4}+; *Pt.* מַעֲמִיד 2 Ch 18^{34} (but v. **Hoph.**);—**1.** *station, set*, c. acc. Ju 16^{25} (בֵּין); for duty Nu 11^{24} (E; סְבִיבֹת), 1 K 12^{32} (ב loc.), 2 Ch 19^{5} (*id.*), Ne 13^{11} (עַל־עָמְדָם), Is 21^{6}+ (Ne 4^{7a} read perhaps **Qal**, so Perles$^{Anal.\,65}$), c. עַל *against* Ne 4^{3}. **2.** *cause to stand firm* ψ 18^{34} = 2 S 22^{34} (c. עַל loc.); *maintain* (opp. overthrow) Ex 9^{16} (J), 1 K 15^{4}, cf. Pr 29^{4}. **3.** *cause to stand up, set up, erect*, c. acc. עַל־רַגְלַי + Ez 2^{2} 3^{24}, so עַל־עָמְדִי Dn 8^{18}; temple Ezr 2^{68} (עַל loc.), cf. 2 Ch 24^{13} (עַל loc., of repairs); esp. doors Ne 3^{1} + 7 t. Ne; Asherim 2 Ch 33^{19}, cf. 25^{14}. **4.** + לִפְנֵי *present* one *before* king Gn 47^{7} (P), י׳ (in sanctuary) Lv 14^{11} + 3 t. P, + (of goat) Lv 16^{7}, priest Lv 27^{8} + 4 t. P, + (of beast) Lv 27^{11}. **5.** *appoint* Ne 7^{3} 1 Ch 15^{17}+ (late); c. עַל *over* Ne 13^{9}+, c. inf. purpose 6^{7}+, c. 2 acc. 1 Ch 15^{16}; = assign (land) to (ל) 2 Ch 33^{8} (‖ 2 K 21^{8} נָתַן); *appoint* courses of priests 8^{14} 31^{2}, cf. Ne 13^{30}; *ordain* commandments, עַל pers. Ne 10^{33}, cf. 2 Ch 30^{5}; *establish* עַד־הָעוֹלָם 1 Ch 17^{14} (ב loc.), cf. 2 Ch 9^{8} ψ 148^{6}; c. acc. of covenant ψ 105^{10} = 1 Ch 16^{17} (ל pers. + ל rei); c. חָזוֹן *vision* Dn 11^{14} (= fulfil, earlier הֵקִים). †**6.** other meanings: **a.** ע׳ אֶת־פָּנָיו 2 K 8^{11} *have a fixed look.* **b.** c. acc. + ב + רַגְלַי loc. ψ 31^{9} (fig.). **c.** *make to stand* (in a covt.; v. ‖ 2 K 23^{3}) 2 Ch 34^{32}. **d.** *restore* waste places Ezr 9^{9}. **e.** + לְפָנֶיהָ Est 4^{5}, i.e. *make servant to.* **f.** *cause* wind *to arise* ψ 107[25]. **g.** =*raise* an army Dn 11[11.13].— 2 Ch 18[34] v. **Hoph.**; ψ 30[8] v. עֹז; Ez 29[7] v. מָעַד.

†**Hoph.** *Impf.* 3 ms. יָעֳמַד־ Lv 16[10] *be presented* (of goat), + לִפְנֵי י׳; *Pt.* הָיָה מָעֳמָד 1 K 22[35] *he was caused to stand*, i. e. propped up, in (ב) his chariot, so rd. also ‖ 2 Ch 18[34] (as 𝔊), for MT מַעֲמִיד.—On *Pf.* הֶעֱמַדְתִּי v. עֹז ψ 30[8].

5977 †[עֹ֫מֶד] **n.[m.] standing-place**;—only sf. after prep.: וַיָּקוּמוּ עַל־עָמְדָם Ne 9[3] *they stood up in their place* (later equiv. of תַּחְתָּם), 8[7] (no vb.); c. עָמַד 2 Ch 30[16] 35[10], ע׳ עַל־עָמְדוֹ 34[31]; וָאַעֲמִדֵם עַל־עָמְדָם Ne 13[11], so עַל־עָמְדִי Dn 8[18]; עֲמֹד עַל־עָמְדֶךָ 10[11]. וַיָּבֹא אֵצֶל עָמְדִי v[17].

5979 †[עֶמְדָּה] **n.f. standing-ground**;—sf. יִקַּח מִכֶּם עֶמְדָּתוֹ Mi 1[11]; text dub. v. Now.

5982 **עַמּוּד, עַמֻּד** $_{110}$ **n.m.**[1 K 7,15] **pillar, column**;—עַמּוּד abs. 1 K 7[15]+, cstr. Ex 13[21]+; עַמֻּד abs. Je 52[21], cstr. Nu 14[14]; sf. עַמּוּדוֹ 2 Ch 23[13]; pl. עַמּוּדִים 1 K 7[16]+, less oft. עַמֻּ׳ v[21]+; cstr. עַמּוּדֵי Ex 26[32]+, less oft. עַמֻּ׳ 38[17]+; sf. עַמּוּדָיו Ex 36[38]+, עַמֻּדָיו 27[10]+, etc.;—**1.** *pillar*, supporting house Ju 16[25.26.29]; *pillars* in tabern. Ex 27[10.11.17] 36[38] Nu 3[37]+27 t. Ex Nu (P), + עַמּוּדֵי שִׁטִּים *pillars of acacia* wood Ex 26[32.37] 36[36]; *pillars* in Sol.'s palace 1 K 7[2.3.6], אוּלָם הָע׳ v[6], עַמּוּדֵי אֲרָזִים v[2] *pillars of cedar* (P); in Ezek.'s temple Ez 42[6.6]; ע׳ שֵׁשׁ Est 1[6] (in palace), Ct 5[15] (sim.). **2.** two bronze pillars—1 K 7[15] 2 K 25[13]=Je 52[17]—before temple 1 K 7[15.15]+14 t. 1 K 7, +2 K 25[16.17.17]=Je 52[20.21.21], Je 27[19] 1 Ch 18[8] 2 Ch 3[15.17]+5 t. Ch; perh. one of these was הָע׳ by which king stood in temple 2 K 11[14]=2 Ch 23[13], 2 K 23[3]; >ע׳ here=*standing-place, platform* Thes al.; two pillars bef. Ezek.'s temple Ez 40[49]. **3.** *columns, uprights*, of silver Ct 3[10] (litter). **4.** ע׳ עָשָׁן Ju 20[40] *column of smoke*: ע׳ (הֶ)עָנָן Ex 13[21.22] (J)+6 t. JE, hence Ne 9[12.19] ψ 99[7]; ‖ ע׳ (הָ)אֵשׁ Ex 13[21.22] (J), Nu 14[14] (JE), Ne 9[12.19]; ע׳ אֵשׁ וְעָנָן Ex 14[24] (J), all of the theoph. at time of Exodus. **5. a.** ע׳ בַּרְזֶל Je 1[18] (fig. of proph.). **b.** poet. of pillars of earth Jb 9[6] ψ 75[4], of heaven Jb 26[11]. **c.** of wisdom's house Pr 9[1].

4612 †[מַעֲמָד] **n.[m.] office, function, service**;—**1.** *station, office, post* מַעֲמָדְךָ Is 22[19] (‖ מַצָּבְךָ), עַל־מַעֲמָדָם 2 Ch 35[15] *at their post.* **2.** *office, function* 1 Ch 23[28]. **3.** *service*, prob. specif. *waiting* at table (strictly *mode of standing*), cstr. מַעֲמַד מְשָׁרְתָיו 1 K 10[5]=2 Ch 9[4].

†מָעֳמָד **n.[m.] standing-ground, foothold** ψ 69[3] (in fig.). 4613

עִמָּדִי v. עִם infr. sub עמם. p. 767 5973

עמה (√of foll.; cf. As. *emû, be united, associated; emûtu, family, family connexion;* NH עָמִית=BH (rare)).

†[עָמִית] **n.m.**[Lv 18,20] **associate, fellow, relation** (perh. orig. f. abstr. *association*, cf. פֶּחָה);—alw. sf.: גֶּבֶר עֲמִיתִי Zc 13[7] *a man* (who is) *my fellow;* elsewhere only Lv: עֲמִיתוֹ 5[21.21]; recipr. אִישׁ בַּעֲמִיתוֹ 19[11] 24[19], cf. 25[17]; עֲמִיתְךָ 18[20], עֲמִיתֶךָ 19[15.17] 25[14.14.15]. 5997

עַמִּיאֵל and similar n.pr. v. sub I. עמם. p. 770 5988

†**עָמַל** **vb. labour, toil** (NH *id.;* Ar. عَمِلَ *labour, make;* Sab. עמל *work* (? n. or vb.) CIS[iv. No. 250]; Aram. עֲמַל, ܥܡܠ; Zinj. עמל; As. *nîmelu, gain, possessions*);—**Qal** *Pf.* 3 ms. ע׳ Ec 2[21]; 3 fs. עָמְלָה Pr 16[26]; 2 ms. עָמַלְתָּ Jon 4[10]; 1 s. עָמַלְתִּי Ec 2[11]+2 t.; 3 pl. עָמְלוּ ψ 127[1]; *Impf.* 3 ms. יַעֲמֹל Ec 1[3]+3 t.;—*labour* (very late): in building ψ 127[1]; tillage, c. בְּ Jon 4[10]; gen., c. בְּ Ec 2[21], c. לְ Pr 16[26] Ec 5[15], c. לְ+inf. 8[17]; עֲמָלוֹ שֶׁיַּעֲמֹל 1[3] 5[17], cf. 2[11.19.20]. 5998

†I. **עָמָל** **n.m.**[Jb 4,8] **f.**[Ec 10,15] (against Albr[ZAW xvi (1896), 113], v. Kö[Synt. § 249 m]) **trouble, labour, toil** (on this form as abstr. v. Lag[BN 143] Ba[NB 105]);—ע׳ Nu 23[21]+; cstr. עֲמַל Ju 10[16]+; sf. עֲמָלִי Gn 41[51]+, etc.;—**1.** *trouble* (‖ *sorrow*): one's own suffering, עָמָל וְיָגוֹן Je 20[18]; עָנִי ψ 10[14]; ע׳ וָכַעַס ψ 10[14]; עָנִי וע׳ Dt 26[7] ψ 25[18]; ע׳ וָאָוֶן 90[10]; ‖ אָוֶן Nu 23[21] Jb 5[6]; ‖ שָׁוְא Jb 7[3]; ע׳ נפשו Is 53[11]; ע׳ בְּעֵינָי ψ 73[16]; אדם לע׳ Jb 3[10]; ע׳ מְנַחֲמֵי 16[2]; וַיַּסְתֵּר ע׳ מֵעֵינָי 5[7]; יוּלָּד ψ 73[5]; בע׳ אנוש אינימו Jb 11[16]; שכח ע׳ Gn 41[51] (E); נַשַּׁנִי ע׳ Pr 31[7]; לא זכר ע׳ Ju 10[16]. תקצר נפשו בע׳ **2.** *trouble, mischief*, as done to others: ‖ שֹׁד Pr 24[2]; יֹצֵר ע׳ ψ 94[20]; ע׳ וָאָוֶן ψ 7[17]; יָשׁוּב ע׳ בְּראֹשׁוֹ 10[7]; ‖ רַע Hb 1[13]; און וע׳ 55[11]; ‖ אָוֶן Is 10[1] 59[4] Hb 1[3] ψ 7[15] Jb 4[8] 15[35]; עֲמַל שְׂפָתֵימוֹ ψ 140[10] *mischief of their lips.* **3.** *toil, labour* (late in Heb.): Ec 2[10.10.21.24] 3[13] 4[4.6.8.9] 5[14.18] 6[7] 8[15] 10[15]; c. עָמַל (q. v.) 1[3] 2[11.19.20] 5[17]; ע׳ אֲשֶׁר עָמַל 9[9]; ע׳ שֶׁאֲנִי (שֶׁהוּא) עָמֵל 2[18.22]; =fruit of labour, ע׳ לְאֻמִּים יִירָשׁוּ ψ 105[44]; וַיַּכְנַע בע׳ לִבָּם 107[12] *he humbled their mind by toil.*

†II. **עָמָל** **n.pr.m.** name in Asher 1 Ch 7[35], 6000 𝔊 Αμαα, 𝔊L Αλαμ.

6001 †I. עָמֵל **n.m.**$^{Pr 16, 26}$ **labourer, sufferer**;—'ע Pr 16^{26}+2 t.; pl. עֲמֵלִים Ju 5^{26};—**1.** *labourer, workman:* Ju 5^{26} Pr 16^{26}. **2.** *sufferer,* Jb 3^{20} (‖ מָרֵי נֶפֶשׁ), 20^{22}.

5998, 6001 †II. עָמֵל **adj. verb.** toiling, only Ec, as pred.;—Ec 2$^{18.22}$ 3^{9} 4^{8} 9^{9}.

6002 עֲמָלֵק$_{39}$ **n.pr.gent. Amalek** (on ָ v. Lag$^{BN 162}$ Ba$^{NB 160}$);—ancient people Nu 24$^{20.20}$, S. of Canaan—in Negeb 13^{29} (all JE), fierce and war-like Bedawin (cf. GASm$^{Geogr. 282}$ GFM$^{Ju 6, 3.33}$), foes of Isr. during Exodus Ex 17^{8}+6 t. Ex 17 (E), Dt 25$^{17.19}$; later marauders in Isr. territory Ju 3^{13} 6$^{3.33}$ 7^{12} 10^{12}, defeated by Saul 1 S 14^{48} 15^{2}+9 t. 1 S 14, 28^{18}, and by David 30^{18} (cf. **adj. gent.** infr.), 2 S 8^{12}=1 Ch 18^{11}, cf. ψ 83^{8}; also 'הָע 2 S 1^{1} (where read עֲמָלֵק or הָעֲמָלֵקִי, v. Comm.); 'ע 1 Ch 4^{43}; as grandson of Esau Gn 36^{12} (P)=1 Ch 1^{36}, Gn 36^{16}; appar. connected with Ephr. territory Ju 5^{14} (cf. 12^{15} infr.; yet GFM conj. עֵמֶק).—On Amalek v. Nö$^{Amalekites (1864)}$; Ency. Bi. s.v.

6003 †עֲמָלֵקִי **adj.gent.** 1 S 30^{13} 2 S 1^{13}, also (as pred.) v^{8}; coll.=(*the*) *Amalekites* 1 S 15$^{6.15}$ 30^{1}, elsewh. c. art. 'הָע Nu 14$^{25.43.45}$ (J; all+הַכְּנַעֲנִי), 1 S 27^{8}; 'שְׂדֵה הָע Gn 14^{7}; 'הַר הָע Ju 12^{15} (in Ephraim); rd. 'הָע also Ju 1^{16} (for הָעָם) Bu GFM, >עֲמָלֵק Hollenb Mey Kit^{Kau}; on 2 S 1^{1} v. foreg.

† I. עָמַם **vb.** (√ of foll. cf. Ar. عَمَّ *be comprehensive, include;* عَمٌّ *company;* also *paternal uncle;* perhaps As. *ummanu, people;* Sab. עם either (*a*) *people,* or (*b*) *paternal uncle* CIS$^{iv. p. 20}$; pl. sf. אעממהו=(*b*) Mordtm$^{Himj. Inschr. 45.70}$; also often in n.pr. CIS$^{iv. No. 5, 1. 99, 7}$ etc., Prät$^{Neue Beitr. 25}$ Hom$^{Chrest. 12, 133; A. und A. 6}$ We$^{GGN 1893, 480}$). p. 770

5971 I. עַם, עָם$_{1840}$ **n.m.**$^{Gn 11, 6}$ (v. infr.) **people** (NH *id., plebeian, common man;* 𝔗 עַמָּא *people,* pl. *peoples, tribes,* etc.; Syr. ܥܡܐ; Ar. عَمٌّ v. supr.; orig. mng. prob. *those united, connected, related,* cf. We$^{GGN 1893, 480}$);—abs. עַם Gn 11^{6}+, עָם Ju 9^{36}+, הָעָם Jos 8^{11}+; cstr. עַם Nu 21^{29}+; sf. עַמִּי Ex 3^{7}+, עַמְּךָ 22^{27}+, etc.; pl. עַמִּים Is 2^{3}+, עֲמָמִים (cf. BAram.) Ne 9^{22}; cstr. עַמֵּי 1 K 8^{43}+, עַמְמֵי Ne 9^{24}; pl. c. sf. v. II. עַם;—(Thes cites foll. as **f.** וְחַטָּאת עַמֶּךָ Ex 5^{16} [but corrupt and unintellig.; read perh. וְחַטָּאתָ לְעַ', so 𝔊 𝔖 Di]; Ju 18^{7} [but יֹשֶׁבֶת must agree with lost word *city,* or the like, v. GFM]; Je 8^{5} [but read שׁוֹבֵב for שׁוֹבֵבָה Gie]);—**1.** *a people, nation* (sts. ‖ גּוֹי), n. coll. (sg. Ex 21^{8} Jos 17$^{14.15.17}$ 2 S 17^{29}+oft., or pl. Ex 20^{15} 24^{2} Je 5^{31}+oft., or both in same clause Ex 1^{20} 2 S 13^{24}): עַם אֶחָד=all mankind Gn 11^{6} (J); peoples in gen. 27^{29} (J; ‖ לְאֻמִּים), Ex 19^{5} (E), Dt 2^{25} 4^{6}+oft. Dt, Ne 13^{24}+oft.; קְהַל עַמִּים Gn 28^{3} (P) *an assembly* (multitude) *of peoples,* 48^{4} (P), Ez 23^{24} 32^{3} (+רַבִּים); one's own people Je 46^{16} ψ 45^{11}
Ru 1$^{10.15.16.16}$+ (on עַמִּי נָדִיב Ct 6^{12} v. esp. Bu); 5993
particular peoples, Egypt Gn 41^{40} (E), Ex 1^{22} (E), Ne 9^{10}+; עַם־אֲרָם Am 1^{5}; עַם־כְּמוֹשׁ (i.e. Moab) Nu 21^{29} (JE), Je 48^{46}; but esp. Isr. Ex 1^{20} (E)+oft.; 'עַם־בְּנֵי יִשׂ v^{9} (J); called עַ' יהוה Nu 11^{29} (E), 1 S 2^{24}+, and (by 'י) עַמִּי Ex 3^{7} 5^{1} (J)+oft. (all periods); קְהַל עַם־הָאֱלֹהִים Ju 20^{2}, עַם־הַקָּהָל Lv 16^{33} (P), קְהַל עָם ψ 107^{32}; esp. הָעָם הַזֶּה (oft. in contempt or disgust) Nu 11$^{1.12.13}$+; fig. of ants Pr 30^{25}, the *shaphan* v^{26}, locusts Jo 2^{2}, cf. לְעָם לְצִיִּים ψ 74^{14} (where rd. לְעַם צִיִּים Hup-Now).—On Ju 1^{16} v. עֲמָלֵקִי. **2.**=smaller units, e.g. **a.** inhab. of a city Gn 19^{4} (J), 1 S 9$^{12.13}$ Je 29$^{16.25}$ 2 Ch 31^{4}+ (Je 8^{5} del. 'יְרוּשׁ 𝔊 Gie Co Rothst). **b.** inhab. of a locality Je 37^{12} [appar. not=tribe, Dt 33^{3} rd. עַמּוֹ 𝔊 Di Dr, Ho 10^{14} Ju 5$^{8.14}$ rd. בְּעָרֶיךָ We Now; v. sub **d**]. **c.** retainers, followers Gn 14^{16} 32^{8} 33^{15} 35^{6} Ju 3^{18} 8^{5} 2 S 15^{17} Je 41$^{13.14}$+. **d.** people bearing arms 1 S 11^{11} 1 K 20^{10}+; עַ' כָּבֵד Nu 20^{20} (JE), i.e. a powerful force; עַם הַצָּבָא Nu 31^{32} (P), עַ' הַמִּלְחָמָה Jos 8$^{1.3.11}$ 10^{7} 11^{7} (all JE); so prob. Ju 5^{8} *a* (fighting) *band;* perh. also v^{14} (rd. sg.? v. GFM Bu). **3.**=common people Je 21^{7} 22^{4}, Lv 4^{27} (opp. ruler v^{22}), Ne 5^{1} (opp. יְהוּדִים), 7^{5} (opp. rulers). **4.** *people* in gen., *persons* Gn 50^{20} (E), so appar. כָּל־הָעָם אֲשֶׁר וגו' Ex 33^{16} (J), Nu 11^{34} (J), Jos 5$^{5.5}$ (D), Ju 9^{36} (as sg.), v^{37} (as pl.), Je 36^{9}; persons labouring 1 K 9^{23}; superior persons Jb 12^{2} (iron.); עַם עוֹלָם Ez 26^{30} *people of long ago* (now in She'ôl). **5.** phrases are: **a.** בְּנֵי עַמּוֹ (עַמְּךָ, עַמִּי, עַמָּהּ) *members of one's people, compatriots, fellow-countrymen,* etc. Nu 22^{5} (E), Gn 23^{11} (P) Lv 19^{18} (H), Ju 14$^{16.17}$ Ez 33$^{2.12}$+. **b.** בְּנֵי הָעָם=*common people* (v. **3**) 2 K 23^{6} Je 26^{23}+; *people* in gen. שַׁעַר בְּנֵי הָעָם Je 17^{19} i.e. *public gate* 2 Ch 35$^{5.12}$. **c.** עַם הָאָרֶץ *the people* at large, as a body 2 K 11$^{14.18.19.20}$ 15^{5} 16^{15} 21$^{24.24}$+, Je 37^{2} 44^{21} Lv 20^{2} (H), Gn 23$^{7.12.13}$ (P); common people Je 34^{19}, cf. דַּלַּת עַ' הא' 2 K 24^{14}; disting. from prince Ez 45^{22} 46$^{3.9}$, from priests Hg 2^{4} Zc 7^{5}; =Canaanites Nu 14^{9} (JE), cf. עַמֵּי הָאָרֶץ 1 Ch 5^{25}; mixed post-exil. population Ezr 4^{4}. **d.** עַמֵּי הָאָרֶץ usu. *peoples of the earth* Jos 4^{24} (D), 2 Ch 32^{19}+; of heathen peoples about and in Pal. after exile Ezr 10$^{2.11}$; traders Ne 10^{31}; עַמֵּי הָאֲרָצוֹת 9^{30} 10^{29} 2 Ch 32^{13}. **e.** מִשְׁפְּחוֹת עַמִּים ψ 96^{7}=1 Ch 16^{28} (cf. ψ 22^{28}).

f. בַּת־עַמִּי = people personif. Is 22^{4} Je 4^{11} + 7 t. Je + 6^{14} (van d. H.; om. בַּת Baer Gi), La 2^{11} 3^{48} $4^{3.6.10}$; בְּתוּלַת בַּת־עַמִּי Je 14^{17}. **g.** designations of Isr. are: עַם־קָדוֹשׁ Dt 7^{6} + 3 t., ע׳ קְדֹשִׁים Dn 8^{24}, ע׳ (ה)קֹּדֶשׁ Is 62^{12} 63^{18} Dn 12^{7}; ע׳ סְגֻלָּה Dt 7^{6} 14^{2} 26^{18}. **h.** of foreign (non-Isr.) peoples: ע׳ נָכְרִי Ex 21^{8} (E), ע׳ אַחֵר Dt 28^{32}, and esp. from language, ע׳ עִמְקֵי שָׂפָה Ez 3^{5} cf. v^{6}, כִּלְשׁוֹן עַם וָעָם Ne 13^{24} cf. Est $1^{22.22}$ 3^{12}, ע׳ לֹעֵז ψ 114^{1}. **i.** עַם עֶבְרָתִי Is 10^{6}, ע׳ חֶרְמִי 34^{11}, ע׳־מִבְחָרָיו Dn 11^{15}, עַמֵּי הַתֹּעֵבוֹת הָאֵלֶּה Ezr 9^{14}; לֹא עַם בִּינוֹת Is 27^{11}.—For עַם־עוֹלָם Is 44^{7} read (מִי הִשְׁמִיעַ מֵעוֹלָם (אֹתִיּוֹת) Oort Du Kit Che^{Hpt} cf. Perles$^{Anal. 40, 64}$.

5973 **עִם prep. with** (Aram. עִם, ܥܡ, Sab. עם DHM$^{Epigr. Denkm. 12}$ Hom$^{Chrest. 51}$; cf. Ar. مَعْ, مَعَ,
5978 (but v. Prät$^{BAS. i. 26}$)), sf. עִמִּי$_{46}$ and עִמָּדִי$_{45}$ (prob. akin to Ar. عِنْدٌ *side*, عِنْدَ *beside*: cf. √עמד), without difference of meaning (עמי in Pent. Gn 31^{31} $39^{7.12.14}$ Ex 33^{12} Lv $26^{21.23.27.40}$ [H] Nu 22^{19}; Jos–K. 13 t.; ψ 42^{9} 86^{17} Jb 10^{17} Ru 1^{11} Est 7^{8}; in Dn 7 t., Ezr Ne Ch 11 t.: עמדי in Pent. Gn [JE] 14 t., Ex 17^{2} Lv 25^{23} Dt 5^{28} $32^{34.39}$; Ju S 7 t.; ψ 23^{4} 50^{11} 55^{19} 101^{6}; Jb 14 t., Ru 1^{8}); עִמְּךָ, עִמְּכָה + 1 S 1^{26}, עִמָּךְ; עִמּוֹ, עִמָּהּ; עִמָּנוּ; עִמָּכֶם; עִמָּם$_{27}$ (Gn 18^{16}, etc.: Gn–K 20 t.; Ne 13^{25}; not Ezr Ch), and עִמָּהֶם$_{23}$ (chiefly late: Nu 22^{12} Dt 29^{16} (v^{24} עמם), Jon 1^{3} Jb 1^{4}, and 19 t. Ne Ezr Ch):—**1.** of fellowship and companionship (Lat. *cum*), as Gn 13^{1} ולוט עמו and Lot *with* him, 18^{16} 19^{30} 24^{54} הוא והאנשים אשר עמו, וכל ישׂראל עמו Jos 7^{24} *al.*; + oft. Peculiar to Ch Ezr are clauses introd. by ועמהם . . . 1 Ch 12^{34} 13^{2} 15^{18} +, Ezr $8^{13.14}$ (Aram. 5^{2}) +; so ועמו . . . 1 Ch 12^{28} 2 Ch 17^{14-18} 26^{17} Ezr $8^{3-12.33}$. Coupling substantives, *together with*, chiefly in poetry: Dt 12^{23} לא תאכל הנפשׁ עם הבשׂר, Jos 11^{21} Ju 16^{3} Ec 7^{11}; 2 S 1^{24} שָׁנִי עִם עֲדָנִים, Dt 32^{14} עִם חֵלֶב כרים, $v^{14.24.25}$ Am 4^{10} Is 25^{11} 34^{7} Je 6^{11} 51^{40} Na 3^{12} ψ 66^{15} אעשׂה בקר עם עתודים, 81^{3} 83^{8} 87^{4} 89^{14} 104^{25} +, Ct 1^{11} $4^{13.13}$ כפרים עם נרדים, $v^{14.14}$ $5^{1.1.1}$. Unusually, Est 9^{25} אמר עם הספר he ordered *in conjunction with* writing, in a written order. Poet. or late uses: ψ 42^{9} ובלילה שִׁירֹה עמי, ψ 89^{22} אשׁר יָדִי תִּכּוֹן עמו, v^{25}; in Jb of the companionship of sufferings or prosperity, 6^{4} חִצֵּי שַׁדַּי עמדי, 17^{2} אם לא הֲתֻלִים עמדי, 29^{6} וְצוּר יָצוּק עִמָּדִי פלגי שׁמן, v^{20} כבודי חָדָשׁ עמדי, 2 Ch 14^{5} ואין עמו מלחמה, 16^{19} יֵשׁ עמך מלחמות, 28^{10} עִמָּכֶם אֲשָׁמוֹת. Hence, in partic. **a.** of *aid*, Ex 23^{5} Dt 22^{4}; 1 Ch 12^{19}; esp. of God, Gn 21^{22} אלהים עמך, 26^{3} ואהיה עמך, v^{33} $31^{3.5}$ Ex 3^{12} Jos 1^{5} Is 8^{10} כי עמנו אל ψ 23^{4} $46^{8.12}$ Jb 29^{5} + oft. (cf. אֵת, Gn $39^{2.3.21.23}$ Is 43^{5} +): so הִתְחַזֵּק עם 1 Ch 11^{10} 2 Ch 16^{9} Dn 10^{21}, עָזַר עם 1 Ch 12^{21}, כי גם ידם עם דוד 1 S 22^{17}, 2 S 3^{12} 1 Ch 4^{10} (cf. Ex 23^{1}, and II. אֵת **1 a**). *With the help of* (= Gk. σύν), 1 S 14^{45} כי עם אלהים עשׂה היום הזה, Dn 11^{30} (rare).

b. Of actions done jointly *with* another, as ירשׁ עם inherit *with*, Gn 21^{10}, כרת ברית עם 26^{28} + oft., חָלַק (חִלֵּק) עם to share *with* Jos 22^{8} Is 53^{12} +; cf. Dt 10^{9} חֵלֶק וְנַחֲלָה עִם אֶחָיו, 18^{1}.

c. If the common action be of the nature of a contest or combat, עִם is *with* in the sense of *against*: so often with נִלְחַם *to fight*, נִשְׁפַּט *to dispute*, נֶאֱבַק *to wrestle*, רִיב *to strive* (see these verbs), Gn 26^{20} 30^{8} 32^{29}; בּא בְּמִשְׁפָּט עם to enter into judgment *with* Is 3^{14} +, Jb 14^{3} (הֵבִיא), רִיב לי׳ עִם Hos 4^{1} +; hence, without a verb expressing the idea explicitly, ψ 94^{16} מי יקום לי עִם מְרֵעִים *in the struggle with* evil-doers? v^{b} 55^{19} כי בְרַבִּים היו עמדי for as many are they *in combat with* me, Jb 9^{14} אֶבְחֲרָה דְבָרַי עמו *in the contest with* him, $10^{17\,b}$ 16^{21}; perhaps צָדַק עִם 9^{2} 25^{4} (cf. **4 b** *end*).

d. Of dealing *with* a person, or of the relation in which one stands *with*, or *towards*, another: as עשׂה חסד עם to do kindness *with* Gn 24^{12} + oft. (in 1 pers. observe that in this phr. עמדי, not עמי, is regul. used, Gn 19^{19} 20^{13} 40^{14} 1 S 20^{14} 2 S 10^{2} [‖ 1 Ch 19^{2} עמי: here only], *al.*), עשׂה טוב עם Gn 26^{29} +, v. also 20^{9} 31^{29} Dt 33^{21} Ju 15^{3} Jb 10^{12} 13^{20} 42^{8} ψ 86^{17} (cf. אִתְּכֶם Dt 1^{30} 10^{21}; and Aram. Dn 3^{32}), 119^{124} 126^{2} (1 S 12^{24}), Jb 33^{29}; הֵיטִיב עם Gn $32^{10.13}$ +, הֵרַע עִם 31^{7}; רָצָה עם be well pleased *with* ψ 50^{18} Jb 34^{9}; דִּבֶּר עם to speak *with* (subj. usu. God) Ex 19^{9} + (v. דִּבֶּר **3 e**), hence דָּבָר עִם Ju $18^{7.28}$ 2 S 3^{17} 1 K 1^{7} Jb 15^{11} דָּבָר לָאַט עמך a word (spoken) gently *with* thee, cf. 11^{5} ויפתח שׂפתיו עמך; יֵאָמֵן עם 2 Ch 1^{9}: and with adjj. תמים עם perfect *with* (i.e. *toward*) Dt 18^{13} ψ 18^{24}, שָׁלֵם עם 1 K 8^{61} +; cf. וְלִבָּם לֹא נָכוֹן עִמּוֹ ψ 78^{37}, 2 S 21^{4} 23^{5} 1 K 3^{6} (עמך), Mi 6^{8} הַצְנֵעַ לֶכֶת עִם אֱלֹהֶיךָ, ψ 73^{22} *toward* thee, 1 Ch 19^{6} Hos 12^{1} (?); also הָלַךְ קְרִי עִם Lv $26^{21\,ff.}$ (7 t.), מַמְרִים הֱיִיתֶם עם Dt $9^{7.24}$ 31^{27}, 2 Ch 16^{10} 26^{19} ψ 85^{5} Jb $10^{17\,a}$.

e. Of a common lot, Gn 18^{23} האף תספה צדיק עם רשׁע *together with* the wicked, v^{25} Jb $3^{14.15}$ Is 38^{11} ψ 26^{9} אל תאסף עם חטאים נפשׁי, v^{b} $28^{3.3}$, 69^{29} Jb 30^{1} 1 Ch 24^{5}; hence *like*, ψ 73^{5} ועם אדם לא יְנֻגָּעוּ *with* (i.e. *like*) men (in general),

106^{6} חטאנו עם אבותינו, Ec 2^{16} ואיך ימות הֶחָכָם עם הכסיל i.e. *like* the fool.

f. Of equality or resemblance generally (poet.), Jb 9^{26} חָלְפוּ עִם אֳנִיּוֹת אֵבֶה they pass by *with*, i.e. as swiftly as, skiffs of reed, 37^{18} תרקיע עמו שחקים i.e. *like* him, 40^{15} אשר עשיתי עמך; so נִמְשַׁל עִם ψ 28^{1} 143^{7}, נֶחְשַׁב עִם 88^{5}.

†**g.** Of *time*, = *as long as*, ψ 72^{5} יִירָאוּךָ עִם שֶׁמֶשׁ *as long as* the sun *endureth* (cf. Aram. Dn 3^{33} 4^{31}; also Ovid. *Am.* i. 15, 16 *cum* sole et luna semper Aratus erit); *at the time of* (?) 2 Ch 21^{19} (but rd. perh. מֵחֳלָיו); and c. inf. (late), Ezr 1^{11} עִם הֵעָלוֹת הַגּוֹלָה (cf. ἅμα τῷ sq. inf. Ju 3^{21} 9^{33}; also עם Ecclus 40^{14}).

2. Of a locality, *close to, beside:* †Gn 25^{11} וישב יצחק עם באר לחי ראי *beside* the well of, etc., 35^{4} תַּחַת הָאֵלָה אשר עם שכם (so, after אשר, Jos 7^{2} Ju 9^{6} 18^{22} 2 S 13^{23}), Jos 19^{46} (?), Ju 18^{3} הֵמָּה עִם בֵּית מִיכָה (so 19^{11} 2 S 20^{8}), 1 S 10^{2} 2 S 6^{7} וַיָּמָת שָׁם עִם אֲרוֹן הא׳, 19^{38} 24^{16} 1 K 1^{9} 1 Ch 13^{14} *by* the house of O., in its own house (v. Be), 21^{15} (2 S 24^{16}), 26^{16} (cf. אֵת **2**). By a *person*, Dt 5^{28} וְאַתָּה עֲמֹד פֹּה עמדי *by me*, 1 S 1^{26} הַנִּצֶּבֶת עִמְּכָה +; of one living *near* another, Ex 22^{24} Lv $25^{35.36.39.47}$.

3. Of persons, עִם is spec. **a.** *in the house* or *family* or *service of* (*apud, chez*): Gn 23^{4} גֵּר וְתוֹשָׁב עמך (fig. of ׳י Lv 25^{23} ψ 39^{13}), 27^{44} 29^{14} וַיֵּשֶׁב עִמּוֹ, v^{25} עבדתי עמך I have served *with* thee (so v^{30}, cf. Dt 15^{16}), 31^{38} Lv $25^{6.40.40.50.53}$ Dt 22^{2} 23^{17} Ju 17^{10} 2 S 19^{34} 1 K 11^{22}; cf. 1 S 2^{21} עם ׳י i.e. at his sanctuary.

b. *In the possession of* (Lat. *penes*): Gn 24^{25} straw, etc., is עִמָּנוּ, 31^{32} Dt 17^{19} והיתה עמו *with him, at his side*, 29^{16} Jb 28^{14} וְיָם אָמַר אֵין עִמָּדִי; = *stored up with*, Dt 32^{34} כָּמֻס עִמָּדִי, Jb 27^{13} (but rd. here prob. מֵאֵל; cf. 20^{29}); of ethical or mental attributes, 1 S 25^{25} וּנְבָלָה עִמּוֹ, Jb 12^{13} עִמּוֹ חָכְמָה וּגְבוּרָה, v^{16} 25^{2} ψ 130^{7} 2 Ch $19^{3.7}$. Cf. fig. ψ 36^{10} כִּי עִמְּךָ מְקוֹר חַיִּים.

c. *In the custody* or *care of*, 1 S 9^{23} שִׂים אֹתָהּ עִמָּךְ; 22^{23} כִּי מִשְׁמֶרֶת אַתָּה עִמָּדִי: cf. Jb 17^{3} עָרְבֵנִי עִמָּךְ be surety for me *with thyself*.

d. *Beside* = *except*, Dt 32^{39} אֵין אלהים עִמָּדִי, ψ 73^{25} ועמך לא חפצתי בארץ and *beside thee* I delight not (in aught that is) upon earth (al. *in comparison of* thee, **1 f**), 2 Ch 14^{10} וְאֵין עִמְּךָ לַעְזוֹר there is none *beside thee* to help, 20^{6}; perh. Hos 9^{8} (Hi Ke; but very dub., v. Comm.). Cf. אֵת **1 b**.

e. *With* = *friendly with*, Gn 31^{2} כי איננו עמי (syn. v^{5} אֶל *towards*), 2 K 10^{15} לְבָבִי עִם לְבָבְךָ, Pr 23^{7} וְלִבּוֹ בַּל עִמָּךְ.

4. Idiom. of a *thought* or *purpose* present *with* one:—†**a.** עִם לְבַב פ׳, esp. in Dt. and the later Deut. style, Dt 8^{5} וְיָדַעְתָּ עִם לְבָבֶךָ thou shalt know *with* thy heart, 15^{9} פן יהיה דבר עם לבבך בליעל a wicked thought *with* thy heart, Jos 14^{7} I brought back word כאשר עם לבבי; ויהי עם לְבַב פ׳ היה, esp. of a purpose, 1 K 8^{17} ויהי עם לבב דוד לִבְנוֹת וגו׳ i.e. it was David's *purpose* to build, etc., $v^{18.18}$ 1 K 10^{2} (= 2 Ch $6^{7.8.8}$ 9^{1}), 1 Ch 22^{7} 28^{2} (both based on 1 K 8^{17}, etc.), 2 Ch 1^{11} 24^{4} 29^{10}; rather differently, to *muse* or *talk with* one's heart, ψ 77^{7} Ec 1^{16}.

†**b.** עִם alone, = in one's *consciousness*, whether of knowledge or memory or purpose (cf. אֵת **3 b**; عِنْدَ W $^{AG ii. § 66}$): Nu 14^{24} עֵקֶב הָיְתָה רוּחַ אַחֶרֶת עִמּוֹ i.e. operating in his mind, 1 K 11^{11} יען אשר היתה זאת עמך, 1 Ch 28^{12} the pattern of all אשר היה בָרוּחַ עמו that was in spirit (i.e. mentally) *with* him, ψ 50^{11} וְזִיז שָׂדַי עִמָּדִי is *with* me (i.e. is known to me; ‖ ידעתי), prob. also 73^{23} 139^{18} (= in thy thought and care); Jb 9^{35} לא כן אנכי עמדי not so am I *with myself* (my consciousness—or conscience—does not tell me that I need dread him), 10^{13} ידעתי כי זאת עמך i.e. that this was thy purpose (‖ אֵלֶּה צָפַנְתָּ בִלְבָבֶךָ), 15^{9} ולא עמנו הוא and is not *with us* (= in our knowledge; ‖ וְלֹא נֵדָע), 23^{10} כי ידע דרך עמדי the way *of which I am conscious* (De; Ew Di the way *attending* me, my usual way), v^{14} וְכָהֵנָּה רַבּוֹת עִמּוֹ i.e. he has many such purposes, 27^{11} אֲשֶׁר עִם שַׁדַּי לֹא אֲכַחֵד i.e. his purposes or principles of action. Also sts. *in the judgment* or *estimation of*, 1 S 2^{26} טוֹב עִם, 2 S 6^{22} נִכְבַּד עִם, perh. צָדַק עִם Jb 9^{2} 25^{4} (Ges Bu; but Ew as **1 c**, Hi De *beside, in comparison of*).

†**5.** Metaph. *together with* = *in spite of, notwithstanding* Ne 5^{18} וְעִם זֶה (cf. مَعَ W $^{AG ii. § 57}$; in Heb. בְּ is the more usual syn.).—In 1 S 16^{12} אַדְמוֹנִי עִם יְפֵה עֵינַיִם (cf. 17^{42} עִם יְפֵה מַרְאֶה), if text correct, יפה must be a neuter subst., *with* beauty of eyes; but rd. prob. (Gr Bu) עֶלֶם *a youth* (17^{56} 20^{22}) for עם (v. HPS; Che $^{Expos. T. x. 521}$ אַדְמוֹנִי עֶצֶם, cf. La 4^{7}).

מֵעִם $_{72}$ *from with* or *beside* (= παρά with a gen.: cf. מֵאֵת): hence **a.** after verbs of departing, taking, removing, etc., Gn 13^{14} אַחֲרֵי הִפָּרֶד־לוֹט מֵעִמּוֹ, 26^{16} לֵךְ מֵעִמָּנוּ, 1 S $10^{2.9}$ 14^{17} מי הלך מעמנו, 2 S 1^{2}; 1 S 16^{14} ורוח י׳ סרה מעם שאול, 18^{12}; 2 K 2^{9} בטרם אֶלָּקַח מעמך; 2 S 15^{28} עד בּוֹא דָּבָר מֵעִמָּכֶם; of heart turning מעם י׳ Dt 29^{17} 1 K 11^{9}; after שׁאל *to ask*, Ex 22^{13} Dt 10^{12} מה י׳

שָׁאַל מֵעִמְּךָ, 1 S 1^{17} 20^{28} (Niph.), Is 7^{11}+; דרשׁ *to require*, Dt 18^{19} 23^{22}, 1 K 14^{5} (to *inquire*); יצא מֵעִם פרעה *from* (being) *with* Ph. Ex 8$^{8.25.26}$ 9^{33}+: cf. 2 S 3^{26}, 1 S 18^{13} ויסירהו שאול מעמו; and מֵעִם פְּנֵי Gn 44^{29} Jb 1^{12}. †Sq. a word denoting a place, Gn 48^{12} וַיּוֹצֵא יוֹסֵף אֹתָם מֵעִם בִּרְכָּיו, Ex 21^{14} מֵעִם מִזְבְּחִי (cf. 1 S 2^{33}), Ju 9^{37} מֵעִם טַבּוּר הארץ, 1 S 20^{34} מֵעִם הַשֻּׁלְחָן; Jb 28^{4} מֵעִם גָּר *away from, far from* (si vera l.).

†**b.** Gn 24^{27} אשר לא עזב חסדו מעם אֲדֹנִי (cf. with הכרית 1 S 20^{15}, הסיר 2 S 7^{15} 1 Ch 17^{13} (∥ 2 S 7^{15} מִן), הפיר ψ 89^{34}); Ru 4^{10} לֹא־יִכָּרֵת שֵׁם מֵעִם.

†**c.** *From the possession*, or *custody*, *of* (cf. עִם **3 b, c**): so with גזל Gn 31^{31}, ערב to take in pledge 44^{32}, גנב Ex 22^{11}, יצא (subj. a slave; cf. עִם **3 a**) Lv 25^{41} Dt 15^{16} (cf. with שִׁלַּח חָפְשִׁי Dt 15$^{12.13.18}$ Je 34^{14}, הִצִּיל Dt 23^{16}), לקח 2 S 3^{15}, קנה 24^{21}.

†**d.** Expressing *origination* or *authorship:* 1 S 20^{7} כִּי כָלְתָה הָרָעָה מֵעִמּוֹ, v$^{9.33}$ (cf. מֵאֵת Est 7^{17}); esp. of י׳ (cf. מֵאֵת **c**), Gn 41^{32} נָכוֹן הַדָּבָר מֵעִם הא׳ is established *from*, on the part of, God, 1 K 2^{33} שָׁלוֹם . . . מעם י׳, 12^{15} (2 Ch 10^{15}) כִּי הָיְתָה סִבָּה מעם י׳, Is 8^{18} signs and portents מעם י׳, 28^{29} גם זאת מעם י׳ יצאה, 29^{6} ψ 121^{2} עֶזְרִי מעם י׳, Ru 2^{12}. And of a judgment proceeding *from* any one: 2 S 3^{28} נקי מעם י׳ = *pronounced* guiltless *by* י׳, Jb 34^{33} הֲמֵעִמְּךָ *at thy judgment* shall he requite? (cf. מִן **2 d** *end*).

6005 †עִמָּנוּאֵל† **n.pr.m. Immanuēl** (*with us is*
410, 5973 *God*);—ע׳ Is 7^{14} van d. H. Baer; עִמָּנוּ אֵל Gi;—name of child, symbolizing presence of י׳ to deliver his people (on interpret. v. Comm.)—עִמָּנוּ אֵל 8$^{8.10}$ is declaration of trust and confidence, *with us is God!* (cf. ψ 46$^{8.12}$); v. עִם.

5971 †II. [עַם] **n.[m.] kinsman** (on father's side) (Ar. عَمٌّ *paternal uncle*, etc., v. I. עמם; cf. perh. TelAm. *ammu, kinsmen* (?); on Nab. עם *ancestor* cf. Lzb^{151,499}; v. also esp. Nes$^{Eg\ 187}$, ZAW xvi (1896), 322 f. Krenkel$^{ib.\ viii\ (1888),\ 280–84}$);—sf. עַמִּי in בֶּן־עַמִּי (q.v.), and n.pr. sqq.; elsewhere pl. sf. עַמֶּיךָ Nu 27^{13} 31^{2} (Lv 19^{16} read עִמְּךָ 𝔊 Sam), + (poss.) עֲמָמֶיךָ Ju 5^{14}; עַמָּיו Gn 25^{8} + 15 t., עַמֶּיהָ 17^{14} + 3 t.; read עַמִּי (for MT עַמִּי, I. עַם; cf. Krenkel$^{l.c.\ 281}$) Gn 49^{29} and perh. Ju 14^{3} (cf. Lv 21^{14}); acc. to Buhl Kit also 2 K 4^{13};—*father's kinsmen:* וַיֵּאָסֶף אֶל־עַמָּיו Gn 25^{8} (of joining kinsmen in Sheʾôl), so v^{17} 35^{29} 49^{33} Nu 20^{24} Dt 32^{50}, cf. Gn 49^{29} (v. supr.), Nu 27^{13} 31^{2} Dt 32^{50} (all P); וְנִכְרְתָה הַנֶּפֶשׁ מֵעַמֶּיהָ Gn 17^{4} (severed from living kinsmen), so Lv 7$^{20.21.25.27}$ 19^{8} 23^{29} Nu 9^{13}; מִקֶּרֶב עַמֶּיהָ Ex 31^{14}, cf. 30$^{33.38}$ Lv 17^{9} (all PH); מֵעַמָּיו יִקַּח אִשָּׁה 21^{14} (H), and perh. Ju 14^{3} (sim. I. עַם: [ם—, ה—] מִקֶּרֶב עַמּוֹ Lv 17$^{4.10}$ 18^{29}+); other combin. Ju 5^{14} (si vera l., read perh. בַּעֲמָקֶךָ, v. I. עַם **2 d**), Lv 21$^{1.4.15}$ (H), Ez 18^{18} and (perh.) 2 K 4^{13}.—בֶּן־עַמִּי (v. p. 122 b) perh. = *son of my kinsman;* on n.pr. c. עַם v. Gray$^{Prop.\ N.\ 41\ ff.}$.

†I. [עֻמָּה] **n.f. juxtaposition**, but only in 5980
st. c. with force of a **prep. close by, side by side with, parallel to, agreeing with, corresponding to**;—st. c. עֻמַּת, exc. Ec 5^{15} always c. לְ, sf. לְעֻמָּתוֹ, once pl. cstr. לְעֻמּוֹת Ez 45^{7};—**a.** *close by, side by side with:* Ex 25^{27} (37^{14}), 28^{27} (39^{20}), Lv 3^{9} לְעֻמַּת הֶעָצֶה יְסִירֶנָּה shall take it away *close by* the backbone; esp. of what is *parallel*, Ez 42^{7} the wall *alongside of* the chambers; of the contiguous portions in Ezek.'s division of the land, *alongside of* each other, Ez 45$^{6.7}$ 48$^{13.18.18.21}$; of movement in parallel lines, 2 S 16^{13} Shimei was going along לְעֻמָּתוֹ *parallel with* him, v^{13} Ez 1^{20} וְהָאוֹפַנִּים יִנָּשְׂאוּ, v^{21} 3^{13} 10^{19} 11^{22}; 3^{8} נָתַתִּי פָנֶיךָ חֲזָקִים לְעֻמַּת פְּנֵיהֶם, לְעֻמָּתָם *by the side of* their face (which, as antagonism is implied, = *against*, RV), v^{8}. **b.** *agreeing with, corresponding to* (a common result of juxtaposition), Ex 38^{18} a screen five cubits high לעמת קלעי החצר *agreeing with* (RV *answerable unto*) the hangings of the court (in height), Ez 40^{18}; prob. also 1 Ch 26^{16} Ne 12^{24} מִשְׁמָר לְ׳ מִשְׁמָר ward *corresponding to* ward. **c.** *correspondingly to*, 1 Ch 24^{31} they also cast lots לְעֻמַּת אֲחֵיהֶם *correspondingly to* their brethren, v^{b} the head, *correspondingly to* his younger brother, 26^{12} to these . . . belonged charges *correspondingly to* (in common with) their brethren. **d.** before a sentence (Ges^{§155n}), 1 Ch 25^{8} (strangely) לְעֻמַּת כַּקָּטֹן כַּגָּדוֹל (v. Ke) *correspondingly to* (the principle) *of* as the small so the great; Ec 5^{15} כָּל־עֻמַּת שֶׁבָּא *quite exactly as* he came, so shall he go (but Lambert RÉJ xxxi. 47, Rahlfs$^{Th.\ Lt.-z.\ 1896,\ 587}$ כִּלְעֻמַּת). **e.** מִלְּעֻמַּת (v. מִן **1 c, 9 a**) 1 K 7^{20} *close beside.*

†II. עֻמָּה **n.pr.loc.** Jos 19^{30}, v. עַכּוֹ. 5981

עַמּוֹן$_{106}$ **n.pr.gent. Ammon**, 𝔊 Αμμαν, 5983
Αμμων (As. *Bît Ammanu* COT$^{Gloss.}$);—always (except 1 S 11^{11} [where however 𝔊 rds. בְּנֵי ע׳], ψ 83^{8}, which have ע׳ alone) בְּנֵי עַמּוֹן, connected by J with בֶּן־עַמִּי son of Lot Gn 19^{38} (and meaning of name doubtless sought herein by J; cf. II. עַם); people apparently akin to Isr., but usu.

hostile, dwelling E. of Jordan, NE. of Moab, between Arnon and Jabbok: Nu 21$^{24.24}$ (JE), Dt 2$^{19.19.37}$ 3$^{11.16}$ Jos 12^{2} 13^{10} (D), v^{25} (P), Ju 3^{13} 10^{6}+25 t. Ju 10–12, 1 S 11^{11} 12^{12} 14^{47} 2 S 8^{12} 10^{1}+14 t. 2 S 10–12, 17^{27} 1 K 11$^{7.33}$ 2 K 23^{13} 24^{2} 1 Ch 18^{11}+20 t. Ch, Am 1^{13} Is 11^{14} Je 9^{25} +9 t. Je, Zp 2$^{8.9}$ Ez 21$^{25.33}$+5 t. Ez 25, Dn 11^{41}. —Vid. Che^{Ammon} in Ency. Bib.

5984 †עַמּוֹנִי, עַמֹּנִי **adj. gent.** **Ammonite**;—abs. ms. עַמּוֹנִי as subst. Dt 23^{4} *an Ammonite* (generic), so עַמֹּנִי Ne 13^{1}; הָעַמּוֹנִי of individual 1 S 11$^{1.2}$ 2 S 23^{37} = 1 Ch 11^{39}, Ne 2^{19}, so הָעַמֹּנִי 2^{10} 3^{35}; fs. הָעַמֹּנִית 1 K 14^{21} = 2 Ch 12^{13}, 1 K 14^{31},
5985 so הָעַמּוֹנִית 2 Ch 24^{26}; הָעַמֹּנִי as subst. coll. Ezr 9^{1}; mpl. as subst. עַמֹּנִים 1 K 11^{5}, הָעַ׳ Dt 2^{20} Ne 4^{1}, הָעַמּ׳ 2 Ch 26^{8} (on 20^{1} v. מְעוּנִים); fpl. as adj. עַמֳּנִיֹּת 1 K 11^{1}, so Ne 13^{23} Qr, Kt עמוניות.

5988 †עַמִּיאֵל **n.pr.m.** (*my kinsman is God*, Gray$^{Prop. N. 254}$);—𝔊 Αμ(με)ιηλ: **1.** E. Jordan name 2 S 9$^{4.5}$ 17^{27}. **2.** a Danite Nu 13^{12} (P). **3.** David's father-in-law 1 Ch 3^{5} (= אֱלִיעָם 2 S 11^{3}). **4.** son of Obed Edom 1 Ch 26^{5}.

5989 †עַמִּיהוּד **n.pr.m.** (*my kinsman is majesty*);—𝔊 (Σ)εμιουδ, Αμιουδ, etc.: **1.** a Geshurite 2 S
5991 13^{37} Qr (> Kt עֲמִיחוּר, cf. Dr al., Gray$^{Prop. N. 43}$). **2.** an Ephraimite Nu 1^{10} 2^{18} 7$^{48.53}$ 10^{22} (all P), 1 Ch 7^{26}. **3.** a Simeonite Nu 34^{20}. **4.** a Naphtalite Nu 34^{28}. **5.** a Judahite 1 Ch 9^{4}.

5990 †עַמִּיזָבָד **n.pr.m.** (*my kinsman hath bestowed*; cf. זְבַדְיָה, זַבְדִּיאֵל, יְהוֹזָבָד, אֶלְזָבָד, זָבָד, and, esp. on Palm. equiv., v. Gray$^{Prop. N. 223 f.}$ also Lzb^{265} Cook$^{46 f.}$);—son of Benaiah 1 Ch 27^{6}, 𝔊 Λαιβαζαθ, A Αμιραζαθ, 𝔊L Αμειναζαβαδ.

5991 עמיחור 2 S 13^{37} Kt v. עַמִּיהוּד. above

5992 †עַמִּינָדָב **n.pr.m.** (*my kinsman is noble*);—𝔊 Αμ(ε)ιναδαβ: **1.** Aaron's father-in-law Ex 6^{23} Nu 1^{7} 2^{3} 7$^{12.17}$ 10^{14} (all P), Ru 4$^{19.20}$ 1 Ch 2$^{10.10}$. **2.** Levites: **a.** 1 Ch 6^{7}. **b.** 15$^{10.11}$.

5996 †עַמִּישַׁדָּי **n.pr.m.** (*my kinsman is Shaddai*);—a Danite Nu 1^{12} 2^{25} 7$^{66.71}$ 10^{25}, 𝔊 Αμ(ε)ισαδαι, 𝔊L Αμισαδε.

6004 †II. [עָמַם] **vb. darken, dim** (NH *id.*; Ar. غَمَّ *cover, veil, conceal*; 𝔗 עֲמַם *grow dark*);—**Qal** *Pf.* 3 pl. sf. עֲמָמֻהוּ Ez 31^{8} dub., but prob. (as Thes) cedars *did not eclipse him*; עֲמָמוּךָ 28^{3} no secret *do they hold dark* (= is held dark) for thee (Ges$^{§ 117 x}$). **Hoph.** *Impf.* 3 ms. יוּעַם זָהָב La 4^{1} (fig.) *how is the gold dimmed!* cf. Bu.

עַמְמֵי, עֲמָמִים v. I. עַם supr. p. 766 5971

עִמָּנוּאֵל v. sub עִם supr. p. 769 6005

†[עָמַס, ?עָמַשׂ] **vb. 1. load. 2. carry** 6006
a load (NH *id.*; Ph. עמס *carry*; cf. poss. Ar. عَمِسَ *gravis et obscurus fuit dies* (Frey));—**Qal** *Impf.* 3 ms. וַיַּעֲמֹס Gn 44^{13}, יַעֲמָס־ ψ 68^{20}; *Pt. act.* עֹמְסִים Ne 13^{15}; עֹמְשִׂים 4^{11} (but v. infr.); sf. עֹמְסֶיהָ Zc 12^{3}; *pass.* עֲמֻסִים Is 46^{3}, עֲמוּסוֹת v^{1};—**1.** *load* (obj. om.) upon (עַל) ass Gn 44^{13} (E), Ne 13^{15}; so abs. 4^{11}, lit., si vera l. (v. Be-Ry Ryle); but rd. prob. חֲמֻשִׁים Ry^{Kau}. **2.** *carry a load* ψ 68^{20} (י׳, for (ל) his people), *carry as a load* Zc 12^{3} (fig.), pass. Is 46^{1} (lit.), v^{3} (fig.).

†עָמוֹס **n.pr.m. Amos** the prophet;—Am 5986
1^{1} 7$^{8.10.11.12.14}$ 8^{2}, 𝔊 Αμως.

†עֲמַסְיָה **n.pr.m.** name in Judah 2 Ch 17^{16}, 6007
𝔊 Μασαιας, 𝔊L Αμασιας (cf. Ph. אשמנעמס, בעלעמס CIS$^{I. 139, 169, 719}$, v. also Gray$^{Prop. N. 296 f.}$).

†מַעֲמָסָה **n.f. load, burden**;—אֶבֶן מ׳ Zc 4614
12^{3} *a stone of burden* = heavy stone, hard to lift.

†עַמְעָד **n.pr.loc.** in Asher, Jos 19^{26}, 𝔊 6008
Αμιηλ, A Αμαδ, 𝔊L Αλφααδ.

†[עָמֹק, Lag$^{BN 28}$] **vb. be deep** (NH in 6009
deriv.; Ar. عَمُقَ; Eth. ዐመቀ: prob. As. [*emêḳu*] III. 2 *implore* (earnestly; 'from *bottom* of one's soul'), *emûḳu, might, nîmeḳu, wisdom* (? as unfathomable); 𝔗 in deriv.; Syr. in der. spec.);—**Qal** *Pf.* 3 mpl. עָמְקוּ ψ 92^{6} (of י׳'s designs; cf. As. supr.). **Hiph.** *make deep*: *Pf.* 3 ms. (symbol.) הֶעְמִיק הִרְחִב Is 30^{33} (sc. Tophet; van d. H. הֶעֱמִיק, and so in foll.); 3 mpl. הֶעְמִיקוּ Ho 5^{2} the pit of Shittim(?) *have they made deep* (reading שַׁחַת הַשִּׁטִּים We Now, cf. Che Gu^{Kau}); הֶעְמִיקוּ סָרָה Is 31^{6} (fig.) *they have made deep (their) apostasy*; sq. vb., with adverbial force הֶ׳ שִׁחֵתוּ Ho 9^{9} = *they are in the depth of corruption* (v. שחת); *Imv.* mpl. הַעְמִיקוּ (Ges$^{§ 63 o}$), sq. inf. Je 49$^{8.30}$ *make deep to dwell* (of hiding, so most; > Gie *take an abject seat*, as 13^{18} 48^{18}); *Pt.* הַמַּעֲמִיקִים לַסְתִּר Is 29^{15} *they who deeply hide* fr. י׳ (their) counsel; *Inf. abs.* הַעְמֵק Is 7^{11} = Imv. *make deep* (ask a sign in the depths of Sheʾôl, reading שְׁאֹלָה; opp. הַגְבֵּהַּ).

עֵמֶק$_{70}$ **n.m.**$^{Mi 1, 4}$ **vale** (prop. *deepening, depth*, 6010
v. GASm$^{Geogr. 384 f. 654 f.}$; cf. נַחַל, גַּיְא, בִּקְעָה);—ע׳ abs. Jos 8^{13}+, cstr. Gn 14^{17}+; sf. עִמְקֵךְ Je

49^{4}, עִמְקָם 47^{5} (but v. infr.); pl. עֲמָקִים Mi 1^{4}, sf. עֲמָקַיִךְ Is 22^{7};—*vale, valley, lowland,* opp. הֶהָרִים Mi 1^{4}, amid mts., e.g. about Jerus. Is 22^{7} Je 31^{40}, so perh. ע׳ הַמֶּלֶךְ = ע׳ שָׁוֵה Gn 14^{17} v^{17} 2 S 18^{18}, cf. ע׳ חֶבְרוֹן Gn 37^{14} (J), ע׳ בְּגִבְעוֹן Is 28^{21}, Jos 8^{13} (JE), ע׳ הָאֵלָה 1 S $17^{2.19}$ 21^{10} (perh. *Wady es-Sant,* in Shephelah, W. of Bethlehem, GASm$^{\text{Geogr. 226}}$); ע׳ אֲשֶׁר לְבֵית רְחוֹב Ju 18^{28} in extreme north; in Moab Je 48^{8} (‖ [opp.?] מִישׁוֹר); or wider, e.g. Ju 5^{15} (scene of Sisera's defeat; rd. perh. ע׳ also for עֲמָלֵק v^{14} GFM), ע׳ יִזְרְעֶאל Ju 6^{33} Ho 1^{5} Jos 17^{16} (JE), cf. Ju $7^{1.8.12}$ 1 S 31^{7} = 1 Ch 10^{7}, these all perh. narrow ends of plain (cf. GASm$^{\text{l.c.}}$), but v. 1 K 20^{28} (opp. הֶהָרִים; ‖ מִישׁוֹר v^{23}; = *open country,* cf. Aphek v^{26}); of Jordan-valley Jos $13^{19.27}$ (P); of maritime plain (opp. הָהָר) Ju $1^{19.34}$; fit for chariots, so also אֶרֶץ הָע׳ Jos 17^{16} (P), cf. Jb 39^{21}; יֹשֶׁבֶת הָע׳ Je 21^{13}, cf. Nu 14^{25} (v. Gie Di); cultivated 1 S 6^{13} Je $49^{4.4}$ Jb 39^{10}, fertile 1 Ch 27^{29} ψ 65^{14} Ct 2^{1}; v. also עָכוֹר, סֻכּוֹת, יְהוֹשָׁפָט, חָרוּץ, II. בְּרָכָה, בָּכָא, אַיָּלוֹן, בֵּית הָע׳; שִׁדִּים, רְפָאִים, קְצִיץ v. p. 112 a.—For עִמְקָם Je 47^{5} rd. עֲנָקִם *Anakim* 𝔊 Thes Hi Gf Gie Co Rothst; so also (more dub.) 1 Ch 12^{16} (van d. H. v^{15}) Gf Gie, where otherwise הָע׳ = *people of valleys.*

6011 †עֹ֫מֶק **n.[m.]** **depth**;—abs. Pr 25^{3}; pl. cstr. עִמְקֵי שְׁאוֹל 9^{18} (Kö$^{\text{ii. 1, 32}}$).

6012 †[עָמֵק] **adj.** **deep, unfathomable**;—pl. cstr. עִמְקֵי שָׂפָה (Ges$^{\S\,93\,\text{ii}}$) i.e. *unintelligible of speech* Is 33^{19} Ez $3^{5.6}$.—Pr 9^{18} v. עֹמֶק.

6013 עָמֹק$_{17}$ **adj.** **deep** (cf. Ba$^{\text{NB}\,\S\,23\,\text{b}}$);—**1.** ע׳ lit. Lv 13^{3} + 6 t. Lv 13; f. עֲמֻקָּה of cup Ez 23^{32}, trench Pr 22^{14} 23^{27} (all 3 in sim.); ע׳ מִשְּׁאוֹל Jb 11^{8} (fig.); pl. מַיִם עֲמֻקִּים (sim.) Pr 18^{4} 20^{5}. **2.** = *unsearchable* עָמֹק עָמֹק ψ 64^{7} Ec $7^{24.24}$; pl. עֲמֻקּוֹת (Baer עֲמוּקוֹת, van d. H. עֲמֻקּוֹת) Jb 12^{22}.

5987 †עָמוֹק **n.pr.m.** a priest Ne $12^{7.20}$, Αμουκ.

4615 †מַעֲמַקִּים **n.m.pl.** **depths**;—abs. מ׳ ψ 130^{1} (fig.); cstr. lit. מַעֲמַקֵּי־יָם Is 51^{10}; fig. מ׳ מַיִם Ez 27^{34} (fall of Tyre), ψ $69^{3.15}$ (distress).

I. עמר (√ of foll.; mng. dub., perh. related to Ar. غَمَرَ *be abundant* (of water), *surpass, overtop;* NH עָמִיר, עוֹמֶר = BH; 𝔗 עוּמְרָא, עֲמִירָא = BH I. עֹמֶר).

6016 †I. עֹ֫מֶר **n.m.**$^{\text{Lv 23, 11}}$ **sheaf** (*swath,* row of fallen grain, Wetzst$^{\text{Z. f. Ethnol. 1873, 273 (Syr. Dreschtafel)}}$, ag. him Vogelstein$^{\text{Landwirthschaft in Pal. 61}}$ who trans. *heap of sheaves*);—ע׳ abs. Dt 24^{19} Lv $23^{11.12.15}$, cstr. v^{10}; fig. of food (abs.) Jb 24^{10}; pl. עֳמָרִים lit. Ru $2^{7.15}$.

†II. עֹ֫מֶר **n.m.**$^{\text{Ex 16, 22}}$ **omer** (cf. Ar. غُمَرٌ *small drinking cup* or *bowl;* relation to I. ע׳ obscure);—a measure, only Ex 16;—the measure itself v$^{18.32.33}$; amount measured v$^{16.22}$; = $\frac{1}{10}$ ephah v^{36}; 𝔊 γόμορ. 6016

†עָמִיר **n.[m.]** **swath, row of fallen grain** 5995
(*hay,* as Mishn., acc. to Vogelstein$^{\text{l. c. 74 f.}}$ (who is then compelled to rd. עֹמֶר Mi 4^{12}), cf. Syr. ܥܡܝܪܐ *grass,* Schwally$^{\text{Idiot. 69}}$);—Am 2^{13} (on cart), Je 9^{21} (falling behind reaper), Mi 4^{12} (brought to threshing-floor), Zc 12^{6} (inflammable).

†[עִמֵּר] **vb. Pi. denom. bind sheaves** (NH 6014
id., so 𝔗$^{\psi\,129,7}$, cf. Chr Pal Aram. Schwally$^{\text{Idiot. 69}}$);—*Pt.* מְעַמֵּר ψ 129^{7} (in sim.; ‖ קוֹצֵר).

†II. [עָמַר] **vb. Hithp. deal tyrannically** 6014
with (ב) (Ar. غَمِرَ *cherish enmity, rancour, malice,* III. *plunge* into a conflict, غِمْرٌ *rancour, malice*);—*Pf.* 3 ms. וְהִתְעַמֶּר־ consec. Dt 24^{7}; *Impf.* 2 ms. תִּתְעַמֵּר 21^{14}.

†עֲמֹרָה$_{19}$ **n.pr.loc.** **Gomorrah,** Γομορρα 6017
(ג = غ; √ II. עמר acc. to Lag$^{\text{BN 54}}$);—alw. c. סְדֹם q.v.; Gn 10^{19} + 8 t. Gn, in sim. Am 4^{11} Is 1^{9} 13^{19} Dt 29^{22} Je 49^{18} 50^{40} Zp 2^{9}, cf. Dt 32^{32}; fig. of iniquity Is 1^{10} Je 23^{14}.

III. עמר (√ of foll.; cf. Ar. عَمِرَ, عَمَرَ *live, live long;* also *worship;* n.pr. عُمَرُ etc.; RS$^{\text{K 266}}$ prop. mng. *worshipper,* עָמְרִי *worshipper of* י׳ (cf. We$^{\text{Skizzen iii. 165}}$), against him Nö$^{\text{ZMG xl (1886), 185}}$, who cp. meaning *live,* عُمْرٌ, عَمْرٌ *life*).

עָמְרִי$_{18}$ **n.pr.m.** **1. Omri,** king of Israel 6018
(MI$^{4.5.7}$ עמרי; in As. *Ḫumri* COT$^{\text{Gloss.}}$);—1 K 16^{16} + 11 t. 1 K 16, 2 K 8^{26} = 2 Ch 22^{2}, Mi 6^{16}, 𝔊 (Ζ)αμβρ(ε)ι. **2. a.** name in Benj. 1 Ch 7^{8}. **b.** in Judah 9^{4}. **c.** in Issachar 27^{18}.

עַמְרָם$_{14}$ **n.pr.m.** (√ עמר Nö$^{\text{ZMG xl (1886), 185}}$; 6019
poss. עַם + רָם Thes, cf. Gray$^{\text{Prop. N. 45, 47, 51}}$);—**1.** father of Moses Ex $6^{18.20.20}$ + 4 t. P, 1 Ch $5^{28.29}$ + 4 t. Ch; Αμ(β)ραμ[ν]. **2.** Ezr 10^{34}.

†עַמְרָמִי **adj. gent.** of **1**, c. art. as n.coll. 6020
Nu 3^{27} 1 Ch 26^{23}.

עמשׁ v. עמס. p. 770 6006

עֲמָשָׂא$_{16}$ **n.pr.m.** (cf. עמס, עמשׁ? or read 6021
עַמִּישַׁי (II. עַם + יִשַׁי), We$^{\text{Isr. u. Jüd. Gesch. 24}}$, cf. Gray

Prop. N. 44, 323);—**1.** Absalom's general 2 S 17$^{25.25}$ 19^{14} + 8 t. 2 S 20, 1 K 2$^{5.32}$ 1 Ch 2$^{17.17}$, 𝔊 Αμεσσ(α)ει, 𝔊L Αμεσσα. **2.** Ephraimite 2 Ch 28^{12}.

6022 † עֲמָשַׂי **n.pr.m.** (cf. foreg.);—**1.** warrior of David 1 Ch 12^{19} (van d. H. v^{18}), Αμασαι, perh. = אֲבִישַׁי (2 S 23^{18}). **2.** Levites: **a.** 1 Ch 6$^{10.20}$ (עֲמָשָׂ֑י). **b.** 2 Ch 29^{12}. **c.** priest 1 Ch 15^{24}.

6023 † עֲמַשְׁסַי **n.pr.m.** (prob. textual error for foreg., Ol ^{§277}, cf. Thes^{1044});—a priest Ne 11^{13}, Αμασεια [-σαι], = מַעְשַׂי 1 Ch 9^{12} (Μαασαια [-σει]).

ענב (√ of foll.; cf. NH עֵנָב = BH; Ar. عِنَبٌ *id.;* Sab. אנעב *vineyards* SabDenkm^{47}; Mordtm$^{ZMG\ xli\ (1887),\ 309,\ 364}$; 𝔗 עִנְּבָא; perh. also As. *inbu, fruit* (and not = אֵב q.v.), cf. Hom$^{A.\ und\ A.\ 94}$).

6025 † עֵנָב **n.m.**$^{Gn\ 40,\ 11}$ **grape(s)** (on formation cf. Lag$^{BN\ 153}$);—ע׳ abs. Dt 32^{14} (coll.); elsewhere pl. עֲנָבִים Gn 40^{10} +; cstr. עִנְּבֵי (Ges $^{§20\ h}$) Lv 25^{5} Dt 32^{32}; sf. עֲנָבֵמוֹ v^{32};—*grapes* Gn 40$^{10.11}$ (E), Am 9^{13} (all as yielding juice for drink), Ho 9^{10} (sim.), Is 5$^{2.4}$ (parable), Je 8^{13} Ne 13^{15} Lv 25^{5} (H); מִשְׁרַת ע׳ Nu 6^{3} (P), poet. דַּם־ע׳ Gn 49^{11} Dt 32^{14}; בִּכּוּרֵי ע׳ Nu 13^{20}, אֶשְׁכּוֹל ע׳ v^{23} (JE); eaten Dt 23^{25}, so ע׳ לַחִים וִיבֵשִׁים Nu 6^{3}; אֲשִׁישֵׁי ע׳ Ho 3^{1} *raisin-cakes;* ע׳ רוֹשׁ Dt 32^{32} *grapes of poison.*

6024 † עֲנָב **n.pr.loc.** in hill-country of Judah Jos 11^{21} 15^{50}, Αναβ(ωθ), Ανωβ[ν], mod. *ʿAnab,* 18½ miles SW. from Hebron, Buhl$^{Geogr.\ 164}$.

6036 † עָנוּב **n.pr.m.** 1 Ch 4^{8}, Εννων, 𝔊L Ανωβ.

6026 † [עָנַג, Lag$^{BN\ 31}$] **vb. be soft, delicate, dainty** (NH *id.* Pi. *make soft, pliable, live* or *spend in enjoyment;* Ar. غَنِجَ *use amorous behaviour, affect langour*);—**Pu.** *Pt.* f. הַמְּעֻנָּגָה Je 6^{2} *daintily bred,* fig. of Jerusalem. **Hithp. 1.** *be of dainty habit, Inf. cstr.* הִתְעַנֵּג Dt 28^{56} (woman, ‖ רֹךְ). **2.** *take exquisite delight, Pf.* 3 pl. וְהִתְעַנְּגוּ consec. ψ 37^{11} (עַל rei); 2 mpl. וְהִתְעַנַּגְתֶּם consec. Is 66^{11} (מִן rei); *Impf.* 3 ms. יִתְעַנָּג Jb 27^{10}; 2 ms. תִּתְעַנַּג Is 58^{14}, תִּתְעַנָּג Jb 22^{26} (all c. [עַל־י׳ [שַׁדַּי); 3 fs. תִּתְעַנַּג Is 55^{2} (ב rei); *Imv.* ms. הִתְעַנַּג עַל־י׳ ψ 37^{4}. **3.** c. עַל, in bad sense, *make merry over, make sport of, Impf.* 2 mpl. עַל־מִי תִּתְעַנָּגוּ Is 57^{4}.

6027 † עֹנֶג **n.[m.] daintiness, exquisite delight;**—הֵיכְלֵי ע׳ Is 13^{22}; וְקָרָאתָ לַשַּׁבָּת ע׳ 58^{13}.

6028 † עָנֹג **adj. dainty;**—הָע׳ Dt 28^{54} man; הָעֲנֻגָּה v^{56} woman; Is 47^{1} (Bab. personif.); all ‖ רַכ[ה].

† תַּעֲנוּג **n.[m.] daintiness, luxury, exquisite delight;**—**1.** *luxury:* ת׳ Pr 19^{10}; else- 8588
where pl.; cstr. תַּעֲנֻגוֹת Ec 2^{8}. **2.** sf. בְּנֵי תַּעֲנוּגָיִךְ Mi 1^{16} *thy dainty sons;* בֵּית תַּעֲנֻגֶיהָ 2^{9} *her* (their) *dainty house(s),* >of tender love (rdg. בְּנֵי 2^{9}) We Now. **3.** *delight* of love, pl. abs. בַּתַּעֲנוּגִים Ct 7^{7} (Perles$^{Anal.\ 22\ f.}$ conj. בַּת עַמִּינָדָב).

† [עָנַד] **vb. bind around, upon** (cf. Ar. عَنَدَ *turn aside* fr. way; Syr. ܥܢܕ *defecit, defuit;* 6029
cf. also עִמָּדִי (for עִמִּי));—**Qal** *Impf.* 1 s. אֶעֶנְדֶנּוּ לִי Jb 31^{36} (obj. garland, in fig.); *Imv.* sf. עָנְדֵם Pr 6^{21} (fig.; ‖ קָשַׁר).

† מַעֲדַנּוֹת **n.f.pl. bonds, bands;** so appar. 4575
הַתְקַשֵּׁר מ׳ כִּימָה Jb 38^{31} (by metath. or err. from √ ענד, v. Di Bu).—1 S 15^{32} v. מ׳ p. 588 supr.

I. עָנָה $_{316}$ **vb. answer, respond** (NH *id.,* 6030
respond, make response; 𝔗 עֲנָא; Syr. ܥܢܐ; OAram. Palm. ענה; cf. Ar. عَنَا, عنى *intend* by saying);—**Qal** *Pf.* 3 ms. ע׳ Mi 6^{5} +; sf. עָנָנִי 1 S 28^{15} +, עָנָךְ Is 30^{19} Je 23^{37}, עָנָהוּ 1 S 9^{17} +; 1 s. עָנִיתִי Ho 14^{9}, etc.; *Impf.* 3 ms. יַעֲנֶה Gn 41^{16} +, וַיַּעַן Am 7^{14} +, sf. יַעֲנֵנִי Jb 20^{3} +, etc.; *Imv.* עֲנֵה Mi 6^{3} Pr 26^{5} etc.; *Inf. cstr.* עֲנוֹת Gn 45^{3} + [2 S 22^{36} v. עֲנָוָה]; *Pt.* עֹנֶה Ju 19^{28} +, etc.;—**1.** *answer, respond to* sthg. said, actual or implied, Ju 8^{8} 1 S 4^{20} Jb 9^{15} +; esp. **a.** of men, c. acc. pers. Gn 45^{3} (E), Ju 5^{29} 2 K 18^{36} = Is 36^{21} Jb 5^{1} + very oft. (c. 110 t.); specif. *be responsive,* i.e. *answer kindly,* grant request 1 K 12^{7} (sf. pers.); = *be amenable, docile* (toward י׳) Ho 2^{17} (of Isr. in fig.); seldom and late, c. acc. of thing replied to, Jb 32^{12} 33^{13} (De Di Bu), 40^{2}. **b.** of God answering (graciously): usu. c. acc. pers.; by oracle 1 S 14^{37} 28$^{6.15}$ +, fig. Hb 2^{11}; by deed 1 S 7^{9} 1 K 18$^{37.37}$, cf. בָּאֵשׁ v^{24} 1 Ch 21^{26}, and esp. Ho 2$^{23.24}$ 14^{9}, v. also Mi 3^{4} Is 41^{17} 49^{8} Je 33^{3} Jb 12^{4} +, esp. ψψ, e.g. 3^{5} 4^{2} 20^{2} + 33 t., etc. (in all c. 77 t.). **c.** rarely c. acc., or cl., of answer: אלהים יַעֲ׳ אֶת־שְׁלוֹם פַּרְעֹה Gn 41^{16}, Jb 15^{2} Pr 18^{23}; Ne 8^{6} they *responded, Amen!* 2 S 19^{43} *they made reply against* Isr. (c. עַל *against,* only here), + quoted answer; c. acc. pers. + answer 1 S 20^{28} *Jonathan answered Saul, David asked leave,* etc.; c. 2 acc. (c. 20 t.) 2 K 18^{36} = Is 36^{21}, Jb 23^{5} +; so = *grant, vouchsafe to,* נוֹרָאוֹת תַּעֲנֵנוּ ψ 65^{6} *terrible things dost thou* [י׳] *vouchsafe to us.* **d.** oft. + אָמַר Gn 18^{27} Abr. *answered and said,* Ex 4^{1} (J), 19^{8} (E), Jb 4^{1} 6^{1} etc.; + אָמַר אֶל־ Gn 27^{39} + 16 t.; + א׳ לְ v^{37} + 8 t.; ע׳ + acc. pers. + אמר, 1 S 9^{8} *he answered Saul and said,* + 23 t. (in all c. 130 t.); seldom + לֵאמֹר † Nu 32^{31} (P),

ע׳ + acc. pers. | לא׳ Gn 23$^{5.10.14}$ (P), 41^{16} 42^{22} (E), Jos 1^{16} (D) †. **e.** seldom + דָּבָר Jos 22^{21} (P), 2 K 1$^{10.11.12}$; ע׳ + acc. pers. + ד׳ Gn 34^{13} (P). **2.** **a.** *respond* to an occasion, speak in view of circumstances: 1 S 9^{17} (acc. pers. + quot.), Ju 18^{14} (+ אָמַר), Nu 11^{28} (JE; + *id.*), 2 K 1^{11} (+ *id.*), + 19 t. **b.** fig. יַעֲנֶה אֶת־הַכֹּל Ec 10^{19} money *meets all demands.* †**3.** **a.** specif. *respond* as a witness, *testify*, so perh. pt. עֹנֶה (abs.) Mal 2^{12} (in good sense); c. בְּ pers. = *in the case of* = *for* Gn 30^{33}; usu. *against*, 1 S 12^{3} 2 S 1^{16} Is 3^{9} 59^{12} Mi 6^{3} Je 14^{7} Nu 35^{30} (P), Ru 1^{21} (> Be *be occupied with*, II. ענה; Vrss Luth Kit^{Kau} עִנָּה *humiliate*); c. בְּפָנָיו Ho 5^{5} 7^{10} Jb 16^{8}; c. לְפָנָיו Dt 31^{21} (+ לְעֵד *as witness*); c. בְּ pers. + acc. of charge, סָרָה 19^{16}, of false witness שֶׁקֶר v^{18}, עֵד־שֶׁקֶר Ex 20^{16} (Ginsb v^{13}), || Dt 5^{17}, Pr 25^{18}: abs. (bad implic.) Ex 23^{2} (E; עַל *concerning*). **b.** less oft. *make response* as one accused (*respondent*) Jb 9$^{14.15}$. †**Niph.** **1.** *make answer*, subj. י׳, c. לְ pers., *Pf.* 1 s. נַעֲנֵיתִי Ez 14^{4}; *Pt.* נַעֲנֶה v^{7} (**Qal** not in Ez). **2.** *be answered: Impf.* 3 ms. יֵעָנֶה, **a.** Jb 11^{2} (subj. words). **b.** of man = *receive answer* Pr 21^{13}, so 1 s. אֵעָנֶה Jb 19^{7}. †**Hiph.** *Pt.* מַעֲנֶה בְּשִׂמְחַת לִבּוֹ Ec 5^{19}, wholly dub.; Hi (God) *causes* (all things) *to respond in the joy of his heart;* De *answers to the joy*, etc.; de Jong Wild *occupies him* (II. עָנָה) *with the joy*, etc.

5772 †[עֹנָה] **n.f. cohabitation** (NH עוֹנָה *time*, also = BH; poss. *response* or *correspondence*, *commerce*, from above √; or else euphemist., specific *time*, SS (cf. Ba$^{ES 17}$, from √ أنى); Thes from עון *dwell*);—sf. עֹנָתָהּ Ex 21^{10} (E)
5771 i.e. her marriage rights.—Ho 10^{10} v. עָוֺן.

6256 עֵת$_{297}$ **n.f.**$^{Am 5,13}$ and (seldom, mostly late) **m.**$^{Ezr 10,14}$ **time** (NH *id.;* Ph. עת; As. *inu, ittu, time;* Talm. עִנְתָּא; clearly fr. a √ ענה, but doubtful whether I. (ע׳);—abs. ע׳ Ho 10^{12}+, cstr. ע׳ Gn 24^{12}+, עֶת־ Lv 15^{25} + 5 t.; sf. עִתּוֹ Ho 2^{11}+, etc.; pl., late, עִתִּים 1 Ch 12^{32}+, sf. עִתֶּיךָ Is 33^{6}; עִתּוֹת ψ 9^{10} 10^{1}, sf. עִתֹּתָי 31^{16};—ע׳ only twice P, once H;—**1.** *time* of an event, etc.: **a.** usu. (213 t.) c. prep.: c. בְּ (142 t.), esp. בָּע׳ הַהִוא Gn 21^{22} (E) *in that time*, 38^{1} (J), Nu 22^{4} (E), Dt 1^{9} + 14 t. Dt; בָּע׳ הַהִיא Jos 5^{2} Am 5^{13} Dn 12$^{1.1}$ + (69 t., not in P); בָּע׳ הַזֹּאת Est 4^{14}, בָּעִתִּים הָהֵם 2 Ch 15^{5} Dn 11^{14}; בְּכָל־עֵת *at all times* Ex 18$^{22.26}$ (E), Lv 16^{2} (P) ψ 34^{2}+; = *continually* Pr 8^{30}, בְּכָל־עֵת אֲשֶׁר Est 5^{13} *as long as* I see Mordecai; c. לְ (31 t.; cf. לְ **6**, p. 516 supr.), 2 S 11^{1} + *at the time*, but Ez 12^{27} *for distant times*, cf. לְעֵת כָּזֹאת Est 4^{14}, etc.; c. כְּ (21 t.; cf. כ **1 a**, p. 453 supr.), †מָחָר כָּע׳ הַזֹּאת Jos 11^{6} (JE) *to-morrow about this time*, usu. כָּע׳ מָחָר (Kö$^{Synt. 401 o}$) Ex 9^{18} (J), 1 S 9^{16} (cf. Dr), 20^{12} 1 K 19^{2} 20^{6} 2 K 7$^{1.18}$ 10^{6}†; כָּעֵת חַיָּה v. p. 312; †כָּעֵת הָרִאשׁוֹן Is 8^{23} *at the former time;* כָּעֵת alone Nu 23^{23} (JE) *at this time* = *now* (prob., cf. Di), Ju 13^{23} 21^{22}†, etc.; c. מִן (8 t.), מִן הָעֵת הַהִא Ne 13^{21}, etc.; c. עַד (12 t.), מֵעֵת עַד־הָע׳ הַהִיא Ne 6^{1} *up to that time*, מֵעֵת עַד־עֵת Ez 4$^{10.11}$, etc. (5 t. Dn); c. אֶל־ מֵעֵת אֶל־עֵת 1 Ch 9^{25}. **b.** oft. cstr. defined by n.foll.: בְּעֵת צָהֳרַיִם Je 20^{16}, לְעֵת (הָ)עֶרֶב 2 S 11^{12} Gn 8^{11} 24^{11} (both J), כְּעֵת מִנְחַת Is 17^{14} Zc 14^{7}, עַד־עֵת הָעָרֶב Jos 8^{29} (JE), עֶרֶב Dn 9^{21}, redundantly לְעֶת־יוֹם בְּיוֹם 1 Ch 12^{22}, ע׳ זִקְנָה ψ 71^{9}, ע׳ (ה)קָצִיר Je 50^{16} 51^{33}, ע׳ הַזָּמִיר Ct 2^{12}, 1 K 11^{4} 15^{23}, בְּע׳ אַפְּךָ Je 18^{23} = לְע׳ פָּנֶיךָ ψ 21^{10} (of anger), לְעִתּוֹת בַּצָּרָה 9^{10} 10^{1} *at times of destitution* (v. בַּצָּרָה), etc. **c.** sq. inf. לְע׳ בּוֹא הַשֶּׁמֶשׁ Jos 10^{27} (JE), 2 Ch 18^{34}, בְּע׳ קָרְאָם Je 11^{14a} (rd. בְּעֵת also v^{b}, Gie), etc. **d.** sq. cl. c. vb. fin. (poet. or late) Dt 32^{35} Jb 6^{17} 2 Ch 20^{22} 24^{11} 29^{27} + (cf. **2 c**). **2.** **a.** = *usual time:* לְע׳ צֵאת 2 S 11^{1} *at the time of* kings' *going forth* = 1 Ch 20^{1}; בְּעֵת יַחֵם Gn 31^{10}; עֵת לֶדֶת Jb 39$^{1.2}$. **b.** *proper, suitable time:* rain בְּעִתּוֹ Dt 11^{14} Je 5^{24}+, cf. Lv 26^{4} (H), also ψ 1^{3} 104^{27} 145^{15} Pr 15^{23} Is 60^{22} Ec 3^{11}; עֵת מִלְחָמָה v^{8}, ע׳ שָׁלוֹם v^{8}; sq. inf. Ho 10^{12}, הַעֵת לָקַחַת 2 K 5^{26} *is it a time to take money?* Hg 1^{4}, עֵת־בֵּית י׳ לְהִבָּנוֹת v^{2} (v^{a} read עַתָּ בָּא Hi We Now al.); עֵת לַעֲשׂוֹת ψ 119^{126}, cf. Ec 3$^{2-8}$ (26 t.); abs. כִּי עֵת Ho 13^{13} (Hi We al.; Gu^{Kau} gives עַתָּ; > Now כָּעֵת); abs. c. neg. Jb 22^{16} Ec 7^{17}; hence (late) יוֹדְעֵי בִינָה לָעִתִּים 1 Ch 12^{32}, יֹדְעֵי הָעִתִּים Est 1^{13} i.e. astrologers, etc. **c.** *appointed time*, בְּעֵת תֵּת וגו׳ 1 S 18^{19} *at the appointed time of giving*, Ez 7$^{7.12}$ Is 13^{22}, ע׳ פְּקֻדָּתָם Je 8^{12} 10^{15} = 51^{18}, 46^{21} 50^{27} cf. (c. vb. fin.) 6^{15} 49^{8} 50^{31}, ע׳ אַרְצוֹ Je 27^{7}, ע׳ גּוֹיִם Ez 30^{3}, לְעִתִּים מְזֻמָּנִים Ezr 10^{14} Ne 10^{35} cf. 13^{31}; עַד־ע׳ מוֹעֵד 2 S 24^{15}, ψ 103^{14} (|| מוֹעֵד), etc.; cf. עֵת וּמִשְׁפָּט Ec 8$^{5.6}$ (for *time of judgment*), עִתּוֹ 9^{12}; esp. לְעֵת קֵץ Dn 8^{7} cf. 11$^{35.40}$ 12$^{4.9}$, בְּע׳ עֲוֺן קֵץ Ez 21$^{30.34}$ cf. 35^{5}; לְקֵץ הָעִתִּים Dn 11^{13}. **d.** as uncertain עֵת וָפֶגַע Ec 9^{11}. **3.** = *experiences, fortunes*, pl. אֱמוּנַת עִתֶּיךָ Is 33^{6}, ψ 31^{16}; הָעִתִּים אֲשֶׁר עָבְרוּ עָלָיו 1 Ch 29^{30}. †**4.** *occurrence, occasion* (= פַּעַם), רַבּוֹת עִתִּים Ne 9^{28} *great numbers of times* (= very often).

†[עֵת] קָצִין **n.pr.loc.** on border of Zebulun, 6278
only c. ה loc., עִתָּה ק׳ Jos 19^{13}; site unknown.

עַתָּה$_{435}$ (also Ez 23^{43} ψ 74^{6} עת Kt, Qr עַתָּה), 6258
וְעַתָּה Gn 32^{5}+, **adv.** of time, now (prop. acc.

of [ʿint], עֵת (Kö$^{ii. 260}$), *at the time*, in partic. of
the present time, i. e. *now*; cf. Germ. *zur Zeit*,
Ar. أَلْآنَ *at the time*, i. e. *now*);—*now*: **1. a.**
Gn 12^{19} ועתה הנה אשתך and *now*, behold thy
wife, 22^{12} כי עתה ידעתי *now* I know (so Ex 18^{11}
Ju 17^{13} 1 K 17^{24} [עַתָּה זֶה], ψ 20^{7}), 26$^{22.29}$ 27^{36}
31$^{13.28}$, etc., Ex 5^{5} הן רבים עתה עם הארץ; whether
in opp. to past time, as Gn 32^{11} Jos 14^{11} כְּכֹחִי
אָז וּכְכֹחִי עָתָּה, Ju 11^{8} 1 K 12^{4} Is 1^{21} ועתה מרצחים,
16^{14} Ho 2^{9} כִּי טוֹב לִי אָז מֵעָתָּה, 13^{2}, Jb 30^{1}+, or
to future, as Nu 24^{17} אֶרְאֶנּוּ ולא עתה, Ju 8^{6} הֲכַף
זֶבַח וגו׳ עַתָּה־בְּיָדֶךָ, 1 S 2^{16} כִּי עַתָּה תִתֵּן; = *after*
all Nu 22^{38} Ju 8^{2}; = *now at last* 2 S 24^{16} 1 K
19^{4} 2 K 19^{25} Ho 7^{2} Je 4^{12}; and in the phr. מעתה
ועד עולם †Is 9^{6} 59^{21} Mi 4^{7} (v. infr.), ψ 113^{2} 115^{18}
121^{8} 125^{2} 131^{3}. **b.** of the imminent or impending future: Gn 19^{9} עַתָּה נָרַע לְךָ מֵהֶם, 29^{32}
כי עתה יאהבני אישי, v^{34} Ex 6^{1} עתה תראה, Nu 11^{23}
22^{4} 2 S 20^{6} Is 33^{10} (ψ 12^{6}), 43^{19} 49^{19} Am 6^{7} לכן
עתה יִגְלוּ, Is 49^{19} Mi 7$^{4.10}$ Dn 10^{20}; and esp. ἀσυνδέτως in Hos, introducing a punishment, Ho 4^{16}
עתה יִרְעֵם י׳ וגו׳ 5^{7} 8$^{8.13}$ (Je 14^{10}), 10^{2}. **c.** of a
time *ideally* present (= *then*, from our point
of view): Is 29^{22} לא עתה יבוש יעקב, v^{b} Ho 10^{3}
Mi 4$^{9.10.11.14}$ 5^{3}. **d.** describing a present state
= *as things are*: 1 S 8^{5} thou art old, etc., עתה
שִׂימָה לנו מלך, 9^{6} 13^{12} 14^{30} 25^{7b} 27^{1} *now* I shall
be swept away one day, etc., 2 K 18$^{20.25}$ Jb 6^{21}
14^{16} 16^{7}. **e.** with an Imv., as an encouragement, implying that the time has come for the
exhortation or advice to be followed, Gn 31^{13}
עתה קום צא, Ex 18^{19} עתה שְׁמַע בקולי, Nu 22^{11}
Dt 2^{13} Is 30^{8}.

2088 **2.** Phrases: **a.** עַתָּה זֶה (זֶה **4 h**) †1 K 17^{24}
2 K 5^{22}. **b.** ועתה and, *now*, or *now*, therefore
(וְ **4**), drawing a conclusion, esp. (cf. **1 e**) a
practical one, from what has been stated: Gn
3^{22} *and now* (since man has once been disobedient), lest he put forth his hand, etc.,
20$^{7.23}$ וְעַתָּה הִשָּׁבְעָה לִּי הֵנָּה, 27$^{3.8}$ ועתה בני שְׁמַע
בקולי, 30^{30} 31$^{16.44}$ 37^{20}+oft., Is 5$^{3.5}$ 36^{8} ψ 2^{10};
Gn 11^{6} ועתה לֹא־יִבָּצֵר מֵהֶם וגו׳, 31^{30} 45^{8} 2 S 19^{11}
2009 ψ 39^{8} ועתה מַה־קִּוִּיתִי אֲדֹנָי, Is 52^{5}. **c.** וְעַתָּה הִנֵּה
stating the ground on which some conclusion
or action is to be based, Ex 3^{9} Jo 14$^{10.10}$ 1 S 12^{2}
24^{21} 1 K 1^{18} Je 40^{4} (with ועתה usu. repeated
after the הנה-clause). †**d.** גם עתה Gn 44^{10}
1 S 12^{16} 1 K 14^{14} Jo 2^{12} Jb 16^{19}. †**e.** מֵעַתָּה
from now, henceforth, Je 3^{4} Is 48^{6} Dn 10^{17} (acc.
to some, here = from *just now*), 2 Ch 16^{9}; מעתה
5704 ועד עולם, v. supr. **1 a** *end*. **f.** עַד־עַתָּה *until*
now, Gn 32^{5} וָאֵחַר עַד־ע׳, Dt 12^{9} לא באתם עד ע׳
אל הנחלה (opp. to the fut.), 2 K 13^{23}; esp. after
clause with מִן, 46^{34} מִנְּעוּרֵינוּ וְעַד־ע׳ (2 S 19^{8} Ez
4^{14}), Ex 9^{18} 2 K 8^{6} Ru 2^{7}. **g.** כִּי עַתָּה *for in* 3588
this case, in our idiom, *for then* (עתה pointing
to a condition assumed as a possible contingency; cf. Dr$^{§ 141, 142}$); †(*a*) Ex 9^{15} כי עתה
שלחתי וגו׳ for *then* (if the intention expressed
in v^{14} had not existed) *I should have* put forth
my hand, etc., Nu 22^{29} כי עתה הֲרַגְתִּיךָ, 1 S 13^{13}
Jb 3^{13}; sq. impf. Jb 6^{3} for *then* (if it were
weighed, v^{2}) it would be heavier, etc., 13^{19} *for*
then would I be silent and die; (*b*) after a
protasis, *surely then* Gn 31^{42}+ (see כִּי **1 d** *b*,
p. 472).—*Note.* Read כְּמוֹ עַתָּ (𝔊𝔙) *as now*, for
כְּמוֹ עֵת Ez 16^{57}, עַתְּ נִשְׁבַּרְתְּ (𝔊𝔖𝔙) *now art thou*
broken! for עֵת נִשְׁבֶּרֶת Ez 27^{34}, and prob. עַתָּ בָּא
(Hi We Kö Now, cf. 𝔊𝔖) for עֶת־בֹּא Hg 1^{2};
also עַתָּה for אַתָּה 1 K 1^{20}, and אַתָּה for עַתָּה
v$^{18 b}$ 2 S 18^{3}.

†עַתַּי **n.pr.m.** (Ι)εθθει **1.** of Judah 1 Ch 2^{35} 6262
(עַתָּי), v^{36}. **2.** of Gad 12^{11}. **3.** 2 Ch 11^{20}

†עִתִּי **adj. timely, ready** (Gk. ὡραῖος);— 6261
אִישׁ ע׳ Lv 16^{21} *a man* who is *in readiness*.

יַעַן$_{96}$ prop. **subst., purpose, intention**, but 3282
always used as **prep.** or **conj., on account of,**
because (for יַעֲנֶה, of the form יִצְהָר, etc., Sta
§ 259 Kö$^{ii. 403}$; cf. عَنَى *mean, intend*):—**1.** as **prep.,**
rarely with a subst., †Ez 5^{9} יַעַן תּוֹעֲבוֹתַיִךְ, Hg
1^{9} יַעַן מֶה, v^{9} יַעַן בֵּיתִי; with a ptcp. Ez 36^{13}
יען אמרים *because of men saying* to you (but rd.
prob. אָמְרָם, Co Toy Berthol); freq. with inf. c.,
1 K 21^{20} יַעַן הִתְמַכֶּרְךָ *on account of* thy having
sold thyself, Am 5^{11} Is 30^{12} 37^{29} (= 2 K 19^{28})
יַעַן הִתְרַגֶּזְךָ אֵלַי, Je 5^{14} 7^{13} 23^{38} 48^{7}, and oft.
(c. 18 t.) in Ezek., as 5^{7} (rd. יַעַן הֲמָרְתְכֶם), 13$^{8.22}$
25$^{3.6.8.12}$.

2. As **conj.**: **a.** יַעַן אֲשֶׁר (32 t.), usu. with 834
pf., as Gn 22^{16} יען אשר עשית זאת *because that*
thou hast done this, Dt 1^{36} (Jos 14^{14}), Ju 2^{20}
1 S 30^{22} 1 K 3^{11} 8^{18} Je 19^{4} 25^{8} 29^{23} (not Is)+;
with impf. (in frequent. sense) Ez 44^{12}. †**b.**
יַעַן כִּי, Nu 11^{20} יַעַן כִּי מְאַסְתֶּם אֶת־י׳, 1 K 13^{21} 21^{29} 3588
Is 3^{16} 7^{5} 8^{6} 29^{13}. **c.** יַעַן alone (23 t.), with pf.
Nu 20^{12} יַעַן לֹא הֶאֱמַנְתֶּם בִּי, 1 S 15^{23} 1 K 14^{13} 20^{42}
2 K 22^{19} Ho 8^{1} Is 61^{1} 65^{12} 66^{4}; with impf. (freq.)
†Ez 34^{21}; of the fut. †Ez 12^{12} *because* he shall
not see, etc., (but 𝔊 Co Kau Berthol לְמַעַן אשר
לֹא יִרְאֶה לָעַיִן): usu. the vb. follows immediately,
but Ezek. sometimes puts the obj. first for emph.,
5^{11} יַעַן אֶת־מִקְדָּשִׁי טִמֵּאת, 20$^{16.24}$ 36^{6}, cf. 34^{21}.

†**3.** יַ֫עַן וּבְיַ֫עַן, q. d. *because and by the cause* (that), sq. perf., Lv 26^{43} (H) יען וביען בְּמִשְׁפָּטַי מָאָ֑סוּ, Ez 13^{10}; יַ֫עַן בְּיַ֫עַן sq. inf., Ez 36^{3}. (In all, reckoning יען (ו)ביען once each, 93 t., of which 20 are in 1–2 K, 11 in Je, 38 in Ez; and only 9 in Gn–2 S.)

4617 **מַעֲנֶה†** **n.m.**$^{Pr\,15,1}$ **answer, response**;—abs. מ׳־רַךְ Pr 15^{1} *a gentle answer;* cstr. מַעֲנֵה פִּיו v^{23}, cf. מ׳ לָשׁוֹן 16^{1} (i.e. ability to answer); מ׳ אֱלֹהִים Mi 3^{7} i.e. *response* for guidance; abs. also Pr 29^{19} *response*=obedience; Jb 32$^{3.5}$ *reply*, refutation; sf. לַמַּעֲנֵהוּ 16^{4}=for its purpose, that for which it *answers* (v. Toy).

4616 **[מַ֫עַן]** **subst.** purpose, intent, only with לְ, in **לְמַ֫עַן**$_{271}$ **prep.** and **conj. for the sake of, on account of, to the intent** or **in order that** (abbrev. from מַעֲנֶה: cf. מַ֫עַל; Kö$^{ii.\,116}$);—with sf. לְמַעַנְךָ, לְמַעֲנִי, and לְמַעַנְכֶם;—**1. prep.**:—**a.** Gn 18^{24} wilt thou . . . not spare the place למען חמשים הצדיקים *for the sake of* the 50 righteous? Dt 30^{6} ל׳ חַיֶּיךָ *for thy life's sake*, 1 K 8^{41} the foreigner who comes from afar ל׳ שְׁמֶךָ, Is 43^{14} לְמַעַנְכֶם שִׁלַּחְתִּי בָבֶ֫לָה, 45^{4} 62^{1} ל׳ ציון, 63^{17} ל׳ עבדיך, 65^{8} Ez 36$^{22.22}$ Jb 18^{4} ψ 122$^{8.9}$; לְמַעַן דָּוִד (עַבְדִּי ד׳), i.e. for the sake of David's memory, and the promises given to him, †1 K 11$^{12.13.32.34}$ 15^{4} 2 K 8^{19} 19^{34} (=Is 37^{35}), 20^{6} (all D^{2}); לְמַעֲנִי (of י׳) *for my own sake*, i.e. to vindicate my name, †2 K 19^{34} (=Is 37^{35}), 20^{6} Is 43^{25} 48^{11} לְמַעֲנִי לְמַעֲנִי אֶעֱשֶׂה, so לְמַעַנְךָ Dn 9^{19}, ל׳ אֲדֹנָי v^{17}; לְמַעַן שְׁמוֹ (שְׁמִי, שִׁמְךָ) י׳ is said (or entreated) to act i.e. to maintain his reputation, or character, †ψ 23^{3} 25^{11} 31^{4} 79^{9} 106^{8} 109^{21} 143^{11} Je 14$^{7.21}$ Ez 20$^{9.14.22.44}$ Is 48^{9}; simil. ל׳ חַסְדֶּךָ (i.e. to maintain it consistently) †ψ 6^{5} 44^{27}, ל׳ טוּבְךָ †25^{7}, ל׳ צִדְקוֹ †Is 42^{21}.

b. *In view of, on account of* (but not expressing causation distinctly, like מִן **2 f,** or מִפְּנֵי), Dt 3^{26} ויתעבר י׳ בי לְמַעַנְכֶם *on your account*, 1 K 11^{39} ל׳ זאת *in view of this*, ל׳ שׁוֹרְרָי *on account of* my watchful foes, †ψ 5^{9} 27^{11}, ל׳ צורריך ψ 8^{3}, simil. 69^{19}; 48^{12} (97^{8}) ישמח הר ציון . . . ל׳ משפטיך *in view of* thy judgments.

c. Sq. inf. Gn 18^{19} לְמַעַן הָבִיא י׳ *for the purpose of* J.'s bringing=*to the intent that* J. *might* bring, 37^{22} ל׳ הַצִּיל *in order to* rescue, 50^{20} Ex 1^{11} 9^{16} 10^{1}, etc., Dt 2^{30} 6^{23}, etc., 2 K 10^{19}, Je 7$^{10.18}$ 11^{5} 50^{34} (on הִרְגִּיעַ, v. עַד **2 a** *b*), Ez 14^{5} 21^{15} 22^{6}, etc., 36^{3} (v. p. 176), + oft. (Kö$^{iii.\,595\,f.}$). Onoo, ploon., לְמַעַן לָמוּג לֵב Ez 21^{20} (cf. בַּעֲבוּר לְ 1 Ch 19^{3}; but rd. prob. הַמּוּג).

2. Conj. (sq. impf.):—**a.** לְמַעַן אֲשֶׁר Gn 18^{19} 834
I have known him ל׳ אשר יְצַוֶּה *to the end that* he might command, etc., Dt 27^{3} Jos 3^{4} 2 S 13^{5} Je 42^{6}; more oft. **b.** without אשׁר, as Gn 12^{13} לְמַעַן יִיטַב לִי, 27^{25} Ex 4^{5} ל׳ יאמינו, 8$^{6.18}$ 9^{29} 10^{2} Is 5^{19} 23^{16} ψ 9^{15} 30^{13} 48^{14} + oft. (Kö$^{iii.\,571}$).

c. Sq. לֹא: (*a*) ל׳ אשר לֹא †Nu 17^{5} Dt 20^{18} Ez 31^{14} 36^{30} 46^{18}; (*b*) ל׳ לֹא †Ez 14^{11} 19^{9} 25^{10} 26^{20} Zech 12^{7} ψ 119$^{11.80}$ 125^{3} (Kö$^{iii.\,574}$. Less common than לְבִלְתִּי or מִן with inf., or פֶּן).

Note 1.—לְמַעַן is always *in order that*, never merely *so that* (ἐκβατικῶς); but sts., in rhetorical passages, the issue of a line of action, though really undesigned, is represented by it ironically as if it were designed: Dt 29^{18} (v. Dr) וְהִתְבָּרֵךְ בִּלְבָבוֹ . . . ל׳ סְפוֹת וגו׳ and he congratulate himself . . . *in order to* sweep away the moistened with the dry (i.e. to destroy all together), Is 30^{1} 44^{9} בל יראו ובל ידעו ל׳ יֵבֹשׁוּ *in order that they may be* put to shame, Je 7^{18} ל׳ הַכְעִיסֵנִי v^{19} ל׳ בֹּשֶׁת פְּנֵיהֶם, 27$^{10.15}$ 32^{29} Ho 8^{4} their silver, etc., they have made into idols ל׳ יִכָּרֵת *in order that* it may be cut off (of course, not the *real* purpose of the idolatry), Am 2^{7} Mi 6^{16}: cf. ψ 51^{6} (v. Comm.) *in order that* thou mightest be just when thou judgest (*sc.* by manifesting thy justice in judgment on my sin). Cf. لِ Qor 28^{7} (Fl$^{Kl.\,Schr.\,i.\,397\,f.}$).

Note 2.—In Jos 4^{24} for the anom. ל׳ יְרָאתֶם, rd. inf. ל׳ יִרְאָתָם *in order that they* might fear (Dr$^{§\,14\,Obs.}$): Neh 6^{13} לְמַעַן שָׂכוּר הוּא לְמַעַן אִירָא (si vera l.) the first ל׳ points forwards, *to this intent* was he hired, *to the intent that* I should be afraid.—On Pr 16^{4}, v. מַעֲנֶה above 4617

†II. **[עָנָה]** **vb. be occupied, busied with** 6031
(בְּ), only Ec (perh. Aram. loan-word; Syr. ܥܢܳܐ *be occupied with*, ܥܶܢܝܳܢܳܐ *occupation, affair;* cf. Ar. عَنَا, عنى *concern one*, also *be occupied* by; Ecclus 42$^{8\,marg.}$);—**Qal** *Inf.* עֲנוֹת Ec 1^{13} 3^{10}.

עִנְיָן† **n.m.**$^{Ec\,1,13}$ **occupation, task**, only Ec 6045
(Aram. loan-word Lag$^{BN\,205}$; common in NH);—ע׳ abs. Ec 2^{26} 3^{10} 5^{2} 8^{16}; sf. כַּעַס עִנְיָנוֹ 2^{23} *his task is* (sheer) *vexation;* עִנְיַן רָע 1^{13} *an evil* (worthless) *task*, so 4^{8} (Mass. עִנְיַן as if cstr., v. Baer^{1,13} but Kö$^{ii.\,1,\,99}$), and, in weakened sense, 5^{13} *a bad business, bad affair.*

4618 †מַעֲנָה **n.f. place for task** (?), specif. **field for ploughing**;—pl. sf. לְמַעֲנוֹתָם ψ 129^{3} Kt *they have extended their ploughing-grounds* (Qr מַעֲנִיתָם); sg. מַעֲנָה only 1 S 14^{14}, where text corrupt and meaning dub. v. Comm.

4618 מַעֲנִית ψ 129^{3} Qr v. foregoing.

6031 †III. [עָנָה] **vb. be bowed down, afflicted** (NH *id.*; MI Pi. ויענו 1^{5}, אענו 1^{6}; As. *enû*, *thwart, frustrate, do violence to*; Ar. عنو, عَنَا, *be lowly, submissive*, v. Rahlfs עָנִי und עָנָו in d. Psalmen (1892), 67 ff.; 𝔗 עֲנֵי Pa. *oppress*; Syr. Ethpe. *humble oneself*, and deriv.);—**Qal** *Pf.* 1 s. עָנִיתִי ψ 116^{10}; *Impf.* 3 ms. יַעֲנֶה Is 25^{5} 31^{4}, etc.;—**1.** *be put down* or *become low*, of song of triumph Is 25^{5} (others as **Hiph.** *he putteth down*, ‖ תַּכְנִיעַ). **2.** *be depressed, downcast* Is 31^{4} (of lion; ‖ יֵחָת). **3.** *be afflicted* ψ 116^{10} 119^{67} Zc 10^{2}. **Niph.** *Pf.* 1 s. נַעֲנֵיתִי ψ 119^{107}; *Inf. cstr.* לֵעָנֹת (perh. rd. as Qal Ges §51 l) Ex 10^{3}; *Pt.* נַעֲנֶה Is 53^{7}; fs. נַעֲנָה 58^{10};—**1.** *humble oneself* מִפָּנַי Ex 10^{3}. **2.** *be afflicted* ψ 119^{107} Is 53^{7} 58^{10}. **Piel.** *Pf.* 3 ms. עִנָּה Dt 22^{24} + 5 t.; 2 ms. עִנִּיתָ ψ 88^{8}; 1 s. עִנֵּיתִי ψ 35^{13}, sf. וְעִנִּתִךְ consec. Na 1^{12}, etc.; *Impf.* יְעַנֶּה Jb 37^{23}, etc.; *Imv.* עַנּוּ Ju 19^{24}; *Inf. abs.* עַנֵּה Ex 22^{22}; *cstr.* עַנּוֹת Is 58^{5} +, etc.; *Pt.* pl. sf. מְעַנַּיִךְ Is 60^{14} Zp 3^{19};—**1.** *humble, mishandle, afflict*: individual Gn 16^{6} 31^{50} (J) Ex $22^{21.22.22}$ (E) Jb 30^{11}; by imprisonment and bonds Ju $16^{5.6.19}$ ψ 105^{18}; a nation by war or in bondage Gn 15^{13} (J) Ex $1^{11.12}$ Nu $24^{24.24}$ (E) Dt 26^{6} 1 S 12^{8} (inserting וַיְעַנּוּם מִצְרַיִם, so 𝔊 Dr Bu Kit HPS [cf. Th We]), 2 S 7^{10} 2 K 17^{20} ψ 94^{5} Is 60^{14} Zp 3^{19}; dynasty of David ψ 89^{23}. **2.** *humble*, a woman by cohabit., Gn 34^{2} (J) Dt 21^{14} $22^{24.29}$ Ju 19^{24} 20^{5} 2 S $13^{12.14.22.32}$ Ez $22^{10.11}$ La 5^{11}. **3.** *afflict* as a discipline (God agent) Dt $8^{2.3.16}$ 1 K 11^{39} ψ 88^{8} 90^{15} 119^{75} Is 64^{11} Na $1^{12.12}$ La 3^{33}. **4.** *humble, weaken*, obj. כֹּחַ ψ 102^{24}; משפט Jb 37^{23} (cf. Talm. עִנָּה דִּין); נֶפֶשׁ *oneself*, by fasting Lv $16^{29.31}$ $23^{27.32}$ Nu 29^{7} (P) ψ 35^{13} Is $58^{3.5}$; by an oath Nu 30^{14} (P). **Pu.** *Pf.* 1 s. עֻנֵּיתִי ψ 119^{71}; *Impf.* 3 fs. תְּעֻנֶּה Lv 23^{29}; *Inf. cstr.* sf. עֻנּוֹתוֹ ψ 132^{1}; *Pt.* מְעֻנֶּה Is 53^{4};—**1.** *be afflicted*, in discipline by God ψ 119^{71} 132^{1} Is 53^{4}. **2.** *be humbled* by fasting Lv 23^{29} (P). **Hiph.** *Impf.* 2 ms. sf. תַּעֲנֵם 1 K 8^{35} = 2 Ch 6^{26} *afflict*, in discipline. **Hithp.** *Pf.* 3 ms. הִתְעַנָּה 1 K 2^{26}; 2 ms. הִתְעַנִּיתָ v^{26}; *Impf.* 3 mpl. יִתְעַנּוּ ψ 107^{17}; *Imv.* הִתְעַנִּי Gn 16^{9}; *Inf. cstr.* הִתְעַנּוֹת Ez 8^{21} Dn 10^{12};—**1.** *humble oneself* (c. תַּחַת יָדֶיהָ) Gn 16^{9} (J). **2.** *be afflicted*, by men 1 K $2^{26.26}$; by God in discipline ψ 107^{17}. **3.** *humble oneself* in fasting Ezr 8^{21} Dn 10^{12}.

†עָנָו (?; Lag BN 48) **n.m. poor, afflicted,** 6035
humble, meek;—עָנָו Nu 12^{3} (Kt; Qr עָנָיו is to ensure the ָ acc. to Di Kö ii. 1, 76); elsewh. pl. עֲנָוִים Is 29^{19} + 11 t. + Kt עֲנָוִים Is 32^{7} ψ 9^{19} (Qr עֲנִיִּים); Qr עֲנָוִים ψ 9^{13} 10^{12} Pr 3^{34} 14^{21} 16^{19} (Kt עניים); cstr. עַנְוֵי Zp 2^{3} + 2 t., + Kt ענוי (Qr עֲנִיֵּי) Am 8^{4} (so Jb 24^{4} van d. H.; but עֲנִיֵּי Kt and Qr Baer Ginsb)—these forms shew confusion
with עָנִי, which is perh. only another form of עָנָו 6041
(otherwise Rahlfs op. cit. 62 f. Dr 'Poor' in Hastings DB;
עָנָו = *humble, meek*, עָנִי = pass. *humbled, afflicted*); 6041
—**1.** *poor, needy* Pr 14^{21} (Qr). **2.** *poor and weak*, oppressed by rich and powerful Am 2^{7} Is 29^{19} 32^{7} (Kt); ענוי (ה)ארץ ψ 76^{10} Is 11^{4} Zp 2^{3} Am 8^{4} (Kt), Jb 24^{4}. **3.** *poor, weak and afflicted* Israel (usu. rendered *meek*) ψ 10^{17} 22^{27} $25^{9.9}$ 34^{3} 37^{11} 69^{33} (עָנִי **3**, also in all these ψψ), 147^{6} 149^{4} Is 61^{1} (‖ נשברי לב, cf. 66^{2} עָנִי **3**), ψ 9^{19} (Kt) v^{13} 10^{12} (Qr). **4.** *humble, lowly, meek* Nu 12^{3} (Moses); Pr 3^{34} 16^{19} (both Qr).

†עֲנָוָה **n.f. humility**;—ע׳ Pr 15^{33} + 3 t.; 6037-38
עַנְוָה־ (contr. because of Maqqeph, see Br MP) ψ 45^{5}; עַנְוַתְךָ ψ 18^{36} (= עֲנֹתְךָ 2 S 22^{36} v. I. ענה; rd. עֶזְרָתְךָ Ol We);—**1.** *humility, meekness* ψ 45^{5} (dub.), Pr 15^{33} 18^{12} 22^{4} Zp 2^{3} (prob. gloss, v. We Now). **2.** *condescension* ψ 18^{36} (dub., v. supr.).

†עֱנוּת **n.f. affliction**;—ψ 22^{25}; Che JBL xv 6039
(1896), 198 prop. צַעֲקַת *cry* [cf. 𝔊𝔙𝔗], (צ dropped out after ץ).

†עָנִי **adj. poor, afflicted, humble**;—ע׳ Dt 6041
24^{12} + 51 t.; pl. עֲנִיִּים Is 3^{15} + 6 t.; cstr. עֲנִיֵּי Is 10^{2} + 4 t. (v. also Kt and Qr sub עָנָו supr.); sf. עֲנִיֶּיךָ ψ 72^{2} 74^{19}, עֲנִיֶּךָ Dt 15^{11}, עֲנִיָּו Is 49^{13}; fs. עֲנִיָּה Is 51^{21} 54^{11} (+ Is 10^{30} MT, but rd. עֲנִיָּה, v. I. ענה);—**1.** *poor, needy*, ‖ אביון Dt 15^{11} $24^{14.15}$ Pr 31^{20}, ‖ יתום Jb 24^{9} Ex 22^{24} (E), Dt 24^{12}; having right to gleanings Lv 19^{10} 23^{22} (H); יְמֵי ע׳ Pr 15^{15}, cf. Pr 14^{21} (Kt). **2.** *poor and weak*, oppressed by the rich and powerful Is $3^{14.15}$ 32^{7} (Qr), 58^{7} 29^{12} $36^{6.15}$ Pr 30^{14} Ec 6^{8} Ez 18^{17} Zc 7^{10} Jb 24^{4}, also Am 8^{4} (Qr); ‖ דל Jb 34^{28} Pr 22^{22}; עֲנִיֵּי עַמִּי Is 10^{2}; עני ואביון Jb 24^{14} Pr 31^{9} Je 22^{16} Ez 16^{49} 18^{12} 22^{29}. **3.** *poor, weak, afflicted* Israel, or *pious* in Israel *afflicted* by wicked nations or the wicked in Israel itself ψ $10^{2.9.9}$ 14^{6} (dub., cf. ψ 53^{6}) 102^{1} (or n.pr.), Is 14^{32} Hb 3^{14}; of Zion, עֲנִיָּה Is 51^{21} 54^{11}; שד ע׳ ψ 12^{6}; יחיד וע׳ 25^{16}; עני ואביון 35^{10} 37^{14} 40^{18} = 70^{6}, 74^{21} 86^{1} $109^{16.22}$, pl. Is 41^{17}; עני וְכוֹאֵב ψ 69^{30}; ע׳ וָרָשׁ 82^{3}; עֱנוּת ע׳

22[26]; ע׳ וְגֹוֵעַ 88[16]; || דל Is 26[6] Zp 3[12]; ע׳ וּנְכֵה־רוּחַ Is 66[2];—Zc 11[7.11] v. II. כְּנַעֲנִי;—God does not forget them ψ 9[13.19] 10[12] (Kt) 74[19], but has compassion on them Is 49[13], saves ψ 34[7], delivers 35[10], and bestows various favours 68[11] 140[13], the king also judges 72[2.4], and delivers 72[12]. **4.** *humble, lowly,* Zc 9[9] (victorious king); opp. לֵצִים Pr 3[34] (Kt); opp. גֵּאִים 16[19] (Kt); עם עני opp. עינים רמות ψ 18[28] = 2 S 22[28].

6040 † עֳנִי **n.m. affliction, poverty**;—ע׳ Ex 3[7]+; עֳנִי Dt 16[3]+; עׇנְיִי ψ 107[41], עוני 2 S 16[12] (Kt, but rd. עָנְיִי; > Qr עֵינִי!); sf. עׇנְיִי Gn 31[42]+, עׇנְיֵךְ 16[11], etc.;—**1.** *affliction,* Jb 36[15.21] ψ 44[25] 88[10] 107[41] 119[50.92] La 1[3] 3[19]; ארץ ע׳ Gn 41[52] (E); יְמֵי ע׳ Jb 30[16.27] La 1[7]; כּוּר ע׳ Is 48[10]; חַבְלֵי ע׳ Jb 36[8]; אֲסִירֵי ע׳ ψ 107[10]; בְּנֵי ע׳ Pr 31[5]; ראה ע׳ Gn 31[42] (E), Ex 3[7] 4[31] (J), Dt 26[7] 2 K 14[26] Ne 9[9] Jb 10[15] ψ 9[14] 25[18] 31[8] 119[153] La 1[9] 3[1], ins. also before עַמִּי 1 S 9[16 b] 𝔊 Th We Dr Kit Bu HPS; ראה בע׳ Gn 29[32] (J), 1 S 1[11] 2 S 16[12] (v. supr.); שמע ע׳ Gn 16[11] (J); העלה מע׳ Ex 3[17] (J); לחם עני Dt 16[3]. **2.** *poverty,* בְּעָנְיִי הכינותי זהב 1 Ch 22[14].

8589 † [תַּעֲנִית] **n.f. humiliation,** by fasting (cf. √**Pi. Hithp.**; NH ת׳ = *fasting*), sf. תַּעֲנִיתִי Ez 9[5].

6030 † IV. עָנָה **vb. sing** (Ar. غَنَّى *sing, chant,* غِنَآء *singing, chanting,* etc.; Syr. ܥܢܳܐ *sing responsively,* ܥܽܘܢܺܝܬܳܐ *hymn, refrain;* poss. As. *enû, resound* (?); Egypt. *anni* is loan-word acc. to Bondi[80]);—**Qal** *Pf.* 3 ms. וְעָנוּ consec. Je 51[14]; *Impf.* 3 ms. יַעֲנֶה Je 25[30]; 3 fs. וַתַּעַן Ex 15[21]; 3 fpl. וַתַּעֲנֶינָה 1 S 18[7], etc.; *Imv.* עֱנוּ Nu 21[17] ψ 147[7]; *Inf. cstr.* עֲנוֹת Ex 32[18.18];—*sing, utter tunefully,* Ex 15[21] (E) *and Miriam sang to* (ל) *them;* of uttering shout (הֵידָד), as in vintage Je 25[30] (י׳ subj.; + אֶל־ pers.), in attack 51[14] (+ עַל־ pers.); קול עֲנוֹת גְּבוּרָה (חֲלוּשָׁה) Ex 32[18.18] (E); c. ל rei vel pers. laudat. Nu 21[17] (JE; well); ψ 147[7] (י׳; || זַמְּרוּ), Ezr 3[11]; + אָמַר 1 S 18[7] *the women sang, and said;* יַעֲנוּ בִמְּחֹלוֹת לֵאמֹר 21[12] 29[5]; c. acc. rei laudat. ψ 119[172] (cf. || v[171]).—Is 14[22] v. עון. **Pi.** intens.: *Imv.* עַנּוּ־לָהּ Is 27[2] *sing sweetly of it; Inf.* קוֹל עַנּוֹת Ex 32[18] (E) *the sound of distinct singing;* cf. לְעַנּוֹת ψ 88[1].

6034 עֲנָה 12 **n.pr.m.** Horites:—**1.** Gn 36[2] (read הַחֹרִי for הַחִוִּי v. Di) v[14.18.20.25.25.29] = 1 Ch 1[38.41]. **2.** ('nephew' of **1**) Gn 36[24.24] = 1 Ch 1[40].—Ανα, Α(ι)να(ν) (cf. n.pr.m. עַן, Safa, Hal[JAs 7, x. 374]).

6042 ענו Kt v. עֻנִּי. עֲנוֹק v. I. עֲנָק. below, p. 778

עָנֵז (√ of foll.; Kö[ii. 1, 38] cp. Ar. عَنَزَ *turn aside,* whence [fr. movements] عَنْز *goat,* cf. As. *enzu;* Syr. ܥܶܙܳܐ, ostr. ܥܢܙܐ; also ܥܰܢܙܳܐ; ܥܰܢܳܙܳܐ *goat-herd;* Ph. Palm. עז; NH עֵז (rare)).

עֵז 74 **n.f.**[Gn 15, 9] **she-goat**;—abs. ע׳ Gn 15[9]+ 5795
6 t.; pl. עִזִּים 27[9]+65 t.; sf. עִזֶּיךָ 31[38];—†**1.** as property Gn 30[32.33.35] (J), 31[15.38] (E), 1 S 25[2]. **2.** as food: גְּדִיֵי (גְּדִי) עִזִּים *kid(s) of she-goats* Gn 27[9.16] (J) + 7 t., שְׂעִיר עִזִּים 37[31] (J) *a buck of goats, he-goat,* שֵׂה עִזִּים Dt 14[4] *a(n individual) goat;* cf. Lv 7[23] (P; fat forbidden); also חֲלֵב ע׳ Pr 27[27] *goats' milk.* **3.** as sacrificial victim, chiefly P: **a.** in gen. Lv 22[27] (H), Nu 15[11]. †**b.** in בְּרִית Gn 15[9] (JE; cf. v[18]). †**c.** פֶּסַח Ex 12[5] (שֶׂה), בְּנֵי עִזִּים 2 Ch 35[7]. †**d.** עוֹלָה Lv 22[19] (H), 1[10] Nu 28[30] (שְׂעִיר ע׳). †**e.** זֶבַח שְׁלָמִים Lv 3[12] 17[3] (H; cf. v[5]), אִשֶּׁה Nu 18[17] (בְּכוֹר ע׳). **f.** חַטָּאת, שְׂעִיר ע׳ Ez 43[22] 45[23] Lv 4[23]+3 t. Lv, Nu 7[16]+ 19 t. Nu; שְׂעִירַת עִזִּים *a single she-goat* Lv 4[28] 5[6]; צְפִירֵי עִזִּים 2 Ch 29[21] *he-goats.* **4.** עִזִּים = *goats'* hair, as material 1 S 19[13.16] Ex 25[4] + 6 t. P (35[26] obj. of טָוּוּ!). †**5.** in sim. חֲשִׂפֵי עִזִּים 1 K 20[27] (v. [חָשִׂיף]); כְּעֵדֶר הָע׳ Ct 4[1] 6[5], of flowing, undulating hair. †**6.** צְפִיר הָע׳ Dn 8[5.8] *he-goat* in vision.

† עֻנִּי **n.pr.m.** Levites:—**1.** 1 Ch 15[18.20], Ωνει, 6042
𝔊L Ανανιας. **2.** Ne 12[9] Qr (Kt ענו), Ιανα(ι).

† עֲנָיָה **n.pr.m.** Ne 8[4] 10[23], Ανανια(ς). 6043

עָנִיר v. עָנָו sub III. ענה. עֲנִים v. p. 745.

עַיִן v. II. [ענה]. עֵין גַּנִּים v. עֲנֵם.

† עֲנָמִים **n.pr.gent.** in (or near) Egypt Gn 6047
10[13] = 1 Ch 1[11], Αινειαμιειμ, Αινεμετιειμ, etc.; form dub. and locality unknown, v. conj. in Di.

† עֲנַמֶּלֶךְ **n.pr.div.** of סְפַרְוַיִם (q.v.) 2 K 17[31], 6048
Ανημελεχ (om. 𝔊L); = As. *Anu-malik* acc. to Schr[COT ad loc.], but dub., v. Kit[ad loc.] and reff.; Che[Expos. Times, June, 1898, 429] rds. ענומלך, and ins. also 2 K 19[37] (bef. אלהיו); cf. also Hal cited sub עֲנָת.

I. ענן (√ of foll., perh. orig. *cover,* as Sab. ענן = ظلّ (Heb. צלל), DHM[Epigr. Denkm. 26 f.]; or < Ar. عَنَّ *appear, present oneself,* specif. *intervene as an obstacle* (Lane; cf. Lag[BN 103]), hence عَنَان *clouds, as intervening,* and so *obstructing;* cf. NH עָנָן *cloud* = BH (rare), vb. denom. Pi. עִנֵּן as BH; 𝔗 עֲנָנָא, Syr. ܥܢܳܢܳܐ *clouds*).

I. עָנָן 87 **n.m.**[Ex 19, 16] **cloud-mass, cloud**;— 6051
(הָע׳) abs. Ex 19[9]+; cstr. עֲנַן Ho 6[4]+; sf. עֲנָנְךָ

Nu 14^{14}, עֲנָנוֹ Jb 26^{9} 37^{15}; pl. עֲנָנִים Je 4^{13};—**1.** *cloud-mass:* **a.** esp. of theophanic cloud (58 t.), chiefly at Exodus in JE (less oft. P), usu. עַמּוּד הֶעָ׳ Ex 13$^{21.22}$+ (v. עמּוּד), but also ע׳ alone Ex 34^{5} cf. 14^{20} (J), Nu 10^{34} 11^{25} 14^{14} (all JE); עַב־הֶעָ׳ Ex 19^{9}, ע׳ כָּבֵד v^{16} (E); ע׳ in P Ex 16^{10} 24^{15}+ 23 t.; also Dt 1^{33} 4^{11} 5^{19}, ψ 78^{14} 105^{39}; in temple 1 K 8$^{10.11}$ = 2 Ch 5$^{13.14}$, cf. Ez 1^{4} 10$^{3.4}$; hence in gen. ψ 97^{2}, as symbol of protection Is 4^{5}; as a barrier La 3^{44}; cf. וע׳ אֲבַק רַגְלָיו Na 1^{3}. **b.** of rain-bow cloud Gn 9$^{13.14.14.16}$ (P), Ez 1^{28} (sim.). **c.** עֲנַן־בֹּקֶר Ho 6^{4} 13^{3} (sim. of transitoriness; on phenom. in Pal. v. Chaplin[PEQ. 1883, 19]), cf. Is 44^{22} Jb 7^{9} (both *id.*); sim. of invasion Ez 38$^{9.16}$, pl. Je 4^{13}. **d.** poet. in various connex. Jb 26$^{8.9}$ 38^{9}; c. אוֹר as thunder-cloud 37$^{11.15}$. **e.** symbol. of gloom Ez 30^{18} 32^{7}; יוֹם ע׳ וַעֲרָפֶל Zp 1^{15} Ez 34^{12} Jo 2^{2}, cf. Ez 30^{3} (all of day of י׳). †**2.** ע׳ קְטֹרֶת Lv 16^{13} (P) *cloud of incense*, so Ez 8^{11} (del. ע׳ 𝔊 Co Berthol, not Toy).

6049 †[עָנַן] **vb. denom. Pi.** *Inf. cstr.* sf. c. acc. cogn. בְּעַנְנִי ע׳ עַל־הָאָרֶץ Gn 9^{14} (P) *when I bring clouds*, etc.

6053 † עֲנָנָה **n.f.** cloud (Ges[§ 122t]) Jb 3^{5}.

6049 †II. [עָנַן] **vb. Pō'.** practise soothsaying (prob. denom., but orig. meaning dub.; connex. with I. עָנָן (De[Is 2, 6]) now gen. abandoned; Löw[ZMG xxxi (1877), 539] cp. עַיִן *eye*, so We[Skizzen iii. 148] (but v. infr.); RS[JPhil xiv (1885), 119 f.] cp. Ar. غَنَّة *nasal twang, hum of insects*, whence diviners as *crooning;* Ew Gerber[31] of diviner as interpreting *hum* of insects, *whisper* of leaves, etc.; We[Heid. 2, 204] now cp. عَنَّ *appear*, i.e. *dealers in phenomena*);—*Pf.* 3 ms. consec. וְעוֹנֵן 2 K 21^{6} = 2 Ch 33^{6}; *Impf.* 2 mpl. וְלֹא תְעוֹנֵנוּ Lv 19^{26} (H); *Pt.* as subst. מְעוֹנֵן Dt 18^{10} (forbidden), pl. מְעֹנְנִים v^{14}, מְעוֹ׳ Mi 5^{11}, אֵלוֹן מְעוֹנְנִים Ju 9^{37} (v. I. אֵלוֹן; seat of an oracle, cf. RS[Sem i. 179, 2nd ed. 196]); also (without מְ, cf. Sta[§ 233] Kö[i. 349]) עֹנְנִים Is 2^{6}, sf. עֹנְנֵיכֶם Je 27^{9}; fs. in בְּנֵי עֹנְנָה Is 57^{3} *sons of a soothsaying woman*, fig. of apostates.—Vid. כִּשֵּׁף, II. [נָחַשׁ], [קָסַם].

6052 †II. עָנָן **n.pr.m.** Ne 10^{27}, Ηναμ, Η(ι)ναν (cf. n.pr.m. Sab. ענן SabDenkm[30]; Palm. ענני).

6054 † עֲנָנִי **n.pr.m.** 1 Ch 3^{24}, Μανει, Ανανι(ας).

6055 † עֲנַנְיָה **n.pr. 1. m.** Ne 3^{23}, Ανανια(ς). **2. loc.** Ne 11^{32}, Ανανια, Ανια; perh. mod. *Beit Ḥanîna*, c. 4 miles NNW. from Jerusalem, cf. Buhl[Geogr. 167].

עָנַף (√ of foll.; meaning unknown; NH עָנָף = BH, 𝔗 עַנְפָּא (both rare), Syr. ܥܢܦܐ).

† עָנָף **n.[m.]** branch(es), bough(s);—usu. 6057
sg. coll., abs. ע׳ *branches* of vine Ez 17^{8}, pl. only sf. עֲנָפֶיהָ ψ 80^{11} (both in fig.); *boughs* of tree, cstr. עֲנַף Lv 23^{40}, sf. (as if from *עֶנֶף Kö[ii. 1, 74]) עַנְפְּכֶם Ez 36^{8}; sg. abs. (in fig.) Mal 3^{19}, of cedar Ez 17^{23} 31^{3}.

†[עָנֵף] **adj.** full of branches;—fs. עֲנֵפָה 6058
Ez 19^{10} (of vine, in fig.).

עָנַק (√ of foll., mng. dub.; cf. Ar. عُنُقٌ, *neck*, 𝔗 עוּנְקָא; also עִינְקָא *necklace*, Syr. ܥܢܩܐ; Eth. ዐንቅ: *gem;* vbs. denom. in Ar., Eth., NH).

†I. עֲנָק **n.[m.]** neck, only in **epith. gent.** 6061
בְּנֵי הָעֲנָק *long-necked* (tall) *men*, early giant people about Hebron and in Philistia, Ενακ, Εναχ, Jos 15^{14} (JE) = Ju 1^{20}, without art. Nu 13^{33} (JE), Dt 9^{2}; also יְלִידֵי הָעֲ׳ Nu 13$^{22.28}$ Jos 15^{14} (all JE);
called also עֲנָקִים *long-necks*, Ενακειμ, Jos 14$^{12.15}$ 6062
(JE), 11$^{21.22}$ (D), Dt 2$^{10.11.21}$+ Je 47^{5} (rd. עֲנָקִים for MT עִמְקָם), and perh. 1 Ch 12^{16} (v. עֵמֶק *ad fin.*);
בְּנֵי עֲנָקִים 1^{28} (𝔊 γίγαντες, cf. Nu 13^{33}), 9^{2}; עֲנָק 6061
later (erron.) as eponym. ancestor of Anaḳim Jos 15^{13} = עֲנוֹק 21^{11} (both P).—Vid. esp. Mey[ZAW i (1881), 139] GFM[Ju 1, 10, 20] Che[Ency. Bib. Anak].

†II. עֲנָק **n.m.**[Ct 4, 9] necklace, neck-pendant 6060
(Aramaism acc. to Lag[BN 175]);—abs. ע׳ Ct 4^{9} appar. part of necklace, perh. *neck-pendant;* pl. עֲנָקוֹת Ju 8^{26} (ornament of camels), עֲנָקִים Pr 1^{9} (of youth; in fig.).

†[עָנַק] **vb. denom.** serve as necklace;— 6059
Qal 3 fs. sf. עֲנָקַתְמוֹ ψ 73^{6} pride *is necklace for them.* **Hiph.** *Impf.* and *Inf. abs.* הַעֲנֵיק תַּעֲנִיק לוֹ Dt 15^{14} *thou shalt make a rich necklace for him* fr. thy flock, etc., fig. for *richly load him.*

† עָנֵר **n.pr. 1.** appar. **m.** ally of Abram Gn 6063
14$^{13.24}$, Αυναν; cf. אֶשְׁכּוֹל, מַמְרֵא. **2. loc.** in Manasseh 1 Ch 6^{55} Αμαρ, 𝔊L Ανηρ.

ענשׁ (√ of foll.; mng. dub.; cf. (as denom.) Ph. Niph. נענ[ש] *be fined* CIS[i. 165, 20], Palm. ענושותא *treasurership;* v. also NH עוֹנֶשׁ *punishment*, עָנַשׁ *punish* (in general)).

† עֹנֶשׁ **n.[m.]** indemnity, fine;—וַיִּתֶּן־ע׳ 6066
עַל־הָאָרֶץ 2 K 23^{33}; of individual נֹשֵׂא ע׳ Pr 19^{19}.

†[עָנַשׁ] **vb. denom.** (Gerber[61 f.]) fine, 6064
mulct;—**Qal** *Pf.* consec. וְעָנְשׁוּ Dt 22^{19} (2 acc.); *Impf.* וַיַּעֲנֹשׁ 2 Ch 36^{3} (2 acc.; ∥ 2 K 23^{33} supr.); *Inf. cstr.* עֲנוֹשׁ Pr 17^{26} (לְ pers.); = *punish* (in gen.) עֲנָשׁ־ 21^{11}; *Pt. pass.* עֲנוּשִׁים Am 2^{8} *those fined,*

mulcted. **Niph.** *Impf.* + **Qal** *Inf. abs.* עָנוֹשׁ יֵעָנֵשׁ Ex 21²² (E) *he shall be strictly fined;* more gen. *Pf.* נֶעֶנָשׁוּ Pr 22³ *be mulcted, punished* = 27¹².

6067 †עֲנָת **n.pr.m.** father of Shamgar Ju 3³¹ 5⁶,
1042-43 Αναθ (Δειναχ, Κεναθ);—v. also בֵּית עֲנוֹת, בֵּ׳ עֲנָת (cf. Tel Am. n.pr. *Anati*, Wkl[125, 43]; As. n.pr. deae *Anatu* (Jastr[Rel. Bab. 158]; hence) in Syria and Ph.—also Egypt—ענת (Muss-Arnolt[JBL xi (1892), 80] Pietschmann[Phön. 149 f.] Hal[JAs. 7, x (1877), 374; xiii (1879), 208])).

6068 †עֲנָתוֹת and (1 K 2²⁶) עֲנָתֹת **n.pr.** Αναθωθ; **1. loc.** (cf. goddess *Anat*, ref. sub foregoing);—Is 10³⁰ 1 K 2²⁶ Je 1¹ 11^{21.23} 32^{7.8.9} Jos 21¹⁸ (P), 1 Ch 6⁴⁵ Ezr 2²³ = Ne 7²⁷, Ne 11³²; mod. *ʿAnâtâ*, c. 3 miles NNE. from Jerusalem, cf. Buhl[Geogr. 175] GASm[Geogr. 315]. **2. m. a.** 1 Ch 7⁸. **b.** Ne 10²⁰.

6069 †עַנְּתֹתִי **adj. gent.** of foreg.;—הָע׳ Je 29²⁷ 1 Ch 12³ 2 S 23²⁷ = הָעֲנְּתוֹתִי 1 Ch 11²⁸ 27¹².

6070 †עַנְתֹתִיָּה **n. pr. m.** Benjamite 1 Ch 8²⁴, Ανωθαιθ, Αναθωθ(ι)α.

6072 †[עָסַס] **vb. press, crush,** by treading, **tread down** (NH עֲסִיסִית *crushed* wheat; cf. Ar. عَسَّ *go the rounds,* [*tramp*], *prowl;* Syr. ܥܣ *explore,* v. Brockelmann);—**Qal** *Pf.* 2 mpl. fig. וְעַסּוֹתֶם רְשָׁעִים Mal 3²¹ (consec.).

6071 †עָסִיס **n.m.**[Jo 1, 5] **sweet wine** (prop. *pressed out* juice);—abs. ע׳ Am 9¹³ (v. Dr and reff.), Jo 1⁵ 4¹⁸; in sim. Is 49²⁶; cstr. עֲסִיס רִמֹּנִי Ct 8².

6073 †עפאים Kt, עֳפָיִם Qr **n.[m.]pl. foliage** (cf. Ges[§ 93 z]; Aram. loan-word, ℑ עִפְיָא *foliage,* Syr. ܥܘܦܝܐ *flower, branch*);—ψ 104¹².

6075 †I. עָפַל **vb. swell** (?; so Thes; inferred fr. deriv.; Ar. عَفَلٌ is a *tumour* in the vulva or anus, عَفِلَ appar. denom. (cf. II. עֹפֶל) v. As. *uplu,* prob. *tumour* (Dl[HWB 7] *ublu,* but v. Jen[Th Lz 1895, 250]));—**Pu.** *Pf.* 3 fs. עֻפְּלָה Hb 2⁴ acc. to MT (subj. נַפְשׁוֹ, cf. GASm); but subst. needed, Brd[SK 1889, 121] הַמְעֻלָּף, We Now הָעַוָּל, cf. Gu[Kau].—**Hiph.** v. II. עפל. below

6076-77 †I. עֹפֶל **n.[m.] mound, hill,** only as acropolis;—ע׳ abs. 2 K 5²⁴+, cstr. Mi 4⁸;—fortified mound or hill within city, of Jerus. (cf. Rob[BR i. 267] Gu[ZPV v (1882), 326]) Mi 4⁸ Is 32¹⁴; S. end of eastern hill Ne 3²⁶ 11²¹ 2 Ch 33¹⁴ חוֹמַת הָע׳ Ne 3²⁷ 2 Ch 27³ (cf. חמת העפל in קרחה MI^{21.22}); of Samaria 2 K 5²⁴.

6076 †II. [עֹפֶל] **n.m.**[1 S 6, 4] **tumour**;—only pl. Kt (בָּ)עֳפָלִים Dt 28²⁷ 1 S 5^{6.9.12}; cstr. עָפְלֵי 6⁴; sf. עָפְלֵיכֶם v⁵; Qr in all טְחֹרִים (ב)טְחֹרִים, טְחֹרֵי, טְחֹרֵיכֶם, v. [טְחוֹר]. p. 373 2890

†II. [עָפַל] **vb.** perhaps **be heedless** (Ar. 6075
عَفَلَ *be heedless, neglectful, inadvertent*);—**Hiph.** *shew heedlessness, Impf.* 3 mpl. וַיַּעְפִּלוּ לַעֲלוֹת Nu 14⁴⁴ (JE) *they shewed heedlessness in going up* (went up heedlessly), so de Dieu, cited (and allowed) by Di Buhl[Lex]; > Thes al. *shewed presumption* (I. עפל, this sense dub.).

†עָפְנִי **n.pr.loc.** in Benj., הָע׳ Jos 18²⁴, 6078
𝔊L Αφνη.

עפעף v. עוף. p. 733 6079

I. עפר (√ of foll.; mng. dub.; cf. Ar. عَفَرٌ *dust,* As. *epru, epiru,* Tel Am. *ḫaparu* and *aparu* (Canaan. glosses); ℑ עַפְרָא, Syr. ܥܦܪܐ; NH עָפָר = BH).

†עָפָר **n.m.**[Lv 14, 42] **dry earth, dust**;—abs. ע׳ 6083
Gn 2⁷+, cstr. עֲפַר Gn 13¹⁶+; sf. עֲפָרֵךְ Ez 26¹², עֲפָרוֹ Dt 9²¹, etc.; pl. cstr. עַפְרֹת Jb 28⁶ Pr 8²⁶;—**1.** lit.: **a.** *dry, loose earth,* thrown (in malice) 2 S 16¹³ (‖אֲבָנִים); וַיַּעֲלוּ ע׳ עַל־רֹאשׁ Jos 7⁶ (JE; sign of grief), so Ez 27³⁰ La 2¹⁰, and (c. זָרַק) Jb 2¹²; loose earth (on surface of ground) 1 K 18³⁸ Am 2⁷ Mi 1¹⁰ Is 34^{7.9} Lv 17¹³ (H) Ez 24⁷ (in fig.), Nu 5¹⁷ Jb 14¹⁹ 38³⁸ 39¹⁴, Gn 26¹⁵ (R), made into siege works Hb 1¹⁰; of sand-storm Dt 28²⁴ (+ אָבָק); as serpent's food, token of punishment and humiliation, Gn 3¹⁴ (J) Is 65²⁵ (cf. Mi 7¹⁷ **2 e** infr.); זֹחֲלֵי ע׳ Dt 32²⁴ (poem; cf. **2 e**). **b.** specif. as material of human body Gn 2⁷ 3¹⁹ (J), Ec 3²⁰, cf. Jb 4¹⁹ 8¹⁹ ψ 103¹⁴, to which it returns (שׁוּב אֶל־) Gn 3¹⁹ Jb 10⁹ ψ 104²⁹ Ec 3²⁰; so (c. עַל) Jb 34¹⁵ Ec 12⁷. **c.** = surface of ground Ex 8^{12.13.13} (P; ע׳ הָאָרֶץ), Jb 19²⁵ Is 25¹² 26⁵ (both ‖ אֶרֶץ), surface of (whole) earth Jb 41²⁵, מְחִלּוֹת ע׳ Is 2¹⁹ (for hiding), so ע׳ alone v¹⁰, cf. חֹרֵי ע׳ Jb 30⁶; = *soil,* Jb 5⁶ 14⁸. **d.** *powder* of anything pulverized Dt 9^{21.21} (cf. דַּק ‖ Ex 32²⁰), 2 K 23^{6.6.12.15}, so in sim. 2 S 22⁴³ = ψ 18⁴³, hence = ashes v⁴ Nu 19¹⁷. **e.** *debris,* of ruined city 1 K 20¹⁰ Ez 26^{4.12} Ne 3³⁴ 4⁴ ψ 102¹⁵. The foll. are late: **f.** earth of the grave: לְע׳ אֶשְׁכָּב Jb 7²¹, so (c. עַל) 20¹¹ 21²⁶, cf. 17¹⁶; יוֹרְדֵי ע׳ ψ 22³⁰, שֹׁכְנֵי ע׳ Is 26¹⁹, יְשֵׁנֵי אַדְמַת־ע׳ Dn 12²; עֲפַר־מָוֶת ψ 22¹⁶; ע׳ in fig. ψ 30¹⁰. **g.** *mortar* (i. e. dried mud) for plastering houses Lv 14^{41.42.45} (P). **h.** (iron-) *ore* Jb 28²; עַפְרֹת זָהָב v⁶ *gold-dust* (but v. סַפִּיר). **i.** material of earth Is 40¹², cf. רֹאשׁ עַפְרוֹת תֵּבֵל Pr 8²⁶ *the first of the earth-*

particles of the world. **2.** fig.: **a.** of abundance Gn 13[16.16] 28[14] (all J) 2 Ch 1[9] Jb 27[16] ψ 78[27] (‖ חוֹל יַמִּים), cf. עֲפַר יַעֲקֹב Nu 23[10] (JE); with added idea of commonness, worthlessness Zp 1[17] Zc 9[3]. **b.** of worthlessness (alone) Jb 22[24]. **c.** sim. of the scattered, dispersed 2 K 13[7]; כֶּעָ׳ Is 41[2] (so van d. H. Ginsb; Baer כֶּעָ׳; on meaning v. Du Che, rdg. יִתֵּן תְּשִׁימֵם for יִתֵּן). **d.** of self-abasement Gn 18[27] (+ אֵפֶר), וְנִחַמְתִּי עַל־ע׳ וָאֵפֶר Jb 42[6], יִתֵּן בֶּעָ׳ פִּיהוּ La 3[29]. **e.** of humiliation (sitting or lying in dust) Is 47[1] cf. 29[4.4], Jb 16[15] 40[13] ψ 7[6] 44[26] 119[25], sim. Jb 30[19]; licking dust ψ 72[9] Is 49[23] Mi 7[17], cf. TelAm. *tikalu ipra* (of enemies, v. Wkl[Altor. Forsch. iii. 291]; also of serpent **1 a** supr.); of י׳ raising from the dust 1 S 2[8] = ψ 113[7], 1 K 16[2]; of lifting oneself Is 52[2].

6080 † [עָפַר] **vb. denom. Pi.** וְעִפַּר בֶּעָפָר 2 S 16[13] *and kept dusting* (him) *with dust* (throwing [lumps of] dry earth at him).

II. עפר (√ of foll.; cf. Ar. غُفْرٌ *young of mountain-goat*, NH עוֹפֶר *young* of animals).

6082 † עֹפֶר **n.m.**[Ct 4, 5] **young hart, stag**;—cstr. עֹ׳ הָאַיָּלִים (‖ צְבִי) Ct 2[9.17] 8[14]; pl. abs. עֳפָרִים תְּאוֹמֵי צְבִיָּה 4[5] 7[4] (all in sim.).

6081 † עֵפֶר **n.pr.m.** Αφερ, etc.;—**1.** 'son' of Midian Gn 25[4] = 1 Ch 1[33] (𝔊L Γοφερ). **2.** in Judah 1 Ch 4[17] (A Γαφερ). **3.** in Manasseh 5[24].

1036 עַפְרָה v. בֵּית לְעַ׳ p. 112 supr.

6084 † עָפְרָה **n.pr. 1. loc.: a.** in Benj. Jos 18[23] (P), Αφαρ, etc.; 1 S 13[7] Γοφερα; prob. = עֶפְרוֹן **2** and אֶפְרַיִם **6**; perh. mod. *eṭ-Ṭayyibeh*, c. 4 miles NE. from Bethel, cf. GASm[Geogr. 252] Buhl[Geogr. 177]. **b.** in Manasseh, Εφραθα: Ju 6[11] 8[27]; cstr. עָפְרַת אֲבִי הָעֶזְרִי 6[24], but עָפְרָה וגו׳ 8[32]; c. ה loc. עָפְרָתָה Ju 9[5]. **2. m.** in Judah 1 Ch 4[14], Γοφερα, 𝔊L Εφραθ.

6085 † עֶפְרוֹן **n.pr.** Εφρων:—**1. m.** Hittite, Abr.'s time, acc. to Gn 23[8.10.10.13.16.17] 49[29], עֶפְרֹן 23[6] 25[9] 49[30] 50[13] (all P). **2. loc.** 2 Ch 13[19] Kt (עֶפְרַיִן Qr), cf. עָפְרָה **1 a.** **3. mont.** הַר־ע׳, on N. border of Judah Jos 15[9].

6085 עֶפְרַיִן 2 Ch 13[19] Qr v. עֶפְרוֹן **2.** above

5777 † עֹפֶרֶת **n.m.**[Je 6, 29 (si vera l. Qr)] **lead** (√ dub.; prob. foreign word; cf. 𝔗 אֲבָרָא *lead*, Syr. ܐܒܪܐ, and (as Aram. loan-word) Ar. أَبَارٌ [v. Dozy], Frä [152]; perh. also As. *abaru*, a metal, *magnesite* acc. to Hilpr[Assyriaca i (1894), 80 ff.] Hpt[ib. 83]);—כִּכַּר ע׳ Zc 5[7] *a round weight* (disc) *of lead*, אֶבֶן־הָעֹ׳ v[5]; with other metals (v. בְּדִיל): עֹ׳ Ez 22[18.20] 27[12], הָעֹפָרֶת Nu 31[22] (P); עֹפָ׳ also Jb 19[24] (with which chiselled letters are filled acc. to Di and most; Bu rds. בְּעֹ׳ *in* [a tablet of] *lead*); also (as flux) Je 6[29] (rdg. Qr; so Gf Co; emend. Gie); עֹ׳ in sim. Ex 15[10] (song).

עֵפָתָה v. עֵיפָה sub II. עוּף. עֵץ v. II. עצה. 5890, 6086
p. 734, 781

† I. [עָצַב] **vb. hurt, pain, grieve** (NH 6087
Nithp. and in deriv.; 𝔗 עֲצַב *be in pain* (rare); Eth. ዐጸበ: *be hard, difficult*; Lag[BN 50, cf. 201] cp. Ar. غَضِبَ *be angry*, but dub.);—**Qal** *Pf.* 3 ms. sf. עֲצָבוֹ 1 K 1[6] his father *had* not *pained him* (𝔊 Klo Gr עֲצָרוֹ, but v. Benz); ins. עָצַב (with other words) 2 S 13[21] 𝔊 Ew Th We Kit Bu HPS; *Inf. cstr.* sf. לְבִלְתִּי עָצְבִּי 1 Ch 4[10] *that* it (רָעָה) *may not pain me; Pt. pass.* cstr. עֲצוּבַת רוּחַ Is 54[6] *hurt in spirit* (of Zion under fig. of deserted wife). **Niph.** *Pf.* 3 ms. נֶעְצַב 1 S 20[34] *be pained* for (אֶל pers.; del. 𝔊 HPS); נֶעֱצַב 2 S 19[3] the king *is in pain* (is grieving) for (עַל pers.); *Impf.* 3 ms. יֵעָצֵב 1 S 20[3] lest *he be pained;* + בָּהֶם instr. Ec 10[9] *shall be hurt* by them (i. e. אֲבָנִים; only here of physical pain); 2 mpl. תֵּעָצְבוּ Gn 45[5] *be* not *grieved* (+ יִחַר; sq. כִּי *that* ye sold me), cf. Ne 8[10.11] (abs.) *do not grieve.* **Pi.** *Pf.* 3 pl. עִצְּבוּ c. acc. Is 63[10] *they vexed* his holy spirit (+ מָרוּ); *Impf.* 3 mpl. דְּבָרַי יְעַצֵּבוּ ψ 56[6] *my affairs they vex* (Thes al.), but improb., < Che בִּדְבַר יְעַ׳ *with speech they vex* (me). **Hiph.** *Impf.* 3 mpl. sf. יַעֲצִיבוּהוּ ψ 78[40] *they used to cause him* [י׳] *pain.* **Hithp.** *Impf.* 3 ms. וַיִּתְעַצֵּב אֶל־לִבּוֹ Gn 6[6] *and he was vexed to his heart* (of י׳; ‖ וַיִּנָּחֶם); 3 mpl. וַיִּתְעַצְּבוּ Gn 34[7] (+ וַיִּחַר, sq. clause with כִּי).

† I. עֶצֶב **n.[m.] pain, hurt, toil**;—**1.** ע׳ 6089
pain Gn 3[16] (of travail), Pr 10[22]. **2.** *hurt* (of mind), דְּבַר־ע׳ Pr 15[1] *a word that hurts* (opp. מַעֲנֶה־רַךְ). **3.** *toil* Pr 14[23]; pl. לֶחֶם הָעֲצָבִים ψ 127[2] *bread of* (gained by) *toils;* sf. עֲצָבֶיךָ Pr 5[10].

† I. עֹצֶב **n.[m.] pain**;—ע׳ 1 Ch 4[9] (of 6090
travail); דֶּרֶךְ־ע׳ ψ 139[24] *hurtful way* (of any wicked habit; > 𝔗 Thes *way of idolatry;* II. עֹצֶב); sf. עָצְבְּךָ Is 14[3] of the *pain* of exile.

† [עָצֵב, > עַצָּב] **n.[m.] toiler** (prop. *suf-* 6092
ferer; less well עֶצֶב *toil* Thes Kö[ii. 1, 29] al.);—pl. sf. עַצְּבֵיכֶם תִּנְגֹּשׂוּ Is 58[3] (d. f. dirim. Ges[§ 20 h]) *your toilers ye drive on;* Klo Che עֲבֹט בְּיֶדְכֶם (cf. Vrss in part) *money lent on pledge* ye exact.

6094 †[עַצֶּ֫בֶת] **n.f.** hurt, injury, pain;—עַצָּ֑בֶת Pr 10^{10} he that winketh with the eye causeth *hurt* (stirs up strife, etc.); cstr. עַצְּבַת־לֵב *pain of heart* 15^{13} (opp. לֵב שָׂמֵחַ); pl. sf. עַצְּבֹתָי Jb 9^{28} *my pains*, so rd. perh. also 7^{15} (for MT עַצְמוֹתָי); עַצְּבוֹתָם ψ 16^{4} (due to idolatry; > *idols* 𝔗 𝔙 We al.); מְחַבֵּשׁ לְעַ׳ 147^{3} *binding up their hurts*.

6093 †עִצָּבוֹן **n.[m.]** pain, toil;—עִ׳ abs. Gn 3^{17} *toil;* cstr. עִצְּבוֹן יָדֵינוּ 5^{29} (both of agriculture); sf. עִצְּבוֹנֵךְ 3^{16} (of travail; all J).

4620 †מַעֲצֵבָה **n.f.** place of pain (> simply *pain*);—לְמַ׳ תִּשְׁכָּבוּן Is 50^{11} *in* (constr. praegn.) *a place of pain shall ye lie down*.

6087 † II. [עָצַב] **vb. Pi.** shape, fashion (NH Pi. *stretch* child *into shape;* Buhl^{Lex} cp. عَصَبَ *cut, cut off* [whence idea of *carving, fashioning*]);—**Pi.** *Pf.* יָדֶיךָ עִצְּבוּנִי וַיַּעֲשׂוּנִי Jb 10^{8} *thy hands shaped me*, etc. **Hiph.** *Inf. cstr.* לְהַעֲצִבָה Je 44^{19}, but rd. בָהּ-, *to fashion her*, i.e. make images of her (poss. denom. from עָצָב).

6089 † II. עֶ֫צֶב **n.m.** vessel (as *fashioned*);—עֶ׳ נִבְזֶה וגו׳ Je 22^{28} *a vessel despised*, etc. (fig. of Coniah = Jehoiachin).

6090 † II. [עֹ֫צֶב] **n.m.** idol;—sf. עָצְבִּי Is 48^{5}.

6091 †[עָצָב] **n.[m.]** idol;—always pl. עֲצַבִּים (Ges$^{§ 93ee}$): Ho 4^{17} 8^{6} (כַּסְפָּם וּזְהָבָם), 13^{2} (מַסֵּכָה ‖ כַּסְפָּם), 14^{9} Zc 13^{2} 2 Ch 24^{18} (+ אֲשֵׁרִים); cstr. עֲצַבֵּי ψ 106^{38} 135^{15} (כֶּסֶף וְזָהָב); sf. עֲצַבֶּיהָ Is 10^{11} (‖ אֱלִילֶיהָ), Je 50^{2} (‖ גִּלּוּלֶיהָ), Mi 1^{7}; עֲצַבֵּיהֶם 1 S 31^{9} = 1 Ch 10^{9}, 2 S 5^{21} (but read אֱלֹהֵיהֶם as ‖ 1 Ch 14^{12}, so 𝔊 We Dr al.), Is 46^{1} ψ 106^{36} 115^{4} (כֶּסֶף וְזָהָב).

עצד (√ of foll.; cf. Ar. عَضَدَ *lop trees with a* مِعْضَد, a kind of *reaping-hook;* Eth. ዐፀደ:, ዐፀደ: *reap*, ማዕፀድ:, ማዕፀድ: *sickle;* NH מַעֲצָד *axe* (smaller than כַּשִּׁיל Levy$^{NHWB\ ii.\ 423}$).

4621 †מַעֲצָד **n.[m.]** axe;—Je 10^{3}; in Is 44^{12} prob. del. (so Du Che^{Hpt} Skinner).

6095 † I. [עָצָה] **vb.** shut (Ar. (و et ى) غَضَا IV. *shut* eyes; Eth. ዐፀወ: *shut* door);—**Qal** *Pt. act.* עֹצֶה עֵינָיו Pr 16^{30} *he that shuts his eyes* (SS cp. עצם [Is 29^{10}], which Gr reads).

II. **עצה** (√ of foll.; meaning dub.; cf. Sab. עצם *wood* DHM$^{ZMG\ xxxvii\ (1883),\ 341,\ 412}$, Ar. غِضَةٌ, orig. عِضَهَةٌ nom. unit. of عِضَاهٌ *large, thorny trees* (v. Lane; also Nö$^{GGA\ 1862,\ 544;\ ZMG\ xxxii\ (1878),\ 406}$ Lag $^{BN\ 158\ f.}$); Eth. ዕፅ: *tree, wood;* As. *iṣ(ṣ)u;* Ph. עץ *wood;* NH = BH; Aram. אָע (init. א by dissim.); Ba$^{NB\ §\ 2,\ c.1}$ thinks originally bilit.).

עֵץ$_{329}$ **n.m.** $^{Gn\ 2,\ 9}$ tree, trees, wood;—עֵ׳ abs. 6086
Gn 3^{3} +, cstr. 3^{24} +, עֶץ־ 2^{16} +; sf. עֵצְךָ Dt 28^{42}, etc.; pl. עֵצִים Ju 9^{8} +, cstr. עֲצֵי Is 7^{2} +, sf. עֵצֶיךָ Dt 29^{10}, עֵצֵינוּ La 5^{4}, etc.;—**1.** (c. 150 t.) **a.** a standing *tree* Gn 18$^{4.8}$ (J) +, Ex 15^{25} (J; of shrub?), Je 17^{18} = ψ 1^{3} (sim.); to be felled Dt 19^{5} 2 K 6^{6}; הָעֵצִים (appar. incl. vine and bramble) in allegory Ju 9^{8} + 6 t. Ju 9; עֵץ הַחַיִּים † Gn 2^{9} 3$^{22.24}$ (J), cf. עֵ׳ חַיִּים, fig. of source of (life and) happiness † Pr 3^{18} 11^{30} 13^{12} 15^{4}; עֵ׳ הַדַּעַת טוֹב וָרָע Gn 2$^{9.16}$ (J); עֲצֵי (ה)יַּעַר Is 7^{2} (sim.), 44^{14} Ez 15^{2} +; עֲצֵי הַשָּׂדֶה Is 55^{12} Ez 17^{24} (fig.), +; עֲצֵי לְבָנוֹן 2 Ch 2^{7}; עֲצֵי־מַיִם † Ez 31^{14}; עֲצֵי י׳ † ψ 104^{16}; עֲצֵי עֵדֶן † Ez 31$^{9.16.18.18}$; עֲצֵי לְבוֹנָה Ct 4^{14}; of vine עֵץ הַגֶּפֶן † Ez 15$^{2.6}$; תַּחַת כָּל־עֵץ רַעֲנָן place of illicit worship † Dt 12^{2} Je 2^{20} 3$^{6.13}$ 1 K 14^{23} 2 K 16^{4} 17^{10} Ez 6^{13} Is 57^{5} 2 Ch 28^{4}, cf. עַל־עֵץ רַעֲנָן Je 17^{2}; כָּל־עֵץ עָבֹת Ez 20^{28}. **b.** coll. *trees*, עֵץ־הַגָּן Gn 2^{16} 3$^{1.2.8}$ (all J); usu. later, עֵ׳ 1$^{12.29.29}$ (P), +; עֵץ פְּרִי *fruit*-bearing *trees* Gn 1^{11} (P), ψ 148^{9}, cf. Ec 2^{5}, פְּרִי עֵץ Ex 10^{15} (J), Ez 36^{30} Lv 23^{40} (H), cf. Jo 2^{22}; עֵץ־מַאֲכָל Dt 20^{20} Lv 19^{23} (H), Ez 47^{12} Ne 9^{25}; עֵץ הַזַּיִת Hg 2^{19} *olive trees*, עֵץ שֶׁמֶן Ne 8^{15}, עֵץ־שָׁמֶן Is 41^{19}; סִבְכֵי־עֵץ ψ 74^{5} *thicket of trees;* עֵץ הַשָּׂדֶה Ex 9^{25} (J), +; עֵץ הַיַּעַר † Ez 15^{6}, cf. Is 10^{19} 44^{23}; כִּימֵי הָעֵץ Is 65^{22} (sim. of great age). **c.** pl. of *trees* felled for building, 1 K 5$^{20.32}$ (+ אֲבָנִים); עֲצֵי אֲרָזִים 2 S 5^{11} = 1 Ch 14^{1} + 7 t.; עֲצֵי בְרוֹשִׁים 1 K 5$^{22.24}$ 9^{11}; עֲצֵי אַלְמֻגִּים (אַלְגּ׳), v. אַלְגּ׳ p. 38 supr. **2.** (c. 175 t.; c. 120 t. pl., to denote *pieces* [or articles] *of wood*) **a.** *wood*, as material; for building, 2 K 12^{13} (+ אַבְנֵי מַחְצֵב), 22^{6} = 2 Ch 34^{11} (both + *id.*), Ne 2^{8} +; עֲצֵי שֶׁמֶן 1 K 6$^{23.31.33}$ cf. v^{32}; עֲצֵי־גֹפֶר Gn 6^{14} (Noah's ark), עֲצֵי שִׁטִּים Ex 25$^{5.10}$ + 20 t. Ex (of tabern. and its furniture; all P) Dt 10^{3}; מִגְדַּל־עֵץ Ne 8^{4}; מוֹטֹת עֵץ Je 28^{13} (in fig.; opp. מֹ׳ בַרְזֶל); כְּלִי־עֵץ *article of wood* Lv 11^{32} 15^{12} Nu 31^{20}, cf. 35^{18} (all P). Hence **b.** עֵצִים = *articles of wood* Ex 7^{19} (P; ‖ אֲבָנִים), 1 Ch 29^{2}; so עֲצֵי בְרוֹשִׁים 2 S 6^{5} (but v. בְּרוֹשׁ *ad fin.*); specif. הָעֵץ = helve of axe Dt 19^{5}; עֵץ חֲנִית(וֹ) 1 S 17^{7} Qr (Kt חֵץ) = 1 Ch 20^{5}, 2 S 21^{19} 23^{7}; עֲצֵי הָעֲגָלָה 1 S 6^{14} (i.e. wood of which cart was made), עֲצֵי הָאֲשֵׁרָה Ju 6^{26}; esp. *timbers* of a house Zc 5^{4} Hb 2^{11} Lv 14^{45}, of a city 1 K 15^{22} = 2 Ch 16^{5}, Ez 26^{12}; עֵץ of *pole* on which bodies of slain (criminals and others) were exposed (perhaps orig. *tree*) Gn 40^{19} (E), Jos 8$^{29.29}$ 10$^{26.26.27}$ (all JE),

Dt 21$^{22.23}$; late (in Pers.) used for executing criminals (? by hanging = *gallows*), תָּלָה עַל־עֵץ Est 2^{23} + 8 t. Est. †**c.** of idols, עֵץ וָאֶבֶן Dt 4^{28} 28$^{36.64}$ 29^{16} 2 K 19^{18} = Is 37^{19}, Ez 20^{32}, cf. Je 2^{27} 3^{9} Hb 2^{19}; so עֵץ alone Ho 4^{12} Is 40^{20}, cf. 44^{19} 45^{20}; אֲשֵׁרָה כָּל־עֵץ Dt 16^{21}. **d.** (fire-)*wood* Jos 9$^{23.27}$ (J), v^{21} (P), Dt 19^{5} Is 30^{33} +, rd. עֵצִים also Ez 24^{5} (for MT עצמים) Bö Ew Sm Co Berthol Toy; esp. for sacrifices 1 K 18$^{23.23}$ +, Gn 22$^{7.9.9}$ Lv 1^{7} + 6 t. Lv (all P), 2 S 24^{22} ‖ 1 Ch 21^{23}, +; עֲצֵי עוֹלָה Gn 22$^{3.6}$ (P). **e.** עֵץ (הָ)אֶרֶז *cedar-wood*, used in purifications Lv 14$^{4.6.49.51.52}$ Nu 19^{6} (all P). **f.** פִּשְׁתֵּי הָעֵץ Jos 2^{6} *woody-flax*, i.e. flax on the stalk.—Je 10^{8} Gie prop. הֶבֶל מֹעֲצֹתָו for MT הֲבָלִים עֵץ הוּא.—מֹאֶסֶת כָּל־עֵץ Ez 21^{15} is dub., Sm prop. מָאַסְתְּ כָּל־עֵץ, Co מֹאֲסֵי כָּל־עֹז, Berthol וּמְאַסֵּף כָּל־עֵז; Siegf^{Kau} Toy leave untranslated.

6097 †II. עֵצָה **n.f. coll. trees** Je 6^{6}, but rd. עֵצָהּ (עֵץ c. sf. 3 fs.), so Orient. Codd. 𝔊 𝔖 𝔙 𝔗 Hi Gf Gie.—I. עֵצָה v. sub יָעַץ.

III. עצה (√ of foll.; meaning dub.; cf. As. *eṣên-ṣêri*, *eṣên of the back*, prob. *spine*; Ar. عَصًا *os cruris*, Lane^{2068c} *bone of the shank*, عُصْعُص *os caudae coccygisve*).

6096 †עָצֶה **n.[m.]** either **spine** or **os sacrum**, bone close to fat-tail, הֶעָ׳ Lv 3^{9}.

IV. עצה (√ of foll.; Lag$^{BN 157}$ cp. غَضْيَاءُ *a land abounding with the trees called* غَضًا).

6100 †עֶצְיוֹן גֶּבֶר **n.pr.loc.** usu. Γασιων [Γεσ.] Γαβερ, near Elath at head of Gulf of Aḳaba 1 K 9^{26} = 2 Ch 8^{17}, עֶ׳ גָּ֑בֶר 1 K 22^{49} = 2 Ch 20^{36}; עֶצְיֹן גָּבֶר Dt 2^{8} Nu 33$^{35.36}$ (P).

6101 †[עָצַל] **vb. Niph. be sluggish** (NH in der. species, and deriv.; cf. Ar. عَظِلَ III. *stick fast in coitu*, Lane^{2086}; Syr. ܥܛܠ *be stupid*);—*Impf.* 2 mpl. אַל־תֵּעָצְלוּ לָלֶכֶת Ju 18^{9} *be not sluggish in going*.

6102 עָצֵל$_{14}$ **adj. sluggish, lazy**;—alw. עָ׳ abs.;—אִישׁ־עָ׳ Pr 24^{30}; elsewhere subst. *sluggard* Pr 6$^{6.9}$ + 10 t. Pr + הֶעָ׳ 10^{26}.

6103 †עַצְלָה **n.f. sluggishness**;—עָ׳ Pr 19^{15}; du. intens. עֲצַלְתַּיִם Ec 10^{18} *double* (i.e. great) *sluggishness* (so Thes De al.; rd. then perhaps עַצְלְתַיִם; > fr. עָצֵל *a sluggish pair*, i.e. hands Ew al.), but improb.; ‖ שִׁפְלוּת יָדַיִם, whence Bi conj. עַצְלוּת, Siegf עַצְלַת יָדַיִם.

†עַצְלוּת **n.f. id.**;—לֶחֶם עַ׳ Pr 31^{27}. 6104

†I. [עָצַם, cf. Lag$^{BN 31}$], עָצַם **vb. be vast, mighty, numerous** (NH Nithp. *contend strenuously*, and in deriv.; Ph. in עצמת *mighty deeds*, עצמם *bones*; Ar. عَظُمَ *be great* in bone, or anything, عَظْمٌ *bones*; Eth. ዐፀም: *id.*; Aram. עִטְמָא, ܥܛܡܐ *thigh*);—**Qal** *Pf.* 3 ms. וְעָצַם consec. Dn 8^{24} 11^{23}; 2 ms. עָצַמְתָּ Gn 26^{16}; 3 pl. עָצְמוּ Is 31^{1} +, עָצֵמוּ ψ 38^{20}; *Impf.* 3 mpl. וַיַּעַצְמוּ Ex 1$^{7.20}$; *Inf. cstr.* עָצְמַת Is 47^{9}; sf. עָצְמוֹ Dn 8^{8};—**1.** *be mighty*, Gn 26^{16} (J; c. מִן comp.), Dn 8$^{8.24}$ 11^{23}. **2.** *be numerous*, ‖ רַבּוּ etc., Is 31^{1}, בְּעָצְמַת חֲבָרַיִךְ מְאֹד 47^{9}, Je 5^{6} 30$^{14.15}$ Ex 1^{7} (P), v^{20} (J), ψ 38^{20} 69^{5}; c. מִן comp. Je 15^{8} ψ 40$^{6.13}$; alone 139^{17}. **Hiph.** *make strong*, *Impf.* 3 ms. sf. וַיַּעֲצִמֵהוּ ψ 105^{24} + מִן comp. 6105

†עֹצֶם **n.[m.] might, bones**;—**1.** *might*, cstr. עֹ׳ יָדִי Dt 8^{17}, עֹ׳ יָדְךָ Jb 30^{21}; sf. עָצְמָה Na 3^{9} (Ges$^{§ 93e}$); + בְּעֹ׳ רוּחוֹ Is 11^{15} (Thes al.; for MT בַּעְיָם ר׳). **2.** *bones* (coll.): sf. עָצְמִי ψ 139^{15} = *my frame*. 6108

†עָצְמָה **n.f. might**;—Is 40^{29} (‖ כֹּחַ). 6109

I. עֶצֶם$_{125}$ **n.f.**$^{ψ 35, 10}$ (c. pron. masc. Ez 37$^{5.6}$ etc., cf. Albr.$^{ZAW xvi (1896), 73}$) **bone, substance, self**;—abs. עֶ׳ Gn 2^{23} +; עֶצֶם Pr 15^{30} 16^{24}; cstr. עֶצֶם Ex 24^{10} +; sf. עַצְמִי Jb 19^{20} +, etc.; pl. עֲצָמוֹת 2 K 23^{16} +; cstr. עַצְמוֹת Jos 24^{32} +; sf. עַצְמֹתַי Jb 4^{14} +, etc.; also עֲצָמִים Ez 24^{4} +, sf. עֲצָמַי Gn 2^{23} +, etc.;—**1.** *bone*: **a.** of living pers. Mi 3$^{2.3}$ (hyperb.), Jb 10^{11} 19^{20} La 4^{8} ψ 102^{6} Ec 11^{5} +; fig. of close relationship †עֶצֶם מֵעֲצָמַי Gn 2^{23}, cf. 29^{14} (both J), Ju 9^{2} 2 S 5^{1} = 1 Ch 11^{1}, 2 S 19$^{13.14}$ (all + בָּשָׂר). **b.** עֶ׳ + בָּשָׂר = *body*, Jb 2^{5}; pl. = *bodily frame* Je 20^{9} (sim.), *limbs, members*, לַעֲצָמֶיהָ Ju 9^{29} i.e. *limb by limb* (GFM); as seat of vigour Jb 20^{11}, etc. **c.** (poet.) as seat of disease and pain Jb 30$^{17.30}$ and (esp. of personif. Isr.) ψ 22^{15} 31^{11} 102^{4} La 1^{13} Hb 3^{16} +. **d.** pl. as representing entire person = one's whole being, (esp. of personif. Isr.) ψ 6^{3} (‖ נַפְשִׁי v^{4}), 35^{10} (‖ נַפְשִׁי v^{9}), Is 66^{14}; of individ. (incl. physical and moral) Pr 3^{8} 14^{30} 15^{30} 16^{24}. **e.** sg. = *external body* La 4^{7} Ew Th al., but dub.; Bi Bu *bones* (= branches) of coral (פְּנִינִים); Löhr עוֹרָם *their skin*. **f.** esp. of dead Nu 19$^{16.18}$ (P), Ez 37^{1} +; oft. (pl.) = *remains* Am 6^{10} Gn 50^{25} Ex 13$^{19.19}$ Jos 24^{32} (all E) +. **2.** *bone* of animal Ex 12^{46} Nu 9^{12} (both P); Ez 24$^{4.5}$ (symbol.); of (living) hippopot. Jb 40^{18}. †**3.** sg. *substance, self* (cf. גֶּרֶם **3**): כְּעֶ׳ הַשָּׁמַיִם Ex 24^{10} (JE), 6106 *like the substance of the sky* = the sky itself; בְּעֶ׳ תֻּמּוֹ Jb 21^{23} i.e. full prosperity; esp. בְּעֶ׳ הַיּוֹם הַזֶּה Ez 24^{2} *this selfsame day,* בְּעֶ׳ וגו׳ 24^{2} 40^{1} Gn 7^{13} 17$^{23.26}$ Ex 12$^{17.41.51}$ Lv 23$^{21.28.29.30}$ Dt 32^{48} Jos 5^{11} (all P), עַד־עֶ׳ וגו׳ Ez 2^{3} Lv 23^{14} (P), Jos 10^{27} (R).—Ez 24^{5a} rd. הָעֵצִים (Bö Ew al.); v^{10} del. הָעֲצָמוֹת (Co Toy); Jb 7^{15} rd. מֵעַצְבוֹתַי (Reiske Me Bu Du al.); ψ 53^{6} rd. perh. מְעֻצַּת (cf. ‖ ψ 14^{6} Bae; v. Hup Che al.); 69^{5} rd. מֵעַצְמוֹתַי (for MT מַצְמִיתַי), 𝔊 Ol Che Bae al.

6107 †II. עֶ֫צֶם **n.pr.loc.** Ασομ, etc., in Negeb of Judah, עֶ֫צֶם Jos 15^{29}, Simeon 19^{3} 1 Ch 4^{29} (עָ֑צֶם).

6099 עָצוּם$_{31}$ **adj. mighty, numerous**;—עָ׳ Gn 18^{18}+, pl. עֲצוּמִים Is 8^{7}+, עֲצֻמִים Mi 4^{3}+; sf. עֲצוּמָיו ψ 10^{10};—**1.** *mighty*, esp. of people, *strong* in numbers (oft. ‖ רַב, גָּדוֹל) Gn 18^{18} Ex 1^{9}+3 t. JE; Dt 4^{38}+6 t. D, Mi 4$^{3.7}$ Zc 8^{22} Is 60^{22} (opp. צָעִיר), of locusts Jo 1^{6} 2$^{2.5}$, cf. v^{11}; so of חַיִל Dn 11^{25}; עַם לֹא עָצוּם, i.e. feeble Pr 30^{26} (of the שְׁפַנִּים); less oft. of individ. מְלָכִים עֲ׳ ψ 135^{10}; of waters Is 8^{7}; עָ׳ alone Pr 18^{18} *the mighty*, Dn 8^{24}; ψ 10^{10} *his mighty ones* (i.e. claws, of lion, so Ew De Che Bae al.). **2.** *numerous, countless* (all ‖ רַב): Am 5^{12} ψ 35^{18}; as subst. = *many*
6110 Is 53^{12} Pr 7^{26}.—Is 41^{21} v. עֲצֻמָה sub III. עצם below.

8592 †[תַּעֲצֻמָה]† **n.f.** might;—pl. intens. עֹז וְתַעֲצֻמוֹת ψ 68^{36} *strength and abundant might.*

6111 †עַצְמוֹן† **n.pr.loc.** Ασε(λ)μωνα, on extreme S. border of Canaan, Nu 34^{5}, c. ה loc. עַצְמֹ֫נָה v^{4}, עַצְמ֫וֹנָה Jos 15^{4}.

6105 †II. [עָצַם] **vb.** shut the eyes (NH Hiph.; poss. connex. with Syr. ܥܰܡܶܨ = *id.*, Ar. غَمَضَ, غَمَّضَ IV (on ض = ܨ v. Nö $^{ZMG\ xxxii\ (1878),\ 406}$); NH עִמֵּץ *close* eyes of dead; cf. Ba $^{ES\ 5f.}$);—**Qal** *Pt.* וְעֹצֵם עֵינָיו מִן Is 33^{15} *shutteth his eyes from* seeing. **Pi.** *Impf.* 3 ms. וַיְעַצֵּם אֶת־עֵינֵיכֶם Is 29^{10}
6095 *he hath tightly shut your eyes* (cf. I. עצה).

III. עצם (√of foll., si vera l.; cf. Ar. عَصَمَ *defend, protect,* عِصْمَةٌ *defence*, v. Du and cf. Thes; > De Di al. *your mighty things,*
6099 strong arguments (fr. עָצוּם, sub I. עצם, which foll. perhaps imitates in vocalization)).

6110 †[עֲצֻמָה]† **n.f. defence**;—pl. sf. עֲצֻמוֹתֵיכֶם (so Baer Ginsb; van d. H. עַצְ׳) Is 41^{21} *bring forward your defences,* defensive arguments (Che ^{Hpt} עַצְּבוֹתֵיכֶם *your idols*, after Gr, [so Lo
6099 Klo explain עֲצֻ׳, as *mightiest* aid, I. עצם]).

5719, 6112 עֲצְנוֹ(ה) 2 S 23^{8}, v. 1. עֲדִינוֹ sub I. עדן. p. 726

עָצַר$_{46}$ **vb. restrain, retain** (NH *id.*; cf. 6113
prob. As. *eṣêru, retain, restrain*, Dl $^{HWB\ 199}$ Jäger $^{BAS\ i.\ 483}$ Zehnpfund $^{ib.\ 500}$; Eth. **ዐጸረ:** *press*, Ar. عَصَرَ; 𝔗 עֲצַר, Syr. ܥܨܰܪ *id.*);—**Qal** *Pf.* 3 ms. עָ׳ Gn 20^{18}+, sf. עֲצָרַנִי 16^{2}; 1 s. עָצַרְתִּי Dn 10$^{8.16}$, etc.; *Impf.* 3 ms. יַעְצֹר 1 S 9^{17}+, יַעְצָר־ 2 Ch 2^{5}; sf. יַעַצָרְכָה 1 K 18^{44}, etc.; *Inf. abs.* עָצֹר Gn 20^{18}, *cstr.* לַעְצֹר 2 Ch 22^{9}, וַעְצֹר Jb 4^{2} (Ges ^{§28b}); *Pt. pass.* עָצוּר Je 33^{1}+, etc.;—**1.** *restrain*, c. acc. pers. Gn 16^{2} (J; + מִן, i.e. prevent), עָצֹר עָצַר בְּעַד כָּל־רֶחֶם 20^{18} (E), cf. abs. Is 66^{9} (opp. מוֹלִיד); sq. inf. 2 K 4^{24}; c. acc. pers. alone 1 K 18^{44} *hinder, stop*; c. acc. of sky (hindering rain) Dt 11^{17} 2 Ch 7^{13}; pt. pass. abs. *shut up*, or *hindered* (for reasons not given) Je 36^{5} Ne 6^{10} (? by a vow, or by ceremonial uncleanness, cf. RS $^{Sem\ i.\ 436\ f.,\ 2nd\ ed.\ 455\ f.}$); = *shut up* (c. בְּ, in prison) 2 K 17^{4}, pt. pass. Je 33^{1} 39^{15}, fig. 20^{9}; on עָצוּר וְעָזוּב (5 t.), v. I. עזב; עֲצֻרָה לָנוּ 1 S 21^{6} women have been *kept away* with ref. to us (cf. RS $^{l.c.}$); עָצוּר מִפְּנֵי 1 Ch 12^{1} *kept away from before* Saul; = *detain*, c. acc. Ju 13$^{15.16}$; in Jb c. בְּ, עָ׳ בְּמִלִּין 4^{2}, cf. 29^{9}, so בַּמַּיִם 12^{5}; עָ׳ בְּעַמִּי 1 S 9^{17} is *rule over*, etc. (si vera l.); ins. also (with other words) 10^{1} 𝔊 We Dr al. **2.** (late) *retain*, c. acc. כֹּחַ 2 Ch 13^{20} 22^{9} Dn 10$^{8.16}$ 11^{6}; + inf. = *be able to* 1 Ch 29^{14} 2 Ch 2^{5}; om. כֹּחַ 14^{10} (+ עִמְּךָ), 20^{37} (+ inf.). †**Niph.** *be restrained, stayed*, of plague: Pf. 3 fs. נֶעֶצָ֑רָה Nu 17^{15}; *Impf.* 3 fs. תֵּעָצַר 2 S 24^{21} = 1 Ch 21^{22}, וַתֵּעָצַר Nu 17^{13} 25^{8} (P) 2 S 24^{25} ψ 106^{30}; *be shut up* (of sky), *Inf. cstr.* בְּהֵעָצֵר 1 K 8^{35} = 2 Ch 6^{26}; *be under restraint* or *detention Pt.* נֶעְצָר 1 S 21^{8} + לִפְנֵי י׳ (? i.e. kept by a vow, cf. HPS and Ne 6^{10} supr.).

†עֶ֫צֶר† **n.[m.] restraint** (?), only יוֹרֵשׁ עֶ׳ Ju 6114
18^{7} *a possessor of restraint*, i.e. ruler, but 𝔊 𝔙 *wealth*, so Thes al., text very dub., cf. GFM; Bu conj. that עֶ׳ combines readings אֹצֶר and עֹשֶׁר.

†עֹ֫צֶר **n.[m.] restraint, coercion**;—עֹ׳ abs.: 6115
מֵעֹ׳ וּמִמִּשְׁפָּט Is 53^{8} *from* (as a result of) *coercion and judgment* he was taken off; cstr. עֹ׳ רָעָה ψ 107^{39}; עֹ׳ רָחַם Pr 30^{16} *restraint of womb*, barrenness (so ψ 107^{39} Perles $^{Anal.\ 85}$).

†עֲצָרָה, עֲצֶ֫רֶת **n.f. assembly** (? as *confined*, 6116
held in);—abs. עֲצָרָה Is 1^{13}+2 t.; עֲצֶ֫רֶת Dt 16^{8}+3 t., עֲצָ֑רֶת 2 Ch 7^{9}; cstr. עֲצֶ֫רֶת Je 9^{1}; pl. sf. עַצְּרֹתֵיכֶם Am 5^{21};—**1.** sacred *assembly*, rejected by י׳, Is 1^{13} and (at Bethel, etc.) Am 5^{21}; for Baal 2 K 10^{20}; Dt 16^{8} (last day of Maṣṣoth), Lv 23^{36} (P), Nu 29^{35} (P), Ne 8^{18} (all of day after

feast of booths), cf. 2 Ch 7[9] [NH of feast of weeks, 𝔗 עֲצַרְתָּא Jos[Ant. iii.10,6] Ἀσάρτα]; occasional, Jo 1[14] 2[15]. **2.** *assemblage, company* (in gen.), ע׳ בֹּגְדִים Je 9[1] *an assemblage of deceivers* (Gr עֲדַת; Che חֶבְרַת).

4622 † מַעְצוֹר **n.[m.]** restraint, hindrance;—מ׳ 1 S 14[6] sq. inf., י׳ has no *hindrance* in delivering.

4623 † מַעְצָר **n.[m.]** restraint, control;—מ׳ Pr 25[28] a man whose spirit is without *control*.

עקב (√ of foll., meaning dub.: Thes assumes *be protuberant*, whence both עָקֵב *heel*, and II. עָקֹב *hilly*).

6119 †I. עָקֵב **n.m.** heel, footprint, hinder-part (Arab. عَقِبٌ *heel*, fig. *end* (of a month), عُقْبَةٌ *mark, sign, trace;* Aram. עִקְּבָא, ܥܩܒܐ *heel, footprint*, fig. *trace, mark* (cf. Wsd 2[4] 𝔖, Ecclus 13[26] 𝔥𝔖), also *end, extremity*);—ע׳ abs. Gn 3[15] +, cstr. עֲקֵב 25[26], pl. cstr. עִקְּבֵי Ct 1[8], עִקְּבֵי Gn 49[17] Ju 5[22], עִקְּבוֹת ψ 77[20] 89[52], etc.;—**a.** *heel*, of man, Gn 25[26] וְיָדוֹ אֹחֶזֶת בַּעֲקֵב אָחִיו, as obj. of attack from behind, 3[15] וְאַתָּה תְּשׁוּפֶנּוּ עָקֵב, Jb 18[9] יֹאחֵז בְּע׳ פָּח, Je 13[22] נֶחְמְסוּ עֲקֵבָיִךְ are treated violently, i. e. are rudely exposed (|| נִגְלוּ שׁוּלַיִךְ); as instrument of attack, ψ 41[10] הִגְדִּיל עָלַי ע׳ hath *made great the heel against me*, i. e. given me insidiously a great fall (fig. for, taken some cruel advantage of me; cf. ὑποσκελίζω); of an animal, Gn 49[17] הַנֹּשֵׁךְ עִקְּבֵי סוּס, Ju 5[22]. **b.** *mark of heel, footprint*, Ct 1[8] צְאִי־לָךְ בְּעִקְבֵי הַצֹּאן, ψ 56[7] יִשְׁמֹרוּ עֲקֵבַי they mark my *footprints*, i. e. watch me insidiously wherever I go, 89[52] אֲשֶׁר חֵרְפוּ עִקְּבוֹת מְשִׁיחֶךָ i. e. followed him mockingly, of י׳ (fig.) ψ 77[20] עִקְּבוֹתֶיךָ לֹא נֹדָעוּ thy *footprints* were not known (the waters closing over them). **c.** *hinder-part, rear* (of a troop of men), Gn 49[19] וְהוּא יָגֻד עָקֵב׃ (rd. עֲקֵבָם ׃ אָשֵׁר) he will troop on *their rear*, Jos 8[13] עֲקֵבָם (cf. Di).

6117 † עָקַב **vb.** follow at the heel, fig. assail insidiously, circumvent, overreach (denom. from עָקֵב; cf. Ar. عَقَبَ *follow* (at the heel), *succeed*, III. *bring consequence on*, i. e. *punish*, Qor 22[59], IV. *make to follow*, i. e. *reward* or *punish*, عَاقِبَةٌ *end, final lot* 6[11], *reward* 6[136]; ܥܩܒ *hold back* (rare), *follow*, Pa. *investigate, search out*: Eth. ዐቀበ፡ is *keep, guard*);—**Qal** *Pf.* 3 ms. Ho 12[4] בַּבֶּטֶן עָקַב אֶת־אָחִיו he *attacked* his brother *at the heel* (cf. Gn 25[26] sub עָקֵב); *Impf.* 3 ms. Gn 27[36] הֲכִי קָרָא שְׁמוֹ יַעֲקֹב וַיַּעְקְבֵנִי זֶה פַעֲמַיִם and he hath *overreached* me now twice; + *Inf. abs.* Je 9[3] כָּל־אָח עָקוֹב יַעְקֹב surely *overreacheth* (|| רָכִיל יַהֲלֹךְ). [𝔊 πτερνίζω, to attack *with* the heel; but this dub. In 'supplant,' also, the fig. is a different one.] **Pi.** Jb 37[4] וְלֹא יְעַקְּבֵם, dub.; poss. *attack at the heel* (cf. זִנֵּב), hence fig. *hold back;* more prob. rd. וְלֹא יְעַכְּבֵם *holdeth* them not *back* (sc. בְּרָקָיו his lightnings), when his voice is heard, from עִכֵּב *to hold back* (common in NH; 𝔗 עַכֵּב).

†II. עָקֵב **adj. verb.** overreacher, ψ 49[6] 6120
עֲוֹן עֲקֵבַי יְסֻבֵּנִי i. e. of those who would take some insidious advantage of me.

†I. עָקֹב **adj. 1.** insidious, deceitful, Je 6121
17[9] עָקֹב הַלֵּב מִכֹּל. **2.** foot-tracked (denom. from I. עָקֵב) Ho 6[8] גִּלְעָד קִרְיַת פֹּעֲלֵי אָוֶן עֲקֻבָּה מִדָּם.

†II. עָקֹב **adj.** steep, hilly (v. √; cf. عَقَبَةٌ 6121
difficult mountain path, Qor 90[11]; ዐቀብ፡ *hill*);—Is 40[4] והיה הֶעָקֹב לְמִישׁוֹר let the *steep ground* (Ch) become a plain (|| הָרְכָסִים). Cf. Ecclus 6[20].

† עָקְבָּה **n.f.** insidiousness, 2 K 10[19] וְיֵהוּא 6122
עָשָׂה בְעׇ׳.

† עֵקֶב **n.[m.]** consequence, usu. as **adv.** 6118
acc. as a consequence of, because (that), also reward, end (v. sub עָקֵב; and cf. عَقِبٌ *heel*, fig. *consequence, result*);—**1.** Is 5[23] מַצְדִּיקֵי רָשָׁע עֵקֶב שֹׁחַד (adv. acc.) *in consequence of* a bribe, ψ 40[16] (= 70[4]) עַל עֵקֶב בָּשְׁתָּם (pleon.) *according to the consequence of* their shame, i. e. *in consequence of* the disgrace falling upon them. Hence as **conj.** עֵקֶב אֲשֶׁר *as a consequence of* (the fact) *that, because*, Gn 22[18] ע׳ אֲשֶׁר שָׁמַעְתָּ בְּקֹלִי, 26[5] 2 S 12[6]; so עֵקֶב כִּי 2 S 12[10] Am 4[12] ע׳ כִּי זאת אעשה לך; עֵקֶב alone, Nu 14[24], and (sq. impf.) Dt 7[12] ע׳ תשמעון *in consequence of* your hearkening, etc., 8[20]. **2.** *consequence* = *gain, reward*, ψ 19[12] בְּשָׁמְרָם עֵקֶב רָב, Pr 22[4] עֵקֶב עֲנָוָה (וְ)יִרְאַת י׳ עֹשֶׁר וגו׳. **3.** *end* (of time), adv. acc., ψ 119[33] וְאֶצְּרֶנָּה ע׳ *to the end*, v[112] לְעוֹלָם ע׳ (cf. Ecclus 16[3]; 𝔗 עִקְּבָא (rare)).

† עַקּוּב **n.pr.m.** 𝔊B usu. (Ἰ)ακουν[μ], A 𝔊L 6126
Ακ(κ)ουβ:—**1.** descendant of David 1 Ch 3[24]. **2.** heads of post-exilic families: **a.** Ezr 2[42] = Ne 7[45]. **b.** Ezr 2[45] (si vera l.). **3.** Levites: **a.** 1 Ch 9[17]. **b.** Ne 8[7]. **c.** Ne 11[19] 12[25].

יַעֲקֹב[344], יַעֲקוֹב[5] **n.pr.m.** et **gent.** Jacob, 3290
Ιακωβ, son of Isaac and Rebekah, father of tribes of Isr. (expl. fr. עָקֵב *heel* Gn 25[26] Ho 12[4], i.e. *supplanter;* cp. with עָקַב *overreach* Gn 27[36]; *one closely following* acc. to Lag[BN 127]; connexion

with Pal. city (?) called in Egyptian *Y'kb'ara* (i.e. יַעֲקֹב־אֵל) is obscure; cf. Mey $^{ZAW\ vi.\ 1\ ff.}$ WMM $^{As.\ u.\ Eur.\ 162\ ff.}$ Jen $^{ZA\ x\ (1895-6),\ 347\ ff.}$; v. also Bab. n.pr.m. *Ya'ḳubilu*, Pinches in Hom $^{AHT\ 61,96,112}$; hence OT יַעֲקֹב perhaps orig. יעקבאל or the like, cf. Palm. n.pr. (עתעקב, בלעקב);—יַעֲקוֹב Je 30^{18} + 3 t. Je, Lv 26^{42}; יַעֲקֹב 215 t. Hex. (chiefly JE; 180 t. Gn, once Lv, etc.), 34 t. ψ, 42 t. Is (27 t. 40–66), etc.;—**1.** as **n.pr.m.** Gn 25^{26} + 205 t. (+אַבְרָהָם, יִצְחָק 19 t.); also בֵּית יַעֲ׳ of people (v. בַּיִת **5 d** (γ)), עֵין יַעֲ׳ (v. בֵּן **1 j** (β)), זֶרַע יַעֲ׳ (v. זֶרַע **4 f**), בְּנֵי יַעֲ׳ (v. עַיִן), etc. **2.** as **n.pr.gent.** (c. 100 t.; poet. and proph.) Nu $24^{5.19}$ Dt 32^{9} ψ 44^{5} Is 10^{21} 17^{4} Je 10^{25} 30^{7}+; ‖ יִשְׂרָאֵל Nu 23^{7} Dt 33^{10} Is 14^{1} ψ 14^{7} + c. 35 t.; specif. of N. Isr. Am $7^{2.5}$ Ho 12^{13} (+ 10^{11} 12^{3} prob., v. Now), Mi $1^{5.5}$ Is 9^{7}; of Judah Mi $3^{1.8}$ Ob ^{10} Is 65^{9} Mal 2^{12} + al. post-exilic; אֱלֹהֵי יַעֲ׳ v. גְּאוֹן יַעֲ׳ +; אֵל יַעֲ׳ ψ 146^{5}, ψ 114^{7}+; אֱלֹהֵי יַעֲ׳ 2 S 23^{1} Is 2^{3}=Mi 4^{2} + 9 t. ψψ, + ψ 24^{6} (א׳ יַעֲ׳ for MT יַעֲ׳ alone), so 𝔊 𝔖 𝔙 Ew Ol Hup Bae We Che al.; read א׳ יַעֲ׳ also prob. 2 S 23^{2} (for צוּר יִשׂ׳ ‖ א׳ יִשׂ׳) 𝔙 HPS; קְדוֹשׁ יַעֲ׳ Is 29^{23} (‖ א׳ יִשׂ׳) מֶלֶךְ יַעֲ׳ 41^{21} (‖ יהוה).—On יַעֲקֹב v. esp. Dr 'Jacob' in Hastings $^{Dict.\ Bib.\ ii.\ 526\ ff.}$.

3291 †יַעֲקֹבָה **n.pr.m.** Simeonite 1 Ch 4^{36} Ιωκαβα, A Ιακαβα, 𝔊L Ιεκεβα.

6123 †I. [עָקַד] **vb. bind** (NH *id.*, *bind bent limbs together;* Ar. عَقَدَ *tie, tie fast;* Eth. ዐቀደ: Syr. ܥܩܰܕ and esp. ܥܰܩܶܕ *bend, twist;* 𝔗 עֲקַד as NH; also *kneel*, cf. Chr. Pal., Schwally $^{Idiot.\ 71}$);—**Qal** *Impf.* וַיַּעֲקֹד אֶת־יִצְחָק Gn 22^{9}.

1044 עֵקֶד **n.[m.]** ? binding, cf. בֵּית ע׳ הָרֹעִים p. 112.

II. עקד (√ of foll.; usu. identif. with I, whence עָקֹד *striped with bands*, but dubious; Lag $^{BN\ 31}$ vocalizes √ עקד).

6124 †עָקֹד **adj.** striped, streaked;—of Jacob's goats and sheep; as subst. ע׳ Gn 30^{40} (coll.), pl. עֲקֻדִּים $31^{8.8}$; pl. as attrib. $30^{35.39}$, pred. $31^{10.12}$.

6125 †[עָקָה] **n.f.** ψ 55^{4} v. עוק p. 734.

עקה (√ of foll.; cf. Ar. عَقَا *hinder*).

4624 †מַעֲקֶה **n.[m.]** parapet;—Dt 22^{8}.

6127 †[עָקַל] **vb. bend, twist** (NH esp. in deriv.; 𝔗 in deriv.; Syr. ܥܩܰܠ *twist*, in der. spec.; Ar. عَقَلَ *bind* camel's folded fore-shank and arm *together*);—**Pu.** *be bent out of shape, crooked, Pt.* fig. מִשְׁפָּט מְעֻקָּל Hb 1^{4} *crooked justice.*

†[עֲקַלְקַל] **adj. intens.** crooked;—fpl. 6128
אֳרָחוֹת עֲקַלְקַלּוֹת Ju 5^{6} i.e. roundabout paths (GFM); sf. עֲקַלְקַלּוֹתָם ψ 125^{5} *their crookednesses.*

†עֲקַלָּתוֹן **adj.** crooked (acc. to Sm $^{ZAW\ iv.\ 213}$ 6129
constellation *Draco*);—לִוְיָתָן נָחָשׁ ע׳ Is 27^{1}.

†עֲקָן **n.pr.m.** in Edom;—וַע׳ Gn 36^{27}, 6130
(Ι)ουκαμ, = יַעֲקָן 1 Ch 1^{42}, Ωυαν, Ιαακαν, etc. (v. 3292
Lag $^{BN\ 84\ Anm.**}$; also בְּנֵי־יַעֲקָן and בְּאֵרֹת בְּ׳ יַעֲ׳). 885, 1142

עקר (√ of foll.; mng. dub.; cf. Aram. עִקָּרָא, ܥܶܩܳܪܳܐ *root;* Eth. ዐቀር: *medicine;* Ar. vb. appar. denom. عَقَرَ *extirpate*, 𝔗 עֲקַר *id.;* NH עָקַר=BH).

†I. עֵקֶר **n.m.** offshoot, member (? from 6133
root);—cstr. ע׳ מִשְׁפַּחַת גֵּר Lv 23^{47} *a member of a sojourner's family.* below

†[עָקַר] **vb. denom.** pluck or root up;— 6131
Qal *Inf. cstr.* לַעֲקוֹר c. acc. Ec 3^{2} (opp. נָטַע). 5193
Niph. *Impf.* 3 fs. עֶקְרוֹן תֵּעָקֵר Zp 2^{4} (word-play).

†עִקֵּר **vb. Pi. denom.** (from עֵקֶר or other 6131
like word = (*root-sinew*), *hamstring*);—**hamstring** horses (on Arab. funeral usage, with camel and horse v. We $^{Heid.\ 2,\ 181}$): *Pf.* 3 ms. ע׳ Jos 11^{9}, *Impf.* 3 ms. וַיְעַקֵּר 2 S 8^{4}=1 Ch 18^{4}, 2 ms. תְּעַקֵּר Jos 11^{6} all c. acc.; *Pf.* 3 mpl. עִקְּרוּ שׁוֹר Gn 49^{6} *they hamstrung an ox.*

†עָקָר **adj.** barren;—ע׳ of male Dt 7^{14}, עֲקָרָה 6135
of female v ^{14} (mankind and beasts), Ex 23^{26} (E; female); elsewhere of women Gn 11^{30} 25^{21} 29^{31} (all J), Ju $13^{2.3}$ 1 S 2^{5} Jb 24^{21} ψ 113^{9} (עֲקֶרֶת cstr.); of personif. Zion Is 54^{1}.

†II. עֵקֶר **n.pr.m.** in Judah 1 Ch 2^{27}, Ακορ, Ικαρ. 6134

†עַקְרָב **n.m.** scorpion (appar. quadrilit.; 6137
NH *id.;* As. *akrabu;* Eth. ዐቅራብ: ; Ar. عَقْرَبٌ; 𝔗 עַקְרַבָּא);—abs. עַקְרָב Dt 8^{15} (coll.; of wilderness), pl. עַקְרַבִּים Ez 2^{6} (fig. of enemies); יִסַּר בָּע׳ 1 K $12^{11.14}$=2 Ch $10^{11.14}$, i.e. scourges with points, stings.—Vid. also מַעֲלֵה עַקְרַבִּים p. 751 4610

עֶקְרוֹן 22 **n.pr.loc. Eḳrôn**, Ακκαρων (in As. 6138
Amkarruna COT $^{Gloss.}$, Dl $^{Pa\ 289}$ who prop. עַקָּרוֹן); —Philistine city, one of the famous five, Am 1^{8} Jos 13^{3} (D) + 4 t. Jos (P), Ju 1^{18} 1 S $5^{10.10}$ + 5 t. 1 S; 2 K $1^{2.3.6.16}$ Je 25^{20} Zp 2^{4} Zc $9^{5.7}$; mod. *'Âḳir* Rob $^{BR\ i.\ 227\ ff.}$ GASm $^{Geogr.\ 193}$ Buhl $^{Geogr.\ 187\ f.}$.

†עֶקְרוֹנִי **adj. gent.** of foregoing, c. art.= 6139
subst. the *Eḳrônite* Jos 13^{3} (D); pl. הָעֶקְרֹנִים 1 S 5^{10}.

6140 †[עָקַשׁ] **vb.** twist (NH *id.* (rare));—**Niph.** *Pt.* cstr. נֶעְקַשׁ דְּרָכַיִם Pr 28^{18} *one crooked in ways* (< pl., cf. Toy). **Pi.** *Pf.* 3 pl. עִקְּשׁוּ לָהֶם Is 59^{8} *their paths they have twisted.* *Impf.* 3 mpl. יְעַקֵּשׁוּ Mi 3^{9} all that is straight *they make crooked; Pt* מְעַקֵּשׁ דְּרָכָיו Pr 10^{9} (cf. **Niph.**). **Hiph.** *Impf.* וַיַּעְקְשֵׁנִי Jb 9^{20} (Ges$^{§ 53 n}$) *he hath declared me crooked,* devious (in life).

6141 † I. עִקֵּשׁ **adj. twisted, perverted**;—abs. דּוֹר ע׳ וּפְתַלְתֹּל Dt 32^{5} *a generation twisted and crooked,* לֵבָב ע׳ ψ 101^{4}; as n.m. (of one devious in life) *the perverted* 2 S 22^{27} = ψ 18^{27}, Pr 22^{5}, of things 8^{8}; cstr. ע׳ דְּרָכַיִם 28^{6}, ע׳ שְׂפָתָיו 19^{1}, עִקֶּשׁ־לֵב 17^{20}; pl. אָרְחֹתֵיהֶם עִקְּשִׁים 2^{15} *whose ways are twisted;* cstr. עִקְּשֵׁי־לֵב 11^{20}.

6142 † II. עִקֵּשׁ **n.pr.m.** a Tekoan 2 S 23^{26} = 1 Ch 11^{28}, 1 Ch 27^{9}; Εισκα, Εκκις, etc.

6143 † עִקְּשׁוּת **n.f. crookedness**:—cstr. ע׳ פֶּה *crookedness of mouth* Pr 4^{24} 6^{12} (cf. עִקֵּשׁ 19^{1}).

4625 †[מַעֲקָשׁ] **n.[m.] twisted, crooked place**;—pl. מַעֲקַשִּׁים Is 42^{16} (opp. מִישׁוֹר).

6144 † I. עָר **n.pr.loc.** in Moab, S. of Arnon (Ηρ Nu 21^{15}, elsewhere chiefly Αροηρ);—ע׳ Nu 21^{15} Dt 2$^{9.18.29}$; עָר מוֹאָב Nu 21^{28} Is 15^{1};—usually interpreted as capital *city* (עָר = עִיר) of Moab (DHM$^{ZMG\ xxxvii\ (1883),\ 398}$ cp. Sab. ער *fortified height,* cf. Mordtm$^{Him.\ Inschr.\ 29}$ Hal$^{Ét.\ Sab.\ 159}$, so Ar. اَلْعِرُّ, dial. of Yemen); Buhl$^{Geogr.\ 269\ f.}$ thinks name of *district* S. of Arnon.

6145 † II. עָר **n.m.** only 2 t.: עָרֶךָ 1 S 28^{16} (v. Dr); rd. צָרֶךָ *thine adversary* Klo HPS (al. as altern. with foll.) > עִם רֵעֶךָ 𝔊 𝔖 𝔗 Th Bu Kit (?) al.; עָרֶיךָ ψ 139^{20} is very dub.; Hup עָלֶיךָ, Ol Che al. שְׁמֶךָ; Bae leaves untranslated.

6147 עָר v. I. עוּר. p. 735

I. ערב (✓of foll.; prob. *עָרַב *mix;* NH עָרַב *mix;* so 𝔗 Pa. (oft.), Syr. ܥܪܰܒ *mix* (rarely, in der. forms), ܥܽܘܪܳܒܳܐ *mixture*).

6154 † I. עֵרֶב **n.m.**$^{Ex\ 12,\ 38}$ **mixture, mixed company**;—heterogeneous body attached to a people; to Israel Ex 12^{38}(E), Ne 13^{3}; to Egyptians Je 25^{20}(𝔙 joins to v^{19}, so Gie); to Chaldeans 50^{37}; in Je 25^{24} del. וְאֵת . . . . הָעֶרֶב as doublet (so Gie, cf. 𝔊); in 1 K 10^{15} rd. עֲרָב (as ‖ 2 Ch 9^{14}, so Benz Kit al.); Ez 30^{5} rd. prob. *id.* (Co).

II. עֵרֶב **n.[m.] woof** (as *mixed,* interwoven, 6154
with warp);—Lv 13^{48} + 8 t. 13 (all opp. שְׁתִי *warp*), cf. GFM$^{PAOS\ 1889,\ clxxviii}$.

עָרֹב **n.m.**$^{Ex\ 8,\ 20}$ prob. **swarm** (*mixture,* from 6157
incessant, involved motion; Lag$^{BN\ 112}$ doubts);—of plague of stinging flies, coming in a *swarm* (v. Di^{Ex}) Ex 8$^{17.17}$ + 5 t. 8 (J), ψ 78^{45} 105^{31}.

† II. עָרַב **vb. take on pledge, give in** 6148
pledge, exchange (NH *go surety for* (rare); Ph. ערב *surety;* OAram. ערבא *pledge;* 𝔗 עֲרַב, Syr. ܥܪܰܒ, *go surety for;* usu. identified with I. ערב—*mix, exchange, pledge*—but quite uncertain; cf. Buhl^{Lex} Lag$^{BN\ 203}$);—**Qal** *Pf.* 3 ms. ע׳ Gn 44^{32} + 4 t.; 2 ms. עָרַבְתָּ Pr 6^{1}; *Impf.* 1 s. sf. אֶעֶרְבֶנּוּ Gn 43^{9}; *Imv.* עֲרֹב ψ 119^{122}, sf. עָרְבֵנִי Is 38^{14}, so Jb 17^{3} (but v. infr.); *Inf. cstr.* לַעֲרֹב Ez 27^{9}; *Pt.* עֹרֵב Pr 17^{18}, etc.;—**1.** c. acc. pers. *take on pledge,* i. e. *go surety for* the safety of, Gn 43^{9}(J), 44^{32}(J; + מֵעִם pers.); for the debts of Pr 11^{15} 20^{16} 27^{13}; of God Is 38^{14} *go surety for me,* ψ 119^{122}, so Jb 17^{3} (si vera l., v. עֵרָבוֹן); acc. pers. om., ע׳ לְ Pr 6^{1} *go surety to* one (in behalf of another, ‖ תָּקַע לַזָּר כַּפֶּיךָ); c. acc. rei Pr 22^{26} (‖ תֹּקְעֵי־כָף). **2.** *give in pledge,* c. acc. rei Ne 5^{3} (i. e. mortgage), fig. ע׳ אֶת־לִבּוֹ Je 30^{21} so ע׳ עֲרֻבָּה לִפְנֵי רֵעֵהוּ Pr 17^{18} (‖ תֹּקֵעַ כָּף). **3.** *exchange* (in trade), c. acc. cogn. מַעֲרָבֵךְ Ez 27$^{9.27}$. **Hithp. 1.** recipr.: *Imv.* הִתְעָרֶב נָא אֶת־אֲדֹנִי 2 K 18^{23} *exchange pledges* (make a bargain) *with my lord* = Is 36^{8}. **2. a.** *have fellowship* with, בְּ pers., *Pf.* 3 pl. הִתְעָרְבוּ Ezr 9^{2}; *Impf.* 3 mpl. וַיִּתְעָרְבוּ ψ 106^{35}; 2 ms. תִּתְעָרַב c. לְ pers. Pr 20^{19}, c. עִם pers. 24^{21}. **b.** *share* in, בְּ rei, 3 ms. יִתְעָרַב Pr 14^{10} in his joy no other *shares.*

† עֲרֻבָּה **n.f. thing exchanged, pledge,** 6161
token;—sf. עֲרֻבָּתָם 1 S 17^{18} = *a token from them,* i. e. response, token of welfare, Th Dr al.; abs. as acc. cogn. עָרַב ע׳ Pr 17^{18} *give a pledge.*

† עֵרָבוֹן **n.[m.] pledge**;—נָתַן ע׳ *give a* 6162
pledge Gn 38$^{17.18}$, לָקַח ע׳ v^{20} (all J), *receive* (back) *a pledge* (when condition is fulfilled).—Jb 17^{3} rd. perh. עֶרְבֹנִי (for MT עָרְבֵנִי), as obj. of שִׂימָה *set my pledge* (*a surety for me*), so Beer Bu al.

† I. [מַעֲרָב] **n.m.** usu. **coll. articles of ex-** 4627
change, merchandise (only of Tyre, Ez 27);—sf. מַעֲרָבֵךְ v$^{13.17.19.25.27\ a.34}$; as acc. cogn. c. עָרַב v$^{9.27}$; pl. sf. מַעֲרָבַיִךְ v^{33} perh. *thy* (diverse) *wares* (DHM$^{VOJ\ viii\ (1894),\ 4}$ prop., ingeniously, meaning *imports,* deriving fr. V. ערב *enter,* but improb.).

8594 †[תַּעֲרֻבָה] **n.f.** pledge; only pl. in phr. בְּנֵי הַתַּעֲרֻבוֹת 2 K 14[14] i.e. *hostages* = 2 Ch 25[24].

6149 †III. [עָרֵב] **vb. be sweet, pleasing** (NH *id.* (rare); Hiph. Impf. יעריבו Ecclus 40[21]; 𝔗 עָרִיב adj. *pleasant, sweet*);—**Qal** *Pf.* 3 fs. עָֽרְבָה Je 31[26] my sleep *was sweet* to me (לִי), וְע׳ שְׁנָתְךָ consec. Pr 3[24]; of offering לא ע׳ לי׳ Mal 3[4]; 2 fs. עָרַבְתְּ Ez 16[37] c. עַל pers., to whom *thou wast pleasing;* 3 pl. לֹא עָרְבוּ לִי Je 6[20] (of sacrif.); *Impf.* 3 ms. יֶעֱרַב עָלָיו שִׂיחִי ψ 104[34] *let my meditation be pleasing unto him!* 3 fs. תֶּעֱרַב לְ Pr 13[19] (of realized wish); 3 mpl. לֹא יֶעֶרְבוּ לוֹ Ho 9[4] (of sacrifice; but Kue Che We GASm Now read יַעַרְכוּ).

6156 †עָרֵב **adj.** sweet, pleasant;—ע׳ לָאִישׁ לֶחֶם שָׁקֶר Pr 20[17]; קוֹלֵךְ ע׳ Ct 2[14].

IV. **ערב** (√of foll.; poss. *be arid;* Thes cp. Eth. **ዐረረ:** *be arid, sterile,* so Baentsch[Die Wüste (1883). 17], but dub.; Syr. ܥܪܒܐ = BH; Ar. العَرَبَة n.pr. of depression S. of Dead Sea).

6152 †עֲרָב **n.[m.]** desert-plateau, steppe (cf. Che[Intr. Is. 129]);—בַּעְרַב בַּעֲרָב (si vera l.) Is 21[13.13] *in the steppe* (of what we know as N. Arabia); but in v[b] Vrss Lo Che Gu[Kau] al. בָּעֶרֶב *in the evening.*

6163 †עֲרָבִי **n. gent.** of foregoing, steppe-dweller;—Is 13[20]; כַּעֲרָבִי בַּמִּדְבָּר Je 3[2].

6152 †עֲרָב **n.pr. gent. coll.** steppe-dwellers of N. Arabia (Wetzst[ZVölkerpsych. vii. 463 f.]; extended later (so Herod[ii. 11] etc.) to whole peninsula, cf. Ar. العَرَبُ *the Arabs,* Bedúwy *the people,* Doughty[Arab. Deserta, i. 224]; Sab. ערבן, ערב, אערב CIS[iv. p. 123], As. *Aribu, Arubu, Arabi,* people in N. Arabia, Dl[Pa 295 f. 304 f.] COT[Je 25, 24]; also *Urbi* Dl[Pa 305 f.] of nomad 'Arab' tribes);—מַלְכֵי ע׳ הַשֹּׁכְנִים בַּמִּדְבָּר Je 25[24] (v. I. עֵרֶב), 2 Ch 9[14] + ‖ 1 K 10[15] (v. *id.*); ע׳ also Ez 27[21] + 30[5] (v. *id.*); v. esp. Nö[Arabia] in Ency. Bib.

6163 †עֲרָבִי **adj. gent.** Arabian (in strictly ethnographic sense, Nö[l.c.]);—הָע׳ as subst. Ne 2[19] Geshem *the Arabian,* so 6[1]; pl. הָעֲרָבִים Ne 4[1] 2 Ch 21[16] 22[1]; also (written as NH) הערביים 26[7] (Qr הָעֲרָבִים), and even הָעֲרָבִיאִים 17[11].

6160 I. עֲרָבָה[61] **n.f.** desert-plain, steppe;—abs. ע׳ 2 S 4[7] +, sf. עַרְבָתָהּ Is 51[3]; pl. עֲרָבוֹת Je 5[6] ψ 68[5], cstr. עַרְבוֹת 2 K 25[5] +, עַרְבֹת Je 52[8];—**1.** earliest use: **a.** arid steppe W. of Dead Sea (in S. Judah) 1 S 23[24], also Ez 47[8] Is 51[3], whence name יָם הָע׳ Jos 3[16] (JE ‖ יָם הַמֶּלַח), also 2 K 14[25] Dt 4[49], and (‖*id.*) 3[17] Jos 12[3] (D); נַחַל הָעֲרָבָה Am 6[14] must be E. of Dead Sea, si vera l., but rd. prob. נַחַל נ׳ מִצְרַיִם v. **b.** Jordan-valley W. of river + adjacent plain; near ford (opp. Jericho) 2 S 2[29], cf. Jos 8[14] (JE); also Dt 11[30] 2 K 25[4] = Je 39[4] = 52[7];—2 S 15[28] 17[16] v. עֲבָרָה. **c.** Jordan-valley E. of river 2 S 4[7]. **2.** in D: **a.** esp. of E. Jordan plain Dt 1[1] (prob.) Jos 12[1.3], E. half of Jordan-valley Dt 3[17] 4[49]; of entire Jordan-valley (between כִּנֶּרֶת and Dead Sea, mod. *El-Ghôr, the Depression*) Dt 1[7] Jos 11[2.16]; W. Jordan plain only Jos 12[8]; depression S. of Dead Sea (mod. *Wady el-'Arabah*) Dt 2[8]. **3.** in P always pl. cstr. עַרְבוֹת מוֹאָב (E. Jordan) Nu 22[1] + 11 t. (v. מוֹאָב); ע׳ יְרֵחוֹ (W. Jordan) Jos 4[13] 5[10], also 2 K 25[5] = Je 39[5] = 52[8]. **4.** appar. N. Arabian desert Is 40[3] 41[19]. **5.** in gen. *the steppe* (oft. ‖ מִדְבָּר), Je 17[6] 50[12] Is 33[9] 35[1.6] Jb 24[5] 39[6] ψ 68[5]; זְאֵב עֲרָבוֹת Je 5[6] (fig. of invader); cf. description of Exodus אֶרֶץ עֲרָבָה וְשׁוּחָה Je 2[6]; in sim., of a *plain,* of future land of Judah Zc 14[10].—Vid. Dr[Dt 1, 1 and reff.] Buhl[Geogr. 111].

עַרְבָתִי v. בֵּית הָעֲרָבָה. p. 112 6164

V. **ערב** (√of foll.; cf. As. *erêbu, enter, go in; erêb šamši, sunset;* Ar. غَرَبَ *set* (distinct fr. غَرَبَ *depart,* = Sab. ערב *withdraw,* acc. to DHM[Epigr. Denkm. 27]), غَرْبٌ *place of sunset, west;* Sab. מערבי, מערבם [not ע!] *west, western,* CIS[iv. p. 199] DHM[l.c.]; Eth. **ዐረበ:** *set* (of heavenly bodies), so Syr. ܥܪܒ; ܡܥܪܒܐ *evening* (Lag[BN 64 f.]); Zinj. מערב *west;* NH עֶרֶב = BH. Hence also Εὐρώπη, *Europe,* Lewy[Fremdw. 139]).

עֶ֫רֶב[131] **n.[m.** 1 S 20[5] del. הַשְּׁלִשִׁית v. We 6153
Dr al.] (sun)**set, evening**;—abs. ע׳ 2 K 2[16] +, עָרֶב Ex 12[18] +; cstr. עֶרֶב Pr 7[9]; du. עַרְבַּיִם Ex 30[8] + 4 t., -בָּיִם 12[16] + 5 t. (all P);—**1. a.** *evening,* orig. sun*set,* and hence perh. לְעֵת ע׳ *at the time of* sunset †Gn 8[11] (J), 24[11] (J; ‖ לְעֵת צֵאת הַשֹּׁאֲבֹת), 2 S 11[2] Is 17[14] and (of the day of י׳) Zc 14[7], עֵת הָע׳ Jos 8[29] (JE)†; usu. ע׳ alone = *time of sunset, evening:* בָּע׳ *in the evening* Gn 19[1] (J), 29[23] (E), Ex 12[18] (P), Dt 16[6] (+ כְּבוֹא הַשֶּׁמֶשׁ), 1 K 22[35] (cf. ‖ 2 Ch 18[34] where + לְעֵת בּוֹא הַשָּׁמֶשׁ) + 20 t. + בָּע׳(־)בָּע׳ 2 Ch 13[11.11] = *every evening;* לָע׳ *at evening* only late: †1 Ch 16[40] 23[30] 2 Ch 2[3] Ezr 3[3] ψ 59[7.15] 90[6] Ec 11[6]†; לִפְנוֹת ע׳ *at the turn of evening* †Gn 24[63] (J), Dt 23[12]; ע׳ as adv. acc. Ec 16[6] (P), ψ 55[18]; as marking duration of impurity, in phr. עַד־הָע׳ Lv 11[24] + 30 t. P + Lv 22[6] (H); of Day of Atonement מֵע׳

עַד־ע׳ 23^{32} (P). **b.** du. in phrase (only P) בֵּין הָעַרְבַּיִם *between the two evenings,* i.e. prob. between sunset and dark (v. Thes [various views fully given]; otherwise Di$^{Ex\ 12,6}$; on form as poss. only expanded pl. v. Ges$^{§\ 88\ c}$), †Ex 12^{6} 16^{12} $29^{39.41}$ 30^{8} Lv 23^{5} Nu $9^{3.5.11}$ $28^{4.8}$†. **c.** other phrases are: צִלְלֵי ע׳ Je 6^{4} (dist. fr. צָהֳרַיִם and לַיְלָה v^{5}), מִנְחַת (הָ)ע׳ †2 K 16^{15} Ezr $9^{4.5}$ ψ 141^{2} Dn 9^{21}†; זְאֵבֵי ע׳ v. I. זְאֵב; for all combin. with בֹּקֶר *morning,* v. ב׳ **1 d, e.** **2.** (late poet.) = *night,* עֶרֶב Jb 7^{4}; cf. בְּנֶשֶׁף בְּעֶרֶב יוֹם Pr 7^{9} (‖ בְּאִישׁוֹן לַיְלָה וַאֲפֵלָה).

6150 †[עָרַב] **vb. denom.** become evening; **grow dark** (?);—**Qal** *Inf. cstr.* רָפָה הַיּוֹם לַעֲרוֹב Ju 19^{9}, but rd. prob. נָטָה הַיּוֹם לַעֲרֹב 𝔊L GFM; *Pf.* 3 fs. fig. עָרְבָה Is 24^{11} all joy *has grown dark,* but rd. עָבְרָה *has passed away* Lo Gr Perles$^{Anal.\ 91}$ Che^{Hpt} al. **Hiph.** *Inf. abs.* הַשְׁכֵּם וְהַעֲרֵב 1 S 17^{16} *doing it* at morning and *at evening.*

4628 †II. מַעֲרָב **n.[m.]** **west** (late) (place of sun*set*);—מִמַּעֲרָבָה (= בָה־, cf. De Ges$^{§\ 91e}$) Is 45^{6} *from its setting-place* (opp. מִמִּזְרַח־שֶׁמֶשׁ); מַעֲרָב opp. מִזְרָח also 43^{5} 59^{19} ψ 103^{12} 107^{3}, so לְמ׳ *westward* 1 Ch 7^{28} 12^{16} (van d. H. v^{15}), $26^{16.18}$; מ׳ opp. מוֹצָא ψ 75^{7}; מִן־הַמַּעֲרָב (alone) Dn 8^{5}; c. ה loc. מַעֲרָבָה 1 Ch 26^{30} *westward,* sq. לְ = *to the west of* 2 Ch 32^{30} 33^{14}, מִמ׳ לְגִבְעָה Ju 20^{33} acc.

4629 to 𝔊 (not B) 𝔙 Be GFM al. (v. [מַעֲרֶה]).

VI. **ערב** (√of foll.; cf. Ar. غَرَبَ *be black,* غُرَابٌ *crow* (raven, rook, etc.); As. *âribu, êribu;* Aram. ܥܘܪܒܐ, עוּרְבָּא, all *crow, raven*).

6158-59 †עֹרֵב **n.m.**$^{Lv\ 11,15}$ **raven;**—הָע׳ Gn 8^{7} (J), Lv 11^{15} (H) = Dt 14^{14} Jb 38^{41}; כָּעוֹרֵב Ct 5^{11} black *as the raven;* בְּנֵי עֹרֵב ψ 147^{9} *young ravens;* pl. abs. הָעֹרְבִים 1 K $17^{4.6}$; cstr. עֹרְבֵי־נַחַל Pr 30^{17}.

6155 †II. [עֲרָבָה] **n.[f.]** **poplar** (*populus Euphratica* = Ar. غَرَبٌ We in De$^{Gn\ (4),\ 568}$ Kersten $^{ZPV\ ii.\ 209}$ De$^{Is\ (4)\ 44,\ 4}$ Löw$^{p.\ 300\ Anm.}$; NH עֲרָבָה; √obscure);—pl. abs. עֲרָבִים עַל־יִבְלֵי־מָיִם Is 44^{4}, cf. ψ 137^{2}; cstr. עַרְבֵי־נָחַל Lv 23^{40} (H), Jb 40^{22}; נַחַל־הָעֲרָבִים Is 15^{7} (a wady in Moab; identification dub., v. conjectures in Buhl$^{Geogr.\ 124}$).

6165 †[עָרַג] **vb.** **long for** (cf. Ar. عَرَجَ *ascend,* II. *bend, incline* toward (على); عَرِيجٌ *high, elevated;* Eth. **ዐርገ:** *ascend;* NH עֲרוּגָה = BH);—**Qal** *Impf.* 3 fs. תַּעֲרֹג ψ 42^{2} (of stag, c. עַל rei in sim.); c. אֶל, of longing for God v^{2} (subj. נַפְשִׁי), so תַּעֲרוֹג Jo 1^{20} (of beasts, craving water).

†[עֲרוּגָה] **n.f.** **garden terrace** or **bed;**— 6170
cstr. עֲרוּגַת הַבֹּשֶׂם Ct 5^{13} *bed of balsam* (sim.); pl. cstr. עֲרֻגוֹת הַבּ׳ 6^{2}, ע׳ מַטָּעָהּ Ez 17^{7} i.e. where the vine was planted, עֲרֻגֹת צִמְחָהּ v^{10} (all fig.).

† I. עֲרָד **n.pr.loc.** Can. city in the Negeb, 6166
Αραδ (Egypt. *ʿa-ru-dâ* WMM$^{As.\ u.\ Eur.\ 168,\ 170}$);—Ju 1^{16}, מֶלֶךְ־ע׳ Nu 21^{1} (JE) = 33^{40}, Jos 12^{14} (D, Α(ι)ραθ, A 𝔊L Αδερ); prob. mod. *Tel Arad,* 16½ miles S. of Hebron; cf. GFM$^{Ju\ 1,\ 16}$ Buhl$^{Geogr.\ 182}$.

† II. עֵרֶד **n.pr.m.** Benjamite 1 Ch 8^{15}, Ωρηρ, 6166
A Αρωδ, 𝔊L Αραδ.

†[עָרָה] **vb.** **be naked, bare** (Ar. عَرِيَ *be* 6168
naked; Ph. ערה [Pi.] *lay bare* (cf. Bloch Lzb); As. *ûru, nakedness,* also *desert waste* (cf. [עָרָה] infr.) Jäger$^{BAS\ ii.\ 282}$ and reff.; NH עֶרְוָה = BH, 𝔗 עִירְיָתָא; Syr. ܥܪܛܠܝܬܐ in Lexx);—**Pi.** *Pf.* 3 ms. עֵרָה Is 22^{6} Zp 2^{14}; *Impf.* 3 ms. יְעָרֶה Is 3^{17}; 3 fs. וַתְּעַר Gn 24^{20}; 2 ms. juss. תְּעַר ψ 141^{8}; 3 mpl. וַיְעָרוּ 2 Ch 24^{11}; *Imv.* mpl. עָרוּ ψ $137^{7.7}$; *Inf. abs.* עָרוֹת Hb 3^{13} (Ges$^{§\ 75\ n}$);—**1.** *lay bare* Is 3^{17} 22^{6} Zp 2^{14} (indef. subj.); of laying foundations bare, i.e. tearing down walls, etc. Hb 3^{13} (yet on text v. Now), abs. עָרוּ עָרוּ ψ $137^{7.7}$. **2.** *lay bare* by removing contents, *empty,* water-jar Gn 24^{20} (J; + אֶל loc.), chest 2 Ch 24^{11}. **3.** *pour out,* אַל־תְּעַר נַפְשִׁי ψ 141^{8} (i.e. slay). **Hiph.** *Pf.* 3 ms. הֶעֱרָה: **1.** *make naked,* of sexual offences Lv $20^{18.19}$ (both ‖ גִּלָּה). **2.** *pour out,* הֶע׳ לַמָּוֶת נַפְשׁוֹ Is 53^{12} (fig. for *slay,* cf. **Qal 3**). **Niph.** pass. of **Hiph. 2**: 3 ms. יֵעָרֶה עָלֵינוּ רוּחַ Is 32^{15} (fig.) until *there be poured upon us a spirit* from on high. **Hithp. 1.** *Impf.* 2 fs. תִּתְעָרִי La 4^{21} *thou shalt make thyself naked* (of Edom under fig. of drunken woman). **2.** *Pt.* מִתְעָרֶה ψ 37^{35} usu. *pouring himself,* i.e. *spreading himself out* like a tree (Bae doubts; Du מִתְעַלֶּה *lifting himself up,* cf. 𝔊).

†[עָרָה] **n.f.** **bare place;**—pl. עָרוֹת Is 19^{7} 6169
(si vera interpr.; > 𝔊 ἄχ(ε)ι, Ki Saad *reeds*).

עֶרְוָה$_{54}$ **n.f.** **nakedness, pudenda;**—abs. 6172
ע׳ Ex 28^{42} Lv 18^{6}; usu. cstr. עֶרְוַת Gn 9^{22}+, sf. עֶרְוָתֶךָ Ex 20^{23} (Ginsb), Lv 18^{10}; עֶרְוָתֵךְ Is 47^{3}+; תוֹ־ Lv 20^{17}, תָהּ־ 18^{7}+; sf. 3 fpl. עֶרְוָתָן v$^{9.10}$;—**1.** *pudenda,* of man, רָאָה ע׳ implying shameful exposure Gn $9^{22.23}$ (J); mostly of woman: fig. of Jerus. (c. רָאָה) La 1^{8} Ez 16^{37}; usu. c. גלה: lit. תִּגָּלֶה ע׳ i.e. be exposed to view Ex 20^{23} (Ginsb; van d. H. v^{26}; E), so, as shameful punishment,

fig. of Egypt Is 20^{4} (gloss acc. to Du Cho Di Kit), Bab. 47^{3}, of Jerus. Ez 16^{37} 23$^{10.29}$ (עֶרְוַת זְנוּנַיִךְ; all three obj. of act. vb.); chiefly euphem. for cohabit., גִּלָּה ע׳ Lv 18^{6}+ (v. גלה **Pi. 1 a**); fig. of Jerus. (vb. pass.) Ez 16^{36}; רָאָה ע׳ in same meaning Lv 20$^{17.17}$ (H; of both sexes); ע׳ also 18$^{8.10.16}$ (H); כִּסָּה ע׳ *cover nakedness* Gn 9^{23} (J), Ex 28^{42} (P; בְּשַׂר ע׳), Ho 2^{11} (fig. of Isr.), Ez 16^{8} (of Jerus.); reviling words are לְבשֶׁת ע׳ אִמֶּךָ 1 S 20^{30} (cf. Doughty[Arab. Deserta i. 269]). **2.** עֶרְוַת דָּבָר *nakedness of a thing*, i.e. prob. *indecency, improper behaviour* Dt 23^{15} 24^{1} (v. Dr). **3.** fig. ע׳ הָאָרֶץ Gn 42$^{9.12}$ (E), i.e. its exposed, undefended parts (Ar. عَوْرَةٌ).

6181 **† עֶרְיָה$_{6}$ n.f. nakedness**;—alw. abs. ע׳;—ע׳־בֹשֶׁת Mi 1^{11} (in) *nakedness*, (in) *shame* (fig. of town Shaphir); of Jerus. עֵרֹם וְע׳ Ez 16^{7}+3 t. (v. עֵירֹם sub II. עור); of bow Hb 3^{9} (v. II. עור).

4626, 4629 **† [מַעֲרֶה], מַ֫עַר n.[m.] bare, naked place** (hence Μαραθών, Marathon, acc. to Lewy[Fremdw. 144]);—**1.** *bare place*, or *space*: cstr. מִמַּעֲרֵה־גָבַע Ju 20^{33} *bare* (open) *space* of Geba' (si vera l.; but v. II. מַעֲרָב); כְּמַעַר־אִישׁ 1 K 7^{36} *according to the clear space on each* (plate, v. לוּחַ). **2.** sf. מַעְרֵךְ Na 3^{5} fig. of Nineveh (*pudenda* exposed in shameful punishment; cf. עֶרְוָה).

4638 **† מַעֲרָת n. pr. loc.** in Judah Jos 15^{59}, Μαγαρωθ, A 𝔊L Μα(α)ρωθ.

8593 **† תַּ֫עַר† n.m.** [ψ 52, 4] and (Is 7^{20}) **f. razor, sheath**;—**1. a.** *razor*, abs. יְגַלַּח בְּת׳ Is 7^{20} (fig.); subj. of לֹא יַעֲבֹר עַל־רֹאשׁ Nu 6^{5}, obj. of הֶעֱבִיר עַל־ 8^{7} (P), cf. cstr. ת׳ הַגַּלָּבִים Ez 5^{1}; abs. כְּת׳ מְלֻטָּשׁ ψ 52^{4} (sim. of tongue). **b.** cstr. ת׳ הַסֹּפֵר Je 36^{23} =*penknife*. **2.** *sheath*, always sf. of sword: בְּתַעְרָהּ 2 S 20^{8}; of drawing sword, שָׁלַף מִתּ׳ 1 S 17^{51}, הוֹצִיא מִתּ׳ Ez 21$^{8.10}$, תֵּצֵא מִתּ׳ v^{9}; of sheathing, הֵאָסְפִי אֶל־תַּעְרֵךְ Je 47^{6}; הָשֵׁב אֶל־תַּעְרָהּ Ez 21^{35}.

6171 **† עָרוֹד n.[m.] wild ass** (prob. Aram. loan-word (=Heb. פֶּרֶא), 𝔗 עֲרָדָא, עֲרוֹדָא; Syr. ܥܪܕܐ; Mand. אראדא, cf. Hom[NS 133]);—Jb 39^{5}.

6186 **† עָרַךְ vb. arrange or set in order** (NH *id.*; also *roll* dough, 𝔗 עֲרַךְ *id.*; Ph. ערכת CIS[No. 132, 4] *valuation*, Bloch, but dub.; Ar. عَرَكَ III. *contend* in battle, مَعْرَكٌ, مَعْرَكَةٌ *battle-ground*);—**Qal** *Pf.* 3 ms. ע׳ Jb 32^{14} 2 Ch 13^{3}, וְע׳ consec. Lv 1^{12} 6^{5}; עָרַכְתִּי Nu 23^{4}+, etc.; *Impf.* 3 ms. יַעֲרֹךְ Ex 27^{21}+, etc.; *Imv.* עֶרְכָה Jb 33^{5}, עִרְכוּ Je 46^{3} 50^{14}; *Inf. abs.* עָרֹךְ Is 21^{5}; *cstr.* עֲרֹךְ Ju 20^{22}+; *Pt. act.* pl. עֹרְכִים Is 65^{11}, etc.; *pass.* עָרוּךְ Je 6^{23}+, cstr. עֲרוּךְ Jo 2^{5}, etc.;—not in D;—**1. a.** *arrange in order*, seven altars Nu 23^{4}, i.e. I have built seven altars *in a row* (cf. בנה v^{1}), flax-stalks Jos 2^{6} (both JE); esp. **b.** *set* or *lay in order*, as wood Gn 22^{9} (E), 1 K 18^{33}, cf. Tophet Is 30^{33}, Lv 1^{7}; offerings Lv 1$^{8.12}$ 6^{5}; lamp(s) Ex 27^{21} Lv 24$^{3.4}$ (all P), lamp (fig. of dynasty) ψ 132^{17}; 'shew'-bread Ex 40$^{4.23}$ (upon [עַל] sacred שֻׁלְחָן; both c. acc. cogn.), Lv 24^{8} (P). **c.** in common life (cf. RS[Sem i. 183 f., 2nd ed. 200 f.]), *arrange* a table (i.e. dishes in order upon it), שֻׁלְחָן Is 21^{5} Pr 9^{2} (fig. of wisdom), Ez 23^{41} (of Jerus. in fig.); ψ 23^{5} 78^{19} (fig.; subj. God); in idolatr. worship Is 65^{11}. **d.** *arrange* a battle, i.e. draw up in battle order, ע׳ מִלְחָמָה Ju 20^{22} 1 S 17^{8} 2 S 10^{8} = 1 Ch 19^{9}, 1 Ch 12^{37} (van d. H. v^{36}), 2 Ch 14^{9}, עֹרְכֵי מִלְחָמָה 1 Ch 12$^{34.36}$ (van d. H. v$^{33.35}$); עֲרוּךְ מ׳ Jo 2^{5}; + אֵת *with*, i.e. *against* Ju 20^{20} Gn 14^{8}, עִם 2 Ch 13^{3}; + לִקְרַאת 1 S 17^{2} 1 Ch 19$^{17 b}$; ע׳ מַעֲרָכָה לִקְרַאת 1 S 17^{21}; עָרוּךְ כְּאִישׁ לַמִּלְחָמָה Je 6^{23} 50^{42}; obj. om. Ju 20$^{22.33}$, + לִקְרַאת 1 S 4^{2} 2 S 10$^{9.10}$ = 1 Ch 19$^{10.11}$, 2 S 10^{17}; + אֶל *against* Ju 20^{30} Je 50^{14} 1 Ch 19$^{17 a}$, לְ *against* Je 50^{9};—Jb 6^{4} read יַעַבְרוּנִי Di Bu Du. **e.** *arrange* weapons of army *in order* for battle Je 46^{3}, 1 Ch 12^{9} (van d. H. v^{8}). **f.** *arrange* words (מִלִּין) Jb 32^{14} (+ אֶל *against*), so (obj. om.) 33^{5} (+ לְפָנַי), 37^{19} ψ 5^{4} (prob.; > of arranging a sacrifice); cf. *recount* things *in order*, יַעַרְכֶהָ לִי Is 44^{7}. **g.** *state in order, set forth* a legal case Jb 13^{18} 23^{4}, so prob. (obj. om.) of God ψ 50^{21} (+ לְעֵינֶיךָ), and (pass. of בְּרִית) 2 S 23^{5} (cf. Dr).—הֲיַעֲרֹךְ שׁוּעֲךָ Jb 36^{19} is difficult: Di *will he set thy cry* (שׁוּעֲךָ) *in order?* Bi (for לֹא) הֲיֵעָרֵךְ שׁ׳ לוֹ *shall thy cry be set in order unto him?* (sense good, although **Niph.** not found); v. al. in Di. **2. a.** *compare* (as result of arranging in order): מַה־דְּמוּת תַּע־לוֹ Is 40^{18} *what likeness will ye compare to him?* אֵין עֲרֹךְ אֵלֶיךָ ψ 40^{6}. **b.** intrans. *be comparable*, c. לְ, ψ 89^{7} (‖ דָּמָה), c. sf. of thing compared Jb 28$^{17.19}$.

עֵ֫רֶךְ$_{33}$ n.m. [Lv 27, 25] **order, row, estimate**;— 6187
cstr. ע׳ Ju 17^{10} Ex 40^{23}; sf. עֶרְכִּי ψ 55^{14}, עֶרְכְּךָ Lv 5^{15}+, etc.;—**1.** *order, row*, ע׳ בְּגָדִים Ju 17^{10} *a* (complete) *suit of clothes* (laid out in order), 𝔊^{B} στολὴν ἱματίων; ע׳ לֶחֶם Ex 40^{23} i.e. loaves arranged in a row, so ע׳ alone v^{4} (P); עֶרְכּוֹ Jb 41^{4} *his symmetry* (v. חִין sub חנן). **2.** *estimate, valuation*, made by ordering, classifying: אִישׁ

כְּעֶרְכּוֹ 2 K 23[35]; in 12[5] read עֶרֶךְ (for MT עוֹבֵר) *money of a man's valuation* 𝔊 Benz Kit, and prob. del. כֶּסֶף נַפְשׁוֹת עֶרְכּוֹ (כ׳ עֶרֶךְ נ׳?) Kit) as gloss (Sta ZAW v (1885), 288 f.); כְּעֶרְכִּי ψ 55[14] a man *acc. to my valuation*, fig. for *my equal;* elsewhere P, of priest's valuation of trespass-offering Lv 5[15.18.25], vows, and redemption-money 27[2.3.3.4] + 17 t. 27 (כֶּסֶף עֶרְכְּךָ v[15.19], מִכְסַת הָעֶרְכְּךָ v[23] [del. הָ], cf. v[23b] [del. *id.*]), Nu 18[16].—Jb 28[13] read דַּרְכָּהּ 𝔊 Di al.

6186 †[עָרַךְ] **vb. denom. Hiph.** value (for taxation), tax (from עֵרֶךְ **2**);—*Pf.* 3 ms. הֶעֱרִיךְ אֶת־הָאָרֶץ 2 K 23[35]; in P, וְהֶע׳ consec., c. acc. pers. Lv 27[8.12] c. sf. v[14]; *Impf.* יַעֲרִיךְ v[14]; sf. יַעֲרִיכֶנּוּ v[8].

4633 †[מַעֲרָךְ] **n.[m.]** arrangement;—pl. cstr. מַעַרְכֵי־לֵב Pr 16[1] to man belong *arrangements* (plans) *of the mind* (cf. לֵב **3**).

4634 †מַעֲרָכָה **n.f.** row, rank, battle-line;—**1. a.** מ׳ *battle-line* 1 S 4[2.12.16.16]; וַיָּרָץ הַמּ׳ 17[22] *and he ran to the battle-line*, so v[28] (on ref. here to Isr.'s line cf. HPS), עֹרְכֵי מ׳ v[21]; מ׳ לִקְרַאת מ׳ 1 Ch 12[39] (van d. H. v[38]); nearly = battle הַחַיִל הַיֹּצֵא אֶל־הַמּ׳ 1 S 17[20]. **b.** pl. *ranks* = army; cstr. מַעַרְכוֹת יִשׂ׳ 1 S 17[10.45], מַעַרְכֹת יִשׂ׳ v[8]; מ׳ אֱלֹהִים חַיִּים v[26.36]; מ׳ פְּלִשְׁתִּים 23[3] and 17[23] Qr,
4630 so 𝔊[A] (v. om. B) 𝔙 𝔗; sg. 𝔊L 𝔖 (> Kt מערות). **2.** נֵרוֹת הַמַּעֲרָכָה Ex 39[37] *lamps of the row*, i.e. arranged in a row.

4635 †מַעֲרֶכֶת **n.f.** row, line;—only of the rows of 'shew'-bread; abs. מ׳ Lv 24[7], מַעֲרֶכֶת v[6] (P); elsewh. Chr: לֶחֶם הַמּ׳ 1 Ch 9[32] 23[29] Ne 10[34], שֻׁלְחַן הַמּ׳ 2 Ch 29[18], cf. 1 Ch 28[16]; cstr. מַעֲרֶכֶת לֶחֶם 2 Ch 13[11] *the row of bread*, so מ׳ תָּמִיד 2[3] *the row of continuity*, bread continually present in rows; pl. abs. שְׁתַּיִם מַעֲרָכוֹת Lv 24[6].

ערל (√ of foll.; meaning dub.; cf. Ar. غُرْلَةٌ *foreskin;* Aram. עוּרְלְתָא, ܥܘܪܠܬܐ; NH = BH; also Egypt. *karnaθà* Brugsch ÄZ 1876, 128 Krall SB der Wiener Ak., hist.-phil. Cl. cxvi (1888), 659 f.).

6190 עָרְלָה 16 **n.f.** foreskin;—ע׳ Gn 34[14] Je 9[24]; cstr. עָרְלַת Ex 4[25] Dt 10[16], etc.; pl. הָעֲרָלוֹת (not עֲ) Jos 5[3] (Kö ii. 1, 158); cstr. עָרְלוֹת Je 4[4] + 2 t.; עָרְלֹתֵיהֶם 1 S 18[27];—*foreskin* 1 S 18[25.27] 2 S 3[14], cf. גִּבְעַת הָעֲרָלוֹת Jos 5[3] *hill of the foreskins*, near Gilgal; of circumcision, כרת ע׳ Ex 4[25] (J), בְּשַׂר ע׳ Gn 17[11] + 5 t. P (v. II. מול), אִישׁ אֲשֶׁר לוֹ ע׳ Gn 34[14] (P), i.e. one uncircumcised; cf. Je 9[24]; fig. of fruit trees, עָרְלָתוֹ Lv 19[23] (P; v. [עָרַל]); fig. of heart, ע׳ לבב Dt 10[16] Je 4[4].

†[עָרַל] **vb. denom.** count as foreskin, 6188
i.e. as uncircumcised;—**Qal** *Pf.* 2 mpl., c. acc. cogn. וַעֲרַלְתֶּם עָרְלָתוֹ Lv 19[23] *ye shall regard* its fruit *as uncircumcised*, and not eat it (for three years) (> SS *remove its foreskin* (its fruit), as 𝔙, cf. 𝔊 περικαθαριεῖτε τὴν ἀκαθαρσίαν αὐτοῦ). **Niph.** *Imv.* הֵעָרֵל Hb 2[16] *be counted uncircumcised*, i.e. be object of mockery; but dub., read probably הֵרָעֵל *reel* (𝔊 𝔖 We Now Buhl Lex).

†עָרֵל 35 **adj.** having foreskin, i.e. uncir- 6189
cumcised;—ע׳ Ex 12[48] + 5 t.; cstr. עֶרֶל Ez 44[9.9]; עֲרַל Ex 6[12.30]; f. עֲרֵלָה Je 6[10]; pl. עֲרֵלִים Lv 19[23] + 20 t.; cstr. עַרְלֵי Je 9[25] + 2 t.;—*uncircumcised person* Ex 12[48] Jos 5[7] (P), Philistines Ju 14[3] 15[18] 1 S 14[6] 17[26.36] 31[4] 2 S 1[20] 1 Ch 10[4]; of other nations Is 52[1] Je 9[25]; esp. as slain Ez 28[10] 31[18] 32[19] + 9 t. 32; in v[27] rd. מֵעוֹלָם so Hi and most (v. on meaning Toy[31, 18]); עָרֵל זָכָר *uncircumcised male* Gn 17[14] (P); ע׳ בָּשָׂר Ez 44[7.9] *uncircumcised of flesh;* fig. of fruit trees Lv 19[23] (cf. [עָרַל] supr.); ע׳ שְׂפָתַיִם fig. of incapacity to speak Ex 6[12.30]; of character, ע׳ לב Je 9[25] Ez 44[7.9], cf. לְבָבָם הֶעָרֵל Lv 26[41] (P), עֲרֵלָה אָזְנָם Je 6[10] *their ear is uncircumcised* (unreceptive).

עָרוֹם, עָרֹם, עֵרֹם v. II. עור. p. 735f 5903, 6174

†I. [עָרַם] **vb. Niph.** be heaped up (cf. 6192
Sab. אערמהו, pl. of [ערם] *dam*, so Ar. عَرِمٌ, cf. DHM ZMG xxx (1876), 676; VOJ i. 25 who cp. BH עֲרֵמָה, Ar. عَرَمَةٌ (which Frä[135] thinks Aram. loan-word), cf. ܥܪܡ Pa. *heap up;* > Wetzst Zeitschr. für Ethnol. 1873, 279 (Syr. Dreschtafel) who cp. عَرَمَ *strip* [whence עַרְמוֹן infr.], and thinks עֲרֵמָה = *bare heap*);—*Pf.* 3 pl. נֶעֶרְמוּ מַיִם Ex 15[8].

†עֲרֵמָה **n.f.** heap;—abs. ע׳ Ru 3[7]; cstr. 6194
עֲרֵמַת Hg 2[16] Ct 7[3]; pl. עֲרֵמוֹת abs. Ne 13[15] +, cstr. 3[34]; abs. עֲרֵמִים Je 50[26];—*heap* of rubbish (עָפָר) Ne 3[34]; ע׳ = ruin-heap Je 50[26]; = grain-heap (of threshed grain, عَرَمَةٌ unthreshed, acc. to Wetzst l.c.), Hg 2[16] Ne 13[15] Ru 3[7]; ע׳ חִטִּים Ct 7[3]; of grain and fruit 2 Ch 31[6.6.7.8.9].

II. **ערם** (√ of foll.; cf. Ar. عَرَمَ *strip* flesh from bone (to eat it), *strip* leaves from trees (said of camels); عُرَامٌ *bark* of tree (stripped off)).

†עַרְמוֹן **n.[m.]** plane-tree (as *stripped* of 6196
bark);—ע׳ Gn 30[37] (J); pl. עַרְמֹנִים Ez 31[8].

4000 מַעֲרַמֵּיהֶם 2 Ch 28^{15} v. sub II. עור. p. 736

6191 †[עָרַם] Lag[BN 31]] **vb. be shrewd, crafty** (NH *id.*, Hiph.; Ar. عَرَمَ, عَرِمَ, عَرُمَ *be ill-natured, cross;* 𝔗 adj. עָרִים *shrewd*, Syr. ܥܪܝܡ *id.*, and vb. in der. spec. (Pe. in Lexx.));—**Qal** *Inf. abs.* in עָרֹם יַעְרִם 1 S 23^{22} *he is exceedingly crafty.* **Hiph.** *Impf. be crafty*, 3 ms. יַעְרִם 1 S 23^{22}; *be* or *become shrewd* יַעְרִם Pr 15^{5} 19^{25}; all these **Qal** Impf. in ◌ַ acc. to Ba[ZMG xliii (1889), 180] so Ges[§ 63 n] Buhl[Lex], but perh. rd. יֶעְרַם as **Qal**; true **Hiph.** in 3 mpl. יַעֲרִימוּ סוֹד ψ 83^{4} *they make crafty* (their) *counsel* against thy people.

6193 †[עֹרֶם] **n.[m.] craftiness**;—sf. בְּעָרְמָם Jb 5^{13} (possibly from עָרְמָה Ges[§ 91 e] al.).

6195 †עָרְמָה **n.f. craftiness, prudence**;—**1.** בְּע׳ *craftily* Ex 21^{14} (E), Jos 9^{4} (JE). **2.** ע׳ in Pr, in good sense, *prudence* Pr 1^{4} $8^{5.12}$.

6175 †עָרוּם **adj. crafty, shrewd, sensible**;—**1.** *crafty*, ע׳ as pred., of serpent Gn 3^{1}; pl. as subst. מַחְשְׁבוֹת עֲרוּמִים Jb 5^{12}, לְשׁוֹן ע׳ 15^{5}. **2.** in Pr, in good sense (opp. פֶּתִי, כְּסִיל, אֱוִיל); as attrib. אָדָם עָרוּם Pr 12^{23} *a shrewd* or *sensible man;* ע׳ as subst. = *id.*, v^{16} 13^{16}, so חָכְמַת ע׳ v^{8}; = *prudent man* 14^{15} 22^{3} 27^{12}; pl. עֲרוּמִים 14^{18}.

6197-98 עֵרָן, עֵרָנִי v. sub I. עור. p. 735

ערס (√ of foll.).

6182 †[עֲרִיסָה] **n.f.** meaning dub., usu. **coarse meal**; 𝔊 AV RV **dough**, so Toy (with ?) (NH עַרְסָן *barley-meal;* Syr. ܥܪܣܢܐ (in Lexx) *hulled barley*, or (cf. Lag[GGN 1889, 301 f.]) *wheat*); > Sm[Ez] Co[Ez] **kneading-trough** (so NH עֲרֵיסָה Jastr; appar. secondary, עֲרִיסָה also [*bed*], *cradle*, v. ערש);—only רֵאשִׁית עֲרִסֹתֵיכֶם Ez 44^{30}, ר׳ עֲרִיסֹתֵינוּ Ne 10^{38}; ר׳ עֲרִסֹתֵיכֶם Nu $15^{20.21}$ (P).

6176-77, 6199 עֲרוֹעֵר, עֲרֹעֵר, עֲרֹעֵר, עַרְעָר, עַרְעָר v. II. ערר. p. 792

I. ערף (√ of foll.; meaning dub.; NH עוֹרֶף = BH; Ar. عُرْفٌ *mane* of horse, also part of *neck* where hair grows, etc.).

6203 †עֹרֶף **n.m.**[Dt 31, 27] **back of neck, neck**;—ע׳ abs. Jos 7^{12}+; cstr. Gn 49^{8}+; sf. עָרְפִּי Jb 16^{12}, עָרְפְּךָ Dt 31^{27}, etc.;—**1.** *back of neck* of fleeing foe יָדְךָ בְּע׳ וגו׳ Gn 49^{8} (poem in J), cf. וְאָחַז בְּעָרְפִּי Jb 16^{12} (fig.); Ex 23^{27} (E), ψ 18^{41} = 2 S 22^{41}; *turn* (פָּנָה, הָפַךְ) *one's back before* (לִפְנֵי) a foe Jos $7^{8.12}$ (JE), abs. Je 48^{39}; fig. of apostasy פָּנָה ע׳ אֶל Je 2^{27} 32^{33} (opp. פָּנָה פָנִים) abs. וַיִּתְּנוּ ע׳ 2 Ch 29^{6}; of י׳'s disfavour ע׳ וְלֹא פָנִים אֶרְאֵם Je 18^{17} *with the back and not the face will I look at them.* **2.** fig. in קְשֵׁה־ע׳ *stiff of neck*, i.e. *obstinate*, of Isr. Ex 32^{8} $33^{3.5}$ 34^{9} (all JE), Dt $9^{6.13}$; עָרְפְּךָ הַקָּשֶׁה Dt 31^{27}; with vb. הִקְשָׁה ע׳ i.e. be obstinate, intractable 10^{16} Je 7^{26} 17^{23} 19^{15} 2 K $17^{14.14}$ Ne $9^{16.17.29}$ 2 Ch 30^{8}; cf. גִּיד בַּרְזֶל ע׳ Is 48^{4} (|| קָשֶׁה אָתָּה); הִקְשָׁה ע׳ of individual 2 Ch 36^{13} Pr 29^{1}. **3.** of bird: nip its head מִמּוּל עָרְפּוֹ Lv 5^{8} (P).

†[עָרַף] **vb. denom. break the neck** of an animal;—**Qal** *Pf.* 2 ms. sf. וַעֲרַפְתּוֹ consec. Ex 13^{13} 34^{20} (JE), 3 pl. וְעָרְפוּ־שָׁם אֶת־הָעֶגְלָה consec. Dt 21^{4}; *Pt. act.* עוֹרֵף כֶּלֶב Is 66^{3}; *pass.* הָעֶגְלָה הָעֲרוּפָה Dt 21^{6}; *Impf.* 3 ms. יַעֲרֹף Ho 10^{2} fig. of breaking down altars. 6202

†עָרְפָּה **n.pr.f.** sister-in-law of Ruth, Ru $1^{4.14}$, Ορφα. 6204

†II. [עָרַף] **vb. drip, drop** (cf. Ar. غَرَفَ *lade out water with the hand* (as with ladle), cf. Ph. ערפת *portico* (whence rain *drips*) v. Hoffm[Abh. d. GGW xxxvi, May, 1889, 12 f.]; cf. also Ar. غُرْفَةٌ *upper-room;* מערף ענן Ecclus 43^{22} *the dropping of a cloud*, As. *irpu, irpitu, cloud(s)*);—**Qal** *Impf.* 3 mpl. שָׁמָיו יַעַרְפוּ־טָל Dt 33^{28} *his heavens drop dew;* fig., of speech, intrans., יַעֲרֹף כַּמָּטָר לִקְחִי 32^{2} *let my teaching drop like the rain* (|| תִּזַּל כַּטַּל אִמְרָתִי).—Cf. רָעַף. 6201

†[עָרִיף] **n.[m.] cloud**;—pl. sf. בַּעֲרִיפֶיהָ Is 5^{30} (Perles[JQ 1899, 689] prop. בְּעַד יָפְיָהּ, referring sf. to ארץ, and cp. ψ 139^{11}). 6183

†עֲרָפֶל **n.m. cloud, heavy cloud** (perh. fr. above √ + ל afform.; NH = BH; Syr. ܥܪܦܠܐ; 𝔗 עֲרָפִילָא; Mand. ארפילא Nö[M 126, 128]; on vocaliz. v. Ba[NB 160] and against him Schwally[ZAW x (1890), 178] who prop. עַרְפֶּל);—ע׳ in which God dwells Ex 20^{18} (Gi; van d. H. v^{21}), 1 K 8^{12} = 2 Ch 6^{1}; + עָנָן Dt 4^{11} (also חֹשֶׁךְ), 5^{19} ψ 97^{2}; Jb 22^{13} v. בַּעַד; ע׳ תַּחַת רַגְלָיו 2 S 22^{10} = ψ 18^{10}; as swaddling-bands of sea Jb 38^{9}; fig. of misery Is 60^{2} (|| חֹשֶׁךְ); of י׳'s judgment Je 13^{16} (|| צַלְמָוֶת), as a past day יוֹם עָנָן וַע׳ Ez 34^{12} = (of future day of י׳) Zp 1^{15} (|| יוֹם חֹשֶׁךְ וַאֲפֵלָה) = Jo 2^{2} (|| *id.*). 6205

†[עָרַץ] **vb. cause to tremble, tremble** (in terror, or awe) (cf. Ar. عَرَصَ *quiver, flicker;* Syr. ܥܪܨ *come upon suddenly* or *violently*, PS s.v. *passim;* cf. Egypt. *'u-ra-dau(t), they terrified* (= ערצו) WMM[As. u. Eur. 76]);—**Qal** *Impf.* 2 ms. 6206

תַּעֲרֹץ Dt 7[21]+; 2 fs. תַּעֲרֹצִי Is 47[12]; 1 s. אֶעֱרוֹץ
Jb 31[34], etc.; *Inf. cstr.* עֲרֹץ Is 2[19]+;—**1.** *cause
to tremble* (i.e. strike with awe) c. acc. הָאָרֶץ
Is 2[19.21] (subj. 'י; ins. prob. also v[10]); הֶעָלֶה נִדָּף
'תַּע Jb 13[25] *wilt thou strike with awe the driven
leaf?* abs. *cause trembling = inspire awe* Is 47[12]
(of Bab.), ψ 10[18]. **2.** intrans. *tremble, feel
dread* (D), Dt 1[29] 7[21] 20[3] 31[6] Jos 1[9]; c. acc. Jb
31[34] because *I stood in awe of* the great multitude. **Niph.** *Pt.* אֵל נַעֲרָץ ψ 89[8] *El, terrible*
in the company of the holy ones (‖נוֹרָא).
Hiph. 1. *regard*, or *treat, with awe, as awful:*
2 mpl. וְלֹא תַעֲרִיצוּ Is 8[12] (acc. מוֹרָאוֹ); 3 mpl.
יַעֲרִיצוּ 29[23] acc. 'אֶת־אֱלֹהֵי יִשׂ. **2.** *inspire with
awe* (cf. **Qal 2**);—*Pt.* sf. הוּא מַעֲרִצְכֶם Is 8[13] *he*
shall be *your awe-inspirer.*

6178 †[עָרוּץ] **adj.** **dreadful** (prop. Pt. pass.)
cstr. בַּעֲרוּץ נְחָלִים Jb 30[6] *in the* (most) *dreadful
of ravines.*

6184 †עָרִיץ **adj. awe-inspiring, terror-strik-
ing**;—'ע of 'י, כְּגִבּוֹר עָרִיץ Je 20[11]; pl. as subst.
עָרִיצִים, in bad sense of formidable adversaries,
personal, Je 15[21] (‖רָעִים), Jb 6[23] (‖צָר), and
national, ψ 54[5] (‖זָרִים), = 'עֲדַת ע 86[14] (‖זֵדִים),
'הֲמוֹן ע Is 29[5] (‖זָרַיִךְ); esp. of Chaldeans Is 13[11],
cstr. עָרִיצֵי גוֹיִם *most terrifying of the nations*
Ez 28[7] (‖זָרִים) 30[11] 31[12] (‖זָרִים), 32[12]; so (prob.)
sg. עָרִיץ Is 49[25] (rd. 'ע also for צַדִּיק v[24], so Lo
Ew Che Gr al.); without specif. ref. גּוֹיִם עָרִיצִים
Is 25[3] *awe-inspiring nations* (Du Che take 'ע
as subst.), 'רוּחַ ע v[4] (del. as gloss Di al.), 'זְמִיר ע
v[5] (del. verse as gloss Du Che); late, of wicked
in gen., as *ruthless* 'רָאִיתִי רָשָׁע ע ψ 37[35] *I have
seen a wicked man ruthless;* as subst., Is 29[20]
(‖לֵץ), Jb 15[20] (‖רשע), pl. 27[13] (‖*id.*), Pr 11[16];
rd. also עָרִיצ(ים) Is 11[4] (for MT אֶרֶץ), so Che
Br[MP] Du Gr al. (‖רָשָׁע).

4637 †מַעֲרָצָה **n.f. awful shock, crash**;—Is
10[33], of 'י's lopping off (tree-)crown (fig.).

6207 †[עָרַק] **vb. gnaw** (Ar. عَرَقَ *id.;* Syr. ܥܪܩ
Pa.);—**Qal** *Pt.* pl. הָעֹרְקִים צִיָּה Jb 30[3] *they who
gnaw the dry* (ground; fig. of scanty subsist-
ence); sf. עֹרְקַי v[17] *my gnawing* (pains) *do not sleep.*

6208 †עַרְקִי **adj. gent.** **Arkite**, inhabitant of city
ʿ*Arka* (As. *Arka* COT[Gloss.] Dl[Pa 282], Tel Am.
Irkat(a), Egypt. *Arkantu*, cf. As. n.gent. *Irka-
natai* COT[Gloss.], Ency. Bib.[i. 310]);—only 'הָע as
n.coll. Gn 10[17], τὸν Ἀρουκαῖον, = 1 Ch 1[15], A *id.*,
𝔊L τὸν Αρακει: mod. ʿ*Arḳa*, near Mediterranean,
c. 60 miles N. of Beirut (cf. Ency. Bib.[l. c.]).

I. ערר (√of foll.; on this [and not עור]
v. Nö[ZMG xxxii (1878). 404] Lag[Symm. ii. 91 f.]; cf. Palm.
מערתא *sepulchre*).

מְעָרָה **n.f. cave**;—abs. 'מ Gn 19[30]+; cstr. 4631
מְעָרַת 23[19]+; pl. מְעָרוֹת Ju 6[2]+, cstr. *id.* Is
2[19];—*cave*, esp. as place of sojourn or refuge
Gn 19[30] (J), 1 S 24[3.3.7.8.10] (Ginsb; v[4.8.9.11] van d.H.
Baer), 1 K 19[1.13], Ez 33[27] Jos 10[16] (מ' בַּמַּקֵּדָה)+
7 t. Jos 10, Ju 6[2] 1 S 13[6] 1 K 18[4.13], cf. ψ 57[1]
142[1]; מְעָרוֹת צֻרִים Is 2[19], hence מ' פָּרִצִים Je 7[11]
robbers' cave; Is 32[14] *den* (of wild beasts);—
מ' עֲדֻלָּם 1 S 22[1] 2 S 23[13], whence in ‖ 1 Ch 11[15],
rd. prob. 'מְצֻדַת ע or מְצָדָה We, cf. Dr, Bu Kit
HPS;—as burial place, מ' הַמַּכְפֵּלָה Gn 23[9]+
(v. מַכְפֵּלָה) = 'מ alone 23[11.17.20] 49[29.32] (all P).
מ' אֲשֶׁר לַצִּידֹנִים Jos 13[4] (D), cave-region in 4632
Lebanon E. of Sidon, mod. *Mughâr Ğezzîn*,
acc. to most, but dub.; perhaps, rather, near
Tyre Buhl[MDPV 1895, 55].

†II. [עָרַר] **vb. strip oneself** (‖ form of 6209
ערה, II. עור);—**Qal** *Imv.* עֹרָה Is 32[11] (‖פְּשֹׁטָה;
acc. to Ges[§ 110 k] Hi De al. ms. with fpl. subj.;
acc. to Ew[§ 226 a] Du Di al. fpl., shortened from
ערנה etc.). **Pōʿ.** *Pf.* 3 pl. עֹרְרוּ אַרְמְנוֹתֶיהָ Is
23[13] *they have laid bare* (the foundations of)
her palaces, i.e. destroyed them; so **Pilp.** *Inf.
abs.* + **Hithpalp.** *Impf.* 3 fs. עַרְעֵר תִּתְעַרְעַר Je
51[58] *be laid utterly bare*, cf. ערה **Pi. 1.**

†עֲרִירִי **adj. stripped**, specif. **childless**;— 6185
'ע Gn 15[2] (JE), Je 22[30]; pl. עֲרִירִים Lv 20[20.21] (H).

†עַרְעָר **adj. stripped, destitute**;—'הָע as 6199
subst. ψ 102[18] *the prayer of the destitute.*—Je
17[6] v. עֲרוֹעֵר. below 6176

†I. עֲרוֹעֵר **n.[m.]** prob. a tree or bush; 6176
juniper? (Ar. عَرْعَرٌ *juniper* (or *cypress*? v. Lane),
so Tristr[NHB 358] Rob[BR ii. 124]; on format. v. Lag
[BN 162] Ba[NB 160]);—עֲרוֹעֵר בַּמִּדְבָּר Je 48[6], +17[6],
where rd. prob. עֲרֹעֵר בָּעֲרָבָה (for MT עַרְעָר;
>Gf al. conversely, rd. עַרְעָר 48[6]).

†II. עֲרֹעֵר, עֲרוֹעֵר, עֲרֹעֵר **n.pr.loc.** 6177
Αροηρ, MI[26] ערער;—**1.** city on N. bank of Arnon,
S. limit of E. Jordan Isr., עֲרֹעֵר Nu 32[34] (JE),
Dt 2[36] 3[12] 4[48] Jos 12[2] (D) 2 K 10[33] 1 Ch 5[8]; עֲרוֹעֵר
Jos 13[9] (D), v[16] (P), 2 S 24[5]; Moabitish Je 48[19]
(cf. MI[26]); once עַרְעוֹר Ju 11[26]; mod. ʿ*Arʿâir* Buhl

Geogr. 269, Tristr Moab 129 ff. **2.** city near Rabbah in Ammon, עֲרֹעֵר Ju 11^{33}, עֲרוֹ׳ Jos 13^{25} (P), site unknown. **3.** city in S. Judah, עֲרֹעֵר 1 S 30^{28} (𝔊 Αροηρ + Αμμαδει, latter orig. acc. to We, indicating form ערערה; 𝔊L Ραγουηλ); + Jos
5735 15^{22} rdg. ע׳ (or עַרְעָרָה) for MT עַדְעָדָה, 𝔊B Αρουηλ, We 1 S 30, 28 (cf. Dr HPS), Di ad loc. Benn Steuern; poss. *'Ar'âra* c. 9 miles S. of E. from Beersheba, but cf. Buhl Geogr. 183.—Is 17^{2} rd. עָרֶיהָ עֲדֵי עַד 𝔊 Lo Lag Sem. i. 30 Che Buhl Lex al. (for MT עָרֵי עֲרֹעֵר). —Vid. also Che Ency. Bib. 317.

6200 †עֲרֹעֵרִי† **adj. gent.** of foreg.; הָע׳ 1 Ch 11^{44}.

ערשׂ (√ of foll.; cf. Ar. عَرْش *booth, shed, throne*, عَرِيش *grape-trellis*, woman's (camel-) *saddle*; Eth. **ዐረሽ:** *booth* (? also **ዐራት:** *bed*); As. *iršu, bed, couch*; NH עֲרִיסָה *cradle*, 𝔗 עַרְסָא, Syr. ܥܪܣܐ, Palm. ערשא; the common idea is appar. that of a *wooden structure, frame*, cf. Nö ZMG xl (1886), 737).

6210 †עֶרֶשׂ† **n.f.** Jb 7, 13 **couch, divan**;—cstr. ע׳ Dt 3^{11} +; abs. עָרֶשׂ Am 3^{12}; sf. עַרְשִׂי Jb 7^{13} +, etc.; pl. sf. עַרְשׂוֹתָם Am 6^{4};—*couch, divan*, Am 3^{12} 6^{4} (‖מִטּוֹת), + 2 S 17^{28} (rd. עַרְשׂת מִשְׁכָּב Klo Ne Marg. 18 HPS, cf. 𝔊); for lying at night Jb 7^{13} ψ 6^{7} (‖מִטָּה), Pr 7^{16}, עֶרֶשׂ יְצוּעָי ψ 132^{3} *the couch of* (consisting in) *my bed*; couch of sickness ψ 41^{4}; marriage couch Ct 1^{16}; perhaps transf. to sarcophagus, as last couch עַרְשׂוֹ עֶרֶשׂ בַּרְזֶל Dt 3^{11} (v. Dr).

ערשׁ (√ of foll.; meaning unknown).

3298 †יַעֲרֶשְׁיָה† **n. pr. m.** Benjamite 1 Ch 8^{27}, Ιασαραια, A Ιαρασια, 𝔊L Ιερσια.

עשׂב (√ of foll.; mng. dub.; cf. As. *ešêbu* [*bear fruit*], II. 1, causat. (Dl Pr 87), *išbu*, perh. = H; Ar. عَشِبَ is *be dry*, but عُشْب *fresh, juicy herbage*; NH = BH, cf. 𝔗 עִסְבָּא, Syr. ܥܣܒܐ, Palm. עשביא).

6212 †עֵשֶׂב† **n.m.** Gn 1, 11 **herb, herbage**;—ע׳ abs. Dt 11^{15} +; cstr. Gn 2^{5} +; sf. עֶשְׂבָּם Is 42^{15}; pl. cstr. עִשְּׂבוֹת (d.f. dirim.) Pr 27^{25};—*herb, herbage*, in oldest use oft. gen. (therefore incl. grass [דֶּשֶׁא]): ע׳ הַשָּׂדֶה Ex 9^{22} (E), Gn 2^{5} (+ שִׂיחַ) Ex 9^{25} (+ עֵץ), 10^{15} (+ *id*; all J) Am 7^{2}, so ע׳ הָאָרֶץ Ex 10^{12} (E), + פְּרִי הָעֵץ v^{15} (J), whence ψ 105^{35}; appar. gen. also in ע׳ הארץ Jb 5^{25} ψ 72^{16}, ע׳ alone 92^{8}; ע׳ כָּל־הַשָּׂדֶה Je 12^{14}, ע׳ alone Dt 32^{2} (‖דֶּשֶׁא), Is 42^{15} ψ 102$^{5.12}$, and Dt 29^{22} Mi 5^{6} Pr 19^{12}; hence ע׳ as food for cattle Dt 11^{15} ψ 106^{20} cf. Je 14^{6} Zc 10^{1}; עִשְּׂבוֹת הָרִים Pr 27^{25} (‖דֶּשֶׁא, חָצִיר); but as human food (hence excluding חָצִיר) ע׳ הַשָּׂדֶה Gn 3^{18} (J); esp. P Gn 1^{29} (+ עֵץ), יֶרֶק ע׳ v^{30} 9^{3}, hence ע׳ ψ 104^{14} (‖ חָצִיר for cattle); ע׳ disting. fr. דֶּשֶׁא, עֵץ also Gn 1$^{11.12}$, ע׳ שָׂדֶה + דֶּשֶׁא חָצִיר 2 K 19^{26} + Is 37^{27}.

I. **עָשָׂה** $_{2622}$ **vb.** do, make (NH = BH; MI 23. 26 עשתי, l. 3. 9 ואעש, l. 24 Imv. עשו; OH n.pr. עשיו, מעשיהו, אלעשה; not Aram., and not certainly found in S. Sem. lang.; on Sab. v. esp. DHM SB Berl. Ak. 1886, 849);—**Qal** $_{2524}$ *Pf.* 3 ms. Gn 3^{1} +, sf. עָשָׂהוּ Ho 8^{6} +; 3 fs. עָשְׂתָה Dt 22^{21} +, וְעָשְׂת consec. Lv 25^{21}; 2 ms. עָשִׂיתָ Gn 3^{14} +, etc.; *Impf.* 3 ms. יַעֲשֶׂה Gn 18^{25} +, וַיַּעֲשֶׂה 1 K 16^{25} + 3 t., וַיַּעַשׂ Is 5^{2} +; יַעֲשֶׂה Is 64^{3}, 2 ms. תַּעֲשֶׂה 1 S 10^{8}, תַּעֲשֶׂה Gn 26^{29} Jos 7^{9}, juss. (c. אַל) תַּעַשׂ Gn 22^{12} +, תַּעֲשֶׂה 2 S 13^{12} Je 40^{16} Qr (Kt תַּעַשׂ); 1 s. אֶעֱשֶׂה Gn 2^{18} +, וָאֶעֱשֶׂה Ez 20^{14} Dn 8^{27}, וָאַעַשׂ Dt 10^{3} + 4 t. Ez; etc.; *Imv.* ms. עֲשֵׂה Ju 10^{15} +; fs. עֲשִׂי Je 6^{26} +, etc.; *Inf. abs.* עָשֹׂה 44^{17} +; עָשׂוֹ 7^{5} + 2 t. (4^{18} van d. H. עָשׂוֹ); cstr. עֲשׂוֹת Gn 2^{4} +, עֲשֹׂה 50^{20} + 2 t., עֲשׂוֹ 31^{28}, sf. עֲשׂתוֹ 41^{32} +, עֲשֹׂהוּ + Ex 18^{18}, etc.; *Pt. act.* עֹשֶׂה Is 5^{5} +, sf. הָעֹשׂוֹ Jb 40^{19} (but v. infr.); pl. עֹשִׂים Gn 24^{49} +; sf. עֹשָׂי Jb 35^{10} (yet v. Ges §124 k), etc.; *pass.* עָשׂוּי Ex 3^{16} +, הֶעָשׂוּ Jb 41^{25} (Ges §75 k); f. עֲשׂוּיָה Ez 21^{20} +, etc.;—**I. 1.** *do* (1560 + t.): **a.** (1) c. acc. act. Gn 3^{14} (J) 20^{10} (E) + oft.; *do* right in eyes of י׳ 2 K 12^{3} 14^{13} +, evil 8$^{18.27}$ + (cf. 1. עַיִן **3 c**); *do* God's commands, statutes, etc., Dt 16^{12} 30^{8}, Nu 15^{39} (P); ע׳ חַיִל 1 S 14^{48} + *do might*, i.e. mightily, valiantly; Pr 31^{29} *do efficiency*, i.e. efficiently; = commit (offence) Lv 20^{13} (H), Dt 20^{18}; sq. מִן part., וְעָשָׂה מֵאַחַת מֵהֵנָּה Lv 4^{2} *and shall do a single one of them* (things prohibited; v. מִן **3 b** (*d*)), cf. וְעָשׂוּ אַחַת מִכָּל־מִצְוֹת י׳ v$^{13.22}$ 5^{17} (all P); *do* = *perform* a work, c. acc. cogn. מַעֲשֶׂה Ex 18^{20} 23^{12} (E), also (י׳ subj.) Dt 11^{7} Dn 9^{14} Ec 3^{11}; c. acc. מְלָאכָה Gn 2$^{2.2}$ (J), Ex 20$^{9.10}$ = Dt 9^{13} (10 Words); c. acc. דְּרָכֶיךָ + Is 58^{13}; ע׳ מְלוּכָה עַל 1 K 21^{7} = *exercise sovereignty over*; of י׳ performing signs (אֹתֹת) Jos 24^{17} (E), Nu 14$^{11.22}$ (JE), Dt 11^{3}, so Moses Ex 4^{17} and (מֹפְתִים) v^{21}. (2) *do* something to one (לְ pers.) Gn 20^{9} (E), Ju 9^{56} +; c. עַל reflex. Je 26^{19} *do evil against ourselves*; esp. י׳ subj., c. לְ, *do* good to Ex 18^{9} (E), 2 K 8^{66}, or evil Gn 42^{28} (E); in phr. *so may God do to me*, etc. 1 S 3^{17} 2 K 6^{31} + (v. יסף **Hiph. 1**). (3) *do* something for one (לְ pers.) Gn 30^{31} 1 K 11^{8} +, dir. obj. om. 1 S 20^{4}; + לְ rei Ju 21$^{7.16}$ *what shall* *we do for them, for wives?* c. עַל pers. Ne 5[19]; c. dat. eth. (ל) 1 S 10[7]; c. לְ, of י׳ doing kindness for 1 S 22[3]; executing vengeance for Ju 11[36] (+ מִן of enemy); י׳ doing a sign (אות) for †Ju 6[17] (elsewhere נָתַן אוֹת לְ), cf. עֲשֵׂה־עִמִּי אוֹת לְטוֹבָה ψ 86[17]. (4) do something (in relation or intercourse) with (אֶת pers.), י׳ subj. Dt 1[30] *all that he did with you,* 10[21] (cf. ψ 86[17] supr.), human subj. 2 Ch 24[24] (obj. שְׁפָטִים), Ru 2[11]. (5) seldom c. ב, usu. of executing judgment upon 1 S 28[18] Is 48[14], more gen. Est 1[15] *what shall we do with the queen?* also, subj. י׳, Ez 25[11] 28[26] ψ 149[7.9] Nu 33[4] (on false gods); in good sense, ע׳ חֲסָדִים בְּ׳ Ne 13[14]. (6) of י׳ *doing* the justice (מִשְׁפָּט) of any one, i.e. maintaining his cause 1 K 8[45.49] ψ 9[5]. (7) c. adv. *do thus,* כֹּה, Jos 6[14] (JE), *acc. to,* כְּ, Gn 6[22] (P), 18[21] (J), 1 K 2[6]; *acc. as,* כַּאֲשֶׁר Gn 27[19] (J); Ex 1[17] (E) +; c. בְּ of manner, Ju 9[16 a], Ez 8[18] 25[15]. **b.** *work* for (ל rei) Gn 30[30] (J); c. ל pers. 1 S 14[6] Ez 29[20] (for י׳); *work* in (ב) gold or other material 1 K 7[14] 2 Ch 2[6.13] Ex 31[4.5] 35[32] (all P); c. בָּהּ (i.e. בָּעֲבֹדָה) Ex 5[9] (J) *in toil; work* with (עִם) God 1 S 14[45], so prob. of God's working with (אֶת) Moses and Aaron 1 S 12[6] (usu. *appoint*); c. אֶת *with* (of pers. in whose company, in whose field) Ru 2[19.19] (gleaning); work בְּחֵפֶץ כַּפֶּיהָ Pr 31[13]; without prep. Ex 36[1] Ne 3[28]. **2.** *deal* with, c. עִם, 2 Ch 2[2] Dn 1[13] (כַּאֲשֶׁר *acc. as*); c. אֶת, Ez 20[44] ψ 109[21]; Ez 22[14] Zp 3[19] (perh.; Gr Now ins. כָּלָה, v. **II 1 g**), + בְּ Je 21[2], + בְּ of manner Ez 23[25.29]; c. לְ pers. + בְּ 25[12]; c. בְּ pers., Je 18[23] Dn 11[7], + כְּ *acc. to* Ne 9[24] Est 3[11]. **3.** oft. in phr., *do* kindness (חֶסֶד) with: c. עִם (עִמָּדִי) Gn 19[19] 24[12.14] (J), Ju 1[24] 8[35] 1 S 15[6] 2 S 2[5] 10[2] = 1 Ch 19[2] +; c. עַל, 1 S 20[8] (but rd. עִם Vrss We Dr al.); abs., ψ 109[16]; obj. אֱמֶת + חֶסֶד, c. עִם, Jos 2[14] (JE) Ju 9[19] 2 S 2[6]; c. אֶת *with,* Gn 24[49] 32[11] 47[29] (all J); c. לְ, Ex 20[6] = Dt 5[10], 2 S 22[51] = ψ 18[51]; so ע׳ טוֹב, c. עִם, Gn 26[29] (J), cf. Ju 8[35] 9[16]; c. אֶת *with,* 1 S 24[19] 2 S 2[6]. **4.** abs. *act, act with effect,* esp. of י׳, 1 K 8[32.39] Je 14[7] Ez 20[9.14.22] ψ 22[32] 37[5] 52[11] Dn 9[19]; of men 2 Ch 31[21] Dn 8[12.24] 11[28.30.32]; c. ל pers. Ez 31[11].

II. 1. *make* (670 + t.): **a.** c. obj. concr., ark Gn 8[6], altar 13[4], idols Ju 18[24.31] +, etc. **b.** oft. of God's making (creating) Gn 3[1] (J), 1[7.16.25] (P), Ne 9[6] Jb 9[9] Pr 8[26] 2 Ch 2[11] ψ 95[5] +; making man ψ 100[3] 119[73] (made by God's hands), in the womb Jb 31[15.15]; making, constituting, nation Dt 26[19] 32[6.15]; pt. sf. עֹשֵׂהוּ *his Maker* Is 17[7] Pr 14[31] 17[5] (הָעֹשׂוֹ Jb 40[19] is improb., most rd. הֶעָשׂוּי, with various interpr. of foll. words); עֹשֵׂךְ Is 51[13], עֹשֵׂנִי Jb 32[23] (Ginsb; v[22] van d. H. Baer), עֹשֵׂנוּ ψ 95[6]; so appar. pt. pl. עֹשָׂי Jb 35[10], עֹשַׂיִךְ Is 54[5] (Ges [§ 124 k] expl. as sg.). **c.** *make* something, c. לְ reflex., *make for thee* Ex 20[4] Dt 9[12] 10[1] +, for (ל) another 1 S 2[19] 2 S 7[11] 1 K 2[24] +; obj. מִשְׁתֶּה *banquet* Gn 40[20] Est 5[4], also (no ל) Gn 29[22] (E) Ju 14[10] Est 5[5.12] and (fig., י׳ subj.) Is 25[6]; c. ל rei, Dt 22[8]; c. ל of animal Gn 33[17] (J). **d.** *make* a name (שֵׁם) for oneself (ל) 2 S 7[9] 1 Ch 17[8], also (no ל) 2 S 8[13]; a new heart for oneself (ל) Ez 18[31]. **e.** *make* war with (אֶת) Gn 14[2] Jos 11[18] (D); c. עִם, Dt 20[12.20] 1 Ch 5[10.19]; abs. 1 Ch 22[8]; c. ל reflex. Pr 24[6]; pt. עֹשֵׂה מִלְחָמָה 2 Ch 11[1] 26[11.13]; *make* peace, c. ל pers. Jos 9[15] (J); ע׳ אִתִּי בְרָכָה 2 K 18[31] *make an agreement with me.* **f.** c. ב, ע׳ פֶּרֶץ בְּ׳ Ju 21[15] י׳ *brought a catastrophe upon* (cf. פרץ). **g.** c. 2 acc., *make* something out of (acc. mater.) Ex 25[18] 28[13] 37[17.24] Ct 3[10] Dt 10[3] +; *make* something into something (Ges [§ 117 ii]) Ho 8[4] Gn 27[9] Ju 17[4] Nu 11[8] 17[3] ψ 104[4]; *make* something כָּלָה, i.e. utterly destroy it Na 1[8] Zp 1[18] Ez 20[17] Ne 9[31]; c. pt. pass. as 2nd acc. Ex 38[7] *they made it* נְבוּב לֻחֹת *hollow with boards,* 39[9]; but also c. acc. + לְ, Ho 2[10] gold they made into (ל) the Baal, Ju 8[27] Ex 27[3] (P), Dt 9[14] Je 37[15] Ez 4[9] Is 44[17.19]; *make* something for (ל pers.), + מִן of material Ct 3[9]. **2.** *produce, yield:* of grain, yielding meal Ho 8[7.7], vineyard, grapes Is 5[2.2.4.4.10], tree, fruit 2 K 19[30] = Is 37[31], Ho 9[16] Je 12[2] 17[8] Ez 17[23] (all fig.), Gn 1[11.12] (P); branches Jb 14[9] and (fig.) Ez 17[8]; land, fruit Lv 25[21] cf. Hb 3[17], abs. Gn 41[47]; of seed Is 5[10], vine, shoots Ez 17[6] (fig.); of cows, *yielding* milk Is 7[22]; hippop. producing fat Jb 15[27]. **3.** *prepare,* esp. of dressing and cooking food, Gn 18[7.8] Ju 6[19] 13[5] 1 S 25[18] (pass.), 2 S 12[4.4] Gn 27[14.17.31] 2 S 13[5.7] 1 K 17[12] Ex 12[39] (+ ל reflex.); a bullock for sacrifice (v. infr.) 1 K 18[23.25.26]; כְּלִי גוֹלָה Ez 12[3] (+ ל reflex.); a chamber Ne 13[7]; *prepare* to build (+ ל pers. and inf.). **4.** *make* offering, e.g. עוֹלָה Ju 13[16] Je 33[18] Lv 16[24], עוֹלָה וָזֶבַח 2 K 5[17] (+ ל dei), הַחַטָּאת Lv 14[19], אִשֶּׁה Nu 15[3.14], various offerings 1 K 8[64] Lv 9[22] Ez 45[17] 46[2] +; + לי׳ *to* י׳ Lv 17[9] +; also c. acc. of thing sacrificed (perh. orig. *prepare* or *provide,* v. supr.) Ez 43[25.25] 46[15] Lv 14[30] 15[15.30] 16[9] Nu 6[11.17] ψ 66[15] (+ ל dei) +; abs. = *offer sacrifice* Ex 10[25] (E + לי׳), to (ל) heathen gods 2 K 17[32]. **5.** *attend to, put in order:* pare (the nails) Dt 21[12]; wash (feet) 2 S 19[25]; trim (beard) v[25] (cf. Fr. *faire la barbe,* Ger. *die Haare machen*). **6.** *observe, celebrate,* religious festival, e.g. passover Ex 12^{48} Nu 9$^{4.6.13}$ Jos 5^{10}, also (+ לי׳) Ex 12^{48} Nu 9$^{10.14}$ (all P), Dt 16^{1}+; sabbath Ex 31^{16} Dt 5^{15}; feast of weeks 16^{10}, booths 16^{13}, Purim Est 9$^{21.27}$, etc. **7.** *acquire* property of various kinds (cf. 'make money') Gn 12^{5} 31^{1} (J), Is 15^{7} Je 17^{11} 48^{36} Dt 8^{18} Ez 22^{13} 28$^{4.4}$ 38^{12} 2 Ch 32^{29} Ec 2^{8}; + ל reflex. Dt 8^{17} 2 S 15^{1} 1 K 1^{5}; of fruits from vineyards, etc. ψ 107^{37}. **8.** *appoint* priests 1 K 12^{31} 13^{33} 2 Ch 2^{17} (all + מִן source), a feast 1 K 12$^{32.33}$ (+ ל pers.); *ordain* a sacrifice Nu 28^{6}, a festal day ψ 118^{24}; *institute,* אוב וְיִדְּעֹנִי *ghost and familiar spirit* 2 K 21^{6} = 2 Ch 33^{6} (cf. Dr$^{Dt 18, 11}$). **9.** *bring about,* of י׳'s effecting a deliverance Ex 14^{13} (לָכֶם), 1 S 11^{13} 2 S 23^{10} (ins. also ‖ 1 Ch 11^{13} Dr), v^{12}; *cause,* sq. cl. c. שֶׁ Ec 3^{14}. **10.** *use,* וְע׳ לִמְלַאכְתּוֹ 1 S 8^{16}; pass. Ex 38^{24} **11.** *spend, pass,* days of life Ec 6^{12}.

Niph.$_{97}$ *Pf.* 3 ms. נַעֲשָׂה Ju 16^{11}+; 3 fs. נֶעֶשְׂתָה 2 S 17^{23}+, etc.; *Impf.* 3 ms. יֵעָשֶׂה Gn 29^{26}+, 3 fs. c. ו subord. וְתֵעָשׂ Est 5^{6} 7^{2} 9^{12} (Ges$^{§ 109 f}$), etc.; *Inf. cstr.* הֵעָשׂוֹת Est 9$^{1.14}$, etc.; *Pt.* נַעֲשֶׂה Ne 5^{18}, etc.;—**1.** *be done* (pass. of **Qal I 1**): **a.** subj. מְלָאכָה Ju 16^{11} (c. ב instr.), Ne 6^{16} (c. מֵאֵת אֱלֹהִים), v^{9} Ex 12^{16} + 4 t.; subj. om. Ez 44^{14}, indef. Est 4^{1}; c. כֵּן 9^{14}; *be done,* כַּתּוֹרָה Ezr 10^{3}; *be committed,* of offence, Dt 13^{15} Nu 15^{24} Ec 4^{1} + 3 t.; c. neg. *not* (yet) *done,* i.e. future Is 46^{10}; *be accomplished, performed, fulfilled* Ez 12$^{35.38}$ Dn 11^{36} Est 5^{5} 7^{2} 9^{12}; *be executed, carried out,* of sentence Ec 8^{11}, decree Est 9^{1}; *be followed,* of counsel 2 S 17^{23}; nearly = *occur* Ec 1$^{9.9.13}$ 9$^{3.6}$, subj. מַעֲשֶׂה 1^{14} 2^{17} 4^{3} 8$^{9.17}$, subj. הֶבֶל v^{14}, עִנְיָן v^{15}. **b.** *Impf.* c. neg., *is* (*are*) *not done,* not acc. to usage, of flagrant offences Gn 20^{9} (E), 29^{26} (c. כֵּן), 34^{7} (both J), 2 S 13^{12} (כֵּן); hence (P) *not to be done,* forbidden by י׳ Lv 4$^{2.13.22.27}$ 5^{17}. **c.** *be done to,* c. ל of animal 1 S 11^{7} (כֹּה); ל pers. Ex 2^{4} (E) 21^{31} (E; כַּמִּשְׁפָּט), Is 3^{11} Je 5^{13} (כֹּה), Lv 24^{19} (H; כֵּן), Nu 15^{34} (P) + 8 t.; *be done for,* ל pers. Ju 11^{37} Est 6^{3}, עִם pers. v^{3}; ל rei Nu 15^{11} (כָּכָה). **d.** *be done* upon, against (ב) Dn 9^{12}. †**2.** (pass. of **Qal II**): **a.** *be made,* of concr. things 1 K 10^{20} = 2 Ch 9^{19} (throne), Je 3^{16} (ark), 2 K 12^{14} Ez 43^{18} Ex 25^{31} Nu 4^{36} (P); c. acc. mat. Lv 2^{7}. **b.** *be produced* from (מִן) vine Nu 6^{4}. **c.** *be prepared,* of food Ex 12^{16} Lv 6^{14} 7^{9} (all P), Ne 5$^{18.18}$. **d.** *be offered,* מִנְחָה Lv 2$^{8.11}$, kid Nu 28$^{15.24}$. **e.** *be observed,* passover 2 K 24$^{22.23}$ (ל dei) = 2 Ch 35$^{18.19}$; Purim Est 9^{28}. **f.** *be used* Lv 7^{24} (P), + ל rei 13^{51} (P) Ez 15$^{5.5}$.

†**Pu.** *Pf.* 1 s. עֻשֵּׂיתִי ψ 139^{15} *I was made.*

עֲשָׂהאֵל$_{18}$ **n.pr.m.** Ασαηλ, 𝔊L Ασσαηλ (on 6214
this and foll. cf. אֶלְעָשָׂה);—**1.** brother of Joab and Abishai 2 S 2$^{18.18}$ + 7 t. 2, + 3$^{27.30}$ 23^{24} 1 Ch 2^{16} 11^{26} 27^{7}. **2.** Levites: **a.** 2 Ch 17^{8} (Ιασειηλ, Ασιηλ). **b.** 31^{13}. **3.** post-exil. name Ezr 10^{15}.

†עֲשִׂיאֵל **n.pr.m.** Simeonite 1 Ch 4^{35}, Ασιηλ. 6221

†עֲשָׂיָה **n.pr.m.** Ασαιας, etc.; 𝔊L in Kgs. 6222
Αζαριας;—**1.** servant of Josiah 2 K 22$^{12.14}$ = 2 Ch 34^{20}. **2.** Simeonite 1 Ch 4^{36}. **3.** Levites: **a.** 6^{15} 15$^{6.11}$. **b.** 9^{5}.

†(ו)יעשׂו Kt, (ו)יַעֲשָׂי Qr, **n.pr.m.** one with 3299
foreign wife Ezr 10^{37}, 𝔊 καὶ ἐποίησαν.

†יַעֲשִׂיאֵל **n.pr.m.** **1.** hero of David 1 Ch 3300
11^{47}, (Ι)εσσιηλ. **2.** Benjamite ruler 27^{21}, Ασειηρ, 𝔊L Ιασσιηλ.

מַעֲשֶׂה$_{233}$ **n.m.**$^{Gn 20, 9}$ **deed, work**;—abs. מ׳ 4639
Gn 44^{15}+, cstr. מַעֲשֵׂה Is 5^{12}+; sf. מַעֲשֵׂהוּ Ju 13^{12}+, etc.; pl. מַעֲשִׂים Gn 20^{9}+; cstr. מַעֲשֵׂי Je 1^{16}+; sf. מַעֲשָׂיו 1 S 19^{4} (or sg., so Dr)+, etc.;—oft. acc. cogn. c. עשׂה;—**1. a.** (1) *deed, thing done* by man Nu 16^{28} (JE), 1 K 13^{11} Is 26^{12};—1 S 20^{19} is obscure; (2) implic. evil Gn 44^{15} (J), Ex 23^{24} (E), Ne 6^{14} + 8 t., + sg. coll. *doing*(*s*) Mi 6^{16} Lv 18$^{3.3}$ (H), 2 Ch 17^{4}, מ׳ יְדֵיהֶם La 3^{64} Hg 2^{14}, Jb 33^{17} (rdg. מִמַּעֲשֵׂהוּ 𝔊 Di Siegf Bu), Ez 16^{30} (*behaviour*); explic. מַעֲשֵׂינוּ הָרָעִים Ezr 9^{13} cf. Ec 4^{3} 8$^{11.14}$, מַעֲשֵׂי־אָוֶן Is 59^{6}; specif. of idolatr. practices, מ׳ יְדֵיכֶם sg. Dt 31^{29} Je 25$^{6.7}$ 32^{30}, pl. 44^{8}, cf. sg. 1 K 16^{7} 2 K 22^{17} = 2 Ch 34^{25}; (3) implic. right, praiseworthy 1 S 19^{4} 2 K 23^{19} Jon 3^{10} Pr 31^{31}; of duty in gen. הַמּ׳ אֲשֶׁר יַעֲשׂוּן Ex 18^{20} (E) = *what they are to do;* explic. Ec 4^{4} 8^{14}; (4) as basis of judgment (good or bad) Is 66^{18} ψ 33^{15} 62^{13} Ec 12^{14}, מ׳ יְדֵיהֶם Je 25^{14}. **b.** (1) *work, labour,* husbandry Ex 23^{16} (E), Gn 5^{29} (J), Ju 19^{16}, מ׳ יְדֵיכֶם Hg 2^{17}; enforced labour of Isr. in Egypt Ex 5$^{5.13}$ (J); in gen. 23^{12} (E); also of product of labour 23^{16}, cf. Is 65^{22} Ec 5^{5}; שֵׁשֶׁת יְמֵי הַמּ׳ Ez 46^{1} *the six working-days;* of religious work, מ׳ עֲבֹדַת בֵּית הָא׳ 1 Ch 23^{28}, cf. מ׳ 2 Ch 31^{21}; (2) *business, pursuit,* Gn 46^{33} 47^{3} (J), Ju 13^{12} 1 S 25^{2} Is 54^{16}; in gen., *occupation* Is 29^{15} Ec 2$^{4.11}$ 3$^{17.22}$ 8^{9} 9$^{7.10}$; (3) *undertaking, enterprise* Is 19$^{14.15}$ Dt 15^{10}; מ׳ יָדְךָ Dt 2^{7} + 5 t. Dt, 2 Ch 32^{30} Jb 1^{10} ψ 28^{4}, מ׳ יָדֵינוּ ψ 90$^{17.17}$; (4) *achievement* Je 48^{7} Est 10^{2}; (5) in weakened sense, מַעֲשֶׂיךָ Pr 16^{3} *thine affairs;* nearly = *occurrences* Ec 1^{14} (pl.), 2^{17} 8^{17} (sg.). **c.** *deed*(*s*), *work*(*s*) of י׳, esp. in deliverance and in judgment, Ju 2$^{7.10}$ Jos 24^{31} (D), ψ 33^{4} + 21 t., + מ׳ יָדָיו

etc. Is 5^{12} ψ 28^{5} 92^{5}+4 t.; מ׳ הָאֱלֹהִים in gen. Ec 7^{13} 8^{17} 11^{5} cf. 3^{11}. **2. a.** (1) *work, thing made*, by man, מ׳ אֹפֶה Gn 40^{17} (E) *baker's work;* מ׳ יְדֵי יוֹצֵר La 4^{2}; oft. of furnishings of tabern., מ׳ חֹשֵׁב Ex 26^{1}+7 t., מ׳ רֹקֵם 26^{36}+5 t., מ׳ אֹרֵג 28^{32}+2 t., מ׳ חָרָשׁ 28^{11}, cf. מ׳ יְדֵי אָמָּן Ct 7^{2}; of holy oil, etc. מ׳ רֹקֵחַ Ex 30^{25}+2 t. (ins. רֹקֵחַ perh. also 2 Ch 16^{14}); hence מ׳=*work of art* Is 3^{24} (of coiffure), cf. כְּלִי מ׳ Nu 31^{51}; sq. n. of material, pattern, etc., מ׳ עִזִּים v^{20} (i.e. goats' hair), v. also Ex 27^{4} 28^{14}+; in temple, מ׳ שְׂבָכָה 1 K 7^{17}, מ׳ שׁוּשַׁן v^{19}, etc.; מ׳ צַעֲצֻעִים 2 Ch 3^{10}, cf. מ׳ הַחֲבִתִּים 1 Ch 9^{31} *the work of* (consisting in) *bread-wafers; =materials* of (prepared for) הָעוֹלָה 2 Ch 4^{6}; in theoph. מ׳ לִבְנַת הַסַּפִּיר Ex 24^{10} (J); מ׳ of ships 2 Ch 20^{37}; in gen. Is 29^{16}; Ez 27$^{16.18}$ = *thy manufactures, wares;* מַעֲשַׂי ψ 45^{2}=*my verses* (ποίημα, *poem*); (2) *workmanship* Ez 1$^{16.16}$ (v^{16a} del. Co Toy) 1 K 7^{8} Ex 28^{8}+ 11 t.; (3) מ׳ יְדֵי אָדָם of idols (contemptuously) Dt 4^{28} 2 K 19^{18}=Is 37^{19}=2 Ch 32^{19}, ψ 115^{4} 135^{15}, cf. Is 2^{8} (מ׳ יָדָיו), Ho 14^{4} Mi 5^{12} Je 1^{16}; so (יְדֵי) מ׳ חָרָשׁ Dt 27^{15} Je 10$^{3.9}$, cf. Ho 13^{2}; מ׳ חֲכָמִים Je 10^{9}; מ׳ תַּעְתֻּעִים v^{15} 51^{18}; appar. also מַעֲשֵׂהֶם Is 41^{29} cf. 57^{12} Ez 6^{6}; מ׳ יָדָיו of altars Is 17^{8}. **b.** *work* (made by) God Ex 32^{16} (E); esp. (poet. and late), of created things, ψ 103^{22} 104^{24}+4 t. ψ; מ׳ אֶצְבְּעֹתֶיךָ 8^{4}, מ׳ יָדֶיךָ 102^{26} (both of heavens), cf. 19^{2} (heavenly bodies), 8^{7} (animals); of man Jb 14^{15} 34^{19}, cf. לָדַעַת כָּל־אַנְשֵׁי מַעֲשֵׂהוּ 37^{7} (but rd. prob. אנשים 𝔅 Ol Di al.); of a nation Is 19^{25} 60^{21} 64^{7}; of weights Pr 16^{11} (but rd. perh. הַמֶּלֶךְ for י׳ Gr Toy). **c.** *product* of olive-tree, מ׳ זַיִת Hb 3^{17}; fig. *product of righteousness* Is 32^{17}.

4640-41 †מַעֲשַׂי, -יָה, מַעֲשֵׂיָהוּ **n.pr.m.** (*work of* י׳; cf. n. pr. מעשיהו on Isr. seal, Cl-Gann, v. Lzb^{315});—Μα(α)σσαια(ς), etc., 𝔊^{B} Ezr 10^{21} Μαση λ:—**1.** priest, Je.'s time, מַעֲשֵׂיָה Je 21^{1} 29^{25} 37^{3}; perh. 35^{4} (-יָהוּ). **2.** 29^{21}. מַעֲשֵׂיָהוּ **3.** Levites: **a.** 1 Ch 15$^{18.20}$. **b.** 2 Ch 23^{1}. **4.** officials: **a.** 26^{11}. **b.** 34^{8}. **5.** son of Ahaz 28^{7}. **6.** Levite 1 Ch 6^{25} rdg. מַעֲשֵׂיָה for MT בַּעֲשֵׂיָה q.v., cf. Kit. מַעֲשֵׂיָה of various post-exil. men: **7.** Ne 3^{23} (Μαδασηλ, A Μαασιου). **8. a.** 8$^{4.7}$. **b.** 10^{26}. **c.** 11^{5}. **d.** v^{7}. **e.** 12^{41}. **f.** v^{42}. **9. a.** Ezr 10^{18}. **b.** v^{21} (Μασαηλ, Μασειας). **c.** v^{22}. **d.** v^{30}. **10.** מַעֲשַׂי (van d. H. מַעֲשַׂי) Μα(α)σαι(α), a priest 1 Ch 9^{12}.

6213 †II. [עָשָׂה] **vb. Pi.** press, squeeze (NH עָשָׂה Pi. *compel;* 𝔗 עַסִּי Pa. *crush, gnash* (teeth); cf. Ar. غَشِيَ *compress* a woman);—*Pf.* 3 pl. עִשּׂוּ דַּדֵּי בְּתוּלֵיהֶם Ez 23$^{3.8}$ (unchaste act); *Inf. cstr.* בַּעְשׂוֹת . . . דַּדַּיִךְ v^{21} rd. Pi. בְּעַשּׂוֹת (Ew Co Toy, al.).

עֵשָׂו$_{97}$ **n.pr.m.** Esau, Ησαυ;—*Esau*, elder son of Isaac Gn 25$^{25.26}$+7 t. 25, 26^{34} 27^{1}+24 t. 27, 28, 32^{4}+15 t. 32, 33, 35, Jos 24$^{4.4}$ Mal 1$^{2.3}$ 1 Ch 1^{34}; identif. with אֱדוֹם Gn 36$^{1.8.19}$, ancestor of Edomites v$^{9.43}$, cf. 1 Ch 1^{35}; dwelling in Mt. Seir Gn 36^{8} (25 t. in all, Gn 36) Dt 2^{5} Jos 24^{4}; בְּנֵי עֵשָׂו = Edomites Dt 2$^{4.8.12.22.29}$; עֵשָׂו = Edom Je 49^{8} Ob^{6}, בֵּית עֵשָׂו v$^{18.18}$, הַר עֵשָׂו v$^{8.9.19.21}$. 6215

†[עָשַׂק] **vb. Hithp.** contend (perh. orig. *cling* to (in strife), cf. Ar. عَشِقَ *cling* with love (Lag$^{BN\ 143}$); Syr. ܥܣܩ, Ethpa. *be difficult* (i.e. *indignant, hostile*); NH עָסַק, 𝔗 עֲסַק, *busy oneself*, NH עֵסֶק *business, occupation*);—*Pf.* 3 pl. הִתְעַשְּׂקוּ עִמּוֹ Gn 26^{20} *they contended with him.* 6229

†עֵשֶׂק **n.pr.font.** in SW. Pal. Gn 26^{20} (expl. as *contention*);—locality unknown, 𝔊 Ἀδικία. 6230

עשׂר (√ of foll.; appar. *gather, unite*, cf. Ar. عَشِيرٌ *kinsman*, عَشِيرَةٌ *tribe*, مَعْشَرٌ *assembly;* hence *ten = collection, union*).

עֶשֶׂר, עֲשָׂרָה$_{176}$ **n.m.** and **f.** ten (NH=BH; perh. MI^{33} עשר; Ph. עשר, עסר, עשרת, etc.; Ar. عَشْرٌ, عَشَرَةٌ; Sab. עשר SabDenkm$^{No. 11\ b, 1.5,6}$, עשרת and cpds. Hom$^{Chrest. 48}$; Eth. ዐሥሩ: ዐሠርቱ; As. *ešertu;* 𝔗 עֲסַר, עֲשַׂר; עַסְרָא, עַשְׂרָא; Syr. ܥܣܪ, ܥܣܪܐ; Nab. עשר, all = *ten;* Palm. עשרתא *the Ten* (rulers));—**m.** (c. **n.f.**) עֶשֶׂר 2 S 15^{16}+53 t. (abs. and cstr. usu. indistinguishable); עֶשֶׂר 1 K 7^{43} 1 Ch 6^{46}; **f.** (c. **n.m.**): abs. עֲשָׂרָה Gn 24^{10}+ 69 t.; cstr. (prob.) עֲשֶׂרֶת 1 S 17^{18}+46 t.; f.pl. עֲשָׂרֹת Ex 18^{21}+2 t.;—on pl. עֶשְׂרִים, 20, v. infr.;—†**1.** *a ten*, only f.pl. *tens* in phr. שָׂרֵי ע׳ *captains of tens* Ex 18$^{21.25}$ (E), Dt 1^{15}. **2.** *ten*, enumerating pers. or things, usually without other num.: **a.** עֶשֶׂר bef. n.f.pl., Gn 45^{23}+43 t.; after n. †1 K 7$^{27.43}$+late passages Jos 15^{57} 21$^{5.26}$ (all P), 1 Ch 6^{46} 2 Ch 4^{7}; bef. בָּאַמָּה = *ten cubits* †1 K 6$^{3.25.26}$ 7$^{23.24}$. **b.** עֲשָׂרָה bef. n.m.pl., Gn 45^{23} + 25 t. (incl. ע׳ אֲלָפִים = 10,000 2 S 18^{3} 2 K 24^{14} Kt, עֲשֶׂרֶת Qr); bef. n. coll. בָּקָר 1 K 5^{3}, רֶכֶב 2 K 13^{7}; also ע׳ לֶחֶם הַזֶּה 1 S 17^{17} *these ten loaves*, cf. 1 K 14^{3}; ע׳ אֶלֶף Ez 45^{1} rd. עֶשְׂרִים א׳ 𝔊 Hi Co Berthol Toy; after n.m.pl. †Gn 32$^{16.16}$ 43^{3} (all E), Jos 17^{5} (JE), Nu 29^{23} (P), 1 K 7^{43} 2 Ch 4$^{6.8}$ Dn 1$^{12.14.15}$+; after n. coll. צאן 2 Ch 30^{24}; n. om., sc. *men*, † Gn 18^{32} (J) Am 5^{3} Ezr 8^{4}; sc. *shekels* (weight) Gn 24^{22} (J) Nu 7^{14}+13 t. Nu 7 6235 6242

(ע׳ זָהָב); ע׳ כֶּסֶף (sc. *shekels*, value) 2 S 18[11]; sc. *measures* (of grain) Hg 2[16]; c. art. *the ten* Gn 18[32] (J; sc. *men*), Ne 11[1] (*id.* = *every ten*); as pred. Ex 27[12.12] = 38[12.12] (all P)†. **c.** עֲשֶׂרֶת bef. n.m.pl. Ex 34[28] + 18 t., + בַּעֲשֶׂרֶת הַיָּמִים 1 S 25[38] (on art. cf. Weir in Dr, but dub.; prob. om., so 𝔊 We Bu), + ע׳ אֲלָפִים = 10,000 Ju 1[4] + 26 t.; n. om. ע׳ כֶּסֶף (sc. *shekels*) Ju 17[10]. †**3.** rarely + other num.: **a.** עֶשֶׂר after larger num., מֵאָה וָע׳ שָׁנִים Gn 50[22.26] Jos 24[29] (all E), Ju 2[8]. **b.** ע׳ before larger num. עֶשֶׂר שָׁנִים וּתְשַׁע מֵאוֹת שָׁנָה Gn 5[14] (P). **c.** עֲשָׂרָה after larger num., מֵאָה וַעֲשָׂרָה הַזְּכָרִים Ezr 8[12], cf. (n. preceding) 1[10]. **d.** עֲשָׂרָה after smaller num., שִׁבְעָה שְׁקָלִים וַעֲשָׂרָה הַכָּסֶף Je 32[9] = *seventeen shekels;* before smaller num. + n. sg. עֲשָׂרָה וַחֲמִשָּׁה שֶׁקֶל Ez 45[12], but rd. חֲמִשִּׁים, joining עֲשָׂרָה to preceding, 𝔊[A] Hi Co al.

6240 **עָשָׂר**$_{203}$, **עֶשְׂרֵה**$_{144}$ **n. ten**, only after units to make num. 11–19, both cardinal and ordinal; עֶשְׂרֵה c. **n.f.**, עָשָׂר c. **n.m.**, thus: **1.** *eleven:* **a.** אַחַד עָשָׂר (c. n.m.) Gn 32[23] + 2 t. **b.** אַחַת עֶשְׂרֵה (c. n.f.) 2 K 23[36] + 7 t.; also = *eleventh* 1 K 6[38] 2 K 9[29]. **c.** עַשְׁתֵּי עָשָׂר (c. n.m.) Nu 29[20]; ord. Dt 1[3] + 7 t. **d.** עַשְׁתֵּי עֶשְׂרֵה (c. n.f.) Ex 26[7] + 4 t.; ord. Je 1[3] + 4 t. **2.** *twelve:* **a.** שְׁנֵי(ם) עָשָׂר (c. n.m.) Gn 35[22] + 80 t.; ord. 1 K 19[19] + 12 t. **b.** שְׁתֵּי(ם) עֶשְׂרֵה (c. n.f.) Ex 24[4] + 31 t.; ord. 2 K 8[25] + 6 t. **3.** *thirteen:* **a.** שְׁלֹשָׁה עָשָׂר (c. n.m.) Nu 29[14] + 2 t.; ord. Est 3[12] + 7 t. **b.** שְׁלֹשׁ עֶשְׂרֵה (c. n.f.) 1 K 7[1] + 9 t.; ord. Gn 14[4] + 2 t. **4.** *fourteen:* **a.** אַרְבָּעָה עָשָׂר Gn 46[22] + 13 t.; ord. Ex 12[6] + 17 t. **b.** אַרְבַּע עֶשְׂרֵה Gn 31[41] + 5 t.; ord. 2 K 18[13] + 3 t. **5.** *fifteen:* **a.** חֲמִשָּׁה עָשָׂר Ho 3[2] + 3 t.; ord. Ex 16[1] + 14 t. †**b.** חֲמֵשֶׁת עָשָׂר Ju 8[10] 2 S 19[18]. **c.** חֲמֵשׁ עֶשְׂרֵה 2 K 14[17] + 9 t.; ord. †2 K 14[23] 2 Ch 15[10].—Vid. also עֶשֶׂר **2 d.** **6.** *sixteen:* **a.** שִׁשָּׁה עָשָׂר Ex 26[25] + 6 t.; ord. 1 Ch 24[14] + 2 t. **b.** שֵׁשׁ עֶשְׂרֵה Gn 46[18] + 13 t. **7.** *seventeen:* **a.** שִׁבְעָה עָשָׂר 1 Ch 7[11] + 2 t.; ord. Gn 7[11] + 3 t. **b.** שְׁבַע עֶשְׂרֵה Gn 37[2] + 4 t.; ord. 1 K 22[52] 2 K 16[1].—Vid. also עֶשֶׂר **3 d.** **8.** *eighteen:* **a.** שְׁמֹנָה (שְׁמֹנַת) עָשָׂר Gn 14[4] + 10 t.; ord. †1 Ch 24[15] 25[25]. **b.** שְׁמֹנֶה עֶשְׂרֵה Ju 3[14] + 6 t.; ord. 1 K 15[1] + 8 t. †**9.** *nineteen:* **a.** תִּשְׁעָה עָשָׂר 2 S 2[30]; ord. 1 Ch 24[16] 25[26]. **b.** תְּשַׁע עֶשְׂרֵה Gn 11[25] Jos 19[38]; ord. 2 K 25[8] = Je 52[12].

These num. usually take sg. of the nouns most often used, אִישׁ, יוֹם, שָׁנָה, חֹדֶשׁ, cf. (sts.) אַמָּה, etc.; otherwise pl.; rarely (late usage) they follow noun, which is then usu. pl., e.g. Nu 29[30] Jos 15[51] (P), Ezr 8[35.35] Est 3[13] 8[5], etc. (even שָׁנִים שְׁתֵּים עֶשְׂרֵה Na 5[14]), but שָׁנָה precedes ordinal 1 K 6[38], שְׁנַת 15[1] + 8 t., so יוֹם (c. ord.) 2 Ch 29[17] + 5 t. Est 9; also יוֹם and שָׁנָה (שְׁנַת) both precede and foll. ordinal Nu 7[72.78] 2 K 8[25] 9[29] 14[23] 16[1] Je 32[1] 2 K 25[8] = Je 52[12].—Vid. also Kö[ii. 1, 211 ff.] Da[Synt. § 37 a, also R. 1, 2] Ges[§§ 92 d, e, 134], and esp. Herner[Synt. d. Zahlwörter im AT (1893)]; on form in הֵ— (prob for יֵ—), Ol[§ 110] Kö[ii. 1, 427] W[SG 138].

†[**עָשַׂר**] **vb. denom. take the tenth of, tithe**;—**Qal** *Impf.* 3 ms. יַעְשֹׂר 1 S 8[15.17] (c. acc. of thing tithed). **Pi.** *Impf.* + *Inf. abs. give a tenth of*, c. acc. rei: 2 ms. עַשֵּׂר תְּעַשֵּׂר Dt 14[22]; 1 s. עַשֵּׂר אֲעַשְּׂרֶנּוּ לָךְ Gn 28[22] (P); *Pt. taking the tenth*, הַמְעַשְּׂרִים Ne 10[38]. **Hiph.** (so usu. expl.) *Inf.* לַעְשֵׂר Dt 26[12] c. acc. cogn. i.e. *taking, reckoning, tithe*, but Inf. cstr. with ַ— improb., < rd. לְעַשֵּׂר **Pi.**; בַּעְשֵׂר Ne 10[39] abs., i.e. *receiving tithes*, but read prob. בַּעְשֹׂר **Qal** (on anom. points, see Ges[§ 53 k] Dr[Dt 26, 12]). 6237

†**עָשׂוֹר**, and (Ex 12[3]) **עָשֹׂר n.[m.] a ten, decade**;—**1.** usu. of days: **a.** *a period of ten days* Gn 24[55] (J). **b.** in phr., בֶּעָשׂוֹר (עָשֹׂר) לַחֹדֶשׁ *on the tenth day of the month* Lv 25[9] (H), Ez 20[1] 24[1] 40[1] Ex 12[3] Lv 16[29] 23[27] Nu 29[7] Jos 4[19] (all P), 2 K 25[1] = Je 52[4], Je 52[12] (*seventh day* in ‖ 2 K 25[8]). **2.** of strings of instr.: נֵבֶל ע׳ *harp, a ten*(-stringed one) ψ 33[2] 144[9]; ע׳ alone ψ 92[4] upon *a ten*(-stringed instrument). 6218

עֶשְׂרִים$_{315}$ **n. pl. indecl.** (a) **twenty** (ancient pl. of עֶשֶׂר Prä[BAS i. 376]; NH = BH; Ar. عِشْرُونَ; As. *ešrâ;* Sab. עשרי Hom[Chrest. 48]; Eth. ዕሥራ፡; Aram. עשרין, ܥܣܪܝܢ; Nab. (עשרין);—**I.** as cardinal: **1.** without other num.: **a.** usu. sq. n.s. (esp. שָׁנָה, אִישׁ, אַמָּה, etc.) Gn 31[38] 1 S 14[14] Ex 38[18] + 64 t., + עֶשְׂרִים אֶלֶף 20,000 1 Ch 18[4] + 7 t. + Ez 45[1] (rdg. עֶשְׂרִים אֶלֶף, v. עֶשֶׂר **2 b**). **b.** sq. n.pl. 2 S 3[20] Ex 36[23.24.25] + 4 t. †**c.** sq. n.s. coll. 1 K 5[3]. **d.** n.pl. precedes Gn 32[15.15.16] 2 Ch 3[3] + 6 t. **e.** n. om. Gn 18[31.31] (הָע׳), 1 K 6[2] + 6 t., as pred. Ex 27[10.10.11.11] + 4 t. †**f.** + בָּאַמָּה Zc 5[12]. **2.** + other num.: **a.** c. units, usu. 20 + (c. וְ) unit + n.s. Ju 10[2.3] 1 K 14[20] + 58 t. (incl. 20 + 1 × 1000, etc., 27 t.); n. om. Jos 15[32] + 2 t. pred.; less oft. unit + 20 + n.s. Gn 11[24] Ex 38[24] Nu 8[24] (all P) + 27 t.; unit + 20 + בָּאַמָּה Ez 40[21] Ex 26[2] 36[9] (both P). **b.** 20 + unit + n.pl. Nu 7[8.8] (P), 1 Ch 2[22] + 3 t. Chr. †**c.** n.pl. + 20 + unit Jos 19[30] 1 Ch 12[29] (van d. H. v[28]). **d.** c. hundreds, 20 usu. foll.; sq. n.s. 1 K 9[14] Gn 6[3] Dt 31[2] + 7 t.; n. om. 2 Ch 3[4] Ezr 2[32] = Ne 7[35]; 20 + 100 (n. om.) 6242 6235 6235

Nu 7^{86}. **e.** n.pl. + 100 + 20 1 Ch 15$^{5.6}$;—cf. further מֵאָה. **II.** as ordinal: **1.** 20 alone, בִּשְׁנַת ע׳ *in the twentieth year* 1 K 15^{9} + 4 t.; n. om. Nu 10^{11} + 3 t. **2. a.** 20 + unit + ns. Ez 29^{17} 40^{1}. **b.** ns. + 20 + unit Hg 1^{15} 2 Ch 7^{10} +; ns. + unit + 20 Ex 12^{8}; בִּשְׁנַת + 20 + unit 1 K 16^{10}, etc.—Vid. reff. sub עֶשֶׂר.

6224 עֲשִׂירִי $_{20}$ **m.**, עֲשִׂירִיָּה, and עֲשִׂירִית $_{8}$ **f.** **adj. num. ord.** tenth;—**1.** דּוֹר עֲשִׂירִי Dt 23$^{3.4}$; בַּיּוֹם הָעֲ׳ Nu 7^{66} (P); הַחֹדֶשׁ הָעֲ׳ Gn 8^{5} (P) Ez 24^{1} + 5 t.; בַּחֹדֶשׁ הָעֲשִׂרִי Je 39^{1}; ח׳ om. הָעֲשִׂירִי Gn 8^{5} (P), בָּעֲשִׂרִי Ez 29^{1} 33^{21}; other nouns om. הָעֲשִׂירִי 1 Ch 12^{13} 25^{17} 27^{13}, הָעֲשִׂרִי 24^{11}; בַּשָּׁנָה הָעֲשִׂרִית Ez 29^{1}, בַּשׁ׳ הָעֲשִׂרִית Je 32^{1}. **2.** as subst. *a tenth part*: f. abs. עֲשִׂרִיָּה Is 6^{13}; f. cstr. עֲשִׂירִית הָאֵיפָה Nu 28^{5}, עֲשִׂירִת Ex 16^{36}, עֲשִׂרִת Lv 5^{11} 6^{13} Nu 5^{15}; עֲשִׂרִית הַחֹמֶר Ez 45^{11}; m. abs. הָעֲשִׂרִי Lv 27^{32} *the tithe* (i.e. of cattle, etc.).

6241 עִשָּׂרוֹן $_{33}$ **n.m.** $^{Lv\ 14,\ 10}$ tenth part (of ephah; cf. 𝔊 δέκατον τοῦ οἰφί Nu 15^{4}, and עֲשִׂירִת הָאֵיפָה 28^{5}; i.e. = עֹמֶר, v. further Benz$^{Arch.\ 182}$ Now$^{Arch.\ i.\ 203}$);—abs. ע׳ Lv 14^{21} +, עִשָּׂרֹן Ex 29^{40} Nu 28^{13}; pl. עֶשְׂרֹנִים Nu 28^{9} +;—only P (H), as measure of סֹלֶת used in meal-offering Ex 29^{40} Lv 14^{10} + 3 t. Lv (H only 23^{17}); Nu 15^{4} + 26 t. Nu, incl. distributive עִשָּׂרוֹן עִשָּׂר(ו)ן 28^{13} + 4 t.

4643 †מַעֲשֵׂר **n.m.** $^{Nu\ 18,\ 28}$ tenth part, tithe;—abs. מ׳ Nu 18^{26} +; cstr. מַעְשַׂר Lv 27^{30} +, מַעֲשַׂר Ne 10^{39} (bef. הַמַּעֲשֵׂר); sf. מַעַשְׂרוֹ Lv 27^{31}; pl. abs. מַעַשְׂרוֹת Ne 12^{44}; sf. מַעְשְׂרֹתֵיכֶם Am 4^{4} + 3 t.;—**1.** *tenth part* of ḥomer Ez 45^{11}, of bath v^{14}. **2.** *tithe, payment of tenth part*: c. מִן rei Gn 14^{20} Nu 18^{26}; usu. cstr. bef. n. rei Dt 12^{17} 14$^{23.28}$ 26^{12} Lv 27$^{30.32}$ 2 Ch 31$^{5.6.6}$ Ne 10$^{38.39}$ 13$^{5.12}$; abs. Nu 18$^{21.26.26}$ Mal 3$^{8.10}$ 2 Ch 31^{12} Ne 10^{39} 12^{44}; שְׁנַת הַמַּ׳ Dt 26^{12} *the year of the tithe* (i.e. of tithing); c. genit. pers. paying tithe Am 4^{4} Dt 12$^{6.11}$ Lv 27^{31} Nu 18$^{24.28}$.—Cf. RS$^{Sem.\ i.\ 228\ ff.;\ 2nd\ ed.\ 245\ ff.;\ Proph.\ Lect.\ ii.\ N.}$ Now$^{Arch.\ i.\ 313;\ ii.\ 257\ f.}$ Benz$^{Arch.\ 309,\ 460\ f.}$ Dr$^{Dt.\ 168\ ff.}$

5906 I. עָשׁ Jb 9^{9} prob. error for עיש, v. עַיִשׁ p. 747

6211 II. עָשׁ v. עשׁשׁ. p. 799

6220 †עַשְׁוָת **n.pr.m.** in Asher 1 Ch 7^{33}, Ασειθ, Ασουαθ.

עשׁן (√of foll.; cf. Ar. عَثَنَ *ascend*, Lag$^{BN\ 51}$ (plausibly); v. عَثَنٌ, عُثَانٌ *smoke*; also Syr. ܥܘܬܢܐ (Nö$^{§\ 116}$), ܐܬܘܢܐ, from √ *ܥܬܢ acc. to Hoffm$^{LCB\ 1882,\ 320}$; vb. denom. in Ar. NH).

†I. עָשָׁן **n.m.** $^{Ex\ 19,\ 18}$ smoke;—abs. ע׳ Ju 6227
20^{38} +, cstr. עֲשַׁן Jos 8$^{20.21}$, עֶשֶׁן Ex 19^{18}; sf. עֲשָׁנוֹ Ex 19^{18}, עֲשָׁנָהּ Is 34^{10};—**1. a.** of burning city Jos 8$^{20.21}$ Ju 20$^{38.40}$, cf. Na 2^{14}; heralding a foe Is 14^{31}. **b.** in fig. of destruction of Isr. Is 9^{17}, Edom 34^{10}. **c.** sim. of dust-cloud Ct 3^{6}; of transitoriness Ho 13^{3} Is 51^{6} ψ 37^{20} (rdg. כֶּע׳, as 𝔊 𝔖 𝔙), 68^{3} 102^{4}; sim. of the unpleasant, Pr 10^{26}. **d.** breath of crocodile Jb 41^{12}. **2. a.** attending theoph., תַּנּוּר ע׳ Gn 15^{17}; of mt. Ex 19^{18}, cf. sim. כְּעֶ׳ הַכִּבְשָׁן v^{18}; Is 6^{4}, also 4^{5} Jo 3^{3}. **b.** of God's anger, ע׳ בְּאַפּוֹ 2 S 22^{9} = ψ 18^{9}; so prob. also Is 65^{5}.

†עָשַׁן **vb. denom.** smoke, be wroth;— 6225
Qal 1. a. *smoke*, *Pf.* 3 ms. ע׳ of mt. Ex 19^{18}, so *Impf.* 3 mpl. יֶעֱשָׁנוּ (at touch of י׳) ψ 104^{32} 144^{5}. **b.** fig., 3 ms. יֶעְשַׁן אַף־י׳, c. ב *against*, Dt 29^{19} ψ 74^{1}. Hence **2.** subj. pers., *fume*, i.e. *be wroth*, *Pf.* 2 ms. עָשַׁנְתָּ בּ׳ ψ 80^{5}.

†עָשֵׁן **adj.** smoking;—ע׳ of mt. Ex 20^{18} 6226
(Gi v^{15}); pl. הָאוּדִים הָעֲשֵׁנִים Is 7^{4} *the smoking firebrands* (dying out; in fig.).

†II. עָשָׁן **n.pr.loc.** in Shephelah of Judah 6228
Jos 15^{42}, in Simeon acc. to 19^{7} 1 Ch 4^{32}, Levit. city 6^{44}; Ασαν, etc.; = בּוֹר עָשָׁן, q.v. p. 92 supr.

†עָשַׁק **vb.** oppress, wrong, extort (𝔗 6231
עֲשַׁק = BH, so OAram. עשק; Syr. ܥܫܩ *accuse, slander*; As. adj. *ešḳu, strong*; Ar. عَسْقٌ *roughness, injustice*);—**Qal** *Pf.* ע׳ Lv 5^{21} Ez 18^{18}; 2 ms. sf. עֲשַׁקְתָּנוּ 1 S 12^{4}, etc.; *Impf.* 3 ms. sf. יַעַשְׁקֵנִי ψ 119^{122}; 2 ms. תַּעֲשֹׁק Lv 19^{13} +, etc.; *Inf. cstr.* עֲשֹׁק Ho 12^{8}, sf. עָשְׁקָם 1 Ch 16^{21} ψ 105^{14}; *Pt. act.* עשֵׁק Pr 14^{31} +, fpl. הָעֹשְׁקוֹת Am 4^{1}, etc.; *pass.* עָשׁוּק Dt 28^{29} +, etc.;—**1.** *oppress, wrong* (oft. by extortion, ‖ גָּזַל), c. acc. pers. 1 S 12$^{3.4}$ Mi 2^{2} Lv 5^{21} 19^{13}; esp. the poor and helpless Am 4^{1} Dt 24^{14} Je 7^{6} Ez 22^{29} Zc 7^{10} Pr 14^{31} 22^{16} 28^{3} Ec 4^{1}; also c. acc. cogn. ע׳ עֹשֶׁק (וְ)גָזֵל גָּזֵל Ez 18^{18} *practise extortion*, 22^{29}, *take by extortion* Lv 5^{23} and (c. acc. rei) Mal 3^{5}; abs. Ho 12^{8} *practise extortion*; Jb 10^{3} *deal tyrannically* (of God); pt. *oppressor, extortioner* Je 21^{12} ψ 72^{4} Ec 4^{1}; pt. pass. as subst. *the oppressed* ψ 103^{6} 146^{7}. **2.** *oppress* a nation Is 52^{4}, cf. ψ 105^{14} = 1 Ch 16^{21}, ψ 119^{122}, pt. act. *oppressor* v^{121}, pt. pass. *oppressed* Je 50^{33}, in predict. ע׳ וְגָזוּל Dt 28^{29}, ע׳ וְרָצוּץ v^{33} Ho 5^{11}. **3.** dub. are: יַעֲשֹׁק נָהָר Jb 40^{23} *a river oppresses* him, i.e. rushes violently upon him (sc. the hippopot.; Du יָשֹׁק, fr. שׁוּק; > Gunk Bu יִשְׁקַע ישׁקע *falls, sinks*); עָשֻׁק בְּדַם נֶפֶשׁ

Pr 28^{17} *oppressed* (? *burdened*) with the blood of a person. **Pu.** *Pt.* f. הַמְעֻשָּׁקָה Is 23^{12} *crushed* (of conquered Sidon under fig. of woman).

6233 † עֹשֶׁק **n.m.** $^{\text{Ec 7, 7}}$ **oppression, extortion**;—ע׳ abs. Je 6^{6}+, cstr. ψ 119^{134} Ec 5^{7};—**1.** Je 6^{6} 22^{17} Ez 22$^{7.12}$ ψ 73^{8}; c. genit. subj. 119^{134}, obj. Ec 5^{7}; as acc. cogn. c. עָשַׁק (q.v.) Ez 18^{18} 22^{29}. **2.** national *oppression*, Is 54^{14}. **3.** concr., *gain of extortion* ψ 62^{11}, so perh. Ec 7^{7}; as acc. cogn. Lv 5^{23} (‖ גָּזֵל).—Is 30^{12} 59^{13} rd. עִקֵּשׁ Lag Gr al.

6232 † עֵשֶׁק **n.pr.m.** Benjamite 1 Ch 8^{39}, Ασηλ, Ασεκ.

6234 † עָשְׁקָה **n.f. oppression, distress**;—עָשְׁקָה־לִּי Is 38^{14} (cf. Ges $^{\text{§§ 9 v, 48 l}}$) *oppression to me!* = I am oppressed, distressed.

6216 † עָשׁוֹק **n.[m.] oppressor, extortioner**;—
6233 Je 22^{3} (= עָשׁוֹק 21^{12}).

6217 † עֲשׁוּקִים **n.pl.abstr. oppression, extortion**;—ע׳ Am 3^{9} Jb 35^{9}, עֲשֻׁקִים Ec 4^{1}.

4642 † [מַעֲשַׁקָּה] **n.f. extortionate act**;—pl. abs. רַב מַעֲשַׁקּוֹת Pr 28^{16} *great in extortions;* בֶּצַע מ׳ Is 33^{15} *gain of extortions.*

6238 † [עָשַׁר] **vb. be** or **become rich** (NH in der. spec., and deriv.; Aram. עֲתַר, ܥܬܪ; cf. Ar. غَثَرَ *abound with herbage,* غُثْرَةٌ *abundance,* of herbage, goods, etc.);—**Qal** *Pf.* 1 s. עָשַׁרְתִּי Ho 12^{9} *I have become rich; Impf.* 3 ms. יַעֲשַׁר Jb 15^{29} *he shall not be rich.*—1 K 22^{49} rd. עָשָׂה. **Hiph. 1.** *make rich,* c. acc. pers.: *Pf.* 1 s. הֶעֱשַׁרְתִּי Gn 14^{23}; 2 fs. הֶעֱשַׁרְתְּ Ez 27^{33} (of personif. Tyre; + בְּרֹב הוֹנַיִךְ); *Impf.* 3 ms. sf. יַעְשְׁרֶנּוּ (Ges $^{\text{§ 61 g}}$), + acc. cogn. עֹשֶׁר; 2 ms. sf. רַבַּת תַּעְשְׁרֶנָּה ψ 65^{10} *thou dost greatly enrich it* (the land); obj. om. 3 fs. תַּעֲשִׁיר Pr 10^{22}, so *Pt.* מַעֲשִׁיר 1 S 2^{7} י׳ *maketh rich* (opp. מוֹרִישׁ). **2.** *gain riches,* abs.: *Impf.* 3 ms. יַעֲשִׁר ψ 49^{17}, יַעֲשִׁיר Pr 21^{17}
6239 Dn 11^{2} (+ acc. cogn. עֹשֶׁר); 3 fs. תַּעֲשִׁיר Pr 10^{4}; 1 s. ואעשר וָאַעֲשִׁר Zc 11^{5} (Gi Kt; van d. H. Baer וָאַעְשִׁר); 3 mpl. וַיַּעֲשִׁירוּ Je 5^{27}; *Inf. cstr.* לְהַעֲשִׁיר Pr 23^{4} 28^{20}. **Hithp.** *Pt.* מִתְעַשֵּׁר Pr 13^{7} *one enriching himself.*

6239 עֹשֶׁר$_{37}$ **n.m.** $^{\text{1 S 17, 25}}$ **riches**;—ע׳ abs. Gn 31^{16}+ 27 t., cstr. Est 1^{4}; sf. עָשְׁרוֹ Je 9^{22}+5 t., עָשְׁרָם ψ 49^{7} Pr 14^{24}; + (or ‖) כָּבוֹד 1 K 3^{13} Pr 3^{16}+9 t.; עָשָׂה ע׳ Je 17^{11}, cf. Eng. 'make money.'

6223 עָשִׁיר$_{23}$ **adj. et n. rich**;—abs. ע׳ Ex 30^{15}+ 19 t.; pl. abs. עֲשִׁירִים Ec 10^{6}; cstr. עֲשִׁירֵי ψ 45^{13}; sf. עֲשִׁירֶיהָ Mi 6^{12};—**adj. m.** 2 S 12$^{1.4}$ (opp. רָאשׁ), Ru 3^{10} (opp. דַּל); usu. **n.m.** *the rich,* opp. דַּל, Pr 10^{15}+3 t.; opp. רָשׁ 2 S 12^{2} Pr 14^{20}+4 t.; opp. אֶבְיוֹן ψ 49^{3}; alone Je 9^{22} Mi 6^{12}+5 t., + עֲשִׁירֵי עָם ψ 45^{13}; ע׳ Is 53^{9} is prob. crpt., cf. ‖ רְשָׁעִים; Bö Ry Di-Kit עֹשֵׂי רָע; Krochm Gr Che^{Hpt} conj. רְשָׁעִים for ע׳, and פֹּשְׁעִים for ר׳.

† [עָשֵׁשׁ] **vb. waste away** (cf. As. *ašašu,* 6244
moth; Ar. عُثَّ *moth*(-worm), عَثَّ *eat* (of moth; ? denom.); acc. to De $^{\text{ψ 6, 8}}$ al. עָשֵׁשׁ is denom. from עָשׁ, prop. *be moth-eaten,* but improb.);—**Qal** *Pf.* 3 fs. עָשְׁשָׁה מִכַּעַס עֵינִי ψ 6^{8} *my eye is wasted from grief,* = 31^{10} (בְּכַעַס; + בִּטְנִי, נַפְשִׁי); 3 pl. עֲצָמַי עָשֵׁשׁוּ v^{11}.

† II. עָשׁ **n.m.** $^{\text{Is 50, 9}}$ **moth** (as *waster, con-* 6211
sumer);—ע׳ abs., Ho 5^{12} (‖ רָקָב), Is 50^{9} 51^{8}; in sim. ψ 39^{12}; כְּבֶגֶד אֲכָלוֹ עָשׁ Jb 13^{28}; symbol of fragility Jb 4^{19}.—27^{10} read prob. עַכָּבִישׁ q.v.

† I. [עָשַׁת] **vb. be smooth** or **shiny** (?), 6245
si vera l. (cf. עֶשֶׁת);—only **Qal** *Pf.* 3 pl. שָׁמְנוּ עָשְׁתוּ Je 5^{28} (fig.) *they have grown fat, they are smooth* (or *shine,* from fat); doubtful word, Thes conj. עָשְׁרוּ *have grown rich* (cf. 𝔊 𝔖 𝔗), so Gie (but וַיַּעֲשִׁירוּ precedes, v^{27}).

† עֶשֶׁת **n.[m.] plate** (as *smooth, shiny?* 6247
NH *id., lump* or *bar* of metal);—cstr. ע׳ שֵׁן Ct 5^{14} *a plate of ivory* (Löw in Buhl^{Lex} Bu).

† עָשׁוֹת **adj. smooth?**—only בַּרְזֶל ע׳ Ez 27^{19} 6219
as merchandise of Tyre; Co עֲשׁוּת, i.e. pt. pass., from √עשת *forge,* or *work skilfully;* Toy *iron skilfully wrought;* all dubious.

† II. [עָשַׁת] **vb. Hithp. think** (Arama- 6245
ism: BAram. Pt. עֲשִׁית, 𝔗 אִתְעַשַּׁת);—**Hithp.** *Impf.* 3 ms. יִתְעַשֵּׁת א׳ לָנוּ Jon 1^{6} perhaps *God will give a thought to us* (cf. חשב ψ 40^{18}).

† עַשְׁתּוּת (van d. H. ־וֹת) **n.f. thought**;— 6248
cstr. ע׳ שַׁאֲנָן Jb 12^{5} (־וֹת would be pl., fr. *עֶשֶׁת).

† [עֶשְׁתֹּנָה] **n.f. id.** (Aram.: 𝔗 עֶשְׁתּוֹנִין; cstr. 6250
עשתוני Ecclus 3^{24});—pl. sf. אָבְדוּ עֶשְׁתֹּנֹתָיו ψ 146^{4}.

† עַשְׁתֵּי$_{19}$ **n.num. one** (As. *išten, one; išten* 6249
ešrit, eleven; Dl $^{\text{§ 75}}$, TelAm. [*iš-*]*tit, first time;* v. Gie $^{\text{ZAW i (1881), 226}}$ Ges $^{\text{§ 97 e}}$ Kö $^{\text{ii. 1, 212}}$ and reff.);—only + עָשָׂר, עֶשְׂרֵה (q.v.) = *eleven, eleventh,* Je 1^{3} 39^{2} = 52^{5} = 2 K 25^{2}, Ez 26^{1} 40^{49} Zc 1^{7} Ex 26$^{7.8}$ 36$^{14.15}$ Nu 7^{72} 29^{20} (all P), Dt 1^{3} 1 Ch 12^{13} 24^{12} 25^{18} 27^{14}.

6253 †עַשְׁתֹּ֫רֶת **n.pr.deae.** ʿ**Aštōreth**, < ʿ**Aštart**, ʿ**Aštéreth** (v. infr.) (MI[17] עשתר כמש; Ph. עשתרת (+ oft. in n.pr.), n.pr. עבד עשתר Cook[Acad. Jan. 18, 1896] Sab. n. pr. dei עתּתר v. esp. Os[ZMG xx (1866), 279 f.] DHM[ib. xxxvii (1883), 376] Fell[Sab. Götternamen, ZMG liv (1900), 231 ff., esp. 237 ff.]; As. *Ištar;* OAram. Palm. עתר (= עתּתר) in n. pr.; in Egypt. ʿ*astirati* WMM[As. u. Eur. 313]; Gk. Ἀστάρτη; on other Gk. equivalents (e.g. Ἀφροδίτη) cf. Lewy[Fremdw. 148, 186 f. 250]);— ֹ ְ prob. artificial, to suggest בֹּשֶׁת, orig. ־תֶּ֫רֶת, ־תָּרְתְּ, cf. *Ištar*, Ασταρτη, etc.; ע׳ 1 K 11[5] + 2 t.; pl. ־תָּרוֹת Ju 2[13] + 3 t. + ־רֹת 1 S 7[4]; 1 S 31[10] rd. prob. sg. (Dr al.);—ʿ*Aštart*, ʿ*Aštereth* (Ασταρτη, pl. Ασταρται, but Ju 10[6] 1 S 7[4] Ασταρωθ), ancient Sem. goddess (with male counterpart in Moab., Sab. and appar. Ph.); Phoenician deity, עשתרת אֱלֹהֵי צִדֹנִים 1 K 11[5.33], ע׳ שִׁקֻּץ צ׳ 2 K 23[13];
1045 so prob. בֵּית ע׳ 1 S 31[10] (rdg. sg.; v. esp. Dr); elsewhere pl., of various local goddesses, called עַשְׁתָּרוֹת (cf. As. *ilâni u ištarat = gods and Ištars* (i.e. goddesses), usu. + בעל(ים), as Canaanitish deities Ju 2[13] 10[6] 1 S 7[4] 12[10]; ‖ אֱלֹהֵי הַנֵּכָר 7[3].—Vid. esp. Dr[Ashtoreth] in Hast[DB]; on *Ištar* Jastr[Rel. Bab. pass. esp. 202 f.]; on ʿ*Athtar* Bae[Rel. 117 f.]; on Ph. ʿ*Aštart* Pietschm[Gesch. Phön. 184 f.]; on ʿ*Ashtoreth* Barton[JBL x (1891), 73 ff.] GFM[Ency. Bib.]

1045 I. עַשְׁתָּרוֹת v. foregoing.

6251 †II. [עַשְׁתְּרוֹת] **n.pl.f.** only cstr. in phr. עַשְׁתְּר(ו)ת צֹאנֶךָ Dt 7[13] 28[4.18.51] (all ‖ שְׁגַר אֲלָפֶיךָ) usu. interpr. either as **a.** = *ewes* (Thes) or as **b.** = *young* (cf. *veneres gregis;* in either case with ref. to ʿ*Aštart* as goddess of fecundity; RS[Sem. i. 292, 457 f., 2nd ed. 310, 476 f.], adopting **b**, thinks one type of ʿAšt. in Canaan had form of sheep, so Dr[Dt 7, 13]); cf. also عَثْرِى as name of land fertilized by dew and rain We[Skizzen iii. 170].

6252 †III. עַשְׁתָּרוֹת **n.pr.loc.** Ασταρωθ, etc., E. of Jordan (name from worship of diff. forms of ʿAštart; in Egypt. ʿ*astiratu*, as E. Jordan loc. WMM[As. u. Eur. 162, 313]; cf. TelAm. n.pr.loc. *Aštarti*);—in Bashan (near Edrei) Dt 1[4] (־רֹת), Jos 12[4] 13[12.31] (all + אֶדְרֶעִי), 9[10] 1 Ch 6[56] = עַשְׁתְּרֹת בְּעֶשְׁתְּרָה (i.e. בֵּית עַשְׁתְּרָה) Jos 21[27]; also
6255 עַשְׁתְּרֹת קַרְנַיִם Gn 14[5] (𝔊 Ασταρωθ Καρναιν, cf. GFM[JBL xvi (1897), 155 f.] who expl. name as ʿ*Ashtereth of the two-peaked mt.*); cf. further, קַרְנַיִם Am 6[13];—site prob. either *Tel ʿAštara*, 21 miles E. of Sea of Galilee, or *Muzeirib*, 8 miles further S.; poss. both occur in OT; cf. esp. Dr[Ashtaroth] in Hast[DB] Di[Gn 14, 5] Buhl[Geogr. 248 ff.] GASm[Ency. Bib. 335 f.]

†עַשְׁתְּרָתִי **adj.gent.** of foreg. הָע׳ 1 Ch 11[44]. 6254

עֵת v. I. ענה. p. 773 6256

†I. [עָתַד] **vb.** be ready (NH adj. עָתִיד 6257
future (as prepared); Ar. عَتُدَ *be ready, prepared* (also *great, bulky*); Syr. ܥܬܰܕ, 𝔗 in der. spec. and deriv.);—**Pi.** *Imv.* ms. sf. וְעַתְּדָהּ Pr 24[27] *and make it ready* i.e. thy work (‖ הָכֵן). **Hithp.** *Pf.* 3 pl. הִתְעַתְּדוּ לְגַלִּים Jb 15[28] which [houses] *were prepared* (destined) *for* (i.e. to be) *heaps* of ruin.

†עָתִיד, [עָתוּד] **adj.** ready, prepared;— 6259, 6264
1. abs. עָתִיד לַכִּידוֹר Jb 15[24] a king *ready for the onset;* pl. עֲתִדִים לַיּוֹם Est 3[14] *ready for the day,* so 8[13] Qr (Kt עתודים). **2.** *ready* = skilled הָעֲתִידִים עֹרֵר Jb 3[8] *those skilled in rousing* Leviathan. **3.** *prepared* = impending (cf. NH = *future*), fpl. וְחָשׁ עֲתִדֹת Dt 32[35] *the impending things are hastening* (‖ קָרוֹב יוֹם אֵידָם). **4.** *prepared* = stored up, ועתידתיהם Is 10[13] Kt (Qr וַעֲתוּדֹתֵיהֶם, to differentiate it from above) *and their stores* have I plundered.

[עַתּוּד]₂₉ **n.m.**[Gn 31, 10] he-goat (NH = BH; 6260
As. *atudû;* Ar. عَتُودٌ *young he-goat;* relation to above √ not clear; Thes *well-developed*, cp. Ar. عَتَدٌ *horse fit for running* (cf. √ mng. *great*, i.e. perh. *full-grown*); acc. to Hom[NS 247 f.] animal *ready* to fight);—only pl. עַתּוּדִים Is 1[11] + 13 t.; עַתֻּדִים Gn 31[10] + 13 t.; cstr. עַתּוּדֵי Is 34[6];—as property Gn 31[10.12] Ez 27[21] Pr 27[26], food Dt 32[14]; as leaders of flock Je 50[8] (sim.), hence fig. of princes and chief men Is 14[9] Ez 34[17], v. also infr.; as sacrif. victims Is 1[11] Nu 7[17] + 12 t. Nu 7, ψ 66[15] and (iron.) 50[9.13]; fig. of people and princes in י׳'s great sacrifice Is 34[6] Je 51[40] (sim.), Ez 39[18], and (idea of sacrif. dropped) Zc 10[3].

עַתָּה, עַתַּי, עִתִּי v. עֵת sub I. ענה. p. 773f 6258, 6261-62

†עֲתָיָה **n.pr.m.** Ne 11[4], Αθεα, 𝔊L Αθαρασθας (very dub.); = עוּתַי 1 Ch 9[4]. p. 736 6265, 5793

†עֲתָךְ **n.pr.loc.** in Judah 1 S 30[30] 𝔊[A] Αθαγ, 𝔊L Ναγεβ; HPS prop. עֲרָד; v. עֶתֶר. p. 801 6269, 6281

עתל (√ of foll.; perh. = As. *atâlu, grow great*, cf. *etellu, great, exalted;* so Che[Expos. Times, vii. 484, 568; viii. 48]).

†עֲתַלְיָ֫הוּ, עֲתַלְיָה(וּ) **n.pr.f.** et **m.** (? י׳ *is exalted*);—**1. f.** Athaliah, daughter of Ahab and Jezebel, mother of Ahaziah king of Judah; 6270-71

Γοθολια: עֲתַלְיָהוּ 2 K 8^{26} 11$^{2.20}$ — 2 Ch 22$^{2.10.11}$ 23$^{12.13.21}$ 24^{7}; עֲתַלְיָה 2 K 11$^{1.3.13.14}$ 2 Ch 22^{12}. **2. m. a.** 1 Ch 8^{26} Ογοθολια. **b.** Ezr 8^{7} Αθελει, A Αθλια; 𝔊L Γοθονίου (genit.). **c.** עַתְלַי one with foreign wife Ezr 10^{28}, Θαλι, A Οθαλι.

6272 †[עָתַם] **vb.** dub.; **Niph.** *Pf.* 3 ms. נֶעְתַּם אָרֶץ Is 9^{18} (غَتَمَ is *be clogged in speech,* غَتْمٌ *suffocating heat,* مَغْتُومٌ *burned by heat;* hence Thes *scorched,* but derived sense dub.; v. RS$^{\text{JPhil. xiii. 61 f.}}$);—read perhaps נִצְּתָה (√יצת) *is burned up,* cf. RS$^{\text{l.c.}}$, Krochm Kit Che^{Hpt}.

6273 †עָתְנִי **n.pr.m.** Levite 1 Ch 26^{7}, Γοονει, (Γ)οθνι.

6274 †עָתְנִיאֵל **n.pr.m.** son of Ḳenaz, a hero in Isr., Γοθονιηλ, Jos 15^{17} Ju 1^{13} 3$^{9.11}$ 1 Ch 4$^{13.13}$; name of family 27^{15}.

6275 †[עָתַק] **vb. move, proceed, advance** (NH Hiph.; As. *etêḳu* as H., also trans. *bring, move;* Ar. عَتَقَ, عَتُقَ *precede, pass forth, become free, grow old;* Aram. ܥܬܩ, עֲתֵק *grow old,* Palm. adj. עתק *old*);—**Qal** *Pf.* 3 fs. עָתְקָה ψ 6^{8}, 3 pl. עָתְקוּ Jb 21^{7}; *Impf.* 3 ms. יֶעְתַּק Jb 14^{18} 18^{4};—**1.** *move* וְצוּר יֶע׳ מִמְּקֹמוֹ Jb 14^{18}, so 18^{4}. **2.** *advance* (in years; Aramaic sense) 21^{7} (‖יִחְיוּ); hence = grow old and weak ψ 6^{8} (of eye, ‖עָשְׁשָׁה). **Hiph.** *Pf.* 3 pl. הֶעְתִּיקוּ Jb 32^{16} (Gi; van d. H. Baer v^{15}), Pr 25^{1}; *Impf.* 3 ms. וַיַּעְתֵּק Gn 12^{8} 26^{22}; *Pt.* מַעְתִּיק Jb 9^{5};—**1.** *move forward* (sc. tent) = proceed Gn 12^{8} (מִשָּׁם, ה loc.), 26^{22} (מִשָּׁם); so fig. Jb 32^{16} (v. supr.) words *have moved away* from them (מֵהֶם), but v. prob. gloss (Bu al.). **2.** Jb 9^{5} *he who removeth mountains.* **3.** very late Pr 25^{1} *transcribe* (*remove* from one book or roll to another; 𝔊 ἐξεγράψαντο, 𝔙 *transtulerunt;* so in mediaeval Heb.: Zunz$^{\text{ZMG xxv (1871). 447 f. = Ges. Schr. iii. 66 f.}}$).

6277 †עָתָק **adj. forward, arrogant** (of speech) (Thes *free* (v. Ar.), *unrestrained*);—1 S 2^{3} ψ 31^{19} 94^{4}; so also 75^{6} (cf. צַוָּאר).

6276 †עָתֵק **adj.** Thes (*ancient* and so) **valuable;** < **advanced, eminent, surpassing** (cf. عتيق *preceding,* hence *surpassing, choice* Lane ^{1947});—הוֹן ע׳ Pr 8^{18} *eminent wealth.*

6266 †עָתִיק **adj. eminent, surpassing, choice** (v. עָתֵק);—מְכַסֶּה ע׳ Is 23^{18} *choice attire.*

†[עַתִּיק] **adj. removed, old;**—**1.** *removed,* 6267
עַתִּיקֵי מִשָּׁדָיִם Is 28^{9} i.e. weaned (‖ גְּמוּלֵי מֵחָלָב; on cstr. v. Ges$^{\S 130a}$). **2.** *old, ancient* (Aramaism: ܥܬܝܩ, עַתִּיק, *old*), הַדְּבָרִים עַתִּיקִים 1 Ch 4^{22}.

†I. [עָתַר] **vb. pray, supplicate** (always to God) (cf. Ar. عَتَرَ *slaughter for sacrifice* De$^{\text{Gn (4) 381}}$ We$^{\text{Skizzen iii. 115, 166; Held. (2), 118, 142}}$; RS$^{\text{Sem i. 210 f.; 2nd ed., 227 f.}}$);—**Qal** *Impf.* 3 ms. וַיֶּעְתַּר לי׳ Gn 25^{21}, אֶל־י׳ Ex 8^{26} 10^{18} Ju 13^{8}; יֶעְתַּר אֶל־אֱלוֹהַּ Jb 33^{26}. **Niph.** *be supplicated, entreated* (and grant entreaty; always of God), usu. c. לְ of worshipper (v. לְ **5 d**): *Pf.* 3 ms. consec. וְנֶעְתַּר לָהֶם Is 19^{22}; *Impf.* 3 ms. וַיֵּעָתֶר לוֹ Gn 25^{21} 2 Ch 33^{13}, וַיֵּעָתֵר לָנוּ Ezr 8^{23}; c. לָאָרֶץ *for the land* 2 S 21^{14} 24^{25}; *Inf. abs.* וְנַעְתּוֹר לָהֶם 1 Ch 5^{20}; *cstr.* (as subst.) הֵעָתֶר־לוֹ 2 Ch 33^{19}. **Hiph. = Qal,** *make supplication,* c. לְ, אֶל: *Pf.* וְהַעְתַּרְתִּי אֶל־י׳ Ex 8^{25}; *Impf.* 2 ms. תַּעְתִּיר אֵלָיו Jb 22^{27}; *Imv.* mpl. הַעְתִּירוּ אֶל־י׳ Ex 8^{4} 9^{28}, לי׳ 10^{17}; also c. לְ pers. *in behalf of* whom, *Impf.* 1 s. אַעְתִּיר לְךָ Ex 8^{5}, so *Imv.* הַעְתִּירוּ, c. בַּעֲדִי v^{24}. 6279

†I. [עָתָר] **n.[m.] suppliant, worshipper** (?; so usu., but dub.);—only pl. sf. עֲתָרַי Zp 3^{10}. 6282

†II. [עָתַר] **vb. be abundant,** si vera l. (as Aram. loan-word; עֲתַר, ܥܬܪ, *be rich* = Heb. עָשַׁר);—**Niph.** *Pt.* fpl. נַעְתָּרוֹת Pr 27^{6} (of enemy's kisses; De *excessive;* opp. נֶאֱמָנִים); Toy prop. נֶעְקָשׁוֹת, or נַעֲוֹת, *crooked, hypocritical.* **Hiph.** *Pf.* 2 mpl. הַעְתַּרְתֶּם עָלַי דִּבְרֵיכֶם Ez 35^{13} *ye have multiplied against me your words* (‖ וַתַּגְדִּילוּ עָלַי בְּפִיכֶם), del. as gloss Co after 𝔊, Toy reads sg., and thinks verb due to Aramaizing scribe. 6280

†עֲתֶרֶת **n.f. abundance** (Aramaism, si vera l.);—cstr. Je 33^{6} I will reveal to them *abundance* of peace, etc. (corrupt acc. to Gie Buhl^{Lex}; Vrss. render variously). 6283

†עֶתֶר **n.pr.loc.** (√dub.);—in Judah Jos 15^{42} (Ιθακ; A𝔊L Αθερ), in Simeon 19^{7} (Ιεθερ; in both sq. עָשָׁן); perhaps = עָתָךְ q.v.; perhaps (Conder$^{\text{Survey iii. 261}}$) *ʿAtr,* c. 2 miles NW. of *Beit Jibrin* (cf. GASm$^{\text{Geogr., Map}}$). 6281 6269

III. עתר (√of following).

†II. [עָתָר] **n.[m.] odour** (si vera l.) (so Vrss.);—cstr. עֲתַר Ez 8^{11}, of incense. 6282

ף, פ

ף, פּ, פ, *Pê*, seventeenth letter; used as numeral 80 in postB.Hebrew.

6311 **פא** v. פה. p. 805

6284 † **[פָּאָה]** **vb.** perh. (si vera l.) **cleave in pieces** (Ar. (فأو, فأى) فَأَا *cleave, split* (head, bowl, etc.); Sab. פעי DHM $^{ZMG\ xxx\ (1876),\ 701\ f.}$);—**Hiph.** *Impf.* 1 s. sf. אַפְאֵיהֶם Dt 32^{26} *I* [י׳] *will cleave them in pieces* (poss. point אַפְ׳, i.e. **Qal**; on other views v. Dr; rd. perh. אֲפִיצֵם 𝔊 Gr).

6285 **פֵּאָה** $_{86}$ **n.f. corner, side** (*part cut off*, 'Abschnitt,' acc. to Schröter in Me $^{Archiv.\ i.\ 461}$ Ba $^{ZMG\ xli\ (1887),\ 615}$ Buhl^{Lex}, but perh. bilit., Nö$^{M.485}$ Sta^{§185}, and not fr. √פאה; cf. Ar. فِئَةٌ *company*, etc. (Nö$^{l.c.}$); As. *pâtu, side, edge, border*, v. esp. Meissn$^{Suppl.74}$; NH=BH, Aram. פְּאתָא, ܦܐܬܐ);—abs. פ׳ Je 9^{25}+4 t.; cstr. פְּאַת Am 3^{12}+77 t.; pl. abs. פֵּאֹת Ex 25^{26} 37^{23}; du. cstr. פַּאֲתֵי Nu 24^{17} (but read prob. פְּאַת as ‖ Je 48^{45});—†**1.** *corner* of divan Am 3^{12}; table Ex 25^{26} 37^{23}; field Lv 19^{9} 23^{22} (H); land (prob.) וַתַּחְלְקֵם לְפֵאָה Ne 9^{22}, i.e. into every corner; פ׳ רֹאשְׁכֶם Lv 19^{27} (i.e. *your temples*), פ׳ זְקָנֶךָ v^{27} cf. 21^{5} (all H); קְצוּצֵי פֵאָה *those clipped on the temples* Je 9^{25} 25^{23} 49^{32} (epith. of Arab. tribes, Herod.^{iii,8} WMM$^{As.\ u.\ Eur.\ 140\ f.}$ We$^{Skizzen\ iii.\ 119;\ Heid.\ 2,198}$); *temples of Moab* (under fig. of man) Nu 24^{17} (JE) Je 48^{45}. **2.** *side*: **a.** usu. of Ezekiel's temple, the tabern., the holy city and the land, or its subdivisions (only Ez 41–48 [47 t.] and P [26 t.]): in plur. פְּאַת קָדִימ(ה) *East side* Ez 47^{18}+17 t. Ez, =פ׳ קֵדְמָה Ex 27^{13}+3 t. P and Ez 45^{7} (v. Co Toy); פ׳ נֶגֶב צָפוֹנ(ה) *North side* Ez 47^{15} Ex 26^{20}+9 t.; פ׳ נֶגְבָּה (נֶגְבָּה) *South side* Ez $47^{19.19}$ Ex 27^{9}+8 t.; פ׳ יָם (יָמָּה) *West side* Ez 45^{7} Ex 27^{12}+21 t. + פ׳ דֶּרֶךְ־הַיָּם Ez 41^{12} (also פ׳ קָדִים הַיָּם 48^{1}); abs. only לִפְאָה הָאֶחָת Ex 27^{9}. **b.** פְּאַת פָּנָיו Lv 13^{41} *side* (border) *of his face* (forehead and temples; P).

6371 **פאם** v. פימה. p. 810

6286 † I. **[פָּאַר]** **vb. Pi. beautify, glorify**;—*Pf.* 3 ms. sf. פֵּאֲרָךְ (obj. Isr.) Is 55^{5} 60^{9}; c. acc. of temple; *Impf.* 1 s. אֲפָאֵר 60^{7}; *Inf. cstr.* פָּאֵר v^{13} Ezr 7^{27}; so פָּאֵר עֲנָוִים בִּישׁוּעָה ψ 149^{4}. **Hithp. 1.** *glorify oneself*, c. עַל pers.: =boast, *Impf.* 3 ms. יִתְפָּאֵר Ju 7^{2} Is 10^{15}; as polite address to king, *Imv.* ms. הִתְפָּאֵר Ex 8^{5} (J), *assume the honour over me* (to decide) *when*, etc. **2.** *get glory to oneself, be glorified, by means of* (ב), of י׳, בְּיִשְׂרָאֵל יִתְפָּאָר Is 44^{23}, so 1 s. אֶתְפָּאָר 49^{3}; of people [by י׳], *Inf. cstr.* הִתְפָּאֵר 60^{21} 61^{3}.

† **פְּאֵר** **n.m.** $^{Ez\ 44,\ 18}$ **head-dress, turban** 6287
(? orig. *ornament*);—abs. פ׳ of bridegroom Is 61^{10}, sign of joy v^{3} (opp. mourning, and so) פְּאֵרְךָ Ez 24^{17}, pl. sf. פְּאֵרֵכֶם v^{23} (worn by men of position); of priests פַּאֲרֵי פִשְׁתִּים Ez 44^{18}, פ׳ הַמִּגְבָּעֹת שֵׁשׁ Ex 39^{28} (P); pl. abs. פְּאֵרִים Is 3^{20} (of luxurious women).

† **תִּפְאָרָה** **n.f. beauty, glory**;—ת׳ Is 28^{5} 8597
Je 48^{17}; elsewh. abs. and cstr. תִּפְאֶרֶת Is 3^{18}+20 t.; תִּפְאָרֶת Pr 28^{12}+6 t.; sf. תִּפְאַרְתִּי Is 46^{13}+20 t. sf.;—**1.** *beauty, finery* Is 3^{18}; of garments 52^{1}; jewels Ez $16^{17.39}$ 23^{26}, cf. 2 Ch 3^{6}; flock Je 13^{20}; a man Is 44^{13}; city of Samaria $28^{1.4}$; diadem v^{5}. **2.** *glory*: **a.** of rank: apparel of h.p. Ex $28^{2.40}$ (P); עֲטֶרֶת ת׳ *crown of glory* Pr 4^{9} 16^{31} Is 62^{3} Je 13^{18} Ez 16^{12} 23^{42}; greatness of monarch Est 1^{4}; house of David and inhabitants of Jerus. Zc $12^{7.7}$. **b.** of renown לְשֵׁם ולת׳ Dt 26^{19} 1 Ch 22^{5} Je 13^{11} 33^{9}. **c.** attribute of י׳ ψ 71^{8} 1 Ch 29^{11}; שֵׁם ת׳ Is 63^{14} 1 Ch 29^{13}; עֹז ת׳ ψ 89^{18}; זְרוֹעַ ת׳ Is 63^{12}; hence ת׳ in י׳'s sanctuary ψ 96^{6}, בֵּית תִּפְאַרְתִּי Is 60^{7} cf. 63^{15} (of heavenly temple), 64^{10}; ת׳ as י׳'s gift to Isr. 46^{13} cf. 60^{19} (also ψ 89^{18} supr.); of future fruit of land 4^{2}; design. of ark of י׳ ψ 78^{61}. **3. a.** *honour* of nation Isr. La 2^{1}. **b.** *glorying, boasting*, of individ., Is 20^{5} Pr 17^{6} 19^{11} 20^{29} 28^{12}; warrior Ju 4^{9}; monarchs Is 10^{12}; nations Is 13^{19} Ez 24^{25}, מַקֵּל ת׳ *rod* (*sceptre*) *of glorying* Je 48^{17} (others **1**).

II. **פאר** (doubtful √).

† **[פֹּארָה]** **n.f. bough**;—pl., all in fig.: of 6288
vine, abs. פֹּארוֹת Ez 17^{6} (Baer פֹּראוֹת); of cedar, sf. פֹּארֹתָו 31^{5} (Kt; ־ָיו Qr); פֹּארֹתָיו v^{6}, פֹּראֹתָיו $v^{8.12.13}$.

† **פארה** Kt., **פֻּרָה** Qr **n.f.coll. boughs** 6288,6333
Is 10^{33} (van d. H. Baer פֻּארָה). 6288

† **[פֵּאֵר]** **vb. denom. Pi. go over the** 6286
boughs;—*Impf.* 2 ms. תְּפָאֵר Dt 24^{20} *thou shalt not go over the boughs* after thee (i.e. glean).

† **פָּארוּר** **n.[m.]** mng. dub.; only קִבְּצוּ פ׳ 6289
Na 2^{11} Jo 2^{6}; Thes, all faces *gather a glow* (*glow* with dread, fr. assumed √פאר), so We

Now; AE Hi al. *gather in* (their) *beauty* (√I. פאר; grow pale); Vrss AV *gather blackness* (fr. פָּרוּר *a pot!*), v. Dr; all very uncertain.

6290 †פָּארָן **n.pr.loc.** **Paran**, Φαραν (cf. n.pr. פארן Sin. Inscr.);—usu. מִדְבַּר פ׳ home of Ishmael Gn 21[21] (E), traversed by Isr. in Exodus Nu 12[16] (E), 10[12] 13[2.26] (all P); it lay NE. fr. (the traditional) Sinai, with Gulf of Akaba and the ʿArabah as its E. border; in the same region was הַר פ׳ Dt 33[2] Hb 3[3],—perh. coast-range of mts. along W. shore of Gulf of Akaba; פ׳ alone 1 K 11[18.18] (betw. Midian and Egypt); Dt 1[1] (loc. dub.).—1 S 25[1] v. ii. מָעוֹן sub עון.—Vid. Rob[BR i. 177 f.] Palmer[Desert of Exodus, 284 ff.], Di Dr[Dt].

פגג (√of foll.; mng. dub.; NH פַּגָּה *unripe fig*, pl. פַּגִּין; so Syr. ܦܓܐ in Lexx; Ar. فِجٌّ *unripe fruit;* 𝔗 פַּגָּא *unripe grape;* cf. Post in Hastings[DB. 'Fig'] Tristr[NHB 352] Löw[p. 391]).

6291 †[פַּגָּה] **n.f.** (cf. NH) **early fig**;—pl. sf. פַּגֶּיהָ Ct 2[13].

פגל (√of foll.; mng. dub.; Ar. فَجَلَ, فَجُلَ (فَجِلَ) is *be thick and soft, flaccid;* NH פִּגּוּל = BH, cf. Levy[NHWB s.v.]).

6292 †פִּגּוּל **n.m.**[Lv 7, 18] **foul thing, refuse**, but only as term. techn. of unclean sacrificial flesh;—it is פ׳ if eaten on third day Lv 7[18] (P), 19[7] (H); cf. בְּשַׂר פ׳ Ez 4[14] (undefined); pl. מְרַק פִּגֻּלִים Is 65[4] *broth of refuse things* (Kt פרק), RS[Sem i. 325, 2nd ed. 343] thinks of flesh with the blood; Du[ad loc.] of mice and other unclean animals.

6293 †פָּגַע **vb. meet, encounter, reach** (NH *id.;* Aram. פְּגַע, ܦܓܥ; poss. akin to Ar. فَجَأَ, فَجِئَ *happen to, light upon;* فَجَعَ is *pain, afflict*);—**Qal** *Pf.* 3 ms. פ׳ 1 K 2[32]+, sf. וּפְגָעוֹ consec. Am 5[19], etc.; *Impf.* 3 ms. וַיִּפְגַּע Gn 28[11]+; 1 pl. נִפְגַּע Jb 21[15], etc.; *Imv.* ms. פְּגַע Ju 8[21]+; mpl. פִּגְעוּ Gn 23[8]; *Inf. cstr.* לִפְגֹּעַ 1 S 22[17], sf. פִּגְעוֹ Nu 35[19.21];—**1.** *meet, light upon*, c. acc. pers. 1 S 10[5] Ex 5[20] (J), c. sf. pers. Am 5[19]; פ׳ שׁוֹר Ex 23[4]; c. בְּ pers. Gn 32[2] (E), Nu 35[19.21] (P); c. בְּ loc. Gn 28[11] (E). **2.** *meet*, with kindness, c. acc. pers. Is 64[5] (subj. י׳), so 47[3] acc. to Ew De Di al.; Che[Hpt] אֶפְרַע (reading, with Du, אמר for אָדָם). **3.** *encounter* with hostility, *fall upon* c. בְּ pers. Jos 2[16] (JE), Ju 8[21] 15[12] 18[25] 1 S 22[17.18.18] 2 S 1[15] 1 K 2[25.29.31.32.34.46] Ru 2[22]; of God, c. acc. (sf.), + בְּ instr. Ex 5[3]. **4.** *encounter* with request, *entreat*, c. בְּ pers. Je 7[16] Jb 21[15], sq. cl. Je 27[18] Ru 1[16], + לְ pers. on whose behalf Gn 23[8]. **5.** *strike, touch*, of boundary, c. בְּ loc. Jos 16[7] 19[11.22.26.27.34.34], cf. 17[10]; c. אֶל loc. 19[11]. **Hiph.** **1.** *cause to light upon*, *Pf.* 3 ms. הִפְגִּיעַ c. acc. rei + בְּ pers. Is 53[6]. **2.** *cause one* (acc.) *to entreat* 1 s. הִפְגַּעְתִּי (בְּ pers.) Je 15[11] (otherwise Gie; Co del. v. as gloss). **3.** *make entreaty*, 3 pl. הִפְגְּעוּ Je 36[25] c. בְּ pers.; more gen. *interpose*, *Impf.* 3 ms. יַפְגִּיעַ Is 53[12], c. לְ pers. in whose behalf; *Pt.* מַפְגִּיעַ 59[16] *one interposing.* **4.** *make attack*, only *Pt.* Jb 36[32] *assailant*, but Ol Bu Du al. מִפְגָּע *mark.*

†פֶּגַע **n.m.** **occurrence, chance**;—abs. פ׳ 1 K 5[18] evil *occurrence;* Ec 9[11] time and *chance.* 6294

†מִפְגָּע **n.[m.]** **thing hit, mark**;—לָמָּה שַׂמְתַּנִי לְמִ׳ לָךְ Jb 7[20] (cf. also פָּגַע **Hiph. 1**). 4645

†פַּגְעִיאֵל **n.m.** Asherite, Φαγαιηλ, -εηλ;—Nu 1[13] 2[27] 7[72.77] 10[26]. 6295

†[פָּגַר] **vb. Pi. be exhausted, faint** (𝔗 פַּגַּר der. spec. *tear down, destroy;* As. *pagru, body, corpse;* NH פֶּגֶר = BH; Aram. פִּגְרָא, ܦܓܪܐ; Palm. פגר; Mand. פאגרא Nö[M § 89]);—*Pf.* 3 pl. פִּגְּרוּ מִן *they were too faint* to go, etc. 1 S 30[10.21]. 6296

†פֶּגֶר **n.m.**[Is 14, 19] **corpse, carcass**;—abs. פ׳ Is 14[19]+, פָּגֶר Na 3[3]; cstr. פֶּגֶר 1 S 17[46]; pl. פְּגָרִים 2 K 19[35]+; cstr. פִּגְרֵי Je 33[5]; sf. פִּגְרֵיכֶם Lv 26[30]+, etc.;—**1.** of men, sg. Is 14[19]; usu. pl. 34[3] 66[24] Je 31[40] 33[5] 41[9] Ez 6[5] 43[7.9] Lv 26[30] Nu 14[29.32.33] 2 Ch 20[24],—v[25] rd. prob. בְּגָדִים, so 𝔊 (?), 𝔙 Be Krochm Kau Kit;—פְּגָרִים מֵתִים 2 K 19[35] = Is 37[36]; sg. coll. 1 S 17[46], רַב־הַפֶּגֶר Am 8[3], כֹּבֶד־פ׳ Na 3[3]; fig. of idols פִּגְרֵי גִּלּוּלֵיכֶם Lv 26[30]. **2.** of animals Gn 15[11]. 6297

†[פָּגַשׁ] **vb. meet, encounter** (syn. פָּגַע);—**Qal** *Pf.* 1 s. פָּגָשְׁתִּי Gn 33[8]; 3 pl. consec. וּפָגְשׁוּ Is 34[14]; *Impf.* 3 ms. sf. יִפְגָּשְׁךָ Gn 32[18] (Gi; Baer יִפְגָּשְׁךָ; van d. H. יִפְגָּשְׁךָ), וַיִּפְגְּשֵׁהוּ Ex 4[24.27]; 3 fs. וַתִּפְגֹּשׁ 1 S 25[20] (rd. prob. וַתִּפְגּשׁ Ges[§ 47 k], cf. van d. H), etc.; *Inf. abs.* פָּגוֹשׁ Pr 17[12]; *cstr.* פְּגֹשׁ Je 41[6];—*meet*, c. acc. Gn 33[8] 1 S 25[20] Is 34[14] Je 41[6], so c. sf. Gn 32[18] Ex 4[24.27] 2 S 2[13]; *meet, encounter*, of bear, c. בְּ pers. Pr 17[12], of י׳ (like a bear) Ho 13[8] (c. sf. pers.). **Niph.** *meet together, each other*, *Pf.* 3 pl. נִפְגָּשׁוּ Pr 22[2] 29[13], fig. of חֶסֶד וֶאֱמֶת ψ 85[11]. **Pi.** intens. *Impf.* 3 mpl. יְפַגְּשׁוּ חֹשֶׁךְ Jb 5[14] *they keep encountering darkness* in the daytime. 6298

6299 †פָּדָה **vb.** ransom (NH in deriv.; Ph. in n.pr.; As. *padû*, *id.*, Ar. فَدَى; Eth. ፈደየ:; Min. פדית *redeemed* or *purchased land* Mordt Beitr.23);—**Qal** *Pf.* 3 ms. פָּדָה Lv 27^{27}+; sf. פָּדְךָ Jb 5^{20}; 2 ms. פָּדִיתָ Dt 9^{26}+, etc.; *Impf.* יִפְדֶּה ψ 49^{8}+, etc.; *Imv.* פְּדֵה ψ 25^{22}; sf. פְּדֵנִי ψ 26^{11} + 3 t.; *Inf. abs.* פָּדֹה Nu 18^{15} ψ 49^{8}; *cstr.* לִפְדּוֹת 2 S 7^{23} = 1 Ch 17^{2}; *Pt. act.* פּוֹדֶה ψ 34^{23}; sf. פֹּדְךָ
6302 Dt 13^{6}; *pass.* pl. cstr. פְּדוּיֵי Is 35^{10} 51^{11} Nu 3^{49}; also abs. פְּדוּיִם Nu 3^{51} (Qr; Kt פדים), cstr. פְּדוּיֵי v^{46}; sf. פְּדוּיָו Nu 18^{16} (all n. abstr. acc. to Di Kö ii.1,138, v. פְּדוּיִם, פְּדֻיִם infr.);—*ransom*: **1.** for an assessed price Ex $13^{13.15}$ 34^{20} (J), Lv 27^{27} Nu $3^{46.48.49.51}$ $18^{15.16.17}$ (P). **2.** fr. violence and death 1 S 14^{45} Jb 6^{23} ψ 49^{8}. **3.** God subj. (underlying thought of payment): **a.** fr. Egypt, c. מִן, מִבֵּית עֲבָדִים Dt 7^{8} 13^{6} Mi 6^{4}; מִנִּי־צָר ψ 78^{42}; ממצרים 2 S 7^{23} (but del. פָּדִיתָ Gei Urschr.288 We Dr al.) = 1 Ch 17^{21}; מִשָּׁם Dt 24^{18}; abs. Dt 9^{26} 15^{15} 21^{8} Ne 1^{10}. **b.** from exile, Je 31^{11} Zc 10^{8}; פְּדוּיֵי י׳ יְשֻׁבוּן Is 35^{10} = 51^{11}. **c.** in gen. Ho 7^{13}; מִכֹּל צָרוֹתָיו ψ 25^{22}; מִכֹּל עֲוֹנֹתָיו ψ 130^{8}. **d.** c. acc. individ. ψ 26^{11} 31^{6} 44^{27} 69^{19}; Abraham Is 29^{22}; פ׳ נפש ψ 34^{23} 71^{23}; + מכל צרה 2 S 4^{9} 1 K 1^{29}; מֵעֲבֹר בַּשָּׁחַת Jb 33^{28}; מִקְּרָב־לִי ψ 55^{19}; מִמָּוֶת Jb 5^{20}; מיד שאול ψ 49^{16} Ho 13^{14}; מֵעֹשֶׁק אָדָם ψ 119^{134}; מִכַּף עָרִיצִים Je 15^{21}. **Niph.** *Pf.* 3 fs. (+ **Hoph.** *Inf. abs.*) הָפְדֵּה לֹא נִפְדָּתָה Lv 19^{20} *she hath not been at all ransomed* (from bondage); *Impf.* יִפָּדֶה Lv 27^{29} (from ban); 3 fs. צִיּוֹן בְּמִשְׁפָּט תִּפָּדֶה Is 1^{27}. **Hiph.** *Pf.* 3 ms. sf. וְהֶפְדָּהּ Ex 21^{8} *he shall let her be ransomed*. **Hiph.** *Inf. abs.* v. **Niph.**

6302 †פְּדוּיִם **n.[m.]pl.abstr.** ransom;—so rd.
6306 perh. Nu 3^{49} for MT פִּדְיוֹם, Sam. פדוים; cstr. פְּדוּיֵי v^{48}; for other poss. cases v. **Qal** *Pt. pass.*

6303 †פָּדוֹן **n.pr.m.** (*ransom*; cf. Ph. פדי) head of family of Nethinim Ezr 2^{44} Ne 7^{47}; Φαδων.

6304 †פְּדוּת **n.f.** ransom; פ׳ ψ 111^{9} + 2 t.; פְּדֻת Ex 8^{19};—fr. exile Is 50^{2}; fr. iniquities ψ 130^{7}; in gen. ψ 111^{9}, שַׂמְתִּי פְדֻת בֵּין עַמִּי וּבֵין עַמֶּךָ Ex 8^{19} *I will set a ransom* (distinguishing) *between my people and thy people* 𝔗, but improb. and text dub.; 𝔊𝔖𝔙 *set a distinction* (rdg. what?).

6306 †פִּדְיוֹם **n.m.** ransom;—Nu 3^{49}, rd. prob. פְּדוּיִם (so Sam.); פְּדֻיִם v^{51} Kt (Qr פְּדוּיִם);—v.
6299, 6302 פדה **Qal** *Pt. pass.*, and פְּדוּיִם supr.

6306 †פִּדְיוֹן **n.m.** id.;—פ׳ נֶפֶשׁ Ex 21^{30} (E), ψ 49^{9}.

6300 †פְּדַהְאֵל **n.pr.m.** (*Ēl hath ransomed*; cf. Ph. בעלפדה; As. *Pudu-ilu*, *Pudi-ilu* COT Gloss.);—prince of Naphtali Nu 34^{28}; Φαδαηλ.

†פְּדָהצוּר **n.pr.m.** (*the Rock hath ransomed*) 6301
Manassite, Nu 1^{10} 2^{20} $7^{54.59}$ 10^{23} Φαδασσουρ.

†פְּדָיָה, פְּדָיָהוּ **n.pr.m.** (י׳ *hath ransomed*; 6305
in late As. *Padâma*, Hilpr Univ. Pa. Exp. ix. 27, 68);—פְּדָיָה: **1.** father-in-law of Josiah 2 K 23^{36}, but 𝔊 Εδειλ (𝔊L Ιερεμιας, fr. v^{31}). **2.** father of Zerub. 1 Ch $3^{18.19}$. **3. a.** Ne 3^{25}. **b.** 8^{4}. **4.** Benjamite Ne 11^{7}. **5.** Levite Ne 13^{13}. **6.** פְּדָיָהוּ, Manassite 1 Ch 27^{20}—𝔊 (exc. **1**) Φα(λ)δαιας, etc.

פַּדָּן 11 **n.pr.loc.** (?*garden, field*; cf. 𝔗 פַּדָּנָא 6307
yoke, span of oxen; Syr. ܦܕܢܐ *yoke*, whence, as loan-wd. Ar. فَدَّانٌ Frä 129; As. *padanu*, =*road*, and also *garden*, etc. (in word-lists, v. KAT 2, 612); also Nö Aram. in Ency. Bib.);—פ׳ Gn 48^{7}, abbrev. fr. פַּדַּן־אֲרָם (? = *garden, field of* [*in*] *Aram*; conj. by many that שְׂדֵה אֲרָם Ho 12^{13} is Heb. transl., cf. Di Gn 25, 20) 25^{20} + 5 t.; פַּדֶּנָה א׳ $28^{2f.}$ (v. אֲרָם **b**; all P); 𝔊 Μεσοποταμία (Συρίας); perh. *Paddânâ*, near Haran (and *Tel Faddān* of Arab. geogr.), v. Nö l.c.

†[פָּדַע] **vb.** dub., only *Imv.* ms. sf. פְּדָעֵהוּ 6308
Jb 33^{24} a mng. like *deliver him* needed, Codd. Bu Du פְּרָעֵהוּ; < rd. פְּדֵהוּ (פדה) Ew Di SS.

†[פֶּדֶר] **n.[m.]** suet, of עֹלָה (so Vrss NH: 6309
√ unknown);—abs. פָּדֶר Lv 1^{8} 8^{20}; sf. פִּדְרוֹ 1^{12}.

פֶּה 485 **n.m.** Jos 9, 2 mouth (prob. bilit. [פי, פו] 6310, 6366
Sta § 183; NH = BH; Ph. לפי *acc. to*; As. *pû*, *mouth*; Ar. فُوهٌ, فَاهٌ, فِيهٌ; Eth. አፍ:; Syr. ܠܦܘܡ *acc. to*; but also Ar. فَمٌ, فُمٌ, فِمٌ, BAram. פֻּם, 𝔗 פּוּמָא; Syr. ܦܘܡܐ; Mand. פומא Nö M § 87);—abs. פ׳ Ex 4^{10}+, cstr. פִּי Is 1^{20}+; sf. 1 s. פִּי Gn 45^{12}+, 2 ms. פִּיךָ 41^{40}+, 3 ms. פִּיו 25^{28}+, פִּיהוּ Ex 4^{15}+, 3 mpl. פִּיהֶם Ju 7^{6}+, פִּימוֹ ψ 17^{10} + 2 t., etc.; pl.
פִּיּוֹת Pr 5^{4}, פֵּיוֹת (שְׁנֵי) Ju 3^{16}, פִּיפִיּוֹת Is 41^{15} ψ 149^{6}; 6374
פִּים 1 S 13^{21} (corrupt, v. Dr al.);—**1. a.** *mouth*, of man, organ of eating and drinking Gn 25^{28} Ju 7^{6} 1 S $14^{26.27}$ Ne 9^{20} Pr 19^{24} = 26^{15}+; fig. as finding things sweet Jb 20^{12} ψ 119^{103}; fig. of earth Gn 4^{11}, swallowing Korah, etc. Nu $16^{30.32}$ 26^{10} Dt 11^{6}; fig. also of She'ôl, וּפָעֲרָה פִיהָ Is 5^{14}, cf. ψ 69^{16}. **b.** external organ, וַיָּשֶׂם פִּיו עַל־פִּיו 2 K 4^{34} Pr 30^{20}; of kissing 1 K 19^{18} Ct 1^{2}; וַתִּשַּׁק יָדִי לְפִי Jb 31^{27}; cf. phr. שִׂים יָד עַל־פֶּה (of keeping silence) Ju 18^{19} Mi 7^{16} Jb 21^{5}, cf. 29^{9} 40^{4} Pr 30^{32}; of mocking triumph פ׳ עַל פָּעֲרוּ עָלַי בְּפִיהֶם Jb 16^{10}; הִרְחִיב פ׳ עַל ψ 35^{21} Is 57^{4}, also רָחַב פִּי עַל 1 S 2^{1}. **c.** of י׳ in theoph., sending out fire 2 S 22^{9} = ψ 18^{9}. **2. a.** much

oftener, as organ of speech, of man: פ׳ speaks Gn 45^{12} 2 S 1^{16} Is 9^{16} Jb 9^{20} 15$^{5.6}$ ψ 37^{30}+; speak בְּמוֹ־פִי Jb 19^{16}; open פ׳, אֶל־י׳ פ׳ Ju 11$^{35.36}$, abs. Jb 3^{1} 33^{2}+; shut פ׳ (be silent) Is 52^{15}, cf. חָשַׂךְ פ׳ Jb 7^{11}, and (of iniquity, personif.) קָפְצָה פ׳ Jb 5^{16} ψ 107^{42}; guard פ׳, Pr 13^{3} (נָצַר), 21^{23} (שָׁמַר), cf. שָׁמַר פִּתְחֵי פ׳ Mi 7^{5}, also ψ 39^{2} (v. שׁמר); words, etc., are in (ב) mouth 2 S 17^{5} 18^{25} Dt 30^{14} 1 K 17^{24}; שִׂים דְּבָרִים בְּפ׳ 2 S 14$^{3.19}$ Ex 4^{15}, also (God subj.) Nu 22^{38} 23$^{12.16}$+; of utterance יָצָא מִפּ׳ Ju 11^{36} Nu 30^{3} 32^{24} Jos 6^{10}+; depart fr. mouth (cease to be mentioned) מוּשׁ מִפּ׳ Jos 1^{8} Is 59^{21}, cf. נִכְרַת מִפּ׳ Je 7^{28}, לֹא יִשָּׁמַע עַל־פִּיךָ Ex 23^{13}; אִמְרֵי פ׳ Dt 32^{1} *words of my mouth*, so Jb 8^{2} ψ 19^{15} 54^{4}; דִּבְרֵי פ׳ ψ 36^{4} Ec 10^{12}; of agency, בְּפ׳ *by the mouth of* 2 Ch 36$^{21.22}$=מִפּ׳ Ezr 1^{1}; דִּבֶּר פִּיו עִם־פִּיו Je 32^{4} *speak mouth to mouth*=34^{3}; פ׳=*speech, sayings* Is 29^{13} ψ 49^{14} Ec 10^{3}; כְּבַד פ׳ Ex 4^{10} *heavy of speech* (not eloquent); אֶהְיֶה עִם־פ׳ v$^{12.15}$, i.e. aid thee in speaking; יִהְיֶה־לְּךָ לְפ׳ v^{16} *he shall be mouth for thee;* מִפִּיו יִקְרָא אֵלַי Je 36^{18}, i.e. dictate; כָּתַב מִפּ׳ v. כָּתַב **1 b** (3); bad qualities ascribed to it, עִקְּשׁוּת פ׳ Pr 4^{24} 6^{12}; פִּי תַהְפֻּכוֹת 8^{13}; פֶּה חָלָק 26^{28}; אַל־תַּגְדֵּל פ׳ Ob^{12}, cf. Mi 6^{12} Ez 35^{13}. **b.** as laughing Jb 8^{21} ψ 126^{2}; panting 119^{131}. **c.** of God; his mouth speaks Is 1^{20} 40^{5} Je 9^{11}+; he speaks בְּפ׳ 1 K 8$^{15.24}$; wd. proceeds מִפּ׳ Dt 8^{3} Is 45^{23}+; פֶּה אֶל־פֶּה אֲדַבֶּר בּוֹ Nu 12^{8}; he creates בְּרוּחַ פִּיו ψ 33^{6}; he executes judgment בְּשֵׁבֶט פִּיו Is 11^{4}; esp.=*command:* עָבַר אֶת־פִּי י׳ 1 S 15^{24} Nu 14^{41}, cf. 22^{18} Pr 8^{29}; מָרָה (אֶת־) פ׳ 1 S 12$^{14.15}$ Nu 20^{24} 1 K 13^{21}+; cf. **6 d**. **d.** of idols, ψ 115^{5} 136$^{16.17}$. **e.** of musical instr.=sound Am 6^{5} (cf. **6 d**). **3.** of animals: bird Gn 8^{11} (carrying), Is 10^{14} (chirping); ass Nu 22^{28} (speaking); bear, lion 1 S 17^{35} (seizing), Am 3^{12} (*id.*), hippop. Jb 40^{23} (drinking), crocod. 41$^{11.13}$ (breathing flame); also of human foes, under fig. of ravenous beasts ψ 22^{22} Ez 21^{27} 34^{10}; פָּצָה פ׳ עַל ψ 22^{14} La 2^{16} 3^{46}; hence of *edge* of sword, חֶרֶב פִּיּוֹת Pr 5^{4} *a sword with edges* (in sim.), =ח׳ פִּיפִיּוֹת ψ 149^{6}; cf. Ju 3^{16}; v. also **6 c** (2), infr.; בַּעַל פִּיפִיּוֹת Is 41^{15}, of מוֹרַג. **4.** *mouth*=opening, orifice; of well Gn 29$^{2.3.3.8.10}$; cave Jos 10$^{18.22.27}$; ravine, abyss Je 48^{28} (si vera l., cf. Gie); also of Sheʾôl ψ 141^{7}; of a sack Gn 42^{27} 43$^{12.21}$ 44$^{1.2.8}$; ephah Zc 5^{8}; high-priest's robe Ex 28^{32} + 5 t., cf. prob. ψ 133^{2}; tunic Jb 30^{18}; of a round opening also 1 K 7$^{31.31.31}$ (on text and meaning v. Benz Kit); of *mouth* of Nile Is 19^{7} (others *brink*); gate of city Pr 8^{3} (but rd. perhaps לִפְנֵי, v. Toy). **5. a.** *extremity, end* פֶּה לָפֶה *from end to end*, of a temple 2 K 10^{21}; city 21^{16}, מִפֶּה אֶל־פֶּה of land Ezr 9^{11}. **b.** =portion, פִּי שְׁנַיִם †Dt 21^{17} 2 K 2^{9} Zc 13^{8}. **6.** with preps.:— **a.** אֶל פִּי, v. infr. **d** (2). **b.** כְּפִי: (*a*) *acc. to the command of*, 1 Ch 12^{23}; (*b*) *acc. to the mouth of*, i.e. *in proportion to* (cf. As. *ki-i pi-i*, Dl$^{HWB 525}$), †Ex 16^{21} they gathered it אִישׁ כְּפִי אָכְלוֹ each *in proportion to* his eating (v$^{16.18}$ לְפִי), Lv 25^{52} כְּפִי שָׁנָיו *acc. to* the number of his years (cf. v^{16} לְפִי); Nu 6^{21} 7^{5} אִישׁ כְּפִי עֲבֹדָתוֹ (so 2 Ch 31^{2}), 7$^{7.8}$ 35^{8} (all P); Jb 33^{6} הֶן־אֲנִי כְפִיךָ לָאֵל I am *in the proportion of* thee as regards God, i.e. I stand towards God even as thou dost. As **conj.**, כְּפִי אֲשֶׁר, †Ml 2^{9} כְּפִי אֲשֶׁר אֵינְכֶם שֹׁמְרִים אֶת־דְּרָכַי *acc. as* ye do not keep, etc.; and without אשׁר Zc 2^{4} כְּפִי אִישׁ־לֹא נָשָׂא רֹאשׁוֹ *in such proportion that* none did lift up his head (but We Now אֲשֶׁר for אִישׁ, that it, Judah, did not, etc.). **c.** לְפִי, nearly i.q. כְּפִי (v. לְ **5 i** *b*), but more common (cf. Aram. לְפוּם, ܠܦܘܡ): (1) † Gn 47^{12} לְפִי הַטָּף, Ex 12^{4} ye shall compute אִישׁ לְפִי אָכְלוֹ each *acc. to* his eating (acc. to the quantity which his family will consume), 16$^{16.18}$ Lv 25^{16} לְפִי רֹב הַשָּׁנִים, v$^{16.51}$ 27^{16} לְפִי זַרְעוֹ, Nu 26^{54} Jos 18^{4} 1 K 17^{1} except לְפִי דְבָרִי, Ho 10^{12} קִצְרוּ לְפִי חֶסֶד (|| לִצְדָקָה), Pr 12^{8} 27^{21}: sq. inf. Nu 9^{17} לְפִי הֵעָלוֹת הֶעָנָן = *acc. as* the cloud was lifted up, Je 29^{10}. (2) in the phr. לְפִי חֶרֶב *acc. to the mouth*, or *measure*, of the sword, i.e. as the sword devours, without quarter, Gn 34^{26} Ex 17^{13} Nu 21^{24}+oft. **d.** עַל פִּי: (1) *acc. to* (עַל **1 f** *a*) *the mouth of*, i.e. (*a*) the command of, Gn 41^{40} 45^{21} Ex 17^{1} 38^{21} Nu 3$^{16.39}$ +(esp. P), 2 K 23^{35}; (*β*) the evidence or sentence of, Dt 17^{6} עַל־פִּי עֵד אֶחָד, 19^{15} 21^{5} (on עַל־פִּי הַנֶּבֶל Am 6^{5}, v. **2 e** supr.). (2) *acc. to the measure of, in accordance with*, † Gn 43^{7} we told him על פי הדברים האלה *acc. to* these words (i.e. the questions Joseph asked), Ex 34^{27} *in accordance with* these words, Lv 27^{8} עַל־פִּי אֲשֶׁר תַּשִּׂיג יַד הַנֹּדֵר *acc. to* what the hand of the vower can reach to, v^{18} (cf. לְפִי 25$^{16.51}$), Dt 17$^{10.11}$ 2 S 13^{32} (but v. שׁוּמָה), Pr 22^{6} חֲנֹךְ לַנַּעַר עַל פִּי דַרְכּוֹ. In the same sense אֶל פִּי, †Jos 15^{13} 17^{4} 21^{3}.

פֹּה$_{58}$, and (Ez 40–41, 23 out of 35 t.) **פּוֹ**, 6311
also †Jb 38^{11b} **פֹּא**, **adv.loc.** here, hither (prob. from the same demonst. √ found in ف *so, then* (oft. in apod.), אַף, אֵפוֹא: cf. Kö$^{ii. 1, 247 f., 243, 331 f.}$):—**1.** *here:* **a.** Gn 19^{12} עֹד מִי־לְךָ פֹה whom hast thou still *here?* 22^{5} שְׁבוּ לָכֶם פֹּה,

40[15] Nu 22[8] 32[16] Dt 5[28] 12[8] Ju 4[20] הֲיֵשׁ פֹּה אִישׁ, 2 K 3[11], etc.; asked in some surprise, Ju 18[3] מַה־לְּךָ פֹה = what is thy business *here?* simil. †1 K 19[9.13] Is 22[16] 52[5] וְעַתָּה מַה־לִּי־פֹה. Cf. the syn. כֹּה, בָּזֶה **2.** **b.** עַד־פֹּה †Jb 38[11a]. **c.** מִפֹּה or מִפּוֹ, only Ez 40–41, and always (exc. 40[12a], where it must be supplied with 𝔊 𝔖) repeated, *on this side . . . on that side* (cf. מִזֶּה . . . מִזֶּה), Ez 40[10.10.12b.b.21.21], etc. **d.** with the interrog. אֵי, אֵיפֹה *where?* v. p. 33. †**2.** after a verb of motion, *hither*, 1 S 16[11] עַד־בֹּאוֹ פֹה, Ezr 4[2].

6312 †פּוּאָה, פֻּוָּה **n.pr.m.** in Issachar, Φουα, etc.;—פּוּאָה Ju 10[1] (v. GFM), 1 Ch 7[1]; פֻּוָּה Gn 46[13] Nu 26[3].

6324 †פּוּנִי **adj.gent.** of פֻּוָּה, c. art. Nu 26[23]; rd. פֻּוָּנִי? or (Φουαει) פֻּוִּי?—𝔊 L Φουλαΐ.

6313 †[פּוּג] **vb.** grow numb (Ar. فَاجَ *grow cool;* Syr. ܦܳܓ *be cold;* 𝔗 פוג *cease, be helpless;* NH *id. vanish*);—**Qal** *Impf.* 3 ms. וַיָּפָג לִבּוֹ Gn 45[26]; 3 fs. תָּפוּג ψ 77[3] of hand (si vera l., v. נגר), i.e. drop helpless; Hb 1[4] of תּוֹרָה, i.e. be ineffective. **Niph.** *Pf.* 1 s. נְפוּגוֹתִי וְנִדְכֵּיתִי ψ 38[9] *I am benumbed and crushed* (fig.); rd. prob. also אָפוּגָה ψ 88[16] (for MT ἅπ. λεγ. אָפוּנָה), Ol Hup Dy Gr Che אָפוּגָה.

6314 †פּוּגַת (Ges[§ 80 f]) **n.f.** benumbing (fig.), cessation;—אַל־תִּתְּנִי פ׳ לָךְ La 2[18] *grant thyself no benumbing* (rd. prob. פּוּגוֹת).

2014 †[הֲפוּגָה] **n.f.** id.;—pl. מֵאֵין הֲפֻגוֹת La 3[49] (of weeping; form very strange, rd. prob. פֻּגוֹת),

6315 †[פּוּחַ] **vb.** breathe, blow (NH פּוּחַ *blow out;* Ar. (فوخ), فَاخَ = Heb., so Aram. פּוּחַ, ܦܳܚ);—**Qal** *Impf.* 3 ms. יָפוּחַ הַיּוֹם Ct 2[17] 4[6] until *the day breathes*, i.e. grows cool. **Hiph.** *Impf.* 3 ms. יָפִיחַ ψ 10[5]+; יָפִחַ Pr 14[25]; וְיָפֵחַ Hb 2[3], etc.; *Imv.* fs. הָפִיחִי Ct 4[16];—**1.** *cause* garden (acc.) *to exhale* (sc. odours) Ct 4[16]. **2. a.** *puff, snort*, against, בְּ pers., ψ 10[5]. **b.** עַל pers., Ez 21[36] with the fire of my wrath *will I blow against thee.* **c.** *excite, inflame* city Pr 29[8]. **d.** c. לוֹ ψ 12[6] *puff, =pant for it* (so most; Thes Hi al. *against whom men puff;* Bae אֹפִיעַ לוֹ *I will shine forth to him*); לַקֵּץ Hb 2[3] the vision *panteth* (hasteth) *towards the end* (so most). **3.** *breathe out, utter*, כְּזָבִים Pr 6[19] 14[5.25] 19[5.9], אֱמוּנָה 12[17].

6368 †פִּיחַ **n.[m.]** soot, 𝔊 αἰθάλη (?*wafted* about);—cstr. פ׳ (הַ)כִּבְשָׁן Ex 9[8.10] (P) *furnace-soot.*

†פּוּט **n.pr.gent.** prob. **Libyans,** or Lib. 6316
tribe; usu. named with African peoples: Na 3[9] Je 46[9] Ez 27[10] 30[5] 38[5] (𝔊 usu. Λίβυες); Gn 10[6] (P) = 1 Ch 1[8] (Φουδ); + Is 66[19] (for MT פּוּל; 𝔊 Φουδ),—vid. Di[Gn 10, 6] Jen[ZA x. 325 ff.].

†פּוּטִיאֵל **n.pr.m.** Eleazar's father-in-law 6317
Ex 6[25], Φουτιηλ.

†פּוֹטִיפַר **n.pr.m.** Joseph's master (abbrev. 6318
fr. foll.);—Gn 37[36] (E), 39[1] (R[J]), Πετεφρης, etc.

†פּוֹטִי פֶרַע **n.pr.m.** priest of On, Joseph's 6319
father-in-law (Egypt. *P'-dì-p'-R'*, i.e. *he whom the Ra gave*, v. Sethe[De aleph prosthetico in ling. aeg. (1892), 31]; Dr in Hastings[DB]);—Gn 41[45.50] (E), 46[20] (P), Πετεφρης, A Πετρεφης.

†פּוּךְ **n.[m.]** antimony, stibium (NH = 6320
BH; cf. poss. Ar. فَكَّ *open, separate;* Syr. ܦܟ *pulverize;* but פּוּךְ perh. foreign word);—black mineral powder, for increasing brilliance of eyes by darkening edges of lids; וַתָּשֶׂם בַּפּ׳ עֵינֶיהָ 2 K 9[30], תִּקְרְעִי וגו׳ Je 4[30]; (on practice in Arab. v. We[GGN, 1893, 443]; in Egypt, Lane[Mod. Egypt. ed. 5, i. 45 f.]); fig. Is 54[11] of dark cement setting off precious stones (but We[DLZ, Aug. 2, 1890] Che[Hpt] al. rd. נֹפֶךְ q.v.); אַבְנֵי פ׳ 1 Ch 29[2] are perh. stones of brilliant hue of antimony.—Cf. n.pr. קֶרֶן הַפּוּךְ, 7163
and כָּחַל. p. 471, 902 3583

†פּוֹל **n.[m.]coll.** beans (NH = BH; Ar. 6321
فُول; Eth. ፉል: 𝔗 פּוֹלָא);—2 S 17[28] Ez 4[9], 𝔊 κύαμος.

†פּוּל **n.pr.m.** = תִּגְלַת פִּלְאֶסֶר (q.v.) (As. 6322
Pulu; Babylonian name of TP, Schr[SBAk 1887, 592; KB ii, 287, cf. 277] Tiele[Gesch. 266 f.]; cf. (through Pers. trad., EMey[Entstehung, 30]) Πῶρος, Canon of Ptol. KAT[2, 490]); 2 K 15[19.19] 1 Ch 5[26], Φουα[λ].—Is 66[19], v. פוט.

†[פּוּן] **vb.** (?); only אָפוּנָה ψ 88[16]; rd. prob. 6323, 6437
אָפוּגָה, v. פוג, אָפוּנָה.

פּוּנֹה 2 Ch 25[23] v. פִּנָּה. p. 819, פּוּנִי v. פּוּאָה. 6312, 6324,
above 6438

†פּוּנֹן **n.pr.loc.** 2nd station of Isr. fr. Hor 6325
Nu 33[42.43], Φ(ε)ινω; betw. Petra and Zoar, famous for mines, Gk. Φινων, Φαινων Euseb[Onom. ed. Lag. 299, 85], v. also Ritter[Erdkunde, Asien. xiv. 125 ff.] Seetzen[Reise iii, 17] (*Kálaêt Phenân*); perh. = Edom. n.pr.m. פִּינֹן q.v.

†פּוּעָה **n.pr.f.** a midwife Ex 1[15], Φουα. 6326

†I. [פּוּץ] **vb.** be dispersed, scattered 6327
(NH = BH; perh. akin to Ar. فَضَّ *break asunder, scatter*);—**Qal** *Impf.* 3 mpl. יָפוּצוּ ψ 68[2], יָפֻצוּ Ez 48[16]+; 3 fpl. וַתְּפוּצֶינָה Ez 34[5]+, וּתְפוּצֶינָה Zc 13[7], etc.; *Imv.* mpl. פֹּצוּ 1 S 14[34]; *Pt.*

pass. pl. st. פּוּצַי Zp 3[10] (v. infr.); *be dispersed, disperse*, בָּעָם 1 S 14[34]; *be scattered*, of enemies 1 S 11[11] Nu 10[35] ψ 68[2]; of Isr. (among nations) under fig. of flock Ez 34[5.5] Zc 13[7]; בַּת־פּוּצַי Zp 3[10] is prob. crpt., and v[9.10] gloss v. Schwally[ZAW x (1890), 203] Now Da; of besieging army 2 S 20[22] (מֵעַל הָעִיר); people from (מִן) possessions Ez 46[18]; men (from Babel) Gn 11[4] (עַל loc.). **Niph.** *Pf.* 3 fs. נָפוֹצָה Je 10[21], 3 pl. נָפֹצוּ Gn 10[18] +, 2 mpl. נְפֹצֹתֶם Ez 11[17] +, etc.; *Pt.* f. נְפוֹצֶת 2 S 18[8] Qr (> Kt נפצות) cf. Dr al.; pl. נְפוֹצִים, נְפֹצִים 1 K 22[17], 2 Ch 18[16];—**1.** *be scattered*, of army 2 K 25[5] (מֵעַל pers.) = Je 52[8], 1 K 22[17] (אֶל loc.) = 2 Ch 18[16] (עַל), cf. Je 40[15] (abs.); of dispersed Isr. c. בְּ loc. Ez 11[17] 20[34.41] 28[25], as flock Je 10[21] Ez 34[6] (עַל loc.), v[12] (שָׁם); Egyptians 29[13] (שָׁמָּה); of battle *scattered* over country by defeat 2 S 18[8]. **2.** *be spread abroad*, of peoples Gn 10[18].

Hiph. *Pf.* 3 ms. consec. וְהֵפִיץ Dt 4[27] +, 1 s. consec. וַהֲפִיצוֹתִי Ez 22[15], etc.; *Impf.* 3 ms. יָפִיץ Jb 37[11], וַיָּפֶץ Gn 11[8] +, etc.; *Imv.* ms. הָפֵץ Jb 40[11]; *Inf. cstr.* לְהָפִיץ Ez 20[23], etc.;—**1.** trans. *scatter:* **a.** c. acc. pers. Gn 11[8.9] (עַל loc.), Is 41[16] Hb 3[14]; c. בְּ Gn 49[7]; Isr. among (בְּ) nations Dt 4[27] 28[64] Je 9[15] Ez 11[16] 12[15] 20[23] 22[15] 36[19] Ne 1[8]; c. שׁמ(ה) Dt 30[3] Je 30[11]; c. אֶל loc. Ez 34[21]; abs. Je 13[24] 18[17], under fig. of flock Je 23[1.2]; Gr rds. אֲפִיצֵם also Dt 32[26] (v. [פאה]); Egyptians (c. בְּ) Ez 29[12] 30[23.26]; inhab. of earth Is 24[1]. **b.** c. acc. rei, arrows (fig. for lightnings) 2 S 22[15] = ψ 18[15], ψ 144[6]; cloud Jb 37[11]; הָפֵץ עֶבְרוֹת אַפֶּךָ 40[11] (i.e. lightnings?); seed Is 28[25]. **c.** וֶהֱפִיצֻהוּ Jb 18[11] *and drive him* (si vera l., vid. conj. in Bu). **2.** intrans., *scatter*, c. בְּ loc. Ex 5[12], c. מֵעַל pers. 1 S 13[8]; of wind Jb 38[24] (עַל loc.).

4650 †מֵפִיץ **n.m.** scatterer, disperser;—Na 2[2] (si vera l.), but rd. perh. מַפֵּץ *club, hammer* JD Mich We Now; so also Pr 25[18], cf. Toy.

8600 †[תְּפוֹצָה] assumed as sg. of **n.f.pl.** sf. וּתְפוֹצוֹתֵיכֶם Je 25[34] (so van d. H) *your dispersions* (𝔙 al.); but Baer Gi ־תִיכֶם, expl. as **vb. Tiph.** 1 s. Thes al., so (rdg. תְּפִיצוֹתִיכֶם) Hi Gf Kö[i. 471]; word corrupt; Gr וְנִפַּצְתִּיכֶם, Gie וְנִפַּצְתֶּם.

6327 †II. פּוּץ **vb.** flow, overflow (Ar. فَاضَ *flow*, cf. Ba[ES 69]);—**Qal** *Impf.* 3 mpl. יָפוּצוּ Pr 5[16] of springs, fig. for sources of pleasure; 3 fpl. תְּפוּצֶנָה עָרַי מִטּוֹב Zc 1[17] *my cities shall overflow with good.*

6328 †I. [פּוּק] **vb.** reel, totter;—**Qal** *Pf.* 3 pl. פָּקוּ פְּלִילִיָּה Is 28[7] *they reel* (drunken, in giving) *judgment* (‖ שָׁגוּ, תָּעוּ, etc.); rd. prob. also *Impf.* 3 fs. תָּפוּק Am 2[13] *tottereth* (v. עוק). **Hiph.** *Impf.* **1.** *totter:* 3 ms. יָפִיק Je 10[4] (of idol). **2.** rd. prob. also *Pt.* מֵפִיק Am 2[13] *cause tottering* (v. עוק).

†פּוּקָה **n.f.** tottering, staggering;—fig. for qualm of conscience 1 S 25[31] (+ מִכְשׁוֹל לֵב, v. Dr). 6330

†פִּק, פִּיק **n.[m.]** id. lit.;—פִּק בִּרְכַּיִם Na 2[11] *tottering of knees* (so Baer Gi; פִּיק van d. H). 6375

†II. פּוּק **vb. Hiph.** bring out, furnish, promote (NH *id.*; appar. akin to Aram. נְפַק *go forth*, Aph. *bring forth, produce*);—**1.** *produce, furnish:* *Impf.* (juss.) וְתָפֵק לָרָעֵב Is 58[10] c. נַפְשֶׁךָ (rd. perh. לַחְמְךָ v. Che[Hpt]); *Pt.* מְפִיקִים מִזַּן אֶל־זַן ψ 144[13] (v. זַן). **2.** *bring out, elicit, obtain*, c. acc.; יָפִיק Pr 3[13], + מִן pers., וַיָּפֶק 8[35] 18[22] (all ‖ מצא), 12[2]. **3.** זְמָמוֹ אַל־תָּפֵק ψ 140[9] *his device do not promote.* 6329

†פּוּר **n.m.** lot (NH = BH; perh. As. loan-word fr. *puru, buru, stone* Jen[ZA x. 339 f.] and in Wild[Est p. 173 f.]);—expl. by הַגּוֹרָל Est 3[7] 9[24]; שֵׁם הַפּוּר v[26] explains name of feast פּוּרִים v[26]; יְמֵי הַפֻּרִים *days of Purim* v[28.31]; אִגֶּרֶת הַפּ׳ v[29], דִּבְרֵי הַפּ׳ v[32].—Vid. on *Purim* esp. Now[Arch. ii. 194 ff.] and reff. 6332

I. פור (√ of foll.; poss. *foam*, cf. Ar. (فور), قَارَ, *boil, ferment;* Syr. ܦܘܪ, Ethpe., of anger).

†פּוּרָה **n.f.** wine-press;—פּ׳ דָּרַכְתִּי Is 63[3] (v. דָּרַךְ **3**); disting. fr. יֶקֶב, and perh. part of it, Hg 2[16] (rdg. מְפּ׳, so Sm Now; usu. *measure* of juice from one filling of the פּ׳, v. Ke). 6333

†פָּרוּר **n.[m.]** pot (Thes fr. *boiling*, dub.; otherwise Kö[ii. 1, 151]);—*pot* (earthen? v. פרור Ecclus 13[2], Gk. χύτρα, opp. λέβης; Syr. ܦܘܪܐ, ܩܘܠܐ ܕܦܚܪܐ *jar of the potter*, opp. ܩܣܛܐ), for boiling Nu 11[8] (JE), 1 S 2[14], cf. Ju 6[19] (𝔊 χύτρα, κύθρα). 6517

II. פור v. II. פרר. p. 830

†פּוֹרָתָא **n.pr.m.** son of Haman Est 9[8], Φαραδαθα, Βαρδαθα. 6334

†I. [פּוּשׁ] **vb.** appar. spring about, **Qal** *Pf.* 3 pl. consec. וּפָשׁוּ פָּרָשָׁיו Hb 1[8] (but prob. del. וּפָשׁוּ as dittogr. v. Now); 2 mpl. consec. וּפִשְׁתֶּם Mal 3[20], *Impf.* 2 mpl. תָּפוּשׁוּ Je 50[11] Qr (so 𝔊; > Kt תפושי), in both, sim. of gambolling calves. 6335

†II. [פּוּשׁ] **vb. Niph.** be scattered;—3 pl. נָפֹשׁוּ עַמְּךָ עַל־הֶהָרִים Na 3[18] (rd. prob. נָפֹצוּ). 6335

†פּוּתִי **adj.gent.** c. art. הַפּ׳ 1 Ch 2[53], a family in Judah; Μειφειθειμ, A Ηφιθειν, 𝔊L Αφφουθι. 6336

6337 פַּז v. I. פזז. below

6338 †I. [פָּזַז] vb. **Hoph.** be refined (?) (dub. √);—*Pt.* זָהָב מוּפָז 1 K 10^{18} *refined gold* (si vera l.; 𝔊 δόκιμος, ‖ 2 Ch 9^{17} טָהוֹר).

6337 †פַּז **n.m.**$^{ψ 19, 11}$ refined, pure gold (Talm. פִּיזָא; 𝔗 פִּיזּוּזָא);—עֲטֶרֶת פָּז ψ 21^{4}; in compar. of value or beauty: La 4^{2}, אַדְנֵי־פ׳ Ct 5^{15}; ‖ (or +) זהב Jb 28^{17} (כְּלִי־פ׳), ψ 19^{11} (+רָב), 119^{127}; ‖ כֶּתֶם Is 13^{12}, cf. כֶּתֶם פ׳ Ct 5^{11}; +חָרוּץ Pr 8^{19}.

6339 †II. [פָּזַז] **vb.** be supple, agile (Talm. (rare) פִּיזָא *hasty*; Ar. فَزَّ *be frightened, excited*; Syr. (Lexx.) ܦܙ *leap*, ܦܙܝܙܐ *agile*, etc.);—**Qal** *Impf.* 3 mpl. וַיָּפֹזּוּ Gn 49^{24}, of arms. **Pi.** *shew agility, leap* (in dance), *Pt.* מְפַזֵּז וּמְכַרְכֵּר 2 S 6^{16}.

6340 †[פָּזַר] **vb.** scatter (usually regarded as secondary form of בזר q.v.; NH *id.* Pi. (opp. כנס = כנש), Niph.; Ar. فَزَرَ *rend, slit*, also *separate, disperse*);—**Qal** *Pt. pass.* f. שֶׂה פְזוּרָה Je 50^{17} *a scattered sheep* is Israel (i.e. driven off, isolated). **Niph.** *Pf.* 3 pl. נִפְּזְרוּ ψ 141^{7} our bones *are scattered* לְפִי שְׁאוֹל. **Pi.** *Pf.* 3 ms. פִּזַּר ψ 53^{6} 112^{9}, etc.; *Impf.* 3 ms. יְפַזֵּר 147^{16}; 2 fs. וַתְּפַזְּרִי Je 3^{13}; *Pt.* מְפַזֵּר Pr 11^{24};—*scatter* ψ 89^{11} 53^{6} 147^{16} (all subj. י׳), Jo 4^{2}; obj. דְּרָכַיִךְ Je 3^{13}, of Isr. running hither and thither to strange gods; abs. of spending money ψ 112^{9} (alms), Pr 11^{24}. **Pu.** *Pt.* מְפֻזָּר Est 3^{8} *scattered*, of Isr.

6341 I, II. פַּח v. פחח. p. 809

6342 †פָּחַד **vb.** dread, be in dread, in awe (NH Hithp. (rare), Ecclus 41^{12} Imv. פחד על *fear for*; 𝔗 פַּחְדָּא n.);—**Qal** *Pf.* 3 ms. פָּחַד ψ 119^{161}, וּפ׳ consec. Is 19^{16} 60^{5}; 1 s. פָּחַדְתִּי Jb 3^{25}, etc.; *Impf.* 3 ms. יִפְחַד Is 19^{17}; 2 ms. תִּפְחַד Dt 28^{67}+, etc.;—**1.** *be in dread*, abs. Dt 28^{66} Is 12^{2} 33^{14} 44$^{8.11}$ ψ 78^{53} Pr 3^{24}; לֹא פ׳ Je 36^{24} sign of callousness; c. acc. cogn. פַּחַד Dt 28^{67} Jb 3^{25} ψ 14^{5} = 53^{6}; c. מִן pers. Is 19^{17} Jb 23^{15} ψ 27^{1} (‖ יָרֵא), cf. 119^{161}, and (c. מִפְּנֵי) Is 19^{16}; c. עַל rei Je 33^{9} (+רָגְזוּ); c. אֶל, pregn., *turn in dread* to each other Je 36^{16}, submitting to י׳ Ho 3^{5} Mi 7^{17} (‖ יָרֵא). **2.** *be in awe* (at י׳'s favour), abs., Is 60^{5}. **Pi.** *be in great dread*, *Impf.* 2 ms. וַתְּפַחֵד Is 51^{13}, c. מִפְּנֵי rei; *Pt.* abs. מְפַחֵד Pr 28^{14} *deeply dreading* (sc. sin). **Hiph.** *Pf.* 3 ms. הִפְחִיד Jb 4^{14} *filled* my bones *with dread*.

6343 I. פַּחַד $_{49}$ **n.m.** $^{1 S 11, 7}$ **dread**;—פ׳ abs. Gn 31^{42}+, cstr. 1 S 11^{7}+, sf. פַּחְדְּךָ Dt 2^{25} ψ 119^{120}, פַּחְדּוֹ Jb 13^{11} 1 Ch 14^{17}, etc.; pl. פְּחָדִים Jb 15^{21}:—**1.** *dread*, פ׳ י׳, i.e. before י׳, oft. (not alw.) terrifying, unfitting for action, †Is 2$^{10.19.21}$ 1 S 11^{7} 2 Ch 14^{13} 17^{10}, so פ׳ אֱלֹהִים + 20^{29}, c. sf. Jb 13^{11} ψ 119^{120} *trembleth for dread of thee*; c. genit. obj. Isr., †Dt 2^{25} (‖ יִרְאָה), 11^{25} (‖ מוֹרָא), ψ 105^{38} Est 8^{17} 9^{2}, פ׳ אוֹיֵב †ψ 64^{2}, of individual †1 Ch 14^{17} Est 9^{3}; c. genit. obj. rei Pr 1^{33}; abs., in gen., Ex 15^{16} (song; ‖ אֵימָתָה), Jb 4^{14} (‖ רְעָדָה), Je 30^{5} (‖ קוֹל חֲרָדָה)+; as acc. cogn. c. פָּחַד ψ 14^{5}+ (v. פָּחַד); c. genit. subj. †Pr 1$^{26.27}$ (both ‖ אֵיד) Dt 28^{67}. **2.** = *object of dread* †ψ 31^{12} 36^{2}, פ׳ אֵלִי Jb 31^{23}; פַּחַד פָּחַדְתִּי †Jb 3^{25}; מִקּוֹל הַפַּחַד † Is 24^{18} *sound of the disaster*, for מִפְּנֵי הַפּ׳ of orig. Je 48^{44}, but קוֹל פְּחָדִים †Jb 15^{21} = a sound of terrors; פ׳ פִּתְאֹם 22^{10} Pr 3^{25}. **3.** as design. dei †פ׳ יִצְחָק Gn 31^{42} (‖ אֱלֹהֵי אַבְרָהָם), so v^{53} (‖ *id.*; both E).

6345 †[פַּחְדָּה] **n.f. dread**, religious **awe**, sf. לֹא פַחְדָּתִי אֵלַיִךְ Je 2^{19} no *awe of me* (came) *unto thee*.

6344 †II. [פַּחַד] **n.[m.] thigh** (prob. loan-word (through Aram., otherwise ז = ذ) from Ar. فَخِذٌ *thigh* and (cf. We$^{GGN, 1893, 479}$) *sub-tribe*, Palm. פחד *tribe*);—גִּידֵי פַחֲדוֹ Jb 40^{17} Kt *the sinews of his thigh* (Qr פַּחֲדָיו), of hippopotamus.

6346 פֶּחָה $_{28}$ **n.m.** $^{2 K 18, 24}$ **governor** (loan-word fr. As. *paḫâti* [abbrev. from *bel paḫâti*], *lord of a district*; cf. perh. OAram. פחי *governor*);—abs. הַפּ׳ Ne 5^{14}, cstr. פַּחַת Hg 1^{1}+, פַּחַת־ 2^{21}; sf. פֶּחָתְךָ Mal 1^{8}, פֶּחָם Ne 5^{14} (but read prob. פֶּחָה); pl. abs. פַּחוֹת 1 K 20^{24}+; cstr. פַּחוֹת 10^{15} = 2 Ch 9^{14}, פַּחֲוֹת Ezr 8^{36}+; sf. פַּחוֹתֶיהָ Je 51$^{28.57}$;—as Assyr. captains 2 K 18^{24} = Is 36^{9} (< del. פ׳, cf. Sta$^{ZAW vi (1886), 182}$ al.), cf. Ez 23$^{6.12}$; of Babylon Je 51$^{23.57}$, and Bab. allies Ez 23^{23}; of Media Je 51^{28}; Pers. *governor* of עֵבֶר הַנָּהָר, i.e. in Pal., Hg 1$^{1.14}$ 2$^{2.21}$ Ne 2$^{7.9}$ + 8 t.; Pers. *satraps* in gen. Est 3^{12} 8^{9} 9^{3}; applied (by late writer) to Sol.'s *governors* 1 K 10^{15} = 2 Ch 9^{14}; Benhadad's *captains* 1 K 20^{24} (del. v., Sta al.).—Cf. BAram.

6348 †[פָּחַז] **vb. be wanton, reckless** (NH *id.* (rare); Ar. فَخَزَ *be haughty, boastful, reckless*; 𝔗 פְּחַז, Syr. ܦܚܙ *be lascivious*, in der. spec. and deriv.);—**Qal** *Pt.* אֲנָשִׁים רֵיקִים וּפֹחֲזִים Ju 9^{4}; of prophets Zp 3^{4} *extravagant* (‖ אַנְשֵׁי בֹּגְדוֹת).

6349 †פַּחַז **n.[m.] wantonness, recklessness, unbridled license**;—Gn 49^{4}, abstr. for concr. (+ כַּמַּיִם *like* [boiling, or overflowing] *water*).

6350 †[פַּחֲזוּת] **n.f. recklessness, extravagance**;—sf. ־תָם Je 23^{32} of prophets.

פחח (√of foll.; meaning dub.; cf. Aram. פַּחָא, ܦܚܳܐ, whence (Frä ^{119}) Ar. فَخّ as loan-word).

6341 †I. **פַּח n.m.** $^{\psi 124, 7}$ **bird-trap** (cf. Wilkinson $^{\text{Egyptians (1878) ii, 103, 109 f.}}$ Dr $^{\text{Am 3, 5}}$ Hoffm $^{\text{ZAW iii (1883), 101}}$);—פ׳ abs. Ho 5^{1}+, פָּ֑ח Je 48^{44}+; cstr. פַּח Ho 9^{8}+; pl. פַּחִים Je 18^{22}+;—**1.** lit. יַעֲלֶה פ׳ Am 3^{5b} (as metaph.; v^{a} del. פ׳), Pr 7^{23} Ec 9^{12} (c. אָחוּז; both in sim.). **2.** usually fig. (sts. ‖ רֶשֶׁת, מוֹקֵשׁ, צַמִּים): **a.** of calamities and plots, פ׳ יָקוֹשׁ Ho 9^{8}, cf. ψ 91^{3} 124^{7}; פ׳ alone Je 48^{43} = Is 24^{17}, Jb 22^{10} ψ 124^{7} Pr 22^{5}; טָמַן פ׳ לְ Je 18^{22} ψ 140^{6} 142^{4}; 119^{110}, יָקֹשׁ פ׳ לְ 141^{9}; יֹאחֵז בְּעָקֵב פ׳ נָתַן פ׳ לְ Jb 18^{9}; יִלָּכֵד בַּפּ׳ Je 48^{44} = Is 24^{18}. **b.** = source or agent of calamity Ho 5^{1} Jos 23^{13} (D), Is 8^{14} ψ 69^{23}.

6352 —ψ 11^{6} v. פֶּחָם. below

6351 †[**פָּחַח**] **vb. Hiph. denom. ensnare**; *Inf. abs.* הָפֵחַ בְּלָּם Is 42^{22}, c. בְּ loc. *an ensnaring* [i.e. men have ensnared] *them all in*, etc.

6341 †II. [**פַּח**] **n.[m.] plate** of metal; pl. רִקֻּעֵי פַּחִים Nu 17^{3}; cstr. וַיְרַקְּעוּ אֶת־פַּחֵי הַזָּהָב Ex 39^{3}.

פחם (√of foll.; cf. prob. Ar. فَحُمَ *be black*, NH פֶּחָם *id.* (in der. spec.), פֶּחָם = BH; Ar. فَحْمٌ *charcoal*; As. *pêntu* (= **pêmtu*) glowing *coal*; Syr. ܦܚܡܐ in Lexx).

6352 †**פֶּחָם n.[m.] coal** (coll.); abs. פ׳, as inflammable, פ׳ לְגֶחָלִים Pr 26^{21} (*charcoal for embers*, Toy); of glowing coal Is 44^{12}, אֵשׁ פ׳ 54^{16}; ψ 11^{6} for MT פַּחִים אֵשׁ read פַּחַם אֵשׁ (or פַּחֲמֵי) *coals of fire* (‖ גָּפְרִית), so Ew al.

פחת (√of foll.; cf. Ar. فَحَتَ *cut off*, VII. *be perforated* (of roof); Syr. ܦܚܬ Pa. *pierce, break through*, ܦܚܬܐ *pit, chasm*; NH פָּחַת *dig, hollow out*, also *diminish*).

6354 †**פַּ֫חַת n.m.** $^{2 S 18, 17}$ (in 17^{9} rd. בְּאַחַד) **pit**;—פ׳ abs. Je 48^{43}+, פָּ֑חַת v^{28}; pl. פְּחָתִים 2 S 17^{9};—*pit*, 2 S 17^{9} 18^{17} Je 48^{28} (Gie qu. text); fig. of calamity פַּחַד וָפ׳ וָפָ֑ח Je 48^{43} cf. v$^{44.44}$ = Is 24^{17} cf. v$^{18.18}$ and La 3^{47}.

6356 †**פְּחֶ֫תֶת n.f.** a **boring** or **eating out**;—Lv 13^{55}, of leprous decay in garment.

6355 †**פַּחַת מוֹאָב n.pr.m.** post-exil. name;—בְּנֵי־פ׳ מ׳ Ne 3^{11} (Φααβ[θ]μωαβ, 𝔊L Ερωμαθ), בְּנֵי־פ׳ מ׳ Ezr 2^{6} = Ne 7^{11}, Ezr 8^{4} (all Φααθμωαβ, etc.), 10^{30}; פ׳ מ׳ Ne 10^{15} (both Φααδ[θ]μωαβ, etc.).

6357 †**פִּטְדָה n.f.** (**m.** acc. to Albr $^{\text{ZAW xvi (1896), 108}}$) **topaz** or **chrysolite** (acc. to 𝔊 τοπάζιον, 𝔙 *topazius*, etc.; prob. foreign word, cf. Skr. *pîta* (prop. *yellow*));—named with other precious stones Ez 28^{13} Ex 28^{17} = 39^{10}; cstr. פִּטְדַת־כּוּשׁ Jb 28^{19}.—Vid. Plin $^{\text{NH xxxvii. 8 (32)}}$, Houghton in Sm $^{\text{DB, Topaz}}$ Ri $^{\text{HWB, Edelstein}}$.

†**פַּטִּישׁ n.m.** $^{\text{Je 50, 23}}$ **forge-hammer**;—(NH = BH; Aram. loan-word acc. to Frä ^{85}, and so Ar. فِطِّيس (cf. Ar. trad. in Lane), v. 𝔗 פַּטִּישָׁא; but Lag $^{\text{BN 103}}$ cp. فِطِّيسَةٌ *swine's snout*, Syr. ܦܛܝܫ *flat-nosed*);—פ׳ abs. Is 41^{7} Je 23^{29}; cstr. 50^{23} fig. of Bab. as destroyer. 6360

†**פָּטַר vb. separate, remove, set free** (NH *depart, set free*, Niph. also *die*; Ph. פטר CIS $^{102a, 2}$ *depart* (*die?*); As. *paṭâru, split, break through, ipṭiru, ransom*, Tel Am. *escape, set free* (perh. Canaanit.); Ar. فَطَرَ *cleave, split*, also *create*; Eth. ፈጠረ: *create, fabricate*; Aram. פְּטַר, ܦܛܰܪ *withdraw, depart*);—**Qal** *Pf.* 3 ms. פ׳ 2 Ch 23^{8}; *Impf.* 3 ms. וַיִּפְטַר 1 S 19^{10}; *Pt. act.* פּוֹטֵר Pr 17^{14}; *pass.* פְּטוּרִים 1 Ch 9^{33} Qr (Kt פטירים); cstr. פְּטוּרֵי 1 K $6^{18.29.32}$, פְּטֻרֵי v^{35};—**1.** intrans. *remove* oneself, specif. *escape* 1 S 19^{10} (מִפְּנֵי, cf. Dr). **2.** trans. *set free* fr. duty 2 Ch 23^{8} (acc. pers.), so pass. 1 Ch 9^{33} Qr (Kt פטירים adj. or Aram. pt., same mng.); פ׳ מַיִם Pr 17^{14} *set free, let out*; pass. פְּטוּרֵי צִצִּים term. techn. of ornament in temple, dub., usually *out-spread* (garlands) *of flowers* 1 K $6^{18.29.32.35}$. **Hiph.** *Impf.* 3 ms. יַפְטִירוּ בְשָׂפָה ψ 22^{8} *they separate with the lip*, i.e. open mouth wide (insultingly). 6362

6358

6359

†**פֶּ֫טֶר n.[m.] that which separates, first opens**;—cstr., פ׳ רֶחֶם i.e. firstborn, of man and beast, Ez 20^{26} Ex $13^{12.15}$ 34^{19} Nu 18^{15}; appos. בְּכוֹר Ex 13^{2} Nu 3^{12}; רֶחֶם om. Ex $13^{12.13}$ $34^{19.20}$. 6363

†[**פִּטְרָה**] **n.f.** id., פִּטְרַת כָּל־רֶחֶם Nu 8^{16}. 6363

פטיר 1 Ch 9^{33} Kt v. פטר **2.** 6362

פִּי v. פֶּה. p. 804 6310

†**פִּי־בֶ֫סֶת n.pr.loc.** in Egypt (*Pabast*, Eb $^{\text{GS 495}}$, or *Per-Bastet*, Griffith $^{\text{Hastings DB iii. 874}}$, '*House of Bast(et)*' orig. *Pĕi-wbaste* acc. to Steind $^{\text{BAS i. 350}}$, cf. Naville $^{\text{Bubastis 44, 46, 48, 56}}$, Gk. Βούβαστις (Herod.), Βούβαστος (Diod. Sic.));—Ez 30^{17} 𝔊 Βουβάστου (genit.), mod. *Tel-Basṭa*, near Zaḳaziḳ, c. 30 miles NNE. fr. Cairo.—Vid. Herod. $^{\text{ii. 59 f., 67, 137 f., 166}}$ Diod. $^{\text{xvi. 49, 51}}$ Naville $^{\text{l.c.; Trans. Vict. Inst. xxiii. 137 ff.}}$ 6364

†**פִּי הַחִירֹת n.pr.loc.** on E. border of Egypt, Ex $14^{2.9}$ (𝔊 ἡ ἔπαυλις), Nu 33^{7} (Ε(π)ιρωθ) + v^{8} (read מִפִּי ה׳ Sam 𝔖 𝔙 𝔗, or מִפְּנֵי פִּי ה׳, for MT מִפְּנֵי ה׳, cf. Di). Site unknown. 6367

פּוּד, פִּיד (√of foll.; cf. Ar. فود, فَادَ *die*, فيد, فَادَ *pass away, be exhausted* (of property)).

6365 †**פִּיד** **n.[m.]** ruin, disaster;—abs. Jb 12^{5}; cstr. 31^{29} Pr 24^{22}; sf. פִּידוֹ Jb 30^{24} + 21^{20} (for כִּיד).

6310, 6268 **פִּיּוֹת, פֵּיוֹת** v. פֶּה. **פִּיהַ** v. פוח. p. 804, 806

6369 †**פִּיכֹל** **n.pr.m.** captain of Abimelech of Gerar Gn 21$^{22.32}$ 26^{26}, Φικολ, 𝔊L Φιχολ.

6370 **פִּילֶגֶשׁ** v. פִּלֶגֶשׁ. p. 811

פִּים, perh. < **פאם** (√of foll., cf. Ar. فَأَمَ *fill*, II. *make wide*, IV. *become full* (of fat); hence (Thes al.) foll., by syncope of א, cf. Ges$^{§ 19k}$).

6371 †**פִּימָה** **n.f. superabundance** (of fat);—פ׳ Jb 15^{27} (‖ חֶלְבּוֹ).

6372 **פִּינְחָס**$_{25}$ **n.pr.m.** (Egypt. *Pe-nehasi, the negro*, acc. to Lauth$^{Moses (1868), 71, ZMG xxv (1871), 139 f.}$ cf. Nes$^{Eg 112, AJSL xiii (1897) 174}$ Baen$^{Ex 6, 25}$, yet v. Di);—**1.** grandson of Aaron, Φ(ε)ινεες, Ex 6^{25} Nu 25^{7} + 16 t. †**2.** son of Eli 1 S 1^{3} († פִּנְחָס), 2^{34} 4$^{4.11.17.19}$ 14^{3}.

6373 †**פִּינֹן** **n.pr.m.** Edomite Gn 36^{41} 1 Ch 1^{52}, Φινες, Φινων, Φινα;—cf. פּוּנֹן.

6374-75 **פִּיפִיּוֹת** v. פֶּה. **פִּיק** v. I. פוק. p. 804, 807

6376 †**פִּישׁוֹן** **n.pr.fl.** (Thes sub פוש, cf. esp. Nes$^{Marg. 5}$, but dub.);—one of the rivers of Eden Gn 2^{11}, Φ(ε)ισων, (on theories of identif. v. Comm., also reff. sub גִּיחוֹן).

6377 †**פִּיתוֹן** **n.pr.m.** descendant of Saul 1 Ch 8^{35} = פִּיתֹן 9^{41}, Φιθων, Φαιθων, 𝔊L Φιθωθ.

פכך (√of foll.; cf. NH פַּךְ *flask*, also פִּכְפֵּךְ *trickle*, denom., or < onomatop.).

6378 †**פַּךְ** **n.m.**$^{2 K 9, 1}$ **vial, flask**;—cstr. פ׳ הַשֶּׁמֶן, for anointing, 1 S 10^{1} 2 K 9$^{1.3}$.

6379 †**פָּכָה** **vb. Pi.** trickle, perh. denom.;—*Pt.* pl. מַיִם מְפַכִּים מִן Ez 47^{2} *water trickling on* the south side.

6380 †**פֹּכֶרֶת הַצְּבָיִים** **n.pr.m.** (*bindress* [Aram.; perh. *binder* (fem. of office)] of *the gazelles*);—head of post-exilic family, בְּנֵי פ׳ ה׳ Ezr 2^{57} = Ne 7^{59} (הַצְּבָיִים), υἱοὶ Φασραθ υἱοὶ Ασεβωειν (Φακαραθ, Σαβαειμ, etc.).

פלא (√of foll.; *separate* from the ordinary, *distinguish* acc. to Thes Gerber^{212}, cf. פלה).

6382 †**פֶּלֶא** **n.m.** wonder (NH *id.*; as *unusual, extraordinary*);—פ׳ Ex 15^{11} + 6 t.; sf. פִּלְאֲךָ ψ 89^{6}; פִּלְאֶךָ 77^{12} 88^{13}, pl. פְּלָאִים La 1^{9}; fpl. פְּלָאוֹת ψ 119^{129} Dn 12^{6};—**1.** *wonder:* extraordinary, hard to be understood, God's dealings with His people Is 29^{14}; the testimonies of the Law ψ 119^{129}; פֶּלֶא יוֹעֵץ Is 9^{5} *marvel of a counsellor* (Baer פֶּלֶא), *wonderful counsellor* (of Mess. king); pl. as adv. acc. וַתֵּרֶד פ׳ La 1^{9} *she* (Jerus.) *hath come down marvellously.* **2.** *wonder:* of God's acts of judgment and redemption ψ 77^{12} 88^{13} 89^{6}; עֹשֵׂה פ׳ Ex 15^{11} Is 25^{1} ψ 77^{15} 78^{12} 88^{11}; of extraord. trials קֵץ הפ׳ Dn 12^{6}.

[**פָּלָא**]$_{71}$ **vb. denom. Niph.** etc., be sur- 6381
passing, extraordinary (cf. Gerber^{212});—**Niph.** *Pf.* 3 fs. נִפְלְאת ψ 118^{23} (Ges$^{§ 44 f}$); נִפְלְאַתָה 2 S 1^{26} (Kö$^{i. 610 f., 614}$ Ges$^{§ 75 oo}$); 3 pl. נִפְלְאוּ Pr 30^{18}; *Impf.* יִפָּלֵא Dt 17^{8} + 6 t.; *Pt.* mpl. נִפְלָאִים ψ 139^{14}; fs. נִפְלֵאת Dt 30^{11}; pl. נִפְלָאוֹת Jos 3^{5} +; sf. נִפְלְאֹתַי Ex 3^{20}, etc.;—†**1.** *be beyond one's power, difficult* to do, לעשׂות 2 S 13^{2}; בְּעֵינֵי פ׳ Zc 8$^{6.6}$; c. מִן pers. *too difficult for* Dt 30^{11}, for י׳ Gn 18^{14} (J) Je 32$^{17.27}$. †**2.** *be difficult* to understand; c. מִן pers. *too difficult for* ψ 131^{1} Pr 30^{18} Jb 42^{3}, to decide Dt 17^{8}. Esp. †**3. a.** *be extraordinary, wonderful*, 2 S 1^{26} ψ 119^{18}; of God's acts, נ׳ בְּעֵינֵינוּ 118^{23}, cf. 139^{14}. **b.** *Pt.* as subst. *marvellous things* Jb 37^{14} (acts of God), Dn 11^{36} (presumptuous words); as adv. *wondrously* Jb 37^{5} Dn 8^{24}. **4.** נִפְלָאוֹת = *wonderful acts* of י׳ in judgment and redemption, Ex 3^{20} (J) Ju 6^{13} Je 21^{2} 1 Ch 16$^{9.24}$ ψ 9^{2} 26^{7} + 15 t. ψψ; also עשׂה נ׳ Ex 34^{10} Jos 3^{5} (J) Jb 5^{9} = 9^{10}, + 9 t. Chr ψψ; הראה נ׳ Mi 7^{15} ψ 78^{11}. †**Pi.** *Inf.* cstr. לְפַלֵּא נֶדֶר *make a special votive offering*, Lv 22^{21} Nu 15$^{3.8}$ (P). **Hiph.** *Pf.* 3 ms. הִפְלִיא ψ 31^{22} 2 Ch 26^{15}; הִפְלָא Is 28^{29}; וְהִפְלָא consec. Dt 28^{59} (Ges$^{§ 75 oo}$); *Impf.* יַפְלִא Lv 27^{2} Nu 6^{2}; *Inf. abs.* הַפְלֵא Is 29^{14} 2 Ch 2^{8}; cstr. הַפְלִיא Is 29^{14} Jo 2^{26}; *Pt.* מַפְלִא Ju 13^{19};—**1.** *do a hard or difficult thing:* הפ׳ (לִנְדֹּר) נֶדֶר *make a hard vow* Lv 27^{2} Nu 6^{2} (cf. **Pi.**). **2.** *make wonderful, do wondrously:* of God, הפ׳ מַכּוֹת *make plagues wonderful* (exceptional), Dt 28^{59}; הפ׳ עֵצָה Is 28^{29} *make counsel wondrous*, 29^{14} *do wonderfully with people*, הַפְלֵא וָפֶלֶא +; עשׂה עמכם לה׳ Jo 2^{26} *dealt with you doing wondrously;* הפ׳ חַסְדּוֹ לִי ψ 31^{22}; הפ׳ לְהֵעָזֵר 2 Ch 26^{15} *did marvellously in receiving help;* of the temple גָּדוֹל וְהַפְלֵא 2 Ch 2^{8} (Kö$^{Synt. § 318 e}$). **3.** of God, מַפְלִא לַעֲשׂוֹת Ju 13^{19} *working wonders in doing.* †**Hithp.** *Impf.* תִּתְפַּלָּא בִי Jb 10^{16} *thou dost shew thyself marvellous* (act inexplicably) *against me.*

6396 †פַּלּוּא **n.pr.m.** (DHM[Epigr. Denkm. 9. 1] cp. Lihy. n.pr. פלה);—son of Reuben Gn 46^{9} Ex 6^{14} Nu $26^{5.8}$ 1 Ch 5^{3}, Φαλλου(ς), etc.; v. also פֶּלֶת.

6384 †פַּלֻּאִי **adj. gent.** of foregoing, c. art. as n. coll., Nu 26^{5}.

6383 [פִּלְיא] v. following.

6383 †[פִּלְאִי] **adj. wonderful, incomprehensible**;—**m.** פלאי (i.e. פִּלְאִי) Kt, Ju 13^{18} (name of מַלְאַךְ י׳; > Qr (פֶּלִי(א)); **f.** פלאיה דַעַת מִמֶּנִּי (i.e. פְּלִאִיָּה) ψ 139^{6} God's knowledge; > Qr פְּלִיאָה.

6411 †פְּלָאיָה **n.pr.m.** Ne 8^{7} 10^{11}, 𝔊L Φαλαιας.

6411 †פְּלָיָה **n.pr.m.** (late As. *Pi-lâma* Hilpr [Univ. Pa. Exp. ix. 68]);—1 Ch 3^{24}, Φαρα, Φαλαια, Φαδια.

4652 †[מִפְלָאָה] **n.f. wondrous work** (si vera l.);—pl. cstr. מִפְלְאוֹת Jb 37^{16} (of providence; but read probably נִפְלְאוֹת Bu SS, cf. Di).

6385 †[פָּלַג] **vb. split, divide** (NH chiefly in secondary meanings and deriv.; Ar. فَلَجَ *divide, split;* Aram. פְּלַג, ܦܠܓ *divide;* Eth. ፈለግ: *ravine, stream;* As. *palgu, canal*);—**Niph.** *Pf.* 3 fs. נִפְלְגָה Gn 10^{25} the earth *was divided*. **Pi. 1.** *Pf.* 3 ms. פִּלַּג Jb 38^{25} *cleave* a channel for rain. **2.** *Imv.* ms. פַּלַּג (Ges [§ 52 n]) ψ 55^{10} *divide* their speech (their counsels).

6388 †I. פֶּלֶג **n.m.**[ψ 65, 10] (cleft) **channel,** (artif.) **canal**;—usu. pl. פְּלָגִים Is 30^{25} (+ יִבְלֵי־מָיִם); cstr. פַּלְגֵי־מַיִם ψ 1^{3}, sim. Is 32^{2} Pr 21^{1}, metaph. 5^{16}, of tears La 3^{48} ψ 119^{136}; פְּלָגָיו ψ 46^{5} (i.e. irrigating canals fr. river, metaph.); פַּלְגֵי־שָׁמֶן Jb 29^{6} (fig. of prosperity); sg. פֶּלֶג אֱלֹהִים ψ 65^{10}, poet. of channel for rain (cf. Jb 38^{25}).

6389 †II. פֶּלֶג **n.pr.m.** son of Eber, Φαλεκ, 𝔊L Φαλεγ: Gn 10^{25} $11^{17.18.19}$ 1 Ch $1^{19.25}$, פָּלֶג Gn 11^{16}.

6390 †[פְּלַגָּה] **n.f. 1. stream. 2. division**;—pl. פְּלַגּוֹת: **1.** *streams* Jb 20^{17}. **2.** *divisions, sections* of tribe, פ׳ cstr. Ju $5^{15.16}$ (read perhaps פְּלֻגּוֹת, v. following), > *streams.*

6391 †[פְּלֻגָּה] **n.f. division** (= מַחֲלֹקֶת q.v.), of priests, for service;—pl. cstr. פְּלֻגּוֹת 2 Ch 35^{5}.

4653 †[מִפְלַגָּה] **n.f. id.**; pl. abs. מִפְלַגּוֹת 2 Ch 35^{12}.

6370 פִּילֶגֶשׁ, פִּלֶגֶשׁ 37 **n.f. concubine** (NH *id.;* 𝔗[Jer] פִּילַקְתָּא (פַּלְקְתָּא), perhaps influenced by Gk. παλλακή, παλλακίς (prop. *young girl*), Lat. *pellex;* orig. Gk. word acc. to Sta[G. i. 380], cf. also Lewy [Fremdw. 66 f.]; on poss. Hittite origin v. Jen[ZMG xlviii (1894), 468 ff.]);—פ׳ abs. 2 S 3^{7}, cstr. 21^{11}, פִּי׳ abs. Gn 36^{12} Ju 19^{1}, cstr. Gn 35^{22} + 4 t.; sf. פִּילַגְשׁוֹ 22^{24} +, -שְׁהוּ Ju 19^{24}; -שִׁי 20^{4} + 2 t.; pl. פִּלַגְשִׁים 2 S 5^{13} + 2 t., פִּי׳ Gn 25^{6} + 5 t.; cstr. פִּלַגְשֵׁי 2 S $16^{21.22}$; sf. פִּילַגְשָׁיו 2 Ch 11^{21}, פִּלַגְשֶׁיךָ 2 S 19^{6}, פִּלַגְשֵׁיהֶם Ez 23^{20};—**1.** *concubine* Gn 22^{24} 25^{6} 35^{22} 36^{12} Ju 8^{31} 19^{1} + 10 t. Ju 19, 20, 2 S $3^{7.7}$ + 7 t. 2 S, 1 K 11^{3} 1 Ch 1^{32} + 6 t. Ch, Est 2^{14} Ct $6^{8.9}$. **2.** either = *paramour* (perhaps contempt.; ὁ πάλλαξ = *youth*), or < *concubinage* Ez 23^{20} (fig. of Jerusalem doting on Babylon).

†[פְּלָדָה] **n.f.** usu. **iron, steel** (origin dub.; 6393
steel in Ar. is فُولَاذ, فَالُوذ, but Vulg. Ar. بُولَاد; Syr. ܦܠܕ (in Lexx); loan-wd. fr. Pers. پُولَاد acc. to Lag[Ges. Abh. 75], cf. Nö[ZMG xxx (1876), 769], but uncertain, cf. Now and reff.);—pl. [abs.!] בְּאֵשׁ־פְּלָדֹת הָרֶכֶב Na 2^{4} > כָּאֵשׁ פ׳ וגו׳ We Now, *like fire the steel* (fittings) *of the chariots.*

†פִּלְדָּשׁ **n.pr.m.** Nahorite Gn 22^{22}, Φαλδας. 6394

†[פָּלָה] **vb. Niph. be separated, distinct** 6395
(‖ form of פלא q.v.; cf. Ar. فلو, فَلَا *separate from sucking, wean;* Eth. ፈለየ: *separate, distinguish*);—**1.** *Pf.* 1 pl. consec. וְנִפְלִינוּ Ex 33^{16} *and we shall be distinct,* c. מִן pers. **2.** 1 s. נִפְלֵיתִי ψ 139^{14} *I am wonderful* (viz. in bodily stature etc.); < Vrss Hup-Now Bae We ־תָ *thou* [י׳] *art wonderful* (פלא **3**). **Hiph.** *Pf.* 3 ms. הִפְלָה ψ 4^{4}, וְה׳ consec. Ex 9^{4}; 1 s. וְהִפְלֵיתִי consec. 8^{18}; *Impf.* 3 ms. יַפְלֶה 11^{7}; *Imv.* ms. הַפְלֵה ψ 17^{7};—of י׳, *make separate,* c. acc. Ex 8^{18} (by treating differently); *set apart* ψ 4^{4}, but perh. read חֶסֶד לִי (for MT חָסִיד לוֹ), *hath made wonderful* (his) *kindness to me* (Dy Gr Che We Du [Bae 'perh.']), so 17^{7} (cf. 31^{22}); *distinguish* between, בֵּין rei, Ex 9^{4}, בֵּין pers. 11^{7}.

†I. פְּלֹנִי **pron. a certain one**; Gk. ὁ, ἡ δεῖνα 6423
(acc. to Thes from above √, through an unused noun פָּלֹן, prop. *one defined, a particular one:* NH *id.;* Aram. ܦܠܢ, f. ܦܠܢܝܬܐ; Arab. فُلَانٌ W[AG i. § 353 R. c], voc. فُلُ Siegf[ZWTh xxvii. 355]; As. *pulpul* Hpt[BAS i. 114]), always joined with אַלְמֹנִי (prop. *one not mentioned*) in the sense of 'ein *gewisser* verschwiegener' (Ew[§ 106 c, 2] Sta[§ 150 b]), '*a certain* unnamed *one,*' i.e. *such a one;* Ru 4^{1} שְׁבָה־פֹּה פְּלֹנִי אַלְמֹנִי sit down here, *such a one* (Gk. ὦ οὗτος; Ar. يَا فُلُ); in the phr. מְקוֹם פ׳ א׳ the place of *such a one* = *such and such* a place, 1 S 21^{3}

2 K 6^{8}. From פ׳ א׳ arose by contraction (or
6422 conflation, Perles$^{Anal. 82}$) ויאמר . . . פַּלְמֹנִי †Dn 8^{13}
לַפּ׳ הַמְדַבֵּר to *that certain one* who spake.—II.
6397 פְּלֹנִי v. p. 813.

6398 †[פָּלַח] **vb. cleave** (Ar. فَلَحَ *cleave;* Aram.
פְּלַח (usu.), ܦܠܚ, are *till, work, serve* [=עָבַד]);
—**Qal** *Pt.* פֹּלֵחַ ψ 141^{7} of *cleaving*, ploughing,
(בקע||) בָּאָרֶץ. **Pi.** *Impf.* **1.** *cleave open, through,*
3 ms. יְפַלַּח of piercing kidneys Jb 16^{13}, liver
Pr 7^{23} (both fig.); וַיְפַלַּח אֶל 2 K 4^{39} of cutting
up (fruit) into pot. **2.** *cause to cleave open,*
3 fpl. יַלְדֵיהֶן תְּפַלַּחְנָה Jb 39^{3} of animals bringing
forth young, rd. perh. תְּפַלֵּטְנָה (21^{10}).

6400 †פֶּלַח **n.f.**$^{Jb 41, 16}$ **cleavage, mill-stone** (mill
cleft betw. the stones? cf. GFM^{Ju}; 𝔗 פִּלְחָא);—
פ׳ abs. Jb 41^{16}, elsewh. cstr.;—**1. a.** *mill-stone,*
פ׳ רֶכֶב *mill-stone of riding*, i.e. upper stone,
wh. is turned (cf. רֶכֶב), Ju 9^{53} 2 S 11^{21}; פ׳ תַּחְתִּית
Jb 41^{16} *lower mill-stone* (sim. of hardness). **b.**
פ׳ דְּבֵלָה 1 S 30^{12} *a cake of figs* (from shape?).
2. *cleavage, split*, hence *slice* פ׳ הָרִמּוֹן Ct 4^{3}
=6^{7} sim. of human temple (from colour, cf.
Wetzst in De$^{Comm. Excurs. A}$).

6401 †פִּלְחָא (Baer פִּלְחָה) **n.pr.m.** post-exilic
name Ne 10^{25}; Φαδαεις, 𝔊L Φαλλαει.

6403 †[פָּלַט] **vb. escape** (NH *id.;* Ph. in n.pr.;
Ar. فلت IV. *escape*, Vulg. Ar. فلط; OAram. פלט
Pa. *rescue*, 𝔗 פַּלֵּט, Syr. ܦܠܛ);—**Qal** *Pf.* 3 pl.
consec. וּפָלְטוּ Ez 7^{16} *and* (if) escapers of them
escape. **Pi.** causat.: *Impf.* 3 ms. sf. יְפַלְּטֵם;
2 ms. תְּפַלֵּט Mi 6^{14}, etc.; *Imv.* ms. פַּלְּטָה ψ 17^{13},
etc.; *Pt.* sf. מְפַלְטִי 18^{3}+;—**1.** *bring into security*
Mi 6^{14}; esp. of י׳, *deliver*, c. acc. pers., ψ 22$^{5.9}$
31^{2} 37^{40} 71^{2} (+הִצִּיל), 82^{4} 91^{14}; + מִן *from* 2 S 22^{44}
=ψ 18^{44}, ψ 18^{49} (מוֹצִיא || 2 S 22^{49}), 17^{13} 37^{40} 43^{1}
71^{4}; pt. c. sf., *my deliverer* 2 S 22^{2}=ψ 18^{3}, ψ 40^{18}
70^{6} 144^{2}. **2.** *cause to escape, cast forth,*
of cow calving Jb 21^{10} (cf. [מָלַט] **Hiph.**,
also 𝔗 *vomit* out, and so ܦܠܛ). **3.** appar.
intrans. *be delivered*, c. מִן Jb 23^{7}, but dub.; Bu
Qal ('perh.'); 𝔊 Du read מִשְׁפָּטִי as obj. (but
elsewhere י׳ subj. of **Pi.**). **Hiph.** *bring into
security; Impf.* 3 ms. יַפְלִיט Is 5^{29} of Assyria,
under fig. of lion, carrying off prey (opp. הִצִּיל);
2 ms. תַּפְלִיט Mi 6^{14} (cf. **Pi. 1**).

6404 †פֶּלֶט **n.pr.m. 1.** 1 Ch 2^{47}, Φαλεκ[γ, τ].
2. 1 Ch 12^{3}, Ιωφαλητ, Φαλετ, etc.—Vid. בֵּית פָּלֶט.

I. פַּלְטִי **adj. gent.** v. בֵּית פֶּלֶט.

†פַּלֵּט **n.[m.]** deliverance (si vera l., prop. 6405
Inf. of foregoing);—ψ 32^{7} רָנֵּי פ׳ *shouts of deliverance* (dub., v. Comm.); עַל־אָוֶן פַּלֶּט־לָמוֹ 56^{8}, read
פַּלֶּס־ (Ew Hup al.) *for* (their) *iniquity weigh* to
them (retribution), or עַל־אָוֶן אֵין פַּלֶּט־ Bae.

†פָּלִיט **n.m.**$^{Am 9,1}$ **escaped one, fugitive;**— 6412
פ׳ abs. 2 K 9^{15}+; pl. cstr. פְּלִיטֵי Ju 12^{4}+; sf.
פְּלִיטָיו Ob^{14}, etc.;—Am 9^{1} 2 K 9^{15} Gn 14^{13} Ez
24$^{26.27}$ 33^{21} (+מִן loc.), v^{22}; שָׂרִיד וּפ׳ Jos 8^{22} Je
42^{17}; פ׳ וְשָׂרִיד 44^{14} La 2^{22}; c. genit. subj. Ju 12^{5}
fugitives of Ephr. (del. in v^{4}, see GFM), so c.
sf. Ez 6^{9} 7^{16} Ob^{14}; c. genit. obj., *escaped of*, i.e.
from Is 45^{20}, so פְּלִיטֵי חֶרֶב Je 44^{28} Ez 6^{8}.

†[פָּלֵיט] **n.m. id.**;—pl. פְּלִיטִם Nu 21^{29} (as 6412
appos., or adj.), ־ִים Is 66^{19}; פְּלֵטִים Je 44^{14},
+ מִן *from* 50^{28} 51^{50}.

†פְּלֵיטָה **n.f. escape** (on form cf. Ba$^{NB 144,}$ 6413
^{166});—abs. פ׳ Gn 32^{9}+, פְּלֵטָה Ex 10^{5}+; cstr.
פְּלֵיטַת 2 K 19^{30}+;—**1.** *escape, deliverance* Gn
45^{7} (E) Je 25^{35}. **2.** elsewh. prob. alw. *escaped
remnant:* **a.** of green things (fr. locusts) Ex
10^{5} (J) Jo 2^{3}. **b.** of pers. Gn 32^{9} (J) Ju 21^{17}
Is 15^{9} Je 50^{29} 1 Ch 4^{43} 2 Ch 12^{7} 20^{24} 30^{6} Ezr 9^{8}
Dn 11^{42}; + מִפְּנֵי 2 S 15^{14}. **c.** specif. of *those* of
Judah *escaped* fr. Assyr. 2 K 19$^{30.31}$ (+מִן) = Is
37$^{31.32}$, cf. Is 10^{20}; fr. Bab. Ne 1^{2} Ezr 9$^{13.14.15}$, cf. Ez
14^{22}; after י׳'s future judgment Is 4^{2} Ob^{17} Jo 3^{5}.

†II. פַּלְטִי **n.pr.m.** Φαλτει (perh. abbrev. fr. 6406
פַּלְטִיאֵל);—**1.** Benjamite Nu 13^{9}. **2.** second
husband of Michal 1 S 25^{44} (=פַּלְטִיאֵל 2 S 3^{15}).

†פִּלְטַי **n.pr.m.** priest Ne 12^{17}, Φελητει, etc. 6408

†פַּלְטִיאֵל **n. pr. m.** Φαλτ(ε)ιηλ: **1.** Nu 6409
34^{26}. **2.** 2 S 3^{15} (=פַּלְטִי 1 S 25^{44}), 𝔊L Φαλτιου.

†פְּלַטְיָה, פְּלַטְיָהוּ **n.pr.m.** Φαλτιας, Φα- 6410
λεττι(α), etc.:—**1.** ־יָהוּ, a prince of people Ez
11$^{1.13}$. **2.** ־יָה, grandson of Zerub. 1 Ch 3^{21},
perh.=Ne 10^{23}. **3.** ־יָה, Simeonite 1 Ch 4^{42}.

†יַפְלֵט **n.pr.m.** Asherite (on form cf. Ba^{NB} 3310
$^{144, 166}$);—1 Ch 7$^{33.33}$, also v^{32} (Gi יַפְלֵט); Ιφαμηλ,
Αφαληκ, etc., A Ιαφαλητ.

†יַפְלֵטִי **adj. gent.** c. art. as n. coll. הַיּ׳ *the* 3311
Japhlites Jos 16^{3}, family or clan on SW. border
of Ephraim; Απταλειμ, A Ιεφαλθι, 𝔊L Ιεφλητι.

†מִפְלָט **n.[m.] escape** (Hup Bae) or **place** 4655
of escape (We Du);—ψ 55^{9} si vera l.; 𝔊 Che
מְפַלֵּט *deliverer*.

6383, 6411 **פְּלִיָּה, פְּלִי** v. פלא p. 811

פלך (√of foll.; cf. Ar. فَلَكَ II. *be round* (esp. *hemispherical*), فَلْكَةٌ *whirl* of spindle, so As. *pilakku;* NH = BH; 𝔗 פִּלְכָּא *circuit, district;* As. also *pilku, district*).

6418 †**פֶּלֶךְ** **n.[m.] 1. whirl of spindle. 2. district** (prop. *circle, circuit*);—abs. פ׳ 2 S 3^{29}, פָּלֶךְ Pr 31^{19}; cstr. פֶּלֶךְ Ne 3^{9}+; sf. פִּלְכּוֹ v^{17};—**1.** *whirl of spindle,* 2 S 3^{29} (prob., v. Dr), Pr 31^{19} (‖ כִּישׁוֹר). **2.** *district,* Ne 3$^{9.12.14.15.16.17.17.18}$.

6419 **[פָּלַל]**$_{84}$ **vb.** prob. **intervene, interpose** (hence both *arbitrate, judge,* and *intercede, pray,* cf. Dr$^{1\,S\,2,25}$; NH פלל (rare), נתפלל, *pray,* פִּילּוּל *act of prayer,* פְּלִילָה *judicial matter;*—otherwise We$^{Heid.\,(2),\,126}$ who conj. der. for הִתְפַּלֵּל from Ar. فَلَّ *notch edge* (of sword, etc.), i.e. *cut oneself* in worship);—†**Pi.** *mediate, judge: Pf.* 3 ms. consec., *arbitrate,* sf. וּפִלְלוֹ 1 S 2^{25} (but read prob. 3 pl. וּפִלְלוּ We Dr al., word-play with יִתְפ׳ foll.); 2 fs. פִּלַּלְתְּ Ez 16^{52} *mediate for* (ל pers.) viz., through thine own sins; 1 s. פִּלָּלְתִּי Gn 48^{11} (E; poss. denom. from פליל) *I did* not *judge* (have the opinion, expect) to see, etc.; *Impf.* 3 ms. וַיְפַלֵּל ψ 106^{30} (abs.) *he interposed* (by slaying offender). **Hithp.**$_{80}$ *Pf.* 3 ms. הִתְפַּלֵּל 1 K 8^{42}; 1 s. הִתְפַּלָּלְתִּי 1 S 1^{27}, etc.; *Impf.* יִתְפַּלֵּל ψ 32^{6}+; יִתְפַּלֶּל־ 1 S 2^{25}; 1 s. אֶתְפַּלָּל ψ 5^{3}, etc.; *Imv.* הִתְפַּלֵּל Nu 21^{7}+, etc.; *Inf. cstr.* הִתְפַּלֵּל Ez 10^{1}+, etc.; *Pt.* מִתְפַּלֵּל Je 42^{4}+, etc.;—**1.** specif. *intercede* (with י׳), c. בעד, *on behalf of* Gn 20^{7} Nu 21^{7} (E) Dt 9^{20} 1 S 12^{23}+6 t.; c. לְ, 1 S 2^{25}; אֶל־יהוה Nu 11^{2} 21^{7} (JE) Dt 9^{26}; c. אל־יהוה + בעד 1 S 7^{5} Je 29^{7}+4 t.; אל־האלהים Gn 20^{17} (E); c. על *for* 2 Ch 30^{18} Jb 42^{8} (late). **2.** gen. *pray,* c. אֶל, unto idol Is 44^{17} 45^{20}; unto Israel v^{14}; בוא אל־מקדש להתפ׳ 16^{12}. **3.** *pray* (to י׳), abs. 1 K 8^{33} 2 K 6^{17} Ezr 10^{1} Dn 9^{20} 2 Ch 6^{24} 7$^{1.11}$, c. אֶל־י׳ 1 S 1^{26} 8^{6} 2 K 4^{33} 6^{18} 20^{2} = Is 38^{2} = 2 Ch 32^{24}, +10 t.; הִתְפ׳ תפלה אֶל־י׳ 2 S 7^{27} 1 K 8^{54}; על יהוה 1 S 1^{10} (rd. אֶל); לִפְנֵי 1 S 1^{12} 1 K 8^{28}+5 t.; c. לְ Dn 9^{4}; c. אֶל of thing prayed for 1 S 1^{27}; c. אֶל *against* 2 K 19^{20} = Is 37^{21} (read עַל); עַל־זֹאת *because of this* 2 Ch 32^{20} ψ 32^{6}; c. אֶל loc.: אֶל־הַמָּקוֹם 1 K 8$^{29.30.35}$ = 2 Ch 6$^{20.21.26}$; אֶל־הַבַּיִת 1 K 8^{42} = 2 Ch 6^{32}; c. acc. דֶּרֶךְ הָעִיר 1 K 8^{44} = 2 Ch 6^{34}; דֶּרֶךְ אַרְצָם 1 K 8^{48} = 2 Ch 6^{38}. **4.** of *poetical, liturgical* prayer, abs. 1 S 2^{1}, c. אֶל Jon 2^{2}.

8605 **תְּפִלָּה** **n.f. prayer;**—ת׳ Is 1^{15}+, cstr. תְּפִלַּת ψ 80^{5}+; sf. תְּפִלָּתִי 4^{2}+, etc.; pl. תְּפִלּוֹת 72^{20};—**1. a.** *prayer,* 1 K 8^{38} = 2 Ch 6^{29}, Is 1^{15} ψ 35^{13} 80^{5}+. **b.** *pray a prayer,* הִתְפּ׳ ת׳ 2 S 7^{27} 1 K 8^{54} (cf. v$^{28.29}$ = 2 Ch 6$^{19.20}$); דִּבֶּר בַּתּ׳ Dn 9^{21}; specif. of intercession, נשׂא ת׳, c. בְּעַד *in behalf of* 2 K 19^{4} = Is 37^{4} Je 7^{16} 11^{14}. **c.** ת׳ אֶל־אֱלֹהִים 2 Ch 33^{18}, לְאֵל ψ 42^{9}, cf. 69^{14}; c. vb. + לפני 88^{3} 141^{2}; ת׳ תְּקַדְּמֶךָּ 88^{14}. **d.** בית ת׳ Is 56$^{7.7}$ *house of prayer* (temple); c. vb. + אל־היכל + אֶל־י׳ Jon 2^{8}; c. vb. + למעון קדשו 2 Ch 30^{27}. **e.** *hear prayer* is שמע (אֶת־) ת׳ 1 K 8$^{45.49}$ = 2 Ch 6$^{35.39}$, 1 K 9^{3} ψ 4^{2} 39^{13}+9 t.; שמע אֶל־ת׳ 1 K 8$^{28.29}$ = 2 Ch 6$^{19.20}$, Ne 1^{6} Dn 9^{17}; פנה אל ת׳ 1 K 8^{28} = 2 Ch 6^{19}, ψ 102^{18}; אָזְנֶיךָ קַשֻּׁבוֹת לת׳ 2 Ch 6^{40} 7^{15}, cf. Ne 1^{11} (אֶל); הַקְשִׁיבָה ת׳ ψ 61^{2}; הַאֲזִינָה ת׳ 17^{1} 55^{2} 86^{6}; הִקְשִׁיב בְּקוֹל ת׳ 66^{19}; לקח ת׳ 6^{10}; cf. 66^{20} 102^{18b}. **2.** in ψ-titles, poetic, liturgical prayer ψ 17^{1} 86^{1} 90^{1} 102^{1} 142^{1} Hb 3^{1}; of Davidic Psalter, תפלות דוד ψ 72^{20}.

†**פָּלָל** **n.pr.m.** a wall-builder Ne 3^{25}, Φαλαλ, 𝔊^{א} Φαλακ, A Φαλαξ, 𝔊^{L} Φαλλη. 6420

†**[פָּלִיל]** **n.m. judge;** pl. פְּלִלִים Dt 32^{31} our enemies being *judges, umpires;* עָוֺן פ׳ Jb 31^{11}, rd. עֲוֺן פ׳ acc. to Di Siegf, cf. De; < עָוֺן פְּלִילִי as v^{28}, so Bu Du; בִּפְלִלִים Ex 21^{22}, rd. perh. בַּנְּפָלִים *for the abortion* Bu$^{ZAW\ xi\ (1891),\ 107}$, cf. also Di-Ry. 6414

†**פְּלִילָה** **n.f. office of judge or umpire;**—עשׂי פ׳ (Qr עֲשׂוּ) Is 16^{3} *do an umpire's office.* 6415

†**פְּלִילִי** **adj. for a judge, calling for judgment;**—עָוֺן פ׳ Jb 31^{28} (on v^{11} see פָּלִיל; Kue$^{Ond.\ (2)\ 161}$ reads עֲוֺן פְּלִילִים in both v^{11} and v^{28}). 6416

†**פְּלִילִיָּה** **n.f. the giving a decision;**—פ׳ Is 28^{7} (of priests). 6417

†**פְּלַלְיָה** **n.pr.m.** (י׳ *hath interposed*);—priest Ne 11^{12}, Φαλ(λ)αλια(ς). 6421

†**אֶפְלָל** **n.pr.m.** in Judah 1 Ch 2$^{37.37}$, Αφαμηλ, etc., 𝔊^{L} Αφαλλ. 654

פַּלְמֹנִי v. I. פְּלֹנִי sub פלה. p. 811 6422-23

†II. **פְּלוֹנִי, פְּלֹנִי** **adj. gent.** erron.: c. art. הַפְּלוֹנִי 1 Ch 11^{27} 27^{10} read הַפַּלְטִי as 2 S 23^{26} (v. בֵּית פֶּלֶט); הַפְּלֹנִי 1 Ch 11^{36} read הַגִּלֹנִי, as 2 S 23^{34}. 6397
—I. פְּלֹנִי v. פלה. p. 811 6423

פלס, פלשׂ (√of foll.; ? *be even, balance*).

†**פֶּלֶס** **n.[m.] balance, scale;**—lit. Pr 16^{11}, fig. Is 40^{11} (in both ‖ מֹאזְנַיִם). 6425

6424 †[פִּלֵּס] **vb. Pi. denom.** weigh, make level (Ph. פלס Pi. *make level* (?) in n.pr.);—*Impf.* 3 ms. יְפַלֵּס ψ 78[20]; 2 mpl. תְּפַלֵּסוּן ψ 58[3] (v. infr.), etc.; *Imv.* ms. פַּלֵּס Pr 4[26]; *Pt.* מְפַלֵּס 5[11];—**1.** *weigh out* חֲמַס יְדֵיכֶם תְּפ׳ ψ 58[3] (fig.; but read perh. חָמָס יְדֵיכֶם תְּפַלֵּסְנָה *violence do your hands weigh out*, so 𝔊 𝔖 𝔗 Bae Kau We). **2.** *make level*, smooth (cf. Gerber[32]), c. acc. of path (fig.), מַעְגָּל Pr 4[26] 5[21] Is 26[7], נָתִיב ψ 78[50], אֹרַח Pr 5[6].

4657 †[מִפְלָשׂ] **n.[m.]** swaying, poising;—מִפְלְשֵׂי־עָב Jb 37[16]; Bu (plausibly) מִפְרְשֵׂי, as 36[29].

6426 †[פָּלַץ] **vb. Hithp.** shudder;—*Impf.* 3 mpl. יִתְפַּלָּצוּן Jb 9[6] its (earth's) pillars *shudder*.

6427 †פַּלָּצוּת **n.f.** shuddering;—פ׳ abs. Jb 21[6] Is 21[4] Ez 7[18] ψ 55[6].

4656 †מִפְלֶצֶת **n.f.** horrid thing (thing *to shudder at*);—עָשְׂתָה מ׳ לָאֲשֵׁרָה 1 K 15[13] (of some abominable object of idolatry, not precisely known), so sf. מִפְלַצְתָּהּ v[13] = 2 Ch 15[16.16].

8606 †[תִּפְלֶצֶת] **n.f.** shuddering, horror;—sf. תִּפְלַצְתְּךָ Je 49[16] *horror at thee!* (exclam.); not quite certain, v. Gie.

6424 פלשׂ v. פלס. above

6428 †[פָּלַשׁ] **vb. Hithp.** act of mourning, poss. **roll in** (dust, etc.; weakened fr. *burrow into*) (NH Pi. *break open*, or *through;* As. *palâšu, dig a hole;* Syr. ܦܠܫ *dig* or *break through;* but connexion dub., Vrss mostly *besprinkle oneself*, Aq *roll oneself*);—*Pf.* 1 s. עָפָר הִתְפַּלָּשְׁתִּי Mi 1[10] Kt (Qr *Imv.* פַּלָּשִׁי-, others mpl. פַּלָּשׁוּ-); *Impf.* 3 mpl. בָּאֵפֶר יִתְפַּלָּשׁוּ Ez 27[30], so *Imv.* fs. הִתְפַּלְּשִׁי בָאֵפֶר Je 6[26] (cf. Mi 1[10] Qr); abs., mpl. הִתְפַּלְּשׁוּ 25[34].

6429 †פְּלֶשֶׁת **n.pr.terr.** Philistia, poet. and late;—(יֹשְׁבֵי) פְּלָשֶׁת Ex 15[14] (Φυλιστιειμ; elsewh. (οἱ) ἀλλόφυλοι), Jo 4[4], elsewhere פְּלֶשֶׁת Is 14[29.31] ψ 60[10] = 108[10], 83[8] 87[4]; As. *Palastu, Pilistu*, COT[Gn 10, 14] Dl[Pa 288 f.] Gk. Παλαιστίνη Herod.[ii. 104, 106, vii. 89] Jos[Ant. i. 6, 2] (also Φυλιστίνου); v. Rel[Pal. 73 f.]

6430 פְּלִשְׁתִּי [288] **adj.gent.** Philistine, (οἱ) Φυλιστιειμ, and (not in Hex) (ὁ) ἀλλόφυλος, (οἱ) ἀλλόφυλοι;—only as subst.: הַפּ׳ *the Philistine* (Goliath) slain by David 1 S 17[8] + 27 t. 17, 18[6] 19[5] 21[10] 22[10]; one slain by Abishai 2 S 21[17]; elsewhere pl. *the Philistines* [255], usu. פְּלִשְׁתִּים without art., rarely הַפּ׳ 1 S 4[7] 7[13] + (esp. c. prep. בַּפּ׳ v[13] +, and then perh. due to punctuators), Gn 10[14] = 1 Ch 1[12], Gn 26[14.15.18] Ju 3[31] + 33 t. Ju, 1 S 4[1.1] + 118 t. 1 S, 2 S 1[20] + 28 t. 2 S, +; אֶרֶץ פ׳ Gn 21[32.34] + 12 t.; שְׂדֵה פ׳ 1 S 6[1] 27[7.11]; מֶלֶךְ פ׳ Gn 26[1.8]; שָׂרֵי פ׳ 1 S 18[30] + 5 t.; סַרְנֵי פ׳ Jos 13[3] Ju 3[3] + 13 t.; יָם פ׳ Ex 23[31]; אֱלֹהֵי פ׳ Ju 10[6].—Cf. כַּפְתּוֹר, II. כְּרֵתִי. On Philistines v. also WMM[As. u. Eur. 387 f.] Evans[Cretan Pictographs, 100 ff.] Schwally[ZWT xxxiv. 103 f., 255]

†פֶּלֶת **n. pr. m. 1.** Reubenite Nu 16[1], 6431
Φαλεθ[κ]; rd. prob. פַּלּוּא (q. v.) so Gf Dr al. **2.** Judahite 1 Ch 2[33], Θαλεθ, Φαλεθ[ατ].

†פְּלֵתִי **adj.gent.** from unknown n.pr.; only 6432
c. art. as n. coll. with הַכְּרֵתִי (q.v.) of David's guard 2 S 8[18] 15[18] 20[7.23] 1 K 1[38.44] 1 Ch 18[17].

פֶּן־ [133] (alw. with Makkeph) **conj.** (averting, 6435
or deprecating), **lest** (origin dub.: Thes Kö[ii. 334] from פָּנָה, prop. subst. cstr. in accus. *for the aversion of;* but פָּנָה is intrans.: Nö[M. 474] cps. the enclitic particle פוּן in 𝔗, *then*, ἄν, 'etwa,' thinking that a part. with the mng. 'es möchte etwa,' spoken in a tone of alarm, might readily acquire a deprecatory force);—*lest:* **1.** with *impf.* Gn 3[3] ye shall not eat thereof ... פֶּן־תְּמֻתוּן *lest* ye die, 11[4] let us build a city פֶּן־נָפוּץ *lest* we be scattered, 19[15.17.19] 38[23] 45[11] Ex 1[10] 23[29.33] etc., 2 K 10[23] (sq. יֵשׁ), Is 6[10] 27[3] 28[22] 48[5.7] ψ 2[12] 7[3] etc.; oft. after הִשָּׁמֶר־לְךָ *take heed to thyself* Gn 24[6] 31[24], and esp. in Dt, as 4[9.23] 6[12] 8[11] al.; after a vb. of fearing Gn 32[12], and once, even, of swearing Ju 15[12]; deprecating pathetically, Gn 44[34] how shall I go up, etc.? *lest* I look upon the evil that will befal my father. Once, unusually, preceding the principal clause, Pr 5[6] אֹרַח חַיִּים פֶּן־תְּפַלֵּס *lest* she should make level the path of life, her ways are unstable, etc. (Ew Be Now; v. also Toy). Note esp. **a.** the idiom כִּי אָמַר (אָמַרְתִּי) פֶּן־ *for he* (*I*) *said, Lest ...*, implying always that some precaution has been taken to avert the dreaded contingency, †Gn 26[9] for I said, Lest I die on account of her (to obviate which, Isaac had called Rebecca his sister), 31[31] 38[11] 42[4] Ex 13[17] Nu 16[34] 1 S 13[19] 27[11] (לֵאמֹר), ψ 38[17]; with כי אמר implied Gn 26[7]; cf., with an aposiop., 3[22] and now, *lest* he put forth his hand, etc. (implying that measures are taken to prevent this, see v[23]): cf. Tob 8[9]. **b.** פֶּן־ at the beg. of a sentence, with a dissuasive force, (Beware) *lest:* †Is 36[18] פֶּן־יַסִּית אֶתְכֶם חזקיהו (beware) *lest* Hezekiah deceive you, Dt 29[17.17] (sq. יֵשׁ), Je 51[46] Jb 32[13] 36[18]. **2.** with

Pf., the result feared being conceived as having possibly already taken place; †2 S 20^{6} pursue after him, פֶּן־מָצָא לוֹ . . . וְהִצִּיל *lest he have found* him fenced cities, etc. (but the tense of והציל makes יִמְצָא prob., Dr^{Sm} Bu Kö$^{iii. 486}$), 2 K 2^{16} פֶּן־נְשָׂאוֹ רוּחַ י׳ וַיַּשְׁלִכֵהוּ וגו׳.

6436 †פַּנַּג **n.[m.]** unknown word, appar. some kind of food; חִטֵּי מִנִּית וּפ׳ וּדְבַשׁ וגו׳ Ez 27^{17}; Vrss conject.; Co prop. וְדוֹנַג, so Hoffm$^{Ph. Inschr. 15}$ Krae Berthol ('perhaps').

6437 פָּנָה$_{135}$ **vb. turn** (NH *id.*; Syr. ܦܢܳܐ, 𝔗 פְּנָא; Eth. ፈነወ: Ar. فَنِيَ *pass away, banish;* cf. Sab. פנה (variously) e.g. CIS$^{iv. Nos. 1, 37, 40}$; As. *pânu, face*, Ph. פנם, MI$^{13, 18}$ לפני, sf. מפני 1^{19});—**Qal**$_{117}$ *Pf.* 3 ms. פ׳ Je 6^{4}+, 2 ms. פָּנִיתָ 2 S 9^{8}, etc.; *Impf.* 3 ms. יִפְנֶה 1 S 13^{17}+, וַיִּפֶן Ex 2^{12}+, 3 fs. וַתֵּפֶן 1 K 10^{13}, 1 s. וָאֵפֶן Dt 9^{15} 10^{5}, 1 pl. וַנֵּפֶן 2^{1}+, etc.; *Imv.* ms. פְּנֵה ψ 25^{16}+, etc.; *Inf. abs.* פָּנֹה Hg 1^{9}; cstr. לִפְנוֹת Gn 24^{63}+, etc.; *Pt.* פֹּנֶה Dt 29^{17}+, etc.;—**1.** †**a.** *turn* toward, אֶל pers., lit., Ju 6^{14} Is 13^{14}=Je 50^{16}, Jb 21^{5} (i.e. attentively); cf. of branches Ez 17^{6} (in allegory); c. עַל of direction Gn 24^{49}; fig. c. אֶל־י׳ (in worship), Is 45^{22}, other gods Ho 3^{1} Dt 31$^{18.20}$ Lv 19^{4}; for help Lv 19^{31} 20^{6} Jb 5^{1}; אֶל־אָוֶן 36^{21}; c. acc. הַמָּקוֹם אֲשֶׁר יִפְנֶה Ez 10^{11}; c. ה loc. 1 K 17^{3} Dt 2^{3} (+לָכֶם dat. eth.), Ct 6^{1}; c. דֶּרֶךְ 1 S 13$^{18.18}$ Jb 24^{18}, אֶל־ד׳ Ju 20^{42} 1 S 13^{17}; fig. לְדַרְכּוֹ Is 53^{6} 56^{11}; c. acc. כֹּל אֲשֶׁר־יִפְנֶה 1 S 14^{47}, so, +שָׁם, fig. 1 K 2^{3}, i.e. whatever thou undertakest, אֶל־כָּל־אֲשֶׁר יִפְנֶה Pr 17^{8}. †**b.** *turn* from, מִן loc. Gn 18^{22}, fig., of heart, c. מֵעִם י׳ Dt 29^{17}, abs.=*turn away* 30^{17}; in phr. פ׳ עֹרֶף *turn* (with) *the back* (cf. ראה עֹרֶף Je 18^{17}), +לִפְנֵי, Jos 7^{12} (of flight), fig., +אֶל־י׳, Je 2^{27} 32^{33}. **c.** *turn* and do a thing, lit. (esp. +vb. of motion) Nu 21^{33} Dt 1$^{7.24}$ Ju 18^{21} 1 K 10^{13} +17 t.; to do a thing (inf.) †Ec 2^{12}. †**d.** *turn, decline*, of day Je 6^{4}, days of life ψ 90^{9}. †**e.** *turn toward, approach*, of evening, לִפְנוֹת עָרֶב Gn 24^{63} Dt 23^{12}; of morning, לִפ׳ (הַ)בֹּקֶר Ex 14^{27} Ju 19^{26} ψ 46^{6} (fig.). †**2. a.** *turn and look, look*, lit., אֶל pers. Nu 12^{10} 2 Ch 20^{24} 26^{20}, וַיִּפֶן כֹּה וָכֹה Ex 2^{12}; c. לְמַעְלָה Is 8^{21}; abs. *look* (back) 2 Ch 13^{14}; c. אַחֲרֵי *look behind one* (and see, or say), Jos 8^{20} Ju 20^{40} 2 S 1^{7} 2^{20} 2 K 2^{24}, *look after* another Ez 29^{16} (fig. for seek alliance with); c. אֶל of direction Ex 16^{10} Nu 17^{7}. **b.** of inanimate things, *face*, c. אֶל loc. Jos 15^{7}, usu. of facing points of compass, c. ה loc. 1 K 7$^{25.25.25.25}$=2 Ch 4$^{4.4.4.4}$, Jos 15^{2} Ez 8^{3} 46^{19}, but also c. קָדִים 43^{17} 44^{1} 46$^{1.12}$ 47^{2}, cf. 43^{1}. **c.** esp. fig. *look* at, אֶל־ pers., *regard*, (1) graciously 2 S 9^{8}; of י׳ Ez 36^{9} Lv 26^{9} 2 K 13^{23} ψ 40^{5}, +חָנַן 25^{16} 69^{17} 86^{16} 119^{132}; c. אֶל־תְּפִלָּה 1 K 8^{28}=2 Ch 6^{19}, ψ 102^{18}, אֶל־מִנְחָה Nu 16^{15} Mal 2^{13}; (2) sternly, אֶל־קְשִׁי הָעָם Dt 9^{27}. **d.** *look* for (אֶל rei)=expect Hg 1^{9}. **e.** fig. *look* at (ב rei)=consider Ec 2^{11}.—2 Ch 25^{23} v. פִּנָּה. †**Pi.** *Pf.* 3 ms. פִּנָּה Zp 3^{15}, etc.; *Imv.* mpl. פַּנּוּ Is 40^{3}+ 2 t.;—*turn away, put out of the way*, c. acc. pers. Zp 3^{15} (‖ הֵסִיר); hence *make clear*, c. acc. הַבַּיִת, i.e. clear away things scattered about, make orderly, Germ. 'aufräumen,' Gn 24^{31}; *empty* it Lv 14^{36}; fig., c. acc. דֶּרֶךְ *make clear*, free from obstacles, Is 40^{3} 57^{14} 62^{10} Mal 3^{1}; acc. om. *clear away* (ground) before it, i.e. to plant it ψ 80^{10} (fig.). †**Hiph.** (esp. Je) *Pf.* 3 ms. הִפְנָה Je 48^{39}, 3 fs. הִפְנְתָה 49^{24}, etc.; *Impf.* וַיֶּפֶן Ju 15^{4}; *Inf. cstr.* sf. הַפְנֹתוֹ 1 S 10^{9}; *Pt.* מַפְנֶה Na 2^{9};—**1.** *turn*, c. acc. וַיֶּפֶן זָנָב אֶל־זָנָב Ju 15^{4}, עֹרֶף Je 48^{39} (cf. הפך Jos 7^{8}), שִׁכְמוֹ לָלֶכֶת 1 S 10^{9}. **2.** *make a turn, shew* (signs of) *turning*, +נָסוּ Je 46^{21}, לָנוּס 49^{24}; opp. נָסוּ 46^{5}, cf. Na 2^{9}; +אֶל pers. 47^{3}. †**Hoph.** *Imv.* mpl. הָפְנוּ Je 49^{8} (Ges$^{§ 46 a, N.}$) *be ye turned back!* (in flight, +נֻסוּ); *Pt.* מָפְנֶה צָפוֹנָה Ez 9^{2} the gate . . . *which is faced northward* (cf. **Qal 2 b**).

[פָּנֶה], pl. פָּנִים$_{2123}$ **n.m.**$^{Pr 25, 23}$ and (Ez 21^{21} 6440
=*edge;* on 2 S 10^{9} v. infr.) **f. face,** also **faces** (as *turned* toward one);—pl. abs. פָּנִים Gn 32^{31}+; cstr. פְּנֵי 2 S 14^{32}+; sf. 1 s. פָּנַי Gn 43^{3}+; 3 ms. פָּנָיו Gn 4^{5}+, פָּנֵימוֹ ψ 11^{7} (Kö$^{ii. 1, 446}$); 2 mpl. פְּנֵיכֶם Gn 40^{7}+, etc.;—usu. c. vb. pl., Gn 4$^{5.6}$ Ex 33^{14}+; c. vb. sg. La 4^{16} (through influence of intervening י׳, Ges$^{§ 146 a}$), Pr 15^{14} (but read פִּי, as Qr, v. פֶּה);—**I. 1.** *face, faces* (Je 30^{6} Ez 27^{35}+, cf. 1^{6} 10$^{14.21}$ etc.): **a.** lit., of man Gn 43^{31} 2 S 19^{5} 1 K 19^{13} Lv 13^{41} Dn 8^{18} 10$^{9.15}$+; עוֹר פ׳ Ex 35$^{29.30.35}$; pale (from alarm) Is 29^{22} Je 30^{6}, flushed Is 13^{8} Ez 21^{3}, cf. Na 2^{11} Jo 2^{6}; tearful Is 25^{8} Jb 16^{16}; sad, פ׳ רעים Gn 40^{7}, cf. Ne 2$^{2.3}$, also רֹעַ פ׳ Ec 7^{3} i.e. sadness; יֵיטִב פ׳ Pr 15^{13} *maketh glad the face;* נָפְלוּ פָנֶיךָ Gn 4$^{5.6}$ why *is thy face fallen* (in displeasure), cf. 1 S 1^{18} (rdg. הִפִּילָה, נָפְלוּ, or נָפְלָה); covered with shame Ez 7^{18}, whence fig. of confusion, discomfiture Je 51^{51} ψ 69^{8} 83^{17}, etc. **b.** of י׳ Ex 33^{20}, cf. v^{23}. **c.** פָּנִים אֶל־פָּנִים *face to face*, of seeing (God) Gn 32^{31}, cf. Ju 6^{22}, knowing Dt 34^{10}, judging Ez 20^{35}, speaking Ex 33^{11}, and so פ׳ בְּפ׳ Dt 5^{4}; נִתְרָאֶה פָנִים 2 K 14^{8} *see each other* (in the) *face*=meet each other

in battle, cf. v^{11}=2 Ch 25$^{17.21}$. **d.** of relations with 'י: הֵרִים פ' Ezr 9^{6}, in worship (v. also נשׂא); in spiritual sense Je 2^{27} 32^{33} (פָּנָה אֵלַי עֹרֶף וְלֹא פָנִים); נָתַן אֶת־פ' לִדְרוֹשׁ י' 2 Ch 20^{3}; נָתַן פ' אֶל־אֲדֹנָי Dn 9^{3}; הַבָּנִים קְשֵׁי פָנִים Ez 2^{4}. **e.** of 'י himself, לֹא יָסִיר פָּנִים מִכֶּם 2 Ch 30^{9}; פְּנֵי י' בְּעֹשֵׂי רָע ψ 34^{17}; גַּעֲרַת פָּנֶיךָ 80^{17}.—Vid. further sub **7**. **2. a.**=*presence, person,* of 'י Ex 33$^{14.15}$, בְּפָנָיו Dt 4^{37}, מַלְאַךְ פָּנָיו Is 63^{9}; לֶחֶם הַפָּנִים, v. לֶחֶם; of 'י's angry presence La 4^{16} ψ 21^{10}; of Absalom 2 S 17^{11}; in weakened sense, nearly=sf. (cf. נפשׁ **4 a**), Pr 7^{15}. †**b.** c. ראה technically, *see* one's *face,* i.e. appear before one, in one's presence: before a man Gn 32^{21} (+3 other uses of 'פ), (God, c. יראה pointed as **Niph.,** v. **II 2**); esp. as privilege, = have access to, man of rank Gn 43$^{3.5}$ 44$^{23.26}$, king Ex 10$^{28.28}$ cf. v^{29} (all J), 2 S 14$^{24.24.28.32}$ cf. 3$^{13.13}$; רֹאֵי פְּנֵי הַמֶּלֶךְ 2 K 25^{19}= Je 52^{25}, Est 1^{14}; implying favour of person seen, man Gn 33^{10}(J), God v^{10}, cf. Jb 33^{26} (Hiph.), and, c. חזה, ψ 11^{7} 17^{15}. **3.** *face* of seraphim Is 6^{2}, cherubim Ex 25$^{20.20}$=37$^{9.9}$, Ez 1$^{8.11}$ 2 Ch 3^{13}+. **4.** *face* of animals, פְּנֵי הַצֹּאן Gn 30^{40}; פ' אַרְיֵה וּפ' שׁוֹר וּפ' נֶשֶׁר Ez 1^{10} (in descr. of cherubim), cf. 10^{14}; פ' אַרְיֵה also 1 Ch 12^{8} (fig.), פ' כְפִיר Ez 41^{19}; פַּתְחֵי פ' Jb 41^{6} of crocodile. **5.** *face* (=*surface*) of ground (הָאֲדָמָה) Gn 2^{6} 4^{14} 7^{4} ψ 104^{30}+, so פ' הָאָרֶץ Gn 1^{29} 7^{3} 8^{9} 11$^{4.8.9}$ 19^{28} Is 24^{1}, פ' תֵבֵל Is 14^{21} 27^{6}; of a field Pr 24^{31}; פ' תְהוֹם Gn 1$^{2.2}$ Jb 38^{30}, פ' הַמַּיִם Gn 7^{18}; פ' רְקִיעַ הַשָּׁמַיִם 1^{20}; פ' כִסֵּה Jb 26^{9} i.e. of God's throne (but Bu reads כֶּסֶה *full moon*); פ' הַלּוֹט Is 25^{7} v. [לוט]; פ' לְבוּשׁוֹ Jb 41^{5} *the expanse of his* [the crocodile's] *coat; front* (esp. Ezek.), of house Ez 41^{14} 47^{1}, פ' הַקֹּדֶשׁ 41^{21}; of gate 40$^{6.20.22}$ 42^{15} 43^{4}; of chamber 40$^{44.44.45.46}$; of pot (סִיר) Je 1^{13}; פ' הַמִּלְחָמָה 2 S 10^{9} *battle-front* =1 Ch 19^{10} (vb. agrees with 'הַמִּ in gender, Ges^{§146a}); =*van* of locust-army Jo 2^{20} (opp. סֹפוֹ); *front,* i.e. *edge,* of sword Ez 21^{21}, of axe Ec 10^{10}; =condition, state of a thing, as denoted by its *appearance;* of flock Pr 27^{23}; פ' הַדָּבָר 2 S 14^{20} *the appearance* (situation, attitude) *of the affair.* **6.** as **adv.loc.** מִפָּנִים וּמֵאָחוֹר 2 S 10^{9} *before and behind*=פ' וְא' 1 Ch 19^{10}, also Ez 2^{10} 2 Ch 13^{14}; פְּנֵי *toward* Ct 7^{5}, also *in front* (to the East?) *of* 2 Ch 20^{16} (v. לִפְנֵי **d** infr.); לְפָנִים *forward* Je 7^{24} (opp. לְאָחוֹר); מִלִּפְנִים 1 K 6^{29} v. פְּנִימָה; **adv. temp.** לְפָנִים *formerly* Dt 2$^{12.20}$ Jos 11^{10} Ju 1$^{10.11.13}$ +12 t.; מִלְּפָנִים Is 41^{26} *from beforetime* (‖ מֵרֹאשׁ). **7.** for other phrases see: אור **vb. Hiph. 5**; אוֹר **n. 10**; בּוֹשׁ **Hiph.**; בקשׁ **Pi. 3**; בֹּשֶׁת **1,** p. 102; [הַכָּרָה], p. 648; הָדָר **2**; זָעַם **Niph.**; זָעַף **1**; חָבַשׁ **1 a**; I. חָדָה; I. חָוַר; חָזַק **Pi. 5**; II. חלה; IV. חמר; חָפָה; טָחַן; יָעַד **Hoph.**; יְשׁוּעָה **3,** p. 447; כּוּן **Hiph. 3**; כִּפֶּר **1,** p. 497; כָּסָה **Pi. 1, 2**; מָאוֹר, p. 22; מְזַמָּה p. 169; I. מוּל; מַשָּׂא, p. 673; [נָבַט] **Hiph. 3**; נֶגֶד **1, 2 c**; נֹכַח; נָכַר **Hiph.**; נָפַל **3 b,** and **Hiph. 5**; נָשָׂא **1 b** (3); נָתַן **2 b**; סָבַב **Hiph. 1 a**; סָתַר **Hiph. 2**; I. עֵבֶר **2**; עָזַז, עַז **Hiph.**; עָמַד **Hiph. 6 a**; II. עָמָה; [צָרַב]; [קָדַם] **Pi.**; שִׂים; שׁוּב **Hiph.**; שִׁית; II. שָׁנָה **Pi.**; תֹּפֶת.

II. פְּנֵי, with prepositions:—**1.** אֶל־פְּנֵי: **a.** *to the presence of,* Ex 23^{17} pregn. יֵרָאֶה . . . אֶל־פְּנֵי הָאָדֹן shall appear (coming) to *the presence of* (= before) 'י (‖ 34^{23} אֶת־פְּנֵי הָא'); c. יָצָא = *to confront* 2 Ch 19^{2}. **b.** *to the front of,* after a vb. of motion, Lv 6^{7} הַקְרֵב אֹתָהּ . . . אֶל־פְּנֵי הַמִּזְבֵּחַ, 9^{5} 16^{2} Nu 17^{8} 20^{10}. **c.** *towards* or *on the front of* (אֶל = עַל: see p. 41), Ez 41$^{4.12.15.25}$ 42$^{2.3.7.10.13}$ 45^{7} 48^{21}. **d.** *on to the surface of,* Lv 14^{53} וְשִׁלַּח . . . אֶל־פְּנֵי הַשָּׂדֶה, Ez 16^{5}.

†**2.** אֶת־פְּנֵי *close by* (II. אֵת) *the face* or *front of:* hence **a.** *in the presence of,* 1 S 2^{11} אֶת־פ' עֵלִי 1 K 12^{6} who stood אֶת־פ' שְׁלֹמֹה (cf. לִפְנֵי 10^{8}), Est 1^{10} Pr 17^{24}; pregn. (nisi וַיִּנָּחֵם leg., 𝔖 𝔗 We Dr al.) 1 S 22^{4}. Spec. אֶת־פְּנֵי י' Gn 19^{13} (1 S 2^{17}), v^{27} 1 S 2^{18}; and with נִרְאָה of the appearance of all males at the three annual חַגִּים, Ex 34^{23} יֵרָאֶה כָּל־זְכוּרְךָ אֶת־פ' הָאָדֹן, v^{24} Dt 16^{16} (cf. Dr), 31^{11} 1 S 1^{22} (‖ אל־פ' י' Ex 23^{17}); so פָּנַי alone Ex 23^{15}=34^{20} (לֹא יֵרָאוּ פָנַי רֵיקָם), Is 1^{12}, פָּנֶיךָ ψ 42^{3} (acc. to many, as Ges^{Thes} Di$^{Ex 23, 15}$ Che$^{Is 1, 12, crit. n.}$, the vb. in all these passages was originally **Qal,** afterwards pointed as **Niph.** to avoid the expression *see the face of* 'י); אֶת־פָּנֶיךָ *in thy presence* ψ 16^{10} 21^{7} 140^{14}. **b.** *in front of,* Gn 33^{18} וַיִּחַן אֶת־פ' הָעִיר, Lv 4^{6} לִפְנֵי י' אֶת־פ' פָּרֹכֶת הַקֹּדֶשׁ, v^{17}.—מֵאֵת פְּנֵי *from before,* v. II. אֵת **4 a.**

3. בִּפְנֵי: †(*a*) *in the face of,* mostly in partic. phrases, with hostile import: thus, with יָרַק *to spit* Nu 12^{14} Dt 25^{9}; התיצב *to make a stand* Dt 7^{24} 11^{25}, and עמד Jos 10^{8}, לֹא יַעֲמֹד אִישׁ בְּפָנֶיךָ 21^{42} 23^{9}; עָנָה *to answer* (give evidence) *against,* Ho 5^{5} וענה גאון ישׂראל בפניו, 7^{10} Jb 16^{8}; וְנָקֹטּוּ בִּפְנֵיהֶם = feel loathing *against* their own selves, Ez 6^{9}, so 20^{43} 36^{31}. †(*b*) *in front of,* Ez 42^{12}.

4. לִפְנֵי, prop. *at the face* or *front of,* the most general word for *in the presence of, before:* as 3942
Gn 18^{22} עֹמֵד לִפְנֵי אַבְרָהָם, Ex 4^{21} 11^{10} 2 S 2^{14} Pr 17^{18} + oft.; after a vb. of motion, Gn 47^{2} וַיַּצִּגֵם לִפְנֵי פ' and set them *before* Ph., 27^{20} כִּי הִקְרָה י'

לְפָנַי lit. made (it) to meet *before* me (cf. 24^{12}), Ex 29^{10} Pr 18^{16} etc. In partic.,

a. With the implication of (*a*) *under the eye* or *oversight of*, Dt 25^{2} 1 S 3^{1}. (*b*) *under the eye and regard of*, Gn 17^{18} לוּ יִשְׁמָעֵאל יִחְיֶה לְפָנֶיךָ, Ho 6^{2} Is 53^{2} ψ 61^{8}; cf. Je 30^{20} 31^{36} Is 66^{22} ψ 102^{29}: also 1 S 2^{28} 2 S 19^{14}. (*c*) fig. for *in* (or *into*) *the full* (mental) *view of*, Gn 6^{13} קֵץ כָּל־בָּשָׂר בָּא לְפָנַי is come in *before me*, La 1^{22} תָּבֹא כָל־רָעָתָם לְפָנֶיךָ, Jon 1^{2} עָלְתָה לְפָנָי (cf. אֶל Gn 18^{21} Ex 2^{23}), Is 65^{6} כְּתוּבָה לְפָנָי, Je 2^{22} נִכְתָּם עֲוֹנֵךְ לְפָנַי (cf. נֶגְדִּי Is 47^{12}). (*d*) *openly before*, 1 S 12^{2} הִתְהַלַּכְתִּי לְפָנֵי, and with collat. idea of deserving (and receiving) regard 2^{35}, esp. לפני י׳ Gn 17^{1} al. (v. p. 236^{a}). (*e*) *in presence of* the moon or sun, ψ 72$^{5.17}$, i.e. as long as they endure. (*f*) *free before, at the disposal of*, Gn 13^{9} הֲלֹא כָל־הָאָרֶץ לְפָנֶיךָ (cf. 20^{15} 34^{10} 47^{6} Je 40^{4} 2 Ch 14^{6}), 24^{51} Ct 8^{12}. (*g*) *in the sight* (estimation) *of*, Gn 7^{1} thee have I seen to be just *before* me, 10^{9} a mighty hunter *before* י׳, Dt 24^{4} תּוֹעֵבָה לִ׳ י׳, v^{13} צְדָקָה לִ׳ י׳, 1 S 20^{1b}, אָרוּר לִ׳ י׳ Jos 6^{26} 1 S 26^{19}, לְרָצוֹן לִ׳ י׳ acceptable *before* י׳, Lv 1^{3}+, ψ 19^{15}; 2 K 5^{1} a great man לִפְנֵי אֲדֹנָיו, Pr 14^{12} ψ 143^{2}; וַיִּיטַב לִ׳ (late syn. of earlier בְּעֵינֵי) †Ne 2$^{5.6}$ Est 5^{14}; טוֹב לִ׳ Ec 2^{26} 7^{26}; cf. also נָתַן לְרַחֲמִים לִפְנֵי, v. רַחֲמִים. (*h*) לִפְנֵי י׳, spec. of acts done with a solemn sense of י׳'s presence, often, but not always, at a sanctuary: Gn 27^{7} that I may eat and bless thee *before* י׳, before I die, Ex 18^{12} to eat bread *before* God, Dt 1^{45} ye wept *before* י׳, 6^{25} 12^{7} (to eat, so v^{18} 14$^{23.26}$ 15^{20}), v^{12} (rejoice, so v^{18} 27^{7} Is 9^{2}), Jos 18^{6} 24^{1} Ju 11^{11} 20$^{23.26}$ 21^{2} 1 S 7^{6} 10^{19} 11^{15} 12^{7} 15^{33} 23^{18} 2 S 5^{3} 7^{18} 21^{9}; and constantly in P, as Ex 16$^{9.33.34}$ Lv 1$^{5.11}$ 3$^{1.7}$ etc.; of residents in Jerus. Is 23^{18}. So in הָלַךְ לִ׳ י׳ 1 K 2^{4} al. (v. p. 234^{b} **c**).

b. In other phrases:—(*a*) עָמַד לִפְנֵי *to stand before*, i.e. *wait upon, be in attendance on*, Dt 1^{38} al. (v. עָמַד **1 e**). Simil. הָיָה לִפְנֵי 1 S 19^{7} (cf. 29^{8}), 2 K 5^{2}; עָבַד לִ׳ 2 S 16^{19}. (*b*) הִשְׁתַּחֲוָה לִפְנֵי *to bow down before*, Gn 23^{12} Dt 26^{10} 2 K 18^{22} al. (v. sub שָׁחָה; also נָפַל **3 b**): so with הִתְפַּלֵּל *to pray* 1 S 1^{12}+; cf. הלך לפני 1 K 12^{30} 1 Ch 21^{30}. (*c*) *to be smitten* (נִגַּף) *before* a foe; v. נָגַף Niph. [contrast נוּס מִפְּנֵי: infr. **6 a**]. So with נָפַל 1 S 14^{13}; נָתַן (in helplessness or flight), esp. in Dt, as 1$^{8.21}$ 7$^{2.23}$ Jos 10^{12} 11^{6}+(Dr$^{\text{Dt lxxxii}}$): cf. Ju 4^{15} 2 S 5^{20} Is 45^{1} Je 1^{17}. (*d*) עָמַד לִפְנֵי *to stand* (make a stand) *before* (not quite so strong as עָ׳ בִּפְנֵי, supr. **3**), Ex 9^{11} Ju 2^{14} 2 K 10^{4} Je 49^{19} ψ 76^{8} 147^{17} Na 1^{6}; so with הִתְיַצֵּב Dt 9^{2} Jos 1^{5} Jb 41^{2}, קוּם Jos 7$^{12.13}$. (*e*) in hostile sense (rare), יָצָא לִפְנֵי go forth *to face* 1 Ch 14^{8} 2 Ch 14^{9}. (*f*) שִׂים (נָתַן) לִפְנֵי, of food, to set or place *before*, Gn 18^{8} 24^{33}+. (*g*) נָתַן לִפְנֵי to *set before*, i.e. propound for acceptance or choice, usu. of laws (esp. Dt Je), Dt 4^{8} 11$^{26.32}$ 30$^{1.15.19}$ 1 K 9^{6} (D^{2}), Je 9^{12} 21^{8} 26^{4} 44^{10} Dn 9^{10}, cf. Ez 23^{24} (place at disposal of): so with שִׂים Ex 19^{7} 21^{1}.

c. With reference to *position*: (*a*) *in front of, before*, esp. with vbs. of motion (with which נֶגֶד is hardly used), Gn 32^{21} בַּמִּנְחָה הַהֹלֶכֶת לְפָנָי that goeth *before* me, 33^{14} the cattle אֲשֶׁר לְפָנַי, Ex 17^{5} 23^{20} etc.; in the description of a march or procession, Ex 13$^{21.22}$ Nu 10^{33} Is 52^{12} 58^{8}+; 2 S 3^{31} and wail *before* Abner (before his bier); of flocks before a shepherd Gn 32^{18}; of captives or booty driven before a conqueror 1 S 30^{20} (rd. וַיְנַהֲגוּ לְפָנָיו We Dr), Is 8^{4} 40^{10}=62^{11} וּפְעֻלָּתוֹ לְפָנָיו his recompence (i.e. his newly-recovered people, regarded as his prize of war) *before* him, Am 9^{4} La 1$^{5.6}$. (*b*) of a leader, etc.=*at the head of*, Dt 10^{11} Ju 9^{39} 1 S 8^{20} Mi 1^{13} al.; cf. בא ויצא לפני (העם) Nu 27^{17} 1 S 18$^{13.16}$ 2 Ch 1^{10}; Ec 4^{16} *before* whom (at whose head) he was. (*c*) denoting superiority, *before, above*, Gn 48^{20} וַיָּשֶׂם את־אפרים לפני מנשה, Jb 34^{19}.

d. Of *places* (not very common): Ex 14^{2} *before* Pi-haḥiroth . . ., *before* Baal-ẓephon, Nu 33^{7b}, Gn 23^{17} אשר לִ׳ מַמְרֵא (usu. על פני מ׳: v. **7 a** *d*), 1 Ch 19^{7} Ne 8$^{1.3}$; *before* the temple, veil, altar, etc., Ex 16^{34}+ לִ׳ הָעֵדֻת, 30^{6}+ לִ׳ הַפָּרֹכֶת, 40$^{5.6}$ Nu 3^{38} 7^{10} al. (all P), 1 K 6^{21} 7^{49}+.

e. Of time, *before*: Am 1^{1} לפני הָרָעַשׁ *before* the earthquake, Gn 29^{26} 30^{30} לְפָנָי *before* me (i.e. before I came to thee), Ex 10^{14} לפניו לא היה כן *before* it there was not the like, Nu 13^{22} 1 K 16$^{25.30}$ מִכֹּל אֲשֶׁר לְפָנָיו, Is 43^{10} 48^{7} Pr 8^{25} Jb 15^{7} etc. Sq. inf., Gn 13^{10} לִפְנֵי שַׁחֵת י׳ *before* י׳'s destroying, etc., 27^{7} לִפְנֵי מוֹתִי, 36^{31} 1 S 9^{15}+. Once, in late Heb., לִפְנֵי מִזֶּה *before* this Ne 13^{4}.

f. *In the manner of, like* (rare and dub.), 1 S 1^{16} אַל־תִּתֵּן אֶת־אֲמָתְךָ לִפְנֵי בַּת־בְּלִיַּעַל *like* a worthless woman, Jb 3^{24} *like* my food, 4^{19} they are crushed *like* the moth (cf. Lat. *pro*).

5. מִלִּפְנֵי$_{73}$ *from before*:—**a.** *from the presence of* (properly, from a position *before* a person or object: to be distinguished from מִפְּנֵי; v. **6**): (*a*) Gn 41^{46} ויצא יוסף מִלִּפְנֵי פ׳ *from before* Ph., 47^{10} 2 K 5^{27} 6^{32}+; מלִ׳ י׳ Gn 4^{6} Cain went forth *from before* י׳, Jon 1$^{3.10}$; spec. of the sanctuary, Lv 9^{24} ותצא אש מלפני י׳ (so 10^{2}), קֶצֶף Nu 17^{11} (cf. 2 Ch 19^{2}), with לָקַח etc. Lv 16^{12} Nu 17^{24} 20^{9}, 1 S 21^{7} the shew-bread that was removed *from before* י׳; *from before* a place 1 K 8^{54} Ezr 10^{6}

2 Ch 1^{13}. (*b*) of taking, etc., *from before* a person, Gn 23^{4} to bury my dead *from before* me, v^{8} Ex 36^{3} Dt 17^{18} וכתב לו מִשְׁנֵה התורה הזאת מל׳ הכהנים *from* (the copy) *before* the priests, 28^{31} נָזוֹל מלפניך. (*c*) with בקשׁ Est 4^{8} [cf. מִן קֳדָם Dn 2^{18}]; and to express the idea of *proceeding* from a person, Est 1^{19} [cf. Dn 2^{15}], Ec 10^{5}; 1 Ch 29^{12} מלפניך הָעֹשֶׁר והכבוד מלפניך (cf. Acts 3^{19}); ψ 17^{2} יֵצֵא מִשְׁפָּטִי. (*d*) of cutting off, etc., *from before* י׳ (cf. לִפְנֵי **a** *b*, *c*), Lv 22^{3} 1 K 8^{25} לֹא־יִכָּרֵת לְךָ אִישׁ מִלְּפָנַי, Je 31^{36} 33^{18} Is 48^{19}: ψ 51^{13} אַל־תַּשְׁלִיכֵנִי מִלְּפָנֶיךָ (cf. **8 a**); Je 16^{17} לֹא נִסְתְּרוּ מִלְּפָנַי, 18^{23} Ne 3^{37}. (*e*) of expelling *from before* an invader, Ex 23^{28} Dt 9^{4} 11^{23} 31^{3}+ (but much less common than מִפְּנֵי).

†**b.** (Chiefly late) to express the *source* or *cause*, with the force of the לְ weakened, in cases where the earlier language would have used מִפְּנֵי: with vbs. of fearing, 1 S 18^{12} Ec 3^{14} 8$^{12.13}$; 1 Ch 16^{30} חִילוּ מִלְּפָנָיו [‖ ψ 96^{9} מפניו], ψ 114$^{7.7}$; Est 7^{6}; 2 Ch 32^{7} (+מפני); failing, etc., Is 57^{16} ψ 97^{5}; being humbled, 1 K 21^{29} (+מפני), 2 Ch 32$^{12.23}$ 34^{27} [‖ 2 K 22^{19} מפני], 36^{12}; crying for help 1 S 8^{18} [cf. מפני Ex 3^{7}], singing 1 Ch 16^{33} [‖ ψ 96^{13} לפני], fleeing 19^{18} [‖ 2 S 10^{18} מִפְּנֵי]. †**c.** of time, once, = לִפְנֵי Ec 1^{10}.—With the later usages of מל׳, cf. מִן קֳדָם in BAram. and 𝔗 (Dr Sm lxx–lxxi, lxxiii); v. also Kö$^{ii. 320}$.

6. מִפְּנֵי *from the face* or *presence of*, *from before*, Ex 14^{19} וַיִּסַּע עמוד הענן מִפְּנֵיהֶם removed *from before* them, Is 30^{11} Ho 11^{2}; so **a.** (oft. with suggestion of causation (v. מִן **2 d, e, f**), *because of*, *for fear of* [so AV RV Ju 9^{21} 1 S 21^{11} 23^{26} Je 35$^{11.11}$ 37^{11} 41^{9} 50^{16}]) after vbs. of hiding Gn 3^{8} 4^{14} Is 2^{10} (cf. v$^{19.21}$); and esp. of escaping, Ju 9^{21} (Thes 'bene 𝔙 *ob metum* A.'), 1 S 18^{11} 19^{10} 23^{26}, or fleeing, Ex 4^{3} 14^{25} 1 S 17^{24}+oft. (v. בָּרַח and נוּס), and expelling, destroying, etc. Ex 23^{30} אֲגָרְשֶׁנּוּ מִפָּנֶיךָ I will expel them *from before* thee, 34$^{11.24}$ אוֹרִישׁ גּוֹיִם מִפָּנֶיךָ (v. הוֹרִישׁ), Lv 18^{24} Dt 8^{20} Am 2^{9} ψ 89^{24}+oft. (as though clearing the way for Israel, for Israel's sake: cf. Is 63^{12} בּוֹקֵעַ מַיִם מִפְּנֵיהֶם, Jos 2^{10} 4^{23}). Pregn. Is 17^{9} כַּעֲזוּבַת . . . אשר עזבו מפני בני ישׂר׳ which they forsook (fleeing) *from before*, etc. **b.** implying causation more distinctly, ψ 9^{4} יאבדו מפניך perish *from before* thee or *at thy presence*, Dt 7^{20}: very oft. with vbs. of fearing, as חיל, יגר, גור, ירא, ערץ, פחד, קוץ Ex 9^{30} Nu 22$^{3.3}$ Dt 1^{17} Je 5^{22} etc. (mostly when the object inspiring fear is a person: when it is a thing, מִן alone is preferred; but see Dt 5^{5} 9^{19}); of being alarmed or dismayed Gn 45^{3} Jos 2^{9} Je 1^{17} Jb 23^{15}, etc.; of humbling oneself Ex 10^{3} Ju 11^{33}+; with other words, to indicate the *external ground* of an action or effect, as הַס מִפָּנָיו be silent *at* (i.e. *because of*) his presence Zp 1^{7} Hb 2^{20}; Ju 5^{5} the mts. flowed מפני י׳ *at the presence of* י׳, Is 63^{19} Je 4^{26} Na 1^{5}, ψ 68^{3} as wax melteth מפני אשׁ; Dt 20^{19}; Is 19^{1}; 26^{17} כן היינו מפניך so were we *through thy presence* (more than לפניך,—implying that their state was *due to* י׳); קום מפני to rise up *at the presence of* Gn 31^{35} Lv 19^{32}. (N.B. In **a, b,** freq. rendered *before* in AV RV, and so confused with לפני; but the מִן retains always its full force in the Heb.) **c.** of the *cause*, whether nearer or more remote: (*a*) Gn 6^{13} מָלְאָה הָאָרֶץ חָמָס מִפְּנֵיהֶם *because of* them (i.e. occasioned by them), 27^{4} I loathe my life *because of* the daughters of Heth, 36^{7} the land could not support them *because of* their cattle, 41^{31} 47^{13} Ex 3^{7} their cry *by reason of* their taskmasters, 8^{20} תִּשָּׁחֵת הָאָרֶץ מִפְּנֵי הֶעָרֹב, 9^{11} Jos 2^{11} 23^{3} Ju 2^{18} 6^{6} 1 K 5^{17} 8^{11}+oft.; Is 10^{27} (RVm), Je 15^{17} ψ 38$^{4.6}$, etc.; Je 4^{4}+ מִפְּנֵי רֹעַ מַעַלְלֵיכֶם *by reason of* the evil of your doings, 7^{12} 9^{6} 13^{17} 14^{16} 23^{9}+oft. (*b*) stating the reason for which a thing is *not* done (Lat. *prae*), 1 K 8^{11} Jb 37^{19}. †(*c*) with אֲשֶׁר as a **conj.,** twice, *because that*, Ex 19^{18} Je 44^{23}.—Nu 33^{8} v. פִּי הַחִירֹת.

7. עַל־פְּנֵי (cf. Ph. עַל פְּנֵ, עלת פְּנֵ, Lzb^{352}) has different meanings according to the different senses of the noun and the prep.:—

a. From the sense of *face* or *front*: (*a*) *in front of* (more definite and distinct than לפני): ψ 18^{43} as dust *before* the wind (cf. לפני 35^{5} 83^{14}+), Gn 32^{22} the present passed on על־פניו *in front of* him, Ex 33^{19} אעביר כל־טובי על־פניך, 2 S 15$^{18.23}$ (read על־פניו: v. Dr), Jb 4^{15}; = *in the sight of*, Lv 10^{3} ועל־פני כל העם אֶכָּבֵד, Je 6^{7} עַל־פָּנַי תָּמִיד חֳלִי וּמַכָּה, 13^{26} (cf. Na 3^{5}), ψ 9^{20} יִשָּׁפְטוּ גוים על־פניך *before* thee: defiantly, Jb 1^{11} אם־לא על־פניך יְבָרְכֶךָּ will renounce thee *to thy face*, 6^{28} ועל־פניכם אם אֲכַזֵּב, 21^{31}; to die *in the presence of* any one (= in his lifetime) †Gn 11^{28} Nu 3^{4}. (*b*) *before*, to the exclusion of another, i.e. *in preference to*, Dt 21^{16}, and perh. (Ew $^{§217 l}$) Ex 20^{3} (Dt 5^{7}) לא יהיה לך אלהים אחרים על־פני (Thes al. as *c*). (*c*) *in addition to*, Jb 16^{14} פֶּרֶץ עַל־פְּנֵי־פָרֶץ יִפְרְצֵנִי. (*d*) of localities, *in front of*, mostly (but not always: v. GFM$^{Ju., p. 351}$) = *east of*, 1 K 6^{3} the porch *in front of*, etc., v^{3} 7^{6} 8^{8} 2 Ch 3^{17} Ez 42^{8}; Gn 16^{12} על־פני כל־אחיו ישׁכן (cf. 25^{18b}), perh. (Di al.) with collateral idea of defiance; עַל־פ׳ מַמְרֵא 23^{19} (50^{13}), Ex 16^{14}; oft. in . . . אשׁר על־פני Gn 25^{9} (49^{30}), מצרים v^{18a} (Jos 13^{3} 1 S 15^{7}), Nu 21^{11} 33^{7a}, ירחו Dt 32^{49} (34^{1}), Jos 13$^{3.25}$ 15^{8} (18^{16}), 17^{7} 18^{14} 19^{11} Ju 16^{3} 1 S 24^{3} (prob.), 26$^{1.3}$ 2 S 2^{24} 1 K

11^{7} (the Mt. of Olives, E. of Jerus.; so 2 K 23^{13} Zc 14^{4}), 17$^{3.5}$.—Gn 1^{20} let fowl fly על־פני רקיע השמים *in front of* the firmament of heaven, viz. as looked up to from below, i.e. between the firmament and the earth. (*e*) with vbs. implying direction, *over towards*, Gn 18^{16} וישקף על־פני סדם, 19^{28}; Nu 21^{20} (23^{28}) נשקפה על־פני הישימן *overlooking;* to sprinkle *against the front of* Lv 16^{14}; in a hostile sense (rare), Na 2^{2} עָלָה מֵפִיץ עַל־פָּנַיִךְ, ψ 21^{13} Ez 32^{10}.

b. From the sense of *surface*, Gn 1^{2} על־פני תהום *upon the face* of the deep, Ex 16^{14} על־פ׳ המדבר: oft. in the phrases על־פני (כל) הארץ Gn 1^{29} 7^{3}+, and (more freq.) על־פני האדמה *on the face* of the ground 6^{1} 7^{23} etc.; על פני השדה Lv 17^{5} Nu 19^{16} 1 S 14^{25}+; after vbs. of motion, 11^{4} lest we be scattered *over the face* of all the earth, v$^{8.9}$ Ex 32^{20} Lv 14^{7} (v^{53} אל), Is 18^{2} 19^{8} Am 5^{8} Ez 32^{4} Jb 5^{10}+.

8. מֵעַל־פְּנֵי: **a.** *from before the face of,* Gn 23^{3} Abraham rose up מֵעַל פְּנֵי מֵתוֹ *from before* his dead, i.e. from mourning before or beside it; †מֵעַל פני (פניו)† *from before my* (*his*) *face,* oft. in K Je of the rejection of Isr. or the temple, as with שִׁלַּח 1 K 9^{7} (‖ 2 Ch 7^{20} השליך), Je 15^{1}, השליך 2 K 13^{23} 24^{20} (Je 52^{3}), Je 7^{15}, נטש Je 23^{39}, הסיר 2 K 17$^{18.23}$ 23^{27} 24^{3} Je 32^{31}. **b.** *from off the surface of,* oft. in the phrase מֵעַל פְּנֵי הָאֲדָמָה, with verbs of cutting off, removing, expelling, etc., †Gn 4^{14} 6^{7} 7^{4} 8^{8} Ex 32^{12} Dt 6^{15} 1 S 20^{15} 1 K 9^{7} 13^{34} Am 9^{8} Je 28^{16} Zp 1$^{2.3}$.

6441 †פְּנִ֫ימָה† **adv.** (ה loc.) **1. towards the (in-)side. 2. within** (lit. *faceward*, fr. point of view of one entering by opposite door);—of a building, usu. temple: **1.** after vb. of motion Lv 10^{18} 2 Ch 29^{18}, and (after הִגִּיד) 2 K 7^{11}, also לִפ׳ Ez 41^{3} 2 Ch 29^{16}. **2.** פ׳ 1 K 6^{18}, also לִפ׳ v^{30}, so read also v^{29} (for MT מִלִּפְנִים, v. Kmp^{Kau} Kit Benz), Ez 40$^{16.16}$, also ψ 45^{14} MT, i.e. within the house, but Krochm Gr Che al. (plausibly) פְּנִינִים, q.v.; מִפּ׳ 1 K 6$^{19.21}$=2 Ch 3^{4}.

6442 פְּנִימִי$_{32}$ **adj. inner**;—פ׳ 1 K 6^{27}+; f. פְּנִימִית v^{36}+; mpl. פְּנִימִים 1 Ch 28^{11}; fpl. פְּנִימִיּוֹת 2 Ch 4^{22};—alw. c. art., and alw. of parts of building, usu. temple: 1 K 6^{27} 7^{12}+; esp. Ez 8$^{3.16}$ 10^{3}+ 21 t. 40–46; as subst. בַּפְּנִימִי 41^{17} *on the inside* (but dub., v. Co al.); אֶל־הַפְּנִימִית 42^{4} *toward the inside* (del. 𝔊 𝔖 Co Toy al.).

3942 לִפְנַי 1 K 6^{17}, Ew ^{§164a} Ke as adj., *anterior,*
6440 but rd., with 𝔊, לִפְנֵי הַדְּבִיר Th Sta Kit al.

6439 †פְּנוּאֵל **n.pr.** (*face of God,* cf. GFM $^{Ju 8, 8}$; late As. *Panîli* Hilpr $^{Univ. Pa. Exp. ix. 68}$);—Φανουηλ, but in Gn εἶδος (τοῦ) Θεοῦ: **1. loc.** E. of Jordan, near Jabbok Gn 32^{32} Ju 8$^{8.8.9.17}$ 1 K 12^{25}=פְּנִיאֵל Gn 32^{31}: site unknown; v. esp. Paine $^{Bib. Sac. 1878, 481 ff.}$ **2. m. a.** in Judah 1 Ch 4^{4}. **b.** in Benjamin 1 Ch 8^{25} Qr (Kt פניאל).

3312 יְפֻנֶּה$_{16}$ **n.pr.m.** (on form cf. Lag$^{BN 134}$);—**1.** father of Caleb Nu 13^{6} 14^{6} Jos 14$^{6.13}$ 1 Ch 4^{15}+ 10 t., Ιεφοννη. **2.** Asherite 1 Ch 7^{38}, Ιφινα, A Ιεφιηλ, 𝔊L Ιεφοννη.

6372, 6439 פִּנְחָס v. פִּינְחָס. פְּנִיאֵל, פְּנוּאֵל v. פנה above, p. 810

6440, 6443 פְּנִינִים v. פְּנִינִים. פָּנִים, etc., v. פנה below, p. 815

פנן (√ of foll.; appar. ‖ form of פנה).

6434, 6438 פִּנָּה$_{28}$ **n.f. corner**;—abs. פ׳ 2 K 14^{13}+, cstr. פִּנַּת Je 31^{40}+; sf. פִּנָּתָהּ Jb 38^{9}, פִּנָּהּ Pr 7^{8} (Ges ^{§91e}); pl. abs. פִּנּוֹת Zp 1^{16} 2 Ch 26^{15}, פִּנִּים Zc 14^{10}; cstr. פִּנּוֹת 1 K 7^{34}+, etc.;—**1. a.** *corner,* of square objects 1 K 7^{34}+v^{30} (rd. פִּנּוֹתָיו for פַּעֲמֹתָיו, cf. Kit), Ex 27^{2} 38^{2} Ez 43^{20} 45^{19}; of house Jb 1^{19}, roof Pr 7^{12} 21^{9}=25^{24}; אֶבֶן לְפִ׳ Je 51^{26} i.e. a corner-stone; אֶבֶן פ׳ of earth Jb 38^{9}; cf. (fig.) ψ 118^{22}, and (אבן om.) Is 28^{16}; פ׳=street-*corner* 2 Ch 28^{24}. **b.** specif. of wall of Jerus., Ne 3^{24} (in SE.), v$^{31.32}$ (NE.); שַׁעַר הַפִּ׳ 2 K 14^{13}+‖ 2 Ch 25^{23} 𝔊 𝔖 𝔗 and most (for MT שׁ׳ הַפּוֹנֶה), + (v. שַׁעַר); הַפִּנּוֹת appar. with battlements 2 Ch 26^{15}; of cities in gen. הַפִּ׳ הַגְּבֹהוֹת Zp 1^{16}; of the nations 3^{6}. **2.** fig. of chief, ruler as *corner* (support or defence), Ju 20^{2} 1 S 14^{38} Is 19^{13} (rd. perhaps pl.); Zc 10^{4} (+יָתֵד q.v.).

6443 †פְּנִינִים **n.[f.]pl. corals** (? as *branching,* cf. Ar. فَنَنٌ *branch* of tree; so Mich Thes al.; >*pearls* Bo$^{Hieroz. 601}$ Di^{Jb} after Ra al.);—פ׳ fig. of value Pr 20^{15}; usu. מִפּ׳, comp. Jb 28^{18} Pr 3^{15} (Kt מפניים), 8^{11} 31^{10} (all of value), La 4^{7} (of red colour); + ψ 45^{14} (perh.; for פְּנִימָה, q.v.).

6444 †פְּנִנָּה **n.pr.f.** (prop. sg. of foregoing?) wife of Elkanah 1 S 1$^{2.2.4}$, Φεννανα.

6445 †[פִּנֵּק] **vb. Pi.** indulge, pamper (NH Pi.; cf. Ecclus 14^{16}; Ar. فَنَّقَ II.; Aram. פנק, ܦܢܩ Pa.);—Pt. מְפַנֵּק Pr 29^{21} *one pampering* a servant.

658, 6446 [פַּס] v. פסס. פַּס דַּמִּים v. אֶפֶס ד׳. p. 67, 821

6448 †פָּסַג **vb. Pi.** dub.; if correct, **pass between** (NH Pi. *split, cut off,* also=BH; 𝔗 פְּסַג *cut in two*);—*Imv.* mpl. פַּסְּגוּ ψ 48^{14} *pass between* her palaces; Gr Che פַּקְּדוּ; Du conj. 'possibly' פִּסְעוּ *step,* cp. [NH פָּסַע] Aram. פְּסַע *step,* cf. [פָּשַׂע].

6449 †פִּסְגָּה **n.pr.mont. Pisgah** (prob. *cleft*, fr. a natural feature of mt.; Dr $^{Dt\,3,17}$);—alw. הַפּ׳:
798 ראשׁ הַפּ׳ Nu 21^{20} 23^{14} Dt 3^{27} 34^{1}; אַשְׁדֹּת הַפּ׳ 3^{17} 4^{49} Jos 12^{3} 13^{20}; mt. in Moab, on NE. shore of Dead Sea, exact loc. unknown (cf. *Fešḫa* as a cliff on NW. shore, v. Di $^{Nu\,21,20}$); Φασγα Dt 3^{17} +, τ. λαξευτήν 4^{49}, Λελαξευμένου Nu 21^{20} +.

6451 [פָּסָה] v. פסס. p. 821

6452 †I. **פָּסַח** **vb. pass** or **spring over**;—**Qal** *Pf.* 3 ms. פ׳ Ex 12^{27}, וּפ׳ consec. v^{23} (J); 1 s. וּפָסַחְתִּי v^{13} (P), all c. עַל, of י׳ *passing over* (sparing) houses of Isr.; *Inf. abs.* פָּסֹחַ Is 31^{5} *a passing over* (sc. עַל־יְרוּשָׁלַםִ).

6453 †פֶּסַח **n.m. passover** (usu. (Thes and most) from I. פסח, with reference to Ex 12^{13} etc.; Reuss $^{Gesch.\,AT\,\S\,58}$ *passing over* into new year; Schaefer $^{Passah\text{-}Mazzoth\,(1900),\,346}$ cp. As. *pašâḫu*, *soothe*, *placate* [deity], < *be soothed*, Pi. trans., Jen $^{ZA\,iv\,(1889),\,275}$ Zim $^{Bab.\,Rel.\,i\,(1896),\,Gloss.;\,ii\,(1899),\,92}$; Schwally $^{Idiot.\,124}$ fr. II. פסח, of sacred dance);—abs. פ׳ Ex 12^{11} +; פָּסַח v^{21} +; pl. פְּסָחִים 2 Ch 30^{17} + 3 t.;—**1.** *sacrifice of passover*, involving communion-meal, hence a species of peace-offering (cf. 1. זֶבַח **II. 2**), זֶבַח פ׳ הוא לי׳ Ex 12^{27} (J), cf. v^{11} (P); זֶבַח פ׳ Dt 16$^{2.5.6}$; אכל הפ׳ 2 Ch 30^{18}; the special feature lay in the application of blood to homes to consecrate them; cf. sim. Bab. rite of purification Zim $^{ib.\,ii.\,126\text{-}7}$. **2.** *the animal victim of the passover*: שׁחט פ׳ Ex 12^{21} (J) 2 Ch 30^{15} 35$^{1.6.11}$ Ez 6^{20}, cf. 2 Ch 30^{17}; בשׁל הפ׳ באשׁ 2 Ch 35^{13}; לפסחים 2 Ch 35$^{7.8.9}$. [Passover animals (cf. Br $^{Hex.\,206}$) were צֹאן *flock* Ex 12^{21} (J), שֶׂה v$^{3.4.5}$, incl. כֶּבֶשׂ and עֵז v^{5} (P); צאן ובקר Dt 16^{2}; large numbers of all these (שֶׂה not used) in Josiah's passover, acc. to 2 Ch 35$^{7.8.9}$, but evident mingling of whole burnt-offerings for the passover with special passover victim.] **3.** *festival of the passover*: חג הפ׳ Ex 34^{25} (J); (ה)פ׳ Lv 23^{5} Nu 28^{16} 33^{3} Jos 5^{11} (P) Ez 45^{21}; חֻקַּת הפ׳ Ex 12^{43} Nu 9$^{12.14}$ (P); עשׂה פ׳ Ex 12^{48} Nu 9$^{2.4.5.6.10.13.14}$ Jos 5^{10} (P) Dt 16^{1} 2 K 23$^{21.22.23}$ 2 Ch 30$^{1.2.5}$ 35$^{1.16.17.18.18.19}$ Ezr 6^{19}; it was held in month הָאָבִיב Dt 16^{1}, בָּעֶרֶב v^{6}; on 14th day Jos 5^{10} (P), of 1st month Ez 45^{21}; בֵּין הערבים (Ex 12^{6}) Lv 23^{5} Nu 9^{5} (P); if impossible at that time, then on 14th of 2nd month Nu 9$^{10.12}$. [No ref. to פֶּסַח in E; J subordinates it to מַצּוֹת (the great feast of JE); in D it predom. over מצות; P makes it first in importance (Br $^{Hex.\,195\,f.}$).]

8607 †תִּפְסַח **n.pr.loc.** on Euphrates (prob. *ford* (though Lag $^{BN\,131}$ doubts); Lewy $^{Fremdw.\,146}$ cp. Λάμψακος (on Bosphorus), expl. as לַפֶּסַח);—1 K 5^{4}, NE. limit of Sol.'s dominion; =Gk Θάψακος Xen $^{Anab.\,i.\,4}$ etc.; identif. with *Kal'at Dibse*, at the great easterly bend of the river, c. Lat. 35° 55′ N, Long. 38° 20′ E, JPPeters $^{Nation,\,May\,23,\,1889;\,Nippur\,i.\,96\,ff.}$

†II. [**פָּסַח**] **vb. limp** (Thes sub I. פ׳, but 6452
dub.; Ar. فَسَخَ is *dislocate;* acc. to Gerber ^{73} II. פ׳ is denom. fr. פִּסֵּחַ [and this sub I. פ׳?]);—**Qal** *Pt.* pl. פֹּסְחִים עַל־שְׁתֵּי הַסְּעִפִּים 1 K 18^{21} fig. (v. [סְעִפָּה]). **Niph.** *Impf.* 3 ms. וַיִּפָּסֵחַ וַיִּפֹּל 2 S 4^{4} *and he fell and was made limping* (lame). **Pi.** *Impf.* 3 mpl. וַיְפַסְּחוּ עַל־הַמִּזְבֵּחַ 1 K 18^{26} *they went limping* (along by the altar), i.e. prob. in their dance, v. Kit Pietschm $^{Phön.\,220}$ (Gr ויפסעו [=וַיִּפְשְׂעוּ] *stepped*).

†פָּסֵחַ **n.pr.m.** (*limper*);—**1.** in Judah 1 Ch 6454
4^{12}, Βεσσηε, Φεσση, etc. **2.** head of post-ex. family Ezr 2^{49} = Ne 7^{51}, Φισον, etc., 𝔊L Φασσα. **3.** father of wall-builder Ne 3^{6}, Φασεκ, Φεσσε.

†פִּסֵּחַ **adj. lame**;—abs. פ׳ 2 S 9^{13} +; pl. 6455
פִּסְחִים 5^{6} +;—as attrib. Lv 21^{18} (+ עִוֵּר); pred. 2 S 19^{27}, פ׳ שְׁתֵּי רַגְלָיו 9^{13} *lame as to both his feet;* cf. also (of animal) Dt 15^{21} (+ עִוֵּר); as subst. 2 S 5$^{6.8.8}$ Je 31^{8} Mal 1$^{8.13}$ Jb 29^{15} (all + עִוֵּר), also Is 33^{23} 35^{6} Pr 26^{7}.

†פָּסַךְ (van d. H. פָּסַךְ) **n.pr.m.** Asherite 6457
1 Ch 7^{33}, Βαισηχι, A Φεσηχι, 𝔊L Φασεχ.

†**פָּסַל** **vb. hew, hew into shape** (NH Pi. 6458
hew off boughs; Aram. פְּסַל, ܦܣܠ = BH; Nab. פסלא *stone-cutter*);—**Qal** *Pf.* 3 ms. sf. פְּסָלוֹ Hb 2^{18}; *Impf.* 3 ms. וַיִּפְסֹל Ex 34^{4}, etc.; *Imv.* ms. פְּסָל־ Ex 34^{1} Dt 10^{1};—*hew out* stone tablets Ex 34$^{1.4}$ Dt 10$^{1.3}$; building-stones 1 K 5^{32}; c. cogn. acc. (sf. referring to פֶּסֶל) Hb 2^{18}.

פֶּסֶל$_{31}$ **n.m.** $^{Hb\,2,18}$ **idol, image**;—abs. פ׳ Ju 6459
17^{3} +, פָּסֶל Is 42^{17}; cstr. פֶּסֶל Ju 18^{31} +; sf. פִּסְלִי Is 48^{5}, etc.; pl. supplied by פְּסִילִים, v. foll.;—*idol*, as likeness of man or animal Ex 20^{4} = Dt 5^{8}, Dt 4$^{16.23.25}$, also 27^{15} 2 K 21^{7} 2 Ch 33^{7} Is 42^{17} 44^{9} 48^{5} Na 1^{14} Hb 2^{18} (of wood or stone, cf. v^{19}); of metal Ju 17$^{3.4}$ + 6 t. 18 (cf. GFM), Is 40^{19} 44^{10} (c. נָסַךְ), Je 10^{14} 51^{17} (c. צוֹרֵף); of wood Is 40^{20} 44$^{15.17}$ 45^{20}.

[פָּסִיל]$_{23}$ **n.m.** $^{Dt\,7,25}$ **id.**;—pl. (פֶּסֶל serving 6456
as sg.) פְּסִילִים Ju 3^{19} +; פְּסִלִים Ho 11^{2} +; cstr. פְּסִילֵי Je 51^{47} +; sf. פְּסִילֶיךָ Mi 5^{12}, etc.;—*idols*, Ho 11^{2} Is 10^{10} + 10 t., + (of wood, c. שָׂרַף) Dt

7$^{5.25}$, so (c. גָּדַע) 12^{3}; of stone Is 21^{9} (c. שִׁבֵּר), Ju 3$^{19.26}$ (cf. GFM), stone or metal Mi 1^{7} 2 Ch 34^{7} (כִּתַּת), cf. v$^{3.4}$; (sheathed with) silver Is 30^{22}.

I. **פסס** (√of foll.; perh. cp. פשה *spread;* cf. Ph.(Pu.) פס *tablet;* Aram. פַּסָּא, ܦܣܐ, = BH).

6446 †[**פַּס**] **n.[m.] flat** of hand or foot (palm, sole);—only כְּתֹנֶת פַּסִּים tunic reaching to palms and soles (v. כ׳) Gn 37$^{3.23.32}$ 2 S 13$^{18.19}$ (cf. Dr).

6451 †[**פִּסָּה**] **n.f.** dub.; if correct, prob. **abundance, plenty** (? prop. *spread out*);— cstr. פִּסַּת בַּר ψ 72^{16}; Lag Gr Che al. read שִׁפְעַת.

6461 †II. [**פָּסַס**] **vb. disappear, vanish** (si vera l., cf. As. *pasâsu, do away, blot out* (esp. sins));—**Qal** *Pf.* 3 pl. פַּסּוּ מִן ψ 12^{2} the faithful *have vanished* (Che Dr) *from* (among) . . . men; Lag$^{\text{Proph. Chald. xlvi}}$ Gr We Du read אָפְסוּ (Is 16^{4}).

6462 †**פִּסְפָּה** **n.pr.m.** Asherite 1 Ch 7^{38}, Φασφα(ι).

6463 †[**פָּעָה**] **vb. groan** (onomatop. acc. to Thes; NH Hiph. *bleat,* so Ar. بغى, بعى Dozy; Aram. פְּעָא, ܦܥܐ *bleat*);—*Impf.* 1 s. אֶפְעֶה כַּיּוֹלֵדָה Is 42^{14} (of י׳ straining himself to deliver Isr., + אֶשֹּׁם [נשם], אֶשְׁאַף).—[אֶפַע] Is 41^{24}, v. p. 67.

660 †**אֶפְעֶה** **n.[m.]** a kind of **viper** (Thes 'a flando et sibilando;' cf. Ar. أَفْعَى *viper,* Eth. **አፍዖት:** *id.*);—א׳ Is 30^{6} 59^{5}, לְשׁוֹן א׳ Jb 20^{16}.

6464 †**פָּעוּ, פָּעִי** **n.pr.loc.** in Edom, פָּעוּ Gn 36^{39} = פָּעִי 1 Ch 1^{50}; Φογωρ, 𝔊L Ch Φαουα.

6466 **פָּעַל** $_{57}$ **vb. do, make** (poet. for עָשָׂה) (NH פּוֹעֵל *workman,* cf. J Aram.; Ph. פעל = BH (oft.); Ar. فَعَلَ *id.;* OAram. פעל; Syr. in der. spec. and deriv.);—**Qal** *Pf.* 3 ms. Dt 32^{27}+, פָּעַל אֵל Nu 23^{23}, 2 ms. פָּעַלְתָּ Ex 15^{17}+, etc.; *Impf.* 3 ms. יִפְעַל Jb 22^{17}+; 2 ms. תִּפְעָל־ 35^{6}, etc.; *Inf. cstr.* לְפָעֳלָם Jb 37^{12} (v. infr.); *Pt. act.* פֹּעֵל ψ 15^{2}+, pl. cstr. פֹּעֲלֵי 5^{6}+, etc.;—**1.** *do:* **a.** of God, c. acc. (abstr.) Nu 23^{23} Dt 32^{27} Jb 33^{29}, יְשׁוּעוֹת ψ 74^{12}; + ל pers. ψ 31^{20} 68^{29} Is 26^{12} Jb 22^{17}; c. acc. cogn. פֹּעַל ψ 44^{2} Hb 1^{5}; acc. om. Is 43^{13}, cf. 41^{4}. **b.** of men, c. acc. ψ 11^{3} Jb 11^{8}, + ל pers. (God) 7^{20}, + ב pers. (God) 35^{6}; esp. of doing evil, שָׁקֶר Ho 7^{1}, עָוֶל Jb 34^{32}, עַוְלָה 36^{23} ψ 58^{3} 119^{3}, אָוֶן Pr 30^{20}, esp. פֹּעֲלֵי אָוֶן Ho 6^{8} Is 31^{2} Jb 31^{3} 34$^{8.22}$ ψ 5^{6} + 15 t. ψ, Pr 10^{29} 21^{15}, פֹּעֲלֵי רָע Mi 2^{1}; rarely of doing right, c. acc. מִשְׁפָּטוֹ Zp 2^{3}, צֶדֶק ψ 15^{2}. **c.** of clouds, c. acc. Jb 37^{12} (disregarding ‸). **2.** *make:* **a.** of God, c. acc. concr. Ex 15^{17}; + ל rei Pr 16^{4}, ל of 2nd obj. ψ 7^{16}; פֹּעֲלִי Jb 36^{3} *my Maker.* **b.** of man, c. acc. concr. Is 44$^{12.15}$; acc. om. 44^{12} ψ 7^{16}.—Is 1^{31} v. פֹּעַל.

פֹּעַל $_{37}$ **n.m.**$^{\text{Pr 20, 11}}$ **doing, deed, work** (poet. and late, nearly = מַעֲשֶׂה);—פ׳ abs. Hb 1^{1} ψ 44^{2}, cstr. Dt 33^{11}+; sf. פָּעֳלוֹ 32^{4}+, פֹּעֲלוֹ Is 1^{31} (Kö ii. 1, 35, 493 Ges$^{\S 93 q}$, v. infr.), Je 22^{13}; פָּעָלְכֶם Is 41^{24}, etc.; pl. פְּעָלִים 2 S 23^{20} 1 Ch 11^{22};—**1.** *deed, thing done:* **a.** of God, פָּעֳלוֹ his work in providence Dt 32^{4} Is 5^{12} Jb 36^{24}; in deliverance ψ 44^{2} (as acc. cogn.), 77^{13} + 5 t.; in judgment 64^{10} 95^{9}, as acc. cogn. Hb 1^{5}. **b.** of false gods Is 41^{24}. **c.** of men, daily toil Jb 24^{5} ψ 104^{23}; specif. act Ru 2^{12}; פ׳ יָדָיו of sacrificing Dt 33^{11}; pl. of *achievements* 2 S 23^{20} = 1 Ch 11^{32}; action as having moral quality Jb 34^{11} Pr 20^{11} 24$^{12.29}$, evil implied Je 25^{14} 50^{29} Jb 36^{9} ψ 28^{4}, פ׳ כַּפָּיו 9^{17}; פ׳ חָמָס Is 59^{6}; good action Pr 21^{8}. **2.** *work, thing made:* **a.** by hands of God Is 45$^{9.11}$ (of men). **b.** by man Is 1^{31} (i. e. prob. his idol Ges Che$^{\text{Comm.}}$ Di al.; > read בַּעֲלוֹ Lag$^{\text{Sem. i. 5}}$ Sta ZAW iii (1883), 12 f.). **3.** *wages of work* Je 22^{13} Jb 7^{2}. **4.** *acquisition* of treasures Pr 21^{6}. 6467

†[**פְּעֻלָּה**] **n.f. work, recompence** (poet. and late);—cstr. פְּעֻלַּת Lv 19^{13}+, sf. פְּעֻלָּתִי Is 49^{4}, etc.; pl. cstr. פְּעֻלּוֹת ψ 17^{4}, ־לֹּת 28^{5};—**1.** *work:* **a.** pl. *deeds of* י׳ ψ 28^{5}. **b.** of men, ψ 17^{4} (pl.); toil, suffering Je 31^{16}; good action 2 Ch 15^{7}, wicked Is 65^{7}, פ׳ שָׁקֶר Pr 11^{18}. **2.** *wages* (as earned by work) Lv 19^{13} Pr 10^{16} (‖ תְּבוּאָה), Ez 29^{20}; *reward* (from י׳) Is 49^{4} 61^{8}; prob. fig. of people won back by י׳ in warfare 40^{10} 62^{11} (‖ שָׂכָר); of punishment, ψ 109^{20}. 6468

†**פְּעֻלְּתַי** **n.pr.m.** Levite 1 Ch 26^{5}, Ιαφθοσλααθι, A Φολλαθι, 𝔊L Φελλαθι. 6469

†[**מִפְעָל**] **n.[m.] work, thing made** (by י׳);—pl. sf. מִפְעָלָיו Pr 8^{22}. 4659

†[**מִפְעָלָה**] **n.[f.] deed** (of י׳);—pl. cstr. מִפְעֲלוֹת י׳ ψ 46^{9}, מ׳ אֱלֹהִים 66^{5}. 4659

†[**פָּעַם**] **vb. thrust, impel** (prob. orig. *strike, hit,* v. deriv., and Ph. פעם *foot*);—**Qal** *Inf. cstr.* sf. לְפַעֲמוֹ Ju 13^{25} the spirit of י׳ began *to impel him.* **Niph.** *be disturbed, Pf.* 1 s. נִפְעַמְתִּי ψ 77^{5}; *Impf.* 3 fs. וַתִּפָּעֶם רוּחוֹ Gn 41^{8} Dn 2^{3}; so **Hithp.** *Impf.* 3 fs. וַתִּתְפָּעֶם רוּחוֹ Dn 2^{1}. 6470

פַּעַם $_{118}$ **n.f.**$^{\text{Ex 8, 28}}$ (masc. only Ju 16^{28} [text suspicious, v. GFM Albr$^{\text{ZAW xvi (1896), 76}}$ Kö$^{\text{Synt.} \S 248 m}$], 2 S 23^{8} [< Qr fem.], 1 K 7^{30} [crpt., v. infr.]) **beat,** 6471 foot, anvil, occurrence;—abs. פ׳ Gn 2^{23}+; פַּעַם 46^{30}+; du. פַּעֲמַיִם Gn 27^{36}+, etc.; pl. פְּעָמִים 33^{3}+; also (concr.) cstr. פַּעֲמֵי Ju 5^{28}+; sf. פְּעָמַי ψ 57^{7} 119^{133}, etc.; פַּעֲמֹתָיו (only **1 c**) Ex 25^{12} + 2 t.;—**1. a.** poet., *hoof-beat* Ju 5^{28}; late, of human *footfall, footstep*, fig. ψ 17^{5} (‖ אֲשֻׁרַי), 119^{133}; וְיָשֵׂם לְדֶרֶךְ פְּעָמָיו 85^{14}. **b.** *foot*, fig., 57^{7} 58^{11} 74^{3} 140^{5} Pr 29^{5}; lit. Is 26^{6} (‖ רֶגֶל), Ct 7^{2}; בְּכַף פ׳ 2 K 19^{24}=Is 37^{25}. **c.** *foot*, of ark Ex 25^{12} 37^{3} (P).—פַּעֲמֹתָיו 1 K 7^{30} read פִּנּוֹתָיו (cf. v^{34}). **2.**=*anvil* (struck by hammer) Is 41^{7}. **3.** *occurrence, time* (orig. *stroke, beat*): **a.** פ׳ אֶחָת [אַחַת] *one time, once* Jos 6$^{3.11.14}$ (JE), 10^{42} (D) + 3 t. + 2 S 23^{8} Qr (>Kt אחד); פַּעֲמַיִם *twice* Gn 41^{32} + 6 t.; פ׳ Na 1^{9} *second time;* אַרְבַּע פ׳ Ne 6^{4} *four times;* חָמֵשׁ אוֹ שֵׁשׁ פ׳ 2 K 13^{19}, cf. פ׳ חֲמִישִׁית Ne 6^{5}; also c. שָׁלֹשׁ, שֶׁבַע, q.v.; (זֶה) עֶשֶׂר פ׳ Nu 14^{22} (JE) Ne 4^{6} Jb 19^{3}, all indef.=over and over; indef. also פַּעַם וּשְׁתַּיִם Ne 13^{20} *once and* [i.e. or] *twice;* פַּעֲמַיִם שָׁלוֹשׁ Jb 33^{29} *twice* (or) *thrice;* מֵאָה פְּעָמִים 2 S 24^{3}=1 Ch 21^{3}, אֶלֶף פ׳ Dt 1^{11}; פ׳ רַבּוֹת ψ 106^{43} Ec 7^{22}; עַד־כַּמֶּה פְּעָמִים 1 K 22^{16}=2 Ch 18^{15}. **b.** כְּפַעַם־בְּפַעַם *as time on time*, i.e. as formerly, as usual, Nu 24^{1} (E) Ju 16^{20} 20$^{30.31}$ 1 S 3^{10} (cf. Dr) 20^{25}. **c.** (גַּם) בַּפַּעַם הַזֹּאת *at this repetition* (this time) also Ex 8^{28} 9^{14} (J) + 3 t.; גַּם בַּפ׳ הַהִוא Dt 9^{19} 10^{10}. **d.** הַפַּעַם (Hex only J): (1)=*this once* Gn 18^{32}, אַךְ הַפ׳ Ex 10^{17} Ju 6^{39}, רַק־הַפ׳ v^{39}, אַךְ הַפ׳ הַזֶּה 16^{28} (הַזֶּה dub., v. supr.); (2)=*now at length* Gn 2^{23} 29$^{34.35}$ 30^{20} 46^{30} Ju 15^{3} 16^{18}, cf. also Ex 9^{27} *now at length* (it is clear that) *I have sinned.* **e.** פַּעַם . . . פַּעַם Pr 7^{12} *now . . . now, at one time . . . at another.*

6472 †פַּעֲמֹן **n.[m.]** bell, on high-p.'s robe (from its *stroke, beat*);—פ׳ abs. Ex 39$^{26.26}$; cstr. פ׳ זָהָב 28$^{34.34}$; pl. הַפַּעֲמֹנִים 39^{25}, cstr. פַּעֲמֹנֵי זָהָב 28^{33} 39^{25}.

צָפְנַת פַּעְנֵחַ v. צָפְנַת פ׳.

6473 †[פָּעַר] **vb. open wide** (the mouth) (NH rarely = BH, usu. *open* bowels, go to stool; cf. JAram. פְּעַר; Ar. فَغَرَ and Syr. ܦܥܰܪ=BH, ܦܽܥܪܳܐ *chasm*);—**Qal** *Pf.* of voracious greed, fig. 3 fs. וּפָעֲרָה פִּיהָ Is 5^{14} (of Sheʾôl), 3 pl. פָּעֲרוּ עָלַי בְּפִיהֶם (Ges $^{§ 119q}$) Jb 16^{10}; of eager desire (good sense), פִּיהֶם פָּעֲרוּ 29^{23}, פִּי־פָעַרְתִּי ψ 119^{131}.

6474 †פַּעֲרַי **n.pr.m.** 2 S 23^{35} (cf. Ph. n.pr.m. פער)=נַעֲרַי q.v.

6465 †פְּעוֹר **n.pr.** Φογωρ: **1. mont.** in Moab (appar. from some √פער);—Nu 23^{28} cf. (בֵּית פ׳, בַּעַל פ׳ and reff.; also) Buhl $^{Geogr. 122}$ Dr $^{Dt 3, 29}$; [𝔊 Jos 15$^{59a [60]}$ gives a Φαγωρ with Bethlehem; v. also 𝔊 for פְּעִי, פָּעוּ]. **2. dei** (appar.) Nu 25$^{18.18}$ (cf. בַּעַל פ׳ v$^{3.5}$), 31^{16} Jos 22^{17}.

†[פָּצָה] **vb. part, open** (Ar. فَصَى I, II. *separate, remove;* Aram. פְּצָא esp. *set free,* ܦܰܨܝ Pa. *set free*);—**Qal** *Pf.* 3 fs. פָּצְתָה Gn 4^{11}+, 2 ms. פָּצִיתָ Ju 11^{36}, etc.; *Impf.* 3 ms. יִפְצֶה Jb 35^{16}; *Imv.* ms. פְּצֵה Ez 2^{8}, sf. פְּצֵנִי ψ 144$^{7.11}$; *Pt.* פֹּצֶה Is 10^{14}, פּוֹ׳ ψ 144^{10};—**1.** *open* mouth: **a.** to swallow, fig. of ground, הָאֲדָמָה Gn 4^{11} (J), Nu 16^{30} (JE), הָאָרֶץ Dt 11^{6}; of enemies, + עַל pers. La 2^{16} 3^{46} ψ 22^{14}; lit. Ez 2^{8}. **b.** to speak Ju 11$^{35.36}$ (utter a vow, + אֶל־י׳); Jb 35^{16}; hence= *utter*, אֲשֶׁר פָּצוּ שְׂפָתָי ψ 66^{14}; of bird chirping פֹּצֶה פֶּה Is 10^{14} (in fig.). **2.** *snatch away, set free* (Aram. loan-word), only ψ 144, + הִצִּיל c. מִן v$^{7.11}$; פ׳ c. מִן v^{10}. 6475

† פָּצַח **vb. cause to break** or **burst forth, break forth with** (cf. Ar. فَضَخَ *break, crush;* Eth. ፈጽሐ: *shatter;* Syr. ܦܨܰܚ is *be joyous, hilarious*);—**Qal** *Pf.* 3 pl. פָּצְחוּ רִנָּה Is 14^{7} *they have broken forth with joyous shout; Impf.* יִפְצְחוּ רִנָּה 55^{12} (of mts.); *Imv.* fs. פִּצְחִי רִנָּה 54^{1} (of Zion); mpl. פִּצְחוּ ר׳ 44^{23} 49^{13} Qr (>Kt יפצחו; of mts.); abs. פִּצְחוּ Is 52^{9} ψ 98^{4} (both + רַנְּנוּ). **Pi.** *break* bones *in pieces*: *Pf.* 3 pl. פִּצֵּחוּ Mi 3^{3}. 6476

†[פָּצַל] **vb. Pi. peel** (NH Pi. *split, divide;* so Ar. فَصَلَ, JAram. (Talm.) פְּצַל, Syr. ܦܨܰܠ; akin to בצל q.v.);—*Pf.* 3 ms. פִּצֵּל Gn 30^{38} (obj. rods); *Impf.* 3 ms. וַיְפַצֵּל v^{37} (c. acc. cogn.). 6478

†[פְּצָלָה] **n.f.pl. peeled spot or stripe**;— pl. פְּצָלוֹת לְבָנוֹת Gn 30^{37} (as acc. cogn.). 6479

†[פָּצַם] **vb. split open** (Ar. فَصَمَ *crack;* 𝔗 פְּצַם Je 22^{14}, *cut out,* make, window);—**Qal** *Pf.* 2 ms. sf. of earth, פְּצַמְתָּהּ ψ 60^{4} (subj. God). 6480

†[פָּצַע] **vb. bruise, wound by bruising** (NH *split, bruise;* Ar. فَصَعَ *squeeze* a ripe date, *rub;* Aram. פְּצַע *split*);—**Qal** *Pf.* 3 pl. sf. הִכּוּנִי פְצָעוּנִי Ct 5^{7}; *Inf. abs.* הַכֵּה וּפָצֹעַ 1 K 20^{37} *a smiting and a bruising* (him); *Pt. pass.* cstr. פְּצוּעַ־דַּכָּה Dt 23^{2} *one wounded by crushing.* 6481

†פֶּצַע **n.m.** $^{Pr 27, 6}$ **bruise, wound**;—abs. פ׳ Ex 21^{25} Is 1^{6} (fig.), Pr 20^{30}, פָּצַע Ex 21^{25}; sf. פִּצְעִי Gn 4^{23}; pl. פְּצָעִים Pr 23^{29}; fig. also cstr. פִּצְעֵי 27^{6} and sf. פְּצָעַי Jb 9^{17}. 6482

†[פָּצַץ] **vb. break** (Ar. فَضَّ *break, break asunder;* Nab. פצץ *break asunder;* Syr. ܦܰܨ 6327

crush);—**Pō'.** *Impf.* 3 ms. יְפֹצֵץ סָלַע Je 23^{29} a hammer which *shatters rock.* **Pilp.** *Impf.* 3 ms. sf. וַיְפַצְפְּצֵנִי Jb 16^{12} *he* [God] *dashed me in pieces* (fig.).

6483 † פִּצֵּץ only הַפִּ׳ **n.pr.m.** priestly name 1 Ch 24^{15}; τῷ Φεταια, Α Αφεσση, 𝔊L Αφεσσει.

1048 פִּצֵּץ v. בֵּית פַּצֵּץ p. 112.

6484 † [פָּצַר] **vb. push, press** (perh. related, by transp., to Ar. فَرَضَ *appoint, prescribe,* As. *parṣu, command,* cf. Ba$^{\text{ZMG xliii (1889), 188}}$);—**Qal** *Impf.* 3 ms. וַיִּפְצַר Gn 19^{3}+, 3 mpl. וַיִּפְצְרוּ v^{9} 2 K 2^{17};—*push, press,* upon (בְּ pers.) physically Gn 19^{9}; =*urge* v^{3} 33^{11} Ju 19^{7} 2 K 2^{17}, + inf. 5^{16}; read also prob. וַיִּפְצַר־בּוֹ 2 S 13$^{25.27}$ 2 K 5^{23} (for וַיִּפְרָץ־), וַיִּפְצְרוּ־בוֹ 1 S 28^{23} (for וַיִּפְרְצוּ־), Tanchum (cf. The), Weir in Dr$^{\text{1 S 28, 23}}$ Kit$^{\text{id.}}$ Bu HPS Löhr. **Hiph.** *Inf. abs.* הַפְצַר 1 S 15^{23} *to display pushing* (i.e. arrogance, presumption; ‖ מְרִי; cf. Dr).

6477 † פְּצִירָה appar. **n.f.** fr. √פצר, 1 S 13^{21}; dub.; prob. incurably crpt.; AV *file* fr. 𝔗𝔖 Rabb., Ke *bluntness;* both lack philol. ground; v. esp. Dr.

6375 פַּק v. פִּיק. p. 807

6485 פָּקַד$_{303}$ **vb. attend to, visit, muster, appoint** (NH *id., visit, enjoin;* Ph. פקד *attend to, provide;* As. *paḳâdu* = BH; Ar. فَقَدَ *lose, miss;* also (Dozy) *give heed, attention, to;* Eth. ፈቀደ: *visit, muster, desire, need,* etc.; Nab. פקד *command* (Cook), so 𝔗 פְּקַד Pa., Syr. ܦܩܶܕ, also *visit*);—**Qal**$_{234}$ *Pf.* 3 ms. פ׳ Ex 4^{31}+; 1 s. פָּקַדְתִּי 3^{16}+, etc.; *Impf.* 3 ms. יִפְקֹד Gn 50^{24}+, etc.; *Imv.* ms. פְּקֹד Nu 3^{15}+, etc.; *Inf. abs.* פָּקֹד Gn 50^{24}+; *cstr.* לִפְקֹד 2 S 24^{4}+, etc.; *Pt. act.* פֹּקֵד Ex 20^{5}+; *pass.* (הַ)פְּקֻדִים 30^{14}+, cstr. פְּקוּדֵי Nu 31^{14}+, etc.;—**A. 1. a.** *pay attention to, observe* (with care, practical interest), of י׳ c. acc. pers. + rei Ex 3^{16} (J), c. acc. pers. 4^{31} (J; ‖ רָאָה), ψ 8^{5} (with providence, cf. פְּקֻדָּה Jb 10^{12}; ‖ זָכַר); c. acc. rei 1 S 15^{2} ψ 80^{15} (‖ רְאֵה, הַבֵּט), La 4^{22} (‖ גִּלָּה עַל), יִזְכֹּר עֲוֹנָם וְיִפְקֹד חַטֹּאתָם Ho 8^{13} = 9^{9} = Je 14^{10}; 1 S 17^{18} *observe thy brothers as to well-being* (לְשָׁלוֹם; i.e. see how they fare). **b.** *attend to,* in act, *see to,* c. acc. pers. 2 K 9^{34}; acc. of sheep Je 23^{2} (in fig.); cf. Zc 10^{3b} 11^{16}. **c.** *seek* (with interest, desire), seek י׳ Is 26^{16}; in bad sense, *look about for* Ez 23^{21}. Hence **d.** *seek in vain, need, miss, lack* (cf. **Niph.,** and Ar. Eth. supr.), c. acc. pers. 1 S 20^{6} Is 34^{16}, rei 1 S 25^{15} Je 3^{16}. **2.** specif. *visit,* c. acc., for different purposes: with (בְּ) a present Ju 15^{1}; esp. of י׳, *visit graciously* Gn 21^{1} 50$^{24.25}$ = Ex 13^{19} (all E), Is 23^{17} Je 15^{15} (‖ זָכַר), 27^{22} 29^{10} ψ 8^{5} (‖ זָכַר) 65^{10}+; בִּישׁוּעָתֶךָ 106^{4} (‖ זָכַר); *visit* to search, test, acc. pers. Jb 7^{18} (‖ בָּחַן), ψ 17^{3} (‖ *id.*; obj. om.), abs. Jb 31^{14}; to punish Je 6^{15} 49^{8} 50^{31} ψ 59^{6}; acc. pers. om. Ex 32^{34a} Is 26^{14}, c. עַל rei (of sin) Je 5$^{9.29}$ 9^{8} (here + בְּ pers.); acc. rei ψ 89^{33}; abs., of י׳'s anger Jb 35^{15}. **3.** c. עַל pers., *visit upon,* י׳ subj., + acc. rei (of sin) Am 3$^{2.14}$ Ho 1^{4} 2^{15} Ex 20^{5} 34^{7} Dt 5^{9} + 10 t.; acc. rei om., =*punish* Is 10^{12} Je 9^{24} 11^{22} 13^{21} + 10 t. Je, + 8 t.; + כְּ rei Ho 12^{3} Je 21^{14}; + cl. of sin Ho 4^{14}; c. אֶל pers. Je 50$^{18.18}$, אֶל + עַל 46^{18}; indef. subj. c. עַל of vineyard = *injure* Is 27^{3}. **4.** *pass in review, muster* (nearly = *number*), c. acc., 1 S 11^{8} 13^{15} 2 S 24$^{2.4}$ + 11 t. + Nu 1$^{3.19.44.49}$ + 16 t. Nu (P); acc. om. 1 S 14$^{17.17}$ Nu 3^{42}; obj. נָוֶה Jb 5^{24}; esp. pt. pass., persons or things *mustered* (*numbered*), Ex 30$^{12.13.14}$ 38$^{25.26}$ Nu 1$^{21.22}$ + 67 t. Nu, + 1 Ch 23^{24}. **B.** *appoint:* **1.** c. acc. pers. + אִתָּם Gn 40^{4}, + עַל pers. over whom Je 15^{3} 51^{27} Nu 27^{16}, + אֶל (for עַל) Je 49^{19} = 50^{44}; c. acc. pers. alone Nu 3^{10}, + בְּרֹאשׁ הָעָם Dt 20^{9}; *pt. pass.* pl. *appointed ones, officers,* of (fighting) host Nu 31$^{14.48}$ 2 K 11^{15} 2 Ch 23^{14}. **2.** c. acc. rei, *appoint, assign,* + עַל pers. to whom, Nu 4^{27} (on text v. Di); c. acc. rei only, v^{32}; cf. Jb 34^{13} 36^{23}; *lay upon* (עַל pers.) *as a charge,* Zp 3^{7} (rdg. מֵעֵינֶיהָ, 𝔊 We Now, for מְעוֹנָהּ); + inf. 2 Ch 36^{23} = Ezr 1^{2}; =*deposit,* c. acc. rei + בְּ loc., 2 K 5^{24} (cf. פִּקָּדוֹן). †**Niph.** *Pf.* 3 ms. נִפְקַד 1 S 25^{7}+; 2 ms. וְנִפְקַדְתָּ 20^{18}; *Impf.* 3 ms. יִפָּקֵד v^{18}+, etc.; *Inf.* הִפָּקֵד *abs.* 1 K 20^{39}; *cstr.* Ju 21^{3};—**1.** *be* (*sought,* i.e. *needed*) *missed, lacking* 1 S 20^{18}+ v^{19} (𝔊, for MT תֵּרֵד, We Dr al.), 25^{7} 1 K 20^{39} (+ inf. abs.), 2 K 10$^{19.19}$ Je 23^{4} (Gr Gie conj. יִפְחָדוּ), + מִן part. Ju 21^{3} 1 S 25^{21} 2 S 2^{30} Nu 31^{49}; of seat 1 S 20^{18}, place v$^{25.27}$ (i.e. *be empty*). **2.** *be visited* (graciously) Ez 38^{8} Is 24^{22}, cf. 29^{6} (בְּ accomp.; v. Di). **3.** *be visited upon,* עַל pers., Nu 16^{29} (subj. פְּקֻדָּה); בַּל יִפָּ׳ רָע Pr 19^{23} *evil shall not be visited* (sc. upon him; rd. perh. שֶׁבֶר עָלָיו for יָלִין שָׂבֵעַ v. Toy). **4.** *be appointed* Ne 7^{1}, + עַל 12^{44}. †**Pi.** (intens.) *muster* a host, *Pt.* מְפַקֵּד Is 13^{4} (of י׳). †**Pu.** *be passed in review, Pf.* 3 ms. פֻּקַּד Ex 38^{21}; *be caused to miss,* deprived of, 1 s. פֻּקַּדְתִּי Is 38^{10} c. acc. rei. †**Hithp.** *be mustered, Pf.* 3 pl. הִתְפָּקְדוּ Ju 20$^{15.17}$; *Impf.* 3 ms. וַיִּתְפָּקֵד 21^{9}; 3 mpl. 20^{15} (on form v. Ges$^{\text{§54 l}}$). †**Hothp.** *id., Pf.* 3 pl. הָתְפָּקְדוּ 1 K 20^{27} Nu 1^{47} 2^{33} 26^{62} (Ges$^{\text{l.c.}}$). **Hiph.**$_{29}$ *Pf.* 3 ms. הִפְקִיד Gn 39^{5}+, 2 ms. sf. הִפְקַדְתּוֹ 1 S 29^{4}, etc.; *Impf.* 3 ms. יַפְקִיד Is 10^{28}, etc.; *Imv.* ms. הַפְקֵד Nu 1^{50} ψ 109^{6}, etc.;—**1.** c. acc. pers., *set* (*over*), *make overseer,* 2 K 25^{23}; + עַל Gn 39^{4} Je 1^{10} Nu 1^{50} + 8 t., fig., acc. of punishment, Lv 26^{16}; + ב Je 40^{5} + 3 t.; + ב and על Gn 39^{5}; + ל 1 K 11^{28}; + אֲשֶׁר שָׁם ב 1 S 29^{4} *where thou hast stationed him*, ins. also v^{10} 𝔊 The We Dr al.; + אִתּוֹ Je 40^{7}, cf. 41^{10}. **2.** c. acc. rei (implic.), **a.** *commit, entrust* (cf. פִּקָּדוֹן), עַל־יַד פ׳ 1 K 14^{27} = 2 Ch 12^{10}; c. acc. רוּחִי + בְּיָדְךָ ψ 31^{6}. **b.** *deposit*, c. acc. rei + ב loc. Je 36^{20}, + ל loc. Is 10^{28}; acc. pers. (Jer. as prisoner) + ב loc. Je 37^{21}. †**Hoph. 1.** *be visited* in punishment, *Pf.* 3 ms. הָפְקַד Je 6^{6} (impers.; but 𝔊 ψευδής, read הַשֶּׁקֶר JDMich, הַפֶּרֶק Gie). **2.** *be deposited*, אִתּוֹ Lv 5^{23} (subj. הַפִּקָּדוֹן). **3.** *be made overseer*, *Pt.* (הַ)מֻּפְקָדִים, c. בֵּית 2 K 22^{9} 12^{12} Qr (Kt הפקדים); בְּבֵית י׳ 22^{5} (Qr del. ב), 2 Ch 34^{10}; c. עַל pers. 2 Ch 34^{12}; abs. v^{17}.

6486 פְּקֻדָּה $_{32}$ **n.f. oversight, mustering, visitation, store**;—abs. פ׳ Ho 9^{7} 1 Ch 23^{11}; cstr. פְּקֻדַּת Nu 3^{32} +; sf. פְּקֻדָּתוֹ 109^{8}, etc.; pl. פְּקֻדּ(וֹ)ת Je 52^{11} +;—**1.** *visitation*: **a.** = punishment Ho 9^{7} Is 10^{3} Mi 7^{4} Ez 9^{1} Nu 16^{29} (P), esp. in עֵת(שְׁנַת) פְּקֻדָּתָם Je 8^{12} 10^{15} + 6 t. Je (cf. עֵת c. פָּקַד 6^{15} 49^{8} 50^{31}), בֵּית הַפ׳ = prison 52^{11}. **b.** gracious visitation, providence Jb 10^{12}. **2. a.** *oversight, charge* Nu 4^{16} (P), also 3^{36} (P; redund.), 1 Ch 26^{30}; = *office* 2 Ch 23^{18}. **b.** *overseer* (abstr. for concr.), 2 K 11^{8} Ez 44^{11} (c. אֶל rei), Nu 3^{32} (P); coll. = magistracy Is 60^{17} (Lag$^{BN\ 151}$), cf. 2 Ch 24^{11}. **c.** *class of officers* 1 Ch 23^{11} 24$^{3.19}$. **d.** *charge* = thing entrusted Nu 4^{16} (P). **3.** *mustering* 2 Ch 17^{14} 26^{11}. **4.** *store*, things laid up, Is 15^{7} ψ 109^{8} (perh.; Hup We$^{Skizzen\ vi.\ 184}$ al. *office*).

6485 †[פְּקוּדִים] **n.pl.[m.] abstr. musterings, i.e. expenses**;—cstr. פְּקוּדֵי Ex 38^{21} (v. Di).

6496 †פָּקִיד **n.m. commissioner, deputy, overseer**;—abs. פ׳ Je 20^{1} +; cstr. פְּקִיד 2 Ch 24^{11} Ne 11^{22}; sf. פְּקִידוֹ Ju 9^{28}; pl. פְּקִדִים Gn 41^{34} Je 29^{26}, פְּקִידִים 2 Ch 31^{13} Est 2^{3};—*commissioner*, for special duty Gn 41^{34} (E), Est 2^{3}; permanent *deputy* of king Ju 9^{28}, of priest 2 Ch 24^{11}, of Levites 31^{13}; *overseer, one in charge* of men, c. עַל of soldiers 2 K 25^{19} = Je 52^{25}, Benjamites Ne 11^{9}, priests v^{14}; abs., without עַל, Je 29^{26} (of priest in temple, reading פָּקִיד Vrss. Gie), cf. 20^{1} (v. נָגִיד **3**); c. sf. of Levites Ne 11^{22}, singers 12^{42}.

6488 †פְּקִדֻת **n.f. oversight**;—בַּעַל פ׳ Je 37^{13} *sentinel*.

6490 [פִּקּוּד]$_{24}$ **n.m.**$^{ψ19.9}$ precept (of י׳; prop. *thing appointed, charge*, cf. √**B 2**), in ψψ (cf. Syr. ܦܘܩܕܢܐ, ܦܘܩܕܐ);—only pl. cstr. פִּקּוּדֵי י׳ ψ 19^{9}, and sf. פִּקּוּדָיו 111^{7}, פִּקֻּדָיו 103^{18}; elsewh. פִּקּוּדֶיךָ 119$^{15.27}$ + 10 t. 119 + v^{128} (for MT פִּקּוּדֵי כֹל, 𝔊 𝔙 and most); פִּקֻּדֶיךָ v$^{4.45}$ + 6 t. 119.

†פִּקָּדוֹן **n.m.**$^{Lv\ 5,\ 23}$ **deposit, store** (cf. √**Qal** 6487
B2; **Hiph. 2**);—פ׳ abs., of grain stored against famine Gn 41^{36}; thing left in trust Lv 5$^{21.23}$.

†מִפְקָד **n. [m.] muster, appointment,** 4662-63
appointed place;—abs. מ׳ only in שַׁעַר הַמִּ׳ Ne 3^{31}, v. I. שַׁעַר; cstr. מִפְקַד: **1.** *muster* of people 2 S 24^{9} = 1 Ch 21^{5}. **2.** *appointment* of (by) Hezekiah 2 Ch 31^{13}. **3.** *appointed place* of (in) temple Ez 43^{21} (Krae *watch, guard-house*; Kö$^{ii.\ 1,\ 93}$ conj. מוֹקֵד).

†פְּקוֹד **n.pr. gent. et terr.** a people in 6489
Bab. army Ez 23^{23} (Φακουκ; A και Φουδ); יוֹשְׁבֵי פ׳ Je 50^{21}; = As. *Puḳûdu*, tribe in SE. Babylonia, bordering Elam Wkl$^{Sargon\ i.\ 241}$ Schr$^{COT\ Je}$ Dl$^{Pa\ 240\ f.}$

†פָּקַח **vb. open** eyes and (once) ears (NH 6491
id., *open* (and remove) rubbish heap, sq. עַל *look to, attend to*; Ar. فَقَّحَ *blossom*, II. *open eyes*; JAram פְּקַח *open* eyes, etc.; Syr. ܦܩܚ *blossom*);—**Qal** *Pf.* 3 ms. פ׳ Jb 27^{19}; 2 ms. פָּקַחְתָּ 14^{3}; *Impf.* 3 ms. וַיִּפְקַח Gn 21^{19} +; 1 s. אֶפְקַח Zc 12^{4}; *Imv.* ms. פְּקַח 2 K 6^{17} +, so Dn 9^{18} Qr (Kt פקחה); *Inf. abs.* פָּקוֹחַ Is 42^{20}; cstr. לִפְקֹחַ v^{7}; *Pt. act.* פֹּקֵחַ ψ 146^{8}; *pass.* fpl. פְּקֻחוֹת Je 32^{19};—**1.** *open* eyes: **a.** one's own 2 K 4^{35} Jb 27^{19} Pr 20^{13}; 2 K 19^{16} = Is 37^{17} Dn 9^{18}; + עַל Je 32^{19} Zc 12^{4} Jb 14^{3}. **b.** eyes of others Gn 21^{19} 2 K 6$^{17.17.20.20}$ Is 42^{7} ψ 146^{8};—for details v. עַיִן **1 j.** **2.** *open* ears = hear Is 42^{20} (without understanding; fig. of Isr.). **Niph.** *Pf.* 3 pl. consec. וְנִפְקְחוּ Gn 3^{5}; *Impf.* 3 fpl. תִּפָּקַחְנָה Is 35^{5}, וַתִּ׳ Gn 3^{7};—*be opened*, of eyes; fig., so as to know good and evil Gn 3$^{5.7}$; opp. blindness (fig.) Is 35^{5}.

†פִּקֵּחַ **adj. seeing**;—פ׳ Ex 4^{11} (opp. עִוֵּר); 6493
pl. פִּקְחִים, fig., 23^{8} *clear-sighted ones* (cf. [עִוֵּר]).

†פְּקַח־קוֹחַ, rd. פְּקַחְקוֹחַ **n.[m.] opening** (of 6495
eyes; cf. Comm., Ges$^{§\ 85\ n}$, prop. *wide*, or *complete, opening*);—לַאֲסוּרִים Is 61^{1}, fig. of freeing fr. dark prison; but 𝔊 Che^{Hpt} read לַעִוְרִים, cf. Di-Kit.

†פֶּקַח **n.pr.m.** usurping king of Israel, 6492
Φακεε (*opening* (? of eyes), or cf. Syr. ܦܩܚܐ *flower*; cf. n.pr.m. פקח, פקחי, on old Isr. seals; in As. *Pakaḥa* (acc.) Schr$^{COT\ 2\ K\ 15,\ 30}$);—2 K 15$^{25.27.29.30.31.32.37}$ 16$^{1.5}$ Is 7^{1} 2 Ch 28^{6}.

†פְּקַחְיָה **n.pr.m.** king of Israel (י׳ *hath* 6494
opened the eyes);—2 K 15$^{22.23.26}$, Φακεσιας, Φακειας.

פקע (√of foll., mng. dub.; NH פָּקַע *split, spring off;* cf. 𝔗 Ithpe., Syr. ܦܩܥ *burst, crash;* NH פְּקַעַת is *ball, roll,* פְּקִיעַ *wick,* הִפְקִיעַ denom.; Ar. فَقَعَ is *be yellow,* also *break wind,* II. *crack* finger-joints, etc.; Ecclus 46[17] פקע *crash;* 𝔗 פְּקַע *roll noisily;* Syr. ܦܩܥܐ *crash, crack*).

6497 †פְּקָעִים **n.m.** [1 K 7, 24] **pl.** carved wood or metal ornaments, either **ball-**, **knob**-shaped (Löw [p. 332 f.]) or **gourd**-shaped (so most; cf. foll.; Syr. ܦܩܥܬܐ *flowers* [Lexx]);—1 K 6[18] 7[24.24].

6498 †פַּקֻּעֹת **n.**[f.]**pl. gourds** (*wild cucumbers, citrullus colocynthis,* with purgative properties, acc. to Post [Hastings DB ii. 250] De [Ri HWB 278 f.] 𝔊 κολοκυνθίς; >*momordica* (or *ecballium*) *elaterium,* which is not a *vine;* cf. Syr. ܦܩܘܥܐ, fruit of *colocynthis* (or the similar *cucumis prophetarum*), Löw [l. c.] Brock);—cstr. פ׳ שָׂדֶה 2 K 4[39].

6499 פַּר v. פרר. p. 830

6500, 6509 I. **פרא** v. **Hiph.** *Impf.* יַפְרִיא sub פרה. p. 826

II. **פרא** (√of foll.; Jen [Cosmol. 110] cp. Talm. פרא *run;* Ar. فَرَأٌ, فَرَاءٌ *wild ass,* Hom [NS 123]; As. *parû, mule* (*wild ass* is *purîmu*)).

6501 †פֶּרֶא **n.m.** [Jb 39, 5] (**m.** et **f.** Je 2[24], but **f.** prob. erron., cf. Kö [Synt. 157] Albr [ZAW xvi (1896), 68]) **wild ass** (prob. from swiftness);—פ׳ abs. Ho 8[9]+ (so Je 2[24] Gi; van d. H. Baer פֶּרֶה), cstr. Gn 16[12]; pl. פְּרָאִים Je 14[6]+;—*wild ass* Je 14[6] Jb 6[5] 39[5] Is 32[14] ψ 104[11]; עַיִר פ׳ Jb 11[12] *wild ass's colt;* פ׳ אָדָם Gn 16[12] (J) *a wild ass of a man* (Ishmael as a free nomad); fig. of wilfulness Ho 8[9] (v. I. בָּדָד); of lust Je 2[24] (i.e. Israel's love of idolatry); of poor desert-dwellers Jb 24[5].

6502 †פִּרְאָם **n.pr.m.** Canaanite king of Jarmuth Jos 10[3], Φειδων, 𝔊L Φεδαμ, A Φεραμ.

6288, 6503 פֹּארָת v. פֹּארָה. פַּרְבָּר v. [פַּרְוָר]. p. 802, 826

6504 †I. [**פָּרַד**] **vb. divide** (NH *id., divide, separate;* so Syr. in der. spec. and deriv.; Ar. فَرَدَ *be single, sole,* also (Dozy) *unfold, unroll*);—**Qal** *Pt. pass.* fpl. פְּרֻדוֹת Ez 1[11] *divided,* i.e. spread, of wings. **Niph.** *Pf.* 3 pl. נִפְרְדוּ Gn 10[5.32], נִפְרָדוּ 2 S 1[23]; *Impf.* יִפָּרֵד Gn 2[10] Pr 19[4], etc.; *Imv.* ms. הִפָּרֶד נָא Gn 13[9]; *Inf. cstr.* הִפָּרֵד־לוֹט v[14]; *Pt.* נִפְרָד Ju 4[11] Pr 18[1], נִפְרָדִים Ne 4[13];—**1.** *divide, separate* (intrans.), Gn 2[10] (of river, *dividing* into branches); of one man *separating* from another, c. מֵעַל 13[9.11], מֵעִם v[14] (all J), from others, מִן Ju 4[11]; recipr. Gn 25[23] (J; of sons of Rebekah representing nations, c. מִמֵּעַיִךְ in constr. praegn. [Ges [§ 119 ff]], i.e. divided (hostile) from birth); abs. Pr 18[1]; of peoples separating from (מִן) parent stock 10[5.32] (P). **2.** *be divided, separated,* 2 S 1[23] Ne 4[13]; of loss of friendship Pr 19[4]. **Pi.** *Impf.* 3 ms. יְפָרֵדוּ Ho 4[14] *make a separation,* i.e. go apart (in company with [עִם] harlots, cf. RS [Sem. i. 436, 2nd ed. 455]). **Pu.** *Pt. divided,* עַם ... מְפֻזָּר וּמְפֹרָד בֵּין הָעַמִּים Est 3[8]. **Hiph.** *Pf.* 3 ms. הִפְרִיד Gn 30[40]; *Impf.* יַפְרִיד Ru 1[17] Pr 18[18], 3 mpl. וַיַּפְרִדוּ 2 K 2[11]; *Inf. cstr.* sf. בְּהַפְרִידוֹ Dt 32[8]; *Pt.* מַפְרִיד Pr 16[28] 17[9];—**1.** *divide, separate* Gn 30[40] (JE) Dt 32[8], of separating friends Pr 16[28] 17[9]. **2.** *make a division, separation,* between (בֵּין), 2 K 2[11] Ru 1[17]; of parting disputants (c. בֵּין) Pr 18[18]. **Hithp.** *Pf.* 3 pl. וְהִתְפָּרְדוּ ψ 22[15]; *Impf.* יִתְפָּרְדוּ 92[10], -רָדוּ Jb 4[11] 41[9];—*be divided, separated, from each other;* of scales of crocodile (c. neg.) Jb 41[9], of bones, = be loosened at the joint, ψ 22[15] (fig. of helplessness); = be dispersed Jb 4[11] ψ 92[10].

†[פְּרֻדָה] **n.f. grain** of seed (?) (prop., si vera l., the *separated;* cf. Syr. ܦܪܕܐ, ܦܪܕܬܐ, Talm. פְּרִידָא, *pebble, berry*);—only pl. פְּרֻדוֹת Jo 1[17]. 6507

†פְּרוּדָא **n.pr.m.** post-exil. name Ezr 2[55] (Φαδουρα), = פְּרִידָא Ne 7[57] (Φερειδα; 𝔊L as Ezr). 6514

II. **פרד** (√of foll.; cf. Syr. ܦܪܕ *flee, flee away,* so 𝔗 der. spec.; NH פֶּרֶד = BH).

†פֶּרֶד **n.m.** [2 S 18, 9] **mule;**—פ׳ abs. 2 S 18[9.9.9]+, sf. פִּרְדּוֹ 13[29]; pl. פְּרָדִים 1 K 10[25]+; פִּרְדֵיהֶם Ezr 2[66] = Ne 7[68] (van d. H.; Gi Baer in marg.);—*mule,* ridden by princes 2 S 13[29], in battle 18[9.9.9]; cf. (later, + horses, etc.) Zc 14[15] Is 66[20]; royal gift 1 K 10[25] = 2 Ch 9[24]; royal property 1 K 18[5]; in trade of Tyre Ez 27[14]; beast of burden, מַשָּׂא צֶמֶד פְּרָדִים 2 K 5[17] *the load of a pair of mules,* of earth, 1 Ch 12[40]; property of returning exiles Ezr 2[66] = Ne 7[68]; as refractory ψ 32[9] (in sim.). 6505

†פִּרְדָּה **n.f. she-mule;**—פ׳ ridden by king 1 K 1[33], cstr. פִּרְדַּת הַמֶּלֶךְ v[38.44]. 6506

†פַּרְדֵּס **n.**[m.] **preserve, park** (loan-word from Zend *pairi-daêza, enclosure,* Spieg Haug in Ew [Jahrb. v. 162 f.], cf. Spieg [Avesta i. 293]; Pers. پاليز, *pâlêz* Lag [Ges. Abh. 75, 211], Kurd. *parês* Nö [ZMG xxxvi (1882), 182]; hence Arm. *partêz* Lag [Arm. Stud. § 1878], late As. *pardisu* Meissn [ZA vi. 290], Ar. فِرْدَوْس; Gk. παράδεισος; cf. also Dl [Pa 95 ff.] Di [Gn 2, 8]);—הַפ׳ Ne 2[8] (containing trees); cstr. פַּרְדֵּס רִמּוֹנִים Ct 4[13] (fruit-trees and costly plants); pl. פַּרְדֵּסִים Ec 2[5] (+ גַּנּוֹת). 6508

6509 †[פָּרָה] **vb.** bear fruit, be fruitful (NH =BH **1**, פְּרִי=BH; Ph. פר *fruit*; Eth. ፈረየ: ፈረየ: *blossom, bear fruit*; As. *pir'u, posterity*; cf. also ᵀפֵּרָא, Syr. ܦܐܪܐ *fruit*, and Ba$^{ZMG\ xli\ (1887).\ 604}$);—**Qal** *Pf.* 3 pl. פָּרוּ Ex 1^{7}; 1 pl. consec. וּפָרִינוּ Gn 26^{22}, etc.; *Impf.* 3 ms. יִפְרֶה Is 11^{1}, etc.; *Imv.* ms. פְּרֵה Gn 35^{11}, mpl. פְּרוּ 1^{22}+; *Pt. act.* פֹּרֶה Dt 29^{17}, f. פֹּרִיָּה Ez 19^{10} Is 17^{6}, פֹּרָת (Ges ^{§80g}; for *פֹּרִיַּת Lag$^{BN\ 81}$) Gn 49$^{22.22}$;—**1.** of men and animals, Ex 23^{30} (E) Gn 26^{22} (J); esp. +רבה Je 3^{16} 23^{3} Ez 36^{11} Gn 35^{11} 47^{27} (P), and שָׁרַץ (P) Gn 8^{17} 9^{7} Ex 1^{7}, פְּרוּ וּרְבוּ וּמִלְאוּ וגו׳ Gn 1$^{22.28}$ 9^{1}. **2.** of vine, גֶּפֶן פֹּרִיָּה Is 32^{12} *fruitful vine*, so ψ 128^{3} (sim. of wife); cf. (in fig. of Isr.) Ez 19^{10}; in Mess. prediction Is 11^{1} a shoot from his [Jesse's] roots *shall bear fruit;* c. acc. שֹׁרֶשׁ פֹּ׳ רֹאשׁ fig., Dt 29^{17} *a root bearing gall* (as its fruit); יִפְרוּ יֶשַׁע Is 45^{8} is dub., read perh. 3 fs. תֵּפֶר *let earth be fruitful in salvation* (Oort al.); *Pt.* f., as subst., הַפֹּרִיָּה *the fruit-bearer*, poet. for tree, Is 17^{6} (cf. [סָעִיף] **2**); so בֵּן פֹּרָת Gn 49$^{22.22}$ Joseph is *son of a fruit-bearer*, i.e. a fruitful bough. **Hiph. 1.** *cause to bear fruit*, **2.** *make fruitful*, subj. ׳י, c. acc. of man or people: **1.** *Pf.* 3 ms. sf. הִפְרַנִי Gn 41^{52} (E). **2.** in P, וְהִפְרֵתִי Gn 17$^{6.20}$ (־רֵיתִי), +הִרְבָּה Lv 26^{9} (H); *Impf.* 3 ms. juss. יַפְרְךָ וְיַרְבֶּךָ Gn 28^{3}, וַיֶּפֶר ψ 105^{24}; *Pt.* הִנְנִי מַפְרְךָ וְהִרְבִּיתִךָ Gn 48^{4}. **3.** *shew fruitfulness, bear fruit* (Ges $^{§53\ c,}$
6500 $^{d,\ g}$): *Impf.* 3 ms. יַפְרִיא Ho 13^{15} (as if from פרא).
6529 פְּרִי$_{119}$ **n.m.**$^{Ho\ 14,9}$ **fruit**;—abs. ׳פ Ho 9^{16}+, פֶּרִי Je 12^{12}+; esp. cstr. פְּרִי Gn 4^{3}+; sf. פִּרְיִי Pr 8^{19}, פֶּרְיְךָ Ho 14^{9}, פִּרְיוֹ Gn 3^{6}+, וּפֶרְיְכֶם Ez 36^{8}, פִּרְיָהֶם Am 9^{14}, פִּרְיָם La 2^{20}+, פִּרְיָמוֹ ψ 21^{11}, פִּרְיָהֶן Je 29^{28}, פִּרְיָהּ v^{5}, etc.;—**1.** פְּרִי הָאֲדָמָה Gn 4^{3} (J), *fruit of the ground*, of produce in gen., so Dt 7^{13}+9 t. Dt+3 t.; פ׳ הָאָרֶץ Nu 13$^{20.26.27}$ (JE)+5 t., cf. Ez 25^{4}; *fruit* of vineyard 2 K 19^{29}=Is 37^{30}, Zc 8^{12} Is 65^{21} Ct 8$^{11.12}$, in fig. Ho 10$^{1.1}$+5 t.+Ez 17^{14} (but del. 𝔊 Co al.); esp. פ׳ הָעֵץ Gn 3$^{2.3.6}$ Ex 10^{15} (all J) + 21 t., also, in fig., Am 2^{9} Ho 9^{16} + 4 t. + Ez 17^{23} (read פֹּארָה *branches* Co al.); of gardens Am 9^{14} Je 29$^{5.28}$, fig. Ct 4$^{12.16}$; עֵץ פְּרִי is *fruit-tree* Gn 1^{11} ψ 148^{9}, cf. Ec 2^{5}; אֶרֶץ פְּרִי ψ 107^{34}; פְּרִי תְבוּאָה v^{37} *fruit of* (consisting in) *a crop;* ψ 72^{16} is dub.; Che Du interpr. as **2**; Bae prop. יִפְרוּ. **2.**=*offspring: fruit* of womb (בֶּטֶן) Gn 30^{2} Dt 7^{13}+9 t., cf. La 2^{20} ψ 21^{11}; of cattle (בְּהֵמָה) Dt 28$^{4.11.51}$ 30^{9}; of serpent, fig. of power conquering Philistia Is 14^{29}. **3.** fig. of *fruit* of actions, i.e. their consequences: good Is 3^{10} ψ 58^{12}; bad Ho 10^{13} Pr 1^{31} Mi 7^{13}, of thoughts Je 6^{19}; of result of removing sin Is 27^{9}; result of labour (*fruit* of hands) Pr 31$^{16.31}$; product of works of ׳י ψ 104^{13}, of wisdom Pr 8^{19}; פ׳ צְדָקָה Am 6^{12}, cf. פ׳ צַדִּיק Pr 11^{30} (rd. צֶדֶק 𝔊 Hi Toy); of doings (i.e. course of life, or character) Je 17^{10} 21^{14} 32^{19}; פ׳ פִּי־אִישׁ i.e. speech Pr 12^{14} 13^{2} 18^{20}; *fruit* of arrogance Is 10^{12} is arrogant speech; *fruit* of tongue Pr 18^{21}= consequences of speech.

I, II. פָּרָה v. III. פרר. פֶּרֶה v. פֶּרֶא. 6501, p. 825, 831 6510-11

[פֵּרָה], פֵּרוֹת Is 2^{20} v. [חֲפַרְפָּרָה] p. 344. 2661, 6512

†פָּרָה **n.pr.m.** Ju 7$^{10.11}$, Φαρα. 6513

†פַּרְוָיִם **n.pr.loc.** זְהַב פ׳ 2 Ch 3^{6}, Φαρουαιμ; 6516
in Arabia? Sprenger$^{Alte\ Geogr.\ Ar.\ 54\ f.}$ identif. with *Farwa* in Yemen, Gl$^{Skizze\ ii.\ 347}$ (less prob.) with *Sûk el Farwain* in Yemama (Nejd).

†[פַּרְוָר] **n.[m.]** structure (colonnade?) 6503
attached to W. side of Solomon's temple; pl. פַּרְוָרִים 2 K 23^{11}; appar. same word in sg. פַּרְבָּר 1 Ch 26$^{18.18}$ (all c. art.) (Thes cp. Pers. فرور *open kiosk, summer-house* (lit. *light-bearer*), whence perhaps ׳פ as loan-word, cf. Mishn. פַּרְוָר, פַּרְוָאר, ᵀפַּרְוָרָא *suburb* (made up of *villas, summer-houses* Thes); ׳פ then post-ex. insertion in 2 K 23^{11}; cf. further Dr in Hastings^{DB}).

†[פֶּרֶז or פָּרָז] **n.[m.]** פְּרָזָו Hb 3^{14}, text and 6518
meaning dub.; *warriors* (𝔙ᵀ) or *leaders* (𝔊 δυναστῶν, cf. 𝔖 Thes We) would suit context.

פרז (√of foll.; cf. Ar. فرز *remove, separate*, فرز *depressed ground between hills;* NH הִפְרִיז *extend* border, exceed limit; פְּרוּז=BH פְּרָזִי).

†[פְּרָזָה] **n.f.** open region, hamlet;—only 6519
pl. פְּרָזוֹת: אֶרֶץ פ׳ Ez 38^{11} *a land of hamlets* (opp. חוֹמָה, etc.); פ׳ תֵּשֵׁב יְרוּשָׁלַםִ Zc 2^{8} *as open regions shall Jerusalem sit* (יָשַׁב **4**); עָרֵי הַפּ׳ Est 9^{19} (opp.
שׁוּשָׁן v^{18}); perh. Ju 5^{7} (׳פ for פְּרָזוֹן, cf. 𝔖ᵀGFM). 6520

†פְּרָזִי **n.[m.]** hamlet-dweller;—coll. c. 6521
art. כֹּפֶר הַפּ׳ 1 S 6^{18} (opp. עִיר מִבְצָר), עָרֵי הַפּ׳ Dt 3^{5} (opp. עָרִים בְּצֻרֹת חוֹמָה וגו׳); pl. הַפְּרָזִים Est 9^{19} Qr (Kt הפרוזים).

†פְּרָזוֹן **n.[m.]** dub.; ׳פ Ju 5^{7}; sf. פִּרְזוֹנוֹ v^{11} 6520
(Lag$^{BN\ 119}$), poss. coll. *rural population, rustics*, Bachm Bu (the latter as gen. obj. after צִדְקֹת *righteous acts to the peasants*); >𝔊 Thes Be
leaders and *leadership* (cf. [פֶּרֶז]); text very 6518
uncertain; on v^{7} see [פְּרָזָה] supr. 6519

6522 פְּרִזִּי $_{23}$ **adj.gent. Perizzite** (poss., but not certainly, connected with above √);—only הַפּ׳ as n.pr.coll. ὁ (οἱ) Φερεζαῖος (-αῖοι), of ancient inhab. of Canaan, + הַכְּנַעֲנִי [q.v.] Gn 13[7] 34[30] (J), Ju 1[4.5]; also in list of peoples dispossessed by Israel Gn 15[20] Ex 3[8] + 17 t.

6524 †I. **פָּרַח** **vb. bud, sprout, shoot** (NH Hiph. = BH **Hiph. 2**; Ecclus פרח **Qal** = *flourish*, **Hiph.** causat., 49[10] 40[19]; Ar. فَرَّخَ II. *hatch*, also *sprout*, فَرْخٌ *young* of bird (v. אֶפְרֹחַ infr.), *twig*, *sprout*; As. *pirḫu*, n. *sprout*;—on mng. cf. GFM [JBL x (1891), 57]);—**Qal** *Pf.* 3 ms. פ׳ Ez 7[10] +, etc.; *Impf.* 3 ms. יִפְרַח Ho 14[6] +, 3 fpl. תִּפְרַחְנָה Is 66[14], etc.; *Inf. abs.* פָּרֹחַ 35[2]; cstr. בִּפְרֹחַ ψ 92[8]; *Pt.f.* פֹּרַחַת Gn 40[10];—*bud, sprout, send out shoots*, of vine Gn 40[10] (E), Ho 14[8] (sim.), Ct 6[11] 7[13]; fig-tree Hb 3[17] (< 𝔊 We Now תִּפְרֶה); rods Nu 17[20.23]; metaph. of restored Isr. Ho 14[6] Is 27[6], cf. of bones Is 66[14] (כַּדֶּשֶׁא); of righteous ψ 72[7] 92[13] Pr 11[28]; of wicked (כְּמוֹ עֵשֶׂב) ψ 92[8]; also of steppe (עֲרָבָה) Is 35[1], פָּרֹחַ תִּפְרַח v[2]; fig. of judgment Ho 10[4] (כָּרֹאשׁ; but on text v. Now); of זָדוֹן (q.v. p. 268) Ez 7[10]. **Hiph.** *Pf.* 1 s. הִפְרַחְתִּי Ez 17[24]; *Impf.* יַפְרִחַ Jb 14[9], etc.;—**1.** *cause to bud* or *sprout*, c. acc. עֵץ Ez 17[24], זֶרַע Is 17[11], both fig. **2.** *shew buds, sprouts*, of tree Jb 14[9]; fig. of righteous ψ 92[14]; = flourish, of אֹהֶל יְשָׁרִים, Pr 14[11] (all **Qal** in ־ acc. to Ba [ZMG xliii (1889), 180 f.]).

6525 †פֶּרַח **n.m.** [Na 1, 4] **bud, sprout**;—abs. פ׳ Is 18[5] +, פָּרַח Ex 25[33] 37[19]; cstr. פֶּרַח Na 1[4] +; sf. פִּרְחָהּ Nu 8[4], פִּרְחָם Is 5[24]; pl. sf. פְּרָחֶיהָ Ex 25[31] +;—*bud*, Is 5[24], of vine 18[5] (both fig.), Nu 17[23]; פ׳ לְבָנוֹן Na 1[4] *the sprout of Lebanon* (i.e. of its cedars); of bud-shaped ornament in temple 1 K 7[26] (פ׳ שׁוֹשָׁן) v[49] = 2 Ch 4[5] (פ׳ שׁוֹשַׁנָּה) v[21]; in tabern. Ex 25[31.33.33.34] 37[17.19.19.20] Nu 8[4].

6526 †פִּרְחַח **n.m. coll. brood** (? as *offshoot, offspring*);—פ׳ Jb 30[12], i.e. the wretched crowd.

667 †[אֶפְרֹחַ] **n.m.** [Jb 39, 30] **young one, pl. young ones, young,** of birds (Eth. አፍሮት፡ *id.*);—אֶפְרֹחִים Dt 22[6.6]; sf. אֶפְרֹחָיו Jb 39[30], אֶפְרֹחֶיהָ ψ 84[4].

6524 †II. **פָּרַח** **vb. break out,** of leprosy and like eruptions (in P) (usu. taken as = I. פ׳, but dub.; NH *id.*, also *decay, ferment* Vogelst [Landwirthschaft 22]; Syr. ܦܪܰܚ *spread*, of leprosy, etc.; NS. ܦܘܪܚܢܐ *leprous spots*);—**Qal** *Pf.* 3 ms. פ׳ Lv 13[39] (of בֹּהַק), וּפ׳ consec. 14[43] (of נֶגַע); of צָרַעַת, 3 fs. פָּרְחָה 13[20.25], also *Impf.* 3 fs. + *Inf. abs.* פָּרוֹחַ תִּפְרַח v[12], and *Pt.* f. פֹּרַחַת v[42]; of שְׁחִין *Pt.* m. פֹּרֵחַ Ex 9[9.10].

†III. [**פָּרַח**] **vb. fly**, Aramaism, si vera l. 6524
(NH *id.*, esp. *fly away*; Aram. פְּרַח, ܦܪܰܚ *fly*; ܦܪܰܚܬܐ *insect, bird*);—**Qal** *Pt.* fpl. לְפֹרְחוֹת Ez 13[20.20] *for* (like ?) *flying things*, i. e. birds, but del. 𝔊 𝔖 Hi Siegf in v[a] (where prob. ins. from v[b]); Co Toy Berthol Krae in v[a.b].

†פָּרוּחַ **n.pr.m.** in Issachar 1 K 4[17], 𝔊 6515
Φουασουδ, A Φαρρου, 𝔊L Βαρσαουχ.

†[**פָּרַט**] **vb.** very dub., **Qal** *Pt.* pl. 6527
הַפֹּרְטִים עַל־פִּי הַנָּבֶל Am 6[5] (NH *break off, divide*, so Syr. ܦܪܰܛ; NH פְּרוּטָה, Aram. פְּרִיטָא, *small coin, change*, hence) AW Ra AE Ki *divide* words into parts (in singing), AV *chant;* and Thes *scatter* (cf. פֶּרֶט) empty words; poss. also would be *stammer* (of broken speech; said contemptuously):—(Ar. فَرَطَ is *precede, act hastily*, IV. *act extravagantly, talk immoderately* (v. further Dr [Am. 236]), hence) AW (as altern.) *improvise carelessly, idly*.

†פֶּרֶט **n.[m.] the broken off,** i.e. fallen 6528
grapes;—cstr. פ׳ כַּרְמְךָ Lv 19[10].

פְּרִי v. פרה.

I. **פרך** (√ of foll.; NH פָּרַךְ *rub, chafe, crumble*; As. *parâku, display violence*; Ar. فَرَكَ *rub and press*, also *hate violently*; Aram. פְּרַךְ, ܦܪܰܟ *rub, crumble*).

†פֶּרֶךְ **n.[m.] harshness, severity**;—in 6531
phr. בְּפ׳ Lv 25[53], בְּפָרֶךְ v[43.46] (H P), Ez 34[4] (all c. רדה *rule harshly*); Ex 1[13] (c. וַיַּעֲבִדוּ), v[14] (c. עֲבֹדָה; both P).

II. **פרך** (√ of foll.; cf. As. *parâku, bar, shut off; parakku, apartment, shrine;* Syr. ܦܶܪܟܳܐ *shrine* (v. RS [JPhil 13, 283]); v. also Muss-Arnolt [JBL xi (1892), 77] Kö [ii. 1, 201]).

פָּרֹכֶת $_{25}$ **n.f. curtain,** before Most Holy 6532
Place, in tabern. (P) (prop. *that which habitually shuts off*, i.e. **parrâku* (Lag [BN 88]) Kö [ii. 1, 201]);—פ׳ abs. Ex 26[31] + 17 t. P; cstr. פ׳ הַמָּסָךְ Ex 35[12] 39[34] 40[21] Nu 4[5], פ׳ הַקֹּדֶשׁ Lv 4[6], פ׳ הָעֵדוּת 24[3]; in temple 2 Ch 3[14].

†[**פָּרַם**] **vb. tear, rend garment** (NH = 6533
BH; Ar. فَرَمَ *chop up* onions, etc. (Landberg [Prov. 421]); Syr. ܦܪܰܡ *cut, rend*);—always c. בְּגָדִים:

Qal *Impf.* 3 ms. יִפְרֹם Lv 21[10] (H), 2 mpl. תִּפְרֹמוּ 10[6] (P); *Pt. pass.* pl. פְּרֻמִים 13[45] (P).

6534 †פַּרְמַשְׁתָּא **n.pr.m.** son of Haman Est 9[9], Μαρμασιμ(ν)α.

6535 †פַּרְנָךְ **n. pr. m.** of Zebulun Nu 34[25], Φαρ(α)ναχ.

6539 פָּרַס [28] **n.pr.terr. Persia,** Περσῶν (genit.), Dn 11[2] τῇ Περσίδι (𝔊 et Θ), 2 Ch 36[20] Μήδων (OPers. *Pârsa, Persian, Persia,* Spieg[APK 231], NPers. پَارْسِ, فَارْسِ; Ar. فَارِسُ);—פ׳ 2 Ch 36[22]+, פָּרָס v[20]+;—in late lit., 2 Ch 36[20], v[22.22.23]=Ezr 1[1.1.2], Dn 10[1]+11 t. Ezr Dn+(c. מָדַי) Est 1[3.14.18.19] 10[2] Dn 8[20]; פ׳ Ez 27[10] 38[5] is doubted by Toy (who, 27[10], rds. כּוּשׁ, after Gr), but Krae defends.

6542 †פַּרְסִי **adj. gent. Persian**;—הַפּ׳ Ne 12[22].

6536 †[פָּרַס, erron. פָּרַשׂ Nö[ZA i. 417]] **vb. break in two, divide** (NH in der. forms; As. *parâsu, divide, hinder;* Ar. فَرَسَ *break* neck, etc.; Syr. ܦܪܣܐ *hoof,* 𝔗 פַּרְסְתָא (v. פַּרְסָה infr.); cf. Nö [ZA i. 417 f.]);—**Qal** *Pf.* 3 pl. וּפָרְשׂוּ Mi 3[3] *they have broken up* bones, as in kettle (? rd. Impf. וַיִּפְרְשׂוּ Nö[l. c.]); *Inf. abs.* פָּרֹס לָרָעֵב לַחְמֶךָ Is 58[7] *a breaking for the hungry thy bread,* so *Impf.* 3 mpl. יִפְרְסוּ יפ׳ לָהֶם אֶל־אֵבֶל Je 16[7] (לֶחֶם om.; but read לֶחֶם לָהֶם Gie, cf. [in part] 𝔊 𝔙 Gf); *Pt.* פֹּרֵשׂ לָהֶם La 4[4] (acc. לֶחֶם om.). **Hiph.** *Pf.* 3 fs. הִפְרִיסָה Lv 11[6], etc.; *Impf.* 3 ms. יַפְרִיס v[5]; *Pt.* מַפְרִיס v[4]+, מַפְרֶסֶת v[3]+, etc.;—**1.** c. acc. פַּרְסָה *divide hoof,* i. e. have divided hoof (>denom. *have hoofs*), Dt 14[6.7.8] and ‖ Lv 11[3.4.5.6.7], so also Lv 11[26]; מַפְרִיסֵי הַפּ׳ Dt 14[7]=מַפְרִיסֵי הַפּ׳ Lv 11[4] (H). **2.** pt. abs. denom. ψ 69[32] *having hoofs* (+מַקְרִן).

6538 †פֶּרֶס **n.[m.]** a bird of prey, perh. **bearded vulture** (*gypaetus barbatus*), '**ossifrage**' (Tristr [NHB 171; FFP 94]; from *tearing* its prey);—forbidden as food Dt 14[12]=Lv 11[13] (H).

6541 פַּרְסָה [21] **n.f. hoof** (prob. orig. *divided* hoof; cf. Nö[ZA i (1886), 417], later of any hoof (v. **2** infr.), even Aram. of foot-sole of dove 𝔗[Onk Gn 8, 9], and of men (Je 47[3]+), cf. Nö[l. c.]);—פ׳ abs. Ex 10[26]+; pl. פְּרָס(וֹ)ת Dt 14[6] Lv 11[3]; cstr. *id.* Is 5[28]+; sf. פַּרְסֹתַיִךְ Mi 4[13], פַּרְסֵיהֶן Zc 11[16];—**1.** of ruminants Ex 10[26] (E; meton. for animal itself), Mi 4[13] (fig. of Zion), Ez 32[13] Zc 11[16] (fig.); esp. שֶׁסַע פ׳ (שְׁתֵּי) Dt 14[6]=Lv 11[3], Lv 11[7], and c. פָּרַס **Hiph.** (q.v.) v[3]+10 t. Lv 11 Dt 14. **2.** of horses (not *divided*) Is 5[28] Ez 26[11] (so 𝔗 𝔖), Je 47[3].

I. פרע (√of foll.; cf. perh. Ar. فَرَعَ *overtop,* fig. *excel;* فَرْعٌ *noble, eminent man;* Sab. פרע *be lofty* Os[ZMG xix (1865), 178 f.], פרע *highest part* SabDenkm[90], fig. *best,* DHM[ib., 32 f.] CIS[iv. No. 2. l. 13], esp. of *offering* DHM[ZMG xxxvii (1883), 341 ff.] (cf. Ar. فَرَعٌ *firstling offered to gods*)).

I. פֶּרַע **n.[m.]** leader (?);—pl. abs. בִּפְרֹעַ פְּרָעוֹת Ju 5[2] *for the leading of the leaders* (𝔊[A] Be Bu al., but uncertain; 𝔊[B] Symm, cf. We[Isr. u. Jüd. Gesch. (2), 97; Heid. (2), 123] al., *for the loosing of locks* [II. פֶּרַע], in vow of war; on these and other views v. esp. GFM[ad loc.]; conj. also by Lambert[RÉJ xxiv. 140] Grimme[ZMG l (1896), 572] Che[JQ, July 1899, 561] [reading ברכו]); cstr. מֵרֹאשׁ פַּרְעוֹת אוֹיֵב Dt 32[42] *from the head of leaders of the foe* 𝔊 Di Steuern al.; Kn Ke Dr al. *from the long-haired heads of the foe.* 6545

†[פָּרַע] **vb. denom. act as leader, lead** (?);—only Inf. cstr. בִּפְרֹעַ Ju 5[2], v. supr. 6544

†פִּרְעָתוֹן **n.pr.loc.** in Ephr. (? =*height;* cf. Sab. n.pr. יהפרע *he makes lofty* Os[l. c.]);—Ju 12[15], Φαραθωμ, A 𝔊L Φρααθων; perh. mod. *Far'atâ,* c. 6 miles WSW. from Nablus, cf. Buhl [Geogr. 206] (GASm[Geogr. 355] prop. top of *Wady Farah* NE. from Nablus). 6552

†פִּרְעָתוֹנִי **adj.gent.** of foregoing, Ju 12[13.15], 1 Ch 27[14] cf. פִּרְעָתֹנִי 2 S 23[30]=1 Ch 11[31]. 6553

II. פרע (√of foll.; cf. Syr. ܦܪܥ *sprout;* As. *pir'u, sprout, progeny, pirtu, hair of head;* late Ar. فَرَعَ *sprout* (Schroeter in Me[Archiv. i. 176] Dozy[ii. 256]), فَرْعٌ *long hair* of woman;—on this and foll. √ v. Schulthess[Hom. Wurz. 56] Nö[ZMG liv (1900), 154]).

†II. פֶּרַע **n.[m.]** long hair of head, **locks**;—פ׳ abs. Ez 44[20]; cstr. פ׳ שְׂעַר רֹאשׁוֹ Nu 6[5] (P).—Ju 5[2] Dt 32[42], v. I. פֶּרַע. above 6545 6546

†III. פָּרַע **vb. let go, let alone** (NH *id. unbind* (hair), *uncover;* Ar. فَرَغَ *be empty, vacant, unoccupied* (c. من rei), Syr. ܦܪܥ *uncover;* 𝔗 פְּרַע =NH);—**Qal** *Pf.* 3 ms. consec. וּפָרַע Nu 5[18]; sf. פְּרָעֹה (Ges[§7 b, c]) Ex 32[25]; *Impf.* 3 ms. יִפְרָע Lv 21[10], etc.; *Imv.* ms. sf. פְּרָעֵהוּ Pr 4[15]; *Inf. cstr.* פְּרֹעַ Ju 5[2]; *Pt. act.* פּוֹרֵעַ Pr 13[18] 15[32]; *pass.* פָּרוּעַ Lv 13[45], פָּרֻעַ Ez 32[25];—**1.** *let go, let loose,* people, i.e. remove restraint from them, Ex 32[25.25] (E); cf. Jb 15[4] Che[JQ, July 1897, 577] (תִּפְרַע for תִּגְרַע); *unbind* head (by removing turban, sign of mourning) Lv 10[6] 21[10] (forbidden to priests); 6544

also 13^{45} (leper), Nu 5^{18} (woman; all c. ראשׁ; v. Now$^{Arch. ii. 114}$; >denom. from פֶּרַע Gerber^{18} al.). **2.** *let alone*=avoid Pr 4^{15}; =neglect 1^{25} 8^{33} 13^{18} 15^{32}; abs. = refrain Ez 24^{14}.—Ju 5^{2} v. I. פֶּרַע. **Niph.** *Impf.* 3 ms. יִפָּרַע עָם Pr 29^{18} *the people is let loose,* lacks restraint. **Hiph.** *Pf.* 3 ms. הִפְרִיעַ 2 Ch 28^{19}; *Impf.* 2 mpl. תַּפְרִיעוּ Ex 5^{4};—**1.** *cause* people *to refrain,* מִמַּעֲשָׂיו Ex 5^{4}. **2.** *shew lack of restraint* 2 Ch 28^{19}.

6547 **פַּרְעֹה** $_{275}$ **n.m. Pharaoh,** Φαραω, title of Egyptian kings (Egypt. *pr-ʿo, great house,* of royal court, and (in new kingdom) of king Griffith$^{Hastings DB}$ Mey$^{Gesch. Alt. i. 59}$ Steind$^{BAS i. 343}$; in As. *pir'u* acc. to most, cf. COT$^{Gloss.}$ Steind$^{l.c.}$, but v. Wkl$^{MVAG, 1898, 3 f.}$);—פ׳ Gn 12$^{15.15.15.17}$ + 212 t. Hex (mostly JE, rarely DP), 1 S 2^{27} 6^{6} 1 K 3^{1} 11^{1} + 19 t. K, Is 19$^{11.11}$ + 3 t., Je 25^{19} + 10 t., Ez 17^{17} + 12 t., Ne 9^{10} 1 Ch 4^{18} 2 Ch 8^{11} ψ 135^{9} 136^{15} Ct 1^{9}; + מֶלֶךְ מִצְרַיִם (not early) Je 25^{19} 46^{17} Dt 7^{8} 11^{3} Ez 29$^{2.3}$ 30$^{21.22}$ 31^{2} 1 K 3^{1} 9^{16} 11^{18} 2 K 17^{7} 18^{21} = Is 36^{6}, Gn 41^{46} (E), Ex 6$^{11.13.27.29}$ 14^{8} (all P); c.n.pr. פ׳ חָפְרַע Je 44^{30}, פ׳ נְכֹה 46^{2} 2 K 23$^{29.33.34.35}$.

6550 †I. **פַּרְעֹשׁ** **n.m. flea** (As. *puršuʾu, paršuʾu;* on transp. of, v. Hom$^{A. u. A. i. 21}$);—fig. of insignificance 1 S 24^{15}; 26^{20} נַפְשִׁי 𝔊 Th We Dr al.

6551 †II. **פַּרְעֹשׁ** **n.pr.m.** Φορος, Φαρες, etc. (flea; cf. Gray$^{Prop. N. 94}$);—**1.** head of post-ex. family Ezr 2^{3} = Ne 7^{8}, Ezr 8^{3} 10^{25} Ne 3^{25}. **2.** Ne 10^{15}.

6554 †**פַּרְפַּר** **n.pr.flum.** near Damascus 2 K 5^{12}, (A) φαρφαρ; A Φαρφαρα; perh. mod. *ʿAwaj,* S. of Damascus Rob$^{BR iii. 447 f.}$.

6555 †I. **פָּרַץ** **vb. break through** (NH *id.;* JAram. פְּרַץ *id.;* perh. As. *parâṣu* (v. Dl^{HWB}); Ar. فَرَضَ *cut, slit,* also *hit*);—**Qal** *Pf.* 3 ms. פָּרַץ 2 S 5^{20} +; 2 ms. sf. פְּרַצְתָּנוּ ψ 60^{3}, etc.; *Impf.* 3 ms. יִפְרֹץ Ex 1^{12} 19^{22}, יִפְרָץ־ v^{24}, וַיִּפְרֹץ Gn 30^{30} +, etc.; *Inf. abs.* פָּרוֹץ Is 5^{5}; cstr. פְּרֹץ 2 Ch 31^{5}, פְּרוֹץ Ec 3^{3}; *Pt. act.* פֹּרֵץ Mi 2^{13} Ec 10^{8}; *pass.* fs. פְּרוּצָה 2 Ch 32^{5} Pr 25^{28}; mpl. פְּרֻצִים Ne 4^{1}, + הֵם פְּרוּצִים 2^{13} Qr (>Kt המפרוצים);—*break through:* **1.** *break* or *burst out,* from womb Gn 38^{29} (J; c. acc. cogn.); from enclosure Mi 2^{13}. **2.** *break through, down* (from without), c. acc. גָּדֵר Is 5^{5} ψ 80^{13} 89^{41} Ec 10^{8}; חוֹמָה Ne 3^{35} 2 Ch 26^{6}, cf. pt. pass. Ne 2^{13} 2 Ch 32^{5}; c. בְּחוֹמָה = *make a breach in* 2 K 14^{13} = 2 Ch 25^{23}; עִיר פְּרוּצָה Pr 25^{28}; abs., opp. בָּנָה Ec 3^{3}; הַפֹּרֵץ Mi 2^{13}; הַפְּרוּצִים Ne 4^{1} *the part broken down.* **3.** *break into,* c. acc. בֵּית י׳ 2 Ch 24^{7}. **4.** *break open,* a mining shaft Jb 28^{4}. **5.** *break up, break in pieces,* c. acc. מַעֲשֶׂיךָ 2 Ch 20^{37} (|| וַיִּשָּׁבְרוּ אֳנִיּוֹת). **6.** *break out* (violently) *upon,* of י׳ in sudden judgment, c. acc. pers. 2 S 5^{20} = 1 Ch 14^{11}, ψ 60^{3}; c. בְּ pers. Ex 19$^{22.24}$ (J), 1 Ch 15^{13}, so of plague ψ 106^{29}; of י׳, c. acc. cogn. פֶּרֶץ + בְּ pers. 2 S 6^{8} = 1 Ch 13^{11}; c. acc. cogn. + sf. Jb 16^{14}. **7.** *use violence,* abs. Ho 4^{2}. **8.** *break over* [limits], *increase,* וַיִּפְרֹץ לָרֹב Gn 30^{30} (J), 1 Ch 4^{38}; + ה loc. Gn 28^{14} (J); abs. 30^{43} (J), Ex 1^{12} (J; + רָבָה), Ho 4^{10} Is 54^{3}, פָּרַץ בָּאָרֶץ Jb 1^{10}. **9.** *burst open,* intrans., of wine-vats Pr 3^{10} (c. acc. mat. תִּירוֹשׁ). **10.** *spread,* i.e. become known, of הַדָּבָר 2 Ch 31^{5}.—1 Ch 13^{2} is prob. corrupt, v. Kau, who (after SS) conj. נֶחֶרְצָה; פ׳ in 2 Ch 11^{23} is appar. *distribute* (c. מִן partit.), but dubious.—1 S 28^{23} 2 S 13$^{25.27}$ 2 K 5^{23} v. פצר. **Niph.** *Pt.* אֵין חָזוֹן נִפְרָץ 1 S 3^{1} *no vision spread abroad* (i.e. general, or frequent, cf. **Qal 10**; || דְּבַר י׳ הָיָה יָקָר), but text dubious. **Pu.** *Pt.* f. מְפֹרָצֶת Ne 1^{3} (of wall). **Hithp.** *Pt.* pl. הַמִּתְפָּרְצִים 1 S 25^{10} slaves *who break away,* each from (מִפְּנֵי) his master.

†I. **פֶּרֶץ** **n.m.**$^{Jb 30, 14}$ **bursting forth, breach;** 6556
abs. פ׳ Ju 21^{15} +, פָּרֶץ Gn 38^{29} +; cstr. פֶּרֶץ 2 S
5^{20} +; pl. פְּרָצִים Am 4^{3} +, פְּרָצוֹת Ez 13^{5}, sf. פִּרְצֵיהֶן 6559
Am 9^{11} (פִּרְצֶיהָ We Now);—**1.** *bursting forth, outburst,* of water 2 S 5^{20} = 1 Ch 14^{11}; fr. womb Gn 38^{29} (J). **2.** *breach* in wall Am 4^{3} 1 K 11^{27} Ne 6^{1} ψ 144^{14}, Jb 30^{14}; so (c. גָּדַר, i.e. repair) Am 9^{11} Is 58^{12}; fig. of effort to avert calamity, עָלָה בַּפְּרָצוֹת Ez 13^{5} (|| גָּדַר), עָמַד בַּפֶּרֶץ 22^{30} (|| id.), cf. ψ 106^{23}, by instruction and (esp.) intercession. **3.** *broken wall,* פ׳ נֹפֵל Is 30^{13}. **4.** fig. of *outburst* of י׳'s wrath, acc. cogn. c. פָּרַץ 2 S 6^{8} = 1 Ch 13^{11}, Jb 16^{14} (פֶּרֶץ עַל־פְּנֵי־פָרֶץ); עָשָׂה פ׳ בְּ Ju 21^{15}.

†II. **פֶּרֶץ** **n.pr. 1. m.** son of Judah and 6557
Tamar, Φαρες;—פ׳ Gn 46^{12} +, פָּרֶץ 38^{29} + 3 t.;—Gn 38^{29} 46$^{12.12}$ Nu 26$^{20.21}$ Ru 4$^{12.18.18}$ 1 Ch 2$^{4.5}$ 4^{1} 9^{4}
27^{3} Ne 11$^{4.6}$. **2. loc.** in **a.** פ׳ עֻזָּה near Jerus. 6560
2 S 6^{8} = 2 Ch 13^{11}. **b.** הַר פְּרָצִים Is 28^{21}, perh. =
בַּעַל פ׳ q.v. p. 128.—Cf. רִמֹּן פֶּרֶץ. p. 942 7428

†**פַּרְצִי** **adj. gent.** of II. פֶּרֶץ **1,** c. art. as 6558
n.coll. Nu 26^{20}.

†**פָּרִיץ** **n.m. violent one** (robber, mur- 6530
derer);—פ׳ שֹׁפֵךְ דָּם Ez 18^{10}; אָרְחוֹת פ׳ ψ 17^{4}; pl. פָּרִיצִים Ez 7^{22}, מְעָרַת פָּרִצִים Je 7^{11}; cstr. בְּנֵי פָּרִיצֵי עַמְּךָ Dn 11^{14}; of wild beast, פְּרִיץ חַיּוֹת Is 35^{9}.

II. **פרץ** (√ of foll.; cf. Ar. فَرَضَ *notch, make mark by notching;* فُرْضَةٌ *gap* by which boats ascend, unload, or are stationed; فِرَاضٌ *mouth* of river or inlet).

4664 †[מִפְרָץ] **n.[m.] landing-place**:—וְעַל מִפְרָצָיו יִשְׁכּוֹן Ju 5[17] (cf. GFM).

6561 †[פָּרַק] **vb. tear apart, away** (NH *remove* (load, etc.), Pi. *separate, take to pieces;* Ar. فَرَقَ *split, divide;* 𝔗 פְּרַק esp. *redeem, rescue;* Syr. ܦܪܰܩ *withdraw* (intrans.), also *remove, rescue;* Eth. ፈረቀ: *set free*);—**Qal** *Pf.* 2 ms. וּפָרַקְתָּ Gn 27[40]; *Impf.* 3 ms. sf. וַיִּפְרְקֵנוּ ψ 136[24]; *Pt. act.* פֹּרֵק La 5[8] ψ 7[3] *tear away* yoke from off (מֵעַל) neck Gn 27[40] (J); *snatch* from (מִן) foes, = *rescue* (Aram.) La 5[8] ψ 136[24]; so abs. ψ 7[3] (prefixing (וְ)אֵין), 𝔊 𝔖 Che Du We), > Hup Bae al. *snatch away* as prey. **Pi.** *Impf.* 3 ms. יְפָרֵק Zc 11[16] *he shall tear off* their hoofs; *Imv.* mpl. פָּרְקוּ Ex 32[2] (E) *tear off* the golden ear-rings; *Pt.* מְפָרֵק 1 K 19[11] a great wind *rending* mts. (‖ מְשַׁבֵּר). **Hithp.** *tear off* (for, i.e. from, oneself Ges[§ 54 f]); *Impf.* 3 mpl. וַיִּתְפָּרְקוּ Ex 32[3] (E), c. acc. אֶת־נִזְמֵי הַזָּהָב; *Imv.* mpl. הִתְפָּרְקוּ v[24] (E; obj. om.); pass. *be broken off, Pf.* 3 pl. הִתְפָּרְקוּ Ez 19[12] (branches).

6563 †פֶּרֶק **n.[m.]** **1. parting of ways**, Ob[14]. **2. plunder** (as *snatched away*), Na 3[1].

6564 †[פָּרָק] **n.[m.] fragment**;—cstr. פְּרַק פִּגֻּלִים Is 65[4] Kt, but read מְרַק, v. מָרָק.

4665 †[מַפְרֶקֶת] **n.f. neck** (*dividing* head from body);—sf. וַתִּשָּׁבֵר מַפְרַקְתּוֹ 1 S 4[18].

6331, 6565 †I. [פָּרַר] **vb. Hiph. break, frustrate** (NH Pi. *crumble;* JAram. פְּרַר; As. *parâru, destroy;* II. *shatter;* Liḥy. והפרו *destroy*, DHM Epigr. Denkm., No. 21, 7);—*Pf.* 3 ms. הֵפֵר Is 33[8] +, הֵפַר Gn 17[14] Nu 15[31]; also metaplastic form הֵפִיר Ez 17[19] ψ 33[10] (Ges[§ 67 v]); 2 ms. וְהֵפַרְתָּה 2 S 15[34], etc.; *Impf.* 3 ms. יָפֵר Nu 30[13] +, וַיָּפֶר Ne 4[9], etc.; also 1 s. אָפִיר ψ 89[34] (Ges[l.c.]); *Imv.* ms. הָפֵר 2 Ch 16[3] ψ 85[5], הָפֵרָה 1 K 15[19]; *Inf. abs.* הָפֵר Pr 15[22] +; cstr. לְהָפֵר 2 S 17[14] +, לְהָפִיר Zc 11[10], sf. לְהַפְרְכֶם Lv 26[15] (Ges[§ 67 dd]); *Pt.* מֵפֵר Is 44[25] Jb 5[12];—**1.** *break, violate*, esp. c. acc. בְּרִית: **a.** of ׳י Ju 2[1] Je 14[21] Lv 26[44] Zc 11[10]. **b.** of men violating covenant with ׳י Je 11[10] 31[32] Dt 31[16.20] Lv 26[15] Ez 44[7] Gn 17[14] Is 24[5], cf. Je 33[20]. **c.** of men breaking compact, league (with men), Is 33[8] 1 K 15[19] = 2 Ch 16[3], Ez 17[15.16.18.19]. **d.** of destroying the אַחֲוָה between Judah and Israel Zc 11[14]. **e.** of breaking ׳י's מִצְוָה Nu 15[31] Ezr 9[14], תּוֹרָה ψ 119[126]. **2.** *frustrate, make ineffectual:* **a.** counsel (עֵצָה) 2 S 15[34] 17[14] Ezr 4[5]; ׳י subj. Ne 4[9] ψ 33[10]; of man frustrating ׳י's counsel Is 14[27], so, c. acc. מִשְׁפָּט Jb 40[8]; c. acc. מַחֲשָׁבוֹת in gen., of men Pr 15[22], ׳י subj. Jb 5[12], so, c. acc. אתות Is 44[25]. **b.** *make* vow (נֶדֶר) *ineffectual, annul* it Ne 30[9.14] (opp. הֵקִים), v[13], also (Impf. + Inf. abs.) v[13.16]. **c.** of annulling (godly) fear Jb 15[4]; חַסְדִּי לֹא אָפִיר מֵעִמּוֹ ψ 89[34] rd. prob. אָסִיר Ol Che Bae al.; הָפֵר כַּעַסְךָ 85[4] (rd. הָסֵר 𝔊 Bi Che). **d.** וְתָפֵר הָאֲבִיּוֹנָה Ec 12[5] is dub.: De Wild al. *fails* (to excite [?< וְתֻפַר **Hoph.** *is made ineffectual*]); Ew *bursts* (Siegf וְתִפָּר); but caper-berry not dehiscent (Post Flora of Syr. 106 ff. M'Lean-Dyer Ency. Bib. 696): Post Letter, July 28, 1901 *breaks up* (by shrivelling), fig. of failing sexual power; Aq from פרה *bear fruit* (cf. GFM JBL x (1891), 60); Perles Anal. 30 וְתִפְרַח. **Hoph.** *Impf.* **1.** *be frustrated*, 3 fs. וְתֻפַר Is 8[10] (of עֵצָה). **2.** *be broken*, of covenant, 3 fs. תֻּפַר Je 33[21]; וַתֻּפַר Zc 11[11]; so Is 28[18] (read וְתֻפַר for וְכֻפַּר, v. כ׳). **Pilp.** *Impf.* 3 ms. sf. וַיְפַרְפְּרֵנִי Jb 16[12] *he hath shattered me.*

†II. [פָּרַר] **vb. split, divide** (so ψ 74[13] 6331, 6565
seems to require [but √ פור SS is possible], cf. Ar. فَرْفَرَ *split, tear, rend;* perh. = I.; > Buhl Lex. *shake, quake*, citing Ar. قَرْقَرَ *shake*, Aram. ܦܰܪܦܰܪ, אִתְפַּרְפַּר, cf. NH פִּרְפֵּר);—**Qal** *Inf. abs.* + **Hithpō'.** *Pf.* 3 fs. פּוֹר הִתְפּוֹרְרָה אֶרֶץ Is 24[19] *split* or *cracked through is the earth* (Che Heb. Hpt. פרוק התפרקה). **Pō'ēl** *Pf.* 2 ms. פּוֹרַרְתָּ ψ 74[13] *thou* [׳י] *didst divide* the sea.

III. פרר (√ of foll.; cf. NH פַּר, פָּרָה = BH; Ar. فُرَارٌ *young* of ewe, cow, or goat; Syr. ܦܪܳܐ *ewe* (cf. Nö ZMG xl (1886), 734), and so As. *parru*, acc. to Jen and Zim ZA iii. 202).

פַּר 132 **n.m.** Gn 32, 16 **young bull, steer**;—abs. 6499
פ׳ Nu 7[15] +, פָּר ψ 50[9], alw. הַפָּר 1 S 1[25] +; cstr. פַּר (הַ)חַטָּאת Ex 29[36] +; pl. פָּרִים Gn 32[16] +; sf. פָּרֶיהָ Je 50[27];—*steer* [v. esp. פַּר בֶּן־בָּקָר Lv 4[3] + 6 t.; פ׳ אֶחָד ב״ב Ex 29[1] + 12 t. Nu 7, cf. 8[8]; פ׳ ב״ב אֶחָד Nu 15[24] + 3 t., cf. Ez 43[23] 45[18] 46[6]; pl. פָּרִים בְּנֵי־ב׳ Nu 28[11] + 4 t.; v. בֵּן, בָּקָר]: **1.** as gift Gn 32[16] (E); fig. of fierce enemies ψ 22[13]. **2.** elsewh. as sacrificial victims: **a.** in peace-offering Ex 24[5] (E; Covenant Code), 1 S 1[24] (rd. פַּר for פָּרִים 𝔊 𝔖 Th We Dr al.), v[25] Nu 7[88] (P), 2 Ch 30[24.24]. **b.** burnt-offering Ju 6[25.25] (on text cf. GFM), v[26.28] 1 K 18[23.23.23.25.26.33]; Ez 43[23] + 5 t. Ez, Nu 7[15.21] + 46 t. Nu (P), 1 Ch 15[26] 29[21] Ezr 8[35] Jb 42[8] ψ 50[9] 51[21]; Lv 23[18] (gloss, Dr-Wh). **c.** sin-offering Ez 43[19] + 5 t. Ez, Ex 29[1.3.10.10.11.12.14.36] cf. 2 Ch 13[9] 29[21], Lv 4[3.4.4.4] + 25 t. Lv (P), Nu 8[8]; —both **b.** and **c.** Nu 8[12]. **d.** more gen. Is 1[11] ψ 69[32]. **e.** fig. פָּרִים שְׂפָתֵינוּ Ho 14[3] we will pay (as with) *bullocks, our lips*, but read פְּרִי 𝔊 We

Now, cf. Che. **f.** of princes and warriors slain by ׳י, under fig. of sacrifice Is 34^{7} Je 50^{27} Ez 39^{18}.

6510 I. פָּרָה$_{26}$ **n.f. heifer, cow**;—abs. ׳פ Is 11^{7}+; sf. פָּרָתוֹ Jb 21^{10}; pl. פָּרוֹת Gn 32^{16}+, פָּרֹת 41^{26}; cstr. פָּרוֹת Am 4^{1};—as gift Gn 32^{16}; in Pharaoh's dream 41$^{2.3.3}$ + 8 t. 41; drawing cart 1 S 6$^{7.12.14}$ + ׳פ׳ עָלוֹת v$^{7.10}$ *cows giving suck*, milch cows; ׳פ calving Jb 21^{10}, grazing Is 11^{7}; פ׳ אֲדֻמָּה *red heifer* Nu 19^{2}, cf. v$^{5.6.9.10}$; sim. of stubbornness Ho 4^{16}; פָּרוֹת הַבָּשָׁן Am 4^{1}, fig. of luxurious women.

6511 †II. פָּרָה **n.pr.loc.** in Benj., ׳הַפּ Jos 18^{23}, Φαρα, Αφρα.

6566 †פָּרַשׂ **vb. spread out, spread** (NH *id.*; Ar. فَرَشَ; 𝔗 פְּרַס (rare), Syr. ܦܪܣ; cf. As. *parašu, fly* (der. spec.; prop. *spread* [wings]); v. also Nö$^{ZA\ i.\ 417}$);—**Qal** *Pf.* 3 ms. ׳פ La 1^{10}+; 2 ms. וּפָרַשְׂתָּ Jb 11^{13} Ru 3^{9}, etc.; *Impf.* 3 ms. יִפְרֹשׂ Dt 32^{11}+; 3 fs. וַתִּפְרֹשׂ 2 S 17^{19}, etc.; *Pt. act.* פּוֹרֵשׂ Pr 29^{5}, etc.; *pass.* פָּרֻשׂ Jo 2^{2}; fs. פְּרוּשָׂה Ho 5^{1}; pl. פְּרֻשׂוֹת 1 K 8^{54};—**1.** *spread out* a garment (שִׂמְלָה) Ju 8^{25}, + לִפְנֵי pers. Dt 22^{17};—wings 32^{11} 1 K 6^{27} (rd. כַּנְפֵיהֶם 𝔊 Sta Kmp Kit Benz), + עַל Je 49^{22} (fig.), + אֶל 48^{40} 1 K 8^{7} = 2 Ch 5^{8} (עַל), + לְ Jb 39^{26}, לְמַעְלָה Ex 25^{20} 37^{9}; wings om. 1 Ch 28^{18} and perhaps 2 Ch 3^{13} (del. כַּנְפֵי Be); of ׳פ׳ עָלָיו אוֹרוֹ, Jb 36^{30}; *spread out* writing, לִפְנֵי ׳י pers. 2 K 19^{14} = Is 37^{14}, Ez 2^{10}; sail Is 33^{23}; fishing-net, מִכְמֶרֶת Is 19^{8} (עַל loc.); net (רֶשֶׁת) as snare, fig. Ho 5^{1} (עַל loc.), ψ 140^{6}, לְרַגְלַי La 1^{13}, c. עַל pers. Ho 7^{12} (of ׳י), Ez 12^{13} = 17^{20}, 19^{8} 32^{3}, עַל־פְּעָמָיו Pr 29^{5}; ׳פ׳ כַּפַּיִם in prayer, + אֶל Ex 9$^{29.33}$ (J), 1 K 8^{38} = 2 Ch 6^{29}, Ezr 9^{5} Jb 11^{13}, + לְ ψ 44^{21}, + הַשָּׁמַיִם 1 K 8^{22} = 2 Ch 6^{13} (הַשָּׁמָיְמָה), 1 K 8^{54}, no complem. 2 Ch 6^{12}; of almsgiving, כַּפָּהּ פָּרְשָׂה לֶעָנִי Pr 31^{20}; ׳פ׳ יָד, c. עַל rei, La 1^{10} of enemy's greed (si vera l., v. Bu); *spread out* = display וּכְסִיל יִפְרֹשׂ אִוֶּלֶת Pr 13^{16}. **2.** *spread* covering over 2 S 17^{19} (עַל־פְּנֵי + מָסָךְ rei), הַמִּכְבָּר over (עַל) face of another 2 K 8^{15}, כָּנָף *skirt*, עַל pers. Ru 3^{9} Ez 16^{8} (fig. of ׳י); בֶּגֶד c. עַל rei Nu 4$^{7.8.11.13}$, c. מִלְמַעְלָה v^{6}; כִּסּוּי c. עַל rei v^{14}; אֶת־הָאֹהֶל, c. עַל־הַמִּשְׁכָּן Ex 40^{19}; שַׁחַר פָּרֻשׂ עַל־הֶהָרִים Jo 2^{2}; of ׳י, פ׳ עָנָן לְמָסָךְ ψ 105^{39}.—Mi 3^{3} La 4^{4} v. פָּרַס. **Niph.** *Impf.* 3 mpl. יִפָּרֵשׂוּ Ez 17^{21} *they shall be scattered* לְכָל־רוּחַ; 34^{12} read prob. *Pt.* צֹאן נִפְרָשׁוֹת (for ־שׁוֹת, Hä Krae; on emend. of context v. esp. Toy Krae). **Pi.** *Pf.* 3 ms. consec. וּפֵרַשׂ Is 25^{11}, etc.; *Impf.* 3 ms. יְפָרֵשׂ v^{11}, 3 fs. תְּפָרֵשׂ Je 4^{31}; *Inf. cstr.* פָּרֵשׂ ψ 68^{15}, sf. פָּרִשְׂכֶם Is 1^{15};—**1.** *spread out*: **a.** c. acc. כַּפַּיִם in prayer Is 1^{15} Je 4^{31}, so c. יָדַיִם ψ 143^{6} (אֶל־י׳), and of ׳י entreating people Is 65^{2} (אֶל); פ׳ צִיּוֹן בְּיָדֶיהָ La 1^{17}. **b.** *spread out* hands as in swimming Is 25^{11}, and (יָדַיִם om.) v^{11}. **2.** = *scatter*, (?) subj. ׳י, c. acc. pers. Zc 2^{10} (𝔊 We Now קִבַּצְתִּי מִן, yet v. GASm); ψ 68^{15}, in doubtful connexion.

†[מִפְרָשׂ] **n.[m.] spreading out, thing spread**;—sf. מִפְרָשֵׂךְ Ez 27^{7} *thy spread* (canvas, as sail, cf. vb. Is 33^{23}); pl. cstr. מִפְרְשֵׂי עָב Jb 36^{29}, so perhaps 37^{16} (for מִפְלְשֵׂי). 4666

†פַּרְשֵׁז (Baer, ־שֵׁ van d. H. Gi), *Inf. abs.* **Pi'lēl** (Ges$^{§ 56}$) from פָּרַשׂ (si vera l.), פ׳ עָלָיו עֲנָנוֹ Jb 26^{9} *a spreading his cloud upon it* (but Bu Du al. read פָּרַשׂ, פֵּרַשׂ, or פָּרֹשׂ). 6576

†I. [פָּרַשׁ] **vb. make distinct, declare** (NH *separate oneself*, Pi. *separate, explain*, so Aram. פָּרֵשׁ, esp. Pa.; Syr. ܦܪܫ *separate, distinguish, explain*, cf. Mand., Nö$^{M\ 221}$);—**Qal** *Inf. cstr.* לִפְרֹשׁ לָהֶם עַל־פִּי ׳י Lv 24^{12} (P) *to declare distinctly to them.* **Niph.** *Pt.* נִפְרָשׁוֹת Ez 34^{12} read prob. ־שׂוֹת, v. פרשׂ. **Pu.** *Pf.* 3 ms. פֹּרַשׁ Nu 15^{34} (P) what should be done to him *had* not *been distinctly declared; Pt.* מְפֹרָשׁ Ne 8^{8} *made distinct* (cf. BAram Ezr 4^{18}), v. Be-Ry Kö$^{Einl.\ 99}$, > *interpreted*, Ke al., Berliner$^{T.Onk.\ ii.\ 74}$. 6567

†[פָּרָשָׁה] **n.f. exact statement**;—cstr. פָּרָשַׁת הַכֶּסֶף Est 4^{7}, פ׳ גְּדֻלַּת מָרְדֳּכַי 10^{2}. 6575

†II. [פָּרַשׁ] **vb. Hiph. pierce, sting** (?) (cf. As. *paruššu, staff* (which pierces); Aram. פרשׁא, ܦܪܫܐ (in Lexx) *ox-goad*);—*Impf.* 3 ms. יַפְרִשׁ Pr 23^{32} (כְּנָחָשׁ יִשָּׁךְ ‖ כְּצִפְעֹנִי), of wine. 6567

III. פרשׁ (√ of foll.; cf. Aram. פְּרַת Pa. (rare) *cause to break* or *burst forth* (a serpent its brood), פַּרְתָּא *dung;* Syr. ܦܪܬ Pa. *rip open*, ܦܪܬܐ = I. פֶּרֶשׁ; Ar. فَرَثَ IV. *rip open* stomach, *and scatter* contents (cf. VII), فَرْثٌ = I. פֶּרֶשׁ).

†I. פֶּרֶשׁ **n.[m.] fæcal matter found in intestines of victim**;—׳פ abs. Mal 2^{3}; cstr. v^{3}; sf. פִּרְשׁוֹ Ex 29^{14} Lv 4^{11} 8^{17}; פִּרְשָׁהּ Nu 19^{5}; פִּרְשָׁם Lv 16^{27} (all P). 6569

†II. פֶּרֶשׁ **n.pr.m.** Manassite 1 Ch 7^{16}, A 𝔊L Φαρες. 6570

IV. פרשׁ (√ of foll.; mng. dub.; against Lag$^{BN\ 50}$ (*horse*, one that *breaks* the ground, Ar. فَرَسٌ) v. Frä^{94}, cf. also Nö$^{ZMG\ xl\ (1886),\ 737}$).

6571 †II. [פָּרָשׁ] **n.[m.]** **horse, steed** (less common synon. of סוּס (> explained away by Schwally[ZAW viii (1888). 191]); Ar. فَرَسٌ *horse, mare* (oft.), so Eth. ፈረስ:, cf. Sab. פרס *horse*, Mordtm[Him. Inschr. 70]);—pl. פָּרָשִׁים (erron. for *פְּרָשִׁים Kö[ii. 1. 89]) Ez 27[14]+, sf. פָּרָשָׁיו Is 28[28] 1 S 8[11];—*steeds* Ez 27[14] (+ סוּסִים, פְּרָדִים), from Togarmah; sim. of swiftness Jo 2[4] (‖ סוּסִים); prob. also Is 28[28] Je 46[4] (‖ סוּסִים, cf. Gf Gie), and perhaps וְשָׂם לוֹ בְּמֶרְכַּבְתּוֹ וּבְפָרָשָׁיו וְרָצוּ וגו׳ 1 S 8[11] (kg.subj.).

6571 †III. פָּרָשׁ **n.m.**[Na 3, 3] **horseman** (i.e. *parrâš*, cf. Ges[§ 84 b b]; Ar. فَارِسٌ; Eth. ፈረስ:; Aram. פָּרָשׁ, ܦܳܪܫܳܐ);—abs. פ׳ Na 3[3] Je 4[29], also פָּרָשׁ Ez 26[10] (as if cstr. Kö[Synt. § 337 s]); pl. פָּרָשִׁים Gn 50[9]+; sf. פָּרָשָׁיו Ex 14[9]+;—*horseman*, usu. pl., esp. + רֶכֶב *chariotry*: Egyptian Gn 50[9] (J), Jos 24[6] (E), Ex 14[9.17.18.23.26.28] (all P), 15[19] (song), Is 31[1] 2 K 18[24] = Is 36[9], 2 Ch 12[3] cf. 16[8]; Philistine 1 S 13[5] 2 S 1[6] (del. בַּעֲלֵי 𝔊 We Dr Bu HPS); Aramæan 2 S 10[18] (but read prob. אִישׁ, cf. ‖ 1 Ch 19[18], We Dr al.), and (+ אִישׁ רַגְלִי) 2 S 8[4] = 1 Ch 18[4], cf. 1 Ch 19[6]; also עַל־סוּס וּפָרָשִׁים 1 K 20[20] (si vera l.); Isr., of Adonijah 1 K 1[5] (+ רֶכֶב, חֲמִשִּׁים אִישׁ רָצִים); Solomon + רֶכֶב 9[19.22] 10[26.26] = 2 Ch 8[6.9] 1[14.14], prob. also 1 K 5[6] (+ סוּסִים לְמֶרְכָּבוֹ) = 2 Ch 9[25] (+ סוּסִים וּמֶרְכָּבוֹת); Jehoahaz 2 K 13[7] (+ רַגְלִי, רֶכֶב); fig. of Elijah 2 K 2[12], of Elisha 13[14]; + סוּסִים Ho 1[7]; Assyrian Is 22[6.7] (+ רֶכֶב), cf. Na 3[3], פ׳ רֹכְבֵי סוּסִים Ez 23[6.12]; Babylonian Hb 1[8.8] Je 4[29] (+ רֹמֵה קֶשֶׁת), Ez 26[7] (+ סוּס, רֶכֶב), v[10] (+ גַלְגַּל וָרֶכֶב), Scythian (Gog) 38[4] (+ סוּסִים); Persian Is 21[7.9] (צֶמֶד פ׳), Ne 2[9] Ezr 8[22]; of king of north Dn 11[40] (+ רֶכֶב).

6572 †פַּרְשֶׁגֶן **n.m.** **copy** (loan-word from Persian through Aram., v. BAram.);—cstr. פ׳ הַנִּשְׁתְּוָן Ezr 7[11], cf. פַּתְשֶׁגֶן.

6574 †פַּרְשְׁדֹנָה **n.[m.]** only וַיֵּצֵא הַפ׳ Ju 3[22], read perh. פֶּרֶשׁ *fæces* (𝔙 𝔗 Nö[Untersuch. 180] Bu GFM).

6576 פַּרְשֵׁז v. פַּרְשֵׁז sub פרשׁ. p. 832

6577 †פַּרְשַׁנְדָּתָא **n.pr.m.** a son of Haman Est 9[7], Φαρσαν και Νεσταιν, Φαρσανεσταν, etc.

6578 †פְּרָת **n.pr. flum.** **Euphrates**, Ευφρατης (As. *Purattu* Dl[Pa 169 ff.], whence OPers. *Ufrâtu*, Spieg[APK 211]);—the greatest river of W. Asia; פ׳ Gn 2[14], נְהַר פ׳ 15[18] (both secondary phrases in J), נְהַר פ׳ also 2 S 8[3] (Qr, v. נָהָר), Je 46[2.6.10] Dt 1[7] 11[24] Jos 1[4] (D), 2 K 23[29] 24[7] 1 Ch 5[9] 18[3]; נהר om. Je 13[4.5.6.7] (where Ew Hi Marti, after Schick[ZPV iii. 11], think of some other פְּרָת, but Gf Gie and most defend *Euphrates*), 51[63] 2 Ch 35[20] (cf. Gn 2[14] supr.); name not certainly attested before D Je; on earlier הַנָּהָר for this river v. נ׳.

פְּרָת Gn 42[22] v. [פָּרָה]. p. 826 6509

†פַּרְתְּמִים **n.m.pl.** **nobles** (loan-word from 6579
OPers. *fratama*, *first*, Spieg[APK 232], cf. Skr. *prathama*; Lag[Arm. Stud. § 2289]);—הַפ׳ Est 1[3] 6[9] Dn 1[3].

פָּשָׂה[21] **vb.** **spread**, intrans. (NH פָּסָה *id.*; 6581
Ar. فَشَا (فشو) *be divulged, spread, be extensive*);—**Qal** *Pf.* 3 ms. פ׳ Lv 13[5]+, 3 fs. פָּשְׂתָה v[8], פָּשָׂתָה v[23]; *Impf.* 3 ms. יִפְשֶׂה v[35], 3 fs. תִּפְשֶׂה v[7]+; *Inf. abs.* פָּשֹׂה v[7]+;—only Lv 13, 14, of leprosy and like eruptions: c. בָּעוֹר, בַּבֶּגֶד, etc., Lv 13[5]+7 t. 13, 14[39.44.48] + בָּעוֹר (תִּפ׳) פָּשֹׂה יִפְשֶׂה 13[7.22.27.35]; abs. v[23.32.55].

†[פָּשַׂע] **vb.** **step, march** (NH פָּסַע; 6585
Aram. פְּסַע, ܦܣܰܥ);—**Qal** *Impf.* 1 s. אֶפְשְׂעָה (Ges[§ 10h]) Is 27[4], c. בְּ *against*.

†פֶּשַׂע **n.[m.]** **step**; כְּפ׳ בֵּינִי וּבֵין הַמָּוֶת 1 S 20[3]. 6587

†מִפְשָׂעָה **n.f.** **stepping-region** of body, 4667
hip or **buttock**; עַד־הַמּ׳ 1 Ch 19[4] (= שְׁתוֹתֵיהֶם ‖ 2 S 10[4]).

†[פָּשַׂק] **vb.** **part, open wide** (NH פָּסַק, 6589
Aram. פְּסַק, ܦܣܰܩ, all *cut, sever, cleave*);—**Qal** *Pt.* פֹּשֵׂק שְׂפָתָיו Pr 13[3] i.e. one talkative. **Pi.** *Impf.* 2 fs. וַתְּפַשְּׂקִי אֶת־רַגְלַיִךְ Ez 16[25] (c. לְ pers.; sensu obsc.).

†פַּשׁ **n.[m.]** Jb 35[15] si vera l. from √פשׁשׁ 6580
(cf. Ar. فَسِيسٌ *weak* in mind or body, فَسْفَاسٌ *very stupid*);—i.e. **folly**; but read פֶּשַׁע (𝔊 Theod Symm 𝔙 Di Bae[Kau] Du).

†[פָּשַׁח] **vb. Pi.** **tear in pieces** (NH פָּשַׁח; 6582
Aram. פְּשַׁח 1 S 15[33] (Agag), ܦܫܰܚ, ܦܰܫܰܚ);—*Impf.* 3 ms. sf. וַיְפַשְּׁחֵנִי La 3[11] (of lion, in fig.).

†פַּשְׁחוּר **n.pr.m.** Πασχωρ, Φα(δα)σσουρ, 6583
etc.: **1.** Je 20[1.2.3.3.6]. **2.** 21[1] 38[1b] Ne 11[12], cf. 1 Ch 9[12]. **3.** Ne 10[4]. **4.** father of one Gedaliah Je 38[1a]. **5.** head of post-exil. family Ezr 2[38] = Ne 7[41], Ezr 10[22]. Cf. Mey[Entstehung 169 f.].

†פָּשַׁט **vb.** **strip off, make a dash, raid** 6584
(cf. As. *pašâṭu*, *expunge, obliterate*; NH פָּשַׁט, Aram. פְּשַׁט, ܦܫܰܛ, are *stretch out, extend, make plain*, so Ar. بَسَطَ);—**Qal** *Pf.* 3 ms. פ׳ Ho 7[1]+, 2 ms. וּפָשַׁטְתָּ Ju 9[33], etc.; *Impf.* 3 ms. וַיִּפְשֹׁט 1 S 19[24]; 3 mpl. יִפְשֹׁטוּ Ez 26[1], etc.; *Imv.* ms. פְּשֹׁטָה Is 32[11];

Pt. pl. פֹּשְׁטִים Ne 4^{17};—**1.** *strip off, put off*, one's garment (acc.) 1 S 19^{24} Ez 26^{16} 44^{19} Lv 6^{4} (opp. לָבַשׁ), 16^{23} (*id.*; both P), Ne 4^{17} Ct 5^{3}; acc. om. Is 32^{11}; of locusts Na 3^{16} *stripping off* (sheaths of wings, cf. Da Dr$^{Am. 85}$). **2.** *put off* (one's shelter), i.e. *make a dash* (from a sheltered place), c. אֶל Ju 20^{37}, abs. 9^{44}; esp. of marauding foray, Ho 7^{1}, c. עַל *against* Ju 9$^{33.44}$ 1 S 23^{27} 30^{14} (ins. עַל cf. 𝔊 We Dr al.), Jb 1^{17}, c. אֶל 1 S 27^{8} 30^{1}, c. בְּ 1 Ch 14$^{9.13}$ 2 Ch 25^{13} 28^{18}; in 1 S 27^{10} rd. אָן (for אַל־), We Dr al. **Pi.** *Inf. cstr.* לְפַשֵּׁט, c. acc. pers. 1 S 31^{8} *to strip the slain* = 1 Ch 10^{8}; abs. *only to strip* (sc. the slain) 2 S 23^{10} (ins. also ‖ 1 Ch 11^{13} Dr). **Hiph.** *Pf.* 3 ms. הִפְשִׁיט Jb 19^{9}; 3 mpl. sf. וְהִפְשִׁיטוּךְ Ez 23^{26}, etc.; *Impf.* 3 ms. וַיַּפְשֵׁט Nu 20^{28}; 1 s. sf. אַפְשִׁיטֶנָּה Ho 2^{5}; 2 mpl. תַּפְשִׁטוּן Mi 2^{8}, etc.; *Imv.* הַפְשֵׁט Nu 20^{26}; *Inf. cstr.* הַפְשִׁיט 2 Ch 29^{34}; *Pt.* pl. מַפְשִׁיטִים 35^{11};—**1.** *strip* one *of* garment (2 acc.) Gn 37^{23} (E), Nu 20$^{26.28}$ (opp. הִלְבִּישׁ), Ez 16^{39} 23^{26}; c. acc. pers. alone 1 Ch 10^{9}; Ho 2^{5} *strip* her (sf.) naked (עֲרֻמָּה). **2.** *strip off*, acc. כֵּלָיו 1 S 31^{9}, clothing Jb 22^{6}; c. acc. אֶדֶר + מִמּוּל Mi 2^{8}; c. acc. עוֹר + מֵעַל 3^{3}, cf. (acc. כְּבוֹדִי) Jb 19^{9}. **3.** *flay*, c. acc. הָעֹלָה Lv 1^{6} 2 Ch 29^{34}; acc. om. 35^{11}. **Hithp.** *Impf.* 3 ms. וַיִּתְפַּשֵּׁט 1 S 18^{4} *he stripped himself of* his garment (acc.).

6586 †פָּשַׁע **vb.** rebel, transgress (NH *id.*; Syr. [Syriac] is *be terrified*, [Syriac] *tepid, insipid*);—**Qal** *Pf.* 3 ms. פ׳ 2 K 3^{7}+, 2 fs. פָּשַׁעַתְּ Zp 3^{11}; פָּשָׁעַתְּ Je 3^{13}, etc.; *Impf.* יִפְשַׁע Pr 28^{21} + 8 t. Impf.; *Imv.* mpl. פִּשְׁעוּ Am 4^{4}; *Inf. abs.* פָּשֹׁעַ Is 59^{13}; cstr. פְּשֹׁעַ Am 4^{4} Ez 10^{13}; *Pt.* פֹּשֵׁעַ Is 48^{8}; פֹּשְׁעִים Is 1^{28}+, etc.;—**1.** *rebel, revolt*, of nations, c. בְּ *against*, 1 K 12^{19} 2 K 1^{1} 3$^{5.7}$ 2 Ch 10^{19}; abs. 2 K 8^{22}, מִתַּחַת יַד v$^{20.22}$ 2 Ch 21$^{8.10.10}$; פָּשְׁעוּ בִי Is 1^{2} (Isr. under fig. of י׳'s sons). **2.** *transgress* against God, abs. Is 1^{28} 46^{8} 48^{8} 53$^{12.12}$ Ho 14^{10} Am 4$^{4.4}$ La 3^{42} Dn 8^{23} ψ 37^{38} 51^{15}, *for* (עַל) *a bit of bread* Pr 28^{21}; בַּדָּבָר הַזֶּה Ezr 10^{13} *in this thing*; עַל תּוֹרָתִי פ׳ ב׳ Ho 8^{1}; elsewhere c. בְּ *against* God: Is 43^{27} 59^{13} 66^{24} Je 2$^{8.29}$ 3^{13} 33^{8} Ez 2^{3} 20^{38} Ho 7^{13}; פְּשָׁעִים אשר פ׳ ב 1 K 8^{50} Ez 18^{31}; עלילות אשר פ׳ ב Zp 3^{11}. **Niph.** *Pf.* 3 ms. אָח נִפְשָׁע (van d. H. *Pt.* נִפְשָׁע) *a brother* (who has been) *offended* Pr 18^{19}, but very dubious, cf. Toy.

6588 †פֶּשַׁע **n.m.**$^{ψ 19,14}$ transgression;—abs. פ׳ Ex 22^{8}+, פָּשַׁע Pr 10^{19}+; cstr. פֶּשַׁע Gn 50^{17}+; sf. פִּשְׁעִי Gn 31^{36} + 14 t. sfs.; pl. פְּשָׁעִים Pr 10^{12}; cstr. פִּשְׁעֵי Am 1^{3}+, etc.;—**1.** *transgression* against individuals Gn 31^{36} 50$^{17.17}$ Ex 22^{8} (E), 1 S 24^{12} 25^{28} Pr 10^{19} 17^{19} 28^{24} 29$^{6.16.22}$; פ׳ שְׂפָתַיִם 12^{13}; על כל־פשעים תְּכַסֶּה אַהֲבָה 10^{12}, cf. 17^{9} 19^{11} 28^{13}. **2.** of nation, against nation: Am 1$^{3.6.9.11.13}$ 2^{1}; of land Pr 28^{2}. Elsewh. **3.** against God: **a.** in gen., ‖ חטאת Is 58^{1} 59^{12} Mi 1$^{5.5.13}$ 3^{8} Am 5^{12}; ‖ עון Ez 21^{29} ψ 107^{17}; עשׂה פ׳ Ez 18$^{22.28}$; בְּיוֹם פ׳ 33^{12}; רַבּוּ פ׳ Is 59^{12} Jb 35^{6} Je 5^{6} (?); יֹסִיף על חטאתו פ׳ Jb 34^{37} *he addeth transgression unto his sin*; יַלְדֵי פ׳ Is 57^{4}; personified as evil spirit, נאם פשע ψ 36^{2}. **b.** as recognized by sinner; he knows it ψ 51^{5}, makes known concerning it to י׳ 32^{5}, does not cover it (כסה) Jb 31^{33}; turns from it Is 59^{20} Ez 18^{30}; casts it away from him Ez 18^{31}. **c.** God deals with it: by visiting it (פקד) Am 3^{14} ψ 89^{33}, dealing with one according to it, עשׂה כ Ez 39^{24}, making it known to sinner Jb 13^{23} 36^{9}; punishing in various ways: מִפּ׳ *because of* it Is 53$^{5.8}$; c. עַל, *acc. to* it Am 2$^{4.6}$ La 1$^{5.22}$; *for* it, c. ב Is 50^{1}; על פ׳ La 1^{14} *yoke of transgression*; personified, וַיְשַׁלְּחֵם בְּיַד פ׳ Jb 8^{4}; he does not grant forgiveness to it, לא נשׂא ל׳ Ex 23^{21} Jos 24^{19} (E). **d.** God forgives (נשׂא) it Ex 34^{7} Nu 14^{18} (J), Jb 7^{21}, cf. ψ 32^{1}; pardons (סלח) 1 K 8^{50}; passes over (עבר על, cf. Pr 19^{11}) Mi 7^{18}; removes (הרחיק) ψ 103^{12}; covers over (כפר) 65^{4};—cf. (of priest) וְכִפֶּר עַל־הַקֹּדֶשׁ מִפּ׳ Lv 16^{16}, and confession of פ׳ over (עַל) goat v^{21};—God blots out (מחה) Is 43^{25} 44^{22} ψ 51^{3}; וּפ׳ אַל־תִּזְכֹּר 25^{7}; delivers from, הציל מן 39^{9}.—Jb 35^{15} read פֶּשַׁע for פַּשׁ q. v. **4.** *guilt of transgression* (cf. עון **2**), בְּלִי פ׳ *without* (guilt of) transgression Jb 33^{9} 34^{6}; לא פ׳ ψ 59^{4}; כבד פ׳ עלינו Ez 33^{10}; עליה פ׳ Is 24^{20}; בְּרֹב פ׳ ψ 5^{11}; נקיתי מפ׳ 19^{14}; יִטַּמְּאוּ בְּכָל־פ׳ *defile themselves with all (the guilt of) their transgressions* Ez 14^{11} 37^{23}; חָתֻם בִּצְרוֹר פ׳ Jb 14^{17}. **5.** *punishment for transgression*, Dn 8$^{12.13}$ 9^{24}, cf. עון **3**. **6.** *offering for transgression*, האתן בכורי פשעי Mi 6^{7} *shall I give my first-born as an offering for my transgression* (cf. חטאת **4**).

†פֵּשֶׁר **n.[m.]** solution, interpretation 6592
(loan-word from Aram. פִּשְׁרָא);—cstr. פ׳ Ec 8^{1}.

†[פֵּשֶׁת] **n.[m.]** flax, linen (√dub.; NH 6593
פִּשְׁתָּן, Pun. Φοιστ; Löw$^{p. 233}$);—sf. פִּשְׁתִּי Ho 2$^{7.11}$; elsewhere pl. פִּשְׁתִּים Ju 15^{14}+, cstr. פִּשְׁתֵּי Jos 2^{6};—**1.** *flax*, after gathering, פִּשְׁתֵּי הָעֵץ Jos 2^{6} (JE, v. עֵץ **2 f**); inflammable Ju 15^{14} (sim.); as natural product (+ צֶמֶר) Ho 2$^{7.11}$; as material, פְּתִיל פ׳ Ez 40^{3}; of various garments Je 13^{1} Ez 44$^{17.18.18}$, + צֶמֶר Dt 22^{11} Lv 13$^{47.48.52.59}$ (P), cf. Pr 31^{13}; עֹבְדֵי פ׳ שְׂרִיקוֹת Is 19^{9} (v. [שָׂרִיק]).

6594 †פִּשְׁתָּה **n.f. flax**;—פ׳: **1.** growing Ex $9^{31.31}$ (J). **2.** =wick Is 42^{3} 43^{17} (in sim.).

6595 פַּת v. פתת. p. 837

6596 †[פֹּת] **n.[f.]** pl. הַפֹּתוֹת לְדַלְתוֹת הַבַּיִת 1 K 7^{50} i.e. prob. the *sockets* above and below, in which the door-pivots turned (performing office of mod. hinges); sg. sf. פָּתְהֵן Is 3^{17} (Ges ^{§91f}), prob., si vera l., *their secret parts, cardo femina* (so Thes and most); but read perh. חָרְפָּתְהֵן Bachm $^{SK. 1894, 650}$ Kit (in Di) Marti; > פַּאתְהֵן Sta $^{ZAW vi (1886), 336}$, cf. 𝔅 Di.

6612 פְּתָאִים v. I. פֶּתִי sub I. פתה. below

6597 פִּתְאֹם v. פֶּתַע. p. 837

6598 †[פַּת־בַּג] (read always [פַּתְבַּג]) **n.[m.] portion** (of food) for king, **delicacies** (Pers. loan-word, cf. Skr. *prati-bhâga*, Zend [*pati-baga*; whence] Gk. translit. *ποτί-βαζις*, Syr. ܦܰܬܒܰܓ; Gildem $^{ZKM iv. 213 f.}$ Lag $^{Ges. Abh. 73}$ Bev ^{Dn} Dr ^{Dn});—cstr. פַּת־בַּג הַמֶּלֶךְ Dn $1^{5.8.13.15}$, sf. פַּת־בָּגָם v^{16}, אֹכְלֵי פַת־בָּגוֹ 11^{26}.

6599 †פִּתְגָם **n.m. edict, decree** (Pers. loan-wd., OPers. *patigâma* (*patigam, come to, arrive*), NPers. *paigâm, message*; v. Gildem $^{ZKM iv. 214}$ Mey $^{Entstehung 23}$; Aram. פִּתְגָּמָא, ܦܶܬܓܳܡܳܐ, *word, command*, BAram. = BH);—cstr. פ׳ הַמֶּלֶךְ Est 1^{20}; c. genit. obj. פ׳ מַעֲשֵׂה הָרָעָה Ec 8^{11} (appar. f., cf. De; but Hi Albr $^{ZAW xvi (1896), 115}$ read נַעֲשֶׂה for נַעֲשָׂה).

6601 [פָּתָה] **vb. be spacious, wide, open** (Aram. פְּתָא *be spacious*, ܦܬܳܐ *be spacious, abundant*; cf. Ar. فَتُوَ, فَتِيَ *be youthful, in prime of life*, فَتًى *young man, one in prime of life* (development of various meanings from √ not wholly clear, cf. Nö $^{ZMG xl (1886), 735}$));—**Qal** *Pt.* פֹּתֶה Pr 20^{19} poss. *one open* as to lips, but v. פָּתָה denom. infr. **Hiph.** *Impf.* 3 ms. juss. יַפְתְּ א׳ לְיֶפֶת Gn 9^{27} *may God make wide for Japhet* (give him an extensive inheritance).—*Pf.* poss. Pr 24^{28} (reading וְהִפְתִּיתָ בִּשְׂפָתֶיךָ, *make wide with* (open wide) *thy lips*, for MT וַהֲפִתִּיתָ בִּשׂ׳, so SS; but cf. פָּתָה denom. **Pi.**).

6612 †פֶּתִי [for פֶּתִי Lag $^{BN 52}$ Ba $^{ZMG xlii (1888), 353; NB 320}$] **adj. simple,** poss. as **open-minded**;—פֶּתִי Pr 9^{4}+, פֶּתִי ψ 19^{8}+; pl. פְּתָאִים (Ges ^{§93x}) 116^{6}+6 t. Pr; פְּתָיִים 119^{130} Pr 22^{3}; פְּתָיִם $1^{22.32}$; —*simple*, as subst. concr.: open to the instruction of wisdom or folly, Pr $9^{4.16}$; believing every word 14^{15}; lacking עָרְמָה 1^{4} 8^{5} 19^{25}; needing בין ψ 119^{130}, חכמה 19^{8} Pr 21^{11}; in good sense, שׁמר פתאים י׳ ψ 116^{6} *'* *preserveth the simple-minded;* but usu. tendency to bad sense; love פתי פתאים Pr 1^{22}; inherit אִוֶּלֶת 14^{18}, are easily enticed, misled and go back 1^{32} 7^{7} 9^{6} 22^{3}=27^{12}; they need atonement Ez 45^{20} (‖ שׁגה).

†[פְּתִי] **n.f. simplicity** (i.e. lack of wisdom), 6612
עַד־מָתַי פְּתָיִם תְּאֵהֲבוּ־פֶתִי Pr 1^{22}.

†פְּתַיּוּת **n.f.** id. Pr 9^{13} (Toy conj. מְפַתָּה). 6615

†[פָּתָה] **vb. denom. be simple** (NH Pi. 6601
entice);—**Qal** *Impf.* 3 ms. יִפְתֶּה Dt 11^{16}; וַיִּפְתְּ Jb 31^{27}; *Pt.* פֹּתֶה Jb 5^{2} Pr 20^{19}; f. פּוֹתָה Ho 7^{11};— **1.** *be open-minded* (?), *simple* Jb 5^{2}; יוֹנָה פוֹתָה Ho 7^{11} *silly dove;* פֹּתֶה שְׂפָתָיו Pr 20^{19} *one foolish as to his lips* (most, *openeth wide his lips*). **2.** *be enticed, deceived* Dt 11^{16} Jb 31^{27}. **Niph.** *Pf.* 3 ms. נִפְתָּה Jb 31^{9}; *Impf.* 1 s. וָאֶפָּת Je 20^{7};— *be deceived* Je 20^{7}; c. עַל *enticed unto* Jb 31^{9}. **Piel** *Pf.* 2 ms. פִּתִּיתָ Pr 24^{28}; sf. פִּתִּיתַנִי Je 20^{7}; 1 s. פִּתֵּיתִי Ez 14^{9}; *Impf.* 3 ms. יְפַתֶּה Ex 22^{15}+, etc.; *Imv.* פַּתִּי Ju 14^{15} 16^{5}; *Inf. cstr.* sf. פַּתֹּתְךָ 2 S 3^{25}; *Pt.* sf. מְפַתֶּיהָ (Ges ^{§93ss}) Ho 2^{16};—**1.** *persuade*, woman Ho 2^{16} (fig., י׳ subj.), *seduce*, virgin Ex 22^{16}; *entice*, husband Ju 14^{15} 16^{5}; a man to sin Pr 1^{10} 16^{29}. **2.** *deceive*, 2 S 3^{25} Pr 24^{28} (yet cf. √**Hiph.** supr.); subj. י׳, obj. proph., Je 20^{7} Ez 14^{9}, cf. 1 K $22^{20.21.22}$=2 Ch $18^{19.20.21}$; obj. י׳, ψ 78^{36}. **Pual** *Impf.* 3 ms. יְפֻתֶּה: **1.** *be persuaded*, Pr 25^{15}. **2.** *be deceived*, Je 20^{10}; by י׳, Ez 14^{9}.

†יֶפֶת **n.pr.m.** third son of Noah, *Ιαφεθ*;— 3315
יֶפֶת: יַפְתְּ א׳ לְיֶפֶת Gn 9^{27} (J), 7^{13}, 10^{2} (P)=1 Ch 1^{4}, Gn 9^{23} 10^{21} (J); יָפֶת 9^{18} (J), 5^{32} 6^{10} 10^{1} (P), 1 Ch 1^{5}.

†פְּתוּאֵל **n.pr.m.** father of prophet Joel 6602
Jo 1^{1} (𝔊 *Βαθουηλ*, i. e. בְּתוּאֵל).

†פְּתוֹר **n.pr.loc.** home of Balaam;—c. ה 6604
loc. פְּתוֹרָה Nu 22^{5}, *Φαθουρα*, A *Βαθουρα*; פ׳ אֲרַם נַהֲרַיִם Dt 23^{5}, but om. פ׳ 𝔊;—cf. As. *Pitru* (on W. bank of upper Euphr.) Schr $^{KGF 220; COT Nu 22, 5}$ Dl $^{Pa 269}$ Dr $^{Hastings DB}$; Eg. *Pe-d-ru* WMM $^{As. u. Eur. 291}$.

[פְּתוֹת] v. פתת. p. 837 6626

†I. פָּתַח **vb. open** (NH *id.*; Ph. פתח; 6605
As. *pitû, patû*; Sab. פתח Os $^{ZMG xix (1865), 197}$; Ar. فَتَحَ; Eth. ፈተሐ:; Aram. פְּתַח, ܦܬܰܚ; Nab. Palm. פתח);—**Qal** *Pf.* 3 ms. פ׳ 2 K 15^{16}+, etc.; *Impf.* 3 ms. יִפְתַּח Ex 21^{33}+; 3 mpl. sf. יִפְתָּחוּם Ne 13^{19}, etc.; *Imv.* ms. פְּתַח 2 K 13^{17}+; fs. פִּתְחִי

Ct 5^{2}; mpl. פִּתְחוּ Jos 10^{22}+; *Inf. abs.* פָּתֹחַ Dt 15^{8}+; cstr. לִפְתֹּחַ Ez 21^{27}+; *Pt. act.* פֹּתֵחַ Ju 3^{25}+; *pass.* פָּתוּחַ Je 5^{16}+, etc.;—*open* sack, שַׂק, Gn 42^{27} (E), אַמְתַּחַת 43^{21} 44^{11} (J), skin-bottle (נֹאוד) Ju 4^{19}, hamper (תֵּבָה) Ex 2^{6} (E), pit (בּוֹר) 21^{33} (E; i.e. uncover it), mouth (פִּי) of cave Jos 10^{22} (JE), grave Ez $37^{12.13}$ (to bring forth dead), cf. (in fig.) Je 5^{16} ψ 5^{10}; כְּלִי פָּתוּחַ Nu 19^{15} (P) *open vessel;* door (דֶּלֶת; sts. opp. סָגַר) Ju 3^{25} + v^{25} (obj. om.), 19^{27} 1 S 3^{15} 2 K $9^{3.10}$ 2 Ch 29^{3} Jb 31^{32} (c. לְ pers.); fig. of Leb. Zc 11^{1}; דַּלְתֵי שָׁמַיִם ψ 78^{23} (of י׳, sending rain); ד׳ = city-gates Ne 13^{19} Is 45^{1} (‖ שְׁעָרִים; י׳ subj., c. לְפָנָיו); ד׳ om. Ct $5^{2.5.6}$; gate (שַׁעַר), of land Na 3^{13} (Inf. abs. + Impf. **Niph.** q.v.), cf. Ez 25^{9}, שַׁעַר of temple (-court) Ez 46^{12} (c. לְ pers.), ψ 118^{19} (*id.*), city Is 26^{2}, obj. om. Dt 20^{11} 2 K 15^{16}; window, חַלּוֹן, 2 K $13^{17.17}$, אֲרֻבּוֹת הַשָּׁמַיִם (by י׳ sending rain) Gn 8^{6} (J), Mal 3^{10}; city Je 13^{19}, עִיר פְּתוּחָה Jos 8^{17} (JE); abs. פ׳ וְלֹא סגר Is $22^{22.22}$;—14^{17} is dubious, Gr Perles[Anal. 28. 42] Kit (in Di) read לַאֲסִירָיו לֹא־פ׳; > Bu Che Marti אֲסִירָיו לֹא פּתח אִישׁ בֵּית־הַכֶּלֶא לְבֵיתוֹ; storehouse, armoury Gn 41^{56} Je 50^{25} (of י׳), Je 50^{26} (for destruction), fig. of sky, for rain Dt 28^{12} (c. לְ pers.; of י׳), cf. *open* בַּר, expose for sale, Am 8^{5}; *open* womb, i.e. grant offspring Gn 29^{31} 30^{22} (J); *open* mouth (פֶּה) to cry, speak Ez 21^{27} Jb 3^{1} Dn 10^{16}, hence = speak Is $53^{7.7}$ Jb 33^{2} ψ 39^{10} 78^{2} (בְּמָשָׁל), 109^{2} (c. עַל pers.), Pr 24^{7} 31^{8} (c. לְ pers.), v$^{9.26}$ (בְּחָכְמָה); ψ 49^{5} either *utter, declare, propound* riddle, or *open up, expound;* have power of speech ψ 38^{14}; of י׳ giving power of (prophetic) speech Ez 3^{27} 33^{22}, giving speech to ass Nu 22^{28} (J); *open* mouth, to eat Ez 3^{2}, of earth, to swallow up, Nu 16^{32} 26^{10}, cf. (פֶּה om.) ψ 106^{17}; *open* lips, to speak Jb 11^{5} (c. עִם pers.), 32^{20} (Gi v^{21}); of י׳ opening man's lips ψ 51^{17}, man's ear Is 50^{5} (As. *uznâ puttû*); of eyes only pt. pass., c. אֶל 1 K 8^{29} = 2 Ch 6^{20}, 1 K 8^{52} Ne 1^{6}, c. לְ 2 Ch 6^{40} (by zeugma), 7^{15} (all of י׳'s favour); *open* hand, in giving Dt $15^{8.11}$ (c. לְ pers., + inf. abs.), of י׳ ψ 104^{28} 145^{16}; book Ne $8^{5.5}$, letter 6^{5}; *open* river (channel) Is 41^{18} (of י׳), rock, letting out water, ψ 105^{41} (*id.*); *open* sword, = draw it Ez 21^{33} ψ 37^{14}; of root שָׁרְשִׁי פָתוּחַ אֱלֵי־מָיִם Jb 29^{19}, i.e. with no obstacle intervening.—תִּפְתַּח אֶרֶץ Is 45^{8} is dub.; verb not elsewhere intrans.; Du Che[Hpt] Marti prop. רַחֲמָה as obj.; Gr Kit (in Di) read תִּפָּתַח. **Niph.** *Pf.* 3 ms. נִפְתַּח Is 5^{27}, etc.; *Impf.* 3 ms. יִפָּתַח Ez 24^{27}, יִפָּתֵחַ 44^{2}+, etc.; *Inf. cstr.* הִפָּתֵחַ Is 51^{14}; *Pt.* נִפְתָּח Zc 13^{1};—*be opened,* of girdle Is 5^{27} (i.e. loosened), cf. of captive 51^{14}, and, of calamity, Je 1^{14} *be let loose* (c. עַל pers.); gates Na 2^{7} 3^{13} (of land, *thrown open* to (לְ) enemy), Ez 44^{2} $46^{1.1}$ Ne 7^{3}; impers. of man shut in by God Jb 12^{14}; of windows of heaven Gn 7^{11} (P), cf. Is 24^{18} (of future destruction); the heavens themselves Ez 1^{1} (for visions); fountain Zc 13^{1}; wine(-skin, c. neg.) Jb 32^{19}; mouth, in speech 24^{27} 33^{22}; ears Is 35^{5}. **Pi.** *Pf.* 3 ms. פִּתַּח Jb 30^{11}+, פִּתֵּחַ 12^{18}+, etc.; *Impf.* 3 ms. יְפַתַּח Is 28^{24}, 1 s. אֲפַתֵּחַ Is 45^{1}, etc.; *Inf. abs.* פַּתֵּחַ Is 58^{6}; cstr., *id.* ψ 102^{21}; *Pt.* מְפַתֵּחַ 1 K 20^{11};—*loose:* **1.** *free,* i.e. ungird, camels Gn 24^{32} (J): loins of kings Is 45^{1} (i.e. disarm them); *set free,* c. sf. pers. ψ 105^{20}, Je 40^{4} (c. מִן); c. acc. בְּנֵי תְמוּתָה ψ 102^{21}. **2.** *loosen* (and remove) sack-cloth Is 20^{2} (c. מֵעַל), ψ 30^{12}; armour 1 K 20^{11} (obj. om.; opp. חָגַר); bonds Jb 12^{18} ψ 116^{16}, cf. Is 58^{6} Jb 39^{5}; cord 30^{11} 38^{31}; *loosen* ground Is 28^{24} (in tillage; cf. Vogelst[Landwirthschaft 38], As. *puttû*). **3.** *open* gates Is 60^{11}, doors Jb 41^{6} (fig. of crocodile's jaws); ear Is 48^{8} (rd. prob. either פִּתַּחְתִּי, פָּתַחְתִּי [𝔊 Du Marti], or נִפְתְּחָה [Gr Che Kit in Di]; buds Ct 7^{13} (of blossom; obj. om.; or intrans., as sts. Ar. فَتَّحَ, v. Dozy). **Hithp.** *Imv.* mpl. התפתחו Is 52^{2} Kt < Qr fs. הִתְפַּתְּחִי (so 𝔊; of personif. Jerus.) *loosen thee* (Ges[§ 54 f]) *the fetters of thy neck.*

פֶּ֫תַח $_{164}$ **n.m.**[Ez 8, 8] (**f.** 2 S 17^{9} but We reads 6607
אַחַד for אַחַת, and so Albr[ZAW xvi (1896), 86]) **opening, doorway, entrance**;—abs. פ׳ Gn 4^{7}+, פָּ֑תַח 19^{11}+, הַפֶּ֫תְחָה v^{6}; cstr. פֶּתַח 18^{1}+; sf. פִּתְחוֹ Pr 17^{19}, פִּתְחָהּ Ez 40^{38}; pl. פְּתָחִים 1 K 7^{5} Pr 8^{3}; cstr. פִּתְחֵי ψ 24^{7}+; sf. פְּתָחָ֑י Pr 8^{34}, etc.;—*doorway* of nomad's tent, פ׳ הָאֹהֶל Gn $18^{1.2.10}$ (J), Ex $33^{8.10}$ (E), Nu 11^{10} 16^{27} (JE), Ju 4^{20}, cf. (without הָאֹהֶל) Gn 4^{7} (in fig.), Jb $31^{9.34}$; of sacred tent, פ׳ הָאֹהֶל Ex $33^{9.10}$ Nu 12^{5} (E), 26^{36} 36^{37} 39^{38} (P), Dt 31^{15}, usu. (P) פ׳ אֹהֶל מוֹעֵד Ex 29^{4} + 6 t. Ex + $40^{6.29}$ (פ׳ מִשְׁכַּן אֹהֶל מ׳), Lv 1^{3} + 22 t. Lv, Nu 3^{25} + 11 t. Nu, Jos 19^{51} 1 S 2^{22}, cf. 1 Ch 9^{21}; פ׳ הַמִּשְׁכָּן Ex 35^{15}, cf. $40^{5.28}$ (all P); of court Nu 3^{26} cf. 4^{26} and (of temple) Ez 8^{7}; *doorway* of (private) house Gn $19^{6.11.11}$ + 22 t., cf. Ct 7^{14}; in Pr 17^{19} Frankenb Toy rd. פִּיו for פִּתְחוֹ; of temple 1 K 6^{33} Ez 8^{16}, so פ׳ הַבַּיִת Ez 47^{1} 2 Ch 4^{22}; פ׳ הַדְּבִיר 1 K 6^{31}, פ׳ הַצֵּלָע v^{8} Ez 41^{11} cf. v$^{11.11}$; pl. 1 K 7^{5}; various doorways in Ezek.'s temple Ez $40^{13.13}$ + 13 t. 40–42 (v. also infr.); doorway of ark Gn 6^{16} (P); of tower Ju 9^{52}; in wall Ez 8^{8}; *opening* (mouth) of cave 1 K 19^{13}; פ׳ הַשַּׁעַר *opening,* i.e.

doorway, of gate Ez 40^{11}; of city פ׳ שַׁעַר הָעִיר, i.e. the outer aperture of the gate Jos 8^{29} 20^{4} Ju 9$^{35.44}$ Je 1^{15} (pl.), cf. 19^{2} 1 K 22^{10}=2 Ch 18^{9}, 2 K 23^{8} Pr 1^{21}; so פ׳ הַשַּׁעַר Ju 9^{40} 2 S 10^{8} 11^{23} 2 K 7^{3} 10^{8}, and (of farm or village) Ju 18$^{16.17}$; so פ׳ הָעִיר 1 K 17^{20} 1 Ch 19^{6} (=2 S 10^{8} supr.), cf. Gn 38^{14}; pl. of city gates themselves (poet.) Is 3^{26} (personif.), פִּתְחֵי עוֹלָם ψ 24$^{7.9}$ פ׳ נְדִיבִים 13^{2}; (|| שְׁעָרִים); cf. fig. שְׁמֹר פִּתְחֵי־פִיךָ Mi 7^{5}; also פ׳ שַׁעַר בֵּית י׳ Je 36^{10} Ez 8^{14} 10^{19} cf. 8^{3} 11^{1} 40^{4} 46^{3}, פ׳ שׁ׳ י׳ Je 26^{10}; פְּתָחֶיהָ Mi 5^{6} of *entrances* to a country; fig. פ׳ תִּקְוָה Ho 2^{17} *doorway of hope.*

6608 †פֵּתַח **n.m. opening, unfolding**;—cstr. פ׳ דְּבָרֶיךָ יָאִיר ψ 119^{130}, so 𝔊 and most; >Symm Jer Bae פֶּתַח (=*thy words as a doorway*).

6610 †פִּתְחוֹן **n.[m.] opening**;—cstr. פִּתְחוֹן פֶּה *opening of mouth* in speech or song Ez 16^{63} 29^{21}.

6609 †[פְּתִיחָה] **n.[f.] drawn sword**;—pl. פְּתִחוֹת ψ 55^{22} (fig. of words; cf. Ez 21^{33} ψ 37^{14}).

6611 †פְּתַחְיָה **n.pr.m. 1.** priest 1 Ch 24^{16}, Εζεκηλ, Φεθεια, etc. **2.** Levite Ezr 10^{23} Ne 9^{5}, Φαθαια, Φεθεια(ς), etc. **3.** Judahite Ne 11^{24}, Παθαια, Φαθαια.

3316 †יִפְתָּח **n.pr. 1. m. Jephthah**, Ιεφθαε (*he* [God] *openeth*);—Ju 11$^{1.1}$+26 t. 11, 12, 1 S 12^{11}. **2. loc.** in the שְׁפֵלָה Jos 15^{43} (P), A 𝔊L Ιεφθα.

3317 †יִפְתַּח־אֵל **n.pr.loc.** (*God openeth*; cf. Sab. n.pr.m. יפתחאל Hal^{148,1});—in גֵּי יִפ׳ (Γαιφαηλ, Γαι και Φθαιηλ, A 𝔊L Γαι (Ι)εφθαηλ), valley betw. Zebulun and Asher Jos 19$^{14.27}$ (P); prob. near *Jêfât* (*Jotapata*), and perhaps upper part of *Wady ʿAbellîn*, v. Buhl$^{Geogr. 109, 223}$.

4669 †[מִפְתָּח] **n.[m.] opening, utterance**;—cstr. מִפְתַּח שְׂפָתַי Pr 8^{6} i.e. that with which my lips open.

4668 †מַפְתֵּחַ **n.m. key** (*opening instrument*);—מ׳ abs. Ju 3^{25} 1 Ch 9^{27}; cstr. Is 22^{22} (fig.).

5318 †נֶפְתּוֹחַ **n.pr.loc.** Μαφθω, Ναφθω, in מֵי נ׳ Jos 15^{9} 18^{15} (P), on border of Judah and Benj.; usu. identif. with spring *Liftâ*, near Jerus. to the NW., v. Buhl$^{Geogr. 101}$. נַפְתֻּחִים v. p. 661.

6612, 6615 פְּתָיוּת, פְּתִי v. sub פתה. p. 834

6605 †II. [פָּתַח] **vb. Pi. engrave** (NH Pi. *id.*, פִּתּוּחַ=BH, and so 𝔗; As. *patâḫu, bore, penetrate;* cf. perh. Ar. فَتْخَةٌ, فَتَخَةٌ *ring* (cf. Frä^{252}));—*Pf.* 3 ms. פִּתַּח 2 Ch 3^{7}, etc.; *Impf.* 3 ms. וַיְפַתַּח 1 K 7^{36}; 2 ms. תְּפַתַּח Ex 28^{11}; *Inf. cstr.* לְפַתֵּחַ 2 Ch 2$^{6.13}$; *Pt.* מְפַתֵּחַ Zc 3^{9};—*engrave*, c. acc. + עַל, on metal 1 K 7^{36} 2 Ch 3^{7} Ex 28^{36} (acc. cogn. פִּתּוּחֵי חוֹתָם), on stone v^{9}; c. acc. אֶבֶן + acc. cogn. v^{11} (all P); c. acc. cogn. only, Zc 3^{9} (on stone), and, in gen., 2 Ch 2$^{6.13}$. **Pu.** *Pt.* fpl. מְפֻתָּחֹת פִּתּוּחֵי חוֹתָם Ex 39^{9} (P) *stones engraved with the engravings of a signet.*

6603 †פִּתּוּחַ **n.m. engraving**;—abs. פ׳ 2 Ch 2^{13}; sf. פִּתֻּחָהּ Zc 3^{9}; elsewhere pl. פִּתּוּחִים 2 Ch 2^{6}, etc.;—on (wood overlaid with) metal, פִּתּוּחֵי מִקְלְעוֹת כְּרוּבִים 1 K 6^{29} (see v$^{21.22}$), in temple, so ψ 74^{6}; on stone Zc 3^{9}, esp. פִּתּוּחֵי חֹתָם Ex 28$^{11.21.36}$ 39$^{6.14.30}$; in gen. 2 Ch 2$^{6.13}$.

6614 †פְּתִיגִיל **n.[m.] rich robe**(?) (prob. foreign word);—פ׳ abs. Is 3^{24}, 𝔊 χιτὼν μεσοπόρφυρος, 𝔙 *fascia pectoralis.*

6617 †[פָּתַל] **vb. twist** (NH Pi. and deriv.; Ar. فَتَلَ; Eth. ፈተለ:; Aram. פְּתַל, chiefly deriv., in fig. senses; Syr. ܦܬܠ);—**Niph.** *Pf.* 1 s. נִפְתַּלְתִּי עִם Gn 30^{8} *I have wrestled* (lit. twisted myself) *with; Pt.* עֲצַת נִפְתָּלִים Jb 5^{13} *the plan of the tortuous;* נִפְתָּל וְעִקֵּשׁ Pr 8^{8} anything *tortuous and twisted.* **Hithp.** *Impf.* 2 ms. עִם־עִקֵּשׁ תִּתְפַּתָּל ψ 18^{27} *with the twisted thou dost deal tortuously*=2 S 22^{27} (so rd. for imposs. תִּתַּפָּל).

6616 †פְּתִיל **n.m.**$^{Ju 16, 9}$ **cord, thread** (*twisted*);—abs. פ׳ Nu 19^{15}; cstr. פְּתִיל Ju 16^{9}+; sf. פְּתִילֶךָ Gn 38^{18}; pl. פְּתִילִים v^{25}, פְּתִילִם Ex 39^{3};—*cord* (from which seal was hung) Gn 38$^{18.25}$ (J), פ׳ נְעֹרֶת Ju 16^{9} (sim.), פ׳ פִּשְׁתִּים Ez 40^{3} (as measuring line); פ׳ תְּכֵלֶת, for fastening, Ex 28$^{28.37}$ 39$^{21.31}$ Nu 15^{38}, cf. פָּתִיל alone 19^{15} (perh. gloss, v. Di); *threads* (of gold) in ephod Ex 39^{3} (all P).

6618 †פְּתַלְתֹּל **adj. tortuous**;—דּוֹר עִקֵּשׁ וּפ׳ Dt 32^{5}.

5319 †[נַפְתּוּלִים] **n.[m.] pl. wrestlings** (cf. √ **Niph.** *Pf.*);—cstr. נַפְתּוּלֵי א׳ Gn 30^{8} *wrestlings of God,* i.e. mighty wrestlings.

5321 נַפְתָּלִי$_{51}$ **n.pr.m. et trib. Naphtali**, Νεφθαλει(μ), etc. (interpr. as *my wrestling* Gn 30^{8}; perhaps orig. *crafty, cunning one*);—**1.** second son of Jacob and Bilhah Gn 30^{8} (J), 35^{25} 46^{24} (P), 1 Ch 2^{2}, cf. Gn 49^{21} (poem). **2.** as a tribe of Isr.: **a.** Ju 1^{33} 4^{10} 5^{18} Dt 33$^{23.23}$+; so (Hex, only P) בְּנֵי נ׳ Ju 4^{6} Nu 1^{42}+6 t., מַטֵּה נ׳ Nu 2^{29} 1 K 7^{14} +5 t., מַטֵּה בְנֵי נ׳ Nu 10^{27} 34^{28} Jos 19^{39}; שַׁעַר נ׳

Ez 48[34] (in now Jerus.); אֶרֶץ נ׳ 1 K 15[20] 2 K 15[29], cf. Is 8[23]; גְּבוּל נ׳ Ju 4[6]; הַר נ׳ Jos 20[7]; קֶדֶשׁ נ׳ Ez 48[4], יָמָּה נ׳ v[3]; עָרֵי נ׳ 2 Ch 16[4]. **b.** as territorial name Dt 34[2] (JE) 1 K 4[15] 1 Ch 12[41] (van d. H. v[40]), 2 Ch 34[6]; Ju 6[35] 7[23] might be **a** or **b**.

6619 †פִּתֹם **n.pr.loc.** Pithom, Π(ε)ιθω, A Πιθωμ (Egypt. *Patum, Per-Atum, house of* (god) *Atum*) one of the עָרֵי מִסְכְּנוֹת built by Isr. for Pharaoh Ex 1[11]; identif. by Naville with *Tel el-Maskhûta*, near E. end of Wady Tumilat, Naville[Pithom, 1885] Di-Ry[ad loc.] Di[SBAk, 1885, 889 ff.] Bäd[Egypt (4), 159].

פתן (√ of foll.; mng. dub.; Hilpr[Bab. Exped. Univ. Pennsylv. ix (1898), 53], cp. As. *patânu*, '*protect*,' whence two foll., 'serpent' as *protector*, and 'threshold' as *asylum*; plausible, but exact meaning of *patânu* still uncertain).

6620 †פֶּתֶן **n.m.**[ψ 68, 5] a venomous serpent, perh. **cobra** (פתן Ecclus 39[30]; Aram. פִּתְנָא, ܦܬܢܐ, whence perh. Ar. بَثَن);—only poet.: pl. רֹאשׁ פְּתָנִים Dt 32[33] (|| חֲמַת תַּנִּינִם), Jb 20[16], מְרוֹרַת פ׳ v[14]; sg. פֶּתֶן ψ 91[13] (|| תַּנִּין), פ׳ חֵרֵשׁ 58[5], חֻר פֶּתֶן Is 11[8].

4670 †מִפְתָּן **n.[m.]** threshold (cf. NH פָּתִין *cross-beam*; ? Ar. فَيْتَن *carpenter*);—abs. מ׳ 1 S 5[4] Zp 1[9]; cstr. מִפְתַּן דָּגוֹן 1 S 5[5], מ׳ הַבַּיִת Ez 9[3] 10[4.18] 47[1], מ׳ הַשַּׁעַר 46[2].

6621 †פֶּתַע **subst.** suddenness (√ unknown: cf. As. *ina pitti, ina pittimma, in suddenness, instantly*, Dl[HWB 553]):—Nu 35[22] . . . וְאִם־בְּפֶתַע הֲדָפוֹ if he have thrust him *in suddenness*, before he is aware what he has done (i.e. accidentally); + פִּתְאֹם Nu 6[9], וכי ימות מת עליו בפתע פתאם i.e. very suddenly; לְפֶתַע *according to* (לְ, p. 516b) *suddenness*, Is 29[5] והיה לפתע פתאם = *at an instant*, suddenly, 30[13] אשׁר פתאם לפתע יבוא שִׁבְרָהּ. As adv. acc., *suddenly*, Pr 6[15] (= 29[1]) פֶּתַע יִשָּׁבֵר, Hb 2[7].

6597 †פִּתְאֹם, once ψ 64[8] (v. Baer) פִּתְאוֹם **subst.** suddenness, usu. as **adv. acc. suddenly** (from פֶּתַע, with the term. ם- (cf. שִׁלְשֹׁם), and with ע weakened to א: Sta[§ 295] Kö[ii. 255 f.] Ba[NB § 216 b]);—Nu 12[4] ויאמר י׳ פ׳ אל־משׁה, Jos 10[9] 11[7]; esp. of calamity, invasion, etc., coming *suddenly*, Is 47[11] 48[3] Je 4[20] פ׳ שֻׁדְּדוּ אֹהָלַי, 6[26] 15[8] 18[22] 51[8] ψ 64[5] פ׳ יֹרֻהוּ וְלֹא יִירָאוּ, v[8] Jb 5[3] 9[23] Ec 9[12] Pr 6[15] 24[22]; also 7[22] Mal 3[1]; thrice with פֶּתַע (q.v.). As a gen. †Pr 3[25] אל־תירא מִפַּחַד פ׳ of the terror of *suddenness*, i.e. the *sudden* terror, Jb 22[10]; and with בְּ, *in suddenness*, †2 Ch 29[36] בפ׳ היה הדבר.

†פָּתַר **vb.** interpret (dream), only Gn 40, 41 (NH *id.*, JAram. פְּתַר; appar. = Aram. פְּשַׁר, ܦܫܪ, *dissolve*, fig. *solve, interpret*, cf. פֵּשֶׁר);— 6622

Qal *Pf.* 3 ms. פָּתַר, c. לְ pers. Gn 40[22] 41[13]; abs. 40[16] 41[12]; c. acc. rei: *Impf.* 3 ms. וַיִּפְתָּר־לָנוּ פָּתַר 41[12]; *Inf. cstr.* לִפְתֹּר 41[15]; *Pt. act.* פֹּתֵר 40[8] 41[15], פֹּ׳ 41[8].

†פִּתְרוֹן [Kö[ii. 1, 154]] **n.m.** interpretation (of a dream), only Gn 40, 41;—cstr. פִּתְרוֹן Gn 40[5] 41[11]; sf. פִּתְרֹנוֹ 40[12.18]; pl. פִּתְרֹנִים v[8]. 6623

†פַּתְרוֹס **n.pr.terr.** = Upper Egypt, Παθουρης, Φαθουρης, etc. (Egypt. *p(ě)-tě-res, south land*, in As. *Paturisi*, Erman[ZAW x (1890), 118 f.] Steind[BAS i. 344] WMM[Hastings DB]; also (on As.) Schr[KGF 283 f.] Dl[Pa 310]);—alw. in connexion with מִצְרַיִם, etc.: Is 11[11] Je 44[15] Ez 30[14], אֶרֶץ פ׳ Je 44[1] Ez 29[14]; מִפַּתְרֹס prop. also ψ 68[31] (for מִתְרַפֵּס) Ne[JBL x (1891), 152] (plausibly), cf. Che[ib. xi (1892), 125] Kau[ψψ crit. n.]. 6624

†פַּתְרֻסִים **adj. gent. pl.** of foregoing, as subst. Gn 10[14] = 1 Ch 1[12]. 6625

†פַּתְשֶׁגֶן **n.m.** copy (= פַּרְשֶׁגֶן q.v.);—cstr. פ׳ (הַ)כְּתָב Est 3[14] 4[8] 8[13]. 6572

†[פָּתַת] **vb.** break up, crumble (NH *id.*; Ar. فَتَّ; Eth. ፈተተ:; Syr. ܦܬ);—**Qal** *Inf. abs.* of bread of מִנְחָה: פָּתוֹת אֹתָהּ פִּתִּים Lv 2[6]. 6626

†פַּת **n.f.**[Pr 17, 1] fragment, bit, morsel of bread;—abs. פ׳ חֲרֵבָה Pr 17[1] *a dry morsel*; cstr. פַּת־לֶחֶם Gn 18[5] Ju 19[5] 1 S 2[36] 28[22] 1 K 17[11] Pr 28[21]; sf. פִּתִּי Jb 31[17], פִּתְּךָ Pr 23[8], פִּתֵּךְ Ru 2[14], פִּתּוֹ 2 S 12[3]; pl. פִּתִּים Lv 2[6] 6[14]; in sim. ψ 147[17]. 6595

†[פָּתוֹת] **n.[m.]** id.;—pl. cstr. פְּתוֹתֵי לֶחֶם Ez 13[19]. 6595

צ

צ, ץ, *Ṣādê*, eighteenth letter; used as numeral 90 in post B.Hebrew.

6627, 6674-75 [צָאָה], צֹאָה, [צֹאִי] v. צוא. p. 844

6628 †צֶאֱלִים **n.m.pl.** a kind of lotus (*Rhamnus* (more exactly *Zizyphus*), *Lotus* [Linn.], *thorny lotus* (not sacred *Nymphaea Lotus*); Saad. ضَالٌ, cf. AW De$^{Job\ 2}$, Syr. ܨܐܠܐ, v. Löw$^{p.\ 275}$);—Jb 40$^{21.22}$.

צאן (√of foll.; Dl$^{Pr\ 87\ f.;\ HWB}$ cp. As. *ṣênu*, adj., *good, docile*; Thes (cf. Lag$^{BN\ 136}$) cp. יָצָא [as πρόβατον from προβαίνω]; As. *ṣênu*=BH צֹאן, and so NH *id.*, MI^{31} צאן; Ar. ضَأْنٌ *id.*; TelAm *ṣunu* is Canaanitish acc. to Zim$^{ZA\ vi\ (1891),\ 156}$; Aram. עָנָא, ܥܢܐ, and perhaps Palm. ענא).

6629 **צֹאן** $_{273}$ **n. coll. f.** $^{Gn\ 30,\ 36}$ (poss. **m.** v$^{39\ a}$+, Kö$^{Synt.\ §\ 247\ g}$, but dub., v$^{39\ b}$ c. vb. fpl., as usually; in 1 S 15^{14} join הַזֶּה with קוֹל; v. further Albr $^{ZAW\ xv\ (1895),\ 316\ ff.}$) **small cattle, sheep and goats, flock, flocks**;—צ׳ abs. Gn 4^{2}+, cstr. 29^{9}+; sf. צֹאנוֹ 4^{4}+; צֹאנֵנוּ Ex 10^{9}, צֹאונֵנוּ ψ 144^{13}; as pl. צֹאנֵינוּ Ne 10^{37} van d. H. Gi (not Baer; very late, si vera l.), etc.;—**1.** lit. **a.** *small cattle*, usu. of sheep and goats in one flock (Rob$^{BR\ i.\ 477}$) Gn 30$^{31.32}$+; sheep specified also 21^{28} (כִּבְשֹׂת הַצּ׳), 31^{28} (אֵילֵי צ׳)+; sheep only 1 S 25^{2} (+עִזִּים); goats specified Gn 27^{9} Je 50^{8}; צ׳ as yielding (1) animals for food Am 6^{4} (כָּרִים), 1 S 14^{32} 2 S 12^{4} Ne 5^{18}+; צ׳ מַאֲכָל ψ 44^{12} (in sim.); (2) wool Gn 31^{19}+ (v. [גָּזַז], גֵּז); (3) milk, חֲלֵב צ׳ Dt 32^{14} (? goats' milk, cf. Pr 27^{27}); (4) sacrif. victims Gn 4^{4} (J), Lv 1$^{2.10}$ 3^{6} Nu 15^{3} (all P), 22^{40} (E), Dt 12$^{6.17.21}$+oft.; so צֹאן קָדָשִׁים Ez 36$^{38\ a}$, cf. בְּכוֹרֵי בְקָרֵינוּ וְצֹאנֵינוּ Ne 10^{37}; in gen. as property (oft. +בָּקָר, etc.) Gn 12^{16} 13^{5} 24^{35} Jb 1^{3} 42^{12}+oft. (v. also II. [עַשְׁתְּרוֹת]); gift Gn 20^{14} 21^{27} 38^{17} (goat), Dt 15^{14} 2 Ch 17^{11}; booty 1 S 15$^{9.15}$+. **b.** צ׳ sts. of a definite number of animals (i. e. as pl. of שֶׂה, etc.): two Is 7^{21}, four Ex 21^{37} (larger numbers v. 1 S 25$^{2.5.18}$ Nu 31$^{32.36}$ Ne 5^{18} Jb 1^{3} 42^{12} supr.).—Vid. also בֵּן **7 b**; מַרְבֵּץ, מִכְלָה, גְּדֵרָה, שַׁעַר, רֹעֶה, כֶּלֶב; עֵדֶר, נָוֶה. **2.** sim. of multitude Ez 36$^{37.38}$, cf. ψ 107^{41}; of children Jb 21^{11}; of dead, with death as shepherd ψ 49^{15}; of (shepherdless) Isr. Nu 27^{17} 1 K 22^{17}=2 Ch 18^{16}, Zc 10^{2} 13^{7}, wandering in sin Is 53^{6}; of Isr. led by י׳ ψ 77^{21} 78^{52} 80^{2}, cf. Zc 9^{16} (on text v. We Now); Ez 34^{12}; of Isr. in distress, כְּצ׳ טִבְחָה ψ 44^{23}, cf. (of wicked) צ׳ לְטִבְחָה Je 12^{3}; of scattered Bab. Is 13^{14}. **3.** metaph. of multitude, צ׳ אָדָם Ez 36^{38}; of Isr. 2 S 24^{17}=1 Ch 21^{17}, Je 23$^{1.2.3}$ Ez 24^{5}, and esp. sustained fig. 34$^{2.3}$+17 t. 34, also Zc 11$^{7.17}$; צ׳ אֹבְדוֹת Je 50^{6}, צ׳ תִּפְאַרְתֵּךְ 13^{20}; of Isr. under י׳'s care, צ׳ מַרְעִיתֶךָ (ـ׳, ـוֹ) ψ 74^{1} 79^{13} 100^{3} Ez 34^{31}, also צ׳ יָדוֹ ψ 95^{7} (|| עַם־מַרְעִיתוֹ; rd. perh. עַם יָדוֹ, צ׳ מַרְעִיתוֹ, so Che al.); צ׳ נַחֲלָתֶךָ Mi 7^{14}; also in combinations: אַדִּירֵי הַצּ׳ Je 25$^{34.35.36}$, צ׳ הַהֲרֵגָה Zc 11$^{4.7}$ (cf. ψ 44^{23}), עֲנִיֵּי הַצּ׳ v$^{7.11}$ (all of Isr.); of Edom צְעִירֵי הַצּ׳ Je 49^{20} 50^{45}.

†**צַאֲנָן** **n.pr.loc.** Mi 1^{11} Σεννααρ [ν], perh.= 6630
צְנָן in the Shephelah of Judah Jos 15^{37}, Σεννα(μ). 6799

[צֶאֱצָא] v. יצא. I, II. צָב v. I, II. צבב. 6631-31
p. 425, 839

†[**צָבָא**] **vb. wage war, serve** (Sab. צבא *wage war with*, also n. *army, campaign* Hom$^{Chrest.\ 125}$ CIS$^{iv.\ 299,\ 1.\ 2}$ DHM$^{VOJ\ i.\ 28}$; Eth. ፀብአ: (>ጸብአ:) *wage war*; As. *ṣâbu, man, soldier*; Nö$^{ZMG\ xl\ (1886),\ 726}$ al. cp. (on account of Sab. Eth. ץ) Ar. ضَبَأَ *conceal oneself*, hence *lie in wait*; this is phonetically suitable, but better in mng. would be صَبَأَ *go* or *come forth* (against one), etc., so Thes Lag$^{BN\ 21}$; Frä^{232} cp. صَبِيٌّ *young man*);—**Qal** *Pf.* 3 mpl. צָבְאוּ Ex 38^{8} Zc 14^{12}; *Impf.* 3 mpl. יִצְבְּאוּ Nu 31^{7}; *Inf. cstr.* לִצְבֹּא Is 31^{4}; לִצְבֹא Nu 4^{23} 8^{24}; *Pt.* pl. צֹבְאִים Nu 31^{42} Is 29$^{7.8}$; sf. צֹבֶיהָ Is 29^{7} (Ges$^{§\ 75\ oo}$; Di צָרֶיהָ); fpl. צֹבְאֹת Ex 38^{8}; צֹבְאוֹת 1 S 2^{22};—**1.** *wage war, fight*, c. עַל *against*, Nu 31^{7} (P) Is 29$^{7.8}$ 31^{4} Zc 14^{12}, c. sf. Is 29^{7} (?); abs. Nu 31^{42} (P). **2.** *serve* at sacred tent, Levites, c. acc. צָבָא Nu 4^{23} 8^{24} (P); women Ex 38$^{8.8}$ (P) 1 S 2^{22}. **Hiph.** *Pt.* הַמַּצְבִּא אֶת־עַם וגו׳ 2 K 25^{19}=Je 52^{25} *muster*. 6633

צָבָא $_{485}$ **n.m.** $^{2\ Ch\ 28,\ 9}$ (poss. **f.** Is 40^{2} Dn 8^{12}, but v. Albr$^{ZAW\ xv\ (1895),\ 319}$; Bev^{Dn}) **army, war, warfare**;—abs. צ׳ Nu 1^{3}+ (מִצָּבָה Zc 9^{8} v. p. 663 a); cstr. צְבָא Nu 10^{15}+; sf. צְבָאִי Jb 14^{14}; צְבָאֲךָ Ju 9^{29}; צְבָאָיו ψ 103^{21} 148^{2} (Kt צבאו; so read prob. in both), etc.; pl. צְבָאוֹת Nu 20^{9}+278 t.; cstr. צִבְאוֹת Ex 12^{41}+2 t.; sf. צִבְאֹתַי 7^{4}; צִבְאֹתָם 6^{26}+, etc.;—**1.** *army, host*: **a.** organized for war Ju 8^{6} 9^{29} (J) Is 34^{2} Je 51^{3} 2 Ch 28^{9}; צְבָאוֹ *his host* Nu 2$^{4.6}$+10 t. 2 (P), לְצִבְאֹתָם 1$^{3.52}$ 2$^{3.9}$+11 t. 2, 10, 33^{1} (P); אַלְפֵי הַצּ׳ 31^{48} (P); צ׳ ישׂראל 2 Ch 25^{7}; חֵיל (ה)צ׳ 1 Ch 20^{1} 2 Ch 26^{13}; גְּדוּדֵי צ׳ 6635

1 Ch 7^{4}; כל־הצבא 2 S 3^{23} 10^{7} 1 Ch 19^{8} 2 Ch 26^{14}; שַׂר (ה)צ׳ *captain of* (the) *host* Gn 21$^{22.32}$ (E) 26^{26} (J) Ju 4$^{2.7}$ 1 S 12^{9} + 21 t.; שָׂרֵי (ה)צבא 1 K 1^{25} (but rd. שַׂר), 1 Ch 25^{1} 26^{26} 2 Ch 33^{11}; שָׂרִים בצ׳ 1 Ch 12^{22}; שָׂרֵי (ה)צבאות Dt 20^{9} 1 K 2^{5} 1 Ch 27^{3}; עַל (ה)צ׳ מַלְכֵי צבאות ψ 68^{13}; רָאשֵׁי הצ׳ 1 Ch 12^{14}; *over the host* (as captain) Nu 10$^{14.15}$ + 10 t. Nu 10 (P), 2 S 8^{16} = 1 Ch 18^{15}, 2 S 17^{25} 1 K 2^{35} 4^{4}; אל־ כל הצ׳ 2 S 20^{23} (אל for עַל); עַל־צִבְאֹתָם Ex 6^{26} 12^{51} (P); הוציא צבאות *lead out armies* Ex 7^{4} 12^{17} (P); יצא צ׳ *army goes forth* (to war) Ex 12^{41} 1 Ch 7^{11}; לֹא תֵצֵא בְּצִבְאוֹתֵינוּ ψ 44^{10}, of י׳ going *with our armies* = 60^{12} = 108^{12}; fig. of great number, צבא רב 68^{12}.—On חֲלִיפוֹת וְצָבָא Jb 10^{17} v. Di; Bu prop. תַּחֲלִף צְבָאֲ(ךָ) i.e. *thou dost renew* (*thine*) *army* against me. **b.** *host* (organized body) of angels (cf. Lu 2^{13}), (כל) צבא השמים *all the host of heaven* 1 K 22^{19} = 2 Ch 18^{18}, Ne 9^{6}; כל צבאיו ψ 103^{21} 148^{2}; צבא הַמָּרוֹם Is 24^{21} *host of the high* (angel-princes; ‖ earthly monarchs); צבא השמים Dn 8^{10}, הצבא v^{10} (al. v^{b} fig. of Israel); שׂר צ׳ י׳ *captain of the host of* י׳ Jos 5$^{14.15}$ (theophanic angel); שׂר הצבא Dn 8^{11} (angel-prince of Israel, others, God). **c.** of sun, moon and stars, כל צבא השמים Dt 4^{19} 17^{3} 2 K 17^{16} 21$^{3.5}$ = 2 Ch 33$^{3.5}$, 2 K 23$^{4.5}$ Je 8^{2} 19^{13} (all as objects of worship), Is 34^{4}; צ׳ השמים Je 33^{22} Zp 1^{5}; כל צבאם Ne 9^{6} ψ 33^{6} Is 34^{4} 45^{12}; צבאם Is 40^{26}.—Je 3^{19} v. I. צְבִי. **d.** of the entire creation, כל צבאם Gn 2^{1}. **2.** *war, warfare, service:* יָצָא צָבָא *go out to war* Nu 1$^{3.20}$ + 12 t. Nu 1, 26^{2} (P) 1 Ch 5^{18} 7^{11} 12$^{33.36}$ 2 Ch 25^{5} 26^{11}; יצא בצ׳ Nu 31^{36} (P) Dt 24^{5}; יצא לצ׳ Nu 31$^{27.28}$ (P); עלה לצ׳ *go up to war* Jos 22$^{12.33}$ (P); בא מצ׳ *come from war* Nu 31^{14} 2 Ch 28^{12}; קבץ לצ׳ 1 S 28^{1}; שלח לצ׳ Nu 31$^{4.6.6}$ (P); התיחשׂם בצ׳ 1 Ch 7^{40}; צ׳ תְּנָתֵן Dn 8^{12}; אַנְשֵׁי (ה)צ׳ *men of war* Nu 31$^{21.53}$ (P) 1 Ch 12^{8}, cf. עַם הצ׳ Nu 31^{32} (P); v. also II. חלץ; גִּבּוֹרֵי חַיִל לצ׳ 1 Ch 12^{25}; כְּלֵי צ׳ 1 Ch 12^{37} *instruments of war.* **3.** *service:* **a.** of Levites in sacred places Nu 4$^{3.23.30.35.39.43}$ 8$^{24.25}$; קֹדֶשׁ וְצָבָא Dn 8^{13} (al. as v^{11}, **1 b**). **b.** of *hard service* of troubled life Jb 7^{1} 14^{14} Is 40^{2} Dn 10^{1}. **4.** צְבָאוֹת, in name of י׳ as God of war, prob. first in time of warlike David (some connect with sacred ark, but ark older), explained יהוה צבאות אֱלֹהֵי מערכות ישׂראל 1 S 17^{45} י׳ *Sebaoth God of the battle array of Israel* (the thought of angels and stars as army of God is later); **a.** earliest form c. art.: י׳ אֱלֹהֵי הַצְּבָאוֹת Am 3^{13} 6^{14} 9^{5} (אֱלֹהֵי om. by error, cf. We), Ho 12^{6}. **b.** without art., definite by usage, י׳ אֱלֹהֵי צְבָאוֹת 2 S 5^{10} Am 5$^{14.15.16}$ 6^{8} 1 K 19$^{10.14}$ Je 5^{14} 15^{16} ψ 89^{9}; י׳ אֱלֹהֵי צְבָאוֹת אֱלֹהֵי יִשְׂרָאֵל Je 35^{17} 38^{17} 44^{7} 1 S 7^{27} = 1 Ch 17^{24}, Is 21^{10} 37^{16}; 1st אֱלֹהֵי om. Je 7$^{3.21}$ + 30 t. Je; Zp 2^{9}; י׳ אלהים צ׳ אלהי ישׂראל ψ 59^{6} (אלהים variant of י׳); י׳ א׳ צ׳ שְׁמוֹ *God of hosts his name* Am 4^{13} 5^{27}, later reduced to י׳ צ׳ שְׁמוֹ Is 47^{4} 48^{2} 51^{15} 54^{5} Je 10^{16} 31^{35} + 6 t. Je. **c.** as n.pr. *Sebaoth:* י׳ צבאות, י׳ *Sebaoth* (*Lord of hosts,* Vrss, owing to Qr אֲדֹנָי, but this never cstr. אֲדֹנָי; al. י׳ *of hosts,* but < names in appos., since י׳ is n.pr.; צ׳ for earlier אלהי צ׳; cf. Σαβαωθ Ja 5^{4} Rom 9^{29}): 1 S 1$^{3.11}$ 4^{4} 15^{2} 17^{45} 2 S 6$^{2.18}$ 7$^{8.26}$ 1 K 18^{15} 2 K 3^{14} 19^{31} 1 Ch 11^{9} 17^{7} ψ 24^{10} + 6 t. ψψ, Mi 4^{4} Na 2^{14} 3^{5} Hb 2^{13} Zp 2^{10} Is 1^{9} 2^{12} 5$^{7.9.16.24}$ + 35 t. Is 6–39, Is^{2} only 44^{6} 45^{13}, Je 6$^{6.9}$ 8^{3} 9$^{6.16}$ + 26 t. Je, Hg 1$^{2.5}$ + 12 t. Hg, Zc 1$^{3.3.3.4}$ + 40 t. Zc 1–8, 9^{15} + 8 t. 10–14, Mal 1$^{4.6.8}$ + 21 t. Mal; האדון י׳ צ׳ Is 1^{24} + 4 t. Is (incl. 10^{16} Baer Gi > van d. H. אֲדֹנָי for י׳); אֲדֹנָי י׳ צ׳ 3^{15} + (on these phr. v. אָדוֹן **1, 6**); אלהים צ׳ (א׳) later Qr for orig. י׳) ψ 80$^{8.15}$; י׳ אלהים צ׳ (earlier י׳ + later [inserted] א׳) ψ 80$^{5.20}$ 84^{9}.—Cf. Driver Hastings DB (1900), Lord of Hosts and reff., Löhr Amos (Beihefte zur ZAW iv (1900), 38–67).

צְבָאִים, צְבָאוֹת, צְבָאוֹת v. further I, II. צְבִי. p. 840 6643

צְבָאִים v. צְבִיִּים. p. 840 6636

I. **צבב** (√ of foll.; cf. As. *ṣumbu* (= **ṣubbu*), *cart;* 𝔗 צִיבָא *low, covered wagon*).

†I. צָב **n.[m.]** litter;—abs. צ׳, in עֶגְלֹת צָב 6632
Nu 7^{3}, prob. *litter-wagons,* i.e. wagons covered, like palanquin; pl. צַבִּים Is 66^{20} *litters* (on Vrss cf. Di^{Nu}).

II. **צבב** (√ of foll.; cf. Ar. ضَبَّ *cleave to ground;* NH צָב = BH, Syr. ܥܒܐ in Lexx; Ar. ضَبّ is a large lizard, v. esp. Seetzen Reisen iii. 436 ff.).

†II. צָב **n.[m.] lizard,** as unclean, Lv 11^{29}. 6632

†צֹבֵבָה **n.pr.m.** in Judah, הַצּ׳ 1 Ch 4^{8}, 6637
Σαβαθα, A Σωβηβα, 𝔊^{L} Σαβηβα.

†I. [צָבָה] **vb. swell, swell up** (NH 6638
id.);—**Qal** *Pf.* 3 fs. consec. וְצָבְתָה Nu 5^{27}; appar. **Hiph.** *Inf. cstr.* לַצְבּוֹת v^{22}, < read **Qal** לִצְבּוֹת Di Ol$^{§ 78 c}$ Sta$^{§ 114 a, 2}$; both of adulteress' belly.—צֹבִיָּה Is 29^{7} v. צבא.

†[צָבֶה] **adj. swelling, swollen**;—f. צָבָה 6639
Nu 5^{21} (as foregoing).

II. **צבה** (√ of foll.; meaning dub.; Dl$^{Pr 159}$ Buhl al. cp. Ar. صبا *lean, incline* (esp. III.), fig. *incline* toward (الى), *yearn* for, As. *ṣabû,* Aram. צְבָא, ܨܒܳܐ, all *desire,* etc.).

6643 †I. צְבִי n.m.[2S1,19] beauty, honour;—abs. צ׳ 2 S 1[19]+, צְבִי Dn 8[9]; cstr. צְבִי Is 13[19]+; pl. cstr. צְבָאוֹת Je 3[19] (so 𝔗 Ki Thes Hi Gf Ol[§145b] Kö[ii.1,584] al.; > fr. צבא 𝔙 Gie al.);—**1. a.** *beauty, decoration,* צ׳ עֶדְיוֹ, of silver and gold Ez 7[20], of products of soil Is 4[2] (predict.). **b.** elsewhere in fig.: of drunkard's chaplet, צ׳ תִּפְאַרְתּוֹ Is 28[1.4] (fig. of Samaria); עֲטֶרֶת צ׳ v[5] (of י׳); הַצּ׳ 2 S 1[19] (Saul and Jonathan); גְּאוֹן כָּל־צ׳, of Tyre Is 23[9]; צ׳ מַמְלָכוֹת 13[19] (of Bab.); of land of Isr. (Judah), צְבִי הִיא לְכָל־הָאֲרָצוֹת Ez 20[6.15], נַחֲלַת צְבִי צִבְאוֹת גּוֹיִם Je 3[19] (v. supr.) *heritage of the beauty of beauties of the nations,* i.e. most beauteous heritage; הַצּ׳ esp. of Jerus. and temple Dn 8[9] (Bev), cf. אֶרֶץ הַצּ׳ 11[16.41] (v. Dr), הַר צ׳־קֹדֶשׁ v[45] (i.e. temple-hill); of cities of Moab, צ׳ אֶרֶץ Ez 25[9]. **2.** = *honour,* צ׳ לַצַּדִּיק Is 24[16].—Ez 26[20] rd. וְתִתְיַצְּבִי for וְנָתַתִּי צְבִי, so 𝔊 Co Berthol Toy Krae al.

III. צבה (√of foll.; NH צְבִי, צְבִיָּה = BH; so As. *ṣabîtu,* Ar. ظَبْيٌ, Aram. טַבְיָה, ܛܒܝܐ).

6643 †II. צְבִי n.m.[Is13,14] gazelle;—צ׳ abs. Dt 12[15]+; pl. צְבָיִם 2 S 2[18], צְבָאִים 1 Ch 12[9] (Gi Baer; van d. H. v[8]), צְבָאוֹת Ct 2[7] 3[5];—*gazelle,* allowed as food Dt 14[5], cf. 12[15.22] (although not for sacrif., Dr; all + אַיָּל), so 15[22] (+ אַיָּל, יַחְמוּר, etc.), v. 1 K 5[3]; sim. of swiftness 2 S 2[18] 1 Ch 12[9] v. supr., Pr 6[5]; of grace and beauty Ct 2[9.17] 8[14] (cf. Jacob Arab. Dichter iv. 20f.); hence used in adjuration 2[7] 3[5] (+ אילות); צ׳ מֻדָּח Is 13[14], sim. of fugitives.

6646 † צְבִיָּה n.f. id.;—תְּאוֹמֵי צ׳ Ct 4[5] = 7[4].

6644 †צִבְיָא n.pr.m. in Benjamin 1 Ch 8[9], Ιεβια, A Σεβια, 𝔊L Σαβια.

6645 †צִבְיָה n.pr.f. (= צְבִיָּה *gazelle,* cf. Sta [§192b]);—mother of Jehoash of Judah 2 K 12[2], Αβια = 2 Ch 24[1], Αβια, 𝔊L Σαβια.

6636 †צְבֹיִים n.pr.loc. near Sodom, Gn 14[2.8] Dt 29[22] = צְבֹיִם Gn 10[19] = צְבֹאִים Ho 11[8] Kt (צְבוֹיִם Qr); Σεβωειμ.

6642 †[צָבַט] vb. reach, hold out, to (לְ pers.) (prop. *grasp, hold,* so NH (rare), בֵּית הַצְּבִיטָה *handle* (of jug); Ar. ضَبَطَ *hold firmly, seize;* Eth. ፀበጠ: *grasp firmly*);—**Qal** *Impf.* 3 ms. וַיִּצְבָּט־לָהּ Ru 2[14] (acc. rei).

I. צבע (√of foll.; NH צֶבַע *dye;* As. *ṣibûtum, ṣubâtu, dyed stuff* (v. Zehnpf[BAS i. 519]); Ar. صَبَغَ, Aram. צְבַע, ܨܒܥ, all *dip, dye*).

†צֶבַע n.[m.] dye, dyed stuff;—cstr. צ׳ רִקְמָתַיִם Ju 5[30] (perhaps del. צ׳, cf. GFM); pl. שְׁלַל צְבָעִים *booty of dyed stuffs* v[30.30]. 6648

†צָבוּעַ adj. coloured, variegated (prop. pt. pass.);—עַיִט צ׳ Je 12[9] *a variegated bird of prey.* 6641

II. צבע (√of foll.; cf. Ar. صَبَعَ *point* Lag[BN 20.21] إِصْبَعٌ, *finger,* Sab. אצבע DHM[ZMG xxxvii (1883), 375]; Eth. አጽባዕት: NH = BH; Aram. אֶצְבְּעָא, ܨܒܥܐ, Mand. צבאתא Nö[M36]; Dl[Pr172] Kö[ii. 1,96] cp. As. *ṣibû* II. *surround firmly*).

אֶצְבַּע 31 n.f.[Lv14,6] finger;—א׳ abs. Is 58[9], cstr. Ex 8[15]+; sf. אֶצְבָּעוֹ Lv 4[6]+; pl. אֶצְבָּעוֹת Je 52[21], cstr. אֶצְבְּעֹת 2 S 21[20]+, etc.;—**1.** *finger,* esp. **a.** *forefinger,* of priest, applying blood (P), Ex 29[12] Lv 4[6.17.25] + 8 t.; applying oil 14[16.16.27]. **b.** שְׁלֹחַ א׳ of any one Is 58[9], sign of contempt. **c.** of God, as writing Ex 31[18] (E) Dt 9[10]; = *act* of God Ex 8[15] (J). **d.** pl. of all the fingers 2 S 21[20a]; fingers in gen. Is 2[8] 17[8] 59[3] ψ 144[1], Pr 7[3] Ct 5[5]; of י׳ ψ 8[4]; מֹרֶה בְא׳ Pr 6[13] (of contempt. gesture); as measure of thickness, Je 52[21] *four fingers.* **2.** *toes:* אֶצְבְּעֹת רַגְלָיו 2 S 21[20b], lit. *fingers of his feet,* cf. א׳ ‖ 1 Ch 20[6] = fingers and toes. 676

III. צבע (perhaps √of foll.; cf. Ar. ضبع *limp* (so Lag[BN20]), whence ضَبُعٌ *hyena,* Syr. ܐܦܥܐ *id.,* NH צָבוּעַ).

†צִבְעוֹן n.pr.m. a Horite (*hyena;* RS[K219]; Gray[Prop. N. 95] and reff.);—Gn 36[2.14.20] (in these gloss acc. to Di Holz), v[24.24.29] 1 Ch 1[38.40], Σεβεγων. 6649

†צְבֹעִים n.pr.loc. in Benj.;—גֵּי הצ׳ (perh. *valley of hyenas,* so Thes, cf. Lag[BN 36] Gray[l. c.]);—1 S 13[18] (acc. to Buhl[Geogr. 98] = *Wady el-Kelt,* between Jerus. and Jericho), Σαμειν, 𝔊L Σαβαιν; cf. צ׳ Ne 11[34], A Σεβοειμ, 𝔊L Σεβωειν. 6650

†[צָבַר] vb. heap up (NH *id.;* Aram. צְבַר; Syr. ܨܒܪ is *prate, chatter, rave;* Ar. صَبَرَ is *collect, bind together;* cf. further Dozy);—**Qal** *Impf.* 3 ms. יִצְבֹּר Gn 41[35] ψ 39[7]; 3 fs. וַתִּצְבָּר־ Zc 9[3], etc.;—*heap up,* in great quantity: **c.** acc. corn Gn 41[35.49] (E), dead frogs Ex 8[10] (J), dust Hb 1[10], silver like dust Zc 9[3] Jb 27[16], cf. (obj. om.) ψ 39[7]. 6651

†[צִבּוּר] n.m. heap;—only pl. שְׁנֵי צִבֻּרִים 2 K 10[8] *two heaps* (of heads). 6652

צבת (√of foll.; NH צָבַת *bind, unite;* As. *ṣabâtu, grasp, take;* Talm. צְבַת *join,* and der.).

6653 †צְבָתִים n.[m.] pl. bundles of grain Ru 2[16] (Vogelst[Landwirthschaft 61] *swaths* [grasped and] lifted for binding).

צדד (√ of foll.; cf. Ar. صَدَّ *turn away*, then *shun, alienate;* NH BAram. צַד = BH; Ar. صَدَدٌ *vicinity*, صَدَدَ *in front of, in the vicinity of;* Aram. צַד, צִיד *by, apud*).

6654 †צַד n.m.[Ex 25, 32] **side**;—צַד abs. Ez 34[21] Is 60[4], cstr. 2 S 2[16]+; sf. צִדָּהּ Gn 6[16]+, etc.; for צִדָּה 1 S 20[20] rd. צִדָּה (or צִדּוֹ; cf. Dr, > צִדָּה); pl. צִדִּים Ju 2[3], rd. prob. צֵדִיכֶם as Nu 33[55] Jos 23[13]; cstr. צִדֵּי Ex 26[13], etc.;—*side*, of man 2 S 2[16] Nu 33[55] (H) Jos 23[13] (D), Ju 2[3] (prob. rd. context as Nu 33[55] GFM; Dl[Pr 75] cp. As. *ṣaddu, snare, trap*); of one lying Ez 4[4.6.9], מִצִּדְּךָ אֶל־צִדֶּךָ v[8] *turn from side to side;* children carried עַל־צ׳ (i.e. prob. on hip) Is 60[4] 66[12]; of cattle Ez 34[21] (in fig.); of things 1 S 20[20] (cf. Dr), Gn 6[16] Ex 25[32.32.32] = 37[18.18.18], 26[13] 30[4] = 37[27], Dt 31[26] (all P); מִצַּד *at the side of*, c. gen. pers. 1 S 20[25] Ru 2[14], so מִצִּדְּךָ ψ 91[7]; c. gen. loc. Jos 3[16] 12[9], מִצַּד הָהָר 2 S 13[34]; מִצַּד הָהָר מִזֶּה 1 S 23[26 bis] *on this side* of the hill and on *that side;* c. sf. rei מִצִּדּוֹ 1 S 6[8].

6657 †[צְדָד, צְדָדָה] **n.pr.loc.** on N. border of Canaan, c. ה loc., צְדָדָה Nu 34[8] (Σαραδακ, Sam. צרדה), Ez 47[15] (Σελδαμμα), rd. prob. צְרָדָה; perh. *Khirbet Ṣerādā*, N. of Abil, E. of *Merj ʿAjûn* toward Hermon (lat. c. 33°25′ N., long. c. 35°35′ E.), so van Kasteren[Rev. Bibl., 1895, 30], cf. Buhl[Geogr. 67].

6661 †צִדִּים **n.pr.loc.** in Naphtali, הַצ׳ Jos 19[35] (𝔊 τῶν Τυρίων).

6658 †I. **צָדָה** vb. **lie in wait** (NH *id.*, rare; cf. (si vera l.) BAram. צְדָא Dn 3[14]);—**Qal** *Pf.* 3 ms. צ׳ Ex 21[13] (E; abs.); *Pt.* c. acc. וְאַתָּה צֹדֶה אֶת־נַפְשִׁי לְקַחְתָּהּ 1 S 24[11] (Gi; v[12] van d. H. Baer).

6660 †צְדִיָּה **n.f. lying-in-wait;**—(ב)צ׳ Nu 35[20.22] i.e. with malicious intent (P).

6658 † II. [צָדָה] **vb. lay waste** (NH *id.* (rare), Aram. צְדִי, ܨܕܐ, صَدِيَ *id.*);—**Niph.** *Pf.* 3 pl. נִצְדּוּ עָרֵיהֶם Zp 3[6] *their cities are laid waste.*

6720, 6722 צֵדָה v. צֵידָה, sub II. צוד. צִדֹנִית v. צִידֹנִי p. 845, 851

צדק (√ of foll.; NH, Aram. in deriv.; cf. Ar. صَدَقَ *speak the truth* (also صَدْقٌ *hard, even, straight, perfect*); Sab. צדק *just*, epith. of king Mordtm[ZMG xxx (1876), 37] Hom[Chrest. 125]; usu. *excellent* DHM[ZMG xxix (1875), 595, 599] CIS[iv. p. 176]; also verb *favour, endow* (one with something) CIS[iv. No. 198, 1.4] DHM[l. c.] Mordtm[Him. Inschr. 70 f.]; Ph. צדק adj. *just, right*, TelAm (Can.) *ṣaduḳ, innocent;* OAram. צדק n. *righteousness, loyalty*, Nab. אצדק adj. *authorized*, Palm. זדקתא εὐσεβής; Saho *sadak, be true, clear* Reinisch[Saho Spr. (1890) 312]; Eth. ጸድቀ: *be just, righteous*, so NH צדק Pi. Hiph., Aram. צְדִיק, ܙܕܩ; cf. Kau[Deriv. d. St. צדק (1881)] HPS[צדק etc. Presb. Rev., 1882, 165 ff.] Gerber[206 ff.]).

†צֶדֶק n.m. [Is 1, 21] **rightness, righteousness**;—צ׳ Lv 19[36] + 87 t.; צִדְקִי Is 41[10] + 8 t., etc.;—**1.** *what is right, just, normal; rightness, justness*, of weights and measures, אֶבֶן, אֵיפָה שְׁלֵמָה וָצֶדֶק Dt 25[15] *a perfect and a just weight, ephah;* בַּת צ׳, הִין צ׳, אֵיפַת צ׳, אַבְנֵי צ׳; מֹאזְנֵי צ׳ Lv 19[36] (H) Jb 31[6] Ez 45[10]; מַעְגְּלֵי צ׳ *right paths* ψ 23[3]; זִבְחֵי צ׳ *right peace-offerings* Dt 33[19] ψ 4[6] 51[21]. **2.** *righteousness*, in government: **a.** of judges, rulers, kings, שפט בצ׳ Lv 19[15] (H); שפט צ׳ Dt 1[16] Pr 31[9]; משפט צ׳ Dt 16[18]; רדף צ׳ v[20]; חוקק צ׳ Pr 8[15]; מלך לצ׳ Is 32[1]; דבר צ׳ ψ 58[2]; also Pr 25[5] ψ 94[15] Ec 5[7]. **b.** of law, as מִשְׁפְּטֵי Is 58[2] ψ 119[7.62.75.106.160] (𝔊, but MT מִשְׁפַּט), v[164]; as עֵדוֹת v[138.144]; as מִצְוֹת v[172]. **c.** of Davidic king, Messiah Is 11[4.5] 16[5] ψ 45[5], דין בצ׳ 72[2]. **d.** of Jerus., as seat of just government, עִיר הַצֶּדֶק Is 1[26] *city of righteousness;* נְוֵה צ׳ Je 31[23] 50[7] (poss. these reflect an orig. god צֶדֶק, v. מַלְכִּי צֶדֶק); צ׳ יָלִין בָּהּ Is 1[21] *righteousness used to lodge in her;* cf. מְקוֹם הצ׳ Ec 3[16] *the place of righteousness.* **e.** of God's attribute as sovereign Jb 36[3], husband of Israel Ho 2[21]; צ׳ his personif. agent ψ 85[11.12.14], foundation of his throne 89[15] = 97[2]; in his government ψ 9[9] 65[6] 96[13] = 98[9], promise Is 45[19], administration of justice Jb 8[3] Je 11[20] ψ 7[18] 48[11] 50[6] = 97[6], vindication of his people 9[5] 35[24.28]; raising up Cyrus Is 45[13], calling his servant 42[6]; אֱלֹהֵי צִדְקִי ψ 4[2] God *of my righteousness* (who vindicates me); his צ׳ is everlasting 119[142]. **3.** *righteousness, justice*, in a case or cause Jb 6[29] 8[6] 29[14] ψ 35[27] Is 59[4]; God שפט כצ׳ ψ 7[9] *judges according to righteousness;* גמל כצ׳ 18[21]; השיב כצ׳ v[25]; שמע צ׳ 17[1]; הוציא צ׳ 37[6]. **4.** *rightness*, in speech, דבר צ׳ ψ 52[5] (opp. שֶׁקֶר); יַגִּיד צ׳ Pr 12[17]; בצ׳ כל אמרי פי 8[8]; שִׂפְתֵי צ׳ 16[13]. **5.** *righteousness*, as ethically right Jb 35[2] ψ 17[15] 45[8] Pr 1[3] 2[9] Ec 7[15] Je 22[13] Ez 3[20] Ho 10[12] (read פְּרִי צ׳, so 𝔊 We Now); פעל צ׳ ψ 15[2]; למד צ׳ Is 26[6.10]; בקש צ׳ Zp 2[3]; רדף צ׳ Is 51[1]; ידע צ׳ v[7]. **6.** *righteousness* as vindicated, 6664

justification in controversy with enemies and troubles, *deliverance, victory, prosperity:* **a.** of God as covenant-keeping, in redemption, בִּימִין צִדְקִי Is 41^{10}, ‖ יֶשַׁע 45^{8} 51^{5}, cf. 42^{21}; בשׂר צ׳ ψ 40^{10}; אִמְרַת צ׳
3072 119^{123}. **b.** in name יהוה צִדְקֵנוּ, of Messianic king (vindicating people's cause and giving victory) Je 23^{6}; of city 33^{16}. **c.** of people as enjoying צ׳ of salvation, ‖ יְשׁוּעָה Is 62^{1}; ‖ כָּבוֹד 58^{8} 62^{2}; כהנים יִלְבְּשׁוּ צ׳ ψ 132^{9}; שַׁעֲרֵי צ׳ 118^{19}; אֵילֵי הצ׳ Is 61^{3}. **d.** of Cyrus, צ׳ יִקְרָאֵהוּ לְרַגְלוֹ Is 41^{2} (who) *in victory calleth him at every step* (Che[Hpt] *on whose steps attends victory*, so Di Du).

6666 צְדָקָה 157 **n.f.** righteousness;—abs. צ׳ Gn 15^{6} + 81 t.; cstr. צִדְקַת Dt 33^{21} + 5 t.; sf. צִדְקָתִי Gn 30^{33} +, etc.; pl. צְדָקוֹת Is 33^{15} + 3 t.; cstr. צִדְקוֹת Ju 5^{11} +; sf. צִדְקֹתֶיךָ Dn 9^{16}, etc.;—**1.** *righteousness*, in government: **a.** of judge, ruler, king: ‖ משׁפט Is 5^{7} 9^{6} Am 5^{7} 6^{12}; משׁפט וצ׳ עשׂה 2 S 8^{15}, *D. executed justice and righteousness* = 1 Ch 18^{14}, cf. 1 K 10^{9} = 2 Ch 9^{8}, Je $22^{3.15}$ 33^{15} Ez 45^{9}; בצ׳ יִכּוֹן כִּסֵּא Pr 16^{12}, cf. Is 54^{14}; נֹגְשַׂיִךְ צ׳; מַעֲשֵׂה הצ׳, עֲבֹדַת הצ׳ Is 32^{17}, cf. v^{16}; Is 60^{17}. **b.** of law, ‖ מִשְׁפָּטִים, צִדְקַת י׳ Dt 33^{21}. **c.** of Davidic king, Messiah, ‖ מִשְׁפָּט, ψ $72^{1.3}$ Is 9^{6} Je 23^{5} 33^{15}. **2.** God's attribute as sovereign ψ 36^{7} 71^{19}; in government, עשׂה משׁפט וצ׳ 99^{4} Je 9^{23}; administering justice Jb 37^{23}; punishment Is 1^{27} 5^{16} 10^{22} 28^{17} Dn 9^{7}; vindication of his people Mi 7^{9}. **3.** *righteousness*, in a case or cause, בצדקתי החזקתי Jb 27^{6} *on my righteousness I hold fast;* מה ישׁ לי עוד צ׳ 2 S 19^{29} *what right have I yet?* of God's judgments, הגיד צ׳ Is 57^{12} (iron.); השׁיב צ׳ 1 S 26^{23} Jb 33^{26}; השׁיב כצ׳, 2 S 22^{25}, גמל v^{21}, נתן 1 K 8^{32} = 2 Ch 6^{23}. **4.** *righteousness* = *truthfulness*, באמת ובצ׳ Is 48^{1} Zc 8^{8}; in word Is 45^{23} 63^{1}, oath Je 4^{2}. **5.** *righteousness*, as ethically right: Gn 30^{33} (J) Dt 6^{25} Is 33^{5} 41^{18} Ez $14^{14.20}$ Pr 10^{2} $11^{4.5.18.19}$ + 17 t., + צִדְקַת (ה)צַדִּיק(ים) Is 5^{23} Ez 18^{20} 33^{12}; צ׳ ישׁרים Pr 11^{6}; אֹרַח צ׳ 8^{20} 12^{28}; דֶּרֶךְ צ׳ 16^{31}; עשׂה צ׳ *do righteousness* ψ 106^{3} Is 56^{1} 58^{2} Ez 18^{22}; עשׂה משׁפט וצ׳ Ez 18^{5} + 6 t. Ez; עשׂה צ׳ ומשׁפט Gn 18^{19} (J) Pr 21^{3}; רדף צ׳ Pr 15^{9} 21^{21}; הלך באמת ובצ׳ 1 K 3^{6}; חשׁב לו (ל)צ׳ Gn 15^{6} (JE) *imputed to him (for) righteousness*, ψ 106^{31}; צ׳ וָחֶסֶד Pr $21^{21.21}$ (del. 𝔊[AB] Toy). **6.** *righteousness* as vindicated, *justification, salvation*, etc. (cf. צֶדֶק **6**): **a.** of God, ‖ יֶשַׁע, תְּשׁוּעָה, יְשׁוּעָה Is 45^{8} 46^{13} 51^{6} + 7 t. Is²; ‖ בְּרָכָה ψ 24^{5}; ‖ נַחֲלָה Is 54^{17}; ‖ חֶסֶד ψ 36^{11} 103^{17}; שֶׁמֶשׁ צ׳ Mal 3^{20} *sun of righteousness* (with healing); בְּצ׳, י׳ delivers, guides, exalts his people ψ 5^{9} 31^{2} 71^{2} 89^{17} 119^{40} $143^{1.11}$; אַל־יָבֹאוּ בְּצִדְקָתֶךָ 69^{28} (of wicked); as acc. after verbs of declaring, etc., his *saving (delivering) righteousness* 22^{32} 40^{11} 51^{16} $71^{15.16.24}$ 98^{2} 145^{7}; also יִוָּדַע צ׳ 88^{13}; צ׳ עֹמֶדֶת לָעַד *his righteousness endureth* for ever 111^{3} cf. 119^{142}. **b.** of people, = *prosperity*, ‖ הון, עשׁר Pr 8^{18}; מוֹרֶה לצ׳ *early rain for prosperity* Jo 2^{23}. **7.** pl. *righteous acts:* **a.** of God Ju $5^{11.11}$ 1 S 12^{7} Mi 6^{5}; vindication of right ψ 103^{6}; redemptive Is 45^{24} Dn 9^{16}. **b.** of man's moral conduct Is 64^{5} Je 51^{10}, also prob. Ez 3^{20} 18^{24} 33^{13} (Kt sg.) ψ 11^{7} (? gloss), Dn 9^{18}; as adv. acc., הֹלֵךְ צְדָקוֹת Is 33^{15}.

†[צָדֵק, צָדֹק] **vb. denom.** be just, 6663
righteous;—**Qal** *Pf.* 3 fs. צָדְקָה Gn 38^{26}; 2 ms. צָדַקְתָּ Jb 33^{12} 35^{7}, etc.; *Impf.* 3 ms. יִצְדַּק Jb 9^{2}+; יִצְדָּק Jb 4^{17} 11^{2}; 3 fpl. תִּצְדַּקְנָה Ez 16^{52} (𝔊 Co תְּצַדֵּקִין, not Berthol Toy Krae), etc.;—**1.** *have a just cause, be in the right*, Jb $9^{15.20}$ 13^{18} 34^{5}; in complaint Jb 33^{12}; c. מִן pers. Gn 38^{26} (J; of Tamar). **2.** *be justified*, in one's plea Jb 11^{2}; c. עִם (man with God) 9^{2} 25^{4}; בי׳ Is 45^{25}; by witnesses 43^{9}; by acquittal ψ 143^{2} Is 43^{26}; by condemnation of opponent Jb 40^{8}. **3.** *be just:* of God, in his government, in charging with sin ψ 51^{6}; of מִשְׁפְּטֵי־י׳ 19^{10}. **4.** *be just, righteous*, in conduct and character: of men Jb 10^{15} 15^{14} 22^{3} 35^{7}, c. מִן comp., Jb 4^{17} (more than God; Dr *at God's hand*, מִן **2 d**), Ez 16^{52} (< 𝔊 Co **Pi.**). **Niph.** *Pf.* 3 ms. וְנִצְדַּק קֹדֶשׁ consec. Dn 8^{14} *the holy place shall be put right*, in a right condition (Marti[Kau] Buhl SS; Bev Dr Marti[Comm.] *be justified*, its cause vindicated). **Pi.** *Pf.* 3 fs. צִדְּקָה Je 3^{11}; *Impf.* 2 fs. תְּצַדְּקִי Ez 16^{51}; *Inf. cstr.* sf. צַדְּקֶךָ Jb 33^{32}; צַדְּקָתֵךְ (Ges §52p) Ez 16^{52}; צַדְּקוֹ Jb 32^{2};—*justify:* עַל צַדְּקוֹ נַפְשׁוֹ מֵאֱלֹהִים Jb 32^{2} *because he justified himself rather than God* (cf. **Qal 1**); *make to appear righteous* Je 3^{11} Ez $16^{51.52}$ (all c. מִן comp.); חָפַצְתִּי צַדְּקֶךָ Jb 33^{32} *I desire to justify thee* (in thy plea, cf. **Qal 2**). **Hiph.** *Pf.* 1 s. sf. הִצְדַּקְתִּיו 2 S 15^{4}; 3 mpl. הִצְדִּיקוּ Dt 25^{1}; *Impf.* 3 ms. יַצְדִּיק Is 53^{11}; 1 s. אַצְדִּיק Ex 23^{7} Jb 27^{5}; *Inf. cstr.* הַצְדִּיק 1 K 8^{32} = 2 Ch 6^{23}; *Imv.* mpl. הַצְדִּיקוּ ψ 82^{3}; *Pt.* מַצְדִּיק Pr 17^{15}, etc.;—**1.** *do justice*, in administering law 2 S 15^{4} ψ 82^{3}. **2.** *declare righteous, justify*, c. acc. (ה)צַדִּיק Dt 25^{1} 1 K 8^{32} = 2 Ch 6^{23}; רָשָׁע Ex 23^{7} (E) Is 5^{23} Pr 17^{15}; *justify* accusers, by recognizing charge as just Jb 27^{5}. **3.** *justify, vindicate the cause of, save*, c. acc., Is 50^{8} (of God), c. לְ of obj. Is 53^{11} (of servant

of ׳י). **4.** *make righteous, turn to righteousness,* Dn 12^{3}, cf. Aboth $5^{20.27}$ Bev. **Hithp.** *Impf.* 1 pl. נִצְטַדָּק Gn 44^{16} (J) how *shall we justify ourselves,* clear ourselves from suspicion?

6662 צַדִּיק$_{206}$ **adj. just, righteous**; — abs. ׳צ Gn 6^{9}+; pl. צַדִּיקִים Ex 23^{8}+, etc.;—**1.** *just, righteous,* in government: **a.** of Davidic king 2 S 23^{3}; צֶמַח Je 23^{5} Zc 9^{9} (‖ *victorious*). **b.** of judges, Ez 23^{45} Pr 29^{2} (v. Toy; Kau questions this meaning in all these). **c.** of law, מִשְׁפָּטִים צ׳ Dt 4^{8}. **d.** of God Dt 32^{4} ψ 119^{137} 129^{4} Jb 34^{17}, opp. Pharaoh Ex 9^{27} (J); in discrimination Je 12^{1} Zp 3^{5} ψ $7^{10.12}$ 11^{7}; condemnation 2 Ch 12^{6} Dn 9^{14} La 1^{18} Ezr 9^{15} Ne 9^{33}; redemption Is 45^{21} ψ 116^{5}; keeping promises Ne 9^{8}; in all his ways ψ 145^{17}. **2.** *just* in one's cause, *right:* Ex $23^{7.8}$ (E) Dt 16^{19} 25^{1} 1 K 8^{32} = 2 Ch 6^{23}, Is 5^{23} 29^{21} Jb 32^{1} 36^{7} Pr $17^{15.26}$ $18^{5.17}$ 24^{24} Am 2^{6} 5^{12} Hb $1^{4.13}$; right in law, not under penalty 2 S 4^{11} 1 K 2^{32}; innocent of specif. offence 2 K 10^{9}; c. מִן comp. 1 S 24^{18}. **3.** *just, righteous,* in conduct and character: **a.** towards God Gn 7^{1} $18^{23.24.24.25.25.26.28}$ (J) 20^{4} (E), Hb 2^{4} Mal 3^{18}. **b.** in gen., ethically: ψ 5^{13} 7^{10} $11^{3.5}$ + 21 t. ψψ (+ infr.), Pr 2^{20} 3^{33} 4^{18} 9^{9} + 56 t. Pr, Ec 3^{17} + 7 t. Ec, Is 3^{10} $57^{1.1}$ Je 20^{12} La 4^{13} Ez $3^{20.21.21}$ + 12 t. Ez, Ho 14^{10}; ‖ תמים Gn 6^{9} (P) Jb 12^{4}; ‖ נָקִי Jb 17^{9} 22^{19} 27^{17} ψ 94^{21}; ‖ יִשְׁרֵי לֵב ψ 32^{11} 64^{11} 97^{11}. **4.** *righteous,* as justified and vindicated by ׳י, esp. servant of ׳י Is 53^{11}, so his people, usu. pl. Is 60^{21} ψ 33^{1} + 8 t. ψψ (v. also supr.); אָהֳלֵי צ׳ 118^{15} *tents of the righteous;* גּוֹרַל צ׳ 125^{3}; עֲדַת צ׳ 1^{5}; דֶּרֶךְ צ׳ v^{6}; sg. coll. $34^{20.22}$ 75^{11} Is 24^{16} $26^{7.7}$; גּוֹי צַדִּיק v^{2} (‖ שֹׁמֵר אֱמֻנִים). **5.** *right, correct,* Is 41^{26} (cf. אֱמֶת 43^{9}); *lawful* שְׁבִי צ׳ 49^{24} EV; but rd. עָרִיץ.

6659 צָדוֹק, and (1 K 1^{26}) צָדֹק$_{54}$ **n.pr.m.** (*just, righteous;* cf. Sab. n. pr. צדק CIS$^{\text{iv, No. 287, l. 2.11.15}}$ etc., DHM$^{\text{Hof Museum, No. 32}}$);—Σαδωκ, Σαδδουκ (cf. Lag$^{\text{BN 225 ff.}}$):—**1.**$_{48}$ priests: **a.** David's time 2 S 8^{17} = 1 Ch 18^{16}, 2 S $15^{24.25}$ + 23 t. S K Ch, + (Sol.'s time) 1 K 2^{35} = 1 Ch 29^{22}, 1 K $4^{2.4}$; ancestor of בְּנֵי צָדוֹק Ez 40^{46} 44^{15} 48^{11}, זֶרַע צ׳ 43^{19}, בֵּית צ׳ 2 Ch 31^{10}; descendant of Eleazar 1 Ch $5^{34.34}$ + 5 t. Ch. **b.** 1 Ch $5^{38.38}$, poss. = **c.** 1 Ch 9^{11} Ne 11^{11}. †**2.** father-in-law of Uzziah 2 K 15^{33} = 2 Ch 27^{11}. †**3.** two wall-builders: **a.** Ne 3^{4}. **b.** v^{29}; perh. = **c.** 10^{22}, and **d.** צ׳ הַסּוֹפֵר 13^{13}.

6667 צִדְקִיָּהוּ$_{56}$, ־יָּה$_{7}$ **n.pr.m.** (׳י *is righteousness;* cf. Sab. צדקאל DHM$^{\text{ib., on No. 32}}$);—Σεδεκια(ς): **1.** last king of Judah, מַתַּנְיָה, changed to צ׳: ־יָּהוּ 2 K $24^{17.18.20}$ $25^{2.7.7}$ = 2 Ch $36^{10.11}$, 1 Ch 3^{15} Je 1^{3} $21^{1.3.7}$ + 37 t. Je; ־יָּה †Je 27^{12} 28^{1} 29^{3} 49^{34}. †**2.** false prophets: **a.** under Ahab, ־יָּהוּ 1 K 22^{24} = 2 Ch $18^{10.20}$; ־יָּה 1 K 22^{11}. **b.** ־יָּהוּ Jerem.'s time, Je $29^{21.22}$. †**3.** ־יָּהוּ prince, Jerem.'s time, Je 36^{12}. †**4.** ־יָּה, priest, Nehem.'s time, Ne 10^{2} (𝔊L Σεχενιας). †**5.** ־יָּה, son of Jehoiachin, acc. to 1 Ch 3^{16}, but prob. gloss, Be SS, cf. Kit.

†[צָהֵב, צָהֹב, cf. Lag$^{\text{BN 31}}$] **vb. gleam** (NH *id.* (of face, bronze, etc.); Ar. صَهِبَ *be red*);—**Hoph.** *Pt.* נְחֹשֶׁת מֻצְהָב Ezr 8^{27} *polished bronze* (so NH and—appar. Hebraism—𝔗 2 Ch 4^{16}). 6668

†צָהֹב **adj. gleaming, yellow** (of hair);— שֵׂעָר צ׳ Lv $13^{30.32.36}$ (opp. שֵׂ׳ שָׁחֹר v$^{31.37}$). 6669

†I. [צָהַל] **vb. neigh, cry shrilly** (Ar. صَهَلَ *neigh,* Syr. ܨܗܠ *id.;* 𝔗 Est 8^{15} = BH);— 6670
Qal *Pf.* 3 fs. צָהֲלָה Est 8^{15}; 3 pl. צָהֲלוּ Is 24^{14}; *Impf.* 3 mpl. יִצְהָלוּ Je 5^{8}; 2 fs. תצהלי 50^{11} Kt, Qr 2 mpl. תִּצְהֲלוּ and so Vrss; *Imv.* fs. צַהֲלִי Is 10^{30} +; mpl. צַהֲלוּ Je 31^{7};—**1.** *neigh,* of men under fig. of stallions; c. אֶל *unto* (in desire) Je 5^{8}, of profligate Judaeans; abs. 50^{11} of arrogant Chaldeans. **2.** *cry shrilly,* in distress Is 10^{30} (c. adv. acc. קוֹלֵךְ); usu. joy, praise (‖ רָנַן) 12^{6} 54^{1}, c. ב *at, over,* Je 31^{7} Is 24^{14}; + שִׂמְחָה Est 8^{15}.

†[מִצְהָלָה] **n.f. neighing**;—pl. cstr. קוֹל 4684
מִצְהֲלוֹת אַבִּירָיו Je 8^{16} (‖ נַחְרַת סוּסָיו); sf. מִצְהֲלוֹתַיִךְ 13^{27} of idolatrous Judah, under fig. of mare desiring stallion (‖ זִמַּת זְנוּתֵךְ, נְאָפַיִךְ).

†II. [צָהַל] **vb. Hiph. make shining** (NH *id.* (rare); ‖ form of צהר, denom. fr. צהרים);—*Inf. cstr.* לְהַצְהִיל פָּנִים מִשָּׁמֶן ψ 104^{15}. 6670

צהר (√of foll.; cf. Ar. ظَهَرَ *appear, mount,* ظَهْرٌ *back,* ظَهِيرَةٌ *midday;* As. *ṣêru* (TelAm. *zu'ru,* etc.), *back;* Aram. טִיהֲרָא, ܛܗܪܐ MI^{15} הצהרם, *midday;* Lag$^{\text{BN 129}}$; > Kö$^{\text{ii. 1, 93}}$ (cf. Thes) = *shine,* ‖ זהר, NH Hiph. (rare), for this is in Aram. צהר (rare)); הִצְהִיר Ecclus 43^{3} is denom. from צהרים.

†I. [צֹהַר] **n.[m.]** only pl. צָהֳרַיִם **midday, noon,** Dt 28^{29}+, צָהֳרָיִם Gn 43^{16}+ (when sun *mounts* its highest; on form as expanded pl. (not du.) v. Ges$^{\S\ 88\ c}$ and reff.);—usu. **1.** *noon* as a specif. time of day, 1 K 18^{29}; esp. בַּצ׳ *at noon* Gn $43^{16.25}$ Am 8^{9} 1 K 18^{27} 20^{16} Ct 1^{7} (resting-time for flock), Je 6^{4} (opp. evening); בְּעֵת צ׳ Je 20^{16} (dist. fr. morning) as time of supposed security Je 15^{8} Zp 2^{4}; also מֵהַבֹּקֶר וְעַד הַצ׳ 1 K 18^{26}, 6672

עד־הצ׳ 2 K 4^{20}; without ב, as adv., צ׳ as time of prayer ψ 55^{18} (+ עֶרֶב, בֹּקֶר); as time of wasting קֶטֶב ψ 91^{6}; מִשְׁכַּב הַצ׳ 2 S 4^{5} *noonday repose.* **2.** *noon*, as bright, sim. of happiness, blessing, Is 58^{10} (opp. אֲפֵלָה), ψ 37^{6} (|| כָּאוֹר); cf. Jb 11^{17} (Ges[§ 133 e]); v. also בְּתוֹךְ הַצ׳ Is 16^{3} (opp. צִלֵּךְ); בַּצ׳ Dt 28^{29} Is 59^{10} Jb 5^{14}.

6672 †II. **צֹהַר** **n.f.** prob. **roof** (cf. Ar. As. TelAm. *back;* > Thes Di al. *light*, window);—צ׳ תַּעֲשֶׂה לַתֵּבָה Gn 6^{16}.

3323 †I. **יִצְהָר** **n.[m.] fresh oil** (newly *appeared*, cf. 'Ausbruch' Lag[BN 129] Kö[ii. 1, 93]; > Thes al. that which *shines*);—abs. יִצ׳ Ho 2^{10}+, sf. יִצְהָרְךָ Dt 7^{13}+;—*fresh oil*, as product of land, in unmanufactured state, usu. + דָּגָן, תִּירוֹשׁ, etc., rich possession, gift of י׳ Ho $2^{10.24}$ Je 31^{12} Dt 7^{13} 11^{14} Jo $2^{19.24}$, so חֵלֶב יִצ׳ Nu 18^{12}; Dt 28^{51} Hg 1^{11} 2 Ch 32^{28} Ne 5^{11}; tithed Dt 12^{17} 14^{23}; firstfruits for priest 18^{4} Ne 10^{38} cf. v^{40} 13^{5} (tithe for Levites), v^{12}, for priest and Levite 2 Ch 31^{5}; זֵית יִצ׳ 2 K 18^{32} *oil-olive*, i.e. oil-yielding olive-trees, cf. יִצ׳ alone Jo 1^{10}; יִצ׳ as *anointing oil* only in בְּנֵי הַיִּצ׳ Zc 4^{14}, i.e. anointed ones.

6671 †[צָהַר] **vb.denom.** fr. foreg., **Hiph. press out oil**;—*Impf.* 3 mpl. יַצְהִירוּ Jb 24^{11}.

3324 †II. **יִצְהָר** **n.pr.m.** Ισ(σ)ααρ: Levite, son of Kohath Ex $6^{18.21}$ Nu 3^{19} 16^{1} 1 Ch 5^{28} $6^{3.23}$ $23^{12.18}$.

3325 †**יִצְהָרִי** **adj.gent.** of foreg., c. art. as subst. coll. הַיִּצ׳ Nu 3^{27} 1 Ch 24^{22} $26^{23.29}$.

6673 **צַו** v. **צוה**. p. 846

צוא (√of foll.; cf. Syr. ܨܐܐ *be foul*, Eth. **ጸአ**: ; prob. also Ar. وَضِىَ *be polluted;* Dl[Pr 160] Kö[ii. 1, 162] cp. also As. *ṣi'*, *destroy, ruin;* NH צוֹאָה = BH; Aram. צָאתָא, ܨܐܬܐ, *filth*).

6627 †[**צֵאָה**] **n.f. filth**, specif. **human excrement**;—sf. צֵאָתֶךָ Dt 23^{14}; cstr. בְּגֶלְלֵי צֵאת הָאָדָם Ez 4^{12} (as fuel; cf. [גֵּל] p. 165 supr.).

6675 †**צֹאָה** **n.f. filth**;—abs. צ׳ Is 28^{8} (of drunkards' vomit, cf. קִיא); צ׳ fig. of iniquity, cstr. צֹאַת Is 4^{4}, sf. צֹאָתוֹ Pr 30^{12}; specif. of human *excrement* (= [צֵאָה]) sf. צֹאָתָם 2 K 18^{27} = Is 36^{12}
2716 (both Qr; Kt חר(א)יהם, cf. [חֲרָא] p. 351 supr.).

6674 †[**צֹאִי**] **adj. filthy**;—pl. צוֹאִים Zc 3^{3}, צֹאִים v^{4} (both of garments).

6677 **צַוָּאר** v. I. **צור**. p. 848

2578, 6678 †**צוֹבָא, צוֹבָה, צֹבָה** **n.pr.terr.** Σουβα, rarely Σωβα(λ): an Aramaean kingdom, time of (Saul and) David אֲרַם צוֹבָא 2 S $10^{6.8}$ (elsewhere צוֹבָה), אֲרַם צוֹבָה ψ 60^{2} (title); הֲדַדְעֶזֶר מֶלֶךְ צ׳ 2 S $8^{3.5.12}$ = 1 Ch $18^{3.5}$, 1 K 11^{23} 1 Ch 18^{9}; צ׳ also 19^{6};
חֲמַת צ׳ 2 Ch 8^{3}; orig. home of one of David's 2578
heroes 2 S 23^{36} (perh. rd. also for n.pr.m. מִבְחָר || 1 Ch 11^{38}, cf. Dr); מַלְכֵי צ׳ 1 S 14^{47} (only here in Saul's time); Nö[ARAM, in Ency. Bib., cf. ZMG xxv (1871), 113 ff.] places between Hamath and Damascus (about *Ḥums*, Emesa), and so Dl[Pa 279 f.], who cp. As. city *Ṣubitu*, cf. Schr[COT. 2 S 8, 3].

†I. **צוּד** **vb. hunt** (NH *id.* (rare), מְצוּדָה 6679
= BH; As. *ṣâdu*, *hunt*, so Ar. صَادَ (صيد), Aram. צוּד, צִיד, ܨܕ (ܨܘܕ?); OAram. צידא *hunting*);—**Qal** *Pf.* 3 pl. צָדוּ La 4^{18}; sf. צָדוּנִי 3^{52}, וְצָדוּם consec. Je 16^{16}; *Impf.* 3 ms. יָצוּד Lv 17^{13}, etc.; *Imv.* ms. צוּדָה Gn 27^{3}; *Inf. abs.* צוֹד La 3^{52}; *cstr.* לָצוּד Gn 27^{5}; *Pt.* הַצָּד v^{33};—*hunt*, c. acc. 1. צַיִד Gn 27^{3} Qr (> Kt צידה), v$^{5.33}$ (all J), צֵיד חַיָּה Lv 17^{13} (H); טֶרֶף Jb 38^{39}; c. acc. pers. Mi 7^{2} (+ חֵרֶם, instr.), Je 16^{16} (+ מֵעַל), Jb 10^{16}, צוֹד צָדוּנִי כַּצִּפּוֹר La 3^{52}, subj. evil ψ 140^{12}; c. acc. צְעָדֵינוּ La 4^{18}, נֶפֶשׁ יְקָרָה Pr 6^{26}.—Ho 9^{13} rd. prob. לָצוּד (or לְצַיִד), for MT לְצוֹר, v. צֹר. **Pō'l.** *hunt* (keenly, eagerly?), *Impf.* 2 fpl. תְּצוֹדֵדְנָה Ez 13^{18}; *Inf.cstr.* לְצוֹדֵד v^{18}; *Pt.* fpl. מְצֹדְדוֹת v$^{20.20}$, all c. acc. נְפָשׁוֹת (of magic arts, necromancy, etc.).

†I. **צַיִד** **n.m. hunting, game**;—abs. צ׳ 6718
Gn 10^{9}+, צָיִד 27^{3} (Qr; > Kt צידה), Ne 13^{15}, cstr. צֵיד Gn 27^{25}; sf. צֵידִי v^{19}, etc.;—**1.** *hunting* Gn 27^{30}; יֹדֵעַ צ׳ 25^{27}, גִּבֹּר־צ׳ $10^{9.9}$, (all J). **2.** *game* hunted and taken (cf. Ba[NB 161]), Gn 25^{28} 27^{3} (v. supr.) v$^{5.7.19.25.31.33}$ (all J), cf. Pr 12^{27}; צֵיד חַיָּה אוֹ עוֹף Lv 17^{13} (H).

†[**צַיָּד**] **n.m. hunter**;—pl. צַיָּדִים Je 16^{16}. 6719

†**מְצָד, מְצַד** **n.f.**[Je 48, 41] **fastness, stronghold** 4679
(prop. *hunting-place*?);—abs. מְצָד 1 Ch 11^{7} 12^{16}, מְצַד 12^{8}; pl. abs. מְצָדוֹת 1 S 23^{14}+, cstr. *id.* v^{29} (Gi, 24^{1} van d. H. Baer), Is 33^{16};—**1.** *mountain-fastness* Ju 6^{2} 1 S $23^{14.19.29}$ (v. supr.), Ez 33^{27} 1 Ch $12^{8.16}$; מְצָדוֹת סְלָעִים Is 33^{16}. **2.** more gen., *stronghold* Je 48^{41} 51^{30} Ez 19^{9} (Baer Gi; van d. H. מְצוֹדוֹת *id.* [II. מְצוֹדָה] Ew Hi-Sm Da al.; *nets* [I. מְצוֹדָה] Krae; del. Co Oort Toy); citadel of Jerusalem 1 Ch 11^{7}.

†I. [**מָצוֹד**] **n.m.** in pl., dub., usu. **siege-** 4685
works;—מְצוֹדִים גְּדֹלִים Ec 9^{14}, but read מְצוּרִים Wkl[Altor. Forsch. iv. 353], v. מָצוֹר **2**, p. 849 a.

†II. [**מָצוֹד**] **n.[m.] hunting implement,** 4685
specif. net (cf. Syr. ܡܨܕܬܐ, 𝔗 מְצַדְתָּא, *net*);—

only fig.: cstr מְצוֹד רָעִים Pr 12^{12} (but text dub., v. conj. in Toy); sf. מְצוּדוֹ Jb 19^{6} (of God as Job's hunter); pl. מְצוֹדִים וַחֲרָמִים לִבָּהּ Ec 7^{26} (of woman).

4685 †I. מְצוֹדָה **n.f. net**;—מ׳ Ec 9^{12} for fish (in
4679 sim.);—pl. Ez 19^{9} v. מְצָד supr. p. 844

4686 †I. מְצוּדָה **n.f. net, prey**;—abs. מ׳ Ez 13^{21} ψ 66^{11}; sf. מְצוּדָתִי Ez 12^{13} 17^{20};—**1.** *net*, in fig. of י׳'s judgment, Ez 12^{13} 17^{20} (both ‖ רֶשֶׁת), ψ 66^{11}. **2.** *prey* Ez 13^{21} (fig.).

4685 †II. [מְצוֹדָה] **n.f. fastness, stronghold**;—sf. מְצֹדָתָהּ Is 29^{7} (of Ariel);—pl. Ez 19^{9} v. מְצָד.

4686 †II. מְצוּדָה **n.f. fastness, stronghold**;—abs. מ׳ 1 S 22^{4}+, מְצֻדָה 2 S 5^{9}, cstr. מְצֻדַת v^{7}; sf. מְצוּדָתִי ψ 18^{3}+, מְצֻדָתִי 2 S 22^{2}; pl. מְצוּדוֹת ψ 31^{3};—*fastness* of David, 1 S 22$^{4.5}$ 24^{23} (Gi v^{22}) 2 S 5^{17} 23^{14} = 1 Ch 11^{16}; rd. also מְצֻדַת עֲדֻלָּם 1 S 22^{1} 2 S 23^{13} 1 Ch 11^{15}, for MT מְעָרַת (v. מְעָרָה p. 792 b); of Jerus., מְצֻדַת צִיּוֹן 2 S 5^{7} = 1 Ch 11^{5}, cf. 2 S 5^{9}; home of eagle Jb 39^{28} (+שֶׁן־סֶלַע); elsewhere fig. of י׳ ψ 18^{3} = 2 S 22^{2}, ψ 31^{4} 71^{3} (all + סַלְעִי), 91^{2} (+ מַחְסִי), 144^{2} (+ חַסְדִּי, but this dub., Krochm Gr Che חֶסְנִי, Dy חִזְקִי, Du סַלְעִי; poss. is מַחְסִי); also בֵּית מְצוּדוֹת 31^{3}.

II. **צוד** (√ of foll.; relation to I. צוד dub.; cf. As. *ṣidîtu*, Ar. زَادَ (و), Aram. זְוָדָה, ܙܘܳܕܳܐ, Palm. זוד, all *provisions* (esp. for journey); in Thes = I. צוד; on *game* as early food of nomads v. RS$^{\text{Sem. i. 205; 2nd ed. 222 f.}}$ cf. Doughty$^{\text{Arab. Des. i. 70, 326, 562}}$; ז (Ar. Aram.) is then secondary).

6718 †II. [צַיִד] **n.[m.] provision, food**;—abs. צַיִד Ne 13^{15}; sf. צֵידוֹ Jb 38^{41}, etc.;—*provision* taken on journey Jos 9^{14}, לֶחֶם צֵידָם v^{5} (both JE); more gen. (late), *food, food-supply*, Ne 13^{15}
6718 ψ 132^{15}, of raven Jb 38^{41}.—I. צַיִד v. צוד. p. 844

6720 †צֵידָה **n.f. id.**;—abs. צ׳ Jos 9^{11} + 2 t., צֵדָה Gn 42^{25} + 5 t.;—*provision* for journey, march, Gn 42^{25} 45^{21} Ex 12^{39} (all E), Jos 1^{11} (D), 9^{11} (JE), Ju 7^{8} (text dub. cf. GFM), 20^{10} 1 S 22^{10}; *supply*
6718 *of food* ψ 78^{25}.—Gn 27^{3} v. I. צַיִד, sub צוד.

6679 †[צִיד] **vb. denom. Hithp. supply oneself with provisions, take as one's provision**;—*Pf.* 1 pl. הִצְטַיַּדְנוּ Jos 9^{12} this bread *we took as our provision*; *Impf.* 3 mpl. וַיִּצְטַיָּדוּ v^{4} (so rd. for MT וַיִּצְטַיָּרוּ, Codd Vrss Thes al.), abs.

6680 [צָוָה]$_{485}$ **vb. Pi. lay charge (upon), give charge (to), charge, command, order** (Ba $^{\text{ZMG xli (1887), 641}}$ Gerber^{124} cp. Ar. وَصَى *combine*, II. *enjoin*, IV. *charge*; وَصِيَّةٌ *injunction, command*; Thes cp. Syr. ܨܘܳܐ, *erect*, ܨܘܳܝܳܐ, *stone-heap*, Ar. صُوَّةٌ *guide-stone*, cf. Schulth^{57}; Gerber makes Heb. vb. denom. fr. מִצְוָה, but vb. is much earlier);—*Pf.* 3 ms. צִוָּה Gn 6^{22}+; sf. צִוַּנִי Dt 4^{5}+; צִוְּךָ Dt 4^{23}+; צִוָּהוּ Gn 7^{5}+, etc.; 1 s. צִוִּיתִי Ex 29^{35} + 29 t., צִוֵּיתִי Lv 8^{31} + 4 t., etc.; *Impf.* 3 ms. יְצַוֶּה Gn 18^{19} + 8 t.; יְצַו Dt 28^{8}; וַיְצַו Gn 2^{16}+; sf. וַיְצַוֵּךְ 1 Ch 22^{12}, etc.; 1 s. וָאֲצַוֶּה Ezr 8^{17} Qr (> Kt ואוצאה); 3 mpl. וַיְצַוּוּ Gn 50^{16}+, etc.; *Inf. cstr.* צַוֺּת 2 S 18^{5}+, etc.; *Imv.* ms. צַוֵּה Jos 4^{16} + 2 t.; צַו Lv 6^{2} + 9 t.; mpl. צַוּוּ Jos 1^{11} 4^{3}; *Pt.* מְצַוֶּה Nu 32^{25}+; cstr. מְצַוֵּה Is 55^{4}, etc.; f. מְצַוָּה Gn 27^{8};—**1. a.** *lay charge upon*, c. עַל pers., Gn 2^{16} (J) 28^{6} (P) 1 K 2^{43} 11^{11} Am 2^{12} Je 35^{6} + 6 t.; עַל rei, עַל הֶעָבִים אֲצַוֶּה מֵהַמְטִיר Is 5^{6}, cf. Jb 36^{32}, צ׳ עַל־חָגָב 2 Ch 7^{13}. **b.** *give charge to, command to* c. לְ pers. Ex 1^{22} (E) 1 S 20^{29} 1 Ch 22^{17} Is 13^{3} Jer 32^{23} ψ 105^{8} תּוֹרָה צ׳ לָנוּ מֹשֶׁה Dt 33^{4}, cf. Ne 9^{14}; צַו לְבֵיתֶךָ 2 K 20^{1} *give charge to thy household* (in preparation for death) = Is 38^{1} (cf. NH, B.Bath.$^{151\,b}$, צַוָּאָה '*verbal will*' Id$^{147\,a}$). **c.** *give charge unto*, c. אֶל pers. Ex 16^{34} (P), 1 K 11^{10}; וַיְצַו אֶל־בֵּיתוֹ 2 S 17^{23} (cf. **b**). **d.** *give charge over, appoint*, c. acc. pers. + עַל rei, Ne 7^{2} 1 Ch 22^{12}, צ׳ (לִהְיוֹת) נָגִיד עַל *appoint* one (to be) ruler over 2 S 6^{21} 1 K 1^{35}; c. לנגיד 1 S 13^{14} 25^{30}; שפטים על 2 S 7^{11} = 1 Ch 17^{10}; c. inf. (no עַל) לִרְעוֹת עמי 2 S 7^{7} = 1 Ch 17^{6}; וְצִוִּיתָה אתו לְעֵינֵיהֶם Nu 27^{19} (P) *and thou shalt install him in their sight*, cf. v^{23} (P). **e.** *give* one *charge, command* (oft. עַל *concerning*), Gn 12^{20} (J), Nu 8^{22} (P), 2 S 14^{8} 18^{5} Je 7^{22} 39^{11} Is 45^{12} (AV RV Che Ry^{Kau}; > Ges Ew Di Du al. as **d**), 10^{6} (al. *against*), Na 1^{14} (al. *id.*); c. לְ Nu 9^{8} 32^{28} (P), ψ 91^{11} La 1^{17} Est 3^{2}; c. אֶל Is 23^{11} Je 47^{7}. **2.** *charge, command*: **a.** c. acc. pers. + rei, oft., esp. of the law: Deut. phrases are אשר אנכי מצוך Ex 34^{11} (J), Dt 4^{40} 6$^{2.6}$ + 18 t. Dt, cf. 15^{15}; אשר אנכי מצוה אתכם Dt 4$^{2.2}$ + 9 t. Dt; †הַדֶּרֶךְ אשר צ׳ Dt 13^{6} Ex 32^{8} (E) Dt 5^{30} 9$^{12.16}$ 11^{28} 31^{29}. **b.** c. acc. pers. + obj. clause, e.g., Inf. Gn 50^{2}+; ו consec. Pf. 18^{19} (J), Nu 35^{2} (P); ו consec. Impf. 2 S 4^{12} 1 K 2^{46}; weak ו c. Impf. Ex 27^{20} (P) Jos 4^{16}; Imv. Jos 1^{9} 1 S 18^{22}. **c.** acc. pers., acc. rei om., Ex 18^{23} (E) Gn 49^{33} (P)+; obj. given after לֵאמֹר Gn 26^{11} 32$^{18.20}$ Lv 6^{2}+; וַיֹּאמֶר, etc., Gn 28^{1} 49^{29}+. **d.** acc. rei, acc. pers. om., צ׳ לעולם בריתו ψ 111^{9}; †זֶה הַדָּבָר אֲשֶׁר צ׳ י׳, Ex 16$^{16.32}$ 35^{4} Lv 8^{5} 9^{6} 17^{2} Nu 30^{2} 36^{6} (P); obj. cl., Lv 8^{34} (P), 13^{54} (P); Gn 42^{25}

(E), 1 K 5^{20}; Ju 4^{6}. **e.** abs. Gn 50^{16} (E), La 3^{37}. **3.** *charge, command*, acc. pers. in phr. כַּאֲשֶׁר צ׳ Ex 23^{15} (E) Gn 7^{9} (P)+; ככל אשר צ׳ Gn 7^{5} (J) Ex 29^{35} (P)+; כאשר צ׳ י׳ מֹשֶׁה Ex 12$^{28.50}$ 39$^{1.5}$ +37 t. P; ככל אשר צ׳ י׳ משה 39$^{32.42}$+5 t. P; †לכל אשר צ׳ Jos 1^{18} 22^{2} Je 35^{8}; acc. pers. om. כאשר צ׳ Ex 7^{10} Nu 32^{25} (P)+; ככל אשר צ׳ 2 K 11^{9}=2 Ch 23^{8}+; †לכל אשר צ׳ Ex 36^{1} (P). †**4.** *charge*, with command to others, *commission*, **a.** acc. pers. + אֶל pers. (sts. + acc. rei) Ex 6^{13} 25^{22} Lv 27^{34} (P) Dt 1^{3} Je 27^{4} Est 4^{10}; acc. pers. om. Gn 50^{16} (E) Est 3^{12} 8^{9}. **b.** בְּיַד of agent, + אֶל, Nu 15^{23} 36^{13} (P); אֶל om. Lv 8^{36} (P), Ezr 9^{11} Ne 8^{14}. **c.** acc. pers. + עַל for אֶל Ezr 8^{17} 1 Ch 22^{13} Mal 3^{22} Est 4^{5}. **d.** c. acc. rei, וצ׳ בִּרְכָתִי לָ Lv 25^{21} (P) *and I will command my blessing to you*, c. אִתְּךָ Dt 28^{8}, cf. ψ 133^{3}; צ׳ חסדו 42^{9}, בֹּקֶר Jb 38^{12}, חֶרֶב, נָחָשׁ Am 9$^{3.4}$. †**5.** *command, appoint, ordain*, of divine act: in creation Is 45^{12} ψ 33^{9} 148^{5}, providence 2 S 17^{14} Am 6^{11} 9^{9} Jb 37^{12} ψ 78^{23} Is 34^{16}, redemption ψ 7^{7} 44^{5} 68^{29} 71^{3}; so of idol Is 48^{5} (|| עשׂה). †**Pu.** *Pf.* 3 ms. צֻוָּה Nu 3^{16} 36^{2}; 2 ms. צֻוֵּיתָה Gn 45^{19}, etc.; *Impf.* 3 ms. יְצֻוֶּה Ex 34^{34};—*be commanded*, i.e. receive command, subj. pers., Gn 45^{19} (E), c. בְּ by whom Nu 36^{2} (P); אשר צ׳ Ex 34^{34} (P), כִּי־כֵן צ׳ Lv 8^{35} 10^{13} (P), כאשר צ׳ Nu 3^{16} (P) Ez 12^{7} 24^{18} 37^{7}.

6725 †צִיּוּן **n.m. sign-post, monument** (NH *id.* (צִיֵּן Pi. denom.); prob. from √ in orig. physical sense, v. esp. Ar. صُوَّةٌ, صَوَّانٌ Syr. ܨܘܝܐ, cf. Schulth$^{Hom. Wurz. 57}$ Kö$^{ii. 1, 154}$; > √צין Buhl);—abs. צ׳, grave-stone 2 K 23^{17}; sign-post Ez 39^{15}; guide-posts, pl. צִיֻּנִים Je 31^{21} (|| תַּמְרוּרִים).

4687 מִצְוָה $_{181}$ **n.f. commandment**;—מ׳ Pr 6^{23}+; cstr. מִצְוַת Jos 22^{3}+; sf. מִצְוָתְךָ Dt 26^{13} ψ 119^{96}, מִצְוָתוֹ Nu 15^{31}; pl. מִצְוֹת abs. Lv 26^{14}+ (מצוות Ne 9^{14}); cstr. 4^{2}+; sf. מִצְוֹתַי Gn 26^{5}+, etc.;—not used before D and Je; in Je only of man's commands; not Ez nor Minor Proph., exc. Mal;—**1.** *commandment*, of man: king, 1 K 2^{43} 2 K 18^{36}=Is 36^{21}, 2 Ch 8^{15}+14 t.; מ׳ אב Je 35$^{14.16.18}$ Pr 6^{20}; מ׳ אנשים Is 29^{13}; pl. only Je 35^{18} Pr 10^{8} Ne 10^{33}; המצוה, *the order* (title of property) Je 32^{11}. **2.** of God: **a.** sg. *the commandment*, code of law: 2 Ch 8^{13} Ezr 10^{3} ψ 19^{9}; esp. of D שמר המ׳ Dt 8$^{1.2}$+5 t. D; עשׂה המ׳ Dt 6^{25} 15^{5}; (ה)מ׳ אשר צוה Dt 26^{13} 30^{11} 31^{5}; סוּר מִן המ׳ Dt 17^{20}; מ׳ הַסֵּפֶר Nu 15^{31} (P); || תּוֹרָה Ex 24^{12} (R^{D}) Jos 22^{5} (D) 2 Ch 14^{3} 31^{21}; + מִשְׁפָּטִים, חֻקִּים Dt 5^{28} 6^{1}+. **b.** pl. of *commands* of D and later codes c. 2 pl. (*ye shall, shall not;* Br$^{Hex. new ed., 246 ff.}$), Lv 4^{2}+5 t. P, Is 48^{18}+25 t. (late; esp. ψ 119, 20 t.); שמר מ׳ Ex 20^{6} (R) Lv 22^{31} (H) Dt 4^{2}+10 t. D, 1 K 14^{8} 2 K 18^{6}+5 t.; עשׂה מ׳ Lv 26^{14} (H)+5 t.; שמע מ׳ Dt 11^{13}+4 t.; המ׳ אשר צוה Lv 27^{34} (H); עבר מ׳ Dt 26^{13} 2 Ch 24^{20}; עזב מ׳ 1 K 18^{18} 2 K 17^{16} Ezr 9^{10}; הפר מ׳ Ezr 9^{14}; in combinations, esp. by Redactors and late writers; order various: (1) with חֻקִּים Ex 15^{26} (R^{D}) Dt 4^{40} Ezr 7^{11}+; ח׳+משפטים Dt 26^{17} 1 K 8^{58} Ne 1^{7} 10^{30}; +משפטים, תורות Ne 9^{13}; +תורה Ne 9^{14}; +עדות Dt 6^{17} 1 Ch 29^{19} 2 Ch 34^{31}. (2) with חֻקּוֹת Lv 26^{3} (H) Dt 6^{2} 10^{13}+9 t.; ח׳+משפטים Lv 26^{15} Dt 8^{11} 11^{1} 30^{16} 1 K 6^{12}+תורה, משפטים ψ 89^{32}, +משפטים, עֵדוֹת 1 K 2^{3}; +תורות Gn 26^{5} (R^{D}); +עדות 2 K 23^{3}. (3) with משפטים Nu 36^{13} (P) 1 Ch 28^{7} Ne 9^{29} Dn 9^{5}; with תורות Ex 16^{28} (R), with ערות Ne 9^{34}. **c.** of special *commands* of God 1 S 13^{13} 1 K 13^{21} 2 Ch 29^{25} Ne 13^{5} Mal 2$^{1.4}$ Jb 23^{12}. **3.** *commandment*, sg., of code of wisdom Pr 19^{16}, || תורה 6^{23}, || דבר 13^{13}; pl. of special commands 2^{1} 3^{1} 4^{4} 7$^{1.2}$.

†צַו appar. **n.[m.]**, dub. word;—in הָלַךְ 6673
אַחֲרֵי־צָו Ho 5^{11} usu. *command, ordinance;* < 𝔊𝔖 Che Now GASm שָׁוְא; elsewh. only צַו לָצָו צַו לָצָו (|| קַו לָקָו קַו לָקָו), Is 28^{10} in mocking mimicry of Is.'s words, and, v^{13}, of the unintelligible speech of י׳'s foreign agents of judgment; Ges Che$^{Comm.}$ al. (cf. AV RV) render *command upon command;* Ew Di (carpenter's) *rule* (+קַו=*line and rule*), fr. √צָוָה (whence צַו); Du Che^{Hpt} explain as mocking sounds without sense.

†[צָוַח] **vb. cry aloud** (NH *id.;* so As. 6681
ṣâḫu (?), Ar. (صيح), صَاحَ, Aram. צְוַח, ܨܘܚ; Eth. ጸውዐ: *call*);—**Qal** *Impf.* 3 mpl. יִצְוָחוּ Is 42^{11} (in joy, || יָרֹנּוּ).

†צְוָחָה **n.f. outcry**;—in distress, grief, abs. 6682
צ׳ ψ 144^{14}; cstr. צִוְחַת Je 14^{2}; sf. צִוְחָתֵךְ 46^{12}; abs. also Is 24^{11} (c. עַל *for, because of*).

צול (√of foll., cf. *miṣwal* (in Syria), a stone-lined hollow, or basin, for washing grain, Wetzst$^{Siebe ZPV xiv (1891), 3}$).

†צוּלָה **n.f. ocean-deep**;—Is 44^{27}. 6683

†[מְצוֹלָה], מְצוּלָה **n.f. depth, deep**;— 4688
abs. מְצוּלָה Jb 41^{23}+; pl. abs. מְצוֹלֹת Ex 15^{5} Ne 9^{11}, מְצֻלוֹת ψ 88^{7}; cstr. מְצוּלוֹת Zc 10^{11}, מְצֻלוֹת Mi 7^{19} ψ 68^{23};—*depth*, pl. מ׳ יָם *depths of the sea* Mi 7^{19} ψ 68^{23}; abs. Ex 15^{5} (of Red Sea) Ne 9^{11}

(*id.*); fig. of deep distress ψ 88[7] (בּוֹר תַּחְתִּיּוֹת ‖); מ׳ יְאֹר Zc 10[11] (i.e. of Nile); sg. = *the deep sea, deep*, ψ 107[24] Jon 2[4] Jb 41[23] (in hyperb. descript. of crocodile); *depth* of marsh, swamp, בִּיוֵן מ׳ ψ 69[3] *in mire of (the) depth*, fig. of distress (מַעֲמַקֵּי־מַיִם ‖), cf. מ׳ alone v[16] (בְּאֵר ‖).

4699 †מְצֻלָּה **n.f.** dub. word: Zc 1[8] the myrtles which are בַּמּ׳, appar. some locality about Jerus., called *the basin, hollow;* GASm *glen* or *valley-bottom;* poss. is מְצֻלָּה < מְצִלָּה, *shadow* (III. צלל).

6684 †[צוּם] **vb. abstain from food, fast** (NH *id.;* Ar. (صوم) صَامَ, Eth. ጾመ: Aram. צוּם, ܨܳܡ);—**Qal** *Pf.* 2 ms. צַמְתָּ 2 S 12[21]; 2 mpl. צַמְתֶּם Zc 7[5], sf. צַמְתֻּנִי v[5]; *Impf.* 3 ms. וַיָּצָם 2 S 12[16], וַיָּצוֹם 1 K 21[27]; 1 s. אָצוּם Est 4[16], etc.; *Imv.* mpl. צוּמוּ v[16]; *Inf. abs.* צוֹם Zc 7[5]; *Pt.* צָם 2 S 12[23] Ne 1[4];—*fast*, in mourning the dead 1 S 31[13] = 1 Ch 10[12], 2 S 1[12]; in worship (contrition, intercession, etc.) Ju 20[26] 1 S 7[6] 2 S 12[16] (c. acc. cogn. צוֹם; ‖ בִּקֵּשׁ), v[23] and (+ בָּכָה), v[21.22] (q.v. for explanation), Je 14[12] Zc 7[5] (+ סָפוֹד), הֲצוֹם צַמְתֻּנִי v[5] (Ges § 117 x) *was it at all unto me* [׳י] *that ye fasted?* וָאֱהִי צָם Ne 1[4] (periphr. conj.; + מִתְפַּלֵּל), cf. Ezr 8[23] (+ בִּקֵּשׁ), Est 4[16] (c. עַל pers. *for* whom), v[16], Is 58[3] (עִנִּינוּ נַפְשֵׁנוּ ‖), v[4] (c. לְ rei), v[4]; once in disappointment and vexation 1 K 21[27].

6685 †צוֹם **n.m.**[Is 58, 5] **fasting, fast**;—צ׳ abs. 2 S 12[16]+, cstr. Zc 8[19] (4 t.); sf. צֹמְכֶם Is 58[3]; pl. צוֹמוֹת Est 9[31];—*fast*, as acc. cogn. 2 S 12[16]; public observance 1 K 21[9.12] 2 Ch 20[3] Ezr 8[21] Je 36[9] Jon 3[5] (all obj. of קָרָא *proclaim*), cf. Jo 1[14] 2[15] (both obj. of קִדְּשׁוּ); יוֹם צוֹם Je 36[6], יוֹם צֹמְכֶם Is 58[3], cf. v[5] (יוֹם עַנּוֹת אָדָם נַפְשׁוֹ ‖), v[5.6]; of periodic fasts Zc 8[19.19.19.19] Est 9[31]; act or state of fasting, נֶאֶסְפוּ בְצ׳ וּבְשַׂקִּים Ne 9[1] cf. Jo 2[12] Dn 9[3] Est 4[3]; עִנֵּיתִי בַצ׳ נַפְשִׁי ψ 35[13] cf. 69[11] (on וָאֶבְכֶּה v. Che Bae); causing physical weakness 109[24].

צוע (√of foll.; cf. Ar. صاغ *form, fashion*).

6816 †צַעֲצֻעִים **n.[m.]pl. things formed, images**; מַעֲשֵׂה צ׳ 2 Ch 3[10] *image work* (of cherubim).

6687 †[צוּף] **vb. flow, overflow, [float]** (NH *id.;* so Aram. טוּף, ܛܳܦ;—Ar. طَوْف *skin-raft* is loan-wd. Frä[220]);—**Qal** *Pf.* 3 pl. צָפוּ־מַיִם עַל־רֹאשִׁי La 3[54] (fig.). **Hiph. 1.** *Pf. cause to flow over*, הֵצִיף אֶת־מֵי יַם־סוּף עַל־פְּנֵיהֶם Dt 11[4]. **2.** *cause to float: Impf.* 3 ms. וַיָּצֶף הַבַּרְזֶל 2 K 6[6].

6688 †I. צוּף **n.m.** (honey-)comb (as *exuding* honey);—only fig.: cstr. צוּף־דְּבַשׁ Pr 16[24]; pl. צוּפִים ψ 19[11] (+ נֹפֶת, דְּבַשׁ), 𝔊 κηρίον, κηρία, 𝔙 *favus*.

†II. צוּף **n.m.** Ephr. ancestor of Elkanah and Samuel, בֶּן־צ׳ 1 S 1[1] (ἐν Ναυειβ, 𝔊L υἱοῦ Σωφ), 1 Ch 6[20] Qr 𝔊 𝔙 (Kt צִיף); appar. = צוֹפַי v[11] (Levite), Σουφ(ει): hence prob. אֶרֶץ צוּף 1 S 9[5] (in Benj., τὴν (γῆν) Σ(ε)ιφ(α)). 6689

†צוּפִי **adj.gent. Ṣuphite**;—so read prob. for צוֹפִים 1 S 1[1] (We Klo Dr and most mod., after 𝔊 Σ(ε)ιφα, A Σωφιμ). 6689 7436

†[צָפָה] **n.f. out-flow**;—sf. צָפָתֵךְ Ez 32[6] *thine outflow* (flowing blood), Co Bthl Toy Krae. 6824

צוֹפַי = II. צוּף. צוֹפִים v. צוּפִי. above 6689, 7436

†I. [צִיץ, צוּץ] **vb. 1. blossom. 2. shine, sparkle** (perh. orig. meaning of √, but connex. of **1, 2.** dub.) (NH *id.* Hiph., fig. senses, צִיץ n. = BH);—**Qal** *Pf.* **1.** 3 ms. צָץ הַמַּטֶּה Ez 7[10] (fig.; ‖ פָּרַח הַזָּדוֹן); *Impf.* 3 ms. יָצִיץ ψ 90[6] (of grass, חָצִיר), 103[15] (man under fig. of flower), fig. יָצִיץ וּפָרַח יִשׂ׳ Is 27[6]; 3 mpl. יָצִיצוּ ψ 72[16], וַיָּצִיצוּ 92[8] (‖ פָּרַח; both fig. of men =) *flourish*. **2.** *shine, gleam:* of crown (נֵזֶר) ψ 132[18]. **Hiph.** *Impf.* 3 ms. וַיָּצֵץ צִיץ Nu 17[23] *it put forth blossoms* (of rod; — perhaps from ‖ וַיֹּצֵא פֶרַח). 6692

†I. צִיץ **n.m.**[Is 28, 1] **1. blossom, flower. 2. shining thing**;—צ׳ abs. Is 42[7]+, cstr. v[6]+; pl. צִצִּים 1 K 6[18] + 3 t. 6 (on form v. Kö[II. 1, 60]);—**1.** *blossom, flower*, Nu 17[23] (P; of Aaron's rod); (fig. of man Is 40[7.8] (both נָבֵל צ׳; ‖ חָצִיר), cf. sim. צִיץ הַשָּׂדֶה v[6] (‖ *id.*), ψ 103[15], and צ׳ alone Jb 14[2]; צ׳ נֹבֵל Is 28[1] (fig. of Samaria), so prob. also v[4] (for MT צִיצַת נ׳; so Marti); פְּטוּרֵי צִצִּים, as ornaments of temple 1 K 6[18.29.32.35]. **2.** *shining thing*, plate of gold, constituting the diadem on front of high priest's mitre, Lv 8[9] Ex 28[36] 39[30] (all P).—II, III. צִיץ, v. p. 851 infr. 6731 6733 6731-32

צִיצַת Is 28[4], v. I. צִיץ supr. 6733

†II. [צוּץ] **vb. Hiph. gaze, peep** (NH Hiph. *gaze* (rare); Aram. צִיץ *gaze*);—*Pt.* מֵצִיץ מִן־הַחֲרַכִּים Ct 2[9] (v. ח׳, p. 355). 6692

†I. [צוּק] **vb. Hiph. constrain, bring into straits, press upon** (NH צוּק *be distressed* (rare), Hiph. = BH; Ar. (ى) ضَاقَ *be narrow, tight*, so Eth. ጸቀ:; Aram. עִיק, ܥܳܩ; Chr Pal. ܥܘܩ);—*Pf.* 3 fs. הֱצִיקַתְהוּ Ju 16[16], sf. הֱצִיקַתְהוּ 14[17], ־נִי Jb 32[18] (Gi v[19]); 1 s. וַהֲצִיקוֹתִי consec. Is 29[2]; *Impf.* 3 ms. יָצִיק Dt 28[53] + 2 t.; 3 mpl. יְצִיקוּ Je 19[9]; *Pt.* מֵצִיק Is 51[13.13], pl. מְצִיקִים 29[7];—*bring into straits*, by importunity c. לְ pers. Ju 16[16], c. sf. pers. 14[17]; *constrain* (to speak) Jb 32[18] 6693

(sf. pers.); elsewhere of *bringing into straits* a city or people, c. לְ, Is $29^{2.7}$, so 7^{6} (reading וּנְצִיקֶנָּה for MT וּנְקִיצֶנָּה), Thes Che Du Gr Marti, cf. formula בְּמָצוֹר וּבְמָצוֹק אֲשֶׁר יָצ׳ לְ Dt $28^{53.55.57}$ Je 19^{9}; pt. abs. הַמֵּצִיק Is $51^{13.13}$ *the oppressor.*

6695 †צוֹק **n.[m.]** si vera l., **constraint, distress**;—וּבְצוֹק הָעִתִּים Dn 9^{25} usu. *in distressful times;* Gr וּבְקֵץ וגו׳ (so 𝔊 [v^{27}] 𝔖), as beginning of v^{26}, omitting וְ in וְאחרי (cf. Bev Marti).

6695 †צוּקָה **n.f. pressure, distress**;—national Is 8^{22} (+צָרָה), cf. אֶרֶץ צָרָה וְצ׳ 30^{6}; personal צָרָה וְצ׳ Pr 1^{27}.

4164 †II. מוּצָק, מוּצַק **n.[m.] constraint, distress**;—abs. מוּצָק Is 8^{23} *distress;* abs. also מוּצָק Jb 36^{16}, of distress as *constraint* (opp. רַחַב); רֹחַב מַיִם בְּמוּצָק 37^{10}, lit. *in constraint* (i.e.

4165 frozen).—I. מוּצָק v. יצק. p. 427

4689 †מָצוֹק **n.[m.] straitness, straits, stress**;—alw. abs. מ׳;—כָּל־אִישׁ מ׳ 1 S 22^{2} *every man of straits* (in straits); בְּמָצוֹר וּבְמ׳ Dt $28^{53.55.57}$ Je 19^{9} (all of national *straits*); צַר־וּמ׳ מְצָאוּנִי ψ 119^{143}; perh. rd. מָצוֹק also 32^{6}, for מצא רק, cf. Du Br.

4691 †מְצוּקָה **n.f.** id.;—abs. יוֹם צַר וּמ׳ Jb 15^{24}; צָרָה וּמ׳ Zp 1^{15}; pl. sf., of י׳ delivering מִמְּצוּקוֹתַי ψ 25^{17}, מִמְּצוּקוֹתֵיהֶם etc., $107^{6.13.19.28}$.

6694 †II. [צוּק] **vb. pour out, melt** (‖ יצק);—**Qal** *Pf.* 3 pl. (acc. to Thes al.) צָקוּן Is 26^{16}, but v. infr.; *Impf.* 3 ms. וְאֶבֶן יָצוּק נְחוּשָׁה Jb 28^{2} (rd. perh. יְצֻקוּ, v. Bu) *and stone* (ore, *men*) *melt it into copper;* צוּר יָצוּק עִמָּדִי פַּלְגֵי־שָׁמֶן Jb 29^{6} *the rock used to pour out beside me streams of oil.*—Is 26^{16} (as above) must mean *they poured out* (uttered) a whisper (לַחַשׁ; i.e. prayer); but form most improb.; Koppe Gr Di Du al. prop. צֹקֶן לַחַשׁ (from assumed צֹקֶן, I. צוק)=*constraint of* (like that of) *magic;* <Houb Kit צָעֲקוּ בְלַחַץ, or Che[Hpt] צָעַקְנוּ מִלַּחַץ כִּי מוּסָרְךָ לָנוּ וגו׳.

4690 †[מָצוּק] **n.m. molten support, pillar**;—pl. cstr. מְצֻקֵי אֶרֶץ 1 S 2^{8} *the supports of the earth* are י׳'s;—מָצוּק 14^{5} ('as a pillar,' 'steep,' etc.) is difficult (cf. HPS); del. with 𝔊 Th Dr Bu.

I. **צור** (√ of foll.; cf. possibly Ar. صَارَ (و) *cause to incline, lean;* NH=BH (rare), so Aram. ܨܘܪܐ (cf. Kö[ii. 1, 90]), (צַוְּרָא).

6677 †צַוָּאר **n.m.**[ψ 75, 6] **neck, back of neck**;—abs. צ׳ Is 8^{8}+, cstr. צַוַּאר Je 28^{10}+3 t. 28; sf. צַוָּארִי La 1^{14}, צַוָּרָם Ne 3^{5}, etc.; pl. cstr. צַוְּארֵי Ju 8^{21}+; sf. צַוָּארָיו Gn 27^{16}+, צַוְּארֵיכֶם Je 27^{12}, צַוְּארֹתֵיכֶם† Mi 2^{3};—**1.** *neck*, esp. *back of neck*, of man, wearing chain as ornament Gn 41^{42}(E), so of woman Ct 1^{10}, cf. Ju 5^{30} (rd. perh. צַוָּארַי for ־רֵי), elsewh. in Gn usu. pl. intens., of individual, נָפַל עַל־צ׳ 45^{14} (E), 46^{29} 33^{4} (Qr; Kt sg.), so בָּכָה עַל־צ׳ 45^{14} 46^{29} (all J); חֶלְקַת צַוָּארָיו 27^{16} *smooth part of neck* (J); neck of beautiful woman Ct 4^{4} 7^{5}; neck as pressed by foot of conqueror Jos $10^{24.24}$ (JE); place of yoke Gn 27^{40} (sg.; J), Dt 28^{48} Is 10^{27} Je $27^{2.8.11.12}$ $28^{10.11.12.14}$ 30^{8}; of transgressions as yoke La 1^{14}; place of bonds Is 52^{2}; of bearing load, Ne 3^{5} (fig.), hence calamity as burden Mi 2^{3}; neck as smitten with sword Ez 21^{34}; עַד־צ׳ as measurement of height (depth; in fig.) Is 8^{8} 30^{8} Hb 3^{13}; בְּצ׳ עָתָק fig. ψ 75^{6} speak not with *arrogant neck* (si vera l.; but rd. perh. בְּצוּר *against the Rock,* 𝔊 κατὰ τοῦ θεοῦ, Bae Hup-Now Che Kau); of wicked, rushing against God Jb 15^{26}.—עַל־צַוָּארֵנוּ נִרְדָּפְנוּ La 5^{5} is dubious; Matthes Löhr Bae עֹל עַל־וגו׳; Bu עֹל צַו׳, and הֻרְדַּפְנוּ or יֶהֶדְפֵנוּ for נִר׳. **2.** *neck* of animals, camels (wearing ornaments) Ju $8^{21.26}$; heifer Ho 10^{11} (i.e. place of yoke, in fig. of Ephr.); horse Jb 39^{19}, crocodile 41^{14}.

†[צַוְּרוֹן] **n.[m.] pl. necklace**;—sf. אַחַד עֲנָק מִצַּוְּרֹנָיִךְ Ct 4^{9}. 6677

II. **צוּר vb. confine, bind, besiege** (NH *id., wrap* (rare); Aram. צוּר *besiege, beleaguer*);—**Qal** *Pf.* 2 ms. וְצַרְתָּ Dt 14^{25}, etc.; *Impf.* 3 ms. וַיָּצַר 1 K 20^{1}+, 2 ms. תָּצוּר Dt 20^{19}, etc.; *Imv.* fs. צוּרִי Is 21^{2} (after עֲלִי Kö[i. 444], cf. Ges[§72 s]); *Inf. cstr.* לָצוּר 1 S 23^{8}; *Pt.* pl. צָרִים 1 K 15^{27}+;—**1.** *confine, secure* (‖ I. צרר), acc. rei+בְּ of receptacle Dt 14^{25} 2 K 5^{23} Ez 5^{3}; complem. om. 2 K 12^{11}. **2.** *shut in, besiege*, c. עַל of city 2 S 11^{1} 1 K 15^{27} 16^{17} 20^{1} 2 K $6^{24.25}$ 17^{5} 18^{9} 24^{11} Is 29^{3} (+acc. of siege-works), Je 32^{2} 37^{5} 39^{9} Dt 20^{12} Ez 4^{3} Dn 1^{1}; c. עַל pers. (within city) 2 S 20^{15} 2 K 16^{5} Je $21^{4.9}$; c. אֶל of city (for עַל) Dt 20^{19}; c. אֶל pers. 1 S 23^{8}; c. אֵת of city only 1 Ch 20^{1} (‖ 2 S 11^{1} supr.); abs. Is 21^{2}.—הִנָּם צָרִים אֶת־הָעִיר עָלֶיךָ Ju 9^{31} is corrupt; Frankenb[Richterbuch 28] Bu GFM[Hpt] Now מְעִרִים *inciting* against. **3.** *shut up, enclose:* נָצוּר עָלֶיהָ לוּחַ אָרֶז Ct 8^{9} (עַל of maid [under fig. of door]+acc. mater., cf. Is 29^{3} supr.); c. sf. pers. ψ 139^{5} (fig., י׳ subj.).

†מָצוֹר **n.[m.] siege-enclosure, siege, entrenchment**;—alw. מ׳ abs., exc. cstr. מְצוֹר Ez 4^{7}, sf. מְצוֹרֵךְ v^{8};—**1.** *siege* מ׳ שָׂם עָלֵינוּ Mi 4^{14} *he hath* 4692

laid siege to us, cf. בּוֹא בַמּ׳ וְנָתַתָּ עָלֶיהָ מ׳ Ez 4^{2}; בּוֹא בַמּ׳
is *come into a state of siege* Dt 20^{19} 2 K 24^{10} 25^{2}
Je 52^{5}, cf. וְהָיְתָה בַמּ׳ Ez 4^{3}; יוֹשֶׁבֶתִי בַּמּ׳ Je 10^{17};
מְצוֹר יְרוּ׳ Ez 4^{7} *siege of Jerus.*, but also מ׳ עַל־יְרוּ׳
Zc 12^{2}; יְמֵי מ׳ of duration of siege Ez 4^{8} 5^{2};
בְּמ׳ וּבְמָצוֹק Na 3^{14} *water for a siege*; in phr. מֵי מ׳
in the siege and stress Dt $28^{53.55.57}$ Je 19^{9}. **2.**
enclosure, i.e. *siege-works* Dt 20^{20}; late=*rampart* Zc 9^{3}, עִיר מ׳ *entrenched city* ψ 31^{22} (al. *besieged*), 60^{11} (‖ 108^{11} ע׳ מִבְצָר), cf. 2 Ch 8^{5}; עָרִים לְמ׳
11^{5}, יֹשְׁבִים בְּמ׳ בִּירוּשָׁלָ‍ִם 32^{10}; מ׳ Hb 2^{1} acc. to
most (‖ מִשְׁמֶרֶת); but We der. fr. נצר, i.e. *watch-
tower*, Now conj. מִצְפֶּה (cf. וַאֲצַפֶּה foll.); > Buhl
4693 conj. מְצָד.—מ׳ **n.pr.terr.** v. p. 566.

4694 †מְצוּרָה **n.f. siege-works, rampart**;—
abs. מ׳ Na 2^{2} 2 Ch 14^{5}; pl. מְצוּרוֹת 2 Ch
11^{11}+, מְצֻרֹת Is 29^{3}, etc.;—**1.** *siege-works* Is
29^{3}. **2.** *rampart* נָצוֹר מ׳ Na 2^{2} *guard the
rampart!* (‖ צַפֵּה דֶרֶךְ; We Now der. fr. נצר,
i.e. *keep watch!*), 2 Ch 11^{11}, עָרֵי מְצוּרָה 14^{5} *fortified* cities, so עָרֵי (הַ)מְּצוּרוֹת $v^{10.23}$ 12^{4} 21^{3}.

6696 †III. [צוּר] **vb. shew hostility to, treat
as foe** (c. acc. pers.) (akin to II. צרר, to which
SS assign the forms, but cf. Ar. ضَارَ (ى) *act
unjustly*, also *defraud*; Syr. ܥܪܬܐ, *rival wife*);
—**Qal** *Pf.* 1 s. וְצַרְתִּי אֶת־צֹרְרֶיךָ Ex 23^{22} (subj.
י׳; ‖ וְאָיַבְתִּי אֶת־אֹיְבֶיךָ); *Impf.* 2 ms. אַל־תָּצַר
אֶת־מוֹאָב Dt 2^{9}; 2 mpl. sf. אַל־תְּצֻרֵם v^{19}; *Pt.*
הַצָּרִים אוֹתָם Est 8^{11}.

6696 †IV. [צוּר] **vb. fashion, delineate** (NH
id.; so Aram. צוּר, ܨܘܪ, ܨܪ; ܨܘܪܬܐ *picture*, Sab.
צור, pl. צורת Hom$^{\text{Chrest. 125}}$ Mordtm$^{\text{Him. Inschr. 14.15}}$;
Ar. صُورَةٌ is loan-word acc. to Frä^{272});—*Pf.*
2 ms. וְצַרְתָּ Ez 43^{11} (for MT צוּרַת) acc. to 𝔊 We
Sm Co Toy Berthol Krae, *and thou shalt de-
lineate* the house (cf. הַגֵּד v^{10}, הוֹדַע וּכְתֹב v^{11});
Impf. 3 ms. וַיָּצַר אֹתוֹ בַּחֶרֶט Ex 32^{4} (E) *and
fashioned it* [the gold] *with a graving-tool*;
וַיָּצַר אֶת־שְׁנֵי הָעַמּוּדִים 1 K 7^{15} (+acc. mater.), rd.
וַיִּצֹק (יצק), so 𝔊 SS Kit Benz cf. Th; 1 s. sf.
3335 אצורך Je 1^{5} Kt, v. יצר. p. 427

6699 †[צוּרָה] **n.f. form, fashion**;—cstr. צוּרַת
Ez 43^{11} v. foreg.; sf. צוּרָתוֹ v^{11} (𝔊 מְצֻוֹתָיו, so Co,
or תּוֹרֹתָיו, so Berthol Krae; Toy as MT); so
also Kt $v^{11.11}$ (Qr pl. sf. צוּרֹתָיו) 2nd of these del.
as dittogr. all moderns; 1st rd. as Kt Co
Berthol, as Qr Toy; sg. sf. צוּרָם (Ges$^{\S\ 91\text{e}}$ Kö$^{\text{ii. 1, 440}}$)
ψ 49^{15} Qr (Kt צירם) *their form* (of the dead).

†I. [צִיר] **n.m.** image;—pl. צִירִים Is 45^{16}= 6736
idols; sg. sf. צירם ψ 49^{5} Kt *their form* (v. צוּרָה above). 6699

V. **צור** (√ of foll.; ‖ III. צרר; cf. Sl$^{3.6}$ צַר,
rock, Aram. טוּרָא, ܛܘܪܐ *hill*, so Palm. pl. טוריא).

†I. **צוּר** **n.m.**$^{\text{Jb 29,6}}$ **rock, cliff**;—צ׳ abs. Ex 6697
17^{6}+, cstr. Dt 8^{15}+; sf. צוּרִי 2 S 22^{3}, etc.; pl.
צֻרִים Nu 23^{9}+, צוּרוֹת Jb 28^{10}; cstr. צוּרֵי 1 S 24^{3}
(Gi v^{2});—**1. a.** *rocky wall, cliff*, Ex $17^{6.6}$ (E),
Dt 8^{15} (צ׳ הַחַלָּמִישׁ), Is $48^{21.21}$ ψ $78^{15.20}$ 105^{41} 114^{8}
(‖ חַלָּמִישׁ); בּוֹא בַצ׳ Is 2^{10}, בִּמְעָרוֹת צֻרִים v^{19},
בְּנִקְרוֹת הַצ׳ v^{21}, cf. Ex $33^{21.22}$ (JE); yielding
honey (from its clefts) ψ 81^{17} (cf. Dt 32^{13}; Dy
Perles$^{\text{Anal. 34}}$ We rd. צוּף); as look-out Nu 23^{9}
(JE), home of goats 1 S 24^{3} (Gi v^{2}), snow-
covered Je 18^{14}; bearing (olives for) oil Dt 32^{13}
(חַלְמִישׁ צ׳), Jb 29^{6}; resort of homeless 24^{8},
pierced by miners 28^{10}, cf. perh. שִׁית בְּצ׳ נְחָלִים
אוֹפִיר 22^{24} *deposit* (thy) gold *in the rock* of the
wadys (most sub צֹר *pebble*); as quarry, fig. of
Abr. as ancestor of Isr. Is 51^{1}; place of security
1 Ch 11^{15}, צ׳ הַמִּישׁוֹר Je 21^{13} (of city), fig. ψ 27^{5}
61^{3}; symb. of firmness Na 1^{6} Jb 14^{18} 18^{4}; enduring material 19^{24}. **b.** *rock* with flat surface
2 S 21^{10} Pr 30^{19}. **c.** *block of stone, boulder* Ju
6^{21} 13^{19} (as altar); cf. צוּר מִכְשׁוֹל Is 8^{14} (‖ אֶבֶן
נֶגֶף). **d.** *rock* with specif. name, צ׳ עוֹרֵב Ju 7^{25}
Is 10^{26}. **2. a.** fig. of God (33 t.) as support
and defence of his people (oft. ‖ אֱלֹהִים, י׳, etc.),
צ׳ מָעוֹן ψ 71^{3}, צ׳ עֻזִּי 62^{8}, צ׳ מָעוֹז ψ 31^{3}, צ׳ מָעֻזֵּךְ Is 17^{10},
71^{3}, צ׳ יְשֻׁעָתוֹ Dt 32^{15} cf. 2 S $22^{47\text{b}}$ (but del., v.
‖ ψ 18^{47}), ψ 89^{27} 95^{1}, צ׳ וִישׁוּעָתִי $62^{3.7}$, צ׳ מַחְסִי 94^{22},
צ׳ יִשְׂרָאֵל Is 30^{29} 2 S 23^{3} (personif.), צוּרִי ψ $18^{3.47}$
=2 S $22^{3.47\text{a}}$, ψ 19^{15} 28^{1} 92^{16} 144^{1}, צ׳ לְבָבִי 73^{26},
צוּרֵנוּ Dt 32^{31}, צוּרָם v^{30} ψ 78^{35}; c. בְּ essent. בְּיָהּ י׳
צ׳ עוֹלָמִים Is 26^{4} (cf. ψ 62^{8}; v. ב **I. 7 c**); as **n.pr.
dei** (*the*) *Rock* Dt $32^{4.18}$ (צ׳ יְלָדְךָ), v^{37} Hb 1^{12}, +
(perh.) ψ 75^{6} (rd. בַּצּוּר, v. צַוָּאר; v. also פְּדָהצוּר).
b. of a heathen god Dt 32^{31}, cf. Is 44^{8}, מִי צוּר
מִבַּלְעֲדֵי א׳ 2 S 22^{32} ‖ ψ 18^{32}, cf. 1 S 2^{2}.—Vid. also
בֵּית צוּר and חֶלְקַת הַצֻּרִים.—ψ 89^{44} v. צַר sub
III. צרר, 49^{15} v. צוּרָה sub III. צוּר. above 6699

†II. **צוּר** **n.pr.m.** Σουρ (*Rock*);—**1.** a prince 6698
of Midian Nu 25^{15} 31^{8} Jos 13^{21}. **2.** Gibeonite 1 Ch 8^{30} 9^{36}.

†**צוּרִיאֵל** **n.pr.m.** (*my rock is Ēl*);—a 6700
Levite Nu 3^{35}, Σουριηλ.

†**צוּרִישַׁדָּי** **n.pr.m.** Σουρ(ε)ισαδαι[ε] (*my rock* 6701
is Shadday);—a Simeonite Nu 1^{6} 2^{12} $7^{36.41}$ 10^{19}.

6677,6865 צוֹר *Tyre* v. צֹר. צֻוְּרֹנִים צַוָּר v. צַוָּאר. p. 862
3341,6702 [צוּת] **Hiph.** Is 27^{4} v. יצת. p. 428
6703,6727 צַח v. צחח. צִחָא v. צִיחָא. below, p. 851

צחה (√of foll.; Ar. (و)ضحى *be cloudless*, so Eth. ጸሐወ: Aram. צְחָא, צְחִי *be thirsty*).

6704 †[צִחֶה] **adj. intens. parched** (cf. Ges ^{§84bc});—cstr. צִחֵה צָמָא Is 5^{13} *parched with thirst.*

6705 †[צָחַח] **vb. be dazzling** (𝔗 צַחְצַח *polish;* Syr. ܨܚ *be scorched*, Aph. *declare in writing* (make clear), ܨܚܨܚܐ *clarus, lucidus, fulgidus;* صَحْصَحَانٌ, صَحْصَحٌ, *smooth, plain*);—**Qal** *Pf.* 3 pl. צַחוּ מֵחָלָב La 4^{7} (‖ זַכּוּ מִשֶּׁלֶג), *they are more dazzling* (i.e. *whiter*) *than milk* (of effeminate skin).

6703 †צַח **adj. dazzling, glowing, clear;**—חֹם צַח Is 18^{4} *glowing heat;* רוּחַ צַח Je 4^{11} *glowing wind;* דּוֹדִי צַח וְאָדוֹם Ct 5^{10} *my beloved is dazzling* (*white*) *and ruddy* (cf. La 4^{7}); fpl. לְדַבֵּר צָחוֹת Is 32^{4} *to speak clear* (words), *clearly.*

6706 †[צְחִיחַ] **n.[m.] shining, glaring, surface** cstr. צְחִיחַ סֶלַע i.e. a smooth, bare, rock Ez 24$^{7.8}$
6708 26$^{4.14}$; pl. בַּצְּחִיחִים Ne 4^{7} Qr (Kt בַּצְּחְחִיִּים), *in glaring, bare places* (?).

6707 †צְחִיחָה **n.f. scorched land**;—צ׳ ψ 68^{7}.

6710 †[צַחְצָחָה] **n.[f.] scorched region**;—pl. צַחְצָחוֹת Is 58^{11}.

צחן (√of foll.; NH צַחֲנָה=BH; Aram. צַחֲנְתָּא *stinking fluid*, ܨܚܢ, ܨܚܢܐ *foul*).

6709 †[צַחֲנָה] **n.f. stench**;—sf. צַחֲנָתוֹ Jo 2^{20} (‖ בָּאְשׁוֹ).—Cf. עפר צחנה Ecclus 11^{12}.

6711 †[צָחַק] **vb. laugh** (Ar. ضَحِكَ, *laugh*, Syr. ܓܚܟ, cf. Ba $^{ES 34}$; v. also שׂחק);—**Qal** *Pf.* 3 fs. צָחֲקָה Gn 18^{13}, etc.; *Impf.* 3 ms. יִצְחַק־ Gn 21^{6}, וַיִּצְחָק 17^{17}; 3 fs. וַתִּצְחַק 18^{12};—*laugh*, Gn 18$^{12.13.15.15}$ (J), 17^{17} (P); c. לְ *at, concerning*, 21^{6}. **Pi.** *Impf.* וַיְצַחֵק Ju 16^{25}; *Inf. cstr.* לְצַחֵק Ex 32^{6}, לְצַחֶק בָּנוּ (בִּי) Gn 39$^{14.17}$; *Pt.* מְצַחֵק Gn 19^{14} 26^{8}, מְצַחֵק 21^{9};—**1.** *jest* Gn 19^{14} (J). **2.** *sport, play* Gn 21^{9} (E) Ex 32^{6} (J); *make sport for* Ju 16^{25} (וִישַׂחֶק־לָנוּ ‖ לִפְנֵי); *toy with* (אֶת), of conjugal caresses Gn 26^{8} (cf. Doughty $^{Arab. Des. i. 231}$), *make a toy of*, c. בְּ, 39$^{14.17}$ (all J).

6712 †צְחֹק **n.[m.] laughter**;—צְחֹק עָשָׂה לִי א׳ Gn 21^{6} (E) *laughter hath God caused for me;* =*laughing-stock*, תִּהְיֶה לִצ׳ וּלְלַעַג Ez 23^{32} (del. 𝔊^{B} Hi Co Berthol Siegf Krae; not Toy).

יִצְחָק$_{108}$, יִשְׂחָק$_{4}$ **n.pr.m.** Ισαακ: **Isaac,** son 3327, 3446
of Abr. and Sarah (*he laugheth*, cf. play upon name Gn 18$^{12 f.}$ (J), 21^{6} (E), 17$^{17.19}$ (P); 26^{8} (J));—יִצְחָק Gn 21$^{3.4.5}$ (E)+, 24$^{62.63.67}$ (J)+, 17$^{19.21}$ (P)+, (80 t. Gn, 9 t. Ex, 7 t. Dt), Lv 26^{42} Nu 32^{11} Jos 24$^{3.4}$, 1 K 18^{36} 2 Ch 13^{23} 1 Ch 1$^{28.34.34}$ 16^{16} 29^{18} 2 Ch 30^{6}; †יִשְׂחָק Je 33^{26} ψ 105^{9}, and (=Israel) בָּמוֹת יִשְׂחָק Am 7^{9}, בֵּית יִשְׂחָק v^{16}.

צחר (√of foll.; cf. Ar. صَحَرَ xi. *dry up, become yellow* [parched by sun], صُحْرَةٌ *reddish-gray colour* (v. Müll $^{Königsb. Stud. i. 6}$)).

†[צַחַר] **n.[m.] reddish-gray, tawny;**— 6713
צֶמֶר צַחַר Ez 27^{18} *wool of reddish-gray, tawny wool*, or (Hi-Sm Krae), *of* land *Ṣachar* (si vera l.; Co del. צחר as dittogr.).

†[צָחֹר] **adj. tawny**;—fpl. אֲתֹנוֹת צְחֹרוֹת 6715
Ju 5^{10}.

†צֹחַר **n.pr.m. 1.** father of Ephron the 6714
Hittite Gn 23^{8} 25^{9}, Σααρ. **2.** son of Simeon Gn 46^{10} Ex 6^{15}, Σααρ. **3.** name in Judah 1 Ch
4^{7} Qr (וְצֹחַר; Kt יצחר), Σααρ, 𝔊L Εισαρ. 3328

יִצְחָר 1 Ch 4^{7} Kt, v. foregoing. 3328

†I. צִי **n.m.** $^{Is 33, 21}$ **ship** (loan-word from Egypt. 6716
t'aī, acc. to Bondi ^{66}, cf. Erman $^{ZMG xlvi (1892). 123}$ DHM $^{VOJ viii. 7, 165}$);—abs. צִי אַדִּיר Is 33^{21} *a majestic ship;* pl. צִים Nu 24^{24} (JE), Ez 30^{9} (בַּצִּ׳; but 𝔊 σπεύδοντες, cf. 𝔖, whence Co Berthol אָצִים).

†II. [צִי] **n.m.** $^{Je 50, 39}$ a wild beast, prop. either 6728
desert-dweller (denom. from צִיָּה, so most), or **crier, yelper** (√*צוה=ضوى [*yelp*, Dozy], Ba $^{NB 188}$, cf. Ew $^{§146g, note}$);—in any case a specif. animal, but not certainly identif.; Bo $^{Hieroz. i, lib. 3, §14}$, cp. Ar. ضَيْوَنٌ *wild cat;*—pl. צִיִּים Is 13^{21} (f. אִיִּים v^{22}), 23^{13} 34^{14} (+אִיִּים), Je 50^{39} (*id.;* all betokening desolation); לְעָם לְצִיִּים ψ 74^{14} (rd. לְעַמְלְצֵי ים Hup-Now Bae); appar. of people 72^{9}, but prob. corrupt, Ol conj. צָרִים (‖ אֹיְבָיו), and so most moderns.

צִיבָא and (2 S 16^{4}) צִבָא$_{16}$ **n.pr.m.** Σ(ε)ιβα: 6717
servant of Saul's house, 2 S 9$^{2.2}$ + 14 t. 9, 16, 19.

†צִידוֹן and (Gn 10$^{15.19}$ 49^{3}) צִידֹן **n.pr.loc.** 6721
Sîdôn, Σιδων, ancient Phoenician city, on coast N. of Tyre (in As. *Sidun(n)u*, COT ^{Gloss}; TelAm. *Ṣiduna*, Ph. צדן, OAram. צידן; in Egypt. *Di-(d)u-na*, WMM $^{As. u. Eur. 184}$);—'first-born' of

Canaan Gn 10^{15} = 1 Ch 1^{13}, northern limit of
7237 Canaanite Gn 10^{19}, cf. 49^{13}; defined as צ׳ רַבָּה Jos 11^{8} (so 19^{28} infr.); also Ju 1^{31} 10^{6} (אֱלֹהֵי צ׳), 18^{28} 1 K 17^{9}; named with Tyre Jos 19^{28} (cf. v^{29}), 2 S 24^{6} (cf. v^{7}), Is 23$^{2.4}$ and בְּתוּלַת בַּת־צ׳ v^{12} (cf. v^{5}, etc.), Je 25^{22} 27^{3} 47^{4} Ez 27^{8} 28$^{21.22}$ (cf. v$^{2.12}$), Zc 9^{2} Jo 4^{4}.—Vid. Pietsch$^{Phöniz. 54 ff.}$ Prutz$^{Aus Phönicien (1876), 98 ff.}$ Rob$^{BR ii. 478 ff.}$ de Luynes$^{Voyage à la Mer Morte i. 18 ff., and Pl. vi-xi.}$ Bd$^{Pal 3 (1898), 313 ff.}$

6722 † צִידֹנִי **adj. gent.** of foregoing;—צ׳ Ju 3^{3} Ez 32^{30}; elsewhere pl. צִידֹנִים Dt 3^{9} +, צִידוֹנִים Ju 10^{12}, צִדֹנִים 18^{7} + 3 t.; fpl. צִדְנִיֹּת 1 K 11^{1};—as subst. = *Sidonians*, coll. c. art. Ez 32^{30} Ju 3^{3}; in earlier lit. appar. = *Phoenicians* Dt 3^{9} Jos 13$^{4.6}$ Ju 3^{3} 10^{12} 18$^{7.7}$ 1 K 5^{20} (= Tyre v^{15}), 16^{31} (if, [Jos$^{Ant. viii. 13, 1}$] Ethb. was king of Tyre also), Ez 32^{30}; also עַשְׁתֹּרֶת אֱלֹהֵי צ׳ 1 K 11$^{5.33}$, cf. 2 K 23^{13}; named with Tyrians 1 Ch 22^{4} Ezr 3^{7}.

צוה, ציה (√ of foll.; Ar. صَوَى *be parched*, so Aram. צְוֵי, צְוָא (not 𝔗), ܨܘܳܐ (chiefly in Lexx)).

6723 † צִיָּה **n.f. dryness, drought**;—abs. צ׳ Ho 2^{5} +; pl. צִיּוֹת ψ 105^{41};—*drought* Jb 24^{19} (|| חֹם); elsewh. of land (oft. || מִדְבָּר, עֲרָבָה, etc.): אֶרֶץ צ׳ *land of drought, desert* Ho 2^{5} (sim.), Je 2^{6} 50^{12} (fig.), 51^{43} Is 41^{18} 53^{2} (in sim.), ψ 107^{35}; + צָמָא Ez 19^{13} (fig.), + שְׁמָמָה Jo 2^{20}, + עָיֵף ψ 63^{2} (fig.); צ׳ = *desert* Is 35^{1} Zp 2^{13} Jb 30^{3} ψ 78^{17}; pl. 105^{41}.

6724 † צָיוֹן **n.[m.] dryness, parched ground** (on format. v. Lag$^{BN 204}$);—בְּצ׳, כְּחֹרֶב בְּצ׳ Is 25^{5}, 32^{2} (|| אֶרֶץ עֲיֵפָה; both in sim.).

6726 צִיּוֹן$_{154}$ **n.pr.loc.** Σ(ε)ιων; **Ṣîyyôn, Zion** (Syr. ܨܶܗܝܽܘܢ, older form, acc. to Lag$^{BN 84, cf. 198}$);—צ׳ 2 S 5^{7} +; צִיּוֹנָה Je 4^{6};—stronghold (of Jebusites), מְצֻדַת צ׳ captured by David, and made his residence 2 S 5^{7} = 1 Ch 11^{5} (both + הִיא עִיר דָּוִד), on S. part of E. hill of Jerusalem, distinct from site of temple 1 K 8^{1} = 2 Ch 5^{2} (both מֵעִיר ד׳ הִיא צ׳), not elsewh. in narrative, but often in poets and proph.: as name of Jerus., from political point of view (sts. = inhabitants), Am 6^{1} (|| הַר־שֹׁמְרוֹן), || יְרוּשָׁלַםִ Mi 3$^{10.12}$ = Je 26^{18}, Is 4^{3} 30^{19} 40^{9} 41^{27} 52^{1} 62^{1} 64^{9} Zp 3^{16} Zc 1$^{14.17}$ ψ 51^{20} and (בַּת־צ׳) Is 52^{2} Mi 4^{8} (|| בַּת־יְרוּשׁ׳), La 2^{13} (|| *id.*), also (יוֹשֶׁבֶת צ׳) Je 51^{35}; = Jerus. also Is 14^{32} 33^{5} +, so esp. in phr. בְּנוֹת צ׳ Is 3$^{16.17}$ 4^{4} Ct 3^{11}, בְּנֵי צ׳ La 4^{2} Jo 2^{23} ψ 149^{2} (|| יִשְׂרָאֵל), cf. Zc 9^{13}, יָלְדָה צ׳ אֶת־בָּנֶיהָ Is 66^{8}, and even הַר־צ׳ 2 K 19^{31} = Is 37^{32} (both || יְרוּשׁ׳), Is 29^{8} (|| אֲרִיאֵל v^{7}), Ob$^{17.21}$ ψ 48^{12} (|| בְּנוֹת יְהוּדָה), 125^{1}; so also הַר־בַּת צ׳ Is 16^{1} and 10^{32} Qr (Kt בית || גִּבְעַת־יְרוּשׁ׳); cf. מְרוֹם־צ׳ Je 31^{12}; in foll. הַר־צ׳ might refer to temple-hill Is 10^{12} (+ יְרוּשׁ׳), 31^{4} (+ גִּבְעָתָהּ = יְרוּשׁ׳ v^{5}), La 5^{18} Jo 3^{5} (+ יְרוּשׁ׳); specif. of Jerus. as abode of י׳ and place of his worship Am 1^{2} Is 31^{9} Zc 8^{3} Mi 4^{2} = Is 2^{3}, Jo 4^{16} ψ 102^{22} 135^{21} 147^{12} (all || יְרוּשׁ׳), 76^{3} (|| שָׁלֵם); partic. of sanctuary 20^{3} (|| קֹדֶשׁ), 14^{7} = 53^{7} +; of Jerus. הַר־צ׳ ψ 48^{3} (|| קִרְיַת מֶלֶךְ רָב), 78^{68} (|| שֵׁבֶט יְהוּדָה), Is 24^{23} (|| יְרוּשׁ׳), etc.; הַרְרֵי צ׳ in same sense † ψ 133^{3}; particularly of sanctuary Is 4^{5} and (|| הַר־קָדְשִׁי) Jo 2^{1} 4^{17}; הַר־צ׳ קָדְשִׁי ψ 2^{6} is seat of king.—Vid. also הַר־צ׳, בַּת־צ׳, יֹשֶׁבֶת צ׳, sub יָשַׁב, הַר, בַּת.

צִיּוֹן v. ציה. צִיּוּן v. צוה. above, p. 846 6724-25

† צִיחָא **n.pr.m.** an overseer of Nethinim 6727
Ne 11^{21}, who are called בְּנֵי צִיחָא Ezr 2^{43} = בְּנֵי צִחָא Ne 7^{46}; Σηα, Σιααυ, Σιαλ, Σουλαι, etc.

צִיִּים, צִים v. I, II. צִי. צִין **n.pr.loc.** v. צִן. p. 850, 856 6716, 6728, 6790

צִינֹק v. צנק. צִיעֹר v. צער. p, 857, 859 6729-30

צִיף v. II. צוף. I. צִיץ, צִיצָה v. I. [צוּץ]. p. 847 6689, 6733

† II. צִיץ **n.[m.]** meaning dubious; only in 6731
תְּנוּ־צִיץ לְמוֹאָב Je 48^{9} usu. (after AW Ra Ki al.) *wings* (coll.) (cf. Aram. צִיץ *wing, fin*, Thes Gf al.); cf. Perles$^{Anal. 46}$, who reads נוֹצִין (wing-) *feathers* (as in Aram.); 𝔊 σημεῖα, whence Gie *sign-post*, rdg. צִיּוּן,—or נֵס,—(indicating flight).

† III. צִיץ **n.pr.loc.** in מַעֲלֵה הַצּ׳ 2 Ch 20^{16}; 6732
ה perh. radical, cf. *Wady Ḥaṣâṣâ*, and plateau *Ḥaṣâṣâ*, N. of Engedi, Buhl$^{Geogr. 97}$; 𝔊 Ασαε, 𝔊L τῆς ἐξοχῆς Ασισα.

† צִיצִת **n.f. tassel, lock** (√ dub.; NH *id.*, 6734
so 𝔗 צִיצִיתָא, Syr. ܨܝܨܝܬܐ; cf. Ar. نَاصِيَةٌ *hair on forehead*);—צ׳ abs. Nu 15$^{38.39}$ *tassel* on flowing ends (כְּנָפַיִם) of garments, cstr. צ׳ הַכָּנָף v^{38} (v. Kennedy$^{Hast. DB ii. 69, FRINGES}$); צ׳ רֹאשִׁי Ez 8^{3} *lock* of hair on forehead.

צִיקְלַג v. צִקְלַג. p. 862 6860

I. ציר (√ of foll.; cf. صَارَ (ى) *become, attain to, go*; perh. Sab. (Min.) ציר (*cause to become*), *form* Hom$^{Chrest. 125}$);—on Hithp. Jos 9^{4} v. ציד.

† II. צִיר **n.m.**$^{Pr 25, 13}$ **envoy, messenger**;—צ׳ 6735, 6737
abs. Je 49^{14} +, cstr. Pr 13^{17}; pl. צִירִים Is 18^{2}; sf. צִרַיִךְ 57^{9};—*envoy*, from Cush Is 18^{2}, from apostate Isr. 57^{9}; from י׳ Je 49^{14} = Ob^{1}; *messenger* in gen. צִיר אֱמוּנִים Pr 13^{17}, צ׳ נֶאֱמָן 25^{13}.—

I. צִיר v. IV. צור. p. 849 6736

II. **צִיר** (√of foll.; ? *turn, revolve;* NH צִיר *pivot* (of door), *hinge*, so Ar. صَائِرٌ (cf. سَيَّارٌ, Dozy$^{i. 712 b}$); perh. As. *ṣirru;* Aram. צִירְתָּא, ܨܝܪܳܐ).

6735 † III. **[צִיר] n.[m.] pivot** (of door), **hinge**;—sf. הַדֶּלֶת תִּסּוֹב עַל־צִירָהּ Pr 26^{14} (in ‖ of sluggard).

6735 † IV. **[צִיר] n.[m.] pang** (prop. *writhing*);—pl. צִירִים Is 13^{8} 21^{3}; cstr. צִירֵי 21^{3}; sf. צִירַי Dn 10^{16}, צִרֶיהָ 1 S 4^{19};—*pangs* of childbirth 1 S 4^{19}, so (sim.) Is 21^{3}; and, of terror, 13^{8} (+ חֲבָלִים), 21^{3}; in gen., of physical effects of mental distress Dn 10^{16}.

6738,6741 צֵל, צִלָּה v. III. צלל. p. 852

6740 † **[צָלָה] vb. roast** flesh (NH *id.;* so Ar. صَلَى (ى), Eth. ጸለወ:);—**Qal** *Impf.* 3 ms. יִצְלֶה צָלִי Is 44^{16} *he roasteth a roast;* 1 s. אֶצְלֶה בָשָׂר v^{19}; *Inf. cstr.* לִצְלוֹת 1 S 2^{15} give flesh (בָּשָׂר) *to roast.*

6748 † **צָלִי adj.** et **n.m. roasted, roast**;—cstr. (as adj.) צְלִי־אֵשׁ (P) of flesh (בָּשָׂר) Ex 12$^{8.9}$ (opp. מְבֻשָּׁל בַּמָּיִם); abs. as subst. cogn. Is 44^{16} v. [צָלָה].

6743 † I. **[צָלַח] vb. rush**;—(Thes al. cp. 𝔗 צְלַח, Syr. ܨܠܰܚ, *cleave, penetrate,* then *advance,* v. foll.);—**Qal** *Pf.* 3 fs. וְצָלְחָה consec. 1 S 10^{6}; 3 pl. וְצָלְחוּ 2 S 19^{18}; *Impf.* 3 ms. יִצְלַח Am 5^{6} (v. infr.), 3 fs. וַתִּצְלַח Ju 14^{6}+;—*rush,* וְצָ׳ הַיַּרְדֵּן 2 S 19^{18} *they rushed into the Jordan* (dub., v. Dr HPS), יִצְ׳ כָּאֵשׁ בֵּית יוֹסֵף Am 5^{6} lest *he rush like fire upon the house of Joseph* (or *O house,* etc. GASm; Now conj. יָצִית בָּאֵשׁ); esp. of sudden possession by (אֱלֹהִים) רוּחַ י׳, c. עַל pers. Ju 14^{6} the Spirit ... *rushed upon* him, so v^{19} 15^{14} 1 S 10$^{6.10}$ 11^{6}; c. אֶל pers. 16^{13} and (of רוּחַ א׳ רָעָה) 18^{10}.

6743 † II. **[צָלַח, צָלֵחַ] vb. advance, prosper** (NH *id.;* Ph. Pi. causat. in n.pr.; Ar. صَلَحَ *be in good condition,* cf. Sab. הצלח Sab Denkm^{93}; Aram. צְלַח, ܨܠܰܚ, *prosper*);—**Qal** *Pf.* 3 fs. צָלְחָה Je 12^{1}; *Impf.* 3 ms. יִצְלַח Je 13^{7}+, etc.; *Imv.* ms. צְלַח;—*prosper,* of way of wicked Je 12^{1}, cf. Nu 14^{41} Is 53^{10} 54^{17} Ez 17$^{9.10}$ Dn 11^{27}; c. לְ rei, = *be good for* anything Je 13$^{7.10}$ Ez 15^{4}; subj. pers., abs., Je 22$^{30.30}$ Ez 17^{15}, ψ 45^{5} *be successful!* וַתִּצְלְחִי לִמְלוּכָה Ez 16^{13} *and thou didst prosper to royalty* (dub.; del. 𝔊 Co Toy; > Sta ZAW vi (1886). 337 f. Krae לִמְלָאכָה i.e. harlotry). **Hiph.** *Pf.* 3 ms. הִצְלִיחַ Gn 24^{21}, 2 ms. וְהִצְלַחְתָּ 1 Ch 22^{11}, etc.; *Impf.* 3 ms. יַצְלִיחַ Ne 2^{20}+, וַיַּצְלַח 1 Ch 29^{23} 2 Ch 32^{30}, etc.; *Imv.* ms. הַצְלַח 1 K 22^{12}+, הַצְלִיחָה Ne 1^{11}, ־יָה ψ 118^{25}, etc.; *Pt.* מַצְלִיחַ Gn 24^{42}+;—**1.** *make prosperous, bring to successful issue,* of י׳, c. acc. of man's way (דֶּרֶךְ), Gn 24$^{21.40.42.56}$ (J), c. acc. rei Gn 39$^{3.23}$ (J), c. acc. pers. 2 Ch 26^{5}, c. לְ pers. Ne 1^{11} 2^{20}; abs. *send success* ψ 118^{25}; human subj. c. acc. דֶּרֶךְ Dt 28^{29} Jos 1^{8} (D), Is 48^{15} ψ 37^{7}, so prob. 1^{3} (al. sub **2**), 2 Ch 7^{11}; c. acc. מִרְמָה Dn 8^{25}. **2.** *shew, experience, prosperity,* of men 1 K 22$^{12.15}$ = 2 Ch 18$^{11.14}$, Je 2^{37} (+ לְ pers. in ref. to whom) 5^{28} 32^{5} 1 Ch 22$^{11.13}$ 29^{23} 2 Ch 13^{12} 14^{6} 20^{20} 24^{20} 31^{21} 32^{30} (בְּכָל־מַעֲשֵׂהוּ), Pr 28^{13} Dn 8^{12} (of horn), v^{24} 11^{36}; אִישׁ מַצְלִיחַ Gn 39^{2} (J) *a prosperous man;* subj. דֶּרֶךְ Ju 18^{5} (cf. ψ 1^{3} supr.), י׳'s word Is 55^{11}.

III. **צלח** (√of foll.; NH צְלֹחִית = BH; cf. Aram. צְלוֹחִיתָא, ܨܠܘܚܺܝܬܳܐ (in Lexx) *flat dish;* Eth. ጸሕል: Amhar. ጽንሓ: ጽና: (v. Prä$^{Amh. Spr. § 65 c}$); Ar. صَحْنٌ, all *bowl, dish;* v. Frä$^{63.170}$).

† **[צֵלָחָה] n.[f.] pot** for cooking;—pl. צֵלָחוֹת 6745
2 Ch 35^{13} (+ סִירוֹת, דְּוָדִים).

† **צַלַּחַת n.f. dish**;—2 K 21^{13} (sim.), צַלַּחַת 6747
Pr 19^{24} 26^{15} (v. טמן).

† **צְלֹחִית n.f. jar**;—צְ׳ חֲדָשָׁה 2 K 2^{20}. 6746

צָלִי v. צלה. above 6748

† I. **[צָלַל] vb. tingle, quiver** (NH צִלְצֵל 6750
whirr (rare); Ar. صَلَّ, صَلْصَلَ; 𝔗 צְלַל; Syr. ܨܠ);—*Pf.* 3 pl. צָלֲלוּ Hb 3^{16}; *Impf.* 3 fpl. תְּצִלֶּינָה 1 S 3^{11}, תְּצִלֶּנָה (Ges$^{§ 67 g}$) 2 K 21^{12} Je 19^{3};—*tingle,* of ears, at horrid sound 1 S 3^{11} 2 K 21^{12} Je 19^{3} (all of dreadful news); of lips, *quiver* in terror Hb 3^{16}.

I. **[צְלָצַל] n.[m.] whirring, buzzing**;— 6767
cstr. אֶרֶץ צִלְצַל כְּנָפָיִם Is 18^{1} *land of buzzing of* (insects') *wings* (so prob.; other views v. in Di).

† II. **[צִלְצַל] n.[m.] spear** (fr. *whizzing*);— 6767
cstr. צִלְצַל דָּגִים Jb 40^{31} *fish-spear, harpoon.*

† **צְלָצַל n.m.** a **whirring locust** (cf. As. 6767
ṣarṣaru, Ar. صَرْصَرٌ, Syr. ܨܪܨܘܪܳܐ, ܨܳܪܨܳܪܳܐ; Lag Ges. Abh. 145, N. 9);—Dt 28^{42} (devouring; not identif.; Tr$^{NHB 313}$).

† **צֶלְצְלִים n.m.pl.** musical instr. of per- 6767
cussion, **cymbals** (with *clashing* sound; NH צִלְצַל, Aram. צִלְצְלִין, ܨܶܠܨܠܳܐ);—צְ׳ 2 S 6^{5} (+ מְנַעַנְעִים, q.v.; ‖ 1 Ch 13^{8} מְצִלְתַּיִם); cstr. צִלְצְלֵי־שֵׁמַע

ψ 150⁵, צ׳ תְּרוּעָה v⁵;—cf. Now[Arch. i. 272 f.] Benz[Arch. 277] We[ψψ Eng. Tr. 232].

4698 †[מְצִלָּה] **n.f.** **bell** (fr. *tinkling*);—pl. cstr. מְצִלּוֹת הַסּוּס Zc 14²⁰.

4700 †מְצִלְתַּיִם **n.f.du.** **cymbals** (appar. later equiv. of צֶלְצְלִים where v. reff.);—מ׳ 1 Ch 13⁸ (‖2 S 6⁵ v. צֶלְצְלִים), 15¹⁹ 16⁵·⁴² 25⁶ 2 Ch 5¹²·¹³ 29²⁵ Ezr 3¹⁰ Ne 12²⁷; -תָּיִם 1 Ch 15¹⁶·²⁸ 25¹.

6749 †II. [צָלַל] **vb.** **sink, be submerged** (NH *id.;* As. *ṣalâlu, sink down, sink to rest,* II. *launch* (Hpt[Prol. Assyr. Gr. liii; BAS i. 127; Ball, Gen. 53]); Eth. ጸለለ: *float,* cf. Nes[Mar. x]: Aram. צְלַל, ܨܠ, are *filter, clarify*);—**Qal** *Pf.* 3 pl. צָלְלוּ כַּעוֹפֶרֶת בְּמַיִם Ex 15¹⁰.

6751 †III. [צָלַל] **vb.** **be or grow dark** (cf. Ar. ظَلَّ *be black,* ظِلّ *shade;* Eth. ጸለለ: *be dark;* As. *ṣillu, shade, ṣalâlu,* Pi. *roof over,* so Sab. טלל [II.], טלת *ceiling, roof,* Hom[Chrest. 125], cf. Palm. תטלילא; OAram. טלל *overshadow,* Aram. טְלָלָא, ܛܶܠܳܠܳܐ *shadow*);—**Qal** *Pf.* 3 pl. צָלְלוּ שַׁעֲרֵי יר׳ Ne 13¹⁹ *the gates of Jerusalem grew dark,* i.e. evening came on. **Hiph.** *Pt.* חֹרֶשׁ מֵצַל Ez 31³ *a shadowing wood* (but del. 𝔊 Co Toy Krae).

6738 †צֵל **n.m.**[ψ 144, 4] **shadow**;—צ׳ abs. 2 K 20⁹+, cstr. Gn 19⁸+; sf. צִלְּךָ ψ 121⁵, צִלּוֹ Ez 31⁶+, also צִלְלוֹ Jb 40²², etc.; pl. צְלָלִים Ct 2¹⁷ 4⁶; cstr. צִלְלֵי Je 6⁴;—**1.** *shadow* on dial 2 K 20⁹·¹⁰·¹⁰·¹¹ ‖Is 38⁸; צִלְלֵי־עָרֶב Je 6⁴, cf. Ct 2¹⁷ 4⁶; of mt. Ju 9³⁶. **2.** *shadow, shade,* as protection (fr. sun): of branches, Ju 9¹⁵ (in allegory), Ho 4¹³
6752 Jb 40²² Jon 4⁵·⁶ and (in fig.) Ho 14⁸ Ez 17²³ 31⁶·¹²·¹⁷ ψ 80¹¹ Ct 2³ (of refreshment, delight); of rock Is 32² (sim.); צ׳ קֹרָתִי Gn 19⁸ *shadow of my roof;* of cloud Is 25⁴ and (fig. of י׳'s protection) 4⁶ 25⁴, so prob. 16³; צ׳ כְּנָפֶיךָ *shadow of thy wings,* fig. of י׳'s protection ψ 17⁸ 36⁸ 57² 63⁸; *shade,* in gen., Jb 7², fig. of י׳ ψ 121⁵; hence = *protection, defence,* of city (wall) Je 48⁴⁵; of י׳ Nu 14⁹ (JE), ψ 91¹ (v. also n.pr. בְּצַלְאֵל), cf. צֵל יָדוֹ Is 49² (covering prophet, under fig. of sword), 51¹⁶ (covering people); of human ally Is 30²·³, of king La 4²⁰; also of wisdom Ec 7¹², money v¹².—בְּצִלָּהּ Is 34¹⁵ appar. ref. to קִפּוֹז, but improb.; rd. perh. בֵּיצֶהָ *her eggs* Du Che[Hpt] (Che[Heb Hpt] transp. וּבָקְעָה וְדָגְרָה). **3.** *shadow* as symb. of transitoriness of life Jb 8⁹ 14² ψ 144⁴ (כְּצֵל עוֹבֵר), Ec 6¹² 8¹³; כְּצֵל נָטוּי of an individ. life near its end ψ 102¹², so כְּצֵל כִּנְטוֹתוֹ 109²³; in sim. of emaciated members, וִיצֻרַי כַּצֵּל Jb 17⁷.

†צִלָּה **n.pr.f.** wife of Lam. Gn 4¹⁹·²²·²³, Σελλα. 6741

†צִלְּתַי **n.pr.m.** (Thes expl. as צֵלֶת יָהּ);— 6769
1. Benj., 1 Ch 8²⁰, Σελαθ(ε)ι. **2.** צִלְּתַי, Manassite, 1 Ch 12²¹ (van d.H. v²⁰), Σεμαθει, Σιλαθα, etc.

†צַלְמָוֶת **n.** [**m.**] **death-shadow, deep** 6757
shadow, poet. (prob. = צֵל + מָוֶת, 𝔊 (usu.) σκιὰ θανάτου, cf. 𝔖 𝔙, so Thes Schwally[Leben n. d. Tode, 194], v. esp. Nö[ZAW xvii (1897), 183 ff.]; Ew Br and most mod. (after older comm.) rd. צַלְמוּת *darkness, deep darkness,* cp. Ar. ظَلِمَ IV, As. [*ṣalâmu*], Eth. ጸልመ: *be black, dark*);—*death-shadow,* oft. ‖ חֹשֶׁךְ, לַיְלָה, etc., and opp. בֹּקֶר, אוֹר. **1.** = *deep shadow, darkness* (cf. אַרְזֵי אֵל, הַרְרֵי אֵל): Am 5⁸ Jb 3⁵ 12²² 24¹⁷ ᵃ 28³ 34²²; of eyes heavy with weeping 16¹⁶; בַּלְהוֹת צ׳ 24¹⁷ ᵇ *terrors of the darkness.* **2.** fig. **a.** of distress Je 13¹⁶ ψ 107¹⁰·¹⁴; אֶרֶץ צ׳ Is 9¹. **b.** of extreme danger Je 2⁶ ψ 23⁴ 44²⁰. **3.** characterizing world of the dead, אֶרֶץ חֹשֶׁךְ וצ׳ Jb 10²¹, כְּמוֹ אֹפֶל צ׳ v²² (text dub., v. Bu Du); שַׁעֲרֵי צ׳ 38¹⁷ (𝔊 πυλωροὶ δὲ ᾅδου; ‖ שַׁעֲרֵי־מָוֶת).

צִלְלוֹ, צְלָלִים, צִלְלֵי v. צֵל. above 6738

†הַצְלֶלְפּוֹנִי **n.pr.f.** in Judah (*give shade,* 6753
thou *that turnest to me!*) 1 Ch 4³, Εσηλεββων, etc.

IV. צלל (√ of foll.; meaning dub.; Eth. መጸለት: is *unleavened bread* (Di[1257] as *pure,* unfermented, cf. ܨܠ sub II. צלל), more prob. would be designation of shape).

†צְלוּל Kt, צְלִיל Qr **n.m.** **cake, round** 6742
loaf;—צ׳ לֶחֶם שְׂעֹרִים Ju 7¹³ (cf. GFM).

צלם (√ of foll.; Nö[ZMG xl (1886), 733 f.] cp. Ar. صَلَمَ, *cut off* (e.g. an ear, a nose);—NH צֶלֶם = BH, so As. *ṣalmu,* Sab. צלם Gildemeister[ZMG xxiv (1870), 180] CIS[iv, no. 2, l. 4], Aram. צַלְמָא, ܨܠܡܐ, OAram. צלמא, so Nab. Palm. (also צלמתא of woman's statue)).

†צֶלֶם **n.m.**[Ez 16, 17] **image** (something *cut out,* 6754
cf. פֶּסֶל; Nö 'Schnitzbild');—צ׳ abs. ψ 39⁷, cstr. Gn 1²⁷+; sf. צַלְמוֹ v²⁷ 5³, צַלְמֵנוּ 1²⁶, צַלְמָם ψ 73²⁰; pl. cstr. צַלְמֵי 1 S 6⁵·⁵+, sf. צְלָמָיו 2 K 11¹⁸ 2 Ch 23¹⁷, צַלְמֵיכֶם Am 5²⁶;—**1.** *images* of tumours and mice (of gold) 1 S 6⁵·⁵·¹¹; esp. of heathen gods Am 5²⁶ (text dub.; del. We as gloss, cf. GASm Dr), 2 K 11¹⁸ = 2 Ch 23¹⁷ (both c. vb. שִׁבְּרוּ), Ez 7²⁰, so צ׳ זָכָר 16¹⁷ (i.e. in male form, acc. to fig. of harlotry for idolatry); צַלְמֵי מַסֵּכֹתָם Nu 33⁵² *their molten images;* of painted pictures of men Ez 23¹⁴. **2.** *image, likeness,* of resem-

blance, בְּצ׳ (בָּרָא) עָשָׂה, of God's making man in his own image, Gn 1[26] (||כִּדְמוּתֵנוּ), v[27.27] 9[6], בְּצ׳ 5[3] (||בִּדְמוּתוֹ; all P). **3.** fig. = *mere, empty, image, semblance,* בְּצ׳ ψ 39[7] *as* (ב essentiae) *a* (mere) *semblance man walks about;* צַלְמָם תִּבְזֶה 73[20] *thou wilt despise their semblance.*

6756 †I. צַלְמוֹן **n.pr.mont.** **1.** הַר־צ׳ Ju 9[48] near Shechem, not identif., cf. GFM, Buhl[Geogr. 100]; Ερμων (erron.). **2.** snow-capped mt. ψ 68[14], prob. E. of Jordan (in Ḥauran acc. to Wetzst, cf. Buhl[Geogr. 118]), Σελμων.

6756 †II. צַלְמוֹן **n.pr.m.** a hero of David 2 S 23[28] (= עִילַי 1 Ch 11[29]), (Σ)ελλω, 𝔊 L Ελιμαν.

6757 צַלְמָוֶת v. III. צלל. p. 853

6758 †צַלְמֹנָה **n.pr.loc.** station of Isr. in wilderness Nu 33[41.42], Σελμωνα.

6759 צַלְמֻנָּע[12] **n.pr.m.** a king of Midian, + זֶבַח, Ju 8[5] + 10 t. Ju 8, ψ 83[12], Σελμανα, Σαλμ.

I. צלע (√of foll.; cf. Ar. ضَلَعَ, *decline, deviate,* ضَلِعٌ *curved;* NH צֶלַע = BH, so Ar. ضِلَعٌ, As. *ṣêlu,* BAram. עֲלַע, עִילְעָא, Syr. ܐܠܥܐ).

6763 צֵלָע[41] **n.f.** (**m.** 1 K 6[34], and appar. Ex 26[26]) **rib, side**;—abs. צ׳ Gn 2[22] +, cstr. צֶלַע Ex 26[26] +, also צְלַע 2 S 16[13]; sf. צַלְעוֹ Ex 25[12] +; pl. צְלָעִים 1 K 6[34], צְלָעוֹת v[3] +; cstr. צַלְעֹת Ez 41[26] +; sf. צַלְעֹתָיו Gn 2[21] +;—**1.** *rib* of man Gn 2[21.22] (J). **2.** *rib* of hill, i.e. ridge, or terrace 2 S 16[13]. **3.** *side-chambers* or *cells* (enclosing temple like ribs) 1 K 6[5.6] (rd. הַצ׳ for היצוע, v. [יָצִיעַ]), 7[3], so of Ezek.'s temple Ez 41[5] + 10 t. 41 (on text v. Co Toy Krae). **4.** *ribs* of cedar and fir, i.e. *planks, boards* (pl.), of temple wall 1 K 6[15.16], floor v[15]. **5.** *leaves* of door v[34]. **6.** (in P) *side,* of ark (אָרוֹן) Ex 25[12.12.14] = 37[3.3.5]; of tabern. (מִשְׁכָּן) 26[20] (|| פֵּאָה v[18]), v[26.27.27] = 36[25] (|| פ׳ v[23]), v[31.32], 26[35.35]; of altar 27[7] = 38[7], 30[4] = 37[27].—Je 20[10] Jb 18[12] v. צֶלַע sub II. צלע.

6762 †צֵלַע **n.pr.loc.** in Benj. Jos 18[28], A 𝔊L Σελα[(ε)λαφ]; burial-place of Saul 2 S 21[14] (צֶלַע), ἐν τῇ πλευρᾷ; poss. = TelAm. *Zilu,* so Zim[ZA vi. 258] Jastr[JBL xi (1892), 105] (Wkl, however, thinks of סלע).

6760 †II. [צָלַע] **vb.** limp (Ar. ظَلَعَ, Aram. טלע Aph.);—**Qal** *Pt.* צֹלֵעַ עַל־יְרֵכוֹ Gn 32[32] (J; of Jacob); f. הַצֹּלֵעָה as subst., of personif. Judah as flock [צֹאן] Mi 4[6.7] Zp 3[19].

†צֶלַע **n.** [**m.**] **limping, stumbling**;—fig. 6761
of calamity, abs. לְצ׳ ψ 38[18] *I am ready* (נָכוֹן) *for stumbling* (and falling); sf. בְּצַלְעִי ψ 35[15] *at my stumbling;* שֹׁמְרֵי צ׳ Je 20[10] *watchers of my stumbling;* אֵיד נָכוֹן לְצַלְעוֹ Jb 18[12] *ruin is ready for his stumbling.*—Vid. also צֶלַע cstr.

†צָלָף **n.pr.m.** (NH *caper-plant*);—father 6764
of a wall-builder Ne 3[30], Σελε(φ), etc.

†צְלָפְחָד **n.pr.m.** of Manasseh, Nu 26[33.33] 6765
27[1.7] 36[2.6.10.11] Jos 17[3] 1 Ch 7[15.15], Σαλπααδ, etc.

†צֶלְצַח **n.pr.loc.** in Benj. 1 S 10[2] (si vera l.; 6766
prob. crpt. (Dr); HPS conj. מִצֶּלַע, cf. 2 S 21[14]).

I, II. [צִלְצַל], צִלְצַל, צֶלְצְלִים v. I. צלל. p. 852 6767

†צֶלֶק **n.pr.m.** Ammonite hero of David 2 S 6768
23[37] = 1 Ch 11[39], Ελιε, Σελ(λ)η(κ), Σαλααδ, etc.

צִלְּתַי v. III. צלל. p. 853 6769

†[צָמֵא] **vb. be thirsty** (NH = BH (rare); 6770
so Ar. ظَمِئَ, Eth. ጸምአ: As. *ṣûmu, thirst,* etc.);—**Qal** *Pf.* 3 fs. צָמְאָה ψ 42[3] 63[2]; 2 fs. וְצָמִת consec. Ru 2[9] (Ges[§ 75 qq]); 1 s. צָמֵתִי Ju 4[19] (Ges[§ 74 k]); 3 pl. צָמְאוּ Is 28[21]; *Impf.* 3 ms. וַיִּצְמָא Ex 17[3] Ju 15[18]; 3 mpl. יִצְמָאוּ Is 49[10], וַיִּצ׳ Jb 24[11]; 2 mpl. תִּצְמָאוּ Is 65[13];—*be thirsty* Ju 4[19] 15[18] Ru 2[9] Is 48[21] 49[10] (|| יִרְעָבוּ), 65[13] (|| תִּרְעָבוּ) Jb 24[11]; c. ל rei, Ex 17[3] (E); fig. צָמְאָה נַפְשִׁי לֵאלֹהִים ψ 42[3] *my soul thirsteth for God,* cf. 63[2].

†צָמָא **n.** [**m.**] thirst;—abs. צ׳ Ex 17[3] +, sf. 6772
צְמָאִי ψ 69[22], etc.;—Ex 17[3] (E), Ju 15[18] Ho 2[5] Am 8[13] La 4[4] Ne 9[20] ψ 69[22]; || רָעָב Is 5[13] (van d. H. צָמָה), Dt 28[48] Ne 9[15] 2 Ch 32[11]; of wild asses ψ 104[11], of fish וְתָמֹת בַּצ׳ Is 50[2], but rd. perh. (or בַּצְּמָאָה) וּבְהֶמְתָּם בַּצָּמָא Gunk[Schöpf. 98] Che[Hpt] Marti (cf. Is 44[3] sub foll.); fig. of grief of exile Is 41[17], cf. אֶרֶץ צִיָּה וְצָמָא Ez 19[13]; c. ל, *thirst for* water Am 8[11].—בַּצ׳ Je 48[18] is prob. corrupt; read perhaps לָאָרֶץ (Gie), or בֶּעָפָר.

†צָמֵא **adj.** thirsty;—abs. צ׳ Is 21[14] +; fs. 6771
צְמֵאָה Dt 29[18]; pl. צְמֵאִים ψ 107[5];—*thirsty,* usu. + (or ||) רָעֵב: 2 S 17[29] Pr 25[21] ψ 107[5], as subst. *thirsty one* Is 29[8] 32[6]; so also 21[14], and (fig. of thirst for י׳'s favour) 55[1]; צָמֵא 44[3] = *thirsty land* (Gunk[l. c.] prop. צְמֵאָה); הָרָוָה אֶת־הַצְּמֵאָה Dt 29[18] *the watered* (plant, herbage) *with the thirsty,* fig. of entire people.

†צִמְאָה **n.f.** parched condition;—Je 2[25] 6773
spare thy throat מִצ׳, *from being parched* (in fig.).

6774 †צִמָּאוֹן **n.[m.]** **thirsty ground**;—abs. צ׳ Dt 8[15] Is 35[7] ψ 107[33].

6775 †[צָמַד] **vb.** **bind, join** (Ar. ضمد *bind, wind*, specif. of girl with two lovers We[GGN 1893, 470]; *fasten* (cattle) to yoke Dozy, مِضْمَد *yoke, Id.*; As. *ṣamâdu, bind, harness*, so Eth. ፀመደ: and III. *be attached, attach oneself*, specif. *be* (religiously) *devoted*; Aram. צְמַד, ܨܡܰܕ, *bind*);—**Niph.** *Impf.* 3 ms. וַיִּצָּמֶד Nu 25[3]; 3 mpl. וַיִּצָּמְדוּ ψ 106[28]; *Pt.* pl. נִצְמָדִים Nu 25[5]; *join, attach, oneself* to (ל) Baal Peor, i.e. adopt his worship Nu 25[3.5] (JE), whence ψ 106[28]. **Pu.** *Pt.* f. מְצֻמֶּדֶת 2 S 20[8] a sword *bound* upon (עַל) his loins. **Hiph.** *Impf.* 3 fs. תַּצְמִיד מִרְמָה ψ 50[19] *thy tongue combineth* (fitteth together, frameth) *deceit* (>denom. fr. צֶמֶד Gerber[170]).

6776 †צֶמֶד **n.m.**[1 K 19, 19] **couple, pair**;—צ׳ cstr. Ju 19[3]+; sf. צִמְדּוֹ Je 51[23]; pl. צְמָדִים 1 K 19[19] 2 K 9[25] (but v. infr.); cstr. צִמְדֵּי Is 5[10] (Ges[§ 93m]);—**1.** *couple, pair*, usu. of animals, צ׳ חֲמֹרִים Ju 19[3.10] 2 S 16[1]; צ׳ (הַ)בָּקָר *span of oxen* 1 S 11[7] 1 K 19[21], pl. of more than one span v[19] (ploughing), Jb 1[3] 42[12]; צֶמֶד פְּרָדִים 2 K 5[17]; צ׳ פָּרָשִׁים Is 21[7.9] *a pair of horsemen;* pl. also of one pair of riders 2 K 9[25] (but rd. prob. צֶמֶד, so Kit); צ׳ alone = *span* (of oxen) Je 51[23]. **2.** a measure of land (only square measure in OT) like *acre;* orig. appar. what a *span* can plough (in a day; v. Now[Arch. i. 202] Benz[Arch. 208]; cf. mod. *faddan*, = what can be ploughed in a season Schumacher[ZPV xii (1889), 163 f., Across Jordan 22], or in a day Bergheim[PEQ. 1894, 192], Ency. Bib.[ACRE]), צ׳ שָׂדֶה 1 S 14[14] (on text v. Dr HPS); צִמְדֵּי־כֶרֶם Is 5[10].

6781 †I. צָמִיד **n.m.**[Gn 24, 22] **bracelet** (*bound* on wrist);—abs. צ׳ Nu 31[50]; pl. צְמִידִים Gn 24[22]+;—*bracelet* Gn 24[22.30.47] (J), Nu 31[50] (P); in fig. Ez 16[11] 23[42].

6781 †II. צָמִיד **n.[m.]** **cover,** of vessel, Nu 19[15].

6777 צַמָּה v. צמם. p. 855

6779 †צָמַח **vb.** **sprout, spring up** (NH *id.*, so 𝔗 צְמַח; Syr. ܨܡܰܚ *spring* or *shine forth*, ܨܶܡܚܳܐ *shining*, also *sprout;* Ph. צמח *posterity*);—**Qal** *Pf.* 3 ms. צָמַח־בּוֹ Lv 13[37]; 3 pl. וְצָמְחוּ consec. Is 44[4]; *Impf.* 3 ms. יִצְמַח Jb 5[6], 3 fpl. תִּצְמַחְנָה Is 42[9], etc.; *Pt.* צֹמֵחַ Ex 10[5], צוֹמֵחַ Ec 2[6]; fpl. צֹמְחוֹת Gn 41[6.23];—*sprout, spring up:* **1.** of plants, trees, etc. Gn 2[5] Ex 10[5] (both J), Gn 41[6.23] (E), Ez 17[6] (in fig.); once (late) יַעַר צוֹמֵחַ עֵצִים Ec 2[6] *wood sprouting with trees* (full of growing trees); fig. of future ruler (v. צֶמַח) Zc 6[12], posterity Is 44[4], cf. Jb 8[19], trouble (עָמָל) 5[6], truth (אֱמֶת) ψ 85[12], restoration (אֲרֻכָתְךָ) Is 58[8], future events Is 42[9]. **2.** of hair Lv 13[37] (P; cf. **Pi.**). **Pi.** *grow abundantly*, always of hair;—Pf. 3 ms. צִמַּח Ez 16[7] (in fig.): *Impf.* 3 ms. יְצַמַּח 2 S 10[5] = 1 Ch 19[5] (of beard); *Inf. cstr.* לְצַמֵּחַ Ju 16[22] (Samson's hair). **Hiph.** *Pf.* 3 ms. sf. וְהִצְמִיחָהּ Is 55[10]; *Impf.* 3 ms. יַצְמִיחַ 2 S 23[5] Is 61[11], וַיַּצְמַח Gn 2[9], etc.; *Inf. cstr.* לְהַצְמִיחַ Jb 38[27]; *Pt.* מַצְמִיחַ ψ 104[14] 147[8];—**1.** *cause to grow*, c. acc. of plant, subj. י׳ Gn 2[9] ψ 104[14], cf. Jb 38[27], c. 2 acc. ψ 147[8] *who causeth mts. to sprout grass;* fig., obj. צֶמַח צְדָקָה Je 33[15]; *horn* (קֶרֶן) of Isr. Ez 29[21], of David ψ 132[17]; righteousness, etc. Is 61[11b]; cf. also 2 S 23[5] (if interrog., v. Dr Bu; otherwise HPS); subj. ground Gn 3[18] cf. Is 61[11a] (sim.), Dt 29[22] (obj. om.); also (fig.) Is 45[8] (cf. Di Kit). **2.** of rain, *cause* the earth *to sprout* (abs.), Is 55[10].

†צֶמַח **n.m.**[Je 23, 5] **sprout, growth**;—abs. צ׳ 6780
Ho 8[7]+, צָמַח Zc 3[8]; cstr. צֶמַח Gn 19[25]+; sf. צִמְחָהּ Ez 17[9]+;—**1.** coll. *sprouting, growth*, צ׳ הָאֲדָמָה Gn 19[25] (J), צ׳ הַשָּׂדֶה Ez 16[7] (sim.), cf. Is 61[11] ψ 65[11]; so צ׳ יהוה Is 4[2], צ׳ abs. Ho 8[7]; *growth* (=foliage) of vine, טַרְפֵּי צ׳ Ez 17[9]. **2.** process of *growth*, of vine, עֲרֻגוֹת צִמְחָהּ Ez 17[10] = *the beds where it grew.* **3.** future ruler, under fig. of *sprout* from Davidic tree (cf. ψ 132[17]) וַהֲקִמֹתִי לְדָוִד צ׳ צַדִּיק Je 23[5] *a righteous sprout, shoot,* = אַצְמִיחַ לְדָוִד צ׳ צְדָקָה 33[15]; hence (as n.pr.) עַבְדִּי צ׳ Ze 3[8], of Zerub. אִישׁ צ׳ שְׁמוֹ 6[12].

צַמִּים v. צמם. צְמִיתֻת v. צמת. below, p. 856 6782-83

צמם (√ of foll.; cf. Ar. ضَمَّ *draw together*, or ضَمَّ *bandage* (a wound), *be compact;* NH צִמְצֵם *press;* 𝔗[Jer] Palp. Ithpalp. *veil* (? denom.)).

†צַמָּה **n.f.** **woman's veil**; sf. צַמָּתֵךְ;—Is 6777
47[2] Ct 4[1.3] 6[7].

†צַמִּים **n.m.** doubtful word, usu. **snare, trap** 6782
(fr. || פַּח Jb 18[9]);—וְשָׁאַף צ׳ חֵילָם Jb 5[5] *and a snare snappeth at his wealth* (so Bu Bev[JPhil. xxvi. 304 f.]; Vrss Di Du and most mod. צְמֵאִים, or צָמֵא, *the thirsty*, sometimes with change of וְשָׁאַף); 18[9] (|| פַּח; Che[JQ ix (1897), 578] צִירִים *pangs*, cf. Is 13[8]).

†[צָמַק] **vb.** **dry up, shrivel** (NH *id.;* 6784
𝔗[J] Nu 6[3] צְמִיקִין, for יְבֵשִׁים);—**Qal** *Pt. act.* pl. שָׁדַיִם צֹמְקִים Ho 9[14] *shrivelling breasts* (of women; || רֶחֶם מַשְׁכִּיל).

6778 †[צִמּוּק] **n.m.**$^{1 S 30, 12}$ **bunch of raisins** (*dried grapes*);—pl. צִמֻּקִים 1 S 25^{18} 30^{12}, צִמּוּקִים 2 S 16^{1} 1 Ch 12^{41} (van d. H. v^{40}).

צמר (√of foll.; NH צֶמֶר = BH; Eth. ፀምር: Aram. עֲמַרָא, ܥܡܪܐ; Palm. עמרא).

6785 †צֶ֫מֶר **n.m.**$^{Ez 44, 17}$ **wool**;—abs. צ׳ Is 1^{18}, צָ֫מֶר Lv 13^{48}; cstr. צֶ֫מֶר Ez 27^{18} (v. infr.); sf. צַמְרִי Ho $2^{7.11}$;—*wool* (usu. c. (פִּשְׁתִּי(ם *flax, linen*): in natural state גִּזַּת הַצ׳ Ju 6^{37}, אֵילִים צ׳ 2 K 3^{4} (but constr. difficult, and צ׳ perhaps gloss); Ho $2^{7.11}$ (as gift of value); white Is 1^{18} (sim.; ‖ שֶׁלֶג), sim. of snow ψ 147^{16} (from white flakes); *white* (?) *wool* as merchandise Ez 27^{18} (צ׳ צַ֫חַר, but on text v. צַ֫חַר), Pr 31^{12}; prey of moth Is 51^{8} (sim.); made up into garments Dt 22^{11}, בֶּגֶד צ׳ Lv $13^{47.59}$ cf. $v^{48.52}$; בֶּגֶד om. Ez 34^{3} 44^{17}.

6788 †צַמֶּ֫רֶת **n.f.** **tree-top** (poss. from *woolly*, feathery, appearance);—צ׳ cstr., of cedar (in fig.) Ez $17^{3.22}$, so sf. צַמַּרְתּוֹ $31^{3.10}$; of tall trees in gen., צַמַּרְתָּם v^{14}.

6786 †צְמָרִי **adj. gent.** c. art. as subst. coll. (people of the city called *Ṣimirra* by As., COT^{Gn} Dl$^{Pa 281 f.}$, Egypt. *D̲a-(m)-ma-ra* WMM$^{As. u. Eur. 187}$; Tel Am. *Ṣumur* acc. to Zim$^{ZPV xiii (1890), 145}$ Jastr$^{JBL xii (1893), 63}$; Gk. τὰ Σίμυρα, etc., e.g. Strabo$^{xvi. 2, 12}$, >Wkl$^{MVG 1896, 203 f., cf. Tel Am. 40*}$ thinks צ׳, Σίμυρα, = As. *Zimarra*, distinct from *Ṣimirra-Ṣumur*);—הַצ׳ Gn 10^{18} = 1 Ch 1^{16}, 𝔊 τὸν Σαμαραῖον; Ez 27^{11} Co rds. וּצְמָרִים for וְגַמָּדִים (q.v.); Toy Krae retain וְג׳;—cf. mod. *Ṣumra*, N. of Tripoli and S. of Ruad (Arvad), v. Pietschm$^{Phön. 39}$ Bäd$^{Pal. 3 (1898), 407}$.

6787 †צְמָרַ֫יִם **n.pr.loc.** **1.** in Benj. Jos 18^{22}, Σαρα, A Σεμριμ, 𝔊L Σαμαρειμ, perh. *Es-samra*, N. of Jericho Buhl$^{Geogr. 180}$. **2.** הַר־צ׳ mt. in Ephraim 2 Ch 13^{4}, Σομορων, unknown.

6789 †[צָמַת] **vb. put an end to, exterminate**, poet. and (in **Qal, Pi.**) hyperb. (prop. *compress*, NH *id.*, *press together*; Ar. صَمَتَ is *be silent*, II, IV. *make speechless, silence*; Syr. ܨܡܬ *be silent* (in Lexx));—**Qal** *Pf.* 3 pl. צָמְתוּ . . . חַיָּי La 3^{53} *they have put an end to my life* (Bu conj. **Pi.**). **Niph.** *be ended, annihilated*; *Pf.* 1 s. נִצְמַתִּי מִפְּנֵי־חֹשֶׁךְ Jb 23^{17} *I am* [not] *annihilated because of* (the) *darkness*; 3 pl. נִצְמָתוּ Jb 6^{17} (of dried-up brooks). **Pi.** *Pf.* 3 fs. sf. צִמְּתַתְנִי ψ 119^{139} קִנְאָתִי *hath put an end to me* (it is so intense). **Pilēl** *Pf.* 3 pl. sf. צִמְּתוּתֻנִי (but rd. צִמְּתוּנִי Ges$^{§ 55 d}$, or צִמְּתַתְנִי Hi [Ges$^{§ 145 k}$]; cf. Bae) ψ 88^{17} thine alarms *have annihilated me*. **Hiph.** *Pf.* 2 ms. הִצְמַתָּה ψ 73^{27}; *Impf.* 3 ms. sf. יַצְמִיתֵם ψ $94^{23.23}$; 2 ms. תַּצְמִית ψ 143^{12}, etc.; *Imv.* ms. sf. הַצְמִיתֵם ψ 54^{7}; *Pt.* pl. sf. מַצְמִיתַי ψ 69^{5};—*exterminate, annihilate*, c. acc. pers., subj. Psalmist ψ 18^{41} = 2 S 22^{41} (read as in ψ), $101^{5.8}$; his foes ψ 69^{5}; י׳ 54^{7} 73^{27} $94^{23.23}$ 143^{12}.

†צְמִיתֻת **n.f.** **completion, finality**, only in phr. לַצ׳, לִצ׳ = *in perpetuity*, of alienation of land; לִצְמִתֻת Lv 25^{23}, לַצְּמִיתֻת v^{30} (P). 6783

†צִן **n.pr.loc.** Σ(ε)ιν; name of wilderness S. of Canaan, where lay Kadesh Barnea, c. ה loc. צִ֫נָה Nu 34^{4} (where Lag$^{BN 47}$ חצן), Jos 15^{3} (van d. H. צִ֫נָּה in Jos); elsewh. מִדְבַּר־צִן Nu 13^{21} 20^{1} $27^{14.14}$ 33^{36} 34^{3} Dt 32^{51} Jos 15^{1} (all P). 6790

[צֵן], I, II, III. צִנָּה, v. I, II, III. צנן. below 6791, 6793

†צֹנֶה, [צֹנֶא] [**n.m.**] **flocks** (‖ form of צֹאן q.v.);—abs. צֹנֶה ψ 8^{8}; sf. צֹנַאֲכֶם Nu 32^{24} (JE). 6792

†[צָנַח] **vb. descend** (meaning inferred fr. context);—**Qal** *Impf.* 3 fs. וַתִּצְנַח מֵעַל הַחֲמוֹר Ju 1^{14} = Jos 15^{18} *and she descended* (alighted) *from the ass*; וַתִּ׳ בָּאָרֶץ Ju 4^{21} *and it* (the tent-peg) *went down into the ground*. 6795

†[צָנַם] **vb. dry up, harden** (cf. Aram. צוּנְמָא, ܨܘܢܡܐ, *stone*);—**Qal** *Pt. pass.* fpl. צְנֻמוֹת Gn 41^{23} (E) of ears of grain. 6798

I. **צנן** (√of foll.; meaning obscure).

†[צֵן] **n.**[**m.**] **thorn**? **barb**?;—pl. צִנִּים Pr 22^{5} (+ פַּחִים); וְאֶל־מִצִּנִּים Jb 5^{5} *from* (behind) *thorns* (a protecting thorn hedge, so Di), but very dub.; Che$^{JQ July, 1897, 576}$ del. as doublet of צַמִּים; Bev$^{JPhil. xxvi. 305}$ prop. וְאֹנָם צִנִּים [*and* as to *their wealth, barbs* (? barbed spears) *take* it]. 6791

†I. [צִנָּה] **n. f.** appar. **hook**, or **barb** (of fishing-spear ?);—pl. צִנּוֹת Am 4^{2} (‖ סִירוֹת דּוּגָה). 6793

†[צָנִין] **n.**[**m.**] **thorn, prick**;—pl. צְנִינִם Nu 33^{55} (P; ‖ שִׂכִּים), צְנִנִים Jos 23^{13} (D; both fig.). 6796

II. **צנן** (√of foll.; NH צָנַן *be cold*, so JAram. צְנַן; 𝔗 צִינְתָא *cold*).

†II. [צִנָּה] **n.f. coolness**;—cstr. צִנַּת־שֶׁלֶג Pr 25^{13} *coolness of snow* (צינת רוח צפון Ecclus 43^{20}). 6793

III. **צנן** (√of foll.; Thes (so Di^{Lex}) cp. Ar. صَانَ *preserve, keep*, Eth. ጸወነ: *protect*, but dub.).

6793 †III. צִנָּה **n.f.** large **shield** (*covering* whole body);—abs. צ׳ 1 S 17⁷+; pl. צִנּוֹת 2 Ch 11¹²; —*shield*, larger than מָגֵן 1 K 10¹⁶·¹⁶ (cf. v¹⁷)= 2 Ch 9¹⁵·¹⁵; נֹשֵׂא (הַ)צִּנָּה 1 S 17⁷·⁴¹ (הָאִישׁ נ׳ הַצ׳), 2 Ch 14⁷, נֹשְׂאֵי צ׳ 1 Ch 12²⁵ (van d. H. v²⁴); עִרְכוּ מָגֵן וְצִנָּה Je 46³, cf. עֹרְכֵי צ׳ 1 Ch 12⁹ (van d. H. v⁸); הַחֲזֵק מָגֵן וְצ׳ ψ 35²; אֹחֵז רֹמַח וְצ׳ 2 Ch 25⁵; הֵקִים עָלַיִךְ צ׳ Ez 26⁸; + מָגֵן also 23²⁴ 38⁴ 39⁹; צ׳ 1 Ch 12³⁵ (van d. H. v³⁴) 2 Ch 11¹²; sim. of י׳'s favour ψ 5¹³; fig. of י׳'s faithfulness 91⁴.

6803 † צִנְצֶנֶת **n.f. jar**, or like receptacle (so Vrss and context; perh. from above √; >*basket*= 𝔗 Talm. צִנָּא);—Ex 16³³ (P).

6799 צָנָן v. צַאֲנָן. p. 838

6800 †[צָנַע] **vb. be modest, humble** (perhaps prop. *be retired*, NH Hiph. *keep close, reserve, preserve*, so 𝔗 אַצְנַע; צְנִיעַ *retiring, modest*);—**Hiph.** *Inf.abs.* הַצְנֵעַ לֶכֶת Mi 6⁸ *a making humble to walk* = shewing a humble walk (with God).

†[צָנוּעַ] **adj. modest** (on format. cf. Ba NB § 31 d);—pl. צְנוּעִים Pr 11² (v. Toy; opp. זָדוֹן).

6801 †[צָנַף] **vb. wrap, or wind up, together** (cf. Ar. صَنِفَةٌ *hem* of garment, 𝔗ᴶ צְנָפָא *skirt* (=כָּנָף); מִצְנְפָא, ܡܨܢܦܬܐ *turban*, ChrPal. ܨܢܦܐ *tassel*);—**Qal** *Impf.* 3 ms. יִצְנֹף Lv 16⁴ *he shall wind* (his head) with (ב) the turban (מִצְנֶפֶת q.v.); sf., + *Inf. abs.* and acc. cogn. צָנוֹף יִצְנָפְךָ צְנֵפָה Is 22¹⁸ *he will wind thee entirely up* (with) *a winding* (under fig. of ball, to be driven far off, in exile).—צנוף Is 62³ v. following.

6797 † צָנִיף **n.m.** Zc 3,5 **turban**;—abs. צ׳ Zc 3⁵·⁵ (for h. priest) and (fig. of righteousness) Jb 29¹⁴; cstr. צְנִיף מְלוּכָה Is 62³ Qr *royal turban* (Kt צנוף); pl. הַצְּנִיפוֹת Is 3²³ (of women's turbans).

6802 † צְנֵפָה **n.f. winding**;—Is 22¹⁸, v. [צנף].

4701 † מִצְנֶפֶת **n.f. turban** of high priest;—abs. מ׳ Ez 21³¹, מִצְנֶפֶת Ex 28³⁷ 29⁶; cstr. מִצְנֶפֶת Lv 16⁴;—*turban* of linen Ex 28⁴·³⁷·³⁷·³⁹ 29⁶·⁶ 39²⁸·³¹ Lv 8⁹·⁹ 16⁴; sign of royalty Ez 21³¹.

צנק (√of foll.; cf. Sam. ࠑࠍࠒ *shut up* or *in*, and perh. Eth. ጸቅለ: *hedge about*, Prä BAS i. 374; cf. also Ar. زَنَقَ *bind, restrain, straighten*, Syr. ܙܢܩ (in Lexx; usu. *throw*)).

6729 † צִינֹק **n.[m.] pillory**;—Je 29²⁶ (‖ מַהְפֶּכֶת).

צנר (√of foll.; NH צִנּוֹר = BH (also *hinge-socket*), and so 𝔗 צִינוֹרָא (rare)).

† צִנּוֹר **n. m. pipe, spout, conduit** (so NH);—abs. וְיִגַּע בַּצִּנּוֹר 2 S 5⁸ (i.e., si vera l., of Jerus., but very dubious, cf. Dr HPS); pl. sf. קוֹל צִנּוֹרֶיךָ ψ 42⁸ *the sound of thy* (water-) *spouts* fig., of sluices of heaven opened, cf. פֶּלֶג, אֲרֻבָּה. 6794

† צַנְתְּרוֹת **n. m. pl.** cstr. **pipes** feeding lamps with oil Zc 4¹² (in vision) (formation by inserting ת acc. to Bö § 300 b Kö ii. 1, 201). 6804

†[צָעַד] **vb. step, march** (NH *id.* (rare); 6805
Ar. صَعِدَ *ascend*);—**Qal** *Pf.* 3 fs. צָעֲדָה Gn 49²² (but on text v. infr.); 3 pl. צָעֲדוּ 2 S 6¹³; *Impf.* 3 ms. יִצְעַד Pr 7⁸, etc.; *Inf. cstr.* sf. בְּצַעְדְּךָ Ju 5⁴, בְּצַעְדְּךָ ψ 68⁸;—*step, march*, of י׳ Ju 5⁴ ψ 68⁸ (c. ב loc.), Hb 3¹² (c. acc. אֶרֶץ); rd. prob. also צֹעֵד Is 63¹ (for MT צֹעֶה, v. צעה); of men, c. acc. cogn. צְעָדִים 2 S 6¹³ *they had gone six steps*; c. acc. דֶּרֶךְ *step* a certain way Pr 7⁸; of idols, לֹא יִצְעָדוּ Je 10⁵.—בָּנוֹת צָעֲדָה עֲלֵי־שׁוּר Gn 49²² is dubious: usu. (its) *daughters* (twigs of bough) *have climbed* over the wall (on sg. vb. v. Ges § 145 k; others think ָה old fpl. ending, e. g. Nö ZMG xxxviii (1884), 411 JPPeters Hbr iii (1887), 111; v (1888), 199; conject. emend. of text v. in Ball Hpt Holz). **Hiph.** *Impf.* 3 fs. sf. וְתַצְעִדֵהוּ Jb 18¹⁴ *and it* (an unseen power Di; disease Du, rdg. וְיַצ׳) *makes him march*, c. ל pers.

†[צַעַד] **n.m.** 2 S 6,13 **step, pace**;—abs. צַעַד Pr 30²⁹; sf. צַעֲדוֹ Je 10³ Pr 6⁹, etc.; pl. cstr. צַעֲדֵי Jb 18⁷; sf. צְעָדַי Jb 31⁴, etc.;—**1.** lit. *step, pace*, 2 S 6¹³, תַּרְחִיב צַעֲדִי תַּחְתָּי 2 S 22³⁷ = ψ 18³⁷, i.e. givest me firm footing, מֵיטִיבֵי צ׳ Pr 30²⁹ = *making a good step*, stately in march; La 4¹⁸ (‖ לֶכֶת). **2.** *step, steps*, in fig. of course of life, fortune: sg. לֹא יֵצַר צ׳ Pr 4¹²; ‖ דֶּרֶךְ Je 10²³ Pr 16⁹; pl. Jb 14¹⁶ 31⁴ 34²¹, צַעֲדֵי אוֹנוֹ 18⁷ (cf. Pr 4¹² supr.); מִסְפַּר־צְעָדַי אַגִּידֶנּוּ 31³⁷; of harlot Pr 5⁵ fig., שְׁאוֹל צְעָדֶיהָ יִתְמֹכוּ. 6806

†I. צְעָדָה **n.f. marching**;—קוֹל צ׳ 2 S 5²⁴ *the sound of marching* = 1 Ch 14¹⁵. 6807

[מִצְעָד] **n. [m.] step**;—pl. sf. בְּמִצְעָדָיו Dn 11⁴³ i. e. at his heels, in his train; cstr., fig. of course of life, מִצְעֲדֵי־גֶבֶר ψ 37²³ (‖ דַּרְכּוֹ), Pr 20²⁴. 4703

II. צעד (√of foll.; meaning unknown).

†II. [צְעָדָה] **n.f. armlet**, band clasping upper arm (so SS al.; most *step-chain*, from I. צעד);—pl. הַצְּעָדוֹת Is 3²⁰ (ladies' finery); read הַצ׳ also 2 K 11¹² (for MT הָעֵדוּת) We Bl. Einl. 4, 258 = Comp. (2), 361 Kmp SS Kit Benz. 6807

685 †אֶצְעָדָה **n.f.** id.;—abs. 'א Nu 31^{50} (+צָמִיד, *bracelet*); 'הַצְּעָדָה א' אֲשֶׁר עַל־זְרֹעוֹ 2 S 1^{10} (read הַצְּעָדָה We Dr Bu HPS, cf. 2 K 11^{12} supr.).

6808 †[צָעָה] **vb.** stoop, bend, incline (Ar. صَغَا (ى, و) *incline, lean*, cf. also صَغِيَ);—**Qal** *Pt.* **1.** צֹעֶה Is 51^{14} *one stooping* (under a burden), 63^{1} *bending* (forward or backward; fr. abundant strength), but read prob. צֹעֵד *marching* (Lo Gr Che Du Di-Kit al.); f. אַתְּ צֹעָה זֹנָה Je 2^{20} (in sensu obscoeno). **2.** trans. (=**Pi.** q.v.) pl. צֹעִים Je 48^{12} *men inclining, tipping* a vessel, to empty it. **Pi.** *Pf.* 3 pl. sf. וְצֵעֻהוּ Je 48^{12} I will send tippers *and they shall tip him over* (Moab, under fig. of vessel).

6813 †[צָעַן] **vb.** wander, travel (Ar. ظَعَنَ *journey, go away;* prob. connected with As. *ṣênu*, Eth. ጸዐነ:, Aram. טְעַן, Palm. טען, all *load* (beast, etc.)=Heb. טָעַן †Gn 45^{17}; Aram. טְעַן, ܛܥܢ also *bear, carry*);—**Qal** *Impf.* 3 ms. יִצְעַן Is 33^{20} *travel*, i. e. be removed, of tent (+יִסַּע).

6814 †צֹעַן **n.pr.loc.** Τανις: **Tanis**, in Egypt (Egypt. *Ḏa'nĕ(t)* Steind$^{BAS 600}$, in As. *Ṣi'inu, Sa'anu* Ib$^{id. 598 ff.}$ Dl$^{Pa 315}$); it was built 7 years after Hebron acc. to Nu 13^{22}; Is 19$^{11.13}$ 30^{4} Ez 30^{14} ψ 78$^{12.43}$; mod. *Ṣân*, in NW. part of Delta; v. also Eb$^{GS 512 ff.}$ Bd$^{Lower Eg. 3 (1895), 228}$ Petrie$^{Tanis (1885)}$.

6815 †צַעֲנַנִּים **n.pr.loc.** only c. בְּ, pointed as prep., and so most (but ב perh. radical, v. GFM); on border of Naphtali, near Ḳedesh;—'בְּצ Jos 19^{33} (Βεσεμεειν, Σεεναναιμ, etc.) + Ju 4^{11} Qr (Kt בצענים), 𝔊 πλεονεκτούντων (√בָּצַע), ἀναπαυομένων.

צעף (√of foll.; cf. Ar. ضَعَّفَ III. *make double*, ضِعْفٌ *double;* Eth. ፀዐፈ: *fold, double*, so Aram. עוּף, ܥܘܦ, ܥܛܦ *double* (for ܐܥܛܦ =צָעִיף), cf. 𝔗 עִיפָא for Heb. צָעִיף (prop. *a double* or *folded thing*); v. esp. Lag$^{Sem. i. 23 ff.}$).

6809 †צָעִיף **n.[m.]** wrapper, shawl, or veil;—abs. 'צ Gn 24^{65} 38^{14}; sf. צְעִיפָהּ v^{19} (all J).

6816 צַעֲצֻעִים v. צוע. p. 847

6817 †צָעַק **vb.** cry, cry out, call (||זָעַק; NH *id.;* Ar. صَعَقَ, perhaps orig. *sound as thunder*, cf. صَاعِقَةٌ *thunderbolt*, صَعِيق *bellow* (of bull));—**Qal** *Pf.* 3 ms. 'צ 1 K 20^{39} La 2^{18}, 3 fs. צָעֲקָה Dt 22^{24}+, etc.; *Impf.* יִצְעַק Ex 23^{22}+, etc.; *Imv.* fs. צַעֲקִי Je 22^{20}, וּצְעָקִי v^{20}; fpl. צְעַקְנָה 49^{3}; *Inf. abs.* צָעֹק Ex 22^{22}; cstr. לִצְעֹק 2 K 8^{3}; *Pt.* fs. abs. צֹעֶקֶת 2 K 8^{5}; mpl. צֹעֲקִים Gn 4^{10} Ex 5^{8};—**1.** *cry, cry out*, for help, usu. c. אֶל pers.;—**a.** unto man Gn 41^{55} (E; +לְ rei), Nu 11^{3} (JE), 1 K 20^{39} 2 K 6^{26} 8^{3} (+אֶל rei), v^{5} (+עַל rei); sq. אמר Ex 5^{15} (J), 2 K 4^{1} and (אֶל pers. om.) Ex 5^{8} (J), 2 K 4^{40} 6^{5}. **b.** esp. unto 'י: Gn 4^{10} Ex 8^{8} (+עַל־דְּבַר rei), 14$^{10.15}$ 15^{25} 17^{4} 22^{22} (צָעֹק יִצְעַק), v^{26} Nu 12^{13} 20^{16} Jos 24^{7} (all JE), Ju 4^{3} 10^{12} Dt 26^{7} Is 19^{20} (+מִפְּנֵי rei), La 2^{18} Ne 9^{27} ψ 107$^{6.28}$; קוֹלִי ... נֶגְדֶּךָ 77^{2}, cf. 34^{18}; c. לי' 2 Ch 13^{14}, אֶל־א' וְאֶצְעָקָה ψ 88^{2}. **c.** *cry* unto (אֶל) idol Is 46^{7}. **2.** abs. *cry, cry out*, in distress, need;—Gn 27^{34} (J; c. acc. cogn.), Dt 22$^{24.27}$ Is 33^{7} (|| בָּכָה), 65^{14} (|| הֵילִיל, opp. רָנַן; c. מִן rei), Je 22$^{20.20}$ (|| נָתַן קוֹל), 49^{3} (|| הֵילִיל), Jb 35^{12}; c. obj. חָמָס Jb 19^{7} (|| אֲשַׁוַּע). **3.** *make outcry, clamour*, Is 42^{2} (+יִשָּׂא, יַשְׁמִיעַ קוֹלוֹ). **Niph.** *be summoned* (i.e. to arms), abs.; *Impf.* 3 ms. וַיִּצָּעֵק Ju 7$^{23.24}$ 12^{1}, so 3 mpl. וַיִּצָּעֲקוּ 10^{17} 2 K 3^{21}, sq. אַחֲרֵי שָׁאוּל+acc. loc. 1 S 13^{4}. **Pi.** *Pt.* מְצַעֵק *cry aloud*, in grief, 2 K 2^{12}. **Hiph.** *call together* וַיַּצְעֵק אֶת־הָעָם אֶל־י' הַמִּצְפָּה 1 S 10^{17}.

†צְעָקָה **n.f.** cry, outcry (older form of זְעָקָה);—abs. 'צ Gn 27^{34}+; cstr. צַעֲקַת Ex 3^{9}+; 6818
sf. צַעֲקָתוֹ 1 S 9^{16}+, etc.;—**1.** *outcry* against (Sodom) Gn 18^{21} 19^{13} (both J). **2.** *cry of distress*, esp. as *heard* by 'י Ex 3^{7} (J), 22^{22} (E), cf. Is 5^{7} Jb 27^{9} 34^{28} ψ 9^{13}; צ' בָּאָה אֵלַי Ex 3^{9} (E), 1 S 9^{16}, cf. Jb 34^{28}; צ' גְּדֹלָה Ex 11^{6} 12^{30} (both J), Ne 5^{1}; as acc. cogn. Gn 27^{34} (J); קוֹל צ' 1 S 4^{14} Je 25^{36} (|| יְלָלָה), Zp 1^{10} (|| *id.*, + שֶׁבֶר גדול), Je 48^{3} (|| שֹׁד וָשֶׁבֶר גדול), cf. 49^{21}; צַעֲקַת שֶׁבֶר 48^{5} (|| בְּכִי).

†[צָעַר] **vb.** be, or grow, insignificant 6819
(|| זער; NH *id.*, As. *ṣeḫêru*, *be small*, Ar. صَغُرَ *id.;* Syr. ܙܥܪ *be insignificant, despicable;* 𝔗 צְעַר trans. *despise, revile*);—**Qal** *Impf.* (opp. כָּבֵד), 3 mpl. יִצְעֲרוּ Jb 14^{21}, יִצְעָרוּ Je 30^{19}; *Pt.* as subst. הַצֹּעֲרִים Zc 13^{7} (i.e. sheep, in fig., cf. Now).

†צֹעַר, צוֹעַר **n.pr.loc.** Zoar (understood 6820
as *insignificance*, cf. Gn 19^{20});—Σηγωρ, 𝔊 L Σιγωρ, but Gn 13^{10} Je 48^{34} Ζογορ(α); on 𝔊 cf. further Lag$^{BN 54 f.}$: city at SE. end of Dead Sea,
צֹעַר Gn 13^{10} 14$^{2.8}$ (both=בֶּלַע), Dt 34^{3} Is 15^{5} Je 1106
48^{34}; צוֹעַר Gn 19$^{22.30.30}$; c. ה loc., צֹעֲרָה v^{23} + Je 48^{4} (for MT צעוריה), 𝔊 Ζογορα, JDMich Ew Gf Gie al.—Cf. Buhl$^{Geogr. 271. 274}$ GASm$^{Geogr. 506 f. 678 (App.)}$.

6810 †I. צָעִיר **adj.** little, insignificant, young;
—abs. צָעִיר Gn 25[23]+; f. צְעִירָה Gn 19[31]+; צְעִרָה
1 S 9[21]; mpl. צְעִירִים Jb 30[1]; sf. צְעִירֶיהָ Je 48[4]
Qr (Kt צעוריה; but v. צָעַר); צְעִירֵיהֶם Je 14[3]
(Kt צעוריהם), etc.;—**1. a.** *little*, with idea of
insignificance Ju 6[15] (‖ הַדַּל), cf. 1 S 9[21] (‖ קְטַנֵּי),
Mi 5[1] ψ 68[28] Is 60[22] (opp. גוי עצום); of horn in
vision Dn 8[9], rd. prob. אחרת צעירה for אחת
4704 מִצְּעִירָה, cf. Bev Dr; צְעִירֵי הַצֹּאן Je 49[20] 50[45] (fig.
of helpless captives). **b.** *insignificant, mean*,
ψ 119[141] (‖ נִבְזֶה), Je 14[3] (as subst.); on Je 48[4]
v. צָעַר. **2.** more oft. of age, *young* (usu.
c. art. the *younger, youngest*, as subst.), of son
(brother), opp. הַבְּכוֹר Gn 43[33] 48[14] (both J), Jos
6[26] 1 K 16[34], opp. רַב Gn 25[23] (J), cf. צ׳ אני
לְיָמִים ואתם יְשִׁישִׁים Jb 32[6]; of daughter (sister),
opp. הַבְּכִירָה Gn 19[31.34.35.38] (J) 29[26] (E);—here
belongs also צְעִירִים מִמֶּנִּי לימים Jb 30[1], si vera l.;
GHBWr Siegf Bu del. ממני לימים; 𝔊 ἐλάχιστοι;
put then under **1 b.**

6811 †II. [צָעִיר] **n.pr.loc.** prob. on border of
Edom, צָעִירָה 2 K 8[21], εἰς Σειωρ (𝔊L ἐκ Σιωρ).

6812 †[צְעִירָה] **n.f.** youth;—sf. כִּצְעִרָתוֹ Gn 43[33]
(J; opp. כִּבְכֹרָתוֹ).—On adj. צְעִירָה v. foregoing;
צעוריה Je 48[4], צעוריהם Je 14[3], v. צָעִיר, צָעַר.

6686 †צוּעָר **n.pr.m.** Σωγαρ, in Issachar (*little
one*);—alw. in נְתַנְאֵל בֶּן־צ׳ Nu 1[8] 2[5] 7[18.23] 10[15].

6730 †צִיעֹר **n.pr.loc.** Σωρθ, A𝔊L Σιωρ, Jos 15[54],
prob. *Ṣâʿîr*, 5 m. NNE. fr. Hebron, Buhl [Geogr. 158].

4705 †I. מִצְעָר **n.m.** a small thing (‖ מִזְעָר);—**1.**
abs. מ׳ *a small thing*, of city Gn 19[20.20] (J); of
Job's fortunes, רֵאשִׁיתְךָ מ׳ Jb 8[7] (opp. יִשְׂגֶּה מְאֹד);
cstr. מִצְעַר אֲנָשִׁים 2 Ch 24[24] *a few men;* of time
לַמּ׳ Is 63[18] *for the* [*a*] *little while.*—ψ 42[7] v. II. מ׳.

4706 †II. מִצְעָר **n.pr.mont.** near Hermon, הַר מ׳
ψ 42[7] *mt.* (of) *Miṣʿar* (perh. orig. *littleness*), not
identified; so De Now Du Dr GASm [Geogr. 477];
others *mt. of littleness, little mt.*, so 𝔊 𝔙 Hi
Che Bae We al. (interpr. then usu. of Zion).

6821 †צָפַד **vb. draw together, contract** (NH
id., trans.; Ar. صَفَدَ *bind fast, shackle*, cf. Nö
[M § 46] who cp. Mand. סאפטים *fetters*);—**Qal** *Pf.*
3 ms. צ׳ La 4[8] their skin *contracteth, shrivelleth*,
upon (עַל) their bones.

6824 צָפָה Ez 32[6] v. צוּף. p. 847

6822 I. [צָפָה] [37] **vb. look out** or **about, spy,
keep watch** (NH *id.*, Pi. *hope;* Eth. ሰፈወ:
III. *hope*);—**Qal** [28] *Impf.* 3 ms. juss. יִצֶף בֵּינִי
וּבֵינֶךָ Gn 31[49] (J) *may* י׳ *keep watch between
me and thee* (that the covenant be kept=
עד א׳ וגו׳ v[50]); 3 fpl. עֵינָיו בַּגּוֹיִם תִּצְפֶּינָה ψ 66[9]
*his eyes keep watch upon the nations; Pt.
act.* צוֹפֶה רָשָׁע לַצַּדִּיק ψ 37[32] *a wicked man
spieth upon the righteous;* Ct 7[5] the town
which looketh toward (פְּנֵי) Damascus; f. צוֹפִיָּה
Pr 31[27] *she keepeth watch* of (c. acc.); pl. עֵינֵי י׳
צֹפוֹת רָעִים וְטוֹבִים Pr 15[3]; elsewh. as subst. *watchman*, abs. צֹפֶה 2 S 13[34]+; pl. צֹפִים 1 S 14[16]+, 6839
sf. צֹפָיו Is 56[10] Qr (Kt צפו), צֹפַיִךְ Is 52[8];—1 S
14[16] 2 S 13[34]+8 t. SK, Ez 33[2.6.6] Is 52[8], so in
שְׂדֵה צֹפִים Nu 23[14] (JE); fig. of prophets Ho 9[8]
Je 6[17] Ez 3[17] 33[7] Is 56[10];—צוֹפִים 1 S 1[1] v. צוֹפִי; 6839
Pt. pass. צָפוּ (Codd. and Qr צָפוּי), Jb 15[22] *spied out*
(and brought) *to* (אֱלֵי) the sword (Ew Bi Perles
[Anal. 29] צָפוּן cf. Di Bu). †**Pi.** *Pf.* 1 pl. צִפִּינוּ La
4[17]; *Impf.* 1 s. אֲצַפֶּה Mi 7[7]+; *Imv.* ms. צַפֵּה
Na 2[2], fs. צַפִּי Je 48[19]; *Pt.* מְצַפֶּה 1 S 4[13], Is 21[6];
pl. sf. מְצַפַּיִךְ Mi 7[4];—*watch* (*closely*), אֶל־דֶּרֶךְ
צ׳־דֶּרֶךְ Je 48[19], עִמְדִי וְצ׳ Na 2[2]; +אֶל of person
expected La 4[17]; fig. בַּי׳ אֲצַפֶּה Mi 7[7]; abs. lit.
1 S 4[13]; fig. Hb 2[1] *I will look forth*, to see
(לִרְאוֹת) what he will say; ψ 5[4] *I will look out*
(expectantly); pt. as n.=*watchman* Is 21[6] Mi 7[4].

†צְפִי, צְפוֹ **n.pr.m.** Σωφαρ: in Edom (? *gaze,* 6825
gazing);—צְפוֹ Gn 36[11.15]+v[43] (ins. prob. after
עירם; cf. Lag [Sept. Stud. ii. 10, i. 178; 37, i. 270] Nes [Mar. 12])=
צְפִי 1 Ch 1[36].

צְפוֹן, צְפוֹנִי v. צִפְיוֹן. below, p. 128, 861 1189, 6828, 6830-31

†[צְפִיָּה] **n.f.** outlook-post (?);—sf. בְּצִפִּיָּתֵנוּ 6836
צִפִּינוּ La 4[17] (Ba [NB 139]; Bi [for both] בְּצַפּוֹתֵנוּ).

†צִפְיוֹן **n.pr.m.** Σαφων: son of Gad (? *gaze*);— 6837
Gn 46[16],=צְפוֹן Nu 26[15] (v. בַּעַל צ׳). p. 128 1189, 6827

†I. צְפוֹנִי **adj. gent.** of צְפוֹן (v. foregoing); c. 6831
art. as subst. coll. Nu 26[15].—II. צ׳ v. צפן. p. 861 6830

†I. מִצְפֶּה **n.m. 1.** watch-tower, Is 21[8]. 4707
2. outlook-point, 2 Ch 20[24] on high ground.

†II. מִצְפֶּה **n.pr.loc. 1.** הַמּ׳ in Shephelah of 4708
Judah Jos 15[38], Μασ(σ)ηφα. **2.** מִצְפֵּה־מוֹאָב
1 S 22[3], Μασσηφα. **3.** מִצְפֵּה גִלְעָד Ju 11[29.29]
(ἡ σκοπιά) prob.=רָמַת הַמּ׳ Jos 13[26] Μασ(ση)φα 7434
and perh. מִצְפָּה **2.**—Jos 11[8] 18[26] v. מִצְפָּה **3, 4.**

מִצְפָּה [38] **n.pr.loc.** (prop. *outlook-point* or 4709
-height; c. art. (exc. Ho 5[1]));—†**1.** in Gilead, expl.
as name given to Laban's cairn, N. of Jabbok

Gn 31^{49} (on text v. Ball Holz; 𝔊 ἡ ὅρασις). †**2.** prob. S. of Jabbok, Ju 10^{17} (ἡ σκοπιά), 11$^{11.34}$ (Μασσηφα; so 𝔊L 10^{17}), Ho 5^{1} (ἡ σκοπιά); appar. = II. מִצְפֶּה **3**, Buhl$^{Geogr. 262}$ (-פֶּה, -פָּה, seem to interchange); site unknown; v. conj. in Buhl$^{l.c.}$, cf. GASm$^{Geogr. 586}$. †**3.** near Hermon, אֶרֶץ הַמּ׳ Jos 11^{3}, Μασευμαν, Μασσηφα(θ), = בִּקְעַת־מִצְפֶּה v^{8}, Μασσωχ, Μασσηφα; v. Buhl$^{Geogr. 240}$. **4.** old sacred place in Benj., Μασσηφα, etc.;—הַמּ׳ Ju 20^{1}+, הַמִּצְפָּ֫תָה 1 S 7^{5}+;—Ju 20$^{1.3}$ 21$^{1.5.8}$ 1 S 7^{5} + 7 t. 1 S 7, 10, 1 K 15^{22} = 2 Ch 16^{6}, 2 K 25$^{23.25}$ Je 40^{10} + 12 t. 40, 41, Ne 3$^{7.15.19}$; = הַמִּצְפֶּה Jos 18^{26};—mod. *Nabî Samwîl*, 5 miles NW. of Jerusalem, v. Buhl$^{Geogr. 167 f.}$.

6823 II. [צָפָה]$_{47}$ **vb.** lay out, lay over (NH Pi. = BH);—**Qal** *Inf. abs.* צָפֹה הַצָּפִית Is 21^{5} *they lay out the rug!* or the like, so most moderns, v. צָפִית. **Pi.** *overlay, plate: Pf.* 3 ms. צִפָּה 1 K 6^{15}+; 2 ms. וְצִפִּיתָ Ex 25^{11}+; *Impf.* 3 ms. וַיְצַף 1 K 6^{20}+, sf. וַיְצַפֵּהוּ v^{20}+; 2 ms. תְּצַפֶּה Ex 29^{29}; 3 mpl. וַיְצַפּוּ 2 Ch 3^{10}, etc.;—*overlay*, esp. *plate* sthg. *with* metal (gold, bronze), usu. 2 acc.: 1 K 6$^{20.20}$ + 6 t. 1 K 6, + 10^{18}, ‖ 2 Ch 3$^{4.10}$ 4^{9} 9^{17}, Ex 25$^{11.13}$ + 21 t. Ex 25–38 (all P); *overlay, stud with* precious stones, 2 acc. 2 Ch 3^{6}; also *plate*, acc. mater. om., 1 K 6^{15} 2 K 18^{16} Ex 25^{11} 38^{28}; acc. dir. obj. om. 1 K 6$^{32.35}$; c. acc. + בְּ mater. v^{15} *overlaid the floor of the house with timbers.* †**Pu.** *Pt.* מְצֻפֶּה Pr 26^{23} impure silver (Toy) *laid over* (עַל) a sherd; pl. מְצֻפִּים זָהָב Ex 26^{32}, pillars *overlaid with gold.*

6826 †צִפּוּי **n.[m.]** metal **plating**;—of idols Is 30^{22}, capitals Ex 38$^{17.19}$, altar Nu 17$^{3.4}$.

6844 †צָפִית **n.f. rug, carpet** (*laid out*);—צָפֹה הַצָּפִית Is 21^{5}, so now most, v. esp. Che$^{Intr. Is. 126}$; > *watch, outlook* (I. צפה), Ges De al.

6858 †צֶ֫פֶת **n.f.** appar. **plated capital** of pillar 2 Ch 3^{15}.

צפח (√ of foll.; cf. Ar. صَفَحَ II. *make wide, broad;* صَفِيحَة *anything broad* (stone, plank, sheathing, plating), Syr. ܨܦܝܚܐ *plating;* also Eth. ሰፍሐ: *spread out, extend;* Sab. (Liḥ.) הצפחת, אצפחת, *platform*, DHM$^{Epigr. Denkm. 84. 86}$; but (transp.) Ar. صَحْفَة, *wide bowl*, cf. Frä^{63}).

6835 †צַפַּ֫חַת **n.f. jar, jug,** of flat or broad shape;—abs. צַפַּ֫חַת 1 K 17^{12}; cstr. צַפַּ֫חַת 1 S 26^{11}+;—*jar* or *jug* for water 1 S 26$^{11.12.16}$ 1 K 19^{6}; for oil 1 K 17$^{12.14.16}$ (on masc. verb חָסֵר v. Ew$^{§ 317c}$, but prob. rd. חָסֵרָה SS Albr$^{ZAW\ xvi\ (1896),\ 89}$, cf. v^{14}).

†צַפִּיחִת **n.f. flat cake, wafer;**—Ex 16^{31}. 6838

†צוֹפַח **n.pr.m.** in Asher, 1 Ch 7^{35}, צוֹפָה v^{36}, 6690
Σωχαθ, Σωφας[ρ], 𝔊L Σουφα.

צְפִי, צְפִיָּה, צְפִיּוֹן v. I. צפה. p. 859 6825, 6836-37

צָפִית v. II. צפה. above 6844

†**צָפַן** **vb.** hide, treasure up (NH *id.;* 6845
TelAm. *ṣapânu; set*, of sun);—**Qal** *Pf.* 3 ms. צ׳ Pr 27^{16}: 2 ms. צָפַנְתָּ Jb 10^{13}+, etc.; *Impf.* יִצְפֹּן Jb 21^{19} + Pr 2^{7} Qr (Kt וצפן), sf. יִצְפְּנֵנִי ψ 27^{5}, etc.; *Pt. act.* pl. sf. צֹפְנֶיהָ Pr 27^{16}; *pass.* צָפוּן Pr. 13^{22}+, ψ 17^{14} Kt; f. צְפוּנָה Ho 13^{12}, etc.;—**1.** trans. *hide*, c. acc. pers. Ex 2^{2} (E), Jos 2^{4} (JE), of *hiding* a quarrelsome woman, like hiding wind Pr 27$^{16.16}$ (si vera l.; cf. Toy); of י׳'s *hiding* his servants (from evil) ψ 27^{5} 31^{21}: = *treasure up* a thing, Pr 10^{14}, + אִתָּךְ *with thyself*, in thine own keeping 2^{1} = 7^{1}, in (בְּ) the heart Jb 10^{13} (subj. י׳; of secret purposes), ψ 119^{11}, cf. Jb 23^{12}; + לְ pers. Pr 13^{22} Ct 7^{14}, subj. י׳ Jb 21^{19} *reserve* penalty; blessings ψ 31^{20} Pr 2^{7}; + מִן Jb 17^{4} *thou* [God] *hast treasured up* their heart *away from* understanding, kept it therefrom; pass., of sin Ho 13^{12} (abs.; ‖ צָרוּר); read poss. צָפוּן for צָפוּ Jb 15^{22} *treasured up* for (אֱלֵי) the sword (v. I. צפה); צָפוּן = *treasured, cherished place* (i.e. Jerusalem) Ez 7^{22}; = *treasure* ψ 17^{14} Qr (Kt צפינך, v. צפין), Jb 20^{26} (on dub. text v. Bu); pl. of י׳'s *treasured ones*, his saints ψ 83^{4}. **2.** intrans. *lie hid, lurk*, abs. ψ 56^{7}, c. לְ pers. Pr 1$^{11.18}$ and (of eyes of wicked) ψ 10^{8}. **Niph.** *Pf.* 3 ms. נִצְפַּן Je 16^{17} *be hidden* from before (מִנֶּגֶד) י׳'s eyes (‖ נִסְתְּרוּ); 3 pl. נִצְפְּנוּ Jb 24^{1} + מִשַּׁדַּי *stored up on the part of Shadday; stored up* for (לְ) one 15^{20}. **Hiph.** *hide*, = **Qal**: *Impf.* 2 ms. sf. תַּצְפִּנֵנִי Jb 14^{13}, c. בְּ loc.; 3 mpl. יצפינו ψ 56^{7} Kt (but < Qr v. **Qal**); *Inf. cstr.* sf. הַצְפִּינוֹ (Ges$^{§ 20h}$) Ex 2^{3} *to hide him.*

†[צָפִין] **n.[m.] treasure;**—sf. צְפִינְךָ ψ 17^{14} 6840
Kt < צְפוּנְךָ Qr, v. צפן pt. pass. 6845

I. צָפוֹן$_{153}$ **n.f.**$^{Is\ 43,6}$ **north** (as the *hidden*, 6828
dark; cf. Thes Lewy$^{Fremdw. 188 f.}$; perh. Ph. צפל *north*);—abs. צ׳ Je 26^{26}+, צָפֹ֫נָה *northward* Gn 13^{14}+, oftener צָפ֫וֹנָה Je 3^{12}+, also צָפוֹן = צָפוֹנָה Je 1^{13}+ (after preps. and st. cstr.; cf. Ges$^{§ 90e}$); cstr. מִצְּפוֹן לְ Jos 8^{11}+, also מִצְּפוֹן 19^{14} Gi (cf. Benn; van d. H. Baer מִצְּ׳), מִצְּפ֫וֹנָה לְ Ju 21^{19}; (צ׳ occurs oftenest in Ez [46 t.], Jos [25 t.], Je [25 t.], Dn [9 t.]);—*north* (opp. S., E., W.)

Gn 13^{14} 28^{14} (both J), Ex 27^{11} (P), +; פְּאַת צ׳ *north side* Ex 26^{20} Jos 15^{5}+ (v. פֵּאָה); so צֶלַע צ׳ Ex 26^{35}, רוּחַ הַצּ׳ Ez 42^{17}, cf. עַל־יֶרֶךְ הַמִּזְבֵּחַ צָפֹונָה 2 K 16^{14}; גְּבוּל צ׳ Nu 34$^{7.9}$ *north boundary;* יַרְכְּתֵי צ׳ *remote parts of north* Is 14^{13} (as divine abode), Ez 38$^{6.15}$+ (v. [יַרְכָה]); שַׁעַר הַצּ׳ Ez 40^{35}+, פֶּתַח צ׳ 42^{2}; רוּחַ צ׳ Pr 25^{23} *north wind*, and so צ׳ alone Ct 4^{16}; *toward the north* is צָפֹונָה Jos 13^{3}+ (v. also supr.), and אֶל־צָפוֹן Ec 1^{6}, אֶל־הַצּ׳ Ez 42^{1}, ד׳ צָפוֹנָה v^{20}, דֶּרֶךְ הַצָּפוֹן 40^{23}, לַצָּפוֹן 8^{14}, אֶל־הַצָּפֹונָה 8$^{5.5}$+, etc.; esp. (in Je Ez etc.) of quarter whence invaders were to come, e.g. Assyr. Is 14^{31}, cf. Zp 2^{13}, Babylonians Je 6$^{1.22}$ 15^{12} 46$^{20.24}$ (עַם־צ׳), 47^{2}, Ez 26^{7}, Cyrus against Bab. Is 41^{25}, cf. Je 50$^{3.9.41}$ 51^{48}; more vaguely, Je 1$^{14.15}$ (מַמְלְכוֹת צ׳), 4^{6} 10^{22} 13^{20} 25$^{9.26}$ (מַלְכֵי הַצּ׳); of Gog's host Ez 38$^{6.15}$ 39^{2}; נְסִיכֵי צ׳ 32^{30} (appar. of nearer [Aramæan?] princes); אֶרֶץ צ׳ Je 31^{8} is region of Carchemish, but Zc 2^{10} 6$^{6.8.8}$ of Babylon; מֵאֶרֶץ צ׳ (sts.+other countries) the exiles and dispersed are to return Je 3^{18} 16^{15}=23^{8}, 31^{8}, cf. Is 43^{6} 49^{12}; מֶלֶךְ הַצּ׳ Dn 11$^{6.7.8.11.13.15.40}$ denotes successive Seleucidae.

6830 †II. צְפוֹנִי **adj.** from foregoing, northern (so most);—c. art. as **n.m. northern one, northerner,** invader from north Jo 2^{20} (of locust-swarm, cf. We Now Dr, GASm$^{Proph. ii. 397}$).

6831 —I. צְפוֹנִי v. צִפְיוֹן sub I. צפה. p. 859

6829 †II. צָפוֹן **n.pr.loc.** on E. bank of Jordan, in tribe of Gad, צ׳ Jos 13^{27} (Σαφαν[ων]), צָפֹונָה Ju 12^{1} (βοῤῥᾶν, 𝔊L Σεφηνα); acc. to Talm. = mod. *Amateh*, N. of Jabbok, GFM Buhl$^{Geogr. 259}$ (who doubts); *Ṣapuna* appears Tel Am Wkl$^{No. 174}$.

1189,6828 צְפוֹן, in בַּעַל צְפוֹן (q.v.), perhaps n.pr.dei, Bae$^{Rel. 22}$ Nö$^{ZMG\ xlii\ (1888),\ 472}$ Gray$^{Prop. N. 134}$.

6846 †צְפַנְיָה(וּ) **n.pr.m.** Σοφονιας (י׳ *hath treasured;* OHeb. צפניהו, Ph. צפנבעל);—**1.** priest, ־יָה Je 21^{1} 22$^{25.29}$ 52^{24} = ־יָהוּ 2 K 25^{18} (𝔊L Σαφανιας), Je 37^{3}. Elsewhere ־יָה: **2.** the prophet Zp 1^{1}. **3.** a Judæan Zc 6$^{10.14}$. **4.** ancestor of Heman 1 Ch 6^{21} (Σαφανιας; = אוּרִיאֵל v^{9}).

4710 †[מַצְפּוֹן] **n.[m.] hidden treasure, treasure**;—sf. מַצְפֻּנָיו Ob^{6} *his treasures.*

6847 †צָפְנַת פַּעְנֵחַ **n.pr.m.** (< vocaliz. *Ṣapnĕtĕph ʿōnḥ*, i.e. *the god speaks and he lives*, Egypt. *D̠(d)-pnt(r)-ĕf-ʿnḥ* (*D̠ĕ-pnutĕ-ef-ʿōnḥ*), v. Steind$^{ÄZ\ 1889,\ 41\ f.;\ 1892,\ 50\ ff.}$, so Eb$^{Smith\ DB\ (2),\ 1798\ b}$ Brugsch, v. Dr$^{Hast.\ ii.\ 775\ a\ n.\ §}$, Crum$^{ib.\ i.\ 665\ b}$ Griffith$^{ib.\ iii.\ 819\ b}$);—Egypt. name given to Joseph Gn 41^{45}, Ψονθομφανηχ, 𝔊L Ψομ΄.

I. צפע (√of following; meaning dub., perh. *hiss*, onomatop., so Thes; NH צִפְעוֹן = BH).

†צֶ֫פַע **n.m.** a (poisonous) serpent (from *hissing?*);—Is 14^{29}; usu. taken as = following. 6848

†צִפְעֹנִי **n.m.** *id.*;—abs. צ׳ Is 11^{8} (‖ פֶּתֶן), 6848
בֵּיצֵי צ׳ 59^{5}; כְּצִפְעֹנִי Pr 23^{32} (sim.; ‖ נָחָשׁ); pl. צִפְעֹנִים Je 8^{17} (app. ‖ נְחָשִׁים); identif. dub.; Tristr$^{NHB\ 275}$ ('poss.') *daboia xanthina*, a venomous viper, but vipers do not lay eggs Furrer$^{Ri\ HWB\ 2,\ 1423}$; Furrer proposes *ailurophis vivax.*

II. צפע (√of foll.; cf. Ar. صَفَعَ *cacavit*, صَفْعٌ, Eth. ፀፍዕ: *excrement*).

†[צָפִיעַ] **n.[m.] dung** of cattle;—pl. cstr. צְפִיעֵי הַבָּקָר Ez 4^{15} Qr (opp. גֶּלְלֵי הָאָדָם), so Co Toy al., > Kt צפועי. 6832

III. צפע (√of foll.; meaning unknown).

†[צְפִיעָה] **n.f.** dub.; appar., fr. context, **offshoot**;—pl. הַצְּפִיעוֹת Is 22^{24} (fig.; ‖ הַצֶּאֱצָאִים). 6849

†[צָפַף] **vb. Pilp. chirp, peep** (onomatop.; NH Pilp. *id.*; JAram. צַפְצֵף *chirp;* Ar. صُفْصُفٌ *sparrow*, etc.);—*Impf.* 3 fs. תְּצַפְצֵף Is 29^{4}, 1 s. אֲצַפְצֵף 38^{14}; *Pt.* מְצַפְצֵף 10^{14}, pl. הַמְצַפְצְפִים 8^{19};—*chirp, peep:* **1.** of birds Is 10^{14} (fig. of conquered peoples); of mourning, כְּסוּס . . . אֲצ׳ 38^{14} (‖ אֶהְגֶּה כַּיּוֹנָה). **2.** of spirits, ghosts Is 8^{19} (+ הַמַּהְגִּים), מֵעָפָר אִמְרָתֵךְ תְּצ׳ 29^{4} (like a spirit's). 6850

†צַפְצָפָה **n.f.** a kind of **willow** (?onomatop., from *rustling;* NH *id.*; Ar. صَفْصَافٌ);—Ez 17^{5}. 6851

†I. [צָפַר] **vb.** dub.;—*Impf.* 3 ms. יָשֹׁב וְיִצְפֹּר מֵהַר הַגִּלְעָד Ju 7^{3} *let him return and* (Vrss) *let him depart*, AV *depart early* (as Ki, fr. Aram. צפרא, ܨܦܪܐ *morning*, improb.), wholly uncertain; Gr וַיַּעֲבֹר; on difficulty of מֵהַר הַגּ׳ v. גִּלְעָד **2**, and GFM, who conj. וַיִּצְרְפֵם גִּדְעוֹן and so *Gideon put them to the test* (cf. v^{4}), so Bu Now (cf. Dr$^{Hast.\ ii.\ 176\ n}$). 6852

II. צפר (√of foll.; cf. Ar. صَفَرَ *peep, twitter, whistle* (usu. of bird; onomatop.); As. *ṣapâru* is *cry, howl;* NH צִפּוֹר = BH, so Ph. צפר, 𝔗 צִפַּר, Syr. ܨܶܦܪܳܐ, Mand. ציפרא, ציפאר Nö$^{M\ §\ 102}$; also Ar. عُصْفُورٌ *sparrow*, etc., and (perh.) As. *iṣṣuru, bird*).

I. צִפּוֹר, צִפֹּר$_{40}$ **n.f.**$^{Am\ 3,\ 5}$ (**m.** ψ 102^{8}, cf. Kö$^{Synt.\ §\ 252\ a}$, so 104^{17}, yet cf. Albr$^{ZAW\ xvi\ (1896),\ 71}$), **bird**;—abs. צִפּוֹר Ho 11^{11} + 15 t., צִפֹּר Gn 15^{10}+ 6833

11 t., cstr. צִפּוֹר Dt 4^{17} + 5 t., צִפֹּר ψ 8^{9}; pl. צִפֳּרִים Lv 14^{4} + 5 t.;—**1.** single *bird*, Am 3^{5} Ho 11^{11} (sim.; ‖ יוֹנָה), La 3^{52} Jb 40^{29} ψ 102^{8} 124^{7} Pr 6^{5} 7^{23} 26^{2} 27^{8} (all sim.), Lv 14^{5} + 10 t. Lv 14; כָּל־צ׳ כָּנָף Dt 4^{17}, קַן־צ׳ טְהוֹרָה 14^{11} (כל distrib.); כָּל־צ׳ 22^{6} *bird's nest*, קוֹל הַצ׳ Ec 12^{4}; pl. Is 31^{5} (sim.), Ne 5^{18} Lv 14^{4} (שְׁתֵּי צִפֳּרִים, in purif.; cf. We Heid. 2.171 RS Sem. i. 402, 2nd ed. 422), v^{49} (*id.*), ψ 104^{17} Ec 9^{12}. **2.** less oft. coll., either def. Gn 15^{10} (two), or indef. ψ 11^{1} (fig.), צִפֹּר שָׁמַיִם 8^{9}, esp. צ׳ (כָּל־)כָּנָף Ez 39^{17} ψ 148^{10}, כֹּל צ׳ כָּל־כָּנָף 17^{23} Gn 7^{14}, also redund. c. עַיִט, עֵיט צ׳ כָּל־כָּנָף Ez 39^{4} *birds of prey of all kinds*.

6834 †II. צִפּוֹר **n.pr.m.** father of Balak, king of Moab (*bird; perh. specif. sparrow*, cf. Gray Prop. N. 94; Palm. n.pr.m. צפרא);—צ׳ Nu $22^{2.4.16}$ Jos 24^{9} Ju 11^{25}, צִפֹּר Nu 22^{10} 23^{18}; Σεπφωρ.

6855 †צִפֹּרָה **n.pr.f.** wife of Moses (*bird*);—Ex 2^{21} 4^{25} 18^{2}; Σεπφωρα (cf. Lag BN 90 Anm.*).

III. צפר (√of following; cf. Ar. ضَفَرَ *plait, braid*, Eth. ፀፈረ: *id.*; NH צְפִירָה = *rim* of basket).

6843 †צְפִירָה **n.f. plait, chaplet**;—abs. צ׳ Ez 7^{7}, צְפִרָה v^{10}; cstr. צְפִירַת Is 28^{5};—*chaplet, coronet, diadem*, צ׳ תִּפְאָרָה Is 28^{5} (fig. of י׳; ‖ עֲטֶרֶת צְבִי).—צ׳ Ez $7^{7.10}$ is dub.; AV *morning* (as Ki, fr. Aram.) is unsuitable; most (after AW دَوْر) *doom, fate* (as *coming round* upon one, cf. RV Da Toy), but v. Dr Hast. ii. 176 n; *diadem* is possible v^{10} (‖ הַמַּטֶּה; of royal house of Judah Co Berthol; or of Jerus. Krae), but not v^{7}; conj. in Co Berthol Krae.

IV. צפר (√of foll.; mng. dub.; NH = BH; so Ar. ظُفْر, ظُفُر, Eth. ጽፍር:, As. *ṣupru*; Aram. טְפַר, טוּפְרָא, ܛܦܪܐ, all *nail*).

6856 †צִפֹּרֶן **n.[m.]** nail (of finger), **stylus-point**;—cstr. צ׳ Je 17^{1}; pl. sf. צִפָּרְנֶיהָ Dt 21^{12};—**1.** *finger-nail* Dt 21^{12} (cf. RS K 178; Sem. i. 407, 2nd ed. 428 We Heid. 2.171). **2.** transf., בְּצ׳ שָׁמִיר Je 17^{1} *with a point of diamond* (cf. Plin NH 37, 4).

V. צפר (√of foll.; cf. Aram. צְפִירָא, ܨܦܝܪܐ = צָפִיר; perh. cp. Ar. ضَفَرَ *leap* (but ز = ض?)).

6842 †צָפִיר **n.m. he-goat** (late);—abs. צ׳ Dn $8^{5.21}$; cstr. צְפִיר הָעִזִּים $v^{5.8}$ (all in vision, symbol. of Alex.); pl. cstr. (lit.) צְפִירֵי עִזִּים 2 Ch 29^{21}, צְפִירֵי חַטָּאת Ezr 8^{35} *he-goats for a sin-offering*.

6691 †צֹפַר and (Jb 2^{11}) צוֹפַר **n.pr.m.** Job's third friend, צ׳ הַנַּעֲמָתִי Jb 2^{11} 11^{1} 20^{1} 42^{9}; Σωφαρ.

†צְפַרְדֵּעַ **n.f.** Ex 8, 2 (cf. also Albr ZAW xv (1895), 322 Ges §§ 135 o, 145 o) **frogs** (Ar. ضِفْدِع, etc.; Aram. עוּרְדְּעָנַיָּא, אוּרְדְּעָא, ܥܘܪܕܥܐ);—*frogs*, coll. Ex 8^{2} ψ 78^{45}; pl. צְפַרְדְּעִים Ex $7^{27.28.29}$ $8^{1.3.4.5.7.8.9}$ ψ 105^{30}. 6854

צֶפֶת v. II. צפה. p. 860 6858

†צְפַת **n.pr.loc.** Σεφεκ[ρ]: Canaanite city Ju 1^{17} = חָרְמָה q. v.; identif. by many (v. esp. Palmer Desert of Exod. 374 ff.) with *Sebaita* (c. Lat. 30° 54′ N., Long. 34° 40′ E.), by Rob BR ii. 181 with pass *eṣ-Ṣŭfâh*, further E.; against both v. GFM. 6857

†צְפָתָה **n.pr.loc.** in Judah (van d. H. צְפָתָה, so Kit); בְּגֵיא צ׳ לְמָרֵשָׁה 2 Ch 14^{9}; 𝔊 κατὰ βορρᾶν, whence Hi al. prop. צָפֹנָה, so Buhl Lex. 6859

צִצִּים v. I. צִיץ sub I. צוץ. p. 847 6731

צָקוּן Is 26^{16} v. II. צוק. p. 848 6694

†צִקְלַג and (1 Ch $12^{1.21}$ צִיק׳) **n. pr. loc.** 6860
(צִקְלָג 1 S 27^{6a} +, צִקְלָג 2 S 2^{1}, צִיקְלַג 1 Ch 12^{1});—assigned to Judah Jos 15^{31}, to Simeon 19^{5}; Philistine city given to David 1 S $27^{6.6}$ $30^{1.1.1.14.26}$ 2 S 1^{1} 4^{10} 1 Ch 4^{30} $12^{1.21}$ (van d. H. v^{20}); Σεκελακ, Σικελαγ, etc.; usually identified with *Zuheilikah*, 19 miles SW. from Bêt Jibrin, 11 miles ESE. from Gaza (cf. Buhl Geogr. 185).

†[צִקְלֹן] **n.[m.]** doubtful word;—sf. בְּצִקְלֹנוֹ 2 K 4^{42} 𝔖 𝔗 *garment*; 𝔊 om., but A βακελλεθ, Arm. *bakelaθ*, whence Lag Armen. Stud. § 333, M. i. 212 reads (plausibly) בְּקִלְעָתוֹ *in his wallet*, Ar. قَلْعَةٌ, قِلْعَةٌ, and so 𝔙 *pera*. 6861

I, II, III, IV. צַר, II. צֹר, v. I, II, III. צרר. p. 865-66 6862, 6864

†צֵר **n.pr.loc.** in Naphtali, Jos 19^{35}; Τυρος. 6863

†I. צֹר, צוֹר **n.pr.loc.** Τυρος: **Tyre**, famous Phoenician city (Ph. צר; As. *Ṣurru*, so TelAm; Egypt. *Ḏa-(ʾ)ra*, *Ḏa-ru* WMM As. u. Eur. 185);—צֹר 2 S 24^{7} + 32 t., צוֹר 1 K 5^{15} + 8 t. (Gi);—city of Hiram, friend of David and Sol. 2 S 5^{11} 1 K 5^{15} $9^{11.12}$ 1 Ch 14^{1} 2 Ch $2^{2.10}$; of artif. Hiram 1 K 7^{13}; בַּת־צֹר ψ 45^{13} of city personif. (another view in Che); צ׳ also in name of Ph. fortress, מִבְצַר־צ׳ 2 S 24^{7}, עִיר מ׳ צ׳ Jos 19^{29} (P); threatened by proph. Am $1^{9.10}$ and (with esp. ref. to commercial greatness) Is 23^{1} (מַשָּׂא צֹר), $v^{5.8.15.15.17}$ Je 25^{22} (מַלְכֵי־צֹר), 27^{3} (מֶלֶךְ צֹר), 47^{4} Ez $26^{2.3.4.7.15}$ $27^{2.3.3.8.32}$, 28^{2} (נְגִיד צֹר), v^{12} (מֶלֶךְ צוֹר); besieged by Nebuch. $29^{18.18}$; cf. Zc $9^{2.3}$ Jo 4^{4} ψ 83^{8} (יֹשְׁבֵי צ׳); of Tyrians as proselytes ψ 87^{4} (predict.);—לְצוֹר Ho 9^{13} is prob. corrupt, read לְצוּד or לְצַיִד 𝔊 We GASm,

cf. Now.—צ׳ oft. + צִידוֹן q. v.;—see, on Tyre, Pietschm[Phön. 60 ff.] Rob[BR ii. 461 ff.] de Luynes[Voyage à la Mer Morte (1874) i. 28 ff., and Pl. xiii-xviii] Bd[Pal. 3 (1898), 307 ff.].—

6864 II. צֹר (*flint, knife*) v. III. צרר. p. 866

6876 †צֹרִי **adj. gent. Tyrian**;—אִישׁ צ׳ 1 K 7[14] = 2 Ch 2[13]; pl. as subst. הַצֹּרִים *the Tyrians* 1 Ch 22[4] Ezr 3[7] (both + הַצִּידֹנִים), Ne 13[16].

6866 †[צָרַב] **vb. burn, scorch** (As. *ṣarâbu, burn;* Frä[ZA iii. 52] Ba[ES 32] cp. Ar. صَرِمَ *be kindled, blaze;* cf. also זרב);—**Niph.** *Pf.* 3 pl. consec. וְנִצְרְבוּ Ez 21[3] all faces *shall be scorched.*

6867 †[צָרָב] **adj. burning, scorching** (= *צָרֹב Thes al.);—כְּאֵשׁ צָרָבֶת Pr 16[27] (sim. of words).

6867 †צָרֶבֶת **n.f. scab, scar,** of a sore (lit. *a burning, scorching*);—cstr. צָרֶבֶת הַשְּׁחִין הִוא Lv 13[23]; צ׳ הַמִּכְוָה הִוא v[28].

6868 †צְרֵדָה **n.pr.loc.** home of Jerob. 1 K 11[26],

6891 Σαρειρα, A Σαριδα; v. [צְרֵדָה] צָרְתָן. p. 866

6868, 6891 צְרֵדָתָה 2 Ch 4[17] v. צָרְתָן. p. 866

6869 I, II. צָרָה v. I, II. צרר. p. 865

צרה (√ of foll.; cf. Ar. ضَرَا (و, ى) of vein, *run blood, bleed,* ضَرْوٌ an odorif. tree, or its gum, cf. Hom[A. und A. i. 4], Sab. צרו SabDenkm[83]; (Syr. ܨܪܘܐ *fructus pini,* etc. is loan-word); NH = BH; as to form cp. Gk. στύραξ (hardly ‖ in meaning, Lag[M. i. 234, 384], v. Ency. Bib. infr.), cf. Lewy[Fremdw. 41]).

6875 †צְרִי and (Gn 37[25]) צֳרִי(ו) **n.[m.]** a kind of **balsam,** as merchandise Gn 37[25] (J), Ez 27[17], gift Gn 43[11] (J), medicament Je 8[22] 46[11] 51[8] (for national disaster, in fig.);—ThDyer-M'Lean in Ency. Bib.[Balm] think a resin, like (not necess. =) gum of mastic-tree, *pistacia lentiscus* (otherwise Post[Hastings DB]).

6874 †צְרִי **n.pr.m.** a musician, 1 Ch 25[3] (Σ)ουρ(ε)ι, = יִצְרִי (q.v.) v[11] (Ιεσδρει, 𝔊L Ασειρηλα).

6870 †צְרוּיָה **n.pr.f.** Σαρουια: mother of Abishai, Joab and Asahel;—צ׳ 1 S 26[6]+, צְרֻיָה 2 S 14[1] 16[10] 23[37];—acc. to 1 Ch 2[16a] she was David's sister; called אֵם יוֹאָב 2 S 17[25]; elsewh. after cstr. בֶּן (בְּנֵי): בֶּן־צ׳ of Abishai 1 S 26[6] 2 S 16[9] 18[2] 19[22] 21[17] 1 Ch 18[12]; of Joab 2 S 2[13] 8[16] = 1 Ch 18[15], 2 S 14[1] 23[18] and v[37] = 1 Ch 11[39], 1 K 1[7] 2[5.22] 1 Ch 11[6] 26[28] 27[24]; pl. of all three 2 S 2[18] 1 Ch 2[16]; Abishai and Joab 2 S 3[39] 16[10] 19[23].

†I. צָרַח **vb. cry, roar** (NH *id., cry* (of 6873
raven); As. *ṣarâḫu, cry aloud,* Ar. صَرَخَ, Eth. ጸርኀ: 𝔗 צְרַח Aph. (of bear), Syr. ܨܪܚ esp. Aph. and deriv.);—**Qal** *Pt. act.* מַר צֹרֵחַ שָׁם גִּבּוֹר Zp 1[14] *bitterly roareth there a hero,* but abrupt in context and improb.; Gr (in part after 𝔊) conj. קוֹל י׳ יִצְרַח כַּגִּבּוֹר (cf. **Hiph.**). **Hiph.** *Impf.* 3 ms. יַצְרִיחַ Is 42[13] *utter a roar* (of י׳, going to battle; ‖ יָרִיעַ).

II. צרח (√ of foll.; cf. Ar. ضَرَحَ *dig* a ضَرِيحٌ, also *cleave* the ground, *rend open;* ضَرِيحٌ *sepulchral chamber* (with niches for bodies); Nab. צריחה (cf. Nö in Eut[Nab. Inschr. 55] Dr[Sm. 76])).

†צְרִיחַ **n.[m.]** perh. **excavation, underground chamber**;—צ׳ abs. Ju 9[49], cstr. v[46]; pl. 6877
צְרִחִים 1 S 13[6];—used as hiding-places 1 S 13[6] (+ בֹּרוֹת, סְלָעִים, חֲוָחִים, מְעָרוֹת); as refuge Ju 9[46] (where connected with shrine), v[49] (Vrss *stronghold;* on uncertainty of meaning v. GFM).

צֹרִי v. I. צֹר. צֳרִי, צְרִי, צְרִיָה v. צרה. 6865, 6870,
above, p. 862 6875

צרך (√ of foll.; NH צָרַךְ *have need of;* Ar. ضَرَكَ *be needy,* so Aram. צְרַךְ, ܨܪܟ (צ, ܨ = ض!); ChrPal. ܨܘܪܟܐ χρεία).

†[צֹרֶךְ] **n.[m.]** need (Aram.);—sf. כְּכָל־צָרְכֶּךָ 6878
2 Ch 2[15] *according to all thy need,* cf. Ecclus 8[9] + often.

צרע (√ of foll.; cf. perh. Ar. ضَرَعَ *throw down, prostrate;* Sab. צרע *humble oneself,* DHM[Hofm. No. 6, l. 8] Mordtm[Him. Inschr. 71]; vbs. denom. in NH 𝔗).

צָרַעַת[35] **n.f. leprosy**;—abs. צ׳ Dt 24[8]+, 6883
צָרָעַת Lv 13[2]+; cstr. צָרַעַת 2 K 5[27]+; sf. צָרַעְתּוֹ 2 K 5[3.6.7];—*leprosy* 2 K 5[3.6.7.27] 2 Ch 26[19]; elsewhere only in laws: נֶגַע צ׳ Dt 24[8], and Lv 13, 14 (P; 29 t.): תּוֹרַת הַצ׳ 14[57]; specif. of **a.** human disease (as above) נֶגַע צ׳ Lv 13[2] + 8 t.; without נ׳ 13[8] + 10 t. **b.** *leprosy* in a garment 13[47.49.51.52.59] (תּוֹרַת נֶגַע צ׳ בֶּגֶד). **c.** in house 14[34] (נֶגַע צ׳), v[44]; house or garment v[55].—Exact meaning of **b.** and **c.** dub., perh. some fungus or mould; v. esp. Di Dr-Wh Baen.

†[צָרַע] **vb. denom.,** only in pass., **be struck** 6879
with leprosy, leprous;—**Qal** *Pt. pass.* אִישׁ צָרוּעַ Lv 13[44]; elsewh. as subst., = *leper,* v[45] 14[3] Nu 5[2] (all P), Lv 22[4] (H). **Pu.** *Pt.* מְצֹרָע 2 S 3[29]+, מְצוֹרָע 2 Ch 26[20]; pl. מְצֹרָעִים 2 K 7[3.8];

f. מְצֹרַ֫עַת Ex 4^{6}+, מְצֹרָ֫עַת Nu 12^{10};—*leprous*, of hand Ex 4^{6} (J), of pers. Nu 12$^{10.10}$ (E), 2 K 5^{27} 2 Ch 26^{20}; אֲנָשִׁים מְצֹרָעִים 2 K 7^{3}; as subst.=*leper* 2 S 3^{29} 2 K 5$^{1.11}$ 7^{8} 15^{5}=2 Ch 26^{21a}, 2 Ch 26$^{21b, 23}$; תּוֹרַת הַמְּצֹרָע Lv 14^{2}.

6880 †צִרְעָה **n.f.coll. hornets** (? as *wounding, prostrating;* NH=BH);—allies of Isr.;—הַצּ׳ Ex 23^{28} Jos 24^{12} (both E), Dt 7^{20}.

6871 †צְרוּעָה **n.f.** mother of Jeroboam 1 K 11^{26}, 𝔊^{A} Σαρουα.

6881 †צָרְעָה **n.pr.loc.** Σαραα, etc. (cf. also Lag $^{BN 85}$), in the Shephelah of Judah (Tel Am. *Ṣarḫa*, named with *Aialuna*, Ajalon);—Jos 15^{33}, but assigned to Dan 19^{41}; Ju 13$^{2.25}$ 16^{31} 18$^{2.8.11}$ 2 Ch 11^{10} Ne 11^{29}; mod. *Ṣarʿa*, 15 miles W. from Jerus., cf. GASm$^{Geogr. 218}$ Buhl$^{Geogr. 195}$.

6882 †צָרְעִי v. foll.

6882 †צָרְעָתִי **adj. gent.** c. art. as n. coll. הַצּ׳ 1 Ch 2^{53} 4^{2}=הַצָּרְעִי 2^{54}.

6884 †צָרַף **vb. smelt, refine, test** (NH *id.;* Ph. מצרף *smelter;* As. *ṣurrupu, refined, ṣarpu, silver, naṣraptu, crucible;* Ar. صَرْفٌ is *pure, unmixed* (esp. of wine); very doubtful is Sab. צרף *silver, money*, cf. Mordtm$^{Him. Inschr. pp. 14, 29}$ CIS$^{iv, No. 291, l. 1}$);—**Qal** *Pf.* 3 ms. צ׳ Je 6^{29}, sf. צְרָפָ֑תְהוּ ψ 105^{19}; 2 ms. sf. צְרַפְתָּנִי ψ 17^{3}, etc.; *Impf.* 1 s. אֶצְרֹף Is 1^{25}, sf. אֶצְרְפֶנּוּ Ju 7^{4}; *Imv.* ms. צרופה ψ 26^{2} Kt, צָרְפָה Qr; *Inf. abs.* צָרוֹף Je 6^{29}; *cstr.* לִצְרוֹף Dn 11^{35}, etc.; *Pt. act.* sf. צוֹרְפָם Je 9^{6}, etc.; *pass.* צָרוּף ψ 12^{7}, etc.;—**1.** *smelt, refine:* Je 6$^{29.29}$ *in vain hath he smelted continually* (inf. abs.; fig. of purifying people); so *smelt away* Is 1^{25} (acc. of dross; fig.); of silver Zc 13^{9} ψ 66^{10}, כֶּסֶף צָרוּף בַּעֲלִיל 12^{7} (all sim.); of אִמְרַת י׳ ψ 18^{31}=2 S 22^{31}, ψ 119^{140} Pr 30^{5} (אִמְרַת אֱלוֹהַּ); *refine* (men, by trials) Dn 11^{35} (+ לְלַבֵּן, לְבָרֵר). **2.** *test* Ju 7^{4} *I will test them* (the warriors) *for thee* (י׳ subj.);—perh. also v^{3} (v. I. צפר); more gen., of י׳'s *testing, trying* (the hearts of) men (oft. ‖ בָּחַן) Je 9^{6} Is 48^{10} Zc 13^{9} ψ 26^{2} 66^{10}. **3.** *test* (and prove true) a man (subj. י׳'s saying) ψ 105^{19}. **4.** *Pt. act.* as **n.** *smelter, refiner*, hence=*goldsmith* Ju 17^{4} Je 10$^{9.14}$ 51^{17} Is 40$^{19.19}$ (but perhaps del. v^{b}, cf. Du Che Marti), 41^{7} 46^{6} Pr 25^{4}; as a guild Ne 3$^{8.32}$. **Niph.** *Impf.* 3 mpl. יִצָּֽרְפוּ Dn 12^{10} many *shall be refined* (by suffering; + יִתְלַבְּנוּ, יִתְבָּֽרְרוּ). **Pi.** *Pt.* מְצָרֵף as **n.** *a refiner*, כְּאֵשׁ מ׳ Mal 3^{2} (sim. of י׳), cf. מְ׳ alone v^{3} (+ מְטַהֵר כֶּסֶף).

†צֹרְפִי **n. [m.] coll. goldsmiths**;—only 6885
בֶּן־הַצ׳ Ne 3^{31} i.e. *belonging to the goldsmiths*, a member of their guild.

†צָרְפַת **n.pr.loc.** Σαρεπτα: on coast S. of 6886
Sidon (? *smelting*-place; on strange form cf. Lag$^{BN 84}$; As. *Ṣariptu* Dl$^{Pa 284}$ COT$^{1 K 17, 9}$; Egypt. *Ḏa-ꞽra-pu-tꞽ* WMM$^{As. u. Eur. 184}$);—צ׳ Ob^{20}; צָרְפָ֫תָה 1 K 17$^{9.10}$ (so Gi; פַ֫תָה- van d. H. Baer); mod. *Ṣarfend* Rob$^{BR ii. 474 ff.}$ Pietschm$^{Phön. 58 f.}$.

†מַצְרֵף **n.[m.] crucible** (prop. *place* or *in-* 4715
strument of refining); מ׳ לַכֶּסֶף וְכוּר לַזָּהָב Pr 17^{3} 27^{21}.

†I. צָרַר **vb. bind, tie up, be restricted,** 3334, 6887
narrow, scant, cramped (NH *id.;* Ar. صَرَّ *bind, tie up;* so Aram. צְרַר, ܨܪ);—**A.** trans.: **Qal** *Pf.* 3 ms. צָרַר Ho 4^{19} Pr 30^{4}; *Imv.* צוֹר Is 8^{16}; *Inf. cstr.* צְרוֹר Pr 26^{8} (?); *Pt. act.* צֹרֵר Jb 26^{8}; *pass.* צָרוּר Ho 13^{12}, f. צְרוּרָה 1 S 25^{29}; fpl. צְרֻרֹת Ex 12^{34} 2 S 20^{3};—*bind* or *tie up*, of kneading-troughs Ex 12^{34} (E); fig. of a life preserved by י׳, נֶפֶשׁ צְרוּרָה בִּצְרוֹר הַחַיִּים 1 S 25^{29}; of preserving prophetic teaching Is 8^{16}; of retention of guilt Ho 13^{12}; of י׳'s *binding* waters in (a garment of) cloud Pr 30^{4} Jb 26^{8}; =*shut up* 2 S 20^{3};—צָרַר רוּחַ אוֹתָהּ בִּכְנָפֶיהָ Ho 4^{19} (si vera l.) pregn., *the wind hath wrapped her up in its wings*, to carry her off; כִּצְרוֹר אֶבֶן Pr 26^{8} *like the tying up of a stone*, but unintellig. in context (v. Toy). **Pu.** *Pt.* pl. מְצֹרָרִים Jos 9^{4} *tied up* (mended by tying), of old wine-skins. **B.** intrans.: **Qal** *Pf.* 3 fs. צָ֫רָה Is 28^{20}; *Impf.* 3 ms. יֵצֶר Pr 4^{12}, יֵ֫צֶר לוֹ Jb 20^{22}, וַיֵּ֫צֶר Gn 32^{8}+, etc.;—*be scant, cramped, in straits;* of scanty bed-covering Is 28^{20} (in fig.); of land too small for (מִן) its people Is 49^{19}+Jos 19^{47} (for וַיֵּצֵא) Dr$^{Expos. Jan. 1887, 59}$ Benn, cf. 𝔊; of steps = *be cramped*, or impeded, Pr 4^{12} Jb 18^{7} (both in fig.); esp. impers. c. לְ pers., וַיֵּ֫צֶר לוֹ Gn 32^{8} *and it was narrow for him*=he was in straits, distress, so Ju 2^{15} 2 S 13^{2} Jb 20^{22}, also 3 fs. וַתֵּ֫צֶר לְ Ju 10^{9} 1 S 30^{6} (v. Dr). **Hiph.** *Pf.* 3 ms. וְהֵצַר Dt 28$^{52.52}$ consec.; 1 s. וַהֲצֵרֹתִי Je 10^{18} Zp 1^{17}; *Impf.* 3 ms. יָצַר־לוֹ 1 K 8^{37}=2 Ch 6^{28}, וַיָּ֫צַר 2 Ch 28^{20}; 3 mpl. וַיָּצֵרוּ Ne 9^{27}; *Inf. cstr.* הָצֵר 2 Ch 28^{22} 33^{12};—*make narrow* for, *press hard* upon, *cause distress* to, c. לְ pers., Je 10^{18} (subj. י׳), Zp 1^{17} (subj. *id.*); Dt 28$^{52.52}$ 1 K 8^{37}=2 Ch 6^{28}, Ne 9^{27} (all subj. foe), 2 Ch 28^{20} (subj. TP); indef. subj. 2 Ch 28^{22} (but rd. כִּי אִם לְצָרָה לוֹ, and join to v^{21}, opp. לְעֶזְרָה לוֹ, 𝔊 Kit Buhl^{Lex}), 33^{12}.

6862 †I. צַר adj. narrow, tight;—abs. צ׳ 2 K 6^{1}+; צָר Nu 22^{26}+; f. צָרָה Pr 23^{27};—*narrow*, מָקוֹם צָר Nu 22^{26}, צַר מִמֶּנּוּ 2 K 6^{1} *too narrow for us*, cf. צַר־לִי הַמָּקוֹם Is 49^{20} (of land of Judah after exile); בְּאֵר צָרָה Pr 23^{27} (fig. of harlot; i.e. rescue difficult; ‖ שׁוּחָה עֲמֻקָּה); כַּנָּהָר צָר Is 59^{19} *like a contracted* (and hence swift, powerful) *river* (sim. of י׳; Klo נְהַר מָצוֹר, Che^{Hpt} נ׳ מְצֹר, both 'of Egypt'); סָגוּר חוֹתָם צָר Jb 41^{7} (of scaly back of crocodile), usu. closely joined (as) *with tight seal* (𝔊 Me Bi Hoffm Bu Du חוֹתַם צֹר *with seal of flint*, but why specify material?); בְּיוֹם צָרָה צַר כֹּחֶכָה Pr 24^{10} *thy strength will be narrow*, limited (si vera l., cf. Toy).

6862 †II. צַר n.[m.] straits, distress;—abs. צ׳ Jb 15^{24}+, also c. art. בַּצַּר Ho 5^{15}+, צָר ψ 4^{2}+;—*straits, distress* Is 5^{30} Jb 15^{24} ψ 32^{7} 60^{13} 108^{13} 119^{143}; צַר־וּמָצוֹק; עֵת־צ׳ Jb 38^{23}, cf. בַּצַּר Is 26^{16}, בַּצָּר ψ 4^{2}; צ׳־רוּחִי Jb 7^{11} *distress of my spirit;* לֶחֶם צַר Is 30^{20}; לֹא צָר Is 63^{9} usu. *he* (י׳) *had distress* (rdg. לוֹ Qr), but 𝔊 οὐ πρέσβυς, Du Che^{Hpt} al. לֹא צִר, *no messenger* and (or) angel, (but) his own face, etc. Instead of sf. directly appended, לְ sf. is used (only after בְּ): בַּצַּר־לִי *in my distress* ψ 18^{7} = 2 S 22^{7}, ψ 66^{14}, so בְּיוֹם צַר(־)לִי 59^{17} 102^{3}; בַּצַּר לְךָ Dt 4^{30} (prob. orig. meant as בְּצַר, or בְּצֹר [inf.], Dr; so) בַּצַּר־לוֹ Is 25^{4} 2 Ch 15^{4}, בַּצַּר לָהֶם Ho 5^{15} ψ 107$^{6.13.19.28}$, also (after רָאָה) 106^{44}—צַר 1 S 2^{32} is corrupt, cf. Dr.

6869 I. צָרָה$_{72}$ n.f. id.;—abs. צ׳ 1 S 26^{24}+, צָרָתָה ψ 120^{1} (Ges^{§90g}); cstr. צָרַת Gn 42^{21}; sf. צָרָתִי 35^{3}+, צָרַתְכֶם Ju 10^{14}, etc.; pl. צָרוֹת abs. Is 65^{16}+; sf. צָרֹתֵיכֶם 1 S 10^{19}, etc.;—*straits, distress*, Gn 42^{21} (E), 1 S 26^{24} 2 S 4^{9} 1 K 1^{29} Is 8^{22} Jb 5^{19} 27^{9}; esp. ψψ (24 t.), e.g. 22^{12} 25^{17} (v. רחב), v^{22} 31^{8} 34$^{17.18}$; specif. of travail, צָרָה וַחֲבָלִים Je 49^{24} (sim.), cf. 4^{31} (Gie צְוָחָה, after 𝔊); צָרַת נַפְשׁוֹ Gn 42^{21} (E); בְּיוֹם צָרָתִי 35^{3} (E), ψ 77^{3} 86^{7}, cf. 2 K 19^{3} = Is 37^{3}, ψ 20^{2} 50^{15} Pr 24^{10} 25^{19} Je 16^{19} Ob$^{12.14}$ Na 1^{7} Hb 3^{16}, יוֹם צ׳ וּמְצוּקָה Zp 1^{15}; בְּעֵת־צָרַתְכֶם Ju 10^{14}, cf. Ne 9^{27} ψ 37^{39} Is 33^{2} Je 14^{8} 15^{11} 30^{7} Dn 12^{1}; also בַּצָּרָה ψ 81^{8}, בְּצָרָה 91^{15} Ne 9^{37}, בְּצָרוֹת ψ 46^{2}, etc.; רָעוֹת וְצָרוֹת Dt 31$^{17.21}$ cf. 1 S 10^{19} ψ 71^{20}, צָרָה וְצוּקָה Pr 1^{27}, אֶרֶץ צ׳ וְצ׳ Is 30^{6}; c. לְ (poet.), בַּצָּרָתָה לִּי ψ 120^{1} *in my distress*, מִצָּרָה לִי Jon 2^{3}.—צָרָה Zc 10^{11}, rd. מִצְרַיִם [or מָצוֹר] We Now GASm; צָרָה Klo$^{ThLz, 1879, 566}$ Sta$^{ZAW\ i\ (1881), 22}$; ψ 9^{10} 10^{1} v. בַּצָּרָה.

6887 †[צָרַר] vb. denom. Hiph. suffer distress (specif. of travail, cf. Je 4^{31} 49^{24});—*Pt.* אִשָּׁה לֵב מְצֵרָה (in sim.) Je 48^{41} 49^{22}.

†I. צְרוֹר n.m. $^{Hg\ 1,6}$ bundle, parcel, pouch, 6872
bag (prop. *a binding*, i.e. sthg. bound up);—צ׳ abs. Am 9^{9}+, cstr. Gn 42^{35}+; pl. cstr. צְרֹרוֹת v^{35};—*bundle* or *pouch* (purse) of money 42$^{35.35}$ (E), Pr 7^{20}; צ׳ הַמֹּר Ct 1^{13} (fig. of lover); צְרוּרָה בִּצ׳ הַחַיִּים 1 S 25^{29} (fig.; v. I. צרר); חָתֻם בִּצ׳ פִּשְׁעִי Jb 14^{17} (i.e. hidden, forgotten Hi Bu al.; > al. *treasured up*), צ׳ נָקוּב Hg 1^{6} (v. I. נקב).

†מֵצַר n.[m.] straits, distress;—abs. מִן־ 4712
הַמֵּצַר קָרָאתִי ψ 118^{5}; pl. הַמְּצָרִים La 1^{3} *the distresses*, of conquered Judah; cstr. מְצָרֵי שְׁאוֹל ψ 116^{3} *the straits* of Sheol, i.e. the worst possible (‖ חֶבְלֵי־מָוֶת).

† II. צָרַר vb. shew hostility toward, vex 6887
(NH צַר *foe;* Ar. ضَرَّ *harm, damage,* Sab. צר *war, foe* Mordtm$^{Him.\ Inschr.\ 60.71}$ SabDenkm^{24} CIS$^{iv.\ 174,\ l.\ 6}$ Hom$^{Chrest.\ 125}$; Eth. ፀረረ: *be hostile,* in der. spec. and deriv.; As. *ṣarâru, be hostile, ṣarru, foe;* Ar. ضَرَّةٌ, As. *ṣirritu*, Syr. ܥܪܬܐ, all = *rival-wife*, so (? Heb. infl.) 𝔗 צָרְתָא 1 S 1^{6}; v. esp. Lag Deceased Wife's Sister, GGN, 1882, No. 13; = Ml. 125 ff. Dr$^{1\ S\ 1,\ 6}$);—**Qal** *Pf.* 3 pl. וְצָרֲרוּ Nu 33^{55} consec., sf. צְרָרוּנִי ψ 129$^{1.2}$; *Impf.* 3 ms. יָצֹר Is 11^{13}; *Inf. abs.* צָרוֹר Nu 25^{17}; *Pt. act.* צֹרֵר 10^{9}, pl. sf. צֹרְרַי ψ 31^{12}+, etc.;—*shew hostility toward, treat with enmity, vex, harass,* c. acc. pers. Is 11^{13} Nu 10^{9} 25^{17}; once c. לְ pers. v^{18}; also pt. as subst. (cstr. or c. sf.) *vexer, harasser,* Am 5^{12} Is 11^{13} Ex 23^{22} (E), ψ 6^{8} 7$^{5.7}$ 8^{3} 10^{5} 23^{5} 31^{12} 42^{11} 69^{20} 74$^{4.23}$ 143^{12} Est 3^{10} 8^{1} 9$^{10.24}$.—Lv 18^{18} v. [צָרַר] sub II. צָרָה, infr.

III. צַר$_{68}$ n.m. $^{Nu\ 10,9}$ adversary, foe;—abs. צָר 6862
Am 3^{11}+, even c. art. הַצַּר Nu 10^{9}, but also הַצָּר Est 7^{4}; צָר Zc 8^{10}+; pl. צָרִים La 1^{7}; cstr. צָרֵי Ezr 4^{1}+ Is 9^{10} (but read prob. צָרוֹ or צָרָיו, cf. Di-Kit Che^{Hpt}; al. שָׂרֵי), Je 48^{5} (del. 𝔊 Hi Gie), Ez 30^{16} (but 𝔊 Sm וְנָפֹצוּ, so Berthol; Co וְנִפְרְצוּ, so Toy; Krae יָעוּף); sf. צָרַי ψ 3^{2}, צָרֵיהֶם Ez 39^{23}, צָרֵימוֹ Dt 32^{27}, etc.;—*adversary, foe,* Am 3^{11} Gn 14^{20} Nu 10^{9} (P), 24^{8} (JE) Dt 32^{27} 33^{7} Jos 5^{13} (JE), 2 S 24^{13} Is 9^{10} (v. supr.), Zc 8^{10} Ezr 4^{1} Ne 4^{5} Est 7^{6} (אִישׁ צַר וְאוֹיֵב), + 21 t., + ψ 3^{2} 13^{5} 27^{2} 78^{42}, + 13 t. ψψ, + (of י׳'s foes) 78^{66} 97^{3}; + (of י׳'s foes) also Is 1^{24} 26^{11} 59^{18} 64^{1} Je 46^{10} Na 1^{2} Dt 32$^{41.43}$ Jb 19^{11}.—Je 48^{5} Ez 30^{16} v. supr.

†II. [צָרָה] n.f. vexer, rival-wife (v. reff. 6869
sub √; also Ecclus 37^{11});—sf. צָרָתָהּ 1 S 1^{6}.

†[צָרַר] vb.denom. make a rival-wife;— 6887
Qal *Inf. cstr.* לִצְרֹר Lv 18^{18} *to make* [her] *a rival-wife* (Lag$^{GGN,\ 1882,\ 406}$ Dr-Wh^{Lv} Baen$^{l.v}$).

III. צרר (√of foll.; cf. Ar. ظَرَّ *be sharp* (? denom.), ظُرَرٌ, ظِرٌّ *sharp-edged hard stone*, As. *ṣurtu*, appar. *knife* RJHarper BAS ii. 435; Syr. ܛܰܪܳܢܳܐ *rock, stone, flint*).

6862 †IV. צַר **n.[m.]** hard pebble, **flint**;—כַּצַּר
6864 Is 5[28] (sim. of horses' hoofs; read perhaps כצֹּר).

6864 †II. צֹר **n.[m.]** id.;—צ׳ used as knife Ex 4[25]; in comp., כְּשָׁמִיר חָזָק מִצּ׳ Ez 3[9]; pl. חַרְבוֹת צֻרִים Jos 5[2.3] *knives of flint*.—צוּר חַרְבּוֹ ψ 89[44] is dub., צ׳ usu. taken as = צֹר, and then either *flint of his sword* (i.e. sword sharp as flint, Bae), or *edge* (like flint) *of his sword* (most); We leaves untransl.; חֶלְקַת הַצֻּרִים v. I. חֶלְקָה.—Jb 22[24] v.
6697, 6865 I. צוּר sub V. צוּר. I. צֹר v. p. 862. p. 849

6872 †II. צְרוֹר **n.m.** pebble;—צ׳ 2 S 17[13]; also Am 9[9] (where perhaps fig. for grain of wheat, in metaph. of winnowed Isr., cf. Dr Now al.; > pebble retained in sieve Preuschen ZAW xv (1895), 24, cf. on custom Wetzst ZPV xiv (1891), 2 f.). p. 865

†III. צְרוֹר **n.pr.m.** grandfather of Ḳish 6872
1 S 9[1], Αρεδ, 𝔊L Σαρα.

†[צְרֵרָה] **n.pr.loc.** צְרֵרָתָה Ju 7[22] (Γαραγαθα, 6888
𝔊L καὶ ἦν συνηγμένη), usu. thought corrupt for
צְרֵדָתָה, and in any case prob. = צָרְתָן, q.v. (GFM). 6868, 6891

†צֶרֶת **n.pr.m.** in Judah 1 Ch 4[7], Αρεθ, A 6889
Σαρεθ, 𝔊L Σαρηθ.

†צֶרֶת הַשַּׁחַר **n.pr.loc.** assigned to Reuben 6890
Jos 13[19], Σεραδα και Σειων, 𝔊L Σαρθ; cf. mod. *eṣ-Sara*, on spur of Mt. *ʿAṭṭârûs*, E. of Dead Sea Buhl Geogr. 268.

†צָרְתָן **n.pr.loc.** in Jordan valley, near 6891
ford, Buhl Geogr. 181; exact site unknown; Jos 3[16] (Καθιαιρειν, 𝔊L Καριαθιαρειμ), 1 K 7[46] (Σειρα, 𝔊L
Σαρθαν) = צְרֵדָתָה 2 Ch 4[17] (Αναμε [i.e. ἀνὰ μέσον] 6868
σιρδαθαι; Σα(ρι)δαθα; is Chr right?); צָרְתָנָה 1 K
4[12] (Σεσαθαν, 𝔊L Σαρθαν)—cf. צְרֵרָתָה Ju 7[22], 6888
appar. same place; identity with צְרֵדָה 1 K 11[26] 6868
is usually assumed, but not proven.

ק

ק, *Kôph*, 19th letter; = 100 in postB. Heb.

6892 [קָא] v. קיא. קָאם v. קום.

6893 †קָאַת, קָאָת **n.[f.]** a bird, usu. **pelican** (cf. 𝔊 Lv Dt ψ, 𝔙 ψ (der. by Thes from [קוא], קיא (v. Kö ii. 1, 173, and, on ת, Ges § 80 g), as *throwing up* food from its crop for its young); but sea-fowl improb. in ψ Is; NH קָאת, 𝔗 קָאתָא *id.*);—abs. הַקָּאָת Lv 11[18] = Dt 14[17], as unclean; קָאַת (van d. H. Gi; Baer קָאָת) Is 34[11] Zp 2[14], as inhabiting ruins; cstr. קְאַת מִדְבָּר ψ 102[7], sim. of loneliness.

6894 קַב v. I. קבב. below

I. קבב (√of foll.; cf. Ar. قُبَّةٌ *arch, dome* (hence '*al-cove*'), *vaulted tent*, esp. *tent of honour* Goldziher ZMG xlvii (1893), 74 f. Jacob Beduinenleben (2) 86, 245; Syr. ܩܒܘܒܬܐ *vault, dome*, ܩܘܒܬܐ *id.*, *vaulted tent* PS 3466 b; so NH קוּבָּה, specif. *lupanar*; 𝔗 קוּבְּתָא *vault* (esp. *vaulted* heavens); perh. also As. *kabâbu, shield*).

6894 †קַב **n.[m.]** kab (NH *id.*; Syr. ܩܒܐ; Talm. קַבָּא);—a measure of capacity, BH only dry measure, רֹבַע הַקַּב 2 K 6[25] ¼ *kab*; on size of קַב = 4 לֹג = ⅙ סְאָה = ⅙ הִין = c. 2 litres v. Now Arch. i. 202 f. Benz Arch. 182.

†קֻבָּה **n.f.** large vaulted tent;—abs. Nu 6898
25[8] (P) Ke al. Zimri's *princely tent*; > Thes al. *large tent* used as *lupanar* (cf. NH).

†II. [קָבַב] **vb.** utter a curse against, 6895
curse (cf. [ב]יקו Ecclus 41[7]);—**Qal** *curse*, c. acc., usu. pers.: *Pf.* 3 ms. sf. קַבֹּה (Ges § 58 d) Nu 23[8]; 2 ms. sf. consec. וְקַבֹּתוֹ v[27]; *Impf.* 3 ms. וַיִּקֹּב (Ges § 67 g) Lv 24[11] (c. acc. אֶת־הַשֵּׁם); 2 ms. sf. תִּקֳּבֶנּוּ Nu 23[25] (+ Inf. abs.); 1 s. אֶקֹּב v[8] (obj. om.); וָאֶקּוֹב נָוֵהוּ Jb 5[3] (prob. corrupt; 𝔊 Du rd. וַיִּרְקַב, cf. Me Bi Siegf Beer; וַיִּפָּקֵד Bu; וַיּוּקַּב Che JQ July, 1897, 575; וַיִּבַּק Bev JPhil. xxvi. 308 (cf. Is 24[1.3] Je 51[2] Na 2[3])); 3 mpl. sf. יִקְּבֻהוּ Jb 3[8] Pr 11[26] 24[24]; *Imv.* ms. קָבָה־לִּי (Ges § 67 p Kö i. 329 ff.) Nu 22[11.17], sf. 3 ms. וְקָבְנוֹ־לִי (Ges § 67 o) 23[13] (all JE; all + לִי as dat. comm., so also v[27] vid. *Pf.* supr.); *Inf. abs.* קֹב v[25] (+ Impf.); *Inf. cstr.* לָקֹב v[11] 24[10].

קבה (√of foll. (cf. Dl Pr 113 Kö ii. 1, 185): Ar. قِبَّةٌ *echinus*, i.e. *stomachi pars pelliculata*; Syr. ܩܒܐ is *collect, contain*, water, ܡܩܒܐ (ܩܒ׳) *cistern*; Eth. ቀበወ: *have dropsy*; NH קֵבָה = BH).

6896-97 קֵבָה, sf. קֵבָתָהּ (Kö$^{i.6.}$ cf. Ges^{§10h}) **n.f. stomach, belly**;—**1.** abs. הַקּ׳ of sacrificial victim, assigned to priest Dt 18^{3}, 𝔊 τὸ ἔνυστρον, i.e. *fourth stomach* of ruminants (cf. Dr), 𝔙 *ventriculum*. **2.** sf. of woman, appar. more gen., *belly* Nu 25^{8} (P).

6901 †[קָבַל] **vb. Pi. receive, take** (late) (Aram. loan-word (and in Aram. denom.) Gerber^{32}, cf. Aram. (לְ)קֳבֵיל *in front*, ܠܘܩܒܠ *opposite*, BAram. לָקֳבֵל *before*, OAram. Palm. לקבל *over against*, Nab. *id.*, *in view of*; also Sab. לקבל *in view of* CIS$^{iv. No.79, ll.2.4.5.8}$, As. *ḳablu, encounter*; verbs are: Sab. קבל *accept*, DHM$^{ZMG xxix (1875), 615; xxx (1876), 672}$; Ar. قَبِلَ *be in front, opposite*, قَبِلَ *accept, admit*; Eth. ቀበለ:, esp. III. 2, *go to meet, accept*; NH קִבֵּל *accuse*, Pi.=BH; Aram. קַבֵּל, ܩܰܒܶܠ *receive*);—*Pf.* 3 ms. קִבֵּל Est 4^{4}+ (9^{27} Qr קִבְּלוּ); 3 pl. קִבְּלוּ Ezr 8^{30}; *Impf.* 3 ms. sf. וַיְקַבְּלֵם 1 Ch 12^{19} (v^{18} van d. H.); 3 mpl. וַיְקַבְּלוּ 2 Ch 29$^{16.22}$; 1 pl. נְקַבֵּל Jb 2$^{10.10}$; *Imv.* ms. קַבֵּל Pr 19^{20}, קַבֶּל־ 1 Ch 21^{11};—**1.** *take*, c. acc. rei 2 Ch 29^{22} Ezr 8^{30}; acc. om. 2 Ch 29^{16}, + לְ reflex. = choose 1 Ch 21^{11}; *receive*, c. acc. pers. 12^{19} (van d. H. v^{18}). **2.** *accept*, c. acc. rei Jb 2$^{10.10}$; ק׳ מוּסָר Pr 19^{20}; acc. om. Est 4^{4}. **3.** *accept, assume*, an obligation, sq. cl., Est 9^{23}, sq. inf. v^{27} (+ עַל reflex.). **Hiph.** *Pt.* fpl. מַקְבִּילֹת *shew oppositeness*, i.e. correspond, one to (אֶל) another Ex 26^{5} 36^{12} (both P).

6904 †[קֹבֶל] **n.[m.] 1. something in front**, spec. an **attacking-engine** (cf. قُبُلٌ *front*; ܩܰܒܶܠ, *advance* to attack, so הקביל Ecclus 12^{5}), Ez 26^{9} מְחִי קָבָלּוֹ the stroke of his *attacking-engine* (on the form *ḳobollô*, from קֹבֶל for *ḳŭbŭl*, see Ol^{§169} Kö$^{ii. 68 f.}$; and cf. קָטְנִּי from קֹטֶן for *ḳŭṭŭn*, קָרְבְּכֶם, קָטָבְךָ; and on the בָּ, Ges^{§93q}).
6905 **2.** cstr. קָבָל־עָם (*ḳobol*) 2 K 15^{10}, explained formerly as *before* the people, i.e. publicly (cf. BAram קֳבֵל *before*); but the Aram. is surprising, and הָעָם needed: rd. בְּיִבְלְעָם *in Ibleam*, with 𝔊L (confirming earlier conj. of Gr$^{G ii. 1.99}$ Sta$^{G i. 575}$), Dr Klo Benz Kit al.

6906 †קָבַע **vb.** dub., perhaps **rob** (syn. גזל, so Rabb. (rare), v. De$^{Pr 22, 23}$);—**Qal** *Pf.* 3 ms. consec. וְקָבַע Pr 22^{23}, subj. י׳, c. acc. pers.+rei; c. acc. pers. alone 1 pl. בַּמֶּה קְבַעֲנוּךָ Mal 3^{8} (obj. י׳); *Impf.* 3 ms. הֲיִקְבַּע אָדָם אֱלֹהִים v^{8}; *Pt. act.* אַתֶּם קֹבְעִים אֹתִי v$^{8.9}$; sf. קֹבְעֵיהֶם Pr 22^{23} *those robbing them*.—In Mal 𝔊 We עָקַב *circumvent*.

†קֻבַּעַת **n.f. cup** (perhaps loan-word from 6907
As. [*ḳabu'tu*], pl. *ḳabûâtê*, prob. *cups, goblets*; cf. Ar. قُبْعَةٌ *flower-cup, calyx*);—cstr. ק׳ כּוֹס הַתַּרְעֵלָה Is 51^{17} cf. v^{22} (both fig., and כּוֹס in both prob. explanatory gloss, v. Comm.).

קָבַץ$_{127}$ **vb. gather, collect** (syn. אָסַף) 6908
(Ar. قَبَضَ *grasp, seize*; Sab. קבץ *harvest*, in דק׳, attrib. of ʿAttar, acc. to Fell$^{ZMG liv (1900), 237 f.}$; Eth. ቀበጸ: is *fail, despair*; NH קִבֵּץ=BH);—†**Qal** *Pf.* 3 ms. ק׳ 1 K 20^{1}; *Impf.* 3 ms. יִקְבָּץ־ ψ 41^{7}, וַיִּקְבֹּץ Gn 41^{48}+, etc.; *Imv.* ms. קְבֹץ 1 K 18^{19}, mpl. קִבְצוּ 1 S 7^{5}+; *Inf. cstr.* sf. לְקָבְצִי Zp 3^{8}; *Pt. act.* קֹבֵץ Ez 22^{19} Pr 13^{11}; *pass.* pl. קְבוּצִים Ne 5^{16};—*gather, collect*: **1.** c. acc. rei, grain Gn 41$^{35.48}$ (E), booty Dt 13^{17} (+ אֶל loc.), money 2 Ch 24^{5} (+ מִן pers.), so Ez 16^{31} (Gr Toy Krae, rdg. לְקַבֵּץ fr. לְקַלֵּס, cf. 𝔊 𝔖 Symm); acc. om. קֹבֵץ Pr 13^{11} *one gathering* by degrees; fig. לִבּוֹ יִקְ׳־אָוֶן לוֹ ψ 41^{7} *his heart gathereth wickedness to itself*. **2.** usu. c. acc. pers. *gather, assemble*, + ה loc. 1 S 7^{5} 29^{1} (for battle); + אֶל loc. 1 K 18^{20} Ezr 8^{15} Est 2^{3}; + אֶל pers. 2 S 3^{21} Hb 2^{5} (in fig.; ‖ אָסַף); + עַל (=אֶל) pers. 1 K 11^{24}; + אֶל pers. et loc. 1 K 18^{19} 2 Ch 32^{6}; + מִן loc. 2 Ch 23^{2}, cf. Ezr 7^{28}; acc. pers. alone 1 K 22^{6}=2 Ch 18^{5}, 2 K 10^{18}, Ne 7^{5} (+inf. purpose), Jo 2^{16} (‖ אָסַף), 2 Ch 15^{9} 24^{5} 25^{5}; pass. c. עַל + שָׁם of work Ne 5^{16}; for י׳'s judgment Zp 3^{8} (‖ אָסַף), Ez 22^{20} cf. v^{19} (+ אֶל־תּוֹךְ; fig. of metals into furnace); specif. for war, battle, Ju 12^{4} 1 S 28^{1} 2 S 2^{30} 1 K 20^{1} 2 K 6^{24}; + לַצָּבָא 1 S 28^{1} (29^{1} v. supr.). †**Niph.** *Pf.* 3 pl. נִקְבְּצוּ Jos 10^{6}+, etc.; *Impf.* 2 ms. תִּקָּבֵץ Ez 29^{5}; 3 mpl. וַיִּקָּבְצוּ 1 S 7^{6}+, etc.; *Imv.* mpl. הִקָּבְצוּ Gn 49^{2}+; *Inf. cstr.* הִקָּבֵץ Ezr 10^{7}+; *Pt.* pl. נִקְבָּצִים Je 40^{15}, sf. נִקְבָּצָיו Is 56^{8};—**1.** intrans. *assemble, gather* 1 S 25^{1} Gn 49^{2} Is 45^{20} 48^{14} 49^{18} 60^{4} Jo 4^{11} 2 Ch 20^{4} (+inf. purpose) 32^{4}; for war 1 S 28^{4} Jos 10^{6} (c. אֶל *against*); c. ה loc. 1 S 7^{6}, acc. loc. Ezr 10$^{7.9}$ 2 Ch 15^{10}; c. אֶל pers. *unto* Je 40^{15} 1 Ch 13^{2} Ezr 10^{1} Ne 4^{14}, cf. 2 Ch 13^{7} (עַל for אֶל); אֶל pers.+ה loc. 1 Ch 11^{1}; c. יַחְדָּו Ho 2^{2} Is 43^{9} (‖אָסַף), ψ 102^{23}; of birds and beasts Is 34^{15} (c. שָׁם), Ez 39^{17}. **2.** pass. *be gathered* Is 60^{7} (of flocks, + לְ pers.), Est 2^{8} (+ אֶל loc.), v^{19}; pt. c. sf. pers. Is 56^{8}; Ez 29^{5} (‖ אסף) rd. תִּקָּבֵר Hi (not Sm) Co Berthol Toy Krae. **Pi.** 51

Pf. 3 ms. sf. וְקִבֶּצְךָ Dt 30^{3} consec., קִבְּצָם Mi 4^{12} ψ 107^{3}, קִבְּצָן Is 34^{16}; 3 fs. קִבָּצָה Mi 1^{7}, etc.; *Impf.* יְקַבֵּץ Is 11^{12} 40^{11}, etc.; *Imv.* ms. sf. קַבְּצֵנוּ 1 Ch 16^{35}, ψ 106^{47}; *Inf. abs.* קַבֵּץ Mi 2^{12}; *cstr.* קַבֵּץ Is 66^{18} etc.; *Pt.* מְקַבֵּץ Na 3^{18}+, etc.;—*gather together:* **1.** usu. of ׳י *gathering* his dispersed people (acc.), sts. under fig. of flock: Mi 2^{12}+inf. abs. (‖ אָסֹף), 4^{6} Zp 3$^{19.20}$ Je 31^{10} Zc 10^{8} Is 54^{7} 56^{8a}, cf. also 40^{11}; c. acc.+ מִן loc. Dt 30$^{3.4}$ Je 23^{3} 29^{14} 31^{8} 32^{37} Ez 11^{17}+6 t. Ez+ 37^{21} (מִסָּבִיב), Is 11^{12} 43^{5} Zc 10^{10} Ne 1^{9} ψ 106^{47}, cf. ‖ 1 Ch 16^{35}, ψ 107^{3}; acc.+ עַל pers. Is 56^{8b} (cf. **Niph.** *Pt.*);=(*gather* and) restrain Ho 8^{10} (c. acc. alone); of ׳י *gathering* dispersed Egyptians, acc.+ מִן loc. Ez 29^{13}; *gathering* the nations (acc.) for judgment Mi 4^{12} Is 66^{18} Jo 4^{2}; *gathering* lovers of Jerus. (under fig. of harlot) Ez 16$^{37.37}$ (עַל + מִסָּבִיב pers. *against*); *gathering* beasts into Edom Is 34^{16}. **2.** men subj.: מִצְרַיִם תְּקַבְּצֵם מֹף תְּקַבְּרֵם Ho 9^{6} (cf. Ez 29^{5} **Niph.**, supr.), Ne 13^{11}; c. acc. rei Mi 1^{7} (+ מִן), Is 22^{9} 62^{9} Pr 28^{8}; אֵין מְקַבֵּץ *none that gathereth* Is 13^{14} (acc. om.), Na 3^{18} (*id.*), Je 49^{5} (sq. לַנֹּדֵד, cf. ל **3** ad fin.). **3.** perh. (*gather* and so) *take away* (= אָסַף **4**), Na 2^{11} Jo 2^{6}, v. פָּארוּר. **Pu.** *Pt.* מְקֻבֶּצֶת Ez 38^{8} (c. מִן) of land (for people) of Isr. †**Hithp.** *gather together* (intrans.), *be gathered together*. *Pf.* 3 pl. הִתְקַבְּצוּ Ju 9^{47} 1 S 7^{7} (+ ה loc.); *Impf.* 3 mpl. וַיִּתְקַבְּצוּ 1 S 8^{2} 22^{2} (+ אֶל pers.), יִתְק׳ Is 44^{11}; for battle, war, *Imv.* mpl. הִתְקַבְּצוּ Je 49^{14}; *Impf.* also Jos 9^{2} (c. יַחְדָּו, + inf. purpose), + אַחֲרֵי pers. 2 S 2^{25}.

6899 †[קִבּוּץ] **n.m.** (si vera l.) **heap**;—pl. sf. קִבּוּצַיִךְ Is 57^{13} *thy heaps* (of idols); but read perh. שִׁקּוּצַיִךְ Weir in Che, Che^{Hpt} Kit-Di Marti.

6910 †[קְבֻצָה] **n.f. a gathering**;—cstr. קְבֻצַת כֶּסֶף . . . אֶל־תּוֹךְ כּוּר Ez 22^{20} (after קבץ אֶתְכֶם, sq. אֶקְבֹּץ).

3343,6909 †קַבְצְאֵל, [יְקַבְצְאֵל] **n. pr. loc.** in S. of Judah (*gathering of Ēl*, or *Ēl gathereth*, cf. Sab., of *ʿAttar*, sub √supr.);—ק׳ Jos 15^{21} 2 S 23^{20}= 1 Ch 11^{22}, Καβ(ε)σεηλ, etc.; וּבִיקַב׳ Ne 11^{25}, 𝔊L Καβσεηλ.

6911 †קִבְצַיִם **n.pr.loc.** (Thes *two heaps*);—Levite city in Ephr. Jos 21^{22} (𝔊^{B} om., A Καβσαειμ, 𝔊L Καβσεμ), = יָקְמְעָם [q.v. sub קום] 1 Ch 6^{53}.

6912 קָבַר$_{132}$ **vb. bury** (NH *id.*; Ph. קבר, *bury*, קבר *tomb*; Ar. قَبَرَ, As. *ḳibêru*, Aram. קְבַר, ܩܒܰܪ, Nab. קבר, all *bury*; Palm. Nab. קברא *tomb*, so Sab. קבר Hom$^{Chrest. 126}$, Liḥy. קבר *bury*, DHM$^{Epigr. Denkm. No. 35, 2, 3}$, cf. (מקבר(הם *burial-place* CIS$^{iv, No. 20, 1. 2, 4}$);—**Qal**$_{86}$ *Pf.* 3 ms. ק׳ Gn 23^{19}; 2 ms. sf. consec. וּקְבַרְתַּנִי 47^{30}, etc.; *Impf.* 3 ms. וַיִּקְבֹּר Dt 34^{6} 2 K 21^{26}, etc.; *Imv.* קְבֹר Gn 23^{6}+, etc.; *Inf. abs.* קָבוֹר Dt 21^{23}; *cstr.* לִקְבּוֹר Je 19^{11}+, etc.; *Pt. act.* קֹבֵר 2 K 9^{10}+, etc.; *pass.* קָבוּר 1 K 13^{31}, pl. קְבֻרִים Ec 8^{10} *bury*, acc. pers., bones, etc., usu. c. בּ loc., 2 S 2^{32} 1 K 13$^{31.31}$ Gn 23^{6} Jos 24$^{30.32.32}$ Ju 2^{9}+33 t.; c. בֵּיתוֹ loc. 2 Ch 33^{20} (בְּגַן־בֵּיתוֹ ‖ 2 K 21^{18}, also בְּבֵיתוֹ 1 S 25^{1} 1 K 2^{34}); c. שָׁם Nu 11^{34}, תַּחַת 1 S 31^{13}= 1 Ch 10^{12}; pregn. c. אֶל loc. Gn 23^{19} 25^{9} Ez 39^{15}; אֶל־אֲבֹתָי Gn 49^{29}; cf. עִם־אֲבֹתָיו 2 K 12^{22} 15^{7} 2 Ch 25^{28} 26^{23} (v. also **Niph.**, and תָּבוֹא אֶל־אֲבֹתֶיךָ Gn 15^{15}); c. שָׁמָּה Gn 23^{13} 49$^{31.31.31}$ 50^{5}; c. acc. pers. alone 2 S 2$^{4.5}$+22 t.; + מִלְּפָנַי Gn 23$^{4.8}$; pass. Ec 8^{10}; acc. om. 2 K 9^{10}+3 t.+ (c. בּ) 2 S 4^{12}. **Niph.**$_{39}$ *Impf.* 3 ms. יִקָּבֵר Je 22^{19}, etc.;—*be buried* Gn 15^{15} Je 8^{2} 16$^{4.6}$ 25^{33} (+ אסף), so rd. perh. Ez 29^{5} for תִּקָּבֵץ (+ *id.*); קְבוּרַת חֲמוֹר יִקּ׳ Je 22^{19}; usu. c. בּ loc. Gn 35^{19} Ju 8^{32}+6 t. Ju, 2 S 17^{23} 1 K 2$^{10.34}$+16 t. K Ch (+ עִם־אֲבֹתָיו 1 K 14^{31} 15^{24}+6 t.; עִם־מַלְכֵי יִשְׂר׳ 2 K 13^{13} 14^{16}); c. שָׁם Nu 20^{1}+3 t.; c. מִתַּחַת, תַּחַת Gn 35^{8}. †**Pi.** *bury* (in masses), c. acc.: *Impf.* 3 fs. sf. תְּקַבְּרֵם Ho 9^{6}; *Inf. cstr.* לְקַבֵּר 1 K 11^{15}; *Pt.* pl. מְקַבְּרִים Nu 33^{4} Ez 39^{14}; as n. intens., of office, *burier*, sg. מְקַבֵּר Je 14^{16}, pl. הַמְ׳ Ez 39^{15}. †**Pu.** *Pf.* 3 ms. שָׁמָּה קֻבַּר אַבְרָהָם Gn 25^{10}.

קֶבֶר$_{67}$ **n.m.** $^{1 K 13, 31}$ **grave, sepulchre**;—abs. 6913
ק׳ Gn 23^{4}+, קָבֶר 1 K 14^{13}+; cstr. קֶבֶר Ju 8^{32}+; sf. קִבְרִי Gn 50^{5}, etc.; pl. קְבָרִים Ex 14^{11}+, cstr. קִבְרֵי Je 26^{23}+, sf. קִבְרֵיהֶם 8^{1}; also קְבָרוֹת Jb 21^{32}, cstr. קִבְרוֹת Ne 2^{3}+, sf. קִבְרֹתָיו Ez 32^{22} 2 Ch 16^{14}, etc.;—*grave, sepulchre*, Ju 8^{32} 2 S 2^{32} 1 K 13^{22}+; אֲחֻזַּת ק׳ Gn 23$^{4.9.30}$ 49^{30} 50^{13}; hewn out (חָצַב) Is 22$^{16.16}$; מִבֶּטֶן לַקֶּבֶר אוּבָל Jb 10^{19}; fig. וַתְּהִי־לִי אִמִּי ק׳ Je 20^{17}; שֹׁכְבֵי ק׳ ψ 88^{6} the slain *lying in grave;* הַיֹּשְׁבִים בַּקְּבָרִים Is 65^{4} *they who sit in the tombs* (occult rite, prob. in necromancy, etc., cf. Che and RS$^{Sem. i. 180 ff.; 2nd ed. 197 ff.}$); קֶבֶר בְּנֵי הָעָם 2 K 23^{6} i.e. burial-place of common people, so קִבְרֵי בְּנֵי הָעָם Je 26^{23}; pl. intens. Jb 17^{1}, also of stately (royal) sepulchre 2 K 22^{20}= 2 Ch 34^{28}, Ne 3^{16} 2 Ch 16^{14} cf. 35^{24}; Jb 21^{32}; conceived as in lower world Ez 32$^{22.23.25.26}$, ‖ אֲבַדּוֹן ψ 88^{12}; ψ 49^{12} rd. קִבְרָם for קִרְבָּם Vrss and most; ק׳ פָּתוּחַ sim. of quiver Je 5^{16}; fig. ק׳ פ׳ גְּרֹנָם ψ 5^{10}; of exile Ez 37$^{12.12.13.13}$.

6914 †קִבְרוֹת הַתַּאֲוָה **n.pr.loc.** Μνήματα (τῆς) ἐπιθυμίας: **a** station in wilderness (*the graves of desire,* cf. Nu 11^{34} and תַּאֲוָה p. 16 supr.);— Nu 11$^{34.35}$, קִבְרֹת הַתּ׳ 33$^{16.17}$ Dt 9^{22}.

6900 †[קְבֻרָה], and (4 t.) קְבוּרָה **n.f. grave, burial**;—abs. קְבוּרָה Is 14^{20} + 2 t.; cstr. קְבוּרַת Je 22^{19}, קְבֻרַת Gn 35^{20}+; sf. קְבֻרָתוֹ Dt 34^{6}+;— **1.** *grave* Gn 35$^{20.20}$ 47^{30} Dt 34^{6} 1 S 10^{2} 2 K 9^{28} 21^{26} 23^{30} Ez 32$^{23.24}$; שְׂדֵה הַקּ׳ 2 Ch 26^{23}. **2.** *burial,* Is 14^{20} Ec 6^{3}; קְבוּרַת חֲמוֹר Je 22^{19}.

6896-97 קַבְתָּהּ v. קֵבָה. p. 867

6915 †I. [קָדַד] **vb. bow down** (As. (including TelAm.) *ḳadâdu, bow down*); — **Qal** *Impf.* 3 ms. וַיִּקֹּד Gn 24^{26}+, etc.;—usu. + וַיִּשְׁתַּחוּ etc.; in worship of ׳י Gn 24$^{26.48}$ Ex 4^{31} 12^{27} 34^{8} Nu 22^{31} 2 Ch 20^{18} 29^{30} Ne 8^{6}; homage to man of rank Gn 43^{28}, king 1 S 24^{9} (Gi v^{8}), 28^{14} 1 K 1$^{16.31}$; to ׳י + king 1 Ch 29^{20}.

II. קדד (√of foll.; mng. dub.; NH קָדְקֹד = BH; As. *ḳaḳḳadu* = קָדְקֹד; cf. JAram.).

6936 †קָדְקֹד **n.[m.] head, crown of head**;—׳ק abs. Dt 33^{20} Je 2^{16}, cstr. Is 3^{17}+; sf. קָדְקֳדוֹ 2 S 14^{25} Jb 2^{7}; קָדְקֳדֶךָ Dt 28^{35};—esp. poet. Gn 49^{26} = Dt 33^{16}, ψ 7^{17}, ׳ק שֵׂעָר 68^{22} *hairy crown* or *scalp* (all ‖ רֹאשׁ), Is 3^{17} Je 2^{16} 48^{45} (‖ פֵּאָה), so rd. also Nu 24^{17} for וְקַרְקַר (‖ *id.*), v. Ew Di Pat al., Dt 33^{20}; in prose only מִכַּף רֶגֶל וְעַד־ק׳ Dt 28^{35} 2 S 14^{25} Jb 2^{7}.

6916 †קִדָּה **n.f.** a spice, usu. **cassia** (𝔖 𝔙 𝔗 cf. Di^{Ex}; √dub.; perh. foreign word);—merchandise Ez 27^{19}; ingredient of sacred oil Ex 30^{24} (P):—cf. Dioscor.$^{De\ Mater.\ Med.\ i.\ 12}$ (κασσία = ἡ κιττώ), Theophr$^{Hist.\ Plant.\ ix.\ 5}$ Plin$^{NH\ xii.\ 19\ (42\ ff.)}$; v. also Schröd$^{Ph.\ Spr.\ 126}$ Lewy$^{Fremdw.\ 36}$.

6919 †[קָדַח] **vb. be kindled, kindle** (NH *id.*, also *bore,* Aram. קְדַח, ܩܕܚ *bore, kindle;* Ar. قَدَحَ *strike fire* (with flint, etc.); Ph. מקדח is *lamp-lighter* (in temple) acc. to CIS$^{i,\ No.\ 352,\ l.\ 3}$); —**Qal 1.** *be kindled: Pf.* 3 fs. אֵשׁ קָדְחָה בְאַפִּי Dt 32^{22} Je 15^{14} 17^{4} (rdg. קָדְחָה for קְדַחְתֶּם), all of ׳י's wrath. **2.** act. *kindle; Inf. cstr.* כִּקְדֹחַ אֵשׁ הֲמָסִים Is 64^{1} (v. [הֶמֶס]); *Pt.* קֹדְחֵי אֵשׁ 50^{11}.

6920 †קַדַּחַת **n.f. fever**;—Dt 28^{22} Lv 26^{16}.

688 †אֶקְדָּח **n.[m.]** perh. **fiery glow, sparkle**; אַבְנֵי אֶקְדָּח Is 54^{12} i.e. carbuncles (?);—𝔊 λίθους κρυστάλλου, 𝔙 *lapides sculptos,* Aq Theod Sym.

קדם (√of foll.; *be before, in front,* cf. As. *ḳudmu, front, former time;* Ar. قَدُمَ *precede* (so Eth. ቀደመ:), IV, v. *be bold and foremost in attack* (קֶדֶם **1 a**); Sab. קדם *begin* Hom$^{Chrest.\ 126}$, *march forth, advance,* CIS$^{iv,\ No.\ 79,\ l.\ 9}$ Sab Denkm$^{No.\ 9,\ l.\ 2.4.6.7.8.9}$, (הו)קדמ *front* CIS$^{iv,\ No.\ 276,\ l.\ 2}$; Ph. בקדם *as formerly* (?); OAram. קדם *before,* so Palm. Nab.; BAram. 𝔗 קֳדָם *before;* Syr. ܩܕܡ *precede;* NH קָדַם *be in front*).

†קֶדֶם **n.[m.] front, east, aforetime**;— 6924
abs. ׳ק Dt 33^{27}+, קֵדֶם Ju 8^{10}+; cstr. קֶדֶם Pr 8^{22}; once pl. cstr. קַדְמֵי v^{23};—**1.** loc. **a.** *front,* מִקּ׳ Is 9^{11} *from the front* (i.e. East), *in front* (opp. מֵאָחוֹר), אָחוֹר וָק׳ ψ 139^{5} *behind and before;* ק׳ אֶהֱלֹךְ Jb 23^{8} *I go forward* (opp. אָחוֹר). **b.** *East:* הַר־הַקּ׳ Gn 10^{30} (J) *mount of the East;* בְּנֵי־ק׳ = dwellers in the E., tribes E. or NE. of Canaan Gn 29^{1} (E), Ju 6$^{3.33}$ 7^{12} 8^{10} 1 K 5^{10} Is 11^{14} Je 49^{28} Ez 25$^{4.10}$ Jb 1^{3}; הַרְרֵי ק׳ Nu 23^{7}, v. Di Sachau$^{Reise\ (1883),\ 159\ ff.\ 165\ ff.}$ Dr in Hast.^{PETHOR}; אֶרֶץ ק׳ Gn 25^{6} (J); מָלְאוּ מִקֶּדֶם Is 2^{6} *they are full from the E.* (ins. prob. קֶסֶם, מִקְסָם, or < קֹסְמִים before מִקּ׳, cf. Lo De Du Che^{Hpt} Di-Kit); elsewh. מִקּ׳ = *eastward:* (1) *in the E.* Gn 2^{8}; (2) *on the E.* (side) 12^{8} (J) Zc 14^{4}; מִקּ׳ לְ *on the E. of* Gn 3^{24} (J), 12^{8} (J), Nu 34^{11} (P), Jos 7^{2} (JE), Ju 8^{11} Ez 11^{23} Jon 4^{5}; (3) *eastward,* c. vb. of motion Gn 11^{2} 13^{11} (both J). **2.** temp., *ancient time, aforetime:* **a.** הַרְרֵי ק׳ Dt 33^{15} *ancient mts.,* cf. אֱלֹהֵי ק׳ v^{27}, בִּימֵי־ק׳ Is 19^{11}, בִּשְׁמֵי שְׁמֵי־ק׳ ψ 68^{34}. **b.** בִּימֵי ק׳ ψ 44^{2} *in ancient days;* cf. מִימֵי ק׳ *from of old* Is 23^{7} Mi 7^{20} La 1^{7} 2^{17}, Is 37^{26} = לְמִימֵי ק׳ 2 K 19^{25} (v. מִן **9b** (2)); כִּימֵי ק׳ Is 51^{9} Je 46^{26}; יַרְחֵי ק׳ Jb 29^{2} *months of old.* **c.** מִקּ׳ *from of old* Mi 5^{1} Is 45^{21} 46^{10} Hb 1^{12} Ne 12^{46} ψ 74^{12} 77^{12}; מִנִּי־ק׳ 78^{2} *springing out of, derived from, ancient times* (cf. Dr); יָמִים מִקּ׳ 77^{6} 143^{5} *days from of old.* **d.** ק׳ alone, as adv. *anciently, of old* ψ 74^{2} 119^{152}; כְּקּ׳ Je 30^{20} La 5^{21}; יֹשֵׁב ק׳ ψ 55^{20} *he that sitteth* (enthroned from) *of old.* **e.** *beginning,* מִקַּדְמֵי־אָרֶץ Pr 8^{23} *from the beginnings of the earth;* ק׳ מִפְעָלָיו Pr 8^{22} *the beginning of his works* (‖ רֵאשִׁית).

†[קָדַם] **vb. Pi. denom.** (Gerber ^{130}) **come** 6923
or be in front, meet;—*Pf.* 1 s. קִדַּמְתִּי Jon 4^{2} ψ 119^{147}; 3 pl. קִדְּמוּ Dt 23^{5}+, etc.; *Impf.* 3 ms. sf. יְקַדְּמֵנִי ψ 59^{11}; 3 fs. sf. תְּקַדְּמֶךָּ ψ 88^{14}; 1 s. אֲקַדֵּם Mi 6^{6}; *Imv.* ms. קַדְּמָה ψ 17^{13};—**1. a.** *meet, confront* (with hostility) c. acc. pers. 2 S 22$^{6.19}$ = ψ 18$^{6.19}$, Jb 30^{27}, c. acc. פָּנָיו ψ 17^{13}; of hostile approach to city (acc.) 2 K 19^{32} = Is 37^{33}

(+adv. acc.). **b.** *come to meet* one (acc.) as friend, with (ב) sthg. Is 21^{14} Dt 23^{5} Ne 13^{2}, so, as worshippers (acc. of ׳י), Mi 6$^{6.6}$; c. acc. pers. +rei ψ 21^{4}, so 59^{11} Kt 𝔊 𝔙 (acc. pers. alone Qr), acc. pers. alone ψ 79^{8}; acc. ׳פני י 88^{14}, acc. פָּנָיו (of ׳י) 95^{2}, cf. חֶסֶד וֶאֱמֶת יְקַדְּמוּ פָנֶיךָ 89^{15} (viz., to join themselves to thee). **c.** *meet, receive,* acc. pers., Jb 3^{12}. **2. a.** *go before, in front* ψ 68^{26}. **b.** *be in front,* 1 S 20^{25} (rd. וַיְקַדֵּם for וַיָּקָם) 𝔊 Ew Th We Dr al. **3.** *be beforehand,* c. ב temp. ψ 119^{147}; + inf. cstr. Jon 4^{2}; *anticipate, forestall,* c. acc. rei ψ 119^{148}. **Hiph.** **1.** *Impf.* 3 fs. תַּקְדִּים (We Now GASm תְּקַדֵּם) Am 9^{10} *calamity . . . shall not come in front about us* (בַּעֲדֵינוּ). **2.** *Pf.* 3 ms. sf. הִקְדִּימַנִי Jb 41^{3} who *has anticipated me* [God]? 𝔊 Me Bi Bu *confronted me* (rdg. וַיִּשְׁלָם for foll. וַאֲשַׁלֵּם); Du יְקַדְּמֶנּוּ *confronted him* (the crocodile).

6924 †[קֵדֶם], c. ה loc. I. קֵ֫דְמָה **adv. eastward, to, toward, the E.**;—Gn 25^{6} (J), Lv 1^{16} 16^{14} Nu 34$^{3.11.15}$ Jos 19$^{12.13}$ (all P), 1 K 7^{39} = 2 Ch 4^{10}, 1 K 17^{3} 2 K 13^{17} Ez 8$^{16.16}$; + N, S, W, Gn 13^{14} 28^{14} (both J), Nu 2^{3} 3^{38} 10^{5} (N, W, in 𝔊), 34^{10} (all P); also as **n.** after פְּאַת = *E. side,* Ex 27^{13} 38^{13} (both P), + W Ez 45^{7} (del. Co; rd. קֶדֶם Berthol Toy Krae), + N, S, W, Nu 35^{5} Jos 18^{20} so גְּבוּל ק׳ 15^{5} (all P).

6927 †[קַדְמָה] **n.f. antiquity, former state**;— **1.** *antiquity, beginning,* sf. קַדְמָתָהּ Is 23^{7} (of Tyre). **2.** *former state,* sf. קַדְמָתָן Ez 16$^{55.55}$, קַדְמַתְכֶן v^{55}; pl. sf. קַדְמוֹתֵיכֶם 36^{11}. **3.** cstr. sg. = **conj.** *before* (temp.; Aram.) שֶׁקַּדְמַת שָׁלַף ψ 129^{6}.

6926 †[קִדְמָה] **n. f. front, East**; — only cstr. קִדְמַת as prep.: **1.** *in front of, over against* (cf. Nö[ZMG xxxiii (1879), 532]), Gn 2^{14} (i.e. from standpoint of writer; really, on geogr. grounds, = W. of; yet v. Di[ed. 6]), 4^{16} (both J). **2.** *on the E. of,* Ez 39^{11}; 1 S 13^{5} may be either.

6929 †II. קֵ֫דְמָה **n.pr.m.** Κεδ(ε)μα, son of Ishmael
6924 Gn 25^{15} = 1 Ch 1^{31}.—I. ק׳ v. [קֵדֶם]. above

6921 קָדִים$_{69}$ **n.m.**[Ho 13, 15] **East, east wind**;—abs. ק׳ Gn 41^{6}+; c. ה loc. קָדִ֫ימָה Ez 11^{1}+, קָדְמָה 48^{4}+;—†**1.** (apart from Ez) *East,* esp. רוּחַ (הַ)ק׳ *wind of the East, east wind,* oft. as violent and scorching, from desert on SE., = Ar. *sirocco* (شرقية *eastern*), cf. Dr[Am 4, 9]: Ex 10$^{13.13}$ (JE), 14^{21} (J), Je 18^{17} (sim.), Jon 4^{8} ψ 48^{8}; also ק׳ (רוּחַ om.) = *east wind* Gn 41$^{6.23.27}$ (E), Ho 12^{2} 13^{15} Is 27^{8} Jb 15^{2} 27^{21} 38^{24} ψ 78^{26}.—קָדִ֫ימָה Hb 1^{9} is dub., usu. *eastward,* i.e. *forward,* but text prob. corrupt, cf. We Now Da, GASm prop. מְקַדִּים (v. also [מְגַמָּה] p. 169 supr.). **2.** in Ez (52 t.): **a.** *East* רוּחַ הַק׳ *east wind* 17^{10} 19^{12} 27^{26}; *east side* 42^{16} (+N, S, W); שַׁעַר הַק׳ 40^{44} (+N, S); פְּאַת ק׳ 47^{18}, +W 48$^{6.7.8}$, cf. v^{1} (פ׳ ק׳ הַיָּם; but rd. מִפּ׳ ק׳ וְעַד פ׳ יָמָּה 𝔊 Co Toy al.), + N,S,W, v^{16}; דֶּרֶךְ הַק׳ i.e. *toward the E.* 40^{10} + 7 t., מִד׳ הַק׳ 43^{2}; לַק׳ 40^{23} *eastward* (+N) 41^{14}; מֵהַק׳ 42^{9} *on the East.* **b.** קָדִ֫ימָה = *East*: דֶּרֶךְ הַק׳ 40^{6}; גְּבוּל קָדִימָה 45^{7} 48^{21} (+W); פְּאַת קָדִימָה 47^{18}, + W 48^{3} + 8 t., + N,S,W, v^{32}. **c.** as adv. קָדִ֫ימָה *eastward* 11^{1} 44^{1} 47^{1}; +W 45^{7} (del. Berthol Krae), 48^{18}, + N,S,W, v$^{10.17}$; also (הַ)קָּדִים *eastward* 40^{19} 43^{17} 46$^{1.12}$ 47$^{1.3}$, + N v^{2}.

†קְדוּמִים **n.[m.] pl.** only נַחַל ק׳ Ju 5^{21}, 6917
meaning dub.; 𝔊^{A} n.pr. Καδησειμ, 𝔊L Καδημειμ;
𝔊^{B} ἀρχαίων, so 𝔗, AV *ancient* river (lit. *of*
antiquity), Bachm al.; Be al. *of attack* (cf. קָדַם 6923
1 a); v. further GFM Bu Now Cook[Ency. Bib. 2683].

†[קַדְמוֹן] **adj. eastern**; — fs. הַגְּלִילָה 6930
הַקַּדְמוֹנָה Ez 47^{8} *the eastern circuit.*

†I. קַדְמֹנִי **adj. former, eastern** (on format. 6931
v. Lag[BN 195] Ba[NB, § 227 d]); — abs. ק׳ 1 S 24^{14} (Gi v^{13}), Jo 2^{20}; -מוֹנִי Ez 10^{19}+; mpl. קַדְמֹנִים Jb 18^{20}, -מוֹנִים Ez 38^{17}; fpl. קַדְמֹנִיּוֹת Is 43^{18} Mal 3^{4};— **1.** *former, ancient,* יָמִים ק׳ Ez 38^{17} *former days;* שָׁנִים ק׳ Mal 3^{4} (|| יְמֵי עוֹלָם): fpl. as n., *former things* Is 43^{18} (|| רִאשֹׁנוֹת); ms. as n. coll. מְשַׁל הַקַּדְמֹנִי 1 S 24^{14} *a proverb of the ancients.* **2.** *eastern:* of שַׁעַר Ez 10^{19} 11^{1}, יָם (i.e. Dead Sea) 47^{18} and (opp. הַיָּם הָאַחֲרוֹן) Zc 14^{8} Jo 2^{20}; mpl. as n. *Easterns, those of the E.* (opp. W) Jb 18^{20} (so Ew De Hi Di Bae Du; Vrss *earlier* and *later,* so Da al. [both future], Bu *former* generations [now in Sheʾôl], and future).

†II. קַדְמֹנִי **adj.gent.** c. art. הַק׳, as n.pr.coll. 6935
(*Easterners*);—Gn 15^{19} *the Kadmonites* (in list of peoples); τοὺς Κελμωναίους, 𝔊L Κεδμωναίους.

†קְדֵמוֹת **n.pr.loc.** in Reuben (Moab) Κεδ(α)- 6932
μωθ, Καδημωθ, etc.; Jos 13^{18}, -מוֹת 21^{37} 1 Ch 6^{64}; hence מִדְבַּר קְדֵמוֹת Dt 2^{26} of contiguous desert; —ק׳ lay N. of upper Arnon; not identified; Buhl[Geogr. 268] conj. *Umm-er-raṣâṣ,* c. 10 m. ENE. from Dibon (cf. Tristr[Moab 140 ff.] Bd[Pal. 3 (1898), 177]).

†קַדְמִיאֵל **n.pr.m.** Καδμιηλ, 𝔊L Κεδμιηλ; 6934
Levite name (*Ēl is the ancient one;* cf. Sab. אלקדם DHM[ZMG xxvii (1883), 374]);—Ezr 2^{40} = Ne 7^{43}, Ezr 3^{9} Ne 9$^{4.5}$ 10^{10} 12$^{8.24}$.

6836 קָדְקֹד v. II. קדד. p. 869

6937 †קָדַר **vb. be dark** (*dull-coloured*, cf. Ar. قَذِرَ *be dirty* (on ذ=ד v. Nö$^{ZMG\ xl\ (1886),\ 729}$); NH Hiph. (of face) *shew gloom;* 𝔗^{J} קְדַר *be dark*);—**Qal** *Pf.* consec. וְקָדַר Mi 3^{6}; 1 s. קָדַרְתִּי Je 8^{21}, etc.; *Pt.* קֹדֵר ψ 35^{14}+; pl. קֹדְרִים Jb 5^{11} 6^{16};—*be dark*, of sky Je 4^{28} (leaden-coloured, as with clouds, v. Hithp.), of sun and moon Jo 2^{10} 4^{15}; fig. of lack of revelation from י׳, וְק׳ עֲלֵיהֶם הַיּוֹם Mi 3^{6}; of turbid stream Jb 6^{16}; fig. of mourning (prob. *be squalid*, of neglected person and dress of mourner, cf. 2 S 19^{25}) Je 8^{21} 14^{2} (לָאָרֶץ, metaph. of gates); Jb 5^{11} 30^{28} (בְּלֹא חַמָּה), ψ 35^{14} 38^{7} 42^{10} 43^{2}. **Hiph. 1.** *darken: Pf.* 1 s. consec. וְהִקְדַּרְתִּי Ez 32^{7} (obj. stars), cf. *Impf.* 1 s. sf. אַקְדִּירֵם עָלֶיךָ 32^{8}. **2.** *cause to mourn* וָאַקְדִּר עָלָיו לְבָנוֹן 31^{15}. **Hithp.** *Pf.* 3 pl. וְהַשָּׁמַיִם הִתְקַדְּרוּ עָבִים 1 K 18^{45} *and the heavens grew dark with clouds.*

6940 †קַדְרוּת **n.f. darkness, gloom**;—אַלְבִּישׁ שָׁמַיִם ק׳ Is 50^{3} (cf. √, Je 4^{28} 1 K 18^{45}; ‖ שַׂק).

6941 †קְדֹרַנִּית **adv. as mourners**;—Mal 3^{14}.

6938 †קֵדָר **n.pr.gent.** (*swarthy? black*-tented?); Κηδαρ: **1.** tribe of nomads in Arab. desert Is 21^{16} 42^{11} (c. vb. fem.), 60^{7}, Je 2^{10} 49$^{28.28}$ Ez 27^{21}; בְּנֵי־ק׳ Is 21^{17}; אָהֳלֵי ק׳ ψ 120^{5} Ct 1^{5} (made of black goat-skins Jacob$^{Beduinenleben\ (2),\ 41}$ or black woven stuff Doughty$^{Arab.\ Des.\ i.\ 224\ f.}$; sim. of swarthy hue). **2.** ancestor of **1**, son of Ishmael, Gn 25^{13}=1 Ch 1^{29}.—Cf. As. *Ḳidru* COT$^{Gn\ 25,13}$, Plin$^{NH\ v.\ 11\ (12)}$ *Cedrei;* also Sab. tribe-name קדר Hal^{623} (cf. DHM$^{ZMG\ xxxvii\ (1883),\ 14}$).

6939 †קִדְרוֹן **n.pr.** of wady just E. of Jerusalem (Thes. *turbidus*);—נַחַל ק׳ 2 S 15^{23} 1 K 2^{37}; usu. as place for refuse 1 K 15^{13}=2 Ch 15^{16}, 2 K 23$^{6.6.12}$ 2 Ch 29^{16} 30^{14}, Je 31^{40}; so שַׁדְמוֹת ק׳ 2 K 23^{4}; Κεδρων; cf. Rob$^{Phys.\ Geogr.\ 87\ ff.}$ Buhl$^{Geogr.\ 93}$ Bd$^{Pal.\ 3\ (1898),\ 94}$.

קדשׁ (√ of foll.; poss. orig. idea of *separation, withdrawal* (Baud$^{Studien,\ ii}$ Nö$^{LCB\ Mar.\ 22,\ 1879,\ 361}$ RS$^{Sem.\ i.\ 140;\ 2nd\ ed.\ 150}$); NH=BH; Ph. קדש *holy*, מקדש *sanctuary;* As. *ḳadâšu* II. 1, *cleanse* (Meissn$^{Suppl.\ 84}$), also *ḳadištu, hierodule* consecrated to Ištar (cf. AJerem$^{Izdubar\ 59\ f.}$); Ar. قُدْسُ n.pr.mont. (Nö$^{l.c.}$ RS$^{Proph.\ v.,\ N.\ 9}$); in Ar. otherwise under infl. of Heb., so Eth.; cf. 𝔗 קדש in der. spec. and deriv., Syr. ܩܰܕܶܫ *consecrate*, etc.; Palm. קדש *id.;* Aram. קְדָשָׁא, ܩܕܫܐ (ear- or nose-) *ring*, (orig. *holy* thing, Nö$^{l.c.}$);—on whole subj. v. Baud Nö RS (reff. above), also HPS$^{Presb.\ Rev.\ 1881,\ 588\ ff.}$; diff. fr. חרם v. GFM$^{Ju.\ p.\ 36}$).

קֹדֶשׁ 469 **n.m. apartness, sacredness** (opp. 6944
חֹל Lv 10^{10} + 4 t. Ez);—abs. ק׳ Ex 3^{5}+; קוֹדֶשׁ Dn 11^{30}; cstr. קֹדֶשׁ Ex 30^{36}+; sf. קָדְשִׁי Lv 20^{3}+, etc.; pl. קֳדָשִׁים Ex 29^{37}+, הַקֳּדָשִׁים 26^{33}+; cstr. קָדְשֵׁי Lv 22^{15}+; sf. קָדָשַׁי Ez 22^{8}+ 3 t., קָדָשֶׁיךָ †Dt 12^{26}, קֳדָשָׁיו Nu 5^{10} 2 K 12^{19}, קָדָשָׁיו +2 Ch 15^{18}, etc.;—**1.** *apartness, sacredness, holiness*, of God: **a.** of divine activity, syn. majesty, בַּקֹּדֶשׁ (of victory), Ex 15^{11} (song) ψ 68^{18} 77^{14}; זְרוֹעַ ק׳ *holy arm* Is 52^{10} ψ 98^{1}. **b.** to attest his word as inviolable נשבע בק׳ Am 4^{2} ψ 89^{36}; cf. דִּבְרֵי ק׳ Je 23^{9}, דְּבַר ק׳ ψ 105^{42}. **c.** of his name as sacred, inviolable, separate from all defilement, etc.: שֵׁם קָדְשִׁי Lv 20^{3} 22$^{2.32}$ (P), Am 2^{7} 1 Ch 16$^{10.35}$ 29^{16}+9 t. Ez, 5 t. ψψ; זֵכֶר ק׳ ψ 30^{5}=97^{12}; and so **d.** רוּחַ קָדְשׁוֹ *his holy Spirit* Is 63$^{10.11}$, cf. ψ 51^{13}. **2.** of places set apart as sacred by God's presence: †**a.** heavenly abode; מְעוֹן ק׳ Dt 26^{15} Je 25^{30} Zc 2^{17} 2 Ch 30^{27} ψ 68^{6}; הֵיכַל ק׳ Mi 1^{2} Hb 2^{20} Jon 2$^{5.8}$ ψ 11^{4}; מְרוֹם ק׳ ψ 102^{20}; זְבוּל ק׳ Is 63^{15}; שְׁמֵי ק׳ ψ 20^{7} כסא ק׳ 47^{9}; בְּקָדְשׁוֹ 150^{1}. †**b.** on earth: אַדְמַת ק׳ Ex 3^{5} (E), cf. Jos 5^{15} (JE) 2 Ch 8^{11}; הַר ק׳ אלהים Ez 28^{14} (cf. p. 249 b). **c.** (only P and Ch) the tabernacle and its courts Ex 40^{9} Nu 3^{28}+; tabernacle by itself Ex 38^{24} Lv 10^{4}+; court Lv 10$^{17.18}$+ (so קדש הקדשים †Nu 18^{10}); the outer room (specific designation; הַקּ׳) Ex 26^{33} 28^{29}+; inner room Lv 4^{6} 16^{2}+, but specif. design. קדש הקדשים Ex 26$^{33.34}$ 1 Ch 6^{34}; שֶׁקֶל הַקּ׳ *shekel of the sanctuary* Ex 30^{13}+24 t. P. **d.** the temple and its precincts 2 Ch 29^{7} Dn 8^{13}+; שָׂרֵי ק׳ Is 43^{28} 1 Ch 24^{5}; דבר בְּקָדְשׁוֹ ψ 60^{8}=108^{8} (oracle; al. *by his holiness*, as נשבעתי בקדשי 89^{36}), temple by itself 2 Ch 29^{5}; †בית (ה)ק׳ Is 64^{10} 1 Ch 29^{3}; †הֵיכַל קדשך ψ 5^{8}=138^{2}, 79^{1}; הַקּ׳ outer room 1 K 8^{10}=2 Ch 5^{11}; courts of priests Ez 42^{14} 44$^{27.27}$; †חצרות קדשי Is 62^{9}; inner room Ez 41$^{21.23}$, specif. †דְּבִיר קדשך ψ 28^{2}; †קדש הקדשים 1 K 6^{16} 7^{50} 8^{6} 2 Ch 3$^{8.10}$ 4^{22} 5^{7} Ez 41^{4}; †לִשְׁכוֹת הַקּ׳ Ez 42^{13} 44^{19} 46^{19} (v. לִשְׁכָּה **1 c**). †**e.** Jerus. and its hills: מקום קדשו Ezr 9^{8}, עיר הק׳ Is 48^{2} 52^{1} Ne 11$^{1.18}$, ע׳ קדשך Dn 9^{24}, הר (ה)ק׳ Is 11^{9}+6 t. Is$^{2.3}$, Je 31^{23} Ez 20^{40} Jo 2^{1} 4^{17} Ob^{16} Zp 3^{11} Zc 8^{3} Dn 9$^{16.20}$ 11^{45}+6 t. ψψ; גְּבוּל ק׳ ψ 78^{54}, הַרְרֵי ק׳ 87^{1} prob. also 110^{3}, ק׳ of city and suburbs in Mess. future Je 31^{40} Jo 4^{17}. Cf. **f.** ק׳ קדשים (ה)קדש of Zion Ob^{17} ψ 20^{3} 24^{3} 63^{3} 68^{25},

Ez 43[12]; נְוֵה ק׳ Ex 15[13] of Zion (or Shiloh). **g.** of holy land Zp 3[4], אדמת הק׳ Zc 2[16], עָרֵי קדשׁך Is 64[9]; future portion of priests ק׳ Ez 45[1.1] + 11 t. Ez; קדשׁ קדשׁים Ez 45[3] 48[12]; of Levites קדשׁ Ez 48[14]. **3.** things consecrated at sacred places: **a.** furniture of tabern. †קדשׁ (ה)קדשׁים Ex 30[10.29] Nu 4[4.19]; altar of burnt-offering Ex 29[37] 40[10] Dn 9[24]; ארון הק׳ 2 Ch 35[3]. **b.** sacrifices of animals Nu 18[17] Ez 36[38] 2 Ch 29[33]; sacrificial food Lv 21[22 b] Nu 5[9] +; †קדשׁ (ה)קדשׁים Lv 2[3.10] 6[10.18.22] 7[1.6] 10[12.17] 14[13] Nu 18[9.9] (all P), Ez 42[13.13] 2 Ch 31[14] Ezr 2[63] = Ne 7[65]; tithe was קדשׁ Lv 27[30] +, also first loaves of new harvest Lv 23[20]; fruit of trees of 4th year Lv 19[24]. **c.** any consecrated thing: ‖ vows Dt 12[26] Pr 20[25] +, house Lv 27[14], field Lv 27[21.23]; treasures consecrated to treasury of tabern. or temple Jos 6[19] (E) 1 K 7[51] +; consecrated things in gen. Ex 28[38] (P), Ez 20[40] 22[8] +; these may be †קדשׁ (ה)קדשׁים Ez 44[13], so חֵרֶם Lv 27[28]. **d.** anointing oil of priest Ex 30[25.25] + 5 t. (P), ψ 89[21]; incense Ex 30[35.37], ק׳ קדשׁים v[36]; shew-bread 1 S 21[5], קדשׁ (ה)ק׳ Lv 24[9] cf. 21[22a] (P); foretold of common articles, ק׳ לי׳ Zc 14[20.21]. On ק׳ הקדשׁים v. also Di[Ex 26, 33 Lv 21, 22] We[Comp. 160 f.] Dr[Dn 9, 24]. **4.** persons sacred by connex. with sacred places: **a.** priests Lv 21[6] 2 Ch 23[6] 31[18] Ezr 8[28], garments of priesthood Ex 28[2.4] + 7 t. Ex, Lv 16[4.32] Ez 42[14], specif. of h. priest כתנת ק׳ Lv 16[4], נֵזֶר הק׳ Ex 29[6] 39[30] Lv 8[9]; inscription on head piece קדשׁ ליהוה Ex 28[36] 39[30]. **b.** of Israel, קדשׁ לי׳ Je 2[3], היתה לקדשׁו ψ 114[2], עם (ה)קדשׁ Is 62[12] Dn 12[7], עם קדשׁך Is 63[18]; זֶרַע (ה)קדשׁ Is 6[13] Ezr 9[2]; אַנְשֵׁי קדשׁ Ex 22[30] (R), and so spoil for their use Is 23[18]; holy adornment הַדְרַת ק׳ 1 Ch 16[29] 2 Ch 20[21] ψ 29[2] 96[9]; הַדְרֵי ק׳ ψ 110[3] (but rd. הַרְרֵי see **2 e**; הָדָר **1**); covt. between God and his people ברית ק׳ Dn 11[28.30.30]. **5.** times consecrated to worship: שׁבת Ex 16[23] 31[14.15] 35[2] (P) Ne 9[14]; of שׁבת also יום ק׳ Is 58[13]; disting. fr. שׁבת Ne 10[32]; יובל Lv 25[12] (P); assembly called at stated times for worship מקרא(י) ק׳ Ex 12[16.16] + 17 t. Lv 23 Nu 28 (all P). †**6.** of things and persons ceremonially cleansed, and so separated as sacred; things 1 S 21[6]; flesh Je 11[15] Mal 2[11]; priests cleanse thus, 1 Ch 23[13.28]; בין (ה)קדשׁ לחל Ez 22[26] 42[20] 44[23]; בין הק׳ ובין החל Lv 10[10]; דֶּרֶךְ הק׳ Is 35[8] way of the clean; שְׂאוּ יְדֵכֶם ק׳ ψ 134[2]; לְבֵיתְךָ נַאֲוָה־ק׳ ψ 93[5].—*Note:* מֵרִבְבֹת קֹדֶשׁ Dt 33[2] is lit. *from myriads of sacredness, sacred myriads;* but ‖ suggests n.pr.loc., 𝔊 *σὺν μυριάσιν* Καδής, < מִמְּרִבַת קָדֵשׁ *from Meribah Kadesh* Di Buhl Steuern.; or (מִן om.) *to M. Kadesh*
We[Prol. 364; 3rd ed. 359; Hist. 344]; v. קָדֵשׁ and Dr[Dt.]. p. 873f 6946

†קָדוֹשׁ **adj.** sacred, holy;—abs. ק׳ Ex 6918
19[6] +; קָדֹשׁ Ex 29[31] +; cstr. קְדוֹשׁ Is 1[4] +; קְדֹשׁ Is 49[7] + 2 t.; sf. קְדֹשִׁי Hb 1[12]; קְדוֹשׁוֹ Is 10[17] 49[7] קְדוֹשְׁכֶם Is 43[15]; pl. קְדוֹשִׁים Ho 12[1] + 2 t., קְדֹשִׁים Lv 11[44] + 16 t.; sf. קְדֹשָׁיו Dt 33[3] ψ 34[10], קְדֹשָׁו Jb 15[15];—**1.** of God, as separate, apart, and so *sacred, holy:* **a.** exalted on theophanic throne Is 6[3.3.3], ψ 22[4]; heavenly throne Is 57[15]; in victory 5[16] 1 S 2[2] ψ 99[3] (‖נוֹרָא), v[5.9]; ק׳ וְנוֹרָא שְׁמוֹ 111[9]. **b.** separate from human infirmity, impurity, and sin: Jos 24[19] (E), 1 S 6[20] Hb 1[12]; כי קדושׁ אני Lv 11[44.45] 19[2] 20[26] 21[8] (H); קדושׁ בְּקִרְבְּךָ Ho 11[9]; ק׳ בישׂראל Ez 39[7]. **c.** קְדוֹשׁ יִשְׂרָאֵל = divine name (originating fr. *trisagion,* Is 6[3]) Is 1[4] 5[19.24] 10[20] 12[6] 17[7] 29[19] 30[11.12.15] 31[1]; Is[2] 41[14.16.20] 43[3.14] 45[11] 47[4] 48[17] 49[7] 54[5] 55[5] 60[9.14] elsewhere only 2 K 19[22] = Is 37[23], Je 50[29] 51[5] ψ 71[22] 78[41] 89[19]; ק׳ יעקב Is 29[23], קְדוֹשׁוֹ 10[17] 49[7], קְדוֹשְׁכֶם 43[15]; קָדוֹשׁ 40[25] Hb 3[3] Jb 6[10], pl. intens. קד(ו)שׁים Ho 12[1] Pr 9[10] 30[3]. **2. a.** of place, *sacred, holy,* chambers of priests Ez 42[13], camp of Isr. Dt 23[15], + מָרוֹם of heaven Is 57[15] (but of י׳ Du Ry, and [rdg. בְּק׳ *as holy,* ב essent.] Klo Che Marti); in foll. (oft. defect.) pointing dub., rd. prob. קֹדֶשׁ **2**: מק(ו)ם ק׳ of the court of tabernacle, Ex 29[31] Lv 6[9.19.20] 7[6] 10[13] 16[24] 24[9] (P), of Jerusalem Ec 8[10]; ק׳ מִשְׁכְּנֵי עליון ψ 46[5]; ק׳ הֵיכָלֶךָ 65[5]. **b.** persons: priests Lv 21[7.8] Nu 16[5.7] (P), Aaron ψ 106[16], Levites 2 Ch 35[3], prophet 2 K 4[9], Nazirite Nu 6[5.8] (P), Isr. גּוֹי ק׳ Ex 19[6] (E), עם ק׳ Dt 7[6] 14[2.21] 26[19] 28[9]; כָּל־הָעֵדָה Nu 16[3] (P); remnant in Jerus. Is 4[3]; קדשׁים *sacred* Lv 11[44.45] 19[2] 20[7.26] 21[6] Nu 15[40]; קדשׁים *sacred ones, saints* Dt 33[3] (song), ψ 16[3] 34[10] Dn 8[24]. **c.** angels, ψ 89[6.8] Jb 5[1] 15[15] Zc 14[5] Dn 8[13.13]. **d.** מים קדשׁים Nu 5[17] *holy water.* **e.** time הַיּוֹם ק׳ (לי׳) Ne 8[9.10.11];
קְדוֹשׁ י׳ Is 58[13], of Sabbath.—(Cf. BAram. קַדִּישׁ). 6922

†קָדַשׁ **vb. denom.** be set apart, conse- 6942
crated (Gerber[238 ff.]);—**Qal** *Pf.* 3 ms. ק׳ Ex 29[21]; sf. קִדַּשְׁתִּיךָ Is 65[5]; 3 mpl. קָדֵשׁוּ Nu 17[2]; *Impf.* 3 ms. יִקְדַּשׁ 1 S 21[6]; יִקְדָּשׁ Ex 29[37] +, etc.;—**1.** *be set apart, consecrated,* hallowed, of shew-bread 1 S 21[6] (dub. passage, but cf. esp. RS[Sem. i. 436; 2nd ed. 455] [also Dr[Sm. 293]], who prop. יֻקְדַּשׁ); Aaron and his sons by blood Ex 29[21] (P); other persons Is 65[5] (Di; but **Pi.** Gei RS[Sem. i. 431; 2nd ed. 451] Che Du Buhl). **2.** *be hallowed,* by contact with sacred things, and so tabooed from

profane use, or forfeited to sanctuary Ex 29[37] 30[29] Lv 6[11.20] Nu 17[2.3] (P), Hg 2[12]. **3.** *consecrated, tabooed* (supr.) Dt 22[9] (law against mixtures). **Niph.** *Pf.* 3 ms. נִקְדַּשׁ Is 5[16] Ex 29[43], etc.; *Impf.* 3 ms. וַיִּקָּדֵשׁ Nu 20[13]; 1 s. אֶקָּדֵשׁ Lv 10[3]; *Inf. cstr.* sf. הִקָּדְשִׁי Ez 36[23] 38[16];—**1.** *shew oneself sacred, majestic:* c. בְּ pers., + לְעֵינֵי Ez 20[41] 28[25] 36[23] 38[16] 39[27]; c. בְּ Is 5[16] Ez 28[22], cf. Nu 20[13] (P). **2.** *be honoured* or *treated as sacred* ‖ נכבד Lv 10[3] (P); opp. חלל שׁם Lv 22[32] (P). **3.** *be consecrated, dedicated,* by כבוד י׳ Ex 29[43] (P). **Pi.** *Pf.* 3 ms. קִדַּשׁ Nu 6[11] 1 K 8[64], etc.; *Impf.* 3 ms. יְקַדֵּשׁ Gn 2[3] +, etc.; *Imv.* ms. קַדֵּשׁ Jos 7[13]; קַדֶּשׁ־ Ex 13[2], etc.; *Inf. cstr.* קַדֵּשׁ Ex 29[1] +, etc.; *Pt.* מְקַדֵּשׁ Ex 37[28]; sf. מְקַדִּשְׁכֶם Ex 31[13] +, etc.;—**1.** *set apart as sacred, consecrate, dedicate:* **a.** places: Sinai Ex 19[23] (J), altar, etc., Ex 29[36.37] 30[29] (P), tabern., etc. Ex 40[9.10.11] Lv 8[10.11.15] Nu 7[1.1] (P); tent of meeting Ex 29[44] (P); place of sacrifice 1 K 8[64] = 2 Ch 7[7]; gate Ne 3[1.1];—Ez 7[24] v. מִקְדָּשׁ infr. **b.** wave-offering Ex 29[27] (P). **c.** persons: priests Ex 28[3.41] 29[1.33.44] 30[30] 40[13] Lv 8[12.30]; firstborn Ex 13[2] (P); keepers of ark 1 S 7[1]. †**d.** 7th day (by God) Gn 2[3] Ex 20[11] (P). **2.** *observe as holy, keep sacred:* feasts, Sabbath Ex 20[8] = Dt 5[12] (Decal.), Je 17[22.24.27] Ez 20[20] 44[24] Ne 13[22]; fast Jo 1[14] 2[15]; year of Jubilee Lv 25[10] (P); so עצרה לבעל 2 K 10[20]. **3.** *honour as sacred, hallow:* **a.** God Dt 32[51], his name Ez 36[23]. **b.** priest Lv 21[8] (H). **4.** *consecrate* by purification: **a.** places, house of י׳ 2 Ch 29[5.17.17], altar מִטֻּמְאֹת Lv 16[19]. **b.** people העם Jos 7[13] (J), Ez 44[19] 46[20]; by washing Ex 19[10.14] (E); קהל for fast Jo 2[16]; Nazirite Nu 6[11] (P), sons of Job Jb 1[5]; family for sacrif. 1 S 16[5]. **c.** war, or warriors, fr. custom of opening campaign by sacrifice, ק׳ מִלְחָמָה (עַל) Je 6[4] Jo 4[9] Mi 3[5]; Je 22[7] 51[27.28]. **d.** of God, keeping his people pure and sacred: אני יהוה מְקַדֵּשׁ Ex 31[13] Lv 20[8] 21[8.15.23] 22[9.16.32] (H), Ez 20[12] 37[28]. **Pu.** *Pt.* מְקֻדָּשׁ Ez 48[11], etc.;—*consecrated, dedicated:* priests 2 Ch 26[18] Ez 48[11] (rd. pl.), things 2 Ch 31[6], feasts Ezr 3[5], warriors Is 13[3]. **Hiph.** *Pf.* 3 ms. הִקְדִּישׁ Zp 1[7] +, etc.; *Impf.* יַקְדִּישׁ Lv 27[16] + 4 t., יַקְדִּשׁ Lv 27[14], etc.; *Imv.* sf. הַקְדִּשֵׁם Je 12[3]; *Inf. abs.* הַקְדֵּשׁ Ju 17[3]; *cstr.* הַקְדִּישׁ 2 Ch 2[3] +, etc.; *Pt.* מַקְדִּישׁ Lv 27[15] +, etc. **1.** *set apart, devote, consecrate:* **a.** places, temple 2 Ch 2[3], city Jos 20[7] (P). **b.** things Ex 28[38] Lv 22[2.3] (P) 2 K 12[19] 1 Ch 23[13] 26[26.27.28.28] Ne 12[47.47]; money Ju 17[3.3]; spoil 2 S 8[11.11] = 1 Ch 18[11]; field Lv 27[16.17.18.19.22] (H); house Lv 27[14.15] (H); firstlings Dt 15[19] (D) Lv 27[26] (H). **c.** of God: *consecrate* temple 1 K 9[3.7] = 2 Ch 7[16.20], 2 Ch 30[8] 36[14]; prophet Je 1[5]; firstborn Nu 3[13] 8[17] (P); devote wicked (as sheep) for sacrifice Je 12[3]. **2.** *regard,* or *treat, as sacred, hallow:* God Is 8[13] 29[23.23]; + לְעֵינֵי pers. Nu 20[12] 27[14]. **3.** *consecrate* by purification: vessels 2 Ch 29[19]; persons for passover 30[17]; guests for sacrif. feast Zp 1[7] (God subj.). **Hithp.** *Pf.* 1 s. הִתְקַדִּשְׁתִּי Ez 38[23], 2 mpl. (consec.) -דִּשְׁתֶּם Lv 11[44] 20[7], 3 pl. הִתְקַדָּשׁוּ 2 Ch 5[11] 30[17], etc.; *Impf.* 3 ms. יִתְקַדְּשׁוּ 2 Ch 29[34] +; יִתְקַדָּשׁוּ Ex 19[22]; *Imv.* mpl. הִתְקַדְּשׁוּ Nu 11[18] +; הִתְקַדָּשׁוּ Jos 3[5]; *Inf. cstr.* הִתְקַדֵּשׁ 2 Ch 29[34]; הִתְקַדֶּשׁ־ Is 30[29]; *Pt.* fs. מִתְקַדֶּשֶׁת 2 S 11[4]; pl. מִתְקַדְּשִׁים Is 66[17];—**1.** *keep oneself apart* from unclean things Lv 11[44] 20[7] (P). **2.** of God, *cause himself to be hallowed,* לְעֵינֵי גּוֹיִם Ez 38[23]. **3.** *be observed as holy,* of feast Is 30[29]. **4.** *consecrate oneself* by purification, of priests and Levites Ex 19[22] (J), 1 Ch 15[12.14] 2 Ch 5[11] 29[5.15.34.34] 30[3.15.24] 31[18] 35[6]; of people Nu 11[18] Jos 3[5] 7[13] (J) 1 S 16[5] 2 Ch 30[17] Is 66[17]; woman 2 S 11[4] *she having (just) purified herself* מִטֻּמְאָתָהּ RS[K. 276] Dr HPS.

†I. קָדֵשׁ **n.m.** **temple-prostitute** (man) (cf. 6945
RS[Proph. ii, N. 19], and v. As. sub √);—ק׳ Dt 23[18];
coll. 1 K 14[24] 22[47]; pl. קְדֵשִׁים 15[12] 2 K 23[7] Jb 36[14];
also f. קְדֵשָׁה (woman) Dt 23[18]; pl. קְדֵשׁוֹת Ho 4[14]; 6948
=*harlot,* fs. Gn 38[21.21.22] (J).

†קֶ֫דֶשׁ **n.pr.loc.** (*sanctuary*) Καδης: **1.** in 6943
Galilee Jos 20[7] 21[32] (P), 1 Ch 6[61]; Naphtali Jos 19[37] (P), ק׳ נַפְתָּלִי Ju 4[6]; = קֶדֶשׁ alone Jos 12[22] (D; with king); Ju 4[9.10] + v[11] (where poss. different place on sea of Galilee, v. GFM[Ju 117, 119]), also 2 K 15[29]; TelAm. *Ḳidši;* Eg. *Ḳdšě* WMM[As. u. Eur. 173, 217]; mod. *Kades,* NW. of Lake Huleh; v. Rob[BR iii. 366 ff.] Survey[WP i. 226 ff.] Buhl[Geogr. 235 f.]. **2.** Κεδες: city of refuge in Issachar 1 Ch 6[57] = קִשְׁיוֹן Jos 21[28]; poss. *Tel Abu Kudeis* [Survey[WP i. 69]], c. 2 miles SE. from *Lejjun* (*Megiddo*): cf. Buhl[Geogr. 209]. **3.** Καδης: in S. Judah; Jos 15[23] (P) (= II. קָדֵשׁ **1**? if so, then Mass. distinction from קֶדֶשׁ in N. was here neglected).

†II. קָדֵשׁ **n.pr.loc.** (*sacred;* but perh. orig. 6946-47
קֶדֶשׁ, and pointing artif. to disting. fr. ק׳ in N);
—**1.** Καδης: in S. of Judah Gn 16[14] (J), 20[1] (E), in מִדְבַּר פָּארָן Nu 13[26] (P), specif. מ׳ צִן 20[1] 33[36], cf. מ׳ קָדֵשׁ ψ 29[8]; on W. border of Edom Nu 20[16] (E), 33[37] (P), cf. 20[14] (E), v[22] (P), Ju 11[16.17] (hence Rob[BR ii. 175, 194] sought it at *ʿAin Weibeh,* in W. of Arabah); long abode of Isr. during Exod. Dt 1[46]; מֵי מְרִיבַת ק׳ Nu 27[14] (cf. 20[1-13]),
Dt 32[51] (P), Ez 47[19] (rd. מְרִיבַת), 48[28], cf. Dt 33[2] 6944

5880,6944, (v. קֹדֶשׁ ad fin.); cf. עֵין מִשְׁפָּט Gn 14[7]; ק׳ בַּרְנֵעַ=
6947 (meaning of ב׳ unknown; 𝔊 K. (τοῦ) βαρνη);—
Nu 32[8] (J), Dt 1[2.19] 2[14] 9[23] Jos 10[41] 14[6] (D), Nu
34[4] Jos 15[3] (P);—mod. *'Ain Ḳadîs* (*Ḳudais*,
قُدَيْس), c. 50 miles S. of Beersheba, JRowlands
(1842) v. GWilliams[Holy City, 464 f.], and especially
HCTrumbull (1881) [Kadesh Barnea, 238–321]. **2.**
Hittite capital on the Orontes, N. of Damascus,
towards Hamath (Eg. *Ḳdš*, *Ḳdšu*, *Ḳdšĕ*, WMM
[As. u. Eur. 213 ff.]);—2 S 24[6] 𝔊L We Dr Kit Bu Löhr,
8483 rdg. א׳ תַּחְתִּים חָדְשִׁי for MT אֶרֶץ הַחִתִּים קָדֵשָׁה
(הַחִתִּים already Hi[Gesch. Isr. i. 29]; קֶדְשָׁה Th, קֶדֶשְׁה
Klo, of קֶדֶשׁ in Napht.); HPS doubts.

4720 מִקְדָּשׁ[74] **n.m.**[Am 7, 9] **sacred place, sanctuary**;—מ׳ Ex 25[8]+; מִקְּדָשׁ 15[17] (Ges[§ 20 h] Kö
[ii. 1, 471]); cstr. מִקְדַּשׁ Lv 16[33]+; sf. מִקְדָּשִׁי Lv 20[3]+,
etc., מִקְדְּשׁוֹ Nu 18[29] (Kö[ii. 1, 97]); pl. מִקְדָּשִׁים Ez 21[7],
cstr. מִקְדְּשֵׁי Je 51[51]+2 t.; sf. מִקְדָּשַׁי Lv 21[23];
מְקַדְשֵׁיהֶם Ez 7[24] (on anomalous pointing v. Ew
[§ 215 a] Hi-Sm; but prob. **Pi.** *Pt.* was in mind,
Ges[§ 93 oo Anm.]; < rd. מִקְדְּשֵׁיהֶם); etc.;—**1.** old Isr.
sanctuaries: of י׳ at Shechem Jos 24[26] (E); prob.
also Ex 15[17] (i.e. Shiloh); pl. of sanct. to be
destroyed by י׳ Lv 26[31] (H); מִקְדְּשֵׁי יִשׂ׳ in N. Isr.
Am 7[9]; מִקְדַּשׁ־מֶלֶךְ v[13] (Bethel). **2.** of the
nations: Moab Is 16[12] pl. of Tyre Ez 28[18] (Co Toy
[not Berthol Krae] read קָדְשְׁךָ *thy sanctity*).
3. tabernacle and its precincts Ex 25[8] (P)+;
מִקְדַּשׁ הַקֹּדֶשׁ Lv 16[33], pl. 21[23]. **4.** temple and
precincts 1 Ch 22[19] Is 63[18] ψ 74[7]+; בֵּית מִקְדָּשָׁם
2 Ch 36[17], מקדש הבית Ez 48[21], מְכוֹן מ׳ Dn 8[11]; pl.
of many sacred places in and about the temple,
מִקְדְּשֵׁי בית י׳ Je 51[51]; מִקְדְּשֵׁי אֵל ψ 73[17]. Doubtful
are: מִמִּקְדָּשֶׁיךָ ψ 68[36] (𝔊 ἐν τοῖς ὁσίοις αὐτοῦ;
𝔙 *de sanctuario*; SS מִקְּדָשֶׁךָ); מִקְדָּשִׁים Ez 21[7]
(𝔊 Co Berthol Buhl מִקְדָּשָׁם; Toy Krae מִקְדָּשֶׁיהָ;
‖ יְרוּשָׁלַםִ); וּמִקְדָּשׁ לַמִּקְדָּשׁ Ez 45[4 b] (Co, after 𝔊,
[לְבָתִּים] וּלְמִגְרָשִׁים; Toy [לְבָתֵּי] מִפְקַד לְקָדְשָׁם, cf.
Krae לְמִגְרָשׁ). **5.** י׳ will become לְמ׳ for his
people Ez 11[16] (Br[MP 268]), so appar. Is 8[14] (but
gloss Du Che[Hpt] Marti; Lag[Sem. i. 16] מִקֹּשׁ i.e.
stumbling-block [he cp. Syr. ܢܩܫ *strike*]). **6.**
of י׳'s future sanct., מ׳ בתוכם לעולם Ez 37[26.28].—
(מִכָּל־חֶלְבּוֹ) אֶת־מִקְדְּשׁוֹ (מִמֶּנּוּ) Nu 18[29] *even the
hallowed part thereof* AV RV, but this not the
meaning of מ׳; Ew[§ 255 c] assumes מַקְדֵּשׁ* in this
6944 sense; < rd. קָדְשׁוֹ (v. קֹדֶשׁ **3 d**), מ being dittogr.
p. 872
6949 †[קָהָה] **vb.** be blunt, dull (NH *id.*;
Aram. קְהָא, ܩܗܐ);—**Qal** *Impf.* 3 fpl. תִּקְהֶינָה
Je 31[29.30] Ez 18[2] (all of teeth). **Pi.** in sense of
Qal: *Pf.* 3 ms. קֵהָה Ec 10[10] *if the iron be blunt.*

†[קִהָיוֹן] **n.**[**m.**] **bluntness** (Lag[BN 201]);— 5356
rd. perh. cstr. קִהְיוֹן Am 4[6] (for נִקְיוֹן; v. נָקִיּוֹן). 5356
p. 667
קהל (√ of following; cf. Sab. קהל, קהלת
assembly, congregation DHM[ZMG xxx (1876), 685] Hom
[Chrest. 127]; Saho *kahal, come together, assemble*
Reinisch[Saho Spr. 210]; Syr. ܩܗܠ *assemble*, ChrPal.
ܩܗܠܐ, λαός; NH Hiph.=BH; Lag[BN 51] cp. Ar.
قَهَلَ *rebuke*, and conj. קָהָל='Rügegericht').

קָהָל[123] **n.m.**[Ez 38, 15] **assembly, convocation,** 6951
congregation;—abs. ק׳ Je 31[8]+; cstr. קְהַל Ex
12[6]+; sf. קְהָלְךָ Ez 38[13], etc.; pl. sf. קְהָלֶיךָ Ez
38[7];—**1.** *assembly* specially convoked: †**a.** for
evil counsel, ‖ סוד Gn 49[6] (poem); ק׳ מרעים
ψ 26[5]; for civil affairs Pr 5[14] (v. Toy), 26[26] Jb
30[28] (Di *publice*). **b.** for war or invasion,
Nu 22[4] (E), Ju 20[2] 21[5.8] 1 S 17[47] Ez 16[40] 38[7] (pl.
only here), + 8 t. Ez; ק׳ גדול (‖ חיל רב) Ez 38[15];
ק׳ רב (‖ חיל גדול) 17[17] 38[4]; ק׳ גוים Je 50[9];
ק׳ עמים Ez 23[24] 32[3]. **c.** *company* of returning
exiles, Je 31[8] Ezr 2[64]=Ne 7[66]. **d.** for religious
purposes, to hear words of י׳ at Horeb Dt 5[19],
ביום הק׳ Dt 9[10] 10[4] (gloss, not in 𝔊), 18[16]; word
of Jer. Je 26[17] 44[15]; for feasts, fasts and worship
2 Ch 20[5] 30[25.25] Ne 5[13] Jo 2[16] ψ 107[32]; ק׳ רב 22[26]
+4 t.; ק׳ גדול 2 Ch 30[13]; וַיֵּאָסְפוּ . . . ק׳ לרב מְאֹד
1 K 8[65]=2 Ch 7[8]; בתוך (ה)ק׳ 2 Ch 20[14] ψ 22[23].
2. *congregation*, as organized body: **a.** of Isr.:
ק׳ יהוה Mi 2[5] Nu 16[3] 20[4] (P), 1 Ch 28[8]; (בא בק׳ (י׳
Dt 23[2.3.3.4.4.9] Ne 13[1] La 1[10]; כל ק׳ ישׂראל Dt 31[30]
Jos 8[35] (D) Lv 16[17] (P) 1 K 8[14.14.22.55]=2 Ch 6[3.3.12.13],
1 K 12[3] 1 Ch 13[2]; כל ק׳ עדת ישׂראל Ex 12[6] (𝔊
rds. בני before יִשׂ׳), Nu 14[5] (P; 𝔊 συναγωγή; MT
prob. conflation); כל הק׳ כל עם הק׳ Lv 16[33]; הק׳
Ex 16[3] (P) 1 Ch 13[4]+12 t. Ch; הק׳ Lv 4[13.14.21]
+8 t. Nu (P), 8 t. 2 Ch. **b.** restored community in Jerus. Ezr 10[12.14] Ne 8[2.17]; ק׳ הַגּוֹלָה Ezr
10[8]; later the better part of it, ק׳ חסידים ψ 149[1].
c. of angels, ק׳ קדשים ψ 89[6]. **d.** more gen.:
company, assembled multitude, ק׳ גוים Gn 35[11]
(P), ק׳ עמים Gn 28[3] 48[4] (P), ק׳ רפאים Pr 21[16].

†[קָהַל] **vb. denom.** (Gerber[107 f.]) **assemble** 6950
as a קָהָל;—**Niph.** *Pf.* 3 mpl. נִקְהֲלוּ Est 9[2]+
3 t.; *Impf.* 3 ms. וַיִּקָּהֵל Ex 32[1] Je 26[9]; 3 mpl.
וַיִּקָּהֲלוּ 2 S 20[14] Qr (Kt ויקלהו, cf. HPS), etc.; *Inf.* 7035
cstr. הִקָּהֵל Nu 17[7] Est 8[11]; *Pt.* pl. נִקְהָלִים Ez
38[7];—*assemble as a* קָהָל: **1. a.** for conflict or
war 2 S 20[14] (Qr; v. supr.), Est 8[11] 9[2.15.16.18]; c.
עַל pers. Ez 38[7], acc. loc. Jos 22[12] Ju 20[1]. **b.**
rebellion, c. עַל pers. Nu 16[3] 17[7] 20[2] (P), poss.

also Ex 32¹ (J; most, *unto* Aaron). **2.** for religious purpose: to erect tent of meeting, acc. loc. Jos 18¹ (P); hear word of 'י, c. אֶל loc. Lv 8⁴ (P), ב loc. + אֶל pers. Je 26⁹; for festival, אֶל pers. 1 K 8²=2 Ch 5³; לְ loc. 2 Ch 20²⁶. **Hiph.** *Pf.* 2 ms. הִקְהַלְתָּ Ez 38¹³, וְהִקְהַלְתָּ Nu 8⁹; 3 mpl. הִקְהִילוּ 1¹⁸; *Impf.* 3 ms. יַקְהִיל Jb 11¹⁰; אָז יַקְהֵל 1 K 8¹ = יַקְהֵל 2 Ch 5²; וַיַּקְהֵל Ex 35¹ + (**Qal** *Impf.* in *i* acc. to Ba[NB p. 147]); pl. וַיַּקְהִלוּ Nu 20¹⁰; *Imv.* ms. הַקְהֵל Lv 8³ +, etc.; *Inf. cstr.* הַקְהִיל Nu 10⁷; — *summon an assembly*: **1. a.** for judgment Jb 11¹⁰. **b.** for war 1 K 12²¹ = 2 Ch 11¹, Ez 38¹³. **2.** for *religious purposes*: c. acc. אֶת־הַקָּהָל Nu 10⁷, + אֶל loc. 20¹⁰, c. acc. (כָּל־)הָעֵדָה Ex 35¹ Nu 1¹⁸ 8⁹ 20⁸ (P), + אֶל loc. Lv 8³ Nu 16¹⁹ (P); c. acc. הָעָם Dt 4¹⁰ 31¹²; כָּל־יִשְׂרָאֵל 1 Ch 13⁵ 15³; elders of tribes Dt 31²⁸, of Isr. 1 K 8¹ = 2 Ch 5²; princes of Isr. 1 Ch 28¹.

6952 †קְהִלָּה **n.f. assembly, congregation**;— abs. 'ק Ne 5⁷; cstr. קְהִלַּת Dt 33⁴ (poem).

6953 †קֹהֶלֶת, (†קוֹהֶלֶת Ec 12⁸) **n.m.** [Ec 1, 2] **collector** (of sentences), or (AV RV) **preacher** (*concionator* Jer.: ἐκκλησιαστής 𝔊 (member of an ἐκκλησία); fem. either of office, Ges[§122r] De Now Che, cf. סֹפֶרֶת Ezr 2⁵⁵; خَلِيفَةٌ, *Khalif;* Germ. *Majestät, Excellenz;* or as in Ar. with intensive force, one realizing the idea in its completeness (cf. جَمَّاعَةٌ *great collector,* بَاقِرَةٌ *deep investigator* (formed like קֹהֶלֶת), W[AG i. § 233 R. c] v. Dr[Intr. 466]; RVm *great orator*): hence either *convener*, or *great collector* (of sentences), cf. בַּעֲלֵי אֲסֻפּוֹת Ec 12¹¹, בקש ק׳ למצא דברי חפץ v¹⁰ (but Kö[Einl. 428] Dr[l. c.] al. *speaker in assembly*, Plumptre *debater*));—'ק a king in Jerus., son of David, prob. = Sol., the pseudonym of book of Ec.: Ec 1¹, v² (appos. of אֲנִי), called חכם 12⁹, cf. v¹⁰; אמר ק׳ 1², אמר הק׳ 12⁸ + 7²⁷ for MT אמרה ק׳.

6954 †קְהֵלָתָה **n.pr.** (*assembly*) station of Isr. in wilderness Nu 33²²·²³ (P); 𝔊 Μακελλαθ.

4721 †[מַקְהֵל] **n.[m.] assembly**, for worship, pl.: poss. **choirs**, מַקְהֵלִים ψ 26¹², מַקְהֵלוֹת 68²⁷.

4722 †מַקְהֵלֹת **n.pr.loc.** (*place of assembly*);— station of Isr. in Exod. Nu 33²⁵·²⁶ (P); 𝔊 Μακηλωθ.

6955 קְהָת 30 **n.pr.m.** Κααθ: son of Levi Gn 46¹¹ Ex 6¹⁶ Nu 3¹⁷ 1 Ch 5²⁷ 6¹ 23⁶, cf. Ex 6¹⁸ Nu 26⁵⁸ and בֶּן־ק׳ Nu 16¹ 1 Ch 6²³; בְּנֵי ק׳ Ex 6¹⁸ + 4 t. Ch; as a division of Levites Nu 3¹⁹·²⁹ + 9 t.; מִשְׁפְּחוֹת ב׳ ק׳ Jos 21²⁰·²⁶ 1 Ch 6⁵¹, מִשְׁפַּחַת לִב׳ ק׳ v⁵⁵.— Van d. H. has קֳהָת Nu 3¹⁹ + 7 t.

†קְהָתִי **adj. gent.** of foreg., c. art. 'הַק as subst. coll.: מִשְׁפַּחַת (-וֹת) הַקּ׳ Nu 26⁵⁷ + 8 t.; בְּנֵי הַקּ׳ Nu 4³⁴ 1 Ch 6¹⁸ 2 Ch 29¹²; pl. הַקְּהָתִים Nu 10²¹ and בְּנֵי הַקּ׳ 2 Ch 20¹⁹ 34¹².—Van d. H. has הַקֳּהָתִי(ם) Nu 3²⁷ 10²¹ + 6 t. 6956

I. קַו only in קַו לָקָו Is 28¹⁰·¹⁰·¹³·¹³, mimicry of Isaiah's words, perh. senseless, v. צַו p. 846. 6957

II. קַו v. I. קוה. p. 876 6957

†קוֹבַע **n.[m.] helmet** (word of peculiar form, and dub. √; prob. foreign word; cf. Eth. ቆብዕ: *turban, tiara, cowl,* so Syr. ܩܘܒܥܐ; 𝔗 קוּבְעָא *turban*);—abs. 'ק Ez 23²⁴; cstr. קוֹבַע נְחֹשֶׁת 1 S 17³⁸.—Cf. also כּוֹבַע. 6959

קוא only in מִקְוֵא v. II. מִקְוֶה sub II. קוה. p. 876 4723

†קְוֵה, or קְוֵא **n.pr.terr.** Kuë in Cilicia 4723
(cf. KAT[2. 257]); מִקְוֵה *from Kuë*, for MT מִקְוֵה 1 K 4723
10²⁸·²⁸ and ‖ מִקְוֵא 2 Ch 1¹⁶·¹⁶; so Wkl[Alttest. Unters. 173] 4723
Gr Benz Kit, cf. 𝔊 ἐκ Θεκουε (also ἐκ Κωα Field Hexapla i. 616), 𝔙 *de Coa*, Κωδ Lag[Onom. 273], Jer *Coa* Id.[ibid. 111].

†I. [קָוָה] **vb. wait for** (prob. orig. *twist, stretch,* then of *tension* of enduring, waiting: As. *ḳu'û* II, 1. *wait*, *ḳû*, *cord;* Ar. قَوِيَ *be strong*, قُوَّةٌ *strength*, also *strand* of rope; Syr. ܩܘܐ *endure, remain, await*, ܩܘܐ̈ *threads*, so 𝔗 קוּיָן spider's *threads, web*);—**Qal** *Pt.* pl. *those waiting for* ('י): cstr. קֹוֵי י׳ ψ 37⁹; so Is 40³¹ van d. H., and Kt Baer Gi (Qr קוֹיֵי); sf. קֹוָי 49²³, קֹוֶיךָ ψ 25³ 69⁷; קֹוָיו La 3³⁵ Qr (Kt קוו, i.e. קֹוָו). **Pi.** *Pf.* 3 fs. קִוְּתָה ψ 130⁵; 1 s. קִוִּיתִי Gn 49¹⁸ + 5 t., וְק׳ Is 5⁴, קִוֵּיתִי consec. 8¹⁷; sf. קִוִּיתִיךָ ψ 25²¹; 3 pl. קִוּוּ ψ 56⁷ +, etc.; *Impf.* יְקַוֶּה Mi 5⁶ Jb 7², juss. יְקַו Jb 3⁹, וַיְקַו Is 5²·⁷, etc.; *Imv.* ms. קַוֵּה Ho 12⁷ +; *Inf. abs.* קַוֹּה ψ 40², קַוֵּה Je 8¹⁵ 14¹⁹;— **1.** *wait*, or *look eagerly, for*, c. לְ rei Is 5⁷ 59⁹·¹¹ Je 8¹⁵, 13¹⁶ 14¹⁹ Jb 3⁹ 6¹⁹; לִישׁוּעָתְךָ Gn 49¹⁸; c. acc. rei La 2¹⁶ (sf.), Jb 7² 30²⁶ ψ 39⁸; obj. rei om. Is 64²; sq. inf. Is 5²·⁴ ψ 69²¹; abs. Jb 17¹³; c. acc. 'י Is 26⁸ (sf.), ψ 25⁵·²¹ (sf.), 40² (+ inf. abs.), 130⁵, acc. om. v⁵, acc. שִׁמְךָ ψ 52¹¹ (but rd. prob. אֲחַוֶּה, Hi Che Bae al., v. III. חוה); c. לְ of 'י Is 8¹⁷ 25⁹·⁹ 33² 60⁹ (but rd. prob. צִיִּים יִקָּווּ *ships shall gather* (II. קוה), so Du Che[Hpt] Di-Kit Marti, cf. Skinner (also Luzz Gei Oort), Je 14²² Pr 20²²; c. אֶל־י׳ אֶל־אֱלֹהִים Ho 12⁷, Is 51⁵ ψ 27¹⁴·¹⁴ 37³⁴. **2.** *lie in wait for*, sq. נַפְשִׁי ψ 56⁷; sq. לְ pers. ψ 119⁹⁵ (+ inf. purpose). **3.** *wait* (*linger*) *for* c. לְ of man Mi 5⁶ (‖ יְיַחֵל).

6957 †II. קַו **n.m.**[Zc 1, 16] line (cf. Kö[ii. 1, 40 Anm. 2]);—
6961 abs. קַו Ez 47[3] + Zc 1[16] Qr (Kt קוה), קָו Is 34[17] +; cstr. קַו 2 K 21[13] +;—measuring-*line* (ק׳ מִדָּה Je 31[39]): 1 K 7[23] (Qr; Kt קוה, v. infr.) = 2 Ch 4[2], Ez 47[3]; for marking off a possession in land Is 34[17] (fig.); esp. נָטָה ק׳ עַל, in building, Jb 38[5] (fig. of earth), Zc 1[16] (יִבָּנֶה ‖ יִנָּטֶה; so יָצָא ק׳ Je 31[39] (Qr; Kt קוה); נָטָה ק׳ of designing idol Is 44[13]; marking off for destruction, נָטָה ק׳ עַל 2 K 21[13] Is 34[11] (קַו־תֹהוּ ‖ אַבְנֵי־בֹהוּ), נ׳ ק׳ La 2[8]; so וְשַׂמְתִּי מִשְׁפָּט לְקָו Is 28[17].—קַוָּם ψ 19[5] (AV *their line*, fig. of their domain) rd. prob. קֹלָם *their sound*, Capp. Ol Che and now most. Is 18[2.7] v. קוקו
6957 infr.; 28[10.13] v. I. קַו.

6957, 6961 †קוה **n.m.** Kt = II. קַו Qr; abs. (קֹוֶה, or קָוֶה) Zc 1[16]; cstr. (קְוֵה, or קְוֵה) 1 K 7[23] Je 31[39].

6979 †קַוְקַו (or קַו־קַו, קְוַקְוַ) **n.[m.]** might(?);—
6957, 6978 so read (acc. to most) for קַו־קָו, in phrase גּוֹי ק׳ Is 18[2.7] i.e. *a mighty nation* (cf. Ar. قُوَّةٌ *strength*; v. (on redupl.) Ges[§ 123 e]); > RV '*meting out*'
6957 conquered lands, lit. 'of line, line' (II. קַו).

4723 †I. מִקְוֶה **n.[m.]** hope;—abs. מ׳ 1 Ch 29[15] Ezr 10[2]; cstr. in phr. מִקְוֵה יִשְׂרָאֵל, epithet of י׳, Je 14[8] 17[13], cf. 50[7].

8615 †I. [תִּקְוָה] **n.f.** cord (cf. √*ad init.*);— cstr. תִּקְוַת (חוּט) הַשָּׁנִי Jos 2[18.21].

8615 †II. תִּקְוָה 34 **n.f.** hope;—abs. ת׳ Ho 2[17] +; cstr. תִּקְוַת Jb 8[13] +; sf. תִּקְוָתִי 6[8] +, etc.;—**1.** *hope*, Je 31[17] La 3[29] Jb 5[16] 7[6] 11[18.20] 14[7.19] 17[15a] 19[10] ψ 62[6] Pr 19[18] 26[12] 29[20] Ru 1[12]; פֶּתַח ת׳ Ho 2[17]; אֲסִירֵי הַתּ׳ Zc 9[12] (i.e. with hope of deliverance). **2.** = ground of hope Jb 4[6] ψ 71[5] (cf. 62[6]). **3.** *things hoped for, outcome*, Ez 19[5] 37[11] Jb 6[8] 8[13] 17[15b] (but rd. טוֹבָתִי 𝔊 Me Bi Siegf Beer Bu Du), 27[8] ψ 9[19] Pr 10[28] 11[7.23] 23[18] 24[14] (del. Toy as gloss); אַחֲרִית וְת׳ Je 29[11] (i.e. by hendyadis, the hoped-for future).

8616 †III. תִּקְוָה **n.pr.m.** (*hope*; cf. Lag[BN 131]);— **1.** father-in-law of Huldah 2 K 22[14], Θεκουαν,
8445 A 𝔊L Θεκ(κ)ουε (= תוקהת 2 Ch 34[22] Kt [Qr תָּקְהַת], Καθουαλ, A Θακουαθ, 𝔊L Θεκωε). **2.** post-ex. name Ezr 10[15], Ελκεια, A 𝔊L Θεκουε.

6960 †II. [קָוָה] **vb.** collect (NH Hiph. *collect*);—**Niph.** *be collected*, *Pf.* 3 pl. וְנִקְווּ consec. Je 3[17] (of nations); *Impf.* 3 mpl. יִקָּווּ Gn 1[9] (P; of waters; both c. אֶל loc.); so prob. of ships (c. לְ pers.) Is 60[9] (for MT יְקַוּוּ), v. I. קוה **Pi. 1.**

†II. [מִקְוֶה] **n.[m.]** collection, collected mass (P);—cstr. מִקְוֵה Gn 1[10] (מִקְוֶה also v[9], for מָקוֹם, acc. to 𝔊 Ball), Ex 7[19] Lv 11[36], all of water. —מ׳ 1 K 10[28.28] = מִקְוֵא 2 Ch 1[16] (*company* of merchants; *drove* of horses), v. קֹוֶה. p. 875 4723

†מִקְוָה **n.f.** reservoir;—Is 22[11]. 4724

קוֹחַ v. פְּקַח־קוֹחַ. p. 824 6495

†[קוּט] **vb.** feel a loathing (‖ form of קוּץ q.v.);—**Qal** *Impf.* 1 s. אָקוּט בְּדוֹר ψ 95[10] *I felt a loathing at* the generation. **Niph.** *Pf.* 2 mpl. consec. וּנְקֹטֹתֶם בִּפְנֵיכֶם Ez 20[43] *ye shall feel loathing against your faces* (at yourselves), c. בְּ rei, so 36[31] (עַל rei); metapl. (as if from קטט) 3 pl. consec. וְנָקֹטּוּ בִּפְנֵיהֶם Ez 6[9] (אֶל rei, for עַל, + לְ rei, for which Co בְּ, Krae בְּ or עַל); also 3 fs. נָקְטָה נַפְשִׁי בְּ Jb 10[1] (as if from נקט*; on both forms v. Ges[§§ 67 dd, 72 dd]). **Hithpō'l.** *id.* *Impf.* 1 s. אֶתְקוֹטָט בְּ ψ 139[21] (We אֶתְקוֹמֵם); abs. וָאֶתְקוֹטָטָה 119[158].—Ez 16[47] v. קָט; Jb 8[14] v. foll. 5354, 6962 6990 5354 6985 p. 881

†[קוּט] dub. **vb. intrans.,** assumed mng. break, snap (supposed to be akin to Ar. قَطَّ *cut, cut off, pare, trim* [whence Buhl assumes √קטט]), to account for יָקוֹט Jb 8[14], either as **Qal** *Impf.* 3 ms. whose hope *snappeth*; or as **n.[m.]** = *fragile thing* (‖ בֵּית עַכָּבִישׁ; cf. Di Bu); prob. crpt.; Du Beer rd. קוּרִים, Bu conj. קְרֵי קַיִט [Aramaism for ק׳ קַיִץ]. 6962 6990

קול (√of foll.; As. *kâlu, speak, call, cry* (TelAm. *lament*), *kûlu, speech*; Ar. قَالَ (و) *say*, قَوْلٌ *word*; Eth. ቃል: *sound, voice*, and so Aram. קָלָא, ܩܳܠܳܐ; Ph. קל *voice*, so NPun. קאל, sf. קולא; SI[2] *sound, voice*; NH קוֹל *noise*, בַּת קוֹל = *echo*).

קוֹל (sts., c. pref. et suff., קֹל) 506 **n.m.**[Gn 39, 14] sound, voice;—abs. קוֹל Gn 4[10] + (הַקֹּל 27[22] 45[16]); cstr. קוֹל 3[8] + (וְקֹל Ex 19[16], לְקֹל 4[8.8]); sf. קוֹלִי 1 S 26[17] +, קוֹלְךָ Ju 18[25] +, etc. (קֹלִי Gn 22[18], קֹלֶךָ Ex 3[18], etc.); pl. (usu. of thunder) קֹלֹת Ex 9[23] + 4 t., קוֹלֹת 20[18] (Gi v[15]), קלות 1 S 2[17] + 5 t.;—**1.** *sound:* esp. **a.** of human voice Jos 6[10] 2 K 7[10]; in speech Gn 27[22.22] 1 S 1[13] 24[17] 26[17.17]; recognized (הִכִּיר) v[17] Je 18[3]; יְפֵה ק׳ Ez 33[32] *pleasant of voice*, cf. Ct 2[14.14] 8[13]; in singing Ex 32[18] 2 S 19[36] Is 52[8], calling Ju 9[7], shouting Ex 32[17] 1 S 4[6.6] 1 K 1[40] Ezr 3[13], rejoicing Je 7[34.34.34.34] = 16[9] 25[10] 33[11], praise ψ 66[8] 26[7] Jo 2[10], laughter Je 30[19], weeping Gn 21[16] Ju 2[4] 1 S 11[4] Ru 1[9.14] Ezr 3[13], outcry Gn 39[15.18] 1 S 4[14] Je 8[19], distress, lament Je 9[18] Ez 27[30] Zc 11[3] ψ 102[6], 6963

supplication ψ 28$^{2.6}$ 31^{23} 86^{6}; adv. ק׳ אֶחָד *with one voice* Ex 24^{3} 2 Ch 5^{13}, ק׳ גָּדוֹל *loud voice* 2 S 15^{23}+ (cf. בְּק׳ ג׳ Gn 39^{14} 1 S 28^{12}+), ק׳ רָם †Dt 27^{14}; נָשָׂא ק׳ Gn 21^{16}+ (v. נָשָׂא **1 b** (5)), הֵרִים ק׳ 39^{15}+ (v. רום **Hiph.**); on ק׳ as independ. nom., sq. subj. + vb. of calling ψ 3^{5} 27^{7} 142^{2} v. Ges$^{§144\,m}$. **b.** of י׳ Gn 3$^{8.10}$ Is 6^{8} Ex 19^{19} 1 K 19^{13} Mi 6^{9} Ez 10^{5} (cf. also **2 b**) +; adv. ק׳ גָּדוֹל Dt 5^{19} Ez 9^{1}; ק׳ דְּמָמָה דַקָּה 1 K 19^{12}. **c.** of seraph Is 6^{4}. **d.** of angel Dn 8^{16} (ק׳ אָדָם i.e. in human speech, cf. Bev); ק׳ דְּבָרָיו 10$^{6.9.9}$. **e.** of animals: bleating of sheep 1 S 15^{14}, lowing of cattle v^{14} Je 9^{9}, neighing of horses 8^{16}, roaring of lion Am 3^{4} Je 2^{15}+, hissing of serpent 46^{22} (in sim.), singing of birds Na 2^{8} Zp 2^{14} ψ 104^{12} Ct 2^{12} Ec 12^{4}. **f.** exclamation, at beginning of cl., *a sound of...!=hark!* Gn 4^{10} Is 13^{4} 40^{3} 52^{8} Je 4^{15} 10^{22} 50^{28} Ct 2^{8} 5^{2} (Ges^{§146b}). **2.** *sound:* **a.** of instrument, esp. ק׳ (הַ)שּׁוֹפָר Ex 9^{16} 20^{18} (Gi v^{15}) Am 2^{2} 1 K 1^{41}+, חֲצֹצְרוֹת וגו׳ 2 Ch 5^{13}, כִּנּוֹר Ez 26^{13}, עוּגָב Jb 21^{12}; of פַּעֲמֹנִים on high priest's robe Ex 28^{35}. **b.** thunder-clap or peal (cf. Dr 1 S 12^{17}), קוֹל י׳ (or קוֹלוֹ) Am 1^{2} Is 30$^{30.31}$ Je 10^{13}=51^{16}, Jo 2^{11} 4^{16} ψ 18^{14}=2 S 22^{14}, ψ 29$^{3-5.7-9}$ 46^{7} Jb 37^{4} (cf. 1 S 7^{10} ψ 77$^{18.19}$ 104^{7}), so esp. pl. abs. (v. supr.) †Ex 9$^{23.28.29.33.34}$ 19^{16} 20^{18} (Gi v^{15}), 1 S 7^{10} 12$^{17.18}$ Jb 28^{26}=38^{25}. **c.** קוֹל רַגְלֶיהָ 1 K 14^{6} cf. 2 K 6^{32}, and (prob.) Gn 3^{8}; also ק׳ (הַ)צְּעָדָה 2 S 5^{24}=1 Ch 14^{15}; of runners 2 K 11^{13} 2 Ch 23^{12}. **d.** stamping of hoofs Je 47^{3} Ez 26^{10} (+ chariots, etc.), cf. 1 K 1^{41}. **e.** of chariots Na 3^{2} Jo 2^{5}; wheels Ez 3^{13}; whip Na 3^{2}. **f.** of sea, and great waters Hb 3^{10} Ez 1^{24} 43^{2} ψ 93$^{3.4}$, cf. Je 50^{42} (in sim.); ק׳ צִנּוֹרֶיךָ ψ 42^{8}. **g.** earthquake Ez 37^{7}. **h.** a fall Je 49^{21} Ez 26^{15} 31^{16}. **i.** of a multitude 1 S 4^{14} Is 13^{4} Ez 23^{42}. **j.** din of war Ex 32^{17} Je 50$^{22.46}$ 51^{55} La 2^{7}. **k.** of wings Ez 1^{24} 3^{13} 10^{5}. **l.** flame Jo 2^{5}; crackling of thorns Ec 7^{6}; rustling of leaves Lv 26^{36}. **m.** millstones Je 25^{10} Ec 12^{4}. **3.** of articulate speech, thing said: **a.** (1) oft. of human advice, command, entreaty Gn 3^{17} 4^{23} Ex 3^{18} 4$^{1.9}$ Dt 1^{45} 21$^{18.18.20}$ 1 S 2^{25} 8$^{7.9}$ 2 S 12^{18}; ק׳ דִּבְרֵיכֶם Dt 1^{34} 5^{25}; even of written words 2 K 10^{6}; so also ק׳ הָאֹת Ex 4$^{8.8}$ *voice* (teaching) *of the sign.* (2) of a report Gn 45^{16} Ec 10^{20}. (3) of a proclamation Ex 36^{6} (P), 2 Ch 24^{9} 30^{5} 36^{22}=Ezr 1^{1}, Ezr 10^{7} Ne 8^{15}. (4) ק׳ אָלָה Lv 5^{1} *utterance of adjuration.* **b.** oft. (esp. Dt Je) of words of י׳ Gn 22^{18} 26^{5} Ex 5^{2} 15^{26} 19^{5} Dt 8^{20} 9^{23} 13$^{5.19}$+, Ju 2^{20} 6^{10} 1 S 12$^{14.15}$ 15$^{1.19.20.22}$ Je 3$^{13.25}$ 7^{23}+; of מַלְאַךְ י׳ Ex
6963 23$^{21.22}$.—קֹל Je 3^{9} v. sub קלל. p. 887

6964 †קוֹלָיָה **n.pr.m.** (*voice of* י׳);—**1.** father of proph Ahab Je 29^{21}. **2.** Benjamite Ne 11^{7}; Κωδια, A Κωλεια, 𝔊L Κολεια. Prob. also **3.** Levite Ezr 10^{23}, MT קְלָיָה but 𝔊 Κωλεια, A Κωλαια (cf. Gray$^{\text{Prop. N. 297}}$).

קוּם$_{628}$ **vb. arise, stand up, stand**;—(NH in der. spec. and deriv.; Ph. Hiph. Pt. and מקם *place;* Ar. قَامَ (و) *stand, rise,* Eth. ቆመ: *stand, stop;* Sab. מקם, *place,* Hom$^{\text{Chrest. 127}}$; Aram. קוּם, ܩܘܡ=BH, so OAram. Nab. קום; Palm. Aph. אקים *erect* statue; cf. prob. As. *kumu* (*k*=כ), *place, dwelling, kum, kêmu, in place of,* and perh. *kaiamânu, enduring, constant* (v. כִּיּוּן); Thes cp. also Sam. ࠒࠅࠌ, *live,* cf. esp. 𝔗 Pa.);—**Qal**$_{460}$ *Pf.* 3 ms. קָם 1 S 17^{48}+, וְקָאם consec. Ho 10^{14} (Ges$^{§72\,p}$); 2 ms. קַמְתָּ 2 S 12^{21}, etc.; *Impf.* 3 ms. יָקוּם Ex 21^{19}, juss. יָקֹם Gn 27^{31}, וְיָקָם (לָךְ) Jb 22^{28} (Ges$^{§109\,h}$ Dr$^{§152(3)}$); וַיָּקָם Gn 4^{8}+, etc.; *Imv.* ms. קוּם Gn 13^{17}+, fpl. קֹמְנָה Is 32^{9}, etc.; *Inf. abs.* קוֹם Je 44^{29}; *cstr.* קוּם Am 5^{2}+, etc.; *Pt.* fs. קָמָה Mi 7^{6}; mpl. קָמִים 2 S 18^{31}+, הַקּוֹמִים 2 K 16^{17} (Ges$^{§72\,p}$), etc.;—**1.** *arise:* מִתַּחְתָּיו Ex 10^{23} (E). Specif.: **a.** after lying down (sleep, sickness, mourning, etc.), 1 S 3$^{6.8}$ 2 S 12^{21} Ex 21^{19} Gn 19$^{33.35}$ 31^{17} Ru 3^{14} Ec 12^{4}+50 t.; fr. lying dead, וַיָּקָם עַל־רַגְלָיו 2 K 13^{21}, cf. Jb 14^{12} Is 26$^{14.19}$ ψ 88^{11}; after falling Am 5^{2} 8^{14} Je 8^{4} 25^{27}+4 t. (chiefly fig.); after being smitten, wounded, etc. ψ 18^{39} ‖ 2 S 22^{39}, Is 27^{9} (of Asherim, etc.), 43^{17}+4 t.; from sitting, reclining, esp. at meals Gn 25^{34} 1 S 1^{9} 20^{34} (מֵעִם הַשֻּׁלְחָן; v^{25} see קֶדֶם), Est 7^{7} (+ אֶל in constr. praegn.), but also Ju 3^{20} (מֵעַל), 2 S 2$^{14.14.15}$, Jon 3^{6} (מִכִּסְאוֹ), + 11 t., + (*arise*=stand up, in respect), Gn 19^{1} (+ לִקְרָאתָם), 31^{35} (מִפָּנֶיךָ), Lv 19^{32} (מִפְּנֵי), Is 49^{7} Jb 29^{8}; + וַיִּשְׁתַּחוּ 2 K 2^{19}, cf. Gn 23^{7} Ex 33^{10} 1 S 20^{41} 25^{41};—(v. also **e**); from kneeling (מִן, + מִלִּפְנֵי loc.) 1 K 8^{54}, fr. obeisance 1 S 24^{42} Est 8^{4}; from bending over (עַל) dead Gn 23^{3} (P). **b.** out of (מִן) a condition, state, Ezr 9^{5}. **c.** of bear *rising* עַל pers., 1 S 17^{35}. **d.** *arise* (+ stand) Ex 33^{8} ψ 20^{9} (fig. of success, prosperity), Jb 24^{22} (*id.*), +; of sheaf Gn 37^{7}; of waters Jos 3^{16} (נֵד־אֶחָד). **e.** constr. praegn. *arise* (and stand) for a purpose Nu 11^{32} (E); *over,* עַל pers., 2 S 12^{17}. **f.** *arise* as prelim. to formal speech Ju 20^{8} Mi 6^{1} Je 1^{17} 1 Ch 28^{2} (עַל־רַגְלָיו), Pr 31^{28} Jb 30^{28}+5 t.; to testify (against) Dt 19$^{15.16}$ (both בְּ pers.), ψ 27^{12} 35^{11}, cf. also וַיָּקָם בִּי Jb 16^{8} (of כַּחַשׁ q.v.; Bu כַּעַשׂ); to vindicate Jb 19^{25} (עַל־עָפָר); to rd. aloud Ne 9^{3} (עַל־עָמְדָם); to bless people 2 Ch 30^{27} (priests). **g.** to listen to God's 6965

word Nu 23^{18} Is 32^{9}; to praise God 2 Ch 20^{19} Ne $9^{4.5}$. **h.** of noise, tumult Ho 10^{14}; of light Jb 25^{3} (עַל pers.). **2.** *arise*, in hostile sense (oft. with idea of suddenness); c. עַל pers. Dt 19^{11} (out of ambush), 22^{26} Ju 9^{18} 20^{5} ψ 27^{3} (of war), Ob^{1} (לַמִּלְחָמָה), + 11 t., + Jb 30^{12} (acc. to Bu, rdg. עָלַי for עַל־יָמִין), + (of י׳) Am 7^{9} (ב instr.), Is 14^{22} 31^{2}; c. אֶל pers. Gn 4^{8} 1 S 22^{13} 24^{8} (Gi v^{7}); c. ב pers. Mi 7^{6} ψ 27^{12} (false witness), Mi 7^{6}; c. עִם pers. ψ 94^{16} (‖ יִתְיַצֵּב); v. esp. pt. c. sf. = *those rising up against me* (thee, etc.) Ex 15^{7} 32^{25} Dt 33^{11} + 8 t. + ψ 109^{28} (rd. קָמַי יֵבֹשׁוּ 𝔊 𝔙 Bae We Du, cf. Hup Dr); c. מִן *from, out of* Jos $8^{7.19}$ Ju $9^{35.43}$ 20^{33}; = *revolt* Nu 16^{2} (לִפְנֵי pers.), 2 K 12^{21} 2 Ch 13^{6}, cf. Hb 2^{7}. **3.** *arise*, abs., = become powerful Pr $28^{12.28}$. **4.** *arise* = come on the scene, appear, of leader, prophet, king Ju $5^{7.7}$ $10^{1.3}$ Dt 13^{2} 34^{10} Ex 1^{8} 2 K 23^{25}; of years of famine Gn 41^{30}; c. אַחֲרֵי pers. Dt 29^{21} Ju 2^{10} 1 K 3^{12}; c. תַּחַת, *in place of*, 1 K 8^{20} = 2 Ch 6^{10}, Nu 32^{14}; c. עַל־מַמְלֶכֶת 2 Ch 21^{4}; c. מִן Nu 24^{17} (sceptre out of Isr.); of calamity, Na 1^{9} Pr 24^{22}; מִצָּהֳרַיִם יָקוּם חָלֶד Jb 11^{17} i.e. to shine upon thee. **5.** *arise* for, i.e. to become, c. ל rei; בְּיוֹם קוּמִי לְעַד Zp 3^{8} (read לְעֵד, *for a witness*, 𝔊 𝔖 We Now GASm cf. Da); הֶחָמָס קָם לְמַטֵּה־רֶשַׁע Ez 7^{11} (but dub.; Co Berthol Krae קָמֵל). **6. a.** *arise* for action, esp. of י׳ arising [from his throne], + inf. Is $2^{19.21}$; for judgment ψ 76^{10} (לַמִּשְׁפָּט), Jb 31^{14}; oft. Imv. Nu 10^{35} Je 2^{27} ψ 3^{8} + 8 t. ψψ + 2 Ch 6^{41} (c. לְנוּחֶךָ), ψ 132^{8} (c. לִמְנוּחָתֶךָ); Impf. Is 28^{21} + 4 t.; Imv. also of men, *arise! up!* i.e. act! Ju 4^{14} Ezr 10^{4}, of idols Je 2^{28}; Impf. of the tongue (personified) Is 54^{17} (אִתָּךְ לַמִּשְׁפָּט). **b.** *arise* (out of inaction), introducing some specific deed Gn 21^{18} Ex 32^{1} Ju 5^{12} $8^{20.21}$ Je 49^{14} (לַמִּלְחָמָה), Ob^{1} (קוּמוּ וְנָקוּמָה עָלֶיהָ לַמִּלְחָמָה), + 37 t. **c.** esp. *arise* = start, make a move, to go somewhere, Gn 13^{17} $19^{14.15}$ 1 S 9^{3} Jon 1^{3} (in flight), 3^{3} + 110 t. **7.** *stand:* esp. fig. **a.** = *maintain oneself* Jos $7^{12.13}$ (JE; לִפְנֵי pers.), Am $7^{2.5}$ Na 1^{6} La 1^{14} ψ 1^{5} 24^{3} Jb 41^{18} (of sword), of courage (רוּחַ) Jos 2^{11} (D; בְּאִישׁ, + לִפְנֵי pers.). **b.** = *be established, confirmed*, of kingdom 1 S 24^{21} (בְּיָדְךָ; Gi v^{20}); of purchase Lv 27^{19}, c. ל pers. *be assured to* 25^{30} Gn $23^{17.20}$ (all P). **c.** *stand, endure* 1 S 13^{14} Jb 8^{15} (‖ עָמַד), 15^{29}. **d.** = *be fixed*, of price, Lv $27^{14.17}$. **e.** = *be valid*, of vows, Nu $30^{5.5}$ + 6 t. Nu 30 + v^{10} (c. עַל pers.; all P). **f.** = *be proven* Dt 19^{15}. **g.** = *be fulfilled* Je 44^{29} (impf. + inf. abs.; עַל pers.), Jb 22^{28} (ל pers.); of י׳'s purpose Je 51^{29} (עַל pers.), Is 14^{24} Pr 19^{21}, cf. Je 44^{28} Is 40^{8} 46^{10}; of human plans, *succeed* Is 7^{7} 8^{10} 28^{18} Pr 15^{22}. **h.** *persist*, עַל־נְדִיבוֹת יָקוּם Is 32^{8} lit. *on noble things doth he take his stand.* **i.** יָקוּם עַל־שֵׁם אָחִיו Dt 25^{6} *he shall stand upon the name of his* dead *brother*, represent him. **j.** of eyes, = *be set, fixed*, without vision 1 S 4^{15} 1 K 14^{4} (עַיִן **1 i**). †**Pi.** *Pf.* 3 ms. קִיַּם Est $9^{31.32}$; 3 pl. קִיְּמוּ v$^{27.31}$; *Impf.* 1 s. וָאֲקַיֵּמָה ψ 119^{106}; *Imv.* ms. sf. קַיְּמֵנִי v^{28}; *Inf. cstr.* לְקַיֵּם Ez 13^{6} +;—late (Aram.): **1.** *fulfil*, Ez 13^{6} ψ 119^{106}. **2. a.** *confirm, ratify*, Ru 4^{7}. **b.** *confirm, establish*, of י׳ ψ 119^{28} (c. sf. acc.). **c.** *impose*, an obligation, עַל pers. Est $9^{21.31b}$, עַל reflex. v$^{27.31c}$; c. acc. rei v$^{29.31a.32}$. †**Pōʿl.** *raise up:* *Impf.* 2 ms. תְּקוֹמֵם Is 58^{2}; 1 s. אֲקוֹמֵם 44^{26}; 3 mpl. יְקוֹמֵמוּ 61^{4} (all of rebuilding);—יְקוֹמֵם Mi 2^{8}, rd. תְּקוּמוּ We Now, or קָמִים GASm Buhl. †**Hithpōʿl.** *raise oneself*, = *rise up:* *Pt.* fs. מִתְקוֹמָמָה Jb 20^{27} (לְ pers. *against*); ms. sf. -מְמִי 27^{7} *one rising up against me* (‖ אֹיְבִי); pl. abs. -מְמִים ψ 17^{7}; sf. -מְמַי 59^{2}; v. also 139^{21}, reading
וּבְמִתְקוֹמְמֶיךָ (for MT וּבִתְק׳ ‖ מְשַׂנְאֶיךָ); see also 8618
קוּט. **Hiph.** $_{146}$ *Pf.* 3 ms. הֵקִים Jos 4^{9} +; 2 ms. 6962
הֲקֵמֹתָ, וַהֲקֵמֹתָ Ex 26^{30} Dt 27^{2}; 1 s. הֲקִימֹתִי 1 S 15^{13}, Gn 9^{17} +, etc.; *Impf.* 3 ms. יָקִים Dt 18^{15} +; juss. יָקֵם 1 S 1^{23} +; וַיָּקֶם Ju 2^{16} +; 2 fpl. תְּקִימֶנָה Je 44^{25}, etc.; *Imv.* ms. הָקֵם 2 S 7^{25} +, etc.; *Inf. abs.* הָקֵים Je 44^{25}, הָקֵם Dt 22^{4} Ju 7^{19}; cstr. הָקִים 2 S 3^{10} +, etc.; *Pt.* מֵקִים Am 6^{14} +, etc.;—†**1.** *cause to arise, raise:* **a.** the prostrate (acc. pers. vel rei) 2 S 12^{17} (מִן־הָאָרֶץ), Dt 22^{4} (הָקֵם תָּקִים עִמּוֹ), ψ 41^{11} Ec $4^{10.10}$; fig. Am 5^{2} $9^{11.11}$ Ho 6^{2} Is 49^{8} 1 S 2^{8} = ψ 113^{7} (‖ הֵרִים), Jb 4^{4}, Je 50^{32}. **b.** from throne (מִן) Is 14^{9}. **c.** *lift up* shield (צִנָּה) against (עַל) Ez 26^{8}. **d.** fig. *raise* (to dignity, power) Is 49^{6}. **2.** †**a.** *raise, set up*, stones Jos 4^{9} (JE; בְּתוֹךְ loc.), v^{20} (JE; ב loc.), 24^{26} (E; שָׁם, תַּחַת loc.), Dt 27^{2}; pillars 1 K $7^{21.21.21}$ ‖ 2 Ch 3^{17} Ex 40^{18} (P); פֶּסֶל, מַצֵּבָה Ju 18^{30} (ל reflex.), Lv 26^{1} Dt 16^{22}; throne, fig., 2 S 3^{10}, king Dt 28^{36} (both c. עַל *over*). **b.** *erect, build:* Is 23^{13} Ex 26^{30}; heap of stones over (עַל) Jos 7^{26} 8^{29}; altar 2 S 24^{18} (לי׳) ‖ 1 Ch 21^{18} (*id.*), 1 K 16^{32} (לבעל), 2 K 21^{3} (*id.*) = 2 Ch 33^{3} (לבעלים); curtains Je 10^{20} (of Judah's tent, in fig.); tabern., etc., Ex $40^{2.18.33}$ + 4 t. Nu; *erect* against (עַל) Is 29^{3}. †**c.** fig. of setting up law ψ 78^{5} (עֵדוּת; ‖ שִׂים). †**3.** *raise up* = bring on the scene: c. acc., sons in place of (תַּחַת) fathers Jos 5^{7}, אַחֲרֵי 2 S 7^{12} = 1 Ch 17^{11}, 1 K 15^{4}; *raise up* זֶרַע לְאָחִיךָ Gn 38^{8} (J); judges Ju $2^{16.18}$

(לָהֶם), cf. 3[9.15] (both ל pers.); king Je 30[9], צֶמַח צַדִּיק 23[5], prophet Je 29[15] Dt 18[15.18], priest 1 S 2[35] (all ל pers.); shepherds, etc. Mi 5[5] (עַל *against*), Zc 11[16]; לְהָקִים לְאָחִיו שֵׁם Dt 25[7]; plant of name Ez 34[29] (ל pers.); evil (רָעָה) 2 S 12[11] (עַל *against*). †**4. a.** *raise up* = rouse, stir up (lion, in fig.) Gn 49[9] (poem) = Nu 24[9] (JE). **b.** *instigate*, c. acc. pers. + עַל *against* Am 6[14] 1 S 22[8]; + ל pers. 1 K 11[14.23]; c. acc. alone Hb 1[6]. †**5.** *raise up* = constitute, הֲקִים־אֹתְךָ . . . לוֹ לְעָם Dt 29[12] cf. 28[9] Jb 16[12]; וָאָקִים מִבְּנֵיכֶם לִנְבִיאִים Am 2[11]; יָקֵם סְעָרָה לִדְמָמָה ψ 107[29] (cf. **Qal 5**). **6.** *cause to stand:* †**a.** *set, station*, sentinels Ju 7[19] (הָקֵם הֵקִימוּ), Je 51[12], cf. 6[17] (עַל pers.), 23[4] Ez 34[23]; *set* feet on (עַל) rock ψ 40[3]. †**b.** *cause to hold one's ground* ψ 89[44] (בַּמִּלְחָמָה). †**c.** *establish* throne 2 Ch 7[18], כָּל־אַפְסֵי־אָרֶץ Pr 30[4]. †**d.** *establish* (make, ratify) covenant, of ׳י, c. אֵת (prep.) pers. Gn 6[18] 9[9.11] 17[19.21] Ex 6[4] (all P), Ez 16[62]; c. בֵּין . . . בֵּין Gn 9[17] 17[7] (both P); c. ל pers. Ez 16[60]. †**e.** = *make binding*, a vow Nu 30[14.15.15]. **f.** = *carry out, give effect to* (Dr [Sm. 1, 23]), oath, covenant, vow, word, plan, command, of man 1 S 15[11.13] + 6 t.; of ׳י Gn 26[3] Lv 26[9] 1 S 1[23] 1 K 6[12] Dt 8[18] Je 23[20] + 18 t. †**g.** לְהָקִים שֵׁם־הַמֵּת עַל־נַחֲלָתוֹ Ru 4[5.10] *to cause the dead man's name to stand upon his inheritance* (cf. **Qal 7 i**). †**Hoph.** *Pf.* 3 ms. הֻקַם עָל 2 S 23[1] *be raised up* (on הֻקַּם van d. H., v. Dr); הוּקַם *be set up* Ex 40[17] (of tabern.); הוּקַם אֶת־דִּבְרֵי פ׳ Je 35[14] *be held upright* (Ges [§121 a]), i.e. observed, obeyed.

6967 **קוֹמָה, קֹמָה** $_{45}$ **n.f. height**;—abs. קוֹמָה Ex 38[18] +, קֹמָה 27[18]; cstr. קוֹמַת 1 K 6[26] +; sf. קוֹמָתוֹ 7[23] +, קֹמָתוֹ Ex 25[10] +, etc.;—**1.** *height*, of pers., *stature* 1 S 16[7] Ez 13[18] Ct 7[8]; מְלֹא־קוֹמָתוֹ 1 S 28[20] *his full length.* **2.** of tree 2 K 19[23] = Is 37[24]; in fig. Is 10[33] Ez 31[3.5.10.14]; of vine (fig.) Ez 19[11] and שִׁפְלַת ק׳ 17[6] *low of height.* **3.** of artificial structures: temple, its parts, furnishings, etc., 1 K 6[2] + 12 t. 1 K 6, 7, 2 K 25[17.17] = Je 52[21.22], 2 Ch 4[1.2] 6[13]; a wall Ez 40[5]; tabern. and furnishings Ex 25[10.23] + 8 t. Ex (all P); Noah's ark Gn 6[15] (P).

7054 †**קָמָה** **n.f. standing grain**;—abs. ק׳ Ex 22[5] +; cstr. קָמַת Dt 23[26.26]; pl. cstr. קָמוֹת Ju 15[5]; —*standing grain* (mature) Ex 22[5] (E), Dt 16[9] 23[26.26] Ju 15[5.5] Is 17[5]; לִפְנֵי ק׳ 2 K 19[26] = Is 37[27] (i.e. before maturity); in fig. Ho 8[7].—Cf. Vogelst [Landwirthsch. 51]

†[**קִים**] **n.m. adversary** (prop. *uprising, insurgent* [Kö [ii. 1, 60]], cf. √**Qal 2**);—sf. קִימָנוּ (Kö [ii. 1, 442]) Jb 22[20], but prob. corrupt; Ges [§91 f], Du קָמֵ(י)נוּ (Pt. sf.) Me Bu יְקֻמָם, Perles [Anal. 59] קִנְיָנָם. 7009

†[**קִימָה**] **n.f. rising up**;—sf. קִימָתָם La 3[63] (opp. שִׁבְתָּם). 7012

†**קָמוֹן** **n.pr.loc.** Ju 10[5], Ραμνων, A Ραμμω (𝔊L Καλκων); in Gilead Jos [Ant. v. 7, 6] (Καμων); prob. = Καμουν of Polyb [v. 70, 12] (named next after Πελλα); Buhl [Geogr. 256] thinks of *Ḳumêm, Ḳamm* (Schumacher [Northern Ajlûn 137 f.]), between Jarmuk and Jabbok, W. of *Irbid.* 7056

†**קוֹמְמִיּוּת** **n.f. uprightness**;—only as adv. Lv 26[13] made you go *upright*, i.e. as freemen. 6968

אַלְקוּם v. supr. p. 39. 510

†**יְקוּם** **n.[m.] substance, existence** כָּל־הַיְקוּם = *all that subsists* Gn 7[4.23] (man and animal), in more limited sense Dt 11[6]. 3351

†**יָקִים** **n.pr.m.** (*he lifteth up;* cf. Sab. n.pr. יהקם Hal [151]);—Ιακειμ, A (24[12]) Ελιακειμ: **1.** Benjamite 1 Ch 8[19]. **2.** Levite 24[12]. 3356

†**תְּקוּמָה** **n.f. standing, power to stand** (cf. √**Qal 7 a**);—abs. ת׳ Lv 26[37] (c. לִפְנֵי pers.). 8617

†[**תְּקוֹמֵם**], וּבִתְקוֹמְמֶיךָ ψ 139[21], v. √, **Hithpōʿl.** p. 878 6965, 8618

מָקוֹם, מָקֹם (Ex 29[31], etc.) $_{399}$ **n.m.** [Gn 19, 13] (but v. infr.), **standing-place, place**;—abs. מ׳ Ex 21[13] +; cstr. מְקוֹם Gn 12[6] + (oft. before אֲשֶׁר 39[20] +); sf. מְקוֹמוֹ 1 S 3[2] +, מְקֹמוֹ Gn 18[33] +, etc.; pl. usu. מְקֹמוֹת Ju 19[13] +, מְקוֹמוֹת 1 S 7[16] Je 29[14], מְקוֹמֹתֵיכֶם 2 S 17[9] + 2 t.; sf. ־מֹת Am 4[6], etc. [appar. **f.** (not Gn 18[24], where עִיר is in mind, but) Jb 20[9] (emend. v. Comm.), and Codd. (either Kt or Qr) Ju 19[13] 2 S 17[9.12]; mostly expl. away by Albr [ZAW xvi (1896), 53]];—**1. a.** *standing-place* Ex 3[5] (E), Jos 5[15] Ex 33[21] Nu 23[13.27] (all JE), Gn 19[27] (J), Jos 3[3] (D), of מַצֵּבוֹת, etc., 2 K 23[14], of ark (place where it is set, stands) 1 K 8[7] = 2 Ch 5[8], earth Is 13[13] Jb 9[6], rock Jb 14[18] 18[4]; cf. 38[12.19]. **b.** *station*, where soldiers are placed Jos 8[19] (JE), Ju 20[33.33]; *post* in battle 2 S 11[16]. **c.** *post, office* 1 K 20[24] Ec 10[4]. **2. a.** *place* where a thing belongs Gn 29[3] (J), Jos 4[18] (JE), 1 S 5[3] Is 46[7] Jb 6[17] 37[1] (of the heart), Ec 1[5]; esp. of ark 1 S 5[11] + 9 t.; of pers. = destination Ju 11[19]. **b.** esp. (1) *place of human abode* Gn 13[14] 20[13] Ju 7[7] 1 S 2[20] + 42 t., + מְקוֹם אָהֳלֶךָ Is 54[2]. (2) of ׳י's abode Ho 5[15], in heaven 4725

Mi 1^{3} Is 26^{21} 1 K 8^{30} = 2 Ch 6^{21}. (3) lair of lion (fig.) Je 4^{7}. **3.** *place* = **a.** *city* Gn 18$^{24.26}$ 20^{11} Dt 21^{19} (‖ עִיר) 2 K 18^{25} + 39 t. (1 S 7^{16} הַמְּקֹדָשִׁים 𝔊, cf. We HPS). **b.** of land: Canaan Ex 23^{20} 1 S 12^{8} Je 16$^{2.3}$ (‖ אֶרֶץ) + 17 t. (12 t. Je); Philistia 1 S 14^{46}; Egypt Je 44^{29}; appos. מְדִינָה Est 4^{3}, = עִיר + מְדִינָה 8^{17}. **c.** plot, parcel, of ground Is 7^{23}; מְקוֹם הַגֹּרֶן 1 Ch 21^{22}, cf. v^{25} 2 Ch 3^{1}. **d.** land, region Nu 20^{5} 32^{1}; Che (privately) prop. בִּמְקֹם בְּקָעוֹת ψ 84^{7} (for בְּעֵמֶק הַבָּכָא; cf. Is 41^{18}). **4.** in gen., *place, locality, spot* Gn 28$^{16.17}$ Ju 2^{5} Am 4^{6} Ne 4$^{6.7.14}$ + (221 t. in all); מְקוֹם פְּלֹנִי אַלְמֹנִי *place of such a one* † 1 S 21^{3} 2 K 6^{8}; בְּכָל־הַמָּקוֹם אֲשֶׁר Ex 20^{24} (E; Gi v^{21}) *in all places that;* בְּכָל־מ׳ Nu 18^{31} = *anywhere*, cf. Dt 12^{13}; = *everywhere* Pr 15^{3} Mal 1^{11}, cf. Am 8^{3}; מ׳ צַר Nu 22^{26} *narrow place;* מ׳ Ne 2^{14} (passable) *place;* in partic.: *place* at banquet † 1 S 9^{22} 20$^{25.27}$; sleeping-*place*, couch, † 1 S 3$^{2.9}$ Ru 4^{10}; מְקוֹם הַחֵצִי 1 S 20^{37} i.e. where arrow fell; = haunt, lurking-place 1 S 23^{22} 2 S 17$^{9.12}$; מְקוֹם תַּנִּים ψ 44^{20} *place of jackals*, i.e. desert; מ׳ הַמֻּנָּח Ez 41$^{11 b}$ *place of the uncovered space*, portion (cf. הַמֻּנָּח alone v$^{11 a}$); מ׳ הַשֶּׁבֶת of seat of Sol.'s throne 1 K 10^{19} = 2 Ch 9^{18}; מ׳ אֶחָד where waters were collected Gn 1^{9} (𝔊 Ball מִקְוֶה), ψ 104^{8}; destination of dead Ec 3^{20} 6^{6}; מ׳ = resting-*place* Jb 16^{18}; מ׳ נֶאֱמָן *sure place*, for a peg (securely fastened) Is 22$^{23.25}$ (fig., cf. Ezr 9^{8}); of places, spots, on the body: leprous spot † 2 K 5^{11}; מ׳ הַשְּׁחִין † Lv 13^{19} *place of the boil;* esp. of shrine, sanctuary (cf. We$^{1 S 7, 16}$), מְקוֹם שְׁכֶם Gn 12^{6} (J; v. Di Holz), so of Bethel Gn 13^{3} (J), v^{4} (J; מְקוֹם הַמִּזְבֵּחַ), 28^{19} (J), v$^{11.11.11}$ (E), 22$^{3.4.9.14}$ (E), +; of idolatrous shrines Dt 12$^{2.3}$ Ez 6^{13} 2 Ch 33^{19}; esp. of temple: הַמּ׳ אֲשֶׁר יִבְחַר (י׳ אֱלֹהֵיכֶם בּוֹ) Dt 12$^{5.14}$ 14$^{23.25}$ 15^{20} 16$^{2.6}$ 17^{8} 18^{6} + 13 t. Dt + Jos 9^{27} (D), Ne 1^{9}; מ׳ 1 K 8$^{29.29.30.35}$ = 2 Ch 6$^{20.20.21.26}$ Je 27^{22} +; מ׳ שֵׁם־י׳ צְבָאוֹת הַר־צִיּוֹן Is 18^{7}; מ׳ מִקְדָּשִׁי Ez 43^{7}; מ׳ מִקְדָּשֵׁנוּ Je 17^{12}; מ׳ כִּסְאִי Is 60^{13}; מ׳ קָדְשׁוֹ † Ezr 9^{8} ψ 24^{3}, etc.; of tabern. מ׳ הַקֹּדֶשׁ Lv 10^{17} 14^{30}; מ׳ קָדוֹשׁ in or about tabern., Ex 29^{31} Lv 6$^{9.19.20}$ + (all P), מ׳ קָדוֹשׁ Ec 8^{10}. Note esp. † מְקוֹם before rel. cl., c. אֲשֶׁר Gn 39^{20} 40^{3} Ez 6^{13} Est 4^{3} 8^{17}, c. שֶׁ Ec 1^{7} 3^{16}, rel. om. Jb 18^{21}; also בִּמְ׳ אֲשֶׁר Ho 2^{1} 2 S 15^{21} 1 K 21^{19} Je 22^{12} Ez 21^{35} Ne 4^{14} Lv 4$^{24.33}$ 6^{18} 7^{2} 14^{13} Nu 9^{17} (Ges$^{§ 130 c}$). † **5. a.** *space, room*, Gn 24$^{23.25.31}$ (J), Is 5^{8} cf. 28^{8}, Je 7^{32} 19^{11}. **b.** *space, distance*, between (בֵּין) 1 S 26^{13}. † **6.** *region, quarter, direction* Ez 10^{11}; מִמּ׳ אַחֵר Est 4^{14} *from another quarter*, source. † **7.** peculiar uses are: **a.** נָתַן מ׳ לְ Ju 20^{36} *give place* (yield ground) *to*. Perh. **b.** בִּמְ׳ אֲשֶׁר יֵאָמֵר Ho 2^{1} *instead of* its being said (cf. תַּחַת); מְקוֹם נְהָרִים Is 33^{21} *instead of* rivers (i.e. a substitute for them).—מְקוֹמָהּ Na 1^{8} (‖ אֹיְבָיו) rd. בְּקָמָיו or בְּקָ׳ Buhl$^{ZAW v (1885), 181}$, מִתְקוֹמְמָו We, מְקָמָיו Now (all = *his adversaries*, cf. GASm).

† יְקַמְיָה **n.pr.m.** in Judah (= יָקֻם יָהּ acc. to 3359
Ol$^{§ 277 h, 2}$);—**1.** 1 Ch 2$^{41.41}$, Ιεχεμειας, A Ιεκομιας, 𝔊L Ιακεμιας. **2.** 3^{18}, Ιεκενια, 𝔊L Ιεκεμια.

† יְקַמְעָם **n.pr.m.** (= יָקֻם עָם acc. to Ol 3360
$^{§ 277 i}$; meaning then *may kinsman establish*, cf. Gray$^{Prop. N. 46 f. 59}$);—a Levite 1 Ch 23^{19} 24^{23}, Ικεμιας, Ιοκομ (24^{23}), etc., 𝔊L Ιακαμιας.

† יָקְמְעָם **n.pr.loc.** (perh. = יְקָמְעָם i.e. יָקֻם 3361
עָם Ol$^{§ 277 k, 3}$; = *let the people be established?* cf. Gray$^{Prop. N. 218}$);—in N. Isr. 1 K 4^{12}, Λουκαμ, 𝔊L Ουκαμ; poss. = mod. *Tel Ḳaimûn*, N. of Megiddo, Buhl$^{Geogr. 210}$; city of refuge in Ephr. 1 Ch 6^{53} (= קִבְצַיִם [q.v.] Jos 21^{22}), Ικααμ, Ιεκμααν, etc.

קוֹנֵן v. קין. p. 884 6969

† קוֹעַ **n.pr.gent.** named with Bab., Chald., 6970
Assyr., (פְּקוֹד וְ)שׁוֹעַ וְקֹ׳ Ez 23^{23} *Šôʿa and Ḳôʿa;* identif. by Dl$^{Pa 235}$ with As. *Sutû, Kutû* (abbrev. *Su* (? v. שׁוֹעַ) and [by infer.] *Ku*), E. of Tigris, on border of Elam and Media; cf. COT$^{Ez 23, 23}$ Dr$^{Hast. iii, Koa}$; but קוֹעַ = *Kutû* now doubted by Wkl$^{Altor. Forsch. ii. 2 (1899), 54}$.

† [קוֹף] **n.[m.]** ape, so Vrss, 𝔊 πίθηκοι (om. 6971
𝔊^{B} in K) (foreign word; prob. = Skr. *kapi, id.;* Egypt. as loan-word *gôfē* WMM$^{As. u. Eur. 95}$, *gi'f* Erman$^{ZMG xlvi (1892), 121}$; Gk. κῆβος, κῆπος is of Eg. orig. acc. to Lewy$^{Fremdw. 6}$);—pl. קֹפִים 1 K 10^{22} = קוֹפִים 2 Ch 9^{21}, brought to Sol. [from SE.] by Phoenician fleet; cf. Ar. prov. '*donum regionis Jemen simiae sunt,*' Freytag$^{Provv. iii. 3160}$.

קוף (√ of foll.; appar. = II. נקף, *go around*). 5362
p. 668
† [תְּקוּפָה] **n.f. coming round, circuit;**— 8622
cstr. תְּקוּפַת הַשָּׁנָה Ex 34^{22} (JE), adv., *at the circuit* (completion) *of the year*, so לִתְ׳ הַשָּׁנָה 2 Ch 24^{23}; = pl. cstr. לִתְקֻפוֹת הַיָּמִים 1 S 1^{20}; sg. sf. of finished *circuit* of sun ψ 19^{7} (opp. מוֹצָאוֹ; cf. of moon, בתקופתו Ecclus 43^{7}).

† I. [קוּץ] **vb. feel a loathing, abhorrence,** 6973
sickening dread (‖ √ of קוט; 𝔗 קוּץ *id.;* for connex. of meanings cf. Aram. קְנַט *loathe*, قَنِطَ *fear*);—**Qal** *Pf.* 3 fs. קָצָה Nu 21^{5}; 1 s. קַצְתִּי Gn 27^{46}; *Impf.* 3 ms. וַיָּקָץ Nu 22^{3} 1 K 11^{25} (but v. infr.); 2 ms. juss. תָּקֹץ Pr 3^{11}; 1 s. וָאָקֻץ Lv

20[23]; 3 mpl. וַיָּקֻצוּ Ex 1[12]; *Pt.* קָץ Is 7[16];—**1.** *feel a loathing* at, *abhor*, c. ב rei Nu 21[5] (JE), Gn 27[46] (P), Pr 3[11] (‖ מָאַס); c. ב pers. Lv 20[23] (H; subj. 'י); so 1 K 11[25], but Kit (after 𝔖, cf. 𝔊) prop. וַיָּצֶק (√ צוק **Hiph.** *distress*). **2.** *feel a sickening dread*, c. מִפְּנֵי pers. Ex 1[12] (J), Nu 22[3] (E), Is 7[16]. **Hiph.** *Impf.* 1 pl. sf. נְקִיצֶנָּה Is 7[6] (sf. of Judah) *let us cause her sickening dread*, but weak, rd. נְצִיקֶנָּה (√צוק) Thes Che Du Gr Marti.—Other **Hiph.** forms v. קיץ.

II. קוץ (√of foll.; cf. perh. NH, 𝔗, קוּץ *cut off;* NH קוֹץ=BH).

6975 †I. קוֹץ **n.m.** [Ez 28, 24] **thornbush, thorn**;—abs. 'ק Gn 3[18]+; pl. קֹצִים Ex 22[5]+, קוֹצִים Is 33[12]+; cstr. קוֹצֵי Ju 8[7.16]; — **1.** *thornbush*, +דַּרְדַּר (q.v.) Gn 3[18] (J), Ho 10[8]; +שָׁמִיר Is 32[13]; + בַּרְקָנִים (q.v.), ק' הַמִּדְבָּר Ju 8[7.16]; 'ק alone Ex 22[5] (E); כְּאֵשׁ קוֹצִים ψ 118[12] (sim. of foes); in various fig., Is 33[12] Je 4[3] 12[13]. **2.** *thorn*, fig, Ez 28[24] (c. מַכְאִב, v. כאב; ‖ סִלּוֹן q.v.); sim. כְּקֹ' מֻנָד 2 S 23[6] (Perles[Anal. 53] conj. מִין, but v. also נוד **Hoph.**).

6976 †II. קוֹץ **n.pr.m.** **1.** name in Judah 1 Ch 4[8], Κωε, Κως. **2.** הַקֹּ': priest 1 Ch 24[10], Κως, A 𝔊L Ακκως; Ezr 2[61]=Ne 7[63], Ne 3[4.21], Ακ(κ)ους, -ως.

6977 †[קְוֻצּוֹת] **n.f.pl.** locks of hair (√obscure; NH *id.;* Syr. ܩܘܨܬܐ, ܩܘܨܬܐ PS[3556]; Ar. قُصَّةٌ *hair over forehead*);—sf. קְוֻצּוֹתַי Ct 5[2], -תָיו v[11].

6979 †I. [קוּר] **vb.** bore, dig (Ar. قَارَ (و) *cut a round hole in, scoop out*);—**Qal** *Pf.* 1 s. קַרְתִּי 2 K 19[24] *I have dug* (sc. a well)=Is 37[25] (Meinh conj. כָּרִתִי).—**Hiph.**, **Pilp.**, v. I, II. קרר.

4726 †מָקוֹר **n.m.** [Zc 13, 1] **spring, fountain** (app. orig. *well*);—abs. 'מ Zc 13[1] Pr 25[26]; cstr. מְקוֹר Je 2[13]+, מְקֹר Lv 12[7] 20[18]; sf. מְקוֹרוֹ Ho 13[15], etc.;—**1.** *spring* of water: **a.** fig., of 'י, מ' מַיִם חַיִּים Je 2[13] 17[13], cf. מ' חַיִּים ψ 36[10]; מ' חַיִּים (more gen.), Pr 10[11] 13[14] 14[27] 16[22]+18[4] (so rd. for מ' חָכְמָה 𝔊 Heb Codd Toy). **b.** fig. of purification Ez 13[1]. **c.** מְקוֹר מָשְׁחָת Pr 25[26] (fig.; +מַעְיָן). **d.** fig. of source of life and vigour Ho 13[15] Je 51[36]; of a nation's orig. source, stock ψ 68[27] (Kay Che, of temple); source of joy Pr 5[18] (fig. of wife; ‖ אֵשֶׁת). **2.** fig. of eye, מְקוֹר דִּמְעָה, Je 8[23]. **3.** *source* of menstruous blood, מְ' דָּמֶיהָ Lv 20[18], so מְקֹרָהּ v[18] (H). **4.** =*flow* of blood after child-birth מְ' דָּמֶיהָ 12[7] (P).

II. קור (√of foll.; cf. Ar. قَارَ (و) v. *turn, twist* (of serpent), قُوَّرٌ a kind of *rope*).

†[קוּר] **n.m.** [Is 59, 6] **thread, film**;—pl. cstr. קוּרֵי עַכָּבִישׁ Is 59[5] they weave *spider-threads*, fig. of machinations of wicked, so sf. קוּרֵיהֶם v[6]. 6980

קוֹרֵא v. קרא. קוֹרָה v. קרה. p. 896, 900 6981-82

†[קוֹשׁ] **vb.** lay bait or lure (‖ √of יקשׁ);—**Qal** *Impf.* 3 mpl. יְקֹשׁוּן Is 29[21], c. לְ pers. (fig.). 6983

†קוּשָׁיָהוּ **n.pr.m.** (form dub.; Kit[Hpt] 'קִישׁ, cf. 6[29] and 𝔊; Pei[ZAW xvii (1897), 348] finds here a god *Ḳûs*, but very precarious);—Levite, 1 Ch 15[17], (υἱὸς) Κ(ε)ισαίου,=קִישִׁי 6[29], Κεισαι[ν], 𝔊L Κουσει. 6984 7029

קַח, קָח, קַחַת etc., v. לקח. p. 542 3947

†קָט Ez 16[47] (כִּמְעַט ק'), dub.; Ki *only* (Ar. قط); del. 𝔊 𝔖 Thes Hi Co Berthol, Toy זאת, Perles [Anal. 30] קָטֹן; Krae conj. כִּי־אִם עָסַפְתְּ, for כמעטקט. 6985

קטב (√of foll.; cf. 𝔗 קְטַב *cut off* (rare); in Ar. قَطَبَ *id.*, ط said to be for ض, v. Lane).

†קֶטֶב, [קֹטֶב] **n.m.** [Dt 32, 24] **destruction**;—of pestilence, abs. 'ק Dt 32[24] (‖ רֶשֶׁף), ψ 91[6] (‖ דֶּבֶר), so sf. (of Sheʾôl) קָטָבְךָ (Ges [§ 93 q]) Ho 13[14] (‖ of מָוֶת, דְּבָרֶיךָ); more gen., שַׁעַר קֹטֶב Is 28[2]. 6986-87

†[קָטַל] **vb.** **slay** (poet. and late) (Ar. قَتَلَ, Eth. ቀተለ: Sab. קתל Hom[Chrest. 126], all *slay* (orig. form with ת; changed later, after ק); Aram. קְטַל, ܩܛܠ; OAram. קטל, כטל, קתל);—**Qal** *Impf.* c. acc. pers., 3 ms. יִקְטָל־ Jb 24[14]; sf., subj. God, יִקְטְלֵנִי 13[15]; of God also 2 ms. תִּקְטֹל ψ 139[19]. 6991

†[קֶטֶל] **n.[m.]** slaughter;—מִקָּטֶל MT Ob[9], but join to v[10] (then מִקֶּטֶל), 𝔊 We Now GASm. 6993

†[קָטֹן, Lag [BN 26.31]] **vb.** **be small, insignificant** (NH Hiph. and deriv.; JAram. in deriv., Syr. ܩܛܢ; OAram. קטין *insignificant;* Ar. قَطِينٌ *parum edens;* Eth. ቀጠነ: *be thin*, chiefly in deriv.; prob. also As. *ḳuttinnu*, *small, younger*, Zehnpf [BAS i. 505] (otherwise Dl [HWB 323]); Meissn [Suppl.] *ḳatânu*, *be short* (of hair), cf. Bez [ZA viii, 141 f.]);—**Qal** *Pf.* 1 s. קָטֹנְתִּי Gn 32[11], c. מִן comp., *I am too insignificant for* all the kindnesses; *Impf.* 3 fs. וַתִּקְטַן זֹאת בְּעֵינֶיךָ 2 S 7[19]=1 Ch 17[17]. **Hiph.** lit. *Inf. cstr.* לְהַקְטִין Am 8[5] *making* ephah *small*. 6994

†I. קָטָן **adj.** small, young, unimportant;—abs. 'ק Gn 9[24]+; sf. קְטַנָּם (Kö [ii. 1, 74]) Je 6[13]+; 6996

fs. קְטַנָּה Gn 29^{16}+; mpl. קְטַנִּים 2 K 18^{24}+; cstr. קְטַנֵּי 1 S 9^{21} (v. Dr; We conj. ־נִּי, old cstr., cf. HPS), Pr 30^{24}; fpl. קְטַנּוֹת Ez 16^{61}+;—**1.** *small:* esp. **a.** of children, youth=*young*, Gn 44^{20} (J) 2 S 9^{12} 1 K 11^{17} 2 K 2^{23} 5^{2}, of sister Ct 8^{8}; =*younger*, of two children (oft. opp. גדול), Gn 9^{24} 27$^{15.42}$ (all J), 29$^{16.18}$ (E), 1 S 14^{49} (f.; opp. הַבְּכִירָה); of *younger* sister Ju 15^{2}, so (fig.) Ez 16^{46} and (+מִן comp.) v^{61}; brother 1 Ch 24^{31}; הַקּ׳ *youngest* son (of several) 1 S 16^{11} 17^{14}; +גָּדוֹל = *young and old* (v. קָטֹן **1**) Je 16^{6} cf. 2 Ch 31^{15} 34^{30}. **b.** of things: utterance Nu 22^{18} (E), weight Dt 25$^{13.14}$, vessels 2 Ch 36^{18}, animals ψ 104^{25} (all opp. גדול); cf. also 2 S 12^{3} 1 K 2^{20} 17^{13} 18^{44} 2 K 4^{10} Ez 43^{14} (opp. גדול), Pr 30^{24} Ct 2^{15}, + prob. Ez 46^{22} (v. II. [קָטַר]); כְּלֵי הַקָּטָן Is 22^{24} the vessels *of small size* (fig.). **2.** *small:* **a.** with added idea of weakness, pers. 2 K 18^{24}=Is 36^{9}, city Ec 9^{14}. **b.**=*insignificant*, (1) tribe 1 S 9^{21}; (2) pers. (+גדול;=all persons) Je 6^{13} 31^{34} Jon 3^{5} ψ 115^{13} Est 1$^{5.20}$, cf. 1 Ch 12^{14} (van d. H. v^{13}); (3) in gen., יוֹם קְטַנּוֹת Zc 4^{10} *day of small things.*—Vid. also קָטֹן.

6997 †II. קָטָן **n.pr.m.** (*the small*);—הַקּ׳, post-ex. name Ezr 8^{12}, Ακ(κ)αταν.

6996 קָטֹן$_{54}$ **adj. small, insignificant**;—abs. ק׳ 1 S 2^{19}+; cstr. קְטֹן 2 Ch 21^{17};—f., pl. and sf. supplied by קָטָן;—**1.** *small:* esp. **a.** of youth =*young*, נַעַר ק׳ 1 S 20^{35} 1 K 3^{7} 2 K 5^{14} Is 11^{6}; =*younger* of two brothers, Gn 48^{19} (E) Ju 1^{13} 3^{9} (+מִן comp.); הַקּ׳ *youngest* brother Gn 42^{13}+ 10 t. Gn (JE), son Ju 9^{5} 2 Ch 22^{1}, so קְטֹן בָּנָיו 21^{17}; +גדול = *young and old* (v. קָטָן **1**), i.e. everybody Gn 19^{11} (J), 1 S 5^{9} 30^{2}+ (of pers. and things) v^{19}. **b.** of things 1 S 2^{19} 1 K 8^{64} (+מִן comp.), Am 6^{11} Is 54^{7}; opp. גָּדוֹל 1 S 22^{15} 25^{36} Gn 1^{16} (P). **2.** = *unimportant*, things, Ex 18$^{22.26}$ (E), 1 S 20^{2} (all opp. גדול); pers.,=*feeble* Am 7$^{2.5}$; =*insignificant* Je 49^{15} Ob^{2} (both ‖ בָּזוּי), Is 60^{22} (‖ צָעִיר); ק׳ בְּעֵינֶיךָ 1 S 15^{17}; esp. +גָּדוֹל = low and high,=everybody, Dt 1^{17} 1 K 22^{31} = 2 Ch 18^{30}, Je 8^{10} Jb 3^{19}, +8 t.—Vid. also קָטָן.

6995 †[קֹטֶן] **n.m.** little (finger);—sf. קָטְנִּי (=קְטַנִּי van d. H. in Ch; cf. Kö $^{ii. 69}$ Ges $^{§ 93q}$), 1 K 12^{10}=2 Ch 10^{10}.

6998 [קָטַף] **vb. pluck off** (twigs, etc.), or out (NH=BH; Ar. قَطَفَ *pluck* grapes; ℑ קְטַף, Syr. ܩܛܦ; cf. As. *ḳatâpu*, appar. *pluck off*);—**Qal** *Pf.* 3 ms. קָטַף Ez 17^{4} *he* [i.e. eagle, in fig.] *plucked off* twigs; 2 ms. וְקָטַפְתָּ Dt 23^{26} (ears of grain, בְּיָדֶךָ); *Impf.* 1 s. אֶקְטֹף Ez 17^{22} (subj. י׳; acc. + מִן *from*); *Pt.* mpl. הַקֹּטְפִים Jb 30^{4} *they who pluck out* the mallow. **Niph.** *Impf.* 3 ms. יִקָּטֵף Jb 8^{12} *it is not plucked off.*

I. קטר (√of foll.; cf. As. *ḳutru* (with ת) *smoke;* Talm. ℑ קוּטְרָא, קִיטְרָא (thick) *smoke;* Ar. قَتَرَ *smoke* (said of fire); usu. *exhale odour* (esp. of roast meat); As. *ḳutrinnu*, *incense-offering;* Sab. מקטר *censer* CIS $^{iv, nos. 26, l. 6; 30, l. 4}$; Eth. ቀተረ: *incense;* Egypt. *ḳatalθa* Bondi $^{74 ff.}$, *ḳataruti̥* WMM $^{As. u. Eur. 97}$ = קְטֹרֶת, קְטָרוֹת; NH [קָטַר] *smoke* (said of incense)).

†קִיטוֹר (Lag $^{BN 182}$) **n.m. thick smoke**;— 7008
קִיטֹר Gn 19$^{28.28}$ (J), ־טוֹר ψ 119^{83}; 148^{8} (fig. of clouds in thunderstorm; Vrss. appar. קֶרַח, cf. Du).

†קְטוֹרָה **n.m. smoke of sacrifice**;—abs. 6988
Dt 33^{10} (E; Di al. of *incense*).

†קְטוּרָה **n.pr.f.** a wife of Abraham, after 6989
Sarah's death, Gn 25$^{1.4}$ 1 Ch 1$^{32.33}$; Χεττουρα.

קְטֹרֶת$_{60}$ **n.f. smoke, odour of** (burning) 7004
sacrifice, incense;—ק׳ abs. Ex 30^{1}+; cstr. 25^{6}+; sf. קְטָרְתִּי Ez 16^{18} 23^{41};—**1.** *sweet smoke of sacrifice*, ‖ מנחה Is 1^{13} ψ 141^{2}, ק׳ אֵילִים 66^{15}, לְהַקְטִיר ק׳ 1 S 2^{28} (?). **2.** *incense*, ק׳ (ה)סמים Ex 25^{6} 30^{7} 31^{11} 40^{27}+9 t.; ק׳ תמיד Ex 30^{8}, ק׳ רֹקַח v^{35}, הק׳ alone v^{37} Lv 16^{13} Nu 16^{35} 17^{12}; so ק׳ 16$^{7.17.18}$ 17$^{5.11}$ 2 Ch 29^{7}, ק׳ זָרָה Ex 30^{9}, ענן הק׳ Lv 16^{13} Ez 8^{11}, also of אשׁ זרה Lv 10^{1} (illegal worship); in offering of the princes Nu 7^{14}+ 11 t. 7, cf. v^{86}. Altar of incense is מזבח מקטר ק׳ Ex 30^{1}, מ׳ הק׳ 1 Ch 28^{18}, מ׳ הזהב לק׳ Ex 40^{5}, מ׳ ק׳ הסמים Lv 4^{7}, מ׳ הק׳ Ex 30^{27}+6 t. **3.** *perfume*, ‖ שֶׁמֶן Ez 16^{18} 23^{41} Pr 27^{9}.

[קָטַר]$_{115}$ **vb. denom. Pi. Hiph. make** 6999
sacrifices smoke, send them up in smoke (prop. *produce* קְטֹרֶת, v. Sta $^{ZAW vi (1886), 298 f.}$);—**Pi.**$_{42}$ *Pf.* 3 mpl. קִטְּרוּ Je 19^{13}+, קִטַּרְתֶּם Je 44$^{21.23}$; *Impf.* 3 ms. יְקַטֵּר Hb 1^{16}+; 3 mpl. יְקַטֵּרוּן Ho 11^{2}, etc.; *Inf. abs.* קַטֵּר 1 S 2^{16}+; *cstr.* Je 11^{13}+, *Pt.* pl. מְקַטְּרִים Is 65^{3}+, etc.;—*make sacrifices smoke*, offer them by burning: to י׳, 1 S 2^{16} (where prob. rd. יַקְטִירוּן [and so v^{15}] Sta $^{l.c. 299}$): elsewhere to other gods or in illegal worship, Je 44^{23}; c. acc. קִטֵּר (but see this, infr.) Je 44^{21} (here [and al. in some other passages] of *incense*), תּוֹדָה Am 4^{5}; place is usu. c. בְּ, e.g. בַּבָּמוֹת 2 K 17^{11} 23^{5}; עוֹד הָעָם מְזַבְּחִים וּמְקַטְּרִים בַּבָּמוֹת 1 K 22^{44} 2 K 12^{4} 14^{4} 15$^{4.35}$ (R), cf. 2 K

16^{4} = 2 Ch 28^{4} (cf. RS$^{\text{Sem. i. 471; 2nd ed. 490}}$); הַבּ׳ אֲשֶׁר קִטְּרוּ שָׁמָּה 2 K 23^{8}; c. עַל e.g. על הגבעות Ho 4^{13}, על גג(ו)ת Je 19^{13} 32^{20}, על הלבנים Is 65^{3}, על ההרים v^{7}; c. לְ of deity, Ho 11^{2} Je 1^{16} + 14 t. Je (+ 19^{13} 32^{29} supr.), Hb 1^{16} 2 K 22^{17} 23^{5} 2 Ch 25^{14} 28^{25} 34^{25} Qr (> Kt **Hiph.**), to the brazen serpent 2 K 18^{4}. **Pu.** *Pt.* מְקֻטֶּרֶת מֹר וגו׳ Ct 3^{6} *fumigated with myrrh*, etc. (Aq. 𝔙 Schlottm מְקֻטֹּרֶת). **Hiph.**$_{71}$ *Pf.* 3 ms. הִקְטִיר Lv 9^{10} +; 2 ms. הִקְטַרְתָּ Ex 29$^{13.18.25}$, etc.; *Impf.* 3 ms. יַקְטִיר Lv 4^{26} 16^{25}, וַיַּקְטֵר Ex 40^{27} +, etc.: *Imv.* ms. הַקְטֵר 2 K 16^{15}; *Inf. abs.* הַקְטֵיר 1 K 9^{25}; *cstr.* לְהַקְטִיר Ex 30^{20} +; *Pt.* מַקְטִיר Je 33^{18} +, etc. **1.** *make sacrifices smoke,* usu. **a.** in worship of י׳: abs. 1 K 12^{33} 13^{1} 2 Ch 29^{11}; c. acc. חלב Lv 17^{6} Nu 18^{17} 1 S 2$^{15.16}$, עלת 2 K 16$^{13.15}$ 2 Ch 13^{11}, אִשֶּׁה Ex 30^{20} Lv 2^{11} Nu 18^{17}, מנחה Je 33^{18}; רֹאשׁ, etc., Lv 8^{20} אַזְכָּרָה Lv 2^{16}, חלבי השלמים Lv 6^{5}; קטרת 1 S 2^{28}; on 1 K 9^{25} v. Klo Benz; place is על מזבח Lv 4^{10} + 5 t., הַמִּזְבֵּחָה Ex 29$^{13.18.25}$ + 23 t. Lv, Nu 5^{26} (all P); c. הַמִּזְבֵּחַ (acc.) Lv 6^{8}; בַּבָּמוֹת 1 K 3^{3}; בגיא בן הִנֹּם 2 Ch 28^{3}. **b.** less oft. in worship of other gods, לאלהיהן (gods of Sol.'s wives) 1 K 11^{8}, לאלהיו (of Moab) Je 48^{35}, להם (Baalim) Ho 2^{15};—2 Ch 34^{25} rd. Qr **Qal**. **2.** *cause incense to smoke, offer incense* abs. 2 Ch 2^{5} 26$^{18.18.19}$; c. עַל of altar 2 Ch 26^{16} Ex 30^{7} 40^{27}; c. acc. יַקְטִירֶנָּה 30$^{7.8}$, קטרת סמים 30^{7} 40^{27} 2 Ch 2^{3}, קטרת תמיד Ex 30^{8}, הק׳ קטרת Nu 17^{5} 2 Ch 29^{7}. **3.** *make smoke* upon (על) both altars (of burnt-offering and of incense) 1 Ch 6^{34}, cf. also 23^{13}. **Hoph.** *be made to smoke* as a sacrifice: *Impf.* 3 fs. תָּקְטָר Lv 6^{15}, *Pt.* מֻקְטָר Mal 1^{11} (Ew Ke al. [Ges $^{\S 121 b}$]; We Now rd. מ׳ לִשְׁמִי מִנְחָה; but v. מֻקְטָר).

7002 †קְטֹר (Ol$^{\S 182e}$) **n.f. incense**;—Je 44^{21} (on gender v. Albr$^{\text{ZAW xvi (1896), 100}}$, who reads אֹתָהּ for אֹתָם, and so Rothst^{Kau} Gie; Gie also קְטֹרֶת).

4729 †[מִקְטָר, מִקְטֵר] **n.m. place of sacrificial smoke**;—cstr. מִזְבֵּחַ מִקְטַר קְטֹרֶת Ex 30^{1} *altar, place of offering incense* (SS Kau Buhl^{13} al. n. act. *burning*).

6999 †מֻקְטָר **n.m. incense**;—abs. מ׳ Mal 1^{11} (Thes Hi Marti^{Kau} GASm Kö$^{\text{iii, §307}}$).

4730 †מִקְטֶרֶת **n.f. censer**;—מ׳ abs. 2 Ch 26^{19}; sf. מִקְטַרְתּוֹ Ez 8^{11}.

6999 †[מְקַטְּרָה] **n.f. incense-altar**;—pl. abs. מְקַטְּרוֹת 2 Ch 30^{14}.

7000 †II. [קָטַר] **vb.** dubious word; si vera l. appar. = **shut in, enclose** (𝔗 קְטַר, Syr. ܩܛܪ *bind*, ܩܛܪܐ *chain*);—**Qal** *Pt. pass.* pl. חֲצֵרוֹת קְטֻרוֹת Ez 46^{22} *enclosed courts* (cf. interpr. in Levy^{NHWB}, and ܕܪܬܐ ܩܛܝܪܬܐ PS^{3589}), but rd. prob. קְטַנּוֹת *small*, 𝔊 𝔖 Co Toy Berthol Krae.

†קִטְרוֹן **n.pr.loc.** in Zebulun Ju 1^{30}, Κεδρων, 7003
A Χεβρων; = קַטָּת Jos 19^{15}? site unknown. 7005

†קַטָּת **n.pr.loc.** in Zebulun Jos 19^{15}, Καταναθ, 7005
A Κατταθ, 𝔊L Κοτταθ;—v. קִטְרוֹן. above 7003

†[קִיא Nö$^{\text{ZMG xxxvii (1883), 539}}$] **vb. vomit up,** 6958
spue out, disgorge (NH *id.*, Hiph.; As. *ḳâ'u, spit* Meissn$^{\text{Suppl. 83}}$; Ar. قَاءَ *vomit;* Eth. [ቀየአ፡] ቂእ፡ *vomit*);—**Qal** *Pt.* f. קָאָה Lv 18^{28}, but read prob. קָ֫אָה, *Pf.* 3 fs. (Di Baen); *Impf.* (**Qal** or **Hiph.**) 3 ms. וַיָּקֵא Jon 2^{11}, sf. וַיְקִיאֶנּוּ Jb 20^{15}; 3 fs. תָּקִיא Lv 18^{28} 20^{22}, וַתָּקִא 18^{25}; 2 ms. sf. תְּקִיאֶנָּה Pr 23^{8}; **Hiph.** *Pf.* sf. consec. וַהֲקֵאתוֹ 25^{16}; all *vomit up*:—c. acc., lit. Pr 23^{8} 25^{16} Jon 2^{11}; fig. of land casting out inhab. Lv 18$^{25.28.28}$ 20^{22} (all H); of *disgorging* riches Jb 20^{15}.

†[קֵא] **n.** [**m.**] **what is vomited up, vomit** 6892
(v. Ba$^{\text{NB 79}}$);—sf. קֵאוֹ Pr 26^{11} (of dog).

†קִיא **n.m. id.** (v. Ba$^{\text{NB 80}}$);—abs. ק׳ Is 28^{8}; 6892
sf. קִיאוֹ Is 19^{14} (sim.); fig. Je 48^{26} (of Moab).

†[קָיָה] **vb.** vomit (si vera l. = קִיא, Ges$^{\S 76 h}$ 6958, 7006
Kö$^{\text{ii. 1, 586}}$);—**Qal** *Imv.* mpl. וּקְיוּ Je 25^{27} Qr (Kt וקוו), be drunken *and vomit* (? err. for וְקִיאוּ).

קִיטוֹר v. קטר. קִים, קִימָה v. קום. p. 879, 882 7008-09, 7012
קִימוֹשׁ v. קִמּוֹשׁ. p. 888 7057

קין (√ of foll.; cf. Ar. قَانَ *fit together, fabricate* (*make artificially*), *forge* (cf. Wetzst$^{\text{Syr. Dreschtafel (1873) 297}}$), whence قَيْنٌ *worker in iron*, As. *ḳinai* (Meissn$^{\text{ZA viii (1893), 82}}$), 𝔗 קֵינָאָה, Syr. ܩܝܢܐ, Palm. קיניא (pl.) *metal-worker*, cf. BH תּוּבַל קַיִן; also Ar. قَيْنَةٌ *slave-girl,* and *woman-singer, lute-player* (fr. skill); cf. Eth. ቀኒ፡ *song, singing,* Syr. ܩܝܢܬܐ, *hymn, elegy;* Ar. vb. IV Dozy; NH קִינָה = BH; cf. also Bu$^{\text{ZAW ii (1882), 28}}$).

†I. [קַ֫יִן] **n.** [**m.**] **spear** 𝔊 and most;—sf. קֵינוֹ 7013
2 S 21^{16}; < rd. קוֹבָעוֹ (cf. 1 S 17^{38}) Klo Bu HPS al.

†II. קַ֫יִן **n.pr. 1. gent.** (v. Sta$^{\text{G i. 131 f.}}$ Mey 7014
$^{\text{Entstehung 115}}$; cf. Ar. n.pr.fam. قَيْن; Nab. Sin. n.pr.m. et. f. קינו; tribe of *smiths?*);—tribe of Moses' father-in-law Ju 4^{11} (cf. קֵינִי 1^{16}), Καινα, 𝔊L Κειν; akin to Midian (Nu 10^{29} P), settled among Amal. in S. of Canaan (v. קֵינִי);

prophesied against by Balaam Nu 24^{22} (קַיִן; JE);—v. also קֵינִי. **2. loc.** הַקַּיִן, in S. Judah (a settlement of II. ק׳ **1**?);—Jos 15^{57}, [Ζακαν]αειμ, A [Ζανω] Ακειμ, 𝔊L [Ζανου] Ακεν; poss. = *Yŭkîn* SE. from Hebron [Rob[BR ii. 85]] (v. Buhl[Geogr. 162 f.]
7016 who, however, cp. קִינָה v^{22}).

7016 † I. קִינָה **n.pr.loc.** in S. Judah (a settlement of II. קַיִן **1**?), Jos 15^{22}, Ικαμ, A 𝔊L Κ(ε)ινα.

7014 † III. קַיִן **n.pr.m. Cain**, Καιν, eldest son of Adam and Eve (expl. Gn 4^{1} fr. קָנָה *acquire;* but in fact = II. ק׳, as *heros eponymos*, acc. to We[Comp. 11] Sta[G 285 ff.] Bu[Urg. 193] Holz[Gn 50 f.] esp. Sta[ZAW xiv (1894), 250 ff.; xv (1895), 157 ff.], Che[Ency. Bib. Cain]);—ק׳ Gn $4^{1.2.3.5.5.8.8.9.13.15.15.16.17}$, קָיִן $v^{6.24.25}$ (all J).

7017 † קֵינִי **adj.gent.** of II. קַיִן **1** (q.v.), חֶבֶר הַקּ׳ (dwelling in N. Isr.), ὁ Κειναῖος, Ju $4^{11.17.17}$ 5^{24} (against WMM Jen, who ref. ק׳ here to city *Kîn* near Megiddo, mentioned by Egypt., v. esp. Bu Now on 4^{11}); rd. prob. also חֹבָב הַקּ׳ 1^{16} (for בְּנֵי ק׳; so Bu GFM; 𝔊 οἱ υἱοὶ Ιωθορ τοῦ Κειναίου); elsewhere as **n. gent. coll.** הַקּ׳ settled among Amal., Nu 24^{21} (JE; v. II. קַיִן **1**), 1 S 15^{6}—= קֵינִי v^{6} (We Bu Kit קַיִן, HPS הַקֵּינִי);—הַקּ׳ also 27^{10} 30^{29} (B 𝔊L Κενεζ(ε)ι = קְנִזִּי; A Κηνει, Κειναῖος); Gn 15^{19} (list of peoples; R); = הַקִּינִים 1 Ch 2^{55} (Κ(ε)ιναῖοι), related to Rechabites.

7018 † קֵינָן **n.pr.m.** a Sethite (Sab. n. pr. dei קינן CIS[iv, no. 8, 1. 2]);—Gn $5^{9.10.12.13.14}$ 1 Ch 1^{2}, Καιναν.

7015 † II. קִינָה **n.f. elegy, dirge**;—abs. ק׳ 2 S 1^{17}+; pl. קִינִים Ez 2^{10} (but rd. קינה Co—not Berthol Toy Krae), קִינוֹת 2 Ch 35^{25}; sf. קִינוֹתֵיהֶם v^{25};—*elegy, dirge* 2 S 1^{17} Ez $19^{14.14}$ 32^{16}, pl. 2 Ch 35^{25}; sg. ‖ אֵבֶל Am 8^{10}, ‖ הֶגֶה וָהִי Ez 2^{10}, נשׂא ק׳ Je 7^{29}, c. עַל *for*, Am 5^{1} Je 9^{9} Ez 26^{17} 27^{2} 28^{12} 32^{2}; c. אֶל Ez 19^{1} 27^{32}; למד ק׳ Je 9^{19} (‖ נְהִי); pl. as collection of written dirges 2 Ch 35^{25}.—Bu[ZAW ii (1882), 1 ff., cf. iii (1883), 299 ff.] thinks *Kina* rhythm always 3 + 2 tone-beats, but book La (Heb. קִינוֹת) is in all parts pentam., 3 + 2 varying sts. with 2 + 3, yet always 5 in line, with caesura; of other קִינוֹת, Am 5^{2} Ez $19^{2 ff.}$ $26^{17 b ff.}$ are pent., 2 S $1^{19 ff.}$ $3^{33 f.}$ tetr., Ez $27^{3 ff.}$ $28^{12 ff.}$ $32^{2 ff.}$ hex.; v. Br[Gen. Intr. 379 ff.].

6969 † [קוֹנֵן] **vb. denom. Pō῾l.** chant a קִינָה;—*Pf.* 3 pl. consec. וְקוֹנְנוּ Ez 27^{32} (עַל pers.), sf. (cogn.) וְקוֹנְנוּהָ 32^{16}; *Impf.* 3 ms. וַיְקֹנֵן 2 S 1^{17} (c. acc. cogn. + עַל pers.), cf. (עַל pers. only), 2 Ch 35^{25} and (אֶל pers.) 2 S 3^{33}; 3 fpl. תְּקוֹנֵנָּה c. acc. cogn., Ez 32^{16}, + עַל pers. v^{16}; *Pt.* as subst. Je 9^{16} (professional) *wailing women*.

† I. [קִיץ] **vb. Hiph.** awake (‖ form of 6974
יקץ; NH in Hiph. (rare));—*Pf.* 3 ms. הֵקִיץ 2 K 4^{31} Ez 7^{6}; 2 ms. וַהֲקִיצוֹתָ consec. Pr 6^{22}, etc.; *Impf.* 1 s. אָקִיץ Pr 23^{35}; 3 mpl. יָקִיצוּ Je 51^{39}+; *Imv.* ms. הָקִיצָה Hb 2^{19}+; mpl. הָקִיצוּ Is 26^{19} Jo 1^{5}; *Inf. cstr.* הָקִיץ ψ 17^{15} 73^{20}; *Pt.* מֵקִיץ 1 S 26^{12};—*shew signs of waking, awake:* **1.** from sleep, **a.** 1 S 26^{12} Is $29^{8.8}$ ψ 3^{6} 73^{20} 139^{18} Pr 6^{22} (doubtful line, v. Toy). **b.** of י׳ ψ 44^{24} *awake* [fr. sleep] to activity, so 35^{23} (c. ל rei), 59^{6} (c. inf. purpose). **c.** fr. ecstatic sleep of proph. Je 31^{26}. **2.** fr. sleep of death, c. neg. 2 K 4^{31} Je $51^{39.57}$ Jb 14^{12}; of resurrection Is 26^{19} Dn 12^{2}. **3.** from stupor (of drunkenness) Jo 1^{5} Pr 23^{35}. **4.** of inanimate thing Hb 2^{19}; cf. בָּא הַקֵּץ הֵקִיץ אֵלָיִךְ Ez 7^{6} *the end cometh, it hath awaked unto thee* (Co del. הֵקִיץ, but the word-play favours it).—ψ 17^{15} is put by Thes Ol Hup Du al. sub **1 a**; Ew De Che sub **2**; We sub **1 b**; Calv Now: from night of distress and helplessness, and so Bae (psalmist representing Isr.).

II. קיץ (√ of foll.; usu. taken as = I. קִיץ, but connex. not clear; cf. Ar. قَيْظٌ *vehement heat of summer, late summer* (We[Skizzen iii, 90]), قَاظَ *be vehemently hot;* Sab. קים *summer* Mordtm[Him. Inschr. 71]; NH קַיִץ = BH, so 𝔗 קַיְטָא, Syr. ܩܝܛܐ; OAram. (Zinj.) כיצא *summer*).

† קַיִץ **n.m.**[Je 8, 20] **summer, summer-fruit** (cf. 6972,
Gk. θέρος in both meanings);—abs. ק׳ Gn 8^{22}+; 7019
קָיִץ Am 3^{15}+; sf. קֵיצֵךְ Is 16^{9} Je 48^{32};—**1.** *summer*-season, opp. חֹרֶף Gn 8^{22} (J), Am 3^{15} Zc 14^{8} ψ 74^{17}; ‖ קָצִיר Je 8^{20} Pr 6^{8} 10^{5} 26^{1}, also (without קָצִיר) 30^{25}; as fruit harvest Is 28^{4}; time of drought ψ 32^{4} (fig.). **2.** *summer-fruit* 2 S $16^{1.2}$ Am $8^{1.2}$ Je $40^{10.12}$ also, ‖ בָּצִיר, 48^{32} Mi 7^{1} (in sim.), but ‖ קציר Is 16^{9} (assim. to ק of קַיִץ; rd. prob. בציר).

קִיצוֹן v. קצץ. p. 894 7020

† קִיקָיוֹן **n.m.**[Jon 4, 6] a plant (cf. As. *kuk-* 7021
kânîtum (כ) a garden-plant, Dl[HWB 327]);—usu. **ricinus** (R. *communis*, Linn. = *castor-oil tree;* cf. Dioscor.[iv. 164] κίκι (Egypt.) = κρότων [*castor-oil tree*]; Talm. שֶׁמֶן קִיק; v. esp. Löw[p. 353 f.]); perh. < **bottle-gourd** (𝔊 κολόκυνθα; i.e. *cucurbita lagenaria*, a vine growing and withering rapidly, Post in Hastings[DB ii. 250]);—Jon $4^{6.6.7.9.10}$.

קִיקָלוֹן v. קלל. p. 887 7022

7023 1. קִיר [74] **n.m.** [ψ 62, 4] **wall** (√unknown);—abs. ק׳ Nu 22[25]+, קִר Is 22[5]; cstr. קִיר 1 K 6[5]+; pl. קִירוֹת 1 K 6[16]+, cstr. *id.*, v[5]+; sf. קִירֹתָיו Ex 30[3]+, etc.;—*wall*, esp. as flat surface: **1.** usu. of house or chamber: **a.** inner surface, Am 5[19] 1 S 18[11]+9 t., +(of temple) 1 K 6[15 a]+ v[15 b] (but rd. קוֹרוֹת *beams*, with 𝔊 The Kit Benz), v[16.27.27]+6 t. †**b.** outer surface, 2 K 9[33] Ez 33[30] Is 59[10] (in sim.); so זֶרֶם קִיר Is 25[4] (but Lo Kn Gr Di Du Che[Hpt] al. rd. קֹר; JP Peters [JBL xi (1892), 46] prop. בָּרָד [as 28[2]]); of temple 1 K 6[5.5.6], cf. Ez 41[6.6]. †**c.** both inner and outer v[17.20.25]. †**d.** indeterminate, 12[5.7.12] 23[14]. †**e.** thickness specified, Ez 41[5.9.12.13] (of Ezekiel's temple). †**f.** as enclosing, 2 K 4[10] (of עֲלִיָּה, q.v.); as separating Ez 43[8]. †**2.** *wall* of (temple-)court Ez 8[7.8.8] (in vision); of vineyard Nu 22[25.25] (J), of city 35[4] (P), cf. ק׳ חַחוֹמָה Jos 2[15] (JE) *the* (inner) *surface of the wall.* †**3.** more gen., 1 K 5[13], and (in phr. מַשְׁתִּין בְּקִיר) 1 S 25[22.34] 1 K 14[10] 16[11] 21[21] 2 K 9[8]; in fig. Ez 13[12.14] (appar. fem., but city Jerus. prob. in mind, cf. Albr[ZAW xvi (1896), 85] Kö[ii. 2, 175]), v[15.15] (‖ חַיִץ v[10]), ק׳ נָטוּי ψ 62[4]; אֶבֶן ק׳ 2 S 5[11] = ק׳ 1 Ch 14[1], cf. Hb 2[11] (fig.); קִיר בַּרְזֶל Ez 4[3] (symbol.).—Is 22[5] is dub.: usu. *wall* (so even Du Che[Hpt]
7024 Marti), but ref. not clear; Ew Che[Comm.] III. קִיר; Klo Brd Wkl[Alttest. Unters. 177] קוֹעַ, so WMM[Hast. DB Kir], but v. Dr[ib. Koa]. †**4.** of flat side of altar Ez 41[22] Ex 30[3] 37[26] Lv 1[15] 5[9] (all P). †**5.** קִירוֹת לִבִּי Je 4[19] *walls of my heart* (as seat of pain).

7024 †II. קִיר in **n.pr.loc.** of Moabite cities (cf. קר = *city* MI[11.12.24], pl. קרן l.[29]);—𝔊 usu. om., or reads τὸ τεῖχος;—**1.** ק׳ מוֹאָב Is 15[1], poss.
7025 *Rabba*, S. of Arnon, v. Buhl[Geogr. 270]. **2.** ק׳ חֶ֫רֶשׂ Je 48[31.36], ק׳ חֶ֫רֶשׂ Is 16[11] = ק׳ חֲרֶשֶׂת Is 16[7], 2 K 3[25] (Gi ק׳ חֲרָשֶׂת), perh. *Kerak*, S. of Rabba, v. Buhl[ib.], and cp. (on Kerak) Palmer[Des. of Ex. ii. 472] Dowling[PEQ, Oct. 1896, 327], esp. Mauss in de Luynes [Voyage à la Mer Morte (1864), ii. 106 ff., iii (Atlas, ad fin.), 13 pl.]

7024 †III. קִיר **n.pr.terr. et gent.** ק׳ orig. house of Aram Am 9[7]; קִ֫ירָה as place of exile Am 1[5] 2 K 16[9] (𝔊 τὴν πόλιν); קִיר as people in As. army Is 22[6] (v[5] vid. 1. קִיר ad fin.).—Location dub., v. conspectus of older views Dr[Am 1,5]; plausible is some tribe in S. Babylonia, E. of Tigris Wkl [AT Unters. 178], cf. Hal[RÉJ xi. 60];—WMM[Hast. DB Kir]
7023 everywhere del., or em. קוֹעַ, but v. 1. קִיר **3.** above

7026 קֵירֹס = קֵרֹס. p. 902

†קִישׁ **n.pr.m.** (prob. *קַיִשׁ, Ar. قَيْس, Aram. 7027
קישא, Nö[ZMG xl (1886), 167]; orig. n.pr.dei as Ar. قيس, wh. now only in n.pr. pers. We[Held. 2. 67]);—K(ε)ις: **1.** father of Saul 1 S 9[1.3.3] 10[11.21] 14[51] 2 S 21[14] 1 Ch 8[30.33] (where read אֲבִנֵר, Be Kau Kit), v[33] = 9[36.39] (read as above), v[39] 12[1] 26[28]. **2.** Levites: **a.** 1 Ch 23[21.22] 24[29.29]. **b.** 2 Ch 29[12]. **3.** ancestor of Mordecai Est 2[5] (Κεισαίου).

†קִישׁוֹן **n.pr.** of wady running NW. through 7028
plain of Megiddo (Esdraelon), K(ε)ισων (?*stream of* (god) *Kish* RS[Sem. i. 155; 2nd ed. 170]);—alw. נַחַל ק׳ Ju 4[7.13] 5[21.21] ψ 83[10], also 1 K 18[40]; mod. *Nahr-el-Muḳaṭṭaʿ*; v. Buhl[Geogr. 106, 209], GASm[Geogr. 382].

קִישִׁי v. קוּשָׁיָהוּ sub קוש. p. 881 6984, 7029

קַל, קֹל v. קלל. (קֹל *voice*, v. קול). p. 876,886-87 6963, 7031

קלה 2 S 20[14] Kt, v. קהל. p. 874 7035

†I. [קָלָה] **vb. roast, parch** (NH קָלָה *id.* 7033
(rare), קָלִי = BH; As. *kalû*, II. 1, III. 1 *burn, consume* Meissn[Suppl. 84]; Sab. קלאתם *conflagratio, aestus* Os [4.1.19.20] CIS[iv. No. 74, l. 20]; Ar. قَلَى *fry* or *roast* wheat; Eth. ቀለወ: ቀለየ: *burn, fry*, so 𝔗 קְלָא, Syr. ܩܠܐ);—**Qal** *Pf.* 3 ms. sf. קָלָם בָּאֵשׁ Je 29[22] (acc. pers.) *he roasted them with fire*; *Pt. pass.* אָבִיב קָלוּי בָּאֵשׁ Lv 2[14] (P) grain *parched* with fire; so קָלוּי alone, as common food, Jos 5[11] (P), v. קָלִי. **Niph.** *Pt.* נִקְלֶה as n. ψ 38[8] my loins are filled *with burning* (Vrss Bae *with contempt*, II. קלה).

†קָלִי **n.m.** [1 S 17, 17] **parched** grain, a common 7039
food (Rob[BR ii. 50] Anderlind[ZPV ix. 3]);—abs. ק׳ 1 S 25[18] 2 S 17[28 a]+ v[28 b] (but dittogr., del. 𝔊 𝔖 and Comm.), Lv 23[14] (P), Ru 2[14]; = קָלִיא 1 S 17[17].

†II. [קָלָה] **vb. Niph. be lightly esteemed,** 7034
dishonoured (‖ form of קלל; cf. NH קָלוֹן, 𝔗 קְלָנָא, *disgrace, shame*);—*Pf.* 3 ms. consec. וְנִקְלָה Is 16[14] Dt 25[3]; *Pt.* נִקְלֶה Is 3[5]+2 t.;—*be lightly esteemed*, held of little account, Is 16[14] (glory of Moab); אִישׁ רָשׁ וְנִקְלֶה 1 S 18[23]; so (Pt. as subst.) Is 3[5] (opp. נִכְבָּד), Pr 12[9] (opp. מִתְכַּבֵּד); more positively, *be dishonoured*, degraded, Dt 25[3] (לְעֵינֶיךָ). **Hiph.** *treat with contempt, dishonour, Pt.* מַקְלֶה אָבִיו וגו׳ Dt 27[16] *one dishonouring* [i.e. opp. כַּבֵּד of 5th Command].

†קָלוֹן **n.m.** [Pr 11, 2] **ignominy, dishonour**;— 7036
abs. ק׳ Ho 4[7]+; cstr. קְלוֹן Is 22[18]; sf. קְלוֹנֵךְ Je 13[26]+;—**1.** of national *ignominy* Ho 4[7.18] (dub. line, v. Che Now), Je 46[12] (rd. prob. קוֹלֵךְ, so 𝔊

Gie Co[Hpt]), Hb 2^{16} ψ 83^{17}; of nation under fig. of woman, = pudenda, Je 13^{26} Na 3^{5} (‖ מַעְרֵךְ). **2.** personal *dishonour, disgrace,* of Shebna, as *disgrace* to his lord's house Is 22^{18}(opp. כְּבוֹדֶךָ); individ., Jb 10^{25} Pr 3^{35} (opp. כָּבוֹד), 6^{33} 9^{7} 11^{2} 12^{16} 13^{18} (opp. יְכֻבָּד), 18^{3} 22^{10}.

7037 †קַלַּחַת† **n.f. caldron** (Erman[ZMG xlvi (1892), 121] cp. Egypt. *krḥt, pot,* cf. OCopt. *ǵalaḥt* Lag[BN 88], wh. has come back as loan-wd. WMM[As. u. Eur. 94]);—abs. ק׳ 1 S 2^{14} (+ פָּרוּר, דּוּד, כִּיּוֹר); קַלָּחַת Mi 3^{3} (‖ סִיר).

I. קלט (√ of foll.; NH קָלַט *take up, in, harbour,* so 𝔗 קְלַט; Ba[ES 36] cp. Ar. قَلْتٌ reservoir with ת, cf. קטל, קטן).

4733 †מִקְלָט† **n.[m.] refuge, asylum** (P Ch);—עָרֵי מ׳ *asylum-cities* Nu $35^{11.13.14}$, עָרֵי הַמּ׳ Nu 35^{6} Jos 20^{2}, so 1 Ch $6^{42.52}$ (but rd. עִיר הַמּ׳, acc. to ‖ Jos $21^{13.21}$, so Be Kau Kit), לְמ׳ (after הָיָה) Nu $35^{12.15}$ Jos 20^{3}; cstr. in phr. עִיר מִקְלַט הָרֹצֵחַ Jos $21^{13.21.27.32.38}$ (Gi; v^{36} van d. H. Baer); sf. of refugee, עִיר מִקְלָטוֹ Nu $35^{25.26.27.28.32}$.

7038 †II. [קָלַט] **vb. be stunted** (? = I. ק׳; prop. *be drawn in?* cf. Ar. قُلَاطٌ *very short*);—**Qal** *Pt. pass.* שָׂרוּעַ וְקָלוּט Lv 22^{23} sacrif. animal, overgrown or *stunted.*

7042 †קְלִיטָא† **n.pr.m.** Levite, Ne 8^{7} 10^{11} (𝔊L in
7041 both Καλλιτας) Ezr 10^{23} (where called also קְלָיָה, v. קוֹלָיָה), Κωλιεν, A Κωλιτας, 𝔊L as Ne.

7039-41 קָלִי(א) v. I. קלה. קַלַּי v. קלל. קְלָיָה
7042 v. קְלִיטָא. p. 885, 887, above

7043 [קָלַל] $_{82}$ **vb. be slight, swift, trifling** (prob. orig. *be light;* NH [קָלַל], קַל, קִלֵּל = BH; As. *ḳalâlu* II. *despise, dishonour;* so Tel Am (appar. Canaanism); Ar. قَلَّ *be small, scanty;* Sab. קללם *scanty* Hal[143.8 f.] (cf. Fell[ZMG liv (1900), 246]); Eth. ቀለለ: *be light, small, easy;* II. *despise;* 𝔗 קְלַל, Syr. ܩܰܠ, = BH; also (v. **Pilp.**, etc.) Ar. قَلْقَلَ *shake,* ቈልቈለ: *vibrate, whirl* (of sword), ቀልቀለ: v. *be shaken;*—Schwally[ZAW xi (1891), 170 ff.] thinks *shake* original, v. מַקֵּל);—†**Qal** *Pf.* 2 ms. קַלּוֹתָ Na 1^{14}; 1 s. קַלֹּתִי Jb 40^{4}; 3 pl. קַלּוּ Gn 8^{11}+; *Impf.* 3 fs. וַתֵּקַל 16^{4}; 1 s. וָאֵקַל v^{5}; 3 mpl. יֵקַלּוּ 1 S 2^{30};—**1.** *be slight,* of water, *be abated,* fr. off (מֵעַל) earth Gn $8^{8.11}$ (J). **2.** *be swift,* c. מִן comp., of warriors 2 S 1^{23}, horses Je 4^{13} Hb 1^{8}; one's days Jb 7^{6} 9^{25}. **3.** *trifling,* i.e. of little account, of pers., Gn $16^{4.5}$ (J; both c. בְּעֵינֶיהָ); 1 S 2^{30} (opp. אֲכַבֵּד). †**Niph.** *Pf.* 3 ms. נָקַל (Ges[§ 67 t]) 2 K 20^{10}+, וְנָקַל consec. 2 K 3^{18}; נָקָל Pr 14^{6}; 1 s. consec. וּנְקַלֹּתִי 2 S 6^{22}; *Impf.* 3 mpl. יִקַּלּוּ Is 30^{16}; *Pt.* f. (עַל־)נְקַלָּה Je 6^{14} + 2 t.;—**1.** *shew oneself swift* Is 30^{16} (‖ עַל־קַל נִרְכָּב). **2.** *appear trifling,* 1 S 18^{23} (בְּעֵינֵיכֶם; Inf. subj., cf. Dr), c. מִן comp. *be too trifling* Is 49^{6}, esp. of sin 1 K 16^{31} (Inf. subj.), and (c. מִן comp.) Ez 8^{17}; *easy* 2 K 3^{18} (בְּעֵינֵי), 20^{10} (c. Inf.), Pr 14^{6}; *Pt.* (as subst.) c. עַל in adv. phr. עַל־נְקַלָּה *lightly* i.e. superficially, Je 6^{14} 8^{11}. **3.** *be lightly esteemed* 2 S 6^{22} (‖ שָׁפָל; opp. אִכָּבֵדָה). **Pi.** $_{40}$ *Pf.* 3 ms. קִלֵּל 2 S 19^{22}+, etc.; *Impf.* יְקַלֵּל Lv 20^{9}+, etc.; *Imv.* ms. קַלֵּל 2 S 16^{10}; *Inf. cstr.* קַלֵּל Gn 8^{21} Jos 24^{9}, etc.; *Pt.* מְקַלֵּל Ex 21^{17}+; sf. כֻּלֹּה מקללוני Je 15^{10}, rd. מְקַלְלֽוּנִי! (Baer); err. for כֻּלְּהֶם קִלְלוּנִי JDMich Gf Gie Du al., etc.;—*curse* (prop. *make contemptible*): **1.** c. acc. pers. homin. Ex 21^{17} (E), Gn 12^{3} (J), Lv 19^{14} (H), Ju 9^{27} 2 S 16^{9} + 16 t.; קִלְלַנִי קְלָלָה 1 K 2^{8}; obj. om. 2 S $16^{5.7.10.11.13}$ ψ 62^{5} 109^{28} (opp. בֵּרֵךְ); acc. pers. + בְּ of oath 1 S 17^{43} 2 K 2^{24}; c. בְּ of oath alone Is 8^{21}. **2.** c. acc. dei Ex 22^{27} (E), Lv 24^{15} (H), 1 S 3^{13} (rdg. אֱלֹהִים for לָהֶם, 𝔊 Comm.), + (obj. om.) Lv $24^{11.14.23}$. **3.** c. acc. rei Gn 8^{21} (י׳ subj.), Jb 3^{1}. †**Pu.** *Impf.* 3 ms. יְקֻלָּל Is 65^{20} *be cursed* by death; 3 fs. תְּקֻלַּל Jb 24^{18} their portion *is cursed; Pt.* pl. sf. מְקֻלָּלָיו ψ 37^{22} *those cursed by him* (opp. מְבֹרָכָיו). †**Hiph.** *Pf.* 3 ms. הֵקַל Is 8^{23}; 2 ms. sf. הֱקִלֹּתַנִי 2 S 19^{44} (van d. H. -הַ); 3 pl. הֵקַלּוּ Ez 22^{7}; *Impf.* 3 ms. יָקֵל 1 S 6^{5}; *Imv.* ms. הָקֵל Ex 18^{22}+; *Inf. cstr. id.*, Is 23^{9} Jon 1^{5};—**1.** *make light, lighten,* יָקֵל אֶת־יָדוֹ מֵעֲלֵיכֶם 1 S 6^{5} *he will lighten his hand from upon you;* c. מֵעַל pers. alone, *make light from upon* one, lighten one's burden Ex 18^{22} (E), Jon 1^{5} 1 K 12^{10} = 2 Ch 10^{10}; + מִן partit. 1 K $12^{4.9}$ = 2 Ch $10^{4.9}$. **2.** *treat with contempt,* acc. pers. 2 S 19^{44} Is 23^{9} Ez 22^{7}; dir. caus. *bring contempt, dishonour* Is 8^{23} (opp. הִכְבִּיד). †**Pilp.** *Pf.* 3 ms. **1.** *shake* קִלְקַל בַּחִצִּים Ez 21^{26} (in divination). **2.** (peculiarly) *whet* Ec 10^{10} (prop. move quickly to and fro). †**Hithpalp.** reflex. of **1**: *Pf.* 3 pl. הִתְקַלְקָלוּ Je 4^{24} hills *shook themselves,* shook.

קַל **adj. light, swift, fleet;**—ms. ק׳ Am 7031
2^{15}+, קַל v^{14}; fs. קַלָּה Je 2^{23}; pl. קַלִּים Is 18^{2}+;—ק׳ קַל בְּרַגְלָיו *light with his feet* Am 2^{15} 2 S 2^{18};

alone, *swift*, messengers Is 18[2], pursuers La 4[19] (מִן comp.), camel Je 2[23], cloud Is 19[1]; of swift vanishing of wicked Jb 24[18] (Bu קַלּוֹ for קַל הוּא); as subst. Am 2[14] Je 46[6] Ec 9[11], = *swift* (horse) Is 30[16]; קַל as adv., *swiftly* (+ מְהֵרָה) Is 5[26] Jo 4[4].

6963 †קֹל† **n.[m.] lightness, frivolity** (so Vrss Ki Gie; Gf thinks = קָלוֹן; > = *voice*);—מִקֹּל
6963 זְנוּתָהּ Je 3[9].—קֹל *voice*, v. קוֹל. p. 876

7044 †קָלָל† **adj. burnished** (fr. *light, quick* movement of rubbing?);—נְחֹשֶׁת ק׳ *burnished brass* Ez 1[7] Dn 10[6] (so most; Co, Ez, קָלוֹת, in prefixing כַּנְפֵיהֶם fr. v[8]; Dn then follows crpt. Ez.

7045 קְלָלָה [33] **n.f. curse**;—abs. ק׳ Gn 27[12] +; cstr. קִלְלַת Ju 9[57] +; sf. קִלְלָתְךָ Gn 27[13], קִלְלָתוֹ 2 S 16[12] (van d. H. Kt קללתי, so We Dr Löhr); pl. קְלָלוֹת Dt 28[15.45];—*curse*, Gn 27[12.13] (J); oft. opp. בְּרָכָה, Dt 11[26.28] 23[6] = Ne 13[2], + 8 t. Dt., Jos 8[34] (D), Ju 9[57] ψ 109[17.18] Pr 27[14]; קִלְלַת חִנָּם Pr 26[2] *a groundless curse*, cf. 2 S 16[12]; קְלָלָה נִמְרֶצֶת 1 K 2[8] *a grievous curse*; = a formula of cursing Je 29[22]; = *object of curse*, קִלְלַת אֱלֹהִים תָּלוּי Dt 21[23], שַׁמָּה וּקְלָלָה 2 K 22[19], cf. Je 24[9] 25[18] + 6 t. Je, Zc 8[13].

7040 †קַלַּי† **n.pr.m.** priest Ne 12[20], 𝔊L Καλμει.

7052 †קְלֹקֵל† **adj. contemptible, worthless** (cf. Ol[§ 189 f] Ba[NB 160]);—בַּלֶּחֶם הַקְּ׳ Nu 21[5] (JE).

7022 †קִיקָלוֹן† **n. [m.] disgrace**;—Hb 2[16], si vera l. intens. Ol[§ 82 c] Kö[ii. 130, 497], but dub. (v. We Now GASm).

7046 †[קָלַס] **vb. mock, scoff** (Ecclus 11[4] תקלס, text by Adler[JQ xii (1900), 470]);—**Pi.** *Inf. cstr.* לְקַלֵּס אֶתְנָן Ez 16[31] *to scoff at hire* (of Jerusalem under fig. of harlot), but 𝔊 𝔖 Symm *collect*, rd. לְקַבֵּץ Gr Toy Krae (or לְלַקֵּט, Co). **Hithp.** *mock, deride*, c. ב pers., *Impf.* 3 ms. יִתְקַלָּס Hb 1[10]; 3 mpl. יִתְקַלְּסוּ Ez 22[5], וַיִּת׳ 2 K 2[23].

7047 †קֶלֶס† **n.[m.] derision**, i.e., object of it, ‖ חֶרְפָּה;—Je 20[8], + לַעַג ψ 44[14] 79[4].

7048 †קַלָּסָה† **n.f.** id., ‖ *id.*;—Ez 22[4].

7049 †I. [קָלַע] **vb. sling, hurl forth** (Thes cp. Ar. قَلِعَ *sit insecurely* (v. also Frä[224], Socin in Buhl[Lex 13]), *waver*, whence قِلْعٌ *sail* (loan-wd. Frä[l.c.]), JAram. קַלְעָא *id.*, BH NH קֶלַע *curtain*; thence *hurl, sling*; but this perh. denom. (Socin[l.c.]) fr. قُلَاعَةٌ *loosened clod*, cf. Syr. ܩܠܥܬܐ *id.* (Nö in Frä[l.c.]); Ar. مِقْلَعٌ *sling*, Eth. ሞቅሎዕ: *id.*; 𝔗 קְלַע vb. *sling*, Syr. n. ܩܠܥܐ *sling*);—**Qal** *Pt.* קֹלֵעַ בָּאֶבֶן אֶל־ Ju 20[16] *one slinging* (*with*) *a stone at* a hair; קוֹ׳ c. acc. pers. Je 10[18] *I will sling forth* the inhabitants. **Pi.** *Impf.* 3 ms. וַיְקַלַּע 1 S 17[49] *and he slang* (sc. the stone); sf. יְקַלְּעֶנָּה 25[29] *he shall sling away* (life of enemy).

†I. קֶלַע **n.[m.] sling**;—abs. ק׳ 1 S 17[50], 7050
כַּף הַקָּלַע 25[29] *hollow of the sling* (fig.); sf. קַלְעוֹ 17[40]; אַבְנֵי־קֶלַע Jb 41[20] *sling-stones*, so א׳ קְלָעִים 2 Ch 26[14]; א׳־קֶלַע Zc 9[15] is difficult: Marti[Kau] כְּא׳־ק׳; We Now בְּנֵי ק׳ *sons of* ——?

†[קַלָּע] **n.m. slinger**;—pl. קַלָּעִים 2 K 3[25]. 7051

II. [קֶלַע] [15] **n.[m.] curtain, hanging** (P);— 7050
pl. abs. קְלָעִים Ex 27[9] + 7 t. Ex; cstr. קַלְעֵי 35[17] + 4 t. Ex, Nu 3[26] 4[26].—1 K 6[34 b] read צְלָעִים.

† II. קָלַע **vb. carve**;—**Qal** *Pf.* 3 ms. ק׳: 7049
c. 2 acc., *carve walls with*, 1 K 6[29]; c. acc. cogn. + עַל v[32]; c. acc. of thing carved v[35].

†מִקְלַעַת† **n.f. carving**;—cstr. מ׳ 1 K 6[18]; 4734
pl. abs. מִקְלָעוֹת 7[31]; cstr. מִקְלְעוֹת (after קָלַע) 6[29.32].

קִלְקֵל v. קלל. above 7052

†קִלְּשׁוֹן doubtful word, in phrase וְלִשְׁלֹשׁ ק׳ 7053
1 S 13[21] (poss. would be *fine point*, cf. Aram. קלשׁ *be thin*, hence שׁ׳ ק׳ *tridens*, E.V. *forks*, but against anal., v. esp. Dr).

קָמָה v. קוּם. p. 879 7054

†קְמוּאֵל **n.pr.m.** Καμουηλ: **1.** son of Nahor 7055
Gn 22[21]. **2.** Ephraimite Nu 34[24]. **3.** Levite 1 Ch 27[17] (B Σαμουηλ, A Καμ., 𝔊L Κεμ.).

קָמוֹן v. קוּם. p. 879 7056

קמח (✓ of foll.; As. *ḳamû*, perh. *crush, grind*; *kêmu* (= *ḳemû*?), *flour*; NH = BH, so 𝔗 קִמְחָא, Syr. ܩܡܚܐ; Vulg. Ar. قَمْح *wheat*; Eth. ቀምሕ: *produce, fruit, vegetables*; cf. Egypt. *kamāḥ*, Bondi[77], *ḳmḥ*, a kind of bread, Erman[ZMG xlvi (1892), 120]).

†קֶמַח **n.[m.] flour, meal**;—abs. ק׳ 1 S 7058
1[24] +, קָמַח Is 47[2]; cstr. קֶמַח Nu 5[15];—Ju 6[19] (material for unleavened cakes), 1 S 1[24] 28[24] 2 K 4[41]; defined by סֹלֶת (q.v.) Gn 18[6], disting. fr. סֹלֶת 1 K 5[2]; of barley (שְׂעֹרִים) Nu 5[15] (P), but 2 S 17[28] + חִטִּים, שְׂעֹרִים, קָלִי; + other articles of

food 1 Ch 12^{41} (van d. H. v^{40}); kept in a) כַּד 1 K 17$^{12.14.16}$; made by grinding Is 47^{2}; צֶמַח בְּלִי יַעֲשֶׂה ק׳ Ho 8^{7}.

7059 †[קָמַט] **vb. seize** (NH *id., seize, grasp, press together*; Ar. قمط *bind together*; Aram. קְמַט=BH; ܩܡܛ *seize, compress*);—**Qal** *Impf.* 2 ms. sf. וַתִּקְמְטֵנִי Jb 16^{8} *and thou didst seize me.* **Pu.** *be snatched* (untimely) *Pf.* 3 pl. קֻמְּטוּ Jb 22^{16}.

7060 †[קָמֵל] **vb. be decayed** (Syr. ܩܡܠ *be mouldy, decay*);—**Qal** *Pf.* 3 ms. קָמֵל Is 33^{9} *Lebanon mouldereth*; 3 pl. קָמֵלוּ 19^{6} (of קָנֶה וָסוּף).

7061 †קָמַץ **vb. enclose with the hand, grasp** (NH *id.*=BH; 𝔗 קְמַץ; As. *ḳimṣu, kinṣu*, is a part of the body occurring in pairs, Meissn Suppl. 84);—**Qal** *Pf.* 3 ms. consec. וְקָמַץ Lv 2^{2} 5^{12} (both c. acc. קֻמְצוֹ מְלֹא + מִן of source), Nu 5^{26} (c. acc. + מִן of source; all P).

7062 †[קֹמֶץ] **n.[m.] closed hand, fist**;—sf. מְלֹא קֻמְצוֹ *his fist-full* Lv 2^{2} 5^{12}; take up בְּק׳ 6^{8} *in his fist* (all P); pl. לִקְמָצִים Gn 41^{47} the earth yielded *by handfuls* (i.e. abundantly; E, acc. to most; P, Ball Holz, who questions text).

קמשׁ (√of following; meaning unknown).

7057 †קִמּוֹשׁ **n.m.** Ho 9,6 **coll. thistles** or **nettles** (𝔊 ἄκανθαι, cf. Ki; 𝔙 *urtica*);—abs. ק׳, sign of desolation, Ho 9^{6} (> van d. H. קִימֹשׁ; cf. Baer De Complut. Var. 28; || חוֹחַ), Is 34^{13} (+ חוֹחַ, סִירִים); pl.
7063 (c. נ ins., Thes Nö M 169, Anm. 3 Löw 194 Anm.) קִמְּשֹׂנִים Pr 24^{31} (> van d. H. קִמְּשׁוֹנִים; || חֲרֻלִּים).

7064 קֵן v. קנן. p. 890

קנא (√of foll.; Ar. قنأ *become intensely red* (or *black*), with dye; NH קִנְאָה *jealousy*; Syr. ܩܢܐ *lividus fuit*, ܛܢܢܐ *zeal, envy* (rare); vb. denom. NH קִנֵּא, Aram. קַנֵּא, Eth. ቀንአ: all *be jealous, zealous*).

7068 †קִנְאָה **n.f. ardour, zeal, jealousy** (from colour produced in face by deep emotion);—abs. ק׳ Nu 5^{14}+; cstr. קִנְאַת Is 9^{6}; sf. קִנְאָתִי Nu 25^{11}+, etc.; pl. קְנָאֹת Nu 5$^{15.18.25.29}$;—**1.** *ardour of jealousy* of husband Pr 6^{34} 27^{4}; רוּחַ ק׳ *jealous disposition* Nu 5$^{14.14.30}$ (P); offering for jealousy, מנחת ק׳ v$^{15.18.25}$ (P); תּוֹרַת הק׳ v^{29} (P); of *rivalry* Ec 4^{4} 9^{6}; Ephr. against Judah Is 11^{13}; *ardent love*, || אהבה Ct 8^{6}. **2.** ardour of *zeal*: **a.** of men for God Nu 25$^{11.11}$ (P) 2 K 10^{16}; for the house of י׳ ψ 69^{10}. **b.** of God for his people, esp. in battle Is 42^{13} 63^{15} Zc 1^{14} 8^{2}; מְעִיל ק׳ Is 59^{17}; ק׳ י׳ תעשׂה זאת 9^{6} 37^{32} = 2 K 19^{31}. **3.** ardour of *anger*: **a.** of men against adversaries ψ 119^{139} Jb 5^{2} (|| כַּעַשׂ), Pr 14^{30} (opp. לֵב מַרְפֵּא). **b.** of God against men, || חֵמָה Ez 5^{13} 16$^{38.42}$ 23^{25} 36^{6}; || עֶבְרָה 38^{19}; || אַף Dt 29^{19} Ez 35^{11}; + אֵשׁ Is 26^{11} Ez 36^{5} Zp 1^{18} 3^{8} ψ 79^{5}; סֶמֶל הַק׳ הַמַּקְנֶה Ez 8^{3} *the anger-image provoking to anger*; ס׳ הק׳ alone v^{5}.

†[קָנָא] **vb.denom. Pi.** be jealous, zealous 7065
(Gerber 131);—*Pf.* 3 ms. קִנֵּא Nu 25^{13}+; 1 s. קִנֵּאתִי Zc 1^{14}+etc.; *Impf.* יְקַנֵּא Is 11^{13} Pr 23^{17}, etc.; *Inf. abs.* קַנֹּא 1 K 19$^{10.14}$; *cstr.* sf. קַנְאוֹ Nu 25^{11}; קַנֹּאתוֹ 2 S 21^{2}; *Pt.* מְקַנֵּא Nu 11^{29};—**1.** *be jealous of*, c. acc. אֶת־אִשְׁתּוֹ Nu 5$^{14.14.30}$ (P); in rivalry Is 11^{13}. **2.** *be envious of*, c. בְּ pers., Gn 30^{1} (E), 37^{11} (J) ψ 37^{1} 73^{3} Pr 3^{31} 23^{17} 24$^{1.19}$; c. acc. pers. Gn 26^{14} (J), Ez 31^{9}; c. לְ pers. ψ 106^{16}. **3.** *be zealous* for: **a.** of man, c. לְ pers. Nu 11^{29} (J), 2 S 21^{2}; for God Nu 25^{13} (P), 1 K 19$^{10.14}$; קנאה ק׳ Nu 25^{11} (P). **b.** of God, לְשֵׁם קָדְשִׁי Ez 39^{25}, לְאַרְצוֹ Jo 2^{18}, לירושׁ׳ Zc 1^{14}, לְצִיּוֹן Zc 8$^{2.2}$. **4.** *excite to jealous anger*, c. בְּ instr. Dt 32$^{21\,a}$ (dub.; probably הִקְנִאוּנִי; cf. v$^{16.21\,b}$), 1 K 14^{22}. **Hiph.** *provoke to jealous anger*: *Impf.* 3 mpl. sf. יַקְנִאֻהוּ Dt 32^{16}; יַקְנִיאוּהוּ ψ 78^{58} (|| וַיַּכְעִיסוּהוּ); 1 s. אַקְנִיאֵם Dt 32$^{21\,b}$; *Pt.* metapl. מַקְנֶה Ez 8^{3} (Ges §75 q, del. Co).

†קַנָּא **adj. jealous**;—only of God: אֵל קַנָּא 7067
Ex 20^{5} (J) = Dt 5^{9} (as punishing those who hate him), Ex 34^{14} (J), Dt 4^{24} 6^{15} (demanding exclusive service); קַנָּא שְׁמוֹ Ex 34^{14} (J).

†קַנּוֹא **adj.** id.;—אֵל קַנּוֹא Jos 24^{19} (E) (cf. 7072
Dt 6^{15} supr.), Nah 1^{2} (|| נֹקֵם).

I. קָנָה 84 **vb. get, acquire** (NH=BH; Ph. 7069
(Pun.) מקנא, *property* [in cattle]; As. *ḳanû, gain, acquire*, Meissn Suppl. 85; Ar. قنا (و, ى) *acquire, procure*; Sab. קני *acquire, possess*, CIS iv, no. 89, 5.6, קני n. *property* Id ib. no. 3, 8. 29, 3; Eth. ቀነየ: *acquire, subjugate*; Aram. קְנָא, ܩܢܐ, *acquire*);—**Qal** 81 *Pf.* 3 ms. ק׳ Gn 25^{10}+; sf. קָנְךָ Dt 32^{6}, קָנָהוּ Lv 27^{24}; 3 fs. קָנְתָה ψ 78^{54}; 2 ms. קָנִיתָ Ex 15^{16}+, etc.; *Impf.* 3 ms. יִקְנֶה Lv 22^{11}+, וַיִּקֶן Gn 33^{19}+, etc.; *Imv.* ms. קְנֵה Gn 47^{19}+; *Inf. abs.* קָנֹה Lv 25^{14} 1 Ch 21^{24}, קָנוֹ 2 S 24^{24}; *cstr.* קְנֹה Pr 16^{16}, קְנוֹת Pr 16^{16}+, etc.; *Pt.* קֹנֶה Dt 28^{68}, קוֹנֶה Pr 15^{32}+, etc.;—†**1.** *get, acquire* (all poet.): **a.** of God as originating, creating, קֹנֵה שָׁמַיִם וָאָרֶץ Gn 14$^{19.22}$, Dt 32^{6} (Isr.),

ψ 139^{13} (כִּלְיֹתָי); Pr 8^{22} (חכמה q.v.). **b.** of God as victoriously redeeming his people Ex 15^{16} Is 11^{11} ψ 74^{2} (|| גָּאַל); obj. הַר־זֶה 78^{54}. **c.** of Eve, acquiring קָנִיתִי אֶת־י׳ (i.e. *with the help of*), Gn 4^{1} (J). **d.** of acquiring wisdom, knowledge (only Pr): Pr 1^{5} 4$^{5.5.7.7}$ 15^{32} 16$^{16.16}$ 17^{16} 18^{15} 19^{8} 23^{23}. **2.** elsewhere *buy* Ex 21^{2} (E), Gn 47^{22} (J), 50^{13} (P), Lv 27^{24} (H), Dt 28^{68} Is 24^{2} Je 13^{1} Ez 7^{12} Pr 20^{14}+; קֹנֶה *owner*, as purchaser Lv 25^{30} (P) Is 1^{3} Zc 11^{5}+. **Niph.** *be bought: Pf.* 3 ms. נִקְנָה Je 32^{43}; *Impf.* 3 mpl. יִקָּנוּ v^{15}. **Hiph.** *Pf.* 3 ms. sf. אָדָם הִקְנַנִי Zc 13^{5}; AV makes denom. of מִקְנֶה *cattle;* Thes RV Marti[Kau] Buhl *caused* (one) *to purchase me,* i.e. *made me a bondman;* < We Now GASm read אֲדָמָה קִנְיָנִי.—*Pt.* מַקְנֶה v. קנא.

7075 †קִנְיָן **n.[m.] thing got or acquired, acquisition** (Aramaism, Lag[BN 205]); abs. ק׳ Ez 38$^{12.13}$; cstr. קִנְיַן Lv 22^{11}; sf. קִנְיָנְךָ Pr 4^{7}+, etc.;—**1.** *thing acquired* by purchase קִנְיַן כֶּסֶף Lv 22^{11} (H; cf. מִקְנָה); of property Gn 34^{23} 36^{6} Jos 14^{4} (all P), Ez 38$^{12.13}$ (in all disting. fr. מִקְנֶה cattle); || בַּיִת ψ 105^{21}; מִקְנֵה קִנְיָנוֹ Gn 31^{18} (P; prob. doublet, 𝔊 om.); בְּכָל־קִנְיָנְךָ קְנֵה בִינָה Pr 4^{7} *with* (or *at the price of*) *all that thou hast acquired, get understanding.* **2.** mere gen.: coll. *creatures* 𝔊 κτίσις ψ 104^{24} (cf. √**1 a**).

4735 מִקְנֶה$_{76}$ **n. m.** [Ex 10,26] **cattle**;—abs. מ׳ Gn 46^{32}+; cstr. מִקְנֵה Gn 13^{7}+; sf. מִקְנֵהוּ Gn 3^{18}+, מִקְנֶיךָ Is 30^{23} (Ges[§ 93 ss]), etc.; pl. sf. (but v. Kö[ii.112f.]) מִקְנַי Ex 17^{3}+, מִקְנֵיכֶם Gn 47^{16}+, etc.;—**1.** *cattle* in gen., including cows, sheep, horses, asses, camels (any or all of them), as purchasable domestic animals, Gn 47$^{16.16.17.17}$ Ex 9^{3}+ (J), 10^{26} (E), Dt 3^{19} (not in P), Jb 1^{3} ψ 78^{48} Je 9^{9} 1 Ch 5^{21}+; so prob. ישֵׁב אֹהֶל וּמִקְנֶה Gn 4^{20} (J) of nomads, מִקְנֵה הַבְּהֵמָה Gn 47^{18} (J). **2.** specif. of cows, sheep, and goats in herds and flocks Gn 13^{2} (J), 31^{9} (E), v^{18} 36^{7} 46^{6} Nu 32^{1} (all P), Is 30^{23}+; אַנְשֵׁי מ׳ Gn 46$^{32.34}$ (J), שָׂרֵי מ׳ Gn 47^{6} (P), cf. 1 Ch 28^{1}; רֹעֵי מ׳ Gn 13$^{7.7}$ (J); disting. from בְּהֵמָה Nu 31^{9} (P), 32^{26} 2 K 3^{17}; fr. קנין Jos 14^{4} (P) Ez 38$^{12.13}$; from both Gn 34^{23} 36^{6} (P); מ׳ צאן ובקר 2 Ch 32^{29} מ׳ בקר וצאן Ec 2^{7}; מ׳ צאן ומ׳ בקר Gn 26^{14} 47^{17} (J); sheep only Gn 29^{7} (J) Nu 32^{16} (E).—מִקְנֶה הַשָּׂדֶה Gn 49^{32} (P) rd. מִקְנַת; מִקְנֶה אַף עַל עוֹלֶה Jb 36^{33} rd. מַקְנֶה (**Hiph.** *Pt.*), or מְקַנֵּא (**Pi.** *Pt.*) metapl. fr. קנא, Hi Bö Di Du; 1 S 30^{20} del. הַמּ׳ 𝔊 We Dr al., v. esp. HPS.

4736 †מִקְנָה **n.f. purchase**;—abs. מ׳ Gn 23^{18}+; cstr. מִקְנַת Gn 17^{12}+; sf. מִקְנָתוֹ Lv 25^{16}+;—**1.** *purchase,* מִקְנַת כֶּסֶף Gn 17$^{12.13.23.27}$ Ex 12^{44} (all P); סֵפֶר הַמּ׳ *document of purchase* Je 32$^{11.12.12.14.16}$. **2.** *purchase-price,* Lv 25$^{16.16.51}$ 27^{22} (P). **3.** *possession* (gained by purchase), לְמִקְנָה Gn 23^{18} (P).

†מִקְנֵיָהוּ **n.pr.m.** (*possession of* י׳);— 4737
Levit. musician 1 Ch 15$^{18.21}$, Μακ(κ)ελλ(ει)α, Μακενια(ς), Μακκανια(ς).

II. קנה (√of foll.; cf. As. *ḳanû, reed;* Ar. قَنَاةٌ *spear-shaft;* Eth. **ቀኖት፡** *goad;* NH קָנֶה, Aram. קַנְיָא, ܩܢܝܐ, all = BH. Hence Gk. κάννα, κάνης, also κάνεον *basket* (Lewy[Fremdw. 99]), Lat. *canna*).

קָנֶה$_{62}$ **n.m.** [Gn 41,5] **stalk, reed**;—abs. ק׳ 1 K 7070
14^{15}+; cstr. קְנֵה Ez 40^{3}+; sf. קָנָהּ Ex 25^{31} 37^{17} = קָנָהּ (Ges[§ 91 e]) Jb 31^{22}; pl. קָנִים Ex 25^{32}+; cstr. קְנֵי 37^{18}+; sf. קְנֹתָם 25^{36} 37^{22};—†**1.** *stalk* of grain Gn 41$^{5.22}$ (E). †**2.** *water-plant, reed,* 1 K 14^{15} Is 19^{6} (+ סוּף), 35^{7} (+ גֹּמֶא); coll., חַיַּת ק׳ ψ 68^{31} *beasts of* (*the*) *reeds* (dwelling among them), cf. בְּסֵתֶר ק׳ וּבִצָּה Jb 40^{21}; מִשְׁעֶנֶת הַקּ׳ הָרָצוּץ 2 K 18^{21} = Is 36^{6}, מִשׁ׳ ק׳ Ez 29^{6}, all fig. of weak support; cf. ק׳ רָצוּץ Is 42^{3} (spared by עבד י׳). †**3.** *calamus,* aromatic reed, ק׳ הַטּוֹב Je 6^{20} (Ges[§ 126 w]), ק׳־בֹשֶׂם Ex 30^{23} (P); ק׳ alone Ez 27^{19} Is 43^{24} Ct 4^{14}. **4.** derived meanings: †**a.** *measuring-rod,* קְנֵה הַמִּדָּה Ez 40$^{3.5}$ (6 cubits long, v. אַמָּה) 42$^{16.16.17.18.19}$. **b.** unit of measure, *reed* (of 6 cubits, as As. *ḳanû*) Ez 40$^{5.5}$ + 10 t. 40, 42, + מְלוֹ הַקּ׳ 41^{8} *full reed* (emphat.). †**c.** *beam* of scales, for scales themselves Is 46^{6}. †**d.** *shaft* of lamp-stand Ex 25^{31} = 37^{17} (P). **e.** *branches* thereof, Ex 25$^{32.32.32}$ = 37$^{18.18.18}$ + 16 t. 25, 37 (all P). †**f.** *shoulder-joint,* Jb 31^{22} (|| שְׁכֶם).

†קָנָה **n.pr. 1.** of wady between Ephr. and 7071
Manass., נַחַל ק׳ Jos 16^{8} 17^{9} (both P), Κα(ρα)να, Καναι, etc.; identif. by Rob[BR iii. 135] with *Wady Ḳânah,* S. and SW. of Nablûs, cf. Buhl[Geogr. 101, 105]. **2. loc.** in Asher, 19^{28}, Καν(θ)α(ν), etc.; prob. *Ḳâna,* SE. fr. Tyre Rob[BR ii. 455 f.] Buhl[229], Egypt. *Ka'nô* WMM[As. u. Eur. 181], and perhaps Tel Am. *Ḳanû.*

†קְנַז **n.pr.m.** in Edom, Κενεζ: son of Eliphaz 7073
Gn 36^{11} = 1 Ch 1^{36}, Gn 36^{15} cf. v^{42} = 1 Ch 1^{53}, and father of Othniel Jos 15^{17} Ju 1^{13} 3$^{9.11}$ (v. Di[Gn] Bu[RS 9, Comm. Ju 1, 13] GFM[Ju 1, 13 ff.] Mey[Entstehung 115 f.]).

†קְנִזִּי **adj. gent.,** c. art. הַקּ׳, of Caleb Nu 7074
32^{12} Jos 14$^{6.14}$ (all JE); as n.coll. Gn 15^{19} (in list; appar. S. Canaanitish people).

קֵנִי v. קֵינִי. p. 884 7017

7076 † קִנָּמוֹן **n.m.** cinnamon (prob. foreign wd., coming with the thing from remote E., cf. M'Lean-ThDyer[Ency. Bib. s.v.]; cp. with Malay *kainamanis* by Röd[Thes. Add. 111], *kāyŭ mānĭs* Lewy[Fremdw. 37], but only *kāyu, wood*, given by Scott[Mal. Words in Eng. JAOS xvii, xviii (1896, 1897)]; Gk. κιννάμων from Heb. (against Lag[BN 199]));—fragrant bark used as spice: abs. ק׳ Pr 7[17] Ct 4[14]; cstr. קִנְּמָן־בֶּשֶׂם Ex 30[23] (P) *cinnamon of sweet odour*.—Vid. also Houghton-Tr[Smith DB s.v.] Post[Hastings DB s.v.].

קנן (√of foll.; mng.? NH קֵן *nest*, As. *ḳinnu, ḳannu, nest, family;* Aram. קִנָּא, ܩܶܢܳܐ *nest*).

7064 קֵן **n.m.**[Dt 22, 6] nest;—abs. ק׳ Is 10[14]+; cstr. קַן־ Dt 22[6]; sf. קִנּוֹ 32[11]+, etc.; pl. קִנִּים Gn 6[14];—**1.** *nest*, of bird Dt 22[6] Jb 39[27]; in sim. Is 10[14] Pr 27[8], of *nestlings* Dt 32[11] Is 16[2] (קֵן מְשֻׁלָּח), perhaps also עִם־קִנִּי Jb 29[18], but difficult, Che[JQ July, 1897, 578] prop. זֹקֶן or בְּזִקְנִי (cf. 𝔊); *nest* on high, of rock-dwellings Nu 24[21] (JE) Je 49[16] Ob[4]; fig. of Chaldeans' secure abode Hb 2[9]; temple as secure home for Isr. ψ 84[4] (fig. of swallow). **2.** *cells*, like nests, in Noah's ark Gn 6[14] (P; read prob. קִנִּים קִנִּים, so Lag Ol Bu[Urg. 255] Di Holz Gunk).

7077 †[קִנֵּן] **vb. denom. Pi.** make a nest, nest;—*Pf.* 3 fs. קִנְּנָה Is 34[15]; 3 pl. קִנְּנוּ Ez 31[6] (in fig.); *Impf.* 3 ms. יְקַנֵּנוּ ψ 104[17]; 3 fs. תְּקַנֵּן Je 48[28] (sim.). **Pu.** *Pt.* fs. מקננתי (Ges[§ 90 l]) Je 22[23] Kt (Qr מְקֻנַּנְתְּ; cf. Ges[§ 80 d]) (thou) *who art nested* in the cedars (fig.).

קנץ (√of foll., si vera l.; cf. Ar. قَنَصَ *catch, capture, ensnare*).

7078 †[קֶנֶץ] **n.[m.]** snare, net (si vera l.);—pl. cstr. (Ges[§ 130 a]) עַד־אָנָה תְּשִׂימוּן קִנְצֵי לְמִלִּין Jb 18[2] *how long will ye lay snares for words* (catch at words, talk without knowledge)? so Castle JDMich and most, but sense strange; Vrss transl. *end*, so Thes al. (expl. קנצי [very dub.] as Aram.), rd. then קֵץ (with sg. vb., after 𝔊), Me Bi Siegf Du, and del. עַד־אָנָה Du.

7079 † קְנָת **n.pr.loc.** Κααθ, Κα(α)ναθ, E. of Jordan Nu 32[42] (JE) 1 Ch 2[23]; perh. *Ḳanawat* on W. slope of Hauran mountains (Buhl[Geogr. 252]).

קסם (√of foll.; appar. orig. *divide, assign* (deity), Ar. قَسَمَ *divide, distribute*, x. *get a part allotted to oneself*, especially by drawing lots [with headless arrows] at a sanctuary (cf. esp. Ez 21[26.27]); iv. أَقْسَمَ *swear;* v. also Eth. ቀሰመ: iv. *use divination*, so 𝔗 קְסַם, Syr. ܩܣܰܡ; קִיסְמָא *divination;* see esp. RS[JPhil. xiii (1885), 276 ff.], We[Skizzen iii. 127 f. 167; Heid. 2. 132 ff.] Dr[Dt 18. 10]).

† קֶסֶם **n.[m.]** divination;—abs. ק׳ Nu 7081
23[23]+, קָסֶם Ez 21[26]; cstr. קֶסֶם 13[6]; pl. קְסָמִים Dt 18[10]+;—**1.** of the nations: Balaam, Nu 23[23] (poem in JE; ‖ נַחַשׁ; c. ב *against;* as acc. cogn. לִקְסָם־ק׳ Ez 21[26]; ק׳ as instr. of divination בִּימִינוֹ v[27]; so of elders of Moab and Midian, קְסָמִים בְּיָדָם, Nu 22[7] (E).—Is 2[6] v. [קָסַם]. **2.** of false proph. ק׳ כָּזָב Ez 13[6] (but v. [קָסַם]); ק׳ as acc. cogn. Ez 13[23] (< Co Berthol Krae כָּזָב as v[9] 21[34] 22[28]); ק׳ אֱלִיל (so Gf for MT וֶאֱלוֹל) Je 14[14] (all ‖ חזה שוא or שקר); קֹסֵם קְסָמִים prohibited Dt 18[10] 2 K 17[17]; reprobated 1 S 15[23] (poem; ‖ תרפים). **3.** in good sense ק׳ עַל שִׂפְתֵי מֶלֶךְ Pr 16[10] (king's lips as oracle).

†[קָסַם] **vb.denom.** practise divination;— 7080
Qal *Impf.* 3 mpl. יִקְסְמוּ 2 K 17[17], יִקְסֹמוּ Mi 3[11]; 2 fs. תִּקְסַמְנָה Ez 13[23]; *Imv.* fs. קָסֳמִי 1 S 28[8] Qr (Kt קסומי); *Inf. cstr.* קְסֹם Mi 3[6] (Buhl קֶסֶם), קְסָם־ Ez 21[26.34] קְסוֹם־ Ez 21[28] (read קֶסֶם Co Buhl), esp. *Pt.* קֹסֵם Dt 18[10] Is 3[2], etc.;—**1.** of diviners of the nations, Balaam, Jos 13[22] (D), Philist. 1 S 6[2] (‖ כהנים), Bab. Is 44[25] (‖ חכמים) Ez 21[26] cf. ק׳ שוא Ez 21[28] (but rd. קֶסֶם), + Is 2[6] (ins. prob. קֹסְמִים, > קֶסֶם, or מִקְסָם; v. קֶדֶם **1 b**); of Can. necromancers בָּאוֹב 1 S 28[8]; ‖ מְעֹנְנִים Dt 18[14]; of Ammonites ק׳ כָּזָב Ez 21[34] (+ ל pers.). **2.** false proph. of Isr. ‖ חזה Mi 3[6] (? קֶסֶם; ‖ חזון), v[7]; Is 3[2] (+ נביא; cf. v[3]), ‖ נביאים Je 27[9] 29[8], בְּכֶסֶף Mi 3[11], ‖ חזה שקר Zc 10[2]; ‖ חזה שוא: ק׳ קֶסֶם Ez 13[23] (but v. קֶסֶם), ק׳ כָּזָב Ez 13[9] 22[28], + 13[6] (rd. וְיִקְסְמוּ, or [Co Berthol] inf. abs. וְקָסֹם, Vrss. Toy). **3.** ק׳ קְסָמִים prohibited Dt 18[10] 2 K 17[17].

†[מִקְסָם] **n.[m.]** divination; cstr. מִקְסַם 4738
חָלָק Ez 12[24] (‖ חזון שוא); מִקְסַם כָּזָב Ez 13[7] (‖ מחזה שוא).

†[קָסַס] **vb. Pō'.** strip off (so context 7082
requires; verb otherwise unknown);—*Impf.* 3 ms. וְאֶת־פִּרְיָהּ יְקוֹסֵס Ez 17[9] *and its fruit shall he* not *strip off*?

קֶסֶת v. קשה. p. 903 7083

קְעִילָה[18] **n.pr.loc.** Κεειλα: in Judah, to- 7084
ward Philistines, ק׳ 1 S 23[1]+13 t. 23 (קְעִלָה, v[3.13]); Jos 15[44] (P), cf. 2 Ch 4[19] (geneal. scheme); post-ex. פֶּלֶךְ קְעִילָה Ne 3[17.18]; mod. *Ḳîlā*, c. 8 m. NW. from Hebron, GASm[Geogr. 230] Buhl[Geogr. 193]; cl. TelAm. *Ḳilti* Wkl[No. 165, 11, 18, etc.].

קעקע (√of foll.; NH קִעְקַע usu. *pull, tear* (or *cut*) *down, off*, Levy[NHWB] Ecclus 10[15] (cf. Frä[ZAW xxi (1901), 192]); also, as to Lv 19[28], *incise*, appar. reduplicated fr. a √קוע (Thes) or קעע).

7085 †קַעֲקַע **n.[m.] incision, imprintment, tattoo**; Lv 19[28] (H), v. כְּתֹבֶת (RS[Sem. i. 316; 2nd ed. 324]).

קער (√of foll.; cf. Ar. قَعُرَ *be deep*, of well, قَعَّرَ *come to bottom* of well, vessel, also *make* well *deep*; II. *hollow out* (Dozy); قَعِيرٌ *deep*, of well, bowl; Nab. קער *hollow* or *carve out* (Sachau[SB Ak, 1896, 1057]); Syr. ܡܩܥܪܬܐ, *calyx, acorn-cup, well*; Bondi[60] cp. Egypt. *māqaār, bottom part* of oven).

7086 קְעָרָה[17] **n.f. dish, platter** (P) (NH *id.*);—abs. ק׳ Nu 7[85]; cstr. קַעֲרַת־כֶּסֶף Nu 7[13] + 11 t. 7; pl. cstr. קַעֲרֹת כֶּסֶף 7[84], all of dedication gifts; as utensils in tabern. pl. abs. קְעָרֹת 4[7], sf. קְעָרֹתָיו Ex 25[29] 37[16].

8258 †[שְׁקַעֲרוּרָה] **n.f. depression, hollow** (on format. v. Ges[§ 55 l]);—pl. שְׁקַעֲרוּרֹת Lv 14[37] in wall.

7087 †[קָפָא] **vb. thicken, condense, congeal** (cf. Syr. ܩܦܐ *heap up, collect*);—**Qal** *Pf.* 3 pl. קָפְאוּ תְהֹמֹת Ex 15[8] (song) *the deeps were condensed*, became firm walls; *Impf.* יקפאון Zc 14[6] Kt (i.e. יְקִפָּאוּן [poss. is also יְקִפְּאוּן **Niph.**]) Thes al. glorious(?) ones [stars] *shall contract* (dwindle), but rd. Qr וְקִפָּאוֹן v. foll. *Pt.* הַקֹּפְאִים עַל־שִׁמְרֵיהֶם Zp 1[12] the men *who are thickening on their lees* (easy-going men, under figure of undisturbed wine). **Hiph.** *Impf.* 2 ms. sf. תַּקְפִּיאֵנִי Jb 10[10] *didst thou not curdle me* like cheese (of formation of foetus)?

3368, 7087 †קִפָּאוֹן **n.[m.] congelation**;—Zc 14[6] Qr
7087 [> Kt v. √**Qal** *Impf.*], so 𝔊 𝔖 Symm We Now
3368 (with other change, but see GASm), v. יָקָר. p. 429

7088 †[קָפַד] **vb. Pi. gather together, roll up** (Ar. قَفَدَ *wind* turban *snugly*; Aram. קְפַד, ܩܦܕ, Ithpe. *be drawn in, together*; also קוּפְדָּא, ܩܘܦܕܐ, *porcupine*; so Ar. (د) قُنْفُذٌ (cf. Lag[BN 182]), Eth. ቀንፈዝ:);—*Pf.* 1 s. קִפַּדְתִּי Is 38[12] *I have rolled up*, like a weaver, my life (i.e. finished it; Buhl[Lex 13] תָּ- [of ׳י], but 3 ms. foll. of ׳י).

7090 †קִפֹּד **n.[m.] porcupine** (fr. *rolling* itself *together*; 𝔊 ἐχῖνοι (alw. pl.), 𝔙 *ericius*, Bo[Hieroz. iii. cap. 36] Post[Hastings DB BITTERN]; > (from context) *bittern* Tr[NHB 243] Hi Che Gu[Kau]; v. discussion by M'Lean-Shipley[Ency. Bib. BITTERN]);—ק׳ as haunting desolate places, Is 14[23] Zp 2[14], קִפּוֹד Is 34[11].

†[קְפָדָה] **n.[f.**, Albr[ZAW xvi (1896), 116] cf. Sta[§ 303a]] **shuddering** (cf. ܩܦܕ, of skin, = סָמַר ψ 119[120], v. Thes);—abs. קְפָדָה־בָא Ez 7[25] (read בָּאָה Co Krae, and on tone v. Ges[§ 29 e]). 7089

קפז (√of foll.; cf. Ar. قَفَزَ *leap, spring*; so 𝔗 קְפַז (rare), v. Syr. ܩܦܙ *id.*, ܩܦܘܙܐ *weasel*).

†קִפּוֹז **n.f. arrow-snake** (Ar. قِفَّازَةٌ, so Bo[Hieroz. Pars post. iii. cap. 11] (citing Avicenna[ii. 139, 16], cf. Thes Lag[BN 89]), and most moderns; cf. Dozy[ii. 383] PS[1375 ad fin.]; = ἀκοντίας Aelian[Hist. Anim. vi. 18, viii. 13], called ק׳ as *leaping* from trees on passers-by; but ag. this v. Houghton[Acad. Apr. 24, 1886, 292 f.] (arrow-snake does not incubate) Post[Hast. DB iii. 637] who conj. an owl (as AV));—Is 34[15], token of desolation. 7091

†קָפַץ **vb. draw together, shut** (NH = BH; Ar. قَفَصَ *collect, conjoin, tie*; Syr. ܩܦܨ *draw together, contract, withdraw* (cf. Nö[M 47: ZMG xxxiii (1879), 516]); 𝔗 קְפַץ *hasten* (double oneself up in running), Pi. *hop, spring*);—**Qal** *Pf.* 3 ms. ק׳ ψ 77[10], etc.; *Impf.* 2 ms. תִּקְפֹּץ Dt 15[7]; 3 mpl. יִקְפְּצוּ Is 52[15];—*shut* hand Dt 15[7] (c. מִן *away from*, so as not to lend; opp. פתח v[8]); mouth, in astonishment Is 52[15], in abject silence Jb 5[16] ψ 107[42]; fig. ק׳ רַחֲמָיו 77[10] *shut up his compassion.* **Niph.** *Impf.* 3 ms. יִקָּפְצוּן Jb 24[24] si vera l., *they draw themselves together*, of contraction in death (cf. Di Bu; Ol יִקָּבְצוּן *are gathered in*). **Pi.** *Pt.* מְקַפֵּץ עַל־הַגְּבָעוֹת Ct 2[8] *springing* (i.e. making repeated contractions of body, in taking leaps) *upon the hills* (|| מְדַלֵּג). 7092

קֵץ v. קצץ. p. 893 7093

[קָצַב] **vb. cut off, shear** (?) (NH קָצַב *decide, determine*, **Pi.** *chop* meat; Palm. קצבא *butcher*, so Syr. ܩܨܒܐ, JAram. קַצָּבָא, and Ar. قَصَّابٌ as loan-word Frä[258]; Ar. قَضَبَ also is *cut off* a branch);—**Qal** *Impf.* 3 ms. וַיִּקְצָב־עֵץ 2 K 6[6] *he cut off a stick*; *Pt. pass.* fpl. עֵדֶר הַקְּצוּבוֹת Ct 4[2] *a flock of* (sheep) *that are shorn* (?). 7094

†קֶצֶב **n.m.**[1 K 6, 25] **1. cut, shape; 2. extremity**;—**1.** ק׳ abs., *shape* of cherubim 1 K 6[25] (+ מִדָּה), of bases 7[37] (+ *id.*). **2.** *extremity*, pl. cstr. קִצְבֵי הָרִים Jon 2[7] *the extremities* (bottoms) *of* (the) *mountains* (= קצבי הרים Ecclus 16[19]). 7095

†I. [קָצָה] **vb. cut off** (NH *id.*, *separate*, Ph. קצה *cut off, exterminate*; Aram. קְצָא, ܩܨܐ *break off* (e.g. bread); Ar. قَصَا *be remote*, قُصْيَا *remote extremity*);—**Qal** *Inf.* קְצוֹת עַמִּים Hb 2[10] *cutting off* many *peoples*; Vrss קְצוֹתָ (√קצץ); 7096

Gr Now conj. הֲצִיקוֹתָ. **Pi.** *Inf. cstr.* לְקַצּוֹת בְּ 2 K 10^{32} *to cut off in Israel;* read prob. לִקְצֹף *to be angry with,* 𝔗 Hi Che[Crit. n. Is 14, 6 (in Comm.)] Kmp[Kau] Kit Benz, 𝔙 Gr לְקוּץ; *Pt.* מְקַצֶּה רַגְלַיִם Pr 26^{6} (fig.). **Hiph.** *Pf.* 3 pl. הִקְצוּ Lv 14^{41}, acc. *dust; Inf. cstr.* הִקְצוֹת v^{43}, acc. *house,* in both appar.=קָצַע *scrape, scrape off* (q.v., v$^{41\,a}$), and so prob. read, viz. הִקְצִיעַ, הִקְצְעוּ, RS[JPhil. xvi (1888), 72] Dr-Wh Di-Ry Baen.

7097 קָצֶה$_{92}$ **n.[m.] end, extremity,** only sg.: abs. ק׳ Gn 19^{4}+3 t.; cstr. קְצֵה Ju 6^{21}+; sf. קָצֵהוּ Gn 47^{21}+4 t.; (מִ)קְּצֵיהֶם Ez 33^{2} (sg.; Ges[§ 93 ss]); pl. (cstr.) supplied by קְצוֹת, v. foll.;—**1.** *end,* of staff Ju 6^{21}, rod 1 S 14$^{27.43}$, curtains Ex 26^{5}=36^{12} (P; cf. קָצָה); of conduit Is 7^{3}, river,=*mouth* v^{18} (prob.), Jos 15$^{5.5}$ 18^{19}; of field Gn 23^{9}, valley Jos 15^{8}, tribe v^{21}, sea v^{2} Nu 34^{3} (all P); of territory (גְּבוּל) Nu 20^{16} (JE; just *without*), 22^{36} (E; just *within*), cf. Ez 25^{9} (al. sub **3**); מִקְּ׳ גְּבוּל־מִצְרַיִם וְעַד־קָצֵהוּ Gn 47^{21} (J); cf. מִן־הַקּ׳ אֶל־הַקּ׳ Ex 26^{28} = 36^{33} (of side of tabern.); מִקְּצֵה צָפוֹנָה Ez 48^{1} *at the northern extremity,* cf. מִקּ׳ תֵּימָן Jos 15^{1} (P); of earth, מִקּ׳ (הָ)אָרֶץ Is 5^{26} 43^{6} Dt 28^{49} (all ‖ מֵרָחוֹק), Is 42^{10}+4 t.;+phr. מִקּ׳ (הָ)אָרֶץ וְעַד־ק׳ הָאָרֶץ Dt 13^{8} 28^{64} Je 25^{33}, of land 12^{12} (cf. Is 26^{15}); of earth, abbrev. אֶל־ק׳ עַד־ק׳ הָא׳ 25^{31} Is 48^{20} 49^{6} ψ 46^{10}, בִּק׳ הָא׳ Is 62^{11}; of earth, בִּק׳ תֵּבֵל ‖ בִּק׳־אָרֶץ Pr 17^{24}, ψ 19^{5}; מִקּ׳ הַשָּׁמַיִם Is 13^{5} (‖ מֵאֶרֶץ מֶרְחָק), ψ 19^{7} לְמִק׳ הַשׁ׳ (‖ עַל־קְצוֹתָם), בִּק׳ הַשׁ׳ Dt 30^{4}=Ne 1^{9}; וְעַד־ק׳ הַשׁ׳ Dt 4^{32}. **2.** *border, outskirts,* of city 1 S 9^{27} 14^{2} Jos 4^{19} 18^{15}, camp Nu 11^{1} (JE); esp. to one approaching Ju 7$^{17.19}$ 2 K 7$^{5.8}$, so of armed force Ju 7^{11}, people Nu 22^{41} (E), 23^{13} (JE; emphat. אֶפֶס ק׳, opp. כֻּלּוֹ), mt. Ex 19^{12} (E), Jos 18^{16} (JE); see also 3^{8} (D), v^{15} (JE), Ex 13^{20}=Nu 33^{6}, Ex 16^{35} Nu 33^{37} Jos 13^{27} (all P), Ru 3^{7}. †**3.** condensed term for what is included within extremities,=the whole: מִקּ׳ אֶחָיו Gn 47^{2} (J), cf. Ez 33^{2}; abs. מִקָּצֶה Gn 19^{4} (J)=in (its) entirety; =on all sides, Je 51^{31}+50^{26} (מִקָּצֶה for מִקֵּץ, Gie); so מִקָּצֵהוּ Is 56^{11} Di, but om. מִקּ׳ 𝔊 Du Che Marti. **4.** מִקְצֵה *at the end of* a certain time Jos 9^{16} (JE), 2 S 24^{8}+8 t.

7098 †קָצָה **n.f. et** (pl.) **m.**[Ex 25, 18] **end** (pl. 4 t. **f.** [c. num. masc.], Albr[ZAW xvi (1896), 93] changes gender of num. in all, or regards as irregular agreement in gender (Ges[§ 97 c]); otherwise Kö[ii. 1, 61, 176]);—abs. ק׳ Ex 25^{19}+; pl. cstr. קְצוֹת 1 K 12^{31}+; sf. קְצוֹתָיו Ex 27^{4}+ (so also Ex 37^{8} 39^{4} Qr; Kt קצוותו, cf. קְצָת infr.), etc.;—**1.** *end,* sg. of כַּפֹּרֶת in tabern. Ex 25$^{19.19}$=37$^{8.8}$; of curtain 26^{4}=36^{11}; elsewh. pl., ק׳ הַכַּפֹּרֶת 25^{18}=37^{7}, cf. 25^{19}=37^{8}; of ephod 28^{7}=39^{4}, breast-plate 28$^{23.24.26}$=39$^{16.17.19}$, chains 28^{25}=39^{18}, grating 27^{4} (appar.=*corners*); *tips* of wings 1 K 6$^{24.24}$; of vine Ez 15^{4}; ק׳ הָאָרֶץ *ends of the earth* Is 40^{28} 41$^{5.9}$ Jb 28^{24}; אַרְבַּע ק׳ הַשָּׁמַיִם Je 49^{36}, cf. ψ 19^{7}; ק׳ דְּרָכָיו Jb 26^{14}, i.e. the mere edge, minute part, of his doings. **2.** מִקְצוֹת הָעָם =*from the whole of* (fr. among) *the people,* 1 K 12^{31} 13^{33}, cf. Ju 18^{2} 2 K 17^{32} (v. also Ecclus 16^{17}, and קָצֶה **3**).

†קֵצֶה (Baer קָצֶה) **n.[m.]** end (on ֶ— Ba[NB § 12 a], and [on ה] Kö[ii. 1, 65]);—only אֵין ק׳, usu. +לְ, *no end to* (of), Is 2$^{7.7}$ Na 2^{10} 3^{3}; abs. אֵין קֵצֶה v^{9}. 7097

†[קָצוּ] **n.[m.] end, boundary** (on form Kö[ii. 1, 61]);—only pl. cstr. קַצְוֵי־אֶרֶץ *ends of the earth* ψ 48^{11} 65^{6}; *boundaries of the land* Is 26^{15}. 7099

†קְצָת **n.f. end** (Lag[BN 10] Ges[§ 95 n]);—cstr. ק׳ Ne 7^{69} (Gi Baer, v^{70} van d. H.)+; sf. קְצָתָם Dn 1^{5}; pl. abs. קְצוֹת Ex 38^{5} ψ 65^{9} (+perh. קצוותו Ex 37^{8} 39^{4} Kt. v. קָצָה; Kö[ii. 1, 61] der. these pl. forms fr. [קָצוּ]);—**1.** *end,* of *corners* of grating Ex 38^{5} (‖ קְצוֹתָיו 27^{4}), cf. Ex 37^{8} 39^{4} supr. (all P); *ends* of earth ψ 65^{9}. **2.** מִקְצָת (some) *from the end of, some of* (מִן **3 b**) Ne 7^{69} (so NH), Dn 1^{2}. **3.** מִקּ׳ *at the end of* a certain time Dn 1$^{5.15.18}$. 7117

II. קצה (√of foll. (Ol[§ 215 h] Kö[ii. 1, 405]); cf. Ar. قَضَى *decide judicially, decree,* قَاضٍ *Ḳaḍi*).

†קָצִין **n.m.**[Dn 11, 18] **chief, ruler** (prop. *decider,* cf. Dr[Dn 11, 8]);—abs. ק׳ Ju 11^{6}+; cstr. קְצִין Is 3^{7}; pl. cstr. קְצִינֵי Is 1^{10}+; sf. קְצִינַיִךְ Is 22^{3};—**1.** *chief, commander* in war Jos 10^{24} (JE), Ju 11$^{6.11}$ (‖ ראשׁ), Dn 11^{18}. **2.** *dictator,* Is 3$^{6.7}$. **3.** more gen., *ruler,* man in authority, Is 1^{10} 22^{3} Mi 3$^{1.9}$; of ants, אֵין ק׳ Pr 6^{7} (+שֹׁטֵר, מֹשֵׁל).—Pr 25^{15} read probably קֶצֶף (Toy). 7101

קְצוֹת v. קְצָת. above 7117

קצח (√of foll.; mng. unknown; NH קֶצַח =BH; Ar. قَزَح, قِزْح *seeds used for seasoning*).

†קֶצַח **n.m.**[Is 28, 27] **black cumin** (*Nigella sativa* Linn.; 𝔊 μελάνθιον, 𝔙 *gith, id.;* cf. Tr[NHB 444; Smith DB 2nd ed. Fitches] Post[Hastings DB id.]);—plant with small black acrid seeds, used as condiment: abs. ק׳ Is 28$^{25.27.27}$. 7100

I. קָצַע **vb. scrape, scrape off** (NH *id.,* also קְצִיעָה=BH, 𝔗 קְצִיעֲתָא, Ar. قُضَاعٌ *fine dust*);—**Hiph.** *id. Impf.* 3 ms. אֶת־הַבַּיִת יַקְצִעַ Lv 14^{41}. 7106

7102 †I. [קְצִיעָה] **n.f.** **cassia**, a *powdered* bark, like cinnamon (hence Gk. κασία, Lat. *casia*, Lewy[Fremdw. 37]);—pl. קְצִיעוֹת (מֹר וַאֲהָלוֹת) ψ 45[9] (Che now תּוּגְצָק *are shed*, v. in [Ency. Bib. Cassia, n.]).

7103 †II. קְצִיעָה **n.pr.f.** (*cassia*, fr. fragrance);—Job's second daughter Jb 42[14], Κασ(σ)ιαν (acc.).

4741 †[מַקְצֻעָה] **n.[f.]** **scraping tool**, used in fashioning idols;—pl. בַּמַּקְצֻעוֹת Is 44[13].

†II. קצע (√ of foll.; cf. Aram. קְטַע, ܩܛܥ *cut off*, also Ar. قطع *break off* (if for قطع, RS[JPhil. xvi. 74]), مقطع *place where something is cut off* or *ends abruptly* RS[infr.]; Sab. קצע appar. *cut off*, or the like, Sab Denkm[91]).

4740 מִקְצֹעַ **n.m.**[Ez 46, 21] **place of corner-structure, (inner) corner-buttress** (as (place of) *cutting off* of an inner angle if √ rightly expl.; v. RS[l.c. 71-81]);—abs. מ׳ Ne 3[19]+, -צוֹעַ- Ne 3[20]+; cstr. -צֹעַ- Ez 46[21.21]; pl. abs. מִקְצֹעֹת Ex 26[24] 36[29], cstr. -עוֹת- Ez 46[22], מִקְצוֹעֵי v[21], also מִקְצֹעֹת Ex 26[23] 36[28] Di (not **Pu.** *Pt.* fr. קָצַע Thes Buhl[Lex 13] al.), but rd. prob. מִקְצֹעֹת, so SS Baen; sf. מִקְצוֹעֹתָיו Ez 41[22];—*corner-post* of altar Ez 41[22], tabern. Ex 26[23.24]=36[28.29]; (inner) *buttress-place* of court, where the small corner-courts were, Ez 46[21.21.21.22]; of inner (rock-?) *buttress* at NE. corner of wall of Jerus., הַמּ׳, nearly=n.pr., Ne 3[19.20.25], also (disting. fr. פִּנָּה) v[24] 2 Ch 26[9].

4742, 7102 קָצַע **vb. denom.** **Hoph.** *Pt.* מְהֻקְצָעוֹת (Ew[§192d] Ol[§78c] Ges[§53 q.s.]) Ez 46[22] *cornered? set in corners?* del. with M (cf. Ol) 𝔊 𝔖 𝔙 Hi Kö[I. 1, 294] Co Berthol Toy Krae.—Ex 26[23] 36[28] v. מִקְצֹעַ.

7107 †I. קָצַף **vb.** **be wroth** (NH *id.*, Hiph. *make wrathful* (rare); Syr. ܩܨܦ *be wrathful*, also *be anxious, fearful*);—**Qal** *Pf.* 3 ms. ק׳ Gn 41[10]+, etc.; *Impf.* 3 ms. יִקְצֹף Lv 10[6]+, etc.; *Inf. cstr.* קְצֹף Is 54[9]; *Pt.* קֹצֵף Zc 1[15];—*be wroth*: **1.** of God; abs. Dt 1[34] Is 57[16.17.17] 64[4.8] Zc 1[15]; c. עַל *against*, Lv 10[6] Nu 16[22] (P), Dt 9[19] Is 47[6] 54[9] La 5[22] Zc 1[2.15] Ec 5[5]; c. אֶל Jos 22[18] (P). **2.** of man; abs. Est 1[12] 2[21] 2 K 5[11]; c. עַל Gn 40[2] 41[10] (E), Ex 16[20] Lv 10[16] Nu 31[14] (P), Je 37[15] 1 S 29[4] 2 K 13[19]. **Hiph.** *Pf.* 2 ms. הִקְצַפְתָּ Dt 9[7]; 2 mpl. הִקְצַפְתֶּם v[8]; *Impf.* 3 mpl. יַקְצִיפוּ ψ 106[32]; *Inf. cstr.* הַקְצִיף Zc 8[14]; *Pt.* pl. מַקְצִפִים Dt 9[22];—*provoke to wrath*, c. acc. י׳ Dt 9[7.8.22] Zc 8[14]; so (acc. om.) ψ 106[32]. **Hithp.** *put oneself in a rage*: *Pf.* 3 ms. consec. וְהִתְקַצַּף Is 8[21], of hard-pressed people.

†I. קֶ֫צֶף **n.m.**[2 K 3, 27] **wrath**;—abs. ק׳ Nu 1[53]+; 7110
קֶצֶף Jos 22[20]+; cstr. קְצֶף Je 50[13]+; sf. קִצְפִּי Is 60[10]; קִצְפְּךָ ψ 38[2], קִצְפְּךָ 102[11], קִצְפּוֹ Je 10[10];—**1.** of God: abs. Nu 17[11] (P), Dt 29[27] Is 60[10] Je 10[10] 21[5] 32[37] 50[13] ψ 38[2] 102[11] Zc 7[12]; c. עַל *against* Nu 1[53] 18[5] Jos 9[20] 22[20] (P), 2 K 3[27] 1 Ch 27[24] 2 Ch 19[2.10] 24[18] 29[8] 32[25.26] Is 34[2] Zc 1[2.15]; בְּשֶׁצֶף ק׳ Is 54[8]. **2.** of man (late), Est 1[18] Ec 5[16].—Ho 10[7] v. II. קֶצֶף.

II. קצף (√ of foll.; Ar. قصف *break, snap off*).

†קְצָפָה **n.f.** **a snapping** or **splintering** (on 7111
abstr. formation v. Ba[NB 87]);—Jo 1[7] (of fig-tree; ‖ שַׁמָּה).

†II. קֶ֫צֶף **n.[m.]** prob. **splinter**;—only כְּק׳ 7110
עַל־פְּנֵי־מָיִם Ho 10[7] (sim. of helpless king).

[קָצַץ] **vb.** **cut off** (NH *id.*, also קֵץ *end*; 7112
As. *kaṣâṣu, hew off, cut off, kiṣṣatu, boundary-stone*, Belser[BAS ii. 120, 139], cf. Hilpr[Assyriaca i. 12]; Ar.
قصّ *cut, clip, cut off*; Aram. קְצַץ, ܩܨ *cut off*, 7113
קִיצָא *end*);—**Qal** *Pf.* 2 ms. consec. וְקַצֹּתָה Dt 25[12] (acc. כַּפָּהּ); *Pt. pass.* pl. cstr. קְצוּצֵי פֵאָה Je 9[25] 25[23] 49[32] (v. פֵּאָה **1**). **Pi.** *Pf.* 3 ms. קִצֵּץ ψ 129[4], וְק׳ consec. Ex 39[3] ψ 46[10], קִצֵּץ 2 K 18[16]; *Impf.* וַיְקַצֵּץ 16[17]+, etc.;—*cut* or *hew off*, thumbs, toes, Ju 1[6], hands and feet 2 S 4[12]; *cut in two*, spear (חֲנִית) ψ 46[10], threads Ex 39[3] (P), cords ψ 129[4] (fig.); *cut in pieces*, vessels (of gold) 2 K 24[13] 2 Ch 28[24]; bases (הַמְּכֹנוֹת) 2 K 16[17] (so Kit Benz, transposing הַמִּסְגְּרוֹת), doors 2 K 18[16] (both, for the sake of metal sheathing). **Pu.** *Pt.* pl. מְקֻצָּצִים Ju 1[7] *hewn off* (as v[6] supr.).

קֵץ[68] **n.m.**[Ez 7, 6] **end**;—ק׳ abs. Am 8[2]+, cstr. 7093
Gn 4[3]+, עֵת־ Dn 8[17]; sf. קִצּוֹ Is 37[24]+, קִצָּה ‖ 2 K 19[23], etc.;—**1.** *end*, usu. of time, esp. in phr. מִקֵּץ *at the end of* a definite time Gn 8[6] (J), 41[1] (E), 16[3] (P) + 15 t., + מִקֵּץ הֱיוֹת Est 2[12]; indef. Gn 4[3] (J) 1 K 17[7] Je 13[6]; so (late) לְקֵץ of indef. time 2 Ch 18[2] Ne 13[6] Dn 11[6.13]; defin. כְּעֵת צֵאת הַקֵּ׳ לְיָמִים שְׁנַיִם 2 Ch 21[19]; *end* of life, of a people Am 8[2] Ez 7[2.2.3.6.6] Je 51[13] La 4[18.18], cf. (of all flesh) Gn 6[13] (P); of individ. Jb 6[11] ψ 39[5] (‖ מִדַּת יָמַי), Dn 9[26a] 11[45]; in eschatol. sense, עֵת עֲוֺן קֵץ *time of final punishment* (Toy) Ez 21[30.34] 35[5]; לְקֵץ Hb 2[3] *to the end*; esp. Dn, of time of Antiochus' persecution, foll. by A.'s death, עֵת קֵץ *time of the end* 8[17] 11[35.40] 12[4.9], מוֹעֵד ק׳ 8[19]; cf. ק׳ הַיָּמִין 12[13], ק׳ alone 9[26b] 12[13]; *end*, cessation, abs. לְמוֹעֵד ק׳ 11[27]; ק׳ הַפְּלָאוֹת 12[6], of words Jb 16[3], darkness 28[3],

perfection ψ 119^{96}; אֵין ק׳ *no end*, of peace Is 9^{6}, iniquities Jb 22^{5}, toil Ec 4^{8}, עֲשׂוֹת סְפָרִים 12^{12}. **2.** *end*, in space, מְלוֹן קִצֹּה 2 K 19^{23} *its remotest lodging-place* = Is 37^{24} (v. מָלוֹן p. 533); אֵין ק׳, of multitude Ec 4^{16}.—Je 50^{26} v. קָצֶה **3.**

7104 †קְצִיץ **n.pr.loc.** (fr. above √?);—only in עֵמֶק ק׳ in Benj., Jos 18^{21}, Αμεκαυεις, etc.

7020 †[קִיצוֹן] **adj. at the end, outermost**;—fs. קִיצֹנָה, of curtain (יְרִיעָה) Ex 26$^{4.10a}$ = 36$^{11.17a}$; ins. also prob. 26^{10b} = 36^{17b} so Kit (in Di) Baen.

7114 †[קָצַר], I. קָצֵר (Ges^{§44c} Sta^{§384,2}) **vb. be short** (NH קָצֵר *short*, קִצֵּר *shorten*; Ar. قَصَّرَ *shorten*, قَصُرَ *be short*, c. عَنْ *come short of*; JAram. קְצַר *be short*);—**Qal** *Pf.* 3 ms. קָצַר Is 28^{20} Mi 2^{7} (SS קצר fr. adj. קָצֵר); 3 fs. קָצְרָה Is 50^{2} 59^{1}; *Impf.* 3 fs. תִּקְצַר Jb 21^{4}+, 3 fpl. תִּקְצֹרְנָה Pr 10^{27}; *Inf. abs.* קָצוֹר Is 50^{2}; *Pt. pass.* fpl. קְצֻרוֹת Ez 42^{5};—*be short*, of bed Is 28^{20} (fig.), of לְשָׁכוֹת Ez 42^{5}; esp. (fig.) of יַד י׳, i.e. be ineffective, powerless Nu 11^{23} (JE), c. מִן comp. Is 50^{2} (+inf. abs.), 59^{1}; c. נֶפֶשׁ, רוּחַ, = *be impatient* (opp. [אָרַךְ] **Hiph. 1** (c)): וַתִּק׳ נֶפֶשׁ הָעָם Nu 21^{4b}(JE), of utter discouragement, cf. (of רוּחַ) Jb 21^{4}; וַתִּק׳ נַפְשׁוֹ Ju 16^{16} i.e. he was worn out (by importunity), so of proph. (representing י׳) Zc 11^{8} (ב pers.) reach limit of patience with, endurance of; of י׳ Ju 10^{16} (ב rei); ק׳ רוּחַ י׳ Mi 2^{7} (v. supr.); ק׳ of time †Pr 10^{27} (years of wicked). **Pi.** *shorten Pf.* 3 ms. קִצַּר יָמַי ψ 102^{24}. **Hiph.** *id.*, *Pf.* 3 ms. הִקְצַרְתָּ יְמֵי וגו׳ ψ 89^{46}.

7116 †[קָצֵר] **adj. short**;— in phr. קִצְרֵי־יָד 2 K 19^{26} *short of hand*, feeble, = Is 37^{27}; fig. קְצַר־אַפַּיִם Pr 14^{7} = *impatient*, so קְצַר רוּחַ v^{29} (opp. אֶרֶךְ אַפַּיִם); of time קְצַר יָמִים †Jb 14^{1} *short-lived*.

7115 †קֹצֶר **n.[m.] shortness**;—cstr. ק׳ רוּחַ Ex 6^{9} (P) = *impatience*.

7114 †II. [קָצַר] **vb. reap, harvest** (NH *id.*, also קָצִיר *harvest*; cf. As. *kaṣâru, join together, collect*; v. Dl$^{Pr\ 166f.}$ Zehnpf$^{BAS\ I.503}$ (not Syr. ܩܛܪ *bind*, Eth. ቀጸረ: [ቀፀረ:] *constringere*, v. Nö$^{ZMG\ xl\ (1886).\ 735}$));—**Qal** *Pf.* 3 pl. קָצְרוּ Je 12^{13}, etc.; *Impf.* 3 ms. יִקְצוֹר Is 17^{5} Ec 11^{4}+ Pr 22^{8} Kt (Qr יִקְצָר־); 3 mpl. יִקְצֹרוּן Ru 2^{9}, etc.; *Imv.* mpl. קִצְרוּ Ho 10^{12}+; *Inf. cstr.* לִקְצֹר 1 S 8^{12}+; sf. קֻצְרְךָ Lv 23^{22}, קֻצְרְכֶם 19^{9} 23^{22}; *Pt.* קוֹצֵר Je 9^{21}+, etc.:—*reap*, c. acc. of crop: acc. cogn. קָצִיר 1 S 6^{13} 8^{12} (+חָרִשׁ), Lv 19^{9} 23$^{10.22}$ (all H) Dt 24^{19}; acc. of grain Is 17^{5} (fig.; ‖ אָסַף), Jb 24^{6} (Qr; Kt vid.
Hiph.), cf. Lv 25^{5} (H), v^{11} (P; + זָרַע), so (obj. om.) 2 K 19^{29} = Is 37^{30}, Mi 6^{15} (opp. זָרַע), Lv 19^{9b} 23^{22b} Ru 2^{9} Ec 11^{4} (+זָרַע); obj. קֹצִים Je 12^{13}
(opp. זָרַע); *Pt.* = *reaper* Am 9^{13} (+ חוֹרֵשׁ), Je 9^{21}
(sim.), ψ 129^{7} (‖ מְעַמֵּר), + Is 17^{5} (for קָצִיר, so 7105
Buhl$^{Lex\ 13}$ Marti); pl. 2 K 4^{18} Ru 2$^{3.4.5.6.7.14}$; fig. of reaping fruits of righteousness Ho 10^{12} (+זָרַע), of evil Ho 8^{7} (both + זָרַע), 10^{13} (+חָרַשׁ), Jb 4^{8} (+חָרַשׁ, זָרַע), Pr 22^{8}; ψ 126^{5} they that sow (זָרַע) in tears *shall reap* in joy. **Hiph.** *Impf.* יקצירו Jb 24^{6} Kt (< Qr יִקְצוֹרוּ, v. supr.).

†I. קָצִיר **n.m.**$^{Je\ 8,20}$ **harvesting, harvest** (cf. 7105
Lag$^{BN\ 173}$);— abs. ק׳ Gn 45^{6}+, cstr. קְצִיר Ju 15^{1}+; sf. קְצִירְךָ Lv 19^{9}+, etc.;—*harvest*: **1.** process of *harvesting*, Gn 45^{6} (E; +חָרִישׁ), Ru 2^{21}. **2.** *what is reaped, harvested, crop*, spec. of grain: Gn 8^{22} (+זֶרַע; J), Is 17^{11} (fig.; cf. נוד; ‖ זֶרַע), ק׳ יְאֹר 23^{3} (‖ *id.*) i.e. exported grain of Egypt; ק׳ חִטִּים Ex 34^{22} (JE), ins. also 2 S 24^{15} (𝔊 Th We Dr al.), לֶקֶט ק׳ Lv 19^{9b} 23^{22b}; ק׳ as eaten Je 5^{17} Jb 5^{5} (but rd. here קָצְרוּ 𝔊 Me Bu al., cf. Bev$^{JPhil.\ xxvi.304}$); as acc. cogn. c. קָצַר 1 S 8^{12} Dn 24^{19} Lv 19^{9a} 23$^{10.10.22a}$ סְפִיחַ ק׳ Lv 25^{5} (all H), ק׳ חִטִּים 1 S 6^{13}; of ripe grain Is 1^{11} (ק׳ שָׂדֶה), 4^{13} (בָּשֵׁל ק׳); fig. of punishment Ho 6^{11}; of vintage Is 16^{9} (‖ קַיִץ; rd. prob. בָּצִיר as ‖ Je 48^{32}, Buhl$^{Lex\ 13}$). **3.** *time of harvest*, Ex 34^{21} (+חָרִישׁ; JE), 2 S 21^{10} (23^{13} rd. הַצּוּר as ‖ 1 Ch 11^{15}, so 𝔊L Th We and most), Is 9^{2} (sim.), 18^{5} (fig.), Je 5^{24}, ‖ קַיִץ 8^{20} Pr 6^{8} 10^{5} 26^{1} (sim.); opp. חֹרֶף 20^{4}; יְמֵי ק׳ Jos 3^{21} (JE), 2 S 21^{9a}, יוֹם ק׳ Pr 25^{13} (sim.), עֵת(־הַ)ק׳ Je 50^{16} 51^{33} (fig.); of *wheat-harvest*, יְמֵי ק׳ חִטִּים Gn 30^{14} (J), Ju 15^{1}, without יְמֵי Ru 2^{23b}, הֲלוֹא ק׳־ח׳ הַיּוֹם 1 S 12^{17}; *barley harvest*, ק׳ (הַ)שְּׂעֹרִים 2 S 21^{9b} Ru 1^{22} 2^{23a}; חֹם קָצִיר Is 18^{4}; חַג הַקּ׳ Ex 23^{16} (E). On harvest in Pal. v. Vogelst$^{Landwirthsch.\ 57\ ff.}$ Hayman$^{Smith\ DB\ Agriculture}$.
—Is 17^{5} rd. קֹצֵר, v. קָצַר. 7114

†II. קָצִיר **n.m.**$^{Is\ 27,11}$ usually coll., **boughs,** 7105
branches (connex. with above √dub.);—abs. ק׳ Jb 14^{9}; sf. קְצִירִי Jb 29^{19} (in fig.; ‖ שָׁרְשִׁי), קְצִירוֹ 18^{16} (fig.; ‖ *id.*); קְצִירָהּ Is 27^{11}; pl. sf. קְצִירֶיהָ ψ 80^{12}.

קְצָת v. I. קצה. p. 892 7117

קַר, קֹר v. I. קרר. קִר v. I. קִיר. p. 885, 903 7023, 7119-20

I. קָרָא^{724} **vb. call, proclaim, read** (NH 7121
id., *read aloud, read*; Ph. קרא *call*; Ar. قَرَأَ *read aloud, recite* (the 'Ḳor'ân'), القُرْآن *the Ḳor'ān*; Aram. קְרָא, ܩܪܐ *call*, etc., so OAram.

קרא, Nab. *id.*, Palm. *id.*, קרה);—**Qal** $_{655}$ *Pf.* ק׳ Gn 11^{9}+, 3 fs. consec. וְקָרָאת Is 7^{14} (Ges^{§74g}); 2 ms. קָרָאתָ Ju 12^{1}+, etc.; *Impf.* 3 ms. יִקְרָא Gn 2^{19}+; sf. יִקְרָאוֹ Je 23^{6}, אֵהוּ- Is 41^{2}+; 1 s. אֶקְרָא Dt 32^{3}+, וָאֶקְרָאֶה 1 S 28^{15} (Ges^{§48d} Nes$^{Marg. 15}$); 3 fpl. וַתִּקְרֶאנָה Ru 4$^{17.17}$, וַתִּקְרֶאןָ Nu 25^{2}; 2 fpl. תִּקְרֶאנָה Ru 1$^{20.21}$, etc.; *Imv.* ms. קְרָא Ju 7^{3}+, sf. קְרָאֵנִי ψ 50^{15}, etc.; *Inf. cstr.* קְרֹא 1 S 3^{6}+, קְרֹאות (Baer -אֹת) Ju 8^{1} (Ges^{§74h}); sf. קָרְאִי ψ 4^{2}+, etc.; *Pt. act.* קוֹרֵא Am 5^{8}+, קֹרֵא Je 1^{15}+; pl. קֹרְאִים ψ 99^{6} (Ges$^{§§74l; 75oo}$); *pass.* קָרוּא Est 5^{12}; pl. קְרֻאִים 1 S 9^{22} Ez 23^{23}, קְרֻאִים 1 S 9^{13}+; cstr. קְרוּאֵי Nu 1^{16} Qr (Kt קריאי), 26^{9} Kt (Qr קְרִיאֵי, v. קָרִיא);—**1. a.** *call, cry, utter a loud sound,* Ju 9^{7} 2 S 18^{25} (in v^{28} read וַיִּקְרַב We, confirmed by 𝔊L, so Dr and all recent Comm.), Je 4^{6} Dn 8^{16} (all+אמר), 2 K 7^{11} (on text v. Kit Benz), Is 6^{4}; for help Gn 39$^{15.18}$ (J); of pleading in court Is 59^{4} (ב of manner); explicitly בְּקוֹל גָּדוֹל Gn 39^{14} (J), 1 K 18$^{27.28}$ 2 K 18^{28}=Is 36^{13}=2 Ch 32^{18}, קוֹל גָּדוֹל Ez 9^{1}(+בְּאָזְנַי); c. אַחֲרֵי pers. 1 S 20^{37} (+אָמַר), 24^{8} (Gi; v^{9} van d. H. Baer; +לֵאמֹר), Je 12^{6}. **b.** *call, cry,* obj. in orat. recta Ju 7^{20} 1 S 3^{4} (rd. שְׁמוּאֵל שְׁמוּאֵל; 𝔊 Th We Dr Kit Bu HPS), v^{6} (cf. 𝔊), v^{8} (agst. accents), v^{10} (v. שְׁמוּאֵל), 20^{38} 2 S 20^{16} 2 K 11^{14} Je 20^{8} Lv 13^{45}; =utter, speak Je 36^{18}; of command Gn 45^{1} (E). **2. a.** *call unto* some one: אֶל pers. (oft.+אָמַר; sts. c. מִן loc.), Gn 3^{9} 19^{5} Ex 3^{4} Is 6^{3}+oft.; c. עַל (for אֶל) of satyrs Is 34^{14} (so Vrss Ges Che$^{Comm.}$ al. >recent Comm. from II. קרא or קָרָה which (in Qal) alw. take accus.); unto (אֶל) י׳ (God), in praise †ψ 66^{17} 1 Ch 4^{10}, usu. for help, Ju 15^{18} 1 S 12$^{17.18}$ Ho 7^{7} ψ 3^{5} 4^{4}+, +עַל pers. *against* Dt 15^{9} 24^{15}; to (ל) י׳ (God) †Jb 14^{14} ψ 57^{3} 141^{1}; to (ל) a servant (for service) 2 K 4^{36} Jb 19^{16}, so (אֶל) 2 S 1^{15}; *call* to (ל) one Je 3^{4} (+orat. rect.), La 4^{15} (*id.*), Pr 2^{3} (לַבִּינָה); subj. י׳ Mi 6^{9} Je 35^{17}. **b.** *cry* for help, abs., (poet. and late) Zc 7^{13} Is 58^{9} 65^{24} Jb 5^{1} 9^{16} Pr 21^{13} ψ 4^{2} 20^{10}+10 t. ψψ (147^{9} of young ravens); בְּאָזְנֵי Ez 8^{18}. **c.** ק׳ בְּשֵׁם י׳ *call with name of* י׳ (i.e. use it in invocation): Gn 4^{26} 12^{8} 2 K 5^{11} Je 10^{25}=ψ 79^{6}+16 t. (1 K 18^{24} of specif. appeal to י׳ to display his power), +Is 65^{1} (v. **Pu.**); with name of Baal †1 K 18$^{24.25.26}$. **d.** late, c. acc. dei Is 43^{22} ψ 14^{4}+4 t. ψψ; abs. ψ 116^{2}. **3.** *proclaim:* **a.** c. acc. rei procl. Am 4^{5} Gn 41^{43} Dt 15^{2} Je 31^{6} Lv 25^{10}+; ק׳ צוֹם *proclaim a fast* 1 K 21$^{9.12}$ Je 36^{9}+, ק׳ מוֹעֲדֵי י׳ Lv 23$^{2.4}$; ק׳ sq. orat. rect. Ex 34^{6}, etc.; sq. ל pers. Je 34$^{8.15.17.17}$ Is 61^{1}, עַל pers. (*against, concerning*) 1 K 13$^{4.32}$ Je 49^{29} La 1^{15}; *proclaim* peace to (ל pers.) Ju 21^{13}; cf. ק׳ אֵלֶיהָ לְשָׁלוֹם Dt 20^{10}; ק׳ c. acc. cogn. מִקְרָא Is 1^{13}, הַקְּרִיאָה Jon 3^{2} (+אֶל). **b.** ק׳ שֵׁם י׳ Dt 32^{3} ψ 99^{6}; so (earlier) ק׳ בְּשֵׁם י׳ Ex 33^{19} 34^{5} (JE); cf. ק׳ בְּשֵׁם יַעֲקֹב Is 44^{5} (but read יִקָּרֵא, Lo Che and most). **c.** ק׳ בְּשׁ׳ עֲלֵי ψ 49^{12} *proclaim* (*with*) *name over* landed estates, claim possession (Hup Bae); *proclaim* one's own name Ru 4^{11} = become famous; pt. pass. *proclaimed,* i.e. renowned Ez 23^{23}. **d.** abs. *make proclamation* (sts. +אָמַר, לֵאמֹר) Ju 7^{3} Je 2^{2} (בְּאָזְנֵי) Zc 1$^{14.17}$ Jon 3^{4} Is 40$^{3.6}$+, c. עַל *concerning* Ne 6^{7}, *against* 1 K 13^{2} Jon 1^{2}. †**4. a.** *read aloud,* oft. בְּאָזְנֵי, less oft. לִפְנֵי, c. ב of roll, book Je 36$^{6.8.14}$ Ne 8$^{3.8}$ 9^{3} 2 Ch 34^{18}, +acc. of words Je 36$^{8.10}$; obj. om. Ex 24^{7} (E) Je 36^{15}; c. acc. of roll, book v$^{15.21}$ 51^{63} 2 K 22^{10} 2 Ch 34^{24}, of letter (סֵפֶר), writing 2 K 5^{7} Is 29$^{11.12}$ Je 29^{29}, columns of manuscript Je 36^{23}; c. acc. of words Jos 8$^{34.35}$ Je 36^{6} 51^{61} 2 K 23^{2}=2 Ch 34^{30}, cf. Dt 31^{11}. **b.** *read,* to oneself, in (ב) a roll, book, Dt 17^{19} Ne 8^{18}, so of vision written on tablets Hb 2^{2}; c. acc. of letter (סֵפֶר) 2 K 19^{14} = Is 37^{14}, book 2 K 22^{8}; abs. Is 34^{16}. **c.** *read,* for hear read, 2 K 22^{16}. **5.** *summon:* usu. **a.** c. ל pers.: Gn 12^{18} 20$^{8.9}$ Nu 22$^{5.20.37}$ Ju 8^{1} 1 S 3$^{5.6.8.8}$+oft. (c. 100 t.), +ל reflex. 1 K 1$^{28.32}$, +אֶל loc. Ex 19^{20}, +אֶל pers. 2 S 9^{2}, + inf. purpose Jos 24^{9} Ju 12^{1} 14^{16} 1 S 28^{15}, +מִן loc. Ho 11^{1} Ju 4^{6}; +בִּשְׁמֶךָ Is 45^{4} *summon* by thy name; specif. *summon*=*invite* (esp. to feast) Ex 34^{15} Ju 14^{15} (+inf. purpose) 1 S 16^{3} (+בַּזָּבַח, rd. prob. לַזּ׳ v. HPS), v^{5} (+לַזּ׳), 1 K 1$^{9.26}$+ (c. 17 t.). **b.** c. אֶל pers. Ex 10^{24} Jos 4^{4} 10^{24} 1 K 13^{21}+ (c. 20 t.); אֶל pers.+ל pers. (diff. persons in same relation) Ex 8^{21} Je 42^{8}; =*call for* (demand to see), c. אֶל pers. 2 K 18^{18}; c. ל rei=demand, require Pr 18^{6} cf. 27^{16} (prob. corrupt, v. Toy). **c.** c. acc. pers. Gn 41$^{8.14}$ Ex 2^{7} (+ל pers.), v^{7} Am 5^{16} (+אֶל rei), Is 13^{3} (ל rei), 1 S 3^{16} 22^{11}+ (c. 33 t.), ins. וַיִּקְרָא in this sense also 2 S 15^{12} 𝔊L We Dr and most; +inf. purpose Nu 24^{10}, ק׳ מִמִּזְרָח עַיִט Is 46^{11}; in weakened sense (to bring response, or bring pers. near) Ct 5^{6}; specif. *invite,* 1 S 9^{24} (but corrupt, v. esp. HPS), 1 K 1^{9} (also+ל, MT), v^{10} 12^{20} (+אֶל loc.), Dt 33^{19} (acc. loc.); אֲנִי קָרוּא לָהּ Est 5^{12}, pt. pass. elsewh. pl., *invited ones, guests* 1 S 9$^{13.22}$ 2 S 15^{11} 1 K 1$^{41.49}$ Zp 1^{7} Pr 9^{18}; *invite* or *summon* (acc. pers.) for help, succour, Ho 7^{11}; usu. obj. י׳ (poet. and late) Je 29^{12} 2 S 22$^{4.7}$= ψ 18$^{4.7}$ Is 55^{6} La 3^{57} Jb 27^{10} ψ 50^{15} 86^{5}+8 t. ψψ, acc. שֵׁם י׳ La 3^{55}; acc. חכמה Pr 1^{28}. **d.** abs. *call, summon* Am 7^{4} (+ל rei), Is 22^{12} (*id.*), 1 S 3$^{5.6}$

Zc 7[13]; subj. ׳י (God) Is 52[2] 65[12] 66[4] Jb 13[22] 14[15], קְרוּאֵי הָעֵדָה Nu 1[17] Qr (Kt קְרִיאֵי), 26[9] Kt (Qr קְרִיאֵי !). **e.** *call and commission, appoint,* acc. pers., Is 48[15] 49[1], + בְּשֵׁם *by name, specifically,* Ex 31[2] 35[30] Is 43[1] 45[3]. **f.** *call and endow* (with privilege) Is 51[2] 54[6] 55[5]. **6.** *call=name:* **a.** (early and most common usage), *call* one's name (שֵׁם) so and so, 2 acc.: of pers. Gn 3[20] 4[25.26] 5[2.3.29] + 34 t. Gn, Ex 2[10.22] Ho 1[4.6.9] Is 7[14] 8[3] 9[5] + 10 t. (Je 46[17] read קִרְאוּ שֵׁם 𝔊 Gie al.); of places, etc., Gn 4[17] 11[9] + 17 t. Gn, Ju 1[17.26] 2[5] 15[19] 18[29] + 21 t. **b.** c. acc. of appellation only, Ez 39[11]. **c.** acc. pers. vel loc. + acc. appell. Ho 2[18] Dt 3[14] Je 23[6] Is 58[5] Nu 32[41]. **d.** acc. pers. + cl. ψ 89[27]. **e.** = *give name to,* acc. appell. + ל pers. (loc., vel rei): (1) pers. Ho 2[18] Gn 35[18] 1 S 4[21] Je 3[19] 30[17] 33[16] + 9 t.; (2) loc., vel rei, Ju 18[12] 2 S 2[16] 5[9] 6[8] Jos 22[34] (name lost, 𝔖 Heb. Codd. ins. עֵד; cf. Di Steuern), Gn 1[5.5.8] 2[19.19] Ex 33[7] + 30 t. + Jb 17[14] (ל + sentence incl. name). **f.** c. בְּשֵׁם + ל Is 40[26], cf. 65[11] (שֵׁם אַחֵר), ψ 147[4] (שֵׁמוֹת), Ru 4[17] (לֵאמֹר + שֵׁם), Gn 2[20] 26[18.18] (all c. שֵׁם). **g.** c. ל rei + עַל־שֵׁם 2 S 18[18]. **h.** *call by* (ב) names the names (acc.) of cities Nu 32[38]; *call* to (ל) city, + appell., + בִּשְׁמוֹ v[42]. **i.** *call* cities (acc.) בְּשֵׁם, i.e. specify them, Jos 21[9] 1 Ch 6[50] (בְּשֵׁמוֹת). †**Niph.** *Pf.* 3 ms. נִקְרָא Je 4[20] +, 1 s. נִקְרֵאתִי Est 4[11], etc.; *Impf.* 3 ms. יִקָּרֵא Gn 2[23] +, וַיִּקָּרֵא Ez 20[29] +, etc.; *Pt.* נִקְרָא Is 43[7] Je 44[26]; pl. נִקְרָאִים Is 48[1] Est 6[1];—**1.** reflex., מֵעִיר הַקֹּדֶשׁ נִק׳ Is 48[2] *from the holy city they call themselves.* **2.** pass. *be called:* **a.** *be proclaimed* (cf. **Qal 3**), of שֵׁם י׳ Je 44[26] (בְּפֶה instr.); of man's name = be famous Ru 4[14]; = be announced Je 4[20]. **b.** *be read aloud* (cf. **Qal 4**): impers. c. ב of book, + בְּאָזְנֵי Ne 13[1]; subj. records Est 6[1] (לִפְנֵי). **c.** *be summoned* (cf. **Qal 5**): Is 31[4] (עַל *against*); Est 3[12] 4[11.11] 8[9]; + בְּשֵׁם, i.e. specifically, 2[14]. **d.** *be named* (cf. **Qal 6**): (1) appell. subj. + ל pers. Gn 2[23] *to her shall be called 'woman,'* 1 S 9[9] Is 32[5] 62[4.12] Pr 16[21]; + ל loc. 2 S 18[18] Is 1[26] 35[8] Je 19[6]. (2) וְנִקְרָא שְׁמוֹ וגו׳ Dt 25[10], so Gn 35[10] Dn 10[1] Ez 20[29] (of place); אֶת־שִׁמְךָ Ez 20[29]. (3) וְנִקְרְאָה יְרוּשׁ׳ וגו׳ Zc 8[3], so of land Dt 3[13], temple Is 56[7]. (4) esp. נִקְרָא שֵׁם י׳ עַל, denoting ownership, of pers. Je 15[16], people Dt 28[10] Je 14[9] Am 9[12] Is 63[19] 2 Ch 7[14], ark 2 S 6[2] (del. 2nd שֵׁם 𝔊 We Dr al.), = 1 Ch 13[6] (adding עָלָיו Oettli Kau; > Kit[Hpt] שְׁמוֹ שָׁם), temple 1 K 8[43] = 2 Ch 6[33], Je 7[10.11.14.30] 32[34] 34[15], city Je 25[29] Dn 9[18], city + people v[19]; so name of man 2 S 12[28], as given to his wife Is 4[1]. (5) be called עַל שֵׁם, i.e. reckoned to, Gn 48[6] Is 54[5] 61[6]; עַל־שֵׁבֶט 1 Ch 23[14], cf. Ezr 2[61] = Ne 7[63]. (6) *be called* בְּשֵׁם Is 43[7] 48[1]. (7) בְּיִצְחָק יִקּ׳ לְךָ זָרַע Gn 21[12], i.e. in (through) יִצ׳ shall seed be reckoned to thee; וְיִקָּרֵא בָהֶם שְׁמִי 48[16] *through them shall my name be called,* i.e. perpetuated. (8) *be named* = mentioned, of pers. Is 14[20]. (9) subj. שֵׁם Ec 6[10], i.e. thing is known. †**Pu.** (Ez and Is[2]) *Pf.* 3 ms. קֹרָא *be called,* subj. appell. + ל pers. vel rei = *be named,* Is 48[8] Ez 10[13] (קוֹ׳); וְקֹרָא consec. Is 58[12] 61[3] 62[2] (שֵׁם חָדָשׁ); גּוֹי לֹא קֹרָא בִּשְׁמִי 65[1] (< קָרָא or קֹרֵא [**Qal 2 c**], Vrss Lo Ew Che Di al.); *be called and privileged* (cf. **Qal 5 f**), *Pt.* יִשׂ׳ מְקֹרָאִי 48[12].

†I. קֹרֵא **n.m.** [Je 17,11] usu. partridge (fr. *call- 7124
ing;* v. Gray in FFP[123] Post[Hastings DB s.v.] Tristr[Moab 129, 144 f.]; otherwise Bo[Hieroz. Pt. 2, 81 ff.; ed. Rosenm. vol. ii. 632 ff.]);—1 S 26[20] Je 17[11], cf. עֵין הַקּוֹ׳ Ju 15[19].

†II. קוֹרֵא **n. pr. m.** Κωρηβ, Κωρη, etc.; 6981
Levites: **1.** 1 Ch 9[19] 26[1] (קֹרֵא). **2.** 2 Ch 31[4].

†[קָרִיא] **adj.** called, summoned; — pl. 7148
cstr. as subst.; קְרִיאֵי מוֹעֵד Nu 16[2] *the summoned ones of assembly,* term. techn. for representatives, councillors; so קְרִיאֵי הָעֵדָה 1[16] Kt (Qr קְרוּאֵי), 26[9] Qr (Kt קרואי ! cf. √**Qal 5 d**).

†קְרִיאָה **n.f.** proclamation; — Jon 3[2]. 7150

מִקְרָא 23 **n.m.** [Ex 12,16] convocation, convok- 4744
ing, reading;—מ׳ abs. Is 1[13] Ne 8[8]; cstr. Ex 12[16] +; pl. cstr. מִקְרָאֵי Lv 23[2] +; sf. מִקְרָאֶהָ (Ges[§ 91 k]) Is 4[5];—**1.** *convocation, sacred assembly* Is 1[13] (after קְרֹא), 4[5]; usu. explicitly מ׳ קֹדֶשׁ, term. techn. in P for religious gathering on Sabbath and certain sacred days, Ex 12[16.16] + 14 t. Lv 23 Nu 28, 29, + (pl.) Lv 23[2.4.37]. **2.** (n. verbi, as Aram. Inf., Ges[§ 45 e, cf. 115 d]) *convoking,* מ׳ הָעֵדָה Nu 10[2]. **3.** *reading* Ne 8[8].

II. [קָרָא] 137 **vb. encounter, befall** (‖ form 7122
of קָרָה, q.v.; SI[4] לקרת *to meet, opposite;* Ar. قَرَأَ, *put part to part;* Min. קרא *set opposite,* Hom[Chrest. 127]);—**Qal** 131 *Pf.* 5 3 ms. sf. קְרָאַנִי Je 13[22] Jb 4[2]; 3 fs. קָרָאת Dt 31[29] Je 44[23], etc.; *Impf.* 4 3 ms. יִקְרָא Gn 49[1], sf. יִקְרָאֵנוּ Gn 42[4]; 3 fpl. וַתִּקְרֶאנָה Lv 10[19]; Ex 1[10] rd. 3 fs. sf. תִּקְרָאֵנוּ (Sam
Vrss Di Ges[§ 47 k] So[Kau] Baen); *Inf. cstr.* 121 לִקְרַאת 7125
(Ges[§ 19 k] Ol[§ 137]), Gn 15[10] +, etc.; *Pt.* fpl. sf. קֹרְאֹתַיִךְ Is 51[19];—**1.** *meet, encounter,* only inf. cstr. לִקְרַאת oft. = prep. *toward, against* (Kö[ii. 1, 317]), almost always c. acc. pers., after vb. of motion, Is 7[3] Gn 19[1] 24[17] Ju 4[18.22] 1 K 2[8] +; in war, battle,

Ju 7^{24} $20^{25.31}$ 1 S 4^{1} 1 K 20^{27}+, after עָרַךְ 2 S $10^{9.10.17}$+, ψ 35^{3} v. I. סגר **2 b**; לְחַזֵּק לִבָּם לִקְ׳ הַמִּלְחָמָה Jos 11^{20} *to harden their heart to encounter the war* with Isr.; after הִנֵּה (without vb. of motion), †1 S 10^{10} 2 S 15^{32} 16^{1} 1 K 18^{7} Pr 7^{10}; in constr. prægn. וַיִּשְׂמַח לִקְ׳ Ju 19^{3} *he rejoiced to meet him*, + 1 S 6^{13} (𝔊 We Dr al.); חרד לִקְ׳ 1 S 16^{4} 21^{2}; so c. שׁאג Ju 14^{5}, הריע 15^{14}, מצא 2 K 10^{15}, נצב Ex 5^{20} 7^{15} Nu 22^{34}, etc.; redund. יִקָּרֶה י׳ לִקְ׳ Nu 23^{3}; implic. of *helping*, Is 21^{14} ψ 59^{5} (fig.); לִקְ׳ נְחָשִׁים Nu 24^{1} he did not go *to encounter* (in expectation of) *signs of divination*; in metaph. Is 14^{9}, לִקְ׳ אֱלֹהֶיךָ Am 4^{12}. **2.** fig. *befall* c. acc. pers., bad sense Gn $42^{4.38}$ Dt 31^{29} Je 13^{22} 44^{23} Is 51^{19} Jb 4^{14} Lv 10^{19}; of war Ex 1^{10} (v. supr.); in gen., Gn 49^{1}. **Niph.** *meet unexpectedly; Pf.* 3 ms. נִקְרָא, c. עַל pers. Ex 5^{3}; *Impf.* 3 ms. וַיִּקָּרֵא, c. לִפְנֵי pers. 2 S 18^{9}; *Pf.* 20^{1}, c. שָׁם, *chanced to be there; Impf.* of bird's nest Dt 22^{6} (לְפָנֶיךָ); *Inf. abs.* נִקְרֹא v. קרה. **Hiph.** *Impf.* 2 ms. וַתַּקְרֵא Je 32^{23} *thou didst cause* all this evil *to befall* them (acc. pers. et rei).

7122, 7125 [קְרָאת], לִקְרַאת *to meet*, v. II. קרא p. 896

7126 I. [קָרֵב, קָרַב] $_{279}$ **vb.** come near, approach (NH *approach, be offered*; As. *ḳarâbu, approach*; Ar. قَرُبَ, قَرِبَ *be near, approach*; so Eth. ቀረበ: Sab. קרב *approach* a woman (sexually, v. **1 a** infr.), DHM Hofmus. No. 6. l. 2, but also gen. ד רחק וקרב *he who is far and he who is near* CIS iv, no. 95, 7. 8 cf. SabDenkm No. 12, 9, 10; Aram. קְרֵב, ܩܪܶܒ, *approach*; also, =*oblation*, Sab. קרבן DHM ZMG xxx (1876), 672 Ar. قُرْبَان, OAram. קרבן, 𝔗 קוּרְבָּנָא, Syr. ܩܘܪܒܢܐ; cf. As. *kurbannu* (כ), Dl HWB 351);—**Qal** $_{93}$ *Pf.* 3 ms. קָ׳ Gn 20^{4}+; 3 fs. קָרְבָה Zp 3^{2}, etc.; *Impf.* 3 ms. יִקְרַב Gn 37^{18}+etc.; *Imv.* ms. קְרַב 2 S 20^{16}+, קָרְבָה ψ 69^{19}; mpl. קִרְבוּ Ex 16^{9}; *Inf. abs.* קָרוֹב Ec 4^{17} De Siegf Ol § 249 c Sta § 642 c Kö i. 175; *cstr.* קְרֹב ψ 27^{2} 32^{9}, לְקָרְבָה Ex 36^{2}, etc.;—*approach*: **1. a.** c. אֶל pers. (27 t.) Gn 37^{18} Nu 18^{4} Mal 3^{5} (+לַמִּשְׁפָּט), Jon 1^{6}+; in kindness 1 K 2^{7}, of י׳ to help ψ 69^{19}; for war, battle, Ex 14^{20} Ju 20^{24}; unto God †1 S 14^{36} (+הֲלֹם), Zp 3^{2}, י׳ †Ez 44^{15} Is 48^{16}; *approach* sexually, of man, †Gn 20^{4} Is 8^{3} Dt 22^{14} Lv $18^{6.14.19}$ (H) Ez 18^{6}; of woman †Lv 20^{16} (אֶל of beast); קְ׳ אֵלֶיךָ Is 65^{5} =*keep to thyself* (|| אַל־תִּגַּשׁ־בִּי); c. עַל pers., in hostility, ψ 27^{2} (+inf. purpose), so prob. ψ 55^{19} מִקְּרָב־לִי *that none may approach me* (קְ׳ inf. cstr., so Che Bae Dr, > n.=*battle*). **b.** אֶל loc. Ex 32^{19} Dt 2^{37} 20^{10} Jos 8^{5} Pr 5^{8}; אֶל rei Jos 3^{3} Ez 42^{14} 44^{16} Lv 22^{3} (H), Ex 36^{2}+5 t. P; עַל־הַמִּזְבֵּחַ 2 K 16^{12}; אֶל־הַמִּלְחָמָה Dt 20^{2}. †**c.** לִפְנֵי pers. (י׳) Ex 16^{9} Lv 16^{1} ψ 119^{169} (of cry); before men Nu 9^{6} Jos 17^{4}. †**d.** מוּל gent. Dt 2^{19}. †**e.** בְּ loc. Ju 19^{13} ψ 91^{10} (of evil). †**f.** לְ loc. Jb 33^{22}; adv. loc. הֲלֹם Ex 3^{5}, הֵנָּה Is 57^{3} (cf. **g**, 2 S 20^{16}). †**g.** *draw near* for a purpose, c. Inf. 1 S 17^{48} 2 S 15^{5} Dt 25^{11} Ex 12^{48} Lv 21^{17} Nu 17^{5} Is 34^{1} Ec 4^{17}, + (Inf. om.) Lv 21^{18}; c. וְ subord. 2 S 20^{16} (+עַד־הֵנָּה); c. לַמִּשְׁפָּט Is 41^{1} (cf. **a.** Mal 3^{5}); + Imv. Dt 5^{24} Jos 10^{24} Lv 10^{4}, + Impf. Jos 10^{24} Lv 10^{5}. **h.** abs. (15 t.) Jos $7^{14.14.14}$ (technically of approach to sanctuary, for trial by lot), Is 5^{19} (of י׳'s counsel), 41^{5}+, La 3^{57} (of י׳, to help); וַתִּקְ׳ הַמִּלְחָמָה 1 K 20^{29} i.e. the battle was joined; of calamities Ez 9^{1}, קָ׳ קִצֵּנוּ La 4^{18}. †**2.** of time, *draw near*, Gn 27^{41} Dt 15^{9} Ez 12^{23}; spec. קְ׳ יְמֵי פ׳ לָמוּת Gn 47^{29} Dt 31^{14} 1 K 2^{1}. †**Niph.** *Pf.* 3 ms. consec. וְנִקְרַב אֶל־הָאֱלֹהִים Ex 22^{7} *he shall be brought unto God* (at the sanctuary), also (abs., reflex.) 2 mpl. consec. וְנִקְרַבְתֶּם Jos 7^{14} (cf. **Qal 1 h**). †**Pi.** *Pf.* 1 s. קֵרַבְתִּי Is 46^{13}; 3 pl. קֵרְבוּ Ho 7^{6} (v. infr.), Ez 36^{8}; *Impf.* 2 ms. וּתְקָרֵב ψ 65^{5}; 1 s. sf. אֲקָרְבֶנּוּ Jb 31^{37}; *Imv.* ms. קָרֵב Ez 37^{17}; mpl. קָרְבוּ Is 41^{21};—*cause to approach, bring near*: **1.** in space, acc. rei+אֶל Ez 37^{17}; =*receive*, acc. pers. Jb 31^{37} (Thes Du; most *approach majestically, march up to*), acc. om. ψ 65^{5}; קָ׳ רִיבְכֶם Is 41^{21} *bring on your suit!* **2.** in time, קֵ׳ צִדְקָתִי Is 46^{13} (of י׳), קֵ׳ לָבוֹא Ez 36^{8} *they have brought near to come, brought their coming near*, it is at hand (cf. **Hiph.** Gn 12^{11}).—Ho 7^{6} rd. בָּעֲרוּ for קֵרְבוּ (קִרְבָּם) RS Proph. iv, N. 19), cf. 𝔊 Now. **Hiph.** $_{177}$ *Pf.* 3 ms. הִקְרִיב Gn 12^{11}+, -רִב Nu 7^{19}; 2 ms. וְהִקְרַבְתָּ Ex 29^{3}+, etc.; *Impf.* 3 ms. יַקְרִיב Ez 44^{27}+, -רֵב 46^{4}; וַיַּקְרֵב Ju 3^{17}+; 1 pl. וַנַּקְרֵב Nu 31^{50}, etc.; *Imv.* ms. הַקְרֵב Nu 3^{6}+, etc.; *Inf. abs.* הַקְרֵב Lv 6^{7}; cstr. הַקְרִיב Ju 3^{18}+, etc.; *Pt.* מַקְרִיב Lv 3^{1}+, etc.;—**1. a.** *bring near, bring, present*, c. acc. rei, Ju 5^{25} (+בְּסֵפֶל), cf. Ex 29^{3} (+בַּסָּל); tribute ψ 72^{10}; מִנְחָה Ju 3^{17} (+לְ pers.), v ^{18}; cf. (לְ pers.) Mal 1^{8}; שָׂדֶה בְשָׂדֶה יַקְ׳ Is 5^{8} i.e. *join, incorporate*; pregn., c. מִן loc. 2 K 16^{14} (v. RS Sem. i. 466 ff., 2nd ed. 486 ff.); acc. of case, affair, †Dt 1^{17} (+אֶל pers.), Nu 27^{5} (+לִפְנֵי י׳); c. acc. pers.: + אֶל pers. Nu 15^{33} 25^{6} Jos 8^{23}, + אֶל reflex.

Ex 28[1], + אֶת (prep.) reflex. Nu 18[2]; abs., of pers., *make an approach* Ex 14[10]. **b.** of time, הִקְרִיב לָבוֹא Gn 12[11]; תַּקְרִיב לָלֶדֶת Is 26[17]; וַתַּקְרִיבִי יָמַיִךְ Ez 22[4]. **2.** as term. techn. (c. 158 t.), chiefly in Ez HP, *bring near*, of presenting, dedicating, or offering to י׳: †**a.** c. acc. pers., (1) Aaron and his sons, and Levites, sts. c. אֶל, לִפְנֵי, pers. or loc., Ex 29[4.8] 40[12.14] Lv 3[6] 7[35] 8[6.13.24] Nu 8[9.10] 16[5.5.9.10], cf. (of prince, subj. י׳) Je 30[21]; (2) for selection by lot Jos 7[16.17.17.18] 1 S 10[20.21]; (3) for ordeal of מֵי הַמָּרִים Nu 5[16]. **b.** usually (c. 142 t.) c. acc. of offering, with or without further complement (לִפְנֵי י׳, לי׳, לִפְנֵי אֶל loc., rarely אֶל, ל, of priest, etc.): (1) animal-offering Lv 3[7.12] 8[18.22] (all + סָמַךְ of offerer), Ex 29[10] Lv 1[15] 4[3.14]+, etc.; (2) זֶבַח Lv 7[16]; עֹלָה Nu 29[13.36]; אִשֶּׁה Lv 3[3.14] 23[8.25]+; †(3) blood Lv 1[5] (+זָרַק), 7[33] 9[9]; (4) מִנְחָה Lv 2[8] 6[7] 7[12] 23[16] Nu 5[25] 6[16] 15[9]; לֶחֶם אֱלֹהָיו Lv 21[6.8.17.21], etc.; (5) incense Nu 16[35], censer v[17] 17[3.4]; אֵשׁ זָרָה Lv 10[1] Nu 3[4] 26[61]; (6) esp. c. acc. cogn. קָרְבָּן Lv 1[2.2.14] 2[1.4] 22[18] Nu 7[10.11] 31[50] + (c. 33 t.); (7) acc. om. 2 Ch 35[12]. **c.** abs. *make an offering* Nu 7[2.18].

7131 †קָרֵב **adj. vb.** approaching;—abs. ק׳ 1 S 17[41]+; pl. קְרֵבִים Ez 40[46] 45[4];—*approaching:* **1.** as pred., הֹלֵךְ וְק׳ אֶל־דָּוִד 1 S 17[41], אַתֶּם קְרֵבִים לַמִּלְחָמָה Dt 20[3]; abs. הָלוֹךְ וְק׳ 2 S 18[25]; c. art. as subst., 1 K 5[7] (+אֶל־שֻׁלְחָן), Nu 17[28.28] (+אֶל־מִשְׁכַּן י׳). **2.** c. art., *approaching* י׳, temple or tabern., for service, c. לְשָׁרֵת Ez 40[46] (+אֶל־י׳), 45[4]; abs. הַזָּר הַקּ׳ Nu 1[51] 3[10.38] 18[7].

7128 †קְרָב **n.[m.]** battle, war (hostile *approach;* Aramaism = ܩܪܒܐ, קְרָב, cf. Lag[BN 175]);—abs. ק׳ Zc 14[3]+; pl. קְרָבוֹת ψ 68[31];—‖ מִלְחָמָה Jb 38[23] ψ 144[1]; יוֹם ק׳ Zc 14[3] ψ 78[9]; כְּלֵי ק׳ Ec 9[18]; *his heart was war* ψ 55[22] (v[19] v. √ **Qal 1 a**); pl. ψ 68[31] peoples that delight in *battles.*—2 S 17[11] read בְּקִרְבָּם 𝔊 𝔖 𝔙 Th Dr and most.

7132 †[קִרְבָה Lag[BN 82] Kö[i. 174]] **n.f.** approach;—cstr. in phr. קִרְבַת אֱלֹהִים *approach to God* (Che[Intr. Is. 325]) Is 58[2] ψ 73[28].

7138 †קָרֹב, קָרוֹב[78] **adj.** near;—abs. קָרֹב Ex 12[4]+, -וֹב 2 S 19[43]+; pl. קְרֹבִים 1 K 8[59], קְרוֹבִים Is 33[13]+; fpl. קְרֹבוֹת Ez 22[5], etc.;—*near* (oft. opp. רָחוֹק): **1.** of city Gn 19[20] (+לָנוּס שָׁמָּה), Je 48[24], הַקּ׳ Dt 21[3] *the nearest* (+אֶל), cf. (of elders) v[6]; of land 1 K 8[46] = 2 Ch 6[36]; road Ex 13[17]; =contiguous, כֶּרֶם 1 K 21[2] (+אֵצֶל בֵּיתִי). **2.** of pers.: **a.** + אֶל pers. Gn 45[10] Dt 13[8] 22[2] Jos 9[16] 1 Ch 12[41] (van d. H. v[40]); הַקּ׳ אֶל Ex 12[4] *the nearest to;* c. sf. קְרֹבוֹ Ex 32[27], i.e. *his neighbour.* **b.** abs. (opp. or + רחוק, oft. = *near and far*, i.e. all without distinction), Ez 6[12] Is 57[19] Pr 27[10]; pl. Is 33[13] Je 25[26] Dn 9[7] Est 9[20] Ez 22[5]; ק׳ of distress, personif., ψ 22[12].—Ez 23[5.12] Co Berthol read קְרוּאִים *famous;* Toy רַבִּים (cf. Je 39[13]); Hpt in Toy Krae conj. קְרוֹדִים (As. *ḳurâdu, warrior*). **c.** of near relationship, + אֶל pers. 2 S 19[43] Lv 21[2.3] 25[25] (all H), Nu 27[11] (P); ל pers. Ne 13[4] Ru 2[20]; + מִן comp. 3[12]; of intimacy, קְרוֹבַי Jb 19[14] (‖ מְיֻדָּעַי), ψ 38[12] (‖ אֹהֲבַי וְרֵעַי); קְרֹבוֹ ψ 15[3] (‖ רֵעֵהוּ); *near*, in office, Est 1[14]. **d.** *near* to י׳, עַם קְרֹבוֹ ψ 148[14] (Rie Bae קְרֹבָיו *the people of those near him*). **e.** *near* to י׳ in ceremon. function, c. אֶל Ez 43[19], c. ל 42[13], sf. Lv 10[3]. **f.** of God (י׳), + אֶל pers. Dt 4[7] 30[14]; ל pers. ψ 34[19] 145[18]; abs. Je 12[2] Is 50[8] 55[6] ψ 119[151]; אֱלֹהֵי מִקָּרֹב Je 23[23] *a God from near by* (opp. אֱ׳ מֵרָחוֹק); ק׳ of צֶדֶק י׳ Is 51[5], יֶשַׁע י׳ ψ 85[10] (+ל pers.);—ק׳ שְׁמֶךָ ψ 75[2], read קֹרְאֵי בְּשׁ׳ Dy Che Gr Dr, cf. Bae 𝔊 𝔖 Du. **g.** of word, + אֶל pers. Dt 30[14]; prayer, + אֶל־י׳ 1 K 8[59]. **3.** of time: ק׳ יוֹם אֵידָם Dt 32[35]; esp. of יוֹם י׳ Zp 1[7.14.14] Ez 30[3] (perh. del. as 𝔊 Co Krae), v[3] Is 13[6] Ob[15] Jo 1[15] 2[1] 4[14], cf. Ez 7[7]; + inf. ק׳ אֵיד־מוֹאָב לָבוֹא Je 48[16], cf. Is 13[22] 56[1]; מְחִתָּה ק׳ Pr 10[14] *imminent ruin;* מִקָּרֹב Dt 32[17] *recently*, so Ez 11[3] 𝔊 𝔙 Co Siegf Berthol (for MT + בְּקָרוֹב); Ez 7[8] *soon;* Jb 20[5] *of the briefest.*—אוֹר ק׳ מִפְּנֵי חֹשֶׁךְ Jb 17[12] is dub.; Thes (my) *light is near to* (prope abest a, as Ar. قَرُبَ مِن, but not proven in Heb.) *darkness;* Di *light* (they say) *is near* (breaking away) *from darkness*, will soon leave it behind; Bu אוֹר קְרוֹבָם פֶּן־יֶחְשַׁךְ *the light of their intimate friend shall not* (?) *grow dark.*

קָרְבָּן[80] **n.m.**[Lv 6, 13] offering, oblation (As. *ḳurbannu, id.*, appar. alw. with כ, Dl[HWB 351]);— 7133
abs. ק׳ Lv 1[2]+; cstr. קָרְבַּן 2[1]+; sf. קָרְבָּנִי Nu 28[2]; pl. sf. קָרְבְּנֵיהֶם Lv 7[38];—*offering, oblation*, gen. term for all kinds of offering (only Ez Lv Nu [HP]): animal Lv 1[2.3.10]+, vegetable 2[1.1.5]+, articles of gold Nu 31[50], silver 7[13]+, etc.; as acc. cogn. after הִקְרִיב Lv 1[2.2] 3[14] Nu 6[14]+ (v. √ **Hiph. 2 b** (5)); cstr. ק׳ מִנְחָה Lv 2[1.4.13], ק׳ רֵאשִׁית v[12], ק׳ אִשֶּׁה 22[27]; ק׳ י׳ Nu 9[7.13] (cf. 31[50]).

†[קֻרְבָּן] **n.[m.]** offering;—cstr. קֻרְבַּן הָעֵצִים 7133
wood-offering for second temple Ne 10[35] 13[31].

II. **קרב** (√of foll.; cf. As. *kirbu, midst;* NH [קֶרֶב] pl. *entrails* (rare); MI[23, 24] בקרב *in the midst of* the city; perh. also Ar. قَلْبٌ *heart*).

7130 **קֶ֫רֶב** [227] **n.**[**m.**] **inward part, midst**;—ק׳ abs. Ex 29^{13} + (only **3**); cstr. Gn 45^{6}+; sf. קִרְבִּי Jos 9^{7}+, 3 fpl. קִרְבֶּנָה Gn 41^{21}, -בֶּנָה v^{21} (Ges[§ 91 f.] Kö[ii. 1, 488 N. 1]), etc.; pl. only (sf.) קְרָבַי ψ 103^{1};—usu. c. prep. (בְּק׳ 143 t., מִק׳ 43 t.);—**1.** †**a.** *inward part* of human body, physical sense, בְּק׳ *within* one's body Gn 25^{22} (J), cf. 18^{12} (J), 1 S 25^{37} Je 23^{9} Jb 20^{14} (|| בְּמֵעָיו), cf. Is 19^{1} (of nation personif.); *into* his body ψ 109^{18} (sim.); as seat of life (וְ)תָשָׁב נֶפֶשׁ־הַיֶּלֶד עַל־קִרְבּוֹ 1 K $17^{21.22}$, cf. (of idol) Hb 2^{19} (v. also **2**). †**b.** = belly, of kine אֶל־ק׳ Gn $41^{21.21}$. **c.** of city (בְּק׳ *within it,* מִק׳ etc.) Gn 18^{24} Ju 18^{7} Am 3^{9} + 18 t. cf. Is 25^{11}; בְּק׳ חוצות Is 5^{25}. **d.** of house ψ $101^{2.7}$; temple 48^{10}; בְּק׳ מוֹעֲדֶךָ 74^{4}. **e.** of land (earth) Gn 45^{6} 48^{16} Am 2^{3} Is 5^{8} 24^{13} (|| בְּתוֹךְ הָעַמִּים), + 10 t. (בְּק׳, מִק׳). **f.** of a number of pers., בְּק׳ *in the midst, among,* מִק׳ *from among:* esp. (1) people (96 t.; 80 t. as sg. coll., 15 t. pl.), Am 7^{8} Gn 24^{3} Ex 23^{25} Dt 31^{17} Je 46^{21} 1 S 4^{3} Jos 7^{12} Ju 10^{16}+, בְּק׳ יִשׂ׳ Dt 17^{20}+, בְּק׳ מִק׳ גּוֹי + בְּק׳ הַכְּנַעֲנִי Ju $1^{32.33}$ 3^{5}, בֵּית יִשׂ׳ Am 7^{10}; Dt 4^{34}, etc. (2) הַמַּחֲנֶה (מִק׳) בְּק׳ Jos 1^{11} Nu 14^{44} + 6 t. †(3) בְּק׳ אָחִיו Dt 18^{2} 1 S 16^{13}, and (מִק׳) Dt 17^{15} 18^{18}. †(4) מִק׳ עַמֶּיהָ Ex 31^{14} (II. עַם). (5) בְּק׳ אֹיְבֶיךָ ψ 110^{2}, cf. (of wicked) 55^{16}; בְּק׳ חֲכָמִים Pr 15^{31}. (6) בְּק׳ אֱלֹהִים יִשְׁפֹּט ψ 82^{1}. (7) בְּק׳ הַמִּלְחָמָה 1 K 20^{39} *into the midst of the battle,* the thick of the fight; בְּק׳ צָרָה ψ 138^{7}. †(8) of nations, בְּק׳ הַגּוֹיִם Dt 29^{15}, מִק׳ חוקך הָעַמִּים La 3^{45}, cf. Jos 24^{17} Mi $5^{6.7}$. **g.** ψ 74^{11} (Qr חֵיקְךָ) thy hand *fr. within thy bosom,* (anthrop. of י׳; v. I. כלה **Pi. 2 c**). †**h.** of a period of time, בְּק׳ שָׁנִים Hb $3^{2.2}$. †**2.** of inward part of man; **a.** as seat of thought and emotion: בְּק׳ 1 K 3^{28} Je 4^{14} 9^{7} Pr 26^{24} ψ 62^{5} 94^{19}; || בְּלֵב Pr 14^{33}, עַל־לֵב Je 31^{33}; seat of לֵב ψ 39^{4} 55^{5} 109^{22} La 1^{20}, of רוּחַ Ez 11^{19} $36^{26.27}$ Zc 12^{1} Is 26^{9} ψ 51^{12}, cf. Is $19^{3.14}$; בְּק׳ לִבִּי ψ 36^{2} (rd. לִבּוֹ Vrss Hup Now Che Bae al.). **b.** as faculty of thought and emotion, subj. (no prep.) Is 16^{11} (|| מֵעַי), ψ 64^{7} (|| לֵב) 5^{10}; כָּל־קְרָבַי 103^{1} (only here pl.; || נַפְשִׁי).—49^{12} rd. קִבְרָם 𝔊 𝔖 𝔗, or קְבָרָם, Ew Gr Ol Bi Che Bae al. (for קִרְבָּם). †**3.** term. techn. in P of *entrails* of sacrificial animals (Di[Lv 1, 9] Dr-Wh[Lv, pl. facing p. 4]), Ex 12^{9} $29^{13.17.22}$ Lv $1^{9.13}$ $3^{3.3.9.9.14.14}$ $4^{8.8.11}$ 7^{3} $8^{16.21.25}$ 9^{14}.

† [קַרְדֹּם] **n.**[**m.**] axe (√unknown; cf. NH קַרְדֹּם *double hoe,* one side of which could split wood, Vogelst[Landwirthsch. 37]; Ar. قَدُّوم, قَدُوم *adze* is loan-wd. acc. to Frä[84]);—sf. קַרְדֻּמּוֹ 1 S 13^{20}+ Ju 9^{48} (so prob. rd. for הַקַּרְדֻּמּוֹת, A 𝔊L τ. ἀξίνην, GFM Bu Now); pl. קַרְדֻּמִּים 1 S 13^{21}, קַרְדֻּמּוֹת Je 46^{22} ψ 74^{5}. 7134

קָרָה *cold,* v. קרר. p. 903 7135

† [**קָרָה**] **vb. encounter, meet, befall** 7136 (|| II. קָרָא; NH קָרָה *meet* (rare), קְרִי *misfortune,* specif. (nocturnal) *pollution,* and so Aram. קְרִיוּתָא, ܩܶܪܝܳܐ; Ar. قرا (و) is *go, seek earnestly,* قَرَى *receive hospitably* as guest; Eth. II. 3, **አቅረየ፡** *present, offer as sacrifice*);—**Qal** *Pf.* 3 ms. sf. קָרְךָ Dt 25^{18}, (וְ)קָרָהוּ Gn 44^{29}+; *Impf.* 3 ms. יִקְרֶה Ec 9^{11} + Dn 10^{14} Kt (Qr יִקְרָא), וַיִּקֶר Ru 2^{3}, sf. יִקְרְךָ Nu 11^{23}, יִקְרֵךְ 1 S 28^{10} (d. f. dirim.); *Pt.* fpl. קֹרֹת Gn 42^{29};—**1.** *encounter, meet,* acc. pers. Dt 25^{18}, cf. (acc. rei) וַיִּקֶר מִקְרֶהָ חֶלְקַת וגו׳ Ru 2^{3} *her chance lighted upon a field,* etc. **2.** *befall,* acc. pers., subj. evil Gn 44^{29} (J), 1 S 28^{10}, י׳'s word Nu 11^{23} (JE), indef. Gn 42^{29} (J) Is 41^{22} (abs.) Est 4^{7} 6^{13} Dn 10^{14} (לְ pers.); עֵת וָפֶגַע יִק׳ אֶת־כֻּלָּם Ec 9^{11}; subj. מִקְרֶה 2^{14}, cf. v^{15}. **Niph.** *Pf.* 3 ms. נִקְרָה Ex 3^{18}; 1 s. נִקְרֵיתִי 2 S 1^{6}; *Impf.* 3 ms. יִקָּרֶה Nu 23^{3}, וַיִּקָּר $v^{4.16}$; 1 s. אִקָּרֶה v^{15};—**1.** *encounter, meet* without pre-arrangement, usu. of י׳ (God): c. עַל pers. Ex 3^{18} (J), אֶל pers. Nu $23^{4.16}$; לִקְרָאתִי יִק׳ י׳ v^{3} (all JE); obj. י׳ (om.) v^{15}. **2.** *chance to be present,* בְּ loc., 2 S 1^{6} (+ Inf. abs. נִקְרֹא). **Hiph. 1.** of י׳, *cause* (the right thing, good fortune) *to occur,* c. לִפְנֵי pers.; *Pf.* 3 ms. הִקְרָה Gn 27^{20}; *Imv.* ms. הַקְרֵה 24^{12} (both J). **2.** of Israel, *Pf.* 2 mpl. consec. וְהִקְרִיתֶם לָכֶם עָרִים Nu 35^{11} ye shall (*cause* cities *to occur* rightly *for yourselves,* i. e.) *select* cities *as suitable.*

† [**קָרֶה**] **n.**[**m.**] **chance, accident**;—cstr. 7137 מִקְּרֵה לָיְלָה Dt 23^{11} *by reason of the chance of the night* (i.e. nocturnal pollution, cf. Lv 15^{16}).

† [**קְרִי**] **n.**[**m.**] **opposition, contrariness**;— 7147 only (בְּ)קֶרִי in Lv 26, as adv. modifier of הָלַךְ (in fig. sense), + עִם pers., of Isr.'s relation to י׳: תֵּלְכוּ עִמִּי קֶרִי Lv 26^{21} *if ye walk with me contrariwise,* so v^{23}, בְּקֶרִי $v^{27.40}$; י׳ subj., וְהָלַכְתִּי עִמָּכֶם בְּקֶרִי v^{24}, so v^{41} and (בַּחֲמַת ק׳) *in wrath of opposition*) v^{28}.

† **מִקְרֶה** **n.m.**[1 S 6, 9] **accident, chance, fortune**;—abs. מ׳ 1 S 6^{9}+; cstr. מִקְרֵה Ec 2^{15} (so 4745

read also 3$^{19.19}$ with 𝔊 Ruët^{Kau} Wild, for MT מִקְרֶה);—**1.** *accident, chance,* 1 S 6^{9} 20^{26}; c. קָרָה Ru 2^{3} (v. ק׳ **1**). **2.** in Ec, *fortune, fate,* מ׳ אֶחָד יִקְרֶה אֶת־כֻּלָּם Ec 2^{14} cf. v^{15}, 3$^{19.19.19}$ 9$^{2.3}$.

6982 †קוֹרָה **n.f. rafter, beam** (prop. a thing *meeting,* fitting into, another);—sf. קֹרָתִי Gn 19^{8} (J)=*my roof-tree;* pl. קֹרוֹת *rafters,* abs. 2 Ch 3^{7}, cstr. ‖ 1 K 6^{15b} (reading קוֹרוֹת הַסִּפֻּן 𝔊 Th Kit Benz, for MT קִירוֹת), + 7^{7b} (reading הַקּוֹרוֹת for הַקַּרְקַע, v. ק׳); Ct 1^{17} (‖ רחיטנו Kt, רָהִיטֵנוּ Qr); more gen. *beam,* sg. abs. קוֹרָה 2 K 6$^{2.5}$.

7136 †[קָרָה] **vb. denom. Pi.** lay the beams of, furnish with beams;—c. acc. of the building: *Pf.* 3 pl. sf. קֵרוּהוּ Ne 3$^{3.6}$; *Inf. cstr.* לְקָרוֹת Ne 2^{8} 2 Ch 34^{11}; *Pt.* הַמְקָרֶה ψ 104^{3} (fig.).

4746 †מְקָרֶה **n.[m.]** beam-work;—Ec 10^{18}.

7151 †קִרְיָה **n.f. town, city** (syn. of עִיר, chiefly poet., and in the higher style; perhaps from above √ as *meeting*-place of men; cf. n.pr.loc. MI^{13} קרית, l.^{10} קריתן; JAram. קִרְיָה);—abs. ק׳ Is 1^{21}+; cstr. קִרְיַת Nu 21^{28}+;—**1.** in gen. Dt 2^{36} 3^{4}. **2.** of specif. towns, Ho 6^{8} (גִּלְעָד, 𝔊$^{Codd.}$ Γαλγαλα, cf. Now); קִרְיַת סִיחֹן Nu 21^{28}; Damascus, ק׳ מְשׂוֹשִׂי Je 49^{25} (‖ עִיר תְּהִלָּה); esp. of Jerus. Mi 4^{10} Is 29^{1} 33^{20}, רְחֹבוֹת ק׳ La 2^{11}, ק׳ מֶלֶךְ רָב ψ 48^{3}, city for inhab. 1 K 1$^{41.45}$, ק׳ נֶאֱמָנָה Is 1$^{21.26}$ (‖ עִיר הַצֶּדֶק), ק׳ עַלִּיזָה 22^{2} (‖ עִיר הוֹמִיָּה), 32^{13}. **3.** in Is 24–26 coll., i.e. denoting various, representative, cities, ק׳ תֹּהוּ 24^{10}, ק׳ בְּצוּרָה 25^{2}, ק׳ גּוֹיִם עָרִיצִים v^{3}, ק׳ נִשְׂגָּבָה 26^{5}; so prob. Hb 2$^{8.17}$. **4.** indef., Hb 2^{12} (‖ עִיר); Pr 29^{8}, ק׳ עֹז 18^{19} *a city of strength,* so ק׳ עֻזּוֹ 10^{15} (in fig.)=18^{11}(*id.*);=inhab., 11^{10}, ק׳ הֲמוֹן Jb 39^{7}.

7157 קִרְיַת v. קִרְיַת יְעָרִים. above

7156 †קִרְיָתַיִם **n.pr.loc.** Καριαθαιμ (perh. *double city* (du.), yet in gen. on ־ַיִם in n.pr.loc. v. Ges$^{§ 88 c}$);—**1.** in Moab (MI^{10}) Je 48^{1} (־תָיִם), v^{23}, so קִרְיָתָיְמָה Ez 25^{9} Qr (Kt קריתמה); Reubenite city acc. to Nu 32^{37} (־תָיִם) Jos 13^{9}; שָׁוֵה קִרְיָתָיִם Gn 14^{5} *plain of Ḳiryathaim* (v. שָׁוֵה); mod. *Ḳurêyât,* c. 1¼ m. SE. from (Mt.) ʿAṭṭarus (עֲטָרוֹת), and 6¾ m. NNW. from Dibon; GASm$^{Geogr. 567 f.}$ Buhl$^{Geogr. 267}$. **2.** Levit. city in Naphtali 1 Ch 6^{61},
7178 =קַרְתָּן ‖ Jos 21^{32} (Θεμμων, 𝔊L Καρθαν).

7153 †קִרְיַת אַרְבַּע **n.pr.loc.** older name of Hebron; πόλις Αρβο(κ), Καρ(ι)αθαρβοκ, etc. (prob. =*fourfold city* (otherwise Jos 14^{15} 15^{13} 21^{11}), v. esp. GFM);—Jos 14^{15} (JED), Ju 1^{10b} (ק׳ אַרְבַּע), also Gn 23^{2} Jos 15$^{13.54}$ 20^{7} 21^{11} (all P); ק׳ הָא׳
Gn 35^{27} (P) Ne 11^{25}.—Vid. חֶבְרוֹן. p. 289 2275

†קִרְיַת בַּעַל v. קִרְיַת יְעָרִים. below 7154

†קִרְיַת חֻצוֹת **n.pr.loc.** in Moab, πόλεις 7155
ἐπαύλεων, Nu 22^{39}, site unknown.

†קִרְיַת יְעָרִים **n.pr.loc.** πόλ(ε)ις Ιαρειμ[ν], 7157
Καριαθιαρειμ, etc. (*city of forests*);—city of the Gibeonites Jos 9^{17}, assigned to Judah Jos 15^{60} cf. Ju 18$^{12.12}$, on border of Benj. Jos 15^{9} (הַר יְעָרִים v^{10}, 𝔊 πόλιν Ιαρειν, v. יְעָרִים), 18^{14}, assigned to Benj. v^{28} (יְעָרִים om. by text. err. before עָרִים, v. 𝔊); near Beth Shemesh 1 S 6^{21}, long the abode of ark 7$^{1.2}$ 1 Ch 13$^{5.6}$ 2 Ch 1^{4}; named in genealogical list 1 Ch 2$^{50.52.53}$; named also Ne 7^{29} = ק׳ עָרִים Ezr 2^{25} (read יְעָרִים); c. art. ק׳ הַיְּעָרִים Je 26^{20}; abbreviated (in poet.) (שְׂדֵי־)
יָעַר ψ 132^{6}; called also קִרְיַת־בַּעַל (Καριαθβααλ) 7154
Jos 15^{60} 18^{14} + v^{15} (where read for ק׳ יְעָרִים, so 𝔊 Di Benn Steuern); this abbrev. into בַּעֲלָה, 15$^{9.10}$ [(Ιε)βααλ], also v$^{11.29}$, and מִבַּעֲלֵי יְהוּדָה 2 S 6^{2} (rd. בַּעַל יְה׳, or בַּעֲלַת יְה׳), בַּעֲלָתָה ‖ 1 Ch 13^{6} (v. on these II. בַּעֲלָה). Identif. uncertain; Rob$^{BR\ ii.\ 11}$ conj. *Ḳiryat el-ʿEnab,* 8 m. + W. of Jerusalem (cf. Καριαθιαρειμ Lag$^{Onom. 271}$); ʿ*Erma* (Henderson$^{Pal. 85, 112, 210}$ Conder$^{Survey\ Mem.\ iii.\ 43\ ff.}$), cf. GASm$^{Geogr. 225 f.}$ Buhl$^{Geogr. 166 f.}$

קִרְיַת־סַנָּה v. foll. ק׳ עָרִים v. foreg. 7157-58

†קִרְיַת־סֵפֶר **n.pr.loc.** πόλις (τῶν) γραμμάτων, 7158
+(𝔊^{B} Ju 1^{11}) Καριασσωφαρ: ancient name of דְּבִיר (v. II. ד׳ **2 c**) (perh. ק׳־סֵפֶר *scribe-town,* cf. 𝔊 supr., also 𝔖 and Egyptian *Baʿ-ṯitu-pa-ïra, house of scribe,* WMM$^{As. u. Eur. 174}$ Buhl$^{Geogr. 274}$, cf. GFM^{Ju});—Jos 15$^{15.16}$ Ju 1$^{11.12}$; another name is ק׳־סַנָּה Jos 15^{49} (but 𝔊 πόλις γραμμάτων, hence rd. perh. ק׳־ספר, so Steuern), in S. Judah; on site (prob. *Dhoherîye,* 5 h. SW. from Hebron) v. II. דְּבִיר **2 c** and Buhl$^{Geogr. 164}$.

†[קֶרֶת] **n.f. town, city** (late poet.) (cf. Ph. 7176
קרת חדשת n.pr.loc. in Cyprus, also=*Carthage,* and perhaps *Cirta, Tigranocerta;* cp. Thes);—always קָ֫רֶת;—of Job's city, Jb 29^{7}; indef. Pr 8^{3} 9$^{3.14}$; city as a corporate body of men 11^{11}.

†קַרְתָּה **n.pr.loc.** Καδης, Καριθα, etc.: Levit. 7177
city in Zebulun Jos 21^{34}, site unknown.

קַרְתָּן v. קִרְיָתַיִם **2.** above 7178

7152 †קְרִיּוֹת **n.pr.loc.** (formed as pl. intens. fr. קִרְיָה?);—**1.** in Judah Jos 15^{25} (αἱ πόλεις; whence, as supposed, Judas אִישׁ קְרִיּוֹת), perh. *Ḳaryatên*, c. 12 m. S. of Hebron, Buhl$^{Geogr. 182}$. **2.** in Moab, Καριωθ, αἱ πόλεις; MI^{13} קרית: Je 48^{24}, הַקּ׳ v^{41} Am 2^{2}; perh. = Ραββαθ Μωαβ = Μοαβ = Αρεοπολις (Euseb., v. Lag$^{Onom. 277, 60 al.}$), mod. *Rabba*, c. 11 m. S. of Arnon, cf. Buhl$^{Geogr. 270}$.

7139 †I [קָרַח] **vb. make bald,** or **a baldness,** usu. (by mourners) for the dead, cf. RS$^{Sem. i. 306, 2nd ed. 324}$ (Arab. parallels) (NH *id.* Hiph. *shew baldness;* Ar. قَرَحَ *wound, make sores,* قُرْحَةٌ *whiteness in face* of horse (but قَرِعَ *be bald,* أَقْرَعُ *bald*); Eth. ቀረሐ: *make bald* (rare); Aram. קְרַח, ܩܪܰܚ, chiefly deriv. (and der. meanings); cf. Sin. n.pr.m. קרחו, קרחה; MI$^{3.21.24.25}$ n.pr.loc. קרחה);—**Qal** *Impf.* 3 mpl. יִקְרְחוּ קָרְחָה בְּרֹאשָׁם Lv 21^{5} Qr (> Kt יקרחה; ‖ יְגַלֵּחוּ cf. Dt 14^{1}); *Imv.* fs. קָרְחִי וָגֹזִּי עַל Mi 1^{16} *make a baldness . . . for.* **Niph.** *Impf.* 3 ms. יִקָּרֵחַ לָהֶם Je 16^{6} men *shall* not *make themselves bald for them.* **Hiph.** *Pf.* 3 pl. consec. וְהִקְרִיחוּ אֵלַיִךְ קָרְחָה Ez 27^{31} *and they shall make a baldness* (cf. **Qal**) *for thee.* **Hoph.** *Pt.* כָּל־רֹאשׁ מֻקְרָח Ez 29^{18} *every head made bald* (by carrying load).

7142 †קֵרֵחַ **adj. bald;**—Lv 13^{40} (distinct fr. גִּבֵּחַ v^{41}); **n.m.** 2 K 2$^{23.23}$.

7144 †קָרְחָה **n.f. baldness, bald spot,** made as sign of mourning;—abs. ק׳ Is 3^{24}+; sf. קָרְחָתֵךְ Mi 1^{16};—*bald spot,* עַל־כָּל־ראשׁ Am 8^{10}, בְּכָל־ר׳ Is 15^{2} Ez 7^{18}; ק׳ בְּרֹאשׁ Lv 21^{5} (acc. cogn.); כָּל־ראשׁ ק׳ Je 48^{37}; ק׳ כַּנֶּשֶׁר Mi 1^{16}; בֵּין עֵינֵיכֶם Dt 14^{1}; opp. מַעֲשֶׂה מִקְשֶׁה Is 3^{24}; also Je 47^{5} and (acc. cogn.) Ez 27^{31}.

7146 †קָרַחַת **n.f. baldness of head;**—abs. ק׳ Lv 13^{42a}; sf. קָרַחְתּוֹ v^{42} +;—*baldness of head* (alw. opp. גַּבַּחַת *baldness of forehead*), Lv 13$^{42.42.43.55}$.

7143 קָרֵחַ$_{14}$ **n.pr.m.** in Judah (*bald one*);—2 K 25^{23}, Καρηθ, 𝔊L Καρηε; Je 40^{8} + 12 t. Je, Καρηε.

7141 קֹרַח$_{37}$ **n.pr.m.** Κορε (**baldness?**);—**1.** Edomite name: **a.** Gn 36$^{5.14.18}$ 1 Ch 1^{35}. **b.** Gn 36^{16} (not Sam.; prob. gloss fr. v^{18} Di Kau Ball al.; Holz hesitates). **2.** Levite, rebel ag. Moses, Nu 16^{1} + 10 t. 16, 17, 26$^{9.10}$ 27^{3}; in geneal. lists Ex 6$^{21.24}$ 1 Ch 6$^{7.22}$; בֶּן־ק׳ 9^{19}; בְּנֵי־ק׳ Nu 26^{11}; esp. לִבְנֵי־ק׳ as company of ψ-collectors (or singers), in titles: ψ 42^{1} 44^{1} 45^{1} 46^{1} 47^{1} 48^{1} 49^{1} 84^{1} 85^{1} 87^{1} 88^{1}. **3.** a 'son' of Hebron, i.e. Judahite clan 1 Ch 2^{43} Κορεε, etc.

†קָרְחִי **adj. gent.** of קֹרַח **2**; alw. c. art.; 7145
1 Ch 9^{31}; as subst. coll. Ex 6^{24} Nu 26^{58}; pl. הַקָּרְחִים 1 Ch 9^{19} 12^{7} (van d. H. v^{6}), 26^{1}; בְּנֵי הַקָּרְחִי v^{19}; בְּנֵי הַקָּרְחִים 2 Ch 20^{19}.

II. קרח (√ of foll.; meaning unknown).

†קֶרַח **n.m.**$^{Jb 38, 29}$ **frost, ice;**—abs. ק׳ Gn 7140
31^{40}+, קָרַח Jb 6^{16}+; sf. קַרְחוֹ ψ 147^{17};—**1.** *frost* of night (opp. חֹרֶב of day), Gn 31^{40} (E), Je 36^{30}. **2.** *ice,* Jb 6^{16} 37^{10} 38^{29} (‖ כְּפֹר *hoar-frost*), מַשְׁלִיךְ ק׳ כְפִתִּים ψ 147^{17} (Hup al. think of hail, but v. Bae; ‖ קָרָה *cold,* שֶׁלֶג, כְּפוֹר v^{16}); probably also כְּעֵין ק׳ Ez 1^{22} (so Krae; most *crystal,* after 𝔊).

קְרִי, קִרְיָה, קִרְיַת, קְרִיּוֹת, etc., v. קרה. 7147, 7151-52,
p. 899-900, above 7157

†[קָרַם] **vb. spread** or **lay** something over 7159
(NH *id.* *form a crust,* so Hiph. יקרים על Ecclus 43^{20}; Aram. קְרַם, ܩܪܰܡ, *incrust, overlay*);—**Qal** *Pf.* 1 s. וְקָרַמְתִּי עֲלֵיכֶם עוֹר Ez 37^{6} *I will spread skin over you* (i.e. the dry bones); *Impf.* 3 ms. וַיִּקְרַם עֲלֵיהֶם עוֹר v^{8} (so Gi van d. H.; Baer וַיִּקָּרַם, of which conflicting explan. Ges$^{§§ 9 u, 29 i}$), indef. subj. instead of pass.; but rd. **Niph.** וַיִּקָּרֵם 𝔖 (cf. 𝔙) Co Berthol Toy Krae.

קרן (√ of foll.; mng. dub.; cf. As. *ḳarnu,* Ar. قَرْنٌ, Eth. ቀርን: NH קֶרֶן, Ph. קרן, Aram. קַרְנָא, ܩܰܪܢܳܐ, all *horn;* Sab. קרן *spur* of mt. (?) Hom$^{Chrest. 127}$; v. also Ar. قَرْنٌ *part of man's head where horns are in beasts,* قُرْنَةٌ *corner, extremity,* of anything Frey, *horn* of uterus, Lane).

†קֶרֶן$_{75}$ **n.f.**$^{Je 48, 25}$ **horn;**—abs. ק׳ Is 5^{1}+, קָרֶן 7161
ψ 75^{5}; cstr. קֶרֶן Jos 6^{5}+; sf. קַרְנִי 1 S 2^{1} ψ 92^{11}, etc.; du. קַרְנַיִם Hb 3^{4}, קְרָנַיִם Dn 8$^{3.6}$, -נַיִם v$^{3.20}$; cstr. קַרְנֵי 1 K 22^{11}+, sf. קַרְנָיו Gn 22^{13} Dt 33^{17}, קַרְנָיו Dn 8^{7}, קַרְנֵיכֶם Ez 34^{21}; pl. (usu. in der. senses) קְרָנוֹת Ez 43^{15}+; cstr. קַרְנֹת Ex 29^{12}+, sf. קַרְנֹתָיו 27^{2}+, etc.;—*horn:* †**1. a.** of ram (אַיִל) Gn 22^{13}, so in Daniel's vision Dn 8$^{3.3.6.7.20}$, and (of goat) v$^{5.8.9.21}$; of oppressors in Isr. (under fig. of rams) Ez 34^{21}, so of nations Zc 2$^{2.4.4.4}$; of רְאֵם Dt 33^{17} ψ 22^{22} (both fig., cf. 92^{11}); of Zion under fig. of threshing-ox Mi 4^{13}; ק׳ בַּרְזֶל 1 K 22^{11} = 2 Ch 18^{10} (symbol.); seen in Zech.'s vision Zc 2^{1}. **b.** used as oil-flask 1 S 16$^{1.13}$ 1 K 1^{39} (cf. קֶרֶן הַפּוּךְ infr.). **c.** ק׳ הַיּוֹבֵל, as wind-instr. Jos 6^{5} (cf. שׁוֹפָר). **d.** קַרְנוֹת שֵׁן Ez 27^{15} (from curved shape of tusks). †**2.** fig., of pers., symbol of strength Dt 33^{17}, ק׳ יִשְׁעִי 2 S 22^{3} =

ψ 18^{3} (of 'י as deliverer); others sub **3** or **4**; esp. as lifted up (רום, as of a lordly animal, cf. Dr$^{1S2.1}$), denoting increase of might, dignity 1 S 2$^{1.10}$ La 2^{17} ψ 75^{11} 89$^{18.25}$ 92^{11} 112^{9}, so perh. 1 Ch 25^{5} (v. Kau; >Be *blow loudly* [cf. **1 c**]), + לְעַמּוֹ ψ 148^{14} (subj. 'י); also haughtiness, arrogance 75$^{5.6}$; opp. גָּדַע ק׳ *hew off horns*, i.e. reduce, humiliate, La 2^{3} ψ 75^{11}, pass. Je 48^{25}, so וְעֹלַלְתִּי בֶעָפָר קַרְנִי Jb 16^{15}; אַצְמִיחַ ק׳ לְבֵית יִשׂ׳ Ez 29^{21} is appar. of restoration of might (as ψ 148^{14} supr., c. וַיָּרֶם), but אַצְ׳ ק׳ לְדָוִד ψ 132^{17} of raising up individual ruler of Davidic line. **3.** of altar, horn-like projections at corners (26 t.), Am 3^{14} Je 17^{1} Ez 43$^{15.20}$ ψ 118^{27} Ex 27^{22} + 8 t. Ex, Lv 4$^{7.18}$ + 6 t. Lv (all P); as sanctuary, refuge 1 K 1$^{50.51}$ 2^{28}. †**4.** *hill* (so in Ar., *peak, isolated hill*, cf. Ges) Is 5^{1}. †**5.** קַרְנַיִם מִיָּדוֹ לוֹ Hb 3^{4} *rays at his side(s) had he* (of lightning-flashes in theoph., cf. Now Da).—Am 6^{13} v. קַרְנַיִם n.pr.loc.

7160 †**קָרַן vb. Qal denom.** of קֶרֶן **5, send out rays**;—*Pf.* 3 ms. קָרַן עוֹר פָּנָיו Ex 34$^{29.30.35}$ (P). **Hiph. denom.** of קֶרֶן **1 a, display** (grow) **horns** (be fully developed), *Pt.* פָּר מַקְרִן מַפְרִיס ψ 69^{32}.

7163 †**קֶרֶן הַפּוּךְ n.pr.f.** (*horn of antimony*, i.e. *beautifier*, v. פּוּךְ);—Job's third daughter Jb 42^{14}.

7161 †**קַרְנַיִם n.pr.loc.** conquered by Isr. Am 6^{13} (so Gr We Now GASm, cf. also לֹא דְבָר p. 520 supr.; 𝔊 and most sub קֶרֶן **2**); prob. in Bashan, = Καρναιν 1 Macc 5$^{43.44}$, Καρνιον 2 Macc 12^{21}; also in
6252 עַשְׁתְּרֹת ק׳ Gn 14^{5} (v. III. עַשְׁתָּרוֹת p. 800 supr.).

7164 †[**קָרַס**] **vb. bend down, stoop, crouch** (intrans.) (cf. perh. Ar. قُرْصٌ *disc, round cake*; cp. NH קַרְסֹל, קַרְצוֹל, 𝔗 קַרְסוּלָא, קַרְצוּלָא all *ankle*);—**Qal** *Pf.* 3 pl. קָרְסוּ Is 46^{2}; *Pt.* קֹרֵס v^{1} (both + כָּרַע); of vanquished gods of Babylon.

7165 †[**קֶרֶס**] **n.**[**m.**] hook, on edge of curtains of tabern., matching the loops (לֻלָאֹת, v. [לוּלַי]); pl. קְרָסִים Ex 26$^{6.11}$ = 36$^{13.18}$, 26^{33}; cstr. קַרְסֵי זָהָב v^{6} = 36^{13}, ק׳ נְחֹשֶׁת 26^{11} = 36^{18}; sf. קְרָסָיו 35^{11} = 39^{33}.

7166 †[**קַרְסֹל**] **n.**[**f.** Albr$^{ZAW\ xvi\ (1896),\ 77}$] **ankle** (cf.
7165 𝔊 𝔙 2 S 22^{37}; = קֶרֶס + ל v. Kö$^{ii.1,121}$; pl. sf. קַרְסֻלָּי 2 S 22^{37} = ψ 18^{37}).

7026 †**קֵרֹס n.pr.m.** post-ex., Ezr 2^{44}, Καδης, A Κηραος; = קֵירֹס Ne 7^{47}, Κειρα(ς), 𝔊L (both) Κορες.

7167 **קָרַע**$_{63}$ **vb. tear** (NH *id.*; Ar. قَرَعَ *strike* head, bell, etc., *beat* drum, *box* ear, *gnash* teeth (Frey Dozy); also *impugn, censure*);—**Qal** *Pf.* 3 ms. ק׳ 1 S 15^{28}+, etc.; *Impf.* 3 ms. וַיִּקְרַע Gn 37^{29}+; 1 s. sf. אֶקְרָעֶנָּה 1 K 11^{12}, etc.; *Imv.* mpl. קִרְעוּ 2 S 3^{31} Jo 2^{13}; *Inf. abs.* קָרֹעַ 1 K 11^{11}; cstr. לִקְרוֹעַ Ec 3^{7}, sf. קָרְעִי Ezr 9^{5}; *Pt. act.* קֹרֵעַ 1 K 11^{31}; *pass.* קָרוּעַ 2 S 15^{32}, etc.;—*tear, rend:* **1. a.** usu. (39 t.) of *rending* garment in (1) sign of grief, distress: בֶּגֶד (29 t.) Gn 37$^{29.34}$ 44^{13} 2 S 13^{19}+; ק׳ לְבַבְכֶם וְאַל ב׳ Jo 2^{13}; ק׳ ב׳ לִשְׁנַיִם קְרָעִים 2 K 2^{12}, pt. pass. ק׳ בְּגָדָיו 2 S 1^{2}; cstr. קְרֻעֵי ב׳ *torn of garments* (pers. *with torn garments*) 2 S 13^{31} (but read קָרְעוּ ב׳ 𝔊 𝔙 Th We al.), 2 K 18^{37} = Is 36^{22}, Je 41^{5}; מְעִיל †Jb 1^{20} 2^{12} Ezr 9^{3} (+ בֶּגֶד), כֻּתֹּנֶת 2 S 13^{19}, קָרוּעַ כֻּתָּנְתּוֹ 2 S 15^{32} (Ges$^{\S 121\ d}$); שִׂמְלָה †Gn 37^{34} 44^{13} Jos 7^{6}; pt. pass. † מַדָּיו קְרֻעִים 1 S 4^{12}; †(2) as symbolic act, ק׳ שַׂלְמָה שְׁנֵים עָשָׂר 1 K 11^{30}; †(3) abs. עֵת לִקְרוֹעַ וְעֵת לִתְפּוֹר קְרָעִים Ec 3^{7}. **b.** *tear* away or out: veils Ez 13^{21}, fillets from (מֵעַל) arms v^{20}, mark of leprosy out of (מִן) garment Lv 13^{56}. †**2.** *tear away* sovereignty (under fig. of garment), subj. 'י, מֵעַל pers. 1 S 15^{28} 1 K 11^{11}, also מִיַּד 1 S 28^{17} 1 K 11$^{12.31}$, מִן 14^{8}, abs. 11^{13}; c. acc. מֵעַל + יִשׂ׳ 2 K 17^{21}. †**3.** *tear, rend asunder:* **a.** book with (ב) knife Je 36^{23}. **b.** = *make wide, large*, eyes, with (ב) stibium Je 4^{30}; windows, וק׳ לוֹ חַלּוֹנָ[י] 22^{14}. **c.** *rend open* heavens, and descend, of 'י, Is 63^{19}. †**4.** *tear, rend*, of wild beasts: 'י as fierce bear Ho 13^{8} (obj. סְגוֹר לִבָּם); fig. of human foes ψ 35^{15} (acc. pers. om.), so Hup al., but (fr. context) Ol Bae We al. *malign, rail* (cf. Ar. supr.); >Gr al. קָרְאוּ. †**Niph.** *be rent*, of garment (מְעִיל), *Impf.* 3 ms. וַיִּקָּרַע 1 S 15^{27}, יִקָּרֵעַ Ex 28^{32} 39^{23}; *be rent, split asunder*, of altar 1 K 13$^{3.5}$.

†[**קֶרַע**] **n.m.**$^{1\ K\ 11,\ 30}$ **torn piece** of garment, 7168
rag;—pl. קְרָעִים 1 K 11^{30} he tore it into twelve *pieces*, v^{31} 2 K 2^{12}; *rags* Pr 23^{31} (sign of poverty).

†[**קָרַץ**] **vb. nip, pinch** (NH קָרַץ *cut* dough, 7169
compress lips, קֶרֶץ *piece of bread*; As. *karâṣu, nip off, gnaw*, Ar. قَرَصَ *pinch*; Eth. ቀረጸ: *incise*; Syr. ܩܪܨܐ *nail* [v. also BAram]; cf. Frä$^{35\ f.}$);—**Qal** *Impf.* 3 mpl. יִקְרְצוּ־עָיִן ψ 35^{19} *let them not pinch the eye*, i.e. wink maliciously, so *Pt. act.* קֹרֵץ ע׳ Pr 10^{10}, ק׳ בְּעֵינוֹ 6^{13}; also ק׳ שְׂפָתָיו 16^{30} *pinching his lips* (i.e. compressing, as NH, or biting, gnawing, cf. As.). **Pu.** *Pf.* 1 s. מֵחֹמֶר קֹרַצְתִּי Jb 33^{6} *from clay I was nipped off* (cf. As. *ṭiṭa iḳtariṣ, he nipped off clay*, to form Eabani).

7171 †קֶ֫רֶץ **n.m.** dub. word, appar. **nipping,** concr. **nipper** usu. interpr. (since Hi) of a nipping or stinging insect (cf. Aram. קָרוֹצָא, Ar. قَارِصٌ *biting insect*); e.g. *gadfly* (cf. Thes[Add. 111]), fig. of Nebuchadr. ק׳ מִצָּפוֹן בָּא Je 46^{20} *a gadfly cometh from the north;* 𝔙 (Aq Symm) *stimulator,* i.e. קֹרֵץ; Thes al., more gen., *excidium.*

7172 †I. קַרְקַע **n.**[**m.**] **floor** (prob. redupl. fr. a √קרר, or קור; NH *id., ground,* so 𝔗 קַרְקְעָא, קַרְקָעִיתָא; appar.=As. *ḳakḳaru, ground, earth,* Ar. قَرْقَرٌ *terra aequabilis mollisque;* cf. Kö[ii. 1, 91]);—abs. ק׳ 1 K 6^{16} 7^{7a}, קָ֑ע- v^{7b} (v. infr.); cstr. קַרְקַע Nu 5^{17}+;—*floor* of temple 1 K $6^{15.15.16.30}$ 7^{7a}; v^{7b} read prob. הַקּוֹרוֹת *rafters* (cf. 6^{15} and קוֹרָה) 𝔖 𝔙 Th Sta Kmp[Kau] Benz; *(earth)-floor* of tabern. Nu 5^{17}; קַרְקַע הַיָּם Am 9^3 *the floor,* bottom *of the sea.*

7173 †II. קַרְקַע **n.pr.loc.** (*floor*);—c. art. + ה loc., הַקַּרְקָ֫עָה Jos 15^{13}, on extreme S. border of Judah; τὴν κατὰ δυσμὰς Καδης.

7174 †קַרְקֹר **n.pr.loc.** E. of Jordan, Ju 8^{10}, site unknown; Καρκαρ.

6936 קַרְקַר Nu 24^{17} read קָדְקֹד q.v. p. 869

6979 †I. [קָרַר] **vb. be cold** (Ar. قَرَّ *be cold,* so Eth. ቀረረ: Syr. ܩܰܪ; 𝔗 Ithpa. is *cool oneself* (rare); Levy cp. also NH Nithp. נִתְקָרֵר *grow calm* [i.e. cool]);—**Hiph.** *make* or *keep cool: Pf.* 3 fs. הֵקֵ֫רָה, fig., Je 6^{7b} Jerus. *keepeth* her wickedness *cool,* fresh; *Inf. cstr.* metapl. הָקִיר (Ges[§ 67 v]) v^{7a}, of בּוֹר *keeping* water *cool* (sim.).

7179 †קַר **adj. cool;**—cstr. (fig.) וְקַר־רוּחַ Pr 17^{27} (Kt) *cool of spirit,* i.e. calm, self-possessed (Qr
3368 יְקַר־); pl. קָרִים of water Je 18^{14} Pr 25^{25}. p. 429

7120 †קֹר **n.**[**m.**] **cold;**—abs. Gn 8^{22} (חֹם).

7135 †קָרָה **n.f. id.;**—abs. בְּיוֹם ק׳ Na 3^{17} *a day of coldness,* cold day, so Pr 25^{20}; ק׳ alone, *cold* of night Jb 24^7; in gen., due to winds 37^9 (מְזָרִים v. זרה **Pi.**; yet Voigt Bu, attractively, מִמְּזָוִים (cf. ψ 144^{10}) *out of storehouses* [‖ חֶדֶר]); וְקָרוֹת מִי יַעֲמֹד ψ לִפְנֵי קָרָתוֹ 147^{17}, + pl. Zc 14^6 (rd. וְקִרָה,
3368 v. יָקָר). p. 429

4747 †מְקֵרָה **n.f. coolness;**—abs. מ׳ of chamber: עֲלִיַּת הַמּ׳ Ju 3^{20}=חֲדַר הַמּ׳ v^{24}.

6979 †II. [קָרַר] **vb. Pilp. tear down** (?) (NH קַרְקֵר *tear down* wall);—only *Pt.* מְקַרְקַר קִר Is 22^5 usu. (men are) *tearing down wall(s),* but v. I. קִיר **3** *ad fin.*

קרשׁ (√of foll.; cf. NH קָרַשׁ *be(come) firm, solid,* קֶרֶשׁ *board* (rare)).

קֶ֫רֶשׁ 51 **n.m.**[Ex 26, 16] **board, boards;**—abs. ק׳ 7175
Ex 26^{18}+, קָ֑רֶשׁ v^{20}+; sf. קְרָשֵׁךְ Ez 27^6; pl. קְרָשִׁים v^{15}+; cstr. קַרְשֵׁי v^{26}+; sf. קְרָשָׁיו 35^{11}+;—†**1.** coll. *boards,* of deck Ez 27^6 (of Tyre under fig. of ship). **2.** *board* of tabern. Ex $26^{15.16.16}$ + 45 t. 26–40; Nu 3^{36} 4^{31} (all P).

קֶ֫רֶת v. קרה. p. 900 7176

קשׂה (√of foll., meaning dub.; cf. Ar. قَشْوَةٌ *basket of palm-leaves;* Eth. ቀሡት: *urn, jar;* NH קְסָוָה=BH קשׂוה, cf. 𝔗 קְסָוָתָא, or קסתות; Talm. קִסְטָא, קֶסֶט a measure, Syr. ܩܶܣܛܳܐ *jar,* (ט after ק), Nö[SB Ak. 1882, 1179] Frä[63, 205] Brock[s.v.]).

†[קַשְׂוָה, Kö[ii. 1, 165]] **n.f.** a kind of **jug, jar,** 7184
utensil of tabern. and (Ch) temple;—pl. קְשָׂוֹת Ex 37^{16} 1 Ch 28^{19}; cstr. קְשׂוֹת הַנָּ֑סֶךְ Nu 4^7 *jars of the drink-offering;* sf. (of table) Ex 25^{29}.

†קֶ֫סֶת (for קֶשֶׂת) **n.**[**f.**] **pot** (for ink), **ink-** 7183
horn;—cstr. ק׳ הַסֹּפֵר Ez $9^{2.3}$, abs. הַקֶּ֫סֶת v^{11}.

קשׂט (√of foll.; meaning dub.).

†קְשִׂיטָה **n.f.** unit of (unknown) value, 7192
perh. weight: Gn 33^{19} ‖ Jos 24^{32} (both E), Jb 42^{11}.

קשׂשׂ (√of following; NH קַשְׂקֶשֶׂת *scale;* cf. Ar. قَشَّ *skim off fat,* IV. *scale off* (Berggren), اقشّ *be healed from small-pox,* etc. (Muḥiṭ; i.e. scale off), cf. قَشَّ *get well* from leanness, Frey (Ḳam Golius); also *sweep* (up débris) Dozy[ii. 347]).

†קַשְׂקֶ֫שֶׂת **n.f. scale** of fish, etc.;—of water- 7193
animals having סְנַפִּיר וְק׳ *fin and scale* Dt $14^{9.10}$ =Lv $11^{9.10.12}$; pl. קַשְׂקַשִּׂים, of scale-armour 1 S 17^5; pl. sf. קַשְׂקְשֹׂתֶיךָ Ez $29^{4.4}$ (of Pharaoh under fig. of crocodile).

קַשׂ v. קשׁשׁ. p. 905 7179

קשׁא (√of foll.; cf. Ar. قِثَّاءٌ, Eth. ቀሥጳ: NH קִשּׁוּת, Pun. κισσου Löw[p. 408], all *cucumber(s)* (Löw[p. 330]), so prob. As. *ḳiššû;* cf. Syr. ܩܰܛܳܐ *id.* (Lexx), 𝔗[Jer I.] Nu 11^5 pl. קַטַּיָּא (ט for ת after ק); Gk. σίκυος, σικύη Lag[Arm. Stud. § 1975; M ii. 356] Lewy[Fremdw. 30]).

†[קִשֻּׁאָה, Löw[p. 330]] **n.f. cucumber;**—pl. 7180
קִשֻּׁאִים Nu 11^5.

†I. מִקְשָׁה **n.f. place, field, of cucumbers,** 4750
Is 1^8; so Je 10^5 Gf Gie al. (cf. Baruch 6^{70}).

7181 [קָשַׁב]$_{46}$ **vb.** **incline, attend,** of ears;—†**Qal** *Impf.* 3 fpl. תִּקְשַׁבְנָה Is 32^{3} (subj. אזנים). **Hiph.** *Pf.* 3 ms. הִקְשִׁיב Je 23^{18} ψ 66^{19}, etc.; *Impf.* 3 ms. יַקְשֵׁב Is 42^{23}, etc.; *Imv.* ms. הַקְשֵׁב Jb 33^{21}, esp. הַקְשִׁיבָה ψ 5^{3}+, etc.; *Inf. cstr.* הַקְשִׁיב 1 S 15^{22}+; *Pt.* מַקְשִׁיב Pr 1^{24}+, pl. מַקְשִׁיבִים Ct 8^{13};—*give attention* (sts.+שָׁמַע); abs. Ho 5^{1} 1 S 15^{22} Is 10^{30} 28^{23} 34^{1} 49^{1} Mi 1^{2}+12 t.; +אֶל pers. Je 18^{19} Zc 1^{4} Is 51^{4} (‖ הַאֲזִינוּ), לְ pers. ψ 55^{3}; +אֶל rei Je 18^{18} Ne 9^{34} ψ 142^{7}, עַל rei Je 6^{19} Pr 17^{4} 29^{12}, לְ rei Je 6^{17} Is 48^{18} Pr 4^{20} 5^{1} 7^{24} ψ 5^{3} Ct 8^{13}, בְּ rei ψ 66^{19} 86^{6}; also c. acc. rei Je 23^{18} Jb 13^{6} ψ 17^{1} 61^{2}; acc. cogn. Is 21^{7}; appar.=*cause to attend,* c. acc. אָזְנֶךָ Pr 2^{2} (+לְ rei), ψ 10^{17}, but usage would be so late and rare that אָזְנֶךָ is prob. subj. rei (Ges^{§144m} Da$^{Synt. §109, R. 3}$).

7182 †קֶ֫שֶׁב **n.m.** **attentiveness**;—קָ֑שֶׁב as sign of life 2 K 4^{31}, of a living deity 1 K 18^{29}; as acc. cogn. וְהִקְשִׁיב קֶשֶׁב רַב־קָשֶׁב Is 21^{7} *he shall attend an attentiveness* (give close attention),—*abundance of attentiveness* (cf. 63^{7} ψ 145^{7}).

7183 †[קַשָּׁב] **adj.** **attentive**;—fs. תְּהִי נָא אָזְנְךָ קַשֶּׁבֶת Ne 1^{6}, +אֶל rei v^{11}.

7183 †[קַשֻּׁב] **adj.** id.;—fpl. קַשֻּׁבוֹת, of אָזְנַיִם, 2 Ch 6^{40} 7^{15} ψ 130^{2}, all+לְ rei.

7185 I. [קָשָׁה] **vb.** **be hard, severe, fierce** (NH קָשָׁה *be severe;* Ar. قَسَا (ى) *be hard, dry,* III. *endure, struggle against, severity;* Aram. קְשָׁא, ܩܫܐ *be hard, difficult;* JAram. קְשֵׁי, קַשְׁיָה adj. *hard*);—**Qal** *Pf.* 3 fs. קָשְׁתָה 1 S 5^{7}, קָשָׁתָה Gn 49^{7}; *Impf.* 3 ms. יִקְשֶׁה Dt 1^{17} 15^{18}, וַיִּ֫קֶשׁ 2 S 19^{44};—**1.** *be hard, difficult* Dt 1^{17} (of a legal case; מִן compar.). **2.** *be hard, severe,* ק׳ יָדוֹ עָלֵינוּ 1 S 5^{7} (of י׳, in judgment); יִק׳ בְעֵינֶךָ Dt 15^{18} *it shall not be hard in thine eyes* (seem a severe trial, an injustice); of wrath Gn 49^{7} (poem in J; ‖ עַז); of fierce words 2 S 19^{44}. **Niph.** *Pt.* נִקְשֶׁה Is 8^{21} *hardly bestead, hard pressed.* **Pi.** *Impf.* 3 fs. וַתְּקַשׁ בְּלִדְתָּהּ Gn 35^{16} (E) *she made hard in her bearing* (had severe labour). **Hiph.** *Pf.* 3 ms. הִקְשָׁה Ex 13^{15}+, etc.; *Impf.* 3 ms. וַיַּ֫קֶשׁ 2 Ch 36^{13}; 3 mpl. וַיַּקְשׁוּ Je 7^{26}+, etc.; *Inf. cstr.* sf. בְּהַקְשֹׁתָהּ Gn 35^{17}; *Pt.* מַקְשֶׁה Pr 28^{14} 29^{1};—**1.** *make difficult, difficulty:* הִקְשָׁה לְשַׁלְּחֵנוּ Ex 13^{15} Pharaoh *made difficulty about sending us away;* of travail Gn 35^{17} (E; as **Pi.**); הִקְשִׁיתָ לִשְׁאוֹל 2 K 2^{10} *thou hast made hard to ask,* asked a hard thing. **2.** *make severe, burdensome,* yoke imposed by king 1 K 12^{4}=2 Ch 10^{4}. **3.** **a.** *make hard, stiff, stubborn,* fig. of obstinacy: וַיַּקְשׁוּ אֶת־עָרְפָּם 2 K 17^{14} *they stiffened their neck,* so Je 7^{26} 17^{23} 19^{15} Dt 10^{16} 2 Ch 30^{8} 36^{13} Ne 9$^{16.17.29}$ Pr 29^{1}; אַל־תַּקְשׁוּ לְבַבְכֶם ψ 95^{8}, cf. Pr 28^{14}; subj. י׳, אַקְשֶׁה אֶת־לֵב פ׳ Ex 7^{3} (P), acc. אֶת־רוּחוֹ Dt 2^{30}. **b.** *shew stubbornness* Jb 9^{4} (c. אֶל pers. [י׳]).

†קָשֶׁה **adj.** **hard, severe**;—abs. ק׳ Ex 7186
18^{26}+; cstr. 32^{9}+; fs. קָשָׁה Dt 26^{6}+; cstr. קְשַׁת 1 S 1^{15}; mpl. קָשִׁים 2 S 3^{39}; cstr. קְשֵׁי Ez 2^{4} 3^{7}; fpl. קָשׁוֹת Gn 42$^{7.30}$;—**1.** *hard, difficult,* of a legal question (דָּבָר) Ex 18^{26} (E). **2. a.** *severe,* of battle 2 S 2^{17}, wind Is 27^{8}, servitude (עֲבֹדָה) 1 K 12^{4}=2 Ch 10^{4}, Dt 26^{6} Is 14^{3} Ex 1^{14} 6^{9} (both P); as n.coll. הִרְאִיתָ עַמְּךָ קָשָׁה ψ 60^{5} *thou hast made thy people see severe things;* קְשֵׁה יוֹם Jb 30^{25} i.e. one whose time (life) is hard, so 1 S 1^{15} (reading קְשַׁת יוֹם for ק׳ רוּחַ, 𝔊 Th We Dr al.); *severe, rough,* of lord (אֲדֹנִים) Is 19^{4}, cf. 2 S 3^{39} (c. מִן comp. [מִמֶּנּוּ ? v. HPS]); הָלוֹךְ וְקָשָׁה עַל־ Ju 4^{24} the hand of the sons of Israel went on *being more and more severe* upon Jabin; *fierce, relentless,* of י׳'s sword Is 27^{1} (in fig.); *rough, rude* 1 S 25^{3}; *severe things,* of language Gn 42$^{7.30}$ (E; c. דִּבֵּר), 1 S 20^{10} 1 K 12^{13}=2 Ch 10^{13} (all c. עָנָה); וְאָנֹכִי שָׁלוּחַ אֵלֶיךָ קָשָׁה 1 K 14^{6} *I am commissioned with a severe (message) unto thee* (Ges$^{§121 d. N. 2}$ Da$^{Synt. §§75 (d), 80}$); חָזוּת קָשָׁה Is 21^{2}. **b.** *fierce, intense, vehement,* of קִנְאָה Ct 8^{6} (‖ עַזָּה; cf. Gn 49^{7}). **3.** עַם־קְשֵׁה־עֹרֶף *a people stiff of neck, stubborn,* Ex 32^{9} 33$^{3.5}$ 34^{9} (all JE), Dt 9$^{6.13}$; עָרְפְּךָ הַקָּשֶׁה 31^{27}; cf. דַּרְכָּם הַקָּשָׁה Ju 2^{19}; קְשֵׁי פָנִים Ez 2^{4} (+חִזְקֵי־לֵב), קְשֵׁי־לֵב 3^{7} (+חִזְקֵי־מֵצַח); ק׳ alone=*stubborn* Is 48^{4}.

†קְשִׁי **n.[m.]** **stubbornness**;—cstr. Dt 9^{27}. 7190

†קִשְׁיוֹן **n.pr.loc.** Levit. city in Issachar, 7191
Jos 19^{20} 21^{28} (in ‖ 1 Ch 6^{57} קֶדֶשׁ q.v.); Κεισων, 6943
𝔊L Κεσιων, A Κεσ', Κισ'. p. 873

II. קשה (√ of foll. mng. dub.; Thes *decorticavit,*=Ar. قشا; then *tornavit,* but ش = שׁ ?).

†מִקְשֶׁה **n.[m.]** an artistic hair arrange- 4748
ment; ? **turner's work,** Is 3^{24}, so most.

†II. מִקְשָׁה **n.f.** perhaps **hammered work,** 4749
only of metals (orig. *turner's work* ?);—abs. מ׳, of cherubim in tabern. Ex 25^{18} 37^{7}, lamp-
stand 25$^{31.36}$ 37$^{17.22}$ Nu 8$^{4.4}$, clarions 10^{2}.—I. מ׳ 4750
v. קשא.

7188 †[קָשַׁח] **vb. Hiph. 1.** **make hard.** **2.** **treat hardly** (Ar. قسح *be hard, firm, tough;* Sab. קסח *hardness, severity, cruelty,* SabDenkm [57]);—**1.** *make hard, stubborn, Impf.* 2 ms. תַּקְשִׁיחַ (subj. ′י), c. acc. לֵב Is 63^{17} (+ מִיִּרְאָתֶךָ). **2.** *treat hardly, roughly* (of ostrich), *Pf.* 3 ms. הִקְשִׁיחַ Jb 39^{16} (c. acc. בָּנֶיהָ; rd. 3 fs. הִקְשִׁיחָה Hi Siegf Du); < (Di) *Inf. abs.* (Ges[§ 113z]) הַקְשִׁיחַ Ew, or *Impf.* 3 fs. תַּקְשִׁיחַ Hirz Bae[Kau] Bu.

7189 †קֹשֶׁט **n.** [**m.** ?] **bow**;—ψ 60^{6}, Aram. form of קֶשֶׁת, q.v. (ט for ת after ק).

קשט (√of foll.; cf. Palm. קשט *succeed;* Aram. קְשׁוֹט, קֻשְׁטָא *right, truth;* Syr. ܩܘܫܛܐ *id.,* ChrPalAram. ܩܫܝܛ *true,* Mand. כשט *be true,* v. Schwally[Idiot. 86]; Ar. قِسْطٌ *equity, justice* is loan-word (v. Frä[206])).

7189 †קֹשְׁטְ **n.m. truth**;—Pr 22^{21} (acc. to Toy Aram. gloss to foll. אִמְרֵי אֱמֶת).

7190-91 קִשְׁיוֹן, קְשִׁי, v. I. קשה. p. 904

7194 †קָשַׁר **vb. bind, league together, conspire** (NH *id., bind, join,* קֶשֶׁר *knot;* 𝔗 קְטַר, Syr. ܩܛܪ *bind* (ט for ת after ק) Nö[ZMG xl. 735], who cp. also ('perh.') Ar. قَسَرَ *force* to do a thing, Eth. ቀጸረ: *bind*);—**Qal** *Pf.* 3 ms. קָשַׁר Am 7^{10} 1 K 16^{16}; 2 ms. sf. וּקְשַׁרְתָּם consec. Dt 6^{8}, etc.; *Impf.* 3 ms. וַיִּקְשֹׁר 1 K 15^{27}+, וַיִּקְשְׁרוּ־ 2 K 15^{30}, etc.; *Imv.* ms. sf. קָשְׁרֵם Pr 3^{3}+; *Pt. act.* pl. קֹשְׁרִים 2 S 15^{31}+; *pass.* fs. קְשׁוּרָה Gn 44^{30} Pr 22^{15}; pl. קְשֻׁרִים Gn 30^{42};—**1.** *bind:* **a.** lit., c. acc. rei + עַל Gn 38^{28} (J), Je 51^{63}, + בְּ, Jos 2$^{18.21}$ (JE); *bind, confine,* c. acc. רֵים Jb 39^{10} (+ בְּתֶלֶם), acc. of crocod. 40^{29}. **b.** fig., c. acc. + עַל Dt 6^{8} 11^{18} Pr 3^{3} 6^{21} 7^{3} (all of religious and moral precepts); c. בְּ, נַפְשׁוֹ קְשׁוּרָה בְנַפְשׁוֹ Gn 44^{30} *his life is bound up with his* [viz. the boy's] *life* (J; of strong affection); אִוֶּלֶת ק׳ בְלֶב־נָעַר Pr 22^{15}. **c.** pt. pass. *vigorous* (prop. well-*knit;* opp. עֲטֻפִים) Gn 30^{42} (J). **2.** *league together, conspire:* c. עַל pers. *against* 1 S 22$^{8.13}$ Am 7^{10} 1 K 15^{27} 16^{9} 2 K 10^{9} 15$^{10.25}$, 21$^{23.24}$ = 2 Ch 33$^{24.25}$, 2 Ch 24^{21}; c. acc. cogn. קֶשֶׁר, 1 K 16^{20} 2 K 12^{21} 15^{15}, + עַל pers. 14^{19} = 2 Ch 25^{27}, 2 K 15^{30}; abs. 1 K 16^{16} Ne 4^{2} (+ inf. purpose); c. עִם, *together with,* 2 S 15^{31}. **Niph.** *Pf.* 3 fs. נִקְשְׁרָה 1 S 18^{1} *the life of Jonathan was bound up with the life of D.* (**Qal 1 b**); *Impf.* 3 fs. וַתִּקָּשֵׁר כָּל־הַחוֹמָה Ne 3^{38} *all the wall was joined together* (the circuit complete). **Pi.** *Impf.* **1.** *bind on* (as ornament), 2 fs. sf. וּתְקַשְּׁרִים Is 49^{18} (fig.; ‖ תִּלְבָּשִׁי). **2.** *bind fast,* 2 ms. (הַ)תְקַשֵּׁר מַעֲדַנּוֹת כִּימָה Jb 38^{31} *canst thou bind fast the bands of the Pleiades?* **Pu.** *Pt.* הַצֹּאן הַמְקֻשָּׁרוֹת Gn 30^{41} (J), = **Qal 1 c.** **Hithp.** *conspire: Pf.* 3 pl. הִתְקַשְּׁרוּ עַל־ 2 Ch 24^{25} (‖ 2 K 12^{21} **Qal 2**); *Impf.* 3 ms. וַיִּתְקַשֵּׁר אֶל־ 2 K 9^{14}; *Pt.* pl. הַמִּתְקַשְּׁרִים עָלָיו 2 Ch 24^{26}.

†קֶשֶׁר **n.m.**[2 S 15,12] **conspiracy**;—abs. ק׳ 2 S 7195
15^{12}+, קָשֶׁר 2 K 11^{14}+; cstr. קֶשֶׁר Ez 22^{25} (but v. infr.); sf. קִשְׁרוֹ 1 K 16^{20} 2 K 15^{15};—*conspiracy* 2 S 15^{12}; as acc. cogn. c. קָשַׁר 1 K 16^{20} 2 K 12^{21} 14^{19} = 2 Ch 25^{27}, 2 K 15$^{15.30}$; וַיִּמָּצֵא ק׳ בְּהוֹשֵׁעַ 2 K 17^{4}, נִמְצָא ק׳ בְּאִישׁ וגו׳ Je 11^{9}; as exclam. 2 K 11$^{14.14}$ = 2 Ch 23$^{13.13}$, Is 8$^{12.12}$ (Gr Lag Che[Comm.] Gu[Kau] al. קֹדֶשׁ or קָדֹשׁ); קֶשֶׁר נְבִיאֶיהָ Ez 22^{25}, < rd. אֲשֶׁר נְשִׂיאֶיהָ Co Toy Krae al. (after 𝔊).

†קִשֻּׁרִים **n.** [**m.**] **pl. bands, sashes,** or other woman's ornament that is *bound on:*—abs. ק׳ 7196
Is 3^{20}; sf. קִשֻּׁרֶיהָ Je 2^{32} (‖ עֶדְיָהּ; cf. √**Pi.** Is 49^{18}).

I. **קשש** (√of foll.; cf. 𝔗 קְשַׁשׁ *be old* (orig. *be dried up*?), Syr. ܩܫ *be old;* JAram. קַשִּׁישׁ *old;* Palm. קשישא name of office, perh. *elder;* NH קַשׁ *stubble, straw* (Löw[p. 160]), so Syr. ܩܫܐ, 𝔗 קַשָּׁא (Ex 15^{7} Is 40^{24}); Ar. قَشّ is loan-word Frä[137]).

†קַשׁ **n.m.**[Na 1,10] **stubble, chaff**;—abs. ק׳ 7179
Ex 5^{12}+, קָשׁ 15^{7};—lit. as acc. cogn. לְקֹשֵׁשׁ ק׳ לַתֶּבֶן Ex 5^{12} (J); in sim., as inflammable, 15^{7} Is 5^{24} 47^{14} Na 1^{10} Jo 2^{5}, so in metaph. Is 33^{11} Ob ^{18} Mal 3^{19}; in sim., as driven by wind Is 40^{24} 41^{2} Je 13^{24} ψ 83^{14}; fig. of the worthless Jb 13^{25}, of harmless trifles 41$^{20.21}$.

†[קָשַׁשׁ] **vb. denom. Pō. gather stubble**;— 7197
Pf. 3 pl. consec. וְקֹשְׁשׁוּ Ex 5^{7}; *Inf. cstr.* לְקֹשֵׁשׁ v^{12}; *Pt.* מְקֹשֵׁשׁ Nu 15$^{32.33}$, f. מְקֹשֶׁשֶׁת 1 K 17$^{10.12}$;—*gather stubble,* c. acc. cogn. קַשׁ Ex 5^{12} (לַתֶּבֶן); also c. acc. תֶּבֶן v^{7} (both J); c. acc. עֵצִים as firewood Nu 15$^{32.33}$ (P), 1 K 17$^{10.12}$.

†II. [קָשַׁשׁ] doubtful **vb.,** only **Qal** *Imv.* 7197
+ **Hithpō.** *Imv.,* הִתְקוֹשְׁשׁוּ וָקוֹשּׁוּ Zp 2^{1}; AV RV *gather yourselves together, yea gather together,* from foregoing (cf. Vrss), but this only denom. in specif. mng. *gather stubble, sticks,* etc.; read prob. with Gr Bu[SK 1893, 396] al. הִתְבּוֹשְׁשׁוּ וָבוֹשׁוּ.

†קֶשֶׁת **n.f.**[Gn 9,14] (appar. **m.** 2 S 1^{22} but v. 7198
Albr[ZAW xvi (1896) 91]) **bow** (orig. √ perh. קוש, mng. unknown; NH *id.;* As. *ḳaštu;* Eth. ቀስት:

Ar. قَوْسٌ, pl. قِسِيٌّ, قُسِيٌّ, etc.; 𝔗 קַשְׁתָּא and (ט for ק after ת) קוּשְׁטָא (rare), all *bow*, קַשָּׁתָא *bowman;* Syr. ܩܫܬܐ *bow*, ܩܫܳܬܳܐ *bowman;* OAram. קשת *bow*, Mand. כשטא (Frä^{206}); Palm. קשטא *bowman*);—abs. ק׳ Ho 1^{7}+, קָֽשֶׁת Je 46^{9}+; cstr. קֶ֫שֶׁת Ho 1^{5}+; sf. קַשְׁתִּי Gn 48^{22}+, etc.; pl. abs. קְשָׁתוֹת 2 Ch 26^{14}+; sf. קַשְּׁתֹתָיו (Ges$^{§ 20 h}$) Is 5^{28}, קַשְּׁתוֹתָם Je 51^{56} ψ 37^{15}, קַשְּׁתֹתֵיהֶם Ne 4^{7} (קַשְּׁתוֹתָיו etc., van d. H. [exc. ψ 37^{15}]);—**1.** *bow:* **a.** for hunting Gn 27^{3} (J; + תְּלִי). **b.** battle: + (or ‖) חֶרֶב, Gn 48^{22} Jos 24^{12} (both E), Ho 1^{7} 2^{20} 1 S 18^{4} (+ חֲגֹרוֹ), 2 S 1^{22} 2 K 6^{22} Is 41^{2} Ne 4^{7} (+ רָמְחֵיהֶם), Zc 9^{13} (fig. of Judah as י׳'s bow), ψ 37^{15} (fig.), 44^{7} (+ or ‖ חֶרֶב also infr.); + (or ‖) חִצִּים Is 7^{24} 2 K 13$^{15.15}$ Ez 39$^{3.9}$ 1 Ch 12^{2a}; cf. רִשְׁפֵי ק׳ ψ 76^{4} = arrow (+ מָגֵן וְחֶרֶב) so בֶּן ק׳ Jb 41^{20} (cf. La 3^{13} Jb 5^{7}); + חֲנִית ψ 46^{10}, + כִּידוֹן Je 6^{23} 50^{42}; + various weapons Ne 4^{10} 2 Ch 26^{14}; alone Is 13^{18} (context corrupt), 22^{3} Je 51^{56} Hb 3^{9} (of י׳ as *warrior*); ק׳ מִלְחָמָה Zc 9^{10} 10^{4}; in sim. כְּקֶ׳ רְמִיָּה *like a bow of deception* Ho 7^{16} ψ 78^{57} (i.e. one that misses its aim; al. *slack bow*). **c.** ק׳ coll. = *bow(-men), archers* Is 21^{17}. **d.** phrases are: הַמּוֹרִים אֲנָשִׁים בַּקֶּ׳ 1 S 31^{3} *archers, bowmen* (but dub.; Dr Kit Löhr tr., הַמּ׳ א׳; We Bu del. א׳, as ‖ 1 Ch 10^{3}; HPS Now del. א׳ (הַמּוֹרִים בַּקֶּ׳ 1 Ch 10^{3}); מְטַחֲוֵי ק׳ Gn 21^{16} (v. [טָחָה]), רֹמֵה ק׳ Je 4^{29}, cf. perh. Gn 21^{21} v. קַשָּׁת; נֹשְׁקֵי ק׳ ‖ (v. II. נָשַׁק) 1 Ch 12^{2b} 2 Ch 17^{17}, נ׳ רוֹמֵי ק׳ ψ 78^{9}; תֹּפֵשׂ הַקֶּ׳ Am 2^{15} *one grasping the bow*, (v. Je 46^{9} infr.) v. also מִלֵּא יָדוֹ בַּקֶּ׳ 2 K 9^{24}, הַרְכֵּב יָדְךָ עַל־הַקֶּ׳ 13^{16}; דָּרַךְ ק׳ *bend* (lit. *tread) the bow*, Is 5^{28} (pt. pass), 21^{15} (*id.;* ‖ חֶרֶב), Je 50$^{14.29}$ 51^{3} 1 Ch 5^{18} 8^{40} 2 Ch 14^{7}; ψ 37^{14} (‖ חֶרֶב), in fig. 11^{2} (‖ חֵץ), and, of God, La 2^{4} 3^{12} ψ 7^{13} (‖ חֶרֶב); תֹּפְשֵׂי דֹּרְכֵי ק׳ Je 46^{9}; cf. (fig.) וַיַּדְרְכוּ אֶת־לְשׁוֹנָם קַשְׁתָּם Je 9^{2}; also וְנִחֲתָה ק׳ נְחוּשָׁה ψ 18^{35} = 2 S 22^{35} (rd. וְנִחֲתָה for וְנִחַת); מָשַׁךְ בַּקֶּ׳ *draw the bow* 1 K 22^{34} = 2 Ch 18^{33}, Is 66^{19}. **e.** *bow* (passing over into) fig. of *might*, Gn 49^{24} (poem), 1 S 2^{4} Ho 1^{5} Je 49^{35} Jb 29^{20} (cf. ψ 37^{15}, **b.** supr.). **f.** ק׳ נְחוּשָׁה fig. of divine judgment Jb 20^{24} (‖ נֵשֶׁק בַּרְזֶל). **2.** *rainbow:* כְּמַרְאֵה הַקֶּ׳ אֲשֶׁר יִהְיֶה בֶעָנָן בְּיוֹם הַגֶּשֶׁם Ez 1^{28}; Gn 9$^{13.14.16}$ (P).—וַיֹּאמֶר לְלַמֵּד בְּנֵי־יְהוּדָה קָשֶׁת 2 S 1^{18} is corrupt; 𝔊 al. om.; We Now think misplaced gloss on v^{6}; v. further HPS.

† קַשָּׁת **n.m.** bowman (si vera l.);—וַיְהִי 7199
רֹבֶה ק׳ Gn 21^{20} *and he became, growing up, a bowman;* but ר׳ then superfluous (om. 𝔊), after וַיִּגְדָּל v^{a}; Kn Di רֹבֵה קָשֶׁת (= רֹמֵה ק׳ Je 4^{29}, which Ball reads here), cf. Holz Gunk.

ר

ר *Rêš*, 20th letter; = 200 in post B. Heb.

1676,7201 **רָאָה** Dt 14^{13} textual error; v. דָּאָה. p. 178

7200 **רָאָה**$_{1315}$ **vb. see** (NH *id.;* MI^{4} וארא, הראני 1^{7}, cf. רית *spectacle* 1^{12}; Sab. ראי *see, expect*, DHM$^{ZMG\ xxix\ (1875),\ 596,\ 599}$; Ar. رَأَى *see*, so Eth. ርእየ: 𝔗 רֵיוָא, רֵו human *appearance, features*, etc. (cf. Heb. רְאִי **2**));—**Qal**$_{1141}$ *Pf.* 3 ms. ר׳ Gn 29^{10}+, sf. רָאָהוּ consec. Ex 4^{14}, וְרָאֲךָ 2 K 2^{12}+; 3 fs. רָאֲתָה Gn 38^{14}, sf. רָאָתְךָ Jb 42^{5}; 2 ms. רָאִיתָ Gn 20^{10}+, etc.; *Impf.* 3 ms. יִרְאֶה 22^{8}+, juss. יֵרֶא Gn 41^{33} (Baer Gi, Ges$^{§ 75 p, hh}$ Kö$^{I.561}$; van d. H. יֵרֶא), יֵ֫רֶא Ex 5^{21}+, וַיַּרְא Gn 18^{2}+ (1 S 19^{20} read pl. 𝔊 Comm., i.e. וַיִּרְאוּ Dr$^{Sm\ lxiii}$), sf. יִרְאֵנִי Ex 33^{20}, וַיִּרְאֵנִי 2 S 1^{7}; 3 fs. תִּרְאֶה Lv 20^{17} Jb 33^{28}, juss. תֵּרֶא Mi 7^{10} Zc 9^{5} (Baer Gi, cf. Ges Kö supr.; van d. H. תֵּרֶא), וַתֵּ֫רֶא Gn 3^{6}+; 1 s. אֶרְאֶה 21^{16}+, וָאֵ֫רֶא 31^{10}+, etc.; *Imv.* רְאֵה 27^{27}+, etc.; *Inf.*
abs. רָאֹה Ex 3^{7}+, רָאוֹ Gn 26^{28} Is 6^{9}; cstr. רְאֹה
Gn 48^{11}, רְאוֹת Ex 10^{28}+, רַאֲוָה Ez 28^{17}, etc.; *Pt.* 7207
act. רֹאֶה Gn 13^{15}+, etc.; *pass.* רְאֻיוֹת (Baer Gi; 7203
van d. H. רְאוּיוֹת):—**1. a.** *see*, subj. עַיִן, עֵינַיִם, c. acc. pers. Is 6^{5} 30^{20} Je 42^{2} + 5 t. Jb Pr; subj. pers., c. acc. pers. Gn 12$^{12.15}$+ (מִי רָאָהוּ 1 S 23^{22}, rd. הַמְּהֵרָה 𝔊 Th We al. [not HPS]); רֹאִי 16^{13} (pt. sf., cf. בְּאֵר לַחַי רֹאִי v^{14}, p. 91 supr.); acc. of God 32^{31} (פָּנִים אֶל־פָּנִים); acc. pers. om. 18^{2} 19^{1}+; c. acc. פְּנֵי 31^{2} 46^{30} 48^{11} Ex 33^{20}, opp. אֶת־אֲחֹרָי v^{23}; c. acc. פְּנֵי specif. of having access to man of rank Gn 43$^{3.5}$+ (v. [פָּנֶה] **2 b**). **b.** *see*, c. acc. rei: subj. עַיִן, עֵינַיִם Jos 24^{7} (E) 1 S 24^{11} (van d. H. Baer; v^{10} Gi), Dt 3^{21} + 5 t. Dt, +; וְעֵינָיו אֶת־עֵינָיו תִּרְאֶינָה Je 32^{4}, cf. 34^{3}; acc. om. 2 S 24^{3} Dt 21^{7} + 9 t. (לִרְאוֹת 1 S 6^{13} rd. לִקְרָאתוֹ 𝔊 We Dr Kit Bu HPS Now); subj. pers. Gn 13^{15} 31^{12} + very oft.; c. acc. cogn. מַרְאֶה Ex 3^{3} + 7 t., מַרְאָה Dn 10$^{7.7.8}$, חָזוֹן 8^{15}, חֶזְיֹנוֹת Jo 3^{1}; hence *see* abs. =

receive revelation, Is 30[10] (|| חזה), cf. Ez 13[3] and
v. 1. רֹאֶה; c. acc. עֶרְוָה, v. ע׳, p. 788 f.; *see* war,
i.e. see it impending Ex 13[17] (E); ר׳ אֶת־הַקּוֹלֹת
וְאֶת־הַלַּפִּידִים 20[18] (Gi v[15]); רֹאֵי הַשָּׁמֶשׁ Ec 7[11] *those
who see the sun*=living men; acc. rei om. Ex
22[9] 2 S 13[5]+, וָאֶרְאֶה בֶּחָזוֹן Dn 8[2.2] (abs.); לֹא יֵדְעוּ
וְלֹא יִרְאוּ Ne 4[5]; עֵינֵי רֹאִים Is 32[3], מְקוֹם רֹאִים Jb
34[26]; c. adv. or adv. phr. instead of acc. rei:
כָּהֵנָּה Gn 41[19] cf. Is 66[8], Ez 1[27.27], כַּאֲשֶׁר 2 K 2[19]
2 Ch 29[8] 30[7] Jb 4[8] Ez 16[50] Dn 1[13], כֵּן ψ 48[9]. **2.**
see, sq. acc.+cl. or phr. of closer design.: (1)
+epex. cl. c. כִּי, acc. pers. Gn 6[2] *saw* them *that
they were fair*, 12[4] (both J), Ex 2[2] 32[25] (both E),
1 K 11[28], acc. of face+*id.* Gn 31[5] (E), Ex 34[25]
(P); acc. rei Gn 49[15] (poem), Is 22[9] Gn 1[4] (P),
Ec 2[24] 4[4] and prob. 2 K 14[26] (rdg. כִּי מַר הוּא);
(2) ר׳ כָּל־הַבָּא עָלָיו וְעָמָד 2 S 20[12]; (3)+adj.
(incl. pt.), acc. pers. Gn 7[1] (J), Am 9[1] 2 S 18[10]
+39 t. (Je 46[5] del. ר׳ 𝔊 Gie), +acc. אֲשֶׁר Ex
14[13.13] (J); acc. rei, †Ex 23[5] 33[10] (both E), Dt
22[4] Ez 33[3.6] Dn 1[10] 8[4.6.7]; †(4)+מָה, acc. rei
Nu 13[18] (JE), Hg 2[3]; †(5)+prep. phr., acc.
pers. Ex 5[19] (J), Zc 4[10] Ec 10[7] Est 5[9]; acc. rei
בִּכְבוֹדוֹ+ Hg 2[3], +ב pers. Je 23[13.14], +כ pers.
Ju 9[36], כ rei 2 S 18[27]; (6) acc. pers.+adv. acc.
+כ pers. Je 30[6]. **3.** *see*, so as to learn to
know: c. acc. pers. Dt 33[9] (|| יָדַע, הִכִּיר); c. acc.
rei Dt 1[19.31] 11[2] Jb 11[11] (|| יָדַע), ψ 16[10] 49[10]; =have
experience of, Je 5[12] 14[13] 20[18] 42[14] Zp 3[15] ψ 89[49]
Ec 5[17], שֵׁנָה בְּעֵינָיו אֵינֶנּוּ רֹאֶה Ec 8[16]; מָה רָאִיתָ Gn
20[10] i.e. *what hast thou encountered, that . . . ?*
Bacher ZAW xix (1899), 345 ff.; Terminol. 177 f. **4.** abs. *see*,
have (power of) *vision*, Gn 27[1] (J), 48[10] (E),
1 S 3[2] 4[15] 1 K 14[4], miraculous 2 K 6[17.17.20.20];
denied of idols Dt 4[28] ψ 115[5] 135[16]; fig. of
spiritual vision Is 6[10] 29[18] 42[18] 44[18] Je 5[21] Dt 29[3]
Ez 12[2.2] ψ 40[13] 69[24]; עַיִן רֹאָה Pr 20[12].—1 S 14[27]
rd. Qr v. אור. **5.** *see*=perceive: **a.** sq. cl.
c. כִּי, Ex 3[4] 8[11] Gn 1[10.12]+oft. (1 S 23[15] rd. וַיִּרָא *and
he feared* We Dr Kit Bu HPS Now); om. כִּי (late)
†La 1[10] ψ 49[11] Ec 3[16]; sq. מָה of indirect question
Gn 2[19] (J), 37[20] (E), Ju 9[48] Dt 32[20] Je 7[17] 33[24]
Ez 8[6] Jon 4[5]+; בַּמָּה Ju 16[5] cf. 1 S 14[38], כַּמָּה Zc 2[6]
ψ 35[17]; sq. מִי of indirect question 1 S 14[17] Is 40[26]
La 2[20] (+הַבִּיטָה); sq. אֵי 1 S 26[16], אֵיכֹה 2 K 6[13],
אֵיפֹה Je 3[2]; sq. cl. c. הֲ *whether*, Gn 8[8] 18[21] Nu
11[23] (all J), Ex 4[18] (E), ψ 14[2] 53[3] Ct 6[11b] Est 3[4],
אִם *whether* Je 30[6] La 1[12] ψ 139[24] Ct 7[13], אֲשֶׁר
that or *how* 1 S 18[15], אֵי Ec 2[3], שֶׁ *that* v[13], שֶׁ 3[18].
b. c. acc. צָרַת נַפְשׁוֹ Gn 42[21] (i.e. saw it by outward signs), cf. Ho 5[13]. [*Note*, under **5** (rarely
in other cases, and only S K Je), †Imv.+ידע
Imv.: דַּע וּרְאֵה 1 S 24[12] 2 S 24[13] 1 K 20[22]; דְּעִי וּרְאִי
1 S 25[17] Je 2[19]; דְּעוּ וּרְאוּ 1 S 12[17] 14[38] 23[22] 1 K
20[7] 2 K 5[7]; in reverse order, רְאוּ וּדְעוּ 1 S 23[23]
Je 5[1].] **6.** *look at, see*, by direct volition:
a. subj. men, c. acc. rei, Gn 9[22.23] (J), 42[9.12] (E),
Lv 13[3.15]+; c. acc. of land=reconnoitre Jos 2[1];
look at sun, etc., for worship †Dt 4[19] Jb 31[26];
=inspect 1 K 9[12] Lv 14[36.36]; c. acc. pers. Nu
24[20.21] (JE), Ex 2[25] Lv 13[3.5] (all P), 1 S 9[16]+,
(1 S 19[15] HPS prop. אֶל־בֵּית for לִרְאוֹת); c. prep.
ר׳ אַחֲרֵי רֹאִי Gn 16[13] (J) *I have looked after one
seeing me* (interpr. v. Di). **b.** subj. God, c. acc.
rei Gn 9[16] (P); =inspect 11[5] (J); *look at* with
favour, acc. pers. Jb 37[24] ψ 138[6]; so perh. fig.,
subj. man, *regard*, c. acc. אָוֶן ψ 66[18] (Hup-Now;
Che Bae Dr al. *intend*); *look* with pleasure (acc.
om., +מִן *by reason of, as a fruit of*) Is 53[11]
(si vera l.; ins. acc. אור 𝔊 Houb Klo Du Che [Hpt]
Kit [perh.], with Hiph. יַרְאֶה 𝔊 Du Che [Hpt],
rescues from travail his soul, *makes it see light*).
c. without acc., *look, take a look*, etc. (of man
and God; oft.+(וְ)הִנֵּה), Gn 8[13] 18[2] Ex 3[2] Lv 13[8]
La 3[50] (מִן loc.), Gn 13[14] (מִן loc.+ה loc.), Dt 3[27]
Ez 40[4] 44[5] (all בְּעֵינֶיךָ), +oft.; peculiarly, מִמֶּנִּי
תִּרְאוּ וְכֵן תַּעֲשׂוּ Ju 7[17] (cf. GFM). **d.** *look after,
see after, learn about*, c. acc. rei Gn 37[14] (J), c.
acc. pers.=visit (go to *see*) 1 S 15[35] 20[29] 2 S 13[5.6]
2 K 8[29]=2 Ch 22[6], 2 K 9[16], cf. Ez 20[28], עֵין רֹאִי
Jb 7[8] (Di Bu al.). **e.** *observe, watch*, abs., 1 S
6[9.16] 17[28] Ec 8[16] (|| ידע). **f.** *look upon*=endure
to see, c. acc. rei Hb 1[13] (|| הַבִּיט). **g.** *look out,
find out*, acc. pers. 2 K 9[2], Gn 41[33] (E), +ל pers.
1 S 16[17]; *select*, acc. pers.+מִן *from among* 2 K
10[3], +ב among+ל pers. 1 S 16[1]; *provide, furnish*, c. acc. rei Dt 33[21] (poem), +ל pers. Gn 22[8] 3070
(E), cf. abs. י׳ יִרְאֶה as n.pr.loc.=י׳ *seeth* v[14a] (E;
? read יֵרָאֶה, cf. v[b], **Niph.** and Di); רְאֻיוֹת Est 2[9]
looked out=suitable (as oft. NH). **h.** *look
at*=concern oneself about, acc. rei (+בְּיָדוֹ)
Gn 39[23] (J). **7.** of mental observation: **a.**
Imv. see! observe! consider! exclam. (nearly
=הִנֵּה), sq. cl.: Gn 27[27] 31[50] *see! God is witness*
39[14] 41[41] Ex 4[21] Dt 1[8]+; sq. nom. independ.
2 S 24[22] (|| 1 Ch 21[23] sq. cl.). **b.** *look at*, i.e.
inquire into, a matter, acc. rei om., of י׳, 1 S
24[16] (Gi v[15]). **c.** *give attention to*, acc. rei, Je 2[31],
abs. *give attention!* 2 S 13[28] 2 K 6[32] Ex 25[40]
ψ 45[11]; *take heed to*, acc. rei, 1 K 12[16]=2 Ch 10[16];
abs. *take heed!* Ex 10[10], +פֶּן 2 K 10[23]. **d.**
discern, לִבִּי ר׳ חָכְמָה Ec 1[16], ר׳ טוֹב 3[13]. **e.** *distinguish*, c. בֵּין...לְ of pers. Mal 3[18]. **f.** *consider,
reflect*, Ec 7[14] (sq. cl. orat. rect.). †**8. a.** c. ב, lit.,
look into, hence *look at* with interest (Germ.

'sich vertiefen in'): (1) *gaze at* 1 S 6^{19} (on
context v. We Dr HPS), so as to become
acquainted with Gn 34^{1} (P); so as to find out
Ec 3^{22}; *inspect* liver (for omens) Ez 21^{26}; somewhat weakened = *behold* Jb 3^{9} 2 Ch 7^{3} ψ 64^{9}.
(2) *look at* with kindness, helpfulness, of 'י,
בְּעֳנִי Gn 29^{32} 1 S 1^{11} (+inf. abs.), 2 S 16^{12}, בַּצַּר
ψ 106^{44}. (3) upon a spectacle causing anger
Ex 2^{11} (E), grief Gn 21^{16} (E), 44^{34} Nu 11^{15} (both
J), 2 K 22^{20} (subj. עֵינַיִם) = 2 Ch 34^{28}, Est 8$^{6.6}$,
abhorrence Is 66^{24}. (4) *gaze at* with appre-
hension Ec 11^{4}. (5) with joy, pleasure, 2 K
10^{16} Mi 7^{9} Je 29^{32} Is 52^{8} (עַיִן בְּעַיִן, cf. **Niph.** Nu
14^{14}), Jb 20^{17} 33^{28} ψ 54^{9} 106^{5} 128^{5} Ct 3^{11} 6^{11a}
Ec 2^{1}. (6) esp. with exultation, triumph =
feast eyes upon, sts. *gloat over* (fallen enemies),
7207 Ju 16^{27} Mi 7^{10} Ez 28^{17} Ob$^{12.13}$ ψ 22^{18} 112^{8} 118^{7}.
b. c. אֶל pers. Is 17^{7} (subj. עֵינַיִם || שָׁעָה עַל);
עַל pers. Ex 5^{21} (J); ר׳ עַל־הָאָבְנָיִם Ex 1^{16} v. [אֹבֶן]
and Comm., also Spiegelb $^{ZA\ xiv\ (June\ 1900),\ 269\ ff.}$ **c.**
c. ל, מִי 1 S 16^{7}, הָאָדָם יִר׳ לַעֵינַיִם וַיהוה יִר׳ לַלֵּבָב
וּרְאִיתַנִי כְּתוֹר הָאָדָם ψ 64^{6}.—Corrupt is יִרְאֶה־לָּמוֹ
1 Ch 17^{17} (and || וְזֹאת תּוֹרַת הָאָדָם 2 S 7^{19}), read
וַתַּרְאֵנִי (with other changes) We Dr Kau Bu HPS
Now; Ez 12^{12} read prob. **Niph.** 𝔊 Hi Co Krae;
Mi 6^{9} read prob. יִרְאָה cf. Now GASm. **Niph.**
Pf. 3 ms. נִרְאָה Gn 48^{3}+, etc.; *Impf.* 3 ms. יֵרָאֶה
Gn 22^{14}+, juss. יֵרָא Ex 34^{3} Lv 9^{6}, וַיֵּרָא Gn 12^{7}+;
1 s. וָאֵרָא Ex 6^{3}, etc.; *Imv.* ms. הֵרָאֵה 1 K 18^{1};
Inf. cstr. לְהֵרָאוֹת 1 S 17^{17}+, לֵרָאוֹת Is 1^{12}+ 2 t.,
הֵרָאֹה Ju 13^{21} 1 S 3^{21}, etc.;—**1.** *appear*, esp. **a.**
of 'י (God): c. אֶל pers. Gn 12$^{7.7}$+6 t. J, Gn 35^{1}
(E), v^{9} 48^{3} Ex 6^{3} (בְּאֵל שַׁדָּי, ב essent.), Lv 9^{4} (all
P), 1 K 3^{5} 9$^{2.2}$= 2 Ch 7^{12}, 1 K 11^{9}; c. ל pers. Je
31^{3} 2 Ch 1^{7} 3^{1} (ins. 'י 𝔊 Kau Kit); abs. Gn 22^{14}
in the mt. where 'י *appeareth* (prob., Di Sta $^{G\ i.\ 450}$ Dr $^{Hast.\ DB\ ii.\ 563}$; E), Nu 14^{14} (JE; עַיִן בְּעַיִן,
v. Is 52^{8} **Qal 8 a** (5)), Lv 16^{2} (P; ב loc. + עַל),
1 S 3^{21} (ב loc.), 2 S 22^{11} (וַיֵּרָא < עַל־כַּנְפֵי־רוּחַ || ψ
18^{11}), +5 t.; of מַלְאַךְ י׳, c. אֶל pers. Ex 3^{2} (E),
Ju 13^{21}; of כְּבוֹד י׳; c. אֶל pers. Lv 9$^{6.23}$ Nu 14^{10}
(ב loc.), 16^{19} 20^{6} (all P), Ju 6^{12} 13^{3}; עַל pers. Is
60^{2}; abs. Ex 16^{10} (ב loc.), Nu 17^{7} (both P).
b. *appear*, of man, = *present oneself*: c. אֶל pers.
Gn 46^{29} (J), Ju 13^{10} 1 K 18$^{1.2.15}$ Lv 13$^{7.7.19}$, אֶל of
God ψ 84^{8} (ב loc.), אֶל־פְּנֵי הָאָדֹן Ex 23^{17} (E);
abs. Is 16^{12} (del. as dittogr. Lo Du Che ^{Hpt} Marti
al.); esp. (Mass.) sq. (אֶת־)פְּנֵי of 'י, rendered
appear before 'י: so וְנִרְאָה 1 S 1^{22}, יֵרָאֶה Ex 34^{23}
(JE), Dt 16^{16}, וְאֵרָאֶה ψ 42^{3}, יֵרָאוּ Ex 23^{15} (E),
34^{20} (JE), Dt 16^{16}, לֵרָאוֹת Ex 34^{24} (JE), Dt 31^{11}
Is 1^{12}; read prob. in all **Qal** (v. [פָּנֶה] II. **2**).

c. *appear*, of things: late (Hex only P), abs. Gn 1^{9} 8^{5}, c. ב loc. 9^{14} Lv 13$^{14.57}$; elsewhere poet. ψ 18^{16}= 2 S 22^{16}, ψ 90^{16} Pr 27^{25} (of דֶּשֶׁא), Ct 2^{12} (ב loc.; of blossoms); subj. מַרְאֵיהֶם Dn 1^{15} (+adj. pred.), v^{13} (+לְפָנֶיךָ); subj. חָזוֹן, c. אֶל pers. Dn 8$^{1.1}$; subj. כְּנֶגַע Lv 14^{35} (c. ל pers.). **2.** *be seen*: **a.** subj. rei, 1 K 10^{12}= 2 Ch 9^{11} (where כָּהֵם subj.) Ez 19^{11}, of sins 21^{29} (|| הִגָּלוֹת), subj. כָּזֹאת Ju 19^{30}, כְּאֶבֶן etc. Ez 10^{1}. **b.** subj. pers. 2 S 17^{17} (+לָבוֹא) *be seen to come*. **c.** *be seen* = occur 2 K 23^{24} (ב loc.); = exist, + ל pers. Ex 13$^{7.7}$ (JE), Dt 16^{4}, cf. Ez 10^{8}; = be present, + ב loc. Ju 5^{8} Ex 34^{3} (JE). **3.** *be visible*, Ex 33^{23} (JE; subj. 'י's face), אֵין אֶבֶן נִרְאָה 1 K 6^{18}, 8$^{8.8}$= 2 Ch 5$^{9.9}$, Je 13^{26} Is 47^{3}. †**Pu.** *Pf.* 3 pl. עַצְמֹתָיו לֹא רֻאּוּ Jb 33^{21} (Baer Gi; d. f. Ki Kö $^{i.\ 41,\ 563}$, Mappiḳ Ges $^{§\ 14\ d}$; van d. H. רֻאוּ), appar. *his bones are not seen, detected*; De *which were* (formerly) *not seen*; Di *are insignificant* ('unscheinbar'), so Bae; prob. corrupt, Bu נָאוּ, Du del. as doublet. †**Hithp.** recipr. *look at each other*: *Impf.* 2 mpl. לָמָּה תִּתְרָאוּ Gn 42^{1} (E); techn. 3 mpl. וַיִּתְרָאוּ פָנִים 2 K 14^{11}= 2 Ch 25^{21} *and they looked each other in the face*, i.e. met in combat, so 1 pl. נִתְרָאֶה פ׳ 2 K 14^{8}= 2 Ch 25^{17}, cf. (perhaps) 2 K 23^{29}, where Wkl Benz conj. כְּהִתְרָאוֹת אִתּוֹ (or **Niph.** כְּהֵרָאוֹת אִתּוֹ) for MT כִּרְאֹתוֹ אֹתוֹ. **Hiph.** $_{62}$ *Pf.* 3 ms. הֶרְאָה Gn 41^{28}+, sf. הִרְאַנִי Am 7^{1}+, הֶרְאָנִי Ez 11^{25}, הֶרְאָנוּ Dt 5^{21} Ju 13^{23}, הָרְאֵךָ Dt 4^{36}; 1 s. וְהִרְאִיתִי Na 3^{5} (Ges $^{§\ 53\ p}$), sf. הֶרְאִיתִיךָ Dt 34^{4}, הִרְאִיתִים Is 39^{4} cf. || 2 K 20^{15}, etc.; *Impf.* 3 ms. יַרְאֶה Is 30^{30}, וַיַּרְא 2 K 11^{4}, sf. יַרְאֵנִי Nu 23^{3} ψ 59^{11}; 1 s. sf. אַרְאֶךָּ Gn 12^{1}+, etc.; *Imv.* ms. sf. הַרְאֵנִי Ex 33^{18}, etc.; *Inf. cstr.* הַרְאוֹת Dt 3^{24}+, sf. לְרַאֹתְכֶם Dt 1^{33}, הַרְאוֹתְכָה Ez 40^{4}, etc.; *Pt.* מַרְאֶה Ex 25^{9} Ez 40^{4};—**1. a.** *cause one to see* something, *shew*: (1) subj. man, c. acc. pers. + rei, Nu 13^{26b} (JE), Ju 1$^{24.25}$ 2 K 20$^{13.13.15}$= Is 39$^{2.2.4}$+4 t., acc. rei om. Ez 40^{4} Est 4^{8}, acc. refl. נַפְשׁוֹ + acc. rei Ec 2^{24}; מִי יַרְאֵנוּ טוֹב ψ 4^{7}, acc. pers. om., = *exhibit* Est 1^{4}; c. 2 acc. pers. Ju 4^{22} 2 K 11^{4}. (2) especially subj. 'י (God), c. acc. pers. + rei, Gn 12^{1} Ex 9^{16} (both J), Gn 41^{28} 48^{11} (both E), Ex 33^{18} Dt 34^{1b} (both JE), Dt 3^{24} 4^{36} 5^{21} Jos 5^{6} (D), Ex 25^{9} (P), Ju 13^{23}+5 t. + (of revelation to prophets) Nu 23^{3} (JE), Je 38^{21} Ez 11^{25}, also, c. acc. rei cogn., Nu 8^{4} (P), acc. rei om. Dt 34^{4} (JE), acc. pers. om. = *exhibit*, Is 30^{30}; of visions, 'י subj., c. acc. pers. + כֹּה Am 7$^{1.4.7}$ 8^{1}, + כַּאֲשֶׁר Ex 27^{8} (P), c. acc. pers. only = *cause to see* [a vision] Je 24^{1}; c. 2 acc. pers. + appos. 2 K 8^{13}, acc. pers. + cl. c. כִּי v^{10}. (3) subj. angel, acc. pers.

+rei, of revelation to prophet Zc 2^{3} 3^{1}; acc. pers. + cl. c. מָה Zc 1^{9}. **b.** *cause to experience* something, c. acc. pers. + rei, subj. 'י, Hb 1^{3} ψ 60^{5} 71^{20} 85^{8}. †**2.** *cause to look intently at, to behold*, c. acc. pers. + ב rei (cf. **Qal 8**), subj. 'י: **a.** *cause to gaze at*, with joy ψ 50^{23} 91^{16}. **b.** in exultation, *cause to feast one's eyes upon*, fallen enemies ψ 59^{11} (cf. MI^{7}). **c.** in weakened sense, *cause to behold* Dt 1^{33} (cf. Dr). †**Hoph. 1.** *be caused to see, be shewn*: *Pf.* 2 ms. הָרְאֵיתָ, subj. man, acc. rei, Ex 26^{30} (P; ב loc.); so *Pt.* מָרְאֶה 25^{40} (P; ב loc.); sq. inf. אַתָּה הָרְאֵתָ לָדַעַת כִּי Dt 4^{35}. **2.** *be exhibited to*, subj. rei, acc. pers., *Pf.* 3 ms. consec. וְהָרְאָה אֶת־הַכֹּהֵן Lv 13^{49} (P).

7202 †[רָאֶה] **adj. seeing**, assumed by Thes al. to explain cstr. וּרְאֵה עָנְיִי Jb 10^{15}, but improb.; Mass. appar. intended *Imv.* (unsuitable); Ew al. וְרֹאֶה; Di Bu Du (after Lag Gei) רְוֵה עָנְיִ *drenched* (i.e. sated) *with affliction*.

7203 †I. רֹאֶה **n.[m.]** seer, c. art. הָר׳ (exc. 2 S 15^{27});—old name for נָבִיא 1 S 9^{9b}, used of Sam. $v^{9a.11.18.19}$ and (as archaism) 1 Ch 9^{22} 26^{28} 29^{29}; of חֲנָנִי 2 Ch $16^{7.10}$; הֲרוֹאֶה appar. of Zadok 2 S 15^{27}, but crpt. (conj. in We Dr); pl. (c. prep.) לָרֹאִים Is 30^{10} *the seers*, as a class.

7203 †II. רֹאֶה **n.[m.]** prophetic **vision** שָׁגוּ בָּר׳ Is 28^{7} *they reel in* (their) *vision* (|| פָּקוּ פְּלִילִיָּה).

7204,7211 †III. רֹאֶה **n.pr.m.** 1 Ch 2^{52}, v. רְאָיָה infr.

7200,7207 †רַאֲוָה Ez 28^{17} v. √ **Qal** *Inf.*, and **8 a** (6).
p. 906-08

7212 †רְאוּת **n.f.** look;—cstr. רְאוּת עֵינָיו Ec 5^{10}
7212 Qr (Kt ראית).

7209 †רְאִי **n.m.** mirror;—כִּר׳ מוּצָק Jb 37^{18} (sim.).

7210 †רֳאִי **n.[m.]** looking, seeing, sight;—**1.** *seeing*, אֵל ר׳ Gn 16^{13a} *a God of seeing* (= who sees). **2.** *appearance* (= מַרְאֶה), טוֹב רֳאִי 1 S 16^{12}; מֵרֹאִי Jb 33^{21} *without* (healthy, fair) *appearance*. **3.** *sight*, (warning-) *spectacle*, כְּרֹאִי Na 3^{6}.—ר׳ Gn 16^{13b} Jb 7^{8} is **Qal** *Pt.* sf.

7212 ראית v. רְאוּת above

4759 †I. מַרְאָה **n.f. vision**, as means of revelation: מ׳ abs. Nu 12^{6} (E), 1 S 3^{15} Dn 10^{16}, as acc. cogn. $v^{7.7.8}$; appar. pl. abs. מַרְאוֹת Ez 43^{3}, but rd. מַרְאֵה הָרֶכֶב 𝔊 Co Berthol Siegf Krae, or del. Toy Krae (as altern.); cstr. מַרְאֹת הַלַּיְלָה Gn 46^{2} (E), מַרְאוֹת אֱלֹהִים Ez 1^{1} 8^{3} 40^{2}.

†II. [מַרְאָה] **n.f.** mirror (so Vrss; as 4759
place, or *instrument, of seeing* (oneself));—pl. cstr. מַרְאֹת הַצֹּבְאֹת Ex 38^{8} (P) *the mirrors of the serving-women* (v. Di).

מַרְאֶה 102 **n.m.** Ex 3,3 **sight, appearance,** 4758
vision;—מ׳ abs. Gn 12^{11}+; cstr. מַרְאֵה Dt 28^{34}+; sf. מַרְאֵהוּ Jo 2^{4}+, מַרְאֶהָ Lv 13^{4}+; appar. pl. cstr. מַרְאֵי Ec 11^{9} (Kö ii. 1, 112), sf. (prob. in fact sg. Ges §93 ss) מַרְאַיִךְ Ct $2^{14.14}$, מַרְאֵיהֶן Na 2^{5}+, etc.;—**1.** †**a.** *sight, phenomenon, spectacle* Ex 3^{3} (J). **b.** *appearance* נֶחְמָד לְמ׳ Gn 2^{9} (J) *desirable in appearance*, גָּדוֹל לְמ׳ Jos 22^{10}; *appearance* of man (or woman), Ju $13^{6.6}$ (angel), Is 52^{14} (servant of 'י), Ct 5^{15} Dn 8^{15} 10^{18}; = outward person (opp. inner man) 1 S 16^{7}; visible form Ct $2^{14.14}$ Dn $1^{13.13.15}$; בְּמ׳ Nu 12^{8} (E; so rd. Sam 𝔊 𝔖 𝔗 Di, for MT מַרְאֶה), i.e. in personal presence (< Ew Pat^{Hpt} (לֹא בְמ׳); כְּמַרְאֵה סוּסִים מַרְאֵהוּ Jo 2^{4}; of crocod. Jb 41^{2}; מ׳ כְּבוֹד י׳ Ex 24^{17} (P), מ׳ הַנֶּגַע Lv 13^{3}, מ׳־אֵשׁ Nu $9^{15.16}$, מ׳ בָּרָק Dn 10^{6}+; esp. Ez *appearance* pers. vel rei (27 t., sts. redundant), $1^{5.13.26}$ 8^{2} 10^{1}+, מִמ׳ מָתְנָיו $1^{27.27}$ 8^{2} (|| מִמָּתְנָיו); of beauty יְפֵה מַרְאֶה *fair of appearance* Gn 39^{6} (J; + יְפֵה־תֹאַר), cf. 1 S 17^{42} (rd. עֶלֶם [q.v.] for עִם); fem. (אִשָּׁה) יְפַת־מ׳ Gn 12^{11} (J), 29^{17} (E; יְפַת תֹּאַר +), 2 S 14^{27}; of kine יְפוֹת (הַ)מ׳ Gn $41^{2.4}$ (E), opp. רָעוֹת (הַ)מ׳ $v^{3.4}$, מַרְאֵיהֶן רַע v^{21} (all E); of women also טֹבַת מ׳ Gn 24^{16} 26^{7} (both J), 2 S 11^{2} Est 1^{11} $2^{3.7}$, טוֹבוֹת מ׳ 2^{2}; of boys טוֹבֵי מ׳ Dn 1^{4}, cf. מ׳ alone in לֹא־מ׳ וְנֶחְמְדֵהוּ (of suffering servant of 'י) Is 53^{2}; אִישׁ מ׳ 2 S 23^{21} (but rd. as || 1 Ch 11^{23} אִישׁ מִדָּה We Dr al.). †**c.** *appearance, sight, vision* Nu 8^{4} (P). †**2.** in gen. *what is seen*, מ׳ עֵינָיו Is 11^{3} i.e. what his outward eyes see (cf. 1 S 16^{7} **1 b**), לְמ׳ עֵינֶיהָ Ez 23^{16}, מ׳ עֵינֶיךָ אֲשֶׁר תִּרְאֶה Dt $28^{34.67}$, לְכָל־מ׳ עֵינֵי הַכֹּהֵן Lv 13^{12} (P). †**3.** specif. *a* (supernat.) *vision* (in Ez Dn; oft. acc. cogn. c. ראה): Ez 8^{4} 11^{24} $43^{3.3.3}$, rd. also מַרְאֵה הָרֶכֶב v^{3} (for מַרְאוֹת v. I. מַרְאָה supr.); בַּמ׳ 11^{24}; Dn $8^{16.27}$ 9^{23} 10^{1}; מ׳ הָעֶרֶב וְהַבֹּקֶר 8^{26}. †**4.** *sight, vision* = power of seeing (and enjoying), lato ı מ׳ עֵינַיִם Ec 6^{9}, הַלֵּךְ בְּדַרְכֵי לִבְּךָ וּבְמַ׳ עֵינֶיךָ 11^{9}.

†יְרִאִיָּה **n.pr.m.** (rd. יְרִאִיָּה; 'י *seeth*);— 3376
officer, Jeremiah's time, Je $37^{13.14}$, Σαρουια(ς).

†רְאָיָה **n.pr.m.** ('י *hath seen*);—**1.** Judaite 7211
1 Ch 4^{2} (Ρε..α, A Ρεια, 𝔊L Ρεαα), = III. הָרֹאֶה 2^{52} (crpt.; Αι.. A Αραα). **2.** Reubenite 1 Ch 5^{5}, Ρηχα, 𝔊L .αια. **3.** post-ex. name Ezr 2^{47} (Ρεηλ, A 𝔊L Ρε.α) = Ne 7^{50} (Ραεα, A 𝔊L Ρααια).

7205 **רְאוּבֵן** 71 **n.pr.m.** **Reuben**, Ρουβην[ιν] (*behold a son!* but Gn 29[32] makes = רָאָה בְּעָנְיִי (!); Jos[Ant. i. 19, 7 al.] Ρουβηλος, 𝔖 ܪܘܒܝܠ, ר׳ then perh. = Ar. رِيبَال *lion*, cf. Di);—**1.** eldest son of Jacob and Leah Gn 29[32] 30[14] + 11 t. Gn, Ex 1[2] 1 Ch 2[1]; as head of family or clan Ex 6[14.14] Nu 1[20] 26[5] (all P), 1 Ch 5[1.3], cf. בְּנֵי אֱלִיאָב בֶּן־רְא׳ Dt 11[6]. **2.** as name of clan or tribe Ju 5[15.16] Dt 27[13] Jos 18[7] (+ גָּד; both D), Dt 33[6] (poem), Ez 48[6.7.31] Nu 1[5] (P); so מַטֵּה ר׳ Nu 1[21] 13[4] Jos 20[8] 21[7] (all P), 1 Ch 6[48.63], מַחֲנֵה ר׳ Nu 2[10.16] 10[18] (all P); בְּנֵי ר׳, as tribe, Nu 16[1b] 32[37] (both JE), 2[10] 7[20] 26[5] Jos 13[23.23] (all P), also (+ Gad and oft. Manasseh) Nu 32[1.2.6.25] (JE), Jos 4[12] (D), Nu 32[29.31.33] Jos 22[9] + 11 t. 22 (all P), cf. 1 Ch 5[18]; בֶּן־ר׳ as tribe Jos 15[6] 18[7] (both P), מַטֵּה בְנֵי־ר׳ 13[15] (P).

7206 †**רְאוּבֵנִי** **adj. gent.** of foreg.; of individ. 1 Ch 11[42a]; c. art. as subst. coll. הָרְאוּבֵנִי Nu 26[7] 34[14] (both P), Jos 13[8] (D; + הַגָּדִי), 2 K 10[33] (+ *id.* + הַמְנַשִּׁי), 1 Ch 12[38] (van d. H. v[37]; + הַגָּדִי + חֲצִי שֵׁבֶט מְנַשֶּׁה), 26[32] (*id.*); לָרְאוּבֵנִי 1 Ch 5[6] 27[16], + וְלַגָּדִי (+ sts. חֲצִי שֵׁבֶט מ׳) Dt 3[12.16] 29[7] Jos 1[12] 12[6] 22[1] (all D), 1 Ch 5[26], cf. Dt 4[43].

7209-12 **רְאוּת, רְאִי, רֹאִי, רְאָיָה, רְאִית** v. ראה. p. 909

7214, 7223 **רְאֵים** v. רְאֵם. **רִאישׁוֹן** v. רִאשׁוֹן. p. 911, below

7213 †[**רָאַם**] **vb.** (Mass Thes al.) **rise** (si vera l., ‖ form of רום);—**Qal** *Pf.* 3 fs. רָאֲמָה Zc

7311, 7414 14[10], but < rd. רָאֲמָה = רָמָה (√ רום), Ges[§ 72 p].

7214 †**רְאֵם** **n.m.**[Jb 39, 10] **wild ox** (As. *rêmu* Dl HWB 603 (ראם), Houghton[TSBA v (1877), 336 ff., and illustr. bef. p. 33] Schr[KGF 135 ff., 530] Hom[NS 257 ff., 410, 436 f.] Dr[Dt 33, 17]; on strength and ferocity, Plin[NH viii. 21]; Aram. רְאֵמָא, רֵימָא, רֵימָנָא, ܪܶܐܡܳܐ (Lag[BN 58]); Ar. رِئْم is *white antelope*, antilope leucoryx; 𝔊 (erron.) μονοκέρως (Is 34[7] ἁδροι), 𝔙 *unicornis*, and (oftener) *rhinoceros*);—abs. ר׳ Nu 23[22] +, רְאֵים ψ 92[11], רֵים Jb 39[9.10]; pl. רְאֵמִים Is 34[7] ψ 29[6], רֵמִים 22[22] (v. Baer);—*wild ox*, as fierce and strong Jb 39[9.10]; sim. of strength of Isr., כְּתוֹעֲפוֹת ר׳ לוֹ Nu 23[22] = 24[8] (JE), וַתָּרֶם כִּרְאֵים קַרְנִי ψ 92[11]; so fig. of Joseph, קַרְנֵי ר׳ קַרְנָיו Dt 33[17]; fig. of princes of Edom Is 34[7] (+ פָּרִים עִם אַבִּירִים); of powerful foes, מִקַּרְנֵי רֵמִים ψ 22[22]; in sim. of skipping, leaping, בֶּן־רְאֵמִים ψ 29[6] (‖ עֵגֶל).

7208 †**רְאוּמָה** **n.pr.f.** concubine of Nahor Gn 22[23] (J); A Ρεηρα, 𝔊L Ρεημα.

†I. **רָאמוֹת** **n.[f.pl.]** usu. **corals** (so Ki; 7215
black corals Thes (פְּנִינִים = *red corals*); cf. Ar. رَأْمَةٌ *sea-shell*, We[Heid. 2. 163]);—as costly Jb 28[18], as merchandise, רָאמֹת Ez 27[16];—רָאמוֹת לֶאֱוִיל חָכְמוֹת Pr 24[7], reading and sense dub., v. Toy.

רָאמָה, II. **רָאמוֹת**, **רָאמַת** v. רום, II. רמה. 7213, 7216,
above, p. 728, 926, 928 7414, 7418

רָאשׁ *poor*, **רֵאשׁ** *poverty*, v. רוש. p. 930 7326, 7389

I. **רֹאשׁ** 599 **n.m.**[Lv 13, 45] **head** (common Sem. 7218
word; earliest form *ra'š, Ar. رَأْس, Sab. ראס Prä[ZMG xxix (1875), 425] Mordtm[Him. Inschr. 31]; Eth. ርእስ: Amh. ራስ: hence (*a* heightened) As. *rêšu* (rarely *râšu*), Aram. רֵישָׁא (Egypt. Aram. ראש Cooke[North-Sem. Inscr. 404]), ܪܺܫܳܐ, mod. (*Ma'lûla*) *raïša*, Huart[JAs xii (1878), 491] Duval[id. xiii (1879), 464]; Palm. רשא, Lzb[366], cf. BH רִאשׁוֹן, רֵאשִׁית; fr. *ra'š, also BH *רָאשׁ, ראוש (Lag[Symm. i. 113]), TelAm. *rušu(nu)* Wkl[189, 18] (gloss to *kakkadunu*), NH = BH; SI[6] ראש, Ph. רש, ראש (in n.pr.), Pun. *rus* (in n.pr. loc.) Schröd[Ph. Spr. 133], ראשת *choicest, chief*; on MI[20] (sf.) רשה, l.[28] ש[ר], cf. Sm. u. So[14] Nö[LCB Jan. 8, 1887, 60]);—ר׳ abs. Gn 3[15] +, cstr. 40[20] +; sf. רֹאשִׁי v[16] +, etc.; pl. רָאשִׁים (for *רְאָשִׁים Nö[GGA 1884, 1019]) Ex 18[25] +; cstr. רָאשֵׁי Ho 7[13] + [מְרַאֲשֹׁתֵי 7226
1 S 26[12] v. מְרַאֲשׁוֹת infr.]; sf. רָאשֵׁינוּ 1 Ch 12[19], 4763
רָאשֵׁיכֶם Is 29[10] +, etc.;—**1. a.** (c. 230 t.) *head*, of human being; man Gn 40[16.17] + oft., לְר׳ גֶּבֶר Ju 5[30] *for the head of a man*, i.e. *for each man, per capita;* woman 2 K 9[30] Dt 21[12] Nu 5[18] Est 2[17]; boy 2 K 4[19.19] Gn 48[14.14] +; of י׳, under fig. of armed man ψ 60[9] = 108[9]; of idol 1 S 5[4]; of gates, personif. ψ 24[7.9]. **b.** *head*, of animals: of serpent Gn 3[15], dog 2 S 3[8], ass 2 K 6[25], of הַחַיָּה in Ez 1[22] cf. v[22.26], of הַכְּרֻבִים 10[1] cf. v[11]; of sea-monsters, לִוְיָתָן Jb 40[31] ψ 74[14], תַּנִּינִים v[13]; esp. of animals for sacrifice Ex 12[9] 29[15.19] Lv 1[4.8.12.15] 3[2.8] + 18 t. P; in phr. ר׳ וְזָנָב Is 9[13] (fig. of noble and commoner) cf. v[14] 19[15], so (fig. of relative dignity, power, influence) Dt 28[13.44]. **2. a.** *top* (88 t.): of mt., הַר, Gn 8[5] Ex 19[20.20] 24[17] 34[2] + 34 t.; hill, גִּבְעָה, Ex 17[9.10] (E), 2 S 8[25]; ר׳ גַּיְא Pr 8[2] + 1[21] Toy (for MT הֹמִיּוֹת), ר׳ מְרוֹמִים ר׳ שְׁמָנִים Is 28[1.4]; of rocks, צֻרִים, Nu 23[9] (JE), crag, סֶלַע, 2 Ch 25[12.12]; tower Gn 11[4] (J), stronghold Ju 6[26], ladder Gn 28[12] (E), tree 2 S 5[24] = 1 Ch 14[15], bough Is 17[6] cf. Ez 17[4.22], mast (?; חִבֵּל) Pr 23[34] (otherwise Toy); of ears of grain, שִׁבֹּלֶת Jb 24[24], of stone Gn 28[18] (E), bed, מִטָּה, 47[31] (J), throne, ר׳ עָגוֹל לְכִסֵּה 1 K 10[19], tabern., or its wall, Ex 26[24] = 36[29] (P); pillar (= capital) 1 K 7[16.17] + 13 t., מְכוֹנָה v[35.35], lampstand Zc 4[2.2], h.p.'s robe, מְעִיל, Ex 28[32] (P), ר׳ פִּנָּה ψ 118[22] *top of* (the)

corner, i.e. most conspicuous stone (fig.); =*tip, end*, of staves 1 K 8^{8}=2 Ch 5^{9}, of sceptre Est 5^{2}. **b.** *height* of stars Jb 22^{12} (‖ גֹּבַהּ שָׁמַיִם). **3.** $_{171}$ **a.** *head = chief* (man) Ju 10^{18} $11^{8.9.11}$ Ex 18^{25} (E), Nu 1^{16} (P), Dt 1^{15} Ho 2^{2} Mi 3^{1}+oft.; appar. combined with idea of *first* in a series 1 Ch 12^{10} (van d. H. v^{9}, series of 11); of God 2 Ch 13^{12}. †**b.** =*chief* (city) Jos 11^{10} (D), cf. (of city and king) Is $7^{8.8.9.9}$. †**c.** *chief* nation Je 31^{7}. †**d.** =*chief* (place, position) 1 S 9^{22} 1 K $21^{9.12}$ Dt 20^{9} 1 Ch 4^{42} (cf. also **5**). **e.** כֹּהֵן הָרֹאשׁ *chief priest* 2 K 25^{18}=Je 52^{24}, 2 Ch 19^{11} 24^{11} 26^{20}, הַכֹּהֵן רֹאשׁ 1 Ch 27^{5}, הַכֹּ׳ הָר׳ 2 Ch 31^{10} Ezr 7^{5}; ר׳ alone 2 Ch 24^{6}; רָאשֵׁי הַכֹּהֲנִים Ne 12^{7}. **f.** esp.=*head* of a family (P Chr); רָאשֵׁי בֵּית (rare רֹאשׁ) אֲבוֹתָ(ם) Ex 6^{14} Nu 7^{2} 17^{18} Jos 22^{14} 1 Ch 5^{24} $7^{7.9}$; ר׳ בֵּית הָאָבוֹת v^{40}; ר׳ לְבֵית אֲבֹתָיו Nu 1^{4}, cf. 1 Ch $5^{15.24}$ 7^{2} 9^{13} 24^{4}; ר׳ אֲבוֹת Nu 25^{15}; ר׳ אֻמּוֹת בֵּית־אָב הָעֵדָה 31^{26} cf. 32^{28} Jos 14^{1} 21^{1}; ר׳ אֲבוֹת הַלְוִיִּם Ex 6^{25} Jos 21^{1}; ר׳ (הָ)אָבוֹת לַלְוִיִּם 1 Ch $9^{33.34}$ 15^{12}, cf. Nu 36^{1} Jos 19^{51} 1 Ch $8^{6.13}$ $23^{9.24}$+10 t. Chr.; abs. ר׳ (הָ)אָבוֹת 1 Ch $8^{10.28}$ 9^{9} 26^{32} 27^{1} 2 Ch 1^{2}+8 t. Ezr Ne (Chr); רָאשִׁים לְאָבוֹת Ezr 8^{1}; ר׳ אֲבֹתֵיהֶם Ne 11^{13}; so also ר׳ alone 1 Ch $5^{7.12}$ 7^{3} 8^{28}+; appar. combined with idea of *first* in a series 23^{8} (series of 3), v^{11} (of 4), v^{19} (of 3), v^{20} (of 2). †**4. a.** *head=front*, leader's place Mi 2^{13} 2 Ch 20^{27}, cf. Am 6^{7}. **b.** of time, *beginning*, of night-watch Ju 7^{19} La 2^{19}; abs. מֵרֹאשׁ *from the beginning* Is 40^{21} $41^{4.26}$ (‖ מִלְּפָנִים), 48^{16} Pr 8^{23} (‖ מֵעוֹלָם), Ec 3^{11} (‖ עַד־סוֹף); *first* of months Ex 12^{2} (‖ רִאשׁוֹן), Nu 10^{10} 28^{11} (all P); בְּרֹאשׁ 1 Ch 16^{7} *at first*. **c.** of things, river-*heads* Gn 2^{10} (J); ר׳ עַפְרוֹת תֵּבֵל Pr 8^{26}. **5.** *chief, choicest, best*, of spices, בשׂמ(ים), Ez 27^{22} Ex 30^{23} (P), Ct 4^{14}; ר׳ שִׂמְחָתִי ψ 137^{6} *the choicest of my joy*. †**6.** *head = division* of army, *company, band:* Ju $7^{16.20}$ $9^{34.37.43.44.44}$ 1 S 11^{11} $13^{17.17.18.18}$ Jb 1^{17}. **7.** =*sum*, esp. in phr. נָשָׂא אֶת־ר׳ בְּנֵי־יִשׂ׳ Ex 30^{12} *take the sum of, enumerate*, cf. Nu $1^{2.49}$ $4^{2.22}$ 26^{2} $31^{26.49}$; בְּרֹאשׁוֹ Lv 5^{24} *in its sum*, i.e. in full, so Nu 5^{7} (all P); of י׳'s thoughts ψ 139^{17}; cf. רֹאשׁ דְּבָרְךָ אֱמֶת 119^{160}. **8.** other phr. are: נָשָׂא אֶת־רֹאשׁ פ׳ v. נָשָׂא **Qal 1 b** (2); יָרוּם רֹאשִׁי עַל־אֹיְבַי ψ 27^{6}, י׳ מֵרִים רֹאשִׁי 3^{4} (ψ 110^{7} 140^{10} v. רום); *shake the head*, v. נוע **Hiph.**, cf. יָנִיד בְּרֹאשׁוֹ Je 8^{16}, מְנוֹד רֹאשׁ ψ 44^{15}; נָתַן דַּרְכּוֹ בְּרֹאשׁ, i.e. requite, v. נתן **Qal 2 b** ad fin.; יָשׁוּב גְּמֻלְךָ בְּר׳ Ob ^{15}, cf. ψ 7^{17} 1 K 2^{33} (sub דָּם **2 i**), and (c. עַל־ר׳) Est 9^{25}, הֵשִׁיב רָעָה בְּרֹאשׁ Ju 9^{57} 1 S 25^{39} 1 K 2^{44}, cf. Jo $4^{4.7}$; 1 K 2^{32} (sub דָּם **2 i**), cf. Ne 3^{36} (אֶל־רֹאשָׁם), v. also 2 S 3^{29} sub I. חול **3**; see,
7219-20 further, דָּם **2 i**; Dn 1^{10} v. חוב **Pi.**

†[רֵאשָׁה] **n.f.** beginning-time, early 7221
time;—pl. sf. רֵאשֹׁתֵיכֶם Ez 36^{11} (cf. רֹאשׁ **4 b**).

†רֹאשָׁה **n.f.** top;—appos. הָאֶבֶן הָר׳ Zc 4^{7} 7222
i.e. the topmost stone.

רִאשׁוֹן $_{182}$ **adj. former, first, chief** (*i* 7223
heightened fr. orig. *a*, v. √);—abs. ר׳ Ho 2^{19}+, רִשׁ׳ Ex 12^{15}+, רִישׁוֹן Jb 8^{8}, cstr. רִאשׁוֹן Jb 15^{7} Qr (Kt ראישון, and so always Cod. Sam. Pent., v. Kö$^{ii. 1, 225 n}$); f. רִאשֹׁנָה Ju 20^{37}+ (Jos 21^{10} Kt ראישנה, v. supr.); mpl. רִאשֹׁנִים Ex 34^{1}+, fpl. רִאשֹׁנוֹת Is 41^{22}+, etc.;—**1.** *former:* **a.** in time, *former* of two Gn 25^{25} (J), 41^{20} (E), Dt $10^{1.2.3.4.10}$ 24^{4}, cf. Ho 2^{9}, Lv 4^{21} 9^{15} (both P), Ju 20^{39} 2 K 1^{14} Hg $2^{3.9}$ Ezr 3^{12}+; more gen. *former, previous*, Nu 21^{26} (JE), Mi 4^{8} 2 K $17^{34.40}$ Zc 1^{4} $7^{7.12}$ 8^{11} Ne 5^{15} Ec 1^{10} ψ 79^{8}+; כָּעֵת הָר׳ Is 8^{23}; דִּבְרֵי דויד הָר׳ †1 Ch 29^{29} *the doings of David, the former* and the latter (הָאַחֲרֹנִים), cf. †2 Ch 9^{29} 12^{15} 16^{11} 20^{34} 25^{26} 26^{22} 28^{26} 35^{27}; *early* days of harvest 2 S 21^{9}; רִאשֹׁנִים as subst., *former persons*, ancestors, men of old, Dt 19^{14} Lv 26^{45} (H), Ec 1^{11} (opp. אַחֲרֹנִים); (הָ)רִאשֹׁנוֹת as subst. the *former things*, i.e. past events Is 41^{22} $43^{9.18}$ 46^{9} 48^{3}, earlier predictions 42^{9}. **b.** loc., *foremost*, of two 2 S 18^{27}. **2.** *first:* **a.** in time, הַמַּכָּה הָר׳ 1 S 14^{14} *the first slaughter* (prelim. to general carnage); וְלֹא־הָיָה דְּבָרִי ר׳ 2 S 19^{44} *was not my word first?* ר׳ in appos. with pers. subj. †2 S 19^{21} I am come *as first*, cf. perh. Is 41^{27} (ins. אָמַרְתִּי Ges De < read הִגַּדְתִּים for הִנֵּה הִנָּם, Che^{Hpt} Kit^{Di}), and הָר׳ Je 50^{17} (opp. הָאַחֲרוֹן), Is 43^{27}; ר׳ abs., *first* of mankind Jb 15^{17}; abs. of י׳, *I* (am the) *first* Is 41^{4} (+אֶת־אַחֲרֹנִים), + אַחֲרוֹן 44^{6} 48^{12}; abs. of time, מֵרִאשׁוֹן Je 17^{12} *from the beginning;* esp. *first* of a def. series (sts. opp. אַחֲרוֹן), *first* day of feast Dt 16^{4} Ex $12^{15.15.16}$+5 t. P (H), Ne 8^{18}; usu. *first* month (חֹדֶשׁ) Ex $40^{2.17}$ Lv 23^{5}+6 t. P, 1 Ch 12^{16} (van d. H. v^{15})+10 t. Ch Ezr, Est 3^{7} Dn 10^{4}, חֹדֶשׁ om. Gn 8^{13} Ex $12^{2.18}$ Nu 9^{5} (all P) Ez 29^{17} 30^{20} $45^{18.21}$, so Jo 2^{23}, but rd. כְּבָרִאשׁוֹנָה (**3 a**) 𝔊 𝔖 We Now and Dr. **b.** *first* in degree, *chief:* יַד הַשָּׂרִים . . . רִאשֹׁנָה Ezr 9^{2} *the hand of the princes . . . has been first* in this trespass; 1 Ch 18^{17} Dn 10^{13} (cf. Est 1^{14} infr.). †**3. a.** fem. c. prep. as adv. phr.: (1) of time, בָּרִאשֹׁנָה Gn 13^{4} (J), =*before, formerly*, so Jos $8^{5.6}$ (JE), 2 S 7^{10} 20^{18} Je 7^{12} Is 52^{4}, לָר׳=*before, formerly*, Gn 28^{19} (J), Ju 18^{29}; so כְּבָר׳ *as formerly* Ju 20^{32} 1 K 13^{6} Is 1^{26} Je $33^{7.11}$, = בָּר׳ Dt 9^{15} Dn 11^{29} (opp. כָּאַחֲרוֹנָה); בָּר׳=*at first*, first of all, Dt 13^{10} 17^{7}

Nu 10[13] (P) Jos 8[33] (D), 1 K 17[13] 20[9] Zc 12[7] Pr 20[21] (opp. אַחֲרִיתָהּ), 1 Ch 11[6.6] 17[9] Ne 7[5]; לְמַבָּרִאשׁוֹנָה 1 Ch 15[13] (=לְמַה־בָּר׳) *for what was at first*, etc. (מָה **1 e**); (2) loc., בָּר׳, i.e. *at the head* of an army 1 K 20[17], a procession Nu 10[14] (P), cf. Is 60[9]. **b.** רִאשֹׁנָה alone as adv.: (1) of time, *first* Gn 38[28] (J), 1 K 18[25] Je 16[18] Lv 5[8] Nu 2[9] Jos 21[10] (all P), Is 65[7] (Ew De Che Di Du Skinner, >adj. Ges Hi Kn); (2) of place Gn 33[2] (J); (3) of degree, rank, Est 1[14].

7224 †[רִאשֹׁנִי] **adj.** first;—fs. הַשָּׁנָה הָרִאשֹׁנִית Je 25[1] *the first year;* but rd. ־נָה, Gie Du Kö[ii. 1, 225].

4763, 7226 רַאֲשׁוֹת 1 S 26[12] v. מְרַאֲשׁוֹת infr.

7225 †רֵאשִׁית **n.f.** beginning, chief (for *רְאִשִׁית Nö[GGA 1884, 1019], cf. Holz[Hex 465]; Syr. ܪܺܫܺܝܬܳܐ);—abs. ר׳ Dt 33[21]+, cstr. ר׳ Gn 10[10]+, רֵשִׁית Dt 11[12]; sf. רֵאשִׁיתוֹ Ec 7[8], רֵאשִׁתוֹ Jb 42[12], etc.;—**1. a.** *beginning*, of kingdom Gn 10[10] (J), year Dt 11[12], reign Je 26[1] 27[1] 28[1] 49[34]; =first phase, step, or element in course of events Is 46[10] (opp. אַחֲרִית); of a thing (דָּבָר) Ec 7[8] (opp. *id.*); of sin Mi 1[13], strife Pr 17[14], wisdom ψ 111[10], knowledge Pr 1[7]; *thy beginning* Jb 8[7]=thine early life, so *his beginning* 42[12] (both opp. אַחֲרִית); ר׳ before cl., בְּר׳ בָּרָא א׳ Gn 1[1] *in the beginning when God created* (>abs. *in the beginning God created*); ר׳ אוֹנִי 49[3] (poem) *beginning* (first product) *of my manly vigour* (‖ כֹּחִי, בְּכֹרִי), so Dt 21[17] ψ 78[51] (both ‖ בְּכוֹר), 105[36]; cf. ר׳ דַּרְכֵי אֵל Jb 40[19] (of hippopot.), ר׳ דַּרְכּוֹ Pr 8[22] (of wisdom);=first season (of a tree) Ho 9[10]; ר׳ גּוֹיִם Nu 24[20] (JE), *first, earliest, of nations.* **b.** *first* of fruits Ex 23[19] (E), 34[26] (JE), Dt 26[2.10] Ez 44[30a], of harvest Lv 23[10] (H), grain Dt 18[4] 2 Ch 31[5], dough Nu 15[20.21] (P), Ez 44[30b] Ne 10[38], wool Dt 18[4]; of כָּל־תְּבוּאָתֶךָ Pr 3[9]; Israel is ר׳ תְּבוּאָתֹה Je 2[3] (i.e. of י׳'s increase); ר׳=*first-fruits* Lv 2[12] (P), Nu 18[12] (P), Ne 12[44]; ר׳ הָאָרֶץ Ez 48[14]. **2.** *first, chief,* Am 6[1]; ר׳ גְּבוּרָתָם Je 49[35] (of bows); so appar. ר׳ בְּנֵי עַמּוֹן Dn 11[41], i.e. the principal part of them (Buhl Marti conj. שְׁאֵרִית, after 𝔖); ר׳ מַשְׂאוֹתֵיכֶם Ez 20[40], i.e. your chief oblations; ר׳ שְׁמָנִים Am 6[6], i.e. choice oils; =choice part, of land Dt 33[21], offering 1 S 2[29], הַחֵרֶם 15[21]; abs. *chief thing* Pr 4[7] (of wisdom).

4762 מָרֵשָׁה, מָרֵאשָׁה **n.pr.loc.** v. p. 601.

4761, 4763 †[מְרַאֲשׁוֹת] **n.[f.]pl. denom.** place at the head, head-place;—only sf. מְרַאֲשֹׁתָיו as adv. *at his head-place* (of one lying down) Gn 28[11.18] (E), 1 S 19[13.16] 1 K 19[6]; so Qr 1 S 26[7.11.16] (Kt מראשתו); in v[12] read מִמְּרַאֲשֹׁתָיו 𝔊 We Dr HPS, for MT מְרַאֲשֹׁתֵי שָׁאוּל; מְרַאֲשׁוֹתֵיכֶם Je 13[18] 7226 (*head-tires* AV[m] RV), rd. מֵרָאשֵׁיכֶם, *from your heads*, 𝔊 𝔖 𝔙 Gie Buhl Co[Hpt] (cf., already, Thes).

†II. רֹאשׁ and (†Dt 32[32]) רוֹשׁ **n.m.**[Dt 32, 33] 7219 a bitter and poisonous herb, then **venom**, alw. fig.;—**1.** a bitter and poisonous herb, +(or ‖) לַעֲנָה Dt 29[17] La 3[19], so (מֵי רֹאשׁ) מֵי ר׳ Je 9[14] 23[15]; (without ל׳) 8[14]; עִנְּבֵי־רוֹשׁ Dt 32[32] (‖ מְרֹרֹת); וּפָרַח כָּרֹאשׁ ר׳ רֹאשׁ וּתְלָאָה La 3[5]; ר׳ alone ψ 69[22]; הֲפַכְתֶּם לְר׳ מִשְׁפָּט מִשְׁפָּט Ho 10[4], Am 6[12]. **2.** *venom*, of serpents, ר׳ פְּתָנִים Dt 32[33] Jb 20[16].

†III. רֹאשׁ **n.m.** son of Benj.;—Gn 46[21], Ρως. 7220

†IV. רֹאשׁ **n.pr.gent.** Rôsh (so 𝔊 and 7220 most; >*chief* Ew Sm al. (𝔙 *principem capitis Mosoch*);—only in phr. גּוֹג (אֶרֶץ מָגוֹג) נְשִׂיא רֹאשׁ מֶשֶׁךְ וְתֻבָל Ez 38[2.3] 39[1], Ρως; not identified.

I, II. רַב, רֹב v. I. רבב. III. רַב v. II. רבב. 7227-28, p. 912f, 914 7230

רַב v. ריב. p. 936 7378

†I. [רָבַב] **vb.** be or become, many, much 7231 (NH רַב esp. *lord, master,* רַבִּי *my master, teacher;* MI[5] adj. pl. רבן; Ph. רב, f. רבת; As. [*rabâbu*], *rabbu;* Ar. رَبَّ *rear, increase* (act.; رُبٌّ *thick juice*, cf. NH רְבָב *grease*, is thought by Buhl al. to indicate original mng. *be thick*), رَبٌّ *lord, owner, master;* Sab. רב esp. in n.pr., רבאל, רבבם, רבשמסם, etc., CIS[iv. nos. 285, 3; 286, 1; 287, 12], etc.; Liḥy. רבה *its lord* DHM[Epigr. Denkm. Ar. 232]; Eth. ረበበ: *expand, spread* (intrans.); Aram. רַב, ܪܰܒ *great, chief*, so OAram. Nab. Palm. רב, Lzb[366] Cook[107]);—**Qal** *Pf.* 3 fs. consec. וְרַבָּה Ex 23[29] Is 6[12], רַבָּה Gn 18[20] (Ho 9[7] rd. וְרֹב הַמַּשְׂטֵמָה [for MT וְרַבָּה מ׳] 𝔊 We Now); elsewh. only 3 pl. רַבּוּ 1 S 25[10]+, רָבּוּ Je 46[23]+2 t. [other forms supplied by רבה q.v.]; *Inf. cstr.* רֹב Gn 6[1] Jos 9[13] Lv 25[16] (‖ מְעֹט), sf. רֻבְּכֶם Dt 7[7], and perh. רֻבָּם Ho 4[7] (cf. רֹב infr.);—**1.** *be (become) many*, pers. Gn 6[1] (J) Ex 23[29] (E; v. supr.), 1 S 25[10] Ho 4[7] (perh.), Is 66[16] ψ 3[2] 25[19] 38[20] Ec 5[10], +מִן comp. Je 46[23] Dt 7[7] ψ 69[5]; of things Is 22[9] ψ 4[8] 104[24], years Lv 25[16] (P), sins Je 5[6] 14[7] Is 59[12] Jb 35[6]. **2.** *become great*, Gn 18[20] (J), Is 6[12]; *be long*, of journey, Jos 9[13].—**Pu.** v. [רָבַב] **denom.** p. 914, 1127 7231

I. רַב[429] **adj.** much, many, great;—ms. 7227 abs. ר׳ Gn 24[25]+, רָב Gn 33[9]+, also רָב 2 Ch 20[2], רָב 28[8], רָב Ezr 10[13], etc.; cstr. רַב Ex 34[6]+; fs. רַבָּה Nu 11[33]+; cstr. רַבַּת Ez 22[5]+, רַבָּתִי (Ges[§ 90 k 1]) La 1[1.1]; mpl. abs. רַבִּים Ex 23[2.2]+, cstr. v. II. רַב;

fpl. abs. רַבּוֹת Gn 30^{43}+;—[often both as pred. and as attrib.; as attrib. preceding n. (infl. of usage for numerals? Kö$^{Synt. § 334 κ}$ Ges$^{§ 132 b}$): רַב Is 63^{7} ψ 145^{7} (but read prob. רַב־, רֹב; in Is 21^{7} ר׳ is pred.), רַבִּים Je 16^{16} ψ 32^{10} 89^{51} (on context Bö^{NÄ} Bae, also Hup), Pr 7^{26} 1 Ch 28^{5}, רַבּוֹת Ne 9^{28} Pr 31^{29}];—**1.** (oft. opp. מְעַט) **a.** (1) *much:* of substances, gold 1 K 10^{2} ψ 19^{11}, silver (money) 2 K 12^{11} = 2 Ch 24^{11}, bronze 1 Ch 18^{8}, wine Est 1^{7}; of other quantities, e.g. spoil 2 S 3^{22}, property 2 Ch 32^{29}, seed Dt 28^{38}, etc.; רַב שֶׁיִּהְיוּ Ec 6^{3b} *be it much that* his days *amount to;* (2) esp. of collectives, *numerous,* עַם־רַב Jos 11^{4} 2 S 13^{34}, עֲבֻדָּה רַבָּה Gn 26^{14} Jb 1^{3}, מִקְנֶה רַב Dt 3^{19}+, etc. **b.** pl. *many:* pers. Ex 5^{5} Ju 8^{30} 9^{40} 1 K 4^{20} 11^{1}+, things Gn 30^{43} Am 5^{12} Dt 31^{17}+; n. om. רַבּוֹת Dn 11^{41} (sc. lands; rd. רִבּוֹת *myriads* Kmp Bev Behrm Marti Prince); יָמִים רַבִּים *many days* (a long time) Gn 21^{34} 37^{24} + 28 t., שָׁנִים רַבּוֹת Ne 9^{30} Ec 6^{3a}, אִם עוֹד רַבּוֹת בַּשָּׁנִים Lv 25^{51}; רַבּוֹת עִתִּים Ne 9^{28} *many times* (v. supr.) = פְּעָמִים רַבּוֹת ψ 106^{43} Ec 7^{22}; מַכָּה רַבָּה Dt 25^{3} *many blows;* מַיִם רַבִּים *many waters* Nu 20^{11} 24^{7} + 27 t., cf. Is 8^{7}; etc. **c.** רַב as subst. coll. pers. Ex 19^{21}, also (opp. מְעַט) 1 S 14^{6} Nu 13^{18} 26$^{54.56}$ 33^{54} 35^{8}; so רַבַּת (Ges$^{§ 130 a}$) 2 Ch 30$^{17.18}$, and (rei; = *much*) Ez 24^{12}; רַב cstr. before abstr. (= רֹב) Is 21^{7} 63^{7} ψ 145^{7}; esp. pl. רַבִּים of pers. Ex 23$^{2.2}$ + 37 t. + בַּת־רַבִּים Ct 7^{5} (v. p. 123). †**d.** cstr. = *abounding in,* רַב־בְּרָכוֹת Pr 28^{20}, רַב־חֶסֶד (v. I. חֶסֶד **3**), רַב־כֹּחַ ψ 147^{5}, רַב־מְאֵרוֹת Pr 28^{27}, רַב הַמְּהוּמָה Ez 22^{5}, רַב־נוֹצָה 17^{7}, רַב־הָעֲלִילִיָּה Je 32^{19}, רַב־פְּעָלִים 2 S 23^{20} = 1 Ch 11^{22}, רַב־פָּשַׁע Pr 29^{22}, רַב־תְּבוּנָה 14^{29}; רַבַּת אוֹצָרֹת Je 51^{13}, רַבַּת בָּנִים 1 S 2^{5}, רַבָּתִי עָם La 1^{1} (Ges$^{§ 90 l}$). †**e.** + מִן comp. = *more numerous than* Ex 1^{9} Nu 22^{15} Jos 10^{11} Ju 16^{30} 2 K 6^{16} Is 54^{1} 1 Ch 24^{4} 2 Ch 32^{7} Dn 11^{13}; sq. inf., *too many to* Gn 36^{7} Ju 7^{2} (cf. v^{4}); vid. also foll. †**f.** רַב = *abundant, enough* Gn 24^{25} 33^{9}; as exclam. *enough!* Gn 45^{28} 2 S 24^{16} = 1 Ch 21^{15}, 1 K 19^{4}, so (+ מִן inf.) Ex 9^{28} (מִן **6 d**); רַב־לָךְ (with implication of excess) Dt 3^{26} (let it) *suffice thee!* so רַב־לָכֶם Ez 45^{9}, also Nu 16$^{3.7}$ = ye assume too much! + inf. *it is enough for you to* Dt 1^{6} 2^{3} (i.e. you have done it enough), so + מִן inf. 1 K 12^{28}, מִן subst. Ez 44^{6}. †**g.** as adv. *much, exceedingly* (only ψψ), רַב ψ 123^{3}, רָב ψ 18^{15} (Hup De Che al.; HPS$^{2 S 22,15}$ conj. רָמָה; om. ‖ 2 S 22^{15}); רַבָּה ψ 62^{3} 78^{15} 89^{8} (𝔊 Bae רַב הוּא); רַבַּת (Aramaism, cf. Syr. ܪܰܒܳܐ, ܪܰܒܬ݂ܳܐ, Nö$^{§ 155 A}$ W$^{SG 135}$) ψ 65^{10} 120^{6} (= long enough), 123^{4} 129$^{1.2}$. **2.** less oft. *great:* **a.** of space 1 S 26^{13}, the deep Am 7^{4} Gn 7^{11} Is 51^{10} ψ 36^{7} (fig.), city La 1^{1} (רַבָּתִי בַגּוֹיִם Ges$^{§ 90 l}$),—v. also צִידוֹן, חֲמָת;—plague Nu 11^{33}, empire Est 1^{20}, goodness ψ 31^{20}, wickedness Gn 6^{5}, etc. **b.** specif. *strong* (opp. אֵין כֹּחַ) 2 Ch 14^{10}; רַב לְהוֹשִׁיעַ Is 63^{1}; so רַבִּים as subst. Is 53^{12} (‖ עֲצוּמִים). †**c.** *major natu* Gn 25^{23} (opp. צָעִיר); רַבִּים as subst. *grandævi,* Jb 32^{9}. †**d.** + מִן comp. *greater than* Dt 7$^{1.17}$ 9^{14} 20^{1}; *too great for* Jos 19^{9} 1 K 19^{7}.—Pr 26^{10} is hopelessly corrupt, v. Toy.

II. רַב$_{49}$ **n.m.** chief (As.-Bab. influence, cf. 7227
rab Dl$^{HWB 609 b}$; BAram. רַב);—cstr. ר׳ Je 39^{9}+;
pl. cstr. רַבֵּי 39^{13} 41^{1} (but v. infr.);—esp. רַב־
טַבָּחִים *chief of guardsmen* (v. טַבָּח), only as title
of Bab. officer Je 39$^{9.10}$ + 15 t. Je, 7 t. ‖ 2 K 25
(cf. שַׂר הַטּ׳ in Gn [JE]); also † רַב הַחֹבֵל Jon 1^{6}
chief of the sailors, i.e. captain; †in gen. כָּל־רַב
בֵּיתוֹ Est 1^{8}, † רַב־סָרִיסָיו Dn 1^{3} (v. סָרִיס), and so רַבֵּי
מֶלֶךְ בָּבֶל Je 39^{13}, רַבֵּי הַמֶּלֶךְ 41^{1} (late gloss; om.
𝔊 and ‖ 2 K 25^{25}, so Hi Gf Gie). †The foll.
titles of As.-Bab. officers are prob. loan-words
in Heb.: רַב־מָג Je 39$^{3.13}$ usu. *chief soothsayer* 7248
(v. מָג), but = *rab-mugi* [? *chief of princes*]
Pinches$^{Hast. DB. RAB-MAG}$; רַב־סָרִיס (cf. OAram. 7249
[Nineveh] רב סרס Lzb^{366}), 2 K 18^{17} (As.; not
in ‖ Is 36^{2}), Je 39$^{3.13}$ (Bab.), usu. *chief eunuch,*
but = *rabû-ša-rêši, chief of the heads* (the principal men) Wkl$^{Unters. z. altor. Gesch., 1889, Excurs. v, p. 138}$
(actually found as *rubû-ša-ri-ešu* Pinches$^{Acad. June 25, 1892, 618}$), Pinches$^{Hast. DB. RAB-SARIS}$; רַב־שָׁקֵה (van 8248
d. H. רַבְשָׁקֵה) *chief of the officers* (?) (so prob. As. 7262
rab-ŠAḲ; *šaḳû = high one;* COT$^{2 K 18,17}$ KB$^{ii. 23}$
Dl$^{HWB 685 a}$ Tiele$^{Bab.-As. Gesch. 497.513}$ Pinches$^{Hast. DB. iv. 191}$), 2 K 18$^{17.19.26.27.28.37}$ 19$^{4.8}$ = Is 36$^{2.4.11.12.13.22}$ 37$^{4.8}$.

†רַבָּה **n.pr.loc.** Rabba (prop. *great* or 7237
populous, sc. city);—**1.** capital of Ammonites:
explicitly, רַבַּת בְּנֵי עַמּוֹן 2 S 12$^{26.27}$ 17^{27} Dt 3^{11} Je 49^{2} Ez 21^{25}; רַבָּה alone 2 S 11^{1} ‖ 1 Ch 20$^{1.1}$, Am 1^{14} Je 49^{3} Ez 25^{5} Jos 13^{25} (P); c. ה loc. רַבָּתָה 2 S 12^{29}; in Gk. period *Philadelphia,* Lag$^{Onom. 215, 94; 219, 82}$ (but Ραββατάμανα Polyb$^{v. 71. 4}$), mod. ʿ*Ammân,* 13½ m. NE. from Heshbon, 28½ m. E. of Jordan; cf. Buhl$^{Geogr. 260}$;—𝔊 Ραββαθ, Ραββα. **2.** הָרַבָּה, city in Judah Jos 15^{60} (P), site unknown;—𝔊 Σωθηβα, A 𝔊L Αρεββα.

רֹב$_{151}$ **n.m.**$^{Jb 11, 2}$ multitude, abundance, 7230
greatness;—abs. ר׳ Gn 16^{10}+, רוֹב 1 Ch 4^{38} 2 Ch 31^{10} + Jb 33^{19} Qr (Kt רִיב); cstr. רֹב Ex 15^{7} + (רָב־) Jb 37^{23} Baer Gi), רָב־ Jb 23^{6}+; 2 K 19^{23} and pl. cstr. רֻבֵּי Ho 8^{12} v. infr.;—**1.** *multitude*

(c. 125 t.): of pers. Ho 10^{13} Pr 14^{28} 20^{6} Est 10^{3}+; of things Is 1^{11} 47^{12} Ez 27^{18} Lv 27^{16} Pr 10^{19} Jb 11^{2}+; = *great quantity, abundance* Gn 27^{28} Ho 9^{7} + oft. (2 K 19^{23} Qr [= Is 37^{24} Kt], > Kt רכב; 2 Ch 24^{27} Kt ורב, > Qr יִרֶב), + (of time) רֹב שָׁנִים Jb 32^{8} (Gi; v^{7} van d. H., Baer), בְּרֹב יָמִים Ec 11^{1}; = *whole number* (of bones) Jb 4^{14} 33^{19} (Qr; Kt וריב); esp. לָרֹב *in respect of, for, multitude,* in sim., like sand, stars, etc., Jos 11^{4} (JE), 1 S 13^{5} 2 S 17^{11} + 10 t.; = *abundantly,* c. vb. (= הַרְבֵּה) Gn 30^{30} (J), 48^{16} (E), 1 K 1$^{19.25}$ 10^{10}; usu. late Ne 9^{25} Jb 26^{3} Zc 14^{14} 1 Ch 4^{30} 2 Ch 9^{9} (‖ הַרְבֵּה 1 K 10^{10}) + 23 t. Ch; as pred. c. הָיָה 1 Ch 22^{14}; = *in great numbers,* 2 Ch 30$^{5.24}$; nearly = adj. (c. subst.; = רַב) 9^{1} (‖ רַב 1 K 10^{2}), 16^{8} 24^{24} 30^{13}; מֵרֹב *from multitude of,* Dt 7^{7} 28^{47} + 14 t.; abs. *from (for) mult.* 1 K 7^{47}, Gn 16^{10} 32^{13} (J), 1 K 3^{8} 8^{5} = 2 Ch 5^{6}. **2.** *greatness* (c. 26 t.): מֵר׳ שִׂיחִי 1 S 1^{16}, רֹב חַסְדֶּךָ Ne 13^{22} ψ 5^{8} 69^{14}, cf. 106^{45}, ר׳ כֹּחַ Is 63^{1} Jb 23^{6} 30^{18} ψ 33^{16}, etc.; read רֹב prob. also (for רַב) Is 63^{7} ψ 145^{7}; = *length* of journey (cf. vb. Jos 9^{13}) בְּרֹב דַּרְכֵּךְ Is 57^{10}; Ho 8^{12} Qr רֻבֵּי תוֹרָתִי = *greatnesses* [great things], or *numerous things,* of my law, but form dubious, read perhaps רֹב תּוֹרֹתַי (sub **1**), so We (cf. 𝔊); Gr al. דִּבְרֵי; > Kt רבו, v. רִבּוֹ.—Lv 25^{16}
7231 Dt 7^{7} Ho 4^{7}, v. √. p. 912

7233 †רְבָבָה **n.f. multitude, myriad, ten thousand** (Kö$^{ii. 1, 221}$);—abs. ר׳ Gn 24^{60}+; sf. רִבְבָתוֹ Kt 1 S 18^{7} + 2 t. (Qr רִבְבֹתָיו); pl. abs. רְבָבוֹת 1 S 18^{8}; cstr. רִבְבוֹת Mi 6^{7}+, רִבֲבוֹת Dt 33^{17}; sf. v. supr. Qr;—*myriad,* 10,000: of great number of pers., indef. Gn 24^{60} (J; אַלְפֵי רְבָבָה *thousands of myriads*), Dt 33^{2} (poem; מֵרִבְבֹת קֹדֶשׁ, but v. קֹדֶשׁ, ad fin.), ψ 3^{7} Ct 5^{10}; רִבְבוֹת אַלְפֵי יִשׂ׳ Nu 10^{36}, cf. Dt 33^{17} (poem);—רְבָבָה Ez 16^{7} rd. רְבִי 𝔊 Co Berthol Krae;—more precisely: (100, 1000), 10,000, Ju 20^{10}; opp. 2, Dt 32^{30} (poem), opp. 100, Lv 26^{8} (H), opp. 1000, 1 S 18$^{7.8}$ 21^{12} 29^{5} ψ 91^{7}; so of things, Mi 6^{7}.

7239 †רִבּוֹא, רִבּוֹ **n.f.** $^{Ezr 2, 64}$ **ten thousand, myriad** (later (Aramaizing) synonym of foregoing; perh. for Aram. רִבּוֹ(ת), Kö$^{ii. 1, 221 f.}$, but Palm. רבו Lzb^{367});—abs. רִבּוֹ 1 Ch 29$^{7.7}$ Jon 4^{11} (? cstr.), + cstr. Ho 8^{12} Kt (v. infr.); רִבּוֹא Ezr 2^{64} = Ne 7^{66}, Ne 7^{71} (van d. H. v^{72}); du. רִבֹּתַיִם ψ 68^{18}; pl. רִבּוֹת Ne 7^{70} (van d. H. v^{71}), רִבֹּאוֹת Ezr 2^{69} Dn 11^{12};—*ten thousand;* of pers., 4 × 10,000 + 2000 + 3 × 100 + 60 Ezr 2^{64} = Ne 7^{66}; 12 × 10,000 + n. Jon 4^{11}; indef. Dn 11^{12} *he shall cast down myriads;* rd. רִבּוֹת also v^{41} (for MT רַבּוֹת) Kmp Bev Behrm Marti Prince; of things, esp. units of value, n. + 10,000 1 Ch 29^{7}, n. + 6 × 10,000 + 1000 Ezr 2^{69} ‖ n. + 2 × 10,000 Ne 7$^{70.71}$ (v. supr.); 10,000 + 8 × 1000 + n. 1 Ch 29^{7}; indef. רֶכֶב אֱלֹהִים רִבֹּתַיִם ψ 68^{18} (‖ אלפים);—רִבּוֹ תוֹרָתִי Ho 8^{12} (Kt; 10,000 [precepts] *of my instruction*) would be only early instance, v. רֹב. 7231

†רַבִּית **n.pr.loc.** in Issachar;—הָר׳ Jos 19^{20}; 7245
mod. *Râbâ,* c. 13 m. NE. from Nablûs, cf. Buhl Geogr.^{204};—𝔊 Δαβειρων, A 𝔊L Ραββωθ.

†רְבִיבִים **n.m.** $^{Je 3, 3}$ **pl. copious showers,** 7241
causing fertility;—ר׳ Dt 32^{2} + 3 t., רְבִבִים Je 14^{22}, רְבִבִם 3^{3};—*copious showers,* Je 3^{3} (+ מַלְקוֹשׁ), יִתְּנוּ ר׳ 14^{22} (‖ מִנְּשָׁמַיִם), ר׳ ψ 65^{11}; sim., of penetrating, pervasive infl. of prophetic words Dt 32^{2} (‖ שְׂעִירִם, also מָטָר, טַל), of Jacob Mi 5^{6} (‖ טַל), of future king ψ 72^{6} (‖ מָטָר).

יָרָבְעָם ^{104} **n.pr.m. Jeroboam,** Ιεροβοαμ (prob. 3379
= יָרֹב + עָם *the people increaseth* Thes Kit$^{1 K 11, 26}$ al.; cf. also Gray$^{Prop. N. 59; Ency. Bib. i. 139 f.}$; > √ ריב *the people contendeth,* or (*the god*) *'Amm contendeth* Nbr$^{Stud. Bib. i. 225}$, cf. Che$^{JQ. July, 1899, 559; Ency. Bib.}$);—**1.** $_{90}$ (K Ch), leader of revolt of N. Isr. (10th cent.), and first king 1 K 11^{26} 12$^{2.2.20}$, etc., ‖ 2 Ch 10$^{2.2.3.12}$, etc., 1 K 13$^{1.4.33}$+; (specif. יר׳ בֶּן־נְבָט 1 K 11^{26} + 23 t.); in later times (under Deut. infl.) as sinful and author of Isr.'s sin 1 K 15^{30} 16$^{2.7.19.26.31}$ + 15 t. †**2.** son of Jehoash of N. Isr. (8th cent.) and 13th king 2 K 13^{13} 14$^{16.23.27.28.29}$ 15$^{1.8}$ Ho 1^{1} Am 1^{1} 7$^{9.10.11}$; prob. also 1 Ch 5^{17}.

†II. [רָבַב] **vb.** shoot;—**Qal** *Pf.* 3 pl. וָרֹבּוּ 7232
(Ges$^{§ 67 m}$) Gn 49^{23} abs. (בַּעֲלֵי חִצִּים in ‖ l.; Sam. וַיְרִיבֻהוּ, so perh. 𝔊 ἐλοιδόρουν).—רָב ψ 18^{15} (חִצָּיו
in ‖ l.), v. I. רַב **1 g.** p. 912 7227

†III. [רַב] **n.m. archer;**—pl. רַבִּים Je 50^{29} 7228
(‖ דֹּרְכֵי קֶשֶׁת; Gie רֹבִים, II. רבה), sf. רַבָּיו Jb 16^{13} (in fig.; Bö al. רֹבָיו; Vrss. Ew al. *his missiles*).

I. רבד (√ of foll.; cf. Ar. رَبَدَ *confine, tie.*)

†רָבִיד **n.[m.]** chain, ornament for neck;— 7242
abs. ר׳ Ez 16^{11}; cstr. רְבִד הַזָּהָב Gn 41^{42} (E).

†II. [רָבַד] **vb. be-spread, deck** (cf. Ar. 7234
رَبَدَ v. *shew patches of colour, become clouded* (of sky); NH רֹבֶד *pavement, paved terrace,* 𝔗 רוֹבְדָא *pavement*);—**Qal** *Pf.* 1 s. מַרְבַדִּים רָבַדְתִּי עַרְשִׂי Pr 7^{16} *with spreads* (coverlets) *have I bespread my couch;* read also *Impf.* 3 ms. וַיִּרְבְּדוּ לְשָׁאוּל 1 S 9^{25} 𝔊 Th We Dr al. (for MT וַיְדַבֵּר עִם שׁ׳), obj. om.

4765 †[מַרְבַד] **n.[m.]** spread, coverlet;—only pl. abs. מַרְבַדִּים (Kö$^{II. 1, 97, 471}$) Pr 7^{16} 31^{22}.

7235 I. [רָבָה]$_{225}$ **vb.** be, or become, much, many, great (NH *id.;* As. *rabû, be great, grow;* Ar. رَبَا, Aram. רְבָא, ܪܒܐ, all *grow, increase*);—†**Qal**$_{59}$ *Pf.* 3 fs. רָבְתָה 1 S 14^{30}; 2 ms. וְרָבִיתָ consec. Dt 30^{16}; 3 pl. רָבוּ Ezr 9^{6}+, etc.; *Impf.* 3 ms. יִרְבֶּה Dt 8^{13}+, juss. יִרֶב Gn 1^{22}+ 2 Ch 24^{27} Qr (< ורב Kt, v. רֹב **1**), וַיִּרֶב Ex 1^{20}; 3 fs. תִּרְבֶּה Dt 7^{22} Dn 12^{4}, וַתֵּרֶב Gn 43^{34} 1 K 5^{10}; 3 mpl. יִרְבּוּ Dt 11^{31}+, יִרְבּוּן ψ 139^{18}, יִרְבְּיֻן Dt 8^{13}, etc.; *Imv.* ms. וּרְבֵה Gn 35^{11}; *Inf. cstr.* רְבוֹת Ex 11^{9}+;—*Pt.* רֹבֶה v. II. רבה;—**1.** *become many, numerous:* **a.** of a people, Ex 1$^{10.12}$ (J), v^{20} (E), Dt 6^{3} 8^{1} 30^{16} Zc 10^{8} 1 Ch 5^{23}; רָבוּ לְמָעְלָה 23^{17}; esp.+פרה *be fruitful and multiply* Je 3^{16} 23^{3} (fig. of flock), Gn 47$^{27\,b}$ (P), Ex 1^{7} (P), ψ 107^{38}, also (of man and beast) Ez 36^{11}; of children Jb 27^{14}; בִּרְבוֹת צ׳ צַדִּיקִים Pr 28^{28}, Pr 29^{2} (Toy רְדוֹת *rule,* ‖ מְשֹׁל), בר׳ רְשָׁעִים v^{16} (Toy *id.*). **b.** of animals Dt 7^{22} (+עַל pers.), 8^{13} 1 Ch 5^{9}; +פרה Gn 1^{22} 8^{17} (both P; cf. Ez 36^{11} supr.). **c.** of things Dt 8$^{13.13}$ Ez 31^{5} Ex 11^{9} (P), Ec 5^{10}; of sins Ezr 9^{6} (+לְמַעְלָה), Pr 29^{16}; +מִן comp. ψ 16^{4} 139^{18}; of days Gn 38^{12} (J), Dt 11^{21} 1 S 7^{2} Pr 9^{11}, years of life 4^{10}; of waters Gn 7^{17} (J), v^{18} (P). **2. a.** *be great:* (1) of things, Gn 43^{24} (J; + מִן comp.), 1 S 14^{30}; of way=*be long* Dt 19^{6} and (מִן comp. pers.) 14^{24} *be too long for;* of wisdom 1 K 5^{10} (מִן comp.). (2) of pers., יִרְבֶּה אֱלֹהִים מֵאֱנוֹשׁ Jb 33^{12} i.e. is too great for (De al.); has loftier, nobler thoughts (Di Bu), but no ‖. **b.** *grow great* (Aramaism): (1) of pers.,=grow up Ez 16^{7} (+גָּדַל), Jb 39^{4}. (2) of glory ψ 49^{17}, knowledge Dn 12^{4}.—2 Ch 24^{27} v. supr. †**Pi.**$_{4}$ *make large, increase;*—*Imv.* ms. רַבֵּה צְבָאֲךָ Ju 9^{29} *enlarge thy host;* *Pf.* 2 ms. רִבִּיתָ בִּמְחִירֵיהֶם ψ 44^{13} *thou hast* not *made great with their price* (set a high price; so Ew De Che al.); or *increased* (sc. thy wealth) *by their price* (Hup Bae); = *bring up, rear* (children) La 2^{22} (+טפח), whelps Ez 19^{2} (in fig.). **Hiph.**$_{162}$ *Pf.* 3 ms. הִרְבָּה Ho 8^{11}+, sf. וְהִרְבְּךָ consec. Dt 30^{5}; 2 ms. הִרְבִּיתָ Is 9^{2}+, 1 s. הִרְבֵּיתִי Ho 2^{10}+, etc.; *Impf.* יַרְבֶּה 12^{2}+, וַיֶּרֶב 2 S 18^{8} La 2^{5}, etc.; *Imv.* ms. הַרְבֵּה Ez 24^{10}, הֶרֶב Ju 20^{38}+ψ 51^{4} Qr (הרבה Kt, Inf. abs.), etc.; fs. הַרְבִּי Is 23^{16}, mpl. הַרְבּוּ Am 4^{4} Gn 34^{12}; *Inf. abs.* הַרְבֵּה 15^{1}+, הַרְבָּה (Ba$^{NB\,90, 91}$) 3^{16} 16^{10} 22^{17}; *cstr.* הַרְבּוֹת Dt 28^{63}+ (2 S 14^{11} Kt הרבית; Am 4^{9} Pr 25^{27} v. infr.); *Pt.* מַרְבֶּה Ex 16^{17}+, cstr. מַרְבֵּה Lv 11^{42}, etc.;—**1.** *make much,* or *many:* **a.** obj. pers. (or a people), *multiply, increase* Gn 16^{10} 17^{20} Is 9^{2}+; Ez 36^{10} (+עַל pers.), v^{11} (man and beast; +*id.*); Dt 30^{5} (+מִן comp. pers.); +פרה Hiph. Gn 28^{3} 48^{4} (both P); הִרְבָּה כּוֹשֵׁל Je 46^{16}=*he made many stumble;* =*have many* 1 Ch 7^{4} 8^{40} 23^{11}. **b.** obj. animals Dt 17$^{16.16}$ (cf. Ez 36^{11} supr.). **c.** obj. things Ho 2^{10} 8$^{11.14}$ Gn 3^{16}+; הַרְבּוּ עָלַי מְאֹד מֹהַר וּמַתָּן 34^{12}; opp. הִמְעִיט Lv 26^{16} Nu 26^{54} 33^{54}; obj. words Ec 10^{14} (v. Jb 34^{37} sub **2**), cf. Is 1^{15} Jb 40^{27}, הַרְבִּי שִׁיר Is 23^{16}; obj. days Jb 29^{18} (like sand); = *use many* (medicines) Je 46^{11}; *have many* (feet) Lv 11^{42}; *bring abundantly* 2 Ch 31^{5}; *yield abundantly* Ne 9^{37}; c. לְ of obj. Ho 10^{1} (לְ **3 a**); obj. om. Hb 2^{6} Pr 22^{16}, also (opp. מעט [usu. Hiph.]) Ex 16$^{17.18}$ 30^{15} Nu 35^{8} (all P), Pr 13^{11}. †**d.** (1) sq. inf., *make much to do, do much in respect of,* = do much, abundantly, greatly, often, etc. (Dr$^{181, 12}$): הַרְבּוּ לִפְשֹׁעַ Am 4^{4}=*transgress greatly,* so Ezr 10^{13}, cf. 2 K 21^{6}=2 Ch 33^{6}; further, Is 55^{7} Ex 36^{5} 2 Ch 36^{14} ψ 78^{38}, also 2 S 14^{11} (Kt מהרבית, Qr מֵהַרְבַּת, rd. prob. מֵהַרְבּוֹת Dr$^{reff.}$ Ges$^{§\,75\,ff.}$ Th-Löhr); +מִן comp. 18^{8}; 1 S 1^{12}=*pray a long time;* Ju 20^{38} del. הֶרֶב as dittogr. of הארב Be Bu GFM. (2) sq. vb. fin. (Dr^{Sm} Ges$^{§\,120\,g}$), אַל־תַּרְבּוּ תְדַבְּרוּ 1 S 2^{3} i.e. *talk not so much;* cf. ψ 51^{4}. **e.** the Inf. abs. (Ol$^{§\,191\,b}$ Kö$^{II. 1, 555}$ Ges$^{§\,75\,ff.}$) is used: (1) הַרְבָּה אַרְבֶּה *I will greatly increase* Gn 3^{16} 16^{10} 22^{17} (all J; Ges$^{§\,113\,n}$); (2) וְהַרְבֵּה carrying on inf. cstr. Ez 21^{20}; (3) הַרְבֵּה as adv. (c. vbs. and [Ec 7^{16}] adj.), *greatly, exceedingly,* etc., esp. ה׳ מְאֹד Gn 41^{49} (E), 1 S 26^{21} 2 S 12^{30}=1 Ch 20^{2}, Jos 13^{1} (D), 2 K 21^{16} Ne 2^{2}; perh. also 1 K 5^{9} 10^{10} (both c. נָתַן), v^{11} (c. הֵבִיא), Je 40^{12} (c. אָסַף), 2 Ch 14^{12} (c. נָשָׂא); הַרְבֵּה alone 2 K 10^{18} (opp. מְעַט), Ne 3^{33} Ec 1^{16} 5^{19} 7$^{16.17}$ ψ 51^{4} Kt (Qr הֶרֶב Imv.); (4) as adj. attrib. (Kö$^{Synt.\,§\,318\,e}$), ה׳ מְאֹד Dt 3^{5} Jos 22^{8} (D; ‖ רַב־מְאֹד), 2 S 8^{8} (רַבָּה מְאֹד in ‖ 1 Ch 18^{8}), 12^{2} Is 30^{33} 2 Ch 32^{27}; so הַרְבֵּה alone Ne 4$^{4.13}$ (+רְחָבָה), Ezr 10^{1} (preceding n., cf. 1. רַב), Ec 2^{7} 5$^{6.16}$ (rdg. כעס as n., Ew De Hi-Now al.), 6^{11} 9^{18} 11$^{8\,a}$ 12$^{9.12.12}$, הַרְבּוֹת alone Pr 25^{27} (Toy reads הַרְבֵּה); הַרְבֵּה מְאֹד as pred. Gn 15^{1} (J; Sam. אַרְבֶּה), Ec 11$^{8\,b}$ ψ 130^{7} (adv. Bae); (5) הַרְבֵּה as n. concr. (Kö$^{Synt.\,§\,318\,a}$) 2 S 1^{4} Je 42^{2} (-בָּה van d. H.), c. מִן comp., 2 Ch 25^{9} Jon 4^{11}; as obj. (or adv.), opp. מְעַט Hg 1$^{6.9}$ Ec 5^{11}; late in adv. phr. (לְהַרְבֵּה (מְאֹד †Ne 5^{18} 2 Ch 11^{12} 16^{8}; הַרְבּוֹת as n. Am 4^{9} (rd. prob. הֶחֱרַבְתִּי We Now). †**2.** *make great,* obj. pers. 2 S 22^{36}=ψ 18^{36};

enlarge border 1 Ch 4[10]; perhaps also Jb 34[37] *make words great*, presumptuous, against God (לְאֵל; so Buhl[Lex]; most *make many words*, **1 c**).

697 †אַרְבֶּה **n.m.** [Ex 10, 19] a kind of **locust** (usu. interp. as *the multitudinous*, but Dl[HWB 126] as = As. *âribu, êribu, êribû, locust-swarm*, from ארב *devastate*);—alw. abs. א׳(הָ);—usu. coll. *locust-swarm*, in sim. of swarm of invaders Ju 6[5] 7[12]; oft. appar. the common species (|| other species, cf. לְמִינוֹ Lv 11[22]): Je 46[23] Na 3[15] (sim. of multitude; || יֶלֶק); as destructive Ex 10[4.12.13.14.14.19a] (all J), ψ 105[34] (|| יֶלֶק), Dt 28[38] (vb. חסל), 1 K 8[37] = 2 Ch 6[28], ψ 78[46] (all + חָסִיל), Jo 1[4.4] (|| גָּזָם, יֶלֶק, חָסִיל), 2[25] (|| *id.*); as disappearing suddenly (sim.) Na 3[17] (|| גּוֹב גּוֹבָי); as edible Lv 11[22] (H; || סָלְעָם, חָגָב, חַרְגֹּל); as well organized Pr 30[27] (cf. Jo 2[7.8]); of single locust, א׳ אֶחָד Ex 10[19b] (J), as leaping (sim.) Jb 39[20], as shaken out of garment (sim.) ψ 109[23] (v. II. נָעַר).—Cf. Dr[Jo 82 ff.].

4766 †מַרְבֶּה **n.[m.] 1. abundance**;—abs. מ׳ Is 33[23], as adv., *in abundance*. **2. increase**(?), cstr. לְםַרְבֵּה (sic) 9[6] *for the increase* of the dominion (take לם as dittogr. of foregoing, and read רַבָּה, 𝔊 Gr Che Kit Buhl[Lex] Marti; Du לְמַרְבֵּה, in view of following לְשָׁלוֹם).

4767 †מַרְבָּה **n.f. much**;—only מ׳ לְהָכִיל Ez 23[32] *much to contain*, i.e. which contains much; but read מַרְבָּה Hiph. Pt. Hi-Sm Co Berthol Krae (v. √ **Hiph. 1 d** (1)).

4768 †מַרְבִּית **n.f. increase, great number, greatness**;—מ׳ abs. Lv 25[37]; cstr. 1 S 2[33] + 2 t.; sf. מַרְבִּיתָם 1 Ch 12[30] (van d.H. v[29]);—**1.** *increase*, concr.: **a.** of family 1 S 2[33]. **b.** *increment, interest, usury*, Lv 25[37] (H; of food-stuffs, || נֶשֶׁךְ, of money; מ׳ of money Egypt. Aram., opp. ראש *principal*, Cooke[North-Sem. Inscr. 404]). **2.** *great number*: of people 2 Ch 30[18]; c. sf. = the greater part of them, 1 Ch 12[30] (v. supr.). **3.** *greatness*, of wisdom 2 Ch 9[6].

8635 †תַּרְבּוּת **n.f. increase, brood**;—cstr. in phr. ת׳ אֲנָשִׁים חַטָּאִים Nu 32[14] *a brood* (contempt.) *of sinful men* (cf. מַרְבִּית 1 S 2[33]).

8636 †תַּרְבִּית **n.f. increment, interest, usury** (= מַרְבִּית **1 b**; cf. (on both) Ar. رَبَا IV. *take usury*, رِبًا *interest, usury*, Syr. ܬܰܪܒܺܝܬܳܐ; Saalschütz Mos. Recht (ii. 1848), 859 Hoelemann Letzte Bibelstud. (1885), 297 f. Di[Lv 25, 36] Benn[Hast. DB Debt]);—alw. abs. ת׳: + נֶשֶׁךְ Lv 25[36] (H), Ez 18[17] 22[12] Pr 28[8]; || *id.* Ez 18[8.13].

†II. [רָבָה] **vb. shoot** (cf. II. רָבַב, I. 7235
רָמָה);—only **Qal** *Pt.* רֹבֶה קַשָּׁת Gn 21[20] < רֹבֶה קֶשֶׁת, Kn Di al., but read prob. רֹמֵה ק׳ Ol Ball, *one shooting* the bow.

רְבִיבִים, רְבִית, רִבּוֹ(א), רַבָּה v. I. רבב. 7237, 7239,
p. 913-14 7245

† [רָבַךְ] **vb. mix, stir** (Ar. رَبَكَ *mix*, 7246
mingle; NH רְבִיכָה, 𝔗 רְבִיכָא [for BH מֻרְבֶּכֶת], (dough) *mixed*, or *stirred*);—**Hoph.** *Pt.* f. as term. techn. in sacrif., alw. of סֹלֶת *well mixed*, מֻרְבֶּכֶת Lv 6[14] 7[12], הַמֻּרְבָּכֶת 1 Ch 23[29].

†רִבְלָה **n.pr.loc. 1.** ר׳ in land of Hamath 7247
2 K 23[33] 25[21] = Je 52[27], Je 39[6]; c. ה loc., רִבְלָתָה 2 K 25[6.20] = Je 52[26], also ('in land of Hamath') Je 39[5] 52[9]; בְּרִבְלָתָה v[10]; read רִבְלָתָה also Ez 6[14] (for MT דִּבְ׳, v. [דִּבְלָה]); 𝔊 usu. Δεβλαθα (also Ez 6[14]); mod. *Ribla* on Orontes, Rob[BR ii. 507; iii. 543 ff.] Bd[Pal 3. 405]. **2.** הָרִבְלָה (מִשְׁפָם) Nu 34[11], on NE. border of land of Isr., certainly not so far N. as **1**, but site unknown; 𝔊 ἀπὸ Σεπφαμαρ Βηλα, whence Di al. conj. הַרִבְּלָה, but not *Harmel*, 8 m. SW. from ר׳ **1** (Wetzst[ZAW iii (1883), 274 f.]), see Dr[Hast. DB].

רַב־סָרִיס, רַב־מָג v. II. רַב. p. 913 7248-49

I. רבע (√ of following; v. [רָבַע], רֶבַע, רֹבַע etc., infr.; also in ling. cogn.).

1. אַרְבַּע, אַרְבָּעָה [316] **n.m.** et **f. four** (NH 702
= BH; MI[8] ארבען = 40; Ph. ארבע, Pun. ארבעת, *four*; so As. *arba'u* (rarely *irba'*), *irbitti*; Ar. أَرْبَعَةٌ, أَرْبَعٌ; Sab. ארבעת CIS[iv, no. 232. 2] Hom Chrest. 47; Eth. አርባዕ: አርባዕቱ: Aram. אַרְבַּע, אַרְבְּעָה, ܐܰܪܒܰܥ, ܐܰܪܒܥܳܐ; Nab. ארבע, Palm. ארבע, ארבעא, Lzb[367]);—**m.**[148] (c. **n.f.**) אַרְבַּע (abs. vel cstr.) Ex 21[37] +; also אַרְבַּע Lv 11[20] +; note (Baer Gi) Jos 21[18] + 6 t. Jos 21 (van d.H. אַרְבַּע); in Pr 30[18] read **f.** with Qr; **f.** (c. **n.m.**) abs. אַרְבָּעָה Gn 2[10] + 125 t. + Pr 30[18] (v. supr.); cstr. אַרְבַּעַת 1 S 4[2] + 29 t., incl. Ez 7[2] (but rd. **m.** Kt); sf. אַרְבַּעְתָּם Ez 1[8] + 5 t. Ez, אַרְבַּעְתָּן 1[10.10] (but rd.
prob. תָּם-, Krae), v[16.18]; du. אַרְבַּעְתָּיִם 2 S 12[6], v. 706
1 d; pl. אַרְבָּעִים = 40, v. infr.;—*four* (in Hex. 108 t., chiefly P, 98 t.; Ez 52 t., Ch 47 t.):—**1.** without other num.: **a.** אַרְבַּע (1) before n.fpl. Je 15[3] Ex 25[12] (P) + 101 t., incl. א׳ אַמּוֹת Dt 3[11] + 5 t. (but also † א׳ בָּאַמָּה *four* (*in*) *cubit*(*s*) Ex 26[2.8] 36[9] 1 K 7[27.27.38]), and א׳ מֵאוֹת = 400 Gn 11[13] + 55 t. (2) א׳ bef. du. רַגְלַיִם Lv 11[23], רַגְלָיו Ex 25[26]. †(3) bef. collective, א׳ צֹאן Ex 21[37] (E); א׳ רִבּוֹא = 40,000 Ezr 2[64] = Ne 7[66]. †(4) rare

and late, after n.fpl. עָרִים א׳ Jos 19^{7} (P); after n. fs. cstr. בִּשְׁנַת א׳ לְ 1 K 22^{41} Zc 7^{1} 2 Ch 3^{2}.—קִרְיַת א׳, v. this, and II. אַרְבַּע infr. †(5) n. om. Ez 43$^{15\,b}$ Pr 30$^{15.18}$ (Kt, v. supr.), v^{21} Dn 8$^{8.22}$; עַל־אַרְבַּע (sc. רגלים)=*on all fours* Lv 11$^{20.21.27.42}$. **b.** אַרְבָּעָה (1) bef. n. mpl. Gn 2^{10} (J), 14^{9} Ex 25^{34} + 21 t., + (וְ)א׳ חֳדָשִׁים יָמִים Ju 19^{2} 1 S 27^{7}; also א׳ א׳ פָּנִים distrib. Ez 10^{21}. †(2) late, after n. mpl. 1 Ch 23^{10}. (3) n. om., Am 1$^{3.6.9}$ + 15 t., + (as pred. of n. mpl.) †Ex 27$^{16.16}$ 38$^{19.19}$; also בְּא׳, (sc. יוֹם) †Zc 7^{1}= ordinal, *on the fourth* (day). **c.** אַרְבַּעַת (1) bef. n. mpl. Ju 11^{40} 1 K 7^{32} + 11 t. (not Ez 7^{2}, v. supr.), + א׳ אֲלָפִים = 4000, 1 S 4^{2} + 14 t. †(2) bef. coll. הַבָּקָר Nu 7^{7}. †(3) n. om. 2 S 21^{22}. †(4) c. sf., after n. pl., =*the four of them*, Ez 1$^{8.10.10.10}$ + 6 t. Ez, Dn 1^{17} *these boys, the four of them.* **d.** du. אַרְבַּעְתָּיִם 2 S 12^{6} =*four-fold* Ges $^{§\,98\,h}$ Kö $^{ii.\,1,\,227}$, but read שִׁבְעָתָיִם 𝔊 Th We Klo Dr Kmp Bu HPS. **2.** with other num.: **a.** (1) אַרְבַּע עֶשְׂרֵה=*14*, (*a*) before n. fs., א׳ ע׳ שָׁנָה Gn 31^{41}, + (as ordinal, =*14th*) 14^{5} 2 K 18^{13}=Is 36^{1}, Ez 40^{1}. (*β*) after n. fpl. עָרִים א׳ ע׳ Jos 15^{36} + 8 t., נָשִׁים א׳ ע׳ 2 Ch 13^{21}. (2) אַרְבָּעָה עָשָׂר = *14*, (*a*) before n. ms. Nu 17^{14} (14 × 1000), Jb 42^{12}; esp. (as ord.) א׳ ע׳ יוֹם *14th day* Ex 12$^{6.18}$ + 7 t. (*β*) bef. n. mpl. Nu 29^{15}. (*γ*) after n. mpl. Nu 29$^{13.17}$ + 6 t. (*δ*) after n. ms. Est 9$^{15.19.21}$, all=*14th.* (*ε*) א׳ ע׳ pred. of נֶפֶשׁ Gn 46^{22}. (*ζ*) א׳ ע׳=*14th* (sc. day) Lv 23^{15} 2 Ch 30^{15} + 6 t. **b.** 20 + (וְ) 4 + n. s. 1 K 15^{33} 1 Ch 23^{4} + 13 t. 1 Ch 27; + n. pl. †Nu 7^{88}; n. om. 2 S 21^{20}, pred. ‖ 1 Ch 20^{6}, Ne 7^{23}; 4 + 20 + n. s. Nu 25^{9}; =*24th*, יוֹם ע׳ וְא׳ Hg 1$^{15.18}$ Zc 1^{7} Ne 9^{1} Dn 10^{4}, יוֹם om. Hg 2$^{10.20}$, and (א׳ וְע׳) 1 Ch 24^{18} 25^{31}†. **c.** other tens + 4, 1 Ch 7^{7} 5^{18} (+ n. s.), Ezr 2^{15} + 7 t.; 4 + tens + שָׁנָה Gn 11^{16}, + אֶלֶף 1000 Nu 1$^{27.29}$ 2$^{4.6}$ 26$^{25.43}$.—Vid. Kö $^{ii.1,\,§\,106}$.

704 †II. אַרְבַּע n.pr.m. (called הָאָדָם הַגָּדוֹל בָּעֲנָקִים Jos 14^{15}, אֲבִי הָעֲנָק 15^{13} cf. 21^{11}), inferred (erron.)
7153 from n.pr.loc. קִרְיַת א׳ (q. v.). p. 900

705 אַרְבָּעִים $_{136}$ **n.pl. indecl.** a **forty**;—**1.** sine num. al.: **a.** usu. appos. bef. n., esp. שָׁנָה, יוֹם (sing.): אַרְבָּעִים שָׁנָה Ju 3^{11} 1 S 4^{18} Am 2^{10} 5^{25} + 29 t.; א׳ יוֹם Gn 7^{17} 1 K 19^{8} Jon 3^{4} + 6 t., א׳ יוֹם וְא׳ לַיְלָה Gn 7$^{4.12}$ Ex 24^{18} + 7 t.; also א׳ בַּת †1 K 7^{38}, א׳ גָּמָל †2 K 8^{9}, א׳ אַמָּה †Ez 41^{2} and (אַמָּה om.) 46^{22}, but א׳ בָּאַמָּה †1 K 6^{17} (v. אַמָּה); א׳ אֶלֶף Nu 1^{33} 2^{19} 26^{18} Jos 4^{13} Ju 5^{8} 2 S 10^{18} 1 K 5^{6} 1 Ch 12^{37} (van d.H. v^{36}), 19^{18} (v. also infr.); rarely sq. n.pl., א׳ בָּנִים Ju 12^{14}, א׳ אֲדָנִים Ex 26$^{19.21}$ 36$^{24.26}$ (P).—(As round no. Gn 7^{17} Ju 3^{11} 5^{31} 8^{28} 1 S 4^{18} +). **b.** after n. pl., פָּרוֹת א׳ Gn 32^{16} (E), שְׁקָלִים א׳ Ne 5^{15}. **c.** n. om. Gn 18^{29}, הָא׳ v^{29}; א׳ יַכֶּנּוּ Dt 25^{3} *forty (blows) may he smite him.* **2.** c. num. al.: **a.** before unit, + n. s., 40 + 1 שָׁנָה 1 K 14^{21} 15^{10}, 2 K 14^{23}; 40 + 2 שָׁנָה 2 Ch 22^{2}, אִישׁ 2 K 10^{14}, עִיר Nu 35^{6}, אֶלֶף Ju 12^{6}; 40 + 5 שָׁנָה Jos 14^{10} (JE), etc. (12 t.); + n.pl. יְלָדִים 2 K 2^{24}; after n. pl. הָעַמּוּדִים + 40 + 5 1 K 7^{3}; n. om. 40 + 5 Gn 18^{28}, cf. Ezr 2^{24}=Ne 7^{28}. **b.** after unit, 9 + 40 שָׁנָה Lv 25^{8} (H); 1 + 40 אֶלֶף Nu 1^{41} 2^{28}, etc. (9 t. Nu, P). **c.** c. hundreds, 40 שָׁנָה + 800 שָׁנָה Gn 5^{13} (P); 100 + 40 שָׁנָה Jb 42^{16}; + units, 7 שָׁנִים + 40 + 100 שָׁנָה Gn 47^{28} (P); but (Ezr Ne, mostly pred., without n.), 900 + 40 + 5 Ezr 2^{8}, cf. v^{25} Ne 7^{62}, and (א׳ without וְ) 600, 40 + 2 Ezr 2^{10}, v. also ‖ Ne 7^{15}, Ezr 2^{34}=Ne 7^{36}, Ezr 2^{66}=Ne 7^{68} (ver. om. Baer Gi), Ne 7$^{13.29.44}$; 1000, 200, 40 + 7 Ezr 2^{38}=Ne 7^{41}; n.pl. 200 + 40 + 5 Ne 7^{67}, n.pl. 200, 40 + 2 11^{13}; also n. s. נֶפֶשׁ 700, 40 + 5 Je 52^{30}. **3.** as ordinal, בְּא׳ שָׁנָה Dt 1^{3} *in the fortieth year;* also בִּשְׁנַת הָא׳ Nu 33^{38} 1 Ch 26^{31}; בִּשְׁנַת א׳ וְאַחַת 2 Ch 16^{13} *in the forty-first year.*

†[רָבַע] **vb.denom.,** only *Pt.pass.* **squared,** 7251
square;—**Qal** *Pt. pass.* רָבוּעַ *square,* of altar Ex 27^{1} 30^{2} 37^{25} 38^{1}, cf. Ez 43^{16}; breastplate 30^{2} 39^{9}; pl. רְבֻעִים, of doorways, etc. [on text v. Kit Benz] 1 K 7^{5}; fs. רְבֻעָה as subst.=*a square* Ez 41^{21} (acc. Co Toy, om. מְזוּזַת, and joining ר׳ to v^{20}; Krae reads מְזוּזֹת רְבֻעֹת, cf. 1 K 6^{33}, רְבִיעִי **2**). **Pu.** *Pt. square,* מְרֻבָּע Ez 45^{2}, of piece of land; fs. מְרֻבַּעַת 40^{47}, of court; fpl. מְרֻבָּעוֹת 1 K 7^{31} (opp. עֲגֻלּוֹת), of borders of bases (cf. Sab. רבעתם, a kind of square building, Sab-Denkm ^{31}).

†I. רֶבַע **n.m.** $^{Ez\,1,\,8}$ **1. fourth part. 2.** pl. 7253
four sides;—**1.** ר׳ cstr., *fourth part,* of shekel 1 S 9^{8}, of hin Ex 29^{40}. **2.** in Ez, pl. sf. *four sides* (אַרְבַּעַת always preceding): רִבְעָיו Ez 43^{16}, רִבְעֵיהֶם v^{17}; רִבְעֵיהֶם 1^{8} 10^{11}, -הֶן 1^{17}.

†רֹבַע **n.[m.]** fourth part;—ר׳ cstr.; of 7255
Israel Nu 23^{10}; of a kab 2 K 6^{25}.

†רְבִיעִי **m.,** רְבִיעִית **f., adj. num. ordin.** 7243
fourth;—**m.** רְבִיעִי Gn 2^{14} + 29 t., רְבִעִי 1 Ch 24^{8} 26^{11}; pl. רְבִיעִים 2 K 15^{12}, רְבִעִים 10^{30}; **f.** abs. רְבִיעִית 1 K 6^{1} + 3 t., רְבִעִת Lv 19^{29}, רְבִעִית 1 K 6^{37} + 6 t. + 1 K 6^{33} (v. infr.); cstr. רְבִיעִית Nu 15^{5}, רְבִעִת Ex 29^{40} + 4 t., רְבִעִית Nu 15^{4} + 2 t.;—*fourth,* usu. הָר׳: **1. m.** Gn 2^{14} 15^{16} (JE), also (esp. of days, months, sons, etc.) Gn 1^{19} Ex 28^{20} 39^{13} Nu 7^{30} 29^{23} Jos 19^{17} (all P), Ju 19^{5} Je 39^{2} 52^{6} 1 Ch 27$^{7\,b}$ 2 Ch 20^{26} Ezr 8^{33}; n. om. 2 S 3^{4}=

1 Ch 3^{2}, 1 Ch 2^{14} 3^{15} 8^{2} 12^{10} 23^{19} $24^{8.23}$ 25^{11} $26^{2.4.11}$ 27^{7a} Ezr 10^{14} Dn 11^{2}; sc. חֹדֶשׁ Ez 1^{1} Zc 8^{19}; pl. in בְּנֵי רְבִ(י)עִים *sons of fourth* (*ones*), i. e. to the fourth generation, 2 K 10^{30} 15^{12} (cf. [רִבֵּעַ], and [OAram. Nērab] בני רבע Cook[107]). **2. f.** of years, 1 K $6^{1.37}$ 2 K 18^{9} Je 25^{1} 28^{1} 36^{1} 45^{1} 46^{2} 51^{59} Zc 6^{3} Lv 19^{24} (H); מֵאַת רְבִעִית 1 K 6^{33}, rd. מְזֻזֹת רְבֻעוֹת 𝔊 𝔙 Th Sta Kmp Kit Benz Bur. **3.** רְבִיעִית Ez 48^{20} *four square* (rd. poss. רְבוּעָה). **4.** רְבִ(י)עִ(י)ת as n.=*fourth part*, cstr., ר׳ הַהִין Lv 23^{13} (H), Ex 29^{40} Nu $15^{4.5}$ $28^{5.7.14}$; ר׳ הַיּוֹם Ne 9^{3a}; so abs. (הַיּוֹם om.) v^{3b}.

7256 †[רִבֵּעַ] **adj. pertaining to the fourth** (in a series);—pl. in phr. עַל־שִׁלֵּשִׁים וְעַל־רִבֵּעִים, i. e. those belonging to the 3rd and 4th generations, Ex 20^{5} (E) = Dt 5^{9}, Ex 34^{17} (J), Nu 14^{18} (JE), cf. **1** supr.

7250 †II. [רָבַע] **vb. lie stretched out, lie down** (Aram. form of רָבַץ (q.v.); NH רבע usu. of copulation, chiefly unnatural; yet cf. also Sab. רבע *abide, encamp, settle*, DHM[ZMG xxix (1875), 593], Ar. رَبَعَ *abide, dwell*)—**Qal** only *Inf.*: sf.
7252 רִבְעִי ψ 139^{3} *my lying down* (for repose, opp. אָרְחִי); elsewh. (H) for copulation (woman with beast) לְרִבְעָה אֹתָהּ Lv 20^{16}, but read אִתָּהּ (sf. of beast) Dr-Wh Kö[Synt. 226 e], cf. Bae Berthol (and Dr[2 S 13,14]); לְרִבְעָהּ 18^{23}, rd. לְרִבְעָה (compl. om.; v. *id.*). **Hiph.** *Impf.* 2 ms. בְּהֶמְתְּךָ לֹא תַרְבִּיעַ כִּלְאַיִם Lv 19^{19} (H) *thy cattle thou shalt not cause to* (let) *lie down* (i. e. breed) in *two kinds*.

7254 †II. רֶבַע **n.m.** a king of Midian Nu 31^{8} Jos 13^{21}; Ροβοκ, Ροβε(κ).

7257 †רָבַץ **vb. stretch oneself out, lie down, lie stretched out** (NH = BH; As. *rabâṣu*, *lie, dwell*; *rubṣu* (in word-lists), *stall*, also *womb* (cf. II. רבע supr.); Ar. رَبَضَ *lie down on the breast, stretch oneself out*, مرابض, Sab. מרבצן CIS[iv, no. 5, 2]; 𝔗 רְבַע *lie stretched out*, Syr. ܪܒܥ, ChrPal ܪܒܥ *recline at meals*, Schwally[Idiot. 87]);—**Qal** *Pf.* 3 ms. ר׳ Gn 49^{9}, 3 fs. consec. וְרָבְצָה Dt 29^{19}, רָבָצָה Ez 19^{2}, etc.; *Impf.* 3 ms. יִרְבַּץ Is 11^{6} 27^{10}; 3 fs. וַתִּרְבַּץ Nu 22^{27}; 3 mpl. יִרְבְּצוּ 11^{7}, 14^{30}, יִרְבָּצוּן Zp 2^{7} ψ 104^{22}; 3 fpl. תִּרְבַּצְנָה Ez 34^{14}; *Pt.* רֹבֵץ Ex 23^{5} + 3 t.; f. רֹבֶצֶת Gn 49^{25} + 2 t.; mpl. רֹבְצִים 29^{2};—*lie down, lie:* of domestic animals, ass Ex 23^{5} (E; under heavy burden), Nu 22^{27} (Je; in obstructed path), Gn 49^{14} (at ease; poet., in sim.); sheep, in repose, 29^{2} (J), Is 17^{2} Zp 2^{14}; fig. of people Ez 34^{14}; calf, in repose Is 27^{10}; of wild beasts, lion, in lair, Gn 49^{9} (poem in J; fig.), ψ 104^{22}; = make lair, abode Ez 19^{2} (fig.), so of צִיִּים Is 13^{21}, תַּנִּין Ez 29^{3} (fig.); leopard (with kid) Is 11^{6}, cf. v^{7}; = brood, of mother-bird Dt 22^{6} (עַל־הָאֶפְרֹחִים); of man, in repose Is 14^{30} Jb 11^{19}, cf. Zp 2^{7} 3^{13} (fig. of flock perhaps impl., cf. Ez 34^{14} supr.); of the deep, תְּהוֹם רֹבֶצֶת תָּחַת Gn 49^{25} Dt 33^{13}; fig. of curse Dt 29^{19} (ב pers.); of sin, לַפֶּתַח חַטָּאת רֹבֵץ Gn 4^{7} *at the door sin makes its lair*. **Hiph.** *Impf.* 3 ms. sf. יַרְבִּיצֵנִי ψ 23^{2}, 2 ms. תַּרְבִּיץ Ct 1^{7}, etc.; *Pt.* מַרְבִּיץ Is 54^{11}, pl. מַרְבִּצִים Je 33^{12};—*cause to lie down*, or *lie*, acc. of flock (for repose) Je 33^{12}, also (fig.) ψ 23^{2} Ez 34^{15}; acc. of flock om. Is 13^{10} Ct 1^{7}; of *laying* stones Is 54^{11}.

†רֵבֶץ **n.** [**m.**] **(place of) lying down, resting- or dwelling-place**;—cstr. ר׳ בָּקָר Is 65^{10} 7258
(|| נְוֵה צֹאן); sf. בִּנְוֵה תַנִּים רִבְצָהּ 35^{7} (cf. Ges[§ 145 m], but Du רִבְצָה, sc. flock); רִבְצָם Je 50^{6} (people as sheep); of man, רִבְצוֹ Pr 24^{15} (|| נְוֵה צַדִּיק).

†מַרְבֵּץ **n.** [**m.**] id.;—of wild beasts, מ׳ לַחַיָּה 4769
Zp 2^{15} (sign of desolation, || שַׁמָּה); of flock, cstr. מִרְבַּץ־צֹאן Ez 25^{5} (|| נְוֵה גְמַלִּים).

רבק

(√of following; cf. Ar. رَبَقَ *tie fast*; 𝔗 רִיבְקָא *stall*).

†מַרְבֵּק **n.** [**m.**] **stall** (lit. *tying-place*);— 4770
עֲגָלִים מִתּוֹךְ מ׳ Am 6^{4} *calves out of the stall* (where they were fattened); עֵגֶל־מ׳ 1 S 28^{24} i.e. a stall-fed, fatted, calf; so כְּעֶגְלֵי מ׳ Mal 3^{20} (sim. of prosperity), Je 46^{21} (sim. of well-fed and arrogant mercenaries).

רִבְקָה 30 **n. pr. f. Rebekah**, daughter of 7259
Bethuel and wife of Isaac, Gn 22^{23} 24^{15} + 24 t. 24, 25, 26, 27; 28^{5} 29^{12} 35^{8} 49^{31};—𝔊 Ρεβεκκα.

רַב־שָׁקֵה v. II. רַב sub רבב. p. 913 7227, 7262

רגב

(√of following).

†[רֶגֶב] **n.m.** clod of earth;—pl. רְגָבִים יְדֻבָּקוּ 7263
Jb 38^{38} *clods are joined together*; cstr. רִגְבֵי נָחַל 21^{33} *clods of* (the) *wady*.

†אַרְגָּב **n.m. heap, mound** (prob.);—so 68, 5045
read 1 S 20^{19} (for אבן), v^{41} (for נגב), 𝔊 (αργαβ, 68, 5045
εργαβ), Th We Klo Dr Kit Bu HPS.

†אַרְגֹּב **n.pr. 1. loc.** (*heap*, or *region of* 709
clods; '*glebe*' GASm[G 551]);—always חֶבֶל א׳ Dt $3^{4.14}$ 1 K 4^{13}, ח׳ הָא׳ Dt 3^{13}, = *measured region of Argōb*; some well-defined district of Bashan (appar. identif. with חַוֹּת יָאִיר Dt 3^{14} [where ח׳ י׳

in Bashan, so Jos 13^{30}], but this a harmonistic correction; ח׳ י׳ in fact in Gilead [Nu 32^{41} Ju 10^{4}], and disting. from אַרְגֹּב 1 K 4^{13} cf. Dt 3^{13}); exact loc. dubious, GASm$^{l.c.}$ and esp. Dr$^{Dt\ 3,4}$; Buhl$^{Geogr.\ 18}$ thinks of *Ṣuwet*, S. of Upper Yarmuk, a border district between Bashan and Gilead.—Αργοβ; 1 K 4^{13} Ερεβαταμ, 𝔊L Ραγαβαν, A Εργαβ. **2. m.** 2 K 15^{25}, Αργοβ; dub.; v. Klo Kit Benz Bur.

7264 †**רָגַז** **vb. be agitated, quiver, quake, be excited, perturbed** (Ph. Iph. (+ Inf. abs. Qal) *disquiet, disturb*, Inscr. Tabn.$^{4.6.7}$; NH Hiph. *provoke to wrath*; رجز *tremble* (with rage, fear, Dozy); v, viii, *rumble* (of thunder, Frey), رُجَز *a trembling disease* (of camels), etc.; Aram. רְגַז *tremble, rage*, ܪܓܙ *be enraged;* Zinj. רגז *wrath*, Lzb^{367});—**Qal** *Pf.* 3 ms. consec. וְרָגַז Pr 29^{9}, 3 fs. רָגְזָה Is 14^{9}+, etc.; *Impf.* 3 ms. יִרְגַּז 2 S 7^{10} 1 Ch 17^{9}, 2 fs. וַתִּרְגְּזִי Ez 16^{43} (but v. infr.); 3 mpl. יִרְגְּזוּן Hb 3^{7}, יִרְגָּזוּן Ex 15^{14}, etc.; *Imv.* ms. רְגָזָה (Ges$^{§\ 48\ i}$) Is 32^{11}, mpl. רִגְזוּ ψ 4^{5};—*quake*, subj. אֶרֶץ 1 S 14^{15} Am 8^{8} (עַל rei), ψ 77^{19} (+ רָעַשׁ), Jo 2^{10} (לְפָנָי) of locusts; ‖ רעשׁ), Pr 30^{21} (תַּחַת pers.); subj. מוֹסְדֵי הָרִים ψ 18^{8} (‖ רעשׁ), = 2 S 22^{8} (מוֹסְדוֹת הַשָּׁמַיִם; ‖ *id.*); הֶהָרִים Is 5^{25}; תְּהֹמוֹת ψ 77^{17}; of tent-curtains Hb 3^{7} (fig. of terror of tent-dwellers); of people, in dread, c. מִפְּנֵי pers. Dt 2^{25} (‖ חול), Is 64^{1}; c. עַל rei Je 33^{9} (+ פָּחַד); abs., Ex 15^{14} (‖ חִיל אָחַז וגו׳), ψ 99^{1} Jo 2^{1}; pregn. = *come quivering* Mi 7^{17} (מִן loc.); of pers., in fear, awe, Gn 45^{24} (ב loc.), Is 32^{11} (‖ חָרַד), v^{10} ψ 4^{5}, Hb 3^{16} (תַּחְתַּי), cf. of בִּטְנִי Hb 3^{16}; of Israel, = *be disquieted*, 2 S 7^{10} = 1 Ch 17^{9}; *be excited, perturbed*, of pers. 2 S 19^{1} (by grief; cf. Dr), שְׁאוֹל Is 14^{9} (surprise; לְ pers.); in rage, c. לְ *at*, Ez 16^{43} (of Jerus. personif.; but rd. **Hiph.** (i.e. *didst enrage me*) 𝔊𝔖𝔙𝔗 Hi Sm Co Berthol Toy Krae); prob. also וְרָ׳ וְשָׂחַק Pr 29^{9}; of י׳ Is 28^{21}. **Hiph.** *Pf.* 3 ms. הִרְגִּיז Is 23^{11}; 2 ms. sf. הִרְגַּזְתַּנִי 1 S 28^{15}; *Impf.* 1 s. אַרְגִּיז Is 13^{13}; *Inf. cstr.* הַרְגִּיז (Ges$^{§\ 53\ l}$) Je 50^{34}; *Pt.* מַרְגִּיז Is 14^{16} Jb 9^{6}, pl. cstr. מַרְגִּיזֵי 12^{6};—*cause to quake, disquiet, enrage*: *cause* earth *to quake* Is 14^{16} (fig.; ‖ רעשׁ), Jb 9^{6} *shake earth* מִמְּקוֹמָהּ; heavens Is 13^{13} (‖ רעשׁ); kingdoms 23^{11}; *cause disquiet*, c. לְ pers., Je 50^{34} (‖ רגע); = disturb 1 S 28^{15} (cf. Ph. תרגזן, Inscr. Tabn.^{4} Dr$^{Sm\ xxviii}$); = enrage, provoke, מַרְגִּיזֵי אֵל Jb 12^{6}; so also prob. Ez 16^{43} (rdg. תַּרְגִּזִי לִי), v. **Qal** ad fin. **Hithp.** *excite oneself*, only *Inf. cstr.* sf. הִתְרַגֶּזְךָ אלי *thine exciting thyself* (to rage) against me, 2 K 19$^{27.28}$ = Is 37$^{28.29}$.

†**רֹגֶז** **n.m.** $^{Jb\ 3,26}$ **agitation, excitement, raging**;—ר׳ abs. Hb 3^{2}+, cstr. Jb 37^{2}; sf. רָגְזְךָ Is 14^{3};—*raging* Jb 3^{17}; *disquiet, turmoil* Is 14^{3} Jb 3^{26} 14^{1}; *raging, wrath* Hb 3^{2}; ר׳ קֹלוֹ Jb 37^{2} *rumbling of his voice* (i.e. thunder); of *excitement* of warhorse, בְּרַעַשׁ וְרֹגֶז 39^{24}. 7267

†**רַגְזָה** **n.f. a quivering, quaking**;—ר׳ Ez 12^{18} (‖ רַעַשׁ). 7269

†**רַגָּז** **adj. quivering, quaking**;—לֵב ר׳ Dt 28^{65} *a quaking heart.* 7268

†**אַרְגַּז** **n.m. box, chest,** or like receptacle (cf. Ar. رِجَازَةٌ *a kind of* (camel-)*vehicle for women*, also *a garment containing stones*, etc., as balance, makeweight (at side of *haudaj*); from above √, as *swaying*? Syr. ܪܓܙܐ *sack*, Talm. אַרְגָּז *chest, coffin*);—הָא׳ 1 S 6$^{8.11.15}$, cf. HPS. 712

רֶגֶל $_{247}$ **n.f.** $^{Dt\ 8,4}$ (on sf. m. Ct 5^{3} v. Kö$^{Synt.\ §\ 14}$ Albr$^{ZAW\ (xvi,\ 1896,\ 76)\ xv\ (1895),\ 316\ f.}$), **foot** (NH *id.*; Ar. رِجْلٌ *leg, foot;* Aram. רַגְלָא, ܪܓܠܐ *foot*; Palm. sf. רגלה Lzb^{368}; transp. Zinj. (pl. cstr.) לגרי Id$^{ib.}$, Mand. ליגרא Nö$^{M\ 102}$; cf. Eth. ሰረገላ: *vehicle* Di^{347});—abs. ר׳ Ex 21^{24}+, רָגֶל v^{24}+; cstr. רֶגֶל Nu 22^{25}+; sf. רַגְלִי Gn 30^{30}+, etc.; du. רַגְלַיִם Is 28^{3}+, רַגְלָיִם 2 S 4^{4}+; cstr. רַגְלֵי Gn 24^{32}+; sf. רַגְלַי Nu 20^{19}+, רַגְלֶיךָ Ex 3^{5}+, etc.; pl. רְגָלִים 23^{14}+ 3 t. (v. **2** infr.);—**1.** *foot*: **a.** human, Gn 18^{4} 19^{2}+ 10 t. of washing feet (רחץ); Ex 3^{5} 4^{25}+ oft.; in fig. Dt 32^{35} 1 S 2^{9} Je 2^{25} Jb 12^{5}+ oft.; ר׳ גַּאֲוָה ψ 36^{12} *foot of pride*; הֲדֹם לְר׳ 110^{1}; מִכַּף ר׳ + כַּף ר׳ *sole of foot* Dt 2^{5} 11^{24} 28$^{56.65}$+ 6 t., וְעַד ראשׁ Is 1^{6}, cf. (וְעַד קדקד) 2 S 14^{25} Dt 28^{35} Jb 2^{7}; also מֵראשׁ וְעַד ר׳ Lv 13^{12}; שָׁרְשֵׁי ר׳ Jb 13^{27}, v. שֹׁרֶשׁ; אֶצְבְּעוֹת ר׳ 2 S 21^{20} = *toes*, בֹּהֶן ר׳ = *great toe* Ju 1$^{6.7}$ Ex 29^{20}+ 6 t. Lv; ר׳ = *leg* 1 S 17^{6} (v. also **f.** ad fin.). †**b.** anthrop. of God, Ex 24^{10} 2 S 22^{10} = ψ 18^{10}, Na 1^{3} Hb 3^{5} Is 60^{13} Zc 14^{4}; כַּפּוֹת ר׳ Ez 43^{7}; הֲדֹם ר׳ Is 66^{1} La 2^{1} 1 Ch 28^{2} ψ 99^{5} 132^{7}. †**c.** of seraphim Is 6^{2}, Ezekiel's חיות Ez 1$^{7.7}$ and (כַּף ר׳) v^{7}, cherubim 2 Ch 3^{13}; idols ψ 115^{7}. **d.** of animals: dove, כַּף ר׳ Gn 8^{9} (J); שֶׁרֶץ עוֹף Lv 11$^{21.23}$, שֶׁרֶץ v^{42}; calf, כַּף ר׳ Ez 1^{7} (in sim.), בְּהֵמָה 29^{11}; Pharaoh under fig. of תַּנִּים 32^{2}; prob. of beast also Jb 39^{15}, indef. Is 28^{3} (in fig.). **e.** of table Ex 25^{26} 37^{13} (P). **f.** phrases: +לְר׳ (לְ **5 i**) *acc. to the pace of* Gn 33$^{14.14}$ (J; as fast as cattle, children, can go); *at one's guidance* Dt 33^{3}; *at one's foot*, i.e. at every step Gn 30^{30} (J), Is 41^{2}, cf. Jb 18^{11} (v. I. [פוץ] **Hiph.**); הלך לְר׳ 1 S 25^{42}, i.e. went where 7272

she went, cf. 2 S $15^{15.17.18}$; + בְּר׳ *on* one's *feet*, on
foot, Nu 20^{19} (JE), Dt 2^{28} Ju $4^{15.17}$ ψ 66^6, שַׁלַּח בְּר׳
Ju 5^{15} (v. שׁלח), cf. Jb 18^8 (and בְּרַגְלֵי שִׁלְּחוֹ 30^{12});
הָעָם, הַיְקוּם, הַבְּהֵמָה) אֲשֶׁר בְּר׳), i.e. which follow
one, hence obey or belong to one, Ex 11^8 (J),
Ju 4^{10} 8^5 1 K 20^{10} Dt 11^6 2 K 3^9, הַמִּתְהַלְּכִים בְּר׳,
1 S 25^{27}; נָשָׂא ר׳ + Gn 29^1 (E) = set out, but
יָרִים אֶת־ר׳ + 41^{44} (E) *lift the foot*, i.e. make a
movement, do anything; †euphemism מֵסִיךְ אֶת־ר׳
Ju 3^{24}, cf. 1 S 24^3 (Gi; van d. H. Baer v^4; v. I.
[סָכַךְ] **Hiph.**); וַתְּפַשְּׂקִי אֶת־ר׳ לְ Ez 16^{25} (v. פשׂק);
הַיּוֹצֵאת מִבֵּין ר׳ Dt 28^{57} (v. יצא **1 h**); מֵימֵי ר׳ Qr
2 K 18^{27} = Is 36^{12} (Kt שׁיניהם; v. מַיִם **3**); שַׂעַר
הָר׳ Is 7^{20}, i.e. hair of the private parts. †**2.**
pl. only in phr. שָׁלֹשׁ רְגָלִים *three times* (feet, paces,
cf. פַּעַם) Ex 23^{14} (E), Nu $22^{28.32.33}$ (J).

7270 †רָגַל **vb. denom.** foot it, go about;—**Qal**
go about (maliciously, *as slanderer;* cf. Ar.
مُشَّاءٌ and سَاعٍ *slanderer*, from √√ مَشَى *walk*
along, سَعَى *walk quickly*), *slander*, *Pf.* 3 ms.
לֹא־ר׳ עַל־לְשֹׁנוֹ ψ 15^3 *he takes no slander upon*
his tongue (‖ דֹּבֵר אֱמֶת v^2). **Pi.** *Impf.* 3 ms.
וַיְרַגֵּל 2 S 19^{28}, 3 mpl. וַיְרַגְּלוּ Dt 1^{24} Jos 7^2; *Imv.*
mpl. רַגְּלוּ Jos 7^2; *Inf. cstr.* לְרַגֵּל Nu 21^{32} + 5 t.;
sf. לְרַגְּלָהּ 2 S 10^3; *Pt.* pl. מְרַגְּלִים Gn 42^9 + 11 t.;
—**1.** *slander* (cf. **Qal**), וַיְר׳ בְּעַבְדְּךָ אֶל 2 S 19^{28}.
2. *go about as explorer, spy*, c. acc. loc. Nu 21^{32}
Jos 6^{25} $7^{2.2}$ 14^7 (all JE), Ju 18^2 (‖ חָקַר), $v^{14.17}$ 2 S
10^3 (‖ חָקַר), 1 Ch 19^3, so also pt. Gn 42^{30} (E),
Jos 6^{22} (JE); pt., acc. om., as adj., אֲנָשִׁים מְרַגְּלִים
Jos 2^1, cf. 6^{23} (both JE); as subst., *spies* 1 S 26^4
2 S 15^{10}, and so perh. (as pred.) Gn $42^{9.11.14.16.31.34}$
8637 (all E). **Tiph.** *Pf.* 1 s. תִּרְגַּלְתִּי לְאֶפְרַיִם Ho 11^3
I taught Ephr. *to walk* (si vera l.; v. Ges $^{\S 55h}$).
רֹגֵל (*treader, fuller* (cf. כבס), so Thes SS al.)
5883 v. עֵין ר׳, II. עַיִן **c.** p. 745

7273 †רַגְלִי **adj.** on foot;—אִישׁ ר׳ (after num.)
footmen, esp. foot-soldiers, Ju 20^2 2 S 8^4 = 1 Ch
18^4, 1 Ch 19^{18} (פָּרָשִׁים in ‖ 2 S 10^{18}); elsewhere
ר׳ as subst., usu. coll., of Isr. at Exod. Ex 12^{37}
Nu 11^{21} (both JE); = foot-soldiery 1 S 4^{10} 15^4
2 S 10^6 1 K 20^{29} 2 K 13^7; n.pl. רַגְלִים *footmen*,
men on foot Je 12^5 (opp. הַסּוּסִים).

4772 †[מַרְגְּלוֹת] **n.[f.] pl. denom.** place of
the feet, feet (cf. [מְרַאֲשׁוֹת] sub I. ראשׁ);—sf.
מַרְגְּלֹתָיו *place of his feet* Ru $3^{4.7}$; adv. = *at his*
feet v^8 + v^{14} Qr (Kt מרגלתו); = *his feet* Dn 10^6
(opp. וְרֹעֹתָיו).

†רֹגְלִים **n.pr.loc.** (place of *fullers*, v. רֹגֵל 7274
supr.);—in Gilead, 2 S 17^{27} 19^{32}; unknown;
𝔊 Ρωγελ(λ)ειμ, 𝔊L Ρακαβειν.

†[רָגַם] **vb.** stone, kill by stoning 7275
(denom.? cf. סקל; or orig. = *throw, hurl*? NH
רָגַם *throw at* (rare); Ar. رَجَمَ *throw stones at*,
stone, also (from accompaniment of stone-throwing) *revile, curse*, cf. Eth. ረገመ: *curse*, We$^{Heid.}$
$^{2.\,111,\,250}$; Aram. רְגַם, ܪܓܡ *stone*);—**Qal** *Pf.* 3 pl.
consec. וְרָגְמוּ Lv 24^{14} + 2 t., sf. וּרְגָמֻהוּ Dt 21^{21};
Impf. 3 mpl. יִרְגְּמוּ Lv $20^{16.27}$, וַיִּר׳ Jos 7^{25} + 4 t.;
sf. יִרְגְּמֻהוּ Lv 20^2, וַיִּר׳ 2 Ch 24^{21}; *Inf. abs.* רָגוֹם
Lv 24^{16} Nu 15^{35}; *cstr.* לִרְגּוֹם 14^{10};—*stone*, c. acc.
pers. + בָּאֲבָנִים Dt 21^{21} (D), Nu 14^{10} $15^{35.36}$ (P),
+ בָּאֶבֶן Ez 16^{40} Lv $20^{2.27}$ (H); + acc. אֶבֶן Jos 7^{25}
(JE), Lv 24^{23} (P), 2 Ch 24^{21}; c. ב pers. + acc. אֶבֶן
1 K 12^{18} = 2 Ch 10^{18}; c. עַל pers. + acc. אֶבֶן Ez
23^{47}; c. acc. pers. alone Lv 24^{14} (P); c. ב pers.
alone, רָגוֹם יִרְגְּמוּ־בוֹ v^{16} (P).—Syn. סקל q.v. p. 709 5619

†[רִגְמָה] **n.f.** heap (of stones, then) crowd 7277
(of people; si vera l.);—sf. רִגְמָתָם ψ 68^{28}, but
read probably רִגְשָׁתָם, v. [רִגְשָׁה]. p. 921 7285

†מַרְגֵּמָה **n.f.** sling (?; implement of 4773
hurling stone? so 𝔊 al.; Thes al. *stone-heap*);—
כִּצְרוֹר אֶבֶן בְּמ׳ Pr 26^8, v. esp. Toy.

†רֶגֶם **n.pr.m.** (Thes cp. Ar. رَجْمٌ *friend;* 7276
v. also Sab. רגם Hal ^{63,4});—1 Ch 2^{47}, Ραγεμ, Ρεγεμ,
𝔊L Ρεγμα.

†רֶגֶם מֶלֶךְ **n.pr.m.** exilic, Zc 7^2; Αρβεσεερ 7278
ὁ βασιλεύς.

†רָגַן **vb.** murmur, whisper (NH *id.*; 𝔗 7279
Ithpe. *backbite, slander*);—**1.** *murmur* (rebelliously): **Qal** *Pt.* pl. רוֹגְנִים Is 29^{24} *murmurers;*
Niph. *Impf.* 3 mpl. וַיֵּרָגְנוּ ψ 106^{25} *and they murmured* in their tents, so 2 mpl. וַתֵּרָגְנוּ Dt 1^{27}.
2. *whisper* (maliciously), *backbite, slander:*
Niph. *Pt.* נִרְגָּן *backbiter* Pr 16^{28} 18^8 $26^{20.22}$. 5372

†I. רָגַע **vb.** disturb (NH Hiph. *move to* 7280
and fro; perh. transp. from Ar. رَعَجَ *disturb*,
Ba$^{ES\,8}$);—**Qal** *Pf.* Jb 26^{12} בְּכֹחוֹ רָגַע הַיָּם; *Pt.*
cstr. (Ges$^{65d,\,116g,\,x}$), Je 31^{35} = Is 51^{15} רֹגַע הַיָּם
וַיֶּהֱמוּ גַלָּיו. **Hiph.** denom. from רֶגַע *make a*
twinkling, only 1 s. Impf. cohort. וְעַד אַרְגִּיעָה
לְשׁוֹן שָׁקֶר and *while I would twinkle* (= *only*
for a moment: cf. Jb 20^5) is the false tongue
(opp. תִּכּוֹן לָעַד), Pr 12^{19} (cf. De); and כִּי אַרְגִּיעָה

אֲרִיצֶנּוּ מֵעָלֶיהָ *I will twinkle and* (=I will *in a moment*, Ges[§ 120 g]; cf. Hi) chase them away from it, Je 49^{19}=50^{44}. (Ba[§ 86] as subst.=רֶגַע, of the very rare type *'aqtîl;* ה- as Ges[§ 90 f].)

7281 †רֶ֫גַע **n.m. a moment** (NH *id.;* 𝔗 רִיגְעָא Ec 9^{12}: prob. properly a *movement*, i. e. *twinkling*, of the eye; cf. *momentum*, i. e. *movimentum*);—abs. ר׳, רֶגַע Nu 16^{21}+, pl. רְגָעִים;—**a.** ψ 30^{6} ר׳ בְּאַפּוֹ a *moment* (passes) in his anger (opp. חיים ברצונו); Is 54^{7} בְּר׳ קָטֹן during *a little moment*. **b.** usu. in adv. phrases:—(*a*) as adv. acc., (*a*) Ex 33^{5} ר׳ אֶחָד *for one moment*, so ר׳ alone Is 54^{8}; repeated Je $18^{7.9}$ רֶגַע . . . רֶגַע *at one moment . . . at another moment;* (*β*) *in a moment, suddenly*, ψ 6^{11} יָשֻׁבוּ יֵבֹשׁוּ רָגַע, Je 4^{20} Is 47^{9} Jb 34^{20}. (*b*) בְּרֶגַע *in a moment* Jb 21^{13} וּבְר׳ שְׁאוֹל יֵחָתּוּ (of a quick and painless death; but see 34^{20} ψ 73^{19}: Hoffm Buhl Beer Bu Du [cf. 𝔊 ἐν ἀναπαύσει, 𝔗 בְּמַרְגּוֹעָא] take רֶגַע (or rd. רֹגַע) as subst. [✓ II. רגע] *in tranquillity*, of a peaceful death). So (*c*) כְּר׳ Nu 16^{21}=17^{10} וַאֲכַלֶּה אֹתָם כְּרָגַע, ψ 73^{19}. (*d*) כְּמוֹ ר׳ La 4^{6}. (*e*) עֲדֵי רָגַע while *a moment* lasts Jb 20^{5}. (*f*) כִּמְעַט ר׳ *like* the littleness of *a moment*=*for* a little *moment* Is 26^{20} Ezr 9^{8}. (*g*) pl. לִרְגָעִים *by moments, at every moment*, Is 27^{3} Ez 26^{16} וְחָרְדוּ לִ׳ (so 32^{10}), Jb 7^{18} (‖ לִבְקָרִים).

7280 †II. רָגַע **vb. be at rest, repose** (prob.=Ar. رَجَعَ *return*, prop. *return to rest*, after wanderings, etc.);—**Niph.** *Imv.* 2 fs. Je 47^{6} (of sword) be gathered into thy scabbard, הֵרָגְעִי וָדֹמִּי *repose*, and be still. **Hiph. a.** trans. *give rest to;*—*Inf. cstr.* Je 31^{2} הָלוֹךְ לְהַרְגִּיעוֹ I will go to *give him* (Isr.) *rest*, 50^{34} לְמַעַן הִרְגִּיעַ את־הארץ (on הִ׳, v. Ges[§ 531] Dr[Dt 7, 24]; read prob. הַ׳); Is 51^{4} וּמשפטי לאור עמים אַרְגִּיעַ usu. I will *cause* my judgment (religion) *to repose* as, etc. (i. e. I will establish it; cf. שִׂים 42^{4}); but metaph. strange: hence Bachm Che Marti (joining to v^{5}) צִדְקִי (< אָקְרֵב 46^{13}) אַרְגִּיעַ אַקְרִיב *in a moment* (I. רָגַע Hiph.) will I bring near, etc., Du הִרְגִּיעַ קָרֵב, Oort Ry Kit בְּרֶגַע קָרֵב (cf. 𝔊 ἐγγίζει ταχύ). **b.** intrans. *rest, repose*, Dt 28^{65} ובגוים ההם לא תַרְגִּיעַ, Is 34^{14} שָׁם הִרְגִּיעָה לִּילִית. So Ecclus 36^{31}.

7282 †רָגֵעַ **adj. restful, quiet,** ψ 35^{20} וְעַל רִגְעֵי־אֶרֶץ דִּבְרֵי מִרְמוֹת יַחֲשֹׁבוּן, of the peaceful worshippers of י׳.

4771 †מַרְגּוֹעַ **n.[m.] rest** (poet.), Je 6^{16} וּמִצְאוּ מ׳ לְנַפְשְׁכֶם.

†מַרְגֵּעָה **n.f. rest, repose** (poet.), Is 28^{12} 47..
אֲשֶׁר אָמַר זֹאת הַמְּ׳ ‖ הַמְּנוּחָה) וְלֹא אָבוּא שְׁמוֹעַ).

†III. רָגַע **vb. harden** (Eth. ረግዐ: *coagulate, congeal:* poss. a special development of ✓ رَجَعَ, v. II. ר׳);—Jb 7^{5} עוֹרִי רָגַע וַיִּמָּאֵס my skin *hardens*, and (then) runs again (II. מָאַס), of the ulcers in elephantiasis. 7280

†[רָגַשׁ] **vb. be in tumult or commotion** (Ar. رَجَسَ *make a vehement noise;* BAram. Aram. רְגַשׁ, ܪܓܫ *be disturbed, in tumult* (𝔗 Ithp. often for הָמָה, as ψ 46^{6}, שָׁאָה Is $17^{12 f.}$; ܪܶܓܫܳܐ for הָמוֹן *ibid.*); but Syr. usu. *perceive*, so NH Hiph., but Hithp. *fall stormily upon*);—**Qal** *Pf.* 3 pl. ψ 2^{1} רָגְשׁוּ why do the nations *throng tumultuously?* 7283

†[רֶ֫גֶשׁ] **n.[m.]** throng;—בְּרָגֶשׁ נְהַלֵּךְ ψ 55^{15} used to walk *in the throng* (cf. הָמוֹן 42^{5}, also to בית אלהים). 7285

†[רִגְשָׁה] **n.f.** throng;—cstr. רִגְשַׁת פֹּעֲלֵי אָוֶן ψ 64^{3}; so (of worshippers, cf. רֶגֶשׁ) 68^{28}, reading רִגְשָׁתָם for רִגְמָתָם, Hup Pe Bi Che Bae Dr. 7285

†[רָדַד] **vb. beat out,** fig. **beat down, subdue** (NH Pi. *stamp* or *beat down, make flat, spread out;* 𝔗 רְדַד *beat out;* cf. prob. Ar. رَدَّ *repel, reject* (Nö[M 75]); As. *radâdu* is *pursue* (rare));—**Qal,** fig., *beat down: Inf. cstr.* לְרַד לְפָנָיו גּוֹיִם Is 45^{1}; *Pt. act.* הָרוֹדֵד עַמִּי תַחְתָּי ψ 144^{2};—so also *Impf.* יָרֹד Is 41^{2} acc. Ew al. (for MT יַרְדְּ, v. I. רדה **Hiph.**).—Ju 19^{11} rd. יָרַד. **Hiph.** lit. *beat out: Impf.* 3 ms. וַיְּרַד עַל־הַכְּרוּבִים . . . אֶת־הַזָּהָב 1 K 6^{32} *and beat out the gold upon the cherubim* (covered them with beaten gold). 7286

†[רְדִיד] **n.[m.] wide wrapper,** or **large veil** (𝔗[Jer] רְדִידָא (esp. for Heb. צָעִיף); Syr. ܪܕܝܕܐ, appar. *veil;* Ar. رِدَآء is *wrapper*);—sf. רְדִידִי Ct 5^{7}; pl. הָרְדִידִים Is 3^{23} (in list of women's finery). 7289

†רַדַּי **n.pr.m.** fifth son of Jesse, acc. to 1 Ch 2^{14}; Ζαδδαι, A Ραδδαι, 𝔊L Ρεδαι. 7288

†I. [רָדָה] **vb. have dominion, rule, dominate** (NH רָדָה, 𝔗[Jon] רְדָא, *chastise;* Ar. رَدَى *tread, trample;* Syr. ܪܕܐ *chastise*, also (and so As. *radû*) *go, flow*);—**Qal** *Pf.* 3 pl. consec. וְרָדוּ Is 14^{2} Lv 26^{17}; 2 mpl. רְדִיתֶם Ez 34^{4}; *Impf.* 3 ms. sf. יִרְדֶּנּוּ Lv 25^{53}, וַיִּרְדֶּנָּה La 1^{13}, juss. וְיֵרְדְּ Nu 24^{19} ψ 72^{8}; 2 ms. תִּרְדֶּה Lv $25^{43.46}$, etc.; *Imv.* 7287

ms. רְדֵה ψ 110[2]; mpl. רְדוּ Gn 1[28] (Jo 4[13] v. ירד); *Inf. cstr.* רְדוֹת Ez 29[15]; *Pt.* רֹדֶה 1 K 5[4] Is 14[6]; sf. רֹדֵם ψ 68[28]; pl. הָרֹדִים 1 K 5[30] + 2 t.;—*have dominion, rule*, over, usu. c. ב pers. vel pop. 1 K 5[4.30] 9[23] = 2 Ch 8[10], Is 14[2] Lv 25[43.46.53] 26[17] Ez 29[15] Ne 9[28] ψ 49[15]; ב of fish, etc., Gn 1[26.28]; בְּקֶרֶב ψ 110[2]; c. acc. pers. Ez 34[4] Is 14[6] (perh. + acc. cogn., v. [מִרְדָּה] infr.); acc. om. Nu 24[19] (מִיַּעֲקֹב), Je 5[31] (+ עַל־יְדֵיהֶם, v. יָד **5 h** (2); vid. also ingenious conj. sub II. רדה; but < Gr יוֹרוּ *teach*), ψ 72[8]; for וַיִּרְדֶּנָּה La 1[13] *and it* (the fire) *prevailed against them* (my bones), read perh. יְרָדָהּ into my bones *it descended* (Bu).—רֹדֵם ψ 68[28] is dub.; Grill Hup-Now Che Du קִדֵּם. יְרַד Ju 5[13.13] v. יָרַד. **Hiph.** *Impf.* 3 ms. וּמְלָכִים יַרְדְּ Is 41[2] *and kings he causeth* (him) *to dominate;* but apoc. form strange, read יָרֹד (√ רדד q.v.) Ew Di Du; יַחֲרִד 𝔊 Klo Che.

4783 †[מִרְדָּה] **n.f.** dominion;—as acc. cogn.
מִרְדַּת בְּלִי חָשָׂךְ Is 14[6], cstr. bef. cl. (Ges[§ 130 d]; so
4783 most for MT מֻרְדָּף q.v. sub רדף). p. 923

7287 †II. רָדָה **vb.** scrape out (NH *id., scrape*
or *draw off, out* (bread from oven));—**Qal** *Pf.* 3 ms. ר׳ הַדְּבַשׁ Ju 14[9b] out of the carcass *he scraped the honey* (v. GFM); sf. וַיִּרְדֵּהוּ אֶל־כַּפָּיו v[9a] *he scraped it out into his palms;* Buhl[Lex] Du also ר׳ עַל־יְדֵיהֶם Je 5[31], sc. gifts, money, fig. for making gain (most I. רדה q.v.).

7288 רַדַּי **n.pr.** v. רדד. p. 921

7290 †[רָדַם] **vb. Niph.** be in, or fall into,
heavy sleep (NH *id.;* cf. Ar. رَدَمَ *stop up* (door, gap, etc.), whence perh. *be deaf* (stopped up) to sounds, etc.);—*Pf.* 3 ms. נִרְדַּם Ju 4[21]; 1 s. נִרְדַּמְתִּי Dn 8[8]; *Impf.* 3 ms. וַיֵּרָדֵם Jon 1[5]; *Pt.* נִרְדָּם Pr 10[5] + 3 t.;—*be* or *fall fast asleep:* Ju 4[21] Jon 1[5] (after וַיִּשְׁכַּב), v[6] (pt., Ges[§ 120 b] Da[Synt. § 70 (a)]); pt. as subst. נִרְדָּם בַּקָּצִיר Pr 10[5]; of sleep of death ψ 76[7]; stunning effect of awe and dread Dn 8[18] 10[9] (both + אַרְצָה [וּפָנַי] עַל־פָּנַי).

8639 †תַּרְדֵּמָה **n.f.** deep sleep;—abs. ת׳ Gn
2[21]+; cstr. תַּרְדֵּמַת 1 S 26[12];—*deep sleep*, usu. c. נָפַל + עַל pers., and usu. by supernat. agency: ת׳ נָפְלָה עַל ... וַיַּפֵּל י׳ א׳ ת׳ עַל Gn 2[21] (J; 𝔊 ἔκστασις), 15[12] (J; 𝔊 *id.*), Jb 4[13] = 33[15] (𝔊 [δεινὸς] φόβος), so תַּרְדֵּמַת י׳ 1 S 26[12] (𝔊 θάμβος), result of slothfulness (עַל and pers. om.) Pr 19[15]; fig. for insensibility of spirit, נָסַךְ עֲלֵיכֶם י׳ רוּחַ ת׳ Is 29[10].

1719, 1721 †רֹדָן **n. pr. loc.** vel **gent. Rhodes,**
Rhodians, so read, בְּנֵי ר׳, Ez 27[15] (for MT
1719 בְּנֵי דְּדָן, v. ד׳ **1**), 𝔊 Sta Co Berthol Toy Krae.
p. 187

†רוֹדָנִים **n.pr.gent.pl. Rhodians;**—1 Ch 1721
1[7], Ῥόδιοι; and so ∥ Gn 10[4] (for דֹּדָנִים p. 187). 1721

רָדַף 141 **vb. pursue, chase, persecute** 7291
(NH *id.*, Aram. רְדַף, ܪܕܰܦ; Ar. رَدِفَ; Sab. רדף *id.*, SabDenkm[No. 7, l. 2]);—**Qal** 128 *Pf.* 3 ms. ר׳ Ju 4[16]+; 1 s. וְרָדַפְתִּי Je 29[18], etc.; *Impf.* יִרְדֹּף Dt 19[6]+, יִרַדֹּף ψ 7[6] (appar. to give choice of Qal or Pi, Ki JHMich Bae al.; Ges[§ 63 n] expl. as developed from יִרְדֹּף, cf. Ol[§ 236 e], and, further, Kö[i. 160]), sf. יִרְדָּפְךָ Ez 35[6.6], etc.; *Imv.* ms. רְדֹף Gn 44[4]+, sf. רָדְפֵהוּ ψ 34[15]; mpl. רִדְפוּ Ju 3[28]+; *Inf. cstr.* לִרְדֹּף Jos 8[16]+, מִרְדֹּף 1 S 23[28] 2 S 18[16], sf. רָדְפִי ψ 38[21] Qr, רדופי Kt, etc.; *Pt.* רֹדֵף Ju 4[22]+, pl. רֹדְפִים 8[4]+;—**1. a.** *pursue* (sts. + הִשִּׂיג): lit. c. אַחֲרֵי pers., in order to overtake Gn 44[4] (J), 2 K 5[21]; esp. with hostile purpose Gn 31[23] (+ הִדְבִּיק), 35[5] Jos 24[6] (all E), 2[5.7.7] 8[16.16.17] 10[19] (JE), Dt 11[4] 19[6] Jos 20[5] (all D), Ex 14[4.8.9] (P), Ju 1[6] 2 S 20[6.7.10.13] 2 K 9[27] + 17 t., + 2 K 25[5] (אַחַר), + Ju 4[16] (אַחֲרֵי הָרֶכֶב); + רִדְפוּ אַחֲרַי Ju 3[28] = *follow me* (as leader; but this meaning not elsewhere; rd. רְדוּ 𝔊 Kit GFM). **b.** lit., c. acc. pers., *put to flight, chase* (defeated foe; sts. c. הִשִּׂיג): Am 1[11] Ho 8[3] Dt 32[30] (poem; ∥ הֵנִיס), 28[22.45] Jos 23[10] (D), Lv 26[8.8] (H); וְרָדַף אֹתָם קוֹל עָלֶה נִדָּף v[36a] (H); Jos 7[5] 8[24] 10[10] 11[8] (all JE), Gn 14[15] Dt 1[44] Ju 4[22] Is 41[3] + 13 t. + Ju 7[25] (rd. אֶת־ for אֶל־, 𝔊 𝔙 𝔗 GFM Bu Now). †**c.** lit., acc. om. Ju 8[4] 1 S 30[8] (+ הִשִּׂיג), v[10] Gn 14[14] Ex 14[23] (P), 15[9] (poem; + הִשִּׂיג), Lv 26[36b.37] (H), Pr 28[1]; esp. pt. pl. הָר׳ *the pursuers* Jos 2[16.16.22.22] Ne 9[11] Is 30[16], so הָרֹדֵף Jos 8[20] La 1[6]. †**d.** *chase, hunt*, partridge (קֹרֵא) 1 S 26[20] (in sim.; ∥ בִּקֵּשׁ). †**e.** *pursue*, in fig., Je 20[11] La 4[19], רִדְפוּ וְתִפְשׂוּהוּ ψ 71[11], cf. La 1[3]; ψ 7[6] (+ הִשִּׂיג; v. supr.); esp. subj. י׳, *pursue* (fig. of punishment, judgment), c. acc. pers. Je 29[18] (בַּחֶרֶב), La 3[43] and (בְּאַף) v[66], ψ 83[16] (בִּסַעֲרֶךָ); אֶת־קַשׁ יָבֵשׁ תִּרְדֹּף Jb 13[25] (∥ תַּעֲרוֹץ); רֹדְפָם, of מַלְאַךְ י׳, ψ 35[6]. †**f.** fig. *persecute, harass*, c. acc. pers. Dt 30[7] Jb 19[22] (כְּמוֹ־אֵל), ψ 69[27] 109[16] 119[86.161]; c. acc. נַפְשִׁי 143[3], c. acc. נְדִבָתִי Jb 30[15] (but subj. obscure; read perh. תֵּרָדֵף Bu; Du תִּנָּדֵף); c. לְ pers. Jb 19[28]; pt. as subst. Je 15[15] 17[18] ψ 7[2] 31[16] (∥ אוֹיְבַי; We מְרַדְּפַי for רֹדְפַי), 35[3] 119[84.157] (+ צָרַי), 142[7]. †**g.** *pursue, dog*, subj. דָּם, c. acc. pers. Ez 35[6.6] (del v[a] 𝔊 Co Toy Krae); in good sense, *attend closely upon*, טוֹב וָחֶסֶד יִרְדְּפוּנִי ψ 23[6]. †**2.** fig. *follow after, aim to secure:* in bad sense, c. acc. שַׁלְמֹנִים Is 1[23], שֵׁכָר 5[11], ר׳ קָדִים Ho 12[2], רֹדְפֵי זִמָּה ψ 119[150]; good

sense, c. inf. לָדַעַת אֶת־י׳ Ho 6[3], c. acc. צֶדֶק Dt 16[20] Is 51[1] (|| מְבַקְשֵׁי י׳), צְדָקָה וָחָסֶד Pr 21[21], שָׁלוֹם ψ 34[15] (|| בַּקֵּשׁ), טוֹב 38[21]. †**Niph.** pass.: *Pf.* 1 pl. עַל־צַוָּארֵנוּ נִרְדָּפְנוּ La 5[5] *upon our neck* (i.e. closely) *we are pursued* (improb., cf. Bu); perh. *Impf.* 3 fs. תִּרְדֹּף Jb 30[15] Bu (for תִּרְדֹּף); *Pt.* א׳ יְבַקֵּשׁ אֶת־נִרְדָּף Ec 3[15] *God seeketh the pursued* (i.e. what has disappeared, is past, but dub.). †**Pi.** *Pf.* 3 fs. consec. וְרִדְּפָה Ho 2[9]; *Impf.* 3 ms. יְרַדֶּף־ Na 1[8] (ψ 7[6] v. **Qal**); 3 fs. תְּרַדֵּף Pr 13[21]; *Pt.* מְרַדֵּף 11[19] +;—*pursue ardently*, c. acc. pers. Ho 2[9] (in fig.); fig. also וְאֹיְבָיו יְר׳ חֹשֶׁךְ Na 1[8] (Gunk[ZAW xiii (1893), 230], plausibly, יֶהְדֹּף), cf. Pr 13[31]; elsewhere pt., in Pr: *aim (eagerly) to secure*, c. acc. רָעָה 11[19], רֵיקִים 12[11] 28[19], אֲמָרִים 19[7] (mng. dub., v. Toy); in good sense, צְדָקָה 15[9]. †**Pu.** *Pf.* 3 ms. consec. וְרֻדַּף כְּמֹץ הָרִים Is 17[13] *it shall be chased away like chaff of the mountains* (||וְנָס). †**Hiph.** *Pf.* 3 ms. sf. הִרְדִּיפֻהוּ Ju 20[43] usu. *they chased him* (Benj., coll.), but strange after כִּתְּרוּ *surrounded* (still stranger after כתתו or כרתו 𝔊), and why Hiph.? GFM conj. dittogr. of הִדְרִיכֻהוּ foll.; the reverse conjectured by Bu Now.

4783 †מֻרְדָּף **n.[m.]** persecution (si vera l.)
7291 (formed like **Hoph.** *Pt.*);—Is 14[6], but 𝔗 Thes and most מִרְדַּת q.v. p. 922

7292 †[רָהַב] **vb.** act stormily, boisterously, arrogantly (Ecclus 13[8], NH *id.*, Hiph. *make proud* (rare), 𝔗 רְהַב *be arrogant*; As. *ra'âbu*, *storm at* (angrily); Ar. رَهِبَ *be alarmed, frightened;* Syr. ܪܗܒ, Pe. Pt. *trembling, hastening*, Aph. *terrify, hasten*);—**Qal** *Impf.* 3 mpl. יִרְהֲבוּ הַנַּעַר Is 3[5] (|| וְנִגַּשׂ) בַּזָּקֵן *storm against* (𝔊 προσκόψει); *Imv.* רְהַב רֵעֶ(י)ךָ Pr 6[3] *beset, importune, thy friend* (Perles[Anal. 61] conj. רְהַן *give surety*, cf. NH הרהין). **Hiph.** *Pf.* 3 mpl. sf. הִרְהִיבֻנִי Ct 6[5], of eyes, dub.: *alarm me* Hi Ew Bu, *awe me* Gi, *disturb, confuse me*, Oettli Dr[Intr. 419 (446)] Buhl; *Impf.* 2 ms. sf. תַּרְהִבֵנִי ψ 138[3] (subj. י׳), Buhl Bae Dr *thou makest me proud, bold* (Thes De Che denom. of רֹהַב).

7295 †[רָהָב] **adj.** proud, defiant (si vera l.);—pl. אֶל־רְהָבִים ψ 40[5] *unto the proud;* but read prob. הבלים (cf. 𝔊 ματαιότητας).

7296 †[רֹהַב] **n.[m.]** Thes al. pride, i.e. obj. of pride;—sf. רָהְבָּם ψ 90[10] (cf. ἡ ἀλαζονία τοῦ βίου 1 Jn 2[16]); < 𝔊 𝔙 *their width, extent* (רָחְבָּם).

†רַהַב **n.[m.]** lit. storm, arrogance, but 7293-94
only as names, v. infr.;—abs. ר׳ Is 30[7], רָהַב Jb 9[13] +;—**1.** mythical sea monster (cf. Barton[JAOS xv. 1 (1891), 22 f.]): עֹזְרֵי ר׳ Jb 9[13]; || יָם 26[12] ψ 89[11]; || תַּנִּין Is 51[9]. **2.** emblemat. name of Egypt, רַהַב וּבָבֶל ψ 87[4]; || מצרים Is 30[7].

מַרְהֵבָה **n.f.** boisterous, raging, behaviour;—Is 14[4]; so read (for MT מַדְהֵבָה) Thes and most, after 𝔊; || נגשׂ (cf. 3[5]). 4062

רהג (√of foll.; Ar. رَهَجَ is *raise* (dust, a tumult, conflict, etc.), Lane).

†רָהְגָּה Qr, רוהגה Kt, **n.pr.m.** in Asher 7303
1 Ch 7[34]; A Ογα, 𝔊L Ραγουε.

†[רָהָה] **vb.** dub., appar. **fear**;—**Qal** 7297
Impf. 2 mpl. אַל־תִּפְחֲדוּ וְאַל־תִּרְהוּ Is 44[8]; Thes תִּרְהוּ, but no √ ירה; Ew Brd Buhl[Lex 13] תִּרְאוּ (יָרֵא); > Lag Gr Che[Hpt] תִּרְהֲבוּ (in Syr. sense).

I. רהט (√of foll., prob. *collect, gather*, cf. Ar. رَهْطٌ I, VIII. *be collected, congregated*, cf. Nö[ZA xii. 186]; 𝔗 רָטְיָא = רְהָטִים, Gn 30[38.41] Ex 2[16]; Syr. ܪܗܛܐ is appar. *conduit*, also *reservoir* (?); As. *râṭu*, *vessel* for water, provisions, etc.).

†I. [רַהַט] **n.[m.]** trough (where water 7298
is *collected* ?);—for watering cattle;—pl. רְהָטִים Gn 30[38.41] Ex 2[16] (all J).

II. רהט (√of two foll.; perhaps Aram. רְהַט = רוּץ *run, flow*).

II. [רַהַט] **n.[m.]** dub., Thes and most **lock** 7298
of hair (? fr. *flowing* down);—pl. רְהָטִים Ct 7[6].

†[רָהִיט] **n.m. coll.** rafters ? boards ? (as 7351
strips *running* between beams ? so Bu conj.; cf. Syr. ܪܗܛܐ *boards* (?), Nö in Bu);—sf. רָהִיטֵנוּ Ct 1[17] Qr (Kt רחיטנו; Codd. רח׳ Baer[p. 46] Kö[ii. 1, 149]), || קֹרוֹת.

רוֹב v. רֹב sub רבב. [רוּב] v. ריב. p. 913, 936 7230, 7378

†רוד **vb.** wander restlessly, roam (cf. 7300
Ar. رَادَ (و) *go to and fro* [Nö[ZMG xxxvii (1883), 539]], Eth. ሬደ: *run upon, invade, attack*);—**Qal** *Pf.* 3 ms. עֹד רָד עִם אֵל Ho 12[1], fig., crpt., 𝔊 appar. עַתָּ יְדָעָם, We עֹדֵר דַּעַת *lacks knowledge*, Now יָדַע, Bewer[JBL xxi (1902), 108 f.] עֹד יְדָעָם; 1 pl. רַדְנוּ Je 2[31] fig. of Isr.; read וָרַדְתִּי perh. Ju 11[37] lit., v. ירד **1 g.** **Hiph.** *shew restlessness: Impf.* 2 ms. כַּאֲשֶׁר תָּרִיד Gn 27[40] (dub. Nö[l. c. 540]); 1 s. אָרִיד בְּשִׂיחִי ψ 55[3] *I shew restlessness* (?) *in my murmuring.*

4788 †[מָרוּד, Kö ii. 1, 127 f.] **n.[m.] restlessness, straying** (?);—sf. עָנְיִי וּמְרוּדִי La 3[19]; pl. sf. יְמֵי עָנְיָהּ וּמְרוּדֶיהָ La 1[7] (rd. prob. מְרוּדָהּ Nö ZMG xxxvii (1883), 539); pl. וַעֲנִיִּים מְרוּדִים Is 58[7], usu. concr. *the wandering* (homeless) *poor* (Di thinks old Qal pass. Pt.; Che Comm. rds. Hoph. מוּרָדִים; Buhl Lex Hiph. מְרִידִים; Kö ii. 1, 128 takes MT as abstr. for concr. [appos. of ע׳]; so Du Che Hpt [ע׳ gloss], read perhaps pt. רָדִים (מ dittogr.)).

7301 †[רָוָה] **vb. be saturated, drink one's fill** (NH in der. spec.; Ar. رَوِىَ; Eth. ረወየ: Aram. רְוִי, ܪܘܳܐ);—**Qal** *Pf.* 3 fs. consec. וְרָוְתָה מִדָּמָם Je 46[10], fig. of sword (|| אָכְלָה, שָׂבְעָה); *Impf.* 3 mpl. יִרְוְיֻן מִדֶּשֶׁן בֵּיתֶךָ ψ 36[9] (Ges § 75 u) fig. of men (|| תַּשְׁקֵם); 1 pl. נִרְוֶה דֹדִים Pr 7[18] *we will take our fill of love* (|| נִתְעַלְּסָה). **Pi.** *Pf.* 3 fs. רִוְּתָה Is 34[5], ר׳ consec. v[7]; 1 s. consec. וְרִוֵּיתִי Je 31[14]; *Impf.* 1 s. sf. אֲרַיָּוֵךְ Is 16[9] (read prob. אֲרַוֵּיךְ Margolis Am. J. Sem. Lang., Oct. 1902, 48, vid. also Kö i. 589 f.; > אֲרַיָּוֵךְ Sta § 634 e Ges § 75 dd); 3 mpl. sf. יְרַוֻּךָ Pr 5[19]; *Inf. abs.* רַוֵּה ψ 65[11] (Ges § 113 z);—**1.** intens. *be intoxicated, drunk* Is 34[5], fig. of sword; + מִדָּם v[7], of land (|| יְדֻשַּׁן). **2.** causat., *drench, water abundantly*, c. acc. תְּלָמֶיהָ (subj. י׳); Is 16[9] c. acc. pers. + דִּמְעָתִי material; *saturate* (fig.), *sate*, ור׳ נֶפֶשׁ הַכֹּהֲנִים דָּשֶׁן Je 31[14] (|| שׂבע); sexually, דַּדֶּיהָ יְרַוֻּךָ Pr 5[19]. **Hiph.** *Pf.* 3 ms. הִרְוָה Is 55[10], sf. הִרְוַנִי La 3[15]; 2 ms. sf. הִרְוִיתָנִי Is 43[24]; 1 s. הִרְוֵיתִי Je 31[25]; *Pt.* מַרְוֶה Pr 11[25];—*saturate, water*, c. acc. ארץ Is 55[10] (subj. גֶּשֶׁם, שֶׁלֶג); *cause to drink* (fig.), c. acc. pers. et rei (לַעֲנָה) La 3[15] (|| הִשְׂבִּיעַנִי); c. acc. pers. only (נֶפֶשׁ) Je 31[25] (|| מִלֵּאתִי), abs. Pr 11[25]; of Isr. satisfying י׳, חֵלֶב זְבָחִים Is 43[24]. **Hoph.** *Impf.* יוֹרֶא (יוּרֶה?) Pr 11[25] v. Toy and ירא p. 432.

7377 †רִי **n.[m.] moisture** (for *רְוִי Sta § 117 c, or *רִוְיִ Kö ii. 1, 64; cf. II. כִּי);—abs. בְּרִי יַטְרִיחַ עָב Jb 37[11].

7302 †רָוֶה **adj. watered**;—ms. ר׳, of garden גַּן (in sim.) Je 31[12] Is 58[11]; fs. הָרָוָה Dt 29[18] (opp. הַצְּמֵאָה; appar. of herbage, in proverb. expression for *everything*); perhaps also cstr. רְוֵה Jb 10[15] = *sated* with affliction (for רְאֵה), v. [רָאֶה].

7310 †רְוָיָה **n.f. saturation** (Lag BN 51, 150);—abs. כּוֹסִי ר׳ ψ 23[5] (fig.), i. e. is well-filled Ges § 141 c; in gen. לָר׳ 66[12], but Vrss and most mod. לָרְוָחָה *to* (a place of) *relief*.

7303 רוהגה v. רָהֲגָה sub רהג. p. 923

רוח (√of foll.; prob. *breathe, blow* (v. Gerber[46]); cf. Syr. ܪܘܰܚ *breathe*; Ar. رَاحَ *be windy*; Eth. ረሐ: *flabello ventilare, ventulum facere*; Ar. رِيحٌ *breath, wind, spirit*, رُوحٌ *soul, spirit*; NH רוּחַ, Aram. רוּחָא, ܪܘܚܳܐ *wind, breath, spirit*; also NH רֵיחַ, Aram. רֵיחָא, ܪܺܝܚܳܐ, all *odour*; NH רֵיחַ, רוּחַ (usu. Hiph.), 𝔗 Syr. Aph., all *smell*).

רוּחַ 378 **n.f.** Gn 41, 8 (less oft. **m.** Ex 10, 13+) **breath, wind, spirit**;—abs. ר׳ Gn 8[1]+, רוּחָה Je 52[23]; cstr. רוּחַ Gn 6[17]+; sf. רוּחִי v[3]+, רוּחֲךָ ψ 104[30]+, etc.; pl. רוּחוֹת v[4]+, רֻחוֹת Je 49[36], רוּחֹת Nu 16[22] 27[16] (v. Br רוח in O.T., JBL xix (1900), 132 ff., full statement of all passages);—†**1.** *breath* of mouth or nostrils (33 t.): **a.** רוּחַ פִּיו Jb 15[30] *breath of his mouth*, cf. 19[17]; רוּחַ אַפֵּינוּ La 4[20] (fig. of king), of idols לֹא רוּחַ בָּם Je 10[14] = 51[17], Hb 2[19] ψ 135[17]; cf. Jb 9[18]. **b.** as mere breath: cf. **2 e.** לְרוּחַ אִמְרֵי Jb 16[3] i. e. windy words; דִּבְרֵי־רוּחַ Jb 6[26], הַנְּבִיאִים יִהְיוּ לְרוּחַ Je 5[13]. **c.** as word of command: (1) of God: (נעשׂו) בְּרוּחַ פִּיו כָּל־צְבָאָם ψ 33[6], cf. Is 34[16] (|| פֶּה); (2) of Messianic king: בְּרוּחַ שְׂפָתָיו יָמִית רָשָׁע Is 11[4]. **d.** as hard breathing through the nostrils in anger: (1) of God: מֵרוּחַ אַפּוֹ יִכְלוּ Jb 4[9] Ex 15[8] (poem), 2 S 22[16] = ψ 18[16], Is 30[28] 59[19]; (2) of man: רוּחַ עָרִיצִים Is 25[4]. **e.** as sign and symbol of life: רוּחַ חַיִּים *breath of life* Gn 6[17] 7[15] (P); נִשְׁמַת רוּחַ חַיִּים בְּאַפָּיו Gn 7[22] (P); Ez 37[5], cf. v[6.8.9.9.9.10.14] (*breath* or *spirit*), Ec 3[19]. **2.** *wind* (117 t.): **a.** *wind* of heaven: Gn 8[1] (P) Ex 15[10] (E) Nu 11[31] (J) 1 K 18[45]+, Je 10[13], thence 51[16] ψ 135[7]; רוּחַ י׳ Ho 13[15] Is 40[7], cf. Jb 26[13] (Di Bu); †רוּחַ (ה)קָּדִים *east wind* Ex 10[13.13] 14[21] (J) ψ 48[8] Je 18[17] Ez 17[10] 19[12] 27[26] Jon 4[8]; †ר׳ צָפוֹן *north wind* Pr 25[23]; †ר׳ יָם *sea wind* (west wind) Ex 10[19] (J); †ר׳ הַיּוֹם *day wind*, evening wind Gn 3[8] (J; cf. Ct 2[17] 4[6]); †אַרְבַּע רוּחוֹת *four winds* Je 49[36] Ez 37[9] (quarters?) Dn 8[8] 11[4] (fig. quarters; cf. **b**), Zc 2[10] 6[5]; רוּחַ סְעָרָה *storm wind* ψ 107[25] 148[8] Ez 1[4] (ר׳ סְעָרוֹת), 13[11.13]; רוּחַ סֹעָה *rushing wind* ψ 55[9] (read poss. סערה Hup); בַּעְיָם רוּחוֹ Is 11[15] (read בְּעֹצֶם ר׳, v. עֲיָם, עֹצֶם), etc.; wind personif.: כַּנְפֵי רוּחַ 2 S 22[11] = ψ 18[11], 104[3], cf. Ho 4[19] ψ 104[4]. **b.** *quarter* (of wind), *side*: רוּחַ הַקָּדִים Ez 42[16] *east side*; רוּחַ הַצָּפוֹן v[17] *north side*; רוּחַ הַדָּרוֹם v[18] *south side*; רוּחַ הַיָּם v[19] *west side*; אַרְבַּע רוּחוֹת v[20] 1 Ch 9[24] *four sides*; רוּחָה Je 52[23] *on the sides*. **c.** *breath of air*: רוּחַ לֹא יָבֹא בֵינֵיהֶם Je 14[6]; שָׁאֲפוּ רוּחַ כַּתַּנִּים Jb 41[8]. **d.** *air, gas*, from womb (dub.): כְּמוֹ 7307

רוּחֲכֶם אֵשׁ תֹּאכַלְכֶם (RV יָלַדְנוּ רוּחַ Is 26^{18} (Di, e);
breath) Is 33^{11} (Du, **3 c**). **e.** *vain, empty
thing*: רוּחַ חַיָּי Jb 7^{7} *my life is wind*; דַּעַת רוּחַ
15^{2}; רוּחַ וָתֹהוּ נִסְכֵּיהֶם Is 41^{29}; רְעוּת רוּחַ *striving
for wind* Ec 1^{14} 2$^{11.17.26}$ 4$^{4.6}$ 6^{9}; cf. 1^{17} 4^{16} 5^{15}.
†**3.** *spirit*, as that which breathes quickly *in
animation or agitation* = *temper, disposition*
5315 (76 t.; so, distinctively, as compared with נֶפֶשׁ
3824 and לֵבָב): **a.** *spirit, animation, vivacity, vigour*:
מַה־זֶּה רוּחֲךָ 1 K 10^{5} = 2 Ch 9^{4}; לֹא הָיָה בָהּ עוֹד רוּחַ
וַתָּשָׁב רוּחוֹ 1 K 21^{5}; וַתְּחִי רוּחַ Gn 45^{27} (E); סָרָה
Ju 15^{19} 1 S 30^{12}. **b.** *courage*: לֹא הָיָה בָם עוֹד ר׳
Jos 5^{1}; וְנָבְקָה ר׳ מִצְרַיִם ψ 76^{13}; יִבְצֹר ר׳ נְגִידִים
Is 19^{3}; לֹא קָמָה תתעטף רוּחִי ψ 77^{4} 142^{4} 143^{4};
עוֹד ר׳ Jos 2^{11}; ר׳ אִישׁ יְכַלְכֵּל מַחֲלֵהוּ Pr 18^{14}. **c.**
temper, esp. *anger*: אָז רוּחַ רָעָה בֵּין וגו׳ Ju 9^{23};
8^{3}; רָפְתָה רוּחָם מֹשֵׁל בְּרוּחוֹ Pr 16^{32}, cf. 25^{28} 29^{11}
Jb 15^{13}; הֵנִיחוּ אֶת־רוּחִי Zc 6^{8}; Ec 7^{9} 10^{4}. **d.** *impatience* or *patience*: קֹצֶר רוּחַ Ex 6^{9} (P) *impatience*,
hastiness of temper, cf. (of י׳) Mi 2^{7}; קְצַר־רוּחַ
Pr 14^{29} (|| אֶרֶךְ אַפַּיִם); הֱצִיקַתְנִי רוּחַ בִּטְנִי Jb 32^{18}
(Du *breath*; Di Bu *divine spirit*, cf. v^{8}); אִם
הֲקָצַר רוּחַ י׳ Mi 2^{7}; מַדּוּעַ לֹא־תִקְצַר רוּחִי Jb 21^{4};
אֶרֶךְ ר׳ Ec 7^{8}. **e.** *spirit, disposition*, as troubled,
bitter, or discontented; וַתִּפָּעֶם רוּח(וֹ) (*his*)
spirit was troubled Gn 41^{8} (E) Dn 2^{3}, cf. v^{1};
מֹרַת רוּחַ Gn 26^{35} (P) *bitterness of spirit*; עֲצוּבַת ר׳
Is 54^{6}, cf. Ez 3^{14} Jb 6^{4}. **f.** as crushed: וְכֵהָתָה
כָּל־רוּחַ Ez 21^{12}, cf. Is 61^{3} Pr 15$^{4.13}$ 17^{22} 18^{14} ψ 143^{7}.
g. *disposition* of various kinds, oft. *unaccountable
and uncontrollable impulse*: הֵעִיר אֶת־רוּחַ 1 Ch
5$^{26.26}$ 2 Ch 21^{16} 36^{22} Ezr 1$^{1.5}$ Je 51^{11} Hg 1$^{14.14.14}$; הִנְנִי
נ(וֹ)תֵן בּוֹ רוּחַ 2 K 19^{7} = Is 37^{7}; Nu 14^{24} (J; v. עִם
4 b), Mal 2$^{15.15.16}$ Dt 2^{30}; רוּחַ קִנְאָה *jealous disposition* Nu 5$^{14.14.30}$ (P); רוּחַ זְנוּנִים Ho 4^{12} 5^{4}; רוּחַ
עִוְעִים Is 19^{14}; רוּחַ מִשְׁפָּט 28^{6}; אִישׁ אֲשֶׁר רוּחַ אֱלֹהִים
בּוֹ (administrative) Gn 41^{38} (E); קַר רוּחַ אִישׁ תְּבוּנָה
Pr 17^{27}. **h.** *prophetic spirit*: יְהוֹשֻׁעַ אִישׁ אֲשֶׁר־
רוּחַ בּוֹ Nu 27^{18} (P; or **g**, as Gn 41^{38}); רוּחַ אֵלִיָּהוּ
עַל־אֱלִישָׁע 2 K 2^{15}, cf. v^{9}; רוּחַ תַּרְדֵּמָה *spirit of
deep sleep* (ecstatic, cf. Gn 2^{21} 15^{12}, but Di al. **g**,
as Is 19^{14}) Is 29^{10}; Mi 2^{11}; רוּחַ הַטֻּמְאָה Zc 13^{2} (of
lying proph.), cf. Ez 13^{3}. †**4.** *spirit* of the
1320 living, breathing being, dwelling in the בָּשָׂר of
5315 men and animals, || נֶפֶשׁ (35 t.): **a.** gift and
creation of God: יֹצֵר רוּחַ אָדָם בְּקִרְבּוֹ Zc 12^{1};
רוּחַ אֱלוֹהַּ בְּאַפִּי Jb 27^{3}, cf. Is 42^{5}. **b.** God pre-
serves it: פְּקֻדָּתְךָ שָׁמְרָה רוּחִי Jb 10^{12}, cf. 12^{10};
תֹּכֵן רוּחוֹת Nu 16^{22} 27^{16} (P); אֱלֹהֵי הָרוּחֹת לְכָל בָּשָׂר
Pr 16^{2}. **c.** it is therefore God's spirit: Gn 6^{3}
(J; v. דִּין ad fin.). **d.** it departs at death:

ψ 78^{39} (Dr *a wind* that passeth *away* **2 e**);
חַיֵּי רוּחִי Is 38^{16} (Di *principle of life*), ψ 146^{4};
esp. 104$^{29.30}$ Jb 17^{1} 34^{14} (cf. v^{15}), Is 57^{16} Ec 8$^{8.8}$
(*wind* Wild); אֵינְךָ יוֹדֵעַ מַה־דֶּרֶךְ הָרוּחַ Ec 11^{5}, cf.
3^{21}; over ag. הָרוּחַ תָּשׁוּב אֶל־הָאֱלֹהִים אֲשֶׁר נְתָנָהּ
12^{7}; בְּיָדְךָ אַפְקִיד רוּחִי ψ 31^{6}. **e.** disembodied
being (dub., Di Du *breath of wind*): וְרוּחַ עַל־פָּנַי
יַחֲלֹף Jb 4^{15}. †**5.** *spirit* as seat of emotion
= נֶפֶשׁ: **a.** *desire* (poss. **3 g**), Is 26^{9} (|| נֶפֶשׁ). 5315
b. *sorrow, trouble* (prob. **3 e**), Jb 7^{11} (|| נֶפֶשׁ).—
1 S 1^{15} v. קָשֶׁה. †**6.** occasionally (and late)
= seat or organ of mental acts, || לֵב, or synon. 3820
with it: רוּחַ חָכְמָה Ex 28^{3} Dt 34^{9} (both P; prob.
3 g); תֹּעֵי רוּחַ Is 29^{24}, cf. Jb 20^{3} (Hi Bu Du *wind*
of Job's words), ψ 77^{7} (𝔊 Sym 𝔖 Jer troubled
disposition); רוּחַ יהוה Is 40^{13}; come into *mind* Ez
11^{5}, 20^{32} (cf. לֵב Is 65^{17} Je 3^{16} +); 1 Ch 28^{12}. †**7.**
rarely of the will; also = לֵב: רוּחַ נָכוֹן ψ 51^{12} 3820
(= לֵב נָכוֹן 57$^{8.8}$ +); רוּחַ נְדִיבָה v^{14}; נְדָבָה רוּחוֹ Ex
35^{21} (P; cf. נְדִיב לֵב Ex 35$^{5.22}$ (P) 2 Ch 29^{31}).
†**8.** רוּחַ esp. of moral character; also = לֵב: 3820
רוּחַ חֲדָשָׁה Ez 11^{19} 18^{31} 36^{26}; רוּחִי v^{27} Is 59^{21}
(|| דְּבָרַי, רוּחִי; but prob. prophetic spirit **9 b**);
דַּכְּאֵי רוּחַ Is 66^{2}; נְכֵה רוּחַ Ez 18^{31} 36^{26}; לֵב חָדָשׁ
ψ 34^{19} (cf. לֵב נִדְכָּאִים Is 57^{15}); מִשֵּׁבֶר רוּחַ Is 65^{14}
(cf. **3 f**); רוּחַ נִשְׁבָּרָה ψ 51^{19} (|| לֵב נִשְׁבָּר, cf.
נִשְׁבְּרֵי לֵב 34^{19} Is 61^{1}); ψ 32^{2} Pr 11^{13} 16^{18} ψ 78^{8}
Ec 7^{8} (cf. גְּבַהּ לֵב Pr 16^{5}); שְׁפַל רוּחַ Pr 16^{19} 29^{23}
Is 57^{15}; רוּחַ שְׁפָלִים v^{15} (cf. **3 f**). †**9.** *spirit
of God* (94 t.; not D or Je or any Deut. writer;
conception of its activity in inspiring prophecy
prob. discredited from abuse by false prophets,
v. נבא, נביא): **a.** as inspiring ecstatic state of
prophecy, Nu 11$^{17.25.25.26.29}$ (J), 1 S 10$^{6.10}$ (cf. v^{5}),
19$^{20.23}$; as inciting to deeds of frenzy, in the
ecstatic state; hence conceived as ר׳ אֱלֹהִים רָעָה
1 S 16$^{15.15.16}$, ר׳ רָעָה מֵאֵת י׳ v^{14} = צלח ר׳ א׳ רָעָה
18^{10} (other narrative) = ר׳ י׳ רָעָה 19^{9}; ר׳ א׳ 16^{23}
= רוּחַ הָרָעָה v^{23}, cf. הָרוּחַ 1 K 22^{21} = ר׳ שֶׁקֶר v$^{22.23}$
= 2 Ch 18$^{20.21.22}$ = רוּחַ י׳ 1 K 22^{24} = 2 Ch 18^{23}; cf.
also (in earlier prophets) אִישׁ הָרוּחַ, i. e. one
possessed by the spirit in the ecstatic state,
|| הַנָּבִיא Ho 9^{7}; רוּחַ י׳ Mi 3^{8} (|| כֹּחַ) is prob. gloss
(We Now); וְלֹא רוּחִי Is 30^{1}; רוּחַ dealing with
Ezek.: Ez 2^{2} 3$^{12.14.24}$ 8^{3} 11$^{1.5.24}$ (Co gloss), 37^{1} 43^{5}
(all implying ecstatic state of vision), cf. Elijah
1 K 18^{12} 2 K 2^{16}. **b.** *spirit* as impelling proph.
to utter instruction or warning (higher and later
conception): transition prob. Nu 24^{2} 2 S 23^{2}
1 Ch 12^{18}; elsewhere in Ch.: 2 Ch 15^{1} 20^{14} 24^{20};
distinctly in Is^{2}, 48^{16}, cf. 61^{1}; so of ancient

prophets, Zc 7^{12} Ne 9^{30}, cf., of future prophetic gift, Jo 3$^{1.2}$. **c.** imparting warlike energy, and executive and administrative power: (1) to וַתְּהִי רוּחַ ,מְלָכִים ,מוֹשִׁיעִים ,שֹׁפְטִים, of ancient Isr.: עַל ר׳ י׳ Ju 3^{10} 11^{29}, cf. 6^{34} 13^{25} 14$^{6.19}$ 15^{14} 1 S 11^{6} 16$^{13.14}$; so also עַד יֵעָרֶה עָלֵינוּ רוּחַ מִמָּרוֹם Is 32^{15}; (2) resting upon Messianic king: Is 11$^{2.2.2}$; upon servant of י׳, 42^{1}. **d.** late, as endowing men with various gifts: technical skill Ex 31^{3} 35^{31} (P); understanding Jb 32^{8} (|| נִשְׁמַת שַׁדַּי); poured out by divine wisdom Pr 1^{23}. **e.** as energy of life: רוּחַ אֱלֹהִים מְרַחֶפֶת עַל־פְּנֵי הַמָּיִם Gn 1^{2} (P); רוּחַ אֵל עָשָׂתְנִי Jb 33^{4} (|| נִשְׁמַת שַׁדַּי); as vital power, opp. בָּשָׂר: Is 31^{3}; in cherubic chariot: Ez 1^{12}, cf. v$^{20.21}$ 10^{17}; reviving Israel Ez 39^{29} Zc 12^{10} Is 44^{3}. **f.** = ancient angel of the presence and later Shekina: ר׳ קָדְשׁוֹ Is 63$^{10.11}$ = ר׳ י׳ v^{14} (= מַלְאַךְ פָּנָיו v^{9}), cf. ψ 106^{33}; so also ר׳ קָדְשְׁךָ ψ 51^{13} (in national prayer), cf. Ne 9^{20} ψ 143^{10}; proph. of restoration conceive of the divine spirit as standing in their midst and about to fulfil all divine promises: רוּחִי עֹמֶדֶת בְּתוֹכְכֶם Hg 2^{5}, Zc 4^{6}; this conception culminates in רוּחַ = divine Presence, and as such omnipresent, ψ 139^{7} (|| פָּנֶיךָ; cf. v^{8}).

7381 **רֵיחַ** $_{58}$ **n.m.** $^{\text{Je 48, 11}}$ **scent, odour** (prop. *breath*);—abs. Ct 2^{13}+, usu. cstr. Gn 8^{21}+; sf. רֵיחוֹ Je 48^{11} Ct 1^{12}, רֵיחֵנוּ Ex 5^{21};—**1.** *scent, odour*, of plants and fields Gn 27^{27} (JE) Ct 1^{12} 2^{3} 4^{11} 7^{14} Ho 14^{7}, of ointments Ct 1^{3} 4^{10}, of pers. and garments Gn 27$^{27.27}$ (JE) Ct 4^{11} 7^{9}, of water Jb 14^{9}; fig. of influence, reputation Ex 5^{21} (J) Je 48^{11}. **2.** term. techn., רֵיחַ נִיחֹחַ *odour of soothing* (to God), tranquillizing odour (of ascending sacrifices, v. נִיחֹחַ) Gn 8^{21} (J), elsewh. Ez 6^{13} 16^{19} 20$^{28.41}$ and P: Ex 29$^{18.25.41}$ Lv 1^{9} + 16 t. Lv, Nu 15^{3} + 17 t. Nu.

7306 †[**רִיחַ**] **vb. denom. Hiph.** (?), **smell, perceive odour**;—*Impf.* 3 ms. יָרִיחַ Jb 39^{25}, יָרַח 1 S 26^{19} + 2 t.; וַיָּרַח Gn 8^{21}; 3 mpl. יְרִיחוּן ψ 115^{6}, יְרִיחֻן Dt 4^{28}, etc.; *Inf. cstr.* הָרִיחַ Ex 30^{38}, etc.;—*smell*, c. acc. Gn 8^{21} 27^{27} (JE), 1 S 26^{19}; abs. Dt 4^{28} ψ 115^{6}; metaph. בַּהֲרִיחוֹ אֵשׁ Ju 16^{9}, יָרִיחַ מִלְחָמָה Jb 39^{25} the horse *scenteth battle;* c. ב Ex 30^{38} Lv 26^{31} (both P); metaph. = *delight in* Am 5^{21} Is 11^{3} (prob. dittogr. Br $^{\text{MP 202}}$).

7304 †**רָוַח** **vb. be wide, spacious** (NH *id.*, *extend* (intrans.), רֶוַח *wide space;* Ar. رَوِحَ *be wide* (between thighs), and deriv.; cf. perhaps Eth. ረዐወ: *make open, open* (der. spec.; Di^{293}); Aram. רְוַח *be wide* (usu. fig. as Heb.), رْوَس, ܪܘܰܚ *be wide, enlarged*);—**Qal** *Pf.* 3 ms. ר׳, sq. לְ pers. 1 S 16^{23} fig. there *was enlargement, relief*, for Saul; *Impf.* 3 ms. יִרְוַח לִי Jb 32^{20} that *there may be relief* for me. **Pu.** *Pt.* pl. מְרֻוָּחִים Je 22^{14} *spacious* (of rooms; || בֵּית מִדּוֹת).

†**רֶוַח** **n.m. 1. space, interval** Gn 32^{17} (E; 7305
בֵּין . . . וּבֵין). **2. respite, relief**, Est 4^{14}.

†**רְוָחָה** **n.f. respite, relief**;—abs. ר׳ Ex 8^{11} 7309
(J); sf. רַוְחָתִי La 3^{56} (Ew Löhr Bu $^{\text{Comm.}}$ צְוָחָתִי *my outcry;* then del. שַׁוְעָתִי as gloss); rd. לָרְוָחָה also for MT לָרְוָיָה ψ 66^{12} (v. sub רוה).

רְוָיָה v. רוה. p. 924 7310

†**רוּם** **vb. be high, exalted, rise** (OHeb., 7311
Ph., OAram., Palm., all in n.pr.; Sab. in רים epith. dei et regis Fell $^{\text{ZMG liv (1900), 25 f.}}$ also in n.pr. Mordtm $^{\text{ib. xxx (1876), 36}}$ SabDenkm $^{\text{No. 14, 1. 1}}$; Ar. رَامَ *be high*, dial. of Oman (Jayakar $^{\text{JA xxi. 813, 875}}$) and Zanzibar (Prä $^{\text{ZMG xxxiv (1880), 218}}$); Eth. in deriv.; Aram. רָם, ܪܳܡ (very often in der. spec. and deriv.));—**Qal** *Pf.* 3 ms. consec. וְרָם Dt 8^{14}+;
3 fs. רָמָה 1 S 2^{1}+; וְרָאֲמָה Zc 14^{10} v. רָאַם; 3 pl. 7213
רָמוּ Pr 30^{13} ψ 131^{1}, רָמּוּ Jb 22^{12} (Baer Gi; Ges $^{\text{§ 20 i}}$); *Impf.* יָרוּם Is 30^{18}+, juss. יָרֹם Nu 24^{7}, וַיָּרָם Ho 13^{6} Ez 10^{4} [וַיָּרֻם Ex 16^{20} v. רמם]; 3 mpl. יְרֻמוּן Is 49^{11}, etc.; *Imv.* ms. רוּמָה ψ 21^{4}+; *Inf. cstr.* רוּם Dt 17^{20} Ez 10^{16}, כְּרֻם ψ 12^{9} [Bae conj. כְּרֻם], sf. רוּמָם Ez 10^{17} (Ges $^{\text{§ 72 q}}$); *Pt.* רָם Is 6^{1}+, pl. רָמִים 2^{13}+, cstr. רָמֵי 10^{33}, etc.;—**1. a.** *be high*, lit. rock (in fig.) ψ 61^{3} (מִן comp.); *be* (*set on*) *high*, רָמּוּ Jb 22^{12} (of stars), esp. pt., = adj., in gen. Is 2^{12} (+ גֵּאֶה), of mts. v^{14} Dt 12^{2}, hill Ez 6^{13} 20^{28} 34^{6}, throne Is 6^{1}, trees = *tall* 2^{13} Ez 17^{22}, cf. (in fig.) Is 10^{33} (רָמֵי הַקּוֹמָה); human stature Dt 1^{28} (מִן comp.), 2$^{10.21}$ 9^{2}; רָמִים ψ 78^{69} *heights* (of heaven; || אֶרֶץ); רָמִים of inhab. of heavens Jb 21^{22}. **b.** esp. of י׳, רָם וְנִשָּׂא Is 57^{15}, cf. ψ 138^{6}, + עַל־כָּל־הָעַמִּים 99^{2}, גּוֹיִם 113^{4}. **2.** *be raised, uplifted:* **a.** of highway Is 49^{11} (*made high*, put in order); voice, Dt 27^{14} (pt. = adj.) *uplifted.* **b.** fig.: of hand, symbol of might, Dt 32^{27}, + עַל pers. Mi 5^{8}; of Isr. in Exodus בְּיָד רָמָה Ex 14^{8} Nu 33^{3} (both P); of י׳'s hand Is 26^{11} ψ 89^{14} (|| תָּעֹז); fig. of presumption Nu 15^{30} (P); זְרוֹעַ רָמָה of might Jb 38^{15}; of eyes, fig. of arrogance Pr 6^{17} 30^{13} ψ 131^{1} (|| גָּבַהּ לִבִּי), so 18^{28}, but || 2 S 22^{28} of pers.; of heart, fig. of reckless elation, Ho 13^{6} Dt 8^{14} Ez 31^{10} (גָּבַהְתָּ || בְּגָבְהוֹ, בְּקוֹמָה) Dn 11^{12}, + מִן pers. Dt 17^{20}; of horn, fig.

of triumph 1 S 2[1] (song), ψ 89[25] (v[18] see **Hiph.**), 112[9], so head 27[6] (+ עַל pers.), 140[9] (join ירומו to v[10], but read יָרִימוּ Che, cf. Hup-Now). **c.** of pers., *be exalted* (in fig.), king Nu 24[7] (JE; + מִן comp.; ‖ תִּנַּשֵּׂא); of God (י׳, i.e. shew his exaltation) Is 30[18] 2 S 22[47] = ψ 18[47], ψ 21[14] 46[11.11], + עַל־(הַ)שָּׁמַיִם 57[6.12] 108[6]; עֶבֶד י׳ Is 52[13], י׳'s people ψ 89[17]; rebellious 66[7] (Qr; Kt Hiph.: *shew exaltation*); worthlessness (personif.) ψ 12[9]; of city Pr 11[11]. **3.** *be lifted, rise,* of ark, מֵעַל־הארץ Gn 7[17] (J), so of cherubim Ez 10[16], cf. v[17]; כְּבוֹד י׳ v[4] (מֵעַל הַכְּרוּב).—Pr 24[7] v. I. רָאמוֹת p. 910b. **Pōlēl** *Pf.* 3 fs. sf. רֹמְמָתְהוּ Ez 31[4]; 1 s. רוֹמַמְתִּי Is 1[2] 23[4]; *Impf.* 3 ms. יְרוֹמֵם Ho 11[7], sf. יְרוֹמְמֵנִי ψ 27[5], וִירוֹמִמְךָ 37[34]; 1 s. sf. וַאֲרֹמְמֶנְהוּ Ex 15[2] (Ges §58 i), etc. (אֲרוֹמָם v. **Hithpō'l.**); *Imv.* mpl. רוֹמְמוּ ψ 99[5.9]; *Inf. cstr.* לְרוֹמֵם Ezr 9[9]; *Pt.*
7319 מְרוֹמֵם 1 S 2[7], sf. מְרוֹמְמִי ψ 9[14], f. רוֹמֵמָה ψ 118[16] (מ om., Hup-Now Bae; cf. Kö I. 454);—**1. a.** *raise, rear,* children Is 1[2] 23[4] (both ‖ גִּדֵּל). **b.** *cause* tree *to grow,* subj. תְּהוֹם Ez 31[4] (‖ גִּדֵּל). **c.** *rear, erect,* temple Ezr 9[9]. **2.** *lift up:* **a.** in fig., acc. pers., subj. י׳ ψ 27[5] (+ בְּצוּר); + מִן comp. 2 S 22[49] = ψ 18[49], + מִן *from* 9[14]; acc. om. Ho 11[7] (si vera l., cf. We Now). **b.** *raise* waves of sea, subj. wind, ψ 107[25]. **c.** *exalt,* acc. pers., subj. י׳ Jb 17[4] (read perh. תְּרֹמֵם, so Bu, cf. Di), ψ 37[34] (+ לָרֶשֶׁת אָרֶץ); acc. om. 1 S 2[7] ψ 118[16] (in victory); subj. wisdom, acc. pers. Pr 4[8], cf. צְדָקָה תְּרוֹמֵם־גּוֹי 14[34]. **3.** *exalt, extol,* acc. י׳, ψ 30[2], ‖ הִלֵּל Is 25[1] ψ 118[28], ‖ אוֹדֶה ‖ הִשְׁתַּחֲווּ 99[5.9], שֵׁם י׳ 107[32], ‖ בֵּרַךְ 145[1], ‖ אַנְוֵהוּ Ex 15[2]; acc. ψ 34[4] (‖ גִּדֵּל). **Pōlal** *Impf.* 3 fpl. תְּרוֹמַמְנָה ψ 75[11] *be lifted up,* of horns (cf. **Qal 2 b**); *Pf.* 3 ms. וְרוֹמַם 66[17] *and he was extolled* (so Ki al.; but v. רוֹמָם infr.); *Pt.* מְרוֹמַם Ne 9[5] *extolled,* of י׳'s name (cf. **Pōlēl 3**), + עַל־כָּל־בְּרָכָה וגו׳. **Hiph.** *Pf.* 3 ms. הֵרִים 1 K 11[27]+; 2 ms. הֲרִימוֹתָ 2 K 19[22] ψ 89[43], וַהֲרֵמֹתָ Nu 31[28]; 2 mpl. consec. וַהֲרֵמֹתֶם 18[26], etc.; *Impf.* 3 ms. יָרִים Gn 41[44]+, juss. יָרֵם Nu 17[2] 1 S 2[10], וַיָּרֶם Ex 7[20]+, sf. וַיְרִימֶהָ Gn 31[45], etc.; *Imv.* ms. הָרֵם Ex 14[16] Is 58[1], הָרִימָה ψ 74[3], etc.; *Inf. cstr.* הָרִים Is 10[15]+, sf. הֲרִימִי Gn 39[18], etc.; *Pt.* מֵרִים Ex 35[24]+, etc.;—**1. a.** (1) *raise, lift,* c. acc., hand Ex 17[11] (E), Nu 20[11] (P), + אֶל־י׳ (in oath) Gn 14[22] cf. (אֶל־הַשָּׁמַיִם) Dn 12[7], + בְּ pers. *against* 1 K 11[26.27]; feet, פְּעָמִים ψ 74[3], i.e. run (+ לְ dir.); hand or foot Gn 41[44] (E), i.e. make any movement (hyperb.); head ψ 110[7] (As. *ullû rêšu* Dl HWB 62 a), cf. יָרִימוּ 140[9] (so rd., v. **Qal 2 b**); face, אֶל־י׳ Ezr 9[6]; hand of another, subj. י׳, fig. of giving strength to, ψ 89[43], so head 3[4]; c. acc. of rod Is 10[15] Ex 14[16] (P), הָרִים בַּמַּטֶּה 7[20] (E); rod subj., c. acc. rei Is 10[15]. (2) *raise* poor אֶבְיוֹן, c. מִן loc. 1 S 2[8] ψ 113[7]. **b.** *lift up* voice Gn 39[15.18] (J; both + קָרָא), Is 40[9.9] (acc. om.), 58[1] Ezr 3[12]; + בִּתְרוּעָה Ez 21[27], בַּחֲצֹצְרוֹת 2 Ch 5[13]; + לְ pers. Is 13[2], לָעָב Jb 38[34], + עַל pers. *against* 2 K 19[22] = Is 37[23]; הָרִים בְּקוֹל 1 Ch 15[16]. **c.** (take into one's hand and) *lift, take up,* stone Jos 4[5] (JE; עַל־שִׁכְמוֹ), leg (of sacrif. meal) 1 S 9[24], mantle 2 K 2[13], axe 6[7] (acc. om.), yoke Ho 11[4] (עַל־לְחֵיהֶם), censers Nu 17[2] (P; + מִבֵּין), ashes Lv 6[3]. **d.** *set up, erect,* stone as מַצֵּבָה Gn 31[45] (E); standard, + אֶל of people Is 49[22], עַל 62[10]. **e.** *set on high,* throne, מִמַּעַל לְכוֹכְבֵי אֵל Is 14[13]; nest (subj. נֶשֶׁר) Jb 39[27]. **f.** *lift up, exalt,* c. acc. pers., subj. י׳ 1 K 14[7] 16[2] ψ 89[20] (all c. מִן), ψ 75[8] (opp. יַשְׁפִּיל); subj. קָלוֹן Pr 3[35], cf. 14[29]; c. acc. קֶרֶן, in both good and bad sense (cf. **Qal 2 b**) 1 S 2[10] La 2[17] (לַמָּרוֹם), ψ 89[18] (Kt; Qr **Qal**), 92[11] 148[14] ψ 75[5.6]; but 1 Ch 25[5] *sound the horn;* inf. = *exaltation* ψ 75[7]; 66[7] v. **Qal 2 c.** **2.** *lift up* and take away, *remove,* c. acc. הָעֲטָרָה Ez 21[31] (‖ הָסִיר); acc. rei + מִן loc. Is 57[14], Lv 2[9] 4[8.19] 6[8]; = do away with, גְּרֻשֹׁתֵיכֶם Ez 45[9] (מֵעַל of people), הַתָּמִיד Dn 8[11] (Kt; Qr **Hoph.**); = set apart, מֶכֶס Nu 31[28] (מִן pers.). **3.** *lift off and present, contribute, offer:* **a.** to י׳, c. acc. cogn. תְּרוּמָה, Ez 45[13] 48[8.20] Nu 15[20.20] (P), Ex 35[24] (P); + לי׳ Ez 45[1] 48[9] Nu 15[19] 18[19.24] 31[52]; תְּרוּמַת י׳ 18[26] (+ מִן rei), v[28.29] (all P); ת׳ בֵּית־א׳ Ezr 8[25]. **b.** c. acc. rei, + לי׳ Lv 22[15]. **c.** *contribute,* acc. rei, לְ pers. (for sacrif.), 2 Ch 30[24.24] 35[7.8] (acc. om.), v[9]. **Hoph.** *Pf.* 3 ms. הוּרַם Ex 29[27], הֻרַם Dn 8[11] Qr (Kt **Hiph.**); *Impf.* 3 ms. יוּרָם Lv 4[10]; —*be taken off* from (מִן) Lv 4[10] (P), cf. Ex 29[27] (P; ‖ הוּנַף); *be abolished* Dn 8[11] Qr (cf. **Hiph. 2**); Bev (after 𝔊) ins. *Pt.* מוּרָם after הַתָּמִיד v[13]. **Hithpō'l.** *Impf.* 3 ms. וְיִתְרוֹמֵם וְיִתְגַּדֵּל עַל־כָּל־אֵל Dn 11[36] *and he shall exalt and magnify himself above,* etc.; 1 s. (ת assim.) אֵרוֹמָם Is 33[10] (Ges §54 c Kö I. 454) *I will raise myself* (+ אֶנָּשֵׂא, אָקוּם).

†רוּם, רֻם **n.[m.]** **height, haughtiness** 7312
(prop. inf.);—abs. ר׳, **1.** *height, loftiness,* שָׁמַיִם לָרוּם וָאָרֶץ לָעֹמֶק Pr 25[3]; cstr. רוּם עֵינַיִם fig. of *haughtiness* Is 10[12] (‖ גֹּדֶל לֵבָב), Pr 21[4] (‖ רְחַב־לֵב); so רָם לִבּוֹ Je 48[29] (‖ גָּבְהוֹ, גְּאוֹנוֹ, גַּאֲוָתוֹ); then alone: **2.** *haughtiness,* רוּם אֲנָשִׁים Is 2[11.17] (both ‖ גַּבְהוּת).

†רוֹם **adv. on high,** of direction (cf. מָרוֹם 7315
2) רוֹם יָדֵיהוּ נָשָׂא Hb 3[10] (subj. תְּהוֹם).

7316 † רוּמָה **n.pr.loc.** מִן־ר׳ 2 K 23^{36}; (ἐκ) Κρουμα, A Ρυμα, 𝔊L Λοβεννα; poss. = [אֲרוּמָה] Ju 9^{41} (q. l. perh. also v^{31}, see GFM), yet cf. Kit Benz.

7317 † רוֹמָה **adv.** **haughtily,** לֹא תֵלְכוּ ר׳ Mi 2^{3}.

7410 † רָם **n.pr.m. 1. a.** an ancestor of David, Ru $4^{19.19}$, brother of Jerachmeel 1 Ch $2^{9.10}$. **b.** son of J. 1 Ch $2^{25.27}$.—Αρραν, Ραμ, etc. **2.** name of Elihu's family, Jb 32^{2} (Ραμ[α], Αραμ), dub., cf. Bu.

7413 † I. רָמָה **n.f. height, high-place**;—abs. ר׳ as term. techn. (cf. בָּמָה), = *shrine* (for illicit worship): Ez 16^{25}; ‖ גַּב $v^{21.31.39}$; so perh. 1 S 22^{6}, but rd. prob. בָּמָה, 𝔊 Βαμα (A Ραμμα), HPS.

7414 II. רָמָה **n.pr.loc.** usu. c. art. הָר׳ **the Height, Rama,** הָרָמָה (exc. Je 31^{15} Ne 11^{33}): **1.** in Benj., on border of Ephr., Ho 5^{8} 1 K $15^{17.21.22}$ = 2 Ch $16^{1.5.6}$, Ju 4^{5} 19^{3} Is 10^{29} Je 31^{15} 40^{1} Jos 18^{25} (P), Ezr 2^{26} = Ne 7^{30}, prob. also Ne 11^{33}; 𝔊 usu. Ραμα; mod. *er-Râm*, 5 miles N. of Jerus., Buhl $^{Geogr. 172}$. **2.** in hill-country of Ephr. (= **1**?), home of Samuel 1 S 1^{19} 2^{11} 7^{17} 8^{4} 15^{34} 16^{13} $19^{18.22a}$ (all c.
7436 ה loc., הָרָמָתָה), $v^{19.22 b.23.23}$ 20^{1} 25^{1} 28^{3}, = הָרָמָתַיִם 1 1^{1}
7436 (v. צוֹפִי); 𝔊 Αρμαθαιμ, Ραμα; perhaps (if distinct from **1**) = *Beit-Rima*, 13 miles ENE. of Lydda (GASm $^{Geogr. 254}$ Buhl $^{Geogr. 170}$); or *Râm-allah*, 3 m. SW. of Bethel (Ew $^{Hist. ii. 421}$ al.) [cf. also Ἀριμαθαία Mt 27^{57} +]. **3.** in Asher Jos 19^{29} (P), Ραμα; perh. *Râmiye*, c. 12 miles E. of Ladder of Tyre Rob $^{BR iii. 79}$ Buhl $^{Geogr. 231}$. **4.** in Naphtali, Jos 19^{36} (P), Αραηλ, A 𝔊L Ραμα; mod. *Râmeh*, c. 8 miles WSW. of Safed Buhl $^{Geogr. 222}$. **5.** (בְּ)רָמָה 2 K 8^{29} = 2 Ch 22^{6} (Ρεμμωθ, Ραμωθ; 𝔊L
7216 Ραμαθ Γαλ.), v. רָמוֹת **1**.—Vid. Dr $^{Hast. DB. RAMAH}$ p. 847

7435 † רָמָתִי **adj. gent.** (of what Rama?), c. art. הָרָ׳ 1 Ch 27^{27}; ὁ ἐκ Ραηλ; A ὁ Ῥαμαθαῖος.

7418 רָ(א)מַת **n.pr.loc.** cstr., in combin.: **1.**
7437 רָמַת לֶחִי Ju 15^{17}, v. II. לְחִי p. 534. **2.** רָמַת
7434 הַמִּצְפֶּה Jos 13^{26} (P), in Gilead, on N. border of Gad; Αραβωθ [A Ραμωθ, 𝔊L Ραμεθ] κατὰ τὴν Μασ(ση)φα; = II. מִצְפֶּה **3**; on (dub.) identif.
7418 cf. GASm $^{Geogr. 586 f.}$ Buhl $^{Geogr. 262}$. **3.** רָאמַת נֶגֶב Jos 19^{8} (P), Βαμεθ [A 𝔊L Ιαμεθ] κατὰ λίβα
1192, 7418 (= בַּעֲלַת־בְּאֵר v^{8}, q.v. p. 128); prob. = רָמוֹת־נֶגֶב 1 S 30^{27}, Ραμα νότου; site dub., v. Dr $^{Hast. DB. RAMAH}$.

7216 רָ(א)מוֹת $_{26}$ **n.pr. 1. loc. Heights, Ramôth**;—**a.** in Gilead, רָמֹת בַּגִּלְעָד Jos 21^{38} (Gi; van d. H. Baer v^{36}; P), רָאמוֹת בַּגּ׳ (of Gad) Dt 4^{43} 1 Ch 6^{65}, רָאמֹת בַּגּ׳ Jos 20^{8} (P), Ραμωθ [Jos
7433 20^{8} Αρημωθ] ἐν (τῇ) Γαλααδ; usu. רָמֹת ג׳ (Ρεμμαθ [Ερεμαθ, Ραμωθ, Ραμα(θ)] Γαλ., etc.) 1 K 4^{13} + 19 t. K Ch (v. גִּלְעָד **1 d**); = II. רָמָה **5**, q.v.; site dub.; 1568, 7414
Onom. (Lag $^{287.91}$) 15 m. W. of Philadelphia [Jer Ib. $^{145.31}$ says E!], hence Di $^{Gn 31, 54}$ Buhl $^{G. 261 f.}$ conj. *el-Jal'aud*, c. 17 Eng. m. NW. of Phil., and 3 m. S. of Yabbok; SMerrill $^{E. of Jordan, 284 ff.; Hast. DB. RAMOTH G.}$ conj. (on gen. grounds) *Jerash*, c. 28 m. N. of Phil.; GASm $^{G. 586}$ some place just S. of Yarmuk, cf. GACooke in Dr $^{Dt Add. xviii f.}$, q.v. esp. against *es-Salṭ* (Seetzen al.). †**b.** רָמוֹת־נֶגֶב 1 S 30^{27}, 7418
v. רָ(א)מַת **3**. †**c.** רָאמוֹת, Levit. city in Issachar
1 Ch 6^{58} (Δαβωρ, 𝔊L Ραμωθ), prob. = רֶמֶת Jos 19^{21} 7432
(P; Ρεμμας, A Ραμαθ), and יַרְמוּת **2**, Jos 21^{29}, q.v. p. 438 (v. also Di $^{Jos 19, 21}$). **2. m.** (וְ)רָמוֹת Ezr 10^{29} Qr (Kt ירמות) v. יְרֵימוֹת **5 c**, p. 438. 3406

רָמָתַיִם **n.pr.loc.** הָר׳ 1 S 1^{1}, v. II. רָמָה **2.** above 7414, 7436

† [רָמוּת] **n.f. height, lofty stature**;—sf. 7419
רָמוּתֶךָ Ez 32^{5}.

† רוֹמָם **n. [m.] extolling, praise**;— = *song* 7318
of praise (to י׳) ψ 66^{17}, so read with van d. H., cf. Thes Hup-Now Che Bae Buhl ^{Lex}; > Ki Baer Gi vb. **Pōʿlal,** רוֹמַם; pl. cstr. רוֹמְמוֹת אֵל 149^{6}.

† [רוֹמֵמוּת] **n.f. uplifting, arising**;—sf. 7319, 7427
מֵרוֹמְמֻתֶךָ Is 33^{3} *at thine arising.*

† רֹמַמְתִּי עֶזֶר as **n.pr.m.** (*I have made* 7320
lofty help; cf. גִּדַּלְתִּי and reff.);—son of Heman 1 Ch 25^{4}, ר׳ עָזֶר v^{3}.

רֶמֶת v. רָ(א)מוֹת **1 c.** above 7216, 7432

† מָרוֹם **n.m.** $^{Ec 10, 6}$ **height** (poet.);—abs. מ׳ 4791
Mi 6^{6} +; cstr. מְרוֹם 2 K 19^{23} +; pl. מְרוֹמִים Is 33^{16} +; cstr. מְרוֹמֵי Ju 5^{18}; sf. מְרוֹמָיו Jb 25^{2};—**1.** *height, elevation* (concr.), *elevated place*: מְרוֹם שִׁבְתּוֹ Ob ^{3} (cf. Now), בְּרֹאשׁ מְרֹמִים Pr 8^{2}; מְרוֹמֵי שָׂדֶה Jb 5^{18}, מְרוֹם גִּבְעָה in ‖ Je 49^{16}; מ׳ הָרִים *top of mts.* 2 K 19^{23} = Is $37^{24 a}$, מ׳ קִצּוֹ $v^{24 b}$; מ׳ עָזָּה Je 51^{53} (of Bab.); specif. of Zion, מ׳ Je 17^{12}, מ׳ בְּהָרֵי מ׳ יִשׂ׳ 31^{12}, בְּהַר מ׳ יִשְׂרָאֵל Ez 17^{23} 20^{40}, צִיּוֹן 34^{14}; indef., Hb 2^{9} (in fig.), לָשׂוּם שְׁפָלִים לְמ׳ Jb 5^{11}; בַּמְּרוֹמִים רַבִּים Ec 10^{6} (of high office, rank; opp. שָׁפֵל); יֹשְׁבֵי מָרוֹם Is 26^{5}, i.e. in (supposed) security, cf. מְרוֹמִים יִשְׁכֹּן 33^{16} ‖ מְצָדוֹת סְלָעִים; בַּמ׳ לַמ׳ *on high* (Germ. *in die Höhe*) ψ 75^{6}, so Jb 39^{18}, adv. = *in a high place* Is 22^{16}. **2.** מ׳ alone = *height* of heaven: אֱלֹהֵי מָרוֹם Mi 6^{6}; 2 S 22^{17} = ψ 18^{17}, Is $24^{21.21}$ 32^{15} 57^{15} 58^{4} La 1^{13} ψ 7^{8} 68^{19} 71^{19} 93^{4} 144^{7}, pl. Jb 25^{2}; ‖ שָׁמַיִם, מ׳ קָדְשׁוֹ ψ 102^{20}, מְרוֹמִים Jb 16^{19} ψ 148^{1}; ‖ מְעוֹן קָדְשׁוֹ Je 25^{30}, ‖ מָעַל Jb 31^{2} (pl.), opp. מוֹסְדֵי אֶרֶץ Is 24^{18};

as pred. of ׳י ψ 92^{9} cf. 10^{5}; as adv. (i.e. in heaven) Is 33^{5}; ׳לַמּ *toward heaven* Is 38^{14} 40^{26}, 37^{23} = 2 K 19^{22}; ׳מִמּ in fig. ψ 73^{8} they speak (as if) *from the sky*, from heaven (i.e. so arrogantly). **3.** ׳מ adv. fig., = *proudly* ψ 56^{3} (so Gei Hup-Now al., cf. Che, but dub.), Bae *in high station;* Du reads מָרוֹם (יוֹם to v^{4}; as dittogr.?). **4.** fig. of nobles (coll.) מְרוֹם עַם־הָאָרֶץ Is 24^{4}.

8641 **תְּרוּמָה** **n.f. contribution, offering,** for sacred uses (not certain before Dt.; chiefly Ez P and late) (prop. something *lifted off, separated*);—abs. ׳ת Ez 45^{13}+; cstr. תְּרוּמַת Ex 30^{14}+; sf. תְּרוּמָתִי 25^{2}, ־מַתְכֶם Nu 18^{27}, ־מָתָם Ex 29^{28}; pl. תְּרוּמוֹת Na 12^{44} Pr 29^{4}, ־מֹת 2 S 1^{21} Nu 18^{19}; sf. תְּרוּמֹתַי v^{8}, etc.;—**1.** earliest use: contrib. of products of soil for ׳י, תְּרוּמַת יֶדְכֶם Dt $12^{6.11}$, cf. v^{17}; also Ez 20^{40} Nu $15^{19.20.21}$. **2.** contrib. for prince, in Ezekiel's scheme: Ez $45^{13.16}$ **3.** tract of land to be set apart for temple, and for use of priests and Levites, in Ezek.'s scheme: Ez 45^{1} $48^{8.9.20a.21b}$; called ׳ת הַקֹּדֶשׁ $45^{6.7.7}$ $48^{10.18.18.20b.21a.21c}$; ׳ת הָאָרֶץ קֹדֶשׁ קָדָשִׁים v^{12}. **4.** contrib. to ׳י, set apart for priests, Ez 44^{30} Lv 22^{12} Nu 5^{9} $18^{8.11.19}$ 2 Ch $31^{10.12.14}$; specif.: **a.** of cakes and cereals Lv 7^{14} Ne $10^{38.40}$ (also for Levites), 12^{44} (*id.*), 13^{5}; cf. וּשְׂדֵי תְּרוּמוֹת 2 S 1^{21}, i.e. (si vera l.) fields yielding sacred imposts, but very dub.; 𝔊L ὄρη θανάτου, cf. We; JPPet JBL xii (1893), 54 prop. שׁ׳ (הָרֵי) מָוֶת ה׳ as gloss; HPS שְׂדוֹת הַמָּוֶת; > Sta וּשְׂדֵי עֲרֵמוֹת; v. also Dr. **b.** of animal sacrif., the thigh, שׁוֹק הַתּ׳ Ex 29^{27} Lv 7^{34} $10^{14.15}$ Nu 6^{20}. **c.** priests' share of Levites' tithe, Nu $18^{26.27.28.28.29}$. **d.** of booty Nu $31^{29.41.52}$. **e.** tithe for Levites 18^{24}. **5.** materials for tabern., sacred garments, etc., Ex $25^{2.2.3}$ $35^{5.5.21.24.24}$ $36^{3.6}$; for temple Ezr 8^{25}. **6.** half-shekel for maintaining service of sanctuary Ex $30^{13.14.15}$. **7.** late, *contribution*, in gen., אִישׁ תְּרוּמוֹת Pr 29^{4} *a man of contributions*, i.e. demanding them, = man of exactions.—׳ת Is 40^{20} of idol-image (si vera l.), so still Di-Kit; rd. perh. תְּמוּנָה 𝔊 (ὁμοίωμα v^{19}) Du; other conj. in Che^{Hpt}, v. also III. [סָכַן].—Vbs. c. ׳ת are: הֵרִים Ez 45^{1} + 14 t., הֵבִיא Dt 12^{6} + 9 t., נָתַן Ez 44^{30} + 9 t., לָקַח Ex $25^{2.2}$ + 4 t., הִקְרִיב Lv 7^{14} Nu 5^{9}.—Vid. Dr Dt 12, 6; Hast. DB iii. 588.

8642 **תְּרוּמִיָּה**† **n.f. denom. what belongs to a contribution, attendant or secondary contribution, subdivision** (on form. v. Kö ii. 1, 204; strictly adj. (used as subst.), Ges § 86 h);—׳ת מִתְּרוּמַת הָאָרֶץ Ez 48^{12}, of strip of land for priests in Ezekiel's scheme (but rd. prob. תְּרוּמָה).

†[רוּן] **vb. overcome** (cf. Ar. رَانَ (ى), c. 7442
على or ب pers., *overcome*, e.g. of wine);—assumed in Heb. by Thes (after 𝔊) and most mod. to explain **Hithpō'.** *Pt.* כְּגִבּוֹר מִתְרוֹנֵן מִיָּיִן ψ 78^{65} *like a hero overcome by wine* (cf. ‖ v^{a});
AV RV De Che al. *shout* (√רנן), cf. 𝔗; so 7442
Hup-Now, with altern. conj. מִתְעוֹרֵר, and this sense more suitable (cf. Luzzatto Il Pentateuco iii (1874),
162 (Lv 21, 7) Perles^{79}).—Pr 29^{6} v. רנן, רוץ. p. 930, 943 7323, 7442

†[רוּעַ] **vb. Hiph.** $_{40}$ **1. raise a shout. 2.** 7321
give a blast with clarion or horn (NH *id.*, Hiph.; Thes cp. Ar. رَغَا *utter a grumbling cry*);—*Pf.* 3 mpl. הֵרִיעוּ Ju 15^{14} Ezr 3^{11}, הֵרֵעוּ 1 S 17^{20}, etc.; *Impf.* 3 ms. יָרִיעַ Is 42^{13} ψ 41^{12}, וַיָּרַע Jos 6^{20}, etc.; *Imv.* fs. הָרִיעִי Zc 9^{9}; mpl. הָרִיעוּ Jos 6^{10}+; *Inf. cstr.* הָרִיעַ 2 Ch $13^{12.15}$; *Pt.* pl. מְרִיעִים Ezr 3^{13};—**1.** *shout a war-cry*, or *alarm of battle*, Jos $6^{10.10.10.16.20}$ Ju 7^{21} 1 S 17^{52} Is 42^{13} 2 Ch $13^{15.15}$; הריע תְּרוּעָה Jos $6^{5.20}$; לקראת Ju 15^{14}; בַּמִּלְחָמָה 1 S 17^{20}. **2.** *sound a signal for war* or *march:* c. חֲצֹצְרוֹת Nu $10^{7.9}$ (P); ‖ תקע שׁוֹפָר Ho 5^{8}, cf. Jo 2^{1}; c. על *against* 2 Ch 13^{12}; so also prob. Jb 30^{5} (against a thief). **3.** *shout in triumph* over enemies: c. עַל, Je 50^{15} ψ 41^{12}; abs. Zp 3^{14} (‖ רנן). **4.** *shout in applause:* abs. 1 S 10^{24} Zc 9^{9}, cf. (of angels) Jb 38^{7}. **5.** *shout* with religious impulse: הר׳ תְּרוּעָה 1 S 4^{5} Ezr $3^{11.13}$; so in public worship with music and sacrifice, c. לְ, to God ψ 47^{2} 66^{1} 81^{2} $95^{1.2}$ 98^{4} 100^{1}, לפני 98^{6}; in joy, תַּחְתִּיּוֹת אֶרֶץ Is 44^{23} (‖ רָנּוּ שָׁמַיִם). **6.** *cry out in distress*, Is 15^{4} (but Du Bu יָרֹעוּ *tremble*); לָמָּה תָרִיעִי רֵעַ Mi 4^{9} (of Zion under fig. of woman, but perh. read לָמָּה תֵּרֹעִי רֹעַ *why art thou broken all to pieces?* as Pr 11^{15}). **Pō'lal.** *Impf.* 3 ms. impers. לֹא יְרֹעָע Is 16^{10} *a shout shall not be uttered* (of joy in harvest; ‖ יְרֹנָּן). **Hithpō'l.** *Impf.* 1 s. אֶתְרוֹעָע ψ 108^{10}; 3 mpl. יִתְרוֹעֲעוּ 65^{14}; *Imv.* fs. הִתְרוֹעֲעִי 60^{10};—**1.** *shout in triumph:* c. על ψ 60^{10} (subj. Phil.; iron.) ‖ 108^{10} (subj. ׳י). **2.** *shout for joy*, ψ 65^{14} (meadows, valleys; ‖ שׁיר).

†I. רֵעַ **n.verb. shouting, roar,** but dub.;— 7452
קוֹל הָעָם בְּרֵעֹה Ex 32^{17} (E) *sound of the people as they shouted* (read Inf. cstr. בְּרֵעֹה for בַּהֲרִיעוֹ, cf. √**5**); יַגִּיד עָלָיו רֵעוֹ Jb 36^{33} *the roar thereof telleth of him* (< רַעְמוֹ *his thunder*, so Bu); לָמָּה תָרִיעִי רֵעַ Mi 4^{9} *why criest thou out with a crying?*
i.e. so loudly (but v. √**6**).—II. III. רֵעַ v. רעה. 7453-54
p. 945f

†תְּרוּעָה **n.f. shout or blast of war, alarm,** 8643
or joy;—׳ת Lv 23^{24}+; cstr. תְּרוּעַת Je 4^{19}+;—

1. *alarm* of war, *war-cry*, Jos 6$^{5.20}$ Je 20^{16} Ez 21^{27} Am 1^{14} 2^{2} Zp 1^{16} Jb 39^{25}; ת׳ מִלְחָמָה Je 4^{19} 49^{2}; ת׳ מֶלֶךְ *battle-cry of king* Nu 23^{21} (poem in JE). **2.** *blast* for march: תקע ת׳ Nu 10$^{5.6.6}$ (P; with חֲצֹצְרוֹת; hence) חֲצֹצְרוֹת הַתּ׳ Nu 31^{6} (P) 2 Ch 13^{12}; on day of atonement שׁוֹפַר ת׳ Lv 25^{9} (H); 1st of mo. זִכְרוֹן ת׳ 23^{24} (P; בַּחֹדֶשׁ הַשְּׁבִיעִי בְּאֶחָד לַחֹדֶשׁ), יוֹם ת׳ Nu 29^{1} (P); gen. צִלְצְלֵי ת׳ ψ 150^{5}. **3.** *shout of joy* with religious impulse, 1 S 4$^{5.6.6}$ 2 S 6^{15} = 1 Ch 15^{28}, 2 Ch 15^{14} Ezr 3$^{11.12.13}$; קוֹל ת׳ הַשִּׂמְחָה Ezr 3^{13}; in public worship gen. Jb 33^{26}; esp. + musical service ψ 33^{3} 47^{6}; יֹדְעֵי ת׳, 27^{6} זִבְחֵי ת׳; 89^{16}. **4.** *shout of joy*, in gen. Jb 8^{21} (|| שְׂחוֹק).

רוף (√ of foll.; = רפא).

8644 †תְּרוּפָה **n.f. healing**;—Ez 47^{12}.

7323 †**רוּץ vb. run** (NH *id.* (rare); Eth. ሮጸ: Zinj. *Pf.* 1 s. רצת; = Aram. רְהַט, ܪܗܛ (W$^{SG 47}$)); cf. As. *râṣu, be helpful* (i.e. *run* to help?));—**Qal** *Pf.* 3 ms. רָץ Gn 18^{7}; 2 ms. רַצְתָּה Je 12^{5}, etc.; *Impf.* יָרוּץ Hb 2^{2}+, יָרֻץ Jb 16^{14}, וַיָּרָץ Gn 18^{2}+, וַיָּ֫רָץ 2 S 18^{21}; 1 s. sf. ארוצם Je 50^{44} Kt (but < Qr Hiph., v. infr.), etc. [v. also רצץ]; *Imv.* ms. רוּץ 2 S 18^{23} 2 K 4^{26}, רֻץ 1 S 20^{36} Zc 2^{8}; *Inf. cstr.* לָרוּץ 1 S 20^{6}+; *Pt.* רָץ 2 S 18^{22}+, pl. רָצִים 1 S 22^{17}+, רָצִין 2 K 11^{13} (Ges $^{§ 87e}$);—**1.** *run*, c. אֶל loc. Gn 18^{7} 24^{20} (both J), Nu 17^{12} (P), אֶל pers. Gn 24^{29} (J; + ה loc.), 1 S 3^{5} Is 55^{5} (fig.), with hostility, *against*, Jb 15^{26} (fig.), so goat against ram Dn 8^{6}, עַל pers., *against* Jb 16^{14}; ה loc. also Jos 7^{22}, לְבֵיתוֹ Hg 1^{9}, לָרַע Is 59^{7} Pr 1^{16}; acc. loc. 1 S 20^{6} 17$^{22.48}$ (+ לִקְרַאת); ב loc. *on* (ב II. **2**), of horses Am 6^{12}, locusts Jo 2^{9}; *into* Pr 18^{10} (fig.); מִן loc. 1 S 4^{12}, so MT 2 K 23^{12} (= *he went quickly thence*, but text perh. corrupt, v. Kit Benz, and cf. **Hiph.** infr.); אַחֲרֵי pers. 2 S 18^{22} 1 K 19^{20} 2 K 5$^{20.21}$ Ct 1^{4}, עַד pers. 2 K 4^{22}; לִפְנֵי pers. 2 S 15^{1} 1 K 1^{5} (both of royal escort, *out-runners*), 18^{46} (+ עַד loc.), לִפְנֵי rei 1 S 8^{11}; אֵת pers. accomp. Je 12^{5}; c. acc. of way, אֹרַח ψ 19^{6}, דֶּרֶךְ 2 S 18^{23} ψ 119^{32} (fig.); as prelim., + inf. לִקְרַאת *run to meet* Gn 18^{2} 24^{17} 29^{13} 33^{4} (all J), 2 K 4^{26} Je 51^{31}, + vb. fin. Gn 24^{28} 29^{12} (both J), Nu 11^{27} Jos 8^{19} (both JE), Ju 7^{21} 13^{10} 1 S 10^{23} 17^{51} 2 S 18^{19} ψ 59^{5}; as imv. + imv. 1 S 20^{36} Zc 2^{8}; abs. 1 S 20^{36} Is 40^{31} 2 Ch 23^{12} (v. **2 a**), Pr 4^{12} 6^{18} (of feet), of locusts Jo 2$^{4.7}$; specif., *run* as messenger 2 S 18$^{21.22.23.23.24.26.26}$, fig. of prophet's activity Je 23^{21}, of י׳'s word ψ 147^{15}; fig. of reading smoothly, יָרוּץ קוֹרֵא בוֹ Hb 2^{2}.—ψ 18^{30} = 2 S 22^{30} read אָרֻץ (for אָרוּץ, אָרֻץ), √ רצץ Ew Ol Che Bae al. **2.**
Pt. as subst.: **a.** pl. הָרָצִים *the runners* (prop. *out-runners*, as royal escort, cf. vb. 2 S 15^{1} 1 K 1^{5}; then) of royal body-guard 1 S 22^{17} 1 K 14$^{27.28.28}$ = 2 Ch 12$^{10.11.28}$, 2 K 10$^{25.25}$ 11$^{4.6.11.19.19}$.—הָרָצִין (הָעָם) v^{13} is gloss (Kit Benz; whence [easier] הָעָם
הָרָצִים 2 Ch 23^{12} v. **1**).—Pr 29^{6} for יָרֻן Pinsk 7442
Toy favour יָרוּץ. **b.** *runner* = (royal messenger, post, late), רָץ Je 51$^{31.31}$ (|| מַגִּיד), cf. Jb 9^{25} (as swift); הָרָצִים 2 Ch 30$^{6.10}$ Est 3$^{13.15}$, riders הָר׳ רֹכְבֵי הָרֶכֶשׁ 8^{10}, הָר׳ בַּסּוּסִים v^{14}. **Pō'lēl** *Impf.* 3 mpl. יְרוֹצֵצוּ Na 2^{5} *they run swiftly, dart* (like lightning; of chariots). **Hiph.** *cause to run*: **1.** *bring*, or *move, quickly*, *Impf.* 3 mpl. sf. וַיְרִיצֻהוּ, מִן loc. Gn 41^{14} (E), rd. perh. also 3 ms. וַיָּרֶץ 2 K 23^{12} (acc. om.; for MT וַיָּרָץ v. **Qal**); ל pers., acc. rei om. וַיָּרִיצוּ 2 Ch 35^{13}; *Imv.* ms. הָרֵץ 1 S 17^{17} (+ acc. loc., ל pers.); *Impf.* 3 fs. תָּרִיץ יָדָיו ψ 68^{32} *quickly stretch out* hands, לֵאלֹהִים (viz. with offerings). **2.** c. מֵעַל = *drive away from*, 1 s., sf. 3 ms., אֲרִיצֶנּוּ Je 49^{19}, so read prob. also in || 50^{44} (Qr אֲרִיצֵם, > Kt ארוצם).

†מֵרוֹץ **n.[m.] running, race**;—abs. Ec 9^{11}. 4793

†I. [מְרוּצָה] **n.f. 1. running. 2. course** 4794
(of life):—**1.** *running, mode, style, of running*, cstr. מְרוּצַת 2 S 18^{27}, מְרֻצַת v^{27}. **2.** *course* (of life), sf. מְרוּצָתָם Je 8^{6} (Qr; > Kt pl. מרצותם),
23^{10}.—II. מְרוּצָה Je 22^{17} v. sub רצץ. 4835, 7533

רוֹשׁ *poison*, Dt 32^{32}, v. II. רֹאשׁ. p. 912 7219

[רוּשׁ or רִישׁ]$_{24}$ **vb. be in want, poor** 7326
(related to ירשׁ [cf. **Qal 3, Niph. Hiph. 3**]? 3426
so Thes);—**Qal** *Pf.* 3 pl. כְּפִירִים רָשׁוּ וְרָעֵבוּ ψ 34^{11} p. 439f
young lions are in want and hunger; elsewhere *Pt.* רָשׁ 1 S 18^{23} + 16 t., רָאשׁ 2 S 12^{1} + 2 t.; pl. רָשִׁים Pr 22^{7}, רָאשִׁים 13^{23};—(oft. opp. עָשִׁיר): as adj. 1 S 18^{23} 2 S 12$^{1.4}$ Pr 28^{3} Ec 4^{14}; as subst. = *poor man (men)*, 2 S 12^{3} ψ 82^{3} Ec 5^{7}, esp. Pr 10^{4} 13$^{8.23}$ + 12 t. Pr. **Hithpō'lēl** *Pt.* מִתְרוֹשֵׁשׁ Pr 13^{7} *one impoverishing himself* (opp. מִתְעַשֵּׁר; cf. Pôʿl.
רוֹשֵׁשׁ Ecclus 11^{12} 13^{5}).—Je 5^{17} Mal 1^{4} v. רשׁשׁ. 7567

†רִישׁ, רֵישׁ, רֵאשׁ **n.m. poverty**, only Pr;— 7389
רִישׁ 28^{19}, sf. רִישׁוֹ 31^{7}; רֵישׁ 13^{18}, sf. רֵישֶׁךָ 24^{34} (|| מַחְסֹרֶךָ), רֵישָׁם 10^{15} (opp. עָשִׁיר); רֵאשׁ 30^{8} (opp. עֹשֶׁר), sf. רֵאשֶׁךָ 6^{11} (= 24^{34}, || *id.*).

רוּת **n.pr.f.** v. sub רעה. p. 946 7327

†רָזָה **vb. be or grow lean** (Ar. رَزِىَ *grow* 7329
thin and weak);—**Qal** *Pf.* 3 ms. רָזָה Zp 2^{11} obj. false gods, appar. *make lean* (𝔙 *attenuavit*; 𝔊

is ἐξολεθρεύσει), but sense strange, < רָזָה (v. Ar. supr.), yet even this very doubtful. **Niph.** *be made lean*, *Impf.* 3 ms. מִשְׁמַן בְּשָׂרוֹ יֵרָזֶה Is 17[4].

7330 †[רָזֶה] **adj. lean** (on formation cf. Lag [BN 49]);—fs. רָזָה, Ez 24[20] (of שֶׂה; opp. בְּרִיאָה), of land, = barren, Nu 13[20] (JE; opp. שְׁמֵנָה).

7334 †רָזִי **n.[m.] leanness, wasting**;—רָזִי־לִי Is 24[16.16] *to me, wasting!* (opp. צְבִי).

7332 †I. רָזוֹן **n.[m.] leanness, wasting, scantness**;—abs. ר׳: **1.** *leanness* Is 10[16] (fig.; opp. מִשְׁמַנָּיו). **2.** *wasting*, i.e. wasting disease, ψ 106[15] (cf. Bae). **3.** אֵיפַת ר׳ Mi 6[10] *ephah*

7333 *of scantness*, scant measure.—II. רָזוֹן v. רזן. below

רזה (? *cry out*, cf. Talm. מְרַזֵּחַ *bewailed*).

4797-98 †מַרְזֵחַ **n.m.**[Am 6,7] **cry** (𝔗 מַרְזְחָא *mourning-feast*; Ph. מרזח a rel. festival (> usu. a month), cf. Palm., ClGann Littm, v. GACooke [Inscr. 95. 121 f. 303] and reff.; Lzb [Ephem. i. 47 f. 343 f.]);—**1.** *mourning cry* (or *feast*? Talm. מַרְזֵיחָא), abs. בֵּית מ׳ Je 16[5] i.e. house of mourning (‖ נוד, ספד). **2.** *cry of revelry*, cstr. מִרְזַח סְרוּחִים Am 6[7].

7334 רָזִי v. רזה. above

7335 †[רָזַם] **vb. wink, flash** (of eyes) (transp. [text. err.?] for Ar. رَمَزَ, Aram. רְמַז, ܪܡܙ; so NH רָמַז (rare), רֶמֶז *sign, intimation*);—**Qal** *Impf.* 3 mpl. וּמַה־יִּרְזְמוּן עֵינֶיךָ Jb 15[12] (Codd. ירמזון) *why do thine eyes flash* (in wrath)? but possibly read יְרוּמוּן (Pr 6[17] 30[13], etc., cf. Bu).

7336 †[רָזַן, ? earlier רָזוֹן, so Lag [BN 31]] **vb. be weighty, judicious, commanding** (Ar. رَزُنَ *be weighty, grave, firm of judgment*; NH רוֹזֵן = BH, so רוזנים Ecclus 44[4]);—only **Qal** *Pt.* pl. as subst., *rulers, potentates*, ‖ מְלָכִים : רֹזְנִים Ju 5[3] Hb 1[10], ר׳ ψ 2[2] Pr 8[15] 31[4], ‖ שֹׁפְטֵי אֶרֶץ Is 40[23].

7333 †II. רָזוֹן **n.m. potentate**;—abs. ר׳ Pr 14[28]

7332 (‖ מֶלֶךְ).—I. רָזוֹן v. sub רזה supr.

7331 †רְזוֹן **n. pr. m.** founder of kingdom of Damascus, Solomon's time, 1 K 11[23]; 𝔊 (v[14]) Εσρωμ [A v[23] Ραζων]; identified with חֶזְיוֹן 15[18] by Th Klo (reading חזרון), but cf. Kit Benz.

7337 †רָחַב [? also רָחֹב, so Lag [BN 31]; cf. also Id [ib. 52 f.]] **vb. be, or grow, wide, large** (NH in der. spec. (rare) and deriv.; Ar. رَحُبَ, Eth. ርሒበ: Sab. in epith. dei Fell [ZMG liv (1900), 249], and n.pr. CIS [iv, no. 1, 3] etc.; As. in *rêbitu, open place*; Aram. רְחַב in deriv.);—**Qal** *Pf.* 3 ms. ר׳ פִּי 1 S 2[1], + עַל *against* (i.e. to devour, in fig.; cf. **Hiph.**); consec. וּפָחַד וְר׳ לְבָבֵךְ Is 60[5] *be widened, enlarged*, relieved, and expanded with joy (cf. **Hiph. 2**); 3 fs. וְרָחֲבָה וְנָסְבָה Ez 41[7] prob. err., Co רָחֲבָה וְנוֹסְפָה, Toy וְהִרְחִב נוֹסֵף, Krae וַיֹּסִפוּ רָחֳבוֹ [? וְ]. **Niph.** *Pt.* as adj. כַּר נִרְחָב Is 30[23] *a broad, roomy, pasture*. **Hiph.** *Pf.* 3 ms. הִרְחִיב Gn 26[22] Hb 2[5], הִרְחִב Is 30[33]; 2 ms. הִרְחַבְתָּ ψ 4[2], etc.; *Impf.* 3 ms. יַרְחִיב Dt 12[20] +, etc.; *Imv.* ms. הַרְחֶב־ ψ 81[11] (cf. also 25[17] infr.); fs. הַרְחִיבִי Is 54[2], הַרְחִיבִי Mi 1[16]; *Inf. cstr.* הַרְחִיב Am 1[13]; *Pt.* מַרְחִיב Dt 33[20];—**1.** *make large*, c. acc. baldness Mi 1[16] (sign of mourning), fun. pile Is 30[33] (acc. om.; + הֶעְמִיק); *make wide*, acc. couch Is 57[8] (fig.). **2.** *enlarge* limit of territory (גְּבוּל) Am 1[13] Ex 34[24] (J), Dt 12[20] 19[8], so מַר׳ גָּד 33[20], cf. הַר׳ מְקוֹם אָהֳלֵךְ Is 54[2] (fig.); also abs. + לְ pers., הִר׳ י׳ לָנוּ Gn 26[22] (J), and (fig. of deliverance), בַּצָּר הִר׳ לִי ψ 4[2]; מַתָּן אָדָם יַר׳ לוֹ Pr 18[16] *a man's gift makes room for him*, gives access to patron; of י׳'s *enlarging* the heart (לִבִּי) ψ 119[32] (cf. **Qal**); צָרוֹת לְבָבִי הִרְחִיבוּ מ׳ ψ 25[17] rd. prob. (with most) Imv. הַרְחֵ(י)ב וּמ׳ (Bae הִרְחִיבוּ, *alarm*, cf. Ct 6[5]); c. acc. צַעֲדִי *my step, stride* ψ 18[37] = 2 S 22[37] (i.e. givest me firm footing and vigorous step, cf. צַעַד **2**); *enlarge* mouth, open it wide, c. עַל pers. *against* Is 57[4] ψ 35[21] (cf. **Qal**); without עַל, as a young bird to receive food, fig., ψ 81[11]; הִר׳ שְׁאוֹל נַפְשָׁהּ Is 5[14] (‖ פָּעֲרָה פִיהָ; נֶפֶשׁ **5 c**), cf. Hb 2[5].

†רַחַב **n.[m., not f.** Jb 36[16] Albr [ZAW xvi (1896), 94] Di Bu] **breadth, broad expanse**;—abs. ר׳ Jb 36[16] (opp. צַר); pl. cstr. intens. רַחֲבֵי־אָרֶץ 38[18] *the broad expanse of earth*. 7338

רֹחַב[101] **n.[m.] breadth, width**;—ר׳ abs. Ez 42[2] +, cstr. 1 K 6[3] +; sf. רָחְבּוֹ Ex 25[10] +, -בָּהּ Gn 6[15] +, רָחְבָּן Ez 42[11];—*breadth*, of land, + אֹרֶךְ = whole extent, expanse, Gn 13[17] (J), so ר׳ alone Is 8[8]; ר׳ מַיִם Jb 37[10]; fig. ר׳ לֵב *largeness of understanding* (like sand of sea-shore) 1 K 5[9]; *breadth*, = thickness, of wall גֶּדֶר Ez 42[10]; elsewh. only in measurements *width, breadth* (Dt 3[11], K 10 t., Ez 54 t., Zc 2[6] 5[2], P 23 t., Ch 6 t.; ‖ אֹרֶךְ 1 K 7[6] + 63 t., + קוֹמָה 6[2] + 14 t., + גֹּבַהּ † Ez 40[42] 2 Ch 3[4]; ‖ קוֹמָה alone † 1 K 7[27] Ez 40[5]): of buildings, etc., 1 K 6[2.3.3.6.6.6] +, Ez 41[1.1.1.5.7] +, altar Ex 27[1] = 38[1], ark, תֵּבָה, Gn 6[15], אָרוֹן Ex 25[10] = 37[1], etc.; of area, the עֶרֶשׂ of Og Dt 3[11], the תְּרוּמָה of land Ez 45[1.3.5.6] +, of court Ex 27[12.13.18]; of city Zc 2[6]; of roll 5[2]; of curtain Ex 26[2.8] +, 7341 etc.; of wall (קִיר),=*thickness*, Ez 41[9.12] (cf. 42[10] supr.); of doorway 40[11] 41[2.3], etc.

7342 I. רָחָב adj. wide, broad;—abs. ר׳ Jb 30[14]; cstr. רְחַב Pr 21[4]+; fs. רְחָבָה Ex 3[8]+; cstr. רַחֲבַת Gn 34[21]+; mpl. cstr. רַחֲבֵי Is 33[21];—*wide, broad, spacious,* of land Ex 3[8] (J), Ne 9[35], רַחֲבַת יָדַיִם, etc., Gn 34[21]+6 t., v. יָד **3 d**; ר׳ מִנֵּי־יָם Jb 11[9] (of greatness of God, ‖ אֲרֻכָּה מֵאֶרֶץ); בָּרְחָבָה as subst. ψ 119[45] *in a wide, roomy, space* (fig.); פֶּרֶץ ר׳ Jb 30[14] (sim.); of cup Ez 23[32] (in fig.; +הָעֲמֻקָּה); of wall (=*thick*) Je 51[58]; specif., in Jerusalem (as n.pr.) הַחוֹמָה הָר׳ Ne 3[8] 12[38]; fig. *extensive,* of work, undertaking, מְלָאכָה, Ne 4[13] (+הַרְבֵּה); of י׳'s commandment ψ 119[96] (i.e. unlimited, measureless); רְחַב לֵבָב 101[5] i.e. *exultant, arrogant* (‖ גְּבַהּ־עֵינַיִם), so ר׳ לֵב Pr 21[4] (‖ רוּם־ע׳); רְחַב נֶפֶשׁ Pr 28[25] i.e. *greedy* (cf. רחב אולת Ecclus 47[23c], in play on רְחַבְעָם).

7343 †II. רָחָב n.pr.f. harlot in Jericho;—Jos 2[1.3] 6[17.23.25] (all JE); Ραаβ (so Heb 3[11] Jas 2[25], but Mt 1[5] Ραχαβ).

7339 †I. רְחוֹב n.f.[Dn 9, 25] [not **m.** Zc 8[5] Albr[ZAW xvi (1896), 51] cf. Ges[§ 145 p, t, u]] **broad open place, plaza** (Lag[BN 178] Ba[NB 142]);—ר׳ abs. Gn 19[2]+, cstr. Ju 19[17]+, רְחֹב v[15] 2 S 21[12]; sf. רְחֹבָהּ Dt 13[17] ψ 55[12]; pl. abs. רְחֹבוֹת Am 5[16]+, cstr. *id.* Zc 8[4]+ (v. also רְחֹבוֹת n.pr., infr.); sf. רְחֹבֹתֶיהָ Is 15[3]+, etc.;—*broad open place* in city (usu. near gate, Ne 8[1.3.16.16] 2 Ch 32[6] Jb 29[7]; ‖ חוּץ Je 5[1]+8 t., דֶּרֶךְ Pr 26[13], שְׁוָקִים Ct 3[2]), for various private and public uses Gn 19[2] (J), Ju 19[15.17.20] Dt 13[17] 2 S 21[12] Je 5[1] Ez 16[24.31] Ne 8[16.16] Is 59[14] ψ 55[12] Jb 29[7], essential part of city Dn 9[25]; for lamentations Am 5[16] Is 15[3] Je 48[38], ר׳ הָעִיר אֲשֶׁר לִפְנֵי שַׁעַר הַמֶּלֶךְ Est 4[6] (cf. v[1 f.]), cf. Je 9[20] 49[26] 50[30] La 2[11.12], ψ 144[14], assemblies 2 Ch 29[4] 32[6] Ezr 10[9] (ר׳ בֵּית הָא׳), Ne 8[1.3], proclamations Est 6[9.11], speeches Pr 1[20]; social life Zc 8[4.5.5] La 4[18] Pr 5[16] 7[12], cf. 22[13] 26[13], Ct 3[3]; ר׳ in Na 2[5] is appar. outside city (cf. As. *rêbit Ninâ,* etc.).

7340 †II. רְחֹב, רְחוֹב n.pr. Ρааβ, Ρоωβ, etc.: **1.** (cf. Lag[BN 56 f.]) **loc.**: **a.** towards Hamath, רְחוֹב 2 S 10[8] (𝔊L Βαιθρααβ), רְחֹב Nu 13[21] (P);=בֵּית ר׳ q.v. p. 112 (also 𝔊 1 S 14[47] Βαιθεωρ, 𝔊L Βαιθροωβι). **b.** רְחֹב in Asher: (1) Jos 19[28] (P); (2) [perh.= (1)], v[30] (P), Ju 1[31], Levit. city Jos 21[31] (P)= 1 Ch 6[60]; Egypt. *Raḥubu,* N. of Kishon, WMM[As. u. Eur. 153]. **2. m.**: **a.** Aram. name, רְחֹב 2 S 8[3.12]. **b.** post-exilic Levite, רְחוֹב Ne 10[12].

†רְחֹבוֹת **n. pr. loc. 1.** רְחֹבֹת עִיר near Nineveh Gn 10[11] (J), τὴν Ροωβως[θ] πόλιν; Dl[Pa 261] cf. As. *rêbit Ninâ,* but v. COT[Gn 10, 11]. **2.** רְחֹבוֹת, name of well Gn 26[22] (J), Εὐρυχωρία (cf. interpr. v[22]); Palmer[Desert 296 f.] identif. with er-Ruḥaibeh (in Wady R.) c. 45 m. SW. of Hebron, N. of lat. 31°. **3.** ר׳ הַנָּהָר, home of a king of Edom Gn 36[37] (P)=1 Ch 1[48], Ροωβωθ τῆς παρὰ ποταμόν, P. τοῦ ποταμοῦ (i.e. on Euphrates? here improb.; conj. in Di Holz Wkl[Gesch. Isr. i. 192]). 7344

†רְחַבְיָה(וּ) **n.pr.m.** son of Eliezer and grandson of Moses: רְחַבְיָה 1 Ch 23[17.17] (Ρααβια) =-יָהוּ 26[25] (Ρα(α)βιας, 𝔊L Αβια), appar. also 24[21.21] (Ρααβια, Αβια). 7345

רְחַבְעָם **n.pr.m. Rehoboam** (word-play on רחב Ecclus 47[23c]);—king of Judah, son of Solomon; Ροβοαμ: 1 K 11[43] 12[1.3.6]+16 t. 1 K 12, 14, +15[6] ‖ 2 Ch 9[31] 10[1.3.6]+21 t. 2 Ch 10, 11, 12, +13[7.7]; also 1 Ch 3[10]. 7346

†מֶרְחָב **n.**[**m.**] **broad, roomy, place**;—abs. מ׳, of pasture Ho 4[16] (in sim.); fig. of freedom from distress and anxiety 2 S 22[20]=ψ 18[20], ψ 31[9] 118[5] (MT cstr. in מֶרְחַבְיָה *spacious place of Yah,* i.e. extraordinarily spacious, < מֶרְחָב יָהּ, יָהּ being subj. of vb.); pl. cstr. מֶרְחֲבֵי־אֶרֶץ Hb 1[6] *expanses of the earth.* 4800

רחה (√of foll.; mng. unknown; NH= BH; Ar. رَحًى *handmill* (cf. Wetzst[Siebe, ZPV xiv (1891), 4]); Aram. רֵיחְיָא, ܪܚܝܐ; Lag[BN 157] Ba[NB 9, 21]).

†[רֵחֶה] **n.**[**m.**], only **du.** רֵחַיִם (hand-)**mill** (prob. = *two mill-stones*);—ר׳ abs., common household utensil, turned by maids, Ex 11[5] (הָרֵחָיִם; J), female slaves Is 47[1] (c. טָחַן, q.v.); ר׳ וָרֶכֶב Nu 11[8] (J); טָחַן בָּר׳ Dt 24[6] (v. רכב); קוֹל ר׳ as sound of family life Je 25[10]. 7347

רחיטנו Ct 1[17] Kt, v. [רָהִיט] sub רהט. p. 923 7351

רֵחַיִם v. רחה. above 7347

רחל (√of foll.; mng.?; cf. NH רָחֵל (pl. ־ים, ־ות), Ar. رِخْل, رَخِل, Aram. רַחְלָא, all *ewe*; cf. perh. As. *laḫru* (transp.; vid. on רֶגֶל)).

†I. רָחֵל **n.f.**[Is 53, 7] **ewe**;—abs. ר׳ Is 53[7] (in sim., ‖ שֶׂה); pl. רְחֵלִים Gn 32[15] (E; + אֵילִים, עִזִּים), Ct 6[6] (in sim.); sf. רְחֵלֶיךָ וְעִזֶּיךָ Gn 31[38] (E). 7353

II. רָחֵל **n.pr.f.** (*ewe,* RS[K 219]);—**Rachel,** Ραχηλ, daughter of Laban and wife of Jacob: Gn 29[6.9.10.11.28.29.30]+36 t. Gn (JE 37 t., P 6 t.), 7354

קְבֻרַת(־)ר׳ 35[20] (JE), 1 S 10[2] (cf. אֶפְרָתָה **1**, p. 68; on site vid. Dr[Hast. DB Rachel]); ר׳ (in fig.) Je 31[15]; ר׳ Ru 4[11] (in sim.).

I. **רחם** (√of foll.; orig. meaning dub.; Thes *be soft*, so Gerber[126], cp. Ar. رَخُمَ *be soft, gentle* (but خ orig. cons.?); Dl[HWB 604 b] *be wide*; cf. As. *rîmu*, *rêmu*, Ar. رَحِمٌ, NH רֶחֶם, Aram. רַחְמָא, ܪܚܡܐ, all *womb*; MI[17] רחמת *female captives*; vbs. (connexion with רֶחֶם not wholly clear, cf. Nö[ZMG xl (1886), 151 f.], v. רַחֲמִים): As. *râmu*, *love, compassionate*, Ar. رَحِمَ *have compassion*, also رَخِمَ *be inclined toward, affectionate to* (=رحم acc. to Ar. authorities, v. Lane); Sab. epith. dei רחמנן *Compassionate* (= Ar. اَلرَّحْمَانُ), CIS[iv. no. 6, 3] Fell[ZMG liv (1900), 252] who cp. epith. רחם *id.*; cf. NH רִחֵם Pi.; Thes cp. Eth. መሐረ: (transp.) *have compassion*, but v. Prät[BAS i. 21] and reff.; Aram. רְחֵם, ܪܚܶܡ, Palm. רחם, all *love* (common); Nab. Palm. רחם *friend*).

7356, †רֶחֶם, רַ֫חַם **n.m.**[Ho 9, 14] womb (**f.** Je 20[17],
7358 unless הָרַת a noun, cf. Albr[ZAW xvi. 81] SS);—abs. ר׳ Gn 20[18]+, רַ֫חַם Ju 5[30], רָ֑חֶם Je 20[17]+, רָ֑חַם Gn 49[25]+; cstr. רֶ֫חֶם Nu 12[12] Jb 3[11]; sf. רַחְמָהּ Gn 29[31]+, רַחְמָהּ Je 20[17] (Ges[§ 91 e]; >f.
7356, abs. Kö[ii. 1, 159]); du. רַחֲמָתַיִם Ju 5[30];—**1.** *womb*,
7361 Gn 49[25] (J) Je 20[17] Jb 24[20]; מֵרֶחֶם i.e. from birth Je 20[17] ψ 22[11] 58[4] Jb 3[11] (מִנִּי), Is 46[3], fig. ψ 110[3]; בְּרֶחֶם Jb 31[15]; יצא מֵר׳ *go forth from womb* in birth Je 1[5] 20[18] Jb 38[8], cf. 10[18]; מֵר׳ אֵם Nu 12[12] (E); פתח ר׳ *open the womb*, in order to childbirth Gn 29[31] 30[22] (JE); כָּל־פֶּטֶר רחם *all that first opens womb* (of men and animals) Ex 13[12.15] 34[19] (J) Nu 18[15] (P) Ez 20[26]; פטר ר׳ Nu 3[12] (P), פִּטְרַת כל ר׳ Nu 8[16]; פטר כל ר׳ Ex 13[2] (P); on the other hand, ר׳ מַשְׁכִּיל Ho 9[14] *miscarrying womb*; עֹצֶר ר׳ Pr 30[16] *restraint* (i.e. barrenness) *of womb* (so ψ 107[36] Perles Anal. 85); עָצַר בְּעַד ר׳ (of God) Gn 20[18] (E); סָגַר ר׳ (בְּעַד) 1 S 1[5.6], preventing childbirth. **2.** *womb-man, woman-slave*: רַחַם רַחֲמָתַיִם Ju 5[30] *a woman, two women*.

7356 †רַחֲמִים **n.m.**[2 S 24, 14] **abs. pl. intens.** compassion (acc. to many denom. from רֶחֶם, orig. *brotherhood, brotherly feeling*, of those born from same womb, v. Nö[ZMG xl (1886), 151 (yet v. 152)] We[GGN 1893, 475] Gerber[126], or *motherly feeling* Kö[ii. 1, 34]);—abs. ר׳ Gn 43[14]+; cstr. רַחֲמֵי Pr 12[10]; sf. רַחֲמָיו La 3[22] (Baer Gi; van d. H. Qr, Kt רחמו), 2 S 24[14] Qr (>Kt רחמו), etc.;—**1.** *compassion*: usu. of God Is 63[7.15] ψ 77[10] 79[8] 119[77] Zc 1[16] Dn 9[9] Ne 9[28]; c. רבים 2 S 24[14] = 1 Ch 21[13], Ne 9[19.27.31] ψ 119[156] Dn 9[18]; גדולים Is 54[7]; ‖ חסד ψ 40[12] 103[4] Ho 2[21] Je 16[5]; חסדים ψ 25[6]; כרֹב רחמיךָ ψ 51[3] 69[17]; c. על rei 145[9]; נתן ר׳ ל Dt 13[18] Je 42[12]; לֹא כָלוּ ר׳ La 3[22]. **2.** of man, Am 1[11] Pr 12[10]; עָשָׂה ר׳ Zc 7[9]; נָתַן לִפְ׳ ר׳ לִפְנֵי Gn 43[14] (R); נתן פ׳ לר׳ לִפְנֵי 1 K 8[50] Ne 1[11] Dn 1[9] ψ 106[46], cf. 2 Ch 30[9]; שׂם ר׳ ל Is 47[6]; נִכְמְרוּ ר׳ אל Gn 43[30] (J), c. על 2 K 3[26].

†[רָחַם] **vb. denom.** love. **Pi.** have compassion;—**Qal** *Impf.* 1 s. sf. אֶרְחָמְךָ ψ 18[2] *I love thee* (perhaps gloss; v. not in ‖ 2 S 22[2]; Hi Ch SS Gerber read אֲרֹמִמְךָ). **Pi.** *Pf.* 3 ms. רִחַם ψ 103[13]+; sf. וְרִחַמְךָ consec. Dt 13[18], etc.; *Impf.* 3 ms. יְרַחֵם Is 9[16]+; sf. יְרַחֲמֵהוּ Is 55[7], etc.; *Inf. abs.* רַחֵם Je 31[20] Hb 3[2]; cstr. רַחֵם Is 49[15] ψ 103[13]; sf. רַחֶמְכֶם Is 30[18]; *Pt.* מְרַחֵם ψ 116[5], etc.;—*have compassion, compassionate*;—**1.** usu. of God: c. acc. of his people, Ex 33[19.19] (J) Dt 13[18] 30[3] 2 K 13[23] Is 9[16] 14[1] 27[11] 30[18] 49[10.13] 54[8.10] 55[7] 60[10] Je 12[15] 30[18] 31[20.20] 33[26] Ez 39[25] Ho 1[6.7] 2[6.25] Mi 7[19] Zc 1[12] 10[6] ψ 102[14]; c. על 103[13]; abs. Je 13[14] Hb 3[2] ψ 116[5] La 3[32]. **2.** of man, usu. a conqueror: c. acc. 1 K 8[50] Je 42[12]; abs. 6[23] 21[7] 50[42]; elsewhere of children, c. acc. Is 13[18] 49[15]; c. על ψ 103[13]. **Pu.** *Pf.* 3 fs. רֻחָ֑מָה Ho 2[3.25] (Ges[§ 152 a N.] Kö[i. 270]);—*Impf.* 3 ms. יְרֻחָם Ho 14[4]; יְרֻחָ֑ם Pr 28[13]; *be shewn compassion, compassionated*: of orphans Ho 14[4]; children of Israel wife of Yahweh 2[3.25] (cf. לֹא־ר׳ 1[6.8], p. 520); penitent sinner Pr 28[13].

†רַחוּם **adj.** compassionate;—always of God: אֵל רַחוּם Dt 4[31], ר׳ וְחַנּוּן Ex 34[6] (J) = ψ 86[15] 103[8]; later חַנּוּן ור׳ 2 Ch 30[9] Ne 9[17.31] Jo 2[13] Jon 4[2] ψ 111[4] 112[4] 145[8]; והוא ר׳ 78[38]. 7349

†[רַחֲמָנִי] **adj.** id.;—pl. f. נָשִׁים רַחֲמָנִיּוֹת La 4[10] *compassionate women*. 7362

†רַ֫חַם **n.pr.m.** (*girl*(-like)?);—in Judah, 1 Ch 2[44]; Ραμεε, A Ραεμʹ, 𝔊L Ρααμ. 7357

רֻחָמָה in לֹא ר׳ n.pr.f., v. p. 520. 3819

†רְחוּם, רְחֻם **n. pr. m.** (*compassion*, or *softness, gentleness*?);—post-exilic name: **1.** with Zerub.: **a.** רְחוּם Ezr 2[2], A Ιρεουμʹ, 𝔊L Ναουμ (= נְחוּם ‖ Ne 7[7]). **b.** priest, רְחֻם Ne 12[3] Ρεουμ (= חָרִם v[15], cf. 7[42] = Ezr 2[39], Ezr 10[21], v. חָרִם **3 a**). **2.** רְחוּם, with Neh.: **a.** Levite Ne 3[17], Βασουθ, אA𝔊L Ραουμ. **b.** Ne 10[26], Ρα[ε]ουμ. 7348

3395 †יְרֹחָם **n.pr.m.** (*may he be compassionated*; cf. Lag[BN 134]);—**1.** father of Elkanah, grandf. of Sam., Ephraimite 1 S 1[1] (Ιερεμε[ι]ηλ, A Ιεροαμ); Levite 1 Ch 6[12.19] (Ιδαερ, Ηααλ; A Ιεροβοαμ, Ιερεαμ; 𝔊L Ιεραμαηλ). **2.** Benjamites: **a.** 1 Ch 8[27] Ιρααμ, etc. (appar. = יְרֵמוֹת v[14]). **b.** 9[8], 𝔊 *id.* (= **a**?). **3.** priests: **a.** 1 Ch 9[12], Ι(ε)ρααμ, etc. **b.** Ne 11[11], Ι(ε)ροαμ. **4.** father of a hero of David 1 Ch 12[8] (van d. H. v[7]), Ρααμ, A 𝔊L Ιεροαμ. **5.** Danite 1 Ch 27[22], Ιωραμ (𝔊L as **4**). **6.** father of a captain with Jehoiada, 2 Ch 23[1], Ιωραμ.

3396 †יְרַחְמְאֵל **n.pr.m.** (*may Ēl have compassion*) Ιεραμεηλ, etc.;—**1.** name in Judah 1 Ch 2[9.25.26.27.33.42] (cf. **adj. gent.** foll.). **2.** son of king Jehoiakim Je 36[26]. **3.** Levite, 1 Ch 24[29].

3397 †יְרַחְמְאֵלִי **adj.gent.** (earlier than foregoing; as tribal name bef. n.pr.m. [For radical view of relations of יְרַח׳, (with many text. emendations), v. Che[Ency. Bib. JERACHM.]]);—הַיְר׳ as subst. coll., נֶגֶב הַיר׳ 1 S 27[10] *the Negeb of the Yeraḥmeelites* (in S. Judah), (νότον) Ιεσμεγα, A Ισραμηλει, 𝔊L Αερμων; עָרֵי הַיר׳ 30[29], τοῦ Ισραηλ, A Ιεραμηλει (cf. **1** supr., and Gray[Prop. N. 214, 265, 307]).

II. רחם (√ of foll.; cf. Ar. رَخَمٌ *vulture*; n. unit. رَخَمَةٌ).

7360 †רָחָם **n.[m.]** carrion-vulture;—abs. הָר׳ Lv 11[18] (Sam. רחמה; so perh. read) = הָרָחָמָה ‖ Dt 14[17] (on accent v. Dr; cf. Ges[§ 90 f]).

7360 †רָחָמָה **n.[m.]** id.; Dt 14[17], v. foregoing.

רחן (appar. √ of foll.; meaning dubious).

8647 †תִּרְחֲנָה **n.pr.** [**m.**? **f.**?] child of Caleb 1 Ch 2[48]; Θαραμ, A Θαρχνα, 𝔊L Θαρaανα.

7363 †I. [רָחַף] **vb. grow soft, relax** (cf. Ar. رَخُفَ *be soft*);—**Qal** *Pf.* 3 pl. רָחֲפוּ Je 23[9] (bones of one appalled).

7363 †II. רָחַף **vb. Pi. hover** (NH *id.*, cf. Grünbaum[ZMG xxxix (1885). 607]; Syr. Pa. ܪܰܚܶܦ *move gently*, also *cherish*, and *brood*, cf. Thes[s.v.]; connexion with I. ר׳ dub.);—**Pi.** *Impf.* 3 ms. יְרַחֵף עַל Dt 32[11] (poem) of vulture *hovering* over young; *Pt.* רוּחַ א׳ מְרַחֶפֶת עַל־פְּנֵי הַמָּיִם Gn 1[2] (P); *hovering* over face of waters, or perh. (v. Syr.) *brooding* (and fertilizing), so Jer[Quaest. in Gen. ed. Lag. 4] (reading '*marahaefeth*'), cf. Di Gunk.

7364 רָחַץ [72] **vb. wash, wash off, away, bathe** (NH = BH; Ar. رَحَضَ (also of garments); Eth. ረሐፀ:, ረሐፀ: *sweat*; cf. As. *raḫâṣu*, *overflow*, *flood* (on *ḫ* = ح v. Nö[ZMG xl (1886). 727]));—**Qal** [69] *Pf.* 3 ms. ר׳ Is 4[4]+, etc.; *Impf.* 3 ms. יִרְחַץ Dt 23[12]+ etc.; *Imv.* ms. רְחַץ 2 S 11[8] 2 K 5[13]; mpl. רַחֲצוּ Gn 18[4]+; *Inf. cstr.* רְחֹץ Gn 24[32]+, לִרְחֹצָה Ex 30[18]+; *Pt.* fs. רֹחֶצֶת 2 S 11[2], fpl. רֹחֲצוֹת Ct 5[12];—**1.** trans. *wash* (with water), c. acc. feet (רגלים; בַּמַּיִם oft. expr.), Gn 18[4] 19[2] 24[32] 43[24] (all J), Ju 19[21] 1 S 25[41] 2 S 11[8] Ct 5[3]; פְּעָמָיו יִר׳ בְּדַם הָרָשָׁע ψ 58[11] (fig. of righteous, at י׳'s vengeance); c. acc. hands (יָדַיִם) Dt 21[6] (+ עַל *over*, in ceremonial, to express innocence), hence fig. אֶר׳ כַּפַּי בְּנִקָּיוֹן ψ 26[6] 73[13]; hands and feet Ex 30[19] (+ מִן of laver), v[21] 40[31] (+ מִן *id.*; all P); c. acc. face (פָּנָיו) Gn 43[31] (J); c. acc. pers. Ez 16[9] Ex 29[4] 40[12] Lv 8[6] (all P), acc. בְּשָׂרוֹ (oft. ‖ כבּס of garments), Lv 14[9] 15[13] + 9 t. P (H); c. acc. of parts of sacrificial victim Ex 29[17] Lv 1[9.13] 8[21] 9[14]; *wash off, away*, c. acc. of filth Is 4[4] (fig.). **2.** intrans. *wash, bathe* (oneself): Ex 2[5] (E), 2 S 11[2] 12[20] 1 K 22[38] 2 K 5[10.12.13] Is 1[16] Ez 23[40] (+ לְ pers. for whom), Ru 3[3] Lv 14[8] + 14 t. P (oft. ‖ כבּס); + בְּ of laver 2 Ch 4[6.6]; of eyes, *bathed* in milk (בֶּחָלָב) Ct 5[12] (fig.); Jb 29[6] (fig.), v. הָלִיךְ. †**Pu.** *Pf.* 3 ms. רֻחָץ Pr 30[12] *be washed* (+ מִן of filth, fig.); 2 fs. בְּמַיִם לֹא רֻחַצְתְּ Ez 16[4] (in fig.). †**Hithp.** *Pf.* 1 s. הִתְרָחַצְתִּי בְמוֹ שָׁלֶג Jb 9[30] if *I washed myself in snow* (fig.).

†[רַחַץ] **n.[m.]** washing, fig.;—only sf. in סִיר רַחְצִי ψ 60[10] Moab is *my wash-pot* = 108[10]. 7366

†רַחְצָה **n.f.** id., lit.;—עָלוּ מִן־הָר׳, of sheep, Ct 4[2] 6[6] (in sim.). 7367

†רָחַק **vb.** be, or become, far, distant 7368 (NH = BH; As. esp. adj. *rûḳu*, *far*; cf. Ar. رَحِيقٌ *choice wine* (i.e. from a distance) Frä[158]; Eth. ርሕቀ: *be far*, Sab. רחק CIS[iv, nos. 95, 98]; Aram. רְחֵק, רְחֵיק, and (oft. in der. spec. and deriv.) ܪܚܩ);—**Qal** *Pf.* 3 ms. ר׳ Is 59[9] La 1[16], etc.; *Impf.* 3 ms. יִרְחַק Dt 12[21]+, etc.; *Imv.* fs. רַחֲקִי Is 54[14], mpl. רַחֲקוּ Ez 11[15] < *Pf.* רָחֲקוּ Ra Hi Sm Co Toy Krae; *Inf. cstr.* רְחֹק ψ 103[12] Ec 3[5], לְרָחֳקָה Ez 8[6];—*be far, distant*: c. מִן pers., of place Dt 12[21] 14[24], of pers., = neglect, abandon, Pr 19[7], esp. in ψψ, of י׳, ψ 22[12.20] (מִן pers. om.), 35[22] 38[22] 71[12]; of utter absence, or non-existence La 1[16], cf. Is 49[19] (abs.), subj. justice Is 59[9] (opp. הִשִּׂיג), cf. v[11] (‖ אַיִן), subj. blessing ψ 109[17]; subj. עֲצַת רְשָׁעִים Jb 21[16] 22[18]; c. מֵעַל pers. (י׳), of Isr. (fig.) Je 2[5], cf. Ez 44[10]; = *far from* (land of) י׳ 11[15] (v. supr.; Krae ins. אֶרֶץ); c. מֵעַל loc. Ez 8[6] (of י׳),

מִן loc. (E. from W.) ψ 103^{12}; c. מִן rei (fig.): תּוֹרָֽתְךָ 119^{150} (opp. קרב); מֵעֹשֶׁק מִיֶּשַׁע Jb 5^{14}, Is 54^{14}, cf. Pr 22^{5}; =*wholly abstain from* Ex 23^{7} (E), so (מִן inf.) Ec 3^{5}; abs. of י׳'s righteousness, with ref. to time Is 46^{13} (‖ אחר; opp. קרב).—יִרְחַק־חֹק Mi 7^{11} *boundary shall become distant*, i.e. territory be enlarged (? crpt., cf. We Now); ירחק חֶבֶל הַכֶּסֶף Kt Ec 12^{6} *be removed?* Qr יֵרָתֵק *be joined?* 𝔊 ἀνατραπῇ, 𝔙 *rumpatur*, cf. 𝔖, rd. prob. יִנָּתֵק Pfannk Thes Ew De Siegf Buhl^{Lex}. **Pi.** *Pf.* 3 ms. רִחַק Is 6^{12}, of י׳, *send far away*, acc. pers.; of people, לִבּוֹ ר׳ 29^{13}, c. מִן of י׳; 2 ms. רִחַקְתָּ 26^{15} *thou hast far extended* (c. acc.) all the ends (boundaries) of the land; *Impf.* 3 mpl. יְרַחֲקוּ אֶת־זְנוּתָם Ez 43^{9}. **Hiph.** *Pf.* 3 ms. הִרְחִיק Jb 19^{13} ψ 103^{12}, 1 s. sf. הִרְחַקְתִּים Ez 11^{16}, etc.; *Impf.* 3 ms. sf. יַרְחִיקֶנָּה Pr 22^{15}, 2 ms. תַּרְחִיק Jb 22^{23}, etc.; *Imv.* ms. הַרְחֵק Pr 4^{24}+2 t., הַרְחֶק־ Jb 13^{21}, sf. הַרְחִיקֵהוּ 11^{14}; *Inf. abs.* הַרְחֵק Gn 21^{16}+, *cstr.* הַרְחִיק Je 27^{10}, sf. הַרְחִיקָם Jo 4^{6};—**1.** dir. caus. *make*, or *exhibit, distance, be gone far*, subj. pers.: Gn 44^{4} (J), c. מִן loc. Jos 8^{4} (JE), Ju 18^{22}; sq. inf. cstr. הַרְחֵק לֹא תַר׳ לָלֶכֶת Ex 8^{24} (J), cf. ψ 55^{8}; Inf. abs. as adv. = *at a distance* Gn 21^{16} (E), c. מִן loc. Ex 33^{7} (E), Jos 3^{16} (JE; הַר׳ מְאֹד מִן, Qr; >Kt ב for מן). **2.** indir. caus. *remove, put far away*, c. acc. pers. + מֵעַל of land Je 27^{10}, cf. Jo 4^{6}, + מֵעַל pers. Jb 19^{13} and (acc. הַצְּפוֹנִי) Jo 2^{20}, + מִן pers. ψ 88$^{9.19}$; + בַּגּוֹיִם Ez 11^{16}; c. acc. כַּף + מֵעַל pers. Jb 13^{21}, c. acc. דַּרְכֵּךְ + *id.* Pr 5^{8}; c. acc. of sin + מִן pers. 4^{24} Jb 11^{14} (מִן pers. om.); Pr 22^{15} 30^{8} ψ 103^{12}; + מִן loc. Jb 22^{23}.

7369 † [רָחֵק] **adj. verb.** removing, departing;—pl. sf., as subst., רְחֵקֶיךָ ψ 73^{27} *those departing from thee* (i.e. from י׳).

7350 † רָחֹק, רָחוֹק **adj.** distant, far, et **n.m.**$^{\text{Jos 3,4}}$ distance (Lag$^{\text{BN 31}}$);—abs. רָחֹק Ex 2^{4}+, רָחוֹק Ez 6^{12}+; fs. רְחֹקָה Dt 30^{11}+, רְחוֹקָה Jos 9^{6}+; mpl. רְחֹקִים Dt 13^{8}+, etc., fpl. abs. רְחֹקוֹת Je 48^{24}+, etc.;—oft. opp. קָרוֹב: **1. adj. a.** of space: *distant*, land Jos 9$^{6.9}$ (+מְאֹד), Dt 29^{21} 1 K 8$^{41.46}$=2 Ch 6$^{32.36}$, 2 K 20^{14}=Is 39^{3}, אִיִּים ר׳ Is 66^{19}+perh. ψ 65^{6} (Che We read אִיִּם for יָם; Weir in Che גּוֹיִם; MT makes ר׳=*distant ones*, people); c. מִן pers., of peoples Jos 9^{22} (JE), Ju 18^{7}, persons Ez 22^{5} Ne 4^{13} Pr 15^{29} (י׳, fig.), cf. Je 12^{2} (*id.*), cities Dt 20^{15}, so (מִן loc.) Ju 18^{28}; abs. of people Jo 4^{8}, persons Is 33^{13} 57^{19} Je 25^{26} Ez 6^{12} Zc 6^{15} Pr 27^{10} Dn 9^{7} Est 9^{20}, cities Je 48^{24}, trees ψ 56^{1} (title; v. יוֹנָה *ad fin.*, p. 401), of *distant* journey Nu 9^{10} (P); fig., רָחוֹק pred. (indef.) Ec 7^{24}, of י׳'s מִצְוָה Dt 30^{11}; c. מִן pers. (i.e. absent from, lacking to), of salvation ψ 119^{155}, wisdom Ec 7^{23}; of pers. c. מִן of act or quality Is 46^{12} ψ 22^{2}; of price, c. מִן comp. = *far beyond* Pr 31^{10}. **b.** of time: לְעִתִּים רְחוֹקוֹת Ez 12^{27}. **2. n.m.** always sing.: **a.** of space: *distance* Jos 3^{4} (D); elsewhere c. prep.: (1) מֵר׳ *from a distance*, c. verbs implying motion, physical or mental: look Gn 24^{4} (E) 37^{18} (J) Jb 2^{12} 36^{25}; bring Dt 28^{49} Is 43^{6} 60^{9}, cf. Je 46^{27}; come Is 49^{12} 60^{4} Hb 1^{8}; hear Is 49^{1}; smell Jb 39^{25}; remember Je 51^{50}; understand ψ 139^{2}; prob. also worship Ex 24^{1} (J); (2) מֵר׳ *at a distance* (מִן **1 c**) Ex 2^{4} (E), 20$^{18.21}$ (E; Gi v$^{15.18}$), 1 S 26^{13} 2 K 2^{7} Is 5^{26} 59^{14} ψ 38^{12}, cf. אֱלֹהֵי מֵר׳ Je 23^{23} *a God afar off* (on cstr. cf. Ges$^{\text{§ 130 a}}$; <read אלהים ר׳ Gie, cf. 𝔊); (3) מֵר׳ *to a distance* (מִן **1 c**) Is 22^{3} 23^{7} Pr 7^{19}; (4) בְּר׳ *at a distance* ψ 10^{1}; עַד־ר׳ *to a distance* Mi 4^{3}; also c. two prepp.: (5) לְמֵר׳ *from* (מִן **9 b**), Jb 36^{3} 39^{29}; (6) עַד־מֵר׳ (III. עַד **I. 1 a**) *to a distance* Is 57^{9}+Ne 12^{43} van d. H. (עַד om. Baer Gi); even (7) עַד־לְמֵר׳ (עַד III.) 2 Ch 26^{15} Ezr 3^{13}. **b.** of time, מֵר׳ *long ago* Is 22^{11}, c. noun=*ancient, of long standing* 25^{1}; לְמֵר׳ *long ago* 2 K 19^{25}=Is 37^{26}; *from afar* 2 S 7^{19}=1 Ch 17^{17}.

† מֶרְחָק **n.m.** distant place, distance;— 4801
abs. מ׳ Is 10^{3}+, מֶרְחָק ψ 138^{6}; pl. מֶרְחַקִּים Zc 10^{9}, מֵר׳ Is 33^{17} Je 8^{19}, cstr. מֶרְחַקֵּי־ Is 8^{9};—*distant place, far country* Is 8^{9} Zc 10^{9}; often c. אֶרֶץ: א׳ (ה)מֶּרְחָק *land of distance*, distant land Is 13^{5} 46^{11} Je 4^{16} 6^{20} Pr 25^{25}, so c. pl. א׳ מרחקים Je 8^{19}, *land of distances*, i.e. of wide extent, Is 33^{17}; מִמּ׳ *from far* Is 10^{3} 30^{27} Je 5^{15} Ez 23^{40} Pr 31^{14}; fig. ψ 138^{6}; מִמּ׳ *at a distance* Je 31^{10}, *to a distance* Is 17^{13}.—בֵּית הַמּ׳ v. p. 112. 1023

† רָחַשׁ **vb.** keep moving, stir (NH *stir*, 7370
move, esp. of lips in speech, also, in expl. of מרחשת, of *stewing, boiling*; Aram. רְחֵישׁ, ܪܚܫ, ܪܚܫ, *creep, move, flutter*, ܪܚܫܐ *reptile*);—**Qal** *Pf.* 3 ms. ר׳ לִבִּי דָּבָר טוֹב ψ 45^{2} *is astir*.

† מַרְחֶשֶׁת **n.f.** stew-pan, sauce-pan (so 4802
NH; v. esp. Levy$^{\text{NHWB iii. 69 b}}$, and cf. NH רָחוּשׁ Id$^{\text{ib. iv. 443 a}}$);—מִנְחַת מ׳ Lv 2^{7}, כָּל־[מִנְחָה] נַעֲשָׂה בַּמּ׳ 7^{9}.

† רַחַת **n.[f.]** winnowing-shovel, or the 7371
like (√unknown; Thes fr. רוח=*ventilabrum*, cf. Nö$^{\text{ZMG xl (1886), 728}}$; Wetzst in De$^{\text{Is (2), 709}}$ fr. רחה = رَخُوَ *be soft, loose, friable*, etc., cf. Kö$^{\text{ii. 1, 177}}$; NH=BH, Ar. رَحْتٌ is prob. loan-wd. Nö$^{\text{l.c.}}$);—זֹרֶה בָר׳ וּבַמִּזְרֶה Is 30^{24}.

7372 †[רָטֹב, רָטֵב Lag[BN 31]] **vb. be moist** (NH *id.*; As. *raṭâbu*, II. *moisten;* Ar. رَطِبَ, Eth. ረጥበ: Aram. רְטַב, رطب, all *be moist*);—**Qal** *Impf.* 3 ms. מִזֶּרֶם הָרִים יִרְטָבוּ Jb 24^{8}.

7373 †רָטֹב **adj. moist, juicy, fresh**;—ר׳ הוּא לִפְנֵי־שָׁמֶשׁ Jb 8^{16}.

3399 †[רָטָה] **vb.** (dub.) **wring out** (NH=BH (si vera l., v. Levy[NHWB iv. 444] and reff.));—**Qal** *Impf.* 3 ms. sf. יִרְטֵנִי Jb 16^{11} upon the hands of wicked men *he wrings me out*, but read prob.
3399 יְרִ׳, ירט √ (Di Bu Du al.), q. v. p. 437

רטט (Aram. רְטַט *tremble*, rare, der. spec.).

7374 †רֶטֶט **n.[m.] trembling, panic** (Ba[NB § 20 a] Kö[ii. 1, 42]);—abs. ר׳ הֶחֱזִיקָה Je 49^{24} *she hath seized panic*, but < הֶחֱזִיקָהּ (Gie), *panic hath seized her.*

7375 †**רֻטֲפַשׁ vb. quadril. intrans. grow fresh** (Ges[§ 56]; si vera l., transp. טרפשׁ [expanded
2954 from טָפַשׁ *be wide, loose, delicate*, cf. esp. As. *tapâšu, be fat*, Zim[BP 99 A] Frä[ZA iii. 55]], cf. Talm. טַרְפְּשָׁא *fatty membrane*, Syr. ܛܪܦܫܐ PS[1527] *thin flesh;* Ar. طَرْفَشَ *be convalescent;* but ר׳ perh. not orig.);—*Pf.* pass. רֻטֲפַשׁ בְּשָׂרוֹ מִנֹּעַר Jb 33^{25} *his flesh hath grown fresher than*, etc.; rd. perh. טפשׁ Altschüller[ZAW vi (1886), 212], יטפשׁ Bi Bu cf. Du.

7376 †[רָטַשׁ] **vb. Pi. dash in pieces** (cf. ℑ רְטַשׁ **cast away, reject**; but possibly akin to לָטַשׁ);—**Pi.** *Impf.* 2 ms. תְּרַטֵּשׁ 2 K 8^{12} their children *thou wilt dash in pieces;* 3 fpl. קְשָׁתוֹת נְעָרִים תְּרַטַּשְׁנָה Is 13^{18}, but prob. crpt., Du conj. נְעָרוֹת תְּרַטַּשְׁנָה, cf. Che. **Pu.** *Pf.* 3 fs. אֵם עַל־בָּנִים רֻטָּשָׁה Ho 10^{14}; *Impf.* 3 mpl. יְרֻטְּשׁוּ Is 13^{16} Na 3^{10}, יְרֻטָּשׁוּ Ho 14^{1}, all of children.

7377 רִי v. רוה. p. 924

7378 †**רִיב** [Nö[ZMG xxxvii (1883), 530, 534] Ges[§ 73 b]] **vb. strive, contend** (cf. Ar. رَابَ (ى) *agitate* (the mind), رَيْبٌ *disquiet;* cf. also Syr. ܪܳܒ *cry, shout*, Aph. also *quarrel noisily*, ܪܘܼܒܵܐ *shouting, clamour* (v. Nö[l. c.]); on Sab. n.pr. ריב=Ar. رِياب v. DHM[ib. 14]);—**Qal** *Pf.* 3 ms. רָב Ju 11^{25} 1 S 25^{29}; 2 ms. רַבֹתָ La 3^{58}, רִיבוֹתָ Jb 33^{13}, etc.; *Impf.* 3 ms. יָרִיב Ju 6^{31}+, juss. יָרֵב Ho 4^{4} 1 S 24^{16}, יָרֶב לוֹ(בּוֹ) Ju $6^{31.32}$; וַיָּרֶב Gn 31^{36}+; 2 ms. תרוב Pr 3^{30} Kt, תָּרִיב Qr; 3 mpl. יְרִיבֻן Ex 21^{18}, etc.; *Imv.* ms. רִיב Mi 6^{1} Pr 25^{9}, רִיבָה ψ 35^{1}+, mpl. רִיבוּ Is 1^{17} Ho 2^{4}; *Inf. abs.* רוֹב Ju 11^{25}, רֹב Jb 40^{2}; רִיב Je 50^{34} (Ges[§ 73 d] Kö[i. 509] Ba[NB 80]); *cstr.* רִיב Is 3^{13} Jb 9^{3}+ Ju 21^{22} Qr (Kt רוב), רִב Am 7^{4} Pr 25^{8}; *Pt.* רָב Is 19^{20}+;—*strive:* **1.** involving bodily struggle Ex 21^{18} (sc. one with another; E); public hostilities, יָדָיו רָב לוֹ Dt 33^{7} (with) *his hands he strove for it*, c. עִם of Israel, הֲרוֹב רָב Ju 11^{25} (‖ נִלְחַם). **2.** with words, c. בְּ pers. Gn 31^{36} (E), Ex 17^{2a} (J) Ju 6^{32}, so (in fig.) Ho 2^{4} cf. v^{4}; oft.=*quarrel*, c. עִם pers., Gn 26^{20} Ex 17^{2b} Nu 20^{3} (all J), Ne 13^{25}; subj. God Jb 9^{3} 13^{19} 23^{6}; also 40^{2} (עִם of God; on inf. abs. v. Ges[§ 114 ee]), in gen. Pr 3^{30}; c. אֶת pers. Ju 8^{1} Ne 5^{7} $13^{11.17}$, subj. י׳ Is 49^{25} (cf. I. יָרִיב infr.), ψ 35^{1} (‖ לְחַם); אֶת of י׳ Is 45^{9} (pt. *one striving*), Nu 20^{13} (P); c. עַל rei Gn $26^{21.22}$; abs.=*find fault* Ho 4^{4} (‖ הוֹכִיחַ). Esp. **3.** *conduct a* (legal) *case, suit*, usu. fig., י׳ subj.; Is 3^{13} (‖ דִּין), 57^{16} (‖ קָצַף), ψ 103^{9} (נָטַר [אַף]), cf. קֹרֵא לָרִב בָּאֵשׁ Am 7^{4}; c. acc. pers. with whom (unfriendly sense), Jb 10^{2} Is 27^{8}; c. acc. cogn. רִיב in good sense, =take one's part, 1 S 24^{15} (Gi; v^{16} van d. H. Baer; ‖ שָׁפַט), Mi 7^{9} Je 50^{34} (רִיב יָרִיב אֶת־רִיבָם, inf. cstr.=inf. abs., v. supr.), 51^{36} (‖ נקם), La 3^{58} Pr 22^{23} ψ 43^{1} (+ מִגּוֹי; ‖ שָׁפַט), 119^{154} (+ גָּאַל), also 74^{22} (God, his own cause); + מִיַּד pers. against whom 1 S 25^{39} (of vengeance); + אֶת pers. against whom Pr 23^{11}, so (without acc. cogn.) Is 50^{8} Je $2^{9.9}$; cf. אֶת־הֶהָרִים Mi 6^{1} (II. אֵת **1 c**; 𝔊 πρός, whence We Now אֶל־ *in the presence of*, but on רִיב אֶל v. **4**); ר׳=*plead*, c. לְ pers. for whom Ju $6^{31.31.31}$ Jb 13^{8}, c. acc. pers. for whom Is 1^{17}, of God 51^{22}, cf. Dt 33^{8} (obscure, v. Dr); of human disputes Pr 25^{8}, רִיבְךָ ר׳ אֶת־רֵעֶךָ v^{9}. **4.** =*make complaint*, c. אֶל pers. unto and against whom Ju 21^{22} Je 2^{29} 12^{1} Jb 33^{13}. **Hiph.** *Pt.* sf. מריבו 1 S 2^{10} Kt (Qr מְרִיבָיו), i.e. (those) *displaying contention against him* (י׳), cf. pl. cstr. וְעַמְּךָ כִּמְרִיבֵי כֹהֵן Ho 4^{4}, obscure; RS[Proph. 406] מָרוּ בִי *thy people have rebelled against me, O priest!* BeckWü We GASm הַכֹּ׳ as voc., and [by some] וְעַמִּי כִּכְמָרָיו הַכֹּהֵן joined to v^{5}); Hermann[SK, 1879, 516] וְעַמְּךָ מְרִיבֵי הַכֹּ׳, cf. Oort (רִיבִי); Ruben[Crit. Rem. ad loc.] וְעַמִּי כָּמוֹךָ הַכֹּ׳, so Now.—וַיָּרֶב 1 S 15^{5} v. ארב **Hiph.** p. 70 693

7379 **רִיב** n.m.[Is 1, 23] **strife, dispute**;—abs. ר׳ Gn 13^{7}+, רִב Ex 23^{2}+; cstr. רִיב 17^{7}+; sf. רִיבִי 1 S 24^{16}+, רִבְכֶם Jb 31^{13} (or inf.?), etc.; pl. רִיבֹת Dt 17^{8}; cstr. רִיבֵי 2 S 22^{44}+ 2 t., רִבוֹת Jb 13^{6};—*strife, quarrel:* †**1.** in words, Ex 17^{7} (J), Dt 1^{12}, about pasturage Gn 13^{7} (J; = מְרִיבָה v^{8}), in gen. Pr 15^{18} 17^{14} 20^{3} $26^{17.21}$ 30^{33}, + מָדוֹן Hb 1^{3}, so וְחֵי־ר׳ Pr 17^{1}; fig. ר׳ עֲצָמָיו Jb 33^{19} Kt (Qr רוֹב, i.e. רֹב q. v.); ר׳ לְשֹׁנוֹת ψ 31^{21}, cf. Is 58^{4} Pr 18^{6};

ר׳ אִישׁ Je 15[10] (+ א׳ מָדוֹן). †**2.** of public hostilities 2 S 22[44] = ψ 18[44], cf. אִישׁ רִיב Ju 12[2], אַנְשֵׁי רִיבֶךָ Is 41[11]; ‖ חָמָס ψ 55[10]. **3.** 39 esp. *dispute, controversy, case at law:* Ex 23[2.3.6] (E), Dt 21[5] (+ נֶגַע), 25[1] 2 S 15[2.4] (‖ מִשְׁפָּט), + 10 t., + (of י׳) Ho 4[1] 12[3] Mi 6[2.2] Je 25[31] Ez 44[24] La 3[36]; as acc. cogn., *case, cause* Mi 7[9] Je 50[34] + 8 t. (v. √ **3**), רִיבֵי נַפְשִׁי La 3[58]; רִיב חֶרְפָּתִי 1 S 25[39], + דִּבְרֵי רִיבֹת Dt 17[8] *matters of controversy;* ר׳ 19[17] *dispute* as to guilt; אִישׁ רִיבִי Jb 31[35] = *accuser.* †**4.** *plea:* Pr 18[17], רִבוֹת שְׂפָתַי Jb 13[6] *pleadings of my lips.*

7380 †רִיבַי **n.pr.m.** in Benj., 2 S 23[29] (Ρειβα, Ερıβα)
3403 = 1 Ch 11[31] (Ρεβιε, Ρηβαι, Ριβατ, etc.); cf. יְרִיבַי below.

3377 †יָרֵב **n.m. epith.** of Assyrian king (prop., si vera l., vb. = *let him contend,* or (one who) *contends*);—only מֶלֶךְ י׳ Ho 5[13] 10[6], i.e. TP. III; WMM[ZAW xvii (1897), 335] prop. מַלְכִּי רָב (י- old nom. termin.) = As. *šarru rabbu;* Che[Expos., Nov. 1897, 364] מלך רב; Che[Ency. Bib. JAREB] conj. מלך ערבי, *Arabian king;* cf., further, Comm., Schr[COT, ad loc.] J A Selbie [Hastings DB, JAREB] and reff.

3401 †I. [יָרִיב] **n.[m.] opponent, adversary** (Ges[§ 85d]);—sf. (of Zion), יְרִיבֵךְ Is 49[25] (𝔊 רִיבֵךְ, so Du); cf. pl. sf. יְרִיבַי ψ 35[1] (‖ לֹחֲמָי); of personal opponent, יְרִיבָי Je 18[19] (𝔊 רִיבִי, so Gie).

3402 †II. יָרִיב **n.pr.m.** (*he contendeth* or *taketh* (our) *part, conducteth* (our) *case;* cf. Sab. ירב Hal[615]);—**1.** son of Simeon 1 Ch 4[24], Ιαρειν[μ, β],
3199 = יָכִין **1**, v. sub כון. **2.** post-ex. names, Ιαρειμ[β], etc.: **a.** Ezr 8[16], perhaps = **b.** 10[18].

3403 †[יְרִיבַי] **n.pr.m.** a hero of David (OAram. יריבי CIS[ii. 70 (biling.)] ‖ As. *Iribai*);—c. ו, וִירִיבַי 1 Ch 11[46], Ιαριβει, 𝔊L Ιαρειβ.

4808 †I. מְרִיבָה **n.f. strife, contention;**—abs. מ׳, of quarrel between herdsmen Gn 13[8] (J); cstr. מְרִיבַת הָעֵדָה, of people's strife with Moses at Kadesh Nu 27[14] (P), cf. II. מ׳ **2.**

4809 †II. מְרִיבָה **n.pr.loc.** (*place of strife*);—**1.** at Rephidim, מַסָּה וּמ׳ Ex 17[7] (J), Λοιδόρησις. **2.** at Kadesh, esp. in מֵי מְרִיבָה *water of M.* (𝔊 ὕδωρ ἀντιλογίας) Dt 33[8] Nu 20[13] (P) ψ 81[8] 106[32], also (𝔊 ὕδωρ τῆς λοιδορίας, 𝔊L as above)
6946 Nu 20[24] (P); מ׳ cstr. in מֵי מְרִיבַת קָדֵשׁ (𝔊 ὕδωρ ἀντιλογίας [ἐν] Καδης) Nu 27[14] Dt 32[51] (both P), and (𝔊 ὕδωρ Βαριμωθ Καδης) Ez 48[28]; so מֵי מְרִיבוֹת קָדֵשׁ ק׳ 47[19] (𝔊 ὕδωρ Μαριμωθ Καδης); Dt 33[2] v. *ad fin.;* מְרִיבָה alone, only ψ 95[8] (παραπικρασμός; ‖ יוֹם מַסָּה).

יְרֻבַּעַל 14 **n.pr.m.** name given to Gideon 3378
(acc. to Ju 6[32], where expl. as *let Baal contend* (cf. Dr[2 S 4, 4] Kö[ii. 1, 467]); Impf. ירוב not elsewhere [yet תרוב Pr 3[30] Kt, and Inf. cstr. רוב Ju 21[23] Kt], hence We[Sm 31] expl. as = יְרוּבַעַל, √ ירה, cf. יְרִיאֵל, יְרוּאֵל (p. 436 b), so GFM[Ju] Bu[Ju] Now[Ju]);—Ju 6[32] 7[1] 8[29.35] 9[1] + 8 t. 9 (-בַּעַל 9[24.57]), 1 S 12[11];
= יְרֻבֶּשֶׁת + 2 S 11[21] (v. בֹּשֶׁת **2**, sub בושׁ); Ιεροβααλ 3380
(usu.; so 𝔊L 1 S 12[11] 2 S 11[21], where 𝔊B Ιεροβοαμ).
—יָרָבְעָם, v. רבב. p. 914 3379

†יְרֻבֶּשֶׁת 2 S 11[21] v. foregoing. 3380

†מְרִיב בַּעַל **n.pr.m.** (*Baal is* (our, my, his) 4807
advocate(?), cf. Nes[Eg. 120] Dr[2 S 4, 4]; but Gray[Prop. N. 201] thinks מרי בעל orig. form = *hero of Baal*);—**1.** son of Jonathan 1 Ch 8[34], מ׳ בָּעַל v[34] 9[40] =
מְרִי־בַעַל (err.?) v[40] = מְפִיבֹשֶׁת (later change, v. 4648, 4810
בֹּשֶׁת sub בושׁ) 2 S 4[4] 9[6.6.10.11.12.12.13] 16[1.4] 19[26.31] 21[7], מְפִבֹשֶׁת 16[25] (called בֶּן־שָׁאוּל); 𝔊 in 2 S Μεμφιβοσθε, in 1 Ch (usu.) Μεριβααλ; 𝔊L Μεμφιβααλ
in 2 S (exc. 4[1.2] etc., where not in 𝔥). **2.** מְפִבֹשֶׁת 4648
son of Saul and Rispah, acc. to 2 S 21[8], 𝔊 (incl. 𝔊L) Μεμφιβοσθε.

רִיחַ, רֵיחַ v. רוח. רִים v. רְאֵם. p. 910, 926 7214, 7381

[רֵיעַ] v. II. רֵעַ sub רעה. רִיעַ v. ריע. p. 929, 945 7321, 7453

ריף (√ of following; meaning unknown).

†[רִיפָה] **n.[f.]** dub.; some grain or fruit 7383
(such as was spread out to dry (2 S), and also pounded (Pr); 𝔙[2 S] *as if drying barley-groats,* 𝔊L παλάθας, *cakes of preserved fruit,* cf. preparation of 'apricot-cheese' Wetzst [ZPV xiv. 2] Nes[Marg. 18], who cites also Almkvist [Kl. Beitr. zur Lexicogr. des Vulg. Ar. Actes, 419]);—pl. abs. רִפוֹת 2 S 17[19], רִיפוֹת Pr 27[22].

†רִיפַת **n. pr. gent.** 'son' of Gomer (of 7384
Japhet);—Gn 10[3] (P; > ‖ 1 Ch 1[6] דִּיפַת q.v.); 7384
Joseph. makes = Paphlagonians; Bo Lag[Ges. Abh. 255] cp. river Ῥῆβας (Arrian[Peripl. 12, 3]) = *Rhebas* (Plin[NH vi. 4]), on Thracian Bosphorus, but v. Di. p. 193

†[רִיק] **vb. Hiph.** make empty, empty 7324
out (Ar. رَاقَ (ى) *pour out, forth,* intrans. (of water, blood, etc.); Aram. רִיק *empty, pour,* ﻭ in deriv.; As. *rêḳu, empty*);—*Pf.* 1 s. הֲרִיקֹתִי Lv 26[33] Mal 3[10]; 3 pl. הֵרִיקוּ Ez 28[7] 30[11]; *Impf.* 3 ms. יָרִיק Hb 1[17], וַיָּרֶק Gn 14[14] (but v. infr.); *Imv.* ms. הָרֵק ψ 35[3]; *Inf. cstr.* הָרִיק Is 32[6]; *Pt.* pl. מְרִיקִים Gn 42[35] Zc 4[12];—**1.** *empty* vessels Gn 42[35] (E) Je 48[12]; *keep empty,* לְהָרִיק נֶפֶשׁ רָעֵב

Is 32^{6} (i.e. keep hungry). **2.** *pour out* or *down*, rain Mal 3^{10} Ec 11^{3}, oil Zc 4^{12}. **3.** *empty out* (i.e. *draw*) sword (cf. As. *kakkê ittabbaku* [pass.], Dl$^{HWB\,699\,b}$) Ex 15^{9} (poem), Lv 26^{33} (H), Ez 5$^{2.12}$ 12^{14} 28^{7} 30^{11}; prob. also Hb 1^{17} (חרבו for חרמו Gie We Now); of lance ψ 35^{3}; cf. (si vera l.) וירק חניכיו Gn 14^{14} (R) *led forth*, < Sam. וַיָּדָק (Aram. דּוּק Aph. *look*) i.e. *mustered* 𝔊 cf. Di al., ויפקד Ball.—In ψ 18^{43} 𝔊 𝔖 Hup-Now Bae rd. אֲדָקֵם; so ‖ 2 S 22^{43} MT; but De Dr < אֲרִיקֵם (v. דקק). **Hoph.** *be emptied out* from vessel: *Pf.* 3 ms. הוּרַק Je 48^{11}; *Impf.* 2 ms. תּוּרַק Ct 1^{3} (al. 3 fs.; of ointment, in sim.); cf. also Am 6^{6}, where Oort מוּרְקֵי for מִזְרְקֵי.

7386 † [רִיק], רֵק **adj. empty, vain**;—m. abs. רֵק Gn 37^{24} + 2 t.; f. רֵקָה Ez 24^{11} Is 29^{8}; mpl. רֵ(י)קִים Ju 7^{16} +; fpl. רֵקוֹת Gn 41^{27};— **1.** *empty*, of vessels 2 K 4^{3} Ju 7^{16} Ez 24^{11} + (prob.)
7385 Je 14^{3} (רֵיקִים for רֵיקָם), 51^{34} (רִיק for רֵיק); of pit Gn 37^{24} (J), lap Ne 5^{13}, ears of grain Gn 41^{27} (E; דַּקּוֹת v$^{6.7.23.24}$); רֵקָה נַפְשׁוֹ Is 29^{8} (cf. 32^{6} √ **1**). **2.** *empty, idle, worthless*, ethically; אנשים ריקים *worthless fellows* Ju 9^{4} 11^{3} 2 Ch 13^{7}, so הָרֵקִים alone (as subst.) 2 S 6^{20}; מְרַדֵּף רֵיקִים Pr 12^{11} AV RV of persons; < *vain, unprofitable things*, 28^{19} (v. Toy); דָּבָר ר׳ מִן Dt 32^{47} (D) *a thing too empty* (of significance) for you; + (prob.) ψ 4^{3} (רֵיק for MT רִיק) *love an empty thing* (‖ כזב), of abortive course of action.

7385 † רִיק **n.[m.] emptiness, vanity**;—chiefly in adv. phr. לְרִיק Is 49^{4} Jb 39^{16} *in vain* (of labour without benefit), so לָר׳ Lv 26$^{16.20}$ (H), Is 65^{23}; and as adv. acc. רִיק Is 30^{7} ψ 73^{13}, prob. also 2^{1} (most = *empty scheme* as רֵיק **2**) cf. ψ 4^{3} (rd. prob. רֵיק);
7386 בְּדֵי רִיק Je 51^{58} = Hb 2^{13}.—Je 51^{34} v. רֵיק **1.** above

7387 † רֵיקָם **adv. emptily, vainly**; — **1.** *in empty condition, empty* = with empty hands; c. vb. of sending Gn 31^{42} (E), Dt 15^{13} 1 S 6^{3} Jb 22^{9}; of going forth Ex 3^{21}, returning Ru 1^{21} 3^{17}; = without an offering, לֹא יֵרָאוּ פָנַי ר׳ Ex 23^{15} (E) = 34^{20} (J), more fully Dt 16^{16} (cf. [פָּנֶה] II. **2,** ראה **Niph. 1 b**). **2.** *in vain, without effect:* c. שׁוּב 2 S 1^{22} (poem), Is 55^{11} Je 14^{3} (but v. רֵיק **1**), 50^{9}; prob. also צוֹרְרַי ר׳ ψ 7^{5} *those who were my adversaries in vain* (without success); הַבּוֹגְדִים ר׳ 25^{3} that *deal treacherously in vain* (in both most *without cause*).

7325 † [רִיר] **vb. flow** (like slime);—(Aram. רִירָא, ܪܳܝܪܳܐ *saliva, spittle;* cf. Ar. رَالَ *slaver, slobber*);—**Qal** *Pf.* 3 ms. רָר בְּשָׂרוֹ אֶת־זוֹבוֹ Lv 15^{3} *his flesh* (בָּשָׂר **3**) *flows with his issue.*

† רִיר **n.m. slimy juice, spittle**;—cstr. בְּרִיר 7388
חַלָּמוּת Jb 6^{6} *in the juice of* ח׳ (al. *slime of yolk*, i.e. white of egg); sf. רִירוֹ 1 S 21^{14} *his spittle.*

רֵישׁ, רִישׁ v. רוּשׁ. רִישׁוֹן v. ראשׁון. p. 930 7223, 7389

רַךְ, רֹךְ v. רכך. p. 940 7390-91

† רָכַב **vb. mount and ride, ride** (NH = 7392
BH; As. *rakâbu*, Ar. رَكِبَ, Aram. רְכֵיב, ܪܟܶܒ, all *id.;* cf. Zinj. רכב *war-chariot*, n.pr. div. רכבאל (Cook^{108}); Sab. רכבהו = *his rider* Mordtm Him. Inschr. 25 (of horse; but *his trappings* CIS$^{iv,\,no.\,306,\,5}$); Eth. ረከበ: is *attain, acquire*);—**Qal** *Pf.* 3 ms. ר׳ Est 6^{8}; 2 ms. רָכַבְתָּ Nu 22^{30}; 3 pl. רָכְבוּ 1 S 30^{17}; *Impf.* 3 ms. יִרְכַּב Lv 15^{9}, etc.; *Imv.* ms. רְכַב ψ 45^{5}; *Inf. cstr.* לִרְכּוֹב 2 S 16^{2} 2 K 4^{24}; *Pt. act.* רֹכֵב abs. Nu 22^{22} +, cstr. Am 2^{15}; sf. רֹכְבוֹ Gn 49^{17} +; fs. abs. רֹכֶבֶת 1 S 25^{20}; mpl. רֹכְבִים Ju 10^{4} +, etc.;—**1.** *mount, mount and sit,* or *ride,* c. עַל of camel Gn 24^{61} (J), 1 S 30^{17}, of ass (חֲמוֹר) 1 S 25^{42} 25^{20} 2 S 16^{2} (עַל obj. om.), 19^{27} 1 K 13^{13}, of mule (פֶּרֶד) 2 S 13^{29}; abs. of mounting (and riding in) chariot 1 K 18^{45} 2 K 9^{16}. **2.** *ride, be riding,* c. עַל of mule (פֶּרֶד) 2 S 18^{9}, of ass, אָתוֹן Nu 22^{22} (J), so (עַל obj. om.) 2 K 4^{24}, of חֲמוֹר Zc 9^{9}, of horse Zc 1^{8}; c. עַל־מֶרְכָּב (v. מ׳) Lv 15^{9}; c. ב of animal (בְּהֵמָה) Ne 2^{12}; ב of chariotry and horses Je 17^{25} = 22^{4}; abs. (perh. in chariot) ψ 45^{5} *ride on! ride* (habitually) c. עַל of אָתוֹן Nu 22^{30} (J), of עֲיָרִים Ju 10^{4} 12^{14}, of סוּס Ho 14^{4} (fig. of alliance with Egypt), Je 6^{23} 50^{42} Est 6^{8}, Hb 3^{8} (fig. of י׳; poss. add sf. ref. to יָם, cf. Dt 33^{26}), עַל־קַל (‖ סוּס) Is 30^{16}; of י׳, עַל־כְּרוּב 2 S 22^{11} = ψ 18^{11}, עַל־עָב קַל Is 19^{1}, c. acc. שָׁמַיִם *ride through* Dt 33^{26}, but also c. ב loc. *in, through,* ψ 68$^{5.34}$. **3.** pt. רֹכֵב etc., as subst., *rider:* רֹכְבֵי אֲתֹנוֹת Ju 5^{10}; ר׳ (ה)סוּס Am 2^{15} 2 K 9$^{18.19}$ Ez 23^{23} 38^{15} Zc 10^{5}, so (appos. פָּרָשִׁים) Ez 23$^{6.12}$; sf. of סוּס Gn 49^{17} Ex 15$^{1.21}$ Je 51^{21a} Zc 12^{4} Jb 39^{18} Hg 2^{22b}; עַל of סוּס 2 K 18^{23} = Is 36^{8}; רֹכְבֵי רֶכֶשׁ Est 8$^{10.14}$; sf. of chariot Je 51^{21b} Hg 2^{22}. **Hiph.** *Pf.* 2 ms. הִרְכַּבְתָּ ψ 66^{12}, etc.; *Impf.* 3 ms. וַיַּרְכֵּב Gn 41^{43} 2 K 13^{16}, sf. יַרְכִּבֵהוּ Dt 32^{13}, etc.; *Imv.* ms. הַרְכֵּב 2 K 13^{16};—**1.** *cause to* (*mount and*) *ride:* c. acc. pers. + עַל of חֲמוֹר Ex 4^{20} (J), of פִּרְדָּה 1 K 1$^{33.38.44}$, of סוּס Est 6^{9}, cf. (עַל־סוּס om.) v^{11}; c. acc. pers. + ב of chariot Gn 41^{43} (E), 2 K 10^{16}; ב of chariot om. 2 K 9^{28} 23^{30} = (c. עַל־רֶכֶב) 2 Ch 35^{24}; fig. Jb 30^{22} (sc. on the wind); c. acc. rei + אֶל־עֲגָלָה 2 S 6^{3} = 1 Ch 13^{7}; fig., c. acc. pers. + עַל loc. (על־במותי ארץ) Dt 32^{13} so Is 58^{14}, +

לְרֹאשֵׁנוּ ψ 66^{12} *over our heads.* **2.** *cause to draw* (plough, etc.) Ho 10^{11}, obj. Ephr. under fig. of heifer. **3.** fig. (עַל־הַקֶּשֶׁת) הַרְכֵּב יָדְךָ 2 K 13$^{16.16}$ *cause hand to ride upon* (grasp) *bow.*

7393 רֶכֶב$_{120}$ **n.m.** $^{2 K 13,7}$ [even Na 2^{5}, where read מַרְאֵיהֶם (for -הֶן) We Now Albr$^{ZAW xvi (1896), 90}$] **chariotry, chariot, mill-stone**; appar. also **riders** (cf. Lag$^{BN 151}$);—abs. ר׳ Gn 50^{9}+, רָ֑כֶב 2 S 8^{4}+; cstr. רֶכֶב Ex 14^{9}+; sf. רִכְבִּי Ju 4^{7}+, רִכְבּוֹ 2 K 5^{9}+, רִכְבָּהּ Na 2^{14}; pl. cstr. רִכְבֵי Ct 1^{9};—Ho 10^{13} v. infr.;—**1.**$_{109}$ coll. *chariotry, chariots* [sts. of specific no. 2 K 13^{7} 2 S 8^{4} Ex 14^{7} etc.; often + פָּרָשִׁים, (סוּס(ים)], esp. war-chariots: in Egypt Ex 14^{7} (J), Jos 24^{6} (E)+; early Canaan Jos 11^{4} Ju 4$^{7.13}$ 5^{28} (not sg.; ‖ מַרְכְּבוֹתָיו) +, called ר׳ בַּרְזֶל (i.e. iron-bound, or studded, cf. GFM $^{Ju 1, 19}$ and reff.), †Jos 17$^{16.18}$ Ju 1^{19} 4$^{3.13}$†; Philist., acc. to 1 S 13^{5} 2 S 1^{6}; Aram 8^{4} 10^{18}+; Judah and Israel (from David's time, cf. 8^{4}) 1 K 9$^{19.22}$ 10^{26}+, read also בְּרִכְבְּךָ Ho 10^{13} (for בְּדַרְכְּךָ) 𝔊^{A} We Now GASm; Assyria 2 K 19^{23} = Is 37^{24}, Na 2$^{4.5.14}$ (to be burnt; made mainly of wood); Babyl. Je 47^{3} (on title v^{1}, see Gf Gie), 50^{37} 51^{21} Ez 23^{24}+, etc.; for dignity and display 1 K 1^{5} 2 K 5^{9} Je 17^{25} 22^{4} Is 66^{20}, cf. Gn 50^{9} (J), (cf. also 1 K 9$^{19.22}$ 10^{26}, etc.); fig. of Elijah, ר׳ יִשְׂרָאֵל וּפָרָשָׁיו 2 K 2^{12}, of Elisha 13^{14}; רֶכֶב אֵשׁ 2 K 2^{11} *chariotry of fire* (at Elijah's translation); ר׳ אֵל ψ 68^{18} *chariots of Ēl,* i.e. his heavenly host, cf. vision 2 K 6^{17}, and also 7^{6}; ר׳ meton. for chariot-*horses* 2 S 8^{4} = 1 Ch 18^{4}. †**2.** of single chariot 1 K 22$^{35.38}$ 2 K 9$^{21.21.24}$ 10^{16} 2 Ch 35^{24}, prob. also Ex 14^{6}; pl. רִכְבֵי פַרְעֹה Ct 1^{9}. †**3.** *upper millstone* (as *riding* on the lower) Dt 24^{6} Ju 9^{53} 2 S 11^{21}. **4.** appar. = *riders* (coll.), *troop* (of riders): שְׁנֵי רֶכֶב סוּסִים 2 K 7^{14} *two riders of horses, horsemen* (or *two chariots drawn by horses?*); in foll. text dub.: ר׳ צֶמֶד פָּרָשִׁים ר׳ חֲמוֹר ר׳ גָּמָל Is 21^{7} *riders,* viz. *a pair of horsemen, ass-riders, camel-riders;* cf. ר׳ אִישׁ צֶמֶד פָּרָשִׁים v^{9} i.e. *men riding, a pair of horsemen;* בְּר׳ אָדָם פָּרָשִׁים 22^{6} *with riders* (consisting of) *men, horsemen,* but use of אָדָם very improb.; attractive is *with chariotry of* (drawn by) *steeds* (א׳ as gloss) Du Che^{Hpt} Di-Kit but פ׳ hardly *steeds* here (cf. פ׳ *horsemen,* v^{7}); read perhaps simply בְּר׳ וּפ׳.

7396 †רִכְבָּה **n.f.** act of riding;—לְר׳ Ez 27^{20}.

†רַכָּב **n.m. 1.** charioteer, רַכָּבוֹ 1 K 22^{34} =
7395 הָרַכָּב 2 Ch 18^{33}. **2.** horseman, רַכָּב 2 K 9^{17} (= רֹכֵב (ה)סוּס v$^{18.19}$).

†[רְכוּב] **n.[m.]** chariot (Ba$^{NB 85}$);—sf. 7398
הַשָּׂם עָבִים רְכוּבוֹ ψ 104^{3} (of י׳).

†רֵכָב **n.pr.m.** (*band of riders?* cf. Ar. رِكَابٌ 7394
camels used in journeying);—**1.** Ρηχαβ: **a.** in יְהוֹנָדָב בֶּן־ר׳ (Jehu's time, v. יֵהוּא) 2 K 10$^{15.23}$, whose descendants [or, the members of whose society, RS$^{K 15}$, yet v. Nö$^{ZMG xl (1886), 171}$] were contemp. with Jerem., Je 35$^{6.8.14.16.19}$; 1 Ch 2^{55} הַקִּינִים (v. קֵינִי) are said to be descended fr. *Ḥammath,* אֲבִי בֵית־רֵכָב.—On the asceticism of diff. tribes cf. Diod$^{xix. 94}$ (Nabataeans), Palmer$^{Desert 432}$ (*Kheibarī* Jews in Arabia); v. also Berthol$^{Stellung Isr. zu d. Fremden 80}$. **b.** (perh. = **a**, so EMey$^{Entstehung 147}$) in מַלְכִּיָּה בֶן־ר׳ Ne 3^{14}. **2.** in Benjamin, 2 S 4^{2} (Ρηχαβ), v$^{5.6.9}$ (Ρεκχα; A 𝔊L Ρηχαβ in all).

†[רֵכָבִי] **adj. gent.** of רֵכָב **1**, only pl. הָרֵכָבִים as subst., in בֵּית הָר׳ Je 35$^{2.3.18}$, בְּנֵי בֵית־הָר׳ v^{5}, Αρχαβειν, Ραχαβειν, etc.

†מֶרְכָּב **n.m.** $^{Lv 15, 9}$ chariot, riding-seat 4817
(prop. *riding-place*);—**1.** *chariot* (= foll.), sf. סוּסִים לְמֶרְכָּבוֹ 1 K 5^{6}. **2.** abs. מ׳, prob. *saddle* Lv 15^{9} (P). **3.** מֶרְכָּבוֹ *seat* of litter Ct 3^{10}.

†מֶרְכָּבָה **n.f.** chariot;—abs. מ׳ Ju 4^{15}+, 4818
cstr. מִרְכֶּבֶת †Gn 41^{43}; sf. מֶרְכַּבְתּוֹ 46^{29}+; pl. מַרְכָּבוֹת Zc 6^{1}+; cstr. מַרְכְּבוֹת 2 K 23^{11}+, -בֹת Ex 15^{4}; sf. מַרְכְּבֹתֶיךָ Mi 5^{10} Hb 3^{8}, etc.;—*chariot* (oft. ‖ סוּס(ים), פָּרָשִׁים 1 S 8^{11}): esp. war-chariot, Egypt., Ex 14^{25} (J), 15^{4} (song), 2 Ch 14^{8}; from *Muṣri* in N. Syr. (acc. to Wkl., v. מצרים *ad fin.,* cf. Kit$^{1 K 10, 28}$ Benz$^{ib.}$) 1 K 10^{29} = 2 Ch 1^{17}; Can., Jos 11$^{6.9}$ (JE), Ju 4^{15} (‖ רֶכֶב), 5^{28} (‖ *id.*); Assyr., Is 2^{7} Na 3^{2}; foe from north Je 4^{13}, nations in gen. Hg 2^{22}; Isr. and Jud. 1 K 20^{33} 22^{35} = 2 Ch 18^{34}, 2 K 9^{27} 10^{15} 2 Ch 35^{24} Mi 5^{10}; fig. of י׳'s chariots Is 66^{15} Hb 3^{8}, cf. (in vision) Zc 6$^{1.2.2.3.3}$; מ׳ for dignity and display Gn 41^{43} (E), 46^{29} (J), 1 S 8$^{11.11}$ 2 S 15^{1} 2 K 5$^{21.26}$, מַרְכְּבוֹת כְּבוֹדֶךָ Is 22^{18} (iron.); used in flight 1 K 12^{18} = 2 Ch 10^{18}, Mi 1^{13}; מַרְכְּבוֹת הַשֶּׁמֶשׁ 2 K 23^{11} (idolatrous); הַמּ׳ הַכְּרוּבִים (read מִרְכֶּבֶת הַכּ׳, 𝔊 Benz) 1 Ch 28^{18} (on this conception of cherubim in temple v. Benz); מ׳ in similes: כְּמַעֲשֵׂה אוֹפַן הַמּ׳ 1 K 7^{33}, כְּקוֹל מ׳ Jo 2^{5}; on the obscure מַר׳ עַמִּי נָדִיב Ct 6^{12} *chariots of my people, a prince* (?) v. esp. Bu.

†רֵכָה **n.pr.loc.** in Judah;—1 Ch 4^{12}, Ρηχαβ. 7397

†[רָכַךְ] **vb. be tender, weak, soft** (Ar. 7401
رَقَّ, Aram. רְכַךְ (in der. spec. and deriv.), *id.*);—**Qal** *Pf.* 3 ms. רַךְ 2 K 22^{19} 2 Ch 34^{27};

3 pl. רַכּוּ ψ 55^{22}; *Impf.* יֵרַךְ (Ges[§67p]) Is 7^{4}+;—**1.** *be tender, weak,* of heart: **a.** *be timid, fearful,* ‖ יָרֵא, Is 7^{4} Je 51^{46} Dt 20^{3}. **b.** *be softened, penitent,* ‖ כָּנַע Niph., 2 K 22^{19}=2 Ch 34^{27}. **2.** *be soft,* of treacherous words ψ 55^{22} (c. מִן comp.; ‖ II. חָלַק). **Pu.** *Pf.* 3 fs. רֻכְּכָה Is 1^{6} *it has not been softened,* mollified, with oil (of wound, מַכָּה). **Hiph.** *Pf.* 3 ms. וְאֵל הֵרַךְ לִבִּי Jb 23^{16} (Ges[§67v]), causat. of **Qal 1 a.**

7390 †רַךְ **adj. tender, delicate, soft**;—ר׳ abs. Gn 18^{7}+, cstr. Dt 20^{8} 2 Ch 13^{7}; fs. רַכָּה Dt 28^{56}+; mpl. רַכִּים Gn 33^{13}; fpl. abs. רַכּוֹת 29^{17} Jb 40^{27};—**1.** *tender* of flesh Gn 18^{7} (J; בֶּן־בָּקָר); *tender, delicate,* esp. in body, of children 33^{13} (J), cf. (implying weakness of undeveloped character) 2 S 3^{39}, נַעַר וָרָךְ 1 Ch 22^{5} 29^{1}, רַךְ (וְיָחִיד) Pr 4^{3} ('of tender age,' Toy, q.v.); of man (+ עָנֹג; i.e. delicately nurtured) Dt 28^{54}, so of woman v^{56} (+ עֲנֻגָּה), so, fig. of Bab., Is 47^{1} (+*id.*); רַךְ as subst.=*tender* (twig) Ez 17^{22} (in fig.); *delicate, weak,* of eyes Gn 29^{17} (E). **2.** רַךְ (ה)לֵּבָב *weak of heart,* timid, Dt 20^{8} (+ יָרֵא), 2 Ch 13^{7} (נַעַר). **3.** *soft,* of words, abs. רַכּוֹת Jb 40^{27}= subst., mild, gentle words (‖ תַּחֲנוּנִים); מַעֲנֶה רַךְ Pr 15^{1} (opp. דְּבַר עֶצֶב), לָשׁוֹן רַכָּה 25^{15}.

7391 †רֹךְ **n.[m.] tenderness, delicacy**;—of delicately-nurtured woman, מֵהִתְעַנֵּג וּמֵרֹךְ Dt 28^{56}.

4816 †מֹרֶךְ **n.[m.] weakness** (Kö[ii. 1, 98]);—Lv 26^{36} *I will send* מ׳ *into* (ב) *your heart* (i.e. make you timid, fearful, cf. √ **1 a,** רַךְ **2**).

7402 †[רָכַל] **vb.** prob. **go about,** from one to another (for trade or gossip) (? connected with רגל; cf. Ar. رَكَلَ *kick* a horse, to make him go [? prop. *use the foot,* cf. رِجل ?]; NH רוֹכֵל, Aram. רוֹכְלָא, ܪܰܟܳܠܳܐ *trader,* NH רְכִילוּת *slander* [cf. مَاشٍ *calumniator,* fr. مَشَى *go about,* Qor 2^{19} al.]);—**Qal** *Pt.* רוֹכֵל Ct 3^{6}; fs. cstr. רֹכֶלֶת Ez 27^{3}, sf. רֹכַלְתֵּךְ v$^{20.23}$; mpl. רֹכְלִים 1 K 10^{15}+, etc.;—as subst. =*trafficker, trader:* usu. pl., Na 3^{16} Ez 17^{4} (עִיר ר׳), 27$^{13.15.17.22.22.23a}$ (< del. Toy Krae), v^{24} Ne 3$^{31.32}$ 13^{20} (+ מֹכְרֵי כָל־מִמְכָּר); מִסְחַר הָר׳ 1 K 10^{15} (text dub.; cf. מ׳, p. 695); sg. fig. of Tyre, רֹכֶלֶת הָעַמִּים אֶל־אִיִּים רַבִּים Ez 27^{3}, of a people v$^{20.23b}$ (pl. Mez[Harran 34] Krae, v. also כִּלְמַד); sg. of pers. only אַבְקַת רוֹכֵל Ct 3^{6}.

7404 †[רְכֻלָּה] **n.f. 1. traffic**;—sf. רְכֻלָּתְךָ Ez 28$^{5.16.18}$. **2. merchandise,** רְכֻלָּתֵךְ 26^{12}.

7403 †רָכָל **n.pr.loc.** (*trader?*);—in S. of Judah בְּרָכָל 1 S 30^{29}, 𝔊 ἐν Καρμήλῳ [A Ραχηλ], rd. prob. בְּכַרְמֶל We Dr Bu Kit HPS; v. II. כ׳ **2.**

†רָכִיל **n.[m.] slander, > tale-bearer, in-** 7400
former;—always ר׳ abs.;—הָלַךְ ר׳ Je 9^{3}, ר׳ יַהֲלֹךְ Lv 19^{16} (H), הוֹלֵךְ ר׳ Pr 11^{13} 20^{19}, all of going about *in slander,* as slanderer (Ges[§118q]); הֹלְכֵי ר׳ Je 6^{28} *goers of slander* (slanderous persons) (cf. הָלַךְ, p. 231 f.); אַנְשֵׁי ר׳ Ez 22^{9} *men of slander,* informers.

†[מַרְכֹּלֶת] **n.f.** prob. **place of trade,** 4819
market-place;—sf. בְּמַרְכֻלְתֵּךְ Ez 27^{24} *in thy market-place* (Thes Buhl[Lex] Hi-Sm Krae al.; > בָּם רְכֻלָּתֵךְ 𝔗 Co Berthol, cf. Toy).

†[רָכַס] **vb. bind** (As. *rakâsu, id.;* NH 7405
found, lay foundation (rare); Ar. رَكَسَ *bind with* رِكَاسٌ [rope tying camel's head to forefoot] (Frey); but usu. *turn over, reverse* (Lane));—**Qal** *Impf.* 3 mpl. יִרְכְּסוּ (P) Ex 28^{28}, וַיִּרְכְּסוּ 39^{21}, *bind* חֹשֶׁן by (מִן) its rings to (אֶל) rings of ephod.

†[רֶכֶס] **n.[m.]** dub.; perh. *roughness* (of 7406
ground; ? lit. *binding, knot*); or bound up, impeded, i.e. *the impassable;* or mountain-*chain* (v. Thes);—pl. הָרְכָסִים Is 40^{4} (‖ הֶעָקֹב; opp. בִּקְעָה).

†[רֹכֶס] **n.[m.]** dub., Thes Hup-Now *snare,* 7407
or *band* (Dr *banding together*), or (most) *league, conspiracy* (RV *plottings*); Ol reads deriv. of רכל=*slander,* so (רְכִילֵי) Che Du; Bae despairs;—pl. cstr. רֻכְסֵי־אִישׁ ψ 31^{21} (‖ רִיב לְשֹׁנוֹת).

†רָכַשׁ **vb. collect, gather property,** vb. 7408
only P (rare) (Mand. רכש *gather,* Norberg[Lexid. 231]; As. *rukûšu, property* (Hpt[Hbr iii. 110] *riding anim.*); Aram. רְכַשָׁא, ܪܶܟܫܳܐ = BH רֶכֶשׁ);—**Qal** *Pf.* 3 ms. ר׳, acc. קִנְיָן, Gn 31^{18b} 36^{6}; elsewhere c. acc. cogn. רְכוּשׁ: אֲשֶׁר רָכָשׁ 31^{18a}, 3 pl. רָכְשׁוּ 46^{6}, רָכָשׁוּ 12^{5}.

†רֶכֶשׁ **n.m.**[Est 8, 10] **coll. steeds** (connex. with 7409
√ dub.);—abs. ר׳ Mi 1^{13}+, רָכֶשׁ 1 K 5^{8};—+ סוּסִים 1 K 5^{8}, harnessed to chariot Mi 1^{13}, ridden Est 8^{10} (+ סוּסִים; defined as בְּנֵי הָרַמָּכִים), v^{14}.

†רְכוּשׁ, רְכֻשׁ **n.m.**[Gn 13, 6] **property, goods**;— 7399
abs. רְכוּשׁ Nu 16^{32}+, רְכֻשׁ Gn 14$^{16.21}$; cstr. רְכוּשׁ 2 Ch 35^{7}, רְכֻשׁ Gn 14^{11}; sf. רְכֻשׁוֹ v^{12}+, רְכוּשָׁם 12^{5}+, etc.;—*property, goods,* PRChr Dn Gn 14: **1.** gen. term for movable possessions of all kinds (oft. specif. incl. cattle), Gn 12^{5} 15^{14} Nu 16^{32} 1 Ch 27^{31} 28^{1} 2 Ch 31^{3} 32^{29} Ezr 8^{21} 10^{8}. **2.** used specif. of cattle, flocks, etc. Gn 13^{6} 31^{18} 36^{7} Nu 35^{3} 2 Ch 35^{7}. **3.** of stores, utensils, etc. Gn 46^{6} Ezr 1$^{4.6}$, as camp-baggage Dn 11^{13}, esp. as booty Gn 14$^{11.12.16.16.21}$ 2 Ch 20^{25} 21$^{14.17}$ Dn 11$^{24.28}$.

7214, 7311-12 רָם, רֵם v. רום. רֵם v. רְאֵם. p. 910, 926-28

7411 †I. רָמָה vb. **cast, shoot** (As. *ramû, throw, lay;* Ar. رَمَى *throw, shoot;* Eth. ረመየ: *strike, aim a blow at;* Aram. רְמָא, ܪܡܳܐ *cast, throw*);—**Qal** *Pf.* 3 ms. ר׳, subj. י׳ Ex 15[1.21] (song), c. acc. +בַּיָּם; *Pt.* רֹמֵה קֶשֶׁת Je 4[29] coll. (or read רֹמֵי) *bow-shooters, bowmen,* pl. cstr. נוֹשְׁקֵי רוֹמֵי־ק׳ ψ 78[9] (v. II. נשק); cf. רֹבֶה קַשָּׁת Gn 21[20] (v. II. רבה).

7411 †II. [רָמָה] vb. **Pi.** **beguile, deal treacherously with** (NH in deriv.; 𝔗 רְמָא Pa.; Buhl[Lex] cp. Ar. رَمَى VI. *be sluggish, backward* (of wound), *become putrid, corrupt*);—*Pf.* 3 ms. רִמָּה Pr 26[19], sf. רִמָּנִי 2 S 19[27]; 2 ms. sf. רִמִּיתָנִי Gn 29[25] 1 S 28[12]; 2 fs. sf. רִמִּיתִנִי 19[17], etc.; *Inf. cstr.* sf. לְרַמּוֹתֵנִי 1 Ch 12[18] (van d. H. v[17]);—*beguile, deceive, mislead,* acc. pers., Gn 29[25] (E), Jos 9[22] (JE), 1 S 28[12] 2 S 19[27] Pr 26[19]; *deal treacherously with, betray,* acc. pers., 1 S 19[17] La 1[19], +לְצָרַי 1 Ch 12[17].

7423 †I. רְמִיָּה n.f. **deceit, treachery**;—always abs. ר׳;—*deceit, treachery:* esp. of speech, pred. of לְשׁוֹן Mi 6[12] (‖ שֶׁקֶר), appos. of לָשׁוֹן (or read לְשׁוֹן?) ψ 120[2] (‖ שְׂפַת שֶׁקֶר), v[3]; of man, עֹשֵׂה ר׳ 52[4] *that workest treachery,* 101[7] (‖ דֹּבֵר שְׁקָרִים); also Jb 13[7] 27[4] (both ‖ עַוְלָה); *deception* ψ 32[2] (‖ עָוֹן); in phr. קֶשֶׁת ר׳ *treacherous bow* (sim.) Ho 7[16] ψ 78[57] (failing him who trusts to it).

4820 †II. מִרְמָה n.f. **deceit, treachery**;—abs. מ׳ Am 8[5]+; pl. abs. מִרְמוֹת ψ 10[7]+;—*deceit,* of balances, מֹאזְנֵי מ׳ i.e. *deceptive balances* Am 8[5] (‖ שֶׁקֶר), Ho 12[8] Pr 11[1] (opp. אֶבֶן שְׁלֵמָה), 20[23], אַבְנֵי מ׳ Mi 6[11] (v. [מאזן] p. 24); esp. *treachery, craftiness,* 2 K 9[23], בְּמ׳ *treacherously,* Gn 27[35] (J), and (of crafty speech) 34[13] (P); שִׂפְתֵי מ׳ ψ 17[1] i.e. *treacherous lips,* לְשׁוֹן מ׳ 52[6], פִּי מ׳ 109[2] ψ 24[4] נִשְׁבַּע לְמ׳, דִּבְרֵי מִרְמוֹת 35[20], (לְשׁוֹן שָׁקֶר ‖) (לַשָּׁוְא ‖); cf. Is 53[9] (‖ חָמָס); also Ho 12[1] (‖ כַּחַשׁ), Je 5[27] 9[5.5.7] Zp 1[9] (+ חָמָס), ψ 10[7] (+ תֹּךְ, ‖ עָמָל), 34[14] 36[4] (+ אָוֶן, וָאָוֶן), 38[13] 59[19] 55[12] (+ תֹּךְ), Jb 15[35] 31[5] (‖ שָׁוְא), Pr 12[20] 14[8] 26[24] Dn 8[25]; opp. מִשְׁפָּט Pr 12[5], + עֵד שְׁקָרִים v[17], + יָפִחַ כְּזָבִים 14[25] (Hi Wild Toy read מַדְמֶה for מרמה, but II. דמה not elsewhere Pi); ψ 5[7] אִישׁ דָּמִים וּמ׳ (‖ דֹּבְרֵי כָזָב), cf. 55[24], אִישׁ מ׳ וְעַוְלָה 43[1]; יַעֲשֶׂה מ׳ Dn 11[23].—

4821 I. מִרְמָה n.pr. v. p. 599.

8649 †תַּרְמָה in בְּתּ׳ Ju 9[31] si vera l. *in treachery, treacherously,* but form strange and meaning unsuitable; read poss. (בָּ)אֲרוּמָה n.pr.loc. (q.v.), cf. v[41] and GFM.

תרמות Je 14[14] Kt, v. foll. 8649

†תַּרְמִית n.f. **deceitfulness**;—abs. לְשׁוֹן תּ׳ Zp 3[13] (‖ כָּזָב, עַוְלָה), תַּרְמִת Je 8[5]; cstr. תַּרְמִית לִבָּם 14[14] Qr (>Kt תרבות), תַּרְמִת לִבָּם 23[26] (‖ שֶׁקֶר); sf. ψ 119[118] שֶׁקֶר תַּרְמִיתָם (where 𝔊 𝔖 𝔙 al. תַּרְעִיתָם Aram. *their thought*). 8649

III. רמה (√ of foll.; connex. with II. ר׳ dub.; cf. As. *ramû, grow loose;* II. *loosen*).

†II. רְמִיָּה n.f. **laxness, slackness**;—alw. abs. ר׳;—כַּף ר׳ Pr 10[4] *slack* (negligent, idle) *hand* (opp. יַד חָרוּצִים); ר׳ alone = *slackness* (abstr. for concr. = one who is slack) 12[24] (‖ *id.*), v[27] (v. חרך); נֶפֶשׁ ר׳ 19[15] (‖ עַצְלָה); as adv. עֹשֶׂה מְלֶאכֶת י׳ רְמִיָּה Je 48[10]. 7423

יִרְמְיָה(וּ) [147] n.pr.m. (? י׳ *looseneth,* sc. the womb? cf. As. *ša kirimmaša rummû, whose womb is loosened* Dl[HWB 623]);—**1.**[136] proph., son of Ḥilkiah, of priestly family in ʿAnathôth: יִרְמְיָהוּ Je 1[1.11] 29[27] 36[1.4.4] + 116 t. Je, + 2 Ch 35[25] 36[12.21.22] (יר׳ הַנָּבִיא Je 21[2] + oft.); -יָה Je 27[1] 28[5.6.10.11.12.15] 29[1] Ezr 1[1] Dn 9[2]; Ἰερεμίας. †**2.** יִרְמְיָהוּ, of Libnah, father of Josiah's wife, 2 K 23[31] 24[18] = Je 52[1], Ἰερεμίας. †**3.** -יָהוּ Gadite, David's time 1 Ch 12[13], Ιερεμεια, 𝔊L Ιεραμαου. The foll. all -יָה, 𝔊 Ἰερεμία(s), Ἰερμία(s), etc.: †**4.** Manassite 1 Ch 5[24]. †**5.** Benjamite 12[4]. †**6.** Gadite 12[10]. †**7. a.** priestly name: Ne 12[1.2]. **b.** Ne 10[3], perhaps = 12[34]. 3414

†רַמְיָה n.pr.m. (prop. י׳ *hath loosened?*);—one with foreign wife Ezr 10[25], Ραμιά(s). 7422

I, II. רָמָה v. רום. רִמָּה v. II. רמם. p. 928, 942 7413-15

†I. רִמּוֹן n.m. [Je 52,23] **pomegranate** (foreign word of doubtful origin, cf. Löw[No. 310] Hom [A. u. A. 07 ff.]; Aram. רִמּוֹנָא, רוּמָּנָא, ܪܘܡܳܢܳܐ, Mand. רומאנא Nö[M. 123]; Ar. رُمَّانٌ (Aram. loan-word, Frä[142]), Eth. ሮማን:);—abs. ר׳ 1 S 14[2]+, רִמֹּן Ex 39[26.26]; sf. רִמֹּנִי Ct 8[2]; pl. רִמּוֹנִים 1 K 7[20]+, etc.;—*pomegranate:* **1.** tree 1 S 14[2], oft. + גֶּפֶן, תְּאֵנָה, etc., Nu 20[5] (JE), Dt 8[8] Hg 2[19] Jo 1[12] Ct 4[13] 6[11] 7[13]. **2.** fruit Nu 13[23] (JE; + עֲנָבִים, תְּאֵנִים); עֲסִיס ר׳ Ct 8[2], פֶּלַח הָר׳ (in sim.) 4[3] 6[7]. **3.** ornaments in temple, shaped like pomegranates (cf. رُمَّانَة in mod. Syria = *epaulet,* Almkvist[Kl. Beiträge zur Lexicogr., etc.] Nes[Marg. 12]), 1 K 7[18] (on text cf. Sta[ZAW iii (1883), 154 f.] Kit Benz), v[20.42.42] 7416

‖ 2 Ch 3^{16} 4$^{13.13}$ 2 K 25^{17} = Je 52^{22}, Je 52$^{22.23.23}$; so in tabernacle, Ex 28$^{33.34.34}$ 39$^{24.25.25.26.26}$.

7417 †II. **רִמּוֹן n.pr.dei,** in Aram. (OAram. רמן in n.pr. Lzb^{369} Cook^{108}; As. *Rammânu*, god of wind, rain and storm (Schr$^{COT\ 2\ K\ 5,\ 18}$ Zim$^{KAT\ 3.\ 442\ ff.}$ Muss-Arnolt$^{JBL\ xi\ (1892).\ 172}$ Jastr$^{Rel.Bab.156\ ff.}$); Sab. רמן (CIS$^{iv,\ no.\ 140,\ 209}$ H. Derenb in Kohut-Studies$^{120\ ff.}$); etym. dub.; √רעם *thunder* Schr; √*ramâmu*, *roar* Dl$^{HWB\ 624}$ and most; = I. רִמּוֹן Hom$^{A.\ u.\ A.\ 98}$);—בֵּית ר׳ 2 K 5^{18}, בֵּית רִמּוֹן v$^{18.18}$; Ρεμμαν[θ];—v. also הֲדַדְרִמּוֹן p. 213, טַבְרִמּוֹן p. 372.

7417 †III. **רִמּוֹן n.pr.m.** in Benj., 2 S 4$^{2.5.9}$; Ρεμμων.

7417 †IV. **רִמּוֹן n.pr.loc. 1.** in סֶלַע הָרִמּוֹן *cliff of R.* Ju 20$^{45.47}$, ס׳ רִמּוֹן v^{47} 21^{13}; Ρεμμων; = mod. cliff *Rammôn*, E. from Bethel, Buhl$^{G\ 100}$, cf. GFM$^{Ju\ 20,\ 45}$. **2.** in S. Judah, עַיִן וְר׳ Jos 15^{32}; עַיִן ר׳ 19^{7} (both P), 1 Ch 4^{32}; = ר׳ Zc 14^{10};
5871, 5884 Ρεμμων[θ], etc.; v. III. עַיִן **2**, p. 745, and עֵין רִמּוֹן. **3.** in Zebulun Jos 19^{13} (Ρεμμωνα(μ)), = רִמּוֹנוֹ 1 Ch 6^{62} (Ρεμμων); + Jos 21^{35} (rd. רִמּוֹנָה for דִּמְנָה, Di Benn Steuern); mod. *Rummâne*, c. 6 miles E. of N. from Nazareth (Buhl$^{G\ 221}$).

7428 †**רִמֹּן פָּרֶץ n.pr.loc.** station of Israel in wilderness, Nu 33$^{19.20}$ (P), Ρεμμων, Ραμμων.

7417 רִמּוֹנוֹ 1 Ch 6^{62} see IV. רִמּוֹן **3.** above

7216, 7419 **רָמוֹת**, [רָמוּת] v. רום. p. 928

7420 †**רֹמַח n.[m.] spear, lance** (etym. unknown; Aram. רוּמְחָא, ܪܘܡܚܐ; Ar. رُمْحٌ; Eth. ረምሕ:);—oft. + קֶשֶׁת, מָגֵן, צִנָּה, חֶרֶב, etc.;—abs. ר׳ Ju 5^{8} Nu 25^{7} (P), Ez 39^{9} 1 Ch 12$^{9.25}$ (van d.H. v$^{8.24}$), 2 Ch 14^{7} 25^{5}; pl. רְמָחִים 1 K 18^{28} Je 46^{4} Jo 4^{10} Ne 4$^{10.15}$ 2 Ch 11^{12} 26^{14}; sf. רָמְחֵיהֶם Ne 4^{7}.

761 **הָרַמִּים** 2 Ch 22^{5}, err. for הָאֲרַמִּים, v. אֲרָם. p. 74

7422-23 **רַמְיָה**, I, II. רְמִיָּה v. II. רמה. p. 941

7424 †[**רַמָּךְ**] **n.[f.]** exact meaning dub. (cf. Syr. ܪܡܟܐ *herd*; foreign wd.; Pahlavi *ramak*, NPers. رمه *herd* of sheep, horses, etc., Thes^{1291} Vullers$^{ii.\ 52}$; in NH *mule* born of mare and he-ass);—בְּנֵי הָרַמָּכִים Est 8^{10} usu. *sons of the* (*royal*) *mares*, said of הָרֶכֶשׁ.

רמל (in foll. cpd.; Thes cp. Ar. رَمَّلَ *adorn* with gems; OHeb. רמליהו Lzb^{369}).

7425 †**רְמַלְיָהוּ n.pr.m.** father of Peḳah, king of Israel, בֶּן־ר׳ 2 K 15$^{25.27.30.32.37}$ 16$^{1.5}$ Is 7^{1} 2 Ch 28^{6}; contempt. (פֶּקַח om.) Is 7$^{4.5.9}$ 8^{6}; υἱὸς Ῥομελίου.

†I. [**רָמַם**] **vb. be exalted** (‖form (acc. to 7426
Mas.) of רוּם);—**Qal** *Pf.* 3 pl. רוֹמּוּ מְּעַט וְאֵינֶנּוּ Jb 24^{24} (perhaps pass. form Ges$^{§\ 67\ m}$ Bu; Du רָמוּ);—
Pt. רֹמֵם v. רום **Pōʿl. Niph.** *Impf.* 1 s. אֵרוֹמָם Is 7311
33^{10} (‖ אֶנָּשֵׂא); **Hithpōʿl.** fr. רום Kö$^{i.\ 454}$ Ges$^{§\ 54\ c}$), 3 mpl. וַיֵּרֹמּוּ Ez 10^{15} (of cherubim), יֵרֹמּוּ v^{17}, וַיֵּרֹמּוּ v^{19}; *Imv.* mpl. הֵרֹמּוּ מִתּוֹךְ הָעֵדָה Nu 17^{10} (P). p. 927

II. **רמם** (√of following; cf. Ar. رَمَّ *grow rotten, decay*).

†**רִמָּה n.f. worm** (cause and sign of *decay*);— 7415
abs. ר׳ Ex 16^{24} (P), Is 14^{11} (‖ תּוֹלֵעָה), Jb 7^{5} 17^{14} 21^{26} 24^{20} all indic. corruption, feeding on dead, etc.; hyperb. of insignificant man 25^{6} (‖תּוֹלֵעָה).

†[**רָמַם**] **vb. denom. be wormy**;—*Impf.* 7426
3 ms. (c. acc. result, Ges$^{§\ 121\ d\ N}$) וַיָּרֻם תּוֹלָעִים Ex 16^{20} (Ges$^{§\ 67\ n}$; + וַיִּבְאַשׁ).

רֹמַמְתִּי עֶזֶר v. sub רום. p. 928 7320

†**רָמַס vb. trample** (NH *id.*; JAram. 7429
רְמַס; cf. perh. Syr. ܦܩܣ, Ar. رَفَسَ *kick* (Ba$^{ES\ 33}$ Kö$^{ii.\ 196}$); رَمَسَ is *bury, and conceal grave*);—**Qal** *Pf.* 3 ms. consec. וְר׳ Mi 5^{7}; *Impf.* 3 ms. יִרְמֹס Ez 26^{11} ψ 7^{6}, יִרְמָס־ Is 41^{25}, sf. וַיִּרְמְסֶנָּה 2 K 9^{33}, etc.; *Imv.* fs. רִמְסִי Na 3^{14}; *Inf. cstr.* רְמֹס Is 1^{12}; *Pt.* רֹמֵס Is 16^{4};—*trample*, of men, c. acc. חֲצֵרָי Is 1^{12}, חוּצוֹת Ez 26^{11} (by horses' hoofs), טִיט 41^{25} (in sim.), cf. ר׳ בַּחֹמֶר Na 3^{14}, acc. מִרְעֶה Ez 34^{18} (in fig.); *trample down*, acc. pers., anim., vel rei, 2 K 7$^{17.20}$, so (by horses' hoofs) 9^{33}, יִר׳ לָאָרֶץ חַיָּי ψ 7^{6}; 91^{13} (‖ תִּדְרֹךְ); subj. י׳ Is 63^{3} (fig.; + דָּרַךְ), subj. רֶגֶל Is 26^{6}; subj. beast 2 K 14^{9} (allegory) = 2 Ch 25^{18}, Dn 8^{7} (vision), of horn, v^{10}; abs. of lion, וְר׳ וְטָרַף Mi 5^{7} (sim.); pt. as subst. coll. *tramplers* (i.e. devastators) Is 16^{4}. **Niph.** *be trampled*, *Impf.* 3 fpl. בְּרַגְלַיִם תֵּרָמַסְנָה Is 28^{3} (on subj. cf. Di Du Che^{Hpt} Kö$^{i.\ 183}$).

†**מִרְמָס n.[m.] trampling-place, tramp-** 4823
ling;—abs. מ׳ Mi 7^{10} +, מִרְמַס (Kö$^{ii.\ 1,\ 96}$) Is 10^{6}; cstr. מִרְמַס 7^{25} Ez 34^{19};—**1.** *trampling-place*, מ׳ שֶׂה Is 7^{25} (‖ מִשְׁלַח), מ׳ רַגְלֵיכֶם Ez 34^{19} (fig.). **2.** *trampling*, וְהָיָה לְמ׳ Is 5^{5} *it shall become a trampling*, be trampled down, so Mi 7^{10}, Is 28^{18} והייתם לו למרמס, cf. 10^{6} Dn 8^{13}.

†**רָמַשׂ vb. creep, move lightly, move** 7430
about (chiefly P) (Ar. رَمَشَ *touch gently* (Kam Frey); NH רְמָשִׂים *creeping things* (rare));—**Qal** *Impf.* 3 fs. תִּרְמֹשׂ Gn 9^{2} + 2 t.; *Pt.* רֹמֵשׂ 1^{26} +; fs. רֹמֶשֶׂת Lv 11^{46} + 2 t.;—**1.** subj. ground,

כֹּל אֲשֶׁר ת׳ הָאֲדָמָה *all with which the ground creeps* (teems), i.e. all creeping things, Lv 20^{55} (H), Gn 9^{2} (P). **2.** elsewhere subj. animal: **a.** *creep,* עַל־הָאֲדָמָה Dt 4^{18} Gn 7^{8} (P), עַל־הָאָרֶץ Lv 11^{44} (H), Gn 1^{30} (P); הָרֶמֶשׂ הָרֹמֵשׂ עַל־הָאֲדָמָה Ez 38^{20}, עַל־הָאָרֶץ Gn 1^{26} 7^{14} 8^{17} (all P). **b.** *move lightly, glide about,* of water animals, כָּל־נֶפֶשׁ הַחַיָּה הָרֹמֶשֶׂת (בַּמַּיִם) Lv 11^{46} (H), Gn 1^{21} (P), cf. ψ 69^{35}. **c.** in gen. *move about,* of all land-animals, עַל־הָאָרֶץ Gn 1^{28} 7^{21} 8^{19} (all P); specif. of wild beasts prowling at night ψ 104^{20}.

7431 †רֶמֶשׂ **n.m.**$^{Ez 38, 20}$ **coll. creeping things, moving things**;—ר׳ abs. 1 K 5^{13}+, cstr. Ho 2^{20}+;—**1.** *creeping things* (disting. from בְּהֵמָה, חַיָּה, עוֹף, צִפּוֹר, דָּג) Ho 2^{20} 1 K 5^{13} Ez 8^{10} 38^{20} Gn 1$^{24.25.26}$ 6$^{7.20}$ 7$^{14.23}$ 8$^{17.19}$ (all P), Hb 1^{14} (in sim.) ψ 148^{10}. **2.** of sea animals, *gliding things,* ψ 104^{25}. **3.** *moving things,* of all animals Gn 9^{3} (P).—Cf. Dr$^{Hast. DB Creeping Things}$.

7432, 7435-36 רָמָתַיִם, רָמָתִי, רֶמֶת v. רום. p. 928

7438, 7440-41 רֹן, I, II. רִנָּה v. רנן. below

7439 †[רָנָה] **vb. rattle** (onomatop.?);—**Qal** *Impf.* 3 fs. תִּרְנֶה Jb 39^{23} the quiver *rattleth.*

7442 †[רָנַן] **vb. give a ringing cry** (onomatop.? cf. Ar. رَنَّ *cry aloud,* also *twang* (of bowstring); NH Pi. *murmur, complain,* cf. JAram. (not 𝔗));—**Qal** *Impf.* 3 ms. יָרֹן (Ges^{§67q}) Pr 29^{6}
7323 (but rd. perhaps יָרוּץ, Pinsk Toy, v. רוץ **2**); 3 fs. תָּרֹן Is 35^{6}; 3 mpl. יָרֹנּוּ 24^{14}+, וַיָּר׳ Lv 9^{24}; 3 fpl. תָּרֹנָּה Pr 1^{20} 8^{3}; *Imv.* fs. רָנִּי Is 54^{1}+, רֹנִּי 12^{6}; mpl. רָנּוּ Je 31^{7}+; *Inf. cstr.* בְּרָן־ Jb 38^{7};—*give a ringing cry:* **1.** in joy, exultation, ‖ צָהַל Je 31^{7} (ר׳ שִׂמְחָה), Is 12^{6} 24^{14} (‖ נָשָׂא קוֹל), 54^{1} (+ פָּצַח רִנָּה); ‖ הָרִיעַ Zp 3^{14} (+ שׂמח, עלז), Is 44^{23} Jb 38^{7}; ‖ שָׂמַח Zc 2^{14} ψ 35^{27} Pr 29^{6} (v. supr.); ‖ גִּיל Is 49^{13} (+ הָרִים רִנָּה), ‖ צָוַח 42^{11}; opp. צָעַק (*cry* in distress) 65^{14} (מִן of cause); Lv 9^{24} Is 35^{6} (subj. לָשׁוֹן).—Is 61^{7} is corrupt; read perh. וָרֹק *and spitting,* Klo Che^{Hpt}. **2.** in distress, La 2^{19}. **3.** *cry aloud,* in summons, exhortation (of wisdom) Pr 1^{20} (‖ נָתַן קוֹל), 8^{3}. **Pi.** *Pf.* 3 pl. consec. וְרִנְּנוּ Je 31^{12} 51^{48}; *Impf.* 3 fs. תְּרַנֵּן ψ 51^{16}, 3 mpl. יְרַנְּנוּ 84^{3}+, יְרַנֵּ֫נוּ 5^{12}+; 3 fpl. תְּרַנֵּ֫נָּה 71^{23} (van d. H. תְּרַנֵּנָה), etc.; *Imv.* mpl. רַנְּנוּ Is 52^{9}+; *Inf. abs.*
7444 רַנֵּן ψ 132^{16}, *cstr. id.* Is 35^{2};—*give a ringing cry,* in joy, exultation, esp. in praise to י׳, Je 31^{12} 51^{48} Is 26^{19} 35^{2} (+ גִּילַת, v. גִּילָה), 52^{8} (‖ נָשָׂא קוֹל), v^{9} (+ פָּצַח); elsewh. only ψψ: ψ 5^{12} (‖ עָלַץ, שָׂמַח), 67^{5} 90^{14} 92^{5} (c. בְּ rei; all ‖ שׂ׳ alone); 149^{5} (‖ עָלַז); 98^{4} (‖ הָרִיעַ; + פָּצַח, זִמֵּר), 132^{9} 145^{7}, רַנֵּן יְרַנֵּ֫נוּ 132^{16}; c. acc. of theme 51^{16} 59^{17} (‖ שִׁיר); בְּ rei 20^{6} 63^{8} 89^{13}; c. בי׳ 33^{1}; c. לי׳ 95^{1} (‖ הָרִיעַ), אֶל־אֵל 84^{3}, (מִ)לפני י׳ 96^{12} (‖ עָלַז) = 1 Ch 16^{33} (‖ עָלַץ), ψ 98^{8}; subj. שְׂפָתַיִם 71^{23} (‖ זִמֵּר). **Pu.** *Impf.* 3 ms. impers. לֹא יְרֻנָּן Is 16^{10} *no ringing cry shall be given* (‖ יְרֹעָע). **Hiph.** *Impf. cause to ring out* for joy, 1 s. לֵב אַלְמָנָה אַרְנִן Jb 29^{13}; 2 ms. מוֹצָאֵי בֹקֶר וָעֶרֶב תַּרְנִין ψ 65^{9}; *Imv.* mpl. הַרְנִינוּ *ring out a cry* of joy ψ 32^{11} (‖ שׂמח, גיל), לי׳ 81^{2} (‖ הריע); c. acc. of theme, עַמּוֹ Dt 32^{43} (v. Dr; cf. **Pi.**).—**Hithpo῾l.** ψ 78^{65} cf. רון. p. 929 7442

†[רֹן] **n.[m.] ringing cry**; pl. cstr. רָנֵּי פַלֵּט ψ 32^{7}. 7438

†רְנָנָה **n.f. id.**;—ר׳ abs., of joy Jb 3^{7} ψ 100^{2} (‖ שִׂמְחָה); pl. שִׂפְתֵי רְנָנוֹת 63^{6}; exultation, sg. cstr. רִנְנַת רְשָׁעִים Jb 20^{5} (‖ שִׂמְחָה). 7445

†I. רִנָּה **n.f. ringing cry**;—abs. ר׳ Je 7^{16}+; 7440
sf. רִנָּתִי ψ 17^{1}+, רִנָּתָם Je 14^{12}+;—*ringing cry:* **1.** in entreaty, supplication, to י׳, 1 K 8^{28} = 2 Ch 6^{19}, Je 7^{16} 11^{14} ψ 17^{1} 61^{2} 88^{3} (all + תְּפִלָּה), 106^{44} 119^{169} 142^{7} Je 14^{12}. **2.** in proclamation 1 K 22^{36}. **3.** in joy, esp. praise to י׳, + שִׂמְחָה Is 35^{10} 51^{11} (+ שָׂשׂוֹן); + תְּהִלָּה 2 Ch 20^{22}, + שָׂשׂוֹן ψ 105^{43}, + תּוֹדָה 107^{22}, + עלץ Pr 11^{10}; ‖ שְׂחוֹק ψ 126^{2}; opp. בְּכִי, etc. 30^{6} 126^{6}, cf. v^{5}; קוֹל ר׳ Is 48^{20} ψ 42^{5} (+ תּוֹדָה), 47^{2} 118^{15} (+ יְשׁוּעָה); פָּצַח ר׳ Is 14^{7} 44^{23} 49^{13} 54^{1} 55^{12}; of י׳'s joy over Zion Zp 3^{17};—בָּאֳנִיּוֹת רִנָּתָם Is 43^{14} *in the ships of their ringing cry,* in which they exulted, but dub.; Hi Ew בַּאֲנִיּוֹת (bring down) *into mourning their* ר׳; cf. Kit-Di Du Che^{Hpt} Marti.

†II. רִנָּה **n.pr.m.** in Judah 1 Ch 4^{20}; Ανα, 7441
A Ραννων, 𝔊L Ρεννα.

†רְנָנִים **n.[m.] pl.** bird of **piercing cries,** 7443
i.e. ostrich, acc. to 𝔙 Bo Di and most, כְּנַף ר׳ Jb 39^{13}, but read prob. יְעֵנִים Hoffm Bu Du (as
La 4^{3} Qr), v. [יָעֵן]. p. 419 3283

†רִסָּה **n.pr.loc.** station in wilderness, Nu 33$^{21.22}$; Δεσσα, A Ρεσσα, 𝔊L Δρεσσα. 7446

רסן (√ of following; cf. Ar. رَسَنَ (Frä$^{100 f.}$) = רֶסֶן; 𝔗 רִסְנָא (rare), cf. Dalm^{WB}).

†I. רֶסֶן **n.m.**$^{Is 30, 28}$: **1. halter; 2. jaw**(?);— 7448
1. abs. ר׳ ψ 32^{9} restraining mouth of horse or ass (+ מֶתֶג); fig. of שֵׁם י׳, ר׳ עַל־לְחָיֵי עַמִּים Is 30^{28}; ר׳ מִפָּנַי שִׁלֵּחוּ Jb 30^{11}, i.e. threw off restraint.

2. sf. כֶּפֶל רִסְנוֹ 41^{5} *the double of his jaw,* his double jaws (of croc.), si vera l.; connexion of mngs. strange, ‖ פְּנֵי לְבוּשׁוֹ, whence GHBWright Du conj. סִרְיֹנוֹ.

7449 †II. רֶ֫סֶן **n.pr.loc.** in Assyria, near Nineveh Gn 10^{12}; Δασεμ (prob. = *rêš êni, head of spring;* cf. Dl$^{Pa\ 261}$ COT$^{Gn\ 10,\ 12}$).

7450 †I. [רָסַס] **vb. moisten** (so Aram. רְסַס, ܪܣܣ; Ar. رَشَّ (! ش) *sprinkle*);—**Qal** *Inf. cstr.* שֶׁמֶן לָרֹס אֶת־הַסֹּלֶת Ez 46^{14}.

7447 †I. [רָסִיס] **n.[m.] drop** (of dew);—pl. cstr. רְסִיסֵי לָיְלָה Ct 5^{2} (‖ טַל).

II. רסס (√ of foll.; NH רָסַס Pi. *break, crush;* so Mand. רסס Norberg$^{Lexid.\ 232}$, JAram. רְסַס; cf. Ar. رَسَّ *well stopped up with stones* Hoffm$^{ZAW\ iii\ (1893),\ 115}$).

7447 †II. [רָסִיס] **n.[m.] fragment;**—pl. רְסִיסִים, of houses destroyed Am 6^{11} (‖ בְּקִעִים).

7451-52, 7455 רֹעַ, רַע v. I. רעע. I. רֵעַ v. רוע. p. 929, 947f

7453-54 II, III. רֵעַ v. II. רעה. p. 945f

7456 †רָעֵב **vb. be hungry** (NH *id.* Hiph. and deriv.; As. *rûbatu, hunger;* Ar. رَغُبَ *be roomy, voracious,* رَغِبَ *desire vehemently;* Eth. ርኅበ: *be hungry*);—**Qal** *Pf.* 3 ms. ר׳ Is 9^{19} 44^{12}; 3 pl. רָעֵבוּ ψ 34^{11}; *Impf.* 3 ms. יִרְעַב Is 8^{21}, 1 pl. נִרְעָב Je 42^{14}, etc.;—*be hungry* Is 8^{21} Gn 41^{55} (E; of land, = have famine), Je 42^{14} (לַלֶּחֶם), Is 49^{10} (‖ צמא), 65^{13} (‖ *id.;* opp. אכל), ψ 50^{12} *if I should be hungry* (of י׳), Pr 6^{30} 19^{15}. **Hiph.** *allow* one *to hunger,* subj. י׳: *Impf.* 3 ms. וַיַּרְעִבֶךָ Dt 8^{3} (opp. וַיַּאֲכִלְךָ), יַרְעִיב נֶפֶשׁ Pr 10^{3}.

7458 רָעָב$_{101}$ **n.m.**$^{Gn\ 26,1}$ **famine, hunger;**—abs. ר׳ Gn 12^{10}+; sf. רְעָבָם Ne 9^{15}; **1.** *famine* (in land, nation or city), Gn 12^{10} 26^{1} 41$^{30.31}$ Ex 16^{3} 2 S 21^{1} 24^{13} = 2 K 4^{38} 6^{25}+; שְׁנַת ר׳, שְׁנֵי(ה)ר׳ Gn 41$^{27.30.36}$, v^{50}, but also שֶׁבַע [שָׁלוֹשׁ] שָׁנִים ר׳ 2 S 24^{13} (on gender v. Albr$^{ZAW\ xvi\ (1896),\ 103}$) = 1 Ch 21^{12}; c. חזק (*be*) *severe* Gn 47$^{56.57}$ 1 K 18^{2} 25^{3} = Je 52^{6}, חזק על Gn 47^{20}; c. כָּבֵד 12^{10} 47$^{4.13}$; גָּדוֹל 2 K 6^{25}; זַלְעֲפוֹת ר׳ La 5^{10}; מְזֵי ר׳ Dt 32^{24} + Is 5^{13} (v. [מָזֶה]), תַּחֲלוּאֵי ר׳ Je 14^{18}, חַלְלֵי ר׳ La 5^{10}, אַסְפֵי ר׳ Ez 34^{29}; חִצֵּי הָר׳ 5^{16}; as scourge of י׳ (+ דֶּבֶר, חֶרֶב, etc.; esp. Je Ez), Je 5^{12} 11^{22} 14^{12} 21$^{7.9}$ Ez 5^{2} 6$^{11.12}$+, etc.; fig. of lack of י׳'s word Am 8^{11}. **2.** *hunger,* of individual Je 32^{9} Dt 28^{48} (+ צָמָא, etc.), 2 Ch 32^{11} (+*id.*).

†רָעֵב **adj. hungry;**—abs. ר׳ 2 S 17^{29}+; 7457
fs. רְעֵבָה ψ 107^{9} Pr 27^{7}; mpl. רְעֵבִים 1 S 2^{5}+;—*hungry* (sts. + צָמֵא, עָיֵף), 2 S 17^{29} 2 K 7^{12} Is 8^{21} Pr 25^{21} ψ 107^{5}; נֶפֶשׁ רְעֵבָה v^{9} Pr 27^{7}; as subst. sg. *a hungry man* Is 29^{8} 32^{6} 58$^{7.10}$ Ez 18$^{7.16}$ Jb 5^{5} (Bev$^{JPhil.\ xxvi.\ 304}$ prop. רָעֵב, cf. Ez 7^{15}) 22^{7}, pl. 1 S 2^{5} (opp. שְׂבֵעִים בַּלֶּחֶם), Jb 24^{10} (‖ עָרוֹם), ψ 107^{36} 146^{7}; יְהִי־רָעֵב אֹנוֹ Jb 18^{12} (fig.) *his strength grows hungry,* i.e. fails (𝔙 Ew Di al.); 𝔖 De Bu Du (reading אָוֶן) al. *his trouble grows hungry* (i.e. ravenous for him), but ר׳ never elsewhere in this sense.

†רְעָבוֹן **n.[m.] hunger, lack of food,** 7459
famine;—cstr. רַעֲבוֹן בָּתֵּיכֶם Gn 42$^{19.33}$ (E); abs. בִּימֵי רְעָבוֹן ψ 37^{19}.

†[רָעַד] **vb. tremble, quake** (NH *id.,* 7460
Hiph. *shake* (rare), רְעָדָה *a trembling, shaking;* Ar. رَعَدَ *thunder* (said of sky), VIII. *tremble, quiver;* Eth. ርዕደ: *tremble;* JAram. רְעַד *tremble, shake*);—**Qal** *Impf.* 3 fs. וַתִּרְעָד ψ 104^{32} and it (the earth) *trembleth* at the gaze of י׳, in theoph. **Hiph.** *Pt.* עָמַדְתִּי מַרְעִיד Dn 10^{11} *I stood trembling;* pl. מַרְעִידִים Ezr 10^{9}, c. יָשַׁב.

†רַ֫עַד† **n.m. trembling;**—יִרְאָה וָר׳ יָבֹא בִי 7461
ψ 55^{6}; יֹאחֲזֵמוֹ רָ֑עַד Ex 15^{15}.

†רְעָדָה† **n.f.** id.; subj. of אֲחָזָה Is 33^{14} ψ 48^{7}; 7461
‖ יִרְאָה 2^{11}; ‖ פַּחַד Jb 4^{14}.

I. רָעָה$_{167}$ **vb. pasture, tend, graze** (As. 7462
rê'û, vb. *pasture,* n. *ruler,* TelAm. *ruḫi* (as Canaanism) Wkl$^{No.\ 181,\ 11}$; Ar. رَعَى, Eth. ርዐየ: Aram. רְעָא, ܪܥܐ, all = BH);—**Qal** *Pf.* 3 ms. consec. וְרָעָה Mi 5^{3}+, 1 s. sf. consec. וּרְעִיתִים Ez 34^{13}, 3 pl. sf. consec. וְרָעוּם Je 23^{4}, etc.; *Impf.* 3 ms. יִרְעֶה Is 27^{10}+, juss. יֵרַע Jb 20^{26}, sf. יִרְעֶנָּה ψ 80^{14}, וַיִּרְעֵם ψ 78^{72} (וַיַּר׳ **Hiph.** van d. H.), etc.; *Imv.* ms. רְעֵה Mi 7^{14}+, sf. רְעֵם ψ 28^{9}; fs. רְעִי Ct 1^{8}; mpl. רְעוּ Gn 29^{7}; *Inf. cstr.* לִרְעוֹת 37^{12}+, etc.;
Pt. רֹעֶה 30^{36}+, sf. רֹעִי ψ 23^{1}+; fs. רֹעָה Gn 29^{9} 7473
Pr 25^{19}, etc.;—**1.** trans. **a.** *pasture, tend* (*pascere*), lit., c. acc. צֹאן Gn 30$^{31.36}$ 37^{12} (all J), Ex 3^{1} (E), 1 S 17^{15} 25^{16} Is 61^{5}, acc. of asses Gn 36^{24} (P), kids Ct 1^{8}; acc. (צאן) om. Gn 29^{7} 37^{13} (ב loc.) v^{16} (all J), Ct 1^{7} (‖ הִרְבִּיץ), Jb 24^{2} (𝔊 Me Siegf Bu וְרֹעוֹ);—metaph. גֹּרֶן וָיֶקֶב לֹא יִרְעֵם Ho 9^{2}, but rd. יֵדָעֵם 𝔊 We Now GASm; מָוֶת יִרְעֵם ψ 49^{15}. **b.** fig. of י׳, acc. pers., Gn 48^{15} (E) God, who *shepherded* me; c. acc. of people, as flock Ho 4^{16} Is 40^{11} Mi 7^{14} (בְּשִׁבְטֶךָ), Ez 34^{13} (pregn., c. אֶל loc.), v$^{14.15}$ (+ הִרְבִּיץ), v^{16} ψ 28^{9}. **c.** fig. of ruler, and.

teacher, acc. of people, as flock, 2 S 5[2] = 1 Ch 11[2], 2 S 7[7] = 1 Ch 17[6], ψ 78[72] Je 3[15] 23[2.4] Ez 34[2.3.8.10.23.23] Zc 11[4.7.7.9]; of teaching, שִׂפְתֵי צַדִּיק יִרְעוּ רַבִּים Pr 10[21]; c. ב of people ψ 78[71]; abs. Mi 5[3]; c. acc. pers. reflex. *pastured* (fed, en-
7423 riched) *themselves* Ez 34[2.8.10]. **d.** esp. pt. רֹעֶה, etc., as subst. = *shepherd, herdsman:* (1) lit., רֹעֵה צֹאן Gn 4[2] 46[32.34] 47[3] (all J), רֹעֵה בַּצּ׳ 37[2] (E), 1 S 16[11] 17[34]; רֹעֵי מִקְנֵה Gn 13[7.7] (J); (ה)ר׳ alone,
7473 sg. Am 3[12] + 7 t. (all in sim.); רֹעָה *shepherdess,* Gn 29[9] (J); כְּלִי רֹעֶה אֱוִלִי Zc 11[15] (v. כְּלִי **2 c**), as symbol; pl. (הָ)רֹעִים Am 1[2] Ex 2[17.19] (J), 1 S 21[8] (אַבִּיר הָר׳; Gr Dr Bu Kit Löhr א׳ הָרָצִים; 𝔊 Lag BN 45 HPS אֲבִיל הָעֲיָרִים, but cf. We) + 8 t. + Is 31[4] (sim.), 38[12] (rd. רֹעִים for רֹעִי Perles[29] Du Che Hpt cf. Di), cf. (sf.) Gn 13[8.8] (J); כְּלִי הָרֹעִים 1 S 17[40] (v. כְּלִי **3**);—בֵּית־עֵקֶד הָרֹעִים, v. p. 112. (2) fig. of ruler (as oft. As.; cf. Gk. (Homer) ποιμένα λαῶν), abs. sg. Je 17[16] Zc 10[2] 11[16] 13[7b] + 8 t. Je Ez; sf. of י׳, רֹעִי Is 44[28] (of Cyrus), Zc 13[7 a.17] (rd. רֹעִי הָאֱוִלִי We Now GASm); abs. pl. Is 56[11] Je 2[8] 3[15] Mi 5[4] Zc 10[3] 11[5.8] + 18 t. Je Ez 34, + (of Assyrian leaders) Na 3[18]; רֹעֵי יִשׂ׳ Ez 34[2]; רֹעֵי צֹאנוֹ Is 63[11] (but rd. רֹעֵה [of Moses] 𝔊 𝔗 Di Du al.). (3) epith. of י׳: י׳ רֹעִי ψ 23[1], רֹעֵה יִשׂ׳ 80[2], רֹעֶה אֶבֶן יִשׂ׳ Gn 49[24] (poem in J; rd. cstr. רֹעֵה, cf. Comm.); מֵרֹעֶה אֶחָד Ec 12[11] DeWild, < *president* of assembly of sages Siegf SS. **2.** intrans. *feed, graze:* **a.** lit. of cows, sheep, etc.: c. ב loc. Gn 41[2.18] (E), 1 Ch 27[29]; c. acc. of pasture Is 30[23]; c. עַל loc. Zp 2[7] (עַל־הַיָּם for MT עֲלֵיהֶם, v. Now); אֶל־מוּל loc. Ex 34[3] (J); abs. Is 5[17] 11[7] (|| רבץ; but v. II. רעה infr.) 27[10] (|| *id.*), 65[25] Jon 3[7] Jb 1[14]. **b.** fig. of idolater, Is 44[20] *he feedeth on ashes* (acc.); cf. Ho 12[2] Ephr. *feedeth on wind* (acc.); פִּי כְסִילִים יִר׳ אִוֶּלֶת Pr 15[14] (so Vrss Qr; Kt פני for פי) *the mouth of fools feeds on folly* (Toy; Buhl √ II. רעה, Gerber[162] sub III. רעה); in Ct, c. ב loc., fig. of lover Ct 2[16] 6[2.3]; of breasts (like gazelles) 4[5]. **c.** fig., of Isr. as flock Is 14[30] (|| רבץ), rd. (י—)בְּכָרַי *in my pasture(s)*, for MT בְּכוֹרֵי, Koppe Ew Di Du (otherwise Che Hpt, cf. Marti); Zp 3[13] (|| *id.*); c. עַל־דְּרָכִים Is 49[9]; c. acc. of pasture-land Je 50[19] Mi 7[14] Ez 34[14b] (+ אֶל loc.), v[18.19]; hence *crop, strip,* i.e. devastate, of conqueror, c. acc. of land Mi 5[5], cf. אֶת־יָדוֹ Je 6[3]; so יִרְעוּךְ קָדְקֹד 2[16]; acc. of Isr. under fig. of vine (subj. foes, as beasts) ψ 80[14]. **d.** subj. wind, c. acc. pers. Je 22[22], i.e. drive them away; subj. fire, c. acc. rei, יֵרַע Jb 20[26], but read perh. יֵרַע, **Niph.** (Ol Di Hoffm Siegf Bu; otherwise Du). —רֹעֶה עֲקָרָה 24[21] is difficult; Bu הֵרַע for ר׳; more radical conj. in Du. **Niph.** poss. Jb 20[26], v. **2 d** supr. **Hiph.** ψ 78[72] van d. H., v. **1 c** supr.

רֹעֶה *shepherd,* רֹעָה *shepherdess,* v. √ **1 d.** above 7462, 7473

†רְעִי **n. [m.] pasture;**—עֶשְׂרִים בָּקָר ר׳ 1 K 5[3] 7471
twenty cattle (fr.) *pasture* (v. Ges §131c; Kit בָּקָר).

רֹעִי Is 38[12] Zc 11[17], v. √ **1 d** (1), (2). above 7473

†מִרְעֶה **n.m.** Ez 34,14 **pasturage, pasture;**— 4829
abs. מ׳ Gn 47[4] +; cstr. מִרְעֵה Is 34[14]; sf. מִרְעֵהוּ Jb 39[8], מִרְעֵיכֶם Ez 34[18];—*pasturage,* לְצֹאן Gn 47[4] (J), cf. 1 Ch 4[39.41], also Is 32[14]; מ׳ שָׁמֵן וָטוֹב v[40], cf. (fig.) Ez 34[14.14.18a]; of cattle Jo 1[18], stag La 1[6]; = *pasture,* of wild ass Jb 39[8]; of כְּפִירִים Na 2[12] (but read מְעָרָה *cave,* for מרעה, We Now, || מְעוֹן); יֶתֶר מִרְעֵיכֶם Ez 34[18b] (fig.).

†[מַרְעִית] **n.f. pasturing, shepherding,** 4830
pasturage (alw. fig.);—sf. מַרְעִיתִי Je 23[1] Ez 34[31], מַרְעִיתֶךָ ψ 74[1] 79[13], etc.;—**1.** *pasturing, shepherding,* צֹאן מַרְעִיתִי, of Isr. as flock of י׳, Je 23[1] Ez 34[31], cf. ψ 74[1] 79[13] 100[3] + 95[7] (rd. צ׳ מ׳ וְעַם יָדוֹ, cf. Hup-Now Che). **2.** *pasturage,* Ho 13[6] (Now כְּרְעוֹתָם), Is 49[9] Je 25[36]. **3.** by meton. = *flock* Je 10[21].

†II. [רָעָה] **vb.** prob. **associate with** (cf. 7462
Schulthess 69 ff. but also Nö ZMG liv (1900), 154 f.; As. *ru'a, ruttu, neighbour, fellow* (m. et f.; cf. Jäger BAS i. 483, 486); so Bed. رَاعِي, راعيها *master, owner,* Wallin ZMG v (1851), 9 Jayakar JA xxi. 851; Eth. መርዓ፡ *marriage;* Ar. أُرْعُوَّةٌ, Eth. አርዑት፡ *yoke;* NH רֵעוּת *friendship* is fr. BH רֵעַ);—**Qal** *Imv.* ms. וּרְעֵה אֱמוּנָה ψ 37[3] *cherish faithfulness* (Hup-Now RV Che Du Dr); > *feed securely* (Bae; I. רעה; *feed on* (his) *faithfulness* Am RV); *Pt.* רֹעֶה כְסִילִים Pr 13[20] *one associating with fools,* so ר׳ זוֹלְלִים 28[7], ר׳ זונות 29[3] (Thes al. think these fig. fr. I. רעה, v. **2 b**). **Hithp.** 2 ms. אַל־תִּתְרַע אֶת־בַּעַל אָף Pr 22[24] *do not make companionship with a bad-tempered man;* perhaps also 3 fpl. תִּתְרָעֶינָה Is 11[7] (Lag Or. i. 21; Deceased Wife's Sister 399 Brd Du Che Hpt) cow and bear *shall be each other's companions;* + *Inf. cstr.* הִתְרָעֹת Pr 18[24] (Toy, for MT הִתְרֹעֵעַ) there are [יֵשׁ for אִישׁ] friends
(merely) *to be companions* (v. II. רעע *ad fin.*). 7489

II. רֵעַ 187 **n.m.** Pr 17,17 **friend, companion,** 7453
fellow;—ר׳ abs. 2 S 13[3] +, cstr. 1 Ch 27[33]; sf. רֵעִי Jb 31[9] +, רֵעֲךָ Dt 5[17] +, רֵעֶךָ Ex 2[13] +, also רֵעֶיךָ 2 S 12[11] (sg.; Ges §93ss), רֵעֵהוּ (Ges §84a i) Gn 11[3] + 114 t., רֵעוֹ Je 6[21], רֵעָה 3[30]; pl. רֵעִים Je 3[1] +, cstr. רֵעֵי Jb 2[11]; sf. רֵעָיו 32[3], רֵעֵהוּ (Ges §91k) 42[10]

1 S 30^{26}, etc.;—**1.** *friend, intimate*, Gn $38^{12.20}$ (J), 1 S 30^{26} 2 S 13^{3} 1 K 16^{11} (𝔊 om.); רֵעֲךָ אֲשֶׁר כְּנַפְשְׁךָ Dt 13^{7}, מֶתֶק רֵעֵהוּ Pr 27^{9} (txt. dub., v. Toy); Mi 7^{5} (‖ אַלּוּף), Je 9^{3} (‖ אָח), 19^{9} La 1^{2} (+ אֹהֲבֶיהָ), ψ 35^{14} (‖ אָח) + 3 t. ψψ; esp. Jb 2^{11} 6^{14} + 8 t. Jb, Pr 17^{17} 18^{24} + 8 t. Pr (12^{26} v. מֵרֵעַ infr.), Ct 5^{1} (‖ דּוֹדִים); associates Zc 3^{8}; term. techn. ר׳ הַמֶּלֶךְ 1 Ch 27^{33} (v. רֵעֶה), cf. 2 S $16^{17.17}$; of lover Ct 5^{16} (‖ דּוֹדִי), husband Je 3^{20}, paramours Ho 3^{1} Je 3^{1}; metaph. רֵעַ לִבְנוֹת יַעֲנָה Jb 30^{29} (‖ אָח לְתַנִּים). **2.** in weaker sense, *fellow, fellow-citizen*, even *another person*, with whom one stands in recipr. relations, Ex 2^{13} $20^{16.17.17.17}$ (Gi $v^{13.14.14.14}$) = Dt $5^{17.18.18.18}$, Ex 21^{14} $22^{7.8.10.25}$ (all E), Lv $19^{13.16.18}$ 20^{10} (all H), Dt 4^{42} $15^{2.2}$ + 11 t. Dt, Jos 20^{5} (D), Ju 7^{14} Je 9^{7} 22^{13} 29^{23} Ez $18^{6.11.15}$ $22^{11.12}$ Hb 2^{15} Jb 16^{21} Ru 4^{7} ψ 15^{3} 28^{3} 101^{5} Pr $3^{28.29}$ 6^{1} (‖ זָר!) + 18 t. Pr; שְׁכֵן וְרֵעוֹ Je 6^{21}; 1 S 15^{28} *hath given* (the kingdom) *to thy fellow*, = another than thou, so 28^{17} 2 S 12^{11}; so also אִישׁ . . . רֵעֵהוּ *a* (given, certain) *man* over against *his fellow* (diff. fr. **3**) Ex $21^{18.35}$ $22^{6.9.13}$ 33^{11} (all E), Dt 19^{11} 22^{26} Ju 7^{13} 1 K 8^{31} 20^{35} Je 7^{5} 1 Ch 6^{22} Ru 3^{14} Ec 4^{4}; similarly שָׂעִיר אֶל־רֵעֵהוּ Is 34^{14}. **3.** in recipr. phr. אִישׁ . . . רֵעֵהוּ Gn 11^{3} they said *one* to *another* (אִישׁ distrib.), *each* the speech of *the other* v^{7}, absent *one* from *the other* 31^{49}, cf. 43^{33} (all J), Ex 11^{2} $18^{7.16}$ 32^{27} (all E), Ju 6^{29} 7^{22} 10^{18} 2 S $2^{16.16}$ + 4 t. 1 S, 2 K 3^{23} $7^{3.9}$ 2 Ch 20^{23} Is 3^{5} (‖ אִישׁ בְּאִישׁ), 13^{8} 19^{2} (‖ אִישׁ בְּאָחִיו), 41^{6} Je 5^{8} + 11 t. Je, Ez 33^{26} Zc 3^{10} + 6 t. Zc (11^{6} read רֹעֵהוּ Sta ZAW i (1881). 26), Mal 3^{16} Jon 1^{7}; so of
7452, 7454 things Gn 15^{10} (J).—I. רֵעַ v. רוע. p. 929, below

7463 †רֵעֶה **n.m. friend** (cf. Sta § 184 Lag BN 156 Ba § 12a);—cstr. in term. techn. רֵעֶה הַמֶּלֶךְ (Ges § 93 ll Kö ii. 1, 78 f.) 1 K 4^{5} (= רֵעַ 1 Ch 27^{33}), cf. רֵעֶה דָּוִד 2 S 15^{37} 16^{16}; ins. also 15^{32} (cf. v^{37}) 𝔊 We Dr al.; in simple sense Pr 27^{10} Kt (Qr רֵעַ; cf. Kö l.c.).

7462 †[רָעָה] **vb. denom. Pi. be a special friend**;—*Pf.* 3 ms. מֵרֵעֵהוּ אֲשֶׁר רֵעָה לוֹ Ju 14^{20} his comrade who *had been 'best man'* (GFM) to him.

7464 †[רֵעָה] **n.f. companion, attendant**;—of maidens, pl. sf. רֵעוֹתַי Ju 11^{37} Qr (> Kt רעיתי), רֵעוֹתֶיהָ v^{38} ψ 45^{15}.

7474 †[רַעְיָה] **n.f. companion**;—of beloved bride, sf. רַעְיָתִי Ct $1^{9.15}$ $2^{2.10.13}$ $4^{1.7}$ 5^{2} 6^{4}; so of attendant maidens Ju 11^{37} Kt, but v. foregoing.

7468 †I. רְעוּת **n.f. fellow (-woman)**;—sf. in recipr. phr. אִשָּׁה מֵאֵת רְעוּתָהּ Ex 11^{2} (E) *each from her fellow* (‖ אִישׁ מֵאֵת רֵעֵהוּ, cf. II. רֵעַ **3**); cf. Je 9^{19}; of birds of prey (דַּיּוֹת) Is 34^{15} cf. v^{16}; people under fig. of sheep Zc 11^{9}; רְעוּתָהּ Est 1^{19} = *another than she* (cf. 1 S 15^{28} II. רֵעַ **2**). p. 945 7453

†רוּת **n.pr.f. Ruth** (for רְעוּת, i.e. *friendship*, Syr. ܪܥܘܬ, Thes Lag BN 84, 156; Or. ii. 41 Kö ii. 1, 481);—Moabitess, ancestress of David, Ru $1^{4.14.16.22}$ $2^{2.8.21.22}$ 3^{9} $4^{5.10.13}$; Ρουθ. 7327

†רְעוּ **n.pr.m.** (prop. name of a god, Duval ZA vi. 126 Mez Harrân 23, cf. Hom A. u. A. ii. 208);—son of Peleg: Gn $11^{18.19.20.21}$ (P), 1 Ch 1^{25}; Ραγαυ. 7466

†רְעוּאֵל **n.pr.m.** Ραγουηλ: **1.** Moses' father-in-law Ex 2^{18} (J; 𝔊L Ιοθορ), Nu 10^{29} (JE); elsewhere יִתְרוֹ q.v. **2.** Edomite Gn $36^{4.10.13.17.17}$ (P), ‖ 1 Ch $1^{35.37}$. **3.** Gadite Nu 2^{14}, v. דְּעוּאֵל p. 396. **4.** Benjamite 1 Ch 9^{8}. 7467

†רֵעִי **n.pr.m.** (cf. Palm. n.pr. רעי *friendly* (?) Cook 109);—courtier of David (si vera l.) 1 K 1^{8}; Ρησει, 𝔊L οἱ ἑταῖροι αὐτοῦ. 7472

†[מֵרֵעַ] **n.m. friend, companion** (strange formation; orig. dub.; Wetzst Syr. Dreschtafel, Z. Ethnol. 1873, 289 cp. مرياع *miryâ'*, name of bell-wether among Syr. nomads (prop. [inseparable] *companion*), and der. fr. *ריע, prop. *closely joined;* cf. Gerber 97, 162);—sf. מֵרֵעֵהוּ Gn 26^{26} +, מְרֵעֵהוּ Pr 19^{7}, מֵרֵעֲךָ Ju 15^{2}; pl. מֵרֵעִים 14^{11};—*companion, confidential friend*, Gn 26^{26} (J; cf. רֵעֶה); of bridegroom's escort 14^{11}, 'best man' (GFM) v^{20} $15^{2.6}$; more gen. *friends* (‖ אחים) 2 S 3^{8} Pr 19^{7}; 12^{26} is dub., Död Hi De al. מְרֵעֵהוּ; Toy conj. poss. (יָסֵר) מֵרָעָה, v. further תור. 4828

III. רעה (Aram. רְעָא, ܪܥܐ, *take pleasure* (in), *desire*, = Ar. رضى [Heb. רָצָה], whence Aram. רְעוּתָא *desire*, רַעְיוֹנָא, רַעְיָנָא, ܪܶܥܝܳܢܳܐ, *opinion, thought, disposition*, and following late and Aram. words in Heb., cf. Nö ZMG liv (1900). 155; > De Siegf Qoh. 18 al. from I. רעה **2 b**, cf. Ho 12^{2}, and Ar. رَعَى *watch, regard, respect* (Lane) [Ba NB 46 f. Kau Aramaismen 82 f. derive foll. from I. רעה = *observe, attend to*, specif. *tend sheep*, also *aim at, purpose*]).

†III. [רֵעַ] **n.[m.] purpose, aim**;—sf. רֵעִי ψ 139^{2} (of man), pl. sf. רֵעֶיךָ v^{17} (of Ēl). 7454

†II. רְעוּת **n.f. longing, striving**;—cstr., הֶבֶל וּר׳ רוּחַ Ec 1^{14} $2^{11.17.26}$ 4^{4} 6^{9}; עָמָל וּר׳ רוּחַ 4^{6}. 7469

†רַעְיוֹן **n.[m.] id.**;—cstr., רַעְיוֹן רוּחַ Ec 1^{17}, בְּכָל־עֲמָלוֹ וּבְר׳ לִבּוֹ 2^{22}. הֶבֶל וְר׳ רוּחַ 4^{16} (cf. foreg.), 7475

רֹעָה v. II. רעע.

7477 †[רָעַל] **vb. quiver, shake, reel** (Aram. רְעַל, ܪܥܠ, *quiver, shake, tremble;* Ar. رَعْلٌ *the hanging part* of a sheep's split ear, also (Frey) a kind of *veil* of which a part hangs down in front; أَرْعَلُ *dangling;* Liḥy. has n.pr. רעל DHM[Epigr. Denkm. Ar. 38]);—**Hoph.** *Pf.* 3 pl. הַבְּרֹשִׁים
6188 הָרְעָלוּ Na 2[4] *are made to quiver.* Vid. also [עָרַל].

7478 †רַ֫עַל **n.[m.] reeling**;—only סַף־ר׳ Zc 12[2] *goblet of reeling* (fig. of Jerusalem).

7479 †[רְעָלָה] **n.[f.]** prob. **veil** (cf. Ar. supr.);—pl. הָרְעָלוֹת Is 3[19], in list of finery.

4831 מַרְעֵלָה v. p. 599.

8653 †תַּרְעֵלָה **n.f. reeling** (cf. רַ֫עַל);—כּוֹס הַתּ׳ Is 51[17.22]; יַיִן תּ׳ ψ 60[5] drink *reeling as wine.*

7480 †רְעֵלָיָה **n. pr. m.** companion of Zerub.,
7485 Ezr 2[2] (Ρεελεια, 𝔊L Δεμίου), = רַעַמְיָה Ne 7[7] (Νааμια, א Δαεμια, 𝔊L Δαιμίας, A Ρεελμα).

רעם (√ of foll., prob. onomatop.; Gerber[47] prop. *move violently* as orig. meaning, but ref. to thunderous *sound* everywhere, exc. Ez 27[35] where text dub., v. infr.; cf. Aram. רְעִים, רַעַם n. *thunder,* רְעַם vb. *thunder;* esp. Aph. Ithpa. *utter* (loud) *complaints;* ܪܥܡܐ, ܪܥܡ n. *thunder,* ܪܥܡ vb. *thunder, lament,* cf. NH רָעַם Hiph. *thunder,* Hithp. *complain;* Eth. ረዓም፡ n. *thunder,* As. *rîmu, id.;* Ar. رَغِمَ *vex, dislike,* etc.).

7482 †רַ֫עַם **n.[m.] thunder**;—ascribed to י׳: ר׳ abs. Is 29[6], בְּסֵתֶר רַ֫עַם ψ 81[8] (Baer Gi; i.e. thunder-cloud); sf. קוֹל רַעַמְךָ 77[19] 104[7]; cstr. רַעַם גבורתו Jb 26[14] (fig. of י׳'s display of might; opp. שֵׁמֶץ); fig. of captains, ר׳ שָׂרִים 39[25], i.e. thunderous shouting (+ תְּרוּעָה).

7481 †[רָעַם] **vb. denom. thunder**;—**Qal** *make the sound of thunder, thunder: Impf.* 3 ms. יִרְעַם *let* the sea *thunder* (in praise, ‖ גיל, שׂמח, רנן, מחא כף, הריע, עלז) ψ 96[11] = 1 Ch 16[32], ψ 98[7].—*Pf.* 3 pl. רָעֲמוּ פָּנִים Ez 27[35] is dub.: *faces tremble* (Toy *are convulsed*), or *they tremble* (cf. Hi-Sm Krae; AV RV *are troubled*) *in face,* lacks etym. support (otherwise Gerber[47], but v. √ supr.); 𝔊 𝔖 Co דָּמְעוּ פְּנֵיהֶם. **Hiph.** (Gerber[47]) *thunder, cause thunder;*—*Pf.* 3 ms. הִרְעִים ψ 29[3]; *Impf.* 3 ms. יַרְעֵם (on ـַ v. Kö[i. 210]) ψ 18[14] +; וַיַּרְעֵם 1 S 7[10]; 2 ms. תַּרְעֵם Jb 40[9]; 1 S 1[6] v. infr.;—*thunder,* of י׳ (God) 2[10] 7[10] (both c. עַל pers. *against* whom), ψ 18[14] = 2 S 22[14], ψ 29[3] Jb 37[4.5], cf. 40[9].—הַרְּעִמָהּ 1 S 1[6] is appar. *Inf. cstr. sf.* (Ges[§ 20 h; 22 s]), but not understood by 𝔊 and dub.: AV RV *to make her fret,* cf. Aram. *utter* (loud) *complaints* (Weir in Dr[Sm 291]); perhaps corrupt HPS.

רַעְמָא v. II. רַעְמָה. below 7484

†I. רַעְמָה (Gi[Intr. 127 f.]) **n. f. vibration? quivering** mane? of horse's neck: Jb 39[19] *hast thou clothed his neck (with)* ר׳? so most, but very uncertain. 7483

†II. רַעְמָה, רַעְמָא (Gi[Intr. 124 ff.]) **n. pr. m.** 'son' of Cush, ـָה Gn 10[7.7] = ـָא 1 Ch 1[9.9] (Baer, v. his note; van d. H. Gi ـָה v[b]); Ρεγχμα, Ρεγμα; ـָה as trading people Ez 27[22], Ραμα, Ραγμα. Identified by many with city Ῥεγ(α)μα (Ptol[vi. 7, 14]), Ῥηγμα (Steph. Byz.), in SE. Arabia, on Pers. Gulf (so even DHM[ZMG xxx (1876), 122] Glas[Skizze ii. 251, 325]), but this is رجمة in inscr. (Glas[ib. 252]); < Sab. רעמה near *Meʿîn* in SW. Arabia (Hom[Südar. Chr. 131] Hal[535, 11], cf. DHM[l. c.]), perh. = Ῥαμμανῖται of Strabo[xvi. 4. 24], v. Di[Gn 10, 7]. 7484

רַעַמְיָה (? *thunder of* י׳) Ne 7[7] v. רְעֵלָיָה. 7480, 7485

†רַעְמְסֵס **n. pr. loc.** Ex 1[11] (J), = רַעְמְסֵס Gn 47[11] Ex 12[37] Nu 33[3.5] (all P), **Ramses,** city in Egypt; Ραμεσ(σ)η; built by King Rameses II (hence its name; the king used Israelitish *corvée* acc. to Ex 1[11]), near *Tel el-Maskhuta* (Pithom), but not certainly identified, v. פִּתֹם and reff.; אֶרֶץ ר׳ Gn 47[11] of district round. 7486

†[רָעַן] **vb.** only **Paʿlel be** or **grow luxuriant, fresh, green**;—*Pf.* 3 fs. רַעֲנָנָה (De[Hiob]) Jb 15[32] (of branch, in fig.).

†רַעֲנָן **adj. luxuriant, fresh**;—m. ר׳ Dt 12[2] +; f. רַעֲנָנָה Ct 1[16]; mpl. רַעֲנַנִּים ψ 92[15];—*luxuriant,* of trees: בְּרוֹשׁ Ho 14[9], זַיִת ψ 52[10] (both sim.), Je 11[16] (fig.); sim. also, כְּאֶזְרָח ר׳ ψ 37[35] (but rd. כְּאֶרֶז הַלְּבָנוֹן 𝔊 𝔖 and most); esp. in phrase תַּחַת כָּל־עֵץ ר׳ place of idolatrous rites, Dt 12[2] 1 K 14[23] 2 K 16[4] = 2 Ch 28[4], 2 K 17[10] Je 2[20] 3[6.13] Is 57[5] Ez 6[13]; עַל־עֵץ ר׳ Je 17[2] (ci vera l.); leaf v[8] (fig.); leafy couch Ct 1[16]; *fresh,* oil ψ 92[11]; *fresh, flourishing,* pers. (fig., as trees) v[15] (+ דְּשֵׁנִים). 7488

I. **רעע** (√ of foll.; orig. meaning dub.).

†רֹ֫עַ **n.[m.] badness, evil**;—ר׳ abs. Gn 41[19] + 4 t. Je; cstr. Ho 9[15] + 13 t.;—**1.** *badness, bad quality,* of cattle Gn 41[19] (E), figs Je 24[2.3.8] 29[17]. **2.** *wilfulness,* רֹעַ לבב 1 S 17[28] (Gerber[161] makes **2** and **4** [inf. of] vb.). **3.** ethical, *evil, badness,* only in phr.: רֹעַ מעללים *evil of doings* 7455

Dt 28^{20} Is 1^{16} Je 4^{4} 21^{12} 23$^{2.22}$ 25^{5} 26^{3} 44^{22} Ho 9^{15} ψ 28^{4} (cf. רַע מעללים 1 S 25^{3}). **4.** *sadness,*
7489 ר׳ פָּנִים Ec 7^{3}, ר׳ לֵב Ne 2^{3} (cf. [רָעַע] **2**).

7451 I. רַע$_{226}$ **adj.** bad, evil (distinction from n., and vb. Pf. 3 ms., is sts. not easy, and opinions differ);—ms. רַע Gn 6^{5}+; רָע 31^{24}+; pl. רָעִים 13^{13}+; cstr. רָעֵי Ez 7^{24} (del. Co); fs. רָעָה Gn 37^{2}+37 t. (this form usu. noun), pl. רָעוֹת 28^{8} +14 t.; רָעֹת 41^{27} (18 t. noun);—†**1.** *bad, disagreeable, malignant:* of a woman, רָעָה בְּעֵינֵי Ex 21^{8} (E; perhaps, with changed accent, vb. 3 fs. רָעָה) *disagreeable, unpleasing in the eyes of,* pl. Gn 28^{8} (P); of poisonous herb 2 K 4^{41}, malignant boils Dt 28^{35} Jb 2^{7}, diseases Dt 7^{15} 28^{59} 2 Ch 21^{19} Ec 6^{2}, deadly sword ψ 144^{10}, arrows Ez 5^{16}, severe judgments 14^{21}, wonders Dt 6^{22}; ψ מַלְאֲכֵי רָעִים 78^{49} = fierce messengers (of God; Ew$^{§287 a}$ Ges$^{§130 e}$), wild beasts Gn 37$^{20.33}$ (JE) Lv 26^{6} (H) Ez 5^{17} 14$^{15.21}$ 34^{25}; unclean thing Dt 23^{10}. †**2.** *bad, unpleasant,* giving pain, unhappiness, misery: ימים רעים *evil days* (of trial and hardship) Gn 47^{9} (P) Pr 15^{15}; עִנְיַן רע Ec 1^{13} 5^{13}; עִנְיַן 4^{8}, cf. 2^{17} 9^{3}; הַמַּעֲשֶׂה הָרָע 4^{3}; הדבר הרע *evil report* Ex 33^{4} (J), so דִּבָּה רָעָה Gn 37^{2} (JE) Nu 14^{37} (P), שם רע Dt 22$^{14.19}$ Ne 6^{13}, שְׁמוּעָה רָעָה Je 49^{23} ψ 112^{7}; of things: painful discipline Pr 15^{10}, evil occurrence 1 K 5^{18}, *evil*(-bringing) *net* Ec 9^{12}, instruments Is 32^{7}: כל הדבר הרע Jos 23^{15} (D) *all evil* (injurious) *things;* רַע it is *bad, harmful* Is 3^{11} Je 2^{19}; of speech, דבר, רע או טוב Gn 24^{50} (J) in prov., speak *bad or good* = anything at all, מטוב עד רע 31$^{24.29}$ (E), לְמֵרָע ועד טוב 2 S 13^{22}, of the divine spirit as producing an ecstatic state of frenzy and violence 1 S 16$^{14.15.16.23}$ 18^{10} 19^{9} (see רוּחַ **9**). †**3.** *evil, displeasing* עָשָׂה רָע בְּעֵינֵי סַרְנֵי פְלִשְׁתִּים 1 S 29^{7}. †**4.** *bad of its kind,* land Nu 13^{19} (J), place 20^{5} (JE), waters 2 K 2^{19}, figs Je 24$^{2.3.3.8}$, kine Gn 41$^{3.4.19.20.21.27}$ (E), מום רע Dt 15^{21}, cf. 17^{1}. †**5.** *bad,* i.e. of low value Lv 27$^{10.10.12.14.33}$ (H), cf. Mal 1$^{8.8}$; רַע רַע יֹאמַר הַקּוֹנֶה Pr 20$^{14.14}$. †**6.** רָעֵי + מִן comp., *worse than,* 2 S 19^{8}; as superl., גוֹיִם Ez 7^{24} *worst of nations* (del. Co). †**7.** *sad, unhappy:* לֵב־רָע *sad heart* (cf. opp. יטב, טוב) Pr 25^{20}; of face Gn 40^{7} (E) Ne 2^{2}; רע לְפָנָיו v^{1}. †**8.** חָשַׁב מַחֲשֶׁבֶת (ה)רָעָה *devise evil* (hurtful) *device* Ez 38^{10} Est 9^{25}. †**9.** *bad, unkind,* vicious in disposition or temper: וְלֵב־רָע *when the mind is vicious,* harmful Pr 26^{23}; רַע עָיִן *one evil* of eye Pr 23^{6} 28^{22}; רוּחַ רָעָה Ju 9^{23} *bad temper.*

10. ethically *bad, evil, wicked:* †**a.** in gen., אם טוב ואם רע Ec 12^{14} *whether good or bad.* †**b.** of persons, איש רע 1 S 30^{22}; ψ אדם רע 140^{2}; רָע המן הרע הזה Est 7^{6} *this wicked Haman,* so רָע = *evil man* ψ 10^{15}, Jb 21^{30} Pr 11^{21} 12^{13} 24^{20}, רָעִים = *evil men* Gn 13^{13} (J) Je 6^{29} 15^{21} Ez 30^{12} Jb 35^{12} Pr 4^{14} 12^{12} 14^{19} 15^{3}; רָעוֹת *evil women* Je 2^{33}; שכנים רעים 12^{14} *evil neighbours;* of הַדּוֹר Dt 1^{35}, הָעָם Je 13^{10}; הָעֵדָה Nu 14$^{27.35}$ (P), המשפחה Je 8^{3}; רע בְּעֵינֵי י׳ *wicked* in the eyes of י׳ Gn 38^{7} (JE) = 1 Ch 2^{3}; עָשָׂה הָרַע בְּעֵינֵי י׳ Nu 32^{13} (R) Dt 4^{25} 9^{18} 17^{2} 31^{29} Ju 2^{11}+48 t., +(c. sf. of God) 2 K 21^{15} Is 65^{12} 66^{4} Je 7^{30} 32^{30} ψ 51^{6} 2 S 12^{9}, prob. also Je 18^{10} (read הָרָע for הָרָעָה). **c.** of thoughts, יֵצֶר Gn 6^{5} 8^{21} (J), הַלֵּב הָרָע Je 3^{17} 7^{24} 11^{8} 16^{12} 18^{12}; words, רעות Pr 15^{28}. **d.** *deeds, actions,* עשה (כ)דבר הרע Dt 13^{12} 17^{5} 19^{20} Ne 13^{17}; עשה דברים הרעות Je 3^{5}; ψ דבר רע 64^{6} 141^{4} Ec 8$^{3.5}$; 1 S 2^{23} 2 K 17^{11}; דֶּרֶךְ 1 K 13^{33} Je 18^{11} 23^{22}+11 t.; דרכים 2 K 17^{13} 2 Ch 7^{14} Ez 20^{44} 33^{11} 36^{31} Zc 1^{4}; מעשׂינו Ezr 9^{13}; מעללים Zc 1^{4} Ne 9^{35} (cf. רֹעַ **4**); בֶּצַע רע Hb 2^{9}; מרוצתם Je 23^{10}; (ה)תועבות (ה)רעות Ez 6^{11} 8^{9} (del. Co); ψ כִּי רָעוֹת בִּמְגוּרָם 55^{16} *for evil deeds are in their dwelling.*

II. רַע$_{126}$ **n.m.** $^{Jb\ 30,\ 26}$ evil, distress, misery, 7451
injury, calamity;—abs. רַע Nu 11^{1}+, בְּרָע Ex 5^{19}+, רָע Gn 48^{16}+;—†**1.** *evil, distress, adversity:* יְרֵא רַע *fear evil* ψ 23^{4} Zp 3^{15}; בּוֹרֵא רָע Is 45^{7} (of God), הביא רע 31^{2}; מתאננים רַע Nu 11^{1} (J) *murmuring respecting distress* (see Di); אם טוב ואם רע Je 42^{6} *whether prosperity or adversity;* יום רע Am 6^{3} *day of calamity;* יְמֵי רע ψ 49^{6} 94^{13}; כי טוב קויתי ויבא רע Jb 30^{26}; בְּרָע *in adversity* Ex 5^{19} (E) ψ 10^{6}; יִפֹּל בְּרָע Pr 13^{17}; אֶרְאֶה בְרָע Gn 44^{34} (J); בכל־רע Pr 5^{14}, מכל רע Gn 48^{16} (E) ψ 121^{7}; v. also Mi 1^{12} ψ 140^{12} Jb 5^{19} 31^{29} Pr 12^{21} 19^{23}. †**2.** *evil, injury, wrong:* Hb 2^{9} Jb 2^{10} Pr 21^{10}; עשה רע + עִם pers. Gn 31^{29} (E); ל pers. Je 39^{12}; as obj. of חשב Ho 7^{15}, חרשׁ Pr 6^{14} 12^{20} 14^{22}, ψ השיב 54^{7}, גמל 7^{5} Pr 31^{12}, בקשׁ 17^{11}, ψ אמר 41^{6}, שׁלם 20^{22}, דבר 109^{20}; דבר בְּרָע 73^{8} *speak about injury;* לֹא יִתְנַבֵּא טוב כִּי אִם רָע 1 K 22$^{8.18}$ = 2 Ch (18^{7} לְרָעָה), 18^{17} לְרָע; לרע *for harm, injury* Is 59^{7} Je 7^{6} 25^{7} ψ 56^{6} Pr 1^{16} 21^{12} Ec 8^{9}; רַע יֵרוֹעַ Pr 11^{15} (but rd. רֹעַ Gr SS, v. Toy). **3.** ethical *evil,* Dt 30^{15} 2 S 14^{17} Is 5^{20} Am 5^{14} Mi 7^{3}+10 t.; עשה רע 2 K 21^{9} 2 Ch 12^{14} 33^{9} Ne 9^{28}+8 t.; פֹּעֲלֵי רע Mi 2^{1}; אהב רע 3^{2} (Qr), ψ 52^{5}; שׂנא רע Am 5^{15} ψ 97^{10} Pr 8^{13}; מאס ברע ψ 36^{5}; Is 7$^{15.16}$; בִּעֵר הרע מִן *consume evil from* Dt 13^{6}+8 t. Dt;

לֹא יְגֻרְךָ רָע ψ 5^{5} (adj.=*evil man* Hup De al.); סר מֵרָע ידע טוב ורע Gn 2$^{9.17}$ 3$^{5.22}$ (all J), Dt 1^{39}; Is 59^{15} ψ 34^{15} 37^{27} Pr 3^{7}+8 t.; כי ברע הוא Ex 32^{22} (J) *he is set on evil;* רע מעללים ψ 7^{10}, רע רשעים 1 S 25^{3}, cf. Mi 3^{4} (v. רֹעַ **3**); דִּבְרֵי רָע *deeds of evil* Je 5^{28}; תַּהְפֻּכוֹת רָע Pr 2^{14}; אֹרַח רע ψ 119^{101}; עֲצַת רע Ez 11^{2}; מַחְשְׁבוֹת רע Pr 15^{26}; אִישׁ רע 29^{6}; אַנְשֵׁי רע 28^{5}; אֵשֶׁת רע 6^{24} (but rd. רֵעַ Gr Bi Toy).

7451 רָעָה $_{310}$ **n.f.** evil, misery, distress, injury;—abs. ר׳ Gn 26^{29}+; cstr. רָעַת 6^{5}+; sf. רָעָתִי ψ 35^{4}+; רָעָתְךָ 1 K 2^{44}+; רָעָתֵכִי Je 11^{15} (txt. dub.); רָעַתְכֶם 1 S 12^{17}, etc.; pl. רָעוֹת Dt 31^{17}+; רָעֹת Je 44^{9} Ex 23^{2}; sf. רָעוֹתֵיכֶם 1 S 10^{19}+, etc.;—**1.** *evil, misery, distress:* פַּחַד רָעָה Pr 1^{33}, באה (ה)רעה Ez 7$^{5.5}$; c. עַל Is 47^{11} (read באה for בא), Je 5^{12}+5 t.; c. אֶל Je 2^{3} 51^{60}; †הביא רעה Je 4^{6} 1 K 21^{29}; +אֶל 2 S 17^{14}+8 t. K Je; +עַל 1 K 9^{9}=2 Ch 7^{22}, Je 19^{3}+6 t. Je+8 t.; +אֶל et עַל Je 19^{15} 36^{31}; יוֹם רעה 17$^{17.18}$+5 t.; יְמֵי הרעה †Ec 12^{1} (i.e., spring days, fatal to old people, Wetzst in De$^{\text{Koh. 447}}$); רָעוֹת *evils* Dt 31$^{17.17.21}$ (JE), 32^{23} (poem), ψ 34^{20} 40^{13} 88^{4}; עֵת רָעָה Am 5^{13} Je 2$^{27.28}$+5 t.; †ראה ברעה Nu 11^{15} (JE) Ob^{13} Est 8^{6}; †ראה רעה Je 44^{17} ψ 90^{15} Pr 22^{3}=27^{12}; †יפול ברעה 17^{20} 28^{14}; †בְּרָעָה Gn 44^{29} (J) Pr 14^{32} 24^{16} Ne 1^{3} 1 Ch 7^{23} ψ 107^{26}; ברעותיכם 141^{5}; נִחַם עַל רָעָה Ex 32$^{12.14}$ (J) Je 8^{6}+6 t.; c. אֶל 2 S 24^{16} Je 26$^{3.13.19}$ 42^{10}. **2.** *evil, injury, wrong:* †עשה רעה 2 S 12^{18} Je 26^{19} 41^{11}; c. עִם Gn 26^{29} (J) Ju 15^{3} 2 S 13^{16}; c. את Ju 11^{27}; c. ל 1 S 6^{9} 1 K 2^{44}+4 t.; c. אֶל Je 44^{7}; obj. of vbs. חשב Gn 50^{20} (E) Je 36^{3} 48^{2}+7 t.; †חרשׁ 1 S 23^{9} Pr 3^{29}; הֵשִׁיב Gn 50^{15} (E) Ju 9$^{56.57}$+4 t.; †גמל Gn 50^{17} (E) 1 S 24$^{18(17)}$ Is 3^{9} Pr 3^{30}; בקשׁ Nu 35^{23} (P) 1 S 24$^{10(9)}$ 25^{26}+4 t.; †שִׁלֵּם Gn 44^{4} (J) Je 18^{20} 51^{24} ψ 35^{12} 38^{21}; לְרָעָה *for harm* Gn 31^{52} Ex 23^{2} (E) Dt 29^{20} Ju 2^{15} 2 S 18^{32} Je 21^{10}+8 t. Je, Am 9^{4} Zc 1^{15} Pr 6^{18} Ec 5^{12}; בְּרָעָתֶךָ 2 S 16^{8} *in thy mischief;* בְּרָעָה Ex 32^{12} (J) *for mischief;* רָעָה רַבָּה Ec 2^{21}; רָעָה חוֹלָה Ec 5$^{12.15}$. **3.** *ethical evil,* 1 S 12$^{17.19}$ 24^{10} 20^{18} Is 47^{10} Je 2^{19} +13 t. Je, +18 t., +foll.: עָשָׂה (הָ)רָעָה Gn 39^{9} Dt 31^{18} (J) + 5 t. + Je 18^{10} (Kt, but Qr רע); שׁוּב מרעה Ec 8^{11}; מַעֲשֶׂה רעה אהב רעה Mi 3^{2} (Kt); Je 18^{8} 23^{14} 44^{5}; בִּעֵר רעה מ׳ Ju 20^{13} (v. II. רַע **3**); מפני רָעַת רעתכם Ho 10^{15}; מִפְּנֵי רָעָה Je 7^{12} 44^{3}; בגלל ר׳ Je 11^{17}; על כל ר׳ 1^{16} 32^{32} 33^{5}; מֵר׳ ψ 107^{34} Je 12^{4}; אַנְשֵׁי רָעָה Pr 24^{1}.

7489 [רָעַע] $_{98}$ **vb. denom.** be evil, bad;—†**Qal** *Pf.* 3 ms. רַע Nu 22^{34}+3 t., רָע 11^{10}; 3 fs. רָעָה Dt 15^{9} (Ex 21^{8} v. 1. רַע); *Impf.* 3 ms. יֵרַע (Ges$^{\S 67\,p}$) Gn 21^{12}+; 3 fs. תֵּרַע Dt 28$^{54.56}$; 3 mpl. יֵרְעוּ Ne 2^{3};—**1.** *be displeasing:* רַע בְּעֵינֵי Nu 11^{10} 22^{34} (J), Jos 24^{15} (E), Je 40^{4} Pr 24^{18} (c. וְ consec.) impf. יֵרַע בְּעֵינֵי Gn 21$^{11.12}$ (E), 48^{17} (J), 1 S 8^{6} 18^{8} 2 S 11^{25}; later, וַיֵּרַע אֶל Jon 4^{1} or וירע לְ Ne 2^{10} (intensified by רָעָה גְדוֹלָה, לִי מְאֹד) 13^{8}. **2.** *be sad:* ירע לבב Dt 15^{10} 1 S 1^{8}; יֵרְעוּ פָּנַי Ne 2^{3}. **3.** *be injurious, evil:* וַיֵּרַע לְ ψ 106^{32} *it went ill with* Moses, pers. subj. 2 S 20^{6}; רָעָה עַיִן *be grudging,* c. בְּ pers., Dt 15^{9} 28$^{54.56}$. **4.** *be evil, wicked,* ethically: וַיֵּרַע בְּעֵינֵי י׳ Gn 38^{10} (J) 2 S 11^{27} Is 59^{15}; בְּעֵינֵי אֱלֹהִים 1 Ch 21^{7}. † **Niph.** *suffer hurt:* *Impf.* 3 ms. יֵרוֹעַ (רַע) Pr 11^{15} 13^{20}. **Hiph.** $_{70}$ *Pf.* 3 ms. הֵרַע Ex 5^{23}+; 2 ms. הֲרֵעוֹתָ 1 K 17^{20}, etc.; *Impf.* 3 ms. יָרֵעַ Zp 1^{12}, וַיָּרַע 1 K 16^{25}; 2 ms. תָּרַע ψ 44^{3}+, etc.; *Inf. abs.* הָרֵעַ 1 S 12^{25} 1 Ch 21^{17}; *cstr.* הָרַע Gn 31^{7}+8 t., הָרֵעַ Is 1^{16}+4 t.; *Pt.* מֵרַע Is 9^{16} Pr 17^{4}; pl. מְרֵעִים Is 4827
1^{4}+;—**1.** *do an injury, hurt:* abs. Gn 44^{5} (J), Is 11^{9}=65^{25}, Je 31^{28} Pr 4^{16} 24^{8}; opp. היטיב Is 41^{23} Je 10^{5} Zp 1^{12} (all in prov. phr.=do anything at all, cf. רָע **2**); הרע ל Gn 19^{9} 43^{6} Ex 5$^{22.23}$ Nu 11^{11} (J) 20^{15} Jos 24^{20} (E)+5 t.; c. acc. pers. Nu 16^{15} (J)+4 t.; c. בְּ, 1 Ch 16^{22}=ψ 105^{15} (c. ל), Je 25^{29} ψ 74^{3}; c. עִמָּדִי Gn 31^{7} (E); c. על 1 K 17^{20} *bring evil upon;* swear לְהָרַע,=to one's hurt, ψ 15^{4} Lv 5^{4} (P); Pt.=subst. לְבָבָם לְמֵרָע Dn 11^{27} (shall be) *for mischief.* **2.** *do evil, wickedly:* abs. Gn 19^{7} (J) 1 S 12$^{25.25}$+6 t.; opp. היטיב Je 4^{22} 13^{23}; c. מִן comp., 1 K 14^{9} 16^{25} 2 K 21^{11} Je 7^{26} 16^{12}; c. acc. הֵרֵעוּ מַעַלְלֵיהֶם Mi 3^{4}, cf. 1 S 25^{3}; *Pt.* מֵרַע *evil doer,* Is 9^{16} Pr 17^{4}; pl. Je 20^{13} 23^{14} 4827
ψ 27^{2}+7 t.; זֶרַע מ׳ Is 1^{4} 14^{20}; בית מ׳ 31^{2}; עֲדַת מ׳ ψ 22^{17}; קְהַל מ׳ 26^{5}; סוד מ׳ 64^{3}.

†II. [רָעַע] **vb.** break (Aram. loan-word 7489
=Heb. רָצַץ q.v.);—**Qal** *Pf.* 3 pl. רָעוּ Je 11^{16}; *Impf.* 3 ms. יָרֹעַ Je 15^{12} Jb 34^{24}, 2 ms. sf. תְּרֹעֵם ψ 2^{9} (but v. infr.); *Inf. abs.* רֹעָה Is 24^{19} (del. ה as dittogr. and read רֹעַ, v. **Hithpō̄.**); *Pt.* f. הֲיָרֹעַ בַּרְזֶל רֹעָה (? for רֹעֲעָה) Pr 25^{19}:—**1.** trans. 7465
בַּרְזֶל וגו׳ Je 15^{12} *can one break iron, iron out of the north?* cf. יָרֹעַ כַּבִּירִים Jb 34^{24}; תְּרֹעֵם בְּשֵׁבֶט בַּרְזֶל ψ 2^{9} (but rd. תִּרְעֵם, v. I. רעה, 𝔊 𝔖 𝔙 Hup-Now al.). **2.** intrans. *break=be broken,* of branches Je 11^{16} (in fig.; Gf Or al.; >Hi Gie *are in a sad state,* √I. רעע); שֵׁן רֹעָה Pr 25^{19} *a broken tooth* (רֹעֲעָה=ר׳ ?; Frankenb **Niph.** *Pt.* נְרָעָה, cf. Toy, but Niph. not elsewhere; Vrss רָעָה *bad*).—רֹעוּ Is 8^{9} read דְּעוּ (𝔊 Lo Che al.,

|| הַאֲזִינוּ). **Hithpō'.** *Pf.* 3 fs. + **Qal** *Inf. abs.* (v. supr.) רֹעַ הִתְרֹעֲעָה [הָ]ארץ Is 24[19] *the earth is broken asunder* (|| מוֹט הִתְמוֹטְטָה, פּוֹר הִתְפּוֹרְרָה); also *Inf. cstr.* לְהִתְרוֹעֵעַ Pr 18[24] *will be broken in pieces* (Ges[§114 i]), *ruined,* De al., but < read
7462 לְהִתְרָעוֹת Vrss Toy al., v. II. רעה Hithp. (see, however, Dr[Expos. Times xi (1899-1900), 230f.]).

7491 †[רָעַף] **vb. trickle, drip,** synon. of נזל, II. ערף (cf. Ar. رَعَفَ *flow* (of blood), *bleed* (of the nose));—**Qal** *Impf.* 3 mpl. יִרְעֲפוּ, of clouds Jb 36[28] (c. עֲלֵי pers.; || יִזְּלוּ), c. acc. mat. טַל Pr 3[20]; fig. מַעְגָּלֶיךָ יִרְעֲפוּן דָּשֶׁן ψ 65[12] (i.e. fertilizing rain); subj. of moistened ground, נְאוֹת מִדְבָּר, v[13]. **Hiph.** *Imv.* mpl. הַרְעִיפוּ Is 45[8] *trickle,* O heavens, from above (fig.: || יִזְּלוּ צֶדֶק).

7492 †[רָעַץ] **vb. shatter** (Aram. רְעַץ *smite, shatter;* cf. perh. TelAm. *raḫâṣu,* Wkl[TelAm. 128, 31; 137, 32]);—*Impf.* 3 fs. יְמִינְךָ י׳ תִּרְעַץ אוֹיֵב Ex 15[6]; 3 m. pl. וַיִּרְעֲצוּ Ju 10[8], acc. pers. (of men; || וַיְרֹצְצוּ).

7493 †[רָעַשׁ] **vb. quake, shake,** intr. (NH = BH, so Aram. ܪܥܫ (rare), and (once) רְעַשׁ *toss, rage* (of sea); Ar. رَعَسَ, usu. رَعِشَ, رَعَشَ (loan-word?), *tremble, quiver, quake;* cf. perhaps As. *rêšu, exult*);—**Qal** *Pf.* 3 fs. רָעֲשָׁה Je 8[16] 49[21], רָעָשָׁה Ju 5[4] ψ 68[9]; 3 pl. רָעֲשׁוּ Jo 2[10] +, etc. *Impf.* 3 ms. יִרְעַשׁ ψ 72[16], 3 fpl. תִּרְעַשְׁנָה Ez 26[10], etc.; *Pt.* pl. רֹעֲשִׁים Je 4[24];—*quake, shake,* of earth Ju 5[4] = ψ 68[9], 2 S 22[8] (|| רגז) = ψ 18[8] (|| *id.*), ψ 77[19] (+ רגז), also Is 13[13] (c. מִמְּקוֹמוֹ + עַל־כֵּן, pregn.; || רָגַז), Je 51[29]; c. מִן caus. Je 8[16] 10[10] 49[21]; of מוֹסְדֵי אָרֶץ Is 24[18]; of heavens Jo 2[10] (לְפָנָיו caus.; || רָגְזָה); heavens and earth 4[16]; mts. Je 4[24] Na 1[5] (מִן pers. caus.), ψ 46[4] (ב caus.); walls Ez 26[10] (מִן caus.); אִיִּים v[15] (id.); מִגְרָשׁוֹת 27[28] (ל caus.); הַסִּפִּים Am 9[1]; all living things Ez 38[20] (מִפָּנַי caus.); of waving grain ψ 72[16]. **Niph.** נִרְעֲשָׁה הָאָרֶץ Je 50[46] *is made to quake* (מִקּוֹל). **Hiph.** *Pf.* 2 ms. הִרְעַשְׁתָּה ψ 60[4]; 1 s. הִרְעַשְׁתִּי Ez 31[16]; וְהִר׳ consec. Hg 2[7]; *Impf.* 2 ms. sf. 3 ms. (הֲ)תַרְעִישֶׁנּוּ Jb 39[20]; *Pt.* מַרְעִישׁ Is 14[16] + 2 t.;—**1.** *cause to quake,* subj. י׳, c. acc. of heavens, earth, nations, etc., Hg 2[6.7.21], cf. ψ 60[4]; nations + מִקּוֹל Ez 31[16]; subj. man, c. acc. of kingdoms Is 14[16] (|| מַרְגִּיז). **2.** *cause* (horse) *to spring, leap* (like locust), man subj., Jb 39[20].

7494 †רַעַשׁ **n.m.** [Je 10, 22] **quaking, shaking;**—ר׳ abs. 1 K 19[11] +, cstr. Na 3[2] Jb 41[21];—**1.** specif. *earthquake,* Am 1[1] Zc 14[5] 1 K 19[11.11.12]; fig. of י׳'s judgment Is 29[6] Ez 38[19]; cf. (in vision) קוֹל ר׳ גָּדוֹל 3[12.13]; prob. also 37[7] (𝔊 Thes Co Krae; > *rustling, rattling,* Hi-Sm Toy); hence hyperbol. of shaking of earth by tramping of warriors Is 9[4], by war-chariots Je 47[3], cf. 10[22], or wheels Na 3[2], by war-horse('s hoofs) Jb 39[24] (+ רֹגֶז). **2.** *quaking, trembling,* of pers. Ez 12[18]. **3.** *shaking, quivering,* of dart Jb 41[21] (al. *rushing sound*).

†רָפָא **vb. heal** (NH in deriv.; Ph. רפא, Syr. ܐܣܝ *heal;* on Aram. n.pr. cpd. with רפא v. Nö[ZMG xl (1886), 723] Lzb[369]; Sab. n.pr. אלרפא Langer[1,1] DHM[ZMG xxxvii (1883), 326]; Ar. رَفَأَ (and رَفَا) *darn, mend, repair, pacify;* Eth. ረፈአ: *stitch together, mend;* cf. Küchenmeister[ZWiss. Th. xxx (1887), 257 ff.]);—**Qal** *Pf.* 3 ms. consec. וְר׳ Is 6[10], sf. וּרְפָאָם 19[22], 1 s. sf. consec. וּרְפָאתִיו 57[19], etc.; *Impf.* 3 ms. יִרְפָּא 2 K 20[8] +, sf. יִרְפָּאֵנוּ Ho 6[1], 1 s. אֶרְפָּא Ho 14[5] +, אֶרְפָּה (Ges[§75 pp]) Je 3[22]; 3 fpl. תִּרְפֶּינָה (Id[ib. qq]) Jb 5[18], etc.; *Imv.* ms. רְפָא Nu 12[13], רְפָה (Id[ib. pp]) ψ 60[4], רְפָאָה 41[5], etc.; *Inf. abs.* רָפוֹא Is 19[22]; *cstr.* לִרְפֹּא Ho 5[13], etc.; *Pt.* רֹפֵא 2 K 20[5] +, etc.;—*heal:* **1.** lit., **a.** of God, c. acc. pers. Gn 20[17] (E), ψ 107[20] (sf.), c. ל pers. Nu 12[13] (JE) 2 K 20[5.8]. **b.** of men, abs. Ec 3[3] (opp. הרג); pt. as subst. *healer, physician,* Gn 50[2.2] (J) 2 Ch 16[12]. **2.** fig., *heal* hurts of nation, involving י׳'s (restored) favour (and, often, forgiveness): **a.** subj. י׳, c. sf. pers., Ho 6[1] 11[3] (yet cf. We Now), Ex 15[26] (J), Is 19[22 b] 57[18.19] Je 33[6] ψ 30[3], cf. 6[3]; c. acc. עַם 2 Ch 30[20], c. acc. אֶרֶץ 2 Ch 7[14]; c. ל of nation Ho 7[1], and (indef. subj.) Is 6[10] (lest) *one heal them* (= pass., *they be healed*); c. acc. of hurt, מַחַץ מַכָּתוֹ 30[26], שְׁבָרִים (of land) ψ 60[4], so מְשׁוּבָה Ho 14[5] Je 3[22] (incl. the *consequences* of backsliding); c. ל of hurt ψ 103[3]; acc. nation (personif.) + מִן of hurt Je 30[17] *I will heal thee of thy wounds* (|| אֶרְפָּאֵךְ); abs. Is 19[22 a] (opp. נגף), Dt 32[39] (opp. מחץ); pt. as subst. *healer, physician* Je 8[22]. **b.** human subj., c. ל of nation, Ho 5[13], cf. La 2[13]. **3. a.** fig., *heal* individ. distresses, c. sf. pers. Je 17[14], c. acc. נַפְשִׁי = *me* ψ 41[5], c. ל pers., לִשְׁבוּרֵי לֵב ψ 147[3] (i.e. longing exiles, cf. Is 61[3]); abs. Jb 5[18] (opp. מחץ); pt. as subst. Jb 13[4]. **Niph.** *Pf.* 3 ms. נִרְפָּא Lv 13[37] +, 3 fs. נִרְפָּתָה (Ges[§75 qq]) Je 51[9]; 3 pl. וְנִרְפְּאוּ consec. Ez 47[8]; *Impf.* 2 ms. תֵּרָפֵא Je 51[8]; 3 mpl. יֵרָפְאוּ Ez 47[9.11], וַיֵּרָפוּ (Ges[l.c.]) 2 K 2[22], etc.; *Inf. cstr.* הֵרָפֵא Je 15[18] +, הֵרָפֵה (Id[ib.]) Je 19[11];—*be healed:* **1.** lit., of pers. 1 S 6[3]; + acc. of disease Dt 28[27.35]; subj. disease Lv 13[18.37] 14[3.48]; of (bad) water 7495

2 K 2^{22}, salt waters (prediction), i.e. be made fresh, Ez $47^{8.9.11}$; of (broken) pottery, i.e. be made whole, Je 19^{11} (in sim.). **2.** fig., *be healed:* **a.** of national hurts, subj. city Je $51^{8.9}$; involving forgiveness and י׳'s blessing, impers. c. לְ of people, נִרְפָּא־לָנוּ Is 53^{5} i.e. *healing has come to us.* **b.** of personal distress, subj. pers. Je 17^{14}, subj. the distress 15^{18}. **Pi.** *Pf.* 1 s. רִפֵּאתִי 2 K 2^{21}; 2 mpl. רִפֵּאתֶם Ez 34^{4}; 1 pl. רִפֵּאנוּ Je 51^{9}; *Impf.* 3 ms. יְרַפֵּא Ex 21^{19} Zc 11^{16}, וַיְרַפֵּא 1 K 18^{30}; 3 mpl. וַיְרַפְּאוּ Je 6^{14}, וַיְרַפּוּ (Ges $^{§75\,qq}$) 8^{11}; *Inf. abs.* רַפֵּא Ex 21^{19};—*have healed, heal,* usu. human subj.: **1.** lit., רַפֵּא יְרַפֵּא Ex 21^{19} *he shall have (him) well healed;* c. acc. of altar, =*repair,* 1 K 18^{30}; c. לְ of water (subj. י׳) 2 K 2^{21}. **2.** fig. of healing national defects and hurts, acc. pers., Ez 34^{14} Zc 11^{16}; *work at healing, treat* (acc. of hurt) Je 6^{14} 8^{11} (both עַל־נְקַלָּה, v. [קָלַל] **Niph. 2**), 51^{9}. **Hithp.** *Inf. cstr.* of purpose, לְהִתְרַפֵּא, lit., *in order to get healed,* + מִן of wounds 2 K 8^{29}=9^{15}, so ‖ 2 Ch 22^{6} (rd. with 𝔊 מִן for כִּי, cf. Be Kau Benz).

7498 †I. רָפָא **n.pr.m.** in Benj., 1 Ch 8^{2}, Ραφη[α].—
1051, 7498 II. רָפָא v. רפה.—Vid. also בֵּית ר׳ p. 112. p. 952
7496-97 I, II. רְפָאִים v. sub רפה. p. 952
7498 †I. רָפָה **n.pr.m.** in Saul's line 1 Ch 8^{37}, Ραφαι(α), 𝔊L Αραχα; v. רְפָיָה.—II. ר׳ v. רפה.
7505 †רָפוּא **n.pr.m.** in Benj., Nu 13^{9}, Ραφου[αν].
7499 †[רְפֻאָה] **n.f.** remedy, medicine;—pl. abs. רְפֻאוֹת Ez 30^{21} Je 30^{13}, ־וֹת 46^{11} (all fig.).
7500 †רִפְאוּת **n.f.** healing;—ר׳ abs. Pr 3^{8} (fig.).
7501 †רְפָאֵל **n.pr.m.** Levite, 1 Ch 26^{7}, Ραφαηλ.
7509 †רְפָיָה **n.pr.m.** **1.** in David's family 1 Ch 3^{21}, Ραφαλ, A 𝔊L Ραφαια. **2.** in Simeon, 4^{42}, Ραφαια(ς). **3.** in Issachar, 7^{2}, Ραφαρα, A 𝔊L Ραφαια. **4.** descendant of Saul 9^{43}, Ραφαια, 𝔊L Αραχα (=רָפָה 8^{37}). **5.** post-ex. name Ne 3^{9}, Ραφαια(ς).
3416 †יִרְפְּאֵל **n.pr.loc.** in Benj., Jos 18^{27}, A 𝔊L Ιερφ(α)ηλ; unknown.
4832 †מַרְפֵּא, מַרְפֵּה **n.m.** $^{Ec\,10,\,4}$ **healing, cure, health** (usu. fig.);—abs. מַרְפֵּא Je 14^{19}+, מַרְפֵּה 8^{15}; cstr. מַרְפֵּא Pr 15^{4};—**1.** *healing, cure,* of national woes, Je 8^{15} 14^{19b} (‖ שָׁלוֹם), 36^{6} (+אֲרֻכָה); esp. אֵין לָנוּ מ׳ Je 14^{19a} *there is no cure for us,* עַד לְאֵין מ׳ 2 Ch 36^{16}. **2.** fig. of pers., *health, profit,* Pr 4^{22} (‖ חַיִּים), 12^{18} 13^{17} 16^{24}; with spiritual implic. Mal 3^{20}; אֵין מ׳ Pr 6^{15}=29^{1}; לֵב מ׳ 14^{30} *a mind of health* (healthy, composed, mind), cf. מ׳ alone=*composure* Ec 10^{4}; מ׳ לָשׁוֹן 15^{4} *healing of the tongue,* =a soothing tongue (Toy). **3.** lit., of disease, לְאֵין מ׳ 2 Ch 21^{18}.

†[רָפַד] **vb. spread** (As. *rapâdu, stretch oneself;* Ar. رَفَدَ *prop up, support, aid, give,* cf. **Pi.** infr.; Sab. רפדת pl. *protection, guard,* CIS $^{iv,\,no.\,40,3}$, cf. ארפד *terraces* DHM $^{Hofmus.}$);— **Qal** *Impf.* 3 ms. יִרְפַּד Jb 41^{22} *he* (the crocodile) *spreadeth a threshing-sledge upon the mud* (leaves marks upon it from his scales). **Pi.** *Pf.* 1 s. of couch (fig.) רִפַּדְתִּי יְצוּעָי Jb 17^{13}; then (*spread out* any support, hence) *Imv.* mpl. sf. רַפְּדוּנִי Ct 2^{5} *support me* with apples (‖ סַמְּכוּנִי). 7502

†[רְפִידָה] **n.f.** perh. **support** (cf. Ar. supr.), i.e. back, or arm, of palanquin; sf. רְפִידָתוֹ Ct 3^{10}; 𝔊 ἀνάκλιτον, 𝔙 *reclinatorium.* 7507

†רְפִידִים **n.pr.loc.** station of Isr. at Exodus (in P), Ex 17^{1} 19^{2}; רְפִידִם 17^{8} Nu $33^{14.15}$; Ραφιδειν. 7508
—אַרְפַּד v. p. 75. 774

†רָפָה **vb. sink, relax** (NH *id.,* so Aram. רפא (der. spec.), Zinj. רפה Aph., رَفُهَ; Ar. رَفَاهَةٌ *an easy life* is perhaps akin);—**Qal** *Pf.* 3 ms. Ju 19^{9} (yet v. infr.); 3 fs. רָפְתָה Ju 8^{3} Je 49^{24}, etc.; *Impf.* 3 ms. יִרְפֶּה Is 5^{24}, וַיִּרֶף Ex 4^{26} (v. infr.), etc.;—**1.** *sink down,* of hay in flame Is 5^{24}; *sink, decline,* of day Ju 19^{9} (si vera l.; 𝔊L κέκλικεν, GFM נָטָה [but how expl. the difficult רפה?]). Usu. **2.** *sink, drop* (of wings, v. **Pi.**), of hands, c. מִן Ne 6^{9} *their hands will drop from the work* (in fear); elsewh. abs. fig.=*lose heart, energy,* 2 S 4^{1} Is 13^{7} Je 6^{24} 50^{43} Ez 7^{17} 21^{12} Zp 3^{16}; יָדַיִם om. Je 49^{24}. **3.** *sink, relax, abate,* of temper Ju 8^{3} (+ מֵעַל pers.). **4.** *relax, withdraw,* subj. י׳, מִן pers. Ex 4^{26} (J), i.e. let one alone (but rd. perh. וַיֶּרֶף, v. **Hiph.**). **Niph.** *Pt.* pl. נִרְפִּים *idle* Ex $5^{8.17}$ (J). **Pi.** *Pf.* 3 ms. רִפָּה Jb 12^{21}; *Impf.* 3 fpl. תְּרַפֶּינָה Ez $1^{24.25}$; *Pt.* מְרַפֵּא (Ges $^{§75\,rr}$) Je 38^{4}; pl. מְרַפִּים Ezr 4^{4};—causat.: *let* wings *drop* Ez $1^{24.25}$ (rd. **Qal,** כנפיהם subj., 𝔊 Co Toy Krae al., who del. in v^{25}); loosen and *let drop,* girdle of mighty, fig. for *weaken* them Jb 12^{21}; c. acc. hands, fig. for *enfeeble, dishearten* Je 38^{4} Ezr 4^{4}. **Hiph.** *Impf.,* 3 ms. sf. יַרְפְּךָ Dt 4^{31}+; juss. 2 ms. תֶּרֶף Jos 10^{6}+, etc.; *Imv.* ms. הַרְפֵּה Ju 11^{37} 2 K 4^{27}; הֶרֶף Dt 9^{14}+; mpl. הַרְפּוּ ψ 46^{11}; —causat., **1.** *let drop,* the hand 2 S 24^{16}=1 Ch 21^{15}; fig., + מִן pers., =*abandon,* Jos 10^{6} (JE); 7503

perh. also (יָד om.)=*relax, refrain* Ex 4^{26} (rdg. וַיֶּרֶף, v. **Qal**); acc. rei,=*abandon, forsake*, Ne 6^{3}, so (subj. 'י) ψ 138^{8}; subj. 'י, c. acc. pers., Dt 4^{31} 31$^{6.8}$ Jos 1^{5} (D), 1 Ch 28^{20}. **2.** *let go*, sf. pers., Ct 3^{4} (opp. אחז); fig., acc. (om.) מוּסָר, Pr 4^{13} (opp. החזיק), צְדָקָה Jb 27^{6} (opp. *id.*). **3.** *refrain*, c. מִן pers., =*let* one *alone* Ju 11^{37} Dt 9^{14}, מִן of anger ψ 37^{8}; c. לְ pers. 1 S 11^{3} 2 K 4^{27}; acc. pers. Jb 7^{19}; abs. *let alone*, i.e. do nothing, be quiet, 1 S 15^{16} ψ 46^{11} (cf. Weir in Dr$^{1\,S\,15,16}$).—Je 3^{22} Jb 5^{18} ψ 60^{4} v. רָפָא. **Hithp.** *Pf.* 2 ms. הִתְרַפִּיתָ Pr 24^{10} *hast shewn thyself slack; Pt.* מִתְרַפֶּה 18^{9} *one shewing himself slack*, pl. מִתְרַפִּים Jos 18^{3}.—Vid. also רָפָא *heal.*

7504 †רָפֶה **adj. slack**;—abs. 'ר, of people, Nu 13^{18} (J); cstr. רְפֵה יָדַיִם 2 S 17^{2}, i.e. weak (‖ יָגֵעַ); fpl. יָדַיִם רָפוֹת, fig. of discouragement and fear
7503 Is 35^{3} Jb 4^{3}. Cf. √**Qal 2.** p. 951

7510 †[רִפָּיוֹן Ges$^{§\,85u}$, or רִפְיוֹן Sta$^{§\,296\,d}$ cf. Kö$^{ii.154}$] **n.[m.] sinking**;—cstr. רִפְיוֹן יָדַיִם Je 47^{3} *sinking of hands*, fig. of helpless terror.

7498 †II. רָפָה, II. רָפָא as **n.pr.m.**, alw. c. art. **Hā-Rāphā** (perh. der. fr. n.pr.gent. II. רְפָאִים, q.v.);—הָרָפָה 2 S 21$^{16.18}$, c. prep. 'לְהָ v$^{20.22}$= בִּילִדֵי הָר' לְהָרָפָא 1 Ch 20$^{6.8}$;—only as parent, 'יֻלַּד לְהָר 2 S 21$^{16.18}$ (=מִילִידֵי הָרְפָאִים 1 Ch 20^{4});
7498 v$^{20.22}$ ‖ 1 Ch 20$^{6.8}$.—I. רָפָה v. sub רָפָא. p. 951

7496 †I. רְפָאִים **n.m.**$^{Jb\,26,5}$ **pl. shades, ghosts** (by most connected with above √, as *sunken, powerless, ones*, Sta$^{G.\,i.420}$; Ph. רפאם);—Wisd. Lit. and late, name of dead in Sheʾôl, c. art. 'הָר Jb 26^{5}, elsewhere nearly= n.pr.: 'ר Is 14^{9} (in Sheʾôl), 26^{4} (‖ מֵתִים), ψ 88^{11} (‖ *id.*), Pr 2^{18} (‖ מָוֶת), 9^{18} (in עִמְקֵי שְׁאוֹל), קְהַל רְפָאִים 21^{16}; of righteous Isr. Is 26^{19} *earth shall cast forth* 'ר (‖ מֵתֶיךָ).

7497 †II. רְפָאִים **n.pr.gent.** old race of giants (perh.=I. 'ר, as extinct and *powerless;* v. esp. WRS in Dr$^{Dt\,2,11}$; or as shadowy, vaguely known, Schwally$^{ZAW\,xviii\,(1898),\,127\,ff.}$ v. also Sta$^{l.c.}$);—ancient inhab. of Canaan [W. of Jordan ?], Gn 15^{20} Jos 17^{15} (JE), cf. 1 Ch 20^{4} (v. II. רָפָה supr.); hence 'עֵמֶק ר, plain S. of Jerus. 2 S 5$^{18.22}$ 23^{13} 1 Ch 11^{15} 14^{9} Is 17^{5} Jos 15^{8} 18^{16} (P); 'ר E. of Jordan Dt 2^{11} (‖ עֲנָקִים; tall, cf. v^{10}), v^{20} (‖ *id.*; tall;= Zamzummim); in Bashan, Gn 14^{5}, Og the last of them Dt 3^{11} (of huge size), Jos 12^{4} 13^{12} (D); 'אֶרֶץ ר Dt 2^{20} 3^{13}. 𝔊 Ραφαειν[μ]; οἱ γίγαντες Gn 14^{5} + 4 t.; τῶν Τιτάνων 2 S 5$^{18.22}$ + (𝔊L) 23^{13}.

7383 רִפוֹת v. רִיפָה sub רִיף. p. 937

†רֶפַח **n.pr.m.** in Ephr., 1 Ch 7^{25}, Ραφη[α]. 7506

רְפָיָה **n.pr.m.** v. sub רפא. רִפְיוֹן v. רפה. above, p. 951 7509-10

†רָפַשׂ, רָפַס **vb.** stamp, tread, foul by stamping, treading (NH רָפַס *tread*, Syr. ܪܦܣ; cf. Ar. رَفَسَ *kick*);—**Qal** *Impf.* 2 ms. וַתִּרְפֹּס Ez 32^{2}, c. acc. rivers; 2 mpl. תִּרְפֹּשׂוּן 34^{18}. **Niph.** *Pt.* מַעְיָן נִרְפָּשׂ Pr 25^{26} *a fountain befouled.* **Hithp.** (*stamp oneself down*, then fig.), *Imv.* ms. הִתְרַפֵּס Pr 6^{3} *humble thyself*, become a suppliant (RV^{m} Toy *bestir thyself*, as conject.); *Pt.* מִתְרַפֵּס בְּרַצֵּי כָסֶף ψ 68^{31} *stamping, trampling, down pieces of silver* (?), obscure and prob. crpt., see conjj. in Bae al. and פַּתְרֹס supr., ad fin. 7511, 7515

†[מִרְפָּשׂ?] **n.[m.]** (water) **befouled** (by trampling);—cstr. מִרְפַּשׂ רַגְלֵיכֶם Ez 34^{19}. 4833

†[רַפְסֹדָה] **n.[f.]** raft (etym. dub.; NH once רַפְסוּדוֹת *bench* or *stool* on which feet rest);—pl. רַפְסֹדוֹת 2 Ch 2^{15} (late ‖ for דֹּבְרוֹת 1 K 5^{23}). 7513

†[רָפַף] **vb. Pōʿ.** shake, rock (Aram. רְפַף, ܪܦ *move gently;* Ar. رَفَّ *quiver, flash, throb;* also NH רִפְרֵף *flutter*, Ar. رَفْرَفَ *flutter, flap wings*);—*Impf.* 3 mpl. עַמּוּדֵי שָׁמַיִם יְרוֹפָפוּ Jb 26^{11}. 7322

†[רָפַק] **vb. Hithp. support oneself, lean** (Eth. ረፈቀ: *reclinare, accumbere* ad mensam; cf. Ar. رَفَقَ *be gentle, bind camel's arm to prevent going quickly;* مِرْفَقٌ, NH מַרְפֵּק, J Aram. מַרְפְּקָא, *elbow*);—*Pt.* f. מִתְרַפֶּקֶת Ct 8^{5} (c. עַל pers.). 7514

רפשׂ v. רפס. above 7511, 7515

רפשׁ (√ of foll.; NH רֶפֶשׁ = BH; Schulthess$^{71\,f.}$ cp. Ar. رَفَثَ *talk* or *act obscenely*, and a Syr. ܪܦܫܐ *slag, refuse* (not in PS Brock al.)).

†רֶפֶשׁ **n.[m.]** mire;—Is 57^{20} (+ טִיט). 7516

†[רֶפֶת] **n.[m.]** appar. **stable, stall** (NH *id.;* √dub.; Thes fr. רפף, cf. Ar. رَفٌّ *enclosure for sheep and goats*, but no satisfactory meaning of רפף known);—pl. רְפָתִים Hb 3^{17} (for cattle). 7517

רָץ v. רוץ. [רַץ] v. רצץ. p. 954 7323, 7518

†[רָצָא] **vb.** si vera l., ‖ form of רוץ *run*, *Inf. abs.* רָצוֹא Ez 1^{14}, but rd. יָצוֹא (יָצָאוּ) Hi-Sm Co Toy, cf. Krae Berthol al.; 𝔊 om. verse and most mod. think interpol.—Vid. also רצה. p. 953 7519 7521

†[רָצַד] **vb. Pi. watch** stealthily, or with envious hostility (Ar. رَصَدَ *watch* or *wait* (oft. *lie* 7520

in wait) for; ירצד Ecclus 14^{22} *observe stealthily,* so once Aram. רְצַד Levy$^{NHWB\ iv.\ 464}$);—only *Impf.* 2 mpl. תְּרַצְּדוּן ψ 68^{17} (fig. of mts., c. acc.).

7521 †**רָצָה vb. be pleased with, accept favourably** (NH *id., will, be willing;* Ar. رَضِيَ (orig. و) *be well pleased with,* Nö$^{ZMG\ liv\ (1900),\ 155}$; Sab. רצו *favour* CIS$^{iv,\ no.\ 77,\ 9\ al.}$, cf. Hom$^{Südar.\ Chrest.\ 123}$, רצים *good, acceptable,* CIS$^{iv,\ no.\ 73,\ 9,\ al.}$, of a coin, *good,* Id$^{ib.\ no.\ 21,\ 5}$; Aram. רְעָא, رُعا *have pleasure in,* cf. II. רָעָה supr.);—**Qal** *Pf.* 3 ms. ר׳ Ec 9^7; sf. רָצָם Je 14^{10}; 1 s. וְרָצְאתִי Ez 43^{27} consec. (metapl. Ges$^{§\ 75\ rr}$; Aramaism, Krae; but Co וְרָצִיתִי), etc.; *Impf.* 3 ms. יִרְצֶה ψ 147^{10}+, sf. יִרְצְךָ Mal 1^8; 3 fs. juss. תִּרֶץ Lv 26^{43}; 3 fpl. תִּרְצֶנָה Pr 23^6 Kt (< Qr תִּצֹּרְנָה, √נצר, cf. Toy), etc.; *Imv.* רְצֵה ψ 40^{14} 119^{108}; *Inf. cstr.* רְצוֹת Pr 16^7 ψ 77^8, etc.; *Pt.* רוֹצֶה 147^{11} 149^4, sf. רֹצָם Je 14^{12}; pass. רָצוּי Est 10^3, cstr. רְצוּי Dt 33^{24};—**1.** *be pleased with, favourable to:* **a.** of God, c. acc. pers. Is 42^1 ψ 44^4 147^{11} Jb 33^{26}; c. acc. rei ψ 85^2 1 Ch 29^{17} Pr 16^7 Ec 9^7; c. ב pers. ψ 149^4; ב rei 147^{10} Hg 1^8; abs. ψ 77^8. **b.** of men: c. acc. pers., subj. father Mal 1^8, ‖ אהב Pr 3^{12}; of brother Gn 33^{10} (JE), monarch 2 Ch 10^7; c. acc. rei ψ 62^5 102^{15} Jb 14^6 Pr 23^{26} (but v. supr.); c. בְּ rei 1 Ch 29^3 ψ 49^{14}; עִם pers. Jb 34^9 ψ 50^{18}; pt. pass. רָצוּי *favoured, acceptable to* Dt 33^{24} (poem), Est 10^3. **2.** *accept:* of God, c. acc. pers., sacrificing, 2 S 24^{23} Ho 8^{13} Je $14^{10.12}$ Ez $20^{40.41}$ 43^{27}; c. acc. of sacrifice Dt 33^{11} Mal $1^{10.13}$ ψ 51^{18} 119^{108}; c. בְּ of sacrifice Mi 6^7; abs. Am 5^{22}. **3.** *be pleased:* **a.** *determined,* c. inf. ψ 40^{14}. **b.** c. בּ pers. 1 Ch 28^4. **4.** *make acceptable, satisfy* (by paying off debt), subj. land, paying off its sabbaths (Di Dr al. *accept,* be satisfied with [in payment]) Lv $26^{34.43}$ 2 Ch 36^{21}, c. acc. of guilt incurred (עָוֹן) Lv $26^{41.43}$ (< point all these as **Hiph.**, so SS Gerber). **Niph.** *Pf.* 3 ms. נִרְצָה Lv 1^4 Is 40^2; *Impf.* 3 ms. יֵרָצֶה Lv 7^{18}+, etc.;—**1.** pass. of **Qal 2**, *be accepted,* of sacrifices, c. לְ pers., Lv 1^4 22^{25}; c. לְ of sacrifice $22^{23.27}$; abs. 7^{18} 19^7. **2.** pass. of **Qal 4**: נִרְצָה עֲוֹנָהּ Is 40^2 *her punishment is accepted* (as satisfactory). **Pi.** *Impf.* 3 mpl. יְרַצּוּ Jb 20^{10}, c. acc. דַּלִּים *seek the favour of the poor* (but Bu SS Gerber from רצץ). **Hiph.** *Pf.* 3 fs. וְהִרְצָת (Ges$^{§\ 75\ m}$) consec. Lv 26^{34} *the land shall pay off her sabbaths* (acc.), cf. **Qal 4**. **Hithp.** *Impf.* 3 ms. יִתְרַצֶּה 1 S 29^4 with what *shall he make himself acceptable unto* (אֶל) his lord? + 3 mpl. יִתְרַצּוּ Ho 4^{10} 𝔊 We Now (for MT יפרצו) *they shall* not *have delight.*

†**רָצוֹן n.[m.] goodwill, favour, acceptance, will;**—abs. ר׳ Dt 33^{23}+; cstr. רְצוֹן ψ 145^{19}+; sf. רְצוֹנִי Is 60^{10}, רְצֹנוֹ Dn 8^4+, etc.;—**1.** *goodwill, favour:* **a.** of God, Dt 33^{16} Is 60^{10} ψ 5^{13} $30^{6.8}$ 51^{20} 89^{18} 106^4 Pr 8^{35} 12^2 18^{22}; עֵת ר׳ Is 49^8 ψ 69^{14}; יוֹם ר׳ Is 58^5; שְׁנַת־ר׳ Is 61^2; ‖ בְּרָכָה Dt 33^{23}; opp. תּוֹעֵבָה Pr $11^{1.20}$ 12^{22} 15^8. **b.** of men: in gen. Pr 10^{32} 11^{27} 14^9; of kings v^{35} $16^{13.15}$ 19^{12}. **2.** *acceptance,* of persons, offering sacrifice, לרצון לפני יהוה Ex 28^{38} (P); c. לְ pers. *for acceptance for him before* י׳; c. sf. pers. לרצנו Lv 1^3; abbrev. לְרָצוֹן לָכֶם 22^{20}, לרצנכם 19^5 $22^{19.29}$ 23^{11}, לרצון 22^{21} Is 56^7 Je 6^{20} ψ 19^{15} (of words; cf. Ho 14^3); על רצון Is 60^7 (read לְ, so Codd., v. Gi, also Du), רצון Mal 2^{13}. **3.** *will, desire, pleasure:* **a.** of God, עשה ר׳ *do* his *will* Ezr 10^{11} ψ 40^9 103^{21} 143^{10}. **b.** of man, עשה כרצונו *do according to his will,* exactly as he pleased, Dn 8^4 $11^{3.16.36}$ Ne 9^{24} Est 1^8 9^5, cf. Ne 9^{37}; *desire* ψ $145^{16.19}$ 2 Ch 15^{15}; = self-will Gn 49^6 (poem). 7522

†**תִּרְצָה n.pr.f.** et **loc.** (*pleasure, beauty*);—**1. f.** daughter of Ṣelophehad of Gilead Nu 26^{33} 27^1 36^{11} Jos 17^3; Θερσα. **2. loc.** old Can. city Jos 12^{24}, early cap. of N. Isr. (until Omri) 1 K 14^{17} (תִּרְצָתָה), $15^{21.33}$ $16^{6.8.9.9.15.17.23}$, Θαρσα, usu. Θερσα; Menahem's base of operations 2 K $15^{14.16}$ (Θαρσ(ε)ιλα v^{14}, Euseb$^{Onom.\ 263,\ 62,\ ed.\ Lag}$ cp. Θαρσιλα, village of Samaritans in Batanea, and Buhl$^{Geogr.\ 247}$ conj. *Tesîl,* 20 m. E. of Lake Gennesaret, but this too remote); in sim. of beauty (om. 𝔊) Ct 6^4 (‖ יְרוּשָׁלָ͏ִם);—site not certain; conj. are: *Tallûza,* just N. of Mt. Ebal (Rob$^{BR\ iii.\ 302\ f.}$), *Tayaṣir,* c. 10 m. further NE., > *eṭ-Ṭîre,* S. of Gerizim (see, on these, GASm$^{Geogr.\ 355}$ Buhl$^{Geogr.\ 203}$ Aglen$^{Hast.\ DB.\ s.v.}$). 8656

†**רָצַח vb. murder, slay** (NH (rare, also in deriv.) = BH; cf. Ar. رَضَحَ, رَضَخَ *break, bruise, crush*);—**Qal** *Pf.* 3 ms. consec. וְר׳ Nu 35^{27}, וּרְצָחוֹ Dt 22^{26}; 2 ms. רָצַחְתָּ(ה) 1 K 21^{19}, *Impf.* 3 ms. יִרְצַח Nu 35^{30} Dt 4^{42}; 2 ms. תִּרְצָח(-צַח) Ex 20^{13} = Dt 5^{17}; *Inf. abs.* רָצֹחַ Ho 4^2 Je 7^9; *Pt. act.* רֹצֵחַ Dt 19^3+, רוֹ׳ 4^{42}+;—*murder, slay,* with premeditation, Ex 20^{13} (E) = Dt 5^{17}, Ho 4^2 Je 7^9 1 K 21^{19} (all abs.); c. acc. pers. Dt 22^{26}, unawares Dt 4^{42}; *slay* as avenger Nu $35^{27.30}$ (P; ‖ הֵמִית v$^{19.21}$); esp. pt. as subst. = *slayer, manslayer,* without intent, Dt 4^{42} $19^{3.4.6}$; also in P: Nu $35^{6.11.12.25.26.27.28}$ Jos $20^{3.5.6}$ $21^{13.21.27.32.26}$ (van d. H., Baer, v^{38} Gi; all P); *murderer,* with intent, Nu $35^{16.16.17.17.18.18.19.21.21.30.31}$; 7523

also Jb 24[14]. **Niph.** *Impf.* 1 s. אֵרָצֵחַ Pr 22[13] *I shall be slain; Pt.* fs. as adj. אִשָּׁה הַנִּרְצָחָה Ju 20[4] *the murdered woman.* **Pi.** (intens.) *murder, assassinate:* 3 mpl. יְרַצְּחוּ Ho 6[9] (abs.), יְרַצֵּחוּ ψ 94[6] (acc. pers., ∥ הָרַג); ψ 62[4] v. infr.; *Pt.* מְרַצֵּחַ, as subst. 2 K 6[32] *murderer, assassin;* pl. מְרַצְּחִים Is 1[21] *assassins.* **Pu.** *Impf.*, 2 mpl. תְּרָצְּחוּ ψ 62[4], so Baer Gi, van d. H. תְּרָצְחוּ, but Ben Napht. **Pi.** תְּרַצְּחוּ (Baer[143]), so Vrss Hup-Now De Che Bae al. *ye murder* (or *batter, shatter*).

7524 †רֶצַח **n.[m.] shattering**;—בְּרֶ׳ בְּעַצְמוֹתַי ψ 42[11] *with a shattering in my bones,* fig. of effect of sneering words (Codd. כְּרֶ׳; Ol Gr Che We כְּרָקָב); appar. *slaughter* Ez 21[27], but 𝔊 βοῇ (so ∥ תְּרוּעָה), Co רִנָּה, Houb (in Rosenm) צֶרַח, so Berthol Toy Krae.

7525 †רִצְיָא **n.pr.m.** in Asher 1 Ch 7[39], Ρασ(ε)ια.

7526 †רְצִין **n.pr.m. 1.** king of Aram, Ahaz's time: 2 K 15[37] 16[5.6.9] Is 7[1.4.8] 8[6] 9[10]; Ρα(α)σ(σ)ων, Ρασειν. **2.** Ezr 2[48]=Ne 7[50], Ρα(α)σων.

7527 †רָצַע **vb. bore, pierce** (NH=BH; Ar. رَصَعَ *stab violently*);—**Qal** *Pf.* 3 ms. consec. וְרָ׳ Ex 21[6] (E) he *shall pierce* his ear (acc., בּ instr.).

4836 †מַרְצֵעַ **n.[m.] boring-instrument, awl**;—abs. מ׳ Ex 21[6] (E), Dt 15[17].

7528 †I. [רָצַף] **vb. fit together, fit out,** si vera l. (Ecclus 43[8d] id. Pi. *pave* (fig.; si vera l.); As. *raṣâpu, join together, build;* Ar. رَصَفَ *join together,* cf. DHM[VOJ i. 30], Sab. רצף, רצפם Id[ib.] Hal[JAS, 1872, Juin, 534]; Aram. רְצַף, ܪܨܰܦ, *arrange in a line;* cf. Aram. רִצְפְּתָא, ܪܨܺܝܦܳܐ, NH רִצְפָּה, all = *pavement*);—**Qal** *Pt. pass.* תּוֹכוֹ רָצוּף אַהֲבָה Ct 3[10] *its interior fitted out* (?) *with love* (Gr al. הָבְנִי *ebony*).

7531 †רִצְפָה **n. f. pavement**; — abs. ר׳ Ez
7531 40[17.17]+, cstr. רִצְפַת Est 1[6] (van d. H. רִצְפָּה, -פַּת);—*pavement,* in Ezek.'s temple, Ez 40[17.17.18.18] 42[3]; Sol.'s temple 2 Ch 7[3]; in a palace Est 1[6].

4837 †מַרְצֶפֶת **n.f. id.**;—cstr. מ׳ אֲבָנִים 2 K 16[17].

II. רצף (√ of foll.; prob. *glow,* cf. Ar. رَضَفَ *heated stone,* رَضَفَ *cauterize, roast;* Syr. ܪܶܨܦܳܐ *bread baked in ashes* (coals), cf. Rob[BR i. 485, ii. 117, 262]).

7531 †I. רִצְפָּה **n. f. glowing stone** (or coal) (We[Isr. u. Jüd. Gesch. (3) 83]);—ר׳ abs. Is 6[6]; pl. עֻגַת
7529 רְצָפִים 1 K 19[6] (cf. Syr. supr.).

7530 †רֶצֶף **n.pr.loc.** conquered by Assyr. (As. *Raṣappa,* COT[2 K 19, 12] Schr[KGF 167] Dl[Pa 297]; prob. =Ῥησάφα Ptol[v. 18]);—2 K 19[12]=Is 37[12], Ραφε(ι)ς, Ραφεθ; mod. *Ruṣâfa,* between Palmyra and the Euphrates Dl[l. c.] Peters[Nippur i. 105].

†II. רִצְפָּה **n.pr.f.** concubine of Saul, 2 S 3[7] 7532
21[8.10.11], Ρεσφα.

רְצָפִים v. I. רִצְפָּה. above 7529, 7531

†[רָצַץ] **vb. crush** (NH=BH; Ar. رَضَّ 7533
bruise, bray, crush; Aram. רְעַע, ܪܰܥ *crush, shatter*);—**Qal** *Pf.* 2 ms. sf. רַצּוֹתָנוּ 1 S 12[4]; 1 s. רַצּוֹתִי v[3]; *Impf.* 3 ms. יָרוּץ (Ges[§ 67q]) Is 42[4] (Cod. Bab. יֵרוֹץ, Niph., so SS here and Ec 12[6a]), 3 fs. תָּרוּץ Ec 12[6a], 1 s. אָרֻץ ψ 18[30]=אָרוּץ 2 S 22[30] (v. infr.); *Pt. act.* fpl. רֹצְצוֹת Am 4[1]; *pass.* רָצוּץ Is 42[3]+, cstr. רְצוּץ Ho 5[11]; pl. רְצוּצִים Is 58[6];—*crush:* **1.** lit., **a.** *pt. pass.* in (הַ)קָּנֶה (הָ)רָצוּץ 2 K 18[21]=Is 36[6], Is 42[3] (all metaph. of weak pers.). **b.** impf. intrans. *get crushed* (rd. תֵּרוֹץ ?), of bowl Ec 12[6a] (in metaph.). **2.** fig. *crush, oppress,* acc. pers. 1 S 12[3.4] Am 4[1]; pt. pass. Dt 28[33], as subst. *the oppressed* Is 58[6]; רְצוּץ מִשְׁפָּט Ho 5[11] (We Now רֹצֵץ, i.e. *perverting judgment,* but dub.); intrans. *get crushed* (rd. יֵרוֹץ ?), of servant of י׳, under fig. of wick, Is 42[4] (+ יִכְהֶה) he shall not grow dim or *be crushed out.* **Niph.** *be crushed, broken: Pf.* 3 ms. consec. וְנָרֹץ (Ges[§ 67t]) Ec 12[6b] (of wheel at cistern); *Impf.* 2 ms. תֵּרוֹץ Ez 29[7] (of Pharaoh as reed, cf. **Qal 1 a**); Jb 20[10] rd. perh. יֵרֹצּוּ (for יְרַצּוּ, v. רצה Pi.), *are crushed* (as) poor men, Bu, cf. Hoffm SS Gerber. —Is 42[2] Ec 12[6a] v. **Qal. Pi.** *crush in pieces:* **1.** lit. (in metaph.) *Pf.* 2 ms. רִצַּצְתָּ ψ 74[14] c. acc. rei. **2.** fig. = *grievously oppress,* 3 ms. רִצַּץ Jb 20[19]; *Impf.* 3 ms. וַיְרַצֵּץ מִן הָעָם 2 Ch 16[10]. **Pōʿēl** *Impf.* 3 mpl. וַיְרֹצְצוּ Ju 10[8], acc. pers. (=**Pi. 2**; ∥ רעץ; רצץ here perh. doublet, so GFM[Hpt], cf. Bu Now). **Hiph.** *Impf.* 3 fs. וַתָּרִץ (Kö[i. 352]; Ba[ZMG xliii (1889), 181] thinks **Qal**) Ju 9[53] *she crushed his skull.* **Hithpō.** recipr., *Impf.* 3 mpl. וַיִּתְרֹצְצוּ הַבָּנִים בְּקִרְבָּהּ Gn 25[22] (J) *the children crushed* (thrust, struck) *one another within her.*

†[רַץ] **n.[m.]** usu. **piece, bar** (?), in phr. 7518
מִתְרַפֵּס בְּרַצֵּי כָסֶף ψ 68[31], but very obscure and dub.; Aq. 𝔙 *wheels;* 𝔊 Symm צְרֻפֵי; Che בִּבְצָרֵי כ׳, or בְּבֶצַע כ׳, or (JBL[xi (1892), 125]) בִּרְצֵי כֶסֶף (i.e. mercenaries); Pott We בִּרְצֵי כָזָב; Du בִּרְצֵי סִפֵּף.

†II. מְרוּצָה **n.f. crushing, oppression**;— 4835
Je 22[17] (+הָעֹשֶׁק). p. 930 4794

רַק v. I. רקק; רֵק v. רֵיק; רֹק v. II. רקק. 7386, 7534-36
p. 938, 956

7537 [רָקֵב] **vb.** rot (NH *id.*; Aram. רקב in deriv.);—**Qal** *Impf.* 3 ms. יִרְקָב Is 40^{20} (of tree); fig. שֵׁם רְשָׁעִים יִרְקָב Pr 10^{7} (Krochm al. יוּקָּב *be cursed*, √קבב, cf. Toy).

7538 †רָקָב **n.[m.]** **rottenness, decay** (always fig.);—ר׳ abs.; appar. of ravages of worm, in בֵּית יְהוּדָה, in fig. Ho 5^{12} (‖ עָשׁ), cf. Jb 13^{28} (‖*id.*); elsewhere of decay of bones, *caries* (in fig.), ר׳ בְּעַצְמ׳ Hb 3^{16} Pr 12^{4}, cstr. רְקַב עַצְמ׳ 14^{30}.

7539 †רִקָּבוֹן **n.[m.]** **id.**;—עֵץ ר׳ Jb 41^{19} *wood of rottenness*, =*rotten wood* (in fig.).

7540 †רָקַד **vb.** **skip about** (NH Pi. Hiph.=BH; so Aram. רְקַד Pa., ܪܩܰܕ Pa.; As. *raḳâdu*, *skip, dance*; Ar. رَقَدَ IX. *run with leaps and bounds*, رَقَدَانٌ *leaping up briskly*);—**Qal** *skip about*, *Pf.* 3 mpl. רָקְדוּ ψ 114^{4} (of mts., כְּאֵילִים); *Impf.* 2 mpl. תִּרְקְדוּ v^{6} (id.; both of Sinai quaking at law-giving); *Inf.cstr.* עֵת רְקוֹד Ec 3^{4} a time to mourn (סְפוֹד), and *a time to skip about* (gaily). **Pi.** *dance, leap*: *Impf.* 3 mpl. יְרַקְּדוּ Is 13^{21} (of שְׂעִירִים); יְרַקֵּדוּן Jb 21^{11} (of children; merrily), Jo 2^{5} (of locusts); *Pt.* מְרַקֵּד 1 Ch 15^{29} (of David; =מְפַזֵּז, מְכַרְכֵּר, in ‖ 2 S 6$^{14.16}$); fs. מְרַקֵּדָה Na 3^{2} (of jolting chariots); in 2 S 6^{21a} ins. אֲרַקֵּד *I will dance*, after לִפְנֵי י׳, 𝔊 ThWe Dr Bu HPS (מְרַקֵּד). **Hiph.** *Impf.* 3 ms. sf. וַיַּרְקִידֵם ψ 29^{6} *he* (י׳) *made them skip* like calves (trees, by lightning).

7541-42 רַקָּה v. I. רקק. רַקּוֹן v. II. רקק. p. 956

7543 †[רָקַח] **vb.** **mix, or compound oil, ointment** (perh. denom.; in this case √ meaning unknown; NH has מִרְקַחַת *ointment*; Ph. רקח either *spice-mixer* (Bloch) or *spice-dealer* (Lzb); perh. akin to As. *riḳḳu, spice*, Meissn[Suppl. 90], cf. *rikkê*, Dl[HWB 620]);—**Qal** *Impf.* 3 ms. יִרְקַח Ex 30^{33}; *Pt.* רֹקֵחַ v$^{25.35}$, רוֹ׳ 37^{29} Ec 10^{1}; pl. cstr. רֹקְחֵי 1 Ch 9^{39};—*mix, compound*, Ex 30^{33} (P; כָּמֹהוּ, i.e. anything like the holy oil); pt. as subst. רֹקְחֵי הַמִּרְקַחַת 1 Ch 9^{30} *compounders of the ointment*; as a professional name, *mixer, perfumer*, Ex 30$^{25.35}$ 37^{29} Ec 10^{1}. **Pu.** *Pt.* mpl. מְרֻקָּחִים 2 Ch 16^{14} *mixed as ointment.* **Hiph.** *Inf. abs.* הַרְקַח הַמֶּרְקָחָה Ez 24^{10} (‖ הָתֵם), as Imv., *spice the spicing* (?), i.e. spice (the meat) well, but very dub., Krae prop. הָרֵק הַמָּרָק *empty out the broth.*

7544 †רֶקַח **n.[m.]** **spice**;—יֵין הָר׳ Ct 8^{2} wine, (that is) *spice* (i.e. spiced wine).

7545 †רֹקַח **n.[m.]** **spice-mixture, perfume**;—of holy oil, ר׳ מִרְקַחַת מַעֲשֵׂה רֹקֵחַ Ex 30^{25}; of incense, ר׳ מַעֲשֵׂה רוֹקֵחַ v^{35}.

†[רַקָּח] **n. m.** **ointment-maker, perfumer**;—only in phr. בֶּן־הָרַקָּחִים Ne 3^{8}, i.e. one of the perfumers, i.e. of that guild. 7546

†[רַקָּחָה] **n.f.** (female) **ointment-maker, perfumer**;—pl. רַקָּחוֹת 1 S 8^{13} (+ טַבָּחוֹת, אֹפוֹת). 7548

†[רִקּוּחַ] **n.[m.]** **perfumery**;—pl. sf. רִקֻּחַיִךְ Is 57^{9} *thy perfumeries, unguents.* 7547

†[מֶרְקָח] **n.[m.]** **spice, perfume** (of 4840
cheeks); pl. מֶרְקָחִים Ct 5^{13} (v. also מִגְדָּל **3**). p. 153 4026

†מֶרְקָחָה **n.f.** **1. ointment-pot**, in which ointment is compounded, Jb 41^{23} (fig.). **2. spice-seasoning** (?); as acc. cogn. v. √ **Hiph.** 4841

†מִרְקַחַת **n.f.** **1. ointment-mixture. 2. ointment-pot** (?);—**1.** abs. רֹקְחֵי הַמּ׳ 1 Ch 9^{30}; רֹקַח מ׳ Ex 30^{25}. **2.** בַּמּ׳ 2 Ch 16^{14} *in an ointment-pot* (?), or *as an ointment-mixture.* 4842

†[רָקַם] **vb.** **variegate** (NH *id.*; so Ar. رَقَمَ, Eth. ረቀመ:, cf. 𝔗 רִקְמָתָא, רְקַם *variegated cloth or skin*, Syr. ܪܘܩܡ̈ܐ *freckles*);—**Qal** *Pt. act.* רֹקֵם, as subst. *variegator*, worker (weaver) in colours, c. ב mater. Ex 38^{23}, מְלֶאכֶת חָרָשׁ וְחֹשֵׁב וְר׳ 35^{35}; esp. מַעֲשֵׂה ר׳ *variegator's work* 26^{36} 27^{16} 28^{39} = 36^{37} 38^{18} 39^{29} (all P; all c. mater. exc. 28^{39}). **Pu.** *Pf.* 1 s. רֻקַּמְתִּי ψ 139^{15} *I was skilfully wrought* (woven, ‖ סכך v^{13}). 7551

†רִקְמָה **n.f.** **variegated stuff** (woven or embroidered);—abs. ר׳ Ju 5^{30}+; sf. רִקְמָתֵךְ Ez 16^{18}, ־תָם 26^{16}; du. רִקְמָתַיִם Ju 5^{30}; pl. רְקָמוֹת ψ 45^{15};—(piece of) *variegated stuff*, Ju 5$^{30.30}$, for garments Ez 16$^{10.13}$ 27$^{16.24}$ ψ 45^{15}; explicitly, בִּגְדֵי ר׳ Ez 16^{18} 26^{16}; ר׳ appar. =*variegated work* 27^{7}; fig. of variegated plumage 17^{3}; of variegated stone 1 Ch 29^{2}. 7553

†רֶקֶם **n.pr.** **1. m. a.** a king of Midian Nu 31^{8} (Ροκομ), Jos 13^{21} (Ροβοκ, A Ροκομ, 𝔊 Ορoκομ). **b.** a 'son' of Hebron 1 Ch 2$^{43.44}$, Ρεκομ, Ροκομ, Ρωκημ. **c.** name in Gilead 1 Ch 7^{16}, 𝔊L Ρακαμ. **2. loc.** in Benj., Jos 18^{27}, Νακαν, A𝔊L Ρεκεμ[ν]. 7552

†[רָקַע] **vb.** **beat, stamp, beat out, spread out** (NH *id.*; Hiph., Aram. רְקַע Aph., both *spread out*, and deriv.; Syr. ܪܩܰܥ *press down* (Lk 6^{38} 𝔖), *spread out*, also *consolidate*; Ar. رَقَعَ *patch, put on a patch, repair*, cf. Chr.-Pal. ܡܪܩܥܐ *patch*, ܡܪܩܘܥܝܬܐ *swaddling-bands*, Schwally[Idiot. 90]; Ph. מרקע *platter*, or *bowl*, of gold CIS[I. 90, 1]);—**Qal** *Impf.* 1 s. sf. אֶרְקָעֵם 2 S 7554

22^{43} *I will stamp them down* (prob. gloss to אֲדִקֵּם preceding, cf. Bae$^{\psi 18, 43}$); *Imv.* רְקַע בְּרַגְלְךָ Ez 6^{11} *beat* (stamp) with thy foot, in token of contemptuous pleasure, cf. Da (‖ הַכֵּה בְכַפְּךָ); so *Inf. cstr.* sf. רַקְעֲךָ בְּרֶגֶל 25^{6} (‖ מַחְאֲךָ יָד); *Pt. act.* as subst. cstr. (Ges$^{§ 65 d}$) רֹקַע הָאָרֶץ (i.e. י׳) *he that* (beateth out) *spreadeth out the earth* Is 42^{5}, רֹקַע הָא׳ 44^{24}, רוֹקַע הָא׳ ψ 136^{6}. **Pi.** *Impf.* 3 ms. sf. בַּזָּהָב יְרַקְּעֶנּוּ Is 40^{19} a goldsmith *with gold overlayeth it* (lit. *beateth it out*); 3 mpl. וַיְרַקְּעוּ אֶת־פַּחֵי הַזָּהָב Ex 39^{3} *they beat out the plates of gold;* sf. וַיְרַקְּעוּם צִפּוּי Nu 17^{4} *they beat them out as plating.* **Pu.** *Pt.* כֶּסֶף מְרֻקָּע Je 10^{9} *silver beaten out.* **Hiph.** *Impf.* 2 ms. תַּרְקִיעַ עִמּוֹ לִשְׁחָקִים Jb 37^{18} *canst thou make with* (=like) *him a spreading for clouds* (spread out clouds; cf. רָקִיעַ)?

7549 † רָקִיעַ **n.m.**$^{Gn 1, 6}$ **extended surface,** (solid) **expanse** (as if *beaten out;* cf. Jb 37^{18});—abs. ר׳ Ez 1^{22}+, cstr. ר׳ Gn 1^{14}+;—𝔊 στερέωμα, 𝔙 *firmamentum,* cf. Syr. sub √ supr.;—**1.** (flat) *expanse* (as if of ice, cf. כְּעֵין הַקֶּרַח), as base, support (Wkl$^{Altor. Forsch. iv. 347}$) Ez 1$^{22.23.25}$ (gloss? cf. CoToy), v^{26} (supporting י׳'s throne). Hence (Co$^{Ez 1, 22}$) **2.** the vault of heaven, or 'firmament,' regarded by Hebrews as solid, and supporting 'waters' above it, Gn 1$^{6.7.7.7.8}$ (called שָׁמַיִם; all P), ψ 19^{2} (‖ הַשָּׁמַיִם), זֹהַר הָר׳ Dn 12^{3}; also ר׳ הַשָּׁמַיִם Gn 1$^{14.15.17}$, עַל־פְּנֵי ר׳ הַשּׁ׳ v^{20} (all P).

7555 † [רִקֻּעַ] **n. [m.] expansion;**— pl. cstr. וְעָשׂוּ אֹתָם רִקֻּעֵי פַחִים Nu 17^{3} *expansions of plates,* i.e. they shall be beaten into *broad plates.*

I. רקק (√ of foll.; Ar. رَقَّ *be thin,* also fig. *be weak, slender, scanty,* etc.; Eth. ረቀቀ: *be thin,* ረቂቅ: *thin;* Syr. ܪܩ Pa. Aph. *make thin,* ܪܩܝܩ *thin*).

7534-35 רַק †**1. adj. thin;**—fpl. רַקּוֹת, of kine, Gn

7535 41$^{19.20.27}$ (‖ v$^{3.4}$ דַּקּוֹת). **2.**$_{109}$ **adv.** with restrictive force, **only, altogether, surely** (syn. אַךְ);—**a.** *only,* Gn 14^{24} 41^{40} רַק הַכִּסֵּא אֶגְדַּל מִמֶּךָּ *only* as regards the throne, etc., 47^{22} רַק אַדְמַת הַכֹּהֲנִים לֹא קָנָה, 50^{8} Ex 8^{5} רַק בַּיְאֹר תִּשָּׁאַרְנָה, 10^{17} וְיָסֵר מֵעָלַי רַק הַמָּוֶת הַזֶּה *only* this death, Dt 2^{35} (cf. 20^{14} Jos 8$^{2.27}$), 3^{11} Ju 6^{39} (cf. אַךְ *ib.* Gn 18^{32} Ex 10^{17}), 11^{34} (circ. cl.) רַק הִיא יְחִידָה (there being) *only* she, an only one, 1 S 1^{13} Am 3^{2} רק אתכם ידעתי *only* you have I known, etc., Jb 1$^{15.16.17.19}$ וָאִמָּלְטָה רַק אֲנִי לְבַדִּי I *only,* ψ 91^{8}+ oft. Once strengthening אַךְ, †Nu 12^{2} הֲרַק אַךְ־בְּמֹשֶׁה דִּבֶּר י׳. And separated (as sts. in English) from the word actually emphasized, Pr 13^{10} רַק בְּזָדוֹן יִתֵּן מַצָּה by pride there *only* cometh [נָתַן **1 z**] contention. **b.** prefixed to *sentences,* to add a limitation on sthg. previously expressed (or implied), Gn 19^{8} *only* to these men do nothing, 24^{8} רַק אֶת־בְּנִי לֹא־תָשֵׁב הֵנָּה, Ex 8^{24} I will let you go . . ., *only* go not far, v^{25} Nu 20^{19} *only*—it is nothing—let me pass through on my feet (cf. Dt 2^{28}); esp. in Deut. writers, as Dt 10^{15} 12^{15} 20^{16} 1 K 3$^{2.3}$ (cf. 2 K 12^{4} 14^{4} 15$^{4.35}$), 8^{19} 11^{13} 15$^{14.23}$ 2 K 3^{2} (cf. 14^{3} 17^{2}), etc., Is 4^{1}; emphasizing a command, Dt 4^{9} 12$^{16.23}$ Jos 1$^{7.18}$ 6^{18} 13^{6} 22^{5} (all D^{2}). **c.** emphasizing single words, esp. adjj., *only*=*nought but, altogether,* Gn 6^{5} יֵצֶר מַחְשְׁבֹת לִבּוֹ רַק רַע is *only* evil, i.e. *exclusively* evil, *nought but* evil, Gn 26^{29} עָשִׂינוּ עִמְּךָ רַק טוֹב *nothing but* good, Dt 28^{33} וְהָיִיתָ רַק עָשׁוּק, Is 28^{19} רַק זְוָעָה it shall be *nought but* terror to, etc., 1 K 14^{8} (cf. אַךְ **2 b** β); sq. an adv. Dt 28^{13} וְהָיִיתָ רַק לְמַעְלָה above *only;* sq. a vb., Ju 14^{16} thou dost *but* hate me. †**d.** after a neg., *save, except* (syn. כִּי אִם **2 a**), 1 K 8^{9} (=2 Ch 5^{10}) אֵין בָּאָרוֹן רַק שְׁנֵי לֻחוֹת הָאֲבָנִים, 15^{5} 22^{16} (=2 Ch 18^{15}), 2 K 17^{18}. †**e.** with an affirmative, asseverative force, *only, altogether*=*surely,* Gn 20^{11} רַק אֵין יִרְאַת אלהים במקום הזה, Dt 4^{6} (so EV; but Ges populus *mere* sapiens, so Di), 1 K 21^{25} 2 Ch 28^{10} ψ 32^{6} רַק לְשֵׁטֶף מים רבים אליו לֹא יַגִּיעוּ. †**f.** רַק אִם (רַק prefixed for emph.) *if only, provided only,* Dt 15^{5} רַק אִם שמוע תשמע וג׳, 1 K 8^{25} (=2 Ch 6^{16}) רַק אִם ישמרו בניך דרכם ללכת וג׳, 2 K 21^{8} (=2 Ch 33^{8}).

† רָקִיק **n.m. a thin cake,** (RV) **wafer** (cf. 7550
Ar. رُقَاقَةٌ *a thin round cake of bread*), always of unleavened bread: Ex 29^{23}=Lv 8^{26} ר׳ אֶחָד, רְקִיק מַצָּה אֶחָד Nu 6^{19}, רְקִיקֵי מַצּוֹת Ex 29^{2} Lv 2^{4} 7^{12} Nu 6^{15} (all P), 1 Ch 23^{29}.—𝔊 λάγανον.

† רַקָּה **n.f. the temple** (of the head): Ju 4^{21} 7541
v^{22} 5^{26} וַתִּתְקַע הַיָּתֵד בְּרַקָּתוֹ, וּמָחֲצָה וְחָלְפָה רַקָּתוֹ, Ct 4^{3}=6^{7} כְּפֶלַח הָרִמּוֹן רַקָּתֵךְ.

II. [רָקַק] **vb. spit** (NH, Aram. רְקַק, ܪܩ, 7556
all=BH);—**Qal** *Impf.* 3 ms. יָרֹק Lv 15^{8}, c. בְּ
of pers. spit upon.—Cf. יָרַק. p. 349 3417

† רֹק **n.[m.] spittle;**—abs. ר׳ Is 50^{6} Jb 30^{10} 7536
(both of contemptuous spitting); sf. רֻקִּי 7^{19} while I swallow (בָּלְעִי) *my spittle,* i.e. for the briefest time.

† רַקּוֹן **n.pr.loc.** in Dan, הָר׳ Jos 19^{46}, prob. 7542
doublet of הַיַּרְקוֹן, om. 𝔊 Benn Steuern, cf. Di.

7557 **†רַקַּת n.pr.loc.** in Naphtali, Jos 19^{35}; 𝔊 (Ομαθα) δακεθ, A Ρεκκαθ, 𝔊L Ρακκαθ; a Jewish trad. identified with Tiberias, Talm$^{Jer. Megilla 2 b}$ Nbr$^{Geogr. 208 f.}$ Buhl$^{Geogr. 226}$ GASm$^{Geogr. 447}$.

7326 **רָשׁ** v. רוּשׁ. p. 930

רשה (√ of foll.; cf. NH Hiph. *permit*, Hoph. Ecclus 3^{22}; JAram. רְשָׁא *have power*, Aph. *permit*; OAram. רשי *cause, occasion*, Lzb^{370}, Nab. *allowed*, Id$^{ib.}$; Syr. ܪܫܐ is usu. *blame*; As. *rašû, possess, râšû, creditor*; Ar. رَسَا(و) *be firm*, IV. *make firm*; Eth. ረሰየ: *set, put in, place over, prepare*, etc.; Sab. רשו *servant* of deity JHMordtm$^{ZMG xxx (1876), 31 f.}$).

7558 **†רִשְׁיוֹן n.[m.] permission**;—cstr. ר׳ Ezr 3^{7}.

7225 **רֵשִׁית** v. רֵאשִׁית sub **ראשׁ**. p. 912

7559 **†[רָשַׁם] vb. inscribe, note** (NH *id.*; so Aram. רְשַׁם, ܪܫܡ; Ar. رشم is loan-word Nö ZMG xxix (1875), 327 Frä 137. 250);—**Qal** *Pt. pass.* c. art. as subst. הָרָשׁוּם בִּכְתָב אֱמֶת Dn 10^{21} *that which is inscribed in the writing of truth.*

רשע (√ of foll.; opp. צדק; cf. Ar. رَسِعَ *be loose* (of limbs) Kam Frey; whence perh. *be* (*disjointed*), *ill regulated, abnormal, wicked*; NH רָשָׁע *criminal*, רִשְׁעָה *crime*, vb. Hiph. (denom.) *declare guilty*; Aram. רְשַׁע *be wicked*, ܪܫܥ Aph. *do wickedly*, and deriv.; Eth. ረስዐ: usu. *forget*, less oft. *err, be wicked*, ረሲዕ: *wicked* (loan-word fr. Syr. ܪܫܝܥܐ Schwally$^{ZMG lii (1898), 135}$)).

7563 **רָשָׁע**$_{263}$ **adj. wicked, criminal**;—abs. ר׳ Gn 18^{23}+; pl. רְשָׁעִים Is 13^{11}+; cstr. רִשְׁעֵי ψ 75^{9} + 3 t.; fs. רְשָׁעָה Ez 3^{18} (del. Co), v^{19} (רֶשַׁע Co);—†**1.** usu. as subst., *one guilty of crime*, deserving punishment; sts. also *wicked*; opp. צַדִּיק; רָשָׁע Ex 2^{13} 23^{1} (E), Dt 25^{2} Pr 17^{23} 18^{5} 25^{5} Jb 9$^{22.24}$; coll. Gn 18$^{23.25.25}$ (J) Mi 6^{10} Pr 3^{33} 28^{4}, רשׁעים 1 S 24^{14} Je 5^{26} Pr 19^{28} 20^{26} 29^{12}, אנשׁים רשׁעים 2 S 4^{11} (murderers), רָשָׁע לָמוּת Nu 35^{31} (P) *guilty of death*, מוֹשֵׁל ר׳ Pr 28^{15}, cf. 29^{2}, הִצְדִּיק ר׳ Ex 23^{7} (E) Is 5^{23} Pr 17^{15}; הִרְשִׁיעַ ר׳ Dt 25^{1} 1 K 8^{32} = השׁיב לְרָשָׁע 2 Ch 6^{23}; אמר לר׳ צַדִּיק Pr 24^{24}. **2.** *guilty of hostility* to God or his people, *wicked enemies*: רשׁע sg. ψ 17^{13} + 6 t. ψψ, Is 26^{10}; coll. ψ 9$^{6.17}$ 10^{2} + 6 t. ψψ, Is 11^{4} Hb 3^{13}; רשׁעים ψ 3^{8} 7^{10} 9^{18} + 5 t. ψψ, Is 48^{22} 57$^{20.21}$ Je 25^{31} Ez 21^{34} Mal 3^{21} (+ (poss.) other cases; often hard to decide); specif. of Pharaoh Ex 9^{27} (J), Babylon Is 13^{11} 14^{5}, Chaldeans Hb 1$^{4.13}$; ∥ שֹׂנְאֵי יהוה 2 Ch 19^{2}. **3.** *guilty of sin*, against either God or man, *wicked*: האנשׁים הרשׁעים Nu 16^{26} (J, rebellious Korahites), Mal 3^{18} (not serving י׳), opp. צַדִּיק; sg. indiv. Ez 3$^{18.18}$ 21^{30} 33$^{8.8}$ ψ 11^{5} 32^{10} Pr 9^{7}+; coll. Is 3^{11} Jb 34^{18} 36$^{6.17}$; pl. רשׁעים Is 53^{9} Je 23^{19} = 30^{23}, Zp 1^{3} ψ 26^{5} Pr 10^{3} Ec 8^{10}+; ∥ חסידים 1 S 2^{9} (poem), ψ 12^{9} 50^{16} 97^{10} 145^{20}; ∥ עֹזְבֵי תוֹרָתֶךָ 119^{53}, cf. v^{61}, +; †אדם ר׳ Pr 11^{7} Jb 20^{29} 27^{13}; †אִישׁ ר׳ Pr 21^{29}; מלאך ר׳ 13^{17}; זֶרַע רשׁעים ψ 37^{28}; †עֲצַת רשׁעים 1^{1} Jb 10^{3} 21^{16} 22^{18}; †דֶּרֶךְ רשׁעים Je 12^{1} ψ 1^{6} 146^{9} Pr 4^{19} 12^{26}; דֶּרֶךְ רשׁע 15^{9}; מִדַּרְכּוֹ הָרְשָׁעָה Ez 3$^{18.19}$ (but v. Co, supr.); †רִשְׁעֵי (ה)ארץ ψ 75^{9} 101^{8} 119^{119} Ez 7^{21} (𝔊 Co עריצי).—רָשָׁע is rare before exile; chiefly Ez ψψ WisdLit.

†רֶשַׁע n.m.$^{1 S 24, 14}$ **wickedness**;—abs. ר׳ Mi 7562
6^{10}+, רָשַׁע Ec 3^{16}; cstr. (perh.) רֶשַׁע 7^{25}; sf. רִשְׁעוֹ Dt 9^{27}+, etc.;—**1.** *wickedness*, as violence and crime against civil law Ec 3$^{16.16}$; אֶגְרֹף ר׳ Is 58^{4} *fist of wickedness*; חַרְצֻבּוֹת ר׳ v^{6}; לֶחֶם ר׳ Pr 4^{17}; מַטֵּה ר׳ Ez 7^{11}; מֹאזְנֵי ר׳ Mi 6^{11}; אֹצְרוֹת ר׳ v^{10}, cf. Pr 10^{2}; עשׂות ר׳ 16^{12}; בְּרֶשַׁע ψ 141^{4} Pr 12^{3}; מֵרְשָׁעִים יֵצֵא ר׳ 1 S 24^{14} (proverb). **2.** *wickedness* of enemies: of Egypt Ez 31^{11} (dub. Co; gloss Toy); שֵׁבֶט הר׳ ψ 125^{3} (𝔊 SS רָשָׁע). **3.** *wickedness*, in ethical relations: ∥ חטאת Dt 9^{27} (D^{2}); ∥ עון Je 14^{20}; ∥ עולה Ho 10^{13}; opp. צֶדֶק ψ 45^{8}, אֱמֶת Pr 8^{7}; v. also ψ 5^{5} 10^{15} Jb 34^{10} 35^{8} Ec 7^{25} 8^{8}; אַנְשֵׁי ר׳ Jb 34^{8}; אָהֳלֵי ר׳ ψ 84^{11}; שׁוּב
מֵרִשְׁעוֹ Ez 3^{19} 33^{12} (v. רִשְׁעָה **3**). p. 958 7564

†[רָשַׁע] vb. denom. be wicked, act 7561
wickedly;—**Qal** *Pf.* 1 s. רָשַׁעְתִּי 2 S 22^{22}+, רָשָׁעְנוּ 1 K 8^{47}+; *Impf.* 2 ms. תִּרְשַׁע Ec 7^{17}; 1 s. אֶרְשָׁע Jb 9^{29} 10^{7};—**1.** *be wicked, act wickedly*, 1 K 8^{47} = 2 Ch 6^{37}, Dn 9^{15} Ec 7^{17}; + מֵאֱלֹהָי 2 S 22^{22} (*in departing*) *from my God* = ψ 18^{22}. **2.** *be guilty*, Jb 9^{29} 10$^{7.15}$. **Hiph.** *Pf.* 3 ms. הִרְשִׁיעַ 2 Ch 20^{35}; 3 mpl. הִרְשִׁיעוּ Dt 25^{1} Dn 12^{10}; 1 pl. הִרְשַׁעְנוּ 9^{5}, etc.: *Impf.* 3 ms. יַרְשִׁיעַ Pr 12^{2}+; יַרְשִׁעַ Jb 34^{29}; 3 mpl. יַרְשִׁיעֻן Ex 22^{8}, etc.; *Inf. cstr.* הַרְשִׁיעַ 1 K 8^{32} 2 Ch 22^{3}; *Pt.* מַרְשִׁיעַ Pr 17^{15}; pl. cstr. מַרְשִׁיעֵי Dn 11^{32};—**1.** *condemn as guilty*, in civil relations, c. acc. Ex 22^{8} (E) Dt 25^{1} ψ 94^{21} Jb 34^{17} Pr 17^{15}. **2.** *condemn as guilty*, in ethical and religious relations, c. acc. 1 K 8^{32} Jb 9^{20} 10^{2} 15^{6} 32^{3} 40^{8} ψ 37^{33} Pr 12^{2} Is 50^{9} 54^{17}, abs. Jb 34^{29}. **3.** *act wickedly* (late), in ethics and religion: Jb 34^{12} (denied of י׳), Ne 9^{33} Dn 12^{10} 2 Ch 22^{3}; ∥ חטא ψ 106^{6} Dn 9^{5}; הרשׁיע לעשׂות 2 Ch 20^{35}; מַרְשִׁיעֵי בְרִית Dn 11^{32}.—יַרְשִׁיעַ 1 S 14^{47} read יִוָּשֵׁעַ 𝔊 Capp We Dr Bu HPS.

7564 †רִשְׁעָה **n.f. wickedness**;—abs. ר׳ Is 9^{17}+; cstr. רִשְׁעַת Dt 9^{4}+; sf. רִשְׁעָתוֹ Dt 25^{2}+;—**1.** *wickedness* in civil relations, Dt 25^{2} Pr 13^{6} Is 9^{17}; בְּרִשְׁעָתוֹ יִפֹּל רָשָׁע Pr 11^{5}. **2.** *wickedness* of enemies, גְּבוּל ר׳ Mal 1^{4} (Edom); זאת הר׳ Zc 5^{8} (personif.); לְרִשְׁעָה Ez 5^{6} (del. Co); רִשְׁעַת הגוים Dt $9^{4.5}$. **3.** *wickedness*, ethical and religious, עשׂה ר׳ Mal $3^{15.19}$, שׁוּב מֵרִשְׁעָתוֹ Ez 18^{27} 33^{19}; רִשְׁעַת (הָ)רָשָׁע 18^{20} 33^{12}.

4849 †מִרְשַׁעַת **n.f. wickedness**;—abs. הַמּ׳ 2 Ch 24^{7} Athaliah *the* (embodied) *wickedness*.

3573 רִשְׁעָתַיִם v. כּוּשַׁן ר׳ p. 469.

רשף (√ of foll.; Sam. ࠓࠔࠐ *irritavit, incendit*; NH רֶשֶׁף *flame*, Ecclus 43^{17c} רשף *lightning-flame* (? si vera l.); JAram. רִשְׁפָּא *flame*; רשף as n. pr. div. in OAram. and Ph. Lzb [154. 370] Pietschm [Phön. 150 ff.] EMey [ZMG xxxi (1877), 719] Nö [ib. xlii (1888), 473] Spiegelberg [ZA xiii (1898), 121] Lzb [ib. 328] WMM [As. u. Eur. 311 ff.] GACooke [Inscr. 56 f.]).

7565 †I. רֶ֫שֶׁף **n.m.** [Hb 3, 5] **flame, fire-bolt**;—abs. ר׳ Dt 32^{24}+; pl. רְשָׁפִים ψ 78^{48}, cstr. רִשְׁפֵּי 76^{4}, רִשְׁפֵּי Ct 8^{6}; sf. רְשָׁפֶיהָ v^{6};—**1.** *flame*: ר׳ ר׳ אֵשׁ Ct 8^{6} *its flames* (sc. of קִנְאָה, אַהֲבָה) *are flames of fire*; בְּנֵי ר׳ Jb 5^{7} = *sparks*; ר׳ = pointed *flame* of lightning ψ 78^{48} (|| בָּרָד); ר׳ קָשֶׁת 76^{4} sharp *flames of the bow*, fig. for arrows. **2.** *fire-bolt* of י׳, bringing pestilence and death, Dt 32^{24} (cf. Dr; || קֶטֶב מְרִירִי), Hb 3^{5} (|| דֶּבֶר).

7566 †II. רֶ֫שֶׁף **n.pr.m.** in Ephr., 1 Ch 7^{25}; Σαραφ, A Ρασεφ, 𝔊L Ρασηφ.

7567 †[רָשַׁשׁ] **vb. Pōʿēl beat down, shatter** (Syr. ܪܫ *bruise, grind*);—*Impf.* 3 ms. יְרֹשֵׁשׁ Je 5^{17} one *shall beat down* thy fortified cities. **Pu.** *Pf.* 1 pl. רֻשַּׁשְׁנוּ Mal 1^{4} *we are beaten down*.

7568 רֶ֫שֶׁת *net*, v. ירשׁ. p. 440

7570 †[רָתַח] **vb. boil** (NH *id.*; Ecclus 43^{3} Hiph. *make hot*; Aram. רְתַח, ܪܬܚ *boil*);—**Pi.** *Imv.* ms. רַתַּח causat. Ez 24^{5} *cause to boil*, bring to boiling, c. acc. rei. **Pu.** *Pf.* 3 pl. רֻתְּחוּ Jb 30^{27} my bowels *have been made to boil* without quiet (fig. of violent emotion). **Hiph.** *Impf.* 3 ms. יַרְתִּיחַ כַּסִּיר מְצוּלָה Jb 41^{23} *he* (the crocod.) *maketh the depth boil like the pot.*

†[רֶ֫תַח] **n.[m.] boiling**;—pl. sf. רְתָחֶיהָ 7571
Ez 24^{5}, as acc. cogn. *cause its boilings to boil*, make it boil vigorously; but rd. נְתָחֶיהָ Hi-Sm Co Da (poss.) and all mod. (cf. v$^{4.6}$; || עצמים).

†[רָתַם] **vb. bind, attach** (cf. Ar. رَتِيمَة 7573
thread bound to finger as reminder);—**Qal** *Imv.* ms. רְתֹם הַמֶּרְכָּבָה לָרֶכֶשׁ Mi 1^{13}.

†רֹ֫תֶם **n.m.** [1 K 19, 5] a kind of broom-shrub, 7574
broom-plant, retem (NH *id.*; Ar. رَتَمٌ (on form Lag [BN 152]); 𝔗 רִיתְמָא, all = BH);—abs. ר׳ אֶחָד 1 K 19^{5}, ר׳ אחת v^{4} Kt (אֶחָד Qr); pl. שֹׁרֶשׁ רְתָמִים לַחְמָם Jb 30^{4} (on text v. Bu Che [infr.]); גַּחֲלֵי רְתָמִים ψ 120^{4}, Rob [BR i. 84, 203, 205, 500] Löw [No. 313] Post [Hastings, DB, 'Juniper'] Che [Ency. Bib. 'Juniper'].

†רִתְמָה **n.pr.loc.** station in wilderness, 7575
Nu $33^{18.19}$; Ραθαμα, 𝔊L Ραμαθα.

†[רָתַק] **vb. bind** (Ar. رَتَقَ *close up* and 7576
repair, sew up; Talm. רִיתְקָא *fenced enclosure*);—**Pu.** *Pf.* 3 pl. רֻתְּקוּ בַזִּקִּים Na 3^{10} her great ones *were bound with fetters*. **Niph.** *Impf.* 3 ms. יֵרָתֵק Ec 12^{6} Qr (ירחק Kt), from context = *be snapped, broken*; read prob. יִנָּתֵק (Pfannkuche Thes and mod.).

†[רְתֻקָה] **n.[f.] chain** (?);—pl. cstr. רְתֻקוֹת 7577
כֶּסֶף Is 40^{19}.

†רַתּוֹק **n.[m.] chain** (on form Lag [BN 89]);— 7569
abs. עֲשֵׂה הָר׳ Ez 7^{23}, i.e. for captives, but very dub.; Co עָרֹה וּבָקוֹק, Krae עֲשֵׂי הַבִּתּוֹק (ב׳ = As. *butâḳu, obstruction*); hence perh. also pl. cstr.
רַתּוּקוֹת זָהָב 1 K 6^{21} Qr (Kt רתיקות), *chains of gold* 7572
before the דְּבִיר in temple.

רתיקות, רַתּוּקוֹת v. foregoing. 7569, 7572

רתת (√ of foll.; NH רָתַת, Aram. רְתַת, ܪܬ, all *tremble*; cf. רטט).

†רְתֵת **n.[m.] trembling** (on form Lag 7578
[BN 176] Ba [§ 7 b]);—ר׳ Ho 13^{1} (si vera l.) *when Ephr. spoke trembling* (AV Che al.); Ew al. *spoke terror*; Hi Ke RV *spoke*, there was *trembling*; text dub. (v. Now).

שׂ

שׂ *Sîn*, 21st letter (with שׁ, q.v.).

שׂאר (√of foll.; vb. unknown; cf. NH שְׂאוֹר, סְאוֹר; JAram. סִיאוֹרָא, all *leaven*).

7603 †**שְׂאֹר n.m.** Ex 12, 19 leaven;—abs. 'שׂ Ex 13[7] (J), Dt 16[4] (D), Ex 12[15.19] Lv 2[11] (all P).

5375, **שְׂאֵת** v. נשׂא. **שָׂב** v. שׂיב. p. 670, 966
7867

שׂבך (√of foll.; *interweave;* NH סָבַךְ, der. spec., שְׂבָכָה *hair-net*, etc.; Ar. شَبَكَ *insert, interweave;* Syr. ܣܒܟ *rush in, adhere, embrace, be mixed* with, ܣܒܟܐ *velum reticulatum;* cf. As. *šabikû, headdress,* Dl HWB 638).

7730 †**שׂוֹבֶךְ n.** [**m.**] network of boughs;—cstr. 'שׂ הָאֵלָה 2 S 18[9].

7639 †**שְׂבָכָה n.f.** lattice-work, network;—abs.
7638 'ה 1 K 7[18]+, pl. שְׂבָכוֹת v[41]+, שְׂבָכִים v[17];—**1.** prob. window-*lattice* 2 K 1[2]. **2.** net-ornament on pillars, 1 K 7[17.17] (om. 𝔊 Kit Benz), v[18.20] (crpt., cf. Kit Benz), v[41.42.42] 2 Ch 4[12.13.13] 2 K 25[17.17] ‖ Je 52[22.23]. **3.** *network, toils,* for catching animals (fig.) Jb 18[8] (+ רֶשֶׁת, פַּח, צַמִּים).

7638-39 **שְׂבָכִים** v. שְׂבָכָה. above

7643 †**שְׂבָם n.pr.loc.** Nu 32[3], שִׂבְמָה v[38] Jos 13[19] Is 16[8.9] Je 48[32]; in Moab (Reuben), near Heshbon (cf. also Jerome[Is 16, 8]); Σεβαμα.

7646 **שָׂבַע** [**שָׂבֵעַ**, **שָׂבֵעַ**]$_{96}$ **vb. be sated, satisfied, surfeited** (NH (der. spec.)=BH; so As. *šebû,* Ar. شَبِعَ, Aram. סְבַע, ܣܒܥ, Palm. שבע; the Eth. vb. of same meaning is ጸገበ:);—**Qal**$_{79}$ *Pf.* 3 ms. שָׂבַע 1 Ch 23[1], 'וְשׂ consec. Dt 31[20]; 3 pl. שָׂבֵעוּ Is 9[19], 'ושׂ consec. Dt 14[29] 26[12], etc.; *Impf.* 3 ms. יִשְׂבַּע Pr 12[11]+, 3 mpl. יִשְׂבְּעוּן ψ 104[28], etc.; *Imv.* שְׂבַע־ Pr 20[13]; *Inf. abs.* שָׂבוֹעַ Jo 2[26] 2 Ch 31[10]; cstr. לִשְׂבֹּעַ Ex 16[8] La 5[6], לְשָׂבְעָה Hg 1[6]; **1.** *be sated* (with food), esp. human subj.: **a.** abs., after אָכַל, Ho 4[10] Is 9[19] Dt 8[10], Ex 16[8] (P), + 11 t., cf. Is 44[16] (‖ אָכַל); exposing men to arrogance Dt 6[11] 8[12] 31[20], cf. Ho 13[6.6] (Isr. under fig. of cattle), Je 50[19] (id.; c. ב loc.; ‖ רָעָה *graze*); =have (or get) enough to eat ψ 37[19] 59[16], enough to drink Am 4[8], fig. of sword Je 46[10], of wine Hb 2[5]. **b.** c. acc. of food Je 44[17] La 5[16] Ex 16[12] (P), + 6 t., cf. Ez 39[20] (of beasts, in fig.), of earth, sated with water (rain) Pr 30[16], so of trees (acc. om.) ψ 104[16], fig. of requital Pr 18[20b]. **c.** c. מִן of food Jb 19[22] (fig.); fig. of earth having its fill (of rain) ψ 104[13], and (fig. of requital) Pr 18[20a]; good sense 12[14] (del. טוֹב, so Toy), bad sense 1[31] 14[14]; c. מִן of source Is 66[11] (fig.). **2.** more gen., *be sated,* have desire satisfied: **a.** abs. Ez 16[28.29] (i.e. with harlotry), Je 50[10] (with plunder), Is 53[11] (with a given result); of eyes Pr 27[20], of Sheʾôl and Abaddōn v[20], cf. 30[15]; =have abundance Pr 30[9] (exposure to arrogance). **b.** c. acc., *be satisfied with, have one's fill of:* Je 31[14], cf. ψ 17[15] 63[6], Pr 5[10] Ec 5[9], cf. (eye subj.) 4[8], acc. of sons ψ 17[14] (si vera l., but text dub., v. Ol Du, cf. Bae We), days of life, i.e. reach the full limit (+ זָקֵן) 1 Ch 23[1] 2 Ch 24[15]. **c.** c. ב of goodness ψ 65[5], c. מִן id. Ec 6[3]. **d.** c. ל inf., לֹא־תִשְׂבַּע עַיִן לִרְאוֹת Ec 1[8] (‖ מָלֵא). **3.** *have in excess, be surfeited with:* **a.** lit., with honey (acc.) Pr 25[16]. **b.** fig.=*be weary of,* c. acc. of offerings Is 1[11] (subj. 'י), tossings Jb 7[4], poverty Pr 28[19], shame Hb 2[16], contempt ψ 123[3.4], c. acc. pers. Pr 28[17]. **c.** id., c. ב of troubles ψ 88[4], of reproach La 3[30]. †**Niph.** *Pt.* נִשְׂבָּע *sated* Jb 31[31]. †**Pi.** *satisfy, Impf.* 3 mpl. יְשַׂבֵּעוּ Ez 7[19] *they shall* not *satisfy* their appetite (נַפְשָׁם ‖ מִלֵּא); *Imv.* ms. sf., subj. 'י, שַׂבְּעֵנִי חַסְדֶּךָ ψ 90[14] (2 acc.). †**Hiph.** *Pf.* 3 ms. הִשְׂבִּיעַ ψ 107[9], 'וְה consec. Is 58[11]; 2 fs. הִשְׂבַּעַתְּ Ez 27[33], etc.; *Impf.* 3 ms. sf. יַשְׂבִּעֵנִי Jb 9[18], 2 ms. תַּשְׂבִּיעַ Is 58[10], 1 s. וְאַשְׂבִּעַ Je 5[7], sf. אַשְׂבִּיעֶךָ ψ 81[17] van d. H., אַשְׂבִּיעֲךָ Baer Gi, etc.; *Inf. cstr.* לְהַשְׂבִּיעַ Jb 38[27]; *Pt.* מַשְׂבִּיעַ ψ 103[5] 145[16];—**1. a.** *satisfy* (esp. with material blessings), subj. 'י, c. acc. pers. Je 5[7] (exposing men to arrogance), Is 58[11] (acc. נֶפֶשׁ; of refreshment in drought, ב loc., fig. of help and blessing), ψ 107[9] (acc. נֶפֶשׁ ‖ מִלֵּא), cf. 103[5] (ב instr., on acc. v. עֲדִי); c. acc. of ground Jb 38[27] (i.e. with rain); human subj., c. acc. נֶפֶשׁ Is 58[10]. **b.** c. acc. of food + pers., 'י subj., ψ 81[17] (‖ הֶאֱכִיל), 105[40] 132[15] 147[14]; c. acc. pers. + אֹרֶךְ יָמִים 91[16]. **c.** 'י subj., acc. rei + ל pers., 'מַשׂ לְכָל־חַי רָצוֹן ψ 145[16]. **d.** 'י subj., c. acc. of beasts + מִמֶּךָּ (of Pharaoh, in prophetic fig.) Ez 32[4]. **2.** *enrich,* subj. Tyre, c. acc. gent. Ez 27[33] (‖ הֶעֱשִׁיר). **3.** *sate, glut* (with the undesired), subj. 'י, c. acc. pers. + ב rei La 3[15], acc. pers. + rei Jb 9[18].

†**שָׂבָע n.** [**m.**] satiety, abundance;—abs. 7648
'לָשׂ Ex 16[3]+, cstr. שְׂבַע ψ 16[11], 'לְשׂ Pr 13[25]; sf. שָׂבְעֲךָ Dt 23[25], שָׂבְעָהּ Ru 2[18];—**1.** *satiety,* as to

food Ru 2^{18}; (לֶחֶם) אָכַל לָשֹׂ׳ Ex 16^3 (P), Lv 25^{19} 26^5 (both H), cf. אָכַל ... כְּנַפְשְׁךָ שׂ׳ לָשֹׂ׳ ψ 78^{25}; Dt 23^{25} *eat* grapes *according to thine appetite,* (namely) *thy fill,* cf. אֹכֵל לְשֹׂ׳ נַפְשׁוֹ Pr 13^{25}. **2.** *satisfying abundance,* שׂ׳ שְׂמָחוֹת ψ 16^{11}.

7653-54 †שָׂבְעָה, [שִׂבְעָה] **n.f.** satiety;—abs. שׂ׳ Is 56^{11}+, cstr. שִׂבְעַת־ Ez 16^{49}, sf. שָׂבְעָתֵךְ v^{28};—**1.** as to food, esp. אָכַל לְשֹׂ׳ *eat to satiety, one's fill,* Is 23^{18} Ez 39^{19}; לְשֹׂ׳ also Is 55^2 (fig.); שׂ׳ of dogs 56^{11} (fig.); שׂ׳־לֶחֶם leading to arrogance, as sin of Sodom Ez 16^{49} (+ גָּאוֹן, etc.). **2.** as to carnal desire Ez 16^{28} (fig.).

7647 †שָׂבָע **n.m.** Gn 41, 29 plenty, satiety;—only abs. שׂ׳;—**1.** *plenty,* of bread-stuffs Gn $41^{29.30.31.34.47.53}$ (E), Pr 3^{10}. **2.** *satiety,* Ec 5^{11}.

7649 †שָׂבֵעַ **adj.** sated, satisfied, surfeited;—abs. שׂ׳ Gn 25^8 Pr 19^{23}; cstr. שְׂבַע Dt 33^{23}+; fs. שְׂבֵעָה Pr 27^7; mpl. שְׂבֵעִים 1 S 2^5;—**1. a.** *sated* with food, c. בַּלֶּחֶם 1 S 2^5; נֶפֶשׁ שְׂבֵעָה Pr 27^7 (opp. נ׳ רְעֵבָה); *abounding in* י׳'s favour (שְׂבַע רָצוֹן) Dt 33^{23} (‖ מָלֵא); abs. *satisfied* Pr 19^{23}. **b.** in phr. שְׂבַע יָמִים *satisfied with days,* in a good old age, Gn 35^{29} (P), Jb 42^{17} (both + זָקֵן), 1 Ch 29^{28} (+ בְּשֵׂיבָה טוֹבָה), also abs. שָׂבֵעַ Gn 25^8 (P; + *id.* + זָקֵן). **2.** bad sense, surfeited with trouble, etc.: שְׂבַע רֹגֶז Jb 14^1, שׂ׳ קָלוֹן 10^{15}.

7663 †I. [שָׂבַר] **vb.** inspect, examine (van d. H. שֹׁבֵר [so 𝔊 συντρίβων], but Mas. שׂ׳ v. Norzi; hence connex. with Ar. سَبَرَ *probe* a wound, *try, examine,* improb., and this (acc. to Frä 261) denom. from Aram. loan-word; improb. also is connex. with Aram. סְבַר *think* (cf. foll.), Kau Aram. in AT, 85);—**Qal** *Pt.* שֹׂבֵר, c. ב obj., Ne $2^{13.15}$ I *examined into* the wall, inspected it closely.

7663 †II. [שָׂבַר] **vb. Pi.** wait, hope (Aramaism; cf. Aram. סְבַר *think,* Pa. *hope;* ܣܒܰܪ *believe, hope,* Pa. *think,* Aph. *hope*);—*Pf.* 1 s. שִׂבַּרְתִּי ψ 119^{166}, 3 pl. שִׂבְּרוּ Est 9^1; *Impf.* 3 mpl. יְשַׂבֵּרוּ Is 38^{18}, יְשַׂבֵּרוּ ψ 145^{15}, יְשַׂבֵּרוּן ψ 104^{27}; 2 fpl. תְּשַׂבֵּרְנָה Ru 1^{13};—**1.** *wait* for, לְ pers., Ru 1^{13}. **2.** *hope* for, לְ rei ψ 119^{166}, אֶל rei Is 38^{18}, pers. ψ 104^{27} 145^{15}; לְ inf. Est 9^1 *hope to rule.*

7664 †[שֵׂבֶר] **n.m.** hope;—sf. שִׂבְרִי ψ 119^{116}, שִׂבְרוֹ עַל־י׳ 146^5.

7679 [שָׂגָא] **vb.** grow, grow great (✓only in Job; Aramaism; cf. Aram. סְגִי, סְגָא, ܣܓܳܐ, all *increase, grow great;* OAram. BAram. Palm. שגא(י) *adj. much*);—**Qal** *Impf.* 3 ms. metapl. יִשְׂגֶּא Jb 8^{11} (of plant; metapl. form Ges §75 oo; > van d. H. יִשְׂגֶּה). **Hiph. 1.** *make great,* pt. מַשְׂגִּיא לַגּוֹיִם Jb 12^{23} *he maketh the nations great* (v. **3 b**). **2.** *magnify, laud,* 2 ms. תַּשְׂגִּיא פעלו Jb 36^{24} that *thou magnify his work.*—Vid. שׂגה.

7689 †שַׂגִּיא **adj.** great;—of God, abs. אֵל שַׂגִּיא Jb 36^{20}; cstr. שַׂגִּיא־כֹחַ 37^{24}.

7682 †[שָׂגַב] **vb.** be (inaccessibly) high (cf. 𝔗 שַׂגֵּב Pa. [from Heb.] *exalt*);—**Qal** *Pf.* **1.** 3 fs. שָׂגְבָה Dt 2^{36}, of city, c. מִן, *be* (too) *high* for capture. **2.** 3 mpl. שָׂגְבוּ Jb 5^{11} of pers., *be high* in prosperity. **Niph.** *Pf.* 3 ms. נִשְׂגַּב Is $2^{11.17}$; נִשְׂגָּב Pr 18^{10}; 3 fs. נִשְׂגְּבָה ψ 139^6; *Pt.* נִשְׂגָּב Is 12^4+; fs. נִשְׂגָּבָה Is 26^5+;—**1.** *be high,* walls Is 30^{13} Pr 18^{11}; city Is 26^5; God's knowledge ψ 139^6 (unattainable). **2.** *be* (safely) *set on high,* Pr 18^{10}. **3.** *be exalted,* of God Is $2^{11.17}$ 33^5; his name 12^4 ψ 148^{13}. **Pi.** *Impf.* 3 ms. יְשַׂגֵּב Is 9^{10} ψ 107^{41}; sf. יְשַׂגֶּבְךָ 20^2, etc.;—trans. c. acc.: **1.** *set* (securely) *on high,* ψ 20^2 69^{30} 91^{14}; c. מִן, of foe 59^2, affliction 107^{41}. **2.** *exalt,* in effective hostility, c. עַל, Is 9^{10}. **Pu.** *Impf.* 3 ms. יְשֻׂגָּב Pr 29^{25} *be set* (securely) *on high.* **Hiph.** *Impf.* 3 ms. יַשְׂגִּיב Jb 36^{22} God *acts exaltedly* בְּכֹחוֹ.

7687 †שְׂגוּב **n.pr.m.** (*exalted*);—**1.** son of re-builder of Jericho (Hiel) 1 K 16^{34} Qr (Kt שׂגיב; Ζεγουβ; 𝔊L om. v.). **2.** of Judah 1 Ch $2^{21.22}$ (Σερουχ, 𝔊L Σεγουβ).

4869 †I. מִשְׂגָּב **n.** [**m.** Albr ZAW xvi (1896), 60] **secure height, retreat**;—מ׳ ψ 9^{10}+; cstr. מִשְׂגַּב Is 25^{12}; sf. מִשְׂגַּבִּי ψ 18^3+, etc.;—**1. a.** = stronghold, מִבְצַר מ׳ חוֹמֹתֶיךָ Is 25^{12}. **b.** fig. of security Is 33^{16}. **2.** fig. of God as refuge ψ $9^{10.10}$, 18^3 = 2 S 22^3, ψ $46^{8.12}$ 48^4 $59^{10.17.18}$ $62^{3.7}$ 94^{22} 144^2.

4869 †II. מִשְׂגָּב perh. **n.pr.loc.** in Moab;—הַמּ׳ Je 48^1 (v. Schwally ZAW viii (1888), 196 Albr l. c.), Αμαθ; Gf thinks appell. of Ḳir Moab (v. II. קִיר); most sub I. מ׳ **1.**

7685 †[שָׂגָה] **vb.** grow, increase (late; ‖ form of שׂגא);—**Qal** *Impf.* 3 ms. יִשְׂגֶּה ψ 92^{13} righteous *shall grow great* like cedar (‖ יִפְרָח), cf. Jb 8^7 (opp. מִצְעָר; v^{11} see שׂגא). **Hiph.** *Pf.* 3 pl. הִשְׂגּוּ־חָיִל ψ 73^{12} *they have increased riches.*

5473, 7687 שׂגיב v. שְׂגוּב. שִׂגְשֵׂג v. II. סוג. above, p. 691

7702 †[שִׂדֵּד] **vb. Pi.** harrow (שׂדד *id.* Ecclus 38[25 marg. 26]; cf. As. *šadâdu, draw, drag*);—*Impf.* 3 ms. יְשַׂדֵּד Jb 39[10] (of beast); human subj., c. acc. of ground Is 28[24] (+יְפַתַּח, ‖ יַחֲרֹשׁ); יְשַׂדֶּד־לוֹ Ho 10[11] (‖ יַחֲרוֹשׁ; fig. of Jacob).

7708 †שִׂדִּים **n.[m.] pl.** in **n.pr.loc.** עֵמֶק הַשּׂ׳ *vale of Siddim* Gn 14[3] (identif. with Dead Sea), v[8.10] (=*vale of furrows*? or (Di after Onk Sam) *of fields* (=הַשָּׂדִים); 𝔊 ἡ κοιλὰς [φαραγξ] ἡ ἁλυκή; Renan [Hist. Isr. i. 116; Eng. Tr. i. 98] We [Isr. u. Jüd. Gesch. (3) 101] prop. ע׳ הַשֵּׁדִים *demon-valley*).

שׂדה (√of foll., meaning unknown; foll. plausibly connected with As. *šadû, mountain*, used by people whose *land* was *mountainous* (cf. Ju 5[18] Dt 32[13]+), by JPPeters [JBL xii (1893), 54 f.] and (simultan.) Ba [ES (1893), 65 f.] cf. Wkl [Altor. Forsch. ii (1894), 192]; Jäger [BAS ii. 282] cp. As. *šedtum, pasture-land;* Tel Am. (Canaan. gloss) *šatê* Wkl [Tel Am. 180, 56]; Ph. שד=BH, NH=BH, so Ecclus 40[22]).

7704 †שָׂדַי **n.m.** [ψ 96, 12] **field, land** (rare orig. form of שָׂדֶה (q.v. infr.), only poet.);—abs. שׂ׳ Je 4[17], שָׂדָי Ho 10[4]+;—**1.** cultivated *field* 12[12], also 10[4] (si vera l., but v. Now), yielding food Dt 32[13] La 4[9]; שֹׁמְרֵי שׂ׳ Je 4[17] *keepers, watchmen, of a field.* **2.** home of wild beasts: בַּהֲמוֹת שׂ׳ ψ 8[8] Jo 2[22], חַיְתוֹ שׂ׳ Is 56[9] ψ 104[11], זִיז שׂ׳ 50[11] 80[14]. **3.** plain, opp. mt., Je 18[14] (but dub., Co Du שִׂרְיֹן). **4.** *land*, opp. sea, ψ 96[12] (cf. שָׂדֶה **3**; ‖ תֵּבֵל ψ 98[7]).

7704 שָׂדֶה [318] **n.m.** [Lv 27, 24] id. (ordinary contr. form Ges [§ 84a f]);—abs. שׂ׳ Gn 2[5.5]+; cstr. שְׂדֵה 14[7]+; sf. שָׂדִי Je 32[7.8], שָׂדְךָ Dt 11[15]+, שָׂדֶךָ 24[19] Lv 25[3], etc.; pl. שָׂדוֹת 1 S 22[7]+, cstr. שְׂדוֹת Ne 12[29]; also שְׂדֵי 2 S 1[21] Is 32[12] Ru 1[1]+8 t. (some might be sg.=שְׂדֵה cf. Ba [ZMG xlii (1888), 351] SS Buhl; note, e.g. שְׂדֵי Ru 1[6a],=שְׂדֵה v[b] 4[3]; but v. Kö [ii. 1, 77]); sf. שְׂדֹתֶיהָ Ne 11[30], etc.; also שָׂדֵינוּ שָׂדֶיךָ 1 K 2[26], Mi 2[4];—**1.** open *field*, country: **a.** pasture-land Gn 29[2] 30[16] Ex 9[3] (all J), Dt 11[15] 1 S 11[5]+10 t. J, JE. **b.** unfrequented Gn 24[63.65], exposed to violence 4[8] (J), 2 S 14[6] Dt 21[1] 22[25.27], to wild beasts Ex 22[30] (E), Ez 33[27]. **c.** specif. home of beasts: 2 S 17[8] Je 14[5]; esp. phr. חַיַּת הַשּׂ׳ Gn 2[19.20] 3[1.14] (all J) of beasts in gen., and, of wild beasts, Ex 23[11.29] (E), Ho 2[14.20] 4[3] 13[8] Dt 7[22] Lv 26[22] (H), Jb 5[23] (‖ חַיַּת הָאָרֶץ), +16 t.; בֶּהֱמַת הַשּׂ׳ 1 S 17[44] cf. Jo 1[20]; אַיְלוֹת הַשּׂ׳ Ct 2[7] 3[5], cf. הַצְּבָיִם אֲשֶׁר בַּשּׂ׳ 2 S 2[18]; hunting-ground Gn 25[29] 27[3.5] (all JE), cf. אִישׁ שׂ׳ 25[27] (JE; ‖ אִישׁ יֹדֵעַ צַיִד). **d.** yielding plants and trees: Gn 25[27] (JE), 30[14] (J), Ex 10[5] (JE), 2 K 4[39] Ez 21[2] 39[10]; esp. phr. עֵשֶׂב הַשּׂ׳ Gn 2[5] 3[18] (both J), +6 t.+ע׳ בַּשּׂ׳ Zc 10[1]; שִׂיחַ הַשּׂ׳ Gn 2[5], גֶּפֶן שׂ׳ 2 K 4[39], פַּקֻּעֹת שׂ׳ v[39], צִיץ הַשּׂ׳ Is 40[15] ψ 103[15], צֶמַח הַשּׂ׳ Ez 16[7]; עֵץ הַשּׂ׳ (4 t. עֲצֵי) Ex 9[25] (JE), Dt 20[19] Lv 26[4] (H) Is 55[12]+8 t.; 2 S 1[21] v. תְּרוּמָה, √רום. **e.** stony, אַבְנֵי הַשּׂ׳ Jb 5[23]. **f.** *open country*, outside of walled city Ju 9[32.42.43.44] 19[16] 1 S 19[3] 20[5.11.11.24.35] 2 K 7[12] Mi 4[10]; as battle-ground Jos 8[24] (J), 2 S 10[8]=1 Ch 19[9], 2 S 11[23] 18[6], outside of military camp 1 S 4[2] 14[15]; opp. city (in formula) 1 K 14[11] 16[4] 21[24] Je 14[18] Ez 7[15]; שְׂדֵה אֶרֶץ Lv 25[31]; as site of small town, *country*-town 1 S 27[5] (opp. royal city), cf. 1 Ch 27[25]; of high places, גְּבָעוֹת בַּשּׂ׳ Je 13[27]; quite gen., 1 S 30[11] Je 40[7.13]; including road Ju 20[31] 1 K 11[29] Je 6[25]; disting. from road Nu 22[23] (JE), 2 S 20[12]; outside houses and courtyards Ex 8[9] (P), 1 S 25[15]; בַּשּׂ׳ nearly=*outdoors* Ex 1[14] (P), Ju 13[9]; of surface of country or ground, בַּשּׂ׳ Ex 16[25] (JE; =עַל־פְּנֵי הַמִּדְבָּר v[14]), cf. 1 S 14[25]; so (אֶל) עַל־פְּנֵי הַשּׂ׳ 2 K 9[37] Je 9[22] Ez 29[5] (‖ הַמִּדְבָּרָה), 32[4] 39[5]; same phr. opp. house, comfort, etc., 2 S 11[11] Ez 16[5], opp. city Lv 14[7.53], opp. tent Nu 19[16] (all P), opp. tent of meeting Lv 17[5] (H). **g.** =expanse of country, opp. mt., in phr. מְרוֹמֵי שׂ׳ Ju 5[18]; הֲרָרִי בַּשּׂ׳ Je 17[3] (of Jerus.) is dub.; cf. לְעִי הַשּׂ׳ Mi 1[6] (Je 18[14] v. שָׂדַי). **2.** definite portion of ground, *field, land:* **a.** cultivated ground Gn 37[7] (E), 47[24] (J; זֶרַע הַשָּׂדֶה), Ex 22[4.4.4.5] (E), Lv 27[16.17] (P), Mi 3[12] (in sim.) Ru 2[2]+47 t., +שְׂדֵה טוֹב Ez 17[5], שׂ׳־זָרַע v[8] +שְׂדֵי תְרוּמֹת 2 S 1[21], *good soil.* **b.** as private property, Mi 5[2.4] Is 5[8.8] Gn 47[20] (J), 23[9.11.13] (P)+50 t., +2 Ch 26[23] (as burial-place); also חֶלְקַת (הַ)שּׂ׳, v. חֶלְקָה; and שְׂ׳ צֹפִים, v. צפה. **c.** city-land, adjacent to city (town) and subject to its control: Gn 41[48] (E), Lv 25[34] (P), Jos 21[12] (P)=1 Ch 6[41], Ne 11[25.30] 12[29.44]; specif. of Zoan ψ 78[12.43]. **d.** territory of nation, tribe: Gn 32[4] Nu 21[20] (both JE), Ju 5[4] Ru 1[1.2] Gn 14[7]+13 t.+שְׂדֵה נַחֲלַת יִשׂ׳ Ju 20[6]. **e.** territory of king, 2 S 9[7] 13[30]. **3.** *land*, opp. sea, 1 Ch 16[32] (opp. הַיָּם; =שָׂדַי ψ 96[12]), perhaps also *mainland* Ez 26[6.8] (Co Krae Toy al.; not Sm).

שִׂדִּים v. שׂדד. שְׂדֵרָה v. סדר. above, p. 690 7708, 7713

†שֶׂה **n.m.** [Gn 30, 32] and (less oft.) **f.** [Je 50, 17] **one of a flock, a sheep (or goat)** (As. *šu'u*, Ar. شَاةٌ, pl. شَاءٌ, شِوَاهٌ, etc. (also *wild ox*), cf. Egypt. *sau, sheep* Bondi [65], cf. Id. [Ba NB § 2 b δ]);—abs. שֶׂה Gn 30[32]+, cstr. שֵׂה Is 43[23]+; sf. שֵׂיוֹ Dt 22[1], שֵׂיֵהוּ 1 S 14[34]; not in pl.;—**1.** *a sheep*, or *goat*, nom. unit. of צֹאן: as property Gn 32[32.32] (J; +צֹאן 7716

coll., (עִזִּים, כְּשָׂבִים), Ex 21$^{37.37}$ (+ שׁוֹר, צֹאן coll.), 22^{3} (+ חֲמוֹר, שׁוֹר), v^{8} (*id.*), v^{9} (*id.*; all E); Dt 22^{1}
2089 (+ שׁוֹר), 1 S 17^{34} (זה Kt van d.H. erron., v. Baer Dr), roaming pasture Is 7^{25}, straying ψ 119^{176} (sim.), slaughtered Is 53^{7} (in sim.); + חֲמוֹר, שׁוֹר, Ju 6^{4} 1 S 22^{19} Jos 6^{21} (J), + id. + גָּמָל 1 S 15^{3}; as sacrifice Gn 22$^{7.8}$ (J), Ex 13^{13} Lv 5^{12} 12^{8} Nu 15^{11} (שׂ׳ בַּכְּבָשִׂים אוֹ בָעִזִּים; all P), Dt 18^{3} (+ שׁוֹר), Is 43^{23} 66^{3} (+ שׁוֹר), מִן־הַצֹּאן Ez 45^{15}; cf. Ex 34^{19} (+ שׁוֹר), v^{20} (J), Lv 27^{26} (P; + שׁוֹר); fit for sacrifice Lv 22^{28} (H); unfit v^{23} (H), Dt 17^{1} (both + שׁוֹר); as food 1 S 14^{34} (+ שׁוֹר), שׂ׳ כְּשָׂבִים וְשׂ׳ עִזִּים Dt 14^{4} (+ id.); for passover Ex 12$^{3.3.4.4.5}$ (P); fig. of Isr. Ez 34$^{17.17}$ (‖ עַתּוּדִים, אֵילִים), v$^{20.20.22.22}$. **2.** coll. *flock*: שֶׂה פְזוּרָה Je 50^{17} (= צֹאן אֹבְדוֹת v^{6}).

7717 †[שָׂהֵד] **n.[m.] witness** (Aram. loan-word = Heb. עֵד; √ סָהֵד, ܣܗܕ); — sf. שָׂהֲדִי Jb 16^{19} (‖ עֵדִי). — שָׂהֲדוּתָא Gn 31^{47} v. B Aram. Lex.

שׂהר (√ of foll.; cf. Ar. شَهْرٌ *new moon* (شَهَرَ is *make conspicuous, notorious*); Eth. ሠሀር: *id.*; 𝔗 סִיהֲרָא, Syr. ܣܗܪܐ *moon*; OAram. שהר *moon-god* Lzb^{373}).

7720 †[שַׂהֲרֹן] **n.[m.] moon**, or **crescent**;— only pl. הַשַּׂהֲרֹנִים of (non-Israel.) ornaments of camels Ju 8^{21}, kings v^{26}, women Is 3^{18}, 𝔊 μηνίσκοι, 𝔙 (Is 3^{18}) *lunulae*; on crescent as ornament v. Dozy$^{ii. 760}$ Lane$^{Egypt. ii. 314}$ Perles$^{Anal. 79}$, cf. Frä^{58}.

5375, 7721 **שׂוֹא** v. נשׂא p. 670 a. I, II. **שׂוּג** v. I, II. סוג.

7742 **שׂוּחַ** Gn 24^{63} v. I. שׂוּט. p. 1002

7750 †[שׂוּט] **vb. swerve, fall away** (akin to שָׂטָה q.v.; NH סוט Hiph. is *shake, move away*; As. *šâṭu, rebel*, Meissn^{90}; Eth. ሠጠ: *bring back, restore*; in 𝔗 *apostatize* is סְטָא);—**Qal** *Pt.* pl. cstr. וְשָׂטֵי כָזָב ψ 40^{5} *those falling away to falsehood* (Gunk$^{Schöpf. 40}$ וְשָׂטָה).

7846 †[שֵׂט, סֵט] **n.[m.] swerver, revolter** (?), **deeds that swerve** (fr. the right?);—pl. וְשַׁחֲטָה שֵׂטִים הֶעְמִיקוּ Ho 5^{2} *and revolters have gone deep in slaughter* (or שַׁחַתָה *in corruption*), but dub.; We Bae Now GASm, cf. Gu^{Kau}, וְשַׁחַת הַשִּׁטִּים הֶעְ׳ *and the pit of Shittim they have made deep;* עֲשֹׂה סֵטִים ψ 101^{3} *to do deeds that swerve* I hate.

7753 †I. [שׂוּךְ] **vb. hedge** or **fence up, about**
5526 (= II. סוּךְ, q.v.);—**Qal** *Pf.* 2 ms. שַׂכְתָּ בַעֲדוֹ Jb 1^{10} *hast fenced him about* (protectingly); *Pt.* שָׂךְ Ho 2^{8} I *will hedge up* (obstruct) *thy way* (acc.). p. 692

4881 †[מְשֻׂכָּה] **n.f. hedge** (= מְסוּכָה);— cstr. מְשֻׂכַת חֵדֶק Pr 15^{19} (in sim.).— מְשׂוּכָתוֹ v. III. שׂכך.

II. **שׂוך** (? ‖ II. שׂכך: cf. NH סוֹכָה; Aram. סוֹכְתָא, ܣܘܟܬܐ (ms.), ܣܘܟܐ, סוֹכָא,—all *branch*).

†[שׂוֹךְ] **n.[m.] branch** or **brushwood**;— 7754
sf. 3 ms. שׂוֹכֹה Ju 9^{49} (Ges$^{§ 91e}$; but v. GFM Bu).

†[שׂוֹכָה] **n.f.** id.;—cstr. שׂוֹכַת עֵצִים Ju 9^{48} + 7754
perhaps abs. שׂוֹכָה v^{49} (so 𝔊 Doorn for MT שׂוֹכֹה).

†שׂוֹכֹה, שׂוֹכוֹ **n.pr.loc.** in Judah: **1.** in 7755
Shephelah, שׂוֹכֹה Jos 15^{35} 1 S 17$^{1.1}$ (fr. 𝔊 Σοκχωθ HPS (after We, cf. Dr) conj. שׂכות), שׂוֹכוֹ 2 Ch 11^{7} 28^{18}, perhaps also שֹׂכֹה 1 K 4^{10} (Buhl Benz SS ['perh.']; Th Kit sub **2**); mod. *Eš-Šuwêke*, SSE. fr. Beth Shemesh, in Wady-es-Sanṭ Rob$^{BR i. 494}$ Buhl$^{Geogr. 194}$; Σωχω, Σοκχωθ, etc. **2.** in hill-country, Jos 15^{48} (Kt שׂוכה, Qr שׂוֹכוֹ), prob. also שׂוֹכוֹ 1 Ch 4^{18} ('son' of חֶבֶר); mod. *Šuwêke*, 4 h. S. of חֶבְרוֹן Rob$^{BR ii. 16. 21}$ Buhl$^{Geogr. 164}$; Σωχω(ν).

†שׂוּכָתִים **adj. gent. m. pl.** a family of 7756
scribes 1 Ch 2^{55}; Σωχαθιειμ, 𝔊L Σουχαθειμ.

I. **שׂוּם, שִׂים** 582 **vb. put, place, set** (cf. 7760
Nö$^{ZMG xxxvii (1883), 532}$; NH סוּם Pi. *designate, fix*, שׂוּם Ecclus 45^{5c} 49^{6}; Ph. שם, As. *šâmu, fix, determine;* Sab. שים *set, set up*, SabDenkm$^{No. 7, 1. 6}$ CIS$^{iv. 1}$; Ar. شَامَ (ى) is *insert, sheathe*, also *compute;* Eth. ሠየመ: *put, place;* 𝔗 שׂוּם, Syr. ܣܡ, OAram. שים);—**Qal** *Pf.* 3 ms. שָׂם Gn 21^{14} + (2 Ch 1^{5} rd. שָׂם 𝔊 𝔙 Gi Be Kau Benz), sf. שָׂמוֹ Ez 17^{4} +, שָׂמָהוּ 7^{20}; 3 fs. שָׂמָה 1 S 19^{13}, sf. שָׂמַתְהוּ Ez 19^{5} 24^{7}; 2 ms. שַׂמְתָּ Je 32^{20} +; 3 pl. שָׂמוּ Gn 40^{15} +; 1 pl. שַׂמְנוּ Is 28^{15}, etc.; *Impf.* 3 ms. יָשִׂים Ex 4^{11}, יָשֵׂם Gn 30^{42} +, יָשֵׂם Jb 23^{6}; juss. יָשֵׂם 1 S 22^{15} +; וַיָּשֶׂם Gn 2^{8} +; sf. יְשִׂמֵנִי 2 S 15^{4}, וַיְשִׂימְךָ 1 K 10^{9}; 2 fs. וַתָּשִׂימִי Is 51^{23}; וָאָשִׂים 1 S 28^{21} +, וָאָשִׂימָה Ezr 8^{17} Ju 12^{3} Qr (Kt ואישמה); 2 mpl. תָּשִׂימוּ Gn 32^{17} +, תְּשִׂימוּן Ex 22^{24} +, etc.; *Imv.* ms. שִׂים Gn 24^{2} +, etc.; *Inf. abs.* שׂוֹם Dt 17^{15} +, cstr. שׂוּם 45^{7} +, שִׂים Jb 20^{4} + 2 S 14^{7} Qr (Kt שׂוּם), שׂימו Is 10^{6} Kt (Qr שׂוּמוֹ), etc.; *Pt.* שָׂם Am 7^{8} +, fs. הַשָּׂמָה Is 51^{10} (so rd. for MT הַשָּׂמָה); pl. שָׂמִים Mal 2^{2} +; *pass.* שִׂים Nu 24^{21} (cf. Di), Ob^{4}; f. acc. to most שׂוּמָה 2 S 13^{32} (van d. H. שׂימה Kt), but v. infr.; שִׂמָה ψ 56^{9} Bae Buhl, but most Imv. ms.;—*put, set* (oft. ‖ נָתַן **2**, q.v.), c. acc. pers. vel rei (expr. or impl.): **1. a.** *put, set*, in a place, + שָׁם Gn 2^{8} (J), + acc. loc. 28^{11} (E) + 5 t. +, c. 2 acc. + loc., 2 K 10^{8} *heads* (in) *heaps* at (acc. loc.), cf. Lv 24^{6} (עַל); + בְּ 40^{15} (E), fig. of י׳, *put* his name, בִּירוּשׁ׳ 2 K 21$^{4.7}$ = 2 Ch 33^{7}, cf. c. שָׁם 1 K 9^{3} Dt 12^{5} + 6 t.; esp. בְּ

of receptacle Gn 31^{34} (E), Ex 2^{3} (E), Ju 6^{19} + oft.; sackcloth on (ב) loins Gn 37^{34} (J), 1 K 20^{31}, crown on head Zc 6^{11} Est 1^{17}, shoes on feet Ez 24^{17}; hook, etc., in nose 1 K 19^{28} = Is 37^{29} Jb 40^{26}, incense בְּאַפֶּךָ Dt 33^{10}, i.e. cause thee (׳י) to smell it; feet in stocks (fig.) Jb 13^{27} 33^{11}; knife into throat Pr 23^{2} (fig. of self-restraint, Fl in De); words into mouth Ex 4^{15} (J), Nu 22^{38} (E) + 8 t., + Dt 31^{19} teach to say or sing; into heart Jb 22^{22}, ins. also 1 S 29^{10} 𝔊 Th We Dr Kit Bu HPS; trust in God ψ 78^{7}; (guilt of) blood into house Dt 22^{8}, cf. Ju 9^{24} (עַל pers.; so, c. נָתַן Dt 21^{8} Je 26^{15} Jon 1^{14}); something into hand Ex 4^{21} (E), of wonders, i.e. enable hand to do them; elsewhere = take, of hammer Ju 4^{21}, booty 1 K 20^{6}, so (fig.) *take one's life* (נֶפֶשׁ) *into one's palm* (i.e. risk it) Ju 12^{3} 1 S 19^{5} 28^{21} Jb 13^{14}; put eyes בַּפּוּךְ 2 K 9^{30} (v. פּוּךְ, cf. Is 54^{11}); נֶפֶשׁ (= *person*), בַּחַיִּים ψ 66^{9} (subj. ׳י); *set* men *at* (the use of) implements 2 S 12^{31} (prob., cf. Dr
5493, HPS; > וַיָּשַׂר(ם) *sawed them with*, as ‖ 1 Ch 20^{3},
7787 Th We); 1 K 2^{5} (‖ נתן) is dub.; 𝔊L Klo Kit rd. וַיִּקֹּם; *charge* something *against* (ב pers.; properly *put in*, i.e. attribute, impute, to) 1 S 22^{15} Jb 4^{18}; so, c. לְ pers. Dt 22^{14}, cf. (לְ om.) v^{17}; *put* בְּקֶרֶב Am 7^{8} Is 63^{11}, בְּתוֹךְ Ez 26^{12}. **b.** *put* something *upon* (עַל) Nu 21$^{8.9}$ (E) + oft.; jewels, clothes, on person Gn 24^{17} (J), 41^{42} (E), Lv 8^{8} (P), Ru 3^{3}, turban Zc 3$^{5.5}$ Ex 29^{5} (P), Lv 8^{9} (P), cf. (prep. om.) Jb 24^{15} 36^{13} (fig.), girdle Je 13$^{1.2}$, sackcloth 1 K 21^{27}; שׂ׳ אָדָם עֲלֵי־הָאָרֶץ Jb 20^{4} (of man's creation); of siege and siege engines, עַל = *against*, Mi 4^{14} Ez 4^{2} 23^{24}; *put, lay, upon* (עַל), 2 K 4^{29} +; hand Gn 48^{18} (J) + 3 t., + *upon mouth*, in silence Ju 18^{19} Jb 21^{5}, and awe Mi 7^{16}, so c. לְ Jb 29^{9}, לְמוֹ 40$^{4.40}$, upon (עַל) head 2 S 13^{19} (in despair, cf. Je 2^{37}); acc. of disease Ex 15^{26} (J), so (ב pers.) v^{26} Dt 7^{16}; fig., spirit (עַל) Nu 11^{17} (JE), name 6^{27} (P), duty Jb 37^{15} (?), reproach 1 S 11^{2}, וַיָּשִׂימוּ רָעָה תַּחַת טוֹבָה ψ 109^{5} (𝔊 Bae וַיָּשִׁיבוּ, so, or וַיְשַׁלְּמוּ, Hup Che); שׂ׳ עַל לֵב Ct 8^{6} (sim.), so, fig., = remember, treasure up, Is 42^{25} 47^{7} (‖ זָכַר), + 6 t., c. אֶל 2 S 13^{33} 19^{20} (‖ id.); c. ב 1 S 21^{13}; cf. שׂ׳ בְּאָזְנֵי Ex 17^{14} (E), impress upon. **c.** *put, lay, set,* c. לְ, 2 K 11^{16} *lay* (violent) *hands on* = 2 Ch 23^{15}; *put* end *to* Jb 18^{2} 28^{3}; set לַמָּרוֹם 5^{11}; *render* glory *to* Jos 7^{19} (JE; ‖ נָתַן), Is 42^{12}; *make* covenant *with* 2 S 23^{5}; *set* food *for* Gn 43^{32} (J), 2 S 12^{20}, prep. om. Gn 43^{31} (J), so, c. לִפְנֵי 1 S 9^{24} 28^{22} 2 K 6^{22}; שׂ׳ לִפְנֵי elsewhere Ju 18^{21}, of precedence Gn 48^{20b} (E); *set* laws (as authoritative) לִפְנֵי Ex 19^{7} 21^{1} (both E), Dt 4^{44}; God (as moral ruler) לְנֶגְדָּם ψ 54^{5} 86^{14}; שׂ׳ נֶגֶד also Gn 31^{37} (E), נֹכַח Ez 14$^{4.7}$; לְעֵינֵי Gn 30^{41} (J). **d.** *put*, c. בֵּין Jos 24^{7} (E) + 5 t. (Ex 8^{19} v. פְּדוּת p. 804), + Gn 30^{36} (J), 32^{17} (E), *put* space *between*; c. תַּחַת Ex 17^{12} (E), + 3 t. (Ob ^{7} del. לַחְמְךָ We GASm Now al.) + שׂ׳ יָד תַּחַת יָרֵךְ in oath Gn 24$^{2.9}$ 47^{29} (all J); *put*, c. אֶל loc. 1 S 6$^{11.15}$ 19^{13a} Hb 2^{15}, אֶל pers. Jb 5^{8} *commit unto*; c. אֵצֶל rei Lv 6^{3} (P), מִצַּד rei Dt 31^{26} (P); שׂ׳ עִמָּךְ 1 S 9^{23} *lay up* something *with thee*, reserve it; *put*, c. יַחַד Mi 2^{12} *put together* = collect (‖ קִבֵּץ, אָסַף); without modifier 1 K 18$^{23.23.25}$; Ez 30^{21} *apply* bandage (‖ נָתַן). **2.** *set, direct:* **a.** sword against (ב) Ju 7^{22}; fig. *extend* compassion, לְ pers. Is 47^{6}. **b.** *direct* לֵב (*mind*) *toward*, pay attention to, c. לְ, 1 S 9^{20} Dt 32^{46} Ez 40^{4} 44^{5b}; c. אֶל Ex 9^{21} (J), 1 S 25^{25} 2 S 18$^{3.3}$ Jb 2^{3} 34^{14} (Bu Du del. לֵב and rd. יָשִׁיב רוּחוֹ); c. עַל Hg 1$^{5.7}$ Jb 1^{8}; compl. om. Ez 44^{5a} Hg 2$^{15.18.18}$ Is 41^{22}; Ju 19^{30} read perh. לִבְבְכֶם for לָכֶם (or עֵצָה for עֻצוּ), v. esp. GFM$^{Heb. Hpt.}$; לֵב om., Is 41^{20} (+ הִשְׂכִּיל, יָדַע, רָאָה), c. ב pers. Jb 23^{6} (so Bu, who cps. 4^{20} 24^{12} 34^{23}, but all cases dub.); שִׂים לֵב, c. עַל = *intend* Dn 1^{8} (obj. cl.). **c.** *set* face (פָּנִים) toward (acc. loc.) Gn 31^{21} (E), + לָבוֹא Je 42$^{15.15.17}$ 44^{12}, cf. 2 K 12^{18} Dn 11^{17}; c. אֶל, *toward* or *against* (implying opposition) Ez 6^{2} + 5 t. Ez, c. עַל Ez 29^{2} 35^{2}, c. דֶּרֶךְ of direction 21^{2}; c. ב (fig. of oppos., subj. ׳י): הִנְנִי שָׂם פָּנַי בָּכֶם לְרָעָה Je 44^{11}, cf. 21^{10} Ez 15^{7} (‖ נתן), Lv 20^{5} (P); c. לְ rei (human subj.) Dn 11^{18} Qr (< Kt ישב); c. עַל pers. + לִמְלֹךְ of purpose 1 K 2^{15}; *set* eyes (עֵינַיִם) upon, c. עַל pers. = behold Gn 44^{21} (J), = look after, take care of, Je 39^{12} 40^{4}, לְטוֹבָה 24^{6}, but לְרָעָה Am 9^{4}. **3. a.** *set, ordain*, c. acc. rei Nu 24^{23} (> acc. pers. Di). **b.** *set, establish* a law, statute, + לְ pers. Ex 15^{25} Jos 24^{25} (both E), cf. Pr 8^{29}; + ב loc. Is 42^{4} ψ 78^{5} (‖ הֵקִים), also 81^{6} Je 33^{25} + 2 S 20^{19} (שָׁמוּ) for שְׁלֻמֵי 𝔊 Ew We Kit Bu HPS, cf. Dr); *establish* something as (לְ) law Gn 47^{26} (J), 1 S 30^{25} (+ לְ pers.); *establish* bazaars (as a right), ב loc., 1 K 20^{34}; *appoint* a set time Ex 9^{5} (J), Jb 34^{23} (rdg. מוֹעֵד for עוֹד GHBWr Bu), ins. (perh.) 1 S 13^{8} so Dr Klo HPS (> ins. אמר Th We Bu Kit, after 𝔊 𝔗); a place, + לְ pers. Ex 21^{13} 2 S 7^{10} = 1 Ch 17^{9}, לְ rei 1 K 8^{21} (+ שָׁם). **c.** *set, found* a nation, Is 44^{7} (si vera l.), *establish* it ψ 89^{30} (לָעַד). **d.** *set, appoint* (as ruler, official) + עַל pers. vel gent., Ex 1^{11} 5^{14} 18^{21} (all E), Dt 17$^{14.15.15.15}$ Ju 11^{11} (+ לְ of office), 2 S 17^{25} (+ תַּחַת

instead of) + 6 t. + Gn 47^{6} (J; second acc. = ruler, expressed), 2 S 23^{23} (אֶל), עַל in ‖ 1 Ch 11^{25}; also 2 acc. + ל and ב loc. ψ 105^{21}, ב loc. 2 S 15^{4} 2 Ch 33^{14}, בְּרֹאשׁ *at the head of*, Dt 1^{13}, 2 acc. alone Ct 1^{6}; c. acc. pers. + ל pers. Gn 27^{37} (E), Ho 2^{2} 1 S 8^{5} (+ inf.); + ל of title Gn 45$^{8.9}$ Ex 2^{14} (+ עַל; all E) + 4 t. + Ju 8^{33} (+ ל pers.), + Ez 44^{8} (perh. rd. וַתְּשִׂימוּם Hi Sm Co and most); + ל of purpose Hb 1^{12}; + ב of position, ל pers. 1 S 8^{11}; c. acc. of office alone 1 S 8^{12} (+ ל pers.), so Co Ez 21$^{27\,a}$ (שָׂרִים for כָּרִים, v. כַּר sub כרר), 1 K 20^{24} (+ תחת), cf. 2 Ch 23^{18}, + אֶל, עַל, of task Nu 4^{19} (P); Jb 7^{20} *set me as* (ל) *mark for* (ל) *him*. **e.** *set, constitute, make*, c. כ pers. vel rei, Gn 13^{16} (J) *I will make thy seed as the dust*, 32^{13} (J) 48^{20} (E), Dt 10^{22} Ho 11^{8} + 16 t. + (bad sense) Ho 2^{5} Na 3^{6} 1 K 19^{2}. **f.** *set, determine, fix*, bounds Je 5^{22} (2 acc.) Jb 38$^{5.33}$ ψ 104^{9}; pass. *determined, settled*, + עַל־פֶּה 2 S 13^{32} (but v. II. שׂוּם); *appoint, send*, frogs לְפַרְעֹה Ex 8^{8} (J), c. acc. pers. + עַל *against* 2 K 18^{14}. **4. a.** *set, station*, at a post, etc., acc. pers. Jos 8^{13} (JE), + ב loc. 2 K 10^{24} Je 9^{7} + 5 t., + adv. acc. Gn 33^{2} (J), + בֵּין loc. Jos 8^{12}, + ל (against) and אַחֲרֵי loc. v^{2} (both JE), + ל against Ju 9^{25} (+ עַל loc.), + אֶל against 20$^{29.36}$; doubtful are 1 S 15^{2} (c. ל pers.), 1 K 20$^{12.12}$ (עַל־הָעִיר), where no obj. expr. (in MT); either an obj. has fallen out, or vb. (in techn. military sense), here intrans. or inwardly trans. (Dl$^{ZK\ ii.\ 397}$ *forward! take direction toward;* cf. also [on Sm] We Dr Löhr), or else שׂ׳ is corrupt (cf. HPS^{Sm}). **b.** *put* in position, sacred bread, sword, staves, bars, c. acc. 1 S 21^{7} Ez 21^{27} Nu 4$^{6.8.11.14}$ + 4 t. P, Jb 38^{10}; + עַל Ex 32^{27} (E), 40^{20} (P), מִמַּעַל ל Je 43^{10}, מֵעַל Est 3^{1}; + (various modifiers) 8 t.; *set in place*, תֵּבֵל Jb 34^{13} (De al.), but context favours שָׁמַר Bu; Du שׂ׳ לִבּוֹ בְּתֵבֵל. **c.** *set up* altars 1 K 2^{19} Je 11^{13}, stone as memorial Gn 18^{18} (J), 28^{22} (E), 1 S 7^{12} (cf. הֵקִים Gn 31^{45} +), image, etc. Ju 18^{31} (‖ הֵקִים), Dt 27^{15} 1 K 12^{29} (ב loc., ‖ נָתַן), 2 K 21^{7} (ב loc.) = 2 Ch 33^{7}, cf. ψ 74^{4} Is 57^{8} and, + ב loc., Je 7^{30} 32^{34}; rods before (לְעֵינֵי) cattle Gn 30^{41} (‖ וַיַּצֵּג v^{38}), cf. v^{42}, guide-posts Je 31^{21}, bed 2 K 4^{10} (+ ל pers.). **d.** = plant, wheat Is 28^{25}, tree 41^{19} (ב loc.; ‖ נָתַן), slip Ez 17^{5} (עַל *by*). **e.** *set, fix* (countenance) 2 K 8^{11}, so usu., but acc. om., and sense dub.; read perh. וַיֵּשֶׁם (√שׁמם, cf. e.g. 1 K 9^{8}), so Klo Kmp Kit Benz. **5. a.** *make* a thing, or pers. (acc.), *for, transform into* (ל), Jos 6^{18} (J) make camp לְחֵרֶם, Mi 1^{6} *make Samaria* לְעִי, Gn 21$^{13.18}$ (E), Ex 14^{21} (JE), Mi 4^{7} (both good sense), Is 28^{17} 42$^{15.16}$ + 12 t. Is. (25^{2} rd. עִיר for מֵעִיר Vrss. Comm.), Je 2^{7} + 8 t. Je, + 14 t. + Ju 1^{28} *they made the Can. into the corvée;* וְיָשֵׂם לְדֶרֶךְ פְּעָמָיו ψ 85^{14} *maketh his steps into a way* (so RV Hup Che Dr, but meaning obscure; De Bae *attend to the way of* (לְבּ om.); Schr Hup-Now rd. וְיִשְׁמֹר ד׳); c. 2 acc. Jos 8^{28} (J), 1 S 11^{11} Mi 1^{7} 1 K 5^{23} (prægn. c. עַד loc.), + 29 t. **b.** *make, constitute*, 2 acc., 1 S 8^{1} 18^{13} (+ ל pers.) 22^{7} (לְכֻלְּכֶם, ל of acc.; or < rd. וְכֻלְּכֶם), Is 3^{7} 60^{17} + 6 t., + 1 S 11^{11} *form people in bands*, cf. Jb 1^{17} (one acc., *form bands*), + (acc. pers. om.) Ex 4$^{11\,b}$ (J), cf. (beast, in fig.) Ez 19^{5}; 2 acc. and acc. + ל in same ver., Is 54^{12} *I will make rubies thy pinnacles, and* (transform) *thy gates into carbuncles;* in phr. of naming, שָׂם שְׁמוֹ יִשְׂרָאֵל 2 K 17^{34}, cf. Ju 8^{31} Ne 9^{7}; c. ל, וַיָּשֶׂם לָהֶם שֵׁמוֹת Dn 1^{7}, וַיּ׳ לְדָנִיֵּאל בֵּלְטְשַׁאצַּר v^{7}; *make, fashion*, c. acc. rei + ל pers. Ex 4$^{11\,a}$ (J; י׳ subj.); grave Na 1^{14} (but on text and mng. v. Now Bi$^{SB\ Wiener\ Ak.\ 1894,\ Abh.\ v}$); c. acc. דֶּרֶךְ Is 43^{19} (ב loc.), cf. Ez 21$^{24.25}$ (+ ל inf.); ψ 50^{23} is dub., usu. *order* (one's) *way*, De Dr *prepare way* (which), etc., Gr Che תָּם for שָׂם; *make* name + ל pers. 2 S 7^{23} = 1 Ch 17^{21}, 2 S 14^{7}; *make* for, ל pers. (or *give* to), c. acc. of posterity Gn 45^{7} (E); 1 S 2^{20} rd. prob. יְשַׁלֵּם 𝔊 We Kit Bu HPS, cf. Dr; Ezr 10$^{44\,b}$ is obscure, Gu-Batten del. וַיָּשִׂימוּ and rd. וַיְשַׁלְּחוּ bef. נָשִׁים, cf. 3 Esdr 9^{36} Be-Ry Ryle. **c.** *work, bring to pass*, c. acc. rei, of י׳'s signs, etc., + ב loc. Ex 10^{2} (J), Je 32^{20} Is 66^{19} ψ 46^{9} 78^{43} 105^{27}. **d.** *appoint, give*, acc. rei Nu 6^{26} (P), Is 61^{3} (‖ נָתַן; both c. ל pers.); a pledge Jb 17^{3} (‖ עָרְבֵנִי *go surety for me*, but rd. perh. עֶרְבֹנִי as obj., v. p. 786 b); וְשׂוֹם שֶׂכֶל Ne 8^{8} *giving understanding* (making sense clear). †**Hiph.** *Pf.* 1 s. consec. וַהֲשִׂמֹתִיהוּ Ez 14^{8}, acc. pers. + ל, *I will make him for a sign* (< שׂ for שׁ van d. H., √שׁמם; Co Berthol Toy וַשְׁמֹּתִיהוּ (Qal), Krae וְהִשְׁמַדְתִּיהוּ); *Imv.* fs. הָשִׂימִי 21^{21}, prob. del as dittogr. Co Krae after 𝔊 𝔖 𝔙 𝔗 Nö$^{ZMG\ xxxvii\ (1883),\ 530}$ (> Bö Toy al. הַקְדִּימוּ); *Pt.* מֵשִׂים Jb 4^{20} = **Qal** שׂוּם (לֵב) (v$^{23\,b}$), but phr. dub., and text perh. crpt., v. Me Nö$^{l.\ c.}$ †**Hoph.** *Impf.* 3 ms. וַיּוּשַׂם Gn 24^{33} Qr (Kt ויישם Ges$^{§\ 73\ f}$) *there was set before him* (לְפָנָיו) *to eat*, cf. Ol$^{MB\ Ak.\ 1870,\ 389}$ Kö$^{i.\ 435}$, who read also וַיּוּשַׂם 50^{26} *he was laid* in (ב) a mummy-case (for MT וַיִּישֶׂם), Di$^{(ed.\ 4.5.6)}$ allows this.

†[יְשִׂימְאֵל] **n.pr.m.** Simeonite (*Ēl estab-* 3450
lisheth); — וְיִשׂ׳ 1 Ch 4^{36} (van d. H. Gi; Baer וִישִׂימִיאֵל); 𝔊^{L} Ισμαηλ.

8667 †תְּשׂוּמֶת **n.f.** (deposit, then, cstr. ת׳ יַד) **pledge, security,** Lv 5^{21} (P; ‖ פִּקָּדוֹן).

II. **שׂוּם, שִׂים** (perh. √ of foll.; cf. Ar. شَأَمَ *be inauspicious,* شُؤْمٌ *ill-luck*).

7760 †שׂוּמָה (van d. H. שׂמה Kt) perhaps **n.f. token of unluckiness, scowl**;—2 S 13^{32}, so
8040, Ew$^{G\ iii.\ 234,\ H.\ 172}$ (abbrev. fr. שׂמאל; or emend. שִׂמְמָה)
8057 We RS$^{Ency.\ Brit.\ (9)\ DAVID}$ Kit, cf. Dr HPS.

7787 †[שׂוּר] **vb. saw** (‖ form of נָשַׂר; denom.
4883 fr. מַשּׂוֹר?);—**Qal** *Impf.* 3 ms. וַיָּשַׂר 1 Ch 20^{3} (but
5493 v. שׂים **1 a**).—Ho 9^{12} v. סור; Ju 9^{22} Ho 8^{4} v.
8323 שׂרר; 12^{5} v. שׂרה. p. 673, 693f, 962f, 975, 979

7795 †שׂוֹרָה Is 28^{25} prob. dittogr. for foll. שְׂעֹרָה (Koppe We Che al.; 𝔊 𝔖 om.); > 𝔙 Ges Di al. *in rows* (adv. acc.; but NH שׂוּרָה, Ar. سُورٌ, Lag GGN, 1889, 298; cf. Vogelst$^{Landwirthsch.\ 41}$ who favours ש׳ in Is. More plausible would be some grain, as שורה Zinj. Inscr., Lzb^{374} Sachau$^{Panammu\ 23}$).

7797 †**שׂוּשׂ, שִׂישׂ vb. exult, rejoice** (Nö$^{ZMG\ xxxvii\ (1883),\ 536}$ der. ('perh.') fr. interj., as شَأْشَأْ an enticing call, so Gerber^{20});—**Qal** *Pf.* 3 ms. שָׂשׂ Dt 28^{63}+, 1 s. שַׂשְׂתִּי ψ 119^{14}, etc.; *Impf.* 3 ms. יָשִׂישׂ Dt 28^{63}+, 3 mpl. יְשֻׂשׂוּם Is 35^{1} (Ges$^{§\ 47n}$ Kö$^{i.\ 510}$, but ם erron. Kenn Ol$^{§\ 244\ a}$, prob. dittogr., so Lo Hi Gr Che^{Hpt} Marti), etc.; *Imv.* fs. שִׂישִׂי La 4^{2}, mpl. שִׂישׂוּ Is 65^{18} 66^{10}; *Inf. abs.* שׂוֹשׂ 61^{10}; *cstr.* לָשׂוּשׂ Dt 30^{9};—*exult, display joy,* c. עַל *over,* Dt 28$^{63.63}$ 30$^{9.9}$ Je 32^{41} Is 62^{5} Zp 3^{1}(+בְּשִׂמְחָה; ‖ גִּיל), ψ 119^{162}; c. ב Is 61^{10} (שׂוֹשׂ אָשִׂישׂ), 65^{19} ψ 35^{9} (all ‖ גִּיל); 40^{17} 68^{4} (+ בְּשִׂמְחָה; ‖ עָלַץ), 70^{5} (all ‖ שָׂמַח); 119^{14} Jb 39^{21} (horse), ψ 19^{6} (sun, as athlete); c. כִּי and cl. La 1^{21}; abs. Is 35^{1} 65^{18} (both ‖ גִּיל), 64^{4} (but del. שָׂשׂ וְ 𝔊 Gr Du Che^{Hpt} Marti), 68^{14}; La 4^{21} (‖ שָׂמַח), Jb 3^{22} (‖ שְׂמֵחִים אֱלֵי־גִיל), Is 66^{10} (acc. cogn.; ‖ שָׂמַח, גִּיל).—Ez 21^{15} is crpt., Co rds. לְאַנְשֵׁי (for נָשִׂישׂ), Krae לִנְשִׂיאֵי, other conj. in comm.; on cl. vid. esp. Da Toy$^{Heb.\ Hpt.}$.

8342 †שָׂשׂוֹן, שָׂשֹׂן **n.m.** $^{Is\ 51,\ 3}$ **exultation, rejoicing,** abs. שׂ׳ ψ 45^{8}+, שָׂשֹׂן Est 8^{16}; cstr. שְׂשׂוֹן (Sta$^{§\ 296\ e}$) ψ 51^{14} 119^{111};—*exultation, joy* (esp. in י׳'s favour), Jo 1^{12} Is 12^{3} ψ 51^{14} 105^{43} 119^{111}; שֶׁמֶן שׂ׳ (i.e. with which guests were anointed; fig.) ψ 45^{8} Is 61^{3} (opp. אֵבֶל); שֵׁם שׂ׳ Je 33^{9} (‖ תְּהִלָּה; on text v. Gie Albr$^{ZAW\ xvi\ (1896),\ 115}$); elsewh. ‖ שִׂמְחָה: Je 7^{34} 15^{16} 16^{9} 25^{10} 33^{11} Is 22^{13} (only here condemned as reckless, wanton), 35^{10} 51$^{3.11}$ Zc 8^{19} ψ 51^{10} Est 8$^{16.17}$; ‖ שָׂמַח Je 31^{13} (opp. אֵבֶל).

†מָשׂוֹשׂ **n.m.** $^{Is\ 24,\ 8}$ id.;—abs. מ׳ Is 32^{13}+, 4885
cstr. מְשׂוֹשׂ Jb 8^{19}+; sf. מְשׂוֹשִׂי Je 49^{25}, מְשׂוֹשָׂהּ Ho 2^{13};—*exultation,* in gen., La 5^{15} (opp. אֵבֶל), Is 24^{11} 66^{10} (acc. cogn.); of bridegroom 62^{5}; מ׳ תֻּפִּים 24^{8}, מ׳ כִּנּוֹר v^{8}; בָּתֵּי מ׳ 33^{13}; of Jerus. (as causing joy) 60^{15} ψ 48^{3} La 2^{15}, cf. Je 49^{25} קִרְיַת מְשׂוֹשִׂי (‖ תְּהִלָּה), Is 65^{18} (‖ גִּילָה); מ׳ דַּרְכּוֹ (of godless man) Jb 8^{19}; מ׳ פְּרָאִים Is 32^{14}, i.e. desert.—מ׳ Is 8^{6}, si vera l., is cstr. before prep., but מָסוֹס (מִפְּנֵי), Hi Gie Che Du Kit Marti al.

שִׂחַ v. שִׂיחַ. p. 967 7808

†[שָׂחָה] **vb. swim** (NH סָחוּ *swimming;* 7811
𝔗 סְחָא, Syr. ܣܚܐ *swim, bathe,* also סַחְיָא, סַחְיָנָא, שָׂחְיָנָא *swimmer;* Aph. *wash*);—**Qal** *Pt.* + *Inf. cstr.* כַּאֲשֶׁר יְפָרֵשׂ הַשֹּׂחֶה לִשְׂחוֹת Is 25^{11}. **Hiph.** *Impf.* 1 s. אַשְׂחֶה ψ 6^{7} *I make* my bed *swim* (with my tears; another view sub שִׂיחַ **Qal 1**).

†שָׂחוּ **n.**[**m.**$^{Sta\ §\ 192a}$] **swimming** (on format. 7813
(and tone) Ges$^{§\ 84a\ c}$ Kö$^{ii.\ 1,\ 60.\ 497}$);—מֵי שׂ׳ Ez 47^{5}.

†[שָׂחַט] **vb. squeeze out** (so NH סָחַט, 7818
Aram. סְחַט; Mand. סחט *spread out* Nö$^{M\ 238}$);—**Qal** *Impf.* 1 s. וָאֶשְׂחַט Gn 40^{11} (E; אֶת־הָעֲנָבִים אֶל).

†[שָׂחִיף] **adj.**(?), doubtful (van d. H. שְׂחִיף; 7824
√ unknown);—cstr. שְׂחִיף עֵץ Ez 41^{16} usually *panelled, wainscotted, with wood;* or **n.** *a wainscot of wood,* but Co חִפּוּי, Toy חָפוּי (cstr. חִפּוּי).

†שָׂחַק **vb. laugh** (‖ צחק, q.v.; NH שָׂחַק, 7832
סָחַק; Eth. ሠሐቀ:);—**Qal** *Pf.* 3 ms. וְשָׂ׳ consec. Pr 29^{9}; 3 pl. שָׂחֲקוּ La 1^{7} Jb 30^{1}; *Impf.* 3 ms. יִשְׂחַק Jb 39^{7}+, etc.; *Inf. cstr.* שְׂחוֹק Ju 16^{21} Ec 3^{4};—**1. a.** *laugh* at, usu. in contempt, derision, c. עַל pers. Jb 30^{1} ψ 52^{8}; עַל rei La 1^{7}; c. ל pers. God subj. ψ 37^{13} 59^{9} (‖ לָעַג); c. ל rei vel pers. = have no fear of, Hb 1^{10} Jb 5^{22} Pr 31^{25}, also, fig., of noble animals Jb 39$^{7.18.22}$ 41^{21}; abs., Pr 29^{9} (opp. רָגַז), of י׳ ψ 2^{4} (‖ לָעַג), of wisdom Pr 1^{26} (ב temp.; ‖ *id.*). **b.** c. אֶל pers., appar. of friendly laugh Jb 29^{24}; in gen. Ec 3^{4} (opp. בָּכָה). **2.** *sport, play,* Ju 16^{27}. **Pi.** *Pf.* 1 s. וְשִׂחַקְתִּי 1 S 6^{21}; *Impf.* 3 ms. וַיְשַׂחֶק־ Ju 16^{25}, etc.; *Inf. cstr.* לְשַׂחֶק־ ψ 104^{26}; *Pt.* מְשַׂחֵק Pr 26^{19} 1 Ch 15^{29}, f. מְשַׂחֶקֶת Pr 8$^{30.31}$; pl. מְשַׂחֲקִים 2 S 6^{5}+, מְשַׂחֲקוֹת 1 S 18^{7};—**1.** *make sport,* Ju 16^{25} (ל pers.) 2 S 2^{14} (לִפְנֵי pers.; in tournament), Pr 8^{30} (לִפְנֵי), v^{31} (ב loc.). **2.** *jest,* Pr 26^{19}. **3.** *play:* incl. instr. music, singing and dancing 1 S 18^{7}, c. לִפְנֵי י׳

2 S 6[5] (ב instr.), = 1 Ch 13[8], 2 S 6[21] 1 Ch 15[29] (+ מְרַקֵּד); of merry-making Je 15[17] (|| עָלַז), 30[19] 31[4]; of children's sport Zc 8[5]; of beasts Jb 40[20] ψ 104[26]; of man, *play* with (ב) crocod. Jb 40[29]. **Hiph.** (declar.) *Pt.* pl. מַשְׂחִיקִים 2 Ch 30[10] they *uttered mockery* עֲלֵיהֶם (|| מַלְעִגִים).

7814 †שְׂחֹק, שְׂחוֹק **n.[m.] laughter, derision, sport** (prop. inf. cstr.);—abs. שְׂחֹק Je 48[26]+5 t.; cstr. Ec 7[6]; abs. שְׂחוֹק Je 20[7] + 7 t.;—**1.** *laughter* (joyous) Jb 8[21] (|| תְּרוּעָה), ψ 126[2] (|| רִנָּה), Ec 2[2] (|| שִׂמְחָה), 10[19] (|| שִׂמַּח); as hollow Pr 14[13] (opp. כָּאֵב), Ec 7[3] (opp. כַּעַס), cf. שׂ׳ הַכְּסִיל v[6]. **2.** (object of) *derision*, הָיָה לְשׂ׳, Je 20[7] 48[26.27] (rd. לְשׂ׳ for MT הַשׂ׳ 𝔊 𝔖 𝔙 Gie Du; Co del. vv), v[39] La 3[14]; elsewh. Jb 12[4.4]. **3.** *sport* Pr 10[23].

3446 יִשְׂחָק **n.pr.m.** v. sub צחק. p. 850

4890 †מִשְׂחָק **n.[m.] object of derision**, Hb 1[10].

7846 [שֵׂט], שֵׂטִים v. [שׂוט]. p. 962

7847 †[שָׂטָה] **vb. turn aside** (Aram. סְטָא, ܣܛܐ *id.*; שְׂטָא *stray*; Eth. ሠጠየ: III. *be seduced*, etc.; cf. Dr[JPhil. xi (1882), 205]);—**Qal** *Pf.* 2 fs. שָׂטִית Nu 5[19.20]; *Impf.* 3 fs. תִּשְׂטֶה v[12.29], juss. 3 ms. יֵשְׂטְ Pr 7[25]; *Imv.* ms. שְׂטֵה 4[15];—*turn aside*, of unfaithful wife Nu 5[12] (abs.), + תַּחַת אִישׁ, i.e. while married, v[19] (+ טֻמְאָה adv. acc.), v[20.29] (all P); of youth, fr. (מֵעַל) way of evil woman Pr 4[15], toward (אֶל) her ways 7[25].

7852 †[שָׂטַם] **vb. bear a grudge, cherish animosity, against** (NH שָׂטַם Niph., 𝔗 Gn 27[41] שְׂטַם; perh. akin to שׂטן q.v.);—**Qal** *Impf.* 3 ms. וַיִּשְׂטֹם Gn 27[41], 3 mpl. sf. יִשְׂטְמוּנִי ψ 55[4], etc.;—*cherish animosity against*, acc. pers. Gn 27[41] (J), 49[23] (poem in J), 50[15] (E), + בְּאַף ψ 55[4]; of י׳'s persistent assaults on Job, Jb 16[9] 30[21].

4895 †מַשְׂטֵמָה **n.f. animosity**;—Ho 9[7] + v[8] (del. We, cf. Now).

שׂטן (√of following).

7854 †שָׂטָן **n.m.**[ψ 109,6] **1. adversary. 2. Satan** (NH שָׂטָן, סָטָן; Aram. סָטָנָא, שָׂטָנָא, Syr. ܣܛܢܐ (Hebr.); NH vb. סָטַן, Aram. סְטַן; Ar. شَطَنَ is *be remote*, esp. fr. the truth, and fr. the mercy of God; شَيْطَانٌ *Satan*, Eth. ሰይጣን:);—**1.** *adversary*, in gen., personal or national; הָיָה לְשׂ׳ (ל) Nu 22[22] (JE), 1 S 29[4] (cf. Nes[Marg. 15]), 2 S 19[23], יָצָא לְשׂ׳ Nu 22[32] (JE); שׂ׳ 1 K 5[18] 11[25]; הֵקִים שׂ׳ ל, subj. God 1 K 11[14.23], cf. ψ 109[6] (|| רָשָׁע). **2.** *superhuman adversary*, הַשּׂ׳: **a.** of Job, one of בְּנֵי הָאֱלֹהִים Jb 1[6.7.7.8.9.12.12] 2[1.2.2.3.4.6.7]. **b.** of h. p. of Isr. bef. י׳, Zc 3[1.2.2]; 𝔊 ὁ διάβολος. **c.** as n.pr. שׂ׳ *Satan* 1 Ch 21[1] (interpr. 2 S 24[1]), 𝔊 διάβολος (𝔊 σατάν †1 K 11[14.23]; Σατανᾶς Mt 4[10] Mk 1[13] Lk 10[18] + 33 t. NT).

†[שָׂטַן] **vb.denom.** (Gerber[30]) **be or act as** 7853
adversary;—**Qal** *Impf.* 3 mpl. sf. יִשְׂטְנוּנִי ψ 38[21] 109[4]; *Inf.cstr.* sf. לְשִׂטְנוֹ Zc 3[1]; *Pt.* pl. cstr. שֹׂטְנֵי ψ 71[13], sf. שֹׂטְנַי 109[20], שׂוֹטְנַי v[29].

†I. שִׂטְנָה **n.f. accusation**;—Ezr 4[6]. 7855

†II. שִׂטְנָה **n.pr.putei** (*hostility*) Gn 26[21] (J). 7856

[שִׂיא], שִׂיאֹן v. נשׂא. p. 673 7863, 7865

†שִׂיב **vb. be hoary** (NH שֵׂיבָה *old age*; 7867
As. *šêbu, aged man*; Ar. شَابَ (ى) *become hoary*, Eth. ሢበ: (in deriv.); Aram. סִיב *be old*; ܣܳܒ *grow old*, ܣܰܝܒܽܘܬܳܐ *grey hair*);—**Qal** *Pf.* 1 s. זָקַנְתִּי וָשַׂבְתִּי 1 S 12[2]; *Pt.* שָׂב Jb 15[10] (+ יָשִׁישׁ *aged*).

†[שֵׂיב] **n.[m.]** (hoary) **age**;—sf. שֵׂיבוֹ 1 K 14[4]. 7869

†שֵׂיבָה **n.f. hoary head, old age**;—abs. 7872
שׂ׳ Ho 7[9]+; cstr. שֵׂיבַת Gn 44[31]; sf. שֵׂיבָתִי 42[38] 44[29], etc.;—**1.** *grey hair, hoary head* Ho 7[9] (fig.), Gn 42[38] 44[29.31] (all J), 1 K 2[6.9] Pr 16[31] 20[29]; אִישׁ שׂ׳ Dt 32[25] (opp. יוֹנֵק); || זָקֵן Lv 19[32] (H), || זִקְנָה Is 46[4], + id. ψ 71[18] (in these transition to foll.); fig. of sea Jb 41[24]. **2.** *old age*, שׂ׳ טוֹבָה Gn 15[15] (JE), 25[8] (P), Ju 8[32] 1 Ch 29[28]; שׂ׳ also ψ 92[15] (trees, in fig. of righteous), Ru 4[15], + 2 S 19[34] (𝔊 Ew Th Bu Kit, cf. We Dr HPS, אֶת־שֵׂיבָתְךָ, for אִתְּךָ).

שִׂיג v. I. [סוג]. p. 961 7873

שׂיד (√of foll.: NH סִיד *lime*, סַיָּד *whitewasher*; Aram. סִידָא, ܣܺܝܕܳܐ *lime*, Ar. شِيدٌ (not loan-word, cf. Frä[8])).

†שִׂיד **n.[m.] lime, whitewash**;— always 7875
שׂ׳;—*lime*, produced by burning bones Am 2[1], in sim. Is 33[12]; as *whitewash* Dt 27[2.4].

†[שׂוּד, שִׂיד] **vb. denom. whitewash**;— 7874
Qal *Pf.* 2 ms. וְשַׂדְתָּ אֹתָם בַּשִּׂיד Dt 27[2.4].

שֵׂיו, שֵׂיהוּ v. שֶׂה. p. 691 7716

I. **שׂיח** (√of foll.; NH שִׂיחַ *speak*, שִׂיחָה, סִיחָה *conversation* (oft.); Aram. שִׂיחַ *speak*; Nö[ZMG xxxviii (1883), 538] cp. Ar. شَاحَ (ى) *be eager, diligent*, whence (Buhl) *eager occupation* with sthg. as orig. mng. in Heb., but conjectural).

7879 †שִׂיחַ **n.m.**[ψ 104, 34] complaint, musing;—abs. שׂ׳ 1 K 18[27] Pr 23[29]; sf. שִׂיחִי 1 S 1[16]+, שִׂחִי Jb 23[2], שִׂיחוֹ 2 K 9[11] ψ 102[1];—**1.** *plaint, complaint:* Jb 7[13] 9[27] 10[1] (|| מר נפש), 21[4] 23[2] Pr 23[29] ψ 55[3] שָׁפַךְ שׂ׳ לפני י׳ 102[1] (|| אָהִימָה); קוֹלִי בְּשִׂיחִי 64[2]; 142[3]. Foll. are dub.: **2.** *musing,* 1 K 18[27] (E) of a god, || שִׂיג לוֹ, (so RV; SS '*nachdenken*'; Buhl '*beschäftigt sein*'; AV *talk*); ψ 104[34] of man (Buhl SS. Bae '*Rede,* oder *Gesang*').—Vid. also [שֵׂחַ] infr. **3.** *anxiety, trouble:* מֵרֹב שִׂיחִי 1 S 1[16] (defined in MT by כַּעַס, cf. HPS; so Buhl SS, but perh.=**1**). **4.** *talk:* שִׂיחוֹ 2 K 9[11] (so RV SS, but meaning obscure in context).

7881 †שִׂיחָה **n.f.** id.;—abs. שׂ׳ ψ 119[99] Jb 15[4]; sf. שִׂיחָתִי ψ 119[97];—**1.** *complaint:* שׂ׳ לִפְנֵי־אֵל Jb 15[4] (so Bu al., cf. שִׂיחַ **1** De al. *meditation,* cf. [גָּרַע]). **2.** (obj. of) *musing, study:* תּוֹרָה ψ 119[97]; עֵדוּת v[99].

7878 †שִׂיחַ **vb.denom.** muse, complain, poet. talk (of);—**Qal** *Impf.* 3 ms. יָשִׂיחַ ψ 119[23]; 3 fs. sf. תְּשִׂיחֶךָ Pr 6[22]; 1 s. אָשִׂיחַ ψ 119[78]+, etc.; *Imv.* ms. שִׂיחַ Jb 12[8], mpl. שִׂיחוּ Ju 5[10]+; *Inf. cstr.* שִׂיחַ ψ 119[148];—**1.** *complain:* ψ 55[18] 77[4] (both || הָמָה), Jb 7[11] (בְּמַר נַפְשִׁי), + ψ 6[7] (rd. prob. אָשִׂיחָה for אַשְׂחֶה). **2.** *muse:* עִם־לְבָבִי ψ 77[7]; c. ב, *meditate upon, study,* God's עֲלִילוֹת v[13] (|| הָגָה); אִמְרָה 119[15.78]; חֻקִּים v[23.48]; נִפְלָאוֹת v[27]; פִּקּוּדִים v[148]; c. acc. דִּבְרֵי נִפְלְאֹתֶיךָ 145[5]. **3. a.** *talk* (about), *sing* (of): abs. Ju 5[10] (ode); c. ב rei, ψ 105[2] = 1 Ch 16[9] (|| זַמֵּר, שִׁיר; so SS Gerber, but poss. =**2**, so Dr), ψ 69[13] (ב pers. *against;* || נְגִינוֹת, of mocking words). **b.** c. sf. pers. *talk* (with) Pr 6[22] (del. Toy); c. לְ *speak to* Jb 12[8] (Di '*sprich sinnend*'; Hi Bu rd. שֶׁרֶץ; Kau חַיַּת (so Bu as altern.), Bö al. sub II. שִׂיחַ). **Pôlʿel** *meditate, consider:* *Impf.* 3 ms. יְשׂוֹחֵחַ Is 53[8] (abs.); 1 s.
7751 אֲשׂוֹחֵחַ ψ 143[5] (ב rei; || הָגָה).—Gn 24[63] v. I. שׂוּט.

7808 [שֵׂחַ] **n.[m.]** thought;—sf. מַגִּיד לְאָדָם מַה־שֵּׂחוֹ Am 4[13]; read prob. שִׂחוֹ (against Ba[NB 79, 80]) unless otherwise corrupt.

II. שׂיח (√ of foll.; cf. perh. As. *šâḫu, grow, grow up* (of trees), *šiḫtu,* appar. *a shoot, sprout;* NH = BH; Pun. שח; Syr. ܫܝܚܐ *artemisia Judaica,* cf. Wetzst[Reisebericht 4, 41] Löw[p. 78], so Ar. شِيح Lane[1628] (cf. Lag[BN 159])).

7880 †שִׂיחַ **n.[m.]** bush, shrub, plant;—שׂ׳ abs. coll. Jb 30[4], cstr. שׂ׳ הַשָּׂדֶה Gn 2[5] (J); pl. שִׂיחִים Jb 30[7], אַחַד הַשִּׂיחִם Gn 21[15] (E).

I, II. שִׂים, שִׂימָה etc., v. I, II. שׂום. p. 962 7760

שֵׂךְ, שֻׂכָּה v. IV. שׂכך. שַׂךְ v. II. שׂכך. 7899-900, p. 768 7905

שׂכה (√ of foll.; NH סָכָה *look out,* Aram. סְכָא *look out, hope,* סַכְוָאָה *watchman,* סָכוּתָא (for Heb. מִצְפֶּה) *outlook-point;* ܣܟܐ Pa. *hope for;* Ar. شَكَا (و, ى) is *complain* (i.e. *disclose* grief?), مِشْكَاةٌ *lamp-niche,* Eth. መስኮት: *window*).

†שֶׂכְוִי **n.[m.]** perh. a celestial **appearance,** 7907
phenomenon (Rabb. Thes *mind;* De (after Talm.) *cock* (cf. NH שֶׂכְוִי *cock,* שֶׂכְוִיָּה *hen,* foreign words acc. Dalm), Di 'Wolkengebilde');—abs. שׂ׳ perh. of clouds (cf. || טֻחוֹת) Jb 38[36] (RV[m] *meteor*).

†[שְׂכִיָּה] **n.f.** very dub., only pl. cstr. שְׂכִיּוֹת 7914
הַחֶמְדָּה Is 2[16]: perh. gen. term, 𝔙 *quod visu pulchrum est,* Ges[Comm] 'köstliche Anblicke,' cf. De; others refer to *imagery* (cf. מַשְׂכִּית; as attracting the gaze) Che[Comm] RV Du; *watchtowers* (v. Aram.) Ew Di RV[m]; *standards* (as *conspicuous*) Thes; *ships* (*id.*) (Bennett [private letter], and now Gunk[Schöpfung 50] Che[Hpt] Marti, cf. || אֳנִיּוֹת; SS Bu[Jb 40, 31] prop. ס׳=שְׂפִינֹת *ships*).

†מַשְׂכִּית **n.f. show-piece, figure, ima-** 4906
gination;—abs. מ׳ Lv 26[1], sf. מַשְׂכִּיתוֹ Ez 8[12], מַשְׂכִּתוֹ Pr 18[11]; pl. cstr. מַשְׂכִּיּוֹת Pr 25[11] ψ 73[7], sf. מַשְׂכִּיֹּתָם Nu 33[52];—**1.** *show-piece,* specif. *carved figure,* of idolatrous symbols, Nu 33[52] (P; || צַלְמֵי מַסֵּכֹתָם), אֶבֶן מ׳ Lv 26[1] (|| מַצֵּבָה etc.), חַדְרֵי מ׳ Ez 8[12] (>del. Co); elsewhere מ׳ כֶּסֶף Pr 25[11] *silver carvings.* **2.** *imagination, conceit,* Pr 18[11], מ׳ לֵבָב ψ 73[7].

†שָׂכְיָה (so Baer Gi; var. שָׂכְיָא; van d. H. 7634
שָׂבְיָה; Kit[Hpt] dub.) **n.pr.m.** in Benj. 1 Ch 8[10]; 7634
Σαβια, Σεβια, 𝔊L Σεχια; 𝔖𝔙 *Sechia.*

†שַׂכִּין **n.[m.]** knife (NH סַכִּין; prob. loan- 7915
word (Lewy[Fremdw. 176]) fr. Aram. סַכִּינָא, ܣܟܝܢܐ *id.,* whence also Ar. سِكِّين Nö[M 125] Frä[84]; √ dub.);—abs. שׂ׳ Pr 23[2].

†שֶׂכוּ **n.pr.loc.** (si vera l.) near Ramah 7906
(=*outlook,* Kö[ii. 1, 61]);—1 S 19[22]; WMM[As. u. Eur. 165] cp. *T-ku* in Eg. inscr.; but 𝔊 Σεφ(ε)ι; read שְׁפִי Th We Dr Kit Bu HPS.

I. [שָׂכַךְ] **vb.** cover, lay over, so as to 5526
screen (cf. || √ I. סכך);—**Qal** *Pf.* 1 s. וְשַׂכֹּתִי כַפִּי 5526
עָלֶיךָ Ex 33[22] (JE). p. 696

5526, 7918 † II. [שָׂכַךְ] **vb. weave** (cf. ‖ √ II. סכך); **Po'lel** *Impf.* 2 ms. sf. תְּשֹׂכְכֵנִי Jb 10^{11} with bones and sinews *thou weavest me together.* p. 697

7900 † [שֹׂךְ] **n.[m.] booth, pavilion** (שׂ׳ perh. erron., cf. סֹךְ, סֻכָּה sub II. סכך);—sf. שֻׂכּוֹ La 2^{6} *his* [י׳'s] *pavilion* (‖ מֹעֲדוֹ).

5526, 7753 III. שׂכך (√ of foll.; cf. I. שׂוך, II. סוך). p. 692, 962

4881 † [מְשֻׂכָּה] **n.f. hedge**;—sf. מְשׂוּכָּתוֹ Is 5^{5} (if כּ right); perhaps rd. מְשֻׂכָּה v. sub I. שׂוך. p. 962

5526 IV. שׂכך (√ of foll.; cf. Ar. شَكَّ *pierce, transfix* (Lane ^{1582c}), شِكَّةٌ *weapons;* akin also to شَوْكٌ, Eth. ሦክ: *thorn, spine;* As. *sikkatu, peg,* Syr. ܣܶܟܬܳܐ *nail* do not belong here, cf. Dl $^{\text{Prol. 196}}$).

7899 † [שֵׂךְ] **n.[m.] thorn**;—pl. שִׂכִּים Nu 33^{55} (P; ‖ צְנִינִם).

7905 † [שֻׂכָּה] **n.f. barb, spear**;—pl. שֻׂכּוֹת Jb 40^{31}.

7919 † I. שָׂכַל **vb. be prudent** (Gerber ^{47} denom. fr. שֵׂכֶל, but vb. early; NH סָכַל, Hithp. *shew oneself attentive* (to), *look;* Aram. סְכַל (rare) *understand,* Ithpa. *look* (at), *consider,* Aph. *instruct;* שְׂכַל only Aph. (for Heb. הִשְׂכִּיל), *understand, make wise;* ܣܰܟܶܠ Pa. *teach,* Ethpa. *understand,* etc.; Sam. [Samaritan] Ithpa. *look* (for Heb. הִבִּיט); As. *šiklu, clever, šiklûtu, cleverness,* Meissn $^{\text{Suppl. 93}}$);—**Qal** *Pf.* 3 ms. שׂ׳ 1 S 18^{30} *be prudent, circumspect* (SS HPS); Kit Buhl Gerber al. *prosper.* **Hiph.** *Pf.* 3 ms. הִשְׂכִּיל Je 23^{5} 1 Ch 28^{19}; 1 s. הִשְׂכַּלְתִּי ψ 119^{99}; 3 mpl. הִשְׂכִּילוּ Jb 34^{27}+; *Impf.* יַשְׂכִּיל 1 S 18^{5}+; 2 ms. juss. תַּשְׂכֵּל Dn 9^{25}, etc.; *Imv.* mpl. הַשְׂכִּילוּ ψ 2^{10}; *Inf. abs.* הַשְׂכֵּל Je 9^{23}+; הַשְׂכֵּיל (Ges $^{\S 53k}$) Je 3^{15} Jb 34^{35}; *cstr.* הַשְׂכִּיל Gn 3^{6}+, etc.; *Pt.* מַשְׂכִּיל 1 S 18^{14}+, f. מַשְׂכֶּלֶת Pr 19^{14}; pl. מַשְׂכִּילִים Dn 11^{35}+, etc.; meanings hard to classify: scholars differ greatly;—**1.** *look at:* נֶחְמָד הָעֵץ לְהַשְׂכִּיל Gn 3^{6} (J) *was desirable to look upon* (so 𝔊 Ges De; AV, RV *to make one wise;* Ew Di Buhl SS Dr al. sub **3**). **2.** *give attention to, consider, ponder:* Is 41^{20} 44^{18} Dt 32^{29} ψ 64^{10} 106^{7} Jb 34^{27}; c. לְ Pr 21^{12}; c. אֶל ψ 41^{2} Ne 8^{13}; c. עַל Pr 16^{20}; c. בְּ ψ 101^{2} Dn 9^{13}. **3.** *have insight, comprehension:* Je 9^{23} (‖ יָדַע י׳), ψ 94^{8} (‖ בִּין), 119^{99}, Dn 1^{4} 9^{25} (‖ יָדַע); הַשְׂכֵּ(י)ל as subst. = *insight, understanding:* as י׳'s gift to ruler and teacher, ‖ דֵּעָה Je 3^{15}; ‖ דַּעַת Jb 34^{35}; ‖ מַדָּע Dn 1^{17}; מוּסַר הַשׂ׳ Pr 1^{3}; דֶּרֶךְ הַשׂ׳ 21^{16}. **4.** *cause to consider, give insight, teach:* י׳ subj., acc. rei, 1 Ch 28^{19}, acc. pers. ψ 32^{8} Ne 9^{20}; Gabriel subj., 2 acc. Dn 9^{22}; לֵב חָכָם subj., acc. rei Pr 16^{23}; c. לְ, Pr 21^{11}; הַמַּשְׂכִּילִים שֵׂכֶל טוֹב לי׳ 2 Ch 30^{22} (but Be Ke Benz etc. *who shewed* good *skill,* sc. in music, v ^{21b}); (הַ)מַּשְׂכִּילִים Dn $11^{33.35}$ $12^{3.10}$ *the teachers* (so Ew Hi Bev; Thes Ke Behrm al. *the wise*). **5.** *act circumspectly, prudently:* abs. Am 5^{13} ψ 2^{10} 36^{4}; מַשְׂכִּיל as subst. ψ 14^{2} = 53^{3}, Pr $10^{5.19}$ 14^{35} 15^{24} 17^{2} Jb 22^{2}; אִשָּׁה מַשְׂכָּלֶת Pr 19^{14}.—Je 50^{9} has גִּבּוֹר מַשְׁכִּיל acc. to Mas. (van d. H. Baer Gi), cf. 𝔙, i.e. a child-slaying warrior; but שׂ׳ Hiph. elsewhere only Ho 9^{14}, of miscarriage; 𝔊 𝔖 Ew and most mod. (Gf Gie Rothst) read מַשְׂכִּיל, either *skilful* or *fortunate.* **6.** *prosper, have success* (cf. Dr $^{\text{1 S 18, 5}}$): abs. 1 S 18^{15} Is 52^{13} Je 10^{21} 20^{11} 23^{5} Jos 1^{8} (D); c. בְּ, v ^{7} (D) 1 S $18^{5.14}$ (rd. בְּכָל־ for לְכָל־ Vrss Th HPS al.), cf. 2 K 18^{7}; c. אֶל, Pr 17^{8}. **7.** *cause to prosper:* Dt 29^{8} 1 K 2^{3} (D).

שֶׂכֶל, שֵׂכֶל **n.m. prudence, insight**;—שֵׂ׳ 7922
abs. ψ 111^{10}+, cstr. Pr 19^{11}+; שֶׂ׳ abs. 1 S 25^{3}+; שָׂכֶל Jb 17^{4}; sf. שִׂכְלוֹ Pr 12^{8} Dn 8^{25};—**1.** *prudence, good sense:* טוֹבַת שׂ׳ woman *of good sense* 1 S 25^{3}. **2.** *insight, understanding:* ‖ בִּינָה 1 Ch 22^{12} 2 Ch 2^{11}, cf. Jb 17^{4}; שׂ׳ טוֹב Pr 3^{4} 13^{15} ψ 111^{10} 2 Ch 30^{22}; אִישׁ שׂ׳ Ezr 8^{18}; יוֹעֵץ בְּשׂ׳ 1 Ch 26^{14}; מְקוֹר חַיִּים שׂ׳ בְּעָלָיו Pr 16^{22}; restrains from anger 19^{11}, wins praise 12^{8}, fool despises שׂ׳ מִלִּים 23^{9}; שׂוֹם שׂ׳ Ne 8^{8} (‖ הֵבִין) *set forth* (the) *understanding* (i.e. the meaning). **3.** bad sense, *cunning, craft,* Dn 8^{25}.

† מַשְׂכִּיל **n.m. contemplative poem** (**Hiph.** 4905
2. De al.);—in titles of ψψ 32, 42, 44, 45, 52, 53, 54, 55, 74, 78, 88, 89, 142; also 47^{8} זַמְּרוּ מ׳: > Ges al. *didactic poem* (√**4**); Ew Ri Pe al. *skilful, artistic song* (√**3**); √**2** alone fits all cases.

† II. [שָׂכַל] **vb. Pi. lay crosswise** (so, 7919
and not √ I. שׂ׳, 𝔊 𝔖 𝔙 𝔗 ^{Jon} and mod., cf. Ar. شَكَلَ *bind* legs of beast, *plait* locks of hair);—*Pf.* 3 ms. שִׂכֵּל אֶת־יָדָיו Gn 48^{14} (J); Thes Dr, however, *prudentes fecit,* fr. √ I. שׂ׳.

שִׂכְלוּת Ec 1^{17} v. סִכְלוּת. p. 698 5531

† שָׂכַר **vb. hire** (NH *id.;* Sab. תשכר *hire* 7936
oneself out (?), *recompense* (?) DHM $^{\text{Hofmus. 11}}$; Eth. ሦካር: *hired;* Ar. شَكَرَ *reward, thank,* mod. Pal. شكارة *hired,* of land ploughed by hire, Bergheim $^{\text{PEQ 1894, 196}}$; Palm. שכרא perh. *rewarding* Lzb ^{375});—**Qal** *Pf.* 3 ms. שׂ׳ Dt 23^{5} 2 K 7^{6},

sf. שְׂכָרוֹ Ne 6[12]; 1 s. sf. שְׂכַרְתִּיךָ Gn 30[16]; *Impf.* 3 ms. וַיִּשְׂכֹּר Ju 9[4]+, etc.; *Inf. abs.* שָׂכֹר Gn 30[16]; *cstr.* לִשְׂכֹּר 1 Ch 19[6]; *Pt. act.* שֹׂכֵר Pr 26[10.10], pl. שֹׂכְרִים 2 Ch 24[12] (Ezr 4[5] v. II. סכר); *pass.* שָׂכוּר Ne 6[13];—*hire*, retainers Ju 9[4] (ב pret.), soldiers, etc. 2 S 10[6] = 1 Ch 19[6.7], 2 K 7[6] 2 Ch 25[6] (ב pret.), priest Ju 18[4], artificers Is 46[6] 2 Ch 24[12], husband's favour שָׂכֹר שְׂכַרְתִּיךָ Gn 30[16] (J; ב pret.); Pr 26[10.10] obscure, v. De Now Toy; for evil purpose Dt 23[5] = Ne 13[2] (עַל *against*), Ne 6[12.13]. **Niph.** *hire oneself out, Pf.* בַּלֶּחֶם נִשְׂכָּרוּ 1 S 2[5]. **Hithp.** *earn wages, Pt.* הַמִּשְׂתַּכֵּר Hg 1[6] (as subst.), מ׳ v[6] (as vb., + אֶל loc., constr. praegn.).

7938 †שֶׂכֶר† **n.[m.] hire, wages**;—abs. עֹשֵׂי שׂ׳ Is 19[10] (= שָׂכִיר); cstr. Pr 11[18].

7939 †I. שָׂכָר **n.m.**[Ez 29, 18] **hire, wages,** only sg., not c. art.;—abs. שׂ׳ Nu 18[31]+, cstr. שְׂכַר Dt 15[18]+, sf. שְׂכָרִי Gn 30[18]+, etc.;—**1.** *wages*, of servant, Gn 30[28.32.33] (J), 31[8.8] Ex 2[9] (all E), Dt 15[18] (שׂ׳ שָׂכִיר), 24[15] 1 K 5[20] Zc 8[10] Mal 3[5] (שׂ׳ שָׂכִיר); soldiers Ez 29[18.19]; shepherd (symb.) Zc 11[12.12]; beast Ex 22[14] (E), Zc 8[10]. **2.** = *reward*, for work done, faithfulness, etc., Gn 15[1] (JE), 30[18] (E) in expl. of name יששכר, Nu 18[31] (P), כִּי יֵשׁ שׂ׳ לִפְעֻלָּתֵךְ Je 31[16] (cf. 2 Ch 15[7]), Is 40[10] = 62[11] (fig. of reward of י׳'s labours), ψ 127[3] Ec 4[9] 9[5]. **3.** *passage-money, fare*, Jon 1[3].

7940 †II. שָׂכָר **n.pr.m. 1.** father of hero of Dvd. 1 Ch 11[35], Αχαρ, A Σαχαρ (|| שָׁרָר 2 S 23[33]). **2.** doorkeeper 26[4], Σαχαρ.

7916 †שָׂכִיר **adj. hired**;—abs. שׂ׳ Ex 12[45]+, f.
7917 שְׂכִירָה Is 7[20]; cstr. שְׂכִיר Lv 25[53]; sf. שְׂכִירְךָ v[6]; pl. sf. שְׂכִירֶיהָ Je 46[21];—**1.** *hired*, of beast Ex 22[14] (E), razor Is 7[20] (fig.). **2.** usu. as subst. *hireling, hired labourer* Dt 15[18] 24[14], Lv 19[13] 22[10] 25[6.40.53] (all H), Ex 12[45] Lv 25[50] (both P), Mal 3[5] Jb 7[1.2] 14[6]; כִּשְׁנֵי שׂ׳ Is 16[14] years *like a hireling's years* (reckoned strictly), so 21[16]; *mercenaries* Je 46[21].

3485 יִשָּׂשכָר v. p. 441 supr.

4909 †[מַשְׂכֹּרֶת] **n.f. wages**;—sf.: *wages* of servant, מַשְׂכֻּרְתִּי Gn 31[7.41], ־תֶּךָ 29[15]; = *reward* of faithfulness, ־תֵּךְ Ru 2[12].

7958 †שְׂלָו† **n.f.**[Ex 16, 13] **quail** (prob. foreign word; Ar. سَلْوَى, Syr. ܣܠܘܐ, Sam. [illegible]);—*quail*, *coturnix communis* vel *vulgaris* (Tristr[NHB 229 ff.] FFP 124 Post[Hast. DB. QUAIL], Di[Ex 16, 13]):—abs. coll. Nu 11[32] (J), Ex 16[13] (P), ψ 105[40] (in all Qr שְׂלָיו); pl. שַׂלְוִים Nu 11[31] (J; as if from sg. שַׂלְוָה).

שַׂלְמָא, I. שַׂלְמָה v. שַׂלְמוֹן. below 8007, 8009

II. שַׂלְמָה = שִׂמְלָה v. sub שׂמל. p. 971 8008, 8071

†שַׂלְמוֹן **n.pr.m.** father of Boaz Ru 4[21] 8012
(𝔊 Σαλμαν, A𝔊L -μων), = שַׂלְמָה v[20] (𝔊 *id.*; 8009
rd. prob. ־מוֹן), hence שַׂלְמָא 1 Ch 2[11.11] (Σαλμων), 8007
also (as father of Bethlehem, on identity v. Be Now[Ruth]) v[51.54] (Σαλωμων, 𝔊L Σαμ(α)α)—? rd. שַׂלְמוֹן in all.

†שַׂלְמַי **n.pr.m.** head of post-ex. family;— 8014
שׂ׳ Ezr 2[46] Qr (Kt. שׂמלי [cf. NH n.pr. שַׂמְלַי Dalman, Liḥy. שמל DHM[Epigr. Denkm. Ar. No. 13]];
so Baer; van d. H. Gi Qr שַׁלְמַי; Σαμααν, A𝔊L 8073
Σελαμ(ε)ι) = שַׁלְמַי Ne 7[48] (Σελαμει; א Σαμαει).

†[שָׂלַק] **vb. kindle, burn** (Ecclus 43[4 marg.] 5400
הִסִּיק, v[21.23] הִשִּׂיק, *burn;* Aram. (also BA) סְלֵק *ascend*, Aph. *cause to go up* (in flame), offer sacrifice; ܣܠܩ, Palm. סלק, *ascend*);—**Niph.** *Pf.* 3 fs. אֵשׁ נִשְּׂקָה בְיַעֲקֹב ψ 78[21] *a fire was kindled against Jacob.* **Hiph.** *make a fire, burn: Pf.* 3 pl. consec. וְהִשִּׂיקוּ, c. ב rei; *Impf.* 3 ms. abs. יַשִּׂיק Is 44[15] (both || בִּעֵר).

שְׂמֹאל, שְׂמֹאול (Baer[Jos 1, 7])[54] **n.[m.] the** 8040
left (NH *id.;* As. *šumêlu;* Ar. شِمَالٌ (also شَأْمَلٌ, شَامَلٌ and شَمْأَلٌ *north wind*); OAram. שמאל, Palm. (sf.) סמלך; Syr. ܣܡܠܐ; √dub., ל+שאם Nö[M 128] Hom[A. u. A. i. (1892), 21] Kö[ii. 1. 143, 405], (v. also Thes Dietr[Wortforschung 234]), cf. Ar. شَأَمَ *be unlucky*, شُؤْمَةٌ *left*, شَامٌ, شَأْمٌ *north;* Sab. שאם *north, unlucky* DHM[Epigr. Denkm. 29; Epigr. Denkm. Ar. Nos. 6. 7]; other views in Sta[§ 299] Lag[BN 116]);—שְׂמֹאל abs. Gn 13[9]+, cstr. 48[13] 2 K 23[8]; שְׂמֹאול abs. Nu 20[17]+; sf. שְׂמֹאלֶךָ 2 S 2[21], שְׂמֹאלוֹ Gn 48[13]+, etc.;—opp. יָמִין exc. Gn 14[15] Ju 19[27] 2 K 23[8];—**1.** *left*, region on the left, Gn 13[9] (J); *on the left* is עַל־שׂ׳ 2 K 23[8] Ez 16[46] Zc 4[3.11], עַל־הַשּׂ׳ 1 Ch 6[29] cf. 2 Ch 18[18], also מִשּׂ׳ (*a sinistra*) Ex 14[22.29] (P), 2 S 16[6]+7 t.+מֵהַשּׂ׳ 2 Ch 3[17] Ez 1[10], לִשׂ׳ Ec 10[2], שׂ׳ alone Jb 23[9]; *toward the left* is עַל־שׂ׳ Gn 24[49] (J), 2 S 2[21] Zc 12[6], עַל־הַשּׂ׳ 2 S 2[19], שׂ׳ alone 1 S 6[12] Is 9[20]+13 t. †**2.** יַד־שׂ׳ *left hand*, Ju 3[21] 7[20], so שׂ׳ alone Gn 48[13.13.14] (E), Ju 16[29] Ez 39[3] Jon 4[11] Pr 3[16] Dn 12[7] Ct 2[6] 8[3]. †**3.** = *north* (on *left* of one facing east, cf. אָחוֹר **d**, יָמִין **4**, קֶדֶם **1 b**) Gn 14[15] Jos 19[27] (P); cf. Ez 16[46].

8041 †[שִׂמְאֵל] **vb. denom. Hiph.** take the left (alw. opp. הֵימִין):—*Impf. cohort.* אַשְׂמְאִילָה Gn 13^{9}; 2 mpl. תַּשְׂמְאִילוּ Is 30^{21}; *Imv.* fs. הַשְׂמִילִי (Ges ^{§23f} Kö$^{i.276}$) Ez 21^{21}, cf. *Inf. cstr.* הַשְׂמִיל 2 S 14^{19}; *Pt.* מַשְׂמְאִלִים 1 Ch 12^{2};—**1.** = *go to the left* Gn 13^{9} (J), Ez 21^{21}. **2.** fig. *turn* (aside) *to the left* (fr. true way) 2 S 14^{19} Is 30^{21}. **3.** *use the left hand* 1 Ch 12^{2}.

8042 †שְׂמָאלִי **adj.** left, on the left;—שׂ׳ 1 K 7^{21}+; f. שְׂמָאלִית Lv 14^{15}+;—*left* (usu. opp. יְמָנִי), pillar 1 K 7^{21} = 2 Ch 3^{17}, side of temple 2 K 11^{11} = 2 Ch 23^{10}, side of body Ez 4^{4}, palm Lv 14$^{15.16.26.27}$ (P).

8055 שָׂמַח, שָׂמֵחַ$_{154}$ **vb.** rejoice, be glad (NH *id.*; cf. perh. As. *šamâḫu*, *flourish*, Ar. شَمَخَ *be high, proud;* Pun. n. pr. f. שמחת);—**Qal**$_{126}$ *Pf.* 3 ms. שָׂמַח ψ 16^{9}+; וְשָׂמַח consec. Pr 29^{6}; 3 fs. שָׂמְחָה Est 8^{15}; 2 ms. וְשָׂמַחְתָּ Dt 12^{18}+; 3 mpl. שָׂמְחוּ Ne 12^{43}, etc.; *Impf.* יִשְׂמַח Is 9^{16}+, 3 mpl. יִשְׂמְחוּ 65^{13} ψ 69^{33}, 3 fpl. תִּשְׂמַחְנָה 2 S 1^{20}, etc.; *Imv.* ms. שְׂמַח Dt 33^{18}+, fs. שִׂמְחִי Zp 3^{14}+, שְׂמָחִי Jo 2^{21}, etc.; *Inf. cstr.* שְׂמֹחַ Ez 35^{14}+, etc.; *Pt.* v. שָׂמֵחַ adj.;—24 t. ‖ גיל, less oft. ‖ רָנַן, עָלַז, שׂוּשׂ, etc.;—**1.** in common life: **a.** *rejoice*, c. בּ pers. vel rei *take pleasure in* Ju 9$^{19.19}$ Dt 33^{18} Ec 3^{22}+7 t.+(prob.) בְּכָל־יָמֵינוּ ψ 90^{14} (others בּ temp.), cf. Ec 11^{8}; עַל pers. Is 39^{2}+ ‖ 2 K 20^{13} (וישמח for MT וישמע Vrss mod.), עַל rei Jon 4^{6} 2 Ch 15^{15}; c. cl. temp. Je 41^{13}+6 t.+(of heart) Pr 23^{15}, in one's heart Ex 4^{14} (J); c. כִּי *because* Is 14^{29}+3 t.; c. אֵת *with* Is 66^{10}; c. מִן pers. *get pleasure from* Pr 5^{18}; abs. 1 S 11^{9} Ec 3^{12} Pr 13^{9} (fig. of prosperity; subj. אוֹר; opp. דָּעַךְ), +8 t.; c. לְ rei *at* Jb 21^{12}. **b.** *rejoice* arrogantly, *exult* at, לְ pers., Mi 7^{8} Is 14^{8} Ob^{12} ψ 35$^{19.24}$ 38^{17}, c. אֶל־ rei Ez 25^{6}, בּ rei Jb 31^{29} ψ 35^{15} Pr 24^{17}; abs. Ho 9^{1} (+אֶל־גִּיל), 2 S 1^{20}+3 t., +(said of righteous by Eliphaz) Jb 22^{19}. **2. a.** *rejoice* religiously, c. בּ rei 1 S 2^{1} Dt 12^{7} ψ 21^{2}+7 t.; c. בי׳, etc., Jo 2^{23} ψ 32^{11}+10 t. ψψ+9^{3} (+אֶעֶלְצָה בָךְ); c. עַל rei 2 Ch 29^{36}, עַל inf. 1 Ch 29^{9a}; c. לְמַעַן rei ψ 48^{12}; c. כִּי *because* 119^{74}; abs. Zc 2^{14} 4^{10} Jo 2^{21} 1 Ch 29^{9b} (c. acc. cogn.), 16^{31} (of heavens) = ψ 96^{11}, ψ 97^{1} (isles)+18 t. (12 t. ψψ), +(of heart) Zc 10^{7a} ψ 16^{9} 1 Ch 16^{10}, בְּכָל־לֵב Zp 3^{14} (cf. Ex 4^{14} **1 a** supr.); c. לִפְנֵי י׳ Is 9^{2} and (of joyous feasting etc., at sanctuary) Lv 23^{40} (H), Dt 12$^{12.18}$ 16^{11} 27^{7}, cf. 14^{26} 1 S 11^{15}. **b.** subj. י׳, c. עַל pers. Is 9^{16} (‖ רחם; Perles $^{RÉJ\ xxxv.\ 63}$ *be gentle*, Ar. سَمُحَ), בּ rei ψ 104^{31}. **Pi.** *Pf.* 3 ms. וְשִׂמַּח consec. Dt 24^{5}, sf. שִׂמְּחָהוּ Je 20^{15}, etc.; *Impf.* 3 ms. יְשַׂמַּח ψ 104^{15}+, etc.; *Imv.* ms. שַׂמַּח ψ 86^{4}, שַׂמַּח Pr 27^{11}, etc.; *Inf. abs.* שַׂמֵּחַ Je 20^{15}; *Pt.* מְשַׂמֵּחַ Ju 9^{13}, pl. cstr. מְשַׂמְּחֵי ψ 19^{9};—*cause to rejoice, gladden*, c. acc. pers. (or equiv.), subj. pers. Dt 24^{5} Je 20^{15} (+Inf. abs.), Pr 10^{1} 15^{20} 27^{11} 29^{3} (Ho 7^{3} v. משח **2**); esp. subj. י׳ (God) Je 31^{13} (c. מִן separ.) Is 56^{7} 2 Ch 20^{27} (c. מִן of source, v. **Qal 1 a**), Ezr 6^{22} Ne 12^{43} (+acc. cogn.) ψ 86^{4} 90^{15} 92^{5} (בּ instr.), also, c. לְ pers. *cause to exult at* ψ 30^{2}, *id.* c. עַל pers. La 2^{17}; subj. rei Ju 9^{13} ψ 19^{9} 45^{9} 46^{5} 104^{15} Ec 10^{19} Pr 12^{25} 15^{30} 27^{9}. †**Hiph.** = **Pi.** *Pf.* 2 ms. הִשְׂמַחְתָּ ψ 89^{43} (subj. י׳).

†שָׂמֵחַ **adj. verb.** glad, joyful, merry;— 8056
abs. שׂ׳ Dt 16^{15}+, f. שְׂמֵחָה ψ 119^{9}; pl. שְׂמֵחִים 1 K 1^{45}+, cstr. שְׂמֵחֵי Is 24^{17}, שְׂמֵחֵי ψ 35^{26};—**1. a.** as adj. *joyful, shewing joy*, 1 K 1^{45} Est 5^{9} (+טוֹב לֵב), v^{14}; אֵם שְׂמֵחָה ψ 113^{9}; לֵב שׂ׳ Pr 15^{13} 17^{22}; at feast of tab. Dt 16^{15}, in thankfulness to י׳ ψ 126^{3} (both pred. c. הָיָה), 1 K 8^{66} (+טוֹבֵי לֵב) = 2 Ch 7^{10}. **b.** = pt. 1 K 1^{40} (‖ מְחַלְּלִים *piping*), 4^{20} 2 K 11^{14} (+תֹּקֵעַ בּ) = 2 Ch 23^{13}, מִן rei Ec 2^{10}. **2.** as subst. הַשׂ׳ Am 6^{13} (+לְ rei), Pr 2^{14} (לְ inf.), Jb 3^{22} (+אֱלֵי־גִיל; ‖ יָשִׂישׂוּ); שִׂמְחֵי־לֵב Is 24^{7}; of malicious joy שׂ׳ Pr 17^{5} (לְ rei), שְׂמֵחֵי רָעָתִי ψ 35^{26}.

שִׂמְחָה$_{93}$ **n.f.** joy, gladness, mirth;—abs. 8057
שׂ׳ Gn 31^{27}+, cstr. שִׂמְחַת Is 9^{2}+; sf. שִׂמְחָתִי ψ 137^{6}, etc.; pl. שְׂמָחוֹת ψ 16^{11}, ־ת 45^{16};—**1.** *mirth, gladness*, e.g. in festivity, Gn 31^{27} (E), ψ 137$^{3.6}$, 1 K 1^{40} 1 S 18^{6} Is 9$^{2.2}$ 16^{10} ψ 45^{16}; יוֹם שׂ׳ וּמִשְׁתֶּה Est 9$^{17.18.22}$ cf. (יוֹם om.) v^{19} (+יוֹם טוֹב), v^{22} (‖ יוֹם טוֹב), +5 t., +קוֹל שׂ׳ Je 7^{34} = 16^{9} = 25^{10} = 33^{11}; *joy* of heart Pr 14$^{10.13}$ Ec 5^{19} Ct 3^{11}, cf. (of inward joy) Jon 4^{6} Pr 15^{23} 21^{15}; = *gaiety, pleasure* Is 22^{13} Ec 2$^{1.2.10}$ 8^{15} 9^{7}, בֵּית שׂ׳ 7^{4}; שׂ׳ חָנֵף Jb 20^{5}, of foolish Pr 15^{21} 21^{17}; malicious joy Ez 35^{15} (לְ rei), so בְּכָל־לֵבָב שׂ׳ 36^{5}. **2.**$_{46}$ (esp. ψψ Chr) religious: 2 S 6^{12} ‖ 1 Ch 15$^{16.25}$ Jo 1^{16}+; יוֹם שׂ׳ Nu 10^{10} (P); עָשָׂה שׂ׳ i.e. make a (sacred) festivity 2 Ch 30^{23} Ne 8^{12} 12^{27}; שִׂמְחַת עוֹלָם Is 35^{10} = 51^{11}, 61^{7}; שׂ׳ c. עַל pers. Ne 12^{44}; *joy* of heart Is 30^{29} Je 15^{16}; as gift of י׳ ψ 4^{8} 21^{7}+7 t. +(in mockery) Is 66^{5}. †**3.** *joy* of י׳ Zp 3^{17}. †**4.** *glad result, happy issue* ψ 106^{5} (‖ טוֹבָה), Pr 10^{28} 12^{20} (Gr אֱמֻנָה, Toy מִשְׁפָּט; opp. מִרְמָה).

†שְׂמִיכָה **n.f.** rug or thick coverlet (?);— 8063
abs. Ju 4^{18} (v. GFM).

8300 †I. שָׂרִיד **n.m.**[Je 47, 4] **survivor** (from a defeat, etc.);—abs. שׂ׳ Is 1⁹+; sf. שְׂרִידוֹ Jb 27¹⁵ Kt; pl. שְׂרִידִים Jos 10²⁰ Jo 3⁵; cstr. שְׂרִידֵי Je 31²; sf. שְׂרִידָיו Ob¹⁴ + Jb 27¹⁵ Qr (van d. H. also Kt);—**1.** *survivor* (oft.‖ פָּלִיט): esp. עַד בִּלְתִּי הִשְׁאִיר לוֹ שׂ׳ Nu 21³⁵ Jos 8²² (both JE), Dt 3³ Jos 10³³ 11⁸ 2 K 10¹¹ (all D); more simply, לֹא הִשׁ׳ שׂ׳ Dt 2³⁴ Jos 10^{28.30.37.39.40} (all D); לֹא יִהְיֶה שׂ׳ Je 42¹⁷ 44¹⁴ Ob¹⁸; אֵין שׂ׳ Jb 18¹⁹; וְהֶאֱבִיד שׂ׳ מֵעִיר Nu 24¹⁹ (JE); עַם שְׂרִידֵי חָרֶב Je 31², pl. also Jos 10²⁰ (subj. of שָׂרְדוּ), Jo 3⁵ Ob¹⁴ Jb 27¹⁵ (v. supra); sg. also Ju 5¹³ (obscure, for שׂ׳ לְ rd. perh. יִשְׂרָאֵל GFM Now cf. Bu), Je 47⁴ La 2²². **2.** of things: אֵין שׂ׳ לְאָכְלוֹ Jb 20²¹, i.e. nothing has escaped his greed; (אִישׁ) יֵרַע שׂ׳ בְּאָהֳלוֹ v²⁶.

8301 †II. שָׂרִיד **n.pr.loc.** on border of Zebulun;—עַד־שׂ׳ Jos 19¹⁰ (P; Εσεδεκγωλα, A ἕως Σαρθιδ, 𝔊L Σαρειδ), מִשּׂ׳ v¹² (P; ἀπὸ Σεδδουκ; A Σαριδ).

II. שׂרד (√ of foll., *plait, braid*? (Lag[BN 175 ff.] thinks שׂ׳ Avestan loan-word)).

8278 †שְׂרָד **n.[m.]** perhaps Aram. **plaited** or **braided work** (cf. then Aram. סְרָדָא *lattice-work, net-work* (=BH מִכְבָּר), *textile stuff, curtain* (=BH קְלָעִים), סַרְדּוּתָא *plaited* or *braided work*; NH סָרָד *plaiter*, סָרִיד, סָרוּד *woven-work*; Hom[ZMG xliv (1890), 543] cp. Bab. *šardu, skin*);—alw. abs.: בִּגְדֵי (הַ)שּׂ׳ Ex 31¹⁰ 35¹⁹ 39^{1.49} (all P; all + לְשָׁרֵת בַּקֹּדֶשׁ, and last three + ב׳ הַקֹּדֶשׁ); 𝔊 31¹⁰ τ. στολὰς τ. λειτουργικάς (cf. 39¹ [B v¹³, 𝔊L v¹¹]).

8279 †שֶׂרֶד **n.[m.]** from context, a marking-tool for wood, **stylus** (so Thes al.; connexion with above √ dub.; Lewy[Fremdw. 57 f.] cp. σάρδιον as gem used in gem-cutting);—יְתָאֲרֵהוּ בַשֶּׂרֶד Is 44¹³.

שָׂרָה **n.f. et pr.** v. sub שׂרר.

8280 †I. שָׂרָה **vb. persist, exert oneself, persevere** (Ar. شَرِىَ *persist, persevere*);—**Qal** *Pf.* 3 ms. שׂ׳ אֶת־א׳ Ho 12⁴ *he persevered with God*; 2 ms. שָׂרִיתָ עִם־א׳ וְעִם אֲנָשִׁים Gn 32²⁹ (J).—Ho 12⁵ has *Impf.* וַיָּשַׂר in same meaning, as if from a
7786-87 (non-existent) שׂוּר; < rd. וַיִּשַׂר (apoc. fr. וַיִּשְׂרֶה).—
7795 שׂוֹרָה Is 28²⁵ v. supra, p. 965ᵃ.

3478 יִשְׂרָאֵל 2507 **n.pr.m. et gent. Israel** (*Ēl persisteth, persevereth* (or juss. *Let Ēl persist*) [usu. *contendeth* (Nes[Eg. 60 ff.]) or *Let Ēl contend* (Gray[Prop. N. 218]), but v. Dr[Hast. DB Jacob 530]]; on vocalization v. Lag[BN 131 f.] Kit[1 Ch 4, 16 (Hpt)]; MI[5, +5 t.] ישראל; in Egypt. *Y-si-r-'l* Steindorff[ZAW xvi (1896), 331], cf. Breasted[Bib. World ix (1897), 62 ff.] Paton[Syr. and Pal. 134]; As. *Sir-'-lai* (= יִשְׂרְאֵלִי) Schr[KG 356 ff., 364; COT Gn 36, 31, 1 K 16, 29].—On a poss. relation of יִשׂ׳ to n.pr. שָׂרָה, שָׂרַי v. RS[K 257, 2nd ed. 34];—cf. (שְׂרָיָה(וּ));—Ισραηλ: **1. n.pr.m.** second name of Jacob Gn 32²⁹ + 28 t. Gn (JE), Ex 32¹³ (JE), Ho 12¹³ Ju 18²⁹ Ex 6¹⁴ Nu 1²⁰ 26⁵ (all P), 2 K 17³⁴ 1 Ch 1³⁴ + 8 t. Chr, ψ 105²³; בֵּית יִשׂ׳ Ru 4¹¹; בְּנֵי יִשׂ׳ (lit.) Gn 42⁵ + 3 t. E, 2 t. P + Ex 1⁷ (P; transition to wider use), 1 K 18³¹ 1 Ch 2¹ +; = 12 tribes Ex 28⁹ + 7 t. P; אֱלֹהֵי אַבְרָהָם יִצְחָק וְיִשׂ׳ † 1 K 18³⁶ 1 Ch 29¹⁸ 2 Ch 30⁶. **2. n.pr.gent.** (usu. **m.**[Ju 11, 17 f.] but **f.** 1 S 17²¹ 2 S 24⁹ [not ‖ 1 Ch 21⁵], cf. Dr[ad loc.] Albr[ZAW xvi (1896), 57 f.]): name of Hebrew nation; usu. der. from **1**, but יִשׂ׳ more common in early usage than בְּנֵי יִשׂ׳ (v. בֵּן p. 120ᵇ): **a.** (1) undivided kingdom; יִשׂ׳ Gn 47²⁷ (J), 49⁷ (poem in J) + 108 t. JE, Dt 1¹ 18⁶ 33¹⁰ (poem) + 76 t. D, Gn 34⁷ Ex 12¹⁵ + 42 t. P; Ju 5^{2.7.7} + 104 t. Ju, oft. 1 and 2 S, 1 K 1–12; כָּל־יִשׂ׳ of whole people 2 S 8¹⁵ +, of whole army 11¹ +, opp. Judah 2⁹ + (so also later). (2) יִשׂ׳ = N. tribes, disting. fr. Judah, even before disruption, 2 S 2⁹, cf. v¹⁰ 3¹⁰ 4¹ 5⁵ 12⁷ 20¹ 1 K 1³⁵ 4²⁰ 5⁵ +; so at disruption 12^{16.16.16.18.19}; then usu. of N. kingdom, till its fall, v²⁸ 24^{7.10} + very oft. K, Am 1¹ 2⁶ 3¹⁴ +, Ho 1⁵ 4^{15.15} 5^{3.3.5} +, Mi 1¹³, etc. (3) יִשׂ׳ of S. kingdom, Judah, rarely bef. fall of Samaria Is 1³ 8¹⁸ Mi 1^{14.15}, so בְּנֵי יִשׂ׳ 1 K 12¹⁷; after fall of Sam., יִשׂ׳ (less oft. בְּנֵי יִשׂ׳) occurs of entire people, in reference to past or future 2 K 21⁸ 23²² Is 17⁹ ψ 103⁷ Je 2³ 50^{17.19} +; יִשׂ׳ also = Judah Je 2^{14.31} 4¹ +, Ez 13^{2.4.16} 14^{1.7.9} +, Is 40²⁷ 41⁸ 42²⁴ +, Ezr 2⁵⁹ = Ne 7⁶¹, Ezr 2⁷⁰ 3¹¹ +, Ne 10³⁴ 10³ +, ψ 14^{7.7} = 53^{7.7}, 147² 149² +, etc. (4) usage in Chr: יִשׂ׳ of whole people 1 Ch 2⁷ + 110 t., of N. kingdom 2 Ch 11¹ + 16 t., of Judah 12⁶ 19⁸ + 9 t. (5) יִשׂ׳ personif. as עֶבֶד י׳, Is 44^{1.21} 49³. **b.** בְּנֵי יִשׂ׳, (1) of undiv. people Ex 1¹² (J), 3⁹ (E) + 72 t. JE, Dt 3¹⁸ 10⁶ + 25 t. D, Gn 32³³ + 327 t. P; Ju 1¹ + 60 t. Ju; seld. 1 and 2 Sm, 1 K 1–12; in 13–2 K 25 *pass.* in ref. to older hist. (rarely otherwise). (2) seldom of N. kingdom Am 2¹¹ + 9 t. Am Ho, 2 Ch 13¹² + 7 t. Chr. (3) of Judah (late) Ez 2³ Ne 1^{6.6} Ezr 3¹ Jo 4¹⁶ +, 2 Ch 31⁵. **c.** בֵּית יִשׂ׳ Ex 16³¹ 40³⁸ + 142 t. (v. בַּיִת **5 d** (δ); 81 t. Ez, where = Judah; v. esp. 37¹⁶); שְׁנֵי בָתֵּי יִשׂ׳ Is 8¹⁴. **d.** other phrases, v. sub אִישׁ, אֶרֶץ, בַּת, בְּתוּלָה, גְּבוּל, הַר, כִּסֵּא, מֶלֶךְ, מַטֶּה (נטה), עֵדָה (יעד), עַם, שֵׁבֶט; also (in epith. of י׳) sub אָבִיר, אוֹר, אֱלֹהִים, I. גֹּאֵל, מֶלֶךְ, מִקְוֶה (I. קוה), I. צוּר (V. צור), קָדוֹשׁ, I. רָעָה **1 d** (3). †**e.** יִשׂ׳ = the laity, opp.

priests, etc. (late): Ezr 10[25] Ne 11[3] 1 Ch 9[2]; כָּל־ישׂ׳ Ezr 2[70] 10[5]; בְּנֵי ישׂ׳ 9[1]; הָעָם ישׂ׳ Ne 10[40], cf. שְׁאָר ישׂ׳ 11[20].

3481 †יִשְׂרְאֵלִי adj. gent. of foregoing;—m.
3482 הַיִּשׂ׳ Lv 24[10]; f. הַיִּשְׂרְאֵלִית v[10.11], cf. v[10].—2 S 17[25]
<הַיִּשְׁמְעֵאלִי, 𝔊[A] Th We Dr al. (so ‖ 1 Ch 2[17]).

8304 †שְׂרָיָה(וּ) n.pr.m. (׳י persisteth Dr [Hast. DB. ii. 530 JACOB]);—usu. Σαραια(ς);—שְׂרָיָה: 1. secretary of David 2 S 8[17], but 𝔊[B] Ασα, ‖ שְׁיָא 20[25] Kt
7724 (שְׁוָא Qr), שַׁוְשָׁא 1 Ch 18[16] (in both Ἰησοῦς, 𝔊L Σουσα), שִׁישָׁא 1 K 4[3] (Σαβα, A Σεισα, 𝔊L Σαφατ); orig. in all prob. ששא We Dr Klo (*Sausa*), HPS (שושא), Now (*Šoša*), Bu. **2.** chief priest 2 K 25[18]=Je 52[24]. **3.** a captain 2 K 25[23] Je 40[8] 51[59.59.61]. **4. a.** son of Ḳenaz 1 Ch 4[13.14]. **b.** name in Simeon v[35]. **c.** Levite name 5[40.40]. **5. a.** companion of Zerub. Ezr 2[2]. **b.** father of Ezra 7[1]. **c.** one sealed Ne 10[3]. **d.** priest 11[11] 12[1.12]. **6.** שְׂרָיָהוּ, officer of king Jehoiakim, Je 36[26], τῷ Σαρεα.

II. שׂרה (√of foll.; =*rule*? cf. שׂרר).

4951 †מִשְׂרָה n.f. rule, dominion;—Is 9[5.6].

8294 †שֶׂרַח n.pr.f. (cf. Sab. n.pr.m. שרח Sab. Denkm.[No. 20, l. 1, and p. 72], שרחאל Id.[No. 13, l. 2.12], אלשרח DHM[Epigr. Denkm. Arab. lxxii]);—daughter of Asher Gn 46[17] 1 Ch 7[30], שָׂרַח Nu 26[46]; Σααρ, Σαρ(ρ)α, etc.; 𝔊[B] Nu Καρα.

8295 †[שָׂרַט] vb. incise, scratch (NH *id.*, so Aram. סְרַט Pa (𝔗 1 S 21[14]), ܣܪܛ, ܣܪܛ *scratch*, hence *write* (=χαράσσω); As. *šarâṭu*, *slit up, rend;* Ar. شَرَطَ *slit* ear of camel, شَرْط, شَرَط *sign, mark* (RS[K 214 f.]);—**Qal** *Impf.* 3 mpl. c. acc. cogn. וּבִבְשָׂרָם לֹא יִשְׂרְטוּ שָׂרָטֶת Lv 21[5] *shall make no incision; Inf. abs.* c. **Niph.** *Impf.* 3 mpl. שָׂרוֹט יִשָּׂרֵטוּ Zc 12[3] those loaded with the stone *shall be severely scratched,* lacerated.

8296 †שֶׂרֶט n.[m.] incision;—abs. וְשׂ׳ לָנֶפֶשׁ לֹא תִתְּנוּ בִּבְשַׂרְכֶם Lv 19[28].

8296 †[שָׂרֶטֶת] n.f. id. (Ba[§ 93 α β]);—שָׂרָטֶת Lv 21[5], v. vb. **Qal**.

8297 שָׂרַי v. sub שׂרר. p. 979

8304 שְׂרָיָה(וּ) v. sub I. שׂרה. above

8303 †שִׂרְיוֹן, ־וֹן n.pr.mont. (in As. *Sirara* COT [Dt 3, 9; 1 K 5, 13] Dl [Pa 103 f.]);—Sidonian name of Ḥermon
8303 Dt 3[9] (Σανιωρ); ־יֹן ψ 29[6] (+לְבָנוֹן; van d. H. al. שׁ׳).

8308 †[שָׂרַךְ] vb. twist (so 𝔗 סְרַךְ (=Heb. עִוָּה, עִוֵּת); perhaps akin to שׂרג, סרג; Talm. סָרַךְ is *adhere,* cf. Aram. ܣܪܟ, ܣܪܟ; Ar. شَرِكَ is *share, participate,* but شِرَاكٌ *sandal-thong,* شَرَكٌ *snare*);—**Pi.** *Pt.* fs. מְשָׂרֶכֶת דְּרָכֶיהָ Je 2[23] a swift dromedary *entangling her ways* (galloping aimlessly; fig.).

8288 †[שְׂרוֹךְ] n.[m.] (sandal-)thong (? from above √, as *crossed and twisted* over the foot; on vocalization cf. Ar. *supra*, Ges [§ 84 a n] Ba [NB § 42 e]);—cstr., שְׂ׳־נַעַל Gn 14[23] Is 5[27].

8310 †שַׂרְסְכִים n.pr.m. a prince of Nebuch. Je 39[3], but read prob. שַׁזְבָּן (נְבוֹ), v. Gie Du, cf. p. 613[a] supra; 𝔊 Ναβουσαχαρ, etc.

8311 †[שָׂרַע] vb. extend (Ar. شَرَعَ *point directly at,* also *enter upon* a path (Frä[213] thinks orig. *divide,* then *stretch out, make straight*), شَرَعَةٌ *projecting roof,* أَشْرَعُ *long-nosed* (*torto naso* 𝔙[Lv 21, 18]); Eth. ሠርዐ: *dispose, arrange;* Sab. שרע *arrangement, security* Hom[Chr 124];—but Aram. ܣܪܝܥܐ expl. as *mutilated* Lv 21[18] 22[23] PS[2744], cf. 𝔊 ὠτότμητος);—**Qal** *Pt. pass.* שָׂרוּעַ *extended,* i.e. too long (in a limb or member), of man Lv 21[18], beast 22[23] (v. II. חרם). **Hithp.** *stretch oneself: Inf. cstr.* הִשְׂתָּרֵעַ Is 28[20] (v. מַצָּע p. 427[a]).

8312 שַׂרְעַפִּים v. sub שׂעף. p. 972

8313 שָׂרַף[117] vb. burn (70 t. + בָּאֵשׁ, 2 t. + בְּמוֹ־אֵשׁ) (NH (rare)=BH; As. *šarâpu;* Aram. שְׂרַף (rare); ܣܪܦ is *absorb, consume*);—**Qal** *Pf.* 3 ms. שׂ׳ Jos 11[9]+, 3 fs. sf. שְׂרָפָתַם Is 47[14], etc.; *Impf.* 3 ms. יִשְׂרֹף Nu 19[5]+2 t., more oft. וַיִּשְׂרֹף Ex 32[20]+, 2 mpl. תִּשְׂרְפוּן Dt 7[5]+2 t.; *Inf. abs.* שָׂרוֹף 2 S 23[7]; cstr. שְׂרֹף Je 36[25]+; sf. שָׂרְפוֹ Ju 9[52] Am 2[1]; *Pt. act.* שֹׂרֵף Lv 16[28] Nu 19[8], pl. שֹׂרְפִים 2 K 17[31]; *pass.* mpl. שְׂרֻפִים Nu 17[4]; fs. שְׂרוּפָה 1 S 30[3], שְׂרֻפָה ψ 80[17], pl. שְׂרוּפוֹת Ne 3[24], cstr. שְׂרֻפוֹת Is 1[7];—*burn* (59 t. + בָּאֵשׁ, 2 t. + בְּמוֹ־אֵשׁ): **1.** in making bricks, + לִשְׂרֵפָה Gn 11[3] (J; obj. om.). **2. a.** c. acc. rei, usu. to destroy, e.g. door Ju 9[52], house Ju 12[1] 1 K 16[18] (both c. עַל pers.), Je 39[8] + 11 t., cf. pt. pass. Ne 3[24], city Jos 6[24] 1 S 30[1.14] + 16 t., cf. pt. pass. 1 S 30[3] Is 1[7], chariots Jos 11[6.9] 2 K 23[11] ψ 46[10] (subj. ׳י), idols, etc., Ex 32[20] (acc. om.), Dt 9[21] + 10 t., roll †Je 36[25.27.28.29.32], wood †Is 44[16.19] (both + בְּמוֹ־אֵשׁ), cf. ψ 80[17] (fig.), Je 51[32], hair †Ez 5[4]; bones, to lime (as outrage) †Am 2[1]; upon altars (in desecration) †1 K 13[2] 23[16.20]=2 Ch 34[5]; bodies, as funeral rite †1 S

31^{12} (rare custom, RS[Sem. i. 353; 2nd ed. 372]; but Klo Bu rd. יִשְׂפְּדוּ [=יָם׳]; cf. Benz[Arch. 163; Ency. Bib. DEAD] Now[Arch. i. 188]); שׂ׳ as funeral rite also (obj. om., prob. spices, cf. 2 Ch 16^{14}), †c. לְ pers. mort. Je 34^{5}, + acc. cogn. שְׂרֵפָה 2 Ch 16^{14} (cf. שְׂרֵפָה); in ceremonial of P (never of burning sacrif. on altar, הִקְטִיר, cf. הֶעֱלָה, but) chiefly (14 t.) of consuming refuse, esp. unused portions of victims, etc. (to prevent use), and infected objects, Ex $29^{14.34}$+, sts. מִחוּץ לַמַּחֲנֶה Lv 4^{12} (+ עַל־עֵצִים), $v^{21.21}$ + 4 t., etc., cf. Ez 43^{21}; also of burning red heifer (to produce ashes for purification) Nu $19^{5.5.8}$. †**b.** *burn*, c. acc. pers., (1) as penalty Jos 7^{25} (JE), Ju 14^{15} 15^{6} Lv 20^{14}, cf. Nu 17^{4} (pt. pass.), so, אֵשׁ subj., Is 47^{14}, c. acc. cogn. שְׂרֵפָה Lv 10^{6} (P); (2) as sacrifice, Je 7^{31} 19^{5}; + לְ dei Dt 12^{31} 2 K 17^{31}. †**Niph.** *Impf.* 3 ms. יִשָּׂרֵף Jos 7^{15}+, 3 fpl. תִּשָּׂרַפְנָה Pr 6^{27}, etc.;—*be burned* (11 t. + בָּאֵשׁ): of city Je 38^{17} + v^{23} (read תִּשָּׂרֵף for תִּשְׂרֹף 𝔊 𝔖 𝔗 Hi Ew Gf Gie Du), idols, etc., Mi 1^{7} 1 Ch 14^{12}; ritually (cf. **Qal 2 a** ad fin.) Lv 4^{12} 6^{23} $7^{17.19}$ 13^{52} 19^{6}; of pers., as penalty Gn 38^{24} (J), Jos 7^{15} (JE),
5635 2 S 23^{7} (poet.), Lv 21^{9} (H). †**Pi.** *Pt.* sf. מְסָרְפוֹ Am 6^{10} *his burner*, usu. *one burning him*, but prob. *burning* spices for him, v. Dr and cf. **Qal** supra. †**Pu.** *Pf.* 3 ms. שֹׂרַף, of goat Lv 10^{16} *it was burnt up* (and gone).

8314 †I. **שָׂרָף** **n.m.**[Is 14, 29] **a serpent**, usu. venomous (poss. from above √, from *burning* effect of poison);—abs. שׂ׳ Nu 21^{8} (JE; on Ar. parallels v. Jacob[Ar. Dichter ii. 93, iv. 10 f.]), appos. נָחָשׁ שׂ׳ Dt 8^{15}, pl. הַנְּחָשִׁים הַשְּׂרָפִים Nu 21^{6}; a flying serpent, or *dragon*, שָׂרָף מְעוֹפֵף Is 14^{29} 30^{6}.

8314 †II. **[שָׂרָף]** **n.m.**[Is 6, 2] pl. שְׂרָפִים **seraphim** (prob. akin to I. שׂ׳, as beings orig. mythically conceived with serpents' bodies (serpent-deities, cf. Is 14^{29} 30^{6}), or (Che[Comm.]) personif. of lightning, cf. arts. SERAPHIM, Strachan[Hast. DB] Che[Ency. Bib.]; Di Marti al. cp. also Egypt. guardian-griffins, called *Šerref;* v. also כְּרוּב; on As. *Šarrapu* (*-bu*), epith. of god Nergal, connected by Dl[WB] with √ שָׂרַף, v. שָׁרָב, Zim[KAT 3. 415]);—in OT. majestic beings with six wings, and human hands and voices, attendant upon י׳ Is $6^{2.6}$.

8315 †III. **שָׂרָף** **n.pr.m.** a Judahite;—1 Ch 4^{22}; Σαια, A 𝔊L Σαραφ.

8316 †**שְׂרֵפָה** **n.f.** **burning**;—abs. שׂ׳ Is 9^{4}+, cstr. שְׂרֵפַת Nu 19^{6}+;—לִשׂ׳ of brick-burning Gn 11^{3} (+ שָׂרַף); destructive Am 4^{11} Is 9^{4}, of land Dt 29^{22}, of temple, הָיָה לִשְׂרֵפַת אֵשׁ Is 64^{10}, הַר שׂ׳ Je 51^{25} i.e. a burnt-out volcano (fig. of Bab.); of heifer Nu 19^{6}, cf. v^{17}; of spices (prob.) as funeral rite 2 Ch 16^{14} (as acc. cogn.), 21^{19} (obj. of עָשָׂה), v^{19}; of pers. (penal) Lv 10^{6} (acc. cogn., י׳ subj.), Nu 17^{2}.

†**[מִשְׂרָפָה, מַשְׂרֵפָה?]** **n.[f.]** **a burning**;— 4955
only pl. cstr. מִשְׂרְפוֹת: בְּמִ׳ אֲבוֹתֶיךָ Je 34^{5} (read כְּמִ׳ 𝔊 𝔖 𝔙 Gie Du al.), *like the burnings* (of spices; cf. √**2 a**) *for thy fathers;* מִ׳ שִׂיד Is 33^{12} (fig. of ignominious destruction, cf. Am 2^{1}).

†**מִשְׂרְפוֹת מַיִם** **n.pr.loc.** named with Ṣidon 4956
Jos 11^{8} 13^{6} (appar. near coast); cp. (dub. Buhl[Geogr. 229]) *Mušêrfe*, 14 m. S. of Tyre, v. Di and reff., Guérin[Gal ii. 166 f.].—Μασερων, Μασρεφωθμαειμ, etc.

I. **שׂרק** (NH סָרַק, Aram. סְרַק, ܣܪܰܩ, all *comb, card;* Ar. شَرَقَ *slit* sheep's ear, *pluck* fruit).

†**[שָׂרִיק]** **adj.** **carded, combed**, of flax;— 8305
fpl. פִּשְׁתִּים שְׂרִיקוֹת Is 19^{9}.

II. **שׂרק** (cf. NH סָרָק *light red;* הִשְׂרִיק Ecclus[50, 7; 43, 9 marg.] *shine brightly* (of sun); As. *šarku, red blood;* Ar. شَرَقَ *rise and shine* (of sun), *shew redness,* شَرِقَ *become red* (like blood); Sab. שרק *rise* (of sun), משרק *East,* שרקן epith. dei *the shining* Sab. Denkm.[18, 4] Fell[ZMG liv (1900), 253 f.] cf. Hom[Chr 124]).

†I. **[שָׂרֹק]** **adj.** perh. **sorrel** (? fr. II. שׂ׳, or 8320
cf. أَشْقَرُ *having ruddy tinge* over white, of horses *sorrel* Lane[1581]);—pl. אֲדֻמִּים שְׂרֻקִּים וּלְבָנִים Zc 1^{8}, of horses.

†II. **[שָׂרֹק]** **n.[m.]** **vine-tendrils** (or **clus-** 8291
ters) (from *red* colour ?);—pl. sf. שְׂרוּקֶּיהָ Is 16^{8}.

†I. **שֹׂרֵק** **n.[m.]** choice species of **vine**;— 8321
abs. שׂ׳ Is 5^{2}, שׂוֹ׳ Je 2^{21} (both in fig.).

†II. **שֹׂרֵק** (van d. H. שׂוֹ׳) **n.pr.loc.** in נַחַל שׂ׳ 7796
Ju 16^{4} (prop. *Wady of choice vines*);—𝔊 Σωρηχ[κ]; prob. *Wady Ṣurâr* (GASm[Geogr. 218 ff.]), on N. side of which is ruin *Sûrîk*, ¾ h. W. of *Ṣurʿah* (Ẓorʿah), Survey[iii. 53] GFM[ad loc.].

†**שֹׂרֵקָה** **n.f.** choice **vine**;—Gn 49^{11}. 8321

†**מַשְׂרֵקָה** **n.pr.loc.** in Edom;—מַשׂ׳ Gn 4957
36^{36} = 1 Ch 1^{47}; 𝔊 ἐκ Μασέκκας (𝔊L[Ch] ἐκ Μασερικα); Euseb[Onom. ed. Lag. 277] Μασρηκα.

שׂרר (√ of foll.; mng. dub.; Dl[Pr 92] cp. As. *šarâru, rise in splendour* (of sun, etc.), but dub., cf. Hal[RÉJ xiv (1887), 150]).

8269 **שַׂר** $_{420}$ **n.m. chieftain, chief, ruler, official, captain, prince** (NH esp. of angels; As. *šarru, king*);—abs. שַׂר 2 S 3^{38}+, הַשַּׂר Mi 7^{3}+, שָׂ֑ר Ho 3^{4}+; cstr. שַׂר Ju 4^{2}+; sf. שַׂרְכֶם Dn 10^{21}; pl. שָׂרִים 1 K 4^{2}+; cstr. שָׂרֵי Gn 12^{15}+; sf. שָׂרַי Ju 5^{15} Is 10^{8}, שָׂרֵיכֶם Je 44^{21}, שָׂרֵיהֶם Is 3^{4}+;—**1.** *chieftain, leader:* **a.** pl. of Isr. Nu 21^{18} (poem in JE; ‖ נְדִיבֵ הָעָם), of Issachar Ju 5^{15} (poem); שָׂרֵי גִלְעָד 10^{18} is dub. (we should expect וְשׂ׳, and cf. זִקְנֵי ג׳, instead, 11$^{5-11}$); of Midian 7^{25} 8^{3}; Philistines 1 S 29$^{3.3.4.4.9}$ (appar. = סְרָנִים v$^{2.6.7}$ [We], yet disting. by HPS and [with reserve] Bu; 𝔊 𝔖 𝔙 Th Bu del. in v^{4b}), cf. 18^{30}; poet., of כְּמוֹשׁ (i.e. the leading Moabites) Je 48^{7}, of מלכם (q.v.; i.e. the leading Ammonites) Am 1^{15} = Je 49^{3}. **b.** sg. David as leader of freebooters 1 S 22^{2}; cf. שׂ׳ גְּדוּד 1 K 11^{24}, pl. 2 S 4^{2}. **2.** *vassal, noble, official,* under king (acting, on occasion, as counsellor, commander, etc.): **a.** pl., in Egypt Gn 12^{15} (J) + 3 t. Is + 30^{4} Di Du Skinner (> of foreign embassy [cf. ‖ מַלְאָכָיו] Che al. rdg. [Che$^{\text{Heb. Hpt.}}$ Marti] שָׂרִים), ψ 105^{22}; Moab Nu 22^{8} + 8 t. 22, 23 (JE), Am 2^{3}; Edom Is 34^{12} (‖ חֹרִים); As. 10^{8} 31^{9}; Bab. 21^{5} + 7 t. Je + 2 Ch 32^{31} (but here perhaps vaguely = *authorities*); other nations Je 49^{38} + 17 t. Ezr Est; in gen. Is 49^{7}; *officials, official class,* under kings of Israel: David (only Chr) 1 Ch 22^{17} + 5 t. 1 Ch, Ezr 8^{20}; Sol. 1 K 4^{2}; Jehoiachin 2 K 24$^{12.14}$; Zedek. Je 34^{21} 2 Ch 36^{18}; other kings 19 t. 2 Chr; in gen. Ec 10$^{16.17}$; see also (Judah) Je 1^{18} + 31 t. Je (17^{25a} del. שׂ׳ Gf Che Gie Du), 4 t. La, Ez 17^{12}, Zp 1^{8} (where disting. from בְּנֵי הַמֶּלֶךְ, who are never called שׂ׳); so, in gen., Ne 9$^{32.34}$ Dn 9$^{6.8}$; and (N. Isr.) Ho 3^{4} + 6 t. Ho. **b.** as having powers of magistrate (*ḳadi*) Ex 2^{14} (E. + שֹׁפֵט); under Moses (over groups of 1000, 100, 50, 10) 18^{21} + 7 t. 18 (E), Dt 1$^{15.15.15.15}$; later in Judah Ho 5^{10} (Now reads שָׂרֵי יִשׂ׳), Is 1^{23}, cf. 3$^{4.14}$ 32^{1} Mi 7^{3} (sg.; ‖ שֹׁפֵט), Zp 3^{3} (‖ *id.*), Ez 22^{27}, cf. Pr 8^{16} (‖ נְדִיבִים); 28^{2} read perhaps צָרֶיהָ, v. Toy. **c.** as ruler or magistrate of a district (מְדִינָה), 1 K 20$^{14.15.17.19}$ (cf. Est 1^{3} 8^{9} 9^{3}, שָׂרֵי עַם וָעָם 3^{12}). **d.** as *commandant* of city, שׂ׳ הָעִיר Ju 9^{30}, cf. 1 K 22^{26} = 2 Ch 18^{25}, 2 K 23^{8} 2 Ch 34^{8}; of citadel, שׂ׳ הַבִּירָה Ne 7^{2}; pl. of city *officials,* שׂ׳ סֻכּוֹת Ju 8$^{6.14}$ (disting. from זְקֵנִים), cf. 2 K 10^{1} 2 Ch 29^{20}. **3.** specif. military, = *captain, general:* **a.** שַׂר־(ה)צבא Gn 21$^{22.32}$ (E), 26^{26} (J), 1 S 12^{9} + 23 t., + שׂ׳־צ׳־י׳ Jos 5$^{14.15}$ (JE; צָבָא **1 b**), angel-captain in vision; v. also **8, 9**; שָׂרֵי הַצ׳ 1 K 1^{25} + 3 t. Chr, שָׂרִים בַּצ׳ 1 Ch 12^{22} (Gi Baer; van d. H. v^{21}); שָׂרֵי צְבָאוֹת Dt 20^{9} 1 K 2^{5} 1 Ch 27^{3}; שַׂר־הַחַיִל 2 S 24^{2} (but read וְאֶל־שָׂרֵי as 𝔊L and ‖ 1 Ch 21^{2} Th We Dr HPS Bu), שָׂרֵי (הַ)ח׳ v$^{4.4}$ 2 K 9^{5} 2 Ch 33^{14} Ne 2^{9}, שָׂרֵי הַחֲיָלִים 1 K 15^{20} = 2 Ch 16^{4}, 2 K 25$^{23.26}$ Je 40$^{7.13}$ + 7 t. Je; שָׂרֵי מִלְחָמוֹת 2 Ch 32^{6}; so (ה)שׂר alone 2 S 18^{5} 19^{7} 1 K 9^{22} = 2 Ch 8^{9} 𝔊^{B} Be Kit (שָׂרָיו וְשָׁלִישָׁיו, for MT שָׂרֵי שׂ׳), 2 K 9$^{5.5}$ 1 Ch 11$^{6.21}$ + 9 t., + Jb 39^{25} Dn 11^{5}; שׂ׳ וְגָדוֹל 2 S 3^{38} (of Abner); poss. military fig. also in שַׂר שָׁלוֹם Is 9^{5} (Mess. name). **b.** leading companies of 50 2 K 1$^{9-14}$ Is 3^{3}, of 100 1 S 22^{7} + 16 t. + 8^{12} (reading מֵאוֹת for חֲמִשִּׁים 𝔊 HPS, cf. We; Bu ins. שָׂרֵי מֵאוֹת), of 1000 1 S 17^{18} + 11 t., + שָׂרֵי הָאֲלָפִים וְהַמֵּאוֹת 1 Ch 13^{1} 26^{26} (disting. from שָׂרֵי הַצָּבָא), 27^{1} 29^{6} 2 Ch 1^{2}; also שׂ׳ הָרֶכֶב *captain of the chariotry* 1 K 22$^{31.32.33}$ = 2 Ch 18$^{30.31.32}$ + 3 t. + שָׂרֵי ר׳ וּפָרָשָׁיו 1 K 9^{22} = 2 Ch 8^{9}. **4. a.** *chief, head,* of other official classes: שַׂר הַטַּבָּחִים, Egypt, Gn 37^{36} + 5 t.; שָׂרֵי הָרָצִים 1 K 14^{27} = 2 Ch 12^{10}; שָׂרֵי הַנִּצָּבִים 1 K 5^{30} 9^{23} = 2 Ch 8^{10}; even domestic positions (court of Pharaoh), שַׂר הַמַּשְׁקִים Gn 40^{2} + 5 t., שַׂר הָאוֹפוֹת 40^{2} + 4 t. (all E); שָׂרֵי הַמַּחְלְקוֹת 1 Ch 28^{1}, i.e. of the successive courses of royal military officials; cf. הַשַּׂר 27^{28}; שַׂר הַסָּרִיסִים Dn 1$^{7.8.9.10.11.18}$; שַׂר מְנוּחָה Je 51^{59}. **b.** = *overseer:* שַׂר בֵּית הַסֹּהַר Gn 39$^{21.23}$, שָׂרֵי מִקְנֶה 47^{6} (all J; cf. אַבִּיר הָרֹעִים 1 S 21^{8}), שָׂרֵי מִסִּים Ex 1^{11} (J); cf. 1 Ch 15^{27} 29^{6} 27^{31} 28^{1}.—In 1 Ch 15^{22} read prob. סַר הַמַּשָּׂא (=שַׂר) *overseer of the carrying* (for MT בְּמַשָּׂא יָסֹר בַּמַּשָּׂא), so 𝔊 Benz Kit, Be
יָשַׂר=יָסַר; v. another view יסר **Qal**. **5.** of 3256
religious office: שָׂרֵי הַכֹּהֲנִים Ezr 8$^{24.29}$ 10^{5} 2 Ch 36^{14}; שׂ׳ הַלְוִיִּם 1 Ch 15$^{16.22}$ 2 Ch 35^{9}, cf. 1 Ch 15$^{5.6.7.8.10.16}$; heads of classes or courses of priests, called שָׂרֵי קֹדֶשׁ 1 Ch 24^{5}, שׂ׳ אֱלֹהִים v^{5};—שָׂרֵי ק׳ Is 43^{28} (usu. *consecrated princes,* whether priests, or kings, or both) is prob. corrupt, read perh. שַׁעֲרֵי (Du) or וַיְחַלְּלוּ שָׂרֶיךָ קָדְשִׁי 𝔊 Houb Klo Che^{Hpt} Gr (substantially). **6.** late, of representative leaders of people, tribal heads, שׂ׳ שִׁבְטֵי יִשׂ׳ 1 Ch 27^{22} 29^{6}, cf. 28^{1}; appar. = elders, שׂ׳ הָעָם Ez 11^{1} 2 Ch 24^{23}; שׂ׳ alone, ψ 68$^{28.28.28}$; in post-exilic Jerus. Ezr 9$^{1.2}$ Ne 4^{10} 10^{1} 11^{1} (שָׂרֵי הָעָם), + elders Ezr 10$^{8.14}$; called שָׂרֵי יְהוּדָה Ne 12$^{31.32}$; of district-rulers 3$^{9.12.14.15.16.17.18.19}$; of heads of families, שָׂרֵי הָאָבוֹת Ezr 8^{29} 1 Ch 29^{6} (= רָאשֵׁי הָא׳ 24^{31} 27^{1} Ne 7^{70}). **7.** late, as term of rank and dignity, Is 23^{8} (cf. 'merchant-*princes*'), Jb 3^{15} 29^{9} (‖ נְגִידִים), 34^{19} ψ 45^{17} 82^{7} 148^{11}, opp. עבד(ים) Pr 19^{10} Ec 10^{7}; formidable foes ψ 119$^{23.161}$. **8.** = *patron-angel,* only Dn: שַׂר (מַלְכוּת) פָּרַס 10$^{13.20}$, שׂ׳ יָוָן v^{20}; specif. of מִיכָאֵל v$^{13.21}$ 12^{1}. **9.**

שׁמל (√of foll.; Ar. شَمَلَ *enclose, envelope;* شَمْلَةٌ *cloak,* Lane[1600] Dozy[Vêtements, 59 f., 232 f.]).

8071 †שִׂמְלָה **n.f. wrapper, mantle**;—abs. שׂ׳ Gn 9[23]+, cstr. שִׂמְלַת Dt 21[13] 22[5]; sf. שִׂמְלָֽתְךָ Dt 8[4], etc.; pl. שְׂמָלֹת Gn 45[22.22]+, sf. שִׂמְלֹתָם 44[13]+, etc.;—*wrapper, mantle* (of man or [Ru 3[3]+] woman), usu. square piece of cloth worn as *outer garment* (v. Mackie[Hast. DB. i. 625]; Benz[Ency. Bib. iii. 2932]), Gn 35[2] Ex 22[26] (both E), Dt 8[4] 10[18] 21[13] 22[3] Is 3[6.7] 9[4] 2 S 12[20] Kt, Ru 3[3] Kt (Qr in both pl.); as *covering* in sleep Gn 9[23] (J; cf. Ex 22[26]), bed-covering Dt 22[17]; covering or receptacle for articles Ex 12[34] (E), Ju 8[25] 1 S 21[10], cf. Pr 30[4]; more gen. *garment,* Dt 22[5], *clothes* (pl.) Gn 37[34] 44[13] (J), 41[14] Ex 19[10.14] (all E), Jos 7[6] (JE); as costly gifts Gn 45[22.22] Ex 3[22] 12[35] (all E).

8072 †שַׂמְלָה **n.pr.m.** kg. of Edom Gn 36[36.37] (P; Σαμ(α)λα) = 1 Ch 1[47.48] (Σαμαα, Σαβαα).

8008, II. †שַׂלְמָה **n.f. id.** (transp. from שִׂמְלָה);—
8071 abs. שׂ׳ Ex 22[8]+, cstr. שַׂלְמַת v[25]; sf. שַׂלְמָתוֹ Dt 24[13]; pl. שְׂלָמוֹת Jos 9[5]+, sf. שַׂלְמֹתֵיהֶם v[13], etc.;—*garment* (of man or [Ct 4[11]] woman): *outer garment* Ex 22[8.25] (E), Jos 9[5.13] (JE), Dt 24[13] 1 K 11[29.30] ψ 104[2] (fig.); in gen. *clothes* (pl.) Dt 29[4] Ne 9[21] Jb 9[31] Ct 4[11]; as costly gifts 1 K 10[25] = 2 Ch 9[24]; as booty Jos 22[8] (late).—Mi 2[8] rd. prob. שַׂלְמָה (Roorda, RS[Proph. vii. N. 4]), or שְׁלֵמִים (We Now GASm), *him (those) at peace (with*
8009 *him),* cf. 𝔊𝔖. p. 969

8014 שַׂמְלַי Kt Ezr 2[46] v. שַׁלְמַי p. 969

8041 [שָׂמַל] **Hiph.** v. [שָׂמְאַל] p. 970

8079 †שְׂמָמִית **n.f.** a kind of **lizard** (so 𝔊𝔙𝔗 Lv 11, 30 cf. Str[Pr] (also on שׂ > שׁ));—abs. שׂ׳ Pr 30[28] (cf. Shipley-Cook[Ency. Bib. Lizard]).

שׂמר (appar. √of foll.; meaning dub.).

4548 [מַשְׂמֵר], מַשְׂמְרוֹת, Ec 12[14], v. [מַסְמֵר], p. 702.

8130 **שָׂנֵא** [145] **vb. hate** (NH *id.;* MI[4] שנאי *my foes;* Sab. שנאם *foe* Sab. Denkm.[No. 12, l. 9] cf. Ib.[No. 7, l. 9] CIS[iv, No. 173, l. 6]; Ar. شنأ, شَنِئَ, *hate;* Aram. סְנָא, ܣܢܐ, *id.,* סָנְאָה, ܣܢܳܐ *hater,* etc.; Eth. *hate* is ጸልአ:);—**Qal**[128] *Pf.* 3 ms. שׂ׳ Dt 12[31]+, sf. שְׂנֵאָהּ 2 S 13[15]+; 2 ms. שָׂנֵאתָ ψ 5[6]+, sf. שְׂנֵאתַנִי Ju 14[16], etc.; *Impf.* 3 ms. יִשְׂנָא Pr 13[5] 26[28], sf. יִשְׂנָאֶךָּ 9[8], etc.; Imv. mpl. שִׂנְאוּ Am 9[15] ψ 97[10]; *Inf. abs.* שָׂנֹא Ju 15[2]; *cstr.* שְׂנֹא Gn 37[5]+, שִׂנְאַת Pr 8[13]; *Pt. act.* שֹׂנֵא Dt 4[42]+, שֹׂנַאֲךָ Ex 23[5] Pr 25[21]; pl. cstr. שֹׂנְאֵי Ex 18[21]+, etc.; *pass.* fs. שְׂנוּאָה Gn 29[31]+; mpl. cstr. שְׂנֻאֵי 2 S 5[8] Qr (>Kt שְׂנֻאוּ);—*hate* (oft. opp. אָהֵב): **1.** human; **a.** c. acc. pers. Gn 26[27] (J), 37[5.8] (E), Ju 11[7] 2 S 13[22] Am 5[10] (‖ תִּעֵב) + 17 t. (evil-doers †ψ 26[5] 31[7] 139[21]), + (obj. wife) Ju 14[16] 15[2.2]; + pt. pass., of wife, †Gn 29[31.31] (J), Dt 21[15.15.16.17], cf. Pr 30[23]; fig. of Zion Is 60[15] (+ עֲזוּבָה); specif. of sexual revulsion †2 S 13[15.15] (+ acc. cogn.), Dt 22[13.16] 24[3]; so, obj. man (of Jerus. under fig. of harlot) †Ez 16[37]; pass. שְׂנֻאֵי נֶפֶשׁ דָּוִד 2 S 5[8] (but v. obscure); reflex. (acc. נַפְשׁוֹ) †Pr 29[24], abs. †Ec 3[8]. **b.** c. acc. rei, Ez 35[6] (but rd. בְּדָם אָשַׁמְתְּ 𝔊 𝔖 Co Berthol Toy), Ec 2[17.18], esp. evil Ex 18[21] (E), Mi 3[2] ψ 45[7] + 10 t., virtue, etc. Mi 3[2] Pr 1[22] + 4 t. **2.** subj. י׳; obj. perverse Isr. †Am 6[8] (its palaces), Ho 9[15] Je 12[8]; wickedness ψ 5[6] 11[5]; idolatry and evil Am 5[21] Is 1[14] 61[8] Je 44[4] Mal 2[16] + 5 t. **3.** *Pt. act.*[54] as adj. Is 66[5] (as vb. c. 1 s. pron. 61[8], **2** supr.); usu. subst., Pr 13[24] *one hating his son* (opp. אֹהֵב); elsewhere = *enemy, foe* (usu. cstr. or c. sf.), sg. and pl. (oft. ‖ אֹיֵב, sts. opp. אֹהֵב): foe of man Ex 23[5] (E), Gn 24[60] (J), Lv 26[17] (H)+, nation Ex 1[10] (E), Est 9[1.5.16]+, abs. Pr 26[24] 27[6], (c. 31 t. in all); + לֹא שֹׂנֵא לְ c. pers., *a no-hater to* one Dt 4[42] 19[4.6] Jos 20[5], and (without לֹא) Dt 19[11]; foe of good Mi 3[2], cf. Jb 34[17] + 3 t., of evil †Ex 18[21] Pr 28[1], cf. 15[27]; of suretyship †11[15] (i.e. not giving it); foes of י׳ †Ex 20[5] = Dt 5[9], Dt 7[10.10] 2 Ch 19[2]. †**Niph.** *Impf.* 3 ms. יִשָּׂנֵא Pr 14[17] *is hated,* so v[20] (+ לְ pers. *by,* v. לְ **5 d**). †**Pi.** *Pt.* sf. מְשַׂנְאִי Jb 31[29] ψ 55[13]; pl. cstr. מְשַׂנְאֵי 81[16]; sf. מְשַׂנְאַי 2 S 22[41]+, etc.;—*enemy* (**Qal 3**) ‖ אֹיֵב, צַר, etc.: **1.** personal and national, Jb 31[29] Dt 33[11] (poem), 2 S 22[41] = ψ 18[41], ψ 44[8.11] 55[13] 68[2] 89[24]. **2.** of י׳ Nu 10[35] (J), Dt 32[41] (poem), ψ 81[16] 83[3] 139[21]. **3.** of wisdom Pr 8[36].

†[שָׂנִיא] **adj. hated, held in aversion**;— 8146
fs. הַשְּׂנִיאָה Dt 21[15b] *the hated* (wife; v. √**1 a**); but read probably הַשְּׂנוּאָה (as v[15 a bis, 16]).

†שִׂנְאָה **n.f. hating, hatred**;—abs. שׂ׳ Nu 8135
35[20]+, cstr. שִׂנְאַת Dt 1[27] Pr 25[10]; sf. שִׂנְאָתְךָ Ez 35[11] (pl. -אֹתֶיךָ prob. meant, Kö[ii. 1, § 88] cf. Ol[§ 131 k], but < rd. שִׂנְאָתְךָ 𝔊 Co Berthol Toy, cf. Ges[§ 91 l]), etc.;—*hatred* (sts. opp. אַהֲבָה): **1.** human, Nu 35[20] (P), Ez 23[29] 35[11] Pr 10[12.18] 15[17] 26[26] ψ 109[5] Ec 9[1.6]; דִּבְרֵי שׂ׳ ψ 109[3]; emphatic, שִׂנְאַת חָמָס 25[19], תַּכְלִית שׂ׳ 139[22] (against י׳'s foes),

also (of sexual revulsion) שׂ׳ גְּדוֹלָה 2 S 13[15] (all acc. cogn.). **2.** ׳י's *hating*, as vb., c. acc. pers., Dt 1[27] 9[28].

8149 †שְׂנִיר **n.pr.mont.** Σανειρ: Amorite name of Ḥermon Dt 3[9], whence came cypress-trees Ez 27[5], prob. northern peak(s) of Ḥ. 1 Ch 5[23] Ct 4[8] (where + חֶרְמוֹן); so Ar. سنير, Abulf[ed. Par. 68], Syr. ܣܢܝܪ, Ecclus 24[13] *al.*, As. *Saniru* COT[Dt 3, 9] Dl[Pa 104]. Vid. also Dr[Dt 3, 9] Buhl[Geogr. 110 f. and reff.] [van d. H. erron. ׳שׂ Dt Ct].

שׂעף (√of foll.; Thes al. identif. with סעף *divide* (q.v.), whence foll. as *branching out, involved;* Ba[ES 56] cp. شَغَفَ *strike the* (شَغَافُ) *pericardium*, شَغِفَ *be disquieted* by a thing).

5587 †שְׂעִפִּים **n.[m.]pl. disquietings, = disquieting or excited thoughts**;—׳שׂ Jb 4[13]; sf. שְׂעִפַּי (Baer שְׂעִיפַּי) Jb 20[2] (|| חוּשִׁי).

8312 †[שַׂרְעַפִּים] **n.[m.]pl. disquieting thoughts** (cf. סַרְעַפָּה sub סעף, Ges[§ 85 w]);—sf. שַׂרְעַפַּי ψ 94[19] (appar. of anxious doubts); as secrets ־פַּי, 139[23] (open to ׳י; || לְבָבִי).

I. **שׂער** (√of foll.; cf. Ar. شَعِرَ *be hairy*, شَعَرٌ, شَعْرٌ, *hair*, so NH = BH, Eth. ሥዕርት: Aram. סַעֲרָא or (׳שׂ), ܣܥܪܐ, ܣܥܪܬܐ; As. *šârtu*, *hairy skin;* on Gk. deriv. v. Lewy[Fremdw. 86], Egypt. v. Bondi[64] WMM[99]).

8181 שֵׂעָר 27 **n.m.**[Lv 13, 3] **hair**;—abs. ׳שׂ Gn 25[25]+, cstr. שְׂעַר Ju 16[22]+, שְׂעַר Is 7[20] (Ges[§ 93 hh] Kö[ii. 1. 78]); sf. שְׂעָרֵךְ Ez 16[7], שַׂעְרֵךְ Ct 4[1] 6[5] (Kö[l. c.]); שְׂעָרוֹ Lv 14[8]+, שְׂעָרָהּ v[20], שְׂעָרָה v[4] (Ges[§ 91 e]);—*hair:* **1.** of animals, as material, אַדֶּרֶת שׂ׳ Gn 25[5] (J), Zc 13[4]; prob. also אִישׁ בַּעַל שׂ׳ 2 K 1[8] i.e. a man with a garment of skin. **2.** human: שׂ׳ ראשׁוֹ Ju 16[22] 2 S 14[26] Nu 6[5] (P), cf. v[18] (P); + beard Ezr 9[3]; קָדְקֹד שׂ׳ ψ 68[22]; incl. head, beard, eyebrows Lv 14[8.9.10] (P); שׂ׳ הָרַגְלָיִם Is 7[20] (i.e. of genitals; + ראשׁ, זָקָן; in fig.) long *hair* of woman Ez 16[7] Ct 4[1] 6[5]; *hair* of skin in (leprosy-)marks Lv 13[3] + 10 t. 13 (P).

8185 †שַׂעֲרָה **n.f. a hair**, nom. unit. (Ges[§ 122 t]);—abs. Ju 20[16]: cstr. in phr. מִשַּׂעֲרַת ראשׁוֹ 1 S 14[45] *a single hair of his head*, cf. 2 S 14[11] 1 K 1[52] (v. מִן **3 b** (*d*), Dr[1 S 14, 45]); שׂ׳ בְּשָׂרִי Jb 4[15] (appar. n.coll., 𝔊 𝔙 and most; Buhl prop. pl.); pl. cstr. שַׂעֲרוֹת ראשִׁי ψ 40[13] 69[5] (both as numerous).

8175 †[שָׂעַר] **vb. denom. bristle**, with horror;—**Qal** *Pf.* 3 pl. שָׂעֲרוּ שַׂעַר Ez 27[35] (|| רָעֲמוּ, שָׁמַם עַל);

Impf. 3 mpl. יִשְׂעֲרוּ עָלֶיךָ שַׂעַר 32[10] (|| שָׁמֵם Hiph.); *Imv.* mpl. שַׂעֲרוּ Je 2[12] (|| שֹׁמּוּ עַל־).—Dt 32[17] v. III. שׂער.

8175

†I. שַׂעַר **n.[m.] horror** (prop. *bristling*);—׳שׂ abs., as acc. cogn. Ez 27[35] 32[10] v. foregoing; cf. אָחֲזוּ שׂ׳ Jb 18[20] (|| נָשַׁמּוּ עַל). 8178

†I. שָׂעִר **adj. hairy**;—ms. אִישׁ שׂ׳ Gn 27[11]; fpl. יָדָיו שְׂעִרֹת v[33] (J). 8163

II. שָׂעִיר 53 **n.m.**[Nu 15, 24] **he-goat, buck** (*hairy one*; NH *id.*);—abs. ׳שׂ Lv 4[24]+, cstr. שְׂעִיר Nu 7[16]+; pl. שְׂעִירִם Lv 16[7.8]; cstr. שְׂעִירֵי v[5] Nu 7[87];—*he-goat*, usu. שְׂעִיר(־)עִזִּים *buck of goats* (v. עֵז p. 777): Gn 37[31] (J), Ez 43[22] 45[23] Lv 4[23] 9[3] 23[19] + 20 t. Nu (all P); שְׂעִירֵי ע׳ Lv 16[5] Nu 7[87] (P); ׳שׂ alone = *he-goat* Lv 4[24] + 11 t. Lv 16 (P); שְׂעִיר (הַ)חַטָּאת *he-goat for sin-offering* Ez 43[25] Lv 9[15] + 9 t. Lv Nu; שְׂעִירֵי הַח׳ 2 Ch 29[23]; in Dn 8[21] ׳הַשּׂ is prob. gloss to הַצָּפִיר (cf. Dr). 8163

†I. [שְׂעִירָה] **n.f. she-goat**;—cstr. שְׂעִירַת עִזִּים (lit. *hairy female of goats*) Lv 4[28] 5[6]. 8166

†II. [שְׂעִירָה] **n. pr. loc.,** prob. in SE Ephraim (= *goat*, Thes);—c. ה loc. הַשְּׂעִירָתָה Ju 3[26]; Σε(τ)ειρωθα, 𝔊L Σηρωθα. 8167

†III. שָׂעִיר **n.m. satyr, demon** (with *he-goat's* form, or feet; NH *id.;* cf. Baud[Stud. i. 136 ff.]; *hairy* demons We[Skizzen iii. 135; Heid. 152] RS[Sem. 113, 423; 2nd ed. 120, 441]); abs. ׳שׂ Is 34[14] inhabiting desolate ruins, so pl. שְׂעִירִים 13[21]; name for idols 2 Ch 11[15] and (שְׂעִירִם) Lv 17[7] (H); prob. also בָּמוֹת הַשּׂ׳ 2 K 23[8] (MT הַשְּׁעָרִים) Hoffm[ZAW ii (1882), 175] SS Kmp Klo Kit Benz Bur. 8163

†שְׂעֹרָה **n.f. barley** (*bearded* grain; 𝔊 κριθή, 𝔙 hordeum; NH *id.;* Sab. שערם Glas in Fell[ZMG liv (1900), 256], Ar. شَعِيرٌ; OAram. שערה, 𝔗 סְעָרְתָא, Syr. ܣܥܪܬܐ; Di[260] cp. Eth. ሠገም: *wheat, grain*);—abs. ׳שׂ Ex 9[31]+; usu. pl. שְׂעֹרִים Ho 3[2]+;—*barley*, common grain (oft. || חִטָּה, etc.): **1.** growing, standing, sg. Ex 9[31.31] (J), Dt 8[8] Jb 31[40] Jo 1[11], as sown Is 28[25]; standing, pl. 2 S 14[30] שְׂעוֹ׳ 1 Ch 11[13], reaped קְצִיר (הַ)שְּׂעֹרִים 2 S 21[9] Ru 1[22] 2[23], גֹּרֶן הַשּׂ׳ 3[2]. **2.** pl., the grains, measured, cooked, etc.: Ho 3[2.2] Ez 4[9] 13[19] 45[13] 2 K 7[1.16.18] Je 41[8] 2 Ch 2[9.14] 27[5] Ru 2[17] 3[15.17], 2 S 17[28] 1 K 5[8] (food for horses); זֶרַע חֹמֶר שׂ׳ Lv 27[16] (P); קֶמַח שׂ׳ Nu 5[15], לֶחֶם שׂ׳ Ju 7[13] 2 K 4[42], עֻגַת שׂ׳ Ez 4[12]. 8184

†שְׂעֹרִים **n.pr.m.** priest 1 Ch 24[8]; Σεωρειμ. 8188

8165 †שֵׂעִיר **n.pr.** Sēʿîr (=שָׂעִיר, *goat?* cf. Gray Prop. N. 94; but note play in שֵׂעָר Gn 25^{25}, שָׂעִר 27$^{11.23}$; Nö ZMG xl (1886), 165; Ency. Bib. ii. 1183 cp. n. pr. mont. الاشعر (the 'hairy,' i.e. 'well-wooded,' cf. شَعَار *trees*), n.pr.gent. (orig. n.pr.loc.) الأشْعَر; Lag BN 92 thinks שׂ׳ orig. n.pr.m., but land much earlier in OT.; perh. = Tel Am. land *Šêri*, Zim ZA vi (1891), 257 Jastr JBL xi (1892), 114 Wkl Tel Am. 181, 26 Buhl Edom. 28 f.);—**1.** Σηειρ: **a. terr.** land of Edom, S. of Dead Sea, אַ֫רְצָה שׂ׳ Gn 32^{4} (J; ‖ שְׂדֵה אֱדוֹם), cf. 36^{30} (P); שׂ׳ alone Ju 5^{4} (poem; ‖ *id.*), Nu 24^{18} (JE; ‖ אֱדוֹם), Dt 1^{44} 2$^{4.8.12.22.29}$ 33^{2} Jos 11^{19} (D), Is 21^{11} 2 Ch 20$^{23\,b}$; c. ה loc. שֵׂעִ֫ירָה Gn 33$^{14.16}$ (J), Jos 12^{7} (D). **b.** specif. **mont.** E. of Arabah, הַר־שׂ׳ Jos 24^{4} (E), Gn 36$^{8.9}$ (P), Dt 1^{2} 2$^{1.5}$ Ez 35$^{2.3.7.15}$ 1 Ch 4^{42} 2 Ch 20$^{10.22.23}$; cf. הַרְרָם שׂ׳ Gn 14^{6} (home of הַחֹרִי; on text v. Buhl Edom. 28 Gunk Gn). **c. gent.** Ez 25^{8} = Edom [van d. H. שׂ׳]; but del. 𝔊B Hi Co Berthol Toy Krae. **d.** personif. as **m.** in בְּנֵי־שׂ׳ (v. חֹרִי p. 360; cf. Gn 14^{6}) Gn 36^{20} = 1 Ch 1^{38}, Gn 36^{21} (P; + בְּאֶרֶץ אֱדוֹם); = Edomites 2 Ch 25$^{11.14}$ (‖ אֱדוֹמִים). **2. mont.** in Judah, הַר־שׂ׳ Jos 15^{10} (P), Ασσαρ, A Σηειρ, 𝔊L Σειιρ; Di Buhl G 91 al. cp. hill-ruin *Sârîs* c. 9 miles W. of Jerus. (Rob BR iii. 156).

8175 †II. [שָׂעַר] **vb. sweep** or **whirl away** (of storm-wind) (=סָעַר, q.v.; As. *šâru*, *wind*, Dl HWB 635; > Thes 1334 cp. I. שׂער);—**Qal** *Impf.* 3 ms. sf. יִשְׂעָרֶנּוּ ψ 58^{10} fig. *he* (י׳) *shall sweep it away.* **Niph.** *Pf.* 3 fs. impers. נִשְׂעֲרָה ψ 50^{3} round about him *it is tempestuous* exceedingly. **Pi.** *Impf.* 3 ms. sf. וִישָׂעֲרֵהוּ Jb 27^{21} *and it* [an E. wind] *shall whirl him away* fr. (מִן) his place. **Hithp.** *Impf.* 3 ms. וְיִשְׂתָּעֵר עָלָיו Dn 11^{40} the kg. *shall storm against him.*

5591, 8178 †II. שַׂ֫עַר **n.[m.]** storm (=סַ֫עַר);—only cstr. שַׂ׳ קֶטֶב Is 28^{2} *a storm of destruction* (in sim.; ‖ זֶרֶם בָּרָד).

5591, 8183 †שְׂעָרָה **n.f.** id. (=סְעָרָה);—of way of י׳ בְּסוּפָה וּבִשׂ׳ Na 1^{3}; fig. of י׳'s judgments; אֲשֶׁר־בִּשׂ׳ יְשׁוּפֵנִי Jb 9^{17}.

8175 †III. [שָׂעַר] **vb.** perh. **be acquainted with** (Ar. شَعَرَ *perceive* [Sab. שער *id.*? Hom Chrest. 124]; cf. Aram. סְעַר, ܣܥܰܪ, *visit, inspect*, Ba ES 67 RS in Dr Dt Perles Anal. 79);—**Qal** *Pf.* 3 pl. sf. שְׂעָרוּם Dt 32^{17} new gods, *with whom* your fathers *had* no *acquaintance* (𝔊 εἴδησαν; ‖ יְדָעוּם); usu. *fear*, Thes *revere with awe*, Dr *shudder before*,

8175 [שָׂעַר] denom., although not elsewh. c. acc. pers.

IV. שׂער (assumed as √ of foll.).

†שְׂעִירִים **n.[m.]pl. rain**(-drops), si vera l.; 8164
(so acc. to Vrss and context; Thes cp. II. שַׂ֫עַר; Lag. prop. רְסִיסִים);—כִּשְׂ׳ עֲלֵי־דֶשֶׁא Dt 32^{2} (‖ רְבִיבִים, טַל, מָטָר).

שִׂפְדְּנָה Je 49^{3} Mas., < mod. edd. ס׳ v. ספד. 5594

p. 704

שׂפה (√ of foll.; cf. NH = BH; As. *šaptu*, *lip, edge*; so Syr. ܣܶܦܬܳܐ; Ar. شَفَةٌ *lip*, شَفًا *edge*).

שָׂפָה 176 **n.f.** [**m.** Ex 28^{32}, *edge*, cf. Albr ZAW xvi (1896), 76], **lip, speech, edge**;—abs. שׂ׳ Gn 11^{1}+, cstr. שְׂפַת v^{7}+; sf. שְׂפָתוֹ 1 K 7^{23}+, etc.; oftener du. שְׂפָתַיִם Is 6^{5}+, cstr. שִׂפְתֵי ψ 12^{4}+; sf. שְׂפָתַי Je 17^{16}+, sf. 3 mpl. שְׂפָתֵימוֹ ψ 59^{13} 140$^{4.10}$, etc.; pl. (poet. and late) cstr. שִׂפְתוֹת Ec 10^{12}, sf. שִׂפְתוֹתֶיךָ etc. ψ 45^{3} 59^{8} Is 59^{3} Ct 4$^{3.11}$ 5^{13};—**1.** *lip:* **a.** usu. (c. 108 t.) human organ of speech (oft. ‖ לָשׁוֹן, פֶּה, rarely [only late poetry] חֵךְ: 10 t. Jb; 25 t. ψψ; 45 t. Pr): (1) Is 29^{13} Lv 5^{4} (P), Jb 13^{6} Mal 2^{6} ψ 12^{5} Pr 5^{3}+; דַּל שׂ׳ ψ 141^{3} (v. דַּל); אִישׁ שׂ׳ Jb 11^{2} = a talker, אֱוִיל שׂ׳ Pr 10^{8} = one talking folly, so v^{10} (MT; but v. Toy); טְמֵא שְׂפָתַיִם Is 6$^{5.5}$ cf. v^{7} Dn 10^{16}; עֲרַל שׂ׳ Ex 6$^{12.30}$ (P; unskilled in speech); עִקֵּשׁ שׂ׳ 19^{1}; פֹּתֶה שׂ׳ 20^{19} v. [פָּתָה] p. 834; מוֹצָא שׂ׳ i.e. utterance, Dt 23^{24} Je 17^{16} Nu 30^{13} (P), ψ 89^{35}, רוּחַ שׂ׳ Is 11^{4} (of Mess. kg.), דְּבַר שׂ׳ ψ 59^{13} Pr 14^{23}+, = mere, empty, word 2 K 18^{20} = Is 36^{5}; תְּבוּאַת שׂ׳ Pr 18^{20}, נוּב שׂ׳ Is 57^{19} (thanksgiving), cf. Ho 14^{3} (𝔊𝔖 and most פְּרִי for פָּרִים); of flattery, חֵלֶק שׂ׳ Pr 7^{21}, שְׂפַת חֲלָקוֹת ψ 12$^{3.4}$; cf. שְׂפַת אָוֶן, שִׂפְתֵי מִרְמָה ψ 17^{1}, שֶׁקֶר שׂ׳ 31^{9} + 4 t., Pr 17^{4}; poison beneath (cf. לָשׁוֹן) ψ 140^{4} (fig.); פֶּשַׁע שׂ׳ Pr 12^{13}; לְזוּת שׂ׳ 4^{24}; אֱמֶת שׂ׳ 12^{19}, יֶתֶר שׂ׳ 17^{7}, צֶדֶק שׂ׳ 16^{13}, דַּעַת שׂ׳ 14^{7} 20^{15}; חֵן שׂ׳ 22^{11}; רְנָנוֹת שׂ׳ ψ 63^{5} i.e. lips that shout for joy; שָׂפָה בְרוּרָה Zp 3^{9}; c. vbs.: פָּתַח שׂ׳ (to speak) Jb 11^{5} 30^{20} (Gi v^{21}), cf. ψ 51^{17}, מִפְתַּח שׂ׳ Pr 8^{6}; פָּשַׂק שׂ׳ 13^{3} i.e. prate; שׂ׳ מָלְאוּ זַעַם Is 30^{27}; שׂ׳ subj. of דִּבֵּר Is 59^{3} Pr 24^{2}; נָשָׂא עַל־שׂ׳ ψ 16^{14}; קָרַץ שׂ׳ Pr 16^{30} = backbite; אָטַם שׂ׳ 17^{28} = keep silence, so חָשַׂךְ שׂ׳ 10^{19}, כָּלָא שׂ׳ ψ 40^{10}. †(2) lips moving in speech, c. נוּעַ 1 S 1^{13}, נִיד Jb 16^{5}. †(3) transition to mng. *speech*, עָלָה עַל־שְׂפַת לָשׁוֹן Ez 36^{3}; = ability to speak Jb 12^{20}. †**b.** organ of laughter Jb 8^{21}. †**c.** of insulting grimace הִפְטִיר בְּשׂ׳ ψ 22^{8}. †**d.** quivering in terror Hb 3^{16}. †**e.** feature of beauty Ct 4^{3} (scarlet). **f.** place of bridle 2 K 19^{28} = Is 37^{29} (v. מֶתֶג).

†**g.** receiving kiss Pr 24[26] cf. Ct 4[11] and (in fig.) 7[10]. †**h.** of divine speech, מִצְוַת שׂ׳ Jb 23[12], דְּבַר שׂ׳ ψ 17[4]. †**2.** *language* (v. לָשׁוֹן), Gn 11[1.6.7.7.9] ψ 81[6]; עַם עִמְקֵי שׂ׳ Ez 3[5.6] Is 33[19], לַעֲגֵי שׂ׳ 28[11]; שְׂפַת כְּנַעַן 19[18] (i.e. Hebrew). **3.** *edge: shore* of sea Gn 22[17] (J) + 7 t.; *bank* of river Gn 41[3.17] (E) + 5 t., of wady (נַחַל) Dt 2[36] + 7 t.; *lip* (bank) of אָבֵל מְחוֹלָה Ju 7[22] cf. GASm[G 400]; *brim* of vessel 1 K 7[23.23] + 7 t.; *edge* of altar Ez 43[13]; of curtains (in pairs) Ex 26[4.4] (P) + 6 t.; of חֹשֶׁן, toward ephod 28[26] = 39[19] (P); of round opening in robe (יִהְיֶה) שׂ׳ לְפִיו 28[32] = 39[23] (P).

8222 †שָׂפָם **n.[m.]** moustache (cf. NSyr. ܣܦܡܐ *rete*; on meaning and form v. Thes Ol[408] Kö[ii. 73]);—abs. שׂ׳ Mi 3[7] +, sf. שְׂפָמוֹ 2 S 19[25];—*moustache*: עָשָׂה שׂ׳ 2 S 19[25] (𝔊 μύσταξ) i.e. trim it; עָטָה עַל־שׂ׳ Mi 3[7] Ez 24[17.22] Lv 13[45] (P; v. I. עטה **1**).

4939, 5596 שִׂפְּחָה v. III. ספח. מִשְׂפָּח v. II. ספח. p. 705

8224 שִׂפְמוֹת 1 S 30[28] v. שִׁפ׳. p. 1050

5603, 5606-07 שָׂפַן v. ספן. I. שָׂפַק, שֶׂפֶק v. ספק. p. 706

5606 †II. [שָׂפַק] **vb. suffice** (NH סָפַק *suffice, abound*, so Ecclus 15[18] +; 𝔗 סַפֵּק, סְפִיק, Syr. ܣܦܩ; Ar. شَفِقَ is *be niggardly, scanty*, Lane [1573]);—**Qal** *Impf.* 3 ms. יִשְׂפֹּק 1 K 20[10], subj. dust, c. לְ rei.

5607 †[שֶׂפֶק] **n.[m.]** **sufficiency, plenty**;—sf. שִׂפְקוֹ Jb 20[22] (Baer Gi; ס׳ van d. H.; opp. צרר).

5242 שַׂק v. שׂקק. below

8244 †[שָׂקַד] doubtful **vb.**, Ḳi bind on;—**Niph.** *Pf.* 3 ms. נִשְׂקַד עַל La 1[14] (fig.); rd. perh. נִשְׁקַד עַל *watch is kept upon* 𝔊 𝔖 𝔙 Bu, cf. Thes (v. שקד); other conj. in Löhr Bi.

שׂקק (assumed as √ of foll., but nowhere found).

8242 †שַׂק **n.m.**[Jos 9, 4] **sack, sackcloth** (v. Schwally [ZAW xi (1891), 173] who conj. Egyptian origin; NH סַק *sackcloth* (rare); As. *šakku, sack* (Dl[HWB 687 a]), *sackcloth* (Wkl[Altor. Forsch. vi. 44]); Eth. ሠቅ:=BH; Aram. סַקָּא, ܣܩܐ; Gk. σάκκος Lewy[Fremdw. 87]);—abs. שׂ׳ Gn 37[34] +, שָׂק Je 48[37] +; sf. שַׂקִּי ψ 30[12], etc.; pl. שַׂקִּים Jos 9[4] +, sf. שַׂקֵּיהֶם Gn 42[35];—**1.** *sack*, for grain Gn 42[25.27] (‖ אַמְתַּחַת), v[35.35] (E), Jos 9[4] (JE), perh. also Lv 11[32] (P). **2.** *sackcloth*: **a.** worn in mourning and humiliation (v. Now[Arch. i. 192 f.] SACook[Ency. Bib. s.v.]), either loose garment like sack, or piece of similar material (of rough, dark hair), fastened round body: put (שִׂים) on loins Gn 37[34] (J), 1 K 20[31], on (bare) flesh 21[27] 2 K 6[30], cf. Je 48[37] Jb 16[15] (c. תָּפַר); וְהַעֲלֵיתִי עַל־כָּל־מָתְנַיִם שׂ׳ Am 8[10]; usu. girt on (חָגַר) 2 S 3[31] Is 15[3] 22[12] Je 4[8] 6[26] 49[3] Ez 7[18] 27[31] 1 K 20[32] Jo 1[8], cf. Is 3[24]; כִּסָּה בַשׂ׳ 2 K 19[1.2] = Is 37[1.2], Jon 3[6.8] 1 Ch 21[16], fig. of heavens (cf. קָדַר), אָשִׂים כְּסוּתָם שׂ׳ Is 50[3]; late לָבַשׁ שׂ׳ *put on sackcloth* Jon 3[5] Est 4[1], cf. v[2] ψ 35[13] 69[12]; בְּצוֹם וְשׂ׳ Ne 9[1], cf. Dn 9[3]; פִּתַּח שׂ׳ *loosen sackcloth* Is 20[2] (+ מֵעַל), ψ 30[12] (opp. שִׂמְחָה), הֵסִיר שׂ׳ מֵעַל Est 4[4]. **b.** same garment (or material) spread out (to lie on), 2 S 21[10] (c. הִטָּה), Is 58[5] (c. הִצִּיעַ), cf. Est 4[3]; וַיִּשְׁכַּב בַּשׂ׳ 1 K 21[27], לִינוּ בַשׂ׳ Jo 1[13].

†[שָׂקַר] **vb. Pi.** ogle (Aram. סְקַר *look at* (𝔗 Jb 20[9] 28[7]), סַקְרָנִית *looking about, ogling*; ܣܩܪ *eye* with envy or hatred (e.g. 1 S 18[9] 𝔖); cf. De[Is]);—*Pt.* fpl. מְשַׂקְּרוֹת עֵינַיִם Is 3[16] *ogling of eyes* (women of Jerusalem). 8265

שַׂר v. שׂרר. p. 978 8269

†שַׂרְאֶצֶר **n.pr.m.** in Assyr. (Bab.) (van d. H. 8272
שׂ׳, but v. Baer, and Str[ZMG xxxiii (1879), 302]; in As. 8272
perhaps [*Ašur, Bêl*, or *Nergal*] *šar-uṣur*, [. . .] *protect the king!* COT[2 K 19, 37]; Σαρασα(ρ));—**1.** son of Sennach., 2 K 19[37] = Is 37[38] (Schr[COT l.c.] Wkl[KAT 3, 84] Stevenson[Hast. DB. iv. 476]). **2.** a returned exile Zc 7[2] (Stevenson[ib. 477]).—Cf. also נֵרְגַל שׂ׳ p. 669.

†[שָׂרַג] **vb. Pu.** be intertwined (Talm. 8276
סָרַג Pi. *enmesh, weave around*; Aram. ܣܪܓ *intertwine, involve*, סְרַג *entwine*; Ar. شَرَجَ *set in order, join, weave, mix*);—*Impf.* 3 mpl. יְשֹׂרָגוּ Jb 40[17] *are intertwined* (of sinews of hippopot.). **Hithp.** *Impf.* 3 mpl. יִשְׂתָּרְגוּ La 1[14] *they intertwine themselves* (fig. of פְּשָׁעַי).

†[שָׂרִיג] **n.m.**[Gn 40, 10] **tendril, twig** (from 8299
interlacing; cf. Ar. شَرِيجَة palm-leaf *braid*, etc.; Eth. መሥገርት: *net* (Prä[BASI. 371]); Aram. סְרִיגָא, ܣܪܝܓܐ *network, lattice*);—of vine, pl. שָׂרִיגִם Gn 40[10], שָׂרִגִים v[12]; of fig-tree, sf. שָׂרִיגֶיהָ Jo 1[7].

†שְׂרוּג **n.pr.m.** descendant (i.e. younger 8286
branch) of Peleg Gn 11[20.21.22.23] 1 Ch 1[26]; Σερουχ (𝔊L Ch Σερουγ).

†I. [שָׂרַד] **vb. escape** (Ar. شَرَدَ *take fright*, 8277
shy (of camel or horse), *run away*; Aram. ܣܪܕ *be terrified*, ܣܪܝܕܐ *survivor*);—**Qal** *Pf.* 3 pl. שָׂרְדוּ Jos 10[20] (JE; c. מִן pers.), Benn del. as dittogr.

שַׂר־הַצָּבָא 8[11]=*God* (prob., cf. צָבָא **1 c**; yet v. also צ׳ **1 b**), so שַׂר שָׂרִים v[25].

7786, 8323 †[שָׂרַר] **vb. denom.** (Gerber[20]) **be, or act as, prince, rule**;—**Qal** *Impf.* 3 ms. וַיָּשַׂר עַל־ יִשְׂרָאֵל Ju 9[22] Abim. *ruled over Isr.* three years; 3 mpl. יָשֹׂרוּ ... שָׂרִים Is 32[1] princes *shall govern* (*prince it*) justly (‖ יִמְלָךְ־מֶלֶךְ), cf. Pr 8[16]; *Pt.* לִהְיוֹת ... שֹׂרֵר Est 1[22] *that* every man *should bear rule* בְּבֵיתוֹ. **Hithp.** *Impf.*, 2 ms. + *Inf. abs.* כִּי־תִשְׂתָּרֵר עָלֵינוּ גַּם־הִשְׂתָּרֵר Nu 16[13] *that thou shouldst also keep playing the prince over us.*—

3256, 8269 יָשׂר 1 Ch 15[22] v. יָסַר **Qal** and שַׂר **4 b.** **Hiph.** *Pf.* 3 pl. metapl. הֵשִׂירוּ (Ges[§ 67 v]) Ho 8[4] *they made princes* (abs.; ‖ הִמְלִיכוּ). p. 415f, 978

8282 †I. [שָׂרָה] **n.f. princess, noble lady**;—cstr. שָׂרָתִי (Ges[§ 90 l]) La 1[1]; pl. שָׂרוֹת 1 K 11[3], cstr. *id.* Est 1[18]; sf. שָׂרוֹתֶיהָ Ju 5[29], ־תֵיהֶם Is 49[23];—*princesses* attending Sisera's mother Ju 5[29]; of Sol.'s wives 1 K 11[3], other queens Is 49[23] (‖ מְלָכִים); wives of nobles Est 1[18]; fig. of Jerus. La 1[1].

8283 II. שָׂרָה[37] **n.pr.f.** wife of Abraham (*princess*);—Σαρρα: Gn 17[15] (where formal change from שָׂרַי), v[17.19.21] 21[1b.3] 23[1.1.2.2.19] 25[10.12] 49[31] (all P), 18[6] + 9 t. 18, 21[1a.2a] 24[36.67] (all J), 20[2.2.14.16.18] 21[6.7.9.12] (all E); as ancestress of Hebrews Is 51[2].

†שָׂרַי **n.pr.f.** wife of Abram (Nö[ZMG xlii (1888), 484] Ges[§ 80 l] Kö[ii. 1. 427] make = foregoing, with old fem. ending ־ַי; > Lag[BN 92, Anm.*], emphasizing diff. in 𝔊, der. fr. a √ شرى, and cp. شراة, name of a barren mt.; cf. RS יִשְׂרָאֵל supr., sub I. שׂרה);—𝔊 Σαρα;—Gn 11[30] (J), v[31] (P), 12[5.11.17] 16[1.2.3.5.6.6.8.8] (all J), 17[15] (P); שָׂרָ֑י 11[29] (J), 16[2] (J), 17[15] (P). 8297

שָׂשׂוֹן, שָׂשׂן v. שׂוּשׂ. p. 965 8342

שְׂאֵת v. שְׂאֵת sub נשׂא p. 673[a]. 7613

†שָׂתַם **vb.** usu. **stop up**, in sense of *shut out*, shut ears against (late ‖ form of סָתַם; yet awkward; Ba[ES 9] cp. Ar. شَمَّتَ *frustrate, disappoint*);—**Qal** *Pf.* 3 ms. שׂ׳ תְּפִלָּתִי La 3[8] (> van d. H. שָׂתַם) *he* (י׳) *hath shut out my prayer* (Bu שׂ׳ מִתּ׳ *shut up* [himself] *from*). 5640

†[שָׂתַר] **vb. Niph. burst** or **break out**, of tumours (Ar. شَتَرَ *have inverted*, or *cracked, eyelids*, or *lower lips*; Eth. ሠተረ: *lacerate*; As. [*šatâru*] II. *tear down*; Syr. ܣܬܪ *destroy*, so Sab. שתר Sab. Denkm.[No. 48, l. 2], BAram. סְתַר Ezr 5[12]);—**Niph.** *Impf.* וַיִּשָּׂתְרוּ לָהֶם עפלים 1 S 5[9] and tumours *brake out* to them. 8368

שׁ

שׁ *Šin*, 21st letter (with שׂ); = 300 in post B. Hebrew.

834, 7945 ·שֶׁ, also (†Gn 6[3] [? v. **4 a**], Ju 5[7.7] Ct 1[7] Jb 19[29] [?]) ·שַׁ, שָׁ in שָׁאַתָּה †Ju 6[17], and שְׁ in שְׁהוּא †Ec 2[22], שְׁהֵם †3[18] (elsewhere before gutt. שֶׁ, as שֶׁאֲנִי †Ct 1[6] Ec 2[18], שֶׁאֵין †ψ 146[3], שֶׁהֵם †Ct 6[5] La 4[9], שֶׁעָל †Ju 7[12] 8[26], שֶׁרֹאשִׁי †Ct 5[2]), **rel. part.** who, which, that, etc. (constantly in NH; Aram. of Nerab, Ldzb[371, 445]; As. *sha*; Ph. אש (regularly), also sometimes ש (Ldzb[227 f.]): acc. to Ges Ew[§ 181 b] Ol[p. 439] Sta[§ 176 e], abbrev. from אֲשֶׁר; more prob. (Sperling [v. אֲשֶׁר], Kö[ii. 323 f.])

834 an original demonstr. part.), syn. with אֲשֶׁר, but in usage limited to late Heb., and passages with N. Palest. colouring, viz. †Ju 5[7.7] [אֲשֶׁר v[27]], 6[17] 7[12] 8[26] 2 K 6[11] (v. **4 c**), Jon 1[7.12] 4[10] [אֲשֶׁר 11 t.], ψ 122[3.4] 123[2] 124[1.2.6] 129[6.7] 133[2.3] 135[2.8.10] 136[23] 137[8.9] 144[15] 146[3.5] La 2[15.16] 4[9] 5[18] Ezr 8[20] 1 Ch 5[20] 27[27], Ct (uniformly, except in title 1[1]), Ec (68 t.; אֲשֶׁר 89 t.); also (dub.) Gn 6[3] 49[10] (שֶׁלֹּה 𝔊 𝔖 𝔗), Jb 19[29]; and in the n.pr. (q.v.) מִישָׁאֵל and מְתוּשָׁאֵל.—In usage, ·שֶׁ is in the main

parallel with אֲשֶׁר, viz. **1.** as **pron.** *who, which, whom*, Ju 7[12] כַּחוֹל שֶׁעַל שְׂפַת הַיָּם (cf. חוֹל **c**), ψ 122[3] 124[6] etc.; *him whom, that which*, etc., Ct 1[7] 3[1] 1 Ch 27[27] Ec 1[11] 6[3] וְרַב שֶׁיִּהְיוּ יְמֵי חַיָּיו and much (vb.) is *that which* his days amount to (Hi De al.), v[10]; ·שֶׁ הוּא *that which* 1[9.9]; in the genit., ·אַשְׁרֵי שֶׁ †ψ 137[8.9] 146[5].—On ·מַה־שֶּׁ in Ec = *whatever, what*, v. מָה **1 e b**. **2.** as a connecting link; = *where* (cf. אֲשֶׁר p. 81, and **4 b β**), ·מְקוֹם שֶׁ †Ec 1[7] 11[3] (cf. מְקוֹם אֲשֶׁר Gn 39[20]+: Ges[§ 130 c]), *whither* ψ 122[4] (שֶׁשָּׁם ...), *when* Ct 8[8] Ec 12[3] ·בַּיּוֹם שֶׁ (cf. *ib.* **4 b α**). **3.** as a **conj.** (cf. אֲשֶׁר **8**);—**a.** *that*, after רָאָה Ec 2[13] 3[18], יָדַע 1[17] 2[14] 9[5] Jb 19[29] (? v. p. 192[b]), דִּבֵּר Ec 2[15], אָמַר 834

8[14], עָשָׂה אוֹת Ju 6[17]; as subj. of sentence, Ec 3[13] 5[15]; also in the phrases, (*a*) *what is . . . that?* Ct 5[9] (usu. כִּי; v. מָה **1 d** *b*), מֶה הָיָה שֶׁ׳ how comes it *that . . . ?* Ec 7[10]; (*b*) Ct 3[4] כִּמְעַט שֶׁעָבַרְתִּי מֵהֶם hardly (was it) *that* (Germ. *kaum dass*) I had passed, etc., Ec 7[14] עַל דִּבְרַת שֶׁלֹּא יִמְצָא to the intent *that* . . ., 5[15] כָּל־עֻמַּת שֶׁבָּא exactly *as* . . ., 12[9] יֹתֵר שֶׁ׳ besides that, עַד שֶׁ׳ (עַד שַׁ׳ †Ju 5[7]) until *that* ψ 123[2] Ct 2[7.17] + (v. III. עַד **II 1 a** *a* and *b*; cf. NH *Yoma* 5[1]), *while* 1[12] (ib. **2 d**); עָשָׂה שֶׁ׳ to make or cause *that* . . ., †Ec 3[14] (cf. Ez 36[27]). **b.** involving a reason (cf. אֲשֶׁר **8 c**), *because, since,* Ct 1[6.6] 5[2] Ec 2[18b]. Hence שַׁלָּמָה †Ct 1[7] *since why?* =*lest* (v. מָה **4 d** *b*). **4.**
834 compounds: **a.** בְּשֶׁ׳, i. q. בַּאֲשֶׁר **c** (p. 84[a]) *in that, seeing that,* Ec 2[16]; also (acc. to MT 𝔊 𝔖 Hu De) Gn 6[3] בְּשַׁגַּם הוּא בָשָׂר *because that* he
834 also is flesh; but v. שָׁגַג. **b.** כְּשֶׁ׳, i. q. כַּאֲשֶׁר p. 455:—(*a*) *according as* Ec 5[14] 12[7]; (*b*) *when* (so oft. NH, as *Ab* 1[8.S.S.14]) 9[12] 10[3]. **c.** מִשֶּׁ׳, i.q.
834, 4100 מֵאֲשֶׁר **a** (p. 84[a]), 2 K 6[12] מִי מִשֶּׁלָּנוּ who of *those that* are ours? (but Klo Kamp[Kau] Benz מְגַלֵּנוּ who *betrays us?* cf. 𝔊); Ec 5[4] *than that* (cf. מֵאֲשֶׁר 3[22]), + 2[24] (read מִשֶּׁיֹּאכַל with Ew De, etc.; cf. 3[22]).
834, 7945 **d.** שֶׁל, like לְ אֲשֶׁר (אֲשֶׁר **7 b**), a mark of the genit.: thrice, adding slight emph. to the sf., Ct 1[6]=8[12] כַּרְמִי שֶׁלִּי *my* vineyard (lit. my vineyard, which is mine), 3[7] מִטָּתוֹ שֶׁלִּשְׁלֹמֹה (so oft. in NH, but without any special emphasis, as *Aboth* 1[12] הֱוֵי מתלמידיו של־אהרן be of Aaron's disciples, 2[1] הֱוֵי מתפלל בשלומה של־מלכות, v[2] 3[2] שְׂכָרָן שֶׁל־מִצְוֹת; cf. ܕܝܠ in Syr., as Lk 6[42] ܡ̈ܠܝ ܕܝܠܝ *my* words, Nö[§225]). And with בְּ, בְּשֶׁל lit. *through that which belongs to* or *concerns,* pleon. for *on account of* (a late, unidiom. transl. of Aram. בְּדִיל, from בְּ, דִּי, and לְ, as in Onk Gn 12[13] בדילי *on my account,* 30[27] 39[5] בְּדִיל יוֹסֵף; בְּדִיל מָא *on account of* what? Ju 8[1] 2 S 9[1] 1 K 11[12.39], etc.), Jon 1[7] בְּשֶׁלְּמִי *on account of* whom? (‖ v[8] בַּאֲשֶׁר לְמִי: v. p. 84; prob. a gloss), v[12] בְּשֶׁלִּי *on account of* me (𝔗 בְּדִיל מַן, בְּדִילִי); Ec 8[17] בְּשֶׁל אֲשֶׁר יַעֲמֹל הָאָדָם לְבַקֵּשׁ *on account of* (the fact) *that* (=*seeing that*) man labours, etc. (unidiom. transl. of Aram. בְּדִיל דְּ *because that,* as Gn 6[3] בְּדִיל דְּאִינּוּן, בִּסְרָא 39[9] בְּדִיל דְּאַתְּ אִתְּתֵיהּ [for Heb. בַּאֲשֶׁר אַתְּ אִשְׁתּוֹ]; Palm. בדיל די Ldzb[233],—in Tariff 1[4] (Cooke[N.-Sem. Inscr. 320]) = ἐπειδή).

7722 [שׁא] v. [שׁוֹא]. p. 996

7579 †[שָׁאַב] **vb. draw** (water) (NH *id.*, also *attract;* Aram. שְׁאֵיב, of magnet; Ar. سَابَ *be satisfied with drinking*);—**Qal** *Pf.* 2 mpl. consec. וּשְׁאַבְתֶּם Is 12[3]; *Impf.* 3 fs. וַתִּשְׁאַב Gn 24[20], -אָב v[45]; 1 s. אֶשְׁאָב v[19.44]; 3 mpl. יִשְׁאֲבוּן Ru 2[9], וַיִּשְׁאֲבוּ 1 S 7[6] + 2 t.; *Imv.* fs. שַׁאֲבִי Na 3[14]; *Pt.* ms. שֹׁאֵב Dt 29[10], pl. cstr. שֹׁאֲבֵי Jos 9[21.23.27]; fpl. הַשֹּׁאֲבֹת Gn 24[11];—*draw* water, c. acc. מַיִם Gn 24[13] (J), 1 S 7[6] 9[11], + מִן of source 2 S 23[16]=1 Ch 11[18], Is 12[3] (fig.); מֵי מָצוֹר שַׁ׳ לָךְ Na 3[14]; מַיִם om. Gn 24[20.43.45] and (+ לְ of animals) v[19.20.44] (all J); c. acc. אֲשֶׁר Ru 2[9] drink of *that which* the young men *draw;* Pt. fpl. Gn 24[11] *the water-drawing women;* m. שֹׁאֵב מֵימֶיךָ Dt 29[10] (servile labour, ‖ חֹטֵב עֵצֶיךָ), so mpl. Jos 9[21.23.27] (P; all c. לְ, and all ‖ חֹטְבֵי עֵצִים).

†[מַשְׁאָב] **n.[m.]** appar. **drawing-place** 4857
of water; only pl. מַשְׁאַבִּים Ju 5[11].

†שָׁאַג **vb. roar** (NH *id.;* Ar. ثَأَجَ *low,* 7580
bleat, Frey);—**Qal** *Pf.* 3 ms. שׁ׳ Is 5[29] Kt consec. (>Qr וְיִשְׁאַג), שָׁאַג Am 3[8], etc.; *Impf.* 3 ms. יִשְׁאַג Am 3[4]+, etc.; *Inf. abs.* שָׁאֹג Je 25[30]; *Pt.* שֹׁאֵג Ju 14[5] ψ 22[14], שׁוֹאֵג Ez 22[25], שֹׁאֲגִים Zp 3[3] ψ 104[21];—**1.** *roar,* of lion Ju 14[5] (c. לִקְרָאתוֹ), Am 3[4.8] ψ 104[21] (c. לְ of prey), fig. of invaders and foes Je 2[15] (c. עַל pers.) ψ 22[14], cf. 74[4], sim. Is 5[29] Je 51[38]; fig. of rapacious rulers Zp 3[3] Ez 22[25] (read נְשִׂיאֶיהָ for נְבִיאֶיהָ 𝔊 and mod.); of י׳ (like lion) calling scattered Isr. Ho 11[10.10] (on text of v. see Now); of י׳ roaring in thunder Je 25[30a] = Am 1[2] = Jo 3[16], also Je 25[30] (שָׁאֹג יִשְׁאַג, sq. עַל־נָוֵהוּ); cf. יִשְׁאַג־קוֹל Jb 37[4] (‖ יַרְעֵם). **2.** of human cry in distress ψ 38[9] (c. מִן causat.).

†שְׁאָגָה **n.f. roaring**;—**1.** like lion, abs. 7581
שׁ׳ Is 5[29] (of invaders); of lion, cstr. שַׁאֲגַת Zc 11[3] Jb 4[10] (fig. of wicked), sf. קוֹל שַׁאֲגָתוֹ Ez 19[7] (fig. of conquering king). **2.** human cry in distress, שַׁאֲגָתִי ψ 32[3]; דִּבְרֵי שׁ׳ 22[2], שַׁאֲגֹתָי Jb 3[24].

שָׁאָה v. שׁוֹאָה sub שׁוא. p. 996 7722

†I. [שָׁאָה] **vb. make a din** or **crash,** 7582
crash into ruins (perh. akin to שׁוֹאָה (√שׁוא) *storm, devastation;* > Aram. ܫܝܐ *be deserted,* שְׁהָוְתָא, שְׁהָווא *desert*);—**Qal** *Pf.* 3 pl. שָׁאוּ Is 6[11] until cities *have crashed into ruins;* + perh. Na 1[5] (p. 671[a]). **Niph.** *Impf.* 3 fs. תִּשָּׁאֶה שְׁמָמָה Is 6[11], usu., and the ground *be ruined* into a desolation, but 𝔊 Lo Du Marti תִּשָּׁאֵר *be left* a desol.; 3 mpl. יִשָּׁאוּן Is 17[12] *they are in uproar* (of nations, ‖ יֶהֱמָיוּן), v[13] (but del. as doublet Du Che[Hpt] Marti). **Hiph.** *Inf. cstr.* לְהַשְׁאוֹת Is

37^{26}, = לְהַשׁוֹת 2 K 19^{25} (Ges$^{§ 23 f}$ Kö$^{i. 570}$, who follow van d. H. in giving לְהַשְׁאוֹת as Qr, but v. Baer Gi), *to cause . . .* cities *to crash* into ruined heaps.

7584 †שַׁאֲוָה Kt, שׁוֹאָה Qr, **n.f. devastating storm**;—sim. Pr 1^{27} (|| סוּפָה). V. שׁוֹאָה, √II. שׁוא.

7591 †שְׁאִיָּה **n.f. ruin**;—Is 24^{12} (late).

7588 †שָׁאוֹן **n.m.**$^{Ho 10, 14}$ **roar** (of waters, etc.), **din, crash, uproar**;—abs. ׳שׁ Ho 10^{14}+; cstr. שְׁאוֹן Is 13^{4}+; sf. שְׁאוֹנָהּ 5^{14};—**1.** *roar* of water (waves), Is 17^{12} (|| הָמָה), sim. of noise of invading host, so v^{13}, but del. DuChe^{Hpt} Marti, as doublet; *roar* of this host v^{12} (|| הָמוֹן), cf. שְׁאוֹן קוֹלָם Je 51^{55}; of waves also ψ 65$^{8.8}$; of *din* or *crash* of battle Am 2^{2} Ho 10^{14} ψ 74^{23}; ׳בְּנֵי שׁ Je 48^{45} (i.e. warriors); of battle in which ׳י beats down his foes Je 25^{31}, cf. Is 66^{6}; of gathering hosts Is 13^{4}; ׳שׁ זָרִים 25^{5} (Du Marti, plausibly, גְּאוֹן זֵדִים, as 13^{11}); rd. ׳שׁ also prob. (for שַׁאֲנָן, q.v.) 2 K 19^{28} = Is 37^{29}; in mocking appell. of Pharaoh (Necho), Je 46^{17} ׳פ (𝔊 𝔖 𝔙) קִרְאוּ שֵׁם call ye the name of Ph. a *Crash.* **2.** *uproar* of revellers Is 5^{14} 24^{8}.—׳בּוֹר שׁ ψ 40^{3}, *pit of roaring* (of waters? fig., cf. מַעֲמַקֵּי־מַיִם 69^{3}, where also || יָוֵן); Thes al. *of destruction* (v. √**2**), but against usage of שָׁאוֹן;

7723 > Du prop. בּוֹר שָׁוְא (cf. נָפַת שָׁוְא Is 30^{28}). p. 996

7612 †שֵׁאת **n.f.** doubtful word; perh. (for *שֵׁאֵת) din of battle (= שָׁאוֹן); Thes al. **devastation**, cf. שְׁאִיָּה; either meaning suits ׳הַשּׁ La 3^{47} (|| הַשָּׁבֶר; but We$^{Comp. Hex. 2, 351}$, from II. שׁוא, *desolation*);

8351 contr. (acc. to Thes and most) שֵׁת, in בְּנֵי שֵׁת Nu 24^{17} (J) *sons of* (battle-)*din* (warriors, = בְּנֵי שָׁאוֹן in || Je 48^{45}); Vrss take שֵׁת here as n.pr.; Gray prop. שֵׁת = שְׂאֵת, *pride*, or reading as Je, cf. We$^{Comp. 351}$.

7583 †II. [שָׁאָה] **vb. Hithp. gaze** (appar. || form of שָׁעָה, q.v.);—*Pt.* ms. הָאִישׁ מִשְׁתָּאֵה לָהּ Gn 24^{21} (J) *the man was gazing at her* (Ges$^{§ 130 a}$).

7589 [שָׁאט], שְׁאָט v. II. שׁוּט. p. 1002

7591 שְׁאִיָּה v. I. שׁאה. above

7592 **שָׁאַל**^{170} **vb. ask, inquire** (NH *id.*; As. *šaʾâlu*, Ar. سَأَلَ, Eth. ሰአለ: Sab. מסאל *request, petition*, Hom$^{Chrest. 124}$ Levy-Os$^{ZMG xix (1865), 165}$; Aram. ܫܐܠ, שְׁאֵיל; OAram. Zinj. שאל Ldzb^{371}, Nab. Hiph. *lend* Id$^{ib.}$;—on ׳שׁ cf. Jastr$^{JBL xix (1900), 82 ff.}$);—**Qal** *Pf.* 3 ms. ׳שׁ Ju 5^{25}+, שָׁאֶל Ju 8^{26}+2 t.; consec. וְשָׁאַל לוֹ Nu 27^{21}; sf. וּשְׁאֵלְךָ consec. Gn 32^{18} (Ges$^{§ 64 f}$), וּשְׁאֵלֵךְ consec. Ju 4^{20}; 1 s. sf. שְׁאִלְתִּיו 1 S 1^{20}, שְׁאִלְתִּיהוּ Ju 13^{16}; 3 pl. sf. שְׁאֵלוּנוּ ψ 137^{3}; 2 mpl. שְׁאֶלְתֶּם 1 S 12^{13} (del. 𝔊 Th We Dr and most), Jb 21^{29}, וּשְׁאֶלְתֶּם־ consec. 1 S 25^{5}, etc.; *Impf.* 3 ms. יִשְׁאַל Ex 22^{13}+, etc.; *Imv.* שְׁאַל Is 7^{11}+, שְׁאָלוּנִי Is 45^{11} (> תִּשְׁאָלוּנִי Weir Che al.), etc.; *Inf. abs.* שָׁאוֹל Gn 43^{7}+; cstr. לִשְׁאֹל Ju 1^{14}+, etc.; *Pt. act.* שֹׁאֵל 2 S 3^{13}+, fs. שֹׁאֶלֶת 1 K 2$^{20.22}$, mpl. הַשֹּׁאֲלִים 1 S 8^{10}; *pass.* שָׁאוּל 1^{28} 2 K 6^{5};—**1. a.** *ask, ask for*, acc. rei (vel pers.) Ju 5^{25} 8^{26} 1 K 3^{10} ψ 122^{6} (= pray for) +; ׳שׁ אֶת־נַפְשׁוֹ לָמוּת 1 K 19^{4} Jon 4^{8}, i.e. pray for death, but Jb 31^{30} *demand* the life of another בְּאָלָה *by a curse;* c. לְ pers. 1 K 2$^{22.22}$+ (לְ pers. reflex.) 1 S 12$^{17.19}$+; c. מִן pers. Ju 8^{24} (acc. cogn.), Ezr 8^{22} Zc 10^{1}+; sq. inf. 1 K 3^{11}; sq. cl.: ׳שׁ מָה אֶתֶּן־לָךְ 1 K 3^{5} = 2 Ch 1^{7}, cf. 2 K 2^{9}; c. acc. + מֵאֵת pers. 1 S 8^{10} ψ 27^{4} (from ׳י) +; + מֵעִם pers. Is 7^{11} (from ׳י) +; c. acc. pers. (from whom) + rei †ψ 137^{3}; acc. om. Is 7^{12} 1 S 12^{20} 1 K 2^{20}, c. מִן pers. ψ 2^{8}; abs. Mi 7^{3} ψ 105^{40} (of prayer); הִקְשִׁיתָ לִשְׁאוֹל 2 K 2^{10}, i.e. thou hast asked for a difficult thing.—1 S 2^{20} v. **Hiph. b.** specif. *ask* as a favour, for temporary use, i.e. *borrow* (cf. לָוָה, as matter of business, v. Bu$^{1 S 1, 28}$), Ex 22^{13} (E; acc. rei + מֵעִם pers.), 2 K 4^{3} (acc. rei + מִן of source + לְ pers. reflex.), 6^{5} (pt. pass. abs.); so also (acc. to many), c. acc. rei Ex 3^{22} (+ מִן pers.), 11^{2} 12^{35} (both + מֵאֵת pers.; all E),—it is, however, not clear that there was any pretext of mere temporary use; pt. pass. ׳שָׁאוּל לי 1 S 1^{28} (*lent, granted,*) *made over to* ׳י (in effect pass. of Hiph., q.v.). **c.** in weakened sense, *seek, desire* (late), c. acc. 2 Ch 11^{23} Ec 2^{10} (subj. עֵינַי); Pr 20^{4} in harvest he *shall look* [for a crop], וָאָיִן *and there shall be none.* **2. a.** *inquire of*, c. acc. pers. + לֵאמֹר before inquiry Gn 32^{18} (E), 44^{19} (J)+; c. וְאָמַר Ju 4^{20}, וַיֹּאמֶר, etc., Gn 24^{47} (J), Je 37^{13}; sq. וְאָמַר without acc. pers. Gn 32^{30} (J), cf. 1 S 19^{22}, sq. לֵאמֹר Jos 4^{6} (JE); c. acc. pers. + עַל rei Ne 1^{2}; עַל rei alone, Ec 7^{10} (+ מֵחָכְמָה, i.e. prompted by wisdom); c. acc. pers. + rei (about which) 2 S 14^{18} Is 45^{11}+4 t.; acc. pers. + indir. quest. Ju 13^{6}; c. acc. pers. only, Ju 8^{14} 1 S 25^{8} Dt 32^{7}+, *inquire of* beasts (acc.) Jb 12^{7}; c. acc. rei only, Je 50^{5}; c. לְ pers. = acc. 2 K 8^{6} (Kö$^{Synt. § 289 h}$); c. לְ rei about which Gn 26^{7} (J), 32^{30} (J), Ju 13^{18} 2 S 11^{7} Je 6^{16} Jb 8^{8}, also (+ לאמר before the inquiry) Gn 43^{7} (J), and (sq. direct question) Dt 4^{32}; c. לְ pers. about whom, Gn 43^{27} (J), cf. phr. of greeting, ׳שׁ אִישׁ לְרֵעֵהוּ לְשָׁלוֹם Ex 18^{7} (E) *ask each for* (or about) *his fellow as to welfare*, cf. †Ju 18^{15} 1 S 10^{4} 17^{22} 25^{5} 30^{21} [read וַיִּשְׁאֲלוּ לוֹ 𝔊 𝔖 We Dr HPS Bu] 2 S 8^{10} Je 15^{5} 1 Ch 18^{10}; sq. direct question only, 1 S 17^{56} Je 18^{13} (c. ב loc.), sq. indirect question only (c. אִם) Je 30^{6}; שׁ׳ אֶת־פִּי פ׳ Gn 24^{57} (J); abs. *make inquiry* Dt 13^{15} (+ דָּרַשׁ, חָקַר). †**b.** *inquire of, consult*, deity, oracle, etc. (Jastr JBL xix (1900), 88 ff.), sq. acc. פִּי י׳ Jos 9^{14} (JE), Is 30^{2}, י׳ 65^{1} (‖ בִּקֵּשׁ); elsewhere in Hex only (acc. om.), Nu 27^{21} (P; c. ל pers. for whom, + ב instr.), cf. Jos 19^{50}; also שׁ׳ אוֹב Dt 18^{11} (pt. as subst.; Jäger BAS ii. 292 cp. As. *maššaku ša šâ'ili*, i.e. *skin-vessel of the oracle-seeker*, cf. Jastr JBL xix (1900), 96 ff.); c. acc. of human agent 1 S 28^{16} Je $38^{14.27}$; usu. (ancient usage, chiefly Ju Sm) שׁ׳ בי׳ לֵאמֹר (בְּ perh. orig. local, so GFM, or instr.), Ju 1^{1} 20^{23} 1 S 23^{2} 30^{8} 2 S 2^{1} 5^{19} = 1 Ch 14^{10}; לֵאמֹר om. 1 S 10^{22} (sq. direct question), 22^{10} (ל pers. for whom), 23^{4} 28^{6} 2 S 5^{23} = 1 Ch 14^{14} Ju 20^{27}; שׁ׳ בֵּאלֹהִים Ju 18^{5} 20^{18} 1 S 14^{37} (sq. direct question), also (ל pers. for whom), $22^{13.15}$; שׁ׳ בִּדְבַר הָא׳ 2 S 16^{23}; likewise שׁ׳ בְּעֵצוֹ Ho 4^{12} (i.e. his idol), בַּתְּרָפִים Ez 21^{26}, בָּאוֹב 1 Ch 10^{13}; perh. = *receive as oracle* Dt 18^{16} (מֵעִם י׳), Jastr l.c.. †**Niph.** *ask for oneself* (Ges § 51 e), specif. *ask leave of absence*, c. מִן pers.: *Pf.* 3 ms. + *Inf. abs.* נִשְׁאֹל נִשְׁאַל 1 S 20^{6} (sq. inf.), v^{28} (sq. עַד; ? ins. ל inf. HPS); *Pf.* 1 s. נִשְׁאַלְתִּי מִן־הַמֶּלֶךְ Ne 13^{6} (abs.). †**Pi. 1.** *inquire carefully: Impf.* 3 mpl. + **Qal** *Inf. abs.* שָׁאוֹל יְשַׁאֲלוּ 2 S 20^{18} (Bu prop. **Qal** *Impf.* יִשְׁאֲלוּ), c. ב loc.; on foll. context v. We Dr HPS Bu. **2.** *beg, practise beggary*, *Pf.* 3 pl. וְשִׁאֵלוּ (consec.) ψ 109^{10}. **Hiph.** (prop. *let one ask* [successfully], *give*, or *lend, on request*, then) *grant, make over to* (as a favour, with or without request): *Pf.* 1 s. sf. הִשְׁאִלְתִּהוּ לי׳ 1 S 1^{28} *I have made him over to* י׳ (cf. Dr HPS Bu and **Qal** *Pt. pass.*, ib.); perhaps also read 3 fs. הִשְׁאִילָה לי׳ 2^{20} (whom) *she hath made over to* י׳ (for שָׁאַל לי׳) Bu HPS (after 𝔊 in part; other conj. in Dr); *Impf.* 3 mpl. sf. rei וַיַּשְׁאִלוּם Ex 12^{36} (E) *and they handed them over*.

7594 †שָׁאָל **n.pr.m.** with foreign wife, Ezr 10^{29}, 𝔊 Σαλουια, 𝔊L Ασσαηλ.

7586 †שָׁאוּל **n.pr.m.** (= *asked* (of י׳), cf שְׁאַלְתִּיאֵל infr.; Palm. n.pr. שאילא Lzb 371 Cooke 283);—Σαουλ: **1.** 397 1st king of Isr., 1 S $9^{2.3.3.5}$ (son of Kish, a Benjamite) + 359 t. Sm, 28 t. 1 Chr, ψ 18^{1} 52^{2} 54^{2} 57^{1} 59^{1} (all in titles); גִּבְעַת שׁ׳ Is 10^{29} (and 1 S 11^{4} 15^{34}; 2 S 21^{6} v. II. גִּבְעָה). †**2.** a king of Edom Gn $36^{37.38}$ (P) = 1 Ch $1^{48.49}$. †**3.** a son of Simeon Gn 46^{10} Ex 6^{15} Nu 26^{13} (all P) = 1 Ch 4^{24}. †**4.** a Levite 1 Ch 6^{9}.

†שָׁאוּלִי **adj.gent.** of **3** supra: c. art. = 7587
n.pr.coll. הַשָּׁ׳ Nu 26^{13} (P).

שְׁאָלָה Is 7^{11} v. שְׁאוֹל **1.** below 7585

†שְׁאֵלָה [I. שֵׁלָה] **n.f.** request, thing 7596
asked for;—שְׁא׳ Ju 8^{24}+; sf. שְׁאֵלָתִי 1 S 1^{27}+, שֶׁאֱלָתִי Jb 6^{8}, שְׁאֵלָתֵךְ Est 5^{6}+, שֵׁלָתֵךְ 1 S 1^{17}, שְׁאֵלָתָם ψ 106^{15};—**1.** *request, petition*, Ju 8^{24} 1 K $2^{16.20}$ (both acc. cogn. c. שָׁאַל), Est $5^{6.7}$ (c. נָתַן = *grant*), $7^{2.3}$ 9^{12}. This passes easily into **2.** *thing asked for*, 1 S 2^{20}, c. נָתַן $1^{17.27}$ Est 5^{8} ψ 106^{15};
שׁ׳ תָּבוֹא Jb 6^{8}.—II. שֵׁלָה v. infr. אֶשְׁתָּאֹל n.pr.m., 7956
v. p. 84^{a}. p. 1017

†[מִשְׁאָלָה] **n.f.** request, petition;—pl. 4862
cstr. מִשְׁאֲלֹת לִבֶּךָ ψ 37^{4} (c. נָתַן, of י׳); sf. מִשְׁאֲלוֹתֶיךָ 20^{6} (c. מִלֵּא, of י׳).

†שְׁאַלְתִּיאֵל **n.pr.m.** (*I have asked* (him) 7597
of God; on acc. cf. (late) ψ 137^{3});—first son of Jehoiachin and uncle of Zerubbabel acc. to 1 Ch 3^{17} (cf. $v^{18.19}$); but Z.'s father Hg 1^{1} 2^{23}
Ez $3^{2.8}$ Ne 12^{1} (attempts at explan. in Be Kit 7598
Benz).—Σαλαθιηλ.

†שְׁאוֹל, שְׁאֹל **n.f.** ψ 86, 13 (appar. **m.** Jb 26^{6} 7585
cf. Is 14^{9}, v. Albr ZAW xvi (1896), 51) **She'ôl, underworld** (√dub.; שׁאל, i.e. *place of inquiry* (ref. to necromancy) Jastr Am. JSem. Lang. xiv. 170, cf. JBL xix (1900), 88 ff. (Jerem Leben n. d. Tode 109 '*Ort der Entscheidung*'); Thes Bö De Inf. § 158 Di al. cp. √ שׁעל, whence שֹׁעַל *hollow hand*, etc.; שׁ׳ then = *hollow place*, '*Hölle*,' *hell*; other conj. v. Hup Ps. 6, 6 De Is. 5, 14 Beer Bibl. Hades in Holtzmann Festgabe, 1902, 15; most now refrain from positive etymology (e.g. Buhl); OAram. שאול, Syr. ܫܝܘܠ; As. *šu-alu* is dub.: so read and interpr. Dl Pa 121; Prol. 47. 145 Jastr Am. J. Sem. Lang. xiv. 165 ff. Ency. Bib. s.v.; opp. by Bertin TSBA viii. 269 Jen Kosmol. 223 ff. Zim KAT 3. 636 al.; v. also Muss-Arnolt JBL xi (1892), 169 and reff.);—alw. abs., שְׁאוֹל Dt 32^{22} + 52 t., ־ָה Gn 42^{38} ψ 9^{18}; שְׁאֹל 1 K 2^{6} Jb 17^{16}, ־ָה Gn 37^{35} + 7 t.; + Is 7^{11} (so read for שְׁאָלָה Aq Σ Θ Du Che and now most);—**1.** *the underworld*, שׁ׳ תַּחְתִּית Dt 32^{22}, מִתַּחַת Is 14^{9}; מִשּׁ׳ מָטָּה Pr 15^{24}; ‖ מָוֶת 5^{5} 7^{27} Ct 8^{6} ψ 89^{49}; whither men descend at death, Gn 37^{35} (E), 42^{38} $44^{29.31}$ (J), 1 S 2^{6} 1 K $2^{6.9}$ Jb 7^{9} 21^{13} Is $14^{11.15}$ ψ 88^{4},

and Ḳoraḥ and associates go down alive by 'י's judgment, Nu $16^{30.33}$ (J), cf. ψ 55^{16}; under mts. and sea Jb 26^{6} (cf. v^{5}), 'בֶּטֶן שׁ' Jon 2^{3} (cf. v^{7}); with bars Jb 17^{16} (si vera l.: v. 𝔊 Du); 'פִּי שׁ' ψ 141^{7}; 'שַׁעֲרֵי שׁ' Is 38^{10}; personif. Is $28^{15.18}$ (‖ מות) as insatiable monster 5^{14} Hb 2^{5} Pr 1^{12} 27^{20} 30^{16}; as said (fig.) to have snares, 'חֶבְלֵי שׁ', ψ 18^{6} = 2 S 22^{6}, cf. 'מְצָרֵי שׁ' ψ 116^{3}; opp. (height of) שָׁמַיִם Am 9^{2} Jb 11^{8} ψ 139^{8} + (opp. לְמַעְלָה) Is 7^{11} (v. supra); dark, gloomy, without return Jb 17^{13} (cf. v^{16} 7^{9} 10^{21} 16^{22}; all being alike 3^{17-19} 21^{23-26}); without work or knowledge or wisdom acc. to Ec $9^{5.6.10}$ (cf. Jb 14^{21}, and v. רְפָאִים sub רפה; yet cf. Is $14^{9f.}$). **2.** condition of righteous and wicked disting. in 'שׁ' (later than 1 S 28, esp. in WisdLt): **a.** wicked יָשׁוּבוּ לִשְׁאוֹלָה ψ 9^{18}, 'יִדְּמוּ לִשׁ' 31^{18}; death is their shepherd, without power and honour they waste away $49^{15.15}$; 'שׁ' consumes them as drought water Jb 24^{19}; righteous dread it because no praise or presence of God there (as in temple) ψ 6^{6} (cf. 88^{6}), Is 38^{18}; deliverance from it a blessing ψ 30^{4} 86^{13} Pr 23^{14}. In Ezek. 'שׁ' is land below, place of reproach, abode of uncircumcised Ez $31^{15.16.17}$ $32^{21.27}$. **b.** righteous shall not be abandoned, 'לִשׁ' ψ 16^{10} (‖ שַׁחַת q.v.; opp. אֹרַח חַיִּים, etc., v^{11}, cf. 17^{15}), is ransomed from 'שׁ' 49^{16} (cf. $73^{23.25}$ Is $57^{1.2}$); cf. Job's expectation and desire Jb 14^{13} 17^{13} (cf. 10^{21} $19^{25f.}$). **3.** later distinction of places in 'שׁ': **a.** depths of 'שׁ' for sensualist Pr 9^{18}. **b.** 'שׁ' וַאֲבַדּוֹן Pr 25^{11}, v. אֲבַדּוֹן. [שַׁחַת and בּוֹר, q.v., when ‖ 'שׁ', are usu. in bad sense (ψ 88^{4}); prob. = pit in 'שׁ', > 'שׁ' itself as pit; words at least prepare for local distinctions of postB. Judaism and NT.] **4.** 'שׁ' fig. of extreme degradation in sin Is 57^{9}; as place of exile for Israel Ho $13^{14.14}$ (cf. Is 26^{19}).

7599 †[שָׁאַן] **vb. Pa'l.** (Ges ^{§55d}) **be at ease or at peace, rest securely** (Syr. *pacify*, Eth. ሰላም: *peace*);—*Pf.* 3 ms. שַׁאֲנַן Je 48^{11}, 'וְשׁ' consec. 30^{10}+; 3 pl. שַׁאֲנָנוּ Jb 3^{18};—*be at ease, secure,* undisturbed by ill fortune: 'וְשָׁקַט וְשׁ' וְאֵין מַחֲרִיד Je 30^{10} = 46^{27}; 48^{11} (of Moab); 'שׁ' מִפַּחַד רָעָה Pr 1^{33}; of rest from trouble, etc., in grave Jb 3^{18}.

1052 שַׁאַן v. בֵּית שְׁאָן. p. 112

7600 †שַׁאֲנָן **adj. at ease, secure** (Ba $^{NB §143a}$ Ges ^{§84bk});—abs. 'שׁ' Is 33^{20}; pl. שַׁאֲנַנִּים Am 6^{1}+, שַׁאֲנַנּוֹת Is $32^{9.11.18}$;—**1.** *at ease, secure:* 'נָוֶה שׁ' Is 33^{20} *secure habitation* (of Jerus.), cf. 'מְנוּחוֹת שׁ' 32^{18} (‖ מִבְטַחִים). **2.** as subst., *one at ease,* free from misfortune, Jb 12^{5}. **3.** *at ease,* with collat. idea of *careless, wanton, arrogant,* Am 6^{1} Is $32^{9.11}$ Zc 1^{15} ψ 123^{4}. **4.** as subst. abstr. = *arrogance:* sf. שַׁאֲנַנְךָ 2 K 19^{28} (‖ הִתְרַגֶּזְךָ) = Is 37^{29}, but < שְׁאוֹנְךָ *thine uproar,* Bu $^{ZAW\ xii\ (1892),\ 36}$ Gr Che Marti Kit (perh.), Bur. Cf. שׁלאנן.

שׁאסיך Je 30^{16} Kt v. שׁסה, שׁסס. p. 1042 7601, 8154-55

†I. שָׁאַף **vb. gasp, pant, pant after, long for** (so 𝔗 Jb 7^{2});—**Qal** *Pf.* 3 ms. וְשָׁאַף 7602
consec. Jb 5^{5}, 3 fs. שָׁאֲפָה Je 2^{24}, 3 pl. שָׁאֲפוּ 14^{6}; *Impf.* 3 ms. יִשְׁאַף Jb 7^{2}, etc.; *Pt. act.* שׁוֹאֵף Ec 1^{5};—**1.** *gasp,* as a woman in travail, fig. of 'י, Is 42^{14} (‖ נָשַׁם); *pant after, snuff up* the wind (acc.), of wild ass Je 2^{24} 14^{6}; constr. praegn. 'וְאֶל־מְקוֹמוֹ שׁ' Ec 1^{5} *unto his place he panteth* (comes panting), of sun under fig. of racer. **2.** *gasp* or *pant* with desire ψ 119^{131} (‖ יָאַב); *pant after, be eager for,* c. acc. Jb 5^{5} (cf. צַמִּים p. 855^{b}), 7^{2} (‖ יְקַוֶּה), 36^{20} (but obscure in context).

†II. [שָׁאַף] **vb. crush, trample upon** 7602
(‖ form of שׁוּף (q.v.), if pointing right, cf. Kö $^{i.\ 439}$; We Now read שָׁאפִים, etc., from שׁוּף, cf. Ges ^{§72p}; perh. orig. *pulverize by rubbing,* but also appar. by pounding, stamping, treading, Levy ^{ChWB} שׁוּף, Jastr $^{Dict.}$ שׁאף, שׁוּף;—most make = I. שׁאף, but Vrss render as above);—**Qal** *Pf.* 3 ms. sf. שְׁאָפַנִי ψ 56^{2}, 3 pl. שָׁאֲפוּ v^{3}; *Inf. abs.* שָׁאֹף Ez 36^{3}; *Pt.* sf. שֹׁאֲפִי ψ 57^{4}; pl. שֹׁאֲפִים Am 2^{7} 8^{4};—*trample upon, crush* (the poor, etc.), fig., c. acc. pers. Am 8^{4}; strangely 2^{7} (We Now Marti del. עַל־עֲפַר־אֶרֶץ, which Torrey $^{JBL\ xv\ (1896),\ 152}$ expl. as old doublet, cf. 𝔊𝔖; AV RV *pant after the dust,* etc., hyperb. for extreme avarice, cf. Hi Dr; but Dr thinks 𝔙 poss. original: *crush the heads of the poor upon the dust* [cf. Is 3^{15}], in any case del. בְּ after 'שׁ' *crush*); שַׁמּוֹת וְשׁ' אֶתְכֶם מִסָּבִיב Ez 36^{3}; ψ 56^{2} 57^{4} and (acc. om.) 56^{3}.

I. שָׁאַר 133 **vb. remain, be left over** (syn. 7604
יָתַר) (NH *id.*; 𝔗 שְׁאַר; Sab. סאר *remaining* Hom $^{Chr\ 124}$; Ar. سَأَرَ, سُؤْرٌ *be left over,* Lane, cf. Lag $^{GGN\ 1889,\ 297}$; OAram. שאר *remainder,* Nab. שארית, v. Lzb ^{371} SAC ^{110});—†**Qal** *Pf.* 3 ms. 'שׁ' 1 S 16^{11} the youngest still *remains.* **Niph.** 93 *Pf.* 3 ms. נִשְׁאַר Gn 47^{18}+; 3 fs. נִשְׁאֲרָה Jos 13^{1} Dn 10^{8}, etc.; *Impf.* 3 ms. יִשָּׁאֵר Is $11^{11.16}$, וַיִּשָּׁאֶר Gn 7^{23}, etc.; *Pt.* נִשְׁאָר Gn 32^{9}+, וְנֶאשְׁאַר Ez 9^{8} (read וְנִשְׁאַר Hi Toy Krae, וָאֶשָּׁאֵר Sm; del. 𝔊 Hi Co Siegf Berthol); f. נִשְׁאָרָה 2 K 19^{30} = Is 37^{31}, נִשְׁאֶרֶת Ex 10^{5} 2 Ch 30^{6}, נִשְׁאֶרֶת Jos 13^{2}, etc.;—

1. *be left over* (sts. ‖ נוֹתַר) Ex 8^{27} 10^{19} 14^{28} (all J), Jos 11^{22} (D), Ju 7^{3} 2 S 14^{7}+; in restrictive cl. לֹא נ׳ זוּלַת 2 K 24^{14} *there were left only*, etc., לֹא נ׳ לִפְנֵי אֲדֹנִי בִּלְתִּי אִם וגו׳ Gn 47^{18} (J); sq. acc. adv. (Ges^{§118q}), or appos., Dt 4^{27} Ezr 9^{15}, cf. נ׳ בִּמְתֵי מְעָט Dt 28^{62} (Ges^{§119i}); sts. c. ב loc. Ex 8$^{5.7}$ (J), Je 38^{22}+; c. אֵת (prep. loc.) †Jos 23$^{7.12}$ (D); c. מִן = *be left from* (of) †Ex 10^{5} (J), Dt 3^{11} Jos 13^{12} (D), Is 11$^{11.16}$ Je 8^{3a} (pt.; v^{b} del. הַנּ׳ 𝔊 𝔖 Hi Gf Gie Co), Ne 1$^{2.3}$, נ׳ מְעַט מֵהַרְבֵּה Je 42^{2}; **c.** לְ *to* or *for*, †2 K 10$^{11.17}$ (pt.), Zc 9^{7} 2 Ch 21^{17}, הַנּ׳ לָכֶם מִן־הַבָּרָד Ex 10^{5}, cf. 2 Ch 30^{6} and (ב loc. for ל) Je 21^{7}; c. בְּ, *in, among, of*, †1 S 11^{11} Is 17^{6} Je 34^{7} 37^{10} Lv 26$^{36.39}$ (H; pt.), 25^{52} (P; of years), even הַנּ׳ בַּדָּם 5^{9} (P) *the rest of the blood*; c. עַל †1 S 5^{4}; c. inf. נ׳ לְרִשְׁתָּהּ †Jos 13^{1} (D); = *be left alive, survive*, †Gn 7^{23} (J), Ez 9^{8} (but on text v. supr.); הַנּ׳ = *the survivors*, †Gn 14^{10} 1 S 11^{11} Ez 17^{21}; pt. as term. techn. = *the* (purified) *remainder, remnant* (cf. שְׁאָר, שְׁאֵרִית) Is 4^{3} (ב loc.; ‖ הַנּוֹתָר), 2 Ch 34^{21} (ב loc.).—הַנּ׳ 1 S 9^{24} is dub.; *what is left over*, in polite depreciation, Bu; read הַשְּׁאֵר HPS. **2.** *be left behind*, Ex 10^{26} (E), Nu 11^{26} (JE); c. לְבַדּוֹ Gn 42^{38} (J), cf. Is 49^{21} Dn 10^{8}; of widow Ru 1^{3}, + מִן of the dead v^{5}. †**Hiph.** *Pf.* 3 ms. הִשְׁאִיר Ex 10^{12}+, etc.; *Impf.* 3 ms. יַשְׁאִיר Dt 28^{51}, 1 pl. נַשְׁאֵר 1 S 14^{36} (Ges$^{§48g; 109d}$ Kö$^{p. 466 f.}$), etc.; *Inf. cstr.* הַשְׁאִיר Ezr 9^{8}, v. also infr.;—**1.** *leave over, spare*, c. acc. Ex 10^{12} (E), 2 K 25^{22} Je 49^{9} = Ob^{5}, Jos 11^{14} (D), Ju 6^{4}; אֶסְלַח לַאֲשֶׁר אַשׁ׳ Je 50^{20}; esp. לֹא הִשׁ׳ שָׂרִיד *leave no survivor*, Jos 10^{28}, cf. v$^{30.37.39.40}$ (all D), so עַד־בִּלְתִּי הִשׁ׳ שׂ׳ (sts. c. ל pers.) Nu 21^{35} (E) = Dt 3^{3}, cf. Dt 2^{34} Jos 8^{22} 11^{8} (both JE), 10^{33} (D), 2 K 10^{11}, and מִבְּלִי הִשׁ׳ לוֹ כֹּל Dt 28^{55} (in all these rd. *Inf. cstr.* הַשׁ׳, v. Dr$^{Dt 3, 3; 7, 24}$); c. ב, *among, of*, 1 S 14^{36}, ב loc. 1 K 19^{18} Zp 3^{12} (in both of preserving a pious remnant, cf. שְׁאָר, שְׁאֵרִית), also 2 K 3^{25} (Bur rds. בָּנֶיהָ for אֲבָנֶיהָ, Kit אֲנָשִׁים, cf. Klo Benz); c. לְ pers. Dt 28^{51} 1 K 15^{29} 16^{11} 2 K 13^{7} Ezr 9^{8}; c. מִן, *from, of*, 2 K 10^{14}, מִן part. 1 S 25^{22} 2 K 25^{12} = Je 52^{16}, Je 39^{10}. **2.** *leave* or *keep over* (מִן part.) till morning Nu 9^{12} (P). **3.** תַּשְׁ׳ מֵאָה Am 5^{3} the city *shall have* 100 *left*, cf. v^{3}. **4.** *leave* as a gift, וְהִשׁ׳ אַחֲרָיו בְּרָכָה Jo 2^{14}.—We
7605 Now read וַיִּשְׁאֵר Mal 2^{15}, v. שְׁאָר. below

7605 †שְׁאָר **n.m.** $^{Is 16, 14}$ **rest, residue, remnant** (= יֶתֶר, esp. Is. and late; on form Kö$^{ii. 1, 141}$ Nö$^{Beitr. z. Sem. W. 30}$);—שׁ׳ abs. Is 14^{22}+, cstr. Is 10^{19}+;—*rest, residue, remainder*, of trees Is 10^{19}, silver 2 Ch 24^{14}, city 1 Ch 11^{8}, territory Est 9^{12}; שׁ׳ דִּבְרֵי שְׁלֹמֹה 2 Ch 9^{29} (יֶתֶר in ‖ 1 K 11^{41}, and usu. in like phrase, v. p. 451 f.); of men 1 Ch 16^{41} Ezr 3^{8} 4$^{3.7}$ Ne 10^{29} 11$^{1.20}$ Est 9^{16}; of Moab Is 16^{14}, Aram 17^{3} (= last remnant), archers of Kedar 21^{17}; ‖ posterity, שֵׁם וּשׁ׳ וְנִין וָנֶכֶד Is 14^{22} (of Babylon); שׁ׳ הַבַּעַל Zp 1^{4}, i.e. *Baal, to the last remnant*, vestige (so We al.; 𝔊 שֵׁם, cf. Schwally Now GASm); term. techn. = purified *remnant* of Israel (Gie$^{Beiträge 37 f.}$) Is 10^{20} (‖ פְּלֵיטָה), v$^{21.21.22}$ 11$^{11.16}$ 28^{5}.—וּשׁ׳ רוּחַ לוֹ Mal 2^{15} is obscure; read וַיִּשְׁאֵר ר׳ לָנוּ We Now, cf. GASm.

†שְׁאָר יָשׁוּב **n.pr.m.** of Isaiah's son Is 7^{3} 7610
(= *a remnant shall return*, cf. 10^{21}; 𝔊 ὁ καταλειφθεὶς Ἰασουβ).

†שְׁאֵרִית **n.f. rest, residue, remnant, re-** 7611
mainder (= שְׁאָר);—שׁ׳ abs. 2 S 14^{7}+, cstr. Ez 36^{3}+, שֵׁרִית (Ges^{§23f}) 1 Ch 12^{39} (van d. H. v^{38}); sf. שְׁאֵרִיתְךָ Is 14^{30} Ez 5^{10}, ־תוֹ Is 44^{17}, ־תָם Je 15^{9};—**1.** *rest, what is left*, of wood Is 44^{17}, land 15^{9} (‖ פְּלֵיטָה), Je 47$^{4.5}$ Ez 25^{16}; שׁ׳ חֵמֹת ψ 76^{11} is difficult (Gr [cf. Che] prop. חֲמָת *Hamath*, Du אֻמֹּת *tribes*); *rest* of princes Je 39^{3}, of nations (= the other nations, Toy) Ez 36$^{3.4.5}$; of Israel 1 Ch 12^{39} (van d. H. v^{38}), 2 Ch 34^{9} Ne 7^{71} (van d. H. v^{72}); = last *remnant* of people, Philistines Am 1^{8} (cf. We), Is 14^{30}, Edom Am 9^{12}, Anathoth Je 11^{23}, Ashdod 25^{20}, Babylon 50^{26}, Amalek 1 Ch 4^{43} (+ הַפְּלֵיטָה), Isr. 2 K 21^{14} Je 6^{9} 15^{9}; *remnant* left after catastrophe Am 5^{15} Je 8^{3} 24^{8} 40$^{11.15}$ 41$^{10.16}$ 42$^{2.15.19}$ 43^{5} 44$^{12.14.28}$ Ez 5^{10} 9^{8} 11^{13} Hag 1$^{12.14}$ 2^{2}; even וְשַׂמְתִּי אֶת־הַצֹּלֵעָה לִשׁ׳ Mi 4^{7} (as promise, ‖ גּוֹי עָצוּם, cf. Gie$^{Beiträge, 42 f.}$); = survivors Je 44^{7}, הַשׁ׳ מִן־הַחֶרֶב 2 Ch 36^{20}; = faithful *remnant* of Israel or Judah (term. techn. of proph., cf. שְׁאָר ad fin.), 2 K 19^{4} = Is 37^{4}, 2 K 19^{31} (‖ פְּלֵיטָה) = Is 37^{32} (‖ *id.*), Mi 2^{12} 5$^{6.7}$ 7^{18} Ezr 9^{14} (‖ *id.*), Is 46^{3} Je 23^{3} 31^{7} Zp 2$^{7.9}$ (‖ יֶתֶר), 3^{13} Zc 8$^{6.11.12}$. **2.** *remainder* = descendants (= שְׁאָר Is 14^{22}): Gn 45^{7}, שֵׁם וּשׁ׳ 2 S 14^{7}.

II. **שׁאר** (√ of foll.; cf. As. *šêru*, Pun. שאר, *flesh*, Ar. ثَأْرٌ *blood-revenge*, so Sab. ת̄אר, Sab. Denkm.$^{No. 5, 1.7}$; perhaps orig. *blood* (cf. Je 51^{35}), Nö$^{ZMG xl (1886), 723}$ and Id$^{M 101}$, who cp. Mand. תירתא = ثُؤْرٌ *conscience, mind*, etc., perh. prop. *midriff*, cf. Hoffm$^{infr.}$).

†שְׁאֵר **n.m.** $^{ψ 73, 26}$ **flesh** (perh. orig. the inner 7607
flesh, full of blood, next the bones, cf. Hoffm$^{ZAW iii (1883), 107}$, and בָּשָׂר = (orig.) flesh next the skin);—שׁ׳ abs. ψ 78$^{20.27}$, cstr. Mi 3^{3}+, sf. שְׁאֵרִי

Je 51[35] ψ 73[26], etc.;—**1.** *flesh:* **a.** as food, Ex 21[10] (HPS also 1 S 9[24], for הַנִּשְׁאָר), ψ 78[20] (‖ לֶחֶם), v[27] (‖ עוֹף כָּנָף); fig. Mi 3[2] (‖ עוֹר), v[3] (‖ *id.*), Je 51[35] (‖ דָּם). **b.** fig. for physical power ψ 73[26] (+ לֵבָב), Pr 5[11] (+ בָּשָׂר). **2.** in HP=*flesh-* (=blood-) *relation* (i.e. one near of kin): שְׁאֵר אָבִיךָ Lv 18[12], cf. v[13] 20[19], also 18[17] (read שְׁאֵרְךָ

7608 for שַׁאֲרָה, 𝔊 Ew Dr-Wh; cf. Di Baen); + חַקָּרֹב אֵלָיו 21[2] Nu 27[11]; שׁ׳ בְּשָׂרוֹ Lv 18[6] 25[49]. **3.**=*self*, Pr 11[17] (‖ נֶפֶשׁ).

7607-08 שַׁאֲרָה Lv 18[17] v. שְׁאֵר **2.** above

7609 †שֶׁאֱרָה **n.pr.f.** 'daughter' of Ephraim;—בִּתּוֹ שׁ׳ 1 Ch 7[24] (v. also n.pr.loc. אֻזֵּן שׁ׳ p. 25[a] supr.); 𝔊[B] ἐκείνοις τ. καταλοίποις, but 𝔊L (cf. 𝔊[A]) ἡ θυγάτηρ αὐτοῦ Σαραα.

4863 מִשְׁאֶרֶת v. p. 602[a] supr.

7612 שֵׁאת v. שׁאה. p. 981

7614 †שְׁבָא **n.pr.gent. et terr.** Sh[e]bâ, in SW. Arabia (Sab. סבא DHM[ZMG xxxvii (1883), 9], סבא vb.= *make campaign* Mordt[HI 72] or *expedition* Sab. Denkm.[No. 12, 1. 5, 14]; cf. DSMargoliouth[Hast. DB SHEBA] FB[Ency. Bib. SHEBA] and reff.);—*Sheba:* מַלְכַּת־שׁ׳ 1 K 10[1.4.10.13]=2 Ch 9[1.3.9.12]; מַלְכֵי שׁ׳ ψ 72[10]; famous for trade, רֹכְלֵי שׁ׳ Ez 27[22.23], הֲלִיכֹת שׁ׳ Jb 6[19] (‖ תֵּמָא); yielding costly wares Ez 38[13], זְהַב שׁ׳ ψ 72[15], לְבוֹנָה מִשּׁ׳ Je 6[20] (‖ מֵאֶרֶץ מֶרְחָק, cf. foll.), paying homage and tribute to Israel in future Is 60[6]; descended from (Yoktan and) Shem Gn 10[28] (J)=1 Ch 1[22], from (Yokshan and) Abr. and Ḳetûrâh Gn 25[3] (J?)=1 Ch 1[32] (i.e. a northern branch of Sheba, + דְּדָן, q.v.), but from כּוּשׁ Gn 10[7] (P)=1 Ch 1[9]; marauders, N. Arabia, Jb 1[15].

7615 †[שְׁבָאִי] **adj. gent.** only pl. as subst., אֶל־גּוֹי רָחוֹק ‖ לִשְׁבָאִים (Baer Ginsb שְׁבָאִים) Jo 4[8] cf. Je 6[20] supr.), > 𝔊 Me Now לַשְּׁבִי *into captivity.*

I. **שׁבב** (NH שָׁבַב Pi. *hew;* Ar. سَبَّ *cut,* Aram. (Talm.) שִׁבָּא *splinter,* cf. Mand. dim. שאבוניא Nö[M 140]).

7616 †שְׁבָבִים **n.** [**m.**] **pl.** probably splinters;—שׁ׳ יִהְיֶה עֵגֶל שֹׁמְרוֹן Ho 8[6] (cf. We; Vrss appar. conjecture).

II. **שׁבב** (As. *šabâbu, blaze,* cf. Syr. ܫܒ *burn,* ܫܒܒܐ *ray, flash* (Lexx., cf. PS); Ar. شَبَّ is *blaze up* (cf. Ba[ES 50]), but ש=ش? (Another etymology in Ber[Dn 3, 22])).

7632 †[שָׁבִיב] **n. m.** probably **flame** (BAram. שְׁבִיב);—cstr. וְלֹא יִגַּהּ שְׁבִיב אִשּׁוֹ Jb 18[5] (‖ אוֹר); so Ecclus 8[10] 45[19].

שָׁבָה [47] **vb. take captive** (NH, OAram. *id.;* Ar. سَبَا (سبى); Aram. שְׁבָא, ܫܒܐ);—**Qal** *Pf.* 7617
3 ms. שׁ׳ Je 41[14]; sf. וְשָׁבָם (consec.) 43[12] (but rd. וְשָׁבָה Gie; Du conj. וְשָׁמְמוֹ); 2 ms. שָׁבִיתָ 2 K 6[22] ψ 68[19], etc.; *Impf.* 3 ms. וַיִּשְׁבְּ Nu 21[1] Je 41[10], etc.; *Imv.* ms. וּשְׁבֵה Ju 5[12]; *Inf. cstr.* שְׁבוֹת Ob[11]; *Pt. act.* pl. שֹׁבִים Is 14[2], etc.; *pass.* mpl. שְׁבוּיִם Is 61[1], fpl. cstr. שְׁבֻיוֹת Gn 31[26];—*take captive:* **1. a.** c. acc. pers., Nu 24[22] (JE), 1 S 30[2] 2 K 5[2] 6[22] (+ ב instr.) Je 41[10.10] (but v[10 b] Gie reads וַיִּשְׁבֵּם, cf. 𝔊 Luc), v[14], Gn 34[29] (P), 2 Ch 28[8] (+ מִן part.), + 6 t.; + Je 43[12] appar. c. acc. idols (but v. supra; acc. of land Gie). **b.** acc. חֵילוֹ Ob[11], הָרְכוּשׁ 2 Ch 21[17], cattle, etc., 1 Ch 5[21] 2 Ch 14[14]. **c.** pt. in periphrast. conjug. (וְהָיוּ שֹׁבִים לְשֹׁבֵיהֶם) Is 14[2]; pt. c. sf.=*their captives,* etc., 1 K 8[46]=2 Ch 6[36], Is 14[2] Je 50[33], + 5 t.; pt. pass. Is 61[1]= *captives;* כִּשְׁבֻיוֹת חָרֶב Gn 31[26] my daughters *as captives of the sword.* **2.** c. acc. cogn. שְׁבִי Ju 5[12] *lead captive thy captives,* cf. ψ 68[19] 2 Ch 28[17], so (+ מִן pers.) Nu 21[1] (JE), and (acc. שִׁבְיָה) 2 Ch 28[5.11]; שׁ׳ שִׁבְיוֹ Dt 21[10]=*take him captive.* †**Niph.** *be taken captive: Pf.* 3 ms. נִשְׁבָּה, of man Gn 14[14], of beast Ex 22[9] (E), of עֵדֶר י׳ Je 13[17]; 3 pl. נִשְׁבּוּ, human subj. 1 S 30[3.5] 1 K 8[47]=2 Ch 6[37], Ez 6[9].

†שְׁבִי **n. m.** [Is 49, 24] captivity, captives 7628
(coll.);—שׁ׳ abs. Ex 12[29] +, cstr. Ezr 2[1] +; שְׁבִי Nu 21[1] +; sf. שֶׁבְיְךָ Ju 5[12], שִׁבְיוֹ Dt 21[10], שְׁבִיכֶם Nu 31[19], etc.;—**1.**=state of *captivity,* הָלַךְ בַּשּׁ׳ Am 9[4] Dt 28[41] Na 3[10] Je 20[6] 22[22] 30[16] Ez 12[11] (+ בַּגּוֹלָה), 30[17.18] Is 46[2] La 1[18], = הָלַךְ שְׁבִי v[5]; נָתַן לַשּׁ׳ Ezr 9[7], נָתַן בַּשּׁ׳ ψ 78[61], בַּשְּׁבִי יָבֹא Dn 11[8]; וַאֲשֶׁר לַשְּׁבִי לַשְּׁבִי Je 15[2] 43[11], לָקַח בַּשְּׁבִי Je 48[46]; וְנָשֵׁינוּ בַּשּׁ׳ בִּשְׁבִי 2 Ch 29[9]; instr. of judgment Dn 11[33]; אֶרֶץ שׁ׳ Je 30[10] 46[27] 2 Ch 6[37.38]; phr. of deliverance (only Ezr Ne): נִשְׁאֲרוּ מִן־הַשּׁ׳ Ne 1[2], cf. v[3], הָעֹלִים מִשְּׁבִי הַגּוֹלָה Ezr 2[1]=Ne 7[6], הַשָּׁבִים מִן־הַשּׁ׳ 8[17], הַבָּאִים מֵהַשּׁ׳ Ezr 3[8] 8[35]. **2.** act of *capture,* עִם שׁ׳ סוּסֵיכֶם Am 4[10]; שִׂמְלַת שִׁבְיָהּ Dt 21[13] i. e. garb in which she was captured (> others *captivity* in both: Am 4[10]=*your captive horses;* Dt 21[13] *her captive's garb*). **3.** =*captives* (coll.): Ex 12[29] (J), Nu 31[12.19.26] (man and beast), Is 20[4] (‖ גָּלוּת), 49[24.25] Hb 1[9] + Ez 32[9] 𝔊 al. (v. שֶׁבֶר *ad fin.*); appar. fs. Is 52[2] (but v. שְׁבִי); object of שָׁבָה (q.v.) Ju 5[12] (> שֹׁבְיְךָ 𝔖 JDMich We Bu Now), Nu 21[1] (JE), Dt 21[10] ψ 68[19] 2 Ch 28[17].

†[שָׁבִי **adj.** vel **n.m.** whence] **שִׁבְיָה n.f.** 7628
captive (cf. Rahlfs[ענו u. עני in Psalm., 63]);—שׁ׳ בַּת־צִיּוֹן

Is 52[2b] (Bev[JPhil. xvii (1888), p. 127] ingeniously, שְׁבִי הַבַּת וגו׳, cf. ‖ שְׁבִי v[a], and, on הַבּ׳, La 2[13]); read also שׁ׳ יְרוּשָׁלָ͏ִם v[a] (for שְׁבִי) Oort Bu Du Che[Hpt] Marti.

7633 †**שִׁבְיָה** **n.f. captivity, captives** (coll.), cf. שְׁבִי;—always abs. שׁ׳;—**1.** state of *captivity*, Je 48[46] (of בָּנוֹת ‖ שְׁבִי of בָּנִים); אֶרֶץ שׁ׳ Ne 3[36]. **2.** body of *captives*, Dt 21[11] 32[42] (‖ חָלָל), 2 Ch 28[14.15]; object of שָׁבָה, v[5] (שׁ׳ גדולה), הָשִׁיבוּ הַשּׁ׳ אֲשֶׁר שְׁבִיתֶם v[11].

7622 †**שְׁבוּת, שְׁבִית** **n.f.** id. (√שׁבה 𝔊 Thes SS Preusschen[ZAW xv (1895), 1 ff.] Krae[Ez 16, 53]; > √ שׁוב Ew[JBW v (1852-3), 216 f.; § 165 b] Ol[§ 412, 417] Bö[§ 464] Kue[TTijdschr. vii. 519 ff.] Oort[Ib. xiv. 157] Schwally[ZAW viii (1888), 200] al.; Kö[ii. 1, 166 f., 474; ii. 2, § 329 i] thinks deriv. of שׁבה and שׁוב are confused, cf. Ew[§ 166 b]);—abs. שְׁבִית Nu 21[29]; cstr. שְׁבוּת Ho 6[11]+, sf. שְׁבוּתְךָ Dt 30[3], שְׁבִיתְהֶן Ez 16[53a] (v. infr.), שְׁבוּתֵיכֶם Zp 3[20] (rd. -תְכֶם Now GASm), etc. [MT has שְׁבוּת, etc. 16 t., + Kt (שְׁבִית Qr) Zp 2[7] ψ 85[2] 126[4] + Ez 16[53a] (Gi, but Baer שְׁבִיתְהֶן Kt et Qr, v. his note), + Qr (Kt שבית) Je 29[14] 49[39] Ez 16[53 b, c] + v[d] (but < rd. וְשַׁבְתִּי for וּשְׁבִיו Vrss Comm.), La 2[14] Jb 42[10]; שְׁבִית Kt et Qr Nu 21[29], שְׁבִיתֵךְ Ez 16[53] (but Co Krae שְׁבוּתֵךְ); שְׁבִית prob. earlier Ew[§ 166 b] al. ψ 126[1] rd. prob. שְׁבִית for שִׁיבַת];—**1.** in cl. נָתַן בַּשְּׁבִית Nu 21[29] (JE) *give his daughters into captivity* (or *as captives*, ‖ פְּלֵיטִם of sons, cf. Je 48[46]); cf. (perh.) La 1[7] (v. [מִשְׁבָּת] sub שׁבת). **2.** in phr. *restore the captivity of*, acc. after שׁוּב, הֵשִׁיב, י׳ subj. [vb. **Qal** Dt 30[3] + 15 t., + Ez 16[53d] ψ 126[1] (v. infr.); **Hiph.** Je 32[44] + 5 t., + **Qal** Kt, **Hiph.** Qr, Je 33[26] + 2 t.]: **a.** of Isr. (or Judah) Ho 6[11] (𝔊 joins to 7[1], so, as gloss, We Now), Zp 2[7] 3[20] Dt 30[3] Je 29[14] 30[3.18] (שׁ׳ אָהֳלֵי יַעֲקֹב), 31[23] 32[44] 33[7.7.11] (שׁ׳ הָאָרֶץ), v[26] La 2[14] (subj. proph.), Ez 16[53 a, c, d] (on text v. supr.), 39[25] Am 9[14] Jo 4[1] ψ 14[7] = 53[7], 85[2] 126[1] (v. supr.), v[4]. **b.** of other nations Je 48[47] (cf. v[46]), 49[6.39] Ez 29[14] (cf. v[13]). **c.** appar. in more gen. sense, *restore fortunes* of Sodom Ez 16[53b] (Krae, cf. foll.). **d.** restore fortunes of individuals, Jb 42[10].

7618 †**שְׁבוֹ** **n.**[**f.**] **a precious stone** (relation to above √dub.; = As. *šubû*; 𝔊 𝔙 *agate*);—Ex 28[19] = 39[12] (+ אַחְלָמָה, לֶשֶׁם).

7629 †**שֹׁבִי** **n.pr.m.** appar. Ammonite prince, וְשׁ׳ 2 S 17[27], 𝔊 Ουεσβει, 𝔊L καὶ Ζεφεει.

7630 †**שֹׁבַי** **n.pr.m.** in post-ex. Israel Ezr 2[42] = Ne 7[45], 𝔊[B] Αβαου (Ezr), Σαβει, A (Ezr) 𝔊L Σωβαι.

†**שְׁבוּאֵל, שְׁבָאֵל** **n.pr.m.** son of Gershom 7619
1 Ch 23[16] 26[24] (שְׁבֻ׳), = שׁוּבָאֵל 24[20.20], of Heman 25[4] = שׁוּבָאֵל v[20] (cf. Benz on these lists).—𝔊 in all usu. Σουβαηλ, 𝔊L usu. -βιηλ.

†[**תִּשְׁבֶּה**] **n.pr.loc.** (fr. above √?);—read 8664
prob. מִתִּשְׁבֵּה גִּלְעָד (or תִּשְׁבֵּי) 1 K 17[1] (for MT מִתֹּשָׁבֵי) 𝔊 ἐκ Θεσβῶν (𝔊L Θεσσεβῶν) τῆς Γαλααδ, so Jos; Ew Th We Kmp Benz Kit Burney al.; home of Elijah; v. Kasteren[ZPV xiii (1890), 207 ff.] cp. mod. *Istib*, in mts. of Ajlûn, so Buhl[G 257].

†**תִּשְׁבִּי** **adj.gent.**, אֵלִיָּהוּ הַתּ׳ 1 K 17[1] 21[17.28] 8664
2 K 1[3.8] 9[36];—ὁ Θεσβ(ε)ίτης.

†I. [**שָׁבַח**] **vb. Pi. soothe, still** (Ar. سَبَخَ 7623
be free from care, etc., Jen[ZA i (1886), 188; iv (1889), 268], cp. As. *pašâḫu*, *grow calm*, so Ba[ES 9] Schulth[Lex.]);—**Pi.** *Impf.* 3 ms. sf. יְשַׁבְּחֶנָּה Pr 29[11] *he stilleth it*, i.e. רוּחוֹ *his temper* (Bi Toy read חָשַׂךְ אַפּוֹ); 2 ms. sf. תְּשַׁבְּחֵם ψ 89[10] *thou stillest them*, i.e. waves (‖ גֵּאוּת הַיָּם). **Hiph.** *Pt.* (prob. Mass. error for **Pi.** מְשַׁבֵּחַ) מַשְׁבִּיחַ שְׁאוֹן יַמִּים ψ 65[8] *stilling the roar of the seas.*

†II. [**שָׁבַח**] **vb. Pi. laud, praise** (late 7623
Aramaism, cf. Aram. (incl. OAram.) שׁבח, ܫܒܚ, Pa. *praise;* v. Schwally[Idiot. 91] Schulth[Lex.]);—**1.** *laud, praise* God (י׳): *Impf.* 3 mpl. sf. יְשַׁבְּחוּנְךָ ψ 63[4] (‖ בֵּרֵךְ); *Imv.* fs. שַׁבְּחִי 147[12], mpl. sf. שַׁבְּחוּהוּ 117[1] (both ‖ הִלֵּל); his works, *Impf.* 3 ms. יְשַׁבַּח 145[4] (‖ הִגִּיד). **2.** *commend, congratulate*, the dead, *Inf. abs.* שַׁבֵּחַ Ec 4[2] (Ges[§ 113 gg]; c. מִן comp.); mirth, as best thing, *Pf.* 1 s. שִׁבַּחְתִּי Ec 8[15]. **Hithp.** *boast* of (בְּ): *Inf. cstr.* הִשְׁתַּבֵּחַ ψ 106[47] = 1 Ch 16[35], 𝔊 (ἐγ)καυχᾶσθαι ἐν.

†**יִשְׁבַּח** **n.pr.m.** in Judah (?; cf. Lag[BN 131]);— 3431
1 Ch 4[17]; Μαρεθ, A Ιεσαβα, 𝔊L Ιασαφαρ.

שׁבט (√ of foll.; cf. As. *šabâṭu, smite, slay, šibṭu, rod, sceptre;* NH שֵׁבֶט = BH, also שָׁבַט *beat* (denom.? so Nö[ZMG xl (1886), 736], but too sceptical); Sab. סבטם *rod, blow*, Sab.Denkm.[No. 21, 1.5]; Aram. שִׁבְטָא, ܫܒܛܐ = BH; loan-word in Egypt. demot. *šbṭë*, pl. hierogl. *ša-b-di-y*, WMM[As. u. Eur. 89]; Lewy[Fremdw. 122] cp. σπάθη).

שֵׁבֶט 189 **n.m.** [Nu 24, 17] (**f.** [Ez 21, 15. 18] but corrupt): 7626
1. rod, staff, club, sceptre. 2. tribe;—שׁ׳ abs. Gn 49[10] +, cstr. 1 S 10[20] +; שָׁבֶט Dt 1[23] +; sf. שִׁבְטוֹ Ju 21[24] +, etc.; pl. שְׁבָטִים 1 K 11[31] +, cstr. שִׁבְטֵי Gn 49[16] +, sf. שְׁבָטֶיךָ Dt 12[14] +, etc.;—†**1. a.** *rod, staff* (evidently common article), for

smiting (esp. הִכָּה בַשּׁ׳) Ex 21[20] (E), Mi 4[14] Is 10[15] (in sim.; ‖ מַטֶּה), Pr 10[13] +; שׁ׳ מוּסָר 22[15], cf. 29[15]; for beating (חָבַט) cummin Is 28[27] (‖ מַטֶּה); as (inferior) weapon (opp. חֲנִית) 2 S 23[21] = 1 Ch 11[3] (cf. מַקֵּל 1 S 17[40.43]); fig. of י׳'s chastisement: national Is 10[24] 30[31] (both ‖ מַטֶּה), 14[29], שׁ׳ אַפִּי 10[5], שׁ׳ עֶבְרָתוֹ La 3[1]; individual Jb 9[34] 21[9] (שׁ׳ אֱלוֹהַּ), 37[13], 2 S 7[14] (שׁ׳ אֲנָשִׁים, i.e. not *in-human*), ψ 89[33] (both ‖ נְגָעִים). **b.** *shaft*, i.e. spear, dart, 2 S 18[14], but < read שְׁלָחִים, 𝔊 βέλη, Th We Kit HPS Bu. **c.** shepherd's implement, *club*, ψ 23[4] (‖ מִשְׁעֶנֶת), רְעֵה בְשׁ׳ Mi 7[14] (both fig. of י׳); used in mustering or counting sheep Ez 20[37] (fig.), Lv 27[32] (cf. Je 33[13]), v. Mackie[Hast. DB Rod]. **d.** *truncheon, sceptre*, mark of authority, שׁ׳ סֹפֵר Ju 5[14], שׁ׳ מֹשְׁלִים Is 14[5] (‖ מַטֶּה), Gn 49[10] (poem in J; ‖ מְחֹקֵק), Zc 10[11] ψ 45[7.7] Ez 19[11.14] (made from a branch, מַטֶּה); a ruler is תּוֹמֵךְ שׁ׳ Am 1[5.8]; as symbol of conquest Nu 24[17] (JE); שׁ׳ בַּרְזֶל ψ 2[9] (of Mess. king); שׁ׳ הָרֶשַׁע 125[3]; שׁ׳ עֶבְרָתוֹ Pr 22[8] (si vera l., cf. Frankenb. Toy).—Vid. מַקֵּל, מַטֶּה, מִשְׁעֶנֶת. **2.** $_{145}$ *tribe* (syn. מַטֶּה, q.v. **3**, p. 641[b]), esp. **a.** of (12) tribes of Israel, Gn 49[16.28] (poem in J), Dt 33[5] (poem), Ex 24[4] (E), + oft. [JE 13 t., D 28 t. (מַטֶּה not JED), P 9 t. (cf. Gray[Nu 4, 18]; מ׳ 150 t. + in P); Ju 15 t. (never מ׳), S 14 t. (never מ׳), K 13 t. (מ׳ 2 t.), Chr 15 t. (מ׳ 23 t.), ψψ 7 t. (never מ׳), proph. 16 t. (מ׳ †Hb 3[9], very dub.)]; Ju 20[12] 1 S 9[21] rd. שֵׁבֶט (or שִׁבְטֵי Ges[§ 90 l], We Sta[§ 343 e] Dr, for שִׁבְטֵי), Vrss (GFM[Ju]); שִׁבְטֵי־יָהּ ψ 122[4]; שִׁבְטֵי נַחֲלָתֶךָ Is 63[17]. **b.** sg. of people (of Judah, late) ψ 74[2], but Je 10[16] = 51[19] del. שׁ׳ נ׳ Gf Gie Du. **c.** of subdivision of tribe, שׁ׳ מִשְׁפְּחוֹת וגו׳ Nu 4[18] (P).—2 S 7[7] rd. שֹׁפְטֵי (cf. v[11], ‖ 1 Ch 17[6], Ew Th We Dr HPS Bu al.).

8275 **†שַׁרְבִיט n.m. sceptre** (expanded fr. foreg., Ges[§ 85 w]);—only Est: abs. הַשּׁ׳ 5[2]; cstr. שׁ׳ הַזָּהָב 4[11] 5[2]; שַׁרְבִט הַז׳ 8[4].

7627 **†שְׁבָט n.pr. mens.** Sh[e]bāṭ, 11th month (post-ex.) = Feb.–March; loan-word from Bab. *Šabâṭu* (COT[Ne 1, 1] Dl[WB]), Zc 1[7] (der. fr. *šabâṭu, strike, kill, destroy* (Dl[Prol. 38; WB]), Lyon[Bib. Sacr. Apr. 1884, 384] Jen[ZA iv (1889), 273] Muss-Arn[JBL xi (1892), 171 f.] al., as month of *destroying* rain; another conjecture in Zim[KAT 3. 594 n.]; this month called שבט also in Nab Palm, v. Lzb SAC[111]).

7622, 7628, 7633 שְׁבִי, שִׁבְיָה, שְׁבִית, שְׁבִי v. שׁבה. p. 985f

שׁבל (√of foll.; cf. Ar. سَبَّلَ IV. *cause to hang down*, سَبَلَةٌ *flowing dress*; As. *šubultu*, *sunbultu* (Meissner), Ar. سُنْبُلٌ, سُنْبُلَةٌ (Ba[NB 207]), Eth. ሰብል: Aram. שֻׁבַּלְתָּא, ܫܒܠܬܐ, all *ear* of grain).

†שֹׁבֶל n.[m.] flowing skirt, train;—abs. 7640
חֶשְׂפִּי־שֹׁ׳ Is 47[2] *strip off* (thy) *train*.

†I. שִׁבֹּלֶת n.f. flowing stream;—שׁ׳ abs. 7641
ψ 69[3], as test of dialect Ju 12[6] (cf. סִבֹּלֶת and GFM); cstr. שׁ׳ מַיִם ψ 69[16], שׁ׳ הַנָּהָר Is 27[12].

†II. שִׁבֹּלֶת n.f. ear of grain;—שׁ׳ abs. Jb 7641
24[24] +; pl. שִׁבֳּלִים Gn 41[5] +, cstr. שִׁבֲּלֵי Zc 4[12];—*ear*, Gn 41[5.6.7.7.22.23.24.24.26.27] Is 17[5.5] Ru 2[2] Jb 24[24]; transf. *spike* (Pusey), end of olive bough Zc 4[12].

†[שְׁבִיל, שְׁבוּל] n.[m.] way, path (prop. 7635
as *flowing along, stretching out*? cf. NH שְׁבִיל, Ar. سَبِيلٌ, Aram. שְׁבִילָא);—pl. sf. וּשְׁבִילְךָ בְּמַיִם רַבִּים [Kt שְׁבִילֶיךָ, Qr שְׁבִילְךָ] ψ 77[20] (of י׳; ‖ דַּרְכֶּךָ); cstr. (fig. of course of life) שְׁבוּלֵי עוֹלָם Je 18[15] (Kt; Qr שְׁבִילֵי; ‖ דְּרָכִים).

†שׁוֹבָל n. pr. m. 1. Edomite name Gn 7732
36[20.23.29] = 1 Ch 1[38.40]. **2. a.** in Caleb 1 Ch 2[50.52]. **b.** in Judah 1 Ch 4[1.2].—Σωβα(λ), Σουβαλ.

שַׁבְּלוּל v. בלל. p. 117 7642

שׁבן (√of following; meaning dub.).

†שֶׁבְנָא, שֶׁבְנָה n. pr. m. secretary and 7644
major-domo of Hezekiah; נָא- Is 22[15], 36[22] 37[2] = 2 K 18[37] 19[2]; Is 36[3.11] = נָה- 2 K 18[18.26].—Σομνας.

†שְׁבַנְיָה(וּ) n.pr.m. 1. יָה-: **a.** Levites, 7645
(1) Ne 9[4.5] 10[13], (2) 10[11]; Σεβανια, Σαβανια(ς). **b.** priest Ne 10[5], priestly family 12[14] (𝔊L Σεχενια), = שְׁכַנְיָה v[3] (Σεχενια(ς)), and perh. שְׁכַנְיָהוּ 1 Ch 24[11] (Ισχανια, Σεχενια). **2.** יָהוּ-, priest, 1 Ch 15[24] (Σομνια, 𝔊L Σαβανια).

שׁבס (√of following; meaning ?).

†[שָׁבִיס] n.[m.] front-band (Mishn. *id.*; 7636
Levy[NHWB iv. 498]; al. cp. Ar. شمس, lit. a *sun*, of small glass *neck-ornament* We[Skizzen iii. 145]; Heb. perh. a dimin., v. Ges[§ 86 note]);—pl. הַשְּׁבִיסִים Is 3[18], in list of women's finery.

I. שֶׁבַע, שִׁבְעָה $_{394}$ **n.m. et f. seven** 7651
(NH *id.*, MI[16] שבעת; As. *sibi, sibittu* (Dl[Gr. § 65, 6]; s = שׁ), Ar. سَبْعٌ, سَبْعَةٌ, Sab. סבע Hom[Chr 47, 124], Eth. ሰብዕ: ሰብዐቱ: Ph. (Pun.) שבע, Nab. שבע, שבעה, Palm. שבעא, שבעה; Aram. שִׁבְעָא, שְׁבַע, ܫܒܥ, ܫܒܥܐ; on etym. cf. Lag[BN 37 f.]);—**m.** (c. **n.f.**) abs. שֶׁבַע Gn 41[2] + 115 t.; cstr. שְׁבַע 5[26] + 47 t., esp. P (15 t.) and Chr (20 t.), וְשֶׁבַע 1 K

14^{21}. **f.** (c. **n.m.**) abs. שִׁבְעָה Gn 4^{24} + 100 t.; cstr. שִׁבְעַת 7^{10} + 120 t.; sf. שִׁבְעָתָם 2 S 21^{9} Qr (so Vrss and mod.; v. Dr; > Kt שִׁבְעָתַיִם);—*seven:* **1.** without other num.: **a.** שֶׁבַע, before n.fpl. Gn 21^{28} (J), Ju 16^{13} Is 4^{1} + 80 t., esp. שׁ׳ שָׁנִים Gn 29^{18} (E) + 32 t. (but read שָׁלוֹשׁ for שֶׁבַע 2 S 24^{13a}, cf. $v^{b,c}$, also 𝔊 and ‖ 1 Ch 21^{12}; so Th We Dr Bu HPS Now), שׁ׳ פְּעָמִים Gn 33^{3} (J), Lv 4^{6} (P) + 17 t.; שׁ׳ בָּאַמָּה רָחְבָּהּ 1 K 6^{6}; after noun Ez $40^{20.26}$; n. om. Jb 5^{19} Pr 6^{16}, + (= שׁ׳ פְּעָמִים) Lv $26^{18.21.24.28}$ (H), ψ 119^{64} Pr 24^{16}. **b.** שִׁבְעָה, before n.mpl. Nu $23^{1.1.1}$ (E) + 40 t. + Jb 42^{13} (read שׁ׳ for שִׁבְעָנָה Ges ^{§97c} and most); + (distrib.) שׁ׳ וְשׁ׳ Zc 4^{2}; after n. Gn 7^{4} (J), Ex 25^{37} (P) + 12 t. (P Ch Dn Pr); n. om. 1 S 2^{5} + 9 t., incl. שׁ׳ as ordinal, v. infr.; but read שְׂבָכָה for שִׁבְעָה 1 K $7^{17.17}$ 𝔊 Th Kmp Klo Benz Kit Bur; also שׁ׳ שׁ׳ distrib. = 7 *each* Gn $7^{2.3}$ (J); as pred. Gn 46^{25} (P). **c.** שִׁבְעַת, before n.pl. Nu 23^{4} (E), 8^{2} (P), Ez $45^{23.23}$ Jb $2^{13.13}$ + 97 t., incl. שׁ׳ יָמִים Gn 8^{10} (J), + 88 t. + Ez 45^{21} (rd. שִׁבְעַת for שָׁבֻעוֹת, Vrss and mod.). **d.** = ordinal, שְׁנַת (הַ)שֶּׁבַע Dt 15^{9} 2 K 12^{2} + 3 t., בְּשִׁבְעָה לַחֹדֶשׁ Ez 30^{20}, cf. 45^{20}; לְשִׁבְעַת הַיָּמִים Gn 7^{10} (J), 1 Ch 9^{25}. **2.** †**a.** שְׁבַע עֶשְׂרֵה שָׁנָה 17 *years* Gn 37^{2} + 3 t. + 1 K 14^{21} (וּשְׁבַע וגו׳), also as ordin. בִּשְׁנַת שׁ׳ עֶשׂ׳ 1 K 22^{52}, בִּשְׁנַת שׁ׳ עֶשׂ׳ שָׁנָה 2 K 16^{1}. †**b.** שִׁבְעָה עָשָׂר (sc. הַגּוֹרָל *lot*) 1 Ch 24^{15} 25^{24} (cf. also, + other num., 7^{11} Ezr 2^{39} Ne 7^{42}), + יוֹם 17*th day* Gn 7^{11} 8^{4}; unusual is שׁ׳ שְׁקָלִים וַעֲשָׂרָה הַכֶּסֶף Je 32^{9} 7 *shekels and* 10 *the silver.* **3.** שְׁבַע מֵאוֹת = 700 Ju 8^{26} + 39 t. (but Ne 7^{68} om. Mass. Baer Gi q.v.). **4.** שִׁבְעָה אֶלֶף = 7000 1 K 20^{30} + 2 t.; שִׁבְעַת אֲלָפִים = *id.* 1 K 20^{15} + 15 t.; 57,000 is 7 + 50 × 1000 Nu 1^{31} $2^{8.31}$. **5.** שׁ׳ + other num.: **a.** שׁ׳ follows 18 t.: (1) n.s. after שׁ׳ Ju 8^{14}; also (= ord. num.) Ez 29^{17} + 2 t., שְׁנַת שְׁלֹשִׁים וָשׁ׳ שָׁנָה 2 K 13^{10}, cf. 15^{1}; (2) n.pl. before other num. Ezr 8^{35} Ne $7^{[72],71}$; (3) n.s. cstr. precedes שׁ׳ וָשׁ׳ בִּשְׁנַת עֶשְׂרִים 1 K $16^{10.15}$ (ordin.); (4) n. after each num. Gn 23^{1} 25^{17} (both P), etc. **b.** שׁ׳ precedes 10 t. (P and Est): (1) n.s. after other num. Gn 8^{14} Ex $6^{16.20}$ + 3 t. Est; (2) n. repeated Gn 5^{7} 11^{21} 47^{28}, cf. $5^{25.31}$. **c.** 1000 + 17 Ezr 2^{39} = Ne 7^{42}.—שׁ׳ oft. c. sacred signif.: Gn $21^{28ff.}$ (J), Ex 37^{23} Lv $4^{6.17}$ 8^{11} 14^{27} + (P); as round number Gn 4^{24} (song in J), $29^{18ff.}$ 31^{23} $41^{2ff.}$ (all E), etc.; on bowing 7 t. 33^{3} (J; in great humility), cf. Wkl $^{\text{TelAm. nos. 143, 230, 246}}$ Ne $^{\text{Mar. 11 f.}}$; all these prob. originating with week of seven days; cf. esp. Kö $^{\text{Hast. DB Number, 562 f., 565}}$.

7656 †שִׁבְעָה **n.f. pr. putei,** Gn 26^{33} (J); Ὅρκος; (explanation of name בְּאֵר שֶׁבַע.)

שִׁבְעִים $_{91}$ **n.pl. seventy** (irreg. pl. of שֶׁבַע 7657
Ges $^{§97f, R.1}$);—not decl.:—*seventy* (oft. as round no., cf. Kö $^{\text{Hast. DB Number, 563 a}}$): **1.** without other no.: **a.** before n.s. year Gn 5^{12} + 12 t., man Ju 9^{2} Nu 11^{25} + 7 t., shekel 7^{13} + 11 t., other n. 5 t. **b.** before n.pl. kings Ju 1^{7}, sons 8^{30} 9^{24} 2 K 10^{1}, brothers Ju 9^{56}, asses 12^{14}, palms Ex 15^{27} Nu 33^{9}, males Ezr $8^{7.14}$. **c.** after n.coll. (בָּקָר) 2 Ch 29^{32}, n.pl. Dn 9^{24}. **d.** pred. Gn 46^{27}. **e.** n. om. Ex $24^{1.9}$ (man), Nu 7^{85} (shekel), cf. Ju 9^{4}. **2.** שׁ׳ אֶלֶף = 70,000 2 S 24^{15} + 6 t. **3.** + other num.: **a.** + unit + n.s. Ju 8^{14}; n. om. 70 + 7 (times) Gn 4^{24}, cf. Ezr 2^{40} = Ne 7^{43}, so 2 + 70 Nu 31^{38}; n. pl. + 70 + 7 Ezr 8^{35}; 5 years + 70 year Gn 12^{4}. **b.** 5 + 70 × 1000 (man) Est 9^{16}, cf. Nu 2^{4} 3^{43} 26^{32}; 2 + 70 × 1000 31^{33} (בָּקָר precedes); 70 man, 50 × 1000 man 1 S 6^{19}; 7 + 70 year + 7 × 100 year Gn 5^{31}; n. om. 3 + 70 + 200 Nu 3^{46}. **c.** 70 foll. hundreds: 70 year + 5 years Gn 25^{7}, and (n. om.) 70 + 2 Ezr $2^{3.4}$ = Ne $7^{8.9}$, Ne 11^{19}; + 3 Ezr 2^{36} Ne 7^{39}; 5 + 70 Ezr 2^{5}. **d.** 1000 + 7 × 100 + 5 + 70 shekel Ex 38^{25} and (n. om.) v^{38}.

שְׁבִיעִי **m.** שְׁבִיעִית **f.** $_{97}$ **adj. num. ord.** 7637
seventh;—**m.** שְׁבִיעִי Gn 2^{2} +, שְׁבִעִי Ex 12^{15} +; **f.** שְׁבִיעִית Jos 6^{16} +, -עִת Ex 23^{11} +, שְׁבִעִת 21^{2}, -עִית 1 K 18^{44} 2 Ch 23^{1};—*fifth*, esp. P; always c. art.: **1. m.** 7th day Gn 2^{3} + 47 t.; month (חֹדֶשׁ) 8^{4} + 23 t. + (n. om.) Ez 45^{25} + 3 t.; lot (הַגּוֹרָל) Jos 19^{40} + (n. om.) 1 Ch 24^{10} 25^{14}; n. om. also 1 Ch 2^{15} $26^{3.5}$ (son), 12^{11} (man), 27^{10} (captain). **2. f.** 7th year, 2 K 11^{4} + 7 t. + (n. om.) Ex 21^{2} 23^{11}, also שְׁנַת הַשְּׁבִיעִית (Ges ^{§134p}) Ezr 7^{8}; sabbath Lv 23^{16}; time (פַּעַם) Jos 6^{16} + (n. om.) 1 K 18^{44}.

שִׁבְעָנָה Jb 42^{13} read שִׁבְעָה Ges ^{§97c} and most. 7651, 7658
p. 987

†שִׁבְעָתַיִם **n. f. du. seven-fold, seven** 7659
times (cf. Ges $^{§§97h, 134r}$);—**1.** *seven-fold, seven times as much,* Is 30^{26} Pr 6^{31}; as adv. Gn $4^{15.24}$ ψ 79^{12}. **2.** *seven times,* adv. ψ 12^{7}.—2 S 21^{9} read Qr שִׁבְעָתָם, v. I. שֶׁבַע. p. 987 7651

†שָׁבוּעַ **n.m.** $^{\text{Dn 9, 27}}$ **period of seven** (days, 7620
years), **heptad, week** (on format. v. Lag $^{\text{BN 67}}$);—abs. שׁ׳ Dn $9^{27.27}$; cstr. שְׁבֻעַ Gn $29^{27.28}$; du. שְׁבֻעַיִם Lv 12^{5}; pl. שָׁבֻע(וֹ)ת Ex 34^{22} + 4 t. Dt + (in term. techn.) 2 Ch 8^{13}; late שָׁבֻעִים Dn 9^{24} + 4 t. Dn; cstr. שְׁבֻעֹת Je 5^{24} (Ez 45^{21} read שִׁבְעַת with Vrss and all mod., v. שֶׁבַע); sf. שָׁבֻעֹתֵיכֶם Nu 28^{26};—**1.** *period of seven days* (fr. a given time), *week:* Dt $16^{9.9}$ Lv 12^{5} (P); of marriage feast Gn $29^{27.28}$ (E; cf. Ju 14^{12} Tob 11^{19}); שָׁבֻעִים יָמִים Dn $10^{2.3}$ three *weeks, days* (three weeks long);

ש׳ חֻקּוֹת קָצִיר Je 5^{24} *weeks of statutes* (i.e. weeks appointed by י׳) *for harvest;* term. techn. חַג שָׁבֻעֹת Ex 34^{22} (J) *feast of weeks* (ending seven weeks of harvest), Dt 16$^{10.16}$ 2 Ch 8^{13}, so ש׳ alone Nu 28^{26} (P). **2.** *heptad* or *seven* of years, late, Dn 9$^{24.25.26.27.27}$.—שְׁבֻעֵי שְׁבֻעוֹת Ez 21^{28} v. [שָׁבַע].

7650 [שָׁבַע] $_{186}$ **vb. swear** (prob., so to say, *seven oneself,* or *bind oneself by seven things,* cf. Thes (as altern.), Gerb$^{108ff.}$; NH Niph.=BH; 𝔗 שְׁבַע Ithpe. Aph.; v. also Dr$^{Gn\ 21.28}$ Kö$^{Hast.\ DB\ Number,\ 565}$ RS$^{Sem.\ i.\ 166,\ 2nd\ ed.,\ 182}$ We$^{Reste\ Ar.\ Heid.\ 2,186}$);—**Qal** (acc. to Thes Rob Ges) *Pt. pass.* שְׁבֻעֵי שְׁבֻעוֹת Ez 21^{28} *those sworn with* (=who have sworn) *oaths;* both from שְׁבוּעָה, acc. to Krae, *oaths of oaths* (the most sacred); 𝔊 𝔖 Co om.; both from שָׁבוּעַ, Ew Sm ש׳ ש׳ *weeks on weeks* (plenty of time). **Niph.** *Pf.* 3 ms. נִשְׁבַּע Gn 24^{7}+, etc.; *Impf.* 3 ms. יִשָּׁבַע Lv 5^{24}+, וַיִּשָּׁבַע Gn 24^{9}+; 2 ms. תִּשָּׁבַע Dt 6^{13} 10^{20}; 1 s. אִשָּׁבֵעַ Gn 21^{24}, וָאִשָּׁבַע 1 K 2^{8} Ez 16^{8}, etc.; *Imv.* ms. הִשָּׁבְעָה Gn 21^{23}+, etc.; *Inf. abs.* הִשָּׁבֵעַ Nu 30^{3}, הִשָּׁבֹעַ Je 7^{9}; *cstr.* הִשָּׁבַע Je 12$^{16.16}$+1 S 20^{17} v. infra; *Pt.* נִשְׁבָּע Zc 5^{3}+, etc.;—*swear, take an oath:* **1.** subj. man: **a.** in asseveration, abs. Gn 21$^{24.31}$(E), Ju 21$^{1.18}$ 2 S 21^{2}+; also sq. וַיֹּאמֶר 1 S 20^{3} 1 K 1^{29}, sq. לֵאמֹר 2 S 3^{35} Jos 14^{9} (D); c. acc. cogn. Nu 30^{3} (P; ‖ נָדַר); + לַשֶּׁקֶר Je 5^{2} 7^{9} Lv 5^{24} (P; + עַל rei), Mal 3^{5}; + עַל־שׁ׳ Lv 5^{22} (P); + לְמִרְמָה ψ 24^{4}; sq. inf. Lv 5^{4} (P), ψ 15^{4} 119^{106}; + לְ pers. *take an oath to,* Jos 6^{22} (JE), 9^{20} (P; acc. cogn.) Gn 24^{9} (עַל־הַדָּבָר הַזֶּה+), + לְהִשָּׁבֵעַ, so also 1 S 20^{17} (rd. לְהַשְׁבִּיעַ אֶת־ for אֶל־, 𝔊 𝔙 Th We Dr al.); oath of allegiance (לי׳) Is 19^{18} 45^{23} Zp 1^{5} 2 Ch 15^{14}, cf. (abs.) v^{15} (Jos 23^{7} v. **Hiph.**); also sq. וַיֹּאמֶר 2 K 25^{24}, sq. לֵאמֹר 2 S 21^{17} 1 K 1^{13} Je 40^{9}; sq. פֶּן=*that not* Ju 15^{12}, sq. אִם=*id.* 1 K 1^{51}; + אֶל pers. sq. לֵאמֹר Je 38^{16}; + בי׳ *by* י׳, sq. inf. Ju 21^{7}; + בְּשֵׁם י׳ 1 S 20^{42} Is 48^{1}, cf. Gn 31^{53} (E), Dt 6^{13} 10^{20} Je 12^{16} (+חַי־י׳), Is 65^{16} Zc 5^{4} (לַשָּׁקֶר), Lv 19^{12} (*id.*), ψ 63^{12} Dn 12^{7}; + בי׳ sq. אִם 2 S 19^{8}; + לְ pers. c. בי׳ Jos 9$^{18.19}$ (P; pledge faith), sq. לֵאמֹר 1 S 28^{10} 1 K 1^{30} 2$^{8.23}$, sq. כִּי of obj. cl. Jos 2^{12} (JE), 1 K 1^{17}; + לְ pers. c. בא׳, sq. אִם Gn 21^{23} (E), 1 S 30^{15}; as vb. of quotation + obj. חַי־י׳ Ho 4^{15} Je 4^{2} 1 S 19^{6} (+אִם), + אִם in *orat. recta* ψ 132^{2} (‖ נָדַר); also + בְּלֹא אֱלֹהִים Je 5^{7}, בַּבָּעַל 12^{16}, בְּמַלְכָּם Zp 1^{5}, cf. Am 8^{14} (+וְאָמַר). **b.** *imprecate, curse,* בִּי *by me* ψ 102^{9} (cf. שְׁבוּעָה **1 b**, קְלָלָה). **2.** subj. י׳: *swear,* c. בִּי *by myself* Gn 22^{16} (JE), Je 22^{5} (cl. כִּי), 49^{13} (*id.*), Is 45^{23} (*id.*), c. בְּקָדְשׁוֹ Am 4^{2} (*id.*), cf. ψ 89^{36} (‖ אִם אֲכַזֵּב), cf. also Am 6^{8} 8^{17} Je 44^{26} 51^{14} Is 62^{8}; *swear,* sq. inf. Dt 1^{35} 4^{21} Jos 21^{41} (van d. H. Baer; v^{43} Gi), sq. מִן inf.=*not to* Is 54$^{9.9}$, sq. אִם ψ 90^{10}, sq. לֵאמֹר Dt 1^{34} Is 14^{24} Nu 32^{10} (P); sq. *orat. recta* ψ 110^{4}; c. לְ pers. *take an oath to,* Gn 24^{7} (J), Ex 13^{11} (J), Dt 2^{14} + 7 t. Dt. (acc. cogn. 7^{8} 9^{5}), Ez 16^{8} (‖ בוֹא בִבְרִית), ψ 89^{4} (‖ כָּרַת בְּרִית), v^{50} (בֶּאֱמוּנָתֶךָ), +; לְ pers. + inf. (usu. *to give land*) Ex 13^{5} (J), Dt 1^{8} + 9 t. Dt, Jos 1^{6} 5$^{6.6}$ (all R^{D}), Je 11^{5} (+ acc. cogn.), 32^{22}; לְ pers. + acc. rei (usu. *land*)= *promise by oath to* Gn 50^{24} Ex 33^{1} Nu 11^{12} (all J), 14$^{16.23}$ (JE), 32^{11} (P), Ju 2^{1} Mi 7^{20} Dt 6^{18} + 8 t. Dt (obj. covenant 4^{31} 8^{18}); לְ pers. om. Dt 31^{21}. †**Hiph.** *Perf.* 3 ms. הִשְׁבִּיעַ Ex 13^{19}+, 1 s. הִשְׁבַּעְתִּי Ct 2^{7}+, etc.; *Impf.* 3 ms. וַיַּשְׁבַּע Gn 50^{25}+, sf. וַיַּשְׁבִּעֵנִי Gn 24^{37}, etc.; *Inf. abs.* הַשְׁבֵּעַ Ex 13^{19} 1 S 14^{28}; *cstr.* הַשְׁבִּיעַ 1 S 14^{27} (20^{17} v. **Niph.**); *Pt.* sf. מַשְׁבִּיעֶךָ 1 K 22^{16}=2 Ch 18^{15};—**1.** *cause to take an oath,* subj. always man: c. acc. pers. Gn 50^{6} (J), 1 S 14^{27} 1 K 18^{10} 2 K 11^{4}, + acc. cogn. Jos 2$^{17.20}$ (J), + לֵאמֹר Gn 24^{37} 50^{5} (both J), v^{25} (E), Jos 6^{26} (J; acc. pers. om.), so (Inf. abs. + Pf.) Ex 13^{19} (JE), 1 S 14^{28}, + וְאָמַר Nu 5^{19} and (c. acc. cogn.) v^{21} (both P), + inf. cl. Ne 5^{12} Ezr 10^{5}; + בי׳ *by* י׳ Gn 24^{3} (J; cl. אֲשֶׁר), 1 K 2^{42} (‖ וָאָעִד בְּךָ, + לֵאמֹר), cf. Jos 23^{7} (R^{D}; but read perhaps **Niph.** תִּשָּׁבְעוּ Gr al.; 𝔊 del.), Ne 13^{25} (cl. אִם, *orat. recta*), 2 Ch 36^{13}. **2.** *adjure,* c. acc. pers. 1 K 22^{16}=2 Ch 18^{15} (both + cl. אֲשֶׁר); elsewhere only Ct: 5^{9}, c. cl. מַה־ interrog. v^{8}, c. cl. אִם *that not* 2^{7} 3^{5} (both + בּ of oath), =cl. מַה־ 8^{4} (v. מָה **2 a** (*b*)).—1 S 20^{17} v. **Niph.**

†II. שֶׁבַע **n.pr.m. 1.** in Benj., בֶּן־בִּכְרִי 2 S 7652
20$^{1.2.6.7.10.13.21.22}$; Σαβεε. **2.** in Gad 1 Ch 5^{13}; Σεβεε, A Σωβαθε, 𝔊L Σαβεε.

†III. שֶׁבַע si vera l. **n.pr.loc.** in Simeon, 7652
בְּאֵר־שֶׁבַע וְשֶׁבַע Jos 19^{2}; Σαμαα, 𝔊L Σαβε; prob.
del. וְשׁ׳ Di al. (om. ‖ 1 Ch 4^{23}).—בְּאֵר שׁ׳ v. p. 92^{a}. 884

שֶׁבַע v. in cpds. אֱלִישֶׁבַע, (בַּת־שֶׁבַע), יְהוֹשֶׁבַע. 472,1399, 3089

†שְׁבֻעָה, שְׁבוּעָה **n. f.** (Jos 2^{17} read הַזֹּה 7621
Albr$^{ZAW\ xvi\ (1896),\ 116}$) **oath, curse;**—abs. שְׁבוּ׳ Jos 9^{20}+, שְׁבֻ׳ Gn 26^{3}+; cstr. שְׁבֻעַת Ex 22^{10}+; sf. שְׁבֻעָתִי Gn 24^{8}, etc.; pl. שְׁבֻעוֹת abs. Ez 21^{28}, cstr. Hb 3^{9} [Je 5^{24} Ez 45^{21} v. שָׁבוּעַ];—*oath* [as acc. cogn. c. הִשָּׁבַע etc. Nu 30^{3} + (in rel. cl.) 5 t.]: **1.** of man: **a.** attesting innocence Ex 22^{10} (E), friendship 2 S 21^{7}, promise 1 K 2^{43} (after שָׁמַר *keep;* all שְׁבֻעַת י׳ *oath to* י׳); innocence also Nu 5^{21a}; friendship Ne 6^{18} (בַּעֲלֵי שׁ׳ לוֹ), promise Lv 5^{4}; of vow (‖ נדר) Nu 30$^{3.11.14}$ (שְׁבֻעַת אִסָּר), Jos 9^{20} (all P),

Ne 10^{30} (‖ אָלָה), Ec 9^{2}, of covenant with י׳ 2 Ch 15^{15}, שְׁבוּעַת אֱלֹהִים Ec 8^{2} (prob. of oath of allegiance to king), שְׁבֻעַת שֶׁקֶר Zc 8^{17}; of threat Ju 21^{5} 1 S 14^{26} (𝔊 שְׁבֻעַת י׳); *keep, discharge the oath* is הֵקִים הַשׁ׳ Gn 26^{3} (J), Je 11^{5}; נָקָה מִשׁ׳ *be free, exempt from an oath* Gn 24^{8} (J), cf. Jos 2$^{17.20}$. **b.** = *curse*, Is 65^{15} and (‖ אָלָה) Nu 5^{21} (P), Dn 9^{11}. **2.** *oath* of י׳, in promise, Dt 7^{8} (שָׁמַר in rel. cl.), ‖ covenant (בְּרִית), שְׁבוּעָתוֹ לְיִצְחָק ψ 105^{9} = 1 Ch 16^{16}.—שְׁבֻעוֹת מַטּוֹת Hb 3^{9} very dub.: AV *oaths of the tribes; oaths, rods* of the word, Hi-St.; *sworn* (pt. pass. שָׁבֻעַ) were *the rods* (= chastisements) of (thy) word, GesHiRVm; *heptads of spears* Ew, cf. Da; text prob. corrupt, Now prop. (אַשְׁפָּתֶךָ) שִׂבַּעְתָּ מַטּוֹת *thou hast sated with shafts thy quiver;* Marti (after 𝔊$^{Codd.}$) *thy bow was satiated with shafts;* GASm *thou gluttest* (?) *thy shafts*.—Ez 21^{28} v. √.

7660 †[שָׁבַץ] **vb. Pi.** prob. **weave in chequer or plaited work** (NH שָׁבַץ *ornament* a vessel *with a pattern;* Syr. (lexx.) ܫܒܨ *immiscuit*, ܫܘܒܨܐ *commixtio:* v. also Lag$^{BN 143}$);—**Pi.** *Pf.* 2 ms. וְשִׁבַּצְתָּ Ex 28^{39} (P), *and thou shalt chequer* (or *plait*) the tunic (in) byssus. **Pu.** *Pt.* mpl. מְשֻׁבָּצִים זָהָב Ex 28^{20} (P), *inwoven* (i.e. set in a chequered or plaited mounting) *with gold* (-thread) shall they be (of gems).

7661 †שָׁבָץ **n.m.** (meaning and connexion with above √ dub.);—אֲחָזַנִי הַשׁ׳ 1 S 1^{9} הַשׁ׳ *hath seized me*, i.e. perh. *cramp* (Ew$^{G iii. 147}$ Th Ke, cf. Dr); al. *giddiness* (Thes Klo HPS), as intricacy, confusion; Kit Bu Now leave undecided.

4865 †מִשְׁבְּצ(וֹ)ת **n.f.** $^{Ex 28.25}$ **pl. chequered** (or **plaited**) **work**, usu. of *settings* for gems;—מ׳ זָהָב (i.e. plaited with gold-thread) for two gems on high priest's ephod (P): Ex 28$^{11.13}$ 39$^{6.13.16}$; מ׳ abs. 28$^{14.25.39}$ 39^{18}; מִמִּ׳ ז׳ לְבוּשָׁהּ ψ 45^{14} her clothing is of *chequer work* inwrought with gold; < Krochm Gr Che$^{Comm.}$ פְּנִינִים בְּמִשְׁבְּצוֹת ז׳ לְבוּשָׁהּ (v. פְּנִימָה p. 819 supr.) pearls in *plaited settings* of gold(-thread).

8665 †תַּשְׁבֵּץ **n.** [**m.**] **chequered** (or **plaited**) **work**;—כְּתֹנֶת ת׳ Ex 28^{4}.

שבק (√ of foll.; cf. BAram. 𝔗, שְׁבַק *let go, leave*, so ܫܒܩ; Ar. سَبَقَ *outstrip*).

7733 †שׁוֹבֵק **n.pr.m.** one of those sealed Ne 10^{25}; Σωβηκ, 𝔊L Σωβειρ.

3435 †יִשְׁבָּק **n.pr.m.** son of Abr. and Ḳeṭûrâh, Gn 25^{2} 1 Ch 1^{32}; Ιεσβοκ (B Σοβακ Ch).

שָׁבַר$_{148}$ **vb. break, break in pieces** (NH *id.;* Sab. תבר *break, destroy* DHM$^{Hof. Mus., no. 1, l. 26}$ Mordtm$^{HI 74}$; Ar. ثَبَرَ *restrain, destroy;* Aram. תְּבַר, ܬܒܪ; As. *šabâru, break, break in pieces;* Eth. ሰበረ: *break*);—**Qal**$_{53}$ *Pf.* 3 ms. שׁ׳ 1 K 13^{28} 7665
Is 14^{5}, etc.; *Impf.* 3 ms. יִשְׁבֹּר Je 19^{11}, -בּוֹר- Is 42^{3}; 3 fs. תִּשְׁבָּר־ Pr 25^{15}, etc.; *Imv.* ms. שְׁבֹר ψ 10^{15}, sf. שָׁבְרֵם Je 17^{18}; *Inf. cstr.* לִשְׁבֹּר Gn 19^{9} + 2 t., שְׁבוֹר Je 28^{12}; *Pt. act.* שֹׁבֵר Ez 4^{16} + 2 t.; *pass.* שָׁבוּר Lv 22^{22}, pl. cstr. שְׁבוּרֵי ψ 147^{3};—*break*, lit., obj. earthen vessel Ju 7^{20} Lv 11^{33} (P), Je 19^{11} (in sim.), cf. v^{11} 48^{38} Is 30^{14}, flask Je 19^{10}, gate-bar Am 1^{5} (in metaph.), bow Ho 1^{5} Je 49^{35}, and sword Ho 2^{20} (מִן־הָאָרֶץ), bone of lamb Ex 12^{46} Nu 9^{12} (P), and (in metaph.) Pr 25^{15}, cf. שָׁבוּר i.e. fractured of limb Lv 22^{22} (H), yoke Je 28$^{10.12.13}$, and, in metaph., of deliverance (י׳ subj.) v$^{2.4.11}$ 38^{8} (c. מֵעַל), + 4 t., of rebellion Je 2^{20} 5^{5}, so staff Is 14^{5} + 5 t., reed Is 42^{3}, arm of Pharaoh Ez 30$^{21.22.24}$ cf. ψ 10^{15}; trees (subj. thunder) ψ 29^{5}; *break in, down*, door Gn 19^{9} (J); *rend violently* (of lion), man 1 K 13^{26}, ass v^{28}; *wreck* Tyre (as ship) Ez 27^{26}; fig. *break* pride Lv 26^{19} (H); *crush* (fig.) Is 14^{25} (cf. Je 48^{28} supr.), La 1^{15} Dn 11^{26}; מִשְׁנֶה שִׁבָּרוֹן שׁ׳ Je 17^{18}; *break, rupture*, heart (fig.) ψ 69^{21} + Ez 6^{9} (v. **Niph.** ad fin.), שְׁבוּרֵי לֵב ψ 147^{3}; וָאֶשְׁבֹּר עָלָיו חֻקִּי Jb 38^{10} *broke for it my boundary*, of sea, ref. to abrupt ending of mainland; = *quench* thirst (*frangere sitim*) ψ 104^{11}. **Niph.**$_{57}$ *Pf.* 3 ms. נִשְׁבַּר Ex 22^{9} +, etc.; *Impf.* 3 ms. יִשָּׁבֵר Lv 6^{21} +, 3 fs. וְתִשָּׁבֵר Ec 12^{6}, 2 ms. תִּשָּׁבֵר Ez 29^{7}, -בָר- 32^{28}, etc.; *Inf. cstr.* הִשָּׁבֵר Jon 1^{4}; *Pt.* נִשְׁבָּר ψ 51^{19}, fs. נִשְׁבָּרָה v^{19}, נִשְׁבֶּרֶת Ez 27^{34} +, etc.;—*be broken*, of neck 1 S 4^{18}, bones ψ 34^{21}, gate-bars Je 51^{30}, rod (in fig.) Is 14^{21} Je 48^{17}, idols Ez 6$^{4.6}$, horn Dn 8^{8}, cf. v^{22}, arm Jb 31^{22} (מִקָּנָה), and (in metaph.) Je 48^{25} Jb 38^{15} ψ 37^{17}, cf. Ez 30^{22}, bough Ez 31^{12} Is 27^{11}, cf. (fig.) of wickedness, like a tree Jb 24^{20}, other things ψ 37^{15} Je 50^{23} Ez 29^{7} ψ 124^{7}; cisterns Je 2^{13} (*id.*), pottery Lv 6^{21} 15^{12} (P), Ec 12^{6} (in fig.); = *be maimed, crippled* (have limb broken), of animal Ex 22$^{9.13}$ (E), and (fig.) Ez 34$^{4.16}$ Zc 11^{16}, so (fig. of men stumbling) Is 8^{15} 28^{13}; *be wrecked*, of ships 1 K 22^{49} (rd. Qr נִשְׁבְּרוּ), ‖ 2 Ch 20^{37}, Jon 1^{4}, metaph. of Tyre Ez 27^{34}; fig. *be crushed*, destroyed (pers., warriors, kingdoms, etc.), Je 14^{17} 22^{20} 48^{4} 51^{8} + 10 t.; fig. *be broken*, of heart †Je 23^{9} Is 61^{1} ψ 34^{19} 51^{19}, cf. רוּחַ נִשׁ׳ v^{19}.—Ez 6^{9} rd. prob. וְשִׁבַּרְתִּי (We Sm Berthol Toy Krae); Co בְּשָׁבְרִי. **Pi.**$_{36}$ *Pf.* 3 ms. שִׁבַּר Is 21^{9} +, שִׁבֵּר Ex 9^{25}, etc.; *Impf.* 3 ms. יְשַׁבֵּר ψ 46^{10} +, 2 mpl. תְּשַׁבֵּרוּן Ex 34^{13}, etc.; *Inf. abs.* שַׁבֵּר Ex 23^{24}; *Pt.*

מְשַׁבֵּר 1 K 19^{11};—*shatter, break*, tablets Ex 32^{19} (E), 34^{1} (J), Dt 9^{17} 10^{2}; מַצֵּבוֹת Ex 23^{24} (E; + Inf. abs.), 34^{13} (J) + 7 t.; images 2 K 11^{18} + 3 t.; bronze sea, etc., 2 K 25^{13} = Je 52^{17}; horns Dn 8^{7}; jaws Jb 29^{17} (in fig.); of hail *shattering* trees Ex 9^{25} (J), cf. 1 K 19^{11}; elsewhere subj. 'י, *shattering* gate-bars, etc., weapons Is 45^{2} 38^{13} La 2^{9} 3^{4} ψ 46^{10} 76^{4} 107^{16}, trees 29^{5} 105^{33}, heads of תַּנִּינִים 74^{13}; *wrecking* ships 48^{8}. †**Hiph.** *cause to break out*, i.e. *bring to the birth*, *Impf.* 1 s. הַאֲנִי אַשְׁבִּיר וְלֹא אוֹלִיד Is 66^{9} ('י subj.; cf. מַשְׁבֵּר infr.). †**Hoph.** *be broken, shattered* (in heart), *Pf.* 1 s. עַל־שֶׁבֶר בַּת־עַמִּי הָשְׁבָּרְתִּי Je 8^{21}.

7667 †I. שֶׁבֶר, שֵׁבֶר **n.m.** $^{\text{Je 4, 5}}$ **breaking, fracture, crushing, breach, crash**;—abs. שֶׁבֶר Is 51^{19} +, שָׁבֶר La 3^{47} Pr 17^{19}, cstr. שֶׁבֶר Is 1^{28} +, שֵׁבֶר Am 6^{6} +; sf. שִׁבְרִי Je 10^{19}, etc.; pl. שְׁבָרִים Jos 7^{5} Jb 41^{17} (dub., v. infr.), sf. שְׁבָרֶיהָ ψ 60^{4};—**1.** *breaking* of pottery Is 30^{14}, *fracture* of member, limb Lv 21^{19} 24^{20} (H), esp. fig. of people personif. שׁ׳ יוֹסֵף Am 6^{6}, cf. Is 30^{26} (|| מַחַץ מַכָּתוֹ), Je 8^{21} 10^{19} 14^{17} 30^{12} (|| מַכָּה), v^{15} (|| מַכְאֹב), La 2^{11} 3^{48} 4^{10}, also (c. רפא, רפה *heal*) Je 6^{14} 8^{11} La 2^{13} ψ 60^{4}, cf. Na 3^{19}; of sinners Is 1^{28}; *shattering*, crushing, of wall (in fig.) Is 30^{13}; שׁ׳ גָּדוֹל (|| רָעָה) Je 4^{6} 6^{1}, שׁ׳ עַל־שׁ׳ 4^{20}; שֹׁד וָשׁ׳ Is 59^{7} 60^{18} Je 48^{3}, cf. Is 51^{19}; הַשֵּׁאת וְהַשׁ׳ La 3^{47}; זַעֲקַת שׁ׳ Is 15^{5}, cf. Je 48^{5}; of individ. Pr 16^{18} 17^{19} 18^{12}; fig., שׁ׳ רוּחַ *crushing* of spirit, cf. Pr 15^{4}; so (רוּחַ om.) מִשְּׁבָרִים Jb 41^{17} *from terror*, Di De, cf. Bi, but dub.; Buhl Bu conj. מִשְׁבְּרֵי יָם, Gie מִשְּׁנָיו גִּבֹּרִים, Du מִשְׁמָרִים. **2.** *crashing*, Zp 1^{10} (|| יְלָלָה, קוֹל צְעָקָה), Je 50^{22} (|| מִלְחָמָה), 51^{54} (|| קוֹל זְעָקָה). **3.** *breaking* of a dream, i.e. its interpretation (*solution* of
7671 mystery) Ju 7^{15} (cf. GFM). **4.** הַשְּׁבָרִים Jos 7^{5}, perhaps (Di Benn Steuern) *the quarries*, as n.pr.loc., 𝔙 Sabarim (> 𝔊 𝔖 𝔗 הַשְּׁבָרִם).—שִׁבְרִי Ez 32^{9}, read שִׁבְיְךָ 𝔊 Co Sta Berthol Krae (not Toy).

7669 †II. שֶׁבֶר **n.pr.m.** a Calebite 1 Ch 2^{48}; Σαβερ, A Σεβερ, 𝔊L Σαβαρ.

7665 שָׁבוּר Lv 22^{22} v. √ **Qal.** p. 990

7670 †שִׁבָּרוֹן **n.[m.]** **breaking, crushing**;—fig.; cstr. שִׁבְּרוֹן מָתְנַיִם Ez 21^{11} (emotional distress; || מְרִירוּת), read שִׁבָּ׳ also (for MT שִׁבָּרוֹן) 23^{33} Co Berthol Krae; *crushing* of opponents Je 17^{18}.

4866 †מַשְׁבֵּר **n.[m.]** **place of breach**, i.e. mouth of womb;—בָּאוּ בָנִים עַד־מ׳ וְכֹחַ אַיִן לְלֵדָה 2 K 19^{3} = Is 37^{3} (fig. of helplessness); cstr. מַשְׁבֵּר בָּנִים Ho 13^{13} (fig. of opportunity).

†[מִשְׁבָּר] **n.[m.]** **breaker**, of sea;—pl. cstr. 4867
מִשְׁבְּרֵי־יָם ψ 93^{4} (|| קֹלוֹת מַיִם רַבִּים; in comp. of 'י's majesty); fig. of calamities, מִשְׁבְּרֵי־מָוֶת 2 S 22^{5} (חֶבְלֵי־מָוֶת in || ψ 18^{5}); as sent by 'י, מִשְׁבָּרֶיךָ ψ 88^{8}, מ׳ וְגַלֶּיךָ 42^{8} Jon 2^{4}.—Jb 41^{17} v. I. שֶׁבֶר. 7667 above

†III. שֶׁבֶר **n.[m.]** **corn, grain**, as food stuff 7668
(perh. *broken*, i.e. *threshed*, Hoffm $^{\text{ZAW iii (1883), 122}}$ SS Siegf $^{\text{Ne 10, 32}}$; > Kö $^{\text{ii. 1. 19 n}}$ *breaking out*, i.e. sprouting (as chief fruit of soil); hence NH שִׁבָּרוֹן *price of corn*);—שׁ׳ abs. Gn 42^{1} +; cstr. v^{19}; sf. שִׁבְרָם v^{26}, שִׁבְרוֹ 44^{2};—*corn, grain* $42^{1.2.19.26}$ 43^{2} 44^{2} 47^{14} (acc. cogn.), Am 8^{5} (*id.*); so perh. (for בַּר) Gn 42^{3} Lag $^{\text{BN 230}}$; כָּל־שׁ׳ Ne 10^{32} *all kinds of grain*.

†[שָׁבַר] **vb. denom.** buy grain;—**Qal** 7666
Impf. 2 mpl. תִּשְׁבְּרוּ Dt 2^{6}, 1 pl. נִשְׁבְּרָה Gn 43^{4}; *Imv.* mpl. שִׁבְרוּ 42^{2} +; *Inf. cstr.* לִשְׁבֹּר v^{3} +, לִשְׁבָּר־ v^{7} +; *Pt.* mpl. שֹׁבְרִים 47^{14};—*buy grain* for food Gn 41^{57} (v^{56} v. **Hiph.**), 42^{2} (שֶׁבֶר in v^{a}), v^{5}; c. acc. אֹכֶל v$^{7.10}$ $43^{2.4.20.22}$ 44^{25} Dt 2^{6} (מִן pers.); c. acc. בַּר Gn 42^{3}, שֶׁבֶר 47^{14}; fig. Is 55^{1}, c. acc. יַיִן וְחָלָב v^{1}. **Hiph.** *Impf.* 1 pl. נַשְׁבִּיר Am 8^{6}, etc.; *Pt.* מַשְׁבִּיר Gn 42^{6} Pr 11^{26};—*sell grain* (prop. cause to buy grain), c. לְ pers. Gn 42^{6} + v^{56} (read וַיַּשְׁבֵּר for MT וַיִּשְׁבֹּר Ol Di Gunk), c. acc. שֶׁבֶר Am 8^{5}, מַפַּל בַּר v^{6}, cf. Pr 11^{26}; c. sf. pers. + acc. אֹכֶל + בְּ pret. Dt 2^{28}.

שָׁבַת $_{71}$ **vb.** **cease, desist, rest** (As. *šabâtu*, 7673
prob. *cease, be completed* Dl ^{WB} Zim $^{\text{KAT 3. 593}}$ (Jen $^{\text{ZA iv (1889), 277 f.}}$ is sceptical); Ar. سَبَتَ *cut off, interrupt*; NH has שֶׁבֶת *neglect*, etc., Aram. שִׁבְתָּא *cost of neglect*);—**Qal** $_{27}$ *Pf.* 3 ms. שׁ׳ Gn 2^{3} +; 3 pl. שָׁבְתוּ La 5^{14}, etc.; *Impf.* 3 ms. יִשְׁבּוֹת Ho 7^{4}; יִשְׁבֹּת Pr 22^{10} + 2 t.; 3 fs. תִּשְׁבֹּת Lv 26^{35}; תִּשְׁבַּת v^{34} Ne 6^{3} +, etc.;—**1.** *cease:* (abs. 13 t.) of seasons Gn 8^{22} (J); manna Jos 5^{12} (P), etc., Is $14^{4.4}$ Ne 6^{3} +; c. מִן Ho 7^{4} + 3 t. **2.** *desist* from labour, *rest:* **a.** c. מִן (of God) Gn $2^{2.3}$ (P). **b.** מִן om., בְּ temp. Ex 23^{12} (E), 16^{30} 34^{21} (J), 31^{17} (P); בֶּחָרִישׁ וּבַקָּצִיר שׁ׳ 34^{21} (J; i.e., even in these busy seasons). **c.** land in 7th year Lv $26^{34.35.35}$ (H), 2 Ch 36^{21}.—Lv 23^{32} 25^{2} v. [שָׁבַת] vb. denom. infr. †**Niph.** *Pf.* 3 ms. נִשְׁבַּת Is 17^{3} + 2 t.; pl. נִשְׁבְּתוּ Ez 6^{6};—*cease:* abs. Ez 6^{6} 30^{18} 33^{28}; c. מִן Is 17^{3}. **Hiph.** $_{40}$ *Pf.* 3 ms. הִשְׁבִּית Ru 4^{14} +; 2 ms. הִשְׁבַּתָּ ψ 89^{45} 119^{119}, etc.; *Impf.* 3 ms. יַשְׁבִּית Pr 18^{18} Dn 9^{27}; וַיַּשְׁבֵּת 2 K 23^{11} 2 Ch 16^{5}, etc.; *Inf. cstr.* הַשְׁבִּית ψ 8^{3}; לַשְׁבִּית Am 8^{4} (Ges $^{\text{§ 53 q}}$); *Imv.* mpl. הַשְׁבִּיתוּ Is 30^{11}; *Pt.* מַשְׁבִּית Je 16^{9}

ψ 46[10];—**1.** *cause to cease, put an end to:* c. acc. mirth Ho 2[13], work 2 Ch 16[5] Ne 4[5]; sacrifice Dn 9[27]; war ψ 46[10], cf. Is 13[11] Ez 7[24] Pr 18[18] + 6 t., + הִשׁ׳ קוֹל שָׂשׂוֹן מִן + Je 7[34] 16[9], cf. 48[33]. **2.** = *exterminate, destroy:* c. acc. 2 K 23[5.11] Am 8[4] (Now conj. העשקים), Ho 1[4] ψ 8[3] 119[119]; c. acc. + מִן, Je 36[29], מִן הָאָרֶץ Lv 26[6] (H), Ez 34[25]; אלילים 30[13] Dt 32[26]. **3.** *cause to desist* from: c. מִן Ez 16[41] 34[10] Ex 5[5] (E = give rest from); לְבִלְתִּי inf. Jos 22[25] (P). **4.** *remove* (= הֵסִיר מִן): c. מִן Ez 23[27.48] ψ 89[45] (txt. dub.: rd. הִשְׁבַּתּוֹ [3] 𝔊 Du; מַטֵּה הֹדוֹ Herz Che, v. also sub [טְהָר]); leaven מבתים Ex 12[15] (P); הַשׁ׳ אֶת־ק׳ ישׂר׳ מִפָּנֵינוּ Is 30[11]. **5.** *cause to fail,* let be lacking: salt מֵעַל מִנְחָתֶךָ Lv 2[12] (P); acc. pers. + ל pers. Je 48[35] Ru 4[14].

7674 †II. שֶׁבֶת **n.f.** cessation (dub.) Pr 20[3] (c. מֵרִיב, 𝔊 ἀποστρέφεσθαι = שׁוּב); שִׁבְתּוֹ Ex 21[19] i.e. from work = his loss of time (but Di I. שֶׁבֶת, p. 443 f.).—Is 30[7] perh. = *a sitting still* (indolently) √ישׁב, but prob. crpt., v. Du Che al.

7676 שַׁבָּת [111] **n.f.** [Ex 31.14+] and **m.** [Is 66.2.6] (under infl. of יוֹם in freq. יוֹם הַשׁ׳, Albr [ZAW xvi (1896), 47]) **Sabbath** (= שׁבת + ת; NH שַׁבָּת, Aram. שַׁבְּתָא, ܫܒܬܐ; perh. As. *šabattum* (‖ *um nuḫ libbi, day of rest of heart* (i.e. propitiation) [of deity]: only in lex. tablets); cf. Lotz [Quaest. de hist. Sabbati, 1883] Jen [ZA iv (1889), 274 ff.] (doubts connexion of As. word with Heb. Sabbath) Id [S.S. Times, Jan. 16, 1892, 35 f.] Muss-Arn [JBL xi (1892), 93] Schwally [Idiot. 127]; v. (more recently) Jastr [Am. J. Theol. ii (1898), 332 ff.] Toy [TBL xviii (1899), 190 ff.] Dr [Hast. DB SABBATH (1902)] Zim [KAT3. 592 ff.; ZMG 1904, 199 ff.] [15th day of month so called] [458 ff.]);—abs. שׁ׳ Ex 16[25] + 64 t.; cstr. שַׁבַּת v[23] + 10 t.; sf. שַׁבַּתּוֹ Nu 28[10] + 3 t. sf.; pl. שַׁבָּתוֹת Lv 23[15] + 7 t.; cstr. שַׁבְּתֹת v[38] 25[8.8]; sf. שַׁבְּתוֹתַי Is 56[4] +, etc.;—**1.** *sabbath:* **a.** primitive שׁ׳ ליהוה Ex 16[25] (J), 20[10] = Dt 5[14] (ten words) Lv 23[3] (P); הַשׁ׳ Ex 16[29] (J); בְּיוֹם הַשְּׁבִיעִי שׁ׳ Ex 16[26] (J); on seventh day יוֹם הַשַּׁבָּת 20[8.11] = Dt 5[12.15] (ten words), so throughout; Ex 31[15] + 3 t. P, Je 17[21] Ez 46[4] Ne 10[32] + 9 t., + (‖ new moon) Is 1[13] Ez 46[1] 2 K 4[23] Am 8[5], cf. Is 66[23.23], also חג and מועד Ho 2[13]; time of change of watch in temple 2 K 11[5.7.9.9] = 2 Ch 23[4.8.8]; מיסך הַשׁ׳ (in temple) 2 K 16[18]; orig. observed simply by *abstinence from labour* Ex 20[9.10] = Dt 5[12-14], Ex 23[12] (E), 34[21] (J; Br [Hex. 181-195]). **b.** Deut. reason for day is deliverance fr. Egypt Dt 5[15], hence its consecration, לְקַדְּשׁוֹ v[12] = Ex 20[8]; קדשׁ יום השׁ׳ Je 17[22.24.27] (esp. no load carried), Ez 20[20] 44[24]. **c.** intensified by antith. חלל שׁ׳ Ez 20[13] + 5 t. Ez, cf. Ne 13[18]. Phrases in H: שׁמר (ה)שׁ׳ Lv 19[3.30] 26[2], then P Ex 31[13.14.16]; cf. Is 56[2.4.6]; קדושׁ י׳, יוֹם קָדְשִׁי: 58[13.13] (c. כבד). H also שַׁבְּתֹתֵיכֶם Lv 26[35]; מִמָּחֳרַת הַשׁ׳ 23[11.15.16]; שַׁבְּתוֹתַי 19[3.30] 26[2] Is 56[4], Ez 20[12] 22[26], + 8 t. Ez; ‖ מוֹעֵד La 2[6]. **d.** P gives as basis God's resting Ex 20[11] 31[17]; שׁבתות י׳ Lv 23[38]; שׁ׳ קדשׁ ליהוה Ex 16[23], cf. Ne 9[14], שׁ׳ שׁבתון Ex 31[15] 35[2] Lv 23[3]; עשׂה השׁ׳ Ex 31[16], עֹלַת שׁ׳ בְּשַׁבַּתּוֹ Nu 28[10], cf. Is 66[23]; בְּיוֹם הַשׁ׳ בְּיוֹם הַשׁ׳ Lv 24[8] *on every sabbath,* abbr. שַׁבַּת שַׁבָּת 1 Ch 9[32]; לַשַּׁבָּתוֹת, ‖ מועדים + חֳדָשִׁים 23[31] + 3 t. Chr, Ne 10[34] (ל om. by error); work punished by stoning Nu 15[32.36]; trade prohib. Ne 10[32] 13[15-21]. **2.** *day of atonement* is a שַׁבַּת שַׁבָּתוֹן Lv 16[31] 23[32] (P), cf. שַׁבַּת שַׁבָּת v[32] (P). **3.** *sabbath year,* שַׁבַּת שַׁבָּתוֹן Lv 25[4] (H); שַׁבָּת לַיהוה v[2.4] (H); רצה (הארץ) שַׁבְּתוֹתֶיהָ 26[34.34.43] (H), 2 Ch 36[21]. **4.** = *week* (?): שֶׁבַע שַׁבָּתוֹת Lv 23[15] (H), seven *sabbaths* or *weeks;* שֶׁבַע שַׁבְּתֹת (ה)שָּׁנִים 25[8.8] (H) seven sabbaths or weeks (of years), uncertain (v. Mk 16[2.9] Lk 18[12] Mt 28[1], cf. JAram. usage); poss. שַׁבָּת Is 66[23] = *week* (Du). **5.** שַׁבַּת הָאָרֶץ Lv 25[6] (H) = *produce* in sabbath year (growing of itself).

†[שָׁבַת] **vb. denom.** keep, observe (sab- 7673
bath);—**Qal,** c. acc. cogn.; *Pf.* 3 fs. וְשָׁבְתָה הָאָרֶץ שַׁבָּת לי׳ Lv 25[2]; 2 mpl. מֵעֶרֶב עַד־עֶרֶב תִּשְׁבְּתוּ שַׁבַּתְּכֶם 23[32] (P).

†שַׁבָּתוֹן **n.m.** sabbath observance, sab- 7677
batism;—שׁ׳ Ex 16[23] + 10 t. P; usu. phrase שַׁבַּת שַׁבָּתוֹן *sabbath of sabbatic observance;*—**1.** of weekly sabbath Ex 31[15] 35[2] Lv 23[3] Ex 16[23] (שַׁבָּתוֹן שַׁבַּת קֹדֶשׁ, prob. transp.). **2.** day of atonement Lv 16[31] 23[32]. **3.** sabbatical year Lv 25[4], cf. שְׁנַת שַׁבָּתוֹן v[5]. **4.** שׁ׳ alone of feast of trumpets Lv 23[24], and of first and eighth days of feast of tabernacles v[39.39].

†שַׁבְּתַי **n.pr.** Levite;—Ezr 10[15] Ne 8[7] 11[16]; 7678
Σαβ(β)αθαι, etc.

†[מִשְׁבָּת] **n.[m.]** cessation, annihila- 4868
tion;—pl. sf. עַל־מִשְׁבַּתֶּהָ La 1[7] (𝔊 ἐπὶ κατοικεσίᾳ αὐτῆς = עַל־שִׁבְתָּהּ; Marti [LCB 1895, Mar. 2, 282] עַל־שְׁבִיָּתָהּ *her captivity*).

שׁגא v. שָׁגָה. p. 993 7681

†[שָׁגַג] **vb.** go astray, commit sin or error 7683
(‖ שׁוּג, שׁגה);—**Qal** *Pf.* שָׁגַג Lv 5[18]; *Pt.* שֹׁגֵג Jb 12[16] ψ 119[67]; f. שֹׁגֶגֶת Nu 15[28];—**1.** *err,* mentally Jb 12[16]. **2.** *sin* ignorantly, inad-

vertently, Lv 5^{18} Nu 15^{28} (P), cf. ψ 119^{67}.—בְּשַׁגָּם Gn 6^{3} perhaps *Inf. cstr.* sf., *by reason of their going astray*, v. Ges$^{§ 67 p}$ Ew Dr al.; >Vrss *for that he also* is flesh. אֲבִישַׁג, v. p. 4^{b}.

7684 †שְׁגָגָה **n.f. sin of error, inadvertence**;—abs. ׳שׁ Nu 15^{25}+; sf. שִׁגְגָתוֹ Lv 5^{18}; שִׁגְגָתָם Nu 15^{25};—*error* (opp. sins of intention, or בְּיָד רָמָה) only P Ec: Nu 15^{25}=Ec 5^{5}, cf. Ec 10^{5}; על ׳שׁ Lv 5^{18} Nu 15^{25}; חטא בִּשׁ׳ Lv $4^{2.22.27}$ 5^{15} Nu $15^{27.28}$+ (vb. om.) v^{26}; עשׂה בִּשׁ׳ Lv 4^{22} Nu 15^{29}+ (לִשׁ׳) v^{24}; אכל קֹדֶשׁ בִּשׁ׳ Lv 22^{14}; מַכֵּה־נֶפֶשׁ בִּשׁ׳ of unintended killing Nu $35^{11.15}$=Jos $20^{3.9}$ (‖ in D בִּבְלִי־דַעַת).—1 S 14^{24} v. שׁגה. below

7692 שִׁגָּיוֹן v. p. 993^{b}.

7686 †[שָׁגָה] **vb. go astray, err** (Aram. שְׁגָא, ܫܓܐ *id.*);—**Qal** *Pf.* 1 s. שָׁגִיתִי Jb 6^{24} 19^{4}, etc.; *Impf.* 3 ms. יִשְׁגֶּה Pr 5^{23}, etc.; *Inf. cstr.* שְׁגוֹת 19^{27}; *Pt.* שֹׁגֶה Ez 45^{20} Pr 20^{1}, etc.;—**1.** *err, stray*, of flock Ez 34^{6} (fig.). **2.** *swerve, meander, reel* or *roll*, in drunkenness, ב of drink Is $28^{7.7}$; =*be intoxicated*, Pr 20^{1}; so with (בּ) love $5^{19.20}$; שׁ׳ בָּרֹאֶה Is 28^{7}. **3.** *go astray*, morally, 1 S
7684 26^{21} Pr 5^{23} Jb 6^{24} 19^{4}, + 1 S 14^{24} (rdg. שׁ׳ שְׁגָגָה) Th We Dr Now (after 𝔊; otherwise Bu HPS); c. מִן, of י׳'s commands ψ $119^{21.118}$, מִן of words of knowledge Pr 19^{27}. **4.** specif. *commit sin of ignorance*, inadvertence Lv 4^{13} Nu 15^{22} (P) Ez 45^{20} (cf. שׁגג). **Hiph.** *lead astray*: **1.** lit., *Pt.* מַשְׁגֶּה Dt 27^{18} (בַּדָּרֶךְ). **2.** מַשׁ׳ mentally =*mislead* Jb 12^{16}. **3.** morally, *Pt.* Pr 28^{10} (בְּדֶרֶךְ רָע); *Impf.* 2 ms. sf. תַּשְׁגֵּנִי, c. מִן of God's commands ψ 119^{10}; + perhaps Jb 12^{23} *leadeth* nations *astray* (𝔊𝔖, i.e. וַיַּשְׁגֵּם for וַיַּנְחֵם).

7691 †[שְׁגִיאָה Kö$^{ii. 1. 197}$] **n.f. error**;—pl. abs. שְׁגִיאוֹת ψ 19^{13}; read שְׁגָגוֹת?.

4870' †מִשְׁגֶּה **n.m. mistake** Gn 43^{12} (J).

7681 †שָׁגֵה (שָׁגֵא van d. H.) **n.pr.m.** father of a hero of David 1 Ch 11^{34}.—B Σωλα, A Σαγη, 𝔊L Σαμαια.

7688 †[שָׁגַח] **vb. Hiph. gaze** (NH *id.*, Ecclus 40^{29} 50^{5}; late Rabb. הַשְׁגָּחָה=*providence* (from ψ 33^{14}); JAram. שְׁגַח *gaze, consider*);—c. אֶל־ pers.: *Pf.* 3 ms. הִשְׁגִּיחַ ψ 33^{14} (of י׳; מִן loc.); *Impf.* 3 mpl. רֹאֶיךָ אֵלֶיךָ יַשְׁגִּיחוּ Is 14^{16} *they that see thee, at thee shall they gaze* (‖ אֵלֶיךָ יִתְבּוֹנָנוּ; cf. משגיח על שלחן Ecclus 40^{29}); abs.: *Pt.* מַשְׁגִּיחַ Ct 2^{9} (c. מִן *from* (the outside of) *the windows*).

†שִׁגָּיוֹן doubtful word, ψ 7^{1} (title), Ew De al. 7692
from √שׁגה *go astray, reel*, i.e. wild, passionate song, with rapid changes of rhythm; cf. Lag$^{BN 201 f.}$ who cp. שִׁגָּעוֹן, √שׁגע; 𝔊 ψαλμός, rd. prob. מִזְמוֹר; pl. שִׁגְיֹנוֹת Hb 3^{1} (title), rd. נְגִינוֹת, so 𝔊.

†[שָׁגַל] **vb. violate, ravish** (Mass. think verb obscene, and subst. שָׁכַב);—**Qal** *Impf.* 3 ms. sf. יִשְׁגָּלֶנָּה Dt 28^{30} Kt (Qr יִשְׁכָּבֶנָּה). **Niph.** *Impf.* 3 fpl. תִּשָּׁגַלְנָה Is 13^{16} Zc 14^{2} *women shall be ravished* (both Kt; Qr תִּשָּׁכַבְנָה). **Pu.**<**Qal pass.** (Ges$^{§ 52 e}$) *Pf.* 2 fs. אֵיפֹה לֹא שֻׁגַּלְתְּ Je 3^{2} *where hast thou not been ravished?* (Qr שֻׁכַּבְתְּ). 7693

†שֵׁגָל **n. f.** (queen-)**consort** Ne 2^{6} ψ 45^{10}, + perh. Ju $5^{30 c}$ v. שָׁלָל (Palm. n.pr.f. שגל Lzb^{372} SAC^{111} GACooke^{309}; Thes^{1363} cp. '*queen*,' orig. '*woman*'; but שׁ׳ loan-word acc. to Lag$^{BN 51, 153}$ and not from √[שָׁגַל]). 7694

†[שָׁגַע] **Pu.be mad** (Ar. سَجَعَ *coo*, of male pigeon, *utter long whinny*, of camel (cf. Hoffm$^{ZAW iii (1883), 89}$ RS$^{JPhil. xiv. 119 f.}$ Goldziher$^{Arab. Philol. i. 59 ff.}$ Lag$^{BN 202}$); Eth. ሰገወ: *be mad* (*n* ins., Di^{1055} Ba$^{ES 50}$); As. *šegû, rage, howl*; on meaning in Heb. v. esp. We$^{Skizzen iii. 130}$);—**Pu.** *Pt.* as adj.: pred. וְהָיִיתָ מְשֻׁגָּע Dt 28^{34} *thou shalt be maddened* (מִן because of), fig. for driven to despair; מ׳ of proph., contemptuously Ho 9^{7}, כָּל־אִישׁ מ׳ וּמִתְנַבֵּא Je 29^{26}, as subst. 2 K 9^{11}; pl. מְשֻׁגָּעִים 1 S 21^{16} *madmen*. **Hithp.** *shew madness*; *Pt.* אִישׁ מִשְׁתַּגֵּעַ 1 S 21^{15}; *Inf. cstr.* לְהִשְׁתַּגֵּעַ v^{16}. 7696

†שִׁגָּעוֹן **n.m. madness**;—הִכָּה בְּשׁ׳ Dt 28^{28} *smite with madness*, fig. of wild and helpless panic (‖ תִּמְהוֹן לֵבָב, עִוָּרוֹן), Zc 12^{4} (‖ תִּמָּהוֹן); בְּשׁ׳ 2 K 9^{20} (hyperb.) *madly*. 7697

שׁגר (√of foll.; cf. Aram. שְׁגַר *cast, throw*, Ex 13^{12} 𝔗^{J} *drop* young, ܫܓܪ *misit, demisit* (rare); cf. Dr$^{Dt 7, 13}$).

†שֶׁגֶר **n.** [**f.** Albr$^{ZAW xvi (1896), 70}$] **offspring, young** of beasts (שגר *id.* Ecclus 40^{19}; cf. We$^{Skizzen iii. 170}$);—cstr. ׳שׁ;—כָּל־פֶּטֶר שֶׁגֶר בְּהֵמָה Ex 13^{12} (J; כָּל־פֶּ׳ רֶחֶם precedes); also שְׁגַר אֲלָפֶיךָ Dt 7^{13} $28^{4.18.51}$ (all ‖ עַשְׁתְּרֹת צֹאנֶךָ). 7698

שַׁד, II. שׁד *breast*, v. שׁדה. p. 994 7699

†[שֵׁד] **n.**[**m.**] appar. **demon** (loan-word from As. *šêdu*, a protecting spirit, esp. of bull-colossus, Dl$^{Pa 153 f.; WB 646}$ COT$^{Dt 32, 17}$ Zim$^{KAT 3. 460 f., 455, 649}$; cf. Aram. שֵׁידָא, ܫܐܕܐ *demon*, and (perh.) Ph. 7700

n.pr. גדשר Nö[ZMG xlii (1888), 481] Lzb[249]; orig. √ שוד (=Ar. سَادَ *rule*) acc. to Thes Baud[Sem. Rel. i. 130 ff.] Dl[WB] al.; > Ar. سعد (III, IV *aid*), Hom[ZMG xlvi (1892), 529], against this Zim[l.c.]);—יִזְבְּחוּ לַשֵּׁדִים לֹא אֱלֹהַּ Dt 32^{17} (cf. Dr), ψ 106^{37} (human sacrifice).

7701 I. שֹׁד v. שׁדד. below

7703 **[שָׁדַד]**$_{56}$ **vb. deal violently with, despoil, devastate, ruin** (NH *id.*, Niph.; Ar. سَدَّ *stop up, obstruct, arrest, make firm*; Eth. ሰደደ: *expel*; As. *šadâdu* is *draw, drag*);—**Qal** *Pf.* 3 pl. consec. וְשָׁדְדוּ Ez 32^{12}; sf. שַׁדּוּנִי ψ 17^{9};
7736 *Impf.* 3 ms. יָשׁוּד (metapl., cf. Ges§67q Bae) ψ 91^{6}, sf. יְשָׁדֵּם (Ges§67n) Pr 11^{3} Qr (Kt Pf. ושדם), יְשָׁדְדֵם Je 5^{6}; *Imv.* mpl. שָׁדְדוּ (Ges§67cc) 49^{28}; *Inf. abs.* שָׁדוֹד Mi 2^{4}; cstr. לִשְׁדוֹד Je 47^{4} (Ges§45g), cf. also שֹׁד Ho 10^{14}; *Pt. act.* שֹׁדֵד Je 6^{26}+, etc.; *pass.* שָׁדוּד Ju 5^{27}+, f. שְׁדוּדָה ψ 137^{8};—*violently destroy*, pers., =*slay* Ju 5^{27} (pass.), Je 5^{6} (wolf subj.; ‖ הִכָּה); acc. Philistines 47^{4} (‖ הִכְרִית), v^{4} (subj. י׳); =*devastate*, acc. בָּבֶל (subj. י׳) Je 51^{55}, cf. ψ 137^{8} (rd. prob. הַשֹּׁדֵדָה We Du, cf. Ew Hi הַשָּׁדוּדָה v. Kö[ii. 194]); אֶת־גְּאוֹן מִצְרַיִם Ez 32^{12} (‖ נִשְׁמַד), cf. Ho 10^{14}, אֶת־מַרְעִיתָם Je 25^{36} (subj. י׳), abs. Is 21^{2} (‖ בָּגַד), 33^{1} (on use of pt. v. Ges§120b), pass. v^{1} (‖ בָּגַד), אַתְּ שָׁדוּד Je 4^{30} (Gf Ba[NB 179], but dub.; < Du שְׁדוּדָה); =*despoil*, acc. pers. Je 49^{28}; =*bring* pers. *to ruin* Mi 2^{4} (Inf. abs. + Niph. q.v.), Pr 11^{3}; weaker, *assail* ψ 17^{9}; elsewhere *Pt. act.* as subst. *devastator* (*despoiler*?): of national foes Is 16^{4} 21^{2} 33^{1} Je 6^{26} + 8 t. Je; שׁוֹדְדֵי לַיְלָה Ob^{5} (‖ גַּנָּבִים) del. Now GASm; personal foe Jb 15^{21}; representing wicked in gen. 12^{6} (‖ מַרְגִּיזֵי אֵל). †**Niph.** *Pf.* 1 pl. שָׁדוֹד נְשַׁדֻּנוּ (Ges§67u Kö[i. 342 f.]) *we are utterly ruined.* †**Pi.** *Impf.* 2 ms. אַל־תְּשַׁדֵּד רִבְצוֹ Pr 24^{15} *assault not his dwelling-place* (‖ אַל־תֶּאֱרֹב); *Pt.* as subst. מְשַׁדֶּד־אָב Pr 19^{26} *he who assaults, maltreats* (his) father (‖ יַבְרִיחַ אֵם). †**Pu.** *Pf.* 3 ms. שֻׁדַּד Is 15^{1}+, 3 fs. שֻׁדְּדָה Je 4^{20}+, שֻׁדְּדָה Na 3^{7} (Ges§52q), etc.;—*be devastated*, of city Is 15$^{1.1}$ 23^{1} Je 48^{1} 49^{3} Na 3^{7}, country or nation Je 4^{20}, cf. v^{13} 9^{18} 48$^{15.20}$ 49^{10}, dwellings (אֹהֶל) Je 4^{20} 10^{20}, trees Zc 11^{2} (del. Sta[ZAW i (1881), 25]), cf. v^{33}, strength of ships Is 23^{14}, field (by drought) Jo 1^{10}, crop v^{10}. †**Pō'el** *violently destroy*: *Impf.* 3 ms. יְשֹׁדֵד מַצֵּבוֹתָם Ho 10^{2} (‖ יַעֲרֹף מִזְבְּחוֹתָם). †**Hoph.** *Impf.* (or **Qal** *pass. Impf.*? cf. Ges§53u) *be devastated*: 3 ms. כָּל־מִבְצָרַיִךְ יוּשַּׁד Ho 10^{14} (of Ephr., < We pl. יושדו); 2 ms. תּוּשַּׁד Is 33^{1} (subj. שׁוֹדֵד, v. **Qal**).

†I. **שֹׁד, שׁוֹד** (v. infr.) **n.m. violence, havoc,** 7701
devastation, ruin;—שׁ׳ abs. Ho 7^{13}+; cstr. Is 22^{4}+;—**1.** *violence, havoc*, as social sin: חָמָס וָשֹׁד Am 3^{10} Je 6^{7} 20^{8} Ez 45^{9}, ח׳ וְשׁ׳ Hb 1^{3}, כָּזָב וָשֹׁד Ho 12^{2} (l. וָשָׁוְא, 𝔊 We Marti al.), שׁ׳ וָשֶׁבֶר Is 59^{7} 60^{18} Pr 24^{2} (‖ עָמָל); שׁ׳ רְשָׁעִים Pr 21^{7}; c. genit. obj. שׁ׳ עֲנִיִּים ψ 12^{6}. **2.** *devastation, ruin*, for nation Ho 7^{13}, כְּשֹׁד מִשַּׁדַּי יָבוֹא Is 13^{6} (sim. of יוֹם י׳) = Jo 1^{15}, Is 16^{4} (Lo Gr Che Hpt Marti שֹׁדֵד; ‖ רֹמֵס), 22^{4}, שׁ׳ וָשֶׁבֶר 51^{19} Je 48^{3}; more gen. Am 5$^{9.9}$; for individ. Jb 5^{21} (van d. H. שׁוֹט), v^{22}; for beasts Hb 2^{17} (+ חֲמַס לְבָנוֹן).—Ho 10^{14} v. שדד *Inf.*—מִשֹּׁד (הָלְכוּ) Ho 9^{6} read אַשּׁוּר
We Now Marti.—II. שַׁד, v. שׁדה. below 7699

שַׁדַּי v. infr. אַשְׁדּוֹד v. p. 78; > here, Thes al. 795, 7706

שׁדה (√ of foll.; Ar. ثَدَى *moisten*, ثَدْيٌ *breast*; Aram. pl. תַּדְיָא, ܬܕܝܐ *breasts*; cf. Lag[BN 171]; Heb. n. orig. *שָׂדֶה Ba[NB 9], cf. Id.[ZMG xli (1887), 637]).

†**[שַׁד]** **n.m.**[Ho 9, 14] female **breast**;—abs. שַׁד 7699
La 4^{3}; elsewhere du. שָׁדַיִם Ho 9^{14}+, cstr. שְׁדֵי Ez 23^{21}+, sf. שָׁדַי Ct 1^{13} 8^{10}, שָׁדַיִךְ 4^{5}+, etc.;—*breast*: **1.** of woman Ho 2^{4} Ez 16^{7} 23$^{3.21}$ (שְׁדֵי נְעוּרָיִךְ ‖ דַּדַּיִךְ), v^{34} (> del. 𝔊 Codd. Co;—all these of personif. people), Ct 1^{13} 4^{5} 7$^{4.8.9}$ 8$^{8.10}$; of mother ψ 22^{10}, c. יָנַק *suck* Ct 8^{1} Jb 3^{12} Jo 2^{16}; Ho 9^{14} (v. [צָמַק]); עַתִּיקֵי מִשּׁ׳ Is 28^{9} i.e. those already weaned, mature (‖ גְּמוּלֵי מֵחָלָב).—Is 32^{12} v. [ספד]. **2.** of animal La 4^{3}. **3.** both human and animal, בִּרְכֹת שׁ׳ וָרָחַם Gn 49^{25} (poem in J).

†II. **שֹׁד** **n.m. id.** (cf. the rare Arab. ثُدٌّ, 7699
Lane[333] Ba[ZMG xli. 637]);—שׁ׳ abs., of mother Jb 24^{9}; cstr. (fig., c. יָנַק): שׁ׳ מְלָכִים Is 60^{16}, שׁ׳ תַּנְחֻמֶיהָ 66^{11}, i.e. the consolations of Jerusalem.

†**שְׁדֵיאוּר** **n.pr.m.** in Reuben (read prob. 7707
שְׁדֵי אוּר, שׁ׳ is *flame*, v. Nö[ZMG xv (1860), 809] Ne[Eg. 46] Gray[Prop. N. 169, 197]);—only in אֱלִיצוּר בֶּן־שׁ׳ Nu 1^{5} 2^{10} 7$^{30.35}$ 10^{18} (all P); Σεδιουρ.

†**שִׁדָּה** **n.f.** mng. unknown;—only s. et pl. 7705
שִׁדָּה וְשִׁדּוֹת Ec 2^{8}, apparently appos. of תַּעֲנוּגֹת (𝔊 οἰνοχόον καὶ οἰνοχόας, i.e. שָׁרָה וְשָׁרוֹת, from Aram. שְׁדָא *pour out* [but not spec. of wine]; Aq. κυλίκιον καὶ κυλίκια (cf. 𝔙), prob. fr. same √; Dl[Prol. 97] Kö[ii. 1. 161] Wildeb Siegf cp. As. *šadâdu*, *love* (Siegf 'Haremsperlen'), but this word
lacks evidence; poss. שָׂרָה וְשָׂרוֹת, v. I. שָׂרָה). 8282
p. 979

שַׁדַּי$_{48}$ **n.m. dei** (etym. dub. (1) Aq Sym 7706
Theod ἱκανός; Rabb שֶׁ + דַּי (self-)*sufficient*, no moderns. (2) = *almighty*, √ שׁדד + י = Thes De

Di Sta, or √שדה=שדד, n. intens. Ew^{§155c}, but שדד (q.v.) is *deal violently* not simply *mightily;* cf. 𝔊 παντοκράτωρ 14 (15) t. (but in Pent. אל שׁ׳ is ὁ Θεός μου, σου, etc.), 𝔙 mostly *omnipotens.* (3) < conject. for orig. שַׁדַי (v. שֵׁד) *my sovereign lord*, ‖ אֲדֹנָי, בעלי Nö$^{SBA\ 1880,\ 775;\ ZMG\ xlii\ (1888),\ 481}$; Hoffm$^{Ph.\ Inscr.\ 53}$; used of foreign deities (Dt 32^{17}), and so discredited (cf. בַּעַל).—> other conj., e.g. RS^{OTJC,424} √שדה *pour forth* (God as rain-giver); Dl$^{Pr\ 96\ sq.}$ As. *šadû, high, ilu šâdû'a*, Che$^{Comm.\ Is\ ii.\ 148}$, or *šadû, mountain*, also in n. pr.; v. further Dr$^{Gn\ 404\ ff.}$);—**1.** שַׁדַּי Nu 24$^{4.16}$ (JE, poem), and so as archaism Ru 1$^{20.21}$ ψ 68^{15} 91^{1} Jo 1^{15}=Is 13^{6}, Ez 1^{24} (del. Co); esp. Jb 5^{17}+30 t. Jb (+19^{29} Ew Di, rdg. שׁ׳ for שדין). **2.** אֵל שַׁדַּי Gn 49^{25} (poem; so read for אֵת שׁ׳, v. Sam 𝔊 𝔖 Saad, Heb. Codd.), and so, as archaism, divine name of patriarchs in P, Gn 17^{1} 28^{3} 35^{11} 48^{3} Ex 6^{3}, Gn 43^{14} (R^{P}); so Ez 10^{5} (del. Co; but 𝔊 Σαδδαι).

1779 שַׁדּוּן Jb 19^{29} v. דין p. 192^{b} supra.

שדם (√ of following; meaning unknown).

7709 †[**שְׁדֵמָה**] **n.f. field**;—only pl.: abs. שְׁדֵמוֹת
8309 Hb 3^{17} Je 31^{40} Qr (> Kt השרמות); cstr. שַׁדְמ(וֹ)ת Dt 32^{32}+2 t.;—*fields*, as cultivated Dt 32^{32}, also (c. vb. sg.) Is 16^{8} Hb 3^{17}; as locality 2 K 23^{4}, area Je 31^{40}.—שְׁדֵמָה Is 37^{27} v. שְׁדֵפָה.

7710 †[**שָׁדַף**] **vb. scorch, blight** (NH *id.;* Niph. Hithp. *be blighted;* JAram. שְׁדַף Ithpe. *burn* (up); Ar. سدف IV. *be dark*);—**Qal** *Pt. pass.* cstr., of ears of grain, שְׁדוּפֹת קָדִים Gn 41^{6} *scorched by a sirocco*, so שְׁדֻפוֹת ק׳ v^{23}, שׁ׳ הַקּ׳ v^{27} (all E).

7711 †**שְׁדֵפָה** **n.f. blighted or blasted thing**;— וּשׁ׳ לִפְנֵי קָמָה 2 K 19^{26} *a blasted thing before* (the) *standing grain*, i.e. before maturity (> שְׁדֵמָה *field*, as ‖ Is 37^{27}, cf. Di), but improb.; Th prop. וּשׁ׳ ל׳ קָדִים; Kit שְׁדֻף הַקָּדִים; We (and most since) וּשְׁדֵפָה׃ לִפְנֵי קָמָה וגו׳ (Che: וּשְׁפָיִים, for וּשְׁדֵפָה).

7711 †**שִׁדָּפוֹן** **n.m. blight**, of crops (Lag$^{BN\ 202}$ Vogelst$^{Landwirthsch.\ 56}$);—שׁ׳ abs. + יֵרָקוֹן Am 4^{9}, cf. Hg 2^{17}, Dt 28^{22} 1 K 8^{37}=2 Ch 6^{28}.

7714 †**שַׁדְרַךְ** **n.pr.m.** Bab. name given to חֲנַנְיָה, one of Daniel's comrades Dn 1^{7} (form and mng. dub.; Dl (cf. COT Dr) *Šudur-Aku, command of Aku;* Jen$^{Th\ LZ\ 1895,\ 328}$ thinks Pers. [**Khšatraka*]; Kohler$^{ZA\ iv\ (1889),\ 50}$ conj. מרדך, so Wkl$^{Altor.\ Forsch.\ iii.\ 47.57}$ Zim$^{KAT\ 3.\ 396}$).

שדשׁ (√ of foll.; Sab. סת, סדת, *six* Sab Denkm^{90} Hom$^{Chrest.\ 47.124}$; Ar. سَادِسٌ *sixth* (assim. of last cons.), سِتٌّ, سِتَّةٌ, *six;* Eth. ስስ፡ ሲድስት፡ *six;* As. *sudušu* (*s*!) *six-fold, seššu, sixth;* cf. also Aram. שֵׁית, שִׁתָּא, ܫܬܐ, ܫܬ *six*, Nab. שת, Palm. שתא Ldzb^{383} SAC^{118}).

שֵׁשׁ, שִׁשָּׁה $_{216}$ **n.m.** et **f. six**;—**m.** שֵׁשׁ (c. **n.f.**) Gn 31^{41}+120 t.; **f.** שִׁשָּׁה (c. **n.m.**) 30^{20}+ 39 t.; cstr. שֵׁשֶׁת Ex 23^{12}+30 t. (6+10=16 are additional);—*six* (Hex chiefly P): **1.** no other num.: **a.** bef. n.pl. 75 t.: e.g. שֵׁשׁ שָׁנִים Ex 21^{2} (E)+11 t., שֵׁשׁ אַמּוֹת 1 S 17^{4}+8 t.; שֵׁשׁ בָּאַמָּה †1 K 6^{6}; שִׁשָּׁה בָנִים Gn 30^{20} (E)+2 t.; שֵׁשֶׁת יָמִים Ex 23^{12} (E)+14 t.; after n. (late) †Ex 28^{2} Jos 15$^{59.62}$ (all P), 1 Ch 4^{27} 26^{17} Ne 5^{18}; rarely n. om. Lv 24^{6} (P)+ (distrib. 2 S 21^{20}=1 Ch 20^{6}). **b.** =ordin. שְׁנַת שֵׁשׁ לְחִזְק׳ 2 K 18^{10} (Ges^{§134o}). **2.** 16, c. **n.f.**: שֵׁשׁ עֶשְׂרֵה, bef. נֶפֶשׁ Gn 46^{18} (P), שָׁנָה 2 K 13^{10}+9 t., בָּנוֹת 2 Ch 13^{21}; after עָרִים Jos 15^{41} 19^{22} (P); c. **n.m.** שִׁשָּׁה עָשָׂר, bef. אֲדָנִים Ex 26^{25} 36^{30} (P), also אֶלֶף, 1000, Nu 31^{40}+(P); after בָּנִים 1 Ch 4^{27}, etc.; =ordin. 16*th* 1 Ch 24^{14} 25^{23}+, יוֹם שׁ׳ ע׳ 2 Ch 29^{17}. **3.** 600=שֵׁשׁ מֵאוֹת, Gn 7^{6} (P)+63 t.; 6000=שֵׁשֶׁת אֲלָפִים Nu 3^{34} (P)+ 8 t.; שׁ׳ אֶלֶף Ju 20^{15}+2 t. **4.** c. tens, שׁ׳ foll. Gn 46^{26}+13 t., precedes Nu 31^{44} (P). **5.** שׁ׳ as round no., חָמֵשׁ או־שׁ׳ 2 K 13^{19}, cf. Jb 5^{19} Pr 6^{16}. 8337

שִׁשִּׁי **m.** $_{22}$ **שִׁשִּׁית** **f.** $_{6}$ **adj. num. ordin. sixth**;—(הַ)יוֹם הַשִּׁשִּׁי Gn 1^{31}+5 t., etc.; בַּשָּׁנָה הַשִּׁשִּׁית Lv 25^{21} Ez 8^{1}, etc.; cstr. שִׁשִּׁית הַהִין Ez 4^{11} *6th part of the hin*, cf. 45^{13} 46^{14}; read שׁ׳ also 45^{13b} (v. [שִׁשָּׁה] infra). 8345 8341

שִׁשִּׁים $_{59}$ **n. indecl. sixty**;—bef. n. sg.: city Dt 3^{4}+4 t., cubit 1 K 6^{2} Ez 40^{14}, man 2 K 25^{19} =Je 52^{25}, day Lv 12^{5}, etc.; n.pl. בָּנוֹת 2 Ch 11^{21}, cf. Ct 3^{7}; after n.pl. Nu 7$^{88.88.88}$ 2 Ch 3^{3} 11^{21}+; שִׁשִּׁים אֶלֶף 2 Ch 12^{3}+; שׁ׳ foll. units Gn 5^{15}+ 12 t.; שׁ׳ precedes unit Is 7^{8}+12 t.; שׁ׳ foll. 100 (1000) Ezr 8^{10}+11 t.; precedes Gn 5^{18}+8 t. 8346

†[**שִׁשָּׁה**] **vb. Pi. denom. give sixth part** of (si vera l.);—*Pf.* 2 mpl. consec. וְשִׁשִּׁיתֶם הָאֵיפָה Ez 45^{13} (+ מִן part.), but < read שִׁשִּׁית Vrss and mod. (‖ שִׁשִּׁית v^{a}).—וְשִׁשֵּׁאתִיךָ Ez 39^{2} v. **ששא**. 8341 8338

p. 1058

†**I. שֹׁהַם** **n.m.**$^{Jb\ 28,16}$ a gem, identif. dubious, Vrss vary; *onyx* or *chrysoprasus* Ri$^{HWB2,\ 336\ f.}$, *onyx* Taylor$^{Hast.\ DB\ iii.\ 624}$, *beryl* Ridgeway$^{Ency.\ Bib.\ 545}$, *malachite* Myres$^{ib.\ 4808}$, etc.; cf. also Dr$^{Gn\ 2,12}$ (√ unknown; perh. loan-word, cf. As. *sâmtu* Dl$^{WB\ 488}$);—אֶבֶן הַשֹּׁ׳ Gn 2^{12} (J; + הַבְּדֹלַח), in land 7718

Ḥavilah; אַבְנֵי שׁ׳ Ex 25^{7} 28^{9} $35^{9.27}$ 39^{6} (all P), 1 Ch 29^{2}; אֶבֶן om. Ez 28^{13}, Ex 28^{20} 39^{13} (both P; all in lists of gems); שׁ׳ יָקָר וְסַפִּיר Jb 28^{16}.

7719 †II. **שֹׁהַם n.pr.m.** Levite;—שׁ׳ 1 Ch 24^{27}; Ισ(σ)οαμ, Ιεσσαμ.

7723 **שָׁו** Jb 15^{31} Kt, v. שָׁוְא below

7724 †**שְׁוָא n.pr.m. 1.** Calebite 1 Ch 2^{49}, Σαου, Σουε. **2.** secretary, David's time 2 S 20^{25} Qr (Kt
8304 שיא), Ιησους, A Ισους, 𝔊L Σουσα (v. שְׂרָיָה(וּ) **1**).

p. 976

I. **שׁוא** (√of foll.; cf. Ar. سَآءَ (med. و) *be evil, foul, unseemly*; Eth. ሰዪእ: *baseness*).

7723 †**שָׁוְא n.[m.] emptiness, vanity**;—שׁ׳ abs. Ex 23^{1} + 51 t., שָׁו Jb 15^{31} (Kt);—**1.** *emptiness, nothingness, vanity*: שׁ׳ תְּשׁוּעַת אָדָם ψ 60^{13} *vain* (is) *man's deliverance*, = 108^{13}; שׁ׳ לָכֶם 127^{2} it is *vain* (useless) *for you*; 89^{48} *for* (עַל) *what nothingness* hast thou created man? cf. יַרְחֵי שׁ׳ Jb 7^{3}; הַבְלֵי שׁ׳ ψ 31^{7} (idols) = Jon 2^{9}, cf. Je 18^{15} + Ho 5^{11} 𝔊 (for צָו); מִנְחַת שׁ׳ Is 1^{13} of ineffective offering to י׳; נשׂא לַשּׁ׳ (לא) Ex $20^{7.7}$ *take up* name of God *in vain* (to no good purpose) = Dt $5^{11.11}$, cf. ψ 24^{4} 139^{20} [MT *lifted up in vain* are *thy foes*, but rd. שְׁמֶךָ for עָרֶיךָ, cf. נשׂא **1 b** (7); al. עָלֶיךָ, v. II. עָר]; היה שׁ׳ Ho 12^{12} *become nothing* (We עשׂה שׁ׳, and so **3**); ראה שׁ׳ ψ 119^{37}; *adv.* לַשּׁ׳ *in vain* Je 2^{30} 4^{30} 6^{29} 46^{11}; שׁ׳ ψ $127^{1.1}$ Mal 3^{14}. **2.** *emptiness of speech*, ∥ *lying*, שׁ׳ וּדְבַר כָּזָב Pr 30^{8}; דבר שׁ׳ ψ 12^{3} 41^{7} $144^{8.11}$ Is 59^{4} Ez 13^{8}; אָלוֹת שׁ׳ Ho 10^{4} + 12^{2} 𝔊 We al. (for שׁד); הָלַךְ עִם־שׁ׳ Jb 31^{5} (∥ מִרְמָה); עֵד שׁ׳ Dt 5^{17} (= עֵד שֶׁקֶר Ex 20^{16}); cf. שֵׁמַע שׁ׳ Ex 23^{1} (E); of false (empty) prophecy חֲזוֹן שׁ׳ Ez 12^{24}, חָזוּ שׁ׳ La 2^{14}; v. also Ez $13^{6.7.9.23}$ 21^{34} 22^{28} Jb 35^{13} (or *empty* complaining, sub **1**); קסם שׁ׳ Ez 21^{28}; חֲלֹמוֹת הַשּׁ׳ Zc 10^{2}. **3.** of conduct, *worthlessness* (Buhl sub **1, 2**); מְתֵי שׁ׳ *worthless men* ψ 26^{4} Jb 11^{11}; *worthless* motives (in fig.) חַבְלֵי הַשּׁ׳ Is 5^{18}; נָפַת שׁ׳ 30^{28} (i.e. sifting out the worthless; al. *sieve* of (bringing) *disappointment*); play on meanings in Jb $15^{31.31}$, cf. Dr$^{\text{Job, Psalt. 464}}$.

II. **שׁוא** (√of foll.; prob. ∥ form of שׁאה).

7722 †[**שׁוֹא**] **n.[m.] ravage** (?);—pl. sf. שֹׁאֵיהֶם ψ 35^{17} rescue me from *their ravages* (si vera l.); 𝔊 κακουργία; Ol Dy Gr Che$^{\text{Comm.}}$ plausibly שַׁאֲנָם *their roaring*, cf. v$^{16.17c}$; We Du שַׁאֲנִים.

7722 †**שׁוֹאָה, שֹׁאָה n. f. devastation, ruin, waste**;—abs. שׁוֹ׳ Is 10^{3} +, שֹׁאָה 47^{11} Zp 1^{15} Jb 30^{14} (+ 38^{27} van d. H. Gi, but v. Baer's n.); cstr. שֹׁאַת Pr 3^{25};—**1.** *devastation, ruin*, as coming on pers., Is 10^{3} 47^{11} (Babylon personif.), ψ 35^{8a} 63^{10}; שֹׁאַת רְשָׁעִים Pr 3^{25} (obj. genit.; ∥ פַּחַד); (יוֹם) שׁ׳ וּמְשׁוֹאָה Zp 1^{15}; prob. = *devastating storm*, in sim. Ez 38^{9} (∥ עָנָן), Pr 1^{27} (Qr; Kt שׁאוה; ∥ סוּפָה).—ψ 35^{8b} read prob. שַׁחְתּוֹ *his pit*, 𝔖 We (cf. v^{7}). **2.** concretely, *ruin, waste*, of the desert, Jb 30^{3} (rdg. אֶרֶץ for אֶמֶשׁ Ol; otherwise sub **1**), שׁ׳ וּמְשׁוֹאָה 38^{27} (∥ מִדְבָּר v^{26}); = *ruins* Jb 30^{14}.

†**מְשׁוֹאָה, מְשֹׁאָה n.f. desolation**;—**1.** sg. 4875
only in שֹׁאָה וּמ׳ Zp 1^{15} Jb 30^{3} 38^{27}, v. foregoing; pl. (מַשּׁוּאוֹת, rd.) מְשׁוּאוֹת, so Klo Hup-Now Che$^{\text{Comm.}}$ Bae Du ψ 74^{3} *ruins* (of temple) and 73^{18} *ruins* (of one's life, fig.; but Du here der. fr. נשׁא: *deceptions*, v. p. 674; yet cf. synon. שַׁמָּה v^{19}).

†[**תְּשֻׁאָה**] **n.f. noise** (prop. of devastation, 8663
storm);—MT only pl. תְּשֻׁאוֹת abs. city noises Is 22^{2} (of עִיר הוֹמִיָּה), adv. acc. = (with) *shoutings* Zc 4^{7}; so cstr. ת׳ נוֹגֵשׂ לֹא יִשְׁמָע Jb 39^{7} (subj. wild ass); ת׳ סֻכָּתוֹ 36^{29} (of thunder); read perh. sg. תְּשֻׁוָּה (= תְּשֻׁאָה) Jb 30^{22} Kt, dissolvest me *in* (or, 7738
into) *the roar of the storm* (∥ *make me ride on wind*), so Ew Ol De Di Du Bu al.; > תּוּשִׁיָּה Qr AV *my substance* (?), Du מִתְּשׁ׳ 'ohne Halt' (?).

שׁוּב$_{1056}$ **vb. turn back, return** (NH *id.*; 7725
Hiph. in MI$^{8f.12}$; Sab. תוב, התב, esp. *requite* Os$^{\text{ZMG xix (1865), 198}}$ SabDenkm$^{\text{No. 20, l. 1}}$ Hom$^{\text{Chrest. 122}}$ CIS$^{\text{iv. 81, l. 9}}$, etc.; Ar. ثَابَ *return*, so Aram. תּוּב, ܬܳܒ);—**Qal**$_{685}$ *Pf.* 3 ms. שָׁב Gn 18^{33} +, 3 fs. שָׁבָה Ru 1^{15} +, וְשָׁבַת consec. †Ez 46^{17} (Ges$^{\S 72o}$, but Co Toy Krae וְשָׁבָה), 2 ms. שַׁבְתָּ ψ 85^{2}, etc.; *Impf.* 3 ms. יָשׁוּב Ho 11^{5} + oft., יָשֹׁב ψ 146^{4} La 3^{3}, juss. יָשֹׁב Ju 7^{3} +, וַיָּשָׁב Gn 26^{18} +; 3 fpl. תְּשֻׁבֶןָ Ez $16^{55.55}$, תְּשֻׁבֶינָה v^{55}, etc.; *Imv.* ms. שׁוּב Gn 31^{3} +, שֻׁב Ex 4^{19} 1 K 18^{43}, שׁוּבָה Ho 14^{2} +, fpl. שֹׁבְנָה Ru $1^{8.11.12}$, etc.; *Inf. abs.* שׁוֹב Gn 8^{3} +, *cstr.* שׁוּב Ex 4^{21} +, שֹׁב Jos 2^{16} (Ges$^{\S 72q}$), etc.; *Pt.* שָׁב Gn 43^{18} +, fs. שָׁבָה Ru 1^{22} +, etc.; pass. cstr. שׁוּבֵי Mi 2^{8};—*turn back, return*: **1.** *turn back*, c. מִן loc. Ju 3^{19} 8^{13}, cf. 7^{3}, c. מֵאַחֲרֵי pers., i.e. from following 2 S 11^{15} 1 K 19^{21} Ru 1^{16}, fr. pursuing 2 S $2^{26.30}$ 1 K 22^{33} = 2 Ch 18^{32}; c. מִן of pursuit 1 S 17^{53} 23^{28}, cf. 2 Ch 11^{4}; c. אַחֲרֵי pers., i.e. so as to follow 1 S 15^{31} 2 S 23^{10}; *turn back* in fear, rei Jb 39^{22} (of horse), מִפְּנֵי כֹל Pr 30^{30} (of lion), so abs. (of foes) ψ 6^{11} 56^{10} 70^{4}, in shame La 1^{8}; *turn back* and do so and so: Gn 14^{7} Ex 14^{2}, cf. Nu 33^{7} (עַל loc., both P), Jos 8^{21} (E), 11^{10} (J),

1 Ch 21[20], sq. inf. 2 Ch 20[27]; abs. *turn back* (face about) Ct 7[1.1.1.1] (+vb.); =be repulsed, defeated ψ 9[4], 74[21]; fig. *turn back*, viz. from a promise or a vow Ju 11[35]; c. מִן of service Nu 8[25] (P), i.e. be exempt. **2.** *return, come or go back*, c. מֵעַל pers. 1 S 17[15] (opp. הלך), 2 S 10[14] 2 K 18[14], מִן pers. Jos 10[31] (+בְּשָׁלוֹם), מִן loc., esp. from foreign land 2 K 8[3] 2 Ch 10[2] Ru 1[6.22] 2[6] 4[3] Je 31[16] 40[12] 43[5] 44[28] Ezr 6[21] Ne 8[17], מֵהַכּוֹת Gn 14[17] (JE?), 1 S 17[57] 18[6] 2 S 1[1] 8[13], מֵאַחֲרֵי i.e. from pursuing 1 S 24[2] (Gi v[1]); fig., לֹא שׁ׳ מִנִּי חֹשֶׁךְ Jb 15[22] (v. חֹשֶׁךְ **3 a**); עִבְרוּ וָשׁוּבוּ מִשַּׁעַר לָשַׁעַר Ex 32[27] (J), i.e. *go back and forth from gate to gate*, cf. (abs.) pt. as subst. עֹבֵר וָשָׁב Zc 7[14] 9[8] and (=all persons) Ez 35[7]; also וַיֵּצֵא יָצוֹא וָשׁוֹב Gn 8[7] (J), רָצוֹא וָשׁוֹב Ez 1[14] (del. Hi Co Toy al.; yet v. Krae); Gn 8[3] (J) v. הלך **4 c** (4). **3.** esp. *return unto*: **a.** *go back*, אֶל pers. Nu 23[5.16] (JE), 2 K 1[6] (‖ הָלַךְ, as oft.), Ex 5[22] (J; אֶל־י׳), 32[31] (E; *id.*), Nu 17[15] (P), 2 S 20[22] (+acc. loc.), Je 46[16] (both +אֶל loc.), +17 t.; אֶל loc. also Gn 21[32] 28[21] (both E), 2 S 11[4] Ho 5[15] (of י׳), 2 Ch 19[1] (+בְּשָׁלוֹם, +לְ pers.), Est 2[14] (opp. בוֹא), 7[8] (+מִן loc.), +27 t.; of a dog שׁ׳ עַל־קֵאוֹ Pr 26[11]; לְ loc. Gn 18[33] (J), 1 S 26[25] 29[4] 1 K 19[15] (+ה- loc.), Gn 33[16] (J; לְדַרְכּוֹ, +*id.*), ψ 7[8] (of י׳), +25 t.; לְ pers. †Ru 1[10] (לְעַמֵּךְ); ה- loc. also Gn 44[13] (J), Ex 4[20.21] (R), 13[17] (E), +5 t.; שָׁם (=שָׁמָּה) Je 22[27]; acc. loc. also Ho 8[13] 9[3] 1 S 18[2] 2 S 3[27] 15[27] (+בְּשָׁלוֹם), 2 K 2[25] (+מִן loc.), +15 t.; acc. דֶּרֶךְ Ez 46[9]; acc. pers. †Nu 10[36]; אַחֲרֵי pers. Ru 1[15]; abs. 2 S 3[16] 19[16] (+בוֹא), 1 K 18[43] Je 40[5] (<del. 𝔊 Gie Du), Ez 7[13b] (del. 𝔊 Co Krae al.) +; sq. vb., *go back* and do so and so, Gn 43[2] 1 S 1[19] 29[7] (שׁוּב וָלֵךְ), 1 K 13[22] 2 Ch 18[16] (+בְּשָׁלוֹם), +, (Je 42[10] read יָשׁוֹב Vrss and mod.); sq. inf. purpose Ju 14[8] 2 S 6[20] +10 t. **b.** *come back*, אֶל pers. Gn 8[9] (J; +אֶל loc.), Ex 24[14] (J), 1 S 23[23] +2 S 17[3] (𝔊 Ew Th We Dr HPS Bu), 1 K 12[15] (opp. הָלַךְ) + 9 t. + (in hostility) Ju 20[48]; אֶל loc. also Zc 8[3] (subj. י׳); Jos 22[32] (P) has מֵאֵת pers. + מִן loc. + אֶל loc. + אֶל pers.; אֶל rei Ez 7[13]; עַל pers. †Ne 4[6] Mi 5[2] (be reunited to); עַל loc. †1 K 17[21.22]; לְ loc. Jos 1[15] (R), Zc 1[16] (subj. י׳), 2 Ch 30[9] + (from exile) 5 t.; לְ animal., Jb 39[4]; ה- loc. †Gn 15[16] (E), 50[14] (J); acc. loc. †2 Ch 19[8]; שָׁם Je 20[11] (opp. יָצָא), שָׁמָּה v[27], הֵנָּה 31[8]; abs. Gn 43[10] (J), 2 S 10[5] 2 K 1[5] Is 21[12] (‖ אָתָה), Jb 39[12] (Kt, so Bu Du; of wild ox), +oft.; +בְּשָׁלוֹם Ju 8[9] 1 K 22[28] (שׁוּב תָּשׁוּב) = 2 Ch 18[27], 2 Ch 18[26]; +vb., *come back* and do so and so, †Dt 1[45] 30[8] Je 37[8] 1 K 19[7] 20[5] 2 K 9[36] ψ 60[2] (title), cf. Zc 4[1] Dn 11[10], שׁ׳ לָשֶׁבֶת Nu 35[32] (P), שׁ׳ לָלֶכֶת Ec 5[14]. †**4. a.** of dying, שׁ׳ אֶל־(הֶ)עָפָר Gn 3[19.19] (J), ψ 104[29] Ec 3[20], עַל־עָפָר Jb 34[15]; שׁ׳ לְאַדְמָתוֹ ψ 146[4], cf. אָשׁוּב שָׁמָּה (i.e. בֶּטֶן אִמּוֹ) Jb 1[21] (v. Di Bu, also Ec 5[14]); שׁ׳ לִשְׁאוֹלָה ψ 9[18]; so prob. abs. ψ 90[3] (>come back to life); of (human) dust, שׁ׳ עַל־הָאָרֶץ Ec 12[7]; breath, שׁ׳ אֶל־הָאֱלֹהִים v[7]. **b.** of revival from death, שׁ׳ לְבֵיתוֹ Jb 7[10], abs. 10[21] (opp. הָלַךְ), 16[22] (*id.*), Pr 2[19]; also c. אֶל pers. 2 S 12[13]. †**5.** fig. of human relations: **a.** *return* to leader, king, אֶל pers., Ju 11[8] 1 K 12[27.27]; to divorced wife Je 3[1] (opp. הלך). **b.** =change so as to approach (in purpose, desire), אֶל־ pers. Je 15[19.19]. **c.** *turn*, i.e. resort to, לְ pers. ψ 119[79]. **d.** *return* to a physical condition Jb 33[25] (לְ rei); to a state or course of life, לְ rei Is 23[17] Ez 16[55.55.55] Ne 9[17] ψ 85[9] עַל rei Je 11[10], הֲלוֹם ψ 73[10] (but crpt.); ב Je 8[6] (Du rds. שָׁט for שָׁב). **e.** abs. = change course of action; from good to bad, וַיָּשָׁב וַיִּמְרָד־בּוֹ 2 K 24[1], Je 34[11.16]; bad to good v[15]; so שׁ׳ alone Jb 6[29.29] (prob.; read וְשׁוּבוּ, so Di Da Bu al.; other interpr. De Du al.). **f.** pt. pass. = *averse*, שׁוּבֵי מִלְחָמָה Mi 2[8] (>We Now שְׁבִי *spoil of war*). **6.** fig., specif. of spiritual relations: **a.** *turn back* from God, = *apostatize*, מֵאַחֲרֵי י׳ Nu 14[43] (J), 1 S 15[11] 1 K 9[6] (שׁוּב תְּשֻׁבוּן), Je 3[19], Nu 32[15] Jos 22[16.18.23.29] (all P); abs. (usu. +vb.) Ju 2[19] 8[33] Jos 23[12] (R[D]), Je 8[4] ψ 78[41] 2 Ch 7[19]. **b.** of י׳, *turn away*, מֵאַחֲרֵי pers. Dt 23[15]. **c.** *turn back* to God (=seek penitently), אֶל־י׳ Ho 6[1] 7[10] 14[3] Je 3[7] 1 K 8[33.48] (בְּכָל־לְבָב), +18 t.; אֶל־אֱלֹהִים †Ho 5[4] ψ 51[15], cf. Is 10[21]; עַל־י׳ †2 Ch 15[4] 30[9]; עַד־י׳ Am 4[6.8.9.10.11] Ho 14[2] Is 9[12] +5 t.; עַד־שַׁדַּי †Jb 22[23]; לִי Is 31[6], שׁ׳ נַפְשִׁי לִמְנוּחָיְכִי ψ 116[7]; cf. לַבַּעַל Ho 7[16] (for לֹא עָל, Now, cf. Marti); לְתוֹכַחְתִּי Pr 1[23] (prob. del., v. Toy). **d.** abs. *repent*, Ho 3[15] 11[5] Is 6[10] 10[22] Je 3[7.12.14.22] 4[1] 5[3] +14 t., +pt. as subst. Is 1[27]. **e.** *turn back* from evil, c. מִן (esp. Je Ez) 1 K 8[35] 13[33] Je 15[7] 18[8] +8 t. Je, Ez 3[19] 13[22] +12 t. Ez, +9 t.; cf. שָׁבֵי פֶשַׁע Is 59[20]; שׁוּבוּ וְהָשִׁיבוּ מִן Ez 18[30], so c. מֵעַל 14[6]; from good, c. מִן, †Ez 3[20] 18[24.26] 33[18]. **f.** of י׳, שׁ׳ מֵחֲרוֹן אַפּוֹ Ex 32[12] (JE), Dt 13[18] Jos 7[26] (J), 2 K 23[26] Jon 3[9]; שׁ׳ מִמֶּנּוּ אַף־י׳ Ho 14[5] Je 2[35] 4[8] Nu 25[4] (P), 2 Ch 12[12] 29[10] 30[8], so (man's anger) Gn 27[45] (J) and (abs.) v[44] (E); abs. of אַף־י׳ Is 5[25] 9[11.16.20] 10[4] 12[1] Je 23[20] (opp. יָצָא v[19]), 30[24] Jb 14[13] Dn 9[16]. **g.** of י׳, *return*

(to shew favour), אֶל pers. †Gn 18^{10} (+inf. abs.), v^{14} Zc 1^{3} Mal 3^{7} 2 Ch 30^{6}, abs. Is 63^{17} ψ 80^{15} (‖ פְּקֹד, הַבֵּט), 90^{13}, +vb. Je 12^{15} ψ 6^{5} Jo 2^{14} Jon 3^{9}; also in hostility, +vb. Jos 24^{20} (E), c. inf. purpose Ho 11^{9}. **h.** of י׳, *turn back* from (מִן) judgment Je 4^{28}, אֱמֶת ψ 132^{11}; מֵאַחֲרֵי pers., i.e. cease to bless, Je 32^{40}. **7.** of inanimate things (sts. personified, or treated as things of life): **a.** as perceptibly moving, water Gn 8^{3} (J; מֵעַל loc.), Jos 4^{18} (J; לְ loc.), Ex 14^{26} (P; עַל pers.), v^{28} (P; +vb.), ψ 104^{9} (לְ inf.), sea Ex 14^{27} (J; לְאֵיתָנוֹ); wind ψ 78^{39} (opp. הלך), Ec 1^{6} (עַל loc.); shadow 2 K $20^{9.10}$ (+אֲחֹרַנִּית), ‖ Is 38^{8} (sun on dial), of breath (=revive) Ju 15^{19} 1 S 30^{12} (אֶל pers.); clouds Ec 12^{2} (מִן temp.); rain and snow Is 55^{10} (ה loc.); rolling stone Pr 26^{27}; sword 2 S 1^{22} (מִן rei), Ez 21^{10}, arrow Je 50^{9}; of plague-spot=*re-appear*, Lv 14^{43} (P). **b.** =*be brought back*, Gn 43^{18} (J), 1 S 5^{11} (לְ loc.), hence *be restored*, לְ pers. Ez 46^{17}, so of kingdom 1 K 12^{26}, city 1 S 7^{14} (Ez 35^{9} v. ישׁב **4**), field Lv 27^{24} (P); of animal Dt 28^{31}. **c.** =*be turned into*, לְ rei, Is 29^{17}; = *be turned back into*, עַד rei, Mi 1^{7}. **d.** *return*, fig. of word, (1) Is 45^{23}, c. אֶל pers. 55^{11} (both opp. יָצָא); (2) ψ 35^{13} *my prayer turned upon* (עַל) *my bosom* (was uttered with bowed head, De Bae Du). **e.** *turn away, depart*, of infamy Pr 25^{10}. **f.** *return* (in recompense), of crime, evil, etc., c. בְּרֹאשׁ 1 K 2^{33} Ob^{15} ψ 7^{17}, עַל־רֹאשׁ Est 9^{25}, לְ pers. ψ 54^{7} (Kt; >Qr Hiph.), Pr 12^{14}. **g.** ψ 94^{15} *judgment*(-giving) *shall return to* (עַד) *righteousness* (be in accord therewith). **h.** of boundary, =change (sts. reverse) direction (P), ה- loc. Jos 19^{12} (+מִן loc.), v^{34} (+acc. loc.), acc. loc. also v$^{27.29}$ (+עַד loc.), v^{29}. **i.** *be restored* to healthy condition, of withered hand 1 K $13^{6.6}$ (אֶל pers.), leprous hand Ex 4^{7} (J; c. כְּ comp.), flesh 2 K 5^{10} (לְ pers.), v^{14} Lv 13^{16} (‖ נֶהְפַּךְ לְלָבָן). †**8.** denoting repetition, etc. (Ges$^{§ 120 d g}$): +vb., *return (and) do*= do again, Gn 26^{18} 30^{31} Nu 11^{4} (all J), Ju 19^{7} 1 S $3^{5.6}$ 1 K 13^{33} 19^{6} 2 K $1^{11.13}$ 19^{9} 21^{3}=2 Ch 33^{3}, Je 18^{4} 36^{28} Zc 5^{1} 6^{1} Mal 1^{4} Jb 10^{16} 17^{10} ψ 7^{13} Dn 9^{25}, perh. also 2 Ch 19^{4}; cf. Is 6^{13}=*it, in turn, shall be destroyed* (destruction shall be repeated in its case), La 3^{3} appar.=*do repeatedly;* שׁ׳+ Inf. abs. Ec $4^{1.7}$ 9^{11}; in compar. עוֹד תָּשׁוּב תִּרְאֶה Ez 8^{6} *thou shalt see yet* greater abominations, so v^{13} and (מִן comp.) v^{15}; שׁ׳+Inf. cstr. Dt 24^{4} 30^{9} Jos 5^{2} (R^{D}), Je 36^{28} Ez 8^{17} Ezr 9^{14} Ne 9^{28} Jb 7^{7} Ec 1^{7}; =*reverse* one's action, +vb. Jos 2^{23} (E), Ho 2^{11} 2 K 13^{25} Dt 30^{3} Mi 7^{19} Zc 8^{15} ψ $71^{20.20}$ 85^{7}; =*restore* to original condition by doing, +vb. Dt 23^{14}. **9.** trans., peculiarly, in phr. שׁ׳ שְׁבוּת *restore captivity* of, etc., c. 21 t. (v. שְׁבוּת sub שָׁבָה); שׁ׳ י׳ צִיּוֹן Is 52^{8}, שׁ׳ c. sf. pers. ψ 85^{5}; elsewhere only וְשָׁב י׳ אֶת־גְּאוֹן יַעֲקֹב וגו׳ Na 2^{3}, cf. **Hiph. 6.** †**Pō'l. 1.** *bring back, Pf.* 1 s. וְשֹׁבַבְתִּי, c. acc. pers.+אֶל loc. Je 50^{19} (י׳ subj.), *Inf. cstr.* sf. בְּשׁוֹבְבִי, c. מִן loc. Ez 39^{27} and (fig.) לְשׁוֹבֵב, c. אֶל pers. Is 49^{5}; *Impf.* 2 ms. תְּשׁוֹבֵב לָנוּ ψ 60^{3}=*take us back* into power. **2. a.** fig. *restore, refresh*, 3 ms. נַפְשִׁי יְשׁוֹבֵב ψ 23^{3} (י׳ subj.); cf. **Hiph. 2 b.** **b.** *restore, repair, Pt.* מְשֹׁבֵב נְתִיבוֹת לָשָׁבֶת Is 58^{12}. **3.** *lead away* (enticingly), *Pf.* 1 s. sf. (of Gog), י׳ subj., וְשֹׁבַבְתִּיךָ Ez 38^{4} (del. Co), וְשׁ׳ 39^{2}; so fig. 3 fs. sf. וְדַעְתֵּךְ הִיא שׁוֹבְבָתֶךְ Is 47^{10} (of Bab.);—Je 50^{6} v. **Qal.** **4.** *shew turning=apostatize* (cf. **Hiph. 8**), *Pf.* 3 fs. שׁוֹבְבָה Je 8^{5} (read שׁוֹבֵב, and del. ירושלם, c. 𝔊).—Vid. also שׁוֹבָב infra. †**Pu'l.** *Pt.* f. מְשׁוֹבֶבֶת Ez 38^{8} a land *restored*+מִן rei.—Vid. also שׁוֹבָב infra. **Hiph.**$_{353}$ *Pf.* 3 ms. Gn 41^{13}+; sf. וְהֱשִׁיבְךָ 40^{13}, וֶהֱשִׁיבְךָ Dt 28^{68}; 2 ms. וַהֲשֵׁבֹתָ ψ 85^{4}, וַהֲשֵׁבֹתָ Dt 4^{39} 30^{1}, sf. וַהֲשִׁיבוֹתָם 2 Ch 6^{25}; 1 s. consec. וַהֲשִׁבוֹתִי Am 1^{8}, וַהֲשִׁבֹתִי Nu 22^{8}+, sf. והוֹשְׁבוֹתִים Zc 10^{6} (but rd. וַהֲשִׁבוֹתִים, v. ישׁב **Hiph.**), etc.; *Impf.* 3 ms. יָשִׁיב Ex 21^{34}+, (rd. יָשֵׁב Dn $11^{18.19}$>Qr v^{18} יָשֵׂם), וַיָּשֶׁב Gn 20^{14}+; sf. יְשִׁבֵנִי 2 S 15^{3}+, וַיְשִׁיבֵם 2 Ch 19^{4}+1 S 12^{8} Vrss We Dr al.; 3 fpl. תְּשֵׁבְנָה Jb 20^{10}, etc.; *Imv.* ms. הָשֵׁב Gn 20^{7}+, הָשֵׁיב 2 K 8^{6}, הָשַׁב Is 42^{22}, so הָשַׁב Ez 21^{35} (v. Ke and still Toy; Ew Sm Krae Inf. abs. הָשֵׁב), הֲשִׁיבָה Ju 11^{13}+, etc.; *Inf. abs.* הָשֵׁב Ex 23^{4}+; cstr. הָשִׁיב Gn 42^{35}+, etc.; *Pt.* מֵשִׁיב 20^{7}+, etc.;—*cause to return, bring back:* **1. a.** c. acc. pers.+אֶל loc. Gn 24^{5} (J; הֶהָשֵׁב אָשִׁיב), 28^{15} (J), 42^{37} (E), 48^{21} (E), +; esp. from exile 1 K 8^{34}=2 Ch 6^{25}, Je 27^{22}+5 t. Je; +אֶל pers. 1 K 22^{26}=2 Ch 18^{25}; +עַל loc. Je 16^{15} 23^{3} 24^{6}; +לְ loc. 12^{15}; +acc. loc. 2 S 15^{8} (read הָשֵׁב יְשִׁבֵנִי Vrss Th We Dr al.), Dt 28^{68} Ez 29^{14} 47^{6} 2 Ch 33^{13}, etc.; +מִן loc. Je 41^{16} Zc 10^{10}, מֵאֵת pers. Je 41^{16}, מִן inf. 2 Ch 25^{13}; acc. pers. only Ju 19^{3} 1 K $13^{20.23}$+; *bring back* into bondage, etc., Je $34^{11.16}$; =*allow to return* 15^{19}; acc. pers.+rei (=recover, recapture), 28^{6} (+אֶל loc., מִן loc.); =*recover, rescue*, Gn 14^{16} (acc. pers.+rei), ψ 35^{17} (acc. נַפְשִׁי, מִן rei); acc. rei+ אֶל pers. Gn 44^{8} (J), +עַל pers. Ex 15^{9} (song), Pr 20^{26}; +אֶל loc. 1 K 14^{28}=2 Ch 12^{11}, Je 28^{3} 2 Ch 24^{11}; acc. of hand, אֶל־פֶּה 1 S 14^{27} Pr 19^{24}

26^{15}; esp. of י'’s hand, in judgment, sq. עַל Am 1^{8} Is 1^{25} Zc 13^{7} ψ 81^{15}, also of man's hand Je 6^{9} Ez 38^{12}; +acc. loc. 2 S 15$^{25.29}$; +שָׁם Ne 13^{9}; acc. rei alone Gn 43$^{12.21}$ (both בְּיֶדְכֶם), 14^{16} (=recapture), 1 S 6^{21} 30^{19} 1 K 13^{29} (corpse), Lv 26^{26} (H); c. acc. animal. 1 S 6^{7} (מֵאַחֲרֵי), Ez 34$^{4.16}$ (fig.); shadow on dial 2 K 20^{11}=Is 38^{8}.—Jb 39^{12} v. **Qal 3 b**. **b.** *put back*: acc. rei, stone, עַל־פִּי הַבְּאֵר Gn 29^{3} (J), veil עַל־פָּנָיו Ex 34^{35} (P), Dagon לִמְקוֹמוֹ 1 S 5^{3}, rod לִפְנֵי הָעֵדוּת Nu 17^{25} (P), sword, +אֶל of sheath, 1 Ch 21^{27} Ez 21^{35} (acc. om.); hand אֶל־חֵיק Ex 4$^{7.7}$ (J; opp. הוֹצִיא). **c.** =*draw back*, hand Gn 38^{29} (J), 1 K 13^{4} (opp. שָׁלַח; +אֶל reflex.), Jos 8^{26} (E; opp. נטה), so, fig., י' subj. La 2^{3} (אָחוֹר, מִפְּנֵי), ψ 74^{11}; c. מִן=*refrain from* La 2^{8} Ez 18$^{8.17}$ (i.e. from oppressing), 20^{22} (מִן om.); foot, c. מִן Is 58^{13} (fig.); *draw in* breath Jb 9^{18}. **d.** =*give back, restore*, acc. pers. vel rei: +לְ pers. Gn 20^{14} (E), v^{7} (E; acc. om.), Ex 23^{4} (E; הָשֵׁב תְּשִׁיב), Dt 22^{1} (*id.*; both acc. animal.), 24^{13} (*id.*), Ex 22^{25} (E), Ju 17$^{3.3.4}$ 1 S 12^{3} 2 S 9^{7} Dt 22^{2} (P), Ne 5^{11}, so 2 S 16^{3} 1 K 12^{21}=2 Ch 11^{1} (all acc. of kingdom), c. acc. צְדָקָה Jb 33^{26}; +אֶל pers. Gn 37^{22} (E; acc. pers.); +אֶל loc. 42^{25} (E); acc. rei only, 2 K 8^{6} Ez 18^{7} (read Inf. abs. שׁוּב for חוֹב, Co Toy Krae), 18^{12} 33^{15} Lv 5^{33} (P), Nu 5^{7} (P; +בְּרֹאשׁוֹ=*in full*), ψ 69^{5} (opp. גָּזַל), so of land (or city) Ju 11^{13} 1 K 20^{34} Ne 5^{12}, cf. 2 K 14^{28} (+בְּיִשְׂרָאֵל), 16^{6} (+לַאֲרָם); = win back 2 K 13^{25} 14^{22} (+לְ terr.)=2 Ch 26^{2}, boundary (i.e. re-establish it) 2 K 14^{25}; *restore* ruined city Dn 9^{25} (+לִבְנוֹת), conquered nation ψ 80$^{4.8.20}$; joy, acc.+לְ pers. ψ 51^{14}.—2 S 8^{3} v. יָד **2**.—Acc. pers. only, Gn 20^{7} (E), Is 42^{22}; *restore* to office, acc. pers.+עַל Gn 40$^{13.21}$ (E), אֶל loc. 2 S 19^{12}, acc. pers. only, 2 S 19$^{11.13.44}$, cf. Is 1^{26}; =*pay back* money, Lv 25^{27} (לְ pers.), v$^{51.52}$. **e.** =*relinquish*, c. acc. rei, Jb 20^{10}. **f.**=*give in payment, requital*, c. acc. rei+appos. 1 S 6^{8} (לְ pers.), v^{17} (*id.*; cf. טְחוֹר); also *pay* as tribute (in answer to demand), acc. rei 2 K 17^{3} ψ 72^{10}, +לְ pers. 2 K 3^{4} 2 Ch 27^{5}; *give in exchange* Ez 27^{15}. **g.** *bring* one *back* (from dead) 2 S 12^{23}, so c. מִפִּי מָוֶת Jb 33^{20}; on other hand, אֶל־עָפָר Jb 10^{9}=(acc.) 30^{23}, cf. עַד־דַּכָּא ψ 90^{3}. †**2. a.** *bring back* heart, לֵב, עַל pers. Mal 3^{24}; הֲשִׁיבֵנוּ י' אֵלֶיךָ La 5^{21} (<Bu *restore*, del. אליך); הֵשִׁיב אֶל־י' Ne 9^{26} (cf. v^{29}), 2 Ch 19^{4} 24^{19}, also (מִן of evil) Je 23^{22}, abs. 31^{18}. **b.** acc. נֶפֶשׁ=*refresh* La 1$^{11.16.19}$ ψ 19^{8} Pr 25^{13} Ru 4^{15}. **3.** *bring back* words of people, אֶל־י' Ex 19^{8} (E); then, in gen., *bring back* word, דָּבָר, *report to*, +acc. pers. Gn 37^{14} Nu 13^{26} 22^{8} (all E), Dt 1$^{22.25}$ Jos 14^{7} (R^{D}), 22^{32} (P), +8 t.; =*answer* 1 S 17^{30} 2 S 3^{11} 1 K 12^{6}=2 Ch 10^{6}+6 t., +(acc. מִלִּין) Jb 35^{4}; also (דָּבָר om.) Jb 13^{22} 20^{2} 33$^{5.32}$ 2 Ch 10^{16} Ne 6^{4} (כַּדָּבָר הַזֶּה); acc. אֲמָרִים +לְ pers. Ju 5^{29} Pr 22^{21}; later c. לְ pers. alone 1 S 12^{3}; c. cl. orat. recta, אֶל pers. Est 4$^{13.15}$; similar phrases, Ez 9^{11} Pr 18^{13} 24^{26} 26^{16} Hb 2^{1} Jb 31^{14} 32^{14} (Gi v^{15}), 40^{4}. **4. a.** *bring back* (in retribution, cf. **Qal 7 f**) upon, subj. oft. י', acc. of evil, Ju 9^{56}, בְּרֹאשׁ Ju 9^{5} 1 S 25^{39} 1 K 2^{44} Jo 4$^{4.7}$, עַל־רֹאשׁ 1 K 2^{32}, אֶל־רֹאשׁ Ne 3^{36}; לְ pers. Gn 50^{15} (E), 1 S 6^{3} (הָשֵׁב תָּשִׁיבוּ), v^{4} 25^{31} (*return evil for good*), +, etc.; abs. = *make requital*, לְ pers. 2 Ch 6^{23}+ (כְּ comp.) Ho 12^{3} Pr 24$^{12.29}$; †c. acc. of good, לְ pers. 2 S 16^{12} 26^{23} Zc 9^{12}; c. כְּ comp.+לְ pers. ψ 18$^{21.25}$=2 S 22$^{21.25}$, and (כְּ comp. only) 2 Ch 32^{25}; requite י'’s benefits, acc. rei+לי' ψ 116^{12}, cf. Nu 18^{9} (P). **b.** *pay* as recompense, כֶּסֶף יָשׁ' לִבְעָלָיו Ex 21^{34} (E); so (fig.) of י', לְהָשׁ' בְּחֵמָה אַפּוֹ Is 66^{15}, הֵשׁ' נָקָם לְ Dt 32$^{41.43}$. **5.** *turn back, backward*=repel, defeat, c. אֶת־פְּנֵי 2 K 18^{24}=Is 36^{9}, acc. מִלְחָמָה Is 28^{6}, acc. of sword ψ 89^{44}, acc. pers.+אָחוֹר ψ 44^{11} (+מִנִּי pers.), Is 44^{25} (fig., =refute, confute), fig. of calamity La 1^{13}; =*repulse, hinder* Je 2^{24}, esp. acc. Is 14^{27} (יַד־י'), cf. 43^{13}, Jb 9^{12} 11^{10} 23^{13}; =*reject, refuse*, (אֶת־)פְּנֵי פ' 1 K 2$^{16.17.20.20}$ 2 Ch 6^{42} ψ 132^{10}. †**6. a.** *turn away* face, fig., +מֵעַל rei Ez 14^{6}; acc. pers.+מִן rei Mal 2^{6}; anger of י' (acc.)+מֵעַל pers. Nu 25^{11} (P), Pr 24^{18}, מִן pers. Je 18^{20} Ezr 10^{14}; acc. only, Jb 9^{13} ψ 78^{38} 106^{23}; acc. of human anger Pr 15^{1} 29^{8}. **b.** late, *turn toward*, acc. face, לְ loc. Dn 11$^{18.19}$, acc. foot, אֶל rei ψ 119^{59} (fig.). †**7.** *turn* against, אֶל־אֶל, c. acc. רוּחֲךָ Jb 15^{43}. **8.** הֵשׁ' אֶל־לֵבָב *bring back to mind*, take into consideration, c. acc. La 3^{21}, sq. cl. with כִּי Dt 4^{39} (cf. Dr), obj. om. 30^{1} 1 K 8^{47}=2 Ch 6^{37}, Is 44^{19}, +(עַל) 46^{8}. **9.** הֵשִׁיב אֶת־שְׁבוּת פ' Je 32^{44} 33$^{7.11}$ 49^{6} La 2^{14} Ez 39^{25}+(Qr Hiph., Kt Qal) Je 33^{26} 46^{39} Jo 4^{1} (v. **Qal 9**). †**10.** Hiph. declar., הֵשׁ' מֵעַל Ez 14^{6} = *shew a turning away from* your idols (i.e. turn away), cf. (מִן) 18^{30}, abs. הָשׁ' וִחְיוּ v^{32}; of י', הֵשׁ' מֵחֲרוֹן אַפֶּךָ ψ 85^{4} (but rd. prob. הֲשִׁיבוֹתָה חֲרוֹן א' [**6 a** supra]); perhaps in physical sense Jon 1^{13} (אֶל loc.; We Now sc. אֳנִיָּה, etc.). †**11.** *reverse, revoke*, acc. (sf.) rei, i.e. judgment, Am 1$^{3.6.9.11.13}$ 2$^{1.4.6}$; blessing Nu 23^{20} (poem in E), edict Est 8$^{5.8}$. †**Hoph.** *Pf.* 3 ms. הוּשַׁב Gn

42^{28} my money *has been returned!* cf. *Pt.* הַכֶּסֶף הַמּוּשָׁב 43^{12} (both J); אָשָׁם הַמּ׳ לי׳ Nu 5^8 (P) the *which is restored to* י׳; pl. מוּשָׁבִים Je 27^{16} the vessels *are about to be brought back*, c. מִן loc.; *Impf.* 3 ms. וַיּוּשַׁב אֶת־מֹשֶׁה Ex 10^8 (J; cf. Ges § 121 a, b) *Moses was brought back*, c. אֶל pers.

7729 †שׁוּבָה **n.f. retirement, withdrawal** (from war, etc., cf. Mi 2^8);—Is 30^{15}.

7870 †II. [שִׁיבָה] cstr. שִׁיבַת *restoration* (?) ψ 126^1,
7622,7871† but read שְׁבִית, v. sub שָׁבָה.—I. שִׁיבָה v. יָשַׁב. p. 444, 986

7726 †I. שׁוֹבָב **adj. backturning, recusant, apostate** (perhaps for מְשׁוֹבָב, Pt. Pō'l. Ol § 251 b Ges § 52 s Kö I. 454);—שׁ׳ Is 57^{17}; pl. שׁוּבוּ בָּנִים שׁוֹבָבִים Je $3^{14.22}$.—שׁובבים Je 50^6 Kt < Qr שׁוֹבְבוּם
7725 𝔊 Comm., cf. √ **Pō'l.** p. 998

7727 †II. שׁוֹבָב **n.pr.m.** Σωβαβ, etc.: **1.** son of David 2 S 5^{14} = 1 Ch 14^4, 1 Ch 3^5. **2.** son of Caleb 1 Ch 2^{18}.

7728 †שׁוֹבֵב **adj. backturning, apostate** (perh. for מְשׁוֹ׳, v. I. שׁוֹבָב);—as subst., לְשׁוֹ׳ Mi 2^4 (but read prob. שֹׁבֵינוּ *our captors*); f. הַבַּת הַשּׁוֹבֵבָה Je 31^{22} (of Israel), 49^4 (of Ammon).

3437 †יָשׁוּב **n.pr.m.** usu. Ιασουβ;—**1.** in Issachar Nu 26^{24} (P) 1 Ch 7^1 Qr (Kt ישיב). **2.** one
7610 with foreign wife Ezr 10^{29}.—Is 7^3 v. שְׁאָר יָשׁוּב. p. 984

3432 †יָשֻׁבִי **adj.gent.** of foregoing **1**; c. art. as subst. coll. הַיּ׳ Nu 26^{24}.

3433 †יָשֻׁבִי לֶחֶם **n.pr.m.** in Judah 1 Ch 4^{22}; 𝔊L ἐπέστρεψαν ἑαυτοῖς Λεεμ.

3434 †יָשָׁבְעָם **n.pr.m.** a hero of David;—1 Ch 11^{11}, 12^6, 27^2 (יֹשֵׁב בַּשֶּׁבֶת, q.v. p. 444 supra, in 2 S 23^8, v. Dr); Ιεσεβαδα, Ιεσσεβααλ, Ισβααμ, etc.; rd. in all אִשְׁבַּעַל We al.

3142 †יוּשַׁב חֶסֶד **n.pr.m.** son of Zerubbabel, 1 Ch 3^{20}; Αροβασουκ, 𝔊L Ιωσαβεε.

4878 †[מְשׁוּבָה], מְשֻׁבָה **n.f. turning back, apostasy**;—abs. מְשֻׁבָה Je 3^6+; cstr. מְשׁוּבַת Pr 1^{32}; sf. מְשׁוּבָתָם Ho 14^5; pl. sf. מְשׁוּבֹתֵיכֶם Je 3^{22}, etc.;—*backturning, apostasy*, of Isr., Ho 14^5, מְשׁוּבָתִי 11^7 *apostasy from me* (si vera l.); of Judah Je 2^{19} 3^{22} 5^6 8^5 14^7 (all pl.) + Ez 37^{33} (read מְשׁוּבֹתֵיהֶם for מוֹשׁ׳, 𝔊 Comm.); מ׳ נִצַּחַת Je 8^5 *enduring, perpetual apostasy;* also as n. concr., appos. of foll. word, מְשֻׁבָה יִשׂ׳ Je $3^{6.8.11.12}$ *apostate one, Israel.* Of individual, מְשׁוּבַת פְּתָיִם Pr 1^{32}.

†מְשׁוֹבָב **n. pr. m.** in Simeon, 1 Ch 4^{34}; 4877
Μοσωβαβ, 𝔊L ἐπιστρέφων.

†[תְּשׁוּבָה] **n.f. return, answer**;—**1.** sf. 8666
וּתְשֻׁבָתוֹ הָרָמָתָה 1 S 7^{17} *and his return was* (=he returned) *to Rama.* **2.** esp. cstr. לִתְשׁוּבַת הַשָּׁנָה *at the return of the year*, i. e. of spring, 2 S 11^1 1 K $20^{22.26}$ 2 Ch 36^{10}, לְעֵת תְּשׁ׳ הַשּׁ׳ 1 Ch 20^1 (‖ 2 S 11^1). **3.** *answer*, pl. abs. תְּשֻׁבֹת Jb 34^{36}, sf. תְּשׁוּבֹתֵיכֶם 21^{34}.

שׁוּבָאֵל v. שְׁבוּאֵל (cf. Sab. n.pr. חובאל Os ZMG xix (1865), 198 n. Hal 485 DHM ZMG xxxvii (1883), 16).

†שׁוֹבָךְ **n. pr. m.** Aramaean general, 2 S 7731
$10^{16.18}$ (Σωβακ, 𝔊L Σαβεε), = שׁוֹפַךְ 1 Ch $19^{16.18}$ 7780
(Σωφαρ, Σαφαθ; A Σωφαχ, Σωβαχ, 𝔊L Σωφακ).

שׁוֹבָל **n.pr.** v. שׁבל. p. 987 7732

שׁוֹבֵק, שׁוֹבָק **n.pr.** v. שׁבק. p. 990 7733

שׁוג (√ of following; ‖ form of שׂגג, שׂגה).

†[מְשׁוּגָה] **n.f.** error;—sf. מְשׁוּגָתִי Jb 19^4 4879
(? rd. מְשֻׁגָּתִי).

שׁוּד Jb 5^{21} van d. H., for I. שׁד q.v. sub שׁדד. p. 994 7701

[שׁוּד] vb., יָשׁוּד ψ 91^6 v. שׁדד. p. 994 7703, 7736

†I. שָׁוָה **vb.** (be even, smooth, v. **Pi.,** 7737
hence) **agree with, be like, resemble** (Ar. سوى II. *make even, flat, uniform* (with something else); Aram. שְׁוָא (der. spec.) *be like*, ܫܘܐ *be equal, fit, like*, Pa. *lay out smoothly*, Aph. *make plain, fit, worthy*);—**Qal** *Pf.* 3 ms. לֹא שׁ׳ לִי Jb 33^{27} (si vera l.) *it was not equalled to me*, i. e. (v. infra; acc. to most) *not requited* (so De Di Da, and Is 16^6 𝔗); Bu אֵל לֹא שָׁוָה *God did not requite* (or שִׁלֵּם for שוה); Du לֹא שִׁוָּה כַעֲוֺנִי (cf. 𝔊); *Impf.* 1 s. of י׳, אֶל־מִי ... אֶשְׁוֶה Is 40^{25} *to whom shall I be like?* (‖ תְּדַמְּיוּנִי), implying that he is incomp.; 3 mpl. לֹא יִשְׁווּ־בָהּ Pr 3^{15} *are not comparable with her* (wisdom), so 8^{11}; 2 ms. פֶּן־תִּשְׁוֶה־לּוֹ Pr 26^4 *lest thou be like him* (a fool); *Pt.* שֹׁוֶה בְּ Est 7^4 *is not an equivalent for;* c. לְ, *suitable for* 3^8, so 1^{22} Hi Or Ry Kau (rdg. כָּל שֹׁוֶה עִמּוֹ for כִּלְשׁוֹן עַמּוֹ, but v. Siegf.); *adequate for* 5^{13}. **Pi.** *Pf.* 3 ms. שִׁוָּה Is 28^{25} *he hath levelled* its (the ground's) surface; 1 s. שִׁוִּיתִי וְדוֹמַמְתִּי נַפְשִׁי ψ 131^2 *I have smoothed* (composed) *and stilled my soul;* so, sc. נַפְשִׁי Is 38^{13} 𝔙 Ges De al.; Houb Lo Che Du al. read שִׁוַּעְתִּי *I cried;* acc. מִשְׁפָּטִים 119^{30} *accounted suitable,*

meet (|| דֶּרֶךְ אֱמוּנָה בָחָרְתִּי), Hi, cf. Gr v^{128} (v. **Qal** Est 3^{8}); We ins. לְנֶגְדִּי (II. ׳שׁ, cf. ψ 16^{8}); Zenner Du אִוִּיתִי. **Hiph.** *make like: Impf.* 1 s. מָה אַשְׁוֶה־לָּךְ La 2^{13}(|| אֲדַמֶּה); 2 mpl. לְמִי תְדַמְּיוּנִי וְתַשְׁווּ Is 46^{5} (cf. **Qal** 40^{25}). **Nithp.** (appar.) *Pf.* 3 fs. נִשְׁתָּוָה (for נִשְׁתַּוְּתָה) Pr 27^{15} *are alike*, but read prob. Niph. 3 fs. נִשְׁוָתָה Ges^{§75x} Toy al.—תשוה Jb 30^{22} Kt v. II. שׁוא.

7741 †I. שָׁוֵה **n.[m.]** level plain;—in שָׁוֵה קִרְיָתַיִם
7156 Gn 14^{5} (v. ׳ק p. 900^{a}; ׳ק appos. acc. to Ol^{§277c} Lag$^{BN 43}$; ? rd. (שָׁוֶה); Σαυη.

7740 †II. שָׁוֵה in **n.pr.loc.** עֵמֶק שׁ׳ Gn 14^{17}(v. ׳ע); Σαυη.

3438 †יִשְׁוָה **n.pr.m.** in Asher, Gn 46^{17} = 1 Ch 7^{30}; Ιεσσαι, Ισουα, Ιεσους, etc.

3440 †I. יִשְׁוִי **n.pr.m.** **1.** in Asher, Gn 46^{17} = 1 Ch 7^{30}, Nu 26^{44}; Ιεουλ, Ιουλ, Ισουι, Ιεσου, etc. **2.** a son of Saul 1 S 14^{49}; Ιεσσιου(λ), but read אישבעל as 1 Ch 8^{33} 9^{39} (v. אִישׁ־בֹּשֶׁת p. 36^{a}), cf. We Dr al.

3441 †II. יִשְׁוִי **adj.gent.** of foregoing **1**; c. art. as n. coll. הַיִּ׳, Nu 26^{44}.

7737 †II. [שָׁוָה] **vb. Pi.** set, place (B Aram. Hithpa. 𝔗 שְׁוָא Pa. *set, make* (oft. 𝔗 = שית, שום); Thes al. sub I. ׳שׁ, orig. *set, place*, then *set together*, compare, < weakened fr. orig. *make even, right*, cf. Vulg. Ar. سَوَّى II. *make* (Wahrm, cf. also Ba$^{ES 66}$));—*Pf.* 1 s. שִׁוִּיתִי ψ 16^{8} *I have set* ׳י *before me* (לְנֶגְדִּי); שׁ׳ עֵזֶר עַל 89^{20} *I have placed strength upon* a hero, cf. 21^{6}; *Pt.* מְשַׁוֶּה רַגְלַי כָּ 2 S 22^{34} *setting my feet like* hinds = ψ 18^{34} (cf. 𝔗 שַׁוִּי כְּ Gn 48^{20} Je 29^{22}, for שׂים כְּ);—Is 38^{13} v. I. שׁוה;—*Impf.* = *make, produce*, 3 ms. פְּרִי יְשַׁוֶּה לּוֹ Ho 10^{1} (Israel as vine), si vera l., v. We Now (|| עשׂה פְּרִי Ho 9^{16}, cf. 8^{7}).

7743 †[שׁוּחַ] **vb.** sink down (Buhl disting. this as II. ׳שׁ (Ar. ساخ (و) *sink down*, MI$^{9.23}$ אשוח prob. *depression, excavation, reservoir*, so אשיח Ecclus 50^{3}), and hence שָׁחָה Pr 2^{18}, si vera l., and foll. deriv., from I. ׳שׁ *melt away* (Ar. ساح (ى) *flow and spread, melt away*, Eth. ሰሐ: *cause to dwindle*, ሰሕ: *phthisis*, Aram. שׁוּחַ, ܫܚ *flow* or *melt away, vanish*), whence La 3^{20} ψ 44^{26}; but insuff. evidence for I. ׳שׁ in Heb.);—*sink down*, **Qal** *Pf.* 3 fs. שָׁחָה לֶעָפָר נַפְשֵׁנוּ ψ 44^{26} (|| דָּבְקָה לָאָרֶץ); שָׁחָה אֶל־מָוֶת בֵּיתָהּ (|| אֶל־רְפָאִים) Pr 2^{18}; but ׳ב masc., rd. שָׁחָה, √שחה, Albr$^{ZAW xvi (1896), 82}$, so Toy); *Impf.* 3 fs. תָּשׁוּחַ עָלַי נַפְשִׁי La 3^{20} Qr, **Hiph.** declar. תָּשִׁיחַ Kt, of depression of mind.
—ψ 49^{15} Gr rds. שָׁחוּ for MT שָׁתּוּ but v. שׁתת.— 8371
Hithp. ψ 42, 43 v. שׁחח. p. 1006, 1060 7817

†שׁוּחָה **n.f.** pit;—abs. ׳שׁ Je 2^{6} *land of* 7745
steppe and pits (coll.); fig., כָּרָה שׁ׳ לִי Je 18^{20}, so v^{22} (Qr); עֲמֻקָּה Pr 23^{27} *deep pit* (in fig. of harlot), cf. 22^{14}.

†שִׁיחָה **n.f.** id.;—כרה שׁ׳ Je 18^{22} Kt (Qr 7882
שׁוּחָה), ψ 57^{7}; pl. כ׳ שִׁיחוֹת 119^{85}.

†שַׁחַת **n.f.** pit;—abs. ׳שׁ ψ 7^{16} +; שָׁחַת 16^{10} 7845
+; cstr. שַׁחַת Is 38^{17} ψ 35^{7}; sf. שַׁחְתָּם Ez 19$^{4.8}$ (+ שַׁחְתּוֹ ψ 35^{8b} We);—**1.** *pit*, for catching lion (in fig.) Ez 19$^{4.8}$; fig. פעל שׁ׳ ψ 7^{16}; c. עשׂה 9^{16}; c. כרה 35^{7} (transp. ׳שׁ to v^{b}); c. חפר 94^{13} Pr 26^{27}; + ψ 35^{8b} 𝔊 We (for שׁוֹאָה); טָבַל בַּשׁ׳ Jb 9^{31}. **2.** *pit* of Sh^{e}ʾôl, ירד שׁ׳ Jb 33^{24}; ראה (ה)שׁ׳ ψ 16^{10}(|| שְׁאוֹל), 49^{10}; לַשׁ׳, c. הוֹרִיד Ez 28^{8}, and ψ 55^{24} (לִבְאֵר שׁ׳); קָרֵב Jb 33^{22}; יָמוּת Is 51^{14}; עָבַר בַּשׁ׳ Jb 33^{28}; יָרַד אֶל־שׁ׳ ψ 30^{10}; מִשּׁ׳, c. חשק Is 38^{17} (poem), c. חשׂךְ Jb 33^{18} (מִנִּי־); c. העלה Jon 2^{7}; c. הֵשִׁיב Jb 33^{30} (מִנִּי־); c. גאל ψ 103^{4}; personif. Jb 17^{14} (|| רִמָּה).—׳שׁ here either = שְׁאוֹל (hollow place, cavern), or < = pit in שְׁאוֹל (cf., from Ezek. on, בּוֹר **5**; also אֲבַדּוֹן, p. 2, and עִמְקֵי שְׁאוֹל Pr 9^{18}. This distinction of two parts of שְׁאוֹל became important in Jewish and Christian theology).

†שׁוּחַ **n.pr.m.** son of Abr. and Keturah, 7744
Gn 25^{2} 1 Ch 1^{32}; Σωυε, Σωε, Σουε.—In As. *Šuḫi* is named as Aramaean land on Euphr. (left bank Tiele$^{Gesch. 153}$ < right bank, cf. esp. Schr$^{KG 142 f.}$; it had, however, dependencies on left bank) by TP I. (KB$^{i. 33}$), Ašurnaṣirp. (Id.$^{ib. 99, 101}$).

†II. שׁוּחָה **n.pr.** 'son' of חוּר, 1 Ch 4^{11} (Ασχα, 7746
Σουα), = חוּשָׁה v^{4} (Ωσαν, Ουσα), v. ׳ח.

†שׁוּחִי, שֻׁחִי **adj.gent.** of שׁוּחַ (Hilpr^{Assyriaca} 7747
$^{i (1894), 56}$ cp. As. ^{m}*Su-ḫa-ai*);—בִּלְדַּד הַשּׁוּ׳ Jb 2^{11} 8^{1} 42^{9}; הַשּׁ׳ 18^{1} 25^{1}; ὁ Σαυχ(ε)ιτης, (Σαυχαιων).

†שׁוּחָם **n.pr.m.** in Dan, Nu 26^{42}, Σαμ(ε)ι, 7748
Σαμε; = II. חֻשִׁים, חוּשִׁים Gn 46^{23}, Ασομ.

†שׁוּחָמִי **adj.gent.** of foregoing; c. art. 7749
הַשּׁ׳ as n. coll. Nu 26^{42}.

[יְשׁוֹחָיָה] **n.pr.m.** v. sub שׁחח. p. 1006 3439

†I. שׁוּט **vb.** go or rove about (NH Aram. 7751
שׁוּט *rove, row* (Jon 1^{13}), *swim* (Is 25^{11}), *stroke*,

besmear; v. also שׂוּם);—**Qal** *go* or *rove about: Pf.* 3 pl., abs. שָׁטוּ הָעָם Nu 11[8] (J; gathering manna), so, c. ב loc., *Impf.* 3 mpl. וַיָּשֻׁטוּ 2 S 24[8], *Imv.* ms. שׁוּט־נָא v[2], *Inf. cstr.* שׁוּט Jb 1[7], שֻׁט 2[2] (both ‖ הִתְהַלֵּךְ), perhaps also Gn 24[63] (לָשׂוּט for
7742, 7878 לָשׂוּחַ, so 𝔖 Thes[1322] cf. Di Gunk Dr); Je 8[6] Du reads שָׁט for שָׁב.—*Pt.* שָׁטִים v. שׁוט denom. infr. **Pōʿl.** *go eagerly, quickly, to and fro: Impf.* 3 ms. יְשׁוֹטְטוּ לְבַקֵּשׁ Am 8[12] (‖ וְנָעוּ); abs. יְשֹׁטְטוּ Dn 12[4]; c. ב loc., *Imv.* mpl. שׁוֹטְטוּ Je 5[1], *Pt.* pl. מְשׁוֹטְטִים Zc 4[10], מְשֹׁטְטוֹת 2 Ch 16[9] (both of עֵינֵי י׳). **Hithpōʿl.** *Imv.* fpl., ב loc., הִתְשׁוֹטַטְנָה Je 49[3] *run to and fro.*

7752 †שׁוֹט **n.m.**[Is 28,15] **scourge, whip** (NH *id.*, so Ar. سَوْطٌ, سَاطَ (و) *mix, stir about and beat;* Eth. ሰውጥ: Aram. שׁוֹטָא, ܫܘܛܐ; from foregoing? cf. Germ. *streifen;* or onomat., cf. *swish, switch?*);—שׁ׳ abs. Is 10[26]+, cstr. Jb 5[21]; pl. שׁוֹטִים 1 K 12[11]+;—**1.** *scourge,* for chastisement, 1 K 12[11.14] = 2 Ch 10[11.12] (all c. vb. יִסַּר); fig. of national scourge (wielded by י׳) Is 10[26] 28[15] (Qr;
7885 > Kt שַׁיִט), v[18] (both שׁ׳ שׁוֹטֵף, v. שׁטף), calamity Jb 9[23]; *lash* of (accusing) tongue Jb 5[21] (rd. מִשּׁ׳ as 𝔊). **2.** *whip,* for horse, קוֹל שׁ׳ Na 3[2] i.e. *crack of whip,* שׁ׳ לַסּוּס Pr 26[3] (‖ שֵׁבֶט לְגֵו כְּסִילִים).

7850 †שֹׁטֵט **n.[m.] scourge;**—abs. שׁ׳ בְּצִדֵּיכֶם Jos 23[13] (D; national scourge; < rd. שׁוֹטִים).

7885 †שַׁיִט **n.[m.]** rowing (as *whipping, lashing* the water);—only אֳנִי־שׁ׳ Is 33[21] *rowing ves-*
7752 *sel;*—28[15] Kt v. שׁוֹט. above

7751 †[שׁוּט] **vb.denom. row;**—*Pt.* pl. שָׁטִים *rowers* Ez 27[8.26] (of Tyre as ship).

4880 †מָשׁוֹט **n.[m.]** oar;—תֹּפְשֵׂי מ׳ Ez 27[29].

4880 †[מִשּׁוֹט] **n.[m.]** id.; pl. sf. מִשּׁוֹטַיִךְ Ez 27[6] (Kö[ii. 153], cf. Ges[§ 72 e]), made of oak-trees.

7590 †II. [שׁוּט] **vb. treat with despite,** only Ezek. (Aram. שׁוּט, ܫܛ *despise;* cf. perhaps As. *šâṭu, rebel,* Meissn);—only **Qal** *Pt.*, c. acc. pers.: mpl. (subst.) הַשָּׁאטִים אוֹתָם Ez 28[24.26] (Kö[ii. 1. 108, 346] Ges[§ 72 p]); fpl. בְּנוֹת פְּלִשְׁתִּים הַשָּׁאטוֹת אוֹתָךְ 16[57] (Kö[ib. 189]).

7589 †שְׁאָט **n.[m.] despite, contempt** (expanded fr. שׁוּט supr., Kö[i. 439; ii. 1, 486]);—abs. בִּשְׁ׳ בְּנֶפֶשׁ Ez 25[15] *with despite in* the *soul;* cstr. בִּשְׁ׳ נֶפֶשׁ 36[5]; sf. בְּכָל־שָׁאטְךָ בְּנ׳ 25[6] (Ges[§ 23 c] Kö[ii. 1. 67]).

שׁול (√ of foll.; cf. Ar. سَوِلَ *hang down loose*).

†[שׁוּל] **n.m.**[Is 6,1] **skirt,** of robe;—pl. cstr. 7757
שׁוּלֵי Ex 28[34]+; sf. שׁוּלַיִךְ Na 3[5]+, שׁוּלָיו Is 6[1]+, שׁוּלֶיהָ La 1[9];—*skirts;* of י׳'s train, in vision Is 6[1]; elsewh. of city personif. as woman, in phrase of ignominy, גִּלֵּיתִי שׁ׳ עַל־פָּנַיִךְ Na 3[5], חָשַׂפְתִּי שׁוּלַיִךְ Je 13[26], נִגְלוּ שׁ׳ וגו׳ Je 13[22]; of defilement, טֻמְאָתָהּ בְּשׁ׳ La 1[9]; of high priest's robe Ex 28[33.33.34] = 39[24.25.26] (all P).

שׁוֹלָל v. שׁלל. p. 1021 7758

†שׁוּלַמִּית usually expl. as **adj.gent. f.** 7759
Shulammite;—c. art. as n. הַשּׁ׳ heroine of Song of Songs Ct 7[1.1]; = Shunammite (from שׁוּנֵם, mod. *Sulem*), 𝔊[B] Σουμανεῖτις; but 𝔊[א A] Σουλαμιτις; ? cp. Nab. n.pr.f. שלימת = سُلَيْمَةُ, سَلِيمَةُ, Lzb[376].

†[שׁוּם] **n.[m.] garlic;**—pl. שׁוּמִים Nu 11[5] 7762
(J) (*allium sativum,* Linn, Thes Löw[No. 336] Post[Hast. DB ii. 110] Tristr[NHB 448] (or *allium Ascalonicum,* cf. Buhl, after Tristr[FFP 430]; v. this and Post[Flora 789] for many kinds of *allium*); Ar. ثُومٌ, Aram. תּוּמָא, ܬܘܡܐ, As. *šûmu*).

שֻׁמָתִי v. שָׁמָה infra. p. 1029 8126

†שׁוּנִי **1. n.pr.m.** in Gad, Gn 46[16] Nu 26[15]; 7764-65
Σαυν(ε)ις, Σουνει, Σωυνι. **2. adj.gent.** of **1**, 7765
c. art. = n. coll. Nu 26[15].

†שׁוּנֵם **n.pr.loc.** in Issachar;—Jos 19[18] (P), 7766
1 S 28[4] 2 K 4[8]; Σουναν[μ], Σωμαν, Σουμαν, 𝔊[L] Jos Συνημ; in Egypt. *Ša-n-m-â, Ša-na-ma* WMM[As. u. Eur. 170]; mod. *Sûlem,* N. of *Zerʿîn* (*Jezreel*), Buhl[G 217], cf. GASm[G 400 ff.].

†שׁוּנַמִּית **adj. gent. f.** of foregoing: **1.** 7767
אֲבִישַׁג הַשּׁ׳ 1 K 1[3.15] 2[17.21] (הַשּׁ׳), v[22] (*id.*). **2.** הַשּׁ׳ 2 K 4[12.25.36].

†[שָׁוַע] **vb. Pi. cry out for help** (Gerb[33] 7768
thinks denom. from שַׁוְעָה, and this from √ akin to ישע *deliver*);—*Pf.* 1 s. שִׁוַּעְתִּי ψ 30[3] + 3 t.; *Impf.* 3 fs. תְּשַׁוֵּעַ Jb 24[12]; 2 ms. תְּשַׁוַּע Is 58[9], etc.; *Inf. cstr.* sf. שַׁוְּעִי ψ 28[2] 31[23]; שַׁוְעִי 5[3] (Ol[§ 182 d]), etc.; *Pt.* מְשַׁוֵּעַ 72[12] Jb 29[12];—*cry for help:* abs. ψ 72[12] Jb 19[7] 24[12] 29[12] 30[28] 35[9], + Is 38[13] Houb Lo Che Du al. (for שִׁוִּיתִי); specif. to God ψ 5[3] 18[42] 119[147] Jb 36[13] Is 58[9] Jon 2[3] Hb 1[2] La 3[8]; c. אֶל ψ 18[7] 22[25] 28[2] = 31[23], 30[3] 88[14] + v[2] (rd. with Weir אֱלֹהֵי שִׁוַּעְתִּי יוֹם צָעַקְתִּי), Jb 30[20] 38[41].

†I. שׁוּעַ, [שֶׁוַע?] **n.m. cry for help;**—לְהֶן שׁ׳ 7769,
Jb 30[24] (Bi Di Bu Du לֹא יְשַׁוֵּעַ); שׁוּעֲךָ 36[19] (Bu 7773
Buhl שֶׁוְעֲךָ, Du שִׁיחֲךָ).—I. שׁוּעַ v. p. 447[b]. 7769

7771 †II. שֶׁוַע n.[m.] cry, perhaps *war-cry*, or *cry for help* in war Is 22^{5}.—I. שׁוּעַ v. ישׁע.

7775 †[שַׁוְעָה] **n.f. cry for help**;—cstr. שַׁוְעַת 1 S 5^{12} Je 8^{19}; sf. שַׁוְעָתִי 2 S 22^{7} = ψ 18^{7}, ψ 39^{13} 40^{2} 102^{2} La 3^{56} (gloss on רוחתי Ew al.); שַׁוְעָתָם Ex 2^{23} (P), ψ 34^{16} 145^{19}.

7769, 7771, 7774 I. שׁוֹעַ, I. II. שׁוֹעַ, שׁוֹעָא v. p. 447^{b} supra.

7772 †III. שׁוֹעַ **n.pr.gent.** Ez 23^{23} usu. identified with As. *Sutû*, *Sutî*, nomads of Mesop. and (later) E. of Tigris, Dl$^{Pa\ 234\ ff.}$ COT$^{ad\ loc.}$ Wkl $^{KAT\ 3.\ 22}$ Dr$^{Hast.\ DB\ KoA}$.

7779 †[שׁוּף] **vb. bruise** (NH *id.*, Aram. שׁוּף, שְׁפַף, ܫܦ *rub off, away, grind* (Ex 32^{20} 𝔗𝔓 for טְחַן); v. esp. Dr^{Gn}; > Di al. think ‖ form of I. שׁאף);—**Qal** *Impf.* 3 ms. + 2 ms. הוּא יְשׁוּפְךָ רֹאשׁ וְאַתָּה תְּשׁוּפֶנּוּ עָקֵב Gn 3^{15}; אֲשֶׁר־בִּשְׂעָרָה יְשׁוּפֵנִי Jb 9^{17}; אַךְ חֹשֶׁךְ יְשׁוּפֵנִי ψ 139^{11} mng. unsuitable, read perh. c. Ew al. יְשׂוּכֵּנִי *cover, screen, me.*

7780-81 שׁוֹפָךְ v. שׁוֹבָךְ. שׁוּפָמִי v. שְׁפוּפָם sub שׁפף. p. 1000, 1051

I. שׁוק (√ of foll., meaning dub.; Ar. سَاقَ is *drive* beast, etc., *carry on* affairs; Eth. ሰቀ: *sustain*; cf. Ar. سَاقٌ *leg*, esp. *shank*, Aram. שׁוֹקָא *leg* (rare), ܫܩܐ *leg, thigh*; connexion dub. with As. *suḳu*, *street*, Aram. שׁוּקָא, ܫܘܩܐ, *street*, *market-place* (whence Ar. سُوقٌ loan-word acc. to Frä^{187}; but then ש=س?), Palm. שוק *id.*, Lzb^{373}).

7785 שׁוֹק$_{19}$ **n.**[**f.**$^{Lv\ 7,\ 33}$ cf. Albr$^{ZAW\ xvi\ (1896),\ 76\ f.}$, so Ar., v. Lane W$^{AG,\ §290(b)}$] **leg**;—שׁ׳ abs. 1 S 9^{24}+, cstr. Ex 29^{27}+; du. שֹׁקַיִם Dt 28^{35} Pr 26^{7}, cstr. שׁוֹקֵי ψ 147^{10}, sf. שׁוֹקָיו Ct 5^{15};—*leg*: **1.** of man, specif. lower leg, calf, disting. from thigh, in וַיַּךְ אוֹתָם שׁ׳ עַל־יָרֵךְ Ju 15^{8} *he smote them, leg upon thigh*, i.e. utterly (cf. GFM), Dt 28^{35} (‖ בִּרְכַּיִם), Pr 26^{7} ψ 147^{10} Ct 5^{15}; of woman (city personif.) Is 47^{2}. **2.** of sacrificial animal, specif. upper *leg*, thigh, *hind leg*, portion eaten 1 S 9^{24} (cf. Klein$^{ZPV\ vi\ (1883),\ 98}$, cited also by Nes$^{Marg.\ 13}$), שׁ׳ הַיָּמִין *right thigh* Ex 29^{32} + 6 t. P (v. יָמִין), שׁ׳ הַתְּרוּמָה Lv 7^{34} + 4 t. P, *thigh of contribution* (v. ת׳ p. 929).—𝔊 βραχίων, 𝔙 *armus*, hence AV al. *shoulder*, but v. Di Baen Dr$^{Dt\ 18,\ 3}$.

7784 †שׁוּק **n.m. street** (Aram.; v. √);—שׁ׳ Pr 7^{8} Ec 12$^{4.5}$; pl. שְׁוָקִים Ct 3^{2}.

7783 †II. [שׁוּק] **vb.** prob. **be abundant** (As. *šûḳu*, *abundance*);—**Pōʿl.** *Impf.* 3 ms. sf. וַתְּשֹׁקְקֶהָ ψ 65^{10} *thou* (י׳) hast visited the earth *and given it abundance* (Hup Che al.; > Vrss thought of הִשְׁקָה *irrigate*, so Bae EV). **Hiph.** *Pf.* consec. וְהֵשִׁיקוּ הַיְקָבִים תִּירוֹשׁ Jo 2^{24} *the vats overflow with must*, so (acc. om.) 4^{13}.

III. שׁוק (√ of foll.; Ba$^{ES\ 46}$ cp. Ar. شَاقَ *attract*, *impel*, of desire, affection, شَوْقٌ *desire*, but ش=ש is doubtful; perhaps therefore (cf. Buhl) cp. سَاقَ *drive*, v. I. שׁוק; or rd. תְּשׁוּקָה; on NH שׁוּק, השתוקק, v. Nes$^{ZAW\ xxiv\ (1904),\ 312\ ff.}$).

8669 †[תְּשׁוּקָה] **n.f. longing**;—of woman for man, אֶל־אִישֵׁךְ תְּשׁוּקָתֵךְ Gn 3^{16} (J); of man for woman, אֲנִי לְדוֹדִי וְעָלַי תְּשׁוּקָתוֹ Ct 7^{11}; of beast to devour, fig. אֵלֶיךָ תְּשׁוּקָתוֹ Gn 4^{7} (J). (𝔊 ἀποστροφή Gn, ἐπιστροφή Ct, whence Nes$^{Marg.\ 6}$ prop. תְּשׁוּבָתֵךְ Gn 3^{16}, which Ball^{Hpt} reads in all; but how explain the unusual and striking word in MT?).

7788 †I. [שׁוּר] **vb.** perh. **travel, journey** (As. *šâru*, *pass along, take one's way*, Ar. سَارَ (ى) *go, pass along, journey*, سَيَّارَةٌ *caravan*, Palm. שירתא Lzb^{375} SAC^{113} Cooke^{271}, Syr. ܫܝܪܬܐ (?Ar. loan-wd., Frä^{180}));—**Qal** *Impf.* 2 fs. וַתָּשֻׁרִי לַמֶּלֶךְ בַּשֶּׁמֶן Is 57^{9} *and thou* (the apostate faction) *didst journey to* (the god) *Melek with* (thine) *oil*, i.e. bring, offer it (Che Marti read וַתָּסֻכִי). *Pt.* fpl. שָׁרוֹתַיִךְ Ez 27^{25} ships of Tarshish were *thy travellers* (i.e. traders), but improbable; Krae שָׁרוֹת לָךְ בְּ *journey for thee* with thy wares; Toy רֹכְלַיִךְ בְּ; Co שֵׁרְתוּךְ *served thee.*

8670 †תְּשׁוּרָה **n.f. gift, present**(?) (fr. above √ = thing brought, offered? very dubious);—ת׳ 1 S 9^{7} (meaning inferred from context).

7789 †II. [שׁוּר] **vb. behold, regard** (esp. Jb);—**Qal** *Impf.* 3 ms. יָשׁוּר Je 5^{26}, sf. יְשׁוּרֶנּוּ Jb 34^{29}, etc.; *Imv.* ms. שׁוּר Jb 35^{5};—**1.** *behold*, c. acc. pers. Nu 23^{9} 24^{17} (poems in JE, ‖ רָאָה), לֹא תְשׁוּרֵנִי, subj. eye, Jb 24^{15}, and (=I shall not exist) 7^{8}, cf. 20^{9} (subj. מְקוֹמוֹ), 17^{15}; God object 34^{29} 35^{14}; *look, gaze*, abs., מִן loc. Ct 4^{8}. **2.** *regard* with watchful care (subj. י׳) Ho 14^{9}; so, = *notice*, Jb 35^{13}; *regard, observe*, acc. rei, God's word Jb 33^{14} (Hi De Da al.), so, (reading 2 ms.), Siegf Bu; Du יְשִׁיבֶנּוּ *he* (God) *retracts it not.* **3.** *watch* stealthily, *lie in wait*, כְּנָמֵר עַל־דֶּרֶךְ אָשׁוּר Ho 13^{7} (subj. י׳; Meinh Marti אֶשְׁקֹד; 𝔊𝔖𝔙 We Now al. אַשּׁוּר), Je 5^{26} (subj. wicked).—Jb 33^{27} v. שׁיר.

7790 †I. [שׁוּר] dub. word, only pl. sf. וַתַּבֵּט עֵינִי בְּשׁוּרָי ψ 92[12], read בְּשׁוֹרְרָי (Bae al.) v. foll.

8324 †[שׁוֹרֵר] **n.m.** (insidious) **watcher**, (prop. **Pō'l.** *Pt.*, מְ׳ om., Ges § 52 s);—pl. sf. שׁוֹרְרַי ψ 56[3], שׁוֹרְרָי 5[9] 27[11], שֹׁרְרָי 54[7] 59[11]; 92[12] v. foregoing.

III. **שׁוּר** (√of foll.; Ar. ثَارَ (و) is *become raised, excited, leap, spring;* NH שׁוֹר = BH, = Sab. תור(ן) SabDenkm No. 12, 1. 3 DHM ZMG xxxvii (1883), 329; Ar. ثَوْرٌ, Aram. תּוֹרָא, ܬܘܪܐ; Nab. תורא as n.pr.m. Lzb 384 (Gk. ταῦρος, Lat. *taurus*, Eng. *steer*); As. *šûru*, Eth. ሰር:).

7794 שׁוֹר 78 **n.m.** Ne 5, 18 **a head of cattle, bullock, ox**, etc. (oft. + חֲמוֹר, שֶׂה, etc.);—שׁ׳ abs. Is 1[3]+, cstr. Ex 21[35]+, sf. שׁוֹרוֹ 20[17]+, etc.; pl. שְׁוָרִים Ho 12[2];—usu. a single *head of cattle*, without emphasis on sex (opp. בָּקָר coll. Ex 21[37] Nu 7[3]): as property, spoil of war, etc. Ex 20[17] (E; Gi v[14]) = Dt 5[18], cf. Dt 5[14], Ex 21[33] (E) ‖ Dt 22[4], Ex 21[37.37] (‖ בָּקָר of five head), 22[3.8.9.29] 23[12] (all E), Dt 22[1] Gn 49[6] (poem in J), Dt 28[31] Ju 6[4] 1 S 12[3] Jb 24[3]; as *licking up* (לָחַךְ) grass Nu 22[4] (J), feeding ψ 106[20] (in ref. to golden calf), cf. Is 7[25] 32[20]; lowing Jb 6[5]; as intelligent Is 1[3], vicious (goring נָגַח) Ex 21[28.28.28] + 11 t. Ex 21 (E); used in ploughing Dt 22[10], threshing 25[4], cf. Pr 14[4]; drawing wagon Nu 7[3] (P; opp. בָּקָר coll.); פְּנֵי שׁ׳ Ez 1[10]; specif. of male †Jb 21[10] (opp. פָּרָה), of female †Lv 22[28] (H), perhaps also Nu 18[17] (P), appar. generic Dt 15[19] 33[17] (poem, fig.); rarely coll. Gn 32[6] (+ צֹאן), Ex 34[19]—cf. Lv 27[26] (P)—Jos 6[21] 7[24] (all J), 1 S 15[3] 22[19]; †as slaughtered Pr 7[22], for food 1 S 14[34.34] (but v[b] read אֶת־)אֲשֶׁר) with 𝔊 Th We Dr al.), 1 K 1[19.25] Dt 14[4] Lv 17[3] (H), cf. Ne 5[18] (שׁ׳ אֶחָד), Pr 15[17]; for †sacrifice Ju 6[25] (פַּר־הַשּׁ׳, text strange, cf. GFM), ψ 69[32] (שׁוֹר פָּר, but join פָּר to v[b] Bae), 2 S 6[13] Ho 12[12], Lv 9[4.18] (P), 22[23.27] (H), Nu 15[11] (P), Dt 17[1] 18[3], cf. Lv 7[23] 9[19]; מִשּׁוֹר זֶבַח Lv 4[10] (P); illicit sacrifice Is 66[3].

7791 †II. שׁוּר **n.[m.] wall** (Aram. שׁוּרָא, ܫܘܪܐ);—Gn 49[22] (poem in J), 2 S 22[30] = ψ 18[30]; pl. sf. שׁוּרֹתָם Jb 24[11] *their walls* De Di De, cf. Bu; but
8284 v. שׁוּרָה infra; שָׁרוֹתֶיהָ Je 5[10] = *its walls*, acc. to Vrss AV RV Gf Gie, read then שֻׁ׳, but v. id.

7793 †III. שׁוּר **n.pr.loc.** SW. of Palestine, on E. border of Egypt;—Gn 16[7] (J; דֶּרֶךְ שׁ׳), 20[1] (E), towards Egypt 25[18] (J), 1 S 15[7], שׁוּרָה 27[8]; מִדְבַּר־שׁ׳ Ex 15[22] (J).—Oft. supposed to denote properly the 'wall' or line of fortresses, built by Egyptian kings across isthmus of Suez; but dub.: cf. Dr Hast. DB Shur.

†[שׁוּרָה] **n.f.** prob. **row** of olives or vines 7791
(so Du Buhl al.; cf. NH שׁוּרָה, JAram. שׁוּרְתָא *row*, whence mod. Ar. شورة as loan-word, cf. Vogelst Landwirthschaft 41 f.);—pl. sf. שׁוּרֹתָם Jb 24[11] (al. II. שׁוּר); Bu and Du del. sf.; here also Je 5[10] (reading שֻׁ׳) Du Buhl Dr, *her* (vine-)*rows*, but v. II. שׁוּר.

שַׁוְשָׁא **n.pr.m.** 1 Ch 18[16], v. שְׂרָיָה. 7798

†I. שׁוּשַׁן, שׁוֹשָׁן **n.m.** שׁוֹשַׁנָּה **n.f.** usually 7799
lily, prob. any lily-like flower (Tristr NHB 462 ff. Post Hast. DB Lily Löw No. 323; NH שׁוֹשַׁנָּה, Ar. سَوْسَن (Vulg. سُوسَن), esp. *iris*, Aram. שׁוֹשַׁנְּתָא, ܫܘܫܢܐ (PS 4344), Gk. σοῦσον Lewy Fremdw. 48; orig. loan-word from Egypt. *sššn*, *sôšĕn*, Erman ZMG xlvi (1892), 117);—*lily:* in sim., יִפְרַח כַּשּׁוֹשַׁנָּה Ho 14[7] (of Isr.), כְּשׁוֹ׳ בֵּין הַחוֹחִים Ct 2[2] (sim. of bride), so cstr. שׁוֹשַׁנַּת הָעֲמָקִים v[1] (cf. חֲבַצֶּלֶת); pl. שׁוֹשַׁנִּים 2[16] 4[5] 6[2.3] 7[3] and (fig. of lover's lips) 5[13]; of flower-shaped capitals of pillars, מַעֲשֵׂה שׁוּשַׁן 1 K 7[19], מ׳ שׁוֹשָׁן v[22]; cf. פֶּרַח שׁוֹשָׁן of brim of molten sea v[26], ‖ פ׳ שׁוֹשַׁנָּה 2 Ch 4[5]; elsewh. only ψ-titles:
אֶל־שֹׁשַׁנִּים ψ 45[1] 69[1], עַל־שׁוּשַׁן עֵדוּת 60[1], עַל־שֹׁשַׁנִּים 7802
עֵדוּת 80[1]; meaning not clear, v. Bae et Comm. al.; yet cf. עֵדוּת, sub עוד.

†II. שׁוּשַׁן **n.pr.loc. Susa**, winter residence 7800
of Persian kings; Σουσαν, ἐν Σουσοις (cuneif. *Šûšan* Dl Pa 326 COT Ne 1, 1 Billerbeck Susa Say Hast. DB Shushan);—שׁ׳ הַבִּירָה Ne 1[1] (9th month, כִּסְלֵו), Dn 8[2] (in Elam), Est 1[2.5] 2[3.5.8] 3[15a] 8[14] 9[6.11.12] (12th month, אֲדָר, v[1]); הַבִּ׳ om., שׁוּשָׁן Est 4[8.16] and (month אֲדָר) 9[13.14.15.15.18]; הָעִיר שׁ׳ 3[15b] 8[15].

†שׁוּשַׁק **n.pr.m.** 1 K 14[25] Kt, Qr שִׁישַׁק p. 1011 7895

שׁוּת v. שׁית. p. 1011 7896

†שׁוּתֶלַח **n.pr.m.** in Ephraim, Nu 26[35] 7803
1 Ch 7[21], שׁוּתָלַח v[20] Nu 26[36]; Σουταλα, Σωθαλα, etc., 𝔊L Σουθαλα(αμ).

†שֻׁתַלְחִי **adj.gent.** of foregoing; c. art. 8364
הַשּׁ׳ as subst. coll. Nu 26[35].

†[שָׁזַף] **vb. catch sight of, look on** (of 7805
eye);—**Qal** *Pf.* 3 fs. sf. pers., subj. עַיִן, שְׁזָפַתּוּ Jb 20[9], so (rei) 28[7]; cf. שֶׁשְּׁזָפַתְנִי הַשָּׁמֶשׁ Ct 1[6] *because the sun hath looked on me.*

[שָׁזַר] 21 **vb. Hoph. be twisted** (NH שָׁזַר 7806
twist; cf. Ar. شَزَرَ *look askew at,* also *twist* cord

from the left Ba$^{ES 49}$ (expl. שׂ, for normal שׁ, as dissim. before ז), Jacob$^{Ar. Dichter i. 52}$);—*Pt.* שֵׁשׁ מָשְׁזָר Ex 26$^{1.31.36}$ + 17 t. Ex (P); שֵׁשׁ om. 39^{24}.

7807 שַׁח v. שחח. p. 1006

7809 †[שָׁחַד] **vb. give a present, bribe** (Ecclus 35^{14}; Aram. שְׁחַד, ܫܚܕ *bribe;* perh. also As. *šidê, gifts,* Dl$^{WB 643}$);—**Qal** *Impf.* 2 fs., acc. pers. וַתִּשְׁחֲדִי אוֹתָם Ez 16^{33} *thou didst bribe them* to come (לָבוֹא; ‖ נָתַן נְדָנִים); rd. prob. also *Inf. cstr.* sf. שַׁחֲדָהּ Is 47^{11} *to buy it off* (for MT שַׁחְרָהּ, so Kr Gr Buhl Che$^{Hpt Heb 142}$, cf. Marti; v. Pr 6^{35}); *Imv.* mpl. שִׁחֲדוּ בַעֲדִי (Ges$^{§ 64 a}$) Jb 6^{22} *give a bribe for me.*

7810 †שֹׁחַד **n.m.** present, specif. bribe;—שׁ׳ abs. Is 1^{23} + 22 t.;—*bribe,* usu. to pervert justice, obj. of לָקַח Ex 23^{8a} (E), = Dt 16^{19a}, Dt 10^{17} 1 S 8^3 2 Ch 19^7 ψ 15^5 Pr 17^{23}; + inf., take *bribe* to do something, Dt 27^{25} Ez 22^{12}; אֹהֵב שׁ׳ Is 1^{23}; cf. also 5^{23} 33^{15} Ex 23^{8b} (E) = Dt 16^{19b}, Mi 3^{11} ψ 26^{10} Pr 17^8 21^{14}; אָהֳלֵי־שׁ׳ Jb 15^{34}, i.e. abode of bribe-givers; שׁ׳ Pr 6^{35} (‖ כֹּפֶר) is hush-money, or (poss.) legal compensation (cf. Toy); שׁ׳ elsewh. (c. שָׁלַח) of bribing king to take sides 1 K 15^{19} 2 K 16^8, cf. Is 45^{13} (‖ מְחִיר).

7812 [שָׁחָה]$_{172}$ **vb. bow down** (NH *id.;* JAram. שְׁחִי (rare); akin to שׁוח, שׁחח);—**Qal** *Imv.* fs. שְׁחִי Is 51^{23} *bow down.* **Hiph.** *Impf.* 3 ms. sf. יַשְׁחֶנָּה Pr 12^{25}, fig., anxiety *depresses it* (sc. לֵב; opp. שִׂמַּח). **Hithpaʿlēl**$_{170}$ (Ges$^{§ 75 kk}$) *Pf.* 3 ms. הִשְׁתַּחֲוָה Ez 46^2; 2 ms. הִשְׁתַּחֲוִיתָ Dt 4^{19} + 3 t.; 1 s. הִשְׁתַּחֲוֵיתִי 1 S 16^4 + 2 t.; 3 mpl. הִשְׁתַּחֲווּ Je 8^2, etc.; *Impf.* יִשְׁתַּחֲוֶה 2 S 15^{32} + 3 t.; apoc. יִשְׁתַּחוּ Is 44^{17} +; 3 mpl. יִשְׁתַּחֲווּ Gn 49^8 +; 2 fpl. תִּשְׁתַּחֲוֶיןָ Gn 33^6 37^7, etc.; *Imv.* fs. הִשְׁתַּחֲוִי ψ 45^{12}; mpl. הִשְׁתַּחֲווּ 29^2 +; *Inf. cstr.* הִשְׁתַּחֲוֺת Gn 37^{10} +; sf. הִשְׁתַּחֲוָיָתִי 2 K 5^{18} (but 𝔊 𝔙 and mod. -חֲוֺתוֹ); *Pt.* מִשְׁתַּחֲוֶה 2 K 19^{27}, etc.; מִשְׁתַּחֲוִיתֶם Ez 8^{16}, read -וִים all mod.;—**1.** *bow down, prostrate oneself,* before a monarch or superior, in homage, etc.: **a.** c. לְ, after descriptive cl. (esp. with נפל, קדד, **3 b**, q. v.), 1 S 24^9 Gn 43^{28} (J) 2 S 14$^{4.22}$ Ru 2^{10} 1 K 1^{31} 2 K 4^{37} + 6 t., + (after כָּרַע) Est 3$^{2.2.5}$. **b.** c. לְ, sq. phr. (לפני) על אפים ארצה 2 S 14^{33} 1 K 1^{23}; לאפים Gn 48^{12} (E) 2 S 18^{28}; אפים Gn 42^6 (E) + 4 t.; om. אפים 33^3 (J) + 3 t.; על כַּפּוֹת רַגְלַיִךְ Is 60^{14}. **c.** c. לְ pers. only, Gn 23^7 (P) 27$^{29.29}$ 37^9 (E), 49^8 Ex 11^8 (J) + 8 t.; c. לפני Gn 23^{12} (P); c. אל Is 45^{14} (‖ התפלל); abs. Gn 33$^{6.7.7}$ (J), Ex 18^7 (E) 2 S 9^8 16^4 Is 49^7. **2.** before God, in worship, etc.: **a.** c. לְ, after descriptive phr.: קדד ארצה Ex 34^8 (J); ארצה om. Gn 24$^{26.48}$ (J) + 4 t.; כרע אפים ארצה 2 Ch 7^3; כרע 29^{29}; נפל ארצה Jb 1^{20}; נפל לפני 2 Ch 20^{18}. **b.** sq. phr.: ארצה לְ׳ Ne 8^6; קדד וישׁ׳ לְ׳ אפים ארצה Gn 24^{52} (J); הִשׁ׳ לְ׳ בְּהַדְרַת קֹדֶשׁ ψ 95^6; הִשׁ׳ ונכרעה 29^2 96^9 = 1 Ch 16^{29}; אֶל־הֵיכַל (looking towards) ψ 5^8 138^2; לַהֲדֹם רגלים 99^5 132^7. **c.** c. לְ only: 1 S 1^{28} (but read וַתִּשְׁתַּחֲוֵהוּ 𝔊 and mod.), 15^{25} Je 7^2 ψ 66^4 + 9 t.; c. לפני Dt 26^{10} Is 66^{23} + 4 t.; c. בְּ loc. Is 27^{13}; c. לְ loc. ψ 99^9; abs. Gn 22^5 (E) Ju 7^{15} + 5 t.; acc. loc. Ex 33^{10} (E) Je 26^2 Ez 46^3; לפני (ה)מזבח Is 36^7 = 2 K 18^{22} = 2 Ch 32^{12}; c. על loc. Gn 47^{31} (J) 1 K 1^{47} Ez 46^2; מֵרָחֹק *afar off* Ex 24^1 (E). **d.** before angel in theoph.: after cl. c. נפל, קדד, Jos 5^{14} Nu 22^{31}; sq. אפים ארצה Gn 19^1; ארצה 18^2 (all J). **3.** before other gods: abs. Is 2^{20} 44$^{15.17}$ 46^6; acc. loc. 2 K 5$^{18.18.18}$ 19^{37} = Is 37^{38}; c. לְ, Ex 20^5 = Dt 5^9 (10 words), Ex 23^{24} (E), Nu 25^2 (J), Jos 23^7 (D), Dt 8^{19} 11^{16} 1 K 16^{31} + 34 t.; c. על, Lv 26^1 (H); לפני 2 Ch 25^{14} (‖ קטּר).

†[שְׁחוּת] **n.f. pit** (cf. שַׁחַת from שׁוח);— 7816
sf. בִּשְׁחוּתוֹ הוּא יִפּוֹל Pr 28^{10}.

†[שְׁחִית] **n.f.** id.;—pl. sf. נִלְכַּד בִּשְׁחִיתוֹתָם 7825
La 4^{20}, וִימַלֵּט מִשְּׁ׳ ψ 107^{20}.

שִׁחוֹר v. שִׁיחוֹר. שְׁחוֹר v. I. שׁחר. p. 1007,1009 7815, 7883

†[שָׁחַח] **vb. bow, be bowed down,** 7817
crouch (NH *id.;* TelAm. *šaḫâhu* (Wkl$^{TelAm. Vocab.}$), *prostrate oneself,* prob. Canaanism; As. *šaḫâḫu* is *oppress, torment*);—**Qal** *Pf.* 3 ms. consec. וְשַׁח Is 2$^{11.17}$, 1 s. שַׁחוֹתִי ψ 38^7, שַׁחֹתִי 35^{14}, 3 pl. שַׁחוּ Jb 9^{13}, שַׁחוּ Hb 3^6 Pr 14^{19}; *Impf.* 3 ms. יָשֹׁחַ ψ 10^{10}, 3 mpl. יָשֹׁחוּ Jb 38^{40}, וַיָּשֹׁחוּ ψ 107^{39}; *Inf. cstr.* (= *abs.,* as adv., Ges$^{§ 118 q}$ Kö$^{ii. 2, §§ 221, 402 d}$ cf. also Ba$^{NB 164}$) שְׁחוֹחַ Is 60^{14};—**1.** *be bowed down, prostrated, humbled,* by י׳, Is 2$^{11.17}$ (both ‖ שָׁפֵל), Hb 3^6 (of hills), Jb 9^{13} (תַּחְתָּו שׁ׳), ψ 107^{39} (+ מָעַט); by man 10^{10}. **2.** *bow* in homage, לִפְנֵי pers. Pr 14^{19}; וְהָלְכוּ אֵלַיִךְ שְׁחוֹחַ Is 60^{14} (‖ הִשְׁתַּחֲווּ). **3.** *bow,* of mourner (קֹדֵר), ψ 35^{14} 38^7. **4.** *crouch,* of wild beast in lair Jb 38^{40}. **Niph.** *Impf. be prostrated, humbled:* וַיִּשַּׁח אָדָם Is 2^9 (‖ שָׁפֵל) = 5^{15} (‖ *id.*); *be reduced, weakened,* יִשַּׁחוּ כָּל־בְּנוֹת הַשִּׁיר Ec 12^4; = *proceed humbly,* of words מֵעָפָר Is 29^4 (‖ שָׁפֵל). **Hiph.** *prostrate, lay low,* city, walls, etc.; *Pf.* 3 ms. הֵשַׁח Is 25^{12}

26[5] (both ‖ הִשְׁפִּיל). **Hithpō῾.** *be cast down, despairing: Impf.* 3 fs. תִּשְׁתּוֹחֵח ψ 42[7], 2 fs. תִּשְׁתּוֹחֲחִי v[6.12] 43[5] (all c. subj. נַפְשִׁי).

7807 †**שַׁח** **adj. low, lowly**;— cstr. שַׁח־עֵינַיִם Jb 22[29] *lowly of eyes*, humble.

3439 †[**יְשׁוֹחָיָה**] **n.pr.m.** in Simeon (mng.?);— 'יש 1 Ch 4[36]; Ιασουια, Ιεσουια.

7819-20 **שָׁחַט** [84] **vb. slaughter, beat** (orig. *beat, flay*? cf. As. *šaḫâṭu, flay, take off* dress; Ar. سَحَطَ *slay* (but ح = *ḥ*; is this loan-word in Ar.?); NH = BH, esp. in ritual);—**Qal** *Pf.* 3 ms. 'שׁ Je 39[6]+, sf. וְשָׁחֲטוֹ consec. Lv 3[2], etc.; *Impf.* 3 ms. יִשְׁחַט Lv 4[24]+, 2 fs. וַתִּשְׁחֲטִי Ez 16[21], 3 mpl. sf. וַיִּשְׁחָטוּהוּ Ju 12[6]; *Imv.* mpl. שַׁחֲטוּ Ex 12[21] 2 Ch 35[6]; *Inf. abs.* שָׁחֹט Is 22[13]; cstr. לִשְׁחֹט Gn 22[10], -וֹט Ez 40[39], sf. שַׁחֲטָם (Ges[§ 64 a]) Ez 23[39]; *Pt. act.* שׁוֹחֵט Is 66[3], etc.; *pass.* שָׁחוּט 1 K 10[16]+, etc.;—*slaughter*: **1.** beast for food 1 S 14[32.34.34] Is 22[13] (‖הָרֹג), cf. Lv 17[3.3], for blood Gn 37[31] (E). **2.** usu. (51 t.; Hex only P, 38 t.) term. techn. of *killing* sacrifice (BJacob[ZAW xvii (1897), 51]), 1 S 1[25] Ex 29[11] Lv 1[5.11] 4[24] 9[8] Nu 19[3] 2 Ch 29[22.22.24]+; abs. Ez 40[41] (אֶל loc.); bird Lv 14[5.6.50.51]; beast in illicit sacrifice Is 66[3]; c. acc. of sacrifice (עוֹלָה, אָשָׁם, חַטָּאת, etc.) Ez 40[39] (אֶל loc.), v[42] 44[11] Lv 4[24] 7[2] 14[13]+; passover lamb †Ex 12[6], acc. הַפֶּסַח †v[21] 2 Ch 30[15] 35[1.6.11] Ezr 6[20]. **3.** *slaughter* pers. Ju 12[6] 1 K 18[40] 2 K 10[7.14] (אֶל loc.), 2 K 25[7] = Je 39[6a] = 52[10a], Je 39[6b] = 52[10b], 41[7]; 'י subj. Nu 14[16] (JE); in human sacrifice Gn 22[10] (E), to false gods Ez 16[21] 23[39] Is 57[5]. **4.** pt. pass. = *beaten, hammered*, זָהָב שָׁחוּט 1 K 10[16.17] = 2 Ch 9[15 a.16], of shekels 2 Ch 9[15 b]; so also Je 9[7] Qr חֵץ שָׁחוּט (> Kt שׁוֹחֵט) *hammered* (i.e. sharpened) *arrow*. †**Niph.** *Impf.* 3 ms. יִשָּׁחֵט Nu 11[22] (J) *be slaughtered* for food (subj. beast); 3 fs. תִּשָּׁחֵט Lv 6[18.18] (P) *be slain*, of sacrifice.

7821 †[**שְׁחִיטָה**] **n. f.** act of **slaying**;— cstr. שְׁחִיטַת הַפְּסָחִים 2 Ch 30[17].

7819 †**שַׁחֲטָה** **n.f.** (**Qal** *Inf. cstr.* Kö[i. 263]) doubtful word;—וְשׁ' שֵׂטִים הֶעְמִיקוּ Ho 5[2] RV (cf. AV) *the revolters are gone deep in slaughtering* ['Opferschlächterei' Kö[ii. 1. 590, n. 1]], Ew Now (formerly), Che *in corrupting* (rd. then שַׁחֲתָה); We Now GASm Marti שַׁחַת הַשִּׁטִּים *have made deep the pit of Shittim* (as place of idolatry).

7822,7824 שְׁחִין v. שׁחן. שְׁחִיף v. [שָׁחִיף]. below, p. 965

7823 †**שָׁחִיס** Is 37[30] = סָחִישׁ (in ‖ 2 K 19[29]), q. v. p. 695

†**שׁחל** (√of foll.; Dl[Prol. 34] cp. As. *šaḫâlu, call, proclaim*; perh. both onomatop., as Ar. سَحَلَ *bray* (of ass), cf. Nö[ZMG xl (1886), 725]).

שַׁחַל **n.m. lion** (poet.);—abs. 'שׁ Ho 5[14]+, 7826
שָׁחָל Jb 4[10]+;—*lion*, sim. of 'י, toward Israel Ho 5[14] (‖ כְּפִיר), 13[7] (‖ נָמֵר); of guilty men Jb 4[10] (‖ כְּפִירִים, אַרְיֵה); fig. of foes ψ 91[13] (‖ כְּפִיר); *lion*, as hunted 10[16] (in sim.); lit. Jb 28[8] Pr 26[13].

†**שְׁחֵלֶת** **n. f.** an ingredient of the holy 7827
incense, + נָטָף, חֶלְבְּנָה, Ex 30[34]; 𝔊𝔙 ὄνυξ, *onyx* (whence AV *onycha*), i.e. *unguis odoratus*, the *operculum*, or closing-flap, of certain molluscs, with pungent odour when burnt, v. Thes[1388 f.] Di Shipley-Cook[Ency. Bib. ONYCHA]; so most; KG Jacob[ZMG xliii (1889), 354] prop. *amber*.

שׁחן (√of foll.; cf. Ar. سَخُنَ *be hot*, then *inflamed*; Aram. שְׁחַן, ܫܚܢ *be warm, heat*).

†**שְׁחִין** **n.m. boil**, coll. **eruption**;—on man 7822
2 K 20[7] = Is 38[21], 'שׁ רָע Dt 28[35] Jb 2[7]; possibly leprous Lv 13[18.19.20], צָרֶבֶת הַשׁ' 13[23] (v. 'צ; all P), in Egypt, on man and beast Ex 9[9.10.11.11] (all P), cstr. שְׁחִין מִצְרַיִם Dt 28[27].

שׁחף (√of שַׁחֶפֶת and poss. of שַׁחַף; Ar. سَحَفَ is *pare, peel off*; also *affect with consumption* of lungs; سُحَافٌ *consumption*, so JAram. שַׁחַפְתָּא [for שַׁחֶפֶת]).

†[**שַׁחַף**] **n.[m.]** prob. **sea-mew, gull** (cf. 7828
𝔊𝔙) (from *attenuated* body, Thes); so Post[Hast. DB Cuckow] Tristr[NHB 210 ff.]; *sterna fluviatilis*, or *tern* Id[FFP 135] M'Lean-Shipley[Ency. Bib. Id.];—הַשָּׁחַף Dt 14[15] = Lv 11[16] (P), in list of unclean birds.

†**שַׁחֶפֶת** **n.f.** wasting disease, **consumption** 7829
Dt 28[22] Lv 26[16] (H).

שׁחץ (√of foll.; cf. NH *act proudly*, and deriv.; Aram. שַׁחְצָא *lion* (†ψ 17[12] edd.); Eth. ሥሕጸ: *be insolent*; Ar. شَخَصَ is *rise, be elevated*; شَخِيصٌ *bulky, man of rank*, but ش = שׁ ?).

†[**שַׁחַץ**] **n.[m.]** dignity, pride;—בְּנֵי־הַשָּׁחַץ 7830
i.e. majestic wild beasts Jb 28[8] (‖ שָׁחַל), 41[26].

†**שחצומה** Kt, **שַׁחֲצִימָה** Qr (i.e. [שַׁחֲצִים] 7831
+ ־ָה) **n.pr.loc.** in Issachar Jos 19[22]; ἐπὶ Σαλειμ κατὰ θάλασσαν, A 𝔊L Σασειμα(θ).

†[**שָׁחַק**] **vb. rub away, beat fine, pul-** 7833
verize (so Ar. سَحَقَ, سَحْقٌ *worn garment, thin clouds*; Aram. שְׁחַק, ܫܚܩ *pulverize*; Ecclus

שחק 6^{36} is *go often* (wear by treading), Str cp. *iter terere*);—**Qal** *Pf.* 3 pl. אֲבָנִים שָׁחֲקוּ מַיִם Jb 14^{19} *waters rub away stones;* 2 ms. וְשָׁחַקְתָּ Ex 30^{36} (P; of pulverizing incense, v. דקק **Hiph.**); fig., acc. of foes, *Impf.* 1 s. sf. וְאֶשְׁחָקֵם 2 S 22^{43} (‖ דקק) = ψ 18^{43}.

7834 †שַׁחַק **n.m.** [Pr 3, 20] **dust, cloud** (as fine, thin);—ש׳ abs. ψ $89^{7.38}$, cstr. Is 40^{15}; pl. שְׁחָקִים Dt 33^{26}+;—**1.** *fine dust,* ש׳ מֹאזְנַיִם Is 40^{15} (sim. of insignif.). **2.** (thin) *cloud,* usu. pl. (oft. ‖ שָׁמַיִם), Dt 33^{26} (poem), Is 45^8 Je 51^9 Jb 35^5 36^{28} 37^{21} 38^{37} ψ 36^6 57^{11} 68^{35} 77^{18} 78^{23} 108^5; opp. תְּהוֹם Pr 3^{20} 8^{28}; עָבֵי ש׳ 2 S 22^{12} = ψ 18^{12}; = heavens, sky Jb 37^{18} (c. הִרְקִיעַ), and (sg.) ψ $89^{7.38}$.

7883 שְׁחֹר v. שִׁיחוֹר. p. 1009

7835 †I. שָׁחַר **vb. be black** (NH שָׁחוֹר and deriv., *black, blackness,* etc., Ecclus 25^{17} Hiph. *make black;* Aram. שְׁחַר (Jastr Dalm), Aph. *grow black,* so ܐܘܟܡ, ܫܚܘܪܐ *coal;* Jäger [BAS ii. 295] cp. As. *šûru, coal, šurinnu, fire-pot*);—ש׳, of skin Jb 30^{30}.

7815 †שְׁחוֹר **n.[m.] blackness;**—חָשַׁךְ מִשּׁ׳ תָּאֳרָם La 4^8.

7838 †שָׁחֹר **adj. black;**—ש׳ of hair Lv $13^{31.37}$ (P), so fpl. שְׁחֹרוֹת Ct 5^{11}; of skin, fs. שְׁחוֹרָה 1^5; of horses, mpl. שְׁחֹרִים Zc $6^{2.6}$.

7839 †שַׁחֲרוּת **n.f.** acc. to De[Comm.] Rüetschi[Kau] **blackness,** viz. of hair (so 𝔗), i.e. (RV) *prime of life* (which Wild allows); usu. **dawn** of youth (II. שחר);—Ec 11^{10} (+ יַלְדוּת).

7840 †[שְׁחַרְחֹר Ges[§ 84 b n]] **adj. blackish** (Gann JAS 1883, Fev.-Mars, 156, no. 41, cp. Isr. n.pr. שחרחר on seal

7840 = 'le brun');—f. שְׁחַרְחֹרֶת Ct 1^6.

806 †אַשְׁחוּר **n.pr.m.** in Judah, called א׳ אֲבִי תְקוֹעַ 1 Ch 2^{24} 4^5; Ασχω, Σαρα; A Ασδωδ, Ασχουρ; 𝔊L Ασσωρ, Ασσωρ.

II. שחר (√ of foll.; MI[15] שחרת, Ar. سَحَرٌ, As. *šêru,* NH שַׁחַר, Aram. שַׁחֲרָא all *dawn*).

7837 †שַׁחַר **n.m.** [Gn 19, 15] **dawn;**—abs. ש׳ 1 S 9^{26}+, שָׁחַר Ju 19^{25}+; sf. שַׁחְרָהּ Is 47^{11} (but read prob. שַׁחֲדָהּ);—*dawn,* c. עָלָה *rise* Gn 19^{15} $32^{25.27}$ Jos 6^{15} (all J), Ju 19^{25} 1 S 9^{26} Ne 4^{15} Jon 4^7; opp. עֵיפָה Am 4^{13}; as adv. *at dawn* ψ 57^9 = 108^3; עַפְעַפֵּי־ש׳ Jb 3^9 41^{10}; כַּנְפֵי־ש׳ ψ 139^9; 110^3 rd. prob. רֶחֶם ש׳ (v. מִשְׁחָר infr.); ש׳ also Jb 38^{12}, in sim. Ho 6^3 (but rd. כְּשַׁחֲרֵנוּ כֵּן נִמְצָאֵהוּ as inf., v. following, Gie[Beitr. 208] We Now GASm Marti), Is 58^8 Ct 6^{10}, Jo 2^2 (al. *blackness,* ‖ עָנָן וַעֲרָפֶל); בֶּן־ש׳ Is 14^{12} (of star, fig. of royal splendour;—lit. as myth RS[K 300]); אֵין לוֹ ש׳ Is 8^{20} is obscure, so also בַּשׁ׳ Ho 10^{15} (We *in storm,* i.e. בַּשַּׂעַר).—Is 47^{11} usu., but improbably, *dawn* (origin) of calamity: JHMich Hi Ew Röd (Thes) De Di al. *charm away* (RVm) (Ar. سَحَرَ *enchant* (We[Heid. 2. 159, 200]), سِحْرٌ *enchantment* [= Sab. סחר DHM[Hofmus. 24. 1]]); but v. [שָׁחַד]. p. 1005 7809

†[שָׁחַר] **vb.denom. look early, diligently** 7836 for (late; orig. *look for dawn*);—**Qal** *Pt.* שֹׁחֵר טוֹב Pr 11^{27} (‖ דֹּרֵשׁ, בִּקֵּשׁ), elsewhere **Pi.** c. acc. (sf.) *Pf.* 3 ms. sf. שִׁחֲרוֹ מוּסָר Pr 13^{24} *seeks him early* (with) *discipline* (chastises him betimes); 2 ms. sf. consec. וְשִׁחַרְתַּנִי וְאֵינֶנִּי Jb 7^{21}; lit. *Inf.* לְשַׁחֵר פָּנֶיךָ Pr 7^{15}; of wild asses, *Pt.* מְשַׁחֲרֵי לַטָּרֶף Jb 24^5 (Ges[§ 130 u]) *seeking eagerly for their food;* usu. of *seeking* God (י׳) earnestly, *Pf.* וְשִׁחֲרוּ־אֵל ψ 78^{34} (‖ דָּרַשׁ), *Impf.* 2 ms. תְּשַׁחֵר אֶל־אֵל Jb 8^5 (si vera l.), 3 ms. sf. יְשַׁחֲרֻנְנִי (Ges[§ 60 e]) Ho 5^{15} (‖ בִּקֵּשׁ), + 6^3 (v. שַׁחַר), and, acc. wisdom, Pr 1^{28}, *Pt.* sf. מְשַׁחֲרַי Pr 8^{17}; *seek* with longing, long for (י׳), אֲשַׁחֲרֶךָּ Is 26^9 ψ 63^2.

שַׁחֲרוּת v. I. שָׁחַר. above 7839

†מִשְׁחָר **n.[m.] dawn;**—מֵרֶחֶם מ׳ ψ 110^3, 4891 but מ prob. dittogr., read שַׁחַר (Du, cf. Buhl).

†שְׁחַרְיָה **n.pr.m.** in Benjamin, 1 Ch 8^{26}; 7841 Σα(α)ρ(α)ια.

†שַׁחֲרַיִם **n.pr.m.** in Benjamin, 1 Ch 8^8; 7842 Σααρηλ[μ], 𝔊L Σεωρειν.

[שָׁחַת] [151] **vb.** go to ruin (?), only der. 7843 spec. (NH Hiph. = BH, Ecclus. שחיתה 30^{11} *corrupt act;* Ar. سَحَتَ *extirpate;* Eth. ሰሐጠ: *injure, violate;* TelAm. *šaḫâtu* is *fall* (esp. of city), *be prostrate* (? of land), perh. Canaanism (v. Wkl[TelAm. Vocab.]), As. poss. *šêtu, flee, escape* (cf. אבד); OAram. (Zinj.) שחת *destroy* Lzb[374], Aram. שְׁחַת, ܚܒܠ (assim. of ܚ), *mutilate;*—very improb. Gerber[179] denom. from שַׁחַת);—†**Niph.** *be marred, spoiled, Pf.* 3 ms. נִשְׁחַת, of waistcloth Je 13^7, vessel 18^4; *be injured,* or even (hyperb.) *ruined, Impf.* 3 fs. תִּשָּׁחֵת Ex 8^{20} (J) of land (מִפְּנֵי הֶעָרֹב); *be corrupted, corrupt,* in morals and rel., of earth, *Pf.* 3 fs. נִשְׁחֲתָה Gn 6^{12} (P), *Impf.* 3 fs. וַתִּשָּׁ׳ לִפְנֵי הָא׳ v^{11} (P); so *Pt.* fpl. as adj. נִשְׁחָתוֹת Ez 20^{44}. †**Pi.** *Pf.* 3 ms. שִׁחֵת Ex

32^{7}+, sf. שְׁחֶתְךָ Ho 13^{9}; 2 ms. שִׁחֵתָ Is 14^{20}+, etc.; *Imv.* mpl. שַׁחֲתוּ Je 5^{10}; *Inf. cstr.* שַׁחֵת Gn 13^{10}+, etc.;—**1.** *spoil, ruin,* acc. of eye Ex 21^{26} (E), vineyard Je 12^{10} (fig.), branches Na 2^{3} (fig.), also = *destroy,* acc. pers. 2 S 1^{14} 14^{11} (acc. om.), Ez 5^{16} 20^{17}, כָּל־בָּשָׂר Gn 6^{17} 9^{15} (P), city, fortress, etc., Gn 13^{10} 19$^{13.29}$ (all J), 2 S 24^{16} Je 5^{10} (acc. om.), 48^{18} Ez 26^{4} 43^{3} La 2^{5}, *ruin* temple v^{6}, nation Ho 11^{9} 13^{9} (read perh. שִׁחַתִּךָ Oort Now), land 2 K 19^{12} (Hiph. in ‖ Is 37^{12}), Ju 6^{5} Jos 22^{33} (P), Ez 22^{30} 30^{11}, earth Gn 9^{11} (P); c. לְ obj. (לְ **3 b**), city 1 S 23^{10}, pers. Nu 32^{15} (P); c. acc. רַחֲמָיו Am 1^{11}, *destroyed* (stifled) *his compassion* (or, RS$^{\text{K 28}}$ al., *the bonds of kinship,* v. רַחֲמִים), וְשִׁ׳ בְּרִית Mal 2^{8}, i.e. violate it, v. esp. אַרְצָה (sc. *semen*) Gn 38^{9} (J) *he spoiled* (it) *upon the ground,* made it ineffective, = *waste* words Pr 23^{8}. **2.** *pervert, corrupt,* acc. wisdom Ez 28^{17}, abs. = *deal*
6013 *corruptly,* הֶעֱמִיקוּ שִׁחֵתוּ Ho 9^{9} (cf. [עָמֹק], p. 770^{b};
7743 but We Now read שַׁחֲתוּ, √שׁוּח), Ex 32^{7} (JE), Dt 9^{12}, so שִׁ׳ לוֹ 32^{5}. **Hiph.**$_{103}$ *Pf.* 3 ms. הִשְׁחִית Gn 6^{12}+; 1 s. וְהִשְׁחַתִּי Je 51^{20}, etc.; *Impf.* 3 ms. יַשְׁחִית Dn 8^{24}+, יַשְׁחִת, וַיַּשְׁחֵת Mal 3^{11}+, וַיַּשְׁחֵת 1 Ch 20^{1}; 2 fs. וַתַּשְׁחִתִי Ez 16^{47}, 2 mpl. תַּשְׁחִתוּן Dt 4^{16} 31^{29}; *Imv.* ms. sf. הַשְׁחִיתָהּ 2 K 18^{25} = Is 36^{10}; *Inf. abs.* הַשְׁחֵת Dt 31^{29}; cstr. הַשְׁחִית 1 S 26^{15}+, etc.; *Pt.* מַשְׁחִית Gn 19^{14}+, etc.;—**1.** *spoil, ruin,* acc. crop Ju 6^{4} Mal 3^{11}, trees Dt 20$^{19.20}$ Je 11^{19} (fig.), vessels 2 Ch 36^{19}, houses 34^{11}, palaces Je 6^{5}, cf. Is 65^{8} Lv 19^{27} (H), Ru 4^{6}; הִשׁ׳ דַּיָּם Je 49^{9} thieves *damage as much as they want;* acc. pers. = *ruin, destroy,* 1 S 26$^{9.15}$ Ju 20$^{21.25}$ (+אַ֫רְצָה), v$^{35.42}$ 2 K 13^{23} 2 Ch 24^{23} (+מִן separ.), +12 t., +(acc. pers. om.) Is 51^{13}+4 t., acc. בֵּית דָּוִד 2 Ch 21^{7}, abs. Is 11^{9} = 65^{25}; also *ruin* one (by words) Pr 11^{9}; acc. עַם 2 S 24^{16} Dt 9^{26}; land 1 S 6^{5} Je 36^{29} Dn 11^{17} (v. Dr); city wall 2 S 20^{15} (Ew Th here
7845 denom. from שַׁחַת *they were making a pit;* < 𝔖 We (?) Klo Dr Bu HPS Now מְחַשְּׁבִים *were devising*), La 2^{8}, cities and nations Gn 18$^{28.28}$ (J, acc. om.), 19$^{13.14}$ (J), Is 37^{12} (Pi. in ‖ 2 K 19^{12}), 36$^{10.10}$ = 2 K 18$^{25.25}$ + 11 t. + (Israel personif.) Dt 4^{31} 10^{10} 2 K 8^{19}, pride of Judah Je 13^{9}, earth Je 51^{1}; abs. c. adv. acc. Dn 8^{24} (v. Dr; Bev conj. יְשַׁחֵחַ or יָשִׂיחַ *utter monstrous things*), cf. 1 Ch 21^{12}; Pt. as adj., of lion Je 2^{30}, angel 1 Ch 21^{15}; = *destroyer* Ex 12^{23} (J), Je 22^{7} Is 54^{16}, מ׳ גּוֹיִם Je 4^{7}, רוּחַ מ׳ 51^{1}; sg. coll. (הַמּ׳ Ges$^{\text{§ 126 1}}$; *the destroying band,* cf. Dr Bu Now) 1 S 13^{17} 14^{15} (*spoilers, ravagers*); fig. for snare, trap, Je 5^{26}. †**2.** *pervert, corrupt,* morally, acc. דֶּרֶךְ Gn 6^{12} (P; v.
1870 דֶּרֶךְ **6**), הִשׁ׳ נַפְשׁוֹ Pr 6^{32}, cf. Zp 3^{7}, Ez 23^{11} (מִן comp.); הִשְׁחִיתוּ הִתְעִיבוּ עֲלִילָה ψ 14^{1} = 53^{2}; הַשְׁחֵת תַּשְׁחִ׳ (+vb. of particular act) Dt 4^{16} 31^{29}; declar. = *act corruptly,* Is 1^{4} Dt 4^{25} (+vb. of act), 2 Ch 27^{2}, +מִן comp. Ju 2^{19} Ez 16^{47}; *Pt.* as subst. Je 6^{28}, אִישׁ מַשְׁ׳
Pr 28^{24} (18^{9} v. infra).—אַל־תַּשְׁחֵת *destroy not* 516
(catchword of old song or melody?) in ψ-titles: †57^{1} 58^{1} 59^{1} 75^{1}. †**Hoph.** *Pt.* מָשְׁחָת *spoiled, ruined,* of a spring, מָקוֹר Pr 25^{26} (‖ מַעְיָן נִרְפָּשׂ); as subst. Mal 1^{14} sacrificing *a spoiled thing.*

†מַשְׁחִית **n.[m.]** ruin, destruction;—מ׳ 4889
abs. Je 5^{26}+10 t.;—physical *destruction* Ez 5^{16} 9^{6} 21^{36} 25^{15} Ex 12^{13} (P), 2 Ch 20^{23} 22^{4}; בַּעַל מ׳ Pr 18^{9} = *destroyer;* Dn 10^{8} (disfigurement); הַר־מ׳ Je 51^{25} (fig. of Bab. as destroyer), in 2 K 23^{13} = *mt. of corruption* (where *bamoth* were, S. end of Mt. of Olives, poss. adapted from הַר־מִשְׁחָה so Hoffm$^{\text{ZAW ii (1882), 175}}$ Benz Kit Bur; 𝔙 *mons offensionis*).

†מַשְׁחֵת **n.[m.]** id.;—כְּלִי מַשְׁחֵתוֹ Ez 9^{1}. 4892

†מִשְׁחַת **n.[m.]** disfigurement of face 4893
Is 52^{14}.

†מָשְׁחָת **n.[m.]** corruption (ritual), Lv 4893
22^{25} (H).

שַׁחַת v. שׁוּח. p. 1001 7845

שִׁטָּה$_{27}$ **n.f. acacia,** tree and wood (=שִׁנְטָה*, 7848
Ar. سَنْط, prob. loan-word from Egypt. *šndt, šondet,* Thes^{1452} Erman$^{\text{ZMG xlvi (1892), 120}}$);—growing in dry places; esp. *acacia (mimosa) Nilotica;* cf. Rob$^{\text{BR ii. 20}}$, or *a. seyyâl* Post$^{\text{Flora 298 f. Hast. DB SHITTAH-TREE}}$ Tristr$^{\text{NHB 390 ff.}}$;—שׁ׳ sg. Is 41^{19} (to grow in desert); usually pl., עֲצֵי שִׁטִּים *shiṭṭîm wood,* material of ark, altars, staves, etc., in tabern., Dt 10^{3} Ex 25$^{5.10.13}$ + 19 t. Ex 25–38 (P); עֲצֵי om., עַמּוּדֵי שׁ׳ *pillars of shiṭṭîm* (wood), Ex 26$^{32.37}$ 36^{36} (P).

†שִׁטִּים **n.pr.loc.** alw. הַשִּׁ׳; usu. Σαττειν: 7851
1. E. of Jordan, Jos 2^{1} 3^{1} (E), Mi 6^{5} Nu 25^{1} (P);
= אָבֵל הַשּׁ׳ 33^{49}; on exact site v. Buhl$^{\text{G 116}}$ Gray 63
Nu 25, 1. **2.** נַחַל הַשּׁ׳ Jo 4^{18} (perh. *Wady es-Sanṭ,* W. of Jerus., cf. We Buhl$^{\text{Geogr. 90}}$, and views in Dr).

[שָׁטַח] **vb. spread, spread abroad** (NH 7849
id.; Ar. سَطَحَ *spread out;* so Eth. ሰጠሐ: Aram. שְׁטַח, ܫܛܚ);—**Qal** *Pf.* 3 pl. sf. consec. וּשְׁטָחוּם לַשֶּׁמֶשׁ Je 8^{2} *they shall spread them abroad,* etc., acc. of many separate things, so *Impf.* 3 fs. וַתִּשְׁטַח 2 S 17^{19} (עַל loc.; disting. from פָּרַשׂ *spread*

covering); 3 mpl. + *Inf. abs.* וַיִּשְׁטְחוּ לָהֶם שָׁטוֹחַ Nu 11[32] (J) *they spread* (sc. the quails) *for themselves all abroad* round about the camp (i.e. to dry them; 𝔙 *siccaverunt;* cf. Di Gray); *Pt.* שֹׁטֵחַ לַגּוֹיִם Jb 12[23] *expanding the nations* (cf. ל 3 b). **Pi.** *Pf.* 1 s. שִׁטַּחְתִּי אֵלֶיךָ כַפָּי ψ 88[10] *I have spread out unto thee my palms.*

4894 †[מִשְׁטָח] **n.[m.] spreading-place** (NH for drying figs, etc., (ARSKennedy[Ency. Bib. Fruit, 1568])) ;—cstr. מִשְׁטַח חֲרָמִים Ez 26[5.14].

4894 †מִשְׁטוֹחַ **n.[m.] id.**;—מ׳ לַחֲרָמִים Ez 47[10].

7850 שֹׁטֵט v. שׁוט, שִׁטִּים v. supra. p. 1002

7857 †שָׁטַף **vb. overflow, rinse or wash off** (NH *id.*, so JAram. שְׁטַף; As. *šaṭâpu, overflow,* Ar. سطف *id.*, Cuche);—**Qal** *Pf.* 3 ms. ׳שׁ Is 8[8]+, etc.; *Impf.* 3 ms. וַיִּשְׁטֹף 1 K 22[38], etc.; *Pt.* שׁוֹטֵף Is 10[22]+, pl. שֹׁטְפִים Is 28[2];—**1.** *overflow,* of river Is 8[8] Je 47[2a] (v. נַחַל), Dn 11[10.40], all fig. of invading army, cf. Is 28[15] (qy. by Sta[ThLz. Apr. 1894, 235], Du Marti rd. שׁוֹט שֹׁטֵט), v[18] (v. שׁוט), also (sim. of י׳ in judgment) v[2] (מַיִם), 30[28], of judicial destruction, שׁוֹטֵף צְדָקָה Is 10[22]; c. acc. of land Je 47[2b], pers. (fig.) Is 43[2] (נְהָרוֹת), ψ 69[3] (שִׁבֹּלֶת), v[16] (שׁ׳ מַיִם), 124[4] (מַיִם), cf. Is 28[17] Ct 8[7]; גֶּשֶׁם שׁוֹטֵף *flooding rain* (of י׳'s judgment) Ez 13[11.13] 38[22]; נַחַל שׁוֹטֵף Is 66[12], sim., in good sense.—Abs. Dn 11[26] v. **Niph.**—Fig. of *dashing, rushing* horse, כְּסוּס שׁוֹ׳ בַּמִּלְחָמָה Je 8[6]. **2.** *flow, run,* lit. of נַחַל ψ 78[20] 2 Ch 32[4]. **3.** lit., *rinse* or *wash off,* c. acc. of thing washed 1 K 22[38], יָדָיו שָׁטַף בַּמָּיִם Lv 15[11] (P); of stain Ez 16[9] (רָחַץ ‖ מֵעָלָיִךְ); יִשְׁטֹף בַּמַּיִם עֲפַר־אָרֶץ Jb 14[19]. **Niph.** *Impf.* 3 ms. יִשָּׁטֵף Lv 15[12] *be rinsed out, off* (P; of wooden vessel); 3 mpl. יִשָּׁטְפוּ מִלְּפָנָיו Dn 11[22] *be swept away* (defeated), read prob. יִשָּׁטֵף (for יִשְׁטוֹף), also v[26] (cf. Dr). **Pu.** *Pf.* 3 ms. וּמֹרַק וְשֻׁטַּף בַּמָּיִם Lv 6[21] (P) *it shall be scoured and rinsed.*

7858, 8241 †שֶׁטֶף, שֶׁצֶף n.m.[Na 1, 8] **flood**;—abs. שֶׁטֶף Na 1[8] + 3 t.; cstr. שֶׁ׳ Pr 27[4], שֵׁ׳ ψ 32[6];—*flood,* fig. of י׳'s judgment, שׁ׳ עֹבֵר Na 1[8], cf. Dn 9[26], זְרֹעוֹת הַשּׁ׳ 11[22] (cf. Dr); of calamity, שׁ׳ מַיִם רַבִּים ψ 32[6]; שֶׁטֶף אָף Pr 27[4] *a flood of anger;* so שֶׁצֶף קֶצֶף Is 54[8] (צ for ט bef. foll. צ Ew Di; > Du Che Marti del. שׁ׳ as dittogr.); שֶׁטֶף lit. of rainflood, Jb 38[25].

שׁטר (√ of foll.; As. *šaṭâru, write,* Sab. סטר Hom[Chr 124] DHM[Ep. Denkm. Ar. lii. 2, liv. 2]; Ar. سَطَرَ *rule* (a book), *write,* سَطْرٌ *row, line;* Aram. שְׁטָרָא, ܫܛܪܐ *document,* so Hilpr[Bab. Exp. x. 8] CIS[ii. 67], Nab. Palm. שטר Lzb[374]: Hom[NKZ i. 69] all from As.).

7860 †שֹׁטֵר **n.m. official, officer** (prop. *scribe, secretary*? or fr. original meaning as *arranger, organizer*?);—abs. ׳שׁ Pr 6[7], ׳שׁוֹ 2 Ch 26[11]; pl. שֹׁטְרִים Dt 1[15]+, etc.;—appar. subordinate *officer,* judicial, civil or military (cf. Dr[Dt 1. 15] Gray[Nu 11, 16]): organizing people for marching Jos 1[10] 3[2] (both E), cf. Dt 20[5.8.9]; appointed over Isr. by Egypt. overseers Ex 5[14], cf. v[6.10.15.19] (all J); elsewhere + זְקֵנִים Nu 11[16] (E), Dt 29[9] 31[28]; + שֹׁפְטִים 16[18] 1 Ch 23[4] 26[29], + ז׳ et שֹׁפ׳ Jos 8[33] (R[D]), and (+ רָאשִׁים) 23[2] (R[D]), 24[1] (E, or R[D]); שֹׁט׳ as minor judges also Dt 1[15]; שֹׁט׳ הַמְשָׁרְתִים אֶת־הַמֶּלֶךְ 1 Ch 27[1], chosen from Levites 2 Ch 19[11] 34[13] (+ סוֹפְרִים, שׁוֹעֲרִים); as title of individ. 26[11] (‖ הַסּוֹפֵר); of ant, אֵין־לָהּ קָצִין שֹׁטֵר וּמֹשֵׁל Pr 6[7].

†שִׁטְרַי **n.pr.m.** an official of David, 1 Ch 27[29] Kt (> Qr שִׁרְטַי); Ασαρταις, Σαρται. 7861

†[מִשְׁטָר] **n.m. rule, authority**;—sf. מִשְׁטָרוֹ Jb 38[33] (of heavens over earth). 4896

†שַׁי **n.m. gift** offered as homage (√ dub.; perh. in spite of ש = ش, Ar. شَيْءٌ, vb. *wish,* شَيْءٌ *thing* (weakened fr. *thing desired*); cf. חֵפֶץ 4);—יוֹבִלוּ שַׁי Is 18[7], יֹבִילוּ שׁ׳ ψ 76[12], יוֹבִ׳ שָׁי 68[30]. 7862

שִׁיא **n.pr.m.** 2 S 20[25] Kt, v. שְׁוָא. p. 996 7724, 7864

†שִׁיאוֹן **n.pr.loc.** in Issachar, Jos 19[19], Σιωνα, Σηω. 7866

I. שִׁיבָה v. ישׁב. II. שִׁיבָה v. שׁוב. p. 444, 1000 7870-71

†[שָׁיָה] **vb.** only **Qal** *Impf.* apoc. צוּר יְלָדְךָ תֶּשִׁי Dt 32[18], but < read תִּשֶּׁה (II. נשׁה) *the Rock which begat thee thou forgattest,* Sam. תשא, Di Dr. 7876

†שִׁיזָא **n.pr.m.** in Reuben, 1 Ch 11[42], Σαιζα, Σιζαι. 7877

[שִׂיחַ], שִׂיחָה v. שׂוח. p. 1001 7743, 7882

†שִׁיחוֹר **n.pr.flum.** on border of Egypt, prob. E. branch of Nile;—הַשּׁ׳ Jos 13[3], שׁ׳ מִצְרַיִם 1 Ch 13[5]; clearly = Nile, זֶרַע שִׁחֹר Is 23[3] (‖ קְצִיר יְאוֹר), מֵי שִׁחוֹר Je 2[18]; cf. Dl[Pa 311] Wilson[Hast. DB Shihor] (usu. derived from I. שׁחר, as *black water,* but doubtful). p. 1007 7883, 7835

†שִׁיחוֹר לִבְנָת **n.pr.flum.** in Asher, Jos 19[26]; τῷ Σειων[ρ] καὶ Λαβαναθ; poss. *Nahr ez-Zerḳâ,* S. of Carmel, and just N. of Caesarea, Wilson[Hast. DB Shihor Libnath], but v. Buhl[G 105]. 7884

שִׁית v. I. שׁוּת. p. 1002 7885

שִׁילוֹ, שִׁלוֹ, **n.pr.loc.,** שִׁילֹנִי etc., v. שׁלה. p. 1017-18 7887-88

7886 †שִׁילֹה Gn 49^{10}, appar. **n.**, but prob. = שֶׁלּוֹ *he whose it is*, or *that which belongs to him*, v. infra; views are: (1) שִׁיל (= שִׁלְיָל, NH *embryo*, + sf. ה‍ֹ— = *his son*, 𝔗 Jer Rabb Calv); (2) שִׁלוֹ, שִׁילוֹ n.pr.loc. (q.v.) Herder De and most (until recently); (3) n.pr. of Messiah, AV RV Münster (1534) on basis of Talm Sanh 98^{b}; groundless; (4) Jer שלה = שְׁלִחַ, *qui mittendus est;* (5) שֶׁלֹּה = שֶׁ + לוֹ, 𝔗$^{Onk.}$ *whose is the kingdom,* 𝔖 *whose it is,* so Aphr Ephr 𝔊 *ἕως ἂν ἔλθῃ τὰ ἀποκείμενα αὐτῷ* (Codd. *ᾧ ἀπόκειται*); so Sam. שלה, cf. עַד־בֹּא אֲשֶׁר לוֹ הַמִּשְׁפָּט Ez 21^{32}, Aq Sym Theod Saad; this reading best, but exact transl. not certain; v. Dr$^{JPhil.\ xiv\ (1885),\ 1\ ff.\ Gn.\ 418\ ff.}$ Br$^{MP\ 95\ ff.,\ Intr.\ 238\ ff.}$ Poznański$^{Schiloh\ (1904)}$.

7758 שִׁילל v. שׁלל. p. 1021

7889 †שִׁימוֹן **n.pr.m.** in Judah, 1 Ch 4^{20}, *Σεμ(ε)ιων, Σαμι.*

שׁין (√ of foll.; cf. As. *šânu*, Iphte. *istîn*, *urinate; šînâti* (pl.), *urine;* vb. also Eth. ሸነ: Aram. ܫܝܢ, ܫܝܢ; v. Ar. مَثَانَة *bladder* (Wahrm)).

7890 †[שַׁיִן, שֵׁין] **n.[m.] urine**;—pl. sf. שֵׁינֵיהֶם 2 K 18^{27} = Is 36^{12} (both Kt; Qr מֵימֵי רַגְלֵיהֶם).

8366 †[שָׁתַן] **vb. Hiph. urinate** (secondary √ from above);—*Pt.* מַשְׁתִּין בְּקִיר (i.e. a male person) 1 S 25$^{22.34}$ 1 K 14^{10} 16^{11} 21^{21} 2 K 9^{8} (all of exterminating a family).

שׁיר (√ of foll., cf. Nö$^{ZMG\ xxxvii\ (1883),\ 537}$).

7892 †שִׁיר$_{77}$ **n.m. song** (NH *id.;* so Ecclus 40^{21}+);—שׁ׳ abs. Ju 5^{12}+, cstr. 2 Ch 29^{27}+; sf. שִׁירִי ψ 28^{7}, etc.; pl. שִׁירִים 1 Ch 13^{8} Ct 1^{1}; שָׁרִים Gn 31^{27} Pr 25^{20}; sf. שִׁרֶיךָ Am 5^{23}, etc.;—**1.** lyric *song,* + מָשָׁל 1 K 5^{12}, opp. קִינָה Am 8^{10}; joyous Gn 31^{27} (J) Is 30^{29}; שׁ׳ עגבים Ez 33^{32}; triumphal Ju 5^{12}; love song Ct 1$^{1.1}$ (title שִׁיר הַשִּׁירִים), ψ 45^{1} (שִׁיר יְדִידֹת); noisy Am 5^{23} Ez 26^{13}, in drunken revels Is 24^{9}, cf. 23^{16}; שׁ׳ כסילים Ec 7^{5}; not for sorrow Pr 25^{20} ψ 137$^{3.3}$; בְּנוֹת הַשִּׁיר Ec 12^{4} *songstresses* (prob. birds). **2.** religious *song,* in worship, ‖ תפלה ψ 42^{9}; usu. praise, הלל בשיר 69^{31}; מִשִּׁירִי אֲהוֹדֶנּוּ 28^{7}; שִׁיר תְּהִלָּה וְהוֹדוֹת Ne 12^{46}; שִׁיר י׳ ψ 137^{4} 2 Ch 29^{27}; שִׁיר חדש Is 42^{10} (fresh outburst), + 6 t., v. חָדָשׁ; in ψ-titles, שִׁיר 46^{1}, cf. Is 26^{1}; שִׁיר המעלות *pilgrim songs* ψ 120^{1} + 14 t. (v. II. מַעֲלָה p. 752); מַשְׂכִּיל שִׁיר c. מִזְמוֹר ψ 48^{1} + 12 t. (v. מִזְ׳ p. 274); 45^{1}; (שׁ׳ orig. alone in all except 30^{1} 92^{1} 108^{1}, v. Br$^{JBL\ xviii\ (1899),\ 138}$). **3.** specif. song of Levitical choirs, with musical accomp., 1 Ch 6$^{16.17}$ 13^{8} (so read also ‖ 2 S 6^{5} for בְּרוֹשִׁים, 𝔊 Th and mod., cf. ב׳), 25$^{6.7}$ 2 Ch 23^{18} 29^{28} Ne 12^{27}; כלי (ה)שיר instrument to accompany song 1 Ch 15^{16} + 6 t. (v. כְּלִי **2 b**); cf. Am 6^{5}.

7892 †שִׁירָה **n.f. song** (pl. [שׁ]ירות Ecclus 39^{15});—abs. שׁ׳ Ex 15^{1} + 9 t.; cstr. שִׁירַת Is 5^{1} 23^{15}; pl. cstr. שִׁירוֹת Am 8^{3} (rd. שָׁרוֹת 𝔊 Hoffm ZAW iii (1883) We al.);—*song, ode,* Ex 15^{1} (E), 2 S 22^{1} = ψ 18^{1}, Dt 31$^{19.19.21.22.30}$ 32^{44} Nu 21^{17} (E) Is 5^{1} 23^{15}.

7891 †[שִׁיר]$_{86}$ **vb. sing** (denom. acc. to Nö$^{ZMG\ xxxvii\ (1883),\ 537}$ Gerb^{172}, but, if so, an old one);—**Qal**$_{49}$ *Pf.* 3 ms. שָׁר ψ 7^{1}; *Impf.* 3 ms. יָשִׁיר Ex 15^{1} Nu 21^{17} (read יָשֻׁר Jb 33^{27} for יָשֹׁר, √ II. שׁוּר, so SS Bu Gerb; in this sense also Ew De Di RV and all mod.); 3 fs. וַתָּשַׁר Ju 5^{1}, etc.; *Imv.* mpl. שִׁירוּ Ex 15^{21}+; *Inf. cstr.* לָשׁוּר 1 S 18^{6} Kt (< Qr לָשִׁיר, so Bu; 𝔊^{B} om., cf. Dr Kit^{Kau} HPS Now); *Pt.* שָׁר Pr 25^{20}; pl. שָׁרִים 2 S 19^{36}+; f. שָׁרוֹת 2 S 19^{36} + 2 t. + Am 8^{3} (read for שִׁירוֹת; v. שִׁירָה);—*sing,* c. acc. שִׁיר Is 42^{10} ψ 33^{3} + 5 t.; שִׁירָה Ex 15^{1} Nu 21^{17} (E) Is 5^{1}; שׁ׳ בשרים Pr 25^{20}; מִשִּׁיר צִיּוֹן ψ 137^{3}; שגיון 7^{1} (𝔊 מזמור), תהלה 106^{12}; c. acc. of theme 59^{17} 89^{2}; abs. Ju 5^{1} 1 S 18^{6}; c. לְ ψ 13^{6} 96$^{1.2}$ = 1 Ch 16^{23}, Ex 15$^{1.21}$ Je 20^{13}; ‖ זמר ψ 68$^{5.33}$ 101^{1} 104^{33} 105^{2} = 1 Ch 16^{9}, Ju 5^{3}; + זמר abs. ψ 57^{8} = 108^{2}; c. acc. theme 21^{14}; c. לְ pers. 27^{6}; of nature 65^{14} (after הִתְרוֹעֲעוּ); על אנשים Jb 33^{27} (v. supra); pt. שָׁרִים *singers* 2 S 19^{36} 1 K 10^{12} + 6 t. (Ez 40^{44} read שְׁתַּיִם 𝔊 Hi Co mod.); שָׁרוֹת *songstresses* 2 S 19^{36} 2 Ch 35^{25} Ec 2^{8} + Am 8^{3} (v. supra).—ψ 138^{5} rd. וְיָשִׂיחוּ. **Pōl.**$_{36}$ *Pf.* 3 mpl. שֹׁרְרוּ Jb 36^{24}; *Impf.* 3 ms. יְשׁוֹרֵר Zp 2^{14}; *Pt.* מְשׁוֹרֵר 1 Ch 6^{18} 2 Ch 29^{28}; pl. מְשֹׁרְרִים Ezr 2^{65}+, etc.;—*sing:* birds Zp 2^{14}; men Jb 36^{24}; elsewh. pt. of Levitical singers 1 Ch 6^{18} 9^{33} + 31 t., + fpl. Ezr 2^{65} *songstresses* = Ne 7^{67}. †**Hoph.** *be sung: Impf.* יוּשַׁר הַשִּׁיר הַזֶּה Is 26^{1}.

7893 †שַׁיִשׁ **n.[m.] alabaster** (foreign word? NH *id.;* Aram. שַׁיְשָׁא, ܫܝܫܐ, perhaps As. *šaššu*);—אַבְנֵי־שׁ׳ 1 Ch 29^{2} (material of temple); cf. Patrick$^{Hast.\ DB\ MARBLE}$.

†II. שֵׁשׁ **n.m.** id.;—עַמּוּדֵי שׁ׳ Ct 5^{15} (in fig.), 8336
Est 1^{6a}, material of pavement v^{6b} (v. בַּהַט).—
I. שֵׁשׁ, v. שׁדשׁ. p. 995 8337

7894 †שִׁישָׁא **n.pr.m.** Solomon's time, 1 K 4^{3}, *Σαβα, Σεισα,* 𝔊L *Σαφατ*; cf. שְׂרָיָה.

7895 †שִׁישַׁק **n.pr.m.** king of Egypt, Solomon's
7895 time (10th cent. B.C.), 1 K 11^{40} 14^{25} Qr (Kt שושק), = 2 Ch 12^{2}, 2 Ch 12^{9}, שִׁישָׁק v$^{5.5.7}$; = *Šešonk* I, first king of 22nd dynasty, Blau[ZMG xv (1861), 233 ff.] Steind[BAS i. 351]; = *Sošenk* WMM[As. u. Eur. 166 ff.; Ency. Bib. SHISHAK]; cf. Griffith[Hast. DB SHISHAK]. p. 1004

7896 †שִׁית **vb. put, set** (Nö[Beitr. z. Sem. Sprachwiss. 39 f.]; cf. Ph. שת Lzb[375]; Ecclus שית Pt. pass. 31^{27}(?); v. also (Nö[l. c. 41]) Syr. ܫܘܬܐ *quality, appearance*);—**Qal** *Pf.* 3 ms. שָׁת Gn 4^{25}+, 3 fs. שָׁתָה 1 S 4^{20}+, 2 ms. שַׁתָּה ψ 8^{7}, שַׁתָּ 90^{8}, sf. שַׁתַּנִי $88^{7.9}$, 1 s. שַׁתִּי 73^{28}+; 3 pl. שָׁתוּ Ex 33^{4}+3 t., metapl. שַׁתּוּ ψ 49^{15} 73^{9} (other forms not found); *Impf.* 3 ms. יָשִׁית Ex 21^{22}+, juss. יָשֵׁת Jb 9^{33}, וַיָּשֶׁת Gn 30^{40}+; 3 fs. sf. וַתְּשִׁתֵהוּ Ru 4^{16}, תְּשִׁיתֵמוֹ ψ 21^{10}+, 1 s. sf. אֲשִׁתֶנּוּ 1 K 11^{34}; *Imv.* ms. שִׁית Pr 27^{23}, שִׁיתָה ψ 9^{21} 141^{3}; fs. שִׁיתִי Je 31^{21}, etc.; *Inf. abs.* שׁת Is 22^{7}; *cstr.* שִׁית Jb 30^{1}+; *Pt. pass.* וְשִׁית (Je 13^{16} Qr, but rd. Kt יָשִׁית); sf. שִׁתִּי Ex 10^{1};—**1.** *put, lay* hand upon, עַל, Gn 46^{4} (E), $48^{14.17}$ (J), Jb 9^{33} ψ 139^{5}; c. עִם in evil partnership, Ex 23^{1} (E); *put* ornaments, עַל pers., 33^{4} (J); cf. 1 S 2^{8} Is 15^{9} Jb 22^{24} Ru 3^{15}; *lay* child into (ב) bosom Ru 4^{16}; *put* wisdom, ב loc., Jb 38^{36}, cf. Pr 26^{24}; אָשִׁית עֵצוֹת בְּנַפְשִׁי ψ 13^{3}, i.e. take counsel, plan; מַחְסִי בי׳ ψ 73^{28}; *put* things תַּחַת רַגְלָיו 8^{7}; *lay* (penalty) עַל pers. Ex 21^{22} (E), sin Nu 12^{11} (E), cf. (c. אֲשֶׁר = *where*) ψ 84^{4}; nearly = *give* (נתן), acc. + ל pers. Gn 4^{25} (J; explan. of name שֵׁת), *appoint* ψ 9^{21}. **2. a.** *set, station*, sheep לְבַדּוֹ Gn 30^{40}, cf. לֹא שָׁתָם עַל v^{40} (J); acc. pers. = *appoint* (עַל *over*) 41^{33} (E); *set* לָמוֹ pers. (ל **3 b**) + ב loc. ψ 73^{18}, so (acc.) 88^{7} and (obj. pers. om.) 12^{6}, *set* crown לְרֹאשׁוֹ 21^{4}, *set* one (מִן partit.) לְכִסֵּא 132^{11}; *set* pers. *among* (ב pers.) 2 S 19^{29} Je 3^{19}, cf. (עִם) Jb 30^{1}; *set* watch לְפִי ψ 141^{3}, snares לִי 140^{6}, enmity, בֵּין pers. Gn 3^{15} (J); iniquities לְנֶגְדֶּךָ ψ 90^{8}, cf. 101^{3}; *set, direct* face, אֶל loc. Nu 24^{1} (J), eyes לִנְטוֹת בָּאָרֶץ ψ 17^{11}. **b.** in phr. שׁ׳ לֵב לְ *set* one's *mind to*, give heed, attention (cf. שׂוּם **2 b**), Ex 7^{23} (E), 2 S 13^{20} Je 31^{21} ψ 48^{14} Pr 22^{17} 27^{23}, c. אֶל Jb 7^{17}, abs. 1 S 4^{20} ψ 62^{11}; Pr 24^{32} *I reflected.* **c.** *set, fix*, גְּבוּל Ex 23^{31} (E; c. מִן . . . עַד), תָּשִׁית לִי חֹק Jb 14^{13} wouldst *fix me* a limit, 38^{11} וּפֹא יָשִׁית בִּגְאוֹן גַּלֶּיךָ De al. here *shall one fix* it [the boundary, חֹק, v^{10}] = it *shall be fixed* against, etc.: but explan. very forced: Me Kau יִשָּׁבֵר ג׳, Bi Bu יִשְׁבֹּת ג׳). **3.** *constitute, make* one something, 2 acc., 1 K 11^{34} *I will make him prince*, Is 5^{6} 26^{1} Je 22^{6} ψ 21^{7} 84^{7} 88^{9} (+ לָמוֹ ind. obj.), 110^{1} 2 S 22^{12} ‖ ψ 18^{12}; תְּשִׁיתֵמוֹ שֶׁכֶם 21^{13} = *thou wilt make them* (all) *shoulder*, make them turn their back, flee (cf. 18^{41}); acc. + ל *make* something *into* Je 2^{15} = 50^{3}, 13^{16} ψ 45^{17} (+ ב loc.); acc. + כ comp. *make* one *like* Ho 2^{5} (‖ שִׂים), Is 16^{3} ψ 21^{10} $83^{12.14}$; acc. only, *make, prepare*, feast Je 51^{39}, cf. שָׁת קָצִיר לָךְ Ho 6^{11} (rd. poss. שִׁית, pt. pass.), *make* darkness ψ 104^{20}; = *perform* signs, ב loc. Ex 10^{1} (J). **4.** internally trans., = *take one's stand* (cf. שִׂים **4 a**) הַפָּרָשִׁים שֹׁת שָׁתוּ הַשָּׁעְרָה Is 22^{7}; c. עַל־י׳ (*against*) ψ 3^{7}.—יָשִׁית מִמֶּנִּי Jb 10^{20} (Kt; > Qr *Imv.* וְשִׁית) is dub., יָשֵׁת = יָשִׁית: De *direct* (attention) *away from me*, cf. Di (ellipsis of יָד, פָּנִים, or לֵב), Du (sc. יָד; reads *Imv.*); Lag (so Bu) prop. יִשְׁבֹּת, Siegf (יָדוֹ) יָשֵׁב, 𝔊 Beer (best) שְׁעֵה (7^{19}), with יְמֵי חֶלְדִּי (𝔊 Bu Be Du) for יָמַי יחדל prob. rightly. **Hoph.** (or **Qal** *pass.* Ges[§ 53 u]), *Impf.* 3 ms. יוּשַׁת Ex 21^{30} (E) if a ransom *be imposed* עָלָיו, v^{30}.

† שִׁית **n.m.** garment (Nö[Beiträge, 41 f.], cp. Syr. 7897
ܫܘܬܐ *appearance*, and qu. שֵׁית?);—cstr. שִׁית זוֹנָה Pr 7^{10}; fig. שׁ׳ חָמָס ψ 73^{6} (v. II. עטף).

†I. שֵׁת **n.pr.m.** third son of Adam; Gn 4^{25} 8352
(where expl. from √שִׁית), v^{26} $5^{3.4.6.7.8}$ 1 Ch 1^{1}; 7896
Σηθ.—In כָּל־בְּנֵי־שֵׁת Nu 24^{17} (poem in J), read
prob. שֵׁאת *tumult* (cf. La 3^{47}), or שְׂאֵת (v. sub
נשׂא), cf. Gray.—II. שֵׁת, v. II. שׁתה. p. 1059 8357

†[שֵׁת] **n.m.** (Albr[ZAW xvi (1896), 84]) **foundation,** 8356
stay (of society) (√שִׁית Thes Kö[ii. 1. 172]);—pl. הַשָּׁתוֹת יֵהָרֵסוּן ψ 11^{3} (prob. fig. of established *usages, laws*, etc., 𝔙 *leges*, Sym. *θεσμοί*, so Hup-Now Bae Che[(1888)] al.; > Thes al. of *nobles*); Thes puts here also שָׁתֹתֶיהָ Is 19^{10} (so MT probably intends), which Ew Di Kit then interpret of working-classes, ‖ עֹשֵׂי שֶׂכֶר; but perh. opp. of this, the upper classes, so as to include all ranks of society, Thes De Che[Comm.]; Che[Hpt] Buhl al. שֹׁתֶיהָ *weavers of it* (cf. Du Marti), v. III. שׁתה. p. 1059

†שַׁיִת **n. [m.] coll. thorn-bushes** (connex. 7898
with above √dub.; Dietr[Abh. 73] cp. (improb.) שׁאה *devastate*, שְׁאִיָּה *ruin*, whence שׁ׳ wild, rough growth);—alw. c. שָׁמִיר: abs. שׁ׳ Is $7^{23.24}$ 9^{17} 27^{4} (cf. Du); שָׁיִת 5^{6} 7^{25}; sf. שִׁיתוֹ 10^{17} (fig. of Assyr.).

שָׁכַב (Lag[BN 63])[212] **vb. lie down** (NH = BH; 7901
שכב Ecclus 47^{23} (in death), משכב *bed* 40^{5} $47^{20\,d}$, = *death bed* 46^{19}; Ph. שכב, משכב (v. מ׳ **1** infr.), Lzb[375]; Eth. ሰከበ: *lie*, so Aram. שְׁכַב, ܫܟܒ;

Nab. משכבא *couch;* Ar. سَكَبَ only *pour out* (water, tears), *be poured out* (cf. **Hiph.** infr., and Lag[BN 63])); —**Qal** *Pf.* 3 ms. שׁ׳ Gn 26[10]+, etc.; *Impf.* יִשְׁכַּב Gn 30[15]+, 3 mpl. יִשְׁכְּבֻן 1 S 2[22], יִשְׁכָּבוּן Jos 2[8] Jb 30[17], etc.; *Imv.* ms. שְׁכַב 2 S 13[5] Ez 4[4], שִׁכְבָה Gn 39[7.12], etc.; *Inf. abs.* שָׁכֹב Lv 15[24]; *cstr.* שְׁכַב 1 K 1[21]+, sf. שָׁכְבוֹ Ru 3[4], שָׁכְבָהּ Gn 19[33.35], שָׁכְבְּךָ Dt 6[7]+2 t.; *Pt.* שֹׁכֵב Gn 28[13]+, f. שֹׁכֶבֶת Mi 7[5] Ru 3[8], etc.;—**1.** *lie down* (sometimes opp. הֵקִיץ, קוּם): **a.** Ju 5[27] (prostrated by blow, + נָפַל, כָּרַע). **b.** to sleep, Gn 19[4] (J), 28[11] (E), 1 S 3[5] Dt 7[7] Pr 6[22]+oft.; read וַיִּשְׁכַּב also (for וַיַּשְׁכֵּם) 1 S 9[26] 𝔊 Th We Dr and mod.; שׁ׳+ יָשֵׁן *sleep* 1 K 19[5] ψ 3[6] 4[9], cf. Pr 3[24.24], + נִרְדָּם Jon 1[5]; =*be lying* 1 S 3[2.3] 26[5] (all בְּ loc.), v[7] 4[5] (acc. cogn. noon-repose), 2 S 13[8], cf. שֹׁכֵב בְּלֶב־יָם Pr 23[34], of two lying (together, for warmth) Ec 4[11]; + be sleeping 1 S 26[7]; = *keep lying,* c. עַד Ju 16[3] 1 S 3[15] Ru 3[13] Pr 6[9]; emphasis on *resting,* Lv 26[6] (H), Jb 11[18]; token of mourning, (וְלָן) וְשָׁכַב אָרְצָה 2 S 12[16], cf. 13[31], שׁ׳ בַּשָּׂק 1 K 21[27], שׁ׳ בֵּין שְׁפַתָּיִם ψ 68[14] (of indolence?); fig. of prostration by disease 41[9]; among foes 57[5]; of humiliation Je 3[25]; c. עַל rei: land Gn 28[13] (J), usu. bed 2 S 13[5] 1 K 21[4] Lv 15[4.24.26], cf. v[20], for midday repose 2 S 4[7]. **c.** *lie* on (עַל) one's side Ez 4[4.4.6.9] (symbol.). **d.** *lie,* עַל pers. 1 K 3[19] (fatally), 2 K 4[34] (to revive). **e.** *lie* בְּחֵיק, of lamb (i.e. be cherished) 2 S 12[3], of woman Mi 7[5] (intimacy), 1 K 1[2] (vital warmth); *lie down* for copulation Gn 19[33.35] (of woman, v. **3** infr.; both opp. קוּם). **2.**=*lodge* (for night), (שָׁמָּה) שׁ׳ Jos 2[1] (E), 2 K 4[11], cf. 9[16] (yet perhaps =*lie ill*), Lv 14[47] (בְּ loc.). **3.** of sexual relations, *lie* with: subj. man, c. עִם Gn 30[15.16] 39[7.12.14] (J), Ex 22[15] (E), Dt 22[22]+8 t. Dt., 2 S 11[4.11] 12[11.24] Lv 15[33]; c. אֵת fem. *with* (MT אֹתָהּ, etc., orig. אִתָּהּ, etc., v. Dr[2 S 13,14] and II. אֵת, p. 85[a] supra), Gn 26[10] 34[2.7] 35[22] (all J), 1 S 2[22] (om. 𝔊 and mod.), 2 S 13[14] Ez 23[8] (fig.), Lv 15[24] (שָׁכֹב יִשְׁכַּב), Nu 5[19], also (c. acc. cogn. שִׁכְבַת־זֶרַע) v[13] Lv 15[18] 19[20]; c. acc. (sf.) fem. Dt 28[30] Kt (v. [שָׁגַל]); c. אֵצֶל fem. Gn 39[10] (J); c. אֵת vir. (sodomy), Lv 18[22] 20[13] (both H; c. acc. cogn. מִשְׁכְּבֵי אִשָּׁה); c. עִם־בְּהֵמָה Dt 27[21] Lv 22[18] (H); subj. woman, c. עִם vir. Gn 19[32.34.35] (J) 2 S 13[11]; אֵת vir. Gn 19[33.34] (cf. **1 e** supra). **4. a.** *lie down* in death, Is 14[8] 43[17] (opp. קוּם), Ez 31[18] 32[27.28.29.30] Jb 14[12] (opp. הֵקִיץ, קוּם), וְאֶשְׁקוֹט שׁ׳ 3[12]; *be lying* (dead) Is 51[20] La 2[21]. **b.** esp. in phr. שׁ׳ עִם אֲבוֹתָיו *lie down with his fathers,* of kings 1 K 1[21] 2[10]+35 t. K Ch, cf. Gn 47[30] (J), Dt 31[16], and (c. אֶת) 2 S 7[12]. **c.** in grave, בְּבֵיתוֹ Is 14[18] (opp. מִקִּבְרְךָ), שֹׁכְבֵי קֶבֶר ψ 88[6]; לֶעָפָר Jb 7[21], עַל־ע׳ 20[11] 21[26]; in Sheʾôl Ez 32[21]; in Gehenna(?) Is 50[11]. **5.** fig.=relax: Jb 30[17] *my gnawing pains do not sleep;* =have rest, לֹא שׁ׳ לִבּוֹ Ec 2[23]. †**Niph. Pu.** =*be lain with* (sexually; subj. woman), only as Qr for Kt [שָׁגַל] **Niph. Pu.** q.v. †**Hiph.** *lay, Pf.* 3 fs. הִשְׁכִּיבָה c. acc. puer. + בְּחֵיק 1 K 3[20], so *Impf.* 3 fs. sf. וַתַּשְׁכִּיבֵהוּ v[20], cf. (עַל־מִטָּה) 17[19] 2 K 4[21]; *Inf. abs.* הַשְׁכֵּב אוֹתָם אַרְצָה 2 S 8[2] *making them lie down on ground; Impf.* also *lay* בַּמִּשְׁכָּב 2 Ch 16[14] (of burial); נִבְלֵי שָׁמַיִם מִי יַשְׁכִּיב Jb 38[37] i.e. tip them so that contents may flow out (cf. Ar. سَكَبَ supra). †**Hoph.** *Pt.* מֻשְׁכָּב 2 K 4[32] *laid* עַל־מִטָּה; *Pf.* consec. וְהָשְׁכַּב Ez 32[32] *shall be laid* (in death), c. בְּתוֹךְ et אֶת pers. (*with*); so *Imv.* ms. הָשְׁכְּבָה v[19] (c. אֶת pers. only).

†[שְׁכָבָה] **n.f.** act of lying, layer;—only cstr. שִׁכְבַת, all P;—**1.** act of *lying,* as acc. cogn. c. שכב **3**: שִׁכְבַת־זֶרַע Lv 15[18] a man lies with her *a lying of seed* (in copulation), cf. 19[20] Nu 5[13]; then (=*semen*), תֵּצֵא שִׁכְבַת־זֶרַע Lv 15[16.32] 22[4] (+מִמֶּנּוּ) שׁ׳ ז׳ alone 15[17]. **2.** *layer* of dew, שִׁכְבַת הַטָּל Ex 16[13.14] (P). 7902

†[שְׁכֹבֶת] Lag[BN 179] Ba[NB 144] **n.f.** copulation;—sf., all c. נָתַן: וַיִּתֵּן אֶת־שְׁכָבְתּוֹ Nu 5[20] (P; בְּ fem.); לֹא תִתֵּן שְׁכָבְתְּךָ לְזָרַע Lv 18[20] (אֶל fem.), בְּכָל־בְּהֵמָה לֹא תִתֵּן שׁ׳ v[23], cf. 20[15] (all H). 7903

מִשְׁכָּב[46] **n.m.** [Lv 15, 4] **place of lying, couch; act of lying;**—abs. מ׳ 1 K 1[47]+, cstr. מִשְׁכַּב 2 S 4[5]+; sf. מִשְׁכָּבִי Jb 7[13]+, מִשְׁכַּבְכֶם ψ 4[5]; pl. cstr. מִשְׁכְּבֵי Gn 49[4]+, sf. מִשְׁכְּבוֹתָם Ho 7[14]+, etc.;—**1.** *couch, bed* (37 t.), 2 S 4[11] Ho 7[14] Mi 2[1] 1 K 1[47] Ct 3[1]+; וְנָפַל לְמִ׳ Ex 21[18] (E) *he takes to his bed;* מ׳ נִדָּתָהּ Lv 15[26] (P; v. sub I. נדד); מ׳ as place of copulation Gn 49[4] (poem in J), Is 57[7.8.8] Pr 7[17]; as place of burial Is 57[2] Ez 32[25] 2 Ch 16[14] (v. מ׳ Inscr. Tabnit[8] and perh. Jewish inscr. Cooke[341]). †**2.** *act of lying:* **a.** in gen., חֲדַר מ׳ chamber of *lying down*=bedchamber, Ex 7[28] (E), 2 S 4[7] 2 K 6[12], בְּחַדְרֵי מִשְׁכָּבְךָ Ec 10[20]; והוא שֹׁכֵב את מ׳ הַצָּהֳרָיִם 2 S 4[5] his noonday *siesta;* 17[28] rd. perh. עֲרָשׂת מ׳ couches for *lying down* Klo Bu HPS Now, cf. 𝔊. **b.** (from context) sexually: of woman יָדְעַת (אִישׁ לְ) מִשְׁכַּב זָכָר Ju 21[11.12] Nu 31[17.35] (P); of man שכב מִשְׁכְּבֵי אִשָּׁה Lv 18[22] 20[13] (+אֶת־זָכָר sodomy; H); מ׳ דֹּדִים Ez 23[17]. 4904

7904 †[שָׂכָה, so most] vb. **Hiph.** *Pt.* as adj.
in סוּסִים מוּזָנִים מַשְׁכִּים הָיוּ Je 5[8] usu., *horses . . . roaming at large* they have become (cf. Eth. ሰኰ:);—but mng. *lustful* needed; Aq Theod ἕλκοντες, Jer *trahentes* (sc. *genitalia*), i.e. מֹשְׁכִים; read with Arnheim Du Dr מַאֲשִׁיכִים, i.e. fed *stallions* (lit. *growing* אֲשָׁכִים, Lv 21[20]; cf. מַקְרִן, מַפְרִים).

7911 **שָׁכַח** [102] **vb. forget** (NH *id.*; Ecclus 45[26c]
and (**Pi.**) 11[25.25]; Aram. שְׁכַח, ܫܟܚ is *find*);—**Qal** [86] *Pf.* 3 ms. שׁ׳ ψ 9[13] +, sf. שְׁכֵחָנִי Is 49[14]; 2 fs. שָׁכַחַתְּ Je 13[25]; 1 pl. sf. שְׁכַחֲנוּךָ ψ 44[18], etc.; *Impf.* יִשְׁכַּח Dt 4[31] +, etc.; *Imv.* fs. שִׁכְחִי ψ 45[11]; *Inf. abs.* שָׁכֹחַ; *Pt.* pl. cstr. שֹׁכְחֵי Jb 8[13] ψ 50[22]; —*forget:* **1.** subj. man, **a.** acc. rei Gn 27[45] (E), Dt 4[9] 9[7] (opp. זָכַר) +, =*forget and leave*, ב loc., 24[19]; c. obj. cl. c. כִּי Jb 39[15]; c. מִן inf. ψ 102[5]. **b.** c. acc. pers., involving *forgetting to mention*, Gn 40[23] (E; opp. זכר), *ceasing to care for* Je 30[14] (fig.), Is 49[15.15] (acc. om.), v[15] Jb 19[14] ψ 45[11]; c. acc. Jerusalem 137[5a]; יִשְׁכָּחֵהוּ רֶחֶם Jb 24[20]; abs. ψ 137[5b] תִּשְׁכַּח יְמִינִי: AE Ki supply הַמַּעֲשֶׂה or הַנִּגּוּן (whence AV *her cunning*), but forced: 𝔊 תִּשָּׁכַח; read prob. (Gr Bu al.) תִּכְחַשׁ *let it grow lean* (109[24], cf. Zc 11[17]), or (Che) תְּכַחֵשׁ *let it disappoint* (me), *fail* (Hb 3[17]). **c.** esp. c. acc. י׳ (God), Ho 2[15] 8[14] 13[6] Ju 3[7] 1 S 12[9] Is 17[10] Dt 8[19] (שָׁכֹחַ תִּשׁ׳) + 16 t. (5 t. Dt, 4 t. Je), + ψ 59[12] (acc. om.); also acc. of divine name Je 23[27] (בַּבַּעַל), ψ 44[21]; commands of י׳ Ho 4[6] Dt 26[13] (acc. om.) ψ 119[16] + 7 t. ψ 119, his doings and ways, v[139] 78[7.11] 103[2] 106[13], his covenant Dt 4[23.31] 2 K 17[38] Pr 2[17]; law of wisdom 3[1], sc. acc. בִּינָה 4[6]. **2.** subj. י׳ (God): **a.** acc. pers. Ho 4[6] 1 S 1[11] (opp. זָכַר), La 5[20] Is 49[14] (‖ עָזַב), ψ 10[12] 13[2] 42[10]. **b.** acc. of sins Am 8[7] ψ 10[11] (acc. om.), cry ψ 9[13] (opp. זָכַר), cf., of distress, 44[25]. **c.** voice of foes ψ 74[23]. **d.** sq. inf. ψ 77[10]. †**Niph.** *Pf.* 3 ms. נִשְׁכַּח Ec 9[5], etc.; *Impf.* יִשָּׁכַח ψ 9[19], 3 fs. תִּשָּׁכַח Je 20[11], etc.; *Pt.* fs. נִשְׁכָּחָה Is 23[16], נִשְׁכַּחַת v[15], pl. נִשְׁכָּחִים Jb 28[4];—*be forgotten:* subj. rei Gn 41[30] (E), Dt 31[21] Je 20[11] 23[40] 50[5] Is 65[11]; subj. pers. ψ 9[19] 31[13] Ec 2[16], Tyre Is 23[15.16] (under fig. of harlot), subj. זִכְרָם Ec 9[5]; הַנִּשׁ׳ מִנִּי רָגֶל Jb 28[4]. †**Pi.** *Pf.* 3 ms. שִׁכַּח י׳ וגו׳ La 2[6] י׳ *hath caused to forget* (be forgotten) in Zion assembly and sabbath. †**Hiph.** *Inf.* לְהַשְׁכִּיחַ Je 23[27] *to make* my people *forget* my name (2 acc.). †**Hithp.** *Impf.* 3 mpl. יִשְׁתַּכְּחוּ Ec 8[10] *they were forgotten* in the city.

†[שָׁכֵחַ] **adj.** forgetting, forgetful;—pl. 7913
הַשְּׁכֵחִים אֶת־הַר ק׳ Is 65[11] *they who forget the mt.* of my holiness (‖ עֹזְבֵי י׳); cstr. שְׁכֵחֵי א׳ ψ 9[18] all nations *forgetful of God* (cf. שֹׁכְחֵי pt., Jb 8[13] ψ 50[22]).

†[שָׁכַךְ] **vb.** decrease, abate (NH שְׁכִיכָה 7918
is *allaying* of anger; שִׁכֵּךְ אֹזֶן *soothe, satisfy* the *ear* (so appar. Dalm), i.e. allow it to hear and understand, cf. Levy[NHWB] (and Ar. سَكَّ *be narrow, have small ears, be deaf*, Frä[90]); Ar. سكّ v. *humble oneself*, Wahrm *humiliate*);—**Qal** *Impf.* 3 mpl. וַיָּשֹׁכּוּ Gn 8[1] the waters *abated; Inf. cstr.* כְּשֹׁךְ Est 2[1] when *abated* the king's wrath, so *Pf.* 3 fs. שָׁכָכָה 7[10].—כְּשַׁךְ יְקוּשִׁים Je 5[26] usu. *like the bending, crouching, of fowlers* (this meaning for שַׁךְ dub.; Dr כְּשֶׁר; Du del. יָשׁוּר כשׁ, then rds. מוֹקְשִׁים הִצִּיבוּ בַּשַּׁחַת א׳ יִלְכֹּדוּ:). **Hiph.** *Pf.* 1 s. consec. וַהֲשִׁכֹּתִי מֵעָלַי Nu 17[20] *I will allay from upon me the murmurings* (acc.), etc.

†[שָׁכֹל, שָׁכֵל Lag[BN 26]] **vb. be bereaved** 7921
(=Ar. ثَكِلَ, 𝔗 תְּכֵל, תְּכוֹל; cf. Syr. ܬܟܠܐ *loss of children*);—**Qal** *Pf.* 1 s. כַּאֲשֶׁר שָׁכֹלְתִּי שָׁכָלְתִּי Gn 43[14] (E) *if I am bereaved, I am bereaved* (of father, expr. resignation; on כָּל v. Ges[§ 29 u]); *Impf.* 1 s. אֶשְׁכַּל 27[45] (E), c. acc. pers. *be bereaved* of you both (of mother); 3 fs. תִּשְׁכַּל מִנָּשִׁים אִמֶּךָ 1 S 15[33] *thy mother shall be bereaved above* (more than) *women*. **Pi.** *Pf.* 3 fs. שִׁכְּלָה 1 S 15[33] +, sf. וְשִׁכַּלְתָּהּ Ez 14[15], etc.; *Impf.* 3 fs. תְּשַׁכֵּל Dt 32[25] +, 2 fs. תְּשַׁכְּלִי Ez 36[14] Qr (v. כָּשַׁל **Pi.**); *Inf. cstr.* sf. לְשַׁכְּלָם v[12]; *Pt.* מְשַׁכֵּלָה Ex 23[26], -כֶּלֶת Ez 36[13], -כָּלֶת 2 K 2[19.21];—**1.** *make childless*, acc. of father Gn 42[36] (E), of mothers 1 S 15[33] (subj. חֶרֶב), cf. Ez 5[17] (subj. famine and beasts), and 14[15] (*id.*; obj. land); acc. of people Ho 9[12] (מֵאָדָם), Je 15[7] (+ אִבַּדְתִּי), Ez 36[12], cf. v[13.14] (v. supra); obj. om. (subj. חֶרֶב) Dt 32[25] La 1[20] Ez 21[19] (Co, for תִּכָּפֵל, v. כָּפַל p. 495[b]; otherwise Toy Krae). **2. a.** *cause barrenness*, or abortion, הָאָרֶץ מְשַׁכָּ׳ 2 K 2[19], cf. v[21] (Thes otherwise, v. מִשׁ׳ infra). **b.** *shew barrenness*, or *abortion*, (1) of any female Ex 23[26] (E; + עֲקָרָה), animals Gn 31[38] (E) Jb 21[10]; (2) of vine Mal 3[11]. **Hiph.** *Pt.* רֶחֶם מַשְׁכִּיל (וְשָׁדַיִם צֹמְקִים) Ho 9[14] *miscarrying womb.* —Je 50[9] read מַשְׂכִּיל *successful*, 𝔊 𝔖 Heb Codd. Ew Hi Gf Gie.

†שְׁכוֹל **n. [m.] bereavement, loss of** 7908
children;—לֹא אֵדַע שׁ׳ Is 47[8] (‖ אַלְמָנָה), cf. v[9]; fig. ψ 35[12].

7909 †[שָׁכוּל] **adj.** childless (through bereavement);—fs. שְׁכוּלָה Is 49^{21} (fig. of Zion);—on form v. Ba$^{NB\ 47}$.

7909 †שַׁכּוּל **adj.** bereaved, robbed of offspring (Ba$^{§\ 37c}$);—esp. דֹּב שׁ׳ 2 S 17^{8} Ho 13^{8} Pr 17^{12} (sim. of fierceness); נְשֵׁיהֶם שַׁכֻּלוֹת Je 18^{21}; שַׁכֻּלָה אֵין בָּהֶם Ct 4^{2} (of flock, in sim.)=6^{6}.

7923 †[שִׁכֻּלִים] **n. pl. abstr.** bereavement, childlessness;—בְּנֵי שִׁכֻּלָיִךְ Is 49^{20} i.e. *sons of thee, the bereaved.*

7921 †מְשַׁכֶּלֶת acc. to Thes **n.f. abstr.** barrenness, 2 K 2^{21} (‖מָוֶת); if so, read <כֹּלֶת- Klo Kit;
7921 but probably **Pi.** *Pt.* as v^{19}, cf. Bur. p. 1013

שכם (√of foll., meaning unknown; NH Hiph.=BH; Eth. has denom. ሰከመ: *carry on the shoulder;* Ar. سَكَمَ is *take short steps, from weakness* (Kam Frey)).

7926 I. שְׁכֶם **n.m.** $^{Zp\ 3,9}$ shoulder;—abs. שׁ׳ Gn 48^{22}+, שֶׁכֶם 33^{19}+, שֶׁכֶם ψ 21^{13} (whence orig. *šakm inferred Ol$^{§\ 147\ a\ ad\ fin.}$ Sta$^{§\ 199\ a}$; but ֶ der. from ֶ before כ, Ba$^{NB\ 104}$ Kö$^{ii.\ 1.\ 67,\ 506}$); cstr. שְׁכֶם
7929 Gn 9^{23}; sf. שִׁכְמוֹ 49^{15}+, שִׁכְמָה (for שִׁכְמָהּ Ges$^{§\ 91e}$) Jb 31^{22}, etc.;—**1.** *shoulder* (sometimes incl. back of neck; כתף=*shoulder-blade*): **a.** as bearing burdens, וַיֵּט שׁ׳ לִסְבֹּל Gn 49^{15} (poem in J; Issach. under fig. of ass), cf. 21^{14} (E), 24$^{15.45}$ Ex 12^{34}, also Gn 9^{23} (all J), Jos 4^{5} (E), Ju 9^{48} Is 10^{27} (‖צַוָּאר), 14^{25} (both fig.), ψ 81^{7}, so, metaph., of responsibility of rule Is 9^{5} 22^{22} (symbolized by key), of accusation as (easy) burden Jb 31^{36}; fig. also לְעָבְדוֹ שׁ׳ אֶחָד Zp 3^{9} *to serve him* (with) *one shoulder* (as one man), cf. Syr. ܒܚܕ ܟܬܦܐ. **b.** in statement of Saul's height, מִשִּׁכְמוֹ וָמַעְלָה גָּבֹהַּ מִכָּל־הָעָם 1 S 9^{2}, cf. 10^{23} and (with play on n.pr. loc. שְׁכֶם) נָתַתִּי לְךָ שׁ׳ אַחַד עַל־אַחֶיךָ Gn 48^{22} (E; cf. Dr). **2.** in gen. *back:* כְּהַפְנֹתוֹ שִׁכְמוֹ לָלֶכֶת מֵעִם 1 S 10^{9}; so תְּשִׁיתֵמוֹ שׁ׳ ψ 21^{13}, i.e. make them turn (in flight; cf. וְאֹיְבַי נָתַתָּה לִּי עֹרֶף 18^{41}); as beaten מַטֵּה שׁ׳ Is 9^{3} (‖שֵׁבֶט הַנֹּגֵשׂ בּוֹ); more anatom. כְּתֵפִי מִשּׁ׳ תִפּוֹל Jb 31^{22} *let my shoulder-*
7927 *blade fall from its back.*—Ho 6^{9} v. II. שְׁכֶם. below

7929 שִׁכְמָה v. foregoing.

7927 †II. שְׁכֶם **n.pr.loc.** $_{49}$ et **m.** $_{14}$ (Συχεμ; 𝔊L oft. Σίκιμα Lag$^{BN\ 57}$): **1.** district in N. Palestine (prob. *shoulder* (saddle?) of mount.);—מְקוֹם שׁ׳ Gn 12^{6}, שְׁכֶמָה 37^{14}; = city (שְׁכֶם, שְׁכֶמָה, Ho 6^{9} (שְׁכֶמָה) Jos 24^{1}; עִיר שׁ׳ Gn 33^{18} Ju 8^{31}+20 t. Ju 9 (בַּעֲלֵי שׁ׳ v^{2}+12 t., מִגְדַּל־שׁ׳ ב׳ v$^{46.47}$), Ho 6^{9}+21 t. (עִיר שׁ׳ Gn 33^{18}); city of refuge Jos 20^{7} 21^{21} 1 Ch 6^{52}.—WMM$^{As.\ u.\ Eur.\ 394}$, cp. Egypt. *Sa-ka-mà* (cf. Jen$^{ZA\ x\ (1895)\ 356}$); mod. *Nablûs* (from Rom. name Neapolis); v. Buhl$^{G\ 200\ f.}$ GASm$^{G\ 332\ ff.\ 345}$ Wilson. Hast. DB SHECHEM. **2. n.pr.m.** (on connexion with **1** cf. Ju 9^{28}), 'son' of Ḥamor, also Gn 33^{19} 34^{2} +10 t. 34, Jos 24^{3}.

†שֶׁכֶם **n.pr.m.** in Manasseh (Συχεμ): Nu 7928
26^{31} 1 Ch 7^{19}; בְּנֵי־שׁ׳ Jos 17^{2}.

†שִׁכְמִי **adj. gent.** of שֶׁכֶם, c. art. as n. coll. 7930
הַשּׁ׳ Nu 26^{31}.

[שָׁכַם] $_{65}$ **vb. Hiph. denom.** start, rise, 7925
early (prop. *load backs* of beasts for day's journey);—*Pf.* 3 ms. consec. וְהִשְׁכִּים 2 S 15^{2} Jb 1^{5}, etc.; *Impf.* 3 ms. וַיַּשְׁכֵּם Gn 19^{27}+, 2 ms. תַּשְׁכִּים Ju 9^{33}, etc.; *Imv.* הַשְׁכֵּם Ex 8^{16}+; *Inf. abs.* הַשְׁכֵּם Je 7^{25}+, -כִּים Je 44^{4} Pr 27^{14}, erron. אַשְׁכִּים Je 25^{3} (Ges$^{§\ 53k}$); *Pt.* מַשְׁכִּים Ho 6^{4}+, etc.;—*rise early, make an early start,* of journey (Hex only JE); לְדַרְכְּכֶם Ju 19^{9} (+מָחָר), cf. Ct 7^{13}; +vb. of going Gn 19^{2} (J), standing 2 S 15^{2}, encamping Ju 7^{1}, etc.; +inf. 1 S 15^{12} (cf. Dr), 29^{11} 2 K 6^{15} (לָקוּם), מַשְׁכִּימֵי קוּם ψ 127^{3} (opp. מְאַחֲרֵי שֶׁבֶת); usu. c. בַּבֹּקֶר Gn 19^{27} (J; אֶל־הַמָּקוֹם), 1 S 29$^{10.10}$+27 t., + (hyperbol.) מַשְׁכִּימֵי בַבֹּ׳ שֵׁכָר Is 5^{11} (‖מְאַחֲרֵי בַנֶּשֶׁף); c. מִמָּחֳרָת Ex 32^{6} (E), Ju 6^{28}+3 t.; c. בַּעֲלוֹת הַשַּׁחַר Jos 6^{15} (J), 1 S 19^{26}; וַיְמַהֲרוּ וַיַּשְׁכִּימוּ וַיֵּצְאוּ Jos 8^{14} (J) *they made a quick and early start, and went out;* †Inf. abs. (Ges$^{§\ 113s}$) as adv. הַשְׁ׳ וְהַעֲרֵב 1 S 17^{16} *at early morning and at evening;* esp. of י׳, in Je: הַשׁ׳ וְדַבֵּר=*speaking early and often* 7^{13} 35^{14} and (of Je) 25^{3}, cf. 11^{7} 32^{33}; oft. הַשׁ׳ וְשָׁלוֹחַ=*sending early and often* 7^{25} 24^{4} 26^{5} 29^{19} 35^{14} 44^{4}, also 2 Ch 36^{15}; so vb. fin. הִשְׁכִּימוּ הִשְׁחִיתוּ Zp 3^{7}=*with eagerness they corrupted* (Ges$^{§\ 120g}$); pt. כַּטַּל מַשְׁ׳ הֹלֵךְ Ho 6^{4} *like the dew departing early,*
13^{3} (Ges$^{ib.}$).—1 S 9^{26} read וַיִּשְׁכַּב, v. שׁכב. p. 1011 7901

שָׁכֵן, שָׁכַן $_{129}$ **vb.** settle down, abide, 7931
dwell (NH *id.;* Ecclus 43$^{17\ d}$+; Ph. שכן Lzb^{375}; Aram. שְׁכֵן; Syr. ܫܟܢ, all *dwell;* Ar. سَكَنَ *rest, dwell,* cf. As. *šakânu, set, lay, deposit, set up* (a dwelling), intrans. *be situated* (of city), *maškanu, place, dwelling-place*);—**Qal** *Pf.* 3 ms. שׁ׳ Ex 40^{35}+5 t.; שָׁכֵן Dt 33^{12}+2 t., etc.; *Impf.* 3 ms. יִשְׁכֹּן Gn 16^{12}+; יִשְׁכָּן־ Nu 9^{17}+2 t.; 3 mpl. יִשְׁכֹּנוּ Je 49^{31}; 3 fpl. תִּשְׁכֹּנָּה Ez 17^{23}, etc.; *Imv.* ms. שְׁכֹן Gn 26^{2} ψ 37^{27}; שְׁכָן־ v^{3}; mpl. שִׁכְנוּ

Je 48^{28}; *Inf. cstr.* בִּשְׁכֹּן (Ges ^{§45g}) Gn 35^{22}, לִשְׁכּוֹן 2 Ch 6^{1}, etc.; sf. שָׁכְנִי Ex 29^{46}; שָׁכְנוֹ Dt 12^{5} (but v. **Pi. 1**), etc.; *Pt.* שֹׁכֵן Gn 14^{13}+, שֹׁכְנִי (Ges ^{§90lm}) Dt 33^{16}+3 t.; sf. fs. שֹׁכַנְתִּי Je 51^{13}; *Pt. pass.* appar. pl. cstr. c. art. הַשְּׁכוּנֵי Ju 8^{11} (but corrupt, n.pr.loc. needed, v. GFM):—**1.** *settle down to abide:* **a.** of pers.: encamp Nu 24^{2} (E); settle permanently ψ 102^{29} (abs.: ||יִכּוֹן); ש׳ כמלך Jb 29^{25} (|| ישב); *settle down* (to remain) Ju 5^{17}; תַּחְתָּיו 2 S 7^{10} = 1 Ch 17^{9} (not to be removed); esp. at rest, peace, in security, לבטח Je 23^{6} 33^{16} Dt 33^{12}, cf. בין כתפים v^{12}; ψ 16^{9} (|| שמח); בטח Dt 33^{28} Pr 1^{33}; (ל)בדד Nu 23^{9} (poem) Je 49^{31} Mi 7^{14}; land of Egypt Je 46^{26} (remain undisturbed), so 50^{39} Is 13^{20} (|| תֵּשֵׁב, cf. ישב **4**); c. acc. מרומים 33^{16}; abs. Na 3^{18}, subj. אדירים (We יָשְׁנוּ, Now יִשְׁכְּבוּ; || נָמוּ); Pr 7^{11} *her feet tarry not in her house.* **b.** of animals: כְּלָבִיא Dt 33^{20}; ב loc. Is 34^{11} Jb 37^{8}; שָׁם Is 13^{21}; birds ש׳ תַּחַת (under) Ez 17^{23}, ש׳ בְּצֵל, v^{23}; c. עַל = *upon* 31^{13}, = *by* ψ 104^{12}; c. acc. סֶלַע Jb 39^{28}; abs., of man under fig. of bird, אָעוּפָה וְאֶשְׁכֹּנָה ψ 55^{7}. **c.** things: c. עַל of cloud, Jb 3^{5} *settle down over;* cf. Ex 24^{16} 40^{35} Nu 9$^{17.18.22}$ (all P); c. בְּ 10^{12} (P). **2.** *abide, dwell:* **a.** of men: abs. ψ 37^{27} (לְעוֹלָם); שָׁמָּה Is 65^{9}; c. ב loc. ψ 69^{37} Jb 18^{15} 30^{6} Mi 4^{10} Je 48^{28}+10 t.; לְחוֹף יַמִּים Gn 49^{13}; c. עַל, *by* Ju 5^{17} Je 51^{13}; *upon* ψ 37^{29}; על פני Gn 16^{12} (J); c. עִם *with* ψ 120$^{5.6}$; c. acc. Pr 2^{21} Je 17^{6}+5 t.; מִן . . . עַד Gn 25^{18} (J); שֹׁכְנֵי אָרֶץ Is 18^{3} (|| יֹשְׁבֵי תֵבֵל). **b.** of the dead: שֹׁכְנֵי עָפָר Is 26^{19} (|| רְפָאִים); cf. Jb 26^{5} (|| *id.*), so mortals, שֹׁכְנֵי בָתֵּי חֹמֶר 4^{19}; ש׳ דוּמָה ψ 94^{17} (i.e. שאול). **c.** of God: ש׳ בָּעֲרָפֶל 1 K 8^{12} = 2 Ch 6^{1} (poem); מָרוֹם Is 33^{5}; עַד 57^{15}; מָרוֹם וְקָדוֹשׁ v^{15}; ש׳ סְנֶה Dt 33^{16} (theoph.); בְּאָהֳלֵי־שֵׁם Gn 9^{27} (J, v. Br$^{MP\ 82}$; al. Japheth subj.); בְּתוֹכָם Ex 25^{8} 29^{46} Nu 5^{3} (all P), Ez 43^{9}; c. בְּתוֹךְ elsewh. Ex 29^{45} (P)+6 t.; ב loc. ψ 85^{10}; later בְּצִיּוֹן Jo 4$^{17.21}$; בְּהַר צִיּוֹן Is 8^{18}; ψ 68$^{17.19}$ (abs.) +4 t.; שֹׁכֵן יְרוּשָׁלָ͏ִם ψ 135^{21}. **d.** things: אֹהֶל מוֹעֵד, c. את Lv 16^{16} (P); מִשְׁכַּן י׳ שָׁם Jos 22^{19} (P); אור Jb 38^{19}. **e.** abstr. subj.: מִשְׁפָּט Is 32^{16} (בַּמִּדְבָּר); חָכְמָה, c. acc. עָרְמָה Pr 8^{12}. †**Pi.** *Pf.* 3 ms. שִׁכֵּן ψ 78^{60}; 1 s. שִׁכַּנְתִּי Je 7$^{7.12}$; *Impf.* 1 s. אֲשַׁכְּנָה Je 7^{3}; *Inf. cstr.* שַׁכֵּן Nu 14^{30}+7 t.; sf. שִׁכְנוֹ Dt 12^{5} (so read for MT לְשִׁכְנוֹ, cf. Kö$^{ii.1.21}$);—**1.** *make settle down, establish:* אֹהֶל ש׳ בָּאָדָם ψ 78^{60}; esp. in Dt, לְשַׁכֵּן שְׁמוֹ שָׁם *establish his name there* (cf. *šakan šuma* as Canaanism Wkl$^{TelAm.\ 138\ Rev.\ 20;\ 181.\ 6}$) Dt 12^{11} 14^{23} 16$^{2.6.11}$ 26^{2}, cf. Je 7^{12} Ne 1^{9}; +

לְשׁוּם אֶת־שְׁמוֹ שָׁם לְשִׁכְנוֹ Dt 12^{5} (rd. לְשַׁכְּנוֹ). **2.** 7933
make to dwell: c. acc. pers., ב loc., Nu 14^{30} (J)
Je 7$^{3.7}$. †**Hiph.** *Pf.* 1 s. הִשְׁכַּנְתִּי Ez 32^{4}; *Impf.*
3 ms. juss. יַשְׁכֵּן ψ 7^{6}, וַיַּשְׁכֵּן Gn 3^{24} ψ 78^{55}, etc.;—
1. a. *lay,* ψ 7^{6} כבודי לעפר *lay my honour in the dust* (of death); *place, set,* Gn 3^{24} (J); *place, establish,* אהל מועד at Shilo Jos 18^{1} (P). **b.** *cause* birds *to settle,* עַל Ez 32^{4}. **2.** *cause to dwell,* c. acc. pers., ב loc., ψ 78^{55}; cf. Jb 11^{14}.

†[שֵׁכֶן?] **n.m. dwelling**;—sf. שִׁכְנוֹ Dt 12^{5} 7933
(cf. שכן *dwelling* Ecclus 14^{25}), but v. √ **Pi.** above 7931

†שָׁכֵן **adj. inhabitant, neighbour**;—ש׳ Is 7934
33^{24}+; cstr. שְׁכַן Ho 10^{5}; sf. שְׁכֵנוֹ Ex 12^{4}; שְׁכֵנָיִךְ 2 K 4^{3}, etc.; f. sf. שְׁכֶנְתָּהּ Ex 3^{22}; fpl. שְׁכֵנוֹת Ru 4^{17};—**1.** *inhabitant,* Is 33^{24} Ho 10^{5}. **2.** *neighbour:* woman Ex 3^{22} (E); pl. Ru 4^{17}; man Ex 12^{4} (P) Je 6^{21} Pr 27^{10}, pl. 2 K 4^{3}; of places Dt 1^{7}; nations, to Judah Ez 16^{26} ψ 79^{12}; מָדוֹן לשׁ׳ חֶרְפָּה לִשְׁכֵנֵי(נוּ) 44^{14} 79^{4}, cf. 31^{12}, 89^{42}; 80^{7}; to Edom Je 49^{10}; to Sodom v^{18} 50^{40}; to י׳ 11^{14} (because to his people).

מִשְׁכָּן$_{139}$ **n.m.**$^{Ex\ 26,6}$ **dwelling-place, 'taber-** 4908
nacle';—מ׳ Ex 25^{9}+; cstr. מִשְׁכַּן 38^{21}+, etc.; pl. cstr. מִשְׁכְּנֵי ψ 46^{6} (𝔊 Bae Du מִשְׁכָּנוֹ, < מִשְׁכַּן י׳); sf. מִשְׁכְּנֹתֵיהֶם Ez 25^{4} (< משכנתיהם || טִירוֹתֵיהֶם), מִשְׁכָּנוֹת Hb 1^{6} ψ 132^{5}; cstr. מִשְׁכְּנוֹת 87^{2}+, etc.;—†**1.** *dwelling-place:* מִשְׁכַּן־קֹרַח דָּתָן וַאֲבִירָם Nu 16$^{24.27}$ (P) [but here orig. מִשְׁכַּן י׳; v. Comm.]; poet. = *tomb,* Is 22^{16}. **2.** elsewhere in sg. always of abode of י׳: †**a.** in gen., of temple, מ׳ קְדֹשׁ ψ 46^{5}; מִשְׁכַּן כְּבוֹדֶךָ 26^{8}; מ׳ שְׁמֶךָ 74^{7}. **b.** מִשְׁכָּנוֹ שִׁלוֹ 78^{60}. **c.** הַמּ׳ in P, of י׳'s 'dwelling' (Ex 25^{9} RVm; rendered conventionally 'tabernacle'), of planks lined with vari-coloured tapestry, with a 'tent' (אֹהֶל) over it, filled with כְּבוֹד י׳ Ex 40$^{34.35}$; over it cloud שכן Nu 9$^{18.22}$ (during the wanderings); its plan given by י׳ Ex 25^{9} 26^{30}; disting. from אֹהֶל מוֹעֵד, the 'tent' over it (cf. אֹהֶל **3**), Ex 26$^{7.12.13}$ 36^{14} 40^{19}; †מִשְׁכַּן י׳ Lv 17^{4} (H), Nu 16^{9} 17^{28} 19^{13} 31$^{30.47}$ Jos 22^{19} (v. also **1**), 1 Ch 16^{39} 21^{29} 2 Ch 1^{5} 29^{6}; †מ׳ הָעֵדֻת Ex 38^{21} Nu 1$^{50.53.53}$ 10^{11}; מ׳ אהל מועד Ex 39^{32} 40$^{2.6.29}$ 1 Ch 6^{17}, מִשְׁכַּן בֵּית הָאֱלֹהִים v^{23}, נָשָׂא אֶת־הַמִּשְׁכָּן 23^{26}; cf. מִשְׁכָּן (prob. gloss on אהל), 2 S 7^{6} || 1 Ch 17^{5}, +76 t. P. **3.** pl. מִשְׁכָּנוֹת *dwellings* (only poet.): **a.** of Israel, Nu 24^{5} (poem; || אהלים), Je 30^{18} Is 54^{2}+4 t.; of other nations Je 51^{30} Hb 1^{6}, cf. Ez 25^{4} (v. supra); מ׳ עַוָּל Jb 18^{21}; מ׳ רשעים 21^{28}; of wild

ass 39^{6} (‖ בית); shepherds Ct 1^{8}; = tomb ψ 49^{12} (cf. **1**). **b.** God's abode in Zion Ez 37^{27} ψ 132$^{5.7}$, cf. 43^{3}, 84^{2} (‖ חַצְרוֹת י׳).

7935 †שְׁכַנְיָה(וּ) **n.pr.m.** (*Y. hath taken up his abode*);—שְׁכַנְיָה, Σεχενια(ς), etc.: **1.** descendant of Jehoiakin 1 Ch 3$^{21.22}$ (on context v. Kit), Ezr 8$^{3.5}$. **2.** Ezr 10^{2} (diff. from **1**?). **3.** father of a wall-builder Ne 3^{29}. **4.** father-in-law of Tobiah Ne 6^{18}. **5.** priestly name: **a.** Ne 12^{3} = שְׁכַנְיָהוּ 1 Ch 24^{11}, cf. שְׁכַנְיָה **3** Ne 10^{5} 12^{14}. **b.** שְׁכַנְיָהוּ 2 Ch 31^{15}.

7937 †I. [שָׁכַר] **vb. be, or become, drunk, drunken** (NH *id.*, der. spec. and deriv.; Ecclus 40$^{18.20}$ שכר *strong drink*; Ar. سَكِرَ *be drunken*, also *be full*, سَكَّرَ *fill*; As. *šikaru*, = שֵׁכָר, *šakkûru, drunken*, perhaps also vb. *šakâru*; Eth. ሰክረ: Aram. שִׁכְרָא, ܫܶܟܪܳܐ = שֵׁכָר, esp. *date-wine* (Löw$^{p. 125}$), cf. ܫܟܰܪ *be drunken*, usu. (der. spec.) *defile, deform*, etc.; from שֵׁכָר, Egypt. *ṯà-k-ỉra* WMM$^{As. u. Eur. 102}$, Gk. σίκερα Lewy$^{Fremdw. 81}$);—**Qal** *Pf.* 3 pl. שָׁכְרוּ Is 29^{9}; *Impf.* 3 ms. וַיִּשְׁכָּר Gn 9^{21}, 3 mpl. יִשְׁכְּרוּן Is 49^{26}, etc.; *Imv.* mpl. שִׁכְרוּ Je 25^{27} Ct 5^{1}; *Inf. cstr.* לְשָׁכְרָה Hg 1^{6}; *Pt. pass.* שְׁכֻרַת Is 51^{21} (Ges$^{§ 130 b}$ Lag$^{BN 60}$);—*become drunken* Gn 9^{21} (J), of social drinking 43^{34} (J), Ct 5^{1}, token of plenty Hg 1^{6}; fig. of nations staggering helplessly under calamity Je 25^{27}, 51^{21} (וְלֹא מִיָּיִן), Na 3^{11}; of infatuation Is 29^{9} (וְלֹא יַיִן), of disgrace La 4^{21}, self-destruction, כֶּעָסִיס דָּמָם יִשׁ׳ Is 49^{26}. **Pi.** *make drunken*: *Impf.* 3 ms. sf. וַיְשַׁכְּרֵהוּ 2 S 11^{13}, lit.; fig. 1 s. (sf. of people) וַאֲשַׁכְּרֵם (read וָ׳) Is 63^{6} (subj. י׳) *I made them drunk* in my wrath (but MSS Ges Hi Ew Che Kit Marti al. וָאֲשַׁבְּרֵם *I brake them in pieces*); *Pt.* fs., of Bab., מְשַׁכֶּרֶת כָּל־הָאָרֶץ Je 51^{7}; cf. *Inf. abs.* שַׁכֵּר Hb 2^{15} (i.e. terrorizing nations; read prob. הַשְׁקֵה וְאַף שׁ׳ We Now). **Hiph.** *id.*: *Pf.* 1 s. וְהִשְׁכַּרְתִּי Je 51^{57} (subj. י׳) i.e. make princes helpless, וְהִשְׁכַּרְתִּים v^{39}; *Imv.* mpl. sf. הַשְׁכִּירֻהוּ, obj. Moab, i.e. make helpless and disgraced 48^{26}; *Impf.* 1 s. אַשְׁכִּיר חִצַּי מִדָּם Dt 32^{42}.—Ruben$^{JQ xi (1899), 446}$ prop. מַשְׁכִּירוֹת Ho 7^{5} for משך ידו את. **Hithp.** *Impf.* 2 fs. תִּשְׁתַּכָּרִין 1 S 1^{14} how long *wilt thou make thyself drunken* [a drunken spectacle]?

7941 †שֵׁכָר **n.[m.] intoxicating drink, strong drink** (Ba$^{NB § 71}$);—alw. שׁ׳ abs.; usu. ‖ יַיִן (exc. ψ 69^{13}): Is 29^{9}; usu. condemned, Is 5$^{11.22}$ 28$^{7.7.7}$ 56^{12} (נִסְבְּאָה שׁ׳), Mi 2^{11} 1 S 1^{15} Pr 20^{1}; forbidden to priests on duty Lv 10^{9} (P); not for princes Pr 31^{4}; nor Nazirite Nu 6^{3} Ju 13$^{4.7.14}$, cf. חֹמֶץ שׁ׳ Nu 6^{3}; שׁוֹתֵי שׁ׳ ψ 69^{13} *drunkards*; but שׁ׳ as common drink Dt 29^{5} (opp. to miraculous), allowable in sacrif. meal 14^{26}, commended for weak and weary Pr 31^{4}; נֶסֶךְ שׁ׳ Nu 28^{7} (P; for יַיִן v^{14}+); v. further Kennedy$^{Ency. Bib. iv. 5309 f.}$.—On form cf. Lag$^{M ii. 357; BN 51}$.

†שִׁכֹּר, שִׁכּוֹר **adj. drunken** (Ba$^{NB § 134 b}$);— 7910
abs. שִׁכֹּר 1 S 25^{36}, שִׁכּוֹר 1 K 16^{9}+, f. שִׁכֹּרָה 1 S 1^{13}, pl. שִׁכּוֹרִים Jo 1^{5}, cstr. שִׁכֹּרֵי Is 28$^{1.3}$;—*drunken*: 1 S 25^{36}, אִישׁ שׁ׳ Je 23^{9}, שֹׁתֶה שׁ׳ 1 K 16^{9} *drinking* (and) *drunken*, 20^{16}; as subst. = *drunken one, drunkard* Is 28$^{1.3}$ Pr 26^{9}, pl. Jo 1^{5} (‖ שֹׁתֵי יַיִן); in sim. Is 19^{14} Jb 12^{25} ψ 107^{27}, and (of earth) Is 24^{20}; f. of drunken woman 1 S 1^{13}.

†שִׁכָּרוֹן **n.[m.] drunkenness**;—שׁ׳ only 7943
fig.: Je 13^{13} Ez 23^{33} (Co Berthol Krae שִׁבָּרוֹן, not Toy), both of bewilderment and helplessness under calamity; from drinking blood 39^{19}.—Vid. Lag$^{BN 202, cf. 199}$.

†[שִׁכְּרוֹן] **n.pr.loc.** on NW. border of Judah, 7942
c. ה loc. -וֹנָה Jos 15^{11}, Σοκχωθ, 𝔊L Σαχαρωνα.

II. שכר (√ of foll.; meaning unknown).

†אֶשְׁכָּר **n.[m.] gift**;—abs. אֶ׳ ψ 72^{10} (‖ מִנְחָה); 814
sf. אֶשְׁכָּרֵךְ Ez 27^{15}.

†שַׁל in עַל־הַשַּׁל 2 S 6^{7} is disputed; 𝔊^{B} om.; 7944
A 𝔊L τῇ προπετείᾳ, *for his hastiness* (prob. from Aram.; cf. ܡܶܢ ܫܶܠܝܳܐ = *suddenly*), 𝔙 *temeritate*; 𝔗 על דאשתלי because he *acted in error* (Aram. שְׁלָא, שְׁלִי *err*: v. BAram. שָׁלוּ), hence AV RV *for his error*; <Th We Dr Bu Now fragm. of [עַל [אֲשֶׁר] שָׁלַ[ח יָדוֹ עַל], ‖ 1 Ch 13^{10}.

שֶׁל Ct 1^{6} 3^{7} al.; בְּשֶׁל Ec 8^{17}: v. · שֶׁ **4 d.** p. 980 7945

שַׁלְאֲנָן Jb 21^{23} *lapsus cal.* for שַׁאֲנָן, q.v. (cf. 7946
Perles$^{Anal. 82}$).

†[שָׁלַב] **vb. Pu.** be bound, joined (NH 7947
Pu. = BH; שְׁלִיבָה *rung* of ladder; Aram. שְׁלִיבִין appar. only 1 K 7$^{28.29}$, ܫܰܠܒܳܐ *ravine, narrow path between mountains*; Ar. سَلَبَ is *seize, carry off, by force*);—*Pt.* fpl. מְשֻׁלָּבֹת Ex 26^{17} tenons *joined* each to (אֶל) its fellow, 36^{22} (both P).

שְׁלַבִּים **n.[m.] pl.** joinings of bases (𝔙 7948
juncturae);—בֵּין הַשׁ׳ 1 K 7$^{28.29}$, עַל־הַשְּׁ׳ v^{29}; AV RV *ledges*, <*ribs* (Kit) or *frames* (Benz), joining or binding the parts together.

שׁלג (√of foll., unless loan-word; NH= BH, Ecclus 43[17 c] שׁלגו *his snow;* Ar. ثَلْجٌ, Aram. תַּלְגָּא, ܬܠܓܐ, As. *šalgu*).

7950 †שֶׁ֫לֶג **n.m.**[Is 55, 10] **snow**;—abs. שׁ׳ Is 1[18]+, שָׁ֑לֶג Ex 4[6]+; cstr. שֶׁ֫לֶג Je 18[14];—*snow*, 2 S 23[20] (בְּיוֹם הַשּׁ׳) = 1 Ch 11[22], Jb 6[16] 37[6] (|| גֶּשֶׁם מָטָר), ψ 147[16] 148[8] (+ קִיטוֹר, בָּרָד, אֵשׁ); מֵימֵי שׁ׳ Jb 24[19], cf. 9[30] Qr (בְּמֵי, < Qr בְּמוֹ De Di Bu al., snow as purifying; v. also [מַי]); poet. אֹצְרוֹת שׁ׳ 38[22] (|| א׳ בָּרָד); symb. of cold Pr 31[21]; as moistening, fertilizing Is 55[10] (|| גֶּשֶׁם); on mountains, fig. of normal habit, שׁ׳ לְבָנוֹן Je 18[14]; sim. of whiteness, of leprosy Ex 4[6] (J), Nu 12[10] (E), 2 K 5[27]; c. מִן comp., of fair skin La 4[7] (|| חָלָב); sim. of sins, כַּשּׁ׳ יַלְבִּינוּ Is 1[18], cf. ψ 51[9] (מִן comp.); sim. of refreshment Pr 25[13] (drink cooled by snow, v. reff. in De Toy), of the unfitting כַּשּׁ׳ בַּקַּיִץ 26[1] (|| מָטָר).—On snow in Pal. v. Nicol[Hast. DB Snow].

7949 †[שָׁלַג] **vb. denom. Hiph.** snow;—*Impf.* 3 fs. תַּשְׁלֵג (Ges[§ 109 k]), impers. ψ 68[15] *it snows* on Ṣalmon (meaning obscure).

7951 †I. [שָׁלֵו, שָׁלָה] **vb. be quiet, at ease** (Ecclus 47[13] שׁלוה *prosperity*, 41[1 c] שׁליו *prosperous, at ease;* ܫܠܐ *be tranquil, quiet, cease;* 𝔗 שְׁלֵי, שְׁלָא *be at ease*, then *be careless, thoughtless, go astray* [for Heb. שָׁגָה, שָׁגַג], Aph. *neglect* (God, etc.), BAram. 𝔗 שָׁלוּ *error;* Ar. سَلَا (و) *be forgetful, neglectful, content, free* (fr. anxiety));— **Qal 1.** *be* (have) *quiet: Pf.* 1 s. שָׁלַוְתִּי Jb 3[26]. **2.** *be at ease, prosper*, of wicked, 3 pl. שָׁלוּ Je

7952-53 12[1] La 1[5], also *Impf.* 3 mpl. יִשְׁלָ֫יוּ (Ges[§ 75 u]) Jb 12[6], and (of good) ψ 122[6] (יַשְׁלֶ֫ Jb 27[8] v. II. שׁלה). **Niph.** *Impf.* 2 mpl. תִּשָּׁלוּ juss. 2 Ch 29[11] *be* not *negligent* (easy-going; Germ. 'bequem'). **Hiph.** *Impf.* 2 ms. תַּשְׁלֶה juss. 2 K 4[28] *do* not *mislead* me (cf. תְּכַזֵּב v[16]), strong Aramaism, whence Klo תַּשְׁגֶּה.

7959 †[שָׁלוּ] Ges[§ 84 a c] Lag[BN 142] **n.[m.] ease, prosperity** (Perles[Anal. 80] *delusion;* cf. Aram. שָׁלוּ *error*, sub √, e.g., Gn 43[12]);—sf. שַׁלְוִי

7962 ψ 30[7] (cf. De Bae); < read שַׁלְוָתִי (or שַׁלְוֹתִי Bi), Ol Hup-Now Du al. (> Sta Hup think שׁלוי abbreviated from שׁלותי).

7987 †[שֶׁלִי] **n.[m.] quietness**;—בַּשֶּׁ֫לִי 2 S 3[27], i.e. quietly, privately (cf. ܒܫܠܝܐ often in the same sense PS[4167]).

I. שָׁלָה v. שְׁאֵלָה. p. 982 7596

†II. שֵׁלָה **n.pr.m.** son of Judah, Σηλωμ[ν]: Gn 38[5.11.14.26] (J), 46[12] (P); Nu 26[20] (P), 1 Ch 2[3] 4[21]. 7956

†שֵׁלָנִי **adj.gent.** of foreg.: c. art. as n.coll. הַשּׁ׳ Nu 26[20] (P). So rd. also 1 Ch 9[5] Ne 11[5], v. שִׁילֹנִי. p. 1018 7888, 8023

†שָׁלֵו (Lag[BN 43]), שָׁלֵיו, שְׁלֵיו **adj. quiet, at ease**;—**1.** of pers. *at ease*, שָׁלֵו Jb 16[12], שְׁלֵיו 7961
21[23] (Kö[ii. 1. 83]); of nation, שְׁלֵיו (poss. diminutive Kö[ii. 1. 144]) Je 49[31] (|| יוֹשֵׁב לָבֶטַח); *prosperous*, of city fs. שְׁלֵוָה Zc 7[7]; of wicked, mpl. cstr. וְשַׁלְוֵי עוֹלָם ψ 73[12] (Renan[H. iii. 131] prop. וְשֹׁלְיו עֲוִילִים). **2.** of land, *quiet*, שְׁלֵוָה 1 Ch 4[40] (|| שֹׁקֶטֶת). **3.** in לֹא יָדַע שָׁלֵו בְּבִטְנוֹ Jb 20[20] שׁ׳ is appar. n.abstr. *quiet, ease*, so Di De al., read שַׁלְוָה Siegf Bu, Du (after 𝔊) לֹא שָׁלֵו בְּמַטְמֹנוֹ; שָׁלֵו Ez 23[42] is corrupt, Hi Co Berthol (cf. Da) שָׁרוּ *sang*, Toy שָׁרִים, Krae שִׁרִים.

†שַׁלְוָה **n. f. quietness, ease**;—abs. שׁ׳ 7962
ψ 122[7]+; cstr. שַׁלְוַת Ez 16[49] Pr 1[32]; pl. sf. שַׁלְוֹתַיִךְ Je 22[21] (< שַׁלְוָתֵךְ Vrss Gie);—*quietness, peace*, Pr 17[1] (opp. רִיב), ψ 122[7] (|| שָׁלוֹם); *ease, careless security*, Ez 16[49] (שַׁלְוַת הַשְׁקֵט), Pr 1[32]; *prosperity*, Je 22[21] Dn 8[25] 11[21.24]; בְּשׁ׳ *in* (time of) *security* (of sudden attack), if not *unawares* (Thes Ew Hi Ke al.); cf. ܡܢ ܫܠܝܐ lit. *out of quiet*, i.e. *suddenly, unawares* (e.g. 1 Macc 1[30] =ἐξάπινα), 𝔗 מִן שִׁלְיָא Pr 3[25] 6[15] (=פִּתְאֹם), ψ 30[7] v. [שָׁלוּ]. above 7959

†II. [שָׁלָה] **vb. draw out, extract** (si 7952-53
vera l.; =שָׁלַל; Syr. ܫܠܐ (e.g. Ex 2[10]), 𝔗[Jer] שְׁלִי (e.g. Lv 11[17]));—**Qal** *Impf.* 3 ms. apoc. (Ges[§ 109 k]) כִּי יֵשֶׁל אֱלוֹהַּ נַפְשׁוֹ Jb 27[8] (De); < read יַשֹּׁל, or יָשֹׁל (√שׁלל) Di; Schnurrer We Siegf Bu Du יִשָּׂא אֶל־אֱלוֹהַּ *demandeth;* Perles[Anal. 48] יִשְׁאַל.

†[שִׁלְיָה] **n.f. after-birth** (=Ar. سَلًى, Aram. 7988
ܫܠܝܬܐ, שִׁילְיְתָא);—sf. שִׁלְיָתָהּ Dt 28[57].

†שִׁלֹה, שִׁילוֹ, שִׁלוֹ, שִׁילֹה **n.pr.loc.** (orig. שִׁלוֹן, v. 7887
adj.gent. (otherwise Ba[NB § 224 b]), which also shews that √שׁיל, שׁול, was posited when text of K was fixed, cf. Dr[2 S 15. 12]);—שִׁלוֹ Ju 21[19] 1 S 1[24] 3[21] 14[3] Je 7[14] (on destruction of S. v. We[2 S 8, 17]), 26[9] 41[5], מִשְׁכַּן שׁ׳ ψ 78[60]; שִׁילוֹ Ju 21[21.21] Je 7[12]; שִׁלֹה Jos 18[1.8.9.10] 19[51] 21[2] 22[9.12] (all P or R), Ju 18[31] 21[12] 1 S 1[3.9] 2[14] 3[21] 4[3.4.12] 1 K 2[27] 14[2.4] Je 26[6] (var. שִׁלוֹ

in all these [21 t.] given by Gi as Qr).—Σηλωμ, Σηλω(ν).—Mod. *Seilûn*, c. 9½ m. NNE. of Bethel (Beitîn), Buhl$^{G 173}$ Dr$^{Hast. DB SHILOH}$.

7888,8023 †שִׁילֹנִי†, שִׁילֹנִי etc., **adj. gent.** of foreg.: הַשִּׁילֹנִי of Ahijah 1 K 11^{29} 15^{29}, הַשִּׁלֹנִי 12^{15}; הַשִּׁילוֹנִי 2 Ch 9^{29}; הַשִּׁלוֹנִי 10^{15}; also הַשִּׁילֹנִי (coll.) 1 Ch 9^{5}, in ‖ Ne 11^{5} הַשִּׁלֹנִי without n.pr.m., but in both these read הַשֵּׁ(י)לָנִי, Be Ke Ryle Gu^{Hpt}

7956 Siegf^{Ne} Buhl, etc.; v. II. שֵׁלָה. p. 1017

7957 שַׁלְהֶבֶת v. p. 529^{a} supr.

7971 I. שָׁלַח$_{844}$ **vb. send** (NH *id.*; Ecclus 48^{18}+; Aram. שְׁלַח, ܫܠܰܚ, So^{Buhl} Ba$^{ES 41}$ cp. Ar. سَرَحَ (*r=l*), *send forth, drive* cattle to pasture, *send* messenger, etc., but then diff. √ for I. שֶׁלַח, Ar. سِلَاحٌ, سَلَحٌ *weapon;* As. prob. *šalû* (*send, hurl?*), whence *tešlitu, command*);—**Qal**$_{562}$ *Pf.* 3 ms. שׁ׳ Gn 42^{4}+, 2 ms. sf. שְׁלַחְתַּנִי Ex 5^{22}, etc.; *Impf.* 3 ms. יִשְׁלַח Gn 3^{22}+, 2 fpl. תִּשְׁלַחְנָה Ez 23^{40} (Ju 5^{26} read תִּשְׁלָחֶנָּה? Ob^{3} תִּשְׁלַח יָד? Ges^{§47k}); *Imv.* ms. שְׁלַח 1 S 20^{31}+, mpl. שִׁלְחוּ 2 K 2^{17}; *Inf. abs.* שָׁל(וֹ)חַ Nu 22^{37}+; cstr. שְׁלֹחַ v^{15}+, שְׁלֹחַ Is 58^{9}, sf. שָׁלְחֲךָ Gn 38^{17}, etc.; *Pt. act.* שֹׁלֵחַ Ex 9^{14}+, etc.; שָׁלוּחַ 1 K 14^{6}+, etc.;—**1.** *send:* human subj., esp. **a.** acc. pers. Gn 42^{4} 43^{8} (both J; c. אֵת *with*, pers.) Nu 22^{15} (E)+oft., c. לְ rei for which Je 14^{3}; sq. אֶל pers. Gn 37^{13} (J), 2 S 11^{6} Ne 6^{5}+; rarely c. לְ pers. Gn 32^{19} (J; pass.), אֶל loc. 2 Ch 16^{4}, בְּ loc. 1 S 11^{3}, לְ loc. 1 K 5^{28}, acc. loc. 2 K 22^{3}, ה- loc.+מֵעַל pers. 2 S 13^{17}, מִן loc. Gn 37^{14} (J), Nu 13^{3} (P), etc.; sq. inf. purpose 1 S 25^{14} (+מִן loc.), 2 K 1^{16} Je 40^{14}+, אֶל pers. c. inf. purpose 2 S 10^{3} Je 42^{9}+, c. וְ subord. 2 K 5^{6}, c. vb. fin. actionis Ex 2^{5} (E), *sent her maid and took*, +, etc. (many combinations); acc. pers. alone 24^{5} (E), Jos 7^{22} (E), 2 S 10^{7}+oft. **b.** less oft. acc. rei (sometimes c. בְּיַד of agent), c. אֶל pers. 1 S 16^{20} 2 K 5^{5} 20^{12}+, 1 K 5^{23} (=designate by sending unto), לְ pers. Ju 3^{15} 1 K 5^{22}+, אֶל loc. Est 1^{22}, שָׁמָּה 2 K 6^{14}; +inf. purpose 1 Ch 19^{4} Est 4^{4}; +vb. fin. action. ψ 105^{28}; acc. of kid, alone, Gn 38^{23} also (acc. om.) v^{17}, etc. **c.** very oft. without obj.: +vb. fin. action., *send and do* so and so, Gn 27^{45} (E), 2 K 11^{4} Jb 1^{5}+; c. אֶל pers. Ho 5^{13} 2 S 11^{6}+, esp.+לֵאמֹר Gn 38^{25} (J), 1 K 20^{5} (oft. SK), Je 29^{25}+; c. inf. purpose Gn 32^{6} (J), Nu 21^{32} (J), 1 S 22^{11}+, etc. (and so 1 S 31^{9}, reading וַיְשַׁלְּחוּ, for **Pi.,** Th We Dr Now, not HPS Bu); abs. 2 K 2$^{16.17}$ 2 S 14^{29}; =*send to inquire* 1 K 20^{17}, etc. **2.** *send:* subj. ׳י (God), **a.** acc. pers. Gn 45^{5} (E; לִפְנֵי pers.), 1 S 15^{18} (בְּדֶרֶךְ), +אֶל pers. 2 S 12^{1}; acc. of angel, לִפְנֵי pers. Gn 24^{7} Ex 33^{2} (both J), אֵת *with* Gn 24^{40} (J), etc.; c. acc. pers.=*commission* Ex 3^{12} (E), Ju 6^{14} Is 6^{8} Je 14$^{14.15}$+oft. Je, Zc 2^{13}+; also (c. אֶל pers.) Ex 3^{13} (E), Je 25^{4} Ez 3^{6}+, etc.; esp. of sending prophet, (שָׁלֹחַ), הַשְׁכֵּם וְשָׁלוֹחַ Je 7^{25}+ (v. [שָׁכַם]); acc. pers.+inf. purpose 1 S 15^{1} Je 19^{14}+; +עַד loc. 2 K 2^{2}, acc. loc. v^{4}, ה ָ– loc. v^{6}, etc. **b.** c. acc. rei, plagues Ex 9^{14} (c. אֶל־לֵב, בְּ pers.), fig. arrows 2 S 22^{15}=ψ 18^{15} (+vb.fin. action.), ψ 144^{6}, cf. Je 25^{16} al.; his word Is 9^{7} (בְּ gent.), 55^{11} (אשר *to which*), Zc 7^{12} (בְּ agent.), ψ 107^{20} (+vb. fin. action.), 147^{15} (+acc. אֶרֶץ); acc. help 20^{3} (מִן loc.), light and truth 43^{3} (+vb. fin. action.), cf. 57^{4}. **3.** *stretch out*, esp. acc. hand: **a.** human subj., c. בְּ pers. *against*, Gn 37^{22} (E), 1 S 24^{11} Est 2^{21}+; c. בְּ rei (property of others) Ex 22$^{7.10}$ (E), Est 9^{10}+, בַּחַלָּמִישׁ Jb 28^{9}; c. אֶל pers. *against* Gn 22^{12} (E), 2 S 18^{12}, עַל pers. 1 K 13^{4}, etc.; אֶל rei (for good) 2 S 6^{6} (יָד om.); from outside, inward, Ct 5^{4} (מִן loc.); abs. Jb 30^{24} (read טֹבֵעַ for בְּעִי Di Bi Bu). +inf. purpose 1 S 22^{17} 2 S 1^{14} 1 Ch 13^{9}; +vb.fin. act. Gn 3^{22} (J) Dt 25^{11} Ju 15^{15}+; שׁ׳ אֶצְבַּע Is 58^{9}, in token of scorn; c. acc. of rod 1 S 14^{27}; שִׁלְחוּ מַגָּל Jo 4^{13} *stretch out* (the) *sickle.* **b.** ׳י subj., acc. hand, +אֶל pers. *against* Ex 24^{11} (E), cf. (עַל) ψ 138^{7}; +vb. fin. act. †Ex 3^{20} (JE), 9^{15} (J), Jb 1^{11} 2^{5}; in favour, Je 1^{9}, abs. ψ 144^{7} (מִן loc.), also (pass.) Ez 2^{9} and (acc. תַּבְנִית יָד), 8^{3}. †**c.** acc. hand, subj. angel, +acc. loc., inf. purpose 2 S 24^{16}, cherub, אֶל rei, מִן loc. Ez 10^{7}; adversary, אֶל pers. Jb 1^{12}; subj. angel, acc. rod Ju 6^{21}. **d.** *stretched out, slender*, of tree Gn 49^{21} (poem in J), v. I. אֵלָה supr. p. 18^{b}. **e.** perhaps *extend, direct*, acc. rei Ez 8^{17} (v. זְמוֹרָה supr. p. 274^{b}, also conj. in Toy Krae). **4.** rarely *send away* (v. **Pi.**): human subj., acc. pers. Ju 11^{38} (+acc. temp.), Gn 28^{5} (P). **5.** *let loose* (v. **Pi.**), perhaps only ψ 50^{19} (fig.) *thy mouth hast thou let loose in evil.* †**Niph.** *Inf. abs.* וְנִשְׁלוֹחַ סְפָרִים=*letters were sent* (Ges$^{§114 z gg}$) Est 3^{13} (+אֶל pers., בְּיַד agent., inf. purpose). **Pi.**$_{266}$ *Pf.* 3 ms. שִׁלַּח Ex 8^{28}+, sf. שִׁלַּחֲךָ 1 S 20^{22}, etc.; *Impf.* 3 ms. יְשַׁלַּח Je 3^{1}+, יְשַׁלֵּחַ Is 45^{13} Pr 6^{14}; 1 s. sf. אֲשַׁלְּחֲךָ Gn 32^{27}, אֲשַׁלֵּחֲךָ 2 S 11^{12} 1 K 20^{34}, etc.; *Imv.* ms. שַׁלַּח Ex 4^{23}+, etc.; *Inf. abs.* Dt 22^{7} 1 K 11^{22}; cstr. שַׁלַּח Gn 8^{10}+, שַׁלֵּחַ Ex 7^{27}+, etc.; *Pt.* מְשַׁלֵּחַ Gn 43^{4}+, etc.;—**1.** *send* *off, away,* human subj.: **a.** acc. pers. + לְ loc. Jos 24^{28} (E), Ju 7^{8} 1 S 10^{25} +; + לְ pers. Je 48^{12}; + ה- loc. Ju 12^{9} and (c. inf. purpose) Gn 28^{6} (P); acc. of goat, לַעֲזָאזֵל Lv 16^{10} (ה- loc.), v^{26}; *send out,* different ways, acc. pers., בְּ loc. Ju 19^{29} 20^{6}; *send* into exile, י׳ subj., c. מִן loc. Je 24^{5}, ה- loc. 29^{20}. **b.** *send away, dismiss,* acc. pers. Gn 21^{14} (E), 25^{6} (J; מֵעַל pers.), 2 S 13^{16} +; specif., c. acc. of wife (= *divorce*), Dt 22$^{19.29}$ 24$^{1.3}$ Je 3^{1} +, abs. Mal 2^{16}. **c.** *send away* empty (-handed) רֵיקָם, + acc. pers. Gn 31^{42} (E), Dt 15^{13} Jb 22^{9}. **d.** *send off,* give a 'send-off' (sometimes escort part way), acc. pers., Gn 18^{16} 24^{59} 31^{27} (all J), 1 S 9^{26} 2 K 5^{24} 6^{23}. **e.** acc. rei 1 S 6^{8} Ne 8^{12} +, c. acc. loc. 1 S 5^{10} 6^{3}, אֶל pers. Je 27^{3}, etc. **2. a.** *send away,* subj. י׳, acc. pers. Gn 19^{29} (J; מִתּוֹךְ), 1 K 9^{7} (מֵעַל פְּנֵי). **b.** *give over,* acc. pers. ψ 81^{13} (בְּ of evil). **c.** *cast out,* acc. pers. Je 28^{16} (מֵעַל־פְּנֵי), Lv 18^{24} 20^{23} (both מִפְּנֵי). **d.** *send out, forth,* send on a mission, esp. of י׳, c. acc. of hornet Dt 7^{20}, cf. 28^{20} 32^{24} (all בְּ pers.), serpents Nu 21^{6} (E; בְּ pers.), lions 2 K 17$^{25.26}$ (both *id.*), foes 2 K 24$^{2.2}$ (+ inf. purpose); pestilence Am 4^{10} Ez 28^{23} (בְּ pers.), etc.; also springs into (בְּ) channel ψ 104^{10}. **3.** *let go, set free* (sometimes c. חָפְשִׁי) Ex 4^{23} 5$^{2.2}$ (all JE), 2 S 3$^{21.23.24}$ +; = cease to abuse Ju 19^{25}; + inf. purpose Gn 24^{56} (J), Ex 5^{1} (E; + 10 t. Ex), 1 S 5^{11}; c. acc. of bird Gn 8$^{7.8}$ +; עַל־פְּנֵי הַשָּׂדֶה + Lv 14^{7}, cf. v^{53} (both + מֵאִתּוֹ P); = *let loose,* acc. of beast, Ex 22^{4} (E), Lv 16^{22} (בְּ loc.); acc. of bridle Jb 30^{11} (fig.); metaph. of strife Pr 6$^{14.19}$ 16^{28}; *let loose* waters, subj. י׳, Jb 12^{15}. **4.** *shoot forth* branches, Je 17^{8} ψ 80^{12} Ez 31^{5} (but v. I. שֶׁלַח **2**); cf. of locks (פֶּרַע) Ez 44^{20} = *let grow long.* **5.** *let down,* acc. pers. Je 38^{6} (בְּ instr.), acc. rei v^{11} (*id.* + אֶל pers. et loc.). **6.** *shoot* (acc. of arrow om.), לְשַׁ׳ לִי לְמַטָּרָה 1 S 20^{20}. **7.** phrases: שִׁלַּח (אֶת־)הָעִיר בָּאֵשׁ +Ju 1^{8} 20^{48}, cf. 2 K 8^{12} ψ 74^{7}; but also שׁ׳ אֵשׁ בְּ +Am 1$^{4.7.10.12}$ 2$^{2.5}$ Ho 8^{14} Ez 39^{6}; rare expressions are: וַיְשַׁלְּחֵם בְּיַד־פִּשְׁעָם Jb 8^{4} (God subj.); *stretch out* hand, בְּ rei (for use) Pr 31^{19}, לְ pers. (charity) v^{20}; חֶבְלֵיהֶם תְּשַׁלַּחְנָה Jb 39^{3} (of hinds, bearing); שַׁלַּח לַחְמְךָ עַל־פְּנֵי הַמָּיִם Ec 11^{1}. —רַגְלַי שִׁלֵּחוּ Jb 30^{12} is corrupt; Theod Ew Di רַגְלָם שִׁלֵּחוּ; Me Bu Be al. dittogr. from v^{11b}. **Pu.** *Pf.* 3 ms. שֻׁלַּח Ju 5^{15} Jb 18^{8}, etc.; *Impf.* 3 ms. יְשֻׁלַּח Pr 17^{11}; *Pt.* מְשֻׁלָּח Is 16^{2} +;—*be sent off* (started on journey) Gn 44^{3} (J); with commission, בְּ pers. Ob^{1} Pr 17^{11}, אֶל pers. Dn 10^{11}; *be put away, divorced,* of wife Is 50^{1} (fig.); *be impelled* (?), בְּרַגְלָיו (= *at his heels?*), c. בְּ loc. Ju 5^{15} (vb. dub.), cf. שֻׁלַּח בְּרֶשֶׁת בְּרַגְלָיו Jb 18^{8} *he is hurried into the net with his feet* (? 𝔊 Du שִׁלְּחָה רַגְלוֹ); קֵן מְשֻׁלָּח Is 16^{2} *a driven* (scattered) *nest* (|| עוֹף נוֹדֵד), cf. נָוֶה מְשׁ׳ וְנֶעֱזָב כַּמִּדְבָּר 27^{10}; נַעַר מְשׁ׳ Pr 29^{15} *a boy let loose* (unrestrained). †**Hiph.** *Pf.* 1 s. וְהִשְׁלַחְתִּי *and I* (י׳) *will send* famine, בָּאָרֶץ Am 8^{11}, cf. Ez 14^{13}, wild beasts; בְּ pers. Lv 26^{22} (H); *Pt.* מַשְׁלִיחַ, acc. of flies, בְּ pers. Ex 8^{17} (J); *Inf. cstr.* לְהַשְׁלִיחַ, acc. of foe, בְּ gent. 2 K 15^{37}.

I. שֶׁלַח **n.[m.] missile, weapon, sprout** 7973
(late);—abs. שׁ׳ Jo 2^{8} +, שָׁלַח Ne 4^{11} Jb 33^{18}, sf. שִׁלְחוֹ Ne 4^{17}; pl. שְׁלָחִים 2 Ch 23^{10}, etc.;—**1.** *missile, weapon,* Ne 4^{11} and v^{17} (where הַמַּיִם corrupt; read probably בִּימִינוֹ or בְּיָדוֹ; v. Ryle Be-Ry Berthol), 2 Ch 23^{10} (disting. from חֲנִית, מָגֵן); coll. 32^{5} and עָבַר בַּשׁ׳ Jb 33^{18} 36^{12} (*perish by* or < *rush upon* [and perish]), Jo 2^{8} (v. בְּעַד). **2.** *sprout, shoot* (cf. [שְׁלוּחָה], and √ ψ 80^{12} Je 17^{8}), שְׁלָחַיִךְ פַּרְדֵּס Ct 4^{13} (fig.; meaning? Perles$^{Anal.\ 63}$ prop. שְׁנֵי לְחָיַיִךְ *thy two cheeks*); + prob. Ez 31^{5} (rd. בִּשְׁלָחָיו Co Toy al., or בְּשִׁלְחֵי [with v^{6}] Krae).

†II. שֶׁלַח **n.pr.m.** son of Arphachshad, 7974
Σαλα: שׁ׳ Gn 10^{24b} 11$^{13.14.15}$ 1 Ch 1^{18b}; שָׁלַח Gn 10^{24a} 11^{12} 1 Ch 1$^{18a.24}$.

†III. שֶׁלַח **n.pr.** in בְּרֵכַת הַשׁ׳ Ne 3^{15} = שִׁלֹחַ below. 7975

†שִׁלְחִי **n.pr.m.** father of Jehoshaphat's 7977
mother;—1 K 22^{42} = 2 Ch 20^{31}; Σεμεει, Σαλαλα, Σαλει, etc.

†שִׁלְחִים **n.pr.loc.** in Negeb of Judah 7978
Jos 15^{32}; Σαλη, Σαλεειμ, 𝔊L Σελεειμ.

†שִׁלֹחַ **n.pr.font.** at SE. of Jerus. (connex. 7975
with above √ not certain (Ba$^{NB\ 66}$), ψ 104^{10}
has **Pi.**);—מֵי הַשׁ׳ Is 8^{6}; Σ(ε)ιλωαμ; = III. שֶׁלַח; 7975
mod. *Birket Silwân;* v. Wilson$^{Hast.\ DB\ SILOAM}$ Cond GASm RS$^{Ency.\ Bib.\ JERUSALEM,\ \S\S\ 3.11.18}$ Buhl$^{G\ 139}$; on inscription found in adjacent tunnel v. Dr$^{Sm\ xv\ ff.}$ GACooke$^{15\ ff.}$.

†שִׁלּוּחִים **n.[m.] pl. sending away, part-** 7964
ing gift;—**1.** אַחַר שִׁלּוּחֶיהָ Ex 18^{2} (J) *after she had been sent away.* **2.** שִׁלֻּחִים 1 K 9^{16} he gave (city) as *parting gift* (i.e. dowry) to his daughter; cf. fig. שִׁלּוּחִים Mi 1^{14} thou shalt give *a parting gift* (= say farewell to, lose) Morešeth of Gath.

7976 †[שְׁלוּחָה] **n.f. shoot, branch** (cf. I. שׁלח **2**);—pl. sf. שְׁלוּחֹתֶיהָ Is 16[8], of vine of Sibmah (E. of Jordan).

4916 †מִשְׁלַח **n.[m.] 1. outstretching; 2. place of letting loose**;—מ׳ only cstr.: **1.** בְּכֹל־מ׳ יַד פ׳ *in every outstretching of* one's *hand*, = every undertaking, Dt 12[7.18] 15[10] 23[21] 28[8.20]. **2.** לְמ׳ שׁוֹר וּלְמִרְמַס שֶׂה Is 7[25] (√**Pi. 3** esp. Is 32[20]).

4916 †מִשְׁלוֹחַ **n.[m.] 1. outstretching; 2. sending**;—מ׳ only cstr.: **1.** מ׳ יָדָם Is 11[14] Edom and Moab are *the outstretching of their hand* (that of which they take possession, cf. √**Qal 3**). **2.** מִשְׁלֹחַ מָנוֹת אִישׁ לְרֵעֵהוּ Est 9[19.22] *the sending of portions to each other.*

4917 †מִשְׁלַחַת **n.f. 1. discharge; 2. deputation, sending**;—**1.** abs. אֵין מ׳ בַּמִּלְ׳ Ec 8[8] *there is no discharge in war.* **2.** cstr. מ׳ מַלְאֲכֵי רָעִים ψ 78[49] *a deputation* (or sending) of angels of evil.

II. שׁלח (√of foll.; Ar. سَلَخَ *strip off hide*, سِلَاخَةٌ *piece of hide stripped off*; Aram. שְׁלַח, ܫܠܚ *take off* garment; Ar. سَلْخٌ, Aram. שִׁלְחָא, ܫܠܚܐ *hide*, perh. also Palm. שלחא (pl.? Lzb; Reckend[ZMG xlii (1888), 415] cp. I. שָׁלַח); hence שֻׁלְחָן, q.v. (also NH Ecclus), v. GFM[PAOS 1890, lxx; esp. Ju 1, 7]).

7979 שֻׁלְחָן[71] **n.m.**[Ex 25, 23] **table** (on form of word cf. GFM[l.c.]; prop. (v. supr.) *skin* or *leather mat* spread on ground, v. also, on early Sem. 'table,' Thes[1417] We[Skizzen iv. 157] RS[Sem. i. 184; 2nd ed. 201] Kennedy[Ency. Bib. iii. 2991]);—abs. שׁ׳ 1 S 20[34] +; cstr. שֻׁלְחַן 1 K 5[7] +; sf. שֻׁלְחָנִי Ju 1[7] +, etc.; pl. שֻׁלְחָנוֹת Is 28[8] +, cstr. שֻׁלְחֲנוֹת 1 Ch 28[16.16];—**1.** *table* for king's repast Ju 1[7] (c. תַּחַת), 1 S 20[29.34] 2 S 9[11] (read שׁ׳ דָּוִד 𝔊 Th We Dr and mod.), v[13] 19[29] 1 K 2[7] 5[1] 18[19] 10[5] = 2 Ch 9[4], cf. Is 21[5] (c. עָרַךְ (q.v. **1 c**) *arrange*); c. עַל 2 S 9[7.10.11] Dn 11[27]; for governor Ne 5[17] (c. עַל). **2.** for private use 1 K 13[20] (c. אֶל), Jb 36[16] ψ 23[5] (fig., c. עָרַךְ), cf. 78[19] (*id.*), 128[3], also (in bedroom) 2 K 4[10]; of revellers Is 28[8], cf. ψ 69[23] (fig.), of wisdom (fig.) Pr 9[2]. **3.** esp. Ez P for sacred uses: in tab. Ex 25[23] + 17 t. 25–40, Nu 3[31], שֻׁלְחַן הַפָּנִים Nu 4[7] (cf. 2 Ch 29[18] infr.); הַשּׁ׳ הַטָּהֹר Lv 24[26] (cf. 2 Ch 13[11] infr.); in Sol.'s temple 1 K 7[48] 2 Ch 29[18], also (10 in no.) 4[8.19] 13[11], cf. 1 Ch 28[16.16.16.16], also Ez 23[41] (c. עָרַךְ); in Ezekiel's temple Ez 40[39.39] + 6 t. Ez 40 (8 in no.), 40[42] (of stone, 4 in no.); like altar 41[22], = altar of burnt-offering 44[16]; in second temple, שֻׁלְחַן י׳ Mal 1[7], שׁ׳ אֲדֹנָי v[12]; for idolatrous meal Is 65[11]; fig. of י׳'s sacrif. feast Ez 39[20] (eschatol.).

†שָׁלַט **vb. domineer, be master of** (late) 7980
(NH *id.*; As. *šalâṭu, have power*; Ar. سَلُطَ *overcome, prevail*; سَلِيطٌ *strong, hard*, سُلْطَانٌ *dominion*, also *ruler, sultan*; Eth. **ሠለጠ:** Aram. שְׁלֵט, ܫܠܛ (esp. der. spec.), Nab. שלט, שלטון);—**Qal** *Pf.* 3 ms. שׁ׳ Ec 8[9], etc.; *Impf.* 3 ms. יִשְׁלַט Ec 2[19], etc.; *Inf. cstr.* שְׁלוֹט Est 9[1];—*domineer, lord it* over, עַל pers., Ne 5[15]; בְּ pers. Ec 8[9] (לְרַע לוֹ); בְּ rei 2[19]; *become master* of, בְּ pers. Est 9[1.1]. **Hiph. 1.** *give power of*: *Pf.* 3 ms. sf. pers. וְהִשְׁלִיטוֹ לֶאֱכֹל Ec 5[18], so *Impf.* 3 ms. sf. יַשְׁלִיטֶנּוּ 6[2] (both subj. God). **2.** = **Qal**, *get mastery of*: juss. 3 fs. אַל־תַּשְׁלֶט־בִּי כָּל־אָוֶן ψ 119[133].

†שַׁלִּיט **adj. having mastery, domineer-** 7989
ing;—**1.** *having mastery*: אֵין אָדָם שׁ׳ בָּרוּחַ Ec 8[8]; elsewhere as subst. הַשּׁ׳ *the ruler* 10[5], so (c. עַל־הָאָרֶץ) Gn 42[6] (prob. late substitution for original word of E); pl. as subst. שַׁלִּיטִים Ec 7[19] (specif. of Alex.'s successors Perles[Anal. 42]). **2.** *domineering, imperious*, fs. (Kö[ii. 1. 201]) אִשָּׁה זוֹנָה
שַׁלֶּטֶת Ez 16[30] (Jerusalem personified). 7986

†שִׁלְטוֹן **n.[m.] mastery** (Lag[BN 199]);— 7983
Ec 8[4.8] (c. בְּ).

II. שׁלט (√of foll.; Zehnpf[BAS i. 535, No. 53] cites As. *šalṭu, a shield* of leather).

†[שֶׁלֶט] **n.m.**[2 S 8, 7] **shield** (?);—pl. שְׁלָטִים 2 K 7982
11[10] +, cstr. שִׁלְטֵי 2 S 8[7] +; sf. שִׁלְטֵיהֶם Ez 27[11];—*shields* (so AV RV Thes; al. *quivers*, or [v. esp. Barnes[Expos. T. x, 43 f. (cf. 188)]] *arms, equipment*; Vrss vary; As. *šalṭu* (v. √) seems to be a specif. article), 2 S 8[7] = 1 Ch 18[7], 2 K 11[10] = 2 Ch 23[9] (where + מָגִנּוֹת, but) Ct 4[4] appos. of מָגֵן (q.v. sub גנן), hung on walls, cf. Ez 27[11]; מַלְאוּ הַשּׁ׳ Je 51[11] i.e., perh., put arms through thongs, ready to use them (but v. Barnes[l.c.], and Gie, cf. מלא **Qal 2**).

שַׁלֶּטֶת v. שַׁלִּיט supra. 7986, 7989

[שָׁלַךְ][125] **vb. Hiph.**[112] **throw, fling, cast** 7993
(Ph. שלך in cp. n.pr., meaning dub.; Ar. سَلَكَ is *travel* (or *cause to travel*) *along a road, cause to enter*);—*Pf.* 3 ms. הִשְׁלִיךְ Am 8[3] +; 2 ms. sf. consec. וְהִשְׁלַכְתּוֹ Je 51[63]; 2 fpl. consec. וְהִשְׁלַכְתֶּנָה

Am 4^{3}, etc.; *Impf.* יַשְׁלִיךְ Is 2^{20}, וַיַּשְׁלֵךְ Ju 9^{17}+, etc.; *Imv.* ms. הַשְׁלֵךְ Ex 7^{9} ψ 55^{23}, fs. הַשְׁלִיכִי Je 7^{29}, etc.; *Inf. abs.* הַשְׁלֵךְ Je 22^{19} 36^{23}; cstr. הַשְׁלִיךְ Ec $3^{5.6}$, etc.; *Pt.* מַשְׁלִיךְ Mi 2^{5} ψ 147^{17}, etc.;—**1.** usu. human subj., *throw, cast:* **a.** acc. rei, with many prep.: e.g. אֶל loc. 2 K 23^{12} Ez 5^{4} Zc $5^{8.8}$+, also (acc. rei om.) Ex 15^{25} (J), Nu 19^{6} (P)+; ב loc, Ex 32^{24} (E), Ez 7^{19}+; rarely ל loc. 2 Ch 30^{14} and (acc. om.) 24^{10}; עַל loc. 2 K 23^{6}, ה—ָ loc. Ex $4^{3.3}$, שָׁמָּה Ju 8^{25} 2 K 6^{6} (acc. om.), etc.; esp. of casting dead bodies, אֶל loc. Jos 8^{29} (J), 10^{27} (J), +3 t., ב loc. Am 8^{3} 2 K $9^{25.26}$ 13^{21}, מֵהָלְאָה לְ Je 22^{19}; acc. rei + אֶל pers. 1 K 19^{19} 2 S 20^{22} (acc. om.); acc. rei c. עַל pers. Na 3^{6} Ju 9^{53} 2 S 11^{21} (+מֵעַל), etc.; acc. rei + מִיָּד Ex 32^{19} (E), cf. Dt 9^{17} (מֵעַל); + ל of animal Ex 22^{30} (E), Is 2^{20}, etc. †**b.** c. acc. pers., אֶל of pit Gn 37^{22} (E), Je $38^{6.9}$, ב of pit Gn 37^{20} (E), c. ה loc. v^{24} (E; pit), Ex 1^{22} (J), cf. Am 4^{3} (si vera l.); תַּחַת loc. Gn 21^{15} (E); acc. 'י, fig., c. אַחֲרֵי גַוֶּךָ 1 K 14^{9} (of apostasy), Ez 23^{35}, so 'י's law Ne 9^{26}, words (אַחֲרֵי pers. reflex.) ψ 50^{17}. †**c.** *throw away,* acc. rei Ju 15^{17} (מִיָּדוֹ), 2 K 7^{15} Ez $20^{7.8}$ ψ 2^{3} (מִן reflex.), Ec 3^{5} (opp.=כָּנַס); acc. om. Je 7^{29} Jo 1^{7} (of locusts); abs. Ec 3^{6} (opp. שָׁמַר); acc. of transgr. Ez 18^{31} (fig.; מֵעַל reflex.). †**d.** *cast off, shed,* blossom (like flower) Jb 15^{33}. **e.** *cast down* (late), subj. goat, acc. ram, Dn 8^{7} (אַרְצָה) little horn, acc. אֱמֶת v^{12} (*id.*); acc. pers. (lit.) 2 Ch 25^{12} (מִן loc.), Jb 18^{7} *his* (own) *counsel felleth him;* so prob. Je 9^{18} *they have overthrown* our dwellings (Du reads Hoph.). **f.** fig., ψ 55^{23} *cast* עַל־י' *thy lot.* **2.** 'י subj.: **a.** *cast,* acc. rei, + עַל pers. Jos 10^{11} (E), Jb 27^{22} (acc. rei om.); sandal *upon* Edom ψ 60^{10}=108^{10} (sign of possession); ice (no prep.) 147^{17}. **b.** acc. pers. + ב loc. 2 K 2^{16} (subj. רוּחַ י'), Ne 9^{11} Jon 2^{4} (+ acc. loc.); + אַרְצָה Ez 28^{17} (fig.); אֶל loc. (of exile) Dt 29^{27}; esp. of 'י's rejecting men, acc. pers. + מֵעַל פָּנָיו 2 K 13^{23} 24^{20}, cf. 2 K 17^{20} Je $7^{15.15}$ 52^{3}, also ψ 51^{13} and (without פָּנָיו) 71^{9}; casting sins (acc.) אַחֲרֵי גֵוְךָ Is 38^{17}, ב loc. Mi 7^{19}. **c.** *cast down,* honour of Israel + acc. loc., מִן loc., La 2^{1}; acc. pers. ψ 102^{11} (opp. נָשָׂא). **3.** phrases: הִשׁ' גּוֹרָל †Jos $18^{8.10}$ (R^{D}) *cast lots* ל *in behalf of;* מַשׁ' חֶבֶל בְּגוֹרָל Mi 2^{5} (v. גּוֹרָל **3,** חֶבֶל 1. **2**); וַיַּשְׁלֵךְ נַפְשׁוֹ מִנֶּגֶד Ju 9^{17}, v. נֶגֶד **2 c**; בַּיְאוֹר חַכָּה Is 19^{8} i.e. fishermen; מִשִּׁנָּיו אַשׁ' טָרֶף Jb 29^{17} *out of his teeth I cast the prey.* †**Hoph.** *Pf.* 3 ms. הָשְׁלַךְ Dn 8^{11}; 2 ms. הָשְׁלַכְתָּ Is 14^{19}, etc.; *Impf.* 2 fs. וַתֻּשְׁלְכִי Ez 16^{5}; 3 mpl. יֻשְׁלָכוּ Is 34^{3}; *Pt.* מֻשְׁלָךְ 2 S 20^{21}, etc.;—**1.** *be thrown, cast,* acc. of head, אֶל pers. + בְּעַד of wall 2 S 20^{21}; carcass, ב loc. 1 K $13^{24.25.28}$ Je 14^{16}; לַחֶרֶב 36^{30}. **2.** *be cast forth, out,* abs. of dead Is 34^{3}; מִן of grave 14^{19}; אֶל־פְּנֵי הַשָּׂדֶה Ez 16^{5} (Jerus. personified as infant); עַל־הָאָרֶץ Je 22^{28} (of exile). **3.** *be cast down,* לָאָרֶץ Ez 19^{12} (Isr., fig. of vine); abs. of sanctuary Dn 8^{11}. **4.** metaph., *be cast,* עַל of 'י ψ 22^{11} (i.e. on his protection).

†שָׁלָךְ **n.** [**m.**] bird of prey, prob. **cormorant** 7994
(as *hurling* itself from above;—cf. Thes [1419] Di [Lv] Tristr [NHB 252] McLean-Shipley [Ency. Bib. CORMORANT]);—Dt 14^{17} Lv 11^{17} (P).

†I. שַׁלֶּכֶת **n.f.** felling of tree;—Is 6^{13}. 7995

†II. שַׁלֶּכֶת **n.pr.** of a temple-gate, W. side 7996
(? gate of *casting forth;* yet cf. Kit);—1 Ch 26^{16}.

†I. [שָׁלַל] **vb. draw out** (Ar. سَلَّ *draw,* 7997
esp. sword from scabbard, سَلِيلٌ *drawn sword, new-born child* (cf. Frä [75], but also Schulth [Hom. Wurz. 80 f.]); Talm. שָׁלִיל, ת שְׁלִילָא *embryo* or *abortion*);—*Impf.* 2 mpl. + *Inf. abs.* שֹׁל־תָּשֹׁלּוּ לָהּ מִן וגו' Ru 2^{16} *ye shall by all means draw out for her* from the sheaves.

†שׁוֹלָל **adj. indecl.** (Ges [§ 118 o]) **barefoot** 7758
(appar. *stripped* as to walking; alw. c. הלך);—אֵילְכָה שׁוֹלָל וְעָרוֹם Mi 1^{8} Qr *I will go barefoot and naked* (Kt שׁילל); מוֹלִיךְ יוֹעֲצִים שׁ' Jb 12^{17}, cf. v^{19}.

†II. שָׁלַל **vb. spoil, plunder** (usu. identif. 7997
with I. שׁ'; NH *id.* (Jastr, cf. Dalm); As. *šalâlu, id.;* Hom [Chr 33] cp. Sab. הלל *plunder,* connecting this with Ar. ثَلَّةٌ *a flock of sheep* (or *goats*); then ת שְׁלָלָא *booty,* and (rare) Syr. ܫܠܠܐ are loan-words);—**Qal** *Pf.* 3 ms. consec. וְשׁ' Ez 26^{12}; 2 ms. שַׁלּוֹתָ Hb 2^{8}, etc.; *Impf.* 3 mpl. sf. יְשָׁלּוּךָ v^{8}; cstr. לִשְׁלֹל Is 10^{6}+; *Pt.* pl. שֹׁלְלִים Zc 2^{12}, etc.;—*spoil, plunder* (usu. ‖ בָּזַז), c. acc. cogn. שָׁלָל Is 10^{6} Ez 29^{19} $38^{12.13.13}$, acc. חַיִל *wealth* 26^{12}; acc. pers., שֹׁלְלִים Je 50^{10} Hb 2^{8} Ez 39^{10}, גּוֹיִם רַבִּים Hb 2^{8}, cf. Zc 2^{12}. **Hithpō'.** *Pf.* 3 pl. אֶשְׁתּוֹלְלוּ אַבִּירֵי לֵב (א in אֶשְׁתּ' is Aram., or scribal error: Ges [§ 54 a n., cf. 53 k]) ψ 76^{6} *the stout of heart are spoiled;* *Pt.* מִשְׁתּוֹלֵל Is 59^{15} he that departs from evil *is one despoiled.*

שָׁלָל [75] **n. m.** [1 S 30, 16] **prey, spoil, plunder,** 7998
booty;—abs. שׁ' Gn 49^{27}+; cstr. שְׁלַל Ju 5^{30}+,

sf. שְׁלָלֵךְ Zc 14^{1}, שְׁלַלְכֶם Is 33^{4}, etc.;—†**1.** *prey*, of Benj. as wolf Gn 49^{27} (poem in J; c. חֵלֶק). **2.** *booty, spoil* of war, of all kinds (oft. ‖ בַּז): incl. garments, gold and silver Jos 7^{21} (J), ornaments Ju 8$^{24.25}$, fabrics and women 5^{30a,b}, flocks and herds 1 S 30^{20} Je 49^{32} 2 Ch 15^{11}, + persons Dt 20$^{14.14}$, garments, food and drink 2 Ch 28^{15}, etc. (58 t.; among these) שְׁלַל הֶעָרִים Dt 2^{25} 2 S 12^{30} 1 Ch 20^{2} and (+ cattle in addition) Dt 3^{7}, Jos 8^{27} 11^{14} (both R^{D}), cf. (also of city) Is 8^{4} Dt 13$^{17.17}$ Zc 14^{1} and (+ cattle) Jos 8^{2} (R^{D}), but incl. pers. and cattle Dt 20^{14}, cf. v^{14}; fig. of entire nation Je 50^{10} Ez 7^{21} Zc 2^{13}; ׳שׁ in symbol. n.pr. מַהֵר שָׁלָל וגו׳ Is 8$^{1.3}$, v. supr. p. 555^{a}; ׳שׁ in metaph. of future majesty of עֶבֶד י׳ Is 53^{12}; וְהָיְתָה־לּוֹ נַפְשׁוֹ לְשׁ׳ i.e. life shall be spared, Je 21^{9} 38^{2} 39^{18}, cf. 45^{5}. †**3.** private *plunder* Is 10^{2} (אַלְמָנוֹת שְׁלָלָם), Pr 1^{13} and (perh. in current saying) 16^{19}. †**4.** = *gain* Pr 31^{11}.—לְצַוְּארֵי שׁ׳ Ju 5^{30c} is clearly wrong; meaning dub. (v. esp. GFM); plausible conj. are לְצַוָּארַי שׁ׳ *for my neck as spoil*, Reuss Br al., and לְצַוְּארֵי שֵׁגָל *for the neck of the queen* Ew Be Kit al. (but שֵׁגָל elsewh. late); Now del. שָׁלָל and reads לְצַוָּארָיו.

7999 [שָׁלֵם]$_{103}$ **vb. be complete, sound** (NH *id.* (Jastr), Ph. שלם Pi. *complete, requite*, esp. in n.pr., Lzb^{376} GACooke$^{99, also 81, 111, etc.}$; Ar. سَلِمَ *be safe, secure, free from fault*, II. *make over, resign to*, IV. *resign* or *submit oneself*, esp. to God, whence ptcp. *Muslim*, and inf. *Islām*, prop. *submission* to God; As. *šalâmu, be complete, unharmed, be paid;* Aram. שְׁלֵים, ܫܠܡ *be complete, safe*, 𝔗 *peaceful;* OAram. שלם *reward, repay* (Pa; in n.pr.); cf. Sab. סלם *peace* Hom$^{Chr 124}$, Ar. سِلْمٌ, also سَلَامٌ *safety, security;* As. *šulmu, welfare;* Eth. ሰላም: Di^{322} *security, peace;* Aram. שְׁלָמָא, ܫܠܡܐ *security, welfare*, OAram. שלם Lzb^{376}, esp. = *submission*, in n.pr. RS$^{Sem. 79 f.}$; Bondi^{70} (after Brugsch), cp. *šarmā, greet, do homage*, as loan-word in Egypt.);—**Qal** *Pf.* 3 pl. שָׁלְמוּ Is 60^{20}; *Impf.* 3 ms. וַיִּשְׁלָם Jb 9^{4}; f. תִּשְׁלַם 1 K 7^{51} + 2 t.;—**1.** *be complete, finished, ended:* temple 1 K 7^{51} = 2 Ch 5^{1}; walls of city Ne 6^{15}; of time Is 60^{20}. **2.** *be sound, uninjured*, Jb 9^{4}. **Pi.**$_{89}$ *Pf.* 3 ms. שִׁלַּם Lv 5^{24}+, 1 s. וְשִׁלַּמְתִּי Je 16^{18}+, etc.; *Impf.* 3 ms. יְשַׁלֵּם Ex 21^{34}+; sf. יְשַׁלְּמֶנָּה Lv 24^{18}+, etc.; *Imv.* ms. שַׁלֵּם Ec 5^{3} ψ 50^{14}, etc.; *Inf. abs.* שַׁלֵּם Ex 21^{36}+; cstr. *id.* Pr 22^{27}, etc.; *Pt.* מְשַׁלֵּם Dt 7^{10}+, etc.;—†**1.** *complete, finish*, temple 1 K 9^{25}. †**2.** *make safe*, c. acc. Jb 8^{6}. **3.** *make whole* or *good, restore* thing lost Jo 2^{25}, or stolen Ex 21^{37} (E); pay a debt 2 K 4^{7} ψ 37^{21} Pr 22^{27} Jb 41^{3}; *make compensation*, for injury Lv 24$^{18.21}$ (P); for trespass in sacred things 5^{16} (P). **4.** *make good*, i.e. *pay*, vows, c. acc. נֶדֶר Dt 23^{22} 2 S 15^{7} + 9 t., + (c. לְ to God) ψ 50^{14} 66^{13} 116$^{14.18}$; obj. om. 76^{12}; abs. Is 19^{21}; c. acc. תודות c. לְ to God ψ 56^{13}; פרים שפתינו Ho 14^{3} (v. p. 830^{b}). **5.** *requite, recompense, reward*, good 1 S 24^{20} Ru 2^{12}; evil Is 65^{6} Je 51^{56}; c. לְ pers. Dt 7^{10} + 4 t., + (c. acc. rei) Je 51^{24}; אל pers. Jb 21^{19}; acc. rei Pr 20^{22} Je 16^{18}; שִׁלַּם גְּמוּל לְ Is 59$^{18.18}$ (but v. I. שִׁלֻּם), 66^{6} + (v. גְּמוּל); + שׁ׳ פֹּעַל לְ Jb 34^{11}; שׁ׳ גְּמוּל עַל Jo 4^{4}; עַל חֵיק Is 65^{6}; אֶל־חֵיק Je 32^{18}; †c. לְ pers. and כְּ of deeds, ׳שׁ *reward according to one's works* 2 S 3^{39} + 3 t.; acc. pers. ψ 31^{24}; acc. rei †שׁ׳ רעה תחת טובה Gn 44^{4} (J) ψ 35^{12} 38^{21} (read מְשַׁלְּמֵנִי). **Pu.** *Impf.* 3 ms. יְשֻׁלַּם ψ 65^{2} Je 18^{20}; יְשֻׁלָּם Pr 11^{31} 13^{13};—**1.** *be performed*, of vow ψ 65^{2}. **2.** *be repaid, requited*, Je 18^{20} Pr 11^{31} 13^{13}. **Hiph. 1.** *complete, perform: Impf.* 3 ms. יַשְׁלִים Jb 23^{14} Is 44^{26}, יַשְׁלִם v^{28}. **2.** *make an end of*, 2 ms. sf. תַּשְׁלִימֵנִי Is 38$^{12.13}$ (𝔊 Du Marti *deliver up* to pains, as in Aram.).

שָׁלוֹם$_{237}$ **n.m.**$^{Is. 54, 13}$ **completeness, soundness, welfare, peace** (Lag$^{BN 174}$);—שׁ׳ Gn 29^{6}+; 7965
שָׁלֹם (rare) Ez 13^{16}+; cstr. שְׁלוֹם Gn 37^{14}+; sf. שְׁלוֹמִי ψ 41^{10}+, etc.; pl. (all dub.) שְׁלוֹמִים Je 13^{19} ψ 69^{23}; sf. שְׁלֹמָיו 55^{21};—†**1.** *completeness* in no., הָגְלָת שְׁלוֹמִים Je 13^{19} Judah is *wholly carried captive* (but read גָּלוּת שְׁלֵמָה, cf. Am 1^{6}; so 𝔊 We^{Am} SS Buhl). †**2.** *safety, soundness*, in body, אֵין שָׁלוֹם בַּעֲצָמַי ψ 38^{4}; לְשָׁלוֹם Is 38^{17}; שָׁלוֹם אָהֳלֶךָ (Ges$^{§ 141 c}$) Jb 5^{24} *is safe, secure.* **3.** *welfare, health, prosperity:* †שָׁאַל לְפ׳ לשׁ׳ *ask* one *about welfare* Gn 43^{27} (J), Ex 18^{7} (E), Ju 18^{15} + 7 t., cf. 2 S 11$^{7.7.7}$; pregn. ירד לשלום 2 K 10^{13} *descend* (to ask) *about welfare* of, cf. 1 S 17^{18} Je 38^{4}; הלך לשׁ׳ Ex 4^{18} (E) + 5 t.; עלה לשׁ׳ Gn 44^{17} (J), 1 S 25^{35}; דבר לשׁ׳ Gn 37^{4} (JE); שָׁלוֹם לְ׳ *be well with* Gn 29^{6} 43$^{23.28}$ (J), Ju 6^{23} 19^{20} 1 S 20$^{7.21}$ + 10 t., 2 K 4$^{26.26.26}$; שָׁלוֹם בְּ ψ 122$^{7.8}$ *may it be well in;* abs. as obj. of אָמַר *well, be well*, ׳שׁ Gn 29^{6} (J), 2 S 18^{28} 2 K 9$^{11.17.18.19.22}$ Je 6$^{14.14}$ + 10 t.; הֲשָׁלוֹם אֲבִיכֶם (Ges$^{§ 141 c}$) Gn 43^{27} (J); †שׁ׳ בּ(וֹ)אֶךָ 1 S 16^{4} (v. Dr), 1 K 2^{13}; אֵין שׁ׳ Je 6^{14} + 3 t.; †אין שׁ׳ לרשעים Is 48^{22} 57^{21}; but ראה

122^{6}; שׁאל שׁ׳ פ׳ 72^{7}; רֹב שׁ׳† 37^{11} ψ 73^{3}; שׁ׳ רשׁעים (טוב ‖) דרשׁ שׁ׳ Dt 23^{7} Ezr 9^{12}; שׁ׳ יוֹסִיפוּ לָךְ Pr 3^{2}; בַּשׁ׳ Jb 15^{21} *in time of prosperity*. **4.** *peace, quiet, tranquillity, contentment*, Is 32^{17} (‖ הַשְׁקֵט) בְּשׁ׳ (וָבֶטַח); שָׁכַב בשׁ׳ ψ 4^{9} (to sleep); depart life בְּשׁ׳ *in tranquillity* Gn 15^{15} (R^{JE}), 1 K 2^{6} + 3 t., יָבוֹא Is 57^{2}; בא בשׁ׳ אַחֲרִית לְאִישׁ שׁ׳ ψ 37^{37} Ex 18^{23} (E) *come in contentment*; נְוֵה שׁ׳ ארץ שׁ׳ Je 12^{5}; (‖ מבטחים) Is 32^{18}, cf. Je 25^{37}; שׁ׳ מִפַּחַד Jb 21^{9}; ולשׁלומים לְמוֹקֵשׁ ψ 69^{23} *security*, (let it) *become a trap* (but 𝔊 Aq Sym Theod Jer וּלְשִׁלּוּמִים וּלְמ׳, Du (cf. 𝔗) וּשְׁלָמִים *peace-offerings*, and שֻׁלְחָן v^{a}). †**5.** *peace, friendship*: **a.** human relations: אֱנוֹשׁ שְׁלֹמִי Je 20^{10} *man of my friendship*, cf. 38^{22} Ob^{7} ψ 41^{10}; עֲצַת שׁ׳ בין Zc 6^{13}; יֹעֲצֵי שׁ׳ Pr 12^{20}; (עִם, אֶת) דבר שׁ׳ ψ 28^{3} 35^{20} Je 9^{7}; שׁלח בקשׁ שׁ׳ ψ 34^{15}; ידע שׁ׳ Is 59^{8}; דֶּרֶךְ שׁ׳ v^{8}; בשׁ׳ Gn 26^{29} (J); הלך בשׁ׳ v^{31} (J), 1 S 29^{7} + 4 t.; שׁוב בשׁ׳ 2 S 15^{27}; ‖ צדקה in Mess. reign ψ 72^{3}. **b.** *peace* with God, esp. in covt. relation: Is 54^{10} ברית *covt. of my peace*, cf. Nu 25^{12} (P), Ez 34^{25} 37^{26}, also Mal 2^{5}; שׁ׳ י׳ as name of altar
3073 Ju 6^{24}; י׳ subj. שׂם שׁ׳ לְ Nu 6^{26} (P); בֵּרַךְ בשׁ׳ ψ 29^{11}; חפץ שׁ׳ 35^{27}; עשׂה שׁ׳ לְ Je 33^{9}; אָסַף שׁ׳ Je 16^{5} (‖ חסד); דבר שׁ׳ אֶל ψ 85^{9}; נתן שׁ׳ Hg 2^{9}; מחשׁבות שׁ׳ Je 29^{11}; man subj. עשׂה שׁ׳ לְ Is 27$^{5.5}$; הלך בשׁ׳ Mal 2^{6}. In this sense ‖ צֶדֶק ψ 85^{11}, ‖ צְדָקָה Is 54^{13} 60^{17}, ‖ שִׂמְחָה 55^{12}, is *like a river* 48^{18} 66^{12}; שׁ׳ עַל־יִשְׂרָאֵל ψ 125^{5} 128^{6}, רָב לְאֹהֲבֵי תוֹרָתֶךָ 119^{165}; מוּסַר שׁ׳ Is 53^{5} *chastisement for our peace* (but SS Buhl שְׁלֵמֵנוּ). **6.** *peace* from war: עשׂה שׁ׳ (ל) *make peace* (with) Jos 9^{15} Jb 25^{2}; נתן שׁ׳ בארץ Lv 26^{6} (H); †שׁ׳ בין וּבין Ju 4^{17} 1 S 7^{14} 1 K 5^{26}; †קרא (ל)שׁ׳ Dt 20^{10} Ju 21^{13} Mi 3^{5}; †שׁוב בשׁ׳ Jos 10^{21} (E), Ju 8^{9} 11^{31}; בא בשׁ׳ 2 S 19$^{25.31}$ + 7 t.; †היה שׁ׳ לְ 1 K 5^{4} + 3 t., cf. 2 S 17^{3} (v. Dr); בקשׁ שׁ׳ Ez 7^{25}; מלאכי שׁ׳ Is 33^{7}; נתן שׁ׳ וָשֶׁקֶט 1 Ch 22^{9}; מוֹצֵאת שׁ׳ Ct 8^{10}; †(ו)אמת שׁ׳ Is 39^{8} = 2 K 20^{19} + 3 t., cf. Zc 8^{19}; עֵת שׁ׳ Ec 3^{8}; בְּשׁ׳ 1 K 2^{5} *in time of peace*; שַׂר שׁ׳ Is 9^{5} (Mess. title), cf. זֶה שׁ׳ Mi 5^{4}. **7.** as adj. שְׁלֹמָיו ψ 55^{21} *those at peace with him* (rd. שְׁלֵמָיו Bae Buhl Du, or שְׁלֻמָיו SS; 𝔊 appar. שִׁלּוּמָיו).

8002 **שֶׁ֫לֶם** $_{87}$ **n. [m.] sacrifice for alliance or friendship, 'peace-offering'** (expl. disputed: orig. sacrif. for *alliance* Di; al. *peace-offering* (mark of peace with God), 𝔊$^{Sm. K Pr}$ εἰρηνική, De Sta$^{G i. 496}$ We$^{Held. 71}$ (fellowship between God and worshippers); *welfare-offering*, 𝔊 elsewhere σωτήριον, Ke; *thank-offering* (as due rendered for benefit, or in paying vow, cf. ✓**Pi. 4,** and Pr 7^{14}) Ges Ew Kn; sacred meal its special feature: v. RS$^{Sem. i. 219; 2nd ed. 237}$; Now$^{Arch. ii. 211 f.}$ GFM$^{Ency. Bib. Sacrifice, § 11}$; As. *šulmu* = שֶׁלֶם is cited by JJerem$^{Ency. Bib. Ritual, § 11}$);—cstr. שׁ׳ Am 5^{22}; elsewh. pl. שְׁלָמִים Ex 24^{5} + 69 t.; cstr. שַׁלְמֵי Lv 10^{14}; sf. שְׁלָמֶ֫יךָ Ex 20^{24}, etc.; pl. is abstr. intens. Lv 7^{13} Nu 6^{17} (P) +; pl. of no. Ex 24^{5} (JE), 1 S 11^{15} +; usu. hard to decide; שׁ׳ (in app.) defines זְבָחִים Ex 24^{5} (JE), and so זבח of covt. of Horeb is שׁ׳, as also sacrifice for Saul 1 S 11^{15}; foll. phr. shew שׁ׳ essentially = זבחים in like phr. (v. זבח); שׁ׳ coming to mean ז׳ in all ritual; over against עוֹלוֹת Ex 20^{24} 32^{6} (JE), Lv 6^{5} (P), Dt 27^{7} Jos 8^{31} (D), Ju 20^{26} 21^{4} 1 S 13^{9} 2 S 6$^{17.18}$ 24^{25} 1 K 3^{15} 9^{25} 1 Ch 16$^{1.2}$ 21^{26} 2 Ch 31^{2} Ez 43^{27} 45^{17} 46$^{2.12}$; so in longer lists Lv 9$^{4.22}$ Nu 6^{14} 29^{39} (P), 1 K 8$^{64.64}$ 16^{13} 2 Ch 7^{7} 29^{35} Ez 45$^{15.17}$ 46^{12}; and when שׁ׳ alone Lv 7$^{14.33}$; in P שׁ׳ defines ז׳ in cstr. sg. or pl.: Ex 29^{28} Lv 3^{1} + 34 t. P, Lv 17^{5} 19^{5} 22^{21} 23^{19} (H), so 1 S 10^{8} 1 K 8^{63} 2 Ch 30^{22} 33^{16} Pr 7^{14}; ז׳ שׁ׳ of H and P incl. תודה, נדר, נדבה Lv 7$^{12.16}$, and so זבח תודה שׁ׳ v$^{13.15}$; שׁ׳ disting. from (larger) ז׳ in lists עולות, ז׳, שׁ׳ Jos 22^{27} (P); עלה, ז׳, נדר Nu 15^{8} (P); שׁ׳ disting. from נְדָבָה Ez 46^{12} (where may = either of other two); from נדבות, נדרים Nu 29^{39} (P) (and must then ref. to תודות); from נדר Nu 15^{8} (P); appar. then not disting. from תּוֹדָה, תּוֹדוֹת 2 Ch 33^{16} being probably specification.

†**[שָׁלַם]** **vb. denom. be in covenant of** 7999
peace;—**Qal** *Imv.* שְׁלָם Jb 22^{21} *be at peace* (in covt.); *Pt.* sf. שׁוֹלְמִי ψ 7^{5} i.e. my ally, friend (cf. 41^{10}); *Pt. pass.* cstr. שְׁלֻמֵי 2 S 20^{19}, read שְׁמוּ 𝔊 Ew$^{G iii. 264}$ Dr (cf. We) HPS and mod. **Pu.** *Pt.* מְשֻׁלָּם Is 42^{19} *one in covt. of peace* (with י׳; but 𝔊 מֹשְׁלָם *their ruler*, so Che^{Hpt}; Ges Hi Ew al. *one resigned* (to God), read then מָשְׁלָם, cf. ✓, Ar. iv.; Kroch Grä Marti מְשֻׁלָּחִי). **Hiph.** *Pf.* 3 fs. הִשְׁלִ֫ימָה Jos 10^{4} 11^{19}; 3 mpl. הִשְׁלִ֫ימוּ 10^{1}; *Impf.* יַשְׁלִים Is 44^{26} +, יַשְׁלִם Pr 16^{7}; וַיַּשְׁלֵם 1 K 22^{45}, etc.;—**1.** *make peace* with, אֶת, Jos 10$^{1.4}$ 2 S 10^{19} = 1 Ch 19^{19} (עִם); עִם Dt 20^{12} 1 K 22^{45}; c. אֶל pregn. Jos 11^{19} *submitting unto*. **2.** *cause to be at peace*, אֶת, Pr 16^{7}. **Hoph.** *Pf.* 3 fs. הָשְׁלְמָה Jb 5^{23} *live in peace* with, לְ (‖ ברית).

†I. **שָׁלֵם** **adj. complete, safe, at peace**;— 8003
שׁ׳ Gn 15^{16} +; pl. שְׁלֵמִים Gn 34^{21} Na 1^{12}; f. שְׁלֵמָה Dt 25^{15} +; pl. שְׁלֵמוֹת 27^{6} Jos 8^{31};—**1.** *complete*:

a. *full, perfect:* אֶבֶן שְׁלֵמָה *full weight* Dt 25^{15},
אֵיפָה שׁ׳ v^{15} Pr 11^{1}; of עָוֹן Gn 15^{16} (JE); number of
captives Am 1$^{6.9}$; of army Na 1^{12} (text corrupt;
𝔊 מֹשֵׁל מַיִם, but ?; v. Comm.); of reward Ru 2^{12};
of stones, *whole* (in natural condition, *unhewn*)
Dt 27^{6} Jos 8^{31} (cf. law Ex 20^{25}). **b.** *finished:*
stones for temple 1 K 6^{7}; temple 2 Ch 8^{16}. **2.**
safe, unharmed, of pers. Gn 33^{18} (P; Sam. שלום,
cf. בשלום 28^{21}; not n.pr.loc. as Vrss). **3.** *in*
covt. of peace, friendship, c. אֵת Gn 34^{21} (P);
לֵבָב שָׁלֵם עִם י׳ *a mind at peace with* י׳, keeping
covt. relation, hence *complete, perfect,* 1 K 8^{61} 11^{4}
15$^{3.14}$; c. אֶל 2 Ch 16^{9}, אֶל om. 2 K 20^{3} = Is 38^{3} (לֵב),
1 Ch 12^{38} 2 Ch 15^{17} 19^{9} 25^{2}; לֵב 1 Ch 28^{9} 29^{9}.

8004 †II. שָׁלֵם **n.pr.loc.** abbrev. fr. יְרוּשָׁלַםִ (q.v.),
and perh. (Gunk Dr) intended as archaism Gn
14^{18}, cf. (poet.) ψ 76^{3} (‖ צִיּוֹן); v. Jos$^{\text{Ant. i. 10, 2}}$; 𝔊
Σαλημ and (ψ) εἰρήνη.

8005 †I. שִׁלֵּם **n.[m.]** **recompense** (abstr. Ba
$^{\text{NB 73}}$);—Dt 32^{35} (read with 𝔖𝔊 לְיוֹם שׁ׳ ‖ נָקָם);
so read also (for יְשַׁלֵּם) Is 59$^{18.18}$ Du (otherwise
Che^{Hpt} Di-Kit Marti).

8006 †II. שִׁלֵּם **n.pr.m.** in Naphtali Gn 46^{24} Nu
26^{49}; Συλλημ, Σελλη(μ).

8016 †שִׁלֵּמִי **adj. gent.** as n. coll. הַשּׁ׳ Nu 26^{49}.

8021 †[שַׁלְמֹן] **n.[m.]** **reward, bribe**;—pl.
שַׁלְמֹנִים Is 1^{23} (‖ שֹׁחַד).

7966 †שִׁלּוּם Mi 7^{3}, שִׁלֻּם Ho 9^{7}, **n.[m.]** **requital**;—
pl. שִׁלֻּמִים Is 34^{8};—**1.** *requital, retribution,*
יְמֵי הַשּׁ׳ Ho 9^{7} (‖ פְּקֻדָּה); שְׁנַת שׁ׳ Is 34^{8} (‖ נָקָם).
2. *reward, bribe* Mi 7^{3} שֹׁפֵט בַּשּׁ׳.

8011 †[שִׁלֻּמָה] **n.f.** **requital, retribution**;—
cstr. שִׁלֻּמַת ψ 91^{8}.

7967 †שַׁלּוּם (less oft. שַׁלֻּם) **n.pr.m.** Σελ(λ)ουμ,
Σαλ(λ)ουμ, Σελλημ, etc.;—**1.** king of N. Israel
2 K 15$^{10.13.14.15}$. **2.** son of Josiah, and king
of Judah Je 22^{11} 1 Ch 3^{15} = יְהוֹאָחָז **1**, v. p. 219.
3. husband of Huldah 2 K 22^{14} = 2 Ch 34^{22}, B
𝔊L Σελλημ, A -λουμ. **4.** uncle of Jeremiah
Je 32^{7}. **5.** in Simeon 1 Ch 4^{25}. **6.** in
Jerahmeel 2$^{40.41}$. **7.** in Ephr. 2 Ch 28^{12}. **8.**
in Napht. 1 Ch 7^{13}. **9.** father of a threshold-
keeper Je 35^{4}. **10.** wall-builder Ne 3^{12}. **11.**
priests 1 Ch 5$^{38.39}$ Ezr 7^{2} (ancestor of Ezra, perh.
4918 = מְשֻׁלָּם **7 a**). **12.** Levites: **a.** 1 Ch 9$^{17.17}$,
8018 perh. = v$^{19.31}$, and Ezr 2^{42} ‖ Ne 7^{45} (= שֶׁלֶמְיָה **2**,
4920 מְשֻׁלָּם **8 c**, (מְשֶׁלֶמְיָה(וּ)). **b.** Ezr 10^{24}. **13.** v^{42}.
below

†שַׁלּוּן **n.pr.m.** wall-builder Ne 3^{15} = שַׁלּוּם 7967-68
acc. to Thes. above

†מְשֻׁלָּם **n.pr.m.** Μεσουλαμ, Μοσολλαμ, etc.: 4918
1. grandfather of Shaphan 2 K 22^{3}. **2.** son
of Zerub. 1 Ch 3^{19}. **3.** in Benj.: **a.** 8^{17}, perh.
= **b.** 9^{7}. **c.** v^{8}. **d.** Ne 11^{7}. **4.** in Gad 1 Ch
5^{13}. **5.** wall-builders: **a.** Ne 3$^{4.30}$. **b.** 3^{6}.
6. a chief 10^{21}. **7.** priests (distinctions in
part obscure): **a.** 1 Ch 9^{11} Ne 11^{11} 12^{13} (perh. =
שַׁלּוּם **11**). **b.** 1 Ch 9^{12}. **c.** Ne 10^{8}. **d.** Ne 12^{6}. 7967
e. v^{33}. **8.** Levites: **a.** 2 Ch 34^{12}. **b.** Ezr 8^{16}
10^{15} Ne 8^{4}. **c.** 12^{25} (= שַׁלּוּם **12 a**). **9.** Ezr 10^{29}. 7967
above

†מְשִׁלֵּמוֹת **n.pr.m.** Μοσολαμωθ, etc.: **1.** in 4919
Ephr. 2 Ch 28^{12}. **2.** priest Ne 11^{13} = מְשִׁלֵּמִית 4921
1 Ch 9^{12} (Μασελμωθ, etc.).

†מְשֶׁלֶמְיָה(וּ) **n.pr.m.** Μεσολλαμια, etc.: 4920
Levite -יָה 1 Ch 9^{21}, -יָהוּ (𝔊L Σελεμιας) 26$^{1.2.9}$
(= שֶׁלֶמְיָהוּ **2**, שַׁלּוּם **12 a**). above, p. 1025 7967,
8018

מְשִׁלֵּמִית v. מְשִׁלֵּמוֹת. above 4919,
4921

†מְשֻׁלֶּמֶת **n.pr.f.** mother of king Amon 4922
2 K 21^{9}, Μεσολλαμ, A Μασσαλαμειθ.

שְׁלֹמֹה 293 **n.pr.m.** **Solomon** (Σαλωμων, rarely 8010
Σαλομων, 𝔊L mostly Σολομων; cf. Lag$^{\text{BN 53, 96}}$);—
king of Israel, son of David and Bathsheba 2 S
12^{24} 1 K 1^{11}+ [name 2 t. S; 162 t. K; 109 t.
Ch; 7 t. Ezr Ne]; born in Jerus. 2 S 5^{14} 1 Ch
3^{5} 14^{4}; designated by D. as successor, anointed
and proclaimed before D.'s death 1 K 1$^{30.33.34.39}$+;
king after D.'s death 1 K 2$^{12.17}$ 1 Ch 29^{28} 2 Ch 1^{1}+
[phr. הַמֶּלֶךְ שׁ׳ 1 K 1^{34}+ 36 t. K, 11 t. Ch, Je 52^{20}
Ct 3$^{9.11}$; הַמּ׳ שׁ׳ 1 K 2^{17} 12^{2} 1 Ch 29^{24} 2 Ch 10^{2};
שׁ׳ מֶלֶךְ יְהוּדָה 1 K 12^{23} 2 Ch 11^{3}, מ׳ יִשׂ׳ 2 K 23^{13}
24^{13} 2 Ch 30^{26} 35^{3} Ne 13^{26}]; builder of temple
1 K 5^{22} 6$^{1.2}$ 1 Ch 5^{26}+ oft.; wise 1 K 3^{10} 5$^{9.10.14}$
10$^{1.2.3.4}$ 2 Ch 1$^{7.11}$+; author of proverbs (and
songs) acc. to Proverbs מִשְׁלֵי שׁ׳ 1^{1} 10^{1} 25^{1} (cf.
1 K 5$^{12.13}$), v. also לִשׁ׳ ψ 72^{1} 127^{1} (titles), Ct 1^{1}
(title); of written provision for priests, etc.
2 Ch 35^{4}, cf. 8^{14} Ne 12^{45}; elsewh. (outside of K
Ch) name occurs †Je 52^{20} Ct 1^{5} (Wkl$^{\text{Altor. Forsch. ii. 196}}$
prop. *Šalmaites*, Nab. שלמו Lzb^{376}, cf. Levy
$^{\text{TW ii. 489}}$ Jastr^{1587}), 3$^{7.9.11}$ 8$^{11.12}$, and in phr. בְּנֵי עַבְדֵי
שׁ׳ Ezr 2$^{55.58}$ = Ne 7$^{57.60}$, Ne 11^{3}.

†I. שְׁלֹמוֹת, שְׁלֹמִית (שְׁלוֹ׳ Ezr 8^{10}) **n.pr.m.** 8013,
1. Levites: **a.** -מוֹת 1 Ch 24$^{22.22}$ 26^{26}; -מִית v^{25} 8019
23^{18}; -מוֹת 26^{25} Kt, -מִית Qr, Σαλωμωθ, 𝔊L
Σαλωμιθ. **b.** -מוֹת 1 Ch 23^{9} Kt, -מִית Qr, Αλωθειμ,

Σαλωμ(ε)ιθ. **2.** מִית- son (appar.) of Rehob. 2 Ch 11[20], Εμμωθ, A Σαλημωθ, 𝔊L Σαλωμιθ. **3.** מִית- head of post-ex. family Ezr 8[10], Σαλειμουθ, etc.

8019 †II. **שְׁלֹמִית n.pr.f.** Σαλ(ω)μιθ, etc.: **1.** in Israel Lv 24[11]. **2.** daughter of Zerub. 1 Ch 3[19].

8015 †**שְׁלֹמִי n.pr.m.** in Asher, Nu 34[27]; Σελεμ(ε)ι.

7759 **שׁוּלַמִּית** v. p. 1002.

8017 †**שְׁלֻמִיאֵל n.pr.m.** in Simeon Nu 1[6] 2[12] 7[36.41] 10[19]; Σαλαμιηλ.

8018 †**שֶׁלֶמְיָה(וּ) n.pr.m. 1.** Jeremiah's time; Σελεμιου (genit.): **a.** יָ֫הוּ- Je 36[14]. **b.** יָ֫הוּ v[26]. **c.** יָה- 37[3], יָהוּ- 38[1]. **d.** יָה- 37[13]. **2.** Levite,

7967 יָהוּ- 1 Ch 26[14], τῷ Σαλαμεια, etc., =**שַׁלּוּם 12 a**, q.v. **3.** post-ex. names: **a.** יָה- Ne 3[30], Τελεμια(ς), 𝔊L Σελ'. **b.** יָה- Ne 13[13], priest, Σελεμια(ς) (=**c** or **d**?). **c.** יָה- Ezr 10[39], Σελεμια. **d.** יָהוּ- v[41], 𝔊 *id.*

8020 †**שַׁלְמַן** (van d. H. מַן-) **n.pr.m.** vel **loc.** (cf. Palm. n.pr. שלמן GACooke[299]; Ph. n.pr. div. שלמן Lzb[377] GACooke[42]; As. *Salamanu*, of Moabit. prince COT[Ho 10,14]; n.pr. div. *Šulmanu*, v. foll.);—כְּשֹׁד שׁ׳ בֵּית אַרְבֵאל Ho 10[14], Σαλαμαν (cf. also Field[Hex. ii. 957]);—dub., We Now think= foll. (and cl. ins. after Hosea's time), cf. also Marti; others cp. Moabitish prince, v. supra; Spiegelberg[ZA xiii (1898), 120 f.] suggests n.pr.loc., cp. *Ša-ra-ma-na* in Egypt.

8022 †**שַׁלְמַנְאֶ֫סֶר n.pr.m.** king of Assyria (prop. אסרד-, =As. *Šulman-ašaridu*, '(God) *Šulman is chief*,' Schr[ZK ii (1885), 197 ff.] Muss-Arnolt[JBL xi (1892), 79]);—2 K 17[3]=18[9]; Σαλ(α)μανασ(σ)αρ, 𝔙 Salmanasar. This was שׁ׳ IV, B.C. 727–722, Say[Hast. DB s.v.] Johns[Ency. Bib. s.v.].

7888, 8023-24 **שִׁלֹנִי** v. II. שֵׁלָה. **שַׁלְנִי** v. sub שָׁלוֹ. p. 1017-18

8025 †**שָׁלַף vb. draw out, off** (NH *id., loosen, draw* (nail, sword; Jastr); As. *šalâpu, pluck out, draw* sword; Aram. שְׁלַף *draw* sword, *draw off* shoe, ܫܠܦ *draw* sword, in Lexx. *remove* corselet; Ar. سَلَفَ is *pass, pass away*, سَلَبَ *strip, plunder*, etc.);—**Qal** *Pf.* 3 ms. שׁ׳ Ju 3[22]+; *Impf.* 3 ms. וַיִּשְׁלֹף Ru 4[8], etc.; *Imv.* ms. שְׁלֹף Ju 9[54]+; *Pt. act.* שֹׁלֵף 8[10]+, etc.; *pass.* f. שְׁלוּפָה Nu 22[23]+;—**1.** *draw out* sword from (מִן) wound Ju 3[22], cf. Jb 20[25]; usu. sword from sheath Ju 8[20] 9[54] 1 S 31[4]=1 Ch 10[4], +מִתַּעְרָהּ 1 S 17[51]; וְחַרְבּוֹ שְׁלוּפָה בְּיָדוֹ Nu 22[23.31] Jos 5[13] (all J), 1 Ch 21[16]; elsewhere אִישׁ שֹׁלֵף ח׳ coll. Ju 8[10] 20[2.15.17.46] 2 S 24[9] 2 K 3[26] 1 Ch 21[5.5], cf. Ju 20[35] and (שֹׁלְפֵי ח׳) v[25]. **2.** *draw off* sandal Ru 4[7.8] (cf. I. חלץ **1**; also RS[K 269] Dr[Dt 25,9] Bewer[SK lxxvi (1903), 332]). **3.** *shoot up* (?), i.e. *draw out* blade, of grass on roof ψ 129[6] (cf. Ew Bae al.); Che Dr *is unsheathed* (vb. c. subj. indef.=pass.), with same meaning; Hup-Now prop. שָׁלֵם (with ‖ in Syr.); v. Ortenberg[Textkritik d. Ps. (1861), 30] שֶׁחָלַף, We[Hpt] Du חָלַף (as 90[5.6], v. ח׳ **2**). p. 322 2498

†[**שֶׁ֫לֶף**] **n.pr.m.** son of Joḳṭan;—שָׁ֫לֶף Gn 8026
10[26]=1 Ch 1[20]; Σαλεφ; identif. by Os[ZMG xi (1857), 153 f.] with S. Ar. tribe سُلَف, cf. Mordtm[ZMG xxxix (1885), 228] Glaser[Skizze ii. 425] Hom[Chr 70], and v. Di Dr.

שלשׁ (√ of following; meaning unknown; conj. in Dietr[Wortforsch. 229 n.]; cf. Lag[BN 173]).

שָׁלֹשׁ, שָׁלוֹשׁ, שְׁלֹשָׁה, שְׁלֹשָׁה[430] **n.m. et f. a three, triad** (NH *id.;* שלש SI[2]; שלשן 30 MI[2]; Ph. 7969
שלש; As. *šalaštu, šalaltu;* Sab. שלת Hom[Chr 47, 124], but also תלת, etc., Id.[47; A. u. A. ii. 175] Sab Denkm[No. 31, 8]; Ar. ثَلَاثٌ, ثَلَاثَةٌ; Eth. ሠለስ: ሠለስቱ: Aram. תְּלָתָא, ܬܠܬܐ; Nab. תלת Lzb[377]; Palm. תלת (in תלת מאה) Reckend[ZMG xlii (1888), 408]; v. also Kö[ii. 1. 208]);—**m.** שָׁלֹשׁ (וֹשׁ- rare, chiefly late), c. **n.f.** Am 4[8]+90 t., also cstr. שְׁלֹשׁ Gn 18[6]+65 t. (but 38[24] read perh. שְׁלֹשֶׁת Sam., cf. Di al.), שְׁלָשׁ- Ex 21[11]; **f.** שְׁלֹשָׁה (וֹשָׁה- rare, chiefly late), c. **n.m.** Gn 6[10]+149 t., also cstr. שְׁלֹשֶׁת Am 4[4]+92 t. (3+10=13 are additional; on rare exceptions to rule of gender cf. Ges[§ 97 c]), sf. שְׁלָשְׁתְּכֶם Nu 12[4], שְׁלָשְׁתָּם v[4] Ez 40[10] 41[16];—*three* (Hex chiefly P): **1.** no other num.: **a.** bef. n.pl., שָׁלֹשׁ 51 t., e.g. שׁ׳ אַמּוֹת Ex 27[1]+, שׁ׳ בָּאַמָּה +1 K 7[27], שְׁלֹשָׁה 90 t., e.g. Gn 18[2]+ (so always שְׁלֹשׁ, שְׁלֹשֶׁת; rd. מִשְּׁלֹשֶׁת Gn 38[24] Sam Di; =מִשְּׁ׳, from מִן-); after n. (late: on 1 S 1[24] v. [שְׁלִשׁ]) 1 Ch 25[5] +17 t.; n. om. 1 S 17[14] 2 S 24[12]=42 t. **b.** =ordin. לְשׁ׳ יָמִים Ex 19[5] *on third day;* הַיּוֹם שׁ׳ הַיָּמִים 1 S 9[20], הַיּוֹם הַשׁ׳ 30[13], both=*three days ago;* esp. לְ בִּשְׁנַת שׁ׳ 1 K 15[28]+7 t. (Ges[§ 134 o]). **2.** 13, c. **n.f.**: שְׁלֹשׁ עֶשְׂרֵה שָׁנָה Gn 17[25] 1 K 7[1]+ (as ordin.) Gn 14[4] (+שְׁלֹשׁ-), Je 1[2] 25[3]; before עָרִים Jos 21[19]; after, 19[16]+3 t., before עִיר Jos 21[33] 1 Ch 6[45], אַמּוֹת Ez 40[11]; c. **n.m.** שְׁלֹשָׁה עָשָׂר before פָּרִים Nu 29[14]; after, v[13]; ordin. before יוֹם Est 3[12] 9[1]; after, v[17]; יוֹם om. 3[13] 8[12] 9[18]; גּוֹרָל om. 1 Ch 24[13] 25[20] 26[11]. **3.** 300=שְׁלֹשׁ מֵאוֹת Gn 5[22]+59 t. (1 Ch 11[11] perh. intentional change [HPS[Sm]] from שְׁמֹנֶה ‖ 2 S 23[8], which

certainly orig., Vrss Th We Dr and mod.); 3000 =שְׁלֹשֶׁת אֲלָפִים Ex 32^{28} + 28 t. **4.** c. tens, ׳שׁ foll. Nu 1^{43} + 11 t., precedes Lv 12^{4} + 17 t., + (as ordin.) 3 + 20 Je 52^{30} + 3 t.; 20 + 3 2 K 12^{7} + 2 t. **5.** as round, or conventional, no.: 2 (*or*) 3, Am 4^{8} Dt 17^{6} Jos 7^{3} 2 K 9^{32} Is 17^{6}; 3 (*and*) 4, Pr $30^{15.18.21.29}$; *three days' journey* Ex 3^{18} 5^{3} 8^{23}, etc.

8027 †I. [שָׁלַשׁ] **Pi. denom.** do a third time, **divide into three parts**, etc.;—*Pf.* 2 ms. וְשִׁלַּשְׁתָּ Dt 19^{3} *divide* land *into three parts* (so *Impf.* וַיְשַׁלֵּשׁ אֶת־הָעָם [for MT וַיְשַׁלַּח] 2 S 18^{2} 𝔊L Bu); 1 S 20^{19} *stay three days* (cf. Dr); v^{20} We Dr al. (cf. 𝔊) read אֲשַׁלֵּשׁ בְּ׳ (for שְׁלֹשֶׁת הַ׳)=*I will shoot on the third day with* the arrows (HPS qu.); *Impf.* 3 mpl. וַיְשַׁלֵּשׁוּ 1 K 18^{34}, and *Imv.* mpl. שַׁלֵּשׁוּ v^{34} *do a third time.* **Pu.** *Pt.* מְשֻׁלָּשׁ *three years old* Gn 15^{9} + 1 S 1^{24} (read with 𝔊 Th We etc. בְּפַר מְשֻׁלָּשׁ for בְּפָרִם שְׁלֹשָׁה), f. מְשֻׁלֶּשֶׁת Gn $15^{9.9}$; הַחוּט הַמְשֻׁלָּשׁ Ec 4^{12} *the threefold cord;* fpl. מְשֻׁלָּשׁוֹת Ez 42^{6} *three-storied* chambers.

7992 שְׁלִישִׁי **m.** שְׁלִישִׁית **f. adj. num. ord.** $_{108}$ **third**;—יוֹם שְׁלִישִׁי Gn 1^{13} + 31 t., etc. (64 t., rarely שְׁלִשִׁי); pl. שְׁלִשִׁים (*third* 50, set of messengers, etc.) 1 S 19^{21} 2 K 1^{13} + 4 t.; בַּשָּׁנָה הַשְּׁלִישִׁית 1 K 18^{1} + 4 t., etc. (33 t.; sometimes שְׁלִשִׁית ,שְׁלִשֶׁת, etc.); =*third part, a third* 2 S $18^{2.2.2}$ + 13 t., + (cstr.) Nu 15^{6} + 4 t., + שְׁלִשִׁתֵיךְ (Ges$^{§91 l}$) Ez 5^{12} *third part of thee;* =*third time* 1 S 3^{8}; also שְׁלִישִׁיָּה Is 19^{24} *third* (on par with other two); בַּשְּׁלִישִׁים
5697 Ez 42^{3} *in the thirds*, i.e. *third story;*—עֶגְלַת שׁ׳ 15^{5} Je 48^{34}, v. ׳ע p. 722.—שְׁלִישִׁתָהּ Ez 21^{19} is corrupt and doubtful; Krae prop. וְשֻׁלָּשָׁה the sword shall be doubled *and trebled;* other conj. in Co Toy. 1 S 20^{5} del. ׳הַשּׁ 𝔊 We Dr al., so v^{12}. 2 S 23^{18} read הַשְּׁלֹשִׁם 𝔖 We Dr al.

8032 †שִׁלְשֹׁם and (less oft.) שִׁלְשׁוֹם $_{25}$ **adv.** = **three days ago, specif. day before yesterday** (Kö$^{ii.1.255f.}$ Lag$^{BN 20 Anm.}$ Ba$^{NB §216b}$);—in phr. תְּמוֹל שׁ׳ Ex 5^{8} *yesterday* (and) *day before*, idiomat. for *hitherto*, so Ru 2^{11}, אֶתְמוֹל שׁ׳ 1 S 4^{7}; כִּת׳ שׁ׳ Gn $31^{2.5}$ (E), Ex $5^{7.14}$ (J), 2 K 13^{5}, cf. 1 S 14^{21} 19^{7}; גַּם־ת׳ גַּם־שׁ׳ Ex 4^{10} (J), 2 S 3^{17} 1 Ch 11^{2}, cf. 2 S 5^{2}; מִת׳ שׁ׳ from *aforetime, previously* Ex $21^{29.36}$ (E), Dt 4^{42} $19^{4.6}$ Jos 4^{18} (J), 3^{4} 20^{5} (both R), cf. 1 S 10^{11}; כִּת׳ שׁ׳ 1 S 21^{6} *as formerly* (but Bu מִת׳ שׁ׳=*for some days*).—׳שׁ Pr 22^{20} Kt is difficult; Qr
7991 שָׁלִשִׁים (v. III. שָׁלִישׁ) is imposs.; supply perhaps תְּמוֹל have I not written to thee *heretofore*, etc.?

שְׁלֹשִׁים (very seldom שְׁלוֹשִׁים ,שְׁלֹשִׁם) $_{174}$ **n.** 7970
indecl. thirty;—**1.** bef. n. sg.: אַמָּה Gn 6^{15} + 3 t., +, c. בָּאַמָּה Ex 26^{8} + 3 t.; שָׁנָה 2 S 5^{4} + 12 t. (age of paternity, of Levitical or royal duty, etc.), אִישׁ Ju 14^{19} + 3 t., etc.; bef. n.pl. בָּנִים Ju 10^{4} 12^{9}, אֲנָשִׁים Je 38^{10} (read here prob. שְׁלֹשָׁה Ew Hi Gf al.), less common words Ez 40^{17} Ezr $1^{9.10}$, etc.; after n.pl. Gn 32^{16}, פְּעָמִים שׁ׳ Ez 41^{6}; אֶלֶף שׁ׳ 1 Ch 23^{3}+, אֲלָפִים שׁ׳ Ezr 2^{35} Ne 7^{38}; ׳שׁ foll. units Gn 11^{12} + 14 t., precedes 1 K 22^{42} + 29 t.; ׳שׁ foll. 100 (1000, etc.) Gn 5^{5} + 15 t., precedes 5^{3} + 21 t. **2.** as ordin. (בִּ)שְׁנַת שׁ׳ וְאַחַת שָׁנָה לְ 1 K 16^{23}, cf. v^{29} + 4 t.; שָׁנָה om. Ne 5^{14} + 4 t.; שְׁנַת om. 2 K 25^{27}=Je 52^{31}; בִּשׁ׳ שָׁנָה alone Ez 1^{1}.—1 S 13^{5} read שְׁלֹשֶׁת 𝔊L We Dr al.; 2 S 23^{13} read שְׁלֹשָׁה Qr Vrss Th and mod.; 1 Ch 11^{11} read הַשְּׁלֹשָׁה ,הַשָּׁלִשִׁית 𝔊L Kit Benz al. (so ‖ 2 S 23^{8} for הַשָּׁלִשִׁי).

†I. שָׁלִ(י)שׁ **n.[m.]** **third** (part, i.e. of ephah? dub.), name of a measure;—for dust Is 40^{12}, tears ψ 80^{6} (in fig.), adv. acc. *measure-wise.* 7991

†II. [שָׁלִישׁ] **n.[m.]** pl. שָׁלִשִׁים, a (three-stringed? three-barred? three-cornered?) mus. instr., perhaps a *sistrum* (so 𝔙), or 'triangle' (RVm: cf. Prince$^{EB iii. 3228}$), 1 S 18^{6} (+ בְּתֻפִּים). 7991

†III. שָׁלִישׁ **n.m.** **adjutant** or **officer** (best explained as *third* man (in chariot), v. esp. Hpt$^{BAS iv. 586 f.}$ Bender$^{ZAW xxiii (1903), 19}$ WMM$^{As. u. Eur. 329}$; v. also Kau$^{M. N., DPV, 1904, 10}$; doubted by Di$^{Ex 14, 7}$ Baen$^{ib.}$ Buhl^{14});—abs. ׳שׁ of king's personal attendant at court 2 K $7^{2.17.19}$, sf., military officer of king, שָׁלִשׁוֹ 2 K 9^{25}, שָׁלִשָׁה 15^{25} (on abnormal ◌ָ v. Ges$^{§93 xx}$ Kö$^{ii.1.133, 449, 495}$); pl. שָׁלִשִׁים Ez 23^{15} + (sts. שָׁלִשִׁם, etc.) v^{23} Ex 14^{7} 2 K $10^{25.25}$, + (Qr) 2 S 23^{8} (>Kt שלשי), 1 Ch 11^{11} 12^{19} (v^{18} van d. H.; Kt in both, שלושים), read in all three הַשְּׁלֹשָׁה (רֹאשׁ) *chief of the three* 𝔊L We Dr Bu Now.—שָׁלִשִׁים Pr 22^{20} Qr v. שִׁלְשֹׁם. 8032

†II. [שִׁלֵּשׁ] **adj. pertaining to the third**;—only m.pl. as subst. שִׁלֵּשִׁים *those of third generation* (grandsons); בְּנֵי שׁ׳ Gn 50^{23} (E) *sons of those of third generation*, i.e. great-grandsons (v. Kö$^{SK 1898, 533 ff.}$); עַל־בָּנִים עַל־שׁ׳ וְעַל־רִבֵּעִים Ex 20^{5} (E; v. [רִבֵּעַ])=Dt 5^{9}, Nu 14^{18}, cf. Ex 34^{7} (both J). 8029

†שֶׁלֶשׁ (van d. H. שֶׁלֶשׁ) **n.pr.m.** in Asher, 1 Ch 7^{35}, Ζεμη, A Σελλης, 𝔊L Σελεμ. 8028

8031 †שָׁלִשָׁה **n.pr.loc.** doubtful;—אֶרֶץ־שׁ׳ 1 S 9[4], B 𝔊L Σελχα, A Σαλισσα; ? cf. בַּעַל שָׁלִשָׁה 2 K 4[42].

8030 †שִׁלְשָׁה **n.pr.m.** in Asher, 1 Ch 7[37], Σαλεισα, 𝔊L Σελεμσαν.

7597 †שַׁלְתִּיאֵל **n. pr. m.** (= שְׁאַלְתִּיאֵל Thes Buhl);—father of Zerub. Hg 1[12.14] 2[2]; Σαλαθιηλ.

8033 **שָׁם adv.** there, thither (Ar. ثَمَّ *there*, cf. ثُمَّ *then;* BAram. תַּמָּה, Eg. Aram. תמה S-C Pap. A 4, J 6, 𝔗 תַּמָּן (with demonstr. *n*, cf. אֲרַיִן beside אֲרַי), Syr. ܬܡܢ; Zenj Had. 8 (Cooke 159) (שם);—**1. a.** *there* Gn 2[8.12] 11[2.7.31]+oft.; placed early in sentence for emph., Mi 4[10] שָׁם תִּנָּצֵלִי, Na 3[15] Ez 32[22.24] ψ 104[26]+, ... וְשָׁם Gn 41[12] Ex 15[27] Nu 13[22.33]+, שָׁם ... וְשָׁם Ex 15[25] Dt 12[14] Is 27[10] Jb 3[17]+, וְהִנֵּה שָׁם ... Gn 29[2], כִּי שָׁם ... 11[9] 21[31] 35[7] 2 S 1[21] 15[21]+, אַךְ שָׁם ... Is 34[14.15], גַּם שָׁם ... 23[12] 57[7] ψ 139[10]; resuming a preceding 'where,' Jb 39[30] בַּאֲשֶׁר חֲלָלִים שָׁם הוּא, Ju 5[27] Je 22[12] Ec 11[3], cf. 1[7]. Repeated, שָׁם ... שָׁם *here ... there* Is 28[10.13]. In poetry, pointing to a spot in which a scene is localized vividly in the imagination, ψ 14[5] שָׁם פָּחֲדוּ פַחַד *there* feared they a fear! 36[13], cf. 48[7] 66[6] 132[17]; Hos 6[7] Zp 1[14].—Hb 3[4] read probably (We Now) שָׂם the flashes at his side *made he* the hiding of his power; Ec 3[17] שָׁם = *with God*, in the Divine plan or scheme: but read perh. שָׂם Hi De al. **b.** preceded by the rel., אֲשֶׁר שָׁם *where*, Gn 2[11] Ex 20[21] 1 S 9[10]+, usu. with one or more words between, Gn 13[3.14] 19[27] Ex 29[42] 2 S 11[16] 2 K 23[27]+oft.; after בַּאֲשֶׁר הוּא שָׁם, בַּאֲשֶׁר †Gn 21[17]. With אשר omitted (the rel. being indic. by cstr., Ges § 130 c, d) Ez 39[11] מְקוֹם שָׁם קֶבֶר בְּיִשְׂרָ׳ a place *where* a grave (may be) in Isr., but 𝔊𝔙 Co Or al. read שֵׁם a place *of renown*. **2.** *thither*, after vbs. of motion (= שָׁמָּה, v. **3**), Dt 1[37] לֹא תָבֹא שָׁם, Ju 19[15] 21[10] 1 S 2[14] 9[6] al.; אֲשֶׁר ... שָׁם *whither*, 1 K 18[10] 21[18] 2 K 1[4.6.16] Is 20[6], more oft. in Je Ez, as Je 8[3] 22[27] 23[3.8] 45[5]+, Ez 4[13] 12[16] 36[20.22]+; so שֶׁשָּׁם ψ 122[4]. **3.** with ה loc., שָׁמָּה (shâmmāh): **a.** after vbs. of motion, *thither*, Gn 19[20] לָנוּס שָׁמָּה to flee *thither*, v[22] 20[13] 24[6] 29[3] Dt 1[38]+oft.; = *into it, therein* (of a basket, pit, etc.), Ex 16[33] וְתֶן־שָׁמָּה מְלֹא הָעֹמֶר, 21[33] וְנָפַל שָׁמָּה, 30[18] Ju 8[25] 2 K 12[10]; pregnantly, after a verb implying motion, as *to bury*, Gn 23[13] וְאֶקְבְּרָה אֶת־מֵתִי שָׁמָּה, 25[10] 49[31] 50[5] (all P), נוֹעַד *to meet* Ex 29[42.43] 30[6.36] Nu 17[19] (all P), Jos 2[16] 7[3] Je 13[7] Jo 4[7], perh. Ct 8[5] (? **c**). **b.** אֲשֶׁר ... שָׁמָּה *whither* Gn 20[13] Nu 33[54] Dt 4[5.14]+oft.; *where* 2 K 23[8] 1 Ch 4[41]. **c.** more rarely, i.q. שָׁם *there*, Gn 43[30] וַיֵּבְךְּ שָׁמָּה, Jos 2[1] Ju 16[27] 2 K 4[11] 9[16] Ho 2[17] Is 22[18] 34[15] 65[9] Je 18[2] 27[22] Ez 23[3]
32[29.30] (v[22.24.26] שָׁם), 48[35] י׳ שָׁמָּה, ψ 76[4] 122[5] Ec 3[16]. 3074
4. מִשָּׁם *from there, thence:* **a.** oft. after verbs of departing, taking, etc., Gn 2[10] 11[8.9] 12[8] 18[16] 24[7] 42[2], etc., Nu 13[23] 21[12] 22[41] וַיַּרְא מִשָּׁם, Dt 4[29] וּבִקַּשְׁתֶּם מִשָּׁם, 30[4] Je 37[12] Ho 2[17] Am 9[2.3.4] Jb 39[29]+. Peculiarly, Gn 49[24] מִשָּׁם רֹעֶה אֶבֶן יִשְׂרָ׳ Ges De RVm *from there* [from heaven], (from) the Shepherd (י׳), the Stone (Rock) of Israel, Ew Di Sta *from there* (where is) the Shepherd of (רֹעֶה) the (Bethel-)stone of Israel; but both forced: text dubious; Gunk by the name (מִשֵּׁם; so 𝔖) of the Shepherd, etc. (as Ew Di). **b.** אֲשֶׁר ... מִשָּׁם *whence* Gn 24[5] Nu 23[13]+. **c.** expressing *origin*, Gn 3[23] the ground אֲשֶׁר לֻקַּח מִשָּׁם, 10[14] *whence* (= *from whom*) came forth the Phil., Ju 19[18] מִשָּׁם אָנֹכִי, 1 S 10[12] אִישׁ מִשָּׁם, Is 65[20]. **d.** of the mass, *from* which something is taken or made, Gn 27[9] 30[32] (of צאן), Lv 2[2] וְקָמַץ מִשָּׁם וגו׳ (from the meal, etc., of a מנחה), 1 K 17[13] אַךְ עֲשִׂי לִי מִשָּׁם עֻגָה קְטַנָּה i.e. from the meal and oil, 2 K 7[2.19]: וּמִשָּׁם לֹא תֹאכֵל, Ez 5[3].

I. שֵׁם[864] **n.m.**[2 S 7, 9] name (√unknown; Thes 8034
שׁמה, cf. Ba ZMG xli (1887), 635; Lag BN 160 ושם, Ar. وَسْمٌ *brand, mark*, cf. RS K 213, 303 ff. Kö ii. 1. 104; NH = BH (esp. הַשֵּׁם = יהוה); Ph. שם Lzb[377]; As. *šumu;* Sab. סם Hom Chr 124; Eth. ስም: Ar. اِسْمٌ, أُسْمٌ, سِمٌ, سُمٌ; Aram. שֵׁם, שְׁמָא, also שׁוּם, שֻׁם (Kö ii. 1. 512), ܫܡܐ, ܫܡ, OAram., Palm. שם Lzb[377]);—abs. שׁ׳ Gn 6[4]+; cstr. שׁ׳ Gn 12[8]+, rarely שֶׁם־ 1 S 8[2]+; sf. שְׁמִי Ex 3[15]+, שִׁמְךָ Gn 32[9]+, שְׁמֶךָ 1 K 18[31]+, etc.; pl. שֵׁמוֹת (rarely שְׁמֹת) Gn 2[20]+; cstr. שְׁמוֹת Ex 6[16]+, sf. שְׁמוֹתָם Nu 13[4]+, שְׁמוֹתָן Ez 23[4.4];—*name:* **1.** of river Gn 2[11.13.14], beasts v[19.20], city 26[33] (all J)+; שׁ׳ היום †Ez 24[2], i.e. exact designation of it (+ אֶת־עֶצֶם הַיּ׳ הַזֶּה). **2. a.** usu. of pers.: Gn 4[17.19.19] (J)+; as signif. 1 S 25[25], cf. Pr 21[24]; esp. in phr. וַיְהִי אִישׁ ... וּשְׁמוֹ אֶלְקָנָה 1 S 1[1], cf. 9[1.2], Je 37[13]+28 t.; less oft. as גָּלְיָת שְׁמוֹ 1 S 17[4], cf. Zc 6[12]+5 t. (cf. in As. Krae BAS i. 430); freq. c. קָרָא (q.v. **6**, and **Niph. 2, Pu.**; note here, נִקְרָא שׁ׳ עַל in token of ownership 2 S 12[28] (v. Dr), Is 4[1]); rarely, שִׂים אֶת־שְׁמוֹ אֲבִימֶלֶךְ Ju 8[31], cf. 2 K 17[34] Ne 9[7]; וַיָּשֶׂם לָהֶם שׁ׳ Dn 1[7]; c. יֵאָמֵר Gn 32[29] (J); change of name is without vb., as Gn 17[15] (P), or (usu.) c. יִהְיֶה Gn 35[10] (P) *Isr. shall be thy name*, cf. 17[5] 1 K 18[31] 1 Ch 22[9], also

וַיַּסֵּב אֶת־שְׁמוֹ יְהוֹ׳ 2 K 23^{34} = 2 Ch 36^{4}, cf. 2 K 24^{17}, and (subj. ׳י) מַה־שְּׁמֶךָ Is 56^{5}; שׁ׳ עוֹלָם אֶתֶּן־לוֹ Gn 32^{28}, cf. Ex 3^{13} Pr 30^{4}, מִי שְׁמֶךָ Ju 13^{17}; *be explicitly mentioned* is: וְכֻלָּם בְּשֵׁמוֹת Ezr 10^{16}, נִקְּבוּ בְשׁ׳ Nu 1^{17} 1 Ch 16^{41} 2 Ch 28^{15} 31^{19} Ezr 8^{20}, הַבָּאִים בְּשׁ׳ 1 Ch 4^{38}, וַיָּבֹאוּ הַכְּתוּבִים בְּשׁ׳ v^{41}; of things, וּבְשֵׁמוֹת תִּפְקְדוּ Nu 4^{32} (P), + v^{27} (read בְּשֵׁמֹת 𝔊 Di Baen Gray); יְדַעְתִּיךָ בְּשֵׁם Ex 33^{12} (subj. ׳י), i.e. acknowledge thee, personally (as mine), cf. v^{17} (both J); בְּשׁ׳ פ׳ *as the representative of* 1 S 25$^{5.9}$ 1 K 21^{8} Je 29^{25} Est 2^{22} 3^{12} 8$^{8.8.10}$ (cf. also **3**). **b.** = *reputation;* (1) וַאֲגַדְּלָה שְׁמֶךָ Gn 12^{2} (J), וְעָשִׂתִי לְךָ שׁ׳ גָּדוֹל כְּשֵׁם הַגְּדֹלִים אֲשֶׁר בָּאָרֶץ 2 S 7^{9}; †*make oneself a name* וְנַעֲשֶׂה לָּנוּ שׁ׳ Gn 11^{4} (J), וַיַּעַשׂ לוֹ שׁ׳ 2 S 8^{13}, of ׳י Je 32^{20}, hence Ne 9^{10} Dn 9^{15}, Is 63$^{12.14}$, so c. שׂוּם 2 S 7^{23} = 1 Ch 17^{21}; וַיֵּצֵא לָךְ שֵׁם בַּ׳ Ez 16^{14} (cf. 1 Ch 14^{17}), 2 Ch 26^{15} עַד־לְמֵרָחוֹק, v^{8} וַיֵּלֶךְ שְׁמוֹ עַד־לְ׳; 2 S 23$^{18.22}$; = *fame, glory,* Zp 3$^{19.20}$ Ez 39^{13}.—34^{29} read perh. שָׁלֹם 𝔊 Siegf Be Toy; Co שָׁלֵם; Krae conj. שָׁמֵן; אַנְשֵׁי הַשֵּׁם Gn 6^{4} (J), Nu 16^{2} (J), אַנְשֵׁי שֵׁמוֹת 1 Ch 5^{24} 12^{31} (van d. H. v^{30}); c. neg. בְּנֵי בְלִי־שֵׁם Jb 30^{8}; (2) bad sense, וְהוֹצִא עָלֶיהָ שֵׁם רָע Dt 22^{14}, cf. v^{19} Ne 6^{13}; = *byword* Ez 23^{10}; טְמֵאַת הַשׁ׳ 22^{5}. **c.** esp. as giving a man a kind of posthumous life, esp. in his sons, אֵין־לִי בֵן בַּעֲבוּר הַזְכִּיר שְׁמִי 2 S 18^{18}, לְהָקִים לְאָחִיו שֵׁם בְּ׳ Dt 25^{7}, cf. v^{6} Ru 4$^{5.10}$, without whom it is blotted out, etc., Dt 25^{6}, cf. Nu 27^{4} (P), Ru 4^{10}, so that to destroy one's name = extirpate family (and שֵׁם sts. is ‖ זֶרַע) 1 S 24^{22} (Gi v^{21}), 2 S 14^{7} (‖ שְׁאֵרִית), so of peoples Dt 7^{24} 9^{14} 12^{3} Is 14^{22}+; לֹא יִזָּרַע מִשִּׁמְךָ עוֹד Na 1^{14} (of Nineveh); כֵּן יַעֲמֹד זַרְעֲכֶם וְשִׁמְכֶם Is 66^{22}; more abstr. (‖ זֵכֶר) Jb 18^{17} Pr 10^{7}. **3.** *name,* as designation of God, specif. of ׳י (esp. Je Ez Is$^{2.3}$ ψψ):—first (in Hex) in phr. ק׳ בְּשׁ׳ י׳ Gn 4^{26} (J), *call with,* i.e. use the name ׳י in worship, so 12^{8} 13^{4} 21^{33} 26^{35} + (v. קרא **2 c**); hence, of place of worship, בְּכָל־הַמָּקוֹם אֲשֶׁר אַזְכִּיר אֶת־שְׁמִי Ex 20^{24} (Gi v^{21}); לָשׂוּם [לְשַׁכֵּן] אֶת־שְׁמוֹ שָׁם Dt 12$^{5.11}$+; בָּנָה בַיִת לִשְׁמִי 2 S 7^{13}+oft.; people come לְשׁ׳ י׳ Jos 9^{9} (R^{D}), so לְמַעַן שׁ׳ 1 K 8^{41} = 2 Ch 6^{32}, Is 60^{9}; seek it ψ 83^{17}; *swear with* בְּשׁ׳ י׳ 1 S 20^{42} Dt 6^{13} 10^{20} Lv 19^{12}, cf. (לַשָּׁוְא) Ex 20$^{7.7}$ = Dt 5$^{11.11}$; תָּפַשׂ שׁ׳ י׳ Pr 30^{9}; נִקְרָא שְׁמִי עַל־, etc., in token of ownership (cf. **2 a**), Je 7^{10}+ (v. p. 896^{a}); = his reputation, fame, c. עָשָׂה לוֹ, v. **1 b** (1), cf. Jos 7^{9}; בְּשׁ׳ י׳, i.e. as his representative Ex 5^{23} (J), 1 S 17^{45} Dt 10^{8} 2 S 6^{18} 2 K 2^{24}+ (v. **2 a** ad fin.); esp. as embodying the (revealed) character of ׳י: י׳ שְׁמוֹ Am 5^{8} 9^{6} Je 33^{2}, זֶה שְּׁמִי לְעֹלָם Ex 3^{15} (E; ‖ זִכְרִי; fundamental passage), 6^{3} (P); י׳ (א׳) צְבָאוֹת שְׁמוֹ Am 4^{13} 5^{27} Je 10^{16} 46^{18}+10 t. Je Is^{2}, י׳ קַנָּא שְׁמוֹ Ex 34^{14} (J; cf. 20^{5} Na 1^{2}), שׁ׳ קָדוֹשׁ Is 57^{15}, שׁ׳ [קָדְשִׁי] Am 2^{7} Ez 39^{7} 43^{7} ψ 103^{1}+oft.; hence object of knowledge Is 52^{6} Je 48^{17}, יֹדְעֵי שְׁמֶךָ ψ 9^{11} (‖ דֹּרְשֶׁיךָ), love Is 56^{6}, אֹהֲבֵי שׁ׳ ψ 5^{12} 69^{37} 119^{132}, fear 61^{6}, esp. of praise, etc. (הִזְכִּיר, הִלֵּל, הוֹדָה, בֵּרֵךְ, etc.): לְשִׁמְךָ אֲזַמֵּר 2 S 22^{50} (‖ אוֹדְךָ), and so very oft. ‖ (׳י) = ψ 18^{50}, cf. 1 Ch 16^{10} 29^{13} ψ 45^{18} Is 26^{13} 1 K 8$^{33.35}$ = 2 Ch 6$^{24.26}$ ψ 8$^{2.10}$+; הָבוּ לי׳ כְּבוֹד שְׁמוֹ 29^{2} 96^{8}, and many combinations; opp. חִלֵּל אֶת־שׁ׳ א׳ Lv 18^{21}+, נקב שׁ׳ י׳ 24^{16}, נִאֵץ שׁ׳ ψ 74$^{10.18}$, etc.; הַשֵּׁ׳ הַנִּכְבָּד וְהַנּוֹרָא Dt 28^{58}, cf. Ne 1^{11}; לְמַעַן שְׁמֶךָ, in appeals to ׳י to act acc. to his character Je 14$^{7.21}$ Ez 20$^{9.14}$ Is 48^{9} 66^{5} ψ 25^{11} 31^{4}+; שׁ׳ י׳ is powerful agent, בְּשִׁמְךָ הוֹשִׁיעֵנִי 54^{3} (‖ בִּגְבוּרָתְךָ), cf. 124^{8}; of מַלְאַךְ י׳, ׳י says שְׁמִי בְּקִרְבּוֹ Ex 23^{21} (E); הַשֵּׁם Lv 24^{11} is prob. scribal substitution for word ׳י (already beginning to be thought ineffable, esp. c. וַיִּקֹּב, cf. Gei[Urschr. 273 f.] Di Dr-Wh Baen); on development of this usage, and Jewish use of הַשׁ׳ as personif. or hypostasis, v. Levy[NHWB s.v.] Jastr[s.v.].—קָרוֹב שְׁמֶךָ ψ 75^{2} is striking, but doubtful, < 𝔊 Dy Che Gr Hup-Now קֹרְאֵי שׁ׳, Du קָרְנוּ בְשׁ׳ (= קְרָאנוּ). **4.** of false gods, use forbidden Ex 23^{13} (E), Jos 23^{7} (R^{D}), cf. Ho 2^{19} ψ 16^{4}; speak בְּשֵׁם אלהים אחרים Dt 18^{20}; קָרָא בְשׁ׳ א׳ 1 K 18$^{24.25.26}$; יֵלְכוּ בְשׁ׳ א׳ Mi 4^{5}. **5.** = *memorial, monument* Is 55^{13} (‖ אוֹת; so Che Du > = *fame* Di-Kit), יָד וָשֵׁם טוֹב מִבָּנִים וגו׳ 56^{5} (with word-play on שׁ׳ **1 c**).

†II. שֵׁם **n.pr.m.** first son of Noah;—Gn 5^{32} 8035
6^{10} 7^{13} 10$^{1.22.31}$ 11$^{10.10.11}$ (all P), 9$^{18.23.26.27}$ 10^{21} (all J), 1 Ch 1$^{4.17.24}$; Σημ.

†שֶׁמְאֵבֶר **n.pr.m.** king of Ṣᵉboîm;—Gn 8038
14^{2}, Συμοβορ, 𝔊L Συμορ.

שְׁמוּאֵל$_{140}$ **n.pr.m. Samuel** (= *name of Ēl* 8050
Thes al. (or, *his name is Ēl* Hom[Heb. Trad. 98 f.] Wkl[KAT 3. 225] Now[1 S 1, 20]), cf. רְעוּאֵל, פְּנוּאֵל; v. Dr[1 S 1, 20]; Prät[ZMG 1903, 777 ff.] caritative from יִשְׁמָעֵאל; Palm. שמואל Lzb[377]; v. further Gie[AT Schätzung d. Gottesn. (1901), 102 ff.]);—**1.** great prophet, 11th cent. B.C., Σαμουηλ: 1 S 1^{20} (name expl. as if from שָׁאַל), 1$^{18.21.26}$+125 t. 1 S, 1 Ch 6$^{13.18}$ 9^{22} 11^{3} 26^{28} 29^{29} 2 Ch 35^{18} Je 15^{1} ψ 99^{6}. †**2.** in Simeon, Nu 34^{30} (P), Σαλαμιηλ. †**3.** in Issachar 1 Ch 7^{2}, (Ι)σαμουηλ.

8061 †שְׁמִידָע **n.pr.m.** in Manasseh (*the name knoweth?* cf. Sab. ידעסמהו DHM$^{ZMG\ xxxvii\ (1883),\ 16}$);—Nu 26^{22} (Συμαερ), Jos 17^{2} 1 Ch 7^{19}, Συμαρειμ, etc.; 𝔊L Σαμ(ε)ιδα(ε).

8062 †שְׁמִידָעִי **adj.gent.** as n.coll. הַשּׁ׳ Nu 26^{32}.

8070 †שְׁמִירָמוֹת **n.pr.m.** (here acc. to Thes who qu. *nom. altitudinum,* i.e. perhaps of *heavens*): Levites, Σαμε(ι)ραμωθ: **1.** 1 Ch 15$^{18.20}$ 16^{5}. **2.** 2 Ch 17^{8} Qr (Kt שמרימות).

שׁמא (√of following).

8039 †שִׁמְאָה **n. pr. m.** in Benjamin 1 Ch 8^{32} Σεμαα, Σαμαα, etc.,=following.

8043 †שִׁמְאָם **n.pr.m.**=foreg., 1 Ch 9^{38}, Σαμα(α).

שָׁמָּא v. שַׁמָּה, √שמם. שֶׁמְאֵבֶר v. שֵׁם.

8044 †שַׁמְגַּר **n.pr.m.** a 'judge,' son of Anath, Ju 3^{31} 5^{6}, Σαμα[ε]γαρ (on this name (Hittite?) cf. GFM$^{Ju\ 3,\ 31}$; Nö$^{ZMG\ xlii\ (1888),\ 479}$ conj. שמגר).

8045 [שָׁמַד]$_{90}$ **vb. Niph.** **be exterminated, destroyed** (NH der. spec.; Aram. שְׁמַד Pa. *cause to apostatize* (Jastr); Syr. ܫܡܕ seems disputed (in Lexx.); Nö$^{Eut.\ Nab.\ 32}$ *curse;* Ba$^{ES\ 10}$ cites As. *ašmud, I destroyed;* Gerber^{112} thinks vb. denom.);—*Pf.* 3 ms. consec. וְנִשְׁמַד Ez 32^{12}+, etc.; *Impf.* 3 ms. יִשָּׁמֵד Is 48^{19} Pr 14^{11}; 2 mpl. תִּשָּׁמֵדוּן Dt 4^{26}; *Inf. abs.* הִשָּׁמֵד v^{26}; cstr. sf. הִשָּׁמֶדְךָ Dt 28^{20}, etc.;—†**1.** of pers. *be annihilated, exterminated,* Gn 34^{30} (J), Ju 21^{16} 2 S 21^{5} (+מֵהִתְיַצֵּב בְּ;—but rd. לְהַשְׁמִידֵנוּ 𝔊 Ew We Dr al.), ψ 37^{38} (‖ נִכְרַת), 83^{11}; of people Dt 4^{26} (הִשָּׁמֵד תִּשּׁ׳), 7^{23} 12^{30} (+מִפָּנֶיךָ), 28^{20} (‖ אָבַד), v$^{24.45.51.61}$, Je 48^{42} (+מֵעָם), Ez 33^{12} ψ 92^{8} (+עֲדֵי־עַד), cf. also וְלֹא יִשָּׁמֵד שְׁמוֹ מִלְּפָנָי Is 48^{19} (+יִכָּרֵת; זַרְעֶךָ, etc., in ‖ clause). †**2.** *be destroyed,* of bamoth, Ho 10^{8}, cf. (בֵּית רְשָׁעִים) Pr 14^{11}; *be devastated,* of land, Je 48^{8} (‖ אבד). **Hiph.**$_{69}$ *Pf.* 3 ms. הִשְׁמִיד Dt 2^{22}+, etc.; *Impf.* 3 ms. יַשְׁמִיד Is 13^{9}+, וַיַּשְׁמֵד 1 K 16^{12} 2 K 10^{28}, etc.; *Imv.* ms. הַשְׁמֵד Dt 33^{27}; *Inf. abs.* הַשְׁמֵד Is 14^{23}, ־יד Am 9^{8}; cstr. לְהַשְׁמִיד Jos 9^{24}+, also עַד הִשְׁמִידְךָ+ Dt 7^{24}, ־וֹ 28^{48}, ־ם Jos 11^{14} (but rd. in all הַשׁ׳, as Jos 23^{15}, v. Dr$^{Dt\ 7,\ 24}$), לַשְׁמִד +Is 23^{11}, etc.;—**1.** *annihilate, exterminate:* acc. pers. vel gent., subj. י׳ vel pers. hum., Dt 1^{27} 2^{22} (+מִפְּנֵי pers.), 6^{15} (+מֵעַל־פְּנֵי הָאֲדָמָה), 9^{20}+16 t. Dt, Jos 7^{12} (acc. הַחֵרֶם; +מִקִּרְבְּכֶם), 9^{24}+4 t. Jos (all R^{D}), 2 K 14^{16} 1 K 13^{34} Am 9^{8} Is 13^{9} 26^{14} Est 3$^{6.13}$+23 t.; acc. פִּרְיוֹ וְשָׁרָשָׁיו (fig.) Am 2^{9}, cf. Ez 34^{16} (but Vrss Co Toy al. [not Hi Krae] אֶשְׁמֹר); הַשׁ׳ אֶת־שְׁמִי 1 S 24^{22} (Gi v^{21}), 2 S 22^{38} 1 K 16^{12} ψ 145^{20}; הַשְׁמֵד as subst., Is 14^{23} besom of *extermination;* acc. אֶת־הַבַּעַל 2 K 10^{28}, of extirpating Baal-worship מִיִּשְׂרָאֵל. †**2.** *destroy,* cities Mi 5^{13}, fortresses Is 23^{11}, bamoth Lv 26^{30} (H), Nu 33^{52} (P; ‖ אִבֵּד), חֹזֶק מַמְלְכוֹת הַגּוֹיִם Hg 2^{22}.

שֶׁמֶד **n.pr.m.** 1 Ch 8^{12} Gi Baer, v. שֶׁמֶר. p. 1037 8106

[שָׁמָה] **n.pr.m.** whence the following: 8126

†שָׁמָתִי **adj.gent.** in Caleb, c. art. as n.coll. 8126 הַשּׁ׳ 1 Ch 2^{53}; Ησαμαθειμ[ν], ὁ Σαμαθι.

שׁמה (appar. √of foll.; Sta$^{§\ 324\ a}$; so Thes, cp. Ar. سَمَا be high, lofty (or is this secondary?); Jen$^{Kosmol.\ (1890),\ 6}$ cp. As. *šamû, id.* (>*šamû*=*sparkle,* Id$^{ZK\ ii\ (1885),\ 53}$); cf. Dl^{WB}).

[שָׁמַי] **n.m.**$^{Dt\ 33,\ 28}$ only pl. שָׁמַיִם$_{421}$ (Sta$^{§\ 324\ a}$) 8064 **heavens, sky** (NH *id.;* As. *šamû,* pl. *šamê, šamûtu,* also *šamâmu,* cf. Ph. שמם; Sab. סמה Hom$^{Chr\ 46,\ 124}$; Ar. سَمَاءٌ; Eth. ሰማይ: Aram. שְׁמַיָּא, ܫܡܝܐ; Palm. Nab. שמ(י)ן in n.pr. (cpd. with בעל) Lzb^{153} GACooke^{45}; on pl. form v. Ba$^{ZMG\ xlii\ (1888),\ 341\ f.}$);—abs. שׁ׳ Gn 1^{1}+, ־מַיִם Gn 2^{4}+; הַשָּׁמַיְמָה Ex 9^{8}+; cstr. שְׁמֵי Dt 10^{14}+9 t.; sf. שָׁמֶיךָ ψ 8^{4}+2 t., שָׁמָיו Dt 33^{28}, שְׁמֵיכֶם Lv 26^{19}, c. vb. pl., Ho 2^{23};—**1. a.** *visible heavens, sky,* where stars, etc., are Ju 5^{20} Gn 15^{5} (J), Dt 4^{19} Gn 1$^{14.15.17}$ (P), hence כּוֹכְבֵי הַשּׁ׳ 22^{17} (JE)+9 t. (usu. as countless), (כָּל־)צְבָא הַשּׁ׳ Dt 4^{19} Je 8^{2}+ (צ׳ **1 c**; rarely of angels, צ׳ **1 b**); before which fowl fly Gn 1^{20} (P), cf. Dt 4^{17} Je 8^{7} Pr 30^{19}, עוֹף הַשּׁ׳ Gn 2^{19} (J), 1^{19} (P)+(עוֹף **1**), צִפּוֹר שׁ׳+ψ 8^{9}, נִשְׁרֵי שׁ׳ +La 4^{19}; as רָקִיעַ (q.v.) Gn 1^{8} (P), ψ 19^{2}, with waters beneath and above Gn 1^{9} (P, cf. v^{7}), ψ 148^{4}, darkened with clouds 1 K 18^{45}, cleared by wind Jb 26^{13}; whence comes rain Gn 8^{2} (J), Ju 5^{4} Dt 11^{11}+, and dew Gn 27^{28} (J), v^{39} (E), Dt 33^{28} (poem)+, cf. בִּרְכֹת שׁ׳ +Gn 49^{25} (poem in J), מֶגֶד שׁ׳ +Dt 33^{13} (poem), but also (destructive) fire 2 K 1$^{10.10}$ Jb 1^{16}+ (v. also **2 a** infr.); הֹבְרֵי שׁ׳ Is 47^{13}, i.e. astrologers, cf. אותות הַשּׁ׳ Je 10^{2}; as high Gn 11^{4} (J), Am 9^{2} (opp. שְׁאוֹל), v^{6} (opp. אֶרֶץ)+, עַד־לֵב הַשּׁ׳ Dt 4^{11}; as over all the earth, תַּחַת (כָּל־)הַשּׁ׳ Gn 6^{17} 7^{19} (both P), Dt 2^{25} Ec 1^{13} מִתַּחַת וגו׳ (of extermination) Ex 17^{14} (E), Dt 7^{24} 9^{14}+; specif. of Israel, שָׁמֶיךָ Dt 28^{23}, שְׁמֵיכֶם Lv 26^{19} (H); בֵּין הַשּׁ׳ וּבֵין הָאָרֶץ 2 S 18^{9} (hung from tree), 1 Ch 21^{16} (of angel), cf. Ez 8^{3} (Ezekiel in vision), Zc 5^{9} (flying ephah); מִקְצֵה הַשּׁ׳ וְעַד־קְצֵה

הַשׁ׳ of limits of horizon Dt 4^{32}, cf. 30^{4} Ne 1^{9} ψ 19^{7}; as made by God Je 51^{15} (opp. תֵּבֵל), ψ 8^{4}+; enduring Dt 11^{21} Jb 14^{12} ψ 89^{30}; esp. (הַ)שׁ׳ וְ(הָ)אָרֶץ =universe (cf. in Sab., SabDenkm$^{No. 41. 42, l. 3}$), Dt 3^{24} Gn 1^{1} (P) + (esp. Dt Je Is^{2} ψψ), + הַיָּם Ex 20^{11} Hg 2^{6}, etc., + מַיִם מִתַּחַת לָאָרֶץ Ex 20^{4}=Dt 5^{8}, cf. Pr 30^{4}, etc.; opp. תְּהוֹם Pr 8^{27} (+ אֶרֶץ v^{29}); שׁ׳ חֲדָשִׁים וְהָאָרֶץ חֲדָשָׁה as part of future glory †Is 65^{17} 66^{22}. **b.** phrases are: אֲרֻבּוֹת הַשׁ׳ (letting rain through) †Gn 7^{11} 8^{2} (P), Mal 3^{10} (fig.), cf. הֲיַעֲשֶׂה י׳ א׳ בַּשׁ׳ 2 K 7$^{2.19}$, so דַּלְתֵי שׁ׳ †ψ 78^{23} (for manna), cf. דְּגַן שׁ׳ †v^{24}, לֶחֶם שׁ׳ †105^{40}; מוֹסְדוֹת הַשׁ׳ 2 S 22^{8} (‖ הָאָרֶץ; in ‖ ψ 18^{8} (מ׳ הָרִים), עַמּוּדֵי שׁ׳ Jb 26^{11}, חוּג שׁ׳ 22^{14}; *towards the sky* is הַשָּׁמַיְמָה Jos 8^{20} (J), Ex 9$^{8.10}$ (P), Jb 2^{12} Ju 13^{20} 20^{40} 2 Ch 6^{13}; עַל־הַשָּׁמַיִם Ex 9$^{22.23}$ 10$^{21.22}$ (all E), אֶל־שׁ׳ Dt 32^{40} (poem), Dn 12^{7}, שׁ׳ alone 1 K 8$^{22.54}$ Jb 35^{5} Pr 23^{5}. **2. a.** as abode of God (י׳) 1 K 8$^{30.32}$ + oft., where he sits enthroned ψ 2^{3} Is 66^{1}, etc., cf. רֹכֵב שׁ׳ Dt 33^{26} (poem), ψ 68^{34}, whence he rains brimstone Gn 19^{24} (J), bread Ex 16^{4} (E), cf. Ne 9^{15}, casts hailstones Jos 11^{11} (E), talks with Israel Ex 20^{22} (E; Gi v^{19})+, cf. Gn 21^{17} 22$^{11.15}$ (E), looks down Dt 26^{15}+, hears his people ψ 20^{7} + 10 t. Chr, etc.; he thunders בַּשׁ׳ 1 S 2^{10} ψ 18^{14}, ‖ מִן־שׁ׳ 2 S 22^{14}; he bends (נטה) שׁ׳ to come down v^{10}=ψ 18^{10}, cf. ψ 144^{5} and (*rend*) Is 63^{19}; נִפְתְּחוּ הַשׁ׳ Ez 1^{1} in vision of God, cf. שַׁעַר הַשׁ׳ Gn 28^{17} (E; + בֵּית אֱלֹהִים); though even שְׁמֵי הַשׁ׳ *the highest heavens* cannot hold him †Dt 10^{14} 1 K 8^{27}=2 Ch 6^{18}, 2 Ch 2^{5} Ne 9^{6} ψ 148^{4}, שְׁמֵי שְׁמֵי־קֶדֶם 68^{34}; he is called אֱלֹהֵי הַשׁ׳ (post-ex. title) Ezr 1^{2}=2 Ch 36^{23}, + 11 t. Ezr Ne, Jon 1^{9} (cf. Aram., Dn 2$^{18.19.37.44}$; in Gn 24^{7} add c. 𝔊 וֵאלֹהֵי הָאָרֶץ, as v^{3}), אֵל־הַשׁ׳ ψ 136^{26}; his sword is בַּשׁ׳ Is 34^{5}, but also his חֶסֶד ψ 36^{6}, צֶדֶק 85^{12}, אֱמוּנָה 89^{3}, his word fixed 119^{89}.—שׁ׳ are †שָׁמָיו (of Israel) Dt 33^{28} (poem), †שְׁמֵיכֶם Lv 26^{19}; †שָׁמֶיךָ ψ 8^{4} 144^{5}, †שְׁמֵי י׳ La 3^{66}, †שְׁ׳ קָדְשׁוֹ ψ 20^{7}. †**b.** Elijah taken up הַשׁ׳ in whirlwind 2 K 2^{1}, cf. v^{11}. **3.** הַשׁ׳ personified in various relations Is 1^{2} Je 2^{12} Jb 15^{15} ψ 19^{2} 50^{6}=97^{6}, 89^{6} 148^{4}. †**4.** מְלֶכֶת הַשׁ׳ v. מ׳ p. 573.

8033, 8047 I, II. שַׁמָּה v. שׁמם. שָׁמָּה v. שָׁם. p. 1027, 1031

8049 †**שַׁמְהוּת** **n.pr.m.** captain of Israel 1 Ch 27^{8},

8048 Σαλαωθ, A 𝔊L Σαμαωθ; prob.=II. שַׁמָּה **3 b**, p. 1031

8050 **שְׁמוּאֵל** v. sub שֵׁם. p. 1028

8048, 8054 **שַׁמּוֹת** v. II. שַׁמָּה, √שׁמם. p. 1031

שַׁמַּי v. √שׁמם. **שְׁמִידָע**, -דָעִי v. שֵׁם. p. 1029, 1031 8060-62

שַׁמְלַי Ezr 2^{46}, v. שַׂלְמַי. p. 969 8014, 8073

†[**שָׁמַט**] **vb. let drop** (NH *id.*, *loosen*, 8058
detach, draw away, Niph. *slip off*; Aram. שְׁמַט *loosen, pull away*; ܫܡܛ *draw* sword, *draw* or *pull away*; Ar. سَمَطَ is *hang, suspend*, II. *release* debtor (Ḳam), سِمْطٌ *string* of pearls);—**Qal** *let drop, fall*: *Imv.* mpl. sf. + *Impf.* 3 ms. sf. וַיִּשְׁמְטוּהָ (final ו dittogr.) שִׁמְטוּהוּ 2 K 9^{33} he said, *Let her fall, and they let her fall*; then fig., of letting land rest in seventh year, 2 ms. sf.: תִּשְׁמְטֶנָּה Ex 23^{11} (E); *Pf.* 2 ms. וְשָׁמַטְתָּה Je 17^{4} *thou shalt let drop* thy hand (read יָדְךָ for וּבְךָ JDMich and mod.) from (מִן) thine inheritance, i.e. abandon it; *Inf. abs.* שָׁמוֹט Dt 15^{2} *let fall* (a debt in seventh year; v. מַשֶּׁה p. 674^{b}).—Pf. 3 pl. שָׁמְטוּ הַבָּקָר 2 S 6^{6}=1 Ch 13^{9} is dub., most naturally either *they let the oxen fall* (slip, stumble), or (as 𝔗) *the oxen let it fall* (reading שְׁמָטוֹ, sc. the ark); > Thes *the oxen ran away*; 𝔖 *slipped* (the yoke)? v. further Dr. **Niph.** *Pf.* 3 pl. נִשְׁמְטוּ ψ 141^{6} their judges *have been thrown down*. **Hiph.** 2 ms. (?) juss. (?) תַּשְׁמֵט Dt 15^{3} *thou shalt cause* thy hand *to let drop*, etc.; Ba$^{NB 147}$ **Qal**; < read תִּשְׁמֹט (cf. Dr), יָדְךָ subj.

†**שְׁמִטָּה** **n.f. a letting drop** of exactions, 8059
a (temporary) remitting: תַּעֲשֶׂה שׁ׳ Dt 15^{1} (at end of seven years), v^{2} כִּי קָרָא שׁ׳ לי׳; whence seventh year is שְׁנַת הַשׁ׳ v^{9} 31^{10}.

שְׁמִירָמוֹת v. sub שֵׁם. p. 1029 8070

†[**שָׁמֵם**] **vb. be desolated, appalled** (con- 8074
nex. of mngs. not clear) (NH *id.*; JAram. שְׁמַם Ithp. *be dazed*);—**Qal** *Pf.* 3 fs. שָׁמֵמָה Ez 35^{15}, etc.; *Impf.* 3 ms. יִשֹּׁם 1 K 9^{8}+, 3 mpl. יָשֹׁמּוּ Jb 17^{8} ψ 40^{16}, etc.; *Imv.* mpl. שֹׁמּוּ Je 2^{12}; *Inf. cstr.* (?) metapl. שַׁמּוֹת Ez 36^{3} (Ges$^{§ 67 r}$, but v. infra);—תֵּשַׁם, etc. (v. [יָשַׁם]) are placed here by most; Ez 6^{6} reads תִּישַׁמְנָה, v. Ges$^{§ 67 p dd}$;—*Pt.* שׁוֹמֵם La 3^{11} (v. also **Pō.**); f. שֹׁמֵמָה (Ges$^{§ 84 a s}$) 2 S 13^{20}+; pl. שׁוֹמֵמִין La 1^{14}, etc.;—**1.** *be desolated*, of Tamar 2 S 13^{20} (i.e. deflowered, or deserted; others *appalled*), of pers. elsewhere late La 1^{16}; נְתָנַנִי שֹׁמֵמָה v^{13}, שָׂמַנִי שׁ׳ 3^{11}; pt. as n.f. בְּנֵי שׁוֹמֵמָה Is 54^{1} (opp. בְּעוּלָה) [Dn 8^{13} + v. **Pō.**]; usu. of land, etc. (sts.=*deserted*), Is 49^{8} Ez 33^{28} (מֵאֵין עוֹבֵר), 35^{12} (read שָׁמֵמוּ Qr Co Toy Krae; > Kt שממה), v^{15}; הֶחֳרָבוֹת הַשֹּׁמְמוֹת 36^{4} (‖ הֶעָרִים הַנֶּעֱזָבוֹת); שַׁמּוֹת v^{3} is prob. corrupt, Co שְׁאָט as v^{5}, Hi-Sm

from נשׁם=שׁמה, Toy reads נָשֹׁם, Krae נָשֹׁם;—pt. fpl. as n.=*desolate places* Is 49^{19} 61^{4} (both || חֳרָבוֹת), v^{4} (cf. שְׁמָמָה 62^{4}); =*desolations* Dn 9$^{18.26}$. **2.** *be appalled, awestruck*, usu. at (עַל) judgments on others, Lv 26^{32} (H), Je 2^{12} (v. II. [חָרֵב]), Ez 26^{16} 27^{35} 28^{19} Is 52^{14} Jb 17^{8}, cf. 1 K 9^{8} =2 Ch 7^{21}, Je 18^{16} 19^{8} 49^{17} 50^{13}; on oneself ψ 40^{16} (עַל־עֵקֶב).—Is 42^{14} v. [נשׁם]. **Niph.** *Pf.* 3 fs. נָשַׁמָּה Je 12^{11}+, 3 pl. נָשַׁמּוּ Zp 3^{6}+; *Pt.* f. נְשַׁמָּה Ez 36^{34}+, etc.;—=**Qal**: **1.** *be desolated*, of roads Lv 26^{22} (H), Is 33^{8}, bamoth Am 7^{9} (|| יֶחֱרָבוּ), altars Ez 6^{4}; cf. 25^{3} 32^{15} Zp 3^{6} Zc 7^{14} Jo 1^{17} ψ 69^{26}; of lands Ez 29^{12} 30^{7} 36$^{34.35}$, cities Is 54^{3} (opp. יוֹשִׁיבוּ), cf. Ez 36^{35} Am 9^{14} Je 33^{10}; הַנְּשַׁמָּה Ez 36^{36} *the desolated* (sc. land, in fig.). **2.** *be appalled* Je 4^{9} La 4^{5} Ez 4^{17} 30^{7}, c. עַל rei Jb 18^{20}. **Pō'.** *Pt.* **1.** וָאֵשְׁבָה מְשׁוֹמֵם Ezr 9^{3} *I sat appalled*, cf. v^{4}. **2.** transit. *appalling, causing horror* (Dr$^{Dn\ 150\ f.}$): (הַ)שִּׁקּוּץ מְשֹׁמֵם Dn 11^{31}, + perh. 9$^{27\,a}$ (v. שִׁקּוּץ); so also שִׁקּ׳ שֹׁמֵם 12^{11} (on ׳שׁ v. Ges $^{§\,52\,s}$), הַפֶּשַׁע שֹׁמֵם 8^{13} *the crime causing horror*, and ׳שׁ as n. *horror-causer, appaller*, 9$^{27\,b}$. **Hiph.** *Pf.* 2 ms. הֲשִׁמּוֹתָ Jb 16^{7}, etc.; *Impf.* 3 ms. יַשִּׁים (Ges$^{§\,67\,y}$) Je 49^{20} 50^{45}, 3 mpl. sf. וַיְשִׁמֵּם 1 S 5^{6}, 1 pl. נַשִּׁים Nu 21^{30}, etc.; *Imv.* mpl. הָשַׁמּוּ (Ges $^{§\,67\,v}$) Jb 21^{5}; *Inf. abs.* הַשְׁמֵם Mi 6^{13}; *Pt.* מַשְׁמִים Ez 3^{15};—**1.** *devastate, ravage*, acc. pers. 1 S 5^{6} Ez 20^{26} Ho 2^{14} (fig. of vine), Jb 16^{7}; acc. loc. Lv 26$^{31.32}$ (H), Je 10^{25} Ez 30$^{12.14}$ ψ 79^{7}, so (acc. om.) Nu 21^{30} (poem in JE), Mi 6^{13};—Ez 14^{8} v. שׂים **Hiph.** **2. a.** *appal*, acc. pers., c. עַל *at*, Je 49^{20} 50^{45} Ez 32^{10}. **b.** inwardly trans., וָאֵשֵׁב מַשׁ׳ 3^{15} *shewing horror*, Jb 21^{5} (Bu Niph. הִשַּׁמּוּ). **Hoph.** *Inf. cstr.* כָּל־יְמֵי הָשַּׁמָּה (sc. הָאָרֶץ) Lv 26^{34} (H) *all the days of* (its) *being desolate*, so v^{35} 2 Ch 36^{21}; Aramaizing, בְּהָשַּׁמָּה (Ges$^{§\,67\,y}$) Lv 26^{43}. **Hithpō'.** *Impf.* 3 ms. יִשְׁתּוֹמֵם ψ 143^{4}, etc.;—**1.** *be appalled, astounded*, כִּי *that, because*, Is 59^{16} 63^{5}; עַל rei Dn 8^{27}; בְּתוֹכִי יִשְׁתּ׳ לִבִּי ψ 143^{4} (cf. 1 pl. נשתומם Ecclus 43^{24}). **2.** *cause oneself desolation, ruin*, Ec 7^{16}.

8076 †שָׁמֵם **adj. devastated**;—׳שׁ of sanctuary Dn 9^{17}; f. שְׁמֵמָה of land Je 12^{11}.

8077 שְׁמָמָה$_{55}$ **n.f. a devastation, waste**;—abs. ׳שׁ Ex 23^{29}+; pl. cstr. שִׁמְמוֹת Je 51^{26}+;—*waste*, usu. of land, city, houses, etc., Ex 23^{29} (E), Is 1^{7} (prob. del., with words foll. Stu$^{JP\ Th.\ 1877,\ 714}$ FB $^{JBL\ (1890),\ 84}$), Lv 26^{33} (H), Je 4^{27} + 14 t. Je (|| מֵאֵין אָדָם וגו׳ 32^{43}, מֵאֵין יֹשֵׁב 34^{22}), Ez 6^{14} + 18 t. Ez (35^{7a} read שְׁמָמָה וּמְשַׁמָּה for MT שְׁמָמָה וּשְׁמָמָה, so Hi Co Toy Krae al.) +; of prince, יִלְבַּשׁ שׁ׳ Ez 7^{27}; of idols Mi 1^{7}; כּוֹס שַׁמָּה וּשׁ׳ Ez 23^{33}.—Ez 35^{12}
v. שמם **Qal**. p. 1030 8074

שִׁמְמָה Ez 35^{7} v. foregoing. 8077

†שַׁמָּא **n. pr. m.** in Asher, 1 Ch 7^{37}, 8037
Σεμ(μ)α, etc.

†I. שַׁמָּה **n.f. waste, appalment** (24 t. Je);— 8047
abs. ׳שׁ Je 5^{30}+; pl. abs. שַׁמּוֹת ψ 46^{9};—**1.** *a waste*, of land, city, etc., Ho 5^{9} Is 5^{9} 13^{9} 24^{12} Zc 7^{14} Je 2^{15} 4^{7} 18^{16} 19^{8} 46^{19} 48^{9} 50^{3} 51$^{29.43}$, vine Jo 1^{7}; pers. ψ 73^{19}; כּוֹס שׁ׳ וּשְׁמָמָה Ez 23^{33}. **2.** *appalment, horror*, i.e. occasion of it; of people, land, etc., Dt 28^{37} 2 K 22^{19} Mi 6^{16} Zp 2^{15} Je 5^{30} 25$^{9.11.18.38}$ 29^{18} 44$^{12.22}$ 49$^{13.17}$ 50^{23} 51$^{37.41}$ 2 Ch 29^{8} 30^{7}; שׁ׳ הֶחֱזִקַתְנִי Je 8^{21}.

†II. שַׁמָּה **n.pr.m.** **1.** in Edom Gn 36$^{13.17}$ 8048
1 Ch 1^{37}, usu. Σομε. **2.** third son of Jesse
1 S 16^{9} 17^{13}, Σαμ(μ)α, 𝔊^{L} Σαμαα; v. שִׁמְעָה, שִׁמְעָא, 8092-93
שִׁמְעִי. **3.** Σαμαια(ς), etc., heroes of David: **a.** 8096
2 S 23^{11} (om. accid. || 1 Ch 11^{13} Dr), v^{33}. **b.** v^{25}
=שַׁמּוֹת 1 Ch 11^{27}, Σαμαωθ, Σαμ(μ)ωθ; prob. also 8054
שַׁמְהוּת 1 Ch 27^{8}. p. 1030, 1035 8049

שַׁמּוֹת **n.pr.m.** v. foregoing. 8054

†שַׁמַּי **n.pr.m.** in Judah: **1.** 1 Ch 2$^{28.28.32}$, 8060
Σαμ(μ)αι, etc. **2.** 1 Ch 2$^{44.45}$, Σαμαι. **3.** 1 Ch 4^{17}, Σεμεν, Σεμμαι, Σαμι.

†שִׁמָּמוֹן **n.[m.] appalment, horror** (Ba 8078
$^{NB\ 324,\ 336}$; another view Lag$^{BN\ 202,\ 203}$);—abs. Ez 4^{16} *drink water* בְּשׁ׳, so 12^{19}.

†מְשַׁמָּה **n.f.**=שַׁמָּה;—abs. **1.**=*devastation*, 4923
waste, וְנָתַתִּי אֶת־הָאָרֶץ שְׁמָמָה וּמ׳ Ez 6^{14} 33^{28}, cf. v^{29} 35^{3}, +35^{7a}, v. שְׁמָמָה; pl. מְשַׁמּוֹת Is 15^{16}=Je 48^{34}. **2.** *horror*, וְהָיְתָה חֶרְפָּה . . . וּמ׳ Ez 5^{15}.

שַׁמָּה v. שָׁם. שְׁמָמִית v. שְׂמָמִית. p. 971, 1027 8033, 8079

†I. [שָׁמֵן] **vb. grow fat** (NH Hiph. *id.*, 8080
also שָׁמֵן; Ar. سَمِنَ *be fat;* Aram. ܫܡܢ, esp. der. spec. and deriv.; שְׁמֵין adj. *fat:* As. *šamnu*, *fat;* Ph. (Pun.) שמן *oil*, so Palm. שמנא Lzb^{378}; on relation of meanings Frä^{147});—**Qal** *Pf.* 2 ms. שָׁמַנְתָּ Dt 32^{15} and *Impf.* 3 ms. וַיִּשְׁמַן v^{15} both of Israel (prosperous and arrogant) under fig. of *fat* beast; so *Pf.* 3 pl. שָׁמְנוּ Je 5^{28} (of wicked). **Hiph.** *Impf.* 3 mpl. וַיַּשְׁמִינוּ Ne 9^{25} *were sated and shewed fatness* (inner causat.); *Imv.* ms. הַשְׁמֵן Is 6^{10} *make fat* (dull, unreceptive), לֵב הָעָם הַזֶּה.

8082 †שָׁמֵן **adj. fat, robust**;—שׁ׳ m. Ju 3^{29}+, f. שְׁמֵנָה Gn 49^{20}+;—**1.** *fat, rich*, of food, Gn 49^{20} (poem in J), Is 30^{23} (+דָּשֵׁן), Hb 1^{16} (‖ בְּרִאָה); of land, *fertile* Nu 13^{20} (E), Ne $9^{25.35}$, pasturage Ez 34^{14} 1 Ch 4^{40}. (1 S 15^{9} v. מִשְׁנֶה **3**). **2.** *stout, robust*, of men Ju 3^{29} (‖ אִישׁ חָיִל; v. GFM); f. coll. (fig. of flock) Ez 34^{16} (+הַחֲזָקָה).

4924 †[שָׁמָן] **n.[m.] fat, fertile, place**;—pl. cstr. מִשְׁמַנֵּי הָאָרֶץ (Ges $^{§§ 20a, 93ee}$) Gn 27^{28} (poem in J; מִן partit.), v^{39} (poem in E; מִן priv. acc. to Thes Ew Di Gunk al.; < partit. here as v^{b}, 𝔙 [𝔊 ἀπὸ in both], AV RV Nö $^{Ency. Bib. 1184}$, cf. Dr).

8081 שֶׁ֫מֶן $_{192}$ **n.m.** $^{2 K 20, 13}$ (on appar. **f.** Ct 1^{3} cf. Albr $^{ZAW xvi (1896), 99, 106}$) **fat, oil**;—שׁ׳ abs. Gn 28^{28}+, cstr. Lv 8^{2}+; שֶׁ֫ 2 K 4^{6}+; sf. שַׁמְנִי Ho 2^{7}+, etc.; pl. שְׁמָנִים Am 6^{6}+; sf. שְׁמָנַיִךְ Ct 1^{3}, -נַיִךְ 4^{10};—**1.** *fat, fatness*: קֶרֶן בֶּן־שׁ׳ Is 5^{1} (of fertile slope); pl. גֵּיא־שְׁמָנִים $28^{1.4}$; of food (in fig.) $25^{6.6}$; lit. בְּשָׂרִי כָּחַשׁ מִשָּׁמֶן ψ 109^{24} (cf. צוֹם v^{a}), cf. מִפְּנֵי שׁ׳ Is 10^{27} (in fig., si vera l., mng. obscure; most now emend by conjecture; RS $^{JPh xiii (1885), 62}$ עָלָה מִצְּפוֹן שֹׁדֵד [v. also II. חבל], joining to v^{28}; Du Marti *has gone up from* P*e*ne-Rimmon [??], cf. Di-Kit). **2. a.** *oil*, specif. olive-oil, as rich product Dt 8^{8}+ (v. זַיִת); hence עֵץ שׁ׳ Is 41^{19} *oil-tree*, usu. explained as wild olive, *oleaster*, so Ne 8^{15} (‖ זַיִת), עֲצֵי שׁ׳ *oleaster-wood* 1 K $6^{23.31.32.33}$; once שׁ׳ הַמֹּר Est 2^{2} (v. מֹר p. 600^{b}; מ׳ also in holy anointing oil Ex 30^{23}). **b.** שׁ׳ as staple (condiment) Nu 11^{8} (J; v. לשד), of value 1 K $17^{12.14.16}$ 2 K $2^{4.6.7}$+4 t.; symb. of plenty Dt 32^{13} 33^{24} Jb 29^{6}; ascribed (falsely) to gift of Baals Ho 2^{7}; as royal treasure 2 K 20^{13}=Is 39^{2}, cf. 1 K 5^{25} (שׁ׳ כָּתִית, v. כ׳)=2 Ch $2^{9.14}$+3 t.; tribute Ho 12^{2}, art. of trade Ez 27^{17}; odoriferous Pr 27^{9} Ct 1^{3} 4^{10}, שׁ׳ רוֹקֵחַ Ec 10^{1}, so (fig.) Ct 1^{3} Ec 7^{1}; Pr. 27^{16} is corrupt, v. Toy; sign of luxury Ez 16^{13} Pr 21^{17}, of prosperity Ez 16^{20}. **c.** שׁ׳ as medicament Is 1^{6}; as unguent, for shield 2 S 1^{21}, person Am 6^{6} Mi 6^{15} Dt 28^{40} Ez 16^{9} Est 2^{12} ψ 92^{11} 104^{15}, not for mourner 2 S 14^{2}; on head, token of happiness Ec 9^{8}, of hospitality, דִּשַּׁנְתָּ בַשּׁ׳ רֹאשִׁי ψ 23^{5} (fig.), in sim. 133^{2} 141^{5}. **d.** for anointing king, פַּךְ הַשּׁ׳ 1 S 10^{1} 2 K $9^{1.3}$, cf. v^{6}, c. קֶרֶן 1 S $16^{1.13}$ 1 K 1^{39}; cf. בְּשׁ׳ קָדְשִׁי מְשַׁחְתִּיו ψ 89^{21}. **e.** in various figs., of joy שׁ׳ שָׂשׂוֹן Is 61^{3} ψ 45^{8}; soft words 55^{22} Pr 5^{3}; as penetrating 109^{18}; as clear, transparent Ez 32^{14}. **f.** used in primitive worship, poured on stone Gn 28^{18} (E), 35^{14} (J). **g.** in later ritual: for anointing priests, tabern., altar utensils, etc. (P), made of various ingred., שׁ׳ זַיִת among them, Ex 30^{24}, שׁ׳ הַמִּשְׁחָה 25^{6} Lv $8^{2.10.12}$+11 t.; שׁ׳ מִשְׁחַת־קֹדֶשׁ Ex $30^{25.25}$+2 t.; שׁ׳ מ׳ י׳ Lv 10^{7}, שׁ׳ מ׳ אֱלֹהָיו 21^{12}; שׁ׳ הַקֹּ׳ Nu 35^{25}; שׁ׳ alone Lv 14^{10}+12 t. Lv 14; for lighting Ex 25^{6}+6 t.+שׁ׳ זַיִת זָךְ כָּתִית Ex 27^{20} Lv 24^{2} (v. כָּתִית); poured upon מִנְחָה Lv 2^{1}+5 t., cf. 5^{11} Nu 5^{15}; smeared (v. מָשַׁח) upon wafers Ex 29^{2} Lv 2^{4}+, and cakes (or mixed in the making? cf. בָּלַל) Ex 29^{2} Lv $2^{4.5}$+, so סֹלֶת בַּשׁ׳ Lv 2^{7}, etc. (c. 45 t. in all), חַלַּת לֶחֶם שׁ׳ Ex 29^{23} Lv 8^{26}. **h.** for use in temple 1 Ch 9^{29}. **i.** for תְּרוּמָה in Ezekiel's temple Ez $45^{14.14}$+7 t. 45, 46. †**j.** efficacy denied Mi 6^{7}. †**k.** offered to idols Is 57^{9} Ez $16^{18.19}$ 23^{41}.—Vid. Macalister $^{Hast. DB Oil}$ ARSKennedy $^{Ency. Bib. Oil}$.

†אַשְׁמַנִּים (elative, Ges $^{§§ 85b, 133a}$; on נּ v. Id. 820
$^{§§ 20a, 93ee}$) appar. **n.[m.] pl.** בָּא׳ כַּמֵּתִים Is 59^{10} perhaps: (we are) *among the stout* (RV *lusty*) *like dead men*, cf. Di-Kit; or abstr. *in* (actual) *vigour* (Buhl) > AV (after Jos Ki fr. אָשֵׁם Ho 14^{1} '*be desolate*') *in desolate places* (other conj. v. Che ^{Hpt} Marti).

†[מִשְׁמָן] **n.[m.] fatness**;—cstr. וּמִשְׁמַן 4924
בְּשָׂרוֹ יֵרָזֶה Is 17^{14} (fig.); pl. concr.: *stout, vigorous, ones*, sf. מִשְׁמַנָּיו Is 10^{16} (opp. רָזוֹן; on form v. Ges $^{§ 93pp}$), מִשְׁמַנֵּיהֶם ψ 78^{31}; =*fertile spots*, cstr. מִשְׁמַנֵּי
מְדִינָה Dn 11^{24}. Cf. also 1 S 15^{9}, v. מִשְׁנֶה **3.** p. 1041 4932

†[מַשְׁמָן] **n.[m.] fat piece, tid bit**;—pl. 4924
מַשְׁמַנִּים (Ges $^{l. c.}$) Ne 8^{10} (for eating; ‖ מַמְתַקִּים for drinking).

†מַשְׁמַנָּה (Ges $^{l. c.}$) **n.pr.m.** a hero of David, 4925
1 Ch 12^{11} (v^{10} van d. H., who reads מִשׁ׳); 4925
Μασεμμανη, etc.; 𝔊L Μασαμαννη.

II. שמן, שמני (√ of following; meaning unknown).

שְׁמֹנֶה (less oft. שְׁמוֹנֶה), שְׁמֹנָה $_{109}$ **n.m. et f.** 8083
eight (on ◌ֶ cf. Ba $^{NB 20, 200}$ and (against him) Philippi $^{BAS ii. 364}$; Ar. ثَمَانِيَةٌ, ثَمَانٍ, Sab. (ת)חמני Hom $^{Chr 47, 122}$ DHM $^{ZMG xxxvii (1883), 369 f., 375}$; Aram. תְּמָנֵי, תְּמָנְיָא, ܬܡܢܐ, ܬܡܢܝܐ; Nab. תמונא, Palm. תמניא, Lzb ^{386}; NH=BH; Ph. שמן; Eth. ሰመንቱ: ሰማኒቱ: on As. equiv. v. Dl $^{§ 75}$);—**m.** (c. **n.f.**) alw. abs. שְׁמֹנֶה Ju 3^{8}+40 t.; **f.** (c. **n.m.**) abs. שְׁמֹנָה 1 S 17^{12}+34 t., cstr. שְׁמֹנַת Nu 2^{24}+3 t. (cases of 8+10=18 are additional, v. infr.); pl. שְׁמֹנִים, 80, v. infr.:—**1.** without other num.: **a.** שְׁמֹנֶה card., before n.pl. Ju 3^{8} 1 K 7^{10}+8 t.;

before n.sg. שָׁנָה 1 K 8^{17} (Kt; Qr pl.), 22^{1}; after n.pl. Ez 40^{31}; ordin. בִּשְׁנַת שׁ׳ לְ׳ 2 K 24^{12}, בִּשׁ׳ שָׁנִים לְ׳ 2 Ch 34^{3}. **b.** שְׁמֹנָה card., before n.pl. 1 S 17^{12}+3 t., +(n. om.) Je 14^{15}+2 t., also שׁ׳ אֵלֶּה Gn 22^{23} *these* 8, and, as round no., Mi 5^{4} 7 *and* 8 (i.e. plenty); after n.pl. Nu 29^{29} 2 Ch 29^{17}; ordin., בְּיוֹם שׁ׳ לְ׳ v^{17}. **c.** f. cstr. שְׁמֹנַת יָמִים Gn 17^{12} 21^{4}, שׁ׳ הַבָּקָר Nu 7^{8}. **2.** 8+10=18: **a.** c. **n.f.** שְׁמֹנֶה עֶשְׂרֵה, card.: bef. sg. שָׁנָה Ju 3^{14} +2 t., אַמָּה 1 K 7^{15}+2 t.; after n.pl. 1 Ch 26^{9} 2 Ch 11^{21}; n. om. Ezr 8^{18} Ne 7^{11}; ordin., בִּשְׁנַת שׁ׳ ע׳ לְ׳ 1 K 15^{1}+4 t.; בִּשׁ׳ ע׳ שָׁנָה לְ׳ 2 K 22^{3}+ 2 t.; הַשָּׁנָה שׁ׳ ע׳ שָׁנָה לְ׳ Je 32^{1}. **b.** c. **n.m.** שְׁמֹנָה עָשָׂר card.: bef. sg. אֶלֶף Ju 20^{44}+4 t.+ ψ 60^{2} (title), so read for שְׁנֵים ע׳, cf. 2 S 8^{13}= 1 Ch 18^{12}; before pl. Ezr 8^{9}; n. om. Gn 14^{14}; ordin., n. om. 1 Ch 24^{15} 25^{15}; שְׁמֹנַת עָשָׂר אֶלֶף Ju 20^{25}. **3.** c. other numerals: **a.** שְׁמֹנֶה מֵאוֹת 2 S 23^{8} (so read also ‖ 1 Ch 11^{11} Kit Benz, cf. Th We Dr al.), +16 t. **b.** שְׁמֹנָה אֶלֶף 1 Ch 12^{36} (v^{35} van d. H.), 23^{3}; שְׁמֹנַת אֲלָפִים Nu 2^{24}+3 t. **c.** שׁ׳, card., after tens 1 S 4^{15}+20 t.; before ten, only שׁ׳ וְעֶשְׂרִים בָּאַמָּה Ex 26^{2} 36^{9}; ordin., בִּשְׁנַת שְׁלֹשִׁים וּשׁ׳ שָׁנָה לְ׳ 1 K 16^{29} 2 K 15^{8}.

8066-67 **שְׁמִינִי**, **־ית** $_{31}$ **adj. num. eighth**;—בַּיּוֹם הַשְּׁמִינִי Ex 22^{29}+16 t.; הַחֹדֶשׁ הַשׁ׳ 1 K 6^{38}+4 t.; n.m. om. 1 Ch 24^{10}+4 t.; הַשָּׁנָה הַשְּׁמִינִת Lv 25^{22}; elsewhere only phr., עַל־הַשְּׁמִינִית 1 Ch 15^{21}, and titles ψ 6^{1} 12^{1}, usu. *acc. to the eighth key*, or *on the octave*, but wholly dubious.

8084 **שְׁמֹנִים** $_{38}$ **n.pl.indecl. an eighty**;—without other num.: sq. sg. שָׁנָה ψ 90^{10}+4 t., אִישׁ 2 K 10^{24} Je 41^{5}; sq. n.pl. 2 Ch 26^{17} Ezr 8^{8} Ct 6^{8}; n. om. 2 K 6^{25} 1 Ch 15^{9}; c. other num., card.: שׁ׳ אֶלֶף Nu 2^{9}+6 t.; שׁ׳ foll. units Gn 5^{25}+4 t.; precedes, Gn 16^{16}+4 t.; foll. 100, etc. 1 Ch 25^{7} +6 t.; precedes, Gn 5^{26}+2 t.; ordin., בִּשׁ׳ שָׁנָה וְאַרְבַּע מֵאוֹת שָׁנָה לְ׳ 1 K 6^{1}.

4924 [שְׁמֵנִים] ,שְׁמַנִּי v. שָׁמֵן. p. 1032

8085 **שָׁמַע** $_{1159}$ **vb. hear** (NH *id.*; Ph. שמע Lzb^{378}; As. *šemû*; Ar. سَمِعَ; Sab. סמע, mostly in deriv., esp. epith. div. סמע *he who hears* Hom Chr 124 Fell ZMG liv (1900), 250, 252 DHM Hofmus. No. 10, l. 1; Eth. ሰምዐ: Aram. שְׁמַע, ܫܡܰܥ, OAram. שמע Lzb^{378}; cf. also משמעת MI^{28} *obedience*);—**Qal** $_{1052}$ *Pf.* 3 ms. שׁ׳ Gn 24^{52}+, שָׁמֵעַ Je 36^{13}+3 t.; 2 fs. שָׁמַעַתְּ 1 K 1^{11}+2 t.; 3 pl. שָׁמְעוּ Ju 2^{17}+, etc.; *Impf.* 3 ms. יִשְׁמַע Ex 6^{30}+, 1 s. cohort. אֶשְׁמְעָה Nu 9^{8}, וָאֶשְׁמְעָה (on ־ָ cf. Ges § 10 h; Ol § 65 c qu. reading) Dn 8^{13}; 2 mpl. תִּשְׁמְעוּן Dt 8^{20}+, תִּשְׁמָעוּן Dt 1^{17}, etc.; *Imv.* ms. שְׁמַע Am 7^{16}+, שְׁמָעָה Jb 32^{10}+ (esp. ψψ), שְׁמָעָה Dn 9^{19}; fpl. שְׁמַעְנָה Is 32^{9} Je 9^{19}, שְׁמַעַן Gn 4^{23} (Ges § 46 f), etc.; *Inf. abs.* שָׁמוֹעַ Is 6^{9}+; cstr. שְׁמֹעַ 1 S 15^{22}+; sf. שָׁמְעוֹ Dt 29^{18}+, שָׁמְעָתוֹ Is 30^{19} (Ges § 45 d), etc.; *Pt.* שֹׁמֵעַ Gn 42^{23}+; f. שֹׁמַעַת Gn 18^{10}+, etc.;—**1.** subj. pers. hum. (vel rei personif.): **a.** *hear* (perceive by ear), acc. rei, esp. קוֹל Gn 3^{10} (J)+46 t., דבר(ים) Am 8^{11}+50 t., etc.; acc. חָכְמָה i.e. wise sayings 1 K 5^{14}+4 t.; so any utterance or sound (c. 150 t. in all)+(obj. om.) Dt 4^{33}+32 t.+(cl. temp.) 1 S 14^{27}+6 t.; very rarely c. ב, שׁ׳ בְּסוֹד י׳ Jb 15^{8}; c. obj. cl., כִּי Ex 4^{31}+52 t.+Is 39^{1b} (rd. כִּי שׁ׳ 𝔊 𝔖 ‖ 2 K 20^{12}), אֵת־אֲשֶׁר Jos 2^{10} 5^{1} (both R^{D}), מַה־ Ju 7^{11}+3 t.; without connect. שׁ׳ אֹתָהּ עָשִׂיתִי †2 K 19^{25}=Is 37^{26}; sg. orat. rect. †Is 40^{28} Zc 8^{23}. †**b.** acc. pers.+מְדַבֵּר *hear one speaking* Gn 27^{6} (J), Je 26^{7} Dn 8^{13}, so בֹּכֶה Nu 11^{10} (J), נִבָּא Je 20^{1}, מְקַלֶּלְךָ Ec 7^{21}; occas. pers. om., דְּבָרִים Gn 37^{17} (JE), אֶת־מִדַּבֵּר Ez 2^{2} 43^{6} (v. דבר **Hithp.**); acc. pers. only Dn 12^{7}. †**c.** c. לֵאמֹר only, *hear say* =*hear it said*, 1 S 13^{4} 2 S 19^{3} Dt 13^{13} Jos 22^{11} (P), 1 K 16^{16}; +עַל pers. *concerning* Gn 41^{15} (E), Is 37^{9}; אֶל pers. *id.* 2 K 19^{9}. **d.** *hear of, concerning*: (1) acc. rei, אֵת (כָּל־)אֲשֶׁר Ex 18^{1} 2 K 19^{11}+5 t., דבר(ים) 1 S 3^{11}+4 t., רָעָה Je 19^{3}+5 t., etc.; כַּאֲשֶׁר 1 S 23^{11} ψ 48^{9}, כָּזֹאת Is 66^{8} *hear of anything like this*, כָּאֵלֶּה Je 18^{13}; acc., etc., om. Ju 9^{46}+ 43 t.; (2) less oft. acc. pers. Jb 42^{5}, אֶל pers. Ez 19^{4}, pers. om. Dt 9^{2}; c. ב pers. *hear exultantly* of their fate †ψ 92^{12} (prob. imitated from ‖ הִבִּיט בְּ v^{a}; v. esp. ראה **8 a** (6)). †**e.** *hear*, abs., =have power to hear, 2 S 19^{36} (c. בְּקוֹל), Is 21^{3} 32^{3} Pr 20^{12} Zc 7^{11}; in sim. ψ 38^{15}; c. neg. of idols Dt 4^{28} ψ 115^{6}; fig. (spiritual power) Je 5^{21} Dt 29^{3} Ez 12^{2} Is 42^{20}.—Pr 21^{28} is probably corrupt, v. Toy. **f.** *hear with attention, interest, listen to* (sts. ‖ הֶאֱזִין, הִקְשִׁיב), acc. דבר(ים) (54 t.) Am 4^{1}+, esp. דבר(י) י׳ Nu 12^{6} (JE)+45 t.; אִמְרָה Is 28^{23}, קוֹל v^{23}, זֹאת Mi 3^{9}, etc.; oft. abs. Ju 5^{3}+ 57 t., +(neg.) ψ 38^{14} *pay no attention*; abs. לֵב שֹׁמֵעַ 1 K 3^{9}, אִישׁ שׁוֹמֵעַ Pr 21^{28}. †**g.** *understand* (language), שָׂפָה Gn 11^{7} (J), Is 33^{19}, לָשׁוֹן Dt 28^{49}, דְּבָרִים Ez 3^{6}, מַה־יְדַבֵּר Je 5^{15}, no acc. Gn 42^{23} (E), 2 K 18^{26}=Is 36^{11}. **h.** specif. of *hearing* a (judicial) case, דָּבָר Dt 1^{17}, cf. v^{17}; acc. om. בֵּין pers. v^{16}, of י׳ Ju 11^{10}; c. מִשְׁפָּט 1 K 3^{11}; לִשׁ׳ הַטּוֹב וְהָרָע 2 S 14^{17}, וְשֹׁמֵעַ אֵין לְךָ 15^{3}, cf. Jb 31^{35}.

†**i.** c. acc. pers. in polite address, *hear us (me)!* Gn 23$^{6.8.11.13.15}$ (all P), 1 Ch 28^{2} 2 Ch 13^{4} 15^{2} 20^{20}. **j.** *listen, give heed* (sts. ‖ הִקְשִׁיב), abs., Gn 42^{21} (E) + 18 t., + (usu. ‖ הִטָּה אֹזֶן), Je 7^{13} + 14 t. Je, + (opp. חָדַל) Ez 2^{5} + 3 t. Ez; + שִׂים עַל־לֵב Mal 2^{2}; *hear + do* Dt 5^{24} 2 K 18^{12}, etc.; = *consent, agree,* Gn 37^{27} (J), *grant request* Ju 11^{17}; c. לְ pers. (mostly late) Ju 19^{25} 1 S 30^{24} Jb 15^{17} + 16 t., לי׳ Ho 9^{17} Lv 26$^{14.18.21.27}$; לְדִבְרֵי י׳ 1 S 15^{1}, לְעֵצָה Pr 12^{15}. **k.** c. אֶל pers. + *listen to, yield to* Gn 49^{2} Ju 2^{17} + 69 t. (אֶל־י׳ 15 t., esp. Je 7^{26} + 10 t. Je), עַל pers. 2 K 20^{13}; אֶל־דִּבְרֵי etc., Dt 18^{19} Je 29^{19} + 14 t., עַל־דִּבְרֵי etc., 2 K 22^{13} + 3 t.; very rarely acc. rei 1 S 24^{10} (Gi v^{9}). **l.** שׁ׳ לְקוֹל = *id., obey,* Gn 3^{17} (J) + 11 t. + (לְקוֹל י׳) Ju 2^{20} Ex 15^{26} (JE). **m.** very oft., שׁ׳ בְּקוֹל = *obey* 1 S 8^{7} + 25 t., + שׁ׳ בְּקוֹל י׳ (י׳'s word, etc.) Dt 4^{30} Je 3^{13} + 65 t. (Dt 18 t., Je 18 t.). **n.** *obey,* c. acc. (דבר(ים) Jos 1^{18} + 2 t. + (ד׳ י׳) Je 11^{3} + 5 t. Je, 1 K 12^{24} = 2 Ch 11^{4}, etc.; acc. pers. Ex 6^{12} (P), 2 Ch 28^{11}. **o.** abs. *be obedient* (esp. to י׳) Is 1^{19} Mi 5^{14} Je 12^{17} + 4 t. Je + 7 t. **2.** י׳ (God) subj.: **a.** acc. קול, דברים, etc., Gn 21^{17} (E), 2 K 19$^{4.4.16}$, usually with favour implied Nu 20^{16} Dt 33^{7} +, so esp. acc. תְּפִלָּה, תְּחִנָּה, etc., 1 K 8^{45} ψ 6^{10} +. **b.** obj. cl. כִּי Gn 29^{33} (J). **c.** no obj. (32 t.) Is 59^{2} Je 22^{21}, usu. *hear and forgive, help,* etc., 1 K 8$^{30.32}$ Is 30^{19} +; *hear and be angry* ψ 78^{59}, cf. 55^{20}. **d.** = *be able to hear* Is 59^{1} ψ 94^{9}. **e.** שׁ׳ בְּקוֹל = *hear (and grant)* Gn 30^{6} (J) + 6 t. **f.** *hear and answer,* c. אֶל of cry, etc., Gn 21^{7} 16^{11} 1 K 8^{28} + 8 t.; c. אֶל pers. Dt 3^{26} + 12 t. **g.** c. לְ of utterance Je 18^{19} ψ 61^{6}; לְ pers. Jos 24^{10} (E). **h.** *hear,* acc. pers. + מִתְנוֹדֵד Je 31^{18}; favourably, c. acc. pers. Mi 7^{7} + 3 t., so, + לְ *concerning,* Gn 17^{20} (P); obj. om. 2 K 22^{19} ψ 22^{25} + 3 t. + ψ 34$^{7.18}$ (hear and deliver); c. cl. temp. Je 11^{14}. **Niph.** $_{42}$ *Pf.* 3 ms. נִשְׁמַע Gn 45^{16} +, etc.; *Impf.* 3 ms. יִשָּׁמַע Ex 23^{13} +, יִשָּׁמֵעַ 1 S 1^{13}, etc.; *Inf. cstr.* הִשָּׁמַע Est 2^{8}; *Pt.* f. נִשְׁמַעַת Je 51^{46}, etc.;— **1.** *be heard,* of voice, sound, etc., 1 S 1^{13} 1 K 6^{7} Jb 26^{14} (or 1 pl. **Qal** *Impf.*?); of a report, נִשׁ׳ . . . לֵאמֹר Gn 45^{16} (E); subj. cl., כִּי, Ne 6^{1} (לְ pers.), cf. cl. וְהַיְּהוּדִים חשְׁבִים Ne 6^{6}; v^{7} *be reported,* (לַמֶּלֶךְ) כַּדְּבָרִים הָאֵלֶּה; *be heard,* לִפְנֵי אֱלֹהֶיךָ Dn 10^{12}. **2.** *be heard of,* כָּמֹהוּ Dt 4^{32}. **3.** *be regarded, obeyed,* Ec 9^{17}; in 2 S 22^{45} = ψ 18^{45} it is *be obedient* (לִי), si vera l. (read perh. **Qal**, cf. Now). **4.** וַיִּשׁ׳ בְּקוֹלָם 2 Ch 30^{27} = (favourable) *hearing was granted to their voice.* †**Pi.** *Impf.* 3 ms. וַיְשַׁמַּע 1 S 15^{4} *he caused* the people (acc.) *to hear* (and respond, i.e. he assembled them), so 23^{8} (v. **Hiph. 1 c**). **Hiph.** $_{63}$ *Pf.* 3 ms. הִשְׁמִיעַ 1 K 15^{22} +, etc.; *Impf.* 3 ms. sf. יַשְׁמִעֵנִי Dt 30$^{12.13}$; 2 ms. juss. תַּשְׁמַע Ju 18^{25}, etc.; *Imv.* ms. sf. הַשְׁמִיעֵנִי ψ 143^{8}; fs. sf. הַשְׁמִיעִנִי Ct 2^{14} 8^{13}, etc.; *Inf. cstr.* לַשְׁמִעַ ψ 26^{7} (Ges$^{§ 53 q}$); *Pt.* מַשְׁמִיעַ Je 4^{15} +, etc.;—**1.** of man: **a.** *cause to hear,* acc. pers. + rei Dt 30$^{12.13}$ Ct 2^{14} 8^{13} + 4 t.; obj. rei om. (= *make proclamation to*) 1 K 15^{22}; obj. pers. om. Je 5^{20} +; acc. שָׁלוֹם †Is 52^{7} Na 2^{1} i.e. *proclaim* peace; אָוֶן †Je 4^{15} (מִן loc.); הַשׁ׳ קוֹל *utter a sound* Jos 6^{10} (J; ‖ הֵרִיעַ), cf. Ju 18^{25} (קוֹלֶךָ + עִמָּנוּ), Is 42^{2} 58^{4}; הַשׁ׳ קוֹל תְּהִלָּתוֹ †ψ 66^{8}, בְּקוֹל תוֹדָה †26^{7}. **b.** abs. as musical term, *sound aloud,* בִּמְצִלְתַּיִם לְהַשְׁמִיעַ 1 Ch 15^{19} (perhaps to mark the time, Gr$^{ψ 67}$ De: cf. 16^{5}; also ψ 150^{5} בְּצִלְצְלֵי שָׁמַע), מַשְׁמִיעִים 15$^{16.28}$ 16^{42}, לְהַשׁ׳ קוֹל אֶחָד 2 Ch 5^{13} i.e. prob. in unison (Prince$^{EB iii. 3241}$), Ne 12^{42}. **c.** abs. *make proclamation* (oft. ‖ הִגִּיד), Am 3^{9} 4^{5} Is 41^{26} Je 4^{5} + 6 t. Je. †**d.** הַשְׁמִיעוּ, acc. pers. + אֶל loc. = *summon* Je 50^{29}, עַל loc. 51^{27} (cf. **Pi.**). **2.** י׳ subj.: **a.** *cause to hear,* acc. pers. et rei Dt 4$^{10.36}$ (מִן loc.), 2 K 7^{6} + 4 t.; acc. pers. om. Is 30^{30} + 3 t.; acc. rei om. 44^{8} 48^{5}. †**b.** = *tell,* acc. pers. + כָּזֹאת Ju 13^{23}; acc. pers. only, Is 42^{9}; acc. rei only, 48^{3} Ez 36^{15} (אֵלַיִךְ). †**c.** abs., *make proclamation* Is 43^{12} 62^{11} (אֶל loc.).

†I. [שֶׁמַע] **n.** [**m.**] sound;—הַלְלוּהוּ בְּצִלְצְלֵי 8088
שָׁמַע ψ 150^{5} (‖ תְּרוּעָה).

†II. שֶׁמַע **n.pr.m.** usu. Σαμα(α), Σεμαα (cf. 8087
Sab. n.pr. סמע Hal^{509});—**1.** in Judah 1 Ch 2^{44},
שָׁמַע v^{43}. **2.** in Reuben 5^{8}. **3.** in Benj. 8^{13}
(= שִׁמְעִי v^{21}). **4.** post-ex. Ne 8^{4}, Σαμαιας. 8096

p. 1035

†שֵׁמַע **n.** [**m.**] hearing, report (on form 8088
cf. Lag$^{BN 143}$);—שׁ׳ abs. Is 23^{5}; cstr. v^{5} +; sf. שִׁמְעִי 66^{19}, etc.;—*report,* usu. c. genit. obj.: acc. with שֵׁמַע Gn 29^{13} (J) *the tidings about Jacob,* Is 23^{5} + (c. sf.) Nu 14^{15} (JE), Dt 2^{25} 1 K 10^{1} = 2 Ch 9^{1}, Na 3^{19} Hb 3^{2} Je 37^{5} 50^{43} Is 66^{9}; c. לְ genit. Is 23^{5}; לַעֲדָתָם Ho 7^{12} usu. *according to the report (heard by) their congregation* (!), but inexpl. and prob. corrupt, We Now; Marti (cf. Oettli) (כְּשֵׁמַע עַל־רָעָתָם as gloss) *according to their wickedness;* נָשָׂא שׁ׳ שָׁוְא Ex 23^{1} (E) *take up* (utter) *a false report;* לְשׁ׳ אֹזֶן ψ 18^{45} i.e. as soon as heard of, = *mere report* Jb 42^{5} (opp. personal knowledge), cf. שְׁמֻעָה 28^{22}.

8089 †[שֵׁמַע] **n. m.** $^{Est\ 9,4}$ report; — sf. שָׁמְעוֹ: וַיְהִי שׁ׳ Jos 6^{27}, *the report of him went*, etc.; שָׁמַע שׁ׳ 9^{9} (both R^{D}), Je 6^{24}; וְשׁ׳ הוֹלֵךְ בְּכָל־הַמְּדִינוֹת Est 9^{4}.

8090 †שְׁמַע **n. pr. loc.** in S. Judah, Jos 15^{26}, Σα(λ)μα(α).

8091 †שָׁמָע **n.pr.m.** a hero of David 1 Ch 11^{44}, Σαμαθα, Σαμμα (cf. OSem. שמע on scarab Cl Gann JAs 1883 Fev.-Mars, 135, No. 9; also on seal from Megiddo (1904), cf. Kau Mitth. u. Nachr. DPV, 1904, 2 ff.).

8092 שִׁמְעָא **n.pr.m. 1.** brother of David 2 S
21^{21} Qr (cf. Dr; Kt שמעי) Σεμεει, 𝔊L Σαμαα,
8093 = 1 Ch 20^{7}, third son of Jesse 1 Ch 2^{13}; = שִׁמְעָה
8048 1 S $13^{3.32}$, Σαμα(α), etc., שַׁמָּה (q.v.) 1 S 16^{9} 17^{13}.
8051 **2.** son of David 1 Ch 3^{5} (= שַׁמּוּעַ **1**), Σαμαν, Σαμαα.
3. Levites, Σομεα, Σαμα(α): **a.** 1 Ch 6^{15}. **b.** v ^{24}.

8092-93 שִׁמְעָה **n.pr.m.** v. שִׁמְעָא **1.** above p. 1031

8094 †שְׁמָעָה **n.pr.m.** c. art. הַשּׁ׳ הַגִּבְעָתִי 1 Ch 12^{3}, Αμα, Σαμαα, 𝔊L Ασμα.

8100 †שִׁמְעָת **n.pr.f.** $^{2\ Ch\ 24,\ 26}$ mother of one of Joash's murderers, 2 K 12^{22} (Ιεμουαθ), called Ammonitess 2 Ch 24^{26} (Σαμα(αθ)).

8101 †שִׁמְעָתִים **adj. gent. pl.** as **subst.,** family of scribes 1 Ch 2^{55}, Σαμαθ(ι)ειμ[ν].

8052 †שְׁמוּעָה **n.f.** report;—abs. שׁ׳ 1 S 4^{19}+, שְׁמֻעָה 2^{24}+; cstr. שְׁמֻעַת 2 S 4^{4}; sf. שְׁמֻעָתֵנוּ Is 53^{1}; pl. abs. שְׁמֻעוֹת Dn 11^{44};—**1.** *report*, sts. after שָׁמַע 1 S 2^{24} 4^{19} (= *news*), 1 K 10^{7} = 2 Ch 9^{6}, 2 K 19^{7} = Is 37^{7}, Je 51^{46}; שׁ׳ רָעָה Je 49^{23}, cf. ψ 112^{7}, and שׁ׳ טוֹבָה Pr 15^{30} 25^{25}; *tidings about* Saul 2 S 4^{4}; c. בָּאָה 13^{30} (+ לֵאמֹר), 1 K 2^{28} Ez 21^{12} Je 10^{22}, cf. 51^{46}+ (בָּאָה om.) v ^{46}; תָּבוֹא שׁ׳ אֶל־שׁ׳ Ez 7^{26}; שׁ׳ יְבַהֲלֻהוּ Dn 11^{44}; שְׁמוּעָתֵנוּ Is 53^{1} *the report that reached us*, cf. also Is $28^{9.19}$ Je 49^{14} Ob ^{1} (De Du al. specif. of prophetic message, but v. Gie Beiträge 155 f. We Now Ob 1). **2.** = *mention*, לֹא הָיְתָה סְדֹם לִשׁ׳ בְּפִיךָ Ez 16^{56}.

8051 †שַׁמּוּעַ **n.pr.m. 1.** son of David 2 S 5^{14} =
8092 1 Ch 14^{4}, Σαμμους[ε], Σαμαα (= שִׁמְעָא **2**). **2.** Reubenite, Nu 13^{4}, Σαμουηλ, Σαλαμιηλ, etc. **3.** Levite, Ne 11^{17} (= שְׁמַעְיָה 1 Ch 9^{16}), Σαμουει, etc.; 12^{18} (? same person), 𝔊L Σαμουε.

8095 שִׁמְעוֹן $_{44}$ **n.pr.m.** (cf. n.pr. שמעון in Palm. Lzb ^{378}; meaning doubtful; RS al. cp. سِمْعٌ, said to mean *offspring of hyena and wolf*; v. Hogg EB iv. 4531);—**1.** second son of Jacob and Leah, Συμεων: Gn 29^{33} (name expl. from שָׁמַע), 35^{23} Ex 1^{2} + 14 t. (assoc. esp. with Levi Gn $34^{25.30}$ 49^{5}). **2.** tribal name Ju $1^{3.3.17}$ Nu 1^{6}+; so בְּנֵי שׁ׳ Nu 1^{22} + 7 t., מַטֵּה שׁ׳ Nu 1^{23} 2^{12} 13^{5}; מַטֵּה בְנֵי שׁ׳ 10^{19} 34^{20} Jos $19^{1.8}$ 21^{9} 1 Ch 6^{50}. †**3.** post-ex. Jew with foreign wife Ezr 10^{31}.

†שִׁמְעֹנִי **adj. gent.** c. art. as n. coll., Nu 8099
25^{14} 26^{14} 1 Ch 27^{16}; מַטֵּה הַשּׁ׳ Jos 21^{4}.

I. שִׁמְעִי $_{43}$ **n.pr.m.** usu. Σεμεει: **1.** in Benj.: 8096
a. 2 S $16^{5.7.13}$ $19^{17.19.22.24}$, 1 K 2^{8} + 10 t. 1 K 2. †**b.** 1 K 1^{8}, perh. = 4^{18}. **2.** a Ramathite 1 Ch 27^{27}. †**3.** Levites: **a.** 'son' of Gershon Ex 6^{17} Nu 3^{18} 1 Ch 6^{2} $23^{7.9.10.10}$. **b.** 6^{14}. **c.** v ^{27}. **d.** 25^{17}. **e.** 2 Ch 29^{14}. **f.** $31^{12.13}$. **g.** Ezr 10^{23}. †**4.** brother of Zerub. 1 Ch 3^{19}. †**5.** in Simeon $4^{26.27}$.
†**6.** in Reuben 5^{4}. †**7.** 1 Ch 8^{13} = (II.) שֶׁמַע v ^{13}. 8087
†**8.** post-ex. names: **a.** Ezr 10^{33}. **b.** v ^{38} (cf. **3 g** supr.). †**9.** grandfather of Mordecai
Est 2^{5}. **10.** 2 S 21^{21} Kt (Qr שִׁמְעָא q. v. **1**). 8092

†II. שִׁמְעִי **adj. gent.** of **3 a**;—c. art. as 8097
n. coll. הַשּׁ׳ Nu 3^{21}; cf. Zc 12^{13}.

†שְׁמַעְיָה(וּ) **n.pr.m.** Σαμαιας, etc.: שְׁמַעְיָה, 8098
1. prophet, Rehob.'s time 1 K 12^{22} 2 Ch $12^{5.7.15}$; = ־יָהוּ 11^{2}. **2.** Jer.'s time: **a.** false proph. Je $29^{31.31.32}$ = ־יָהוּ v ^{24}. **b.** ־יָהוּ 36^{12}. **3.** ־יָהוּ a prophet's father 26^{20}. **4.** descendant of Zerub. 1 Ch $3^{22.22}$. **5.** in Simeon 4^{37}. **6.** in Reuben 5^{4}. **7.** Levites: **a.** 1 Ch 9^{14}. **b.** v ^{16} = שַׁמּוּעַ **3**. **c.** $15^{8.11}$. **d.** 24^{6}. **e.** $26^{4.6.7}$. **f.** 2 Ch 29^{14}. **g.** Ezr 8^{16}. **h.** Ne 11^{15}. Also ־יָהוּ **i.** 2 Ch 17^{8}. **j.** 31^{15}. **k.** 35^{9}. **8.** companions of Ezra: **a.** Ezr 8^{13}. **b.** 10^{21}. **c.** v ^{31}. **9.** of Neh.: **a.** Ne 3^{29}. **b.** 6^{10}. **10.** priests: **a.** Ne 10^{9} 12^{42}. **b.** v $^{6.18}$. **c.** v ^{35}. **d.** v ^{36}. **11.** a prince v ^{34}.

אֶשְׁתְּמוֹעַ v. p. 84. 851

ישמעאל יִשְׁמָעֵאל $_{48}$ **n. pr. m.** (*Ēl heareth*; Sab. 3458
ישמעאל Hal ^{187}; on form cf. Lag BN 131);—**1.** son of Abraham and Hagar Gn 16^{11} (name expl. כִּי שָׁמַע י׳ וגו׳), v $^{15.16}$ + 11 t. Gn 17. 25, $28^{9.9}$ 36^{3} 1 Ch $1^{28.29.31}$; Ισμαηλ. **2.** usu. Ισμαηλ: murderer of Gedaliah Je $40^{8.14.15.16}$ + 17 t. Je 41, 2 K $25^{23.25}$ (𝔊L Ισραηλ!). **3.** in Benj. 1 Ch 8^{38} 9^{44}. **4.** in Judah: **a.** 2 Ch 19^{11}. **b.** 23^{1}. **5.** Jew with foreign wife Ezr 10^{22}, Σαμαηλ, A𝔊L Ισμαηλ.

†יִשְׁמְעֵאלִי **adj. gent.** of יִשׁ׳ **1**;—sg. c. art. 3459
הַיִּשׁ׳ 1 Ch 2^{17} + ‖ 2 S 17^{25} (so read for הַיִּשְׂרְאֵלִי, v. Comm.); הַיִּשְׁמְעֵלִי 1 Ch 27^{30}; pl. (הַ)יִּשְׁמְעֵאלִים *Ishmaelites* Gn $37^{25.27.28}$ 39^{1} Ju 8^{24} ψ 83^{7}.

3460 † (ו)יִשְׁמַעְיָה **n.pr.m.** (*'י heareth*);—Σαμαιας: **1.** יָה-, Gibeonite, one of David's heroes 1 Ch 12^{4}. **2.** יָהוּ- in Zebulun 27^{19}.

2045 † הַשְׁמָעוּת **n.f. a causing to hear** (prop. Aramaizing Inf. Hiph.; Ges$^{§53 1}$ Sta^{§304a});—לְהַשׁ׳ אָזְנָיִם Ez 24^{26} *to cause ears to hear*, i.e. bring tidings in person (? rd. מָעַת- Nö$^{ZMG\ lviii\ (1903),\ 416}$).

4926 †I. [מִשְׁמָע] **n.[m.] thing heard**;—cstr. לֹא־לְמִשְׁמַע אָזְנָיו Is 11^{3} *not according to what his ears hear*, not superficially (‖ לְמַרְאֵה עֵינָיו).

4927 †II. מִשְׁמָע **n. pr. m.** Μασ(α)μα(ν): **1.** in Ishmael Gn 25^{14} 1 Ch 1^{30}. **2.** in Simeon 4$^{25.26}$.

4928 † [מִשְׁמַעַת] **n.f. obedient band, body of subjects**;—only sf.: **1.** prob.=*body-guard*, as esp. bound to obedience, מִשְׁמַעְתֶּךָ 1 S 22^{14} captain over *thy guard* (Ew Be^{Ch} Dr Bu Now), cf. תּוֹ- 2 S 23^{23}=1 Ch 11^{25}. **2.** תָּם- Is 11^{14} the sons of Ammon (shall be) *their subjects* (‖ מוֹאָב מִשְׁלוֹחַ יָדָם; cf. משמעת MI^{28}).

שׁמץ (√of foll.; cf. NH שֶׁמֶץ *accusation* (or *suspicion*); Thes cp. Ar. شَمِصَ *speak rapidly* (*and indistinctly*) (Kam Frey); but dub.; *rapidity* seems main idea;—and ש=ش ?).

8102 † שֶׁמֶץ **n.[m.] whisper**;—שׁ׳ abs. Jb 4^{12}; cstr. שׁ׳ דָּבָר 26^{14} *a* (mere) *whisper of a word*, something wholly inadequate.

8103 † שִׁמְצָה **n. f.** (derisive) **whisper, derision**;—שׁ׳ Ex 32^{25} (J).

8104 I. **שָׁמַר**$_{465}$ **vb. keep, watch, preserve** (NH *id.*; Ph. שמר in n.pr. and (Pun.)=*watchman*; Tel Am. *šimiru* is perhaps *overseer* (Canaanism), Wkl$^{No.\ 80,\ l.\ 23}$; Mand. סמירא *preserved* Nö^{M46}; cf. Ar. سَمَرَ *converse by night, stay awake* (v. Lag$^{BN\ 105}$); Ba$^{NB\ 175\ f.;\ ES\ 43}$ infers from ܫܡܪܐ *eyelid* (cf. [שְׁמֻרָה] infr.), and Ar. تَمَلَ *support, aid, protect* (*l*=*r*), that two √√ are combined in Heb.; but proof insuff.);—**Qal**$_{425}$ *Pf.* 3 ms. שׁ׳ Gn 37^{11}+, etc.; *Impf.* 3 ms. יִשְׁמֹר 1 S 2^{9}+, יִשְׁמָר־ Je 5^{24}+, sf. 3 ms. יִשְׁמְרֶנּוּ Ex 21$^{29.36}$; 3 fs. sf. תִּשְׁמוּרֵם Pr 14^{3} (rd. תִּשְׁמְרוּם, v. Ges^{§47g} Toy), etc.; *Imv.* ms. שְׁמֹר Jb 2^{6}+, שָׁמְרָה 1 Ch 29^{18}+; mpl. שִׁמְרוּ Jos 6^{18}+, etc.; *Inf. abs.* שָׁמוֹר Dt 5^{12}+; cstr. שְׁמֹר Gn 3^{24}+, sf. שָׁמְרָהּ 2^{15}, etc.; *Pt. act.* שֹׁמֵר 1 S 1^{12}+, etc.; *pass.* שָׁמוּר Ec 5^{12} (1 S 9^{24} v. infr.), etc.;—[Synon. I. נָטַר, נָצַר, q.v.]: **1. a.** *keep, have charge of*, garden Gn 2^{15} (J), ark 1 S 7^{1}, property in trust Ex 22$^{6.9}$ (E), cf. 1 S 25^{31}; *tend* flock Gn 30^{31} (E), cf. Zc 3^{7} Nu 3^{8} (P); so perh. (obj. om.) Ho 12^{13} (where שׁ׳ chosen for parallelism Now Marti al.); Pt. הֲשֹׁמֵר אָחִי אָנֹכִי Gn 4^{9} (J), שׁ׳ of sheep 1 S 17^{20}, שׁ׳ הַכֵּלִים v^{22}, שׁ׳ הַבְּגָדִים 2 K 22^{14} 2 Ch 34^{22}, שׁ׳ הַנָּשִׁים Est 2$^{3.8.15}$, cf. v^{14}, etc. **b.** *keep, guard*, captives Jos 10^{18} (J), 1 K 20^{39}, דֶּרֶךְ Gn 3^{24} (J); *keep watch and ward*, אֶל pers. for whom 1 S 26^{15} (ψ 59^{10} v. **3** end), עַל pers. v^{16} Pr 6^{22}; בַּנַּעַר 2 S 18^{12} *have a care of* (read לִי for מִי 𝔊 and mod.); in hostile sense, אֶל הָעִיר (in siege) 2 S 11^{16}, עַל חַטָּאתִי Jb 14^{16} (but rd. תַּעֲבֹר c. 𝔊 Ew Di Du al. [not Hi Bu]); abs. c. מֵעַל Ec 5^{7} *watcheth above*, etc. (v. p. 759^{a} **d**); *keep* one's mouth, be prudent of speech †Pr 21^{33}, cf. Mi 7^{5}; *keep*=protect, save, one's life, נֶפֶשׁ †Pr 13^{3} 16^{17} 19^{16} 22^{5}, another's Jb 2^{6}; in Pr, acc. pers., subj. wisdom, 4^{6} *she shall preserve thee*, cf. (+מִן of evil) 6^{24} 7^{5}; esp. Pt. *watch, watchman*, of city Is 21$^{11.11.12}$ 62^{5} (fig.), Ct 3^{3} 5$^{7.7}$ ψ 127^{1}; שׁ׳ הַסַּף (in temple) Je 35^{4}+ (v. סַף), הַשׁ׳ פֶּתַח בֵּית הַמֶּלֶךְ 1 K 14^{27}=2 Ch 12^{10}, שׁ׳ הַשְּׁעָרִים Ne 13^{22}, שֹׁמְרֵי הַבַּיִת (fig.) Ec 12^{3}; שׁ׳ הַבַּיִת *keep the house* (of David's concubines) †2 S 15^{16} 16^{21} 20^{3}; שֹׁמֵר הַכֵּלִים 1 S 17^{22}, שׁ׳ הַבְּגָדִים 2 K 22^{14}, שׁ׳ הַפַּרְדֵּס Ne 2^{8}, שׁ׳ הַנָּשִׁים Est 2$^{3.14.15}$, שֹׁמְרִים abs. Ju 7^{19} Je 51^{12}. **c.** hence *watch for, wait for*, acc. pers. 1 S 19^{11} (to kill him), cf. ψ 59^{1} (title; acc. הַבַּיִת); c. עֲקֵבַי ψ 56^{7}=dog my steps, 71^{10} Je 20^{10}; =watch (suspiciously) Jb 10^{14} 13^{27} 33^{11}; abs. הַשֹּׁמְרִים Ju 1^{24}; *wait for*, נֶשֶׁף Jb 24^{15}, לַבֹּקֶר ψ 130$^{6.6}$. **d.** *watch, observe*, acc. rei 1 S 1^{12} Ec 11^{4} Jb 39^{1} Je 8^{7} (of birds), with intelligence Is 42^{20} ψ 107^{43}; acc. pers. 37^{37} (‖ ראה), Zc 11^{11}; acc. of sin ψ 31^{7} 130^{3}; acc. rei, for the purpose of avoiding, 17^{4}. **2. a.** *keep, retain*, of storing up (food) Gn 41^{35} (E); abs. Ec 3^{6} (opp. הִשְׁלִיךְ); *treasure up* (in memory) Gn 37^{11} (E), cf. Mal 2^{7} 1 Ch 29^{18} Pr 4^{21} (בְּתוֹךְ לְבָבֶךָ), 22^{18} (בְּבִטְנֶךָ); *retain* wrath Am 1^{11} (read שָׁמַר לָנֶצַח We Now GASm Marti; v. also נָטַר **1**)+(anger om.) Je 3^{5} (‖ נטר). **b.** *keep* within bounds, *restrain*, obj. שׁוֹר Ex 21$^{29.36}$ (E); c. acc. hand, מִן of evil Is 56^{2}; fig. *keep thy foot*, c. cl. temp. Ec. 4^{17}; אֶשׁ׳־לְפִי מַחְסוֹם ψ 39^{2} (𝔊 Du al. אָשִׂימָה); appar. reflex. (=**Niph.**), †Jos 6^{18} (+מִן־הַחֵרֶם), poss. sc. נַפְשֹׁתֵיכֶם Di. **3. a.** *observe, celebrate*, acc. of festival, etc., Ex 23^{15} (E), 34^{18} (J), 12^{17}, of day v^{17} (P), of month Dt 16^{1}. **b.** *keep* sabbath †Dt 5^{12} Lv 19$^{3.30}$ 26^{2} (all H), Ex 31$^{13.14.16}$ (P), Is 56^{4}, also (+מֵחַלְּלוֹ) v$^{2.6}$. **c.** of other obligations: *keep* covenant Ez 17^{14}, esp.

covenant of י׳ Dt 29^{8} 1 K 11^{11} + 5 t., י׳ שְׁבֻעַת 1 K 2^{43}, *perform* vow Dt 23^{24}; *keep* commands Je 35^{18} Ez 20^{18}; esp. מִצְוֺת, חֻקִּים, עֲבֹדָה, etc., of י׳ (sts. ‖ נצר), Ex 20^{6} = Dt 5^{10}, Am 2^{4} 1 K 2^{3} ψ 119$^{8.17.34}$ + very oft. (c. 120 t.); י׳ שׁ׳ דֶּרֶךְ Gn 18^{19} (J) + 4 t., י׳ דַּרְכֵי 2 S 22^{22} = ψ 18^{22}, ד׳ י׳ om. Ju 2^{22b}; שׁ׳ אָרְחוֹת צַדִּיקִים Pr 2^{20} (‖ תֵּלֵךְ בְּדֶרֶךְ טוֹבִים), דְּרָכַי (ways of wisdom) 8^{32} (ψ 17^{4} v. **1 d**); *keep, discharge* an office, כְּהֻנָּה Nu 3^{10} 18^{7} (both P), abs. 2 Ch 5^{11}; a function or duty, esp. שׁ׳ מִשְׁמֶרֶת Lv 8^{35} Nu 1^{53} + c. 32 t. (v. מ׳ infr.); acc. of obligation oft. om., esp. D (and R^{D}) *keep and do* Dt 4^{6} 7^{12} + 8 t.; *to do* 5$^{1.29}$ + 16 t. D + 3 t., etc. **d.** *observe* = follow dictates of (prudence, justice, kindness, wisdom) Ho 12^{7} (חֶסֶד וּמִשְׁפָּט), Is 56^{1} Pr 4^{4} 5^{2} 7$^{1.2}$; bad sense, *observe* vanities ψ 31^{7}.—Doubtful are: לִשְׁמֹר abs. Ho 4^{10}, very strange (conj. in We Now Marti); שָׁמוּר 1 S 9^{24}, HPS אַחֲרֵנוּ, cf. Now Bu$^{Comm.}$; ψ 59^{10} read עֻזִּי אֵלֶיךָ אֲזַמֵּרָה (as v^{18}, 𝔖 Che Bae). **4.** sts. י׳ subj.: **a.** *keep, preserve, protect*, acc. pers., + בְּ of way, etc., Gn 28$^{15.20}$ (J), Ex 23^{20} (E; of מַלְאָךְ), ψ 91^{11} (מ׳), Jos 24^{17} (E); acc. pers. (or נפשׁ) only: 1 S 30^{23} Je 31^{9} Nu 6^{24} (P), Jb 29^{2} ψ 16^{1} + 10 t. ψψ; + מִן ψ 121^{7} + 2 t.; acc. רַגְלֵי 1 S 2^{9}, cf. Pr 3^{26} (מִן); *Pt.* שֹׁמְרֶךָ ψ 121$^{3.5}$, cf. v^{4}, etc.; acc. of city 127^{1}. **b.** c. acc. בְּרִית, לְ pers. Dt 7^{12}, + חֶסֶד v^{7} + 5 t., הַשְּׁבֻעָה Dt 7^{8}, etc.; הַשּׁ׳ אֱמֶת לְעוֹלָם ψ 146^{6}; pass. of covenant (י׳ agent) עֲרוּכָה בַכֹּל וּשְׁמֻרָה 2 S 23^{5} (legal terminology, Dr). **5.** *keep, reserve*, weeks of harvest Je 5^{24} (לְ pers.). **Niph.** $_{36}$ *Pf.* 3 ms. נִשְׁמַר 2 S 20^{10}, etc.; *Impf.* 3 fs. תִּשָּׁמֵר Ju 13^{13}; 2 mpl. תִּשָּׁמְרוּ Ex 23^{13}; *Imv.* ms. הִשָּׁמֵר Is 7^{4} (לְךָ) הִשָּׁמֶר Gn 24^{6} +; fs. הִשָּׁמְרִי Ju 13^{4}, etc.;—**1.** *be on one's guard*, c. בַּחֶרֶב 2 S 20^{10} *by reason of the sword*, i.e. against it; c. בְּ temp. 1 S 19^{2}, שָׁם 2 K 6^{10}; *take heed* Ex 23^{13} (E) Dt 2^{4}; c. מִן pers. Ex 23^{21} (E), Je 9^{3}; מִן rei Ju 13^{13} Dt 23^{10}; מִן inf. *take care not to*, etc. Gn 31^{29} (E), 2 K 6^{9}; inf. without מִן Ex 19^{12} (J), but rd. prob. מֵעֲלוֹת; sq. פֶּן *lest* Gn 24^{6} (J) + 11 t. (esp. Dt); c. (וְ)אַל juss. Ex 10^{28} (J), Ju 13^{4} Jb 36^{21}, c. Imv. coörd. Is 7^{4}.—Very oft. Imv. (24 t.), esp. in phr. הִשָּׁמֶר־לְךָ (12 t.), הִשָּׁמְרוּ לָכֶם (3 t.); + לְנַפְשֹׁתֵיכֶם Dt 4^{15} Jos 23^{11} (R^{D}; + inf.); + בְּנַפְ׳ Je 17^{21} appar. בְּ pret. *on peril of your life* (cf. בְּ **III. 3 a**), so perhaps also בְּרוּחֲכֶם Mal 2$^{15.16}$ (We Now). †**2.** *keep oneself, refrain, abstain*, מֵאִשָּׁה 1 S 21^{5}. †**3.** *be kept, guarded*, Ho 12^{14} (cf. שׁ׳ of Jacob v^{13}); be preserved (by י׳) ψ 37^{28} (לְעוֹלָם), but rd. prob. עַוָּלִים (לְעוֹלָם) נִשְׁמָדוּ Hup-Ri(Now) Che Bae Du Dr. †**Pi.** *Pt.* pl. מְשַׁמְּרִים הַבְלֵי־שָׁוְא Jon 2^{9} *those paying regard to false vanities* (cf. Qal ψ 31^{7}). †**Hithp.** *Impf.* 1 s. וָאֶשְׁתַּמֵּר מֵעֲוֺנִי ψ 18^{24} *I kept myself from*, etc. = 2 S 22^{24} (vb. cohort.); 3 ms. וְיִשְׁתַּמֵּר חֻקּוֹת עָמְרִי Mi 6^{16}, but read וַתִּשְׁמֹר *thou keepest, observest*, We Now GASm.

† I. שֶׁמֶר **n. pr. m.** (prop. clan-name, cf. 8106
Sta$^{ZAW\ v\ (1885).\ 166\ f.}$, cf. Sab. שמר Os ^{13}, but NAram.
شمر DHM $^{ZMG\ xxxvii\ (1885).\ 14}$ Sab Denkm ^{30});—
Σεμ(μ)ηρ, etc.: **1.** שׁ׳ orig. owner of hill where
Sam. was built 1 K 16$^{24.24}$. **2.** שָׁמֶר: **a.** Levite
1 Ch 6^{31}. **b.** in Asher 7^{34}, A 𝔊L Σωμηρ; = שֹׁמֵר 7763
v^{32}. **c.** in Benj. 8^{12} van d. H.; > שֶׁמֶד q.v. p. 1029 8106

† שְׁמֻרָה **n.f.** guard, watch;—שִׁיתָה י׳ שׁ׳ 8108
לְפִי ψ 141^{3} (‖ נִצְּרָה עַל־דַּל שְׂפָתָי).

† שֹׁמֵר **n.pr.m.** **1.** father of one of Joash's 7763
murderers 2 K 12^{21}, Σωμηρ, 𝔊L Σεμμηρ (called
שִׁמְרִית q.v., a Moabitess, ‖ 2 Ch 24^{26}). **2.**
Asherite 1 Ch 7^{32}, Σαμηρ, Σωμηρ; = שֶׁמֶר **2 b.** 8106

† שִׁמְרִי **n.pr.m.** usu. Σαμαρει, etc.: **1.** in 8113
Simeon, 1 Ch 4^{37}. **2.** father of a hero of David 1 Ch 11^{45}. **3.** Levites: **a.** 1 Ch 26^{10}. **b.** 2 Ch 29^{13}, Ζαμβρει, Σαμβρι.

† שִׁמְרָת **n.pr.m.** in Benj. 1 Ch 8^{21}, Σαμα- 8119
ραθ, -ρει.

† שִׁמְרִית **n.pr.f.** Moabitish mother of one 8116
of Joash's murderers 2 Ch 24^{26} (**m.** Σομαιωθ, A Σαμαριθ; **f.** 𝔊L Σαμιραμωθ), ‖ שֹׁמֵר n.pr.m. 2 K 12^{21}.

† [שְׁמֻרָה] **n.f.** eye-lid (from its *guarding* 8109
the eye);—pl. cstr. שְׁמֻרוֹת עֵינָי ψ 77^{5}.

† [שִׁמֻּר] **n.[m.]** watching, vigil (so Di; 8107
> *observance*);—pl. לֵיל שִׁמֻּרִים לי׳ Ex 12^{42} *a night of vigils to* י׳, שׁ׳ לְכָל־בְּנֵי יִשׂ׳ v^{42}.

† שְׁמַרְיָה(וּ) **n. pr. m.** (י׳ *has kept, pre-* 8114
served);—Σαμαρ(ε)ια(ς): **1.** ־יָהוּ a hero of David 1 Ch 12^{6} (van d. H. v^{5}). Elsewhere ־יָה: **2.** son of Rehoboam 2 Ch 11^{19}. **3.** contemporaries of Ezra: **a.** Ezr 10^{32}. **b.** v^{41}.

שֹׁמְרוֹן $_{109}$ **n.pr.loc.** capital of N. Isr. from 8111
Omri's time (*belonging to clan* שֶׁמֶר, Sta$^{ZAW\ v\ (1885).\ 165-175}$; originally שָׁמְרוֹן or שָׁמְרַיִן; As. *Samerina* COT$^{1\ K\ 16,\ 24}$);—שׁ׳ 1 K 16^{24} (name expl. as from שֶׁמֶר, orig. owner of site), v$^{28.29.32}$ 20$^{1.10}$ +; שֹׁמְרוֹנָה 1 K 20^{43} 2 K 6^{19} 14^{14}; personified as woman Ez 16$^{46.51.53.55}$ 23$^{4.33}$; king of N. Israel is מֶלֶךְ שׁ׳

1 K 21[1] 2 K 1[3]; מ׳ יִשׂ׳ אֲשֶׁר בְּשׁ׳ 1 K 21[18], cf. מֶלֶךְ עַל־יִשׂ׳ בְּשׁ׳ 22[52]+9 t.; thence name of territory, שְׂדֵה שׁ׳ Ob[19], עָרֵי שׁ׳ 1 K 13[32] (point of view of later editor), 2 K 17[24.26] 23[19]; הָרֵי שׁ׳ Am 3[9] Je 31[5],—cf. הַר־שׁ׳ Am 4[1] 6[1] 1 K 16[24]; perh. שׁ׳ alone Je 23[13] 1 K 18[2] 2 K 7[24.28] 2 Ch 25[13]; חֵיל שׁ׳ Ne 3[34].—𝔊 usu. Σαμαρεια, but 1 K 16[24] Σεμερω, Σαεμερων, Σομορων; =mod. *Sebastieh;* vid. GASm [G 346 ff.] Buhl [G 207 f.] Cowley [Ency. Bib. s. v.] Wilson [Hast. DB s. v.].

8118 †[שֹׁמְרֹנִי] **adj. gent.** Samaritan, only as n.pl. הַשֹּׁמְרֹנִים 2 K 17[29] *the Samaritans.*

8110 †I. שִׁמְרוֹן **n.pr.loc.** Canaanite city, with king: Jos 11[1], in Zebulun 19[15], Συμοων, Σομερων,
8112 etc., =שׁ׳ מְראוֹן 12[20].

8110 †II. שִׁמְרוֹן **n.pr.m.** son of Issachar, Gn 46[13] Nu 24[64] 1 Ch 7[1]; Ζαμβραμ, Σαμβρα, Σεμερων, etc.

8117 †שִׁמְרֹנִי **adj. gent.** of foregoing; c. art. as n.coll. הַשִּׁ׳ Nu 26[24].

821 †אַשְׁמֹ֫רֶת, אַשְׁמוּרָה **n.f. watch** (division of time);—abs. אַשְׁמוּרָה בַלָּ֑יְלָה ψ 90[4]; רֹאשׁ הָאַשְׁמֹרֶת הַתִּיכוֹנָה Ju 7[19]; cstr. אַשְׁמֹרֶת הַבֹּקֶר Ex 14[24] (J), 1 S 11[11]; pl. abs. אַשְׁמֻרוֹת La 19[19] ψ 63[7] 119[148].

3461 †יִשְׁמְרַי **n.pr.m.** in Benj., 1 Ch 8[18], Σαμαρει; A Ιεσαμαρι, 𝔊L Ιασσημαρι.

4929 †מִשְׁמָר **n.[m.]** place of confinement, gaol, prison; late, guard, watch, observance;—abs. מ׳ Gn 42[17]+; cstr. מִשְׁמַר 40[3]+; sf. מִשְׁמָרוֹ Ne 7[3], etc.; pl. sf. ־רָיו 13[14];—**1.** *gaol, prison,* מ׳ בֵּית שַׂר הַטַּבָּחִים Gn 40[3], cf. v[4] (abs.), v[7] 41[10]; 42[17] (abs.), +v[30] (𝔊), בֵּית מִשְׁמַרְכֶם v[19] (all E); *guard-house* in camp Lv 24[12] (H), Nu 15[34] (P). **2.** *guard,* Je 51[12] Ne 4[3.16], אַנְשֵׁי הַמִּ׳ v[17]; *guard-post* 7[3]; fig. of י׳ setting a *guard,* כִּי תָשִׂים עָלַי מ׳ Jb 7[12]; *band of* (Levit.) *guards* or functionaries 1 Ch 26[16] Ne 12[24] (cf. מִשְׁמֶרֶת); *act of guarding,* מִכָּל־מ׳ Pr 4[23] *above all guarding* watch thy heart.—לְמִ׳ Ez 38[7] is doubtful, Hi Co Toy al. *reserve;* Krae לְמֹשֵׁל. **3.** pl. *observances, services,* of temple Ne 13[14].

4931 מִשְׁמֶ֫רֶת [78] **n.f. guard, watch, also charge, function;**—מ׳ abs. 2 S 20[3]+, cstr. 2 K 11[5]+; abs. מִשְׁמָ֑רֶת Ex 16[34]; sf. מִשְׁמַרְתִּי Gn 26[5]+, etc.; pl. מִשְׁמָרוֹת 1 Ch 9[23]+; cstr. מִשְׁמְרוֹת Ne 7[3]; sf. ־רוֹתָם 2 Ch 7[6]+, ־תֵיהֶם 2 Ch 31[17];—†**1.** *guard, watch:* בֵּית מ׳ 2 S 20[3]=*house of detention, confinement;* מ׳ אַתָּה עִמָּדִי 1 S 22[23] i.e. protected, secure; c. שָׁמַר *keep the watch* 2 K 11[5.6.7] 1 Ch 12[30] (van d. H. v[29]); =*post of watch* (fig.) Is 21[8] (‖ מִצְפֶּה), Hb 2[1] (‖ מָצוֹר); pl. =*guards* Ne 7[3] 1 Ch 9[23]. †**2.** *keeping, preserving,* וְהָיָה לָכֶם לְמִ׳ Ex 12[6] i.e. ye shall keep it; הַנִּיחוּ לָכֶם לְמִ׳ 16[23], cf. v[32.33.34] Nu 19[9] (all P). †**3.** *charge, injunction* of י׳, c. שָׁמַר, in gen. Dt 11[1] (+ חֻקּוֹת, מִצְוֹת, מִשְׁפָּטִים), cf. Gn 26[5] 1 K 2[3], and (מ׳ מִצְוַת י׳) Jos 22[3] (all R[D]), Mal 3[14]; of specif. injunctions Lv 18[30] Nu 9[19.23]. †**4. a.** ceremonial *office* or *function* (AV RV usu. *charge*) of priest or Levite (P [esp. Nu], Ez 40, 44, 48, Chr Zc), mostly c. שָׁמַר: מ׳ מִשְׁכַּן הָעֵדוּת Nu 1[53], מ׳ מִשְׁכַּן י׳ 31[30.47], מ׳ הַמִּקְדָּשׁ Ez 44[15] Nu 3[38], מ׳ אֹהֶל מוֹעֵד 18[4] cf. v[3], 1 Ch 23[32], מ׳ הַקֹּדֶשׁ Nu 3[28.32] 18[5] 1 Ch 23[32], מ׳ קָדָשַׁי (of Isr. in gen.) Ez 44[8], מ׳ הַמִּזְבֵּחַ Nu 18[5] Ez 40[46], תְּרוּמֹתָי Nu 18[8], מ׳ הַבַּיִת Ez 40[45] 44[14], מ׳ הַטָּהֳרָה Ne 12[45]; c. genit. (sf.) שׁ׳ מ׳ = *perform the service imposed by, due to,* Lv 8[35] 22[9] Ez 44[8.16] 48[11] Zc 3[7], מ׳ אֱלֹהֵיהֶם Ne 12[45] (of Judah in gen.); מ׳ הָעֵדָה Nu 3[7a], מ׳ בְּנֵי יִשׂ׳ 3[8.38], מ׳ בְּנֵי גֵרְשׁוֹן 3[25], cf. v[7a.31.36] 4[27.28.31.32] 18[3] 1 Ch 23[32]; also, in secular sense, מ׳ בֵּית שָׁאוּל 1 Ch 12[30]; מ׳ מַשָּׂאָם Nu 4[31], כְּלֵי מ׳ מַשָּׂאָם v[32] (v[27] read c. 𝔊 Di Gr Gray, etc. בְּשֵׁמוֹת for בְּמ׳, and perhaps מִשְׁמֶרֶת after אֵת, cf. v[32]); עֲלֵיהֶם מ׳ 1 Ch 9[27] i.e. the duty rested upon them;—25[8] 26[12] v. I. עֻמָּה **c, d** (p. 769 supr.); עַל־מ׳ עֹמְדִים 2 Ch 7[6] were standing *according to* (or *in*) *their offices,* הֶעֱמִיד עַל מ׳ appoint *to their offices* 8[14] 35[2]. **b.** pl. of Levitical *divisions* for service Ne 12[9].

II. שׁמר (√ of foll.; cf. NH שְׁמָרִים=BH, also vb. denom.; 𝔗 שִׁמְרָא; meaning of √ and relation (if any) to I. שׁ׳ obscure; cf. poss. Ar. سَمُرَ *be tawny, dark,* in colour, Lane [1425 a]).

†II. [שֶׁ֫מֶר] **n.m.** [Is 25, 6] only **pl. lees, dregs** 8105
(fig.);—abs. שְׁמָרִים Is 25[6.6] (in both = *wine* matured by resting undisturbed *on the lees*); sf. שֹׁקֵט הוּא אֶל־שְׁמָרָיו Je 48[11] (of Moab's undisturbed life), cf. (of careless men) הַקֹּפְאִים עַל־שִׁמְרֵיהֶם Zp 1[12]; שְׁמָרֶיהָ ψ 75[9] (of י׳'s cup of
judgment). I. שֶׁ֫מֶר p. 1037 8106

III. שׁמר (√ of foll.; mng. dub.; NH שָׁמִיר *diamond,* so Aram. שְׁמִירָא (also *flint*), ܫܡܝܪܐ; Ar. سَمُرٌ = *mimosa gummifera,* Lane [1425 b]).

שׁמור v. III. שָׁמִיר. p. 1039 8053

†I. שָׁמִיר **n.m.** [Ez 3, 9] **thorn(s), adamant,** 8068
flint;—abs. שׁ׳ Is 5[6]+; sf. שְׁמִירוֹ 10[17];—**1.** coll.

thorns, thorn-bushes, token of waste-land, only Is, + שַׁיִת Is 5[6] 7[23.24.25] 27[4]; fig. 9[17] 10[17]; קוֹץ שׁ׳ 32[13]. **2.** *adamant,* as sharp, כְּתוּבָה . . . בְּצִפֹּרֶן שׁ׳ Je 17[1] (|| בְּעֵט בַּרְזֶל); as hard, fig. of prophet's firmness Ez 3[9]; Zc 7[12] fig. of hard heart.

8069 †II. **שָׁמִיר** **n.pr.loc. 1.** in הַר אֶפְרָיִם Ju 10[1.2], Σαμειρ; A 𝔊L Σαμαρεια. **2.** in הַר (יְהוּדָה) Jos 15[48], Σαμειρ; A 𝔊L Σαφειρ.

8053,8068 †III. **שָׁמִיר** **n.pr.m.** Levite, 1 Ch 24[24] Qr,
8053 Σαμηρ, Σεμμηρ (Kt שמור).

שׁמשׁ (√of foll.; mng. unknown; NH= BH; Ph. שמש; As. *šamšu;* Aram. שִׁמְשָׁא, ܫܡܫܐ, OAram., Palm. שמש Lzb[379]; Ar. شَمْسٌ, Sab. שמסם *goddess,* SabDenkm[20.56ff.] DHM[B. u. S. 1032] Wkl[ZMG liv (1900), 408 ff.] RS[K 299] Nö[ZMG xli (1887), 712]).

8121 **שֶׁמֶשׁ** 133 **n.f.**[Ju 19,14] **et m.**[Gn 19,23] (Albr[ZAW xv (1895), 324]) **sun**;—abs. שׁ׳ Jos 10[12]+, שָׁמֶשׁ Ju 20[43]+; sf. שִׁמְשֵׁךְ Is 60[20], שִׁמְשָׁהּ Je 15[9]; pl. sf. שִׁמְשֹׁתַיִךְ Is 54[12];—**1.** *sun,* Gn 37[9] (E; +moon, stars); marking time: as rising (vb. זָרַח q.v.) Ex 22[2] (E)+8 t.+Mal 3[20] (fig. שׁ׳ צְדָקָה, of reward of the faithful, with wings, i.e. rays? Now GASm; or winged sun-disc [cf. We]?); vb. יָצָא Gn 19[23] (J), Is 13[10] Ju 5[31] (sim. of splendour; v. יָצָא **1 f**); setting (vb. בּוֹא) Gn 15[17] (J), Am 8[9]+19 t., וַיְהִי הַשׁ׳ לָבוֹא Gn 15[12] (JE), + שׁ׳ יָדַע מְבוֹאוֹ ψ 104[19] (v. בּוֹא **1 i**, מָבוֹא **2**); as giving daylight Is 60[9]; hot 1 S 11[9] Ne 7[3] Ex 16[21] (P), cf. Is 49[10] Jon 4[8] ψ 121[6]; as ripening crops Dt 33[14] (poem), cf. (fig.) Jb 8[16], tanning the face Ct 1[6]; standing still at Joshua's word Jos 10[12.13a] (poem in J; || יָרֵחַ), v[13b] (J), cf. Hb 3[11] (+יָרֵחַ); casting shadow (on dial), יָרְדָה בְמַעֲלוֹת אָחָז בַּשׁ׳ Is 38[8], וַתָּשָׁב הַשׁ׳ v[8]; set in sky by י׳ Je 31[25] ψ 19[5] 74[16] 136[8], enduring 72[5.17] (cf. עִם **1 g**, p. 768; [פָּנֶה] **II. 4 a** (*e*), p. 817), also 89[37]; personif., called to praise י׳ 148[3] (+יָרֵחַ); to be darkened by י׳'s judgment, Ez 32[7] Jo 2[10] 3[4] 4[15] (cf. Am 8[9] supr., Mi 3[6]). **2.** of direction: מִמִּזְרַח הַשׁ׳ Nu 21[11] (E) *toward sun-rise,=East,* cf. Dt 4[41.47]+16 t. (v. מִזְרָח p. 280); מְבוֹא הַשׁ׳ Dt 11[30]+3 t. (v. מָבוֹא **2**, p. 99). **3.** obj. of worship (usu.+ moon, stars, etc.) 2 K 23[5] Je 8[2] Ez 8[16] Dt 4[19]; horses given to שׁ׳ 2 K 23[11], מַרְכְּבוֹת הַשׁ׳ v[11].—Vid. also בֵּית שׁ׳ p. 112[b]. **4.** other phr.: †**a.** נֶגֶד הַשׁ׳, i.e. *openly, publicly,* 2 S 12[12] Nu 25[4] (P), so לְעֵינֵי הַשׁ׳ 2 S 12[11]. †**b.** fig. of living, רָאָה שׁ׳ Ex 6[5] 7[11] 11[7], opp. תֶּחֱשַׁךְ הַשׁ׳ ψ 58[9], חָזָה שׁ׳ 12[2]. **c.** תַּחַת הַשׁ׳, i.e. on the earth, Ec 1[3]+ 28 t. Ec (cf. Gk. ὑφ' ἡλίῳ, Kue[Ond. iii. 196; Einl. iii. 192]). **5.** *pinnacle,* as *glittering, shining,* pl. Is 54[12] *thy pinnacles, battlements* (of Zion), so perhaps sg. שׁ׳ וּמָגֵן י׳ אֱלֹהִים ψ 84[12] *battlement and shield is* י׳ א׳ (Gr Bae Du Buhl; most *sun,* and so Thes De Che SS; Hup-Now hesitates).

שִׁמְשׁוֹן 38 **n. pr. m. Samson** (As. n.pr. *Šamšânu,* Hilpr[Murâshu 27.70]; on שמש in Ar. n.pr. 8123
trib. cf. Nö[ZMG xl (1886), 166]);—Σαμψων: Ju 13[24] 14[1.3] +35 t. Ju 14, 15, 16.

†**שַׁמְשְׁרַי** **n.pr.m.** in Benj. 1 Ch 8[26], Ισμασαρια, 8125
A Σαμσαρια, 𝔊L Σαμψαια.

שִׁמְתִי v. [שָׁמָה]. p. 1029 8126

שֵׁן, שֶׁן v. בֵּית שְׁאָן. **שֵׁן** v. שנן. p. 112, 1042 1052, 8127, 8129

שְׁנָא v. I. [שָׁנָה]. **שֵׁנָא** v. שָׁנָה √ יָשֵׁן. below, p. 446 8132, 8138, 8142

†**שִׁנְאָב** **n.pr.m.** king of Admah Gn 14[2], 8134
Σενναар (v. שִׁנְעָר v[1], 𝔊 *id.*).

שִׁנְאָן v. sub III. שנה. p. 1041 8136

†**שֶׁנְאַצַּר** **n.pr.m.** uncle of Zerub. 1 Ch 3[18], 8137
Σανεσαρ, 𝔊L Σανασαρ (EMey[Entstehung 77] cp. שֵׁשְׁבַּצַּר, but v. Now[Hg 1, 1]).

שׁנב (√of following; meaning dub.).

†**אֶשְׁנָב** **n.[m.] window-lattice** (אשנב 822
Ecclus 42[11]);—abs. א׳ Ju 5[28]; sf. אֶשְׁנַבִּי Pr 7[6] (both || חַלּוֹן).

†I. **[שָׁנָה]** **vb. change** (NH Pi, etc.; 8138
Ecclus 42[24], etc.; As. *šanû, change,* Aram. שְׁנָא, 8133
Nab. Ethpa. Lzb[379]; Syr. ܫܢܐ, esp. mentally= *grow insane;* cf. (prob.) NH שָׁנָה *year,* =Ph. שת, שנת; MI[2.8] שת; As. *šattu* (cf. Muss-Arnolt JBL xi (1892), 73 n.); Ar. سَنَةٌ; Aram. שַׁתָּא, שְׁנָא, ܫܢܐ, ܫܢܬܐ; OAram., Nab., Palm. שנתא, שנת, שת, שנן Lzb[379 f.]; on *year* from *changing* seasons, v. Philippi[ZMG xxxii (1878), 79 f.] Ba[ZMG xli (1887), 612, 621, 636] (esp. against DHM[VIme Orient. Congr. ii. 1, 452] who proposes bilit. √), cf. Thes; a daring suggestion by Jen[ZA vii (1892), 177]);—**Qal** *Pf.* 1 s. לֹא שָׁנִיתִי Mal 3[6] I am
י׳, *I do not change; Impf.* 3 ms. יִשְׁנֶא (Ges[§ 77 rr]) 8132
La 4[1] how *is* the fine gold *changed* (si vera l.; Löhr[Now] יְשֻׁנָּא; gloss on יועם Bu Löhr); *Inf. cstr.* שְׁנוֹת יְמִין עֶלְיוֹן ψ 77[11] *the right hand of the Highest is changed* (𝔖 𝔙 𝔗 Aq Sym Theod Hup-Now RVm Bae Du We Buhl; AV RV Ew De Che al. *years,* usu. ins. *I will remember*); *Pt.* שׁוֹנִים Est 1[7] *differing, different,* c. מִן, cf. 3[8] (so Ecclus 42[24]);

Pr 24^{21} *those who change* (but dub., v. Toy). **Pi.**
transit., *change, alter*: *Pf.* 3 ms. שִׁנָּה Je 52^{33}
8132 c. acc. garments, = שִׁנָּא (Ges $^{l.c.}$) 2 K 25^{29}; *Impf.*
3 ms. יְשַׁנֶּה דִּין Pr 31^{5} *lest he pervert the judgment*;
וַיְשַׁנּוֹ 1 S 21^{14} (read וַיְשַׁן Ges ^{§75bb}, וַיְשַׁנֶּה We Dr
(and reff.), cf. Bu HPS Now), c. acc. טַעְמוֹ (v.
טַעַם, and As. *šanê têmi, madness*); וַיְשַׁנֶּהָ Est 2^{9},
i.e. *changed her* place לְטוֹב בֵּית הַנָּשִׁים; 1 s.
ψ 89^{35} the utterance of my lips *I will not change*
(‖ לֹא אֲחַלֵּל בְּרִיתִי); *Inf. cstr.* לְשַׁנּוֹת אֶת־דַּרְכֵּךְ Je 2^{36}
i.e. change thy political course; בְּשַׁנּוֹתוֹ אֶת־טַעְמוֹ
ψ 34^{1} (title; cf. 1 S 21^{14} supr.); *Pt.* מְשַׁנֶּה פָנָיו
Jb 14^{20} *altering his face*, i.e. in death (subj. God).
8132 **Pu.** *Impf.* 3 ms. וְעֹז פָּנָיו יְשֻׁנֶּא (Ges ^{§75rr}) Ec 8^{1},
usu. *is changed*, mollified, Siegf יְשֻׂנֵּא *is hated*
(on עֹז פ׳ v. עֹז **4**, √ עזז). **Hithp.** *Pf.* 2 fs.
consec. קוּמִי נָא וְהִשְׁתַּנִּית 1 K 14^{2} *arise, pray, and*
disguise thyself.

8141 שָׁנָה $_{877}$ **n.f.** (on appar. exc. v. Albr $^{ZAW\ xvi\ (1896),}$
^{46}) **year** (etym. v. √);—abs. ש׳ Am 2^{10}+; cstr.
שְׁנַת Gn 41^{50}+; sf. שְׁנָתוֹ Ez 46^{13}+, שְׁנָתָהּ Lv 14^{10}
+2 t.; du. שְׁנָתַיִם Am 1^{1}+, ־תָיִם 1 K 15^{25}+;
pl. שָׁנִים Ex 21^{2}+, cstr. שְׁנֵי Gn 23^{1}+24 t., שְׁנוֹת
Dt 32^{7}+8 t. (poet. and late); sf. שָׁנָיו Lv 25^{52}+
4 t. sf.; שְׁנוֹתַי Is 38^{15} ψ 31^{11}, שְׁנוֹתָם 78^{33}+8 t.
sf.;—*year*, as division of time, Ex 23$^{14.17}$ 3 t.
בַּשָּׁנָה+, etc.; רֵשִׁית הַשׁ׳ Dt 11^{12}, opp. אַחֲרִית הַשׁ׳
v^{12}, צֵאת הַשׁ׳ Ex 23^{16}, תְּקוּפַת הַשׁ׳ 34^{22} 2 Ch 24^{23},
תְּשׁוּבַת הַשׁ׳ 2 S 11^{1}+, etc.; בָּא שָׁנָה 2 K 13^{20}, rd.
כְּבֹא ש׳ 𝔊 Bur, בְּשׁ׳ בארץ ש׳ Kit, cf. בְּשׁ׳ ש׳ =
year by year 1 S 1^{7}+; בַּשָּׁנָה Benz, cf. Ne 10^{33};
so ש׳ ש׳ Dt 14^{22}, ש׳ אַחֲרֵי ש׳ 2 S 21^{1}, בְּכָל־ש׳ וְשׁ׳
Est 9$^{21.27}$; esp. of duration of life; (יְמֵי) שְׁנֵי חַיֵּי פ׳
Gn 23^{1} 25^{7}+(P); שְׁנֵיהֶם Jb 36^{11}+, שְׁנוֹתַי ψ 31^{11}
(‖ חַיַּי), etc.; of God Jb 10^{5} ψ 102$^{25.28}$; in phr.
of age, v. בֵּן **9**, בַּת **9**; indef. שָׁנִים Ez 38^{17} = *for*
years, לְקֵץ ש׳ Dn 11^{6}; זֶה־יָמִים אוֹ זֶה שָׁנִים 1 S 29^{3};
specif. בִּשְׁנַת מוֹת הַמֶּלֶךְ Is 6^{1} 14^{28}, בִּשְׁנַת בֹּא תַרְתָּן
20^{1}, שְׁנַת הַשְּׁמִטָּה Dt 15^{9} 31^{10}, שְׁנַת הַיּוֹבֵל Lv
25^{13}+, etc.; שְׁנֵי שָׂכִיר Is 16^{14} 21^{16} (v. שָׂכִיר);
שְׁנַת פְּקֻדָּתָם Je 11^{23}+2 t.; ש׳ רָצוֹן לי׳ Is 61^{2},
etc.; שְׁנוֹת דֹּר־וָדֹר Dt 32^{7}, cf. Jo 2^{2}; most oft. c.
num. card.: pl. after units, appos., Ex 21^{2}+,
so also שְׁתַּיִם שָׁנִים 2 S 2^{10}+, but du. שְׁנָתַיִם Am 1^{1}
+4 t., שְׁנָתַיִם יָמִים Gn 41^{1}+4 t.; very rarely c.
num. (certainly) cstr. שְׁתֵּי שָׁנִים 1 S 13^{1} (corrupt),
שָׁלֹשׁ ש׳ Lv 25^{21}; 8+שָׁנָה †2 K 22^{1}; before unit
(rare, late) 2 Ch 11$^{17.17}$ Dn 1^{5}; sg. after 11–19,
tens, and hundreds Gn 5$^{3.9}$ 14^{4}+oft.; so 90+9
years 17^{24}+, rarely 30+3 *years* 1 K 2^{11}, etc.;
but אֶלֶף שָׁנִים ψ 90^{4} 1000 *years*, so (+פַּעֲמַיִם)
Ec 6^{6} 1000 *years twice over*; with cp. num. oft.
repeated, 900 *year* + 30 *year* Gn 5^{5}, etc.; 100
year + 70 *year* + 5 *years* 25^{7}, etc.; c. num.
card. = ord., בִּשְׁנַת אַרְבַּע לְ 1 K 22^{41} *in the fourth*
year of, etc., also בִּשְׁנַת חֲמִשִּׁים שָׁנָה לְ 2 K 15^{23},
etc.; but בְּאַרְבַּע עֶשְׂרֵה ש׳ לְ 2 K 18^{13}, etc. (oft.),
and בַּשָּׁנָה הָאַחַת עֶשְׂרֵה 1 K 6^{38}, etc.; also (c. units),
בַּשָּׁנָה הָרְבִיעִת Lv 19^{24}+, etc., +לְ 2 K 17^{6} *the*
ninth year of, etc.; and even (Ges ^{§134p}) בִּשְׁנַת
הַתְּשִׁיעִית לְ 2 K 25^{1}, cf. Ezr 7^{8} Je 46^{2} 51^{59}+(Kt)
28^{1} 32^{1} (Qr בַּשָּׁנָה).

II. שׁנה (√ of foll., meaning dub.; Thes
cp. Ar. سَنَا *shine*, Eth. ሰነየ: = ሠነየ: *be beautiful*,
Di^{251}, cf. Philippi $^{ZAW\ xxxii\ (1878),\ 79}$; but As. *šinîtu*
is dyed cloth).

שָׁנִי $_{42}$ **n.[m.] scarlet** (prop. *coccus ilicis*, 8144
which attaches itself to leaves and twigs of
quercus coccifera; the dried body of female
yields colouring matter; cf. Tristr $^{NHB\ 319}$ Post
$^{Hast.\ DB\ SCARLET}$ M'Lean $^{Ency.\ Bib.\ id.}$);—usu. ש׳: תִּקְוַת
חוּט הַשׁ׳ הַזֶּה Jos 2^{18} *this cord of thread of scarlet*,
ת׳ הַשׁ׳ v^{21}, חוּט הַשׁ׳ Ct 4^{3} (sim. of lips); so (הַ)שׁ׳
alone Gn 38$^{28.30}$ (J), and as material of clothing
2 S 1^{24} Je 4^{30} Pr 31^{21} (pl. שָׁנִים; on order of ll.
v. Toy); pl. also in sim. Is 1^{18} if your sins are like
scarlet (robes); elsewh. (P) תּוֹלַעַת (הַ)שׁ׳ (v. ת׳) of
material for curtain, veil, ephod, etc., Ex 25^{4} 26^{1}
+24 t. Ex; בֶּגֶד ת׳ ש׳ Nu 4^{8} (v. ii. ב׳ **2**); cstr.
שְׁנִי (הַ)ת׳ used in purif., †Lv 14$^{4.6.49.51.52}$ Nu 19^{6}.

†III. שָׁנָה **vb. repeat, do again** (NH *id.*; 8138
Ecclus 42^{1}; Ar. ثَنَى *bend, fold, double*; Aram.
תְּנָא *repeat*, also *teach*, ܬܢܐ; As. *šanû*, esp. Pi.
repeat, relate, cf. Scheil $^{ZA\ v\ (1890),\ 409}$ (Dl thinks
denom.); on ש׳ as √ of שְׁנַיִם *two*, v. Philippi
$^{ZMG\ xxxii\ (1878),\ 77}$ Ba $^{ib.\ xli\ (1887),\ 603}$);—**Qal** *Pf.* 3 ms. ש׳
2 S 20^{10}; *Impf.* 1 s. אֶשְׁנֶה 1 S 26^{8}, etc.; *Imv.*
mpl. שְׁנוּ 1 K 18^{34}; *Pt.* שֹׁנֶה Pr 17^{9} 26^{11};—*do*
again: וְלֹא ש׳ לוֹ . . . וַיַּכֵּהוּ 2 S 20^{10}, cf. 1 S 26^{8};
abs. 1 K 18$^{34.34}$ Ne 13^{21}; = *speak again* Jb 29^{22}
+40^{5} acc. to many moderns (אשנה for MT אענה);
שׁ׳ בְּדָבָר Pr 17^{9} *repeat with a thing*, keep talking
about it (שנות דבר Ecclus 42^{1}); 26^{11} a dullard
repeats with (ב) his folly, does it over again
(learns nothing by experience). **Niph.** *Inf.*
cstr. וְעַל הִשָּׁנוֹת הַחֲלוֹם אֶל־פַּרְעֹה פַּעֲמָיִם Gn 41^{32}
(E) *concerning the dream's being repeated*, etc.

שְׁתַּיִם, שְׁנַיִם (Philippi $^{ZMG\ xlix\ (1895),\ 202}$ Ges 8147
$^{§97b\ note}$) $_{768}$ **n.m. et f. du. two** (NH *id.*; Ph.
אשנם (and שני *second*), Pun. שנם Lzb^{380}; Ar.

إِثْنَانِ, اِثْنَيْ; Sab. תני Hom$^{Chr\ 47}$, Aram. תְּרֵין, ܬܪܶܝܢ (תִּנְיָנָא, ܬܢܝܢܐ second); Nab. תרין, Palm. f. תרתן, תרתיא, Lzb^{388}; As. *šinâ;* on etym. v. √, and esp. Philippi$^{ZMG\ xxxii\ (1878),\ 21-98}$); —**m.** (c. **n.m.**) שְׁנַיִם Am 3^3+; cstr. שְׁנֵי Is 7^{16}+, sf. שְׁנֵיהֶם Gn 2^{25}+, etc.; **f.** (c. **n.f.**) שְׁתַּיִם Am 4^8+; cstr. שְׁתֵּי Gn 4^{19}, וּשְׁתֵּי Is 7^{21}+, etc., מִשְּׁתֵּי Ju 16^{28} (v. GFM); sfs. v. infr. (2+10=12, v. infr.); Hex chiefly P:—*two:* **1.** no other num.: **a.** usu. cstr. before n.pl. (צְמִידִים) שְׁנֵי Gn 24^{22}+194 t.+2 S 23^{20} ‖ 1 Ch 11^{22} (ins. בְּנֵי 𝔊 Th mod., otherwise RS Sem. i. 469, 2nd ed., 488); (נָשִׁים) שְׁתֵּי Gn 4^{19}+132 t., 1 S 10^4 ins. כִּכְּרוֹת Klo HPS Bu Now; Lv 16^{21} read du. יָדָיו Qr, +Ju 16^{28} (v. supr.)+ שְׁתֵּי־אֵלֶּה Is 47^9 *both these things;* before n.sg., שְׁנֵי Ex 16^{22} (Ges$^{§\ 134\ e}$); sf. שְׁנֵיהֶם *the two of them* Gn 2^{25}+62 t., +Pr 24^{22} (>*their years* 𝔖 𝔗 De al.; prob. crpt., v. Toy), שְׁנֵינוּ Gn 31^{37}+2 t., שְׁנֵיכֶם †Gn 27^{45}; שְׁתֵּיהֶם (msf.! Ges$^{§\ 135\ o}$) †Ru 1^{19} 4^{11}, ־ֵהֶן †1 S 25^{43} Ez 23^{13}. **b.** abs. (1) שְׁנַיִם (90 t.), before n.pl. Ju 11^{37}+26 t.; after n.pl. 2 S 1^1 Ex 29^1+21 t. (usu. P Chr), n.sg. (coll.) Gn 46^{27} Nu 7^{17}+11 t. Nu 17; n. om. Gn 7^2 44^{27}+26 t.; שׁ׳ שׁ׳ distrib. Gn 7^9+; לִשׁ׳ cut *in two* †2 K 3^{25} Je 34^{18}; =*double amount* †Ex $22^{3.6.8}$ (E); פִּי שׁ׳ †Dt 21^{17} *double portion,* +בְּרוּחֲךָ †2 K 2^9 *in* (of) *thy spirit,* +בָּהּ †Zc 3^{18}; (2) שְׁתַּיִם (55 t.), bef. n.pl. 1 K 3^{16}+16 t.; after n.pl. (usu. P and late) 2 Ch 24^3+9 t.; n. om., =*two things* †Is 51^{19} Jb 13^{20} Pr 30^7; שְׁתַּיִם=*twice* †2 K 6^{10} Jb 40^5 ψ 62^{12} (or as Pr 30^7), בִּשׁ׳ Jb 33^{14} either so, or *in two ways* RVm (v. De); as ordin. בִּשְׁנַת שְׁתַּיִם לְ 1 K 15^{25}+9 t., etc.; (3) as round number, שְׁנַיִם עֵצִים 1 K 17^{12} *a few sticks* (Germ. 'ein paar'), cf. 2 K 9^{32} Is 17^6; שְׁתַּיִם שָׁלֹשׁ Am 4^8, פַּעַם וּשְׁתָּיִם Ne 13^{20}, cf. Je 3^{14} אֶחָד מֵעִיר וּשְׁנַיִם מִמִּשְׁפָּחָה = a small no.; Ezr 10^{13} *not for one or two days* (but for many), 2 K 6^{10}. **2.** *twelve:* c. **n.m.** שְׁנֵים עָשָׂר Gn 42^{13}+87 t., לִשְׁנֵי עָשָׂר Ex 28^{21}+4 t.; c. **n.f.** שְׁתֵּי עֶשְׂרֵה שְׁתֵּים עֶשְׂרֵה Ex 24^4+34 t., †Ez $32^{1.17}$ 33^{21}; before n.pl. Gn 17^{20} Ex 15^{27}+; after n.pl. Nu $7^{84.84}$+; before n.sg. Ex 28^{21}+, Gn 14^4 (12 *year*)+, etc.; as ord., בְּיוֹם שְׁנֵים עָשָׂר יוֹם Nu 7^{78}, בִּשְׁתֵּי עֶשְׂרֵה שָׁנָה Ez 32^1+, etc. **3.** with larger num.: 10 (etc.)+2, 2 S 8^5 Ju 10^3 +56 t.; 2+10 (etc.) Nu 1^{35} (P), 2 Ch 22^2+18 t. (Kö$^{ii.\ 1.\ 215\ ff.}$ Ges$^{§\ 97\ f.}$); 200+2+30, 1 K 20^{15}; 50+2 as ord. 2 K 15^{27}+2 t.; cf. 2+20, 1 Ch 24^{17}.

8145 שֵׁנִי **m.** שֵׁנִית **f.**$_{157}$ **adj. num. ord.** second;— בַּיּוֹם הַשֵּׁנִי Ex 2^{13}+, etc. (שֵׁנִי 82 t.+Ne 3^{30}, read בַּשָּׁנָה שֵׁנִית; read וְהַשֵּׁנִי also 1 Ch 6^{13} for (וְשׁני); הַשֵּׁנִית Gn 47^{18}+, etc. (שֵׁנִית 72 t.+Ne 3^{30} v. supr.), שִׁבְעַת יָמִים שׁ׳ Lv $13^{5.33.54}$ *a second heptad of days;* שֵׁנִית=*a second time* Gn 22^{15}+16 t.+ (=*again,* of similar—not identical—act, or another point in a series) Ez 4^6 Mal 2^{13}, וְהַשֵּׁנִית 2 S 16^{19}; †mpl. שְׁנִיִּם Nu 2^{16} they shall set out *as second,* but Gn 6^{16} *second stories* (in ark).

מִשְׁנֶה† **n.[m.]** double, copy, second;— 4932
abs. מ׳ Gn 41^{43}+; cstr. מִשְׁנֵה Je 16^{18}+3 t., so read also Dt 15^{18} (van d. H., >־נֶה Gi), Je 17^{18} (Gie Buhl al.); sf. מִשְׁנֵהוּ 1 S 8^2+; pl. מִשְׁנִים 1 Ch 15^{18} (1 S 15^9 Ezr 1^{10} v. infr.);—**1.** (the) *double:* כֶּסֶף מ׳ Gn 43^{12} (J) *money of double amount,* cf. מ׳ כֶּסֶף v^{15} (J), *a double amount* (in) *money* (Ges$^{§\ 131\ q}$); לֶחֶם מ׳ Ex 16^{22} (P); מ׳ עַל אֲשֶׁר וגו׳ v^5 (P) *the double above what* they gathered daily; מִשְׁנֶה שְׂכַר שָׂכִיר Dt 15^{18} (v. Dr); מ׳ עֲוֹנָם Je 16^{18} *the double of their guilt,* 17^{18} (v. supr.); *a double portion* Is $61^{7.7}$ Zc 9^{12}, Jb 42^{10}. **2.** written *copy* of law Dt 17^{18} Jos 8^{32} (D). **3.** *second* in order: **a.** *second rank,* מִרְכֶּבֶת הַמּ׳ Gn 41^{43} (J), רֶכֶב הַמּ׳ 2 Ch 35^{24}; of pers. *one second in rank,* priest next to high-priest, (הַ)מ׳ 2 K 23^4 25^{18}=Je 52^{24}; אֶהְיֶה־לְּךָ לְמ׳ 1 S 23^{17}, מ׳ לַמֶּלֶךְ Est 10^3; מִשְׁנֵה הַמֶּלֶךְ 2 Ch 28^7, 1 Ch 15^{18} 16^5 2 Ch 31^{12}; מ׳ מֵאֶחָיו Ne 11^{17}.—1 S 15^9 read (cf. 𝔖 𝔗) הַמִּשְׁמַנִּים (Ne 8^{10}) Th, הַשְּׁמֵנִים or הַשְּׁמֵנִים We Dr Bu, etc. (Ez 34^{16}); מִשׁ׳ Ezr 1^{10} is appar. corruption of a numeral. **b.** *second in age,* 1 S 8^2 17^{13} 2 S 3^3 1 Ch 5^{12}. **3.** *second quarter, district,* of city, הַמִּשְׁנֶה 2 K 22^{14}= 2 Ch 34^{22}, Zp 1^{10}, cf. הָעִיר מִשְׁנֶה Ne 11^9 over *the city,* viz. the *second quarter.*

שִׁנְאָן† **n.[m.]** repetition (?);—אַלְפֵי שִׁנְאָן 8136
ψ 68^{18} *thousands of repetition,* i.e. *thousands twice-told,* Che; *redoubled,* Dr, i.e. thousands on thousands (Du, reading אֶלֶף, as שִׁנְּאָ c. sf. *removed them,* treating שנאן אדני מסיני בק׳ as gloss).

שֵׁנָה v. יָשֵׁן. שֶׁנְהַבִּים v. √ שׁנן. 8142-43

p. 446, 1042

[שָׁנַן]† **vb.** whet, sharpen (cf. Ar. سَنَّ 8150
id.; Aram. שְׁנִינָא, ܫܢܝܢܐ *sharp,* etc.; Eth. [ሰነነ:] III, 2, ተሰነነ: *contend, litigate;* hence שֵׁן *tooth,* NH *id.,* As. *šinnu,* Ar. سِنٌّ, Eth. ስን: Aram. שִׁנָּא, ܫܶܢܳܐ);—**Qal** *whet, sharpen: Pf.* 1 s. אִם שַׁנּוֹתִי בְּרַק חַרְבִּי (Ges$^{§\ 67\ ee}$) Dt 32^{41}, of י׳'s preparation for judgment; 3 pl. (כַּחֶרֶב) שָׁנְנוּ לְשׁוֹנָם ψ 64^4 140^4 of uttering sharp words; *Pt. pass.* שְׁנוּנִים *sharpened,* of arrows, Is 5^{28} ψ 45^6, fig. of tongue 120^4, of false witness Pr 25^{18}.

Pi. *Pf.* consec. וְשִׁנַּנְתָּם לְבָנֶיךָ Dt 6^{7} i.e. teach the words *incisively*, Germ. 'einschärfen.' **Hithpo̅.** *Impf.* 1 s. ψ 73^{21} in my kidneys אֶשְׁתּוֹנָן *I was pierced* (of poignant envy).

8127 †I. שֵׁן **n.f.**^{182,13} (yet **m.** 1 S 14^{5} cf. Dr) **tooth, ivory**;—שׁ׳ abs. Ex 21^{24}+, cstr. v^{27}+, שֶׁן־ Dt 32^{24}; sf. שִׁנּוֹ Ex 21^{27}; du. שִׁנַּיִם Pr 10^{26}, cstr. שִׁנֵּי Je 31^{29}+; sf. שִׁנֵּיהֶם ψ 124^{6}, שִׁנֵּימוֹ 58^{7}, etc.;—**1.** *tooth*: **a.** of man, Ex $21^{27.27.27}$ (E), Nu 11^{33} (J), Gn 49^{12} (poem in J), Am 4^{6} Ct 4^{2} 6^{6}, שׁ׳ רֹעָה Pr 25^{19}, v. II. רעע **2**; of *lex talionis*, שׁ׳ תַּחַת שׁ׳ Ex 21^{24}(E), Lv 24^{20}(H), שֵׁן בְּשׁ׳ Dt 19^{21}; irritated by acid Pr 10^{26}, dulled by it (in proverb of inherited guilt) Je $31^{29.30}$ Ez 18^{2}; חָרַק שׁ׳ La 2^{16} Jb 16^{9} ψ 35^{16} 112^{10}, v. חָרַק; אֶשָּׂא בְשָׂרִי בְשִׁנָּי Jb 13^{14}=*risk my life* (del. עַל־מָה, dittogr.; ‖ נַפְשִׁי אָשִׂים בְּכַפִּי); בְּעוֹר שִׁנָּי 19^{20}, v. מלט **Hithp.** (other conj. v. Di Bi Bu Du). **b.** of beasts: Dt 32^{24}, crocodile Jb 41^{6}, locusts Jo 1^{6} (teeth of lions); esp. fig. of false prophets Mi 3^{5}, of foes Zc 9^{7}, oppressors Jb 29^{17}, wicked 4^{10} ψ 3^{8} 58^{7} 124^{6}; of their weapons Pr 30^{14} ψ 57^{5}; of Isr. shattered by י׳. **c.** *tooth* of a fork, *tine*, 1 S 2^{13} (cf. Dr $^{Sm. 291}$); of cliff, שֵׁן הַסֶּלַע $14^{4.4}$, cf. Jb 39^{28}, הַשֵּׁן 1 S 14^{5}. **2.** *ivory*, of commerce, קַרְנוֹת שֵׁן Ez 27^{15} (i.e. *tusks* ?); as material, מִטּוֹת שׁ׳ Am 6^{4}, כִּסֵּא־שׁ׳ 1 K 10^{18}=2 Ch 9^{17}, בֵּית הַשׁ׳ 1 K 22^{39}, cf. Am 3^{15}, הֵיכְלֵי שׁ׳ ψ 45^{9}, also Ez 27^{6} Ct 5^{15} 7^{5}.

8129 II. שֵׁן **n.pr.loc.** הַשׁ׳ 1 S 7^{12}, v. יְשָׁנָה p. 446^{a}.

8148 †שְׁנִינָה **n.f. sharp (cutting) word, taunt**;—Dt 28^{37} 1 K 9^{7}=2 Ch 7^{20}, Je 24^{9} (cf. ψ 64^{4} 140^{4}).

8143 †שֶׁנְהַבִּים appar. **n. m. [pl.]**, in list of Solomon's imports, 1 K 10^{22}=2 Ch 9^{21}, AV RV **ivory** (elsewh. שֵׁן alone); hence הַבִּים=*elephants* acc. to Ges (in Thes) Ew Hi Schr $^{ZMG\ xxvii\ (1873), 709}$ COT ^{1K}, cf. 𝔊 (2 Ch, and A in 1 K) ὀδόντων ἐλεφαντίνων, 𝔙 (in 1 K) *dentes elephantorum*, 𝔗; but this very dub.; < rd. Röd ^{Thes} Th Be Che $^{EB\ 1154}$ שֵׁן (וְ)הָבְנִים *ivory* (and) *ebony* (Ez 27^{15}).

8151 †[שָׁנַס] **vb. Pi. gird up** (si vera l.; in Talm. (Aram.) שְׁנַץ=*bind* sandals; NH שְׁנָץ *thong*);—*Impf.* 3 ms. וַיְשַׁנֵּס מָתְנָיו וַיָּרָץ 1 K 18^{46}.

8142, 8153 שְׁנָת ψ 132^{4} v. שֵׁנָה p. 446^{a}.

8152 †שִׁנְעָר **n. pr. loc. Shinar** = Babylonia (=Bab. *Šumêr* acc. to COT $^{Gn\ 11,1}$ al., > denied by Hal $^{Rev.\ Crit.\ 1883,\ 44}$ Jen $^{ZK\ ii\ (1885),\ 419}$; Egypt. *Sangar* (WMM $^{As.\ u.\ Eur.\ 279}$), TelAm. *Šanḫar* (Wkl $^{TelAm.\ 25}$) identif. with שׁ׳ by Mey $^{Egyptiaca\ 63}$; cf., further, Pinches $^{Hast.\ DB\ Shinar}$);—אֶרֶץ שׁ׳ Gn 10^{10} 11^{2} Zc 5^{11} Dn 1^{2}; מֶלֶךְ־שׁ׳ (Amraphel) Gn $14^{2.9}$; שׁ׳ alone Is 11^{11} (as place of diaspora); אַדֶּרֶת שׁ׳ Jos 7^{21}; 𝔊 usu. Σεν(ν)ααρ; Zc 5^{11} (ἐν γῇ) Βαβυλῶνος.

שְׁנַת *sleep*, v. שֵׁנָה sub יָשֵׁן. p. 446 8153

†[שָׁסָה] **vb. spoil, plunder** (rarer syn. of שׁלל, בזז; with this √ WMM $^{As.\ u.\ Eur.\ 131}$ connects Egypt. name of Beduin plunderers *Šôs* [*ša-su, ša-sa*]; connex. doubted by Jen $^{ZA\ x\ (1895),\ 331}$);—**Qal** *Pf.* 3 pl. שָׁסוּ לָמוֹ ψ 44^{11} *they plunder for themselves*; *Impf.* 3 ms. יִשְׁסֶה אוֹצַר וגו׳ Ho 13^{15}; elsewh. *Pt.* שֹׁסִים *plunderers* Ju 2^{14} 2 K 17^{20}; c. acc. loc. 1 S 23^{1}; c. sf. (as obj.) שֹׁסֵהוּ 1 S 14^{48} (prob. pl.=שֹׁסָיו, so Sta $^{p.355}$ Dr Bu, cf. Ges ^{§91k}), שׁוֹסֵינוּ Is 17^{14} (‖ בֹּזְזֵינוּ), שֹׁסֵיהֶם Ju 2^{16}; שֹׁסַיִךְ Je 30^{16} Qr (Kt v. שׁסס ‖ בֹּזְזַיִךְ); cstr. שֹׁסֵי נַחֲלָתִי 8155
50^{11}; *pass.* עַם־בָּזוּז וְשָׁסוּי Is 42^{22}. **Po̅.=Qal** *Pf.* 1 s. שׁוֹשֵׂתִי (Ges ^{§6k}) Is 10^{13}, c. acc. rei; read also prob. *Pt.* מְשׁוֹסֶה Is 42^{24} (‖ בֹּזְזִים), for משוסה 4882
Kt, מְשִׁסָּה Qr; so Du Klo Che ^{Hpt} Marti.

†[שָׁסַס] **vb. id.** (‖ form of שׁסה);—**Qal** 8155
Pf. 3 pl. שַׁסֻּהוּ ψ 89^{42} they *have plundered him*; *Impf.* 3 mpl. וַיָּשֹׁסּוּ Ju 2^{14} (acc. pers.); 1 S 17^{53} (acc. loc.); *Pt.* sf. שֹׁאסַיִךְ Je 30^{16} Kt (Qr v. שׁסה), 8154
Aram. form, Ges ^{§67s}. **Niph.** *be plundered, rifled*, of houses: *Pf.* 3 pl. consec. וְנָשַׁסּוּ Zc 14^{2}; *Impf.* 3 mpl. יִשַּׁסּוּ Is 13^{16}.

†מְשִׁסָּה **n.f. booty, plunder**;—abs. מ׳ 2 K 4933
21^{14}+, so Is 42^{24} Qr (מְשִׁסָּה Gi, מְשִׁיסָּה Baer; Kt משוסה, usu. read מְשׁוּסָּה, < read מְשׁוֹסֶה, v. 4882
שׁסה **Po̅.**); pl. abs. מְשִׁסּוֹת Hb 2^{7};—*plunder, spoil, prey*, usu. הָיָה לִמְ׳ (and ‖ בַּז) 2 K 21^{14} Je 30^{16} Hb 2^{7} Zp 1^{13} (‖ שְׁמָמָה), cf. Is 42^{22} (v^{24} see above).

†[שָׁסַע] **vb. divide, cleave** (NH Pi. *tear* 8156
apart; 𝔗 ^{Jer} Pa. La 3^{11} *tear in pieces* (for 𝔥 פִּשְּׁחַ));—**Qal** *Pt.* (c. acc. cogn. שֶׁסַע): ms. וְשֹׁסַע שֶׁסַע פַּרְסָה Lv 11^{7} (P; on שׁ׳ cf. Lag $^{BN\ 54}$) *cleaving the cleft of the hoof*, i.e. having cloven hoof, so fs. שֹׁסַעַת v^{3}, cf. Dt 14^{6}; שֶׁסַע אֵינֶנָּה שֹׁסַעַת Lv 11^{26} (P); *pass.* הַפַּרְסָה הַשְּׁסוּעָה Dt 14^{7}. **Pi.** *tear in two*, a lion, kid, *Impf.*, *Inf. cstr.* וַיְשַׁסְּעֵהוּ כְּשַׁסַּע הַגְּדִי Ju 14^{6}; a bird (by, or at, its wings), *Pf.* 3 ms. consec. וְשִׁסַּע אֹתוֹ Lv 1^{17} (P); *Impf.* 3 ms. וַיְשַׁסַּע (אֶת־אֲנָשָׁיו בַּדְּבָרִים) 1 S 24^{8} gives too violent a meaning; prob. crpt. for word=*restrain*, or the like Dr HPS, cf. Bu Now (hesitantly).

8156-57 †שֶׁ֫סַע **n.[m.]** cleft;—as acc. cogn. c. [שָׁסַע], q.v.; abs. Lv 11^{26}, cstr. $v^{3.7}$ Dt 14^{6}. p. 1042

8158 †[שִׁסַּף] **vb.** dub.: **Pi.** hew in pieces (Vrss and context);—*Impf.* 3 ms. וַיְשַׁסֵּף 1 S 15^{33}, acc. pers.;—Gr Dr HPS qy. וַיְשַׁסַּע, but improb.

8159 †שָׁעָה **vb. gaze** (steadily, with interest, etc.) (As. *šeʼû, behold, look for, aim at*);—**Qal** *Pf.* 3 ms. שׁ׳ Gn 4^{5}, etc.; *Impf.* 3 ms. יִשְׁעֶה Is $17^{7.8}$, apoc. וַיִּ֫שַׁע Gn 4^{4}, 1 s. אֶשְׁעָה (Ges § 75 l) ψ 119^{117}, etc.; *Imv.* ms. שְׁעֵה Jb 14^{6}; mpl. שְׁעוּ Is 22^{4};—*gaze* at, *regard* (with favour), י׳ subj., c. אֶל Gn $4^{4.5}$ (J); c. מִן pers. = *turn gaze away* Is 22^{4} Jb 7^{19} Thes Ew Che, + prob. 10^{20} (for יָשִׁית), c. מֵעַל pers. 14^{6}; man subj., *regard* God (with trust, devotion), c. עַל Is 17^{7} 31^{1}; c. אֶל rei 17^{8}; c. בְּ of words, statutes, Ex 5^{9} (J) ψ 119^{117}; abs. 3 fpl. תִּשְׁעֶינָה Is 32^{3} *shall* not *behold* makes no sense, read prob. תְּשֹׁעֶינָה (√I. שׁעע, Ew and most); 3 mpl. יִשְׁעוּ 2 S 22^{42} *they look* (about) for help, < as ∥ ψ 18^{42} יְשַׁוְּעוּ. **Hiph.** *Imv.* ms. הָשַׁע מִמֶּנִּי ψ 39^{14} *cause thy gaze to turn away from me* (see also
8173 √I. שׁעע), < **Qal** שְׁעֵה as Jb 14^{6} (cf. 7^{19} Is 22^{4}) Hup Bae Du Ges § 75 gg. **Hithp.** *Impf.* 2 ms. apoc. אַל־תִּשְׁתָּע Is 41^{10} *gaze not about* (in anxiety, ∥ אַל־תִּירָא); 1 pl. וְנִשְׁתָּ֫עָה (Ges § 75 l) v^{23} *let us look at each other* (in rivalry, v. ראה **Hithp.**).

שׁעט (√of following; Ar. ثَعَطَ II. *pound to pieces*).

8161 †[שְׁעָטָה] **n.f. stamping** (of hoofs);—cstr. שַׁעֲטַת פַּרְסוֹת אַבִּירָיו Je 47^{3}.

8162 †שַׁעַטְנֵז **n.m. mixed stuff** (perh. of Egypt. origin; Kn der. from Copt. *saht, woven*, + *nudj, false* (Peyron Lex 224. 133), and thinks orig. שַׁעַטְנֹז; 𝔊 has κίβδηλος, *spurious*);—a kind of cloth forbidden for garments; defined Dt 22^{11} by צֶמֶר וּפִשְׁתִּים יַחְדָּו, and Lv 19^{19} (H) by כִּלְאַיִם.

8165 שֵׂעִיר v. שֵׂעִיר. p. 973

I. **שׁעל** (√of following; NH שַׁעַל *deep, depth*, of sea; Aram. שִׁעֲלָא, שְׁעוֹלָא, ܫܥܠܐ = BH [שֹׁעַל]).

8168 †[שֹׁ֫עַל] **n.[m.] hollow hand, handful**;—**1.** *hollow hand*: sf. בְּשָׁעֳלוֹ Is 40^{12} (fig. of י׳ holding waters). **2.** *handful*: pl. שְׁעָלִים 1 K 20^{10} (dust, in hyperb.); cstr. שַׁעֲלֵי שְׂעֹרִים (as if fr. [שַׁ֫עַל] Kö ii. 1. 35) Ez 13^{19} *handfuls of barley*.

†מִשְׁעוֹל **n.m. hollow way**, road shut in;— 4934
cstr. מ׳ הַכְּרָמִים Nu 22^{24} (JE) i.e. road shut in between vineyards.

II. **שׁעל** (√of foll.; NH שׁוּעָל, שַׁעַל; Ar. ثُعَالٌ, ثُعَالَةٌ; Aram. תַּעֲלָא, ܬܥܠܐ, all = BH שׁוּעָל).

†I. שׁוּעָל **n.m.** Ct 2, 15 fox, perhaps also 7776
jackal;—abs. שׁ׳ Ne 3^{25}; pl. שׁוּעָלִים Ju 15^{4}+, שֻׁ׳ Ez 13^{4} Ct 2^{15b};—*fox* (prob.) Ne 3^{25} Ct $2^{15.15}$; perh. (fr. large no.) *jackal* Ju 15^{4}; as haunting ruins Ez 13^{4} La 5^{18}; eating offal ψ 63^{11}.

†II. שׁוּעָל **n.pr.loc.** district in Israel;— 7777
אֶרֶץ שׁ׳ 1 S 13^{17} (דֶּרֶךְ עָפְרָה); not identified.—Vid. also חֲצַר שׁ׳ p. 347^{b} supr.

†III. שׁוּעָל **n.pr.m.** in Asher;—1 Ch 7^{36}, 7777
Σουλα, A Σουαλ, 𝔊L Σουαν.

†שַׁעַלְבִים **n.pr.loc.** (perh. haunt of *foxes*; 8169
Ar. ثَعْلَبٌ, As. *šêlibu, fox*);—in (orig.) territory of Dan, Ju 1^{35} (cf. GFM, on etym. and site), 1 K 4^{9}, Θαλαβειν, Σαλαβειμ, Ju also αἱ ἀλώπεκες, as doublet, or (A 𝔊L) alone; = שַׁעֲלַבִּין Jos 19^{42}, Σα(α)λαβειν.

שַׁעֲלַבִּין v. foregoing. 8169

†שַׁעַלְבֹנִי **adj.gent.** (of foregoing?);—2 S 8170
23^{32} = 1 Ch 11^{33}; ὁ Σαλβωνείτης, Σαλαβωνι, etc.

†שַׁעֲלִים **n.pr.loc.** district in Israel;— 8171
אֶרֶץ שׁ׳ 1 S 9^{4}, Εασακεμ, A Σααλειμ, 𝔊L Σεγαλειμ; near Michmash Schick ZPV iv. 248; not identified; = שַׁעַלְבִים We Dr Now; cf. II. שׁוּעָל Th HPS Bu.

שׁעם √assumed by Thes for מִשְׁעָם n.pr. q.v.

†[שָׁעַן] **vb. Niph.** lean, support one- 8172
self;—*Pf.* 3 ms. consec. וְנִשְׁעַן Nu 21^{15} Is 10^{20}; 1 pl. נִשְׁעַנּוּ 2 Ch 14^{10}, etc.; *Impf.* 3 ms. יִשָּׁעֵן Jb 8^{15}+, etc.; *Imv.* mpl. הִשָּׁעֲנוּ Gn 18^{4}; *Inf. cstr.* הִשָּׁעֵן Is 10^{20}, sf. הִשָּׁעֶנְךָ 2 Ch $16^{7.8}$, etc.; *Pt.* נִשְׁעָן 2 S 1^{6}+;—*lean*, c. עַל *upon*, 2 S 1^{6} 2 K 5^{18} $7^{2.17}$, *against* pillars Ju 16^{26}, house Jb 8^{15} (fig.); תַּחַת הָעֵץ Gn 18^{4} (J); poet. of cliff, וְנִשׁ׳ לִגְבוּל Nu 21^{15} *leans to* (upon) *the border* of Moab; *lean* (fig. = trust) upon, עַל pers. king Is 10^{20} Ez 29^{7} 2 Ch 16^{7}; עַל־י׳ Mi 3^{11} Is 10^{20} 2 Ch 13^{18} 14^{10} $16^{7.8}$; בֵּאלֹהָיו Is 50^{10}; abs. Jb 24^{23}; עַל־סוּסִים Is 31^{1}; עַל c. n. abstr. 30^{12} Pr 3^{5}.

†אֶשְׁעָן **n.pr.loc.** in hills of Judah Jos 15^{52}, 824
Σομα, 𝔊L Εσαν.

4937 †מִשְׁעָן **n.[m.] support, staff**;—abs. מ׳, fig. of י׳, 2 S 22[19] = ψ 18[19]; cstr. כֹּל מִשְׁעַן־לֶחֶם וְכֹל מִשְׁעַן־מָיִם Is 3[1] (gloss, v. Comm.).

4937 †מַשְׁעֵן **n.m. id.**;—abs. מ׳ וּמַשְׁעֵנָה Is 3[1] fig. *support and staff.*

4938 †מַשְׁעֵנָה **n.f. id.**, v. foregoing (m. et f. to exhaust the category = support of every kind).

4938 †מִשְׁעֶנֶת **n.f. staff**;—abs. Ju 6[21] 2 K 4[31]; cstr. 2 K 18[21]+; sf. מִשְׁעַנְתּוֹ Ex 21[19] Zc 8[4], etc.; pl. sf. מִשְׁעֲנֹתָם Nu 21[18];—*staff*, Ex 21[19] (E) Nu 21[18] (J) Ju 6[21] 2 K 4[29.29.31] Zc 8[4]; fig. of political support, מִשְׁעֶנֶת הַקָּנֶה הָרָצוּץ 2 K 18[21] = Is 36[6], cf. Ez 29[6]; of י׳ as shepherd ψ 23[4] (+ שֵׁבֶט).

8173 †I. [שָׁעַע] **vb. be smeared over, blinded** (Aram. שְׁעַע *smear* (akin to שׁוּעַ *id.*), [illegible] *to smooth*, שְׁעִיעַ *smooth* (of words), *flattering*, [illegible] *smooth* (cf. also [illegible], [illegible] *smear over, close up*));—**Qal** *Imv.* + **Hithpalp.** *Imv.* mpl. הִשְׁתַּעַשְׁעוּ וָשֹׁעוּ Is 29[9] *blind yourselves and be blind!* (|| הִתְמַהְמְהוּ וּתְמָהוּ); > Buhl הִשְׁתָּעוּ וּשְׁעוּ, √שׁעה *look about* (2 S 22[42]); Is 32[3] rd. prob. 3 fpl. תְּשֹׁעֶינָה, of eyes, *be blinded* (v. שׁעה). **Hiph.** *Imv.* ms. וְעֵינָיו הָשַׁע Is 6[10] *and its eyes besmear!*—So perhaps הָשַׁע ψ 39[14] (עֵינֶיךָ om.) was intended by Mas. (but wrongly, v. Ol al.);

8159 see שָׁעָה. p. 1043

8173 †II. [שָׁעַע] **vb. Pilp.**, etc., **sport, take delight in, delight** (usu. made = I. שׁ׳ *smooth over, please;* Buhl cp. Aram. [illegible], Ithpe. *sport, trifle*, Vulg. Ar. مشعشع (loan-word?) Vollers ZMG xlv (1891), 86, l. 3);—**Pilp.** *Pf.* 3 ms. consec. וְשִׁעֲשַׁע Is 29[9] the suckling *shall sport* on (עַל) the cobra's hole; 1 s. שִׁעֲשָׁעְתִּי ψ 119[70] *I take delight in* thy law (acc.; but ? rd. שַׁעֲשֻׁעָי, v[77]); *Impf.* transit. 3 mpl. יְשַׁעַשְׁעוּ ψ 94[19] thy consolations *delight* my soul (acc.). **Palp.** *Impf.* 2 mpl. תְּשָׁעֳשָׁעוּ Is 66[12] upon (עַל) the knees *shall ye be fondled.* **Hithpalp.** *Impf.* 1 s. אֶשְׁתַּעֲשָׁע ψ 119[16] in (בְּ) thy statutes *will I delight myself*, cf. v[47].

8191 †[שַׁעֲשֻׁעִים], -שׁוּעִים **n.[m.] pl. intens. delight** (Ba NB 206);—abs. -שׁוּעִים Je 31[20] Pr 8[30]; sf. -שׁוּעָיו Is 5[7], usu. -שַׁעֲשֻׁעַי Pr 8[31] ψ 119[24], -שַׁעֲשֻׁעַי v[77] + 3 t.;—*delight*, in phr. נְטַע שׁ׳ Is 5[7] *the planting of his delight* (in which he took delight), so יֶלֶד שׁ׳ Je 31[20] (|| בֵּן יַקִּיר); שׁ׳ אֶת־ Pr 8[31] *my delight* (was) *with* the sons of men; elsewhere = *object of delight*, of wisdom v[30]; God's law, etc., ψ 119[24.77.92.143.174].

†שַׁעַף **n.pr.m.** in clan of Caleb, Σαγαε, A Σαγαφ, 𝔊L Σααφ;—**1.** שׁ׳ 1 Ch 2[49]. **2.** שָׁעַף v[47]. 8174

I. שׁער (√ of foll.; Ar. ثَغَرَ *break, break off, through*, ثَغْرٌ *gap, opening;* Eth. ሰበረ: *tear in two, dissolve;* Aram. [illegible] (transp.) *split, divide*, תְּרַע *tear down;* NH שַׁעַר *gate*, so MI[22] שעריה (pl. sf.), Ph. שער Lzb[381]; Tel Am. *šaḫri*, as Canaanism, Wkl[195, l. 16]; Aram. תַּרְעָא, [illegible]; Nab. תרעא Lzb[388];—Egypt. *šaʿār* is loan-word Bondi[70]).

שַׁעַר[373] **n.m.**[2 S 18, 24] (**f.**[Is 14, 31] in personif., Albr ZAW xvi (1896), 86) **gate**;—שׁ׳ abs. Ju 9[40]+, cstr. Gn 22[17]+; c. ה loc., שַׁעְרָה Is 28[6]+; pl. שְׁעָרִים 2 S 18[24]+, cstr. שַׁעֲרֵי 1 S 17[52]+; sf. שְׁעָרֶיךָ Dt 12[15]+, שַׁעֲרֵיהֶם Ez 21[20] 48[34], etc.;—**1. a.** *gate*, entrance to city, shut (סָגַר) by night Jos 2[5.7] (JE), cf. Is 45[1], opened (פָּתַח) by day Ne 7[3], cf. Is 60[11]; for entrance (בּוֹא), and exit (יָצָא) Je 17[19.20.21.24.25.27] La 4[12] Ez 26[10]+; עָבַר שׁ׳ Mi 2[13] *pass out through* (disreg. accents), בֹּא שׁ׳ Is 62[10]; with bars ψ 147[13]; attacked Ez 21[20.27], cf. Is 28[6] Mi 1[9.12] 1 S 17[52]; on Ju 5[8.11] v. Comm.; burned (by foe) Je 1[27] 51[58] Ne 1[3] 2[3.13.17]; as giving control, possession, of city, יָרַשׁ אֵת שׁ׳ אֹיְבָיו Gn 22[17] 24[60] (J); פֶּתַח הַשׁ׳ Ju 9[40]+ (v. פ׳), דַּלְתוֹת הַשׁ׳ 1 S 21[14]+ (v. ד׳ 3); פֶּתַח־הַשׁ׳ Ju 18[16.17] of farm or village; so of camp Ex 32[26.27] (J). In cities, elaborate structure, with roof 2 S 18[24], upper chamber 19[1]; cf. שְׂאוּ שְׁעָרִים רָאשֵׁיכֶם ψ 24[7.9]; write laws בִּשׁ׳ Dt 6[9] (+ עַל־מְזֻזוֹת בֵּיתֶךָ), 11[20] (+ *id.*); אֶל־תּוֹךְ הַשׁ׳ 1 S 9[18], בְּתוֹךְ הַשׁ׳ 2 S 3[27]; לְיַד שׁ׳ as public, 1 S 4[18], + v[13] 𝔊 Th We Dr al., cf. 2 S 15[2] 18[4] Pr 8[3] (|| מְבוֹא פְתָחִים). **b.** particular gates of Jerusalem are: (1) שׁ׳ אֶפְרַיִם 2 K 14[13] || 2 Ch 25[23], Ne 8[16] 12[39]; (2) שׁ׳ הָאַשְׁפֹּת Ne 2[13] 3[14] 12[31] = שׁ׳ הַשְׁפוֹת 3[13]; (3) שׁ׳ בִּנְיָמִן Je 37[13] 38[7] Zc 14[10]; (4) שׁ׳ הַגַּיְא Ne 2[13.15] 3[13] 2 Ch 26[9]; (5) שׁ׳ הַדָּגִים Zp 1[10] Ne 3[3] 12[39] 2 Ch 33[14]; (6) שׁ׳ בֵּין הַחֹמֹתַיִם 2 K 25[4] = Je 52[7], cf. Je 39[4]; (7) שׁ׳ החרסות Je 19[2]; (8) שׁ׳ הַיְשָׁנָה Ne 3[6] 12[39]; (9) שׁ׳ הַמִּזְרָח 3[29]; (10) שׁ׳ הַמַּטָּרָה 12[39]; (11) שׁ׳ הַמַּיִם לַמִּזְרָח 8[1.3.16]; (12) שׁ׳ הַמַּיִם לַמִּזְרָח 3[26], cf. 12[37]; (13) שׁ׳ הַמִּפְקָד 3[31]; (14) שׁ׳ הָעַיִן 2[14] 3[15] 12[37]; 5869 (15) שׁ׳ הַסּוּסִים Je 31[40] Ne 3[28] (cf. **3 b**); (16) שׁ׳ הַפִּנָּה 2 K 14[13] || 2 Ch 25[23] (rd. הַפִּנָּה for הַפּוֹנֶה), Je 31[38] 2 Ch 26[9]; prob. = שׁ׳ הַפִּנִּים Zc 14[10]; (17) שׁ׳ הָרִאשׁוֹן Zc 14[10]; (18) שׁ׳ הצאן Ne 3[1.32] 12[39];—on sites and rel. to each other v. RS-GASm Ency. Bib. JERUSALEM Conder Hast. DB id. Buhl G 133 ff. Bd Pal. s. v. Murray Hd. Bk. s. v. Be-Ry Ne p. 182 ff. Gu ZPV, esp. v (1882), 7 ff.,

8179

viii (1885), 245 ff. Comm.$^{ad\ loc.\ var.}$. **c.** of Ezekiel's holy city, שַׁעֲרֵי הָעִיר Ez 48^{31}, three on each side, named for tribes, $v^{31.31.31.31}$ + 12 t. Ez 48. **2. a.** *gate*=space inside gate, as public meeting-place, market 2 K $7^{1.18}$, place of public well 2 S $23^{15.16}$=1 Ch $11^{17.18}$, where elders, judges, king, sat officially Dt 21^{19} 22^{15} Am $5^{12.15}$ Is 29^{21} 2 S 18^{24} 19^{9} 1 K 22^{10}=2 Ch 18^{9}, Gn 19^{1} (J) Pr 24^{7} Jb 5^{4} 31^{21} Ru $4^{1.11}$ Pr $31^{23.31}$, etc.; of conqueror Je 1^{15}; appar.=רְחוֹב שׁ׳ Gn 19^{2} (J) Ne 8^{16} 1 Ch 9^{16}+ (v. 1. ר׳); Gn 34^{20} (P) one *came unto* gate (בָּא אֶל־), so בָּאֵי שׁ׳ $23^{10.18}$ (P) *those entering the gate*, i.e. having citizens' rights; also *went out* (to), יָצָא שׁ׳ Jb 29^{7} (i.e., in this case, from his own house, outside the city), hence כָּל־יֹצְאֵי שׁ׳ Gn $34^{24.24}$ (P; cf. also הוֹצִיא אֶל־ Dt 21^{19} $22^{15.24}$); hence=body of citizens, כָּל־שׁ׳ עַמִּי Ru 3^{11}. **b.** hence also=city Is 14^{31} (‖ עִיר), ψ 87^{2}, etc. **c.** specif. in Dt, בִּשְׁעָרֶיךָ *in thy gates*, i.e. thy cities, towns, etc., Dt 5^{14}=Ex 20^{10}, Dt $12^{12.15.17.21}$ + 22 t. Dt + 1 K 8^{37} (read בְּאַחַד שׁ׳, cf. Dt 18^{6} 23^{17}, so 𝔊 𝔖 mod.), so ‖ 2 Ch 6^{28}, + (perh.) Je 14^{2} (but 15^{7} Na 3^{13} fig. of *gates* as entrance to land); of private house, שַׁעֲרֵי צַדִּיק Pr 14^{19} (perh. cf. Ju 18^{16} **1 a** supr.). **3. a.** *gate* of royal castle or palace 2 K 9^{31} Je $22^{2.4}$ Ne 2^{8} Est 2^{19} + 10 t. Est; specif. (of king of Judah), שׁ׳ סוּר 2 K 11^{6} =שׁ׳ הַיְסוֹד 2 Ch 23^{5} (v. ס׳, יס׳), שׁ׳ הָרָצִים 2 K 11^{19}, שׁ׳ הַסּוּסִים בֵּית הַמּ׳ 2 Ch 23^{15} הַשׁ׳ אַחַר הָר׳ v^{6}; (=מְבוֹא הַס׳ ‖ 2 K 11^{16}); appar. of official residence, פֶּתַח שׁ׳ יְהוֹשֻׁעַ 2 K 23^{8}. **b.** of temple Je $7^{2.2}$ 1 Ch 9^{23} 16^{42} + 12 t. Ch, incl. שַׁעֲרֵי מַחֲנוֹת י׳ 2 Ch 31^{2} (v. מַחֲנֶה **1**, p. 334), cf. ψ 100^{4} 118^{20}, שַׁעֲרֵי צֶדֶק v^{19}; specif. שׁ׳ בִּנְיָמִין הָעֶלְיוֹן Je 20^{2}, and (om. בְּנ׳) 2 K 15^{35}=2 Ch 27^{3}, Ez 9^{2}, 2 Ch 23^{20}, שׁ׳ הַפְּנִימִית הַפּוֹנָה Je 26^{10} 36^{10}, שׁ׳ (בֵּית) י׳ הֶחָדָשׁ שׁ׳ הַמִּזְבֵּחַ שַׁעַר בֵּית י׳ הַקַּדְמֹנִי Ez 8^{3} cf. v^{14}, 8^{5}, צָפוֹנָה 10^{19} 11^{1}; שׁ׳ שַׁלֶּכֶת 1 Ch 26^{16}; שַׁעַר הַמֶּלֶךְ 1 Ch 9^{18}. **c.** of Ezekiel's temple and courts Ez $40^{3.6}$ $44^{11.17}$ + 67 t. Ez 40–47. **d.** of court of tabern. (P), שׁ׳ הֶחָצֵר Ex 27^{16} 35^{17} + 6 t. Ex + Nu 4^{36}. **4.** fig. זֶה שׁ׳ הַשָּׁמַיִם Gn 28^{17} (E; ‖ בֵּית אֱלֹהִים); pl. שַׁעֲרֵי שְׁאוֹל Is 38^{10}; שׁ׳־מָוֶת Jb 38^{17} ψ 9^{14} 107^{18}; שׁ׳ צַלְמָוֶת Jb 38^{17}.

7778 **שֹׁעֵר** $_{37}$ **n.m. porter** (denom. from 1. שַׁעַר);—abs. שׁוֹ׳ 2 Ch 31^{14}, cstr. שׁ׳ 2 K 7^{10} 1 Ch 9^{21}, + f. שׁוֹעֶרֶת 2 S 4^{6} (for MT [בָּאוּ עַד תּ[וֹךְ) We Dr HPS Bu Now after 𝔊 (Th פְּקִידַת דֶּלֶת); pl. שֹׁעֲרִים 2 K 7^{11}+; cstr. שֹׁעֲרֵי 2 Ch 23^{4};—*porter* of city gate 2 K $7^{10.11}$ (2 S 18^{26} rd. הַשַּׁעַר 𝔊 𝔖 𝔙 Th We Dr and most); *portress* of house 2 S 4^{6} (v. supr.); elsewhere (34 t. Ch Ezr Ne) of gate-keepers in sanctuary 1 Ch $9^{17.18.24}$+; 4,000 in no., 23^{5}; שׁ׳ לָאָרוֹן v^{22}; שֹׁעֲרִים בַּסִּפִּים 9^{21}; פֶּתַח לְאֹהֶל מוֹעֵד $15^{23.24}$; שֹׁעֲרֵי הַסִּפִּים 2 Ch 23^{4}; בְּנֵי הַשֹּׁעֲרִים Ezr 2^{42}.

8187 †**שְׁעַרְיָה** **n.pr.m.** in Benjamin, 1 Ch 8^{38}=9^{44}, Σαρ(α)ια, Σααρια.

8189 †**שַׁעֲרַיִם** **n.pr.loc. 1.** in the Shephelah of Judah (Buhl$^{Geogr. 194}$) Jos 15^{36}, Σακαρειμ, 𝔊L Σεβαρειμ; דֶּרֶךְ שׁ׳ 1 S 17^{52} (𝔊 τῶν πυλῶν). **2.** in the Negeb (Simeon), וּבְשַׁעֲרַיִם 1 Ch 4^{31}, Σεωρειμ, 𝔊L Σααριμ; =שָׁרוּחֶן (q.v.) Jos 19^{6}, and perhaps שִׁלְחִים (in Negeb of Judah) 15^{32}; Buhl$^{Geogr. 185}$.

8176 †II. **שָׁעַר** **vb. calculate, reckon** (NH Pi. JAram. Pa. *put a valuation on, estimate;* JAram. שַׁעֲרָא *interest, market-price;* Ar. سِعْر *market-price* is loan-word Frä ^{189});—**Qal** *Pf.* 3 ms. כְּמוֹ־שׁ׳ בְּנַפְשׁוֹ כֶּן־הוּא Pr 23^{7} *as he has calculated in his soul, so is he*, but dub.: De שֹׁעֵר *as one who calculates;* more radical conj. in Bi Toy.

8180 †II. [**שַׁעַר**] **n.[m.] measure** (prop. *reckoning*);—pl. מֵאָה שְׁעָרִים Gn 26^{12} (J) 100 *measures*, i.e. 100 for one=100-fold.

III. **שער** (√ of following).

8182 †[**שֹׁעָר**] **adj. horrid, disgusting** (Ba$^{NB\ 167}$);—pl. כַּתְּאֵנִים הַשֹּׁעָרִים Je 29^{17} (uneatable).

8186 †**שַׁעֲרוּרָה** **n.f. horror=horrible thing;**—שַׁמָּה וְשׁ׳ Je 5^{30} *an astounding and horrible thing has occurred;* בִּנְבִיאֵי ירוש׳ רָאִיתִי שׁ׳ 23^{14}.

8186 †**שַׁעֲרוּרִיָּה, שַׁעֲרֻרִית** **n.f.** id.;—abs. רָאִיתִי שַׁעֲרוּרִיָּה Ho 6^{10} Qr (> Kt שעריריה); שַׁעֲרֻרִת עָשְׂתָה בְּתוּלַת יִשׁ׳ Je 18^{13}.

8190 †**שַׁעַשְׁגַז** **n.m. pers.** Est 2^{14}, Γαι.

8192 †I. [**שָׁפָה**] **vb. sweep bare** (Ar. سَفَا (ى), of wind, *raise and carry off* dust, أَسْفَى of horse, *scanty* in hair of forelock; NH Pi. *plane off;* Aram. ܫܦܐ Pt. pass. *level* (Is 40^{4}=מִישׁוֹר), *smooth, limpid*, ܫܘܦ *make level, smooth* (and deriv.));—**Niph.** *be wind-swept, bare;* *Pt.* הַר־נִשְׁפֶּה Is 13^{2} *a bare mt.;* **Pu.** *Pf.* consec. וְשֻׁפּוּ עַצְמֹתָיו Jb 33^{21} Qr *his bones are laid bare* (so lean is he; Kt וּשְׁפִי *bareness* are his bones). 8205

8194 †**שְׁפוֹת** (Kö$^{ii. 1. 186}$) **n.f.** dub., perhaps **cream** (as *skimmed off*? cf. Wetzst$^{ZAW\ iii\ (1883),\ 276\ f.}$, who connects with Ar. شُفَافَة *cream*, and this with √ شفا *take off the top* (but ש=ش?); EV *cheese* (after 𝔖𝔗, cf. ARSK$^{EB\ 3091}$));—cstr. שְׁפוֹת בָּקָר 2 S 17^{29} *cream of the herd* (+ דְּבַשׁ וְחֶמְאָה וְצֹאן), cf. Now Bu; 𝔊L HPS *calves*.

8195 †שְׁפוֹ **n.pr.m.** in Edom, Gn 36^{23}, Σωφ, 𝔊L
8195 Σωφαν; =II. שְׁפִי 1 Ch 1^{40}, Σωβ, 𝔊L Σαπφει.

8205 †I. שְׁפִי **n.m.** bareness, smooth or bare
(treeless) height;—**1.** *bareness*, Jb 33^{21} Kt
8192 (v. √). **2.** *bare place, height*: שֶׁפִי Nu 23^{3}
(E), i.e. an outlook-point; pl. שְׁפָיִים Is 41^{18} 49^{9}
Je 3^{21}, שְׁפָיִם 3^{2} 4^{11} (מִדְבָּר ‖), 7^{29}, 12^{12} (בַּמִּדְבָּר), 14^{6}.
p. 1045

827 אַשְׁפָּה *quiver*, vid. s. v. p. 80

3472 †יִשְׁפָּה **n.pr.m.** in Benjamin 1 Ch 8^{16}, Σαφαν, 𝔊L Ιεσφα.—יָשְׁפֵה v. p. 448^{b} supr.

II. שפה (cf. Ar. أُثْفِيَّةٌ *stone* (one of three) supporting kettle, Aram. ܐܬܦܝܐ *tripod*, also תְּפְיָא *fire-jar*; hence perhaps as denom. Heb. [שָׁפַת] q. v., Fra^{63}; cf. ثفى II., Aram. ܐܬܦܝ, תְּפֵי *set on a kettle* or *pot*; v. also GFM$^{Ju\ 5,16}$ RS$^{Sem.\ i.\ 357,\ 2nd\ ed.\ 377}$).

8239 †[שָׁפַת] **vb. denom.** set (on the fire) (NH;
v. √; Sab. שפת = *bestow*, SabDenkm$^{No.\ 8,\ l.\ 15}$);—**Qal**: **1.** *Imv.* ms. שְׁפֹת הַסִּיר 2 K 4^{38} *set on the pot*, so Ez 24^{3}, cf. v^{3} (del. Co, not Krae; Toy allows); later more gen. (subj. י׳): *Impf.* 2 ms. sf. תִּשְׁפְּתֵנִי ψ 22^{16} in the dust of death *thou settest me*. **2.** *ordain, establish*, 2 ms. תִּשְׁפֹּת שָׁלוֹם לָנוּ Is 26^{12}.

830 †אַשְׁפֹּת **n.[m.]** ash-heap(?), refuse-heap,
dung-hill (prob. orig. *fire-place stones*, cf. Ar. sub √);—א׳ abs. as beggars' resting-place 1 S 2^{8} = ψ 113^{7} (both ‖ עָפָר; cf. Jb 2^{8} Wetzst$^{ap.\ De}$); so pl. אַשְׁפַּתּוֹת La 4^{5}; שַׁעַר הָאַשְׁפֹּת Ne 2^{13} 3^{14} 12^{31} = שׁ׳ הַשְׁפוֹת 3^{13} (Ges$^{§\ 35\ d}$).

4942, 8240 †I. שְׁפַתַּיִם **n.[m.]** **du.**: prob. = מִשְׁפְּתַיִם,
infr., q.v.;—בֵּין שׁ׳ ψ 68^{14} (based on Ju 5^{16}?).

8440 II. שְׁפַתַּיִם v. p. 1052 infr.

4942 מִשְׁפְּתַיִם **n.[m.]** **du.** prob. fire-places or
ash-heaps (viz. of the villages or encampments of the tribe) (> Ki Thes and most *sheepfolds*, v. Stu^{Ju});—בֵּין הַמִּשְׁפְּתַיִם Ju 5^{16} (poem; cf. GFM); so (-תַּיִם) Gn 49^{14} (poem in J).

שפח (√ of foll.; cf. Sab. ספח *pour*, also n. מספחת *effusion* (?) DHM$^{VOJ\ ii\ (1888),\ 189}$ Hom$^{Chr\ 124}$; Ar. سَفَحَ *pour out* water, *shed* blood; note (with ref. to etym. of foll. words) phr. سَافَحَهَا *commit fornication with her* (Lane), i.e. *effudit cum ea* (sc. *semen*) Fl in De$^{Jes\ 3,\ 78\ Anm.}$; on Ph. שפח *servant* (?) cf. Hoffm$^{Ph.\ Inscr.\ 18}$ Lzb^{381}).

†שִׁפְחָה **n.f.** maid, maid-servant (syn. 8198
אָמָה, q. v.; orig. = *concubine*? cf. √);—abs. שׁ׳ Gn 16^{1}+; cstr. שִׁפְחַת v^{2}+; sf. שִׁפְחָתִי v^{2}+, etc.; pl. abs. שְׁפָחוֹת 12^{16}+; sf. שִׁפְחֹתֶךָ Ru 2^{13}, etc.;—**1.** lit., *maid, maid-servant*, as belonging to a mistress Gn 16$^{1.3.6.8}$ (PJ) 29$^{24.29}$ (P) ψ 123^{2}, Pr 30^{23} Is 24^{2}; even where concubine of master (cf. אָמָה) Gn 16$^{2.5}$ (PJ) 25^{12} 35$^{25.26}$ (P) 30$^{4.7.9.10.12.18}$ (all JE); less oft. ref. to master 29$^{24.29}$ (J), Ru 2^{13}, of concubine Gn 32^{23}, cf. 33$^{1.2.6}$ (all J); marriageable Lv 19^{20} (H, cf. Ex 11^{5}; not elsewhere in legisl.); in gen., esp. of menial service (never אָמָה) Ex 11^{5} (J) 1 S 25^{41} (opp. אָמָה) 2 S 17^{17} (‖ עֶבֶד) Gn 12^{16} 24^{35} (J) 20^{14} (E) 30^{43} (P) 32^{6} (J; coll.) Dt 28^{68} 1 S 8^{16} 2 K 5^{26} Is 14^{2} Je 34$^{9.10.11.11.16.16}$ Jo 3^{2} Ec 2^{7} 2 Ch 28^{10} Est 7^{4}. **2.** fig. in address, שִׁפְחָתְךָ, etc., of speaker, in token of humility (v. אָמָה) Ru 2^{13} (‖ אָמָה 3^{9}), 1 S 1^{18} (‖ *id.* v^{16}), 25^{27} (‖ v$^{24\,f.}$), 28$^{21.22}$ 2 S 14$^{6.7.12.15.17.19}$ (‖ אָמָה
v$^{15.16}$); 2 K 4$^{2.16}$; not toward God; but v. אָמָה. 519

מִשְׁפָּחָה **n.f.** clan (RS$^{Sem.\ i.\ 258,\ 2nd\ ed.\ 276;\ K\ 149,}$ 4940
303
$^{2nd\ ed.\ 175}$ Ba$^{NB\ §\ 161\ a}$);—abs. מ׳ Am 3^{1}+; cstr. מִשְׁפַּחַת Ju 9^{1}+; sf. מִשְׁפַּחְתִּי Gn 24^{38}+, etc.; pl. מִשְׁפָּחוֹת Na 3^{4}+; cstr. מִשְׁפְּחוֹת Am 3^{2}+; sf. מִשְׁפְּחֹתֵיהֶם Gn 8^{19} + 2 t., usu. -תָם Nu 1^{18} + 84 t., etc.;—**1.** *clan*: **a.** family connexion of individ. Gn 24^{38} (+ בֵּית־אָבִי), v^{40} (+ *id.*), v^{41} (all J; = מוֹלַדְתִּי v^{4}), 2 S 14^{7}, united in sacrifice 1 S 20$^{6.29}$, in passover Ex 12^{21} (JE; cf. Benz$^{Ency.\ Bib.\ Passover,\ §§\ 9,\ 12}$); cf. Lv 20^{5} (H), 25$^{10.41}$ (P), v^{49} (P; defined as מִשְּׁאֵר בְּשָׂרוֹ), non-Heb. v^{47} (H), v^{45} (P), Ju 1^{25}; מִשְׁפְּחוֹתֶיהָ Jos 6^{23} (E or R) is unintelligible, probably del. (cf. Steuern Holz; בֵּית אָבִיהָ in v^{25} [J]), cf. Nu 27$^{4.11}$ (P); מ׳ בֵּית אֲבִי אִמּוֹ Ju 9^{1} *clan of his mother's father-house*; incl. individuals, and included by שֵׁבֶט 1 S 9$^{21.21}$ 10^{21}; with specif. name, in series גֶּבֶר, בַּיִת, מ׳, שֵׁבֶט Jos 7$^{14.14.17\,b,\,c}$ (all J; v$^{17\,a}$ read pl. Di Benn, or < שֵׁבֶט GFM$^{Ju\ 13,\ 2}$; Steuern allows either); cf. Dt 29^{17} Ju 21^{24}, מ׳ אָבִי בְּיִשׂ׳ 1 S 1^{18} (+ חַיַּי, v. II. [חַי]); אִישׁ . . . מִמּ׳ בֵּית־שָׁאוּל 2 S 16^{5}; with name also Ru 2$^{1.3}$ and (non-Isr.) Jb 32^{2}. **b.** in loose, popular sense = tribe, Ju 13^{2} 17^{7} 18^{19}, cf. v^{2} (‖ שֵׁבֶט v^{1}), v^{11} (yet in these two rd. poss. pl., v. GFM). **c.** techn. divisions of people of Isr. Nu 11^{10} (J) Je 2^{4} 31^{1}, cf. 3^{14}; Nu 1$^{2.18}$ 2^{34} 33^{54} (all P), so (post-ex.) Ne 4^{7}: Est 9^{28} (מְדִינָה, מ׳, דוֹר). **d.** usu. (P) techn. divisions of tribes of

Israel, Ex 6$^{14.15.19.25}$ Nu 3^{15}+112 t. Nu (93 t. Nu 26, incl. v^{43} where הַשּׁוּחָמִי appar.=Dan), 34 t. Jos 13–21; also 1 Ch 6$^{4.45}$ 7^{5} Zc 12^{13}; divisions of Gershom, etc. (in Levi) Nu 3$^{18.19.20}$ +41 t. Ex Nu Jos Ch; subdivisions of these divisions (in Levi) Nu 3$^{21.21}$+6 t. Nu 3+4^{18}; cf. (in other tribes) 1 Ch 2^{53} 4$^{2.8.21.27.38}$ 5^{7}; also Zc 12$^{12 b, c 13 b 14 a}$, and (distrib.) v$^{12 a 14 b}$, pleonast. מ׳ מַטֵּה אֲבִיהֶם Nu 36^{6} cf. v^{8}, and (מַטֵּה מ׳ א׳) v^{12}. **e.** late, div. of other peoples 1 Ch 16^{28}=ψ 96^{7}, ψ 22^{28}; in Edom Gn 36^{40} (P). **f.** in wider sense=people, nation; כֹּל מִשְׁפְּחֹת הָאֲדָמָה Am 3^{2} Gn 12^{3} 28^{14} (both J), cf. Je 10^{25} Ez 20^{32} Na 3^{4} (all ‖ גּוֹיִם), Zc 14^{17} Je 1^{15} 25^{9}; as one's posterity Gn 10$^{30.31.32}$ (all P), so prob. v^{5} (P; Di Dr); =all Isr. Am 3^{1}, Judah Mi 2^{3} Je 8^{3} (הַמּ׳ הָרָעָה הַזֹּאת), Isr.+Judah, שְׁתֵּי הַמּ׳ 33^{24}; מִשְׁפַּחַת מִצְרַיִם Zc 14^{18}; cf. ψ 107^{41}. †**2.** =*guild* 1 Ch 2^{55} (of scribes; orig. hereditary in families). †**3.** =*species, kind:* **a.** of judgments Je 15^{3}. **b.** animals Gn 8^{19}(P). †**4.** pl.=*aristocrats* Jb 31^{34} (cf. Eng. 'the classes').

8206 **שֻׁפִּים** **n.pr.m.** v. √שׁפף. p. 1051

8199 **שָׁפַט** $_{185}$ **vb.** judge, govern (NH in deriv.; Ph. שפט=שֹׁפֵט, also in n.pr.; Pun. *sufet* Lzb^{381}; BAram. שָׁפְטִין; As. *šapâtu* (*t*=ת), syn. *dânu* (דִּין), *judge* Dl$^{WB 684}$, *šiptu* (ט), prob. *judgment* [and *šapitu, captain* ?] Jen$^{ZA iv (1889), 278 f.}$; on poss. connexion with Ar. سفط v. Nö$^{ZMG xl (1886), 724}$; on usage of vb. see Ferguson$^{JBL viii (1888), 130 ff.}$);—**Qal** *Pf.* 3 ms. שׁ׳ Ju 16^{31}+, etc.; *Impf.* 3 ms. יִשְׁפֹּט Gn 16^{5}, יִשְׁפּוֹט Is 11^{3}; 3 mpl. יִשְׁפְּטוּ Gn 31^{53}+, יִשְׁפּוּטוּ Ex 18^{26} (Ki יִשְׁפֹּטוּ; cf. Ges$^{§47 g}$), etc.; *Inf. abs.* שָׁפוֹט Gn 19^{9}; cstr. שְׁפֹט Ru 1^{1}, לִשְׁפֹּט Ex 8^{13}+, etc.; *Imv.* שְׁפֹט Pr 31^{9}, שָׁפְטָה ψ 82^{8} La 3^{59}, שִׁפְטוּ Is 1^{17}+, שְׁפֹטוּ Zc 7^{9}, etc.; *Pt.* שֹׁפֵט 1 S 3^{13}+, etc.;—**1.** *act as law-giver, judge, governor* (giving law, deciding controversies and executing law, civil, religious, political, social; both early and late): **a.** of God only, שֹׁפֵט כל הארץ Gn 18^{25} (J), ‖ מְחֹקֵק, מֶלֶךְ Is 33^{22}. **b.** of man, Gn 19$^{9.9}$ (J), Moses deciding cases Ex 18^{13} (E), making known statutes v^{16} (E); so his assistants v$^{22.22.26.26}$ (E), ‖ Dt 1^{16}; of שפטי ישׂראל Nu 25^{5} (executioners); י׳ set שֹׁפְטִים over Isr. Ju 2$^{16.18}$ 2 S 7^{11}=1 Ch 17^{10}, to deliver Isr., שפט ישׂראל Ju 3^{10} 4^{4} 10$^{2.3}$+9 t. Ju, 1 S 4^{18} 7$^{15.16.17}$ 2 K 23^{22}, cf. 1 S 7^{6}; Pt. שֹׁפֵט as subst. also Ju 2$^{17.18.19}$ 1 S 8$^{1.2}$ 2 K 23^{22}; שֹׁפְטֵי יִשׂ׳ 1 Ch 17^{6} (‖ 2 S 7^{7} שִׁבְטֵי), בִּימֵי שְׁפֹט הַשֹּׁפְטִים Ru 1$^{1.1}$ (cf. מוֹשִׁיעִים Ob^{21}); שֹׁפֵט ‖ מֶלֶךְ 1 S 8$^{5.6.20}$ Ho 7^{7} 13^{10}; שֹׁפֵט ישׂראל Mi 4^{14} (=king); king *judges* people 1 K 3$^{9.9}$=2 Ch 1^{10}, 1 K 15^{5}=2 Ch 26^{21}, 2 Ch 1^{11}; abs. 1 K 7^{7} Is 16^{5}; ‖ שָׂרִים Ex 2^{14} (E) Am 2^{3} Zp 3^{3}; ‖ יוֹעֵץ Is 1^{26} Jb 12^{17}, cf. Is 3^{2}; שֹׁפְטֵי אֶרֶץ Is 40^{23} (‖ רוֹזְנִים), Pr 8^{16} (‖ שָׂרִים), ψ 2^{10} 148^{11} (‖ מלכים); שפטינו אשׁר שפטונו Dn 9$^{12.12}$. **2.** specif. *decide controversy*, discriminate betw. persons, in civil, political, domestic and religious questions: **a.** of God ψ 82^{1}: שׁ׳ בֵּין . . . וּבֵין Gn 16^{5} (J; domestic), Ju 11$^{27.27}$ 1 S 24$^{13.16}$ (all of war), Ez 34^{20} (relig.); c. לְ . . . בֵּין Ez 34$^{17.22}$ (relig.); c. בֵּינֵינוּ Gn 31^{53} (E; domestic), Is 2^{4}=Mi 4^{3} (of war); c. בְּ 2 Ch 20^{12} (war); c. acc. 1 K 8^{32}=2 Ch 6^{23}, Ec 3^{17}, condemning wicked and justifying righteous Jb 21^{22} (‖ ידע), 23^{7}; abs. Ex 5^{21} (J) Jb 22^{13}; שׁ׳ צֶדֶק Je 11^{20} ψ 9^{5}; י׳ is שׁוֹפֵט צַדִּיק 7^{12}. **b.** of man, שׁ׳ בֵּין . . . וּבֵין Ex 18^{16} (E) Nu 35^{24} (P) Dt 1^{16} (all civil), Is 5^{3} (relig.); c. acc. Lv 19^{15} (H) Dt 25^{1} (all civil), Ez 20$^{4.4}$ 22$^{2.2}$ 23^{36}; שׁ׳ מִשְׁפָּט Dt 16^{18} 1 K 3^{28} (Sol.); במשפטים Ez 44^{24}, c. לְ 2 Ch 19^{6}; abs. Ez 44^{24} Is 11^{3} (king); influenced by bribes Mi 3^{11} 7^{3} Jb 9^{24}; Absalom desires to decide cases as שֹׁפֵט 2 S 15^{4} (implying lack of such in his time); acc. to 2 Ch 19$^{5.6}$ Jehoshaphat set up שפטים, appar. for the first as judges in this specific sense; code of Dt recognizes them: הַשֹּׁפֵט declares דְּבַר הַמִּשְׁפָּט Dt 17$^{9.12}$ 25^{2}; שפטים + שֹׁטְרִים 16^{18} 1 Ch 23^{4} 26^{29} Jos 8^{33} (+ זְקֵנִים), 23^{2} 24^{1} (D; both + רָאשִׁים, זקנים), + זקנים only Dt 21^{2} Ezr 10^{14}, + כֹּהֲנִים Dt 19$^{17.18}$, שׂרים 2 Ch 1^{2}. **3.** *execute judgment:* **a.** *discriminating*, of man only, מִשְׁפַּט אמת Zc 7^{9}, מֵישָׁרִים שׁ׳ ψ 58^{2} *judge uprightly;* משפט שלום Zc 8^{16}, צֶדֶק Pr 31^{9}, עָוֶל ψ 82^{2}. **b.** *vindicating*, c. acc.: (1) subj. God, יתום ψ 10^{18}, acc. pers. 26^{1} 43^{1} 58^{12} (rd. שֹׁפְטִים for שפטים), שׁ׳ משפט La 3^{59}; מִיַּד *vindicate by delivering from hand of* 1 S 24^{16} 2 S 18$^{19.31}$; שָׁפְטֵנִי כְּצִדְקִי ψ 7^{9}; י׳ כְּצִדְקְךָ 35^{24}. (2) subj. man, c. acc. יתום Is 1$^{17.23}$; דל(ים) 11^{4} Pr 29^{14} ψ 82^{3}; עניי עם 72^{4}; משפט אביונים Je 5^{28}. **c.** *condemning and punishing*, (1) God כְּדַרְכֵי פ׳ *acc. to ways of* Ez 7$^{3.8}$ 18^{30} 24^{14} 33^{20} 36^{19}; במשפטים 7^{27} 23^{24}; משפטי נאפות 16^{38} (=23^{45} of human judges); c. acc. 1 S 3^{13} ψ 51^{6} Is 51^{5} Ez 11$^{10.11}$ 21^{35} 35^{11}. (2) of man, only שֹׁפְטֵי נַפְשׁוֹ ψ 109^{31} and Ez 23^{45} supr., prob. also ψ 141^{6} (corrupt). **d.** *at theophanic advent for final judgment:* God is שֹׁפֵט ψ 50^{6} 75^{8}; שפט הארץ 94^{2}, c. acc. בא לשפט הארץ 96^{13} =1 Ch 16^{33}, ψ 98^{9}; שׁ׳ הארץ 82^{8}; כל הגוים Jo 4^{12}; שׁ׳ עמים ψ 67^{5}; תבל 9^{9} 96^{13}=98^{9}; שׁ׳ מישׁרים

75^{3}. **Niph.** *Pf.* 1 s. נִשְׁפַּטְתִּי Ez 20^{36} + 4 t.; *Impf.* 1 s. אִשָּׁפֵט Ez 20^{36}; אִשָּׁפְטָה 1 S 12^{7}, etc.; *Inf. cstr.* הִשָּׁפֵט 2 Ch 22^{8}; sf. הִשָּׁפְטוֹ ψ 37^{33} 109^{7}; *Pt.* נִשְׁפָּט Is 59^{4} + 4 t.;—**1.** recipr., (Ges ^{§51d}), *enter into controversy, plead:* c. אֶת *with*, of God Je 2^{35} Ez 17^{20} 20$^{35.36.36}$ 38^{22}; of man 1 S 12^{7} (+ וְאַגִּידָה לָכֶם 𝔊 We Dr Bu^{Hpt} Now), Pr 29^{9}; c. עִם, of God Jo 4^{2}, of man 2 Ch 22^{8}; c. לְ, of God Je 25^{31}; נשׁ׳ יחד Is 43^{26} *have controversy together;* באשׁ *by fire* (of God) 66^{16}; באמונה 59^{4}. **2.** pass. *be judged*, ψ 9^{20} 37^{33} 109^{7}. **Pô'el** *Pt.* sf. מְשֹׁפְטִי (dub.; Hi Bu מִשְׁפָּטִי), = *my opponent-at-law* (Ges ^{§55b}) Jb 9^{15}; + Zf 3^{15} ψ 109^{31} We al.

8201 †[שֶׁפֶט] **n.m.** $^{Ex 6, 6}$ **judgment**;—pl. שְׁפָטִים Ex 6^{6} +, sf. שְׁפָטַי Ez 14^{21};—*acts of judgment* (cf. משׁפטים), בשׁפטים גדלים *by great acts of judgment* Ex 6^{6} 7^{4} (P); c. בְּ, עשׂה שׁפטים 12^{12} Nu 33^{4} (P), Ez 5$^{10.15}$ 11^{9} 16^{41} 25^{11} 28$^{22.26}$ 30$^{14.19}$ (all of God); men Ez 16^{41}; c. את, 2 Ch 24^{24} (Syrians against Joash); שׁפטים of God (four: sword, famine, wild beasts, pestilence) Ez 14^{21}; נכונו שׁ׳ ללצים Pr 19^{29} *judgments are prepared for scorners* (𝔊 שְׁבָטִים *rods*, so Perles $^{Anal. 69}$ [or שׁוֹטִים], Toy).

8196 †שְׁפוֹט **n.m.** si vera l. **judgment, act of judgment**;—abs. שׁ׳ 2 Ch 20^{9} (so 𝔊 𝔖, but dub.); pl. שְׁפוּטִים Ez 23^{10} (Toy שְׁפָטִים, Co del.).

8202 †שָׁפָט **n.pr.m.** (*he hath judged*);—usually Σαφατ[θ]: **1.** father of Elisha 1 K 19$^{16.19}$ 2 K 3^{11} 6^{31}. **2.** prince of Simeon Nu 13^{5}. **3.** grandson of Zerub. 1 Ch 3^{22}. **4.** Gaddite chief 5^{12} (Σαβατ, Σαφαμ [ν]). **5.** herdsman of David 27^{29} (Σωφαν, A Σωφατ, 𝔊L Σαφατ).

4941 מִשְׁפָּט$_{422}$ **n. m.** $^{Gn 40, 13}$ **judgment**; — abs. מִשְׁפָּט Ex 21^{31} + 203 t., + לְמִשְׁפָּט Ez 44^{24} (but read Kt לִשְׁפֹּט with 𝔊 𝔗 𝔖 Co al.); cstr. מִשְׁפַּט Ex 23^{6} + 50 t.; sf. מִשְׁפָּטִי Is 40^{27} +; מִשְׁפָּטָם Je 49^{12} +; מִשְׁפָּטָן Nu 27^{5}; pl. מִשְׁפָּטִים Je 4^{12} + 34 t.; sf. מִשְׁפָּטֶיךָ Dt 33^{10} +, etc.;—**1.** *judgment:* **a.** *act of deciding a case:* מ׳ belongeth to God Dt 1^{17}, is from him Pr 16^{33} 29^{26}; אֱלֹהֵי הַמִּ׳ Mal 2^{17}; חשֶׁן מ׳ Ex 28^{15} *the pouch of judgment*, so v$^{29.30}$ (P); worn on heart of Aaron v^{30} (P); שׁפט מ׳ צֶדֶק Dt 16^{18}; הֵבִין מ׳ Jb 32^{9}; 1 K 3^{28}; עשׂה מ׳ 1 K 3^{28}; דְּבַר (ה)מ׳ Dt 17^{9} 2 Ch 19^{6}; רוח מ׳ Is 28^{6}; במשׁפט Lv 19$^{15.35}$ (H) Dt 1^{17} Pr 16^{10} 24^{23}; במ׳ האורים Nu 27^{21} (P); למשׁפט 35^{12} Jos 20^{6} (P) Dt 17^{8} Ju 4^{5} 2 S 15$^{2.6}$ 2 Ch 19^{8} Is 34^{5} 41^{1} 54^{17} 59^{11} Hb 1^{12} Mal 3^{5} ψ 9^{8} 35^{23} 76^{10} 122^{5} Jb 9^{19} (Ez 44^{24} v. supr.). †**b.** *place, court, seat of judgment* Dt 25^{1} 1 K 7^{7} Is 28^{6} Ec 3^{16}. †**c.** *process, procedure, litigation* before judges: הֵבִיא במ׳ Jb 14^{3} Ec 11^{9} 12^{14}; בא במ׳, c. עם Is 3^{14} Jb 22^{4}, c. את ψ 143^{2}, c. יחדו Jb 9^{32}, הלך במ׳ Jb 34^{23}, cf. Ez 34^{16} ψ 112^{5}; pl. דבר משׁפטים, c. את *litigate with* Je 1^{16} 4^{12} 12^{1} 39^{5} = 52^{9}, sg. מִשְׁפָּט in ‖ 2 K 25^{6}, by error. †**d.** *case* or *cause* presented for judgment: בעל מ׳ Is 50^{8}; עָרַךְ מ׳ Jb 13^{18} 23^{4}; שׁמע מ׳ 1 K 3^{11}; שׁפט מ׳ La 3^{59}, cf. Nu 27^{5} (P) 2 S 15^{4}. †**e.** *sentence, decision* of judgment: כן משׁפטך 1 K 20^{40} *thus is thy sentence;* עת ומ׳ Ec 8$^{5.6}$ *time and sentence;* על מ׳ Dt 17^{11} *according to the sentence;* מ׳ מָוֶת 19^{6} 21^{22} Je 26$^{11.16}$; מ׳ דמים Ez 7^{23}, cf. Hb 1$^{4.4}$ ψ 7^{7} 17^{2} Ez 23^{45}; pl. only Ez 16^{68} משׁפטי נאפות; Ho 6^{5} rd. sg. מִשְׁפָּטִי כָאוֹר for מִשְׁפָּטֶיךָ אור after 𝔊 𝔖 𝔗 Ew Hi Che and most mod. †**f.** *execution* of judgment, in gen., עשׂה מ׳, c. בֵּין Je 7^{5} Ez 18^{8}, cf. Dt 32^{41} Zp 3^{5}; c. בְּ *against* ψ 119^{84} 149^{9}; ב om. 9^{17} Ez 39^{21}, מ׳ בא אל Je 48^{21}, ברוח מ׳ Is 4^{4}, מ׳ מואב Je 48^{47}, cf. Is 53^{8} Je 51^{9} Ho 5$^{1.11}$ 10^{4} Jb 36^{17}; pl. Is 26$^{8.9}$ Ez 5^{8} Zp 3^{15} ψ 10^{5}; *in favour of*, עשׂה משׁפטי Mi 7^{9} ψ 9^{5}; מ׳ לעשׁוקים 146^{7}; דין מ׳ והציל Je 21^{12}, cf. Zc 7^{9} 8^{16}; pl. ψ 48^{12} = 97^{8}, 103^{6} 105$^{5.7}$ = 1 Ch 16$^{12.14}$. †**g.** *time of judgment*, לא יקומו במ׳ ψ 1^{5} (late; prob. judgment of the resurrection). **2.** attribute of the שֹׁפֵט, *justice, right, rectitude:* **a.** of God, אלהי מ׳ Is 30^{18}; הֲשֹׁפֵט כָּל־הָאָרֶץ לֹא יַעֲשֶׂה מ׳ Gn 18^{25} (J), cf. Jb 40^{8} Dt 32^{4} ψ 111^{7}; he loves it 33^{5} 37^{28} 99^{4}; צדק ומ׳ Ho 2^{21} ψ 89^{15} = 97^{2}; will not pervert it Jb 8^{3} 34^{12}, cf. 37^{23}; כמשׁפטך ψ 119^{149} (חסדך‖); מִשְׁפָּטְךָ תְּהוֹם רַבָּה 36^{7} (read sg.). **b.** of man: אַשְׁרֵי שֹׁמְרֵי מ׳ ψ 106^{3} (צדקה‖); the tongue of the wise speaketh מ׳ 37^{30}; so of thoughts מ׳ Pr 12^{5}; put on מ׳ as robe Jb 29^{14}, chosen 34^{4}; עשׂה מ׳: God requires that man should do it Mi 6^{8} Is 1^{17} 56^{1}, cf. 61^{8}; it is the joy of the righteous Pr 21^{15}; rulers should know it Mi 3^{1}, cf. Pr 29^{4}; wicked ruler שׂוֹנֵא מ׳ Jb 34^{17}; abhors it Mi 3^{9}, cf. Pr 19^{28} 21^{7} 28^{5}. **3.** *ordinance* promulgated by שֹׁפֵט: 1 S 8$^{9.11}$ 10^{25} (law of king); Levit. ordinances Lv 5^{10} 9^{16} + 13 t. P, 1 Ch 15^{13} 24^{19} 2 Ch 4$^{7.20}$ 8^{14} 35^{13} Ne 8^{18}; חק ומ׳ Ex 15^{25} Jos 24^{25} (E) 1 S 30^{25}, cf. ψ 81^{5}; חקת מ׳ Nu 27^{11} 35^{29} (P); divine law in gen. מ׳ יהוה Je 8^{7}; מ׳ אלהים Is 58^{2} Je 5$^{4.5}$ (‖ דֶּרֶךְ), cf. ψ 25^{9}; ‖ תורה Is 42^{4} 51^{4} Ezr 7^{10}; cf. Zp 2^{3} ψ 119$^{43.160}$; pl. of particular ordinances Dt 33$^{10.21}$ (poem), Is 58^{2} Ez 44^{24} ψ 19^{10} 119^{7} + 16 t., 147^{20}. **4.** *decision* of the שֹׁפֵט in a case of law (v. Br $^{Hex 252 sq.}$): sg. of particular decision of a case Ex 21^{31} (E); pl.

of series of decisions 21^{1} 24^{3} (JE) Dt 7^{12} (D^{2}); in covt. code and D, collection of pentades in conditional or temp. cl., c. כי or אם in D, and subj. in combination, חקים ומשפטים 4$^{1.5.8.14.45}$ +; in code of H and after, in combin. חקות ומשפטים, Lv 18$^{4.5.26}$ 19^{37} +; (the specific type of these laws in H is אִישׁ כִּי, over against נפש כי or אדם כי in code of P, v. Br$^{Hex 254 f.}$); other combin., redactional and later, Lv 26^{46} Nu 36^{13} Dt 30^{16} 2 K 17^{37} 2 Ch 33^{8} Ne 9^{13} ψ 18^{23} 89^{31} 147^{19}. **5.** one's (legal) *right, privilege, due:* מ׳ הַכֹּהֲנִים Dt 18^{3} *due of the priests,* מ׳ הַבְּכֹרָה 21^{17}; מ׳ הַגְּאֻלָּה Je 32^{7} *right of redemption;* מ׳ הַיְרֻשָּׁה v^{8}; הִטָּה מ׳ Ex 23^{6} (E) *wrest right,* so Dt 16^{19} 23^{6} 24^{17} 27^{19} 1 S 8^{3} La 3^{35}, cf. Pr 18^{5}; מ׳ יָתוֹם Dt 10^{18}; מ׳ אביון Ex 23^{6} (E) Je 5^{28} ψ 140^{13}; מ׳ עניים Is 10^{2} Jb 36^{6}; הסיר מ׳ 27^{2} 34^{5}, cf. Is 40^{27} 49^{4}. **6. a.** *proper, fitting, measure* 1 K 5^{8}; *fitness* Is 28^{26}, 40^{14} (of fitness in the order of nature; cf. Di). **b.** *custom, manner:* מ׳ הכהנים 1 S 2^{13} *custom of the priests* (*rightful due,* acc. to ThWe Dr and most); מִשְׁפָּטוֹ 27^{11} *his* (David's) *custom;* מ׳ הגוים 2 K 17^{33} *manner of the nations,* cf. 2 K 17$^{26.27}$ (RS$^{Sem. 1. 24, 2nd ed. 23}$); כמ׳ *after the manner, custom, fashion* (of) Gn 40^{13} Ex 21^{9} (E) Ju 18^{7} 1 K 18^{28} 2 K 11^{14} 17^{34} 1 Ch 6^{17} Ez 42^{11} ψ 119^{132}. †**c.** מה משפט Ju 13^{12} *what manner of* a boy, cf. 2 K 1^{7}. †**d.** *plan* . . . of the tabernacle Ex 26^{30} (P); temple 1 K 6^{38}; palace Je 30^{18}.

8203 †שְׁפַטְיָה(וּ) **n.pr.m.** (*י׳ hath judged, vindicated*);—usu. Σαφατια(ς): **1.** -יָה: **a.** fifth son of David 2 S 3^{4} = 1 Ch 3^{3} (Σαβατεια, A Σαφαθια, 𝔊L Σαφατιας). **b.** contemp. of Jerem. Je 38^{1} (B Σαφανιας). **c.** man of Judah Ne 11^{4}. **d.** chiefs of families of restoration: (1) Ezr 2^{4} = Ne 7^{9}, Ezr 8^{8}; (2) 2^{57} = Ne 7^{59}. **e.** Benjamite 1 Ch 9^{8}. **2.** -יָהוּ: **a.** son of Jehosh. 2 Ch 21^{2}. **b.** hero of David 1 Ch 12^{5}. **c.** Simeonite 27^{16}.

8204 †שִׁפְטָן **n.pr.m.** (*judgment*);—prince of Ephraim Nu 34^{24}; Σαβαθα(ν), 𝔊L Σαφαταν.

I. שְׁפִי v. I. שׁפה. II. שְׁפִי v. שְׁפוֹ sub I. שׁפה.

8206 שֻׁפִּים v. שׁפף. p. 1051

8210 שָׁפַךְ$_{113}$ **vb. pour out, pour** (NH *id.;* As. *šapâku, pour out,* esp. (Dl^{WB} Jen$^{Kosmol. 41}$) earth, to form mound; Ar. سَفَكَ *pour out,* cf. سَبَكَ *melt and pour into mould;* Eth. ሰበከ: Aram. שְׁפַךְ, ܫܦܟ (rare) = BH);—**Qal** *Pf.* 3 ms. שׁ׳ 1 K 2^{31} +; 3 fs. sf. שְׁפָכַתְהוּ Ez 24^{7}, etc.; *Impf.* 3 ms. יִשְׁפֹּךְ 2 K 19^{32} +; 2 ms. sf. 3 ms. תִּשְׁפְּכֶנּוּ Dt 12^{16} +, etc.; *Imv.* ms. שְׁפוֹךְ Ju 6^{20} +, שְׁפָךְ־ ψ 69^{25}; fs. שִׁפְכִי La 2^{19}, etc.; *Inf. cstr.* שְׁפָךְ־ 1 K 18^{28} +, לִשְׁפֹּךְ Is 59^{7} +, etc.; *Pt. act.* שֹׁפֵךְ Gn 9^{6} +, f. שֹׁפֶכֶת Ez 22^{3}, etc.; *pass.* שָׁפוּךְ ψ 79^{10}, שְׁפוּכָה Ez 20$^{33.34}$;—**1.** lit.: **a.** *pour out, pour* water Ex 4^{9} (J; acc. loc.), 1 S 7^{6} (+ לִפְנֵי י׳, unique, symb. of contrition), עַל־פְּנֵי הָאָרֶץ (subj. י׳) Am 5^{8} 9^{6}; blood like water (to flow away and be absorbed), עַל־הָאָרֶץ Dt 12$^{16.24}$ 15^{23}, cf. Lv 17^{13} (H) Ez 24^{7}; also + אֶל loc. Ex 29^{12} Lv 4$^{7.18.25.30.34}$; + עַל pers. reflex. 1 K 18^{28}; *pour out* broth Ju 6^{20}, libation (נֶסֶךְ, to (לְ) false gods) Is 57^{6}; dust Lv 14^{41} (P; אֶל loc.); c. acc. סֹלְלָה *mound* (in siege), = *make by pouring* (earth, orig. from baskets, see esp. As. *šapâku* Dl$^{WB 679 b}$ Jen$^{Kosmol. 41}$), + עַל־ of city 2 K 19^{32} = Is 37^{33}, Je 6^{6} Ez 4^{2} 26^{8}, אֶל־ 2 S 20^{15}; abs. Ez 17^{17} 21^{27} Dn 11^{15}; וַיִּשׁ׳ מֵעָיו אַרְצָה 2 S 20^{10} (by a sword-thrust in the belly), cf. יִשׁ׳ לָאָרֶץ מְרֵרָתִי Jb 16^{13} (metaph., י׳ subj.). **b.** techn., acc. דָּם *shed blood* Gn 37^{22} (E) 9^{6} (P) 1 S 25^{31} Ez 22^{4} + 9 t. Ez, + 15 t. (pass. ψ 79^{10}) + Ez 36^{18} (c. עַל־הָאָרֶץ), 1 Ch 22^{8} (c. אַרְצָה); acc. דָּמִים † 1 K 2^{31} 1 Ch 28^{3} ψ 79^{3} (כַּמַּיִם). **2.** fig.: **a.** י׳ subj., *pour out* anger, etc.: עֲלֵיהֶם אֶשׁ׳ כַּמַּיִם עֶבְרָתִי Ho 5^{10}; שׁ׳ חֲמָתִי עַל Ez 14^{19} + 8 t. Ez, Je 10^{25} Is 42^{25} ψ 79^{6} (אֶל et עַל); acc. ח׳ om. Je 6^{11}; c. בּ loc. La 2^{4}; ח׳ שְׁפוּכָה Ez 20$^{33.34}$; acc. חֲרוֹן אַפּוֹ La 4^{11}; acc. זַעַם (עַל pers.) Ez 21^{36} + 3 t.; acc. בוּז *contempt,* עַל pers., Jb 12^{21} = ψ 107^{40}; *pour* their own wickedness עֲלֵיהֶם Je 14^{16} (i.e. requite it); *pour out* רוּחִי עַל Ez 39^{29}, cf. Zc 12^{10} Jo 3$^{1.2}$. **b.** hum. subj. *pour out* one's heart, etc., כַּמַּיִם לִבֵּךְ La 2^{19}, לְפָנָיו לְבַבְכֶם ψ 62^{9} (i.e. bef. י׳), אֶת־נַפְשִׁי לִפְנֵי י׳ 1 S 1^{15}, עָלַי (reflex.; v. עַל **1 d**) ψ 42^{5}; אֶת־שִׂיחוֹ לִפְנֵי י׳ ψ 102^{1} (title), cf. 142^{3}; in bad sense, וַתִּשְׁפְּכִי אֶת־תַּזְנוּתַיִךְ עַל־ Ez 16^{15}, cf. 23^{8}. †**Niph.** *Pf.* 3 ms. נִשְׁפַּךְ La 2^{11}, etc.; *Impf.* 3 ms. יִשָּׁפֵךְ Gn 9^{6} +, etc.; *Inf. cstr.* הִשָּׁפֵךְ Ez 16^{36};—*be poured out:* of ashes 1 K 13$^{3.5}$, blood (עַל loc.) Dt 12^{27}; *be shed,* of blood Gn 9^{6} (P) Dt 19^{10}; in fig. La 2^{11} *my liver is poured* לָאָרֶץ (cf. **Qal 1 a** *ad fin.*); ψ 22^{15} *I am poured out like water* (nerveless, helpless); subj. נְחֻשְׁתֵּךְ Ez 16^{36} (v. II. [נְחֹשֶׁת]; cf. v^{15} **Qal 2 b**). †**Pu.** *Pf.* 3 ms. consec. וְשֻׁפַּךְ Zp 1^{17} *be poured out* כֶּעָפָר, of blood; שֻׁפַּךְ Nu 35^{33} (P) *be shed,* of blood; 3 fs. שֻׁפְּכָה ψ 73^{2} Kt my steps *were caused to slip* (Qr שֻׁפְּכוּ). †**Hithp.** *Impf.* 3 fs. תִּשְׁתַּפֵּךְ נַפְשִׁי עָלַי Jb 30^{16} *my soul pours itself out upon me* (v. **Qal 2 b**); 3 fpl. תִּשְׁתַּפֵּכְנָה אַבְנֵי־קֹדֶשׁ

La 4^{1} fig. of slaughter; *Inf. cstr.* בְּהִשְׁתַּפֵּךְ נַפְשָׁם
אֶל־חֵיק אִמֹּתָם 2^{12}, i.e. they expire.
8211 †שֶׁ֫פֶךְ **n.[m.]** place of **pouring**;—cstr.
שׁ׳ הַדֶּשֶׁן Lv 4$^{12.12}$ (P).
8212 †שָׁפְכָה **n.f. male organ** (as fluid-duct);—
abs. שׁ׳ כְּרוּת Dt 23^{2} (|| פְּצוּעַ־דַּכָּה).
8213 †שָׁפֵל **vb. be or become low, be abased**
(NH, der. spec.; As. *šapâlu*, der. spec. and
deriv.; Sab. ספל n. *humility* or *lowland* DHM
$^{\text{xxix (1875). 604}}$; Ar. سَفَلَ, سَفِلَ, سَفُلَ *be low* (Lag$^{\text{BN 48}}$));
Aram. שְׁפַל, ܫܦܠ (der. spec.));—**Qal** *Pf.* 3 ms.
שׁ׳ Is 2^{11}; 2 fs. וְשָׁפַלְתְּ 29^{4}, etc.; *Impf.* 3 ms.
וַיִּשְׁפַּל 2^{9} 5^{15}; 3 fpl. תִּשְׁפַּלְנָה 5^{15}, etc.; *Inf. cstr.*
שְׁפַל Ec 12^{4} Pr 16^{19}, v. infr.;—**1.** all Is: *become*
(be brought, laid) *low*, of trees Is 10^{33} (|| נִגְדָּעִים),
mts. 40^{4} (opp. נִשָּׂא), of כָּל־נִשָּׂא 2^{12} (but read, for
שׁ׳, נִשְׂגָּב [Kohler], or גָּבֹהַּ [Lag], so Du Che^{Hpt}
Di-Kit Marti); fig. *be humiliated*, of man 2^{9} 5^{15},
his loftiness 2^{17}, haughty eyes v^{11} (all || שָׁחַח), 5^{15};
of city 32^{19}; as helping vb. (=adv.) וְשׁ׳ מֵאֶרֶץ
תְּדַבֵּרִי 29^{4} *thou shalt speak low out of the ground*
(Ges$^{\text{§ 120 g}}$; || מֵעָפָר תִּשַּׁח אִמְרָתֵךְ). **2.** שְׁפַל־רוּחַ
Pr 16^{9} *to be lowly of spirit*, so Buhl SS Toy al.;
Thes Rob Ges al. sub שָׁפָל. **3.** of sound Ec 12^{4}.
Hiph. *Pf.* 3 ms. הִשְׁפִּיל Is 25^{12}, etc.; *Impf.* 3 ms.
יַשְׁפִּיל ψ 75^{8}, sf. יַשְׁפִּילֶנָּה יַשְׁפִּילָהּ Is 26^{5} (but 2nd
vb. prob. doublet), etc.; *Imv.* mpl. (sf.) הַשְׁפִּילוּ(הוּ)
Jb 40^{11} Je 13^{18}; *Inf. cstr.* sf. הַשְׁפִּילְךָ Pr 25^{7}
(Ez 21^{31} read *abs.* הַשְׁפִּיל || הַגְבֵּהַּ, so Co Krae
Ges$^{\text{§ 113 bb R. 3}}$); *Pt.* מַשְׁפִּיל 1 S 2^{7} ψ 147^{6}; מַשְׁפִּילִי
(Ges$^{\text{§ 90 l}}$) ψ 113^{6};—**1.** usu. fig., ׳י subj., *lay low*,
tree Ez 17^{24} (opp. הִגְבַּהְתִּי); city Is 26^{5} (|| הֵשַׁח);
fortress 25^{12} (+ הֵשַׁח; Du thinks doublet of 26^{5});
humiliate pride v^{11} 13^{11}, cf. Jb 40^{11}; obj. עֵינַיִם
ψ 18^{28}, so read also || 2 S 22^{28}, י׳ מַשׁ׳ אַף־מְרוֹמֵם רָמוֹת
1 S 2^{7}, זֶה יַשׁ׳ וְזֶה יָרִים ψ 147^{6}; רְשָׁעִים 75^{8}, cf.
Ez 21^{31}. **2.** hum. subj. *set* one *in a lower
place* Pr 25^{7}; subj. hum. pride Pr 29^{23}; declar.
Is 57^{9} *thou didst shew abasement* עַד־שְׁאוֹל. **3.**
as helping vb.: + vb. coörd., הַשׁ׳ שֵׁבוּ Je 13^{18}
make low, sit down=take a low seat (Ges$^{\text{§ 120 g}}$);
+ inf. מַשׁ׳ לִרְאוֹת ψ 113^{6} *he who maketh low to look*
upon heaven and earth (i.e. ׳י; || הַמַּגְבִּיהִי לָשָׁבֶת v^{5};
Ges$^{\text{§ 114 m}}$).—הִשְׁפִּילוּ וַתֹּאמֶר גֵּוָה Jb 22^{29} is dub.;
|| יוֹשִׁעַ favours אֱלוֹהַּ as subj., which Bu conj. for
וַתֹּא׳, read then הִשְׁפִּיל, א׳ *hath abased pride*, so
(in part) Du; >*they cast* (thee) *down* (RV);
men are cast down (הַשׁ׳ intrans.; AV, cf. Lag
$^{\text{BN 121}}$); (thy ways) *are brought low* (Ew De Di).

†שֵׁ֫פֶל **n.[m.] low estate, condition**;—abs. 8216
שׁ׳ Ec 10^{6} (opp. מְרוֹמִים); sf. שִׁפְלֵנוּ ψ 136^{23}.
†שִׁפְלָה **n.f. humiliation**;—Is 32^{19} (of city). 8218
שָׁפָל **adj. low**;—abs. שׁ׳ 2 S 6^{22}+, cstr. שְׁפַל 8217
ψ 29^{23}+; fs. שְׁפָלָה Ez 17^{14}+, cstr. שִׁפְלַת v^{6}; pl.
שְׁפָלִים Jb 5^{11};—**1.** *low*, in height, of vine Ez 17^{6},
tree v^{24} (opp. גָּבֹהַּ); שׁ׳ מִן־הָעוֹר Lv 13^{20} *lower*
(deeper) *than the skin* (around it), so v$^{21.26}$, cf.
14^{37}. **2.** of a modest, unambitious kingdom
Ez 17^{14} 29$^{14.15}$; *low* in station Jb 5^{11} (opp. שְׂגָבוּ),
Ez 21^{31} (Ges$^{\text{§ 90 f}}$; rd. הַשְׁפָּלָה). **3.** *humiliated*,
שׁ׳ בְּעֵינָי 2 S 6^{22}; pl. Mal 2^{9} (|| נִבְזִים). **4.** *lowly*,
as subst. ψ 138^{6} (opp. גָּבֹהַּ), רוּחַ שְׁפָלִים Is 57^{15}
(|| נִדְכָּאִים); שְׁפַל רוּחַ v^{15}, Pr 29^{23} (opp. גַּאֲוַת אָדָם),
+ 16^{19} Thes al. (but v. √**Qal 2**).
†שְׁפֵלָה **n.f. lowland**;—alw. abs. שׁ׳ c. art., 8219
exc. sf. שְׁפֵלָתָהּ Jos 11^{16};—*lowland:* **1.** usually
term. techn. of strip W. of Judaean mts. (on
exact limits v. GASm$^{\text{Geogr. 201 ff.; Expos. Dec. 1896, 404 f.}}$
Buhl$^{\text{Geogr. 104}}$ Dr$^{\text{Hast. DB iii. 892 f.}}$): almost alw. disting.
from הָהָר and הַנֶּגֶב, sts. from הָעֲרָבָה, in Dt 1^{7}
Jos 9^{1} (R^{D}) also from חוֹף הַיָּם, cf. Jos 10^{40} 12^{8}
(both R^{D}), Ju 1^{9} (perh. R^{D}, cf. Bu GFM), Jos
15^{33} (P), Je 17^{26} 32^{44} 33^{13} Ob^{19} Zc 7^{7} 2 Ch 26^{10}
(disting. from הַמִּישׁוֹר, table-land E. of Jordan);
region of sycomores 1 K 10^{27}=2 Ch 1^{15} 9^{27}, 1 Ch
27^{28}. **2.** of lowland (near coast) N. of Carmel
Jos 11^{2}; W. of mts. of Ephr. v^{16} (both R^{D}).
†שִׁפְלוּת **n.f. sinking**;—cstr. שׁ׳ יָדַיִם Ec 8220
10^{18} *sinking of hands*, negligence (|| עֲצַלְתַּיִם).
†שָׁפָם **n.pr.m.** in Gad 1 Ch 5^{12}; 𝔊^{B} Σαβατ, 8223
A Σαφαμ, 𝔊L Σαφαν.
†שְׁפָם **n.pr.loc.** on E. border of Israel; שׁ׳ 8221
Nu 34^{10}, שְׁפָ֫מָה v^{11}; 𝔊 Σεπφαμαρ; site unknown.
שְׁפִם v. שֻׁפִּים sub שׁפף. p. 1051 8206
†שִׁפְמוֹת (so Baer with codd. and edd.; 8224
Thes שְׂפ׳; van d. H. Gi שִׂפְ׳);—**n.pr.loc.** in 8224
Negeb 1 S 30^{28}; Σαφει; A Σαφαμως, 𝔊L Σεφειμωθ.
†שִׁפְמִי **adj. gent.** (of foreg.?);—1 Ch 27^{27}. 8225
שׁוּפָמִי **adj. gent.** v. שְׁפוּפָם sub שׁפף. p. 1051 7781
שׁפן (√ of foll.; cf. Ar. ثُفُن Fresnel$^{\text{JAs 1838, 514}}$
Thes^{1467} [usu. called وَبْر or طُبْسُن]).
†I. שָׁפָן **n. m.** $^{\text{Lv 11, 5}}$ rock-badger, *hyrax* 8227
syriacus, AV RV *coney*;—abs. שׁ׳ Dt 14^{7}=Lv

11^{5} (P; unclean animal); living in rocks, pl. שְׁפַנִּים ψ 104^{18} Pr 30^{26}.—Vid. Rob$^{BR\ iii.\ 66,387}$ Tr NHB 75; FFP 1, and Pl. 1 Dr^{Dt} Post$^{Hast.\ DB\ Coney}$ McLean-Shipley$^{Ency.\ Bib.\ Id.}$.

†II. **שָׁפָן** **n.pr.m.** Σαφ(φ)αν: **1.** secretary (הַסֹּפֵר) under Josiah 2 K 22$^{3.8.8.9.10.10.12.14}$ 2 Ch 34$^{8.15.15.16.18.18.20}$. **2.** father of אֲחִיקָם, contemp. of **1** (improb.=**1**): 2 K 22^{12} 25^{22} Je 26^{24} 39^{14} 40$^{5.9.11}$ 41^{2} 43^{6} 2 Ch 34^{20}. **3.** father of אֶלְעָשָׂה Je 29^{3}, perh.=**2.** **4.** father of גְּמַרְיָהוּ 36^{10} (called הַסֹּפֵר), v$^{11.12}$, perh.=**1.** **5.** father of יַאֲזַנְיָהוּ Ez 8^{11}, possibly=**1.**

5855 **שׁוֹפָן** v. עַטְרוֹת p. 743^{a} supr.

3473 †**יִשְׁפָּן** **n.pr.m.** in Benjamin 1 Ch 8^{22}; Ισφαν, A Εσφαν, 𝔊L Ιεσφαν.

שׁפע (√ of foll.; NH שָׁפַע *flow abundantly, be abundant*; 𝔗 שְׁפַע, Syr. ܫܦܥ, *overflow, abound*).

8228 †**שֶׁפַע** **n.[m.]** abundance;—cstr. ׳שׁ Dt 33^{19}.

8229 †[**שִׁפְעָה**], **שִׁפְעַת** **n.f. abundance, quantity**;—appar. abs. שִׁפְעַת 2 K 9^{17}, *a multitude* (of men), (Bur שִׁפְעָה, or שִׁפְעַת אֲנָשִׁים as Klo Benz al.; > 𝔊^{B} Kit עָפָר); cstr. שִׁפְעַת יֵהוּא v^{17} *Jehu's multitude;* cstr., of horses Ez 26^{10}, camels Is 60^{6}; of waters Jb 22^{11} 38^{34}.

8230 †**שִׁפְעִי** **n.pr.m.** in Simeon 1 Ch 4^{37}; Σεφει, 𝔊L Σωφει.

שׁפף (√ of following).

8207 †**שְׁפִיפֹן** **n.[m.] horned snake,** 𝔊 κεράστης (Ar. سُفٌّ, سِفٌّ Frey);—abs. ׳שׁ Gn 49^{17} (‖ נָחָשׁ); =*cerastes cornutus* or *Hasselquistii*, cf. Tr^{NHB} 273 Post$^{Hast.\ DB\ iv.457f.}$ McLean-Shipley$^{Ency.\ Bib.\ iv.4393}$ Dr$^{ad\ loc.}$—שְׁפוּפָם, שְׁפוּפָן vid. s.v.

8197 †**שְׁפוּפָם** **n.pr.m.** in Benjamin;—Nu 26^{39}, Σουταλα, 𝔊L Σοφαν (=מֻפִּים וְחֻפִּים Gn 46^{21}, שֻׁפִּים וְחֻפִּם 1 Ch 7^{12}).

7781 †**שׁוּפָמִי** **adj. gent.** of foregoing, c. art. as n.coll. Nu 26^{39}.

8197 †**שְׁפוּפָן** **n.pr.m.** in Benj. 1 Ch 8^{5}, Σωφαρφακ, A Σωφαν, 𝔊L Σεπφαμ.

8206 †**שֻׁפִּים** **n.pr.m.** **1.** ׳שׁ 1 Ch 7^{15}, Μαμφειν, A Σεφφειμ, 𝔊L Σαφιν, appar.=שֻׁפִּם v^{12}, Σαπφειν, 𝔊L Σαφαν (cf. שְׁפוּפָם, מֻפִּים). **2.** שֻׁפִּים doorkeeper, 1 Ch 26^{16}.

†[**שָׁפַר**] **vb. be beautiful, fair, comely** 8
(Ar. سَفَرَ *remove veil* (of women), *shine;* Aram. שְׁפַר *be pleasing* (v. Dn 6^{2}), ܫܦܪ *be beautiful, bright, pleasing,* ܫܦܝܪ *beautiful*);—**Qal** *Pf.* 3 fs. שָׁפְרָה עָלָי (Aram.) ψ 16^{6} (the) heritage *is beautiful for* (pleasing to) *me* (v. עַל **II. 8**).

†I. [**שֶׁפֶר**] **n.m. beauty, goodliness**;— 823
abs. אִמְרֵי־שָׁפֶר Gn 49^{21} (v. אָמִיר, אֹמֶר). p. 57 534

†II. [**שֶׁפֶר**] **n.pr.mont.** as a station in 823
wilderness;—הַר־שָׁפֶר Nu 33$^{23.24}$ (P); Σαφαρ.

†I. **שִׁפְרָה** **n.f. fairness, clearness,** of sky;— 8235
abs. ׳שׁ Jb 26^{13} by his breath the sky becomes *fair*(*ness*), v. esp. De Di Bu Du; > Che$^{JQ\ 1897,578}$ (after 𝔊) בְּרִיחֵי שָׁמַיִם סִגֵּר הוּא.

†II. **שִׁפְרָה** **n.pr.f.** Hebrew midwife, Ex 8236
1^{15} (E); Σεπφωρα (cf. Lag$^{BN\ 90}$).

†**שָׁפִיר** **n.pr.loc.** in Philist. plain, Mi 1^{11} 8208
(=שָׁמִיר Jos 15^{48}?); 𝔊 καλῶς (!).

אֶשְׁפָּר vid. s.v. p. 80 829

שׁוֹפָר, **שֹׁפָר** $_{72}$ **n.m.** $^{Is\ 27,13}$ **horn**, for blowing 7782
(Aram. שיפורא √ dub.; CAdler$^{PAOS\ 1889,\ clxxi\ ff.}$ cp. As. *šappar*(*u*) a species of wild goat; in any case the ׳שׁ is a curved horn, as of cow or ram, cf. Dr$^{Am\ 2,2}$ (with illustr.));—abs. ׳שׁוֹ 2 S 6^{15}+, ׳שׁ Ex 19^{16}+; cstr. שׁוֹפַר Lv 25^{9}; pl. שׁוֹפָרוֹת Ju 7^{22}+, cstr. שׁוֹפְרוֹת Jos 6^{4}+; sf. שׁוֹפְרֹתֵיהֶם Ju 7^{8};—*horn,* mostly as used in war, rarely, and chiefly late, as sacred instr.: Ho 8^{1} Ju 7$^{8.16}$ Is 58^{1} (sim.) Jb 39^{25} (׳בְּדֵי שׁ, v. דַּי **2 a**); שׁ׳ (הַ)יּוֹבְלִים Jos 6^{4} *rams' horns* (v. יבל), so v$^{6.8.13}$ (all E); קוֹל (הַ)שׁ׳ Ex 19$^{16.19}$ 20^{18} (Gi v^{15}), Jos 6$^{5.20}$ (all E), Am 2^{2}+13 t.; תָּקַע בַּשׁ׳ = *give a blast with the horn,* Ju 3^{27} 6^{34} Jos 6^{4}+9 t. Jos, 1 S 13^{3} 1 K 1$^{34.39}$+9 t., + (׳י subj.) Zc 9^{14}; תָּקַע שׁ׳ Ho 5^{8} Am 3^{6} (vb. Niph.), Je 4^{5}+7 t., + תֹּקְעֵי הַשׁ׳ Jos 6^{9} Qr (Kt תָּקְעוּ); cf. הַשׁ׳ לִתְקוֹעַ Ju 7^{20}, בְּתֵקַע שׁ׳ ψ 150^{3}; also הֶעֱבִיר שׁ׳ תְּרוּעָה Lv 25^{9a} (H), cf. v^{9b} (P), יוֹם שׁ׳ וּתְרוּעָה Zp 1^{16}; used on religious occasions, Jos 6$^{4ff.}$ Lv 25^{9} Jo 2$^{1.15}$ ψ 47^{6} 81^{4} 98^{6} 150^{3} 2 Ch 15^{14}.—On ׳שׁ v. Adler The Shophar (1894) Dr$^{Am\ 2,2}$ Hpt$^{We\ ψψ\ Transl.\ 221f.}$ Abrahams Hast. DB Trumpet.

†[**שפרור** Kt, **שַׁפְרִיר** Qr] **n.[m.]** doubtful, 8237
Thes *splendour* (√ שׁפר; Dl$^{Prol.\ 126}$ cp. As. vb. *šuparruru, spread out* (Id$^{HWB\ 684}$)); appar. of (*brightly-coloured?*) royal *pavilion, canopy,* or poss. *carpet,* sf. נָטָה שפרורו Je 43^{10} (Qr שַׁפְרִירוֹ).

30, 4942, 8239 [שָׁפַת], אַשְׁפֹּת, מִשְׁפְּתַיִם v. II. שׁפה. p. 1046

8240 †II. שְׁפַתַּיִם n.[m.] du. doubtful word: usu. hook-shaped pegs, hooks, so 𝔗 Thes AV RV; abs. 'הַשּׁ Ez 40[43]; < 𝔖 𝔙 Co וּשְׂפָתָם *and their edge*, so Aq Theod Symm and prob. 𝔊, cf.
4942 Hi-Sm, and Krae (וּשְׂפָת).—I. 'שׁ v. √שׁפה. p. 1046

8241 שֶׁצֶף v. שֶׁטֶף sub שׁטף. p. 1009

8245 †שָׁקַד vb. watch, wake (Ph. שקד *be circumspect;* NH שָׁקַד *be insistent;* 𝔗 שְׁקַד = BH);—**Qal** *Pf.* 3 ms. 'שׁ ψ 127[1], שָׁקַדְתִּי Je 31[28] ψ 102[8]; *Impf.* 3 ms. יִשְׁקוֹד Jb 21[32] (Me Bu יִשְׁקְדוּ), וַיִּשְׁקֹד Dn 9[14], 1 s. אֶשְׁקֹד Je 31[28]; *Imv.* mpl. שִׁקְדוּ Ezr 8[29]; *Inf. cstr.* לִשְׁקֹד Pr 8[34]; *Pt. act.* שֹׁקֵד Je 1[12]+; pl. cstr. שֹׁקְדֵי Is 29[20];—**1.** *keep watch* of, *be wakeful* over, 'י subj., עַל pers., to benefit or injure Je 31[28.28] 44[27]; עַל rei, to perform it 1[12] Dn 9[14]; so (men subj.) שֹׁקְדֵי אָוֶן Is 29[20]; of leopard *watching* עַל־עָרֵיהֶם Je 5[6] (to seize prey, fig.); of man *watching* (for admission) at (עַל) wisdom's doors Pr 8[34] (‖ שָׁמַר); 'שׁ וְשִׁמְרוּ = *keep guard* over (עַל) Jb 21[32], cf. (abs.) Ezr 8[29], and (of watchman, שֹׁמֵר) ψ 127[1]. **2.** *be wakeful, wake,* as mourner, sufferer ψ 102[8].—La 1[14] rd. perh. **Niph.** *Pf.* נִשְׁקַד עַל־פְּשָׁעַי (𝔊 Bu) *watch has been kept over my transgressions* (cf. **1** supra), for MT 'נִשְׂקַד עֹל פ.—**Pu.** denom. v. infra.

8247 †שָׁקֵד n.[m.] almond(-tree) (NH *id.;* so called from its early *waking* out of winter's sleep, acc. to Ki Thes Lag[BN 45] al.; Aram. שִׁיגְדָּא, ܫܓܕܐ, ܠܘܙܐ, whence Eth. ሰገድ: cf. Nö[M 39]; cf. Löw[No. 319]);—**1.** *almond,* i.e. the nut, pl. שְׁקֵדִים Gn 43[11] (J; + בָּטְנִים, etc.), Nu 17[23] (P). **2.** *almond-tree* Je 1[11] and (prob.) Ec 12[5].

8246 †[שָׁקַד] vb. Pu. denom.—only *Pt.* pl. in גְּבִעִים מְשֻׁקָּדִים *cups shaped like almond* (blossoms) Ex 25[33.33.34] 37[19.19.20] (all P).

8248 †[שָׁקָה] vb. Hiph. cause to drink water, give to drink (NH Hiph. *id.;* Ar. سَقَى I. *give to drink;* Sab. סקי *be irrigated* Fell[ZMG liv (1900), 246], מסקי *drinks* Hom[Chr 121], מסתקין *id.* DHM[Hofmus., No. 1, 1.7]; Eth. ሰቀየ: *water, irrigate;* As. *šakû* I. = Heb. Hiph., Aram. שְׁקָא, ܫܩܐ Aph.);—for **Qal** v. II. שָׁתָה;—*Pf.* 3 ms. consec. וְהִשְׁקָה Gn 2[6]+, sf. וְהִשְׁקָהּ Nu 5[27]; 2 ms. consec. וְהִשְׁקִיתָ Nu 20[8]+; 1 s. consec. וְהִשְׁקֵיתִי Ez 32[6], etc.; *Impf.* 3 ms. יַשְׁקֶה Nu 5[26], וַיַּשְׁקְ Gn 29[10]+, etc.; *Imv.* ms. sf. הַשְׁקֵהוּ Pr 25[21]; fs. sf. הַשְׁקִינִי Gn 24[43]+; *Inf. cstr.* הַשְׁקוֹת Gn 2[10]+, sf. הַשְׁקֹתוֹ 24[19]; *Pt.* מַשְׁקֶה ψ 104[13], cstr. Hb 2[15] (v. also I., II. מַשְׁקֶה);—**1.** *water, irrigate,* ground: subj. mist Gn 2[6], river v[10] (both J), spring Jo 4[18]; subj. 'י Is 27[3] (כֶּרֶם), Ez 17[7] (גֶּפֶן), both in fig., fig. also 32[6] *water land* מִדָּם; lit. c. מִן of source ψ 104[13] (הָרִים) and (subj. man) Ec 2[6] (יַעַר). **2.** *water, give drink to,* usu. human subj., acc. of beast, Gn 24[14.46.46] 29[2] (מִן of source), v[3.7.8.10] Ex 2[16.17.19] (all J), ψ 104[11] (subj. springs); acc. pers. Gn 21[19] (E), 24[18.19.45] (J), Hb 2[15] (fig.), Is 43[20] ('י subj.), ψ 78[15] (*id.*), 2 Ch 28[15], c. בְּ of vessel Est 1[7]; c. acc. pers. et animal. Nu 20[8] (P); *give* one something *to drink,* acc. pers. + rei (water, wine, etc.), Am 2[12] Gn 19[32.33.34.35] 24[43] (all J), Ju 4[19] 1 S 30[11] 2 S 23[15] = 1 Ch 11[15], Jb 22[7], cf. Ct 8[2] (מִיַּיִן); fig. Je 8[14] 9[14] 16[7] 23[15] 25[15] ψ 69[22], cf. וְנַחַל עֲדָנֶיךָ תַשְׁקֵם 36[9], and וַתַּשְׁקֵמוֹ בִּדְמָעוֹת 80[6]; acc. rei om., lit. Ju 4[19] Ex 32[20] (E), fig. Je 25[17].—Vid. also I. מַשְׁקֶה infra. **Pu.** *Impf.* 3 ms. וּמֹחַ עַצְמוֹתָיו יְשֻׁקֶּה Jb 21[24] *the marrow of his bones is watered,*
8257 (refreshed, invigorated).—נשקה Am 8[8] v. שׁקע. p. 1054.

8250 †שִׁקּוּי n.[m.] drink (Ba[§ 102 d]);—'שׁ לְעַצְמוֹתֶיךָ Pr 3[8] *drink* (fig. for refreshment) *to thy bones*
8249 (cf. vb. **Pu.**); pl. sf. שִׁקּוּיָ (Ol[§ 186 b]) ψ 102[10] (+ לַחְמִי v[a]), שִׁקּוּיָי Ho 2[7].

8268 †שֹׁקֶת, [שֶׁקֶת] n.f. watering-trough (Ges[§ 95 f] Ba[ZMG xli (1887), 605]; Ar. سَاقِيَةٌ *irrigating canal,* سِقَايَةٌ *watering-place, drinking vessel*);—abs. 'הַשּׁ Gn 24[20] (J); pl. cstr. שִׁקֲתוֹת הַמָּיִם 30[38] (J).

4945 †I. מַשְׁקֶה n.m. butler, cup-bearer (prop. *Pt.* **Hiph.** = *one giving drink*);—abs. 'מ Gn 40[5] (E), Ne 1[11], cstr. מַשְׁקֵה Gn 40[1], sf. מַשְׁקֵהוּ v[13], pl. מַשְׁקִים v[2.9.20.21.23] 41[9] (all E); sf. מַשְׁקָיו 1 K 10[5] = 2 Ch 9[4] (> II. 'מ).

4945 †II. מַשְׁקֶה n.m.[Lv 11, 34] irrigation, drink;—abs. 'מ Gn 13[10] Lv 11[34], cstr. מַשְׁקֵה 1 K 10[21]+ 3 t.; sf. מַשְׁקֵהוּ Gn 40[21];—**1.** *irrigation* Gn 13[10] (J; abstr. for concrete, =) *well-irrigated,* of land; Ez 45[15] (< 𝔊 Co Siegf Berthol Toy Krae מִשְׁפְּחוֹת; Gr מִקְנֶה). **2.** *drink* Is 32[6] Lv 11[34]; 'כְּלֵי מ *drinking-vessels* 1 K 10[21] = 2 Ch 9[20]. **3.** = office of butler, *butlership* Gn 40[21] (E).

8252 †שָׁקַט vb. be quiet, undisturbed (𝔗 שְׁקַט (rare); NH שקט is *sink down;* Ar. سَقَطَ is *drop down*);—**Qal** *Pf.* 3 ms. consec. 'וְשׁ

11[5] (P; unclean animal); living in rocks, pl. שְׁפַנִּים ψ 104[18] Pr 30[26].—Vid. Rob[BR iii. 66, 387] Tr[NHB 75; FFP 1, and Pl. 1] Dr[Dt] Post[Hast. DB Coney] McLean-Shipley[Ency. Bib. Id].

†II. שָׁפָן n.pr.m. Σαφ(φ)αν: **1.** secretary (הַסֹּפֵר) under Josiah 2 K 22[3.8.8.9.10.10.12.14] 2 Ch 34[8.15.15.16.18.18.20]. **2.** father of אֲחִיקָם, contemp. of **1** (improb.=**1**): 2 K 22[12] 25[22] Je 26[24] 39[14] 40[5.9.11] 41[2] 43[6] 2 Ch 34[20]. **3.** father of אֶלְעָשָׂה Je 29[3], perh.=**2.** **4.** father of יַאֲזַנְיָהוּ 36[10] (called הַסֹּפֵר), v[11.12], perh.=**1.** **5.** father of יַאֲזַנְיָהוּ Ez 8[11], possibly=**1.**

5855 שׁוֹפָן v. עַטְרוֹת p. 743[a] supr.

3473 †יִשְׁפָּן n.pr.m. in Benjamin 1 Ch 8[22]; Ισφαν, A Εσφαν, 𝔊L Ιεσφαν.

שׁפע (√of foll.; NH שָׁפַע *flow abundantly, be abundant*; 𝔗 שְׁפַע, Syr. ܫܦܥ, *overflow, abound*).

8228 †שֶׁפַע n.[m.] abundance;—cstr. 'שׁ Dt 33[19].

8229 †[שִׁפְעָה], שִׁפְעַת **n.f. abundance, quantity**;—appar. abs. שִׁפְעַת 2 K 9[17], *a multitude* (of men), (Bur שִׁפְעָה, or שִׁפְעַת אֲנָשִׁים as Klo Benz al.; > 𝔊[B] Kit עָפָר); cstr. שִׁפְעַת יֵהוּא v[17] *Jehu's multitude;* cstr., of horses Ez 26[10], camels Is 60[6]; of waters Jb 22[11] 38[34].

8230 †שִׁפְעִי n.pr.m. in Simeon 1 Ch 4[37]; Σεφει, 𝔊L Σωφει.

שׁפף (√of following).

8207 †שְׁפִיפֹן n.[m.] **horned snake**, 𝔊 κεράστης (Ar. سُفٌّ, سِفٌّ Frey);—abs. 'שׁ Gn 49[17] (‖ נָחָשׁ); =*cerastes cornutus* or *Hasselquistii*, cf. Tr[NHB 273] Post[Hast. DB iv. 457 f.] McLean-Shipley[Ency. Bib. iv. 4393] Dr[ad loc.].—שְׁפוּפָם, שְׁפוּפָן vid. s.v.

8197 †שְׁפוּפָם n.pr.m. in Benjamin;—Nu 26[39], Σουταλα, 𝔊L Σοφαν (=מֻפִּים וְחֻפִּים Gn 46[21], שֻׁפִּים וְחֻפִּם 1 Ch 7[12]).

7781 †שׁוּפָמִי adj. gent. of foregoing, c. art. as n.coll. Nu 26[39].

8197 †שְׁפוּפָן n.pr.m. in Benj. 1 Ch 8[5], Σωφαρφακ, A Σωφαν, 𝔊L Σεπφαμ.

8206 †שֻׁפִּים n.pr.m. **1.** 'שׁ 1 Ch 7[15], Μαμφειν, A Σεφφειμ, 𝔊L Σαφιν, appar.=שֻׁפִּם v[12], Σαπφειν, 𝔊L Σαφαν (cf. שְׁפוּפָם, מֻפִּים). **2.** שֻׁפִּים doorkeeper, 1 Ch 26[16].

†[שָׁפַר] **vb. be beautiful, fair, comely** 8231
(Ar. سَفَرَ *remove veil* (of women), *shine;* Aram. שְׁפַר *be pleasing* (v. Dn 6[2]), ܫܦܪ *be beautiful, bright, pleasing,* ܫܦܝܪܐ *beautiful*);—**Qal** *Pf.* 3 fs. שָׁפְרָה עָלָי (Aram.) ψ 16[6] (the) heritage *is beautiful for* (pleasing to) *me* (v. עַל **II. 8**).

†I. [שֶׁפֶר] **n. m. beauty, goodliness**;— 8233
abs. אִמְרֵי־שָׁפֶר Gn 49[21] (v. אָמִיר, אֵמֶר). p. 57 534, 562

†II. [שֶׁפֶר] **n.pr.mont.** as a station in 8234
wilderness;—הַר־שָׁפֶר Nu 33[23.24] (P); Σαφαρ.

†I. שִׁפְרָה **n.f. fairness, clearness,** of sky;— 8235
abs. 'שׁ Jb 26[13] by his breath the sky becomes *fair(ness)*, v. esp. De Di Bu Du; > Che[JQ 1897, 578] (after 𝔊) בְּרִיחֵי שָׁמַיִם סִגֵּר הוּא.

†II. שִׁפְרָה **n.pr.f.** Hebrew midwife, Ex 8236
1[15] (E); Σεπφωρα (cf. Lag[BN 90]).

†שָׁפִיר **n. pr. loc.** in Philist. plain, Mi 1[11] 8208
(=שָׁמִיר Jos 15[48]?); 𝔊 καλῶς (!).

אֶשְׁפָּר vid. s. v. p. 80 829

שׁוֹפָר, **שֹׁפָר** [72] **n.m.** [Is 27, 13] **horn**, for blowing 7782
(Aram. שִׁיפּוּרָא √ dub.; CAdler[PAOS 1889, clxxi ff.] cp. As. *šappar(u)* a species of wild goat; in any case the 'שׁ is a curved horn, as of cow or ram, cf. Dr[Am 2, 2] (with illustr.));—abs. 'שׁוֹ 2 S 6[15]+, 'שׁ Ex 19[16]+; cstr. שׁוֹפַר Lv 25[9]; pl. שׁוֹפָרוֹת Ju 7[22]+, cstr. שׁוֹפְרוֹת Jos 6[4]+; sf. שׁוֹפְרֹתֵיהֶם Ju 7[8];—*horn,* mostly as used in war, rarely, and chiefly late, as sacred instr.: Ho 8[1] Ju 7[8.16] Is 58[1] (sim.) Jb 39[25] ('בְּדֵי שׁ, v. דַּי **2 a**); 'שׁ (הַ)יּוֹבְלִים Jos 6[4] *rams' horns* (v. יבל), so v[6.8.13] (all E); 'קוֹל (הַ)שׁ Ex 19[16.19] 20[18] (Gi v[15]), Jos 6[5.20] (all E), Am 2[2]+13 t.; 'תָּקַע בַּשׁ = *give a blast with the horn,* Ju 3[27] 6[34] Jos 6[4]+9 t. Jos, 1 S 13[3] 1 K 1[34.39]+9 t., + ('שׁ subj.) Zc 9[14]; 'תִּקְעוּ שׁ Ho 5[8] Am 3[6] (vb. Niph.), Je 4[5]+7 t., 'הַשׁ' לִתְקוֹעַ; cf. (תִּקְעוּ Kt) Qr תִּקְעֵי הַשׁ' Jos 6[9] +'הַשׁ Ju 7[20], 'בִּתֵקַע שׁ ψ 150[3]; also 'הֶעֱבִיר שׁ' תְּרוּעָה Lv 25[9 a] (H), cf. v[9 b] (P), 'יוֹם שׁ' וּתְרוּעָה Zp 1[16]; used on religious occasions, Jos 6[4 ff.] Lv 25[9] Jo 2[1.15] ψ 47[6] 81[4] 98[6] 150[3] 2 Ch 15[14].—On 'שׁ v. Adler[The Shophar (1894)] Dr[Am 2, 2] Hpt[We ψψ Transl. 221 f.] Abrahams[Hast. DB Trumpet].

†[שפרור Kt, שַׁפְרִיר Qr] **n.[m.]** doubtful, 8237
Thes *splendour* (√ שׁפר; Dl[Prol. 126] cp. As. vb. *šuparruru, spread out* (Id[HWB 684])); appar. of (*brightly-coloured?*) royal *pavilion, canopy,* or poss. *carpet,* sf. נָטָה שפרורו Je 43[10] (Qr שַׁפְרִירוֹ).

830, 4942, [שָׁפַת], מִשְׁפְּתַיִם, אַשְׁפֹּת v. II. שׁפה.
8239 p. 1046

8240 †II. שְׁפַתַּיִם **n.[m.] du.** doubtful word: usu. **hook-shaped pegs, hooks,** so 𝔗 Thes AV RV; abs. 'וְהַשּׁ Ez 40^{43}; < 𝔖 𝔙 Co וּשְׂפָתָם *and their edge,* so Aq Theod Symm and prob. 𝔊, cf.
4942 Hi-Sm, and Krae (וּשְׂפַת).—I. 'שׁ v. √שׁפה. p. 1046

8241 שֶׁצֶף v. שֶׁטֶף sub שׁטף. p. 1009

8245 †שָׁקַד **vb. watch, wake** (Ph. שקד *be circumspect;* NH שָׁקַד *be insistent;* 𝔗 שְׁקַד = BH);—**Qal** *Pf.* 3 ms. 'שׁ ψ 127^{1}, שָׁקַדְתִּי Je 31^{28} ψ 102^{8}; *Impf.* 3 ms. יִשְׁקוֹד Jb 21^{32} (Me Bu יִשְׁקְדוּ), וַיִּשְׁקֹד Dn 9^{14}, 1 s. אֶשְׁקֹד Je 31^{28}; *Imv.* mpl. שִׁקְדוּ Ezr 8^{29}; *Inf. cstr.* לִשְׁקֹד Pr 8^{34}; *Pt. act.* שֹׁקֵד Je 1^{12}+; pl. cstr. שֹׁקְדֵי Is 29^{20};—**1.** *keep watch* of, *be wakeful* over, 'י subj., עַל pers., to benefit or injure Je $31^{28.28}$ 44^{27}; עַל rei, to perform it 1^{12} Dn 9^{14}; so (men subj.) שֹׁקְדֵי אָוֶן Is 29^{20}; of leopard *watching* עַל־עָרֵיהֶם Je 5^{6} (to seize prey, fig.); of man *watching* (for admission) at (עַל) wisdom's doors Pr 8^{34} (‖ שָׁמַר); = *keep guard* over (עַל) Jb 21^{32}, cf. (abs.) 'שׁ וְשִׁמְרוּ Ezr 8^{29}, and (of watchman, שֹׁמֵר) ψ 127^{1}. **2.** *be wakeful, wake,* as mourner, sufferer ψ 102^{8}.—La 1^{14} rd. perh. **Niph.** *Pf.* נִשְׁקַד עַל־פְּשָׁעַי (𝔊 Bu) *watch has been kept over my transgressions* (cf. **1** supra), for MT 'נִשְׂקַד עֹל פּ.—**Pu.** denom. v. infra.

8247 †שָׁקֵד **n.[m.] almond(-tree)** (NH *id.;* so called from its early *waking* out of winter's sleep, acc. to Ki Thes Lag[BN 45] al.; Aram. שְׁיגְדָּא, ܫܓܕܐ, ܫܓܕ, whence Eth. ሰገድ: cf. Nö[M 39]; cf. Löw[No. 319]);—**1.** *almond,* i.e. the nut, pl. שְׁקֵדִים Gn 43^{11} (J; + בָּטְנִים, etc.), Nu 17^{23} (P). **2.** *almond-tree* Je 1^{11} and (prob.) Ec 12^{5}.

8246 †[שָׁקַד] **vb. Pu. denom.**—only *Pt.* pl. in גְּבִעִים מְשֻׁקָּדִים *cups shaped like almond* (blossoms) Ex $25^{33.33.34}$ $37^{19.19.20}$ (all P).

8248 †[שָׁקָה] **vb. Hiph. cause to drink water, give to drink** (NH Hiph. *id.;* Ar. سَقَى I. *give to drink;* Sab. סקי *be irrigated* Fell[ZMG liv (1900), 246], מסקי *drinks* Hom[Chr 121], מסתקין *id.* DHM[Hofmus., No. 1, l. 7]; Eth. ሰቀየ: *water, irrigate;* As. *šakû* I. = Heb. Hiph., Aram. שְׁקָא, ܫܩܐ Aph.);—for **Qal** v. II. שָׁתָה;—*Pf.* 3 ms. consec. וְהִשְׁקָה Gn 2^{6}+, sf. וְהִשְׁקָהּ Nu 5^{27}; 2 ms. consec. וְהִשְׁקִיתָ Nu 20^{8}+; 1 s. consec. וְהִשְׁקֵיתִי Ez 32^{6}, etc.; *Impf.* 3 ms. יַשְׁקֶה Nu 5^{26}, וַיַּשְׁקְ Gn 29^{10}+, etc.; *Imv.* ms. sf. הַשְׁקֵהוּ Pr 25^{21}; fs. sf. הַשְׁקִינִי Gn 24^{43}+; *Inf. cstr.* הַשְׁקוֹת Gn 2^{10}+, sf. הַשְׁקֹתוֹ 24^{19}; *Pt.* מַשְׁקֶה ψ 104^{13}, cstr. Hb 2^{15} (v. also I., II. מַשְׁקֶה);—**1.** *water, irrigate,* ground: subj. mist Gn 2^{6}, river v^{10} (both J), spring Jo 4^{18}; subj. 'י Is 27^{3} (כֶּרֶם), Ez 17^{7} (גֶּפֶן), both in fig., fig. also 32^{6} *water land* מִדָּם; lit. c. מִן of source ψ 104^{13} (הָרִים) and (subj. man) Ec 2^{6} (יַעַר). **2.** *water, give drink to,* usu. human subj., acc. of beast, Gn $24^{14.46.46}$ 29^{2} (מִן of source), $v^{3.7.8.10}$ Ex $2^{16.17.19}$ (all J), ψ 104^{11} (subj. springs); acc. pers. Gn 21^{19} (E), $24^{18.19.45}$ (J), Hb 2^{15} (fig.), Is 43^{20} ('י subj.), ψ 78^{15} (*id.*), 2 Ch 28^{15}, c. בְּ of vessel Est 1^{7}; c. acc. pers. et animal. Nu 20^{8} (P); *give* one something *to drink,* acc. pers. + rei (water, wine, etc.), Am 2^{12} Gn $19^{32.33.34.35}$ 24^{43} (all J), Ju 4^{19} 1 S 30^{11} 2 S 23^{15} = 1 Ch 11^{15}, Jb 22^{7}, cf. Ct 8^{2} (מִיַּיִן); fig. Je 8^{14} 9^{14} 16^{7} 23^{15} 25^{15} ψ 69^{22}, cf. וְנַחַל עֲדָנֶיךָ תַשְׁקֵם 36^{9}, and וַתַּשְׁקֵמוֹ בִּדְמָעוֹת 80^{6}; acc. rei om., lit. Ju 4^{19} Ex 32^{20} (E), fig. Je 25^{17}.—Vid. also I. מַשְׁקֶה infra. **Pu.** *Impf.* 3 ms. וּמֹחַ עַצְמוֹתָיו יְשֻׁקֶּה Jb 21^{24} *the marrow of his bones is watered,*
(refreshed, invigorated).—נשקה Am 8^{8} v. שׁקע. p. 1054 8257

†שִׁקּוּי **n.[m.] drink** (Ba[§ 102 d]);—'שׁ לְעַצְמוֹתֶיךָ 8250
Pr 3^{8} *drink* (fig. for refreshment) *to thy bones*
(cf. vb. **Pu.**); pl. sf. שִׁקֻּוַי (Ol[§ 186 b]) ψ 102^{10} (+ לֶחֶם 8249
v^{a}), שִׁקּוּיָי Ho 2^{7}.

†שֹׁקֶת, [שֶׁקֶת] **n.f. watering-trough** 8268
(Ges[§ 95 f] Ba[ZMG xli (1887), 605]; Ar. سَاقِيَةٌ *irrigating canal,* سِقَايَةٌ *watering-place, drinking vessel*);—abs. 'הַשּׁ Gn 24^{20} (J); pl. cstr. שִׁקֲתוֹת הַמָּיִם 30^{38} (J).

†I. מַשְׁקֶה **n.m. butler, cup-bearer** (prop. 4945
Pt. **Hiph.** = *one giving drink*);—abs. 'מ Gn 40^{5} (E), Ne 1^{11}, cstr. מַשְׁקֵה Gn 40^{1}, sf. מַשְׁקֵהוּ v^{13}, pl. מַשְׁקִים $v^{2.9.20.21.23}$ 41^{9} (all E); sf. מַשְׁקָיו 1 K 10^{5} = 2 Ch 9^{4} (> II. 'מ).

†II. מַשְׁקֶה **n.m.**[Lv 11, 34] **irrigation, drink**;— 4945
abs. 'מ Gn 13^{10} Lv 11^{34}, cstr. מַשְׁקֵה 1 K 10^{21}+ 3 t.; sf. מַשְׁקֵהוּ Gn 40^{21};—**1.** *irrigation* Gn 13^{10} (J; abstr. for concrete, =) *well-irrigated,* of land; Ez 45^{15} (< 𝔊 Co Siegf Berthol Toy Krae מִשְׁפְּחוֹת; Gr מִקְנֶה). **2.** *drink* Is 32^{6} Lv 11^{34}; 'כְּלֵי מ *drinking-vessels* 1 K 10^{21} = 2 Ch 9^{20}. **3.** = office of butler, *butlership* Gn 40^{21} (E).

†שָׁקַט **vb. be quiet, undisturbed** (𝔗 8252
שְׁקַט (rare); NH שקט is *sink down;* Ar. سَقَطَ is *drop down*);—**Qal** *Pf.* 3 ms. consec. 'וְשׁ

Je 30[10] 46[27], 3 fs. שָׁקְטָה Jos 11[23]+, 2 K 11[20]+; 1 s. שָׁקַטְתִּי Jb 3[26], וְשָׁקַטְתִּי Ez 16[42]; *Impf.* 3 ms. יִשְׁקֹט Ru 3[18]; 2 fs. תִּשְׁקְטִי Je 47[6.7]; 1 s. אֶשְׁקוֹט Is 62[1] Jb 3[13], אשקוטה Is 18[4] Kt, Qr אֶשְׁקֳטָה (Ges[§§ 10 h, 48 c]); *Pt.* שֹׁקֵט Ju 18[7]+, fs. שֹׁקֶטֶת 1 Ch 4[40], שֹׁקָטֶת Zc 1[11]; pl. הַשֹּׁקְטִים Ez 38[11];—*be quiet, undisturbed:* **1.** of land, *at peace,* abs. Ju 3[11.30] 5[31] 8[28] Is 14[7] (+ נָחָה), 2 Ch 13[23]; + מִמִּלְחָמָה Jos 11[23] 14[15] (D?), cf. v[5] (P); שׁ׳ וְשַׁלְוָה 1 Ch 4[40]; of earth, יֹשֶׁבֶת וְשׁ׳ Zc 1[11]; abs. of city 2 K 11[20] = 2 Ch 23[21], kingdom 2 Ch 20[30], + לִפְנֵי pers. 14[4]; of people, שׁ׳ וּבֹטֵחַ *in peace and security* Ju 18[7.27], הַשֹּׁקְטִים יֹשְׁבֵי לָבֶטַח Ez 38[11]; + שַׁאֲנַן Je 30[10] = 46[27]; of Moab, שַׁאֲנַן . . . וְשֹׁקֵט אֶל־שְׁמָרָיו 48[11] *undisturbed upon its lees* (fig. of wine); of Job, *quiet* in death Jb 3[13], *be at rest* (from apprehensions of evil) v[26] (+ שָׁלַוְתִּי, נַחְתִּי). **2.** *be quiet, inactive:* of י׳ + וְאַבִּיטָה Is 18[4] *I will be quiet and gaze,* i.e. gaze as an inactive spectator, ψ 83[2] (‖ חרש, דמה *be silent*); = be pacified Ez 16[42]; of sword of י׳ Je 47[6.7]; of Boaz Ru 3[18] *he will not be quiet* until he has finished the matter; of prophet Is 62[1] (‖ חָשָׁה *be silent*). **Hiph.** *Impf.* 3 ms. יַשְׁקִיט Pr 15[18], יַשְׁקִט Jb 34[29]; *Imv.* ms. הַשְׁקֵט Is 7[4]; *Inf. abs.* הַשְׁקֵט Is 32[17]+; cstr. הַשְׁקִיט ψ 94[13], -קִט Jb 37[17], -קֵט Is 57[20] Je 49[23];—**1.** *shew quietness* (inner causat.), of men Is 7[4] (+ אַל־תִּירָא), of sea Is 57[20] = Je 49[23], earth Jb 37[17] (+ מִדָּרוֹם); hence *Inf. abs.* = subst., *quietness, display of quietness* Is 30[15], עֲבֹדַת הַצְּדָקָה הַשְׁקֵט וָבֶטַח 32[17] *the product of righteousness is quietness and security* (Du Che[Hpt] Marti del. הצ׳ as dittogr. from v[a], read הַמִּשְׁפָּט for הַשְׁקֵט, and del. וְ: *the product of justice is security*); (*presumptuous*) *security,* שַׁלְוַת הַשְׁקֵט Ez 16[49] (of Sodom). **2.** *cause quietness:* subj. י׳ Jb 34[29], לְהַשְׁקִיט לוֹ מִימֵי רָע ψ 94[13]; *pacify, allay,* obj. רִיב Pr 15[18].

8253 †שֶׁקֶט **n.[m.]** quietness;—1 Ch 22[9] (+ שָׁלוֹם).

8254 †שָׁקַל **vb. weigh** (NH *id.;* Ar. ثَقُلَ *be heavy,* ثِقَل *heaviness, weight,* ثَقَل *load,* OAram. תקל *weigh,* Aram. תְּקַל, ܬܩܠ (*weigh*), *pay,* תִּקְלָא *shekel,* but also (OAram. Zinj.) שקל, שקלן Lzb[382]; ܫܩܠ *lift up;* As. *šaḳâlu, weigh, šiḳlu* (appar.) = שֶׁקֶל; Eth. ሰቀለ: *hang up, weigh;* Ph. משקל *weight;* cf. Frä[202], also Gk. σίγλος (𝔊 σίκλος), Lag[M ii. 357] Lewy[Fremdw. 118 f.];—on connex. of mngs. cf. *weigh* trans. and intrans. = Germ. *wägen, wiegen,* also *heave, heavy, heft* (= *weight,* obs. or colloq.));—**Qal** *Pf.* 3 ms. שׁ׳ 2 S 14[26] Is 40[12]; *Impf.* 3 ms. יִשְׁקֹל Ex 22[16], sf. יִשְׁקְלֵנִי Jb 31[6], etc.; *Inf. abs.* שָׁקוֹל Jb 6[2]; cstr. לִשְׁקוֹל Est 4[7]; *Pt. act.* שֹׁקֵל Is 33[18], 2 S 18[12] read perhaps *pass.* שָׁקֻל, v. infra;—**1.** *weigh,* human subj., acc. rei 2 S 14[26] Is 46[6] (ב of scale); fig., י׳ subj. Is 40[12], also (acc. pers.) Jb 31[6] (both c. בְּ of scale); cf. Inf. abs. sub **Niph.**; *weigh* precious metals intrusted to one, לְ pers. Ezr 8[25], עַל־יָדָם v[26], acc. rei om. v[29] (לִפְנֵי of superior). **2.** *weigh out* a price (i.e. pay): acc. of silver Ex 22[16] (E), 1 K 20[39] Zc 11[12] Je 32[10] (ב of scale), Is 55[2] (c. ב, *in exchange for*); + לְ pers. Je 32[9] Gn 23[16] (P); + עַל־כַּפַּי 2 S 18[12] (read perhaps שָׁקֻל, so We Kit[Kau] Bu Buhl), עַל־יְדֵי פ׳ Est 3[9], עַל־גִּנְזֵי הַמֶּלֶךְ 4[7]. **Niph.** *be weighed:* **1.** *Pf.* 3 ms. נִשְׁקַל, subj. rei Ezr 8[33] (pass. of Qal v[25 f.]); *Impf.* 3 ms. fig. (+ **Qal** *Inf. abs.*), לוּ שָׁקוֹל יִשָּׁקֵל כַּעְשִׂי Jb 6[2]. **2.** *be weighed out,* as price, 28[15].

שֶׁקֶל[87] **n.m.** [Lv 27, 6] a weight, **shekel** (orig. = 8255
weight; late Heb. = *coin* GACooke[Inscr. 356]);—abs. שׁ׳ Am 8[5]+, שָׁקֶל Ex 38[29]+; pl. שְׁקָלִים Jos 7[21]+; cstr. שִׁקְלֵי 1 Ch 21[25];—*shekel,* as standard weight Am 8[5]; of weight of bronze armour 1 S 17[5], iron spear-head v[7], + 2 S 21[16 b] (v. מִשְׁקָל), hair 2 S 14[26], food Ez 4[10]; implying value, of wedge of gold Jos 7[21] (JE); of nails in temple (gold) 2 Ch 3[9]; usu. a definite weight of silver (used in payment or valuation) Ex 21[32] (E), Jos 7[21] (JE), 1 S 9[8] 2 S 24[24] 2 K 7[1.1.16.16.18.18] 15[20] Je 32[9] Ez 45[12.12] (v. infra), and (= coin, fr. time of Darius I) Ne 5[15] 10[33] Lv 5[15] 27[3.4.5.5] (all P), + 53 t. P; also מַחֲצִית הַשּׁ׳ Ex 30[13.13.15] 38[26] (= בֶּקַע), all *half-shekel,* atonement-money; cf. שְׁלִישִׁית הַשּׁ׳ Ne 10[33] *one-third;* also רֶבַע שׁ׳ 1 S 9[8] *one-fourth of shekel;* שׁ׳ = 20 גֵּרָה (ג׳ otherwise unknown) Ez 45[12] Ex 30[13] Lv 27[25] Nu 3[47]; 50 שׁ׳ = one maneh Ez 45[12] (read וַחֲמִשִּׁים for וחמשה [and עֲשָׂרָה for עֶשְׂרִים preceding], 𝔊[A] Boeckh Hi-Sm Co Toy Da Krae Berthol); שׁ׳ הַקֹּדֶשׁ Ex 30[13.24] Lv 5[15] Nu 3[47.50] 7[13] + 21 t. P; land estimated in שׁ׳ of gold 1 Ch 21[25]; שׁ׳ also often om. after num.—שׁ׳ was of two standards, one one-half the other; actual weights (and values) varied, but most persistent were: (1) gold, 252⅔ gr. Troy (or 126⅓), mod. equiv. c. £2 1*s.*, or $10; (2) silver, 224½ gr. (nearly ½ oz.) = שׁ׳ הַקֹּדֶשׁ (v. supra), or 112¼, mod. equiv. c. 2*s.* 9*d.*, or 67 c.; שׁ׳ בְּאֶבֶן הַמֶּלֶךְ 2 S 14[26] is dub.; if late (Bu HPS Löhr Now) it prob. ref. to a Bab. or Pers. scale

(cf. S-C [Pap] באבני מלכא oft.); 60 (or 50) ש׳ = 1 mina, 60 minas = 1 talent (v. כִּכָּר, מָנֶה). Vid. esp. ARSKennedy [Hast. DB Weights and Measures, and Money].

4946 †מִשְׁקוֹל **n.[m.] heaviness, weight**;—בְּמ׳ Ez 4[10] *by weight*.

4948 מִשְׁקָל [49] **n.m. id.**;—abs. מ׳ 1 K 25[16]+; cstr. מִשְׁקַל Ju 8[26]+; sf. מִשְׁקָלוֹ Gn 24[22]+, etc.;—*weight* Gn 24[22.22] (J), Jos 7[21] (JE), Ju 8[26] 1 S 17[5] 2 S 12[30] 21[16a] (v[16b] read שֶׁקֶל with 𝔊 [v. esp. 𝔊L] We Dr and mod.), 1 K 7[47] 10[14] Nu 7[13]+ 11 t. Nu 7 (P), 7 t. Chr; of wind Jb 28[25]; בְּמִשְׁקָלוֹ Gn 43[21] (J) *in its* (full) *weight*, cf. מאֹזְנֵי מ׳ Ez 5[1]; בְּמ׳ *by weight* Lv 26[26] 1 Ch 28[14a.18]; בַּמ׳ *id.* Ez 4[16] (of bread), Ezr 8[34] 1 Ch 28[14b.15.15.17.17]; בַּמ׳ Lv 19[35] *in respect to weight*, cf. מ׳ 1 Ch 28[16] *as to weight, in weight*; לֹא־הָיָה מ׳ (i.e. there was too much to be weighed) 2 K 25[16] = Je 52[20], אֵין מ׳ 1 Ch 22[3.14].

4949 †[מִשְׁקֶלֶת], מִשְׁקֹלֶת **n.f. levelling instrument, level** (for horizontal accuracy);—abs. מִשְׁקָלֶת Is 28[17] (fig. of צְדָקָה ‖ קַו); cstr. -קֹלֶת, fig., מ׳ בֵּית אַחְאָב 2 K 21[13].

8256 †[שִׁקְמָה] **n.f. sycomore tree** (NH *id.*, Aram. שִׁיקְמָא, ܫܩܡܐ, Löw [No. 332]; hence Gk. *συκάμινος, mulberry* Lewy [Fremdw. 23]);—pl. abs. שִׁקְמִים Am 7[14]+; sf. שִׁקְמוֹתָם ψ 78[47];—*sycomore, ficus sycomorus* Linn (Tristr [NHB 397 ff.] Post [Flora of Syria 730; Hast. DB s.v.]) a common tree Is 9[9], growing in the Sh^e^phela 1 K 10[27] = 2 Ch 1[15] = 9[27], 1 Ch 27[28]; as property ψ 78[47] (‖ גֶּפֶן); בּוֹלֵס שִׁקְמִים Am 7[14] *a tender of sycomores* (v. [בָּלַס]).

8257 [שָׁקַע] **vb. sink, sink down** (so NH שָׁקַע, Aram. שְׁקַע; Ar. has صَقِعَ *be smitten, prostrated, collapse*);—**Qal** *Pf.* 3 fs. consec. וְשָׁקְעָה Am 9[5] *it shall sink* like the Nile (of land; opp. עָלָה); 3 fs. וַתִּשְׁקַע Nu 11[2] (JE), of fire, *it sank down*, died out; תִּשְׁקַע Je 51[64], of Babylon (like stone in water; opp. קוּם). **Niph.** 3 fs. נִשְׁקְעָה Am 8[8] Qr, of land, *sink* (opp. עָלָה; = **Qal** 9[5]; Kt erron.

8248 נשקה, cf. W [SG 287]). **Hiph.** *Impf.* 1 s. אַשְׁקִיעַ מֵימֵיהֶם Ez 32[14] *I will make their waters sink* (settle, grow clear); 2 ms. וּבְחֶבֶל תַּשְׁקִיעַ לְשֹׁנוֹ Jb 40[25] *with a cord wilt thou make* his tongue *sink* (? pull or press it down; of crocodile; Mich [Suppl. 2349], cited Thes [1477], cp. Sam. ▽ᑭᗯ = חבש *bind*).

4950 [מִשְׁקָע] **n.[m.] what is settled, clarified**

8257 (cf. √ **Hiph.**);—cstr. מִשְׁקַע־מַיִם תִּשְׁתּוּ Ez 34[18] *the clear* (of) *water* ye drink (cf. 32[14] supra).

[שְׁקַעֲרוּרָה] v. קער. p. 891 8258

†I. [שָׁקַף] **vb. Niph. Hiph. overhang,** 8259
look out and down (NH Niph. Hiph. = BH; cf. Aram. שְׁקִיפָא, ܫܩܝܦܐ *rocky pinnacle, rock*, Ar. سَقْفٌ *ceiling, roof, sky* (on connex. of mngs. cf. Ar. أَشْرَفَ *overtop, overlook*, from شَرُفَ *be high*; اِطَّلَعَ *look down upon*, from طَلَعَ *rise*));—**Niph.** *Pf.* 3 fs. נִשְׁקָפָה Ju 5[28]+, וְנִשְׁקָפָה Nu 21[20] (read prob. pt. הַנִּשְׁקָפָה, cf. 23[28], GBG); 1 s. נִשְׁקָפְתִּי Pr 7[6]; *Pt.* נִשְׁקָף Nu 23[28] 1 S 13[18] ψ 85[12]; f. נִשְׁקָפָה Ct 6[10];—*lean over* (and look), *look down*, c. בְּעַד of window, *through* Ju 5[28] 1 S 2[16] = 1 Ch 15[29], Pr 7[6]; abs. *look down, forth* Ct 6[10]; c. מִן of direction whence Je 6[1] ψ 85[12] (both fig.); of mt. *lean over upon* (עַל־פְּנֵי), *overhang* Nu 21[20] 23[28] 1 S 13[18] (read הַגֶּבַע for הגבול We Dr HPS al.). **Hiph.** *Pf.* 3 ms. הִשְׁקִיף ψ 14[2]+; *Impf.* 3 ms. יַשְׁקִיף La 3[50], וַיַּשְׁקֵף Gn 19[28]+, etc.; *Imv.* ms. cohort. הַשְׁקִיפָה Dt 26[15];—*look down* (= **Niph.**): c. בְּעַד of window Gn 26[8] (J), 2 K 9[30], c. אֶל pers. v[32]; *look down* upon, עַל־פְּנֵי, subj. pers. Gn 18[16] 19[28] (both J), abs. וַיַּשׁ׳ וַיַּרְא 2 S 24[20] (וַיַּבֵּט in ‖ 1 Ch 21[21]); esp. subj. י׳, c. אֶל loc. Ex 14[24] (J); c. מִן loc. Dt 26[15] ψ 102[20], + עַל pers. 14[2] = 53[3], + וְיֵרֶא La 3[50].

II. שקף (√of foll.; cf. Aram. שְׁקַף, ܫܩܦ *strike*, whence foll. as that against which the door *strikes*, v. Frä [20]; Ar. سَقَفَ *to ceil* or *roof*, سَقْفٌ *ceiling, roof*).

†[שֶׁקֶף] **n.[m.] frame-work, casing of** 8260
doors (cf. NH שְׁקוֹף *lintel*, Aram. שְׁקוֹף, שַׁקְפָא *threshold*);—שָׁקֶף 1 K 7[5].

†[שְׁקוּף, שָׁקוּף] **n.m.** [1 K 6, 4] **frame, casing** 8261
of windows;—pl. חַלּוֹנֵי שְׁקֻפִים 1 K 6[4] *windows of narrowing frames*, so read also, inserting ש׳, Ez 41[16] (Co Toy; > Krae Berthol read ש׳ for שְׂחִיף v[b]); ש׳ alone 1 K 7[4].

†מַשְׁקוֹף **n.[m.] prob. lintel of door**;—הַמ׳ 4947
Ex 12[7] (P), v[22.23] (J).

שקץ (√of foll.; cf. As. *šikṣu*, appar. a (skin-?) disease; NH Pi. שִׁקֵּץ, Aram. Pa. שַׁקֵּץ *detest*, are denom.; RS [JPhil. xvi. 71 ff.] conj. original meaning *let fall, throw away*, cf. Ar. سَقَطَ *fall, drop down*, but very dubious).

†שֶׁקֶץ **n. m.** [Lv 7, 21] **detestation, detestable** 8263
thing;—ש׳ of the ceremonially unclean Lv 7[21];

creatures forbidden as food: water animals without fins or scales $11^{10.11.12}$, birds of prey, etc., v^{13}, winged creeping things $v^{20.23}$, creeping vermin $v^{41.42}$ (all P), cf. Is 66^{17} (+בְּשַׂר הַחֲזִיר, הָעַכְבָּר); v. RS$^{Sem. i. 275, 2nd ed. 293; K 309 f., 2nd ed. 311 f.}$.—Ez 8^{10} read prob. שִׁקּוּצִים, v. שִׁקּוּץ.

8262 †[שִׁקֵּץ] **vb. Pi. denom.** detest, make detestable;—*Pf.* 3 ms. שִׁקַּץ ψ 22^{25}; *Impf.* 2 mpl. תְּשַׁקְּצוּ Lv 11^{13}+, etc.; *Inf. abs.* שַׁקֵּץ Dt 7^{26};—**1.** *detest*, c. acc. rei Dt 7^{26} (Impf.+Inf. abs.; ‖ תַּעֵב תְּתַעֲבֶנּוּ), Lv $11^{11.13}$ (P); ‖ בָּזָה ψ 22^{25}. **2.** *make detestable*, obj. נַפְשֹׁתֵיכֶם (=reflex.) Lv 11^{43} (P), 20^{25} (H).

8251 †שִׁקּוּץ, שִׁקֻּץ **n.m.**$^{Dn 11, 31}$ **detested thing**;—abs. שִׁקּוּץ Dn 11^{31} 12^{11}, cstr. שִׁקֻּץ 1 K 11^{5}+; pl. שִׁקּוּצִים 2 Ch 15^{8}, שִׁקֻּצִים 2 K 23^{24}; cstr. שִׁקּוּצֵי Ez $20^{7.8}$; sf. שִׁקּוּצֵיהֶם Je 16^{18}+, etc.;—*detested thing*, epith. of Isr. Ho 9^{10} (si vera l.; not elsewhere bef. Dt); of filth Na 3^{6}; appar. of unclean food Zc 9^{7} (as שֶׁקֶץ); of idols (so usu.; oft. ‖ תּוֹעֵבָה, גִּלּוּל, etc.), Dt 29^{16} 2 K 23^{24} Je 4^{1} 7^{30}=32^{34}, 13^{27} 16^{18} Ez 5^{11} 7^{30} $11^{18.20}$ $20^{7.8.30}$ 37^{23}; of idolatrous practices Dn 9^{27}, but rd. prob. as 11^{31} (so 𝔊 Θ), and כַּנּוֹ for כנף (v. Dr); שׁ׳ (מְ)שֹׁמֵם 11^{31} 12^{11} *detested thing causing horror* is the heathen altar erected in temple by Ant. Epiph., with (prob.) a statue of Zeus Olympios=(Ph.) בעלשמם *lord of heaven;* the prophet puts שִׁקּוּץ for בעל, and (מְ)שֹׁמֵם for שָׁמַיִם; cf. Nes$^{ZAW iv (1884), 248}$ Che$^{OP 105}$ Dr^{Dn}.

8264 †[שָׁקַק] **vb.** run, run about, rush (appar. akin to √I. שׁוּק, whence שׁוֹק);—**Qal** *Impf.* 3 mpl. בָּעִיר יָשֹׁקּוּ Jo 2^{9}, of locusts (‖ יְרֻצוּן; > Gr prop. יִסֹּקוּ from סלק); *Pt.* שֹׁקֵק Is 33^{4}, c. ב rei *rush at, upon* (like locusts); of *roving, ranging* bear Pr 28^{15} (unless we read שַׁכּוּל, Toy); fig. of נֶפֶשׁ *longing* for water Is 29^{8} (‖ עָיֵף and, v^{a}, רֵקָה), ψ 107^{9} (‖ רְעֵבָה). **Hithpalp.** *Impf.* 3 mpl. יִשְׁתַּקְשְׁקוּן Na 2^{5}, of chariots, *they rush to and fro.*

4944 †[מַשָּׁק] **n.[m.]** running, rushing;—cstr. מַשַּׁק Is 33^{4}, of locusts.

שׁקר (√of following; *deceive;* Aram. שְׁקַר *deceive*, also n. *deceit*, ܫܩܰܪ Pa. *deceive*, and deriv.; As. *taškirtu* [Dl *-gir-*] *a lie*, so NH שֶׁקֶר, Ar. سُقْر and شُقَّر (loan-word ?)).

8267 שֶׁקֶר $_{113}$ **n.m.** deception, disappointment, falsehood;—שׁ׳ Ex 23^{7}+64 t.; שָׁקֶר Ex 5^{9}+42 t.; pl. שְׁקָרִים ψ 101^{7}+3 t.; sf. שִׁקְרֵיהֶם Je 23^{32};—**1.** *deception*, what deceives, disappoints, and betrays one: a molten image Je 10^{14}=51^{17}; gift Pr 25^{14}; grace of person 31^{30}, etc.; אֹרַח שׁ׳ ψ $119^{104.128}$; דֶּרֶךְ שׁ׳ v^{29}; בטח בשׁ׳ Je 13^{25}; נחל שׁ׳ 16^{19}, cf. also ψ 7^{15} 33^{17} 119^{118} Is 28^{15}; לַשֶּׁקֶר *for disappointment, in vain* 1 S 25^{21} Je 3^{23}. **2.** *deceit, fraud, wrong:* עשׂה (ל)שׁ׳ *do* or *practise fraud, wrong* Ho 7^{1} Je 6^{13} $8^{8.10}$; c. ב, 2 S 18^{13}; פְּעֻלַּת שׁ׳ Pr 11^{18}; לֶחֶם שׁ׳ Pr 20^{17} *food got by fraud;* זֶרַע שׁ׳ Is 57^{4}; עֵט שׁ׳ Je 8^{8}; ילד שׁ׳ ψ 7^{15} (‖ עמל); דרך לשׁון קשׁת שׁ׳ Je 9^{2}; בְּשׁ׳ 3^{10} (‖ בגד), adv. שׁקר *fraudulently, wrongfully* ψ 35^{19} 38^{20} 69^{5} $119^{78.86}$. **3.** injurious *falsehood*, in testimony, esp. in courts: עֵד שֶׁקֶר Ex 20^{16} (E) Dt 19^{18} ψ 27^{12} Pr 6^{19} 14^{5} 25^{18}; עֵד שׁקרים 12^{17} $19^{5.9}$; ענה שׁ׳ Dt 19^{18} *testify falsehood;* שְׁבֻעַת שׁ׳ Zc 8^{17} *false oath;* נשׁבע לשׁ׳ *swear falsely* Je 5^{2}+5 t.; נשׁבע על שׁ׳ Lv 5^{22}; דבר שׁ׳ Mi 6^{12}+ (v. [דָּבַר], דָּבָר); אִמְרֵי שׁ׳ Is 32^{7}; שׂפת(י) שׁ׳ ψ 31^{19} 120^{2} Pr 10^{18} 17^{7}; טפל שׁ׳ Jb 13^{4} ψ 119^{69}, cf. v^{163}; abs. *false!* 2 K 9^{12} Je 37^{14}. **4.** *falsity*, of false or self-deceived *prophets:* נבא שׁ׳ *prophesy falsely* Je 14^{14} $23^{25.26}$ 29^{21}; + ל pers. $27^{10.14.16}$; נ׳ לַשׁ׳ v^{15}; נ׳ בשׁ׳ 5^{31} 20^{6} 29^{9}; מוֹרֶה שׁ׳ Is 9^{14} Hb 2^{18}; חזה שׁ׳ Zc 10^{2}; חֲזוֹן שׁ׳ Je 14^{14}, etc., (+12 t.); רוּחַ שׁ׳ v. p. 925^{b}. **5.** *lie, falsehood*, in gen.: דבר שׁ׳ ψ 101^{7} (‖ רְמִיָּה); דְּבַר שׁ׳ Pr 13^{5}; of מִלִּים Jb 36^{4}; לְשׁוֹן שׁ׳ *false tongue* Pr 6^{17} 12^{19} 21^{6} 26^{28} ψ 109^{2}; of lips Pr 12^{22}; אִישׁ שׁ׳ 17^{4} *liar.*

†[שָׁקַר] **vb. denom.** do or deal falsely;— 8266
Qal *Impf.* 2 ms. תִּשְׁקֹר Gn 21^{23} *thou wilt not do falsely* to me (לִי). **Pi.** *Pf.* 1 pl. שִׁקַּרְנוּ ψ 44^{18}; *Impf.* 3 ms. יְשַׁקֵּר 1 S 15^{29}; 3 mpl. יְשַׁקֵּרוּ Is 63^{8}, etc.;—*deal falsely* 1 S 15^{29} Is 63^{8}, c. ב pers. Lv 19^{11} (‖ כחשׁ); c. ב rei ψ 44^{18} 89^{34}.

שֹׁקֶת, שִׁקְתוֹת v. שׁקה. שֹׁר v. שׁרר. 8268, 8270
p. 1052, 1057
שַׂרְאֶצֶר **n.pr.m.** v. שַׂרְאֶצֶר. p. 974 8272

שׁרב (√of foll., *parch;* NH שָׁרַב *be scorched* (by sun), שָׁרָב *parching heat* (of sun); Ecclus 43^{22} דשׁן שׁרב *parched grass;* Aram. שְׁרִיב, שָׁרָב, ܫܪܰܒ *be parched,* ܫܪܳܒ *heat, drought:* cf. prob. also As. n.pr. div. *Šarrabu* (*-pu*) Zim$^{KAT 3, 415}$; >cp. Ar. سَرَابٌ *mirage* [Rob$^{BR i. 42}$] Ges$^{Is 35, 7}$ al.; see against this esp. Che$^{Introd. Is. 269}$).

†שָׁרָב **n.m. 1.** burning heat; **2.** parched 8273
ground;—only abs.: וְלֹא יַכֵּם שׁ׳ וָשָׁמֶשׁ Is 49^{10}; of ground, הַשּׁ׳ Is 35^{7} (‖ צִמָּאוֹן).

†שֵׁרֵבְיָה **n.pr.m.** a Levite with Ezra (? י׳ 8274

hath sent burning heat; or cp. Syr. ܫܪܒ Pa. *propagavit*);—Σαραβια(ς): Ezr $8^{18.24}$ Ne 8^{7} $9^{4.5}$ 10^{13} $12^{8.24}$.

8275 שַׁרְבִּיט v. שׁבט. p. 987

8281 I. [שָׁרָה] **vb. let loose** (NH *id., dissolve;* As. *šarû*, Pi. *open* (building, for use), *dedicate* it; *tašrîtu, dedication;* OAram. שרה *loose*, so Aram. שְׁרָא, ܫܪܐ; Eth. ፈተወ: *remit, condone*);—**Qal** *Impf.* 3 ms. sf. יִשְׁרֵהוּ Jb 37^{3} *he* (God) *lets*
8293 *it loose* (i.e. the thunder). **Pi.** *Pf.* 1 s. sf. שֵׁרִיתִךָ Je 15^{11} Qr *I will set thee free* (cf. 40^{4} 𝔗 𝔖), but dub.; Kt שרותך (i.e. שָׁרוֹתִךָ, √שׁרר), Thes Gie *I vex thee* [שָׁרַר=צָרַר, very dub.]; Ew al. RV *strengthen thee;* this yields best sense, but as Aram. שׁרר is intrans., read then שֵׁרַרְתִּךָ or הֲשֵׁרוֹתִךָ, Dr; Jerome Rabb rd. שֵׁרִיתְךָ=שְׁאֵרִיתְךָ *thy remnant* (AV).

II. שרה (√of foll.; cf. Ar. ثَرِيَ *be moist;* Aram. תְּרָא, ܬܪܐ *id.;* ܡܪܬܐ *grape-juice;* NH שָׁרָא *soften, dissolve;* whence foll. prop.=*moisture* (Di^{Nu} Dr^{§178} Paterson$^{Nu\ Hpt}$ Gray^{Nu}), and so As. *mešru, succulence* (Hpt $^{Paterson\ Nu}$)).

4952 †[מִשְׁרָה] **n.f. juice**;—cstr. מִשְׁרַת עֲנָבִים Nu 6^{3} (P) *the juice of grapes* (+שֵׁכָר, יַיִן).

III. שרה (√of following; cf. Ar. سِرْوَةٌ, سِرْيَةٌ *short dart*).

8302 †שִׁרְיָה **n.f.** a weapon, perhaps **lance, javelin**;—שׁ׳ Jb 41^{18} (+מַסָּע, חֲנִית, חֶרֶב),—yet 𝔊 θώρακα, 𝔙 *thorax*, i.e. שִׁרְיוֹן.

IV. שרה (√of foll.; meaning dub.; cf. As. *siriyâm, body-armour* (Inscr. of Sennach.), Aram. ܫܪܝܢܐ *id.;* Ecclus 43^{20} *id.;* also Egypt. *tu-ỉ-ra-na, tà-ra-y-na*, WMM$^{As.\ u.\ Eur.\ 102}$).

8302 †שִׁרְיוֹן, שִׁרְיָן **n.[m.] body-armour**;—abs. שִׁרְיוֹן 1 S $17^{5.38}$; שִׁרְיָן (Ges^{§29u}) 1 K 22^{34}=2 Ch 18^{33}, שִׁרְיָן Is 59^{17}; pl. שִׁרְיֹנִים Ne 4^{10}, שִׁרְיֹנוֹת 2 Ch 26^{14};—*body-armour*, perh. more exactly *breast-armour*, Ne 4^{10}; with appendages (הַדְּבָקִים) 1 K 22^{34}=2 Ch 18^{33}; c. vb. לבשׁ 1 S 17^{5}, made of scale-like plates (קַשְׂקַשִּׂים) of bronze v^{5}, named with helmet here, so v^{38} 2 Ch 26^{14} and (fig.) Is 59^{17}.—שׁ׳ n.pr. v. שׁריון.

8285 [שֵׁרָה] *bracelet*, v. שׁרר. p. 1057

8287 †שָׁרוּחֶן **n.pr.loc.** in Simeon;—Jos 19^{6} (𝔊 οἱ ἀγροὶ αὐτῶν, ? rdg. שְׂדֵיהֶן); WMM$^{As.\ u.\ Eur.\ 161,168}$ identif. with Egypt. *Ša-r(a)-ḥa-na.*

שָׁרוֹן **n.pr.loc.** שָׁרוֹנִי **adj.gent.** (†1 Ch 8289-90
27^{29}) v. ישׁר. p. 450, 1124

שׁרות Je 15^{11} v. I. שׁרה; שָׁרוּתֶיהָ Je 5^{10} v. 8281, 8284
II. שׁוּרָה, שׁוּר. above, p. 1004

שִׁרְטַי 1 Ch 27^{29} Qr, v. שִׁטְרַי. p. 1009 7861

†שָׁרַי **n.pr.m.** one with foreign wife Ezr 8298
10^{40}; Σαριου, א Σαρουε, 𝔊L Σαρουα.

שִׁרְיָה v. III. שׁרה. שִׁרְיוֹן v. IV. שׁרה. above 8302

שֵׁרִית v. שְׁאֵרִית. שֵׁרִיתִךָ Je 15^{11} v. I. שׁרה. 7611, 8281
above, p. 984

שְׁרֵמוֹת v. [שְׁדֵמָה] sub שׁדם. p. 995 7709, 8309

שִׁרְיָן v. שִׁרְיוֹן sub IV. שׁרה. above 8302

†שָׁרַץ **vb. swarm, teem** (NH *id.;* Aram. 8317
ܪܚܫ *crawl*, ܫܪܨ=שְׁרַץ, so שִׁרְצָא (rare); Eth. ሠረጸ: *germinate, sprout*);—**Qal** *Pf.* 3 ms. שׁ׳ ψ 105^{30}, שָׁרְצוּ Gn 1^{21}, etc.; *Impf.* 3 ms. יִשְׁרֹץ Ez 47^{9}, etc.; *Imv.* mpl. שִׁרְצוּ Gn 9^{7}; *Pt.* הַשֹּׁרֵץ 7^{21}+, f. הַשֹּׁרֶצֶת Lv 11^{46}; Hex only P:—**1.** *swarm, teem* with (acc. animal.), subj. water Gn $1^{20.21}$, cf. Ex 7^{28}, land ψ 105^{30}. **2.** *swarm*, subj. animal. Gn 8^{17} (+פָּרָה, רָבָה), Ez 47^{9}, הַשֹּׁרֵץ Gn 7^{21} Lv $11^{29.41.42.46}$ (all עַל־הָאָרֶץ), v^{43}; subj. men Gn 9^{7} (+פָּרָה, רָבָה), Ex 1^{7} (*id.*, +עָצַם).

†שֶׁרֶץ **n.m.**$^{Gn\ 7,21}$ **coll. swarmers, swarming things**;—שׁ׳ abs. Lv 11^{29}+, שָׁרֶץ v^{31}; cstr. 8318
v^{20}+;—*swarming things* (H D and P), aquatic Gn 1^{20} Lv 11^{10}; small reptiles and quadrupeds Gn 7^{21} (+עוֹף, בְּהֵמָה, חַיָּה), Lv 5^{2} (+חַיָּה, בְּהֵמָה), 11^{29} (weasel, mouse, lizard), v$^{31.41.42.43}$ (c. cogn. שָׁרַץ), v^{44}, cf. 22^{5}; insects, שׁ׳ הָעוֹף Dt 14^{19}, +הַהֹלֵךְ עַל־אַרְבַּע Lv $11^{20.21}$, cf. v^{23}. Cf. Dr$^{DB\ i.\ 518}$.

†שָׁרַק **vb. hiss,** perh. also **whistle, pipe** 8319
(NH *id., hiss* (dub.), Aram. שְׁרֵיק *id.* 𝔗 Lv $2^{15.16}$, ܫܪܩ *id.;*—from שׁ׳ comes Gk. σῦριγξ acc. to Lag$^{Abh\ GGW\ xxvi.\ 38}$ Lewy$^{Fremdw.\ 165}$);—**Qal** *Pf.* 3 ms. consec. וְשָׁ׳ Is 5^{26}, etc.; *Impf.* 3 ms. יִשְׁרֹק Is 7^{18}+ (Jb 27^{23} read יִשְׁרְקוּ Me Bi Siegf Bu); 1 s. אֶשְׁרְקָה Zc 10^{8};—*hiss*, as signal, לְ pers., fig., י׳ subj.: Is 5^{26} 7^{18} Zc 10^{1}; in derision, עַל civitat., etc. (oft. +שָׁמֵם *be astounded*), Je 19^{8} 49^{17} 50^{13} La 2^{15} (+הֵנִיעַ ראשׁ), Ez 27^{36}; abs. Zp 2^{15} La 2^{16} 1 K 9^{8} (+חָרַק שֵׁן); עַל pers. Jb 27^{23} (c. מִן loc.).

†שְׁרֵקָה **n.f.** (object of derisive) **hissing**;— 8322
always abs. שׁ׳, and always +שַׁמָּה: Je 19^{8} $25^{9.18}$

(קְלָלָה, חָרְבָּה +), 29[18] (חֶרְפָּה, אָלָה +), 51[37] Mi 6[16] (חֶרְפָּה +), 2 Ch 29[8].

8292 †[שְׁרִיקָה] **n.[f.] hissing**, perhaps also **whistling, piping**;—pl. abs. (intens.) שְׁרִיקֹת Je 18[16] Qr *hissing*, in derision, + שַׁמָּה (v. שְׁרֵקָה),
8292 Kt שרוקת; cstr. שְׁרִקוֹת עֲדָרִים Ju 5[16] as signal *hissings* (or whistlings, pipings) *for flocks*.

שרר (√of [שָׁרִיר], שְׁרִירוּת, and perhaps of other words following; OAram. שרר *be firm, sound*, Aram. שְׁרַר *be firm, hard*, ܫܪ *be firm, consistent, substantial, truthful*, ܫܰܪܰܪ *strengthen, confirm*; Aram. and NH שָׁרִיר *firm, hard*; ܫܰܪܺܝܪܽܘܬܳܐ *firmness, strength, constancy*).

8270 †[שֹׁר] **n.[m.] navel-string** (cf. Aram. שׁוֹרָא Ez 16[4] 𝔗, ܫܪܳܐ, Ar. سُرٌّ, all *id.*);—sf. לֹא כָרַּת שָׁרֵּךְ Ez 16[4] (Ges§ 22 s Kö ii. 1. 45) *thy navel-string was not cut*; questioned are: שָׁרֶּךָ Pr 3[8] (De al. *navel*, synechd. for body, ‖ עַצְמוֹתֶיךָ; 𝔊 τῷ σώματί σου, cf. 𝔖, Clericus Bi Frankenberg בְּשָׂרֶךָ, Ew Hi
8326 Kmp al. שְׁאֵרֶךָ, Toy either); שָׁרְרֵךְ Ct 7[3] (𝔊 ὀμφαλός σου; ‖ בִּטְנֵךְ), = שָׁרֵּךְ Thes al.; now oft. interpreted as = *vulva*, cf. Ar. سِرٌّ *secret part*, Hi Stickel Buhl Öttli, noticed also by Thes, but Arabism dub., v. Bu.

8285 †[שֵׁרָה] **n.[f.] bracelet** (Aram. שֵׁירָא *id.*, ܫܺܝܪܳܐ *chain*, Gn 24[22] 𝔖𝔗: Ar. سِوَارٌ *bracelet*, Qor 18[30] [Frä[56]] is said by Lane[1465] to be from the Persian, and, if Sem., would be fr. √سور);—pl. abs. הַשֵּׁרוֹת Is 3[19] (in list of finery).

8325 †שָׁרָר **n.pr.m.** 2 S 23[33] = II. שָׂכָר, q.v.

8306 †[שָׁרִיר] **n.[m.] sinew, muscle** (so context suggests);—pl. cstr. אוֹנוֹ בִּשְׁרִירֵי בִטְנוֹ Jb 40[16] (‖ כֹּחוֹ בְמָתְנָיו).

8307 †שְׁרִירוּת, usu. **שְׁרִרוּת** **n.f. firmness**, always = **stubbornness**; only cstr. שׁ׳, sq. לֵב: שׁ׳ לִבָּם הָרָע Je 9[13] 13[10] 23[17] Dt 29[18] ψ 81[13] (שְׁרִירוּת); Je 3[17] 7[24] 11[8] (שְׁרִי׳), so (לִבּוֹ) 16[12] 18[12].

8331 [שַׁרְשָׁה] Ex 28[22] v. following.

8333 †[שַׁרְשְׁרָה] **n.f.** (in spite of foll. sf. masc. Ex 28[14], Ges§ 135 o Albr ZAW xv (1895), 316, xvi (1896), 96) **chain** (As. *šaršarratu, chain, fetter*; Mishn. שַׁרְשָׁרוֹת, Talm. שַׁרְשׁוּרָא, Syr. ܫܪܫܘܪܬܐ, *chain* or *rope* of palm-leaves, etc., but also NH שַׁלְשֶׁלֶת *chain*, 𝔗 שֵׁישְׁלָא, Syr. ܫܫܠܬܐ [whence Ar. سِلْسِلَةٌ, v. Eth. ሰንሰለ:], (connex. with שַׁר׳ denied by Nö BSSW 56 Anm. 9));—pl. שַׁרְשְׁרֹת, abs. 1 K 7[17] +, -רֹת abs. 2 Ch 3[15], cstr. Ex 28[14] +, שַׁרְשֹׁת v[22] (either abbrev. or textual error);—*chains* of gold, like wreaths, attached to ephod Ex 28[14.14.22] 39[15]; ornaments on pillars at porch of temple 1 K 7[17] (גְּדִלִים מַעֲשֵׂה שׁ׳), ‖ 2 Ch 3[15.16.16].

שרשׁ (appar. √of foll.; Di Jb 40, 16 Buhl al. think = שרשר, √ שרר, cf. שֹׁר, etc., Eth. ሥርው: *nerve, muscle*, whence שֹׁרֶשׁ as root-*fibre*, but word very ancient, and this der. quite unproven; < Schwally ZMG lii (1898), 140 f. cp. Ar. شَرْسٌ (ش by dissimilation), *thorn-bush*, شَرْسٌ *hard, rough, rugged* (of ground), شَرِسٌ *ill-natured, cross*; hence שֹׁרֶשׁ, from *tough, gnarled* root-fibres; NH and Ph. שרש, As. *šuršu*, all *root*, Sab. שרס (v. Ar. supr.) *root, foundation* Hom Chr 124, אשרס *foundation* DHM ZMG xxix (1875), 606; xxxvii (1883), 415; Aram. שׁוֹרְשָׁא, ܫܶܪܫܳܐ *root*).

†**שֹׁרֶשׁ** **n.m.** Dt 29, 17 **root**;—שׁ׳ abs. Dt 29[17] +, 8328
cstr. Is 11[10] +; sf. שָׁרְשִׁי Jb 29[19], etc.; pl. cstr. שָׁרְשֵׁי 13[27] (v. infr.) 36[30], sf. שָׁרָשָׁיו Am 2[9] +, שָׁרָשֶׁיהָ Ez 17[7] +;—**1.** *root* of people under fig. of tree, involving firmness, permanence, Am 2[9] Ho 9[16] 14[6] Is 14[30] 2 K 19[30] = Is 37[31];—שָׁרְשָׁם Ju 5[14] is prob. corrupt, v. GFM;—so of pers. (cf. Ph, Eshmunazar[11] GACooke pp. 30, 36) Is 5[24] Mal 3[19] Jb 8[17] 18[16] 29[19] Pr 12[3.12]; = stock, family Is 11[1.10] Dn 11[7], cf. (of serpent) Is 14[29]; = source or cause Dt 29[17], שׁ׳ דָּבָר Jb 19[28]. **2.** lit. *root* of tree or shrub Je 17[8] (sim.), Ez 31[7] (metaph. of people), Is 53[2] (sim.), Jb 14[8] 30[4]; of vine (metaph. of people) Ez 17[6.7.9.9] ψ 80[10] (acc. cogn. c. שרשׁ **Hiph.**). **3.** *root*, fig. = lowest stratum, of mt. Jb 28[9], of sea 36[30] = bottom (text strange and dub.: Du רָאשֵׁי הָרִים, with אֵדוֹ in v[a]); of feet, שָׁרְשֵׁי רַגְלַי 13[27], i.e. soles Ew Di De Da al. (elsewhere כַּף), Bu place of treading, *footholds*; Du (arbitrarily) שָׁרָשַׁי, del. רגלי.

†[שָׁרַשׁ] **vb. denom. Pi.** = **deal with the** 8327
roots;—**1.** *root up, out*: *Pf.* 3 ms. sf. consec. וְשֵׁרֶשְׁךָ ψ 52[7] *he shall root thee up* from (מִן) the land of the living; of fire (*burn*) roots, *root*: *Impf.* 3 fs. תְּשָׁרֵשׁ בְּ Jb 31[12] fire (fig.) *roots at* all my increase. **Pu.** *Impf.* 3 mpl. יְשֹׁרָשׁוּ 31[8] *be rooted up* (of produce). **2. Poʿēl** *take root*, establish oneself firmly: *Pf.* 3 ms. שֹׁרֵשׁ בָּאָרֶץ גִּזְעָם Is 40[24] (fig. of princes, etc.). **Poʿal** *id.*: *Pf.* 3 mpl. שֹׁרָשׁוּ Je 12[2] (fig. of wicked). **Hiph.** *id.*: *Impf.* 3 ms. יַשְׁרֵשׁ Is 27[6] (fig. of Isr.); 3 fs. וַתַּשְׁרֵשׁ ψ 80[10] (*id.*; c. acc. cogn.); *Pt.* מַשְׁרִישׁ Jb 5[3] (fig. of pers.).

8329 †שַׁרְשׁ **n.pr.m.** in Manasseh (cf. OAram. n.pr. שרש Lzb[383]);—1 Ch 7[16]; Σο[υ]ρος; 𝔊L Φορος.

8331, 8333 [שַׁרְשָׁה], [שַׁרְשְׁרָה] v. שׁרר. p. 1057

8334 [שָׁרַת] [97] **vb. Pi.** **minister, serve** (cf. NH שֵׁרוּת (temple-)*ministry*, Ph. משרת *ministry*, and perhaps vb. שרת *minister*);—**Pi.** *Pf.* 3 ms. שֵׁרֵת Nu 8[26] Dt 18[7]; 3 mpl. שֵׁרְתוּ Nu 3[6]; *Impf.* 3 ms. וַיְשָׁרֶת Gn 39[4], 3 mpl. יְשָׁרְתוּ Nu 3[31]+, etc.; *Inf. cstr.* לְשָׁרֵת Ex 28[35]+, לְשָׁרֶת שָׁם Dt 17[12], etc.; *Pt.* מְשָׁרֵת Nu 11[28]+ (2 S 13[9] v. מַשְׁרֵת, p. 602[a]), f. מְשָׁרֶתֶת 1 K 1[15], etc.;—*serve*: **1.** of ministerial service (opp. menial, עבד): **a.** higher domestic service: Joseph Gn 39[4] 40[4] (JE), Elisha's chief servant 2 K 4[43] 6[15], royal domestics 2 S 13[17.18] 1 K 10[5] 2 Ch 9[4] Est 2[2] 6[3], Abishag 1 K 1[4.15]. **b.** of royal *officers* (late) 1 Ch 27[1] 28[1] 2 Ch 17[19] 22[8] Est 1[10] Pr 29[12]. **c.** Joshua as chief assistant to Moses Ex 24[13] 33[11] (E), Nu 11[28] (J), Jos 1[1] (D), Elisha to Elijah 1 K 19[21]. **d.** of angels to י׳ ψ 103[21], cf. 104[4]. **e.** of kings of nations in proph. Is 60[10]. **2.** usu. of special service in worship: **a.** of Levit. priests, abs. 1 K 8[11] = 2 Ch 5[14]; c. acc. י׳ Dt 10[8] 17[12] 21[5] Je 33[21]+(strangely) מְשָׁרְתֵי אֹתִי v[22]; also Is 60[7] of animals put fig. for those sacrificing them; of foreigners admitted to priesthood Is 61[6], cf. 56[6]; so prob. Samuel conceived as priest 1 S 2[11] 3[1], את פני י׳ 2[18] (פני prob. acc., cf. 𝔊 τῷ προσώπῳ v[11]), שׁ׳ בְּשֵׁם י׳ Dt 18[5.7]. **b.** Levites (P, and late); c. acc. of Aaronic priests Nu 3[6] 8[26] 18[2], c. acc. of י׳ 1 Ch 15[2] 2 Ch 29[11a]; prob. also in ref. to Lev. singer ψ 101[6]; c. acc. tabern. Nu 1[50] (P), congregation 16[9] (P), people Ez 44[11] + v[12] (of idolatry); abs. 1 Ch 16[4] 2 Ch 23[6] 29[11b] 31[2] Ezr 8[17] (pt. as subst., *ministers*); שׁ׳ לִפְנֵי אֲרוֹן בְּרִית י׳ 1 Ch 16[37], שׁ׳ נֶגֶד הַכֹּהֲנִים 2 Ch 8[14]; שׁ׳ c. ב loc. 1 Ch 26[12]; esp. c. בְּ, of sacred vessels Nu 3[31] 4[9.12.14] 2 K 25[14] = Je 52[18]; בַּשִּׁיר 1 Ch 6[17]. **c.** Zadokite priests (Ez), abs. Ez 42[14]+3 t., c. acc. י׳ 40[46]+4 t., cstr. מְשָׁרְתֵי before sacred place 45[4.5] 46[24]. **d.** Aaronic priests, abs. Ex 28[35]+4 t. P; c. acc. י׳ 1 Ch 23[13]; לי׳ 2 Ch 13[10]; מְשָׁרְתֵי י׳ Jo 1[9.13] 2[17], מְשָׁרְתֵי מזבח Jo 1[13], c. בַּקֹּדֶשׁ Ex 28[43]+4 t. P. **e.** of idolatry, c. acc. עץ ואבן Ez 20[32].

8335 †שָׁרֵת **n.m.** religious ministry;—כְּלֵי הַשּׁ׳ *vessels of m.* in tabern. Nu 4[12], temple 2 Ch 24[14].

8154 [שָׁשָׂה] v. [שׁסה] **Pō.** p. 1042

8336-37 I. שֵׁשׁ *six*, v. שׁדשׁ. II. שֵׁשׁ v. שַׁיִשׁ. p. 995, 1010

8336 †III. שֵׁשׁ **n.m.**[Ex 26, 1] byssus (loan-wd. prob. fr. Eg. *šen-suten* Reinisch ap. DHM[VOJ viii (1894). 7] Copt. *šens*, cf. Copt. *šent*, *weave*; v. M'Lean[Ency. Bib. LINEN]; on spinning, weaving, and wearing of linen in Egypt Erman[Aegypten 594 ff.; Eng. Trans. 448 f.]);—always abs. שׁ׳ (שֶׁשִׁי Ez 16[13] is error):—*byssus*, fine Egyptian linen (בּוּץ, q.v., is later synon.), i.e. the linen thread (spun by women Ex 35[25]), and the material woven from it: used for garments Gn 41[42] (E), Ez 16[10.13] (שֶׁשִׁי, read שֵׁשׁ), Pr 31[22]; for sail (in fig. of Tyre as ship) Ez 27[7] (brought from Egypt); elsewhere P, of priestly vestments Ex 28[5.39.39] 39[3.27.28.28]; also שׁ׳ מָשְׁזָר *twisted linen* 28[6.8.15] 39[2.5.8.28.29] + v[24] (read וְשֵׁשׁ מ׳ Sam 𝔊 Bae); שׁ׳ of hangings, etc., in tabern. 25[4] 35[6.23.25.35] 38[23], and so שׁ׳ מָשְׁזָר 26[1.31.36] 27[9.16.18] 36[8.35.37] 38[9.16.18].

8339-40 †[שִׁשֵּׁא] **vb. intens.** appar. **lead on**; so Vrss and context; *Pf.* 1 s. sf. וְשִׁשֵּׁאתִיךָ Ez 39[2] consec., *I* (י׳) *will lead thee on* (acc. of Gog) (form **Pilp.** fr. assumed √שׁאא Ol[§ 253] Sta[§§ 112 a Anm. 2; 464] Hi-Sm Krae Berthol).

8329 †שֵׁשְׁבַּצַּר (Baer Gi; שֵׁשׁ׳ van d. H.) **n.pr.m.** prince of Judah, leader of returning exiles Ezr 1[8.11] (cf. BAram. 5[14.16]); Σαβανασαρ, A Σασαβασσαρος, 𝔊L Σαβασαρης; in 1 Esdr Σαναμασσαρος, etc. (prob. = *Šamaš-bal-uṣur* or *Sin-bal-uṣur* Mey[Entstehung d. Jud. 75 ff., 193] Selbie[Hast. DB, s.v.] Che[Ency. Bib. s.v.] Berthol[Ezr 1, 8] and reff.);—long identified with Zerub., so Be-Ry Ryle, but improbable, v. Sm[Listen 19] Kosters[Herstel 32 f.] Mey[Entstehung l.c.]; Mey[77] al. identify with שֶׁנְאַצַּר 1 Ch 3[18] (against this Now[Hg 1, 1], yet v. Berthol[l.c.]).

8337 [שִׁשָּׁה] v. I. שֵׁשׁ sub שׁדשׁ. p. 995

8343 †שָׁשַׁי **n. pr. m.** Jew with foreign wife Ezr 10[40]; Σεσ(ε)ει.

8344 †שֵׁשַׁי **n.pr.m.** a son of Anak (Aram. form, cf. GFM[Ju]);—Nu 13[22] Jos 15[14] (both JE), Ju 1[10]; Σεσ(σ)ει, Σουσαι, Σουσει.

8345-46 שִׁשִּׁי, שִׁשִּׁים, שִׁשִּׁית v. I. שֵׁשׁ sub שׁדשׁ. p. 995

8347 †שֵׁשַׁךְ **n. pr. terr.** = בָּבֶל (Jer Rabb. and mod.; by *Atbaš* (את׳בשׁ), i.e. disguising name by substituting last letter of alphabet for first, next last for second, etc., cf. Thes);—Je 51[41] and hence (perhaps gloss) 25[26] (v. Gie).

8348 †שֵׁשָׁן **n. pr. m.** in Judah, 1 Ch 2[31.31] (with one son), v[34.34.35] (no sons, but daughters, cf. Benz Kit); Σωσαν[μ], 𝔊L Σισαν.

8349 †שָׁשַׁק (Baer Gi; van d. H. שָׁשָׁק, שָׁשָׁק) **n.pr.m.** in Benjamin, 1 Ch $8^{14.25}$; Σωκηλ, Σωιηκ, A Σωσηκ, 𝔊L Σισαχ (acc. to Simon. (Thes) = שַׁקְשַׁק *one longed for* (√שׁקק)).

8350 †[שָׁשַׁר] **n.[m.] red colour, vermilion** (etym. unknown);—*vermilion*, formerly gained from *kermes* insect (*vermiculus*): מָשׁוּחַ בַּשָּׁשַׁר Je 22^{14} (𝔊 μίλτος, *red ochre*; 𝔙 *sinopis* [from city Sinopis, whence the colour came Plin$^{NH\ xxxv.\ [6]\ 13}$], cf. Thatcher$^{DB\ Colours}$ Canney$^{EB\ Id.}$); חֲקֻקִים בַּשָּׁשַׁר Ez 23^{14}.

8352, 8356 [שָׁת], i. שֵׁת v. שׁית. p. 1011

7612, 8351 ii. שֵׁת v. שֵׁאת sub I. [שׁאה]. p. 981

8357 iii. שֵׁת v. II. שׁתה. below

8354 I. שָׁתָה$_{217}$ **vb. drink** (NH *id.*; As. *šatû*, Eth. ሰትየ: OAram. שתה, Aram. אִשְׁתִּי, שְׁתָא, [ܫܬܐ], ܐܶܫܬܺܝ; Sab. שתי DHM$^{ZMG\ xxxvii\ (1883),\ 403}$ Hom$^{Chr\ 124}$);—**Qal**$_{216}$ *Pf.* 3 ms. שׁ׳ Ex 34^{28}+, 1 s. שָׁתִיתִי 1 S 1^{15}+, etc.; *Impf.* 3 ms. יִשְׁתֶּה Gn 44^{5}+, וַיִּשְׁתֶּה 1 K 19^{8}, usu. וַיֵּשְׁתְּ Gn 9^{21}+; juss. יֵשְׁתְּ 1 K 13^{18}; 3 fs. וַתֵּשְׁתְּ Nu 20^{11}; 2 ms. apoc. תֵּשְׁתְּ Ju 13^{14}+, וַתֵּשְׁתְּ 1 K 13^{22}; 1 s. וָאֵשְׁתְּ Gn 24^{46}; 3 mpl. יִשְׁתָּיוּן ψ 78^{44}, etc.; *Imv.* ms. שְׁתֵה Gn 24^{14}+, etc.; *Inf. abs.* שָׁתֹה Is 21^{5} Je 49^{12} (in 1 S 1^{9} after prep., anom., Ges$^{§\ 113\ e}$, om. 𝔊 Th We Dr and mod.), שָׁתוֹ Je 25^{28}+, שָׁתוֹת Is 22^{13} (Ges$^{§\ 75\ n}$); cstr. שְׁתוֹ †Pr 31^{4}, שְׁתוֹת Je $35^{8.14}$, לִשְׁתֹּת Gn 24^{19}+, sf. שְׁתוֹתוֹ 1 K 13^{33}, לִשְׁתּוֹתָהּ Is 51^{22} etc.; *Pt. act.* שֹׁתֶה Is 29^{8}+, f. שֹׁתָה Jb 6^{4}, etc.;—**1. a.** of man: *drink*, water, wine, etc., Ex 34^{28} (JE), cf. 15^{24} (J), 1 S 30^{12} Am 2^{8} 4^{8} 5^{11} Is 5^{22} $62^{8.9}$ Pr 31^{4}, Ju $13^{4.7.14}$+oft. (2 t. JE; 6 t. D); by measure (short allowance) Ez $4^{11.16}$; milk †Ez 25^{4}, cf. Ct 5^{1}; blood 1 Ch 11^{19} (fig. of water gained by hazard); fig. חֲמָתָם שֹׁתָה רוּחִי Jb 6^{4} *whose venom* [of arrows of י׳] *my spirit drinks up*; acc. + מִן of source †Ex 7^{18} (J), v^{21} (E), 15^{23} (J), Pr 5^{15} (fig.); acc. (of wine, water, etc.) om. Gn $24^{14.14}$ 27^{25} 43^{34} (all J) + 11 t. J, Ex 7^{24} 17^{6} (E), Nu 20^{5} (JE), v^{11} 33^{14} (P), Ju 15^{19}+oft.; acc. שַׁיִן †2 K 18^{27} = Is 36^{12}; מַמְתַקִּים Ne 8^{10}; abs. Ec 2^{24}+; + מִן of source 1 K $17^{4.6}$ ψ 110^{7}, מִכֹּסוֹ 2 S 12^{3}; שׁ׳ בְּמִזְרְקֵי יַיִן †Am 6^{6}, cf. Gn 44^{5}; שׁ׳ בְּיַיִן †Pr 9^{5}; c. מִן partit. Gn 9^{21} Ex 7^{24} Ru 2^{9}, also (fig.) Je 51^{7} (and Jb 21^{20} infra). †**b.** pt. as subst. שֹׁתֵי מַיִם Ez $31^{14.16}$, שׁוֹתֵי יָיִן Jo 1^{5}; שׁוֹתֵי שֵׁכָר ψ 69^{13}. **c.** *drink* wine in sacrificial feast Dt 32^{38} (poem); blood of sacrificial victim ψ 50^{13} (fig. of י׳). **d.** subj. animals Nu 20^{19} Jon 3^{7} (both + men), also (fig.) Ez $34^{18.19}$; acc. (water) om. Gn $24^{19.22}$ $30^{38.38}$. **e.** fig. of drinking cup of י׳'s wrath, שׁ׳ אֶת־כּוֹס חֲמָתוֹ Is 51^{17} (+ מִיַּד י׳), cf. v^{17}, v^{22}, v. also Ez $23^{32.34}$ and (acc. om.) Je $25^{16.26.27}$ + 8 t. Je, Hb 2^{16}; abs. Ob$^{16.16.16}$; acc. שׁ׳ שְׁמָרִים ψ 75^{9}; שׁ׳ מֵחֲמַת שַׁדַּי Jb 21^{20}. †**f.** *drink* blood, fig. of slaughter, Nu 23^{24} (JE; of lion, metaph. of Isr.), Zc 9^{15} (read דָּמָם for הָמוּ 𝔊$^{Codd.}$ Sta Now Marti); so (blood of י׳'s sacrifice) Ez $39^{17.18.19}$. **g.** fig. of wicked deeds: יֵין חֲמָסִים יִשְׁתּוּ Pr 4^{17} (‖ לָחֲמוּ לֶחֶם רֶשַׁע; these are their food and drink), cf. Jb 15^{16} 34^{7}, but Pr 26^{6} appar. = *suffers* violence (cf. De Toy). †**2.** late, = *feast* Est 3^{15} 7^{1} (cf. מִשְׁתֶּה). †**Niph.** *Impf.* 3 ms. יִשָּׁתֶה Lv 11^{34} (P) all which *is* (may be) *drunk*, c. בְּ of vessel.—נִשְׁתָּוָה Pr 27^{15} v. I. שׁוה *ad fin.* For *cause, give, to drink* v. שׁקה.

†i. שְׁתִי **n.[m.] drinking, drinking-bout**;—Ec 10^{17}. 8358

†שְׁתִיָּה **n.f. drinking** (mode or amount) Est 1^{8}. 8360

מִשְׁתֶּה$_{45}$ **n.m.**$^{Gi.\ 21,\ 8}$ **1. feast; 2. drink**;— 4960
abs. מ׳ Gn 19^{3}+; cstr. מִשְׁתֵּה 1 S 25^{36}+; sf. מִשְׁתָּיו Dn 1^{5}+ (Ges$^{§§\ 93\ ss}$), etc.;—**1.** *feast, banquet* (occasion for drinking, drinking-bout), 1 S $25^{36.36}$ Is 5^{12} Je 51^{39} (fig.), Jb 1^{5} Est 2^{18} 5^{14} 8^{17} 9^{19}; lasting seven days Ju $14^{12.17}$ (wedding-feast, cf. Gn 29^{27}, and v. Benz$^{Arch.\ 143;\ Ency.\ Bib.\ 2949}$ Now$^{Arch.\ i.\ 163}$); עָשָׂה מ׳ *give* or *make a feast* (sts. + לְ pers.) Gn 19^{3} 26^{30} (both J), 21^{8} 40^{20} (both E), Ju 14^{10} 2 S 3^{20} 1 K 3^{15} Est 1^{3} + 8 t. Est, Jb 1^{4} + 2 S $13^{27.27}$ 𝔊 Th We Dr and mod.; מִשְׁתֵּה הַיַּיִן Est 5^{6} $7^{2.7}$, בֵּית מִשְׁתֶּה Je 16^{8} Ec 7^{2}, בֵּית מִשְׁתֵּה הַיַּיִן Est 7^{8}; יוֹם מ׳ וְשִׂמְחָה Est $9^{17.18}$, cf. v^{22}; of י׳'s banquet for all peoples Is 25^{6} (fig. of Messianic blessings); fig. also in טוֹב־לֵב מ׳ תָּמִיד Pr 15^{15}. †**2.** *drink* (late): מַאֲכָל וּמ׳ וָשֶׁמֶן Ezr 3^{7}; sf. יֵין מִשְׁתָּיו Dn $1^{5.8}$; מִשְׁתֵּיהֶם v^{16}; מִשְׁתֵּיכֶם v^{10}.

II. שׁתה (√ of foll.; ‖ √ of שׁית; = *set, sit*).

†iii. שֵׁת **n.[m.] seat** (of body), **buttocks** 8357
(cf. NH שֵׁת, Aram. ܫܬܳܐ *foundation*; cf.
[שָׁת] p. 1011; Nö$^{M\ 98}$);—abs. שׁ׳ Is 20^{4}; pl. 8356
sf. שְׁתוֹתֵיהֶם 2 S 10^{4}.

III. שׁתה (√ of foll.; Aram. שְׁתִי, ܫܬܳܐ *weave* (Ju 16^{13} 𝔗 𝔖); ܡܫܬܝܳܐ *textura*; cf. Ar. أَسْتَى, أَسْدَى, *set the warp*).

ii. שְׁתִי$_{8}$ **n.m. warp** (NH *id.*; Ar. سَتًى, 8359
سَدًى *id.*);—always שׁ׳ abs.;—*warp*, the set of

threads drawn lengthwise in loom, through which the shuttle bearing the woof (II. עֵרֶב p. 786) is thrown crosswise; Lv 13[48] + 7 t. Lv 13; cf. GFM [PAOS, Oct. 1889, clxxviii] ARSK [EB WEAVING].

8356 שָׁתוֹת v. [שָׁת] sub שית. p. 1011

8147 שְׁתַּיִם v. שְׁנַיִם sub II. שנה. p. 1040

8362 †[שָׁתַל] **vb. transplant** (NH *id.*; Aram. שְׁתַל, ܫܬܠ; Vulg. Ar. شَتَلَ *plant*, شَتْلَة *slip, cutting*, Dozy (loan-words?) Thes[1488]; As. *šitlu* appar. = *shoot, slip*);—**Qal** *Pf.* 1 s. שָׁתַלְתִּי Ez 17[22]; *Impf.* 1 s. sf. אֶשְׁתָּלֶנּוּ v[23]; *Pt. pass.* שָׁתוּל Je 17[8] = ψ 1[3], etc. (8 t.);—*transplant* (poet.): tree or vine, c. בְּ loc., Ez 17[10.23] 19[13] ψ 92[14]; עַל־מַיִם Ez 19[10] Je 17[8]; ‖ עַל־פַּלְגֵי מָיִם ψ 1[3], עַל־הַר Ez 17[22], אֶל־מַיִם v[8]; לְצוֹר שְׁתוּלָה בְנָוֶה Ho 9[13] is corrupt 𝔊 Che We Now (both in transl.) GASm Harper לְצַיִד שָׁתוּ בָנָיו (or the like; somewhat differently Marti) Ephraim ... *for a prey have they set his sons.*

8363 †[שָׁתִיל] **n.[m.] transplanted shoot, slip**;—pl. cstr. שְׁתִלֵי זֵיתִים ψ 128[3] *slips of olive* (in simile).

†[שָׁתַם] **vb.** dub.; if text correct, **open** 8365
(NH Aram. שתם *open* [vessel]);—only **Qal** *Pt. pass.* cstr. הַגֶּבֶר שְׁתֻם הָעָיִן Nu 24[3.15] (poems in JE) the man *opened of* [mental] *eye*, so 𝔖 Ki Ew al. RVm; 𝔙 Röd Ke Di al. render *closed of* [bodily] *eye*, reading then implicitly שְׂתֻם (cf. סָתַם, שָׂתַם La 3[8]); v. further Gray.

[הִשְׁתִּין, שתן] v. שִׁין. p. 1010 8366

†[שָׁתַק] **vb. be quiet** (late) (NH *id.*, 8367
be silent; Aram. שְׁתַק, שְׁתֵיק, ܫܬܩ *be quiet, silent* (cf. also שקט));—**Qal** *Impf.* 3 ms., of sea יִשְׁתֹּק הַיָּם Jon 1[11.12] (sq. מֵעַל), of quarrel, strife Pr 26[20]; 3 mpl. of persons at sea, יִשְׁתֹּקוּ ψ 107[30].

†שֵׁתָר **n.pr.m.** a prince of Persia Est 1[14]; 8369
Σαρσαθαιος.

†[שָׁתַת] **vb. set, appoint** (poet.) (‖ form 8371
of שית Ges[§ 67 ee]);—**Qal** *Pf.* 3 pl. כַּצֹּאן לִשְׁאוֹל שַׁתּוּ ψ 49[15] *they have been appointed* (lit. they have appointed them, indef. subj.) *like a flock for Shᵉ'ôl*, but Gr rds. שָׁחוּ (שׁוּח), Bae[3] יֵחַתּוּ (נחת); 7743
שַׁתּוּ בַשָּׁמַיִם פִּיהֶם ‖ וּלְשׁוֹנָם תִּהֲלַךְ בָּאָרֶץ 73[9]. p. 1001

ת

ת, ת *Tāw*, 22nd letter; = 400 in postB. Heb.

8372 †תָּא **n.m.**[Ez 40, 21] **chamber** (NH *id.*; perhaps Aramaism, cf. Ar. ثَوَى *dwell*, مَثْوًى *abode* (? akin to أَوَى *turn aside to lodge*, אַוְונָא, ܐܘܢܐ *lodging-place*), Aram. תָּוָן (in Ez 40 תְּוָא, תְּוָיָא), ܬܘܢܐ *room, chamber*);—ת׳ abs. Ez 40[7] +, cstr. 1 K 4[28]; sf. תאו Ez 40[21] Kt (Qr תָּאָיו), so v[29.33.36]; pl. תָּאִים v[7] +; תָּאוֹת v[12]; cstr. תָּאֵי v[10];—*chamber*: תָּא הָרָצִים 1 K 4[28] *chamber of the guards* = 2 Ch 12[11]; in Ezekiel's temple: Ez 40[7.7.10.12.12.13.16.21.29.33.36].

8373 †I. [תָּאַב, תָּאֵב] **vb. long for** (NH *id.*, תַּיאָבוֹן *desire*; Aram. תְּאֵב, תְּאֵיב *long for*; ? secondary √ from אָבָה, or denom. from תַּאֲבָה, and this from אבה, cf. Buhl; but v. Ol[§ 137]);—**Qal** *Pf.* 1 s. תָּאַבְתִּי, c. לְ rei, ψ 119[40.174].

8375 †תַּאֲבָה **n.f. longing**;—ψ 119[20].

8374 II. [תָּאַב] **vb. Pi. loathe, abhor**, v. תעב.

†[תָּאָה] **vb. Pi.** *Impf.* 3 mpl. תְּתָאוּ Nu 34[7.8] 8376
appar. *ye shall mark out* (the boundary), but this (and הִתְאַוִּיתֶם v[10], √ אוה q.v.) very dub., v. Gray, and [תָּאַר]. 8388

†תְּאוֹ **n.m. antelope** (whether *antilope* 8377
leucoryx Tr [NHB 59; FFP 5], or *oryx beatrix* Post [Hast. DB Ox]; on form v. Ol[§ 173 g]);—abs. ת׳ Dt 14[5] (clean animal, cf. Dr); cstr. תוֹא Is 51[20].

תַּאֲוָה v. I. תוה, I. אוה. תַּאֲלָה v. II. אלה. 184, 422,
p. 16, 46, 1063 8379,

תאם (Buhl after Ba[NB § 182 b] prop. وأم III. 8381
agree as √ of following, but dub.; v. As. *tu'âmu*, Ar. تَوْءَم, Syr. ܬܐܡܐ, all *twin*).

†[תּוֹאָם (Kö[ii. 1. 69] תְּאֹם)] **n.m. twin** (NH 8380
id.; cf. Ph. n.pr.m. תאם, Gk. Θωμᾶς = δίδυμος John 20[24]);—pl. abs. of two boys תוֹמִם Gn 25[24] (Ges[§ 23 f.]) תְּאוֹמִים 38[27] (both J); of animals, cstr. תְּאוֹמֵי צְבִיָּה Ct 4[5], תָּאֳמֵי צ׳ 7[4].

†[תָּאַם] **vb. denom. be double**;—**Qal** 8382

Pt. pl. תֹּאֲמִם Ex 26[24] ‖ תּוֹאֲמִים 36[29]; so rd. also (for תַּמִּים) 26[24] 36[29] (both P), cf. Sam Di Baen ARSK [Hast. DB iv. 661]. **Hiph.** *bear twins: Pt.* f. pl. מַתְאִימוֹת Ct 5[2] 6[6].

8385 תֹּאֲנָה, תַּאֲנָה v. III. אנה. p. 58

8384 †תְּאֵנָה **n.f. fig-tree,** (then) **fig** (√dub.; Ar. تِينٌ, Aram. תְּאֵנָא, תִּינְתָא; perhaps Pun. תין (v. Lzb[385]; i.e. תְּיָן Eut, v. DHM [VOJ i. 26]), As. *tittu, a tree;* Lag [M i. 58 ff.] combines ת׳ (precariously) with √(III) אנה *meet opportunely,* with ref. to fructifying of fig by another tree, cf. Hom [Aufsätze u. Abh. i (1892), 100]);—abs. ת׳ Ju 9[10]+; sf. תְּאֵנָתוֹ 1 K 5[5]+, etc.; pl. תְּאֵנִים Nu 13[23]+; cstr. תְּאֵנֵי Je 24[2]; sf. תְּאֵנֵיכֶם Am 4[9];—**1.** *fig-tree* (*ficus carica* Post [Flora 730; Hast. DB, s. v.] Tr [NHB 350] M'Lean-Th-Dyer [Ency. Bib., s. v.]; cf. Löw [§ 335]; oft. + גֶּפֶן): Ju 9[10.11] (in allegory), Am 4[9] Ho 9[10] Na 3[12] 1 K 5[5] 2 K 18[31] = Is 36[16], Mi 4[4] Is 34[4] Pr 27[18]; עֲלֵה ת׳ Gn 3[7] (J) *fig-leaves,* הַתּ׳ חָנְטָה פַגֶּיהָ Ct 2[13]; coll. Nu 20[5] (JE), Ho 2[14] Je 5[17] 8[13] Dt 8[8] Hb 3[17] Hg 2[19] Zc 3[10] Jo 1[7.12] 2[22] ψ 105[33]. **2.** *fig,* alw. pl.: Nu 13[23] (JE), Je 24[1.2.2.3.3.5.8] 29[17] (all symbolic of Judæans), Je 8[13] (אֵין ת׳ בַּתְּאֵנָה), Ne 8[13]; as medicament, דְּבֶלֶת ת׳ 2 K 20[7] = Is 38[21]; תְּאֵנֵי הַבַּכֻּרוֹת Je 24[2] *the figs of early ripeness* (cf. Du).

8383, 8386 תַּאֲנִיָּה v. I. [אנה]. תְּאֻנִים v. I. און. p. 20, 58

8387 †תַּאֲנַת שִׁלֹה **n.pr.loc.** on border of Ephr. Jos 16[6]; Θηνασα καὶ Σελλησα, A Τηναθσηλω, 𝔊L Θηναθασηλω; acc. to Survey [WP ii. 232, 245] Wilson [Hast. DB Taanath-Shiloh] Buhl [Geogr. 202] = mod. *Taʿna,* c. 7 miles ESE. from Nablûs.

8388 †תָּאַר **vb.** appar. **incline** (perh. akin to תור Thes; > Buhl denom. from תֹּאַר, q. v.);—**Qal** *Pf.* 3 ms. ת׳, subj. *boundary:* Jos 18[14], c. ה loc. 15[9b.11]; c. עַל ... מִן v[9a]; c. מִן only, 18[17]; prob. also c. acc. loc. 19[13] (read רִמּוֹנָה וְתָאַר הַנֵּעָה *to Rimmon, and it inclined to Neʿa* Di Steuern

8388 Benn al.). Vid. also [תֵּאֵר] **Pi.** infr.

8389 †תֹּאַר **n.m.** [La 4, 8] **outline, form** (Ph. תאר; acc. to Schwally [Idiot. 100] prop. *something gazed at,* from √תאר = ChrPal Aram. ܬܐܪ *gaze at*);—ת׳ abs. Gn 29[17]+; cstr. Ju 8[18]; sf. תָּאֳרוֹ (Ges [§ 93 q]) Is 52[14], תָּאֳרוֹ 1 S 28[14];—*form,* of woman, יְפַת ת׳ Gn 29[17] (E; + מַרְאֶה, ‖ later צֶלֶם וּדְמוּת 1[26], Lag [Or. ii. 62; BN 149]), Est 2[7] (+*id.*), 1 S 25[3] Dt 21[11]; of man, יְפֵה־ת׳ Gn 39[11] (J; + מַרְאֶה), cf. Is 52[14] (+*id.*), 53[2] (+*id.*, הָדָר), Ju 8[18], so also 1 Ch 17[17]

8447-48 (for MT תור) Klo Perles [Anal. 68]; אִישׁ ת׳ 1 S 16[18], טוֹב־ת׳ 1 K 1[6]; מַה־תָּאֳרוֹ 1 S 28[14]; v. La 4[8] (where by metonymy = *aspect, visage*); of cattle, יְפוֹת ת׳ Gn 41[18] (E), רָעוֹת ת׳ v[19] (E); tree, זַיִת רַעֲנָן יְפֵה פְרִי־ת׳ Je 11[16] (Du יְפֵיפֵה ת׳, v. 46[20]).

†[תֵּאֵר] **vb. Pi. denom.** draw in outline, 8388
trace out;—*Impf.* 3 ms. sf. יְתָאֲרֵהוּ Is 44[13.13] (both c. ב instr.), of shaping idols; for MT 2 mpl. תְּתָאוּ Nu 34[7.8] Che [Ency. Bib. 2109] prop. תְּתָאֲרוּ *ye shall trace out* (the boundary; with וְתֵאַרְתֶּם for וְהִתְאַוִּיתֶם v[10]); v. also תאה, תוה. p. 1060, 1063 8376, 8427

תַּאֲרֵעַ v. תַּחְרֵעַ sub חרע p. 357. 8390

תְּאַשּׁוּר v. sub [אָשֵׁר] p. 81. 8391

†תֵּבָה **n.f. ark** (prop. *chest, box* (cf. NH תֵּבָה); prob. Egypt. loan-word from *T-b-t, chest, coffin* (Brugsch, Erman [ZMG xlvi (1892), 123]); > Bab. word Jen [ZA iv (1889), 272 f.] Hal [JAs., 1888 (Nov.-Dec.), 517]);—abs. ת׳ Gn 7[1]+; cstr. תֵּבַת 6[14] Ex 2[3];—vessel in which infant Moses was laid among reeds v[3] (made of papyrus, גֹּמֶא), v[5] (both E; 𝔊 θῖβις, θήβη, cf. Lewy [Fremdw. 100]); vessel which saved Noah and his family, with animals, during flood (𝔊 κιβωτός): Gn 7[1.7.9.17.23] 8[6.9.9.10.13] 9[18] (all J), 6[14] (made of עֲצֵי גֹפֶר), v[14.15.16.16.18.19] 7[13.15.18] 8[1.4.16.19] 9[10] (all P). 8392

תְּבוּאָה v. בוא. תְּבוּנָה, תְּבוּנָם v. בין. p. 100, 108 8393-94

תּוֹבְנִתוֹ v. בין. תְּבוּסָה v. בוס. p. 101, 103 8394-95

†תָּבוֹר **n.pr. 1. mont.** NE. edge of Great Plain, SW. of Sea of Galilee, on border of Issachar, Zeb. and Napht., mod. *Jebel eṭ-Ṭûr;* cf. Rel [Pal. 331 ff.] Burckhardt [Travels, 332 ff.] Rob [BR iii. 340 f.] Bäd [Pal. Index, s. v.] Buhl [Geogr. 108] GACooke [Ency. Bib., s. v.];—ה(ַ)ר ת׳ Ju 4[6.12.14]; ת׳ alone Ho 5[1] Je 46[18] Jos 19[22.34] (P), ψ 89[13] (+ חֶרְמוֹן); 𝔊 Θαβωρ (so Euseb [Onom.]), but Ho Je Ιταβυριον, and so Jos [Ant. v. 1, 22 [84], BJ iv. 1. 8 [54], etc.] (other Gk. forms v. Cooke [l. c.]). **2. loc.** Ju 8[18] (too far away to be = **1** Be al.), GFM conj. טַבּוּר (9[37]), Bu תֵּבֵץ (9[50]); 𝔊 Θαβωρ. **3. loc.** Levit. city in Zebulun 1 Ch 6[62]; appar. = כִּסְלֹת ת׳ Jos 19[12], and perh. ת׳ v[22] (in Issachar), 3694
𝔊 Θαχχεια, A 𝔊L Θαβωρ. **4. arbor.** in אֵלוֹן ת׳ 1 S 10[3], near Bethel; 𝔊 Θαβωρ. 8396

תּוּבַל v. תֻּבַל. יבל v. תֶּבֶל. בלל v. תֶּבֶל. p. 117, 385, 1063 8397-98, 8422

תַּבְלִית v. [בלה]. תְּבַלֻּל v. בלל. p. 115, 117 8399-400

†תֶּבֶן **n.m.** [Ex 5, 16] **straw** (√unknown; Ges al. cp. בנה (cf. Thes[1492]), but v. Lag [BN 138]; NH = BH; As. *tibnu;* Aram. תִּבְנָא, ܬܒܢܐ, whence Ar. تِبْنٌ as loan-wd. Frä [124]);—abs. ת׳ Gn 24[25]+, 8401

תֶּבֶן Ex 5[10]+;—*straw*, i.e. straw threshed fine: chaff Je 23[28] (opp. בָּר), blown by wind Jb 21[18] (in sim.; || מֹץ), yielding 41[19] (sim.); food for camels Gn 24[25.32] (J), asses Ju 19[19] (all + מִסְפּוֹא), בָּקָר Is 11[7] 65[25], horses 1 K 5[8] (+ שְׂעֹרִים); mixed with clay in brick-making Ex 5[7.7.10.11.12] (opp. קַשׁ), v[13.16.18] (J);—v. further Vogelstein[Landwirthsch. 67].

4963 †מַתְבֵּן **n.[m.] straw-heap**;—מ׳ Is 25[10].

8402 †תִּבְנִי **n.pr.m.** rival of Omri (We[Isr. u. Jüd. Gesch., 3rd ed., 70], cp. Sidon. *Thabnit*);—1 K 16[21.22.22]; Θαμνει, 𝔊L Θαβεννει.

8403-04 תַּבְנִית v. בנה. תַּבְעֵרָה v. בער. p. 125, 129

8405 †תֵּבֵץ **n.pr.loc.** near Shechem: Ju 9[50.50] (תֵּבֶץ; also 8[18] Bu for תָּבוֹר q.v.), 2 S 11[21]; mod. *Ṭûbâs*, 4 h. N. of Shechem Rob[BR iii. 305] Guérin[Sam. i. 357 ff.] Buhl[G 204]; Θηβης, Θαιβαις (in Ju), Θαμασ(ε)ι, 𝔊L Θαμεσσει (in S).

8407 †תִּגְלַת פִּלְאֶסֶר **n.pr.m. Tiglathpileser** (III), king of Assyria (Zinj. תגלתפליסר, תגלתפלסר, GACooke[Inscr. 178. 183. 188]; = As. *Tukulti-apil-êšar-ra* Rost[Keilinschr. TP III (1893), 42] COT[2 K 15, 29]; v. also Pinches[Ency. Bib. TP] Say[Hast. DB. TP]);—2 K 15[29] 16[10] = ת׳ פְּלֶסֶר v[7]; corrupt תִּלְּגַת פִּלְנְאֶסֶר 1 Ch 5[6] 2 Ch 28[20], ת׳ פִּלְנֶסֶר 1 Ch 5[26]; v. also פּוּל;—Αλγαθφελλασαρ, Θαλγαθ[λ]φελλασαρ, Θαλγαβανασαρ, etc., 𝔊L (Kings) Θεγλαφαλασαρ.

8408-09 [תַּגְמוּל] v. גמל. [תִּגְרָה] v. [גרה]. p. 168, 173

8425 †תֹּגַרְמָה, תּוֹ׳ **n.pr.terr.** Gn 10[3] = תּוֹ׳ 1 Ch 1[6]; בֵּית תּוֹ׳ Ez 27[14] 38[6]; Θοργαμα, Θεργ., etc.; it lay in (SW.) Armenia acc. to Di[Gn 10, 2] (and reff.), Dl[Pa 246] (*Til-garimmu*); >NW. Asia Minor (Gk. Τευθρανία) Lag[Ges. Abh. 257; Armen. Stud. § 865; Abh. GGW. xxxv (1888), 142].

8410 תִּדְהָר v. p. 187.

8412 †תַּדְמֹר **n.pr.loc.** built by Solomon, acc. to 1 K 9[18] Qr = 2 Ch 8[4]; *Tadmor* = Palmyra (RS[Ency. Brit. (9) PALMYRA] Mommsen[Röm. Gesch. v. 423], cf. Lag[BN 125]); but read in both places תָּמָר Th RS[l. c.] Mommsen[l. c.] Kmp Benz Kit Bur Reckend[ZMG xlii (1888), 402] Lag[l. c.] GASm[Geogr. 270, N. 2; 580, N. 2]; v. II.
8559 תָּמָר. p. 1071

8413 †תִּדְעָל **n.pr.m.** king allied with Chedorlaomer, called מֶלֶךְ גּוֹיִם Gn 14[1.9]; Θαλγα[λ], 𝔊L Θαργαλ (n.pr. *Tudhula* occurs on late Bab. tablet, Pinches[Trans. Vict. Inst., xxix (1897), 47, 73], Say[Acad. Mar. 21, 1896, 242; Hast. DB TIDAL]; but ident. of pers. unproven, LW King[Hammurabi i (1898), liii] Hpt[Ball Gn 14,1] Che[Ency. Bib. TIDAL]).

תהה (√ of foll.; mng. dub.: Aram. תְּהָא is *rage, roar* (of earth, with ref. to Gn 1[2]), of man, *bluster*; al. cf. Ar. تَاهَ (ى) *go astray*, تِيهٌ *desert waste*, but this very doubtful).

8414 †תֹּהוּ **n.m.**[1 S 12, 21] (Albr[ZAW xvi (1896), 112]) **formlessness, confusion, unreality, emptiness** (primary meaning difficult to seize; Vrss usu. κενόν, οὐδέν, μάταιον, *inane, vacuum, vanum*; cf. Lag[Or. ii. 60; BN 144]);—**1.** *formlessness*, of primaeval earth Gn 1[2] (P), of land reduced to primaeval chaos Je 4[23] (both + וָבֹהוּ *and voidness*), Is 34[11] (קַו־ת׳ || אַבְנֵי בֹהוּ), 45[18] (לֹא ת׳ בְרָאָהּ || לָשֶׁבֶת יְצָרָהּ); 24[10] קִרְיַת־ת׳ *city of chaos* (of ruined city); = *nothingness, empty space*, Jb 26[7] תֹּלֶה אֶרֶץ עַל־ת׳; of empty, trackless *waste* Dt 32[10] (|| מִדְבָּר), Jb 6[18] 12[24] = ψ 107[40]. **2.** fig. of what is *empty, unreal*, as idols 1 S 12[21] (coll.: אַחֲרֵי הַתּ׳ אֲשֶׁר לֹא יוֹעִילוּ), v[21] Is 41[29] רוּחַ וָת׳ נִסְכֵּיהֶם, 44[9] (of idol-makers), groundless arguments or considerations, Is 29[21] וַיַּטּוּ בַתּ׳ צַדִּיק, 59[4] moral unreality or falsehood (בָּטוֹחַ עַל־ת׳ || וְדַבֶּר־שָׁוְא); = *a thing of nought* (cf. Ecclus 41[10] מתהו אל תהו), Is 40[17] (|| אַיִן, אֶפֶס), v[23] שֹׁפְטֵי אֶרֶץ כַּתּ׳ עָשָׂה (|| אַיִן), *worthlessness* 49[4] (לְרִיק יָגַעְתִּי || לְת׳ וְהֶבֶל כֹּחִי כִלֵּיתִי); as adv. acc. 45[19] I said not, תֹּהוּ בַקְּשׁוּנִי seek me *emptily, to no purpose*. Cf. 29[13] 𝔊 וְתֹהוּ for וַתְּהִי.

8417 †תָּהֳלָה **n.f.** error (? si vera l.; √ תהל acc. to Di[Lex. Æth. 522], who cp. Eth. ተሀለ: III. *rove, wander*; Ar. وَهَلَ is *commit error*, cf. Ba[NB § 179, Anm. 3]);—וּבְמַלְאָכָיו יָשִׂים ת׳ Jb 4[18], < rd. תִּפְלָה q.v.

8416, 8418 תְּהִלָּה v. II. הלל. [תַּהֲלוּכָה] v. הלך. p. 237, 239

תהם (prob. √ of following, in view of As. *tiâmtu, tâmtu* (= תְּהוֹם) Dl[HWB 698] Jen[Kosmol. 542] Barton[JAOS xv, 1 ff.], Syr. ܬܗܘܡܐ; all from √ הום Thes Ew[§ 161] Ol[§ 213 d] Sta[§ 264] al.).

8415 †תְּהוֹם **n.f.**[Gn 7, 11 + 7 t.] **et m.**[Jb. 28, 14 + 5 t.] (Albr[ZAW xvi (1896), 62] Kö[ii. 2. 167] Ency. Bib.[DEEP]) **deep, sea, abyss** (almost alw. poet.);—abs. ת׳ Gn 1[2]+; pl. abs. תְּהֹמוֹת ψ 77[17]+, etc., בַּתּ׳ Is 63[13] ψ 106[9] (only here c. art.); cstr. תְּהֹמוֹת 71[20] (but v. **5** infra);—**1.** *deep*, of subterranean waters, Gn 49[25] (poem in J; opp. שָׁמַיִם), Dt 33[13] (opp. *id.*); מַעְיְנוֹת ת׳ רַבָּה Gn 7[11] 8[2] (P; || אֲרֻבֹּת הַשָּׁמַיִם), עִינוֹת ת׳ Pr 8[28] (|| שְׁחָקִים), Jb 28[14] 38[16] (both || יָם); תְּהוֹם רַבָּה Am 7[4] (prob.), ψ 36[7] מִשְׁפָּטֶיךָ ת׳ רַבָּה (opp. צִדְקָתְךָ כְּהַרְרֵי אֵל), Is 51[10] (perh.); so pl. תְּהֹמוֹת, Pr 8[24] (|| מַעְיָנוֹת), 3[20] (opp. שְׁחָקִים), and prob. ψ 33[7] (|| מֵי הַיָּם), 135[6] (+ יַמִּים). **2.** (deep) *sea*, overwhelming Tyre

Ez 26^{19} (‖ הַמַּיִם הָרַבִּים), roaring at theoph. Hb 3^{10}; in gen., ‖ יָם, Jb 38^{30} (פְּנֵי ת׳); ‖ מַיִם Jon 2^{6}; alone Jb 41^{24}; fig., ‖ גַּלִּים, מִשְׁבָּרִים) 42^{8} ת׳ אֶל־ת׳ קוֹרֵא; but poss. here of Jordan, cf. **4**); in pl. = *abysses* of sea, Ex 15$^{5.8}$ (of Red Sea, so) Is 63^{13} ‖ ψ 106^{9}, ψ 77^{17}; also 78^{15} (in sim.), 107^{26} (poet. of hollows of great waves, opp. שָׁמַיִם); vaguely, כָּל־תְּהֹמוֹת ψ 135^{6} 148^{7}. **3.** *primaeval ocean, deep*, in Heb. cosmogony, פְּנֵי ת׳ Gn 1^{2} (P; ‖ פְּנֵי הַמַּיִם), Pr 8^{27} (‖ שָׁמַיִם), ψ 104^{6}.—(Cf., further, Gunk Schöpfung u. Chaos 21 ff. OCWhitehouse Hast. DB Cosmogony Zim KAT3. 492 f., 509 f., 585). **4.** *deep, depth*, of river Ez 31^{4} (Nile; ‖ מַיִם, + נַהֲרֹתֶיהָ), v^{15} (‖ *id.*); pl. of *bursts* of water fertilizing Canaan, יוצאים בבקעה ובהר Dt 8^{7} (+ נַחֲלֵי מַיִם, עֲיָנֹת).—On ψ 42^{8} v. **2.** **5.** *abyss* (si vera l.): תְּהוֹמוֹת הָאָרֶץ = *She'ôl*, ψ 71^{20}, but Ol We תַּחְתִּיּוֹת.

8419-20 [תַּהְפֻּכָה] v. הפך. תָּו v. I. תוה.
below, p. 246

8377, 8380 תוא v. תְּאוֹ. [תוֹאָם] v. תאם. p. 1060

8422 †תֻּבַל **n.pr.terr. et gent.** in E. Asia Minor, perh. nearly = Cappadocia (= As. *Tabalu* Dl Pa 250 f. COT Gn 10, 2, cf. Di Gn 10, 2);—ת׳ Is 66^{19} Ez 27^{13}, תֻּבַל 32^{26}, תֻּבָל Gn 10^{2} = 1 Ch 1^{5}, Ez 38$^{2.3}$ 39^{1}; Θοβελ.

8423 †תּוּבַל(־)קַיִן **n.pr.m.** first worker in metal, acc. to Gn 4$^{22.22}$ (J); Θοβελ.

8394, 8424 תובנתו v. תְּבוּנָה sub בין. תּוּגָה v. יגה. p. 108, 387

8426 תּוֹדָה v. ידה. p. 392

I. תוה (√of foll.; cf. NH תָּאו = BH תָּו, תַּוָּה vb. denom. Pi.; 𝔗 תְּוָא Ez 9^{4}; Levy NHWB iv. 622 derives following from √אוה).

8420 †תָּו **n.m.** mark;—abs. ת׳, *mark* on forehead, sign of exemption fr. judgment Ez 9$^{4.6}$; sf. תָּוִי Jb 31^{35} = *my* (written) *mark* (in attestation).

8379 †[תַּאֲוָה] **n.f.** boundary (as described by a *mark*?);—cstr. תַּאֲוַת גִּבְעֹת עוֹלָם Gn 49^{26} (this
184, 8376 mng. AV RV Ew §186 b [√תָּאָה] De Gn √תאה, אוה, תוה), but < *desire* = *desirable things*, so most.

8427 [תָּוָה] **vb.denom.** make or set a mark;—**Pi.** *Impf.* 3 ms. ויתו Kt, וַיְתָיו Qr 1 S 21^{14} (Ges §75bb) and *he made marks on* (עַל) the doors, but < 𝔊 𝔙 Th We Dr Ges l.c. and most וַיָּתֹף *he drummed* (v. תפף). **Hiph.** וְהִתְוִיתָ תָו עַל־ Ez 9^{4} *set a mark* (acc. cogn.) *upon*.

8428 †II. [תָּוָה] **vb. Hiph.** prob. pain, wound (fig.) (Aram. ܬܘܐ (oft.), תְּוָא (rare) תְּהָא 𝔗^{J}, all *repent*);—*Pf.* 3 pl. וּקְדוֹשׁ יִשׂ׳ הִתְווּ ψ 78^{41} (‖ וַיְנַסּוּ) *the Holy One of Isr. they pained* (𝔊 παρώξυναν).

†תּוֹחַ **n.pr.m.** ancestor of Samuel 1 Ch 6^{19} 8430
[Levite!]; Θειε, Θοουε, 𝔊L Ναaθ; ‖ תֹּחוּ 1 S 1^{1}; 8459
Θοκε, Θοου, 𝔊L Θωε.

תּוֹחֶלֶת v. יחל. p. 404 8431

תּוֹךְ *injury*, v. תֹּךְ sub תכך. p. 1067 8496

תָּוֶךְ 418 **subst.** midst (NH *id.*, also denom. 8432
תִּוֵּךְ; √unknown; not apparently in cognate languages);—abs. תָּוֶךְ Gn 15^{10}+; cstr. תּוֹךְ 1^{6}+; תּוֹכִי, תּוֹכוֹ, etc., 2 fs. תּוֹכֵכִי ψ 116^{19} 135^{9} †, תּוֹכֹה †Ez 48$^{15.21}$, תּוֹכְכֶם Gn 23^{9}+, תּוֹכֲהֶנָה †Ez 16^{53} (Ges §91 f);—*midst*, whether of a space or place, a number of people or things, or of a line: abs. †Ju 16^{29} עַמּוּדֵי הַתָּוֶךְ = the *middle* columns, Je 39^{3} שַׁעַר הַתּ׳; בַּתָּוֶךְ Gn 15^{10} וַיְבַתֵּר, Nu 35^{5} וְהָעִיר בַּתָּוֶךְ, Jos 8^{22} אֵלֶּה בַתּ׳, Ju 15^{4} Is 66^{17} אַחַר אֶחָד בַּתָּוֶךְ; cstr. 1 K 8^{64} קִדַּשׁ הַמֶּלֶךְ אֶת־ תּוֹךְ הֶחָצֵר, Ez 15^{4} וְתוֹכוֹ נָחָר; usu. c. prep., as בְּ (oft. = an emph. *in*, in the very heart and midst of), Gn 1^{6} בְּתוֹךְ הַמַּיִם, 2^{9} בְּת׳ הַגָּן, 9^{21} בְּת׳ אָהֳלֹה, 18^{24} בְּת׳ הָעִיר, 37^{7} בְּת׳ הַשָּׂדֶה, Ex 11^{4} אני יוצא בת׳ מצרים, 39^{3}, Jos 8^{9} בְּת׳ הָעָם, Ju 7^{16} בת׳ הַכַּדִּים, 1 K 3^{20} בְּת׳ הַלַּיְלָה; בְּתוֹכָהּ (of land or city) Nu 13^{32} Is 7^{6}, etc.; in Ez בְּתוֹכֵךְ, בְּתוֹכָהּ, etc., of sins done, or judgment to be wrought, *in the very midst* of Jerusalem, Ez 5$^{8.10}$ 9^{4} 22$^{3.7.9.13}$+; בְּת׳ מֵעַי ψ 22^{15}, 40^{9} תּוֹרָתְךָ בְּת׳ מֵעָי, v^{11} בְּת׳ לִבִּי, cf. Pr 4^{21}; after verbs of motion, = *into* Ex 14^{27} 1 S 9^{14}, = *through* Ex 14^{29} Nu 33^{8} Ez 9^{4} Ne 9^{11}; of a number of persons = *among* (not necess. of the actual *middle*), Gn 40^{20} בְּת׳ עֲבָדָיו, 23^{6} בְּתוֹכֵנוּ, 1 S 10^{10} Jb 1^{6}, etc., בְּתוֹכָם Lv 17$^{8.10.13}$ הַגָּר בְּתוֹכְכֶם +; = *between* (of things arranged by twos) Ex 39^{25}; in P oft. (12 t.) of the divine presence, or dwelling, *in the midst of* Isr., Ex 25^{8} 29$^{45.46}$ Lv 15^{31} 16^{16} + (Carpenter Hex. i. 209, ed. 2, 410; JED in such cases have alw. קֶרֶב), so Ez 37$^{26.28}$ 43$^{7.9}$, cf. Hg 2^{5}; מִן, as Gn 19^{29} מִתּוֹךְ הַהֲפֵכָה, Ex 3^{2} מִתּ׳ הַסְּנֶה, 33^{11} לֹא יָמִישׁ מִתּ׳ הָאֹהֶל, Dt 4^{12} + מִתּ׳ הָאֵשׁ, 1 S 15^{6} רְדוּ מִתּ׳ עֲמָלֵק; = *from among*, as to take, separate, etc., מִתּ׳ הָעָם, מִתּוֹכָם, etc., Ex 7^{5} 28^{1} Nu 3^{12} 4$^{2.18}$ 16$^{21.33}$ 17^{10} 19^{20} (all P)+; אֶל, as Ex 14^{23} וַיָּבֹאוּ . . . אֶל־תּוֹךְ הַיָּם, Lv 11^{33}, Nu 17^{12} וַיָּרָץ, 22^{2} וַהֲבֵאתָהּ אֶל־תּ׳ בֵּיתֶךָ Dt 21^{12}, 19^{6} אֶל־תּ׳ הַקָּהָל 23^{11} 2 S 3^{27} 4^{6} Je 21^{4}+; מֵעַל †Ez 11^{23}.—תוך is used by most writers, occurring c. 8–10 times in many books, but is esp. frequent in P (c. 106 t.) and Ez (116 t.). Syn. קֶרֶב, q.v.

8484 †תִּיכֹן, תִּיכוֹן **adj.** middle;—abs. ת׳ Ex
26^{28}+, fs. תִּ(י)כוֹנָה Ju 7^{19}+, fpl. -נוֹת Ez $42^{5.6}$
(on form, v. הִיצוֹן p. 300, Ges§ 27 x);—Ex 26^{28}=
36^{33} (P) הַבְּרִיחַ הַתִּיכוֹן בְּתוֹךְ הַקְּרָשִׁים the *middle*
bar (holding the 'boards' in their place); Ju 7^{19}
הָאַשְׁמוֹרֶה הַתִּ׳ the *middle* watch (of the night);
of the *middle* story of side-chambers to Temple
1 K $6^{6.8b.b}$ (v^{8a} rd. c. 𝔊 𝔗 הַתַּחְתֹּנָה for הַתִּ׳), Ez
41^{7b} (read c. 𝔊 𝔖 וּמִן־התחתונה יַעֲלוּ לַתִּיכוֹנָה וּמִן־
הַתִּיכוֹנָה עַל־העליונה), $42^{5.6}$, 2 K 20^{4} הָעִיר הַתִּיכֹנָה
(but rd. c. Qr Vrss חָצֵר הַתִּ׳, i.e. the חָצֵר הָאַחֶרֶת,
2694 v. I. חָצֵר **2**).—חָצֵר הַתִּיכוֹן Ez 47^{16}, v. p. 347^{b}.

8433, 8500 תּוֹכֵחָה, תּוֹכַחַת v. יכח. תֻּכִּיִּים v. תֻּכִּ׳. p. 407, 1067

8434-36 תּוֹלָד, [תּוֹלֵדוֹת] v. ילד. תּוֹלוֹן v. תִּילוֹן. p. 410, 1066

8437 †[תּוֹלָל] **n.m.** doubtful word, only pl. sf.
וְתוֹלָלֵינוּ ψ 137^{3}; AV RV *they that wasted us*, cf.
𝔗, but rd. then וְשׁוֹלָלֵינוּ Bae al.; >Thes[596] Hup
De al. *made us wail* (√ילל).

8380, 8551-52 תּוֹמִיךְ v. תמך. תּוֹמִים v. [תּוֹאָם], תאם. p. 1060, 1069

8442, 8487 תּוֹמָן v. II. תֵּימָן sub ימן. תּוֹעָה v. תעה. p. 412, 1073

8443-44 [תּוֹעָפָה] v. II. יעף. [תּוֹצָאָה] v. יצא. p. 419, 426

8445 תוקחת Kt, תָּקְהַת Qr, v. III. תִּקְוָה p. 876.

תוף (√of foll. [Levy NHWB iv. 661, s. v. תופת,
assumes √תפף]; akin to Eth. ተፍአ: *spit*, Aram.
(Talm.) תְּפַף *id.*; Ar. تُفًّا *fie! for shame!* Syr. ܬܘܦ
Aph. (and deriv.) also=*spew out* (BaES 28), but
prob. simply *return*).

8611 †I. תֹּפֶת **n.f.** act of **spitting**;—abs. וְת׳
לְפָנִים Jb 17^{6} *a spitting in the face* do I become,
i.e. men spit in my face (‖ לְמָשָׁל עַמִּים; Perles
8612 Baer Bu מֹפֵת לִפְנֵיהֶם). II. תֹּפֶת v. תפת. p. 1075

8446 †תּוּר **vb. seek out, spy out, explore**
(NH *id.* (rare); perh. orig. *turn* (to or about),
As. *târu*, *turn about, back*, *taiâru* adj. *turning
back*, also *merciful*, and subst. *mercy*; Ar.
تَارَ (و) IV. *go about* (rare), تَوْرٌ *a go-between*);—
Qal *Pf.* 1 s. תַּרְתִּי Ez 20^{6} Ec 2^{3}; 3 pl. תָּרוּ Nu
13^{32}; 2 mpl. תַּרְתֶּם 14^{24}; *Impf.* 3 mpl. יָתֻרוּ 13^{2},
3491 וַיָּתֻרוּ v^{21}; rd. also 3 ms. יָתוּר Jb 39^{8} 𝔙 𝔗 Ew Di
Bu Du and most (for יְתוּר); 2 mpl. תָּתוּרוּ Nu
15^{39}; *Inf. cstr.* תּוּר 10^{33}+; *Pt.* pl. תָּרִים 14^{6},
on 1 K 10^{15} 2 Ch 9^{14} v. infra;—**1.** *seek out, select:*
לָתוּר לָהֶם מְנוּחָה Nu 10^{33} (J, subj. ark of י׳), cf.
Dt 1^{33} (subj. י׳), Ez 20^{6} (*id.*, acc. land); sq. inf.
=*find out how* to do something, ת׳ בְּלִבִּי לְ Ec 2^{3}.
2. *spy out, explore*, acc. of land Nu $13^{2.16.17.21.25.32.32}$
$14^{7.34.36.38}$, acc. of mts. Jb 39^{8} (v. supr.), cf. Pt.
as subj. *explorers, spies* Nu 14^{6} (all P); *explore
mentally*, לָדַעַת וְלָת׳ וּבַקֵּשׁ חָכְמָה Ec 7^{25}, cf. 9^{1} Gr
(ת׳ for בּוּר q.v.), לָת׳ בַּחָכְמָה עַל־ 1^{13} (KueOnd. 2, iii. 196).
3. *go about*, fig. אַחֲרֵי לְבַבְכֶם Nu 15^{39} (P); *Pt.*
אַנְשֵׁי הַתָּרִים 1 K 10^{15} 2 Ch 9^{14}, usually *merchants*
(‖ סֹחֲרִים רֹכְלִים); Kit, after 𝔖 2 Ch, prop. הֶעָרִים
for הַתָּרִים. **Hiph.** *Impf.* 3 mpl. וַיָּתִירוּ בְּבֵית־אֵל
Ju 1^{23} *they made a reconnoisance at Bethel* (Vrss
disagree, Gie וַיִּחֲנוּ, cf. GFM); 3 ms. יָתֵר מְרֵעֵהוּ
צַדִּיק Pr 12^{26} *the righteous searches out* (RV *is
a guide to*) *his friend*, 𝔗 AV *is more excellent
than* (reading יָתֵר), Hi Ew De al. *spies out his
pasture* (מִרְעֵהוּ, in spiritual sense), all dubious;
Toy conjectures יָסֵר מֵרָעָה.

†I. תּוֹר, תֹּר **n.m. plait, turn** (Ar. تَارَةٌ 8447-48
period, succession (περίοδος));—pl. תּוֹרִים *plaits*
(of hair?) Ct 1^{10}, cstr. תּוֹרֵי זָהָב v^{11} *plaits, circlets
of gold*; sg. *turn*, opportunity, cstr. תֹּר נַעֲרָה
Est 2^{12}, cf. v^{15}.—תור אדם 1 Ch 17^{17} is corrupt,
‖ 2 S 7^{19} תּוֹרַת הָאָדָם, also difficult, v. תּוֹרָה **3**, 8451-52
p. 436; Klo PerlesAnal. 68 תֹּאַר, q.v. p. 1061 8389

יְתוּר Jb 39^{8} appar. **n.m.** *a searching*, but v. √. 3491, 8446

II. תּוֹר v. II. תֹּר. p. 1076 8449

תּוֹרָה v. ירה. תּוֹשָׁב v. ישב. p. 435, 444 8451-53

תּוּשִׁיָּה v. ישה. תּוֹתָח Jb 41^{21} v. יתח. p. 444, 450 8454-55

†[תָּזַז] **vb. Hiph. strike away** (𝔗 נְתַז 8456
(rare) *spring forth*; NH נִתַּז *spring, spurt, out*;
Hiph., Aph. *cut off* (head, etc.));—*Pf.* 3 ms.
אֶת־הַנְּטִישׁוֹת הֵסִיר הֵתַז Is 18^{5}.

תַּזְנוּת v. זנה. [תַּחְבֻּלָה] v. I. חבל. p. 276, 287 8457-58

תַּחוּ v. תֹּחַ. תַּחְכְּמֹנִי v. p. 315^{b}. p. 1063 8439, 8459, 8461

תַּחֲלֻאִים v. I. חלא. תְּחִלָּה v. II. חלל p. 321. p. 316 8462-63

תַּחְמָס v. חמס. תֹּחֶלֶת v. תּוֹחֶלֶת sub יחל. p. 329, 404 8431, 8464

תַּחַן v. חנה. I, II. תְּחִנָּה v. I. חנן. p. 334, 337 8465, 8467

תַּחֲנוּן v. חנן. [תַּחֲנָה], תַּחֲנִי v. חנה. p. 334, 337 8466, 8469-70

†תַּחְפַּנְחֵס **n.pr.loc.** Egyptian city Je 8471
$43^{7.8.9}$ 44^{1} 46^{14}, so Je 2^{16} Qr (Kt תחפנס);
=תְּחַפְנְחֵס Ez 30^{18}; Ταφνα(ι)ς [Ταφναι]; identif.
with Gk. *Daphnae*, mod. *Tel Defenneh*, c. 18 m.
ESE. from Tanis, c. 9 m. W. of *El-Ḳanṭara*,
BädEgypt, 5th ed. (1902), 169 PetrieDefenneh (Tanis II), 1888.

8472 †תַּחְפְּנֵיס **n.pr.f.** Egyptian queen;—1 K 11$^{19.20}$, ־נֵס־ v^{20}; Θεκ[χ]εμεινα.

8473 †תַּחְרָא **n.[m.]** prob. (linen) **corselet** (𝔗^{Onk} שריון);—abs. ת׳ Ex 28^{32}, ‖39^{23} (P), in sim.

8474-75 [תַּחֲרָה] v. חרה. תַּחֲרֻע v. חרע. p. 354, 357

8476 †I. תַּחַשׁ **n.m.** taḥaš, a kind of leather or skin, and perh. the animal yielding it (prob. the *dugong*, cf. Ar. تُخَس *dolphin*, Thes^{1500} Di-Ry$^{Ex\ 25,5}$ Post$^{Hast.\ DB\ BADGER}$; As. *taḫšu* (Dl$^{Baer\ Ezech.\ xvi}$), for which Dl$^{Prol.\ 77\ ff.;\ HWB\ 705}$ conj. meaning *sheep*(*skin*); Bondi$^{Egyptiaca\ 1\ ff.}$ cp. Egypt. *tḥś*, *leather;* v. summary of views M'Lean-Shipley$^{Ency.\ Bib.\ BADGERS'\ SKINS}$);—abs. ת׳ Nu 4^{6}+, תָּחַשׁ v^{8}+; pl. תְּחָשִׁים Ex 25^{5}+;—leather used for (woman's) sandals Ez 16^{10}; elsewhere for cover of tabernacle Nu 4^{25}, עוֹר ת׳ v$^{6.8.10.11.12.14}$, עֹרֹת (הַ)תְּחָשִׁים Ex 25^{5} 26^{14} 35$^{7.23}$ 36^{19} 39^{34} (all P).

8477 †II. תַּחַשׁ **n.pr.m.** 'son' of Nahor Gn 22^{24}; Τοχος; identif. by Wkl$^{Mitth.\ d.\ Vorderas.\ Gesellsch.\ 1896,\ 207}$ with *Tiḫesi* (Egypt.), which WMM$^{As.\ u.\ Eur.\ 258}$ puts N. of Kadesh on Orontes.

8478 **תַּחַת** **n.[m.] the under part** (Ar. تَحْتَ *id.*), hence as **adv. accus.** and **prep. underneath, below, instead of** (so Ar. تَحْتَ, Sab. תחת, Eth. ታሕተ: Ph. תחת (Lzb^{385}); BAram. תחות, 𝔗 תְּחוֹת, Palm. in מן לתחת Tariff I^{4} (Cooke^{320}), Syr. ܬܚܝܬ);—**I.** as **adv. accus.** †Gn 49^{25} (=Dt 33^{13}) the deep רֹבֶצֶת תָּחַת that coucheth *beneath;* more usu. with מִן, מִתַּחַת lit. *off* (מִן **1 c**) *the under part*=*beneath*, †Ex 20^{4} (=Dt 5^{8}) בָּאָרֶץ מִתָּחַת (so Dt 4^{39} Jos 2^{11} 1 K 8^{23} [both D^{2}], Is 51^{6}), Dt 33^{27} Ju 7^{8} Am 2^{9} Is 14^{9} Jb 18^{16} Ez 47^{1b}. **II.** as **prep.**; so cstr., and with sf. (usu. in the pl., and so lit. *in the parts underneath*) תַּחְתַּי Hb 3^{16}+, תַּחְתֵּנִי (cf. עוֹדֶנִּי, בַּעֲדֵנִי: Ges$^{§\ 103\ d}$) †2 S 22$^{37.40.48}$ (ψ 18$^{37.40.48}$ תַּחְתָּי); תַּחְתֶּיךָ; תַּחְתָּיו (Kt תחתו †2 S 2^{23} 3^{12} 16^{8} Jb 9^{13}), תַּחְתֶּיהָ Lv 13^{23}+16 t., תַּחְתֶּנָּה (cf. עוֹדֶנָּה, אֵינֶנָּה) †Gn 2^{21}; תַּחְתֵּינוּ †1 S 14^{9} ψ 47^{4}; תַּחְתֵּיכֶם †Jos 2^{14} Am 2^{13}; תַּחְתֵּיהֶם †Nu 16^{31} 1 K 20^{24} 1 Ch 4^{41} 5^{22} 2 Ch 12^{10} (for תַּחְתָּם 1 K 14^{27}), תַּחְתָּם Dt 2^{12}+10 t., תַּחְתֵּיהֶן †Je 28^{13};—**1.** *under, beneath*, Gn 7^{19} תַּחַת כָּל־הַשָּׁמַיִם *under* the whole heaven (so †Dt 2^{25} 4^{19} Jb 28^{24} 37^{3} 41^{3} Dn 9^{12}), 18^{4} ת׳ הָעֵץ, 21^{15} 24^{2}+ oft.; Jb 30^{14} ת׳ שֹׁאָה *under* the crash they roll themselves against me; ת׳ הַשֶּׁמֶשׁ Ec 1$^{3.9.13}$+oft. Ec. (so in Ph., Cooke$^{4.7;\ 5.12}$). With לְ, †2 Ch 4^{3} תַּחַת לוֹ, Ct 2^{6}=8^{3} ת׳ לְרֹאשִׁי. Idiom. **a.** תַּחַת הָהָר *at the foot of* the mt., Ex 24^{4} Dt 4^{11}, so 3^{17} ת׳ אַשְׁדֹּת הַפִּסְגָּה, Jos 11$^{3.17}$+; fig. ψ 18^{37} תַּרְחִיב צַעֲדִי תַחְתָּי thou broadenest my steps *under me*, Jb 36^{16} רַחַב לֹא מוּצָק תַּחְתֶּיךָ (so read for תחתיה, Di Bu) breadth unstraitened is *beneath thee.* **b.** ת׳ הַלָּשׁוֹן, of something held there as a dainty morsel, and ready, when needed, to be brought out, fig. of sweetness Ct 4^{11}, of evil ψ 10^{7} ת׳ לְשׁוֹנוֹ עָמָל וָאָוֶן, Jb 20^{12} (so ψ 140^{4} ת׳ שְׂפָתֵימוֹ), of praise ψ 66^{17} וְרוֹמַם ת׳ לְשׁוֹנִי (syn. בִּגְרוֹנָם 149^{6}). **c.** תַּחַת פ׳: (*a*) of subjection, ψ 18^{40} תַּכְרִיעַ קָמַי תַּחְתָּי, v^{48} (cf. 47^{4} 144^{2}), 45^{6} Jb 9^{13}. (*b*) of a woman, ת׳ אִישָׁהּ, i.e. under his authority, Nu 5$^{19.20.29}$, so Ez 23^{5} תַּחְתָּי being *under me*=being *mine* (fig. of Israel as י׳'s spouse), cf. ὕπανδρος Rom 7^{2}, and تَحْتَ Ḳor 66^{10}. (*c*) of being burdened or oppressed under, Is 24^{5} the earth הָנְפָה ת׳ יֹשְׁבֶיהָ, Pr 30^{21} ת׳ שָׁלוֹשׁ רָגְזָה אֶרֶץ, v$^{22.23}$; Hb 3^{7} ת׳ אָוֶן i.e. (si vera l.) suffering *under* calamity. **d.** ת׳ יַד פ׳, of authority or control, Gn 41^{35} וְיִצְבְּרוּ בָר ת׳ יַד פַּרְעֹה; Ju 3^{30} (cf. ψ 106^{42}), 1 S 21$^{4.5}$ (del. אֶל; dittogr. חל), v^{9} Is 3^{6}. **e.** כֹּל ת׳ רַגְלֵי פ׳, of subjection or conquest, ψ 8^{7} שַׁתָּה ת׳ רַגְלָיו, 18^{39} 47^{4} La 3^{34}, cf. Mal 3^{21}. **2.** *what is under one, the place in which one stands:* hence as accus., **a.** with reflex. pron., idiom., *in one's place, where one stands,* Ex 16^{29} שְׁבוּ אִישׁ תַּחְתָּיו abide every one *in his place,* Lv 13$^{23.28}$ Jos 5^{8} 6$^{5.20}$ Ju 7^{21} 1 S 14^{9} וְעָמַדְנוּ תַחְתֵּינוּ we will *remain where we are,* 2 S 2^{23} וַיָּמָת תַּחְתָּו he died *where he was* (cf. Je 38^{9} [read וּמֵת]), 7^{10} Is 25^{10} 46^{7} Am 2^{13} Hb 3^{16} וְתַחְתַּי אֶרְגָּז I tremble *where I stand,* Zc 12^{6} 14^{10} Jb 36^{20} 40^{12} וַהֲדֹךְ רְשָׁעִים תַּחְתָּם. **b.** in transferred sense, *in place of, instead of:* (*a*) Gn 2^{18} 4^{25} ת׳ הֶבֶל *instead of* Abel, 22^{13} ת׳ בְּנוֹ, 30^{2} הֲת׳ אלהים אנכי (cf. 50^{19}), 44^{33} 2 S 19^{1}+oft.; Jb 16^{4} Is 3^{24} 55^{13} 61$^{3.7}$; of one succeeding to the place of another, וַיִּמְלֹךְ תַּחְתָּיו Gn 36$^{33-39}$ 1 K 8^{20} 11^{43} 14^{20}+oft., Dt 2$^{12.21}$ וַיֵּשְׁבוּ תַחְתָּם, Lv 16^{32} 1 K 2^{35}+; ψ 45^{17} *in place of* thy fathers (whom thou mayest therefore forget) will be thy children. Cf. in Ph. CIS$^{1.3.9}$ (Cooke^{30}). Sq. inf. Is 60^{15} ת׳ הֱיוֹתֵךְ *instead of thy being . . .* Peculiarly Jb 34^{26} (si vera l.)= ***as if they were, like;*** but text very dubious; Bi Bu תַּחַת חֲמָתוֹ רְשָׁעִים his wrath breaketh in pieces the wicked. (*b*) in partic., of things mutually interchanged, *in place of, in exchange* or *return for:* Gn 30^{15} ת׳ דּוּדָאֵי בְנֵךְ *in return for* thy son's love-apples, Ex 21^{23} נֶפֶשׁ ת׳ נָפֶשׁ life *for* life, v$^{24.25.26.27.36.37}$, Jos 2^{14} נַפְשֵׁנוּ תַחְתֵּיכֶם

לָמוּת, 1 S 2^{20} 1 K 20^{39} נפשך ת׳ נפשו, v^{42} (cf. 2 K 10^{24}), 21^{2} Is $43^{3.4}$; often with vbs. of requiting, Gn 44^{4} לָמָּה שִׁלַּמְתֶּם רָעָה ת׳ טוֹבָה why have ye rewarded evil *in exchange for* good? 1 S 25^{21} 2 S 16^{12} 19^{22} ψ 35^{12} יְשַׁלְּמוּנִי רָעָה ת׳ טוֹבָה, 38^{21a} $109^{4.5}$ Pr 17^{13}+; Je 5^{19} תַּחַת מֶה *in return for what?* (cf. עַל־מֶה 22^{8} Dt 29^{23} 1 K 9^{8}). So sq. inf. ψ 38^{21b}. †**3.** as **conj.**: **a.** תַּחַת אֲשֶׁר: (*a*) *instead of that* (Germ. *anstatt dass*), Dt 28^{62} ת׳ א׳ הֱיִיתֶם *instead of that* ye were . . ., *instead of* your being . . ., Ez 36^{34}. (*b*) *in return for* (the fact) *that, because that* (𝔊 ἀνθ᾽ ὧν Am 1^{3}+ oft.), Nu 25^{13} ת׳ אֲשֶׁר קִנֵּא לֵא׳, Dt 21^{14} 22^{29} 28^{47} 1 S 26^{21} 2 K 22^{17} = 2 Ch 34^{25}, Is 53^{12} Je 29^{19} 50^{7} 2 Ch 21^{12}. **b.** תַּחַת כִּי Dt 4^{37} (but? read וַתְּחִי: as end of v^{36}), Pr 1^{29}. Cf. עֵקֶב אֲשֶׁר (כִּי).

III. compounds: —†**1.** אֶל־תַּחַת, after a vb. of motion: **a.** (*in*) *under*, Ju 6^{19} וַיּוֹצֵא אֶל־ ת׳ הָאֵלָה, 1 K 8^{6} (‖ 2 Ch 5^{7}), Je 3^{6} 38^{11} (on 1 S 21^{5} v. **II. 1 d**); after קָרָא Zc 3^{10}: so אֶל־ת׳ לְ׳ Ez 10^{2}. **b.** *into the place of*, Lv 14^{42}. **2.** מִתַּחַת (= ὑπ᾽ ἐκ): **a.** alone, *from under, from beneath*, as מִתַּחַת הַשָּׁמַיִם †Gn 1^{7}, and esp. after such vbs. as שִׁחֵת 6^{17}, מָחָה Ex 17^{14} Dt 9^{14} 25^{19} 29^{19} 2 K 14^{27}, הֶאֱבִיד Dt 7^{24}, cf. La 3^{66}; Ez 47^{1a} מִתּ׳ מִפְתַּן הַבַּיִת, Pr 22^{27} לָמָּה יִקַּח מִשְׁכָּבְךָ מִתַּחְתֶּיךָ; Ex $6^{6.7}$ מִתּ׳ סִבְלוֹת מִצְרַיִם, Ho 4^{12} וַיִּזְנוּ מִתּ׳ אֱלֹהֵיהֶם (cf. **II. 1 c** *a, b*); מִתּ׳ יַד פ׳ (cf. **II. 1 d**) *from under the hand* (power) *of* . . . Ex 18^{10} 2 K $8^{20.22}$ 13^{5} 17^{7}+; מִתַּחְתָּיו (cf. **II. 2 a**) *from his place* Ex 10^{23} Zc 6^{12}. Rarely = תַּחַת or מִתַּחַת לְ׳, Gn 1^{9} (P) Ez 1^{8} 42^{9} 46^{23} Jb 26^{5}. **b.** מִתַּחַת לְ׳ (opp. מִמַּעַל לְ׳) *under, beneath*: Gn 1^{17} הַמַּיִם אֲשֶׁר מִתּ׳ לָרָקִיעַ, Ex 20^{4} הַמַּיִם מִתַּחַת לָאָרֶץ (so Dt 4^{18} 5^{8}), Ju 3^{16} מִתּ׳ לְמַדָּיו, Je 38^{12}+; of locality, †Gn 35^{8} מִתּ׳ לְבֵיתְאֵל, 1 S 7^{11} 1 K 4^{12}. **c.** †לְמִתַּחַת לְ׳ (cf. מִן **9 b**), i.q. מִתַּחַת לְ׳ 1 K 7^{32}.

8481 †תַּחְתּוֹן **adj. lower, lowest**;—abs. ת׳ Jos 16^{3}+, fs. ־תּוֹנָה Is 22^{9}+, fpl. ־תֹּנֹת Ez $42^{5.6}$;—*lower*, Is 22^{9} הַבְּרֵכָה הַתּ׳ the *lower* pool (in Jerus.), of pavement and gate of outer (lower) temple-court Ez $40^{18.19}$ (l. הַשּׁ׳ הַתַּחְתּוֹן), of *lower* ledge (עֲזָרָה) of altar, 43^{14}; of the *lowest* of the three stories of side-chambers surrounding the temple, 1 K 6^{6} הַיָּצוּעַ הַתּ׳, + v^{8a} (v. תִּיכוֹן), Ez 41^{7} (read וּמִן for וְכֵן), $42^{5.6}$; in place-name, בֵּית־חֹרוֹן ת׳ Jos 16^{3} 18^{13} 1 K 9^{17} (‖ 2 Ch 8^{5} הַתּ׳), בֵּית־חֹרוֹן הַתּ׳ 1 Ch 7^{24} 2 Ch 8^{5}.

8482 †תַּחְתִּי **adj.** and **subst.** lower, lowest (places):—fs. תַּחְתִּיָּה †ψ 86^{13}, תַּחְתִּית Ex 19^{17}+; mpl. תַּחְתִּיִּם †Gn 6^{16}; fpl. תַּחְתִּיּוֹת ψ 63^{10}+;—Ex 19^{17} ויתיצבו בְּתַחְתִּית הָהָר in the *lower part* of the mt., Ju 1^{15} = Jos 15^{19} (so read here with 𝔊^{MSS} 𝔖 𝔗 𝔙 for אֵת גֻּלֹּת תַּחְתִּית (גֻּלַּת תַּחְתִּיּוֹת) the *lower* spring, Jb 41^{16} כְּפֶלַח תַּחְתִּית like the *lower* mill-stone, Gn 6^{16} (P) תַּחְתִּיִּם = *lower stories*; of Sheʾôl, Dt 32^{22} עַד שְׁאוֹל תַּחְתִּית to the *lowest* Sheʾôl, ψ 86^{13} מִשְּׁ׳ תַּחְתִּיָּה, so אֶרֶץ תַּחְתִּית the *lowest* earth (or land), i.e. Sh., Ez $31^{14.16.18}$, אֶרֶץ תַּחְתִּיּוֹת the land of *lowest places* 26^{20} $32^{18.24}$, בּוֹר תַּחְתִּיּוֹת the pit of *lowest places* Lam 3^{55} ψ 88^{7}, תַּחְתִּיּוֹת הָאָרֶץ 63^{10} (+ perh. 71^{20}) the *lowest places* of the earth, ת׳ אֶרֶץ Is 44^{23}, and fig. of the dark and hidden interior of the womb ψ 139^{15}.—Ne 4^{7} וָאַעֲמִיד מִתַּחְתִּיּוֹת לַמָּקוֹם and I set (𝔊^{L} *and they stood*) *at parts below* (מִן as in מִתַּחַת לְ׳) the place (where they were to work), so Ke Gu, but text perhaps corrupt (Berthol Sgf).

†II. תַּחַת **n.pr. 1. m. a.** Levite 1 Ch $6^{9.22}$. 8480
b. Ephraimite $7^{20.20}$.—Θααθ, Καaθ, etc. **2. loc.** station in wilderness Nu $33^{26.27}$; Καταaθ.

תַּחְתִּים חָדְשִׁי v. II. קָדֵשׁ **2.** תִּיכוֹן v. תָּוֶךְ. 8483-84
p. 295, 874

†תִּילוֹן **n.pr.m.** in Judah, 1 Ch 4^{20} Qr (Kt 8436
תולון); Ιωνων, A Θιλων, 𝔊L Θωλειμ. 8436

†תֵּימָא **n.pr.terr.** et **gent.** (OAram. תימא 8485
Lzb^{385}; in As. *Têma* Dl$^{\text{Pa 301 f.}}$ Schr$^{\text{KGF 261 ff.}}$;= *south country*, √ ימא (cf. תֵּימָן, √ ימן) acc. to Nö$^{\text{Ency. Bib. Ishmael}}$);—יֹשְׁבֵי אֶרֶץ ת׳ Is 21^{14}, people Je 25^{23}; ת׳ 'son' of Ishmael Gn 25^{15} ‖ 1 Ch 1^{30}; אָרְחוֹת תֵּמָא (l. אֹרְ׳) Jb 6^{19}; Θαιμαν. Mod. *Teyma*, NW. Arabia, Doughty$^{\text{Arab. Des. i, pass., esp. 284-299}}$ Wilson$^{\text{Hast. DB Tema}}$, and on inscr. found there Eut$^{\text{Nab. Inschr. 35}}$ CIS ii, No. 113.114 Nö$^{\text{SBAk. 1884, 813 f.}}$ Hal$^{\text{RÉJ xii, 111 ff.}}$ Cooke$^{\text{195 ff.}}$

I. II. תֵּימָן, תֵּימָנִי, תֵּימְנִי v. ימן. 8486,
8488-89

[תִּימָרָה] v. תמר. p. 1071 8490

†תִּיצִי **adj.gent.** (?): הַתּ׳ 1 Ch 11^{45}, unknown. 8491

תִּירוֹשׁ תִּירשׁ v. ירשׁ. p. 440 8492

†תִּירְיָא **n.pr.m.** in Judah, 1 Ch 4^{16}; Ζαιρα, 8493
A Θηρια, 𝔊L Εθρια.

†תִּירָס **n.pr.terr.** et **gent.** 'son' of Japhet 8494
Gn 10^{2} 1 Ch 1^{5}; Θειρας; identified by Mey$^{\text{Gesch. d. Alt. i. 260}}$ Di Holz Gunk al. with Gk. Τυρσηνοί, Egypt. *Turuša*, on coast of Ægean.

†[תַּיִשׁ] **n.m.** he-goat (NH *id.*; Ar. تَيْس, 8495
Aram. תֵּישָׁא, תַּיְשָׁא, ܬܝܫܐ *id.*; √ unknown);—

abs. תְּיָשׁ Pr 30^{31}; pl. תְּיָשִׁים Gn 30^{35} (J), 32^{15} (E; + עִזִּים *she-goats*), 2 Ch 17^{11}.

8496 תֹּךְ v. תכך. below

8497 †[תָּכָה] **vb.** meaning wholly dub.;—**Pu.** *Pf.* 3 pl. וְהֵם תֻּכּוּ לְרַגְלֶךָ Dt 33^3; *were led* or *assembled* would suit context; v. esp. Dr Berthol.

8498-99 תְּכוּנָה v. כון. p. 467

8500 †תֻּכִּיִּים **n.m.** peacocks (acc. to 𝔗𝔖 Jerome Rabb.; perh. = Malabar *tôgai, tôghai, peacock* Thes[1502]);—1 K 10^{22} = תּוּכִּיִּים 2 Ch 9^{21} + ivory, apes.

תכך (√of foll., cf. pl.; Ar. تَكَّ *overcome* (of wine), *tread under foot;* akin to Aram. [illegible], 𝔗 תּוּךְ (rare) *injure*, ܬܘܟܐ, תּוּכָא (rare) *injury*).

8496 †תֹּךְ, II. תּוֹךְ **n.m. injury, oppression;**—abs. תֹּךְ, + מִרְמָה ψ 10^7 55^{12} (so Gi; Baer תּוֹךְ);
8501 תּוֹךְ, + חָמָס (gloss) 72^{14}; pl. אִישׁ תְּכָכִים Pr 29^{13} *oppressor* (𝔙 *creditor;* cf. איש חמסים 2 S 22^{49} ψ $140^{2.5}$).—I. תּוֹךְ v. תָּוֶךְ.

8501-03 תְּכָכִים v. תֹּךְ. תִּכְלָה, תַּכְלִית v. כלה. above, p. 479

8504 תְּכֵלֶת 48 **n.f. violet, i.e. violet thread and stuff;** 𝔊 usu. ὑάκινθος, ὑακίνθινος; v. Thatcher Hast. DB Colours (NH = BH; 𝔗 תִּכְלָא, תַּכְלָא, תִּכְילְתָּא);—**1.** *violet thread* (spun, Ex 35^{25}; woven, 39^3): **a.** in Ex (P) of hangings of tabern., ephod, etc., ת׳ + אַרְגָּמָן, תּוֹלַעַת שָׁנִי (q.v.; oft. also שֵׁשׁ, זהב), Ex 25^4 26^1 $28^{5.6}$ 28^{33} 35^{25} + 20 t.; of temple hangings (+ כַּרְמִיל, אַרְגְּוָן, אַרְגָּמָן, בּוּץ) 2 Ch $2^{6.13.14}$; loops or cords of ת׳ (alone) Ex 26^4 $28^{28.31.37}$ 36^{11} $39^{21.22.31}$ Nu 15^{38} (all P). **b.** palace hangings in Shushan, + חור Est 1^6. †**2.** *violet stuff, fabric;* לְבוּשֵׁי ת׳ Ez 23^6, גְּלוֹמֵי ת׳ 27^{24}; ת׳ וְאַרְגָּמָן לְבוּשָׁם Je 10^9; also in trade Ez 27^7 (+ שֵׁשׁ בְּרִקְמָה, אַרְגָּמָן), cf. בֶּגֶד ת׳ for covering sacred utensils Nu $4^{6.7.9.11.12}$ (P).

8505 †[תָּכַן] **vb. regulate, measure, estimate** (cf. Aram. Pa. תַּכֵּן (rare) *prepare* (= הֵכִין, כּוֹנֵן); acc. to Ry Syn. d. Wahren u. Guten 33 a secondary √ from כון);—**Qal** *Pt. estimate*, fig.: וְתֹכֵן רוחות י׳ Pr 16^2, so (לִבּוֹת) 21^2 24^{12}. **Niph. 1.** *Pf.* 3 pl. וְלֹא [לוֹ] נִתְכְּנוּ עֲלִלוֹת 1 S 2^3 *by him* (י׳) *are actions estimated.* **2.** *Impf., be adjusted to the standard*, i.e. right, equitable: subj. דֶּרֶךְ (of י׳ and of Israel), 3 ms. יִתָּכֵן Ez $18^{25.25.29.29}$ $33^{17.17.20}$; 3 mpl. יִתָּכְנוּ 18^{29}, יִתָּכֵנוּ v^{25}. **Pi.** *Pf.* 3 ms.: *mete out*, מַיִם תִּכֵּן בְּמִדָּה Jb 28^{25}; וְשָׁמַיִם בַּזֶּרֶת ת׳ Is 40^{12} (‖ מדד, כול); מִי ת׳ אֶת־רוּחַ י׳ v^{13} (v. **Qal**; read poss. הֵכִין or הֵכַן; 1 s. תִּכַּנְתִּי עַמּוּדֶיהָ ψ 75^4 I *regulate* (or *adjust*) her pillars (i.e. of earth). **Pu.** *Pt.* הַכֶּסֶף הַמְתֻכָּן 2 K 12^{12} the silver which was *measured out*.

†I. תֹּכֶן **n.m.** Ez 45, 11 **measurement;**—cstr. ת׳ לְבֵנִים Ex 5^{18} (J) *the measurement*, tale, *of bricks;* abs. Ez 45^{11} *capacity* (of ephah and bath). 8506

†II. תֹּכֶן **n.pr.loc.** in Simeon, 1 Ch 4^{32}; Θοκκα, A Θοχχαν, 𝔊L Ενθεκεμ. 8507

†תָּכְנִית **n.f. measurement, proportion;**—abs. Ez 43^{10} (< read תָּכְנִיתוֹ 𝔊 Ew Hi Co Toy al.); חוֹתֵם ת׳ 28^{12} thou wert *one sealing up* (the) *measure* (RVm), i.e. exhibiting perfect proportion; Codd Sm al. חוֹתַם ת׳ *the seal of* (perfect) *proportion;* but dub., v. Comm. 8508

†מַתְכֹּנֶת **n.f. measurement, tale, proportion;**—**1.** cstr. מ׳ הַלְּבֵנִים Ex 5^8 (J) *the tale of bricks* (cf. I. תֹּכֶן). **2.** sf. -כֻּנְתּוֹ *measurement, proportion*, of ephah and bath Ez 45^{11}; of composition of sacred oil Ex 30^{32}, -תָּהּ v^{37} (P); of temple, *its measurement, proportion* -תּוֹ 2 Ch 24^{13}. 4971

תַּכְרִיךְ v. כרך. תֵּל and cpds. v. תלל. p. 501, 1068 8509-10

†תָּלָא **vb. hang** (‖ form of תלה, Ges § 75 rr);—**Qal** *Pf.* 3 pl. sf. תְּלָאוּם 2 S 21^{12} Qr the Philistines *had hanged them* (Kt תלום; v. Dr); *Pt. pass.* תְּלֻאִים Dt 28^{66} thy life shall be *hung up* before thee, i.e. be in suspense, each moment uncertain.—וְעַמִּי תְלוּאִים לִמְשׁוּבָתִי Ho 11^7 *my people is hung up to my backsliding* is certainly corrupt (AV *bent to backsliding from me*, i.e. hung or swung toward turning from me, cf. GASm, but very dub.); Marti conj. נִלְוִים; Oettli Now² Harper נִלְאָה or הֶלְאַנִי אֶל־עֲצַבִּים *has wearied itself* [*me*] in backsliding. 8511, 8518

[תַּלְאֻבָה] v. לאב. תְּלָאָה v. לאה. p. 520-21 4972, 8514

†תְּלַאשָּׂר **n.pr.loc.** appar. in Mesopot.;—ת׳ 2 K 19^{12} = תְּלַשָּׂר Is 37^{12} (abode of בְּנֵי־עֶדֶן); cf. As. *Til-ašuri* (Esarhaddon) Dl Par. 264 f.; near Edessa Wkl Gesch. Bab. u. As. 269, 335 f.; v. Schr KGF 199 f.; identification not certain, cf. Johns Ency. Bib. Telassar. 8515

תִּלְבֹּשֶׁת v. לבשׁ. תִּלְגַת פִּל׳ v. תִּגְלַת. p. 528, 1062 8407, 8516

†תָּלָה **vb. hang** (NH *id.;* As. Pi. *tullû*, *hang up;* Ar. تَلَّ *let down, dangle* (a rope, etc.); Aram. ܬܠܐ, תְּלָא, ܬܠܐ *hang;* perh. OAram. תלה *id.*, 8518

Lzb[386]; Eth. ተለወ: in derived sense, *be devoted, addicted, to*);—**Qal** *Pf.* 3 ms. ת׳ Gn 40[22]+; 2 ms. וְתָלִיתָ Dt 21[22] consec.; 3 pl. תָּלוּ Est 8[7] 9[14], sf. תלום 2 S 21[12] Kt (Qr v. תלא), etc.; *Impf.* 3 ms. sf. וַיִּתְלֵם Jos 10[26], etc.; *Imv.* mpl. sf. תְּלֻהוּ Est 7[9]; *Inf. cstr.* לִתְלוֹת Ez 15[3] Est 6[4]; *Pt. act.* תֹּלֶה Jb 26[7]; *pass.* תָּלוּי Dt 21[23] + 2 t., pl. תְּלוּיִם Jos 10[26];—*hang*: **1.** *hang up* any object: acc. of hands and feet of slain, + עַל־הַבְּרֵכָה 2 S 4[12]; ת׳ תָּלוּי of Absalom בָּאֵלָה *in the terebinth* 18[10]; c. acc. rei, + עַל Is 22[24] Ez 15[3] Ct 4[4] ψ 137[2]; subj. ׳י, ת׳ אֶרֶץ עַל־בְּלִימָה Jb 26[7]. **2.** specif. *put to death by hanging*, c. acc. pers. Gn 40[22] 41[13] (both E), 2 S 21[12] (cf. תלא), Est 9[14]; abs. תָּלוּי Dt 21[23] *one hanged*; acc. pers. + עַל־עֵץ Gn 40[19] (E), Dt 21[22] Jos 8[29] 10[26.26] (all JE), Est 5[14] 6[4] 7[9.10] 8[7] 9[13.25]. **Niph.** *Pf.* 3 pl. שָׂרִים בְּיָדָם נִתְלוּ La 5[12] *princes have been hung up by their hands*; *Impf.* 3 mpl. וַיִּתָּלוּ עַל־עֵץ Est 2[23] *they were hanged on a tree*; + 3 ms. apoc. וַיִּתֶּל 2 S 18[9] (for וַיִּתֵּן v. נתן; **Hoph.**). **Pi.** *hang up* for display, c. acc. rei: *Pf.* 3 pl. תִּלּוּ Ez 27[10] (ב loc.), v[11] (עַל־חוֹמוֹתַיִךְ).

8522 †[תְּלִי] **n.[m.]** quiver (with its arrows) (as *hanging* from shoulder);—sf. תֶּלְיְךָ וְקַשְׁתֶּךָ Gn 27[3] (J; 𝔊 φαρέτρα, 𝔙 *pharetra*).

8510 תִּלָּה v. תֵּל infra.

3494 †יִתְלָה **n.pr.loc.** in (Southern) Dan Jos 19[42]; Σιλαθα, 𝔊L Ιθλα.

8520 †תֶּלַח **n.pr.m.** in Ephraim;—1 Ch 7[25]; Θαλε(ες), Θαλα.

I. תלל (appar. √of foll.; NH תֵּל *heap*, תְּלוּלִית *hill*; 𝔗J תְּלִיל *lofty*; Ar. تَلٌّ, Syr. ܬܠܐ *mound*; = (perhaps) OAram. תלי CIS[ii, No. 111] Lzb[386] SAC[120]; Jen in Brock[Syr. Lex.] thinks תֵּל As. loan-word from *tîlu, ruin-heap, mound*).

8510 †תֵּל **n.[m.]** mound;—**1.** *mound*, ruin-heap (of city): cstr. תֵּל(־)עוֹלָם Jos 8[28] (JE), Dt 13[17], תֵּל שְׁמָמָה Je 49[2]. **2.** *mound* or hill on which city stood: sf. תִּלָּם Jos 11[13] (D), תִּלָּהּ Je 30[18].

8512 †תֵּל אָבִיב **n.pr.loc.** in Babylonia, on the 'river Chebar,' Ez 3[15].

8521 †תֵּל חַרְשָׁא **n. pr. loc.** in Babylonia;—Ezr 2[59] = Ne 7[61]; Θααρησα, (Θελ)αρησα, etc., 𝔊L Ezr Θαλαα καὶ Ρησα.

8528 †תֵּל מֶלַח **n. pr. loc.** in Babylonia;—Ezr 2[59] = Ne 7[61]; Θερμελεθ, Θελμελεθ[χ].

†תָּלוּל **adj.** exalted, lofty (prop. **Qal** *Pt.* 8524
pass.);—הַר־גָּבֹהַּ ות׳ Ez 17[22] *a high and lofty mt.*

†תַּלְתַּלִּים **n.f.**(?) **pl.** as fig. of woman's 8534
locks, mng. dub.: קְוֻצּוֹתָיו ת׳ שְׁחֹרוֹת כָּעוֹרֵב Ct 5[11]; Thes (from above √) *waving palm-branches*, 𝔊 ἐλάται; NH once, fig., Levy[NHWB iv. 649] *high hills* cf. Jastr[Dict. 1674] *heaps, piles*; but Magnus[Hohes Lied] and Jacob[Stud. Arab. Dichter iv. 21] *envelope* or sheath of spadix of date-palm (with which hair oft. cp. in Ar. poetry Jacob[Ib. iii. 46 f], cf. Ar. تَلْتَلَةٌ *drinking vessel* made of this envelope Lane); so perhaps As. *taltallu* Dl[HWB 708].

†II. [תָּלַל] **vb. Hiph.** mock, deceive, 2048, 8524
trifle with (perhaps akin to Ar. دَلَّ *act coquet-*
tishly; cf. secondary √ [הָתַל] p. 251);—*mock*, 2048
trifle with, c. ב pers.: *Pf.* 3 ms. (בִּי) הֵתֶל Gn 31[7] (E), 2 ms. הֵתַלְתָּ Ju 16[10.13.15]; *Impf.* 3 mpl. יְהָתֵלּוּ Je 9[4], 2 mpl. תְּהָתֵלּוּ Jb 13[9] (on both v. Ges[§ 53 q] Baer[ad loc.]); *Inf. cstr.* Jb 13[19] and (abs.) Ex 8[25] (J). **Hoph.** *Pf.* 3 ms. הוּתַל Is 44[20] a heart (which)
is deceived.—Vid. [הָתַל], הֲתֻלִּים p. 251. 2048-49

תלם (√of foll.; cf. NH תֶּלֶם = BH; Ar. تَلَمٌ, mod. Pal. تِلِم Bergheim[PEF 1894, 195]; Eth. ትልም: Aram. תַּלְמָא; the nearest verbal √ is Ar. ثَلَمَ *break edge* of, *make a breach, gap*, but ت = ث? cf. Frä[131]).

†תֶּלֶם **n.m.**[Jb 31, 38] furrow;—abs. ת׳ Jb 39[10] 8525
(other conj. Du Perles[Anal. 53]); pl. cstr. תַּלְמֵי שָׂדָי Ho 10[4] 12[12]; sf. תְּלָמֶיהָ Jb 31[38] ψ 65[11].—On ploughing in Pal. v. Hogg[Ency. Bib. AGRICULTURE] Vogelstein[Landwirthsch. 25 ff.], on depth of furrow (not more than 8–10 centim.) Id[ib. 36] Anderlind[ZPV ix. 25, 29]; also Benz Arch. s.v.—תְּלָם v. תֵּל supr. 8510

†תַּלְמַי **n.pr.m.** **1.** king of Geshur, father- 8526
in-law of David, 2 S 3[3] 13[37] 1 Ch 3[2]. **2.** a son of 'Anak Nu 13[22] Jos 15[14], תַּלְמָי Ju 1[10]; Θομμει, Θολμει, Θαλαμειν, etc.

תַּלְמִיד v. למד. [תְּלֻנָּה] v. II. לון. 8519, 8527
p. 534, 540

תלע (√of foll.; perhaps *gnaw*, v. מְתַלְּעוֹת infra, and Dl[Pr 113], cf. As. *tultu, worm*).

†I. תּוֹלָע **n.[m.]** worm, scarlet stuff 8438
(dyed with the *coccus ilicis*, v. שָׁנִי, Thatcher[Hast. DB COLOURS]);—**1.** *worm*, only pl. תּוֹלָעִים, in stale manna Ex 16[20] (P). **2.** *scarlet stuff*, abs. sg. תּוֹלָע Is 1[18] (in sim. ‖ שָׁנִים; opp. צֶמֶר); token of luxury La 4[5].

8439 †II. תּוֹלָע **n.pr.m.** in Issachar; a judge of Israel Ju 10¹; assigned to earlier time by Gn 46¹³ Nu 26²³ (both P), 1 Ch 7¹·²·².

8440 †תּוֹלָעִי **adj. gent.** of foregoing; c. art. as n. coll. Nu 26²³.

8438 תּוֹלֵעָה, תּוֹלַעַת 40 **n.f.** worm;—abs. תּוֹלֵעָה Is 14¹¹ Jb 25⁶; תּוֹלַעַת Is 41¹⁴ +, תּוֹלַעַת Dt 28³⁹ Nu 19⁶; cstr. תּוֹלַעַת Ex 25⁴ +; sf. תּוֹלַעְתָּם Is 66²⁴;—**1.** *worm, grub*, vine-weevil Jon 4⁷ Dt 28³⁹ (coll.); devouring the dead Is 14¹¹ (coll.: ‖ רִמָּה), 66²⁴ (coll.); symbol of insignificance 41¹⁴ Jb 25⁶ (‖ רִמָּה), ψ 22⁷. **2.** elsewh. (P) specif., + שָׁנִי (q.v.), of the *coccus ilicis* yielding *scarlet* colour: ת׳(הַ) שְׁנִי Lv 14⁴·⁶·⁴⁹·⁵¹·⁵² Nu 19⁶; of crimson stuff, בֶּגֶד ת׳ שָׁנִי 4⁸; usu. תְּכֵלֶת וְאַרְגָּמָן וְת׳ (הַ)שָּׁנִי וגו׳ Ex 25⁴ 26¹ + 24 t. Ex.

8529 †[תָּלַע] **vb. Pu. denom.** clad in scarlet (v. I. תּוֹלָע **2**; תּוֹלֵעָה **2.**—NH Hiph. denom. is *breed worms*, etc.);—*Pt.* pl. מְתֻלָּעִים Na 2⁴ (‖ מְאָדָּם).

4459, 4973 †מְתַלְּעוֹת **n.f.pl.** teeth (AV RV *jaw-teeth*) (perhaps *gnawers*, v. √);—*teeth, incisors*, late (always ‖ שִׁנַּיִם): cstr. מ׳ Jb 29¹⁷ and (of lion) Jo 1⁶; sf. מְתַלְּעֹתָיו Pr 30¹⁴.

8530 †תַּלְפִּיּוֹת **n.f.pl.** Ges (in Thes) *exitialia, fatal things* (√תלף = Ar. تَلِفَ *perish*);—poet. for *weapons*; many other conj. in Comm.: כְּמִגְדַּל דָּוִיד צַוָּארֵךְ בָּנוּי לְת׳ Ct 4⁴ᵃ, doubtful; Che Expos. Times, ix. 423; JQ, July 1899, 562 שְׁלָטִים *shields*, cf. vᵇ.

8515, 8534 תְּלַשָּׂר v. תְּלַאשָּׂר. תַּלְתַּלִּים v. I. תלל. p. 1067-68

8485, 8535, 8537-38 תֹּם, תָּם, תָּמָה v. תמם. תֵּמָא v. תֵּימָא. p. 1066, 1070

8539 †[תָּמַהּ] **vb.** be astounded, dumbfounded (NH *id.*; so Aram. תְּמַהּ, ܬܡܗ);—**Qal** *Pf.* 3 pl. תָּמְהוּ ψ 48⁶; *Impf.* 2 ms. תִּתְמַהּ Ec 5⁷; 3 mpl. יִתְמָהוּ Jb 26¹¹, etc.; *Imv.* mpl. תְּמָהוּ Is 29⁹ Hb 1⁵;—*be astounded*, Is 29⁹ Hb 1⁵ (v. Hithp.), Je 4⁹ (‖ שׁמם, Niph.), ψ 48⁶; + מִן caus. Jb 26¹¹; + עַל rei at which Ec 5⁷; *look in astonishment* at אִישׁ אֶל־רֵעֵהוּ ת׳ Gn 43³³ (J), Is 13⁸. **Hithp.** *Imv.* mpl. + **Qal** *Imv.* וְהִתַּמְּהוּ תְּמָהוּ Hb 1⁵ (v. supr.), lit. *astonish yourselves, be astounded*, but We **Hithpalp.** הִתְמַהְמְהוּ; Gr rds. inf. abs. תָּמֹהַּ (Marti al. וּתְמָהוּ) for תמהו.

8541 †תִּמָּהוֹן **n.[m.]** bewilderment;—abs. ת׳ Zc 12⁴; cstr. תִּמְהוֹן Dt 28²⁸;—*bewilderment, stupefaction*; ת׳ לֵבָב v²⁸, of those infatuated (v. Dr.); ת׳ alone of bewildered horses Zc 12⁴.

8542 †תַּמּוּז **n.pr.div.** Tammuz (Bab. *Dûzu* (also *Dumuzi*) COT^Ez 8, 14 Zim^KAT³, 397 f. Jastr^Rel. Bab. 482 et pass.; on the phonetic change Hpt^ZA ii. 270, but also Jäger^BAS i. 591);—מְבַכּוֹת אֶת־הַתּ׳ Ez 8¹⁴; ת׳ = Gk. Adonis (אדון); cf. Baud^Rel. Sem. i. 35, 300 f. Dr^Dn 11, 37 Che^Ency. Bib. TAMMUZ Say^Hast. DB ID.

8544-45 תְּמוּנָה v. מין. תְּמוּרָה v. מור. p. 558, 568

8546 תְּמוּתָה v. מות. p. 560

8547 †תֶּמַח **n.pr.m.** head of a Jewish family, Ezr 2⁵³ = Ne 7⁵⁵; 𝔊 Θεμα (Ne Ημαθ), 𝔊L Θεμαα.

8548 תָּמִיד v. מוד p. 556.

8382 תָּמִים Ex 26²⁴ 36²⁹ v. [תָּאַם]. p. 1060f

8551 †[תָּמַךְ] **vb.** grasp, support, attain (Aram. תְּמַךְ Pa. *hold fast*; cf. Ph. and OAram. תמכאל *Ēl hath sustained* Lzb³⁸⁶ SAC¹²¹ Cooke ³⁶¹);—**Qal** *Pf.* 3 fs. תָּמְכָה ψ 63⁹, etc.; *Impf.* 3 ms. יִתְמֹךְ Pr 29²³, 3 mpl. יִתְמֹכוּ Jb 36¹⁷ Pr 5⁵, etc.; *Inf. abs.* תָּמֹךְ ψ 17⁵; cstr. תְּמֹךְ Is 33¹⁵; *Pt.* תּוֹמֵךְ Am 1⁵·⁸, תּוֹמִיךְ ψ 16⁵ (? rd. ־מִיךָ- Ges § 51e, or תֹּמֵךְ, cf. Vrss Du; > Ol תּוֹסִיף, Bi Che תָּמִיד), etc.;—**1.** *grasp, lay hold of*, c. acc. rei Gn 48¹⁷ (E), Pr 31¹⁹ (‖ שִׁלַּח יָד בְּ); acc. pers. (wisdom) Pr 3¹⁸ (‖ מַחֲזִיק); acc. rei (grasp and) *wield* Am 1⁵·⁸; ψ 16⁵ (v. supr.) *thou dost grasp my lot* (i.e. take and cast it for me, cf. mod. Pal. الله يَقوم بجَرَلي *may Allah uphold my lot*, Bergheim^PEF 1894, 194); fig., Jb 36¹⁷ judgment and justice *seize* (thee; but v. obscure and doubtful); Pr 5⁵ her steps *lay hold of* Sheʾôl (keep the path to it); lit., c. בּ rei Is 33¹⁵, בּ pers. Pr 28¹⁷ (or sub **3**; mng. dub.); *lay hold of, attain*, honour, wealth (acc.) Pr 11¹⁶·¹⁶. **2.** *hold up, support*, c. בְּיָדָיו Ex 17² (E); fig., בּ pers. Is 42¹ ψ 41¹³ 63⁹; acc. pers. Is 41¹⁰ (בּ instr.), Pr 29²³ (opp. הִשְׁפִּיל). **3.** *hold, keep*, c. acc. rei Pr 4⁴ let thy heart *keep* my words (‖ שְׁמֹר); *hold firmly* ψ 17⁵ (בּ loc.; opp. נָמֹטּוּ). **Niph.** *Impf.* וּבְחַבְלֵי חַטָּאתוֹ יִתָּמֵךְ Pr 5²² *in the cords of his sin is he seized* (‖ לָכַד).

865, 8543 †תְּמוֹל, (תְּמֹל), אֶתְמוֹל ₂₃, אֶתְמוֹל ₅, † 1 S 10¹¹, אֶתְמוּל † Is 30³³ Mi 2⁸ (v. inf.), **subst.**, used sts. as **adv. acc.**, yesterday, fig. recently, formerly (Aram. אֶתְמָלֵי, תְּמָלֵי, sts. אֶתְמוֹל, ܐܬܡܠ, ܬܡܠ, ܐܬܡܠܝ; Mand. עתמאל Nö^M 202; Eth. ትማልም: As. *timâli, itimâli, ina timâli* (Dl 158, 721); der. dub.; acc. to Me^Gr. Syr. 118 Kö^ii. 264 f. from Ar. تَمَلَّى II. *prolongavit*, IV. *longam vitam*

concessit, مَلًّا *tempus,* المَلَوَان *the two times,* i.e. night and day, in form an inf. of VI. تَمَالٍ; hence prop. *long time,* (past) *time,* specialized to *yesterday*);—*yesterday,* but usually fig.= *recently* or *formerly:* **1.** 2 S 15^{20} תְּמוֹל בּוֹאֶךָ *yesterday* (=*only lately*) was thy coming, Jb 8^{9} תמול אנחנו (of) yesterday (Ges$^{§141 d}$) are we, ψ 90^{4} (genit.) כְּיוֹם אֶתְמוֹל. **2.** usu. in com-
8032 bin. with שִׁלְשֹׁם *yesterday* (and) *the third day,* to express the idea of *formerly:* thus **a.** as *adv. acc.* (*a*) גַּם תְּמוֹל גַּם הַיּוֹם 1 S 20^{27} (lit.), cf. Ex 5^{14} (sub **b**); (*b*) תְּמוֹל שִׁלְשֹׁם Ex 5^{8} Ru 2^{11}, so אֶתְמ׳ שׁ׳ 1 S 4^{7}; (*c*) גַּם ת׳ גַּם שׁ׳ 2 S 3^{17} 1 Ch 11^{2} (‖ 2 S 5^{2} with אֶתְמ׳). **b.** כִּתְמוֹל שִׁלְשֹׁם *as formerly* Gn 31$^{2.5}$ Ex 5^{7} Jos 4^{18} 1 S 21^{6} (but Bu מִתְּ׳, as **c**), 2 K 13^{5}; כְּאֶתְמ׳ שׁ׳ 1 S 14^{21} 19^{7}; Ex 5^{14} כִּת׳ שׁ׳ גַּם תְּמוֹל גַּם הַיּוֹם *as yesterday* (and) *the third day* (=*as formerly*), both yesterday and to-day (=*so more recently*). **c.** מִתְּמוֹל שׁ׳ = (*from*) *aforetime,* Ex 21$^{29.36}$ Jos 3^{4}, וְהוּא לֹא שֹׂנֵא לוֹ מִתְּ׳ שׁ׳, Dt 4^{42} 19$^{4.6}$ Jos 20^{5}; so גַּם מֵאֶתְמוֹל שׁ׳ 1 S 10^{11}; גַּם מִתְּ׳ גַּם מִשּׁ׳ Ex 4^{10}. **3.** מֵאֶתְמוֹל (alone) Is 30^{33} *from yesterday*=*already;* וְאֶתְמוּל עַמִּי Mi 2^{8} corrupt, read וְאַתֶּם לְעַמִּי (WRS, with עַל יָקוּם;
8008 עַמִּי We Now, with תְּקוּמוּ), and v. שַׂלְמָה. p. 971

8552 †[תָּמַם], תַּם **vb. be complete, finished** (Ar. تَمَّ *id.,* Ph. תם, Syr. ܬܡ der. spec. and deriv.; cf. NH=BH (rare), Aram. תְּמִימָא, ܡܫܡܠܝܐ *perfect*);—**Qal** *Pf.* 3 ms. תַּם Gn 47^{18} + 3 t. (+ Qr תַּם מֵאֵשׁ Je 6^{29}); 3 pl. תַּמּוּ Dt 2^{16} +; תָּ֫מּוּ 2 K 7^{13}; 1 pl. תַּמְנוּ (Ges$^{§67 dd}$) Nu 17^{28} ψ 64^{7}; תָּ֫מְנוּ Je 44^{18}; (La 3^{22} rd. תַּמּוּ 𝔗 𝔖 Ew Löhr Bu); *Impf.* 3 ms. יִתֹּם (Ges$^{§67 g}$) Gn 47^{15} Ez 47^{12}; 3 fs. תִּתֹּם Ez 24^{11} (Ges$^{§67 q}$; del. Co), תִּתֹּם Gn 47^{18} 1 K 7^{22}; 1 s. אֵיתָם ψ 19^{14}; 3 mpl. יִתַּ֫מּוּ Nu 14^{35} +, וַיִּתְּמוּ Dt 34^{8}; *Inf. cstr.* תֹּם Lv 25^{29} + 10 t.; תָּם־ Is 18^{5}; sf. תֻּמִּי Je 27^{8} + 7 t. sf.;—**1.** *be finished, completed;* the writing of words Dt 31$^{24.30}$ (v. Dr.; J), Jb 31^{40}; building of temple 1 K 6^{22}, cf. 7^{22}; *fulfilled,* י׳'s command (by obedience) Jos 4^{10} (E); as auxil. + vb. fin.=*completely, wholly, entirely,* תַּמּוּ נִכְרָ֫תוּ Jos 3^{16} (E) *were wholly cut off;* סָפוּ תַּמּוּ ψ 73^{19} *entirely consumed;* sq. ל inf.: תַּמּוּ לעבור *were finished in regard to,* etc., i.e. *were entirely passed over* Jos 3^{17} 4$^{1.11}$ (JE) 2 S 15^{24}; להמול Jos 5^{8} (E) *entirely circumcised,* Nu 17^{28}. **2.** *be finished, come to an end, cease:* the year, Gn 47^{18} (J), Lv 25^{29} (P), Je 1^{3}; the years of י׳ have no end ψ 102^{28}; days of weeping Dt 34^{8} (P), cf. La 4^{22}; also Is 18^{5} La 3^{22}. **3.** *be complete,* of number, 1 S 16^{11}. **4.** *be consumed, exhausted, spent:* silver Gn 47$^{15.18}$ (J); strength Lv 26^{20} (H); lead Je 6^{29} (Qr); bread 37^{21}; fruit Ez 47^{12}; rust 24^{11}. **5.** *be finished, consumed, destroyed:* people Nu 14^{33} (J), v^{35} 17^{28} (P; ‖ מות), 32^{13} (J), Jos 8^{24} 10^{20} (JE), Dt 2$^{14.15.16}$ Jos 5^{6} (D), 1 K 14^{10} 2 K 7^{13} Is 16^{4} Je 14^{15} 24^{10} 27^{8} 36^{23} 44$^{12.12.18.27}$ ψ 9^{7} (but read דַּמּוּ), 104^{35}. **6.** *be complete, sound, unimpaired,* ethically, ψ 19^{14} (‖ נִקָּה; late). **7.** twice, very strangely, si vera l., trans.: ψ 64^{7} תמנו *we have completed* (rd. prob. הֶתְמֹּנוּ); Je 27^{8} עַד־תֻּמִּי אֹתָם בְּיָדוֹ (read with Gr תִּתִּי). **Hiph.** *Pf.* 1 s. הֲתִמֹּתִי Ez 22^{15}; 3 mpl. הֵתַ֫מּוּ 2 S 20^{18}; *Impf.* יַתֵּם 2 K 22^{4}; 2 ms. תַּתֵּם Jb 22^{3} (Ges$^{§67 y}$); *Inf. abs.* הָתֵם Ez 24^{10}; *cstr., id.,* Dn 8^{23} + 9^{24} Qr (v. Dr.); sf. הֲתִמְּךָ (Ges$^{§67 v}$) Is 33^{1};—**1.** *finish, complete, perfect,* a matter 2 S 20^{18} (but **Qal,** *come to an end,* c. ה interrog., We Dr al.); flesh in cooking Ez 24^{10}. **2.** *finish, cease doing* a thing, sq. pt. (Ges$^{§120 b}$), שׁוֹדֵד Is 33^{1}. **3.** *complete, sum up,* c. acc. money 2 K 22^{4} (other conj. Klo Gr Gi); transgressions Dn 8^{23}; sin 9^{24} (Qr; Kt חתם). **4.** *destroy* uncleanness, c. מן *from,* Ez 22^{15}. **5.** causative (of **Qal 6**): acc. דרכיך Jb 22^{3} *make sound thy ways.* **Hithp.** *Impf.* 2 ms. תִּתַּמָּם 2 S 22^{26}, c. עִם *deal in integrity with*=ψ 18^{26} (late, v. **Qal 6**).

†תֹּם **n.[m.] completeness, integrity;**— 8537
תֹּם abs. Pr 10^{29} +; cstr. Jb 4^{6} ψ 78^{72}, cstr. also תָּם־ Pr 13^{6} + 4 t.; sf. תֻּמִּי ψ 26^{1} + 11 t. sf.; pl. תֻּמִּים Ex 28^{30} + 3 t.; sf. תֻּמֶּיךָ Dt 33^{8};—**1.** *completeness, fulness:* כְּתֻמָּם Is 47^{9} *acc. to their full measure;* בְּעֶצֶם תֻּמּוֹ Jb 21^{23} *in his very completeness.* **2.** *innocence, simplicity:* הלכים לתמם 2 S 15^{11}; מָשַׁךְ בַּקֶּשֶׁת לְתֻמּוֹ 1 K 22^{34}=2 Ch 18^{33}, i.e. without definite aim. **3.** *integrity:* תֹּם לֵבָב *integrity of mind* Gn 20$^{5.6}$ (E), 1 K 9^{4} ψ 78^{72} 101^{2}; תָּם־דָּרֶךְ Pr 13^{6} Jb 4^{6}; (הת)הלך בַּתֹּם Pr 10^{9}, בְּתֻמּוֹ 19^{1} 20^{7} 28^{6}, בְּתֻמִּי ψ 26$^{1.11}$; הֹלְכֵי תֹם Pr 2^{7}; בְּתֻמִּי 41^{13}; תֹּם וָיֹשֶׁר ψ 25^{21}; כְּתֻמִּי 7^{9}; מָעוֹז לַתֹּם Pr 10^{29}. **4.** אוּרִים וְתֻמִּים in תֻּמִּים (mng. 8550
dub., v., אורים) Dt 33^{8}, Ex 28^{30} (P) Lv 8^{8} (P), Ezr 2^{63} 224
=Ne 7^{65}; + 1 S 14^{41} (for תָּמִים) We Dr Bu HPS; 8549
also Ho 3^{4} (for תרפים) Che$^{JQ, July 1899, 564}$ and 4^{5} (תֻּמֶּיךָ for אִמֶּךָ) Ruben$^{JQ, April 1899, 44}$ Che$^{l.c.}$.

[תֻּמָּה] **n.f. integrity** (late);—cstr. תֻּמַּת 8538
Pr 11^{3}; sf. תֻּמָּתִי Jb 27^{5} 31^{6}; תֻּמָּתְךָ 2^{9}; תֻּמָּתוֹ v^{3}.

†תָּם **adj. complete;**—ת׳ Gn 25^{27} + 10 t.; 8535

sf. תַּמָּתִי Ct 5^2 6^9 (late, exc. Gn 25^{27});—**1.** *complete, perfect*: in beauty Ct 5^2 6^9; of physical strength ψ 73^4 (rd. לָמוֹ תָּם Ew De Dr$^{Sam. xxxi}$ Che Bae al.). **2.** *sound, wholesome*: אִישׁ תָּם, of Jacob as tent-dweller, opp. Esau, hunter, Gn 25^{27} (J; De *leutseliger Mann*, Di *ruhig, still*, AV RV *plain man*; ת׳ here poss. redactional, =**3**). **3.** *complete, morally innocent, having integrity*: אִישׁ תָּם Jb 1^8 2^3; ת׳ alone 1^1 8^{20} $9^{20.21.22}$
8382 Pr 29^{10} ψ 37^{37} 64^5.—תַּמִּים v. [תָּאֹם]. p. 1060f

8549 **תָּמִים** $_{91}$ **adj. complete, sound**;—ת׳ Gn 6^9+; f. תְּמִימָה Lv 3^9+; cstr. תְּמִים Jb 36^4 37^{16}; pl. תְּמִימִים Ez 43^{25}+; תְּמִימֹת Lv 23^{15}; cstr. תְּמִימֵי ψ 119^1 Pr 11^{20};—†**1.** *complete, whole, entire*, Jb 36^4 תְּמִים דֵּעוֹת, 37^{16}. **2.** *whole, sound, healthful*, of men Pr 1^{12} (‖ חַיִּים); vine Ez 15^5; usu. of sacrif. animals, P; Ex 12^5 + 40 t., so Ez 43^{22} + 10 t. †**3.** *complete, entire*, of time: day Jos 10^{13}; year Lv 25^{30}; sabbaths 23^{15}. †**4.** *sound, wholesome, unimpaired, innocent, having integrity*: of God's way ψ 18^{31} = 2 S 22^{31}; work Dt 32^4; law ψ 19^8; elsewh. of man Gn 6^9 17^1 (P; both ‖ הִתְהַלֵּךְ אֶת (לִפְנֵי) אלהים); ת׳ עם י׳ Dt 18^{13} ψ 18^{24}, c. ל in ‖ 2 S 22^{24}; oft. c. דֶּרֶךְ *way*: תְּמִימֵי דֶרֶךְ ψ 101^2; ת׳ בִּדְרָכֶיךָ Ez 28^{15}; דֶּרֶךְ ת׳ Pr 11^{20} ψ 119^1; וַיַּתֵּן ת׳ || וַיַּתֵּר ת׳ דרכו 2 S 22^{33} ψ 18^{33}; הלך בדרך ת׳ 101^6; דֶּרֶךְ om., הלך תמים Pr 28^{18} ψ 15^2; לב ת׳ 119^{80}; =noun (late), man of *integrity* Pr 11^5 Jb 12^4; pl. Pr 2^{21} 28^{10} ψ 37^{18}. †**5.** as neuter adj. = subst. *what is complete, entirely in accord with truth and fact*: דִּבֶּר ת׳ Am 5^{10}; עֲשִׂיתֶם אִם־בֶּאֱמֶת וּבְת׳ Ju $9^{16.19}$; עִבְדוּ י׳ בְּת׳ וּבֶאֱמֶת Jos 24^{14} (E); *integrity* גֶּבֶר ת׳ ψ 18^{26} (cstr. Ges$^{§ 93s}$; ‖ 2 S 22^{26} גִּבּוֹר), 84^{12}; הֹלְכִים בְּת׳.—
8537 1 S 14^{41} v. תֹּם **4**. p. 1070

4974 †**מְתֹם** **n.[m.] soundness**; in phr. אֵין מְתֹם בּ׳ Is 1^6 ψ $38^{4.8}$; מֵעִיר מְתֹם Ju 20^{48} *from entire city*
4962 (Codd. De Rossi Bu GFM מְתִם, v. מַת and cf. עיר מת(י)ם Dt 2^{34} 3^6 Jb 24^{12}).

8486-87, 8489 **תֵּימָן, תֵּימָנִי** v. תֵּימָן sub ימן. p. 412

8553-54, 8556 **תִּמְנָה, תִּמְנָתָה, תִּמְנִי, תִּמְנַת** v. מנה. p. 584

8555, 8557 **תִּמְנָע** v. מָנַע. **תֶּמֶס** v. מסס. p. 586, 588

תמר (√ of foll.; cf. perh. Ar. إِتْمَأَرَّ *be erect, stiff* (e.g. of lance), so Buhl^{13}, who derives thence תמר *palm-tree*, and also תִּימָרָה, NH תִּמְרָה *column* of smoke, NH תִּמּוּר *rising motion*, etc., but these denom. from תָּמָר Levy^{NHWB} Buhl^{14}; cf. Ar. تَمْرٌ *date*, Eth. ተምር: *id.*, ተመርት: *date-palm*, Aram. תַּמְרָא, ܬܡܪܬܐ *date-palm*, NH תָּמָר *date(-palm)*).

†**תֹּמֶר** **n.m. palm-tree, post**;—cstr. ת׳ דְּבוֹרָה 8560
Ju 4^5 *palm-tree* of Deborah; כְּת׳ מִקְשָׁה Je 10^5 *like a post* (i.e. a *scare-crow*; cf. Bar 6^{70}) *in a cucumber field* (sim. of idol).

†I. **תָּמָר** **n.m. palm-tree, date-palm**, 8558
Phoenix dactylifera;—ת׳ Jo 1^{12}; in sim. of prosperity ψ 92^{13}, of (graceful) stature Ct 7^8, cf. (fig.) v^9; pl. תְּמָרִים in oasis Ex 15^{27} (J), ‖ Nu 33^9 (P); כַּפֹּת ת׳ Lv 23^{40} (H) *palm-branches*, cf. עֲלֵי ת׳ Ne 8^{15}; עִיר הַתְּמָרִים = Jericho Dt 34^3 (JE), 2 Ch 28^{15} Ju 1^{16} 3^{13}.—Vid. Post $^{Hast. DB PALM-TREE}$ M'Lean $^{Ency. Bib. ID.}$ Tr $^{NHB 378 ff.}$ Theob. Fischer $^{Dattelpalme, 1881}$.

II. **תָּמָר** $_{25}$ **n.pr. 1. f.** †**a.** daughter-in-law 8559
of Judah Gn $38^{6.11.11.13.24}$ 1 Ch 2^4 Ru 4^{12}. **b.** daughter of David, sister of Absalom 2 S $13^{1.2}$ + 11 t. 13, 2 Ch 3^9. †**c.** daughter of Absalom 2 S 14^{27}. †**2. loc.** Ez 47^{19} 48^{28}; 1 K 9^{18} Kt (> Qr תַּדְמֹר q.v.), so read also ‖ 2 Ch 8^4 (for MT תַּדְמֹר); site not certain, cf. Buhl $^{G 184}$.—
בַּעַל תָּמָר v. בַּעַל. p. 128 1193

תִּמֹּרָה $_{19}$ **n.f. palm(-tree) figure**, as orna- 8561
ment;—ת׳ Ez 41^{18}+ (van d. H. תִּמֹ׳, so throughout); pl. תִּמֹּרֹת 1 K 6^{29}+ (Gi תִּמֹ׳), תִּמֹּרִים Ez 40^{16}+; sf. תִּימֹרָיו v^{22} Qr (Kt תימרו);—*palm-figure* in Sol.'s temple 1 K $6^{29.32.32.35}$ 7^{36} 2 Ch 3^5; in Ezekiel's temple Ez $40^{16.22.26}$ + 10 t. 40, 41.

†[**תִּימָרָה**] **n.f.** (palm-like) **column** (spread- 8470
ing at top; cf. Ol$^{§ 184b}$);—pl. cstr. תִּימְרוֹת עָשָׁן Jo 3^2 Ct 3^6 (cf. עַמּוּד עָשָׁן in prose Ju 20^{40}).

†II. [**תַּמְרוּר**] **n.m.** pl. תַּמְרוּרִים Je 31^{21}, 8564
doubtful word; sense, and ‖ צִיֻּנִים, require mng. *sign-posts* (= תאמ׳, cf. Ar. تُؤْمُورٌ *sign-post*, √ امر, v. امارٌ *sign*, أَمَرَةٌ *stones* (heaped up) as way-mark; Eth. አመረ: *shew, point out, give sign or signal*);—Gie rejects strange form, reading
תְּמָרִים *palm-trees*, as posts.—I. ת׳ v. מרר. p. 601 8563

תַּמְרוּק, תַּ־רִיק, v. מרק. I. **תַּמְרוּר** v. מרר. 8562-63
p. 600-01
תַּן v. תנן. p. 1072 8565

I. [**תָּנָה**] **vb. hire** (si vera l., akin to 8566
נתן);—**Qal** *Impf.* 3 mpl. יִתְנוּ בַגּוֹיִם Ho 8^{10} *hire* (allies) among the nations; **Hiph.** *Pf.* 3 pl. הִתְנוּ v^9 *have hired* lovers.—We in both יִתְּנוּ *give*: v^9 *give* amorous favours, v^{10} *give* (these), cp. Now Marti Harper.—תְּנָה ψ 8^2 v. נתן **Qal 2 b.**

†**אֶתְנָה** **n.f. hire of a harlot**;—א׳ abs., 866
Ho 2^{14} (in fig. of Israel as adulteress);—on אֶתְנַן
(which We Now Marti read here also) v. II. תנן. 868-69
p. 1072

3496 †יַתְנִיאֵל **n.pr.m.** a Levite (*Ēl hireth*);—1 Ch 26^{2}; Ιενουηλ, 𝔊L Ναθαναηλ.

8567 †II. [תָּנָה] **vb. recount, rehearse** (?) (𝔗 תַּנֵּי, Syr. ܬܢܳܐ, is *recount*, Ar. ثَنَّى II, IV. is *celebrate*, but Heb. ת = Aram. ת = Ar. ث is very dub.);—**Pi.** *Impf.* 3 mpl. יְתַנּוּ Ju 5^{11} *let them recount* (Vrss) the victories of י׳; *Inf. cstr.* תַּנּוֹת 11^{40} *to celebrate* (mod.), or *mourn* (Vrss), c. לְ pers.

8569-70 [תְּנוּאָה] v. [נוא]. תְּנוּבָה v. [נוב]. p. 626

תנך (√of following).

8571 †תְּנוּךְ **n.[m.] tip, i.e. lobe of ear** (𝔊 λοβὸς τοῦ ὠτός, 𝔙 *extremum auriculae*, and so most ancient authorities, cf. Thes [1511]);—cstr. in phr. ת׳ אֹזֶן פ׳ Ex $29^{20.20}$ Lv $8^{23.24}$ $14^{14.17.25.28}$ (all P).

8572-73 תְּנוּמָה v. נום. תְּנוּפָה v. I. נוף. p. 630, 632

8574 †תַּנּוּר **n.m.** [Lv 26, 26] portable **stove** or **fire-pot** (loan-word from As. *tinûru*, *id.*, acc. to DHM [VOJ i. 23] (otherwise Dvořák [ZK i. 155 ff.]); ת׳, a large earthen jar, still in Syria, Wetzst [Verhandl. d. Berl. Anthrop. Gesell., 1882, 467] Whitehouse [Heb. Antiq. 7, 3] ARSK [EB i. 605]; Ar. تَنُّور is loan-word from Aram. תַּנּוּרָא, ܬܢܽܘܪܳܐ, and this from Pers. *tanûra*, acc. to Frä [26]);—ת׳ abs. Ho 7^{4}+, cstr. Gn 15^{17} ψ 21^{10}; pl. תַּנּוּרִים Ne 3^{11} 12^{38};—*fire-pot*, for baking (אָפָה) Ho 7^{4} (read ת׳ בֹּעֵר הֵם אֹפֵהוּ וגו׳, Oort [Th. Tijdschr. 1890, 480 ff.] Albr [ZAW xvi (1896), 88]), cf. $v^{6.7}$ (all in sim.), Ex 7^{28} (J), Lv 2^{4} 7^{9} 26^{26} (P), also (breakable) 11^{35}; ת׳ עָשָׁן Gn 15^{17} (JE) in vision, symbol of י׳'s presence, cf. Is 31^{9} (‖ אוּר); sim. of heat La 5^{10}, of judgment Mal 3^{19}, and so ת׳ אֵשׁ ψ 21^{10}; מִגְדַּל הַתַּנּוּרִים Ne 3^{11} 12^{38} a tower on wall of Jerus.

8575-76 [תַּנְחוּם], תַּנְחֻמֶת, תַּנְחוּמוֹת, [תַּנְחוּם] v. [נחם]. p. 637

I. תנן (√of following; ? akin to II. תנה in sense *lament*, i.e. *howl*).

8565 †[תַּן] **n.[m. et] f.** [La 4, 3] **jackal** (so most; Tr [NHB 109 ff., 263 f.] Shipley-Cook [Ency. Bib. JACKAL]; but *wolf* Post [Hast. DB DRAGON], cf. Che [Is 13, 22] and (rare) Ar. تِينَانٌ);—pl. תַּנִּים Mi 1^{8}+, תַּנִּין La 4^{3} (Ges

8568 [§ 87 e]), לְתַנּוֹת Mal 1^{3} (si vera l.; 𝔊 Thes al. interpret =*dwellings*, Sta Now conjecture נְאוֹת, Marti נָתַתִּי לְ);—*jackal*, howling mournfully in waste places, Mi 1^{8} Jb 30^{29} (both ‖ בְּנוֹת יַעֲנָה), Is 13^{22} (‖ אִיִּים), in desert also 43^{20} (‖ בְּנוֹת יַעֲנָה); deserted sites called נְוֵה ת׳, מְעוֹן ת׳ Je 9^{10} 10^{22} 49^{33} 51^{37}, Is 34^{13} 35^{7}, מְקוֹם ת׳ ψ 44^{20}; ת׳ מִדְבָּר Mal 1^{3} (si vera l., but v. supra); ת׳ as snuffing up wind Je 14^{6}, giving suck La 4^{3}.

†תַּנִּין (erron. תַּנִּים) **n.m.** [Ez 29, 3] **serpent, dragon, sea-monster** (NH *id.* (rare); Ar. تِنِّينٌ, loan-word from Aram. תַּנִּינָא, ܬܢܺܝܢܳܐ Frä [123]; Eth. ተመን:);—abs. ת׳ Ex 7^{9}+, ־ִים Ez 29^{3} 32^{2} (by confusion with pl. of [תַּן]); pl. תַּנִּינִם Gn 1^{21}, etc.;—**1.** *serpent*, Dt 32^{33} (venomous), ψ 91^{13} (‖ פֶּתֶן), Ex $7^{9.10.12}$ (P). **2.** *dragon*, as devourer (sim.) Je 51^{34}; עֵין הַתּ׳ Ne 2^{13}, near Jerus. **3.** *sea-* (or river-) *monster*, Gn 1^{21} (P); fig. Jb 7^{12} ψ 74^{13} (i.e. Egyptians), Is 27^{1} 51^{9} (‖ רַהַב, mythol. personif. of chaos); in summons to praise י׳ ψ 148^{7} (‖ תְּהֹמוֹת).—Vid. Che [Ency. Bib. DRAGON] Gunk [Schöpfung 69 ff.] Barton [JAOS xv. 1 (1891), 23 f.]; personif. of water-spout RS [Sem. i. 161; 2nd ed. 176]; cf. Gk. fish-name θύννος Lewy [Fremdw. 15]. 8577

II. תנן (√of following; apparently ‖ נתן; cf. also I. תנה).

†אֶתְנַן **n.m.** [Ez 16, 34] hire of harlot (= אֶתְנָה);—abs. א׳ Ez $16^{34.41}$, אֶתְנָן Ho 9^{1}+; cstr. אֶתְנַן Dt 23^{19}+; sf. אֶתְנַנָּהּ Is 23^{18}, ־נַּהּ v^{17}; pl. sf. אֶתְנַנֶּיהָ Mi 1^{7a} (We proposes אֲשֵׁרֶיהָ, cf. Now Marti);—harlot's *hire*, Dt 23^{19} (א׳ זוֹנָה); elsewhere in fig.: of idolatrous Israel Ho 9^{1}, Jerus. Ez $16^{31.34.34.41}$, Tyre Is $23^{17.18}$; of costly idols of Samaria Mi $1^{7b.7c}$, cf. v^{7a} (v. supra). 866, 868-69

תִּנְשֶׁמֶת v. [נשם]. p. 675 8580

תעב (√of foll.; תאב (v. [תָּאַב] Am 6^{8}) is erroneous; cf. NH תֹּועֵבָה, תעב Pi; Ph. תעבת, Aram. תּוֹעֵבָא).

תּוֹעֵבָה [117] **n.f. abomination**;—abs. ת׳ Gn 43^{32}+21 t.; תֹּעֵבָה Je 44^{4}; cstr. תּוֹעֲבַת Gn 46^{34}+; pl. תּוֹעֵבוֹת Ez 8^{6}+; cstr. תּוֹעֲבוֹת 6^{11}+, etc.; sf. תּוֹעֲבֹתָיו 2 Ch 36^{8}, etc.;—**1.** ritual sense: **a.** Isr.'s sacrifices, ת׳ מִצְרַיִם (gen. obj.) Ex $8^{22.22}$ (E), cf. Gn 46^{34} (J); ת׳ למצרים 43^{32} (J); ת׳ לְ of physical repugnance ψ 88^{9}. **b.** to God and his people: ת׳ of unclean food Dt 14^{3}; worshipper of idols Is 41^{24}, cf. Je 2^{7}; various objectionable acts: ת׳ לפני י׳ Dt 24^{4}; ת׳ י׳ 7^{25} (חֵרֶם, cf. v^{26}), 17^{1} 18^{12} 22^{5} 23^{19} 27^{15}; offering of children (עשׂה) 12^{31}, cf. Je 32^{35}, also pl. 2 K 16^{3} = 2 Ch 28^{3}, Dt $18^{9.12}$ (+ witchcraft); idolatrous practices (sts. with other illegal acts) עשׂה (כ)ת׳ Dt 13^{15} 17^{4} Ez 16^{50} 18^{12} Mal 2^{11} (intermarriage with idolaters), cf. Je 44^{4}; usu. c. pl. noun Dt 20^{18} 1 K 14^{24} 2 K $21^{2.11}$ 2 Ch 33^{2} 36^{8} Je 7^{10} 44^{22} Ez 8^{6}+12 t. Ez.; cf. תועבות 2 Ch 36^{14} Ezr $9^{1.11.14}$ Ez 5^{9}+18 t. Ez.; 8441 of idols Dt 32^{16}; (תועבה) 2 K 23^{13} Is 44^{19} (cf. Dt 27^{15}); idolatrous objects 2 Ch 34^{33}; ‖ שִׁקּוּצִים Je 16^{18} (R^{JE}) Ez 5^{11} 11$^{18.21}$, (צַלְמֵי ת׳) 7^{20}; ‖ גלולים 14^{6}, cf. 6^{9}; גִּלּוּלֵי ת׳ 16^{36}. **2.** ethical sense: **a.** c. gen. obj. of man, ת׳ שְׂפָתַי Pr 8^{7}, ת׳ מלכים 16^{12}, ת׳ צדיקים 29^{27a}, ת׳ כסילים 13^{19}, ת׳ רָשָׁע 29^{27b}, ת׳ לְאָדָם 24^{9}. **b.** to God and his people: ת׳ of sacrifice of wicked Pr 21^{27} (cf. 15^{8}), his prayers 28^{9} cf. Is 1^{13} (ת׳ לִי), prob. also Je 6^{15}=8^{12} (of various kinds of wickedness); unchastity Lv 18^{22}; c. עשׂה 20^{13} (H) Ez 22^{11} 33^{26}; cf. תועבות Lv 18$^{26.27.29}$ (cf. v^{30}; H), also Pr 26^{25}; ת׳ י׳ Dt 25^{16} Pr 3^{32} + 10 t. Pr., cf. 6^{16}.

8581 †[תָּעַב] **vb. denom. Niph. Pi.**: **Niph.** *Pf.* 3 ms. נִתְעַב 1 Ch 21^{6}; *Pt.* נִתְעָב Is 14^{19} Jb 15^{16};—*be abhorred*: **1.** ritual sense: נֵצֶר נִתְעָב Is 14^{19} *an abhorred* (rejected) *branch* (< נֵץ *vulture*, the unclean scavenger bird); נִתְעָב וְנֶאֱלָח Jb 15^{16} *abhorred and corrupt*, fr. disease (נאלח elsewhere †ψ 14^{3}=53^{4} ‖ התעיב). **2.** ethically: David's census, acc. to 1 Ch 21^{6}. **Pi.** *Pf.* 3 pl. sf. תִּעֲבוּנִי Jb 9^{31} + 2 t.; *Impf.* יְתָעֵב ψ 106^{40} 5^{7} (read 2 ms. תְּתַעֵב); 3 fs. תְּתַעֵב ψ 107^{18}; 2 ms. תְּתַעֵב Dt 23$^{8.8}$, etc.; *Inf. abs.* תַּעֵב Dt 7^{26}; *Pt.* מְתָעֵב Is 49^{7} (but v. infra), + Am 6^{8} (so read for מְתָאֵב Gei $^{Urschrift\ 349}$ We Now Marti Harper); pl. מְתַעֲבִים Mi 3^{9};—**1.** *regard as an abomination, abhor*: **a.** ritual sense: (1) of God; c. acc. of Israel, because of idols ψ 106^{40}. (2) of man: c. acc., of abomination Dt 7$^{26.26}$, cf. 23$^{8.8}$; Job Jb 19^{19} 30^{10}. **b.** ethically: (1) of God; ‖ שׂנא, c. acc.: איש דמים ומרמה ψ 5^{7} (Am 6^{8} v. II. תאב). (2) of man; c. acc. מִשְׁפָּט Mi 3^{9}, דֹּבֵר תָּמִים Am 5^{10} (‖ שׂנא), שֶׁקֶר ψ 119^{163} (‖ שׂנא). **c.** physically: c. acc. כָּל־אֹכֶל ψ 107^{18}. **2.** *cause to be an abomination*: c. acc., ritual sense Ez 16^{25}; Job, from filthy garments Jb 9^{31}; מְתָעֵב גּוֹי Is 49^{7} (‖ בְּזֹה נֶפֶשׁ) (read prob. **Pu.** מְתֹעָב, as Oort SS Bu Du). **Hiph.** *Pf.* 2 fs. הִתְעַבְתְּ Ez 16^{52}; 3 mpl. הִתְעִיבוּ ψ 14^{1}=53^{2}; *Impf.* וַיַּתְעֵב 1 K 21^{26};—*make abominable, do abominably*: **1.** ritual sense: c. acc. rei, Ez 16^{52}; לְ c. inf. 1 K 21^{26}. **2.** ethically: c. acc. עלילה ψ 14^{1}=53^{2} (עול).

8582 †תָּעָה **vb.** err (‖ form of טָעָה, q.v.; Aram. (sts.) תְּעָא, תְּעֵי *id.*; NH=BH (rare));—**Qal** *Pf.* 3 ms. ת׳ Is 21^{4}; 1 s. תָּעִיתִי ψ 119$^{110.176}$, etc.; *Impf.* 3 fs. תֵּתַע Gn 21^{14} Pr 7^{25}; 3 mpl. יִתְעוּ Is 35^{8}+; *Inf. cstr.* תְּעוֹת Ez 44^{10}+; *Pt.* תֹּעֶה Gn 37^{15}+, etc.;—**1.** physically, *wander about*, abs. Ex 23^{4} (E) Is 35^{8} 53^{6} Jb 38^{41} ψ 119^{176}; c. ב loc. Gn 21^{14} 37^{15} (JE), Pr 7^{25} ψ 107^{4}; c. לְ loc. Is 47^{15}; acc. loc. 16^{8}. **2.** of intoxication, c. בְּ of wine Is 28^{7}; מן of wine v^{7}; fig. of perplexity, subj. לבב 21^{4}. **3.** ethically, abs. Ez 44^{10} 48$^{11.11.11}$ ψ 58^{4}, prob. Pr 14^{22} (cf. חוטא v^{21}, but Bu Toy *go astray to ruin*); תֹּעֵי רוח Is 29^{24}, תֹּעֵי לבב ψ 95^{10}; c. מן 119^{110} Pr 21^{16}, מֵאַחֲרֵי Ez 14^{11}, מֵעָלַי Ez 44$^{10.15}$. **Niph. 1.** *be made to wander about*, as a drunkard: *Inf. cstr.* הִתָּעוֹת Is 19^{14}. **2.** ethically: *Pf.* 3 ms. נִתְעָה *be led astray* Jb 15^{31} (c. בשׁוא). **Hiph.** *Pf.* 3 ms. הִתְעָה Ho 4^{12} (We הִתְעָם); *Impf.* וַיֶּתַע 2 Ch 33^{9}; sf. וַיַּתְעֵם Jb 12^{24}+; *Pt.* מַתְעֶה Is 30^{28}+;—**1.** physically: *cause to wander about*: abs. Is 30^{28} (of bridle, in fig.), Pr 10^{17}; Je 50^{6} (acc. of people as sheep); acc. pers. Pr 12^{26}; c. מן loc. Gn 20^{13} (E), ב loc. Jb 12^{24}=ψ 107^{40}. **2.** of intoxication, Is 19$^{13.14}$ Jb 12^{25}. **3.** mentally and morally: *cause to err, mislead*: abs. Is 3^{12} 9^{15} Ho 4^{12}; c. acc. pers. Am 2^{4} Mi 3^{5} 2 K 21^{9}=2 Ch 33^{9}, Je 23$^{13.32}$; c. ב obj. Je 42^{20} (so Gf; Ke al. (so Pr 10^{17}) intr. *err at cost of*; 𝔊 Ew Du Co הֲרֵעֹתֶם); c. מן of י׳ Is 63^{17}.

†תּוֹעָה **n.f. wandering, error**;—**1.** *error* 8442
in morals and religion, c. דִּבֶּר, Is 32^{6}. **2.** *confusion, disturbance*, c. עָשָׂה, Ne 4^{2}.

תֹּעוּ v. תֹּעִי. תְּעוּדָה v. [עוד] p. 730. below 8583-84

†תֹּעִי **n.pr.m.** king of Hamath, 2 S 8$^{9.10.10}$= 8583
תֹּעוּ (which We Dr al. prefer) 1 Ch 18$^{9.10}$.

I, II. תְּעָלָה v. עלה p. 752. 8585

תַּעֲלוּלִים v. I. עלל. p. 760 8586

תַּעֲלֻמָה v. I. [עלם]. תַּעֲנוּג v. [ענג]. 8587-88
p. 761, 772

תַּעֲנִית v. III. [ענה] p. 777. 8589

†תַּעְנַךְ **n.pr.loc.** in Great Plain, [ת׳ Baer 8590
Gi; van d. H. תַּעֲנָךְ, exc. Jos 21^{25} 1 Ch 7^{29}]; 8590
usu. named with Megiddo: old Can. city, Ju 5^{19} Jos 12^{21} (=Egypt. *Ta-ʿ-n-k-â, Ta-ʿa-na-k*, WMM $^{As.\ u.\ Eur.\ 170,\ 195}$); assigned to Manasseh 17^{11} 21^{25} Ju 1^{27} 1 Ch 7^{29} (yet within territory of Issachar Jos 17^{11} 19$^{18\text{ff.}}$); named also 1 K 4^{12}; 𝔊 Θααναχ, Θααναχ, Ταναχ, etc.; =mod. *Taʿannuk*, c. 4½ m. SSE. from *Lejjun* (Megiddo), Rob $^{BR\ iii.\ 117}$ Guérin $^{Sam.\ ii.\ 226\ ff.}$ Buhl $^{G\ 288\ f.}$ Wilson $^{Hast.\ DB\ Taanach}$.

†[תָּעַע] **vb. Pilp. Hithp.** mock (cf. Ar. 8591
تَعْتَعَ *stammer*, also *shake violently*; onomatop.);—**Pilp.** *Pt.* מְתַעְתֵּעַ Gn 27^{12} = subst. *a mocker*. **Hithp.** *Pt.* pl. מִתַּעְתְּעִים 2 Ch 36^{16}, c. ב pers., *mocking at* his prophets (+ בּוֹזִים, מַלְעִבִים).

8595 †תַּעְתֻּעִים† **n.** [m.] **pl. abstr. mockery**;—מַעֲשֵׂה ת׳, epith. of idols, Je 10[15] 51[18] (both+הֶבֶל).

5774,8592 [תַּעֲצֻמָה] v. I. [עצם]. תְּעוּפָה v. II. עוּף. p. 734, 783

8593-94 תַּעַר v. [ערה]. [תַּעֲרֻבָה] v. II. ערב p. 787. p. 789

8595-96 תַּעְתֻּעִים v. [תעע]. תֹּף v. [תפף]. above, below

8597-99 תִּפְאָרָה v. I. [פאר]. I, II, III. תַּפּוּחַ v. [נפח]. p. 656, 802

8600 [תְּפוֹצָה] v. I. [פוץ]. p. 807

8601 †[תֻּפִינִים]† **n.** [m.] **pl.** doubtful word; AV RV *baken pieces* (Thes from √אפה *bake*);—only cstr. תֻּפִינֵי מִנְחַת פִּתִּים Lv 6[14]; text prob. crpt.; rd. תְּפַתֶּנָּה (√פתת), *thou shalt break it* into a meal-offering of pieces, Me[ZWTh vi. 60 f.] (𝔖), Di[ad loc.]

I. **תפל** (√of foll.; NH תָּפֵל, 𝔗 אִיתַּפַּל, in Midr. expl. of Dt 1[1]; on 2 S 22[27] תִּתַּפָּל v. פָּתַל; NH תָּפֵל *unsalted*, of fish, תִּפְלָה=BH; Ar. تَفَلَ is *spit*, تُفْلٌ *spittle*).

8602 †I. תָּפֵל **adj. tasteless, unseasoned**;—abs. ת׳, as subst. Jb 6[6]; fig. of unsatisfying prophecies La 2[14] (+שָׁוְא).

8604 †תִּפְלָה† **n.f.** (moral) **unsavouriness, unseemliness**;—abs. ת׳; *unseemliness*, of men Je 23[13] Jb 24[12]; לֹא נָתַן ת׳ לְא׳ 1[21] *he did not ascribe unseemliness to God;* so read also 4[18] (for MT תָּהֳלָה) Hup Me Bu.

II. **תפל** (√of following; akin to טָפַל).

8602 †II. תָּפֵל **n.** [m.] **whitewash**;—applied to wall, in Ezekiel's vision Ez 13[10.11.14.15]; fig. of false prophet 22[28].

8603 †תֹּפֶל **n.pr.loc.** in, or near, the *ʿArabah;*—Dt 1[1]; =mod. *Ṭafîleh*, 15 m. SE. of Dead Sea Rob[BR ii. 187] v. Burckhardt[Travels 402 f.], but *Ṭ*=ת improb. v. Di Dr; 𝔊 Τοφολ (cf. Lag[BN 54]).

8605-06 תְּפִלָּה v. [פלל]. [תִּפְלֶצֶת] v. [פלץ]. p. 813-14

8607 תִּפְסַח v. I. פסח. p. 820

תפף (√of following; cf. 𝔗 תַּפָּא Ex 15[20] *timbrel*, Ar. دُفٌّ *drum*).

8596 †תֹּף **n.m. timbrel, tambourine**;—abs. ת׳ Gn 31[27]+; pl. תֻּפִּים Ju 11[34]+; sf. תֻּפֶּיךָ Ez 28[13], תֻּפַּיִךְ Je 31[4];—*timbrel,* held and struck with hand, esp. by dancing women, oft. with other musical instr.:—sign of merriment, gladness Gn 31[27] (E) Jb 21[12], revelry Is 5[12]; מְשׂוֹשׂ ת׳ 24[8], cf. Je 31[4] Ez 28[13]; exultation, triumph Ex 15[20.20] (E) Ju 11[34] 1 S 18[6] Is 30[32]; used by prophets in ecstasy 1 S 10[5]; in praise of י׳ 2 S 6[5] ‖ 1 Ch 13[8], ψ 81[3] 149[3] 150[4].—Vid. Prince[EB Music, § 3].

†[תָּפַף] **vb. denom. sound the timbrel, beat**;—**Qal** *Pt.* עֲלָמוֹת תּוֹפֵפוֹת ψ 68[26]; rd. *Impf.* וַיְתָף 1 S 21[14] 𝔊 (v. תוה). **Po'ēl** *Pt.* כְּקוֹל יוֹנִים מְתֹפְפֹת עַל־לִבְבֵהֶן Na 2[8]; >Sta (after 𝔊) מְצַפְצְפוֹת *twittering.* 8608

†[תָּפַר] **vb. sew together** (NH *id.;* Aram. תְּפַר);—**Qal** *Impf.* 3 mpl. וַיִּתְפְּרוּ Gn 3[7] (J) *they sewed together* fig-leaves (acc.); *Pf.* 1 s. תָּפַרְתִּי Jb 16[15], c. acc.+עֲלֵי, *sackcloth I have sewed upon* my skin; *Inf. cstr.* עֵת לִתְפּוֹר Ec 3[6] *a time to sew together* (opp. קְרֹעַ). **Pi.** *Pt.* as subst. f.pl. מְתַפְּרוֹת Ez 13[18] *those who keep sewing,* c. acc.+עַל. 8609

†**תָּפַשׂ** **vb. lay hold of, wield** (=NH תָּפַשׂ, תָּפַס, Aram. תְּפַשׂ, תְּפַס);—**Qal** *Pf.* 3 ms. ת׳ 2 K 14[13]+, sf. consec. וּתְפָשָׂהּ Dt 22[28], etc.; *Impf.* 3 ms. יִתְפֹּשׂ Is 3[6], 1 pl. נִתְפְּשֵׂם 2 K 7[12], etc.; *Imv.* mpl. תִּפְשׂוּ 1 K 18[40], etc.; *Inf. abs.* תָּפֹשׂ Je 34[3]; cstr. תְּפֹשׂ Ez 14[5], לְתָפְשׂ 21[16] 30[21], sf. לְתָפְשָׂהּ Dt 20[19], etc.; *Pt.* תֹּפֵשׂ Gn 4[21]+, cstr. תֹּפְשֵׂי Je 49[16] (Ges[§ 90 l]), etc.;—**1.** *lay hold of, seize* (with the hand), acc. pers., Gn 39[12] (J; +בְּבִגְדוֹ), also (ב pers.) Is 3[6] Dt 21[19] Je 37[14] Ez 29[7] (in fig.; +ב instr.); c. ב rei 1 K 11[30] Dt 9[17]; *arrest, catch,* acc. pers. 1 S 23[26] 1 K 13[4] 18[40.40] Je 26[8] 37[13], 2 K 14[13]=2 Ch 25[23], 2 K 25[6]=Je 52[9], ψ 71[11]; in phrase *catch, capture alive* (חַי), acc. pers. Jos 8[23] (JE), 1 S 15[8] 1 K 20[18.18] 2 K 7[12] 10[14.14]; *seize* city (acc.) Jos 8[8] (JE), 2 K 14[7] 16[9] 18[13]=Is 36[1], Dt 20[9] Je 40[10]; fig. Ez 14[5] *seize* Isr. (acc.) by (ב) their heart (terrorize them); Pr 30[9] *seize* (do violence to) the name (acc.) of my God; תָּפוּשׂ זָהָב Hb 2[19] *grasped* (sheathed) *in gold;* ת׳ מְרוֹם גִּבְעָה Je 49[16] *holding* (occupying) *the height of the hill.* **2.** *grasp* in order to *wield, wield, use skilfully: grasp* sword בַּכָּף Ez 21[16] (acc. om.), cf. 30[21] (ב of sword), and esp. pt.: תֹּפֵשׂ כִּנּוֹר Am 2[15], תֹּפֵשׂ הַקֶּשֶׁת Gn 4[21] (J), ת׳ מַגֵּל Je 50[16], תֹּפְשֵׂי מָגֵן 46[9a] (del. ת׳ v[9b] 𝔊 Gie Co Du), ת׳ מָשׁוֹט Ez 27[29], ת׳ חֲרָבוֹת 38[4]; even ת׳ הַתּוֹרָה Je 2[8] *they that handle* (deal with, are expert in) *the law,* ת׳ הַמִּלְחָמָה Nu 31[27] (P) *those skilled in war.*—Je 34[3] v. infr. **Niph.** *Pf.* 3 ms. נִתְפָּשׂ Ez 19[4], 2 fs. נִתְפַּשְׂתְּ Je 50[24], etc.; *Impf.* 3 fs. וַתִּתָּפֵשׂ 51[41], 2 ms. תִּתָּפֵשׂ Je 34[3] 38[23], etc.; 8610

Inf. cstr. לְהִתָּפֵשׂ Ez 21^{28};—*be seized, arrested, caught* (sts. ‖ נִלְכַּד), subj. pers., Je 38^{23} (ב instr.), 50^{24} (fig. of Bab.), also (c. ב instr.) Ez 12^{13} 17^{20} 19$^{4.8}$ (both fig. of Israel), 21^{29}, and (without ב) v^{28} Nu 5^{13}; + *Inf. abs.* **Qal** תָּפֹשׂ תִּתָּפֵשׂ Je 34^{3}; *be seized*, of fortress, city Je 48^{41} 51^{41} (both ‖ נִלְכַּד), 50^{46}, cf. 51^{32}; fig. ψ 10^{2} *may they be caught in* (ב) *the devices* which they have planned. **Pi.** *Impf.* 2 ms. תְּתַפֵּשׂ Pr 30^{28} a lizard *thou mayest grasp* with the hands (ב);—or rd. תִּתָּפֵשׂ Niph. Impf. 3 fs., v. De Toy.

8611 I. תֹּ֫פֶת v. תוף. p. 1064

8612 †II. תֹּ֫פֶת **n.pr.loc.** in valley of בֶּן־הִנֹּם, S. of Jerusalem (etym. doubtful, v. GFM[Ency. Bib. Molech]; RS[Sem. i. 357, 2nd ed. 372, 377] al. think Aram., = *fire-place*, cf. (שׁפת);—c. art. הַתֹּ׳ 2 K 23^{10} + 5 t., art. om. Je 7^{32} 19$^{11.12}$;—place of sacrificing children Je 7^{31}, cf. v^{32a} 19^{6} (cf. v^{5}), 2 K 23^{10}; to become burial-place Je 7^{32b} 19^{11}; in sim. of desecrated city v$^{12.13}$ (מְקוֹם הַתֹּ׳); scene of a prophecy of Jerem., v^{14};—Ταφες, Ταφεθ (cf. Lag[BN 78]), 𝔊L[2 K 23, 10] Θαφφεθ.—Vid. GFM[l. c.] Salmond[Hast. DB Tophet].

8613 †תׇּפְתֶּה **n.pr.loc.** (si vera l.) id.;—as a place of burning, in fig. of י׳'s judgment on
8612 Assyria Is 30^{33} (Klo Che Buhl Marti al. תֹּפֶת, joining ה to following as interrogative).

8445 תֹּקְהַת Qr, תוקהת Kt, v. III. תִּקְוָה p. 876.

8615-17 I, II, III. תִּקְוָה v. I. [קוה]. תְּקוּמָה v. קום. p. 876
8618, 8622 [תְּקוֹמֵם] -מֵיךָ, v. p. 879. [תְּקוּפָה] v. קוף. p. 880

8626 †[תָּקַן] **vb. become straight** (NH תִּקֵּן *arrange, put right*; Ecclus 47^{9} תיקן *set in order*; As. *takânu, be well ordered*, esp. Pi. as NH; Aram. ܬܩܢ *be established, firm*, Pa. ܬܩܶܢ, תַּקֵּין *fix, arrange, prepare*, etc.; Palm. Pa. *erect*);—**Qal** *Inf. cstr.* לִתְקֹן Ec 1^{15} (opp. מְעֻוָּת *bent*). **Pi.** *Inf. cstr.* לְתַקֵּן 7^{13} *make straight* (opp. עִוָּה); *Pf.* 3 ms. תִּקֵּן 12^{9} *put straight, arrange in order* (proverbs).

8628 תָּקַע^{67} **vb. thrust, clap, give a blow, blast** (NH *id.*; JAram. תְּקַע *strike, blow horn*; Eth. ተቅዐ: *blow* trumpet);—**Qal** *Pf.* 3 ms. תָּ׳ Gn 31^{25} +, 1 s. וְתָקַעְתִּי Ju 7^{18}, etc.; *Impf.* 3 ms. וַיִּתְקַע 3^{37} +, sf. וַיִּתְקָעֵהוּ Ex 10^{19}, etc.; *Imv.* mpl. תִּקְעוּ Ho 5^{8} +; *Inf. abs.* תָּקוֹעַ Jos 6$^{9.13}$; cstr. לִתְקוֹעַ Ju 7^{20}, תְּקֹעַ Is 18^{3}; *Pt. act.* תֹּקֵעַ Pr 17^{18} +, etc.; *pass.* f. תְּקוּעָה Is 22^{25};—**1.** *thrust, drive*, weapon (acc.) into (ב) a person Ju 3^{21} 4^{21} 2 S 18^{14}, peg into (ב) sthg. Is 22$^{23.25}$ (cf. Ju 4^{21}); hence *pitch* a tent (acc.), i.e. drive its pegs: Gn 31^{25a} Je 6^{3} (+ עַל against, in fig.), acc. om. Gn 31^{25b}; *thrust, drive, beat* (strands of hair together) בַּיָּתֵד Ju 16^{14}, ins. also v^{13} (so 𝔊; cf. GFM[Comm. and PAOS Oct. 1889, 176 ff.]); *thrust, drive* locusts seaward (ה loc.), Ex 10^{19} (J); cf. תָּ׳ בְּ 1 S 31^{10} of fastening bodies to wall, and similarly 1 Ch 10^{10} (but rd. in both הוֹקִיעוּ, √יקע Lag We Dr and mod.). **2.** *give a blast, blow* (Germ. 'stossen'), c. ב of instr. (usu. horn or clarion) Jos 6$^{4.8.9.13.13.16.20}$ (JE), Ju 3^{27} 6^{34} 7$^{18.18.19.20}$ + 14 t., + Nu 10$^{3.4.8.10}$ (P; v. חֲצֹצְרָה), also Ez 7^{14} (v. תָּקוֹעַ infr.); תָּ׳ alone Ju 7^{20} Nu 10^{7} (P; opp. הֵרִיעַ *sound an alarm*), c. acc. תְּרוּעָה v$^{5.6.6}$ (P; v. חֲצֹצְרָה); c. acc. of instrument Ju 7^{22} Ho 5^{8} Is 18^{3} Je 4^{5} 6^{1} 51^{27} Jo 2$^{1.15}$ ψ 81^{4}, + תקעו Jos 6^{9} (Kt; Qr תֹּקְעֵי). **3.** *strike, clap* hands; in triumph, תָּ׳ כַּף עָלֶיךָ Na 3^{19}, תָּ׳ כָף ψ 47^{2}; also (late) of gesture ratifying a bargain, specif. pledging oneself to become surety, only Pr. (all ‖ עָרַב): תָּ׳ כַּפֶּיךָ לַזָּר, תָּ׳ כַּף 17^{18} 22^{26}; abs. 11^{15}. †**Niph.** *Impf.* 3 ms. **1.** יִתָּקַע שׁוֹפָר Am 3^{6} if *a horn be blown*, cf. יִתָּ׳ בְּשׁ׳ Is 27^{13} *it shall be blown* (a blast shall be given) on a horn. **2.** מִי־הוּא לְיָדִי יִתָּקֵעַ׃ Jb 17^{3} *who is there that will strike himself* (i.e. pledge himself) *into my hand?*

†תֵּ֫קַע **n.[m.]** blast of horn;—cstr. בְּתֵ׳ שׁוֹפָר 8629
ψ 150^{3} *with horn-blast*.

†תָּקוֹעַ **n.[m.]** a blast-(wind-) instrument 8619
(si vera l.);—abs. תָּקְעוּ בַתָּ׳ Ez 7^{14} (but del. ב, and treat תָּקוֹעַ as inf. abs., so Co and mod.).

†תְּקוֹעַ **n.pr.loc.** in S. Judah (connex. with 8620
above √ dub.);—Am 1^{1} Je 6^{1} 2 Ch 11^{6}, as 'son' of Ashhur 1 Ch 2^{24} 4^{5}; תְּקוֹעָה 2 S 14^{2}; מִדְבַּר תְּ׳ 2 Ch 20^{20}; 𝔊 Θεκωε (also -ουε); mod. *Tekû'a*, c. 5 m. S. of Bethlehem; v. Rob[BR i. 486 f.] Buhl[G 157 f.] Taylor[Hast. DB Tekoa] GASm[Twelve Proph. i. 74 f.] Dr[Am 1, 1].

†תְּקוֹעִי, תְּקֹעִי **adj.gent.** of foregoing: הַתְּ׳ 8621
2 S 23^{26} = 1 Ch 11^{28} 27^{9}; f. הָאִשָּׁה הַתְּקֹעִית 2 S 14$^{4.9}$; pl. as subst. הַתְּקוֹעִים Ne 3$^{5.27}$.

†[תָּקֵף] **vb. prevail over, overpower** 8630
(late; NH *id.*; Aramaism; Aram. תְּקֵיף, ܬܩܶܦ *be strong*; Nab. תקף *authority*; cf. Nö[ZMG xlvii (1893), 102]; Sab. תקף *overpower* SabDenkm[No. 9, l. 13]; Ar. ثَقِفَ *attain to, overtake, overpower*);—**Qal** *Impf.*: 3 ms. sf. יִתְקְפוֹ Ec 4^{12} (Ges[§ 60 d]) if *one overpower him*, so 3 fs. sf. תִּתְקְפֵהוּ Jb 14^{20}; 3 fs. sf. *id.* 15^{24}.

8633 †תֹּ֫קֶף **n. m.** **power, strength, energy** (Aram. תְּקֵף, תְּקוֹף, ܬܘܩܦܐ);—ת׳ abs. Est 9[29]; cstr. Dn 11[17] *the strength of his whole kingdom;* sf. תָּקְפּוֹ Est 10[2] the deeds *of his power* (+ גְּבוּרָתוֹ, etc.).

8623 †תַּקִּיף **adj.** **mighty** (Aram. תַּקִּיף, ܬܩܝܦ);—c. מִן comp. Ec 6[10].

8449 †II. תֹּר, תּוֹר **n.f.**[Lv 5,7] (**m.**[Lv 14,30]) **turtle-dove** (onomatop.);—abs. תֹּר Gn 15[9] (J; + גּוֹזָל), Je 8[7] (as migratory); as sacrif. offering (RS[Sem. i. 202; 2nd ed. 219, 294]) [usu. בֶּן (בְּנֵי) יוֹנָה] Lv 1[14] 5[7.11] 12[6.8] 14[22.30] 15[14.29] Nu 6[10] (all P; cf. also Gn 15[9]); קוֹל הַתּוֹר Ct 2[12]; sf. תּוֹרֶךָ ψ 74[19] (fig. of י׳'s people).—Vid. Tristr[NHB 201 ff.] Shipley-Cook[Ency. Bib. Dove] Post[Hast. DB Turtle-Dove].—

8447-48 I. תֹּר v. I. תּוֹר. p. 1064

8634 †תַּרְאֲלָה **n.pr.loc.** in Benjamin Jos 18[27]; Θαρεηλα, 𝔊L Θεραλα.

8635 תַּרְבּוּת, תַּרְבִּית v. I. [רבה]. p. 916

7270, 8637 תִּרְגַּל v. רָגַל **Tiph.** p. 920

8638 †[תִּרְגֵּם] **vb.quadril.** **interpret, translate** (As. *targumânu, interpreter* (so also TelAm.), perh. from √רגם, cf. رَجَمَ *conjecture, opine* We[Reste Arab. Heid. 207], v. also Dl[HWB 713] Vollers[ZA xii. 138]; NH=BH; Aram. תַּרְגֵּם, ܬܪܓܡ, Ar. تَرْجَمَ);—*Pt. pass.* מְתֻרְגָּם Ez 4[7].—On *Targum* v. Walker[Hast. DB s. v.].

8639 תַּרְדֵּמָה v. [רדם]. p. 922

8640 †תִּרְהָקָה **n.pr.m.** king of Egypt, of Ethiop. dynasty: 2 K 19[9] = Is 37[9]; Θαρακα; 𝔊L Θαρθακ; =Egypt. *T-h-r-ḳ*, As. *Tarku*, Steindorff[BAS i. 345 f.] COT[2 K 19, 9] Wiedemann[Äg. Gesch. 590 ff.] Brugsch[Egypt under Pharaohs (new ed. 1891), 410 ff.] WMM[Ency. Bib. Tirhakah] Griffith[Hast. DB Id.].

8641-43 תְּרוּמָה, תְּרוּמִיָּה v. רום. תְּרוּעָה v. [רוע]. p. 929

8644 תְּרוּפָה v. רוף. p. 930

8645 †תִּרְזָה **n.f.** a tree, AV *cypress,* RV *holm-tree,* but very dub.: Tr[NHB 338] Post[Hast. DB Cypress]; 𝔙 *ilex,* and so M'Lean[Ency. Bib. Cypress];—abs. ת׳ Is 44[14] (+ אַלּוֹן, ‖ אֲרָזִים).

8646 †תֶּ֫רַח **n.pr.** **1. m.** father of Abraham: (a kind of *ibex* RS[K (1st ed.) 220] (cf. As. *turâḫu,* Ar. تَوْرَخ Nö[ZMG xxxiii (1879), 331], Syr. ܬܪܘܚܐ *capra caucasica*), but against this Nö[ZMG xl (1886), 167]; n.pr.div. Jen[ZA vi. 70]);—ת׳ Gn 11[25.26.27.27.28.31.32.32] Jos 24[2]; תָּרַח Gn 11[24] 1 Ch 1[26]; Θαρρα, 𝔊L Θαρα.—Vid. Selbie[Hast. DB Terah]. **2. loc.** station on Exodus journey Nu 33[27.28]; Ταραθ.

תַּרְחֲנָה v. רחן. p. 934 8647

תַּרְמִית, תרמות, תָּרְמָה v. II. [רמה]. p. 941 8649

†תֹּ֫רֶן **n.m.** **mast** (NH *id.;* √unknown; Hoffm[Ph. Inscr. 27 f.] conj. תארן, from ארן, v. אֹרֶן);— 8650
abs. ת׳, of Tyre as ship Ez 27[5]; ת׳ עַל־רֹאשׁ הָהָר Is 30[17] (‖ נֵס), i.e. a (solitary) standard-pole, flag-staff; sf. תָּרְנָם 33[23] (‖ נֵס, חֲבָלִים).

תַּרְעֵלָה v. [רעל]. p. 947 8653

†תִּרְעָתִים **n.pr.m.pl.** a Kenite family, 8654
1 Ch 2[55]; Θαργαθιμ.

†תְּרָפִים **n. m.**[Zc 10, 2] **pl.** (=pl. majest. Nö 8655
ZMG xlii (1888), 476) a kind of idol, obj. of reverence, and means of divination (√and etymol.-mng. dub., cf. GFM[Hast. DB Teraphim] Say[ZA ii. 195] (citing Neubauer, and As. *tarpû, spectre*), al. √רפא, cf. רְפָאִים);—alw. ת׳:—portable and sts. small Gn 31[19.34.35] (called אֱלֹהִים v[30], all E), but in size and shape like a man 1 S 19[13.16]; in household shrine (v. also l. c.) Ju 17[5] (+ אֵפוֹד, cf. GFM[Ju]), 18[14.17] (both + אֵפוֹד, פֶּסֶל, מַסֵּכָה), cf. v[20] (om. מַסֵּכָה), Ho 3[4] (+ א׳ + זֶבַח, מַצֵּבָה); condemned 1 S 15[23] 2 K 23[24] (+ גִּלֻּלִים); used in divining (by king of Bab.), שָׁאַל בַּת׳ Ez 21[26] (+ קִלְקַל בַּחִצִּים, רָאָה בַּכָּבֵד); as giving empty oracles Zc 10[2] (‖ הַקּוֹסְמִים).—Vid. GFM[l. c.] Now[Arch. ii. 23] Sta[Bib. Theol. d. A. T. s. v.].

תִּרְצָה v. רצה. p. 953 8656

†תֶּ֫רֶשׁ **n.pr.m.** eunuch at court of Ahasuerus 8657
(Scheft[53] cp. OIran. *tarša, 'Begierde,'* used as n.pr. in NPers.);—Est 2[21] 6[2]; Θαρ(ρ)ας.

†I. תַּרְשִׁישׁ **n.m.** a precious stone, perhaps 8658
yellow jasper, or other gold-coloured stone (𝔊 Ex 28[20] 39[13] χρυσόλιθος, so Jos[Ant. iii. 7, 5 [168]], v. Petrie[Hast. DB Stones, Precious] Myres[Ency. Bib. Id. § 17] Dr[Dn 10, 6]);—ת׳ כְּעֵין Ez 1[6]; כְּעֵין אֶבֶן ת׳ 10[9]; in list of gems 28[13] Ex 28[20] 39[13]; in sim. of resplendent body Dn 10[6], cf. Ct 5[14].

†II. תַּרְשִׁישׁ **n.pr.** **1. loc.** a distant port, 8659
site not certainly known (Wkl[Altor. Forsch. v. 445]); most *Tartessus* in Spain Thes (after older authorities) Ges[Is i. 719] Mey[Gesch. d. Alt. i, § 281]; other views are: *Tyrseni* (Etruscans) in Italy, WMM[Hast. DB Tarshish], *Phoenicia* Renouf[PSBA xvi. 134 ff.], *Sardinia* Hal[RÉJ xiii. 14]; v. also Ency. Bib.[Tarshish];—

Tarshish, 𝔊 usu. Θαρσ(ε)ις (Is 23[1.14] Καρχήδων=*Carthage*);—esp. in phr.′אֳנִיּוֹת ת *Tarshish-ships* (large, sea-going vessels, *fit* to ply to Tarshish) Is 2[16] (𝔊 πλοῖον θαλάσσης), 23[1.14] 60[9] Ez 27[25] 1 K 22[49], ‖ 2 Ch 20[36.37] (where the ships *go to* ′ת); ′אֳנִי ת 1 K 10[22.22] ‖ 2 Ch 9[21] (אֳנִיּוֹת), + v[21] (ships *go to* ′ת); ′ת alone Is 23[6] Jon 1[3.3] 4[2] (all c. ה loc.), Gn 10[4] ‖ 1 Ch 1[7] (erron. ה loc.), Is 66[19] ψ 72[10] Jon 1[3]; ′בַּת־ת Is 23[10]; trading-port Ez 27[12] 38[13], whence comes silver Je 10[9]. **2. m. a.** in Benjamin 1 Ch 7[10]. **b.** Persian noble Est 1[14]; expl. by Scheft[53] as OIran. *tr̥šus*, ‘*der Gierige*.’

8660 **†תִּרְשָׁתָא n.m.** Tirshathâ, title of Persian governor in Judaea, acc. to Mey[Entstehung d. Jud. 194] al.=*His Excellency* (read *Tarshathâ*) otherwise Lag[Symm. i. 60 (cf. Arm. Stud. §§ 280, 1680)].—As Mey[l.c.], Scheft[93 f.] (*taršta, the feared, revered*) Moss[Hast. DB Tirshatha] Che[Ency. Bib. ID.]; —′הַתּ Ezr 2[63] = Ne 7[65], Ne 7[69] (Baer Gi; v[70] van d. H.); of Nehemiah Ne 8[9] 10[1].

8661 **†תַּרְתָּן n.m.** title of As. general=**field-marshal** (loan-word from As. *tartânu, turtânu* Dl[WB 716] Tiele[Gesch. 495 f.] Pinches[Hast. DB Tartan] Johns[Ency. Bib. ID.]);—Is 20[1] 2 K 18[17] (+ רַב־שָׁקֵה, רַב־סָרִיס); only this last in ‖ Is 36[2]).

8662 **†תַּרְתָּק n.pr.div.** of הָעַוִּים, 2 K 17[31]; Θαρθακ; not identified, cf. Pinches[Hast. DB Tartak].

8667-68 **תְּשׂוּמֶת** v. I. שׂום. **[תְּשֻׁאָה]** v. II. שׁוא. p. 448

8453, 8664 **תּשָׁב** v. תּוֹשָׁב sub ישׁב. **תִּשְׁבִּי** v. שׁבה. p. 444, 986

8665-66 **תַּשְׁבֵּץ** v. [שׁבץ]. **[תְּשׁוּבָה]** v. שׁוב. p. 990, 1000

8663 **תשוה** Jb 30[22] v. [תְּשֻׁאָה] sub II. שׁוא. p. 996

8668 **תְּשֻׁעָה, תְּשׁוּעָה** v. ישׁע. p. 448

8669 **תְּשׁוּקָה** v. III. שׁוק. p. 1003

8454, 8670 **תְּשׁוּרָה** v. I. שׁור. **תֻּשִׁיָּה** v. תּוּשִׁיָּה sub ישׁה. p. 444, 1003

תִּשְׁעָה, תֵּשַׁע₅₈ **n.m. et. f.** a nine, nonad 8672
(NH=BH; As. *tišit* (fem.), *nine, tešû, ninth;* Sab. תסעת *nine*, תסעי *ninety* Hom[Chr 48]; Lihy. תסע DHM[Ep. Denkm. Ar. 52], Ar. تِسْعٌ, Eth. **ተስዑ፡** Aram. תְּשַׁע, ܬܫܥ, Nab. Palm. תשע Lzb[388], Mand. (א for ע; sts. ע pref.) תשא, עשתא Nö[M 188], all *nine*);—**m.** c. **n.f.** abs. תֵּשַׁע Dt 3[11] + 20 t., cstr. תְּשַׁע Ju 4[3] + 18 t.; **f.** c. **n.m.** abs. תִּשְׁעָה 2 S 24[8] + 13 t., cstr. תִּשְׁעַת Jos 13[7] + 2 t. (these include 9 + 10 = 19);—*nine* (Hex chiefly P); **1.** no other num.: **a.** before n.pl. תֵּשַׁע אַמּוֹת Dt 3[11], ′ת שָׁנִים 2 K 17[1] Gn 11[19], ′ת הַיָּדוֹת Ne 11[1], תִּשְׁעָה חֳדָשִׁים 2 S 24[8], תִּשְׁעַת הַשְּׁבָטִים Jos 13[7] (JE?), cf. 14[2] Nu 34[13] (both P); after n.pl. עָרִים תֵּשַׁע Jos 15[44.51] 21[16] (all P), פָּרִים תִּשְׁעָה Nu 29[26] (P); n. om. 1 Ch 3[8]. **b.** =ordin. בְּתִשְׁעָה לַחֹדֶשׁ 2 K 25[3] + 3 t. *on the ninth* (day) *of the month;* שְׁנַת־תֵּשַׁע לְ 18[10] *the ninth year of.* **2.** 9 + 10 = 19, c. **n.f.** תְּשַׁע־עֶשְׂרֵה שָׁנָה Gn 11[25], עָרִים תְּשַׁע־עֶשְׂרֵה Jos 19[38] (both P), as ordinal שְׁנַת תְּשַׁע־עֶשְׂרֵה שָׁנָה לְ 2 K 25[8] ‖ Je 52[12]; c. **n.m.** תִּשְׁעָה עָשָׂר אִישׁ 2 S 2[30], cf. (as ordin., גּוֹרָל om.) 1 Ch 24[16] 25[26]. **3.** 900 = תְּשַׁע מֵאוֹת Ju 4[3] + 14 t. **4.** c. tens (20, 30, etc.): ′ת foll. 2 K 14[2] + 10 t., precedes Gn 11[24] + 6 t., cf. Kö[ii. 1. 215 ff.]

תְּשִׁיעִי, תְּשִׁעִי m. תְּשִׁיעִית f. adj. num. 8671
ord.₁₈ ninth;—בַּיּוֹם הַתְּשִׁיעִי Nu 7[60], ′הַתּ of series of men 1 Ch 12[12] 27[12], of lot 24[11] 25[16]; ′הַחֹדֶשׁ הַתּ Je 36[9.32] Zc 7[1] 1 Ch 27[12] Ezr 10[9], ′ח om. Hg 2[10.18]; הַשָּׁנָה הַתְּשִׁיעִית Lv 25[22] + 3 t., ′בִּשְׁנַת הַתּ (Ges[§ 134 p]) 2 K 17[6] 25[1].

תִּשְׁעִים₂₀ **n. indecl.** ninety (archaic pl., 8673
DHM[ZMG xxxvii (1883). 9 f.] Prät[BAS i. 376], but cf. Ges[§ 97 f.]);—before n. sg.: שָׁנָה Gn 5[9] 17[17] +, אַמָּה Ez 41[12], יוֹם Ez 4[5.9]; less oft. after n.pl. אֵילִים Ezr 8[35], cf. Dn 12[11]; in combination, ′ת precedes units 1 S 4[15] + 7 t.; foll. Gn 5[17.30]; ′ת foll. 100 Ez 4[5.9] + 4 t.

BIBLICAL ARAMAIC

[Dn 2^{4b}–7^{28}; Ezr 4^{8}–6^{18}, 7^{12-26}; Je 10^{11}; Gn $31^{47a\beta}$.]

NOTE.—In the case of words common to Biblical Aramaic and Biblical Hebrew the etymological matter already given with the Hebrew words is not repeated here. The sign ‡ is prefixed to all words peculiar to the Biblical Aramaic. In other cases, except where 𝔗 or Syr. is mentioned alone, it may be understood that the words occur also in the Aramaic of the Targums and in Syriac, even when this is not expressly stated.

2 [אָב] v. אבה. below

3, 4 †[אֵב K[§ 55,5 a) 2]] **n.m. fruit** (BH; √אבב);—
sf. 3 ms. אִנְבֵּהּ (K[§ 11, 4 b)]) Dn $4^{9.11.18}$.

6, 7 †[אֲבַד] **vb. perish** (BH);—**Pe.** *Impf.*
3 mpl. יֵאבַדוּ (not ־וּן v. K[§ 26, 1]) Je 10^{11} *they shall perish*, pass away. **Haph.** (OAram. האבד Lzb[205] Cooke[189]) *destroy*: *Impf.* 2 ms. אַל־תְּהוֹבֵד (K[§ 41 c]) Dn 2^{24} (c. לְ pers.); 3 mpl. יְהוֹבְדוּן v[18] (indef. subj.; acc. pers.); *Inf.* לְהוֹבָדָא v[12.24] (both c. לְ pers.), ־דָה 7^{26} (abs.). **Hoph.** (K[§ 41 c] W[CG 225]) *be destroyed*: *Pf.* 3 ms. הוּבַד 7^{11}.

אבה (assumed as √ of foll.; v. p. 3).

2 †[אַב D[§ 40. 4], אַבָא Id[ib] Me[Chr 165]] **n.m. father**
1 (BH אָב);—**1.** lit. *father*, sf. אֲבִי Dn 5^{13} (v. Behrm Marti), אֲבוּךְ (K[§ 53, 2 a]) v[11.11.11.18] אֲבוּהִי v[2]. **2.** pl. *fathers, ancestors* [אֲבָהָן D[l. c.]], sf. אֲבָהָתִי 2^{23} (Baer ־תַי, but v. K[§ 53, 1]), אֲבָהָתָךְ Ezr 4^{15}, ־תָנָא (Str. ־תַּנָא) 5^{12}.

68, 69 †אֶבֶן **n.f.** [Dn 2, 34] **stone** (BH *id.*);—abs. א׳ Dn 2^{34}+; emph. אַבְנָא v[35];—**1.** *a* (*the*) *stone* Dn $2^{34.35.45}$ 6^{18}. **2.** *stone*, material of idols $5^{4.23}$; of buildings Ezr 5^{8} 6^{4}.

104 †אִגְּרָה (K[§ 50, 3]) **n.f. letter-missive** (late
107 BH אִגֶּרֶת, OAram. אגרת, Palm. אגרתא Lzb[207]);—abs. א׳ Ezr 4^{8} (van d. H. ־רָא); emph. אִגַּרְתָּא 4^{11} 5^{6}.

אֱדַיִן [57] **adv. then, thereupon** (so Eg. Aram. 116
(S-C[Pap. H 1, J 1]), not 𝔗: the usu. Aram. forms are הֵידֵין, ܗܝܕܝܢ, Mand. האידין (Nö[M 207]); from [אֱדַי] = BH אֲזַי (v. אָז) + determ. affix *n* (as in דִּכֵּן, תַּמָּן; in Sab. = post-pos. art., Hom[Chr. § 57]: cf. W[CG 115]), Nö[GGA 1884, 1020]: אֱזַי, [אֱדַי], prob. from same demonstr. √ as זְה, דָּא, דִּי, etc., إِذْ, إِذَا *lo*, إِذًا *well then, in that case*, Eth. ማእዜ: *when?* ይእዜ: *now* (Di[Lex. 197, 1072]), Syr. ܕܶܝܢ (enclitic) *but*);—*then, thereupon*, Dn $2^{15.17.19.25.48}$ 3^{24}+, Ezr $4^{9.23}$ $5^{4.9}$+ (alw., exc. Ezr 5^{5}, at beg. of sentence, introducing new stage of narrative with some emph.); so c. בְּ, בֵּאדַיִן (3 t. Ezr., 26 t. Dn) Dn $2^{14.35.46}$ $3^{3.13.19.21.26}$, etc., Ezr 4^{24} 5^{2} 6^{1}; מִן־אֱדַיִן *from that time* †Ezr 5^{16}.

†אֲדָר (K[§ 57 a]) **n. pr.** 12th month (BH 143-44
id.);—Ezr 6^{15}.

†[אִדַּר K[§ 59 c)]] **n.m. threshing-floor** (𝔗 *id.*, 147
Syr. ܐܶܕܪܳܐ, cf. Chr-Pal. Schulth[Lex. 3]; hence Ar. أَنْدَر as loan-word Frä[136]; conj. on etym. Lag[Ges. Abh. 10] Hoffm[LCB 1882, 320] Jen[ZA vii (1892). 216]);—pl. cstr. אִדְּרֵי־קַיִט Dn 2^{35}.

‡†[אֲדַרְגָּזַר] **n.m. counsellor** (Pers. loan- 148
word = *andarzaghar* Nö[COT Dn 3, 2, Tabari 462] Andr[M 51]* Str[42]* Dr Scheft[ii. 57]; Mey[Entst. J. 25] questions, and thinks military title);—pl. emph. אֲדַרְגָּזְרַיָּא Dn $3^{2.3}$.

149 †אַדְרַזְדָּא **adv.** correctly, exactly (acc. to
Haug[JBW 1853, 152 f.] Scheft[68 f.] from Zend *derez, make
firm*, whence Skr. ptcp. pass. *dṛdha, firm, sure,
suitable*, Zend *dereśta, holding firm*, Pers. *durust,*
230 *whole, complete, correct*; > Nö[KAT² 617] from אָזְדָּא,
q.v.);—Ezr 7[23] יִתְעֲבֵד א׳.

153 אֶדְרָע v. דרע.

אזה (√of foll.; v. BH אוֹת, II. אוה).

852 †[אָת] **n.m.**[Dn 3, 33] sign (alw. as wrought by
God, and alw. c. תמהין *wonders*);—pl. abs. אָתִין
Dn 6[28]; emph. אָתַיָּא 3[32]; sf. אָתוֹהִי v[33].

אול (√of following, BH II. אול, איל).

363 †אִילָן (D[138]) **n.m.**[Dn 4, 7] tree (𝔗 אִילָן, Syr.
ܐܝܠܢܐ; cf. BH אֵלָה, אֵלוֹן, p. 18);—abs. א׳ Dn 4[7];
emph. ־נָא v[8.11.17.20.23].

228 †[אזא] **vb.** make hot, heat (𝔗 *id.* [rare];
cf. Ar. أَزَّ *kindle, burn*);—**Pe.** *Inf.* לְמֵזֵא (K[§ 11, 3b])
Dn 3[19] (ל acc.), sf. לְמֵזְיֵהּ v[19]; *Pt. pass.* אֵזֵה
(K[§ 15e]) v[22].

230 †אַזְדָּא (so Gi, with most MSS.; Baer אָזְדָּא)
adj. sure, assured (Pers. *azda*, Skr. *addhâ*,
'certain' (Kern[ZDMG 1869, 220]); so first Nö[KAT² 617];
confirmed now by Eg. Aram. (RÉS[361, B3]) הן אזד
יתעבד מן if it is made certain (certified) by, etc.;
> 𝔊 Ki AV al. (v. Thes) as vb. *is gone*, or (אָזְדָּא)
is going, from Talm. אֲזַד (=אֲזַל) *go away* (Levy
NHWB[i. 50]); so Scheft[MGWJ 1903, 310] from Zend **azda*
'gone,' ptcp. pass. of *azaiti* 'go');—Dn 2[5] מִלְּתָא
דִּי־אַזְדָּא מִנִּי מִלְּתָא v[8], מִנִּי אַזְדָּא the word is *assured*
on my part (the thing is fully resolved upon by
me: cf. 𝔖 ܩܝܡܐ; IE קִיְּמָא וְאֱמֶת); + 3[14] (v. צְדָא).

235-36 †אֲזַל **vb.** go, go off (BH [rare]);—**Pe.**
Pf. 3 ms. א׳ Dn 2[24] + (אֲזַל v[17] 6[20]); 3 pl. אֲזַלוּ Ezr
4[23]; 1 pl. אֲזַלְנָא 5[8]; *Imv.* ms. (אֱזֶל־אֲחֵת) v[15] (for
אֱזֶל K[§§ 15 e); 38, 1 c)]);—**1.** *go, go off*, c. ל loc. Dn 2[17]
6[19.20] Ezr 4[23] (+ על pers.), 5[8]; *go* and say Dn 2[24],
go (and) put Ezr 5[15].

239, 3976 ## און (√of following; BH II. און, מֹאזְנַיִם).

3977 †מֹאזְנֵא (Baer Gi Str) **n.m.emph.** scale,
balance (cf. also Mand. מוזאניא Nö[M148], Eg.
Aram. מוזנא S-C[G24], Chr-Pal. ܡܘܙܢܐ Schulth
Lex.[5] Nö[BSW 56] Jacob[ZAW xxii (1902), 90]);—Dn 5[27] (van
d. H. du. emph. מֹאזַנְיָא, v. K[§ 51, 1, Anm.] M[33*]).

אחד (√of following; v. BH אֶחָד). 259

†חַד **adj.** one, a;—ms. ח׳ Dn 2[31] +; fs. חֲדָה 2298
Ezr 4[8] +;—**1.** *one* side Dn 7[5]; n. om. 6[3]; חֲדָה
2[9] = *one and invariable (inevitable)*; כַּחֲדָה v[35]
as one, altogether (so S-C[K3] 𝔗, and late BH
כְּאֶחָד Ezr 2[64] +); = ordinal, שְׁנַת חֲדָה *first year*
7[1] Ezr 5[13] 6[3]; ח׳ = *a certain one* (τινά) Dn 7[16]
(c. מִן partit.). **2.** *a* (indef. art.) c. subst.
Dn 2[31] 6[18] 4[16] (v. שָׁעָה), Ezr 4[8] 6[2], חַד שִׁבְעָה Dn
3[19] = *seven-fold* (as Syr.: Nö[§ 241] PS[1194]; cf. Ex 16[5]
𝔖), v. K[§ 66, 2].

אחה (assumed as √of foll.; cf. BH אָח 251
p. 26).

†[אַח] **n. m.** brother;—pl. sf. אחיך Kt 252
(? יָךְ־ K[§ 53, 2, Anm. b)]), אַחָךְ Qr (K[§ 63]) Ezr 7[18] *thy
brethren*, i.e. fellows, associates.

[אַחֲוָיָה] v. [חוה]. [אֲחִידָה] v. חוד. 263, 280

†אַחְמְתָא (orig. ־תָן or ־תָנָא Nö in Streck 307
ZA[15, 368]) **n.pr.loc.** Ecbatana, Ezr 6[2]; capital of
Media, captured by Cyrus (B.C. 550), and then
summer residence of Pers. kings; mod. همدان
Ḥamadân, Spieg[244] Margoliouth[Hast. DB Achmetha],
esp. Brugsch[Reise n. Persien (1862), i. 360-392] (OMed. *Agma-
tana* Dl[Calwer Bib. Lex.]; OPers. *Hañgmatâna* (=*place
of assembling*) Spieg[l. c.], Bab. *Agam(a)tanu*
Beh[60], Bez[p. 26], etc.; Ἀγβάτανα Herod[i. 98]; 𝔊
Ἐκβάτανα 2 Macc 9[3] +; Mey[Gesch. d. Alt. i. § 485] Streck
l. c. 367 f.).

†[אחר] pl. c. אַחֲרֵי, **prep.** after (Cappad. 311
and Eg. Aram. אחר *afterwards* (Lzb[Eph. i. 361] S-C
Pap. C 8), prob. Nab. אחר *after* (Lzb[212] SAC[16]);
Eg. Aram. אחריכם (S-C[Pap. C 8+]); 𝔗 (sts.) אֲחוֹרֵי;
BH אַחַר);—אַחֲרֵי דְנָה *after this* Dn 2[29.45]; c. sf. 310
אַחֲרֵיהֹן 7[24]. Usu. Aram. syn. בָּאתַר, q. v. p. 1083 870

†אָחֳרִי **adj. f.** another: v. אָחֳרָן. below 317, 321

†אחרין Dn 4[5] Kt, וְעַד אחרין עַל קָדָמַי דָּנִיֵּאל; 318
very dub. (v. Comm.); usu. *and unto the last*
(=*at last*) came in, etc.; but word in this sense
unknown: Qr אָחֳרֵין; read perh. (Bev) וְעַד אָחֳרָן
(or ? Kt אַחֲרֵין: cf. ܐܚܪܝܢ) and yet *another* came
in before me.

†אַחֲרִית **n.f. cstr.** end (Hebraism; so (cf. 320
Jacob[ZAW, 1902, 84-6]) Chr-Pal., Schulth[6]);—Dn 2[28]
בְּאַ׳ יוֹמַיָּא (from BH בְּאַ׳ הַיָּמִים p. 31[a]).

†אָחֳרָן **adj. m.** another (Eg. Aram. אחרן 321
S-C[D11+]; Nab. Palm. *id.* (Lzb[212]); 𝔗 אוֹחֲרָן; cf.

Syr. ܐܚܪܢܐ);—Dn 2[11.44] 3[29] 4[5] Kt 5[17] 7[24]. The **f.** in use is אָחֳרִי (Eg. Aram. אחרה, RÉS[246]; 𝔗 Talm. אוֹחְרִי (D[§20.5]); cf. K[§61.5] M[§87d] Nö[Beitr.51]), Dn 2[39] מַלְכוּ א׳, v[39] 7[5.6.8.20].

324 †[אֲחַשְׁדַּרְפְּנִין] **n.m.pl. satraps** (BH ־נִים; cf. M[52*]);—emph. ־נַיָּא Dn 3[2.3.27] 6[2.3.4.5.7.8].

363 אִילָן v. אול. p. 1079

574 †[אֵימְתָן D[§35,16]] **adj.** terrible (𝔗 אֵימְתָן, fr.
367 אֵימְתָא = BH אֵימָה, q.v., √אים);—fs. abs. אֵימְתָנִי (K[§61,5]) Dn 7[7] (on form v. Prät[ZMG lvi (1902), 156] Nö[BSSW 51, Anm. 3]).

383 †אִיתַי (Baer אִתַי, exc. bef. sf., v. Baer[Dn 2, 10]) **part.** there is, are ... (prop. a **subst.** foll. by a gen., v. BH יֵשׁ: Eg. Aram. איתי RÉS[361], S-C[Pap.], Nab. איתי, Palm. אית, 𝔗 Talm. אִית (Dalm[§44,4]), Syr. ܐܝܬ, Sam. ⴰⴻⵜ, Mand. עית, אית
3426 (Nö[M §§ 213. 272]): v. further BH יֵשׁ);—אִיתַי Dn 2[10], sf. אִיתָיךְ 2[26] Kt (Qr אִיתָךְ K[§53, 2 b]), אִיתוֹהִי 2[11], איתינא Kt (i.e. prob. אִיתַיְנָא: K[l. c.]), Qr אִיתָנָא 3[18], אִיתֵיכוֹן v[14.15];—*there is (are)* ..., abs. Dn 2[28] אִיתַי אֱלָהּ בִּשְׁמַיָּא *there is* a God in heaven, v[30] not by wisdom דִּי־אִיתַי בִּי that *is* in me, 3[12] 5[11]; sq. ptcp. or adj. 2[26] הַאִיתָיךְ כָּהֵל *art* thou able ...? 3[15.17]; sq. דִּי, Ezr 5[17] הֵן אִיתַי דִּי if *it is that* ... With neg. לָא אִיתַי (so S-C[D10+]; 𝔗 Syr. Mand. לֵית, ܠܝܬ, Zenj. sf. לישה (Cooke[184]); cf. sub BH יֵשׁ) Dn 2[10] ... לָא אִיתַי אֱנָשׁ דִּי, 3[29] 4[32]; after the subj. 2[11a] 3[25] וַחֲבָל לָא א׳ בְּהוֹן, Ezr 4[16]; sq. ptcp. or adj. Dn 3[14.18]; with pleon. sf., 2[11] דִּי מְדָרְהוֹן עִם־בִּשְׂרָא לָא אִיתוֹהִי.

398-99 †[אֲכַל] **vb.** eat, devour (BH);—**Pe.** *Pf.* 3 mpl. אֲכַלוּ Dn 3[8] 6[25]; *Impf.* 3 ms. יֵאכֻל 4[30]; 3 fs. תֵּאכֻל 7[23]; *Imv.* fs. אֲכֻלִי v[5]; *Pt.* fs. אָכְלָה v[7.19];—**1.** *eat*, of beast, Dn 4[30] (acc. rei). **2.** *devour*, of beast in vision, 7[5] (acc. rei), abs. v[7.19]; hence fig. of kingdom, *devour*, *devastate*, v[23] (acc. of earth). **3.** in phr. א׳ קַרְצֵיהוֹן 3[8] *eat their pieces*, i.e. slander them, cf. 6[25] (v. קְרַץ).

409 †אַל **adv.** of prohibition, do not ..., let
408 not ..., sq. impf. (=BH I. אַל; Zenj. אל (Had[22.23.29]) Cooke[160 f.]; cf. Pehlevi (Nö[GGA, 1884, 1016]); not 𝔗 Syr.);—Dn 2[24] אַל־תְּהוֹבֵד, 4[16] 5[10].

412 †אֵל **demonstr.pron. pl.** these (v. אֵלֶּה infr.), Ezr 5[15] Qr (Kt אֵלֶּה).

†אֱלָהּ [94] **n.m.** god, God (=BH אֱלֹהַּ (p. 43), 426, 433
v. also √I. אלה p. 41);—א׳ abs. Dn 2[28]+, cstr. 421
v[18]+; emph. אֱלָהָא v[20]+; sf. אֱלָהִי 6[23], ־הָךְ Ezr 9[14]+, ־הֵהּ Dn 6[6]+, ־הֲהֹם Ezr 5[5] 7[16], ־הֲהוֹן Dn 3[28.28.29], ־הֲכֹם Ezr 7[17], etc.; pl. abs. אֱלָהִין Dn 2[11]+, emph. ־הַיָּא Je 10[11], cstr. ־הֵי Dn 5[4.23], sf. ־הַי 3[14], etc. [c. pref. לֵאלָהָא Dn 5[23], לֵאלָהָיךְ 3[14], etc.; but not in sg. abs. or cstr., e.g. לֶאֱלָהּ Ezr 5[12], etc.];—**1.** *god*, in gen. Dn 6[8.13]; heathen deities Je 10[11] Dn 2[11] 3[15]+15 t. Dn (made of gold, etc. 5[4.23]), + בַּר־אֱלָהִין 3[25] (v. בַּר). **2.** [73] *God* (of Isr.), Dn 2[28] Ezr 5[2]+; phr. אֱלָהּ יִשׂ׳ Ezr 5[1] 6[14] 7[15]; אֱ׳ יְרוּשְׁלֶם 7[19]; א׳ אֲבָהָתִי Dn 2[23]; א׳ שְׁמַיָּא Ezr 5[11] (+וְאַרְעָא), v[12] 6[9.10] Dn 2[18.19]+6 t. (v. שְׁמַיִן **2 a**); א׳ רַב Dn 2[45]; א׳ אֱלָהִין v[47]; אֱלָהָא עִלָּיָא 3[26.32] 5[18.21]; א׳ חַיָּא 6[21.27]; also בֵּית אֱלָהָא 5[3] Ezr 4[24] 5[2]+16 t. Ezr; עֲבִידַת א׳ Ezr 6[18].

†אֵלֶּה **demonstr. pron. pl.** these (Nab. 429
אלה (Lzb[264] Cooke[241]), Cappad. and Eg. Aram. אלה (Lzb[Eph. i. 323] RÉS[361 A 3] S-C[Pap. E 13, K 13]): prob. therefore not, as used to be supposed, a Hebraism, but a peculiarity of the dialects of Je 10[11] and of Ezr (in which the usu. Aram. form אִלֵּין does not occur): v. further אִלֵּין);—*these*, Je 10[11] 459
Ezr 5[15] Kt.

†אֲלוּ **interj.** lo! (der. uncertain: usu. 431
regarded as by-form of אֲרוּ, q.v.; cf. Eg. Aram. 718
הלו, Cooke[No. 73], RÉS[492 B] = S-C[M b]);—וַאֲלוּ Dn 2[31], חָזֵה הֲוַיְת וַאֲלוּ, 4[7.10] 7[8], always in description of a vision.

†אִלֵּין (אִלֵּן Dn 2[44] 6[7]) **demonstr.pron.pl.** 459
these (pl. of דְּנָה, q.v.: Palm. אלן (Lzb[264] Eph. 1836
i. 343. 345 Cooke[26]); 𝔗 אִילֵין; Mand. עלין (Nö[M 89 f.]); Talm. (with emph. *hâ* prefixed, W[CG 109]) הָאִלֵּין: v. further sub BH אֵלֶּה, and add Eg. Aram. אלו 428
Cooke[26]);—*these*, only Dn: Dn 2[40] דִּי מְרָעַע כָּל־, אֲחַשְׁדַּרְפְּנַיָּא אִלֵּין 6[3], כָּל־אִלֵּין מַלְכְוָתָא, v[44] אִלֵּין (so v.[7]), אִלֵּין חֵיוָתָא 7[17]. p. 1088

†אִלֵּךְ **demonstr. pron. pl.** these (pl. 479
of דֵּךְ, q. v.: Eg. Aram. אלך (Cooke[207] RÉS[361 B] 1791
S-C[Pap. E6+]): with *hâ* prefixed, OSyr. ܗܠܟܘܢ, f. ܗܠܟܝܢ, Nö[§ 67, M § 82] Burkitt[Evang. da-Mepharreshe ii. 42], Chr-Pal. ܗܠܟܘܢ (m. and f.) Schw[Idiot. 24]; cf. Ar. أُولَاكَ, Eth. አልክ: Di[Lex. 1057]: the demonst. affix ךְ as in דֵּךְ, ذَاكَ, etc.; W[CG 110]);—*these*, גֻּבְרַיָּא אִלֵּךְ *these men*, Dn 3[12.13.21.22.23.27] 6[6.12.16.25] Ezr 4[21] 6[8b]; also Ezr 5[9] 6[8a].

505-06 †אֲלַף n.m. 1,000 (=BH II. אֶלֶף);—abs. 'א
(n. pers. precedes) Dn 5[1]; n. om., emph. אַלְפָּא v[1]
the thousand (just mentioned); cstr.+pl.abs. אֶלֶף
אַלְפִּים Dn 7[10] *a thousand thousands* (< Qr אַלְפִין
K[§51,2]).

520-21 †[אַמָּה K[§51,2, Anm. 2]] n.f.[Dn 3,1] cubit (=BH
id.; v. p. 52; Eg. Aram. (pl.) אמן RÉS[246] S-C
[C44]);—pl. אַמִּין (so 𝔗 Syr.) Dn 3[1.1] Ezr 6[3.3].

523-24 †אֻמָּה n.f. nation (BH *id.*, late);—abs. 'א
Dn 3[29]; pl. emph. אֻמַּיָּא 3[4.7.31] 5[19] 6[26] 7[14] Ezr 4[10].

539-40 †[אֲמַן] vb. Haph. trust (BH);—*Pf.*
3 ms. הֵימִן בֵּאלָהֵהּ Dn 6[24]; *Pt. pass.* מְהֵימַן *trusty,
trustworthy*, of pers. 6[5], interpretation 2[45].

560 אמר[71] vb. say, tell, command (BH
559 אָמַר);—Pe. *Pf.* 3 ms. 'א Dn 2[12]+, אֲמַר, 7[1]; 3 fs.
אֲמַרְנָא 5[10] (K[§38,1a]); 1 s. אַמְרֵת 4[5]; 1 pl. אֲמַרְנָא
5[4.9], etc.; *Impf.* 3 ms. יֵאמַר (K[§41]) 2[7]+; 2 mpl.
תֵּאמְרוּן Je 10[11], etc.; *Imv.* ms. אֱמַר 2[4]+; mpl.
אֱמַרוּ 2[9]; *Inf.* לְמֵאמַר v[9], לְמֵמַר Ezr 5[11] (K[§41a]);
Pt. אָמַר Dn 2[5]+oft., pl. אָמְרִין 3[4] Ezr 5[3]+;—1.
say (oft. in phr. *answer and say*): sq. orat. rect.
(only), Dn 2[7.10]+13 t. Dn, Ezr 5[11]; +לְ pers.
Dn 2[5] 3[14]+14 t. Dn [pl. c. indef. subj. for pass.
4[28]], Ezr 5[15]; +קֳדָם pers. Dn 2[9] 5[17] 6[13.14]; +כֵּן 4[11]
7[23], כֵּן c. לְ pers. Ezr 5[3] Dn 2[24.25] 6[7], cf. 7[5]; +כְּנֵמָא
c. לְ pers. Ezr 5[4.9]; +כִּדְנָה c. לְ pers. Je 10[11]; sq.
acc. rei+עַל pers. against whom Dn 3[29]. **2.**
relate, tell: sq. acc. rei Dn 4[6.15] 7[1], +לְ pers.
2[4.9.7] 7[16] (acc. rei om.), +קֳדָם pers. 2[36] 4[4.5]. **3.**
command: sq. inf. 2[12.46]+6 t. Dn; sq. vb. fin.
5[29] 6[17.25]; sq. לְ pers.+or. rect. 3[4] [pl. c. indef.
subj., for pass., K[§76e], so 4[23]].

3983 †מֵאמַר n.[m.] word;—cstr. Dn 4[14] Ezr 6[9].

563 †[אִמַּר] n.m. lamb (As. *immeru* (also=
child; immertu, girl; conj. as to etym. Dl
[Prol. 28] Jen [ZMG xliii (1889), 203; ZA vii. 216] Schwally[Idiot. 114]),
𝔗 אִמְּרָא; Syr. ܐܶܡܪܳܐ, Pun. אמר, Palm. pl. emph.
אמריא Lzb[220] Cooke[Inscr. 120. 337]; Ar. أَمَّرٌ (loan-
word? cf. Frä[107], but also DHM[VOJ i. 24]));—pl.
אִמְּרִין, *lambs*, as sacrif. victims Ezr 6[9.17] 7[17].

4 אִנְבֵּהּ v. אֵב. p. 1078

576 †אֲנָא Dn 2[8] Ezr 6[12] 7[21] in common edd.:
576 v. אֲנָה. below

576, 589 †אֲנָה pr. 1 s. I (=Heb. אֲנִי, q.v.: Zenj.
Cilic. Eg. Aram. אנה (Cooke[182.194.202]; S-C[oft.]),
Nab אנה··· (Lzb[221]); 𝔗 אנא, Syr. ܐܶܢܳܐ);—*I*, Dn 2[30]
4[6.27] 5[16], before a ptcp. 3[25] 4[34], after a ptcp.
(K[§76, 2b]) 2[8] מִן־יַצִּיב יָדַע אֲנָה, v[23] 4[4]; sq. a n.pr.
4[1] אֲנָה נבוכדנצר שְׁלֵה הֲוֵית, v[15.34] 7[15] Ezr 6[12] 7[21],
as nom. pendens, Dn 4[31] 7[28]; emphasizing a sf.
(K[§87,3]) 7[15] Ezr 7[21] (cf. S-C[B8, J12, K3.5]).

†אִנּוּן pr. 3 mpl. they, those (pl. of הוּא: 581
𝔗 אִינּוּן, f. אִינִּין, e.g. Gn 3[7] 6[2]; Syr. ܗܶܢܽܘܢ, ܐܶܢܽܘܢ,
f. ܗܶܢܶܝܢ, ܐܶܢܶܝܢ; Talm. אִינְהוּ, אִינְהִי, אִינְהוֹן (for
אִינְהֵין); Mand. הינון, הינין;—all from הֵן, הוֹן, with
demonstr. syll. אִן, הֵן 'lo,' prefixed, W[CG 98, 106]
Nö[M 86]);—*they, those*, Dn 2[44] מַלְכַיָּא אִנּוּן *those
kings*, 6[25] as accus. רְמוֹ אִנּוּן, 7[17] Kt דִּי אִנּוּן אַרְבַּע
(Qr f. אִנִּין) which are four (Dr[1S 10, 19] K[§87,3]),
Ezr 5[4]...מָה אִנּוּן שְׁמָהָת=*what are the names*...?
(Dr[§201, 3, Obs.], K[l. c.]). Cf. הוּא. p. 1090 1932

†אֲנַחְנָא (Ezr 4[16] אֲנַחְנָה) pr. 1 pl. we 586
(Eg. Aram. RÉS[361] S-C[Pap.] אנחנה; BH אֲנַחְנוּ; 587
W[CG 100 f.]), Dn 3[16.17] Ezr 4[16] (after ptcp.), 5[11].

†אִנִּין they (f.) Dn 7[17] Qr: Kt אִנּוּן, above 581

†[אֲנַס] vb. oppress (BH [late] *con-* 598
strain);—Pe. *Pt.* אָנֵס לָךְ Dn 4[6].

†[אַף, אֲנַף K[§55,4]] n.m. only du. (Schulth 600
[ZAW xxii (1902), 164]) face (BH אַף, √אנף; Aram. of 639
Têma אנפי SAC[23] Lzb[222] Cooke[69, l. 14], so S-C[G19]
and (usu.) 𝔗[J]; אפין 𝔗[Onk Jon], ܐܰܦܶܐ Syr. Chr-Pal.
(Schulth[Lex. 13]); also אפי Palm. Lzb[222] Cooke[p. 339],
Chr-Pal. c. prep. ܠܐܦܝ Schulth[Lex. 14], etc.);—
pl. sf. 3 ms. אַנְפּוֹהִי Dn 2[46] 3[19].

I. אנשׁ (√of foll.; cf. BH II. אנשׁ, I. אֱנוֹשׁ). 582

†אֱנָשׁ n.m. man, mankind;—abs. 'א Dn 606
2[10]+; emph. אֲנָשָׁא v[38]+, so Qr 4[13.14] (>Kt
אנושא K[§57f]); so Nab. אנוש oft. Lzb[222] Cooke[219]
SAC[22]): pl. אֲנָשִׁים 4[14] (Hebraism, M[53*] prop.
אֲנָשָׁא);—**1.** *man*, human being, Dn 2[10] 3[10] 4[13]
5[5.7.7] 6[13.13] 7[4.4.8] Ezr 6[11]; so בַּר־אֱנָשׁ Dn 7[13] *a son
of man*, human being (v. esp. Dr[Dn 102; DB Son of
Man]). **2.** coll. *men, people*, Ezr 4[11] Dn 4[14a.22.
22.29.29.30] 5[21], cf. pl. 4[14]; זְרַע א' 2[43] i.e. human offspring; בְּנֵי אֲנָשָׁא *sons of men*,=men, 2[38] 5[21].

II. אנשׁ (√of foll.; BH III. אנשׁ, אִשָּׁה). 802

†[נְשִׁין] n.f. pl. wives (so Zinj. (Cooke[62, 8]) 5389
cstr. נשי, 𝔗 נְשִׁין, Syr. ܢܶܫܶܐ, Heb. נָשִׁים, Ar. نِسَاءٌ:
on sing. v. BH אִשָּׁה, and add Aram. of Nineveh 802
cstr. אשת (CIS[1.15]), and Eg. Aram. אנתה S-C
[Pap. D 10+]);—pl. sf. נְשֵׁיהוֹן Dn 6[25].

607 ‡אנתה Kt$_{14}$ (i.e. אַנְתָּה, peculiar to
859 BAram.; Qr אַנְתְּ) **pr. 2 ms. thou** (BH אַתָּה p. 61^{b}; Cappad. and Eg. Aram. אנת (Lzb $^{Eph. i. 67}$; S-C$^{A 11+}$, f. אנתי *ib.* $^{D 9, 11, 26+}$), Nerab את (Cooke $^{186.190}$), Palm. אנת (*ib.* ^{308}); 𝔗^{O} את, 𝔗^{J} אנת (D$^{§16.1}$); Syr. ܐܢܬ);—*thou*, Dn 2$^{29.31.37.38}$ etc., Ezr 7^{25}.

608, 859 †אַנְתּוּן **pr. 2 mpl. ye, you** (BH אַתֶּם p. 61^{b}), Dn 2^{8}.

620 †אָסְנַפַּר **n.pr.m. Asnappar,** who transported peoples to Samaria Ezr 4^{10}; Ασενναφαρ, 𝔊L Σαλμανασσάρης; prob.=As. kg. *Ašurbanipal* (B.C. 668–626), i.e. אס(רב)נפל, Gelzer $^{Äg. Zeitsch. 1875, 78}$ COT $^{ad loc.}$ Mey $^{E Jud. 29 f.}$ Zim $^{KAT 3. 351}$ Berthol $^{ad loc.}$ Ency. Bib.^{342}.

629 †אָסְפַּרְנָא **adv. thoroughly,** RV. **with (all) diligence** (Zend *aspĕre, asperenō*, Pers. *siparī, asperī*, all *complete*, Castell [1669], Thes Haug $^{JBW 1853, 154}$ Lag $^{Sem. i. 48}$ Andr$^{Marti, Gl. 53*}$ Scheft $^{MGWJ 1903, 415 (correcting Arisches im AT. 73 f.)}$);—Ezr 5^{8} א׳ מִתְעַבְדָא, 6$^{8.12.13}$ 7$^{17.21.26}$ (cf. OAram. אספרן, on a weight, *complete, correct:* Lzb^{223}, Cooke^{193}).

612, 631 אסר (√ of foll.; BH [אָסַר] *bind*, אֵסוּר *bond*,
632 אִסָּר *binding obligation*).

613 †אֱסוּר **n. [m.] band, bond** (𝔗 אֵיסוּר, אֱסוּר, Syr. ܐܣܘܪ, ܐܣܘܪܐ);—abs. א׳ Dn 4$^{12.20}$ (of iron and bronze, for stump, in Neb.'s vision); pl. abs. אֱסוּרִין Ezr 7^{26} *bonds*=imprisonment.

633 †אֱסָר **n.m. interdict** (as *binding*);—א׳ abs. Dn 6$^{8.13.16}$; cstr. v^{13}; emph. אֱסָרָא v$^{9.10.14}$.

636 †אָע **n.m.** $^{Ezr 5, 8}$ **wood** (so 𝔗, for עֵץ; Eg.
6086 Aram. עק S-C^{H5}; BH עֵץ, √ II. עצה);—**1.** abs. א׳ *timber*, for building Ezr 5^{8} 6^{4}; *beam* v^{11}. **2.** emph. אָעָא *wood*, material of idols Dn 5$^{4.23}$.

637-38 †אַף **conj. also** (BH אַף; Eg. Aram., Palm. אף (S-C$^{Pap.}$ Lzb^{224}); 𝔗 אַף, 𝔗^{J} also אוּף; Syr. ܐܦ);—*also*, always וְאַף Dn 6^{23} Ezr 5$^{10.14}$ 6^{5}.

670 ‡†אֲפָרְסָיֵא (K$^{§52, 2d}$) **n.pr.pl.gent.** Ezr 4^{9}, 𝔊 Ἀφρασαῖοι, A Ἀφαρσαῖοι; Ges $^{Lex. Man.}$ Röd $^{Thes. Add. 107}$ Hoffm $^{ZA ii. 55}$ Mey $^{Enst. J. 38}$ *Persians;* Dl $^{Baer Ezr ix}$ Scheft^{75} *Parsua* (in Media [v. Streck $^{ZA xv. 308 ff.}$]; yet v. COT $^{ad loc.}$); Marquart^{64} (א)סָפְרַיָּא *secretaries* (א dittogr. of preceding); oft. identif. with following, so Andr$^{M 53*}$.

671 ‡†אֲפַרְסְכָיֵא Ezr 5^{6} 6^{6}=(acc. to most)

‡†אֲפַרְסַתְכָיֵא 4^{9}, **n.pr.pl.gent.,** so most 671
hitherto, and still Mey $^{Enst. J. 38 ff.}$ (*Persians*), but many moderns think official title (Hoffm $^{ZA ii. 54}$ Marquart^{64} Jen $^{ThLZ. 1895, 509}$ Ency. Bib. $^{190 f.}$; plausible explanations are: Andr$^{M 53*}$=As. *šuparšak* (v. Muss-Arnolt $^{As. Dict. 1098}$ *šāqū* **3**, *general*, Id $^{AJ Sem. Lang. xx (1904), 186 ff.}$); Scheft^{76}=OIran. *aparasaraka, lesser ruler;* Id $^{MGWJ 47 (1903), 315 f.}$ expl. ־תְּכָיֵא as OPers. **aparaθrāka, lesser governor*).

†אַפְּתֹם or אַפְּתוֹם (so edd.: > Gi Baer 674
[v. p. 102 f.] from MSS, אַפְּתֹם) Ezr 4^{13} וְא׳ מַלְכִים תְּהַנְזִק; of uncertain mng.: Thes Haug $^{JBW 1853, 156}$ *in the end* (from Pehlevi *afdom*, Pers. فدام *end*); Scheft^{79} *treasuries* (from Zend *pathmā*, pl. of *pathma, treasury,* √ *path, to fill up*), will endamage *the treasuries* of kings.

[אֶצְבַּע] v. צבע. אַרְבַּע v. רבע. p. 1109, 1112 677, 703

†[אַרְגְּוָן] **n.m. purple, red-purple** (BH 710-11
id., אַרְגָּמָן);—emph. אַרְגְּוָנָא Dn 5$^{7.16.29}$. 713

ארה (√ of foll.; BH I. ארה, אַרְיֵה). 717, 738

†אַרְיֵה **n.m.** $^{Dn 6, 25b}$ **lion**;—abs. א׳ Dn 7^{4} 744
(sim.); pl. emph. אַרְיָוָתָא (D^{153}) 6$^{8.13.17.20.21.23.25.25.28}$

†אֲרוּ **interj. lo** (of uncertain der.: only 718
BAram. (? Nab., v. CIS$^{ii. 186}$); אֲלוּ, p. 1080, and 431
NH הֲרֵי *see! here!* Ab 3^{4} al., are perh. allied), וַאֲרוּ Dn 7^{2} . . . חָזֵה הֲוֵית וַאֲרוּ, v$^{5.6.7.13}$, always in description of a vision (cf. אֲלוּ).

†[אֹרַח ? as 𝔗 Syr.] **n. [m.?] way** (fig.) 735
(BH);—pl. sf. אָרְחָתָךְ (cf. K$^{§ 51, 2, Anm. 3}$) Dn 5^{23} *thy ways* (the progress and outcome of thine affairs); ־תֵהּ 4^{34} *his ways* (i.e. the course of God's dealings, ‖ מַעְבָדוֹהִי).

אַרְיֵה v. ארה. above 744

†אַרְיוֹךְ **n.pr.m.** in Bab. (BH *id.*, cf. Dl $^{Baer Dn ix}$);—Dn 2$^{14.15.15.24.25}$; Αριωχ(ης).

†I. ארך (√ of foll.; BH [אָרַךְ, אָרֵךְ]). 748-50

†אַרְכָה (Baer$^{Dn 4, 24}$ K$^{§ 54, 3.2}$) **n.f. a length-** 754
ening, prolonging (𝔗);—of time Dn 4^{24} 7^{12}.

II. ארך (√ of foll.; acc. to most, weakened 749
fr. ערך (cf. BH) Be-Ry $^{Ezr 4, 14}$; but אֲרִיךְ loan-word fr. Pers. (OIranian) *āryaka, worthy of an Aryan*, Scheft^{79}).

†אֲרִיךְ **adj.vb. fitting, proper** (א׳ Baer 749
K$^{§ 16, 5}$ M$^{§ 82, Anm. 2}$; van d. H. Gi Str אֲרִיךְ, cf. D$^{WB 39}$; 𝔗 *id.;* orig. *Pt. pass.* K$^{§ 57 b) γ)}$);—Ezr 4^{14}.

755 אַרְכְּבָתָה Dn 5^{6}, v. ברך. p. 1085

756 †אַרְכְּוָיֵ n.pr.gent. people of Erech (BH
751 אֶרֶךְ; so also Mey[EJud. 40]);—pl. emph. Ezr 4^{9} (Qr
אַרְכְּוָיֵא; cf. K[§ 61, 6]).

772, 776 [אֲרַע] $_{21}$ n.[f.] earth (so 𝔗 Syr.;=BH אֶרֶץ,
q.v.);—emph. אַרְעָא Dn $2^{35.39}$ + 16 t. Dn, Ezr 5^{11}
Je 10^{11b}; אַרְעָא (D[§§ 9, 5a; 44, 1n]) = אֲרַע + ־ָא of
direction, *earthward*, i.e. *downward*, אַרְעָא מִנָּךְ
Dn 2^{39} Kt *lower than thou*, i.e. inferior to thee
Qr אֲרַע (cf. 𝔗 אֲרַע מִן Ru 4^{4});—Je 10^{11a} v. [אֲרַק].

773 †[אַרְעִי] n.f.denom. bottom (so 𝔗; cf. also
𝔗 אַרְעָאָה *lower*);—cstr. אַרְעִית Dn 6^{25}.

772, 778 †[אֲרַק] n.[f.] earth (=[אֲרַע]; ארקא Eg.
Aram. S-C[Pap. B 15+oft.] (sts. also ארעא, as ib.[16]),
Ninev. and Bab. Aram. Cooke[192], also Mand.
Nö[M § 66], Zinj., Lzb[227] Cooke[166 (cf. 183)]; ק=ע, as
Zinj. מוקא=מוצא, רקי=רצה, Cooke[166, 185]; cf.
K[§ 7, 2 and Anm. 1] and reff., Cooke[185] Nö[ZMG xlvii (1893), 100;
M § 66] Gunk[Schöpf. 18] Lzb[Eph. i. 223] SAC[JQ, 1903-4, 273]);—
emph. אַרְקָא Je 10^{11a}.

783 †אַרְתַּחְשַׁשְׂתְּא n.pr.m. of king, Ezr $4^{8.11.23}$
783 6^{14}=שַׁסְתְּא- $7^{12.21}$ (BH שַׁשְׂתָּא-; Eg. Aram.
ארתחשסש RÉS[438], S-C[B2+]; v. also Andr[M 54*]
Scheft[i. 79]);—Αρσαρθα, Α(ρ)σαθαθα, Αρθασαθα;
𝔊L Αρταξερξης.

787 †[אֹשׁ K[§ 55, 5c]] n.m.[Ezr 6. 3] foundation (prob.
377 loan-word fr. As. *uššû*, *id.*, √אשׁשׁ (v. BH), so
Zim[KAT 3. 649]; 𝔗 f. אוּשָׁא, NH אוּשָּׁה, Chr-Pal.
ܐܘܫܐ, ܐܫܐ, Schulth[Lex. 19]; Ar. أُسّ: Nö[M 99]);—pl.
emph. אֻשַּׁיָּא Ezr 4^{12} 5^{16}; sf. אֻשּׁוֹהִי 6^{3}.

784-85 †אֶשָּׁא n.[f.] fire (BH אֵשׁ; K[§ 55, 5. 2 b] thinks
emph. fr. onomatop. √אשׁשׁ; D[161] Buhl √אשׁא,
cf. 𝔗 אִשָּׁא, אִישָּׁתָא, Syr. ܐܫܬܐ);—Dn 7^{11}.

787 אֻשַּׁיָּא, אֻשּׁוֹהִי v. [אשׁ]. above

826 †אָשַׁף (K[§ 58a]) n.m. conjurer, enchanter
825 (prob. Bab. loan-word; so BH אַשָּׁף);—abs. א׳
Dn 2^{10}; pl.abs. אָשְׁפִין v^{27} 5^{11}, emph. אָשְׁפַיָּא 4^{4} $5^{7.15}$.

846 ‡†אֻשַּׁרְנָא n.m. meaning and √dub. (K[§ 62]
Buhl[14]);—‖ בַּיְתָא Ezr $5^{3.9}$; most *wall* (𝔖𝔅 *walls*);
M[55*] cp. As. *ašurrû*, *wall*, but ?; Hpt in Gu[Ezr
pp. 34. 63] thinks=[*aširânâ*] fr. As. *ašru*, *sanctuary;*
pointed by Mas. as if=אֻשַּׁיָּא (4^{12} 5^{16}); other
conj. Marquart[44] Scheft[79 f.].

849, 8355 אֶשְׁתַּדּוּר v. שׁדר. אִשְׁתִּיו v. [שְׁתָה]. p. 1114, 1117

†אֲתָא, אֲתָה vb. come (BH poet. 858
אָתָה; Palm. אתי Haph. Lzb[230], Chr-Pal. ܐܬܐ Schulth 857
[Lex.]);—Pe. *Pf.* 3 ms. אֲתָה Ezr 5^{3} Dn 7^{22}; ־ָא
Ezr 5^{16}; 3 mpl. אֲתוֹ 4^{12}; *Imv.* mpl. אֱתוֹ(וְ) Dn 3^{26};
Inf. לְמֵתֵא (K[§ 41c]) v^{2}; *Pt.* אָתֵה 7^{13};—*come*, c. עַל
pers. Ezr 4^{12} (+ ל loc.), 5^{3}; c. ל rei Dn 3^{2}; abs.
v^{26} $7^{13.22}$; sq. vb. fin. act. Ezr 5^{16}. **Haph.** *bring:*
Pf. 3 ms. הַיְתִי (K[l. c.]), Dn 5^{13} (acc. pers. + מִן loc.);
3 mpl. הַיְתִיו, acc. rei 5^{3}, so (ל acc.) v^{23} (+ קֳדָם
pers.), 6^{17} (ל acc. pers.), v^{25} (acc. pers.); *Inf.*
לְהַיְתָיָה (so Eg. Aram. RÉS[361 C]) 3^{13} (ל acc. pers.),
5^{2} (ל acc. rei). **Hêphal** (pass., K[l. c.]) *be brought:*
Pf. 3 fs. הֵיתָיִת (K[§ 47, Beisp. 6], W[CG 225]) subj. rei Dn
6^{18}; 3 mpl. הֵיתָיוּ subj. pers. 3^{13} (+ קֳדָם pers.).

אָת v. אוה. p. 1079 852

†אַתּוּן n.m.[Dn 3, 19] (prob. f. [v. 26]) furnace 861
(prob. loan-word from As. *utûnu*, *atûnu*, *id.*
[also TelAm.], DHM[VOJ i. 23] Buhl; Syr. ܐܬܘܢܐ,
hence Ar. أَتُّون as loan-word Frä[26]; Eth. አቶን:
Di[763]; conj. on etym. in K[§ 59 Anm.] Lag[BN 111]);—
cstr. א׳ Dn $3^{6.11.15.17.20.21.23.26}$; emph. אַתּוּנָא $3^{19.22}$.

אִתַי v. אִיתַי. p. 1080 383

†אֲתַר n.m. place (so Eg. Aram., Nab., 870
Palm.; 𝔗; Syr. ܐܬܪܐ *place;* Zinj. אשר Lzb[229 f.]; Ar.
إِثْرٌ *footstep;* cf. Heb. אֲשׁוּר, and sub אֲשֶׁר);— 834, 838
place: **a.** Dn 2^{35} וְכָל־אֲתַר לָא־הִשְׁתְּכַח לְהוֹן, Ezr
5^{15} וּבֵית אֱלָהָא יִתְבְּנֵא עַל־אַתְרֵהּ, $6^{3.5.7}$. Hence **b.**
בָּאתַר (Dn 7^{6} Baer בָּתַר) *after* (lit. *in the track of:*
so Zinj. באשר (Cooke[160 f., 170]), Palm. 𝔗 בָּתַר, Syr.
ܒܬܪ), בָּאתַר דְּנָה *after this*, Dn $7^{6.7}$, sf. Dn 2^{39}
וּבָתְרָךְ and *after* thee.

אַתְרוּ v. נתר. p. 1103 5426

ב

בְּ prep. in, with, through, etc. (BH בְּ);—
sf. בִּי, בָּךְ Dn 4^{6}+, 3 ms. בֵּהּ 3^{7}+, f. בַּהּ 2^{4} 3^{16}+,
3 pl. בְּהוֹן 3^{25}+;—**1.** *in*, of place, 2^{38} 3^{1} 4^{12} בְּאֱסוּר+;
at Ezr 5^{10}, of time Dn 2^{28} 3^{5} (*at*), 5^{2}+; 4^{12} Ezr 4^{16}
חֲלָק בְּ׳ a share *in* (BH **I. 2**). **2.** *into*, Dn 2^{38}
יְהַב בִּידָךְ, Ezr 5^{12}; עֲדָה בְּ׳ pass *over* or *upon*
Dn 3^{27}. **3.** of the instrument, *by*, *with* Dn
$2^{30.34}$ 3^{4} $4^{12b.24.27}$+; $5^{2.3}$ (Am 6^{6}: BH **III. 2**).
4. of the price (*ib.* **III. 3**), *with*, Ezr $7^{17.18}$.
5. יוֹם בְּיוֹם Ezr 6^{9}=*day by day* (*ib.* **III. 3**, *end;*
so Syr. PS[1577]; cf. ירח בירח S-C[L5], ܡܢ ܟܡܐ

PS [4240]). **6.** *through, on account of* (*ib.* **III. 5**), Ezr 6[14]. **7.** *in the matter of,* Dn 6[6.18]. **8.** after vbs. of *ruling,* Dn 2[38]+, *trusting* 6[24], *looking at* 7[8]; עֲבַד בְּ to do *with* 4[32] Ezr 7[18]. Cf. Lzb [232] K [§ 68].

888 †**בְּאֵשׁ vb.** be evil, bad (so 𝔗; Syr. ܒܐܫ; OAram. באש Lzb [233] SAC [27] Cooke [191]; cf.
887 BH);—**Pe.** *Pf.* 3 ms. impers. ב׳ עֲלוֹהִי Dn 6[15] i.e.
7489 *it was evil* (*displeasing*) *to him* (cf. BH [רעע] **1**).

873 †[**בָּאִישׁ** K [§ 11, 3 b)]] **adj. bad** (so Eg. Aram. Cooke [75. 2]; 𝔗 בִּישׁ, Syr. ܒܝܫ);—fs. emph. וּבְאִישְׁתָּא Ezr 4[12] rebellious *and bad* city (not בְּאוּשְׁתָּא, v. Baer [n.]).

870 **בָּתַר, בָּאתַר** v. אֲתַר. p. 1083

894-95 **בָּבֶל n.pr.loc. Babylon** (BH *id.*);—Dn 2[12]+ 15 t. Dn, 9 t. Ezr.

896 †[**בָּבְלָי**] **adj. gent.** pl. emph. as subst. בָּבְלָיֵא Ezr 4[9] *the Babylonians.*

921 †[**בְּדַר**] **vb. Pa. scatter** (so 𝔗 Syr.; BH
967 [בָּזַר]);—*Imv.* mpl. וּבַדַּרוּ Dn 4[11] (acc. rei).

927 †[**בְּהַל**] **vb. Pa. alarm, dismay** (so usu.
926 𝔗 (not Syr.); BH [בָּהַל]);—*Impf.* 3 ms. sf. יְבַהֲלָךְ Dn 4[16] and 3 mpl. sf. -לְֻנַּנִי- 4[2] 7[15.28] (both juss. Str [§ 13 c] M [§ 52 a]); -לוּךְ 5[10], -לְנָּהּ 4[16], -לוּנֵהּ 5[6]. **Hithpe.** *hasten* (so Pi. in late BH; 𝔗 Ithpe. (rare)); *Inf.* בְּהִתְבְּהָלָה = *in haste* (orig. 'in alarm') Dn 2[25] 3[24] 6[20]. **Hithpa.** *Pt. pass.* מִתְבָּהַל Dn 5[9] was greatly *alarmed.*

924 †**בְּהִילוּ n.f. haste** (𝔗);—בְּב׳ Ezr 4[23] (K [§ 61, 4)]).

בול (assumed as prob. √ of foll., Brock Schulth; Lane [277]).

1079 †**בָּל n.[m.] mind** (Syr. ܒܠ *id.* PS [529]; Ar. بَالٌ *heart*);—abs. שָׂם ב׳ Dn 6[15] (sq. Inf.; cf. Syr. ܣܡ ܒܠ PS [l. c.] Schulth [Lex. 80]).

988-89 †[**בְּטֵל**] **vb. cease** (late BH);—**Pe.** *Pf.* 3 fs. בְּטֵלַת Ezr 4[24], *Pt.* fs. בָּטְלָא v[24] (both of work). **Pa.** *make to cease,* acc. pers.: *Pf.* 3 mpl. בַּטִּלוּ 4[23] 5[5]; *Inf.* לְבַטָּלָא 4[21], acc. pers. om. 6[8].

996-97 †**בֵּין prep. between** (BH [בֵּין, בַּיִן]; 𝔗 בֵּין, בֵּינֵי; Syr. ܒܝܢ, ܒܝܢܬ), Dn 7[5]; c. sf. 3 pl. m. בֵּינֵיהוֹן v[7] Kt (Qr 3 pl. f. בֵּינֵיהֵן).

998-99 ‡†**בִּינָה n.f. understanding** (BH; √ בין; 𝔗 בִּיוּנָא, Syr. ܒܝܘܢܐ);—abs. ב׳ Dn 2[21].

†**בִּירְתָא** (Baer -תָּא) **n.f.** emph. **castle** (so 1001
Egypt. Aram. RÉS [361, A 5; B 1, 2] S-C [Pap. B 3, C 16]+;
Nab. = *temple* CIS [ii. 164. 3]; BH בִּירָה);—Ezr 6[2]. 1002

[**בַּיִת**] $_{44}$ **n.m.** [Ezr 6, 7] **house** (BH בַּיִת);—emph. 1004-05
בַּיְתָא Ezr 5[3]+, -תָה 5[12] 6[15]; cstr. (־) בֵּית 4[24] 5[2]+; sf. בַּיְתִי Dn 4[1] (Baer [n.], cf. M [§ 76 c]; van d. H. Gi בֵּיתִי), בַּיְתֵהּ 2[17]+; pl. sf. בָּתֵּיכוֹן Dn 2[5];—†**1.** *house,* of men: Ezr 6[11.11] Dn 2[5.17] 3[29] 6[11]; of king Ezr 6[4] Dn 4[4], ב׳ מִשְׁתְּיָא 5[10], ב׳ גִּנְזַיָּא דִּי מַלְכָּא Ezr 5[17], cf. 7[20] = ב׳ סִפְרַיָּא וגו׳ 6[1]; ב׳ מַלְכוּ 4[30] *royal residence* (of Bab.). **2.** *house* of God, temple at Jerusalem Dn 5[3.23] Ezr 4[24]+ 28 t. Ezr.

†[**בִּית** D [WB 52]] **vb. denom.** (lodge,) **pass** 956
the night (𝔗 *id.*);—**Pe.** *Pf.* 3 ms. בָּת Dn 6[19].

בָּל v. בול. p. 1084 1079

†[**בְּלָא**] **vb. Pa. wear away, out** (BH 1080
בלה);—*Impf.* 3 ms. יְבַלֵּא Dn 7[25], fig. for *harass* 1086
continually (acc. pers.).

†**בְּלוֹ n.[m.] tribute** (loan-word from As. 1093
biltu, √ובל, acc. to most mod.; but Scheft [80] cp. OIran. *bali, tribute,* OPers. **bari, payment in kind,* so (in Bab. *bara*) Mey [G. d. Altert. iii. 88] Scheft [MGWJ 47 (1903), 316] Buhl [14] 'vielleicht');—abs. מִנְדָּה ב׳ וַהֲלָךְ Ezr 4[13.20] 7[24].

בֵּלְטְשַׁאצַּר $_8$ **n.pr.m.** Bab. name of Daniel 1096
(BH *id.*, p. 117);—Dn 2[26] 4[5]+ 6 t. Dn; Βαλτασαρ. 1095

†**בֵּלְשַׁאצַּר n.pr.m.** king of Bab., acc. to 1113
Dn 5[1.2.9.22.29] (BH *id.*, p. 128) = בֵּלְאשַׁצַּר v[30] 7[1]; 1112
Βαλτασαρ; vid. Bev [Ency. Bib. BELSHAZZAR] Dr [Dn xxviii f.]

†[**בְּנָא, בְּנָה**] **vb. build** (BH בָּנָה);— 1124, 1129
Pe. *Pf.* 3 ms. sf. 3 ms. בְּנָהִי Ezr 5[11]; 1 s. sf. בְּנַיְתַהּ Dn 4[27]; *Impf.* 3 mpl. יִבְנוֹן Ezr 6[7]; *Inf.* לְמִבְנֵא 5[2]+, לְמִבְנְיָה v[9] (rd. לְמִבְנֵא M [§ 64 a] or < לְמִבְנֵה, so S-C [A 3. 64]), לִבְּנֵא (rd. לְמִבְנֵא Str [§ 231] M [l. c.]) v[3.13]; *Pt. act.* pl. בָּנַיִן 4[12]+; *pass.* בְּנֵה 5[11] (v. on forms K [§ 47, Beisp. pass.]);—*build:* c. acc. of temple Ezr 5[2.3.9.11.13.17] 6[7.8], so 5[4] (acc. cogn.); pass. of temple v[11]; c. acc. of city 4[12] Dn 4[27]; abs. Ezr 6[14.14]. **Hithpe.** *be built: Impf.* 3 ms. יִתְבְּנֵא of temple Ezr 5[15] 6[3]; 3 fs. תִּתְבְּנֵא of city v[13.16.21]; *Pt.* מִתְבְּנֵא of temple 5[8] (c. acc. mater.), v[16].

†[**בִּנְיָן**] **n.[m.] a building** (so 𝔗 Syr.);— 1147
emph. בִּנְיָנָא Ezr 5[4].

†**בְּנַס vb. be angry** (𝔗 [J] *id.;* Sam. ࠁࠍࠎ);— 1149
Pe. *Pf.* 3 ms. ב׳ וּקְצַף שַׂגִּיא Dn 2[12].

1156, 1158 †בְּעָא vb. **ask, seek,** only Dn (BH בעה (rare));—**Pe.** *Pf.* 3 ms. ב׳ 2[16.49]; 3 mpl. בְּעוֹ v[13];
1 pl. בְּעֵינָא v[23]; *Impf.* 3 ms. יִבְעֵא 6[8.13]; 1 s. אֶבְעֵא־ 7[16]; *Inf.* לְמִבְעֵא 2[18]; *Pt.* בָּעֵא 6[12.14], pl. בָּעַיִן v[5];—**1.** *ask, request,* c. מִן pers. 2[16] (obj. cl. c. דִּי), v[49] 7[16] (+acc. rei); *ask* of God 2[23] (+*id.*), of God or man 6[8] (+acc. cogn.), v[13]; c. מִן־קֳדָם of God 2[18] (acc. rei); =*pray,* ב׳ וּמִתְחַנַּן קֳדָם א׳ 6[12], ב׳ בָּעוּתֵהּ v[14]. **2.** *seek,* acc. pers. 2[13], acc. rei 6[5]. **Pa.** *Impf.* 3 mpl. יְבַעוֹן (K[§47.3]; M[ad loc.] conj. יִבְעוֹן) 4[33] *resort* (for favours) to, ל pers.

1159 †בָּעוּ (K[§61.4]) **n.f. petition** (𝔗 Syr);—abs.
1156 ב׳ Dn 6[8]; sf. בָּעוּתֵהּ v[14] (both acc. cogn. c. בְּעָא).

1169 †בְּעֵל (K[§54.3]) **n. m. owner, lord** (Syr.
1167 ܒܥܠܐ, used similarly; cf. BH בַּעַל, √בָּעַל; also 𝔗 בְּעֵיל);—cstr. ב׳־טְעֵם Ezr 4[8.9.17] i.e. *commander* (Andr[M56*] as translation of Persian *framātār, commander*).

1236-37 †[בִּקְעָא] **n.f. plain** (𝔗; BH בִּקְעָה, √בקע; cf. Syr. ܦܩܥܬܐ, √ܦܩܥ);—cstr. בְּבִקְעַת דּוּרָא Dn 3[1].

1240 †[בַּקַּר] **vb. Pa. inquire, seek** (only Ezr)
1239 (𝔗 Syr.; v. BH);—*Pf.* 3 mpl. בַּקַּרוּ 4[19] 6[1]; *Impf.* 3 ms. יְבַקַּר 4[15]; *Inf.* לְבַקָּרָה 7[14];—**1.** *inquire,* c. עַל (rei) *concerning* 7[14]; c. subj. indef., =pass., 4[19] *search was made,* so 6[1], 4[15]. **Hithpa.** *Impf.* 3 ms. יִתְבַּקַּר 5[17], impers., *let search be made.*

1247 †I. בַּר **n.m. son** (𝔗 *id.;* Syr. ܒܪ, Mand. ברא Nö[M§148], OAram. Nab. Palm. בר (and בן) Lzb[242 f.]; Sab. בר acc. to Mordtm[VOJ x. 154 f.]; =בֵּן, ן becoming ר, Philippi[ZMG xxxii (1878), 36 ff.] Brock[Syr. Gr. §76] al.; √diff. fr. בן acc. to JHMich Thes K[§63] al.; BH
1121, 1248 בַּר Aramaism for בֵּן);—cstr. ב׳ Dn 3[25]+; sf. בְּרֵהּ 5[22]; pl. cstr. בְּנֵי Ezr 6[9]+; sf. בְּנוֹהִי 6[10] 7[23], בְּנֵיהוֹן Dn 6[25];—**1.** *son(s)* Ezr 5[1.2.2] 6[14] Dn 5[22] 6[25]
1123 Ezr 6[10] 7[23]; בְּנֵי יִשְׂרָאֵל 6[16]=*Israelites,* בְּנֵי גָלוּתָא =*captives* v[16] Dn 2[25] 5[13] 6[14]; בַּר־אֱנָשׁ 7[13] i.e. *one of human kind,* בְּנֵי אֲנָשָׁא *men* 2[38] 5[21]; בַּר־אֱלָהִין 3[25] *a divine* (or angelic) *being* (v. Dr, and cf. BH Gn 6[2] Jb 1[6]); בַּר שְׁנִין וגו׳ 6[1] *a son of* 62 *years*
1121 =62 *years old* (BH בֵּן **9**). **2.** of bullocks, בְּנֵי תוֹרִין Ezr 6[9].

1251 II. בַּר v. ברר. p. 1085

1288-89 †[בְּרַךְ] **vb. kneel, bless** (so BH);—**Pe.** *Pt.* **1.** *act.* בָּרֵךְ עַל־בִּרְכוֹהִי Dn 6[11] *kneeling on his knees* (in prayer). **2.** *pass.* בְּרִיךְ Dn 3[28] *blessed* (be) the God, etc. **Pa.** *bless, praise: Pf.* 3 ms. בָּרִךְ 2[19], 1 s. בָּרְכֵת (K[§39.3]) 4[31], both c. ל of God; *Pt. pass.* מְבָרַךְ 2[20] the name of God (be) *blessed.*

†[בְּרַךְ] **n.[f.] knee**;—pl. sf. בִּרְכוֹהִי Dn 6[11]. 1291

†[אַרְכֻבָּה] **n.f. id.** (by transp.; cf. 𝔗 רְכוּבָא, 755
𝔗[J] אַרְכּוּבְתָא; Chr-Pal. ܐܪܟܘܒܬܐ Schwally[Idiot. 89] (who > expl. from √רכב, cf. Schulth[Lex. 194]); Ar. رُكْبَة *id.*);—pl. sf. אַרְכֻבָּתֵהּ Dn 5[6] *his knees.*

†בְּרַם **adv.** with advers. force, **only,** 1297
nevertheless (der. uncertain: Nö[M 202]=מָא+בַּר, lit. *except what:* 𝔗 בְּרַם oft. for אוּלָם, אַךְ; Syr. ܒܪܡ Ex 9[16] 2 I[21], and in NT for πλήν; Chr-Pal. (ܒܪܡ, ܒܪܡ);—Dn 2[28] 4[12] hew down the tree, etc., בְּרַם . . . שְׁבֻקוּ *only* leave the stump, etc., v[20] 5[17] Ezr 5[13].

ברר (√of foll.; BH ברר, בַּר †Jb 39[4]). 1250, 1305

†II. [בַּר] **n.[m.] open field**;—emph. בָּרָא, 1251
in ב׳ חֵיוַת (=BH חַיַּת הַשָּׂדֶה), Dn 2[38] 4[9.18.20.22.29]; חֵיוְתָא דִּי ב׳ v[12.20].

†בְּשַׂר **n.m. flesh** (𝔗 בְּסַר, Syr. ܒܣܪ; BH 1321
בָּשָׂר, √בשׂר);—abs. ב׳ Dn 7[5] *flesh* (as devoured 1320
by beast); emph. בִּשְׂרָא 2[11] *flesh*=mankind, כָּל־ב׳ 4[9]=all creatures.

†[בַּת] **n.[m.] bath,** liquid measure (𝔗; 1325
perh. loan-word from BH II. בַּת, √בתת);—pl. 1324
abs. בַּתִּין Ezr 7[22.22].

בָּתַר v. sub אֲתַר. p. 1083 870

ג

גאה (prob. √of foll.; BH גָּאָה *rise up*). 1342

†גֵּוָה **n.f. pride** (𝔗 גֵּיוָה; BH גֵּאָה; cf. K[§55, 1 (but also 6 a)]);—abs. בְּגֵ׳ Dn 4[34] *in pride.* 1344, 1467

†[גַּב] **n.[m.]** either **back** (𝔗 גַּב *back, top;* 1355
BH גַּב, √גבב), or < **side** (√גנב, cf. Ar. جَنْبٌ 1354
side, Syr. ܓܒܐ *side,* √ܓܒܒ;—v. also D[WB 65]);—pl. sf. Dn 7[6] Kt wings עַל־גַּבַּיהּ on *its sides* (Bev Behrm Dr; Qr גַּבַּהּ perh. *its back,* so most).

†[גֹּב] **n.m. pit, den of lions** (𝔗 גּוֹב, Syr. 1358
ܓܘܒܐ *pit;* ? cf. BH גֹּב n.pr.loc., √גבב);—cstr. 1359
ג׳ Dn 6[8.25]; גּוֹב v[13]; emph. גֻּבָּא v[17.18.20.21.24.24.25].

גבר (√of foll.; *be strong,* so 𝔗; BH גָּבַר). 1396

1399-400 גְּבַר 21 **n.m.** man (BH);—abs. ג׳ Dn 2[25] 5[11]; pl. abs. גֻּבְרִין (K§54,3e) 3[24.25], also, = *certain* ones, v[8.12.20]; emph. גֻּבְרַיָּא Ezr 4[21] 5[4.10] 6[8] Dn 3[12] +9 t. Dn.

1370 †[גְּבוּרָה] **n.f.** might;—emph. גְּבוּרְתָא (K§§9c); 57b) a) but M§72c) Dn 2[20.23].

1401 †[גִּבָּר] **n.m.** mighty one;—pl. cstr. גִּבָּרֵי־חַיִל Dn 3[20] (=BH גִּבּוֹרֵי חַיִל).

1411 ‡†גְּדָבְרַיָּא **n.m.pl.emph.** Dn 3[2.3], dub.: most think ‖ form of [גְּזָבַר] *treasurer* (or, Mey Entst. J.23, text. err. for גז׳); Gr Bev al. rd. הַדָּבְרַיָּא *ministers* (3[24]); poss. (v. Lag Dr al.) dittogr. for following דְּתָבְרַיָּא.

1414 †[גְּדַד] **vb.** hew down (𝔗J; Syr. (rare);
1413 BH *cut*);—**Pe.** *Imv.* mpl. גֹּדּוּ אִילָנָא (K§46, Beisp. a) Dn 4[11.20].

1459 †[גַּו] **n.m.** midst (Eg. Aram. Nab. Palm.
גו; 𝔗 גַּוִּיו; esp. cstr. מִגּוֹ, לְגוֹ, בְּגוֹ; so Syr. [Syriac]; cf.
1460 BH גֵּו, p. 156);—cstr. גּוֹא (so Nab. Cooke No. 94)
Dn 3[26]+, 7[15] edd., Gi גּוֹ (Baer גּוֹא, v. on 3[6]); sf. 3 ms. גַּוֵּהּ †Ezr 5[7], 3 fs. גַּוַּהּ †4[15] 6[2];—*midst*, alw. c. preps.: **a.** בְּגוֹא (=Heb. בְּתוֹךְ), Dn 3[25], בְּגוֹא נוּרָא, 4[7] 7[15] Ezr 4[15]; 5[7] וְכִדְנָה כְּתִיב בְּגַוֵּהּ, 6[2]. **b.** לְגוֹא Dn 3[6.11.15.21.23.24]. **c.** מִן־גּוֹא Dn 3[26].

1467 גֵּוָה v. גאה. p. 1085

1490 †[גִּזְבַּר] **n.m.** treasurer (Pers. loan-word
1489 (Scheft[81]); 𝔗 Syr. BH; K§64,3; in Bab. *ganzabaru* Peiser ZAW xvii (1897), 347);—pl. emph. גִּזַּבְרַיָּא
1411 Ezr 7[21].—Vid. גְּדָבְרַיָּא. above

1505 †[גְּזַר] **vb.** cut, (divide,) determine (so
1504 𝔗 Syr., in both mngs.; BH usu. *divide*, †Jb Est *decree*);—**Pe.** *Pt. act.* as subst., pl. abs. גָּזְרִין *determiners* (of fate; astrologers or soothsayers) Dn 2[27] 5[11]; emph. גָּזְרַיָּא 4[4] 5[7] (cf. Dr.; Ar. جَزَّار, RS J Phil. xiii (1885), 781). **Hithpe.** *Pf.* 3 fs. הִתְגְּזֶרֶת 2[34] a stone *was cut out*, so אִתְגְּ׳ (K§§23,1; 30,2) v[45] (c. מִן of source).

1510 †[גְּזֵרָה] **n.f.** decree (𝔗 גְּזֵירָא, Syr. [Syriac]);—cstr. גְּזֵרַת Dn 4[14.21].

5085 †[גִּין] c. בְּ, בְּגִין **prep.** on account of (so Galil. Aram., D§47,3), read perh. in 7[15]: v. נִדְנֶה. p. 1102

1528,1615 †[גִּיר] **n.[m.]** chalk, plaster (so 𝔗; BH once, p. 162);—emph. גִּירָא Dn 5[5].

1535 [גַּלְגַּל] v. גלל. below

†[גְּלָה, גְּלָא] **vb.** reveal (BH גָּלָה *un-* 1540-41
cover, reveal);—**Pe.** *reveal* secrets, human agent: *Inf.* לְמִגְלֵא Dn 2[47]; of God, *Pt. act.* גָּלֵא v[22.28.29.47]. **Peʿîl** *Pf.* גְּלִי v[19], גֱּלִי v[30], *revealed* (W CG 225 Nö LCB, 1896, 703);—of secret, c. לְ pers. **Haph.** *take into exile* (BH **Hiph.**), *Pf.* 3 ms. הַגְלִי, c. acc. pers. Ezr 4[10] 5[12] (לְ loc.).

†[גָּלוּ K§61,4] **n.f.** exile;—emph. בְּנֵי גָלוּתָא 1547
i.e. exiles, Ezr 6[16] Dn 2[25] 5[13] 6[14] (cf. BH גּוֹלָה). 1473

גלל (√of following; BH II. גלל; Palm. 1556
גללא Lzb[250] SAC[36] Cooke[334], = στήλη λιθίνη).

†גְּלָל **n.[m.]** rolling;—abs. אֶבֶן גּ׳ Ezr 5[8] 1560
6[4] *stones of rolling*, too heavy for carrying.

†[גַּלְגַּל] **n.m.** wheel (𝔗 BH; Syr. [Syriac]); 1535
—pl. sf. גַּלְגִּלּוֹהִי Dn 7[9] of throne-chariot of God.

†מְגִלָּה **n.f.** (book-)roll (𝔗 BH);—Ezr 6[2]. 4039-40

†[גְּמַר] **vb.** complete (oft. 𝔗 Syr.; rare 1585
BH);—**Pe.** *Pt. pass.* גְּמִיר Ezr 7[12] as adj. *perfect* 1584
(read perh. שְׁלָם ג׳, Torrey Berthol; cf. 5[7]).

†[גְּנַז] **n.m.** Ezr 6,1 treasure (𝔗; v. BH [גְּנָזִים], 1595-96
sub גנז);—pl. emph. גִּנְזַיָּא *treasures* Ezr 6[1], בֵּית ג׳ דִּי מַלְכָּא 5[17], cstr. בֵּית גִּנְזֵי מַלְכָּא 7[20].

†[גַּף] **n.f.** Dn 7,4 wing of bird (𝔗 גַּפָּא, גַּף, 1611
גַּדְפָּא (? D WB 79), Syr. [Syriac]; akin to BH אֲגַף, 102
As. *agappu*? acc. to Nö M77 (cf. Mand. גאדפא, 𝔗 גַּדְפָּא), Id GGA, 1884, 1019, √גדף, Ar. جَدَفَ, جَذَفَ *fly, row* (but this loan-word Frä[227]));—pl. abs. *wings*, גַּפִּין Dn 7[4.6]; sf. גַּפַּיהּ v[4] Kt (Qr sg. גַּפַּהּ).

†[גְּרַם] **n.[m.]** bone (BH גֶּרֶם; Chr-Pal. 1634-35
[Syriac] Schulth Lex. 46);—pl. sf. גַּרְמֵיהוֹן Dn 6[25].

†[גְּשֵׁם] **n.m.** Dn 4,30 body (v. √גשם in BH; 1653, 1655
𝔗J גֻּשְׁמָא, גּוּשְׁמָא (D WB 83), Syr. [Syriac], *body, self*);—*body* of man, sf. גִּשְׁמֵהּ Dn 4[30] 5[21], so pl. sf. גֶּשְׁמֵיהוֹן (K§15a) 3[27.28], both Kt, Qr sg. גֶּשְׁמְהוֹן (K§54,3b).

ד

†דָּא **demonstr. pr. f.** this (=BH זֹה: 1668, 2090
Zinj. Têma, Cappad. Eg. Aram. זא, Nab. דא, Palm. דה (Lzb 264; Eph. I. 323 Cooke 26), 𝔗 דָא: v. further sub BH זֶה. The corresp. masc. is 2088
דְּנָה);—*this*, Dn 4[27] הֲלָא דָא הִיא בָּבֶל רַבְּתָא, 5[6] דָּא לְדָא נָקְשָׁן *one* striking against *another*, similarly 7[3] (cf. זֶה **1 b**), v[8] בְּקַרְנָא־דָא.

1677-78 †דֹּב **n.[m.]** bear (so 𝔗 BH √דבב; Syr. ܕܶܒܳܐ);—abs. ד׳ Dn 7^{5}.

1684, 2076 †[דְּבַח] **vb.** sacrifice (BH זָבַח);—**Pe.** *Pt. act.* pl. דָּבְחִין Ezr 6^{3}, c. acc. דִּבְחִין, v. foll.

1685 †[דְּבַח] **n.[m.]** sacrifice;—pl. abs. דִּבְחִין Ezr 6^{3}.

4056 †[מַדְבַּח] **n.[m.]** altar;—emph. מַדְבְּחָא Ezr 7^{17}.

1692-93 †[דְּבֵק] **vb.** cling (BH);—**Pe.** *Pt.* pl. דָּבְקִין דְּנָה עִם־דְּנָה Dn 2^{43}.

1700-01 †[דִּבְרָה] **n.f.** cause, reason (BH *id.*, √דבר, cf. על דבר Eg. Aram. S-C Pap. B 5.6.8.16);—cstr. in adv. phr. עַל־דִּבְרַת דִּי Dn 2^{30} *for the cause* (to the intent) *that*, 4^{14} (rd. עַל for עד K § 11, 2 Bev).

1722 דְּהַב 23 **n.m.** Dn 2, 32 gold (so 𝔗 Syr.; BH
2091 זָהָב);—abs. ד׳ Dn 2^{32}+, דְּהַב Ezr 7^{15}; emph. דַּהֲבָה 5^{14} 6^{5} 7^{18}, -בָא Dn 2^{35} + 15 t. Dn.

1723 ‡†דהוא Kt, דֶּהָיֵא Qr, acc. to Thes and most **n. pr. gent.** Ezr 4^{9}, v. conj. identif. by Dl Baer Dn x Scheft 81 f.; < read דֶּהוּא *that is*, Hoffm ZA ii. 54 Marquart 64 Mey Entst. J. 36, 𝔊 οἱ εἰσίν.

1752-53 †[דּוּר] **vb.** dwell (v. BH);—**Pe.** *Impf.* 3 fs. of beasts תְּדוּר Dn 4^{18}; 3 mpl. birds יְדֻרוּן v^{9} (Qr f. יְדוּרָן, f. subj., צִפְּרֵי, follows, cf. v^{18} and K § 98, 2 c, Anm. 3); *Pt.* pl. of men, דָּאֲרִין Kt 2^{38} 3^{31} 6^{26} (Qr דָּיְרִין); as subst., cstr. דָּאֲרֵי Kt $4^{32.32}$ (Qr דָּיְרֵי) *dwellers*.

1755, 1859 דָּר **n.[m.]** generation (BH דּוֹר);—abs. in phr. עִם־דָּר וְדָר Dn 3^{33} 4^{31} (is) *with generation and generation*, i.e. endures gen. after gen.

4070 †[מְדוֹר] **n.[m.]** dwelling-place;—sf. מְדֹרָךְ Dn $4^{22.29}$, מְדוֹרֵהּ, 5^{21}.

4070 †[מְדָר] **n.m.** id.;—sf. מְדָרְהוֹן Dn 2^{11}.

8411 †תְּדִירָא **n.f.** continuance (𝔗 *id.*; v. BH
1752 דּוּר);—abs. in phr. בִּת׳ *continually* Dn $6^{17.21}$.

1757 †דּוּרָא **n.pr.loc.** near Bab., only בִּקְעַת ד׳ Dn 3^{1}, 𝔊 τοῦ περιβόλου (Syro-Hex. περίβολον), Θ Δεειρα; *Dûru* is name of several places in Babylonia Dl Par. 216; Baer Dn. p. x, cf. Andr M 58*; Hoffm Pers. Märtyrer 164 f.; name of small river and mounds Opp Expéd. i. 238 f. (v. Dr); improb. expl. as = زور *zôr, depression* (name actually used of lower Euphr. and Tigris valleys) by Wetzst De Jes³ 701 f.; Bab. *dûru* = *wall*.

†[דּוּשׁ] **vb.** tread down (BH);—**Pe.** 1759
Impf. 3 fs. (sf. of earth) תְּדוּשִׁנַּהּ Dn 7^{23}, subj. beast.

‡†[דַּחֲוָה] **n.f.** dub.;—pl. abs. דַּחֲוָן Dn 6^{19}, 1761
Vrss conject.; AV RV *instr. of music* (so AE, assuming meaning *strike* [strings] for דְּחָא
[BH דָּחָה] *thrust;* Saad RVm *dancing-girls;* 1760
Bertholdt al. *concubines* (fr. sens. obsc. of Ar. دَحَى), but then read prob. לְחֵנָן ($5^{2.3.23}$) Marti Prince Dr.

†[דְּחַל] **vb.** fear (so 𝔗 Syr.; BH II. 1763
[זָחַל]);—**Pe.** *Pt. act.* pl. דָּחֲלִין Dn 5^{19}, c. מִן־קֳדָם 2119
of king, 6^{27}, *id.* of God; *pass.* דְּחִיל *terrible* 2^{31}, f. דְּחִילָה $7^{7.19}$. **Pa.** *Impf.* 3 ms. sf. וִידַחֲלִנַּנִי 4^{2} the dream *made me afraid*.

דִּי **part. of relation,** who, which, that, 1768
used also as **mark of gen.** and **conj.** that, because (Aram. of Nineveh, Bab. Zinj. Nerab, Cilicia, Têma, Egypt, זי (Lzb 267. 446 RÉS 361 S-C Pap. A 2+); Nab. Palm. די; 𝔗 דְּ (exc. in cpds., as דִּילִי *mine*, דִּילֵיהּ *his*); Sam. ࠃ; Syr. ܕ; Eth. **H:** *za:* of same origin as Ar. ذُو *possessor of* [cf.
sub BH זֶה]. Properly a demonstr. *that* [cf. זֶה; 2088
in Eth. *ze* is 'this,' *za* 'which']; but this being referred by usage to something preceding becomes equiv. to the relative *who, which,* used,
however, more widely than Heb. אֲשֶׁר);—**1.** as 834
rel. *who, which* (construed like אֲשֶׁר): **a.** Je 10^{11} Dn 2^{11} דִּי מְדָרְהוֹן *whose* dwelling, v^{24} דִּי מַנִּי מַלְכָּא *whom* the king had appointed, v^{26} דִּי שְׁמֵהּ ב׳ *whose* name was B., 4^{5} $5^{12.23}$, etc.; = *that which* 2^{23}; = *him that* Ezr 7^{25}; 6^{15} Dn 7^{17} דִּי אִנּוּן אַרְבַּע *which* are four (v. אִנּוּן). Sq. pron. of 2 ps. (cf. אֲשֶׁר **3**), Dn 2^{37} thou, O king . . . , דִּי . . . יְהַב לָךְ *to whom* . . . hath given, 4^{19}; 4^{6} *as to whom* I know, etc. (cf. אֲשֶׁר **4 d** *end*). Sq. תַּמָּה = *where* Ezr 6^{1}, so דִּי alone 6^{3} Dn 2^{38}; of time, בְּעִדָּנָא דִּי at the time *when*, etc., $3^{5.15}$. With the pred. an inf. c. לְ, Dn 6^{9} כְּתָבָא דִּי לָא לְהַשְׁנָיָה *which* is not to be changed, Ezr 6^{8}; a place- or other determination, Dn 3^{20} valiant men דִּי בְחַיְלֵהּ *that* were in his army, 5^{2} הֵיכְלָא דִּי בִירוּשְׁלֶם, 7^{20} Ezr 4^{24} 5^{6} $6^{2.6}$; cf. Dn 2^{25} 5^{13} 7^{7} Ezr 7^{23}. דִּי לָא = *without*, Ezr 6^{9} 7^{22} (so דְּלָא 𝔗 Gn 15^{2} Ex 21^{11}); cf. Dn $2^{34.45}$. **b.** מָן דִּי, מָה דִּי (cf. in late Heb. מַה־שֶּׁ׳, מָה **1 e** *b*) *whoever, whatever*, so †Dn $3^{6.11}$ מַן־דִּי־לָא יִפֵּל *whoever* does not fall down, 4^{14} לְמַן דִּי יִצְבֵּא to *whomsoever* he willeth, $v^{22.29}$ 5^{21}; מָה דִּי *whatever* (or simply *what*), †Dn 2^{28} מָה דִּי לֶהֱוֵא what will be, $v^{29.29.45}$ Ezr 6^{8} 7^{18}.—Cf. K § 103. **2.** as

mark of the gen., Dn 2^{15} שליטא די מלכא prop. the captain, *that of* the king = *the king's captain* (a genuine Aram. idiom: so 𝔗 דְּ, Syr. ܕ constantly), $v^{19.25.49}$ + oft.: the subst. in such cases may be either in the emph. state (determined), as ll. cc. Ezr 4^{15} 5^{2}, etc., or in the abs. state (undetermined), Dn 5^{5} $7^{4.9.10}$ נְהַר דִּי נוּר; or it may have a pleon. sf., 2^{20} שְׁמֵהּ דִּי אֱלָהָא lit. his name, *that of* God = *God's name*, v^{44} $3^{8.25.26}$ 4^{23}, etc. (so also 𝔗 Syr.). To circumscribe an adj., esp. in specif. of the *material:* Dn 2^{38} thou art רֵאשָׁה דִּי דַהֲבָא the head of gold, v^{39} 3^{1} $5^{7.16}$ Ezr 5^{14} 6^{4}+; as predic. Dn 2^{32} רֵאשֵׁהּ דִּי־דְהַב טָב his head (was) *of* fine gold, v^{33} 7^{19}; with a pron. Dn 2^{20} wisdom and might דִּי־לֵהּ הִיא are *his;* cf. 6^{27} וּמַלְכוּתֵהּ דִּי־לָא תִתְחַבַּל his kingdom (is one) which shall not be destroyed, 7^{14}.—Vid. further K §81. **3.** as **conj.** (cf. אֲשֶׁר **8**): **a.** *that* (*quod*), after vbs. of knowing, Dn $2^{8.9}$, seeing 2^{45} 3^{27}, hearing 5^{14}, etc.; introducing the subject of a sentence, יְדִיעַ ... דִּי ... 3^{18} Ezr 4^{13}; Dn 2^{47} מִן־קְשֹׁט דִּי ... True is it *that* ... (cf. אָמְנָם כִּי Jb 12^{2}). **b.** = *in that, inasmuch as, whereas:* Dn 2^{41} and *whereas* (דִּי) thou sawest, etc. ... it shall be a divided kingdom, v^{43} $4^{20.23}$; as a connecting link = *seeing that, because, for* (cf. אֲשֶׁר **8 c**) $2^{9.20b.23b.47b}$ 4^{15} 6^{24b}. **c.** *that* (*ut*), after vbs. of asking Dn 2^{16}, commanding $3^{10.29}$, expressing a purpose 4^{3} 5^{15} Ezr 4^{15} 6^{10}+; דִּי לָא *that not* (*ne*) Dn 2^{18} 3^{28} 6^{18} (on דִּי לְמָה *lest* Ezr 7^{23}, see מה). **d.** prefixed to direct narr. (like כִּי **1 b**, and sts. אֲשֶׁר **8 a** γ, and ὅτι *recitativum*), Dn 2^{25} and said thus unto him דִּי־הַשְׁכַּחַת (that) I have found, etc., 5^{7} $6^{6.14}$. **4.** with preps. and other prefixes: **a.** כְּדִי (like Heb. כַּאֲשֶׁר; so Eg. Aram. כזי, Palm. Nab. כדי, Lzb 293 SAC Gl 62, 63 Cooke 369 b RÉS 361; 𝔗 כַּד, Syr. ܟܕ); *a. according as*, Dn 2^{43}; *b. so soon as, when*, 3^{7} 5^{20} $6^{11.15}$. **b.** מִן־דִּי: *a. because that*, Dn 3^{22} Ezr 5^{12} (cf. מֵאֲשֶׁר Is 43^{4}); *b. from* (the time) *that, after* (*ex quo*), Dn 4^{23} Ezr 4^{23}. **c.** עַד דִּי *until*, Dn $2^{9.34}$ 4^{30} 7^{22}; = *ere that* 6^{25}. **d.** עַל דִּי Dn 3^{19} is not a conj., but means *above that which* ... **e.** for עַל דִּבְרַת דִּי and כָּל־קֳבֵל דִּי see [דִּבְרָה] and קֳבֵל.

1777-78 †[דִּין] **vb.** judge (BH);—**Pe.** *Pt.* pl. דָּאֲנִין Ezr 7^{25} Kt (Qr דָּיְנִין), sq. ל pers.

1780 †דִּין **n.m.** Ezr 7, 26 judgment;—abs. ד׳ Dn 4^{34} = *justice* (of ways of God); emph. דִּינָה מִתְעֲבֵד מִנֵּהּ Ezr 7^{26} *judgment be executed upon him;* דִּינָא = *judges, court* Dn $7^{10.26}$ + perhaps v^{22} (reading וְד׳ יָתִב וְשָׁלְטָנָא [יְהִב], Ew Bev Kmp Dr); MT however = *judgment was given in favour of* (v. Dr).

†[דַּיָּן] **n.m.** judge;—pl. דַּיָּנִין Ezr 7^{25}. 1782

†[מְדִינָה] **n.f.** (judicial) **district, pro-** 4083
vince (K § 60, 3) d); also BH);—emph. מְדִינְתָּא 4082
(M § 72 c) Ezr 5^{8} 6^{2}; cstr. מְדִינַת Dn $2^{48.49}$ $3^{1.12.30}$
Ezr 7^{16}; pl. abs. מְדִנָן 4^{15}, emph. מְדִינָתָא Dn $3^{2.3}$.

דָּנִיֵּאל **n.pr.m.** Daniel (BH *id.*);—Dn $2^{13.14}$ 1841
+50 t. Dn.

דִּינָיֵא **n.pr.gent.** (?) Ezr 4^{9} (so most, but 1784
Hoffm ZA ii. 55 Marquart 64 Andr M 59* Mey Entst. J. 39
Str 46* read דַּיָּנַיָּא *judges* (as transl. of Pers.
dâtabara), while Scheft 81 (improb.) cp. OIran.
*denya, (the) orthodox, i.e. Persians).

†דֵּךְ **demonstr. pr. m.** this, **f.** דָּךְ; only 1791
Ezr; Dn uses דִּכֵּן (Eg. and Cappad. Aram. זך
(CIS ii. 151 RÉS 361 B S-C Pap. (f. דכא, דכי ib. F 6, 9),
Lzb Eph. i. 67); 𝔗 דֵּיכִי, f. דָּךְ; Ar. ذَاكَ; Eth. ዝኩ:
From דָּא, זֶה, ذَا (f.), with the affix ךְ (W CG 110),
thus lit. = Germ. *dieser da*. The pl. is אִלֵּךְ, 479
q.v.);—*this* (always after its subst.), Ezr 5^{16}
שֵׁשְׁבַּצַּר דֵּךְ, v^{17} בֵּית־אֱלָהָא דֵךְ, $6^{7.8.12}$; f. $4^{13.15.16.16.19.21}$
all קִרְיְתָא דָךְ, 5^{8}. p. 1080

†דִּכֵּן **demonstr. pr. comm.** this, that; 1797
only Dn; Ezr uses דֵּךְ (דֵּךְ + demonstr. affix *n*, 1791
W CG 111);—Dn 2^{31} צַלְמָא ד׳, $7^{20.21}$ קַרְנָא ד׳.

†[דְּכַר] **n.m.** ram (𝔗 דִּכְרָא, Syr. ܕܶܟܪܳܐ *id.*, 1798
also (and primarily) *male*, v. BH זָכָר);—pl. 2145
דִּכְרִין for sacrifice Ezr $6^{9.17}$ 7^{17}.

†[דִּכְרוֹן] **n.[m.]** memorandum, record 1799
(BH זִכָּרוֹן, √זָכַר; cf. Nab. Palm. דכר(ו)ן Lzb 268 2146
SAC 40 Cooke 234+);—emph. דִּכְרוֹנָה Ezr 6^{2}.

†[דָּכְרָן] **n.[m.]** id.;—pl. emph. סְפַר דָּכְרָנַיָּא
Ezr $4^{15.15}$.

†[דְּלַק] **vb.** burn (BH);—**Pe.** *Pt. act.* 1814-15
דָּלִק (K § 29, 1) Dn 7^{9} *burning* fire.

†[דְּמָה] **vb.** be like (BH I. דָּמָה);—**Pe.** 1819, 1821
Pt. act. דָּמֵה Dn 3^{25} (ל pers.); f. דָּמְיָה 7^{5} (לְדֹב).

דְּנָה 57 **demonstr. pr. comm.** this (Zinj. 1836
זן, זנה; Eg. Aram. זנה (S-C Pap. B 17+); זנך (ib. C 6, D 8);
Nab. Palm. דנה (Lzb 264 Cooke 26); 𝔗 דֵּין (e.g.
1 S 10^{27}) and (with הָ, i.e. הָא, ܗܳܐ *ecce*) הָדֵין;
Aram. of Têma הא זא (Cooke 195.198); Syr. ܗܳܢܳܐ
(contr. for הָדְנָא); Mand. האזין; Sab. ذن (Hom
Chrest. 13); Eth. ዝንቱ: all from [דָּה,] זה,
+ demonstr. *n* (W CG 108 f.); fem. BAram. דָּא,
𝔗 דָּא, הָדָה, Syr. ܗܳܕܶܐ, Mand. האזא, Eth. ዛቲ:
without the *n*; the pl. is אִלֵּין, q.v.);—*this:* 459

a. Dn 2[18] רָזָא דְנָה *this* secret, v[28.29.30]+, Ezr 4[11] 5[3.4.9]+; כָּל־דְּנָה Dn 5[22]. **b.** אַחֲרֵי דְנָה *after this* †Dn 2[29.45]; so כְּאתַר דְּנָה †7[6.7]. **c.** כִּדְנָה *like this, thus*, †Je 10[10] (=Heb. כֹּה), Dn 2[10] מִלְּתָא כִדְנָה a word *like this* (cf. כָּזֹאת Est 4[14]), 3[29] Ezr 5[7]. **d.** עַל־דְּנָה *on account of this* †Dn 3[16] Ezr 4[22] 5[5.17] 6[11]; as conj.=*therefore* (cf. Heb. עַל־זֹאת) Ezr 4[14.15].—Vid. also קֳבֵל and קַדְמָה. p. 1080

1751, 1855 †[דְּקַק] **vb.** be shattered, fall to pieces
1854 (BH);—**Pe.** *Pf.* 3 mpl. דָּקוּ Dn 2[35]. **Haph.** *break in pieces: Pf.* 3 fs. הַדֶּקֶת 2[34.45], 3 mpl. הַדִּקוּ 6[25] (all sq. acc.); *Impf.* 3 fs. תַּדִּק 2[40] (abs.), v[44] (acc.); sf. תַּדְּקִנַּהּ 7[23]; *Pt. act.* מְהַדֵּק 2[40] (acc.), f. מַדֱּקָה (K[§ 46, 3 b]) abs. 7[7.19].

1859 דָּר v. דור. p. 1087

1867-68 דָּרְיָוֶשׁ n.pr.m. (BH *id.*; Eg. Aram. דריוהוש RÉS[361] S-C[H 1+]);—**1.** Darius Hystaspis Ezr 4[24] +8 t. Ezr. **2.** 'Darius the Mede' Dn 6[1.2.7.10.26.29].

2220 **דרע** (√of following; BH II. זרע, זְרוֹעַ).

1872 †[דְּרָע] **n.[f.]** arm (so 𝔗 Syr.);—pl. sf. דְּרָעוֹהִי Dn 2[32].

153 †אֶדְרָע (K[§ 60, 1]) **n.[f.]** force (prop. *arm*, 𝔗
248 (rare); BH אֶזְרוֹעַ);—abs. בְּאֶ׳ וְחָיִל Ezr 4[23] *by force and power*, forcibly.

1882 †דָּת **n.f.**[Dn 6, 9] decree, law (Syr.; Pers.
1881 loan-word, v. BH);—ד׳ abs. Dn 6[16] 7[25], cstr. Ezr 7[14]+; emph. דָּתָא Ezr 7[12]+; sf. דָּתְכוֹן Dn 2[9];—**1.** *decree* of king Dn 2[13.15] Ezr 7[26]; c. sf. Dn 2[9] *decree against you.* **2.** unchangeable *law* of Medes and Pers. Dn 6[9.13.16]. **3.** *law* of God (in mouth of non-Jews): Dn 6[6] Ezr 7[12.14.21.26], so (abs.) Dn 7[25]; *laws* of God Ezr 7[25].

1883 †[דְּתֶא] **n.[m.]** grass (so 𝔗 Syr.; BH
1877 דֶּשֶׁא);—emph. דִּתְאָא Dn 4[12.20].

1884 ‡†[דְּתָבַר] **n.m.** judge (loan-word fr. Pers. *dâtabara, law-bearer, judge* (cf. דִּינַיָּא), Andr[M 59*] Mey[Entst. J. 23] Dr[Dn]; in Bab. as *dâtabar(r)i* Hilpr[Bab. Exp. ix. 28]);—pl. emph. דְּתָבְרַיָּא Dn 3[2.3].

ה

הֲ interrog. part. (BH הֲ, q.v.: 𝔗 הֲ; not Syr.: on the vocal., v. K[§ 67, 2]);—Dn 2[26] הַאִיתָךְ *art thou . . . ?* 3[14] הַצְדָּא (Baer Gi; edd. הַצְדָא), 6[21] הַיִכֻל *can he . . . ?* הֲלָא *nonne ?* †3[24] 4[27] 6[13].

†הָא **demonstr. part.** lo! behold! (BH 1888
הֵא (twice); Eg. Aram. and Têma הא (Cooke[195, 1887
198]); 𝔗 הָא; Syr. ܗܳܐ; Mand. הא (Nö[M 81]); Ar. هَا: in Aram. also oft. prefixed to pr. 3 ps. for greater definiteness, as 𝔗 הָהוּא, ܗܳܘ (for *hā-hū*), v. Nö[M 89 f.] W[CG 106 f.]), Dn 3[25].

†הֵא **demonstr. part.,** prefixed idiom. to 1888
כְּ for greater definiteness, lit. *behold like* (BH
הֵא, v. הָא supr.), only in הֵא־כְדִי Dn 2[43] הֵא־כְדִי 1887-88
פַּרְזְלָא לָא מִתְעָרַב *like as* iron doth not mingle with clay (cf. **a.** 𝔗[O] הָא כְמַיָּא Gn 49[4], so 𝔗[Jon] הא כ׳ Is 5[28] 9[4]+oft.; 𝔗[Jer] הֵי כ׳ Gn 26[4.18.22]+oft.; הֵיךְ ψ 2[9] 5[10.13]+, also pleon. הֵיךְ כְּ׳ ψ 22[14.15.17]+ oft. **b.** Palm. הֵיךְ *as* (Lzb[259]), as היך בנמוסא *as* (is) in the law (Cooke[321]; so 𝔗[Jer] ψ 2[9], etc.), הֵיךְ דִּי conj. (like Dn הֵא כְדִי: =Heb. כַּאֲשֶׁר), as היך די גבא *like as* he levied, Cooke[Tariff ii. b 12. 18, c 14. 17. 21. 26] [𝔗[O Jon] for כַּאֲשֶׁר have כְּמָא דְ׳, 𝔗[Jer] הֵיכְמָא דְ׳, 𝔖 ܐܝܟ ܕ]. It is dub. whether הֵא כְדִי belongs to **a** (notice esp. 𝔗[Jon]) or **b**: Schulth[ZAW 1902, 164 f.] to **b**, reading הֵאךְ דִּי (but א rare and late: D[(2) § 45. 1]); Nes[OLtz. 1892, 488] from הֵיךְ (v. BH) *how ?*). 1963

‡†[הַדָּבַר] **n.m.** counsellor, minister 1907
(Pers. loan-word; orig. form and mng. dub., cf. Andr[M 60*] Mey[Entst. J. 23] Dr[Dn 3, 24]);—pl. emph. הַדָּבְרַיָּא Dn 6[8]; cstr. הַדָּבְרֵי 3[27]; sf. הַדָּבְרַי 4[33], הַדָּבְרוֹהִי 3[24].—Vid. גְּדָבְרַיָּא. p. 1086 1411

†[הַדָּם] **n.[m.]** member, limb (loan-word 1917
from Pers. اندام, هندام *id.* Lag[Ges. Abh. 28] Fl[Levy ChWB i. 423 b]); pl. abs. הַדָּמִין תִּתְעַבְדוּן Dn 2[5] *ye shall be made members*, i.e. *dismembered*, so 3[29].

†[הֲדַר] **vb. Pa.** glorify God (𝔗 Syr. BH 1921-22
honour man);—*Impf.* 2 ms. הַדַּרְתָּ Dn 5[23], 1 s. הַדְּרֵת 4[31]; *Pt. act.* מְהַדַּר v[34] (all c. ל pers.).

†[הֲדַר] **n.[m.]** honour, majesty, of kg.;— 1923
emph. הַדְרָא Dn 5[18]; sf. הַדְרִי 4[27.33] (where Behrm plausibly (after Theod.) הַדְרֵת [𝔗 הֲדַר *return*]).

הֲוָה, הֲוָא **vb.** come to pass, become, 1934
be (BH הָיָה);—**Pe.** *Pf.* 3 ms. הֲוָה Dn 4[26]+, 1961
הֲוָא Dn 5[19]+; 2 ms. הֲוַיְתָ Dn 2[31.34], 1 s. הֲוֵית 4[1]+; 3 mpl. הֲווֹ Dn 2[35]+; *Impf.* 3 ms. לֶהֱוֵא (K[§ 47, 1) b] Dr[§ 204 Obs.] Nö[M 215 ff.]; in JAram. as jussive D[§ 61, 1 c]) Dn 2[20]+; 3 fs. תֶּהֱוֵה Dn 4[24]+, —א Ezr 6[8]+, 3 mpl. לֶהֱוֹן Ezr 6[10]+6 t., 3 fpl. לֶהֶוְיָן Dn 5[17]; *Imv.* mpl. הֱווֹ Ezr 4[22], הֱווֹ 6[6];—**1.** *come to pass* Dn 2[28.29.29.45]. **2.** *come into being, arise* Ezr 7[23]; *become, come to be*, c. n.pred. Dn 4[24] 5[29] and (=*represent*) 7[23]; c. כְּ *like* 2[35a], c. ל pred.

v^{35b}, c. adj. pred. Ezr 6^{6}, c. adv. phr. 5^{5} Dn 4^{22}; oft. periphrast., c. pt.: יְדִיעַ לה׳ *let it become known* 3^{18} Ezr 4$^{12.13}$ 5^{8}; so *let it be given* 6$^{8.9}$, also 7^{26} Dn 2^{20}. **3.** *be*, as copula, c. adj. pred. Dn 2$^{40.42}$ 7^{19}; so very often in periphrast. conj. c. pt., ה׳ צָבֵא *wish* 5$^{19.19.19.19}$, חָזֵה ה׳ *behold* 2$^{31.34}$ 7$^{2.4.6}$+, etc.

1932 †הוּא$_{14}$ **m.** הִיא$_{7}$ **f. pron. of 3 s. he,**
1931 **she, it** (=BH הוּא, הִיא; Zinj. and Palm. (once) הא, Palm. (usually) Nab. Eg. Aram. הו, f. הי, Lzb^{257}, S-C$^{Pap. A 1, 12+; A 4, C 9+}$. The pl. is אִנּוּן, q.v.);—*he, she, it*, Dn 2^{21} ... וְהוּא מְהַשְׁנֵא and *he* will change, etc., v$^{22.44}$ 6^{5} 7$^{7.24}$ Ezr 5^{8}; Dn 2^{32} הוּא צַלְמָא *that* image (nom. pend.); 4^{19} אַנְתְּה הוּא thou art *it*. Resuming the subj. with emph. (BH **2 b**) 2^{47} 6^{17}; resuming the subj. in predication (*ib.* **3 b**) 2^{20} חָכְמְתָא וּגְבוּרְתָא דִּי־לֵהּ הִיא *it* is his, v^{28}. Anticipating the subj. (*ib.* **4 a**) 2^{9} חֲדָה הִיא דָתְכוֹן; with a pron. (*ib.* **4 b**) 2^{38} אַנְתְּה הוּא ... *thou art* the head of gold 5^{13}; 3^{15} מַן הוּא אֱלָהּ ... *who is* the god ...? (so pl. אִנּוּן ... Ezr 5^{4}); 4^{27} הֲלָא דָא הִיא ... (*ib.* **4 b** γ); 6^{27} דִּי הוּא ... *who is* ... (*ib.* **2 c**), Ezr 6^{15} (so דִּי אִנּוּן ... Dn 7^{17}). [Cf. in 𝔗 Ex 14^{25} 15^{11} 2 S 20^{19} 24^{17} ψ 43^{2} 63^{4} 66^{3}+.] Affirming existence (BH **6 b**) Dn 4^{21}. Cf. Dr$^{§§ 198-201}$, K$^{§ 87, 3}$.

1965 †[הֵיכַל] **n.m. palace, temple** (As. loan-
1964 word; BH; also Palm. היכלא and הכלא Lzb^{259} SAC^{43});— emph. הֵיכְלָא Ezr 4^{14}+; cstr. הֵיכַל Dn 4^{26}; sf. הֵיכְלִי 4^{1}, ־לֵהּ 6^{19};—**1.** *palace*
4415 of king Dn 4$^{1.26}$ 5^{5} 6^{19} Ezr 4^{14} (v. מְלַח). **2.** *temple*: **a.** in Jerusalem Dn 5$^{2.3}$ Ezr 5$^{14a.15}$ 6$^{5.5}$. **b.** in Babylon 5$^{14b.c}$.

1946, 1981 †[הֲלַךְ] **vb. go** (BH; 𝔗; Syr. only Pa.);—**Pe.** syncop. (so 𝔗 D$^{§ 70, 9}$, Eg. Aram. Cooke^{209}, Impf. S-C$^{D 22, G 25, 28}$) *go*, of men: *Impf.* 3 ms. יְהָךְ (K$^{§ 44 a}$; al. יְהָךְ) Ezr 6^{5}, יְהָךְ 5^{5}; of inanimate things = be brought, 7^{13}; *Inf.* לְמְהָךְ (K$^{l. c.}$; al. ־ְ־ךְ) v^{13}. **Pa.** *Pt.* מְהַלֵּךְ *walking about* Dn 4^{26} (עַל loc.). **Haph.** *id.*: *Pt.* pl. מַהְלְכִין 3^{25} (בְּגוֹא); fig. 4^{34} *walk* in pride (? rd. **Pa.** in these).

1983 †הֲלָךְ (K$^{§ 57 a)}$) **n.[m.] toll**;—Ezr 4$^{13.20}$ 7^{24}.

1994 †הִמּוֹ$_{9}$ (Ezr), הִמּוֹן$_{3}$ (Dn), **pron. 3 pl.**
1992 **they, them** (=BH הֵם, הֵמָּה, q.v., but the more original forms. Eg. Aram. המו CIS$^{145 B 4}$ (Cooke^{207}), $^{149 A 1}$, S-C$^{Pap. C 7, 10+}$; not 𝔗 Syr., which use אִנּוּן, ܐܢܘܢ, ܗܢܘܢ, instead; Ar. هُمْ, هُمُ. The *n* in הִמּוֹן, as in אִלֵּין, דִּין, by the side of אֵלֶּה, זֶה, أُولَاءِ; Nö$^{M 86}$ W$^{CG 106}$);—*they, them*: **a.** as nom. Ezr 5^{11} אֲנַחְנָא הִמּוֹ עַבְדוֹהִי *we are* his servants (constr. as in Syr., Nö$^{§ 312 D}$ Mt 5^{13}, K$^{§ 87, 3}$). **b.** as accus. (in BAram., as in Syr., there being no verbal sf. of 3 pl.; so Eg. Aram. Cooke$^{76 B 4}$, S-C$^{Pap. E 5+}$), Dn 2^{34} והדקת הִמּוֹ and crushed *them*, v^{35} 3^{22} Ezr 4$^{10.23}$ 5$^{5.12.14.14.15}$ 7^{17}.—Comp. אִנּוּן.

†הַמְנִיכָא Qr (Kt המינכא, also [Gi] המוניכא, 2002
etc.) **n.[m.] chain, necklace** (Talm. הַמְנִכָא D$^{WB 108}$; Syr. ܗܡܝܢܟܐ; loan-word from Gk. *μανιάκης* K$^{§ 64, 4}$; or < Pers. *hämyān, girdle* [dimin. would be *hamyānak*] (whence also Gk. *μαν.*, Bev Dr$^{Dn 5, 7}$) Andr$^{M 60*}$ (rdg. הַמְיָנְכָא); v. also Behrm^{ix} Lag$^{Ges. Abh. 40; Arm. Stud. 1420}$; v. Krauss$^{5 f.}$ (who cp. also Talm. מוּנְיָק, מָנְיָק *necklace, bracelet*, Levy$^{NHWB iii. 52 b, 158 b}$ D^{230}));—of gold, Dn 5$^{7.16.29}$.

†הֵן **conj. if, whether** (BH הֵן, q.v.: Zenj. 2005-06
Eg. Aram. (S-C$^{Pap. A 7+}$), Palm. Nab. הן, Mand. הין *if* [𝔗^{OJon} use אם, 𝔗^{Jer} אין, Syr. ܐܢ]);—**1.** *if*, Dn 2^{6} 3$^{15.17}$ 4^{24} 5^{16} Ezr 4$^{13.16}$ 5^{17}, הֵן לָא ... Dn 2$^{5.9}$ 3^{15}; v^{18} הֵן לָא *if not.* **2.** repeated, הֵן ... הֵן *sive ... sive, whether ... or* (cf. BH אִם, **1 b** 1), Ezr 7^{26} (so Palm.$^{Tariff ii. c. 19}$). **3.** in indirect
question, *whether* (cf. אִם, **2 b**), Ezr 5^{17b} 518
יִתְבַּקַּר ... הֵן אִיתַי ...—Vid. also לָהֵן. 3861

הַסֵּק etc., v. סלק Haph. p. 50, 243, 1099

הרהר (√ of foll., 𝔗 הַרְהֵר, NH הִרְהֵר *reflect, brood impurely* D$^{WB 112}$; Syr. ܗܪܗܪ is *injure, irritate, quarrel* PS).

†[הַרְהֹר] **n.[m.] fancy, imagining**;—pl. 2031
abs. הַרְהֹרִין Dn 4^{2} *fancies* (in dream).

ו

וְ, וּ **conj. and** (BH וְ), used mostly as in Heb., except that there is no ו 'consecutive';—*and*, connecting both words (Dn 2^{5}) and sentences (*ib.*). When three or more words are connected together, וְ may connect them all (Dn 2$^{6.10}$ 4^{34} 5^{13}), or only the two last (2^{17} 3^{4} 4^{4} Ezr 6^{9}), or the three last (Dn 2^{37} 3^{21}), or be omitted altogether (2^{27} 5^{11}, cf. 3^{2} Ezr 4^{9}). וְ also connects vbs., in cases where BH would use וַ, as Dn 4^{2} 5^{29} 6$^{17.25}$; in such cases a *pf.* is oft. followed by a *ptcp.*, as Dn 2^{7} עֲנוֹ וְאָמְרִין, so v^{10} 3$^{9.16.24}$+, hence in $2^{5.8.15.20}$ and often read prob. with Nö $^{GGA\ 1884,\ 1021}$ עֲנָה וְאָמַר (for עָנֵה). Special senses:— **a.** *and that* Dn $4^{10.12.20}$ Ezr $6^{8.9}$ (cf. Dn $2^{16.18}$); *and also* Dn 6^{29}; =*with*, 7^{1}. **b.** connecting *contrasted* ideas, *but* Dn 2^{6} $3^{6.18}$ 4^{4}. **c.** =*and so*, Dn 2^{40} 6^{2}, esp. after imv. $2^{4.9.24}$, or impf. 2^{7}. **d.** to express an intention Dn 5^{2} וְיִשְׁתּוֹן *that* they might drink: after a command, etc., even with ptcp. or perf., nearly=*that*, 2^{13} 6^{2} (cf. K $^{§ 102}$). **e.** introducing the pred. (cf. BH **5 c**), Dn 7^{20} וְקַרְנָא דִכֵּן וְעַיְנִין לַהּ and this horn, *it had* eyes; but the case is isolated, and del. prob. ו with Marti.

ז

2084 †[זְבַן] **vb. buy, gain** (𝔗 *id., buy*, Syr. ܙܒܢ, OAram. Nab. Palm. זבן (oft.) Lzb ^{266} SAC ^{47}, cf. As. *zibânîtu, scales*);—**Pe.** *Pt. act.* pl. זָבְנִין Dn 2^{8} time ye (are seeking to) *gain*.

2095 †[זְהַר] **vb. Pe.** *Pt. pass.* pl. זְהִירִין Ezr 4^{22}
2094 be *warned* (𝔗 Syr., cf. BH II. [זָהַר] **Hiph.** *warn*).

2103 †[זוּד] **vb. be presumptuous** (𝔗 ^{J}; v. BH
2102 [זוּד, זִיד]);—**Haph.** *Inf.* לַהֲזָדָה Dn 5^{20} *act presumptuously*.

2109-10 †[זוּן] **vb. feed** (𝔗 זוּן; Syr. ܙܘܢ; cf. BH);—**Hithpe.** *be fed: Impf.* יִתְּזִין (K $^{§ 45, 1 d}$); so in Syr. W $^{CG\ 254}$ Nö $^{LCB,\ 1896,\ 703}$) Dn 4^{9}, מִן of source.

4203 †מָזוֹן (K $^{§ 15a}$) **n.[m.] food** (𝔗 Syr.);—abs. מ׳ Dn $4^{9.18}$.

2111-12 †[זוּעַ] **vb. tremble** (𝔗 Syr.: cf. BH);—**Pe.** *Pt.* pl. זָאֲעִין Kt, Qr זָיְעִין; מִן־קֳדָם pers., Dn 5^{19} 6^{27}.

2122 †[זִיו] **n.m. brightness, splendour** (𝔗 *id.*, Syr. ܙܝܘܐ, perhaps loan-word from As. *zîmu*, chiefly of *countenance*, Dl $^{WB\ 252:\ Pr\ 152}$ Nö $^{ZMG\ xl\ (1886),\ 732}$ Jen $^{ZK\ ii.\ 43}$ Brock $^{Lex.\ Syr.\ 93}$);—sf. זִיוִי Dn 4^{33} *splendour* of royalty; זִיוֵהּ 2^{31} (of image); pl. *brightness* of countenance: sf. זִיוַי 7^{28}, זיויך Kt, זִיוָךְ Qr, 5^{10}, זִיוֹהִי $5^{6.9}$.

2136 †זָכוּ (K $^{§ 61, 4}$) **n.f. purity, innocence** (cf.
2135 BH זָכָה, also 𝔗 דְּכָא, Syr. ܕܟܐ *be clean* (Ar. ذَكَا is *be bright* (of fire), *acute* (of mind), etc.), or Ar. زَكَا *be pure, good*, 𝔗 זְכָא, Syr. ܙܟܐ *be pure, innocent*; are these forms with ז secondary? or ancient ‖?);—abs. ז׳ Dn 6^{13} *innocence* in God's sight.

†זְכַרְיָה **n.pr.m.** prophet (BH *id.*), Ezr 5^{1} 6^{14}. 2148

†זְמַן **n.m.** $^{Dn\ 3,7}$ time (prob. loan-word from 2166
OPers. *zrvan, zarvâna, time, age*, Nö $^{M\ 152}$ Scheft ^{45};
cf. BH (late); and (on change of *v* [*b*] to *m*) 2165
Frä $^{ZA\ iii.\ 52}$; Nab. זמן, Palm. (Nab.) זבן Lzb $^{266.\ 268}$ SAC $^{48.\ 49}$);—abs. ז׳ Dn 2^{16} 7^{12}; emph. זִמְנָא Ezr 5^{3}+; pl. abs. Dn 6^{11}+, emph. זִמְנַיָּא Dn 2^{21};—*time: specified time* Dn 2^{16}; *appointed time* $7^{12.22}$, cf. 2^{21}; בֵּהּ זִמְנָא *at that time* Ezr 5^{3} Dn $3^{7.8}$ 4^{33}; (festival) *seasons* 7^{25}; *time, occurrence*, $6^{11.14}$ *three times in the day*.

†[זְמַן] **vb. denom. Hithpa.** agree to- 2164
gether (𝔗);—*Pf.* 3 mpl. Dn 2^{9} Qr הִזְדְּמִנְתּוּן (D $^{211,\ 2nd\ ed.\ 263}$ M $^{§ 12 a}$; Kt **Haph.** הַזְמִנְתּוּן, v. 𝔗 ^{Onk} Ex 5^{14} D $^{(2)\ 263,\ 403}$), sq. Inf. לְמֵאמַר.

†[זְמָר] **n.[m.] music** (cf. BH I. [זָמַר]);— 2167, 2170
emph. זְמָרָא Dn $3^{5.7.10.15}$.

†[זַמָּר K $^{§ 59 d)}$] **n.m. singer**;—pl. emph. 2171
זַמָּרַיָּא Ezr 7^{24}.

†[זַן] **n.[m.] kind, sort** (𝔗 Syr.; cf. BH);— 2177-78
pl. cstr. זְנֵי זְמָרָא Dn $3^{5.7.10.15}$.

†זְעִק **vb. cry, call** (𝔗 Syr.; cf. BH);—**Pe.** 2199-200
Pf. 3 ms. ז׳ Dn 6^{21} (ב of voice).

זער (𝔗 Syr., *be small*; BH זְעֵיר √זער; Eg. 2191
Aram. זער Cooke ^{213}, Nab. זעירא, Palm. זערא Lzb ^{268} SAC ^{49}).

†[זְעֵיר] **adj. little, small**;—fs. קֶרֶן זְעֵירָה 2192
Dn 7^{8}.

†[זְקַף] **vb. raise, lift up** (𝔗 Syr.; cf. BH 2210-11
(late; rare));—**Pe.** *Pt. pass.* וּזְקִיף יִתְמְחֵא עֲלוֹהִי Ezr 6^{11} *and, lifted up, he be fastened upon it* (sc. the timber erected; ref. prob. to impalement, v. Ryle Berthol).

†זְרֻבָּבֶל **n.pr.m.** (BH *id.*);—Ezr 5^{2}. 2216-17

†זְרַע **n.[m.] seed** (cf. BH I. זרע);—cstr. 2232-34
ז׳ אֲנָשָׁא Dn 2^{43} *seed* (offspring) of men.

ח

†[חֲבַל] **vb. Pa. destroy, hurt** (v. BH 2255
II. חבל);—*Pf.* 3 mpl. sf. חַבְּלוּנִי Dn 6^{23} (of lions); 2254
Imv. mpl. sf. חַבְּלוּהִי 4^{20} (sf. of tree); *Inf.* לְחַבָּלָה Ezr 6^{12} (acc. of temple). **Hithpa.** *be destroyed: Impf.* 3 fs. לָא תִתְחַבַּל Dn 2^{44} 6^{27} 7^{14} (-בָּֽל); all of kingdom of God).

2257 †חֲבָל **n. m.** [Dn 6, 24] **hurt, injury**;—abs. ח׳ Dn 3[25] 6[24], cf. RÉS[362 A 2]; emph. חֲבָלָא Ezr 4[22].

2248 †חֲבוּלָא **n.f. hurtful act, crime**;—abs. ח׳ Dn 6[23].

2269 †[חֲבַר] **n. m. fellow, comrade** (𝔗 Syr.;
2266 v. BH);—pl. sf. חַבְרוֹהִי Dn 2[13.17.18].

2273 †[חַבְרָה] **n.f. fellow**;—pl. sf. חַבְרָתַהּ Dn 7[20] *its fellows* (in vision of horns).

2292 †חַגַּי **n.pr.m. prophet** (BH *id.*);—Ezr 5[1] 6[14].

2298 חֲדָה, חַד v. אחד. p. 1079

2304-05 †חֶדְוָה **n.f. joy** (𝔗 Syr.; v. BH II. חדה);—abs. בְּח׳ Ezr 6[16] *with joy.*

2306 †[חֲדִי], or (K[§ 55, 6 a)]) [חַד] **n. m. breast** (𝔗
2373 Syr.; v. BH II. חזה);—du. (Schulth[ZAW xxii (1902), 164]) sf. חֲדוֹהִי Dn 2[32].

2319, 2323 †חֲדַת **adj. new** (𝔗 Syr.; BH חדשׁ);—ח׳ Ezr 6[4].

חוד (✓of following; 𝔗 חוּד, חוּדִיתָא, *riddle*, v. BH and K[§ 57 b) a)]).

280 †[אֲחִידָה] **n. f. riddle**;—fpl. abs. אֲחִידָן Dn 5[12].

2324 †[חֲוָה] **vb. Pa. Haph.** (M[§ 65c]) **declare**
2331 (𝔗 Syr.; BH III. [חָוָה] (late));—**Pa.** c. acc. פִּשְׁרָא (or equiv.): *Impf.* 3 ms. sf. יְחַוִּנַּנִי (sf. pers. indir. obj.) Dn 5[7], יְחַוִּנַּהּ 2[11] (קֳדָם pers.); 1 s. אֲחַוֵּה 2[24] (ל pers.), 1 pl. נְחַוֵּה v[4]. **Haph.** usu. c. acc. פִּשְׁרָא (or equiv.): *Impf.* 3 ms. יְהַחֲוֵה Dn 5[12]; 2 mpl. תְּהַחֲוֺן 2[6], sf. (of indir. obj.) תְּהַחֲוֻנַּנִי v[9]; 1 pl. נְהַחֲוֵה v[7]; *Imv.* mpl. sf. (of indir. obj.) הַחֲוֺנִי v[6]; *Inf.* לְהַחֲוָיָה v[10] 5[15]; + ל pers. 2[16.27]; c. acc. of signs and wonders 3[32].

263 †[אַחֲוָיָה] **n.f. a declaring** (prop. Inf. Aph., K[§ 60, 1)]);—cstr. אַחֲוָיַת אֲחִידָן Dn 5[12] *the declaring of riddles* (cf. לְהַגִּיד הַחִידָה Ju 14[14f.], Bev).

2338 †[חוּט or חִיט] **vb. repair** (foundations);—**Haph.** *Impf.* 3 mpl. יַחִיטוּ Ezr 4[12] (si vera l. [Nö[GGA, 1884, 1018] Str[§ 13 b]]), rare form for יְחִיטוּן K[§§ 16, 5. 26, 1] M[§ 63 g, Anm.], but perh. read this, and regard as **Qal** (orig. meaning dub.; Ar. خَاطَ is
2339 *sew*, =𝔗 חוּט, Syr. ܚܛ, cf. BH חוּט *thread;* Syr. Pa. also *join together* (so here Schulth[ZAW xxii (1902), 162 Anm.]), cf. Ar. خَيَّطَ *conjunxit* trabes (de Goeje Bibl. Geogr. Arab., Pt. iv (1879), Gloss. 231: cf. Pt. viii (1894), Gloss. p. xx); Frä[ZAW xix (1899), 180] conj. *pull down* and clear away (for rebuilding), cf. *ḫaiaṭu* Dl[WB 274]; Jen [KB vi. 344] cp. As. *ḫâṭu, observe, learn* (Dl[WB] I. חיט), i.e. *examine, test;* Hpt[Gu. Ezr-Ne 62] conj. ✓ חטט *excavate*, cf. Ar. اختطّ *secure* site *by a mark, found* a town; Str[Gr (1905) 40] יְחִיבוּ (after Seybold), cf. Ezr 5[16]; al. conj. *build wall*, denom., cf. Ar. حَائِطٌ *wall* (✓ حوط *guard, surround*)).

†חִוָּר **adj. white** (𝔗 Syr.; BH I. [חָוַר]);— 2357-58
Dn 7[9] (robe).

†חֲזָה **vb. see, behold** (v. BH);—**Pe.** *Pf.* 2370, 2372
3 ms. ח׳ Dn 4[20] 5[1]; 2 ms. חֲזַיְתָ 2[43]+, -תָה 2[41.41]; 1 s. חֲזֵית v[46]+; 2 mpl. חֲזֵיתוֹן 2[8]; **Pe.** *Inf.* לְמֶחֱזֵא Ezr 4[14]; *Pt. act.* חָזֵה Dn 2[31] + 14 t.; pl. חָזַיִן 3[27] 5[23]; *pass.* חֲזֵה 3[19];—**1.** *see*, have sense of sight Dn 5[23]. **2.** *see, behold:* **a.** acc. pers. 3[25], c. ל v[27], acc. rei 5[5]. **b.** *see, witness* dishonour of king (acc.) Ezr 4[14]. **3.** usu. *behold* in dream or vision (oft. pt. in periphrast. conj.), acc. pers., 4[20], acc. rei 2[41.41.43] 4[17], abs. 2[34] 7[4.7.9.11.11.21], + אֲלוּ 2[31] 4[7.10], אֲרוּ 7[2.6.13]; c. obj. cl. 2[8.45]; *behold* a dream, acc. חֵלֶם, 2[26] 4[2.6.15] 7[1]. **4.** pass. = *customary* (*seemly*) Dn 3[19] (so 𝔗 Lv 5[10] al., v. Dr).

†[חֵזוּ] **n.m. vision, appearance**;—emph. 2376
חֶזְוָא (K[§ 55, 6 b)]) Dn 2[19]; sf. -וִי 7[2], -וַהּ v[20]; pl. cstr. חֶזְוֵי 2[28]+;—**1.** *vision* (as mode of revelation) 2[19] (ח׳ דִּי לֵילְיָא), 7[2], so 7[7.13], ח׳ רֵישָׁא 2[28] 4[2.7.10] 7[1.15], ח׳ חֶלְמָא 4[6] (Gie[GGA, 1895, 598] reads אֲחַוֵּא *I will relate*). **2.** *appearance* 7[20].

†[חָזוֹת K[§ 55, 6 b) 2]; rd. perh. -וּת K[§ 61, 4 b), Anm.]] 2379
n. f. sight, visibility (v. Schulth[ZAW xxii (1902), 165 f.]);—sf. חֲזוֹתַהּ Dn 4[8.17].

†[חֲטָי] **n. [m.] sin** (v. BH חטא);—sf. חֲטָיָךְ 2399, 2408
Dn 4[24] (Qr חֲטָאָךְ K[§ 57 a) β)]), < pl. (for חֲטָיָיךְ) Hi Bev Kmp Behrm, cf. ‖ עֲוָיָתָךְ.

†חַטָּיָא **n.f. sin-offering** (BH חַטָּאת **4**; Nab. 2403, 2409
חטיאת *penalty*, acc. to SAC[51]);—abs. ח׳ Ezr 6[17] Kt, Qr חַטָּאָה.

†[חֲיָא] **vb. live** (v. BH חָיָה);—**Pe.** *Imv.* 2418, 2421
לְעָלְמִין חֱיִי *live for ever!* Dn 2[4] 3[9] 5[10] 6[7.22]. **Haph.** *Pt.* מַחֵא (K[§ 11, 3 b) γ)] Hpt[Kmp. Dn. 28]) Dn 5[19] *let live.*

†חַי **adj. living** (BH *id.*);—**1.** of God: 2416-17
abs. ח׳ Dn 4[31], emph. חַיָּא 6[21.27]; men, pl. emph. חַיַּיָּא *the living* 2[30] 4[14]. **2.** pl. as n. abstr. *life* (BH חַיִּים): חַיִּין 7[12]; cstr. חַיֵּי Ezr 6[10].

†חֵיוָא, חֵיוָה **n.f. beast** (BH II. חַיָּה);— 2416, 2423
abs. -ָא Dn 4[13], -ָה 7[5.7]; emph. חֵיוְתָא 7[6.11.19.23], and (coll.) 4[11.12] 5[21]; cstr. (coll.) חֵיוַת בָּרָא 2[38] 4[9.18.20.22.29]; pl. abs. חֵיוָן 7[3], emph. חֵיוָתָא 7[7.12.17].

2429 †חַיִל **n.m. power, strength, army** (v. BH
2428 II. חיל, חול);—**1.** *power:* abs. בְּאֶדְרָע וְחָיִל Ezr
4^{23} *by force and power;* קרא בְּח׳ i.e. *call loudly*
Dn 3^4, בְּחַיִל 4^{11} 5^7; גִּבָּרֵי־ח׳ 3^{20} *mighty men of*
power. **2.** *force, army,* sf. חֵילֵהּ 3^{20}; cstr.
חֵיל שְׁמַיָּא 4^{32} (=BH צְבָא הַשָּׁמַיִם).

2445, 2450 [חַכִּים]$_{14}$ **n.m. wise man** (v. BH חכם);—
pl. abs. חַכִּימִין Dn 2^{21}; elsewhere of the class
possessed of occult learning in Bab. v^{27}, emph.
-מַיָּא v^{13} 5^{15}; cstr. -מֵי $2^{12.14}$ + 7 t. Dn.

2452 †חָכְמָה **n.f. wisdom;**—ח׳ abs. Dn 2^{30} +,
emph. חָכְמְתָא Dn 2^{20} +, cstr. חָכְמַת 5^{11} Ezr 7^{25};—
wisdom, attrib. of God Dn 2^{20}; of gods 5^{11}; of
man 2^{30}; of God imparted to man Ezr 7^{25}
(practical wisdom), Dn 2^{21}; =occult knowledge
(v. foregoing) imparted to men v^{23} $5^{11.14}$.

2493 חֵלֶם$_{22}$ **n.m.** $^{Dn\,4,2}$ **dream** (𝔗 Syr.; v. BH
2472 חֲלוֹם, √ II. חלם);—abs. ח׳ Dn 4^2 7^1; emph.
חֶלְמָא 2^4+; sf. חֶלְמִי 4^6, -מָךְ 2^{28}; pl. חֶלְמִין 5^{12};—
dream, as vehicle of revelation Dn 2^4 + 10 t.,
4^3 + 6 t., 5^{12}; to prophet 7^1.

2498-99 †[חֲלַף] **vb. pass** (over) (v. BH);—**Pe.**
c. עַל pers. *pass over* one (of time): *Impf.* 3 mpl.
יַחְלְפוּן Dn $4^{13.20.22.29}$.

2508 †חֲלָק **n.[m.] portion, possession, lot** (v.
2505 BH);—abs. ח׳ *possession* in land Ezr 4^{16}; sf.
חֲלָקֵהּ Dn $4^{12.20}$, i.e. his appointed lot.

4255 †[מַחְלְקָה] **n.f. class, division,** of priests
4256 and Levites (BH מַחֲלֹקֶת);—pl. sf. מַחְלְקָתְהוֹן
Ezr 6^{18}.

2528 חֱמָא v. יחם. p. 1095

2561-62 †חֲמַר **n.m. wine** (𝔗 Syr.; BH חֶמֶר (poet.
and late), √I. חמר);—abs. ח׳ Ezr 6^9 7^{22}; emph.
חַמְרָא Dn $5^{1.2.4.23}$.

2406, 2591 †[חִנְטָה] **n.f. wheat** (v. BH חִטָּה, √ חָנַט;
Nö $^{LCB,\,1896,\,703}$ cp. Eg. *chnt;* OAram. has חטה, pl.
חטי, Palm. חטא Lzb^{279} SAC^{51});—pl. חִנְטִין Ezr
6^9 7^{22}.

2597-98 †[חֲנֻכָּה] **n. f. dedication** (𝔗; BH *id.*,
√חנך);—cstr. חֲנֻכַּת, of image Dn $3^{2.3}$; temple
Ezr $6^{16.17}$.

2603-04 †[חֲנַן] **vb. shew favour** (v. BH);—**Pa.**
Inf. c. acc. pers. מִחַן (K $^{§46,\,3\,a}$) Dn 4^{24} (cf. BH
Pō̆. Pr 14^{21}). **Hithpa.** *implore favour* (of God;
so BH Hithp.), *Pt.* מִתְחַנַּן Dn 6^{12}.

2608 †חֲנַנְיָה **n.pr.m.** (=BH *id.* **5**);—Dn 2^{17}.

†[חֲסַן] **vb. Haph.** take possession of 2631
(Syr. *be strong, overcome;* 𝔗 *be strong, take*
possession of; Eg. Aram. Haph. החסן *hold pro-*
perty S-C$^{D\,2+}$, cf. BH חסן);—*Pf.* 3 mpl. הֶחֱסִנוּ 2630
(K $^{§38,\,3}$ Kmp $^{ad\,loc}$) Dn 7^{22}; *Impf.* 3 mpl. יַחְסְנוּן
(K $^{§38,\,1b)}$) v^{18} (perhaps point -סִנוּן).

†[חֱסֵן] **n.m.** (royal) **power;**—emph. חִסְנָא 2632
Dn 2^{37}; sf. חִסְנִי 4^{27}.

†חֲסַף **n.[m.] clay, potsherd** (𝔗 *id.;* Chr- 2635
Pal. ܚܣܦܐ *clay vessel,* ܚܣܦܐ pl. *potsherds*
Schulth^{68}, Syr. ܚܣܦܐ *potsherd;* 𝔗 חַצְבָא, NH
חָצָב *clay vessel;* As. *ḫaṣbu, id.;* ܚܨܒܐ *jar* (PS^{1238}),
whence Ar. خزف *pottery* Frä^{169}, but Sab. חסף
jar, acc. to Hom $^{ZMG\,xlvi\,(1892),\,532}$; cf. Eth. ጸሕብ:
jar (transp.; Di^{1265}); v. BH [חַסְפַּס]);—ח׳ abs. 2636
Dn 2^{41} (ח׳ דִּי פֶחָר), חֲסַף $v^{33.42}$; cstr. ח׳ טִינָא $v^{41.43}$;
emph. חַסְפָּא $v^{34.35.43.45}$.

†חַסִּיר **adj. lacking, wanting, deficient** 2627
(cf. BH חָסֵר);—ח׳ Dn 5^{27}. 2637

†[חֲצַף] **vb. Haph. shew insolence,** 2685
harshness (NH חצף **Hiph.** *act insolently,* so
𝔗 Aph.; Syr. ܚܨܦ be audacious);—*Pt.* f.
מְהַחְצְפָה (K $^{§33,\,2\,e)}$) Dn 3^{22} *overbearing* (of command),
מְהַחְצְפָה 2^{15} *harsh* (*id.*).

†[חֲרַב] **vb. be waste** (v. BH II. חרב);— 2717-18
Hoph. *Pf.* הָחָרְבַת Ezr 4^{15} city *was laid waste.*

‡†חַרְטֹם **n.m. magician** (BH *id.*, √I. 2748-49
חרט);—abs. Dn 2^{10}; pl. abs. חַרְטֻמִּין 2^{27} 5^{11};
-מַיָּא $4^{4.6}$.

†[חֲרַךְ] **vb. singe** (𝔗 Syr.; NH חָרַךְ);— 2761
Hithpa. *Pf.* 3 ms. הִתְחָרַךְ Dn 3^{27} (of hair).

†[חֲרַץ] **n.[m.] loin** (v. BH חָלָץ, √ II. 2504, 2783
[חָלָץ]);—sf. חַרְצֵהּ Dn 5^6 the joints of *his loin*
(v. קְטַר).

†[חֲשַׁב] **vb. think, account** (v. BH);— 2803-04
Pe. *Pt. pass.* pl. כְּלָה חֲשִׁיבִין Dn 4^{32} *like those not*
accounted of, of no account, Bev Dr.

†[חֲשַׁח] **vb. need** (As. *ḫašâḫu, crave;* 2818
Syr. ܚܫܚ *in need of;* not 𝔗);—**Pe.** *Pt.* pl.
חָשְׁחִין Dn 3^{16}, sg. Inf. (van d. H., wrongly, חַשׁ׳).

†[חַשְׁחָה] **n.f. thing needed** (Syr. ܚܫܚܬܐ; 2818
Nö in K $^{p.\,175}$);—pl. חַשְׁחָן Ezr 6^9.

†[חַשְׁחוּ] **n.f.coll. things needed, require-** 2819
ment (Syr. *id.*);—cstr. חַשְׁחוּת בֵּית אֱלָהָךְ Ezr 7^{20}.

2822 **חשך** (v. BH חֹשֶׁךְ *darkness*, √חשך).

2816 †[חֲשׁוֹךְ] **n. [m.] darkness**;—emph. חֲשׁוֹכָא Dn 2^{22}.

2827 †[חֲשַׁל] **vb. shatter by a blow** (As. *ḫašâlu, shatter*, perhaps *thresh;* NH חָשַׁל Pi. *shatter:* JAram. חֲשַׁל *forge, hammer*, Syr. ܚܫܠ *forge, furbish;* Buhl[14] cp. ℭ חוּשְׁלָא *barley-groats* (as *pounded, beaten*), and perh. As. *ḫušlu, barley;* Nö[M 135] cp. Ar. حَسَلَ *thrust, drive away* (Frey), ℭ נַחְשׁוֹל *storm(y sea;* cf. in Eng. *beaten, buffetted* by waves; As. loan-word Ba[ZA ii. 117]), Syr. ܚܫܘܠܐ *id.*);—**Pe.** *Pt. act.* חָשֵׁל Dn 2^{40} (acc. rei).

2856-57 †[חֲתַם] **vb. seal** (v. BH);—**Pe.** *Pf.* 3 ms. sf. (of stone) חַתְמַהּ Dn 6^{18} (ב instr.).

ט

2868, 2895 †טְאֵב **vb. be good** (ℭ Syr., v. BH טוב);—**Pe.** *Pf.* 3 ms. ט׳, c. עַל pers. Dn 6^{24} *it was good*
888 *to him=he was glad* (cf. בְּאֵשׁ v^{15}). p. 1084

2869 †טָב **adj. good**;—abs. ט׳ Dn 2^{32} *pure* gold;
2896 =*pleasing* to (עַל pers.) Ezr 5^{17} (cf. 6^{18}, BH טוב **5**).

2876-77 †[טַבָּח] **n. m. guardsman** (v. BH *id.;* √טבח);—pl. emph. טַבָּחַיָּא Dn 2^{14}.

2906 †טוּר **n.m. mountain** (ℭ Syr. Nab., SAC[58]; BH צוּר, √V. צור);—abs. ט׳ Dn 2^{35}; emph. טוּרָא v^{45}.

2908 †טְוָת **adv. fastingly, hungrily** (Syr. ܛܘܬ *id.;* PS[1455]; on etym. cf. Schulth[Hom. Wurz. 32 f.]; on adv. force of f. term. ־ַת, v. Nö[§ 155 A, M 201] W[CG 135]; and cf. רַבַּת ψ 124^{3});—Dn 6^{18}.

2917 †[טִין] **n. [m.] clay** (ℭ *id.;* NH טִינָה, Syr. ܛܝܢܐ, Ar. طِينٌ (yet v. Frä[8]));—emph. חֲסַף טִינָא Dn $2^{41.43}$.

2919-20 †טַל **n. [m.] dew** (v. BH I. טלל);—cstr. טַל שְׁמַיָּא Dn $4^{12.20.22.30}$ 5^{31}.

2927 †[טְלַל] **vb. Haph. have shade** (ℭ Syr.;
2926, 6751 v. BH III. [צָלַל]);—*Impf.* 3 fs. תַּטְלֵל Dn 4^{9} (beasts under tree).

2939 †[טְעַם] **vb. Pa. feed** (Pe. prop. *taste*, v.
2938 BH);—*Impf.* 3 mpl., acc. of grass + לְ pers.: יְטַעֲמוּן Dn $4^{22.29}$, so (sf. pers.) יְטַעֲמוּנֵּהּ 5^{21}.

טְעֵם 30 **n.m.** [Ezr 4, 21] **taste, judgment, com-** 2942
mand (BH טַעַם (late sense));—abs. ט׳ Dn 3^{10}+, 2940
cstr. ט׳ 5^{2} Ezr 6^{14}, טְעֵם (of God, mere scribal dis- 2941
tinction Nö[LCB 1896, 305] Str[§ 8 c] K[Aramaismen 40]) Ezr 6^{14} 7^{23}; emph. טַעְמָא 4^{21}+;—†**1.** Dn 5^{2} in *the taste* of the wine (while they were enjoying it). †**2.** *judgment, discretion*, in reply, הֲתִיב עֵטָא וּט׳ Dn 2^{14} (Pr 26^{16}); in act (pers.) שִׂים ט׳ עַל Dn 3^{12} 6^{14} *shew proper deference* to (עַל). †**3.** *report* (of official), c. הלך Ezr 5^{5}, יהב Dn 6^{3}. **4.** *command*, of God Ezr 6^{14} 7^{23}, of king 6^{14}; שִׂים ט׳ *give command, issue decree* Dn 3^{10} + 3 t., Ezr $4^{19.21.21}$ + 11 t.; בְּעֵל ט׳ *commander* Ezr $4^{8.9.17}$.

†[טְפַר] **n.m. nail, claw** (ℭ טוּפְרָא, Syr. 2953
ܛܦܪܐ; v. BH צִפֹּרֶן, √IV. צפר);—pl. sf. of man 6856
טְפְרוֹהִי Dn 4^{30}; of beast, טפריה (K[§ 53, 2, b)]) 7^{19}, Qr טִפְרַהּ.

†[טְרַד] **vb. chase away** (v. BH);—**Pe.** 2956-57
Pt. act. pl. טָרְדִין, לְ acc. pers. + מִן pers. Dn $4^{22.29}$. **Pe'îl** *Pf.* 3 ms. טְרִיד (W[CG 224]), subj. pers. + מִן 4^{30} 5^{21}.

‡†טַרְפְּלָיֵא **n. pr. gent.** so most, Ezr 4^{9} 2967
(Andreas[M 64*] a title; Hoffm[ZA ii. 55] cp. *Pers. *tarapardа*, i.e. *beyond the bridge;* < Scheft[86] cp. OIran. *tarapâra, beyond the shore* [=*transriparii* Id.[MGWJ 47, 316]] transl. of עֲבַר נַהֲרָא).

י

†[יְבַל] **vb. Haph. bear along, carry** (v. 2987
BH);—*Pf.* 3 ms. הֵיבֵל, acc. rei + לְ loc. Ezr 5^{14} 2986
6^{5}; *Inf.* לְהֵיבָלָה 7^{15}, acc. rei.

†[יַבֶּשֶׁת] **n.f. earth** (so Syr.; ℭ as BH 3007
יַבָּשָׁה *dry land*, √יָבֵשׁ);—emph. יַבֶּשְׁתָּא Dn 2^{10}. 3006

†[יְגַר] **n. [m.] (stone-)heap** (ℭ *id.;* Syr. 3026
ܝܓܪܐ; cf. Eth. ወገረ: *throw together*, ወግር:
mound);—cstr. יְגַר שָׂהֲדוּתָא Gn 31^{47} (=Heb. גַּל־עֵד). 3026

†יַד **n.f.** [Dn 5. 5] **hand** (v. BH);—cstr. י׳ Ezr 3027-28
5^{12}+; emph. יְדָא Dn $5^{5.24}$; sf. יְדִי 3^{15}, יְדָךְ v^{17}, יְדֵהּ Ezr 6^{12}, יְדְהֹם (K[§ 53, 2. a)]) 5^{8}, etc.; du. abs. יְדַיִן Dn $2^{34.45}$;—**1.** *hand* of man Dn $2^{34.45}$ Ezr 5^{8} 6^{12}, and (in vision) Dn $5^{5.5.24}$; fig. בִּידָךְ *in thy possession* Ezr $7^{14.25}$; fig. of God 4^{32}. **2.** *power*, of man Dn 2^{38} $3^{15.17}$ 7^{28} Ezr 5^{12}, of God Dn 5^{23}; of lion 6^{28} (al. *paw*).

3029, 3034 †[יְדָא] **vb. Haph.** praise (v. BH ידה);—*Pt. act.* מְהוֹדֵא Dn 2^{23} (ל dei), מוֹדֵא (K §§33, 2; 43, 1. c)) 6^{11} (קֳדָם dei).

3045-46 †יְדַע **vb.** know (v. BH);—**Pe.** *Pf.* 3 ms. י׳ Dn 5^{21} 6^{11}, 2 ms. יְדַעְתָּ 5^{22}, 1 s. יִדְעֵת 4^{6}; *Impf.* 2 ms. תִּנְדַּע (K § 11, 4. b) δ)) Ezr 4^{15}+, etc.; *Imv.* דַּע ms. (K § 11, 3 a)) Dn 6^{16}; *Pt. act.* יָדַע 2^{8}+; pl. יָדְעִין 5^{23}, etc.; *pass.* יְדִיעַ 4^{12}+;—*know*, c. acc. rei Dn 2^{30} 5^{22}, acc. rei om. Ezr 7^{25}; יָדְעֵי דָּתֵי א׳ v^{25}, יָדְעֵי בִינָה Dn 2^{21}; c. obj. cl. $v^{8.9.22}$ $4^{6.14.23.29}$ 5^{21} $6^{11.16}$ Ezr 4^{15}, so (of God) Dn 4^{22}; *pt. act.* abs. 5^{23} *having capacity of knowledge; pass.* in periphr. conjug., subj. cl. + ל pers. 3^{18} Ezr $4^{12.13}$ 5^{8}. **Haph.** *Pf.* 3 ms. הוֹדַע Dn 2^{15}+, sf. הוֹדְעָךְ v^{29}, 2 ms. sf. הוֹדַעְתַּנִי v^{23}, -תֶּנָה v^{23}, 1 pl. הוֹדַעְנָא Ezr 4^{14}; *Impf.* 3 ms. יְהוֹדַע Dn 2^{25}, sf. יְהוֹדְעִנַּנִי 7^{16}, etc. (v. K § 43 c)); *Inf.* לְהוֹדָעָה 5^{8}, sf. לְהוֹדָעֻתַנִי 4^{15} 5^{16}, etc.; *Pt. act.* pl. מְהוֹדְעִין 4^{4}+;—*cause to know, inform:* ל pers. Ezr 4^{14}, +acc. rei Dn $2^{15.17.25.30}$ 4^{4} $5^{8.17}$, so (sf. pers.) $2^{5.9.26}$ $4^{3.15}$ $5^{15.16}$ 7^{16}, and (subj. God) 2^{23}; ל pers.+obj. cl. Ezr 4^{16} 7^{24}, so (of God) Dn $2^{28.29.45}$, and (sf. pers.) v^{23}; acc. pers. only Ezr 5^{10} 7^{25}.

4486 †מַנְדַּע **n. [m.]** knowledge, power of knowing (𝔗J *id.;* Syr. ܡܕܥܐ, ܡܰܕܥܳܐ; BH
4093 מַדָּע (late); cf. 'Mandâ' = γνῶσις, Nö M xx);—abs. Dn 5^{12}; emph. -דְּעָא 2^{21}; sf. -דְּעִי $4^{31.33}$.

3051-52 †יְהַב **vb.** give (𝔗 Syr.; cf. BH);—**Pe.** *Pf.* 3 ms. י׳ Ezr 5^{12}+; 2 ms. יְהַבְתְּ Dn 2^{23}; 3 mpl. וִיהַבוּ 3^{28}; *Imv.* ms. הַב (K § 11, 3. a)) 5^{17}; *Pt. act.* יָהֵב 2^{21}, pl. יָהֲבִין 6^{3};—**1.** *give*, acc. rei + ל pers. Dn 2^{48} 5^{17}, also (subj. God) $2^{21.23.37.38}$ $5^{18.19}$; *give* report 6^{3} (ל pers.); *give over*, acc. pers. + בְּיַד (יַד **2**) Ezr 5^{12} (subj. God); *give up, surrender* Dn 3^{28} (one's body, acc.). **2.** *place, lay* foundations Ezr 5^{16} (Nab. also *place* Cooke 102, 1. 6 SAC JQ 1904, 274; v. ܝܗܒ **2** Schulth Lex; and ZAW xxii (1902), 162; cf. D WB 171). **Peʿîl** (W CG 224), *be given*, subj. rei, c. ל pers.: 3 ms. יְהִיב Dn $7^{4.6}$, יְהַב $v^{14.22}$, 3 fs. יְהִיבַת 5^{28} $7^{12.27}$; 3 mpl. וִיהִיבוּ Ezr 5^{14}; *be given up* (ל of flame) Dn 7^{11}. **Hithpe.** *Impf.* 3 ms. יִתְיְהֵב Dn 4^{13}, 3 fs. תִּתְיְהִב Ezr 6^{4}; 3 mpl. יִתְיַהֲבוּן Dn 7^{25}; *Pt.* מִתְיְהֵב Ezr 4^{20} 6^{9}, fs. מִתְיַהֲבָא v^{8}, pl. -בִין 7^{19};—**1.** *be given*, subj. rei, ל pers., Dn 4^{13} Ezr 6^{9} 7^{19}; *be given over*, subj. pers. בִּידֵהּ (יַד **2**) Dn 7^{25}. **2.** *be paid*, of cost Ezr 6^{4} (מִן of source), v^{8} (ל pers.), toll 4^{20} (ל pers.).

†יְהוּד **n.pr.terr.** Judah (secondary format. from foll. acc. to M § 68. b Buhl; cf. BH יְהוּדָה);— Dn 5^{13b} Ezr $5^{1.8}$ 7^{14}; בְּנֵי גָלוּתָא דִּי י׳ Dn 2^{25} 5^{13a} 6^{14}. 3061
3063

†[יְהוּדַי] **n.gent.** Jew (BH יְהוּדִי);—pl. abs. יְהוּדָאִין (K § 61, 6)) Dn 3^{12}; emph. יְהוּדָיֵא (Ib. 1b.) v^{8} Ezr $4^{12.23}$ $5^{1.5}$ $6^{7.7.8.14}$. 3062, 3064

†יוֹם **n.m.** Ezr 6, 15 day (v. BH);—abs. י׳ Ezr $6^{9.9.15}$, emph. יוֹמָא Dn $6^{11.14}$; pl. abs. יוֹמִין v^{8}+, emph. יוֹמַיָּא 2^{28}+; cstr. יוֹמֵי 5^{11}, and יוֹמָת (K § 51, 2, Anm. 3) Ezr $4^{15.19}$; sf. יוֹמֵיהוֹן Dn 2^{44};—*day*, as division of time Dn $6^{11.14}$, *day* of month Ezr 6^{15}; thirty days Dn $6^{8.13}$; יוֹם בְּיוֹם Ezr 6^{9} *day by day;* pl. esp. of duration: עַתִּיק י׳ *one aged of days*, aged man Dn $7^{9.13.22}$; עָלְמָא י׳ *days of old* Ezr $4^{15.19}$: of a period: life-time, or reign, of king Dn 2^{44} 5^{11}; לִקְצָת י׳ 4^{31} *at the end of the days* (appointed time), בְּאַחֲרִית י׳ 2^{28} *in the latter part of the* (future) *days*. 3117-18

†יוֹצָדָק **n.pr.m.** Ezr 5^{2} (BH *id.*, √הָיָה). 3136

יזב v. שֵׁיזִב. p. 1115 7804

יחם (√of foll.; v. BH יָחַם, whence חֵמָה). 2534, 3179

†חֱמָא **n.f.** rage;—abs. Dn 3^{19}, ח׳ v^{13}. 2528

†[יְטַב] **vb.** be (good,) pleasing (𝔗; Eg. Aram. Haf. הוטב S-C B 11+; v. BH יטב);—**Pe.** *Impf.* יֵיטַב (K § 43, 2) Ezr 7^{18} (עַל pers., + inf.). 3191

†יְכִל (K § 25. a) β)) **vb.** be able (Dn) (𝔗; Nab. (rare) SAC 60; Eg. Aram. S-C E 8, 11+; Chr-Pal. Schulth 83; BH יָכֹל);—**Pe. 1.** c. Inf. *be able* to do: 3202
3201
Pf. 3 ms. יְכִל Dn 6^{21} (subj. God), 2 ms. יְכֵלְתָּ 2^{47}; *Impf.* 3 ms. יוּכַל (Hebraism, K § 43, 1. Beisp. b)) v^{10}, יִכֻּל 3^{29} (subj. a god), 2 ms. תוכל $5^{16.16}$ (< both Qr תִּכּוּל, K l. c.); *Pt.* יָכִל 3^{17} 4^{34} (both subj. God); pl. יָכְלִין 2^{27} 4^{15} 6^{5}. **2.** *prevail* (BH **2**) *against* (ל), *Pt.* fs. יָכְלָה 7^{21}.

†[יַם] **n.m.** sea (𝔗 Syr.; v. BH יָם, √ימם);— emph. יַמָּא Dn $7^{2.3}$. 3220-21

†[יְסַף] **vb.** add (v. BH);—**Hoph.** (W CG 225) *Pf.* 3 fs. הוּסְפַת (K §§ 15 d); 17, 1; 43, 1. Beisp. c)) Dn 4^{33} *was added*, ל pers. 3254-55

†[יְעַט] **vb.** advise (so JAram.; BH יעץ);—**Ithpa.** *Pf.* 3 mpl. אִתְיָעַטוּ (K §§ 23, 1. Anm.; 39, 5) Dn 6^{8} recipr. *took counsel with each other*, sq. inf. 3272
3289

3272 †[יָעֵט] **n.m.** counsellor (prop. Pt. act.);—pl. sf. יָעֲטֹ֫הִי Ezr 7[14], יָעֲטֹ֫והִי v[15].

2942, 5843 †עֵטָא **n.f.** counsel;—abs. Dn 2[14] (v. טְעֵם **2**). p. 1094

3319 יצא v. שֵׁיצִא. p. 1115

3321 †[יְצַב] **vb. Pa.** make certain, gain certainty (𝔗; cf. BH);—**Pa.** *Inf.* לְיַצָּבָא Dn 7[19], c. עַל *concerning.*

3330 †יַצִּיב **adj.** certain, true (𝔗 *id., firm, native* (=אֶזְרָח));—abs. ׳י Dn 2[8.45], emph. ־בָא 3[24] (K[§ 59. g]); fs. ־בָא 6[13] 7[16];—**1.** *certain, sure* Dn 2[45]; in exclam. 3[24] *undoubtedly!* מִן־יַצִּיב v[8] *of a surety.* **2.** *true* 6[13]; f. as subst. 7[16] *the truth* concerning, עַל rei.

3344-45 †[יְקַד] **vb.** burn (v. BH);—**Pe.** *Pt. act.* f. יָקִדְתָּא Dn 3[6.11.15.17.20.21.23.26].

3346 †[יְקֵדָה] **n.f.** burning;—cstr. לִיקֵדַת אֶשָּׁה Dn 7[11].

3366-67 †[יְקָר] **n.m.** [Dn 2,6] honour (v. BH);—abs. וִיקָר Dn 2[6] 7[14]; cstr. *id.* 4[27], לִיקָר v[33] (K[§ 57. Anm.] Str ־קָר); emph. וִיקָרָא 2[37] 5[18], ־ה v[20].

3358 †[יַקִּיר] **adj.** honourable, difficult;—**1.** *honourable,* emph. יַקִּירָא Ezr 4[10]. **2.** *difficult*
3515 (cf. BH כָּבֵד **adj. 1 d**), fs. יַקִּירָה Dn 2[11].

3390 יְרוּשְׁלֶם [25] **n. pr. loc.** Jerusalem (BH
3389 יְרוּשָׁלַםִ);—Dn 5[2.3] 6[11] Ezr 4[8.12] + 20 t. Ezr.

3391, 3393 †[יְרַח] **n.m.** month (v. BH);—abs. לִירַח אֲדָר Ezr 6[15]; pl. abs. יַרְחִין Dn 4[26].

3410 †[יַרְכָה] **n.f.** thigh, or loin (𝔗; v. BH
3409 ירך);—pl. sf. יַרְכָתֵהּ Dn 2[32].

3478-79 †יִשְׂרָאֵל **n.pr.gent.** Israel (BH *id.*, √I. שָׂרָה);—אֱלָהּ יִשׂ׳ Ezr 5[1] 6[14] 7[15]; מֶלֶךְ לְיִשׂ׳ 5[11]; בְּנֵי יִשׂ׳ 6[16], עַמָּא יִשׂ׳ 7[13].

3442-43 †יֵשׁוּעַ **n.pr.m.** (BH *id.* **3**, p. 221);—Ezr 5[2].

3462, 8142 ישן (√of following; BH יָשֵׁן, שֵׁנָה).

8139 †I. [שְׁנָה] **n.f.** sleep (𝔗 Syr.);—sf. שְׁנְתֵהּ
8140 (K[§ 12 d]) Dn 6[19].—II. [שְׁנָה] v. [שְׁנָא]. p. 1116

853, 3487 †יָת **mark of accus.** (=BH I. אֵת; Palm. ית; Zinj.[Had. 28] c. sf. ותה; Nab. Palm. c. sf. יתה (Lzb[263] Cooke[170]; cf. RÉS[468]); 𝔗 Sam. יָת; Syr. ܝܳܬ (rare); v. further p. 84[b]);—Dn 3[12] דִּי מַנִּיתָ יָתְהוֹן whom thou hast appointed.

3488 †יְתִב (K[§ 25 a) β)]) **vb.** sit, dwell (𝔗 Syr.; v.
3427 BH ישׁב);—**Pe. 1.** *sit, be seated: Pf.* 3 ms. יְתִב Dn 7[9] and (of judgment = the judge) v[10], so *Impf.* 3 ms. יִתִּב (K[§ 43, 1, Beisp. b)], cf. BH יֵשֵׁב) 7[26]. **2.** *dwell, Pt.* pl. abs. יָתְבִין Ezr 4[17] (ב loc.). **Haph.** *cause to dwell: Pf.* 3 ms. הוֹתֵב 4[10] (acc. + ב loc.).

†יַתִּיר **adj.** pre-eminent, surpassing (v. 3493
BH יתר);—ms. abs. ׳י Dn 2[31]; fs. יַתִּירָא 6[4], usu. 3498
־ה 4[33] 5[12.14]; as adv. *exceedingly* 3[22] 7[7.19] (cf. יתיר מתבריך Eut[Sin. 498] wh. Lzb[401] reads יתירית בריך).

כ

כְּ **part.** like, as, about (BH כְּ, q.v.);—*like, as,* Dn 2[40] כְּפַרְזְלָא תַּקִּיפָא, 4[5.32] 5[1] +; *according to* 4[32] וּכְמִצְבְּיֵהּ עָבֵד and *according to* his will he doeth, Ezr 6[9.18] +; *about* (as BH **1 a**: cf. Zinj. Lzb[444] (כשלשן מלכ[ן]), Dn 4[16] כְּשָׁעָה חֲדָה, 6[1]; with inf. (BH **3 b**), 6[21] וּכְמִקְרְבֵהּ לְגֻבָּא and *as* he drew near, etc. Cpds.:—כְּדִי and כְּדְנָה,
v. דִּי and דְּנָה; כַּחֲדָה *together,* v. חַד (sub אחד). p. 453 1768, 1836, 2298

†[כְּדַב] **adj.** false (𝔗 Syr.; v. BH כזב);— 3538, 3576
fs. abs. מִלָּה כִדְבָה Dn 2[9] (> n. appos. K[175] M[66*]).

כְּדִי v. דִּי. p. 1087 1768

†כָּה **adv.** here (BH כֹּה; 𝔗 Mand. כָּא; 3541-42
Chr-Pal. ܟܐ; Syr. with prefixes, as ܠܟܐ *hither,* ܠܐܝܟܐ *where?*);—Dn 7[28] עַד־כָּה סוֹפָא דִּי־מִלְּתָא *hitherto* (cf. Je 48[47] 51[64]) is the end of the matter.

†[כְּהַל] **vb.** be able (𝔗 *id.;* Eg. Aram., 3546
S-C[Pap. A 6, 8, 11+]; Eth. ከሀለ: cf. syn. (יְכִל);—**Pe.** 3202
Pt. act., usu. sq. inf.: abs. כָּהֵל Dn 2[26] 4[15] (inf. om.); pl. abs. כָּהֲלִין 5[8.15].

†[כָּהֵן] **n.m.** priest (v. BH כהן);—emph. 3548-49
כָּהֲנָא Ezr 7[12.21]; pl. emph. ־נַיָּא 6[9.16.18] 7[16.24]; sf. (of Isr.) ־נוֹהִי v[13].

[כַּוָּה Nö[GGA 1884, 1019]] **n.f.** window (𝔗 כַּוְּתָא, 3551
Syr. ܟܘܬܐ, cf. Schulth[Lex. 91] (sub *ܟܘ), hence Ar. كَوَّة, كُوَّة *id.,* as loan-word Frä[13]);—pl. abs. כַּוִּין פְּתִיחָן Dn 6[11] (cf. S-C[J6]).

†[כֹּר] **n.** [**m.**] kôr, a measure of wheat 3734
(BH כֹּר p. 499);—pl. abs. כֹּרִין Ezr 7[22]. 3734

כּוֹרֶשׁ [9] **n.pr.m.** Cyrus (BH *id.*);—Dn 6[28] 3566-67
Ezr 5[13] + 6 t. Ezr.

[כַּכַּר], כַּכְּרִין v. כרר. כֹּל v. כלל. p. 1097-98 3604, 3606

3634-35 †[כְּלַל] **vb.** **complete** (v. BH I. [כָּלַל]; but שַׁכְ׳ perhaps loan-word from As. *šuklulu*, *ušaklil*, *uštaklil*, Dl[WB 331], cf. שֵׁיצִא, שֵׁיזִב and Buhl[14]);—**Shaph.** of building: *Pf.* 3 ms. sf. שַׁכְלְלֵהּ Ezr 5[11] *he finished it;* 3 mpl. שַׁכְלִלוּ 6[14], also (c. acc. rei) 4[12] (Kt שורי אשכללו, read Qr שׁוּרַיָּא שׁ׳); *Inf.* לְהַשְׁכְלָלָה, acc. rei 5[3.9]. **Ishtaph.** *be completed,* of walls; *Impf.* 3 mpl. יִשְׁתַּכְלְלוּן 4[13.16].

3605-06 כֹּל, כָּל־ **n.m.** **the whole, all** (BH כֹּל);—emph. כֹּלָּא Dn 2[40]+, cstr. כֹּל 2[12] 3[2]+, כָּל־ 2[8]+, sf. 3 mpl. כָּלְּהוֹן (so Palm. Lzb[296] Cooke[No. 117, Tariff II b, 18]) †2[38] 7[19] (Qr f. כָּלְּהֵן);—**1.** כֹּל חַכִּימֵי בָבֶל *the whole of* (=*all*) the wise men of B. 3[2.3.5], etc.; 6[2] כל־מלכותא *the whole of* the kingdom, v[4]; c. sf. *the whole of* them, 2[38] 7[19]. **2.** with a sg. noun, understood collectively, *every*, *any*, or with a neg. *none* (BH **1 b**): 3[29] דִּי כָל־עַם אֻמָּה וְלִשָּׁן that *every* people, nation, and language, etc., 6[8] מִן־כָּל־אֱלָהּ of *any* god, Ezr 6[12] כל אנש די *every man who*=*whoever,* Dn 3[10] 5[7] 6[13] Ezr 6[11]; Dn 2[10] כָּל־מֶלֶךְ וְעַם... לא כל מלך שְׁאֵל *no* king hath asked..., v[35] 4[6] 6[5.24]; so כָּל־דִּי (=Heb. כָּל־אֲשֶׁר) *whoever* 6[8] Ezr 7[26], *whatever* v[23], בְּכָל־דִּי *wherever* Dn 2[38] (cf. אֲשֶׁר **4 b** γ). †**3.** emph. כֹּלָּא, used absolutely, as Heb. הַכֹּל (BH **2 b**): Dn 2[40] חָשֵׁל כֹּלָּא crushing *all things*, 4[9.18] וּמָזוֹן לְכֹלָּא־בֵהּ and food *for all* was in it, v[25] כֹּלָּא מְטָא *all* came upon N. (cf. הַכֹּל בָּא Jos 21[43]), Ezr 5[7] שְׁלָמָא כֹלָּא *all* peace (K[§ 83 d]; cf. in Heb. כֻּלּוֹ etc., *after* their noun: BH **1 d** *a*).—

6903 For כָּל־קֳבֵל v. קֳבֵל. p. 1110

3651-52 †כֵּן **adv.** **thus, as follows** (BH כֵּן; 𝔗 כֵּן, Syr. ܟܢ);—usu. c. אֲמַר (אֲמַר, etc.; cf. Eg. Aram. CIS[ii. 149 A 1, B-C 3] RÉS[492 B 5]), Dn 2[24] וְכֵן אֲמַר־לֵהּ, v[25] 4[11] 6[7] 7[5.23] Ezr 5[3]; 6[2] וְכֵן־כְּתִיב בְּגַוַּהּ.

3660 †כְּנֵמָא **adv.** **accordingly, as follows** (der. uncertain: Nö[GGA, 1884, 1021] Marti al. from כֵּן + indef. מָא, *so somewhat, ungefähr so:* v. older improb. view (*as we should say,* from כְּ and נֵאמַר=נֵימָא, cf. Talm. יֵימָא for יֵימַר) in Thes[652]): referring backwards, Ezr 6[13] כְּנֵמָא ... עֲבַדוּ did *accordingly;* referring forwards, 4[8] ... כְּתַבוּ כְנֵמָא wrote a letter... *as follows,* 5[4] (rd. c. 𝔊 אֲמַרוּ; אֲמַרְנָא from v[9], Mey[Entst. 26]), v[9.11].

3673 †[כְּנַשׁ] **vb.** **gather** (𝔗 *id.;* OAram. Palm.

3664 כנש Lzb[298]; Syr. ܟܢܫ; v. also BH [כָּנַס]);—**Pe.** *Inf.* לְמִכְנַשׁ, sq. לְ acc. pers. Dn 3[2]. **Hithpa.** *Pt.* pl. מִתְכַּנְּשִׁין (were) *assembled* 3[3.27].

†[כְּנָת] **n.m.** **associate** (OAram. *id.*, Lzb[298] SAC[65]; S-C[B 6]; Syr. ܟܢܬܐ; Chr-Pal. [ܟܢܬ, ܟܢܬܐ] Schwally[Idiot. 46] Schulth[Lex. 95]; √ appar. כנה K[§ 56, a) β 2] M[§ 74 e]; Buhl makes loan-wd. from As. *kinâtu*, '*Genosse*,' but v. Dl[WB 333] Zim[M. p. 66*]);—*associate*, pl. sf. כְּנָוָתֵהּ Ezr 5[6], ־תְהוֹן 4[9.17.23] 5[3] 6[6.13]. 3675

כסא (v. BH כִּסֵּא *throne*). 3678

†כָּרְסֵא (K[§§ 11, 4 b) e); 62]) **n.m.**[Dn 7, 9a] **throne**;—cstr. כ׳ Dn 5[20]; sf. כָּרְסְיֵהּ 7[9 b]; pl. abs. כָּרְסָוָן 7[9 a]. 3764

כסדי v. כַּשְׂדָּי. p. 1098 3779

†כְּסַף **n.m.**[Ezr 7, 17] **silver** (v. BH);—abs. כ׳ Ezr 7[15]+, כְּסַף Dn 2[32]; emph. כַּסְפָּא v[35]+;—**1.** as material Dn 2[32.35.45] 5[2.4.23] Ezr 5[14] 6[5]. **2.** as money or its equivalent Ezr 7[17], v[15.16.18.22]. 3702

כְּעַן, כְּעֶנֶת, כְּעֶת v. sub ענה. 3705-06

†**כְּפַת** **vb.** **bind** (𝔗 *id.;* NH כָּפַת; Syr. ܟܦܬ *form knots,* ܟܦܬ *twist into a knot,* Ar. كَفَتَ *draw together,* As. [*kapâtu*] II. *bring together*);—**Pe'îl** *Pf.* 3 mpl. כְּפִתוּ (W[CG 224]) Dn 3[21] *they were bound.* **Pa.** *bind: Inf.* לְכַפָּתָה Dn 3[20] (לְ acc. pers.); *Pt. pass.* pl. מְכַפְּתִין *bound* v[23.24]. 3729

†[כְּרָא] **vb.** **Ithpe.** **be distressed** (cf. כַּרְיָא III. adj. *suffering,* כְּרִיוּתָא n. *id.* D[WB 197]; Syr. ܟܪܐ *be short, abridged,* ܟܪܝܐ ܠܝ *it grieved me;* ܟܘܪܗܢܐ *pain, grief;* cf. As. *kûru*, *pain;* also ܟܪܗ (der. spec.) *be ill,* Ar. كَرِهَ *dislike, shrink from*);—*Pf.* 3 ms. אֶתְכְּרִיַּת רוּחִי (K[§ 47. Beisp. 2]) Dn 7[15]. 3735

†[כַּרְבְּלָא] **n.f.** prob. **helmet, cap** (>al. *mantle,* e.g. K[§ 62]; v. Dr) (NH כַּרְבֹּלֶת *comb* of cock; so JAram. כַּרְבַּלְתָּא, Syr. ܟܪܒܠܬܐ; As. *karballatu*, *cap* Andr[M 67*], Muss-Arn[As. Dict. 436 a]; so SAC[JPhil. xxvi. 310 f.], cf. BH [כרבל]);—pl. sf. כַּרְבְּלָתְהוֹן Dn 3[21]. 3737 3736

†[כָּרוֹז] **n.m.** **herald** (loan-word from Gk. κήρυξ, κηρύσσειν (K[§ 64, 4] Krauss[ii. 296 f.]; Nö[GGA 1884, 1019] doubts); 𝔗 *id.*, Syr. ܟܪܘܙܐ (v. Brock), Chr-Pal. [ܟܪܘܙ] Schulth[Lex. 97]; cf. D[§ 37 ad fin.], also K[§ 64, 4] Bev[Dn 5, 29] M[§ 88]);—emph. כָּרוֹזָא Dn 3[4]. 3744

†[כְּרַז] **vb.** **denom.** **Haph.** make proclamation (poss. directly dependent on κηρύξ (D[§ 37, p. 146 (2nd ed. 183)] K[l. c.] M[67*]), but even then formed as denom.; cf. 𝔗 כְּרַז, NH כָּרַז, Syr. ܟܪܙ Af. Ethpe., so Chr-Pal. Schwally[Idiot. 46] Schulth[Lex. 97]);—*Pf.* 3 mpl. הַכְרִזוּ Dn 5[29], c. עַל pers. *concerning.* 3745

3764 **כָּרְסֵא** v. כסא. p. 1097

3603, 3769 **כרר** (√of foll.; cf. BH כרר, כִּכָּר **3**).

3604 †[כַּכַּר]† **n.** [**f.**] **talent**;—pl. abs. כַּכְּרִין Ezr 7^{22}.

3779 †כַּשְׂדַּי **n. pr. gent. Chaldean** (v. BH
3778 כַּשְׂדִּים);—abs. כ׳ Dn 2^{10}; emph. כשדיא Dn 5^{30} Kt (Qr כַּשְׂדָּאָה), כסדיא Ezr 5^{12} Kt (Qr כַּסְדָּאָה); pl. abs. כַּשְׂדָּאִין 3^{8} 5^{11}, emph. כשדיא Kt, כַּשְׂדָּאֵי Qr, Dn 2$^{5.10}$ 4^{4} 5^{7};—**1.** *Chaldean* by race Dn 3^{8} 5^{30} Ezr 5^{12}. **2.** as learned, of the class of Magi (BH כ׳ **1 c**), Dn 2$^{5.10.10}$ 4^{4} 5$^{7.11}$.

3789-90 †כְּתַב **vb. write** (v. BH);—**Pe.** *Pf.* 3 ms. כ׳ Dn 6^{26} לְ pers. + orat. rect., 7^{1} acc. rei; 3 mpl. כְּתַבוּ Ezr 4^{8} acc. אִגְּרָה; 1 pl. נִכְתּוּב 5^{10}, acc. rei; *Pt. act.* abs. fs. כָּתְבָה Dn 5^{5}, subj. יְדָא, fpl. כָּתְבָן v^{5}, subj. אֶצְבְּעָן. **Pe'îl** (W$^{CG\ 224}$) *Pf.* 3 ms. כִּדְנָה כְּתִיב Ezr 5^{7} *thus (it) was written,* so כֵּן כ׳ 6^{2}.

3792 †כְּתָב **n.m.**$^{Dn\ 5,7}$ **writing**;—abs. כְּתָב Ezr 7^{22} (Baer כְּתַב, but v. K$^{§\ 57\ ad\ fin.}$ Str); cstr. כ׳ 6^{18}; emph. כְּתָבָא Dn 5^{8}+, ־ָה 5$^{7.15}$;—**1.** *writing, inscription* (on wall) Dn 5$^{7.8.15.16.17.24.25}$. **2. a.** *written decree* 6$^{9.10.11}$. **b.** *written requirement* Ezr 6^{18} 7^{22}.

3796-97 †כְּתַל† (K$^{§\ 54,\ 3\ a)\ c)\ and\ c)}$) **n.** [**m.**] **wall** (BH כֹּתֶל, √כתל);—cstr. כ׳ Dn 5^{5}; pl. emph. כֻּתְלַיָּא Ezr 5^{8}.

ל

ל prep. to, for, in regard to, at, mark of accus. (BA לְ, and general Aram.);—sf. לִי, לָךְ, לֵהּ, לַהּ Dn 7$^{4.5}$+; לָנָא †Ezr 4^{14}; לְכֹם †5$^{3.9}$ 7^{24} (so Eg. Aram. S-C$^{Pap.\ H\ 12,\ 14+}$), לְכוֹן †Dn 3^{4}; לְהוֹם †Je 10^{11}, לְהֹם †Ezr 5$^{3.4.9.10}$ 6^{9} (so Zinj., Cooke^{184}; Nab., ib.$^{Nos.\ 85,\ 91}$), לְהוֹן †Dn 2^{35} 3^{14} 6^{3} 7^{12} (v^{21} לְהֵן), Ezr 4^{20} 5^{2} (so Palm., Cooke$^{No.\ 110,\ Tariff\ ii.\ c.\ 15\ (p.\ 329)}$);—**1.** *to,* after vbs. of *saying, declaring, writing,* etc., Dn 2$^{4.5.7.19}$ 6$^{21.26}$, etc., *giving* 2$^{16.21}$+, *offering* Ezr 6^{10}; of *going* (Aram. does not use אֶל), usu. to a *place,* 2^{17} לְבַיְתֵהּ אֲזַל, 3^{26} 4^{8} 6^{20}+ oft., rarely to a *person* Ezr 5^{5}; = *towards* Dn 4^{31}; *into* 3$^{6.11}$ 6^{17}+; in address of decree or letter 3^{31} Ezr 5^{7} 7^{12}; to fall or come *to* Dn 4$^{16.18}$ 5^{17} Ezr 5^{7} 7^{20}, be confirmed *to* Dn 4^{23}. **2.** as mark of *accus.* (as oft. in Aram.; cf. in late Heb., BH **3**), Dn 2$^{10.12.14.24}$ + oft., Ezr 7^{25} . . . לְכֹל (cf. אֶת Ju 3^{15} Is 8^{2}). **3.** to become or make *into* (BH **4**) Dn 2^{35} 4^{27}. **4. a.** *with reference to* Ezr 6^{8} לְמָא דִּי, 7^{14} (but rd. prob. וְעַל יְרוּשׁ׳). **b.** *belonging to* Dn 5^{23} לֵהּ, 7$^{4.6.7}$, and in דִּי לֵהּ = *his* 2^{20}+; c. אִיתַי לְ Ezr 4^{16}; הַשְׁכַּח לְ to find (belonging) *to* 2^{35} 6$^{5.6.23}$ (cf. BH מָצָא לְ Dt 22^{14}+). **c.** as periphr. for the *genitive* (BH **5 c**) Dn 7^{1} בִּשְׁנַת חֲדָה לְ׳, Ezr 5^{13} 6$^{3.15.15}$; 5$^{8.11}$. **d.** of the *object* or *purpose, for* (BH **5 g**) Dn 4^{9} וּמָזוֹן לְכֹלָּא־בֵהּ v$^{27.27.33}$ 7^{22} Ezr 6$^{9.17}$ 7$^{19.23}$; *on behalf of* Ezr 6^{10b}. **e.** *according to* (BH **5 i**) Ezr 6^{17} לְמִנְיָן . . . *according to* the number of . . . **5.** of *time, at* Dn 4^{26} . . . לִקְצָת *at the end of* . . ., v^{31}; *to* Dn 2$^{4.44}$+ לְעָלְמִין. **6.** with an *inf.* (BH **7**), after such vbs. as *be able, think, need, agree, command, decree,* Dn 2$^{9.10.12.24}$ 3$^{13.16.19.32}$ 6$^{4.5.8.24}$ Ezr 4$^{21.22}$ 5^{3}+ oft.; =*in order to* Dn 2$^{13.14}$ 3$^{2.20}$, *so as to* 5^{20}. With לָא = *not to be* . . . 6$^{9.16\ end}$ Ezr 6^{8}, v. לָא. Cf. the synopsis Lzb$^{300\ f.}$.

לָא (לָה †Dn 4^{32}) **adv. not** (BH לא; Aram. 3808-09
of Têma, Eg., etc., לא; Nerab ל (Lzb^{301} Cook$^{Gl.\ 67}$); 𝔗 לָא; Syr. ܠܐ);—*not* Je 10^{11} Dn 2$^{5.9.10}$, etc.; before a ptcp. (so rarely in BH, **1 b** *c*), וְכָל־דָּאְרֵי אַרְעָא כְּלָה חֲשִׁיבִין 2$^{27.43}$ 3^{16} 4$^{4.6.15}$+, so v^{32} are *as men not accounted of* (so Bev Behrm Marti, cf. Is 53^{3} 𝔗 בסירין ולא חשיבין; > most 'accounted *as nothing,*' for which no analogy, yet cf. ψ 39^{6} 𝔗); sq. אִיתַי, v. אִיתַי. With inf. and לְ Dn 6^{9} דִּי לָא לְהַשְׁנָיָה which *it is not* to alter = which *is not to be* altered (cf. v^{16}), Ezr 6^{8} (K$^{§\ 67,\ 1}$ Dr$^{§\ 202,\ 2}$; cf. Is 35^{6} 𝔗, D$^{Aram.\ Dialektproben,\ p.\ 1}$). With interr. הֲלָא †Dn 3^{24} 4^{27} 6^{13}.

לאך (√of foll.; BH מַלְאָךְ, לאך). 4397

†[מַלְאַךְ] **n.m. angel** (𝔗 Syr.);—sf. מַלְאֲכֵהּ 4398
Dn 3^{28} 6^{23}.

†לְבַב **n.m.**$^{Dn\ 4,\ 13}$ **heart** (v. BH; so Eg. Aram. 3824-25
S-C$^{B\ 12+}$);—cstr. ל׳ Dn 4^{13} 7^{4}; sf. לִבְבָךְ 2^{30} 5^{22}, ־בֵהּ 4^{13} 5$^{20.21}$.

†[לֵב] **n.** [**m.**] **id.** (BH *id.*; so 𝔗 Syr.; Eg. 3820-21
Aram., Lzb^{301} = Cooke$^{76\ A\ 6}$);—sf. לִבִּי Dn 7^{28}.

†[לְבֵשׁ] **vb. be clothed** (v. BH);—**Pe.** 3847-48
Impf. acc. אַרְגְּוָנָא: 3 ms. יִלְבַּשׁ Dn 5^{7}, 2 ms. תִּלְבַּשׁ v^{16}. **Haph.** *Pf.* 3 mpl. הַלְבִּשׁוּ v^{29} *clothe* one (ל) with (acc.).

†[לְבוּשׁ] **n.m. garment** (BH *id.*);—sf. 3830-31
לְבוּשֵׁהּ Dn 7^{9}; pl. sf. לְבוּשֵׁיהוֹן 3^{21}.

לָה v. לָא. above 3809

3860-61 †I. לָהֵן **conj.** therefore (BH לָהֵן †Ru
1[13.13]; Aram. of Têma להן CIS[ii. 113] = Cooke[195]),
Dn 2[6.9] 4[24] (Lambert[RÉJ. 1904. 273] denies I. לָהֵן, taking
BAram. always as = רַק).

3809,3861 †II. לָהֵן **conj.** except, but (from לָא and
518, 2006, הֵן 'not if' (cf. Heb. אם לא Gn 24[38]); so Nab.
3808 and Eg. Aram. להן Cooke[217. 219, 241] S-C[Pap. C 6, 7+];
lâinnî, however Socin[Arab. Dial. v. Marokko 44, Anm. 103];
𝔗 אִילָהֵין Gn 32[28] 43[3] al.);—**1.** after a neg. (= BH
518, 3588 כִּי אִם, q.v.): **a.** *except* Dn 2[11] 3[28] 6[6.8]. **b.** *but*
(Germ. *sondern*) Dn 2[30]. **2.** without a neg.:
however, but Ezr 5[12]. p. 50

3878-79 †[לֵוִי] **n. gent.** Levite (BH לֵוִי);—pl.
emph. לויא Kt, לֵוָאֵי Qr (K[§§ 61, 6); 52. d]), Ezr 6[16.18]
7[13.24] (all + priests).

3890 †לְוָת **prep.** to, at, beside (der. uncertain;
v. K[128 n.]; perhaps akin to לָוָה ,לְוִי, ܠܘܐ *join*;
𝔗 לְוָת, Syr. ܠܘܬ *to*), c. מִן, Ezr 4[12] the Jews
which came up מִן־לְוָתָךְ *from thee* (*de chez toi*;
cf. ܡܢ ܠܘܬ, מִלְּוָת, e.g. Ex 8[8] 9[33] 𝔖𝔗 = Heb. מֵעִם).

3900 †לְחֶם (K[§ 54, 3. γ]) **n.m. feast** (𝔗 Syr. *bread*,
3899 so BH, q.v. √ II. לחם);—abs. עֲבַד לְ׳ Dn 5[1]
made a feast.

3904 †[לְחֵנָה] **n.f.** concubine (𝔗 לְחֵינְתָא; Fl
Levy NHWB ii. 534 f. cp. Ar. لَخْنَآء, indelicate epithet for
woman; Batten[Ezr 2, 65] cp. Ar. لَحْنٌ *note, tune,
song;* still otherwise Wetzst[De, HL u. Koh. 454]);—
pl. sf. לְחֵנָתָךְ Dn 5[23], ־ָה v[2.3].

3915-16 †[לֵילְיָא] **n.[m.]** night (v. BH לַיְלָה);—
emph. לֵילְיָא Dn 2[19] 5[30] 7[2.7.13].

3956,3961 †לְשָׁן **n.m.**[Dn 3, 7] tongue (𝔗 Syr.; v. BH לָשׁוֹן,
√לשן);—*tongue = language*, fig. for *people*:
abs. עַם אֻמָּה וְלִ׳ ע׳ א׳ Dn 3[29]; pl. emph. וְלִשָּׁנַיָּא
v[4.7.31] 5[19] 6[26] 7[14] (cf. BH לָשׁוֹן **2**, Is 66[18]).

מ

3964, 4101 מָא v. מָה. below

3967, 3969 †מְאָה **n.f.** hundred (v. BH);—abs. מ׳
after noun enum., Ezr 6[17] 7[22.22.22.22], so אַרְבַּע מ׳
6[17], מ׳ וְעֶשְׂרִין Dn 6[1], and du. מָאתַיִן Ezr 6[17].

3977, 3983 מֹאזַנְיָא v. אזן. מֵאמַר v. אמר.
p. 1079, 1081

†[מָאן] **n.m.**[Ezr 7, 19] vessel, utensil (𝔗 מָ(א)ן, 3984
Syr. ܡܐܢܐ, so Chr-Pal., Schulth[Lex. 106]; OAram. מאן,
Ph. מנם; poss. √אנה, v. BH II. אנה, cf. Lag[BN 183] 579
Buhl);—pl., *vessels* of temple at Jerus.: emph.
מָאנַיָּא Ezr 5[14.15] 7[19] Dn 5[23]; cstr. מָאנֵי v[2.3] Ezr 6[5].

מְגִלָּה v. גלל. p. 1086 4040

†[מְגַר] **vb. Pa.** overthrow (𝔗, Syr. 4049
(Lexx.); v. BH (late, rare));—*Impf.* 3 ms. 4048
יְמַגַּר כָּל־מֶלֶךְ Ezr 6[12] (of God).

[מַדְבַּח] v. דבח. מִדָּה v. מִנ׳. p. 1087, 1101 4056, 4061

[מְדוֹר] v. דור. p. 1087 4070

†מָדַי **n.pr. gent. et terr.** Medes, Media 4076-77
(BH *id.*);—**1. gent.** Dn 5[28] 6[9.13.16]. **2. terr.** 4074-77
Ezr 6[2].

מדיא Kt, מָדָאָה Qr (K[§ 61, 6)]) **n. gent.** 4077
Mede;—Dn 6[1].

[מְדִינָה] v. דין. [מְדָר] v. דור. p. 1087-88 4070, 7083

†מָה (מָא †Ezr 6[8]) **pron. interr.** and 3964, 4101
indef. what? (BH מָה; Nab. מה; Zinj. מ;
𝔗 מא; Syr. ܡܢܐ; Ar. مَا: cf. W[CG 124 f.]);—**1.**
what? Dn 4[32] מה עבדת. **2.** *whatever, what*
(cf. BH **1 b** end) Dn 2[22] ידע מה בחשוכא knoweth
what is in darkness, Ezr 6[9]: so מָה דִּי (cf. דִּי **1 b**:
so Nab.; Palm. מדי ,מא די, Lzb[306] Cooke[320, 332])
Dn 2[28.29.29.45] Ezr 6[8] למא די תעבדון with regard
to *what* ye shall do, 7[18] (= *whatsoever*). **3.**
with prefixes: **a.** כְּמָה *how!* Dn 3[33.33]. **b.** לְמָה
why? (cf. BH לָמָּה) Ezr 4[22] be not slack herein:
why should damage grow, etc., virtually = *lest*
damage grow (𝔊 μή ποτε), 7[23] די למה להוא קצף
for why should there be wrath? = *lest* [𝔊 μή ποτε]
there be wrath (cf. 𝔗 דִּילְמָא, Syr. ܕܠܡܐ *lest*:
and v. מָה **4 d** *b*, p. 554[a]). **c.** על־מה *wherefore?* 4100
Dn 2[15].

†מוֹת **n.[m.]** death (𝔗 Syr.; v. BH);— 4191, 4193
abs. Ezr 7[26].

מָזוֹן v. זון. p. 1091 4203

†[מְחָא] **vb.** smite (v. BH II. מָחָה);— 4223, 4229
Pe. *Pf.* 3 fs. מְחַת, לְ rei, Dn 2[34.35] (+ עַל). **Pa.**
Impf. 3 ms. יְמַחֵא בִידֵהּ 4[32], i.e. hinder him (cf.
Ec 8[4] 𝔗; D[Aram. Dialektproben, p. 5]; Talm.: Levy[NHWB s.v.]). **Hithpa.** *Impf.* 3 ms. יִתְמְחֵא Ezr 6[11] *let
him be smitten* (nailed) עֲלֹהִי.

[מַחְלְקָה] v. חלק. p. 1093 4255

4291 †מְטָא, מְטָה **vb.** reach, attain (𝔗 *id.*, Syr. ܡܛܳܐ, cf. Chr-Pal. Schulth$^{Lex. 108}$; Eth. መጠወ: Ar. أَنْطَى (for أَمْطَى) Nö$^{ZMG\ xl\ (1886),\ 736}$; distinct from BH מָצָא, etc., q.v.);—**Pe.** *Pf.* 3 ms. מְטָא Dn 4^{25}, ־ָה $7^{13.22}$; 3 fs. מְטָת 4^{19}, מְטָת v^{21} Qr (Kt, erron., מטית K$^{§ 47,\ Beisp.\ 1)\ a)}$); 3 mpl. מְטוֹ 6^{25}; *Impf.* 3 ms. יִמְטֵא $4^{8.17}$;—**1. a.** *reach, come to* Dn 6^{25} (לְ loc.); *come* unto, as far as 7^{13} (עַד pers.); abs. *arrive* 7^{22} (of time; 𝔊 ἐδόθη; v. Nes$^{MM\ 41}$ who cp. Ar. عَطَى IV. *give*). **b.** *reach, extend*, לְ loc. $4^{8.17.19}$. **2.** c. עַל pers. *come upon, befall* $4^{21.25}$.

4332-33 †מִישָׁאֵל **n.pr.m.** (=BH *id.*, **2**, sub מִי);—Dn 2^{17}.

4335-36 מֵישַׁךְ **n.pr.m.** (BH *id.*);—Dn 2^{49} 3^{12} + 11 t. 3.

4390-91 †[מְלָא] **vb.** fill (v. BH);—**Pe.** *Pf.* 3 fs. מְלָאת Dn 2^{35} (c. acc.). **Hithpe.** *Pf.* 3 ms. הִתְמְלִי חֱמָא 3^{19} *was filled with rage.*

4398,4406 [מַלְאַךְ] v. לאך. מִלָּה v. מלל. below, p. 1098

4416-17 †מְלַח **n.m.** salt (v. BH);—מ׳ abs. Ezr 6^{9} 7^{22} (both for sacrifices), cstr. 4^{14}.

4414-15 †[מְלַח] **vb. denom.** c. acc. cogn., eat salt;—**Pe.** *Pf.* 1 pl. מְלַחְנָא Ezr 4^{14} *we have eaten the salt of the palace* (so most), i.e. have assumed obligations of loyalty, cf. M^{69*} K$^{§ 71,\ 2}$ (and Syr. ܐܬܡܠܚ *be intimate with* PS^{2134}); Str (after Nes$^{MM\ 30\ f.}$) thinks n. c. sf.: *our salt is the salt of the palace.*

4427 I. מלך (√of following, v. BH).

4429-30 מֶלֶךְ$_{178}$ **n.m.** king (general Sem.; v. BH);—מ׳ abs. Dn 2^{10} + 2 t.; cstr. 4^{34} + 6 t.; usu. emph. מַלְכָּא Ezr 4^{8} + 154 t., ־ָה Dn 2^{11}; pl. מַלְכִין Ezr 4^{15} + 9 t., ־ִים 4^{13} (Hebraism, Be-Ry M^{41*}); emph. מַלְכַיָּא Dn 2^{44} + 2 t.;—*king* Dn $2^{4.5}$ + 132 t. Dn, Ezr $4^{8.11}$ + 42 t. Ezr (מֶלֶךְ מַלְכַיָּא of Neb. Dn 2^{37}, of Artax. Ezr 7^{12} [cf. Cooke$^{71.3}$, of Xerxes]; מַלְכִין Dn 7^{17} = kingdoms, cf. מַלְכוּ v^{23}).

4433 †[מַלְכָּה] **n.f.** queen;—emph. מַלְכְּתָא Dn $5^{10.10}$.

4437 †מַלְכוּ **n.f.** royalty, reign, kingdom;—abs. מ׳ Dn 2^{39}+; cstr. מַלְכוּת Ezr 4^{24}+; emph. ־תָא Dn 2^{37}+, ־תָה 2^{44}; sf. ־תִי 4^{15}+, ־תֵהּ 3^{33}+, ־תָךְ 4^{23}+; pl. cstr. מַלְכְוָת 7^{27}; emph. ־וָתָא 2^{44} 7^{23};—**1.** *royalty, kingship, kingly authority:* Dn $4^{23.28.33}$; הֵיכַל מ׳ v^{26}, בֵּית מ׳ v^{27}, כָּרְסֵא מ׳ 5^{20}. **2.** organized (world-) kingdom: $2^{39.39.40.41.42.44}$ $7^{23.23.24.27}$; מ׳ אֲנָשָׁא $4^{14.22.29}$ 5^{21}; of specif. kings 2^{37} $5^{18.28}$ 6^{1}; of God 3^{33} 7^{27} (both מ׳ עָלַם), $2^{44.44}$ 3^{33} 4^{31} 6^{27} 7^{27}; of Mess. $7^{14.14}$; of saints $7^{18.18.22.27}$. **3.** *realm* (territorial) $4^{15.33b}$ $5^{7.11.16.29}$ $6^{2.2.4.8.27}$ Ezr $7^{13.23}$; meton. 6^{5} = administration of realm. **4.** *reign*, time of reigning Dn 5^{26} $6^{29.29}$ Ezr 4^{24} 6^{15}.

II. מלך (√of foll.; As. *malâku, counsel, advise*; 𝔗 מְלַךְ, Syr. ܡܠܟ, Chr-Pal. ܡܠܟ Schulth^{112}; BH II. [מָלַךְ] †Ne 5^{7} as loan-word). 4427

†[מְלַךְ] **n.m. counsel, advice**;—sf. מִלְכִּי 4431
Dn 4^{24} let *my counsel* be acceptable to thee.

†[מַלִּל] **vb. Pa. speak, say** (so 𝔗 Syr.; 4449
cf. BH מלל **Pi.** (rare));—*Pf.* 3 ms. מַלִּל Dn 6^{22} 4448
he spoke with (עִם pers.); acc. of words, *Impf.* 3 ms. יְמַלִּל 7^{25} (c. לְצַד of God); so *Pt. act.* מְמַלִּל v^{8} (van d. H. here מְמַלֱּלָא), v^{20}; f. מְמַלְּלָא (K$^{§ 15\ d)}$) v^{11}.

†מִלָּה **n.f.** word, thing;—abs. מ׳ Dn 2^{9}+, 4406
cstr. מִלַּת v^{10}+; emph. מִלְּתָא v^{5}+, ־ָא v^{8}+; pl. abs. מִלִּין $7^{1.25}$, cstr. מִלֵּי 5^{10}, emph. מִלַּיָּא $7^{11.16}$;—**1.** *word, utterance* Dn 4^{28} 6^{15}, pl. 5^{10} $7^{11.25}$; in bad sense, מ׳ כִדְבָה וּשְׁחִיתָה 2^{9}, מִלַּיָּא רַבְרְבָתָא 7^{11} (cf. רַבְרְבָן alone $v^{8.20}$); *word* of God's judgment 4^{30}; =*command* $2^{5.8}$ $3^{22.28}$ 6^{13}. **2.** *thing, affair, matter:* $2^{10.10.11.15.17.23}$ $5^{15.26}$ $7^{28.28}$, pl. $v^{1.16}$.

†מַן (so Gi, with most MSS., supported by 4479
Syr. ܡܰܢ, Ar. مَنْ; v. K$^{§ 22,\ 1}$), מָן (Baer: v. on Dn 3^{6}), **interr. pron.** who? (OAram. Nab. Palm. מן (Lzb^{312} Cooke^{188}), 𝔗 מַן, Syr. ܡܰܢ, Eth. መኑ: Ar. مَنْ: W$^{CG\ 123}$: BH מִי);—**1.** *who?* Ezr $5^{3.9}$; 4310
strengthened by הוּא, Dn 3^{15} וּמַן־הוּא אֱלָהּ דִּי *who is* the God who ...? (cf. Syr. ܡܰܢܘ contr. from ܡܰܢ ܗܽܘ, and מַנוּ in the Syriacizing 𝔗 to Pr: also BH מִי הוּא, הוּא **4 b** β); so in the pl. Ezr 5^{4} מַן־אִנּוּן שְׁמָהָת *what* (lit. *who*: cf. מִי **1 a**, and Gn 32^{28} Ex 3^{13} 𝔗) are the names of ...? **2.** מַן־דִּי *whosoever* (lit. *who is there that* ...? v. BH מִי **g**) Dn $3^{6.11}$ מַן־דִּי לָא יִפֵּל, 4^{14} וּלְמַן דִּי יִצְבֵּא יִתְּנִנַּהּ to *whomsoever* he willeth, he giveth it, $v^{22.29}$ 5^{21} (so Nab. מן די, Cooke$^{241,\ 325\ ff.}$; 𝔗 מַן דְּ; Syr. ܡܰܢ ܕ; cf. Eg. Aram. S-C$^{Pap.\ K\ 7,\ 12}$ ולמן זי צבית תנתן).

מִן **prep.** from, out of, by, by reason of, 4481
at, more than (BH and general Aram. *id.*);— 4480
rarely assimilated, as in Heb., v. Dn 6^{5} מִצַּד, Ezr 5^{11} 6^{14}; sf. מִנִּי, מִנָּךְ, 3 m. מִנֵּהּ, f. מִנַּהּ †Dn

2^{42} 7^{24}; 3 mpl. מִנְּהוֹן (so Palm.$^{Tariff\ ii.\ a\ 34}$; Nab. Eg. Aram. מנהם, Cooke$^{No.\ 89.6}$, S-C$^{Pap.\ A\ 10}$) †Dn 2$^{33.33.41.41.42.42}$ Kt (Qr each time f. מִנְּהֵן), 6$^{3.3}$;—**1.** of place: **a.** *from*, Dn 4$^{10.11.23}$ 7^{4}+, מִן תַּמָּה †Ezr 6^{6}; fig. *on the side* or *part of* (cf. BH **1 c**) Dn 6^{5} מִצַּד מַלְכוּתָא. **b.** *out of*, Dn 3$^{15.26}$ 5^{2} 7^{3}, etc. **c.** (coming) *from* 2^{35}, *away from*, 2^{45} 4$^{11.22.28}$ Je 10^{11}. **d.** to ask or exact *of* a person, Dn 2$^{16.49}$+; Ezr 7^{26}; to deliver *from* Dn 6^{21}. **2. a.** of the *source* (BH **2 b**), as to be fed *from* Dn 4^{9}; or *author* (*ib.* **d**), מִנִּי שִׂים טְעֵם = *by* me is a decree made, Dn 3^{29} 4^{3} (6^{27} מִן־קֳדָמַי), Ezr 4^{19}+, cf. 5^{17}; מִנִּי = *on my part* Dn 2$^{5.8}$ (v. אַזְדָּא). **b.** of the *immediate cause, as a result of, by*, Dn 4^{22} (= ב v$^{12.20}$), v^{30} 5^{21}: so with a vb. of *fearing* 5^{19}. **c.** of the *remoter cause, by reason of* (BH **2 f**), Dn 5^{19} מִן־רְבוּתָא, 7^{11}; so מִן־דִּי, v. דִּי **3**. **d.** of the *norm* (cf. BH **2 g**) = *at, according to*, Ezr 6^{14} מִן־טַעַם אֱלָהּ יִשׂ׳ *at the decree* of, etc., 7^{23}; Dn 2^{8} מִן־יַצִּיב *according to* certainty, v^{47} מִן־קְשֹׁט. **3.** partitively (BH **3**), Dn 6^{3} חַד מִנְּהוֹן, 7$^{8.16}$; 2^{25} 5^{13}; (some) *of* 2^{41} מִן־נִצְבְּתָא; מִנְּהוֹן ... מִנְּהוֹן *some ... others* of them 2$^{33.41.42a}$; so v^{42b} מִן־קְצָת ... מִנַּהּ. **4.** of time, *from*, Dn 2^{20} (מִן ... וְעַד), Ezr 4$^{15.19}$; v. also אֱדַיִן and דִּי **4**. **5.** in *comparisons*, different *from* Dn 7$^{3.7.19.23.24}$, *beyond, more than* 2$^{30.39}$ 6^{30} 7$^{20\ end}$; 4^{13} לִבְבֵהּ מִן־אֲנָשָׁא יְשַׁנּוֹן let his heart be changed *away from* man's (BH **7 b** *b*; Is 52^{14}). **6.** cpds.:—v. תְּחוֹת, [קַדְמָה], קֳדָם, לְוָת.

4484 מְנֵא v. מנה. below

4061 †מִדָּה, מִנְדָּה (?) **n.f.** tribute (As. loan-
4060 word, cf. BH II. [מִדָּה]);—abs. מִנ׳ Ezr 4^{13} 7^{24}+ 4^{20} Baer (van d. H. Gi Str מִדָּה); cstr. מִדַּת 6^{8}.

4486 מַנְדַּע v. ידע. p. 1095

4483, 4487 †מְנָה **vb.** number, reckon (v. BH);—**Pe.** *Pf.* 3 ms. מ׳ Dn 5^{26} God *has numbered* (the days of) thy kingdom (acc.; i.e. put an end to it);—מְנֵא v. infr. **Pa.** *appoint*, acc. pers.: *Pf.* 3 ms. מַנִּי Dn 2^{24} (+Inf.), v^{49} (ל pers. + עַל rei); 2 ms. מַנִּיתָ 3^{12} (עַל rei); *Imv.* ms. מַנִּי (K$^{§\ 47,\ 3.\ c)}$) Ezr 7^{25}.

4484 †מְנֵא **n.[m.]** maneh, mina, a weight (v.
4487 BH; OAram. מנה SAC^{75} Lzb^{313});—abs. Dn 5$^{25.25.26}$, v. ClGann$^{JAs\ Juillet-Août,\ 1886,\ 36\ ff.}$ Nö$^{ZA\ i.\ 414\ f.}$ Dr al.; its connexion in Dn with מְנָה is due to
6537, 8625 word-play; v. also תְּקֵל, פְּרֵס. p. 1108, 1118

4510 †מִנְיָן **n.[m.]** number;—cstr. מ׳ Ezr 6^{17}.

‡†מִנְחָה **n.f. gift, offering** (BH *id.*, 4503-04
√מנח);—**1.** *oblation*, to God's representative, abs. מ׳ Dn 2^{46}. **2.** techn. *meal-offering*, pl. sf. מִנְחָתְהוֹן Ezr 7^{17}.

מִנְיָן v. מנה. above 4510

†[מְעָא] **n.[m.] pl.** external belly (v. BH 4577
[מֵעֶה] **6**);—sf. מְעוֹהִי Dn 2^{32} (of image in vision). 4578

מַעֲבַד v. עבד. מְעוֹהִי v. [מְעָא]. above, p. 1105 4567, 4577

מֵעָל v. עלל. p. 1106 4606

†מָרֵא **n.m.** lord (𝔗 מָר, c. מָרֵי; Syr. ܡܳܪܝ, e. 4756
ܡܳܪܳܐ, ܡܳܪܝ, Eg. Aram. מרא (RÉS$^{1.361}$); Chr-Pal. ܡܪܐ, etc., Schulth$^{Lex.\ 115}$; OAram. Nab. Palm. מר(א) (Lzb^{316}); cf. n.pr. dei מרנא (μαρνα), god of Gaza, SAC^{77}; also Ar. مَرْءٌ *man*, Sab. מרא *man, lord* Hom$^{Chr\ 127;\ AA\ 293}$ RÉS$^{1.\ 454,\ 2}$);—*lord*: of God, cstr. מ׳ שְׁמַיָּא Dn 5^{23}, מָרֵה מַלְכִין 2^{47}; of king, sf. מָרְאִי Kt (as Nab., SAC$^{l.\ c.}$; K$^{§\ 58,\ 1}$), Qr מָרִי (as Palm., SAC$^{l.\ c.}$) 4$^{16.21}$.

†מְרַד **n.[m.]** rebellion (v. BH);—abs. מ׳ 4776-77
Ezr 4^{19}.

†[מָרָד K$^{§\ 59\ d)}$] **adj.** rebellious;—of city, 4779
f. abs. מָרָדָא Ezr 4^{15}, emph. מָרָדְתָּא (K$^{ib.}$) v^{12}.

מָרֵה v. מָרֵא. above 4756

†[מְרַט] **vb.** pluck (v. BH);—**Pe'îl** *Pf.* 4803-04
3 mpl. מְרִיטוּ Dn 7^{4} *were plucked off* (wings).

†מֹשֶׁה **n.pr.m.** Moses (BH *id.*);—סְפַר מ׳ 4872-73
Ezr 6^{18}.

†מְשַׁח **n.[m.]** oil (v. BH);—abs. Ezr 6^{9} 7^{22}. 4886-87

[מִשְׁכַּב] v. שכב. [מִשְׁכַּן] v. שכן. p. 1115 4903, 4907

[מַשְׁרוֹקִית] v. שרק. [מִשְׁתֵּה] v. שתה. 4953, 4961
p. 1117

[מַתְּנָא] v. נתן. p. 1103 4978

נ

נבא (√of foll.; v. BH *id.*, but esp. Bewer 5012-13
Am. J. Sem. Lang., Jan. 1902 who cp. As. *nabû, tear away, lead forcibly*, hence proph. as (fig.) *carried away* by divine frenzy, ecstasy, cf. 1 S 10$^{6.10}$ 19$^{20.24}$).

†[נְבִיא] **n.m. prophet** (Hebraism? also 5029
𝔗 Syr.; v. BH);—emph. נְבִיאָה Kt, נְבִיָּא Ezr 5^{1} 5030
6^{14}; pl. emph. נְבִיַּאיָּא 5$^{1.2}$.

5017 †[נְבוּאָה] **n.f.** **prophesying**;—cstr. נְבוּאַת
Ezr 6^{14}.

5019-20 נְבוּכַדְנֶצַּר $_{31}$ **n.pr.m.** (=BH ־רֶאצַּר, etc.);—
Dn 2^{28}+23t. Dn, Ezr $5^{12.14}$ 6^{5}; נְבֻכ׳ Dn 3^{3}+3t. Dn.

5023 †נְבִזְבָּה **n.f.** **reward** (so 𝔗 (rare); prob.
Pers. loan-word, Haug [Ew. Jahrb. 1853, 160] prop. OP
**nibagrâ, presentation;* but perh. crpt., v. M[71*]);
—abs. נ׳ Dn 2^{6}; pl. sf. נְבִזְבְּיָתָךְ (al. נְבִזְ׳, נְבִ׳) 5^{17}.

5043 †נֶבְרַשְׁתָּא **n.f. emph.** **the candlestick** (𝔗
id., Syr. ܢܒܪܫܬܐ, NH נִבְרֶשֶׁת; Ar. نِبْرَاس is
loan-word from Aram. Frä[95]; prob. foreign word
K[§62] Fra[95] Bev al.; ? As., cf. Ba[ZA ii. 117]);—Dn 5^{5}.

5047 †[נְגַד] **vb.** **stream, flow** (𝔗 נְגַד, Syr. ܢܓܕ
draw along, lead, 𝔗 also intrans. *move along*
Is 30^{24}, *flow* Dt $33^{13.22}$, נַגְדִּין *streams* Is 44^{4}+);—
Pe. *Pt.* Dn 7^{10} נְהַר דִּי נוּר נָגֵד וְנָפֵק מִן־קֳדָמוֹהִי.

5049 ‡†נֶגֶד **prep.** **in front of, facing** (=BH, v.
5048 √ p. 616b; not elsewhere known in Aram.),
Dn 6^{11} נגד ירושלם.

5053 †[נֹגַהּ] **n.[f.]** **brightness, daylight** (𝔗
5051 Syr.; BH *id.*);—emph. בְּנָגְהָא (K[§54 c), 1]) Dn 6^{20}.

5069 †[נְדַב] **vb.** **Hithpa.** **volunteer, offer**
5068 **freely** (𝔗; BH נָדַב);—*Pf.* 3 mpl. הִתְנַדַּבוּ Ezr
7^{15}; *Inf.* הִתְנַדָּבוּת v^{16}; *Pt.* מִתְנַדַּב v^{13}; pl. ־דְּבִין
v^{16};—**1.** *volunteer*, sq. inf., Ezr 7^{13}. **2.** *give*,
or *offer freely*, v^{15}, acc. rei + לְ of God; v^{16}, c. לְ
of temple; *freewill gift* (inf., prop. *freewill*
giving) v^{16}.

5073 †נִדְבָּךְ **n.m.** **row** or **layer, course** (𝔗 NH
id.; NH also מִדְבָּךְ *id.* (Levy [NHWB iii. 23]), cf.
مِدْمَاكٌ as loan-word Frä[12]; borrowed from As.
nadbaku, mountain-slope acc. to Dl[Pr 150] (cf. Ba
[ZA ii. 115 f.] Hpt[GN 1883, 96; BAS i. 8. 15]), but mng. not very
suitable Nö[ZMG xl (1886), 733] Mey[Entst. 46]);—abs. נ׳
Ezr 6^{4}, pl. נִדְבָּכִין v^{4}.

5074-75 †[נְדַד] **vb.** **flee** (v. BH I. נדד);—**Pe.** *Pf.*
3 fs. שִׁנְתֵּהּ נַדַּת עֲלוֹהִי (K[§46, Beisp. a)]) Dn 6^{19}.

5085 †נִדְנֶה (Mas Baer) **n.[m.]** **sheath** (𝔗 נְדַן,
5084 לְדַן; v. BH (late) נָדָן, Pers. loan-word);—
רוּחִי . . . בְּנ׳ Dn 7^{15} *my spirit in* (its) *sheath*, i.e.
my body; < נִדְנָה emph., or sf. נִדְנַהּ (K[§54. 3. β)]);
or (Nö[GGA. 1884, 1022] Bev) נִדְנַהּ; but expression
at best strange; rd. prob. בְּגִין דְּנָה *on account of*
this (בְּגִין as 𝔗[J]; D[§47. 3 (2nd ed. 47. 10)]), M[72*] cf. Buhl Dr.

†נְהַר $_{14}$ **n.m.** [Dn 7, 10] **river** (v. BH I. נהר);— 5102-03
abs. נ׳ Dn 7^{10}; emph. נַהֲרָה Ezr 4^{10}+, ־ָא 4^{16};—
river, usu. of Euphr., in phr. עֲבַר נ׳ Ezr $4^{10.11.16}$+
10t. Ezr; נ׳ דִּי־נוּר Dn 7^{10} *a river of fire*, in vision.

†[נְהוֹר, נְהִיר] **n.m.** **light** (𝔗 נְהוֹרָא, Syr. 5094
ܢܘܗܪܐ; v. BH II. נהר);—emph. נהירא Kt, < נְהוֹרָא 5102
Qr (cf. 𝔗 Syr.; Nö[LCB 1896, 703]) Dn 2^{22}.

†נַהִירוּ (K[§§16, 5; 61, 4]) **n.f.** **illumination, in-** 5094
sight (Syr. *id.*);—abs. Dn $5^{11.14}$ (both + שָׂכְלְתָנוּ,
חָכְמָה).

†[נוּד] **vb.** **flee** (𝔗 Syr.; cf. [נְדַד] supra 5075, 5111
and BH נוד **1 a**);—**Pe.** *Impf.* 3 fs. תְּנֻד מִן Dn 4^{11}. 5110

†נְוָלִי, נְוָלוּ (K[§61, 4.5]) **n.f.** **refuse-heap** (𝔗 5122
נְוָלִי *dung-heap;* perh. loan-word fr. As. *namâlu*
(*nawâlu*), *ruin*, Jen[KB vi. 363]);—נְוָלוּ Ezr 6^{11}, נְוָלִי
Dn 2^{5} 3^{29}.

נוּר $_{17}$ **n.f.** [Dn 3, 6] **et m.** [7, 9] **fire** (𝔗 Syr.; v. 5135
√ נור BH);—abs. נ׳ Dn 3^{27} $7^{9.9.10}$; emph. נוּרָא 5216
3^{6}+12t. 3.

†[נְזִק] **vb.** **suffer injury** (𝔗 *id.*; As. *nazâku*, 5142
injure; on combin. with Ar. نقص *impair*, v.
Ba[ES 51] Frä[BAS iii. 81]);—**Pe.** *Pt.* נָזִק Dn 6^{3}. **Haph.**
injure: *Impf.* 3 fs. תְּהַנְזִק (K[§33, 2]) Ezr 4^{13} (acc.
pers.). *Pt. act.* f. cstr. מְהַנְזְקַת מַלְכִין v^{15}; *Inf.*
cstr. לְהַנְזָקַת מ׳ v^{22} (K[ib. d)]; M[§48 c] ־קַת).

†נְחָשׁ **n.m.** **copper, bronze** (𝔗 Syr.; BH 5174
נְחוּשָׁה, נְחֹשֶׁת, √ III. נחשׁ);—as material: abs. 5154, 5178
נ׳ Dn 2^{32} $4^{12.20}$ 7^{19}; emph. נְחָשָׁא $2^{35.39.45}$ $5^{4.23}$.

†[נְחֵת] **vb.** **descend** (𝔗 Syr.; v. BH 5181-82
(poet., and late));—**Pe.** *Pt.* נָחִת Dn $4^{10.20}$ (both
מִן־שְׁמַיָּא). **Haph.** *deposit*, בּ loc.: *Impf.* 2 ms.
תַּחֵת (K[§42, b)]) Ezr 6^{5} (Gu[Hpt] reads 3 mpl.); *Imv.*
ms. אֲחֵת (K[§15 d)]) 5^{15} (acc. rei); *Pt. pass.* pl.
מְהַחֲתִין 6^{1} (were) *deposited*. **Hoph.** (W[CG 225]) *be*
deposed: *Pf.* 3 ms. הָנְחַת Dn 5^{20} (מִן־כָּרְסֵא).

†[נְטַל] **vb.** **lift** (𝔗 Syr.; BH (rare));— 5190-91
Pe. *Pf.* 1 s. עַיְנַי לִשְׁמַיָּא נִטְלֵת Dn 4^{31} (As. *naṭâlu*
=*look*). **Pe'il** (W[CG 224]) *be lifted*: *Pf.* 3 fs.
נְטִילַת מִן־אַרְעָא 7^{4}.

†[נְטַר] **vb.** **keep** (𝔗 Syr.; v. BH I. נצר, 5202, 5341
and (rarely) נָטַר);—**Pe.** *Pf.* 1 s. מִלְּתָא בְּלִבִּי 5201
נִטְרֵת Dn 7^{28}.

†[נִיחוֹחַ] **n.[m.]** **soothing, tranquillizing** 5208
(prob. Hebraism, v. BH *id.*, √ נוח (√ also 𝔗 5207
Syr.));—pl. נִיחֹ(וֹ)חִין Ezr 6^{10} Dn 2^{46} i.e. *soothing*
offerings.

5232 †[נְכַס] **n.[m.]**, pl. נִכְסִין **riches, property**
5233 (𝔗 Syr.; Eg. Aram. S-C[E4+]; BH (late));—עֲנָשׁ נ׳ Ezr 7[26] *confiscation of property;* cstr. נִכְסֵי 6[8].

5245-46 †נְמַר **n.[m.]** **leopard** (v. BH);—abs. Dn 7[6].

5255-56 †[נְסַח] **vb. pull away** (𝔗; v. BH);—**Hithpe.** *be pulled away: Impf.* 3 ms. יִתְנְסַח Ezr 6[11] (מִן).

5258, 5260 †נְסַךְ **vb. pour out** (v. BH I. נָסַךְ);—**Pa.** (more gen.): *Inf.* לְנַסָּכָה לֵהּ Dn 2[46] *to offer in sacrifice to him,* c. acc. מִנְחָה וְנִיחֹחִין.

5261 †[נְסַךְ] **n.[m.]** **drink-offering** (𝔗 Syr.; cf.
5262 BH);—pl. sf. נִסְכֵּיהוֹן Ezr 7[17] (+מִנְחָתְהוֹן, etc.).

5267 נסק v. סלק. p. 1104

5307-08 †נְפַל **vb. fall** (v. BH);—**Pe.** *Pf.* 3 ms. נ׳ Dn 2[46]; נְפַל 4[28]; 3 mpl. נְפַלוּ 3[23] + 7[20] Kt (Qr 3 fpl. נְפַלָה, K[§23,2]); *Impf.* 3 ms. יִפֵּל (K[§42]) Dn 3[6]+; 2 mpl. תִּפְּלוּן 3[5.15]; *Pt.* pl. נָפְלִין 3[7];—**1.** *fall,* עַל־אַנְפּוֹהִי Dn 2[46]; *fall down* and do homage 3[5.6.7.10.11.15]; לְ loc. 3[23]; of voice, מִן־שְׁמַיָּא 4[28]. **2.** *fall* by violence 7[20] (c. קֳדָם). **3.** יִפֵּל לָךְ Ezr 7[20] *it shall fall to thee* (thou shalt need) to give (cf. Chr-Pal. Schulth[Lex. 126 and ZAW xxii (1902), 163]).

5312 נְפַק **vb. go,** or **come, out, forth** (𝔗 *id.*, NH נָפַק, Syr. ܢܦܩ, so Chr-Pal. Schulth[Lex. 126], OAram. Nab. Palm. נפק Lzb[324], cf. Ar. نَافِقَاءُ *hole* of field mouse; v. also Aram. נַפְקוּתָא, ܢܦܩܬܐ *outlay,* Eg. Aram. נפקתה Cooke[Inscr. 212], Ar. نَفَقَةٌ *household outlay* (Aram. loan-word Schwally[ZMG lii (1898), 133]));—**Pe.** *Pf.* 3 ms. נ׳ Dn 2[14] *he went out,* c. inf.; 3 fs. נֶפְקַת v[13] decree *went forth* (cf. Lu 2[1]); 3 mpl. נפקו 5[5] Kt (Qr 3 fpl. נְפַקָה, K[§23,2]) fingers *came forth;* c. מִן loc.: *Imv.* mpl. פֻּקוּ (K[§42]) 3[26] *come forth! Pt.* pl. נָפְקִין v[26] (both of men); sg. נָפֵק 7[10] (=*flow out*). **Haph.** *bring forth,* acc. rei + מִן loc.: *Pf.* 3 ms. הַנְפֵּק Ezr 5[14.14] 6[5] Dn 5[2]; 3 mpl. הַנְפִּקוּ v[3] (so Eg. Aram. S-C[Pap. D 15, 17+]).

5313 †[נִפְקָה] **n.f. outlay**;—emph. נִפְקְתָא Ezr 6[4.8].

5324, 5326 †[נִצְבָּה] **n.f. firmness** (v. BH נצב);—emph. נִצְבְּתָא Dn 2[41].

5329-30 †[נְצַח] **vb. Hithpa. distinguish oneself** (v. BH I. נצח);—*Pt.* מִתְנַצַּח Dn 6[4], עַל pers.

5337-38 †[נְצַל] **vb. Haph. rescue, deliver** (v. BH Eg. Aram. הנצל *take away,* S-C[C 10, D 18]);—of God, abs.: *Pt. act.* מַצִּל 6[28], *Inf.* לְהַצָּלָה Dn 3[29]; of man, sf. pers. לְהַצָּלוּתֵהּ 6[15].

5343, 5352 †נְקֵא **adj. clean, pure** (v. BH נקה);—כַּעֲמַר נ׳ Dn 7[9] *like pure wool.*

5367-68 †[נְקַשׁ] **vb. knock** (v. BH (rare));—**Pe.** *Pt. act.* fpl. נָקְשָׁן Dn 5[6] of knees *knocking* דָּא לְדָא.

5375-76 †נְשָׂא **vb. lift, take, carry** (cf. BH; rare in Aram.; v. נְסִי, נְסָא ChWB, NHWB);—**Pe.** *Pf.* 3 ms. נ׳ Dn 2[35] *carry away* (of wind, c. acc. rei); *Imv.* ms. שֵׂא Ezr 5[15] *take* (acc. vessels). **Hithpa.** *make a rising, an insurrection: Pt.* fs. מִתְנַשְּׂאָה Ezr 4[19], עַל pers.

5389 נִשֵׁיהוֹן v. [נָשִׁין] sub II. אנשׁ. p. 1081

5395-97 †[נִשְׁמָה] **n.f. breath** (v. BH, √נשׁם);—sf. נִשְׁמְתָךְ Dn 5[23], i.e. breath of life.

5403 †נְשַׁר **n.m. griffon-vulture** or **eagle** (v.
5404 BH);—abs. נ׳ Dn 7[4]; pl. abs. נִשְׁרִין 4[30].

5407 †[נִשְׁתְּוָן] **n.m.**[Ezr 4, 18] **letter** (prob. Pers.; v.
5406 BH);—emph. נִשְׁתְּוָנָא Ezr 4[18.23] 5[5].

5412 †[נְתִינִין] **n.m.pl. Nethinîn** (prob. loan-
5411, 5414 word from BH נְתִינִים, √נָתַן);—servants of sanctuary, emph. נְתִינַיָּא Ezr 7[24].

5414-15 †[נְתַן] **vb. give** (v. BH; 𝔗 rare; OAram. נתן, Impf. ינתן, so Nab.; Zinj. Palm. יתן; Eg. Aram. Impf. ינתן, אנתן, etc., S-C[Pap. A 7+], pl. sf. תנתנונה ib.[J 9], Inf. למנתן S-C[C 6, 9+]);—**Pe.** *Impf.* 3 ms. יִנְתֵּן (K[§42]) Dn 2[16], sf. יִתְּנִנַּהּ 4[15]+; 2 ms. תִּנְתֵּן Ezr 7[20]; 3 mpl. יִנְתְּנוּן 4[13]; *Inf.* לְמִנְתַּן 7[20];—**1.** *give,* subj. God, c. sf. rei + לְ pers., Dn 4[14.22.29]. **2.** of man, *give, allow,* acc. time, 2[16]. **3.** *give, pay,* acc. rei, Ezr 4[13] 7[20] (+ מִן of source), abs. v[20].

4978 †[מַתְּנָא] **n.f. gift**;—pl. abs. מַתְּנָן Dn 2[6.48]; sf. מַתְּנָתָךְ 5[17].

5426 †[נְתַר] **vb. Haph. strip off** (𝔗 נְתַר *fall off;* Syr. ܢܬܪ; Ar. نَثَرَ *scatter;* As. *našâru, diminish, shorten,* NH נָשַׁר *fall off*);—*Imv.* mpl. אַתַּרוּ (K[§42 b)]) Dn 4[11] (acc. of leaves).

ס

5443 סַבְּכָא v. שַׂבְּכָא. p. 1113

5446 ‡†[סְבַל] **vb.** si vera l. **bear, carry** a load
5445 (v. BH);—**Pō.** *Pt. pass.* אֻשּׁׁהִי מְסוֹבְלִים (K[§36] Nö[GGA, 1884, 1016]) Ezr 6[3] *its foundations* (be) *raised* (Thes al.; W[CG 203, 225]), very dub.; Hpt[Gu ad loc.]

conj. ′אֶשָּׁהִי מְס *his* (God's) *fire-offerings they bring* (As. *zabâlu*), so (hesitantly) Berthol.

5452 †[סְבַר] **vb. think, intend** (𝔗 Syr.; v. BH
7663 II. שׂבר (late));—**Pe.** *Impf.* 3 ms. יִסְבַּר Dn 7^{25},
sq. inf.

5457 †סְגִד **vb. do homage** (by prostration) (𝔗
5456 Syr.; BH (late));—**Pe.** *Pf.* 3 ms. ′ס Dn 2^{46};
Impf. 3 ms. יִסְגֻּד Dn 3^{6}+, 3 mpl. יִסְגְּדוּן 3^{28}, etc.;
Pt. act. pl. סָגְדִין 3^{7}+;—*do homage* לְצֶלֶם Dn
3$^{5.7.10.12.14.15.18}$, ל of false god v^{28}; ′לְצ om., v$^{6.11.15}$;
′לְדָנִיֵּאל ס 2^{46} (perh. as representing God, cf. v^{b},
yet v. Dr).

5460 †[סְגַן] **n.m. prefect** (𝔗 (rare), Eg. Aram.
5461 S-C$^{\text{D 13}}$; v. BH (late), As. loan-word);—pl. abs.
סִגְנִין Dn 2^{48}; emph. סִגְנַיָּא 3$^{2.3.27}$ 6^{8}.

5462-63 †סְגַר **vb. shut** (v. BH);—**Pe.** *Pf.* 3 ms. ′ס
Dn 6^{23} *shut* the lions' mouth (acc.).

5481 †סוּמְפֹּנְיָה **n.f. bag-pipe, or < double pipe
or Pan's pipe** (v. GFM$^{\text{JBL. 1905, 166 ff.}}$) (NH Levy$^{\text{NHWB iii. 492}}$; NH Aram. סִימְפּוֹן is *tube*, esp. *vein, artery* Id$^{\text{ib. 513}}$; loan-word fr. (late) Gk. συμφωνία, Krauss$^{\text{ii. 376, 390}}$ Bev^{41} Dr$^{\text{Dn 3, 5}}$ Nes$^{\text{MM 37}}$ (hence also later Lat. *symphonia*, Ital. *zampogna*), Prince$^{\text{EB 3230}}$);—abs. ′ס Dn 3$^{5.15}$, = סיפניה Kt, סוּפֹּנְיָה Qr v^{10} (Syr. ܣܦܘܢܝܐ *id.*; cf. Palm. ספון = σύμφωνος, *in agreement*, Lzb^{330} GACooke$^{\text{Inscr. 338}}$).

5487 †[סוּף] **vb. be fulfilled** (prop. **ended**) (𝔗
5486 Syr. (oft.); v. BH);—**Pe.** *Pf.* 3 fs. מִלְּתָא סָפַת
Dn 4^{30} (cf. BH I. כָּלָה **Qal 1 c**). **Haph.** *put an
end to: Impf.* 3 fs. תָּסֵף Dn 2^{44} (acc. rei).

5491 †סוֹף **n.[m.] end**;—cstr. ′ס *end* of the earth
Dn 4$^{8.19}$; emph. סוֹפָא 7^{28} *end, conclusion* of the
matter; ′עַד־ס = *for ever* 6^{27} 7^{26}.

5481 סוּמְפֹּנְיָה, סיפניה, סוּפֹּנְיָה v. סוּמְפֹּנְיָה. above

5559 †[סְלִק] **vb. come up** (Aram. loan-word
in BH, q.v.);—**Pe.** *Pf.* 3 fs. סִלְקַת Dn 7^{20}, ת—ַ (!)
v^{8} (K$^{\S\text{ 25 b)}}$); 3 mpl. סְלִקוּ 2^{29} Ezr 4^{12}; *Pt.* fpl. סָלְקָן
Dn 7^{3};—*come up*, מִן pers. Ezr 4^{12}, מִן־יַמָּא Dn 7^{3};
abs. of horn in vision 7$^{8.20}$; fig. of thoughts 2^{29}.
Haph. *lift, take up: Pf.* 3 mpl. הַסִּקוּ (as if from
5267 נסק; K$^{\S\text{ 44 b)}}$) Dn 3^{22}; *Inf.* לְהַנְסָקָה (K$^{\text{l. c.}}$ Str$^{\S\text{ 3 h}}$)
6^{24} (מִן loc.), both c. ל acc. pers. **Hoph.** (W$^{\text{CG 225}}$)
5267 *be taken up: Pf.* 3 ms. הֻסַּק 6^{24} (מִן loc.).

5583 †[סְעַד] **vb. Pa. support, sustain** (𝔗
5582 Zinj.; v. BH);—*Pt. act.* pl. מְסַעֲדִין לְהוֹן Ezr 5^{2}.

†סְפַר **n.m.**$^{\text{Dn 7, 10}}$ **book** (v. BH סֵפֶר);—cstr. 5609, 5612
′ס דָּכְרָנַיָּא Ezr 4$^{15.15}$, ′ס מֹשֶׁה 6^{18}; pl. abs. סִפְרִין
Dn 7^{10} *books* (of records, v. Dr); emph. בֵּית סִפְרַיָּא
Ezr 6^{1} *house of records.*

†[סָפַר] **n.m. secretary, scribe** (𝔗 Syr.; 5613
BH סֹפֵר);—emph. סָפְרָא *the secretary*, Persian 5608
official, Ezr 4$^{8.9.17.23}$; cstr. סָפַר *the scribe* 7$^{12.21}$, of
Ezra as learned in God's law.

†[סַרְבָּל] **n.[m.]** prob. **mantle** (v. esp. SAC 5622
$^{\text{JPhil. xxvi (1899), 307 f.}}$, cf. Andr$^{\text{M 74*}}$, with conj. as to orig. Pers. form; > *trousers;* NH; JAram. *id.*, with both mngs., also *shoes;* Ar. سِرْبَال *mantle* is loan-word Frä^{47}; Egypt. Ar. زربول *shoe* is Gk. loan-word acc. to Vollers$^{\text{ZMG li (1897), 298}}$, cf. Krauss$^{\text{ii. 412}}$);—pl. sf. סַרְבָּלֵיהוֹן Dn 3$^{21.27}$.

†[סָרַךְ] **n.m. chief, overseer** (𝔗 *id.* (= BH 5632
שֹׁטֵר); etym. dub.; prob. with Bev^{Dn} Dr^{Dn} Andr 7860
$^{\text{M 75*}}$, loan-word fr. Pers. *sār* (and **sarak*?), *head,
chief*);—pl. abs. סָרְכִין Dn 6^{3}, emph. סָרְכַיָּא v$^{4.5.7}$,
cstr. סָרְכֵי v^{8}.

†I. [סְתַר] **vb. Pa. hide** (v. BH);—*Pt.* 5641-42
pass. fpl. emph. מְסַתְּרָתָא Dn 2^{22} *the hidden things.*

†II. [סְתַר] **vb. destroy** (Syr. ܣܬܪ; v. 5642
BH שׁתר);—**Pe.** *Pf.* 3 ms. sf. סַתְרֵהּ Ezr 5^{12} 8368
(acc. of temple).

ע

עֲבַד **vb. make, do** (𝔗 Syr. OAram. Nab. 5648
Palm. Eg. Aram. (S-C$^{\text{Pap.}}$; cf. אֲזַדָּא); = BH
עָבַד, q.v., but in mng. ‖ עשׂה);—**Pe.** *Pf.* 3 ms. ′ע 5647
Dn 3^{1}+, 2 ms. עֲבַדְתְּ (K$^{\S\text{ 13, 2}}$) 4^{32}; 1 s. עַבְדֵת 3^{15} 6^{23},
3 mpl. עֲבַדוּ Ezr 6^{13}+; *Impf.* 2 mpl. תַּעַבְדוּן (Baer
K$^{\S\text{ 38, 1. b)}}$; תַּעַבְדוּן Gi Str) Ezr 6^{8} 7^{18}; *Inf.* מֶעְבַּד
(K$^{\S\text{ 15, a) 2)}}$) 4^{22} 7^{18} (מֶעֱבַד); *Pt. act.* עָבֵד 7^{26}+, fs. עָבְדָא
Dn 7^{21}; mpl. עָבְדִין Ezr 4^{15};—**1.** *make*, acc. rei
Dn 3$^{1.15}$ and (of creation) Je 10^{11}; *make* a feast
Dn 5^{1}, war 7^{21} (עִם pers.), ded. of temple Ezr 6^{16}.
2. *do*, acc. of deed, Dn 4^{32} (of God), 6^{23} Ezr 4$^{15.22}$;
do, act, כְּנֵמָא, *thus*, Ezr 6^{13}, כ, *according to*, Dn 7^{18}
and (of God) 4^{32}, abs. 6^{11}; acc. + ב rei Ezr 7^{18} *do
something with*, + עִם pers. 6^{8}; *do, perform*, acc.
of God's law 7^{26}, acc. of signs, etc. (subj. God)
Dn 6^{28} and (+ עִם pers.) 3^{32}. **Hithpe.** *Impf.*
3 ms. יִתְעֲבֵד Ezr 6^{11}+, ד—ִ 6^{12} 7^{21}; 2 mpl. תִּתְעַבְדוּן
Dn 2^{5}; *Pt.* מִתְעֲבֵד Ezr 7^{26}, ־בֵד־ 4^{19}, fs. ־עַבְדָא 5^{8};—

1. *be made into*, c. n. pred., Dn 2^{5} 3^{29} Ezr 6^{11}. **2.** *be done, wrought*, 4^{19}, 5^{8} (subj. עֲבִידְתָּא); *be performed, executed*, of command Ezr 6^{12} 7$^{21.23}$, judgment 7^{26}.

5649 †[עֲבַד D$^{p.105}$, or עֲבֵד K$^{§54, 3. γ)}$] **n.m. slave,**
5650 **servant** (BH עֶבֶד);—cstr. עֲבֵד Dn 6^{21} *servant* of God; pl. sf. of king, עבדיך Kt (K$^{§53 Anm. b)}$), עַבְדָךְ Qr Ezr 4^{11}, עַבְדָךְ Qr Dn 2^{4}; sf. of God, עַבְדוֹהִי, Dn 3$^{26.28}$ Ezr 5^{11}, of king Dn 2^{7}.

5665 †עֲבֵד נְגוֹ **n. pr. m.** comrade of Daniel
5664 (BH *id.*);—Dn 2^{49} 3^{12}+10 t. 3, + עֲבֵד נְגוֹא 3^{29}; =עֲזַרְיָה 2^{17}.

5656, 5673 †[עֲבִידָה] **n.f. work, service** (BH עֲבֹדָה);—emph. עֲבִידְתָּא Ezr 5^{8} Dn 2^{49}, cstr. עֲבִידַת Ezr 4^{24}+;—**1.** *work*, of building temple, Ezr 4^{24} 5^{8} 6^{7}; =*administration* Dn 2^{49} 3^{12}. **2.** *ritual, service*, of God Ezr 6^{18}.

4567 †[מַעְבַד K$^{§60, 3) b)}$] **n.[m.] work** (BH
4566 [מַעְבָּד] †Jb 34^{25}; †𝔗$^{1b.}$; Syr. ܡܥܒܕܐ of magic *works*);—pl. sf. מַעְבָדוֹהִי Dn 4^{34} (sf. of God).

5675 †עֲבַר **n.m. region across, beyond** (v. BH
5676 I. עֵבֶר, √ עבר);—cstr. in phr. עֲבַר(־)נַהֲרָה, i.e. Syria (Scheft^{87}): Ezr 4$^{10.11.17.20}$ 5$^{3.6.6}$ 6$^{6.6.8.13}$ 7$^{21.25}$, ע׳ נהרא 4^{16}. Cf. in Cilic. Aram., Cooke^{346}.

5705 עַד v. עדה. below

5709 †[עֲדָה] **vb. pass on, away** (𝔗 (oft. for
5674, 5710 Heb. עָבַר, Syr.; v. BH I. עָדָה (rare, late));—**Pe.** *Pf.* 3 fs. עֲדָת Dn 3^{27} 4^{28}; *Impf.* 3 ms. יֶעְדֵּה 7^{14}, 3 fs. תֶּעְדֵּה 6^{9};—**1.** *pass on, over*, c. ב pers. Dn 3^{27}. **2.** *pass away*, of kingdom 4^{28} (מִן pers.), 7^{14}; of law 6^{9}. **Haph.** *take away* (so Eg. Aram. S-C^{G35}): *Pf.* 3 mpl. הֶעְדִּיו, acc. rei, Dn 5^{20} (מִן pers.), 7^{12}; *Impf.* 3 mpl. יְהַעְדּוֹן v^{26}; *Pt.* מְהַעְדֵּה 2^{21} *remove, depose* kings, of God.

5705 †עַד$_{35}$ **prep.** and **conj. even to, until** (BH
5704 III. עַד; so 𝔗 Syr. OAram. Nab. Palm. Eg. Aram. (Lzb^{336} S-C^{A5+}));—**1.** *prep.*: **a.** of space, *even to* Dn 7^{13}; עַד־כָּא v^{28}. **b.** of amount, *up to* Ezr 7$^{22 (4 t.)}$. **c.** of time, *until* Dn 2^{20} 6$^{15.27}$ 7$^{18.18.26}$ Ezr 4^{24}; 5^{16} וְעַד־כְּעַן; =our *against* 6^{15} (cf. BH, p. 724^{a} top); *to* (the end of) = *during* Dn 6^{8} עַד יוֹמִין תְּלָתִין, v^{13} 7$^{12.25}$. On עַד־אָחֳרֵין Dn 4^{5} v. אָחֳרֵין; and on עַד־דִּבְרַת דִּי 4^{14} v. [דִּבְרָה]. **2.** *conj.*: **a.** עַד־דִּי *until*, sq. pf. (of past time) Dn 2^{34} 4^{30} 5^{21} 7$^{4.9.11.22}$; sq. impf. (of fut.) 2^{9} 4$^{20.22.29}$.—Dn 6^{25} לָא מְטוֹ . . . עַד דִּי שְׁלִטוּ וגו׳ *up to the time that* . . ., i.e. *ere that*. **b.** עַד alone, Ezr 4^{21} 5^{5}.

†עִדָּן **n.m.**$^{Dn 2,9}$ **time** (𝔗 *id.*, Syr. ܥܕܢܐ, perh. 5732
loan-word from As. *adannu, fixed, appointed*, or *definite, time*; [Ar. عدّان prob. Aram. loan-wd., Schwally$^{ZMG\ liii\ (1899),\ 197}$]);—abs. ע׳ Dn 7^{12}+; emph. עִדָּנָא 2^{8}+; pl. abs. עִדָּנִין 4^{13}+, emph. עִדָּנַיָּא 2^{21};—**1.** in gen., *time*, as duration Dn 2^{8} 7^{12}; involving specif. conditions 2$^{9.21}$; (point of) *time* 3$^{5.15}$. **2.** definite time, =*year* (as mod. Gk. χρόνος, v. EASophocles^{1173}): שִׁבְעָה ע׳ = *seven years*, 4$^{13.20.22.29}$; עִדָּן וְעִדָּנִין וּפְלַג עִדָּן 7^{25} (i.e. 3½ years, v. Dr; perhaps read du. for pl., cf. Bev Gunk$^{Schöpf.\ 201}$).

†עוֹד **adv. still** (BH; S-C^{K13}; 𝔗$^{O\ Jon.}$; Chr- 5750-51
Pal. Schulth$^{143f.}$), Dn 4^{28} עוֹד מִלְּתָא בְּפֻם מַלְכָּא (cf. BH **1 a** *a*).

†[עֲוָיָה] **n.f. iniquity** (BH II. עוה, עָוֺן; cf. 5753, 5758, 5771
𝔗 עֲוָיָא);—pl. sf. עֲוָיָתָךְ (K$^{§56 a) β) 2}$) Dn 4^{24}.

†עוֹף **n.[m.] fowl** (v. BH, √ I. עוף);—ע׳ 5774, 5776
abs. Dn 7^{6} wings of *a fowl*; cstr. 2^{38} coll.

†עוּר **n.[m.] chaff** (JAram. (Talm., rare), 5784
Syr. ܥܘܪܐ; Ar. عائر, عوّار *mote* (in eye, tending to cause *blindness* [עִוֵּר]) acc. to Ar. Lexx., Lane^{2195});—abs. ע׳ Dn 2^{35} (in sim.).

[עִז], עִזִּין v. ענז. p. 1107 5796

†[עִזְקָה] **n.f. signet-ring** (𝔗 Syr.; √ עזק 5824
=*surround*, v. BH);—sf. עִזְקְתֵהּ Dn 6^{18}; pl. cstr. 5823
־קָת v^{18}.

†עֶזְרָא **n.pr.m. Ezra** (BH *id.*);—Ezr 7$^{12.21.25}$. 5830-31

†עֲזַרְיָה **n.pr.m.** comrade of Daniel (BH 5838-39
id.; Dn 1^{6}+);—Dn 2^{17}, = עֲבֵד נְגוֹ v^{49}+.

עֵטָא v. יעט. p. 1096 5843

†[עַיִן] **n.f.**$^{Ezr 5,5}$ **eye** (v. BH I. ע׳);—cstr. עֵין 5869-70
Ezr 5^{5} (of God); pl. (K$^{§51, 1}$) of horn, עַיְנִין Dn 7$^{8.20}$; of man, du. cstr. עַיְנֵי v^{8}, sf. עַיְנַי 4^{31}.

†עִיר **n.m. waking,** or **wakeful, one,** i.e. 5894
angel (√ עיר, cf. Syr. ܥܪ *wake*, ܥܝܪ *waking* 5782
(PS^{2843}), JAram. עִיר, NH עִיר adj. *awake*);—abs. ע׳ Dn 4$^{10.20}$; pl. abs. עִירִין v^{14}; Aq Symm. ἐγρήγορος; cf. Charles$^{Enoch\ i.\ 5;\ xxxix.\ 12;\ also\ p.\ 356}$ Dr$^{ad\ loc.}$; doubtful is the connex. with Ph. *Zophesemim* (Euseb. $^{Praep.\ Evang.\ 10}$), i.e. צפי שמים *watchers of heaven*, as *keeping watch over* or *spying out* (Zim$^{KAT\ 3.\ 629}$ Jerem$^{AT\ im\ Licht\ d.\ AO\ 63}$).

עַל, עֵלָּא v. עלה. עִלָּה v. I. עלל. p. 1106 5922, 5924, 5931

עלה (√ of foll.; v. BH עָלָה). 5927

5928 †[עֲלָת K$^{\S 56, a) \beta) 2}$] **n.f. burnt-offering** (BH עֹלָה; cf. Palm. עלתא *altar*, SAC^{92} Lzb^{341});—pl. abs. עֲלָוָן Ezr 6^{9}.

5943 †[עִלָּי K$^{\S 59\ 1)\ e)}$] **adj. highest**;—alw. emph. עליא Kt, עִלָּאָה Qr, *the Most High* God: אֱלָהָא ע׳ Dn $3^{26.32}$ $5^{18.21}$; ע׳ alone, *the Most High*, $4^{14.21.22.29.31}$ 7^{25} (cf. Nab. n.pr. עליאל Lzb^{341} SAC^{91}).

5945-46 ‡†[עֶלְיוֹן] **adj. id.** (BH *id.*);—pl. of God, קַדִּישֵׁי עֶלְיוֹנִין (double pl., Buhl, as sts. BH, Ges $^{\S 124q}$ Kö$^{\text{ii.1.438f}}$) Dn $7^{18.22.25.27}$.

5952 †[עִלִּי] **n.f. roof-chamber** (cf. Dr; BH
5944 עֲלִיָּה);—sf. עִלִּיתֵהּ Dn 6^{11}.

5922 עַל **prep. upon, over, on account of,**
5921 **above, to, against** (BH and general Aram. *id.*);—sf. 1 s. עֲלַי; 2 ms. עליך Kt (so Eg. Aram., Cooke$^{\text{No. 77, A 5, 6, B 8}}$, S-C$^{\text{Pap. A 3, B 5+}}$), עֲלָךְ, Qr (𝔗 עֲלָךְ, Dalm$^{\S 47, 2}$) Dn 3^{12} + 6 t. Dn, Ezr 7^{18}; 3 ms. עֲלוֹהִי (so Nab. Palm.; Eg. Aram. עלוי S-C$^{\text{A 6+}}$) Dn 3^{28}+, עֲלֹהִי †Ezr 6^{11}; 3 fs. עליה Kt (so Eg. Aram., S-C$^{\text{D 24}}$), עֲלַהּ Qr (so 𝔗) †Dn 4^{14} 5^{21}; 1 pl. עֲלֶינָא †Ezr 4^{12}, עֲלֶינָא 4^{18} 5^{17} Baer (Gi עֲלֶינָא); 3 mpl. עֲלֵיהֹם (so Nab., CIS$^{\text{ii. 226}}$; Eg. Aram., S-C$^{\text{Pap. F 5, 8+}}$) †7^{24}, עֲלֵיהוֹן †$5^{1.3}$;—**1. a.** *upon*, Dn $2^{10.28.46}$ $5^{5.7}$ 6^{11} + oft., 4^{26} עַל־הֵיכַל מַלְכוּתָא (2 S 11^{2}); to be established עַל מַלְכוּתִי 4^{33} (cf. 2 Ch 1^{1}; BH **II. 1**) to lay an impost *upon*, Ezr 7^{24}; to trust *on*, Dn 3^{28}; after a vb. of motion, מְטָא עַל to come *upon*, Dn $4^{21.25}$; of times, to pass *over*, $4^{13.20.22.29}$; Ezr 5^{1} בְּשֻׁם אֱלָהּ יִשְׂרָאֵל עֲלֵיהוֹן i.e. (named) *over* them. **b.** idiom. (as in BH; v. **II. 1 d**) of the pers. who is the *subj.* of an emotion or experience, Dn 5^{9} וְזִיוֹהִי שָׁנַיִן עֲלוֹהִי were changed *upon* him, 7^{28}; 6^{19} וְשִׁנְתֵהּ נַדַּת עֲלוֹהִי (cf. 2^{1}). **c.** *on acc. of* (BH **1 f** *b*), Dn 3^{16} עַל־דְּנָה פִּתְגָם. So in עַל־דְּנָה *on this acc.* †Ezr $4^{15.22}$ 5^{17}, עַל־מָה wherefore? †Dn 2^{15}; and עַל דִּבְרַת דִּי (v. דְּ׳). **d.** *on behalf of* (*ib.* **1 f** *c*), Ezr 6^{17}. **e.** *regarding, concerning* (*ib.* **1 f** *g*), Dn 2^{18} $5^{14.29}$ $6^{6.13}$ Ezr 7^{14} + oft. **2.** *over*, with vbs. of ruling, appointing, etc., Dn $2^{48.49}$ 3^{12} 4^{14}+, Ezr 4^{20} 6^{18}. **3.** in a compar. sense, *above, beyond*, Dn 3^{19} 6^{4}. **4.** expressing *direction*: **a.** *to*, of a person, after a vb. of motion (cf. BH **7 c** *a a*), Dn 2^{24} $4^{31.33}$ $6^{7.16}$ Ezr $4^{12.23}$ + oft.; after to *send* (a letter, etc.) Ezr $4^{11.17.18}$ 5^{6}+, *write* 4^{7}, *prophesy* 5^{1}; of the direction of the mind (*ib.* **7 c** *c*), Dn 3^{12} $6^{14.14.15}$; cf. Ezr 5^{5} וְעֵין אֱלָ׳ הֲוָת עַל (cf. Je 40^{4} and אֶל ψ 34^{16}). **b.** *against*, Dn $3^{19.29}$ 5^{23} $6^{5.6}$+; Ezr 4^{8} 7^{23}. **5.** in such phrases as טְאֵב עַל, שְׁפַר עַל (to be) good or acceptable *to* (as in Syr. and *late* Heb.: v. BH **8**), Ezr 5^{17} אִם עַל מַלְכָּא טָב, $7^{18.18}$ Dn 4^{24} (יִשְׁפַּר), 6^{15} (בְּאֵשׁ), v^{24} (טְאֵב).—Comp. the synopsis of meanings in Lzb^{340}.

†עֵלָּא **adv. above** (from **n.** עַל, with **א-** of 5924
direction, D$^{\S 44.1n.}$; Nab., Eg. Aram., *id.*, Lzb^{341} S-C$^{\text{A 5+}}$; 𝔗 עֵיל, עֵילָּא; Syr. ܥܠ in ܠܥܠ *above*);—Dn 6^{3} עֵלָּא מִנְּהוֹן *above* (*over*) them (cf. Cooke$^{96.2}$, Dt 28^{43} 𝔗).

†עִלָּה **n.f. matter, affair, occasion** (Syr. 5931
ܥܠܬܐ, v. BH I. עלל);—abs. ע׳ Dn $6^{5.5.6}$ (=ground 5953
of accusation).

†[עֲלַל] **vb. go or come in** (𝔗 Syr.; v. BH 5954
III. עלל);—**Pe.** *Pf.* 3 ms. עַל Dn 2^{16}; c. עַל pers. 5953
v^{24}; c. לְבַיְתֵהּ 6^{11}, so 3 fs. עללת Kt, עַלַּת Qr 5^{10}; *Pt.* עללין Kt, עָלִּין Qr, abs. 4^{4} 5^{8}. **Haph.** *bring in*, c. קֳדָם pers.: *Pf.* 3 ms. הַנְעֵל (K$^{\S 11.4.b}$; so Eg. Aram., S-C$^{\text{G 6, 7, 24, 27}}$ הנעלת; cf. D$^{\S 71.7;\ \text{Dial.-Proben, p. 4}}$); Dn 2^{25} (ל acc. pers.), 6^{19} (acc. rei); *Imv.* ms. sf. pers., הַעֵלְנִי 2^{24}; *Inf.* לְהַנְעָלָה 4^{3} (ל acc. pers.); no קֳדָם pers., לְהֶעָלָה 5^{7} (*id.*). **Hoph.** (W$^{\text{CG 225}}$) *be brought*, subj. pers. + קֳדָם pers.: *Pf.* 3 ms. הֻעַל Dn 5^{13}, 3 mpl. הֻעַלּוּ v^{15}.

†[מֶעָל] **n.[m.] going in** (Syr., 𝔗^{J}; 𝔗^{Onk}, 4606
etc., מַעֲלָנָא);—pl. cstr. מֶעָלֵי שִׁמְשָׁא Dn 6^{15} i.e. *sunset* (so read Nö$^{\text{GGA, 1884, 1020}}$ Str M Bev, cf. Syr. ܡܥܠܝ̈, ܡܥܠܢܐ; > van d.H. Gi מֶעָלֵי, Baer מֵעָלֵי; cf. K$^{\S 60,\ \text{Beisp. b)}}$).

†עָלַם **n.[m.] perpetuity, antiquity** (v. 5957
BH III. עלם, עוֹלָם);—ע׳ abs. Dn 3^{33}+, cstr. 7^{18}; 5769
emph. עָלְמָא 2^{20}+; pl. עָלְמִין 2^{4}+, emph. עָלְמַיָּא 2^{44} 7^{18};—*perpetuity* in the future: מַלְכוּת ע׳ Dn 3^{33} 7^{27}, cf. 4^{31} 7^{14}; ע׳ as adv. *for ever* 4^{31}; עַד־עָלְמָא 7^{18} וְעַד־עָלַם עָלְמַיָּא; pl. לְע׳ *for ever* $2^{4.44.44}$ 3^{9} 5^{10} $6^{7.22.27}$; *antiquity*, מִן־יוֹמָת עָלְמָא Ezr $4^{15.19}$; of limitless time both past and future: מִן־ע׳ וְעַד־ע׳ Dn 2^{20}.

†עֵלְמָיֵא **n.gent. pl. Elamites** (cf. BH 5962
עֵילָם);—Ezr 4^{9}. 5867

†[עֲלַע] **n.f. rib** (𝔗 Syr.; v. BH I. צלע, 5967
צֵלָע);—pl. abs. עִלְעִין Dn 7^{5}. 6763

[עֲלָת] v. עלה. above 5928

6567-68 †[פְּרַשׁ] **vb. make distinct** (cf. BH
(chiefly late));—**Pa.** *Pt. pass.* Ezr 4[18] *made
distinct* (BH Ne 8[8]; 𝔗 NH).

6573 †פַּרְשֶׁגֶן **n.m.** [Ezr 4, 23] **copy** (𝔗 -שַׁנְנָא, Syr.
6572 ܦܪܫܓܢ; Aram. loan-word in BH, where also
6572 פַּתְשֶׁגֶן *id.;* loan-word from Pers. (Thes[1133; Add. 108]),
cf. Armen. *patčên, copy,* Gildemeister[ZKM iv. 210]
Lag[Ges. Abh. 79; Armen. Stud. § 1838] Mey[Enst. J. 22] Hoffm[ZA ii.
52], OIran. **paticayan, id.*, acc. to Andr[M 79]*; not
clear whether פר׳ is text. err. for פת׳ (Hoffm[l. c.]),
or from diff. orig. (Andr[l. c.] *paračayan? parica-
yan?*), or from same √ in diff. stage (so appar.
Scheft[52], citing, for both, OBaktr. *fra-sĕn̈hana,
announcement,* OIran. *praśaṃsana, praśāsana,
command,* Ar. *frasasti, command, patisên̈hana,
answer,* OP. **patithan̈hana, announcement, answer*));—cstr. פ׳ Ezr 4[11.23] 5[6].

6590 †[פְּשַׁר] **vb. interpret** (a dream) (𝔗 *id.,*
Syr. ܦܫܪ, perh. Eg.Aram. פשר Lzb[355] SAC[100] (Ar.
فسّر loan-word, v. Frä[263]); As. *pašâru*);—**Pe.**
Inf. לְמִפְשַׁר Dn 5[16], acc. cogn. פִּשְׁרִין. **Pa.** *Pt. act.*
מְפַשַּׁר Dn 5[12], acc. חֶלְמִין.

6591 פְּשַׁר [31] **n.m.** [Dn 2, 45] **interpretation** (of dream)
6592 (cf. BH as loan-word);—cstr. פ׳ Dn 4[3] 5[15.26] 7[16];
emph. פִּשְׁרָא 2[4] + 7 t. Dn, + 4[15.16] Kt (Qr ־ֵהּ);
־ַהּ 2[7] 5[12]; sf. ־ֵהּ 2[5.6.6] + 11 t. Dn, + Qr 4[15.16]
(Kt ־ָא); pl. פִּשְׁרִין 5[16].

6600 †פִּתְגָם **n.m.** [Ezr 6, 11] **command, word, affair**
6599 (Pers.: v. BH);—abs. פ׳ Dn 3[16]; emph. ־מָא Ezr
4[17]+;—*command* Ezr 6[11], *word,* by missive 5[7],
from king 4[17] (both c. שְׁלַח), in answer 5[11] (c.
התיב); weakened, *thing, affair* Dn 3[16] 4[14].

6605-06 †[פְּתַח] **vb. open** (v. BH);—**Pe.** *Pt.
pass.* fpl. פְּתִיחָן Dn 6[11] *opened* (windows). **Peʿîl**
(W[CG 225]) *Pf.* 3 mpl. פְּתִיחוּ 7[10] books *were opened.*

6601 **פתא** (√of foll.; 𝔗 Syr.; BH פתה (rare)).

6613 †[פְּתָי] **n.[m.] breadth** (𝔗 Syr.; Eg. Aram.
RÉS[246] S-C[D4]);—sf. פְּתָיֵהּ Dn 3[1] Ezr 6[3].

צ

6634 †[צְבָא] **vb. be inclined, desire, be
6633 pleased** (𝔗 Syr.; cf. BH II. צבה);—**Pe. 1.**
desire: Pf. 1 s. צְבִית (K[§ 47 Beisp. 1) a)] Nö[GGA, 1884, 1019]
pf. intrans.) Dn 7[19] (c. inf.). **2.** *be pleased,*
will (without hindrance), abs., of God: *Impf.*
3 ms. יִצְבֵּא 4[14 23.29]; *Inf.* sf. מִצְבְּיֵהּ v[32] acc. to
his willing; of Neb.: *Pt. act.* צָבֵא 5[19.19.19.19]

†צְבוּ **n.f. thing, anything** (orig. *purpose*) 6640
(Palm. צבו Lzb[357] SAC[100] Cooke[266], Syr. ܨܒܘܬܐ,
all *thing;* cf. NH חֵפֶץ *thing,* from חָפֵץ *delight in,
crave*);—Dn 6[18].

I. [צְבַע] **vb. dip, wet** (𝔗 Syr.; cf. BH I. 6647
צבע);—**Pa.** *Pt.act.* pl. מְצַבְּעִין Dn 4[22] *wet* thee (ל), 6648
+ מְטַל. **Hithpa.** *Impf.* יִצְטַבַּע (also ־בַּע), *be wet,*
c. בְּטַל 4[12.20], מִטַּל v[30] 5[21].

II. **צבע** (√of foll.; cf. BH II. צבע).

†[אֶצְבַּע] **n.f. 1. finger; 2. toe** (𝔗 Syr.; 677
BH *id.*);—pl. **1.** abs. אֶצְבְּעָן Dn 5[5]. **2.** emph. 676
־ָתָא 2[41]; cstr. ־ָע v[42].

†צַד **n.[m.] side** (very rare in Aram.; perh. 6655
Hebr., v. BH *id.,* √ צדד);—cstr., c. prep.: לְצַד 6654
עליא Dn 7[25], i.e. *against;* מִצ׳ מַלְכוּתָא 6[5], i.e.
arising from, touching.

‡†צְדָא **n.[m.]** usu. (malicious) **purpose** 6656
(Hebraism from BH צְדִיָּה, √ I. צדה);—c. ה in- 6658, 6660
terrog. הַצְדָא Dn 3[14]; < read הַאֻזְדָּא Bev Dr Kmp.

†צִדְקָה **n.f. right doing** (Talm., OAram.; 6665
v. BH צְדָקָה, √ צדק);—צ׳ Dn 4[24]. 6663, 6666

†[צַוַּאר] **n.m. neck** (𝔗 Syr.; v. BH sub I. 6676-77
צור);—sf. צַוְּארָךְ Dn 5[16], צַוְּארֵהּ v[7.29]. 6696

†[צְלָא] **vb. Pa. pray** (orig. *bow* in prayer) 6739
(𝔗 *id., bow,* Pa, *pray,* so Syr. ܨܠܐ and Pa.; As.
sullû, entreat (appar. not of prayer to gods Zim
[KAT 3. 610 f.]); Ar. صَلًا *middle of the back,* صلا II. *pray,*
Eth. ጸለወ: *bow,* ጸለየ: *pray;* Sab. צלות *shrine*
Hom[Chr 125; AA 185]);—*Pt.* מְצַלֵּא Dn 6[11] (abs.); pl.
מְצַלַּיִן (K[§ 47 a)]) Ezr 6[10] (c. ל *in behalf of*).

†[צְלַח] **vb. prosper** (v. BH II. צלח);— 6743-44
Haph. *Pf.* 3 ms. הַצְלַח Dn 3[30] 6[29]; *Pt.* מַצְלַח
Ezr 5[8], pl. ־לְחִין 6[14];—**1.** *cause to prosper* Dn 3[30]
(c. ל pers.). **2.** *shew prosperity, be pros-
perous* 6[29] (of pers.); *have success* (in building)
Ezr 6[14]; *be successful* (of work) 5[8] (בִּידְהֹם).

†צְלֵם [17] **n.m.** [Dn 2, 31] **image** (v. BH צלם);— 6754-55
abs. צ׳ Dn 2[31] 3[1]; cstr. צ׳ 3[19], צְלֵם v[5]+; emph.
צַלְמָא 2[31]+;—*image* Dn 2[31.31.32.34.35] 3[1]+10 t. 3;
צ׳ אַנְפּוֹהִי 3[19] i.e. his expression.

6833, 6853 †[צִפַּר] **n.f.** [Dn 4,18 (cf. K. p.165, Anm. 3)] bird (v. BH II. צפר);—pl. abs. צִפְּרִין Dn 4[30], emph. צִפְּרַיָּא v[11], cstr. צִפֲּרֵי v[9.18].

6841-42 †[צְפִיר] **n.m.** he-goat (v. BH V. צפר);—pl. cstr. צְפִירֵי עִזִּין Ezr 6[17].

ק

קבל (√of following, *be in front of*).

6903 קֳבֵל [T: 29] **subst.** front, as **prep.** in front of, before, because of; sq. דִּי as **conj.** because that (perh. in form a dimin., Bev[Dn 2,8]; 𝔗 קְבֵיל, c. לְ, לִקְבֵיל, sf. לִקְבְלִי, etc., *in front of* (Dalm.[§47,7]); Syr. ܩܽܘܒܳܠܳܐ ,ܩܒܳܠ *aspect*, ܡܶܢ ܩܒܳܠ *in front*, ܠܩܽܘܒܠܳܐ, sf. ܠܩܽܘܒܠܶܗ *in front (of), opposite (to)*, cf. Gn 15[10] 𝔗 𝔖; Palm. לקבל *before* (Cooke [321, cf. 193]));—cstr. לָקֳבֵל Dn 2[8]+, sf. לָקָבְלָךְ †2[31];—†**1.** c. לְ: **a.** Dn 3[3] לק׳ צַלְמָא *before* the image, 2[31] 5[1.5]; *in view of, by reason of,* 5[10] לק׳ מִלֵּי מַלְכָּא *by reason of* the words, etc., Ezr 4[16] לָקֳבֵל דְּנָה (cf. Eg. Aram. לקבל זנה זי, RÉS [361 B5]). **b.** sq. דִּי as **conj.** *because that* Ezr 6[13] (so Palm. CIS[ii. 164]). **2.** c. כֹּל, כָּל־קֳבֵל *in view of, because of* (but read probably כְּלָקֳבֵל *according to the front of,* i.e. *having regard to, because of:* Luzz[Chald. Gr. § 123] Lambert[RÉJ, 1895, 47 f.] Marti[§ 95 d] Nö[LCB, 1896, 703] Nes[OLZ, 1902, 487] Strack[56] al.; cf. BH I. עֻמָּה **d**): **a.** as **prep.** כָּל־קֳבֵל דְּנָה *because of this, therefore,* †Dn 2[12.24] 3[7.8] 6[10] Ezr 7[17]; Dn 3[22] pointing forwards, כָּל־קֳבֵל דְּנָה מִן־דִּי וגו׳ *on this account,* (viz.) because that, etc. **b.** sq. דִּי as **conj.** *because that, inasmuch as,* Dn 2[8] כָּל־קֳבֵל (כְּלָקֳבֵל) דִּי חֲזֵיתוֹן *because* ye see, v[10.41.45]+, Ezr 4[14] 7[14]; Dn 5[22]=*although.* In Dn 2[40] 6[11] taken by 𝔊 (ὃν τρόπον, καθώς), Ges (Thes, not Lex), EwHi as=*according as* (as Ec 5[15] 𝔗 כל קבל דאתא *according as* he came), but not BevBehrm Marti. [Occas. in 𝔗, usu.=*before;* cf. in 𝔗[J] Gn 28[17] 31[32], D[§§ 47.7; 50]].

6901-02 †קַבֵּל **vb. denom. Pa.** receive (BH (late), q. v.; 𝔗 Syr.: prop. *come in front of, come to meet,* cf. Germ. *entgegennehmen*);—*Pf.* 3 ms. קַבֵּל Dn 6[1]; *Impf.* 2 mpl. תְּקַבְּלוּן *ye shall receive* 2[6], 3 mpl. וִיקַבְּלוּן 7[18]; all c. acc. rei.

6925 קֳדָם [T: 42] **prep.** before (so OAram. Nab. Palm. etc. (Lzb[360 f.]), 𝔗 קֳדָם, Syr. ܩܕܳܡ; prop. a subst.
the front, cf. Ar. قُدَّام *the front;* for √ v. BH 6924
קדם);—sf. קֳדָמַי Dn 2[9]+, ־מָ֑י v[6]; קדמיך Kt, קֳדָמָךְ Qr, †5[23] 6[23]; קֳדָמוֹהִי 4[5]+ (cf. Nerab קדמוה, Cooke[189]); 3 fs. קדמיה Kt, קֳדָמַהּ Qr, †7[7.8.20]; קֳדָמֵיהוֹן †4[4];—**1.** *before* (=Heb. לִפְנֵי), esp. in the phrases *to answer, pray, say,* etc., *before* a superior (as more respectful than *to*), Dn 2[9] לְמֵאמַר קֳדָמַי, v[10.11.27] 6[11] (v. Dr), v[12.13.14]; קְרֵי ק׳ Ezr 4[18.23]; 5[23.23]; with שְׁפַר to *seem fair* Dn 3[32] 6[2]; after vbs. of motion, *in before,* Dn 2[24.25] 3[13] 4[3]+; of time 7[7]. †**2.** מִן־קֳדָם *from before* (=מִלִּפְנֵי, but as used in *late* Heb., Est 1[19] 4[8]: p. 818[a]), c. קַבֵּל Dn 2[6], בְּעָא v[18]; of a decree, 6[27] מִן־קֳדָמַי שִׂים טְעֵם (|| מִנִּי 3[29]+), cf. 2[15] Ezr 7[14]; of God, Dn 5[24] מִן־קֳדָמוֹהִי שְׁלִיחַ פַּסָּא דִי־יְדָא, 7[10] (so very oft. in 𝔗, Dr[Sm lxx f., lxxiii]). Also=Heb. מִפְּנֵי, with to *fear* Dn 5[19] 6[27], be *rooted up* 7[8], *fall* v[20].

†[קַדְמָה] **n.f.** former time (cf. BH קַדְמָה, 6927-28
Zinj. קדמה (Cooke[177]), *former state*);—cstr. Dn 6[11] מִן־קַדְמַת דְּנָה = *before this, formerly;* so Ezr 5[11] מִקַּדְמַת דְּ׳. Cf. Gn 28[19] 𝔗[J], Ez 38[17] 𝔗.

†[קַדְמָי] **adj.** former, first (so Nab. Palm. 6933
𝔗 Syr.);—fs. emph. קַדְמָיְתָא *the first* Dn 7[4], fpl. emph. קַרְנַיָּא קַדְמָיָתָא *the former* horns v[8], mpl. emph. קַדְמָיֵא v[24].

קדשׁ (√of foll.; 𝔗 Syr.; v. BH *id.*, קָדוֹשׁ). 6918

†קַדִּישׁ **adj.** holy;—abs. ק׳ Dn 4[10.20]; pl. ־שִׁין 6922
4[5]+, cstr. ־שֵׁי 7[18]+;—gods Dn 4[5.6.15] 5[11]; as subst., of angels 4[10.14.20]; of Isr. (as holy ones, saints) 7[21.22], קַדִּישֵׁי עֶלְיוֹנִין *saints of the Most High* v[18.22.25.27].

קול (√of following; BH קוֹל, קֹל). 6963

†קָל **n.m.** [Dn 4,28] voice (𝔗 Syr.);—ק׳ abs. Dn 7032
4[28] 6[21]; cstr. *sound* of words 7[11], instr. 3[5.7.10.15].

[קוּם] **vb.** arise, stand (v. BH);—**Pe.** *Pf.* 6965-66
3 ms. קָם Dn 3[24], 3 mpl. קָמוּ Ezr 5[2]; *Impf.* 3 ms. יְקוּם Dn 6[20] 7[24], 3 fs. תְּקוּם 2[39.44]; 3 mpl. יְקוּמוּן 7[10.17.24] (יְקֻ׳); *Pt.* קָאֵם 2[31], pl. קאמין Kt, קָיְמִין Qr, 3[3], emph. קָאֲמַיָּא 7[16];—**1.** lit. *arise* Dn 3[24] (i.e. from throne), 6[20] (from bed). **2.** fig.=come on the scene of history: of kingdom 2[39], king 7[17.24] (both מִן of source), v[24]. **3.** *arise* (out of inaction), and build Ezr 5[2], devour Dn 7[5b]. **4.** *stand,* lit., לָקֳבֵל pers. 2[31], cf. 3[3], קֳדָם pers. 7[10]; pt. as n., *those standing* (there) v[16]. **5.** *endure,* of kingdom 2[44]. **Pa.** *set up, establish* an ordinance (קְיָם): *Inf.* לְקַיָּמָה 6[8]. **Haph.** (K[§ 45,4])

Pf. 3 ms. הֲקִים Dn 3[2]+, וַהֲקִים 6[2], sf. הֲקִימֵהּ 5[11], אֲקִימֵהּ 3[1]; 3 fs. הֲקִמַת 7[5]; 2 ms. הֲקֵימְתָּ 3[12.18]; 1 s. הֲקֵימֶת לָא 3[14]; *Impf.* 3 ms. יְהָקִים (K[§ 45, b)) 5[21] 6[16], יְקִים 2[44] 4[14]; *Inf.* sf. לַהֲקָמוּתֵהּ 6[4]; *Pt. act.* מְהָקֵים 2[21];—**1.** *set up*, lit. image 3[1.2.3.3.5.7.12.14.18]; fig. kings 2[21], kingdom v[44]. **2.** *lift up* one side 7[5a] (Dr). **3.** *establish*, c. acc. קְיָם 6[16] (=**Pa.**), אֱסָרָא v[9]. **4.** *appoint* Ezr 6[18], 2 acc. Dn 5[11]; sf. pers.+עַל 6[4], ל acc. pers.+עַל 4[14] 5[21] 6[2]. **Hoph.** *Pf.* 3 fs. הֳקִימַת (variants in Str; cf. K[§ 45, 5]; not Hebraism Nö[GGA 1867, 1784]; W[CG 225, 253]) 7[4] *be made to stand* עַל־רַגְלַיִן.

7010 †קְיָם **n.[m.]** **statute** (Eg. Aram. קימיהם Cooke[209]);—abs. Dn 6[16], cstr. v[8].

7011 †קַיָּם **adj.** **enduring** (cf. Nab. קים (Cooke[217] Lzb קים; SAC, privately, prob. קָיֵם));—abs. ק׳ Dn 6[27] (of God, so oft. 𝔗 NH, cf. Dr); fs. קַיָּמָה 4[23] (of kingdom).

6991-92 †[קְטַל] **vb.** **slay** (𝔗 Syr. (oft.); v. BH (late, rare));—**Pe.** *Pt. act.* קָטֵל Dn 5[19], acc. pers. **Peʿîl** *be slain: Pf.* 3 ms. קְטִיל 5[30], 3 fs. קְטִילַת 7[11]. **Pa.** *slay: Pf.* 3 ms. קַטִּל 3[22] (acc. pers.); *Inf.* לְקַטָּלָה 2[14] (ל acc. pers.). **Hithpe.** *be slain: Inf.* לְהִתְקְטָלָה 2[13]; *Pt.* (=gerundive, K[§ 76, 3]) pl. מִתְקַטְּלִין v[13] were *to be slain*.

קטר (√ of foll.; 𝔗 קְטַר, Syr. ܩܛܰܪ *bind*,
7000 whence קִטְרָא, ܩܶܛܪܳܐ *knot*, etc.; cf. BH II. [קטר]).

7001 †[קְטַר] **n.m.**[Dn 5, 6] **joint, knot**;—lit. pl. cstr. קִטְרֵי Dn 5[6] *joints* of his loin; fig. abs. קִטְרִין v[12.16], usu. *knotty things*, difficulties (Syr. PS[3591]); but prob. of magic *spells, banns* (also Syr. PS[l.c.], cf. Brock[319 b]), so Bev, v. also Dr.

7007 †קַיִט **n.[m.]** **summer** (𝔗 Syr.; v. BH II.
7019 קיץ);—abs. ק׳ Dn 2[35].

7010-11 קַיָּם, קְיָם v. קום. above

7030 †קיתרס Kt, קַתְרֹס Qr, **n.[m.]** **lyre, zither** (also 𝔗; loan-word from Gk. κίθαρις Krauss[i. 193; ii. 573]);—Dn 3[5.7.10.15]; Kmp קִיתָרֹס.

7032 קָל v. קול. p. 1110

7066 †[קְנָא] **vb.** **acquire, buy** (v. BH I.
7069 קנה);—**Pe.** *Impf.* 2 ms. תִּקְנֵא Ezr 7[17] c. acc. rei, +בְּכַסְפָּא.

7097 קצא (√ of following; BH I. קָצָה, קצה).

†קְצָת **n.f.** **end** (so BH (late); 𝔗 (Gn 47[2]); 7117-18
not Syr.; cf. Eg. Aram. RÉS[361 A 4]);—cstr. לִק׳ *at the end of* (months, days) 4[26.31]; מִן־ק׳ מַלְכוּתָא 2[42]=*part of* (|| מִנַּהּ v[d]; cf. BH קְצָת **2**).

†קְצַף **vb.** **be wroth** (Syr.; v. BH I. 7108
קצף);—**Pe.** *Pf.* 3 ms. ק׳ Dn 2[12].

‡†קְצַף **n.[m.]** **wrath** (of God) (only Syr. 7109
ܩܶܨܦܳܐ *sadness, anxiety*, in Lexx.);—abs. ק׳ Ezr 7[23].

קְצָת v. קצא. above 7118

†[קְרָא] **vb.** **call, read out, aloud** (v. BH 7123
I. קרא);—**Pe.** *Impf.* 3 ms. יִקְרֵה Dn 5[7], 1 s. אֶקְרֵא 7121
v[17]; 3 mpl. יִקְרוֹן v[15]; *Inf.* לְמִקְרֵא v[8.16]; *Pt. act.* קָרֵא 3[4]+;—**1.** *call, proclaim,* בְּחַיִל: Dn 3[4] 4[11] 5[7]. **2.** *read out, aloud,* acc. כְּתָבָא 5[7.8.15.16], v[17] (ל pers.). **Peʿîl** (W[CG 225]) *Pf.* 3 ms. קְרִי Ezr 4[18.23] *it was read,* קֳדָם pers. **Hithpe.** *be summoned, Impf.* 3 ms. יִתְקְרֵי Dn 5[12].

†קְרֵב **vb.** **approach** (v. BH I. קרב);— 7126-27
Pe. *Pf.* 3 ms. ק׳ Dn 3[26] (ל loc.); 1 s. קִרְבֵת 7[16] (עַל pers.); abs., 3 mpl. קְרִבוּ Dn 3[8] 6[13]; *Inf.* sf. כְּמִקְרְבֵהּ 6[21] *when he approached,* ל loc. **Pa.** *offer* sacrifice: *Impf.* 2 ms. תְּקָרֵב Ezr 7[17], c. acc. +עַל of altar. **Haph. 1.**=**Pa.**: c. acc. *Pf.* 3 mpl. הַקְרִבוּ Ezr 6[17], *Pt. act.* מְהַקְרְבִין v[10] (ל dei). **2.** *bring near: Pf.* sf. הַקְרְבוּהִי Dn 7[13] (קֳדָם dei).

†קְרָב (K[§ 57 a)]) **n.[m.]** **war** (𝔗 Syr. NH *id.*; 7129
BH as Aramaism);—abs. Dn 7[21]. 7128

†קִרְיָה, ־ָא, **n.f.** **city** (𝔗 Syr.; S-C[A 9+] 7149
קריה; v. BH, √קרה; also Nö[Beitr. 62]);—abs. ־ָה 7151
Ezr 4[10], ־ָא v[15]; emph. קִרְיְתָא v[12.13.15.15.16.19.21]

†קֶרֶן **n.f.**[Dn 7, 8] **horn** (v. BH קרן);—abs. ק׳ 7161-62
Dn 7[8]; emph. קַרְנָא 3[5]+; du. (often!) קַרְנַיִן 7[7]; emph. ־נַיָּא 7[8]+;—**1.** instr. of music, Dn 3[5.7.10.15]. **2.** symbolic, in vision, 7[7.8.8.8.11.20.20.21.24].

[קְרַץ] **n.[m.]** **piece** (𝔗; v. BH קרץ);—pl. 7170-71
sf. קַרְצוֹהִי Dn 6[25], ־צֵיהוֹן 3[8], both in phr. אֲכַלוּ ק׳, i.e. *accuse maliciously* (so 𝔗 Syr. PS[3756] (cf. OAram. אמר כרצי פ׳ Lzb[299] SAC[66] Cooke[205 f.]; כרץ also Mand.), prob. borrowed from As. *karṣe akâlu, malign, slander* (oft.; also TelAm.); cf. also *uktarrizu* Ḫamm[Law 161]; further Ar. أَكَلَ لَحْمَهُ *id.*, and kindred phr.; Eth. በልዐ: ከርሰ: Di[489]).

7187, 7189 †קְשֹׁט **n.[m.]** truth (𝔗 Syr.; v. BH קֹשֶׁט (once, Aramaism));—abs. Dn 4^{34}; מִן־ק׳ 2^{47} *of a truth.*

7030 קַתְרֹס v. קיתרס. p.1111

ר

7200 **ראה** (√of foll.; not Aram.; BH רָאָה *see*).

7299 †[רֵו] **n.m.** appearance (𝔗, rare);—sf. רֵוֵהּ Dn 2^{31} 3^{25}.

7217 †רֵאשׁ **n.m.** $^{Dn\,7,6}$ head (Eg. Aram., S-C$^{Pap.}$;
7218 Palm. רש; 𝔗 רֵישׁ, Syr. ܪܫܐ; BH ראשׁ);—cstr. ר׳ Dn 7^{1}; emph. ־ָה 2^{38}; sf. רֵאשִׁי 4^{2}+, ־ָךְ 2^{28}, ־ֵהּ v^{32}+, ־ַהּ 7^{20}, ־הוֹן 3^{27}; pl. abs. רֵאשִׁין 7^{6}, sf. רָאשֵׁיהֹם (K$^{§§ 53, Anm. b); 63}$ Gu$^{Hpt\,ad\,loc.}$) Ezr 5^{10};—**1.** *head* of man Dn 3^{27}, cf. 7^{9}; in vision: of image 2$^{32.38}$, beast 7$^{6.20}$. **2.** *head* as seat of visions, חֶזְוֵי רֵאשָׁךְ, etc., 2^{28} 4$^{2.7.10}$ 7$^{1.15}$. **3.** =*chief,* בְּר׳ Ezr 5^{10} *in the capacity of their chiefs.* **4.** *sum,* essential content, of matters Dn 7^{1} (Nes$^{MM\,40}$ *beginning*).

7227, 7231, 7239 **רבב** (√of foll.; v. BH I. רבב, רַב, רִבּוֹ).

7229 רַב **adj.** great (𝔗 Syr.);—abs. Dn 2^{31}+, cstr. v^{14}+; emph. m. רַבָּא Ezr 4^{10}+; f. רַבְּתָא
7260 Dn 4^{27}; mpl. redupl. רַבְרְבִין (K$^{§ 59,4}$) 3^{33}, fpl. ־ָן 2^{48}+, emph. ־ָתָא 7$^{11.17}$;—**1.** *great,* lit., of image Dn 2^{31}, rock v^{35}, city 4^{27}, sea 7^{2}, beast v$^{3.17}$, teeth v^{7}, gifts 2^{48}; *great,* imposing, feast 5^{1}, signs 3^{33}, words 7$^{8.11.20}$; c. מִן comp. 7^{20}. **2.** fig. of power, influence, etc.: *great* king 2^{10} Ezr 4^{10} 5^{11} (cf. Zinj. מלכן רברבן Cooke^{183}), God 5^{8} Dn 2^{45}. **3.** as n.=*captain, chief:* רַב טַבָּחַיָּא Dn 2^{14}, ר׳ סִגְנִין v^{48}, ר׳ חַרְטֻמַּיָּא 4^{6} 5^{11}.

7240 †רִבּוֹ (K$^{§ 65,4}$) **n.f.** myriad (𝔗 Syr.);—abs. ר׳+pl. רבון Kt (rd. רִבְּוָן K$^{l.c.}$), רִבְבָן Qr Dn 7^{10} *a myriad myriads.*

7261 †[רַבְרְבָן] **n.m.** lord, noble (cf. 𝔗 Syr.);—pl. sf. רַבְרְבָנַי Dn 4^{33} *my lords* (of Neb.); ־נוֹהִי (of Belshazzar) 5$^{1.2.3.9.10}$, of Darius 6^{18}; ־ניך Kt, ־נָךְ Qr (K$^{§ 53, Anm. b)}$) of Belshazzar v^{23}.

7236 †רְבָה **vb.** grow great (𝔗 Syr.; v. BH I.
7235 רבה);—**Pe.** *Pf.* 3 ms. ר׳ Dn 4^{8}+; 3 fs. רְבַת v^{19}; 2 ms. רְבַיְתָ Kt (>רְבַת Qr K$^{§ 47, Beisp. 1) a)}$) v^{19};—*grow tall and large,* of tree Dn 4$^{8.17}$; *grow long,* of hair v^{30}; fig. *grow great,* of king v^{19}, *increase,* of greatness v^{19}. **Pa.** *make great: Pf.* 3 ms. רַבִּי 2^{48} c. לְ acc. pers.

†רְבוּ **n.f.** greatness (𝔗 Syr.);—abs. ר׳ Dn 7238
4^{33}, emph. רְבוּתָא 5^{18}+, sf. ־ָתָךְ 4^{19};—*greatness* of king Dn 4$^{19.33}$ 5$^{18.19}$; of kingdom 7^{27}.

רבע (v. BH אַרְבַּע, רְבִיעִי, √רבע). 702, 7243

†אַרְבַּע, אַרְבְּעָה **n.m.** et **f.** four;—**1. m.**: 703
bef. **n.fpl.** Dn 7$^{2.3}$; **n.fs.** א׳ מְאָה Ezr 6^{17}; after **n.fpl.** Dn 7^{6}; as pred. אַרְבַּ֫עַ v^{17}. **2. f.**: bef. **n.mpl.** Dn 7$^{6.17}$; after **n.mpl.** 3^{25}.

†[רְבִיעַי] **adj. num. ord.** fourth;—f. abs. 7244
רביעיא Kt, רְבִיעָאָה Qr (K$^{§ 66,1}$) Dn 2^{40} 3^{25} 7$^{7.23}$; emph. רְבִיעָיְתָא v$^{19.23}$.

רַבְרְבִין etc. v. רַב supr. רַבְרְבָן v. רבב. 7229, 7260-61

†[רְגַז] **vb. Haph.** enrage (cf. BH);—*Pf.* 7264-65
3 mpl. הַרְגִּזוּ Ezr 5^{12}, c. acc. לֶאֱלָהּ שְׁמַיָּא.

†רְגַז **n.m.** rage;—abs. Dn 3^{13} (of king). 7266

†[רְגַל] **n.[f.]** foot (v. BH);—*du.* abs. 7271-72
רַגְלַיִן Dn 7^{4}; emph. ־לַ֫יָּא 2$^{41.42}$; sf. ־לוֹהִי v$^{33.34}$, רגליה Kt, רַגְלַהּ Qr (K$^{§ 53, 2, Anm. b)}$) 7$^{7.19}$;—*feet;* in vision, of image Dn 2$^{33.34.41.42}$, of beast 7$^{4.7.19}$.

†[רְגַשׁ] **vb.** be in tumult (𝔗; Syr. (rare; 7284
usu. *feel, perceive*); v. BH (late, rare));—**Haph.** 7283
shew tumultuousness, come thronging: Pf. 3 mpl. הַרְגִּ֫שׁוּ, c. עַל pers. Dn 6$^{7.16}$, abs. v^{12}.

רֵוֵהּ v. [רֵו] sub ראה. above 7299

רוח (√of foll.; v. BH *id.*, רוּחַ, רֵיחַ). 7307, 7381

†רוּחַ **n.f.** $^{Dn\,5,12}$ wind, spirit;—ר׳ abs. Dn 7308
5^{12} 6^{4}, cstr. 4^{5}+, emph. רוּחָא 2^{35}; sf. רוּחִי 7^{15}, ־ֵהּ 5^{20}; pl. cstr. רוּחֵי 7^{2};—**1.** *wind* Dn 2^{35} 7^{2}. **2.** *spirit:* **a.** of man, 5^{20} 7^{15}; as faculty of knowledge, ר׳ יַתִּירָא 5^{12} 6^{4}. **b.** ר׳ אֱלָהִין קַדִּישִׁין 4$^{5.6.15}$ 5^{11}, ר׳ א׳ v^{14}.

†רֵיחַ **n.f.** smell;—cstr. ר׳ נוּר Dn 3^{27}. 7382

†[רוּם] **vb.** rise (v. BH);—**Pe.** *Pt. pass.* 7311, 7313
רִם Dn 5^{20} *lifted up,* of heart, i.e. presumptuous. **Pōʿl.** *extol: Pt.* מְרוֹמֵם 4^{34} (לְ dei). **Haph.** *exalt: Pt.* מָרִים 5^{19} (acc. pers.). **Hithpōʿl.** *lift oneself up* against, 5^{23} (עַל dei).

†[רוּם] **n.m.** $^{Dn\,4,7}$ height;—sf. רוּמֵהּ, of 7314
temple Ezr 6^{3}, image Dn 3^{1}, tree in vision 4$^{7.8.17}$.

†רָז **n.m.** $^{Dn\,2,18}$ secret (𝔗 *id.*, Syr. ܪܐܙ, ܐܪܙܐ, ܐܪܙ, ܪܐܙܐ; 7328
Pers. loan-word; =Phlv. *rāž,* NPers. *rāz* Andr $^{M\,83*}$);—abs. ר׳ Dn 4^{6}, emph. רָזָא 2$^{18.19.27.30.47}$; pl. abs. רָזִין v$^{28.47}$, emph. רָזַיָּא v^{29}.

7348 רְחוּם **n.pr.m.** Persian official Ezr 4^{8} (usu.
7348 expl. from √רחם, v. BH, p. 933; Scheft[92]
thinks poss. orig. רוחם, OIran. n.pr. *rukma*,
=*splendour*).

7359 רַחֲמִין **n.** [**m.**] **pl. intens. compassion**
7356 (BH רַחֲמִים, √I. רחם);—abs. ׳ר Dn 2^{18}.

7365 †[רְחַץ] **vb. trust** (𝔗 *id.*, Chr-Pal. ܪܚܨ
Schwally[Idiot. 126] Schulth[Lex. 193]; As. *raḫâṣu;*
Ar. رَخُصَ II. *have indulgence, permission*);—
Hithpe. *set one's trust* upon (עַל dei) *Pf.* 3 mpl.
הִתְרְחִצוּ Dn 3^{28}.

7350, 7368 רחק (√of following; v. BH רחק, רָחוֹק).

7352 †[רְחִיק] **adj. far**;—pl. abs. רַחִיקִין הֲווֹ מִן־תַּמָּה
Ezr 6^{6}, i.e. keep aloof.

7382 רֵיחַ v. רוח. p. 1112

7411-12 †[רְמָא] **vb. cast, throw** (v. BH I. רמה
(rare));—**Pe.** *Pf.* 3 mpl. רְמוֹ Dn $6^{17.25}$; 1 pl.
רְמֵינָא 3^{24}; *Inf.* לְמִרְמֵא v^{20} Ezr 7^{24};—**1.** *cast*, acc.
pers. + לְ loc. Dn 3^{24} 6^{25}; acc. pers. om. v^{17} 3^{20}.
2. fig. *throw* (burden of) tribute, עַל pers., Ezr
7^{24}. **Pe'il** *Pf.* 3 mpl. רְמִיו (W[CG 225]): **1.** *were
cast*, subj. pers. c. לְ loc., Dn 3^{21}. **2.** *were
placed, set*, 7^{9} (cf. 𝔗 Je 1^{15} Dr, and BH ירה **2**).
Hithpe. *be cast*, subj. pers. c. לְ loc.: *Impf.*
3 ms. יִתְרְמֵא Dn $3^{6.11}$ $6^{8.13}$; 2 mpl. תִּתְרְמוֹן 3^{15}.

7462 רעה (√of following; cf. BH III. רעה).

7470 [רְעוּ] **n.f. good pleasure, will**;—cstr.
רְעוּת of king Ezr 5^{17}, of God 7^{18}.

7476 †[רַעְיוֹן] **n.m.**[Dn 4,16] **thought**;—pl. cstr.
רַעְיוֹנֵי לִבְבָךְ Dn 2^{30}; sf. ־נַי 7^{28}; ־ניך Kt, ־נָךְ Qr
(K[§ 53 Anm. b)]) 2^{29} 5^{10}, רַעְיֹנֹהִי 4^{16} 5^{6}.

7487 †רַעְנַן **adj. flourishing** (perh. loan-word
7488 from BH רַעֲנָן *luxuriant*, √רען);—fig. of pers.
Dn 4^{1} (cf. BH ψ 92^{15}).

7490 †[רְעַע] **vb. crush, shatter** (𝔗 Syr.; v.
7533 BH רצץ);—**Pe.** *Impf.* 3 fs. (וְ)תֵרֹעַ Dn 2^{40} (obj.
om.). **Pa.** *Pt. act.* מְרָעַע 2^{40} (acc. rei).

7511-12 †[רְפַס] **vb. tread, trample** (cf. BH
(late));—**Pe.** *Pt. act.* fs. בְּרַגְלַיהּ רָפְסָה, c. acc. rei
Dn $7^{7.19}$.

7559-60 †רְשַׁם **vb. inscribe, sign** (𝔗 Syr.; v. BH
(once, late));—**Pe.** *Pf.* 3 ms. ׳ר Dn 6^{10}; 2 ms.
רְשַׁמְתָּ v^{13}, רְשַׁמְתָּ v^{14}; *Impf.* 2 ms. (וְ)תִרְשֻׁם v^{9};—
inscribe (prob. with one's name, i.e.) *sign*, acc.
כְּתָבָא Dn $6^{9.10}$, אֱסָר $v^{13.14}$. **Pe'il** *Pf.* 3 ms. רְשִׁים,
subj. כְּתָבָא: **1.** *be inscribed, written*, Dn $5^{24.25}$.
2. *be signed* 6^{11}.

שׂ

†שַׂבְּכָא (>van d. H. ׳ס, v. Baer) **n.** [**f.**] 5443
trigon, mus. instr. (whence prob. Gk. σαμβύκη,
triang. instr. with four strings, v. Thes Lewy
Fremdw. 161 f. Prince[EB 3238] Dr[Dn 3,5]; also BH שְׂבָכָה 7639
lattice-work, √שׂבך, cf. Syr. ܣܒܟܐ);—Dn $3^{5.7.10.15}$.

†[שְׂגָא] **vb. grow great** (𝔗 ׳ס, Syr. ׳ܣ; 7680
v. BH שׂגא (Aramaism in Job));—**Pe.** *Impf.* 7679
3 ms. יִשְׂגֵּא, of injury Ezr 4^{22}; ׳שְׁלָמְכוֹן יִשׂ Dn 3^{31} 6^{26}.

שַׂגִּיא **adj. great, much**;—abs. ׳שׂ Dn 2^{6}+, 7690
fpl. שַׂגִּיאָן 2^{48} Ezr 5^{11};—**1.** *great*, of image Dn 2^{31}
(in vision), height of tree 4^{7} (*id.*); of honour 2^{6}.
2. *much*, fruit $4^{9.18}$, flesh 7^{5}; pl. *many*, years
Ezr 5^{11}, gifts Dn 2^{48}. **3.** as adv. *exceedingly*,
2^{12} 5^{9} $6^{15.24}$ 7^{28}.

†[שָׂהֲדוּ] **n.f. testimony** (√שְׂהֵד = 𝔗 סְהַד 7717
testify, Syr. ܣܗܕ, Ar. شَهِدَ *testify*, cf. BH [שָׂהֵד] 7717
(once, as loan-wd.) K[Aram. 86]; Eg. Aram. pl. שהדיא
witnesses, Cooke[404] S-C[A 15+oft.]);—emph. שָׂהֲדוּתָא
Gn 31^{47} (‖ BH עֵד). 5707

[שׂוּם], שִׂים **vb. set, make** (v. BH; for 7760-61
Pers. infl. on usage cf. Scheft[65]);—**Pe.** *Pf.* 3 ms.
שָׂם Ezr 5^{3}+, sf. שָׂמֵהּ 5^{14}; 2 ms. שַׂמְתָּ Dn 3^{10}; 1 s.
שָׂמֶת טְעֵם Ezr 6^{12}; 3 mpl. שָׂמוּ Dn 3^{12}; *Imv.* mpl.
שִׂימוּ Ezr 4^{21};—**1.** *make*, acc. טְעֵם = *make decree*
Dn 3^{10} Ezr $6^{1.12}$, + vb. fin. v^{3}, + inf. 4^{21} 5^{13} and
(c. לְ pers.) $v^{3.9}$. **2.** *make, appoint*, one's name
Dn 5^{12} (2 acc.), one to office Ezr 5^{14} (2 acc.).
3. *set, fix*, acc. בָּל *mind*, Dn 6^{15} (c. inf.); acc.
טְעֵם 3^{12} 6^{14} *pay* due regard (טְעֵם) to (עַל pers.).
Pe'il 3 ms. מִנִּי שִׂים טְעֵם Ezr 4^{19} *from me a decree
is made*, so 5^{17} $6^{8.11}$ $7^{13.21}$ Dn 3^{29} 4^{3} 6^{27}; lit. 3 fs.
שָׂמַת (rd. prob. שִׂימַת K[§ 45, Beisp. 1. d)]) 6^{18} (of stone,
עַל loc.). **Hithpe.** *be made: Impf.* 3 ms. יִתְּשָׂם
Ezr 4^{24} (of decree, טְעֵם c. מִן agent.); 3 mpl.
יִתְּשָׂמוּן Dn 2^{5} subj. rei + n. pred. *be made into;
Pt.* מִתְּשָׂם Ezr 5^{8} lit. *be set, laid*, of wood, בְּ
of wall.

†שְׂטַר **n.m. side** (Eg. Aram. S-C[A 5]; 𝔗 סְטַר, 7859
סִטְרָא, Syr. ܣܛܪܐ, Chr-Pal. ܣܛܪ Schulth[Lex. 134],
cf. Schwally[Idiot. 62,122]; Ar. شَطْرٌ *half*);—abs. ׳שׂ
Dn 7^{5} (of beast in vision).

7868-69 †[שִׂיב] **vb.** be hoary (v. BH);—**Pe.** *Pt.*
pl. as subst. = *elders*, term. techn., abs. שָׂבֵי יְהוּדָיֵא
Ezr 5^{5} $6^{7.8.14}$; so emph. שָׂבַיָּא 5^{9}.

7920 †[שְׂכַל] **vb. Hithpe.** consider, contem-
7919 plate (v. BH I. שׂכל);—*Pt.* מִשְׂתַּכַּל Dn 7^{8} (ב rei).

7924 †שָׂכְלְתָנוּ (K[§ 61, 4]) **n.f.** insight;—Dn $5^{11.12.14}$.

8131 †[שְׂנָא] **vb.** hate (𝔗 סְנָא, Syr. ܣܢܐ; v.
8130 BH שָׂנֵא);—**Pe.** *Pt.* pl. sf. שׂנאיך Kt, שָׂנְאָךְ Qr
(K[§ 53, 2, Anm. b)]) Dn 4^{16} = *thy foes* (BH **3**, MI⁴ Sab).

8177 †שְׂעַר **n.m.**[Dn 3. 27] hair, of head (𝔗 ס׳, Syr. ܣ׳;
8181 v. BH I. שׂער);—cstr. Dn 3^{27} 7^{9}; sf. שַׂעֲרֵהּ 4^{30}.

שׁ

7592-93 שְׁאֵל **vb.** ask (v. BH);—**Pe.** *Pf.* 3 ms. ש׳
Dn 2^{10}; pl. שְׁאֵלְנָא Ezr $5^{9.10}$; *Impf.* 3 ms. sf. יִשְׁאֲלֶנְכוֹן Ezr 7^{21}; *Pt. act.* שָׁאֵל Dn $2^{11.27}$;—**1.** *ask for, request*, acc. rei Dn 2^{10} (ל pers.), v$^{11.27}$ Ezr 7^{21} (sf. pers.). **2.** *inquire about, for*, acc. rei Ezr 5^{9} (ל pers.); sq. orat. rect. v^{10} (*id.*).

7595 †[שְׁאֵלָה] **n.f.** affair (weakened fr. *question, inquiry*, cf. Dr);—emph. שְׁאֵלְתָא Dn 4^{14}.

7605-06 †שְׁאָר **n.m.**[Ezr 7, 20] rest, remainder (v. BH I. שׁאר; Eg. Aram. n. שאר Cooke[203], vb. ישתאר *be left* (outstanding) Cooke[404] = S-C[L 9], Chr-Pal. ܫܐܪ);—ש׳ abs. Ezr 4^{10}+, cstr. v^{9}+; emph. שְׁאָרָא Dn $7^{7.19}$;—of a thing, *remainder* Ezr $7^{18.20}$; of cities $4^{10.17}$, of persons v$^{9.10.17}$ 6^{16} Dn 2^{18}, of beasts $7^{7.12.19}$.

†שׁבב (√of foll.; cf. BH II. שׁבב).

7631 [שְׁבִיב] **n.[m.]** flame;—emph. שְׁבִיבָא דִּי נוּרָא
Dn 3^{22}; pl. abs. שְׁבִבִין דִּי נוּר 7^{9}.

7624 †[שְׁבַח] **vb. Pa.** laud, praise (𝔗 Syr.;
7623 v. BH II. שׁבח (Aramaism));—*Pf.* 2 ms. שַׁבַּחְתָּ
Dn 5^{23}, 1 s. שַׁבְּחֵת 4^{31}, 3 mpl. שַׁבַּחוּ 5^{4}; *Pt. act.* מְשַׁבַּח 2^{23} 4^{34};—*praise*, c. ל dei Dn 2^{23} $4^{31.34}$; ל of idols $5^{4.23}$.

7625-26 †[שְׁבַט] **n.m.** tribe (BH שֵׁבֶט, √שׁבט);—
pl. cstr. שִׁבְטֵי יִשְׂרָאֵל Ezr 6^{17}.

7655 †[שְׁבַע], only שִׁבְעָה **n.f.** seven (BH
7651 I. שֶׁבַע);—abs. ש׳ bef. **n.m.** pl. Dn $4^{13.20.22.29}$; cstr.
שִׁבְעַת bef. **n.m.** pl. Ezr 7^{14}; חַד שִׁבְעָה עַל־דִּי Dn 3^{19} *seven times above what* (more than), v. חַד, √אחד.

†[שְׁבַק] **vb.** leave, let alone (𝔗 שְׁבַק, Syr. 7662
ܫܒܩ; cf. BH, p. 990);—**Pe.** *Inf.* לְמִשְׁבַּק Dn 4^{23} 7733
leave roots, so *Imv.* mpl. שְׁבֻקוּ v$^{12.20}$ (both c. ב loc.); Ezr 6^{7} *let alone*, c. ל acc. rei. **Hithpe.** *Impf.* 3 fs. תִּשְׁתְּבִק Dn 2^{44} *be left* (of kingdom, + ל gent.).

†[שְׁבַשׁ] **vb. Hithp.** be perplexed (𝔗 7672
id., *entangle, beguile*, NH שָׁבַשׁ *confuse, disarrange*; cf. As. *šabâšu* (*šabasu*), *turn about*; Syr. ܫܒܫ *flatter, allure*, Schulth[Hom. Wurz. 90]; so Mand. Pa. שׁבּשׁ Nö[M 49]; cf. Ar. شَوَّشَ (as loan-word Nö[l. c.]) *confuse*);—*Pt.* pl. מִשְׁתַּבְּשִׁין Dn 5^{9}.

†[שֵׁגָל] **n.f.** (royal) consort (cf. BH *id.*; 7694-95
√unknown Hpt[Gu Ezr-Ne, p. 66] conj. As. *šigrêti, harem-women*);—pl. sf. שֵׁגְלָתָךְ Dn 5^{23}, שֵׁגְלָתֵהּ v$^{2.3}$.

†[שְׁדַר] **vb. Hithpa.** struggle, strive 7712
(𝔗 *id.* Pa. *wrestle*, Ithpa. *be recalcitrant*, also שַׁדֵּל Ithpa. *strive*, and so NH שָׁדַל (ל for ר), Syr. ܫܕܠ *beguile*, esp. Pa., v. Nö[ZMG xl (1886), 735]);—*Pt.* מִשְׁתַּדַּר Dn 6^{15} *he was striving*, sq. Inf.

‡†אֶשְׁתַּדּוּר **n.m.** revolt;—abs. Ezr $4^{15.19}$. 849

שַׁדְרַךְ$_{13}$ **n.pr.m.** (cf. BH *id.*);—Dn 2^{49} 3^{12} 7714-15
+ 11 t. 3.

שׁדת (√of foll.; BH שֵׁשׁ, שׁדשׁ). 8337

†שֵׁת, שֵׁת **n.m.** six;—abs. שֵׁת after **n.f.** 8353
Dn 3^{1}; שְׁנַת־שֵׁת Ezr 6^{15} *year six = sixth year*.

†שִׁתִּין **n. indecl.** sixty;—אַמִּין ש׳ Ezr $6^{3.3}$ 8361
Dn 3^{1}; שְׁנִין ש׳ וְתַרְתֵּין 6^{1}.

†I. [שְׁוָה] **vb.** become like (BH I. שָׁוָה);— 7737, 7739
Pa. *Pf.* 3 mpl. שַׁוִּי Qr (v. ְ foll.; > **Peʿîl** שְׁוִי Kt, v. K[§ 47 Beisp. 3, and p. 175]) Dn 5^{21}, acc. rei, c. עִם.

†II. [שְׁוָה] **vb. Hithpa.** be set, made 7739
(Pa. שַׁוִּי *make*, Cappadoc. Aram. Lzb[Eph. i. 67]; cf.
BH II. [שָׁוָה]);—*Impf.* 3 ms. יִשְׁתַּוֵּה Dn 3^{29}, subj. 7737
rei + acc. *be made into* something (K[§ 84, 3]).

שׁוק (√of following; BH I. שׁוק, שׁוֹק). 7785

†[שָׁק] **n.[m.]** lower leg;—pl. sf. שָׁקוֹהִי Dn 2^{33}. 8243

†[שׁוּר] **n.m.** wall (cf. BH II. שׁוּר *id.*; Eg. 7791-92
Aram. שור RÉS[361 A 5; B 1]);—pl. emph. שׁוּרַיָּא Ezr 4^{16}, א ַ— v^{13}; v^{12} rd. שׁוּרַיָּא ש׳ Qr, for שורי אש׳ Kt.

שׁוּשַׁנְכָיֵא **n. pr. gent. pl.** the Susians, 7801
people of Susa Ezr 4^{9}, v. דהוא (Dl[Pa 327]; sg. [שׁוּשַׁנָךְ] acc. to Scheft[92], = OP **šušana-ka, from Susa*, so (as altern.) Andr[M 85*]; cf. (on Elam. god *Šušinak*) Weissbach[Anzanische Inschr. 136] Jen[VOJ]

[vi.54] Zim[KAT 3.485], and (on *Šušunka* in Elam. inscr., appar. n.pr.terr.) v. Weissb[l. c.] Jen[ZMG lv (1901), 229]).

7844 †[**שְׁחַת**] **vb. corrupt** (𝔗[J] (once), Syr. ܚܒܠ;
7843 BH[שָׁחַת]);—**Pe.** *Pt. pass.* fs. שְׁחִיתָה Dn 2[9] *corrupt* word; as n.=*fault* 6[5.5] (cf. 𝔗 ψ 1 7[3] Ru 4[22]).

7804 †**שֵׁיזִב** **vb. deliver** (prob. **Shaph.** as loan-word from As. *šûzub(u)*, *ušêzib*, *deliver*, √*ezêbu*
5800 (עזב=א[4]), Dl[Pr 140] Hpt[GGN 1883, 91; BAS 1.13] K[§ 43, 1, Anm.]; 𝔗 שֵׁיזִב, Syr. ܫܘܙܒ, Chr-Pal. ܫܘܙܒ Schulth
4898 [Lex. 203], also Nab. שיזב Cooke[255]; cf. n.pr. מְשֵׁיזַבְאֵל BH; OAram. צלמשזב SAC[102]; v. also foll. art.);—*Pf.* 3 ms. שֵׁיזִב Dn 3[28] 6[28]; *Impf.* 3 ms. יְשֵׁיזִב 3[17]; sf. יְשֵׁיזְבִנָּךְ 6[17], ־נְכוֹן 3[15]; *Inf.* sf. לְשֵׁיזָבוּתָךְ 6[21], ־תֵהּ v[15], ־תַנָא 3[17];—*deliver* (usu. c. מִן): Dn 3[17b], ל acc. pers. v[28] 6[28b], sf. pers. 3[15.17a] 6[15.17.21], abs. v[28a].

3319 †**שֵׁיצִיא** Kt, שֵׁיצִי Qr **vb. bring out** (to an end), **finish** (prob. **Shaph.** as loan-word fr. As. *šû-ṣû*, *û-še-ṣû*, *bring out*, √*aṣû* (וצא, BH
3318 יצא, =Aram. יְצָא, cf. Nö[GGA 1884, 1019]), Dl[l. c.] Hpt [l. c.] K[l. c.]; 𝔗 שֵׁיצִי *complete, put an end to*, also *come to an end*, pass. *be finished*, Chr-Pal. ܫܝܨܝ Schulth[Lex. 205]);—*finish* temple: *Pf.* 3 ms. שׁ׳ Ezr 6[15], but read prob. 3 mpl. שֵׁיצִיו K[§ 43, 1 ad fin.] Berthol Gu[Hpt] (so 𝔊𝔙); > *Pf.* pass. Be-Ry.

4904, 7901 **שׁכב** (√of foll.; BH מִשְׁכָּב, שָׁכַב).

4903 †[**מִשְׁכַּב**] **n.[m.] couch, bed**;—sf. מִשְׁכְּבִי Dn 4[2.7.10]; ־ךְ 2[28.29]; ־הּ 7[1].

7912 †[**שְׁכַח**] **vb. Haph.** (K[§ 40, 4] Nö[GGA 1884, 1019]) **find** (𝔗 שְׁכַח *find*, Syr. ܐܫܟܚ, Chr-Pal. ܫܟܚ Schulth[Lex. 205]; Eg.Aram. השכח S-C[E 5], pass. אשתכח RÉS[361 A 2]):—*Pf.* 1 s. הַשְׁכַּחַת Dn 2[25]; 3 mpl. הַשְׁכַּחוּ Ezr 4[19] Dn 6[12]; *Impf.* 2 ms. תְּהַשְׁכַּח Ezr 4[15] 7[16]; *Inf.* לְהַשְׁכָּחָה Dn 6[5.5];—*find*, acc. rei, 6[5] (ל pers.), v[5.6] (ל pers.), v[6] (עַל pers., acc. rei om.), Ezr 7[16] (ב loc.); sq. cl. דִּי 4[15] (ב loc.), v[19]; acc. pers. Dn 2[25]; ל pers. 6[12] (+ pt. action.). **Hithpe.** *Pf.* 3 ms. הִשְׁתְּכַח Dn 2[35]+, 2 ms. ־כַחַתְּ 5[27], 3 fs. ־כַחַת 5[11]+;—*be found*, subj. rei, ב loc., Ezr 6[2]; ב pers. Dn 5[11.12.14] 6[24]; עַל pers. v[5]; ל pers. + קֳדָם pers. v[23]; ל rei 2[35] (v. אֲתַר); subj. pers. 5[27] + חַסִּיר *thou hast been found wanting* (K[§ 85, 3]).

3635 שַׁכְלִלֵה etc., v. כלל. p. 1097

4908, 7931-32 †[**שְׁכַן**] cf. 𝔗] **vb. dwell** (BH מִשְׁכָּן, שָׁכַן);—**Pe.** *Impf.* 3 fpl. יִשְׁכְּנָן Dn 4[18] *dwell*, of birds, ב loc. **Pa.** causat.: *Pf.* 3 ms. שַׁכִּן שְׁמֵהּ תַּמָּה Ezr 6[12], of God, *cause his name to dwell there*.

†[**מִשְׁכַּן**] **n.[m.]** abode, of God;—sf. מִשְׁכְּנֵהּ Ezr 7[15], of Jerusalem. 4907

שׁלו, שׁלה (√of foll.; BH I. שׁלה (late)). 7951

†**שְׁלֵה** **adj.** at ease (Eg.Aram. Cooke[210]);— שׁ׳ הֲוֵית בְּ Dn 4[1] *I was at ease in* my house.— 3[29] v. following. 7954

†**שָׁלוּ** **n.f. neglect, remissness** (𝔗 *id.*);— abs. שׁ׳ Ezr 4[22] 6[9] Dn 6[5] + 3[29] Qr; Kt שלה usu. thought an error for שׁלו; Hi Bev M (perhaps) 7955, 7960
expl. as שְׁלֵה=שְׁאֵלָה=*thing, affair* (4[14]). 7596

†[**שְׁלֵוָה**] **n.f. ease, prosperity**;—sf. שְׁלֵוְתָךְ Dn 4[24]. 7963

†**שְׁלַח** **vb. send** (BH I. שָׁלַח);—**Pe.** *Pf.* 3 ms. שׁ׳ Ezr 4[17]+; 3 mpl. שְׁלַחוּ 4[11]+; 2 mpl. שְׁלַחְתּוּן 4[18]; 1 pl. שְׁלַחְנָא 4[14]; *Impf.* 3 ms. יִשְׁלַח 5[17] 6[12]; *Pt. pass.* שְׁלִיחַ 7[14] Dn 5[24];—*send*, acc. of letter, etc., c. עַל pers. Ezr 4[11.17.18] 5[6.7.17]; abs. 6[13], sq. vb. fin. 4[14], + acc. pers. Dn 3[28] 6[23]; sq. Inf. Dn 3[2]; *send out* hand (acc.) to harm (Inf.); *pass., be sent*, c. מִן־קֳדָם pers.: subj. pers. Ezr 7[14]; subj. פַּסָּא Dn 5[24]. 7971-72

†**שְׁלֵט** **vb. have power, rule** (𝔗 Syr.; BH (q.v.) late);—**Pe.** *Pf.* 3 ms. שׁ׳ Dn 3[27], 3 mpl. שְׁלִטוּ 6[25]; *Impf.* 3 ms. יִשְׁלַט 5[7], 3 fs. תִּשְׁלַט 2[39], 2 ms. תִּשְׁלַט 5[16];—*have power* upon, ב rei, Dn 3[27] (of fire); *fall upon, assault* (𝔗=פְּגַע בְּ), ב pers. 6[25] (of lions); subj. pers. *rule, be ruler*, abs., 5[7.16], subj. kingdom, ב of earth, 2[39]. **Haph.** *make ruler*: *Pf.* 3 ms. sf. הַשְׁלְטָךְ 2[38] (ב pers., etc.); הַשְׁלְטֵהּ v[48] (עַל of province). 7980-81

†**שָׁלְטָן** (K[§ 61, 3, Beisp. a]) **n.m.** [Dn 7 6] **dominion**;— שׁ׳ abs. Dn 7[6.14], cstr. 6[27]+; emph. שָׁלְטָנָא 7[27]; sf. שָׁלְטָנָךְ 4[19], ־נֵהּ 3[33]+, ־נְהוֹן 7[12]; pl. emph. שָׁלְטָנַיָּא 7[27];—**1.** *dominion, sovereignty* (usu. of God): Dn 3[33] 4[19.31.31] 6[27b] 7[6.12.14.14.14.26.27.27]. **2.** *realm* 6[27a]. 7985

†**שַׁלִּיט** **adj. having mastery, ruling**;— abs. שׁ׳ Ezr 7[24]+, emph. ־טָא Dn 2[15]; mpl. שַׁלִּיטִין Ezr 4[20], ־טַן Dn 4[23];—**1.** *having, exercising, mastery*: **a.** of God, sq. ב, Dn 4[14.22.29] 5[21]; abs., of heavens 4[23]. **b.** of kings Ezr 4[20] (ב). **2.** as n.=*ruler* Dn 2[10], *captain* v[15]. **3.** *having authority* to do a thing (Inf.), hence impers.=*it is authorized*, Ezr 7[24] (so oft. in Syr.; cf. S-C [A 11+] אנת שליט למבנה). 7990

†[**שְׁלֵם**] **vb. be complete** (v. BH; Eg. Aram. שלם *pay in full* Cooke[404]=S-C[L 5.7]);—**Pe.** *Pt. pass.* שְׁלִם Ezr 5[16] *finished*, of temple. **Haph.** 7999-8000

Pf. 3 ms. sf. הַשְׁלְמַהּ Dn 5[26] God *has finished it* (the kingdom; brought it to an end); *Imv.* ms. הַשְׁלֵם Ezr 7[19] *render in full*, acc. rei (cf. Syr. Aph., Be-Ry Berthol), sq. קֳדָם dei.

8001 †שְׁלָם **n.m.** [Dn 3, 31] **welfare, prosperity**;—in greetings: abs. Ezr 4[17] *prosperity!* emph. שְׁלָמָא 5[7]; sf. שְׁלָמְכוֹן יִשְׂגֵּא Dn 3[31] 6[26].

8034, 8036 †שֻׁם **n.m.** name (v. BH שֵׁם);—cstr. ש׳ Ezr 5[1]+; sf. שְׁמֵהּ Dn 2[20]+; pl. cstr. שְׁמָהָת Ezr 5[4], sf. ־תְהֹם v[10];—*name*, dei: Dn 2[20] 4[5] Ezr 5[1] 6[12]; vir.: Dn 2[26] 4[15.16] 5[12] (all Dan.), Ezr 5[4.10.10] also v[14], with which cf. S-C [K 4, 5, 8 f., 12 f.]

8046 †[שְׁמַד] **vb. Haph.** destroy (𝔗 Pa. *make*
8045 *apostatize;* cf. BH);—*Inf.* לְהַשְׁמָדָה Dn 7[26] (obj. om., =dominion).

8064-65 †[שְׁמַיִן] **n.m. pl. heavens** (BH [שָׁמַי],
8064 שָׁמַיִם, √ שמה);—alw. emph. שְׁמַיָּא: **1.** visible *sky* Je 10[11] Dn 4[8.10.17.19.20.27.28]; צִפֲּרֵי ש׳ 2[38]; עוֹף ש׳ 4[9.18]; טַל ש׳ v[12.20.22.30] 5[21]; רוּחֵי ש׳ 7[2] *winds of the sky;* עֲנָנֵי ש׳ v[13]; *heavens* + earth = universe Je 10[11], where God shews signs Dn 6[28]. **2.** *heavens* as abode of God Dn 2[28] 4[31], hence, fig., as ruling v[23] (ש׳ sometimes=*God* in NH JAram., D [Worte Jesu 179; Eng. Tr. 218 f.]); as abode of angels v[32] (Dr); elsewh. in phr. אֱלָהּ ש׳ 2[18.19.37.44] Ezr 5[11.12] 6[9.10] 7[12.21.23.23], מֶלֶךְ ש׳ Dn 4[34], מָרֵא ש׳ 5[23].

8075 †[שְׁמַם] **vb. Ethpō'l.** be appalled (𝔗
8074 (rare); v. BH; Chr-Pal. ܫܡ, Schulth[209]);—*Pf.* 3 ms. אֶשְׁתּוֹמַם (K [§ 36]) Dn 4[16].

8085-86 †שְׁמַע **vb. hear** (v. BH);—**Pe.** *Pf.* 3 ms. ש׳ Dn 6[15]; 1 s. שִׁמְעֵת 5[14.16]; *Impf.* 3 ms. יִשְׁמַע 3[10], 2 mpl. תִּשְׁמְעוּן 3[5.15]; *Pt. act.* שָׁמְעִין 3[7] 5[23];—*hear*: =*have sense of hearing* Dn 5[23]; c. acc. of sound 3[5.7.10.15], word 6[15]; c. cl. דִּי + עַל pers. *concerning*, 5[14.16]. **Hithpe.** *shew oneself obedient:* *Impf.* 3 mpl. יִשְׁתַּמְעוּן Dn 7[27], c. לְ pers. (prob.).

8111, 8115 †שָׁמְרַיִן **n.pr.loc.** (BH שֹׁמְרוֹן, I. שָׁמַר);—Ezr 4[7.10].

8121 I. שמשׁ (√of following; BH שֶׁמֶשׁ, שמשׁ).

8122 †[שִׁמְשׁ] **n.** [**m.** so D [WB]] **sun**;—emph. שִׁמְשָׁא Dn 6[15].

8120 †II. [שַׁמֵּשׁ] **vb. Pa.** minister (𝔗 **Pa.** *id.*, תַּשְׁמִישׁ *use;* Palm. שמש, חשמיש, SAC[114, cf. 122] Lzb[379]; Syr. ܫܡܫ, ܫܡܫܐ; Chr-Pal. ܫܡܫ Pa, ܫܡܫܐ; NH שִׁמֵּשׁ, שַׁמָּשׁ, תַּשְׁמִישׁ; Egypt. *šms, servant,* Kopt. *šemše*, cf. WMM in Buhl[14]);—*Impf.* 3 mpl. sf. יְשַׁמְּשׁוּנֵּהּ Dn 7[10] *were ministering to him.*

†שִׁמְשַׁי **n.pr.m.**;—always ש׳ סָפְרָא: Ezr 8124
4[8.9.17.23] (Andr [M 86*] conj. OIran. caritative ששמי, conformed to שמשׁ, cf. Scheft[92], who, however, prefers OBaktr. *simēzhi*=*simaēzhi*, n.pr.).

שֵׁן v. שׁנן. below 8128

[שְׁנָא] **vb. change** (v. BH I. שנה);—**Pe.** *Pf.* 3 mpl. שְׁנוֹ Dn 3[27], sf. שְׁנוֹהִי 5[6] (rd. prob. שְׁנוֹ עֲלוֹהִי); *Impf.* 3 ms. יִשְׁנֵא 7[24], 3 fs. תִּשְׁנֵא 6[18] 7[23]; *Pt. act.* fs. שָׁנְיָא 7[19]; mpl. שָׁנַיִן 5[9], fpl. שָׁנְיָן 7[3];—intrans. *change, be changed:* of garment, by fire Dn 3[27], brightness (זִיו) of face 5[6.9], purpose 6[18]; *be different* from (מִן) 7[3.19.23.24]. **Pa.** *Pf.* 3 mpl. שַׁנִּיו (K [§ 47 e), and Beisp. 3]) Dn 3[28]; *Impf.* 3 mpl. יְשַׁנּוֹן 4[13]; *Pt. pass.* fs. מְשַׁנְּיָא (Baer) 7[7];—trans. *change* Dn 4[13] (לִבְבֵהּ מִן־אֲנָשָׁא); =*frustrate* word of king 3[28]; pt. pass. intrans. *different* 7[7] (מִן). **Ithpa.** *Pf.* 3 mpl. אִשְׁתַּנּוֹ Dn 3[19] Kt (K [§ 47, Beisp. 4]; ־נִּי Nö [GGA 1884, 1019] Str [§ 23 d] M [24*]), > 3 ms. אִשְׁתַּנִּי Qr; *Impf.* 3 ms. יִשְׁתַּנֵּא 2[9], 3 mpl. ־נּוֹ־ (ן om. in pause, K [§ 26, 1], but *modus apocop.* Nö [GGA 1884, 1018], as יְאבַדוּ Je 10[11], יְבַהֲלוּךְ Dn 5[10]; v. also Cooke[166]) 5[10], ־נּוֹן 7[28];—*be changed:* of זִיו Dn 5[10] 7[28] (v. **Pe.**; עַל pers.); צְלֵם אַנְפּוֹהִי 3[19] (*id.*); of time, conditions 2[9]. **Haph.** *Impf.* 3 ms. יְהַשְׁנֵא Ezr 6[11]; *Inf.* לְהַשְׁנָיָה v[12]+; *Pt. act.* מְהַשְׁנֵא Dn 2[21];—trans. *change, alter,* times, etc. (v. **Ithpa.**) Dn 2[21] 7[25]; acc. om. 6[9.16] Ezr 6[12]; *frustrate* edict (v. **Pa.**) 6[11].

†II. [שְׁנָה] **n.f.** year (v. BH שָׁנָה, √ I. 8140
[שָׁנָה]);—cstr. שְׁנַת: ש׳ חֲדָה = *first year* Ezr 5[13] 6[3] Dn 7[1]; ש׳ תַּרְתֵּין Ezr 4[24] *second year;* ש׳ שִׁת 6[15]; pl. שְׁנִין שִׁתִּין וְת׳ Dn 6[1] *62 years;* ש׳ שַׂגִּיאָן
Ezr 5[11].—I. [שְׁנָה] v. ישׁן. p. 1096 8139

שנן (√of following; v. BH [שָׁנַן], שֵׁן). 8127, 8150

†[שֵׁן] **n.[f.] tooth**;—du. (of rows of teeth) 8128
abs. שִׁנַּיִן Dn 7[7];—sf. שניה Kt (K [§ 53, 2. b)]), שִׁנַּהּ Qr, v[5.19] (all of beasts in vision).

†שָׁעָה **n.f. brief time, moment** (𝔗 *id.*, 8160
שַׁעְתָּא, NH שָׁעָה *time, hour;* Syr. ܫܥܬܐ *moment,* then *hour* Brock[369], but Chr-Pal. ܫܥܐ *moment, hour* Schwally [Idiot. 97] Schulth [Lex. 211]; perh.=As. *šattu, duration;* Tel Am. [91, 77] *še-ti, time, hour* (as Canaanism) Wkl [KAT 3. 335]; Ar. سَاعَةٌ, سِعْوٌ *portion* of time, Eth. ሰዓ: *time,* ሰዓት: *hour, time* (Buhl calls Ar. Eth. loan-words, but v. Wkl [l.c.]); √unknown: poss. As. loan-word (v. Wkl [l.c.]); Dl [Pr 39 f.] conj. *שיע = שָׁעָה *look,* hence *moment* = '*Augenblick*,' but vb. ש׳ rather of steady gaze);—*moment:* usu. emph. בַּהּ־שַׁעֲתָא (rd. poss. שָׁ׳ as

𝔗 Syr., M[86*f.] Buhl[14] cf. var. in Str) *in the same moment, forthwith* Dn 3[6.15] 4[30] 5[5]; abs. שָׁעָה חֲדָה 4[16] *for a moment.*

8199-200 ‡†[שְׁפַט] **vb. judge** (BH שָׁפַט);—*Pt.* as n.pl. abs. שָׁפְטִין Ezr 7[25] *judges.*

8209 שַׁפִּיר v. שׁפר. below

8213-14 †[שְׁפֵל] **vb. be low** (v. BH);—**Haph.** *bring low, humble: Pf.* 2 ms. הַשְׁפֵּלְתְּ לִבְבָךְ Dn 5[22] *thou hast* not *humbled thine heart; Impf.* 3 ms. יְהַשְׁפִּל 7[24], *Inf.* לְהַשְׁפָּלָה 4[34], *Pt.* מַשְׁפִּל 5[19], all c. acc. pers. *bring low, put down.*

8215 †שְׁפַל **adj.** low in station;—cstr. שׁ׳ Dn 4[14].

8232 †שְׁפַר **vb. be fair, seemly** (𝔗 Syr.; cf. BH (rare and mostly late); Palm. שפר ל *merit well of,* SAC[117]; Cappad. Aram. שפירא Lzb [Eph. 160]);—**Pe.** *Pf.* 3 ms. שׁ׳, c. קֳדָם pers. *it seemed good to* Dn 3[32] 6[2]; *Impf.* 3 ms. יִשְׁפַּר עַל 4[24] *let* my counsel *be acceptable to* thee.

8209 †שַׁפִּיר **adj. fair, beautiful**;—of foliage Dn 4[9.18].

8238 †[שְׁפַרְפָּר] **n.[m.] dawn** (𝔗 *id.;* redupl. (K[§ 59, 3]) fr. above √?);—emph. שְׁפַרְפָּרָא Dn 6[20].

8243 שָׁק v. שׁוק. p. 1114

8271 †[שְׁרָא] **vb. 1. loosen. 2. abide** (v. BH
8281 I. שׁרה);—**Pe.** *Inf.* לְמִשְׁרֵא Dn 5[16]; rd. מִשׁ׳ also v[12], for מִשְׁ׳ (K[§ 40n] M[87*] al.);—*Pt. pass.* שְׁרֵא (K[§ 47, Beisp.f)]) 2[22]; pl. שְׁרַיִן 3[25];—**1.** *loosen:* lit. pt. pass. *loosed* Dn 3[25] (opp. bound); fig. *loosen* knots, i.e. solve difficulties, 5[12.16]. **2.** *abide* (from *loosening* girths, loads, at encampment; cf. 𝔗 NH [also on pt. pass.]), fig. 2[22] (עִם pers.). **Pa.** *Pf.* 3 mpl. שָׁרִיו Ezr 5[2] *begin* (v. BH III. [חָלַל] **Hiph. 2**), sq. inf. **Hithpa.** *Pt.* mpl. מִשְׁתָּרַיִן Dn 5[6] joints *were loosened* (in fear).

8319 שׁרק (𝔗 שְׁרִיק, Syr. ܫܪܩ, BH שָׁרַק *hiss, whistle* (onomatop.)).

4953 †[מַשְׁרוֹקִי] **n.f. pipe** (cf. Syr. (rare));—emph. מַשְׁרוֹקִיתָא Dn 3[5.7.15], מַשְׁרֹקִ׳ 3[10].

8328, 8330 †[שֹׁרֶשׁ] **n.m.** [Dn 4, 12] **root** (v. BH);—pl. sf. שָׁרְשׁוֹהִי of tree Dn 4[12.20.23].

8332 ‡†שרשו Kt (i.e. שְׁרֹשׁוּ K[§ 61, 4, 5]), Qr שְׁרֹשִׁי **n.f. uprooting, fig. banishment**;—abs. Ezr 7[26].

8353 שֵׁת, שִׁת *six,* v. שׁדת. p. 1114

†[שְׁתָה] **vb. drink** (𝔗 אִשְׁתִּי, שְׁתָא, Syr. 8355
ܐܫܬܝ; v. BH I. שָׁתָה);—**Pe.** *Pf.* 3 mpl. אִשְׁתִּיו 8354
(K[§ 11, 4, a)]) Dn 5[3.4]; *Impf.* 3 mpl. יִשְׁתּוֹן v[2]; *Pt. act.* שָׁתֵה v[1], pl. שָׁתַיִן v[23];—*drink,* acc. wine Dn 5[1.4], + ב of vessel v[23] and (acc. om.) v[2.3].

†[מִשְׁתֵּי so 𝔗] **n.m. feast** (as BH מִשְׁתֶּה);— 4960-61
emph. בֵּית מִשְׁתְּיָא Dn 5[10].

שִׁתִּין *sixty,* v. שׁדת. p. 1114 8361

†שְׁתַר בּוֹזְנַי **n.pr.m.** Pers. official Ezr 5[3.6] 8370
6[6.13]; Σαθαρβουζανα (αι, ε, ης); 𝔊L Σαθραβωζανης (Andr[M 87*] prop. מתרב׳, Gk. Μιθροβουζάνης, = OIran. **Mithrabaužana, Mithra is deliverer* (or the like), so Mey[Entst. J. 32]; Scheft[92f.] OIran. *Šēthrabûzana, empire-delivering;* Wkl [MVAG 1897, 281 f.] conj. a title).

ת

†[תְּבַר] **vb. break** (𝔗 Syr.; BH שָׁבַר);— 7665, 8406
Pe. *Pt. pass.* fs. תְּבִירָה Dn 2[42] *broken in pieces* (kingdom).

תְּדִירָא v. דּוּר. p. 1087 8411

†[תּוּב] **vb. return** (𝔗 Syr.; BH שׁוּב);— 7725, 8421
Pe. *Impf.* 3 ms. יְתוּב, c. עַל pers., of brightness (זִיו) of face Dn 4[33b], of knowledge v[31.33a]. **Haph.** *Pf.* 3 ms. הֲתִיב Dn 2[14]; 3 mpl. sf. הֲתִיבוּנָא Ezr 5[11]; *Impf.* 3 mpl. יַהֲתִיבוּן 6[5], יְתִיבוּן (K[§33, 2]) 5[5]; *Inf.* sf. לַהֲתָבוּתָךְ Dn 3[16];—**1.** *restore,* acc. rei Ezr 6[5]. **2.** *return* (acc. of answer, etc.) 5[5.11] Dn 3[16] (sf. pers.), עֵטָא וּטְעֵם הֲת׳ 2[14].

†תְּוַהּ **vb. be startled, alarmed** (𝔗 *id.,* 8429
Syr. ܬܘܗ);—**Pe.** *Pf.* 3 ms. ת׳ Dn 3[24].

†[תּוֹר] **n.m. bullock** (𝔗 Syr.; BH שׁוֹר, 7794, 8450
√III. שׁור);—pl. abs. תּוֹרִין, for sacrifice Ezr 6[9.17] 7[17]; as eating grass Dn 4[22.29.30] 5[21].

†תְּחוֹת **prep. under** (BH תַּחַת; 𝔗 תְּחוֹת, 8460, 8478-79
Syr. ܬܚܝܬ, ܬܚܘܬ, adv. ܠܬܚܬ; Palm. מן לתחת Cooke[320]);—Dn 7[27] תְּחוֹת כָּל־שְׁמַיָּא (cf. BH **II. 1**); in pl. c. sf. (as BH Syr. 𝔗) 4[9] תְּחֹתוֹהִי (so 𝔗[O] Lv 15[10]: Dalm[§ 47, 2]), v[18]. With מִן, Je 10[11] מִן תְּחוֹת שְׁמַיָּא (cf. BH **III. 2**); sf. Dn 4[11] מִן־תַּחְתּוֹהִי (the form as Syr. adv. supr., unless a Hebraizing punct.).

†תְּלַג **n.[m.] snow** (𝔗 Syr.; BH שֶׁלֶג);— 7950, 8517
abs. ת׳ Dn 7[9] (sim.).

8532 †**תְּלָת** **n.m.**, **תְּלָתָה** **f.**, three (𝔗 Syr.;
7969 BH שָׁלֹשׁ, שְׁלשָׁה);—**m.** תְּלָת bef. **n.f.** pl. Dn 7^{5}; n.f. om. v$^{8.20}$; **f.** תְּלָתָה bef. **n.m.** pl. 7^{24}; after, 3^{24} 6$^{3.11.14}$, so א—ָ Ezr 6^{4}; יוֹם תְּלָתָה 6^{15} *third day;* sf. תְּלָתֵּהוֹן (K$^{§ 65, Anm. 1}$) Dn 3^{23} *the three of them.*

8531 †[**תְּלָת**] **n.[m.]** **a third part** (so 𝔗 תְּלָתָא, תַּלְתָּא, Syr. ܬܘܠܬܐ, Nab. תלת SAC^{121}, Ar. ثُلْثٌ, ثُلُثٌ, As. *šuluštu* (=*šuluštu*) Meissn $^{Suppl. 95}$, cf. Dl^{WB}; v. also M^{88*} Dr$^{Dn 5,7}$);—emph. תַּלְתָּא adv. *as one of three* Dn 5$^{16.29}$ (Bev *the third day*, every three days, v. So in M^{88*}).

8523 ‡†**תַּלְתִּי** **adj. denom.** (only BAram.) as subst. **third** (ruler), i.e. *triumvir* (M^{89*}), cf. foregoing, which possibly is abnormal form of same (K$^{§ 65, 1, Anm. 3}$), Dn 5^{7}.

8523 †[**תְּלִיתַי**] **adj.** **third** (𝔗 תְּלִיתַי, Syr. ܬܠܝܬܝܐ);—f. תְּלִיתָיָא Kt, תְּאָה- Qr (K$^{§ 11, 1 b)}$) Dn 2^{39} *the third kingdom.*

8533 †**תְּלָתִין** **n. indecl. thirty**;—יוֹמִין ת׳ Dn 6$^{8.13}$.

8536 †**תַּמָּה** **adv.** **there** (so Eg. Aram. (RÉS $^{361 B 5}$ [also תנה $^{A 4}$, so Cilic., Cooke$^{68.5}$, cf. Palm. תנן ib.$^{121.3}$, Syr. ܠܬܡܢ] S-C$^{A 4, J 6}$); 𝔗 תַּמָּן, Syr.
8033 ܬܡܢ, v. BH שָׁם);—Ezr 5^{17} 6$^{1.12}$; מִן־ת׳ *thence* 6^{6}.

8540 †[**תְּמַהּ**] **n.m.** **wonder**, as wrought by God (𝔗 Syr.; cf. BH [תָּמַהּ]);—pl. abs. תִּמְהִין Dn 6^{28}; emph. תִּמְהַיָּא 3^{32}, pl. sf. תִּמְהוֹהִי v^{33}.

8145, 8147 **תנא** (𝔗 Syr.; =BH II. שָׁנָה, שְׁנַיִם, שֵׁנִי).

8578 †[**תִּנְיָן**] **adj.** **second**;—fs. תִּנְיָנָה (K$^{§ 66, 1}$) Dn 7^{5}.

8579 †**תִּנְיָנוּת** (K$^{§ 66, 2}$) **adv.** **the second time**;— Dn 2^{7}.

8648 †[**תְּרֵין**] **n.m.**, תַּרְתֵּין (K$^{§ 65, Anm. 1}$) **f.**, **two** (so in Aram. dialects generally (note Nab. f. תרתין over ag. Palm. תרתן Lzb^{388}); v. Philippi$^{ZMG xxxii (1878), 21 ff.}$; **adj.** acc. to M$^{§ 89 b}$);—**m.** only cstr. in תְּרֵי עֲשַׂר *twelve*, after **n.m.** pl. Dn 4^{26} Ezr 6^{17}; **f.** after **n.f.** pl. שְׁנִין שִׁתִּין וְת׳ Dn 6^{1} *years sixty and two;* =ord., שְׁנַת תַּרְתֵּין 4^{24} *second year.*

8614 †**תִּפְתָּיֵא** Kt, תָּאֵי- Qr, **n.m.pl.** name of official Dn 3$^{2.3}$ (so Eg. Aram. RÉS$^{361 B 4}$ דיניא תיפתיא וגושכיא; meaning unknown, conj. in Bev, Behrm, cf. Dr).

[**תַּקִּיף**] v. תְּקֵף. below 8624

†[**תְּקַל**] **vb.** **weigh** (𝔗 Syr.; BH שָׁקַל, 8254,
שֶׁקֶל);—**Peʿîl** *Pf.* 2 ms. תְּקִלְתָּא (W$^{CG 224}$) Dn 5^{27} 8625
thou hast been weighed, ב of scales.

†**תְּקֵל** **n.[m.]** **shekel** (v. BH שֶׁקֶל; 𝔗 8255, 8625
תִּקְלָא);—abs. ת׳ Dn 5$^{25.27}$; v. מְנֵא and reff. p. 1101 4484

†[**תְּקַן**] **vb.** **be in order** (𝔗 Syr.; BH (late));—**Hoph.** *Pf.* 1 s. הָתְקְנַת (W$^{CG 225}$) Dn 4^{33} *I was established,* עַל of kingdom. 8626-27

†[**תְּקֵף**] **vb.** **grow strong** (𝔗 Syr.; BH, q.v., (late));—**Pe.** *Pf.* 3 ms. תְּקֵף, of tree, Dn 4$^{8.17}$; 2 ms. תְּקֵפְתְּ 4^{19}, of king; 3 fs. תִּקְפַת 5^{20} fig. *grow arrogant*, of spirit of man. **Pa.** *make strong, stringent: Inf.* לְתַקָּפָה Dn 6^{8} acc. of interdict. 8630-31

†**תְּקֹף** **n.[m.]** **might**;—cstr. בִּת׳ חִסְנִי Dn 4^{27}, of king. 8632

†[**תְּקֹף**] **n.[m.]** id.;—emph. תָּקְפָּא Dn 2^{37}. 8632

†[**תַּקִּיף**] **adj.** **strong, mighty**;—fs. abs. תַּקִּיפָה, of kingdom, Dn 2^{40} (like iron), v^{42}; א—ָ 7^{7}, of beast; mpl. abs. תַּקִּיפִין, of kings Ezr 4^{20}, God's wonders Dn 3^{33}. 8624

[**תְּרֵין**], **תַּרְתֵּין** *two,* v. **תנא**. above 8648

†**תְּרַע** **n.[m.]** **gate, door** (𝔗 Syr.; BH שַׁעַר, 8179,
√I. שער);—cstr. ת׳: **1.** *door* of furnace Dn 3^{26}. 8651
2. *gate* of king, i.e. palace, court, Dn 2^{49} (cf. Est 2^{19}, v. שַׁעַר **3 a**; also Ar. بَابٌ *gate*, then الباب *the court* of a sovereign; pl. الأبواب *Sublime Porte*, of Turkish court, v. esp. Dozy$^{i. 124}$).

†[**תָּרָע** i.e. *tarrâʿ* K$^{§ 59 d)}$] **n.m.** **porter, door-keeper**, in temple: pl. emph. תָּרָעַיָּא Ezr 7^{24}. 8652

†**תַּתְּנַי** **n.pr.m.** Pers. perfect in Syria;— 8674
Ezr 5$^{3.6}$ 6$^{6.13}$; Θανθανας, Ταν θαναι, A Θαθθαναι; 𝔊L Ταν θαναιος, Σισιννης; Σισιννης also 3 Esdr 6^{3} 7^{26} Jos$^{Ant. xi. 12, 89, etc.}$ (Lag$^{Psalt. Hieron. 162 n.; AS § 1335 n.}$; Mey$^{Entst. J. 32}$ assumes OP **Thithnaya*, or **Thathnaia*); but *Uštanni, Uštanu*, was prefect in Syria under Darius, acc. to contr. tablets, v. Strassm$^{Darius 27, 82}$; names prob. identical; Meissn$^{ZAW xvii (1897), 191 f.}$ reads therefore ושתני (וְשְׁתָּנַי Hpt), cf. Buhl Gu$^{Ezr-Neh. 63}$; Scheft^{94}, however, thinks תתני = תסני = OP *thāsna*, Av. *sāsna* (*teaching*), and this transp. in NBab. *Uštanu*.

ADDENDA ET CORRIGENDA

Page 3^{b}. אָב **9**: see also Ew[Gesch. i. 524. H i. 365] On the force of אָב in proper names (in many prob. a divine title), v. Che[Ency. Bib., Abi, Names with] Nö[ib., Names, §§ 44, 45].

4^{b}. אַבְרָם: Spiegelberg[Randglossen 14] cp. Pal. n.pr. geogr. *ḥkr'ȝ 'ȝbrru* = חקל אברם (c. Eg. art. masc.), in Sheshonk list. As regards etym., Nö[l.c.] al. expl. as 'the father [a divine title] is exalted' (cf. [אֲ]חִירָם, מַלְכִּירָם, יְהוֹרָם).

5^{b}. II. אבל: etym. conject. very dub.; connex. (Lag.) of أَبَلَ *withstand*, with أُبُلٌ *herbage, forage* (sts. *dry*) improb., and of latter with إِبِلٌ *herd of camels* obscure; √ mng. *grow green* unattested; Syr. ܝܰܒܠܶܐ, ܝܰܒܠܳܐ, Talm. יַבְלָא, Pun. ιεβαλ, '*grass*,' appar. = a specific kind of fodder, ἄγρωστις, v. Löw[No. 141] (GFM, privately).

6^{a}. III. אבל, אוּבַל: on this etym., form או׳ needs explanation; GFM (privately) queries whether, if genuine, name may not be theophoric ($x + \bar{\imath}l$), poss. err. for אַדְבְּאֵל; or Aram. Aph. from יבל (which in any case may have influenced pronunciation).

7^{a}. [אֹבֶן] **2**: Spiegelberg[ZA xiv (1900), 269 ff.; Randglossen 19 ff.] expl. as *the two stones* [rd. אַבְנַיִם], i.e. bearing-stool of 'stones' = bricks, tiles.

7^{b}. אַבִּיר **1**: transfer Ju 5^{22} Je 46^{15} to **3** end (but Je 46^{15} many MSS. 𝔊 Aq Symm Theod 𝔙 many moderns read אַבִּירֶךָ *thy bull*, i.e. Apis).

— אַבְרֵךְ: Spiegelberg[Randglossen 14 ff.] expl. as Eg. *'brk = give attention!*

8^{a}. אגא: authority for Ar. vb. أَجَا *flee* is slender, but word occurs as n.pr.mont., and elsewhere (GFM, privately).

— אגד: Aram. א׳ (Talm., once, Levy) prob. Hebraism.

— אגם: Ar. أَجِمَ also = *spoil* (of water); cf. أَجَمَةٌ (أَجَمٌ) = *pool, reed-bed* (also *tangled thicket*, etc.) Lane, and *marsh* Dozy[i. 11].

10^{a}. אֱדוֹם **2, 3**: v. now FBuhl[Gesch. d. Edomiter (1893)].

11^{b}. אֲדֹנִי־בֶזֶק: rd. prob. א׳־צֶדֶק, v. GFM[Ju 1, 5].

13^{b}. I. אהל: Nö[ZMG xl (1886), 154, 720] doubts אֹהֶל = أَهْلٌ = *âlu*; but أَهْلٌ = *dwelling* actually in vulg. Ar. acc. to So[Buhl].

15^{a}. Before אוּאֵל ins. 'או Pr 31^{4} Kt, v. [אַי].'

— אוב: after *return* add 'whence Kö[Off.-begr. ii. 156] Sta[G. i. 504; Bibl. Theol. i. 186] Now[Arch. ii. 273] as *rediens*, "revenant"; but doubtful.'

15^{b}. אֵיד: Bev[JPhil. xxvi. 302] der. from Ar. آدَ *be strong* [also *oppress, burden*], whence مُؤْيِدٌ (or مُؤْيَدٌ) *calamity*.

— אֵד: Ar. derivation very dub.; Dl[W 125, cf. WB 22] KS[2. 4] Hpt[JAOS 1896, 158 ff.] Gunk[Gn 2, 6] Holz[Gn 2, 6] Buhl cp. As. *edû, flood, mass of waters* (√ אדה), *editu, overflow* (for irrigation); 𝔊𝔖𝔙 Aq in Gn 2^{6} have *spring*, 𝔗 *cloud*, so 𝔊 𝔗 Jb 36^{27}; add perh. Jb 36^{30} אֵדוֹ for אוֹרוֹ (Du Dr).

16^{b}. תַּאֲוָה **2**: add Gn 49^{26} (v. p. 1063^{a}).

— II. [אָוָה] end: v. also [תָּאַר], p. 1061^{b}.

17^{b}. II. אול, איל: Ar. أَوَّلٌ, etc., from وَأَلَ, v. Lane.

19^{a}. אַיָּל: Ar. إِيَّلٌ = *ibex* (i.q. وَعْلٌ, وَعِلٌ).

19^{b}. אָוֶן: on etym., cf. also Bev[JPhil. xxvi. 300-2].

20^{b}. אוּפָז: crpt., v. Siegf[ThLz, Nov. 7, 1883, 530]; he expl. מֵאֻ׳ Je 10^{9} as err. for מוּפָז 1 K 10^{18}, and א׳ Dn 10^{5} as borrowed from Je 10^{9}; in Je 10^{9} Gie reads מֵאוֹפִיר, Du either this or מוּפָז (v. פזז); read מֵאוֹפִיר perhaps also Dn 10^{5} (Dr).

— אוֹפִיר: WMM[As. u. Eur. 111] identifies with Egypt. *Pvnt*, on W. coast of Red Sea.

23^{b}. אֵזוֹב: prob. a kind of wild marjoram (*origanum Maru*) Post[Hast. DB Hyssop].

24^{b}. [מאזן], l. 5: after שַׁחַק ins. 'Is 40^{15}.'

25^{a}. III. אָח: Ez 18^{10} אָח is a *vox nihili* (dittogr. from foll. אחד: v. Comm.): in 21^{10} also dub. (𝔊 εὖ), read אַךְ Ew Hi Sm Toy, חַדָּה Co Berthol, אַתְּ Oort Krae.

25ᵇ. אחד **5**: Nu 10^{4} בְּאַחַת is rather '*in one* (of the trumpets)'; Jb 33^{14} it = *in one way;* Pr 28^{18} read prob. with 𝔖 Lag Dys Bi בַּשַּׁחַת; Ju 16^{28} is rather 'vengeance for *one* of my two eyes' (v. GFM). Je 10^{8} בְּאַחַת prob. = *in one, altogether.* אחד **7**: transpose 'abs. Jb 42^{14}' (l. 5) to precede 'Ez 10^{14}' (l. 2).

26ᵇ. On pr. names compounded with אָח, v. reff. given under אָב supr.

— אַחְאָב, ll. 4, 5: read 'Bar Hebraeus[Chron. Ecclesiast. ii. 23]' and del. 'in Euseb.'

— אֲחִיָּהוּ **3**, l. 1: ins. '15^{29}' after '14$^{2.4}$,' and in **4**, l. 1, del. '^{29}.'.

27ᵃ. אֲחִימַן: < אֲחִימָן, v. Norzi[Nu 13, 22] GFM[Ju 1, 10] (after Ven.[1] Mich.).

28ᵇ. אֲחַזְיָהוּ: cf. Ar. اخذ viii, + وَلَدًا = *adopt,* hence perhaps יְ׳ *hath adopted.*

— אָח *fire-pot* is loan-word fr. Eg. *ʿaḥ* acc. to WMM[OLZ 3, 51]; Je 36^{22} rd. וְאֵשׁ הָאָח.

32ᵇ. אֵיךְ **2** end: add Ho 11^{8} acc. to Hi Ke We Marti al.

33ᵃ. IV. אִי Jb 22^{30}: read perhaps אֵל (Me), or אֱלֹהַּ (Ley), with וְתִמָּלֵט in vᵇ.

35ᵇ. אִישׁ, l. 5 from bottom: אֲנָשִׁים Ez 24$^{17.22}$ is textual error; We (ap. Sm) אֲנָשִׁים; Toy[Hpt] אוֹנִים (Ho 9^{4}).

38ᵇ. מַכֹּלֶת: so read also ‖ 2 Ch 2^{9} (MT מַכּוֹת).

— אַלְמוֹדָד: add Glas[Skizze ii. 425, 435].

41ᵇ. אֵלֶּה **c**: in Jos 17^{9} עָרִים הָאֵלֶּה rd. הֶעָרִים, cf. 17^{12} 19$^{8.16.31.48}$, etc.

43ᵃ. אֵל **7**: v. also Brock[ZAW xxvi (1906), 29 ff.] (mng. 'might' very dub.: renders *belongs to the god of (my) hand,* supposing phrase a survival, with orig. mng. forgotten, of ancient idea, found also among other nations, of spirits conferring powers upon particular members of body).

45ᵇ. אֱלִיעָם: < = *Ēl is kinsman* (v. Gray[Ency. Bib. Ammi, Names with] Nö[ib. Names, § 46]).

48ᵇ. I. [אָלַף], l. 5: after 'pers.' ins. 'Jb 15^{5}.'

49ᵃ. At end of II. אֶלֶף ins.: '[אָלַף] **vb. denom. Hiph.** ψ 144^{13} מַאֲלִיפוֹת *producing thousands* (subj. צֹאן).'

— אֶלְקוֹשִׁי: on etymol., and site of place, v. Da[Nahum, etc., 9 ff.] GASm[Twelve Proph. ii. 79 f.].

— At bottom, insert: 'אֶלְתּוֹלַד v. sub I. אַל.'

49ᵇ. אֵם etym.: add '𝔗[Onk. Jon.] אִם, 𝔗[Hag.] אין.'

51ᵃ. 1. אָמוֹן: Je 46^{25} Spiegelberg[Randglossen, 43 ff.] reads נֹא אָמוֹן (as Na 3^{8}) for אָמוֹן נֹא, and finds in both a Thebes in the Delta.

54ᵃ, l. 17: ins. 'Jos' bef. '24^{14}.'

55ᵇ, l. 9: Is 40^{26} read probably אֹמֶץ (𝔊).

57ᵃ. אֱמֹרִי: meaning *mountain-dwellers* very dub.; on א׳ = Eg. *'A-ma-ra* v. WMM[As. u. Eur. 229 ff.], = TelAm. and As. *Amurru,* v. Wkl[TelAm. 36*] Jastr[EB Canaan, § 10] Say[Hast. DB Amorites] al.; cf. also GFM[Ju 4, 5] Dr[Dt 1. 7] Gray[Nu 13, 29].

58ᵇ. III. [אָנָה] **Pu.**: after תְּאֻנָּה ins. 'ψ 91^{10}.'

60ᵃ. [אָנַף, אָנֵף]: in Heb., vb. denom. fr. אַף.

61ᵇ. אָסָא: perhaps apoc. theophoric name, cf. רְפָאֵל.

62ᵇ. אָסַף **Niph. 1** end: add 'so יֵאָסֵף Jb 27^{19}; but read prob. יֹאסִף = יוֹסִף (Ex 5^{7}), 𝔊 𝔖 Ew De Di Du.'

66ᵃ. [אַפֶּדֶן]: Dieulafoy[RÉJ xvi (1888), p. cclxxv f.] makes *apadâna,* more precisely, *throne-room,* cf. Dr[Dn 11, 45].

67ᵃ. אֲפֻנָה: Ar. أَفَنَ in fact = *milk* (camel, etc.) *dry, empty;* مأفون = *empty-headed man;* this does not support *be confused, helpless* (GFM, privately).

67ᵇ. אֲפֵק: now prob. that **1** should include Jos 12^{18} 1 S 4^{1} 29^{1} and 2 K 13^{22} 𝔊L; town not near Jezreel, but at N. end of Philistine plain; cf. 𝔊L[l. c.] We[Comp. 254] Dr[1 S 29, 11] RS[OTJC 2, 435] GASm[Geogr. 400 f.] Buhl[Geogr. 212 (and N.)] Bu[RS 235 f.]; more doubtful are 1 K 20$^{26.30}$ 2 K 13^{17} (Kit[1 K 20, 26]); these, with Jos 19^{30} Ju 1^{31}, might denote an Aphek near Jezreel.

— l. 8 from below: Jb 12^{21} rd. perh. אַבִּירִים Du (v. also Bu).

68ᵃ. אַפִּרְיוֹן: read 'Syr.' for '𝔖,' and 'Talm.' for '𝔗,' thus: 'Syr. ܦܘܪܝܐ (and ܦܘܪܝܘܢ) PS[3073]; Sota 9^{14} and Talm. אַפִּרְיוֹן, Talm. also פּוּרְיָא and פּוּרְיוֹן, Levy[NHWB i. 150, iv. 17].'

68ᵇ. אפת: but Thes[612, Add. 72] del. אפת, and der. מוֹפֵת from √פ״ו, so Ba[NB § 172 c]; v. also, on افت as late by-form of أفك, DBMacdonald[JBL xiv (1895), 58 ff.].

70ᵃ. אָרַב: del. 'also أَرَّبَ *tie* (a knot) Frey.'

71ᵇ. [אֻרְיָה]: Vulg. Ar. آرِيّ = *manger* Moḥiṭ[19, 15] (GFM, privately), cf. Lane[51 c].

— At the end: add 'also pl. אֻוֵרוֹת 2 Ch 32^{28b} (read prob. וַאֲרוֹת לַעֲדָרִים 𝔊 𝔙 Kit Benz al.).'

72ᵃ. אֲרִיאֵל: Du[Is 29. 1] (q.v.) makes **1** = אֲרִיאֵיל, from אָרָה + לְ afform., *hearth* (not + אֵל *hearth of Ēl*).

73ᵃ. אֹרַח, ll. 3, 19: אָרְחִי ψ 139^{3} < *Inf. cstr.,* and ‖ רִבְעִי (*Inf. cstr.* of II. רבע), *not* דרכי, cf. Bae.

73b. אַרְיוֹךְ: on *Rim-Aku* (=*Eri-Aku*?), v. now also Dr[Comm. Gn. 156 ff.]; Zim[KAT 3. 367] thinks identification very dubious.

747 — After אַרְיוֹךְ insert: '†אֲרִיסַי n.pr.m. son of Haman Est 9[9]; Αρσαιος.'

74b. אֲרָם end: add Nö[Ency. Bib. Aram].

77a, l. 13 fr. below: אִשׁ 'm.' is dub.: Nu 16[18] rd. עָלֶיהָ for 2nd עֲלֵיהֶם (𝔊[B]); Je 20[9] v. Ges[§ 132 d]; 48[45] rd. (many MSS., Nu 21[28]) יצאה; ψ 104[4] rd. perh. (Ol Du) לְהָטָה:, or וְלָהַט:; Jb 20[26] v. Ges[§ 145 u (or 121 b)]: cf. Albr[ZAW xvi (1896), 63].

78b. אשה, [אָשְׁיָה]: read 'אשה (√of foll.).'

Also '†[אָשְׁיָה] **n.f. wall, bulwark** (Talm. אָשִׁיתָא (Levy Nö); Mand. אשיתא *wall* Nö[M 113]; 𝔗 pl. sf. אֻשִׁיתָהָא (Dalm[WB] אָשְׁיָתָהָא) Je 50[15], אשיתנא Ct 2[9]; Ar. آسِيَّة *column, support* is loan-word acc. to Frä[11]);—only pl. sf. *bulwarks* of city of Babylon,' etc.

79b. אָשֵׁם, l. 2: for 'أَثِمَ *reum judicavit*,' read 'إِثْمٌ *sin, offence*,' and before 'fault' insert 'requital.' — **Niph.**: after Jo 1[18] add '(si vera l.; Me We al. נָשַׁמּוּ, √שׁמם, cf. Dr[ad loc.]).'

81a. אֲשֵׁרָה: see now also GFM[EB Asherah] Dr[Dt 16, 21] Allen[DB Asherah], all doubtful as to Can. goddess Asherah; question left open by Zim[KAT 3. 436 ff.] (on Sem. goddess *Aširtu-Ašratu* Id.[ib. 432 ff.]); but v. Jerem[AT im Licht d. Alten Orients 207] (name of goddess *Aširat* in letter found at Taanach by Sellin (1902–3) and Id.[ib. 37. 237]) (Oppenheim's find at Ras el-'Ain in Mesop., stone shaft with veiled head as top, supposed to identify *post* with *goddess;* if 2 K 23[7] refers to draped Asherim [v. on text Benz Bur], this even more plausible), Id.[ib. 23, 208 f., 286]. On pictorial representations of *Asherah*-symbol v. WHWard[AJSL xix. 1 (Oct. 1902)].

83b. אֲשֶׁר: **4 b** (γ) transfer Ec 8[4] to בַּאֲשֶׁר **c** (p. 84[a]); and **8 e** add 'In Dt 15[14] also read כַּאֲשֶׁר: note ברכך before.'

85a. For ll. 20, 21, substitute: '(J) וַיּוֹלֶד לַחֲנוֹךְ אֶת־עִירָד, 17[5] (P) לֹא יִקָּרֵא עוֹד אֶת־שִׁמְךָ אַבְרָם *there shall not be called* (=one shall not call) *thy name Abram*, 21[5] (E).'

91b. בְּאֵר לַחַי רֹאִי: לַחַי perhaps orig. 1. לְחִי *jaw(-bone)*; on n.pr.loc. cpd. with לחי, γνάθος, v. 𝔊[Ju 15, 9] We[Prol. 344] Nes[AJSem. Lang. xiii (1897), 176].

92a. בְּאֵרִי: < *the man from Beer*? Nes[l. c.].

94b, l. 8 fr. bottom: Jb 17[16] rd. הַעִמָּדִי (for בַּדֵּי) 𝔊 Du Dr, with נֵחָת in v[b] (for נָחַת).

96a. Before בֹּדֵק, ins.: '†[בָּדַק] **vb. denom. mend fissures** (of);—**Qal** *Inf. cstr.* לְבַדּוֹק 2 Ch 34[10] (+וּלְחַזֵּק; acc. הַבָּיִת).'

101b. בּוֹשׁ: add ref. to עַד־בֹּשׁ *to the point of confusion* †Ju 3[25] (cf. GFM), 2 K 2[17] 8[11].

103a. בֹּזֶק: Nes[AJSL xiii (1897), 176] conj. mng. *gravel*, cf. mod. *Ramle=sand*.

— בָּזֶק: err. in Ju 1[4.5] (v. GFM).

— I. [בָּחַל]: Nö[ZAW xvii (1897), 188] disproves Syr. ܒܚܠ, and adopts the view of Gei[Urschrift 270] (בחל euphem. for a √II. בעל=*loathe*, c. בְּ, assumed (Thes Buhl) for Je 3[14] 31[32]; v. infr. on p. 127[a]).

103b, l. 2 (exc. '—**Qal**') belongs in l. 5.

110b. בית ad fin.: on בְּ as abbrev. בית v. Wetzst[Hauran 110] Kampffmeyer[ZPV xv (1892), 111].

111a. בֵּית־דָּגוֹן: Jerome[Opp. (ed. Vallarsi), iii. 38] defines as *domus tritici*, and says (Id.[ib. 174]): 'sed et usque hodie grandis vicus Capherdago inter Diospolim et Jamniam demonstratur.' [Elsewhere he defines דגון (Id.[ib. 48]) as 'piscis tristitiae'] (HPS, privately).

114b. בִּכּוּרָה: בַּכֻּרוֹת Je 24[2] prob. a diff. word, pl. abstr.=*early ripeness*, cf. Du.

126a. אַבְנֵט: described Jos[Ant. iii. 7, 2] as a sash wound round breast several times, and falling to the feet; in 𝔗𝔖 הֶמְיָן (Pers.) a money-bag wound round body Sta[ThLz, 1894, 236].

— בֹּסֶר: l. 2 read ܒܣܪܐ (PS; syllable ܣ uncertain [Nes, privately]; Polyglotts and Castell have ܒܣܪܐ).

127a. בָּעַל: Je 3[14] 31[32] AW JosKi Thes, comparing Ar. بَعَلَ *be disgusted*, derive from II. בָּעַל **loathe** (sq. בְּ); so Buhl: Gie Du Co in 31[32] read גָּעַלְתִּי (treating 3[14] as I. בָּעַל).

129b. II. [בָּעַר]: **Niph.** Je 10[14]=51[17] rather *stupefied* (by spectacle 10[13]=51[16]).

132b, last line and foll., read: 'in lat. of Shiloh; N. border of Amorites, Nu 21[24] (v. Di), Ju 11[22]; in its upper course it runs S. to N., hence (W.) border of Ammon, Dt 3[16] (cf. 2[37]), Jos 12[2]; mod. *Wady Zerqa* Bd[Pal 181].'

135a. I. בָּרָא: Ar. بَرَأَ prob. loan-word.

137b. בַּרְזִלַּי: no adj. fr. names of metals; perh. Aram., and בַּר=*son*, Nes[ZPV xv. 257; AJSL, Apr. 1897, 173].

141a. 1. בֹּר: Is 1[25] read prob. כַּכֻּר *as in a furnace* (Is 48[10]); there seems no evidence that 'lye' (i.e. water mixed with the burnt ashes of plants containing potash, used formerly for washing) was ever used in refining gold or silver: cf. J. Napier Anc. Workers in Metal (1856), 15, 20, 25 WAW in Smith DB ii. 368; Amer. Rev. Ed. (1871, vol. iii), 1939.

151a. [גָּדַד]: **Hithpo. 1** ad fin., for 'or perh. (cf. גּוּר) sub.' rd. 'We Now Marti Harper (cf. I, II. גּוּר).'

— **2** ad fin., Je 5[7] rd. prob. יִתְגָּרָרוּ ℭ Gie Du al.

152b, l. 13: after 'ψ 18[51]' ins. 'so ‖ 2 S 22[51] (Kt מַגְדִּיל; > Qr מִגְדֹּל).'

— l. 6 from below: cstr. גְּדֹל Ex 15[16] belongs rather sub גֹּדֶל, l. 3, after 'ψ 79[11].'

154b, l. 21: bef. 'sq. two' ins. 'Ez 20[27].'

156a. I. גֵּו: del. 'abs. Jb 30[5].'

161b. [גִּיחַ] **2 b**: rather '*break forth* (with that which is to be born),' but text dub. At end, also, add Ju 20[33].

163b. גָּלוּת: Am 1[6.9] cf. Ob[20.20] and Je 13[19] (ℭ Du Co al.) belong sub **2**=*body of exiles.*

165a. II. גָּלִיל **2**: for '—See also גְּלִילָה *ad fin.*,' rd. '; הַגָּלִילָה **Galilee**, 2 K 15[29] (‖ אֶרֶץ נַפְתָּלִי) Ew§ 173 h n Sta§ 308 a 2 Ges§ 90 f.'

165b, l. 1: del. '2 K 15[29],' and ll. 5b, 6.

— [גִּלּוּל]. Vid. Baud ZMG, 1904, 395 ff. (cps. BAram. גְּלָל (אֶבֶן), Palm. גללא Tariff i. 9 = στήλη λιθίνη; and concludes that it was orig. a designation of the primitive stone menhir or מַצֵּבָה).

168b. גַּם, l. 2: also Zinj. (Lzb[250] Cooke[166]).

175a. I. גָּרַם: l. 1, rd. 'mng. dub.; ? **cut off**, hence **reserve**.'

178b. גְּשׁוּרִי **2**: Jos 13[2] read prob. הַגִּזְרִי We and Dr (on 1 S 27[8]), Mey ZAW i. 126 n GFM Ju 1, 29 n.

184a. עַל־דִּבְרֵי ,עַל־דִּבַר *for the sake of, in reference to*, v. Kö Expositor, Aug. 1902, 142–148; and add for עַל־דִּבַר Nu 25[18.18.18] 31[16] 2 S 18[5], and for עַל־דִּבְרֵי Je 7[22] 2 K 22[13a] = 2 Ch 34[21a], and perh. ψ 7[1].

186a. דָּגוֹן: oldest tradition (Jerome) seems to waver between דָּג *fish* and דָּגָן *grain*, as explan. of דָּגוֹן, v. בית ד׳.

187a. דְּדָן **1**: Je 25[23], transfer to **2**.

189a. דּוּכִיפַת, name of bird: poss. of Egypt. origin, Bondi ZMG l (1896), 292 (Arabic, Ol§ 221 cf. Kö ET ix (1898), 476).

189b. דּוּר *circle, ball*—**1.** *circle:* Du Is 29, 3 thinks noun here also is כַּדּוּר (or כְּדוֹר=כִּידוֹר) *onset* of combatants; Marti כְּדָוִד as ℭ Lo Brd al.

192b, l. 6: on יָדוֹן Gn 6[3] cp. perh. دان *continue, do* something *continually*, in mod. Eg. Ar. (So SK lxvii (1894), 211 f.).

193b. מְדִינָה: cf. also OAram. מדינתא *city*, Palm. מדיתא *city*, sf. מדיתהון, pl. מדינתא SAC[70] Lzb[306] Cooke[266].

218a. יהוה: theories of non-Heb. or non-Sem. origin, opposed (in their older forms) by Bau Rel. i. 181 ff. (v. esp. 230); Dl Pa 162 ff. claimed Bab. origin for יהו, against this Kue National Religions, etc., Note iv (Eng. Trans. 329 ff.) Jastr JBL xiii (1894), 103 f. cf. Hpt BAS i. 170 N; Dl Babel u. Bibel, 46 f., 73 f. makes same claim for יהוה, agst. this v. esp. Hirsch ZAW xxiii (1903), 355 ff. Zim KAT 3. 465 ff.; Spiegelberg ZMG liii (1899), 633 ff. prop. (improb.) Egyptian etymol. for יהוה; further discussions see in Kö EB Names, § 112 and n. 3. 'Jehovah' found in Jacob (? Johann.) Wessel (†1480), acc. to Schwally ThLz, 1905, col. 612.

228b, l. 14 fr. below, rd. אמן for ימן.

229b. [הָלָא]: Mi 4[7] We prop. הַנַּחֲלָה (√חלה) *her that is diseased* (note ‖ הַצֹּלֵעָה, and cf. Ez 34[21]), so Now; Gr הַנִּלְאָה *her that is exhausted;* Marti allows either of these.

231b. הָלַךְ (5) ϵ: לִפְנֵי ה׳ also (less oft.)=*go* (and present oneself) *before* a deity or shrine 1 K 12[30] 1 Ch 21[30] (cf. בוא לפני Ex 28[30], קִדֵּם פְּנֵי ψ 95[2]).

239b. מַהֲלַלְאֵל: rd. מְהַלַּלְאֵל Gray Prop. N. 201.

— l. 6 fr. below: on תְּהִלָּתֶיךָ ψ 9[15] as error for לָּתֶךָ- or לֹּתֶיךָ-, v. Ol§ 131 k; 39 c Sta§ 354 b Hup-Now al. *ad loc.*

241b. הֵמָּה **2** ad fin.: add '—הֵמָּה כִּדְוֵי לַחְמִי Jb 6[7] rd. perh. וְהֵמָה וגו׳ (or וַהֲמָה) it is *loathesome* (√זהם).

242b. הָמוֹן **4**: 2 Ch 11[23] for וַיִּשְׁאַל הֲמוֹן נָשִׁים Perles Anal. 47 prop. וַיִּשָּׂא לָהֶם נ׳ (cf. נשׂא **3 d**).

246b. הרג, l. 5: for '1 S 14[7]' rd. '2 S 14[7].'

248a. II. הָרָה, l. 5: for '1 S 11[5]' rd. '2 S 11[5].'

251b. Bef. התת ins. '† מַהֲתַלּוֹת **n.f.pl.** *deceptions*;—Is 30[10].'

256a. זבי: on Palm. זבי (prob. abbrev. from . . . זבד), v. Lzb[265] Cooke[273, 291].

257a. I. זֶבַח: Ph. זבח of an offering of bread and oil CIS i. 165. 12; 167. 8, cf. RS Sem. 205 (2nd ed. 222).

262b. זָהָב **1**: Jb 37[22] rd. perh. זֹהַר Du and Dr.

265a. I. זִיז: on As. *zîzê, teats*, v. RFHarper AJSL xiv (1897–1898), 174.

269ª. זַכַּי: Nes (privately) suggests that this might be abbrev. fr. זכריה.

271ª, l. 17: *recorder*. Rather, probably, *the* (king's) *reminder*, who brought important business to his notice: cf. Ew [Gesch. iii. 365, H. iii. 267] Ke [2 S 8. 16] Benz [Arch. 310] Now [Arch. i. 308] Kit [1 K 4. 3].

271ª. זָכָר: against Schwally's view see JPeritz [Woman in the Ancient Hebrew Cult, JBL xvii (1898), 111 ff.]

272ª. זִכָּרוֹן: cite also (sub **1**) זִכְרֹנֵיכֶם מִשְׁלֵי־אֵפֶר Jb 13[12] *your memorial words are ashen sayings* (i.e. worthless), cf. Bu Du; Margolis (privately) suggests that 𝔊 seems to have read רְנִיכֶם [רְנַנְכֶם] <?] יִמָּשֵׁל לְאֵפֶר *your exultation shall be like ashes*.

273ª. זָמַם ad fin.: the text of Pr 30[32] is questioned by Frankenberg Toy al.; v. on II. נבל, 614ᵇ infr.

273ᵇ. מְזִמָּה, l. 3: rd. in Je 11[15] altogether עָשְׂתָה מְזִמּוֹת הַנְּדָרִים וּבְשַׂר קֹדֶשׁ יַעֲבִרוּ מֵעָלַיִךְ רָעָתֵךְ.

— זְמָן; Mand. זבאן, v. Nö [M 152]; on OPers. origin v. BAram.

275ª. III. זמר: Ar. ذمر is *urge with chiding, reproof*, ذِمَار *thing involving blame* (if not protected, defended); this hardly supports meaning *choice products* for III. זִמְרָה.

276ᵇ. זַעַם **2** is prob. denom. fr. זַעַם (v. Buhl).

277ᵇ. זָעַק **Niph.**: = *be called out* for military service, pass. of **Hiph. 1**; cf. GFM [Ju 18, 23].

279ª. I. [זָקַק]: perh. prop. *strain* or *filter through*, cf. Jb 36[27] Is 25[6].

279ᵇ. זְרֻבָּבֶל; prob. = Bab. *Zêr-Bâbili* = *offspring of Babylon*, oft. in Inscr. (Mey [E. Jud. v]).

284ᵇ. [זָרַר]: וַיְזוֹרֵר 2 K 4[35] om. 𝔊; Gr Bur think MT arose (by dittogr.) fr. וַיִּנְהַר עַל־הַנַּעַר.

288ª, l. 11 fr. below: rd. 'הַחַיִּים Ec 9[4].'

293ª. חָדַל **2**, l. 2 from end: add 'Jb 10[20] (but rd. here prob. יְמֵי חֶלְדִּי 𝔊 𝔖 Bi Bu Du).'

293ᵇ. [חָדַר]: Ph. is only חדר, חדרת (temple- or sepulchral) *chamber* (Lzb[271] Cooke[126]); Ez 21[19] is best explained from Syr. ܚܕܪ *go about, surround*, ܚܕܪ *around*. It seems uncertain whether חֶדֶר, Ph. חדר *chamber*, Ar. خِدْر *curtain, chamber, tent*, etc., are (ultimately) fr. this √ (as something *surrounding*); or (Buhl) from II. חדר = خَدِرَ II. *conceal behind curtain, conceal, confine*, IV. *conceal oneself*, also *abide, stay, remain behind* (Lane [707 f.]), Eth. ኀደረ: *abide, dwell* (Dr, privately, Nov. 1905).

293ᵇ. חֶדֶר, l. 3: ማኅደር: is not 'chamber,' but (fr. √ ኀደረ: *dwell*) *dwelling-place, abode, tent*.

297ª, l. 11 fr. below: omit 'מְחוֹלֶלֶת Is 51[9]' (which belongs to I. חָלַל).

310ᵇ. חַטּוּשׁ: cf. Nab. חטישו, Cooke[245].

314ª. חֲכִילָה n.pr.loc.; alw. c. art.

321ᵇ. חַלָּמוּת, l. 6: the ref. is to Job's sufferings (from which as little joy comes as from eating unsavoury food, so now Comm. generally), rather than to the unpalatable words of his friends. It is doubtful whether Di's reason for preferring *purslain* to 𝔗 חֶלְמוֹנָא *yolk* of egg (ריר ח׳ *slime of yolk*, i.e. the white of the egg) is convincing, viz. that ancient Hebrews did not keep hens, or that of De, viz. that white of egg is not *slime*, and is not unpalatable; mng. *yolk* preferred also by Da Bu Du.

325ª, l. 12: rd. '+ 25 t. in Ch., + (of royal officials) 1 Ch 28[1].'

326ª. חֶמְאָה: on mode of making *lebben*, by shaking milk in sour milk-skin, v. Doughty [Arab. Des. i. 221, 263; ii. 304, etc.] Thomson [Land and Book ii. 418]. See also ARSK [Ency. Bib. MILK].

— After חֶמְאָה ins. as new article: '+מַחֲמָאֹת **n.f.pl. curd-like things** = smooth, hypocritical, words, only cstr. חָלְקוּ מ׳ פִּיו ψ 55[22] *smooth are the butter-words of his mouth* (Ew De Hup), but read prob. חלק(ו) מֵחֲמָאֹת פיו (פניו) *his mouth* (*face*) *is smoother than curds* (Vrss Ki Thes Ol Che Bae We Du [מֵחֶמְאָה]).'

— l. 2 fr. below: add 'ψ 39[12]' after חֲמוּדוֹ.

329ª, l. 5: after Vog [No. 123 a] ins. '= Cooke [N. Sem. Inscr., No. 136]; Lzb [Ephem. ii (1906), 280].'

339ª, l. 28: after 'Dr)' ins. ', c. אֶת־ Gn 24[49].'

340ᵇ. Bef. חָסֹן ins. '+[חָסַן] **vb.** only **Niph. denom.** *Impf.* 3 ms. יֵחָסֵן Is 23[18] *be treasured up, hoarded* (‖ יֵאָצֵר).'

342ᵇ. II. חפף: cf. Nö [ZMG lvii (1903), 415].

345ᵇ. חֲצִי, l. 16, for מנח rd. נוח, and so seven lines below.

346ᵇ. חֵץ **2**. Here also חֲצָצֶיךָ ψ 77[18].

347ª. I. חָצֵר end: add '42[6] הַחִיצֹנוֹת for הַחֲצֵרוֹת.'

351ª, ll. 1, 2: rd. '1. חֹר, v. II. חור; II, III. חֹר, חַר, v. II, III. חרר.'

— Before I. [חָרֵב] ins. '+[מַחֲרָאָה] **n.f.** only pl. **cloaca, cess-pool**; — מחראות 2 K 10[27] Kt (Qr מוֹצָאוֹת).'

351ᵇ. II. חָרֵב, l. 3: after Zp 2[14] add '(but rd. עֹרֵב, 𝔊 We al.).'

354ᵃ. [חַרְטֹם]: the fact that the word is alw. applied to Egypt. magicians, exc. Dn 2[2] (late), suggests Egypt. origin, but no agreement among Egyptologists: Harkavy [JAs., 1870, Mars-Avril, 169] prop. *χar, speak + tum, hidden = teller of hidden things;* Wied [Samml 44] thinks Heb. word perh. imitating an Egypt. *cher-ṭem-t, he who holds the book;* FCCook ['Speaker's' Comm. i. 279] prop. *cher-tum = bearer of sacred words.*

359ᵃ. I. [חָרַר]: **Niph. 1.** נָחַר Je 6[29] from √נחר *snort, puff*, acc. to Mich Ew Gf Gie al.,—not Du.

359ᵇ. II. [חֹר], l. 2: cf. Nö [ZMG lvii (1903), 416]; and l. 5: del. '6[17] 13[17]' before 'Je 27[20].'

360ᵃ. חרסות, חַרְסִית Je 19[2]: v. Baldensperger [PEF 1904, 136] on the crushing of potsherds in the Valley of Hinnom.

361ᵃ. II. [חָרֵשׁ]: add '**Hithp.** *Impf.* 3 mpl. וַיִּתְחָרְשׁוּ Ju 16[2] *and they kept quiet.*'

369ᵃ. [חָתַת]: יֵחַת Je 21[13] v. נָחֵת.

— ll. 6, 5 fr. below: in Je 14[4] rd. prob. with Du (after 𝔊) Co Dr וְעֹבְדֵי הא׳ חַתּוּ.

371ᵃ. I. טָבַל: add '**Niph.** *Pf.* 3 mpl. נִטְבְּלוּ Jos 3[15] *be dipped*, בְּ of water.'

382ᵃ. טַף: note that the word includes (or implies) *women* as well as children, in foll.: Gn 47[12] Ex 12[37] (E), 10[10.24] (J), Nu 32[16.17] (JE; cf. Di on v[26]).

385ᵇ. תֵּבֵל, l. 12: before '89[12]' ins. 'ψ.'

391ᵇ. יָד end: add, for מִתַּחַת יַד, 2 K 8[20.22] (= 2 Ch 21[8.10]), 13[5] 17[7].

392ᵃ. [יָדָה], l. 12: Palm. ידתא *pious*, read ירתא(נה) SAC[80], also Id. [JQ 1904, 593].

396ᵇ. [יָהַב], l. 1: ? cf. 𝔗 יַהֲבַת ψ 11[6], יְהָבִית Ec 5[10].

402ᵃ. Before יוֹרָה ins. 'יוֹעָשׁ v. sub יהוה; יועם v. II. עמם **Hoph.**'

402ᵇ. Bef. יזע ins. יזן, √of **Pu.** *Pt.* pl. מְיֻזָּנִים Je 5[8] Qr, v. [זון], p. 266ᵃ.

403ᵃ. יַחַד **2** (4): Jb 17[16] rd. נֵחָת for נַחַת (v. Addenda, on pp. 94ᵇ, 629ᵃ); יַחַד here will then belong to (1).

404ᵃ. [יָחַל] **Pi.**: add '**3.** caus. *make to hope* ψ 119[49] (sf. pers.),' and, under **2**, l. 2, del. '[49.]' and ins. 'ψ 147[11].'

405ᵇ, l. 2 fr. below: ins. 'ψ 33[3].'

410ᵃ. Bef. [יָלַל] ins. 'יָלוֹן **n.pr.m.** in Judah 1 Ch 4[17]; 𝔊 Αμων, A 𝔊L Ιαλων.' 3210

410ᵇ. יָם: of Mediterr. in pl. Dn 11[45] [cf. **8 d**] Hi Ke Meinh Bev Dr (world-encircling seas Behrm).

418ᵃ. יָעָה: cf. also Ar. وِعَاءٌ *vessel* Gn 42[25] Saad, cf. Baldensperger [PEF 1904, 53], who cp. Mod. Ar. *waʿâ* (وِعَا).

419ᵃ. Bef. I. [יָעֵף] ins. 'יְעֹעֵרוּ Is 15[5] v. I. [עור] **Pilp.**'

430ᵃ. יָקָר end: Zc 14[6] '*but*' is very dub.; rd. prob. חֹם וְקָרוֹת *there shall be neither heat nor cold*, etc. (We al.).

438ᵃ. יַרְמוּת ad fin.: add 'see רָ(א)מוֹת **1 c**, p. 928ᵇ.'

440ᵇ. תִּירוֹשׁ: on mng., v. ARSK [Ency. Bib. WINE (iv. 5307 f.)].

446ᵃ. Bef. [יָשַׁע] ins. 'יֶשְׁנוֹ v. יֵשׁ.'

450ᵃ. Bef. ישׁשׁ ins. 'שָׁרוֹנִי **adj. gent.** of foregoing, 1 Ch 27[29].'

452ᵇ. יֹתֶרֶת: GFM (Dec. 28, 1899, privately) points out that fat parts are alw. disting. from this; cf. now on יתרת Id. [SACRIFICE EB 4206] and esp. Id. [Oriental. Stud. für Th. Nöldeke (1906), 761], where it is shewn to be the *caudate lobe* of the liver.

458ᵇ. I. [כָּבוֹד]: ψ 45[14] belongs to II. כָּבוֹד **2**; cstr. as Ges [§ 141 d]; v. also כֹּל **1 a** end.

461ᵇ. כִּידוֹר and 462ᵃ. כַּדּוּר: v. note on דּוּר, 189ᵇ.

467ᵇ ad fin.: [כַּוָּן], prob. Bab. loan-word, fr. *kamânu*, cake used in worship of Ištar, Zim [KAT 3. 441].

468ᵃ. I. כור, l. 4: كُورٌ means also a camel's saddle (or 'howdah') with its apparatus, v. Frey Lane.

— I. [כַּר]: for *basket-saddle* read < *camel-palankeen;* the palankeen, or tent-like erection, on the saddle (Burckh [Bedouins and Wahábys, 266] Doughty [Arab. Des. i. 437, ii. 304] Lane [Mod. Egyptians (5) ii. 158] al.), which seems intended here, is distinct from the basket or pannier (in which some women also travelled, Porter [Travels ii. 232]).

489ᵃ. II. כְּנַעֲנִי: add 'pl. sf. כִּנְעָנֶיהָ (si vera l.) Is 23[8] (|| סֹחֲרֶיהָ).'

497ᵃ. I. כפר, on orig. mng. cf. now Dr [Hast. DB PROPITIATION]; also As. *kuppuru, purify* (and deriv. *takpirtu*) Zim [KAT 3. 601 f.] Morgenstern [Sin in Bab. Rel. (MVG, 1905, 3) 44, 122].

498ª, l. 14: others understand מִן as=*away from;* cf. Di[Lv 4, 26], Ri[Sühne 50 f.].

521ª. [לָאָה] end: transpose 'Mi 6^{3}' to follow 'Je 12^{5}.'

523ª. לֵבָב, l. 7: bef. לִבְבֵהֶן ins. 'pl. c. sf.'

525ª, l. 10: after נתן לב לְ rd. 'Ec $1^{13.17}$ 7^{21} $8^{9.16}$ Pr 23^{26} Dn 10^{12}.'

— l. 11: Ne 2^{12} 7^{5} differ from Ec 7^{2} 9^{1} (the 'heart' here not being the subject's).

527ª. לִבְנֶה: named fr. exuding milky (white) gum De Ges al.

546ᵇ. לָשׁוֹן **5**: so As. *lišânu;* v. Meissner [ZAW xxiii (1903), 151 f.] Johns [As. Deeds 2, 281].

555ᵇ, l. 5 fr. below: ins. '22^{1}' after '†Nu'.

556ª. מוג: in view of prevailing fig. use, and of Ar. مَاجَ (موج) *be in tumult, commotion,* of sea, people, *be agitated, perplexed,* it is perh. dub. whether *melt* is orig. meaning; *be moved, agitated* is usu. poss., and even Am 9^{13} ψ 65^{11} (both late), where (esp. Am) *moistening* is suggested, this may be perh. derived fr. *agitating, loosening, dissolving.*

557ᵇ. II. [מוּל], l. 2: after 'cut off' add 'but only seemingly in the dub. passages (v. III. [מָלַל] and Comm.) Jb 14^{2} 18^{16} 24^{24} [MS Levy], ψ 37^{2} 90^{6}.'

560ᵇ. Bef. מוֹתָר ins. '(לְ)מוֹתָם ψ 73^{4} v. [חַרְצֻבָּה] and תָּם **1**.'

568ª. [מִין], del. 'so Syr. (Edessa) ܡܢܬܐ,' ref. due to early text. err. (GFM, privately, Dec. 28, 1899).

571ᵇ. מִלּוֹא: Schwally [ZMG lii (1898), 137] cp. As. *mulu=earthwork, mound, terrace,* Dl[411] M-A[544].

583ᵇ. מִן **9**, l. 2: for מִלְּ in Mish. see e.g. Bab. Mez 7^{10} Kil 8^{1} Ter 8^{11} Pes 1^{6} Taan 2^{7} Yeb 8^{2}; Ec 4^{17} מִלַּעֲשׂוֹת (have no knowledge *so as not* to do evil) is read by Siegfr Wild.

610ᵇ. [נָאַף] **Pi. 1 a**: transpose 'Ez 23^{37}' to foll. 'Ez 16^{32}' sub **b**.

611ª. נבא, v. in BAram. Appendix.

614ᵇ, l. 16: II. [נָבֵל]: **Qal**=*be foolish* †Pr 30^{32} is doubted by Frankenberg Toy (where see various renderings), al., who think text crpt.

617ᵇ. נֶגֶד **2 a**: note that in NH כְּנֶגֶד=*in front of,* Ber 4^{5}, 9^{5} Ab 2^{10}, מכנגד פני Git 7^{7} al.

629ª, l. 16: on Ju 16^{25} (rd. '16^{26}') v. GFM.

629ª. I. נחת **2**: Jb 17^{16} rd. נָחַת (𝔊 Du Dr), √נחת=*descend* (cf. 21^{13}).

635ª, l. 9: Jb 12^{23} rd. prob. וַיַּנִּחֵם *and leaves them* (Je 14^{9}).

637ª, l. 5 from below: נִחוּם<=*comforting, full of comfort* (sc. *is* ׳י ?) cf. ARSK [DB Nahum] Dr[Na 1, 1, Century Bible]).

638ª. I. נחשׁ, l. 2: after 'Thes' ins. 'on assumption that it is i. q. לחשׁ.'

643ᵇ. מַטָּרָה **1**: add Ne 3^{25}.

646ᵇ. מַכָּה, l. 3: after 'etc.;' rd. 'pl. מַכִּים 2 K 8^{29}=9^{15}= 2 Ch 22^{6}; מַכּוֹת abs. Zc 13^{6}+, cstr.,' etc.

648ª, l. 1: Ar. نَكِرَ *be shrewd,* appar. rare, cf. نُكْرٌ *cunning* Lane[2850 a].

648ᵇ. II. נכר, ll. 5 f.: for 'نَكِرَ in sense *be bad, evil,*' etc., rd. 'نَكِرَ *be ignorant of,* Qor 11^{73}; II. *change, alter,* so as not to be known, *disguise* Qor 27^{41}; IV=I, also *deny,* Qor 16^{85} *repudiate.*'

— l. 9: Syr. ܢܟܦ *reject* is rare (twice), and PS prop. ܢܟܪ *alienavit* each time.

— נֵכָר, l. 1: after 'foreign' ins. '(prop. *unknown,* cf. Ar. √).'

650ᵇ. III. מַסָּה: v. Gall [Kultstätten 32] interprets as *place of trial* (ancient judgment-place) and identif. with Ḳadesh, called also (מֵי) מְרִיבָה and עֵין מִשְׁפָּט.

656ª. I. תַּפּוּחַ, v. also Hom [A. u. A. 100, 106, 107]; Tristr [NHB 334 f.] thinks ׳ת=*apricot* (so Id. [Smith DB (2) Apple]); M'Lean-Dyer [EB Apple] makes ׳ת=*quince.*

658ᵇ, l. 7 fr. below: after 'v. Qal' ins. ';=*break up* rafts 1 K 5^{23}.'

663ª. מַצֵּבָה: on this v. also Lagrange [Études Bibl. 197 ff.] and review by Bau [ZMG lvii (1903), 830]; also GFM [EB Massebah] Sta [Bib. Theol. i. § 55] OCWhitehouse [Hast. DB Pillar].

667ª. [נָקָה]: 𝔗 נְקָא Pa.=*cleanse* (with lye) Is 1^{25}; adj. נְקָא *clean* of bread or fruit Gn 40^{16} 𝔗[J I], Dt 6^{3} 𝔗[J II], =*exempt* (BH נָקִי) 1 K 15^{22}.

671ª. נָשָׂא **2 b**, l. 8: after 'cf. v^{23};' ins. '*incur guilt* Ex 28^{43}.'

677ᵇ. נָתַח: rd. נְתָחֶיהָ also Ez 24^{5} for MT רתחיה Hi-Sm Co Berthol Toy Siegf[Kau] Krae Da ('poss.').

691ª. שִׂיג 1 K 18^{27}: om. 𝔊L, dittogr. for שִׂיחַ Klo Bur.

693ª. I. סוּף **2**: cf. also Che [EB Red Sea].

695ᵃ. [סָחַר], l. 3: add '𝔗 אַסְחַר ,סְחַר *go about*, סְחוֹר = Heb. סָבִיב.'

697ᵇ. סֹכֵךְ: transfer to I. [סָכַךְ].

700ᵇ. II. סלל, l. 3: add 'cf. *sull*, a round wicker basket used by women in Palestine for carrying fruit on their heads to market, Baldensperger PEF 1904, 135.'

703ᵇ. סַרְעַפָּה: cf. Syr. ܣܰܪܥܰܦܶܐ *branches*, Ez 31⁵ al. (PS 3956), from √ܣܪܥܦ *propagavit, germinavit.*

711ᵃ. סָתַם: cf. As. *bit sutummu, storehouse, treasury*, Zehnpf BAS i. 531.

713ᵃ. עָבַר **2** end: add Je 25¹⁴ 27⁷ 30⁸.

717ᵇ. עָבַר **3**, l. 7: Jb 14⁵ is *pass over, beyond* (cf. **1 i**).

718ᵇ. עָבַר **Pi 1**: after NH ins. 'מְעֻבֶּרֶת *pregnant*, Yeb 4¹·² 7³ Keth 1⁹'; but note also that in 𝔗ᴶ and Talm. (both Aram. and Heb.) עַבַּר=*conceive*, עִבּוּר *conception*, עוּבַּר *embryo*.

719ᵇ. I. עֵבֶר **1 B** ad fin.: cf. late As. *ebir nari* Schr KB iv. 304, l. 7 fr. below; KAT 3. 188, 437.

721ᵃ. II. [עָבוּר] **1 a**: Je 14⁴ < rd. וְעֹבְדֵי הָאֲדָמָה חַתּוּ Du, cf. 𝔊.

723ᵇ. I. עַד, l. 4: add 'so Gn 49²⁶ (rd. הַרְרֵי עַד for הוֹרַי עַד).'

— II. עַד: cf. 𝔗 עֲדֵי *booty*, Is 10² 33²³+.

735ᵃ, l. 2 fr. below: ins. 'יָעִיר כָּל־חֲמָתוֹ ψ 78³⁸.'

741ᵃ. עֲזַרְיָה occurs also Je 43² = (וְ)יְזַנְיָה 42¹ (v. p. 24ᵇ supra); and as friend of Daniel †Dn 1⁶·⁷·¹¹·¹⁹.

744ᵃ. I. עַיִן **1 j**, l. 8: after 'Jb 14³' ins. 'שִׂים ע׳ עַל Gn 44²¹ (J) Je 39¹² 40⁴, +לטובה 24⁶, +לרעה Am 9⁴'; and in l. 9 for 'v⁴⁰' rd. '2 Ch 6⁴⁰.'

751ᵇ. מַעַל **2 b** (*b*) (γ): Hg 2¹⁵·¹⁸ *and onwards* (as β) is more prob.: v. Now We Kl. Proph. ed. 3 (1898) Marti Dr.

759ᵇ. עֲלָטָה: for '**thick darkness**' rd. < **darkness, dusk,** which suits both passages (Bev, privately).

762ᵃ, l. 7: Is 57¹¹ 𝔊 𝔙 Che Hpt Du Marti rd. מַעְלִם for מֵעוֹלָם, cf. I. [עָלַם] **Hiph.** ψ 10¹.

769ᵃ. II. [עַם] *kinsman*, later development of I. עַם RS K 58; 2nd ed. 72.

769ᵇ. I. [עִמָּה] **c**: ins. 'Ec 7¹⁴ *side by side with, as well as*.'

770ᵇ. [עָמַס etc.] ad fin.: add '**Hiph.** *Pf.* 3 ms. הֶעְמִיס 1 K 12¹¹ *load* upon (acc. rei + עַל pers.) = 2 Ch 10¹¹.

776ᵇ, l. 10 fr. below: bef. '29¹²' ins. 'Jb.'

777ᵃ, l. 3: rd. 'ψ 9¹³ (Kt), v¹⁹ (Qr).'

783ᵇ. עָצַר: cf. As. *uṣurtu, taboo* SAC JA. 1904, 754.

785ᵇ. עַקְרָב: < [**f.**] as in NH Syr. Mand. Ar. (Levy gives Talm. [Aram.] as **m.**, but are rdgs. correct?), Nö (privately).

789ᵃ. עָרוֹד: perh. √عرّد [*run away?*], < √'غرد *schreien* [DHM zu Aṣmaʿī, Farq p. 43] das auch vom Wildesel vorkommt Amra alqais 4. 21, Zuhair 1. 25.'—Nö Fünf Moʿall. ii. 75 (SB Wiener Ak. cxlii).

790ᵃ. מַעֲרָכָה ad fin.: add '**3.** *order, arrangement:* בַּמּ׳ Ju 6²⁶ *in the* (proper or usual) *arrangement* of an altar, cf. עָרַךְ **1 a** Nu 23⁴ of altar.'

792ᵃ. [עָרַק] = Syr. in Lexx., and Pa.; but Syr. usu. *flee*, as 𝔗.

795ᵃ. עָשָׂה **Niph. 2 f**: transpose '+ לְ rei' to follow '*be used*.'

799ᵇ. [עָשֵׁשׁ]: acc. to Jacob ZMG 1901, 142; ZAW 1902, 107 *be dark*, cf. עששא *darkness*, in Chr-Pal.

— [עֶשְׁתֹּנָה]: < [עֶשְׁתּוֹן] Margolis (privately).

806ᵃ. [פּוּג], l. 2 f.: rd. 'Syr. ܦܳܓ *become cold* (Mt 24¹²), *fail, become weak, inefficient;* 𝔗 פּוּג *become cold, fail, be* or (Pa.) *make ineffectual;* NH *id., fail, vanish*.'

807ᵇ. פּוּר: Scheft 49 f. cp. OIran. *fravi*, etc., *progress, fortune, fate, lot.*

809ᵃ. I. פַּח: cf. also Baldensperger PEF 1905, 38 (*paḥ* used now of a trap with a net).

809ᵇ. פָּטַר **Hiph.**: cf. in Syr. PS 3093.

814ᵇ. פֶּן־, l. 1: after 'Makkeph' ins. 'exc. Gn 38²³ 44³⁴ Dt 7²⁵ 32²⁷ [not Gi], Is 27³ Pr 25⁸: Mandelkern Conc. s.v.'

823ᵃ, l. 2: bef. '**Pilp.**' ins. '**Hithpō**ʿ. *Impf.* 3 mpl. וַיִּתְפֹּצְצוּ Hb 3⁶ *and* the eternal mts. *were shattered* (al. √פוץ *were scattered*).'

823ᵇ, l. 1: del. 'ψ 8⁵ (‖ זָכַר)'—already given (correctly) sub **1 a**.

— פָּקַד **Pu.**: Is 38¹⁰ sense dub., Ges *am* (shall be) *missed for;* Hi Di De Che Comm. *am punished, mulcted of.*

828ᵃ. פַּרְנֵךְ: cf. Palm. פרנך Lzb 354 Cooke 298.

834ᵇ. [פָּתָה] **Niph., Pi.**: Je 20⁷ rather *be persuaded, persuade;* **Pu.** Je 20¹⁰ *be beguiled.*

841ᵃ. צַד, l. 12: tr. 'Dt 31²⁶' to follow '*at the side of*.'

— [צָדָה, צָדָד]: del. 'צָדָד,'.

845^{b}, l. 2: for '*erect*' rd. '*heap up* (stones).'

851^{b}. II. צִיץ: Aram. צִיץ *wing* dub. Levy[322 b]; Aram. נוֹצִיץ very rare; but note NH צִיץ *filament, small hair.*

852^{a}. II. ציר: cf. Ar. صار (med. *a*) = *turn* or *incline* one's face or neck, or a bough, etc. Lane[1744].

853^{b}. צַלְמָוֶת: cf. ظُلْمَةٌ *darkness;* We[Kl. Proph. ed. 3, 81] would read fpl. צַלְמוֹת, like ظُلُمَاتٌ Qor 2[16.18], and frequently.

864^{a}. צָרַף, ll. 3, 4: cf. صَرِيف *pure silver*, etc., Schulth[GGA, 1902, 673]; also Zim[GGA, 1899, 250; KAT 3. 650] (Heb., etc., borrowed from As.).

865^{a}. II. צַר: add Jb 36[19].

866^{a}. II. צֹר, l. 7: after חֶלְקַת הצ׳ ins. '2 S 2[16].'

879^{a}. קָמָה: 2 K 19[26]=Is 37[27] dub., < rd. לְפָנַי ... קֻמְךָ and join to v[28]: *before me is thy rising up* and thy sitting down We Bur Du Che[Hpt] al.; cf. sub שְׁדֵפָה.

904^{a}. קָשֶׁב: 2 K 4[31] (so rd.) Baer has קָשֶׁב.

914^{b}. Bef. † רִבִּית ins. art.: '† [רָבַב] **Pu. denom.** fr. preceding:—*Pt.* fpl. מְרֻבָּבוֹת ψ 144[13] *multiplied ten thousand-fold.*'

927^{b}. רום **Hiph. 1 d**, l. 2: bef. '49[22]' ins. 'Is.'

931^{a}. מַרְזֵחַ, l. 4: add 'Lzb[Ephem. ii. 281] ברבנות מרזוחותה די כמרי בל.'

935^{b}. רָחֹק **2 a**: 'ψ 139[2]' transfer to **b**.

939^{a}. רֶכֶב **4**: 2 K 7[14] rd. perh. רֹכְבֵי, cf. 𝔊 and 2 K 9[16] Bur.

945^{a}. I. רָעָה **1 d** (2), l. 3: Je 17[16] fig. of prophet (but Aq Symm 𝔖 Gie Du Co מֵרָעָה).

950^{b}. רַעַשׁ **1** ad fin.: del. 'by warhorse('s hoofs) Jb 39[24] (+ רֹגֶז)', and **3** after '*quivering*' add 'of horse eager to start Jb 39[24] (+ רֹגֶז);'.

951^{a}. רְצִין: As. has *Raṣunnu*, hence rd. perh. רצון, cf. Wkl[KAT 3, 135].

956^{a}. רָקִיעַ **2**: add 'רְקִיעַ עֻזּוֹ ψ 150[1] (sf. ref. to י׳).'

959^{a}. שְׁבָבָה **2**: rd. also 1 K 7[17.17] (for שבעה) Bö Th Sta Klo Kmp Benz Kit Bur.

959^{b}. [שָׂבֵעַ] **Pi.**: Now (after 𝔖 and 𝔊 Codd.) reads שִׂבַּעְתָּ Hb 3[9], for שְׁבֻעוֹת, cf. GASm; Gr Marti שָׂבְעַת (adj. f. cstr.) thy bow is *sated* with shafts. We thinks hopeless.

967^{b}. מַשְׂכִּית **1**: Lv 26[1]: on ancient rock-carvings in Canaan cf. Ghosn-el-Howie[JBL xxiii (1904), 211 ff.]

968^{a}. For 'IV. שׂכך,' etc., substitute: 'IV. [שָׂכַךְ] **Pilp. prick or spur on** (cf. Ar. شَاكَ *pierce* (perh. denom. from) شَوْكٌ *thorn,* شَوْكَةٌ *point* of spear, etc.; Eth. ሦክ: *thorn*);—*prick* or *spur on*, acc. pers.: *Pf.* 1 s. וְסִכְסַכְתִּי Is 19[2] (+ בְּ against); *Impf.* 3 ms. יְסַכְסֵךְ 9[10].'

1076^{a}. תֶּרַח, ll. 2, 4: the deriv. was withdrawn afterwards by RS himself, v. RS[K (2nd ed.) vii]

INDEX

Strong's #	BDB p.	Strong's #	BDB p.	Strong's #	BDB p.	Strong's #	BDB p.	Strong's #	BDB p.
144	1078d	181	15c	215	21a		284b	278	29a
145	12a	182	15c	216	21c		1089b	279	26c
146	12a	183	16a		70b	249	25b	280	1079c
147	1078d	184	16c	217	22a		280c		1092a
148	1078d		1060d	218	22b	250	280d	281	26c
149	1079a		1063b		22d	251	25b	282	26d
150	12c	185	16b	219	21d		26a	283	26d
	204b	186	17a		77a		1079c	284	26d
151	12a	187	23d	220	22d	252	1079c	285	26d
	12c	188	17a		71d	253	25b	286	27a
152	12c	189	16c	221	22b	254	25b	287	27a
153	1079a	190	17a	222	22b		28d	288	27a
	1089a	191	17b	223	22c	255	25b	289	27a
154	12c	192	17b	224	22a		28d	290	27a
	204c	193	17c		1070d	256	25b		591d
155	12b	194	19c	225	22d		26c	291	27b
156	12c	195	19c	226	16d	257	25b	292	27b
	190c		47a		23a		26c	293	27b
157	12c	196	17c	227	23a	258	25c	294	27b
158	13b	197	17c	228	1079a	259	25c	295	27b
159	13b		19d	229	23c		31c	296	27b
160	13b	198	17d	230	1079a		1079c	297	27b
161	13c		19d	231	23c	260	28a	298	27c
162	13c	199	19d	232	25b	261	26a	299	27c
163	13c		48a	233	23b	262	28a	300	27c
164	13c	200	17c	234	23c		296a	301	27c
165	13c	201	57b		272b	263	1079c	302	27c
166	14c	202	20b	235	23c		1092b	303	29a
167	14b	203	20b		1079b	264	27c		317b
168	13d	204	20a	236	1079b	265	29a	304	29a
169	13d		20c	237	23d	266	29a	305	25b
170	14b		58a	238	24b	267	26c	306	29a
171	14b	205	19d	239	24d	268	30c	307	1079c
172	14c		58a		1079b	269	27d	308	29b
173	14c	206	19d	240	24c	270	28a	309	29b
174	14d		122b	241	23d	271	28c	310	29d
175	14d	207	20c	242	25a	272	28c		30c
176	14d	208	20c	243	24d	273	28d		405b
	16b	209	20c	244	24c		403d		1079d
177	15a	210	20c	245	24c	274	28d	311	1079d
178	15a	211	20c	246	25a		306c	312	29c
179	6a	212	66d		279b	275	28d	313	31b
180	6b	213	21a	247	25a	276	28d	314	30d
	385c	214	69d	248	25b	277	26c	315	31b

Strong's #	BDB p.
316	31c
317	1079d
318	1079d
319	31a
320	1079d
321	1079d
322	30d
323	31c
324	1080a
325	31c
326	31c
327	31c
328	31c
	31d
	521b
329	31d
330	32a
331	31d
332	32a
333	32a
334	32a
335	32a
	58b
336	33a
337	33a
338	17b
339	15d
	33b
340	33b
341	33b
342	33c
343	15c
	33d
344	17b
	33d
345	17b
346	32c
	33d
347	33c
348	33b
349	32c
	32d
	33d
350	33b

Strong's #	BDB p.
351	32d
352	17d
	18a
	18b
	33d
353	33d
354	19b
355	19b
356	19a
357	19c
358	19a
	111c
359	19a
360	33d
361	19a
	48a
362	18c
363	1079a
	1080a
364	18c
365	19b
366	33d
367	33d
	1080a
368	33d
	34a
369	33b
	34a
370	32d
	34a
371	35b
372	4c
373	4d
374	35b
375	33a
	35c
376	35c
377	84a
	1083b
378	36b
379	36b
380	36b
	78c
381	35d

Strong's #	BDB p.
382	36a
383	1080a
	1083c
384	36b
	87b
385	16a
	33b
	36b
386	36b
	450d
387	451a
388	450d
389	36c
390	37a
391	37a
	469d
392	37a
	469d
393	37a
	470a
394	37a
	470a
395	37a
	470a
396	38b
397	37a
398	37a
	1080b
399	1080b
400	38a
401	38b
402	38a
403	38c
404	38c
405	38c
406	38d
407	38d
	506d
408	39a
	1080b
409	1080b
410	41d
	42b
	769b

Strong's #	BDB p.
411	41b
412	1080b
413	39b
414	41d
415	42d
416	42c
417	38d
418	38d
419	44d
420	44d
421	46d
	1080c
422	46c
	1060d
423	46d
424	18c
425	18d
426	1080c
427	47c
428	41c
	1080d
429	1080c
430	43b
	218d
	238a
431	1080d
	1082d
432	47a
433	43a
	1080c
434	47b
435	47a
436	18d
437	47c
438	47d
439	18d
	47c
	113d
440	19a
441	48d
	49b
442	47a
443	44d
444	47a

Strong's #	BDB p.
445	44d
446	45a
447	45a
448	45a
	46a
449	44d
	45a
450	45a
451	46d
452	45b
453	45b
454	41b
455	45b
456	45b
457	47b
458	45b
459	1080c
	1080d
	1088d
460	45b
461	45c
462	41b
463	45c
464	45c
465	45c
466	45c
467	45c
	46c
468	45d
469	45d
	46c
470	45d
471	45d
472	45d
	989d
473	47a
474	46a
475	46a
476	46a
477	46a
478	46a
479	1080d
	1088c
480	47d

Strong's #	BDB p.	Strong's #	BDB p.	Strong's #	BDB p.	Strong's #	BDB p.	Strong's #	BDB p.
481	47d		243d	545	53d	580	58c	615	64a
482	48a		474c	546	53d		59a	616	64b
483	48a		1090d	547	52d	581	1081c	617	64b
484	38d		1099a	548	53d	582	60d	618	62a
485	48a	519	51a	549	53d		1081d	619	62a
486	38d		1046c	550	54c	583	60d	620	1082a
	46b	520	51a	551	53d	584	58d	621	62a
487	47d		52a	552	53d	585	58d	622	62a
488	48a		52c	553	54d	586	1081c	623	63a
489	48a		1081a	554	55b	587	58d	624	62b
490	48a	521	51a	555	55b		59c		62c
491	48b		1081a	556	55b		1081c	625	63a
492	48c	522	51a	557	55c	588	58d	626	63b
493	46b		52a	558	55c	589	58d	627	63b
494	46b		52c	559	55c		219a	628	63c
495	48c	523	52c		1081a		1081b	629	1082a
496	46b		1081a	560	1081a	590	58b	630	63c
497	46b	524	1081a	561	57a	591	58b	631	63c
498	46b	525	54c	562	56d	592	58b		1082a
499	46b	526	51b		1051c	593	58b	632	64b
500	46c		54c	563	1081b	594	59d		1082b
501	46c	527	54c	564	57b	595	59a	633	1082b
502	48c	528	51b	565	57a		59d	634	64d
503	48d	529	53c		57b	596	59d	635	64d
504	48c	530	53c	566	57c	597	60a	636	1082b
505	48d	531	55b	567	57b	598	1081c	637	64d
	1081a	532	51b	568	57c	599	60a		210b
506	1081a		54c	569	57d	600	1081c		1082b
507	49b	533	55c	570	57d	601	60b	638	1082b
508	46c	534	57b	571	54a	602	60b	639	60a
509	49b		1051c		57d	603	60c		64d
510	39a	535	51b	572	57d	604	60c		1081d
	49b	536	51c		607c	605	60c	640	65d
	879c	537	51c	573	54c	606	1081d	641	65d
511	46c	538	52c		57d	607	1082a	642	65d
512	49b	539	52d	574	1080a	608	1082a	643	66a
513	39a		1081a	575	33a	609	61d	644	66a
514	49c	540	1081a		57d	610	62a	645	66b
515	49c	541	54d	576	1081b		692a	646	65b
516	1008c		411c	577	58a	611	62a	647	66c
517	51a		412b		58c	612	64a	648	66d
	51c	542	53b	578	58b		1082a	649	60b
518	49c	543	53b	579	58c	613	1082b	650	67d
	210b	544	53b		1099c	614	63b	651	66c

Strong's #	BDB p.	Strong's #	BDB p.	Strong's #	BDB p.	Strong's #	BDB p.	Strong's #	BDB p.
652	66c	685	69d	714	71b	747	1121a	780	76d
653	66c		858a	715	71b	748	73c	781	76d
654	66d	686	69d	716	71b		1082d	782	77a
	813d	687	69d	717	71c	749	1082d	783	77a
655	67a	688	70a		1082c	750	74a		1083a
656	67a		869b	718	1080d		1082d	784	77b
657	67a	689	70a		1082c	751	74b		1083b
	67b	690	70b	719	71c		1083a	785	1083b
658	67c	691	70b	720	71b	752	74a	786	78a
	819d		72a	721	71c	753	73d	787	1083b
659	67c	692	70b	722	71b	754	1082d	788	78a
660	67c		72a	723	71d	755	1083a	789	78a
	821a	693	70b	724	74a		1085c	790	78b
661	67c		936d	725	72b	756	1083a	791	78b
662	67c	694	70c	726	10c	757	74b	792	36b
663	67d	695	70c	727	75b	758	74b		78b
664	68a	696	70c	728	22d		591a	793	78b
665	68a	697	70d		72b	759	74d	794	78b
666	68b		916a		75d	760	74b	795	78b
667	68b	698	70c	729	72c	761	74c		994c
	827b	699	70c		72d		248c	796	78c
668	68b	700	70d	730	72c		942b	797	78c
669	68b	701	70c	731	72d	762	74c	798	820a
670	1082b	702	70d	732	72d	763	74b	799	77d
671	1082b		916d	733	73b		74c	800	77d
	1082c		1112c	734	73a	764	74d	801	77d
672	68c	703	1082c	735	1082d	765	75a	802	61a
	68d		1112c	736	73c	766	75a		78c
673	68d	704	70d	737	73c	767	75a		84b
674	1082c		917b	738	71c	768	58a		1081d
675	69a	705	70d		1082c		75c	803	78c
676	69a		917b	739	72a	769	75a	804	78c
	840c	706	916d	740	72a	770	75a	805	78d
	1109c	707	70d		73c	771	75a		79a
677	1082c	708	71a	741	72a	772	1083a	806	79a
	1109c	709	71a		72b	773	1083a		1007b
678	69c		918d		73c	774	75d	807	79a
679	69c	710	71a	742	71c		951c		92d
680	69b		1082c	743	71c	775	75d	808	84b
681	69a	711	1082c	744	71d	776	75d	809	84b
682	69b	712	71a		1082c		1083a	810	79a
	69c		919c		1082d	777	76c	811	79a
683	69c	713	71a	745	72a	778	1083a	812	79b
684	69d		1082c	746	73c	779	76c	813	79b

Strong's #	BDB p.	Strong's #	BDB p.	Strong's #	BDB p.	Strong's #	BDB p.	Strong's #	BDB p.
814	79b	836	81a	866	1071d		103a	937	100b
	1016d	837	81a		1072c	898	93c	938	100c
815	79b	838	78c	867	87d	899	93d	939	100c
816	79c		81a	868	87d	900	93d	940	100c
817	79d		1083d		1071d	901	93d	941	100c
818	79d	839	81b		1072c	902	94a	942	100c
819	80a	840	77b	869	1071d	903	94a	943	100c
820	80b	841	77b		1072c	904	94b	944	100d
	1032c	842	81b	870	1079d	905	94b		385b
821	80b	843	81b		1083c		94c	945	100d
	1038a	844	77b		1084a		571c	946	100d
822	80b	845	77b		1085d	906	94b		107b
	1039d	846	1083b	871	87d	907	94b	947	100d
823	80b	847	84b	872	91b		95a	948	101b
824	80b	848	84b		99d	908	94b	949	130d
	1043d	849	1083b	873	1084a	909	94b	950	101c
825	80b		1114c	874	91b	910	94d	951	133c
	1083b	850	84c	875	91c	911	95a	952	101c
826	1083b	851	84c	876	91d	912	95a	953	92b
827	80c		1035d	877	92b	913	95d		92d
	251c	852	1079a	878	92a	914	95a		101c
	1046a		1083c	879	91d	915	95c		694c
828	80c	853	84c	880	92a	916	95d		710a
829	80c		1096b	881	92a	917	96a	954	101c
	1051c	854	85c	882	92b	918	96a	955	102a
830	80c	855	87b	883	91d	919	96a	956	1084c
	1046b		88a	884	92a	920	96a	957	102b
	1052a	856	87a		989d	921	1084a		103a
831	80c	857	87b	885	92b	922	96a	958	102b
832	80d		1083c		785c	923	96b	959	102b
833	80d	858	1083c	886	92a	924	1084b	960	102b
834	81c	859	61c	887	1084a	925	97c	961	102c
	84a		61d	888	1084a	926	96b		103a
	455b		87b		1094a		1084b	962	102d
	606b		87c	889	93b	927	1084a	963	102c
	758a		87d	890	93b	928	96d	964	103a
	774d		1082a	891	93b	929	96d	965	103b
	775c	860	87c	892	93b	930	97a	966	103b
	979b	861	1083c	893	93c	931	97b	967	103b
	979d	862	87d	894	93c	932	97b		1084a
	980a	863	87a		1084a	933	97b	968	103b
	1083d	864	87c	895	1084a	934	97b	969	103d
	1087d	865	87c	896	1084a	935	97c	970	104c
835	80d		1069d	897	93c	936	100b	971	103d

Strong's #	BDB p.
972	104c
973	103b
	103c
974	103c
975	103d
976	103d
977	103d
978	104d
	138c
979	104c
980	104c
981	104d
982	105a
983	105b
984	105c
985	105c
986	105c
987	105c
988	105d
	1084b
989	1084b
990	105d
991	106b
992	106b
993	106b
994	106c
995	106c
996	107b
	108a
	126a
	1084b
997	1084b
998	108a
	1084b
999	1084b
1000	101b
1001	1084c
1002	108b
	1084c
1003	108c
1004	108c
	111b
	143d
	476c

Strong's #	BDB p.
	1084c
1005	1084c
1006	110c
1007	110c
1008	110d
1009	70d
	111a
1010	111a
	112a
1011	111a
	111d
	135d
	740a
1012	111a
1013	111b
1014	111b
1015	111b
	179c
1016	111b
1017	111a
1018	111a
1019	111b
1020	111d
1021	111d
1022	112a
1023	112a
	935d
1024	112b
1025	112b
1026	112c
1027	111b
	248b
1028	111c
1029	112d
1030	113a
1031	111c
1032	111c
	357b
	751c
1033	111d
1034	111d
1035	111d
1036	112a
	780b

Strong's #	BDB p.
1037	112a
	571c
1038	112a
	591a
1039	112b
1040	112b
	727a
1041	112b
1042	112b
	779a
1043	112c
	779a
1044	112c
	785b
1045	800a
	800b
1046	112c
1047	112c
1048	112d
	823a
1049	112d
1050	112d
1051	112d
	951a
1052	112d
	983b
	1039c
1053	112d
	746d
1054	113a
1055	113a
1056	113a
1057	113a
1058	113b
1059	113d
1060	114a
1061	114c
1062	114c
1063	114c
1064	114c
1065	113d
1066	114a
1067	114c
1068	114a

Strong's #	BDB p.
1069	114a
1070	114c
1071	114b
1072	114c
1073	114c
1074	114b
1075	114b
1076	114b
1077	114d
	115b
1078	114d
	128c
1079	1084b
	1084c
1080	1084c
1081	114d
	597d
1082	114d
1083	114d
1084	114d
1085	115a
1086	115a
	1084c
1087	115b
1088	115a
1089	117a
1090	117b
1091	117a
1092	117b
1093	1084c
1094	115b
1095	117b
	1084d
1096	1084d
1097	115c
	116a
1098	117d
1099	116a
1100	116a
1101	117b
	117d
1102	117d
1103	118a
1104	118a

Strong's #	BDB p.
1105	118c
1106	118c
	118d
	858d
1107	116b
	118d
1108	118c
1109	118d
1110	118d
	550b
1111	118d
1112	128d
	1084d
1113	1084d
1114	119a
1115	116c
1116	119a
1117	119d
1118	119d
1119	91b
	119d
1120	119d
1121	119d
	122b
	1085b
1122	122a
1123	1085b
1124	1084d
1125	122a
1126	122b
1127	122b
1128	122b
1129	124a
	1084d
1130	122b
1131	125a
1132	122b
1133	122b
	301b
1134	122c
1135	122c
1136	122c
1137	125b
1138	100d

Strong's #	BDB p.	Strong's #	BDB p.	Strong's #	BDB p.	Strong's #	BDB p.	Strong's #	BDB p.
	125a	1173	128b	1209	130a	1248	135a		138c
	125b	1174	128a	1210	131b		1085b	1275	92d
1139	122c	1175	128c	1211	130a	1249	135a		138c
	140c	1176	127d	1212	130b		141a	1276	138c
1140	125b	1177	128a	1213	130b	1250	135a	1277	135d
1141	125c	1178	128a	1214	130b		141b	1278	135c
1142	122c	1179	128a	1215	130c		1085c	1279	135d
	785c	1180	127b	1216	130d	1251	1085b		136a
1143	108a	1181	127b	1217	130d		1085c		138c
1144	122c	1182	128c	1218	130d	1252	101c	1280	138a
1145	122d	1183	128c	1219	130d		141b	1281	138a
	412b	1184	128b	1220	131a	1253	141b	1282	138a
1146	125c	1185	128d	1221	131a	1254	135a	1283	140b
1147	1084d	1186	128b	1222	131a		135d	1284	140b
1148	123a	1187	128b	1223	131a	1255	135d	1285	136b
1149	1084d	1188	128b	1224	131b		597d		138c
1150	126a	1189	128b	1225	131b	1256	135c	1286	42c
1151	122c		859d	1226	131b	1257	135d		136c
1152	126a		861b	1227	131c		141b	1287	138c
	691d	1190	128b		132d	1258	136a		141b
1153	126a	1191	128c	1228	131c	1259	135d	1288	138c
1154	126a	1192	127d		132d	1260	136a		1085b
1155	126a		128c	1229	131c	1261	136a	1289	1085b
1156	1085a		928b		132d	1262	136a	1290	139c
1157	126b	1193	128b	1230	131c	1263	138c	1291	1085c
1158	126d		1071c	1231	131c		140a	1292	140a
	1085a	1194	111a	1232	131c	1264	140b	1293	139c
1159	1085a		128d	1233	132c	1265	137b	1294	139d
1160	129d	1195	128d	1234	131c		141b	1295	140a
1161	130a	1196	128d	1235	132b	1266	137b	1296	140a
1162	126d	1197	128d	1236	1085a		141c	1297	1085c
1163	127a		129c	1237	132c	1267	136a	1298	140b
1164	127a	1198	129d		1085a		137b	1299	140b
	730d	1199	129d	1238	132c	1268	92d	1300	140c
1165	129c	1200	129c	1239	133a		137b	1301	140c
1166	127a	1201	129d		1085b		467b	1302	140d
1167	127b	1202	129d	1240	1085a	1269	137b	1303	140d
	127d	1203	129d	1241	133a	1270	137b	1304	140c
	1085a	1204	129d	1242	133c		1108d		140d
1168	127c	1205	130a	1243	134c	1271	137d	1305	140d
1169	1085a	1206	130a	1244	134c	1272	137d		1085c
1170	127d		130c	1245	134c	1273	104d	1306	141d
1171	128a	1207	130c	1246	135a		138c	1307	92d
1172	128b	1208	131b	1247	1085b	1274	135d		141d

Strong's #	BDB p.
1308	143a
1309	142d
1310	143a
1311	143b
1312	143b
1313	141d
1314	141d
1315	142a
1316	143b
1317	102a
	143c
1318	143c
1319	142a
1320	142b
	925b
	1085c
1321	1085c
1322	102a
	143c
	574c
1323	123a
	143c
1324	143d
	144c
	1085d
1325	1085d
1326	144d
1327	144c
1328	143d
1329	143d
1330	143d
1331	144a
1332	124a
	143d
1333	144a
1334	144a
1335	144a
1336	144b
1337	123d
1338	144c
1339	124a
1340	124a
1341	144b
1342	144b

Strong's #	BDB p.
	1085d
1343	144b
1344	144d
	1085d
1345	145b
1346	144d
1347	144d
1348	145a
1349	145b
1350	145b
1351	146a
1352	146a
1353	145d
1354	146a
	146b
	1085d
1355	1085d
1356	146b
	155d
1357	146a
	146d
1358	1085d
1359	146b
	146c
	1085d
1360	146b
1361	146d
1362	147a
1363	147b
1364	147a
1365	147b
1366	147c
	147d
1367	148b
1368	150a
1369	150b
1370	1086a
1371	147c
1372	147c
1373	146c
	147c
1374	147c
	155d
1375	149b

Strong's #	BDB p.
1376	150c
1377	150c
1378	150d
1379	148b
1380	148b
1381	148c
1382	148c
1383	148b
1384	148c
1385	148c
1386	148d
1387	148d
1388	148d
1389	148d
1390	149b
1391	149c
1392	149c
1393	149c
1394	149b
1395	149b
1396	149c
	1085d
1397	149d
1398	150a
1399	149d
	989d
	1086a
1400	1086a
1401	1086a
1402	150a
1403	150c
1404	150c
1405	146d
	150d
1406	150d
1407	151a
	151b
1408	151c
1409	151c
1410	151a
	151c
1411	1086a
	1086b
	1089d

Strong's #	BDB p.
1412	151a
	151d
	211c
1413	151a
	1086a
1414	1086a
1415	152a
1416	151b
1417	151b
1418	151b
1419	152d
1420	153c
1421	154d
1422	154d
1423	152a
1424	151d
1425	151d
1426	151d
1427	151d
1428	152a
1429	152a
1430	155c
1431	152a
1432	152c
1433	152d
1434	152d
1435	153c
1436	153c
	153d
1437	153d
1438	154b
1439	154c
1440	154c
1441	154c
1442	154c
1443	154d
1444	154d
1445	155a
1446	155b
1447	154d
1448	155a
1449	155b
1450	155b
1451	155b

Strong's #	BDB p.
1452	155b
1453	155b
1454	155c
1455	155c
1456	155c
1457	155c
1458	155c
	156a
1459	1086a
1460	156a
	156b
	1086a
1461	146a
	155c
1462	146d
	147c
	155c
1463	155d
1464	156a
1465	156b
1466	145b
	156a
1467	1085d
	1086b
1468	156d
1469	160a
1470	157a
1471	156c
	157a
	361d
1472	156b
	157a
1473	163c
	1086c
1474	157a
1475	170a
1476	157b
1477	157b
1478	157b
1479	157c
1480	157c
1481	157c
	158c
	158d

Strong's #	BDB p.
1482	158d
1483	158a
	751c
1484	158d
	177c
1485	158a
1486	174a
1487	159a
	162c
1488	159a
	159c
1489	159b
	1086b
1490	1086b
1491	159b
1492	159b
	159c
1493	159b
1494	159c
1495	159c
1496	159b
	159d
1497	159d
1498	160a
1499	160a
1500	160a
1501	160b
1502	160b
1503	160b
1504	160b
	1086b
1505	1086b
1506	160c
1507	160c
1508	160d
1509	160c
1510	1086b
1511	160c
	173d
1512	161a
1513	160d
1514	161a
1515	161a
1516	161a

Strong's #	BDB p.
	360d
	361d
1517	161c
1518	157a
	160d
	161c
1520	161d
1521	161d
1522	160d
	161c
	162a
1523	157a
	162a
1524	162b
1525	162b
1526	162b
1527	162b
	171b
1528	1086b
1529	162c
1530	162c
	164c
1531	165a
1532	162c
1533	162c
1534	162c
	165d
1535	1086b
	1086c
1536	162c
	166a
1537	166a
1538	162c
	166b
1539	162d
1540	162d
	1086c
1541	1086c
1542	162b
	163d
1543	163d
	165a
1544	165c
1545	166b

Strong's #	BDB p.
1546	163c
1547	1086c
1548	164a
1549	163d
1550	165b
1551	165b
1552	165b
1553	165c
1554	164d
1555	163d
1556	94a
	164b
	1086c
1557	165b
1558	164b
1559	165b
1560	1086c
1561	165a
1562	165b
1563	166b
1564	166b
1565	166c
1566	166c
1567	165a
	166d
1568	166d
	928c
1569	167c
1570	167c
1571	167c
	168d
	210b
1572	167c
1573	167d
1574	167d
1575	167d
1576	168b
1577	168c
1578	168c
1579	168a
1580	168a
1581	168c
1582	168d
1583	168c

Strong's #	BDB p.
1584	170a
	1086c
1585	1086c
1586	170a
1587	170b
1588	111b
	170b
	171a
1589	170b
1590	170c
1591	170c
1592	170c
1593	171a
1594	171a
1595	170d
	1086c
1596	1086c
1597	170d
1598	170d
1599	171b
1600	171d
1601	171d
1602	171d
1603	172a
1604	172a
1605	172a
1606	172a
1607	172b
1608	172b
1609	172b
1610	172b
	172c
1611	1086d
1612	172b
1613	172d
1614	172d
1615	162c
	173a
	1086b
1616	158a
	162c
	173a
1617	173a
1618	173a

Strong's #	BDB p.
1619	173a
1620	173a
	176b
1621	173a
	176b
1622	173a
1623	173b
1624	173b
1625	173d
	176a
1626	173d
	176a
1627	159a
	173c
	175c
1628	158c
	173d
1629	173d
1630	173d
1631	173d
1632	175a
1633	175a
1634	175a
	1086d
1635	1086d
1636	175a
1637	175b
	188d
1638	175c
	176b
1639	175c
1640	175d
1641	176a
1642	176b
1643	176c
1644	176c
1645	177a
1646	177a
1647	177a
1648	177a
1649	177b
1650	178a
1651	178c
1652	177d

Strong's #	BDB p.	Strong's #	BDB p.	Strong's #	BDB p.	Strong's #	BDB p.	Strong's #	BDB p.
1653	177c	1686	179b		922b		1087b	1783	192d
	1086d	1687	184b		922c	1756	178d	1784	1088c
1654	177c	1688	184c	1722	1087a		190b	1785	189b
	177d		529a	1723	1087a	1757	1087b		193d
1655	1086d	1689	179c	1724	187a	1758	190b	1786	190c
1656	177d	1690	179b	1725	187b	1759	1087c		193d
1657	177d	1691	179c	1726	187b	1760	190d	1787	190d
1658	177d	1692	179c	1727	187b		191a		193d
1659	178c		1087a	1728	186a		1087c	1788	190d
1660	178c	1693	1087a		187b	1761	1087c		193d
	387c	1694	180a	1729	186a	1762	191a	1789	190d
1661	178c	1695	180a		187b	1763	1087c		193d
	387d	1696	180b	1730	186d	1764	191a	1790	194c
	440c	1697	182a		187c	1765	191b	1791	1080d
1662	387d	1698	184a	1731	188b	1766	191b		1088c
1663	178c	1699	184a	1732	187d	1767	95a	1792	193d
	388a		184c	1733	186d		191b	1793	194b
1664	178c	1700	184a		187d		461d	1794	194b
	388a		1087a	1734	186d		552a	1795	194c
1665	178c	1701	1087a		187d	1768	1087c	1796	194b
	388a	1702	184a	1735	187d		1096c	1797	1088c
1666	178c	1703	184c	1736	188b		1096d	1798	1088d
1667	387d	1704	184c	1737	187d	1769	192a	1799	1088d
1668	1086d	1705	184b	1738	188c	1770	185d	1800	194c
1669	178a	1706	185a	1739	188c		192a		195d
1670	178b	1707	185c	1740	188d	1771	186a	1801	194c
1671	178b	1708	185c	1741	188c		192a	1802	194c
1672	178b	1709	178d	1742	188d	1772	178d	1803	195d
1673	178c		185c	1743	188d		192a	1804	195c
1674	178c	1710	185d	1744	189a	1773	188d	1805	194d
1675	178d	1711	185c	1745	189a		192a	1806	195b
1676	178d	1712	186a	1746	189a	1774	191d	1807	196a
	906b	1713	186a	1747	189b	1775	192a	1808	194d
1677	179a		186b	1748	189b	1776	192a	1809	195c
	187b	1714	186b	1749	200a	1777	189b	1810	196a
	1087a	1715	186b	1750	189b		192a	1811	196a
1678	1087a	1716	186c	1751	1089a		1088b	1812	196a
1679	179a	1717	186d	1752	189c	1778	1088b	1813	196a
1680	179a	1718	186d		1087b	1779	189b	1814	196a
1681	179a	1719	186d	1753	1087b		192c		1088d
1682	184b		187a	1754	189c		995a	1815	1088d
1683	184b		922b		462a	1780	1088b	1816	196b
1684	1087a	1720	187a	1755	189c	1781	193a	1817	194c
1685	1087a	1721	187a		201b	1782	1088c		194d

Strong's #	BDB p.	Strong's #	BDB p.	Strong's #	BDB p.	Strong's #	BDB p.	Strong's #	BDB p.
	195a	1846	200b		1089b	1914	213b	1949	223a
	196b	1847	200b	1878	206a		301b		228d
1818	196b		395c	1879	206c	1915	213b	1950	223b
1819	197d	1848	200c	1880	206b	1916	213b		243a
	1088d	1849	200c	1881	206c	1917	1089d	1951	223b
1820	198c	1850	200c		1089b	1918	213c	1952	223c
1821	1088d	1851	200c	1882	1089b	1919	213c	1953	221d
1822	199a		201a	1883	1089b	1920	213c		223c
1823	198b	1852	200c	1884	1089b	1921	213d	1954	223c
1824	198c		201a	1885	206d		1089d		448a
1825	198b	1853	200c	1886	206d	1922	1089d	1955	448a
1826	198d	1854	200d	1887	210c	1923	1089d	1956	223d
	199b		1089a		1089c	1924	214c		452d
1827	199a	1855	1089a	1888	1089c	1925	214a	1957	223d
1828	199b	1856	201a	1889	210c	1926	214a	1958	223d
1829	199b	1857	201b	1890	210c	1927	214c	1959	212c
1830	199c	1858	201b		396d	1928	214c		223d
1831	199c		204d	1891	211a	1929	214c	1960	224a
1832	199c	1859	1087b	1892	210c	1930	214c		392d
1833	200a		1089a	1893	211a	1931	214d	1961	218b
1834	199d	1860	201b	1894	211b		223d		224a
	204b	1861	201c	1895	211b		1090a		1089d
	217a	1862	201c	1896	211b	1932	1081c	1962	217d
1835	75a	1863	201d		212b		1090a		228a
	192d		205a	1897	211c	1933	216d	1963	228a
	200a	1864	201d	1898	212a		217c		1089c
1836	1080d		204d	1899	211d	1934	1089d	1964	228a
	1088d	1865	204d	1900	212a	1935	213a		1090b
	1096c	1866	204d	1901	211c		217a	1965	1090b
1837	200a	1867	201d	1902	212a	1936	217b	1966	228d
1838	200b		1089a	1903	212b	1937	217b		237d
1839	193a	1868	1089a	1904	212b		217c	1967	228d
1840	193a	1869	201d	1905	212b	1938	217b		243a
	200a	1870	202c		212c		217c	1968	54c
	200b		1008b	1906	212c	1939	217c		228d
1841	1088c	1871	204b		212d	1940	217c	1969	228d
1842	193a	1872	1089a	1907	1089c	1941	217c	1970	229a
	419a	1873	201d	1908	212d	1942	217c	1971	229b
1843	200b		204c	1909	212d	1943	217d		648b
	395b	1874	204c	1910	213a	1944	222d	1972	229b
1844	200b	1875	201d	1911	213a	1945	222d		229c
	395c		205a	1912	213a	1946	1090b	1973	210b
1845	200b	1876	205d	1913	213a	1947	239c		229b
	396a	1877	206a		214c	1948	239c	1974	239b

Strong's #	BDB p.
1975	229c
	534c
1976	229d
	534c
1977	229d
	534c
1978	237b
1979	237b
1980	229d
	539d
	540b
1981	1090b
1982	237a
1983	1090b
1984	237c
	237d
	239c
1985	239b
1986	240c
1987	240c
1988	240d
1989	240d
1990	241a
1991	241a
1992	216d
	241a
	1090b
1993	242a
1994	1090b
1995	242b
1996	155d
	242b
1997	242d
1998	242d
1999	242d
2000	243a
2001	243b
2002	1090c
2003	243b
2004	241d
	243b
	530a
2005	243b
	530a
	1090c
2006	243d
	1090c
	1099a
2007	216d
	241b
	244d
2008	244c
2009	243d
	774b
2010	244d
	629c
2011	244d
2012	245a
2013	245a
	245b
2014	245b
	806b
2015	245b
2016	246a
2017	246a
2018	246b
2019	246b
2020	246c
	665a
2021	246c
2022	219b
	223c
	246d
	249a
	251a
2023	246d
2024	246d
2025	72b
	246d
2026	246d
2027	247c
2028	247c
2029	247c
2030	248a
2031	1090d
2032	248a
2033	248b
	353d
2034	249a
2035	249a
2036	248b
2037	248b
2038	248b
2039	248c
2040	248c
2041	249a
	746d
2042	249a
2043	76d
	210c
	251a
2044	251c
2045	251c
	1036a
2046	251c
	678a
2047	251c
2048	251c
	1068c
2049	251c
	1068c
2050	223c
	251d
2051	255a
2052	255a
2053	255b
2054	255c
2055	255c
2056	255c
	409b
2057	255c
2058	255c
2059	255c
2060	255d
2061	255b
2062	255d
2063	256a
	260a
2064	256a
2065	256b
2066	256b
2067	256c
2068	256c
2069	256c
2070	256a
2071	256b
2072	256b
2073	259c
2074	259d
2075	259d
2076	256d
	1087a
2077	257b
2078	258a
2079	256a
	259b
2080	256b
2081	259b
2082	259c
2083	259d
	560d
2084	1091a
2085	260a
2086	260a
	267d
2087	260a
	268a
2088	260a
	774b
	1086d
	1087c
2089	962a
2090	262b
	1086d
2091	262c
	1087a
2092	263d
2093	263d
2094	263d
	264a
	1091a
2095	1091a
2096	264a
2097	262b
	264c
2098	262b
	264c
2099	264c
2100	264c
2101	264d
2102	264d
	267c
	1091a
2103	1091a
2104	265c
2105	265d
2106	265a
	265d
2107	266a
2108	265d
2109	266a
	402c
	1091b
2110	1091b
2111	266a
	1091b
2112	1091b
2113	266b
2114	266b
	266d
	268b
2115	266d
2116	266d
2117	265b
	267a
2118	267b
2119	267b
	267c
	1087c
2120	267b
2121	268a
2122	1091b
2123	265a
	265c
	268b
2124	265b
	268b
2125	265b
	268b
2126	265b

Strong's #	BDB p.	Strong's #	BDB p.	Strong's #	BDB p.	Strong's #	BDB p.	Strong's #	BDB p.
	268b	2158	274b	2193	276c	2228	280c	2260	287a
2127	266b	2159	274d	2194	276d	2229	281a	2261	287c
	268b	2160	275b	2195	276d	2230	281b	2262	287c
2128	268b	2161	273a	2196	277a	2231	281b	2263	287d
2129	268b	2162	273b	2197	277a	2232	281b	2264	287d
2130	268b	2163	273d	2198	277a		1091d	2265	287d
2131	268b	2164	1091c	2199	277a	2233	282a	2266	251c
	278a	2165	273d		1091c		1091d		287d
	279b		1091c	2200	1091c	2234	1091d		1092a
2132	268b	2166	1091c	2201	277c	2235	283b	2267	288c
2133	268d	2167	274a	2202	277d	2236	284c	2268	288c
2134	269a		1091c	2203	278a	2237	284d	2269	1092a
	269b	2168	274d	2204	278b	2238	284d	2270	288d
2135	269a	2169	275a	2205	278c	2239	284d	2271	289a
	1091b	2170	1091c	2206	278a	2240	285c	2272	289a
2136	1091b	2171	1091c	2207	279a	2241	268d	2273	1092a
2137	269a	2172	274b	2208	279a		285c	2274	288d
	269b	2173	275a	2209	279a	2242	285c	2275	289b
2138	271d	2174	275b	2210	279a	2243	285a		900c
2139	271d	2175	275b		1091d		285c	2276	289c
2140	269b	2176	274b	2211	1091d	2244	285a	2277	288d
2141	269a	2177	275b	2212	279b	2245	285c	2278	289a
2142	269c		1091c	2213	267a	2246	285d	2279	289a
	272c	2178	1091c		279c	2247	285d	2280	289c
	561b	2179	275c	2214	266d	2248	1092a	2281	290a
2143	271a	2180	275b		279c	2249	289c	2282	290b
	271b	2181	266a	2215	279c	2250	289a		290d
2144	271a		275c	2216	279c		289c	2283	290b
2145	271b	2182	276c		1091d	2251	286a		291b
	1088d	2183	276a	2217	1091d	2252	285d	2284	290b
2146	272a	2184	276a	2218	279c		286a	2285	290c
	1088d	2185	275d	2219	279d	2253	285d	2286	290c
2147	271d	2186	276b		561d		286a	2287	290c
2148	272a		276c	2220	283d	2254	286b	2288	291c
	1091c	2187	276c		1089a		287b	2289	292a
2149	273a	2188	276c	2221	283b		1091d	2290	292a
2150	272d		402c	2222	280a	2255	1091d	2291	291b
2151	272d	2189	266b		284b	2256	286c	2292	291b
2152	273a		276c	2223	267a		286d		1092a
2153	273a	2190	266b		280a		287a	2293	291b
2154	273b		276c	2224	280b		287c	2294	291b
2155	273c	2191	277d	2225	280b	2257	1092a	2295	291c
2156	274d		1091d	2226	280b	2258	287a	2296	291c
2157	273d	2192	1091d	2227	280c	2259	287a	2297	26a

Strong's #	BDB p.
	292b
2298	1079c
	1092a
	1096c
2299	292b
2300	292b
	292c
2301	292c
2302	292d
2303	292c
2304	292d
	1092a
2305	1092a
2306	1092a
2307	292c
2308	292d
2309	293b
2310	293b
2311	293b
2312	293b
2313	293c
2314	293c
2315	293c
2316	293c
2317	293d
2318	293d
2319	294a
	1092a
2320	294b
2321	295a
2322	295a
2323	1092a
2324	1092b
2325	295a
2326	295a
2327	295b
2328	295b
2329	295b
2330	295c
2331	296a
	1092b
2332	295c
2333	295d
2334	295d

Strong's #	BDB p.
2335	296a
	302c
	302d
2336	296a
2337	296a
2338	1092b
2339	296c
	1092b
2340	295d
	296c
2341	296c
2342	296d
	298c
	313d
2343	299a
2344	297c
2345	299b
2346	299b
	327b
2347	299b
2348	299c
	342b
2349	299c
2350	299c
2351	299c
2352	301b
	351a
	359d
2353	301a
2354	301a
2355	301a
2356	351a
	359d
2357	301a
	1092c
2358	1092c
2359	301b
2360	213b
	301b
2361	27c
	301b
2362	301c
2363	301c
	301d

Strong's #	BDB p.
2364	302a
2365	302a
2366	302a
	364d
2367	302a
	364d
2368	302a
	368a
2369	302a
	368b
2370	1092c
2371	302a
	303c
2372	302a
	1092c
2373	303d
	1092a
2374	302c
2375	303d
2376	1092c
2377	302d
2378	303a
2379	1092d
2380	303a
2381	303c
2382	303c
2383	303c
2384	303b
2385	304a
2386	306b
2387	306c
2388	304a
2389	305c
2390	304a
	305d
2391	305d
2392	305d
2393	305d
2394	306a
2395	306a
2396	306a
2397	296b
	306c
2398	306c

Strong's #	BDB p.
2399	307d
	1092d
2400	308b
2401	308b
2402	308b
2403	308b
	310d
	1092d
2404	310a
2405	310b
2406	310b
	334d
	1093b
2407	310d
2408	1092d
2409	1092d
2410	310b
2411	310b
2412	310c
2413	310c
2414	310c
2415	310d
2416	310d
	311d
	312c
	312d
	313a
	1092d
2417	1092d
2418	1092d
2419	27d
	310d
	313c
2420	295b
	310d
2421	295c
	310d
	1092d
2422	313a
2423	1092d
2424	313c
2425	310d
2426	298a
	313d

Strong's #	BDB p.
	315d
2427	297d
	313d
2428	298c
	313d
	1093a
2429	1093a
2430	298a
2431	298a
	313d
	316a
2432	298b
2433	313d
	336d
2434	300c
	313d
2435	300b
	313d
2436	300c
	313d
	348d
2437	301b
	313d
2438	27c
	313d
2439	301c
2440	301d
2441	313d
	335a
2442	314a
2443	314a
	335c
2444	314b
2445	1093a
2446	314b
2447	314b
2448	314b
2449	314b
2450	314c
	1093a
2451	315b
2452	1093a
2453	315d
2454	315b

Strong's #	BDB p.	Strong's #	BDB p.	Strong's #	BDB p.	Strong's #	BDB p.	Strong's #	BDB p.
2455	315d	2491	319c		327a	2553	329a	2584	333b
	320d		321a		328d	2554	329b		336d
2456	316a	2492	321b	2525	326a	2555	329c	2585	335c
2457	316a	2493	1093a		328d	2556	329d	2586	337a
2458	316a	2494	321b	2526	325d		330a	2587	337a
2459	316d	2495	321d		328d	2557	329d	2588	333d
2460	317a	2496	321d	2527	326a		330a	2589	335d
2461	316b	2497	298b		328d	2558	330a	2590	334c
2462	317a		322a	2528	1093b	2559	330b		334d
2463	317a	2498	322a		1095c	2560	330b	2591	1093b
2464	317b		1025c	2529	326a		330d	2592	335a
2465	317b		1093a		328a		331a		337a
2466	317c	2499	1093a	2530	326b	2561	330c	2593	335c
2467	317c	2500	322b		326d		1093b	2594	337a
2468	317c	2501	322b	2531	326c	2562	1093b	2595	333d
2469	317c	2502	322c	2532	326c	2563	330c		335a
2470	317c		323a	2533	326d		330d	2596	335b
	318c	2503	323b	2534	326b	2564	330c	2597	1093b
2471	319c	2504	323b		328a	2565	331a	2598	335c
2472	321c		1093d		404b	2566	331c		1093b
	1093a	2505	323c		1095c	2567	332b	2599	335c
2473	298b		325a	2535	328d	2568	331c	2600	335d
	322a		1093b	2536	328a	2569	332b		336c
2474	319d	2506	324a		329b	2570	332d	2601	335d
2475	322b		325b	2537	327d	2571	332d	2602	335d
2476	325d	2507	324c		328a	2572	332b	2603	335d
2477	318d	2508	1093b	2538	328b	2573	332d		337d
2478	319a	2509	325b	2539	328b	2574	333a		1093b
2479	298b	2510	325b	2540	329a	2575	329a	2604	1093b
	319a	2511	325b	2541	330b		333b	2605	336d
2480	319a	2512	325c	2542	330b	2576	329a	2606	337a
2481	316a	2513	324c	2543	331a		329b	2607	337b
	318d		325c	2544	331c	2577	333b	2608	337b
2482	318d	2514	325c	2545	327b	2578	333a		1093b
2483	318b	2515	324c		328a		844b	2609	337d
2484	318d	2516	324c	2546	328a		844c	2610	337d
2485	319d	2517	324d	2547	328a	2579	333a	2611	338a
2486	321a	2518	324d	2548	330a	2580	333b	2612	338a
2487	322b	2519	325c	2549	332c		336b	2613	338b
2488	322d	2520	324d	2550	328a	2581	333b	2614	338b
2489	319a	2521	324d		328b		336d	2615	337b
	456c	2522	325d	2551	328b	2582	333b		338b
2490	319b	2523	325d	2552	328a		337b	2616	338b
	320a	2524	326a		328c	2583	333b		340a

Strong's #	BDB p.
2617	338c
	340a
2618	122c
2619	339d
2620	340a
2621	340b
2622	340b
2623	339c
2624	339d
2625	340c
2626	340d
2627	1093c
2628	340c
2629	340c
2630	340d
	1093c
2631	1093c
2632	1093c
2633	340d
2634	340d
2635	1093c
2636	341a
	1093c
2637	341a
	1093c
2638	341c
2639	341c
2640	341c
2641	341c
2642	341c
2643	341d
	342c
2644	341d
2645	341d
2646	342a
	342c
2647	342a
	342c
2648	342a
2649	342a
2650	342a
	342c
2651	342b
2652	342b
2653	342b
2654	342c
	343c
2655	343a
2656	343a
2657	343b
2658	343c
2659	344a
2660	343d
2661	344a
	344b
	826c
2662	343d
2663	343d
2664	344b
2665	344c
2666	344d
2667	344d
2668	344d
2669	345a
2670	344d
2671	345a
	346b
2672	345a
2673	345b
2674	347d
2675	347d
2676	345c
	346a
2677	345c
	346a
2678	345d
2679	345d
	630a
2680	345d
	630a
2681	347d
2682	348b
2683	346a
2684	346a
2685	1093c
2686	346a
	346d
2687	346b
2688	346c
2689	346d
	348c
2690	348d
2691	346d
	347b
2692	347b
2693	151d
	347c
2694	347c
	1064a
2695	347d
2696	348a
2697	348a
2698	348a
2699	346d
	347b
2700	348a
2701	347c
2702	347c
2703	347c
	745d
2704	347c
	745d
2705	347c
2706	348d
	349b
	350c
2707	348d
2708	349a
	349d
2709	349a
2710	349a
2711	349b
2712	301a
	350c
2713	350c
2714	350d
2715	301c
	351a
	359d
2716	351a
	844b
2717	351a
	351c
	352b
	1093d
2718	1093d
2719	352b
2720	351b
	351d
2721	351b
	351c
2722	352a
2723	352a
2724	351c
2725	351c
2726	353a
2727	353a
2728	353b
2729	353b
2730	353d
2731	353d
2732	354a
2733	248b
	353d
2734	354a
2735	151d
	301b
	351a
2736	354c
	354d
2737	354d
2738	355b
2739	354d
2740	354c
2741	358b
2742	358c
	358d
	359a
2743	358d
2744	354d
	359c
2745	354d
2746	354d
	359c
2747	354d
2748	355a
	1093d
2749	1093d
2750	354c
2751	301a
	355a
2752	355b
	360a
2753	355b
	360a
2754	355a
2755	351a
	355b
2756	358b
2757	358d
2758	361a
2759	362a
2760	355b
2761	1093d
2762	355b
2763	355c
	356d
2764	356a
	357a
2765	356c
2766	356c
2767	356c
2768	356d
2769	356d
2770	357a
2771	357a
	357b
2772	357b
2773	357b
2774	357b
2775	357b
	357c
	360b
2776	357c
	751c
2777	357c
	360b
2778	357c
	358b
2779	358a

Strong's #	BDB p.	Strong's #	BDB p.	Strong's #	BDB p.	Strong's #	BDB p.	Strong's #	BDB p.
2780	358b	2816	1094a	2851	369d		779c	2922	378b
2781	357d	2817	362d	2852	367b	2891	372a	2923	378a
2782	358c	2818	1093d	2853	367c	2892	372d		378b
2783	1093d	2819	1093d	2854	367c	2893	372d	2924	378b
2784	359a	2820	362a	2855	367c	2894	370a	2925	376d
2785	359a	2821	364d	2856	367c	2895	373b	2926	378d
	359b	2822	365a		1094a		405c		1094b
2786	359b		1094a	2857	1094a		1094a	2927	1094b
2787	359b	2823	365b	2858	368b	2896	373c	2928	378d
2788	359c	2824	365b	2859	368c		375a	2929	379a
2789	360a	2825	365b		368d		375c	2930	379a
2790	360b	2826	365b	2860	368c		1094b		380a
	361a	2827	1094a	2861	368d	2897	376a	2931	379d
2791	361c	2828	365c	2862	368d	2898	375c	2932	380a
	361d	2829	365c	2863	369a	2899	375b	2933	380b
2792	361d	2830	365c	2864	369a	2900	375d	2934	380b
2793	361c	2831	365c	2865	369a	2901	376a	2935	380d
2794	360c	2832	365c	2866	369c	2902	376b	2936	380d
2795	361b	2833	365d	2867	369d		377c	2937	380d
2796	360d	2834	362c	2868	1094a	2903	376c	2938	380d
	361d		362d	2869	1094b		377d		1094b
2797	361d	2835	362c	2870	370b	2904	376c	2939	1094b
2798	161b	2836	365d	2871	371b	2905	377a	2940	381a
	360d		366b	2872	371d	2906	1094b		1094c
	361d	2837	366a	2873	370b	2907	377b	2941	1094c
2799	360d	2838	366a	2874	370d	2908	1094b	2942	1094c
2800	360d	2839	366b	2875	370d	2909	377b		1096a
	361d	2840	366b	2876	371a	2910	376b	2943	381b
2801	362a	2841	366b		1094b	2911	377c	2944	381b
2802	362a	2842	366b	2877	1094b	2912	377c	2945	381b
2803	362d	2843	302a	2878	370d	2913	377d		381d
	1093d		366c	2879	367b	2914	377d	2946	381b
2804	1093d	2844	366c		371a	2915	376b	2947	381c
2805	363d		369c	2880	371a		378a	2948	381c
2806	364c	2845	366c	2881	371a	2916	376c	2949	381c
2807	363d		370c	2882	371b		378a	2950	381c
2808	363d	2846	367a	2883	371c	2917	1094b	2951	381d
2809	363d	2847	366c	2884	371d	2918	377a	2952	381d
2810	364a		367b	2885	371c		378a	2953	1094c
2811	364a		369d	2886	372a	2919	378a	2954	382a
2812	364b	2848	367c	2887	372a		378b		936a
2813	364b	2849	369d	2888	372a		1094b	2955	382a
2814	364c	2850	366c	2889	373a	2920	1094b	2956	382a
2815	363d		370c	2890	373a	2921	378a		1094c

Strong's #	BDB p.	Strong's #	BDB p.	Strong's #	BDB p.	Strong's #	BDB p.	Strong's #	BDB p.
2957	1094c	2989	385b	3020	163d	3051	210c		397d
2958	382c	2990	385c		387c		396c		408a
2959	382b		386a	3021	388a		1095b	3082	220d
2960	382b	2991	385d	3022	388b	3052	1095b	3083	220d
2961	382b	2992	386a	3023	388b	3053	396d	3084	415c
2962	382c	2993	386a	3024	388b	3054	397a	3085	221a
2963	382d	2994	386a	3025	388c		397c	3086	221a
2964	383a	2995	125c	3026	1094d	3055	397a	3087	221b
2965	383a		386b	3027	388d	3056	213a	3088	221b
2966	383c	2996	125c		406d		397a	3089	221b
2967	1094c		386b		1094d	3057	397c		989d
2968	383b	2997	125c	3028	1094d	3058	219c	3090	221b
2969	383b		386b	3029	1095a		397a		221c
2970	24d	2998	125d	3030	391d	3059	219d	3091	221c
	383b		386b	3031	185c	3060	219d		448a
2971	22c	2999	132d		391d	3061	1095c	3092	221d
	383b		386b	3032	391d	3062	1095c	3093	397d
2972	22c	3000	140a	3033	392a	3063	397a	3094	239c
	383b		386b	3034	392a		1095c		397d
2973	383b	3001	386b		1095a	3064	397c	3095	240d
2974	383d	3002	386d	3035	392a		1095c		397d
2975	383b	3003	386d	3036	193d	3065	397c	3096	397d
	384b	3004	387a	3037	396a	3066	397c	3097	222a
	456c	3005	142a	3038	393a	3067	397c		398a
2976	384c		386b		393b	3068	217d	3098	222a
2977	78c	3006	387a	3039	391d		397a	3099	219d
	384c		1094d	3040	392a		397d		222a
2978	36b	3007	1094d	3041	392a		398a	3100	222a
	87c	3008	145d		393a	3069	217d	3101	219d
2979	384d		387a	3042	393a		397d		222b
2980	384d	3009	387a	3043	393a	3070	907d	3102	398a
2981	385b	3010	387a		396a	3071	651d	3103	384d
2982	101a	3011	147b	3044	393b	3072	842a		398a
	384d		387a	3045	393b	3073	1023a	3104	385c
2983	101a	3012	153d		1095a	3074	1027c		398a
	384d		387a	3046	1095a	3075	220a	3105	385b
2984	104c	3013	387a	3047	395b	3076	220b		398a
	384d	3014	387c	3048	396a	3077	220b	3106	385b
2985	108a	3015	387b	3049	396b	3078	220c	3107	220a
	384d	3016	388d	3050	219c		408a		222b
2986	384d	3017	158c		238a		487c	3108	222b
	1094d		387c		238b	3079	220c	3109	398a
2987	1094d	3018	388c		239c	3080	220d	3110	220b
2988	385a	3019	388c		396c	3081	220d		222b

Strong's #	BDB p.
3111	220b
	222b
3112	220c
	222c
3113	220c
	222c
3114	220d
	222c
3115	222c
3116	220d
	222c
	398a
3117	398a
	1095c
3118	1095c
3119	401b
3120	75a
	402a
3121	401c
3122	220d
	222c
3123	351a
	401d
3124	402a
3125	402b
3126	413c
3127	413c
3128	401d
3129	220d
	222c
3130	402b
	415c
3131	402b
	415d
3132	402b
	418d
3133	222c
3134	222c
3135	222c
3136	221b
	222c
	1095c
3137	220c
	222d

Strong's #	BDB p.
3138	435c
3139	402b
	435c
3140	436c
3141	221b
	222d
3142	402b
	1000b
3143	444a
3144	402b
	444d
3145	402b
	444d
3146	221d
	222d
3147	222d
3148	452c
3149	402b
3150	402c
	633c
3151	265c
	402c
3152	272c
	402c
3153	24d
	402c
3154	402c
3155	280d
	402c
3156	280d
	402c
3157	283b
	402c
3158	283c
3159	283c
3160	285d
	286a
	402c
3161	402d
3162	403a
	403b
3163	403c
3164	292d
	403d

Strong's #	BDB p.
3165	292d
3166	303c
	403d
3167	303c
	403d
3168	306b
	403d
3169	306a
	306b
	403d
3170	306c
	403d
3171	295d
	313c
	403d
3172	313d
	403d
3173	402d
3174	313d
	403d
3175	404a
3176	403d
3177	404b
3178	404b
3179	404b
	1095c
3180	331c
	405a
3181	327d
	405a
3182	405a
3183	345d
	405a
3184	345d
	405a
3185	345d
	405a
3186	405b
3187	405b
3188	405b
3189	367a
	405c
3190	405c
3191	1095d

Strong's #	BDB p.
3192	406a
3193	406a
3194	398a
	406b
	641a
3195	377b
	406b
	452d
3196	406b
3197	406d
3198	406d
3199	467c
	937b
3200	467c
3201	407b
	1095d
3202	1095d
	1096d
3203	408a
3204	220c
	408a
	467c
	487c
3205	408a
	529a
3206	409b
3207	409c
3208	409c
3209	409c
3210	1124c
3211	409c
3212	229d
3213	410a
3214	410b
3215	410b
3216	410c
	534b
3217	410c
3218	410c
3219	410c
	545a
3220	410d
	1095d
3221	1095d

Strong's #	BDB p.
3222	411b
3223	410c
3224	410d
3225	411c
3226	412c
3227	412a
3228	412b
	412c
3229	410d
	571c
3230	576a
3231	412b
3232	412c
3233	412b
3234	413a
	586b
3235	413a
3236	413a
	598c
3237	413a
3238	402a
	413a
3239	413b
	629c
3240	628d
3241	413b
	630b
3242	413c
3243	413b
	568c
	586b
3244	413d
	676a
3245	413d
3246	414b
3247	414b
3248	414b
3249	693c
3250	416b
3251	414c
3252	414c
3253	414d
	702b
3254	414d

Strong's #	BDB p.
	1095d
3255	1095d
3256	415d
	978d
	979a
3257	416d
	418b
3258	416d
	716d
3259	416d
3260	418a
	723b
3261	418a
3262	418b
3263	418b
	734b
3264	418b
	420c
3265	418b
	418c
	735d
3266	418b
	736b
3267	418b
3268	418c
	739c
	739d
3269	418c
	739d
3270	418c
	741b
3271	418c
3272	1095d
	1096a
3273	418b
3274	418c
	736b
3275	418c
	747c
3276	418c
3277	418d
3278	418d
3279	419a
3280	418d

Strong's #	BDB p.
3281	419a
	761c
3282	419a
	774c
3283	419a
	943d
3284	419a
3285	419b
3286	419b
3287	419b
3288	419b
3289	419c
	1095d
3290	420b
	784d
3291	420b
	785b
3292	420c
	785c
3293	420c
	421a
3294	421a
3295	421a
3296	421a
3297	421b
3298	421b
	793b
3299	421b
	795c
3300	421b
	795c
3301	421b
3302	421b
3303	421c
3304	421d
3305	421d
3306	422a
3307	422a
3308	421d
3309	422b
3310	422a
	812d
3311	812d
3312	422a

Strong's #	BDB p.
	819c
3313	422a
3314	422b
3315	422b
	834d
3316	422b
	836b
3317	422b
	836b
3318	422b
	1115a
3319	1096a
	1115a
3320	426a
3321	1096a
3322	426c
3323	426d
	844a
3324	844b
3325	844b
3326	426d
	427a
3327	426d
	850c
3328	426d
	850d
3329	425c
3330	1096a
3331	426d
3332	427a
3333	427c
3334	864c
3335	427c
	849b
3336	428a
3337	428a
3338	428b
3339	428b
3240	428a
3341	428b
	850a
3342	428c
3343	428c
	868b

Strong's #	BDB p.
3344	428d
	1096a
3345	1096a
3346	1096a
3347	429a
3348	429a
3349	429b
3350	428d
3351	429b
	879c
3352	430c
3353	430c
3354	429a
	429b
3355	429b
3356	879c
3357	430b
3358	1096a
3359	429b
	880c
3360	429b
	880c
3361	429b
	880c
3362	429b
3363	429b
3364	429c
3365	429b
	429c
3366	430b
	1096a
3367	1096a
3368	429d
	891b
	903b
3369	430b
3370	430d
3371	430d
3372	431a
	1108c
3373	431a
	431d
3374	432a
3375	432a

Strong's #	BDB p.
3376	432c
	909d
3377	432c
	937a
3378	432c
	937c
3379	432c
	914c
	937c
3380	432c
	937c
3381	432c
3382	434b
3383	434c
3384	432b
	434d
3385	436c
3386	437b
3387	438d
3388	440b
3389	436c
	1096b
3390	1096b
3391	437b
	1096b
3392	437b
3393	1096b
3394	437a
3395	437b
	934a
3396	437b
	934a
3397	934a
3398	437c
3399	437c
	936a
3400	436c
3401	937a
3402	937b
3403	937a
	937b
3404	436c
3405	437b
	437c

Strong's #	BDB p.	Strong's #	BDB p.	Strong's #	BDB p.	Strong's #	BDB p.	Strong's #	BDB p.
	746d	3437	445a	3464	445d	3497	451a	3537	461c
3406	438b		445b	3465	445d	3498	451a	3538	1096c
	928c		1000a	3466	446a		1096c	3539	461d
3407	438c	3438	445a	3467	223c	3499	451d	3540	462a
3408	438c		1001a		446b		452a	3541	462a
3409	437d	3439	445a	3468	447a	3500	452b		1096d
	1096b		1001d	3469	447d	3501	452b	3542	1096d
3410	1096b		1006a	3470	447d	3502	452b	3543	462c
3411	438a	3440	445a	3471	448c	3503	452b		462d
3412	438b		1001a	3472	448c	3504	452c	3544	462d
3413	438b	3441	445a		1046a	3505	452b	3545	462d
3414	438c		1001a	3473	448c	3506	452d	3546	1096d
	941c	3442	221c		1051a	3507	453c	3547	464c
3415	438c		222d	3474	448c	3508	452c	3548	463a
3416	438c		445a	3475	448c	3509	453c		1096d
	951b		448a		449c	3510	456a	3549	1096d
3417	439a		1096b	3476	448c	3511	456b	3550	464d
	956d	3443	1096b		449c	3512	456c	3551	1096d
3418	438d	3444	447b	3477	449a	3513	457a	3552	464d
3419	438d	3445	445a	3478	441a	3514	458c	3553	464d
3420	439a	3446	850c		975b	3515	458a	3554	464d
3421	439a		966a		1096b		1096b	3555	465a
3422	439a	3447	445a	3479	1096b	3516	458b	3556	456d
3423	439a	3448	36b	3480	441a	3517	459c		465a
3424	440b		445a	3481	976a	3518	459c	3557	465a
3425	440b	3449	445b	3482	976a	3519	458c		480d
3426	441b		674d	3483	449c	3520	458c	3558	484d
	930d	3450	964d	3484	449c		459c	3559	465c
	1080a	3451	445b	3485	441a	3521	459d	3560	467b
3427	442a	3452	445b		969b	3522	460a	3561	467d
	1096b	3453	450a	3486	450a	3523	460d	3562	467b
3428	444a	3454	450b	3487	1096b	3524	460b		487d
3429	444a	3455	441a	3488	1096b	3525	459d	3563	468a
3430	444a	3456	445b	3489	450b	3526	460a	3564	468b
3431	444c	3457	445c	3490	450c	3527	460b	3565	468b
	986d	3458	445c	3491	1064b	3528	460c	3566	468d
3432	444c		1035d		1064d	3529	460c		503c
	1000b	3459	1035d	3492	452d	3530	460c		1096d
3433	1000b	3460	1036a	3493	1096c	3531	460d	3567	1096d
3434	444c	3461	445c	3494	450c	3532	461a	3568	468d
	1000b		1038b		1068b	3533	461b		469a
3435	444c	3462	445c	3495	450d	3534	461c	3569	469a
	990b		1096b	3496	451a	3535	461a	3570	469b
3436	444a	3463	445d		1072a	3536	461c		505b

Strong's #	BDB p.
3571	469a
3572	469b
3573	469b
	958a
3574	469b
	507a
3575	469b
3576	469b
	1096c
3577	469c
3578	469d
3579	469d
3580	469d
3581	470a
	470b
	470c
3582	470b
3583	471a
	806d
3584	471a
3585	471c
3586	471c
3587	465a
	475d
3588	210b
	465a
	471c
	474c
	475c
	758b
	774c
	774d
	1099a
3589	475d
3590	461d
	475d
3591	475d
3592	475d
	647a
3593	461d
	475d
3594	475d
3595	468c
	476a

Strong's #	BDB p.
3596	476a
	647d
3597	476a
3598	465b
	476a
3599	476a
3600	468c
	476a
3601	476a
	507a
3602	462b
	476b
3603	476b
	503a
	1098a
3604	1096d
	1098a
3605	481a
	1097a
3606	1096d
	1097a
3607	476b
	478a
3608	476c
3609	476d
3610	476c
3611	476d
3612	477a
3613	68d
3614	477a
3615	477b
3616	479a
3617	478d
3618	480c
	483c
3619	477b
3620	477b
3621	477b
3622	479a
3623	480c
	483c
3624	480c
3625	480d
3626	480d

Strong's #	BDB p.
3627	479b
	480d
3628	476c
3629	480b
	480d
3630	479a
3631	479a
	480d
3632	483a
3633	465b
	480d
3634	480d
	1097a
3635	1097a
	1115b
3636	483c
3637	483c
3638	484b
3639	484a
3640	484b
3641	484c
3642	484c
3643	158c
	484c
	484d
3644	455d
	484d
3645	484d
3646	485a
3647	485a
3648	485a
3649	485c
3650	485b
3651	467a
	467b
	475c
	485d
	487b
	540c
	1097b
3652	1097b
3653	467b
	487b
	487c

Strong's #	BDB p.
3654	467b
	487b
	487c
	487d
3655	487b
3656	487c
3657	487c
	488a
3658	490a
3659	220c
3660	1097b
3661	488a
3662	487d
3663	487d
3664	488a
	1097b
3665	488b
3666	488c
3667	488c
	488d
3668	489b
3669	489a
	489b
3670	489d
3671	489b
3672	490b
3673	1097b
3674	487c
	490c
3675	1097c
3676	490c
	490d
3677	490c
	492c
3678	490c
	492c
	1097c
3679	505a
3680	491b
3681	492b
	492d
3682	492b
	492d
3683	492d

Strong's #	BDB p.
3684	493a
3685	493a
3686	493b
3687	493a
3688	492d
3689	492d
3690	493a
3691	493b
3692	493b
3693	493b
3694	493b
	1061d
3695	493b
3696	493b
	493c
3697	493c
3698	493c
3699	493c
3700	493d
3701	494a
3702	1097c
3703	494d
3704	492c
	494d
3705	1097c
	1107b
3706	1097c
	1107b
	1107c
	1108a
3707	494d
3708	495b
3709	495b
	496a
3710	495b
3711	495c
3712	495c
	497a
3713	499b
3714	496a
3715	498d
3716	499a
3717	495c
3718	495c

Strong's #	BDB p.	Strong's #	BDB p.	Strong's #	BDB p.	Strong's #	BDB p.	Strong's #	BDB p.
3719	495d	3751	501c	3787	506d	3818	520d	3850	528d
3720	495d	3752	501c	3788	507a	3819	520d	3851	529a
3721	496a	3753	501c	3789	507a		933d	3852	529b
3722	497b		503a		1098a	3820	522c	3853	529c
	498d	3754	501c	3790	1098a		523a	3854	529c
3723	499a	3755	501d	3791	508b		524b	3855	529c
3724	497a	3756	501d	3792	1098a		525d	3856	529c
	498d	3757	502a	3793	508b		925c	3857	529c
	499a	3758	502b	3794	508c		1098d	3858	529d
3725	498c	3759	502a	3795	508c	3821	1098d		532a
3726	499a	3760	502a		510c	3822	522d	3859	529d
3727	498c	3761	502b	3796	508c	3823	525d	3860	242a
3728	499b	3762	502b		1098b	3824	523a		243b
3729	1097c	3763	502b	3797	1098b		925a		530a
3730	499b	3764	1097c	3798	508c		1098d		1099a
3731	499c		1098a	3799	508d	3825	1098d	3861	242a
3732	499c	3765	493c	3800	508d	3826	525d		530a
3733	468b		502b	3801	509a	3827	529b		1090d
	499c	3766	502c	3802	509b	3828	526c		1099a
	503a	3767	502d	3803	509c	3829	526d	3862	530a
3734	499d	3768	502d	3804	509d	3830	528c	3863	520d
	1096d	3769	502d	3805	509d		1098d		530a
3735	1097d		1098a	3806	509d	3831	1098d	3864	526a
3736	499d	3770	503c	3807	510a	3832	526a		530c
	1097d	3771	503c	3808	210b	3833	522d	3865	530d
3737	1097d	3772	503c		518b		526a	3866	530d
3738	456c	3773	503c		529a	3834	525d	3867	530d
	468c	3774	504d		530a	3835	526a		531a
	500a	3775	461a		1098c		527c	3868	531b
3739	500b		505a		1099a	3836	526b	3869	531c
3740	500c	3776	461b	3809	1098c	3837	526c	3870	531c
3741	500b		505a		1098d	3838	526c	3871	531d
	504d	3777	505a		1099a	3839	527b	3872	229d
3742	500c	3778	505a	3810	520d	3840	527c		532a
3743	500c		1098a		529a	3841	526c		751c
3744	1097d	3779	1097c		530d	3842	526b	3873	538a
3745	1097d		1098a	3811	521a	3843	527b	3874	529d
3746	501b	3780	505b	3812	521b	3844	526d		532a
3747	501b	3781	506a	3813	521b	3845	526d	3875	532b
	504d	3782	505b	3814	521b	3846	526d	3876	532b
3748	501b	3783	506a		532a	3847	527d	3877	532b
	504d	3784	506c	3815	522b		1098d	3878	532b
3749	501b	3785	506c	3816	522c	3848	1098d		1099a
3750	501b	3786	506c	3817	522c	3849	528d	3879	1099a

Strong's #	BDB p.	Strong's #	BDB p.	Strong's #	BDB p.	Strong's #	BDB p.	Strong's #	BDB p.
3880	531a	3909	532a	3943	542b		549a	4001	101b
3881	532d		538b	3944	539c		1079b		550a
3882	531b	3910	538b	3945	539b	3977	1079b	4002	550a
3883	533b	3911	538b		539c		1099b		616a
3884	530b	3912	538c	3946	542c	3978	38b	4003	101c
	533b	3913	538b	3947	542c		549a	4004	104d
	533c	3914	531b		881c	3979	38b		550b
3885	533c		538c	3948	544b		549a	4005	104d
	534a	3915	538c	3949	544b	3980	38c	4006	104d
	539b		1099b	3950	544c		549a	4007	550b
3886	534b	3916	1099b	3951	545a	3981	55c		613d
	541d	3917	539b	3952	545a		549a	4008	105a
	542a	3918	539d	3953	545c	3982	57d		550b
3887	534c	3919	534c	3954	545b		549a	4009	105c
	539b		539d	3955	545c	3983	1081b		550b
	542c	3920	539d	3956	546a		1099b	4010	114d
3888	534c	3921	540b		1099b	3984	1099c		550b
3889	534c	3922	540b	3957	545c	3985	549a	4011	125d
	539d	3923	540b	3958	545d	3986	549b		550b
3890	1099a	3924	533b	3959	546a	3987	549b	4012	125d
3891	531c		540c	3960	546d	3988	549b		550b
	534c	3925	540c	3961	1099b		549d	4013	131b
3892	534c	3926	518b	3962	546d		588a		550b
	535a		530c	3963	547c	3989	66b	4014	550b
3893	535a		541a	3964	1099b		549d	4015	138b
3894	535d	3927	541a		1099c	3990	66d		550b
3895	534c	3928	541a	3965	7b		549d	4016	102b
	535a	3929	541a		547a	3991	66d		550b
3896	534d	3930	534b	3966	547a	3992	549d	4017	142a
	535a		541b	3967	547c	3993	70d		550b
3897	535a	3931	541b		549a		550a	4018	143b
3898	535b	3932	541b		1099b	3994	76d		550b
	536d	3933	541c	3968	548c		550a	4019	150d
3899	536d	3934	541d	3969	1099b	3995	95d		550b
	1099a	3935	541d	3970	16c		550a	4020	148b
3900	1099a	3936	541d		548c	3996	99d		550b
3901	535d	3937	541d	3971	548c		550a	4021	149b
3902	537c	3938	542a		558a	3997	99d		550b
3903	537c	3939	542a	3972	548d	3998	100c	4022	550c
3904	1099b	3940	542a	3973	549d		550a	4023	151d
3905	537d	3941	542b	3974	22c	3999	550a		550c
3906	537d	3942	542b		549a	4000	107a	4024	154a
3907	538a		816d	3975	22d		108a	4025	550c
3908	538a		819b	3976	24d		550a	4026	153d

Strong's #	BDB p.	Strong's #	BDB p.	Strong's #	BDB p.	Strong's #	BDB p.	Strong's #	BDB p.
	550c	4050	176b		552b	4095	201c	4116	554d
	955c		551a	4072	191a		552b		555a
4027	154a	4051	550d		551d	4096	204a	4117	555c
4028	154a	4052	175d	4073	191b		258a	4118	555a
4029	154a		551a		551d		552b	4119	555c
4030	550c	4053	175d	4074	552a	4097	205d	4120	555b
4031	156a		551a		1099c		552b	4121	555b
	550c	4054	177b	4075	552a	4098	190c	4122	555b
	550d		551a		1099c		552b	4123	555c
4032	159a	4055	551a	4076	1099c	4099	241a	4124	547a
	550d		551b	4077	1099c	4100	484d		555d
4033	158c	4056	1087a	4078	552a		541a	4125	555d
4034	159a		1099c		553b		547a	4126	100a
	550d	4057	184c	4079	193b		552a		556a
4035	158c		184d		552a		552b	4127	556a
	550d		551a	4080	193c		980a	4128	551b
4036	159a	4058	551a		552a		1099d		556d
	687a	4059	551a	4081	551d	4101	1099b	4129	396b
4037	160d	4060	193c	4082	193d		1099c		552a
	550d		551c		552a	4102	554c		556d
4038	409d		551d		1088c	4103	223b		568a
	550d		1101b	4083	1088c	4104	54d	4130	396b
	618c	4061	1099c	4084	193c		554c		552a
4039	166b		1101b		552a	4105	406b	4131	556d
	550d	4062	551d	4085	189a		554c	4132	557a
	1086c		923c		552a	4106	554c	4133	557b
4040	1086c	4063	551d	4086	199b		555b	4134	557b
	1099c	4064	188c		552a	4107	554c	4135	557d
4041	169d		551d	4087	199b	4108	237b	4136	541a
4042	171c	4065	551d		552a	4109	237b		556a
	689b		623b	4088	199b		554c		557b
	698c	4066	193b		552a	4110	239c	4137	409d
4043	171b		551d	4089	199b		554d		558a
	550d		552a		552a	4111	239d	4138	558a
4044	171c	4067	193c	4090	193b		554d	4139	558a
	550d		551c		552a	4112	240d	4140	410a
4045	172a		551d	4091	193c		554d		558a
	550d	4068	193c		552a	4113	243b	4141	558a
4046	550d	4069	396c	4092	193c		554d		687c
	620a		551d	4093	396b	4114	245c	4142	686d
4047	550d	4070	1087b		552a		246b	4143	414b
4048	550d		1099c		1095b		554d		558a
	1099c	4071	190b	4094	201b	4115	246b	4144	414c
4049	1099c		551d		552a		554d		558a

Strong's #	BDB p.
4145	414c
	558a
4146	414c
4147	64c
	558a
4148	416b
	558a
4149	64c
	588b
4150	417b
	558a
	588d
4151	418a
	558a
4152	418a
	558a
4153	558b
	588c
4154	588c
4155	558b
	734a
4156	420b
	558b
	591d
4157	558b
	734c
4158	422b
	558b
	568c
	592b
4159	68d
	558b
4160	568c
	592b
4161	425c
	558b
	594b
4162	426a
	558b
	594b
4163	426a
	558b
4164	558b
	848a

Strong's #	BDB p.
4165	427c
	558b
	848a
4166	427c
	558b
	595b
4167	558b
4168	428d
	558c
4169	429a
	558c
4170	430c
	558c
4171	558c
4172	432a
	432b
	558d
	559a
	597b
4173	558d
4174	434b
	559a
4175	435a
	435c
	598c
4176	435d
	598c
4177	559a
4178	599a
4179	599a
4180	440c
	559a
4181	440c
	559a
4182	440c
	559a
4183	440d
	559a
	601c
4184	559b
4185	559a
	568c
4186	444b
	559b

Strong's #	BDB p.
4187	559b
	603d
4188	559b
4189	604d
4190	448a
	559b
4191	559b
	607a
	1099d
4192	527c
	761b
	761c
	763a
4193	1099d
4194	560c
4195	560d
4196	560d
4197	561a
4198	561a
4199	561a
4200	265a
	561a
4201	265b
	561a
4202	266a
	561a
4203	1091b
	1099d
4204	561a
	561c
4205	267a
	561a
4206	561a
	561b
4207	272c
	561b
4208	561b
4209	273c
	561b
4210	274c
	561b
4211	275a
	561c
4212	275a

Strong's #	BDB p.
	561c
4213	277d
	561c
4214	280a
	561d
4215	280a
4216	561d
4217	280d
	561d
4218	283c
	561d
4219	284c
	561d
4220	561d
	562d
	568a
4221	561d
	562d
4222	561d
4223	1099d
4224	285c
	561d
4225	289c
	561d
4226	289c
4227	290a
	561d
4228	292b
	561d
4229	562a
	562b
	562c
	562d
	1099d
4230	295b
	562c
4231	562c
4232	562c
	563a
4233	296a
	562d
4234	298b
	562d
4235	562d

Strong's #	BDB p.
4236	303c
	562d
4237	303d
	562d
4238	303d
	562d
4239	562c
	562d
4240	563a
4241	313c
	563a
4242	564b
4243	564b
4244	563a
4245	318b
	563a
4246	298b
	562d
	563a
	563b
4247	320a
	563a
4248	563a
4249	563a
4250	563a
4251	318c
	563a
4252	322c
	563b
4253	322c
	563b
4254	323a
	563b
4255	1093b
	1099d
4256	324d
	563b
	1093b
4257	318d
	563b
4258	563b
4259	563b
4260	563b
4261	326d

Strong's #	BDB p.
	563b
4262	327a
	563b
4263	328c
	563c
4264	334a
	563c
4265	334b
	563c
4266	334b
	563c
4267	338b
	563c
4268	340b
	563c
4269	340d
	563c
4270	341d
	563c
4271	340c
	563c
4272	563c
4273	563d
4274	345b
	563d
4275	345d
	563d
4276	345d
	563d
4277	563d
4278	350d
	563d
4279	563d
4280	351a
	564c
4281	361a
	564c
4282	361a
	564c
4283	564a
	564c
4284	364b
	564c
4285	365b
	564c
4286	362d
	564c
4287	367b
	564c
4288	369d
	564c
4289	367b
	564c
4290	369a
	564c
4291	1100a
4292	370a
	564c
4293	371a
	564c
4294	564c
	641c
4295	564c
	641b
4296	564c
	641d
4297	642a
4298	564c
	642a
4299	376a
	564c
4300	564c
4301	380c
	564c
4302	564c
	642d
4303	381b
	564d
4304	381c
	564d
4305	565a
4306	564d
4307	565a
	643c
4308	382b
4309	565a
4310	566a
	1100d
4311	567d
4312	392a
	568a
4313	438d
	566a
4314	566a
4315	406b
	568a
4316	567d
	568a
4317	567c
	568a
4318	567d
	568a
4319	567c
4320	567c
	568a
4321	567c
	568a
4322	567c
4323	568a
4324	568a
4325	555d
	565a
	568a
4326	568a
4327	558a
	568b
4328	414c
4329	558a
	568c
	697b
4330	568c
4331	568c
4332	567d
	568c
	1100a
4333	1100a
4334	449d
4335	568d
	1100a
4336	1100a
4337	448a
	568d
4338	448a
	568d
4339	449d
	606d
4340	452d
	568d
4341	456b
	568d
4342	460b
	568d
4343	460a
	568d
4344	460a
4345	460d
	568d
4346	460d
	568d
4347	568d
	646d
4348	465a
	568d
4349	467c
	467d
	568d
4350	467d
	568d
	569a
4351	468d
	568d
	569d
4352	568d
4353	569c
4354	569c
4355	568d
4356	476c
	479a
	569a
4357	476c
	479a
	569a
4358	483b
	569a
4359	483b
	569a
4360	483b
	569a
4361	38c
	569a
4362	485a
	569a
4363	485a
	569a
4364	485b
	485c
	569a
4365	485c
	569a
4366	485c
	569a
4367	569a
4368	569a
4369	467d
4370	488b
	569a
4371	493d
	569a
4372	492c
	569a
4373	493d
	569a
4374	492c
	569a
4375	495d
	569a
4376	569a
4377	569c
4378	569d
	648c
4379	500b
	569d
4380	468d
	569d
4381	569d
4382	569d
4383	506a
	569d
4384	506b
	569d

Strong's #	BDB p.	Strong's #	BDB p.	Strong's #	BDB p.	Strong's #	BDB p.	Strong's #	BDB p.
4385	508b	4411	533d	4437	1100b	4466	569d		1101b
	569d		571d	4438	574d		577a	4488	584b
4386	510c	4412	534a	4439	575c	4467	575a	4489	584c
	569d		571d	4440	575c		577a	4490	584b
4387	508d	4413	571d	4441	575c	4468	575c	4491	584d
	569d		576c	4442	575d	4469	577a		624c
4388	509d		1100a	4443	575d		587c	4492	584d
	569d	4414	571d	4444	575d	4470	577a		626a
4389	509d		572a	4445	575d		601b	4493	584d
	569d		1100b	4446	573d	4471	577b		627b
4390	569d	4415	1090b	4447	574c	4472	577a	4494	584d
	1100a		1100b	4448	576a		601b		629c
4391	1100a	4416	1100a		576c	4473	577b	4495	584d
4392	570d	4417	571d		1100c		603d		629d
4393	571a		1100a	4449	1100c	4474	577b	4496	584d
	571d	4418	571d	4450	576c		606a		629d
4394	571b	4419	572a	4451	541a	4475	577b	4497	584d
4395	571b	4420	572a		576d		606a	4498	631a
4396	571b	4421	536a	4452	576d	4476	577b	4499	586a
4397	521c		572b	4453	576d		606c		631a
	571c	4422	572b	4454	577a	4477	577b	4500	644d
	1098d	4423	572d	4455	544b		609a	4501	586b
4398	1098d	4424	572d		544c	4478	577b		633a
	1100a	4425	576c		577a		577c	4502	634d
4399	521d	4426	539c	4456	545b	4479	1100d	4503	585a
	571c		572d		577a	4480	541b		1101c
4400	522b	4427	573d	4457	544c		547a	4504	1101c
	571c		576a		577a		577a	4505	637c
4401	522b		1100b	4458	547a		577c	4506	630a
	571c		1100c		577a		585d	4507	584c
4402	571c	4428	572d	4459	577a		606b	4508	585d
4403	528c		574c		1069a		1100d	4509	568a
	571c		575d	4460	158c	4481	1100d		585d
4404	527c	4429	573a		577a	4482	577c	4510	1101b
	571c		574b	4461	551d		585d		1101c
	576a		1100b		577a	4483	1101b	4511	585d
4405	571c	4430	1100b	4462	558a	4484	1101b	4512	585d
	576b	4431	1100c		577a		1108d		649b
4406	1100a	4432	574c	4463	560d		1118c	4513	586a
	1100c	4433	1100b		577a	4485	584a	4514	586b
4407	571c	4434	540b	4464	561c		618d		653b
4408	572a		576a		577a	4486	1095b	4515	586b
4409	576a	4435	574c	4465	569d		1101b		653b
4410	574c	4436	573c		577a	4487	584a	4516	586b

Strong's #	BDB p.	Strong's #	BDB p.	Strong's #	BDB p.	Strong's #	BDB p.	Strong's #	BDB p.
	654b		697a	4561	416b	4583	589b		752a
4517	586b	4540	587c		416d		732d	4610	751c
	631c		697b		558a	4584	589b		785d
4518	586b	4541	587c		588b		733a	4611	591d
	667d		651a	4562	64b	4585	589b		760b
4519	586b		651b		588b		591d	4612	591d
4520	586d	4542	587c	4563	588b		733a		765b
4521	584a	4543	587d		712c	4586	589b	4613	591d
	584c		698b	4564	588b		590c		765c
	585d	4544	587d		712c	4587	589b	4614	591d
	586d		698c	4565	588b		733b		770c
4522	586d	4545	587c		712c	4588	589b	4615	591d
4523	587a		651c	4566	588b		734a		771b
	588a	4546	587d		716a	4589	589b	4616	541b
4524	587a		700c		1105a		735d		591d
	686d	4547	587d	4567	1101c	4590	589b		775a
	687b		700c		1105a	4591	589b	4617	591d
4525	587a	4548	587d	4568	588b	4592	589d		775a
	689d		601d		716b	4593	599a		775d
4526	587a		702c	4569	588c	4594	590c	4618	591d
	689d		971b		721b		742a		776a
4527	414c	4549	549d	4570	588c	4595	590c	4619	591d
	587b		587d		722d		742c	4620	591d
4528	587b	4550	588a	4571	588c	4596	590c		781a
	690c		652c	4572	588c		730d	4621	591d
4529	587b	4551	588a	4573	558b	4597	590c		781b
4530	587b		652d		588c	4598	591c	4622	591d
	588b	4552	588a	4574	588d	4599	590c		784a
4531	587b		703c		726d		745d	4623	591d
	588a	4553	588a	4575	588d	4600	590c		784a
	650b		704d		726d	4601	590d	4624	591d
4532	587b	4554	588a		772c		591a		785b
	650c		704c	4576	588d	4602	591a	4625	591d
4533	587b	4555	588a		727c	4603	591a		786a
	691d		705d	4577	1101c	4604	591b	4626	591d
4534	587b	4556	588a	4578	588d	4605	591d		789a
	692b		705c		590c		751c	4627	591d
4535	587b	4557	588a		1101c	4606	1101c		786d
	650c		708d	4579	589a		1106d	4628	591d
4536	587b	4558	588a	4580	589b	4607	591d		788a
	695c		709a		728b		751b	4629	591d
4537	587c	4559	588a	4581	589b	4608	591d		788b
4538	587c		709a		731d		751b		789a
4539	587c	4560	588a	4582	590d	4609	591d	4630	592a

Strong's #	BDB p.
	790b
4631	592a
	792c
4632	792c
4633	592a
	790a
4634	592a
	790a
4635	592a
	790b
4636	592a
	736a
	791a
4637	592a
	792b
4638	592a
	789b
4639	592a
	795c
4640	592a
	796b
4641	592a
	796b
4642	592a
	799a
4643	592a
	798b
4644	592a
4645	592a
	803c
4646	592a
	656a
4647	592a
	656b
4648	592b
	937c
4649	592b
4650	592b
	807b
4651	592b
	658c
4652	592b
	811a
4653	592b

Strong's #	BDB p.
	811b
4654	592b
	658c
4655	592b
	812d
4656	592b
	814a
4657	592b
	814a
4658	592b
	658c
4659	592b
	821d
4660	592b
	658d
4661	592b
	659a
4662	592b
	824c
4663	592b
	824c
4664	592b
	830a
4665	592b
	830b
4666	592b
	831c
4667	592b
	832c
4668	592b
	836b
4669	592b
	836b
4670	592b
	837b
4671	558b
	592b
4672	592c
4673	594b
	662d
4674	594b
	663a
4675	594b
	663a

Strong's #	BDB p.
4676	594b
	663a
4677	594b
4678	594b
	663a
4679	594c
	844d
	845a
4680	594c
4681	594c
4682	594c
	595a
4683	594c
	663c
4684	843d
4685	594c
	594d
	844d
	845a
4686	594c
	594d
	845a
4687	594d
	846b
4688	594d
	595a
	846d
4689	594d
	848a
4690	594d
	595b
	848b
4691	594d
	595b
	848a
4692	594d
	848d
4693	594d
	596a
	849a
4694	596a
	849a
4695	594d
	596b

Strong's #	BDB p.
	663c
4696	594d
4697	595a
4698	595a
	853a
4699	847a
4700	595a
	853a
4701	595a
	857b
4702	427a
	595a
4703	595a
	857d
4704	859a
4705	595a
	859b
4706	595a
	859b
4707	859d
4708	595a
	859d
4709	595a
	859d
4710	595a
	861b
4711	595a
4712	595b
	865c
4713	596a
4714	595c
4715	596b
	864c
4716	596b
	597a
4717	666a
4718	596b
	666c
4719	596b
4720	596b
	874a
4721	596b
	875b
4722	596b

Strong's #	BDB p.
	875b
4723	596b
	875c
	876a
	876c
4724	596b
	876c
4725	596b
	596c
	879d
4726	596b
	881b
4727	544c
4728	544c
4729	596b
	883b
4730	596b
	883b
4731	596b
4732	596c
4733	596c
	886a
4734	596c
	887c
4735	596d
	889b
4736	596d
	889b
4737	596d
	889c
4738	596d
	890d
4739	596d
4740	596d
	893a
4741	596d
	893a
4742	596d
	893b
4743	596d
4744	597a
	896d
4745	597a
	899d

Strong's #	BDB p.
4746	597a
	900a
4747	597a
	903b
4748	597a
	904d
4749	597a
	904d
4750	597a
	903d
	904d
4751	597a
	600c
4752	597a
	601c
4753	558d
	597a
	600d
4754	597a
	598a
4755	597a
	600c
4756	1101c
	1101d
4757	596b
	597b
	597d
4758	596b
	597b
	909c
4759	597b
	909b
	909c
4760	597b
4761	912b
4762	597b
	601c
	912b
4763	597b
	910c
	912a
	912b
4764	597b
4765	597b
	915a
4766	597c
	916a
4767	597c
	916b
4768	597c
	916b
4769	597c
	918c
4770	597c
	918d
4771	597c
	921b
4772	597c
	920b
4773	597c
	920c
4774	597c
	921c
4775	597c
4776	597c
	1101c
4777	597c
	597d
	1101c
4778	597d
4779	1101c
4780	597d
4781	597d
4782	598a
4783	598a
	922a
	923a
4784	597b
	598a
	598c
4785	598c
	600d
4786	598c
	601a
4787	598c
	601a
4788	598c
	924a
4789	72d
	598c
4790	598c
4791	598c
	928d
4792	598c
4793	598c
	930c
4794	598c
	599d
	930c
	954d
4795	598c
	599d
4796	598c
4797	931a
4798	598d
	931a
4799	598d
4800	598d
	932c
4801	598d
	935d
4802	598d
	935d
4803	590c
	598d
	1101d
4804	1101d
4805	598b
	599a
4806	597a
4807	565a
	599a
	937c
4808	599a
	937b
4809	599a
	937b
4810	599a
	937c
4811	599a
4812	599a
4813	599b
4814	599b
	601b
4815	599b
	601b
4816	599b
	940b
4817	599b
	939c
4818	599b
	939c
4819	940c
4820	599b
	941b
4821	599b
	941b
4822	599b
4823	599b
	942d
4824	599c
4825	599c
4826	599c
4827	949c
	949d
4828	599c
	946c
4829	599c
	945c
4830	945c
4831	599c
	947a
4832	599c
	951b
4833	599c
	952c
4834	599c
4835	598c
	599d
	930d
	954d
4836	599d
	954b
4837	599d
	954b
4838	599d
4839	600a
	601d
4840	600a
	955c
4841	600a
	955c
4842	600a
	955c
4843	600a
4844	601a
4845	601a
4846	601a
4847	601b
4848	601b
4849	601c
	958a
4850	601c
4851	602a
4852	602a
4853	601d
	672c
	672d
4854	601d
	672d
4855	600d
	601d
	602a
	673d
4856	601d
	673a
4857	602b
	980c
4858	601d
	673a
4859	602a
	673d
4860	602b
	674b
4861	602b
4862	602b
	982c
4863	602b
	985a
4864	601d

Strong's #	BDB p.
5462	688d
	689b
	698c
	1104a
5463	1104a
5464	690a
5465	690a
5466	690b
5467	690a
5468	690b
5469	690c
5470	690c
5471	690c
5472	690d
5473	691b
	960d
5474	689c
5475	691c
5476	691d
5477	691d
5478	492c
	691d
5479	691d
5480	414c
	691d
5481	1104a
	1104b
5482	692b
5483	692b
5484	692d
5485	692d
5486	692d
	1104b
5487	1104b
5488	693a
5489	693b
5490	693a
5491	1104b
5492	693a
	693b
5493	693b
	694c
	963a
	965a

Strong's #	BDB p.
5494	693b
	694c
5495	694c
5496	694c
5497	691d
	694d
5498	694d
5499	695a
5500	691d
	695a
5501	695a
5502	695a
5503	695b
5504	695c
5505	695c
5506	695c
5507	695c
5508	695c
5509	688c
	691a
5510	695d
5511	695d
5512	695d
5513	696b
5514	696a
5515	692b
	696b
5516	696b
5517	696b
5518	696c
5519	697c
5520	697c
5521	697c
5522	696d
5523	697d
5524	696d
5525	696d
5526	692a
	696d
	697b
	697d
	698c
	962b
	967d

Strong's #	BDB p.
	968a
5527	698a
5528	698a
5529	698a
5530	698a
5531	698a
	968d
5532	698b
5533	698b
	698c
5534	698c
5535	698d
5536	698d
	700d
5537	698d
5538	698d
5539	698d
5540	699a
5541	699a
5542	699a
	699d
5543	699a
	699b
5544	699b
5545	699b
5546	699c
5547	699c
5548	699c
5549	699c
5550	700c
5551	700c
5552	700d
5553	700d
5554	701a
5555	325d
	563b
5556	701b
5557	701b
5558	701b
5559	1104b
5560	701c
5561	701c
	702c
5562	701c

Strong's #	BDB p.
5563	701d
5564	701d
5565	702b
5566	702b
5567	651c
	702c
5568	702c
5569	702c
5570	702d
	703a
5571	702d
5572	702d
5573	702d
5574	703a
5575	703a
5576	703a
5577	703b
5578	703a
5579	703b
5580	703b
5581	703b
5582	703c
	1104b
5583	1104b
5584	703c
5585	703d
5586	703d
5587	704a
	972a
5588	704a
5589	703d
5590	704a
5591	704b
	973b
5592	704c
	706b
5593	704c
	706c
5594	704c
	973c
5595	705a
5596	705b
	705c
	974a

Strong's #	BDB p.
5597	705c
5598	705d
	706c
5599	705b
	705c
5600	706b
5601	705d
5602	705d
5603	706a
	974a
5604	706a
5605	706c
5606	706c
	974a
5607	706d
	974a
	974b
5608	707d
	708b
	1104c
5609	1104c
5610	708c
5611	708c
5612	706d
	707c
	708d
	1104c
5613	1104c
5614	709b
5615	707d
	708d
5616	709c
5617	709b
5618	709b
5619	709c
	920c
5620	709d
	711a
5621	709d
5622	1104c
5623	709d
5624	710a
5625	710a
5626	92d

Strong's #	BDB p.	Strong's #	BDB p.	Strong's #	BDB p.	Strong's #	BDB p.	Strong's #	BDB p.
	694c	5655	715a	5689	721d		726b	5744	714d
	710a	5656	715a	5690	721d	5715	726b	5745	716c
5627	694c		1105a	5691	721d		730b	5746	728b
	710a	5657	715c	5692	722a	5716	725d	5747	721d
5628	710a	5658	715c		728a		726b		728b
5629	710b		716c	5693	723a	5717	726a	5748	721d
5630	710b		720d	5694	722d		726b		728b
5631	710b	5659	715c	5695	722a	5718	726a	5749	728c
5632	1104c	5660	715d	5696	722c		726b		729d
5633	710c	5661	715d	5697	722b	5719	726d	5750	723b
	710d	5662	715d		722c		783b		728c
5634	703d	5663	715a		1026b	5720	726d		1105c
	710d	5664	715a	5698	722c	5721	726d	5751	1105c
5635	710d		1105a	5699	722c	5722	726d	5752	723b
	977a	5665	1105a	5700	722d	5723	726b		729c
5636	710d	5666	716a	5701	723a	5724	726b	5753	730c
5637	693c	5667	716b	5702	723a	5725	726b		731c
	710d	5668	721a	5703	723b	5726	726c		1105c
5638	711a	5669	721a		723c	5727	726c	5754	730c
5639	712c	5670	716b	5704	723b	5728	725c		731d
5640	711a	5671	716b		723d		727a	5755	727d
	979c	5672	716a		774b	5729	726c		731d
5641	711b		728a		1105b		727a	5756	731d
	1104c	5673	1105a	5705	1105b	5730	726c	5757	731d
5642	1104c	5674	716d	5706	723b		726d		732a
	1104d		720d		723d	5731	727a	5758	1105c
5643	712a		1105b	5707	723b	5732	1105c	5759	732a
	712c	5675	1105a		729c	5733	726c		732b
5644	712c	5676	719b		1113d		726d	5760	732b
5645	712b		1105a	5708	723b	5734	726c		732d
	716a	5677	720a		726b		726d	5761	731d
	728a	5678	720c	5709	1105b		727a		732a
5646	712b	5679	720b	5710	723c	5735	727a	5762	732a
	728a	5680	720a		725c		793a		743b
5647	712b	5681	720b		1105b	5736	727a	5763	732b
	1104d	5682	720d	5711	725d	5737	727b	5764	732b
5648	1104d	5683	715c	5712	417a		727c	5765	732c
5649	1105a		720d		726b	5738	727d	5766	732b
5650	713d	5684	720d		729d	5739	727c		732c
	1105a	5685	721b	5713	726b	5740	727d		732d
5651	714c	5686	721b		729d	5741	727b		759b
5652	714d	5687	721c		730a	5742	727d		763c
5653	715a	5688	716b	5714	418a	5743	728a	5767	732d
5654	714d		721c		723b		743b	5768	732d

Strong's #	BDB p.	Strong's #	BDB p.	Strong's #	BDB p.	Strong's #	BDB p.	Strong's #	BDB p.
	760c		1107c	5828	740c	5861	743c	5887	745d
5769	732d	5796	1105d	5829	740d	5862	743c	5888	746a
	761d		1107c	5830	740d	5863	743d	5889	746a
	1106d	5797	731d		1105d	5864	743d	5890	734a
5770	745a		736d	5831	1105d	5865	743d		746a
5771	730d		738d	5832	741a		761d		780c
	733b	5798	736d	5833	740d		763a	5891	734a
	773b		738a	5834	741a	5866	743d		746a
	1105c		739b	5835	741c	5867	743d	5892	735c
5772	733b		739c	5836	741b		1106d		746b
	773b	5799	736d	5837	741a	5868	744a		746d
5773	730c	5800	736d	5838	741a	5869	733b	5893	746d
	733b		738a		1105d		744a	5894	1105d
5774	733b		1115a	5839	1105d		745a	5895	736b
	734a	5801	738a	5840	741b		1044d		747a
	746a	5802	738a	5841	738b		1105d	5896	747a
	1074a		739d		741c	5870	1105d	5897	747a
	1105c	5803	738a	5842	741c	5871	745a	5898	746d
5775	733d		739d	5843	1096a		745b	5899	746d
5776	1105c	5804	738a		1105d		745c	5900	747a
5777	780b	5805	737d	5844	741d		942a	5901	747a
5778	734a	5806	738a		742a	5872	745b	5902	747a
	746a	5807	739b	5845	742b	5873	745c	5903	735d
5779	734a	5808	739b	5846	743a	5874	745c		747a
5780	734b	5809	741a	5847	742a	5875	745b		790d
5781	734b	5810	738b	5848	742b	5876	292c	5904	638b
5782	734d	5811	739b		742c		745c		746d
	1105d	5812	739c	5849	742c	5877	745c	5905	746d
5783	735d	5813	739d		742d	5878	353d	5906	747a
5784	1105c	5814	739d	5850	742d		745b		798b
5785	736a	5815	739d	5851	742d		745c	5907	747b
5786	734c	5816	739c	5852	743a	5879	745d	5908	747b
5787	734c	5817	739c	5853	743a	5880	745c	5909	747b
5788	734d	5818	739c	5854	743a		874a	5910	747b
5789	736b	5819	739c	5855	743a	5881	745d	5911	747d
5790	736c	5820	740a		1051a	5882	722d	5912	747c
5791	736c	5821	740a	5856	730c		745c	5913	747c
5792	736c	5822	740a		743b	5883	745b	5914	747c
5793	736d	5823	740a	5857	743b		920b	5915	747c
	800d		1105d		747b	5884	745b	5916	747c
5794	736d	5824	1105d	5858	743b		745c	5917	747c
	738c	5825	740a	5859	743b		942a		747d
5795	736d	5826	740a	5860	743b	5885	745d	5918	747d
	777c	5827	740d		743c	5886	745b	5919	747d

Strong's #	BDB p.
5920	748a
	752b
5921	475c
	591d
	748a
	752b
	752c
	759d
	761b
	763a
	1106a
5922	1105d
	1106a
5923	748a
	760d
5924	1105d
	1106c
5925	748a
5926	748a
5927	748a
	1105d
5928	1106a
	1106d
5929	750a
5930	732d
	750b
	751a
5931	1105d
	1106c
5932	759b
5933	759b
	759d
5934	761c
5935	759b
	759d
5936	763c
5937	759c
5938	759c
5939	759c
5940	750a
	759c
5941	750a
	759c
5942	751a

Strong's #	BDB p.
	759c
5943	1106a
5944	751a
	759c
	1106a
5945	751b
	759c
	1106a
5946	1106a
5947	759c
5948	760d
5949	760a
5950	760b
5951	763c
5952	1106a
5953	759d
	760a
	760c
	1106c
5954	1106c
5955	760a
5956	761a
5957	1106d
5958	761c
5959	761c
5960	761b
5961	761b
	761c
	763a
5962	1106d
5963	761b
5964	761b
5965	763a
5966	763a
5967	1106d
5968	763a
5969	763b
5970	763b
5971	763c
	766b
	769b
	770c
	1107a
5972	1107a

Strong's #	BDB p.
5973	763c
	765c
	767a
	769b
	1107a
5974	1107a
5975	763c
5976	588c
5977	765a
5978	767a
5979	765a
5980	769c
5981	769d
5982	765a
5983	769d
5984	770a
5985	770a
5986	770c
5987	771b
5988	765c
	770a
5989	770a
5990	770b
5991	770a
	770b
5992	770b
5993	766c
5994	1107a
5995	771c
5996	770b
5997	765c
5998	765c
	766a
5999	765d
6000	765d
6001	766a
6002	766a
6003	766a
6004	770b
6005	769b
	770c
6006	770c
	771d
6007	770c

Strong's #	BDB p.
6008	770c
6009	770d
6010	770d
6011	771b
6012	771b
	1107a
6013	771b
	1008a
6014	771c
6015	1107a
6016	771b
	771c
6017	771c
6018	771d
6019	771d
6020	771d
6021	771d
6022	772a
6023	772a
6024	772b
6025	772a
6026	772b
6027	772b
6028	772b
6029	772c
6030	732d
	772c
	777a
	1107a
6031	775d
	776a
	1107c
6032	1107a
6033	1107c
6034	777b
6035	776c
	1107c
6036	772b
6037	776c
6038	776c
6039	776d
6040	777a
6041	776c
	776d

Strong's #	BDB p.
	1107c
6042	777b
	777d
6043	777d
6044	745d
6045	775d
6046	745c
6047	777d
6048	777d
6049	778a
	1107c
6050	1107c
6051	777d
	1107c
6052	778b
6053	778a
6054	778b
6055	778b
6056	1107c
6057	778c
	1107c
6058	778c
6059	778d
6060	778d
6061	778c
6062	778c
6063	778d
6064	778d
6065	1107c
6066	778d
	1107c
6067	779a
6068	779a
6069	779a
6070	779a
6071	779b
6072	779a
6073	779b
	1107c
6074	1107c
6075	779b
	779c
6076	779b
6077	779b

Strong's #	BDB p.	Strong's #	BDB p.	Strong's #	BDB p.	Strong's #	BDB p.	Strong's #	BDB p.
6078	779c	6111	783b		1107d	6185	792d	6218	797c
6079	733d	6112	783b	6150	788a	6186	789b	6219	799d
	779c	6113	783c	6151	1107d		790a	6220	798b
6080	780a	6114	783d	6152	787a	6187	789d	6221	795c
6081	780b	6115	783d		787b	6188	790c	6222	795c
6082	780a	6116	783d	6153	787d		947a	6223	799b
6083	779c	6117	784b	6154	786b	6189	790c	6224	798a
6084	780b	6118	784c		786c	6190	790b	6225	798c
6085	780b	6119	784a	6155	788b	6191	791a	6226	798c
6086	780c	6120	784c	6156	787a	6192	790d	6227	798c
	781c	6121	784c	6157	786c	6193	791a	6228	92d
	1082b	6122	784c	6158	788b	6194	790d		798c
6087	780c	6123	785b	6159	788b	6195	791a	6229	796c
	781a	6124	785b	6160	787b	6196	790d	6230	796c
	1107d	6125	734b	6161	786d	6197	735d	6231	798d
6088	1107d		785b	6162	786d		791b	6232	799a
6089	780d	6126	784d	6163	787b	6198	735d	6233	799a
	781a	6127	785b	6164	112c		791b	6234	799a
6090	780d	6128	785c		787c	6199	791b	6235	796c
	781b	6129	785c	6165	788b		792d		797d
6091	781b	6130	785c	6166	788c	6200	793a		1108a
6092	780d	6131	785c	6167	1107d	6201	791c	6236	1108a
6093	781a	6132	1107d	6168	788c	6202	791c	6237	797c
6094	781a	6133	785c		1107d	6203	791b	6238	799a
6095	781b	6134	785d	6169	788d	6204	791c	6239	799b
	783b	6135	785d	6170	788c	6205	791d	6240	797a
6096	782b	6136	1107d	6171	789b	6206	592a	6241	798a
6097	782a	6137	785d		1107d		791d	6242	796d
6098	420a	6138	785d	6172	788d	6207	792b		797d
6099	783a	6139	785d	6173	1107d	6208	792b	6243	1108a
	783b	6140	786a	6174	736a	6209	792c	6244	799c
6100	782b	6141	786a		790d	6210	793a	6245	799c
6101	782b	6142	786a	6175	791a	6211	747b		799d
6102	782b	6143	786a	6176	791b		798b		1108a
6103	782b	6144	786a		792d		799c	6246	1108a
6104	782c	6145	786b	6177	791b	6211′	1108a	6247	799d
6105	782c		1108a		792d	6212	793b	6248	799d
	783b	6146	1107d	6178	792a		1108a	6249	799d
6106	782c		1108a	6179	735c	6213	793c	6250	799d
6107	783a	6147	735c	6180	735c		796b	6251	800b
6108	782c		786b	6181	789a	6214	795c	6252	800b
6109	782c	6148	786c	6182	791b	6215	796c		902b
6110	783a		1107d	6183	791d	6216	799a	6253	800a
	783b	6149	787a	6184	792a	6217	799a	6254	800c

Strong's #	BDB p.
6255	800b
6256	773b
	800c
6257	800c
	1108a
6258	773d
	800d
	1107b
6259	800c
6260	800c
6261	774c
	800d
6262	774c
	800d
6263	1108a
6264	800c
	1108a
6265	800d
6266	801b
6267	801c
	1108a
6268	810a
	1108a
6269	800d
	801d
6270	800d
6271	800d
6272	801a
6273	801a
6274	801a
6275	801a
	1108a
6276	801b
6277	801b
6278	773d
6279	801c
6280	801d
6281	800d
	801d
6282	801c
	801d
6283	801d
6284	802a
6285	802a

Strong's #	BDB p.
6286	802b
	802d
6287	802c
6288	802d
	825b
6289	802d
6290	803a
6291	803a
6292	803b
6293	803b
6294	803c
6295	803c
6296	803c
6297	803d
6298	803d
6299	804a
	804b
6300	804b
6301	804c
6302	804a
	804b
6303	804b
6304	804b
6305	804c
6306	804b
6307	804c
6308	804c
6309	804d
6310	804d
	809d
	810a
	1108c
6311	802a
	805d
6312	806a
	806d
6313	806a
6314	806b
6315	806b
6316	806c
6317	806c
6318	806c
6319	806c
6320	806c

Strong's #	BDB p.
6321	806d
6322	806d
6323	67a
	806d
6324	806a
	806d
6325	806d
6326	806d
6327	806d
	807b
	822d
6328	807b
6329	807c
6330	807c
6331	830b
	830c
6332	807c
6333	802d
	807d
6334	807d
6335	807d
6336	807d
6337	808a
6338	558b
	808a
6339	808a
6340	808a
6341	808b
	809a
6342	808b
	1108c
6343	808b
6344	808c
6345	808c
6346	808d
	1108b
6347	1108b
6348	808d
6349	808d
6350	808d
6351	809a
6352	809a
	809b
6353	1108b

Strong's #	BDB p.
6354	809b
6355	809b
6356	809b
6357	809b
6358	809c
6359	809c
6360	809c
6361	1108b
6362	809c
	809d
6363	809d
6364	809d
6365	810a
6366	804d
6367	809d
6368	806b
6369	810a
6370	810a
	811b
6371	802b
	810a
6372	810a
	819c
6373	810a
6374	804d
	810a
6375	807c
	810a
	823a
6376	810b
6377	810b
6378	810b
6379	810b
6380	810b
6381	810c
6382	810b
6383	811a
	813a
6384	811a
6385	811a
	1108b
6386	1108b
6387	1108b
6388	811b

Strong's #	BDB p.
6389	811b
6390	811b
6391	811b
6392	1108c
6393	811c
6394	811c
6395	811c
6396	811a
6397	812a
	813d
6398	812a
6399	1108c
6400	812a
6401	812a
6402	1108c
6403	812b
6404	812b
6405	812c
6406	812d
6407	112c
6408	812d
6409	812d
6410	812d
6411	811a
	813a
6412	812c
6413	812c
6414	813c
6415	813d
6416	813d
6417	813d
6418	813a
6419	813a
6420	813c
6421	813d
6422	812a
	813d
6423	811d
	813d
6424	814a
	814b
6425	813d
6426	814a
6427	814a

Strong's #	BDB p.	Strong's #	BDB p.	Strong's #	BDB p.	Strong's #	BDB p.	Strong's #	BDB p.
6428	814b	6460	1108c		826b	6533	827d	6568	1109a
6429	814b	6461	821a	6501	825b	6534	828a	6569	831d
6430	814b	6462	821a		826c	6535	828a	6570	831d
6431	814c	6463	821a	6502	825b	6536	828a	6571	832a
6432	814c	6464	821b	6503	825b		1108d	6572	832b
6433	1108c	6465	822b		826c	6537	1101b		837d
6434	819c	6466	821b	6504	825b		1108d		1109a
6435	814c	6467	821c	6505	825d	6538	828b	6573	1109a
6436	815a	6468	821c	6506	825d	6539	828a	6574	832b
6437	806d	6469	821d	6507	825c		1108d	6575	831d
	815a	6470	821d	6508	825d	6540	1108d	6576	831c
6438	806d	6471	821d	6509	825a	6541	828b		832b
	819c	6472	822b		826a	6542	828a	6577	832b
6439	819c	6473	822b		832c	6543	1108d	6578	832b
6440	542b	6474	822b	6510	826c	6544	828c	6579	832c
	815d	6475	822c		831a		828d	6580	832d
	819b	6476	822c	6511	826c	6545	828c	6581	832c
	819c	6477	823a		831a		828d	6582	832d
6441	542b	6478	822d	6512	344a	6546	828d	6583	832d
	819b	6479	822d		826c	6547	829a	6584	832d
6442	819b	6480	822d	6513	826c	6548	344b	6585	832c
6443	819c	6481	822d	6514	825c	6549	647a	6586	833b
	819d	6482	822d	6515	827c	6550	829a	6587	832c
6444	819d	6483	823a	6516	826c	6551	829b	6588	833b
6445	819d	6484	823a	6517	807d	6552	828c	6589	832d
6446	819d	6485	823a	6518	826d	6553	828d	6590	1109a
	821a		824b	6519	826d	6554	829b	6591	1109a
	1108d	6486	824a	6520	826d	6555	829b	6592	833d
6447	1108c	6487	824c	6521	826d	6556	829c		1109a
	1108d	6488	824b	6522	827a	6557	829d	6593	833d
6448	819d	6489	824c	6523	1108d	6558	829d	6594	834a
6449	820a	6490	824b	6524	827a	6559	829c	6595	834a
6450	67c	6491	824c		827b	6560	829d		837d
6451	820a	6492	824d		827c	6561	830a	6596	834a
	821a	6493	824d	6525	827b		1108d	6597	834a
6452	820a	6494	824d	6526	827b	6562	1108d		837b
	820c	6495	824d		1107b	6563	830a	6598	834a
6453	820a		876c	6527	827c	6564	830a	6599	834a
6454	820c	6496	824b	6528	827c	6565	830b		1109b
6455	820c	6497	825a		1107b		830c	6600	1109b
6456	820d	6498	825a	6529	826b	6566	831a	6601	834b
6457	820d	6499	825a	6530	829d	6567	831c		834c
6458	820d		830d	6531	827d		831d		1109b
6459	820d	6500	825a	6532	827d		1109a	6602	834d

Strong's #	BDB p.	Strong's #	BDB p.	Strong's #	BDB p.	Strong's #	BDB p.	Strong's #	BDB p.
6603	836c		838d	6670	843c		866a	6730	851c
6604	834d	6636	839c		843d	6698	849d		859b
6605	834d		840b	6671	844a	6699	849b	6731	751c
	836b	6637	839d	6672	843d		849c		847c
	1109b	6638	839d		844a		849d		847d
6606	1109b	6639	839d	6673	844b	6700	849d		851c
6607	835d	6640	1109c		846c	6701	849d		862c
6608	836a	6641	840c	6674	838a	6702	850a	6732	847d
6609	836a	6642	840b		844b	6703	850a		851d
6610	836a	6643	839c	6675	838a	6704	850a	6733	847d
6611	836a		840a		844b	6705	850a		851c
6612	834a	6644	840b	6676	1109d	6706	850a	6734	851d
	834b	6645	840b	6677	844b	6707	850b	6735	851d
	834c	6646	840b		848b	6708	850a		852a
	836b	6647	1109c		848c	6709	850b	6736	849c
6613	1109b	6648	840c		850a	6710	850b		851d
6614	836c		1109c		1109d	6711	850b	6737	851d
6615	834c	6649	840d	6678	844b	6712	850b	6738	852a
	836b	6650	840d	6679	844c	6713	850c		853b
6616	836d	6651	840d		845b	6714	850c		853c
6617	836c	6652	840d	6680	845b	6715	850c	6739	1109d
6618	836d	6653	841a	6681	846d	6716	850d	6740	852a
6619	837a	6654	841a	6682	846d		851c	6741	852a
6620	837a		1109c	6683	846d	6717	850d		853c
6621	837b	6655	1109c	6684	847a	6718	844d	6742	853d
6622	837c	6656	1109c	6685	847b		845b	6743	852a
6623	837c	6657	841a	6686	859b	6719	844d		852b
6624	837d	6658	841b	6687	847b	6720	841b		1109d
6625	837d		1109c	6688	847b		845b	6744	1109d
6626	834d	6659	843b	6689	847c	6721	850d	6745	852c
	837d	6660	841b		851c	6722	841b	6746	852d
6627	838a		1109c	6690	860c		851a	6747	852c
	844b	6661	841b	6691	862b	6723	851a	6748	852a
6628	838a	6662	843a	6692	847c	6724	851b		852d
6629	838a	6663	842c		847d		851c	6749	853a
6630	838c		1109d	6693	847d	6725	846b	6750	852d
6631	425c	6664	575d	6694	848b		851c	6751	853a
	838c		841c		862c	6726	851b		1094b
6632	838c	6665	1109d	6695	848a	6727	850a	6752	853b
	839d	6666	842a	6696	848d		851c	6753	853c
6633	838c		1109d		849a	6728	850d	6754	853d
	1109b	6667	843b		849b		851c		1109d
6634	1109b	6668	843c		1109d	6729	851c	6755	1109d
6635	219b	6669	843c	6697	849c		857b	6756	854a

Strong's #	BDB p.	Strong's #	BDB p.	Strong's #	BDB p.	Strong's #	BDB p.	Strong's #	BDB p.
6757	853c	6792	856c	6828	859d	6859	862c	6886	864c
	854a	6793	856c		860d	6860	851d	6887	864c
6758	854a		856d		861b		862c		865b
6759	854a		857a	6829	861b	6861	862d		865c
6760	854b	6794	857c	6830	859d	6862	862d		865d
6761	854c	6795	856c		861a		865a	6888	866c
6762	854b	6796	856d	6831	859d		865d	6889	866c
6763	854b	6797	857b		861b		866a	6890	866c
	1106d	6798	856d	6832	861c		1108a	6891	863a
6764	854c	6799	838c	6833	861d	6863	862d		866c
6765	854c		857a		1110a	6864	862d	6892	866b
6766	854c	6800	857a	6834	862a		863a		883c
6767	852d	6801	857a	6835	860b		866a	6893	866b
	854c	6802	857b	6836	859d	6865	850a	6894	866b
6768	854c	6803	857a		860c		862d	6895	866d
6769	853c	6804	857c		871a		863c	6896	867a
	854c	6805	857c	6837	859d		866a		869a
6770	854c	6806	857d		860c	6866	863a	6897	867a
6771	854d	6807	857d	6838	860c	6867	863a		869a
6772	854d	6808	858a	6839	859c	6868	863a	6898	866d
6773	854d	6809	858b	6840	860d		866c	6899	868b
6774	855a	6810	859a	6841	1110a	6869	863a	6900	869a
6775	855a	6811	859a	6842	862b		865b	6901	867a
6776	855a	6812	859a		1110a		865d		1110b
6777	855b	6813	858a	6843	862a	6870	863b	6902	1110b
	855d	6814	130c	6844	860b		863c	6903	1097b
6778	856a		858a		860c	6871	864a		1110a
6779	855b	6815	858b	6845	860c	6872	865c	6904	867b
6780	855c	6816	847b		860d		866a	6905	867b
6781	855b		858b	6846	861b		866c	6906	867b
6782	855d	6817	858b	6847	861b	6873	863c	6907	867c
6783	855d	6818	858c	6848	861c	6874	863b	6908	867c
	856c	6819	858d	6849	861c	6875	863b	6909	868b
6784	855d	6820	118d	6850	861c		863c	6910	868b
6785	856a		858d	6851	861d	6876	863a	6911	868b
	1107a	6821	859b	6852	861d	6877	863c	6912	868b
6786	856a	6822	859b	6853	1110a	6878	863d	6913	868d
6787	856b	6823	860a	6854	862c	6879	863d	6914	869a
6788	856a	6824	847c	6855	862a	6880	864a	6915	869a
6789	856b		859b	6856	862b	6881	864a	6916	869b
6790	851c	6825	859d		1094c	6882	864a	6917	870c
	856c		860c	6857	862c	6883	863d	6918	872c
6791	856c	6826	860b	6858	860b	6884	864a		1110d
	856d	6827	859d		862c	6885	864c	6919	869b

Strong's #	BDB p.	Strong's #	BDB p.	Strong's #	BDB p.	Strong's #	BDB p.	Strong's #	BDB p.
6920	869b	6948	873d	6979	876a		1111b	7039	885d
6921	870b	6949	874b		881b	7011	1111a		886b
6922	872d	6950	874d		903b		1111b	7040	886b
	1110d	6951	874c	6980	881c	7012	879c		887a
6923	869d	6952	875a	6981	881c		883d	7041	886b
	870c	6953	875a		896c	7013	883d	7042	886b
6924	869c	6954	875b	6982	881c	7014	883d	7043	886b
	870a	6955	875b		900a		884a	7044	887a
	870b	6956	875c	6983	881c	7015	884b	7045	887a
	1110c	6957	875c	6984	881c	7016	884a	7046	887b
6925	1110b		876a		885c	7017	884a	7047	887b
6926	870b		876a	6985	876c		889d	7048	887b
6927	870b	6958	883c		881c	7018	884b	7049	887b
	1110c		883d	6986	881c	7019	884d		887c
6928	1110c	6959	875c	6987	881c		1111b	7050	887c
6929	870b	6960	875c	6988	882c	7020	884d	7051	887c
6930	870c		876b	6989	882c		894a	7052	887b
6931	870c	6961	876a	6990	876c	7021	884d		887d
6932	870d	6962	876c	6991	881d	7022	884d	7053	887d
6933	1110c		878c		1111a		887b	7054	879b
6934	870d	6963	876d	6992	1111a	7023	885a		887d
6935	870d		877b	6993	881d		885b	7055	887d
6936	869a		885c	6994	881d		894d	7056	879c
	903a		887a	6995	882b	7024	885b		887d
6937	871a		1110d	6996	881d	7025	885b	7057	883d
6938	871a	6964	877b		882b	7026	885b		888b
6939	871b	6965	525d	6997	882a		902b	7058	887d
6940	871a		877c	6998	882b	7027	885c	7059	888a
6941	871a		879d	6999	882d	7028	885c	7060	888a
6942	872d		1110d		883b	7029	881c	7061	888a
6943	873d	6966	1110d	7000	883b		885c	7062	888a
	904d	6967	879b		1111b	7030	1111b	7063	888b
6944	871c	6968	879c	7001	1111b		1112a	7064	888b
	873d	6969	880c	7002	883b	7031	885c		890a
	874a		884b	7003	883c		886d	7065	888c
	874b	6970	880c	7004	882c	7032	1110d	7066	1111b
6945	873c	6971	880d	7005	883c		1111b	7067	888d
6946	872c	6972	884d	7006	883d	7033	885c	7068	888b
	873d	6973	880d	7007	1111b	7034	885d	7069	888d
	937b	6974	884c	7008	882c	7035	874d		1111b
6947	140b	6975	881a		883d		885c	7070	889c
	745c	6976	881a	7009	879c	7036	885d	7071	889d
	873d	6977	881b		883d	7037	886a	7072	888d
	874a	6978	876a	7010	1111a	7038	886a	7073	889d

Strong's #	BDB p.
7074	889d
7075	889a
7076	890a
7077	890a
7078	890b
7079	890b
7080	890c
7081	890c
7082	890d
7083	890d
	1099c
7084	890d
7085	891a
7086	891a
7087	891a
	891b
7088	891b
7089	891c
7090	891b
7091	891c
7092	891c
7093	891d
	893d
7094	891d
7095	891d
7096	891d
7097	892a
	892c
	1111b
7098	892b
7099	892c
7100	892d
7101	802d
7102	893a
	893b
7103	893a
7104	894a
7105	894c
	894d
7106	892d
7107	893b
7108	1111c
7109	1111c
7110	893c

Strong's #	BDB p.
7111	893c
7112	893c
7113	893c
7114	894a
	894b
	894d
7115	894b
7116	894b
7117	596d
	892c
	892d
	894d
	1111c
7118	1111c
7119	894d
7120	894d
	903b
7121	894d
	1111c
7122	896d
	897a
7123	1111c
7124	896c
7125	896d
	897a
7126	897b
	1111c
7127	1111c
7128	898b
	1111d
7129	1111d
7130	899a
7131	898a
7132	898b
7133	898d
7134	899c
7135	899c
	903b
7136	899c
	900a
7137	899d
7138	898b
7139	901a
7140	901c

Strong's #	BDB p.
7141	901b
7142	901b
7143	901b
7144	901b
7145	687c
	901c
7146	901b
7147	899d
	901c
7148	896c
7149	1111d
7150	896d
7151	900a
	901c
	1111d
7152	901a
	901c
7153	900b
	917b
7154	900c
7155	900c
7156	900b
	1001a
7157	900b
	900c
	900d
	901c
7158	703a
	707c
	900d
7159	901c
7160	902a
7161	901d
	902b
	1111d
7162	1111d
7163	806c
	902a
7164	902b
7165	902b
7166	902b
7167	902b
7168	902d
7169	902d

Strong's #	BDB p.
7170	1111d
7171	903a
	1111d
7172	903a
7173	903a
7174	903a
7175	903c
7176	900d
	903c
7177	900d
7178	900b
	900d
7179	903b
	903d
	905d
7180	903d
7181	904a
7182	904a
7183	903c
	904a
	904b
7184	903c
7185	904b
7186	904c
7187	1112a
7188	905a
7189	905a
	1112a
7190	904d
	905a
7191	904d
	905a
7192	903d
7193	903d
7194	905a
7195	905c
7196	905c
7197	905d
7198	905d
7199	906c
7200	906b
	909b
	1112a
7201	906b

Strong's #	BDB p.
7202	909a
7203	906d
	909a
	909b
7204	909b
7205	910a
7206	910a
7207	906d
	908a
	909b
7208	910b
7209	909b
	910b
7210	909b
	910b
7211	909b
	909d
	910b
7212	909b
	910b
7213	910b
	910c
	926c
7214	910b
	937c
	941a
7215	910c
7216	910c
	928b
	928d
	942b
7217	1112a
7218	910c
	1112a
7219	911b
	912c
	930d
7220	911b
	912c
7221	911c
7222	911c
7223	910b
	911c
	938c

Strong's #	BDB p.	Strong's #	BDB p.	Strong's #	BDB p.	Strong's #	BDB p.	Strong's #	BDB p.
7224	912a	7245	914c	7279	920d	7311	575d	7338	931d
7225	912a		916c	7280	920d		910b	7339	932a
	957a	7246	916c		921b		926c	7340	932b
7226	910c	7247	916c		921c		941a	7341	931d
	912a	7248	550b	7281	921a		942c	7342	932a
	912c		913c	7282	921b		1112d	7343	932a
7227	912c		916c	7283	921c	7312	927d	7344	932c
	912d	7249	913c		1112c		941a	7345	932c
	913c		916c	7284	1112c	7313	1112d	7346	932c
	914d	7250	918a	7285	920c	7314	1112d	7347	932d
	918d	7251	917c		921c	7315	927d	7348	933d
	1112a	7252	918a	7286	921c	7316	928a		1113a
7228	912c	7253	917d	7287	921d	7317	928a	7349	933d
	914d	7254	918b		922a	7318	928c	7350	935b
7229	1112a	7255	917d	7288	921d	7319	927a		1113a
	1112c	7256	918a		922b		928c	7351	923d
7230	912c	7257	918b	7289	921d	7320	928d		932d
	913d	7258	918c	7290	922b		942c	7352	1113a
	923d	7259	918d	7291	922c	7321	929c	7353	932d
7231	912c	7260	1112b		923b		937c	7354	932d
	912d		1112c	7292	923b	7322	952c	7355	933c
	914b	7261	1112b	7293	923c	7323	929c	7356	933a
	914c		1112c	7294	923c		930a		933b
	1112a	7262	913d	7295	923b		943b		1113a
7232	914d		918d	7296	923b		952d	7357	933d
7233	914b	7263	918d	7297	436c	7324	937d	7358	933a
7234	914d	7264	919a		923c	7325	938b	7359	1113a
7235	915a		1112c	7298	923d	7326	910c	7360	934b
	916c	7265	1112c	7299	1112a		930d	7361	933a
	1112b	7266	1112c		1112d		957a	7362	933d
7236	1112b	7267	919c	7300	923d	7327	930d	7363	934b
7237	851a	7268	919c	7301	924a		946c	7364	934b
	913d	7269	919c	7302	924b	7328	1112d	7365	1113a
	916c	7270	920a	7303	923c	7329	930d	7366	934d
7238	1112c		1076a		924b	7330	931a	7367	934d
7239	914b	7271	1112c	7304	926b	7331	931b	7368	934d
	916c	7272	919c	7305	926c	7332	931a		1113a
	1112a		1112c	7306	926b		931b	7369	935b
7240	1112b	7273	920b	7307	924c	7333	931a	7370	935d
7241	914c	7274	920c		1112d		931b	7371	935d
7242	914d	7275	920c	7308	1112d	7334	931a	7372	936a
7243	917d	7276	920d	7309	926c	7335	931b	7373	936a
	1112c	7277	920c	7310	924b	7336	931b	7374	936a
7244	1112c	7278	920d		926c	7337	931b	7375	936a

Strong's #	BDB p.	Strong's #	BDB p.	Strong's #	BDB p.	Strong's #	BDB p.	Strong's #	BDB p.
7376	936b	7404	940b	7431	943a		946c	7485	947a
7377	138c	7405	940c	7432	928c	7454	929d		947c
	924b	7406	940c		928d		944a	7486	947c
	936b	7407	940c		943a		946b	7487	1113b
7378	912c	7408	940d	7433	928b		946d	7488	947d
	923d	7409	940d	7434	859d	7455	944a		1113b
	936b	7410	928a		928b		947d	7489	945d
7379	936d	7411	941a	7435	928b	7456	944a		948a
7380	937a		1113a		943a	7457	944c		949b
7381	926b	7412	1113a	7436	847c	7458	944b		949d
	937c	7413	928a		928a	7459	944c		1084a
	1112d		941d		928c	7460	944c	7490	1113b
7382	1112d	7414	910b		943a	7461	944c	7491	950a
	1113a		910c	7437	928b		944d	7492	950a
7383	937d		928a	7438	943a	7462	944d	7493	950a
	952b		928c		943c		945c	7494	950b
7384	193d		941d	7439	943a		946b	7495	950c
	937d	7415	941d	7440	943a		950a	7496	951a
7385	938a		942c		943c		1113b		952b
	938b	7416	745c	7441	943a	7463	946b	7497	951a
7386	938a		941d		943d	7464	946b		952b
	938b	7417	942a	7442	929c	7465	949d	7498	951a
	954d		942b		930c	7466	946c		951b
7387	938b	7418	910c		943b	7467	946c		952a
7388	938c		928b		943c	7468	946b		952b
7389	910c		928c	7443	943d	7469	946d	7499	951b
	930d	7419	928c	7444	943b	7470	1113b	7500	951b
	938c		942b	7445	943c	7471	945c	7501	951b
7390	938c	7420	942b	7446	943d	7472	946c	7502	951c
	940a	7421	74c	7447	944a	7473	944d	7503	951c
7391	938c	7422	941d	7448	943d		945a		952a
	940a		942b	7449	944a		945c	7504	952a
7392	938c	7423	941a	7450	944a	7474	946b	7505	951b
7393	939a		941c	7451	944a	7475	946d	7506	952c
7394	939c		942b		948a	7476	1113b	7507	951c
7395	939b		945a		948c	7477	947a	7508	951c
7396	939b	7424	942b		949a	7478	947a	7509	951b
7397	939d	7425	942b	7452	929d	7479	947a		952c
7398	939c	7426	942c		944a	7480	947a	7510	952a
7399	940d	7427	928c		946b		947c		952c
7400	940c	7428	829d	7453	929d	7481	947b	7511	952c
7401	939d		942a		937c	7482	947b		952d
7402	940b	7429	942c		944a	7483	947c		1113b
7403	940b	7430	942d		945d	7484	947c	7512	1113b

Strong's #	BDB p.
7513	952c
7514	952d
7515	952c
	952d
7516	952d
7517	952d
7518	952d
	954d
7519	952d
7520	952d
7521	952d
	953a
7522	953c
7523	953d
7524	954a
7525	954a
7526	954a
7527	954a
7528	954b
7529	954b
	954c
7530	954b
7531	954b
	954c
7532	954c
7533	930d
	954c
	1113b
7534	954d
	956b
7535	954d
	956b
7536	954d
	956d
7537	955a
7538	955a
7539	955a
7540	955a
7541	955b
	956d
7542	955b
	956d
7543	955b
7544	955b

Strong's #	BDB p.
7545	955b
7546	955c
7547	955c
7548	955c
7549	956a
7550	956d
7551	955c
7552	955d
7553	955d
7554	955d
7555	956b
7556	956d
7557	957a
7558	957a
7559	957a
	1113b
7560	1113b
7561	957d
7562	957c
7563	957b
7564	957d
	958a
7565	958b
7566	958b
7567	930d
	958b
7568	440b
	958b
7569	958d
7570	958b
7571	958c
7572	958d
7573	958c
7574	958c
7575	958c
7576	958d
7577	958d
7578	958d
7579	980b
7580	980c
7581	980d
7582	980d
7583	981b
7584	981a

Strong's #	BDB p.
7585	982c
	982d
7586	982b
7587	982c
7588	981a
7589	981b
	1002b
7590	1002b
7591	981a
	981b
7592	981b
	1114a
7593	1114a
7594	982b
7595	1114a
7596	982c
	1017c
	1115c
7597	982c
	1027a
7598	982d
7599	983b
7600	983b
7601	983c
7602	983c
7603	959a
7604	983d
7605	984b
	1114b
7606	1114b
7607	984d
	985a
7608	985a
7609	985a
7610	984c
	1000b
7611	984c
	1056c
7612	981b
	985a
	1059a
7613	673b
	979c
7614	985a

Strong's #	BDB p.
7615	985b
7616	985b
7617	985c
7618	986b
7619	986c
7620	988d
7621	989d
7622	986a
	987b
	1000a
7623	986c
	1114b
7624	1114b
7625	1114b
7626	986d
	1114b
7627	987b
7628	985d
	987b
7629	986b
7630	986b
7631	1114b
7632	985b
7633	986a
	987b
7634	967d
7635	987c
7636	987d
7637	988c
7638	959a
	959b
7639	959a
	959b
	1113c
7640	987c
7641	987c
7642	117d
	987c
7643	959b
7644	987d
7645	987d
7646	959b
7647	960a
7648	959d

Strong's #	BDB p.
7649	960a
7650	989a
7651	987d
	988d
	1114b
7652	989d
7653	960a
7654	960a
7655	1114b
7656	988b
7657	988c
7658	988d
7659	988d
7660	990a
7661	990b
7662	1114c
7663	960b
	1104a
7664	960b
7665	990c
	991b
	1117c
7666	991c
7667	991a
	991c
7668	991c
7669	991b
7670	991b
7671	991b
7672	1114c
7673	991d
	992c
7674	444a
	992a
7675	443d
7676	992a
7677	992d
7678	992d
7679	960b
	1113c
7680	1113c
7681	992d
	993b
7682	960c

Strong's #	BDB p.	Strong's #	BDB p.	Strong's #	BDB p.	Strong's #	BDB p.	Strong's #	BDB p.
	546d	8324	1004a		1059a	8380	1060d	8401	1061d
	1056c	8325	1057a	8353	1114d		1063a	8402	1062a
8290	1056c	8326	1057a		1117b		1064a	8403	125d
8291	977d	8327	1057d	8354	1059a	8381	46d		1062a
8292	1057a	8328	1057c		1117c		1060d	8404	1062a
8293	1056a		1117b	8355	1083b	8382	1060d	8405	1062a
8294	976a	8329	1058a		1117c		1069c	8406	1117c
8295	976b		1058c	8356	1011d		1071a	8407	129c
8296	976b	8330	1117b		1059a	8383	20b		1062a
8297	976b	8331	1057b		1059d		1061b		1067d
	979c		1058a		1060a	8384	1061a	8408	1062b
8298	1056c	8332	1117b	8357	1011d	8385	58c	8409	173d
8299	974d	8333	1057b		1059a		1061a		1062b
8300	975a		1058a		1059d	8386	1061b	8410	187b
8301	975a	8334	1058a	8358	1059c	8387	1061b		1062b
8302	1056b	8335	1058b	8359	1059d	8388	1060d	8411	1087b
	1056c	8336	1010d	8360	1059c		1061b		1117c
8303	976b		1058b	8361	1114d		1061c	8412	1062b
8304	976a		1058c		1117c	8389	1061b	8413	1062b
	976b	8337	995c	8362	1060a		1064c	8414	1062c
	996a		1010d	8363	1060a	8390	357c	8415	1062d
8305	977c		1058b	8364	1004d		1061c	8416	239d
8306	1057b		1058d	8365	1060c	8391	81b		1062d
8307	1057b		1114d	8366	1010b		1061c	8417	1062d
8308	976c	8338	995d		1060c	8392	1061c	8418	237c
8309	995a	8339	1058c	8367	1060c	8393	100a		1062d
	1056c	8340	1058c	8368	979c		1061d	8419	246c
8310	976c	8341	995d		1104d	8394	108a		1063a
8311	976c	8342	965b	8369	1060c		108b	8420	1063a
8312	972a		979c	8370	1117c		1061d		1063b
	976d	8343	1058d	8371	1001c		1063b	8421	1117d
8313	976d	8344	1058d		1060c	8395	101b	8422	1061d
8314	977b	8345	995d	8372	1060b		1061d		1063a
8315	977b		1058d	8373	1060b	8396	58b	8423	1063b
8316	977b	8346	995d	8374	1060b		493b	8424	387b
8317	1056c		1058d	8375	1060b		1061d		1063b
8318	1056d	8347	525d	8376	1060d	8397	117d	8425	1062b
8319	1056d		1058d		1061c		1061d	8426	392d
	1117b	8348	1058d		1063b	8398	385c		1063b
8320	977d	8349	1059a	8377	1060d		1061d	8427	1061c
8321	977d	8350	1059a		1063a	8399	115b		1063b
8322	1056d	8351	981b	8378	16c		1061d	8428	1063b
8323	965a		1059a	8379	1060d	8400	117d	8429	1117d
	979a	8352	1011c		1063b		1061d	8430	1063c

Strong's #	BDB p.	Strong's #	BDB p.	Strong's #	BDB p.	Strong's #	BDB p.	Strong's #	BDB p.
8431	404b		1064d		1065a	8500	1064a	8533	1118a
	1063c	8452	435d	8475	357c		1067a	8534	1068c
	1064d		1064c		1065a	8501	1067a		1069b
8432	1063c		1064d	8476	1065a	8502	479a	8535	1069b
8433	407b	8453	444c	8477	1065a		1067a		1070d
	1064a		1064d	8478	1065a	8503	479b	8536	1118a
8434	410a		1077b		1117d		1067a	8537	1069b
	1064a	8454	444d	8479	1117d	8504	1067a		1070d
8435	410a		1064d	8480	1066c	8505	1067b		1071b
	1064a		1077b	8481	1066b	8506	1067c	8538	1069b
8436	1064a	8455	450c	8482	1066b	8507	1067c		1070d
	1066c		1064d	8483	295a	8508	1067c	8539	1069b
	1066d	8456	1064d		874a	8509	501b	8540	1118b
8437	1064a	8457	276b		1066c		1067c	8541	1069b
8438	1068d		1064d	8484	1064a	8510	1067c	8542	1069c
	1069a	8458	287a		1066c		1068b	8543	1069d
8439	1064d		1064d	8485	1066d		1068d	8544	568b
	1069a	8459	1063c		1069b	8511	1067d		1069c
8440	1046b		1064d	8486	412c	8512	1068b	8545	558c
	1069a	8460	1117d		1066d	8513	521b		1069c
8441	1072d	8461	315d		1071b	8514	520d	8546	560d
8442	1064a		1064d	8487	412d		1067d		1069c
	1073c	8462	321a		1064a	8515	1067d	8547	1069c
8443	419b		1064d		1071b		1069b	8548	556b
	1064a	8463	316a	8488	412d	8516	528d		1069c
8444	426a		1064d		1066d		1067d	8549	1070d
	1064a	8464	329d	8489	412d	8517	1117d		1071a
8445	876b		1064d		1066d	8518	1067d	8550	1070d
	1064b	8465	334c		1071b	8519	534b	8551	1064a
	1075b		1064d	8490	1066d		1068d		1069c
8446	451d	8466	334c	8491	1066d	8520	1068b	8552	1064a
	1064b		1064d	8492	440d	8521	1068b		1070b
	1064d	8467	337c		1066d	8522	1068a	8553	584c
8447	1061b		1064d	8493	432b	8523	1118a		1071b
	1064c	8468	337c		1066d	8524	1068c	8554	584d
	1076a	8469	337c	8494	1066d	8525	1068d		1071b
8448	1061b		1064d	8495	1066d	8526	1068d	8555	586b
	1064c	8470	334c	8496	1063c	8527	541a		1071b
	1076a		1064d		1067a		1068d	8556	584d
8449	1064d		1071d	8497	1067a	8528	1068b		1071b
	1076a	8471	1064d	8498	467d	8529	1069a	8557	588a
8450	1117d	8472	1065a		1067a	8530	1069b		1071b
8451	435d	8473	1065a	8499	467d	8531	1118a	8558	1071c
	1064c	8474	354a		1067a	8532	1118a	8559	1062b

Strong's #	BDB p.	Strong's #	BDB p.	Strong's #	BDB p.	Strong's #	BDB p.	Strong's #	BDB p.
8135	971d	8157	1043a	8190	1045d		1050d		1054c
8136	1039c	8158	1043a	8191	1044b	8225	1050d	8259	1054c
	1041d	8159	1043a	8192	1045d	8226	706a	8260	1054d
8137	1039c		1044b		1046a	8227	1050d	8261	1054d
8138	1039c	8160	1116d	8193	973c	8228	1051a	8262	1055a
	1039d	8161	1043b	8194	1045d	8229	1051a	8263	1054d
	1040d	8162	1043b	8195	1046a	8230	1051b	8264	1055b
8139	1096b	8163	972c	8196	1048a	8231	1051c	8265	974c
	1116d		972d	8197	1051b	8232	1117a	8266	1055d
8140	1096b	8164	973c	8198	1046c	8233	1051c	8267	1055b
	1116d	8165	973a	8199	251c	8234	1051c	8268	1052d
8141	1040a		1043b		1047a	8235	1051c		1055d
8142	446a	8166	972c		1117a	8236	1051c	8269	694a
	1039c	8167	972c	8200	1117a	8237	1051d		974c
	1041d	8168	1043b	8201	1048a	8238	1117a		978a
	1042b	8169	1043c	8202	1048b	8239	1046a		979a
	1096b	8170	1043d	8203	1049b		1052a	8270	1055d
8143	1041d	8171	1043d	8204	1049b	8240	1046b		1057a
	1042b	8172	1043d	8205	1045d		1052a	8271	1117b
8144	1040c	8173	1043a		1046a	8241	1009b	8272	974c
8145	1041b		1044a	8206	1047a		1052a		1055d
	1118b		1044b		1049b	8242	974b	8273	1055d
8146	971d	8174	1044c		1050d	8243	1114d	8274	1055d
8147	1040d	8175	972b		1051b		1117b	8275	987b
	1060a		972c	8207	1051b	8244	974b		1056a
	1118b		973b	8208	1051c	8245	1052a	8276	974d
8148	1042b	8176	1045c	8209	1117a	8246	1052b	8277	974d
8149	972a	8177	1114a	8210	706c	8247	1052b	8278	975a
8150	1041d	8178	972c		1049b	8248	913d	8279	975b
	1116d		973b	8211	1050a		1052b	8280	975b
8151	1042b	8179	745b	8212	1050a		1054b	8281	1056a
8152	1042b		1044c	8213	1050a	8249	1052d		1056c
8153	445c		1118d		1117a	8250	1052c		1117b
	446a	8180	1045c	8214	1117a	8251	1055a	8282	979a
	1042b	8181	972b	8215	1117a	8252	1052d		994d
	1042c		1114a	8216	1050c	8253	1053b	8283	979a
8154	983c	8182	1045d	8217	1050c	8254	1053b	8284	1004b
	1042c	8183	973b	8218	1050c		1118c		1056c
	1042d	8184	972d	8219	1050c	8255	1053c	8285	1056b
	1058b	8185	972b	8220	1050d		1118c		1057b
8155	983c	8186	1045d	8221	1050d	8256	1054a	8286	974d
	1042c	8187	1045c	8222	974a	8257	1052c	8287	1056b
8156	1042d	8188	972d	8223	1050d		1054b	8288	976c
	1043a	8189	1045c	8224	974a	8258	891a	8289	450a

Strong's #	BDB p.
7683	992d
7684	993a
7685	960d
7686	993a
7687	960d
7688	993b
7689	960c
7690	1113c
7691	993b
7692	993a
	993c
7693	993c
7694	993c
	1114c
7695	1114c
7696	993c
7697	993d
7698	993d
7699	993d
	994c
	994d
7700	993d
7701	994a
	994c
	1000c
7702	961a
7703	994a
	1000d
7704	961a
	961b
7705	994d
7706	994c
	994d
7707	994d
7708	961a
	961d
7709	995a
	1056c
7710	995b
7711	995b
7712	1114c
7713	690b
	961d
7714	995b

Strong's #	BDB p.
	1114c
7715	1114c
7716	961d
	966d
7717	962a
	1113c
7718	995d
7719	996a
7720	962a
7721	962b
7722	980b
	980d
	996b
7723	981a
	996a
7724	976a
	996a
	1009d
7725	996d
	1000a
	1117d
7726	1000a
7727	1000a
7728	1000a
7729	1000a
7730	959a
7731	1000c
7732	987c
	1000c
7733	990b
	1000c
	1114c
7734	690d
7735	691b
7736	994a
	1000d
7737	1000d
	1001a
	1114d
7738	996c
7739	1114d
7740	1001a
7741	1001a
7742	962b

Strong's #	BDB p.
	1002a
7743	1001b
	1008a
	1009d
	1060c
7744	1001d
7745	1001c
7746	1001d
7747	1001d
7748	1001d
7749	1001d
7750	962b
7751	967b
	1001d
	1002b
7752	1002a
	1002b
7753	962b
	968a
7754	962c
7755	962c
7756	962c
7757	1002c
7758	1002c
	1010a
	1021d
7759	1002c
	1025a
7760	962c
	965a
	967c
	1113d
7761	1113d
7762	1002c
7763	1037c
7764	1002c
7765	1002c
7766	1002d
7767	1002d
7768	1002d
7769	447d
	575d
	1002d
	1003a

Strong's #	BDB p.
7770	447c
7771	447c
	1003a
7772	447c
	1003a
7773	1002d
7774	447d
	1003a
7775	1003a
7776	1043c
7777	1043c
7778	1045b
7779	1003a
7780	1000c
	1003a
7781	1003a
	1050d
	1051b
7782	1051c
7783	1003b
7784	1003b
7785	1003b
	1114d
7786	975b
	979a
7787	963a
	965a
	975b
7788	1003c
7789	1003d
7790	1004a
7791	1004b
	1004c
	1114d
7792	1114d
7793	1004b
7794	1004a
	1117d
7795	965a
	975b
7796	977d
7797	965a
7798	1004c
7799	1004c

Strong's #	BDB p.
7800	1004d
7801	1114d
7802	1004c
7803	1004d
7804	1095c
	1115a
7805	1004d
7806	1004d
7807	1005a
	1006a
7808	965c
	967b
7809	1005a
	1007c
7810	1005a
7811	965c
7812	1005b
7813	965c
7814	966a
7815	1005d
	1007a
7816	1005c
7817	1001c
	1005d
7818	965c
7819	1006a
	1006b
7820	1006a
7821	1006b
7822	1006b
	1006c
7823	695a
	1006b
7824	965d
	1006b
7825	1005d
7826	1006c
7827	1006c
7828	1006d
7829	1006d
7830	1006d
7831	1006d
7832	965d
7833	1006d